Ancestry in America

First Edition

Ancestry in America

A Comparative City-by-City Guide to over 200 Ethnic Backgrounds -- with Rankings

A UNIVERSAL REFERENCE BOOK

Grey House Publishing

PUBLISHER: Leslie Mackenzie
EDITOR: David Garoogian
EDITORIAL DIRECTOR: Laura Mars-Proietti

PRODUCTION MANAGER: Karen Stevens

MARKETING DIRECTOR: Jessica Moody

A Universal Reference Book
Grey House Publishing, Inc.
185 Millerton Road
Millerton, NY 12546
518.789.8700
FAX 518.789.0545
www.greyhouse.com
e-mail: books @greyhouse.com

First edition

Printed in the USA

Ancestry in America : a comparative guide to over 200 ethnic backgrounds / [ed. David Garoogian] .
3045 p. 27.5 cm.
ISBN: 1-592-37029-2
1. Demography—United States—Statistics—Directories. 2. Ethnic groups—United States—Statistics—Directories. 3. Population research—United States—Directories. 4. United States—Population—Statistics—Directories. I. Garoogian, David. II. Title.
HB3505 .A53 2003
304.6' 0973—dc21

Table of Contents

Introduction

Grey House Publishing is pleased to offer this first edition of *Ancestry in America: A Comparative City-by-City Guide to Over 200 Ethnic Backgrounds – with Rankings*. This brand new title is the latest addition to our Universal Reference demographic and statistical reference works. *Ancestry in America* provides, for the first time in print form, a detailed look at the ethnic makeup of the United States. It was developed as the result of numerous requests from researchers for this data, who were looking for straightforward information that is otherwise time consuming and often difficult to compile.

Compiled from raw 2000 Census data, this reference book includes all places in America with populations over 10,000. The companion CD-ROM gives the same information for all 33,150 places in the country (both incorporated and census designated), regardless of population. See **Explanation of Data** that follows this Introduction for complete and detailed information of the data provided. Both the print and CD versions of *Ancestry in America* are arranged to offer this detailed data in several valuable ways:

Section One – City-by-City Listings
This first section is arranged first by state, then alphabetical by place. For each place, you will find the county it resides in, the type of place (city, town, etc.) and that place's total population. This information is followed by an alphabetical list of ancestries and racial backgrounds, from Acadian/Cajun to Yugoslavian – with up to 217 ethnic categories. Each ethnicity for each place is listed in two ways, by the number of persons who reported it, and by the percentage of the total population. You can see, at a glance, for example, how many people, living in Phoenix, consider themselves to be of Ugandan descent, or what percentage of Los Angeles' total population reported Mexican ancestry.

Section Two – Comparative Ranking Tables
This section is comprised of ranking tables of all ethnic backgrounds. Each table has three parts:

- Top 150 cities with the largest number of persons reporting that particular descent regardless of population. Here you can find out, for example, where in the country are the most persons reporting Armenian descent; the top three are Los Angeles CA, Glendale CA, New York NY.

- Top 150 cities with the highest concentration of that particular descent, based on percentage of that city's population. Here you can find out, for example, where in the country persons reporting Armenian descent make up the largest part of the population, even for places with as few as 50 (or less) people; the top three are Glendale CA, Ridgely MO, Madrid NM.

- Top 150 cities of 10,000 or more population with the highest concentration of that particular decent, based on percentage of that city's population. Here you can find out, for example, where in the country persons reporting Armenian descent make up the largest part of the population; the top three are Glendale CA, Burbank CA, Watertown MA.

Place Index

A master Index includes, in alphabetical order, a complete list of the places included in *Ancestry in America.* This index includes their type, county, state, and the pages in this book they appear on.

Companion CD-ROM

Due to the amount of data in *Ancestry in America: A Comparative City-by-City Guide to Over 200 Ethnic Backgounds – with Rankings*, the printed volume is limited to only the largest places in America – those 4,206 cities with populations of 10,000 or more. The rest of the places, however, can be found on the companion CD-ROM. The CD contains the same information, presented in the same way as the print book, for every incorporated and census designated place (CDP) in America – 33,150 in all. There is no additional charge for the CD, it will be sent to all purchasers of the print book who request it.

Explanation of Data

Places Covered

Section I of this book covers all 4,206 places in the U.S. with populations of 10,000 or more. The ranking tables in Section II are based on all 33,150 places in the U.S (except were noted). Places covered fall into one of the following categories:

19,436 incorporated municipalities. Depending on the state, municipalities are incorporated as either cities, towns, villages, or boroughs. A few municipalities have a form of government combined with another entity (e.g. county) and are listed as "special cities."

5,381 census designated places (CDP). The U.S. Bureau of the Census defines a CDP as "a statistical entity, defined for each decennial census according to Census Bureau guidelines, comprising a densely settled concentration of population that is not within an incorporated place, but is locally identified by a name. CDPs are delineated cooperatively by state and local officials and the Census Bureau, following Census Bureau guidelines. Beginning with Census 2000 there are no size limits."

8,333 minor civil divisions (called towns, townships, districts, gores, locations, and plantations) for the states where the Census Bureau has determined that they serve as general-purpose governments. Those states are Connecticut, Maine, Massachusetts, Michigan, Minnesota, New Hampshire, New Jersey, New York, Pennsylvania, Rhode Island, Vermont, and Wisconsin. In some states incorporated municipalities are part of minor civil divisions and in some states they are independent of them.

Note: Several states have incorporated municipalities and minor civil divisions in the same county with the same name. Those communities are given separate entries (e.g. South Haven, Michigan, in Van Buren County will be listed under both the city and township of South Haven).

Source of Data

The ancestries shown in this book were compiled from three different sections of the 2000 Census: Race; Hispanic Origin; and Ancestry. While the ancestries are sorted alphabetically for ease-of-use, it's important to note the origin of each piece of data. Data for Race and Hispanic Origin was taken from Summary File 1 (SF1) while Ancestry data was taken from Summary File 3 (SF3). The distinction is important because SF1 contains the 100-percent data, which is the information compiled from the questions asked of all people and about every housing unit. SF3 was compiled from a sample of approximately 19 million housing units (about 1 in 6 households) that received the Census 2000 long-form questionnaire.

Ancestries Based on Race

- African-American/Black:
  - Not Hispanic
  - Hispanic
- Alaska Native tribes, specified:
  - Alaska Athabascan
  - Aleut
  - Eskimo
  - Tlingit-Haida
  - All other tribes
- Alaska Native tribes, not specified
- American Indian or Alaska Native tribes, not specified
- American Indian tribes, specified:
  - Apache
  - Blackfeet
  - Cherokee
  - Cheyenne
  - Chickasaw
  - Chippewa
  - Choctaw
  - Colville
  - Comanche
  - Cree
  - Creek
  - Crow
  - Delaware
  - Houma
  - Iroquois
  - Kiowa
  - Latin American Indians
  - Lumbee
  - Menominee
  - Navajo
  - Osage
  - Ottawa
  - Paiute
  - Pima
  - Potawatomi
  - Pueblo
  - Puget Sound Salish
  - Seminole
  - Shoshone
  - Sioux
  - Tohono O'Odham
  - Ute
  - Yakama
  - Yaqui
  - Yuman
  - All other tribes
- American Indian tribes, not specified
- Asian:
  - Bangladeshi
  - Cambodian
  - Chinese, except Taiwanese
  - Filipino
  - Hmong
  - Indian
  - Indonesian
  - Japanese
  - Korean
  - Laotian
  - Malaysian
  - Pakistani
  - Sri Lankan
  - Taiwanese
  - Thai
  - Vietnamese
  - Other Asian, specified
  - Other Asian, not specified
- Hawaii Native/Pacific Islander:
  - Melanesian:
    - Fijian
    - Other Melanesian
  - Micronesian:
    - Guamanian/Chamorro
    - Other Micronesian
  - Polynesian:
    - Native Hawaiian
    - Samoan
    - Tongan
    - Other Polynesian
  - Other Pacific Islander, specified
  - Other Pacific Islander, not specified
- White:
  - Not Hispanic
  - Hispanic

The data on race were derived from answers to the question on race that was asked of all people. The concept of race, as used by the Census Bureau, reflects self-identification by people according to the race or races with which they most closely identify. These categories are sociopolitical constructs and should not be interpreted as being scientific or anthropological in nature. Furthermore, the race categories include both racial and national-origin groups.

If an individual did not provide a race response, the race or races of the householder or other household members were assigned using specific rules of precedence of household relationship. For example, if race was missing for a natural-born child in the household, then either the race or races of the householder, another natural-born child, or the spouse of the householder were assigned. If race was not reported for anyone in the household, the race or races of a householder in a previously processed household were assigned.

African American or Black: A person having origins in any of the Black racial groups of Africa. It includes people who indicate their race as ''Black, African Am., or Negro,'' or provide written entries such as African American, Afro American, Kenyan, Nigerian, or Haitian.

American Indian or Alaska Native: A person having origins in any of the original peoples of North and South America (including Central America) and who maintain tribal affiliation or community attachment. It includes people who classified themselves as described below.

American Indian - Includes people who indicated their race as "American Indian," entered the name of an Indian tribe, or reported such entries as Canadian Indian, French American Indian, or Spanish-American Indian.

Respondents who identified themselves as American Indian were asked to report their enrolled or principal tribe. Therefore, tribal data in tabulations reflect the written entries reported on the questionnaires. Some of the entries (for example, Iroquois, Sioux, Colorado River, and Flathead) represent nations or reservations. The information on tribe is based on self identification and therefore does not reflect any designation of federally or state-recognized tribe. Information on American Indian tribes is presented in summary files. The information for Census 2000 is derived from the American Indian Tribal Classification List for the 1990 census that was updated based on a December 1997 Federal Register Notice, entitled "Indian Entities Recognized and Eligible to Receive Service From the United States Bureau of Indian Affairs," Department of the Interior, Bureau of Indian Affairs, issued by the Office of Management and Budget.

Alaska Native - Includes written responses of Eskimos, Aleuts, and Alaska Indians, as well as entries such as Arctic Slope, Inupiat, Yupik, Alutiiq, Egegik, and Pribilovian. The Alaska tribes are the Alaskan Athabascan, Tlingit, and Haida. The information for Census 2000 is based on the American Indian Tribal Classification List for the 1990 census, which was expanded to list the individual Alaska Native Villages when provided as a written response for race.

Asian: A person having origins in any of the original peoples of the Far East, Southeast Asia, or the Indian subcontinent including, for example, Cambodia, China, India, Japan, Korea, Malaysia, Pakistan, the Philippine Islands, Thailand, and Vietnam. It includes "Asian Indian," "Chinese," "Filipino," "Korean," "Japanese," "Vietnamese," and "Other Asian."

Asian Indian - Includes people who indicated their race as "Asian Indian" or identified themselves as Bengalese, Bharat, Dravidian, East Indian, or Goanese.

Chinese - Includes people who indicate their race as "Chinese" or who identify themselves as Cantonese, or Chinese American.

Filipino - Includes people who indicate their race as "Filipino" or who report entries such as Philipino, Philipine, or Filipino American.

Japanese - Includes people who indicate their race as "Japanese" or who report entries such as Nipponese or Japanese American.

Korean - Includes people who indicate their race as "Korean" or who provide a response of Korean American.

Vietnamese - Includes people who indicate their race as "Vietnamese" or who provide a response of Vietnamese American.

Cambodian - Includes people who provide a response such as Cambodian or Cambodia.

Hmong - Includes people who provide a response such as Hmong, Laohmong, or Mong.

Laotian - Includes people who provide a response such as Laotian, Laos, or Lao.

Thai - Includes people who provide a response such as Thai, Thailand, or Siamese.

Other Asian - Includes people who provide a response of Bangladeshi; Bhutanese; Burmese; Indochinese; Indonesian; Iwo Jiman; Madagascar; Malaysian; Maldivian; Nepalese; Okinawan; Pakistani; Singaporean; Sri Lankan; or Other Asian, specified and Other Asian, not specified.

Native Hawaiian or Other Pacific Islander: A person having origins in any of the original peoples of Hawaii, Guam, Samoa, or other Pacific Islands. It includes people who indicate their race as "Native Hawaiian," "Guamanian or Chamorro," "Samoan," and "Other Pacific Islander."

Native Hawaiian - Includes people who indicate their race as "Native Hawaiian" or who identify themselves as "Part Hawaiian" or "Hawaiian."

Guamanian or Chamorro - Includes people who indicate their race as such, including written entries of Chamorro or Guam.

Samoan - Includes people who indicate their race as "Samoan" or who identify themselves as American Samoan or Western Samoan.

Other Pacific Islander - Includes people who provide a write-in response of a Pacific Islander group, such as Carolinian, Chuukese (Trukese), Fijian, Kosracan, Melanesian, Micronesian, Northern Mariana Islander, Palauan, Papua New Guinean, Pohnpeian, Polynesian, Solomon Islander, Tahitian, Tokelauan, Tongan, Yapese, or Pacific Islander, not specified.

White: A person having origins in any of the original peoples of Europe, the Middle East, or North Africa. It includes people who indicate their race as ''White'' or report entries such as Irish, German, Italian, Lebanese, Near Easterner, Arab, or Polish.

Ancestries Based on Hispanic Origin

Hispanic or Latino:
- Central American:
  - Costa Rican
  - Guatemalan
  - Honduran
  - Nicaraguan
  - Panamanian
  - Salvadoran
  - Other Central American
- Cuban
- Dominican Republic
- Mexican
- Puerto Rican
- South American:
  - Argentinean
  - Bolivian
  - Chilean
  - Colombian
  - Ecuadorian
  - Paraguayan
  - Peruvian
  - Uruguayan
  - Venezuelan
  - Other South American
- Other Hispanic/Latino

The data on the Hispanic or Latino population were derived from answers to a question that was asked of all people. The terms "Spanish," "Hispanic origin," and "Latino" are used interchangeably. Some respondents identify with all three terms while others may identify with only one of these three specific terms. Hispanics or Latinos who identify with the terms "Spanish," "Hispanic," or "Latino" are those who classify themselves in one of the specific Spanish, Hispanic, or Latino categories listed on the questionnaire ("Mexican," "Puerto Rican," or "Cuban") as well as those who indicate that they are "other Spanish/Hispanic/Latino." People who do not identify with one of the specific origins listed on the questionnaire but indicate that they are "other Spanish, Hispanic, or Latino" are those whose origins are from Spain, the Spanish-speaking countries of Central or South America, the Dominican Republic, or people identifying themselves generally as Spanish, Spanish-American, Hispanic, Hispano, Latino, and so on. All write-in responses to the "other Spanish/Hispanic/Latino" category were coded.

Origin can be viewed as the heritage, nationality group, lineage, or country of birth of the person or the person's parents or ancestors before their arrival in the United States. People who identify their origin as Spanish, Hispanic, or Latino may be of any race.

In all cases where the origin of households, families, or occupied housing units is classified as Spanish, Hispanic, or Latino, the origin of the householder is used. If an individual could not provide a Hispanic origin response, their origin was assigned using specific rules of precedence of household relationship. For example, if origin was missing for a natural-born daughter in the household, then either the origin of the householder, another natural-born child, or spouse of the householder was assigned. If Hispanic origin was not reported for anyone in the household, the Hispanic origin of a householder in a previously processed household with the same race was assigned.

Other Ancestries

- Acadian/Cajun
- Afghan
- African, Subsaharan:
  - African
  - Cape Verdean
  - Ethiopian
  - Ghanian
  - Kenyan
  - Liberian
  - Nigerian
  - Senegalese
  - Sierra Leonean
  - Somalian
  - South African
  - Sudanese
  - Ugandan
  - Zairian
  - Zimbabwean
  - Other Subsaharan African
- Albanian
- Alsatian
- Arab:
  - Arab/Arabic
  - Egyptian
  - Iraqi
  - Jordanian
  - Lebanese
  - Moroccan
  - Palestinian
  - Syrian
  - Other Arab
- Armenian
- Assyrian/Chaldean/Syriac
- Australian
- Austrian
- Basque
- Belgian
- Brazilian
- British
- Bulgarian
- Canadian
- Carpatho Rusyn
- Celtic
- Croatian
- Cypriot
- Czech
- Czechoslovakian
- Danish
- Dutch
- Eastern European
- English
- Estonian
- European
- Finnish
- French, except Basque
- French Canadian
- German
- German Russian
- Greek
- Guyanese
- Hungarian
- Icelander
- Iranian
- Irish
- Israeli
- Italian
- Latvian
- Lithuanian
- Luxemburger
- Macedonian
- Maltese
- New Zealander
- Northern European
- Norwegian
- Pennsylvania German
- Polish
- Portuguese
- Romanian
- Russian
- Scandinavian
- Scotch-Irish
- Scottish
- Serbian
- Slavic
- Slovak
- Slovene
- Soviet Union
- Swedish
- Swiss
- Turkish
- Ukrainian
- United States or American
- Welsh
- West Indian, excluding Hispanic:
  - Bahamian
  - Barbadian
  - Belizean
  - Bermudan
  - British West Indian
  - Dutch West Indian
  - Haitian
  - Jamaican
  - Trinidadian and Tobagonian
  - U.S. Virgin Islander
  - West Indian
  - Other West Indian
- Yugoslavian

The data on ancestry were derived from answers to long-form questionnaire Item 10, which was asked of a sample of the population. The data represent self-classification by people according to the ancestry group or groups with which they most closely identify. Ancestry refers to a person's ethnic origin or descent, "roots," heritage, or the place of birth of the person, the person's parents, or their ancestors before their arrival in the United States. Some ethnic identities, such as Egyptian or Polish, can be traced to geographic areas outside the United States, while other ethnicities, such as Pennsylvania German or Cajun, evolved in the United States.

The intent of the ancestry question was not to measure the degree of attachment the respondent had to a particular ethnicity. For example, a response of "Irish" might reflect total involvement in an Irish community or only a memory of ancestors several generations removed from the individual. Also, the question was intended to provide data for groups that were not included in the Hispanic origin and race questions. Official Hispanic origin data come from long-form questionnaire Item 5, and official race data come from long-form questionnaire Item 6. Therefore, although data on all groups are collected, the ancestry data shown in these tabulations are for non-Hispanic and non-race groups.

The ancestry question allowed respondents to report one or more ancestry groups, although only the first two were coded. If a response was in terms of a dual ancestry, for example, "Irish English," the person was assigned two codes, in this case one for Irish and another for English. However, in certain cases, multiple responses such as "French Canadian," "Greek Cypriote," and "Scotch Irish" were assigned a single code reflecting their status as unique groups. If a person reported one of these unique groups in addition to another group, for example, "Scotch Irish English," resulting in three terms, that person received one code for the unique group (Scotch-Irish) and another one for the remaining group (English). If a person reported "English Irish French," only English and Irish were coded. Certain combinations of ancestries where the ancestry group is a part of another, such as "German-Bavarian," were coded as a single ancestry using the more specific group (Bavarian). Also, responses such as "Polish-American" or "Italian-American" were coded and tabulated as a single entry (Polish or Italian).

The Census Bureau accepted "American" as a unique ethnicity if it was given alone, with an ambiguous response, or with state names. If the respondent listed any other ethnic identity such as "Italian-American," generally the "American" portion of the response was not coded. However, distinct groups such as "American Indian," "Mexican American," and "African American" were coded and identified separately because they represented groups who considered themselves different from those who reported as "Indian," "Mexican," or "African," respectively.

Census 2000 tabulations on ancestry are presented using two types of data presentations — one using total people as the base, and the other using total responses as the base. This book uses total responses as the base and includes the total number of ancestries reported and coded. If a person reported a multiple ancestry such as "French Danish," that response was counted twice in the tabulations — once in the French category and again in the Danish category. Thus, the sum of the counts in this type of presentation is not the total population but the total of all responses.

An automated coding system was used for coding ancestry in Census 2000. This greatly reduced the potential for error associated with a clerical review. Specialists with knowledge of the subject matter reviewed, edited, coded, and resolved inconsistent or incomplete responses. The code list used in Census 2000, containing over 1,000 categories, reflects the results of the Census Bureau's experience with the 1990 ancestry question, research, and consultation with many ethnic experts. Many decisions were made to determine the classification of responses. These decisions affected the grouping of the tabulated data. For example, the Italian category includes the responses of Sicilian and Tuscan, as well as a number of other responses.

Although some people consider religious affiliation a component of ethnic identity, the ancestry question was not designed to collect any information concerning religion. Thus, if a religion was given as an answer to the ancestry question, it was listed in the "Other groups" category which is not shown in this book.

Ancestry should not be confused with a person's place of birth, although a person's place of birth and ancestry may be the same.

Section I

In this book, each Section I table shows the name of the place, the county (if a place spans more than one county, the county that holds the majority of the population is shown), and the 2000 population (based on 100-percent data from Summary File 1). Column one displays the ancestry name, column two displays the number of people reporting each ancestry, and column three is the percent of the total population reporting each ancestry. The population figure shown is used to calculate the value in the "%" column for ancestries based on race and Hispanic origin. The sample population figure from Summary File 3 (not shown) is used to calculate the value in the "%" column for all other ancestries.

For ancestries based on race data (White and African American/Black), the value in the "Number" column represents the total number of people who reported each category alone or in combination with one or more other race categories. This number represents the maximum number of people reporting and therefore the individual race categories may add to more than the total population because people may be included in more than one category. Tables P8 and P10 from SF1 were used for these categories.

For ancestries based on race data (American Indian or Alaska Native), the value in the "Number" column represents the total number of people who reported American Indian or Alaska Native alone or in combination with one or more other races, and with one or more tribes reported. This number represents the maximum number of people reporting and therefore the individual ancestries may add to more than the total population because people may be included in more than one category. Tables PCT1 and PCT3 from SF1 were used for these ancestries.

For ancestries based on race data (Asian), the value in the "Number" column represents the total number of people who reported Asian alone or in combination with one or more other races, and with one or more Asian categories. This number represents the maximum number of people reporting and therefore the individual ancestries may add to more than the total population because people may be included in more than one category. Tables PCT5 and PCT7 from SF1 were used for these ancestries.

For ancestries based on race data (Native Hawaiian and Other Pacific Islander), the value in the "Number" column represents the total number of people who reported Native Hawaiian and Other Pacific Islander alone or in combination with one or more other races, and with one or more Native Hawaiian and Other Pacific Islander categories. This number represents the maximum number of people reporting and therefore the individual ancestries may add to more than the total population because people may be included in more than one category. Tables PCT8 and PCT10 from SF1 were used for these ancestries.

The figures in parentheses (only available for ancestries based on race data) show the number of people that reported that particular ancestry alone. For example, in Phoenix, the entry for Korean shows 1,877 in parentheses and 2,462 in the "Number" column. This means that 1,877 people reported being Korean alone and 2,462 people reported being Korean alone or in combination with one or more other races.

For ancestries based on Hispanic Origin, the value in the "Number" column represents the number of people who reported being Mexican, Puerto Rican, Cuban or other Spanish/Hispanic/Latino (all written-in responses were coded). Table PCT11 from SF1 was used for these categories.

For ancestries in the "other" ancestries group, the value in the "Number" column includes multiple ancestries reported. For example, if a person reported a multiple ancestry such as "French Danish," that response was counted twice in the tabulations, once in the French category and again in the Danish category. Thus, the sum of the counts is not the total population but the total of all responses. Table PCT18 from SF3 was used for these categories.

Section II

In Section II of this book, each ancestry has three tables. The first table shows the top 150 places sorted by number (based on all places, regardless of population), the second table shows the top 150 places sorted by percent (based on all places, regardless of population), the third table shows the top 150 places sorted by percent (based on places with populations of 10,000 or more).

Within each table, column one displays the place name, the state, and the county (if a place spans more than one county, the county that holds the majority of the population is shown). Column two displays the number of people reporting each ancestry, and column three is the percent of the total population reporting each ancestry. For tables representing ancestries based on race or Hispanic origin, the 100-percent population figure from SF1 is used to calculate the value in the "%" column. For all other ancestries the sample population figure from SF3 is used to calculate the value in the "%" column.

SECTION ONE:
City-by-City Listings

Alabaster

Place Type: City
County: Shelby
Population: 22,619

Ancestry/Race	Number	%
Acadian/Cajun	8	0.03
African American/Black:	2,287	10.11
Not Hispanic (2,244)	2,280	10.08
Hispanic (6)	7	0.03
African, sub-Saharan:	339	1.46
African	318	1.37
Nigerian	12	0.05
South African	9	0.04
Alaska Native tribes, specified:	1	0.00
Aleut (1)	1	0.00
Am. Ind. or Alaska Nat., not spec.	48	0.21
American Indian tribes, specified:	89	0.39
Apache (1)	2	0.01
Blackfeet (1)	3	0.01
Cherokee (15)	40	0.18
Chickasaw (1)	2	0.01
Chippewa (6)	8	0.04
Choctaw (1)	2	0.01
Creek (10)	14	0.06
Delaware (1)	1	0.00
Houma	1	0.00
Iroquois (1)	1	0.00
Latin American Indians	2	0.01
Navajo (4)	4	0.02
Pueblo	2	0.01
Sioux (1)	3	0.01
All other tribes (1)	4	0.02
American Indian tribes, not spec.	5	0.02
Arab:	37	0.16
Lebanese	37	0.16
Asian:	187	0.83
Bangladeshi (3)	3	0.01
Chinese, ex. Taiwanese (25)	29	0.13
Filipino (21)	23	0.10
Indian (32)	35	0.15
Indonesian (1)	2	0.01
Japanese (8)	23	0.10
Korean (17)	22	0.10
Pakistani (6)	6	0.03
Taiwanese (1)	1	0.00
Thai (5)	8	0.04
Vietnamese (22)	23	0.10
Other Asian, not specified (3)	12	0.05
Austrian	73	0.31
Basque	5	0.02
British	129	0.56
Canadian	23	0.10
Czech	37	0.16
Czechoslovakian	6	0.03
Danish	57	0.25
Dutch	318	1.37
English	3,015	12.99
European	261	1.12
Finnish	18	0.08
French, except Basque	439	1.89
French Canadian	21	0.09
German	2,418	10.42
Greek	24	0.10
Hawaii Native/Pacific Islander:	7	0.03
Polynesian: (2)	4	0.02
Native Hawaiian (2)	4	0.02
Other Pac. Isl., not spec. (2)	3	0.01
Hispanic or Latino:	348	1.54
Central American:	8	0.04
Costa Rican	1	0.00
Panamanian	4	0.02
Salvadoran	1	0.00
Other Central American	2	0.01
Cuban	20	0.09
Dominican Republic	3	0.01
Mexican	212	0.94
Puerto Rican	23	0.10
South American:	33	0.15
Argentinean	4	0.02
Bolivian	1	0.00
Chilean	3	0.01
Colombian	11	0.05
Ecuadorian	8	0.04
Venezuelan	6	0.03
Other Hispanic or Latino	49	0.22
Hungarian	9	0.04
Icelander	11	0.05
Iranian	9	0.04
Irish	2,402	10.35
Italian	628	2.71
Lithuanian	23	0.10
Luxemburger	6	0.03
Northern European	15	0.06
Norwegian	195	0.84
Pennsylvania German	8	0.03
Polish	213	0.92
Portuguese	18	0.08
Romanian	9	0.04
Russian	13	0.06
Scandinavian	19	0.08
Scotch-Irish	510	2.20
Scottish	743	3.20
Serbian	7	0.03
Slavic	9	0.04
Slovak	45	0.19
Swedish	98	0.42
Swiss	58	0.25
Ukrainian	13	0.06
United States or American	3,843	16.56
Welsh	100	0.43
White:	19,983	88.35
Not Hispanic (19,654)	19,782	87.46
Hispanic (185)	201	0.89
Yugoslavian	12	0.05

Albertville

Place Type: City
County: Marshall
Population: 17,247

Ancestry/Race	Number	%
African American/Black:	406	2.35
Not Hispanic (344)	370	2.15
Hispanic (9)	36	0.21
African, sub-Saharan:	17	0.10
African	17	0.10
Am. Ind. or Alaska Nat., not spec.	48	0.28
American Indian tribes, specified:	84	0.49
Apache (1)	1	0.01
Cherokee (26)	56	0.32
Chippewa (3)	3	0.02
Choctaw (1)	1	0.01
Creek (1)	1	0.01
Iroquois (1)	1	0.01
Latin American Indians (6)	20	0.12
All other tribes (1)	1	0.01
American Indian tribes, not spec.	11	0.06
Asian:	65	0.38
Chinese, ex. Taiwanese (15)	16	0.09
Filipino (11)	13	0.08
Indian (1)	4	0.02
Japanese (2)	2	0.01
Korean (3)	5	0.03
Thai (2)	2	0.01
Vietnamese (8)	10	0.06
Other Asian, specified	1	0.01
Other Asian, not specified (3)	12	0.07
British	89	0.51
Canadian	9	0.05
Czech	22	0.13
Czechoslovakian	7	0.04
Dutch	184	1.06
English	1,655	9.53
European	149	0.86
French, except Basque	164	0.94
French Canadian	7	0.04
German	869	5.00
Greek	24	0.14
Hawaii Native/Pacific Islander:	45	0.26
Micronesian: (12)	28	0.16
Guamanian/Chamorro (12)	28	0.16
Polynesian:	8	0.05
Native Hawaiian	8	0.05
Other Pac. Isl., not spec. (5)	9	0.05
Hispanic or Latino:	2,773	16.08
Central American:	323	1.87
Guatemalan	306	1.77
Honduran	9	0.05
Salvadoran	5	0.03
Other Central American	3	0.02
Cuban	9	0.05
Dominican Republic	2	0.01
Mexican	2,222	12.88
Puerto Rican	44	0.26
South American:	4	0.02
Peruvian	1	0.01
Venezuelan	3	0.02
Other Hispanic or Latino	169	0.98
Hungarian	21	0.12
Irish	1,523	8.77
Italian	212	1.22
Polish	47	0.27
Portuguese	9	0.05
Scotch-Irish	260	1.50
Scottish	285	1.64
Slovak	19	0.11
Swedish	39	0.22
Swiss	11	0.06
United States or American	3,939	22.67
Welsh	53	0.31
West Indian, excl. Hispanic:	24	0.14
Haitian	24	0.14
White:	15,046	87.24
Not Hispanic (13,923)	14,020	81.29
Hispanic (936)	1,026	5.95

Alexander City

Place Type: City
County: Tallapoosa
Population: 15,008

Ancestry/Race	Number	%
African American/Black:	4,285	28.55
Not Hispanic (4,251)	4,276	28.49
Hispanic (7)	9	0.06
African, sub-Saharan:	68	0.45
African	68	0.45
Am. Ind. or Alaska Nat., not spec.	13	0.09
American Indian tribes, specified:	26	0.17
Apache	1	0.01
Cherokee (6)	14	0.09
Creek (2)	6	0.04
Seminole	1	0.01
Sioux	2	0.01
All other tribes (2)	2	0.01
American Indian tribes, not spec.	2	0.01
Asian:	63	0.42
Chinese, ex. Taiwanese (8)	8	0.05
Filipino (2)	2	0.01
Indian (12)	18	0.12
Japanese	2	0.01
Korean (5)	5	0.03
Laotian	2	0.01
Taiwanese	3	0.02
Thai (3)	4	0.03
Vietnamese (11)	11	0.07
Other Asian, specified	1	0.01
Other Asian, not specified (1)	7	0.05
British	24	0.16
Canadian	22	0.15
Czech	22	0.15
Czechoslovakian	6	0.04
Danish	7	0.05
Dutch	122	0.82
English	1,297	8.67
European	63	0.42

Notes: 1. Figures in the "Number" column do not add up to the total population due to: a) Ancestry/Race overlap — e.g. persons can report being both White and Irish, b) persons of Hispanic origin can report being any race, c) persons reporting two ancestries are counted in both categories. 2. Numbers in parentheses indicate the number of persons reporting this ancestry/race alone, not in combination with any other ancestry/race. 3. Refer to the Explanation of Data in the front of the book for more detailed information.

Ancestry/Race	Number	%
French, except Basque	149	1.00
German	591	3.95
Greek	14	0.09
Hawaii Native/Pacific Islander:	15	0.10
Polynesian: (2)	5	0.03
Samoan (2)	5	0.03
Other Pac. Isl., specified	1	0.01
Other Pac. Isl., not spec. (1)	9	0.06
Hispanic or Latino:	67	0.45
Central American:	1	0.01
Panamanian	1	0.01
Mexican	32	0.21
Puerto Rican	5	0.03
South American:	1	0.01
Bolivian	1	0.01
Other Hispanic or Latino	28	0.19
Irish	897	6.00
Italian	57	0.38
Polish	10	0.07
Russian	35	0.23
Scotch-Irish	250	1.67
Scottish	314	2.10
Swedish	27	0.18
United States or American	2,590	17.32
Welsh	39	0.26
White:	10,637	70.88
Not Hispanic (10,553)	10,599	70.62
Hispanic (36)	38	0.25

Anniston

Place Type: City
County: Calhoun
Population: 24,276

Ancestry/Race	Number	%
African American/Black:	11,931	49.15
Not Hispanic (11,770)	11,876	48.92
Hispanic (51)	55	0.23
African, sub-Saharan:	300	1.24
African	295	1.22
Nigerian	5	0.02
Alaska Native tribes, specified:	1	0.00
Tlingit-Haida	1	0.00
Am. Ind. or Alaska Nat., not spec.	61	0.25
American Indian tribes, specified:	85	0.35
Apache (2)	3	0.01
Cherokee (24)	52	0.21
Chickasaw (1)	1	0.00
Chippewa (2)	2	0.01
Comanche	6	0.02
Creek (2)	12	0.05
Iroquois (1)	1	0.00
Navajo	1	0.00
Pueblo	1	0.00
Sioux (1)	3	0.01
All other tribes (2)	3	0.01
American Indian tribes, not spec.	6	0.02
Arab:	6	0.02
Lebanese	6	0.02
Asian:	248	1.02
Cambodian (5)	5	0.02
Chinese, ex. Taiwanese (29)	31	0.13
Filipino (24)	31	0.13
Indian (47)	54	0.22
Japanese (7)	18	0.07
Korean (51)	62	0.26
Malaysian	1	0.00
Pakistani (8)	9	0.04
Thai (4)	8	0.03
Vietnamese (8)	11	0.05
Other Asian, not specified (4)	18	0.07
Austrian	18	0.07
Belgian	43	0.18
British	65	0.27
Canadian	30	0.12
Czech	38	0.16
Czechoslovakian	7	0.03
Danish	12	0.05
Dutch	143	0.59
English	1,790	7.39
European	95	0.39
Finnish	43	0.18
French, except Basque	273	1.13
French Canadian	17	0.07
German	1,050	4.33
Greek	21	0.09
Hawaii Native/Pacific Islander:	28	0.12
Micronesian: (2)	2	0.01
Guamanian/Chamorro (2)	2	0.01
Polynesian: (10)	15	0.06
Native Hawaiian (1)	3	0.01
Samoan (9)	12	0.05
Other Pac. Isl., not spec. (6)	11	0.05
Hispanic or Latino:	409	1.68
Central American:	30	0.12
Honduran	6	0.02
Nicaraguan	1	0.00
Panamanian	21	0.09
Salvadoran	2	0.01
Cuban	19	0.08
Dominican Republic	2	0.01
Mexican	216	0.89
Puerto Rican	68	0.28
South American:	10	0.04
Colombian	6	0.02
Peruvian	1	0.00
Venezuelan	3	0.01
Other Hispanic or Latino	64	0.26
Hungarian	14	0.06
Irish	1,433	5.91
Italian	294	1.21
Lithuanian	5	0.02
Norwegian	65	0.27
Polish	114	0.47
Russian	31	0.13
Scandinavian	9	0.04
Scotch-Irish	366	1.51
Scottish	238	0.98
Slavic	5	0.02
Swedish	74	0.31
Swiss	43	0.18
United States or American	2,532	10.45
Welsh	44	0.18
West Indian, excl. Hispanic:	8	0.03
Jamaican	8	0.03
White:	11,971	49.31
Not Hispanic (11,630)	11,767	48.47
Hispanic (195)	204	0.84

Athens

Place Type: City
County: Limestone
Population: 18,967

Ancestry/Race	Number	%
African American/Black:	3,526	18.59
Not Hispanic (3,436)	3,498	18.44
Hispanic (28)	28	0.15
African, sub-Saharan:	312	1.63
African	312	1.63
Alaska Native tribes, specified:	1	0.01
Eskimo (1)	1	0.01
Am. Ind. or Alaska Nat., not spec.	40	0.21
American Indian tribes, specified:	97	0.51
Apache (3)	3	0.02
Cherokee (44)	76	0.40
Choctaw	2	0.01
Creek (5)	6	0.03
Delaware	1	0.01
Latin American Indians (3)	7	0.04
Sioux	2	0.01
American Indian tribes, not spec.	7	0.04
Arab:	7	0.04
Arab/Arabic	7	0.04
Asian:	164	0.86
Chinese, ex. Taiwanese (4)	5	0.03
Filipino (16)	20	0.11
Indian (45)	55	0.29
Japanese (24)	30	0.16
Korean (11)	12	0.06
Thai (6)	6	0.03
Vietnamese (23)	24	0.13
Other Asian, not specified (4)	12	0.06
Belgian	6	0.03
British	61	0.32
Canadian	8	0.04
Czech	6	0.03
Dutch	156	0.82
English	1,734	9.09
European	120	0.63
French, except Basque	184	0.96
French Canadian	13	0.07
German	1,200	6.29
Greek	15	0.08
Hawaii Native/Pacific Islander:	6	0.03
Micronesian: (1)	3	0.02
Guamanian/Chamorro (1)	3	0.02
Polynesian: (1)	2	0.01
Native Hawaiian (1)	2	0.01
Other Pac. Isl., not spec. (1)	1	0.01
Hispanic or Latino:	922	4.86
Central American:	77	0.41
Costa Rican	1	0.01
Guatemalan	69	0.36
Honduran	2	0.01
Panamanian	3	0.02
Salvadoran	2	0.01
Cuban	7	0.04
Dominican Republic	2	0.01
Mexican	736	3.88
Puerto Rican	18	0.09
South American:	6	0.03
Chilean	1	0.01
Colombian	1	0.01
Ecuadorian	1	0.01
Paraguayan	1	0.01
Peruvian	2	0.01
Other Hispanic or Latino	76	0.40
Irish	1,664	8.72
Italian	154	0.81
Latvian	11	0.06
Lithuanian	9	0.05
Norwegian	68	0.36
Polish	46	0.24
Russian	15	0.08
Scotch-Irish	396	2.08
Scottish	263	1.38
Swedish	62	0.32
Swiss	8	0.04
Ukrainian	11	0.06
United States or American	3,548	18.59
Welsh	34	0.18
West Indian, excl. Hispanic:	6	0.03
Other West Indian	6	0.03
White:	14,900	78.56
Not Hispanic (14,245)	14,379	75.81
Hispanic (496)	521	2.75

Auburn

Place Type: City
County: Lee
Population: 42,987

Ancestry/Race	Number	%
Acadian/Cajun	48	0.11
African American/Black:	7,332	17.06
Not Hispanic (7,183)	7,288	16.95
Hispanic (34)	44	0.10
African, sub-Saharan:	485	1.13
African	383	0.89
Ethiopian	6	0.01
Kenyan	7	0.02
Nigerian	58	0.14
South African	6	0.01
Other sub-Saharan African	25	0.06
Am. Ind. or Alaska Nat., not spec.	74	0.17
American Indian tribes, specified:	149	0.35

Notes: 1. Figures in the "Number" column do not add up to the total population due to: a) Ancestry/Race overlap — e.g. persons can report being both White and Irish, b) persons of Hispanic origin can report being any race, c) persons reporting two ancestries are counted in both categories. 2. Numbers in parentheses indicate the number of persons reporting this ancestry/race alone, not in combination with any other ancestry/race. 3. Refer to the Explanation of Data in the front of the book for more detailed information.

Ancestry/Race	Number	%
Apache	2	0.00
Blackfeet	3	0.01
Cherokee (24)	80	0.19
Cheyenne (1)	1	0.00
Chickasaw	3	0.01
Chippewa (1)	1	0.00
Choctaw (5)	16	0.04
Creek (10)	18	0.04
Delaware (1)	1	0.00
Iroquois (1)	3	0.01
Latin American Indians (2)	7	0.02
Navajo	2	0.00
Potawatomi (2)	2	0.00
Seminole	2	0.00
Sioux (1)	1	0.00
All other tribes (7)	7	0.02
American Indian tribes, not spec.	20	0.05
Arab:	217	0.51
Arab/Arabic	33	0.08
Egyptian	8	0.02
Lebanese	111	0.26
Moroccan	10	0.02
Syrian	14	0.03
Other Arab	41	0.10
Armenian	28	0.07
Asian:	1,607	3.74
Bangladeshi (8)	8	0.02
Cambodian (6)	6	0.01
Chinese, ex. Taiwanese (561)	602	1.40
Filipino (44)	67	0.16
Indian (348)	364	0.85
Indonesian (5)	8	0.02
Japanese (48)	78	0.18
Korean (192)	219	0.51
Laotian (9)	10	0.02
Malaysian (2)	12	0.03
Pakistani (15)	15	0.03
Sri Lankan (4)	5	0.01
Taiwanese (29)	37	0.09
Thai (19)	26	0.06
Vietnamese (76)	89	0.21
Other Asian, specified (6)	13	0.03
Other Asian, not specified (22)	48	0.11
Austrian	67	0.16
Belgian	12	0.03
British	476	1.11
Canadian	43	0.10
Croatian	6	0.01
Czech	34	0.08
Czechoslovakian	71	0.17
Danish	72	0.17
Dutch	462	1.08
Eastern European	24	0.06
English	5,215	12.16
Estonian	11	0.03
European	930	2.17
Finnish	22	0.05
French, except Basque	1,288	3.00
French Canadian	176	0.41
German	4,512	10.52
Greek	226	0.53
Guyanese	14	0.03
Hawaii Native/Pacific Islander:	39	0.09
Micronesian: (5)	9	0.02
Guamanian/Chamorro (5)	9	0.02
Polynesian: (10)	12	0.03
Native Hawaiian (5)	6	0.01
Samoan (5)	6	0.01
Other Pac. Isl., specified	2	0.00
Other Pac. Isl., not spec. (2)	16	0.04
Hispanic or Latino:	666	1.55
Central American:	34	0.08
Costa Rican	1	0.00
Guatemalan	11	0.03
Honduran	8	0.02
Nicaraguan	2	0.00
Panamanian	6	0.01
Salvadoran	5	0.01
Other Central American	1	0.00
Cuban	43	0.10
Dominican Republic	6	0.01
Mexican	305	0.71
Puerto Rican	88	0.20
South American:	53	0.12
Argentinean	4	0.01
Bolivian	1	0.00
Chilean	8	0.02
Colombian	17	0.04
Ecuadorian	6	0.01
Paraguayan	1	0.00
Peruvian	6	0.01
Venezuelan	7	0.02
Other South American	3	0.01
Other Hispanic or Latino	137	0.32
Hungarian	131	0.31
Icelander	6	0.01
Iranian	18	0.04
Irish	4,602	10.73
Italian	1,217	2.84
Latvian	11	0.03
Lithuanian	66	0.15
Luxemburger	13	0.03
Macedonian	6	0.01
Northern European	27	0.06
Norwegian	213	0.50
Pennsylvania German	6	0.01
Polish	531	1.24
Portuguese	23	0.05
Romanian	10	0.02
Russian	129	0.30
Scandinavian	52	0.12
Scotch-Irish	1,651	3.85
Scottish	1,603	3.74
Serbian	26	0.06
Slovak	38	0.09
Swedish	322	0.75
Swiss	115	0.27
Turkish	42	0.10
Ukrainian	31	0.07
United States or American	3,336	7.78
Welsh	239	0.56
West Indian, excl. Hispanic:	141	0.33
Bahamian	6	0.01
British West Indian	8	0.02
Haitian	42	0.10
Jamaican	70	0.16
West Indian	15	0.03
White:	33,943	78.96
Not Hispanic (33,188)	33,548	78.04
Hispanic (365)	395	0.92

Bessemer

Place Type: City
County: Jefferson
Population: 29,672

Ancestry/Race	Number	%
African American/Black:	20,758	69.96
Not Hispanic (20,549)	20,661	69.63
Hispanic (89)	97	0.33
African, sub-Saharan:	342	1.14
African	342	1.14
Am. Ind. or Alaska Nat., not spec.	78	0.26
American Indian tribes, specified:	83	0.28
Apache (1)	1	0.00
Blackfeet	1	0.00
Cherokee (35)	60	0.20
Choctaw	1	0.00
Cree	1	0.00
Creek (3)	7	0.02
Latin American Indians (6)	6	0.02
Lumbee (2)	2	0.01
Navajo (1)	2	0.01
All other tribes	2	0.01
American Indian tribes, not spec.	7	0.02
Arab:	38	0.13
Lebanese	21	0.07
Moroccan	8	0.03
Palestinian	9	0.03
Armenian	8	0.03
Asian:	110	0.37
Chinese, ex. Taiwanese (8)	12	0.04
Filipino (4)	9	0.03
Indian (14)	22	0.07
Japanese (5)	11	0.04
Korean (4)	21	0.07
Pakistani (1)	1	0.00
Vietnamese (12)	17	0.06
Other Asian, specified	5	0.02
Other Asian, not specified (4)	12	0.04
Austrian	15	0.05
British	54	0.18
Canadian	31	0.10
Czech	14	0.05
Dutch	151	0.50
English	621	2.07
European	40	0.13
French, except Basque	176	0.59
French Canadian	21	0.07
German	509	1.70
Greek	25	0.08
Hawaii Native/Pacific Islander:	12	0.04
Micronesian: (1)	1	0.00
Guamanian/Chamorro (1)	1	0.00
Polynesian: (2)	4	0.01
Native Hawaiian (2)	4	0.01
Other Pac. Isl., specified	5	0.02
Other Pac. Isl., not spec. (2)	2	0.01
Hispanic or Latino:	338	1.14
Central American:	4	0.01
Panamanian	4	0.01
Cuban	2	0.01
Mexican	206	0.69
Puerto Rican	39	0.13
South American:	5	0.02
Colombian	1	0.00
Venezuelan	4	0.01
Other Hispanic or Latino	82	0.28
Hungarian	7	0.02
Irish	934	3.12
Italian	240	0.80
Norwegian	13	0.04
Pennsylvania German	5	0.02
Polish	27	0.09
Russian	4	0.01
Scandinavian	6	0.02
Scotch-Irish	205	0.68
Scottish	181	0.60
Swedish	13	0.04
Swiss	35	0.12
Turkish	6	0.02
United States or American	2,267	7.57
Welsh	29	0.10
West Indian, excl. Hispanic:	62	0.21
Bahamian	5	0.02
Bermudan	31	0.10
Jamaican	15	0.05
Other West Indian	11	0.04
White:	8,724	29.40
Not Hispanic (8,458)	8,577	28.91
Hispanic (126)	147	0.50

Birmingham

Place Type: City
County: Jefferson
Population: 242,820

Ancestry/Race	Number	%
African American/Black:	179,569	73.95
Not Hispanic (177,709)	178,822	73.64
Hispanic (663)	747	0.31
African, sub-Saharan:	3,519	1.45
African	3,288	1.35
Cape Verdean	8	0.00
Ghanian	6	0.00
Kenyan	52	0.02
Liberian	19	0.01
Nigerian	124	0.05

Notes: 1. Figures in the "Number" column do not add up to the total population due to: a) Ancestry/Race overlap — e.g. persons can report being both White and Irish, b) persons of Hispanic origin can report being any race, c) persons reporting two ancestries are counted in both categories. 2. Numbers in parentheses indicate the number of persons reporting this ancestry/race alone, not in combination with any other ancestry/race. 3. Refer to the Explanation of Data in the front of the book for more detailed information.

Sierra Leonean	15	0.01
Sudanese	7	0.00
Alaska Native tribes, specified:	9	0.00
Alaska Athabascan (1)	1	0.00
Aleut (3)	3	0.00
Eskimo (1)	3	0.00
Tlingit-Haida (1)	2	0.00
Am. Ind. or Alaska Nat., not spec.	507	0.21
Albanian	24	0.01
American Indian tribes, specified:	603	0.25
Apache (4)	11	0.00
Blackfeet (4)	24	0.01
Cherokee (107)	374	0.15
Cheyenne (1)	1	0.00
Chickasaw (2)	3	0.00
Chippewa (1)	3	0.00
Choctaw (4)	26	0.01
Comanche (1)	1	0.00
Creek (28)	80	0.03
Houma (2)	3	0.00
Iroquois	2	0.00
Latin American Indians (8)	20	0.01
Lumbee (2)	2	0.00
Navajo (2)	5	0.00
Pueblo	3	0.00
Seminole (3)	12	0.00
Sioux (3)	13	0.01
Yaqui (1)	1	0.00
All other tribes (10)	19	0.01
American Indian tribes, not spec.	58	0.02
Arab:	743	0.31
Arab/Arabic	45	0.02
Egyptian	34	0.01
Iraqi	12	0.00
Jordanian	10	0.00
Lebanese	498	0.20
Palestinian	106	0.04
Other Arab	38	0.02
Armenian	18	0.01
Asian:	2,397	0.99
Bangladeshi (22)	23	0.01
Cambodian (18)	18	0.01
Chinese, ex. Taiwanese (692)	742	0.31
Filipino (113)	165	0.07
Indian (463)	549	0.23
Indonesian (8)	9	0.00
Japanese (80)	125	0.05
Korean (138)	168	0.07
Laotian (4)	4	0.00
Malaysian (6)	15	0.01
Pakistani (37)	49	0.02
Sri Lankan (3)	6	0.00
Taiwanese (24)	27	0.01
Thai (38)	48	0.02
Vietnamese (213)	247	0.10
Other Asian, specified (6)	46	0.02
Other Asian, not specified (59)	156	0.06
Australian	9	0.00
Austrian	107	0.04
Belgian	32	0.01
British	618	0.25
Bulgarian	7	0.00
Canadian	106	0.04
Celtic	43	0.02
Czech	84	0.03
Czechoslovakian	37	0.02
Danish	99	0.04
Dutch	1,037	0.43
Eastern European	27	0.01
English	7,817	3.22
European	793	0.33
Finnish	31	0.01
French, except Basque	1,561	0.64
French Canadian	151	0.06
German	5,526	2.27
Greek	220	0.09
Hawaii Native/Pacific Islander:	216	0.09
Melanesian: (1)	1	0.00
Fijian (1)	1	0.00
Micronesian: (38)	44	0.02
Guamanian/Chamorro (38)	43	0.02
Other Micronesian	1	0.00
Polynesian: (33)	72	0.03
Native Hawaiian (23)	48	0.02
Samoan (10)	23	0.01
Other Polynesian	1	0.00
Other Pac. Isl., specified	38	0.02
Other Pac. Isl., not spec. (15)	61	0.03
Hispanic or Latino:	3,764	1.55
Central American:	124	0.05
Costa Rican	20	0.01
Guatemalan	16	0.01
Honduran	40	0.02
Nicaraguan	7	0.00
Panamanian	20	0.01
Salvadoran	16	0.01
Other Central American	5	0.00
Cuban	96	0.04
Dominican Republic	2	0.00
Mexican	2,471	1.02
Puerto Rican	250	0.10
South American:	82	0.03
Argentinean	7	0.00
Chilean	7	0.00
Colombian	29	0.01
Ecuadorian	4	0.00
Paraguayan	1	0.00
Peruvian	17	0.01
Venezuelan	9	0.00
Other South American	8	0.00
Other Hispanic or Latino	739	0.30
Hungarian	105	0.04
Iranian	27	0.01
Irish	6,860	2.82
Israeli	9	0.00
Italian	1,911	0.79
Latvian	8	0.00
Lithuanian	44	0.02
Macedonian	10	0.00
New Zealander	16	0.01
Northern European	83	0.03
Norwegian	268	0.11
Polish	636	0.26
Portuguese	45	0.02
Romanian	32	0.01
Russian	320	0.13
Scandinavian	84	0.03
Scotch-Irish	2,573	1.06
Scottish	1,948	0.80
Serbian	9	0.00
Slavic	22	0.01
Slovak	25	0.01
Slovene	16	0.01
Swedish	240	0.10
Swiss	84	0.03
Turkish	18	0.01
Ukrainian	30	0.01
United States or American	9,529	3.92
Welsh	574	0.24
West Indian, excl. Hispanic:	349	0.14
Bahamian	51	0.02
British West Indian	6	0.00
Haitian	24	0.01
Jamaican	200	0.08
Trinidadian and Tobagonian	15	0.01
U.S. Virgin Islander	31	0.01
West Indian	22	0.01
White:	59,732	24.60
Not Hispanic (57,096)	58,215	23.97
Hispanic (1,361)	1,517	0.62
Yugoslavian	41	0.02

Center Point

Place Type: Census Designated Place
County: Jefferson
Population: 22,784

Ancestry/Race	Number	%
Acadian/Cajun	4	0.02
African American/Black:	5,614	24.64
Not Hispanic (5,494)	5,584	24.51
Hispanic (27)	30	0.13
African, sub-Saharan:	214	0.94
African	152	0.67
Nigerian	62	0.27
Am. Ind. or Alaska Nat., not spec.	42	0.18
American Indian tribes, specified:	108	0.47
Cherokee (31)	84	0.37
Chickasaw (2)	2	0.01
Chippewa (1)	2	0.01
Choctaw (1)	1	0.00
Creek (4)	8	0.04
Latin American Indians	2	0.01
Navajo	1	0.00
Sioux (2)	7	0.03
All other tribes (1)	1	0.00
American Indian tribes, not spec.	5	0.02
Arab:	13	0.06
Lebanese	6	0.03
Syrian	7	0.03
Asian:	157	0.69
Chinese, ex. Taiwanese (42)	43	0.19
Filipino (21)	33	0.14
Indian (10)	16	0.07
Indonesian	1	0.00
Japanese (8)	11	0.05
Korean (11)	14	0.06
Malaysian (1)	1	0.00
Pakistani (1)	1	0.00
Taiwanese (1)	1	0.00
Thai	1	0.00
Vietnamese (27)	27	0.12
Other Asian, specified	1	0.00
Other Asian, not specified (4)	7	0.03
Austrian	27	0.12
Belgian	20	0.09
Brazilian	14	0.06
British	46	0.20
Canadian	14	0.06
Danish	15	0.07
Dutch	227	1.00
English	1,849	8.16
European	143	0.63
French, except Basque	488	2.15
French Canadian	102	0.45
German	1,663	7.34
Hawaii Native/Pacific Islander:	12	0.05
Micronesian:	3	0.01
Guamanian/Chamorro	3	0.01
Polynesian: (2)	3	0.01
Native Hawaiian (2)	3	0.01
Other Pac. Isl., not spec. (5)	6	0.03
Hispanic or Latino:	507	2.23
Central American:	38	0.17
Costa Rican	1	0.00
Guatemalan	2	0.01
Honduran	22	0.10
Nicaraguan	3	0.01
Panamanian	5	0.02
Salvadoran	5	0.02
Cuban	5	0.02
Dominican Republic	2	0.01
Mexican	315	1.38
Puerto Rican	46	0.20
South American:	14	0.06
Bolivian	1	0.00
Colombian	11	0.05
Peruvian	2	0.01
Other Hispanic or Latino	87	0.38
Hungarian	18	0.08
Iranian	32	0.14
Irish	2,043	9.02
Italian	376	1.66
Lithuanian	8	0.04
Norwegian	20	0.09
Polish	146	0.64
Portuguese	8	0.04
Russian	22	0.10
Scandinavian	17	0.08

Notes: 1. Figures in the "Number" column do not add up to the total population due to: a) Ancestry/Race overlap — e.g. persons can report being both White and Irish, b) persons of Hispanic origin can report being any race, c) persons reporting two ancestries are counted in both categories. 2. Numbers in parentheses indicate the number of persons reporting this ancestry/race alone, not in combination with any other ancestry/race. 3. Refer to the Explanation of Data in the front of the book for more detailed information.

Scotch-Irish	593	2.62
Scottish	360	1.59
Slovene	20	0.09
Swedish	40	0.18
Swiss	28	0.12
Ukrainian	6	0.03
United States or American	3,240	14.30
Welsh	74	0.33
White:	16,813	73.79
Not Hispanic (16,375)	16,558	72.67
Hispanic (235)	255	1.12

Cullman

Place Type: City
County: Cullman
Population: 13,995

Ancestry/Race	Number	%
African American/Black:	94	0.67
Not Hispanic (45)	80	0.57
Hispanic (5)	14	0.10
African, sub-Saharan:	16	0.11
African	16	0.11
Alaska Native tribes, specified:	1	0.01
Eskimo (1)	1	0.01
Am. Ind. or Alaska Nat., not spec.	37	0.26
American Indian tribes, specified:	85	0.61
Apache (1)	1	0.01
Blackfeet	8	0.06
Cherokee (20)	58	0.41
Chippewa (1)	1	0.01
Choctaw	1	0.01
Creek (5)	6	0.04
Iroquois	1	0.01
Latin American Indians (1)	7	0.05
All other tribes	2	0.01
American Indian tribes, not spec.	4	0.03
Arab:	27	0.19
Egyptian	21	0.15
Lebanese	6	0.04
Asian:	102	0.73
Cambodian (1)	2	0.01
Chinese, ex. Taiwanese (16)	18	0.13
Filipino (3)	7	0.05
Indian (7)	12	0.09
Japanese (4)	10	0.07
Korean (12)	21	0.15
Thai (1)	1	0.01
Vietnamese (17)	19	0.14
Other Asian, not specified (2)	12	0.09
Austrian	24	0.17
British	55	0.39
Canadian	7	0.05
Danish	7	0.05
Dutch	211	1.50
English	1,337	9.52
European	160	1.14
French, except Basque	202	1.44
French Canadian	32	0.23
German	1,962	13.96
Greek	15	0.11
Hawaii Native/Pacific Islander:	11	0.08
Polynesian: (1)	4	0.03
Native Hawaiian	3	0.02
Samoan (1)	1	0.01
Other Pac. Isl., not spec. (5)	7	0.05
Hispanic or Latino:	679	4.85
Central American:	10	0.07
Honduran	6	0.04
Nicaraguan	3	0.02
Panamanian	1	0.01
Cuban	5	0.04
Mexican	555	3.97
Puerto Rican	19	0.14
South American:	10	0.07
Colombian	8	0.06
Ecuadorian	1	0.01
Paraguayan	1	0.01
Other Hispanic or Latino	80	0.57
Hungarian	16	0.11
Irish	1,762	12.54
Italian	302	2.15
Lithuanian	3	0.02
Northern European	17	0.12
Norwegian	61	0.43
Pennsylvania German	12	0.09
Polish	43	0.31
Portuguese	13	0.09
Russian	19	0.14
Scotch-Irish	259	1.84
Scottish	185	1.32
Swedish	60	0.43
Ukrainian	29	0.21
United States or American	3,007	21.40
Welsh	32	0.23
White:	13,676	97.72
Not Hispanic (13,013)	13,158	94.02
Hispanic (483)	518	3.70

Daphne

Place Type: City
County: Baldwin
Population: 16,581

Ancestry/Race	Number	%
African American/Black:	2,093	12.62
Not Hispanic (2,039)	2,076	12.52
Hispanic (9)	17	0.10
African, sub-Saharan:	218	1.29
African	211	1.25
South African	7	0.04
Alaska Native tribes, not specified	1	0.01
Am. Ind. or Alaska Nat., not spec.	24	0.14
American Indian tribes, specified:	79	0.48
Apache (1)	1	0.01
Blackfeet (1)	4	0.02
Cherokee (7)	25	0.15
Chickasaw (1)	1	0.01
Chippewa (2)	2	0.01
Choctaw (7)	9	0.05
Cree	3	0.02
Creek (9)	14	0.08
Houma (1)	1	0.01
Iroquois	2	0.01
Latin American Indians (2)	2	0.01
Lumbee	1	0.01
Potawatomi	1	0.01
Pueblo (5)	5	0.03
Seminole	1	0.01
Sioux	1	0.01
All other tribes (2)	6	0.04
American Indian tribes, not spec.	8	0.05
Arab:	35	0.21
Egyptian	28	0.17
Palestinian	7	0.04
Armenian	8	0.05
Asian:	147	0.89
Chinese, ex. Taiwanese (31)	37	0.22
Filipino (14)	26	0.16
Indian (27)	36	0.22
Indonesian (2)	2	0.01
Japanese (6)	16	0.10
Korean (4)	4	0.02
Taiwanese (7)	7	0.04
Vietnamese (7)	8	0.05
Other Asian, specified	1	0.01
Other Asian, not specified (1)	10	0.06
Austrian	42	0.25
British	204	1.21
Canadian	125	0.74
Croatian	6	0.04
Czech	26	0.15
Czechoslovakian	6	0.04
Danish	98	0.58
Dutch	330	1.96
English	2,044	12.14
European	146	0.87
Finnish	31	0.18
French, except Basque	577	3.43
French Canadian	55	0.33
German	1,966	11.67
Greek	66	0.39
Hawaii Native/Pacific Islander:	5	0.03
Micronesian: (1)	3	0.02
Guamanian/Chamorro (1)	3	0.02
Polynesian:	1	0.01
Other Polynesian	1	0.01
Other Pac. Isl., not spec.	1	0.01
Hispanic or Latino:	254	1.53
Central American:	28	0.17
Costa Rican	3	0.02
Guatemalan	1	0.01
Honduran	7	0.04
Panamanian	8	0.05
Salvadoran	4	0.02
Other Central American	5	0.03
Cuban	39	0.24
Mexican	78	0.47
Puerto Rican	27	0.16
South American:	20	0.12
Bolivian	1	0.01
Colombian	6	0.04
Ecuadorian	2	0.01
Paraguayan	2	0.01
Peruvian	8	0.05
Venezuelan	1	0.01
Other Hispanic or Latino	62	0.37
Hungarian	40	0.24
Iranian	54	0.32
Irish	2,027	12.03
Italian	675	4.01
Lithuanian	9	0.05
Northern European	60	0.36
Norwegian	190	1.13
Polish	446	2.65
Russian	19	0.11
Scandinavian	62	0.37
Scotch-Irish	435	2.58
Scottish	580	3.44
Slovak	42	0.25
Swedish	209	1.24
Turkish	27	0.16
Ukrainian	38	0.23
United States or American	2,127	12.63
Welsh	75	0.45
White:	14,291	86.19
Not Hispanic (13,982)	14,108	85.09
Hispanic (166)	183	1.10
Yugoslavian	6	0.04

Decatur

Place Type: City
County: Morgan
Population: 53,929

Ancestry/Race	Number	%
Acadian/Cajun	3	0.01
African American/Black:	10,803	20.03
Not Hispanic (10,456)	10,694	19.83
Hispanic (92)	109	0.20
African, sub-Saharan:	299	0.55
African	299	0.55
Am. Ind. or Alaska Nat., not spec.	149	0.28
Albanian	22	0.04
American Indian tribes, specified:	449	0.83
Apache (2)	7	0.01
Blackfeet	3	0.01
Cherokee (187)	350	0.65
Chippewa (4)	11	0.02
Choctaw (2)	8	0.01
Comanche (1)	2	0.00
Creek (8)	22	0.04
Delaware (2)	2	0.00
Latin American Indians	6	0.01
Lumbee (7)	10	0.02
Navajo (9)	10	0.02
Osage	2	0.00

Notes: 1. Figures in the "Number" column do not add up to the total population due to: a) Ancestry/Race overlap — e.g. persons can report being both White and Irish, b) persons of Hispanic origin can report being any race, c) persons reporting two ancestries are counted in both categories. 2. Numbers in parentheses indicate the number of persons reporting this ancestry/race alone, not in combination with any other ancestry/race. 3. Refer to the Explanation of Data in the front of the book for more detailed information.

Ancestry/Race	Number	%
Ottawa (1)	1	0.00
Seminole	4	0.01
Shoshone	2	0.00
Sioux	2	0.00
All other tribes (2)	7	0.01
American Indian tribes, not spec.	34	0.06
Arab:	88	0.16
Lebanese	65	0.12
Palestinian	23	0.04
Asian:	497	0.92
Bangladeshi (1)	1	0.00
Cambodian (2)	2	0.00
Chinese, ex. Taiwanese (42)	47	0.09
Filipino (49)	67	0.12
Indian (113)	125	0.23
Indonesian (3)	3	0.01
Japanese (86)	101	0.19
Korean (20)	37	0.07
Laotian (4)	5	0.01
Pakistani (6)	6	0.01
Taiwanese (7)	8	0.01
Thai (6)	10	0.02
Vietnamese (18)	29	0.05
Other Asian, not specified (18)	56	0.10
Australian	6	0.01
Austrian	52	0.10
Belgian	28	0.05
Brazilian	28	0.05
British	160	0.30
Canadian	22	0.04
Celtic	23	0.04
Czech	33	0.06
Czechoslovakian	30	0.06
Danish	39	0.07
Dutch	508	0.94
English	5,357	9.93
European	447	0.83
Finnish	17	0.03
French, except Basque	960	1.78
French Canadian	96	0.18
German	4,633	8.59
Greek	66	0.12
Guyanese	12	0.02
Hawaii Native/Pacific Islander:	83	0.15
Micronesian: (56)	59	0.11
Guamanian/Chamorro (54)	55	0.10
Other Micronesian (2)	4	0.01
Polynesian: (10)	12	0.02
Native Hawaiian (2)	3	0.01
Samoan (7)	8	0.01
Other Polynesian (1)	1	0.00
Other Pac. Isl., not spec. (2)	12	0.02
Hispanic or Latino:	3,040	5.64
Central American:	198	0.37
Guatemalan	185	0.34
Honduran	5	0.01
Nicaraguan	1	0.00
Panamanian	3	0.01
Salvadoran	3	0.01
Other Central American	1	0.00
Cuban	43	0.08
Dominican Republic	3	0.01
Mexican	2,356	4.37
Puerto Rican	54	0.10
South American:	17	0.03
Chilean	1	0.00
Colombian	5	0.01
Ecuadorian	1	0.00
Paraguayan	4	0.01
Peruvian	2	0.00
Venezuelan	4	0.01
Other Hispanic or Latino	369	0.68
Hungarian	58	0.11
Icelander	12	0.02
Iranian	31	0.06
Irish	5,756	10.67
Italian	696	1.29
Lithuanian	62	0.11
Luxemburger	6	0.01
Macedonian	8	0.01
Norwegian	203	0.38
Polish	434	0.80
Portuguese	27	0.05
Romanian	19	0.04
Russian	71	0.13
Scandinavian	16	0.03
Scotch-Irish	1,518	2.81
Scottish	848	1.57
Slavic	27	0.05
Slovak	32	0.06
Swedish	164	0.30
Swiss	44	0.08
Ukrainian	14	0.03
United States or American	8,668	16.07
Welsh	302	0.56
West Indian, excl. Hispanic:	37	0.07
Dutch West Indian	14	0.03
Jamaican	13	0.02
Other West Indian	10	0.02
White:	41,320	76.62
Not Hispanic (39,128)	39,623	73.47
Hispanic (1,586)	1,697	3.15

Dothan

Place Type: City
County: Houston
Population: 57,737

Ancestry/Race	Number	%
Acadian/Cajun	4	0.01
African American/Black:	17,605	30.49
Not Hispanic (17,292)	17,497	30.30
Hispanic (93)	108	0.19
African, sub-Saharan:	478	0.83
African	463	0.80
Ethiopian	6	0.01
South African	9	0.02
Alaska Native tribes, specified:	2	0.00
Aleut	1	0.00
All other tribes (1)	1	0.00
Alaska Native tribes, not specified	1	0.00
Am. Ind. or Alaska Nat., not spec.	124	0.21
American Indian tribes, specified:	253	0.44
Apache (6)	12	0.02
Blackfeet	8	0.01
Cherokee (64)	130	0.23
Cheyenne	2	0.00
Chickasaw	1	0.00
Chippewa (1)	1	0.00
Choctaw (1)	6	0.01
Cree	1	0.00
Creek (17)	49	0.08
Houma (1)	1	0.00
Iroquois	2	0.00
Latin American Indians	2	0.00
Navajo	8	0.01
Seminole (3)	16	0.03
Sioux (4)	4	0.01
Yuman	2	0.00
All other tribes (4)	8	0.01
American Indian tribes, not spec.	11	0.02
Arab:	83	0.14
Jordanian	11	0.02
Lebanese	72	0.12
Armenian	10	0.02
Asian:	611	1.06
Bangladeshi (2)	2	0.00
Chinese, ex. Taiwanese (77)	95	0.16
Filipino (22)	40	0.07
Indian (75)	104	0.18
Indonesian (3)	7	0.01
Japanese (73)	87	0.15
Korean (40)	55	0.10
Laotian (5)	5	0.01
Pakistani (7)	7	0.01
Taiwanese (2)	3	0.01
Thai (3)	7	0.01
Vietnamese (148)	166	0.29
Other Asian, specified	3	0.01
Other Asian, not specified (17)	30	0.05
Australian	15	0.03
Austrian	53	0.09
British	352	0.61
Canadian	74	0.13
Croatian	53	0.09
Czech	86	0.15
Czechoslovakian	35	0.06
Danish	98	0.17
Dutch	459	0.80
English	4,581	7.95
Estonian	9	0.02
European	604	1.05
Finnish	17	0.03
French, except Basque	755	1.31
French Canadian	170	0.29
German	3,246	5.63
Greek	45	0.08
Hawaii Native/Pacific Islander:	42	0.07
Micronesian:	2	0.00
Guamanian/Chamorro	2	0.00
Polynesian: (10)	19	0.03
Native Hawaiian (8)	12	0.02
Samoan (2)	6	0.01
Other Polynesian	1	0.00
Other Pac. Isl., specified	3	0.01
Other Pac. Isl., not spec. (1)	18	0.03
Hispanic or Latino:	764	1.32
Central American:	47	0.08
Costa Rican	3	0.01
Guatemalan	3	0.01
Honduran	5	0.01
Nicaraguan	1	0.00
Panamanian	21	0.04
Salvadoran	6	0.01
Other Central American	8	0.01
Cuban	34	0.06
Dominican Republic	7	0.01
Mexican	345	0.60
Puerto Rican	110	0.19
South American:	46	0.08
Argentinean	5	0.01
Bolivian	4	0.01
Colombian	14	0.02
Ecuadorian	6	0.01
Peruvian	9	0.02
Venezuelan	7	0.01
Other South American	1	0.00
Other Hispanic or Latino	175	0.30
Hungarian	50	0.09
Irish	4,278	7.42
Italian	759	1.32
Lithuanian	15	0.03
Norwegian	168	0.29
Pennsylvania German	4	0.01
Polish	370	0.64
Portuguese	13	0.02
Romanian	20	0.03
Russian	44	0.08
Scandinavian	12	0.02
Scotch-Irish	1,305	2.26
Scottish	796	1.38
Slavic	9	0.02
Slovak	7	0.01
Swedish	224	0.39
Swiss	50	0.09
Turkish	21	0.04
United States or American	10,500	18.21
Welsh	174	0.30
West Indian, excl. Hispanic:	58	0.10
Jamaican	38	0.07
West Indian	14	0.02
Other West Indian	6	0.01
White:	39,302	68.07
Not Hispanic (38,508)	38,882	67.34
Hispanic (365)	420	0.73
Yugoslavian	3	0.01

Notes: 1. Figures in the "Number" column do not add up to the total population due to: a) Ancestry/Race overlap — e.g. persons can report being both White and Irish, b) persons of Hispanic origin can report being any race, c) persons reporting two ancestries are counted in both categories. 2. Numbers in parentheses indicate the number of persons reporting this ancestry/race alone, not in combination with any other ancestry/race. 3. Refer to the Explanation of Data in the front of the book for more detailed information.

Enterprise

Place Type: City
County: Coffee
Population: 21,178

Ancestry/Race	Number	%
African American/Black:	5,012	23.67
Not Hispanic (4,826)	4,954	23.39
Hispanic (35)	58	0.27
African, sub-Saharan:	68	0.32
African	68	0.32
Alaska Native tribes, specified:	3	0.01
Aleut	2	0.01
Tlingit-Haida (1)	1	0.00
Am. Ind. or Alaska Nat., not spec.	56	0.26
American Indian tribes, specified:	150	0.71
Apache	3	0.01
Blackfeet (1)	3	0.01
Cherokee (31)	59	0.28
Chickasaw (3)	3	0.01
Chippewa	1	0.00
Choctaw (4)	6	0.03
Comanche	1	0.00
Cree	1	0.00
Creek (21)	39	0.18
Iroquois (7)	9	0.04
Latin American Indians (2)	2	0.01
Lumbee (1)	2	0.01
Ottawa (1)	1	0.00
Pueblo	1	0.00
Puget Sound Salish (1)	1	0.00
Seminole (2)	6	0.03
Sioux (2)	2	0.01
All other tribes (3)	10	0.05
American Indian tribes, not spec.	14	0.07
Arab:	63	0.30
Egyptian	8	0.04
Lebanese	46	0.22
Other Arab	9	0.04
Asian:	482	2.28
Cambodian (1)	1	0.00
Chinese, ex. Taiwanese (19)	29	0.14
Filipino (34)	68	0.32
Indian (18)	25	0.12
Indonesian (3)	3	0.01
Japanese (25)	43	0.20
Korean (161)	218	1.03
Taiwanese (3)	3	0.01
Thai (5)	9	0.04
Vietnamese (45)	53	0.25
Other Asian, specified	2	0.01
Other Asian, not specified (21)	28	0.13
Belgian	22	0.10
Brazilian	7	0.03
British	124	0.59
Canadian	46	0.22
Croatian	14	0.07
Czech	14	0.07
Czechoslovakian	31	0.15
Danish	129	0.61
Dutch	197	0.93
English	2,075	9.84
Estonian	8	0.04
European	216	1.02
Finnish	54	0.26
French, except Basque	454	2.15
French Canadian	124	0.59
German	2,003	9.50
Greek	16	0.08
Hawaii Native/Pacific Islander:	58	0.27
Micronesian: (7)	14	0.07
Guamanian/Chamorro (6)	12	0.06
Other Micronesian (1)	2	0.01
Polynesian: (20)	33	0.16
Native Hawaiian (13)	22	0.10
Samoan (4)	8	0.04
Other Polynesian (3)	3	0.01
Other Pac. Isl., specified	1	0.00
Other Pac. Isl., not spec. (5)	10	0.05
Hispanic or Latino:	821	3.88
Central American:	73	0.34
Costa Rican	4	0.02
Guatemalan	5	0.02
Honduran	16	0.08
Nicaraguan	8	0.04
Panamanian	31	0.15
Salvadoran	8	0.04
Other Central American	1	0.00
Cuban	28	0.13
Dominican Republic	7	0.03
Mexican	297	1.40
Puerto Rican	239	1.13
South American:	29	0.14
Bolivian	3	0.01
Chilean	1	0.00
Colombian	16	0.08
Ecuadorian	3	0.01
Peruvian	1	0.00
Other South American	5	0.02
Other Hispanic or Latino	148	0.70
Hungarian	64	0.30
Irish	1,651	7.83
Italian	328	1.56
Norwegian	217	1.03
Polish	299	1.42
Portuguese	18	0.09
Russian	60	0.28
Scandinavian	10	0.05
Scotch-Irish	442	2.10
Scottish	511	2.42
Slovak	16	0.08
Swedish	103	0.49
Swiss	21	0.10
Turkish	10	0.05
Ukrainian	36	0.17
United States or American	3,065	14.54
Welsh	73	0.35
West Indian, excl. Hispanic:	30	0.14
Barbadian	9	0.04
Jamaican	21	0.10
White:	15,484	73.11
Not Hispanic (14,692)	14,951	70.60
Hispanic (475)	533	2.52
Yugoslavian	4	0.02

Eufaula

Place Type: City
County: Barbour
Population: 13,908

Ancestry/Race	Number	%
Acadian/Cajun	25	0.18
African American/Black:	5,661	40.70
Not Hispanic (5,596)	5,636	40.52
Hispanic (25)	25	0.18
African, sub-Saharan:	93	0.67
African	93	0.67
Am. Ind. or Alaska Nat., not spec.	29	0.21
American Indian tribes, specified:	36	0.26
Cherokee (15)	21	0.15
Chippewa	1	0.01
Choctaw (4)	4	0.03
Creek (1)	1	0.01
Iroquois	3	0.02
Navajo (1)	2	0.01
Potawatomi (2)	2	0.01
Pueblo (1)	1	0.01
All other tribes (1)	1	0.01
American Indian tribes, not spec.	5	0.04
Asian:	85	0.61
Chinese, ex. Taiwanese (18)	21	0.15
Filipino (1)	1	0.01
Indian (15)	19	0.14
Indonesian	2	0.01
Japanese (5)	10	0.07
Korean (11)	14	0.10
Taiwanese	1	0.01
Thai (8)	8	0.06
Other Asian, specified	1	0.01
Other Asian, not specified (5)	8	0.06
British	109	0.79
Canadian	18	0.13
Danish	21	0.15
Dutch	97	0.70
English	725	5.23
European	121	0.87
French, except Basque	290	2.09
French Canadian	5	0.04
German	525	3.78
Greek	12	0.09
Hawaii Native/Pacific Islander:	9	0.06
Polynesian: (4)	4	0.03
Native Hawaiian (4)	4	0.03
Other Pac. Isl., specified	1	0.01
Other Pac. Isl., not spec. (1)	4	0.03
Hispanic or Latino:	213	1.53
Central American:	3	0.02
Guatemalan	3	0.02
Cuban	4	0.03
Mexican	151	1.09
Puerto Rican	14	0.10
South American:	7	0.05
Colombian	3	0.02
Paraguayan	2	0.01
Uruguayan	2	0.01
Other Hispanic or Latino	34	0.24
Hungarian	4	0.03
Iranian	16	0.12
Irish	681	4.91
Italian	98	0.71
Polish	67	0.48
Romanian	5	0.04
Russian	6	0.04
Scandinavian	15	0.11
Scotch-Irish	235	1.69
Scottish	146	1.05
Swedish	19	0.14
United States or American	2,203	15.88
Welsh	42	0.30
West Indian, excl. Hispanic:	13	0.09
Bahamian	8	0.06
Jamaican	5	0.04
White:	8,039	57.80
Not Hispanic (7,913)	7,980	57.38
Hispanic (54)	59	0.42
Yugoslavian	19	0.14

Fairfield

Place Type: City
County: Jefferson
Population: 12,381

Ancestry/Race	Number	%
African American/Black:	11,215	90.58
Not Hispanic (11,132)	11,175	90.26
Hispanic (39)	40	0.32
African, sub-Saharan:	112	0.90
African	112	0.90
Am. Ind. or Alaska Nat., not spec.	15	0.12
American Indian tribes, specified:	6	0.05
Cherokee (1)	6	0.05
American Indian tribes, not spec.	1	0.01
Arab:	25	0.20
Palestinian	25	0.20
Asian:	35	0.28
Chinese, ex. Taiwanese (1)	3	0.02
Indian (8)	12	0.10
Indonesian	1	0.01
Japanese (1)	2	0.02
Korean (4)	5	0.04
Pakistani (1)	2	0.02
Vietnamese (3)	6	0.05
Other Asian, not specified	4	0.03
British	28	0.23
Dutch	12	0.10
English	156	1.26
European	29	0.23

Notes: 1. Figures in the "Number" column do not add up to the total population due to: a) Ancestry/Race overlap — e.g. persons can report being both White and Irish, b) persons of Hispanic origin can report being any race, c) persons reporting two ancestries are counted in both categories. 2. Numbers in parentheses indicate the number of persons reporting this ancestry/race alone, not in combination with any other ancestry/race. 3. Refer to the Explanation of Data in the front of the book for more detailed information.

French, except Basque	9	0.07
German	55	0.44
Hawaii Native/Pacific Islander:	7	0.06
Polynesian: (2)	5	0.04
Native Hawaiian (1)	4	0.03
Samoan (1)	1	0.01
Other Pac. Isl., not spec.	2	0.02
Hispanic or Latino:	73	0.59
Cuban	8	0.06
Mexican	47	0.38
Other Hispanic or Latino	18	0.15
Irish	73	0.59
Italian	105	0.85
Polish	10	0.08
Scotch-Irish	63	0.51
Scottish	11	0.09
United States or American	160	1.29
Welsh	7	0.06
West Indian, excl. Hispanic:	35	0.28
Dutch West Indian	9	0.07
Jamaican	26	0.21
White:	1,145	9.25
Not Hispanic (1,086)	1,128	9.11
Hispanic (16)	17	0.14

Fairhope

Place Type: City
County: Baldwin
Population: 12,480

Ancestry/Race	Number	%
Afghan	6	0.05
African American/Black:	995	7.97
Not Hispanic (964)	986	7.90
Hispanic (8)	9	0.07
African, sub-Saharan:	27	0.22
African	27	0.22
Am. Ind. or Alaska Nat., not spec.	29	0.23
American Indian tribes, specified:	52	0.42
Cherokee (6)	17	0.14
Choctaw (1)	4	0.03
Cree	1	0.01
Creek (12)	24	0.19
Latin American Indians	2	0.02
Lumbee (2)	3	0.02
Pima	1	0.01
American Indian tribes, not spec.	1	0.01
Arab:	70	0.57
Arab/Arabic	47	0.38
Lebanese	23	0.19
Asian:	108	0.87
Chinese, ex. Taiwanese (15)	17	0.14
Filipino (10)	21	0.17
Indian (12)	13	0.10
Japanese	2	0.02
Korean (6)	7	0.06
Thai (4)	8	0.06
Vietnamese (17)	23	0.18
Other Asian, specified (1)	4	0.03
Other Asian, not specified (7)	13	0.10
Austrian	12	0.10
Belgian	6	0.05
Brazilian	12	0.10
British	137	1.12
Canadian	41	0.34
Celtic	15	0.12
Czech	121	0.99
Czechoslovakian	45	0.37
Danish	53	0.43
Dutch	187	1.53
English	2,283	18.69
European	174	1.42
Finnish	10	0.08
French, except Basque	523	4.28
French Canadian	64	0.52
German	1,367	11.19
Greek	45	0.37
Hawaii Native/Pacific Islander:	10	0.08
Micronesian: (4)	5	0.04
Guamanian/Chamorro (4)	5	0.04
Polynesian: (1)	2	0.02
Native Hawaiian	1	0.01
Samoan (1)	1	0.01
Other Pac. Isl., specified	3	0.02
Hispanic or Latino:	130	1.04
Central American:	14	0.11
Costa Rican	2	0.02
Guatemalan	4	0.03
Honduran	1	0.01
Panamanian	7	0.06
Cuban	4	0.03
Mexican	44	0.35
Puerto Rican	15	0.12
South American:	9	0.07
Argentinean	1	0.01
Chilean	1	0.01
Colombian	3	0.02
Ecuadorian	1	0.01
Paraguayan	1	0.01
Peruvian	2	0.02
Other Hispanic or Latino	44	0.35
Hungarian	27	0.22
Iranian	7	0.06
Irish	1,032	8.45
Italian	388	3.18
Lithuanian	20	0.16
Norwegian	125	1.02
Polish	84	0.69
Russian	40	0.33
Scandinavian	5	0.04
Scotch-Irish	639	5.23
Scottish	412	3.37
Swedish	199	1.63
Swiss	36	0.29
Ukrainian	6	0.05
United States or American	1,268	10.38
Welsh	212	1.74
West Indian, excl. Hispanic:	10	0.08
Other West Indian	10	0.08
White:	11,369	91.10
Not Hispanic (11,176)	11,271	90.31
Hispanic (83)	98	0.79
Yugoslavian	12	0.10

Florence

Place Type: City
County: Lauderdale
Population: 36,264

Ancestry/Race	Number	%
African American/Black:	7,089	19.55
Not Hispanic (6,932)	7,053	19.45
Hispanic (31)	36	0.10
African, sub-Saharan:	155	0.43
African	120	0.33
South African	11	0.03
Other sub-Saharan African	24	0.07
Am. Ind. or Alaska Nat., not spec.	71	0.20
American Indian tribes, specified:	132	0.36
Blackfeet	4	0.01
Cherokee (42)	100	0.28
Cheyenne (3)	3	0.01
Chickasaw (2)	7	0.02
Chippewa (2)	4	0.01
Choctaw	5	0.01
Creek (1)	4	0.01
Crow (1)	1	0.00
Latin American Indians (1)	1	0.00
Ottawa (1)	1	0.00
Sioux	1	0.00
All other tribes (1)	1	0.00
American Indian tribes, not spec.	13	0.04
Arab:	39	0.11
Egyptian	14	0.04
Lebanese	25	0.07
Asian:	289	0.80
Bangladeshi (2)	3	0.01
Chinese, ex. Taiwanese (62)	71	0.20
Filipino (19)	34	0.09
Indian (63)	73	0.20
Japanese (15)	27	0.07
Korean (15)	21	0.06
Pakistani (4)	4	0.01
Sri Lankan (2)	3	0.01
Taiwanese (7)	8	0.02
Thai (1)	1	0.00
Vietnamese (24)	26	0.07
Other Asian, specified (2)	3	0.01
Other Asian, not specified (6)	15	0.04
Austrian	34	0.09
Belgian	25	0.07
British	255	0.70
Bulgarian	6	0.02
Canadian	38	0.10
Celtic	8	0.02
Croatian	7	0.02
Czech	31	0.09
Czechoslovakian	6	0.02
Danish	45	0.12
Dutch	325	0.89
Eastern European	7	0.02
English	3,400	9.33
European	319	0.88
Finnish	25	0.07
French, except Basque	489	1.34
French Canadian	74	0.20
German	2,394	6.57
Greek	26	0.07
Hawaii Native/Pacific Islander:	24	0.07
Melanesian: (1)	3	0.01
Fijian (1)	3	0.01
Micronesian: (3)	6	0.02
Guamanian/Chamorro (3)	6	0.02
Polynesian: (8)	11	0.03
Native Hawaiian (6)	8	0.02
Samoan (1)	2	0.01
Other Polynesian (1)	1	0.00
Other Pac. Isl., specified	1	0.00
Other Pac. Isl., not spec.	3	0.01
Hispanic or Latino:	487	1.34
Central American:	11	0.03
Guatemalan	4	0.01
Honduran	2	0.01
Panamanian	3	0.01
Salvadoran	1	0.00
Other Central American	1	0.00
Cuban	18	0.05
Dominican Republic	7	0.02
Mexican	295	0.81
Puerto Rican	21	0.06
South American:	17	0.05
Chilean	1	0.00
Colombian	11	0.03
Ecuadorian	2	0.01
Peruvian	2	0.01
Uruguayan	1	0.00
Other Hispanic or Latino	118	0.33
Hungarian	34	0.09
Irish	2,987	8.20
Italian	314	0.86
Norwegian	102	0.28
Polish	188	0.52
Portuguese	7	0.02
Romanian	8	0.02
Russian	42	0.12
Scandinavian	6	0.02
Scotch-Irish	1,057	2.90
Scottish	610	1.67
Slavic	36	0.10
Swedish	60	0.16
Swiss	43	0.12
Turkish	43	0.12
Ukrainian	6	0.02
United States or American	7,465	20.49
Welsh	59	0.16
West Indian, excl. Hispanic:	21	0.06
Dutch West Indian	6	0.02
Jamaican	15	0.04

Notes: 1. Figures in the "Number" column do not add up to the total population due to: a) Ancestry/Race overlap — e.g. persons can report being both White and Irish, b) persons of Hispanic origin can report being any race, c) persons reporting two ancestries are counted in both categories. 2. Numbers in parentheses indicate the number of persons reporting this ancestry/race alone, not in combination with any other ancestry/race. 3. Refer to the Explanation of Data in the front of the book for more detailed information.

White:	28,743	79.26
Not Hispanic (28,184)	28,464	78.49
Hispanic (244)	279	0.77

Forestdale

Place Type: Census Designated Place
County: Jefferson
Population: 10,509

Ancestry/Race	Number	%
Acadian/Cajun	24	0.23
African American/Black:	4,842	46.07
Not Hispanic (4,815)	4,831	45.97
Hispanic (11)	11	0.10
African, sub-Saharan:	231	2.18
African	222	2.10
Nigerian	9	0.09
Am. Ind. or Alaska Nat., not spec.	19	0.18
American Indian tribes, specified:	23	0.22
Cherokee (7)	14	0.13
Choctaw (1)	1	0.01
Creek (2)	4	0.04
Iroquois	1	0.01
Lumbee	3	0.03
American Indian tribes, not spec.	5	0.05
Arab:	13	0.12
Lebanese	13	0.12
Asian:	47	0.45
Chinese, ex. Taiwanese (10)	11	0.10
Filipino (5)	5	0.05
Indian (10)	10	0.10
Japanese (1)	3	0.03
Korean (5)	8	0.08
Thai (1)	2	0.02
Vietnamese (3)	4	0.04
Other Asian, not specified (2)	4	0.04
British	17	0.16
Canadian	13	0.12
Celtic	8	0.08
Czech	26	0.25
Czechoslovakian	7	0.07
Dutch	99	0.94
English	623	5.89
European	68	0.64
French, except Basque	124	1.17
French Canadian	16	0.15
German	224	2.12
Hispanic or Latino:	48	0.46
Cuban	2	0.02
Mexican	15	0.14
Puerto Rican	3	0.03
South American:	2	0.02
Bolivian	1	0.01
Ecuadorian	1	0.01
Other Hispanic or Latino	26	0.25
Iranian	7	0.07
Irish	478	4.52
Italian	181	1.71
Norwegian	18	0.17
Polish	19	0.18
Scotch-Irish	142	1.34
Scottish	115	1.09
Swedish	10	0.09
United States or American	1,071	10.12
Welsh	15	0.14
West Indian, excl. Hispanic:	13	0.12
Jamaican	7	0.07
West Indian	6	0.06
White:	5,602	53.31
Not Hispanic (5,536)	5,582	53.12
Hispanic (20)	20	0.19
Yugoslavian	2	0.02

Fort Payne

Place Type: City
County: De Kalb
Population: 12,938

Ancestry/Race	Number	%
African American/Black:	622	4.81
Not Hispanic (570)	601	4.65
Hispanic (16)	21	0.16
African, sub-Saharan:	14	0.11
African	14	0.11
Am. Ind. or Alaska Nat., not spec.	51	0.39
American Indian tribes, specified:	183	1.41
Apache (1)	1	0.01
Blackfeet (2)	7	0.05
Cherokee (52)	145	1.12
Chippewa	2	0.02
Choctaw (1)	1	0.01
Cree	1	0.01
Creek (4)	4	0.03
Crow	3	0.02
Iroquois	2	0.02
Latin American Indians (4)	13	0.10
Navajo	3	0.02
Seminole	1	0.01
American Indian tribes, not spec.	16	0.12
Arab:	45	0.34
Arab/Arabic	17	0.13
Syrian	28	0.21
Armenian	11	0.08
Asian:	98	0.76
Cambodian (1)	5	0.04
Chinese, ex. Taiwanese (8)	13	0.10
Filipino (32)	34	0.26
Indian (8)	17	0.13
Indonesian (2)	3	0.02
Japanese (1)	2	0.02
Korean	1	0.01
Thai (2)	3	0.02
Vietnamese (5)	10	0.08
Other Asian, not specified (7)	10	0.08
Austrian	8	0.06
British	15	0.11
Canadian	40	0.30
Czech	6	0.05
Dutch	166	1.26
English	1,012	7.69
European	49	0.37
French, except Basque	195	1.48
French Canadian	28	0.21
German	648	4.93
Guyanese	7	0.05
Hawaii Native/Pacific Islander:	28	0.22
Micronesian: (17)	18	0.14
Guamanian/Chamorro (17)	18	0.14
Polynesian: (4)	8	0.06
Native Hawaiian (2)	6	0.05
Samoan (2)	2	0.02
Other Pac. Isl., not spec.	2	0.02
Hispanic or Latino:	1,574	12.17
Central American:	395	3.05
Guatemalan	374	2.89
Honduran	6	0.05
Salvadoran	14	0.11
Other Central American	1	0.01
Cuban	3	0.02
Mexican	1,034	7.99
Puerto Rican	22	0.17
South American:	3	0.02
Colombian	3	0.02
Other Hispanic or Latino	117	0.90
Iranian	15	0.11
Irish	1,303	9.91
Italian	149	1.13
Lithuanian	6	0.05
Northern European	58	0.44
Norwegian	26	0.20
Polish	30	0.23
Russian	18	0.14
Scotch-Irish	237	1.80
Scottish	136	1.03
Swedish	9	0.07
Swiss	3	0.02
United States or American	3,236	24.60
Welsh	33	0.25
West Indian, excl. Hispanic:	8	0.06
Bahamian	8	0.06
White:	11,041	85.34
Not Hispanic (10,455)	10,625	82.12
Hispanic (312)	416	3.22

Gadsden

Place Type: City
County: Etowah
Population: 38,978

Ancestry/Race	Number	%
African American/Black:	13,457	34.52
Not Hispanic (13,188)	13,377	34.32
Hispanic (64)	80	0.21
African, sub-Saharan:	468	1.21
African	394	1.01
Ethiopian	8	0.02
Ghanian	54	0.14
Nigerian	12	0.03
Alaska Native tribes, specified:	1	0.00
Eskimo (1)	1	0.00
Am. Ind. or Alaska Nat., not spec.	108	0.28
American Indian tribes, specified:	164	0.42
Apache (1)	3	0.01
Blackfeet (1)	1	0.00
Cherokee (61)	121	0.31
Choctaw (6)	7	0.02
Creek (1)	8	0.02
Iroquois (2)	2	0.01
Latin American Indians (1)	9	0.02
Sioux (3)	6	0.02
Yaqui (1)	1	0.00
All other tribes (3)	6	0.02
American Indian tribes, not spec.	13	0.03
Arab:	33	0.08
Arab/Arabic	8	0.02
Lebanese	8	0.02
Syrian	17	0.04
Armenian	6	0.02
Asian:	274	0.70
Cambodian (1)	1	0.00
Chinese, ex. Taiwanese (20)	24	0.06
Filipino (29)	44	0.11
Indian (56)	64	0.16
Indonesian (6)	12	0.03
Japanese (35)	43	0.11
Korean (17)	22	0.06
Pakistani (1)	3	0.01
Thai (6)	6	0.02
Vietnamese (18)	18	0.05
Other Asian, specified (4)	10	0.03
Other Asian, not specified (12)	27	0.07
Austrian	16	0.04
Brazilian	12	0.03
British	110	0.28
Canadian	6	0.02
Celtic	7	0.02
Croatian	8	0.02
Czech	6	0.02
Danish	24	0.06
Dutch	360	0.93
English	2,569	6.61
European	200	0.51
Finnish	23	0.06
French, except Basque	254	0.65
French Canadian	22	0.06
German	1,347	3.47
Greek	6	0.02
Hawaii Native/Pacific Islander:	64	0.16
Micronesian: (22)	23	0.06
Guamanian/Chamorro (22)	23	0.06
Polynesian: (5)	10	0.03
Native Hawaiian (3)	5	0.01
Samoan (2)	5	0.01
Other Pac. Isl., specified	5	0.01
Other Pac. Isl., not spec. (5)	26	0.07
Hispanic or Latino:	1,039	2.67
Central American:	276	0.71
Guatemalan	223	0.57

Notes: 1. Figures in the "Number" column do not add up to the total population due to: a) Ancestry/Race overlap — e.g. persons can report being both White and Irish, b) persons of Hispanic origin can report being any race, c) persons reporting two ancestries are counted in both categories. 2. Numbers in parentheses indicate the number of persons reporting this ancestry/race alone, not in combination with any other ancestry/race. 3. Refer to the Explanation of Data in the front of the book for more detailed information.

Ancestry/Race	Number	%
Honduran	16	0.04
Panamanian	2	0.01
Salvadoran	30	0.08
Other Central American	5	0.01
Cuban	19	0.05
Dominican Republic	15	0.04
Mexican	411	1.05
Puerto Rican	45	0.12
South American:	63	0.16
Chilean	1	0.00
Colombian	49	0.13
Peruvian	6	0.02
Venezuelan	6	0.02
Other South American	1	0.00
Other Hispanic or Latino	210	0.54
Hungarian	20	0.05
Irish	2,591	6.67
Italian	256	0.66
Lithuanian	12	0.03
New Zealander	8	0.02
Norwegian	41	0.11
Pennsylvania German	16	0.04
Polish	96	0.25
Portuguese	17	0.04
Romanian	6	0.02
Russian	11	0.03
Scandinavian	8	0.02
Scotch-Irish	613	1.58
Scottish	488	1.26
Serbian	4	0.01
Swedish	86	0.22
United States or American	7,492	19.29
Welsh	67	0.17
West Indian, excl. Hispanic:	39	0.10
Dutch West Indian	11	0.03
Haitian	7	0.02
Jamaican	14	0.04
West Indian	7	0.02
White:	24,802	63.63
Not Hispanic (24,016)	24,333	62.43
Hispanic (418)	469	1.20

Gardendale

Place Type: City
County: Jefferson
Population: 11,626

Ancestry/Race	Number	%
African American/Black:	175	1.51
Not Hispanic (172)	175	1.51
African, sub-Saharan:	68	0.58
African	43	0.36
Senegalese	9	0.08
South African	16	0.14
Am. Ind. or Alaska Nat., not spec.	12	0.10
American Indian tribes, specified:	45	0.39
Blackfeet (1)	1	0.01
Cherokee (10)	37	0.32
Chippewa (1)	1	0.01
Choctaw (1)	2	0.02
Creek (1)	4	0.03
Asian:	81	0.70
Chinese, ex. Taiwanese (11)	13	0.11
Filipino (2)	4	0.03
Indian (6)	13	0.11
Japanese (2)	4	0.03
Korean (5)	6	0.05
Laotian (4)	4	0.03
Pakistani (8)	12	0.10
Thai (1)	1	0.01
Vietnamese (19)	20	0.17
Other Asian, not specified	4	0.03
Brazilian	12	0.10
British	14	0.12
Celtic	11	0.09
Danish	24	0.20
Dutch	204	1.73
English	1,044	8.84
European	223	1.89
Finnish	34	0.29
French, except Basque	301	2.55
French Canadian	22	0.19
German	914	7.74
Greek	28	0.24
Hawaii Native/Pacific Islander:	5	0.04
Micronesian: (1)	4	0.03
Other Micronesian (1)	4	0.03
Other Pac. Isl., not spec. (1)	1	0.01
Hispanic or Latino:	75	0.65
Central American:	9	0.08
Costa Rican	1	0.01
Honduran	3	0.03
Nicaraguan	3	0.03
Panamanian	2	0.02
Cuban	4	0.03
Mexican	43	0.37
Puerto Rican	7	0.06
South American:	1	0.01
Uruguayan	1	0.01
Other Hispanic or Latino	11	0.09
Irish	1,093	9.26
Italian	242	2.05
Lithuanian	9	0.08
Luxemburger	7	0.06
Polish	35	0.30
Portuguese	5	0.04
Romanian	15	0.13
Russian	8	0.07
Scandinavian	10	0.08
Scotch-Irish	339	2.87
Scottish	246	2.08
Swedish	10	0.08
United States or American	2,837	24.03
Welsh	97	0.82
White:	11,354	97.66
Not Hispanic (11,243)	11,297	97.17
Hispanic (56)	57	0.49

Hartselle

Place Type: City
County: Morgan
Population: 12,019

Ancestry/Race	Number	%
African American/Black:	646	5.37
Not Hispanic (614)	636	5.29
Hispanic (6)	10	0.08
African, sub-Saharan:	46	0.39
African	36	0.31
Sudanese	10	0.09
Am. Ind. or Alaska Nat., not spec.	34	0.28
American Indian tribes, specified:	152	1.26
Apache	2	0.02
Blackfeet	1	0.01
Cherokee (54)	93	0.77
Chippewa (4)	5	0.04
Choctaw (1)	1	0.01
Creek (1)	8	0.07
Iroquois (1)	1	0.01
Latin American Indians (1)	34	0.28
Osage	1	0.01
All other tribes (3)	6	0.05
American Indian tribes, not spec.	2	0.02
Asian:	53	0.44
Chinese, ex. Taiwanese (9)	11	0.09
Filipino (6)	12	0.10
Indian (15)	17	0.14
Japanese (1)	2	0.02
Korean (3)	5	0.04
Thai (1)	4	0.03
Vietnamese (2)	2	0.02
Belgian	11	0.09
British	19	0.16
Canadian	8	0.07
Celtic	18	0.15
Czechoslovakian	20	0.17
Danish	5	0.04
Dutch	146	1.24
English	1,433	12.18
European	58	0.49
Finnish	25	0.21
French, except Basque	183	1.56
French Canadian	33	0.28
German	813	6.91
Hawaii Native/Pacific Islander:	3	0.02
Polynesian: (2)	3	0.02
Native Hawaiian (2)	3	0.02
Hispanic or Latino:	155	1.29
Central American:	1	0.01
Salvadoran	1	0.01
Cuban	4	0.03
Mexican	107	0.89
Puerto Rican	12	0.10
Other Hispanic or Latino	31	0.26
Irish	1,310	11.14
Italian	153	1.30
Norwegian	73	0.62
Polish	65	0.55
Portuguese	15	0.13
Russian	25	0.21
Scandinavian	23	0.20
Scotch-Irish	302	2.57
Scottish	277	2.35
Swedish	120	1.02
United States or American	2,517	21.40
Welsh	67	0.57
West Indian, excl. Hispanic:	6	0.05
Jamaican	6	0.05
White:	11,202	93.20
Not Hispanic (11,020)	11,129	92.60
Hispanic (67)	73	0.61

Helena

Place Type: City
County: Shelby
Population: 10,296

Ancestry/Race	Number	%
African American/Black:	529	5.14
Not Hispanic (513)	527	5.12
Hispanic (2)	2	0.02
African, sub-Saharan:	8	0.08
African	8	0.08
Alaska Native tribes, specified:	1	0.01
Aleut (1)	1	0.01
Am. Ind. or Alaska Nat., not spec.	3	0.03
American Indian tribes, specified:	40	0.39
Cherokee (10)	20	0.19
Choctaw	5	0.05
Creek (5)	10	0.10
Houma (1)	1	0.01
Ottawa	1	0.01
Shoshone (3)	3	0.03
Arab:	20	0.20
Lebanese	20	0.20
Asian:	82	0.80
Chinese, ex. Taiwanese (20)	22	0.21
Filipino (3)	4	0.04
Indian (17)	17	0.17
Japanese (3)	7	0.07
Korean (11)	13	0.13
Pakistani (1)	1	0.01
Taiwanese (1)	2	0.02
Thai (2)	3	0.03
Vietnamese (4)	4	0.04
Other Asian, not specified (5)	9	0.09
Australian	7	0.07
Austrian	27	0.27
Belgian	9	0.09
British	63	0.62
Canadian	16	0.16
Czech	27	0.27
Dutch	88	0.87
English	1,368	13.48
European	81	0.80
French, except Basque	368	3.63
French Canadian	33	0.33

Notes: 1. Figures in the "Number" column do not add up to the total population due to: a) Ancestry/Race overlap — e.g. persons can report being both White and Irish, b) persons of Hispanic origin can report being any race, c) persons reporting two ancestries are counted in both categories. 2. Numbers in parentheses indicate the number of persons reporting this ancestry/race alone, not in combination with any other ancestry/race. 3. Refer to the Explanation of Data in the front of the book for more detailed information.

German	1,179	11.62
Greek	39	0.38
Hawaii Native/Pacific Islander:	5	0.05
Polynesian: (2)	3	0.03
Native Hawaiian	1	0.01
Samoan (2)	2	0.02
Other Pac. Isl., not spec.	2	0.02
Hispanic or Latino:	103	1.00
Central American:	5	0.05
Costa Rican	2	0.02
Honduran	1	0.01
Nicaraguan	1	0.01
Panamanian	1	0.01
Cuban	9	0.09
Mexican	58	0.56
Puerto Rican	8	0.08
South American:	3	0.03
Chilean	1	0.01
Colombian	2	0.02
Other Hispanic or Latino	20	0.19
Hungarian	25	0.25
Irish	1,166	11.49
Italian	471	4.64
Norwegian	14	0.14
Polish	92	0.91
Portuguese	28	0.28
Russian	7	0.07
Scotch-Irish	333	3.28
Scottish	422	4.16
Swedish	82	0.81
Turkish	10	0.10
Ukrainian	48	0.47
United States or American	1,632	16.08
Welsh	88	0.87
White:	9,651	93.74
Not Hispanic (9,540)	9,584	93.08
Hispanic (61)	67	0.65
Yugoslavian	8	0.08

Homewood

Place Type: City
County: Jefferson
Population: 25,043

Ancestry/Race	Number	%
Acadian/Cajun	4	0.02
African American/Black:	3,911	15.62
Not Hispanic (3,814)	3,890	15.53
Hispanic (17)	21	0.08
African, sub-Saharan:	333	1.34
African	137	0.55
Kenyan	104	0.42
Liberian	18	0.07
Nigerian	25	0.10
Sudanese	18	0.07
Ugandan	10	0.04
Other sub-Saharan African	21	0.08
Alaska Native tribes, specified:	1	0.00
Alaska Athabascan (1)	1	0.00
Am. Ind. or Alaska Nat., not spec.	39	0.16
American Indian tribes, specified:	82	0.33
Apache (7)	7	0.03
Blackfeet	1	0.00
Cherokee (14)	41	0.16
Chickasaw (2)	2	0.01
Choctaw (3)	4	0.02
Cree	1	0.00
Creek (4)	11	0.04
Crow	1	0.00
Delaware	1	0.00
Iroquois	3	0.01
Latin American Indians (1)	2	0.01
Navajo (2)	2	0.01
Pueblo	1	0.00
Sioux	1	0.00
Yaqui	1	0.00
All other tribes (1)	3	0.01
American Indian tribes, not spec.	6	0.02
Arab:	228	0.92
Arab/Arabic	55	0.22
Egyptian	18	0.07
Iraqi	7	0.03
Lebanese	123	0.49
Palestinian	19	0.08
Syrian	6	0.02
Asian:	743	2.97
Bangladeshi (13)	13	0.05
Chinese, ex. Taiwanese (166)	190	0.76
Filipino (17)	26	0.10
Indian (170)	179	0.71
Indonesian	1	0.00
Japanese (38)	52	0.21
Korean (82)	93	0.37
Laotian (1)	1	0.00
Malaysian	1	0.00
Pakistani (20)	22	0.09
Taiwanese (2)	2	0.01
Thai (25)	26	0.10
Vietnamese (74)	79	0.32
Other Asian, specified (18)	20	0.08
Other Asian, not specified (11)	38	0.15
Australian	4	0.02
Austrian	8	0.03
Belgian	7	0.03
Brazilian	56	0.23
British	224	0.90
Bulgarian	8	0.03
Canadian	67	0.27
Celtic	47	0.19
Croatian	41	0.16
Czech	41	0.16
Czechoslovakian	13	0.05
Danish	19	0.08
Dutch	235	0.94
Eastern European	23	0.09
English	4,150	16.68
European	297	1.19
Finnish	44	0.18
French, except Basque	917	3.69
French Canadian	213	0.86
German	2,766	11.12
Greek	164	0.66
Hawaii Native/Pacific Islander:	19	0.08
Micronesian: (5)	5	0.02
Guamanian/Chamorro (5)	5	0.02
Polynesian: (2)	7	0.03
Native Hawaiian (1)	5	0.02
Samoan (1)	2	0.01
Other Pac. Isl., specified	2	0.01
Other Pac. Isl., not spec.	5	0.02
Hispanic or Latino:	702	2.80
Central American:	29	0.12
Guatemalan	3	0.01
Honduran	11	0.04
Nicaraguan	3	0.01
Panamanian	4	0.02
Salvadoran	8	0.03
Cuban	20	0.08
Dominican Republic	6	0.02
Mexican	478	1.91
Puerto Rican	22	0.09
South American:	84	0.34
Argentinean	15	0.06
Chilean	12	0.05
Colombian	10	0.04
Ecuadorian	12	0.05
Paraguayan	1	0.00
Peruvian	28	0.11
Uruguayan	2	0.01
Venezuelan	2	0.01
Other South American	2	0.01
Other Hispanic or Latino	63	0.25
Hungarian	63	0.25
Iranian	30	0.12
Irish	2,673	10.74
Israeli	14	0.06
Italian	863	3.47
Latvian	4	0.02
Lithuanian	30	0.12
Northern European	66	0.27
Norwegian	86	0.35
Polish	217	0.87
Romanian	7	0.03
Russian	143	0.57
Scandinavian	47	0.19
Scotch-Irish	1,183	4.76
Scottish	873	3.51
Slavic	63	0.25
Slovak	11	0.04
Slovene	5	0.02
Swedish	84	0.34
Swiss	40	0.16
Turkish	34	0.14
Ukrainian	21	0.08
United States or American	2,004	8.06
Welsh	138	0.55
West Indian, excl. Hispanic:	50	0.20
British West Indian	6	0.02
Jamaican	31	0.12
Trinidadian and Tobagonian	13	0.05
White:	20,213	80.71
Not Hispanic (19,566)	19,768	78.94
Hispanic (406)	445	1.78
Yugoslavian	7	0.03

Hoover

Place Type: City
County: Jefferson
Population: 62,742

Ancestry/Race	Number	%
Acadian/Cajun	10	0.02
African American/Black:	4,389	7.00
Not Hispanic (4,230)	4,349	6.93
Hispanic (18)	40	0.06
African, sub-Saharan:	260	0.42
African	154	0.25
Kenyan	26	0.04
Liberian	52	0.08
Nigerian	18	0.03
South African	10	0.02
Alaska Native tribes, specified:	2	0.00
Alaska Athabascan	1	0.00
Eskimo	1	0.00
Am. Ind. or Alaska Nat., not spec.	74	0.12
American Indian tribes, specified:	147	0.23
Apache	1	0.00
Cherokee (35)	74	0.12
Chickasaw	4	0.01
Chippewa (2)	9	0.01
Choctaw (2)	10	0.02
Creek (3)	12	0.02
Delaware	1	0.00
Iroquois (1)	1	0.00
Kiowa (1)	1	0.00
Latin American Indians (13)	13	0.02
Lumbee (5)	5	0.01
Pueblo	1	0.00
Puget Sound Salish (1)	1	0.00
Seminole	2	0.00
Sioux (1)	4	0.01
Yaqui	1	0.00
All other tribes (5)	7	0.01
American Indian tribes, not spec.	16	0.03
Arab:	392	0.63
Arab/Arabic	57	0.09
Egyptian	25	0.04
Jordanian	6	0.01
Lebanese	217	0.35
Palestinian	25	0.04
Syrian	8	0.01
Other Arab	54	0.09
Armenian	7	0.01
Asian:	2,095	3.34
Bangladeshi (13)	13	0.02
Chinese, ex. Taiwanese (408)	452	0.72
Filipino (86)	122	0.19
Indian (641)	707	1.13

Notes: 1. Figures in the "Number" column do not add up to the total population due to: a) Ancestry/Race overlap — e.g. persons can report being both White and Irish, b) persons of Hispanic origin can report being any race, c) persons reporting two ancestries are counted in both categories. 2. Numbers in parentheses indicate the number of persons reporting this ancestry/race alone, not in combination with any other ancestry/race. 3. Refer to the Explanation of Data in the front of the book for more detailed information.

Ancestry/Race	Number	%
Indonesian	6	0.01
Japanese (77)	93	0.15
Korean (236)	252	0.40
Laotian (2)	4	0.01
Malaysian	1	0.00
Pakistani (94)	128	0.20
Sri Lankan (8)	14	0.02
Taiwanese (12)	15	0.02
Thai (18)	19	0.03
Vietnamese (162)	171	0.27
Other Asian, specified (9)	12	0.02
Other Asian, not specified (23)	86	0.14
Assyrian/Chaldean/Syriac	8	0.01
Austrian	81	0.13
Basque	11	0.02
Belgian	15	0.02
British	625	1.00
Canadian	147	0.24
Celtic	16	0.03
Croatian	57	0.09
Czech	113	0.18
Czechoslovakian	41	0.07
Danish	152	0.24
Dutch	962	1.54
Eastern European	24	0.04
English	9,569	15.32
Estonian	6	0.01
European	888	1.42
Finnish	83	0.13
French, except Basque	1,535	2.46
French Canadian	265	0.42
German	6,527	10.45
Greek	268	0.43
Hawaii Native/Pacific Islander:	52	0.08
Melanesian:	1	0.00
Fijian	1	0.00
Micronesian: (5)	12	0.02
Guamanian/Chamorro (5)	12	0.02
Polynesian: (9)	22	0.04
Native Hawaiian (4)	12	0.02
Samoan (5)	10	0.02
Other Pac. Isl., specified	1	0.00
Other Pac. Isl., not spec. (7)	16	0.03
Hispanic or Latino:	2,380	3.79
Central American:	133	0.21
Costa Rican	24	0.04
Guatemalan	15	0.02
Honduran	5	0.01
Nicaraguan	7	0.01
Panamanian	11	0.02
Salvadoran	65	0.10
Other Central American	6	0.01
Cuban	74	0.12
Dominican Republic	3	0.00
Mexican	1,724	2.75
Puerto Rican	101	0.16
South American:	117	0.19
Argentinean	21	0.03
Chilean	4	0.01
Colombian	40	0.06
Ecuadorian	14	0.02
Paraguayan	2	0.00
Peruvian	20	0.03
Venezuelan	10	0.02
Other South American	6	0.01
Other Hispanic or Latino	228	0.36
Hungarian	170	0.27
Icelander	6	0.01
Iranian	108	0.17
Irish	6,744	10.79
Israeli	48	0.08
Italian	2,384	3.82
Latvian	18	0.03
Lithuanian	77	0.12
Northern European	42	0.07
Norwegian	318	0.51
Pennsylvania German	8	0.01
Polish	891	1.43
Portuguese	16	0.03
Romanian	16	0.03
Russian	212	0.34
Scandinavian	128	0.20
Scotch-Irish	2,701	4.32
Scottish	2,194	3.51
Slavic	28	0.04
Slovak	60	0.10
Slovene	13	0.02
Swedish	411	0.66
Swiss	180	0.29
Turkish	21	0.03
Ukrainian	112	0.18
United States or American	7,585	12.14
Welsh	537	0.86
West Indian, excl. Hispanic:	123	0.20
Bahamian	19	0.03
British West Indian	8	0.01
Dutch West Indian	4	0.01
Jamaican	74	0.12
Trinidadian and Tobagonian	8	0.01
West Indian	10	0.02
White:	55,540	88.52
Not Hispanic (53,616)	54,064	86.17
Hispanic (1,381)	1,476	2.35
Yugoslavian	51	0.08

Hueytown

Place Type: City
County: Jefferson
Population: 15,364

Ancestry/Race	Number	%
African American/Black:	2,400	15.62
Not Hispanic (2,373)	2,391	15.56
Hispanic (7)	9	0.06
African, sub-Saharan:	37	0.24
African	32	0.21
South African	5	0.03
Am. Ind. or Alaska Nat., not spec.	17	0.11
American Indian tribes, specified:	39	0.25
Blackfeet	1	0.01
Cherokee (13)	24	0.16
Choctaw	1	0.01
Creek (6)	10	0.07
Pueblo (1)	1	0.01
Seminole (1)	2	0.01
Asian:	29	0.19
Chinese, ex. Taiwanese (2)	2	0.01
Filipino (4)	6	0.04
Japanese (2)	3	0.02
Korean	1	0.01
Pakistani (1)	1	0.01
Thai (1)	1	0.01
Vietnamese (8)	11	0.07
Other Asian, not specified (2)	4	0.03
Austrian	6	0.04
British	60	0.39
Canadian	16	0.11
Celtic	5	0.03
Czech	9	0.06
Czechoslovakian	6	0.04
Danish	22	0.14
Dutch	173	1.14
English	1,459	9.59
European	181	1.19
French, except Basque	117	0.77
French Canadian	11	0.07
German	721	4.74
Greek	29	0.19
Hawaii Native/Pacific Islander:	2	0.01
Polynesian:	1	0.01
Native Hawaiian	1	0.01
Other Pac. Isl., not spec.	1	0.01
Hispanic or Latino:	72	0.47
Central American:	1	0.01
Panamanian	1	0.01
Cuban	1	0.01
Mexican	19	0.12
Puerto Rican	9	0.06
South American:	1	0.01
Ecuadorian	1	0.01
Other Hispanic or Latino	41	0.27
Irish	1,064	6.99
Italian	307	2.02
Northern European	6	0.04
Norwegian	41	0.27
Pennsylvania German	6	0.04
Polish	118	0.78
Scandinavian	7	0.05
Scotch-Irish	304	2.00
Scottish	127	0.83
Swedish	8	0.05
Swiss	10	0.07
United States or American	2,935	19.29
Welsh	40	0.26
White:	12,919	84.09
Not Hispanic (12,825)	12,866	83.74
Hispanic (52)	53	0.34

Huntsville

Place Type: City
County: Madison
Population: 158,216

Ancestry/Race	Number	%
Acadian/Cajun	36	0.02
African American/Black:	48,913	30.92
Not Hispanic (47,453)	48,462	30.63
Hispanic (339)	451	0.29
African, sub-Saharan:	1,229	0.78
African	790	0.50
Ethiopian	21	0.01
Ghanian	46	0.03
Kenyan	25	0.02
Liberian	6	0.00
Nigerian	272	0.17
Senegalese	19	0.01
Sudanese	7	0.00
Ugandan	14	0.01
Zairian	9	0.01
Other sub-Saharan African	20	0.01
Alaska Native tribes, specified:	7	0.00
Alaska Athabascan (1)	2	0.00
Aleut	3	0.00
Eskimo (2)	2	0.00
Am. Ind. or Alaska Nat., not spec.	496	0.31
American Indian tribes, specified:	1,561	0.99
Apache (14)	24	0.02
Blackfeet (6)	27	0.02
Cherokee (483)	1,152	0.73
Chickasaw (6)	13	0.01
Chippewa (5)	9	0.01
Choctaw (26)	79	0.05
Comanche (1)	3	0.00
Cree	6	0.00
Creek (13)	53	0.03
Crow	5	0.00
Delaware (6)	10	0.01
Iroquois (5)	15	0.01
Kiowa	2	0.00
Latin American Indians (6)	19	0.01
Lumbee (10)	20	0.01
Navajo (4)	13	0.01
Osage (2)	4	0.00
Ottawa (2)	3	0.00
Pima (1)	1	0.00
Potawatomi (2)	2	0.00
Pueblo (3)	8	0.01
Seminole (5)	13	0.01
Shoshone	3	0.00
Sioux (10)	18	0.01
All other tribes (18)	59	0.04
American Indian tribes, not spec.	99	0.06
Arab:	303	0.19
Arab/Arabic	57	0.04
Egyptian	58	0.04
Lebanese	108	0.07
Moroccan	24	0.02
Syrian	10	0.01

Notes: 1. Figures in the "Number" column do not add up to the total population due to: a) Ancestry/Race overlap — e.g. persons can report being both White and Irish, b) persons of Hispanic origin can report being any race, c) persons reporting two ancestries are counted in both categories. 2. Numbers in parentheses indicate the number of persons reporting this ancestry/race alone, not in combination with any other ancestry/race. 3. Refer to the Explanation of Data in the front of the book for more detailed information.

Other Arab	46	0.03
Armenian	89	0.06
Asian:	4,272	2.70
Bangladeshi (15)	15	0.01
Cambodian (10)	13	0.01
Chinese, ex. Taiwanese (802)	914	0.58
Filipino (213)	322	0.20
Indian (994)	1,063	0.67
Indonesian (14)	23	0.01
Japanese (213)	349	0.22
Korean (692)	837	0.53
Laotian (78)	89	0.06
Malaysian (10)	13	0.01
Pakistani (13)	17	0.01
Sri Lankan (2)	2	0.00
Taiwanese (68)	95	0.06
Thai (55)	82	0.05
Vietnamese (215)	252	0.16
Other Asian, specified (16)	22	0.01
Other Asian, not specified (55)	164	0.10
Austrian	285	0.18
Belgian	77	0.05
British	1,138	0.72
Bulgarian	8	0.01
Canadian	213	0.13
Celtic	93	0.06
Croatian	71	0.04
Czech	243	0.15
Czechoslovakian	245	0.16
Danish	371	0.23
Dutch	1,442	0.91
Eastern European	26	0.02
English	17,031	10.79
Estonian	11	0.01
European	1,667	1.06
Finnish	165	0.10
French, except Basque	2,991	1.89
French Canadian	608	0.39
German	14,157	8.97
German Russian	11	0.01
Greek	309	0.20
Guyanese	55	0.03
Hawaii Native/Pacific Islander:	226	0.14
Melanesian:	1	0.00
Fijian	1	0.00
Micronesian: (40)	55	0.03
Guamanian/Chamorro (34)	48	0.03
Other Micronesian (6)	7	0.00
Polynesian: (38)	99	0.06
Native Hawaiian (32)	82	0.05
Samoan (6)	17	0.01
Other Pac. Isl., specified	2	0.00
Other Pac. Isl., not spec. (7)	69	0.04
Hispanic or Latino:	3,225	2.04
Central American:	156	0.10
Costa Rican	20	0.01
Guatemalan	25	0.02
Honduran	7	0.00
Nicaraguan	11	0.01
Panamanian	77	0.05
Salvadoran	7	0.00
Other Central American	9	0.01
Cuban	137	0.09
Dominican Republic	33	0.02
Mexican	1,640	1.04
Puerto Rican	531	0.34
South American:	127	0.08
Argentinean	13	0.01
Bolivian	2	0.00
Chilean	10	0.01
Colombian	33	0.02
Ecuadorian	12	0.01
Paraguayan	3	0.00
Peruvian	21	0.01
Venezuelan	21	0.01
Other South American	12	0.01
Other Hispanic or Latino	601	0.38
Hungarian	350	0.22
Icelander	9	0.01
Iranian	226	0.14
Irish	12,795	8.10
Israeli	18	0.01
Italian	2,793	1.77
Latvian	6	0.00
Lithuanian	166	0.11
Luxemburger	8	0.01
Macedonian	5	0.00
Maltese	9	0.01
New Zealander	35	0.02
Northern European	116	0.07
Norwegian	875	0.55
Pennsylvania German	4	0.00
Polish	1,667	1.06
Portuguese	93	0.06
Romanian	165	0.10
Russian	464	0.29
Scandinavian	162	0.10
Scotch-Irish	4,793	3.04
Scottish	3,336	2.11
Serbian	27	0.02
Slavic	19	0.01
Slovak	148	0.09
Slovene	7	0.00
Swedish	754	0.48
Swiss	301	0.19
Turkish	109	0.07
Ukrainian	167	0.11
United States or American	18,157	11.50
Welsh	904	0.57
West Indian, excl. Hispanic:	1,272	0.81
Bahamian	77	0.05
Barbadian	53	0.03
Belizean	7	0.00
Bermudan	54	0.03
British West Indian	99	0.06
Dutch West Indian	10	0.01
Haitian	42	0.03
Jamaican	419	0.27
Trinidadian and Tobagonian	166	0.11
U.S. Virgin Islander	47	0.03
West Indian	298	0.19
White:	104,278	65.91
Not Hispanic (100,333)	102,425	64.74
Hispanic (1,665)	1,853	1.17
Yugoslavian	67	0.04

Jasper

Place Type: City
County: Walker
Population: 14,052

Ancestry/Race	Number	%
Acadian/Cajun	9	0.06
African American/Black:	1,987	14.14
Not Hispanic (1,941)	1,961	13.96
Hispanic (24)	26	0.19
African, sub-Saharan:	85	0.60
African	79	0.56
Nigerian	6	0.04
Am. Ind. or Alaska Nat., not spec.	29	0.21
American Indian tribes, specified:	34	0.24
Blackfeet	2	0.01
Cherokee (3)	16	0.11
Choctaw	2	0.01
Creek (4)	4	0.03
Crow (1)	1	0.01
Houma	1	0.01
Navajo (1)	1	0.01
Sioux (1)	4	0.03
All other tribes (3)	3	0.02
American Indian tribes, not spec.	4	0.03
Armenian	5	0.04
Asian:	88	0.63
Chinese, ex. Taiwanese (13)	16	0.11
Filipino (3)	3	0.02
Indian (20)	21	0.15
Japanese	1	0.01
Korean (14)	17	0.12
Pakistani (1)	2	0.01
Thai (1)	1	0.01
Vietnamese (22)	23	0.16
Other Asian, not specified	4	0.03
British	83	0.59
Canadian	10	0.07
Carpatho Rusyn	7	0.05
Czechoslovakian	9	0.06
Danish	6	0.04
Dutch	155	1.10
English	1,050	7.46
European	91	0.65
French, except Basque	47	0.33
French Canadian	9	0.06
German	716	5.09
Greek	35	0.25
Guyanese	22	0.16
Hawaii Native/Pacific Islander:	3	0.02
Polynesian: (3)	3	0.02
Native Hawaiian (3)	3	0.02
Hispanic or Latino:	189	1.35
Central American:	4	0.03
Guatemalan	1	0.01
Honduran	1	0.01
Panamanian	2	0.01
Cuban	3	0.02
Mexican	122	0.87
Puerto Rican	19	0.14
South American:	2	0.01
Colombian	1	0.01
Ecuadorian	1	0.01
Other Hispanic or Latino	39	0.28
Hungarian	23	0.16
Irish	1,453	10.32
Italian	197	1.40
Northern European	6	0.04
Norwegian	18	0.13
Polish	61	0.43
Portuguese	6	0.04
Russian	8	0.06
Scandinavian	7	0.05
Scotch-Irish	349	2.48
Scottish	213	1.51
Swedish	17	0.12
Swiss	9	0.06
United States or American	3,193	22.69
Welsh	51	0.36
West Indian, excl. Hispanic:	10	0.07
Dutch West Indian	5	0.04
Haitian	5	0.04
White:	11,903	84.71
Not Hispanic (11,739)	11,810	84.04
Hispanic (86)	93	0.66
Yugoslavian	9	0.06

Leeds

Place Type: City
County: Jefferson
Population: 10,455

Ancestry/Race	Number	%
African American/Black:	1,691	16.17
Not Hispanic (1,658)	1,686	16.13
Hispanic (5)	5	0.05
African, sub-Saharan:	28	0.26
African	28	0.26
Am. Ind. or Alaska Nat., not spec.	25	0.24
American Indian tribes, specified:	56	0.54
Blackfeet	4	0.04
Cherokee (17)	36	0.34
Creek (4)	14	0.13
Latin American Indians (1)	1	0.01
Sioux (1)	1	0.01
Arab:	21	0.20
Lebanese	21	0.20
Asian:	59	0.56
Chinese, ex. Taiwanese (9)	9	0.09
Filipino	1	0.01
Indian (27)	27	0.26
Japanese (8)	13	0.12

Notes: 1. Figures in the "Number" column do not add up to the total population due to: a) Ancestry/Race overlap — e.g. persons can report being both White and Irish, b) persons of Hispanic origin can report being any race, c) persons reporting two ancestries are counted in both categories. 2. Numbers in parentheses indicate the number of persons reporting this ancestry/race alone, not in combination with any other ancestry/race. 3. Refer to the Explanation of Data in the front of the book for more detailed information.

Korean (2)	2	0.02
Pakistani (1)	2	0.02
Vietnamese (3)	4	0.04
Other Asian, not specified	1	0.01
British	15	0.14
Canadian	40	0.37
Dutch	107	0.99
English	971	9.02
European	129	1.20
French, except Basque	195	1.81
French Canadian	59	0.55
German	769	7.14
Hawaii Native/Pacific Islander:	9	0.09
Micronesian: (2)	3	0.03
Guamanian/Chamorro (2)	3	0.03
Polynesian: (3)	3	0.03
Samoan (3)	3	0.03
Other Pac. Isl., not spec. (3)	3	0.03
Hispanic or Latino:	140	1.34
Central American:	6	0.06
Guatemalan	1	0.01
Honduran	1	0.01
Panamanian	1	0.01
Salvadoran	3	0.03
Cuban	7	0.07
Mexican	86	0.82
Puerto Rican	3	0.03
South American:	3	0.03
Colombian	2	0.02
Paraguayan	1	0.01
Other Hispanic or Latino	35	0.33
Hungarian	21	0.20
Iranian	15	0.14
Irish	1,059	9.83
Italian	336	3.12
Lithuanian	9	0.08
Northern European	39	0.36
Norwegian	6	0.06
Polish	78	0.72
Portuguese	17	0.16
Russian	8	0.07
Scotch-Irish	319	2.96
Scottish	208	1.93
Swedish	77	0.72
Swiss	6	0.06
United States or American	1,950	18.11
Welsh	12	0.11
White:	8,650	82.74
Not Hispanic (8,487)	8,556	81.84
Hispanic (84)	94	0.90

Madison

Place Type: City
County: Madison
Population: 29,329

Ancestry/Race	Number	%
Acadian/Cajun	22	0.08
African American/Black:	3,942	13.44
Not Hispanic (3,796)	3,917	13.36
Hispanic (16)	25	0.09
African, sub-Saharan:	249	0.86
African	158	0.54
Ethiopian	6	0.02
Nigerian	74	0.25
South African	11	0.04
Alaska Native tribes, specified:	4	0.01
Alaska Athabascan	2	0.01
Eskimo	2	0.01
Am. Ind. or Alaska Nat., not spec.	85	0.29
Albanian	9	0.03
Alsatian	7	0.02
American Indian tribes, specified:	300	1.02
Blackfeet	2	0.01
Cherokee (124)	253	0.86
Cheyenne	1	0.00
Chickasaw	1	0.00
Chippewa (2)	5	0.02
Choctaw	5	0.02
Creek (5)	6	0.02
Crow (2)	2	0.01
Delaware (2)	2	0.01
Iroquois (3)	4	0.01
Latin American Indians (4)	7	0.02
Navajo (1)	1	0.00
Seminole	1	0.00
Sioux (1)	2	0.01
All other tribes (4)	8	0.03
American Indian tribes, not spec.	19	0.06
Arab:	214	0.74
Egyptian	25	0.09
Jordanian	35	0.12
Lebanese	64	0.22
Palestinian	12	0.04
Syrian	15	0.05
Other Arab	63	0.22
Armenian	67	0.23
Asian:	1,259	4.29
Bangladeshi (4)	5	0.02
Cambodian (5)	5	0.02
Chinese, ex. Taiwanese (172)	200	0.68
Filipino (59)	81	0.28
Indian (368)	414	1.41
Indonesian	2	0.01
Japanese (56)	96	0.33
Korean (183)	230	0.78
Pakistani (28)	33	0.11
Sri Lankan (2)	2	0.01
Taiwanese (9)	10	0.03
Thai (7)	12	0.04
Vietnamese (100)	111	0.38
Other Asian, specified (2)	11	0.04
Other Asian, not specified (24)	47	0.16
Austrian	85	0.29
Basque	3	0.01
Belgian	55	0.19
British	236	0.81
Bulgarian	18	0.06
Canadian	66	0.23
Czech	76	0.26
Czechoslovakian	32	0.11
Danish	67	0.23
Dutch	408	1.40
English	3,894	13.39
European	530	1.82
Finnish	47	0.16
French, except Basque	803	2.76
French Canadian	95	0.33
German	4,067	13.98
Greek	53	0.18
Hawaii Native/Pacific Islander:	43	0.15
Micronesian: (6)	10	0.03
Guamanian/Chamorro (5)	9	0.03
Other Micronesian (1)	1	0.00
Polynesian: (7)	16	0.05
Native Hawaiian (5)	12	0.04
Samoan (1)	3	0.01
Other Polynesian (1)	1	0.00
Other Pac. Isl., not spec. (5)	17	0.06
Hispanic or Latino:	675	2.30
Central American:	49	0.17
Costa Rican	10	0.03
Guatemalan	11	0.04
Honduran	11	0.04
Nicaraguan	1	0.00
Panamanian	15	0.05
Other Central American	1	0.00
Cuban	35	0.12
Dominican Republic	12	0.04
Mexican	275	0.94
Puerto Rican	163	0.56
South American:	21	0.07
Argentinean	1	0.00
Bolivian	3	0.01
Colombian	7	0.02
Peruvian	1	0.00
Venezuelan	7	0.02
Other South American	2	0.01
Other Hispanic or Latino	120	0.41
Hungarian	60	0.21
Iranian	54	0.19
Irish	3,438	11.82
Italian	871	2.99
Lithuanian	50	0.17
Northern European	12	0.04
Norwegian	325	1.12
Pennsylvania German	10	0.03
Polish	498	1.71
Portuguese	44	0.15
Romanian	49	0.17
Russian	78	0.27
Scandinavian	70	0.24
Scotch-Irish	776	2.67
Scottish	769	2.64
Slavic	16	0.06
Slovak	70	0.24
Swedish	335	1.15
Swiss	63	0.22
Ukrainian	43	0.15
United States or American	3,358	11.54
Welsh	321	1.10
West Indian, excl. Hispanic:	76	0.26
Jamaican	39	0.13
Trinidadian and Tobagonian	37	0.13
White:	23,988	81.79
Not Hispanic (23,053)	23,490	80.09
Hispanic (453)	498	1.70
Yugoslavian	9	0.03

Millbrook

Place Type: City
County: Elmore
Population: 10,386

Ancestry/Race	Number	%
Afghan	13	0.13
African American/Black:	1,817	17.49
Not Hispanic (1,764)	1,803	17.36
Hispanic (13)	14	0.13
African, sub-Saharan:	13	0.13
Sudanese	13	0.13
Am. Ind. or Alaska Nat., not spec.	38	0.37
American Indian tribes, specified:	61	0.59
Cherokee (17)	34	0.33
Chippewa (4)	5	0.05
Creek (4)	11	0.11
Iroquois	2	0.02
Latin American Indians (1)	1	0.01
Lumbee	1	0.01
Osage (2)	2	0.02
Pueblo	1	0.01
Sioux (2)	3	0.03
All other tribes	1	0.01
American Indian tribes, not spec.	16	0.15
Arab:	10	0.10
Iraqi	10	0.10
Asian:	98	0.94
Chinese, ex. Taiwanese (3)	5	0.05
Filipino (15)	24	0.23
Indian (10)	10	0.10
Indonesian (1)	1	0.01
Japanese (6)	13	0.13
Korean (13)	21	0.20
Malaysian	1	0.01
Thai (3)	6	0.06
Vietnamese (3)	5	0.05
Other Asian, not specified (5)	12	0.12
Belgian	8	0.08
British	79	0.77
Canadian	14	0.14
Celtic	9	0.09
Czech	19	0.19
Czechoslovakian	5	0.05
Danish	10	0.10
Dutch	133	1.30
English	854	8.34
European	96	0.94
French, except Basque	223	2.18

Notes: 1. Figures in the "Number" column do not add up to the total population due to: a) Ancestry/Race overlap — e.g. persons can report being both White and Irish, b) persons of Hispanic origin can report being any race, c) persons reporting two ancestries are counted in both categories. 2. Numbers in parentheses indicate the number of persons reporting this ancestry/race alone, not in combination with any other ancestry/race. 3. Refer to the Explanation of Data in the front of the book for more detailed information.

Ancestry/Race	Number	%
French Canadian	45	0.44
German	769	7.51
Greek	31	0.30
Guyanese	8	0.08
Hawaii Native/Pacific Islander:	4	0.04
Micronesian: (2)	2	0.02
Guamanian/Chamorro (2)	2	0.02
Polynesian:	1	0.01
Native Hawaiian	1	0.01
Other Pac. Isl., not spec.	1	0.01
Hispanic or Latino:	150	1.44
Central American:	1	0.01
Nicaraguan	1	0.01
Cuban	1	0.01
Mexican	75	0.72
Puerto Rican	24	0.23
South American:	5	0.05
Argentinean	1	0.01
Colombian	1	0.01
Peruvian	3	0.03
Other Hispanic or Latino	44	0.42
Hungarian	26	0.25
Irish	718	7.01
Italian	155	1.51
Norwegian	85	0.83
Polish	64	0.62
Portuguese	34	0.33
Scandinavian	9	0.09
Scotch-Irish	204	1.99
Scottish	172	1.68
Slavic	16	0.16
Slovak	2	0.02
Slovene	2	0.02
Swedish	31	0.30
Swiss	4	0.04
United States or American	1,802	17.59
Welsh	16	0.16
West Indian, excl. Hispanic:	12	0.12
Dutch West Indian	2	0.02
Jamaican	10	0.10
White:	8,421	81.08
Not Hispanic (8,222)	8,337	80.27
Hispanic (72)	84	0.81

Mobile

Place Type: City
County: Mobile
Population: 198,915

Ancestry/Race	Number	%
Acadian/Cajun	47	0.02
Afghan	7	0.00
African American/Black:	92,888	46.70
Not Hispanic (91,660)	92,425	46.46
Hispanic (408)	463	0.23
African, sub-Saharan:	2,268	1.14
African	2,103	1.06
Cape Verdean	4	0.00
Ethiopian	91	0.05
Ghanian	20	0.01
Nigerian	19	0.01
Senegalese	8	0.00
South African	9	0.00
Sudanese	7	0.00
Zimbabwean	7	0.00
Alaska Native tribes, specified:	6	0.00
Tlingit-Haida (2)	6	0.00
Am. Ind. or Alaska Nat., not spec.	469	0.24
Alsatian	11	0.01
American Indian tribes, specified:	690	0.35
Apache (10)	15	0.01
Blackfeet (3)	16	0.01
Cherokee (65)	229	0.12
Chickasaw (3)	4	0.00
Chippewa (6)	8	0.00
Choctaw (55)	134	0.07
Colville (2)	2	0.00
Comanche	3	0.00
Cree (2)	2	0.00
Creek (84)	163	0.08
Crow (1)	2	0.00
Houma (9)	11	0.01
Iroquois (6)	10	0.01
Kiowa (2)	2	0.00
Latin American Indians (7)	19	0.01
Lumbee (2)	2	0.00
Navajo (3)	7	0.00
Potawatomi (3)	3	0.00
Pueblo (1)	5	0.00
Puget Sound Salish (2)	2	0.00
Seminole	13	0.01
Sioux (2)	9	0.00
Tohono O'Odham	1	0.00
All other tribes (13)	28	0.01
American Indian tribes, not spec.	71	0.04
Arab:	897	0.45
Arab/Arabic	116	0.06
Egyptian	71	0.04
Iraqi	18	0.01
Jordanian	34	0.02
Lebanese	499	0.25
Moroccan	6	0.00
Palestinian	74	0.04
Syrian	16	0.01
Other Arab	63	0.03
Armenian	31	0.02
Asian:	3,565	1.79
Bangladeshi (51)	55	0.03
Cambodian (13)	14	0.01
Chinese, ex. Taiwanese (433)	512	0.26
Filipino (168)	262	0.13
Hmong	1	0.00
Indian (562)	650	0.33
Indonesian (5)	5	0.00
Japanese (90)	145	0.07
Korean (142)	164	0.08
Laotian (47)	58	0.03
Malaysian (36)	43	0.02
Pakistani (89)	105	0.05
Sri Lankan (14)	15	0.01
Taiwanese (6)	7	0.00
Thai (24)	31	0.02
Vietnamese (1,185)	1,285	0.65
Other Asian, specified (11)	34	0.02
Other Asian, not specified (76)	179	0.09
Australian	12	0.01
Austrian	156	0.08
Basque	5	0.00
Belgian	73	0.04
British	765	0.38
Canadian	166	0.08
Celtic	13	0.01
Croatian	133	0.07
Cypriot	9	0.00
Czech	121	0.06
Czechoslovakian	102	0.05
Danish	264	0.13
Dutch	1,401	0.70
Eastern European	64	0.03
English	13,865	6.97
Estonian	9	0.00
European	1,362	0.68
Finnish	90	0.05
French, except Basque	4,763	2.39
French Canadian	472	0.24
German	11,486	5.78
Greek	601	0.30
Guyanese	14	0.01
Hawaii Native/Pacific Islander:	162	0.08
Micronesian: (13)	27	0.01
Guamanian/Chamorro (13)	24	0.01
Other Micronesian	3	0.00
Polynesian: (24)	53	0.03
Native Hawaiian (17)	34	0.02
Samoan (6)	18	0.01
Other Polynesian (1)	1	0.00
Other Pac. Isl., specified	22	0.01
Other Pac. Isl., not spec. (14)	60	0.03
Hispanic or Latino:	2,828	1.42
Central American:	207	0.10
Costa Rican	25	0.01
Guatemalan	42	0.02
Honduran	30	0.02
Nicaraguan	22	0.01
Panamanian	35	0.02
Salvadoran	48	0.02
Other Central American	5	0.00
Cuban	262	0.13
Dominican Republic	13	0.01
Mexican	944	0.47
Puerto Rican	307	0.15
South American:	260	0.13
Argentinean	19	0.01
Bolivian	25	0.01
Chilean	27	0.01
Colombian	66	0.03
Ecuadorian	8	0.00
Paraguayan	9	0.00
Peruvian	57	0.03
Uruguayan	3	0.00
Venezuelan	42	0.02
Other South American	4	0.00
Other Hispanic or Latino	835	0.42
Hungarian	241	0.12
Icelander	15	0.01
Iranian	141	0.07
Irish	13,588	6.83
Israeli	33	0.02
Italian	2,904	1.46
Latvian	7	0.00
Lithuanian	70	0.04
Luxemburger	14	0.01
Maltese	6	0.00
New Zealander	3	0.00
Northern European	64	0.03
Norwegian	687	0.35
Pennsylvania German	26	0.01
Polish	1,097	0.55
Portuguese	55	0.03
Romanian	68	0.03
Russian	350	0.18
Scandinavian	81	0.04
Scotch-Irish	4,197	2.11
Scottish	3,014	1.52
Serbian	21	0.01
Slavic	38	0.02
Slovak	104	0.05
Slovene	17	0.01
Swedish	602	0.30
Swiss	262	0.13
Ukrainian	111	0.06
United States or American	16,873	8.48
Welsh	799	0.40
West Indian, excl. Hispanic:	324	0.16
Bahamian	93	0.05
Barbadian	6	0.00
Bermudan	9	0.00
British West Indian	12	0.01
Dutch West Indian	18	0.01
Haitian	33	0.02
Jamaican	116	0.06
Trinidadian and Tobagonian	5	0.00
West Indian	26	0.01
Other West Indian	6	0.00
White:	101,736	51.15
Not Hispanic (98,965)	100,266	50.41
Hispanic (1,286)	1,470	0.74
Yugoslavian	225	0.11

Montgomery

Place Type: City
County: Montgomery
Population: 201,568

Ancestry/Race	Number	%
Acadian/Cajun	51	0.03
African American/Black:	100,966	50.09
Not Hispanic (99,631)	100,479	49.85

Notes: 1. Figures in the "Number" column do not add up to the total population due to: a) Ancestry/Race overlap — e.g. persons can report being both White and Irish, b) persons of Hispanic origin can report being any race, c) persons reporting two ancestries are counted in both categories. 2. Numbers in parentheses indicate the number of persons reporting this ancestry/race alone, not in combination with any other ancestry/race. 3. Refer to the Explanation of Data in the front of the book for more detailed information.

Hispanic (417)	487	0.24
African, sub-Saharan:	1,946	0.97
African	1,606	0.80
Ethiopian	10	0.00
Liberian	7	0.00
Nigerian	193	0.10
Sierra Leonean	73	0.04
South African	41	0.02
Other sub-Saharan African	16	0.01
Alaska Native tribes, specified:	3	0.00
Alaska Athabascan (3)	3	0.00
Am. Ind. or Alaska Nat., not spec.	377	0.19
Alsatian	26	0.01
American Indian tribes, specified:	627	0.31
Apache (6)	16	0.01
Blackfeet (9)	27	0.01
Cherokee (110)	322	0.16
Cheyenne	1	0.00
Chickasaw	1	0.00
Chippewa (9)	13	0.01
Choctaw (4)	19	0.01
Comanche (2)	4	0.00
Cree	2	0.00
Creek (57)	115	0.06
Crow	6	0.00
Houma (1)	1	0.00
Iroquois (2)	8	0.00
Latin American Indians (9)	25	0.01
Lumbee (4)	7	0.00
Menominee	1	0.00
Navajo	5	0.00
Ottawa (1)	1	0.00
Paiute	1	0.00
Pueblo (4)	8	0.00
Seminole (4)	12	0.01
Shoshone	1	0.00
Sioux (7)	8	0.00
Ute (3)	3	0.00
All other tribes (13)	20	0.01
American Indian tribes, not spec.	125	0.06
Arab:	276	0.14
Egyptian	18	0.01
Lebanese	133	0.07
Moroccan	12	0.01
Palestinian	44	0.02
Syrian	41	0.02
Other Arab	28	0.01
Armenian	44	0.02
Asian:	2,906	1.44
Bangladeshi (13)	13	0.01
Cambodian (13)	18	0.01
Chinese, ex. Taiwanese (387)	446	0.22
Filipino (270)	469	0.23
Indian (440)	518	0.26
Indonesian (10)	11	0.01
Japanese (122)	194	0.10
Korean (240)	359	0.18
Laotian (188)	202	0.10
Malaysian (5)	14	0.01
Pakistani (36)	44	0.02
Sri Lankan (13)	16	0.01
Taiwanese (8)	14	0.01
Thai (91)	119	0.06
Vietnamese (176)	208	0.10
Other Asian, specified (1)	26	0.01
Other Asian, not specified (97)	235	0.12
Australian	62	0.03
Austrian	119	0.06
Belgian	52	0.03
Brazilian	56	0.03
British	958	0.48
Bulgarian	6	0.00
Canadian	127	0.06
Celtic	24	0.01
Croatian	53	0.03
Cypriot	26	0.01
Czech	172	0.09
Czechoslovakian	112	0.06
Danish	204	0.10
Dutch	1,303	0.65
Eastern European	33	0.02
English	13,567	6.73
European	1,571	0.78
Finnish	42	0.02
French, except Basque	2,737	1.36
French Canadian	649	0.32
German	9,170	4.55
German Russian	44	0.02
Greek	211	0.10
Hawaii Native/Pacific Islander:	175	0.09
Micronesian: (19)	30	0.01
Guamanian/Chamorro (16)	27	0.01
Other Micronesian (3)	3	0.00
Polynesian: (43)	79	0.04
Native Hawaiian (24)	48	0.02
Samoan (17)	29	0.01
Tongan (1)	1	0.00
Other Polynesian (1)	1	0.00
Other Pac. Isl., specified	22	0.01
Other Pac. Isl., not spec. (9)	44	0.02
Hispanic or Latino:	2,484	1.23
Central American:	163	0.08
Costa Rican	8	0.00
Guatemalan	36	0.02
Honduran	17	0.01
Nicaraguan	12	0.01
Panamanian	52	0.03
Salvadoran	19	0.01
Other Central American	19	0.01
Cuban	143	0.07
Dominican Republic	22	0.01
Mexican	976	0.48
Puerto Rican	352	0.17
South American:	147	0.07
Argentinean	7	0.00
Bolivian	9	0.00
Chilean	23	0.01
Colombian	64	0.03
Ecuadorian	2	0.00
Paraguayan	2	0.00
Peruvian	22	0.01
Uruguayan	5	0.00
Venezuelan	12	0.01
Other South American	1	0.00
Other Hispanic or Latino	681	0.34
Hungarian	214	0.11
Iranian	18	0.01
Irish	10,934	5.42
Italian	2,218	1.10
Latvian	23	0.01
Lithuanian	115	0.06
Maltese	9	0.00
Northern European	161	0.08
Norwegian	784	0.39
Pennsylvania German	47	0.02
Polish	1,024	0.51
Portuguese	134	0.07
Romanian	62	0.03
Russian	222	0.11
Scandinavian	123	0.06
Scotch-Irish	4,479	2.22
Scottish	3,674	1.82
Serbian	25	0.01
Slavic	35	0.02
Slovak	89	0.04
Slovene	55	0.03
Swedish	835	0.41
Swiss	177	0.09
Turkish	28	0.01
Ukrainian	115	0.06
United States or American	18,878	9.36
Welsh	795	0.39
West Indian, excl. Hispanic:	252	0.12
Barbadian	8	0.00
Belizean	31	0.02
Dutch West Indian	7	0.00
Haitian	14	0.01
Jamaican	159	0.08
Trinidadian and Tobagonian	18	0.01
U.S. Virgin Islander	15	0.01
White:	97,494	48.37
Not Hispanic (94,868)	96,137	47.69
Hispanic (1,217)	1,357	0.67
Yugoslavian	22	0.01

Mountain Brook

Place Type: City
County: Jefferson
Population: 20,604

Ancestry/Race	Number	%
African American/Black:	63	0.31
Not Hispanic (62)	62	0.30
Hispanic (1)	1	0.00
African, sub-Saharan:	60	0.29
African	22	0.10
South African	38	0.18
Am. Ind. or Alaska Nat., not spec.	2	0.01
Albanian	10	0.05
American Indian tribes, specified:	19	0.09
Apache	1	0.00
Cherokee (3)	9	0.04
Choctaw (1)	1	0.00
Creek (2)	4	0.02
Delaware (1)	1	0.00
Latin American Indians	2	0.01
Potawatomi (1)	1	0.00
American Indian tribes, not spec.	1	0.00
Arab:	138	0.66
Arab/Arabic	13	0.06
Egyptian	7	0.03
Lebanese	77	0.37
Palestinian	14	0.07
Syrian	27	0.13
Asian:	165	0.80
Chinese, ex. Taiwanese (38)	41	0.20
Filipino (14)	18	0.09
Indian (22)	27	0.13
Indonesian (1)	3	0.01
Japanese (10)	16	0.08
Korean (23)	27	0.13
Malaysian (1)	1	0.00
Taiwanese	2	0.01
Thai (12)	14	0.07
Vietnamese (7)	8	0.04
Other Asian, not specified (3)	8	0.04
Assyrian/Chaldean/Syriac	10	0.05
Austrian	56	0.27
British	287	1.37
Canadian	53	0.25
Celtic	51	0.24
Czech	72	0.34
Czechoslovakian	10	0.05
Danish	34	0.16
Dutch	230	1.10
Eastern European	106	0.51
English	5,864	27.95
European	415	1.98
Finnish	15	0.07
French, except Basque	629	3.00
French Canadian	67	0.32
German	2,094	9.98
Greek	205	0.98
Hawaii Native/Pacific Islander:	7	0.03
Micronesian: (1)	1	0.00
Guamanian/Chamorro (1)	1	0.00
Polynesian: (3)	3	0.01
Native Hawaiian (2)	2	0.01
Samoan (1)	1	0.00
Other Pac. Isl., not spec.	3	0.01
Hispanic or Latino:	119	0.58
Central American:	23	0.11
Costa Rican	1	0.00
Guatemalan	12	0.06
Honduran	3	0.01
Nicaraguan	7	0.03
Cuban	19	0.09
Mexican	37	0.18
Puerto Rican	7	0.03

Notes: 1. Figures in the "Number" column do not add up to the total population due to: a) Ancestry/Race overlap — e.g. persons can report being both White and Irish, b) persons of Hispanic origin can report being any race, c) persons reporting two ancestries are counted in both categories. 2. Numbers in parentheses indicate the number of persons reporting this ancestry/race alone, not in combination with any other ancestry/race. 3. Refer to the Explanation of Data in the front of the book for more detailed information.

South American:	15	0.07
Chilean	5	0.02
Colombian	6	0.03
Peruvian	1	0.00
Venezuelan	2	0.01
Other South American	1	0.00
Other Hispanic or Latino	18	0.09
Hungarian	79	0.38
Irish	1,700	8.10
Italian	710	3.38
Latvian	23	0.11
Lithuanian	121	0.58
Northern European	38	0.18
Norwegian	183	0.87
Polish	296	1.41
Romanian	19	0.09
Russian	338	1.61
Scandinavian	9	0.04
Scotch-Irish	1,250	5.96
Scottish	1,367	6.51
Slavic	12	0.06
Slovak	33	0.16
Swedish	71	0.34
Swiss	81	0.39
Turkish	48	0.23
Ukrainian	34	0.16
United States or American	1,854	8.84
Welsh	236	1.12
White:	20,360	98.82
Not Hispanic (20,221)	20,255	98.31
Hispanic (103)	105	0.51

Muscle Shoals

Place Type: City
County: Colbert
Population: 11,924

Ancestry/Race	Number	%
African American/Black:	1,726	14.48
Not Hispanic (1,674)	1,708	14.32
Hispanic (15)	18	0.15
African, sub-Saharan:	57	0.47
African	57	0.47
Am. Ind. or Alaska Nat., not spec.	30	0.25
American Indian tribes, specified:	43	0.36
Blackfeet	1	0.01
Cherokee (23)	31	0.26
Chickasaw (2)	2	0.02
Choctaw (4)	4	0.03
All other tribes (4)	5	0.04
American Indian tribes, not spec.	6	0.05
Arab:	12	0.10
Moroccan	12	0.10
Asian:	81	0.68
Bangladeshi (1)	1	0.01
Chinese, ex. Taiwanese (17)	22	0.18
Filipino (3)	5	0.04
Indian (33)	34	0.29
Japanese (2)	2	0.02
Korean (2)	2	0.02
Thai (2)	4	0.03
Vietnamese (4)	4	0.03
Other Asian, specified	2	0.02
Other Asian, not specified (3)	5	0.04
British	28	0.23
Czechoslovakian	15	0.12
Dutch	58	0.48
English	1,152	9.59
European	90	0.75
French, except Basque	154	1.28
German	718	5.98
Greek	65	0.54
Hawaii Native/Pacific Islander:	5	0.04
Other Pac. Isl., specified	2	0.02
Other Pac. Isl., not spec.	3	0.03
Hispanic or Latino:	138	1.16
Central American:	2	0.02
Guatemalan	2	0.02
Cuban	5	0.04
Mexican	73	0.61
Puerto Rican	19	0.16
South American:	5	0.04
Colombian	4	0.03
Venezuelan	1	0.01
Other Hispanic or Latino	34	0.29
Hungarian	26	0.22
Irish	1,195	9.95
Israeli	22	0.18
Italian	91	0.76
Norwegian	86	0.72
Pennsylvania German	6	0.05
Polish	139	1.16
Scotch-Irish	155	1.29
Scottish	113	0.94
Swedish	22	0.18
United States or American	2,852	23.74
Welsh	31	0.26
White:	10,068	84.43
Not Hispanic (9,927)	9,982	83.71
Hispanic (75)	86	0.72

Northport

Place Type: City
County: Tuscaloosa
Population: 19,435

Ancestry/Race	Number	%
African American/Black:	5,098	26.23
Not Hispanic (5,029)	5,067	26.07
Hispanic (29)	31	0.16
African, sub-Saharan:	336	1.76
African	336	1.76
Am. Ind. or Alaska Nat., not spec.	32	0.16
American Indian tribes, specified:	57	0.29
Apache (8)	8	0.04
Blackfeet	1	0.01
Cherokee (10)	33	0.17
Choctaw (5)	5	0.03
Creek (3)	4	0.02
Iroquois (1)	1	0.01
All other tribes (4)	5	0.03
American Indian tribes, not spec.	9	0.05
Arab:	47	0.25
Arab/Arabic	18	0.09
Syrian	9	0.05
Other Arab	20	0.10
Asian:	197	1.01
Chinese, ex. Taiwanese (35)	37	0.19
Filipino (16)	27	0.14
Indian (22)	24	0.12
Japanese (14)	24	0.12
Korean (40)	44	0.23
Pakistani (1)	1	0.01
Taiwanese (6)	6	0.03
Thai	2	0.01
Vietnamese (14)	17	0.09
Other Asian, specified (1)	2	0.01
Other Asian, not specified (6)	13	0.07
Belgian	21	0.11
Brazilian	6	0.03
British	133	0.70
Celtic	57	0.30
Czech	48	0.25
Czechoslovakian	5	0.03
Danish	35	0.18
Dutch	261	1.37
English	1,621	8.49
European	281	1.47
French, except Basque	287	1.50
French Canadian	28	0.15
German	1,264	6.62
Greek	15	0.08
Hawaii Native/Pacific Islander:	37	0.19
Micronesian: (27)	29	0.15
Guamanian/Chamorro (27)	29	0.15
Polynesian: (3)	5	0.03
Native Hawaiian (3)	5	0.03
Other Pac. Isl., specified	1	0.01
Other Pac. Isl., not spec.	2	0.01
Hispanic or Latino:	374	1.92
Central American:	66	0.34
Guatemalan	58	0.30
Honduran	3	0.02
Panamanian	5	0.03
Cuban	8	0.04
Dominican Republic	2	0.01
Mexican	215	1.11
Puerto Rican	17	0.09
South American:	7	0.04
Argentinean	1	0.01
Ecuadorian	1	0.01
Peruvian	1	0.01
Other South American	4	0.02
Other Hispanic or Latino	59	0.30
Hungarian	33	0.17
Irish	1,330	6.97
Italian	95	0.50
Norwegian	71	0.37
Polish	42	0.22
Portuguese	10	0.05
Romanian	8	0.04
Russian	17	0.09
Scandinavian	47	0.25
Scotch-Irish	457	2.39
Scottish	474	2.48
Slovak	7	0.04
Swedish	26	0.14
Swiss	18	0.09
Ukrainian	6	0.03
United States or American	2,608	13.67
Welsh	78	0.41
West Indian, excl. Hispanic:	77	0.40
Jamaican	36	0.19
Trinidadian and Tobagonian	36	0.19
West Indian	5	0.03
White:	13,935	71.70
Not Hispanic (13,696)	13,802	71.02
Hispanic (124)	133	0.68
Yugoslavian	21	0.11

Opelika

Place Type: City
County: Lee
Population: 23,498

Ancestry/Race	Number	%
African American/Black:	10,149	43.19
Not Hispanic (10,034)	10,102	42.99
Hispanic (45)	47	0.20
African, sub-Saharan:	298	1.27
African	273	1.16
Nigerian	25	0.11
Am. Ind. or Alaska Nat., not spec.	46	0.20
American Indian tribes, specified:	67	0.29
Blackfeet (1)	2	0.01
Cherokee (18)	42	0.18
Chippewa (2)	2	0.01
Choctaw	1	0.00
Creek (1)	6	0.03
Houma (2)	2	0.01
Latin American Indians	9	0.04
Yuman (1)	1	0.00
All other tribes (2)	2	0.01
American Indian tribes, not spec.	6	0.03
Arab:	28	0.12
Lebanese	28	0.12
Asian:	278	1.18
Chinese, ex. Taiwanese (12)	16	0.07
Filipino (10)	15	0.06
Indian (30)	34	0.14
Indonesian (1)	1	0.00
Japanese (6)	15	0.06
Korean (31)	40	0.17
Laotian (86)	91	0.39
Pakistani (2)	2	0.01
Thai (10)	10	0.04
Vietnamese (8)	19	0.08

Notes: 1. Figures in the "Number" column do not add up to the total population due to: a) Ancestry/Race overlap — e.g. persons can report being both White and Irish, b) persons of Hispanic origin can report being any race, c) persons reporting two ancestries are counted in both categories. 2. Numbers in parentheses indicate the number of persons reporting this ancestry/race alone, not in combination with any other ancestry/race. 3. Refer to the Explanation of Data in the front of the book for more detailed information.

Ancestry/Race	Number	%
Other Asian, specified	8	0.03
Other Asian, not specified (16)	27	0.11
Australian	13	0.06
British	221	0.94
Canadian	22	0.09
Croatian	22	0.09
Czech	13	0.06
Czechoslovakian	5	0.02
Dutch	173	0.74
English	1,603	6.81
European	199	0.85
Finnish	93	0.40
French, except Basque	296	1.26
French Canadian	32	0.14
German	985	4.19
Hawaii Native/Pacific Islander:	23	0.10
Micronesian: (1)	1	0.00
Guamanian/Chamorro (1)	1	0.00
Polynesian:	9	0.04
Native Hawaiian	3	0.01
Samoan	6	0.03
Other Pac. Isl., specified	2	0.01
Other Pac. Isl., not spec. (1)	11	0.05
Hispanic or Latino:	252	1.07
Central American:	19	0.08
Costa Rican	1	0.00
Guatemalan	13	0.06
Honduran	3	0.01
Panamanian	1	0.00
Salvadoran	1	0.00
Cuban	2	0.01
Dominican Republic	3	0.01
Mexican	114	0.49
Puerto Rican	25	0.11
South American:	11	0.05
Argentinean	5	0.02
Colombian	3	0.01
Uruguayan	3	0.01
Other Hispanic or Latino	78	0.33
Irish	1,257	5.34
Italian	158	0.67
Lithuanian	7	0.03
Northern European	28	0.12
Norwegian	130	0.55
Polish	57	0.24
Russian	22	0.09
Scotch-Irish	552	2.35
Scottish	350	1.49
Serbian	4	0.02
Slavic	2	0.01
Slovak	19	0.08
Swedish	13	0.06
Swiss	41	0.17
United States or American	3,161	13.43
Welsh	63	0.27
West Indian, excl. Hispanic:	40	0.17
British West Indian	33	0.14
Jamaican	7	0.03
White:	13,047	55.52
Not Hispanic (12,797)	12,904	54.92
Hispanic (135)	143	0.61

Oxford

Place Type: City
County: Calhoun
Population: 14,592

Ancestry/Race	Number	%
African American/Black:	1,475	10.11
Not Hispanic (1,440)	1,473	10.09
Hispanic (2)	2	0.01
African, sub-Saharan:	32	0.22
African	32	0.22
Am. Ind. or Alaska Nat., not spec.	20	0.14
American Indian tribes, specified:	85	0.58
Blackfeet (4)	4	0.03
Cherokee (25)	55	0.38
Chippewa (1)	2	0.01
Creek (11)	13	0.09
Latin American Indians (2)	4	0.03
Navajo	3	0.02
Seminole (1)	3	0.02
All other tribes	1	0.01
American Indian tribes, not spec.	5	0.03
Arab:	8	0.05
Lebanese	8	0.05
Asian:	114	0.78
Chinese, ex. Taiwanese (14)	19	0.13
Filipino (8)	14	0.10
Indian (14)	16	0.11
Indonesian (1)	1	0.01
Japanese (19)	20	0.14
Korean (20)	25	0.17
Thai (3)	5	0.03
Vietnamese (10)	10	0.07
Other Asian, not specified (2)	4	0.03
Austrian	8	0.05
Belgian	10	0.07
British	24	0.16
Canadian	22	0.15
Czech	21	0.14
Czechoslovakian	6	0.04
Danish	27	0.18
Dutch	152	1.04
English	1,294	8.82
European	50	0.34
French, except Basque	190	1.30
French Canadian	16	0.11
German	951	6.48
Greek	31	0.21
Hawaii Native/Pacific Islander:	14	0.10
Micronesian: (1)	3	0.02
Other Micronesian (1)	3	0.02
Polynesian: (3)	8	0.05
Native Hawaiian (1)	2	0.01
Samoan (2)	4	0.03
Other Polynesian	2	0.01
Other Pac. Isl., not spec.	3	0.02
Hispanic or Latino:	281	1.93
Central American:	7	0.05
Honduran	3	0.02
Panamanian	3	0.02
Salvadoran	1	0.01
Cuban	5	0.03
Dominican Republic	6	0.04
Mexican	196	1.34
Puerto Rican	23	0.16
South American:	6	0.04
Chilean	1	0.01
Colombian	3	0.02
Other South American	2	0.01
Other Hispanic or Latino	38	0.26
Hungarian	26	0.18
Irish	1,712	11.67
Italian	148	1.01
Norwegian	29	0.20
Polish	27	0.18
Portuguese	29	0.20
Scandinavian	29	0.20
Scotch-Irish	201	1.37
Scottish	276	1.88
Swedish	49	0.33
Ukrainian	20	0.14
United States or American	3,193	21.77
Welsh	103	0.70
White:	12,873	88.22
Not Hispanic (12,610)	12,709	87.10
Hispanic (152)	164	1.12

Ozark

Place Type: City
County: Dale
Population: 15,119

Ancestry/Race	Number	%
African American/Black:	4,350	28.77
Not Hispanic (4,255)	4,322	28.59
Hispanic (24)	28	0.19
African, sub-Saharan:	85	0.56
African	58	0.38
Kenyan	13	0.09
Nigerian	14	0.09
Alaska Native tribes, specified:	2	0.01
Alaska Athabascan (1)	2	0.01
Alaska Native tribes, not specified	1	0.01
Am. Ind. or Alaska Nat., not spec.	53	0.35
American Indian tribes, specified:	159	1.05
Blackfeet (2)	10	0.07
Cherokee (34)	81	0.54
Cheyenne	1	0.01
Chickasaw (1)	4	0.03
Chippewa (4)	5	0.03
Choctaw (3)	5	0.03
Comanche (4)	5	0.03
Creek (17)	26	0.17
Iroquois	2	0.01
Latin American Indians	5	0.03
Navajo (2)	2	0.01
Potawatomi (4)	4	0.03
Shoshone (1)	1	0.01
Sioux (1)	2	0.01
Ute (1)	1	0.01
All other tribes	5	0.03
American Indian tribes, not spec.	13	0.09
Arab:	37	0.24
Lebanese	37	0.24
Asian:	176	1.16
Cambodian (1)	1	0.01
Chinese, ex. Taiwanese (9)	9	0.06
Filipino (7)	21	0.14
Indian (21)	24	0.16
Japanese (18)	30	0.20
Korean (30)	56	0.37
Pakistani (1)	1	0.01
Thai (8)	9	0.06
Vietnamese (3)	6	0.04
Other Asian, specified	1	0.01
Other Asian, not specified (7)	18	0.12
Australian	20	0.13
Basque	7	0.05
Belgian	4	0.03
British	54	0.36
Canadian	23	0.15
Croatian	15	0.10
Czechoslovakian	15	0.10
Danish	25	0.17
Dutch	201	1.33
English	1,226	8.10
European	115	0.76
French, except Basque	259	1.71
French Canadian	114	0.75
German	1,136	7.50
Greek	21	0.14
Hawaii Native/Pacific Islander:	21	0.14
Micronesian: (1)	1	0.01
Guamanian/Chamorro (1)	1	0.01
Polynesian: (6)	10	0.07
Native Hawaiian (6)	8	0.05
Samoan	2	0.01
Other Pac. Isl., specified	1	0.01
Other Pac. Isl., not spec. (1)	9	0.06
Hispanic or Latino:	314	2.08
Central American:	15	0.10
Panamanian	14	0.09
Salvadoran	1	0.01
Cuban	12	0.08
Dominican Republic	15	0.10
Mexican	92	0.61
Puerto Rican	107	0.71
South American:	6	0.04
Colombian	3	0.02
Peruvian	3	0.02
Other Hispanic or Latino	67	0.44
Hungarian	40	0.26
Irish	1,245	8.22
Italian	300	1.98
Norwegian	65	0.43
Polish	158	1.04

Notes: 1. Figures in the "Number" column do not add up to the total population due to: a) Ancestry/Race overlap — e.g. persons can report being both White and Irish, b) persons of Hispanic origin can report being any race, c) persons reporting two ancestries are counted in both categories. 2. Numbers in parentheses indicate the number of persons reporting this ancestry/race alone, not in combination with any other ancestry/race. 3. Refer to the Explanation of Data in the front of the book for more detailed information.

Ancestry/Race	Number	%
Portuguese	7	0.05
Russian	33	0.22
Scotch-Irish	373	2.46
Scottish	234	1.55
Slavic	6	0.04
Swedish	75	0.50
Ukrainian	8	0.05
United States or American	1,825	12.05
Welsh	78	0.52
West Indian, excl. Hispanic:	55	0.36
Jamaican	38	0.25
Trinidadian and Tobagonian	9	0.06
West Indian	8	0.05
White:	10,502	69.46
Not Hispanic (10,138)	10,289	68.05
Hispanic (185)	213	1.41

Pelham

Place Type: City
County: Shelby
Population: 14,369

Ancestry/Race	Number	%
Acadian/Cajun	7	0.05
African American/Black:	591	4.11
Not Hispanic (570)	588	4.09
Hispanic (1)	3	0.02
African, sub-Saharan:	52	0.37
African	9	0.06
Ghanian	11	0.08
Kenyan	32	0.23
Am. Ind. or Alaska Nat., not spec.	36	0.25
Albanian	7	0.05
American Indian tribes, specified:	48	0.33
Blackfeet	1	0.01
Cherokee (16)	24	0.17
Creek (10)	14	0.10
Latin American Indians (4)	5	0.03
Pueblo (1)	1	0.01
Sioux (1)	1	0.01
All other tribes (1)	2	0.01
American Indian tribes, not spec.	4	0.03
Arab:	178	1.26
Arab/Arabic	7	0.05
Jordanian	56	0.40
Lebanese	71	0.50
Palestinian	16	0.11
Syrian	28	0.20
Asian:	305	2.12
Chinese, ex. Taiwanese (32)	44	0.31
Filipino (18)	28	0.19
Indian (52)	59	0.41
Japanese (5)	17	0.12
Korean (46)	48	0.33
Pakistani (25)	46	0.32
Taiwanese (5)	5	0.03
Thai (1)	1	0.01
Vietnamese (48)	50	0.35
Other Asian, not specified (3)	7	0.05
Austrian	30	0.21
British	119	0.84
Canadian	38	0.27
Croatian	7	0.05
Czech	28	0.20
Czechoslovakian	18	0.13
Danish	34	0.24
Dutch	173	1.23
English	1,849	13.11
European	117	0.83
French, except Basque	295	2.09
French Canadian	41	0.29
German	1,426	10.11
Greek	45	0.32
Hawaii Native/Pacific Islander:	2	0.01
Other Pac. Isl., not spec.	2	0.01
Hispanic or Latino:	923	6.42
Central American:	16	0.11
Costa Rican	1	0.01
Guatemalan	1	0.01
Nicaraguan	2	0.01
Salvadoran	10	0.07
Other Central American	2	0.01
Cuban	11	0.08
Mexican	775	5.39
Puerto Rican	15	0.10
South American:	25	0.17
Colombian	7	0.05
Ecuadorian	1	0.01
Paraguayan	2	0.01
Peruvian	10	0.07
Venezuelan	3	0.02
Other South American	2	0.01
Other Hispanic or Latino	81	0.56
Hungarian	10	0.07
Irish	1,617	11.47
Italian	524	3.72
Lithuanian	44	0.31
Northern European	31	0.22
Norwegian	132	0.94
Polish	197	1.40
Russian	28	0.20
Scotch-Irish	512	3.63
Scottish	382	2.71
Slavic	6	0.04
Swedish	41	0.29
Swiss	36	0.26
Ukrainian	9	0.06
United States or American	2,041	14.47
Welsh	111	0.79
White:	13,077	91.01
Not Hispanic (12,473)	12,571	87.49
Hispanic (462)	506	3.52
Yugoslavian	8	0.06

Phenix City

Place Type: City
County: Russell
Population: 28,265

Ancestry/Race	Number	%
African American/Black:	12,794	45.26
Not Hispanic (12,645)	12,719	45.00
Hispanic (65)	75	0.27
African, sub-Saharan:	171	0.60
African	136	0.48
Ghanian	6	0.02
Nigerian	29	0.10
Alaska Native tribes, specified:	1	0.00
Aleut (1)	1	0.00
Am. Ind. or Alaska Nat., not spec.	43	0.15
American Indian tribes, specified:	86	0.30
Apache (1)	2	0.01
Blackfeet (1)	1	0.00
Cherokee (21)	49	0.17
Chickasaw (3)	3	0.01
Choctaw (2)	4	0.01
Comanche	1	0.00
Creek (5)	8	0.03
Navajo (2)	2	0.01
Pueblo	2	0.01
Sioux (3)	5	0.02
Yaqui (2)	2	0.01
All other tribes (3)	7	0.02
Arab:	14	0.05
Lebanese	14	0.05
Armenian	10	0.04
Asian:	224	0.79
Cambodian (3)	3	0.01
Chinese, ex. Taiwanese (19)	28	0.10
Filipino (31)	47	0.17
Hmong (1)	1	0.00
Indian (13)	23	0.08
Japanese (15)	26	0.09
Korean (27)	41	0.15
Malaysian (2)	6	0.02
Pakistani (3)	4	0.01
Taiwanese (4)	4	0.01
Thai (4)	5	0.02
Vietnamese (10)	11	0.04
Other Asian, specified	1	0.00
Other Asian, not specified (11)	24	0.08
Australian	18	0.06
British	46	0.16
Danish	6	0.02
Dutch	186	0.66
English	1,382	4.88
European	125	0.44
French, except Basque	260	0.92
French Canadian	111	0.39
German	988	3.49
Greek	76	0.27
Hawaii Native/Pacific Islander:	18	0.06
Micronesian: (1)	1	0.00
Guamanian/Chamorro (1)	1	0.00
Polynesian: (2)	8	0.03
Native Hawaiian (2)	8	0.03
Other Pac. Isl., specified	1	0.00
Other Pac. Isl., not spec. (3)	8	0.03
Hispanic or Latino:	421	1.49
Central American:	21	0.07
Honduran	3	0.01
Panamanian	18	0.06
Cuban	3	0.01
Dominican Republic	4	0.01
Mexican	149	0.53
Puerto Rican	139	0.49
South American:	11	0.04
Colombian	10	0.04
Peruvian	1	0.00
Other Hispanic or Latino	94	0.33
Hungarian	37	0.13
Irish	1,838	6.49
Italian	370	1.31
New Zealander	12	0.04
Northern European	29	0.10
Norwegian	65	0.23
Polish	81	0.29
Romanian	8	0.03
Russian	25	0.09
Scandinavian	16	0.06
Scotch-Irish	272	0.96
Scottish	243	0.86
Slavic	5	0.02
Swedish	61	0.22
Swiss	10	0.04
Ukrainian	9	0.03
United States or American	4,378	15.45
Welsh	76	0.27
West Indian, excl. Hispanic:	44	0.16
British West Indian	6	0.02
Haitian	7	0.02
Jamaican	21	0.07
U.S. Virgin Islander	10	0.04
White:	15,129	53.53
Not Hispanic (14,788)	14,920	52.79
Hispanic (176)	209	0.74
Yugoslavian	7	0.02

Prattville

Place Type: City
County: Autauga
Population: 24,303

Ancestry/Race	Number	%
Acadian/Cajun	6	0.02
African American/Black:	3,550	14.61
Not Hispanic (3,474)	3,519	14.48
Hispanic (31)	31	0.13
African, sub-Saharan:	91	0.37
African	91	0.37
Am. Ind. or Alaska Nat., not spec.	47	0.19
American Indian tribes, specified:	135	0.56
Apache (1)	1	0.00
Blackfeet (2)	2	0.01
Cherokee (37)	71	0.29
Chippewa (7)	7	0.03
Choctaw (4)	8	0.03

Notes: 1. Figures in the "Number" column do not add up to the total population due to: a) Ancestry/Race overlap — e.g. persons can report being both White and Irish, b) persons of Hispanic origin can report being any race, c) persons reporting two ancestries are counted in both categories. 2. Numbers in parentheses indicate the number of persons reporting this ancestry/race alone, not in combination with any other ancestry/race. 3. Refer to the Explanation of Data in the front of the book for more detailed information.

Ancestry/Race	Number	%
Creek (14)	30	0.12
Houma (1)	1	0.00
Iroquois	1	0.00
Latin American Indians (1)	1	0.00
Navajo (1)	1	0.00
Sioux (1)	2	0.01
All other tribes (8)	10	0.04
American Indian tribes, not spec.	11	0.05
Arab:	20	0.08
Lebanese	9	0.04
Syrian	11	0.05
Asian:	229	0.94
Chinese, ex. Taiwanese (24)	30	0.12
Filipino (19)	40	0.16
Indian (14)	16	0.07
Japanese (29)	46	0.19
Korean (33)	54	0.22
Thai (8)	11	0.05
Vietnamese (17)	18	0.07
Other Asian, specified	2	0.01
Other Asian, not specified (8)	12	0.05
Australian	9	0.04
Austrian	23	0.09
Belgian	6	0.02
Brazilian	10	0.04
British	146	0.60
Canadian	27	0.11
Celtic	8	0.03
Croatian	4	0.02
Czech	29	0.12
Czechoslovakian	9	0.04
Danish	35	0.14
Dutch	292	1.20
English	2,551	10.50
European	275	1.13
French, except Basque	461	1.90
French Canadian	117	0.48
German	2,333	9.60
Greek	43	0.18
Hawaii Native/Pacific Islander:	21	0.09
Micronesian: (6)	6	0.02
Guamanian/Chamorro (6)	6	0.02
Polynesian: (4)	10	0.04
Native Hawaiian (2)	6	0.02
Samoan (2)	4	0.02
Other Pac. Isl., specified	2	0.01
Other Pac. Isl., not spec. (2)	3	0.01
Hispanic or Latino:	416	1.71
Central American:	35	0.14
Costa Rican	6	0.02
Guatemalan	3	0.01
Honduran	10	0.04
Nicaraguan	1	0.00
Panamanian	15	0.06
Cuban	8	0.03
Dominican Republic	3	0.01
Mexican	169	0.70
Puerto Rican	108	0.44
South American:	4	0.02
Bolivian	1	0.00
Colombian	2	0.01
Paraguayan	1	0.00
Other Hispanic or Latino	89	0.37
Hungarian	5	0.02
Irish	2,431	10.01
Italian	421	1.73
Luxemburger	4	0.02
Northern European	21	0.09
Norwegian	66	0.27
Polish	301	1.24
Romanian	20	0.08
Russian	43	0.18
Scandinavian	13	0.05
Scotch-Irish	686	2.82
Scottish	473	1.95
Slavic	8	0.03
Slovak	28	0.12
Slovene	4	0.02
Swedish	99	0.41
Swiss	15	0.06
Ukrainian	11	0.05
United States or American	4,009	16.50
Welsh	98	0.40
West Indian, excl. Hispanic:	17	0.07
Bermudan	4	0.02
Dutch West Indian	13	0.05
White:	20,380	83.86
Not Hispanic (19,941)	20,114	82.76
Hispanic (252)	266	1.09
Yugoslavian	4	0.02

Prichard

Place Type: City
County: Mobile
Population: 28,633

Ancestry/Race	Number	%
Acadian/Cajun	14	0.05
African American/Black:	24,369	85.11
Not Hispanic (24,095)	24,248	84.69
Hispanic (108)	121	0.42
African, sub-Saharan:	292	1.01
African	292	1.01
Am. Ind. or Alaska Nat., not spec.	110	0.38
American Indian tribes, specified:	79	0.28
Apache	1	0.00
Blackfeet	1	0.00
Cherokee (9)	17	0.06
Choctaw (20)	32	0.11
Creek (5)	16	0.06
Iroquois (1)	3	0.01
Navajo (1)	1	0.00
Pueblo	1	0.00
Seminole	1	0.00
Sioux (5)	5	0.02
All other tribes (1)	1	0.00
American Indian tribes, not spec.	12	0.04
Arab:	24	0.08
Syrian	24	0.08
Asian:	87	0.30
Cambodian	1	0.00
Chinese, ex. Taiwanese	13	0.05
Filipino (7)	13	0.05
Indian (4)	15	0.05
Japanese (7)	9	0.03
Korean (2)	3	0.01
Vietnamese (12)	12	0.04
Other Asian, specified	10	0.03
Other Asian, not specified (1)	11	0.04
Belgian	8	0.03
Canadian	35	0.12
Dutch	29	0.10
English	492	1.70
European	22	0.08
French, except Basque	58	0.20
French Canadian	10	0.03
German	273	0.94
Greek	11	0.04
Hawaii Native/Pacific Islander:	20	0.07
Micronesian:	1	0.00
Guamanian/Chamorro	1	0.00
Polynesian: (5)	5	0.02
Native Hawaiian (3)	3	0.01
Samoan (2)	2	0.01
Other Pac. Isl., specified	10	0.03
Other Pac. Isl., not spec. (1)	4	0.01
Hispanic or Latino:	162	0.57
Cuban	9	0.03
Mexican	51	0.18
Puerto Rican	26	0.09
Other Hispanic or Latino	76	0.27
Hungarian	14	0.05
Irish	366	1.27
Italian	30	0.10
Maltese	4	0.01
Norwegian	32	0.11
Polish	18	0.06
Scotch-Irish	114	0.39
Scottish	37	0.13
Swedish	8	0.03
United States or American	1,343	4.65
Welsh	17	0.06
West Indian, excl. Hispanic:	92	0.32
Dutch West Indian	8	0.03
Jamaican	37	0.13
Trinidadian and Tobagonian	17	0.06
U.S. Virgin Islander	9	0.03
West Indian	21	0.07
White:	4,191	14.64
Not Hispanic (4,038)	4,161	14.53
Hispanic (21)	30	0.10

Saks

Place Type: Census Designated Place
County: Calhoun
Population: 10,698

Ancestry/Race	Number	%
Acadian/Cajun	3	0.03
African American/Black:	1,414	13.22
Not Hispanic (1,361)	1,399	13.08
Hispanic (14)	15	0.14
African, sub-Saharan:	21	0.20
African	15	0.14
Zairian	6	0.06
Am. Ind. or Alaska Nat., not spec.	12	0.11
Albanian	5	0.05
American Indian tribes, specified:	49	0.46
Blackfeet (2)	2	0.02
Cherokee (18)	30	0.28
Choctaw (1)	3	0.03
Comanche (1)	1	0.01
Creek (9)	12	0.11
All other tribes (1)	1	0.01
American Indian tribes, not spec.	5	0.05
Arab:	26	0.25
Lebanese	7	0.07
Syrian	19	0.18
Armenian	11	0.10
Asian:	106	0.99
Chinese, ex. Taiwanese (3)	3	0.03
Filipino (16)	20	0.19
Indian	5	0.05
Japanese (2)	4	0.04
Korean (43)	61	0.57
Thai (5)	5	0.05
Vietnamese (5)	7	0.07
Other Asian, not specified (1)	1	0.01
Austrian	17	0.16
British	16	0.15
Celtic	15	0.14
Croatian	12	0.11
Danish	6	0.06
Dutch	283	2.68
English	845	8.01
European	114	1.08
French, except Basque	175	1.66
French Canadian	35	0.33
German	759	7.19
Greek	13	0.12
Hawaii Native/Pacific Islander:	13	0.12
Micronesian: (3)	3	0.03
Guamanian/Chamorro (3)	3	0.03
Polynesian: (4)	9	0.08
Native Hawaiian (3)	6	0.06
Samoan (1)	3	0.03
Other Pac. Isl., not spec. (1)	1	0.01
Hispanic or Latino:	177	1.65
Central American:	11	0.10
Costa Rican	1	0.01
Panamanian	8	0.07
Salvadoran	1	0.01
Other Central American	1	0.01
Cuban	9	0.08
Mexican	72	0.67
Puerto Rican	31	0.29
South American:	11	0.10
Bolivian	1	0.01

Notes: 1. Figures in the "Number" column do not add up to the total population due to: a) Ancestry/Race overlap — e.g. persons can report being both White and Irish, b) persons of Hispanic origin can report being any race, c) persons reporting two ancestries are counted in both categories. 2. Numbers in parentheses indicate the number of persons reporting this ancestry/race alone, not in combination with any other ancestry/race. 3. Refer to the Explanation of Data in the front of the book for more detailed information.

Ancestry/Race	Number	%
Colombian	1	0.01
Venezuelan	9	0.08
Other Hispanic or Latino	43	0.40
Hungarian	11	0.10
Irish	1,000	9.48
Italian	164	1.55
Norwegian	26	0.25
Polish	72	0.68
Portuguese	14	0.13
Romanian	4	0.04
Russian	8	0.08
Scotch-Irish	181	1.72
Scottish	159	1.51
Swedish	6	0.06
Swiss	14	0.13
United States or American	1,941	18.40
Welsh	35	0.33
West Indian, excl. Hispanic:	44	0.42
Dutch West Indian	44	0.42
White:	9,130	85.34
Not Hispanic (8,938)	9,016	84.28
Hispanic (99)	114	1.07

Saraland

Place Type: City
County: Mobile
Population: 12,288

Ancestry/Race	Number	%
African American/Black:	1,140	9.28
Not Hispanic (1,097)	1,134	9.23
Hispanic (5)	6	0.05
African, sub-Saharan:	12	0.10
African	12	0.10
Am. Ind. or Alaska Nat., not spec.	56	0.46
American Indian tribes, specified:	87	0.71
Apache	3	0.02
Cherokee (8)	18	0.15
Choctaw (20)	30	0.24
Creek (11)	27	0.22
Iroquois	1	0.01
Latin American Indians (6)	6	0.05
Potawatomi (1)	1	0.01
All other tribes (1)	1	0.01
American Indian tribes, not spec.	5	0.04
Arab:	8	0.07
Moroccan	8	0.07
Asian:	94	0.76
Chinese, ex. Taiwanese (6)	6	0.05
Filipino (8)	12	0.10
Indian (16)	31	0.25
Indonesian	3	0.02
Japanese (2)	7	0.06
Korean (1)	5	0.04
Laotian	2	0.02
Pakistani (3)	3	0.02
Vietnamese (20)	22	0.18
Other Asian, specified	1	0.01
Other Asian, not specified	2	0.02
Belgian	20	0.17
Canadian	6	0.05
Danish	6	0.05
Dutch	107	0.89
English	893	7.41
European	14	0.12
Finnish	6	0.05
French, except Basque	271	2.25
French Canadian	18	0.15
German	711	5.90
Greek	7	0.06
Hawaii Native/Pacific Islander:	14	0.11
Micronesian: (1)	1	0.01
Guamanian/Chamorro (1)	1	0.01
Polynesian:	3	0.02
Native Hawaiian	2	0.02
Samoan	1	0.01
Other Pac. Isl., specified	1	0.01
Other Pac. Isl., not spec.	9	0.07
Hispanic or Latino:	144	1.17
Central American:	1	0.01
Guatemalan	1	0.01
Cuban	5	0.04
Mexican	84	0.68
Puerto Rican	10	0.08
South American:	2	0.02
Peruvian	1	0.01
Other South American	1	0.01
Other Hispanic or Latino	42	0.34
Irish	1,138	9.45
Italian	156	1.30
Norwegian	71	0.59
Polish	14	0.12
Portuguese	22	0.18
Russian	14	0.12
Scotch-Irish	397	3.30
Scottish	346	2.87
Slovak	6	0.05
Swedish	63	0.52
Swiss	7	0.06
United States or American	2,800	23.25
Welsh	46	0.38
White:	10,986	89.40
Not Hispanic (10,789)	10,895	88.66
Hispanic (86)	91	0.74

Scottsboro

Place Type: City
County: Jackson
Population: 14,762

Ancestry/Race	Number	%
African American/Black:	823	5.58
Not Hispanic (781)	816	5.53
Hispanic (7)	7	0.05
African, sub-Saharan:	41	0.28
African	41	0.28
Am. Ind. or Alaska Nat., not spec.	57	0.39
American Indian tribes, specified:	211	1.43
Apache (1)	1	0.01
Blackfeet (1)	4	0.03
Cherokee (93)	184	1.25
Chippewa (1)	4	0.03
Choctaw (1)	5	0.03
Creek (1)	3	0.02
Sioux (1)	3	0.02
All other tribes (4)	7	0.05
American Indian tribes, not spec.	19	0.13
Arab:	69	0.47
Jordanian	8	0.05
Lebanese	12	0.08
Palestinian	40	0.27
Syrian	9	0.06
Asian:	104	0.70
Cambodian (4)	4	0.03
Chinese, ex. Taiwanese (21)	21	0.14
Filipino (8)	14	0.09
Indian (19)	24	0.16
Japanese (6)	9	0.06
Korean (2)	4	0.03
Pakistani (6)	10	0.07
Vietnamese (7)	9	0.06
Other Asian, specified (1)	1	0.01
Other Asian, not specified (1)	8	0.05
Austrian	7	0.05
Belgian	7	0.05
Brazilian	7	0.05
British	44	0.30
Canadian	7	0.05
Danish	14	0.09
Dutch	180	1.22
English	1,490	10.08
European	72	0.49
Finnish	7	0.05
French, except Basque	183	1.24
French Canadian	30	0.20
German	1,278	8.65
Greek	20	0.14
Hawaii Native/Pacific Islander:	5	0.03
Micronesian: (3)	4	0.03
Guamanian/Chamorro (3)	4	0.03
Polynesian: (1)	1	0.01
Native Hawaiian (1)	1	0.01
Hispanic or Latino:	221	1.50
Central American:	4	0.03
Honduran	4	0.03
Cuban	1	0.01
Mexican	162	1.10
Puerto Rican	10	0.07
South American:	4	0.03
Colombian	2	0.01
Paraguayan	1	0.01
Other South American	1	0.01
Other Hispanic or Latino	40	0.27
Hungarian	14	0.09
Iranian	5	0.03
Irish	1,751	11.85
Italian	244	1.65
Lithuanian	13	0.09
Norwegian	19	0.13
Polish	54	0.37
Romanian	8	0.05
Russian	10	0.07
Scotch-Irish	383	2.59
Scottish	251	1.70
Slavic	42	0.28
Slovak	6	0.04
Swedish	12	0.08
Ukrainian	6	0.04
United States or American	2,921	19.76
Welsh	65	0.44
White:	13,648	92.45
Not Hispanic (13,327)	13,512	91.53
Hispanic (122)	136	0.92

Selma

Place Type: City
County: Dallas
Population: 20,512

Ancestry/Race	Number	%
African American/Black:	14,365	70.03
Not Hispanic (14,242)	14,307	69.75
Hispanic (51)	58	0.28
African, sub-Saharan:	256	1.25
African	214	1.05
Nigerian	16	0.08
Zimbabwean	20	0.10
Other sub-Saharan African	6	0.03
Am. Ind. or Alaska Nat., not spec.	25	0.12
American Indian tribes, specified:	31	0.15
Blackfeet	2	0.01
Cherokee (4)	15	0.07
Choctaw (1)	4	0.02
Creek	2	0.01
Latin American Indians	7	0.03
Navajo (1)	1	0.00
American Indian tribes, not spec.	12	0.06
Asian:	141	0.69
Cambodian (11)	11	0.05
Chinese, ex. Taiwanese (9)	9	0.04
Filipino (10)	12	0.06
Indian (48)	55	0.27
Japanese (10)	12	0.06
Korean (10)	11	0.05
Malaysian (1)	1	0.00
Pakistani (1)	4	0.02
Thai (3)	4	0.02
Vietnamese (7)	7	0.03
Other Asian, specified	6	0.03
Other Asian, not specified (1)	9	0.04
British	8	0.04
Danish	6	0.03
Dutch	91	0.44
English	788	3.85
European	108	0.53
French, except Basque	136	0.66
French Canadian	20	0.10

Notes: 1. Figures in the "Number" column do not add up to the total population due to: a) Ancestry/Race overlap — e.g. persons can report being both White and Irish, b) persons of Hispanic origin can report being any race, c) persons reporting two ancestries are counted in both categories. 2. Numbers in parentheses indicate the number of persons reporting this ancestry/race alone, not in combination with any other ancestry/race. 3. Refer to the Explanation of Data in the front of the book for more detailed information.

German	593	2.90
Hawaii Native/Pacific Islander:	17	0.08
Micronesian: (2)	3	0.01
Other Micronesian (2)	3	0.01
Polynesian:	4	0.02
Native Hawaiian	4	0.02
Other Pac. Isl., specified	6	0.03
Other Pac. Isl., not spec.	4	0.02
Hispanic or Latino:	138	0.67
Central American:	1	0.00
Guatemalan	1	0.00
Cuban	8	0.04
Mexican	65	0.32
Puerto Rican	11	0.05
South American:	3	0.01
Venezuelan	2	0.01
Other South American	1	0.00
Other Hispanic or Latino	50	0.24
Hungarian	22	0.11
Icelander	5	0.02
Irish	611	2.99
Italian	21	0.10
Lithuanian	4	0.02
Norwegian	14	0.07
Polish	32	0.16
Portuguese	10	0.05
Scotch-Irish	285	1.39
Scottish	182	0.89
Slovak	5	0.02
Swedish	35	0.17
Ukrainian	6	0.03
United States or American	1,233	6.03
Welsh	37	0.18
West Indian, excl. Hispanic:	20	0.10
British West Indian	8	0.04
Trinidadian and Tobagonian	12	0.06
White:	5,987	29.19
Not Hispanic (5,875)	5,953	29.02
Hispanic (26)	34	0.17

Smiths

Place Type: Census Designated Place
County: Lee
Population: 21,756

Ancestry/Race	Number	%
African American/Black:	2,813	12.93
Not Hispanic (2,739)	2,791	12.83
Hispanic (17)	22	0.10
African, sub-Saharan:	48	0.22
African	25	0.12
Nigerian	23	0.11
Alaska Native tribes, not specified	1	0.00
Am. Ind. or Alaska Nat., not spec.	38	0.17
American Indian tribes, specified:	137	0.63
Apache (1)	2	0.01
Blackfeet	1	0.00
Cherokee (37)	75	0.34
Chippewa (6)	8	0.04
Choctaw	8	0.04
Comanche	4	0.02
Creek (4)	19	0.09
Iroquois (1)	1	0.00
Latin American Indians (1)	3	0.01
Lumbee (1)	1	0.00
Navajo	1	0.00
Pueblo (6)	6	0.03
Seminole (1)	3	0.01
Sioux	1	0.00
All other tribes (1)	4	0.02
American Indian tribes, not spec.	10	0.05
Arab:	9	0.04
Lebanese	9	0.04
Asian:	139	0.64
Chinese, ex. Taiwanese (1)	5	0.02
Filipino (13)	23	0.11
Indian (8)	10	0.05
Japanese (11)	32	0.15
Korean (27)	36	0.17
Taiwanese (1)	1	0.00
Thai (8)	11	0.05
Vietnamese (8)	9	0.04
Other Asian, not specified (5)	12	0.06
Austrian	16	0.07
Brazilian	9	0.04
British	39	0.18
Canadian	14	0.06
Czech	14	0.06
Czechoslovakian	11	0.05
Dutch	143	0.66
English	1,603	7.42
European	269	1.25
Finnish	33	0.15
French, except Basque	263	1.22
French Canadian	44	0.20
German	1,503	6.96
Greek	24	0.11
Hawaii Native/Pacific Islander:	14	0.06
Micronesian: (1)	3	0.01
Guamanian/Chamorro (1)	3	0.01
Polynesian: (1)	7	0.03
Native Hawaiian (1)	7	0.03
Other Pac. Isl., not spec.	4	0.02
Hispanic or Latino:	453	2.08
Central American:	16	0.07
Guatemalan	1	0.00
Panamanian	12	0.06
Other Central American	3	0.01
Cuban	11	0.05
Dominican Republic	4	0.02
Mexican	105	0.48
Puerto Rican	214	0.98
South American:	9	0.04
Chilean	3	0.01
Ecuadorian	4	0.02
Uruguayan	2	0.01
Other Hispanic or Latino	94	0.43
Hungarian	35	0.16
Irish	2,195	10.16
Italian	319	1.48
Norwegian	115	0.53
Pennsylvania German	11	0.05
Polish	83	0.38
Portuguese	9	0.04
Russian	27	0.12
Scotch-Irish	394	1.82
Scottish	298	1.38
Slovak	8	0.04
Swedish	23	0.11
United States or American	5,156	23.86
Welsh	82	0.38
White:	18,654	85.74
Not Hispanic (18,183)	18,356	84.37
Hispanic (265)	298	1.37

Sylacauga

Place Type: City
County: Talladega
Population: 12,616

Ancestry/Race	Number	%
African American/Black:	3,703	29.35
Not Hispanic (3,629)	3,685	29.21
Hispanic (18)	18	0.14
African, sub-Saharan:	88	0.71
African	88	0.71
Am. Ind. or Alaska Nat., not spec.	25	0.20
American Indian tribes, specified:	47	0.37
Blackfeet (1)	1	0.01
Cherokee (20)	32	0.25
Cheyenne (1)	1	0.01
Choctaw	1	0.01
Creek (2)	8	0.06
Delaware (1)	1	0.01
Iroquois (1)	1	0.01
Seminole	1	0.01
Sioux	1	0.01
American Indian tribes, not spec.	4	0.03
Arab:	7	0.06
Lebanese	7	0.06
Asian:	61	0.48
Chinese, ex. Taiwanese (10)	19	0.15
Filipino (2)	2	0.02
Indian (9)	18	0.14
Indonesian (3)	4	0.03
Japanese (5)	7	0.06
Korean (3)	4	0.03
Thai	1	0.01
Vietnamese (5)	5	0.04
Other Asian, not specified	1	0.01
British	69	0.55
Canadian	10	0.08
Czech	10	0.08
Czechoslovakian	13	0.10
Dutch	121	0.97
English	857	6.89
European	147	1.18
French, except Basque	95	0.76
German	378	3.04
Hawaii Native/Pacific Islander:	12	0.10
Micronesian: (6)	6	0.05
Guamanian/Chamorro (6)	6	0.05
Polynesian: (1)	2	0.02
Native Hawaiian (1)	1	0.01
Samoan	1	0.01
Other Pac. Isl., not spec.	4	0.03
Hispanic or Latino:	123	0.97
Central American:	6	0.05
Salvadoran	6	0.05
Cuban	2	0.02
Dominican Republic	3	0.02
Mexican	60	0.48
Puerto Rican	18	0.14
Other Hispanic or Latino	34	0.27
Irish	643	5.17
Italian	42	0.34
Norwegian	21	0.17
Polish	42	0.34
Russian	16	0.13
Scotch-Irish	243	1.95
Scottish	219	1.76
Swedish	8	0.06
United States or American	2,586	20.78
Welsh	143	1.15
White:	8,819	69.90
Not Hispanic (8,676)	8,759	69.43
Hispanic (51)	60	0.48

Talladega

Place Type: City
County: Talladega
Population: 15,143

Ancestry/Race	Number	%
African American/Black:	6,443	42.55
Not Hispanic (6,375)	6,415	42.36
Hispanic (27)	28	0.18
African, sub-Saharan:	55	0.37
African	55	0.37
Am. Ind. or Alaska Nat., not spec.	33	0.22
American Indian tribes, specified:	33	0.22
Blackfeet	1	0.01
Cherokee (12)	28	0.18
Choctaw	1	0.01
Creek (1)	1	0.01
Sioux (1)	1	0.01
All other tribes	1	0.01
American Indian tribes, not spec.	7	0.05
Asian:	72	0.48
Chinese, ex. Taiwanese (17)	19	0.13
Filipino (7)	15	0.10
Indian (9)	11	0.07
Japanese (1)	1	0.01
Korean (3)	3	0.02
Pakistani (1)	1	0.01
Taiwanese	2	0.01
Thai (1)	2	0.01

Notes: 1. Figures in the "Number" column do not add up to the total population due to: a) Ancestry/Race overlap — e.g. persons can report being both White and Irish, b) persons of Hispanic origin can report being any race, c) persons reporting two ancestries are counted in both categories. 2. Numbers in parentheses indicate the number of persons reporting this ancestry/race alone, not in combination with any other ancestry/race. 3. Refer to the Explanation of Data in the front of the book for more detailed information.

Ancestry/Race	Number	%
Vietnamese (7)	7	0.05
Other Asian, specified	7	0.05
Other Asian, not specified	4	0.03
British	9	0.06
Czech	6	0.04
Danish	26	0.17
Dutch	85	0.57
English	912	6.10
French, except Basque	159	1.06
French Canadian	4	0.03
German	427	2.85
Greek	9	0.06
Hawaii Native/Pacific Islander:	12	0.08
Micronesian: (3)	3	0.02
Guamanian/Chamorro (3)	3	0.02
Other Pac. Isl., specified	7	0.05
Other Pac. Isl., not spec.	2	0.01
Hispanic or Latino:	136	0.90
Mexican	105	0.69
Puerto Rican	5	0.03
South American:	2	0.01
Chilean	1	0.01
Paraguayan	1	0.01
Other Hispanic or Latino	24	0.16
Hungarian	8	0.05
Irish	701	4.69
Italian	59	0.39
Lithuanian	9	0.06
Norwegian	35	0.23
Polish	44	0.29
Scotch-Irish	182	1.22
Scottish	267	1.78
Swedish	22	0.15
Swiss	5	0.03
United States or American	1,944	12.99
Welsh	20	0.13
West Indian, excl. Hispanic:	8	0.05
Jamaican	8	0.05
White:	8,597	56.77
Not Hispanic (8,460)	8,539	56.39
Hispanic (43)	58	0.38

Tillmans Corner

Place Type: Census Designated Place
County: Mobile
Population: 15,685

Ancestry/Race	Number	%
African American/Black:	523	3.33
Not Hispanic (494)	522	3.33
Hispanic (1)	1	0.01
African, sub-Saharan:	30	0.19
African	30	0.19
Alaska Native tribes, specified:	4	0.03
Aleut (3)	4	0.03
Am. Ind. or Alaska Nat., not spec.	55	0.35
American Indian tribes, specified:	124	0.79
Apache (2)	3	0.02
Blackfeet (4)	5	0.03
Cherokee (11)	48	0.31
Choctaw (17)	28	0.18
Creek (18)	28	0.18
Latin American Indians (1)	1	0.01
Lumbee (3)	3	0.02
Seminole (1)	1	0.01
Sioux (3)	4	0.03
All other tribes (2)	3	0.02
American Indian tribes, not spec.	12	0.08
Arab:	68	0.44
Lebanese	53	0.34
Syrian	15	0.10
Asian:	214	1.36
Cambodian (1)	5	0.03
Chinese, ex. Taiwanese (7)	8	0.05
Filipino (13)	34	0.22
Indian (21)	23	0.15
Indonesian (1)	1	0.01
Japanese (3)	11	0.07
Korean (5)	6	0.04
Laotian (3)	7	0.04
Taiwanese (1)	1	0.01
Thai	1	0.01
Vietnamese (88)	106	0.68
Other Asian, specified	4	0.03
Other Asian, not specified (3)	7	0.04
Austrian	6	0.04
British	51	0.33
Canadian	14	0.09
Celtic	23	0.15
Danish	80	0.51
Dutch	264	1.69
English	1,383	8.87
European	169	1.08
Finnish	9	0.06
French, except Basque	584	3.75
French Canadian	134	0.86
German	1,337	8.58
Greek	52	0.33
Hawaii Native/Pacific Islander:	14	0.09
Micronesian:	1	0.01
Guamanian/Chamorro	1	0.01
Polynesian:	6	0.04
Native Hawaiian	6	0.04
Other Pac. Isl., specified	4	0.03
Other Pac. Isl., not spec. (1)	3	0.02
Hispanic or Latino:	192	1.22
Central American:	15	0.10
Honduran	6	0.04
Panamanian	9	0.06
Cuban	9	0.06
Mexican	76	0.48
Puerto Rican	16	0.10
South American:	12	0.08
Bolivian	5	0.03
Chilean	2	0.01
Colombian	4	0.03
Peruvian	1	0.01
Other Hispanic or Latino	64	0.41
Hungarian	8	0.05
Irish	1,591	10.21
Italian	178	1.14
Norwegian	78	0.50
Polish	83	0.53
Portuguese	25	0.16
Russian	19	0.12
Scandinavian	23	0.15
Scotch-Irish	276	1.77
Scottish	235	1.51
Slovak	8	0.05
Swedish	10	0.06
Swiss	9	0.06
Turkish	8	0.05
United States or American	2,807	18.01
Welsh	73	0.47
West Indian, excl. Hispanic:	27	0.17
Dutch West Indian	12	0.08
Jamaican	15	0.10
White:	14,868	94.79
Not Hispanic (14,558)	14,734	93.94
Hispanic (118)	134	0.85
Yugoslavian	19	0.12

Troy

Place Type: City
County: Pike
Population: 13,935

Ancestry/Race	Number	%
African American/Black:	5,441	39.05
Not Hispanic (5,342)	5,405	38.79
Hispanic (31)	36	0.26
African, sub-Saharan:	182	1.32
African	121	0.88
Nigerian	29	0.21
Other sub-Saharan African	32	0.23
Am. Ind. or Alaska Nat., not spec.	42	0.30
American Indian tribes, specified:	61	0.44
Cherokee (2)	23	0.17
Choctaw (3)	4	0.03
Cree (1)	1	0.01
Creek (18)	30	0.22
Iroquois	1	0.01
Navajo (1)	1	0.01
Seminole	1	0.01
American Indian tribes, not spec.	8	0.06
Asian:	132	0.95
Chinese, ex. Taiwanese (29)	33	0.24
Filipino (5)	11	0.08
Indian (17)	19	0.14
Japanese (3)	10	0.07
Korean (25)	33	0.24
Pakistani (4)	4	0.03
Taiwanese (1)	1	0.01
Vietnamese (8)	8	0.06
Other Asian, not specified (1)	13	0.09
Brazilian	17	0.12
British	27	0.20
Canadian	14	0.10
Czechoslovakian	4	0.03
Danish	37	0.27
Dutch	49	0.36
English	1,054	7.64
European	163	1.18
French, except Basque	89	0.64
French Canadian	18	0.13
German	584	4.23
Greek	7	0.05
Hawaii Native/Pacific Islander:	11	0.08
Micronesian:	2	0.01
Guamanian/Chamorro	2	0.01
Polynesian: (1)	7	0.05
Native Hawaiian (1)	7	0.05
Other Pac. Isl., not spec. (1)	2	0.01
Hispanic or Latino:	181	1.30
Central American:	3	0.02
Guatemalan	2	0.01
Panamanian	1	0.01
Cuban	6	0.04
Dominican Republic	3	0.02
Mexican	84	0.60
Puerto Rican	21	0.15
South American:	4	0.03
Bolivian	1	0.01
Colombian	2	0.01
Ecuadorian	1	0.01
Other Hispanic or Latino	60	0.43
Hungarian	11	0.08
Iranian	13	0.09
Irish	687	4.98
Italian	200	1.45
Norwegian	7	0.05
Polish	8	0.06
Russian	25	0.18
Scotch-Irish	232	1.68
Scottish	214	1.55
Slovak	12	0.09
Swedish	11	0.08
Swiss	8	0.06
Turkish	34	0.25
Ukrainian	8	0.06
United States or American	2,087	15.12
Welsh	25	0.18
White:	8,324	59.73
Not Hispanic (8,110)	8,214	58.95
Hispanic (97)	110	0.79

Trussville

Place Type: City
County: Jefferson
Population: 12,924

Ancestry/Race	Number	%
African American/Black:	201	1.56
Not Hispanic (190)	196	1.52
Hispanic (1)	5	0.04
Alaska Native tribes, specified:	4	0.03
Aleut (1)	1	0.01

Notes: 1. Figures in the "Number" column do not add up to the total population due to: a) Ancestry/Race overlap — e.g. persons can report being both White and Irish, b) persons of Hispanic origin can report being any race, c) persons reporting two ancestries are counted in both categories. 2. Numbers in parentheses indicate the number of persons reporting this ancestry/race alone, not in combination with any other ancestry/race. 3. Refer to the Explanation of Data in the front of the book for more detailed information.

Eskimo (3)	3	0.02
Am. Ind. or Alaska Nat., not spec.	14	0.11
American Indian tribes, specified:	56	0.43
Cherokee (25)	36	0.28
Choctaw	1	0.01
Creek	8	0.06
Latin American Indians	8	0.06
Lumbee (2)	2	0.02
All other tribes	1	0.01
American Indian tribes, not spec.	7	0.05
Arab:	24	0.17
Lebanese	24	0.17
Asian:	77	0.60
Chinese, ex. Taiwanese (23)	31	0.24
Filipino (1)	3	0.02
Indian (12)	17	0.13
Japanese (1)	4	0.03
Korean (2)	2	0.02
Malaysian (4)	4	0.03
Pakistani (4)	4	0.03
Taiwanese (1)	1	0.01
Vietnamese (3)	3	0.02
Other Asian, specified (1)	1	0.01
Other Asian, not specified (3)	7	0.05
Austrian	15	0.11
British	92	0.67
Czech	19	0.14
Czechoslovakian	12	0.09
Danish	46	0.34
Dutch	153	1.12
English	1,906	13.89
European	182	1.33
Finnish	8	0.06
French, except Basque	217	1.58
French Canadian	29	0.21
German	1,165	8.49
Greek	10	0.07
Hawaii Native/Pacific Islander:	1	0.01
Other Pac. Isl., not spec. (1)	1	0.01
Hispanic or Latino:	109	0.84
Central American:	1	0.01
Guatemalan	1	0.01
Cuban	5	0.04
Dominican Republic	5	0.04
Mexican	56	0.43
Puerto Rican	14	0.11
South American:	4	0.03
Argentinean	1	0.01
Ecuadorian	2	0.02
Peruvian	1	0.01
Other Hispanic or Latino	24	0.19
Hungarian	43	0.31
Irish	1,832	13.35
Italian	354	2.58
Lithuanian	10	0.07
Norwegian	42	0.31
Polish	30	0.22
Romanian	15	0.11
Russian	16	0.12
Scandinavian	41	0.30
Scotch-Irish	505	3.68
Scottish	273	1.99
Slovak	9	0.07
Swedish	55	0.40
Swiss	26	0.19
Ukrainian	6	0.04
United States or American	2,744	20.00
Welsh	43	0.31
White:	12,574	97.29
Not Hispanic (12,465)	12,525	96.91
Hispanic (42)	49	0.38
Yugoslavian	13	0.09

Tuscaloosa

Place Type: City
County: Tuscaloosa
Population: 77,906

Ancestry/Race	Number	%
Acadian/Cajun	8	0.01
African American/Black:	33,580	43.10
Not Hispanic (33,164)	33,443	42.93
Hispanic (123)	137	0.18
African, sub-Saharan:	777	0.99
African	707	0.90
Nigerian	70	0.09
Alaska Native tribes, specified:	2	0.00
Alaska Athabascan (1)	1	0.00
Aleut	1	0.00
Am. Ind. or Alaska Nat., not spec.	118	0.15
American Indian tribes, specified:	200	0.26
Apache (1)	4	0.01
Blackfeet	7	0.01
Cherokee (32)	89	0.11
Cheyenne	1	0.00
Chickasaw	2	0.00
Chippewa (1)	2	0.00
Choctaw (9)	38	0.05
Creek (11)	25	0.03
Delaware (1)	1	0.00
Houma (1)	1	0.00
Iroquois (3)	4	0.01
Latin American Indians (6)	9	0.01
Lumbee (1)	1	0.00
Navajo (1)	2	0.00
Osage	2	0.00
Paiute (1)	2	0.00
Potawatomi (1)	1	0.00
Seminole (3)	3	0.00
Sioux	1	0.00
All other tribes (2)	5	0.01
American Indian tribes, not spec.	31	0.04
Arab:	171	0.22
Arab/Arabic	47	0.06
Lebanese	70	0.09
Palestinian	8	0.01
Other Arab	46	0.06
Asian:	1,399	1.80
Bangladeshi (8)	9	0.01
Chinese, ex. Taiwanese (448)	480	0.62
Filipino (68)	93	0.12
Hmong	1	0.00
Indian (235)	264	0.34
Indonesian (2)	4	0.01
Japanese (117)	138	0.18
Korean (140)	180	0.23
Laotian (1)	1	0.00
Malaysian (3)	3	0.00
Pakistani (29)	39	0.05
Sri Lankan (1)	1	0.00
Taiwanese (10)	11	0.01
Thai (32)	40	0.05
Vietnamese (38)	44	0.06
Other Asian, specified (1)	19	0.02
Other Asian, not specified (19)	72	0.09
Australian	8	0.01
Austrian	57	0.07
Belgian	58	0.07
British	422	0.54
Canadian	23	0.03
Celtic	16	0.02
Croatian	11	0.01
Czech	87	0.11
Czechoslovakian	48	0.06
Danish	64	0.08
Dutch	759	0.97
Eastern European	11	0.01
English	6,277	8.02
European	1,037	1.32
French, except Basque	1,292	1.65
French Canadian	91	0.12
German	4,433	5.66
Greek	93	0.12
Hawaii Native/Pacific Islander:	52	0.07
Micronesian: (4)	6	0.01
Guamanian/Chamorro (3)	5	0.01
Other Micronesian (1)	1	0.00
Polynesian: (13)	20	0.03
Native Hawaiian (8)	13	0.02
Samoan (4)	6	0.01
Other Polynesian (1)	1	0.00
Other Pac. Isl., specified	16	0.02
Other Pac. Isl., not spec. (2)	10	0.01
Hispanic or Latino:	1,092	1.40
Central American:	42	0.05
Costa Rican	3	0.00
Guatemalan	11	0.01
Honduran	15	0.02
Nicaraguan	2	0.00
Panamanian	7	0.01
Salvadoran	4	0.01
Cuban	56	0.07
Dominican Republic	1	0.00
Mexican	585	0.75
Puerto Rican	96	0.12
South American:	94	0.12
Argentinean	9	0.01
Bolivian	1	0.00
Chilean	1	0.00
Colombian	22	0.03
Ecuadorian	12	0.02
Paraguayan	2	0.00
Peruvian	6	0.01
Venezuelan	39	0.05
Other South American	2	0.00
Other Hispanic or Latino	218	0.28
Hungarian	62	0.08
Iranian	49	0.06
Irish	5,410	6.91
Italian	898	1.15
Lithuanian	33	0.04
Northern European	75	0.10
Norwegian	372	0.48
Polish	492	0.63
Romanian	39	0.05
Russian	131	0.17
Scotch-Irish	1,795	2.29
Scottish	1,494	1.91
Slavic	40	0.05
Slovak	33	0.04
Slovene	36	0.05
Swedish	260	0.33
Swiss	26	0.03
Turkish	14	0.02
Ukrainian	37	0.05
United States or American	5,729	7.32
Welsh	432	0.55
West Indian, excl. Hispanic:	152	0.19
Bahamian	20	0.03
British West Indian	16	0.02
Dutch West Indian	9	0.01
Jamaican	86	0.11
West Indian	21	0.03
White:	42,659	54.76
Not Hispanic (41,667)	42,152	54.11
Hispanic (476)	507	0.65
Yugoslavian	16	0.02

Tuskegee

Place Type: City
County: Macon
Population: 11,846

Ancestry/Race	Number	%
African American/Black:	11,402	96.25
Not Hispanic (11,257)	11,340	95.73
Hispanic (53)	62	0.52
African, sub-Saharan:	298	2.47
African	194	1.61
Ghanian	5	0.04
Liberian	10	0.08
Nigerian	89	0.74
Am. Ind. or Alaska Nat., not spec.	42	0.35
American Indian tribes, specified:	39	0.33
Blackfeet	2	0.02
Cherokee (1)	24	0.20
Chippewa (2)	2	0.02
Choctaw (2)	9	0.08

Notes: 1. Figures in the "Number" column do not add up to the total population due to: a) Ancestry/Race overlap — e.g. persons can report being both White and Irish, b) persons of Hispanic origin can report being any race, c) persons reporting two ancestries are counted in both categories. 2. Numbers in parentheses indicate the number of persons reporting this ancestry/race alone, not in combination with any other ancestry/race. 3. Refer to the Explanation of Data in the front of the book for more detailed information.

Ancestry/Race	Number	%
Iroquois (1)	1	0.01
Navajo (1)	1	0.01
American Indian tribes, not spec.	1	0.01
Asian:	93	0.79
Bangladeshi (16)	16	0.14
Chinese, ex. Taiwanese (7)	8	0.07
Filipino	2	0.02
Indian (54)	58	0.49
Korean	1	0.01
Sri Lankan (1)	1	0.01
Vietnamese (2)	2	0.02
Other Asian, not specified (2)	5	0.04
Canadian	6	0.05
English	33	0.27
French, except Basque	17	0.14
German	14	0.12
German Russian	8	0.07
Greek	5	0.04
Guyanese	8	0.07
Hawaii Native/Pacific Islander:	4	0.03
Other Pac. Isl., not spec. (1)	4	0.03
Hispanic or Latino:	81	0.68
Central American:	4	0.03
Costa Rican	1	0.01
Honduran	1	0.01
Nicaraguan	1	0.01
Salvadoran	1	0.01
Cuban	3	0.03
Dominican Republic	1	0.01
Mexican	22	0.19
Puerto Rican	19	0.16
South American:	2	0.02
Argentinean	1	0.01
Colombian	1	0.01
Other Hispanic or Latino	30	0.25
Irish	29	0.24
Italian	5	0.04
Scotch-Irish	6	0.05
United States or American	78	0.65
West Indian, excl. Hispanic:	63	0.52
Bahamian	12	0.10
Belizean	10	0.08
Dutch West Indian	12	0.10
Jamaican	19	0.16
Trinidadian and Tobagonian	10	0.08
White:	348	2.94
Not Hispanic (298)	333	2.81
Hispanic (9)	15	0.13

Vestavia Hills

Place Type: City
County: Jefferson
Population: 24,476

Ancestry/Race	Number	%
Acadian/Cajun	8	0.03
African American/Black:	481	1.97
Not Hispanic (453)	475	1.94
Hispanic (1)	6	0.02
African, sub-Saharan:	21	0.08
African	21	0.08
Am. Ind. or Alaska Nat., not spec.	22	0.09
American Indian tribes, specified:	69	0.28
Blackfeet	1	0.00
Cherokee (10)	44	0.18
Chickasaw (1)	1	0.00
Choctaw	1	0.00
Creek (1)	6	0.02
Latin American Indians (2)	8	0.03
Lumbee (1)	3	0.01
Osage	1	0.00
Ute	1	0.00
All other tribes (1)	3	0.01
American Indian tribes, not spec.	2	0.01
Arab:	273	1.10
Lebanese	241	0.97
Syrian	28	0.11
Other Arab	4	0.02
Armenian	10	0.04
Asian:	675	2.76
Bangladeshi (2)	4	0.02
Chinese, ex. Taiwanese (234)	250	1.02
Filipino (8)	11	0.04
Indian (235)	246	1.01
Indonesian (3)	8	0.03
Japanese (13)	17	0.07
Korean (37)	46	0.19
Malaysian	1	0.00
Pakistani (1)	7	0.03
Sri Lankan (4)	4	0.02
Taiwanese (17)	17	0.07
Thai (17)	28	0.11
Vietnamese (15)	25	0.10
Other Asian, not specified (8)	11	0.04
Austrian	132	0.53
Brazilian	51	0.21
British	434	1.75
Canadian	33	0.13
Celtic	70	0.28
Czech	27	0.11
Czechoslovakian	23	0.09
Danish	84	0.34
Dutch	246	0.99
Eastern European	9	0.04
English	4,944	19.89
European	373	1.50
Finnish	69	0.28
French, except Basque	746	3.00
French Canadian	25	0.10
German	2,502	10.07
Greek	295	1.19
Hawaii Native/Pacific Islander:	30	0.12
Micronesian: (16)	16	0.07
Guamanian/Chamorro (16)	16	0.07
Polynesian: (8)	8	0.03
Native Hawaiian (5)	5	0.02
Samoan (3)	3	0.01
Other Pac. Isl., not spec.	6	0.02
Hispanic or Latino:	334	1.36
Central American:	8	0.03
Costa Rican	1	0.00
Honduran	1	0.00
Salvadoran	6	0.02
Cuban	27	0.11
Dominican Republic	2	0.01
Mexican	186	0.76
Puerto Rican	34	0.14
South American:	34	0.14
Argentinean	6	0.02
Bolivian	1	0.00
Chilean	1	0.00
Colombian	11	0.04
Ecuadorian	4	0.02
Paraguayan	2	0.01
Peruvian	3	0.01
Uruguayan	2	0.01
Venezuelan	1	0.00
Other South American	3	0.01
Other Hispanic or Latino	43	0.18
Hungarian	67	0.27
Iranian	13	0.05
Irish	2,825	11.37
Italian	1,105	4.45
Latvian	19	0.08
Northern European	38	0.15
Norwegian	213	0.86
Polish	247	0.99
Portuguese	13	0.05
Romanian	34	0.14
Russian	115	0.46
Scandinavian	41	0.16
Scotch-Irish	1,268	5.10
Scottish	1,257	5.06
Serbian	8	0.03
Slovak	6	0.02
Swedish	272	1.09
Swiss	101	0.41
Ukrainian	23	0.09
United States or American	2,846	11.45
Welsh	267	1.07
West Indian, excl. Hispanic:	11	0.04
U.S. Virgin Islander	11	0.04
White:	23,264	95.05
Not Hispanic (22,892)	23,017	94.04
Hispanic (227)	247	1.01

Anchorage

Place Type: Municipality
Borough: Anchorage
Population: 260,283

Ancestry/Race	Number	%
Acadian/Cajun	97	0.04
Afghan	46	0.02
African American/Black:	18,632	7.16
Not Hispanic (14,667)	17,614	6.77
Hispanic (532)	1,018	0.39
African, sub-Saharan:	1,238	0.48
African	1,084	0.42
Cape Verdean	11	0.00
Ethiopian	27	0.01
Nigerian	26	0.01
Sierra Leonean	6	0.00
South African	55	0.02
Other sub-Saharan African	29	0.01
Alaska Native tribes, specified:	16,246	6.24
Alaska Athabascan (2,265)	3,186	1.22
Aleut (2,276)	3,397	1.31
Eskimo (5,607)	7,666	2.95
Tlingit-Haida (1,081)	1,712	0.66
All other tribes (178)	285	0.11
Alaska Native tribes, not specified	1,429	0.55
Am. Ind. or Alaska Nat., not spec.	5,899	2.27
Albanian	271	0.10
Alsatian	6	0.00
American Indian tribes, specified:	4,222	1.62
Apache (48)	129	0.05
Blackfeet (65)	225	0.09
Cherokee (372)	1,296	0.50
Cheyenne (13)	29	0.01
Chickasaw (36)	58	0.02
Chippewa (163)	282	0.11
Choctaw (140)	302	0.12
Colville (14)	20	0.01
Comanche (11)	26	0.01
Cree (5)	17	0.01
Creek (36)	95	0.04
Crow (13)	32	0.01
Delaware (13)	16	0.01
Houma (4)	4	0.00
Iroquois (48)	95	0.04
Kiowa (6)	9	0.00
Latin American Indians (55)	117	0.04
Lumbee (16)	19	0.01
Menominee (17)	26	0.01
Navajo (90)	146	0.06
Osage (10)	33	0.01
Ottawa (1)	7	0.00
Paiute (17)	30	0.01
Pima (5)	8	0.00
Potawatomi (20)	31	0.01
Pueblo (50)	96	0.04
Puget Sound Salish (17)	34	0.01
Seminole (15)	43	0.02
Shoshone (13)	35	0.01
Sioux (112)	239	0.09
Tohono O'Odham (3)	4	0.00
Ute (1)	9	0.00
Yakama (10)	16	0.01
Yaqui (6)	11	0.00
Yuman (8)	12	0.00
All other tribes (360)	671	0.26
American Indian tribes, not spec.	280	0.11
Arab:	556	0.21
Arab/Arabic	48	0.02
Egyptian	59	0.02
Jordanian	9	0.00
Lebanese	212	0.08

Notes: 1. Figures in the "Number" column do not add up to the total population due to: a) Ancestry/Race overlap — e.g. persons can report being both White and Irish, b) persons of Hispanic origin can report being any race, c) persons reporting two ancestries are counted in both categories. 2. Numbers in parentheses indicate the number of persons reporting this ancestry/race alone, not in combination with any other ancestry/race. 3. Refer to the Explanation of Data in the front of the book for more detailed information.

Ancestry/Race	Number	%
Moroccan	43	0.02
Palestinian	55	0.02
Syrian	107	0.04
Other Arab	23	0.01
Armenian	40	0.02
Asian:	18,974	7.29
Bangladeshi (18)	24	0.01
Cambodian (119)	154	0.06
Chinese, ex. Taiwanese (837)	1,371	0.53
Filipino (5,805)	7,481	2.87
Hmong (262)	299	0.11
Indian (453)	593	0.23
Indonesian (24)	58	0.02
Japanese (899)	1,735	0.67
Korean (3,432)	4,084	1.57
Laotian (1,170)	1,385	0.53
Malaysian (4)	21	0.01
Pakistani (47)	67	0.03
Sri Lankan (8)	20	0.01
Taiwanese (33)	43	0.02
Thai (399)	607	0.23
Vietnamese (380)	506	0.19
Other Asian, specified (24)	38	0.01
Other Asian, not specified (241)	488	0.19
Australian	102	0.04
Austrian	724	0.28
Basque	86	0.03
Belgian	208	0.08
Brazilian	55	0.02
British	1,631	0.63
Bulgarian	51	0.02
Canadian	1,072	0.41
Carpatho Rusyn	24	0.01
Celtic	174	0.07
Croatian	313	0.12
Czech	1,104	0.42
Czechoslovakian	400	0.15
Danish	2,239	0.86
Dutch	4,888	1.88
Eastern European	73	0.03
English	26,123	10.04
Estonian	15	0.01
European	3,717	1.43
Finnish	1,328	0.51
French, except Basque	8,842	3.40
French Canadian	2,775	1.07
German	45,770	17.58
German Russian	4	0.00
Greek	843	0.32
Guyanese	11	0.00
Hawaii Native/Pacific Islander:	3,804	1.46
Melanesian: (2)	12	0.00
Fijian (2)	9	0.00
Other Melanesian	3	0.00
Micronesian: (129)	220	0.08
Guamanian/Chamorro (104)	184	0.07
Other Micronesian (25)	36	0.01
Polynesian: (2,048)	3,118	1.20
Native Hawaiian (410)	1,055	0.41
Samoan (1,428)	1,760	0.68
Tongan (179)	231	0.09
Other Polynesian (31)	72	0.03
Other Pac. Isl., specified	1	0.00
Other Pac. Isl., not spec. (147)	453	0.17
Hispanic or Latino:	14,799	5.69
Central American:	618	0.24
Costa Rican	58	0.02
Guatemalan	122	0.05
Honduran	87	0.03
Nicaraguan	31	0.01
Panamanian	120	0.05
Salvadoran	179	0.07
Other Central American	21	0.01
Cuban	343	0.13
Dominican Republic	792	0.30
Mexican	7,246	2.78
Puerto Rican	1,652	0.63
South American:	761	0.29
Argentinean	43	0.02
Bolivian	17	0.01
Chilean	72	0.03
Colombian	287	0.11
Ecuadorian	39	0.01
Paraguayan	12	0.00
Peruvian	216	0.08
Uruguayan	9	0.00
Venezuelan	34	0.01
Other South American	32	0.01
Other Hispanic or Latino	3,387	1.30
Hungarian	1,123	0.43
Icelander	37	0.01
Iranian	44	0.02
Irish	30,031	11.54
Israeli	27	0.01
Italian	8,264	3.18
Latvian	60	0.02
Lithuanian	465	0.18
Luxemburger	23	0.01
Macedonian	55	0.02
Maltese	40	0.02
New Zealander	40	0.02
Northern European	426	0.16
Norwegian	9,988	3.84
Pennsylvania German	98	0.04
Polish	6,103	2.34
Portuguese	919	0.35
Romanian	160	0.06
Russian	3,098	1.19
Scandinavian	1,203	0.46
Scotch-Irish	4,565	1.75
Scottish	6,943	2.67
Serbian	148	0.06
Slavic	121	0.05
Slovak	309	0.12
Slovene	79	0.03
Swedish	6,707	2.58
Swiss	1,018	0.39
Turkish	87	0.03
Ukrainian	563	0.22
United States or American	15,614	6.00
Welsh	2,288	0.88
West Indian, excl. Hispanic:	831	0.32
Bahamian	14	0.01
Barbadian	12	0.00
Belizean	26	0.01
British West Indian	48	0.02
Dutch West Indian	24	0.01
Haitian	24	0.01
Jamaican	432	0.17
Trinidadian and Tobagonian	35	0.01
U.S. Virgin Islander	10	0.00
West Indian	196	0.08
Other West Indian	10	0.00
White:	200,926	77.20
Not Hispanic (181,982)	193,246	74.24
Hispanic (6,027)	7,680	2.95
Yugoslavian	493	0.19

College

Place Type: Census Designated Place
Borough: Fairbanks North Star
Population: 11,402

Ancestry/Race	Number	%
African American/Black:	486	4.26
Not Hispanic (338)	458	4.02
Hispanic (17)	28	0.25
African, sub-Saharan:	23	0.20
African	14	0.12
Ethiopian	9	0.08
Alaska Native tribes, specified:	936	8.21
Alaska Athabascan (396)	500	4.39
Aleut (25)	37	0.32
Eskimo (237)	347	3.04
Tlingit-Haida (28)	46	0.40
All other tribes (4)	6	0.05
Alaska Native tribes, not specified	83	0.73
Am. Ind. or Alaska Nat., not spec.	252	2.21
American Indian tribes, specified:	180	1.58
Apache (3)	9	0.08
Blackfeet	10	0.09
Cherokee (8)	56	0.49
Cheyenne (2)	2	0.02
Chickasaw (1)	6	0.05
Chippewa (3)	5	0.04
Choctaw	18	0.16
Colville (2)	2	0.02
Comanche	2	0.02
Cree (2)	3	0.03
Creek (1)	4	0.04
Delaware (2)	2	0.02
Iroquois (4)	7	0.06
Latin American Indians	1	0.01
Lumbee (1)	1	0.01
Menominee	1	0.01
Navajo (7)	11	0.10
Potawatomi (1)	1	0.01
Pueblo (1)	7	0.06
Puget Sound Salish (1)	3	0.03
Sioux (3)	8	0.07
Yakama (1)	1	0.01
Yaqui	1	0.01
All other tribes (9)	19	0.17
American Indian tribes, not spec.	20	0.18
Armenian	12	0.10
Asian:	505	4.43
Chinese, ex. Taiwanese (92)	114	1.00
Filipino (52)	85	0.75
Indian (46)	55	0.48
Japanese (42)	63	0.55
Korean (92)	123	1.08
Laotian (4)	4	0.04
Malaysian (1)	1	0.01
Pakistani (1)	1	0.01
Taiwanese	3	0.03
Thai (11)	17	0.15
Vietnamese (9)	12	0.11
Other Asian, specified (1)	3	0.03
Other Asian, not specified (8)	24	0.21
Austrian	21	0.18
Belgian	30	0.26
British	119	1.04
Bulgarian	6	0.05
Canadian	35	0.31
Celtic	14	0.12
Croatian	6	0.05
Czech	56	0.49
Czechoslovakian	12	0.10
Danish	215	1.88
Dutch	255	2.23
Eastern European	5	0.04
English	1,417	12.38
European	211	1.84
Finnish	17	0.15
French, except Basque	399	3.48
French Canadian	139	1.21
German	2,328	20.33
Greek	28	0.24
Hawaii Native/Pacific Islander:	30	0.26
Micronesian: (5)	6	0.05
Guamanian/Chamorro (5)	6	0.05
Polynesian: (4)	21	0.18
Native Hawaiian (4)	20	0.18
Samoan	1	0.01
Other Pac. Isl., not spec.	3	0.03
Hispanic or Latino:	396	3.47
Central American:	11	0.10
Costa Rican	1	0.01
Guatemalan	1	0.01
Honduran	2	0.02
Panamanian	7	0.06
Cuban	15	0.13
Dominican Republic	4	0.04
Mexican	220	1.93
Puerto Rican	39	0.34
South American:	11	0.10
Argentinean	4	0.04
Bolivian	5	0.04
Chilean	2	0.02

Notes: 1. Figures in the "Number" column do not add up to the total population due to: a) Ancestry/Race overlap — e.g. persons can report being both White and Irish, b) persons of Hispanic origin can report being any race, c) persons reporting two ancestries are counted in both categories. 2. Numbers in parentheses indicate the number of persons reporting this ancestry/race alone, not in combination with any other ancestry/race. 3. Refer to the Explanation of Data in the front of the book for more detailed information.

Other Hispanic or Latino	96	0.84
Hungarian	62	0.54
Iranian	16	0.14
Irish	1,300	11.35
Italian	408	3.56
Lithuanian	14	0.12
Luxemburger	6	0.05
Northern European	6	0.05
Norwegian	494	4.31
Pennsylvania German	10	0.09
Polish	312	2.72
Portuguese	74	0.65
Russian	152	1.33
Scandinavian	48	0.42
Scotch-Irish	262	2.29
Scottish	304	2.66
Slavic	5	0.04
Slovak	55	0.48
Slovene	6	0.05
Swedish	412	3.60
Swiss	29	0.25
Ukrainian	17	0.15
United States or American	570	4.98
Welsh	152	1.33
West Indian, excl. Hispanic:	13	0.11
Dutch West Indian	6	0.05
U.S. Virgin Islander	7	0.06
White:	9,464	83.00
Not Hispanic (8,677)	9,223	80.89
Hispanic (199)	241	2.11
Yugoslavian	40	0.35

Fairbanks

Place Type: City
Borough: Fairbanks North Star
Population: 30,224

Ancestry/Race	Number	%
Acadian/Cajun	17	0.06
African American/Black:	3,914	12.95
Not Hispanic (3,291)	3,743	12.38
Hispanic (79)	171	0.57
African, sub-Saharan:	203	0.67
African	191	0.63
Nigerian	12	0.04
Alaska Native tribes, specified:	2,581	8.54
Alaska Athabascan (1,472)	1,741	5.76
Aleut (36)	61	0.20
Eskimo (494)	714	2.36
Tlingit-Haida (31)	56	0.19
All other tribes (6)	9	0.03
Alaska Native tribes, not specified	141	0.47
Am. Ind. or Alaska Nat., not spec.	767	2.54
Albanian	5	0.02
American Indian tribes, specified:	616	2.04
Apache (4)	13	0.04
Blackfeet (1)	15	0.05
Cherokee (63)	210	0.69
Cheyenne (1)	6	0.02
Chickasaw (4)	11	0.04
Chippewa (15)	30	0.10
Choctaw (8)	20	0.07
Colville (2)	2	0.01
Comanche	4	0.01
Cree	2	0.01
Creek (5)	11	0.04
Crow (4)	4	0.01
Delaware	1	0.00
Iroquois (11)	22	0.07
Kiowa (1)	3	0.01
Latin American Indians (6)	14	0.05
Lumbee (4)	5	0.02
Menominee (1)	1	0.00
Navajo (20)	31	0.10
Osage (2)	4	0.01
Paiute (2)	2	0.01
Pima (1)	1	0.00
Potawatomi (1)	2	0.01
Pueblo (7)	10	0.03
Puget Sound Salish (1)	1	0.00
Seminole (5)	9	0.03
Shoshone (3)	7	0.02
Sioux (18)	70	0.23
Tohono O'Odham (1)	2	0.01
Ute	1	0.00
Yakama (2)	2	0.01
Yaqui (1)	3	0.01
All other tribes (58)	97	0.32
American Indian tribes, not spec.	33	0.11
Arab:	23	0.08
Lebanese	14	0.05
Syrian	9	0.03
Armenian	5	0.02
Asian:	1,261	4.17
Cambodian (4)	4	0.01
Chinese, ex. Taiwanese (92)	136	0.45
Filipino (206)	334	1.11
Hmong (2)	2	0.01
Indian (47)	64	0.21
Indonesian	2	0.01
Japanese (45)	144	0.48
Korean (284)	392	1.30
Laotian (15)	18	0.06
Pakistani	2	0.01
Sri Lankan	1	0.00
Taiwanese	1	0.00
Thai (54)	77	0.25
Vietnamese (29)	45	0.15
Other Asian, specified	3	0.01
Other Asian, not specified (15)	36	0.12
Australian	29	0.10
Austrian	23	0.08
Basque	77	0.25
Belgian	14	0.05
Brazilian	13	0.04
British	128	0.42
Bulgarian	5	0.02
Canadian	87	0.29
Celtic	28	0.09
Croatian	8	0.03
Czech	118	0.39
Czechoslovakian	97	0.32
Danish	220	0.73
Dutch	537	1.77
English	2,601	8.60
European	182	0.60
Finnish	118	0.39
French, except Basque	665	2.20
French Canadian	335	1.11
German	4,855	16.04
Greek	65	0.21
Hawaii Native/Pacific Islander:	307	1.02
Micronesian: (50)	70	0.23
Guamanian/Chamorro (43)	63	0.21
Other Micronesian (7)	7	0.02
Polynesian: (90)	189	0.63
Native Hawaiian (38)	98	0.32
Samoan (45)	74	0.24
Tongan (6)	9	0.03
Other Polynesian (1)	8	0.03
Other Pac. Isl., specified	1	0.00
Other Pac. Isl., not spec. (16)	47	0.16
Hispanic or Latino:	1,854	6.13
Central American:	104	0.34
Costa Rican	10	0.03
Guatemalan	10	0.03
Honduran	7	0.02
Nicaraguan	4	0.01
Panamanian	54	0.18
Salvadoran	11	0.04
Other Central American	8	0.03
Cuban	46	0.15
Dominican Republic	31	0.10
Mexican	880	2.91
Puerto Rican	348	1.15
South American:	88	0.29
Argentinean	4	0.01
Bolivian	2	0.01
Chilean	4	0.01
Colombian	49	0.16
Ecuadorian	6	0.02
Peruvian	10	0.03
Other South American	13	0.04
Other Hispanic or Latino	357	1.18
Hungarian	88	0.29
Icelander	12	0.04
Irish	3,306	10.93
Israeli	21	0.07
Italian	1,086	3.59
Latvian	6	0.02
Lithuanian	7	0.02
New Zealander	20	0.07
Northern European	34	0.11
Norwegian	1,164	3.85
Pennsylvania German	36	0.12
Polish	548	1.81
Portuguese	157	0.52
Romanian	29	0.10
Russian	248	0.82
Scandinavian	248	0.82
Scotch-Irish	583	1.93
Scottish	627	2.07
Serbian	65	0.21
Slovak	24	0.08
Slovene	13	0.04
Swedish	576	1.90
Swiss	98	0.32
Ukrainian	68	0.22
United States or American	1,777	5.87
Welsh	226	0.75
West Indian, excl. Hispanic:	92	0.30
Haitian	11	0.04
Jamaican	29	0.10
Trinidadian and Tobagonian	21	0.07
U.S. Virgin Islander	13	0.04
West Indian	18	0.06
White:	21,843	72.27
Not Hispanic (19,406)	20,888	69.11
Hispanic (744)	955	3.16
Yugoslavian	24	0.08

Juneau

Place Type: City and Borough
Borough: Juneau
Population: 30,711

Ancestry/Race	Number	%
Acadian/Cajun	7	0.02
African American/Black:	439	1.43
Not Hispanic (235)	415	1.35
Hispanic (13)	24	0.08
African, sub-Saharan:	10	0.03
African	10	0.03
Alaska Native tribes, specified:	4,000	13.02
Alaska Athabascan (63)	170	0.55
Aleut (89)	201	0.65
Eskimo (127)	237	0.77
Tlingit-Haida (2,262)	3,272	10.65
All other tribes (74)	120	0.39
Alaska Native tribes, not specified	163	0.53
Am. Ind. or Alaska Nat., not spec.	616	2.01
American Indian tribes, specified:	530	1.73
Apache (4)	7	0.02
Blackfeet (1)	15	0.05
Cherokee (39)	129	0.42
Cheyenne (2)	8	0.03
Chickasaw (1)	2	0.01
Chippewa (20)	49	0.16
Choctaw (6)	19	0.06
Colville (7)	9	0.03
Comanche (2)	4	0.01
Cree	4	0.01
Creek (10)	17	0.06
Crow (5)	7	0.02
Delaware (1)	7	0.02
Iroquois (6)	9	0.03
Kiowa	1	0.00
Latin American Indians (5)	14	0.05

Notes: 1. Figures in the "Number" column do not add up to the total population due to: a) Ancestry/Race overlap — e.g. persons can report being both White and Irish, b) persons of Hispanic origin can report being any race, c) persons reporting two ancestries are counted in both categories. 2. Numbers in parentheses indicate the number of persons reporting this ancestry/race alone, not in combination with any other ancestry/race. 3. Refer to the Explanation of Data in the front of the book for more detailed information.

Lumbee (2)	6	0.02
Menominee	2	0.01
Navajo (19)	34	0.11
Osage	4	0.01
Ottawa (4)	4	0.01
Paiute	2	0.01
Pima	1	0.00
Potawatomi (6)	8	0.03
Pueblo (13)	17	0.06
Puget Sound Salish (2)	9	0.03
Seminole	5	0.02
Shoshone (1)	3	0.01
Sioux (16)	37	0.12
Ute (3)	3	0.01
Yakama	5	0.02
Yaqui	1	0.00
All other tribes (44)	88	0.29
American Indian tribes, not spec.	18	0.06
Arab:	33	0.11
Palestinian	5	0.02
Syrian	7	0.02
Other Arab	21	0.07
Armenian	5	0.02
Asian:	2,102	6.84
Cambodian (6)	6	0.02
Chinese, ex. Taiwanese (86)	135	0.44
Filipino (1,050)	1,478	4.81
Indian (31)	38	0.12
Indonesian (1)	1	0.00
Japanese (83)	202	0.66
Korean (85)	111	0.36
Laotian (7)	8	0.03
Pakistani (1)	2	0.01
Sri Lankan (1)	1	0.00
Thai (13)	18	0.06
Vietnamese (46)	55	0.18
Other Asian, specified (3)	18	0.06
Other Asian, not specified (8)	29	0.09
Austrian	95	0.31
Basque	25	0.08
Belgian	26	0.08
Brazilian	13	0.04
British	215	0.70
Bulgarian	5	0.02
Canadian	202	0.66
Croatian	65	0.21
Czech	111	0.36
Czechoslovakian	53	0.17
Danish	402	1.31
Dutch	723	2.35
Eastern European	16	0.05
English	4,032	13.13
European	724	2.36
Finnish	247	0.80
French, except Basque	1,178	3.84
French Canadian	258	0.84
German	5,790	18.85
Greek	30	0.10
Hawaii Native/Pacific Islander:	227	0.74
Melanesian: (1)	1	0.00
Fijian (1)	1	0.00
Micronesian: (13)	25	0.08
Guamanian/Chamorro (11)	23	0.07
Other Micronesian (2)	2	0.01
Polynesian: (94)	174	0.57
Native Hawaiian (28)	85	0.28
Samoan (23)	42	0.14
Tongan (41)	44	0.14
Other Polynesian (2)	3	0.01
Other Pac. Isl., specified	10	0.03
Other Pac. Isl., not spec. (8)	17	0.06
Hispanic or Latino:	1,040	3.39
Central American:	21	0.07
Costa Rican	2	0.01
Guatemalan	5	0.02
Honduran	1	0.00
Nicaraguan	10	0.03
Panamanian	1	0.00
Salvadoran	2	0.01
Cuban	6	0.02
Dominican Republic	7	0.02
Mexican	626	2.04
Puerto Rican	87	0.28
South American:	42	0.14
Argentinean	3	0.01
Chilean	8	0.03
Colombian	14	0.05
Ecuadorian	3	0.01
Peruvian	5	0.02
Uruguayan	4	0.01
Venezuelan	1	0.00
Other South American	4	0.01
Other Hispanic or Latino	251	0.82
Hungarian	109	0.35
Icelander	55	0.18
Iranian	16	0.05
Irish	3,996	13.01
Israeli	7	0.02
Italian	1,004	3.27
Latvian	30	0.10
Lithuanian	33	0.11
Maltese	7	0.02
Northern European	79	0.26
Norwegian	1,742	5.67
Pennsylvania German	14	0.05
Polish	449	1.46
Portuguese	74	0.24
Romanian	28	0.09
Russian	281	0.91
Scandinavian	188	0.61
Scotch-Irish	842	2.74
Scottish	1,131	3.68
Serbian	12	0.04
Slavic	11	0.04
Slovak	63	0.21
Swedish	1,185	3.86
Swiss	207	0.67
Ukrainian	75	0.24
United States or American	1,372	4.47
Welsh	284	0.92
West Indian, excl. Hispanic:	44	0.14
Dutch West Indian	8	0.03
Jamaican	29	0.09
Trinidadian and Tobagonian	7	0.02
White:	24,728	80.52
Not Hispanic (22,498)	24,131	78.57
Hispanic (471)	597	1.94
Yugoslavian	115	0.37

Apache Junction

Place Type: City
County: Pinal
Population: 31,814

Ancestry/Race	Number	%
African American/Black:	268	0.84
Not Hispanic (168)	238	0.75
Hispanic (26)	30	0.09
African, sub-Saharan:	48	0.15
African	41	0.13
South African	7	0.02
Alaska Native tribes, specified:	7	0.02
Eskimo (1)	3	0.01
Tlingit-Haida (2)	4	0.01
Alaska Native tribes, not specified	4	0.01
Am. Ind. or Alaska Nat., not spec.	121	0.38
American Indian tribes, specified:	434	1.36
Apache (23)	43	0.14
Blackfeet (1)	8	0.03
Cherokee (40)	117	0.37
Cheyenne	4	0.01
Chickasaw (4)	8	0.03
Chippewa (25)	31	0.10
Choctaw (3)	20	0.06
Comanche (2)	7	0.02
Cree	1	0.00
Creek (5)	5	0.02
Crow	1	0.00
Delaware (1)	3	0.01
Iroquois (2)	5	0.02
Kiowa (1)	1	0.00
Latin American Indians (3)	9	0.03
Lumbee (2)	2	0.01
Menominee (2)	2	0.01
Navajo (49)	63	0.20
Osage (1)	1	0.00
Paiute	1	0.00
Pima (3)	5	0.02
Potawatomi (8)	8	0.03
Pueblo (6)	6	0.02
Puget Sound Salish (3)	3	0.01
Shoshone	1	0.00
Sioux (7)	14	0.04
Tohono O'Odham	12	0.04
Yaqui (4)	16	0.05
Yuman	2	0.01
All other tribes (25)	35	0.11
American Indian tribes, not spec.	26	0.08
Arab:	25	0.08
Lebanese	25	0.08
Asian:	283	0.89
Chinese, ex. Taiwanese (7)	25	0.08
Filipino (83)	127	0.40
Indian (11)	19	0.06
Indonesian	2	0.01
Japanese (17)	36	0.11
Korean (12)	20	0.06
Taiwanese (1)	2	0.01
Thai (13)	22	0.07
Vietnamese (16)	20	0.06
Other Asian, not specified (5)	10	0.03
Australian	27	0.09
Austrian	43	0.14
Basque	23	0.07
Belgian	50	0.16
British	71	0.23
Canadian	97	0.31
Celtic	11	0.04
Czech	146	0.47
Czechoslovakian	46	0.15
Danish	348	1.11
Dutch	688	2.20
English	3,533	11.29
European	170	0.54
Finnish	47	0.15
French, except Basque	1,307	4.18
French Canadian	373	1.19
German	6,327	20.23
Greek	41	0.13
Hawaii Native/Pacific Islander:	66	0.21
Micronesian: (1)	6	0.02
Guamanian/Chamorro (1)	6	0.02
Polynesian: (20)	48	0.15
Native Hawaiian (14)	40	0.13
Samoan (6)	8	0.03
Other Pac. Isl., not spec. (2)	12	0.04
Hispanic or Latino:	2,801	8.80
Central American:	15	0.05
Costa Rican	1	0.00
Guatemalan	3	0.01
Honduran	4	0.01
Panamanian	1	0.00
Salvadoran	4	0.01
Other Central American	2	0.01
Cuban	18	0.06
Dominican Republic	5	0.02
Mexican	2,112	6.64
Puerto Rican	74	0.23
South American:	13	0.04
Argentinean	1	0.00
Bolivian	5	0.02
Colombian	4	0.01
Peruvian	1	0.00
Venezuelan	2	0.01
Other Hispanic or Latino	564	1.77
Hungarian	80	0.26
Irish	4,349	13.90
Italian	1,350	4.32
Latvian	18	0.06

Notes: 1. Figures in the "Number" column do not add up to the total population due to: a) Ancestry/Race overlap — e.g. persons can report being both White and Irish, b) persons of Hispanic origin can report being any race, c) persons reporting two ancestries are counted in both categories. 2. Numbers in parentheses indicate the number of persons reporting this ancestry/race alone, not in combination with any other ancestry/race. 3. Refer to the Explanation of Data in the front of the book for more detailed information.

Ancestry/Race	Number	%
Lithuanian	26	0.08
Luxemburger	9	0.03
Norwegian	1,023	3.27
Pennsylvania German	56	0.18
Polish	925	2.96
Portuguese	130	0.42
Russian	126	0.40
Scandinavian	40	0.13
Scotch-Irish	699	2.23
Scottish	528	1.69
Slavic	32	0.10
Slovak	42	0.13
Slovene	9	0.03
Swedish	604	1.93
Swiss	124	0.40
Turkish	31	0.10
Ukrainian	63	0.20
United States or American	2,135	6.83
Welsh	339	1.08
West Indian, excl. Hispanic:	9	0.03
Jamaican	9	0.03
White:	30,068	94.51
Not Hispanic (27,967)	28,369	89.17
Hispanic (1,511)	1,699	5.34

Avondale

Place Type: City
County: Maricopa
Population: 35,883

Ancestry/Race	Number	%
Afghan	35	0.10
African American/Black:	2,128	5.93
Not Hispanic (1,748)	1,922	5.36
Hispanic (118)	206	0.57
African, sub-Saharan:	112	0.31
African	58	0.16
Cape Verdean	45	0.13
Nigerian	9	0.03
Alaska Native tribes, specified:	4	0.01
Aleut (4)	4	0.01
Am. Ind. or Alaska Nat., not spec.	185	0.52
Albanian	5	0.01
American Indian tribes, specified:	502	1.40
Apache (11)	23	0.06
Blackfeet	4	0.01
Cherokee (14)	59	0.16
Chickasaw (3)	10	0.03
Chippewa (2)	4	0.01
Choctaw (16)	25	0.07
Colville (1)	1	0.00
Comanche (1)	2	0.01
Creek (1)	1	0.00
Crow (1)	1	0.00
Delaware	2	0.01
Iroquois	1	0.00
Latin American Indians (41)	66	0.18
Lumbee (1)	1	0.00
Navajo (68)	93	0.26
Pima (11)	19	0.05
Potawatomi (6)	6	0.02
Pueblo (15)	19	0.05
Sioux (6)	12	0.03
Tohono O'Odham (13)	27	0.08
Yaqui (58)	71	0.20
Yuman (20)	23	0.06
All other tribes (21)	32	0.09
American Indian tribes, not spec.	43	0.12
Arab:	30	0.08
Arab/Arabic	26	0.07
Egyptian	3	0.01
Lebanese	1	0.00
Armenian	59	0.16
Asian:	974	2.71
Cambodian (3)	3	0.01
Chinese, ex. Taiwanese (97)	132	0.37
Filipino (194)	302	0.84
Indian (76)	101	0.28
Japanese (49)	96	0.27
Korean (109)	138	0.38
Laotian (2)	2	0.01
Malaysian (1)	1	0.00
Pakistani (4)	9	0.03
Taiwanese (2)	3	0.01
Thai (19)	28	0.08
Vietnamese (95)	108	0.30
Other Asian, specified (1)	4	0.01
Other Asian, not specified (11)	47	0.13
Australian	8	0.02
Austrian	61	0.17
Basque	36	0.10
Belgian	41	0.11
Brazilian	10	0.03
British	96	0.27
Canadian	119	0.33
Croatian	6	0.02
Czech	147	0.41
Czechoslovakian	63	0.18
Danish	145	0.41
Dutch	468	1.31
English	2,286	6.39
European	328	0.92
Finnish	29	0.08
French, except Basque	699	1.95
French Canadian	236	0.66
German	3,633	10.15
German Russian	8	0.02
Greek	16	0.04
Hawaii Native/Pacific Islander:	112	0.31
Melanesian: (3)	3	0.01
Other Melanesian (3)	3	0.01
Micronesian: (15)	29	0.08
Guamanian/Chamorro (14)	28	0.08
Other Micronesian (1)	1	0.00
Polynesian: (27)	60	0.17
Native Hawaiian (8)	34	0.09
Samoan (19)	26	0.07
Other Pac. Isl., specified	2	0.01
Other Pac. Isl., not spec. (6)	18	0.05
Hispanic or Latino:	16,589	46.23
Central American:	106	0.30
Costa Rican	6	0.02
Guatemalan	27	0.08
Honduran	9	0.03
Nicaraguan	8	0.02
Panamanian	19	0.05
Salvadoran	27	0.08
Other Central American	10	0.03
Cuban	18	0.05
Dominican Republic	12	0.03
Mexican	13,987	38.98
Puerto Rican	175	0.49
South American:	59	0.16
Argentinean	5	0.01
Bolivian	3	0.01
Chilean	5	0.01
Colombian	31	0.09
Ecuadorian	6	0.02
Peruvian	3	0.01
Venezuelan	4	0.01
Other South American	2	0.01
Other Hispanic or Latino	2,232	6.22
Hungarian	111	0.31
Irish	2,937	8.20
Italian	1,122	3.13
Latvian	11	0.03
Lithuanian	32	0.09
Northern European	15	0.04
Norwegian	311	0.87
Pennsylvania German	26	0.07
Polish	506	1.41
Portuguese	81	0.23
Romanian	81	0.23
Russian	58	0.16
Scandinavian	43	0.12
Scotch-Irish	398	1.11
Scottish	285	0.80
Serbian	13	0.04
Slavic	6	0.02
Slovak	30	0.08
Swedish	222	0.62
Swiss	50	0.14
Ukrainian	19	0.05
United States or American	1,639	4.58
Welsh	75	0.21
West Indian, excl. Hispanic:	42	0.12
Belizean	18	0.05
Haitian	8	0.02
Jamaican	4	0.01
West Indian	12	0.03
White:	23,897	66.60
Not Hispanic (15,959)	16,476	45.92
Hispanic (6,745)	7,421	20.68
Yugoslavian	18	0.05

Bullhead City

Place Type: City
County: Mohave
Population: 33,769

Ancestry/Race	Number	%
Acadian/Cajun	7	0.02
African American/Black:	412	1.22
Not Hispanic (317)	378	1.12
Hispanic (23)	34	0.10
African, sub-Saharan:	18	0.05
African	18	0.05
Alaska Native tribes, specified:	10	0.03
Alaska Athabascan (3)	3	0.01
Aleut (2)	6	0.02
Tlingit-Haida (1)	1	0.00
Am. Ind. or Alaska Nat., not spec.	159	0.47
American Indian tribes, specified:	539	1.60
Apache (30)	48	0.14
Blackfeet (6)	17	0.05
Cherokee (48)	133	0.39
Cheyenne (4)	4	0.01
Chickasaw (2)	2	0.01
Chippewa (10)	19	0.06
Choctaw (18)	27	0.08
Comanche (1)	5	0.01
Creek (5)	7	0.02
Crow (1)	2	0.01
Delaware (1)	3	0.01
Iroquois (7)	14	0.04
Latin American Indians (32)	47	0.14
Lumbee	2	0.01
Navajo (42)	55	0.16
Osage	3	0.01
Ottawa (2)	2	0.01
Paiute (3)	3	0.01
Pueblo (7)	14	0.04
Seminole (4)	5	0.01
Shoshone (5)	8	0.02
Sioux (16)	26	0.08
Tohono O'Odham (1)	1	0.00
Ute (1)	4	0.01
Yakama	2	0.01
Yaqui	5	0.01
Yuman (20)	25	0.07
All other tribes (42)	56	0.17
American Indian tribes, not spec.	47	0.14
Arab:	38	0.11
Arab/Arabic	5	0.01
Egyptian	7	0.02
Lebanese	11	0.03
Syrian	15	0.04
Armenian	53	0.16
Asian:	486	1.44
Cambodian (3)	3	0.01
Chinese, ex. Taiwanese (33)	44	0.13
Filipino (119)	153	0.45
Indian (32)	46	0.14
Indonesian	8	0.02
Japanese (47)	68	0.20
Korean (30)	46	0.14
Pakistani (24)	31	0.09
Sri Lankan (1)	1	0.00

Notes: 1. Figures in the "Number" column do not add up to the total population due to: a) Ancestry/Race overlap — e.g. persons can report being both White and Irish, b) persons of Hispanic origin can report being any race, c) persons reporting two ancestries are counted in both categories. 2. Numbers in parentheses indicate the number of persons reporting this ancestry/race alone, not in combination with any other ancestry/race. 3. Refer to the Explanation of Data in the front of the book for more detailed information.

Taiwanese (8)	9	0.03
Thai (21)	24	0.07
Vietnamese (16)	22	0.07
Other Asian, not specified (2)	31	0.09
Australian	9	0.03
Austrian	54	0.16
Basque	5	0.01
Belgian	46	0.14
Brazilian	10	0.03
British	89	0.26
Bulgarian	29	0.09
Canadian	131	0.39
Croatian	23	0.07
Czech	59	0.17
Czechoslovakian	73	0.22
Danish	187	0.55
Dutch	656	1.94
English	3,867	11.42
European	222	0.66
Finnish	73	0.22
French, except Basque	1,194	3.53
French Canadian	252	0.74
German	5,822	17.20
Greek	126	0.37
Hawaii Native/Pacific Islander:	80	0.24
Melanesian: (1)	1	0.00
Fijian (1)	1	0.00
Micronesian: (3)	11	0.03
Guamanian/Chamorro (3)	11	0.03
Polynesian: (18)	51	0.15
Native Hawaiian (15)	42	0.12
Samoan (2)	7	0.02
Tongan (1)	1	0.00
Other Polynesian	1	0.00
Other Pac. Isl., not spec. (3)	17	0.05
Hispanic or Latino:	6,807	20.16
Central American:	70	0.21
Costa Rican	4	0.01
Guatemalan	29	0.09
Nicaraguan	3	0.01
Panamanian	11	0.03
Salvadoran	20	0.06
Other Central American	3	0.01
Cuban	50	0.15
Dominican Republic	3	0.01
Mexican	5,558	16.46
Puerto Rican	78	0.23
South American:	46	0.14
Argentinean	16	0.05
Colombian	7	0.02
Ecuadorian	5	0.01
Peruvian	13	0.04
Venezuelan	1	0.00
Other South American	4	0.01
Other Hispanic or Latino	1,002	2.97
Hungarian	163	0.48
Icelander	17	0.05
Iranian	8	0.02
Irish	4,605	13.60
Italian	1,825	5.39
Lithuanian	27	0.08
Northern European	13	0.04
Norwegian	684	2.02
Pennsylvania German	22	0.06
Polish	687	2.03
Portuguese	206	0.61
Russian	153	0.45
Scandinavian	8	0.02
Scotch-Irish	616	1.82
Scottish	639	1.89
Slavic	39	0.12
Slovak	14	0.04
Slovene	6	0.02
Swedish	512	1.51
Swiss	53	0.16
Turkish	8	0.02
Ukrainian	37	0.11
United States or American	2,041	6.03
Welsh	204	0.60
West Indian, excl. Hispanic:	10	0.03
Dutch West Indian	10	0.03
White:	29,746	88.09
Not Hispanic (25,464)	25,906	76.72
Hispanic (3,432)	3,840	11.37
Yugoslavian	39	0.12

Casa Grande

Place Type: City
County: Pinal
Population: 25,224

Ancestry/Race	Number	%
African American/Black:	1,239	4.91
Not Hispanic (1,020)	1,113	4.41
Hispanic (57)	126	0.50
African, sub-Saharan:	83	0.33
African	57	0.23
Other sub-Saharan African	26	0.10
Am. Ind. or Alaska Nat., not spec.	262	1.04
American Indian tribes, specified:	1,156	4.58
Apache (22)	32	0.13
Blackfeet (6)	6	0.02
Cherokee (2)	39	0.15
Cheyenne	2	0.01
Chickasaw (1)	1	0.00
Chippewa (6)	8	0.03
Choctaw (31)	48	0.19
Comanche	1	0.00
Creek (6)	14	0.06
Iroquois (1)	2	0.01
Kiowa (1)	1	0.00
Latin American Indians (17)	34	0.13
Navajo (44)	65	0.26
Osage (2)	2	0.01
Ottawa (1)	1	0.00
Paiute	1	0.00
Pima (153)	187	0.74
Potawatomi (4)	7	0.03
Pueblo (10)	14	0.06
Seminole (1)	1	0.00
Sioux (11)	18	0.07
Tohono O'Odham (495)	548	2.17
Ute (1)	2	0.01
Yakama (1)	1	0.00
Yaqui (51)	82	0.33
Yuman (8)	11	0.04
All other tribes (21)	28	0.11
American Indian tribes, not spec.	139	0.55
Arab:	97	0.38
Arab/Arabic	20	0.08
Egyptian	18	0.07
Iraqi	40	0.16
Lebanese	11	0.04
Syrian	8	0.03
Asian:	358	1.42
Cambodian (1)	3	0.01
Chinese, ex. Taiwanese (35)	42	0.17
Filipino (111)	129	0.51
Indian (85)	91	0.36
Japanese (17)	26	0.10
Korean (19)	28	0.11
Laotian (2)	2	0.01
Taiwanese (1)	1	0.00
Thai (1)	2	0.01
Vietnamese (18)	20	0.08
Other Asian, specified	1	0.00
Other Asian, not specified (1)	13	0.05
Austrian	42	0.17
Basque	44	0.17
Belgian	14	0.06
Brazilian	15	0.06
British	52	0.21
Canadian	54	0.21
Celtic	10	0.04
Czech	70	0.28
Czechoslovakian	26	0.10
Danish	169	0.67
Dutch	323	1.28
English	2,028	8.01
European	200	0.79
Finnish	43	0.17
French, except Basque	505	1.99
French Canadian	246	0.97
German	3,200	12.64
Greek	40	0.16
Hawaii Native/Pacific Islander:	61	0.24
Micronesian: (7)	7	0.03
Guamanian/Chamorro (6)	6	0.02
Other Micronesian (1)	1	0.00
Polynesian: (16)	28	0.11
Native Hawaiian (7)	14	0.06
Samoan (2)	6	0.02
Tongan (7)	8	0.03
Other Pac. Isl., not spec. (2)	26	0.10
Hispanic or Latino:	9,871	39.13
Central American:	36	0.14
Costa Rican	4	0.02
Guatemalan	7	0.03
Honduran	2	0.01
Nicaraguan	6	0.02
Panamanian	4	0.02
Salvadoran	10	0.04
Other Central American	3	0.01
Cuban	4	0.02
Dominican Republic	3	0.01
Mexican	8,213	32.56
Puerto Rican	50	0.20
South American:	23	0.09
Bolivian	1	0.00
Chilean	8	0.03
Colombian	8	0.03
Ecuadorian	1	0.00
Peruvian	1	0.00
Venezuelan	3	0.01
Other South American	1	0.00
Other Hispanic or Latino	1,542	6.11
Hungarian	125	0.49
Irish	2,192	8.66
Italian	497	1.96
Lithuanian	39	0.15
Northern European	43	0.17
Norwegian	402	1.59
Pennsylvania German	23	0.09
Polish	420	1.66
Portuguese	34	0.13
Russian	37	0.15
Scotch-Irish	257	1.01
Scottish	291	1.15
Slavic	10	0.04
Slovak	15	0.06
Swedish	296	1.17
Swiss	100	0.39
Ukrainian	30	0.12
United States or American	881	3.48
Welsh	153	0.60
West Indian, excl. Hispanic:	10	0.04
Dutch West Indian	10	0.04
White:	17,099	67.79
Not Hispanic (12,707)	12,966	51.40
Hispanic (3,664)	4,133	16.39
Yugoslavian	7	0.03

Casas Adobes

Place Type: Census Designated Place
County: Pima
Population: 54,011

Ancestry/Race	Number	%
Acadian/Cajun	13	0.02
African American/Black:	1,139	2.11
Not Hispanic (837)	1,029	1.91
Hispanic (54)	110	0.20
African, sub-Saharan:	82	0.15
African	27	0.05
Ethiopian	46	0.09
South African	9	0.02
Alaska Native tribes, specified:	8	0.01
Alaska Athabascan (1)	2	0.00

Notes: 1. Figures in the "Number" column do not add up to the total population due to: a) Ancestry/Race overlap — e.g. persons can report being both White and Irish, b) persons of Hispanic origin can report being any race, c) persons reporting two ancestries are counted in both categories. 2. Numbers in parentheses indicate the number of persons reporting this ancestry/race alone, not in combination with any other ancestry/race. 3. Refer to the Explanation of Data in the front of the book for more detailed information.

Ancestry/Race	Number	%
Aleut (2)	2	0.00
Eskimo (1)	1	0.00
Tlingit-Haida	2	0.00
All other tribes	1	0.00
Am. Ind. or Alaska Nat., not spec.	199	0.37
American Indian tribes, specified:	438	0.81
Apache (7)	20	0.04
Blackfeet (1)	3	0.01
Cherokee (38)	110	0.20
Cheyenne (2)	2	0.00
Chickasaw (2)	5	0.01
Chippewa (4)	10	0.02
Choctaw (13)	34	0.06
Colville	3	0.01
Comanche (2)	6	0.01
Cree (1)	1	0.00
Creek (1)	4	0.01
Iroquois (10)	24	0.04
Latin American Indians (17)	24	0.04
Lumbee (5)	7	0.01
Navajo (41)	44	0.08
Osage	2	0.00
Paiute (2)	2	0.00
Pima (5)	6	0.01
Pueblo (5)	8	0.01
Seminole	8	0.01
Sioux (14)	23	0.04
Tohono O'Odham (20)	26	0.05
Yakama (1)	2	0.00
Yaqui (22)	29	0.05
Yuman (4)	4	0.01
All other tribes (20)	31	0.06
American Indian tribes, not spec.	34	0.06
Arab:	293	0.54
Arab/Arabic	51	0.09
Iraqi	9	0.02
Lebanese	138	0.26
Palestinian	25	0.05
Syrian	9	0.02
Other Arab	61	0.11
Armenian	78	0.14
Asian:	1,587	2.94
Cambodian (13)	19	0.04
Chinese, ex. Taiwanese (287)	363	0.67
Filipino (193)	290	0.54
Indian (126)	140	0.26
Indonesian (4)	7	0.01
Japanese (160)	266	0.49
Korean (170)	206	0.38
Laotian (7)	10	0.02
Malaysian (3)	7	0.01
Pakistani (13)	18	0.03
Sri Lankan (7)	7	0.01
Taiwanese (9)	12	0.02
Thai (12)	22	0.04
Vietnamese (123)	159	0.29
Other Asian, specified (7)	12	0.02
Other Asian, not specified (19)	49	0.09
Assyrian/Chaldean/Syriac	13	0.02
Australian	7	0.01
Austrian	234	0.43
Basque	23	0.04
Belgian	114	0.21
Brazilian	36	0.07
British	316	0.59
Bulgarian	20	0.04
Canadian	241	0.45
Celtic	32	0.06
Croatian	109	0.20
Czech	349	0.65
Czechoslovakian	100	0.19
Danish	425	0.79
Dutch	942	1.75
Eastern European	24	0.04
English	7,731	14.34
European	658	1.22
Finnish	192	0.36
French, except Basque	2,414	4.48
French Canadian	541	1.00
German	11,274	20.92
Greek	114	0.21
Hawaii Native/Pacific Islander:	84	0.16
Micronesian: (6)	11	0.02
Guamanian/Chamorro (5)	10	0.02
Other Micronesian (1)	1	0.00
Polynesian: (21)	54	0.10
Native Hawaiian (16)	45	0.08
Samoan (3)	7	0.01
Tongan (1)	1	0.00
Other Polynesian (1)	1	0.00
Other Pac. Isl., specified	2	0.00
Other Pac. Isl., not spec. (5)	17	0.03
Hispanic or Latino:	7,434	13.76
Central American:	93	0.17
Costa Rican	10	0.02
Guatemalan	22	0.04
Honduran	4	0.01
Nicaraguan	18	0.03
Panamanian	19	0.04
Salvadoran	16	0.03
Other Central American	4	0.01
Cuban	55	0.10
Dominican Republic	17	0.03
Mexican	5,598	10.36
Puerto Rican	229	0.42
South American:	123	0.23
Argentinean	20	0.04
Bolivian	6	0.01
Chilean	28	0.05
Colombian	23	0.04
Ecuadorian	7	0.01
Peruvian	26	0.05
Uruguayan	4	0.01
Venezuelan	1	0.00
Other South American	8	0.01
Other Hispanic or Latino	1,319	2.44
Hungarian	504	0.94
Iranian	69	0.13
Irish	7,632	14.16
Israeli	17	0.03
Italian	3,143	5.83
Latvian	18	0.03
Lithuanian	210	0.39
Luxemburger	20	0.04
New Zealander	7	0.01
Northern European	52	0.10
Norwegian	1,307	2.42
Pennsylvania German	10	0.02
Polish	1,874	3.48
Portuguese	168	0.31
Romanian	65	0.12
Russian	702	1.30
Scandinavian	111	0.21
Scotch-Irish	1,387	2.57
Scottish	1,551	2.88
Serbian	9	0.02
Slavic	38	0.07
Slovak	109	0.20
Slovene	65	0.12
Swedish	1,265	2.35
Swiss	334	0.62
Turkish	20	0.04
Ukrainian	208	0.39
United States or American	2,625	4.87
Welsh	605	1.12
West Indian, excl. Hispanic:	25	0.05
Haitian	7	0.01
Jamaican	18	0.03
White:	49,004	90.73
Not Hispanic (43,461)	44,148	81.74
Hispanic (4,428)	4,856	8.99
Yugoslavian	33	0.06

Catalina Foothills

Place Type: Census Designated Place
County: Pima
Population: 53,794

Ancestry/Race	Number	%
Afghan	17	0.03
African American/Black:	855	1.59
Not Hispanic (615)	771	1.43
Hispanic (38)	84	0.16
African, sub-Saharan:	87	0.16
African	61	0.11
Nigerian	10	0.02
South African	16	0.03
Alaska Native tribes, specified:	4	0.01
Aleut (3)	3	0.01
Tlingit-Haida	1	0.00
Am. Ind. or Alaska Nat., not spec.	129	0.24
Albanian	6	0.01
Alsatian	10	0.02
American Indian tribes, specified:	337	0.63
Apache (5)	13	0.02
Blackfeet (8)	15	0.03
Cherokee (26)	74	0.14
Cheyenne	1	0.00
Chickasaw (1)	2	0.00
Chippewa (4)	11	0.02
Choctaw (17)	29	0.05
Comanche (1)	3	0.01
Cree	1	0.00
Creek (9)	12	0.02
Crow (2)	2	0.00
Delaware	1	0.00
Iroquois (6)	9	0.02
Kiowa (1)	1	0.00
Latin American Indians (11)	21	0.04
Lumbee (3)	3	0.01
Navajo (34)	43	0.08
Osage (1)	5	0.01
Potawatomi (1)	2	0.00
Pueblo	3	0.01
Puget Sound Salish (1)	1	0.00
Seminole	3	0.01
Sioux (13)	16	0.03
Tohono O'Odham (10)	13	0.02
Yaqui (15)	24	0.04
Yuman (2)	2	0.00
All other tribes (15)	27	0.05
American Indian tribes, not spec.	25	0.05
Arab:	248	0.46
Arab/Arabic	28	0.05
Egyptian	10	0.02
Lebanese	145	0.27
Syrian	41	0.08
Other Arab	24	0.04
Armenian	88	0.16
Asian:	2,160	4.02
Bangladeshi (4)	4	0.01
Cambodian (14)	17	0.03
Chinese, ex. Taiwanese (551)	648	1.20
Filipino (128)	174	0.32
Indian (371)	425	0.79
Indonesian (6)	7	0.01
Japanese (179)	276	0.51
Korean (263)	312	0.58
Laotian (7)	7	0.01
Malaysian (2)	2	0.00
Pakistani (39)	48	0.09
Sri Lankan (8)	13	0.02
Taiwanese (6)	11	0.02
Thai (17)	30	0.06
Vietnamese (85)	108	0.20
Other Asian, specified (4)	5	0.01
Other Asian, not specified (19)	73	0.14
Assyrian/Chaldean/Syriac	7	0.01
Australian	28	0.05
Austrian	366	0.68
Belgian	111	0.21
Brazilian	13	0.02
British	411	0.77
Bulgarian	7	0.01
Canadian	407	0.76
Croatian	132	0.25
Czech	314	0.59
Czechoslovakian	151	0.28
Danish	423	0.79

Notes: 1. Figures in the "Number" column do not add up to the total population due to: a) Ancestry/Race overlap — e.g. persons can report being both White and Irish, b) persons of Hispanic origin can report being any race, c) persons reporting two ancestries are counted in both categories. 2. Numbers in parentheses indicate the number of persons reporting this ancestry/race alone, not in combination with any other ancestry/race. 3. Refer to the Explanation of Data in the front of the book for more detailed information.

Dutch	1,158	2.16
Eastern European	233	0.44
English	9,346	17.45
European	842	1.57
Finnish	137	0.26
French, except Basque	2,046	3.82
French Canadian	394	0.74
German	11,665	21.78
Greek	420	0.78
Hawaii Native/Pacific Islander:	105	0.20
Melanesian: (2)	4	0.01
Fijian (2)	4	0.01
Micronesian: (16)	25	0.05
Guamanian/Chamorro (16)	25	0.05
Polynesian: (22)	44	0.08
Native Hawaiian (12)	32	0.06
Samoan (9)	10	0.02
Other Polynesian (1)	2	0.00
Other Pac. Isl., not spec. (10)	32	0.06
Hispanic or Latino:	4,062	7.55
Central American:	56	0.10
Costa Rican	10	0.02
Guatemalan	9	0.02
Honduran	5	0.01
Nicaraguan	5	0.01
Panamanian	7	0.01
Salvadoran	15	0.03
Other Central American	5	0.01
Cuban	112	0.21
Dominican Republic	5	0.01
Mexican	2,911	5.41
Puerto Rican	122	0.23
South American:	176	0.33
Argentinean	28	0.05
Bolivian	8	0.01
Chilean	48	0.09
Colombian	36	0.07
Ecuadorian	4	0.01
Peruvian	26	0.05
Uruguayan	1	0.00
Venezuelan	10	0.02
Other South American	15	0.03
Other Hispanic or Latino	680	1.26
Hungarian	577	1.08
Iranian	165	0.31
Irish	7,511	14.02
Israeli	10	0.02
Italian	3,010	5.62
Latvian	16	0.03
Lithuanian	319	0.60
Luxemburger	15	0.03
Macedonian	35	0.07
New Zealander	17	0.03
Northern European	104	0.19
Norwegian	1,351	2.52
Polish	2,360	4.41
Portuguese	187	0.35
Romanian	159	0.30
Russian	2,173	4.06
Scandinavian	146	0.27
Scotch-Irish	1,274	2.38
Scottish	1,846	3.45
Serbian	51	0.10
Slavic	89	0.17
Slovak	118	0.22
Slovene	24	0.04
Swedish	1,428	2.67
Swiss	335	0.63
Turkish	27	0.05
Ukrainian	220	0.41
United States or American	2,496	4.66
Welsh	648	1.21
West Indian, excl. Hispanic:	69	0.13
Belizean	27	0.05
Jamaican	12	0.02
West Indian	22	0.04
Other West Indian	8	0.01
White:	50,026	93.00
Not Hispanic (46,375)	46,998	87.37
Hispanic (2,765)	3,028	5.63
Yugoslavian	167	0.31

Chandler

Place Type: City
County: Maricopa
Population: 176,581

Ancestry/Race	Number	%
Acadian/Cajun	55	0.03
African American/Black:	7,174	4.06
Not Hispanic (5,821)	6,623	3.75
Hispanic (330)	551	0.31
African, sub-Saharan:	844	0.48
African	433	0.25
Cape Verdean	16	0.01
Ethiopian	118	0.07
Ghanian	35	0.02
Liberian	15	0.01
Nigerian	101	0.06
South African	52	0.03
Other sub-Saharan African	74	0.04
Alaska Native tribes, specified:	32	0.02
Alaska Athabascan (1)	2	0.00
Aleut (1)	3	0.00
Eskimo (10)	15	0.01
Tlingit-Haida (4)	10	0.01
All other tribes (2)	2	0.00
Alaska Native tribes, not specified	6	0.00
Am. Ind. or Alaska Nat., not spec.	777	0.44
Albanian	10	0.01
American Indian tribes, specified:	2,344	1.33
Apache (82)	117	0.07
Blackfeet (7)	30	0.02
Cherokee (74)	263	0.15
Cheyenne (5)	7	0.00
Chickasaw (9)	10	0.01
Chippewa (27)	50	0.03
Choctaw (49)	91	0.05
Comanche (2)	10	0.01
Cree (2)	7	0.00
Creek (7)	22	0.01
Crow (1)	5	0.00
Delaware	4	0.00
Iroquois (18)	33	0.02
Kiowa (5)	8	0.00
Latin American Indians (62)	115	0.07
Lumbee (5)	7	0.00
Menominee (5)	7	0.00
Navajo (433)	528	0.30
Osage (3)	6	0.00
Ottawa (1)	2	0.00
Paiute (8)	11	0.01
Pima (259)	328	0.19
Potawatomi (4)	17	0.01
Pueblo (94)	130	0.07
Seminole (2)	8	0.00
Shoshone	1	0.00
Sioux (40)	64	0.04
Tohono O'Odham (57)	79	0.04
Ute (8)	8	0.00
Yaqui (165)	206	0.12
Yuman (22)	40	0.02
All other tribes (74)	130	0.07
American Indian tribes, not spec.	106	0.06
Arab:	1,055	0.60
Arab/Arabic	135	0.08
Egyptian	19	0.01
Iraqi	30	0.02
Jordanian	87	0.05
Lebanese	364	0.21
Moroccan	106	0.06
Palestinian	83	0.05
Syrian	142	0.08
Other Arab	89	0.05
Armenian	117	0.07
Asian:	9,237	5.23
Bangladeshi (77)	82	0.05
Cambodian (141)	181	0.10
Chinese, ex. Taiwanese (1,931)	2,304	1.30
Filipino (1,199)	1,653	0.94
Hmong (2)	2	0.00
Indian (1,578)	1,732	0.98
Indonesian (42)	58	0.03
Japanese (367)	642	0.36
Korean (531)	644	0.36
Laotian (63)	76	0.04
Malaysian (29)	47	0.03
Pakistani (124)	155	0.09
Sri Lankan (27)	39	0.02
Taiwanese (76)	91	0.05
Thai (74)	111	0.06
Vietnamese (918)	1,023	0.58
Other Asian, specified (14)	31	0.02
Other Asian, not specified (86)	366	0.21
Assyrian/Chaldean/Syriac	31	0.02
Australian	40	0.02
Austrian	376	0.21
Basque	30	0.02
Belgian	326	0.18
Brazilian	34	0.02
British	1,105	0.63
Bulgarian	13	0.01
Canadian	570	0.32
Celtic	91	0.05
Croatian	429	0.24
Czech	700	0.40
Czechoslovakian	264	0.15
Danish	1,458	0.83
Dutch	2,995	1.70
Eastern European	29	0.02
English	18,004	10.21
Estonian	8	0.00
European	1,379	0.78
Finnish	660	0.37
French, except Basque	5,201	2.95
French Canadian	1,651	0.94
German	32,987	18.71
Greek	857	0.49
Guyanese	16	0.01
Hawaii Native/Pacific Islander:	568	0.32
Melanesian: (3)	5	0.00
Fijian (3)	5	0.00
Micronesian: (64)	91	0.05
Guamanian/Chamorro (57)	83	0.05
Other Micronesian (7)	8	0.00
Polynesian: (149)	364	0.21
Native Hawaiian (81)	244	0.14
Samoan (42)	77	0.04
Tongan (24)	39	0.02
Other Polynesian (2)	4	0.00
Other Pac. Isl., specified	8	0.00
Other Pac. Isl., not spec. (21)	100	0.06
Hispanic or Latino:	37,059	20.99
Central American:	487	0.28
Costa Rican	72	0.04
Guatemalan	138	0.08
Honduran	33	0.02
Nicaraguan	31	0.02
Panamanian	49	0.03
Salvadoran	134	0.08
Other Central American	30	0.02
Cuban	175	0.10
Dominican Republic	66	0.04
Mexican	29,334	16.61
Puerto Rican	702	0.40
South American:	406	0.23
Argentinean	45	0.03
Bolivian	16	0.01
Chilean	26	0.01
Colombian	133	0.08
Ecuadorian	31	0.02
Paraguayan	2	0.00
Peruvian	82	0.05
Uruguayan	10	0.01
Venezuelan	33	0.02
Other South American	28	0.02
Other Hispanic or Latino	5,889	3.34
Hungarian	839	0.48
Icelander	40	0.02

Notes: 1. Figures in the "Number" column do not add up to the total population due to: a) Ancestry/Race overlap — e.g. persons can report being both White and Irish, b) persons of Hispanic origin can report being any race, c) persons reporting two ancestries are counted in both categories. 2. Numbers in parentheses indicate the number of persons reporting this ancestry/race alone, not in combination with any other ancestry/race. 3. Refer to the Explanation of Data in the front of the book for more detailed information.

Iranian	423	0.24
Irish	20,634	11.70
Israeli	11	0.01
Italian	9,998	5.67
Latvian	17	0.01
Lithuanian	418	0.24
Luxemburger	45	0.03
Macedonian	27	0.02
Maltese	43	0.02
Northern European	116	0.07
Norwegian	4,655	2.64
Pennsylvania German	160	0.09
Polish	5,184	2.94
Portuguese	669	0.38
Romanian	228	0.13
Russian	1,235	0.70
Scandinavian	501	0.28
Scotch-Irish	2,361	1.34
Scottish	3,431	1.95
Serbian	103	0.06
Slavic	66	0.04
Slovak	348	0.20
Slovene	113	0.06
Swedish	4,045	2.29
Swiss	590	0.33
Turkish	147	0.08
Ukrainian	372	0.21
United States or American	7,881	4.47
Welsh	1,272	0.72
West Indian, excl. Hispanic:	242	0.14
Bahamian	18	0.01
British West Indian	15	0.01
Haitian	12	0.01
Jamaican	88	0.05
Trinidadian and Tobagonian	55	0.03
West Indian	37	0.02
Other West Indian	17	0.01
White:	140,714	79.69
Not Hispanic (121,168)	123,728	70.07
Hispanic (15,128)	16,986	9.62
Yugoslavian	286	0.16

Cottonwood-Verde Village

Place Type: Census Designated Place
County: Yavapai
Population: 10,610

Ancestry/Race	Number	%
African American/Black:	57	0.54
Not Hispanic (33)	52	0.49
Hispanic (1)	5	0.05
African, sub-Saharan:	4	0.04
Cape Verdean	4	0.04
Alaska Native tribes, specified:	3	0.03
Aleut (1)	1	0.01
Eskimo (2)	2	0.02
Am. Ind. or Alaska Nat., not spec.	43	0.41
American Indian tribes, specified:	177	1.67
Apache (3)	6	0.06
Blackfeet	2	0.02
Cherokee (7)	26	0.25
Chickasaw	2	0.02
Chippewa (4)	5	0.05
Choctaw (1)	6	0.06
Comanche (1)	1	0.01
Creek	5	0.05
Iroquois	5	0.05
Kiowa (1)	1	0.01
Latin American Indians (4)	8	0.08
Navajo (62)	68	0.64
Osage	2	0.02
Ottawa	1	0.01
Pueblo (3)	6	0.06
Sioux (8)	11	0.10
Yuman (4)	12	0.11
All other tribes (6)	10	0.09
American Indian tribes, not spec.	8	0.08
Arab:	62	0.58
Jordanian	32	0.30
Lebanese	30	0.28
Armenian	5	0.05
Asian:	78	0.74
Chinese, ex. Taiwanese (20)	23	0.22
Filipino (10)	21	0.20
Indian (1)	3	0.03
Indonesian (3)	3	0.03
Japanese (6)	13	0.12
Korean (5)	5	0.05
Thai	2	0.02
Vietnamese (3)	6	0.06
Other Asian, not specified	2	0.02
Australian	10	0.09
Austrian	7	0.07
Belgian	14	0.13
British	57	0.53
Canadian	50	0.47
Croatian	7	0.07
Czech	48	0.45
Czechoslovakian	17	0.16
Danish	101	0.95
Dutch	253	2.37
English	1,523	14.28
European	77	0.72
Finnish	106	0.99
French, except Basque	435	4.08
French Canadian	71	0.67
German	1,789	16.78
Greek	60	0.56
Hawaii Native/Pacific Islander:	18	0.17
Micronesian: (1)	2	0.02
Guamanian/Chamorro (1)	2	0.02
Polynesian: (2)	10	0.09
Native Hawaiian (2)	6	0.06
Samoan	4	0.04
Other Pac. Isl., not spec. (3)	6	0.06
Hispanic or Latino:	1,186	11.18
Central American:	10	0.09
Guatemalan	3	0.03
Salvadoran	7	0.07
Cuban	2	0.02
Mexican	939	8.85
Puerto Rican	8	0.08
South American:	7	0.07
Argentinean	1	0.01
Bolivian	3	0.03
Colombian	3	0.03
Other Hispanic or Latino	220	2.07
Hungarian	49	0.46
Irish	1,608	15.08
Italian	477	4.47
Lithuanian	59	0.55
Norwegian	334	3.13
Polish	204	1.91
Portuguese	53	0.50
Russian	38	0.36
Scandinavian	31	0.29
Scotch-Irish	237	2.22
Scottish	293	2.75
Swedish	239	2.24
Swiss	19	0.18
United States or American	1,360	12.76
Welsh	180	1.69
White:	9,896	93.27
Not Hispanic (9,077)	9,206	86.77
Hispanic (586)	690	6.50

Douglas

Place Type: City
County: Cochise
Population: 14,312

Ancestry/Race	Number	%
African American/Black:	96	0.67
Not Hispanic (54)	57	0.40
Hispanic (16)	39	0.27
Am. Ind. or Alaska Nat., not spec.	53	0.37
American Indian tribes, specified:	141	0.99
Apache (6)	9	0.06
Blackfeet	2	0.01
Cherokee (3)	9	0.06
Choctaw (4)	6	0.04
Latin American Indians (20)	25	0.17
Navajo (37)	44	0.31
Pima (5)	5	0.03
Pueblo (7)	7	0.05
Sioux	3	0.02
Tohono O'Odham (5)	7	0.05
Yaqui (6)	13	0.09
Yuman (5)	5	0.03
All other tribes (3)	6	0.04
American Indian tribes, not spec.	8	0.06
Arab:	45	0.32
Arab/Arabic	16	0.11
Lebanese	29	0.20
Asian:	91	0.64
Chinese, ex. Taiwanese (15)	18	0.13
Filipino (7)	16	0.11
Indian (11)	14	0.10
Japanese (8)	12	0.08
Korean (14)	15	0.10
Taiwanese (1)	2	0.01
Vietnamese (1)	3	0.02
Other Asian, not specified (6)	11	0.08
Austrian	8	0.06
British	24	0.17
Croatian	5	0.04
Czech	12	0.08
Czechoslovakian	11	0.08
Danish	12	0.08
Dutch	60	0.42
English	254	1.79
European	6	0.04
Finnish	9	0.06
French, except Basque	93	0.66
German	321	2.26
Hawaii Native/Pacific Islander:	17	0.12
Micronesian: (7)	7	0.05
Guamanian/Chamorro (5)	5	0.03
Other Micronesian (2)	2	0.01
Polynesian: (2)	6	0.04
Native Hawaiian (2)	6	0.04
Other Pac. Isl., not spec. (3)	4	0.03
Hispanic or Latino:	12,306	85.98
Central American:	12	0.08
Guatemalan	2	0.01
Panamanian	4	0.03
Salvadoran	6	0.04
Cuban	6	0.04
Mexican	10,253	71.64
Puerto Rican	33	0.23
South American:	10	0.07
Argentinean	2	0.01
Chilean	1	0.01
Colombian	2	0.01
Peruvian	4	0.03
Venezuelan	1	0.01
Other Hispanic or Latino	1,992	13.92
Hungarian	17	0.12
Iranian	11	0.08
Irish	275	1.94
Italian	103	0.73
Lithuanian	4	0.03
Northern European	4	0.03
Norwegian	40	0.28
Polish	45	0.32
Russian	10	0.07
Scotch-Irish	39	0.27
Scottish	58	0.41
Serbian	12	0.08
Swedish	58	0.41
Swiss	7	0.05
United States or American	400	2.82
Welsh	4	0.03
White:	9,424	65.85
Not Hispanic (1,731)	1,780	12.44
Hispanic (7,314)	7,644	53.41

Notes: 1. Figures in the "Number" column do not add up to the total population due to: a) Ancestry/Race overlap — e.g. persons can report being both White and Irish, b) persons of Hispanic origin can report being any race, c) persons reporting two ancestries are counted in both categories. 2. Numbers in parentheses indicate the number of persons reporting this ancestry/race alone, not in combination with any other ancestry/race. 3. Refer to the Explanation of Data in the front of the book for more detailed information.

Drexel Heights

Place Type: Census Designated Place
County: Pima
Population: 23,849

Ancestry/Race	Number	%
Acadian/Cajun	19	0.08
African American/Black:	731	3.07
Not Hispanic (593)	667	2.80
Hispanic (32)	64	0.27
African, sub-Saharan:	35	0.15
African	35	0.15
Alaska Native tribes, specified:	9	0.04
Alaska Athabascan	1	0.00
Eskimo (5)	5	0.02
Tlingit-Haida (3)	3	0.01
Am. Ind. or Alaska Nat., not spec.	249	1.04
Albanian	14	0.06
American Indian tribes, specified:	698	2.93
Apache (11)	22	0.09
Blackfeet (3)	6	0.03
Cherokee (27)	49	0.21
Chickasaw	2	0.01
Chippewa (3)	6	0.03
Choctaw (7)	12	0.05
Comanche (2)	2	0.01
Cree	1	0.00
Creek (1)	2	0.01
Houma (3)	3	0.01
Iroquois (1)	3	0.01
Latin American Indians (20)	31	0.13
Navajo (27)	36	0.15
Osage	1	0.00
Ottawa (1)	1	0.00
Paiute (3)	3	0.01
Pima (4)	6	0.03
Pueblo (15)	15	0.06
Seminole (1)	1	0.00
Shoshone (3)	3	0.01
Sioux (4)	7	0.03
Tohono O'Odham (161)	187	0.78
Ute (4)	4	0.02
Yaqui (223)	272	1.14
Yuman (2)	2	0.01
All other tribes (17)	21	0.09
American Indian tribes, not spec.	71	0.30
Arab:	18	0.08
Egyptian	7	0.03
Other Arab	11	0.05
Asian:	341	1.43
Bangladeshi (1)	1	0.00
Cambodian (3)	3	0.01
Chinese, ex. Taiwanese (19)	58	0.24
Filipino (60)	98	0.41
Hmong (3)	3	0.01
Indian (7)	18	0.08
Indonesian (1)	4	0.02
Japanese (23)	39	0.16
Korean (25)	32	0.13
Laotian (22)	28	0.12
Thai (8)	13	0.05
Vietnamese (14)	21	0.09
Other Asian, specified	1	0.00
Other Asian, not specified (3)	22	0.09
Austrian	30	0.13
British	22	0.09
Canadian	10	0.04
Celtic	15	0.06
Croatian	17	0.07
Czech	28	0.12
Czechoslovakian	7	0.03
Danish	24	0.10
Dutch	290	1.22
English	1,416	5.98
European	84	0.35
Finnish	29	0.12
French, except Basque	633	2.67
French Canadian	97	0.41
German	2,594	10.95
Greek	109	0.46
Hawaii Native/Pacific Islander:	51	0.21
Micronesian: (6)	6	0.03
Guamanian/Chamorro (6)	6	0.03
Polynesian: (14)	32	0.13
Native Hawaiian (9)	25	0.10
Samoan (5)	7	0.03
Other Pac. Isl., not spec. (3)	13	0.05
Hispanic or Latino:	14,327	60.07
Central American:	51	0.21
Costa Rican	1	0.00
Guatemalan	8	0.03
Honduran	5	0.02
Nicaraguan	4	0.02
Panamanian	12	0.05
Salvadoran	16	0.07
Other Central American	5	0.02
Cuban	19	0.08
Dominican Republic	1	0.00
Mexican	12,309	51.61
Puerto Rican	58	0.24
South American:	21	0.09
Argentinean	1	0.00
Bolivian	1	0.00
Chilean	1	0.00
Colombian	8	0.03
Ecuadorian	1	0.00
Peruvian	6	0.03
Venezuelan	1	0.00
Other South American	2	0.01
Other Hispanic or Latino	1,868	7.83
Hungarian	114	0.48
Irish	1,720	7.26
Italian	578	2.44
Lithuanian	8	0.03
Luxemburger	10	0.04
Northern European	20	0.08
Norwegian	120	0.51
Polish	243	1.03
Portuguese	63	0.27
Romanian	8	0.03
Russian	30	0.13
Scandinavian	8	0.03
Scotch-Irish	311	1.31
Scottish	150	0.63
Slovak	9	0.04
Swedish	158	0.67
Swiss	16	0.07
Ukrainian	8	0.03
United States or American	585	2.47
Welsh	121	0.51
White:	14,594	61.19
Not Hispanic (7,947)	8,183	34.31
Hispanic (5,920)	6,411	26.88

Eloy

Place Type: City
County: Pinal
Population: 10,375

Ancestry/Race	Number	%
African American/Black:	623	6.00
Not Hispanic (481)	520	5.01
Hispanic (71)	103	0.99
African, sub-Saharan:	86	0.83
African	86	0.83
Am. Ind. or Alaska Nat., not spec.	106	1.02
American Indian tribes, specified:	443	4.27
Apache (2)	13	0.13
Cherokee (5)	11	0.11
Chippewa	1	0.01
Choctaw (4)	9	0.09
Creek (5)	5	0.05
Latin American Indians (33)	40	0.39
Navajo	8	0.08
Pima (16)	21	0.20
Pueblo (3)	3	0.03
Sioux (7)	7	0.07
Tohono O'Odham (222)	255	2.46
Yaqui (50)	66	0.64
All other tribes (1)	4	0.04
American Indian tribes, not spec.	41	0.40
Arab:	14	0.14
Egyptian	5	0.05
Lebanese	9	0.09
Asian:	195	1.88
Chinese, ex. Taiwanese (35)	46	0.44
Filipino (45)	53	0.51
Indian (8)	18	0.17
Indonesian	1	0.01
Japanese (1)	6	0.06
Korean (2)	10	0.10
Laotian (6)	8	0.08
Pakistani (5)	5	0.05
Taiwanese (5)	5	0.05
Thai (1)	1	0.01
Vietnamese (12)	13	0.13
Other Asian, specified (1)	1	0.01
Other Asian, not specified (2)	28	0.27
Belgian	4	0.04
British	7	0.07
Canadian	17	0.16
Celtic	2	0.02
Czechoslovakian	11	0.11
Dutch	42	0.41
English	264	2.56
French, except Basque	39	0.38
French Canadian	34	0.33
German	479	4.65
Hawaii Native/Pacific Islander:	36	0.35
Melanesian: (4)	6	0.06
Fijian (4)	6	0.06
Micronesian: (3)	6	0.06
Guamanian/Chamorro (3)	5	0.05
Other Micronesian	1	0.01
Polynesian: (3)	6	0.06
Samoan (2)	2	0.02
Tongan (1)	3	0.03
Other Polynesian	1	0.01
Other Pac. Isl., not spec. (1)	18	0.17
Hispanic or Latino:	7,717	74.38
Central American:	134	1.29
Guatemalan	63	0.61
Honduran	11	0.11
Nicaraguan	3	0.03
Panamanian	2	0.02
Salvadoran	53	0.51
Other Central American	2	0.02
Cuban	12	0.12
Mexican	6,554	63.17
Puerto Rican	7	0.07
South American:	20	0.19
Argentinean	2	0.02
Colombian	9	0.09
Ecuadorian	1	0.01
Peruvian	6	0.06
Venezuelan	2	0.02
Other Hispanic or Latino	990	9.54
Hungarian	16	0.16
Irish	165	1.60
Italian	32	0.31
Northern European	8	0.08
Norwegian	30	0.29
Polish	5	0.05
Portuguese	28	0.27
Russian	14	0.14
Scotch-Irish	56	0.54
Scottish	61	0.59
Swedish	18	0.17
Swiss	15	0.15
United States or American	268	2.60
Welsh	7	0.07
West Indian, excl. Hispanic:	21	0.20
Haitian	8	0.08
Jamaican	13	0.13
White:	5,822	56.12
Not Hispanic (1,640)	1,721	16.59
Hispanic (3,828)	4,101	39.5

Notes: 1. Figures in the "Number" column do not add up to the total population due to: a) Ancestry/Race overlap — e.g. persons can report being both White and I of Hispanic origin can report being any race, c) persons reporting two ancestries are counted in both categories. 2. Numbers in parentheses indicate the numbe reporting this ancestry/race alone, not in combination with any other ancestry/race. 3. Refer to the Explanation of Data in the front of the book for more det

Flagstaff

Place Type: City
County: Coconino
Population: 52,894

Ancestry/Race	Number	%
Acadian/Cajun	5	0.01
African American/Black:	1,151	2.18
Not Hispanic (866)	1,043	1.97
Hispanic (61)	108	0.20
African, sub-Saharan:	207	0.39
African	153	0.29
Cape Verdean	11	0.02
South African	12	0.02
Other sub-Saharan African	31	0.06
Alaska Native tribes, specified:	17	0.03
Aleut (2)	3	0.01
Eskimo (6)	7	0.01
Tlingit-Haida (6)	7	0.01
Alaska Native tribes, not specified	3	0.01
Am. Ind. or Alaska Nat., not spec.	413	0.78
Alsatian	19	0.04
American Indian tribes, specified:	5,274	9.97
Apache (74)	98	0.19
Blackfeet (3)	13	0.02
Cherokee (32)	120	0.23
Cheyenne (2)	2	0.00
Chickasaw (4)	10	0.02
Chippewa (10)	23	0.04
Choctaw (11)	22	0.04
Comanche (3)	7	0.01
Creek (6)	19	0.04
Crow	1	0.00
Delaware (2)	2	0.00
Iroquois (2)	13	0.02
Kiowa (1)	3	0.01
Latin American Indians (20)	37	0.07
Lumbee (1)	1	0.00
Navajo (3,703)	4,069	7.69
Ottawa (2)	3	0.01
Pima (14)	19	0.04
Potawatomi (2)	5	0.01
Pueblo (485)	608	1.15
Puget Sound Salish (4)	4	0.01
Seminole (1)	3	0.01
Shoshone (1)	1	0.00
Sioux (21)	35	0.07
Tohono O'Odham (7)	17	0.03
Ute (3)	3	0.01
Yaqui (1)	10	0.02
Yuman (39)	50	0.09
All other tribes (51)	76	0.14
American Indian tribes, not spec.	368	0.70
Arab:	139	0.26
Arab/Arabic	6	0.01
Egyptian	18	0.03
Lebanese	69	0.13
Moroccan	17	0.03
Syrian	21	0.04
Other Arab	8	0.02
Armenian	5	0.01
Asian:	925	1.75
Bangladeshi (1)	1	0.00
Cambodian (5)	5	0.01
Chinese, ex. Taiwanese (170)	224	0.42
Filipino (50)	124	0.23
Hmong (1)	1	0.00
Indian (175)	201	0.38
Indonesian (1)	4	0.01
Japanese (81)	130	0.25
Korean (86)	112	0.21
Laoti[illegible]	6	0.01
[illegible]	4	0.01
[illegible]	3	0.01
[illegible]	9	0.02
[illegible]	33	0.06
[illegible]	39	0.07
[illegible]pecified (15)	29	0.05
[illegible]riac	6	0.01
Australian	54	0.10
Austrian	98	0.18
Basque	36	0.07
Belgian	40	0.08
Brazilian	6	0.01
British	369	0.69
Bulgarian	9	0.02
Canadian	188	0.35
Celtic	72	0.14
Croatian	143	0.27
Czech	255	0.48
Czechoslovakian	107	0.20
Danish	614	1.16
Dutch	863	1.62
Eastern European	56	0.11
English	6,444	12.13
European	811	1.53
Finnish	219	0.41
French, except Basque	1,224	2.30
French Canadian	312	0.59
German	8,962	16.87
Greek	127	0.24
Hawaii Native/Pacific Islander:	121	0.23
Melanesian: (1)	3	0.01
Fijian (1)	3	0.01
Micronesian: (17)	22	0.04
Guamanian/Chamorro (5)	10	0.02
Other Micronesian (12)	12	0.02
Polynesian: (42)	84	0.16
Native Hawaiian (34)	70	0.13
Samoan (7)	13	0.02
Other Polynesian (1)	1	0.00
Other Pac. Isl., not spec. (5)	12	0.02
Hispanic or Latino:	8,500	16.07
Central American:	32	0.06
Costa Rican	6	0.01
Guatemalan	3	0.01
Honduran	2	0.00
Nicaraguan	3	0.01
Panamanian	7	0.01
Salvadoran	8	0.02
Other Central American	3	0.01
Cuban	31	0.06
Dominican Republic	8	0.02
Mexican	6,662	12.60
Puerto Rican	127	0.24
South American:	72	0.14
Argentinean	18	0.03
Bolivian	3	0.01
Chilean	7	0.01
Colombian	18	0.03
Peruvian	8	0.02
Uruguayan	6	0.01
Venezuelan	7	0.01
Other South American	5	0.01
Other Hispanic or Latino	1,568	2.96
Hungarian	277	0.52
Icelander	15	0.03
Iranian	29	0.05
Irish	6,177	11.62
Italian	2,417	4.55
Latvian	45	0.08
Lithuanian	98	0.18
Luxemburger	10	0.02
New Zealander	18	0.03
Northern European	79	0.15
Norwegian	1,482	2.79
Pennsylvania German	5	0.01
Polish	1,341	2.52
Portuguese	91	0.17
Romanian	57	0.11
Russian	519	0.98
Scandinavian	220	0.41
Scotch-Irish	901	1.70
Scottish	1,206	2.27
Serbian	6	0.01
Slavic	46	0.09
Slovak	44	0.08
Slovene	25	0.05
Swedish	1,265	2.38
Swiss	224	0.42
Turkish	10	0.02
Ukrainian	120	0.23
United States or American	1,926	3.62
Welsh	671	1.26
West Indian, excl. Hispanic:	55	0.10
Haitian	23	0.04
Jamaican	32	0.06
White:	42,531	80.41
Not Hispanic (36,760)	37,571	71.03
Hispanic (4,454)	4,960	9.38
Yugoslavian	66	0.12

Florence

Place Type: Town
County: Pinal
Population: 17,054

Ancestry/Race	Number	%
African American/Black:	1,615	9.47
Not Hispanic (1,524)	1,557	9.13
Hispanic (39)	58	0.34
African, sub-Saharan:	90	0.52
African	90	0.52
Alaska Native tribes, specified:	2	0.01
Eskimo (1)	1	0.01
Tlingit-Haida (1)	1	0.01
Alaska Native tribes, not specified	1	0.01
Am. Ind. or Alaska Nat., not spec.	388	2.28
American Indian tribes, specified:	406	2.38
Apache (27)	33	0.19
Blackfeet (2)	4	0.02
Cherokee (12)	24	0.14
Chippewa (5)	6	0.04
Choctaw (1)	5	0.03
Comanche (2)	2	0.01
Delaware (1)	1	0.01
Iroquois	1	0.01
Kiowa (1)	1	0.01
Latin American Indians (19)	24	0.14
Lumbee	1	0.01
Navajo (95)	100	0.59
Ottawa (1)	1	0.01
Pima (44)	51	0.30
Pueblo (9)	12	0.07
Seminole (1)	1	0.01
Shoshone (1)	1	0.01
Sioux (5)	7	0.04
Tohono O'Odham (69)	81	0.47
Ute	1	0.01
Yakama (1)	1	0.01
Yaqui (16)	23	0.13
Yuman (9)	12	0.07
All other tribes (10)	13	0.08
American Indian tribes, not spec.	43	0.25
Asian:	195	1.14
Bangladeshi	7	0.04
Chinese, ex. Taiwanese (50)	50	0.29
Filipino (37)	50	0.29
Indian (20)	29	0.17
Indonesian	1	0.01
Japanese (3)	5	0.03
Korean (6)	7	0.04
Pakistani (1)	1	0.01
Thai (2)	2	0.01
Vietnamese (14)	14	0.08
Other Asian, not specified (7)	29	0.17
Australian	13	0.08
Austrian	124	0.72
Basque	7	0.04
Belgian	22	0.13
British	37	0.22
Canadian	20	0.12
Czech	17	0.10
Czechoslovakian	14	0.08
Danish	71	0.41
Dutch	75	0.44
English	843	4.92
Estonian	6	0.03

[illegible]"Number" column do not add up to the total population due to: a) Ancestry/Race overlap — e.g. persons can report being both White and Irish, b) persons [illegible]ort being any race, c) persons reporting two ancestries are counted in both categories. 2. Numbers in parentheses indicate the number of persons [illegible]e alone, not in combination with any other ancestry/race. 3. Refer to the Explanation of Data in the front of the book for more detailed information.

Ancestry/Race	Number	%
European	214	1.25
Finnish	12	0.07
French, except Basque	275	1.60
French Canadian	68	0.40
German	1,316	7.67
German Russian	5	0.03
Hawaii Native/Pacific Islander:	31	0.18
Melanesian:	2	0.01
Fijian	2	0.01
Micronesian: (3)	7	0.04
Guamanian/Chamorro (3)	7	0.04
Polynesian: (4)	7	0.04
Native Hawaiian (1)	2	0.01
Samoan (3)	4	0.02
Tongan	1	0.01
Other Pac. Isl., not spec. (2)	15	0.09
Hispanic or Latino:	6,041	35.42
Central American:	236	1.38
Costa Rican	1	0.01
Guatemalan	77	0.45
Honduran	44	0.26
Nicaraguan	9	0.05
Panamanian	4	0.02
Salvadoran	101	0.59
Cuban	50	0.29
Mexican	4,448	26.08
Puerto Rican	38	0.22
South American:	21	0.12
Colombian	4	0.02
Ecuadorian	9	0.05
Peruvian	3	0.02
Venezuelan	5	0.03
Other Hispanic or Latino	1,248	7.32
Hungarian	1	0.01
Iranian	7	0.04
Irish	1,045	6.09
Italian	267	1.56
Lithuanian	14	0.08
Norwegian	168	0.98
Polish	77	0.45
Portuguese	7	0.04
Russian	26	0.15
Scandinavian	41	0.24
Scotch-Irish	178	1.04
Scottish	139	0.81
Serbian	6	0.03
Slavic	7	0.04
Slovak	8	0.05
Slovene	6	0.03
Swedish	115	0.67
Swiss	52	0.30
Ukrainian	32	0.19
United States or American	446	2.60
Welsh	56	0.33
White:	9,927	58.21
Not Hispanic (8,478)	8,562	50.21
Hispanic (1,263)	1,365	8.00

Flowing Wells

Place Type: Census Designated Place
County: Pima
Population: 15,050

Ancestry/Race	Number	%
African American/Black:	202	1.34
Not Hispanic (120)	177	1.18
Hispanic (14)	25	0.17
African, sub-Saharan:	20	0.13
Ethiopian	12	0.08
South African	8	0.05
Alaska Native tribes, specified:	3	0.02
Eskimo (1)	1	0.01
Tlingit-Haida	2	0.01
Am. Ind. or Alaska Nat., not spec.	82	0.54
American Indian tribes, specified:	289	1.92
Apache (10)	17	0.11
Blackfeet (1)	11	0.07
Cherokee (22)	66	0.44
Cheyenne	3	0.02
Chickasaw (3)	5	0.03
Chippewa (2)	5	0.03
Choctaw	6	0.04
Comanche	1	0.01
Cree (3)	3	0.02
Creek (2)	7	0.05
Delaware (1)	3	0.02
Iroquois (4)	5	0.03
Latin American Indians (12)	19	0.13
Navajo (23)	31	0.21
Osage	1	0.01
Ottawa	1	0.01
Pima (1)	1	0.01
Potawatomi (5)	8	0.05
Pueblo (4)	8	0.05
Seminole (3)	6	0.04
Sioux (6)	12	0.08
Tohono O'Odham (29)	34	0.23
Ute	3	0.02
Yaqui (17)	25	0.17
Yuman (1)	1	0.01
All other tribes (6)	7	0.05
American Indian tribes, not spec.	12	0.08
Arab:	48	0.32
Arab/Arabic	11	0.07
Egyptian	14	0.09
Lebanese	11	0.07
Syrian	12	0.08
Asian:	172	1.14
Chinese, ex. Taiwanese (14)	33	0.22
Filipino (21)	35	0.23
Indian (6)	11	0.07
Japanese (10)	25	0.17
Korean (4)	7	0.05
Laotian (1)	1	0.01
Pakistani (14)	17	0.11
Taiwanese	1	0.01
Thai (3)	10	0.07
Vietnamese (24)	26	0.17
Other Asian, not specified (2)	6	0.04
Austrian	31	0.21
Belgian	48	0.32
British	68	0.45
Canadian	46	0.31
Celtic	16	0.11
Croatian	27	0.18
Czech	30	0.20
Czechoslovakian	15	0.10
Danish	193	1.28
Dutch	310	2.06
English	1,588	10.54
European	141	0.94
Finnish	28	0.19
French, except Basque	451	2.99
French Canadian	83	0.55
German	2,369	15.72
Greek	41	0.27
Hawaii Native/Pacific Islander:	22	0.15
Micronesian: (1)	3	0.02
Guamanian/Chamorro (1)	3	0.02
Polynesian: (4)	9	0.06
Native Hawaiian (3)	7	0.05
Samoan (1)	1	0.01
Other Polynesian	1	0.01
Other Pac. Isl., not spec. (3)	10	0.07
Hispanic or Latino:	3,290	21.86
Central American:	22	0.15
Honduran	3	0.02
Nicaraguan	7	0.05
Panamanian	5	0.03
Salvadoran	2	0.01
Other Central American	5	0.03
Cuban	5	0.03
Mexican	2,744	18.23
Puerto Rican	39	0.26
South American:	8	0.05
Chilean	2	0.01
Colombian	3	0.02
Peruvian	3	0.02
Other Hispanic or Latino	472	3.14
Hungarian	38	0.25
Icelander	21	0.14
Iranian	6	0.04
Irish	1,601	10.62
Italian	855	5.67
Lithuanian	34	0.23
Northern European	15	0.10
Norwegian	378	2.51
Pennsylvania German	19	0.13
Polish	336	2.23
Portuguese	9	0.06
Romanian	18	0.12
Russian	95	0.63
Scandinavian	51	0.34
Scotch-Irish	467	3.10
Scottish	429	2.85
Slavic	10	0.07
Slovak	8	0.05
Swedish	256	1.70
Swiss	34	0.23
Ukrainian	9	0.06
United States or American	915	6.07
Welsh	97	0.64
White:	13,157	87.42
Not Hispanic (11,088)	11,344	75.38
Hispanic (1,586)	1,813	12.05

Fortuna Foothills

Place Type: Census Designated Place
County: Yuma
Population: 20,478

Ancestry/Race	Number	%
African American/Black:	127	0.62
Not Hispanic (76)	111	0.54
Hispanic (15)	16	0.08
Alaska Native tribes, specified:	5	0.02
Alaska Athabascan	1	0.00
Eskimo (2)	2	0.01
Tlingit-Haida (1)	1	0.00
All other tribes (1)	1	0.00
Alaska Native tribes, not specified	2	0.01
Am. Ind. or Alaska Nat., not spec.	62	0.30
American Indian tribes, specified:	144	0.70
Apache (1)	2	0.01
Blackfeet (3)	4	0.02
Cherokee (14)	38	0.19
Chickasaw (4)	7	0.03
Chippewa (6)	7	0.03
Choctaw (3)	4	0.02
Colville (2)	2	0.01
Creek (2)	4	0.02
Delaware (1)	1	0.00
Iroquois (3)	6	0.03
Latin American Indians (8)	13	0.06
Navajo (5)	5	0.02
Osage	1	0.00
Paiute (1)	1	0.00
Pueblo (2)	5	0.02
Puget Sound Salish	1	0.00
Seminole (2)	3	0.01
Sioux (1)	4	0.02
Tohono O'Odham (4)	4	0.02
Ute (1)	1	0.00
Yakama	1	0.00
Yaqui (4)	6	0.03
Yuman (1)	3	0.01
All other tribes (14)	21	0.10
American Indian tribes, not spec.	26	0.13
Arab:	54	0.26
Arab/Arabic	15	0.07
Lebanese	35	0.17
Palestinian	4	0.02
Asian:	149	0.73
Chinese, ex. Taiwanese (22)	31	0.15
Filipino (36)	47	0.23
Indian (15)	21	0.10
Indonesian	1	0.0
Japanese (23)	31	

Notes: 1. Figures in the "Number" column do not add up to the total population due to: a) Ancestry/Race overlap — e.g. persons can report being both White and I of Hispanic origin can report being any race, c) persons reporting two ancestries are counted in both categories. 2. Numbers in parentheses indicate the numbe reporting this ancestry/race alone, not in combination with any other ancestry/race. 3. Refer to the Explanation of Data in the front of the book for more det

Korean (7)	8	0.04
Laotian (1)	2	0.01
Thai (2)	2	0.01
Vietnamese (1)	3	0.01
Other Asian, not specified	3	0.01
Assyrian/Chaldean/Syriac	10	0.05
Australian	36	0.17
Austrian	48	0.23
Basque	19	0.09
Belgian	23	0.11
British	48	0.23
Canadian	138	0.66
Czech	214	1.02
Czechoslovakian	18	0.09
Danish	264	1.26
Dutch	661	3.15
English	3,182	15.19
European	172	0.82
Finnish	75	0.36
French, except Basque	643	3.07
French Canadian	254	1.21
German	3,872	18.48
Greek	3	0.01
Hawaii Native/Pacific Islander:	26	0.13
Micronesian: (4)	4	0.02
Guamanian/Chamorro (4)	4	0.02
Polynesian: (6)	16	0.08
Native Hawaiian (2)	12	0.06
Samoan (4)	4	0.02
Other Pac. Isl., not spec. (5)	6	0.03
Hispanic or Latino:	2,609	12.74
Central American:	16	0.08
Honduran	3	0.01
Nicaraguan	4	0.02
Panamanian	6	0.03
Salvadoran	2	0.01
Other Central American	1	0.00
Cuban	15	0.07
Mexican	2,202	10.75
Puerto Rican	30	0.15
South American:	8	0.04
Colombian	5	0.02
Ecuadorian	2	0.01
Venezuelan	1	0.00
Other Hispanic or Latino	338	1.65
Hungarian	60	0.29
Icelander	6	0.03
Irish	2,190	10.45
Italian	336	1.60
Latvian	29	0.14
Luxemburger	8	0.04
Northern European	14	0.07
Norwegian	914	4.36
Pennsylvania German	17	0.08
Polish	195	0.93
Portuguese	130	0.62
Romanian	6	0.03
Russian	62	0.30
Scandinavian	49	0.23
Scotch-Irish	644	3.07
Scottish	659	3.14
Serbian	11	0.05
Slavic	17	0.08
Slovak	25	0.12
Swedish	535	2.55
Swiss	81	0.39
Ukrainian	47	0.22
United States or American	1,603	7.65
Welsh	245	1.17
White:	18,761	91.62
Not Hispanic (17,361)	17,566	85.78
Hispanic (1,082)	1,195	5.84

Hills

	Number	%
Afghan	35	0.17
African American/Black:	166	0.82
Not Hispanic (118)	163	0.81
Hispanic (1)	3	0.01
African, sub-Saharan:	22	0.11
African	8	0.04
Nigerian	14	0.07
Alaska Native tribes, specified:	6	0.03
Alaska Athabascan (1)	1	0.00
Eskimo (1)	1	0.00
Tlingit-Haida (1)	4	0.02
Am. Ind. or Alaska Nat., not spec.	24	0.12
Alsatian	5	0.02
American Indian tribes, specified:	111	0.55
Apache (12)	12	0.06
Cherokee (3)	18	0.09
Chippewa (2)	5	0.02
Choctaw (2)	4	0.02
Colville (1)	1	0.00
Cree (1)	1	0.00
Creek (4)	6	0.03
Crow	1	0.00
Iroquois (2)	5	0.02
Latin American Indians (5)	5	0.02
Menominee (1)	1	0.00
Navajo (11)	11	0.05
Osage	1	0.00
Pima (1)	2	0.01
Potawatomi (3)	3	0.01
Pueblo (6)	8	0.04
Seminole (1)	1	0.00
Sioux (2)	5	0.02
Ute (1)	1	0.00
Yuman (4)	4	0.02
All other tribes (14)	16	0.08
American Indian tribes, not spec.	8	0.04
Arab:	128	0.63
Arab/Arabic	22	0.11
Egyptian	6	0.03
Lebanese	31	0.15
Moroccan	7	0.03
Syrian	47	0.23
Other Arab	15	0.07
Armenian	18	0.09
Asian:	252	1.25
Chinese, ex. Taiwanese (57)	59	0.29
Filipino (29)	51	0.25
Indian (25)	27	0.13
Indonesian (3)	3	0.01
Japanese (17)	48	0.24
Korean (22)	23	0.11
Laotian	2	0.01
Pakistani (1)	1	0.00
Thai (1)	1	0.00
Vietnamese (22)	28	0.14
Other Asian, specified	1	0.00
Other Asian, not specified (2)	8	0.04
Australian	15	0.07
Austrian	128	0.63
Belgian	72	0.36
Brazilian	41	0.20
British	168	0.83
Bulgarian	7	0.03
Canadian	130	0.64
Croatian	62	0.31
Czech	241	1.19
Czechoslovakian	39	0.19
Danish	233	1.15
Dutch	301	1.49
Eastern European	30	0.15
English	2,986	14.78
European	93	0.46
Finnish	112	0.55
French, except Basque	1,028	5.09
French Canadian	224	1.11
German	5,040	24.95
Greek	191	0.95
Hawaii Native/Pacific Islander:	33	0.16
Micronesian:	3	0.01
Other Micronesian	3	0.01
Polynesian: (12)	24	0.12
Native Hawaiian (6)	16	0.08
Samoan (6)	8	0.04
Other Pac. Isl., not spec.	6	0.03
Hispanic or Latino:	618	3.05
Central American:	19	0.09
Guatemalan	6	0.03
Panamanian	5	0.02
Salvadoran	2	0.01
Other Central American	6	0.03
Cuban	8	0.04
Dominican Republic	1	0.00
Mexican	350	1.73
Puerto Rican	61	0.30
South American:	33	0.16
Argentinean	5	0.02
Chilean	2	0.01
Colombian	4	0.02
Ecuadorian	6	0.03
Peruvian	7	0.03
Uruguayan	6	0.03
Venezuelan	1	0.00
Other South American	2	0.01
Other Hispanic or Latino	146	0.72
Hungarian	248	1.23
Iranian	10	0.05
Irish	2,966	14.68
Israeli	13	0.06
Italian	2,174	10.76
Latvian	6	0.03
Lithuanian	65	0.32
Luxemburger	13	0.06
Macedonian	17	0.08
Maltese	27	0.13
Northern European	50	0.25
Norwegian	784	3.88
Pennsylvania German	8	0.04
Polish	1,215	6.02
Portuguese	35	0.17
Romanian	78	0.39
Russian	231	1.14
Scandinavian	26	0.13
Scotch-Irish	423	2.09
Scottish	562	2.78
Slavic	36	0.18
Slovak	150	0.74
Slovene	62	0.31
Swedish	593	2.94
Swiss	173	0.86
Turkish	10	0.05
Ukrainian	88	0.44
United States or American	806	3.99
Welsh	223	1.10
West Indian, excl. Hispanic:	8	0.04
Jamaican	8	0.04
White:	19,680	97.26
Not Hispanic (19,055)	19,207	94.92
Hispanic (423)	473	2.34
Yugoslavian	62	0.31

Gilbert

Place Type: Town
County: Maricopa
Population: 109,697

Ancestry/Race	Number	%
Afghan	9	0.01
African American/Black:	3,252	2.96
Not Hispanic (2,515)	3,016	2.75
Hispanic (124)	236	0.22
African, sub-Saharan:	219	0.20
African	123	0.11
Nigerian	66	0.06
South African	7	0.01
Other sub-Saharan African	23	0.02
Alaska Native tribes, specified:	12	0.01
Alaska Athabascan (1)	1	0.00
Aleut (4)	6	0.01
Eskimo (1)	2	0.00

Number" column do not add up to the total population due to: a) Ancestry/Race overlap — e.g. persons can report being both White and Irish, b) persons ort being any race, c) persons reporting two ancestries are counted in both categories. 2. Numbers in parentheses indicate the number of persons alone, not in combination with any other ancestry/race. 3. Refer to the Explanation of Data in the front of the book for more detailed information.

Ancestry/Race	Number	%
Tlingit-Haida (3)	3	0.00
Am. Ind. or Alaska Nat., not spec.	267	0.24
American Indian tribes, specified:	918	0.84
Apache (32)	62	0.06
Blackfeet (3)	8	0.01
Cherokee (32)	173	0.16
Cheyenne (1)	3	0.00
Chickasaw (8)	9	0.01
Chippewa (16)	27	0.02
Choctaw (32)	54	0.05
Colville (1)	1	0.00
Comanche (1)	7	0.01
Cree (1)	1	0.00
Creek (13)	25	0.02
Crow (2)	2	0.00
Delaware (3)	4	0.00
Iroquois (9)	20	0.02
Kiowa (5)	5	0.00
Latin American Indians (13)	36	0.03
Navajo (141)	192	0.18
Osage	2	0.00
Ottawa	5	0.00
Paiute (6)	7	0.01
Pima (32)	51	0.05
Potawatomi (5)	5	0.00
Pueblo (38)	50	0.05
Puget Sound Salish (1)	4	0.00
Sioux (25)	50	0.05
Tohono O'Odham (12)	17	0.02
Ute (1)	3	0.00
Yaqui (39)	48	0.04
Yuman (2)	2	0.00
All other tribes (21)	45	0.04
American Indian tribes, not spec.	63	0.06
Arab:	711	0.65
Arab/Arabic	137	0.12
Egyptian	80	0.07
Iraqi	56	0.05
Jordanian	24	0.02
Lebanese	350	0.32
Moroccan	14	0.01
Syrian	26	0.02
Other Arab	24	0.02
Armenian	56	0.05
Asian:	4,961	4.52
Bangladeshi (13)	13	0.01
Cambodian (35)	49	0.04
Chinese, ex. Taiwanese (941)	1,141	1.04
Filipino (758)	1,043	0.95
Indian (614)	673	0.61
Indonesian (21)	29	0.03
Japanese (237)	494	0.45
Korean (467)	557	0.51
Laotian (45)	50	0.05
Malaysian (6)	8	0.01
Pakistani (24)	39	0.04
Sri Lankan (4)	8	0.01
Taiwanese (41)	46	0.04
Thai (90)	119	0.11
Vietnamese (466)	531	0.48
Other Asian, specified (4)	16	0.01
Other Asian, not specified (78)	145	0.13
Assyrian/Chaldean/Syriac	108	0.10
Australian	9	0.01
Austrian	249	0.23
Basque	6	0.01
Belgian	103	0.09
Brazilian	32	0.03
British	567	0.52
Bulgarian	4	0.00
Canadian	532	0.48
Celtic	22	0.02
Croatian	171	0.16
Czech	301	0.27
Czechoslovakian	261	0.24
Danish	1,707	1.55
Dutch	2,119	1.93
Eastern European	24	0.02
English	15,391	14.00
Estonian	8	0.01
European	1,494	1.36
Finnish	271	0.25
French, except Basque	4,075	3.71
French Canadian	1,120	1.02
German	23,504	21.38
Greek	492	0.45
Guyanese	17	0.02
Hawaii Native/Pacific Islander:	325	0.30
Micronesian: (26)	47	0.04
Guamanian/Chamorro (24)	42	0.04
Other Micronesian (2)	5	0.00
Polynesian: (93)	225	0.21
Native Hawaiian (49)	139	0.13
Samoan (22)	50	0.05
Tongan (17)	21	0.02
Other Polynesian (5)	15	0.01
Other Pac. Isl., specified	10	0.01
Other Pac. Isl., not spec. (10)	43	0.04
Hispanic or Latino:	13,026	11.87
Central American:	198	0.18
Costa Rican	27	0.02
Guatemalan	56	0.05
Honduran	33	0.03
Nicaraguan	13	0.01
Panamanian	24	0.02
Salvadoran	36	0.03
Other Central American	9	0.01
Cuban	113	0.10
Dominican Republic	43	0.04
Mexican	9,125	8.32
Puerto Rican	551	0.50
South American:	267	0.24
Argentinean	20	0.02
Bolivian	8	0.01
Chilean	13	0.01
Colombian	90	0.08
Ecuadorian	22	0.02
Paraguayan	1	0.00
Peruvian	62	0.06
Uruguayan	2	0.00
Venezuelan	28	0.03
Other South American	21	0.02
Other Hispanic or Latino	2,729	2.49
Hungarian	483	0.44
Iranian	84	0.08
Irish	13,705	12.47
Israeli	10	0.01
Italian	7,931	7.21
Latvian	7	0.01
Lithuanian	203	0.18
Luxemburger	37	0.03
Macedonian	8	0.01
Maltese	38	0.03
New Zealander	7	0.01
Northern European	111	0.10
Norwegian	3,011	2.74
Pennsylvania German	16	0.01
Polish	4,161	3.78
Portuguese	481	0.44
Romanian	93	0.08
Russian	853	0.78
Scandinavian	491	0.45
Scotch-Irish	1,460	1.33
Scottish	2,944	2.68
Serbian	61	0.06
Slavic	62	0.06
Slovak	313	0.28
Slovene	106	0.10
Swedish	2,571	2.34
Swiss	520	0.47
Turkish	39	0.04
Ukrainian	351	0.32
United States or American	6,157	5.60
Welsh	1,131	1.03
West Indian, excl. Hispanic:	134	0.12
Haitian	58	0.05
Jamaican	68	0.06
Other West Indian	8	0.01
White:	96,743	88.19
Not Hispanic (87,597)	89,286	81.39
Hispanic (6,446)	7,457	6.80
Yugoslavian	267	0.24

Glendale

Place Type: City
County: Maricopa
Population: 218,812

Ancestry/Race	Number	%
African American/Black:	12,011	5.49
Not Hispanic (9,818)	11,206	5.12
Hispanic (452)	805	0.37
African, sub-Saharan:	652	0.30
African	437	0.20
Ethiopian	5	0.00
Ghanian	37	0.02
Nigerian	67	0.03
Sierra Leonean	22	0.01
South African	15	0.01
Sudanese	42	0.02
Zimbabwean	7	0.00
Other sub-Saharan African	20	0.01
Alaska Native tribes, specified:	52	0.02
Alaska Athabascan (3)	4	0.00
Aleut	3	0.00
Eskimo (17)	30	0.01
Tlingit-Haida (13)	15	0.01
Alaska Native tribes, not specified	2	0.00
Am. Ind. or Alaska Nat., not spec.	1,105	0.50
Albanian	13	0.01
American Indian tribes, specified:	3,382	1.55
Apache (124)	196	0.09
Blackfeet (8)	28	0.01
Cherokee (109)	393	0.18
Cheyenne (5)	8	0.00
Chickasaw (18)	32	0.01
Chippewa (38)	71	0.03
Choctaw (49)	118	0.05
Colville (2)	2	0.00
Comanche (3)	15	0.01
Cree	3	0.00
Creek (11)	29	0.01
Crow (1)	3	0.00
Delaware (2)	6	0.00
Iroquois (36)	62	0.03
Kiowa (6)	20	0.01
Latin American Indians (127)	200	0.09
Lumbee (3)	5	0.00
Navajo (1,040)	1,208	0.55
Osage (7)	9	0.00
Ottawa	2	0.00
Paiute (16)	18	0.01
Pima (107)	164	0.07
Potawatomi (10)	20	0.01
Pueblo (151)	195	0.09
Puget Sound Salish (3)	6	0.00
Seminole (3)	9	0.00
Shoshone (13)	26	0.01
Sioux (56)	97	0.04
Tohono O'Odham (61)	95	0.04
Ute (12)	19	0.01
Yakama	3	0.00
Yaqui (40)	75	0.03
Yuman (26)	37	0.02
All other tribes (120)	208	0.10
American Indian tribes, not spec.	241	0.11
Arab:	978	0.45
Arab/Arabic	256	0.12
Egyptian	32	0.01
Iraqi	118	0.05
Jordanian	15	0.01
Lebanese	290	0.13
Moroccan	10	0.00
Palestinian	110	0.05
Syrian	147	0.07
Armenian	100	0.05
Asian:	7,828	3.58
Bangladeshi (8)	8	0.0
Cambodian (115)	136	

Notes: 1. Figures in the "Number" column do not add up to the total population due to: a) Ancestry/Race overlap — e.g. persons can report being both White and [...] of Hispanic origin can report being any race, c) persons reporting two ancestries are counted in both categories. 2. Numbers in parentheses indicate the numbe[...] reporting this ancestry/race alone, not in combination with any other ancestry/race. 3. Refer to the Explanation of Data in the front of the book for more det[...]

Chinese, ex. Taiwanese (1,317)	1,564	0.71
Filipino (1,087)	1,606	0.73
Indian (794)	914	0.42
Indonesian (33)	65	0.03
Japanese (479)	824	0.38
Korean (708)	915	0.42
Laotian (49)	80	0.04
Malaysian (7)	9	0.00
Pakistani (32)	55	0.03
Taiwanese (42)	66	0.03
Thai (179)	252	0.12
Vietnamese (905)	1,009	0.46
Other Asian, specified (33)	37	0.02
Other Asian, not specified (111)	288	0.13
Assyrian/Chaldean/Syriac	268	0.12
Australian	59	0.03
Austrian	507	0.23
Basque	18	0.01
Belgian	239	0.11
Brazilian	78	0.04
British	736	0.34
Bulgarian	49	0.02
Canadian	674	0.31
Celtic	56	0.03
Croatian	295	0.13
Cypriot	8	0.00
Czech	996	0.46
Czechoslovakian	400	0.18
Danish	1,639	0.75
Dutch	3,455	1.58
Eastern European	47	0.02
English	20,069	9.18
Estonian	22	0.01
European	1,935	0.89
Finnish	488	0.22
French, except Basque	6,434	2.94
French Canadian	1,431	0.65
German	36,070	16.50
Greek	650	0.30
Guyanese	12	0.01
Hawaii Native/Pacific Islander:	689	0.31
Melanesian: (2)	2	0.00
Fijian (2)	2	0.00
Micronesian: (78)	123	0.06
Guamanian/Chamorro (68)	105	0.05
Other Micronesian (10)	18	0.01
Polynesian: (155)	382	0.17
Native Hawaiian (94)	263	0.12
Samoan (50)	88	0.04
Tongan (4)	14	0.01
Other Polynesian (7)	17	0.01
Other Pac. Isl., not spec. (51)	182	0.08
Hispanic or Latino:	54,343	24.84
Central American:	633	0.29
Costa Rican	24	0.01
Guatemalan	206	0.09
Honduran	79	0.04
Nicaraguan	29	0.01
Panamanian	60	0.03
Salvadoran	177	0.08
Other Central American	58	0.03
Cuban	202	0.09
Dominican Republic	51	0.02
Mexican	42,874	19.59
Puerto Rican	1,055	0.48
South American:	432	0.20
Argentinean	63	0.03
Bolivian	9	0.00
Chilean	31	0.01
Colombian	144	0.07
Ecuadorian	41	0.02
Peruvian	63	0.03
[illegible]	6	0.00
[illegible]	46	0.02
[illegible] American	29	0.01
[illegible] Latino	9,096	4.16
[illegible]	997	0.46
[illegible]	9	0.00
[illegible]	262	0.12
[illegible]	22,682	10.38
Israeli	53	0.02
Italian	10,927	5.00
Latvian	48	0.02
Lithuanian	382	0.17
Luxemburger	9	0.00
Macedonian	28	0.01
Maltese	29	0.01
Northern European	66	0.03
Norwegian	3,743	1.71
Pennsylvania German	91	0.04
Polish	6,329	2.90
Portuguese	425	0.19
Romanian	825	0.38
Russian	1,412	0.65
Scandinavian	378	0.17
Scotch-Irish	2,503	1.15
Scottish	3,327	1.52
Serbian	133	0.06
Slavic	98	0.04
Slovak	341	0.16
Slovene	127	0.06
Swedish	4,113	1.88
Swiss	765	0.35
Turkish	96	0.04
Ukrainian	470	0.22
United States or American	10,851	4.96
Welsh	1,453	0.66
West Indian, excl. Hispanic:	319	0.15
Bahamian	9	0.00
Belizean	38	0.02
Bermudan	21	0.01
Dutch West Indian	5	0.00
Haitian	67	0.03
Jamaican	121	0.06
Trinidadian and Tobagonian	41	0.02
West Indian	17	0.01
White:	171,720	78.48
Not Hispanic (141,462)	145,107	66.32
Hispanic (23,831)	26,613	12.16
Yugoslavian	415	0.19

Goodyear

Place Type: City
County: Maricopa
Population: 18,911

Ancestry/Race	Number	%
African American/Black:	1,084	5.73
Not Hispanic (962)	1,048	5.54
Hispanic (21)	36	0.19
African, sub-Saharan:	14	0.07
African	14	0.07
Alaska Native tribes, specified:	1	0.01
Aleut (1)	1	0.01
Am. Ind. or Alaska Nat., not spec.	125	0.66
American Indian tribes, specified:	135	0.71
Apache (8)	10	0.05
Blackfeet (3)	4	0.02
Cherokee (4)	18	0.10
Chickasaw (2)	2	0.01
Chippewa (2)	5	0.03
Choctaw (1)	5	0.03
Cree	1	0.01
Creek	1	0.01
Iroquois	2	0.01
Latin American Indians (10)	11	0.06
Lumbee	4	0.02
Navajo (24)	24	0.13
Ottawa	1	0.01
Pima (8)	8	0.04
Potawatomi	2	0.01
Pueblo (4)	9	0.05
Sioux	1	0.01
Tohono O'Odham (4)	4	0.02
Yaqui	1	0.01
Yuman	2	0.01
All other tribes (6)	20	0.11
American Indian tribes, not spec.	24	0.13
Arab:	28	0.15
Arab/Arabic	7	0.04
Egyptian	8	0.04
Lebanese	13	0.07
Armenian	6	0.03
Asian:	479	2.53
Cambodian (1)	2	0.01
Chinese, ex. Taiwanese (82)	119	0.63
Filipino (90)	148	0.78
Indian (16)	29	0.15
Indonesian (3)	6	0.03
Japanese (38)	49	0.26
Korean (34)	43	0.23
Pakistani (2)	2	0.01
Taiwanese (8)	11	0.06
Thai (8)	12	0.06
Vietnamese (17)	20	0.11
Other Asian, specified (6)	6	0.03
Other Asian, not specified (11)	32	0.17
Austrian	33	0.18
Basque	27	0.14
Belgian	44	0.23
British	62	0.33
Canadian	26	0.14
Celtic	13	0.07
Croatian	88	0.47
Czech	85	0.45
Czechoslovakian	7	0.04
Danish	92	0.49
Dutch	332	1.77
English	1,596	8.50
European	74	0.39
Finnish	37	0.20
French, except Basque	552	2.94
French Canadian	128	0.68
German	3,094	16.48
Greek	87	0.46
Hawaii Native/Pacific Islander:	50	0.26
Micronesian: (5)	9	0.05
Guamanian/Chamorro (5)	9	0.05
Polynesian: (9)	31	0.16
Native Hawaiian (5)	19	0.10
Samoan (4)	10	0.05
Other Polynesian	2	0.01
Other Pac. Isl., not spec. (2)	10	0.05
Hispanic or Latino:	3,933	20.80
Central American:	34	0.18
Guatemalan	14	0.07
Honduran	4	0.02
Nicaraguan	2	0.01
Panamanian	6	0.03
Salvadoran	3	0.02
Other Central American	5	0.03
Cuban	13	0.07
Dominican Republic	7	0.04
Mexican	3,155	16.68
Puerto Rican	98	0.52
South American:	30	0.16
Argentinean	4	0.02
Bolivian	1	0.01
Colombian	7	0.04
Ecuadorian	3	0.02
Paraguayan	1	0.01
Peruvian	12	0.06
Venezuelan	2	0.01
Other Hispanic or Latino	596	3.15
Hungarian	120	0.64
Irish	1,840	9.80
Italian	923	4.92
Lithuanian	4	0.02
Luxemburger	8	0.04
Northern European	14	0.07
Norwegian	509	2.71
Polish	515	2.74
Portuguese	90	0.48
Romanian	36	0.19
Russian	112	0.60
Scandinavian	19	0.10
Scotch-Irish	240	1.28
Scottish	271	1.44
Slovak	35	0.19

[illegible] Number" column do not add up to the total population due to: a) Ancestry/Race overlap — e.g. persons can report being both White and Irish, b) persons [illegible] rt being any race, c) persons reporting two ancestries are counted in both categories. 2. Numbers in parentheses indicate the number of persons [illegible] alone, not in combination with any other ancestry/race. 3. Refer to the Explanation of Data in the front of the book for more detailed information.

Slovene	9	0.05
Swedish	260	1.38
Swiss	37	0.20
Ukrainian	23	0.12
United States or American	832	4.43
Welsh	128	0.68
West Indian, excl. Hispanic:	5	0.03
Jamaican	5	0.03
White:	15,259	80.69
Not Hispanic (13,206)	13,448	71.11
Hispanic (1,569)	1,811	9.58
Yugoslavian	36	0.19

Green Valley

Place Type: Census Designated Place
County: Pima
Population: 17,283

Ancestry/Race	Number	%
African American/Black:	45	0.26
Not Hispanic (31)	45	0.26
African, sub-Saharan:	7	0.04
African	7	0.04
Am. Ind. or Alaska Nat., not spec.	16	0.09
American Indian tribes, specified:	56	0.32
Apache	5	0.03
Cherokee (3)	18	0.10
Chickasaw (1)	1	0.01
Chippewa (3)	3	0.02
Choctaw	3	0.02
Cree	1	0.01
Creek (1)	1	0.01
Iroquois (1)	1	0.01
Latin American Indians (2)	4	0.02
Menominee (3)	3	0.02
Potawatomi (1)	1	0.01
Pueblo	2	0.01
Sioux (1)	1	0.01
Ute (1)	1	0.01
Yaqui (1)	2	0.01
All other tribes (5)	9	0.05
American Indian tribes, not spec.	7	0.04
Arab:	26	0.15
Egyptian	17	0.10
Lebanese	9	0.05
Armenian	15	0.09
Asian:	75	0.43
Chinese, ex. Taiwanese (8)	10	0.06
Filipino (11)	16	0.09
Indian (4)	10	0.06
Indonesian	2	0.01
Japanese (19)	23	0.13
Korean (8)	9	0.05
Thai (1)	1	0.01
Vietnamese (3)	4	0.02
Australian	5	0.03
Austrian	80	0.46
Basque	9	0.05
Belgian	52	0.30
British	117	0.67
Bulgarian	9	0.05
Canadian	120	0.69
Celtic	5	0.03
Croatian	32	0.18
Czech	169	0.97
Czechoslovakian	40	0.23
Danish	241	1.39
Dutch	487	2.81
English	4,342	25.05
Estonian	5	0.03
European	159	0.92
Finnish	109	0.63
French, except Basque	869	5.01
French Canadian	192	1.11
German	4,554	26.27
Greek	39	0.22
Hawaii Native/Pacific Islander:	14	0.08
Micronesian: (3)	3	0.02
Guamanian/Chamorro (3)	3	0.02
Polynesian: (4)	7	0.04
Native Hawaiian (2)	2	0.01
Samoan (2)	4	0.02
Other Polynesian	1	0.01
Other Pac. Isl., not spec. (2)	4	0.02
Hispanic or Latino:	394	2.28
Central American:	3	0.02
Panamanian	1	0.01
Other Central American	2	0.01
Cuban	2	0.01
Mexican	289	1.67
Puerto Rican	11	0.06
South American:	6	0.03
Chilean	1	0.01
Colombian	3	0.02
Paraguayan	1	0.01
Other South American	1	0.01
Other Hispanic or Latino	83	0.48
Hungarian	135	0.78
Irish	2,411	13.91
Italian	575	3.32
Latvian	8	0.05
Lithuanian	103	0.59
Northern European	23	0.13
Norwegian	755	4.36
Pennsylvania German	9	0.05
Polish	548	3.16
Portuguese	29	0.17
Russian	121	0.70
Scandinavian	38	0.22
Scotch-Irish	810	4.67
Scottish	714	4.12
Serbian	7	0.04
Slavic	7	0.04
Slovak	41	0.24
Slovene	21	0.12
Swedish	725	4.18
Swiss	194	1.12
Ukrainian	36	0.21
United States or American	936	5.40
Welsh	237	1.37
White:	17,082	98.84
Not Hispanic (16,687)	16,754	96.94
Hispanic (310)	328	1.90
Yugoslavian	21	0.12

Kingman

Place Type: City
County: Mohave
Population: 20,069

Ancestry/Race	Number	%
African American/Black:	151	0.75
Not Hispanic (109)	146	0.73
Hispanic (2)	5	0.02
Alaska Native tribes, specified:	2	0.01
Aleut (1)	1	0.00
Eskimo	1	0.00
Am. Ind. or Alaska Nat., not spec.	112	0.56
American Indian tribes, specified:	430	2.14
Apache (8)	22	0.11
Blackfeet	5	0.02
Cherokee (28)	72	0.36
Cheyenne (1)	2	0.01
Chickasaw (2)	2	0.01
Chippewa (3)	7	0.03
Choctaw (11)	17	0.08
Comanche (1)	2	0.01
Creek	5	0.02
Crow (1)	1	0.00
Delaware (1)	4	0.02
Iroquois (6)	12	0.06
Latin American Indians (9)	24	0.12
Navajo (68)	79	0.39
Osage	1	0.00
Pima (8)	8	0.04
Potawatomi (3)	5	0.02
Pueblo (23)	35	0.17
Puget Sound Salish	1	0.00
Seminole	1	0.00
Shoshone (2)	3	0.01
Sioux (8)	15	0.07
Tohono O'Odham	4	0.02
Yaqui	3	0.01
Yuman (61)	72	0.36
All other tribes (13)	28	0.14
American Indian tribes, not spec.	69	0.34
Arab:	91	0.46
Arab/Arabic	54	0.27
Lebanese	19	0.10
Syrian	10	0.05
Other Arab	8	0.04
Armenian	8	0.04
Asian:	369	1.84
Chinese, ex. Taiwanese (35)	38	0.19
Filipino (60)	94	0.47
Indian (104)	115	0.57
Indonesian (4)	9	0.04
Japanese (14)	23	0.11
Korean (15)	21	0.10
Pakistani (28)	33	0.16
Taiwanese (1)	1	0.00
Thai (7)	7	0.03
Vietnamese (8)	11	0.05
Other Asian, not specified (7)	17	0.08
Austrian	42	0.21
Basque	17	0.09
Belgian	8	0.04
Brazilian	14	0.07
British	42	0.21
Bulgarian	8	0.04
Canadian	22	0.11
Carpatho Rusyn	6	0.03
Celtic	7	0.04
Croatian	18	0.09
Czech	82	0.42
Czechoslovakian	9	0.05
Danish	170	0.86
Dutch	515	2.61
English	2,821	14.28
European	228	1.15
Finnish	65	0.33
French, except Basque	889	4.50
French Canadian	200	1.01
German	4,019	20.34
Greek	28	0.14
Hawaii Native/Pacific Islander:	56	0.28
Melanesian:	1	0.00
Fijian	1	0.00
Micronesian: (10)	14	0.07
Guamanian/Chamorro (6)	10	0.05
Other Micronesian (4)	4	0.02
Polynesian: (17)	32	0.16
Native Hawaiian (14)	26	0.13
Samoan (3)	4	0.02
Tongan	2	0.01
Other Pac. Isl., not spec. (1)	9	0.04
Hispanic or Latino:	1,856	9.25
Central American:	26	0.13
Costa Rican	5	0.02
Guatemalan	9	0.04
Honduran	1	0.00
Nicaraguan	3	0.01
Panamanian	2	0.01
Salvadoran	5	0.02
Other Central American	1	0.00
Cuban	14	0.07
Dominican Republic	3	0.01
Mexican	1,387	6.91
Puerto Rican	52	0.26
South American:	17	0.08
Argentinean	4	0.02
Chilean	2	0.01
Colombian	5	0.02
Peruvian	6	0.03
Other Hispanic or Latino	357	1.78
Hungarian	116	0.59
Iranian	9	0.05
Irish	2,954	14.95

Notes: 1. Figures in the "Number" column do not add up to the total population due to: a) Ancestry/Race overlap — e.g. persons can report being both White and Irish, b) persons of Hispanic origin can report being any race, c) persons reporting two ancestries are counted in both categories. 2. Numbers in parentheses indicate the number of persons reporting this ancestry/race alone, not in combination with any other ancestry/race. 3. Refer to the Explanation of Data in the front of the book for more detailed information.

Italian	691	3.50
Lithuanian	98	0.50
Luxemburger	5	0.03
Northern European	8	0.04
Norwegian	535	2.71
Pennsylvania German	10	0.05
Polish	663	3.36
Romanian	40	0.20
Russian	95	0.48
Scandinavian	53	0.27
Scotch-Irish	358	1.81
Scottish	416	2.11
Serbian	8	0.04
Slavic	7	0.04
Slovak	39	0.20
Slovene	17	0.09
Swedish	394	1.99
Swiss	75	0.38
Ukrainian	29	0.15
United States or American	1,543	7.81
Welsh	189	0.96
West Indian, excl. Hispanic:	8	0.04
Jamaican	8	0.04
White:	18,523	92.30
Not Hispanic (17,119)	17,429	86.85
Hispanic (932)	1,094	5.45
Yugoslavian	65	0.33

Lake Havasu City

Place Type: City
County: Mohave
Population: 41,938

Ancestry/Race	Number	%
African American/Black:	181	0.43
Not Hispanic (127)	170	0.41
Hispanic (2)	11	0.03
African, sub-Saharan:	3	0.01
African	3	0.01
Alaska Native tribes, specified:	7	0.02
Aleut (2)	5	0.01
All other tribes (1)	2	0.00
Alaska Native tribes, not specified	1	0.00
Am. Ind. or Alaska Nat., not spec.	115	0.27
Alsatian	7	0.02
American Indian tribes, specified:	413	0.98
Apache (7)	14	0.03
Blackfeet (8)	18	0.04
Cherokee (50)	126	0.30
Cheyenne (1)	1	0.00
Chickasaw (3)	5	0.01
Chippewa (5)	13	0.03
Choctaw (6)	16	0.04
Comanche	1	0.00
Cree (1)	2	0.00
Creek (3)	7	0.02
Crow (1)	1	0.00
Delaware (2)	3	0.01
Iroquois (5)	11	0.03
Latin American Indians (2)	4	0.01
Menominee (2)	2	0.00
Navajo (18)	26	0.06
Osage (3)	3	0.01
Ottawa (1)	3	0.01
Paiute (9)	11	0.03
Pima (3)	4	0.01
Potawatomi (5)	5	0.01
Pueblo (1)	10	0.02
Seminole (1)	6	0.01
Shoshone (6)	6	0.01
Sioux (17)	26	0.06
Tohono O'Odham	2	0.00
Yakama	1	0.00
Yuman (9)	15	0.04
All other tribes (49)	71	0.17
American Indian tribes, not spec.	20	0.05
Arab:	52	0.12
Lebanese	46	0.11
Syrian	6	0.01
Armenian	35	0.08
Asian:	376	0.90
Cambodian	1	0.00
Chinese, ex. Taiwanese (29)	46	0.11
Filipino (92)	149	0.36
Indian (44)	52	0.12
Indonesian (2)	8	0.02
Japanese (33)	60	0.14
Korean (8)	10	0.02
Sri Lankan (1)	4	0.01
Taiwanese	2	0.00
Thai (3)	6	0.01
Vietnamese (22)	23	0.05
Other Asian, not specified (8)	15	0.04
Australian	7	0.02
Austrian	115	0.27
Belgian	21	0.05
British	135	0.32
Canadian	269	0.64
Croatian	31	0.07
Czech	256	0.61
Czechoslovakian	75	0.18
Danish	504	1.20
Dutch	1,046	2.50
Eastern European	20	0.05
English	6,651	15.89
Estonian	18	0.04
European	242	0.58
Finnish	197	0.47
French, except Basque	1,995	4.77
French Canadian	575	1.37
German	8,945	21.37
Greek	181	0.43
Hawaii Native/Pacific Islander:	83	0.20
Micronesian: (6)	8	0.02
Guamanian/Chamorro (4)	5	0.01
Other Micronesian (2)	3	0.01
Polynesian: (29)	61	0.15
Native Hawaiian (8)	38	0.09
Samoan (20)	22	0.05
Other Polynesian (1)	1	0.00
Other Pac. Isl., not spec. (5)	14	0.03
Hispanic or Latino:	3,298	7.86
Central American:	21	0.05
Honduran	2	0.00
Nicaraguan	1	0.00
Salvadoran	15	0.04
Other Central American	3	0.01
Cuban	32	0.08
Dominican Republic	3	0.01
Mexican	2,612	6.23
Puerto Rican	93	0.22
South American:	64	0.15
Argentinean	20	0.05
Colombian	9	0.02
Ecuadorian	1	0.00
Peruvian	16	0.04
Uruguayan	2	0.00
Venezuelan	4	0.01
Other South American	12	0.03
Other Hispanic or Latino	473	1.13
Hungarian	331	0.79
Icelander	17	0.04
Iranian	9	0.02
Irish	6,095	14.56
Italian	3,019	7.21
Lithuanian	68	0.16
Luxemburger	15	0.04
Maltese	34	0.08
New Zealander	6	0.01
Northern European	21	0.05
Norwegian	1,123	2.68
Pennsylvania German	49	0.12
Polish	1,384	3.31
Portuguese	275	0.66
Romanian	32	0.08
Russian	324	0.77
Scandinavian	126	0.30
Scotch-Irish	920	2.20
Scottish	1,189	2.84
Serbian	6	0.01
Slavic	17	0.04
Slovak	138	0.33
Slovene	26	0.06
Swedish	1,210	2.89
Swiss	115	0.27
Turkish	8	0.02
Ukrainian	131	0.31
United States or American	2,769	6.62
Welsh	347	0.83
West Indian, excl. Hispanic:	8	0.02
Dutch West Indian	8	0.02
White:	40,147	95.73
Not Hispanic (37,550)	37,977	90.56
Hispanic (2,018)	2,170	5.17
Yugoslavian	44	0.11

Marana

Place Type: Town
County: Pima
Population: 13,556

Ancestry/Race	Number	%
African American/Black:	506	3.73
Not Hispanic (381)	465	3.43
Hispanic (11)	41	0.30
African, sub-Saharan:	21	0.16
African	21	0.16
Alaska Native tribes, specified:	5	0.04
Aleut	1	0.01
Tlingit-Haida (1)	4	0.03
Am. Ind. or Alaska Nat., not spec.	59	0.44
American Indian tribes, specified:	316	2.33
Apache (9)	13	0.10
Blackfeet (1)	2	0.01
Cherokee (4)	21	0.15
Chickasaw	2	0.01
Chippewa (2)	4	0.03
Choctaw (3)	3	0.02
Cree	1	0.01
Creek	5	0.04
Delaware (1)	1	0.01
Iroquois (1)	5	0.04
Latin American Indians (17)	23	0.17
Lumbee (3)	7	0.05
Navajo (20)	22	0.16
Osage	1	0.01
Pima (4)	5	0.04
Pueblo (4)	6	0.04
Seminole	3	0.02
Sioux (5)	12	0.09
Tohono O'Odham (30)	35	0.26
Ute (1)	1	0.01
Yaqui (91)	107	0.79
Yuman (3)	5	0.04
All other tribes (22)	32	0.24
American Indian tribes, not spec.	30	0.22
Arab:	55	0.41
Arab/Arabic	8	0.06
Lebanese	33	0.25
Palestinian	5	0.04
Syrian	9	0.07
Asian:	448	3.30
Cambodian (6)	6	0.04
Chinese, ex. Taiwanese (61)	82	0.60
Filipino (57)	79	0.58
Hmong (2)	2	0.01
Indian (25)	29	0.21
Indonesian	3	0.02
Japanese (44)	77	0.57
Korean (34)	48	0.35
Laotian (6)	8	0.06
Malaysian	1	0.01
Pakistani (2)	2	0.01
Taiwanese	2	0.01
Thai (7)	13	0.10
Vietnamese (79)	84	0.62
Other Asian, not specified (3)	12	0.09
Australian	10	0.07

Notes: 1. Figures in the "Number" column do not add up to the total population due to: a) Ancestry/Race overlap — e.g. persons can report being both White and Irish, b) persons of Hispanic origin can report being any race, c) persons reporting two ancestries are counted in both categories. 2. Numbers in parentheses indicate the number of persons reporting this ancestry/race alone, not in combination with any other ancestry/race. 3. Refer to the Explanation of Data in the front of the book for more detailed information.

Austrian	30	0.22
Brazilian	8	0.06
British	64	0.48
Canadian	126	0.94
Celtic	21	0.16
Croatian	15	0.11
Czech	64	0.48
Czechoslovakian	17	0.13
Danish	141	1.05
Dutch	275	2.05
English	1,708	12.71
European	183	1.36
Finnish	49	0.36
French, except Basque	567	4.22
French Canadian	110	0.82
German	2,779	20.67
German Russian	5	0.04
Greek	52	0.39
Guyanese	6	0.04
Hawaii Native/Pacific Islander:	38	0.28
Micronesian: (7)	9	0.07
Guamanian/Chamorro (7)	9	0.07
Polynesian: (11)	20	0.15
Native Hawaiian (10)	16	0.12
Samoan (1)	4	0.03
Other Pac. Isl., not spec. (2)	9	0.07
Hispanic or Latino:	2,663	19.64
Central American:	37	0.27
Costa Rican	1	0.01
Guatemalan	3	0.02
Honduran	4	0.03
Nicaraguan	8	0.06
Panamanian	2	0.01
Salvadoran	19	0.14
Cuban	17	0.13
Dominican Republic	2	0.01
Mexican	2,099	15.48
Puerto Rican	58	0.43
South American:	35	0.26
Argentinean	1	0.01
Bolivian	1	0.01
Chilean	2	0.01
Colombian	11	0.08
Ecuadorian	11	0.08
Peruvian	4	0.03
Venezuelan	3	0.02
Other South American	2	0.01
Other Hispanic or Latino	415	3.06
Hungarian	87	0.65
Irish	1,726	12.84
Italian	666	4.95
Lithuanian	14	0.10
Macedonian	9	0.07
Norwegian	354	2.63
Pennsylvania German	9	0.07
Polish	342	2.54
Portuguese	36	0.27
Romanian	15	0.11
Russian	98	0.73
Scandinavian	7	0.05
Scotch-Irish	367	2.73
Scottish	363	2.70
Serbian	9	0.07
Slavic	19	0.14
Slovene	20	0.15
Swedish	327	2.43
Swiss	41	0.30
Ukrainian	53	0.39
United States or American	471	3.50
Welsh	97	0.72
West Indian, excl. Hispanic:	20	0.15
Jamaican	20	0.15
White:	11,434	84.35
Not Hispanic (9,718)	9,911	73.11
Hispanic (1,376)	1,523	11.23
Yugoslavian	21	0.16

Mesa

Place Type: City
County: Maricopa
Population: 396,375

Ancestry/Race	Number	%
Acadian/Cajun	30	0.01
Afghan	23	0.01
African American/Black:	12,186	3.07
Not Hispanic (9,377)	11,103	2.80
Hispanic (600)	1,083	0.27
African, sub-Saharan:	1,086	0.27
African	939	0.24
Cape Verdean	11	0.00
Ethiopian	30	0.01
Ghanian	9	0.00
Nigerian	40	0.01
Somalian	18	0.00
South African	10	0.00
Zimbabwean	7	0.00
Other sub-Saharan African	22	0.01
Alaska Native tribes, specified:	60	0.02
Alaska Athabascan (7)	7	0.00
Aleut (7)	16	0.00
Eskimo (8)	13	0.00
Tlingit-Haida (11)	16	0.00
All other tribes (8)	8	0.00
Alaska Native tribes, not specified	4	0.00
Am. Ind. or Alaska Nat., not spec.	1,753	0.44
Albanian	7	0.00
Alsatian	7	0.00
American Indian tribes, specified:	7,203	1.82
Apache (330)	470	0.12
Blackfeet (21)	82	0.02
Cherokee (176)	662	0.17
Cheyenne (13)	24	0.01
Chickasaw (11)	42	0.01
Chippewa (56)	101	0.03
Choctaw (88)	193	0.05
Colville (5)	7	0.00
Comanche (10)	22	0.01
Cree (6)	16	0.00
Creek (31)	80	0.02
Crow (9)	14	0.00
Delaware (7)	20	0.01
Iroquois (37)	64	0.02
Kiowa (17)	26	0.01
Latin American Indians (269)	433	0.11
Lumbee (1)	5	0.00
Menominee (4)	8	0.00
Navajo (2,441)	2,780	0.70
Osage (13)	29	0.01
Ottawa (4)	10	0.00
Paiute (13)	21	0.01
Pima (362)	490	0.12
Potawatomi (13)	16	0.00
Pueblo (316)	401	0.10
Puget Sound Salish (2)	7	0.00
Seminole (12)	20	0.01
Shoshone (12)	18	0.00
Sioux (104)	175	0.04
Tohono O'Odham (96)	155	0.04
Ute (19)	29	0.01
Yakama (1)	7	0.00
Yaqui (204)	322	0.08
Yuman (67)	95	0.02
All other tribes (218)	359	0.09
American Indian tribes, not spec.	469	0.12
Arab:	1,109	0.28
Arab/Arabic	275	0.07
Egyptian	112	0.03
Iraqi	68	0.02
Jordanian	34	0.01
Lebanese	332	0.08
Moroccan	5	0.00
Palestinian	41	0.01
Syrian	144	0.04
Other Arab	98	0.02
Armenian	147	0.04
Asian:	8,247	2.08
Bangladeshi (35)	38	0.01
Cambodian (112)	142	0.04
Chinese, ex. Taiwanese (1,074)	1,419	0.36
Filipino (1,337)	2,007	0.51
Hmong (1)	1	0.00
Indian (686)	841	0.21
Indonesian (50)	90	0.02
Japanese (531)	1,017	0.26
Korean (553)	784	0.20
Laotian (46)	57	0.01
Malaysian (3)	5	0.00
Pakistani (33)	49	0.01
Sri Lankan (15)	16	0.00
Taiwanese (45)	68	0.02
Thai (157)	220	0.06
Vietnamese (955)	1,059	0.27
Other Asian, specified (24)	54	0.01
Other Asian, not specified (141)	380	0.10
Assyrian/Chaldean/Syriac	26	0.01
Australian	116	0.03
Austrian	822	0.21
Basque	84	0.02
Belgian	401	0.10
Brazilian	30	0.01
British	1,985	0.50
Bulgarian	98	0.02
Canadian	1,332	0.34
Celtic	94	0.02
Croatian	488	0.12
Czech	1,732	0.44
Czechoslovakian	649	0.16
Danish	5,297	1.33
Dutch	7,461	1.88
Eastern European	88	0.02
English	54,554	13.73
Estonian	19	0.00
European	3,744	0.94
Finnish	860	0.22
French, except Basque	12,835	3.23
French Canadian	2,821	0.71
German	68,647	17.28
German Russian	18	0.00
Greek	1,149	0.29
Guyanese	6	0.00
Hawaii Native/Pacific Islander:	1,679	0.42
Melanesian: (4)	6	0.00
Fijian (4)	6	0.00
Micronesian: (87)	160	0.04
Guamanian/Chamorro (61)	114	0.03
Other Micronesian (26)	46	0.01
Polynesian: (726)	1,259	0.32
Native Hawaiian (176)	481	0.12
Samoan (144)	217	0.05
Tongan (378)	493	0.12
Other Polynesian (28)	68	0.02
Other Pac. Isl., specified	11	0.00
Other Pac. Isl., not spec. (79)	243	0.06
Hispanic or Latino:	78,281	19.75
Central American:	1,136	0.29
Costa Rican	89	0.02
Guatemalan	452	0.11
Honduran	99	0.02
Nicaraguan	72	0.02
Panamanian	64	0.02
Salvadoran	283	0.07
Other Central American	77	0.02
Cuban	398	0.10
Dominican Republic	88	0.02
Mexican	63,519	16.02
Puerto Rican	1,513	0.38
South American:	811	0.20
Argentinean	94	0.02
Bolivian	19	0.00
Chilean	77	0.02
Colombian	214	0.05
Ecuadorian	66	0.02
Paraguayan	2	0.00
Peruvian	196	0.05
Uruguayan	12	0.00

Notes: 1. Figures in the "Number" column do not add up to the total population due to: a) Ancestry/Race overlap — e.g. persons can report being both White and Irish, b) persons of Hispanic origin can report being any race, c) persons reporting two ancestries are counted in both categories. 2. Numbers in parentheses indicate the number of persons reporting this ancestry/race alone, not in combination with any other ancestry/race. 3. Refer to the Explanation of Data in the front of the book for more detailed information.

Ancestry/Race	Number	%
Venezuelan	97	0.02
Other South American	34	0.01
Other Hispanic or Latino	10,816	2.73
Hungarian	1,434	0.36
Icelander	91	0.02
Iranian	289	0.07
Irish	42,830	10.78
Israeli	12	0.00
Italian	17,724	4.46
Latvian	159	0.04
Lithuanian	707	0.18
Luxemburger	53	0.01
Macedonian	51	0.01
Maltese	34	0.01
New Zealander	8	0.00
Northern European	496	0.12
Norwegian	10,709	2.70
Pennsylvania German	225	0.06
Polish	9,974	2.51
Portuguese	812	0.20
Romanian	432	0.11
Russian	1,861	0.47
Scandinavian	1,233	0.31
Scotch-Irish	5,735	1.44
Scottish	9,469	2.38
Serbian	326	0.08
Slavic	167	0.04
Slovak	428	0.11
Slovene	214	0.05
Soviet Union	10	0.00
Swedish	9,152	2.30
Swiss	1,580	0.40
Turkish	164	0.04
Ukrainian	1,043	0.26
United States or American	21,665	5.45
Welsh	3,516	0.89
West Indian, excl. Hispanic:	452	0.11
Barbadian	19	0.00
Belizean	86	0.02
Bermudan	8	0.00
Dutch West Indian	48	0.01
Haitian	60	0.02
Jamaican	158	0.04
Trinidadian and Tobagonian	59	0.01
West Indian	14	0.00
White:	333,223	84.07
Not Hispanic (290,180)	295,371	74.52
Hispanic (33,475)	37,852	9.55
Yugoslavian	532	0.13

Mohave Valley

Place Type: Census Designated Place
County: Mohave
Population: 13,694

Ancestry/Race	Number	%
African American/Black:	78	0.57
Not Hispanic (56)	70	0.51
Hispanic (6)	8	0.06
Alaska Native tribes, specified:	4	0.03
Alaska Athabascan	2	0.01
Aleut (1)	1	0.01
Tlingit-Haida	1	0.01
Am. Ind. or Alaska Nat., not spec.	70	0.51
American Indian tribes, specified:	359	2.62
Apache (4)	10	0.07
Blackfeet (2)	15	0.11
Cherokee (26)	56	0.41
Cheyenne	1	0.01
Chickasaw (10)	16	0.12
Chippewa (1)	4	0.03
Choctaw (8)	18	0.13
Comanche	2	0.01
Cree	2	0.01
Creek (1)	1	0.01
Crow (1)	1	0.01
Iroquois	1	0.01
Latin American Indians (3)	7	0.05
Lumbee (4)	4	0.03
Menominee (1)	1	0.01
Navajo (23)	27	0.20
Osage	2	0.01
Paiute	1	0.01
Pima	1	0.01
Potawatomi (2)	4	0.03
Pueblo (9)	15	0.11
Puget Sound Salish	1	0.01
Sioux (4)	6	0.04
Tohono O'Odham	2	0.01
Ute (1)	1	0.01
Yaqui (6)	8	0.06
Yuman (107)	116	0.85
All other tribes (23)	36	0.26
American Indian tribes, not spec.	37	0.27
Arab:	41	0.30
Lebanese	19	0.14
Syrian	22	0.16
Armenian	30	0.22
Asian:	177	1.29
Cambodian	2	0.01
Chinese, ex. Taiwanese (13)	19	0.14
Filipino (36)	52	0.38
Indian (22)	23	0.17
Indonesian (3)	3	0.02
Japanese (19)	29	0.21
Korean (15)	18	0.13
Malaysian	1	0.01
Thai (5)	5	0.04
Vietnamese (10)	10	0.07
Other Asian, not specified (4)	15	0.11
Austrian	18	0.13
Basque	8	0.06
Belgian	11	0.08
British	35	0.26
Canadian	81	0.60
Celtic	12	0.09
Croatian	9	0.07
Czech	40	0.29
Czechoslovakian	28	0.21
Danish	44	0.32
Dutch	310	2.28
English	1,991	14.67
European	84	0.62
Finnish	24	0.18
French, except Basque	734	5.41
French Canadian	179	1.32
German	2,508	18.47
German Russian	9	0.07
Greek	16	0.12
Hawaii Native/Pacific Islander:	29	0.21
Micronesian: (3)	6	0.04
Guamanian/Chamorro (3)	6	0.04
Polynesian: (12)	20	0.15
Native Hawaiian (12)	18	0.13
Tongan	2	0.01
Other Pac. Isl., not spec. (1)	3	0.02
Hispanic or Latino:	1,640	11.98
Central American:	28	0.20
Costa Rican	2	0.01
Guatemalan	11	0.08
Nicaraguan	4	0.03
Panamanian	10	0.07
Salvadoran	1	0.01
Cuban	8	0.06
Mexican	1,337	9.76
Puerto Rican	26	0.19
South American:	8	0.06
Argentinean	1	0.01
Colombian	2	0.01
Peruvian	4	0.03
Venezuelan	1	0.01
Other Hispanic or Latino	233	1.70
Hungarian	67	0.49
Iranian	22	0.16
Irish	1,812	13.35
Italian	618	4.55
Lithuanian	11	0.08
Luxemburger	10	0.07
Northern European	49	0.36
Norwegian	289	2.13
Pennsylvania German	22	0.16
Polish	360	2.65
Portuguese	72	0.53
Romanian	10	0.07
Russian	101	0.74
Scandinavian	42	0.31
Scotch-Irish	395	2.91
Scottish	263	1.94
Serbian	10	0.07
Swedish	336	2.47
Swiss	30	0.22
Ukrainian	45	0.33
United States or American	805	5.93
Welsh	206	1.52
West Indian, excl. Hispanic:	9	0.07
Dutch West Indian	9	0.07
White:	12,707	92.79
Not Hispanic (11,393)	11,573	84.51
Hispanic (1,040)	1,134	8.28
Yugoslavian	16	0.12

New Kingman-Butler

Place Type: Census Designated Place
County: Mohave
Population: 14,810

Ancestry/Race	Number	%
African American/Black:	112	0.76
Not Hispanic (61)	102	0.69
Hispanic (4)	10	0.07
African, sub-Saharan:	73	0.48
African	66	0.44
South African	7	0.05
Alaska Native tribes, specified:	1	0.01
Eskimo (1)	1	0.01
Alaska Native tribes, not specified	1	0.01
Am. Ind. or Alaska Nat., not spec.	114	0.77
American Indian tribes, specified:	370	2.50
Apache (14)	21	0.14
Blackfeet	17	0.11
Cherokee (37)	109	0.74
Cheyenne (4)	5	0.03
Chickasaw	10	0.07
Chippewa (4)	11	0.07
Choctaw (12)	23	0.16
Comanche (1)	2	0.01
Creek (2)	4	0.03
Delaware	1	0.01
Iroquois (1)	8	0.05
Latin American Indians (6)	9	0.06
Lumbee (1)	1	0.01
Navajo (34)	40	0.27
Osage	1	0.01
Ottawa (1)	1	0.01
Paiute (2)	2	0.01
Pima (2)	3	0.02
Pueblo (14)	18	0.12
Seminole (3)	4	0.03
Shoshone (1)	3	0.02
Sioux (4)	8	0.05
Tohono O'Odham (2)	2	0.01
Yaqui	3	0.02
Yuman (20)	23	0.16
All other tribes (26)	41	0.28
American Indian tribes, not spec.	9	0.06
Arab:	12	0.08
Lebanese	12	0.08
Asian:	126	0.85
Chinese, ex. Taiwanese (2)	17	0.11
Filipino (31)	55	0.37
Indian (2)	6	0.04
Japanese (6)	14	0.09
Korean (10)	14	0.09
Pakistani	1	0.01
Thai (2)	5	0.03
Vietnamese (6)	9	0.06
Other Asian, specified	1	0.01
Other Asian, not specified (3)	4	0.03

Notes: 1. Figures in the "Number" column do not add up to the total population due to: a) Ancestry/Race overlap — e.g. persons can report being both White and Irish, b) persons of Hispanic origin can report being any race, c) persons reporting two ancestries are counted in both categories. 2. Numbers in parentheses indicate the number of persons reporting this ancestry/race alone, not in combination with any other ancestry/race. 3. Refer to the Explanation of Data in the front of the book for more detailed information.

Ancestry/Race	Number	%
Austrian	30	0.20
Basque	10	0.07
Belgian	40	0.26
British	57	0.38
Canadian	47	0.31
Croatian	29	0.19
Czech	29	0.19
Czechoslovakian	32	0.21
Danish	63	0.42
Dutch	493	3.26
English	2,141	14.18
European	86	0.57
Finnish	8	0.05
French, except Basque	672	4.45
French Canadian	158	1.05
German	2,635	17.45
Greek	26	0.17
Hawaii Native/Pacific Islander:	47	0.32
Micronesian: (6)	13	0.09
Guamanian/Chamorro (6)	13	0.09
Polynesian: (11)	28	0.19
Native Hawaiian (10)	24	0.16
Samoan (1)	3	0.02
Other Polynesian	1	0.01
Other Pac. Isl., not spec.	6	0.04
Hispanic or Latino:	1,374	9.28
Central American:	14	0.09
Costa Rican	1	0.01
Guatemalan	5	0.03
Honduran	2	0.01
Nicaraguan	1	0.01
Panamanian	1	0.01
Salvadoran	1	0.01
Other Central American	3	0.02
Cuban	5	0.03
Mexican	980	6.62
Puerto Rican	33	0.22
South American:	6	0.04
Colombian	6	0.04
Other Hispanic or Latino	336	2.27
Hungarian	107	0.71
Irish	2,751	18.22
Israeli	9	0.06
Italian	543	3.60
Lithuanian	51	0.34
Norwegian	273	1.81
Polish	313	2.07
Portuguese	34	0.23
Romanian	13	0.09
Russian	52	0.34
Scandinavian	40	0.26
Scotch-Irish	299	1.98
Scottish	376	2.49
Serbian	34	0.23
Slavic	18	0.12
Slovak	24	0.16
Swedish	178	1.18
Swiss	122	0.81
Turkish	9	0.06
United States or American	1,644	10.89
Welsh	151	1.00
West Indian, excl. Hispanic:	14	0.09
Belizean	14	0.09
White:	13,921	94.00
Not Hispanic (12,784)	13,056	88.16
Hispanic (730)	865	5.84

New River

Place Type: Census Designated Place
County: Maricopa
Population: 10,740

Ancestry/Race	Number	%
African American/Black:	73	0.68
Not Hispanic (45)	65	0.61
Hispanic	8	0.07
Alaska Native tribes, specified:	1	0.01
Aleut (1)	1	0.01
Am. Ind. or Alaska Nat., not spec.	39	0.36
American Indian tribes, specified:	86	0.80
Apache (2)	5	0.05
Blackfeet	2	0.02
Cherokee (7)	30	0.28
Chickasaw	1	0.01
Chippewa (4)	6	0.06
Choctaw	4	0.04
Comanche	2	0.02
Creek	1	0.01
Delaware (1)	1	0.01
Iroquois	1	0.01
Latin American Indians (1)	1	0.01
Navajo (10)	15	0.14
Osage (1)	1	0.01
Pueblo (5)	5	0.05
Puget Sound Salish	3	0.03
Sioux	1	0.01
Yaqui (1)	1	0.01
All other tribes (5)	6	0.06
American Indian tribes, not spec.	5	0.05
Armenian	10	0.09
Asian:	91	0.85
Chinese, ex. Taiwanese (5)	14	0.13
Filipino (24)	37	0.34
Indian (2)	2	0.02
Japanese (6)	19	0.18
Korean (6)	9	0.08
Vietnamese (1)	4	0.04
Other Asian, specified	3	0.03
Other Asian, not specified (2)	3	0.03
Austrian	37	0.34
Belgian	16	0.15
British	44	0.41
Canadian	57	0.53
Croatian	8	0.07
Czech	65	0.60
Czechoslovakian	8	0.07
Danish	98	0.91
Dutch	266	2.47
English	1,333	12.36
European	128	1.19
Finnish	18	0.17
French, except Basque	467	4.33
French Canadian	117	1.09
German	2,566	23.80
Greek	45	0.42
Hawaii Native/Pacific Islander:	14	0.13
Micronesian: (1)	2	0.02
Guamanian/Chamorro (1)	2	0.02
Polynesian: (4)	9	0.08
Native Hawaiian (1)	6	0.06
Tongan (3)	3	0.03
Other Pac. Isl., specified	2	0.02
Other Pac. Isl., not spec.	1	0.01
Hispanic or Latino:	521	4.85
Central American:	7	0.07
Costa Rican	2	0.02
Panamanian	1	0.01
Other Central American	4	0.04
Cuban	12	0.11
Dominican Republic	6	0.06
Mexican	369	3.44
Puerto Rican	13	0.12
South American:	7	0.07
Argentinean	2	0.02
Bolivian	1	0.01
Colombian	1	0.01
Ecuadorian	2	0.02
Peruvian	1	0.01
Other Hispanic or Latino	107	1.00
Hungarian	80	0.74
Irish	1,898	17.61
Italian	447	4.15
Lithuanian	7	0.06
Norwegian	337	3.13
Polish	293	2.72
Portuguese	26	0.24
Romanian	7	0.06
Russian	82	0.76
Scotch-Irish	133	1.23
Scottish	294	2.73
Serbian	8	0.07
Slavic	37	0.34
Slovak	67	0.62
Swedish	250	2.32
Swiss	50	0.46
Ukrainian	13	0.12
United States or American	655	6.08
Welsh	131	1.22
White:	10,431	97.12
Not Hispanic (9,932)	10,039	93.47
Hispanic (364)	392	3.65
Yugoslavian	8	0.07

Nogales

Place Type: City
County: Santa Cruz
Population: 20,878

Ancestry/Race	Number	%
African American/Black:	97	0.46
Not Hispanic (38)	44	0.21
Hispanic (40)	53	0.25
African, sub-Saharan:	25	0.12
African	25	0.12
Alaska Native tribes, specified:	3	0.01
Tlingit-Haida (1)	3	0.01
Am. Ind. or Alaska Nat., not spec.	82	0.39
American Indian tribes, specified:	75	0.36
Apache (1)	7	0.03
Cherokee	8	0.04
Choctaw	1	0.00
Latin American Indians (20)	33	0.16
Pima	5	0.02
Pueblo (1)	1	0.00
Tohono O'Odham	1	0.00
Yaqui (12)	16	0.08
All other tribes (3)	3	0.01
American Indian tribes, not spec.	10	0.05
Arab:	108	0.52
Arab/Arabic	18	0.09
Lebanese	90	0.43
Asian:	94	0.45
Chinese, ex. Taiwanese (11)	21	0.10
Filipino (1)	5	0.02
Indian (22)	24	0.11
Indonesian (1)	1	0.00
Japanese (3)	5	0.02
Korean (19)	19	0.09
Taiwanese (1)	2	0.01
Thai	1	0.00
Vietnamese (7)	7	0.03
Other Asian, not specified (1)	9	0.04
Austrian	15	0.07
Croatian	4	0.02
Czech	3	0.01
Danish	15	0.07
Dutch	23	0.11
English	112	0.54
European	38	0.18
French, except Basque	176	0.84
German	261	1.25
Greek	45	0.22
Hawaii Native/Pacific Islander:	19	0.09
Polynesian: (14)	15	0.07
Native Hawaiian (12)	13	0.06
Samoan (2)	2	0.01
Other Pac. Isl., not spec. (1)	4	0.02
Hispanic or Latino:	19,539	93.59
Central American:	15	0.07
Costa Rican	1	0.00
Honduran	2	0.01
Panamanian	3	0.01
Salvadoran	8	0.04
Other Central American	1	0.00
Cuban	21	0.10
Dominican Republic	2	0.01
Mexican	16,989	81.37
Puerto Rican	17	0.08

Notes: 1. Figures in the "Number" column do not add up to the total population due to: a) Ancestry/Race overlap — e.g. persons can report being both White and Irish, b) persons of Hispanic origin can report being any race, c) persons reporting two ancestries are counted in both categories. 2. Numbers in parentheses indicate the number of persons reporting this ancestry/race alone, not in combination with any other ancestry/race. 3. Refer to the Explanation of Data in the front of the book for more detailed information.

Ancestry/Race	Number	%
South American:	9	0.04
Chilean	3	0.01
Colombian	3	0.01
Peruvian	1	0.00
Venezuelan	2	0.01
Other Hispanic or Latino	2,486	11.91
Hungarian	8	0.04
Iranian	7	0.03
Irish	132	0.63
Italian	156	0.75
Luxemburger	8	0.04
Norwegian	34	0.16
Polish	11	0.05
Portuguese	5	0.02
Romanian	5	0.02
Russian	6	0.03
Scotch-Irish	8	0.04
Scottish	66	0.32
Swedish	23	0.11
United States or American	457	2.19
Welsh	19	0.09
White:	16,802	80.48
Not Hispanic (1,139)	1,168	5.59
Hispanic (15,110)	15,634	74.88
Yugoslavian	7	0.03

Oro Valley

Place Type: Town
County: Pima
Population: 29,700

Ancestry/Race	Number	%
African American/Black:	418	1.41
Not Hispanic (303)	389	1.31
Hispanic (12)	29	0.10
African, sub-Saharan:	6	0.02
African	6	0.02
Alaska Native tribes, specified:	5	0.02
Aleut	3	0.01
Tlingit-Haida (1)	2	0.01
Am. Ind. or Alaska Nat., not spec.	55	0.19
Albanian	19	0.06
American Indian tribes, specified:	148	0.50
Apache (8)	9	0.03
Blackfeet (1)	4	0.01
Cherokee (16)	34	0.11
Chickasaw (1)	2	0.01
Chippewa (1)	7	0.02
Choctaw (5)	8	0.03
Comanche (2)	3	0.01
Cree	2	0.01
Creek (2)	5	0.02
Delaware	1	0.00
Iroquois (3)	5	0.02
Latin American Indians (2)	7	0.02
Navajo (17)	17	0.06
Osage	1	0.00
Potawatomi (4)	4	0.01
Pueblo (3)	6	0.02
Puget Sound Salish	1	0.00
Sioux (2)	4	0.01
Tohono O'Odham (3)	4	0.01
Ute (5)	5	0.02
Yaqui (3)	5	0.02
All other tribes (5)	14	0.05
American Indian tribes, not spec.	13	0.04
Arab:	168	0.57
Egyptian	38	0.13
Jordanian	19	0.06
Lebanese	111	0.37
Armenian	47	0.16
Asian:	736	2.48
Cambodian (1)	1	0.00
Chinese, ex. Taiwanese (142)	180	0.61
Filipino (77)	104	0.35
Indian (109)	124	0.42
Indonesian (4)	12	0.04
Japanese (68)	113	0.38
Korean (84)	95	0.32
Laotian (1)	5	0.02
Pakistani (3)	3	0.01
Taiwanese (3)	3	0.01
Thai (11)	17	0.06
Vietnamese (44)	52	0.18
Other Asian, specified	3	0.01
Other Asian, not specified (13)	24	0.08
Australian	35	0.12
Austrian	148	0.50
Basque	8	0.03
Belgian	32	0.11
Brazilian	17	0.06
British	195	0.66
Canadian	220	0.74
Celtic	15	0.05
Croatian	95	0.32
Czech	164	0.55
Czechoslovakian	72	0.24
Danish	252	0.85
Dutch	628	2.12
Eastern European	40	0.13
English	5,285	17.82
Estonian	9	0.03
European	354	1.19
Finnish	149	0.50
French, except Basque	1,145	3.86
French Canadian	292	0.98
German	7,242	24.42
Greek	89	0.30
Hawaii Native/Pacific Islander:	76	0.26
Micronesian: (5)	7	0.02
Guamanian/Chamorro (5)	7	0.02
Polynesian: (22)	43	0.14
Native Hawaiian (14)	33	0.11
Samoan (8)	8	0.03
Other Polynesian	2	0.01
Other Pac. Isl., not spec. (8)	26	0.09
Hispanic or Latino:	2,218	7.47
Central American:	39	0.13
Costa Rican	8	0.03
Guatemalan	11	0.04
Honduran	6	0.02
Nicaraguan	6	0.02
Panamanian	4	0.01
Salvadoran	4	0.01
Cuban	31	0.10
Dominican Republic	8	0.03
Mexican	1,558	5.25
Puerto Rican	101	0.34
South American:	64	0.22
Argentinean	3	0.01
Bolivian	5	0.02
Chilean	12	0.04
Colombian	7	0.02
Ecuadorian	3	0.01
Peruvian	25	0.08
Uruguayan	4	0.01
Venezuelan	1	0.00
Other South American	4	0.01
Other Hispanic or Latino	417	1.40
Hungarian	322	1.09
Iranian	65	0.22
Irish	4,415	14.88
Italian	2,243	7.56
Latvian	8	0.03
Lithuanian	135	0.46
Luxemburger	32	0.11
Macedonian	10	0.03
Northern European	7	0.02
Norwegian	1,067	3.60
Pennsylvania German	21	0.07
Polish	1,153	3.89
Portuguese	97	0.33
Romanian	81	0.27
Russian	592	2.00
Scandinavian	62	0.21
Scotch-Irish	640	2.16
Scottish	1,207	4.07
Serbian	24	0.08
Slavic	27	0.09
Slovak	87	0.29
Slovene	17	0.06
Swedish	918	3.09
Swiss	222	0.75
Turkish	44	0.15
Ukrainian	162	0.55
United States or American	1,289	4.35
Welsh	372	1.25
West Indian, excl. Hispanic:	49	0.17
Jamaican	38	0.13
West Indian	11	0.04
White:	28,068	94.51
Not Hispanic (26,182)	26,456	89.08
Hispanic (1,470)	1,612	5.43
Yugoslavian	65	0.22

Paradise Valley

Place Type: Town
County: Maricopa
Population: 13,664

Ancestry/Race	Number	%
African American/Black:	129	0.94
Not Hispanic (96)	120	0.88
Hispanic (4)	9	0.07
African, sub-Saharan:	23	0.17
African	8	0.06
South African	15	0.11
Am. Ind. or Alaska Nat., not spec.	6	0.04
American Indian tribes, specified:	35	0.26
Cherokee (2)	10	0.07
Chickasaw (1)	2	0.01
Choctaw (3)	4	0.03
Cree	1	0.01
Creek (3)	3	0.02
Kiowa (1)	1	0.01
Latin American Indians (5)	7	0.05
Navajo (3)	3	0.02
Osage (1)	1	0.01
Pima (1)	1	0.01
Sioux	1	0.01
All other tribes (1)	1	0.01
American Indian tribes, not spec.	6	0.04
Arab:	193	1.42
Arab/Arabic	19	0.14
Egyptian	8	0.06
Lebanese	8	0.06
Palestinian	53	0.39
Syrian	105	0.77
Armenian	13	0.10
Asian:	368	2.69
Cambodian (1)	3	0.02
Chinese, ex. Taiwanese (65)	105	0.77
Filipino (25)	38	0.28
Indian (96)	112	0.82
Japanese (15)	28	0.20
Korean (29)	34	0.25
Laotian (1)	1	0.01
Pakistani (3)	6	0.04
Sri Lankan (1)	1	0.01
Taiwanese (3)	9	0.07
Thai (5)	6	0.04
Vietnamese (6)	6	0.04
Other Asian, specified (1)	2	0.01
Other Asian, not specified (6)	17	0.12
Austrian	72	0.53
Basque	12	0.09
Belgian	9	0.07
Brazilian	18	0.13
British	94	0.69
Canadian	138	1.01
Croatian	86	0.63
Czech	141	1.03
Czechoslovakian	48	0.35
Danish	88	0.65
Dutch	239	1.75
Eastern European	151	1.11
English	2,343	17.19
European	155	1.14

Notes: 1. Figures in the "Number" column do not add up to the total population due to: a) Ancestry/Race overlap — e.g. persons can report being both White and Irish, b) persons of Hispanic origin can report being any race, c) persons reporting two ancestries are counted in both categories. 2. Numbers in parentheses indicate the number of persons reporting this ancestry/race alone, not in combination with any other ancestry/race. 3. Refer to the Explanation of Data in the front of the book for more detailed information.

Ancestry/Race	Number	%
Finnish	27	0.20
French, except Basque	476	3.49
French Canadian	122	0.90
German	2,619	19.22
Greek	202	1.48
Hawaii Native/Pacific Islander:	6	0.04
Micronesian: (3)	3	0.02
Guamanian/Chamorro (3)	3	0.02
Polynesian: (2)	2	0.01
Native Hawaiian (1)	1	0.01
Samoan (1)	1	0.01
Other Pac. Isl., not spec.	1	0.01
Hispanic or Latino:	364	2.66
Central American:	5	0.04
Costa Rican	1	0.01
Guatemalan	1	0.01
Nicaraguan	1	0.01
Panamanian	1	0.01
Other Central American	1	0.01
Cuban	24	0.18
Dominican Republic	3	0.02
Mexican	212	1.55
Puerto Rican	11	0.08
South American:	43	0.31
Argentinean	6	0.04
Colombian	10	0.07
Ecuadorian	8	0.06
Peruvian	7	0.05
Uruguayan	6	0.04
Other South American	6	0.04
Other Hispanic or Latino	66	0.48
Hungarian	120	0.88
Iranian	22	0.16
Irish	1,735	12.73
Israeli	33	0.24
Italian	856	6.28
Latvian	9	0.07
Lithuanian	80	0.59
Luxemburger	12	0.09
Norwegian	402	2.95
Polish	615	4.51
Portuguese	69	0.51
Romanian	32	0.23
Russian	626	4.59
Scandinavian	57	0.42
Scotch-Irish	252	1.85
Scottish	440	3.23
Serbian	31	0.23
Slovak	34	0.25
Slovene	50	0.37
Swedish	433	3.18
Swiss	83	0.61
Turkish	62	0.45
Ukrainian	98	0.72
United States or American	510	3.74
Welsh	211	1.55
West Indian, excl. Hispanic:	9	0.07
Haitian	9	0.07
White:	13,196	96.57
Not Hispanic (12,766)	12,879	94.25
Hispanic (297)	317	2.32
Yugoslavian	15	0.11

Payson

Place Type: Town
County: Gila
Population: 13,620

Ancestry/Race	Number	%
African American/Black:	51	0.37
Not Hispanic (30)	44	0.32
Hispanic (6)	7	0.05
Alaska Native tribes, specified:	5	0.04
Aleut	1	0.01
Eskimo (2)	2	0.01
Tlingit-Haida (2)	2	0.01
Alaska Native tribes, not specified	1	0.01
Am. Ind. or Alaska Nat., not spec.	54	0.40
Albanian	19	0.14
American Indian tribes, specified:	285	2.09
Apache (119)	124	0.91
Blackfeet (1)	5	0.04
Cherokee (14)	35	0.26
Chickasaw (1)	5	0.04
Chippewa (3)	3	0.02
Choctaw (4)	6	0.04
Colville (2)	2	0.01
Comanche	1	0.01
Cree (1)	1	0.01
Iroquois (1)	2	0.01
Latin American Indians (2)	6	0.04
Navajo (27)	37	0.27
Paiute	1	0.01
Pima (8)	11	0.08
Potawatomi (1)	5	0.04
Pueblo (5)	6	0.04
Seminole	3	0.02
Shoshone	4	0.03
Sioux (3)	5	0.04
Ute (1)	1	0.01
Yaqui (5)	7	0.05
Yuman (1)	1	0.01
All other tribes (6)	14	0.10
American Indian tribes, not spec.	3	0.02
Arab:	33	0.24
Arab/Arabic	7	0.05
Lebanese	26	0.19
Asian:	98	0.72
Chinese, ex. Taiwanese (15)	19	0.14
Filipino (9)	12	0.09
Indian (19)	25	0.18
Japanese (13)	18	0.13
Korean (7)	8	0.06
Vietnamese (9)	16	0.12
Australian	8	0.06
Austrian	28	0.20
Belgian	90	0.64
British	46	0.33
Canadian	48	0.34
Celtic	8	0.06
Croatian	21	0.15
Czech	37	0.26
Czechoslovakian	13	0.09
Danish	128	0.91
Dutch	426	3.04
English	2,215	15.80
European	125	0.89
Finnish	30	0.21
French, except Basque	591	4.22
French Canadian	156	1.11
German	3,143	22.42
Greek	6	0.04
Hawaii Native/Pacific Islander:	15	0.11
Micronesian: (1)	1	0.01
Guamanian/Chamorro (1)	1	0.01
Polynesian: (4)	13	0.10
Native Hawaiian (1)	8	0.06
Samoan (3)	4	0.03
Other Polynesian	1	0.01
Other Pac. Isl., not spec. (1)	1	0.01
Hispanic or Latino:	708	5.20
Central American:	3	0.02
Nicaraguan	1	0.01
Salvadoran	2	0.01
Mexican	523	3.84
Puerto Rican	18	0.13
South American:	7	0.05
Chilean	1	0.01
Colombian	2	0.01
Peruvian	1	0.01
Other South American	3	0.02
Other Hispanic or Latino	157	1.15
Hungarian	42	0.30
Icelander	7	0.05
Irish	2,159	15.40
Italian	461	3.29
Lithuanian	21	0.15
Maltese	8	0.06
Norwegian	401	2.86
Polish	363	2.59
Portuguese	19	0.14
Romanian	7	0.05
Russian	24	0.17
Scandinavian	40	0.29
Scotch-Irish	357	2.55
Scottish	431	3.07
Slavic	10	0.07
Slovak	15	0.11
Slovene	7	0.05
Swedish	313	2.23
Swiss	19	0.14
United States or American	860	6.13
Welsh	208	1.48
White:	13,046	95.79
Not Hispanic (12,438)	12,549	92.14
Hispanic (467)	497	3.65
Yugoslavian	23	0.16

Peoria

Place Type: City
County: Maricopa
Population: 108,364

Ancestry/Race	Number	%
Acadian/Cajun	8	0.01
Afghan	16	0.01
African American/Black:	3,538	3.26
Not Hispanic (2,887)	3,330	3.07
Hispanic (125)	208	0.19
African, sub-Saharan:	224	0.21
African	123	0.11
Ethiopian	4	0.00
Nigerian	97	0.09
Alaska Native tribes, specified:	12	0.01
Alaska Athabascan	4	0.00
Aleut (2)	3	0.00
Eskimo	4	0.00
Tlingit-Haida (1)	1	0.00
Alaska Native tribes, not specified	2	0.00
Am. Ind. or Alaska Nat., not spec.	289	0.27
Albanian	53	0.05
Alsatian	28	0.03
American Indian tribes, specified:	928	0.86
Apache (29)	52	0.05
Blackfeet (3)	13	0.01
Cherokee (58)	184	0.17
Cheyenne	5	0.00
Chickasaw (3)	9	0.01
Chippewa (7)	21	0.02
Choctaw (13)	26	0.02
Comanche (2)	6	0.01
Creek (9)	19	0.02
Crow (1)	9	0.01
Delaware (2)	3	0.00
Iroquois (8)	25	0.02
Kiowa (1)	2	0.00
Latin American Indians (24)	41	0.04
Lumbee (1)	5	0.00
Navajo (212)	244	0.23
Osage (1)	11	0.01
Ottawa	2	0.00
Paiute (8)	9	0.01
Pima (5)	11	0.01
Potawatomi (4)	11	0.01
Pueblo (42)	53	0.05
Puget Sound Salish	1	0.00
Seminole (1)	2	0.00
Sioux (12)	33	0.03
Tohono O'Odham (23)	30	0.03
Ute (1)	2	0.00
Yaqui (12)	14	0.01
Yuman (8)	10	0.01
All other tribes (53)	75	0.07
American Indian tribes, not spec.	59	0.05
Arab:	280	0.26
Arab/Arabic	105	0.10
Lebanese	103	0.09
Syrian	18	0.02

Notes: 1. Figures in the "Number" column do not add up to the total population due to: a) Ancestry/Race overlap — e.g. persons can report being both White and Irish, b) persons of Hispanic origin can report being any race, c) persons reporting two ancestries are counted in both categories. 2. Numbers in parentheses indicate the number of persons reporting this ancestry/race alone, not in combination with any other ancestry/race. 3. Refer to the Explanation of Data in the front of the book for more detailed information.

Other Arab	54	0.05
Armenian	29	0.03
Asian:	2,893	2.67
Bangladeshi (4)	4	0.00
Cambodian (45)	58	0.05
Chinese, ex. Taiwanese (350)	501	0.46
Filipino (535)	811	0.75
Hmong (6)	6	0.01
Indian (186)	234	0.22
Indonesian (17)	26	0.02
Japanese (154)	292	0.27
Korean (294)	397	0.37
Laotian (10)	13	0.01
Malaysian (2)	2	0.00
Pakistani (20)	29	0.03
Sri Lankan (1)	1	0.00
Taiwanese (4)	5	0.00
Thai (56)	69	0.06
Vietnamese (296)	345	0.32
Other Asian, specified	7	0.01
Other Asian, not specified (40)	93	0.09
Assyrian/Chaldean/Syriac	143	0.13
Australian	35	0.03
Austrian	263	0.24
Basque	45	0.04
Belgian	93	0.09
British	527	0.49
Bulgarian	19	0.02
Canadian	297	0.27
Croatian	90	0.08
Czech	766	0.71
Czechoslovakian	222	0.20
Danish	979	0.90
Dutch	1,886	1.74
Eastern European	16	0.01
English	12,255	11.30
European	988	0.91
Finnish	375	0.35
French, except Basque	4,039	3.72
French Canadian	934	0.86
German	21,837	20.13
German Russian	11	0.01
Greek	457	0.42
Hawaii Native/Pacific Islander:	299	0.28
Melanesian: (2)	3	0.00
Fijian (1)	2	0.00
Other Melanesian (1)	1	0.00
Micronesian: (31)	60	0.06
Guamanian/Chamorro (28)	55	0.05
Other Micronesian (3)	5	0.00
Polynesian: (72)	180	0.17
Native Hawaiian (40)	121	0.11
Samoan (29)	51	0.05
Tongan (1)	1	0.00
Other Polynesian (2)	7	0.01
Other Pac. Isl., specified	4	0.00
Other Pac. Isl., not spec. (10)	52	0.05
Hispanic or Latino:	16,699	15.41
Central American:	168	0.16
Costa Rican	5	0.00
Guatemalan	61	0.06
Honduran	7	0.01
Nicaraguan	16	0.01
Panamanian	25	0.02
Salvadoran	48	0.04
Other Central American	6	0.01
Cuban	78	0.07
Dominican Republic	12	0.01
Mexican	12,521	11.55
Puerto Rican	434	0.40
South American:	180	0.17
Argentinean	15	0.01
Bolivian	3	0.00
Chilean	25	0.02
Colombian	63	0.06
Ecuadorian	15	0.01
Peruvian	25	0.02
Uruguayan	3	0.00
Venezuelan	21	0.02
Other South American	10	0.01
Other Hispanic or Latino	3,306	3.05
Hungarian	723	0.67
Icelander	40	0.04
Iranian	18	0.02
Irish	13,394	12.35
Italian	6,972	6.43
Latvian	28	0.03
Lithuanian	271	0.25
Luxemburger	35	0.03
Macedonian	6	0.01
Maltese	21	0.02
New Zealander	6	0.01
Northern European	24	0.02
Norwegian	2,927	2.70
Pennsylvania German	56	0.05
Polish	4,075	3.76
Portuguese	287	0.26
Romanian	440	0.41
Russian	1,035	0.95
Scandinavian	199	0.18
Scotch-Irish	1,477	1.36
Scottish	2,016	1.86
Serbian	60	0.06
Slavic	50	0.05
Slovak	218	0.20
Slovene	72	0.07
Swedish	2,535	2.34
Swiss	534	0.49
Turkish	6	0.01
Ukrainian	298	0.27
United States or American	6,041	5.57
Welsh	965	0.89
West Indian, excl. Hispanic:	149	0.14
Bahamian	17	0.02
Barbadian	7	0.01
Belizean	3	0.00
Dutch West Indian	6	0.01
Jamaican	75	0.07
Trinidadian and Tobagonian	19	0.02
West Indian	22	0.02
White:	94,436	87.15
Not Hispanic (84,370)	85,822	79.20
Hispanic (7,680)	8,614	7.95
Yugoslavian	133	0.12

Phoenix

Place Type: City
County: Maricopa
Population: 1,321,045

Ancestry/Race	Number	%
Acadian/Cajun	183	0.01
Afghan	335	0.03
African American/Black:	76,065	5.76
Not Hispanic (63,756)	70,246	5.32
Hispanic (3,660)	5,819	0.44
African, sub-Saharan:	5,963	0.45
African	3,927	0.30
Cape Verdean	49	0.00
Ethiopian	419	0.03
Ghanian	146	0.01
Kenyan	9	0.00
Liberian	28	0.00
Nigerian	572	0.04
Senegalese	19	0.00
Sierra Leonean	29	0.00
Somalian	306	0.02
South African	216	0.02
Sudanese	102	0.01
Ugandan	34	0.00
Zimbabwean	58	0.00
Other sub-Saharan African	49	0.00
Alaska Native tribes, specified:	211	0.02
Alaska Athabascan (20)	34	0.00
Aleut (20)	38	0.00
Eskimo (46)	65	0.00
Tlingit-Haida (43)	65	0.00
All other tribes (5)	9	0.00
Alaska Native tribes, not specified	26	0.00
Am. Ind. or Alaska Nat., not spec.	7,404	0.56
Albanian	592	0.04
Alsatian	46	0.00
American Indian tribes, specified:	26,843	2.03
Apache (1,168)	1,683	0.13
Blackfeet (59)	239	0.02
Cherokee (649)	2,099	0.16
Cheyenne (43)	77	0.01
Chickasaw (89)	194	0.01
Chippewa (242)	408	0.03
Choctaw (267)	561	0.04
Colville (27)	32	0.00
Comanche (55)	88	0.01
Cree (25)	48	0.00
Creek (82)	207	0.02
Crow (13)	32	0.00
Delaware (25)	50	0.00
Houma (2)	6	0.00
Iroquois (139)	274	0.02
Kiowa (55)	82	0.01
Latin American Indians (1,021)	1,595	0.12
Lumbee (10)	17	0.00
Menominee (9)	23	0.00
Navajo (9,034)	10,143	0.77
Osage (24)	65	0.00
Ottawa (15)	20	0.00
Paiute (71)	98	0.01
Pima (1,475)	1,954	0.15
Potawatomi (66)	112	0.01
Pueblo (1,592)	2,089	0.16
Puget Sound Salish (10)	13	0.00
Seminole (21)	52	0.00
Shoshone (42)	67	0.01
Sioux (381)	689	0.05
Tohono O'Odham (798)	1,013	0.08
Ute (31)	48	0.00
Yakama (4)	10	0.00
Yaqui (817)	1,112	0.08
Yuman (296)	398	0.03
All other tribes (811)	1,245	0.09
American Indian tribes, not spec.	1,672	0.13
Arab:	5,172	0.39
Arab/Arabic	1,246	0.09
Egyptian	336	0.03
Iraqi	460	0.03
Jordanian	430	0.03
Lebanese	1,826	0.14
Moroccan	83	0.01
Palestinian	114	0.01
Syrian	442	0.03
Other Arab	235	0.02
Armenian	1,215	0.09
Asian:	34,060	2.58
Bangladeshi (82)	96	0.01
Cambodian (334)	393	0.03
Chinese, ex. Taiwanese (5,656)	6,956	0.53
Filipino (4,757)	6,996	0.53
Hmong (9)	12	0.00
Indian (4,481)	5,169	0.39
Indonesian (107)	220	0.02
Japanese (1,728)	2,989	0.23
Korean (1,877)	2,462	0.19
Laotian (329)	454	0.03
Malaysian (26)	42	0.00
Pakistani (143)	193	0.01
Sri Lankan (72)	88	0.01
Taiwanese (105)	154	0.01
Thai (384)	545	0.04
Vietnamese (5,301)	5,770	0.44
Other Asian, specified (72)	158	0.01
Other Asian, not specified (475)	1,363	0.10
Assyrian/Chaldean/Syriac	822	0.06
Australian	450	0.03
Austrian	3,103	0.23
Basque	327	0.02
Belgian	1,520	0.12
Brazilian	337	0.03
British	4,768	0.36
Bulgarian	506	0.04
Canadian	3,611	0.27

Notes: 1. Figures in the "Number" column do not add up to the total population due to: a) Ancestry/Race overlap — e.g. persons can report being both White and Irish, b) persons of Hispanic origin can report being any race, c) persons reporting two ancestries are counted in both categories. 2. Numbers in parentheses indicate the number of persons reporting this ancestry/race alone, not in combination with any other ancestry/race. 3. Refer to the Explanation of Data in the front of the book for more detailed information.

Carpatho Rusyn	18	0.00
Celtic	335	0.03
Croatian	1,848	0.14
Cypriot	55	0.00
Czech	5,279	0.40
Czechoslovakian	2,424	0.18
Danish	7,129	0.54
Dutch	18,765	1.42
Eastern European	767	0.06
English	105,835	8.01
Estonian	55	0.00
European	8,624	0.65
Finnish	2,620	0.20
French, except Basque	31,941	2.42
French Canadian	7,735	0.59
German	181,124	13.71
German Russian	98	0.01
Greek	4,770	0.36
Guyanese	38	0.00
Hawaii Native/Pacific Islander:	3,554	0.27
Melanesian: (16)	21	0.00
Fijian (15)	20	0.00
Other Melanesian (1)	1	0.00
Micronesian: (449)	662	0.05
Guamanian/Chamorro (358)	551	0.04
Other Micronesian (91)	111	0.01
Polynesian: (1,081)	2,023	0.15
Native Hawaiian (498)	1,185	0.09
Samoan (375)	534	0.04
Tongan (180)	235	0.02
Other Polynesian (28)	69	0.01
Other Pac. Isl., specified	45	0.00
Other Pac. Isl., not spec. (193)	803	0.06
Hispanic or Latino:	449,972	34.06
Central American:	6,085	0.46
Costa Rican	212	0.02
Guatemalan	2,397	0.18
Honduran	624	0.05
Nicaraguan	305	0.02
Panamanian	203	0.02
Salvadoran	1,856	0.14
Other Central American	488	0.04
Cuban	1,952	0.15
Dominican Republic	312	0.02
Mexican	375,096	28.39
Puerto Rican	5,089	0.39
South American:	2,199	0.17
Argentinean	251	0.02
Bolivian	65	0.00
Chilean	126	0.01
Colombian	722	0.05
Ecuadorian	272	0.02
Paraguayan	8	0.00
Peruvian	411	0.03
Uruguayan	42	0.00
Venezuelan	155	0.01
Other South American	147	0.01
Other Hispanic or Latino	59,239	4.48
Hungarian	5,925	0.45
Icelander	158	0.01
Iranian	1,055	0.08
Irish	123,592	9.36
Israeli	372	0.03
Italian	58,578	4.43
Latvian	378	0.03
Lithuanian	2,467	0.19
Luxemburger	202	0.02
Macedonian	171	0.01
Maltese	128	0.01
New Zealander	91	0.01
Northern European	584	0.04
Norwegian	22,052	1.67
Pennsylvania German	514	0.04
Polish	32,050	2.43
Portuguese	2,722	0.21
Romanian	2,975	0.23
Russian	10,601	0.80
Scandinavian	2,542	0.19
Scotch-Irish	15,707	1.19
Scottish	20,873	1.58
Serbian	1,645	0.12
Slavic	590	0.04
Slovak	1,914	0.14
Slovene	425	0.03
Swedish	19,294	1.46
Swiss	3,460	0.26
Turkish	350	0.03
Ukrainian	2,417	0.18
United States or American	53,479	4.05
Welsh	7,728	0.59
West Indian, excl. Hispanic:	1,614	0.12
Bahamian	45	0.00
Barbadian	56	0.00
Belizean	22	0.00
British West Indian	18	0.00
Dutch West Indian	77	0.01
Haitian	173	0.01
Jamaican	696	0.05
Trinidadian and Tobagonian	222	0.02
U.S. Virgin Islander	37	0.00
West Indian	260	0.02
Other West Indian	8	0.00
White:	975,418	73.84
Not Hispanic (736,844)	754,002	57.08
Hispanic (202,009)	221,416	16.76
Yugoslavian	4,559	0.35

Prescott Valley

Place Type: Town
County: Yavapai
Population: 23,535

Ancestry/Race	Number	%
African American/Black:	168	0.71
Not Hispanic (107)	155	0.66
Hispanic (7)	13	0.06
Alaska Native tribes, specified:	5	0.02
Aleut (1)	1	0.00
Eskimo (1)	3	0.01
Tlingit-Haida (1)	1	0.00
Alaska Native tribes, not specified	1	0.00
Am. Ind. or Alaska Nat., not spec.	91	0.39
American Indian tribes, specified:	301	1.28
Apache (14)	24	0.10
Blackfeet (1)	2	0.01
Cherokee (30)	73	0.31
Cheyenne (1)	2	0.01
Chickasaw	4	0.02
Chippewa (7)	10	0.04
Choctaw (16)	20	0.08
Colville (1)	1	0.00
Cree (1)	1	0.00
Creek (4)	9	0.04
Crow (1)	5	0.02
Iroquois (1)	5	0.02
Kiowa (1)	1	0.00
Latin American Indians (7)	10	0.04
Navajo (49)	60	0.25
Osage (1)	1	0.00
Pima (8)	10	0.04
Potawatomi	2	0.01
Pueblo (9)	13	0.06
Seminole	1	0.00
Shoshone	1	0.00
Sioux (6)	8	0.03
Tohono O'Odham (1)	2	0.01
Yaqui (2)	3	0.01
Yuman (3)	5	0.02
All other tribes (15)	28	0.12
American Indian tribes, not spec.	14	0.06
Arab:	31	0.13
Lebanese	24	0.10
Syrian	7	0.03
Armenian	8	0.03
Asian:	263	1.12
Chinese, ex. Taiwanese (19)	45	0.19
Filipino (35)	75	0.32
Indian (13)	22	0.09
Indonesian (5)	6	0.03
Japanese (18)	46	0.20
Korean (14)	25	0.11
Laotian (2)	2	0.01
Taiwanese (1)	1	0.00
Thai (6)	9	0.04
Vietnamese (12)	20	0.08
Other Asian, specified	2	0.01
Other Asian, not specified (1)	10	0.04
Australian	11	0.05
Austrian	70	0.30
Belgian	68	0.29
British	127	0.54
Canadian	83	0.35
Croatian	59	0.25
Czech	160	0.68
Czechoslovakian	60	0.25
Danish	193	0.82
Dutch	556	2.36
English	3,245	13.75
European	100	0.42
Finnish	76	0.32
French, except Basque	1,163	4.93
French Canadian	344	1.46
German	5,481	23.23
Greek	53	0.22
Hawaii Native/Pacific Islander:	70	0.30
Micronesian: (8)	10	0.04
Guamanian/Chamorro (8)	10	0.04
Polynesian: (23)	54	0.23
Native Hawaiian (14)	30	0.13
Samoan (2)	11	0.05
Tongan (6)	6	0.03
Other Polynesian (1)	7	0.03
Other Pac. Isl., not spec. (3)	6	0.03
Hispanic or Latino:	2,617	11.12
Central American:	34	0.14
Costa Rican	1	0.00
Guatemalan	9	0.04
Honduran	8	0.03
Panamanian	1	0.00
Salvadoran	10	0.04
Other Central American	5	0.02
Cuban	8	0.03
Mexican	2,077	8.83
Puerto Rican	47	0.20
South American:	18	0.08
Argentinean	2	0.01
Chilean	5	0.02
Colombian	3	0.01
Ecuadorian	1	0.00
Peruvian	1	0.00
Uruguayan	1	0.00
Venezuelan	5	0.02
Other Hispanic or Latino	433	1.84
Hungarian	131	0.56
Icelander	7	0.03
Irish	3,307	14.01
Italian	1,175	4.98
Lithuanian	47	0.20
Northern European	18	0.08
Norwegian	745	3.16
Pennsylvania German	8	0.03
Polish	566	2.40
Portuguese	82	0.35
Romanian	18	0.08
Russian	103	0.44
Scandinavian	107	0.45
Scotch-Irish	478	2.03
Scottish	627	2.66
Slavic	8	0.03
Slovak	36	0.15
Slovene	73	0.31
Swedish	567	2.40
Swiss	77	0.33
United States or American	1,886	7.99
Welsh	262	1.11
White:	21,928	93.17
Not Hispanic (20,120)	20,434	86.82
Hispanic (1,321)	1,494	6.35
Yugoslavian	45	0.19

Notes: 1. Figures in the "Number" column do not add up to the total population due to: a) Ancestry/Race overlap — e.g. persons can report being both White and Irish, b) persons of Hispanic origin can report being any race, c) persons reporting two ancestries are counted in both categories. 2. Numbers in parentheses indicate the number of persons reporting this ancestry/race alone, not in combination with any other ancestry/race. 3. Refer to the Explanation of Data in the front of the book for more detailed information.

Prescott

Place Type: City
County: Yavapai
Population: 33,938

Ancestry/Race	Number	%
African American/Black:	244	0.72
Not Hispanic (149)	209	0.62
Hispanic (22)	35	0.10
African, sub-Saharan:	25	0.07
African	18	0.05
Kenyan	7	0.02
Alaska Native tribes, specified:	1	0.00
Eskimo (1)	1	0.00
Alaska Native tribes, not specified	3	0.01
Am. Ind. or Alaska Nat., not spec.	162	0.48
Albanian	8	0.02
American Indian tribes, specified:	508	1.50
Apache (19)	27	0.08
Blackfeet (1)	10	0.03
Cherokee (22)	87	0.26
Chickasaw (1)	5	0.01
Chippewa (5)	8	0.02
Choctaw (10)	25	0.07
Cree (1)	1	0.00
Creek (1)	1	0.00
Delaware	4	0.01
Iroquois (2)	6	0.02
Latin American Indians (9)	24	0.07
Navajo (146)	156	0.46
Osage	2	0.01
Ottawa	1	0.00
Paiute (2)	2	0.01
Pima (7)	17	0.05
Potawatomi (4)	4	0.01
Pueblo (27)	32	0.09
Seminole	1	0.00
Shoshone	1	0.00
Sioux (6)	15	0.04
Ute (1)	1	0.00
Yaqui (2)	6	0.02
Yuman (26)	31	0.09
All other tribes (30)	41	0.12
American Indian tribes, not spec.	16	0.05
Arab:	65	0.19
Lebanese	45	0.13
Syrian	20	0.06
Armenian	25	0.07
Asian:	433	1.28
Chinese, ex. Taiwanese (41)	78	0.23
Filipino (52)	83	0.24
Hmong (1)	1	0.00
Indian (50)	68	0.20
Indonesian (5)	5	0.01
Japanese (60)	98	0.29
Korean (32)	42	0.12
Malaysian (1)	1	0.00
Taiwanese (3)	3	0.01
Thai (8)	11	0.03
Vietnamese (19)	22	0.06
Other Asian, specified (1)	2	0.01
Other Asian, not specified (5)	19	0.06
Australian	14	0.04
Austrian	119	0.35
Basque	42	0.12
Belgian	64	0.19
Brazilian	7	0.02
British	191	0.56
Bulgarian	7	0.02
Canadian	63	0.18
Celtic	40	0.12
Croatian	33	0.10
Czech	228	0.66
Czechoslovakian	122	0.35
Danish	351	1.02
Dutch	842	2.45
English	6,255	18.18
European	312	0.91
Finnish	131	0.38
French, except Basque	1,413	4.11
French Canadian	236	0.69
German	7,423	21.57
Greek	158	0.46
Hawaii Native/Pacific Islander:	76	0.22
Melanesian: (1)	1	0.00
Fijian (1)	1	0.00
Micronesian: (7)	11	0.03
Guamanian/Chamorro (7)	11	0.03
Polynesian: (11)	55	0.16
Native Hawaiian (10)	43	0.13
Samoan (1)	10	0.03
Tongan	2	0.01
Other Pac. Isl., not spec. (2)	9	0.03
Hispanic or Latino:	2,773	8.17
Central American:	12	0.04
Costa Rican	2	0.01
Guatemalan	2	0.01
Honduran	3	0.01
Panamanian	3	0.01
Other Central American	2	0.01
Cuban	26	0.08
Dominican Republic	2	0.01
Mexican	2,188	6.45
Puerto Rican	45	0.13
South American:	29	0.09
Argentinean	3	0.01
Chilean	8	0.02
Colombian	7	0.02
Ecuadorian	3	0.01
Paraguayan	1	0.00
Peruvian	2	0.01
Venezuelan	2	0.01
Other South American	3	0.01
Other Hispanic or Latino	471	1.39
Hungarian	197	0.57
Icelander	27	0.08
Iranian	15	0.04
Irish	4,948	14.38
Italian	1,717	4.99
Latvian	8	0.02
Lithuanian	73	0.21
Luxemburger	46	0.13
Macedonian	8	0.02
New Zealander	7	0.02
Northern European	52	0.15
Norwegian	1,084	3.15
Pennsylvania German	2	0.01
Polish	975	2.83
Portuguese	81	0.24
Romanian	51	0.15
Russian	335	0.97
Scandinavian	57	0.17
Scotch-Irish	1,173	3.41
Scottish	1,460	4.24
Serbian	41	0.12
Slavic	33	0.10
Slovak	44	0.13
Slovene	30	0.09
Swedish	983	2.86
Swiss	256	0.74
Turkish	32	0.09
Ukrainian	90	0.26
United States or American	1,643	4.77
Welsh	394	1.14
West Indian, excl. Hispanic:	8	0.02
Dutch West Indian	8	0.02
White:	32,032	94.38
Not Hispanic (29,941)	30,279	89.22
Hispanic (1,597)	1,753	5.17
Yugoslavian	57	0.17

San Luis

Place Type: City
County: Yuma
Population: 15,322

Ancestry/Race	Number	%
African American/Black:	462	3.02
Not Hispanic (438)	439	2.87
Hispanic (14)	23	0.15
African, sub-Saharan:	5	0.03
African	5	0.03
Am. Ind. or Alaska Nat., not spec.	193	1.26
American Indian tribes, specified:	61	0.40
Apache (1)	1	0.01
Latin American Indians (32)	33	0.22
Navajo (1)	1	0.01
Yaqui (5)	10	0.07
All other tribes (16)	16	0.10
American Indian tribes, not spec.	12	0.08
Arab:	4	0.03
Arab/Arabic	4	0.03
Asian:	52	0.34
Chinese, ex. Taiwanese (5)	16	0.10
Filipino (12)	22	0.14
Indian (3)	4	0.03
Korean (2)	2	0.01
Vietnamese (1)	1	0.01
Other Asian, not specified (2)	7	0.05
Assyrian/Chaldean/Syriac	5	0.03
English	12	0.08
French, except Basque	4	0.03
German	17	0.11
Hawaii Native/Pacific Islander:	9	0.06
Micronesian: (1)	3	0.02
Guamanian/Chamorro (1)	3	0.02
Polynesian: (1)	1	0.01
Native Hawaiian (1)	1	0.01
Other Pac. Isl., not spec. (1)	5	0.03
Hispanic or Latino:	13,657	89.13
Central American:	11	0.07
Guatemalan	5	0.03
Salvadoran	3	0.02
Other Central American	3	0.02
Cuban	4	0.03
Mexican	12,717	83.00
Puerto Rican	10	0.07
Other Hispanic or Latino	915	5.97
Irish	3	0.02
Italian	9	0.06
Swiss	4	0.03
United States or American	77	0.50
White:	9,311	60.77
Not Hispanic (1,065)	1,081	7.06
Hispanic (7,942)	8,230	53.71

Scottsdale

Place Type: City
County: Maricopa
Population: 202,705

Ancestry/Race	Number	%
Acadian/Cajun	32	0.02
Afghan	19	0.01
African American/Black:	3,134	1.55
Not Hispanic (2,398)	2,914	1.44
Hispanic (103)	220	0.11
African, sub-Saharan:	313	0.15
African	104	0.05
Kenyan	11	0.01
Nigerian	42	0.02
Somalian	4	0.00
South African	131	0.06
Other sub-Saharan African	21	0.01
Alaska Native tribes, specified:	20	0.01
Alaska Athabascan (6)	7	0.00
Aleut	2	0.00
Eskimo (3)	8	0.00
Tlingit-Haida (1)	2	0.00
All other tribes (1)	1	0.00
Alaska Native tribes, not specified	3	0.00
Am. Ind. or Alaska Nat., not spec.	412	0.20
Albanian	76	0.04
Alsatian	33	0.02
American Indian tribes, specified:	1,540	0.76
Apache (38)	64	0.03
Blackfeet (1)	20	0.01

Notes: 1. Figures in the "Number" column do not add up to the total population due to: a) Ancestry/Race overlap — e.g. persons can report being both White and Irish, b) persons of Hispanic origin can report being any race, c) persons reporting two ancestries are counted in both categories. 2. Numbers in parentheses indicate the number of persons reporting this ancestry/race alone, not in combination with any other ancestry/race. 3. Refer to the Explanation of Data in the front of the book for more detailed information.

Cherokee (58)	246	0.12
Cheyenne (9)	9	0.00
Chickasaw (1)	8	0.00
Chippewa (23)	47	0.02
Choctaw (25)	55	0.03
Colville (3)	5	0.00
Comanche (5)	13	0.01
Cree (2)	5	0.00
Creek (16)	30	0.01
Crow (2)	2	0.00
Delaware (5)	8	0.00
Iroquois (18)	37	0.02
Kiowa (2)	6	0.00
Latin American Indians (53)	66	0.03
Lumbee (4)	4	0.00
Menominee	1	0.00
Navajo (280)	332	0.16
Osage (2)	10	0.00
Ottawa (1)	1	0.00
Paiute (1)	2	0.00
Pima (54)	68	0.03
Potawatomi (2)	9	0.00
Pueblo (70)	101	0.05
Seminole (2)	2	0.00
Shoshone	2	0.00
Sioux (39)	57	0.03
Tohono O'Odham (23)	33	0.02
Ute (3)	7	0.00
Yakama (1)	1	0.00
Yaqui (134)	183	0.09
Yuman (6)	8	0.00
All other tribes (63)	98	0.05
American Indian tribes, not spec.	97	0.05
Arab:	1,345	0.66
Arab/Arabic	208	0.10
Egyptian	157	0.08
Iraqi	50	0.02
Jordanian	115	0.06
Lebanese	483	0.24
Palestinian	120	0.06
Syrian	102	0.05
Other Arab	110	0.05
Armenian	422	0.21
Asian:	5,115	2.52
Bangladeshi (20)	20	0.01
Cambodian (16)	19	0.01
Chinese, ex. Taiwanese (1,076)	1,330	0.66
Filipino (507)	782	0.39
Indian (940)	1,031	0.51
Indonesian (11)	39	0.02
Japanese (453)	686	0.34
Korean (401)	506	0.25
Laotian (12)	13	0.01
Malaysian (5)	8	0.00
Pakistani (33)	41	0.02
Sri Lankan (10)	10	0.00
Taiwanese (43)	60	0.03
Thai (74)	96	0.05
Vietnamese (189)	236	0.12
Other Asian, specified (23)	37	0.02
Other Asian, not specified (83)	201	0.10
Assyrian/Chaldean/Syriac	245	0.12
Australian	191	0.09
Austrian	1,351	0.67
Basque	68	0.03
Belgian	592	0.29
Brazilian	64	0.03
British	1,379	0.68
Bulgarian	55	0.03
Canadian	1,706	0.84
Celtic	42	0.02
Croatian	496	0.24
Czech	1,378	0.68
Czechoslovakian	532	0.26
Danish	2,354	1.16
Dutch	4,081	2.01
Eastern European	470	0.23
English	27,262	13.45
Estonian	47	0.02
European	1,919	0.95
Finnish	572	0.28
French, except Basque	7,445	3.67
French Canadian	1,488	0.73
German	41,695	20.57
German Russian	9	0.00
Greek	1,422	0.70
Guyanese	6	0.00
Hawaii Native/Pacific Islander:	409	0.20
Melanesian: (2)	4	0.00
Fijian (2)	4	0.00
Micronesian: (46)	68	0.03
Guamanian/Chamorro (38)	55	0.03
Other Micronesian (8)	13	0.01
Polynesian: (106)	254	0.13
Native Hawaiian (68)	178	0.09
Samoan (26)	55	0.03
Tongan (3)	5	0.00
Other Polynesian (9)	16	0.01
Other Pac. Isl., specified	7	0.00
Other Pac. Isl., not spec. (13)	76	0.04
Hispanic or Latino:	14,111	6.96
Central American:	175	0.09
Costa Rican	24	0.01
Guatemalan	51	0.03
Honduran	11	0.01
Nicaraguan	19	0.01
Panamanian	19	0.01
Salvadoran	34	0.02
Other Central American	17	0.01
Cuban	222	0.11
Dominican Republic	14	0.01
Mexican	10,108	4.99
Puerto Rican	583	0.29
South American:	500	0.25
Argentinean	61	0.03
Bolivian	13	0.01
Chilean	51	0.03
Colombian	169	0.08
Ecuadorian	45	0.02
Paraguayan	3	0.00
Peruvian	57	0.03
Venezuelan	68	0.03
Other South American	33	0.02
Other Hispanic or Latino	2,509	1.24
Hungarian	1,697	0.84
Icelander	79	0.04
Iranian	620	0.31
Irish	28,482	14.05
Israeli	221	0.11
Italian	17,283	8.52
Latvian	117	0.06
Lithuanian	838	0.41
Luxemburger	108	0.05
Macedonian	25	0.01
Maltese	70	0.03
New Zealander	57	0.03
Northern European	172	0.08
Norwegian	6,401	3.16
Pennsylvania German	71	0.04
Polish	8,905	4.39
Portuguese	630	0.31
Romanian	832	0.41
Russian	5,509	2.72
Scandinavian	574	0.28
Scotch-Irish	4,051	2.00
Scottish	5,948	2.93
Serbian	253	0.12
Slavic	90	0.04
Slovak	838	0.41
Slovene	221	0.11
Swedish	5,907	2.91
Swiss	1,100	0.54
Turkish	90	0.04
Ukrainian	1,049	0.52
United States or American	9,120	4.50
Welsh	2,175	1.07
West Indian, excl. Hispanic:	147	0.07
Bermudan	7	0.00
Haitian	15	0.01
Jamaican	66	0.03
Trinidadian and Tobagonian	27	0.01
U.S. Virgin Islander	9	0.00
West Indian	23	0.01
White:	189,833	93.65
Not Hispanic (178,462)	180,598	89.09
Hispanic (8,421)	9,235	4.56
Yugoslavian	351	0.17

Sedona

Place Type: City
County: Yavapai
Population: 10,192

Ancestry/Race	Number	%
African American/Black:	64	0.63
Not Hispanic (49)	62	0.61
Hispanic (1)	2	0.02
African, sub-Saharan:	40	0.39
African	40	0.39
Alaska Native tribes, specified:	1	0.01
Eskimo (1)	1	0.01
Am. Ind. or Alaska Nat., not spec.	21	0.21
American Indian tribes, specified:	71	0.70
Apache (1)	1	0.01
Blackfeet (1)	1	0.01
Cherokee (4)	17	0.17
Chippewa (5)	6	0.06
Choctaw	3	0.03
Cree (1)	2	0.02
Creek (2)	2	0.02
Crow (1)	1	0.01
Houma (1)	1	0.01
Iroquois (2)	2	0.02
Latin American Indians	5	0.05
Navajo (4)	5	0.05
Ottawa (1)	1	0.01
Pueblo (3)	5	0.05
Puget Sound Salish (2)	2	0.02
Seminole (1)	2	0.02
Sioux (3)	4	0.04
Tohono O'Odham (1)	1	0.01
Ute	1	0.01
Yaqui (1)	1	0.01
All other tribes (2)	8	0.08
American Indian tribes, not spec.	6	0.06
Arab:	40	0.39
Arab/Arabic	15	0.15
Lebanese	25	0.25
Armenian	47	0.46
Asian:	121	1.19
Chinese, ex. Taiwanese (27)	29	0.28
Filipino (12)	15	0.15
Indian (23)	27	0.26
Indonesian	2	0.02
Japanese (19)	26	0.26
Korean (7)	10	0.10
Thai (3)	4	0.04
Vietnamese (4)	4	0.04
Other Asian, specified (1)	1	0.01
Other Asian, not specified	3	0.03
Australian	55	0.54
Austrian	60	0.59
Basque	10	0.10
Belgian	16	0.16
British	42	0.41
Canadian	42	0.41
Celtic	15	0.15
Croatian	19	0.19
Czech	62	0.61
Czechoslovakian	40	0.39
Danish	100	0.98
Dutch	240	2.36
Eastern European	7	0.07
English	1,845	18.13
European	170	1.67
Finnish	36	0.35
French, except Basque	583	5.73
French Canadian	55	0.54
German	2,232	21.93

Notes: 1. Figures in the "Number" column do not add up to the total population due to: a) Ancestry/Race overlap — e.g. persons can report being both White and Irish, b) persons of Hispanic origin can report being any race, c) persons reporting two ancestries are counted in both categories. 2. Numbers in parentheses indicate the number of persons reporting this ancestry/race alone, not in combination with any other ancestry/race. 3. Refer to the Explanation of Data in the front of the book for more detailed information.

Greek	111	1.09
Hawaii Native/Pacific Islander:	18	0.18
Micronesian: (2)	4	0.04
Guamanian/Chamorro (2)	4	0.04
Polynesian: (4)	8	0.08
Native Hawaiian (3)	7	0.07
Samoan (1)	1	0.01
Other Pac. Isl., not spec. (2)	6	0.06
Hispanic or Latino:	907	8.90
Central American:	4	0.04
Salvadoran	4	0.04
Cuban	9	0.09
Dominican Republic	3	0.03
Mexican	793	7.78
Puerto Rican	22	0.22
South American:	7	0.07
Argentinean	2	0.02
Other South American	5	0.05
Other Hispanic or Latino	69	0.68
Hungarian	70	0.69
Irish	1,074	10.55
Italian	484	4.76
Latvian	17	0.17
Lithuanian	37	0.36
Luxemburger	16	0.16
Northern European	17	0.17
Norwegian	379	3.72
Pennsylvania German	18	0.18
Polish	383	3.76
Portuguese	30	0.29
Romanian	29	0.28
Russian	141	1.39
Scandinavian	32	0.31
Scotch-Irish	234	2.30
Scottish	352	3.46
Serbian	9	0.09
Slavic	9	0.09
Slovak	18	0.18
Slovene	29	0.28
Swedish	364	3.58
Swiss	65	0.64
Turkish	16	0.16
Ukrainian	98	0.96
United States or American	444	4.36
Welsh	132	1.30
White:	9,540	93.60
Not Hispanic (8,967)	9,071	89.00
Hispanic (427)	469	4.60

Sierra Vista Southeast

Place Type: Census Designated Place
County: Cochise
Population: 14,348

Ancestry/Race	Number	%
African American/Black:	424	2.96
Not Hispanic (297)	394	2.75
Hispanic (18)	30	0.21
African, sub-Saharan:	27	0.18
African	14	0.09
Ethiopian	4	0.03
South African	9	0.06
Alaska Native tribes, specified:	3	0.02
Alaska Athabascan	1	0.01
Eskimo (1)	1	0.01
Tlingit-Haida (1)	1	0.01
Alaska Native tribes, not specified	5	0.03
Am. Ind. or Alaska Nat., not spec.	92	0.64
American Indian tribes, specified:	267	1.86
Apache (9)	20	0.14
Blackfeet (4)	14	0.10
Cherokee (15)	71	0.49
Cheyenne	3	0.02
Chickasaw	4	0.03
Chippewa (2)	10	0.07
Choctaw (1)	7	0.05
Creek (4)	7	0.05
Crow (3)	4	0.03
Delaware	1	0.01
Iroquois (7)	8	0.06
Latin American Indians (13)	26	0.18
Lumbee (1)	1	0.01
Navajo (14)	26	0.18
Pima (13)	15	0.10
Potawatomi (2)	2	0.01
Pueblo (15)	17	0.12
Shoshone (2)	2	0.01
Sioux (1)	4	0.03
Yaqui (6)	9	0.06
All other tribes (6)	16	0.11
American Indian tribes, not spec.	33	0.23
Arab:	25	0.17
Lebanese	25	0.17
Asian:	422	2.94
Chinese, ex. Taiwanese (23)	38	0.26
Filipino (32)	59	0.41
Indian (8)	15	0.10
Japanese (48)	94	0.66
Korean (93)	136	0.95
Sri Lankan (3)	3	0.02
Taiwanese (1)	1	0.01
Thai (15)	26	0.18
Vietnamese (27)	43	0.30
Other Asian, not specified (4)	7	0.05
Australian	30	0.20
Austrian	23	0.16
Belgian	19	0.13
British	176	1.19
Canadian	41	0.28
Celtic	19	0.13
Croatian	13	0.09
Czech	45	0.30
Czechoslovakian	15	0.10
Danish	48	0.32
Dutch	218	1.47
English	2,275	15.36
European	121	0.82
Finnish	42	0.28
French, except Basque	624	4.21
French Canadian	133	0.90
German	2,925	19.75
Greek	44	0.30
Hawaii Native/Pacific Islander:	98	0.68
Melanesian: (1)	3	0.02
Fijian (1)	3	0.02
Micronesian: (25)	32	0.22
Guamanian/Chamorro (25)	32	0.22
Polynesian: (30)	48	0.33
Native Hawaiian (15)	33	0.23
Samoan (15)	15	0.10
Other Pac. Isl., not spec. (10)	15	0.10
Hispanic or Latino:	2,308	16.09
Central American:	42	0.29
Costa Rican	6	0.04
Guatemalan	10	0.07
Honduran	1	0.01
Nicaraguan	2	0.01
Panamanian	17	0.12
Salvadoran	5	0.03
Other Central American	1	0.01
Cuban	15	0.10
Dominican Republic	2	0.01
Mexican	1,789	12.47
Puerto Rican	98	0.68
South American:	14	0.10
Argentinean	3	0.02
Chilean	3	0.02
Colombian	3	0.02
Ecuadorian	2	0.01
Other South American	3	0.02
Other Hispanic or Latino	348	2.43
Hungarian	43	0.29
Irish	1,799	12.15
Italian	509	3.44
Latvian	10	0.07
Lithuanian	8	0.05
Luxemburger	8	0.05
Northern European	32	0.22
Norwegian	558	3.77
Polish	342	2.31
Portuguese	17	0.11
Romanian	18	0.12
Russian	66	0.45
Scandinavian	27	0.18
Scotch-Irish	337	2.28
Scottish	510	3.44
Serbian	13	0.09
Slavic	8	0.05
Slovak	32	0.22
Swedish	253	1.71
Swiss	26	0.18
Ukrainian	20	0.14
United States or American	1,062	7.17
Welsh	191	1.29
West Indian, excl. Hispanic:	16	0.11
Haitian	8	0.05
Trinidadian and Tobagonian	8	0.05
White:	12,615	87.92
Not Hispanic (10,857)	11,168	77.84
Hispanic (1,264)	1,447	10.09

Sierra Vista

Place Type: City
County: Cochise
Population: 37,775

Ancestry/Race	Number	%
Acadian/Cajun	71	0.19
African American/Black:	4,734	12.53
Not Hispanic (3,943)	4,445	11.77
Hispanic (172)	289	0.77
African, sub-Saharan:	348	0.93
African	321	0.86
Cape Verdean	18	0.05
South African	9	0.02
Alaska Native tribes, specified:	11	0.03
Alaska Athabascan (3)	3	0.01
Aleut (1)	3	0.01
Eskimo (1)	3	0.01
Tlingit-Haida (1)	2	0.01
Alaska Native tribes, not specified	3	0.01
Am. Ind. or Alaska Nat., not spec.	193	0.51
Alsatian	8	0.02
American Indian tribes, specified:	476	1.26
Apache (9)	18	0.05
Blackfeet (4)	20	0.05
Cherokee (55)	156	0.41
Cheyenne (1)	4	0.01
Chickasaw (2)	4	0.01
Chippewa (2)	11	0.03
Choctaw (20)	35	0.09
Colville (1)	1	0.00
Comanche (1)	5	0.01
Cree (8)	8	0.02
Creek (3)	8	0.02
Crow (3)	5	0.01
Delaware (1)	2	0.01
Iroquois (8)	12	0.03
Latin American Indians (9)	22	0.06
Lumbee	2	0.01
Navajo (24)	46	0.12
Osage (3)	5	0.01
Ottawa	1	0.00
Pima (1)	6	0.02
Potawatomi (1)	3	0.01
Pueblo (8)	11	0.03
Seminole (1)	1	0.00
Shoshone (1)	1	0.00
Sioux (11)	26	0.07
Tohono O'Odham (11)	15	0.04
Yaqui (9)	13	0.03
Yuman (2)	3	0.01
All other tribes (17)	32	0.08
American Indian tribes, not spec.	46	0.12
Arab:	57	0.15
Lebanese	21	0.06
Syrian	7	0.02
Other Arab	29	0.08

Notes: 1. Figures in the "Number" column do not add up to the total population due to: a) Ancestry/Race overlap — e.g. persons can report being both White and Irish, b) persons of Hispanic origin can report being any race, c) persons reporting two ancestries are counted in both categories. 2. Numbers in parentheses indicate the number of persons reporting this ancestry/race alone, not in combination with any other ancestry/race. 3. Refer to the Explanation of Data in the front of the book for more detailed information.

Ancestry/Race	Number	%
Armenian	37	0.10
Asian:	2,119	5.61
Bangladeshi	1	0.00
Cambodian (5)	8	0.02
Chinese, ex. Taiwanese (62)	142	0.38
Filipino (320)	508	1.34
Indian (42)	59	0.16
Indonesian (3)	3	0.01
Japanese (168)	302	0.80
Korean (506)	750	1.99
Laotian (3)	4	0.01
Malaysian (1)	3	0.01
Pakistani (1)	1	0.00
Sri Lankan (11)	11	0.03
Taiwanese (9)	10	0.03
Thai (56)	113	0.30
Vietnamese (119)	142	0.38
Other Asian, specified (2)	10	0.03
Other Asian, not specified (20)	52	0.14
Austrian	152	0.41
Basque	17	0.05
Belgian	61	0.16
British	302	0.81
Canadian	92	0.25
Celtic	15	0.04
Croatian	43	0.12
Czech	62	0.17
Czechoslovakian	24	0.06
Danish	158	0.42
Dutch	592	1.59
English	3,971	10.65
Estonian	10	0.03
European	362	0.97
Finnish	123	0.33
French, except Basque	1,110	2.98
French Canadian	308	0.83
German	6,641	17.81
Greek	116	0.31
Hawaii Native/Pacific Islander:	333	0.88
Melanesian: (2)	2	0.01
Fijian (2)	2	0.01
Micronesian: (93)	130	0.34
Guamanian/Chamorro (89)	124	0.33
Other Micronesian (4)	6	0.02
Polynesian: (71)	145	0.38
Native Hawaiian (32)	99	0.26
Samoan (36)	43	0.11
Tongan (1)	1	0.00
Other Polynesian (2)	2	0.01
Other Pac. Isl., specified	2	0.01
Other Pac. Isl., not spec. (5)	54	0.14
Hispanic or Latino:	5,971	15.81
Central American:	154	0.41
Costa Rican	8	0.02
Guatemalan	2	0.01
Honduran	15	0.04
Nicaraguan	8	0.02
Panamanian	91	0.24
Salvadoran	16	0.04
Other Central American	14	0.04
Cuban	37	0.10
Dominican Republic	30	0.08
Mexican	4,116	10.90
Puerto Rican	712	1.88
South American:	55	0.15
Argentinean	2	0.01
Bolivian	1	0.00
Chilean	4	0.01
Colombian	27	0.07
Ecuadorian	6	0.02
Peruvian	10	0.03
Venezuelan	5	0.01
Other Hispanic or Latino	867	2.30
Hungarian	258	0.69
Icelander	18	0.05
Iranian	58	0.16
Irish	3,681	9.87
Israeli	13	0.03
Italian	1,584	4.25
Latvian	7	0.02
Lithuanian	81	0.22
Northern European	27	0.07
Norwegian	678	1.82
Pennsylvania German	36	0.10
Polish	819	2.20
Portuguese	78	0.21
Romanian	29	0.08
Russian	118	0.32
Scandinavian	100	0.27
Scotch-Irish	805	2.16
Scottish	1,086	2.91
Serbian	7	0.02
Slavic	22	0.06
Slovak	33	0.09
Slovene	57	0.15
Swedish	269	0.72
Swiss	110	0.30
Turkish	6	0.02
Ukrainian	69	0.19
United States or American	2,232	5.99
Welsh	256	0.69
West Indian, excl. Hispanic:	58	0.16
Haitian	7	0.02
Jamaican	43	0.12
West Indian	8	0.02
White:	29,192	77.28
Not Hispanic (24,720)	25,800	68.30
Hispanic (2,986)	3,392	8.98
Yugoslavian	10	0.03

Sun City

Place Type: Census Designated Place
County: Maricopa
Population: 38,309

Ancestry/Race	Number	%
African American/Black:	210	0.55
Not Hispanic (193)	205	0.54
Hispanic (3)	5	0.01
Alaska Native tribes, specified:	1	0.00
Alaska Athabascan	1	0.00
Am. Ind. or Alaska Nat., not spec.	33	0.09
Alsatian	6	0.02
American Indian tribes, specified:	89	0.23
Blackfeet	1	0.00
Cherokee (7)	24	0.06
Cheyenne (1)	3	0.01
Chickasaw (2)	3	0.01
Chippewa (1)	9	0.02
Choctaw (3)	6	0.02
Cree (1)	1	0.00
Creek	1	0.00
Crow	1	0.00
Delaware	1	0.00
Iroquois (1)	2	0.01
Latin American Indians	1	0.00
Lumbee (1)	1	0.00
Navajo (1)	1	0.00
Osage	2	0.01
Pima (1)	1	0.00
Potawatomi (4)	5	0.01
Pueblo (2)	3	0.01
Puget Sound Salish (1)	1	0.00
Seminole	2	0.01
Sioux (3)	12	0.03
Tohono O'Odham (1)	1	0.00
All other tribes (4)	7	0.02
American Indian tribes, not spec.	17	0.04
Arab:	86	0.23
Egyptian	15	0.04
Lebanese	38	0.10
Syrian	33	0.09
Asian:	140	0.37
Chinese, ex. Taiwanese (17)	17	0.04
Filipino (18)	25	0.07
Indian (9)	9	0.02
Indonesian (2)	3	0.01
Japanese (51)	61	0.16
Korean (12)	13	0.03
Thai (1)	1	0.00
Vietnamese (5)	5	0.01
Other Asian, specified	1	0.00
Other Asian, not specified	5	0.01
Austrian	236	0.62
Belgian	58	0.15
British	137	0.36
Canadian	154	0.40
Croatian	131	0.34
Czech	493	1.29
Czechoslovakian	133	0.35
Danish	394	1.03
Dutch	940	2.46
English	6,942	18.19
European	146	0.38
Finnish	142	0.37
French, except Basque	1,476	3.87
French Canadian	301	0.79
German	9,212	24.14
Greek	90	0.24
Hawaii Native/Pacific Islander:	15	0.04
Micronesian: (3)	3	0.01
Guamanian/Chamorro (3)	3	0.01
Polynesian: (5)	7	0.02
Native Hawaiian (3)	5	0.01
Samoan (2)	2	0.01
Other Pac. Isl., specified	1	0.00
Other Pac. Isl., not spec. (2)	4	0.01
Hispanic or Latino:	383	1.00
Central American:	2	0.01
Honduran	1	0.00
Panamanian	1	0.00
Cuban	18	0.05
Mexican	201	0.52
Puerto Rican	30	0.08
South American:	7	0.02
Argentinean	1	0.00
Bolivian	2	0.01
Chilean	2	0.01
Peruvian	2	0.01
Other Hispanic or Latino	125	0.33
Hungarian	356	0.93
Icelander	8	0.02
Iranian	6	0.02
Irish	4,706	12.33
Italian	1,454	3.81
Latvian	34	0.09
Lithuanian	195	0.51
Luxemburger	45	0.12
Macedonian	9	0.02
Northern European	9	0.02
Norwegian	1,681	4.41
Pennsylvania German	50	0.13
Polish	1,544	4.05
Portuguese	57	0.15
Romanian	86	0.23
Russian	312	0.82
Scandinavian	84	0.22
Scotch-Irish	1,246	3.27
Scottish	1,120	2.94
Serbian	8	0.02
Slavic	26	0.07
Slovak	189	0.50
Slovene	105	0.28
Swedish	1,402	3.67
Swiss	319	0.84
Ukrainian	140	0.37
United States or American	2,282	5.98
Welsh	542	1.42
White:	37,870	98.85
Not Hispanic (37,420)	37,556	98.03
Hispanic (290)	314	0.82
Yugoslavian	74	0.19

Notes: 1. Figures in the "Number" column do not add up to the total population due to: a) Ancestry/Race overlap — e.g. persons can report being both White and Irish, b) persons of Hispanic origin can report being any race, c) persons reporting two ancestries are counted in both categories. 2. Numbers in parentheses indicate the number of persons reporting this ancestry/race alone, not in combination with any other ancestry/race. 3. Refer to the Explanation of Data in the front of the book for more detailed information.

Sun City West

Place Type: Census Designated Place
County: Maricopa
Population: 26,344

Ancestry/Race	Number	%
African American/Black:	135	0.51
Not Hispanic (129)	135	0.51
Alaska Native tribes, specified:	1	0.00
Tlingit-Haida (1)	1	0.00
Alaska Native tribes, not specified	1	0.00
Am. Ind. or Alaska Nat., not spec.	5	0.02
American Indian tribes, specified:	42	0.16
Apache (1)	2	0.01
Cherokee (6)	19	0.07
Chickasaw	1	0.00
Chippewa	2	0.01
Choctaw (2)	2	0.01
Creek (1)	4	0.02
Delaware	1	0.00
Iroquois	1	0.00
Osage	1	0.00
Seminole	1	0.00
Sioux (2)	4	0.02
All other tribes (1)	4	0.02
American Indian tribes, not spec.	3	0.01
Arab:	36	0.14
Lebanese	18	0.07
Syrian	18	0.07
Armenian	16	0.06
Asian:	116	0.44
Chinese, ex. Taiwanese (23)	28	0.11
Filipino (19)	22	0.08
Indian (6)	6	0.02
Indonesian	1	0.00
Japanese (45)	50	0.19
Korean (1)	4	0.02
Taiwanese (1)	1	0.00
Vietnamese (1)	1	0.00
Other Asian, not specified	3	0.01
Austrian	247	0.94
Belgian	78	0.30
British	124	0.47
Bulgarian	9	0.03
Canadian	166	0.63
Celtic	24	0.09
Croatian	86	0.33
Czech	312	1.19
Czechoslovakian	81	0.31
Danish	352	1.34
Dutch	634	2.41
Eastern European	18	0.07
English	5,333	20.31
European	136	0.52
Finnish	91	0.35
French, except Basque	1,146	4.36
French Canadian	274	1.04
German	6,842	26.05
German Russian	9	0.03
Greek	104	0.40
Hawaii Native/Pacific Islander:	18	0.07
Micronesian: (2)	2	0.01
Guamanian/Chamorro (2)	2	0.01
Polynesian: (6)	14	0.05
Native Hawaiian (4)	11	0.04
Samoan (2)	3	0.01
Other Pac. Isl., not spec. (1)	2	0.01
Hispanic or Latino:	154	0.58
Central American:	2	0.01
Costa Rican	2	0.01
Cuban	4	0.02
Dominican Republic	1	0.00
Mexican	77	0.29
Puerto Rican	14	0.05
South American:	7	0.03
Argentinean	3	0.01
Colombian	1	0.00
Ecuadorian	2	0.01
Other South American	1	0.00
Other Hispanic or Latino	49	0.19
Hungarian	268	1.02
Irish	3,289	12.52
Italian	1,187	4.52
Latvian	8	0.03
Lithuanian	135	0.51
Luxemburger	17	0.06
Macedonian	11	0.04
Maltese	8	0.03
Norwegian	1,238	4.71
Pennsylvania German	17	0.06
Polish	1,255	4.78
Portuguese	32	0.12
Romanian	114	0.43
Russian	371	1.41
Scandinavian	83	0.32
Scotch-Irish	888	3.38
Scottish	1,065	4.05
Serbian	26	0.10
Slavic	17	0.06
Slovak	219	0.83
Slovene	52	0.20
Swedish	1,329	5.06
Swiss	235	0.89
Ukrainian	84	0.32
United States or American	1,215	4.63
Welsh	388	1.48
White:	26,072	98.97
Not Hispanic (25,872)	25,937	98.46
Hispanic (133)	135	0.51
Yugoslavian	45	0.17

Sun Lakes

Place Type: Census Designated Place
County: Maricopa
Population: 11,936

Ancestry/Race	Number	%
African American/Black:	96	0.80
Not Hispanic (93)	96	0.80
Alaska Native tribes, specified:	2	0.02
Aleut	1	0.01
All other tribes	1	0.01
Am. Ind. or Alaska Nat., not spec.	7	0.06
American Indian tribes, specified:	28	0.23
Cherokee (4)	8	0.07
Chickasaw (1)	1	0.01
Chippewa	1	0.01
Choctaw	4	0.03
Creek (1)	2	0.02
Iroquois	1	0.01
Latin American Indians	1	0.01
Lumbee (1)	1	0.01
Osage	1	0.01
Pima (3)	3	0.03
Sioux (2)	3	0.03
Yaqui (1)	1	0.01
All other tribes	1	0.01
American Indian tribes, not spec.	1	0.01
Arab:	27	0.23
Egyptian	10	0.08
Syrian	17	0.14
Armenian	33	0.28
Asian:	50	0.42
Cambodian (1)	1	0.01
Chinese, ex. Taiwanese (10)	13	0.11
Filipino (3)	6	0.05
Indian (2)	2	0.02
Indonesian	1	0.01
Japanese (13)	16	0.13
Korean (5)	5	0.04
Thai (4)	4	0.03
Other Asian, specified	1	0.01
Other Asian, not specified	1	0.01
Austrian	31	0.26
Belgian	42	0.35
British	154	1.29
Canadian	105	0.88
Croatian	21	0.18
Czech	113	0.95
Czechoslovakian	32	0.27
Danish	195	1.63
Dutch	288	2.41
Eastern European	34	0.28
English	2,263	18.94
European	148	1.24
Finnish	45	0.38
French, except Basque	523	4.38
French Canadian	92	0.77
German	2,902	24.29
Greek	50	0.42
Hawaii Native/Pacific Islander:	4	0.03
Polynesian:	1	0.01
Native Hawaiian	1	0.01
Other Pac. Isl., specified	1	0.01
Other Pac. Isl., not spec. (1)	2	0.02
Hispanic or Latino:	112	0.94
Central American:	6	0.05
Guatemalan	4	0.03
Honduran	1	0.01
Panamanian	1	0.01
Cuban	7	0.06
Dominican Republic	1	0.01
Mexican	64	0.54
Puerto Rican	8	0.07
South American:	3	0.03
Peruvian	1	0.01
Venezuelan	1	0.01
Other South American	1	0.01
Other Hispanic or Latino	23	0.19
Hungarian	137	1.15
Icelander	21	0.18
Irish	1,750	14.65
Italian	617	5.16
Latvian	17	0.14
Lithuanian	58	0.49
Luxemburger	11	0.09
Maltese	9	0.08
Norwegian	581	4.86
Pennsylvania German	18	0.15
Polish	481	4.03
Portuguese	38	0.32
Romanian	29	0.24
Russian	204	1.71
Scotch-Irish	354	2.96
Scottish	422	3.53
Serbian	57	0.48
Slavic	15	0.13
Slovak	26	0.22
Slovene	9	0.08
Swedish	516	4.32
Swiss	121	1.01
Ukrainian	53	0.44
United States or American	610	5.11
Welsh	120	1.00
White:	11,770	98.61
Not Hispanic (11,642)	11,669	97.76
Hispanic (99)	101	0.85
Yugoslavian	17	0.14

Surprise

Place Type: City
County: Maricopa
Population: 30,848

Ancestry/Race	Number	%
African American/Black:	937	3.04
Not Hispanic (744)	849	2.75
Hispanic (62)	88	0.29
African, sub-Saharan:	63	0.20
African	58	0.19
South African	5	0.02
Alaska Native tribes, specified:	4	0.01
Aleut (1)	2	0.01
Eskimo (1)	1	0.00
Tlingit-Haida (1)	1	0.00
Am. Ind. or Alaska Nat., not spec.	64	0.21
American Indian tribes, specified:	187	0.61

Notes: 1. Figures in the "Number" column do not add up to the total population due to: a) Ancestry/Race overlap — e.g. persons can report being both White and Irish, b) persons of Hispanic origin can report being any race, c) persons reporting two ancestries are counted in both categories. 2. Numbers in parentheses indicate the number of persons reporting this ancestry/race alone, not in combination with any other ancestry/race. 3. Refer to the Explanation of Data in the front of the book for more detailed information.

Ancestry/Race	Number	%
Apache (3)	3	0.01
Blackfeet (1)	5	0.02
Cherokee (11)	53	0.17
Chickasaw	1	0.00
Chippewa (1)	6	0.02
Choctaw (12)	19	0.06
Creek	4	0.01
Crow (2)	3	0.01
Delaware (1)	2	0.01
Iroquois (1)	2	0.01
Latin American Indians (11)	12	0.04
Lumbee	1	0.00
Navajo (24)	28	0.09
Pima (5)	7	0.02
Potawatomi (1)	2	0.01
Pueblo (4)	5	0.02
Sioux (3)	9	0.03
Tohono O'Odham (1)	3	0.01
Yaqui (4)	4	0.01
Yuman	1	0.00
All other tribes (8)	17	0.06
American Indian tribes, not spec.	13	0.04
Arab:	59	0.19
Lebanese	20	0.06
Moroccan	11	0.04
Syrian	22	0.07
Other Arab	6	0.02
Armenian	31	0.10
Asian:	461	1.49
Bangladeshi	4	0.01
Cambodian (1)	3	0.01
Chinese, ex. Taiwanese (65)	80	0.26
Filipino (92)	136	0.44
Indian (23)	32	0.10
Indonesian (2)	5	0.02
Japanese (39)	59	0.19
Korean (53)	66	0.21
Laotian (2)	4	0.01
Pakistani	4	0.01
Sri Lankan (1)	1	0.00
Taiwanese (1)	1	0.00
Thai (4)	6	0.02
Vietnamese (39)	43	0.14
Other Asian, not specified (7)	17	0.06
Assyrian/Chaldean/Syriac	60	0.19
Australian	5	0.02
Austrian	178	0.58
Basque	13	0.04
Belgian	68	0.22
Brazilian	12	0.04
British	132	0.43
Canadian	94	0.30
Celtic	5	0.02
Croatian	116	0.38
Czech	64	0.21
Czechoslovakian	32	0.10
Danish	231	0.75
Dutch	601	1.95
English	3,603	11.67
European	346	1.12
Finnish	160	0.52
French, except Basque	702	2.27
French Canadian	196	0.63
German	5,546	17.96
Greek	57	0.18
Hawaii Native/Pacific Islander:	31	0.10
Micronesian: (5)	8	0.03
Guamanian/Chamorro (5)	8	0.03
Polynesian: (9)	16	0.05
Native Hawaiian (7)	14	0.05
Samoan (2)	2	0.01
Other Pac. Isl., not spec. (2)	7	0.02
Hispanic or Latino:	7,184	23.29
Central American:	62	0.20
Costa Rican	2	0.01
Guatemalan	27	0.09
Honduran	3	0.01
Nicaraguan	2	0.01
Panamanian	2	0.01
Salvadoran	26	0.08
Cuban	14	0.05
Dominican Republic	2	0.01
Mexican	6,107	19.80
Puerto Rican	113	0.37
South American:	26	0.08
Argentinean	1	0.00
Chilean	5	0.02
Colombian	14	0.05
Peruvian	1	0.00
Venezuelan	4	0.01
Other South American	1	0.00
Other Hispanic or Latino	860	2.79
Hungarian	214	0.69
Irish	3,456	11.19
Israeli	10	0.03
Italian	1,680	5.44
Latvian	19	0.06
Lithuanian	63	0.20
Luxemburger	21	0.07
Maltese	9	0.03
New Zealander	7	0.02
Northern European	17	0.06
Norwegian	718	2.32
Pennsylvania German	7	0.02
Polish	1,008	3.26
Portuguese	88	0.28
Romanian	159	0.51
Russian	209	0.68
Scandinavian	66	0.21
Scotch-Irish	541	1.75
Scottish	507	1.64
Serbian	31	0.10
Slovak	92	0.30
Slovene	18	0.06
Swedish	683	2.21
Swiss	128	0.41
Turkish	10	0.03
Ukrainian	92	0.30
United States or American	1,745	5.65
Welsh	295	0.96
West Indian, excl. Hispanic:	20	0.06
Haitian	20	0.06
White:	27,072	87.76
Not Hispanic (22,136)	22,429	72.71
Hispanic (4,385)	4,643	15.05
Yugoslavian	37	0.12

Tanque Verde

Place Type: Census Designated Place
County: Pima
Population: 16,195

Ancestry/Race	Number	%
Acadian/Cajun	48	0.29
African American/Black:	149	0.92
Not Hispanic (108)	137	0.85
Hispanic (5)	12	0.07
African, sub-Saharan:	28	0.17
Cape Verdean	5	0.03
South African	23	0.14
Alaska Native tribes, specified:	10	0.06
Alaska Athabascan	5	0.03
Aleut (3)	3	0.02
Eskimo	2	0.01
Am. Ind. or Alaska Nat., not spec.	22	0.14
American Indian tribes, specified:	100	0.62
Apache (4)	8	0.05
Blackfeet (1)	1	0.01
Cherokee (9)	26	0.16
Chippewa (4)	5	0.03
Choctaw (4)	6	0.04
Creek (3)	3	0.02
Delaware (3)	4	0.02
Iroquois (1)	1	0.01
Latin American Indians (3)	6	0.04
Navajo (8)	12	0.07
Osage (1)	1	0.01
Potawatomi (4)	4	0.02
Pueblo (2)	3	0.02
Sioux (4)	6	0.04
Tohono O'Odham (3)	3	0.02
Yaqui (2)	2	0.01
All other tribes (4)	9	0.06
American Indian tribes, not spec.	19	0.12
Arab:	27	0.16
Lebanese	15	0.09
Moroccan	6	0.04
Syrian	6	0.04
Armenian	71	0.43
Asian:	310	1.91
Chinese, ex. Taiwanese (67)	88	0.54
Filipino (22)	45	0.28
Indian (31)	34	0.21
Indonesian (1)	6	0.04
Japanese (53)	86	0.53
Korean (23)	37	0.23
Taiwanese (1)	1	0.01
Thai (3)	4	0.02
Vietnamese (5)	7	0.04
Other Asian, specified (1)	1	0.01
Other Asian, not specified	1	0.01
Austrian	72	0.43
Basque	1	0.01
Belgian	62	0.37
Brazilian	8	0.05
British	138	0.83
Canadian	92	0.56
Celtic	39	0.24
Croatian	62	0.37
Czech	167	1.01
Czechoslovakian	94	0.57
Danish	139	0.84
Dutch	434	2.62
Eastern European	39	0.24
English	2,597	15.68
European	291	1.76
Finnish	112	0.68
French, except Basque	514	3.10
French Canadian	167	1.01
German	4,209	25.42
Greek	47	0.28
Hawaii Native/Pacific Islander:	41	0.25
Micronesian: (1)	4	0.02
Guamanian/Chamorro (1)	4	0.02
Polynesian: (10)	26	0.16
Native Hawaiian (5)	21	0.13
Samoan (5)	5	0.03
Other Pac. Isl., not spec. (7)	11	0.07
Hispanic or Latino:	1,180	7.29
Central American:	16	0.10
Costa Rican	3	0.02
Guatemalan	3	0.02
Honduran	6	0.04
Nicaraguan	2	0.01
Panamanian	2	0.01
Cuban	15	0.09
Mexican	859	5.30
Puerto Rican	36	0.22
South American:	24	0.15
Argentinean	5	0.03
Bolivian	1	0.01
Colombian	12	0.07
Ecuadorian	2	0.01
Peruvian	3	0.02
Other South American	1	0.01
Other Hispanic or Latino	230	1.42
Hungarian	70	0.42
Iranian	9	0.05
Irish	2,328	14.06
Italian	1,023	6.18
Latvian	16	0.10
Northern European	16	0.10
Norwegian	665	4.02
Pennsylvania German	12	0.07
Polish	913	5.51
Portuguese	42	0.25
Romanian	35	0.21
Russian	222	1.34
Scandinavian	116	0.70

Notes: 1. Figures in the "Number" column do not add up to the total population due to: a) Ancestry/Race overlap — e.g. persons can report being both White and Irish, b) persons of Hispanic origin can report being any race, c) persons reporting two ancestries are counted in both categories. 2. Numbers in parentheses indicate the number of persons reporting this ancestry/race alone, not in combination with any other ancestry/race. 3. Refer to the Explanation of Data in the front of the book for more detailed information.

Ancestry/Race	Number	%
Scotch-Irish	375	2.26
Scottish	691	4.17
Serbian	16	0.10
Slovak	25	0.15
Swedish	365	2.20
Swiss	107	0.65
Turkish	13	0.08
Ukrainian	99	0.60
United States or American	947	5.72
Welsh	228	1.38
West Indian, excl. Hispanic:	7	0.04
Bermudan	7	0.04
White:	15,522	95.84
Not Hispanic (14,463)	14,603	90.17
Hispanic (806)	919	5.67
Yugoslavian	26	0.16

Tempe

Place Type: City
County: Maricopa
Population: 158,625

Ancestry/Race	Number	%
Acadian/Cajun	16	0.01
African American/Black:	6,908	4.35
Not Hispanic (5,546)	6,441	4.06
Hispanic (255)	467	0.29
African, sub-Saharan:	663	0.42
African	406	0.26
Ethiopian	60	0.04
Ghanian	11	0.01
Nigerian	55	0.03
Senegalese	18	0.01
Sierra Leonean	4	0.00
Somalian	8	0.01
South African	30	0.02
Sudanese	45	0.03
Other sub-Saharan African	26	0.02
Alaska Native tribes, specified:	26	0.02
Alaska Athabascan (2)	2	0.00
Aleut (7)	8	0.01
Eskimo (6)	8	0.01
Tlingit-Haida (5)	5	0.00
All other tribes (3)	3	0.00
Alaska Native tribes, not specified	2	0.00
Am. Ind. or Alaska Nat., not spec.	836	0.53
Albanian	140	0.09
American Indian tribes, specified:	3,242	2.04
Apache (113)	160	0.10
Blackfeet (6)	30	0.02
Cherokee (74)	258	0.16
Cheyenne (6)	10	0.01
Chickasaw (5)	14	0.01
Chippewa (39)	61	0.04
Choctaw (23)	57	0.04
Colville (4)	4	0.00
Comanche (6)	10	0.01
Cree (2)	5	0.00
Creek (8)	22	0.01
Crow (3)	5	0.00
Delaware (6)	9	0.01
Houma (1)	1	0.00
Iroquois (12)	19	0.01
Kiowa (7)	13	0.01
Latin American Indians (86)	145	0.09
Lumbee	2	0.00
Menominee (1)	1	0.00
Navajo (1,231)	1,346	0.85
Osage (1)	2	0.00
Ottawa (2)	3	0.00
Paiute (7)	13	0.01
Pima (86)	111	0.07
Potawatomi (7)	18	0.01
Pueblo (100)	143	0.09
Puget Sound Salish (1)	1	0.00
Seminole (6)	21	0.01
Shoshone (6)	12	0.01
Sioux (70)	107	0.07
Tohono O'Odham (73)	89	0.06
Ute (9)	12	0.01
Yakama (1)	1	0.00
Yaqui (284)	354	0.22
Yuman (29)	39	0.02
All other tribes (87)	144	0.09
American Indian tribes, not spec.	211	0.13
Arab:	1,187	0.75
Arab/Arabic	335	0.21
Egyptian	79	0.05
Jordanian	144	0.09
Lebanese	300	0.19
Moroccan	24	0.02
Palestinian	14	0.01
Syrian	146	0.09
Other Arab	145	0.09
Armenian	139	0.09
Asian:	9,007	5.68
Bangladeshi (61)	71	0.04
Cambodian (218)	261	0.16
Chinese, ex. Taiwanese (2,010)	2,270	1.43
Filipino (535)	853	0.54
Hmong	1	0.00
Indian (1,734)	1,843	1.16
Indonesian (92)	141	0.09
Japanese (536)	758	0.48
Korean (671)	773	0.49
Laotian (74)	92	0.06
Malaysian (18)	21	0.01
Pakistani (96)	142	0.09
Sri Lankan (19)	25	0.02
Taiwanese (125)	149	0.09
Thai (118)	143	0.09
Vietnamese (836)	931	0.59
Other Asian, specified (23)	43	0.03
Other Asian, not specified (237)	490	0.31
Assyrian/Chaldean/Syriac	15	0.01
Australian	56	0.04
Austrian	500	0.32
Basque	63	0.04
Belgian	218	0.14
Brazilian	127	0.08
British	808	0.51
Bulgarian	62	0.04
Canadian	506	0.32
Celtic	161	0.10
Croatian	135	0.09
Cypriot	29	0.02
Czech	880	0.56
Czechoslovakian	368	0.23
Danish	1,417	0.89
Dutch	2,729	1.72
Eastern European	152	0.10
English	17,735	11.19
Estonian	11	0.01
European	2,053	1.30
Finnish	336	0.21
French, except Basque	4,654	2.94
French Canadian	1,137	0.72
German	28,042	17.70
Greek	622	0.39
Hawaii Native/Pacific Islander:	844	0.53
Melanesian: (1)	2	0.00
Fijian (1)	2	0.00
Micronesian: (154)	191	0.12
Guamanian/Chamorro (61)	92	0.06
Other Micronesian (93)	99	0.06
Polynesian: (192)	369	0.23
Native Hawaiian (119)	221	0.14
Samoan (45)	92	0.06
Tongan (22)	41	0.03
Other Polynesian (6)	15	0.01
Other Pac. Isl., specified	6	0.00
Other Pac. Isl., not spec. (98)	276	0.17
Hispanic or Latino:	28,473	17.95
Central American:	328	0.21
Costa Rican	31	0.02
Guatemalan	76	0.05
Honduran	65	0.04
Nicaraguan	40	0.03
Panamanian	34	0.02
Salvadoran	65	0.04
Other Central American	17	0.01
Cuban	180	0.11
Dominican Republic	32	0.02
Mexican	22,178	13.98
Puerto Rican	656	0.41
South American:	542	0.34
Argentinean	71	0.04
Bolivian	20	0.01
Chilean	42	0.03
Colombian	169	0.11
Ecuadorian	68	0.04
Paraguayan	1	0.00
Peruvian	81	0.05
Uruguayan	15	0.01
Venezuelan	47	0.03
Other South American	28	0.02
Other Hispanic or Latino	4,557	2.87
Hungarian	990	0.62
Icelander	27	0.02
Iranian	394	0.25
Irish	18,902	11.93
Israeli	87	0.05
Italian	8,669	5.47
Latvian	128	0.08
Lithuanian	352	0.22
Luxemburger	11	0.01
Macedonian	34	0.02
Maltese	21	0.01
Northern European	127	0.08
Norwegian	4,098	2.59
Pennsylvania German	27	0.02
Polish	4,670	2.95
Portuguese	552	0.35
Romanian	176	0.11
Russian	1,655	1.04
Scandinavian	774	0.49
Scotch-Irish	2,944	1.86
Scottish	3,805	2.40
Serbian	207	0.13
Slavic	100	0.06
Slovak	264	0.17
Slovene	121	0.08
Swedish	3,573	2.26
Swiss	478	0.30
Turkish	128	0.08
Ukrainian	376	0.24
United States or American	6,306	3.98
Welsh	1,319	0.83
West Indian, excl. Hispanic:	242	0.15
Belizean	26	0.02
British West Indian	30	0.02
Dutch West Indian	10	0.01
Haitian	34	0.02
Jamaican	93	0.06
Trinidadian and Tobagonian	45	0.03
West Indian	4	0.00
White:	127,293	80.25
Not Hispanic (110,517)	113,240	71.39
Hispanic (12,435)	14,053	8.86
Yugoslavian	441	0.28

Tucson

Place Type: City
County: Pima
Population: 486,699

Ancestry/Race	Number	%
Acadian/Cajun	32	0.01
Afghan	29	0.01
African American/Black:	24,954	5.13
Not Hispanic (19,795)	22,558	4.63
Hispanic (1,262)	2,396	0.49
African, sub-Saharan:	1,916	0.39
African	1,420	0.29
Ethiopian	64	0.01
Ghanian	27	0.01
Kenyan	10	0.00
Liberian	32	0.01

Notes: 1. Figures in the "Number" column do not add up to the total population due to: a) Ancestry/Race overlap — e.g. persons can report being both White and Irish, b) persons of Hispanic origin can report being any race, c) persons reporting two ancestries are counted in both categories. 2. Numbers in parentheses indicate the number of persons reporting this ancestry/race alone, not in combination with any other ancestry/race. 3. Refer to the Explanation of Data in the front of the book for more detailed information.

Nigerian	121	0.02
Somalian	118	0.02
South African	41	0.01
Sudanese	10	0.00
Other sub-Saharan African	73	0.02
Alaska Native tribes, specified:	70	0.01
Alaska Athabascan (12)	17	0.00
Aleut (5)	8	0.00
Eskimo (22)	31	0.01
Tlingit-Haida (5)	13	0.00
All other tribes (1)	1	0.00
Alaska Native tribes, not specified	11	0.00
Am. Ind. or Alaska Nat., not spec.	3,462	0.71
Albanian	13	0.00
Alsatian	30	0.01
American Indian tribes, specified:	11,031	2.27
Apache (310)	525	0.11
Blackfeet (26)	119	0.02
Cherokee (332)	1,088	0.22
Cheyenne (8)	19	0.00
Chickasaw (20)	54	0.01
Chippewa (93)	157	0.03
Choctaw (102)	198	0.04
Colville (2)	2	0.00
Comanche (10)	30	0.01
Cree (5)	20	0.00
Creek (33)	72	0.01
Crow (10)	15	0.00
Delaware (10)	26	0.01
Houma	1	0.00
Iroquois (48)	113	0.02
Kiowa (5)	11	0.00
Latin American Indians (489)	780	0.16
Lumbee (13)	25	0.01
Menominee (6)	12	0.00
Navajo (1,127)	1,387	0.28
Osage (3)	11	0.00
Ottawa (8)	10	0.00
Paiute (16)	17	0.00
Pima (152)	190	0.04
Potawatomi (17)	30	0.01
Pueblo (206)	300	0.06
Puget Sound Salish	2	0.00
Seminole (9)	23	0.00
Shoshone (12)	19	0.00
Sioux (139)	243	0.05
Tohono O'Odham (2,070)	2,355	0.48
Ute (20)	28	0.01
Yakama (9)	10	0.00
Yaqui (2,028)	2,634	0.54
Yuman (46)	64	0.01
All other tribes (252)	441	0.09
American Indian tribes, not spec.	1,136	0.23
Arab:	1,715	0.35
Arab/Arabic	446	0.09
Egyptian	98	0.02
Jordanian	69	0.01
Lebanese	594	0.12
Moroccan	38	0.01
Palestinian	69	0.01
Syrian	111	0.02
Other Arab	290	0.06
Armenian	331	0.07
Asian:	15,823	3.25
Bangladeshi (22)	25	0.01
Cambodian (63)	72	0.01
Chinese, ex. Taiwanese (2,908)	3,599	0.74
Filipino (1,742)	2,697	0.55
Hmong (1)	1	0.00
Indian (1,336)	1,633	0.34
Indonesian (101)	137	0.03
Japanese (1,085)	1,805	0.37
Korean (1,097)	1,498	0.31
Laotian (207)	262	0.05
Malaysian (19)	28	0.01
Pakistani (107)	144	0.03
Sri Lankan (51)	59	0.01
Taiwanese (88)	116	0.02
Thai (282)	455	0.09
Vietnamese (1,891)	2,148	0.44
Other Asian, specified (35)	88	0.02
Other Asian, not specified (652)	1,056	0.22
Assyrian/Chaldean/Syriac	21	0.00
Australian	178	0.04
Austrian	1,258	0.26
Basque	267	0.05
Belgian	398	0.08
Brazilian	180	0.04
British	2,533	0.52
Bulgarian	35	0.01
Canadian	1,335	0.27
Carpatho Rusyn	10	0.00
Celtic	235	0.05
Croatian	470	0.10
Cypriot	44	0.01
Czech	1,820	0.37
Czechoslovakian	741	0.15
Danish	2,849	0.59
Dutch	6,485	1.33
Eastern European	362	0.07
English	40,147	8.25
Estonian	14	0.00
European	4,388	0.90
Finnish	959	0.20
French, except Basque	13,250	2.72
French Canadian	3,416	0.70
German	69,909	14.37
German Russian	24	0.00
Greek	1,463	0.30
Guyanese	42	0.01
Hawaii Native/Pacific Islander:	1,509	0.31
Melanesian: (4)	8	0.00
Fijian (4)	8	0.00
Micronesian: (301)	413	0.08
Guamanian/Chamorro (210)	300	0.06
Other Micronesian (91)	113	0.02
Polynesian: (400)	765	0.16
Native Hawaiian (239)	509	0.10
Samoan (128)	191	0.04
Tongan (23)	38	0.01
Other Polynesian (10)	27	0.01
Other Pac. Isl., specified	31	0.01
Other Pac. Isl., not spec. (85)	292	0.06
Hispanic or Latino:	173,868	35.72
Central American:	1,272	0.26
Costa Rican	68	0.01
Guatemalan	279	0.06
Honduran	138	0.03
Nicaraguan	137	0.03
Panamanian	256	0.05
Salvadoran	311	0.06
Other Central American	83	0.02
Cuban	640	0.13
Dominican Republic	88	0.02
Mexican	145,234	29.84
Puerto Rican	2,097	0.43
South American:	999	0.21
Argentinean	114	0.02
Bolivian	33	0.01
Chilean	163	0.03
Colombian	246	0.05
Ecuadorian	51	0.01
Paraguayan	14	0.00
Peruvian	209	0.04
Uruguayan	14	0.00
Venezuelan	90	0.02
Other South American	65	0.01
Other Hispanic or Latino	23,538	4.84
Hungarian	2,016	0.41
Icelander	68	0.01
Iranian	426	0.09
Irish	46,811	9.62
Israeli	75	0.02
Italian	19,636	4.04
Latvian	120	0.02
Lithuanian	1,148	0.24
Luxemburger	84	0.02
Macedonian	30	0.01
Maltese	51	0.01
New Zealander	48	0.01
Northern European	327	0.07
Norwegian	8,435	1.73
Pennsylvania German	165	0.03
Polish	10,967	2.25
Portuguese	819	0.17
Romanian	568	0.12
Russian	4,523	0.93
Scandinavian	927	0.19
Scotch-Irish	7,648	1.57
Scottish	9,397	1.93
Serbian	191	0.04
Slavic	285	0.06
Slovak	791	0.16
Slovene	215	0.04
Soviet Union	9	0.00
Swedish	7,792	1.60
Swiss	1,436	0.30
Turkish	358	0.07
Ukrainian	1,017	0.21
United States or American	17,944	3.69
Welsh	3,447	0.71
West Indian, excl. Hispanic:	537	0.11
Bahamian	12	0.00
Barbadian	18	0.00
Belizean	7	0.00
British West Indian	15	0.00
Dutch West Indian	12	0.00
Haitian	99	0.02
Jamaican	251	0.05
Trinidadian and Tobagonian	1	0.00
U.S. Virgin Islander	30	0.01
West Indian	87	0.02
Other West Indian	5	0.00
White:	356,783	73.31
Not Hispanic (263,748)	270,941	55.67
Hispanic (77,676)	85,842	17.64
Yugoslavian	685	0.14

Yuma

Place Type: City
County: Yuma
Population: 77,515

Ancestry/Race	Number	%
Acadian/Cajun	9	0.01
African American/Black:	2,976	3.84
Not Hispanic (2,220)	2,488	3.21
Hispanic (271)	488	0.63
African, sub-Saharan:	243	0.31
African	208	0.27
Ethiopian	18	0.02
Other sub-Saharan African	17	0.02
Alaska Native tribes, specified:	13	0.02
Alaska Athabascan (1)	1	0.00
Aleut (1)	2	0.00
Eskimo (3)	6	0.01
Tlingit-Haida (4)	4	0.01
Alaska Native tribes, not specified	12	0.02
Am. Ind. or Alaska Nat., not spec.	415	0.54
Albanian	7	0.01
American Indian tribes, specified:	1,143	1.47
Apache (36)	54	0.07
Blackfeet (4)	17	0.02
Cherokee (38)	123	0.16
Cheyenne (7)	7	0.01
Chickasaw (6)	13	0.02
Chippewa (3)	12	0.02
Choctaw (20)	57	0.07
Colville	1	0.00
Comanche (11)	13	0.02
Cree (2)	4	0.01
Creek (5)	10	0.01
Crow (1)	6	0.01
Delaware	1	0.00
Houma	1	0.00
Iroquois (14)	20	0.03
Kiowa (4)	4	0.01
Latin American Indians (74)	108	0.14
Lumbee (2)	2	0.00

Notes: 1. Figures in the "Number" column do not add up to the total population due to: a) Ancestry/Race overlap — e.g. persons can report being both White and Irish, b) persons of Hispanic origin can report being any race, c) persons reporting two ancestries are counted in both categories. 2. Numbers in parentheses indicate the number of persons reporting this ancestry/race alone, not in combination with any other ancestry/race. 3. Refer to the Explanation of Data in the front of the book for more detailed information.

Menominee (2)	2	0.00
Navajo (64)	71	0.09
Osage	4	0.01
Ottawa (2)	2	0.00
Paiute (1)	1	0.00
Pima (8)	17	0.02
Pueblo (10)	12	0.02
Puget Sound Salish (3)	3	0.00
Seminole (2)	3	0.00
Shoshone (1)	1	0.00
Sioux (22)	29	0.04
Tohono O'Odham (28)	34	0.04
Ute (2)	2	0.00
Yaqui (58)	94	0.12
Yuman (256)	310	0.40
All other tribes (61)	105	0.14
American Indian tribes, not spec.	158	0.20
Arab:	179	0.23
Arab/Arabic	20	0.03
Egyptian	83	0.11
Iraqi	20	0.03
Lebanese	34	0.04
Syrian	22	0.03
Asian:	1,720	2.22
Cambodian (5)	7	0.01
Chinese, ex. Taiwanese (164)	215	0.28
Filipino (395)	639	0.82
Hmong (2)	4	0.01
Indian (124)	153	0.20
Indonesian (3)	3	0.00
Japanese (118)	233	0.30
Korean (232)	277	0.36
Laotian (3)	6	0.01
Malaysian (1)	1	0.00
Pakistani (9)	14	0.02
Taiwanese (2)	3	0.00
Thai (19)	35	0.05
Vietnamese (53)	66	0.09
Other Asian, specified	6	0.01
Other Asian, not specified (17)	58	0.07
Australian	32	0.04
Austrian	86	0.11
Basque	17	0.02
Belgian	45	0.06
British	246	0.32
Canadian	202	0.26
Celtic	10	0.01
Croatian	47	0.06
Czech	200	0.26
Czechoslovakian	56	0.07
Danish	387	0.50
Dutch	906	1.17
Eastern European	9	0.01
English	5,549	7.16
European	517	0.67
Finnish	151	0.19
French, except Basque	1,622	2.09
French Canadian	345	0.44
German	8,037	10.36
Greek	72	0.09
Hawaii Native/Pacific Islander:	274	0.35
Micronesian: (44)	61	0.08
Guamanian/Chamorro (41)	56	0.07
Other Micronesian (3)	5	0.01
Polynesian: (83)	162	0.21
Native Hawaiian (61)	130	0.17
Samoan (22)	31	0.04
Tongan	1	0.00
Other Pac. Isl., specified	2	0.00
Other Pac. Isl., not spec. (15)	49	0.06
Hispanic or Latino:	35,400	45.67
Central American:	191	0.25
Costa Rican	7	0.01
Guatemalan	22	0.03
Honduran	24	0.03
Nicaraguan	13	0.02
Panamanian	59	0.08
Salvadoran	57	0.07
Other Central American	9	0.01
Cuban	61	0.08
Dominican Republic	21	0.03
Mexican	30,512	39.36
Puerto Rican	422	0.54
South American:	109	0.14
Argentinean	3	0.00
Chilean	9	0.01
Colombian	43	0.06
Ecuadorian	14	0.02
Paraguayan	4	0.01
Peruvian	20	0.03
Uruguayan	5	0.01
Venezuelan	4	0.01
Other South American	7	0.01
Other Hispanic or Latino	4,084	5.27
Hungarian	120	0.15
Icelander	12	0.02
Iranian	11	0.01
Irish	5,734	7.39
Italian	1,609	2.07
Lithuanian	58	0.07
Maltese	26	0.03
Northern European	23	0.03
Norwegian	1,191	1.54
Pennsylvania German	23	0.03
Polish	1,130	1.46
Portuguese	87	0.11
Romanian	51	0.07
Russian	169	0.22
Scandinavian	168	0.22
Scotch-Irish	1,216	1.57
Scottish	1,256	1.62
Slavic	22	0.03
Slovak	62	0.08
Slovene	41	0.05
Swedish	1,002	1.29
Swiss	121	0.16
Ukrainian	147	0.19
United States or American	3,863	4.98
Welsh	230	0.30
West Indian, excl. Hispanic:	56	0.07
Haitian	35	0.05
Jamaican	11	0.01
West Indian	10	0.01
White:	55,549	71.66
Not Hispanic (36,784)	37,701	48.64
Hispanic (16,184)	17,848	23.03
Yugoslavian	17	0.02

Arkadelphia

Place Type: City
County: Clark
Population: 10,912

Ancestry/Race	Number	%
Acadian/Cajun	6	0.06
African American/Black:	2,964	27.16
Not Hispanic (2,879)	2,946	27.00
Hispanic (14)	18	0.16
African, sub-Saharan:	116	1.08
African	96	0.90
Kenyan	20	0.19
Am. Ind. or Alaska Nat., not spec.	48	0.44
American Indian tribes, specified:	73	0.67
Apache	1	0.01
Blackfeet (1)	3	0.03
Cherokee (9)	31	0.28
Chippewa (1)	3	0.03
Choctaw (5)	12	0.11
Comanche (1)	2	0.02
Creek (5)	5	0.05
Houma (1)	1	0.01
Iroquois	4	0.04
Latin American Indians	1	0.01
Navajo (1)	1	0.01
Osage (1)	2	0.02
All other tribes (5)	7	0.06
American Indian tribes, not spec.	4	0.04
Arab:	9	0.08
Lebanese	9	0.08
Asian:	178	1.63
Bangladeshi (6)	6	0.05
Chinese, ex. Taiwanese (44)	50	0.46
Filipino (7)	13	0.12
Indian (19)	19	0.17
Indonesian (1)	2	0.02
Japanese (23)	30	0.27
Korean (4)	8	0.07
Pakistani (1)	1	0.01
Taiwanese (25)	26	0.24
Thai (1)	1	0.01
Vietnamese (6)	7	0.06
Other Asian, specified	1	0.01
Other Asian, not specified (3)	14	0.13
Austrian	27	0.25
Belgian	20	0.19
Brazilian	17	0.16
British	45	0.42
Canadian	13	0.12
Danish	17	0.16
Dutch	172	1.60
English	912	8.50
European	82	0.76
French, except Basque	165	1.54
French Canadian	6	0.06
German	866	8.08
Greek	14	0.13
Hawaii Native/Pacific Islander:	14	0.13
Melanesian:	2	0.02
Other Melanesian	2	0.02
Micronesian:	1	0.01
Guamanian/Chamorro	1	0.01
Polynesian: (6)	9	0.08
Native Hawaiian (2)	2	0.02
Samoan (4)	7	0.06
Other Pac. Isl., specified	1	0.01
Other Pac. Isl., not spec.	1	0.01
Hispanic or Latino:	283	2.59
Central American:	4	0.04
Panamanian	3	0.03
Other Central American	1	0.01
Cuban	6	0.05
Mexican	232	2.13
Puerto Rican	10	0.09
South American:	4	0.04
Argentinean	1	0.01
Colombian	1	0.01
Peruvian	1	0.01
Uruguayan	1	0.01
Other Hispanic or Latino	27	0.25
Irish	888	8.28
Italian	71	0.66
Norwegian	48	0.45
Polish	55	0.51
Portuguese	10	0.09
Russian	6	0.06
Scotch-Irish	287	2.68
Scottish	203	1.89
Swedish	79	0.74
Swiss	20	0.19
United States or American	1,292	12.05
Welsh	85	0.79
West Indian, excl. Hispanic:	7	0.07
Dutch West Indian	7	0.07
White:	7,633	69.95
Not Hispanic (7,419)	7,519	68.91
Hispanic (108)	114	1.04

Bella Vista

Place Type: Census Designated Place
County: Benton
Population: 16,582

Ancestry/Race	Number	%
African American/Black:	44	0.27
Not Hispanic (30)	44	0.27
Alaska Native tribes, specified:	1	0.01
Eskimo (1)	1	0.01
Am. Ind. or Alaska Nat., not spec.	22	0.13

Notes: 1. Figures in the "Number" column do not add up to the total population due to: a) Ancestry/Race overlap — e.g. persons can report being both White and Irish, b) persons of Hispanic origin can report being any race, c) persons reporting two ancestries are counted in both categories. 2. Numbers in parentheses indicate the number of persons reporting this ancestry/race alone, not in combination with any other ancestry/race. 3. Refer to the Explanation of Data in the front of the book for more detailed information.

Alsatian	10	0.06
American Indian tribes, specified:	195	1.18
Apache	2	0.01
Blackfeet	4	0.02
Cherokee (65)	114	0.69
Cheyenne	1	0.01
Chickasaw (1)	2	0.01
Chippewa (1)	5	0.03
Choctaw (10)	20	0.12
Creek (2)	3	0.02
Delaware (2)	2	0.01
Iroquois	2	0.01
Kiowa (4)	4	0.02
Osage (1)	4	0.02
Potawatomi (1)	1	0.01
Sioux (2)	11	0.07
All other tribes (8)	20	0.12
American Indian tribes, not spec.	4	0.02
Armenian	4	0.02
Asian:	57	0.34
Chinese, ex. Taiwanese (7)	7	0.04
Filipino (13)	18	0.11
Indian (10)	11	0.07
Japanese (5)	7	0.04
Korean (6)	6	0.04
Taiwanese (1)	1	0.01
Vietnamese (3)	3	0.02
Other Asian, specified	2	0.01
Other Asian, not specified	2	0.01
Austrian	22	0.13
Basque	10	0.06
Belgian	15	0.09
British	152	0.92
Canadian	10	0.06
Croatian	6	0.04
Czech	190	1.16
Czechoslovakian	33	0.20
Danish	182	1.11
Dutch	410	2.49
English	3,091	18.80
European	105	0.64
Finnish	26	0.16
French, except Basque	542	3.30
French Canadian	104	0.63
German	4,427	26.93
German Russian	9	0.05
Hawaii Native/Pacific Islander:	5	0.03
Micronesian:	2	0.01
Guamanian/Chamorro	2	0.01
Polynesian: (1)	3	0.02
Native Hawaiian (1)	3	0.02
Hispanic or Latino:	168	1.01
Central American:	4	0.02
Panamanian	1	0.01
Salvadoran	3	0.02
Cuban	5	0.03
Mexican	98	0.59
Puerto Rican	10	0.06
South American:	9	0.05
Argentinean	1	0.01
Bolivian	1	0.01
Colombian	6	0.04
Peruvian	1	0.01
Other Hispanic or Latino	42	0.25
Hungarian	29	0.18
Iranian	8	0.05
Irish	2,008	12.21
Italian	292	1.78
Lithuanian	8	0.05
Luxemburger	10	0.06
New Zealander	10	0.06
Norwegian	633	3.85
Pennsylvania German	39	0.24
Polish	418	2.54
Portuguese	8	0.05
Russian	45	0.27
Scandinavian	42	0.26
Scotch-Irish	579	3.52
Scottish	418	2.54
Slovene	10	0.06
Swedish	655	3.98
Swiss	153	0.93
United States or American	1,350	8.21
Welsh	185	1.13
West Indian, excl. Hispanic:	32	0.19
Dutch West Indian	23	0.14
U.S. Virgin Islander	9	0.05
White:	16,356	98.64
Not Hispanic (16,109)	16,221	97.82
Hispanic (119)	135	0.81
Yugoslavian	8	0.05

Benton

Place Type: City
County: Saline
Population: 21,906

Ancestry/Race	Number	%
Acadian/Cajun	19	0.09
African American/Black:	936	4.27
Not Hispanic (886)	925	4.22
Hispanic (8)	11	0.05
African, sub-Saharan:	10	0.05
African	10	0.05
Alaska Native tribes, specified:	3	0.01
Aleut (2)	2	0.01
All other tribes	1	0.00
Am. Ind. or Alaska Nat., not spec.	50	0.23
Albanian	8	0.04
American Indian tribes, specified:	174	0.79
Apache (1)	1	0.00
Blackfeet	7	0.03
Cherokee (22)	78	0.36
Chickasaw (2)	7	0.03
Chippewa (1)	4	0.02
Choctaw (15)	36	0.16
Comanche (2)	4	0.02
Creek (1)	1	0.00
Delaware (1)	2	0.01
Iroquois (3)	3	0.01
Kiowa (4)	7	0.03
Latin American Indians	1	0.00
Lumbee	1	0.00
Navajo (3)	7	0.03
Osage (1)	3	0.01
Ottawa (3)	5	0.02
Potawatomi	1	0.00
Pueblo (1)	2	0.01
Seminole	1	0.00
All other tribes (2)	3	0.01
American Indian tribes, not spec.	20	0.09
Arab:	65	0.29
Palestinian	38	0.17
Syrian	27	0.12
Asian:	184	0.84
Cambodian (1)	2	0.01
Chinese, ex. Taiwanese (17)	21	0.10
Filipino (28)	44	0.20
Indian (21)	25	0.11
Indonesian (1)	2	0.01
Japanese (8)	21	0.10
Korean (24)	32	0.15
Laotian (1)	1	0.00
Sri Lankan (3)	3	0.01
Thai (4)	4	0.02
Vietnamese (8)	13	0.06
Other Asian, specified	4	0.02
Other Asian, not specified (6)	12	0.05
Australian	6	0.03
Austrian	33	0.15
Belgian	6	0.03
British	126	0.57
Canadian	26	0.12
Croatian	34	0.15
Czech	40	0.18
Czechoslovakian	11	0.05
Danish	49	0.22
Dutch	327	1.48
English	1,667	7.56
European	121	0.55
Finnish	14	0.06
French, except Basque	587	2.66
French Canadian	70	0.32
German	2,294	10.41
Greek	54	0.25
Hawaii Native/Pacific Islander:	21	0.10
Polynesian: (10)	16	0.07
Native Hawaiian (5)	11	0.05
Samoan (5)	5	0.02
Other Pac. Isl., specified	4	0.02
Other Pac. Isl., not spec.	1	0.00
Hispanic or Latino:	417	1.90
Central American:	20	0.09
Costa Rican	2	0.01
Guatemalan	4	0.02
Honduran	7	0.03
Nicaraguan	1	0.00
Panamanian	6	0.03
Cuban	10	0.05
Mexican	191	0.87
Puerto Rican	63	0.29
South American:	2	0.01
Colombian	1	0.00
Venezuelan	1	0.00
Other Hispanic or Latino	131	0.60
Hungarian	38	0.17
Irish	2,615	11.87
Italian	371	1.68
Lithuanian	14	0.06
Northern European	6	0.03
Norwegian	83	0.38
Pennsylvania German	5	0.02
Polish	151	0.69
Portuguese	39	0.18
Romanian	14	0.06
Russian	18	0.08
Scandinavian	23	0.10
Scotch-Irish	487	2.21
Scottish	378	1.72
Serbian	25	0.11
Slavic	9	0.04
Slovak	8	0.04
Swedish	134	0.61
Swiss	24	0.11
United States or American	4,157	18.86
Welsh	90	0.41
West Indian, excl. Hispanic:	14	0.06
Dutch West Indian	7	0.03
Haitian	7	0.03
White:	20,618	94.12
Not Hispanic (20,157)	20,378	93.02
Hispanic (211)	240	1.10

Bentonville

Place Type: City
County: Benton
Population: 19,730

Ancestry/Race	Number	%
Acadian/Cajun	16	0.08
African American/Black:	208	1.05
Not Hispanic (165)	197	1.00
Hispanic (9)	11	0.06
Alaska Native tribes, specified:	2	0.01
Tlingit-Haida	2	0.01
Am. Ind. or Alaska Nat., not spec.	69	0.35
American Indian tribes, specified:	362	1.83
Apache	7	0.04
Blackfeet (1)	3	0.02
Cherokee (120)	223	1.13
Chickasaw (6)	7	0.04
Chippewa (3)	6	0.03
Choctaw (17)	36	0.18
Comanche (1)	1	0.01
Creek (15)	22	0.11
Delaware (1)	1	0.01
Iroquois (2)	2	0.01
Latin American Indians (3)	3	0.02

Notes: 1. Figures in the "Number" column do not add up to the total population due to: a) Ancestry/Race overlap — e.g. persons can report being both White and Irish, b) persons of Hispanic origin can report being any race, c) persons reporting two ancestries are counted in both categories. 2. Numbers in parentheses indicate the number of persons reporting this ancestry/race alone, not in combination with any other ancestry/race. 3. Refer to the Explanation of Data in the front of the book for more detailed information.

Ancestry/Race	Number	%
Navajo (1)	5	0.03
Osage (9)	10	0.05
Paiute	1	0.01
Potawatomi (10)	10	0.05
Seminole (2)	3	0.02
Sioux (1)	3	0.02
All other tribes (12)	19	0.10
American Indian tribes, not spec.	9	0.05
Arab:	6	0.03
Lebanese	6	0.03
Asian:	561	2.84
Bangladeshi (4)	4	0.02
Cambodian (1)	1	0.01
Chinese, ex. Taiwanese (53)	63	0.32
Filipino (53)	70	0.35
Indian (110)	115	0.58
Japanese (11)	24	0.12
Korean (18)	23	0.12
Laotian (45)	47	0.24
Malaysian (1)	4	0.02
Pakistani (2)	2	0.01
Sri Lankan (5)	6	0.03
Taiwanese	4	0.02
Thai (2)	3	0.02
Vietnamese (154)	176	0.89
Other Asian, not specified (6)	19	0.10
Austrian	22	0.11
Belgian	47	0.24
Brazilian	10	0.05
British	138	0.70
Canadian	12	0.06
Celtic	16	0.08
Czech	41	0.21
Czechoslovakian	17	0.09
Danish	23	0.12
Dutch	563	2.85
English	2,097	10.62
European	145	0.73
Finnish	12	0.06
French, except Basque	488	2.47
French Canadian	53	0.27
German	3,388	17.15
Greek	12	0.06
Hawaii Native/Pacific Islander:	26	0.13
Micronesian: (5)	5	0.03
Guamanian/Chamorro (4)	4	0.02
Other Micronesian (1)	1	0.01
Polynesian: (1)	11	0.06
Native Hawaiian (1)	8	0.04
Samoan	1	0.01
Other Polynesian	2	0.01
Other Pac. Isl., not spec. (1)	10	0.05
Hispanic or Latino:	1,198	6.07
Central American:	96	0.49
Costa Rican	3	0.02
Guatemalan	13	0.07
Honduran	2	0.01
Panamanian	1	0.01
Salvadoran	77	0.39
Cuban	20	0.10
Dominican Republic	2	0.01
Mexican	764	3.87
Puerto Rican	47	0.24
South American:	37	0.19
Argentinean	1	0.01
Chilean	4	0.02
Colombian	11	0.06
Paraguayan	2	0.01
Peruvian	18	0.09
Other South American	1	0.01
Other Hispanic or Latino	232	1.18
Hungarian	55	0.28
Irish	2,287	11.58
Italian	394	1.99
Lithuanian	6	0.03
Luxemburger	24	0.12
Norwegian	192	0.97
Pennsylvania German	16	0.08
Polish	177	0.90
Portuguese	8	0.04
Russian	16	0.08
Scotch-Irish	392	1.98
Scottish	273	1.38
Swedish	262	1.33
Swiss	31	0.16
Ukrainian	14	0.07
United States or American	2,419	12.25
Welsh	85	0.43
West Indian, excl. Hispanic:	17	0.09
Dutch West Indian	17	0.09
White:	18,250	92.50
Not Hispanic (17,346)	17,589	89.15
Hispanic (593)	661	3.35
Yugoslavian	3	0.02

Blytheville

Place Type: City
County: Mississippi
Population: 18,272

Ancestry/Race	Number	%
African American/Black:	9,693	53.05
Not Hispanic (9,475)	9,638	52.75
Hispanic (53)	55	0.30
African, sub-Saharan:	314	1.72
African	314	1.72
Am. Ind. or Alaska Nat., not spec.	43	0.24
American Indian tribes, specified:	107	0.59
Blackfeet (3)	9	0.05
Cherokee (6)	69	0.38
Chickasaw	3	0.02
Choctaw (3)	16	0.09
Creek	1	0.01
Kiowa (1)	1	0.01
Latin American Indians	3	0.02
Menominee (1)	1	0.01
Pueblo (1)	1	0.01
Sioux (3)	3	0.02
American Indian tribes, not spec.	4	0.02
Arab:	30	0.16
Lebanese	30	0.16
Asian:	145	0.79
Bangladeshi (3)	3	0.02
Chinese, ex. Taiwanese (8)	10	0.05
Filipino (19)	29	0.16
Indian (19)	21	0.11
Japanese (10)	12	0.07
Korean (15)	17	0.09
Thai (3)	3	0.02
Vietnamese (30)	30	0.16
Other Asian, specified	4	0.02
Other Asian, not specified (2)	16	0.09
British	82	0.45
Czech	21	0.12
Czechoslovakian	8	0.04
Dutch	85	0.47
English	979	5.36
European	139	0.76
French, except Basque	169	0.93
French Canadian	23	0.13
German	630	3.45
Greek	18	0.10
Hawaii Native/Pacific Islander:	29	0.16
Micronesian: (3)	5	0.03
Guamanian/Chamorro (3)	5	0.03
Polynesian: (9)	12	0.07
Native Hawaiian (6)	8	0.04
Samoan (3)	4	0.02
Other Pac. Isl., specified	4	0.02
Other Pac. Isl., not spec.	8	0.04
Hispanic or Latino:	239	1.31
Central American:	2	0.01
Salvadoran	2	0.01
Cuban	5	0.03
Mexican	133	0.73
Puerto Rican	17	0.09
Other Hispanic or Latino	82	0.45
Hungarian	24	0.13
Irish	821	4.50
Israeli	8	0.04
Italian	90	0.49
Norwegian	40	0.22
Polish	29	0.16
Russian	10	0.05
Scandinavian	13	0.07
Scotch-Irish	199	1.09
Scottish	147	0.81
Swedish	81	0.44
Swiss	14	0.08
United States or American	2,022	11.08
Welsh	27	0.15
West Indian, excl. Hispanic:	7	0.04
West Indian	7	0.04
White:	8,415	46.05
Not Hispanic (8,151)	8,309	45.47
Hispanic (98)	106	0.58

Cabot

Place Type: City
County: Lonoke
Population: 15,261

Ancestry/Race	Number	%
African American/Black:	78	0.51
Not Hispanic (50)	73	0.48
Hispanic	5	0.03
Alaska Native tribes, specified:	1	0.01
Aleut (1)	1	0.01
Am. Ind. or Alaska Nat., not spec.	33	0.22
American Indian tribes, specified:	111	0.73
Apache	2	0.01
Blackfeet	4	0.03
Cherokee (29)	63	0.41
Chickasaw (1)	5	0.03
Chippewa	1	0.01
Choctaw (11)	15	0.10
Creek	1	0.01
Iroquois	3	0.02
Latin American Indians (1)	1	0.01
Navajo (2)	2	0.01
Osage (1)	2	0.01
Potawatomi (2)	2	0.01
Sioux (1)	2	0.01
Tohono O'Odham (1)	4	0.03
All other tribes (3)	4	0.03
American Indian tribes, not spec.	1	0.01
Arab:	29	0.19
Lebanese	29	0.19
Armenian	7	0.05
Asian:	206	1.35
Chinese, ex. Taiwanese (8)	13	0.09
Filipino (49)	75	0.49
Indian (11)	16	0.10
Japanese (6)	20	0.13
Korean (37)	57	0.37
Taiwanese (1)	1	0.01
Thai	1	0.01
Vietnamese (11)	11	0.07
Other Asian, not specified (11)	12	0.08
Austrian	11	0.07
Belgian	10	0.07
British	126	0.82
Canadian	18	0.12
Czech	35	0.23
Czechoslovakian	24	0.16
Danish	99	0.65
Dutch	264	1.73
English	1,716	11.22
European	188	1.23
Finnish	7	0.05
French, except Basque	431	2.82
French Canadian	112	0.73
German	2,518	16.47
Greek	11	0.07
Hawaii Native/Pacific Islander:	12	0.08
Micronesian: (1)	1	0.01
Guamanian/Chamorro (1)	1	0.01
Polynesian: (4)	10	0.07

Notes: 1. Figures in the "Number" column do not add up to the total population due to: a) Ancestry/Race overlap — e.g. persons can report being both White and Irish, b) persons of Hispanic origin can report being any race, c) persons reporting two ancestries are counted in both categories. 2. Numbers in parentheses indicate the number of persons reporting this ancestry/race alone, not in combination with any other ancestry/race. 3. Refer to the Explanation of Data in the front of the book for more detailed information.

Native Hawaiian (4)	10	0.07
Other Pac. Isl., not spec. (1)	1	0.01
Hispanic or Latino:	286	1.87
Central American:	6	0.04
Costa Rican	4	0.03
Guatemalan	1	0.01
Panamanian	1	0.01
Cuban	1	0.01
Mexican	147	0.96
Puerto Rican	27	0.18
South American:	4	0.03
Argentinean	1	0.01
Colombian	2	0.01
Venezuelan	1	0.01
Other Hispanic or Latino	101	0.66
Hungarian	10	0.07
Irish	2,007	13.13
Italian	292	1.91
Latvian	28	0.18
New Zealander	6	0.04
Northern European	18	0.12
Norwegian	120	0.78
Polish	230	1.50
Portuguese	1	0.01
Russian	28	0.18
Scandinavian	21	0.14
Scotch-Irish	358	2.34
Scottish	374	2.45
Slavic	22	0.14
Slovak	3	0.02
Swedish	102	0.67
Swiss	24	0.16
Turkish	12	0.08
United States or American	2,195	14.36
Welsh	45	0.29
White:	14,924	97.79
Not Hispanic (14,573)	14,728	96.51
Hispanic (163)	196	1.28

Camden

Place Type: City
County: Ouachita
Population: 13,154

Ancestry/Race	Number	%
African American/Black:	6,558	49.86
Not Hispanic (6,475)	6,533	49.67
Hispanic (24)	25	0.19
African, sub-Saharan:	60	0.45
African	60	0.45
Alaska Native tribes, specified:	1	0.01
Aleut (1)	1	0.01
Am. Ind. or Alaska Nat., not spec.	27	0.21
American Indian tribes, specified:	54	0.41
Blackfeet	1	0.01
Cherokee (16)	31	0.24
Chickasaw	1	0.01
Choctaw (2)	6	0.05
Colville	1	0.01
Comanche (1)	1	0.01
Iroquois (2)	4	0.03
Latin American Indians	2	0.02
Potawatomi (3)	3	0.02
Sioux	1	0.01
All other tribes	3	0.02
American Indian tribes, not spec.	1	0.01
Asian:	75	0.57
Chinese, ex. Taiwanese (9)	16	0.12
Filipino (11)	15	0.11
Indian (9)	15	0.11
Japanese (4)	6	0.05
Korean (3)	6	0.05
Vietnamese (12)	14	0.11
Other Asian, specified	2	0.02
Other Asian, not specified (1)	1	0.01
British	12	0.09
Canadian	21	0.16
Celtic	7	0.05
Czech	6	0.05
Dutch	55	0.41
English	612	4.61
European	34	0.26
French, except Basque	205	1.54
French Canadian	59	0.44
German	552	4.16
Greek	4	0.03
Hawaii Native/Pacific Islander:	6	0.05
Micronesian: (1)	1	0.01
Guamanian/Chamorro (1)	1	0.01
Polynesian:	1	0.01
Native Hawaiian	1	0.01
Other Pac. Isl., specified	2	0.02
Other Pac. Isl., not spec. (2)	2	0.02
Hispanic or Latino:	76	0.58
Central American:	1	0.01
Guatemalan	1	0.01
Cuban	3	0.02
Mexican	38	0.29
Puerto Rican	2	0.02
Other Hispanic or Latino	32	0.24
Irish	827	6.23
Italian	95	0.72
Norwegian	24	0.18
Polish	7	0.05
Portuguese	9	0.07
Romanian	14	0.11
Scotch-Irish	230	1.73
Scottish	87	0.66
Swedish	58	0.44
Swiss	23	0.17
United States or American	1,269	9.56
Welsh	23	0.17
White:	6,516	49.54
Not Hispanic (6,405)	6,488	49.32
Hispanic (25)	28	0.21

Conway

Place Type: City
County: Faulkner
Population: 43,167

Ancestry/Race	Number	%
African American/Black:	5,393	12.49
Not Hispanic (5,211)	5,366	12.43
Hispanic (21)	27	0.06
African, sub-Saharan:	335	0.78
African	312	0.72
Ghanian	6	0.01
Nigerian	10	0.02
Other sub-Saharan African	7	0.02
Alaska Native tribes, specified:	1	0.00
Alaska Athabascan	1	0.00
Am. Ind. or Alaska Nat., not spec.	88	0.20
American Indian tribes, specified:	222	0.51
Apache (4)	7	0.02
Blackfeet (2)	6	0.01
Cherokee (51)	136	0.32
Cheyenne	1	0.00
Chickasaw (2)	5	0.01
Chippewa (1)	2	0.00
Choctaw (18)	24	0.06
Cree	1	0.00
Creek (4)	11	0.03
Delaware (1)	1	0.00
Iroquois (4)	4	0.01
Kiowa	3	0.01
Latin American Indians (1)	2	0.00
Navajo	3	0.01
Osage (1)	1	0.00
Paiute (1)	1	0.00
Pueblo (2)	5	0.01
Seminole (1)	1	0.00
All other tribes (6)	8	0.02
American Indian tribes, not spec.	14	0.03
Arab:	85	0.20
Lebanese	85	0.20
Armenian	28	0.06
Asian:	685	1.59
Bangladeshi (12)	12	0.03
Chinese, ex. Taiwanese (169)	195	0.45
Filipino (58)	85	0.20
Indian (76)	86	0.20
Indonesian (8)	10	0.02
Japanese (45)	66	0.15
Korean (47)	75	0.17
Laotian (5)	5	0.01
Malaysian (7)	14	0.03
Pakistani (25)	25	0.06
Taiwanese (8)	9	0.02
Thai (2)	3	0.01
Vietnamese (33)	34	0.08
Other Asian, specified (1)	2	0.00
Other Asian, not specified (38)	64	0.15
Austrian	56	0.13
Belgian	55	0.13
Brazilian	31	0.07
British	203	0.47
Canadian	89	0.21
Celtic	18	0.04
Czech	121	0.28
Czechoslovakian	45	0.10
Danish	87	0.20
Dutch	576	1.33
Eastern European	10	0.02
English	4,293	9.94
European	624	1.44
Finnish	21	0.05
French, except Basque	972	2.25
French Canadian	189	0.44
German	5,751	13.31
Greek	66	0.15
Hawaii Native/Pacific Islander:	38	0.09
Micronesian: (3)	5	0.01
Guamanian/Chamorro (3)	5	0.01
Polynesian: (11)	27	0.06
Native Hawaiian (7)	23	0.05
Samoan (4)	4	0.01
Other Pac. Isl., specified	1	0.00
Other Pac. Isl., not spec.	5	0.01
Hispanic or Latino:	983	2.28
Central American:	37	0.09
Costa Rican	1	0.00
Guatemalan	3	0.01
Honduran	15	0.03
Panamanian	8	0.02
Salvadoran	10	0.02
Cuban	25	0.06
Dominican Republic	5	0.01
Mexican	687	1.59
Puerto Rican	31	0.07
South American:	33	0.08
Argentinean	1	0.00
Bolivian	2	0.00
Chilean	1	0.00
Colombian	13	0.03
Peruvian	7	0.02
Venezuelan	9	0.02
Other Hispanic or Latino	165	0.38
Hungarian	42	0.10
Iranian	9	0.02
Irish	4,426	10.25
Italian	847	1.96
Lithuanian	21	0.05
Maltese	13	0.03
Northern European	22	0.05
Norwegian	354	0.82
Pennsylvania German	19	0.04
Polish	271	0.63
Portuguese	19	0.04
Romanian	25	0.06
Russian	40	0.09
Scandinavian	113	0.26
Scotch-Irish	924	2.14
Scottish	856	1.98
Serbian	11	0.03
Slavic	8	0.02
Slovak	13	0.03
Swedish	279	0.65

Notes: 1. Figures in the "Number" column do not add up to the total population due to: a) Ancestry/Race overlap — e.g. persons can report being both White and Irish, b) persons of Hispanic origin can report being any race, c) persons reporting two ancestries are counted in both categories. 2. Numbers in parentheses indicate the number of persons reporting this ancestry/race alone, not in combination with any other ancestry/race. 3. Refer to the Explanation of Data in the front of the book for more detailed information.

Swiss	414	0.96
Turkish	6	0.01
Ukrainian	43	0.10
United States or American	5,505	12.74
Welsh	219	0.51
West Indian, excl. Hispanic:	26	0.06
Dutch West Indian	8	0.02
Jamaican	18	0.04
White:	36,738	85.11
Not Hispanic (35,817)	36,181	83.82
Hispanic (455)	557	1.29
Yugoslavian	10	0.02

El Dorado

Place Type: City
County: Union
Population: 21,530

Ancestry/Race	Number	%
Acadian/Cajun	29	0.14
African American/Black:	9,628	44.72
Not Hispanic (9,490)	9,603	44.60
Hispanic (22)	25	0.12
African, sub-Saharan:	141	0.66
African	141	0.66
Alaska Native tribes, specified:	3	0.01
Alaska Athabascan (1)	1	0.00
Eskimo (2)	2	0.01
Am. Ind. or Alaska Nat., not spec.	53	0.25
American Indian tribes, specified:	68	0.32
Apache (5)	11	0.05
Blackfeet	1	0.00
Cherokee (13)	30	0.14
Choctaw (3)	9	0.04
Navajo	6	0.03
Potawatomi (1)	2	0.01
Pueblo	1	0.00
Seminole	3	0.01
Sioux	1	0.00
All other tribes (1)	4	0.02
American Indian tribes, not spec.	5	0.02
Arab:	29	0.14
Arab/Arabic	6	0.03
Egyptian	16	0.07
Syrian	7	0.03
Asian:	196	0.91
Chinese, ex. Taiwanese (22)	24	0.11
Filipino (40)	44	0.20
Indian (55)	68	0.32
Japanese (11)	14	0.07
Korean (2)	4	0.02
Pakistani	2	0.01
Thai (1)	1	0.00
Vietnamese (12)	14	0.07
Other Asian, specified	6	0.03
Other Asian, not specified (8)	19	0.09
Austrian	8	0.04
British	73	0.34
Canadian	19	0.09
Czech	21	0.10
Czechoslovakian	7	0.03
Danish	28	0.13
Dutch	115	0.54
English	1,363	6.37
European	92	0.43
French, except Basque	244	1.14
French Canadian	24	0.11
German	750	3.50
Greek	4	0.02
Hawaii Native/Pacific Islander:	30	0.14
Micronesian:	5	0.02
Guamanian/Chamorro	5	0.02
Polynesian: (1)	11	0.05
Native Hawaiian (1)	6	0.03
Samoan	5	0.02
Other Pac. Isl., specified	6	0.03
Other Pac. Isl., not spec. (2)	8	0.04
Hispanic or Latino:	224	1.04
Central American:	12	0.06
Guatemalan	4	0.02
Nicaraguan	3	0.01
Panamanian	1	0.00
Salvadoran	1	0.00
Other Central American	3	0.01
Cuban	12	0.06
Dominican Republic	4	0.02
Mexican	127	0.59
Puerto Rican	16	0.07
South American:	4	0.02
Argentinean	1	0.00
Colombian	2	0.01
Ecuadorian	1	0.00
Other Hispanic or Latino	49	0.23
Irish	1,371	6.41
Italian	138	0.64
Lithuanian	6	0.03
Norwegian	43	0.20
Polish	25	0.12
Scotch-Irish	497	2.32
Scottish	203	0.95
Swedish	33	0.15
Swiss	49	0.23
United States or American	2,569	12.00
Welsh	42	0.20
White:	11,678	54.24
Not Hispanic (11,441)	11,565	53.72
Hispanic (111)	113	0.52

Fayetteville

Place Type: City
County: Washington
Population: 58,047

Ancestry/Race	Number	%
African American/Black:	3,338	5.75
Not Hispanic (2,930)	3,276	5.64
Hispanic (39)	62	0.11
African, sub-Saharan:	305	0.53
African	180	0.31
Ethiopian	13	0.02
Kenyan	31	0.05
Nigerian	68	0.12
South African	7	0.01
Other sub-Saharan African	6	0.01
Alaska Native tribes, specified:	13	0.02
Alaska Athabascan (3)	4	0.01
Eskimo (7)	7	0.01
Tlingit-Haida (2)	2	0.00
Alaska Native tribes, not specified	32	0.06
Am. Ind. or Alaska Nat., not spec.	271	0.47
American Indian tribes, specified:	1,002	1.73
Apache (6)	20	0.03
Blackfeet (2)	15	0.03
Cherokee (349)	641	1.10
Cheyenne	4	0.01
Chickasaw (6)	9	0.02
Chippewa (4)	12	0.02
Choctaw (39)	84	0.14
Comanche (5)	7	0.01
Cree	1	0.00
Creek (18)	30	0.05
Crow	1	0.00
Delaware (4)	7	0.01
Iroquois (8)	13	0.02
Kiowa (1)	1	0.00
Latin American Indians (27)	38	0.07
Lumbee	3	0.01
Menominee	2	0.00
Navajo (10)	20	0.03
Osage (9)	14	0.02
Ottawa (2)	2	0.00
Paiute	1	0.00
Pima (1)	1	0.00
Potawatomi (8)	9	0.02
Puget Sound Salish (1)	1	0.00
Seminole (4)	17	0.03
Shoshone	1	0.00
Sioux (5)	12	0.02
Yakama	1	0.00
Yaqui (2)	2	0.00
All other tribes (26)	33	0.06
American Indian tribes, not spec.	40	0.07
Arab:	167	0.29
Arab/Arabic	27	0.05
Egyptian	26	0.04
Jordanian	12	0.02
Lebanese	66	0.11
Syrian	6	0.01
Other Arab	30	0.05
Armenian	21	0.04
Asian:	1,853	3.19
Bangladeshi (20)	25	0.04
Cambodian (3)	5	0.01
Chinese, ex. Taiwanese (483)	533	0.92
Filipino (70)	99	0.17
Hmong	1	0.00
Indian (219)	254	0.44
Indonesian (27)	37	0.06
Japanese (70)	112	0.19
Korean (130)	150	0.26
Laotian (87)	94	0.16
Malaysian (55)	68	0.12
Pakistani (9)	11	0.02
Sri Lankan (14)	18	0.03
Taiwanese (26)	35	0.06
Thai (14)	23	0.04
Vietnamese (153)	183	0.32
Other Asian, specified (9)	20	0.03
Other Asian, not specified (52)	185	0.32
Austrian	131	0.23
Basque	3	0.01
Belgian	30	0.05
British	294	0.51
Canadian	49	0.08
Celtic	41	0.07
Croatian	24	0.04
Czech	215	0.37
Czechoslovakian	87	0.15
Danish	326	0.56
Dutch	953	1.65
English	7,091	12.27
European	946	1.64
Finnish	72	0.12
French, except Basque	1,866	3.23
French Canadian	156	0.27
German	7,693	13.31
Greek	104	0.18
Hawaii Native/Pacific Islander:	225	0.39
Micronesian: (62)	69	0.12
Guamanian/Chamorro (6)	11	0.02
Other Micronesian (56)	58	0.10
Polynesian: (15)	55	0.09
Native Hawaiian (5)	36	0.06
Samoan (5)	14	0.02
Other Polynesian (5)	5	0.01
Other Pac. Isl., specified	1	0.00
Other Pac. Isl., not spec. (10)	100	0.17
Hispanic or Latino:	2,821	4.86
Central American:	178	0.31
Costa Rican	9	0.02
Guatemalan	16	0.03
Honduran	24	0.04
Nicaraguan	16	0.03
Panamanian	22	0.04
Salvadoran	88	0.15
Other Central American	3	0.01
Cuban	36	0.06
Dominican Republic	5	0.01
Mexican	2,012	3.47
Puerto Rican	64	0.11
South American:	150	0.26
Argentinean	7	0.01
Bolivian	66	0.11
Chilean	11	0.02
Colombian	30	0.05
Ecuadorian	5	0.01
Peruvian	6	0.01
Venezuelan	17	0.03

Notes: 1. Figures in the "Number" column do not add up to the total population due to: a) Ancestry/Race overlap — e.g. persons can report being both White and Irish, b) persons of Hispanic origin can report being any race, c) persons reporting two ancestries are counted in both categories. 2. Numbers in parentheses indicate the number of persons reporting this ancestry/race alone, not in combination with any other ancestry/race. 3. Refer to the Explanation of Data in the front of the book for more detailed information.

Other South American	8	0.01
Other Hispanic or Latino	376	0.65
Hungarian	134	0.23
Iranian	71	0.12
Irish	6,438	11.14
Israeli	15	0.03
Italian	1,290	2.23
Lithuanian	22	0.04
New Zealander	6	0.01
Northern European	113	0.20
Norwegian	551	0.95
Pennsylvania German	1	0.00
Polish	805	1.39
Portuguese	70	0.12
Romanian	41	0.07
Russian	202	0.35
Scandinavian	28	0.05
Scotch-Irish	1,408	2.44
Scottish	1,779	3.08
Serbian	48	0.08
Slavic	9	0.02
Slovak	35	0.06
Slovene	8	0.01
Swedish	747	1.29
Swiss	219	0.38
Turkish	35	0.06
Ukrainian	13	0.02
United States or American	5,597	9.69
Welsh	534	0.92
West Indian, excl. Hispanic:	61	0.11
Bahamian	13	0.02
Dutch West Indian	17	0.03
Haitian	6	0.01
Jamaican	7	0.01
West Indian	18	0.03
White:	51,429	88.60
Not Hispanic (48,769)	49,826	85.84
Hispanic (1,443)	1,603	2.76
Yugoslavian	30	0.05

Forrest City

Place Type: City
County: Saint Francis
Population: 14,774

Ancestry/Race	Number	%
Afghan	8	0.05
African American/Black:	9,079	61.45
Not Hispanic (8,934)	9,001	60.92
Hispanic (68)	78	0.53
African, sub-Saharan:	42	0.28
African	42	0.28
Am. Ind. or Alaska Nat., not spec.	29	0.20
American Indian tribes, specified:	40	0.27
Cherokee (9)	26	0.18
Choctaw	3	0.02
Latin American Indians (1)	1	0.01
Lumbee (1)	1	0.01
Pueblo (1)	1	0.01
Sioux (1)	1	0.01
Tohono O'Odham (1)	1	0.01
All other tribes (1)	6	0.04
American Indian tribes, not spec.	5	0.03
Arab:	21	0.14
Egyptian	2	0.01
Lebanese	19	0.13
Asian:	137	0.93
Cambodian (1)	1	0.01
Chinese, ex. Taiwanese (17)	20	0.14
Filipino (14)	20	0.14
Indian (30)	31	0.21
Japanese (23)	26	0.18
Korean (13)	15	0.10
Laotian (1)	1	0.01
Taiwanese (1)	1	0.01
Thai (2)	2	0.01
Vietnamese	5	0.03
Other Asian, specified (1)	1	0.01
Other Asian, not specified (4)	14	0.09
Austrian	17	0.11
British	7	0.05
Czech	3	0.02
Danish	4	0.03
Dutch	34	0.23
English	450	3.04
European	14	0.09
French, except Basque	154	1.04
French Canadian	16	0.11
German	476	3.22
Hawaii Native/Pacific Islander:	6	0.04
Polynesian:	4	0.03
Native Hawaiian	2	0.01
Samoan	2	0.01
Other Pac. Isl., not spec.	2	0.01
Hispanic or Latino:	1,221	8.26
Central American:	25	0.17
Guatemalan	3	0.02
Honduran	7	0.05
Nicaraguan	1	0.01
Panamanian	9	0.06
Salvadoran	5	0.03
Cuban	21	0.14
Dominican Republic	12	0.08
Mexican	819	5.54
Puerto Rican	29	0.20
South American:	74	0.50
Colombian	66	0.45
Ecuadorian	6	0.04
Venezuelan	2	0.01
Other Hispanic or Latino	241	1.63
Iranian	6	0.04
Irish	437	2.95
Italian	53	0.36
Northern European	13	0.09
Norwegian	20	0.14
Polish	13	0.09
Romanian	7	0.05
Russian	7	0.05
Scotch-Irish	38	0.26
Scottish	101	0.68
Swedish	28	0.19
Ukrainian	8	0.05
United States or American	637	4.30
Welsh	13	0.09
White:	5,545	37.53
Not Hispanic (4,370)	4,445	30.09
Hispanic (877)	1,100	7.45

Fort Smith

Place Type: City
County: Sebastian
Population: 80,268

Ancestry/Race	Number	%
Acadian/Cajun	8	0.01
African American/Black:	7,548	9.40
Not Hispanic (6,874)	7,433	9.26
Hispanic (69)	115	0.14
African, sub-Saharan:	145	0.18
African	145	0.18
Alaska Native tribes, specified:	6	0.01
Alaska Athabascan (1)	1	0.00
Aleut (1)	1	0.00
Tlingit-Haida (1)	2	0.00
All other tribes (2)	2	0.00
Am. Ind. or Alaska Nat., not spec.	482	0.60
American Indian tribes, specified:	2,074	2.58
Apache (4)	29	0.04
Blackfeet (4)	26	0.03
Cherokee (605)	1,242	1.55
Cheyenne (11)	13	0.02
Chickasaw (13)	27	0.03
Chippewa (6)	8	0.01
Choctaw (264)	455	0.57
Comanche (1)	5	0.01
Cree	2	0.00
Creek (32)	59	0.07
Delaware (1)	3	0.00
Iroquois (4)	14	0.02
Kiowa	2	0.00
Latin American Indians (21)	32	0.04
Lumbee (3)	3	0.00
Navajo (3)	3	0.00
Osage (5)	13	0.02
Ottawa	2	0.00
Potawatomi (8)	10	0.01
Pueblo (4)	8	0.01
Seminole (10)	13	0.02
Shoshone	1	0.00
Sioux (5)	13	0.02
Yaqui (1)	1	0.00
All other tribes (58)	90	0.11
American Indian tribes, not spec.	69	0.09
Arab:	227	0.28
Arab/Arabic	48	0.06
Egyptian	51	0.06
Lebanese	66	0.08
Palestinian	20	0.02
Syrian	42	0.05
Armenian	5	0.01
Asian:	4,209	5.24
Bangladeshi (1)	1	0.00
Cambodian (1)	3	0.00
Chinese, ex. Taiwanese (148)	202	0.25
Filipino (81)	143	0.18
Indian (107)	168	0.21
Indonesian (7)	8	0.01
Japanese (36)	76	0.09
Korean (49)	71	0.09
Laotian (1,383)	1,557	1.94
Pakistani (4)	6	0.01
Taiwanese (1)	1	0.00
Thai (51)	69	0.09
Vietnamese (1,641)	1,758	2.19
Other Asian, specified (1)	8	0.01
Other Asian, not specified (82)	138	0.17
Australian	27	0.03
Austrian	65	0.08
Belgian	57	0.07
British	139	0.17
Canadian	107	0.13
Croatian	10	0.01
Czech	171	0.21
Czechoslovakian	54	0.07
Danish	123	0.15
Dutch	1,225	1.52
English	6,591	8.20
European	474	0.59
Finnish	11	0.01
French, except Basque	1,784	2.22
French Canadian	168	0.21
German	9,245	11.50
Greek	204	0.25
Hawaii Native/Pacific Islander:	105	0.13
Melanesian:	2	0.00
Fijian	2	0.00
Micronesian: (24)	29	0.04
Guamanian/Chamorro (22)	27	0.03
Other Micronesian (2)	2	0.00
Polynesian: (4)	18	0.02
Native Hawaiian (3)	16	0.02
Samoan (1)	1	0.00
Other Polynesian	1	0.00
Other Pac. Isl., specified	7	0.01
Other Pac. Isl., not spec. (15)	49	0.06
Hispanic or Latino:	7,048	8.78
Central American:	670	0.83
Costa Rican	3	0.00
Guatemalan	103	0.13
Honduran	53	0.07
Nicaraguan	1	0.00
Panamanian	2	0.00
Salvadoran	491	0.61
Other Central American	17	0.02
Cuban	78	0.10
Dominican Republic	4	0.00
Mexican	5,068	6.31
Puerto Rican	144	0.18

Notes: 1. Figures in the "Number" column do not add up to the total population due to: a) Ancestry/Race overlap — e.g. persons can report being both White and Irish, b) persons of Hispanic origin can report being any race, c) persons reporting two ancestries are counted in both categories. 2. Numbers in parentheses indicate the number of persons reporting this ancestry/race alone, not in combination with any other ancestry/race. 3. Refer to the Explanation of Data in the front of the book for more detailed information.

South American:	49	0.06
Argentinean	3	0.00
Bolivian	2	0.00
Colombian	22	0.03
Ecuadorian	4	0.00
Peruvian	10	0.01
Uruguayan	2	0.00
Venezuelan	2	0.00
Other South American	4	0.00
Other Hispanic or Latino	1,035	1.29
Hungarian	87	0.11
Icelander	10	0.01
Iranian	6	0.01
Irish	9,074	11.28
Italian	1,415	1.76
Latvian	10	0.01
Lithuanian	11	0.01
New Zealander	13	0.02
Northern European	32	0.04
Norwegian	380	0.47
Pennsylvania German	43	0.05
Polish	526	0.65
Portuguese	55	0.07
Romanian	42	0.05
Russian	154	0.19
Scandinavian	62	0.08
Scotch-Irish	1,539	1.91
Scottish	1,033	1.28
Serbian	25	0.03
Slavic	22	0.03
Slovak	24	0.03
Slovene	9	0.01
Swedish	367	0.46
Swiss	156	0.19
Turkish	9	0.01
Ukrainian	43	0.05
United States or American	9,432	11.73
Welsh	317	0.39
West Indian, excl. Hispanic:	272	0.34
Dutch West Indian	216	0.27
Haitian	29	0.04
Jamaican	7	0.01
Trinidadian and Tobagonian	20	0.02
White:	63,868	79.57
Not Hispanic (59,436)	61,085	76.10
Hispanic (2,362)	2,783	3.47
Yugoslavian	27	0.03

Harrison

Place Type: City
County: Boone
Population: 12,152

Ancestry/Race	Number	%
African American/Black:	19	0.16
Not Hispanic (14)	19	0.16
Am. Ind. or Alaska Nat., not spec.	21	0.17
American Indian tribes, specified:	117	0.96
Apache (1)	4	0.03
Blackfeet	5	0.04
Cherokee (30)	59	0.49
Chickasaw (6)	6	0.05
Choctaw (3)	4	0.03
Comanche	3	0.02
Creek (3)	3	0.02
Delaware (1)	5	0.04
Iroquois (1)	1	0.01
Latin American Indians (4)	4	0.03
Potawatomi (1)	2	0.02
Pueblo (1)	2	0.02
Sioux (12)	12	0.10
Ute	1	0.01
All other tribes (4)	6	0.05
American Indian tribes, not spec.	13	0.11
Arab:	34	0.28
Lebanese	18	0.15
Syrian	16	0.13
Asian:	81	0.67
Chinese, ex. Taiwanese (9)	14	0.12
Filipino (26)	34	0.28
Indian (11)	12	0.10
Japanese (4)	4	0.03
Korean (8)	11	0.09
Malaysian (2)	2	0.02
Vietnamese (1)	1	0.01
Other Asian, not specified (1)	3	0.02
Austrian	14	0.11
Brazilian	22	0.18
British	85	0.69
Canadian	30	0.24
Czech	47	0.38
Danish	63	0.51
Dutch	244	1.99
English	1,460	11.91
European	88	0.72
French, except Basque	269	2.19
French Canadian	79	0.64
German	1,529	12.47
Greek	9	0.07
Hawaii Native/Pacific Islander:	9	0.07
Micronesian:	1	0.01
Guamanian/Chamorro	1	0.01
Polynesian: (1)	7	0.06
Native Hawaiian (1)	7	0.06
Other Pac. Isl., not spec. (1)	1	0.01
Hispanic or Latino:	186	1.53
Central American:	6	0.05
Panamanian	2	0.02
Salvadoran	4	0.03
Cuban	4	0.03
Mexican	115	0.95
Puerto Rican	6	0.05
South American:	6	0.05
Argentinean	1	0.01
Colombian	3	0.02
Paraguayan	2	0.02
Other Hispanic or Latino	49	0.40
Hungarian	19	0.15
Irish	1,287	10.50
Italian	198	1.62
Latvian	5	0.04
Norwegian	78	0.64
Polish	67	0.55
Russian	14	0.11
Scandinavian	13	0.11
Scotch-Irish	315	2.57
Scottish	113	0.92
Swedish	74	0.60
Swiss	38	0.31
United States or American	2,729	22.26
Welsh	52	0.42
White:	11,904	97.96
Not Hispanic (11,714)	11,798	97.09
Hispanic (102)	106	0.87

Hope

Place Type: City
County: Hempstead
Population: 10,616

Ancestry/Race	Number	%
African American/Black:	4,668	43.97
Not Hispanic (4,555)	4,624	43.56
Hispanic (28)	44	0.41
African, sub-Saharan:	225	2.14
African	225	2.14
Alaska Native tribes, specified:	2	0.02
Aleut (2)	2	0.02
Am. Ind. or Alaska Nat., not spec.	47	0.44
American Indian tribes, specified:	48	0.45
Blackfeet (1)	5	0.05
Cherokee (8)	26	0.24
Choctaw	3	0.03
Iroquois	1	0.01
Latin American Indians (7)	7	0.07
Pueblo (1)	1	0.01
Yuman (4)	4	0.04
All other tribes	1	0.01
American Indian tribes, not spec.	1	0.01
Asian:	50	0.47
Chinese, ex. Taiwanese (10)	10	0.09
Filipino (6)	10	0.09
Indian (6)	7	0.07
Japanese (3)	6	0.06
Thai (1)	1	0.01
Vietnamese (5)	6	0.06
Other Asian, not specified (1)	10	0.09
Australian	7	0.07
British	33	0.31
Canadian	20	0.19
Czechoslovakian	6	0.06
Dutch	77	0.73
English	503	4.78
European	27	0.26
French, except Basque	131	1.25
German	314	2.99
Hawaii Native/Pacific Islander:	6	0.06
Micronesian: (1)	1	0.01
Guamanian/Chamorro (1)	1	0.01
Polynesian: (2)	2	0.02
Samoan (2)	2	0.02
Other Pac. Isl., not spec.	3	0.03
Hispanic or Latino:	1,431	13.48
Central American:	10	0.09
Costa Rican	3	0.03
Honduran	5	0.05
Salvadoran	1	0.01
Other Central American	1	0.01
Cuban	5	0.05
Mexican	1,282	12.08
Puerto Rican	16	0.15
South American:	5	0.05
Peruvian	5	0.05
Other Hispanic or Latino	113	1.06
Irish	483	4.59
Italian	55	0.52
Polish	44	0.42
Scotch-Irish	66	0.63
Scottish	49	0.47
Swedish	25	0.24
Ukrainian	39	0.37
United States or American	1,139	10.83
Welsh	37	0.35
White:	5,213	49.11
Not Hispanic (4,433)	4,524	42.61
Hispanic (632)	689	6.49

Hot Springs

Place Type: City
County: Garland
Population: 35,750

Ancestry/Race	Number	%
Acadian/Cajun	36	0.10
African American/Black:	6,273	17.55
Not Hispanic (5,990)	6,216	17.39
Hispanic (40)	57	0.16
African, sub-Saharan:	322	0.90
African	307	0.86
Nigerian	15	0.04
Alaska Native tribes, specified:	4	0.01
Eskimo (1)	4	0.01
Alaska Native tribes, not specified	4	0.01
Am. Ind. or Alaska Nat., not spec.	181	0.51
Alsatian	5	0.01
American Indian tribes, specified:	331	0.93
Apache (8)	14	0.04
Blackfeet (1)	16	0.04
Cherokee (63)	190	0.53
Cheyenne (5)	5	0.01
Chickasaw (1)	5	0.01
Chippewa (2)	2	0.01
Choctaw (10)	25	0.07
Comanche (3)	4	0.01
Cree	1	0.00
Creek (3)	9	0.03
Iroquois (4)	9	0.03

Notes: 1. Figures in the "Number" column do not add up to the total population due to: a) Ancestry/Race overlap — e.g. persons can report being both White and Irish, b) persons of Hispanic origin can report being any race, c) persons reporting two ancestries are counted in both categories. 2. Numbers in parentheses indicate the number of persons reporting this ancestry/race alone, not in combination with any other ancestry/race. 3. Refer to the Explanation of Data in the front of the book for more detailed information.

Latin American Indians (5)	8	0.02
Lumbee	1	0.00
Navajo (8)	11	0.03
Osage	4	0.01
Ottawa	1	0.00
Potawatomi (1)	2	0.01
Seminole (3)	3	0.01
Sioux (2)	3	0.01
All other tribes (8)	18	0.05
American Indian tribes, not spec.	23	0.06
Arab:	22	0.06
Lebanese	6	0.02
Syrian	16	0.04
Armenian	6	0.02
Asian:	349	0.98
Chinese, ex. Taiwanese (54)	60	0.17
Filipino (48)	65	0.18
Indian (55)	64	0.18
Japanese (16)	28	0.08
Korean (13)	17	0.05
Sri Lankan (2)	2	0.01
Taiwanese (4)	4	0.01
Thai (3)	3	0.01
Vietnamese (85)	86	0.24
Other Asian, specified	2	0.01
Other Asian, not specified (3)	18	0.05
Australian	8	0.02
Austrian	40	0.11
British	87	0.24
Bulgarian	6	0.02
Canadian	40	0.11
Celtic	5	0.01
Croatian	11	0.03
Czech	137	0.38
Czechoslovakian	23	0.06
Danish	34	0.10
Dutch	685	1.92
English	3,852	10.82
European	250	0.70
Finnish	17	0.05
French, except Basque	886	2.49
French Canadian	120	0.34
German	3,716	10.43
Greek	66	0.19
Hawaii Native/Pacific Islander:	36	0.10
Micronesian: (3)	7	0.02
Guamanian/Chamorro (3)	7	0.02
Polynesian: (14)	23	0.06
Native Hawaiian (6)	11	0.03
Samoan (8)	12	0.03
Other Pac. Isl., specified	2	0.01
Other Pac. Isl., not spec.	4	0.01
Hispanic or Latino:	1,358	3.80
Central American:	84	0.23
Costa Rican	4	0.01
Guatemalan	4	0.01
Honduran	14	0.04
Nicaraguan	1	0.00
Panamanian	2	0.01
Salvadoran	56	0.16
Other Central American	3	0.01
Cuban	37	0.10
Dominican Republic	2	0.01
Mexican	1,009	2.82
Puerto Rican	23	0.06
South American:	8	0.02
Bolivian	1	0.00
Colombian	2	0.01
Ecuadorian	1	0.00
Peruvian	1	0.00
Venezuelan	2	0.01
Other South American	1	0.00
Other Hispanic or Latino	195	0.55
Hungarian	49	0.14
Iranian	29	0.08
Irish	3,976	11.16
Italian	383	1.08
Latvian	17	0.05
Lithuanian	97	0.27
Luxemburger	5	0.01
Macedonian	4	0.01
Norwegian	243	0.68
Pennsylvania German	5	0.01
Polish	325	0.91
Portuguese	5	0.01
Romanian	68	0.19
Russian	51	0.14
Scandinavian	25	0.07
Scotch-Irish	797	2.24
Scottish	668	1.88
Serbian	93	0.26
Slavic	8	0.02
Slovak	28	0.08
Slovene	6	0.02
Swedish	125	0.35
Swiss	28	0.08
Ukrainian	39	0.11
United States or American	4,169	11.71
Welsh	217	0.61
West Indian, excl. Hispanic:	45	0.13
Dutch West Indian	20	0.06
Jamaican	25	0.07
White:	28,794	80.54
Not Hispanic (27,347)	27,859	77.93
Hispanic (847)	935	2.62
Yugoslavian	90	0.25

Jacksonville

Place Type: City
County: Pulaski
Population: 29,916

Ancestry/Race	Number	%
Acadian/Cajun	10	0.03
African American/Black:	7,738	25.87
Not Hispanic (7,357)	7,664	25.62
Hispanic (49)	74	0.25
African, sub-Saharan:	111	0.37
African	111	0.37
Alaska Native tribes, specified:	2	0.01
Eskimo (1)	1	0.00
Tlingit-Haida (1)	1	0.00
Am. Ind. or Alaska Nat., not spec.	86	0.29
American Indian tribes, specified:	222	0.74
Apache (7)	7	0.02
Blackfeet (4)	12	0.04
Cherokee (30)	104	0.35
Chickasaw (2)	4	0.01
Chippewa (3)	8	0.03
Choctaw (16)	26	0.09
Creek (3)	4	0.01
Delaware (1)	1	0.00
Iroquois (1)	2	0.01
Latin American Indians (1)	1	0.00
Lumbee (7)	7	0.02
Navajo (5)	9	0.03
Pima (1)	1	0.00
Pueblo (8)	11	0.04
Seminole (1)	1	0.00
Sioux (4)	6	0.02
Yakama	1	0.00
All other tribes (7)	17	0.06
American Indian tribes, not spec.	34	0.11
Arab:	20	0.07
Lebanese	6	0.02
Syrian	14	0.05
Asian:	854	2.85
Chinese, ex. Taiwanese (27)	48	0.16
Filipino (258)	366	1.22
Indian (40)	46	0.15
Japanese (58)	105	0.35
Korean (102)	138	0.46
Laotian	1	0.00
Malaysian (1)	2	0.01
Pakistani (1)	2	0.01
Taiwanese (4)	6	0.02
Thai (54)	82	0.27
Vietnamese (11)	20	0.07
Other Asian, specified	4	0.01
Other Asian, not specified (25)	34	0.11
Austrian	30	0.10
British	214	0.72
Canadian	13	0.04
Celtic	22	0.07
Czech	33	0.11
Czechoslovakian	13	0.04
Danish	15	0.05
Dutch	432	1.45
Eastern European	8	0.03
English	2,373	7.97
European	225	0.76
Finnish	33	0.11
French, except Basque	798	2.68
French Canadian	185	0.62
German	3,728	12.52
German Russian	17	0.06
Greek	38	0.13
Guyanese	18	0.06
Hawaii Native/Pacific Islander:	73	0.24
Micronesian: (17)	26	0.09
Guamanian/Chamorro (17)	23	0.08
Other Micronesian	3	0.01
Polynesian: (19)	32	0.11
Native Hawaiian (14)	21	0.07
Samoan (5)	11	0.04
Other Pac. Isl., specified	4	0.01
Other Pac. Isl., not spec. (2)	11	0.04
Hispanic or Latino:	1,012	3.38
Central American:	38	0.13
Costa Rican	4	0.01
Guatemalan	4	0.01
Honduran	4	0.01
Nicaraguan	4	0.01
Panamanian	14	0.05
Salvadoran	8	0.03
Cuban	29	0.10
Dominican Republic	3	0.01
Mexican	488	1.63
Puerto Rican	140	0.47
South American:	18	0.06
Bolivian	1	0.00
Chilean	2	0.01
Colombian	4	0.01
Ecuadorian	4	0.01
Paraguayan	1	0.00
Peruvian	6	0.02
Other Hispanic or Latino	296	0.99
Hungarian	20	0.07
Iranian	8	0.03
Irish	3,060	10.27
Italian	727	2.44
Lithuanian	9	0.03
Norwegian	163	0.55
Polish	436	1.46
Portuguese	18	0.06
Romanian	7	0.02
Russian	21	0.07
Scandinavian	14	0.05
Scotch-Irish	543	1.82
Scottish	414	1.39
Serbian	5	0.02
Slavic	7	0.02
Slovak	5	0.02
Slovene	7	0.02
Swedish	135	0.45
Swiss	46	0.15
Ukrainian	6	0.02
United States or American	3,371	11.32
Welsh	98	0.33
West Indian, excl. Hispanic:	84	0.28
Dutch West Indian	15	0.05
Jamaican	64	0.21
West Indian	5	0.02
White:	21,255	71.05
Not Hispanic (20,104)	20,639	68.99
Hispanic (513)	616	2.06
Yugoslavian	10	0.03

Notes: 1. Figures in the "Number" column do not add up to the total population due to: a) Ancestry/Race overlap — e.g. persons can report being both White and Irish, b) persons of Hispanic origin can report being any race, c) persons reporting two ancestries are counted in both categories. 2. Numbers in parentheses indicate the number of persons reporting this ancestry/race alone, not in combination with any other ancestry/race. 3. Refer to the Explanation of Data in the front of the book for more detailed information.

Jonesboro

Place Type: City
County: Craighead
Population: 55,515

Ancestry/Race	Number	%
Acadian/Cajun	24	0.04
African American/Black:	6,434	11.59
Not Hispanic (6,209)	6,380	11.49
Hispanic (50)	54	0.10
African, sub-Saharan:	205	0.37
African	176	0.32
Sierra Leonean	29	0.05
Alaska Native tribes, not specified	1	0.00
Am. Ind. or Alaska Nat., not spec.	149	0.27
Alsatian	9	0.02
American Indian tribes, specified:	270	0.49
Apache (4)	7	0.01
Blackfeet (4)	10	0.02
Cherokee (82)	180	0.32
Chickasaw (1)	3	0.01
Chippewa (2)	3	0.01
Choctaw (11)	19	0.03
Comanche (1)	3	0.01
Creek (1)	1	0.00
Delaware (4)	5	0.01
Houma (1)	1	0.00
Kiowa (2)	3	0.01
Latin American Indians (4)	5	0.01
Menominee	1	0.00
Navajo (4)	5	0.01
Osage (1)	4	0.01
Pima (1)	1	0.00
Potawatomi (1)	1	0.00
Seminole	1	0.00
Sioux (3)	6	0.01
All other tribes (6)	11	0.02
American Indian tribes, not spec.	13	0.02
Arab:	100	0.18
Arab/Arabic	57	0.10
Lebanese	9	0.02
Syrian	7	0.01
Other Arab	27	0.05
Asian:	613	1.10
Bangladeshi (1)	1	0.00
Chinese, ex. Taiwanese (113)	137	0.25
Filipino (53)	84	0.15
Hmong (1)	1	0.00
Indian (76)	92	0.17
Indonesian (2)	3	0.01
Japanese (34)	54	0.10
Korean (62)	75	0.14
Laotian (3)	3	0.01
Malaysian (5)	6	0.01
Pakistani (25)	30	0.05
Sri Lankan (2)	2	0.00
Taiwanese (4)	4	0.01
Thai (19)	27	0.05
Vietnamese (49)	58	0.10
Other Asian, specified	8	0.01
Other Asian, not specified (8)	28	0.05
Austrian	15	0.03
Belgian	9	0.02
British	157	0.28
Bulgarian	7	0.01
Canadian	108	0.19
Celtic	21	0.04
Croatian	21	0.04
Czech	97	0.17
Czechoslovakian	23	0.04
Danish	40	0.07
Dutch	1,009	1.81
English	4,149	7.46
European	557	1.00
French, except Basque	1,028	1.85
French Canadian	104	0.19
German	5,171	9.30
German Russian	9	0.02
Greek	66	0.12
Hawaii Native/Pacific Islander:	46	0.08
Micronesian: (7)	7	0.01
Guamanian/Chamorro (2)	2	0.00
Other Micronesian (5)	5	0.01
Polynesian: (6)	22	0.04
Native Hawaiian (5)	15	0.03
Samoan (1)	5	0.01
Other Polynesian	2	0.00
Other Pac. Isl., specified	3	0.01
Other Pac. Isl., not spec. (3)	14	0.03
Hispanic or Latino:	1,297	2.34
Central American:	24	0.04
Costa Rican	2	0.00
Guatemalan	4	0.01
Honduran	4	0.01
Nicaraguan	1	0.00
Panamanian	6	0.01
Salvadoran	7	0.01
Cuban	20	0.04
Dominican Republic	1	0.00
Mexican	976	1.76
Puerto Rican	37	0.07
South American:	38	0.07
Argentinean	2	0.00
Colombian	23	0.04
Ecuadorian	4	0.01
Peruvian	6	0.01
Venezuelan	3	0.01
Other Hispanic or Latino	201	0.36
Hungarian	72	0.13
Iranian	53	0.10
Irish	5,691	10.23
Italian	823	1.48
Lithuanian	14	0.03
New Zealander	15	0.03
Northern European	18	0.03
Norwegian	112	0.20
Pennsylvania German	12	0.02
Polish	378	0.68
Portuguese	15	0.03
Romanian	17	0.03
Russian	93	0.17
Scandinavian	26	0.05
Scotch-Irish	1,180	2.12
Scottish	702	1.26
Slovak	18	0.03
Swedish	192	0.35
Swiss	39	0.07
Turkish	33	0.06
Ukrainian	29	0.05
United States or American	10,538	18.95
Welsh	273	0.49
West Indian, excl. Hispanic:	26	0.05
Dutch West Indian	9	0.02
Jamaican	9	0.02
West Indian	8	0.01
White:	47,957	86.39
Not Hispanic (46,764)	47,265	85.14
Hispanic (630)	692	1.25
Yugoslavian	69	0.12

Little Rock

Place Type: City
County: Pulaski
Population: 183,133

Ancestry/Race	Number	%
Acadian/Cajun	14	0.01
Afghan	7	0.00
African American/Black:	75,026	40.97
Not Hispanic (73,679)	74,602	40.74
Hispanic (324)	424	0.23
African, sub-Saharan:	3,144	1.71
African	2,660	1.45
Ghanian	73	0.04
Liberian	9	0.00
Nigerian	300	0.16
South African	35	0.02
Ugandan	10	0.01
Other sub-Saharan African	57	0.03
Alaska Native tribes, specified:	7	0.00
Alaska Athabascan (3)	3	0.00
Eskimo (4)	4	0.00
Alaska Native tribes, not specified	1	0.00
Am. Ind. or Alaska Nat., not spec.	454	0.25
Alsatian	7	0.00
American Indian tribes, specified:	793	0.43
Apache (7)	22	0.01
Blackfeet (4)	24	0.01
Cherokee (129)	432	0.24
Cheyenne	1	0.00
Chickasaw (19)	24	0.01
Chippewa (6)	7	0.00
Choctaw (50)	105	0.06
Comanche (3)	6	0.00
Creek (11)	17	0.01
Delaware (8)	12	0.01
Iroquois (3)	3	0.00
Kiowa (2)	2	0.00
Latin American Indians (15)	37	0.02
Lumbee (1)	2	0.00
Navajo (5)	10	0.01
Osage (1)	4	0.00
Paiute (1)	1	0.00
Potawatomi (4)	7	0.00
Pueblo (4)	11	0.01
Seminole (1)	2	0.00
Sioux (4)	16	0.01
Yuman (2)	3	0.00
All other tribes (27)	45	0.02
American Indian tribes, not spec.	72	0.04
Arab:	431	0.23
Arab/Arabic	95	0.05
Egyptian	39	0.02
Iraqi	32	0.02
Jordanian	11	0.01
Lebanese	172	0.09
Syrian	65	0.04
Other Arab	17	0.01
Armenian	35	0.02
Asian:	3,575	1.95
Bangladeshi (9)	12	0.01
Cambodian (2)	2	0.00
Chinese, ex. Taiwanese (739)	832	0.45
Filipino (377)	464	0.25
Hmong (1)	1	0.00
Indian (906)	986	0.54
Indonesian (19)	23	0.01
Japanese (130)	210	0.11
Korean (171)	226	0.12
Laotian (61)	69	0.04
Malaysian (11)	14	0.01
Pakistani (65)	82	0.04
Sri Lankan (16)	20	0.01
Taiwanese (27)	33	0.02
Thai (24)	36	0.02
Vietnamese (328)	355	0.19
Other Asian, specified (8)	25	0.01
Other Asian, not specified (97)	185	0.10
Assyrian/Chaldean/Syriac	68	0.04
Australian	35	0.02
Austrian	168	0.09
Basque	7	0.00
Belgian	35	0.02
British	895	0.49
Canadian	73	0.04
Celtic	51	0.03
Croatian	35	0.02
Czech	305	0.17
Czechoslovakian	246	0.13
Danish	294	0.16
Dutch	1,394	0.76
Eastern European	45	0.02
English	16,116	8.78
European	1,808	0.98
Finnish	68	0.04
French, except Basque	3,735	2.03
French Canadian	300	0.16
German	15,761	8.59

Notes: 1. Figures in the "Number" column do not add up to the total population due to: a) Ancestry/Race overlap — e.g. persons can report being both White and Irish, b) persons of Hispanic origin can report being any race, c) persons reporting two ancestries are counted in both categories. 2. Numbers in parentheses indicate the number of persons reporting this ancestry/race alone, not in combination with any other ancestry/race. 3. Refer to the Explanation of Data in the front of the book for more detailed information.

Greek	336	0.18
Guyanese	22	0.01
Hawaii Native/Pacific Islander:	154	0.08
Micronesian: (17)	22	0.01
Guamanian/Chamorro (16)	19	0.01
Other Micronesian (1)	3	0.00
Polynesian: (35)	70	0.04
Native Hawaiian (26)	55	0.03
Samoan (9)	14	0.01
Other Polynesian	1	0.00
Other Pac. Isl., specified	15	0.01
Other Pac. Isl., not spec. (12)	47	0.03
Hispanic or Latino:	4,889	2.67
Central American:	231	0.13
Costa Rican	1	0.00
Guatemalan	67	0.04
Honduran	34	0.02
Nicaraguan	27	0.01
Panamanian	27	0.01
Salvadoran	60	0.03
Other Central American	15	0.01
Cuban	93	0.05
Mexican	3,373	1.84
Puerto Rican	226	0.12
South American:	128	0.07
Argentinean	22	0.01
Bolivian	4	0.00
Chilean	13	0.01
Colombian	28	0.02
Ecuadorian	15	0.01
Paraguayan	1	0.00
Peruvian	14	0.01
Uruguayan	1	0.00
Venezuelan	21	0.01
Other South American	9	0.00
Other Hispanic or Latino	838	0.46
Hungarian	259	0.14
Icelander	5	0.00
Iranian	98	0.05
Irish	13,364	7.28
Israeli	36	0.02
Italian	2,732	1.49
Latvian	17	0.01
Lithuanian	82	0.04
Luxemburger	8	0.00
New Zealander	133	0.07
Northern European	100	0.05
Norwegian	1,072	0.58
Pennsylvania German	32	0.02
Polish	1,913	1.04
Portuguese	85	0.05
Romanian	89	0.05
Russian	605	0.33
Scandinavian	154	0.08
Scotch-Irish	4,680	2.55
Scottish	3,529	1.92
Serbian	21	0.01
Slavic	12	0.01
Slovak	178	0.10
Slovene	41	0.02
Swedish	1,069	0.58
Swiss	429	0.23
Turkish	81	0.04
Ukrainian	166	0.09
United States or American	14,281	7.78
Welsh	806	0.44
West Indian, excl. Hispanic:	199	0.11
Bahamian	28	0.02
Barbadian	13	0.01
British West Indian	4	0.00
Dutch West Indian	9	0.00
Haitian	63	0.03
Jamaican	68	0.04
Trinidadian and Tobagonian	8	0.00
West Indian	6	0.00
White:	102,705	56.08
Not Hispanic (98,904)	100,532	54.90
Hispanic (1,944)	2,173	1.19
Yugoslavian	45	0.02

Magnolia

Place Type: City
County: Columbia
Population: 10,858

Ancestry/Race	Number	%
African American/Black:	4,331	39.89
Not Hispanic (4,267)	4,321	39.80
Hispanic (9)	10	0.09
African, sub-Saharan:	68	0.63
African	44	0.41
Kenyan	17	0.16
Other sub-Saharan African	7	0.06
Am. Ind. or Alaska Nat., not spec.	32	0.29
Albanian	4	0.04
American Indian tribes, specified:	52	0.48
Apache (1)	5	0.05
Cherokee (6)	20	0.18
Chickasaw	3	0.03
Choctaw (5)	11	0.10
Comanche (3)	3	0.03
Creek	1	0.01
Iroquois (1)	2	0.02
Potawatomi (1)	4	0.04
Sioux	1	0.01
All other tribes (2)	2	0.02
Armenian	4	0.04
Asian:	87	0.80
Bangladeshi	1	0.01
Chinese, ex. Taiwanese (11)	11	0.10
Filipino (3)	6	0.06
Indian (27)	35	0.32
Indonesian (1)	1	0.01
Japanese (4)	4	0.04
Korean (2)	4	0.04
Malaysian (4)	4	0.04
Sri Lankan (3)	3	0.03
Thai (4)	5	0.05
Vietnamese (1)	1	0.01
Other Asian, specified (4)	4	0.04
Other Asian, not specified (6)	8	0.07
Austrian	15	0.14
Czechoslovakian	19	0.18
Danish	30	0.28
Dutch	100	0.92
English	787	7.27
European	98	0.91
French, except Basque	169	1.56
French Canadian	12	0.11
German	474	4.38
Hawaii Native/Pacific Islander:	5	0.05
Polynesian: (2)	4	0.04
Native Hawaiian (1)	3	0.03
Samoan (1)	1	0.01
Other Pac. Isl., not spec.	1	0.01
Hispanic or Latino:	116	1.07
Central American:	4	0.04
Guatemalan	3	0.03
Honduran	1	0.01
Mexican	78	0.72
Puerto Rican	9	0.08
South American:	3	0.03
Peruvian	2	0.02
Venezuelan	1	0.01
Other Hispanic or Latino	22	0.20
Iranian	5	0.05
Irish	871	8.05
Italian	68	0.63
Norwegian	33	0.31
Pennsylvania German	6	0.06
Polish	20	0.18
Portuguese	7	0.06
Scotch-Irish	220	2.03
Scottish	88	0.81
Slavic	10	0.09
Swedish	19	0.18
Swiss	16	0.15
United States or American	1,533	14.17
Welsh	22	0.20
White:	6,390	58.85
Not Hispanic (6,265)	6,322	58.22
Hispanic (59)	68	0.63

Maumelle

Place Type: City
County: Pulaski
Population: 10,557

Ancestry/Race	Number	%
African American/Black:	547	5.18
Not Hispanic (515)	543	5.14
Hispanic (1)	4	0.04
African, sub-Saharan:	108	1.03
African	108	1.03
Alaska Native tribes, specified:	1	0.01
Eskimo (1)	1	0.01
Am. Ind. or Alaska Nat., not spec.	24	0.23
American Indian tribes, specified:	56	0.53
Apache	1	0.01
Blackfeet (1)	1	0.01
Cherokee (26)	37	0.35
Chickasaw	1	0.01
Choctaw (3)	5	0.05
Comanche	1	0.01
Creek (2)	5	0.05
Iroquois (1)	1	0.01
Osage	2	0.02
Potawatomi	1	0.01
All other tribes (1)	1	0.01
American Indian tribes, not spec.	1	0.01
Arab:	8	0.08
Lebanese	8	0.08
Asian:	127	1.20
Chinese, ex. Taiwanese (8)	15	0.14
Filipino (22)	29	0.27
Indian (22)	24	0.23
Japanese (4)	11	0.10
Korean (10)	20	0.19
Laotian	5	0.05
Pakistani (1)	1	0.01
Sri Lankan (2)	2	0.02
Thai (3)	7	0.07
Vietnamese (9)	9	0.09
Other Asian, not specified	4	0.04
Belgian	11	0.10
British	82	0.78
Canadian	23	0.22
Czech	39	0.37
Czechoslovakian	44	0.42
Danish	33	0.31
Dutch	100	0.95
English	1,174	11.17
European	146	1.39
Finnish	19	0.18
French, except Basque	492	4.68
French Canadian	36	0.34
German	1,898	18.06
Greek	7	0.07
Hawaii Native/Pacific Islander:	10	0.09
Micronesian: (1)	3	0.03
Guamanian/Chamorro (1)	3	0.03
Polynesian:	6	0.06
Native Hawaiian	6	0.06
Other Pac. Isl., not spec.	1	0.01
Hispanic or Latino:	187	1.77
Central American:	13	0.12
Costa Rican	1	0.01
Honduran	4	0.04
Nicaraguan	2	0.02
Panamanian	1	0.01
Salvadoran	3	0.03
Other Central American	2	0.02
Cuban	5	0.05
Mexican	87	0.82
Puerto Rican	30	0.28
South American:	10	0.09
Argentinean	7	0.07
Venezuelan	3	0.03

Notes: 1. Figures in the "Number" column do not add up to the total population due to: a) Ancestry/Race overlap — e.g. persons can report being both White and Irish, b) persons of Hispanic origin can report being any race, c) persons reporting two ancestries are counted in both categories. 2. Numbers in parentheses indicate the number of persons reporting this ancestry/race alone, not in combination with any other ancestry/race. 3. Refer to the Explanation of Data in the front of the book for more detailed information.

Ancestry/Race	Number	%
Other Hispanic or Latino	42	0.40
Hungarian	7	0.07
Iranian	6	0.06
Irish	1,572	14.96
Italian	460	4.38
Lithuanian	41	0.39
Norwegian	75	0.71
Polish	169	1.61
Romanian	9	0.09
Russian	23	0.22
Scandinavian	32	0.30
Scotch-Irish	447	4.25
Scottish	363	3.45
Slavic	6	0.06
Slovak	7	0.07
Swedish	131	1.25
Swiss	22	0.21
Turkish	8	0.08
United States or American	1,475	14.04
Welsh	77	0.73
West Indian, excl. Hispanic:	37	0.35
Jamaican	12	0.11
West Indian	25	0.24
White:	9,840	93.21
Not Hispanic (9,635)	9,698	91.86
Hispanic (125)	142	1.35

Mountain Home

Place Type: City
County: Baxter
Population: 11,012

Ancestry/Race	Number	%
African American/Black:	26	0.24
Not Hispanic (20)	26	0.24
African, sub-Saharan:	13	0.12
African	13	0.12
Am. Ind. or Alaska Nat., not spec.	19	0.17
American Indian tribes, specified:	102	0.93
Apache	1	0.01
Blackfeet	2	0.02
Cherokee (17)	55	0.50
Cheyenne (2)	2	0.02
Choctaw (6)	17	0.15
Comanche	1	0.01
Creek (3)	3	0.03
Iroquois (3)	5	0.05
Osage (1)	2	0.02
Sioux (8)	10	0.09
All other tribes (3)	4	0.04
American Indian tribes, not spec.	4	0.04
Arab:	6	0.05
Syrian	6	0.05
Asian:	67	0.61
Chinese, ex. Taiwanese (22)	22	0.20
Filipino (9)	10	0.09
Indian (1)	9	0.08
Japanese (3)	7	0.06
Korean (3)	9	0.08
Taiwanese (2)	4	0.04
Vietnamese (1)	1	0.01
Other Asian, specified	1	0.01
Other Asian, not specified	4	0.04
Austrian	43	0.38
British	8	0.07
Bulgarian	23	0.21
Canadian	8	0.07
Czech	172	1.54
Czechoslovakian	26	0.23
Danish	109	0.97
Dutch	217	1.94
English	1,466	13.10
European	40	0.36
Finnish	21	0.19
French, except Basque	367	3.28
French Canadian	91	0.81
German	2,153	19.23
Greek	14	0.13
Hawaii Native/Pacific Islander:	12	0.11
Micronesian: (1)	3	0.03
Guamanian/Chamorro (1)	3	0.03
Polynesian: (2)	4	0.04
Native Hawaiian	2	0.02
Samoan (2)	2	0.02
Other Pac. Isl., specified	1	0.01
Other Pac. Isl., not spec.	4	0.04
Hispanic or Latino:	132	1.20
Central American:	3	0.03
Costa Rican	2	0.02
Nicaraguan	1	0.01
Mexican	83	0.75
Puerto Rican	8	0.07
South American:	1	0.01
Ecuadorian	1	0.01
Other Hispanic or Latino	37	0.34
Hungarian	5	0.04
Irish	1,228	10.97
Italian	358	3.20
Latvian	10	0.09
Lithuanian	59	0.53
Luxemburger	9	0.08
Northern European	16	0.14
Norwegian	149	1.33
Pennsylvania German	20	0.18
Polish	563	5.03
Romanian	7	0.06
Russian	21	0.19
Scandinavian	43	0.38
Scotch-Irish	357	3.19
Scottish	175	1.56
Slovak	48	0.43
Slovene	17	0.15
Swedish	210	1.88
Swiss	46	0.41
Ukrainian	8	0.07
United States or American	1,252	11.18
Welsh	86	0.77
White:	10,865	98.67
Not Hispanic (10,672)	10,771	97.81
Hispanic (86)	94	0.85
Yugoslavian	7	0.06

North Little Rock

Place Type: City
County: Pulaski
Population: 60,433

Ancestry/Race	Number	%
Acadian/Cajun	11	0.02
African American/Black:	20,896	34.58
Not Hispanic (20,483)	20,818	34.45
Hispanic (52)	78	0.13
African, sub-Saharan:	726	1.20
African	714	1.18
Cape Verdean	12	0.02
Alaska Native tribes, specified:	3	0.00
Alaska Athabascan (2)	2	0.00
Aleut	1	0.00
Alaska Native tribes, not specified	1	0.00
Am. Ind. or Alaska Nat., not spec.	190	0.31
American Indian tribes, specified:	376	0.62
Apache (3)	4	0.01
Blackfeet (8)	19	0.03
Cherokee (80)	223	0.37
Chickasaw	1	0.00
Chippewa (2)	6	0.01
Choctaw (24)	33	0.05
Comanche (1)	2	0.00
Creek (5)	10	0.02
Crow	1	0.00
Delaware (2)	2	0.00
Iroquois (5)	8	0.01
Kiowa	1	0.00
Latin American Indians (4)	7	0.01
Lumbee (1)	5	0.01
Menominee (4)	4	0.01
Navajo (1)	3	0.00
Osage (3)	12	0.02
Ottawa (1)	1	0.00
Potawatomi (4)	5	0.01
Pueblo	1	0.00
Seminole (2)	2	0.00
Shoshone (1)	1	0.00
Sioux (1)	3	0.00
All other tribes (9)	22	0.04
American Indian tribes, not spec.	29	0.05
Arab:	131	0.22
Arab/Arabic	34	0.06
Egyptian	20	0.03
Lebanese	7	0.01
Palestinian	60	0.10
Syrian	10	0.02
Asian:	493	0.82
Bangladeshi	1	0.00
Cambodian (1)	1	0.00
Chinese, ex. Taiwanese (49)	65	0.11
Filipino (52)	86	0.14
Indian (58)	74	0.12
Japanese (20)	35	0.06
Korean (75)	83	0.14
Laotian (4)	4	0.01
Pakistani (2)	2	0.00
Taiwanese (1)	6	0.01
Thai (10)	10	0.02
Vietnamese (52)	67	0.11
Other Asian, specified (1)	25	0.04
Other Asian, not specified (20)	34	0.06
Australian	16	0.03
Austrian	18	0.03
British	149	0.25
Canadian	13	0.02
Celtic	21	0.03
Croatian	9	0.01
Czech	135	0.22
Czechoslovakian	46	0.08
Danish	86	0.14
Dutch	698	1.16
English	5,183	8.58
European	529	0.88
Finnish	29	0.05
French, except Basque	1,123	1.86
French Canadian	157	0.26
German	4,954	8.20
Greek	30	0.05
Hawaii Native/Pacific Islander:	65	0.11
Micronesian: (2)	4	0.01
Guamanian/Chamorro (2)	4	0.01
Polynesian: (16)	33	0.05
Native Hawaiian (12)	23	0.04
Samoan (3)	9	0.01
Other Polynesian (1)	1	0.00
Other Pac. Isl., specified	22	0.04
Other Pac. Isl., not spec. (2)	6	0.01
Hispanic or Latino:	1,463	2.42
Central American:	80	0.13
Costa Rican	3	0.00
Guatemalan	38	0.06
Honduran	7	0.01
Nicaraguan	2	0.00
Panamanian	12	0.02
Salvadoran	11	0.02
Other Central American	7	0.01
Cuban	12	0.02
Mexican	946	1.57
Puerto Rican	94	0.16
South American:	33	0.05
Argentinean	4	0.01
Bolivian	1	0.00
Chilean	21	0.03
Colombian	2	0.00
Peruvian	3	0.00
Uruguayan	1	0.00
Venezuelan	1	0.00
Other Hispanic or Latino	298	0.49
Hungarian	28	0.05
Iranian	51	0.08
Irish	4,891	8.09
Italian	811	1.34

Notes: 1. Figures in the "Number" column do not add up to the total population due to: a) Ancestry/Race overlap — e.g. persons can report being both White and Irish, b) persons of Hispanic origin can report being any race, c) persons reporting two ancestries are counted in both categories. 2. Numbers in parentheses indicate the number of persons reporting this ancestry/race alone, not in combination with any other ancestry/race. 3. Refer to the Explanation of Data in the front of the book for more detailed information.

Latvian	10	0.02
Lithuanian	41	0.07
Luxemburger	13	0.02
Macedonian	11	0.02
Northern European	24	0.04
Norwegian	228	0.38
Polish	636	1.05
Portuguese	10	0.02
Romanian	25	0.04
Russian	138	0.23
Scandinavian	5	0.01
Scotch-Irish	1,290	2.13
Scottish	777	1.29
Serbian	8	0.01
Slavic	28	0.05
Slovak	11	0.02
Swedish	263	0.44
Swiss	198	0.33
Turkish	21	0.03
Ukrainian	75	0.12
United States or American	6,641	10.99
Welsh	360	0.60
West Indian, excl. Hispanic:	167	0.28
British West Indian	34	0.06
Dutch West Indian	19	0.03
Haitian	56	0.09
Jamaican	58	0.10
White:	38,395	63.53
Not Hispanic (37,186)	37,715	62.41
Hispanic (615)	680	1.13
Yugoslavian	14	0.02

Paragould

Place Type: City
County: Greene
Population: 22,017

Ancestry/Race	Number	%
African American/Black:	61	0.28
Not Hispanic (31)	59	0.27
Hispanic	2	0.01
African, sub-Saharan:	11	0.05
African	11	0.05
Alaska Native tribes, specified:	2	0.01
Alaska Athabascan (2)	2	0.01
Am. Ind. or Alaska Nat., not spec.	51	0.23
Albanian	8	0.04
American Indian tribes, specified:	187	0.85
Apache	2	0.01
Blackfeet (1)	12	0.05
Cherokee (47)	129	0.59
Chickasaw (1)	2	0.01
Chippewa (2)	9	0.04
Choctaw (4)	6	0.03
Cree	2	0.01
Creek (4)	9	0.04
Crow	4	0.02
Kiowa	1	0.00
Potawatomi (2)	2	0.01
Seminole	1	0.00
Sioux (1)	5	0.02
All other tribes (2)	3	0.01
American Indian tribes, not spec.	8	0.04
Asian:	73	0.33
Chinese, ex. Taiwanese (6)	7	0.03
Filipino (2)	5	0.02
Indian (10)	15	0.07
Indonesian (1)	7	0.03
Japanese (3)	5	0.02
Korean (7)	8	0.04
Pakistani (4)	4	0.02
Thai (2)	2	0.01
Vietnamese (11)	12	0.05
Other Asian, specified	2	0.01
Other Asian, not specified (2)	6	0.03
Australian	6	0.03
Belgian	16	0.07
British	93	0.42
Canadian	5	0.02
Czech	5	0.02
Danish	45	0.20
Dutch	320	1.45
English	1,807	8.20
European	252	1.14
French, except Basque	387	1.76
French Canadian	87	0.39
German	1,899	8.62
Hawaii Native/Pacific Islander:	13	0.06
Micronesian: (3)	6	0.03
Guamanian/Chamorro (3)	6	0.03
Polynesian: (2)	2	0.01
Native Hawaiian (2)	2	0.01
Other Pac. Isl., specified	2	0.01
Other Pac. Isl., not spec.	3	0.01
Hispanic or Latino:	292	1.33
Central American:	2	0.01
Nicaraguan	2	0.01
Cuban	3	0.01
Mexican	169	0.77
Puerto Rican	13	0.06
Other Hispanic or Latino	105	0.48
Irish	2,212	10.04
Italian	145	0.66
Lithuanian	8	0.04
Norwegian	89	0.40
Polish	94	0.43
Portuguese	8	0.04
Russian	9	0.04
Scotch-Irish	277	1.26
Scottish	169	0.77
Slovak	5	0.02
Swedish	137	0.62
Swiss	44	0.20
Ukrainian	7	0.03
United States or American	4,828	21.91
Welsh	90	0.41
White:	21,700	98.56
Not Hispanic (21,370)	21,530	97.79
Hispanic (157)	170	0.77

Pine Bluff

Place Type: City
County: Jefferson
Population: 55,085

Ancestry/Race	Number	%
Acadian/Cajun	51	0.09
Afghan	6	0.01
African American/Black:	36,495	66.25
Not Hispanic (36,130)	36,340	65.97
Hispanic (145)	155	0.28
African, sub-Saharan:	446	0.82
African	376	0.69
Ghanian	36	0.07
Liberian	10	0.02
Nigerian	14	0.03
Other sub-Saharan African	10	0.02
Alaska Native tribes, specified:	2	0.00
Tlingit-Haida	2	0.00
Alaska Native tribes, not specified	4	0.01
Am. Ind. or Alaska Nat., not spec.	96	0.17
American Indian tribes, specified:	137	0.25
Blackfeet (2)	5	0.01
Cherokee (28)	82	0.15
Chickasaw (3)	7	0.01
Chippewa (1)	1	0.00
Choctaw (4)	16	0.03
Cree	2	0.00
Navajo	2	0.00
Osage (2)	6	0.01
Seminole	5	0.01
Sioux (2)	2	0.00
All other tribes (3)	9	0.02
American Indian tribes, not spec.	20	0.04
Arab:	44	0.08
Egyptian	7	0.01
Lebanese	11	0.02
Syrian	26	0.05
Asian:	505	0.92
Bangladeshi (21)	23	0.04
Chinese, ex. Taiwanese (64)	83	0.15
Filipino (55)	69	0.13
Hmong	1	0.00
Indian (119)	137	0.25
Indonesian	1	0.00
Japanese (53)	62	0.11
Korean (17)	20	0.04
Malaysian (2)	2	0.00
Pakistani (25)	33	0.06
Thai (2)	2	0.00
Vietnamese (28)	29	0.05
Other Asian, specified (1)	10	0.02
Other Asian, not specified (9)	33	0.06
Austrian	6	0.01
Belgian	5	0.01
British	30	0.05
Canadian	10	0.02
Czech	49	0.09
Czechoslovakian	13	0.02
Danish	10	0.02
Dutch	286	0.52
English	1,900	3.48
European	180	0.33
French, except Basque	436	0.80
French Canadian	53	0.10
German	1,565	2.87
Greek	29	0.05
Hawaii Native/Pacific Islander:	54	0.10
Micronesian: (1)	5	0.01
Guamanian/Chamorro (1)	5	0.01
Polynesian: (19)	31	0.06
Native Hawaiian (4)	9	0.02
Samoan (15)	19	0.03
Tongan	2	0.00
Other Polynesian	1	0.00
Other Pac. Isl., specified	7	0.01
Other Pac. Isl., not spec. (1)	11	0.02
Hispanic or Latino:	452	0.82
Central American:	6	0.01
Costa Rican	1	0.00
Honduran	1	0.00
Salvadoran	4	0.01
Cuban	19	0.03
Mexican	246	0.45
Puerto Rican	40	0.07
South American:	5	0.01
Argentinean	1	0.00
Colombian	2	0.00
Peruvian	1	0.00
Venezuelan	1	0.00
Other Hispanic or Latino	136	0.25
Hungarian	33	0.06
Iranian	13	0.02
Irish	1,614	2.96
Italian	420	0.77
Norwegian	47	0.09
Pennsylvania German	24	0.04
Polish	152	0.28
Russian	19	0.03
Scotch-Irish	472	0.86
Scottish	236	0.43
Slovak	8	0.01
Swedish	156	0.29
Swiss	23	0.04
United States or American	3,909	7.16
Welsh	116	0.21
West Indian, excl. Hispanic:	57	0.10
Barbadian	14	0.03
Jamaican	8	0.01
Trinidadian and Tobagonian	29	0.05
Other West Indian	6	0.01
White:	18,069	32.80
Not Hispanic (17,609)	17,872	32.44
Hispanic (184)	197	0.36

Notes: 1. Figures in the "Number" column do not add up to the total population due to: a) Ancestry/Race overlap — e.g. persons can report being both White and Irish, b) persons of Hispanic origin can report being any race, c) persons reporting two ancestries are counted in both categories. 2. Numbers in parentheses indicate the number of persons reporting this ancestry/race alone, not in combination with any other ancestry/race. 3. Refer to the Explanation of Data in the front of the book for more detailed information.

Rogers

Place Type: City
County: Benton
Population: 38,829

Ancestry/Race	Number	%
African American/Black:	255	0.66
Not Hispanic (145)	193	0.50
Hispanic (39)	62	0.16
African, sub-Saharan:	7	0.02
African	7	0.02
Alaska Native tribes, specified:	2	0.01
Aleut (1)	1	0.00
Tlingit-Haida	1	0.00
Am. Ind. or Alaska Nat., not spec.	169	0.44
Albanian	6	0.02
American Indian tribes, specified:	483	1.24
Apache (9)	19	0.05
Blackfeet (1)	6	0.02
Cherokee (146)	259	0.67
Chickasaw (6)	11	0.03
Chippewa (4)	4	0.01
Choctaw (31)	46	0.12
Comanche (1)	4	0.01
Cree	1	0.00
Creek (8)	22	0.06
Crow (1)	1	0.00
Delaware (3)	3	0.01
Kiowa (9)	10	0.03
Latin American Indians (4)	26	0.07
Menominee (1)	1	0.00
Navajo (1)	1	0.00
Osage (4)	6	0.02
Ottawa (1)	1	0.00
Paiute (3)	3	0.01
Potawatomi	3	0.01
Pueblo (1)	1	0.00
Seminole (1)	3	0.01
Sioux (6)	10	0.03
All other tribes (26)	42	0.11
American Indian tribes, not spec.	23	0.06
Arab:	88	0.23
Arab/Arabic	10	0.03
Egyptian	21	0.05
Lebanese	57	0.15
Asian:	668	1.72
Chinese, ex. Taiwanese (48)	54	0.14
Filipino (25)	48	0.12
Indian (76)	84	0.22
Japanese (8)	17	0.04
Korean (53)	77	0.20
Laotian (21)	29	0.07
Malaysian (8)	8	0.02
Pakistani (5)	6	0.02
Taiwanese	1	0.00
Thai (1)	3	0.01
Vietnamese (292)	311	0.80
Other Asian, not specified (15)	30	0.08
Australian	5	0.01
Austrian	21	0.05
Belgian	25	0.06
British	97	0.25
Canadian	22	0.06
Croatian	21	0.05
Czech	66	0.17
Czechoslovakian	60	0.15
Danish	256	0.66
Dutch	672	1.73
Eastern European	6	0.02
English	3,803	9.81
European	183	0.47
Finnish	79	0.20
French, except Basque	971	2.51
French Canadian	161	0.42
German	5,760	14.86
Greek	41	0.11
Hawaii Native/Pacific Islander:	47	0.12
Micronesian: (19)	24	0.06
Guamanian/Chamorro (19)	24	0.06
Polynesian: (10)	18	0.05
Native Hawaiian (7)	14	0.04
Samoan (3)	4	0.01
Other Pac. Isl., not spec.	5	0.01
Hispanic or Latino:	7,490	19.29
Central American:	872	2.25
Costa Rican	12	0.03
Guatemalan	96	0.25
Honduran	17	0.04
Nicaraguan	44	0.11
Panamanian	12	0.03
Salvadoran	661	1.70
Other Central American	30	0.08
Cuban	16	0.04
Dominican Republic	2	0.01
Mexican	5,487	14.13
Puerto Rican	56	0.14
South American:	49	0.13
Bolivian	1	0.00
Chilean	7	0.02
Colombian	4	0.01
Ecuadorian	6	0.02
Peruvian	20	0.05
Venezuelan	7	0.02
Other South American	4	0.01
Other Hispanic or Latino	1,008	2.60
Hungarian	66	0.17
Irish	4,224	10.90
Italian	966	2.49
Lithuanian	22	0.06
Luxemburger	23	0.06
Northern European	5	0.01
Norwegian	497	1.28
Pennsylvania German	18	0.05
Polish	350	0.90
Portuguese	57	0.15
Russian	41	0.11
Scandinavian	93	0.24
Scotch-Irish	788	2.03
Scottish	502	1.30
Slavic	13	0.03
Slovak	14	0.04
Slovene	23	0.06
Swedish	259	0.67
Swiss	153	0.39
Turkish	11	0.03
Ukrainian	17	0.04
United States or American	5,142	13.27
Welsh	220	0.57
West Indian, excl. Hispanic:	98	0.25
Dutch West Indian	95	0.25
Haitian	3	0.01
White:	33,927	87.38
Not Hispanic (29,866)	30,224	77.84
Hispanic (3,430)	3,703	9.54
Yugoslavian	10	0.03

Russellville

Place Type: City
County: Pope
Population: 23,682

Ancestry/Race	Number	%
African American/Black:	1,323	5.59
Not Hispanic (1,214)	1,303	5.50
Hispanic (18)	20	0.08
African, sub-Saharan:	41	0.17
African	41	0.17
Alaska Native tribes, specified:	7	0.03
Aleut	3	0.01
Eskimo	1	0.00
Tlingit-Haida	2	0.01
All other tribes (1)	1	0.00
Am. Ind. or Alaska Nat., not spec.	111	0.47
American Indian tribes, specified:	224	0.95
Apache (3)	7	0.03
Blackfeet (1)	12	0.05
Cherokee (60)	131	0.55
Cheyenne (1)	1	0.00
Chickasaw (4)	11	0.05
Chippewa (1)	1	0.00
Choctaw (16)	25	0.11
Comanche (4)	5	0.02
Cree	3	0.01
Creek (4)	8	0.03
Delaware (1)	4	0.02
Kiowa (2)	2	0.01
Latin American Indians (2)	2	0.01
Osage (1)	3	0.01
Ottawa	1	0.00
Seminole	1	0.00
Yaqui (1)	1	0.00
All other tribes (4)	6	0.03
American Indian tribes, not spec.	11	0.05
Asian:	368	1.55
Bangladeshi (5)	5	0.02
Chinese, ex. Taiwanese (49)	61	0.26
Filipino (6)	20	0.08
Indian (53)	58	0.24
Japanese (21)	34	0.14
Korean (4)	5	0.02
Laotian (38)	55	0.23
Pakistani (13)	13	0.05
Taiwanese (27)	39	0.16
Thai (11)	17	0.07
Vietnamese (35)	39	0.16
Other Asian, not specified (11)	22	0.09
Australian	8	0.03
Austrian	10	0.04
Belgian	34	0.14
British	140	0.59
Canadian	6	0.03
Celtic	8	0.03
Croatian	17	0.07
Czech	86	0.36
Czechoslovakian	15	0.06
Danish	33	0.14
Dutch	398	1.68
English	2,416	10.21
European	252	1.06
Finnish	8	0.03
French, except Basque	626	2.64
French Canadian	102	0.43
German	2,706	11.43
Greek	99	0.42
Hawaii Native/Pacific Islander:	17	0.07
Micronesian: (5)	7	0.03
Guamanian/Chamorro (5)	7	0.03
Polynesian:	3	0.01
Native Hawaiian	3	0.01
Other Pac. Isl., not spec. (1)	7	0.03
Hispanic or Latino:	773	3.26
Central American:	72	0.30
Costa Rican	1	0.00
Guatemalan	5	0.02
Honduran	8	0.03
Nicaraguan	2	0.01
Panamanian	3	0.01
Salvadoran	51	0.22
Other Central American	2	0.01
Cuban	9	0.04
Dominican Republic	1	0.00
Mexican	493	2.08
Puerto Rican	12	0.05
South American:	12	0.05
Argentinean	4	0.02
Colombian	3	0.01
Peruvian	5	0.02
Other Hispanic or Latino	174	0.73
Hungarian	13	0.05
Iranian	15	0.06
Irish	2,485	10.50
Italian	413	1.74
Latvian	7	0.03
Northern European	5	0.02
Norwegian	228	0.96
Polish	232	0.98
Portuguese	35	0.15
Russian	21	0.09

Notes: 1. Figures in the "Number" column do not add up to the total population due to: a) Ancestry/Race overlap — e.g. persons can report being both White and Irish, b) persons of Hispanic origin can report being any race, c) persons reporting two ancestries are counted in both categories. 2. Numbers in parentheses indicate the number of persons reporting this ancestry/race alone, not in combination with any other ancestry/race. 3. Refer to the Explanation of Data in the front of the book for more detailed information.

Scandinavian	17	0.07
Scotch-Irish	485	2.05
Scottish	409	1.73
Slavic	13	0.05
Slovak	35	0.15
Swedish	176	0.74
Swiss	13	0.05
United States or American	3,362	14.20
Welsh	148	0.63
West Indian, excl. Hispanic:	86	0.36
Dutch West Indian	86	0.36
White:	21,535	90.93
Not Hispanic (20,938)	21,189	89.47
Hispanic (313)	346	1.46
Yugoslavian	8	0.03

Searcy

Place Type: City
County: White
Population: 18,928

Ancestry/Race	Number	%
Acadian/Cajun	7	0.04
Afghan	5	0.03
African American/Black:	1,352	7.14
Not Hispanic (1,245)	1,345	7.11
Hispanic (4)	7	0.04
African, sub-Saharan:	22	0.12
African	8	0.04
Nigerian	9	0.05
South African	5	0.03
Am. Ind. or Alaska Nat., not spec.	28	0.15
Albanian	46	0.24
American Indian tribes, specified:	101	0.53
Apache	1	0.01
Blackfeet	1	0.01
Cherokee (19)	63	0.33
Chickasaw	1	0.01
Chippewa (2)	2	0.01
Choctaw (4)	8	0.04
Creek (1)	2	0.01
Delaware	1	0.01
Latin American Indians (1)	1	0.01
Navajo (5)	5	0.03
Potawatomi (2)	2	0.01
All other tribes (10)	14	0.07
American Indian tribes, not spec.	10	0.05
Arab:	34	0.18
Iraqi	10	0.05
Lebanese	24	0.13
Asian:	125	0.66
Chinese, ex. Taiwanese (24)	32	0.17
Filipino (16)	23	0.12
Indian (9)	12	0.06
Indonesian (1)	1	0.01
Japanese (16)	23	0.12
Korean (10)	13	0.07
Laotian (2)	2	0.01
Pakistani (1)	1	0.01
Thai (1)	1	0.01
Vietnamese (13)	13	0.07
Other Asian, specified	1	0.01
Other Asian, not specified (1)	3	0.02
Australian	8	0.04
Austrian	10	0.05
Basque	8	0.04
Belgian	19	0.10
British	164	0.86
Canadian	18	0.09
Celtic	7	0.04
Czech	22	0.12
Czechoslovakian	7	0.04
Danish	18	0.09
Dutch	351	1.85
English	1,865	9.82
European	134	0.71
Finnish	21	0.11
French, except Basque	317	1.67
French Canadian	45	0.24
German	1,926	10.14
Greek	29	0.15
Hawaii Native/Pacific Islander:	22	0.12
Micronesian:	3	0.02
Guamanian/Chamorro	3	0.02
Polynesian: (2)	10	0.05
Native Hawaiian (2)	10	0.05
Other Pac. Isl., specified	1	0.01
Other Pac. Isl., not spec. (2)	8	0.04
Hispanic or Latino:	390	2.06
Central American:	80	0.42
Costa Rican	24	0.13
Guatemalan	15	0.08
Honduran	17	0.09
Nicaraguan	4	0.02
Panamanian	9	0.05
Salvadoran	11	0.06
Cuban	1	0.01
Mexican	214	1.13
Puerto Rican	27	0.14
South American:	10	0.05
Colombian	6	0.03
Peruvian	1	0.01
Venezuelan	3	0.02
Other Hispanic or Latino	58	0.31
Hungarian	91	0.48
Irish	1,759	9.26
Italian	176	0.93
Lithuanian	7	0.04
Norwegian	37	0.19
Polish	197	1.04
Portuguese	4	0.02
Romanian	24	0.13
Russian	5	0.03
Scandinavian	12	0.06
Scotch-Irish	476	2.51
Scottish	321	1.69
Serbian	15	0.08
Slavic	7	0.04
Swedish	63	0.33
Swiss	66	0.35
United States or American	2,664	14.02
Welsh	79	0.42
West Indian, excl. Hispanic:	19	0.10
Dutch West Indian	19	0.10
White:	17,297	91.38
Not Hispanic (16,913)	17,105	90.37
Hispanic (167)	192	1.01
Yugoslavian	30	0.16

Sherwood

Place Type: City
County: Pulaski
Population: 21,511

Ancestry/Race	Number	%
Acadian/Cajun	5	0.02
African American/Black:	2,256	10.49
Not Hispanic (2,168)	2,234	10.39
Hispanic (14)	22	0.10
African, sub-Saharan:	74	0.34
African	65	0.30
South African	9	0.04
Alaska Native tribes, specified:	2	0.01
Alaska Athabascan (1)	1	0.00
Tlingit-Haida (1)	1	0.00
Am. Ind. or Alaska Nat., not spec.	57	0.26
American Indian tribes, specified:	129	0.60
Apache (1)	1	0.00
Blackfeet	2	0.01
Cherokee (40)	72	0.33
Cheyenne (1)	1	0.00
Chickasaw	3	0.01
Chippewa (3)	3	0.01
Choctaw (3)	12	0.06
Creek (1)	2	0.01
Delaware (2)	2	0.01
Iroquois (1)	1	0.00
Latin American Indians (3)	10	0.05
Navajo (1)	1	0.00
Osage (1)	2	0.01
Potawatomi	1	0.00
Seminole (2)	3	0.01
Sioux (3)	7	0.03
All other tribes (6)	6	0.03
American Indian tribes, not spec.	8	0.04
Arab:	66	0.31
Egyptian	8	0.04
Palestinian	48	0.22
Syrian	10	0.05
Armenian	81	0.38
Asian:	291	1.35
Chinese, ex. Taiwanese (25)	43	0.20
Filipino (34)	64	0.30
Indian (26)	27	0.13
Japanese (13)	30	0.14
Korean (57)	74	0.34
Malaysian (1)	1	0.00
Pakistani (3)	4	0.02
Taiwanese (1)	1	0.00
Thai (6)	7	0.03
Vietnamese (27)	34	0.16
Other Asian, specified (1)	2	0.01
Other Asian, not specified (2)	4	0.02
Australian	4	0.02
Belgian	6	0.03
British	33	0.15
Bulgarian	7	0.03
Canadian	15	0.07
Czech	51	0.24
Czechoslovakian	8	0.04
Danish	8	0.04
Dutch	333	1.55
English	2,829	13.13
European	139	0.65
Finnish	25	0.12
French, except Basque	522	2.42
French Canadian	86	0.40
German	3,122	14.49
Greek	32	0.15
Hawaii Native/Pacific Islander:	27	0.13
Micronesian: (2)	4	0.02
Guamanian/Chamorro (2)	4	0.02
Polynesian: (9)	15	0.07
Native Hawaiian (7)	10	0.05
Samoan (2)	5	0.02
Other Pac. Isl., not spec. (2)	8	0.04
Hispanic or Latino:	442	2.05
Central American:	11	0.05
Guatemalan	1	0.00
Honduran	1	0.00
Nicaraguan	1	0.00
Panamanian	5	0.02
Salvadoran	1	0.00
Other Central American	2	0.01
Cuban	12	0.06
Mexican	238	1.11
Puerto Rican	52	0.24
South American:	10	0.05
Argentinean	3	0.01
Bolivian	2	0.01
Colombian	1	0.00
Ecuadorian	1	0.00
Venezuelan	3	0.01
Other Hispanic or Latino	119	0.55
Hungarian	92	0.43
Irish	2,542	11.80
Italian	350	1.62
Lithuanian	19	0.09
Norwegian	108	0.50
Polish	305	1.42
Portuguese	20	0.09
Russian	31	0.14
Scandinavian	16	0.07
Scotch-Irish	535	2.48
Scottish	494	2.29
Swedish	176	0.82
Swiss	57	0.26
Ukrainian	23	0.11

Notes: 1. Figures in the "Number" column do not add up to the total population due to: a) Ancestry/Race overlap — e.g. persons can report being both White and Irish, b) persons of Hispanic origin can report being any race, c) persons reporting two ancestries are counted in both categories. 2. Numbers in parentheses indicate the number of persons reporting this ancestry/race alone, not in combination with any other ancestry/race. 3. Refer to the Explanation of Data in the front of the book for more detailed information.

Ancestry/Race	Number	%
United States or American	3,259	15.13
Welsh	151	0.70
West Indian, excl. Hispanic:	12	0.06
British West Indian	12	0.06
White:	18,818	87.48
Not Hispanic (18,358)	18,558	86.27
Hispanic (216)	260	1.21
Yugoslavian	10	0.05

Siloam Springs

Place Type: City
County: Benton
Population: 10,843

Ancestry/Race	Number	%
Acadian/Cajun	14	0.13
African American/Black:	65	0.60
Not Hispanic (36)	46	0.42
Hispanic (17)	19	0.18
African, sub-Saharan:	7	0.06
African	7	0.06
Alaska Native tribes, specified:	2	0.02
Alaska Athabascan (2)	2	0.02
Am. Ind. or Alaska Nat., not spec.	96	0.89
American Indian tribes, specified:	598	5.52
Cherokee (342)	495	4.57
Chickasaw (5)	5	0.05
Choctaw (17)	31	0.29
Comanche	4	0.04
Creek (10)	21	0.19
Delaware	2	0.02
Iroquois (1)	1	0.01
Kiowa	1	0.01
Latin American Indians (9)	16	0.15
Navajo (1)	1	0.01
Osage (1)	7	0.06
Potawatomi (1)	2	0.02
Pueblo (1)	1	0.01
Seminole	2	0.02
Sioux (2)	2	0.02
All other tribes (1)	7	0.06
American Indian tribes, not spec.	38	0.35
Asian:	130	1.20
Chinese, ex. Taiwanese (12)	17	0.16
Filipino (16)	29	0.27
Indian (16)	21	0.19
Indonesian (6)	6	0.06
Japanese (12)	17	0.16
Korean (15)	22	0.20
Thai (2)	2	0.02
Vietnamese (10)	11	0.10
Other Asian, not specified (1)	5	0.05
Austrian	40	0.37
Basque	15	0.14
Belgian	32	0.30
British	31	0.29
Celtic	25	0.23
Czechoslovakian	8	0.07
Danish	10	0.09
Dutch	229	2.12
English	1,156	10.70
European	254	2.35
French, except Basque	234	2.17
French Canadian	10	0.09
German	1,487	13.76
Greek	5	0.05
Hawaii Native/Pacific Islander:	13	0.12
Micronesian: (1)	1	0.01
Guamanian/Chamorro (1)	1	0.01
Polynesian: (8)	8	0.07
Native Hawaiian (4)	4	0.04
Samoan (4)	4	0.04
Other Pac. Isl., not spec.	4	0.04
Hispanic or Latino:	1,518	14.00
Central American:	262	2.42
Costa Rican	1	0.01
Guatemalan	27	0.25
Honduran	21	0.19
Nicaraguan	1	0.01
Panamanian	6	0.06
Salvadoran	196	1.81
Other Central American	10	0.09
Cuban	13	0.12
Mexican	945	8.72
Puerto Rican	21	0.19
South American:	16	0.15
Bolivian	3	0.03
Colombian	5	0.05
Ecuadorian	8	0.07
Other Hispanic or Latino	261	2.41
Hungarian	19	0.18
Irish	1,007	9.32
Italian	121	1.12
Norwegian	136	1.26
Pennsylvania German	33	0.31
Polish	86	0.80
Romanian	6	0.06
Russian	50	0.46
Scandinavian	17	0.16
Scotch-Irish	178	1.65
Scottish	280	2.59
Swedish	192	1.78
Swiss	28	0.26
Ukrainian	10	0.09
United States or American	1,256	11.63
Welsh	67	0.62
West Indian, excl. Hispanic:	49	0.45
Dutch West Indian	49	0.45
White:	9,594	88.48
Not Hispanic (8,521)	8,748	80.68
Hispanic (719)	846	7.80

Springdale

Place Type: City
County: Washington
Population: 45,798

Ancestry/Race	Number	%
Acadian/Cajun	37	0.08
African American/Black:	490	1.07
Not Hispanic (293)	383	0.84
Hispanic (84)	107	0.23
African, sub-Saharan:	82	0.18
African	82	0.18
Alaska Native tribes, specified:	29	0.06
Aleut (2)	2	0.00
Eskimo (3)	27	0.06
Am. Ind. or Alaska Nat., not spec.	133	0.29
American Indian tribes, specified:	649	1.42
Apache (3)	6	0.01
Blackfeet (2)	3	0.01
Cherokee (207)	409	0.89
Chickasaw (6)	9	0.02
Chippewa (10)	13	0.03
Choctaw (9)	39	0.09
Comanche (2)	6	0.01
Cree	1	0.00
Creek (12)	19	0.04
Delaware (5)	8	0.02
Iroquois (2)	5	0.01
Kiowa (2)	5	0.01
Latin American Indians (37)	48	0.10
Menominee (2)	2	0.00
Navajo (2)	6	0.01
Osage (3)	6	0.01
Ottawa	1	0.00
Paiute (1)	1	0.00
Potawatomi (4)	5	0.01
Pueblo (3)	3	0.01
Puget Sound Salish (5)	5	0.01
Seminole	5	0.01
Sioux (9)	15	0.03
Tohono O'Odham (5)	5	0.01
All other tribes (12)	24	0.05
American Indian tribes, not spec.	25	0.05
Arab:	21	0.05
Lebanese	10	0.02
Moroccan	9	0.02
Other Arab	2	0.00
Asian:	930	2.03
Cambodian (3)	5	0.01
Chinese, ex. Taiwanese (43)	45	0.10
Filipino (59)	84	0.18
Indian (58)	76	0.17
Indonesian (1)	2	0.00
Japanese (19)	28	0.06
Korean (23)	39	0.09
Laotian (444)	484	1.06
Pakistani (4)	4	0.01
Sri Lankan	1	0.00
Taiwanese (4)	4	0.01
Thai (20)	31	0.07
Vietnamese (26)	36	0.08
Other Asian, specified	8	0.02
Other Asian, not specified (54)	83	0.18
Austrian	31	0.07
Belgian	19	0.04
British	140	0.30
Canadian	22	0.05
Czech	83	0.18
Czechoslovakian	64	0.14
Danish	79	0.17
Dutch	891	1.93
Eastern European	23	0.05
English	4,582	9.95
European	385	0.84
Finnish	4	0.01
French, except Basque	1,043	2.26
French Canadian	71	0.15
German	5,171	11.23
Greek	29	0.06
Hawaii Native/Pacific Islander:	904	1.97
Melanesian: (1)	1	0.00
Fijian (1)	1	0.00
Micronesian: (599)	731	1.60
Guamanian/Chamorro (8)	12	0.03
Other Micronesian (591)	719	1.57
Polynesian: (33)	50	0.11
Native Hawaiian (22)	37	0.08
Samoan (11)	13	0.03
Other Pac. Isl., specified	8	0.02
Other Pac. Isl., not spec. (74)	114	0.25
Hispanic or Latino:	9,005	19.66
Central American:	876	1.91
Costa Rican	7	0.02
Guatemalan	76	0.17
Honduran	76	0.17
Nicaraguan	14	0.03
Panamanian	1	0.00
Salvadoran	676	1.48
Other Central American	26	0.06
Cuban	25	0.05
Dominican Republic	7	0.02
Mexican	6,877	15.02
Puerto Rican	59	0.13
South American:	43	0.09
Colombian	16	0.03
Ecuadorian	10	0.02
Paraguayan	1	0.00
Peruvian	8	0.02
Venezuelan	3	0.01
Other South American	5	0.01
Other Hispanic or Latino	1,118	2.44
Hungarian	87	0.19
Icelander	2	0.00
Iranian	1	0.00
Irish	4,852	10.53
Italian	895	1.94
Lithuanian	9	0.02
Northern European	2	0.00
Norwegian	344	0.75
Polish	269	0.58
Portuguese	34	0.07
Russian	104	0.23
Scandinavian	39	0.08
Scotch-Irish	890	1.93
Scottish	613	1.33
Serbian	6	0.01

Notes: 1. Figures in the "Number" column do not add up to the total population due to: a) Ancestry/Race overlap — e.g. persons can report being both White and Irish, b) persons of Hispanic origin can report being any race, c) persons reporting two ancestries are counted in both categories. 2. Numbers in parentheses indicate the number of persons reporting this ancestry/race alone, not in combination with any other ancestry/race. 3. Refer to the Explanation of Data in the front of the book for more detailed information.

Ancestry/Race	Number	%
Slovak	24	0.05
Slovene	4	0.01
Swedish	358	0.78
Swiss	70	0.15
Ukrainian	60	0.13
United States or American	5,897	12.80
Welsh	225	0.49
West Indian, excl. Hispanic:	79	0.17
Dutch West Indian	67	0.15
Haitian	2	0.00
West Indian	10	0.02
White:	38,204	83.42
Not Hispanic (33,926)	34,456	75.23
Hispanic (3,454)	3,748	8.18

Texarkana

Place Type: City
County: Miller
Population: 26,448

Ancestry/Race	Number	%
Acadian/Cajun	9	0.03
Afghan	6	0.02
African American/Black:	8,341	31.54
Not Hispanic (8,163)	8,291	31.35
Hispanic (36)	50	0.19
African, sub-Saharan:	60	0.22
African	50	0.19
Nigerian	10	0.04
Alaska Native tribes, specified:	1	0.00
Alaska Athabascan	1	0.00
Alaska Native tribes, not specified	9	0.03
Am. Ind. or Alaska Nat., not spec.	87	0.33
American Indian tribes, specified:	219	0.83
Apache (1)	3	0.01
Blackfeet	2	0.01
Cherokee (32)	111	0.42
Cheyenne (2)	2	0.01
Chickasaw	2	0.01
Chippewa	2	0.01
Choctaw (27)	56	0.21
Creek (1)	5	0.02
Crow	2	0.01
Latin American Indians (1)	2	0.01
Navajo (6)	6	0.02
Osage	4	0.02
Seminole (1)	2	0.01
Sioux (1)	3	0.01
Yuman (1)	1	0.00
All other tribes (2)	16	0.06
American Indian tribes, not spec.	13	0.05
Asian:	165	0.62
Chinese, ex. Taiwanese (3)	5	0.02
Filipino (21)	33	0.12
Indian (30)	33	0.12
Japanese (3)	9	0.03
Korean (9)	12	0.05
Sri Lankan (1)	1	0.00
Thai (6)	6	0.02
Vietnamese (57)	60	0.23
Other Asian, specified	1	0.00
Other Asian, not specified	5	0.02
Austrian	14	0.05
Brazilian	10	0.04
British	60	0.22
Canadian	34	0.13
Celtic	17	0.06
Czech	12	0.04
Dutch	376	1.40
English	1,499	5.58
European	198	0.74
Finnish	9	0.03
French, except Basque	530	1.97
French Canadian	60	0.22
German	1,774	6.60
Greek	28	0.10
Hawaii Native/Pacific Islander:	14	0.05
Polynesian: (4)	8	0.03
Native Hawaiian (2)	6	0.02
Samoan (2)	2	0.01
Other Pac. Isl., specified	1	0.00
Other Pac. Isl., not spec. (4)	5	0.02
Hispanic or Latino:	472	1.78
Central American:	4	0.02
Costa Rican	1	0.00
Honduran	1	0.00
Panamanian	1	0.00
Salvadoran	1	0.00
Cuban	6	0.02
Mexican	316	1.19
Puerto Rican	19	0.07
South American:	1	0.00
Peruvian	1	0.00
Other Hispanic or Latino	126	0.48
Hungarian	23	0.09
Irish	2,602	9.68
Italian	347	1.29
Norwegian	78	0.29
Polish	91	0.34
Portuguese	8	0.03
Romanian	6	0.02
Russian	33	0.12
Scandinavian	13	0.05
Scotch-Irish	365	1.36
Scottish	405	1.51
Serbian	7	0.03
Slovak	9	0.03
Swedish	81	0.30
Swiss	8	0.03
Ukrainian	13	0.05
United States or American	3,729	13.87
Welsh	58	0.22
West Indian, excl. Hispanic:	30	0.11
Dutch West Indian	30	0.11
White:	17,761	67.15
Not Hispanic (17,191)	17,486	66.11
Hispanic (246)	275	1.04

Van Buren

Place Type: City
County: Crawford
Population: 18,986

Ancestry/Race	Number	%
Acadian/Cajun	8	0.04
African American/Black:	375	1.98
Not Hispanic (311)	364	1.92
Hispanic (1)	11	0.06
African, sub-Saharan:	18	0.10
African	18	0.10
Am. Ind. or Alaska Nat., not spec.	109	0.57
American Indian tribes, specified:	620	3.27
Apache (1)	4	0.02
Blackfeet	2	0.01
Cherokee (215)	443	2.33
Cheyenne (2)	3	0.02
Chickasaw (2)	8	0.04
Chippewa (6)	7	0.04
Choctaw (42)	86	0.45
Creek (5)	7	0.04
Crow	4	0.02
Iroquois (2)	2	0.01
Kiowa (1)	1	0.01
Latin American Indians (4)	7	0.04
Lumbee (3)	3	0.02
Navajo (4)	4	0.02
Osage (2)	9	0.05
Ottawa (4)	4	0.02
Pima (1)	3	0.02
Potawatomi (1)	2	0.01
Pueblo	1	0.01
Seminole (5)	6	0.03
Sioux (1)	2	0.01
All other tribes (7)	12	0.06
American Indian tribes, not spec.	22	0.12
Asian:	640	3.37
Cambodian (6)	6	0.03
Chinese, ex. Taiwanese (17)	26	0.14
Filipino (22)	35	0.18
Indian (15)	25	0.13
Japanese (8)	16	0.08
Korean (33)	46	0.24
Laotian (263)	305	1.61
Thai (3)	10	0.05
Vietnamese (133)	143	0.75
Other Asian, not specified (23)	28	0.15
Austrian	52	0.28
Belgian	24	0.13
British	66	0.35
Czech	44	0.23
Danish	13	0.07
Dutch	409	2.16
Eastern European	8	0.04
English	1,159	6.13
European	111	0.59
French, except Basque	391	2.07
French Canadian	62	0.33
German	2,020	10.69
Greek	42	0.22
Hawaii Native/Pacific Islander:	7	0.04
Micronesian:	1	0.01
Guamanian/Chamorro	1	0.01
Polynesian:	4	0.02
Native Hawaiian	4	0.02
Other Pac. Isl., not spec.	2	0.01
Hispanic or Latino:	1,147	6.04
Central American:	308	1.62
Guatemalan	14	0.07
Honduran	1	0.01
Salvadoran	259	1.36
Other Central American	34	0.18
Cuban	20	0.11
Dominican Republic	2	0.01
Mexican	482	2.54
Puerto Rican	22	0.12
South American:	8	0.04
Colombian	5	0.03
Peruvian	2	0.01
Venezuelan	1	0.01
Other Hispanic or Latino	305	1.61
Irish	2,244	11.87
Italian	308	1.63
Lithuanian	10	0.05
Norwegian	59	0.31
Polish	111	0.59
Portuguese	32	0.17
Russian	8	0.04
Scandinavian	23	0.12
Scotch-Irish	211	1.12
Scottish	171	0.90
Swedish	31	0.16
Ukrainian	40	0.21
United States or American	2,858	15.12
Welsh	67	0.35
West Indian, excl. Hispanic:	36	0.19
Dutch West Indian	36	0.19
White:	17,118	90.16
Not Hispanic (16,152)	16,597	87.42
Hispanic (437)	521	2.74

West Memphis

Place Type: City
County: Crittenden
Population: 27,666

Ancestry/Race	Number	%
Acadian/Cajun	24	0.09
African American/Black:	15,563	56.25
Not Hispanic (15,429)	15,513	56.07
Hispanic (44)	50	0.18
African, sub-Saharan:	177	0.64
African	177	0.64
Am. Ind. or Alaska Nat., not spec.	71	0.26
American Indian tribes, specified:	74	0.27
Blackfeet	2	0.01
Cherokee (19)	43	0.16
Cheyenne (1)	1	0.00

Notes: 1. Figures in the "Number" column do not add up to the total population due to: a) Ancestry/Race overlap — e.g. persons can report being both White and Irish, b) persons of Hispanic origin can report being any race, c) persons reporting two ancestries are counted in both categories. 2. Numbers in parentheses indicate the number of persons reporting this ancestry/race alone, not in combination with any other ancestry/race. 3. Refer to the Explanation of Data in the front of the book for more detailed information.

Chickasaw (3)	3	0.01
Choctaw (2)	12	0.04
Creek (2)	3	0.01
Iroquois	1	0.00
Latin American Indians (1)	1	0.00
Navajo (1)	2	0.01
Potawatomi	1	0.00
Pueblo (1)	1	0.00
Seminole (1)	1	0.00
All other tribes	3	0.01
American Indian tribes, not spec.	11	0.04
Arab:	6	0.02
Lebanese	6	0.02
Asian:	183	0.66
Chinese, ex. Taiwanese (53)	59	0.21
Filipino (20)	22	0.08
Indian (38)	44	0.16
Japanese (3)	3	0.01
Korean (16)	18	0.07
Thai	1	0.00
Vietnamese (11)	12	0.04
Other Asian, specified	10	0.04
Other Asian, not specified (5)	14	0.05
Belgian	8	0.03
British	90	0.32
Celtic	6	0.02
Czechoslovakian	6	0.02
Dutch	149	0.54
English	969	3.49
European	87	0.31
French, except Basque	168	0.61
French Canadian	53	0.19
German	947	3.41
Greek	78	0.28
Hawaii Native/Pacific Islander:	18	0.07
Polynesian: (5)	7	0.03
Native Hawaiian (3)	3	0.01
Samoan (2)	4	0.01
Other Pac. Isl., specified	10	0.04
Other Pac. Isl., not spec.	1	0.00
Hispanic or Latino:	279	1.01
Central American:	6	0.02
Guatemalan	1	0.00
Other Central American	5	0.02
Cuban	5	0.02
Mexican	183	0.66
Puerto Rican	11	0.04
South American:	4	0.01
Colombian	3	0.01
Ecuadorian	1	0.00
Other Hispanic or Latino	70	0.25
Irish	1,169	4.21
Italian	377	1.36
Norwegian	19	0.07
Polish	157	0.57
Scandinavian	6	0.02
Scotch-Irish	451	1.63
Scottish	228	0.82
Swedish	21	0.08
Swiss	9	0.03
United States or American	2,736	9.86
Welsh	26	0.09
West Indian, excl. Hispanic:	29	0.10
Haitian	12	0.04
Jamaican	17	0.06
White:	11,797	42.64
Not Hispanic (11,563)	11,692	42.26
Hispanic (100)	105	0.38

Adelanto

Place Type: City
County: San Bernardino
Population: 18,130

Ancestry/Race	Number	%
Acadian/Cajun	9	0.05
African American/Black:	2,626	14.48
Not Hispanic (2,305)	2,477	13.66
Hispanic (72)	149	0.82
African, sub-Saharan:	169	0.93
African	138	0.76
Nigerian	6	0.03
Other sub-Saharan African	25	0.14
Alaska Native tribes, specified:	1	0.01
Aleut	1	0.01
Am. Ind. or Alaska Nat., not spec.	168	0.93
American Indian tribes, specified:	316	1.74
Apache (14)	35	0.19
Blackfeet (2)	14	0.08
Cherokee (36)	84	0.46
Chickasaw	6	0.03
Chippewa (2)	10	0.06
Choctaw (10)	19	0.10
Creek	1	0.01
Iroquois (1)	4	0.02
Latin American Indians (38)	55	0.30
Lumbee (1)	1	0.01
Menominee	1	0.01
Navajo (10)	14	0.08
Osage (4)	4	0.02
Paiute (4)	4	0.02
Pueblo (3)	18	0.10
Shoshone (1)	1	0.01
Sioux (5)	9	0.05
Tohono O'Odham (4)	4	0.02
Yaqui (9)	10	0.06
Yuman (2)	2	0.01
All other tribes (18)	20	0.11
American Indian tribes, not spec.	41	0.23
Arab:	22	0.12
Arab/Arabic	22	0.12
Armenian	68	0.38
Asian:	524	2.89
Cambodian (30)	58	0.32
Chinese, ex. Taiwanese (2)	28	0.15
Filipino (143)	233	1.29
Indian (13)	35	0.19
Indonesian (1)	6	0.03
Japanese (22)	60	0.33
Korean (6)	14	0.08
Laotian (13)	20	0.11
Pakistani (1)	5	0.03
Thai (14)	19	0.10
Vietnamese (24)	29	0.16
Other Asian, not specified (4)	17	0.09
Australian	17	0.09
Austrian	20	0.11
Belgian	18	0.10
Brazilian	9	0.05
Canadian	26	0.14
Croatian	31	0.17
Czech	23	0.13
Czechoslovakian	51	0.28
Danish	58	0.32
Dutch	66	0.36
English	1,011	5.58
European	95	0.52
Finnish	8	0.04
French, except Basque	436	2.41
French Canadian	47	0.26
German	1,241	6.85
Greek	10	0.06
Hawaii Native/Pacific Islander:	71	0.39
Micronesian: (12)	18	0.10
Guamanian/Chamorro (12)	18	0.10
Polynesian: (16)	43	0.24
Native Hawaiian (8)	34	0.19
Samoan (8)	9	0.05
Other Pac. Isl., not spec. (4)	10	0.06
Hispanic or Latino:	8,299	45.77
Central American:	243	1.34
Costa Rican	7	0.04
Guatemalan	51	0.28
Honduran	8	0.04
Nicaraguan	12	0.07
Panamanian	8	0.04
Salvadoran	113	0.62
Other Central American	44	0.24
Cuban	41	0.23
Mexican	6,415	35.38
Puerto Rican	150	0.83
South American:	68	0.38
Argentinean	13	0.07
Bolivian	3	0.02
Chilean	9	0.05
Colombian	10	0.06
Ecuadorian	4	0.02
Peruvian	20	0.11
Venezuelan	2	0.01
Other South American	7	0.04
Other Hispanic or Latino	1,382	7.62
Hungarian	63	0.35
Iranian	6	0.03
Irish	983	5.43
Italian	633	3.50
Luxemburger	6	0.03
Norwegian	156	0.86
Polish	130	0.72
Portuguese	36	0.20
Russian	34	0.19
Scandinavian	11	0.06
Scotch-Irish	140	0.77
Scottish	131	0.72
Swedish	90	0.50
Ukrainian	27	0.15
United States or American	910	5.03
Welsh	35	0.19
West Indian, excl. Hispanic:	71	0.39
Belizean	65	0.36
Jamaican	6	0.03
White:	10,089	55.65
Not Hispanic (6,616)	6,964	38.41
Hispanic (2,531)	3,125	17.24
Yugoslavian	20	0.11

Agoura Hills

Place Type: City
County: Los Angeles
Population: 20,537

Ancestry/Race	Number	%
African American/Black:	333	1.62
Not Hispanic (268)	318	1.55
Hispanic (4)	15	0.07
African, sub-Saharan:	51	0.25
African	27	0.13
South African	24	0.12
Am. Ind. or Alaska Nat., not spec.	48	0.23
Albanian	23	0.11
American Indian tribes, specified:	88	0.43
Apache (1)	3	0.01
Blackfeet (1)	1	0.00
Cherokee (8)	36	0.18
Cheyenne	1	0.00
Chippewa	2	0.01
Choctaw	1	0.00
Creek	1	0.00
Iroquois	1	0.00
Latin American Indians (12)	15	0.07
Navajo	3	0.01
Potawatomi (1)	1	0.00
Pueblo (1)	2	0.01
Seminole	1	0.00
Sioux (1)	3	0.01
All other tribes (5)	17	0.08
American Indian tribes, not spec.	9	0.04
Arab:	217	1.07
Arab/Arabic	7	0.03
Egyptian	62	0.31
Lebanese	75	0.37
Moroccan	23	0.11
Syrian	25	0.12
Other Arab	25	0.12
Armenian	99	0.49
Asian:	1,642	8.00
Cambodian (4)	4	0.02
Chinese, ex. Taiwanese (375)	450	2.19
Filipino (197)	262	1.28

Notes: 1. Figures in the "Number" column do not add up to the total population due to: a) Ancestry/Race overlap — e.g. persons can report being both White and Irish, b) persons of Hispanic origin can report being any race, c) persons reporting two ancestries are counted in both categories. 2. Numbers in parentheses indicate the number of persons reporting this ancestry/race alone, not in combination with any other ancestry/race. 3. Refer to the Explanation of Data in the front of the book for more detailed information.

Indian (221)	250	1.22
Indonesian (4)	17	0.08
Japanese (164)	253	1.23
Korean (204)	219	1.07
Malaysian (2)	11	0.05
Pakistani (12)	17	0.08
Sri Lankan (3)	4	0.02
Taiwanese (40)	40	0.19
Thai (20)	24	0.12
Vietnamese (42)	46	0.22
Other Asian, specified	4	0.02
Other Asian, not specified (14)	41	0.20
Assyrian/Chaldean/Syriac	20	0.10
Austrian	325	1.60
Basque	19	0.09
Belgian	15	0.07
Brazilian	101	0.50
British	186	0.92
Bulgarian	35	0.17
Canadian	143	0.70
Celtic	26	0.13
Croatian	88	0.43
Czech	107	0.53
Czechoslovakian	47	0.23
Danish	206	1.01
Dutch	315	1.55
Eastern European	297	1.46
English	2,168	10.67
European	503	2.47
Finnish	5	0.02
French, except Basque	743	3.66
French Canadian	135	0.66
German	2,523	12.41
Greek	93	0.46
Hawaii Native/Pacific Islander:	50	0.24
Micronesian:	3	0.01
Guamanian/Chamorro	3	0.01
Polynesian: (12)	24	0.12
Native Hawaiian (10)	20	0.10
Samoan (2)	2	0.01
Other Polynesian	2	0.01
Other Pac. Isl., not spec. (9)	23	0.11
Hispanic or Latino:	1,407	6.85
Central American:	76	0.37
Costa Rican	4	0.02
Guatemalan	26	0.13
Honduran	3	0.01
Nicaraguan	5	0.02
Panamanian	7	0.03
Salvadoran	27	0.13
Other Central American	4	0.02
Cuban	53	0.26
Dominican Republic	3	0.01
Mexican	793	3.86
Puerto Rican	49	0.24
South American:	168	0.82
Argentinean	50	0.24
Bolivian	5	0.02
Chilean	19	0.09
Colombian	25	0.12
Ecuadorian	17	0.08
Paraguayan	4	0.02
Peruvian	33	0.16
Venezuelan	3	0.01
Other South American	12	0.06
Other Hispanic or Latino	265	1.29
Hungarian	345	1.70
Iranian	314	1.54
Irish	2,199	10.82
Israeli	201	0.99
Italian	1,494	7.35
Latvian	38	0.19
Lithuanian	86	0.42
Macedonian	11	0.05
Northern European	8	0.04
Norwegian	354	1.74
Polish	1,374	6.76
Portuguese	110	0.54
Romanian	197	0.97
Russian	1,898	9.34
Scandinavian	146	0.72
Scotch-Irish	283	1.39
Scottish	370	1.82
Serbian	23	0.11
Swedish	485	2.39
Swiss	33	0.16
Turkish	112	0.55
Ukrainian	127	0.62
United States or American	1,419	6.98
Welsh	134	0.66
West Indian, excl. Hispanic:	6	0.03
West Indian	6	0.03
White:	18,385	89.52
Not Hispanic (16,993)	17,419	84.82
Hispanic (865)	966	4.70
Yugoslavian	16	0.08

Alameda

Place Type: City
County: Alameda
Population: 72,259

Ancestry/Race	Number	%
Acadian/Cajun	40	0.06
Afghan	754	1.04
African American/Black:	5,431	7.52
Not Hispanic (4,350)	5,181	7.17
Hispanic (138)	250	0.35
African, sub-Saharan:	978	1.35
African	576	0.80
Cape Verdean	55	0.08
Ethiopian	102	0.14
Kenyan	19	0.03
Nigerian	151	0.21
Somalian	15	0.02
Other sub-Saharan African	60	0.08
Alaska Native tribes, specified:	41	0.06
Alaska Athabascan	2	0.00
Aleut (3)	5	0.01
Eskimo (3)	8	0.01
Tlingit-Haida (6)	21	0.03
All other tribes (1)	5	0.01
Alaska Native tribes, not specified	1	0.00
Am. Ind. or Alaska Nat., not spec.	367	0.51
Albanian	8	0.01
American Indian tribes, specified:	783	1.08
Apache (9)	36	0.05
Blackfeet (10)	50	0.07
Cherokee (37)	210	0.29
Cheyenne (1)	5	0.01
Chickasaw (3)	14	0.02
Chippewa (16)	35	0.05
Choctaw (8)	49	0.07
Colville	1	0.00
Comanche (3)	11	0.02
Cree	7	0.01
Creek (3)	8	0.01
Delaware (2)	4	0.01
Iroquois (3)	14	0.02
Kiowa (4)	5	0.01
Latin American Indians (25)	50	0.07
Navajo (21)	39	0.05
Osage (3)	3	0.00
Paiute (11)	16	0.02
Pima (3)	4	0.01
Potawatomi (3)	5	0.01
Pueblo (8)	11	0.02
Puget Sound Salish	1	0.00
Seminole (3)	13	0.02
Shoshone	3	0.00
Sioux (23)	38	0.05
Tohono O'Odham (6)	10	0.01
Ute	2	0.00
Yakama (2)	2	0.00
Yaqui (5)	9	0.01
All other tribes (72)	128	0.18
American Indian tribes, not spec.	44	0.06
Arab:	434	0.60
Arab/Arabic	73	0.10
Egyptian	5	0.01
Iraqi	16	0.02
Jordanian	12	0.02
Lebanese	105	0.15
Moroccan	33	0.05
Palestinian	116	0.16
Syrian	7	0.01
Other Arab	67	0.09
Armenian	96	0.13
Asian:	21,513	29.77
Bangladeshi (8)	16	0.02
Cambodian (62)	97	0.13
Chinese, ex. Taiwanese (8,067)	8,833	12.22
Filipino (5,428)	6,406	8.87
Hmong (8)	8	0.01
Indian (888)	1,002	1.39
Indonesian (28)	51	0.07
Japanese (831)	1,329	1.84
Korean (1,409)	1,545	2.14
Laotian (24)	40	0.06
Malaysian (5)	14	0.02
Pakistani (43)	57	0.08
Sri Lankan (9)	15	0.02
Taiwanese (48)	53	0.07
Thai (81)	102	0.14
Vietnamese (1,351)	1,529	2.12
Other Asian, specified (25)	39	0.05
Other Asian, not specified (133)	377	0.52
Assyrian/Chaldean/Syriac	6	0.01
Australian	92	0.13
Austrian	169	0.23
Basque	70	0.10
Belgian	40	0.06
Brazilian	80	0.11
British	364	0.50
Bulgarian	17	0.02
Canadian	115	0.16
Celtic	49	0.07
Croatian	79	0.11
Czech	209	0.29
Czechoslovakian	121	0.17
Danish	816	1.13
Dutch	939	1.30
Eastern European	78	0.11
English	6,349	8.79
Estonian	26	0.04
European	986	1.36
Finnish	184	0.25
French, except Basque	1,836	2.54
French Canadian	360	0.50
German	7,883	10.91
German Russian	8	0.01
Greek	366	0.51
Guyanese	10	0.01
Hawaii Native/Pacific Islander:	927	1.28
Melanesian: (1)	1	0.00
Fijian (1)	1	0.00
Micronesian: (161)	263	0.36
Guamanian/Chamorro (157)	257	0.36
Other Micronesian (4)	6	0.01
Polynesian: (234)	489	0.68
Native Hawaiian (104)	294	0.41
Samoan (105)	157	0.22
Tongan (22)	30	0.04
Other Polynesian (3)	8	0.01
Other Pac. Isl., specified	3	0.00
Other Pac. Isl., not spec. (20)	171	0.24
Hispanic or Latino:	6,725	9.31
Central American:	433	0.60
Costa Rican	6	0.01
Guatemalan	80	0.11
Honduran	16	0.02
Nicaraguan	84	0.12
Panamanian	36	0.05
Salvadoran	178	0.25
Other Central American	33	0.05
Cuban	139	0.19
Dominican Republic	21	0.03
Mexican	3,858	5.34
Puerto Rican	413	0.57

Notes: 1. Figures in the "Number" column do not add up to the total population due to: a) Ancestry/Race overlap — e.g. persons can report being both White and Irish, b) persons of Hispanic origin can report being any race, c) persons reporting two ancestries are counted in both categories. 2. Numbers in parentheses indicate the number of persons reporting this ancestry/race alone, not in combination with any other ancestry/race. 3. Refer to the Explanation of Data in the front of the book for more detailed information.

South American:	378	0.52
Argentinean	31	0.04
Bolivian	7	0.01
Chilean	47	0.07
Colombian	68	0.09
Ecuadorian	16	0.02
Paraguayan	2	0.00
Peruvian	130	0.18
Uruguayan	1	0.00
Venezuelan	27	0.04
Other South American	49	0.07
Other Hispanic or Latino	1,483	2.05
Hungarian	323	0.45
Icelander	8	0.01
Iranian	191	0.26
Irish	7,646	10.58
Israeli	25	0.03
Italian	3,852	5.33
Latvian	27	0.04
Lithuanian	135	0.19
Luxemburger	27	0.04
Macedonian	25	0.03
Maltese	16	0.02
New Zealander	21	0.03
Northern European	113	0.16
Norwegian	1,252	1.73
Pennsylvania German	30	0.04
Polish	1,343	1.86
Portuguese	1,056	1.46
Romanian	78	0.11
Russian	941	1.30
Scandinavian	114	0.16
Scotch-Irish	1,070	1.48
Scottish	1,858	2.57
Serbian	19	0.03
Slavic	100	0.14
Slovak	53	0.07
Slovene	26	0.04
Swedish	1,230	1.70
Swiss	352	0.49
Turkish	52	0.07
Ukrainian	163	0.23
United States or American	1,587	2.20
Welsh	488	0.68
West Indian, excl. Hispanic:	116	0.16
British West Indian	6	0.01
Dutch West Indian	11	0.02
Haitian	6	0.01
Jamaican	49	0.07
Trinidadian and Tobagonian	22	0.03
West Indian	22	0.03
White:	44,703	61.86
Not Hispanic (37,921)	40,770	56.42
Hispanic (3,227)	3,933	5.44
Yugoslavian	324	0.45

Alamo

Place Type: Census Designated Place
County: Contra Costa
Population: 15,626

Ancestry/Race	Number	%
African American/Black:	97	0.62
Not Hispanic (72)	95	0.61
Hispanic (2)	2	0.01
Alaska Native tribes, specified:	3	0.02
Aleut	2	0.01
Eskimo (1)	1	0.01
Am. Ind. or Alaska Nat., not spec.	16	0.10
American Indian tribes, specified:	61	0.39
Apache (4)	5	0.03
Blackfeet	1	0.01
Cherokee (10)	25	0.16
Chickasaw	1	0.01
Chippewa	2	0.01
Choctaw (1)	2	0.01
Comanche (1)	1	0.01
Creek (1)	3	0.02
Delaware	2	0.01
Iroquois	1	0.01
Latin American Indians	2	0.01
Osage (1)	2	0.01
Paiute	1	0.01
Sioux	5	0.03
All other tribes (4)	8	0.05
American Indian tribes, not spec.	2	0.01
Arab:	167	1.10
Arab/Arabic	34	0.22
Egyptian	23	0.15
Lebanese	77	0.51
Palestinian	33	0.22
Armenian	229	1.51
Asian:	1,176	7.53
Chinese, ex. Taiwanese (480)	581	3.72
Filipino (114)	183	1.17
Indian (89)	99	0.63
Indonesian (4)	8	0.05
Japanese (92)	143	0.92
Korean (70)	82	0.52
Laotian (3)	3	0.02
Malaysian	5	0.03
Sri Lankan (3)	3	0.02
Taiwanese (20)	23	0.15
Thai (4)	8	0.05
Vietnamese (16)	20	0.13
Other Asian, specified	4	0.03
Other Asian, not specified (3)	14	0.09
Australian	8	0.05
Austrian	114	0.75
Basque	13	0.09
Belgian	18	0.12
British	131	0.87
Canadian	38	0.25
Croatian	17	0.11
Czech	86	0.57
Czechoslovakian	24	0.16
Danish	255	1.68
Dutch	424	2.80
Eastern European	55	0.36
English	2,376	15.69
Estonian	9	0.06
European	221	1.46
Finnish	101	0.67
French, except Basque	621	4.10
French Canadian	159	1.05
German	2,748	18.15
German Russian	6	0.04
Greek	135	0.89
Hawaii Native/Pacific Islander:	44	0.28
Micronesian: (2)	4	0.03
Guamanian/Chamorro (2)	4	0.03
Polynesian: (14)	34	0.22
Native Hawaiian (3)	23	0.15
Tongan (11)	11	0.07
Other Pac. Isl., specified	3	0.02
Other Pac. Isl., not spec. (2)	3	0.02
Hispanic or Latino:	616	3.94
Central American:	35	0.22
Guatemalan	11	0.07
Honduran	1	0.01
Nicaraguan	11	0.07
Panamanian	1	0.01
Salvadoran	4	0.03
Other Central American	7	0.04
Cuban	18	0.12
Dominican Republic	1	0.01
Mexican	340	2.18
Puerto Rican	22	0.14
South American:	49	0.31
Argentinean	9	0.06
Bolivian	1	0.01
Chilean	3	0.02
Colombian	9	0.06
Ecuadorian	2	0.01
Peruvian	11	0.07
Venezuelan	1	0.01
Other South American	13	0.08
Other Hispanic or Latino	151	0.97
Hungarian	134	0.88
Iranian	250	1.65
Irish	2,561	16.91
Israeli	7	0.05
Italian	1,451	9.58
Lithuanian	46	0.30
New Zealander	6	0.04
Northern European	42	0.28
Norwegian	465	3.07
Pennsylvania German	7	0.05
Polish	371	2.45
Portuguese	292	1.93
Romanian	37	0.24
Russian	402	2.65
Scandinavian	27	0.18
Scotch-Irish	345	2.28
Scottish	802	5.30
Slavic	7	0.05
Slovak	21	0.14
Swedish	640	4.23
Swiss	174	1.15
Turkish	19	0.13
Ukrainian	66	0.44
United States or American	498	3.29
Welsh	155	1.02
White:	14,452	92.49
Not Hispanic (13,637)	13,919	89.08
Hispanic (482)	533	3.41
Yugoslavian	69	0.46

Albany

Place Type: City
County: Alameda
Population: 16,444

Ancestry/Race	Number	%
Afghan	23	0.14
African American/Black:	909	5.53
Not Hispanic (644)	835	5.08
Hispanic (31)	74	0.45
African, sub-Saharan:	153	0.93
African	119	0.72
Ethiopian	5	0.03
Sudanese	22	0.13
Other sub-Saharan African	7	0.04
Alaska Native tribes, specified:	1	0.01
Eskimo (1)	1	0.01
Am. Ind. or Alaska Nat., not spec.	70	0.43
American Indian tribes, specified:	156	0.95
Apache	7	0.04
Blackfeet (1)	8	0.05
Cherokee (6)	41	0.25
Chickasaw	4	0.02
Chippewa (2)	5	0.03
Choctaw	7	0.04
Comanche (1)	1	0.01
Creek (1)	1	0.01
Iroquois	3	0.02
Latin American Indians (4)	11	0.07
Lumbee (2)	2	0.01
Navajo (1)	5	0.03
Paiute (1)	1	0.01
Pima (2)	3	0.02
Potawatomi	1	0.01
Pueblo (3)	6	0.04
Puget Sound Salish	1	0.01
Seminole	4	0.02
Sioux (6)	6	0.04
Yakama (2)	2	0.01
Yaqui (4)	4	0.02
All other tribes (15)	33	0.20
American Indian tribes, not spec.	10	0.06
Arab:	191	1.16
Arab/Arabic	77	0.47
Egyptian	54	0.33
Lebanese	37	0.23
Moroccan	6	0.04
Palestinian	10	0.06
Other Arab	7	0.04
Armenian	15	0.09

Notes: 1. Figures in the "Number" column do not add up to the total population due to: a) Ancestry/Race overlap — e.g. persons can report being both White and Irish, b) persons of Hispanic origin can report being any race, c) persons reporting two ancestries are counted in both categories. 2. Numbers in parentheses indicate the number of persons reporting this ancestry/race alone, not in combination with any other ancestry/race. 3. Refer to the Explanation of Data in the front of the book for more detailed information.

Asian:	4,708	28.63
Bangladeshi (7)	7	0.04
Cambodian (12)	18	0.11
Chinese, ex. Taiwanese (2,140)	2,351	14.30
Filipino (178)	270	1.64
Indian (252)	300	1.82
Indonesian (11)	20	0.12
Japanese (501)	654	3.98
Korean (672)	710	4.32
Laotian (5)	11	0.07
Malaysian (1)	6	0.04
Pakistani (13)	22	0.13
Sri Lankan (13)	14	0.09
Taiwanese (81)	97	0.59
Thai (25)	38	0.23
Vietnamese (75)	114	0.69
Other Asian, specified (13)	17	0.10
Other Asian, not specified (33)	59	0.36
Australian	19	0.12
Austrian	84	0.51
Belgian	22	0.13
Brazilian	44	0.27
British	169	1.03
Canadian	46	0.28
Celtic	21	0.13
Croatian	31	0.19
Czech	37	0.23
Czechoslovakian	12	0.07
Danish	124	0.75
Dutch	206	1.25
Eastern European	111	0.68
English	1,586	9.64
Estonian	5	0.03
European	371	2.26
Finnish	103	0.63
French, except Basque	429	2.61
French Canadian	65	0.40
German	1,875	11.40
Greek	63	0.38
Hawaii Native/Pacific Islander:	64	0.39
Melanesian: (1)	6	0.04
Fijian (1)	6	0.04
Micronesian: (6)	9	0.05
Guamanian/Chamorro (6)	8	0.05
Other Micronesian	1	0.01
Polynesian: (10)	22	0.13
Native Hawaiian (4)	16	0.10
Samoan (6)	6	0.04
Other Pac. Isl., specified	2	0.01
Other Pac. Isl., not spec. (5)	25	0.15
Hispanic or Latino:	1,312	7.98
Central American:	83	0.50
Costa Rican	5	0.03
Guatemalan	14	0.09
Honduran	8	0.05
Nicaraguan	20	0.12
Panamanian	5	0.03
Salvadoran	24	0.15
Other Central American	7	0.04
Cuban	25	0.15
Mexican	684	4.16
Puerto Rican	59	0.36
South American:	169	1.03
Argentinean	13	0.08
Bolivian	4	0.02
Chilean	33	0.20
Colombian	16	0.10
Ecuadorian	11	0.07
Paraguayan	1	0.01
Peruvian	49	0.30
Uruguayan	3	0.02
Venezuelan	11	0.07
Other South American	28	0.17
Other Hispanic or Latino	292	1.78
Hungarian	121	0.74
Iranian	221	1.34
Irish	1,694	10.30
Israeli	75	0.46
Italian	907	5.52
Latvian	23	0.14
Lithuanian	31	0.19
Maltese	17	0.10
Northern European	73	0.44
Norwegian	199	1.21
Polish	387	2.35
Portuguese	184	1.12
Romanian	44	0.27
Russian	599	3.64
Scandinavian	57	0.35
Scotch-Irish	207	1.26
Scottish	417	2.54
Serbian	5	0.03
Slavic	13	0.08
Slovene	28	0.17
Swedish	417	2.54
Swiss	94	0.57
Turkish	20	0.12
Ukrainian	52	0.32
United States or American	293	1.78
Welsh	140	0.85
West Indian, excl. Hispanic:	27	0.16
Haitian	10	0.06
Jamaican	11	0.07
West Indian	6	0.04
White:	10,905	66.32
Not Hispanic (9,461)	10,145	61.69
Hispanic (617)	760	4.62
Yugoslavian	6	0.04

Alhambra

Place Type: City
County: Los Angeles
Population: 85,804

Ancestry/Race	Number	%
Acadian/Cajun	5	0.01
Afghan	5	0.01
African American/Black:	1,821	2.12
Not Hispanic (1,255)	1,464	1.71
Hispanic (182)	357	0.42
African, sub-Saharan:	327	0.38
African	241	0.28
Ethiopian	39	0.05
Ghanian	11	0.01
Nigerian	29	0.03
Other sub-Saharan African	7	0.01
Alaska Native tribes, specified:	5	0.01
Aleut (1)	4	0.00
Eskimo	1	0.00
Am. Ind. or Alaska Nat., not spec.	456	0.53
American Indian tribes, specified:	579	0.67
Apache (31)	54	0.06
Blackfeet	10	0.01
Cherokee (26)	87	0.10
Chickasaw (2)	5	0.01
Chippewa (3)	8	0.01
Choctaw (9)	19	0.02
Colville (2)	2	0.00
Comanche	4	0.00
Creek (3)	9	0.01
Crow	3	0.00
Delaware (1)	1	0.00
Iroquois	1	0.00
Latin American Indians (69)	138	0.16
Lumbee (3)	3	0.00
Menominee	2	0.00
Navajo (38)	59	0.07
Osage (3)	4	0.00
Ottawa (1)	1	0.00
Pima (5)	7	0.01
Potawatomi	1	0.00
Pueblo (24)	33	0.04
Seminole (1)	7	0.01
Shoshone (1)	3	0.00
Sioux (10)	20	0.02
Tohono O'Odham (8)	14	0.02
Ute	4	0.00
Yaqui (12)	25	0.03
Yuman (4)	4	0.00
All other tribes (29)	51	0.06
American Indian tribes, not spec.	81	0.09
Arab:	317	0.37
Arab/Arabic	48	0.06
Egyptian	67	0.08
Lebanese	50	0.06
Palestinian	66	0.08
Syrian	53	0.06
Other Arab	33	0.04
Armenian	102	0.12
Asian:	43,951	51.22
Bangladeshi (10)	13	0.02
Cambodian (288)	388	0.45
Chinese, ex. Taiwanese (26,855)	29,139	33.96
Filipino (1,743)	2,078	2.42
Hmong (2)	2	0.00
Indian (518)	613	0.71
Indonesian (304)	475	0.55
Japanese (1,404)	1,758	2.05
Korean (670)	739	0.86
Laotian (24)	33	0.04
Malaysian (55)	91	0.11
Pakistani (31)	34	0.04
Sri Lankan (34)	38	0.04
Taiwanese (1,582)	1,960	2.28
Thai (419)	486	0.57
Vietnamese (4,239)	5,390	6.28
Other Asian, specified (203)	263	0.31
Other Asian, not specified (213)	451	0.53
Assyrian/Chaldean/Syriac	8	0.01
Australian	21	0.02
Austrian	38	0.04
Basque	31	0.04
Belgian	19	0.02
Brazilian	25	0.03
British	113	0.13
Canadian	55	0.06
Celtic	26	0.03
Croatian	37	0.04
Czech	26	0.03
Czechoslovakian	66	0.08
Danish	129	0.15
Dutch	315	0.37
English	1,871	2.18
Estonian	9	0.01
European	201	0.23
Finnish	33	0.04
French, except Basque	786	0.91
French Canadian	106	0.12
German	2,588	3.01
Greek	51	0.06
Hawaii Native/Pacific Islander:	298	0.35
Micronesian: (27)	38	0.04
Guamanian/Chamorro (27)	37	0.04
Other Micronesian	1	0.00
Polynesian: (34)	110	0.13
Native Hawaiian (26)	87	0.10
Samoan (8)	19	0.02
Tongan	1	0.00
Other Polynesian	3	0.00
Other Pac. Isl., specified	2	0.00
Other Pac. Isl., not spec. (25)	148	0.17
Hispanic or Latino:	30,453	35.49
Central American:	1,849	2.15
Costa Rican	91	0.11
Guatemalan	395	0.46
Honduran	67	0.08
Nicaraguan	319	0.37
Panamanian	30	0.03
Salvadoran	723	0.84
Other Central American	224	0.26
Cuban	427	0.50
Dominican Republic	10	0.01
Mexican	22,857	26.64
Puerto Rican	330	0.38
South American:	638	0.74
Argentinean	75	0.09
Bolivian	4	0.00
Chilean	21	0.02
Colombian	156	0.18

Notes: 1. Figures in the "Number" column do not add up to the total population due to: a) Ancestry/Race overlap — e.g. persons can report being both White and Irish, b) persons of Hispanic origin can report being any race, c) persons reporting two ancestries are counted in both categories. 2. Numbers in parentheses indicate the number of persons reporting this ancestry/race alone, not in combination with any other ancestry/race. 3. Refer to the Explanation of Data in the front of the book for more detailed information.

Ecuadorian	120	0.14
Paraguayan	5	0.01
Peruvian	161	0.19
Uruguayan	5	0.01
Venezuelan	17	0.02
Other South American	74	0.09
Other Hispanic or Latino	4,342	5.06
Hungarian	157	0.18
Iranian	44	0.05
Irish	2,131	2.48
Italian	1,770	2.06
Lithuanian	16	0.02
Maltese	24	0.03
Norwegian	266	0.31
Pennsylvania German	10	0.01
Polish	316	0.37
Portuguese	50	0.06
Romanian	89	0.10
Russian	199	0.23
Scandinavian	10	0.01
Scotch-Irish	503	0.59
Scottish	437	0.51
Serbian	18	0.02
Slavic	11	0.01
Slovak	4	0.00
Slovene	28	0.03
Swedish	303	0.35
Swiss	70	0.08
Turkish	33	0.04
Ukrainian	78	0.09
United States or American	993	1.16
Welsh	110	0.13
West Indian, excl. Hispanic:	62	0.07
Belizean	17	0.02
Jamaican	27	0.03
Trinidadian and Tobagonian	6	0.01
West Indian	12	0.01
White:	28,282	32.96
Not Hispanic (11,881)	12,888	15.02
Hispanic (13,877)	15,394	17.94
Yugoslavian	66	0.08

Aliso Viejo

Place Type: Census Designated Place
County: Orange
Population: 40,166

Ancestry/Race	Number	%
Afghan	125	0.31
African American/Black:	1,076	2.68
Not Hispanic (790)	999	2.49
Hispanic (38)	77	0.19
African, sub-Saharan:	97	0.24
African	52	0.13
Nigerian	12	0.03
South African	27	0.07
Zimbabwean	6	0.01
Alaska Native tribes, specified:	6	0.01
Alaska Athabascan (1)	1	0.00
Aleut (1)	1	0.00
Eskimo	2	0.00
Tlingit-Haida (1)	2	0.00
Alaska Native tribes, not specified	1	0.00
Am. Ind. or Alaska Nat., not spec.	110	0.27
American Indian tribes, specified:	260	0.65
Apache (6)	20	0.05
Blackfeet (2)	6	0.01
Cherokee (34)	80	0.20
Cheyenne	1	0.00
Chickasaw (5)	6	0.01
Chippewa (2)	4	0.01
Choctaw (2)	16	0.04
Colville (1)	1	0.00
Creek	7	0.02
Iroquois (1)	3	0.01
Latin American Indians (6)	14	0.03
Lumbee	1	0.00
Navajo (1)	3	0.01
Osage (1)	1	0.00
Paiute	2	0.00
Pima	1	0.00
Potawatomi (4)	4	0.01
Pueblo (2)	7	0.02
Seminole (1)	1	0.00
Sioux (7)	16	0.04
Yaqui	8	0.02
Yuman (1)	1	0.00
All other tribes (27)	57	0.14
American Indian tribes, not spec.	15	0.04
Arab:	666	1.66
Arab/Arabic	36	0.09
Egyptian	201	0.50
Iraqi	22	0.05
Lebanese	250	0.62
Moroccan	31	0.08
Palestinian	82	0.20
Syrian	10	0.02
Other Arab	34	0.08
Armenian	190	0.47
Asian:	5,484	13.65
Bangladeshi	4	0.01
Cambodian (33)	38	0.09
Chinese, ex. Taiwanese (661)	869	2.16
Filipino (955)	1,248	3.11
Indian (408)	453	1.13
Indonesian (41)	72	0.18
Japanese (566)	881	2.19
Korean (645)	713	1.78
Laotian (9)	9	0.02
Pakistani (51)	57	0.14
Sri Lankan (14)	18	0.04
Taiwanese (95)	115	0.29
Thai (50)	66	0.16
Vietnamese (687)	741	1.84
Other Asian, specified (8)	18	0.04
Other Asian, not specified (57)	182	0.45
Australian	20	0.05
Austrian	238	0.59
Basque	43	0.11
Belgian	37	0.09
Brazilian	89	0.22
British	291	0.72
Bulgarian	23	0.06
Canadian	236	0.59
Celtic	9	0.02
Croatian	120	0.30
Czech	154	0.38
Czechoslovakian	89	0.22
Danish	432	1.07
Dutch	699	1.74
Eastern European	27	0.07
English	3,962	9.85
Estonian	7	0.02
European	653	1.62
Finnish	36	0.09
French, except Basque	1,472	3.66
French Canadian	207	0.51
German	6,488	16.13
German Russian	47	0.12
Greek	172	0.43
Hawaii Native/Pacific Islander:	242	0.60
Melanesian: (2)	5	0.01
Fijian (2)	5	0.01
Micronesian: (14)	25	0.06
Guamanian/Chamorro (14)	25	0.06
Polynesian: (61)	157	0.39
Native Hawaiian (39)	122	0.30
Samoan (20)	30	0.07
Tongan (1)	4	0.01
Other Polynesian (1)	1	0.00
Other Pac. Isl., not spec. (10)	55	0.14
Hispanic or Latino:	4,680	11.65
Central American:	114	0.28
Costa Rican	19	0.05
Guatemalan	22	0.05
Honduran	11	0.03
Nicaraguan	13	0.03
Panamanian	13	0.03
Salvadoran	24	0.06
Other Central American	12	0.03
Cuban	141	0.35
Dominican Republic	6	0.01
Mexican	2,857	7.11
Puerto Rican	232	0.58
South American:	438	1.09
Argentinean	86	0.21
Bolivian	17	0.04
Chilean	24	0.06
Colombian	108	0.27
Ecuadorian	32	0.08
Peruvian	102	0.25
Uruguayan	2	0.00
Venezuelan	25	0.06
Other South American	42	0.10
Other Hispanic or Latino	892	2.22
Hungarian	292	0.73
Icelander	9	0.02
Iranian	1,220	3.03
Irish	4,532	11.27
Israeli	33	0.08
Italian	3,336	8.29
Lithuanian	112	0.28
Luxemburger	14	0.03
New Zealander	8	0.02
Northern European	71	0.18
Norwegian	951	2.36
Pennsylvania German	18	0.04
Polish	1,366	3.40
Portuguese	201	0.50
Romanian	101	0.25
Russian	661	1.64
Scandinavian	129	0.32
Scotch-Irish	398	0.99
Scottish	826	2.05
Serbian	9	0.02
Slavic	22	0.05
Slovak	42	0.10
Slovene	6	0.01
Swedish	1,157	2.88
Swiss	108	0.27
Turkish	53	0.13
Ukrainian	208	0.52
United States or American	1,288	3.20
Welsh	379	0.94
West Indian, excl. Hispanic:	70	0.17
British West Indian	8	0.02
Jamaican	52	0.13
Trinidadian and Tobagonian	10	0.02
White:	33,033	82.24
Not Hispanic (28,599)	29,872	74.37
Hispanic (2,796)	3,161	7.87
Yugoslavian	108	0.27

Alpine

Place Type: Census Designated Place
County: San Diego
Population: 13,143

Ancestry/Race	Number	%
Acadian/Cajun	11	0.08
African American/Black:	147	1.12
Not Hispanic (104)	137	1.04
Hispanic (5)	10	0.08
African, sub-Saharan:	4	0.03
African	4	0.03
Alaska Native tribes, specified:	1	0.01
Aleut	1	0.01
Am. Ind. or Alaska Nat., not spec.	67	0.51
American Indian tribes, specified:	169	1.29
Apache (7)	7	0.05
Blackfeet (1)	5	0.04
Cherokee (24)	49	0.37
Chickasaw (6)	8	0.06
Chippewa (2)	2	0.02
Choctaw (3)	6	0.05
Cree (1)	5	0.04
Creek (1)	1	0.01
Crow (1)	1	0.01

Notes: 1. Figures in the "Number" column do not add up to the total population due to: a) Ancestry/Race overlap — e.g. persons can report being both White and Irish, b) persons of Hispanic origin can report being any race, c) persons reporting two ancestries are counted in both categories. 2. Numbers in parentheses indicate the number of persons reporting this ancestry/race alone, not in combination with any other ancestry/race. 3. Refer to the Explanation of Data in the front of the book for more detailed information.

Ancestry/Race	Number	%
Delaware (1)	1	0.01
Iroquois (1)	1	0.01
Latin American Indians (7)	8	0.06
Navajo (5)	5	0.04
Ottawa (1)	1	0.01
Potawatomi (5)	5	0.04
Pueblo (2)	5	0.04
Puget Sound Salish (1)	1	0.01
Seminole (1)	1	0.01
Shoshone (1)	1	0.01
Sioux (3)	8	0.06
Tohono O'Odham (1)	1	0.01
Yuman	1	0.01
All other tribes (30)	46	0.35
American Indian tribes, not spec.	17	0.13
Armenian	9	0.07
Asian:	359	2.73
Cambodian (6)	6	0.05
Chinese, ex. Taiwanese (16)	28	0.21
Filipino (112)	168	1.28
Indian (28)	34	0.26
Indonesian	3	0.02
Japanese (48)	63	0.48
Korean (11)	12	0.09
Laotian (1)	1	0.01
Pakistani (7)	7	0.05
Taiwanese (4)	4	0.03
Thai (11)	18	0.14
Vietnamese (4)	4	0.03
Other Asian, not specified (3)	11	0.08
Austrian	9	0.07
Belgian	18	0.14
British	91	0.69
Canadian	26	0.20
Czech	43	0.33
Czechoslovakian	53	0.40
Danish	122	0.93
Dutch	387	2.94
Eastern European	5	0.04
English	2,065	15.70
European	129	0.98
Finnish	47	0.36
French, except Basque	389	2.96
French Canadian	162	1.23
German	2,411	18.32
Greek	84	0.64
Hawaii Native/Pacific Islander:	66	0.50
Melanesian:	2	0.02
Fijian	2	0.02
Micronesian: (18)	26	0.20
Guamanian/Chamorro (18)	26	0.20
Polynesian: (9)	30	0.23
Native Hawaiian (8)	26	0.20
Samoan (1)	4	0.03
Other Pac. Isl., not spec.	8	0.06
Hispanic or Latino:	1,343	10.22
Central American:	15	0.11
Costa Rican	1	0.01
Guatemalan	4	0.03
Honduran	5	0.04
Panamanian	4	0.03
Salvadoran	1	0.01
Cuban	17	0.13
Mexican	1,000	7.61
Puerto Rican	54	0.41
South American:	13	0.10
Argentinean	5	0.04
Chilean	1	0.01
Colombian	2	0.02
Ecuadorian	4	0.03
Other South American	1	0.01
Other Hispanic or Latino	244	1.86
Hungarian	143	1.09
Icelander	7	0.05
Iranian	30	0.23
Irish	1,858	14.12
Italian	754	5.73
Lithuanian	13	0.10
Northern European	71	0.54
Norwegian	282	2.14
Polish	421	3.20
Portuguese	154	1.17
Romanian	13	0.10
Russian	166	1.26
Scandinavian	37	0.28
Scotch-Irish	288	2.19
Scottish	471	3.58
Serbian	11	0.08
Swedish	390	2.96
Swiss	48	0.36
Ukrainian	19	0.14
United States or American	760	5.78
Welsh	238	1.81
West Indian, excl. Hispanic:	8	0.06
Trinidadian and Tobagonian	8	0.06
White:	12,183	92.70
Not Hispanic (11,074)	11,256	85.64
Hispanic (857)	927	7.05
Yugoslavian	21	0.16

Altadena

Place Type: Census Designated Place
County: Los Angeles
Population: 42,610

Ancestry/Race	Number	%
African American/Black:	14,373	33.73
Not Hispanic (13,112)	13,922	32.67
Hispanic (276)	451	1.06
African, sub-Saharan:	868	2.04
African	702	1.65
Cape Verdean	10	0.02
Kenyan	12	0.03
Liberian	14	0.03
Nigerian	101	0.24
South African	15	0.04
Other sub-Saharan African	14	0.03
Am. Ind. or Alaska Nat., not spec.	274	0.64
American Indian tribes, specified:	496	1.16
Apache (6)	17	0.04
Blackfeet (4)	33	0.08
Cherokee (15)	138	0.32
Cheyenne (2)	2	0.00
Chickasaw (2)	7	0.02
Chippewa (3)	6	0.01
Choctaw (6)	26	0.06
Comanche	2	0.00
Cree	2	0.00
Creek	13	0.03
Delaware (1)	1	0.00
Iroquois (5)	20	0.05
Kiowa	1	0.00
Latin American Indians (41)	58	0.14
Navajo (8)	21	0.05
Osage	1	0.00
Paiute (2)	4	0.01
Pima (3)	3	0.01
Potawatomi (1)	1	0.00
Pueblo (2)	7	0.02
Seminole (2)	14	0.03
Sioux (7)	37	0.09
Tohono O'Odham	6	0.01
Yakama	2	0.00
Yaqui (5)	13	0.03
Yuman (4)	4	0.01
All other tribes (21)	57	0.13
American Indian tribes, not spec.	26	0.06
Arab:	453	1.06
Arab/Arabic	50	0.12
Egyptian	35	0.08
Jordanian	6	0.01
Lebanese	225	0.53
Palestinian	9	0.02
Syrian	77	0.18
Other Arab	51	0.12
Armenian	2,134	5.02
Asian:	2,457	5.77
Bangladeshi	3	0.01
Cambodian (1)	5	0.01
Chinese, ex. Taiwanese (324)	475	1.11
Filipino (474)	614	1.44
Indian (115)	173	0.41
Indonesian (20)	47	0.11
Japanese (505)	692	1.62
Korean (114)	145	0.34
Laotian (5)	6	0.01
Malaysian (3)	8	0.02
Pakistani (11)	17	0.04
Sri Lankan (17)	17	0.04
Taiwanese (5)	8	0.02
Thai (26)	42	0.10
Vietnamese (101)	109	0.26
Other Asian, specified (6)	24	0.06
Other Asian, not specified (28)	72	0.17
Assyrian/Chaldean/Syriac	21	0.05
Australian	44	0.10
Austrian	111	0.26
Basque	14	0.03
Belgian	17	0.04
Brazilian	69	0.16
British	351	0.82
Bulgarian	18	0.04
Canadian	196	0.46
Croatian	18	0.04
Czech	57	0.13
Czechoslovakian	28	0.07
Danish	265	0.62
Dutch	528	1.24
Eastern European	47	0.11
English	3,158	7.42
Estonian	7	0.02
European	448	1.05
Finnish	21	0.05
French, except Basque	714	1.68
French Canadian	105	0.25
German	3,338	7.84
German Russian	6	0.01
Greek	123	0.29
Guyanese	4	0.01
Hawaii Native/Pacific Islander:	138	0.32
Melanesian:	3	0.01
Fijian	3	0.01
Micronesian: (26)	31	0.07
Guamanian/Chamorro (7)	8	0.02
Other Micronesian (19)	23	0.05
Polynesian: (21)	63	0.15
Native Hawaiian (13)	44	0.10
Samoan (5)	16	0.04
Other Polynesian (3)	3	0.01
Other Pac. Isl., specified	8	0.02
Other Pac. Isl., not spec. (8)	33	0.08
Hispanic or Latino:	8,690	20.39
Central American:	683	1.60
Costa Rican	38	0.09
Guatemalan	109	0.26
Honduran	65	0.15
Nicaraguan	41	0.10
Panamanian	36	0.08
Salvadoran	298	0.70
Other Central American	96	0.23
Cuban	129	0.30
Dominican Republic	8	0.02
Mexican	6,194	14.54
Puerto Rican	122	0.29
South American:	239	0.56
Argentinean	36	0.08
Bolivian	9	0.02
Chilean	8	0.02
Colombian	78	0.18
Ecuadorian	31	0.07
Paraguayan	1	0.00
Peruvian	44	0.10
Uruguayan	2	0.00
Venezuelan	16	0.04
Other South American	14	0.03
Other Hispanic or Latino	1,315	3.09
Hungarian	195	0.46
Iranian	51	0.12
Irish	3,144	7.39

Notes: 1. Figures in the "Number" column do not add up to the total population due to: a) Ancestry/Race overlap — e.g. persons can report being both White and Irish, b) persons of Hispanic origin can report being any race, c) persons reporting two ancestries are counted in both categories. 2. Numbers in parentheses indicate the number of persons reporting this ancestry/race alone, not in combination with any other ancestry/race. 3. Refer to the Explanation of Data in the front of the book for more detailed information.

Ancestry/Race	Number	%
Israeli	10	0.02
Italian	1,446	3.40
Latvian	20	0.05
Lithuanian	38	0.09
Luxemburger	5	0.01
Macedonian	9	0.02
Northern European	117	0.27
Norwegian	496	1.17
Polish	430	1.01
Portuguese	75	0.18
Romanian	85	0.20
Russian	369	0.87
Scandinavian	27	0.06
Scotch-Irish	543	1.28
Scottish	806	1.89
Serbian	16	0.04
Slavic	5	0.01
Slovak	22	0.05
Swedish	642	1.51
Swiss	154	0.36
Turkish	18	0.04
Ukrainian	11	0.03
United States or American	1,174	2.76
Welsh	303	0.71
West Indian, excl. Hispanic:	247	0.58
Belizean	14	0.03
British West Indian	17	0.04
Dutch West Indian	8	0.02
Haitian	4	0.01
Jamaican	165	0.39
Trinidadian and Tobagonian	12	0.03
West Indian	27	0.06
White:	22,216	52.14
Not Hispanic (16,848)	18,341	43.04
Hispanic (3,308)	3,875	9.09
Yugoslavian	26	0.06

Alum Rock

Place Type: Census Designated Place
County: Santa Clara
Population: 13,479

Ancestry/Race	Number	%
African American/Black:	375	2.78
Not Hispanic (273)	319	2.37
Hispanic (28)	56	0.42
African, sub-Saharan:	14	0.10
African	14	0.10
Alaska Native tribes, not specified	1	0.01
Am. Ind. or Alaska Nat., not spec.	137	1.02
American Indian tribes, specified:	254	1.88
Apache (18)	37	0.27
Blackfeet	1	0.01
Cherokee (6)	28	0.21
Cheyenne (1)	1	0.01
Chippewa (1)	2	0.01
Choctaw (7)	10	0.07
Creek (1)	2	0.01
Delaware (1)	1	0.01
Latin American Indians (35)	71	0.53
Navajo (3)	15	0.11
Paiute	1	0.01
Pima (3)	3	0.02
Potawatomi (2)	4	0.03
Pueblo (1)	8	0.06
Seminole	1	0.01
Shoshone	1	0.01
Sioux (26)	26	0.19
Tohono O'Odham	3	0.02
Yaqui (8)	9	0.07
All other tribes (16)	30	0.22
American Indian tribes, not spec.	27	0.20
Asian:	1,402	10.40
Cambodian (21)	40	0.30
Chinese, ex. Taiwanese (84)	119	0.88
Filipino (431)	525	3.89
Indian (63)	90	0.67
Indonesian (1)	3	0.02
Japanese (89)	104	0.77
Korean (6)	10	0.07
Laotian (31)	48	0.36
Malaysian	3	0.02
Pakistani (4)	10	0.07
Thai (2)	6	0.04
Vietnamese (394)	416	3.09
Other Asian, specified	1	0.01
Other Asian, not specified (10)	27	0.20
Austrian	51	0.37
Basque	10	0.07
British	84	0.61
Canadian	7	0.05
Danish	18	0.13
Dutch	66	0.48
Eastern European	13	0.09
English	394	2.86
European	44	0.32
French, except Basque	137	0.99
French Canadian	40	0.29
German	455	3.30
Hawaii Native/Pacific Islander:	109	0.81
Micronesian: (9)	17	0.13
Guamanian/Chamorro (9)	16	0.12
Other Micronesian	1	0.01
Polynesian: (33)	61	0.45
Native Hawaiian (6)	32	0.24
Samoan (27)	28	0.21
Other Polynesian	1	0.01
Other Pac. Isl., specified	1	0.01
Other Pac. Isl., not spec. (5)	30	0.22
Hispanic or Latino:	9,029	66.99
Central American:	179	1.33
Guatemalan	16	0.12
Honduran	18	0.13
Nicaraguan	47	0.35
Panamanian	5	0.04
Salvadoran	81	0.60
Other Central American	12	0.09
Cuban	10	0.07
Dominican Republic	1	0.01
Mexican	7,861	58.32
Puerto Rican	86	0.64
South American:	31	0.23
Argentinean	1	0.01
Bolivian	6	0.04
Chilean	3	0.02
Colombian	8	0.06
Ecuadorian	4	0.03
Peruvian	7	0.05
Venezuelan	1	0.01
Other South American	1	0.01
Other Hispanic or Latino	861	6.39
Hungarian	12	0.09
Irish	331	2.40
Italian	432	3.14
Lithuanian	28	0.20
Norwegian	25	0.18
Polish	89	0.65
Portuguese	556	4.04
Russian	13	0.09
Scotch-Irish	37	0.27
Scottish	84	0.61
Serbian	7	0.05
Swedish	48	0.35
Swiss	9	0.07
United States or American	134	0.97
Welsh	25	0.18
West Indian, excl. Hispanic:	25	0.18
Jamaican	13	0.09
West Indian	12	0.09
White:	6,586	48.86
Not Hispanic (2,677)	2,874	21.32
Hispanic (3,273)	3,712	27.54

Anaheim

Place Type: City
County: Orange
Population: 328,014

Ancestry/Race	Number	%
Acadian/Cajun	25	0.01
Afghan	234	0.07
African American/Black:	10,448	3.19
Not Hispanic (7,939)	9,119	2.78
Hispanic (796)	1,329	0.41
African, sub-Saharan:	1,370	0.42
African	638	0.19
Cape Verdean	6	0.00
Ethiopian	314	0.10
Kenyan	55	0.02
Nigerian	84	0.03
Sierra Leonean	32	0.01
Somalian	74	0.02
South African	6	0.00
Sudanese	62	0.02
Other sub-Saharan African	99	0.03
Alaska Native tribes, specified:	15	0.00
Alaska Athabascan (1)	2	0.00
Aleut (6)	6	0.00
Eskimo (3)	3	0.00
Tlingit-Haida (3)	4	0.00
Am. Ind. or Alaska Nat., not spec.	2,123	0.65
Albanian	12	0.00
American Indian tribes, specified:	2,712	0.83
Apache (93)	184	0.06
Blackfeet (21)	73	0.02
Cherokee (174)	576	0.18
Cheyenne (1)	12	0.00
Chickasaw (14)	34	0.01
Chippewa (29)	47	0.01
Choctaw (39)	96	0.03
Colville (2)	4	0.00
Comanche (15)	38	0.01
Cree (4)	9	0.00
Creek (10)	28	0.01
Crow (3)	8	0.00
Delaware (5)	7	0.00
Iroquois (9)	28	0.01
Kiowa (1)	6	0.00
Latin American Indians (524)	733	0.22
Lumbee (1)	6	0.00
Menominee (3)	11	0.00
Navajo (63)	145	0.04
Osage (6)	14	0.00
Ottawa (1)	2	0.00
Paiute (6)	9	0.00
Pima (13)	18	0.01
Potawatomi (10)	21	0.01
Pueblo (57)	83	0.03
Puget Sound Salish (1)	2	0.00
Seminole (3)	11	0.00
Shoshone (8)	17	0.01
Sioux (25)	65	0.02
Tohono O'Odham (5)	9	0.00
Ute (3)	5	0.00
Yakama	3	0.00
Yaqui (27)	55	0.02
Yuman (5)	10	0.00
All other tribes (188)	343	0.10
American Indian tribes, not spec.	319	0.10
Arab:	3,494	1.07
Arab/Arabic	617	0.19
Egyptian	764	0.23
Iraqi	23	0.01
Jordanian	255	0.08
Lebanese	846	0.26
Moroccan	11	0.00
Palestinian	376	0.11
Syrian	341	0.10
Other Arab	261	0.08
Armenian	563	0.17
Asian:	44,343	13.52
Bangladeshi (52)	88	0.03

Notes: 1. Figures in the "Number" column do not add up to the total population due to: a) Ancestry/Race overlap — e.g. persons can report being both White and Irish, b) persons of Hispanic origin can report being any race, c) persons reporting two ancestries are counted in both categories. 2. Numbers in parentheses indicate the number of persons reporting this ancestry/race alone, not in combination with any other ancestry/race. 3. Refer to the Explanation of Data in the front of the book for more detailed information.

Cambodian (415)	509	0.16
Chinese, ex. Taiwanese (4,068)	5,133	1.56
Filipino (8,303)	9,655	2.94
Hmong (88)	89	0.03
Indian (3,986)	4,415	1.35
Indonesian (303)	477	0.15
Japanese (2,346)	3,164	0.96
Korean (6,160)	6,426	1.96
Laotian (677)	799	0.24
Malaysian (32)	65	0.02
Pakistani (432)	601	0.18
Sri Lankan (136)	167	0.05
Taiwanese (712)	832	0.25
Thai (392)	515	0.16
Vietnamese (10,025)	10,559	3.22
Other Asian, specified (47)	57	0.02
Other Asian, not specified (248)	792	0.24
Assyrian/Chaldean/Syriac	223	0.07
Australian	43	0.01
Austrian	669	0.20
Basque	118	0.04
Belgian	272	0.08
Brazilian	131	0.04
British	831	0.25
Bulgarian	53	0.02
Canadian	834	0.25
Carpatho Rusyn	10	0.00
Celtic	52	0.02
Croatian	267	0.08
Czech	510	0.16
Czechoslovakian	355	0.11
Danish	1,394	0.43
Dutch	3,361	1.03
Eastern European	150	0.05
English	17,891	5.47
Estonian	20	0.01
European	2,305	0.70
Finnish	416	0.13
French, except Basque	6,052	1.85
French Canadian	1,217	0.37
German	27,971	8.54
Greek	1,057	0.32
Guyanese	40	0.01
Hawaii Native/Pacific Islander:	2,445	0.75
Melanesian: (30)	30	0.01
Fijian (30)	30	0.01
Micronesian: (178)	302	0.09
Guamanian/Chamorro (176)	299	0.09
Other Micronesian (2)	3	0.00
Polynesian: (1,025)	1,654	0.50
Native Hawaiian (215)	570	0.17
Samoan (690)	888	0.27
Tongan (108)	141	0.04
Other Polynesian (12)	55	0.02
Other Pac. Isl., specified	3	0.00
Other Pac. Isl., not spec. (105)	456	0.14
Hispanic or Latino:	153,374	46.76
Central American:	5,016	1.53
Costa Rican	205	0.06
Guatemalan	1,638	0.50
Honduran	305	0.09
Nicaraguan	313	0.10
Panamanian	90	0.03
Salvadoran	1,992	0.61
Other Central American	473	0.14
Cuban	897	0.27
Dominican Republic	74	0.02
Mexican	126,017	38.42
Puerto Rican	1,306	0.40
South American:	2,406	0.73
Argentinean	277	0.08
Bolivian	110	0.03
Chilean	117	0.04
Colombian	491	0.15
Ecuadorian	222	0.07
Paraguayan	4	0.00
Peruvian	876	0.27
Uruguayan	21	0.01
Venezuelan	51	0.02
Other South American	237	0.07
Other Hispanic or Latino	17,658	5.38
Hungarian	1,008	0.31
Icelander	10	0.00
Iranian	1,597	0.49
Irish	19,691	6.02
Israeli	50	0.02
Italian	10,840	3.31
Latvian	5	0.00
Lithuanian	457	0.14
Luxemburger	43	0.01
Macedonian	9	0.00
Maltese	36	0.01
New Zealander	42	0.01
Northern European	104	0.03
Norwegian	3,093	0.94
Pennsylvania German	71	0.02
Polish	4,250	1.30
Portuguese	866	0.26
Romanian	1,617	0.49
Russian	1,962	0.60
Scandinavian	392	0.12
Scotch-Irish	2,705	0.83
Scottish	3,500	1.07
Serbian	97	0.03
Slavic	100	0.03
Slovak	210	0.06
Slovene	39	0.01
Swedish	3,095	0.95
Swiss	495	0.15
Turkish	128	0.04
Ukrainian	508	0.16
United States or American	10,403	3.18
Welsh	1,267	0.39
West Indian, excl. Hispanic:	428	0.13
Bahamian	8	0.00
Barbadian	8	0.00
Belizean	51	0.02
British West Indian	5	0.00
Dutch West Indian	7	0.00
Haitian	107	0.03
Jamaican	106	0.03
Trinidadian and Tobagonian	40	0.01
West Indian	96	0.03
White:	193,586	59.02
Not Hispanic (117,607)	123,555	37.67
Hispanic (62,020)	70,031	21.35
Yugoslavian	240	0.07

Antioch

Place Type: City
County: Contra Costa
Population: 90,532

Ancestry/Race	Number	%
Acadian/Cajun	8	0.01
Afghan	174	0.19
African American/Black:	10,007	11.05
Not Hispanic (8,551)	9,444	10.43
Hispanic (273)	563	0.62
African, sub-Saharan:	757	0.83
African	601	0.66
Cape Verdean	6	0.01
Ghanian	8	0.01
Liberian	31	0.03
Nigerian	102	0.11
South African	9	0.01
Alaska Native tribes, specified:	9	0.01
Aleut (2)	4	0.00
Eskimo	2	0.00
Tlingit-Haida (1)	3	0.00
Alaska Native tribes, not specified	8	0.01
Am. Ind. or Alaska Nat., not spec.	690	0.76
American Indian tribes, specified:	1,413	1.56
Apache (20)	63	0.07
Blackfeet (11)	53	0.06
Cherokee (134)	542	0.60
Cheyenne (1)	3	0.00
Chickasaw (9)	32	0.04
Chippewa (10)	32	0.04
Choctaw (54)	127	0.14
Comanche (6)	10	0.01
Cree	2	0.00
Creek (13)	31	0.03
Crow (1)	1	0.00
Delaware (1)	10	0.01
Iroquois (6)	18	0.02
Kiowa	1	0.00
Latin American Indians (62)	84	0.09
Lumbee (1)	1	0.00
Navajo (20)	53	0.06
Osage	1	0.00
Ottawa (4)	6	0.01
Paiute (13)	27	0.03
Pima (5)	5	0.01
Potawatomi (5)	7	0.01
Pueblo (5)	18	0.02
Puget Sound Salish (1)	1	0.00
Seminole (1)	8	0.01
Shoshone (4)	6	0.01
Sioux (34)	78	0.09
Tohono O'Odham (2)	2	0.00
Ute (4)	6	0.01
Yaqui (9)	24	0.03
All other tribes (85)	161	0.18
American Indian tribes, not spec.	83	0.09
Arab:	260	0.29
Arab/Arabic	73	0.08
Egyptian	41	0.05
Lebanese	92	0.10
Moroccan	18	0.02
Palestinian	9	0.01
Syrian	10	0.01
Other Arab	17	0.02
Armenian	20	0.02
Asian:	9,054	10.00
Bangladeshi (7)	9	0.01
Cambodian (38)	54	0.06
Chinese, ex. Taiwanese (1,035)	1,474	1.63
Filipino (3,642)	4,775	5.27
Indian (600)	725	0.80
Indonesian (49)	85	0.09
Japanese (265)	584	0.65
Korean (214)	298	0.33
Laotian (12)	17	0.02
Malaysian (3)	11	0.01
Pakistani (82)	103	0.11
Sri Lankan (18)	23	0.03
Taiwanese (13)	19	0.02
Thai (65)	90	0.10
Vietnamese (353)	449	0.50
Other Asian, specified (23)	34	0.04
Other Asian, not specified (57)	304	0.34
Assyrian/Chaldean/Syriac	8	0.01
Australian	87	0.10
Austrian	178	0.20
Basque	74	0.08
Belgian	70	0.08
Brazilian	42	0.05
British	283	0.31
Bulgarian	10	0.01
Canadian	218	0.24
Celtic	88	0.10
Croatian	14	0.02
Czech	80	0.09
Czechoslovakian	52	0.06
Danish	877	0.97
Dutch	1,457	1.60
Eastern European	22	0.02
English	7,543	8.31
European	772	0.85
Finnish	178	0.20
French, except Basque	2,447	2.69
French Canadian	486	0.54
German	12,094	13.32
German Russian	13	0.01
Greek	296	0.33
Hawaii Native/Pacific Islander:	833	0.92
Melanesian: (38)	59	0.07
Fijian (38)	59	0.07

Notes: 1. Figures in the "Number" column do not add up to the total population due to: a) Ancestry/Race overlap — e.g. persons can report being both White and Irish, b) persons of Hispanic origin can report being any race, c) persons reporting two ancestries are counted in both categories. 2. Numbers in parentheses indicate the number of persons reporting this ancestry/race alone, not in combination with any other ancestry/race. 3. Refer to the Explanation of Data in the front of the book for more detailed information.

Micronesian: (110)	176	0.19
Guamanian/Chamorro (100)	165	0.18
Other Micronesian (10)	11	0.01
Polynesian: (168)	431	0.48
Native Hawaiian (82)	291	0.32
Samoan (60)	109	0.12
Tongan (18)	18	0.02
Other Polynesian (8)	13	0.01
Other Pac. Isl., not spec. (42)	167	0.18
Hispanic or Latino:	20,024	22.12
Central American:	1,251	1.38
Costa Rican	30	0.03
Guatemalan	128	0.14
Honduran	32	0.04
Nicaraguan	334	0.37
Panamanian	35	0.04
Salvadoran	536	0.59
Other Central American	156	0.17
Cuban	120	0.13
Dominican Republic	20	0.02
Mexican	13,619	15.04
Puerto Rican	792	0.87
South American:	360	0.40
Argentinean	24	0.03
Bolivian	17	0.02
Chilean	22	0.02
Colombian	62	0.07
Ecuadorian	10	0.01
Paraguayan	3	0.00
Peruvian	177	0.20
Venezuelan	15	0.02
Other South American	30	0.03
Other Hispanic or Latino	3,862	4.27
Hungarian	329	0.36
Iranian	97	0.11
Irish	10,247	11.28
Israeli	20	0.02
Italian	7,477	8.23
Lithuanian	129	0.14
Luxemburger	7	0.01
Maltese	102	0.11
Northern European	67	0.07
Norwegian	1,435	1.58
Pennsylvania German	37	0.04
Polish	1,381	1.52
Portuguese	2,219	2.44
Romanian	56	0.06
Russian	345	0.38
Scandinavian	151	0.17
Scotch-Irish	1,375	1.51
Scottish	1,592	1.75
Serbian	62	0.07
Slavic	39	0.04
Slovak	39	0.04
Slovene	49	0.05
Swedish	1,625	1.79
Swiss	284	0.31
Ukrainian	111	0.12
United States or American	3,550	3.91
Welsh	627	0.69
West Indian, excl. Hispanic:	121	0.13
Belizean	7	0.01
British West Indian	9	0.01
Dutch West Indian	4	0.00
Haitian	36	0.04
Jamaican	25	0.03
West Indian	40	0.04
White:	64,458	71.20
Not Hispanic (50,644)	53,796	59.42
Hispanic (8,504)	10,662	11.78
Yugoslavian	161	0.18

Apple Valley

Place Type: Town
County: San Bernardino
Population: 54,239

Ancestry/Race	Number	%
African American/Black:	4,790	8.83
Not Hispanic (4,141)	4,563	8.41
Hispanic (136)	227	0.42
African, sub-Saharan:	230	0.42
African	199	0.37
Cape Verdean	12	0.02
Ethiopian	19	0.04
Alaska Native tribes, specified:	3	0.01
Aleut (1)	1	0.00
Eskimo (1)	2	0.00
Alaska Native tribes, not specified	5	0.01
Am. Ind. or Alaska Nat., not spec.	251	0.46
American Indian tribes, specified:	960	1.77
Apache (38)	66	0.12
Blackfeet (15)	54	0.10
Cherokee (70)	304	0.56
Cheyenne	9	0.02
Chickasaw (4)	6	0.01
Chippewa (11)	15	0.03
Choctaw (10)	50	0.09
Comanche (3)	18	0.03
Cree (2)	4	0.01
Creek (4)	13	0.02
Crow (1)	1	0.00
Delaware (3)	11	0.02
Iroquois (8)	25	0.05
Kiowa	1	0.00
Latin American Indians (31)	53	0.10
Lumbee (1)	2	0.00
Menominee	1	0.00
Navajo (45)	75	0.14
Osage (6)	14	0.03
Paiute (1)	2	0.00
Pima (13)	16	0.03
Potawatomi (4)	10	0.02
Pueblo (29)	48	0.09
Puget Sound Salish (2)	2	0.00
Seminole (2)	4	0.01
Shoshone (1)	7	0.01
Sioux (11)	36	0.07
Tohono O'Odham	1	0.00
Ute (1)	2	0.00
Yaqui (4)	14	0.03
Yuman (2)	3	0.01
All other tribes (54)	93	0.17
American Indian tribes, not spec.	78	0.14
Arab:	124	0.23
Egyptian	5	0.01
Jordanian	20	0.04
Lebanese	42	0.08
Syrian	57	0.11
Armenian	193	0.36
Asian:	1,654	3.05
Cambodian (21)	21	0.04
Chinese, ex. Taiwanese (93)	151	0.28
Filipino (453)	596	1.10
Indian (199)	217	0.40
Indonesian (11)	28	0.05
Japanese (132)	254	0.47
Korean (126)	156	0.29
Malaysian	5	0.01
Pakistani (8)	14	0.03
Sri Lankan (21)	21	0.04
Taiwanese (16)	25	0.05
Thai (19)	28	0.05
Vietnamese (66)	92	0.17
Other Asian, specified (3)	5	0.01
Other Asian, not specified (18)	41	0.08
Australian	33	0.06
Austrian	101	0.19
Basque	29	0.05
Belgian	38	0.07
British	229	0.42
Canadian	333	0.61
Celtic	33	0.06
Croatian	44	0.08
Czech	165	0.30
Czechoslovakian	88	0.16
Danish	414	0.76
Dutch	1,247	2.30
English	5,778	10.67
Estonian	3	0.01
European	867	1.60
Finnish	42	0.08
French, except Basque	1,743	3.22
French Canadian	387	0.71
German	8,961	16.54
German Russian	7	0.01
Greek	90	0.17
Hawaii Native/Pacific Islander:	224	0.41
Melanesian: (1)	1	0.00
Fijian (1)	1	0.00
Micronesian: (32)	47	0.09
Guamanian/Chamorro (31)	46	0.08
Other Micronesian (1)	1	0.00
Polynesian: (85)	143	0.26
Native Hawaiian (30)	70	0.13
Samoan (55)	68	0.13
Other Polynesian	5	0.01
Other Pac. Isl., not spec. (5)	33	0.06
Hispanic or Latino:	10,067	18.56
Central American:	213	0.39
Costa Rican	15	0.03
Guatemalan	41	0.08
Honduran	26	0.05
Nicaraguan	21	0.04
Panamanian	10	0.02
Salvadoran	76	0.14
Other Central American	24	0.04
Cuban	86	0.16
Dominican Republic	7	0.01
Mexican	7,488	13.81
Puerto Rican	293	0.54
South American:	93	0.17
Argentinean	17	0.03
Chilean	1	0.00
Colombian	16	0.03
Ecuadorian	13	0.02
Peruvian	23	0.04
Uruguayan	1	0.00
Venezuelan	4	0.01
Other South American	18	0.03
Other Hispanic or Latino	1,887	3.48
Hungarian	327	0.60
Icelander	7	0.01
Iranian	23	0.04
Irish	6,132	11.32
Italian	3,241	5.98
Lithuanian	95	0.18
New Zealander	8	0.01
Northern European	10	0.02
Norwegian	944	1.74
Pennsylvania German	70	0.13
Polish	943	1.74
Portuguese	302	0.56
Romanian	71	0.13
Russian	541	1.00
Scandinavian	64	0.12
Scotch-Irish	925	1.71
Scottish	951	1.76
Serbian	29	0.05
Slavic	19	0.04
Slovak	63	0.12
Slovene	24	0.04
Swedish	1,320	2.44
Swiss	147	0.27
Turkish	8	0.01
Ukrainian	86	0.16
United States or American	3,323	6.13
Welsh	625	1.15
West Indian, excl. Hispanic:	169	0.31
Belizean	29	0.05
Bermudan	9	0.02
Dutch West Indian	44	0.08
Jamaican	79	0.15
West Indian	8	0.01
White:	43,527	80.25
Not Hispanic (36,710)	38,113	70.27
Hispanic (4,739)	5,414	9.98
Yugoslavian	55	0.10

Notes: 1. Figures in the "Number" column do not add up to the total population due to: a) Ancestry/Race overlap — e.g. persons can report being both White and Irish, b) persons of Hispanic origin can report being any race, c) persons reporting two ancestries are counted in both categories. 2. Numbers in parentheses indicate the number of persons reporting this ancestry/race alone, not in combination with any other ancestry/race. 3. Refer to the Explanation of Data in the front of the book for more detailed information.

Arcadia

Place Type: City
County: Los Angeles
Population: 53,054

Ancestry/Race	Number	%
Afghan	26	0.05
African American/Black:	772	1.46
Not Hispanic (574)	721	1.36
Hispanic (27)	51	0.10
African, sub-Saharan:	34	0.06
African	20	0.04
Nigerian	8	0.02
South African	6	0.01
Alaska Native tribes, specified:	7	0.01
Alaska Athabascan	2	0.00
Aleut (1)	2	0.00
Tlingit-Haida	3	0.01
Am. Ind. or Alaska Nat., not spec.	152	0.29
Albanian	4	0.01
Alsatian	6	0.01
American Indian tribes, specified:	222	0.42
Apache (6)	16	0.03
Blackfeet (3)	12	0.02
Cherokee (7)	54	0.10
Cheyenne	6	0.01
Chickasaw	4	0.01
Chippewa (1)	4	0.01
Choctaw (6)	10	0.02
Creek (2)	3	0.01
Delaware	1	0.00
Iroquois (2)	3	0.01
Latin American Indians (16)	29	0.05
Lumbee	2	0.00
Navajo (5)	12	0.02
Osage (4)	4	0.01
Paiute	2	0.00
Pima	1	0.00
Potawatomi (2)	2	0.00
Pueblo (3)	5	0.01
Seminole	2	0.00
Shoshone (1)	1	0.00
Sioux (6)	13	0.02
Tohono O'Odham	1	0.00
Ute (1)	1	0.00
Yaqui	4	0.01
All other tribes (20)	30	0.06
American Indian tribes, not spec.	8	0.02
Arab:	639	1.21
Arab/Arabic	87	0.16
Egyptian	275	0.52
Lebanese	177	0.33
Palestinian	65	0.12
Syrian	17	0.03
Other Arab	18	0.03
Armenian	380	0.72
Asian:	25,838	48.70
Bangladeshi (6)	11	0.02
Cambodian (23)	28	0.05
Chinese, ex. Taiwanese (14,008)	14,945	28.17
Filipino (700)	854	1.61
Indian (693)	773	1.46
Indonesian (259)	378	0.71
Japanese (1,117)	1,290	2.43
Korean (1,712)	1,775	3.35
Laotian (3)	6	0.01
Malaysian (20)	27	0.05
Pakistani (56)	60	0.11
Sri Lankan (43)	49	0.09
Taiwanese (4,033)	4,731	8.92
Thai (204)	239	0.45
Vietnamese (264)	326	0.61
Other Asian, specified (74)	93	0.18
Other Asian, not specified (111)	253	0.48
Australian	12	0.02
Austrian	57	0.11
Basque	19	0.04
Belgian	44	0.08
Brazilian	59	0.11
British	248	0.47
Canadian	202	0.38
Carpatho Rusyn	10	0.02
Croatian	160	0.30
Czech	104	0.20
Czechoslovakian	46	0.09
Danish	273	0.52
Dutch	491	0.93
Eastern European	23	0.04
English	4,281	8.08
European	303	0.57
Finnish	56	0.11
French, except Basque	1,080	2.04
French Canadian	154	0.29
German	4,634	8.75
Greek	193	0.36
Hawaii Native/Pacific Islander:	251	0.47
Micronesian: (2)	3	0.01
Guamanian/Chamorro (2)	3	0.01
Polynesian: (25)	56	0.11
Native Hawaiian (11)	35	0.07
Samoan (14)	19	0.04
Other Polynesian	2	0.00
Other Pac. Isl., not spec. (15)	192	0.36
Hispanic or Latino:	5,629	10.61
Central American:	236	0.44
Costa Rican	15	0.03
Guatemalan	71	0.13
Honduran	9	0.02
Nicaraguan	48	0.09
Panamanian	10	0.02
Salvadoran	60	0.11
Other Central American	23	0.04
Cuban	182	0.34
Dominican Republic	6	0.01
Mexican	3,847	7.25
Puerto Rican	104	0.20
South American:	355	0.67
Argentinean	113	0.21
Bolivian	9	0.02
Chilean	23	0.04
Colombian	68	0.13
Ecuadorian	29	0.05
Peruvian	54	0.10
Uruguayan	3	0.01
Venezuelan	11	0.02
Other South American	45	0.08
Other Hispanic or Latino	899	1.69
Hungarian	122	0.23
Iranian	288	0.54
Irish	3,362	6.35
Israeli	34	0.06
Italian	2,697	5.09
Latvian	16	0.03
Lithuanian	115	0.22
Macedonian	5	0.01
Northern European	39	0.07
Norwegian	602	1.14
Pennsylvania German	9	0.02
Polish	821	1.55
Portuguese	41	0.08
Romanian	41	0.08
Russian	431	0.81
Scandinavian	64	0.12
Scotch-Irish	757	1.43
Scottish	902	1.70
Serbian	54	0.10
Slavic	5	0.01
Slovak	31	0.06
Slovene	5	0.01
Swedish	710	1.34
Swiss	157	0.30
Turkish	39	0.07
Ukrainian	173	0.33
United States or American	1,045	1.97
Welsh	245	0.46
West Indian, excl. Hispanic:	49	0.09
Belizean	37	0.07
Bermudan	4	0.01
Haitian	8	0.02
White:	25,406	47.89
Not Hispanic (21,259)	22,122	41.70
Hispanic (2,921)	3,284	6.19
Yugoslavian	131	0.25

Arcata

Place Type: City
County: Humboldt
Population: 16,651

Ancestry/Race	Number	%
African American/Black:	390	2.34
Not Hispanic (247)	358	2.15
Hispanic (12)	32	0.19
African, sub-Saharan:	74	0.44
African	43	0.26
Ethiopian	10	0.06
Nigerian	11	0.07
South African	10	0.06
Alaska Native tribes, specified:	8	0.05
Alaska Athabascan (1)	1	0.01
Aleut (2)	3	0.02
Eskimo (2)	3	0.02
Tlingit-Haida (1)	1	0.01
Alaska Native tribes, not specified	2	0.01
Am. Ind. or Alaska Nat., not spec.	155	0.93
Alsatian	9	0.05
American Indian tribes, specified:	613	3.68
Apache (7)	11	0.07
Blackfeet (2)	13	0.08
Cherokee (24)	120	0.72
Chickasaw (1)	4	0.02
Chippewa (5)	8	0.05
Choctaw (14)	25	0.15
Colville (1)	1	0.01
Comanche (1)	2	0.01
Cree (2)	10	0.06
Creek (1)	4	0.02
Delaware (2)	2	0.01
Iroquois (5)	14	0.08
Latin American Indians (5)	14	0.08
Lumbee (1)	1	0.01
Menominee	1	0.01
Navajo (7)	13	0.08
Osage (2)	2	0.01
Ottawa	1	0.01
Paiute (3)	9	0.05
Potawatomi (1)	4	0.02
Pueblo (4)	4	0.02
Seminole	1	0.01
Shoshone (1)	1	0.01
Sioux (11)	25	0.15
Tohono O'Odham (7)	7	0.04
Ute (1)	3	0.02
Yaqui (3)	6	0.04
Yuman	1	0.01
All other tribes (235)	306	1.84
American Indian tribes, not spec.	36	0.22
Arab:	82	0.49
Arab/Arabic	18	0.11
Iraqi	13	0.08
Lebanese	28	0.17
Moroccan	2	0.01
Palestinian	4	0.02
Syrian	8	0.05
Other Arab	9	0.05
Armenian	16	0.10
Asian:	567	3.41
Cambodian (8)	12	0.07
Chinese, ex. Taiwanese (80)	134	0.80
Filipino (37)	68	0.41
Hmong (25)	33	0.20
Indian (40)	55	0.33
Indonesian (4)	6	0.04
Japanese (88)	146	0.88
Korean (34)	39	0.23
Laotian (3)	3	0.02
Malaysian (2)	3	0.02
Pakistani	3	0.02

Notes: 1. Figures in the "Number" column do not add up to the total population due to: a) Ancestry/Race overlap — e.g. persons can report being both White and Irish, b) persons of Hispanic origin can report being any race, c) persons reporting two ancestries are counted in both categories. 2. Numbers in parentheses indicate the number of persons reporting this ancestry/race alone, not in combination with any other ancestry/race. 3. Refer to the Explanation of Data in the front of the book for more detailed information.

Taiwanese (3)	3	0.02
Thai (6)	10	0.06
Vietnamese (16)	22	0.13
Other Asian, specified (5)	9	0.05
Other Asian, not specified (11)	21	0.13
Australian	6	0.04
Austrian	45	0.27
Basque	33	0.20
Belgian	34	0.20
British	147	0.88
Canadian	55	0.33
Celtic	6	0.04
Croatian	10	0.06
Cypriot	16	0.10
Czech	43	0.26
Czechoslovakian	53	0.32
Danish	209	1.25
Dutch	371	2.22
Eastern European	32	0.19
English	2,177	13.03
European	629	3.76
Finnish	68	0.41
French, except Basque	619	3.70
French Canadian	147	0.88
German	3,034	18.15
Greek	46	0.28
Hawaii Native/Pacific Islander:	80	0.48
Micronesian: (4)	6	0.04
Guamanian/Chamorro (4)	6	0.04
Polynesian: (27)	49	0.29
Native Hawaiian (16)	35	0.21
Samoan (11)	14	0.08
Other Pac. Isl., specified	3	0.02
Other Pac. Isl., not spec. (3)	22	0.13
Hispanic or Latino:	1,202	7.22
Central American:	58	0.35
Costa Rican	6	0.04
Guatemalan	9	0.05
Honduran	1	0.01
Nicaraguan	8	0.05
Panamanian	8	0.05
Salvadoran	18	0.11
Other Central American	8	0.05
Cuban	28	0.17
Dominican Republic	7	0.04
Mexican	784	4.71
Puerto Rican	54	0.32
South American:	67	0.40
Argentinean	4	0.02
Chilean	13	0.08
Colombian	12	0.07
Ecuadorian	6	0.04
Peruvian	17	0.10
Venezuelan	2	0.01
Other South American	13	0.08
Other Hispanic or Latino	204	1.23
Hungarian	62	0.37
Iranian	25	0.15
Irish	2,587	15.48
Israeli	15	0.09
Italian	1,028	6.15
Latvian	13	0.08
Lithuanian	44	0.26
Luxemburger	12	0.07
Maltese	20	0.12
Northern European	56	0.34
Norwegian	490	2.93
Pennsylvania German	8	0.05
Polish	463	2.77
Portuguese	518	3.10
Russian	316	1.89
Scandinavian	129	0.77
Scotch-Irish	496	2.97
Scottish	771	4.61
Slavic	23	0.14
Slovak	15	0.09
Swedish	555	3.32
Swiss	176	1.05
Ukrainian	68	0.41
United States or American	693	4.15
Welsh	186	1.11
West Indian, excl. Hispanic:	13	0.08
Dutch West Indian	3	0.02
West Indian	10	0.06
White:	14,907	89.53
Not Hispanic (13,538)	14,207	85.32
Hispanic (534)	700	4.20
Yugoslavian	18	0.11

Arden-Arcade

Place Type: Census Designated Place
County: Sacramento
Population: 96,025

Ancestry/Race	Number	%
African American/Black:	6,951	7.24
Not Hispanic (5,541)	6,511	6.78
Hispanic (238)	440	0.46
African, sub-Saharan:	732	0.76
African	422	0.44
Cape Verdean	18	0.02
Ethiopian	65	0.07
Kenyan	18	0.02
Liberian	49	0.05
Nigerian	83	0.09
Sierra Leonean	6	0.01
South African	37	0.04
Sudanese	10	0.01
Zairian	15	0.02
Other sub-Saharan African	9	0.01
Alaska Native tribes, specified:	23	0.02
Alaska Athabascan (4)	5	0.01
Aleut (4)	7	0.01
Eskimo (5)	7	0.01
Tlingit-Haida (1)	3	0.00
All other tribes (1)	1	0.00
Alaska Native tribes, not specified	2	0.00
Am. Ind. or Alaska Nat., not spec.	601	0.63
Albanian	6	0.01
Alsatian	7	0.01
American Indian tribes, specified:	1,643	1.71
Apache (34)	64	0.07
Blackfeet (17)	80	0.08
Cherokee (131)	526	0.55
Cheyenne (2)	5	0.01
Chickasaw (13)	19	0.02
Chippewa (22)	51	0.05
Choctaw (23)	89	0.09
Colville (3)	3	0.00
Comanche (2)	8	0.01
Cree (3)	5	0.01
Creek (8)	22	0.02
Crow (2)	4	0.00
Delaware (2)	4	0.00
Iroquois (14)	29	0.03
Kiowa	3	0.00
Latin American Indians (27)	80	0.08
Lumbee	2	0.00
Menominee (2)	6	0.01
Navajo (16)	57	0.06
Osage (3)	12	0.01
Ottawa (6)	10	0.01
Paiute (10)	16	0.02
Pima (1)	11	0.01
Potawatomi (8)	10	0.01
Pueblo (8)	16	0.02
Puget Sound Salish (1)	6	0.01
Seminole (7)	13	0.01
Shoshone (8)	21	0.02
Sioux (32)	70	0.07
Tohono O'Odham (1)	3	0.00
Ute (1)	3	0.00
Yakama (3)	4	0.00
Yaqui (9)	19	0.02
All other tribes (211)	372	0.39
American Indian tribes, not spec.	110	0.11
Arab:	627	0.65
Arab/Arabic	92	0.10
Egyptian	86	0.09
Jordanian	73	0.08
Lebanese	114	0.12
Moroccan	6	0.01
Palestinian	70	0.07
Syrian	89	0.09
Other Arab	97	0.10
Armenian	404	0.42
Asian:	6,189	6.45
Cambodian (37)	44	0.05
Chinese, ex. Taiwanese (877)	1,117	1.16
Filipino (1,064)	1,557	1.62
Hmong (258)	271	0.28
Indian (603)	744	0.77
Indonesian (34)	54	0.06
Japanese (566)	897	0.93
Korean (390)	494	0.51
Laotian (88)	93	0.10
Malaysian (25)	29	0.03
Pakistani (72)	97	0.10
Sri Lankan (15)	15	0.02
Taiwanese (48)	59	0.06
Thai (52)	81	0.08
Vietnamese (380)	421	0.44
Other Asian, specified (12)	18	0.02
Other Asian, not specified (59)	198	0.21
Assyrian/Chaldean/Syriac	64	0.07
Australian	91	0.09
Austrian	264	0.27
Basque	74	0.08
Belgian	83	0.09
Brazilian	15	0.02
British	510	0.53
Bulgarian	42	0.04
Canadian	295	0.31
Celtic	37	0.04
Croatian	205	0.21
Czech	294	0.31
Czechoslovakian	195	0.20
Danish	956	1.00
Dutch	1,694	1.76
Eastern European	80	0.08
English	12,405	12.92
Estonian	11	0.01
European	1,304	1.36
Finnish	223	0.23
French, except Basque	3,596	3.75
French Canadian	704	0.73
German	14,318	14.91
Greek	770	0.80
Hawaii Native/Pacific Islander:	713	0.74
Melanesian: (118)	143	0.15
Fijian (118)	141	0.15
Other Melanesian	2	0.00
Micronesian: (49)	88	0.09
Guamanian/Chamorro (43)	82	0.09
Other Micronesian (6)	6	0.01
Polynesian: (185)	348	0.36
Native Hawaiian (68)	203	0.21
Samoan (64)	80	0.08
Tongan (50)	55	0.06
Other Polynesian (3)	10	0.01
Other Pac. Isl., specified	3	0.00
Other Pac. Isl., not spec. (50)	131	0.14
Hispanic or Latino:	11,501	11.98
Central American:	354	0.37
Costa Rican	23	0.02
Guatemalan	56	0.06
Honduran	33	0.03
Nicaraguan	44	0.05
Panamanian	29	0.03
Salvadoran	138	0.14
Other Central American	31	0.03
Cuban	82	0.09
Dominican Republic	17	0.02
Mexican	8,329	8.67
Puerto Rican	425	0.44
South American:	191	0.20
Argentinean	16	0.02
Bolivian	4	0.00
Chilean	22	0.02

Notes: 1. Figures in the "Number" column do not add up to the total population due to: a) Ancestry/Race overlap — e.g. persons can report being both White and Irish, b) persons of Hispanic origin can report being any race, c) persons reporting two ancestries are counted in both categories. 2. Numbers in parentheses indicate the number of persons reporting this ancestry/race alone, not in combination with any other ancestry/race. 3. Refer to the Explanation of Data in the front of the book for more detailed information.

Ancestry/Race	Number	%
Colombian	26	0.03
Ecuadorian	23	0.02
Paraguayan	2	0.00
Peruvian	62	0.06
Venezuelan	25	0.03
Other South American	11	0.01
Other Hispanic or Latino	2,103	2.19
Hungarian	408	0.42
Icelander	25	0.03
Iranian	475	0.49
Irish	11,488	11.97
Israeli	87	0.09
Italian	5,500	5.73
Latvian	80	0.08
Lithuanian	193	0.20
Luxemburger	18	0.02
Maltese	27	0.03
New Zealander	6	0.01
Northern European	148	0.15
Norwegian	2,131	2.22
Pennsylvania German	51	0.05
Polish	1,626	1.69
Portuguese	1,417	1.48
Romanian	435	0.45
Russian	1,695	1.77
Scandinavian	422	0.44
Scotch-Irish	2,285	2.38
Scottish	2,515	2.62
Serbian	95	0.10
Slavic	43	0.04
Slovak	52	0.05
Slovene	50	0.05
Swedish	1,801	1.88
Swiss	554	0.58
Turkish	30	0.03
Ukrainian	1,365	1.42
United States or American	4,026	4.19
Welsh	957	1.00
West Indian, excl. Hispanic:	161	0.17
British West Indian	29	0.03
Haitian	18	0.02
Jamaican	93	0.10
Trinidadian and Tobagonian	14	0.01
West Indian	7	0.01
White:	78,518	81.77
Not Hispanic (69,620)	72,574	75.58
Hispanic (4,665)	5,944	6.19
Yugoslavian	203	0.21

Arroyo Grande

Place Type: City
County: San Luis Obispo
Population: 15,851

Ancestry/Race	Number	%
African American/Black:	138	0.87
Not Hispanic (93)	121	0.76
Hispanic (6)	17	0.11
Am. Ind. or Alaska Nat., not spec.	50	0.32
American Indian tribes, specified:	172	1.09
Apache (3)	6	0.04
Blackfeet (1)	6	0.04
Cherokee (7)	48	0.30
Chippewa	2	0.01
Choctaw	11	0.07
Cree	3	0.02
Creek (3)	5	0.03
Iroquois (1)	2	0.01
Latin American Indians (6)	14	0.09
Navajo (1)	1	0.01
Osage (4)	5	0.03
Potawatomi	3	0.02
Pueblo (1)	2	0.01
Seminole	5	0.03
Shoshone (1)	2	0.01
Sioux (2)	6	0.04
Yakama	2	0.01
Yaqui (1)	1	0.01
All other tribes (24)	48	0.30
American Indian tribes, not spec.	5	0.03
Arab:	38	0.24
Lebanese	38	0.24
Armenian	31	0.19
Asian:	687	4.33
Cambodian	3	0.02
Chinese, ex. Taiwanese (67)	97	0.61
Filipino (160)	258	1.63
Indian (45)	50	0.32
Indonesian (5)	7	0.04
Japanese (141)	203	1.28
Korean (27)	31	0.20
Laotian (9)	9	0.06
Thai (1)	2	0.01
Vietnamese (8)	10	0.06
Other Asian, not specified (4)	17	0.11
Australian	7	0.04
Austrian	49	0.31
Basque	29	0.18
Belgian	22	0.14
Brazilian	9	0.06
British	144	0.90
Canadian	79	0.49
Celtic	18	0.11
Croatian	34	0.21
Czech	158	0.98
Czechoslovakian	31	0.19
Danish	252	1.57
Dutch	302	1.88
Eastern European	9	0.06
English	2,326	14.49
Estonian	6	0.04
European	145	0.90
Finnish	58	0.36
French, except Basque	545	3.40
French Canadian	130	0.81
German	2,874	17.91
Greek	23	0.14
Hawaii Native/Pacific Islander:	49	0.31
Micronesian: (13)	14	0.09
Guamanian/Chamorro (8)	9	0.06
Other Micronesian (5)	5	0.03
Polynesian: (10)	22	0.14
Native Hawaiian (5)	12	0.08
Samoan (5)	10	0.06
Other Pac. Isl., not spec. (5)	13	0.08
Hispanic or Latino:	1,770	11.17
Central American:	23	0.15
Costa Rican	2	0.01
Guatemalan	7	0.04
Nicaraguan	1	0.01
Panamanian	2	0.01
Salvadoran	10	0.06
Other Central American	1	0.01
Cuban	5	0.03
Mexican	1,365	8.61
Puerto Rican	22	0.14
South American:	25	0.16
Argentinean	7	0.04
Chilean	3	0.02
Colombian	7	0.04
Ecuadorian	2	0.01
Peruvian	3	0.02
Venezuelan	1	0.01
Other South American	2	0.01
Other Hispanic or Latino	330	2.08
Hungarian	38	0.24
Irish	2,255	14.05
Italian	798	4.97
Latvian	46	0.29
Lithuanian	21	0.13
Norwegian	514	3.20
Polish	313	1.95
Portuguese	460	2.87
Romanian	7	0.04
Russian	184	1.15
Scandinavian	93	0.58
Scotch-Irish	386	2.40
Scottish	410	2.55
Serbian	7	0.04
Slavic	14	0.09
Slovak	6	0.04
Slovene	9	0.06
Swedish	454	2.83
Swiss	127	0.79
Turkish	8	0.05
Ukrainian	9	0.06
United States or American	952	5.93
Welsh	225	1.40
West Indian, excl. Hispanic:	8	0.05
Jamaican	8	0.05
White:	14,541	91.74
Not Hispanic (13,109)	13,413	84.62
Hispanic (911)	1,128	7.12

Artesia

Place Type: City
County: Los Angeles
Population: 16,380

Ancestry/Race	Number	%
Afghan	4	0.02
African American/Black:	691	4.22
Not Hispanic (550)	632	3.86
Hispanic (32)	59	0.36
African, sub-Saharan:	60	0.37
African	23	0.14
Ethiopian	37	0.23
Alaska Native tribes, specified:	4	0.02
Tlingit-Haida (4)	4	0.02
Am. Ind. or Alaska Nat., not spec.	119	0.73
American Indian tribes, specified:	110	0.67
Apache (2)	4	0.02
Blackfeet (2)	8	0.05
Cherokee (9)	20	0.12
Chippewa	1	0.01
Choctaw (1)	1	0.01
Iroquois	1	0.01
Latin American Indians (28)	47	0.29
Navajo (5)	5	0.03
Sioux (7)	8	0.05
Tohono O'Odham	2	0.01
Ute (3)	3	0.02
Yaqui (1)	5	0.03
All other tribes (2)	5	0.03
American Indian tribes, not spec.	12	0.07
Arab:	51	0.31
Jordanian	25	0.15
Lebanese	26	0.16
Armenian	10	0.06
Asian:	4,843	29.57
Cambodian (72)	93	0.57
Chinese, ex. Taiwanese (633)	728	4.44
Filipino (1,696)	1,806	11.03
Indian (754)	799	4.88
Indonesian (25)	42	0.26
Japanese (89)	132	0.81
Korean (737)	748	4.57
Laotian (3)	3	0.02
Malaysian (4)	4	0.02
Pakistani (10)	14	0.09
Sri Lankan (5)	12	0.07
Taiwanese (198)	224	1.37
Thai (34)	39	0.24
Vietnamese (120)	148	0.90
Other Asian, specified (4)	8	0.05
Other Asian, not specified (28)	43	0.26
Austrian	4	0.02
Belgian	11	0.07
Brazilian	20	0.12
Canadian	4	0.02
Croatian	6	0.04
Czech	4	0.02
Danish	40	0.24
Dutch	747	4.56
English	406	2.48
European	133	0.81
French, except Basque	143	0.87
French Canadian	61	0.37

Notes: 1. Figures in the "Number" column do not add up to the total population due to: a) Ancestry/Race overlap — e.g. persons can report being both White and Irish, b) persons of Hispanic origin can report being any race, c) persons reporting two ancestries are counted in both categories. 2. Numbers in parentheses indicate the number of persons reporting this ancestry/race alone, not in combination with any other ancestry/race. 3. Refer to the Explanation of Data in the front of the book for more detailed information.

Ancestry/Race	Number	%
German	496	3.03
Guyanese	6	0.04
Hawaii Native/Pacific Islander:	167	1.02
Micronesian: (24)	27	0.16
Guamanian/Chamorro (23)	26	0.16
Other Micronesian (1)	1	0.01
Polynesian: (59)	84	0.51
Native Hawaiian (22)	37	0.23
Samoan (32)	36	0.22
Tongan (4)	4	0.02
Other Polynesian (1)	7	0.04
Other Pac. Isl., not spec. (6)	56	0.34
Hispanic or Latino:	6,272	38.29
Central American:	184	1.12
Costa Rican	36	0.22
Guatemalan	44	0.27
Honduran	5	0.03
Nicaraguan	17	0.10
Panamanian	13	0.08
Salvadoran	57	0.35
Other Central American	12	0.07
Cuban	34	0.21
Dominican Republic	1	0.01
Mexican	5,307	32.40
Puerto Rican	34	0.21
South American:	91	0.56
Argentinean	11	0.07
Bolivian	4	0.02
Chilean	2	0.01
Colombian	6	0.04
Ecuadorian	30	0.18
Peruvian	33	0.20
Venezuelan	2	0.01
Other South American	3	0.02
Other Hispanic or Latino	621	3.79
Irish	400	2.44
Italian	194	1.18
Lithuanian	7	0.04
Norwegian	35	0.21
Polish	37	0.23
Portuguese	1,539	9.40
Scandinavian	19	0.12
Scotch-Irish	54	0.33
Scottish	100	0.61
Swedish	85	0.52
Swiss	15	0.09
Ukrainian	14	0.09
United States or American	237	1.45
Welsh	63	0.38
White:	7,845	47.89
Not Hispanic (4,463)	4,794	29.27
Hispanic (2,773)	3,051	18.63
Yugoslavian	35	0.21

Arvin

Place Type: City
County: Kern
Population: 12,956

Ancestry/Race	Number	%
African American/Black:	166	1.28
Not Hispanic (68)	77	0.59
Hispanic (72)	89	0.69
Alaska Native tribes, specified:	1	0.01
Alaska Athabascan	1	0.01
Am. Ind. or Alaska Nat., not spec.	122	0.94
American Indian tribes, specified:	141	1.09
Cherokee (7)	31	0.24
Choctaw	5	0.04
Comanche (1)	1	0.01
Creek	2	0.02
Latin American Indians (68)	83	0.64
Paiute (3)	3	0.02
Yuman (5)	5	0.04
All other tribes (4)	11	0.08
American Indian tribes, not spec.	25	0.19
Arab:	64	0.49
Arab/Arabic	23	0.18
Other Arab	41	0.32
Asian:	198	1.53
Chinese, ex. Taiwanese (8)	11	0.08
Filipino (46)	58	0.45
Indian (63)	86	0.66
Indonesian	3	0.02
Japanese (7)	8	0.06
Korean	1	0.01
Laotian (18)	18	0.14
Other Asian, specified	1	0.01
Other Asian, not specified (1)	12	0.09
Dutch	15	0.12
English	100	0.77
French, except Basque	13	0.10
German	105	0.81
Greek	20	0.15
Hawaii Native/Pacific Islander:	17	0.13
Micronesian: (7)	7	0.05
Guamanian/Chamorro (7)	7	0.05
Polynesian:	1	0.01
Samoan	1	0.01
Other Pac. Isl., not spec. (8)	9	0.07
Hispanic or Latino:	11,341	87.53
Central American:	45	0.35
Costa Rican	4	0.03
Guatemalan	10	0.08
Honduran	5	0.04
Nicaraguan	1	0.01
Salvadoran	18	0.14
Other Central American	7	0.05
Cuban	6	0.05
Mexican	9,826	75.84
Puerto Rican	66	0.51
South American:	6	0.05
Chilean	1	0.01
Colombian	4	0.03
Other South American	1	0.01
Other Hispanic or Latino	1,392	10.74
Irish	129	1.00
Italian	50	0.39
Norwegian	7	0.05
Polish	7	0.05
Scottish	7	0.05
Swedish	15	0.12
United States or American	332	2.56
Welsh	11	0.08
West Indian, excl. Hispanic:	8	0.06
West Indian	8	0.06
White:	6,348	49.00
Not Hispanic (1,276)	1,339	10.33
Hispanic (4,560)	5,009	38.66

Ashland

Place Type: Census Designated Place
County: Alameda
Population: 20,793

Ancestry/Race	Number	%
Afghan	40	0.19
African American/Black:	4,582	22.04
Not Hispanic (4,067)	4,365	20.99
Hispanic (119)	217	1.04
African, sub-Saharan:	300	1.44
African	245	1.18
Nigerian	55	0.26
Alaska Native tribes, specified:	4	0.02
Eskimo (1)	1	0.00
Tlingit-Haida (1)	3	0.01
Am. Ind. or Alaska Nat., not spec.	245	1.18
American Indian tribes, specified:	372	1.79
Apache (24)	52	0.25
Blackfeet (4)	20	0.10
Cherokee (26)	80	0.38
Cheyenne	2	0.01
Chickasaw (1)	2	0.01
Chippewa (4)	8	0.04
Choctaw (6)	13	0.06
Comanche (1)	8	0.04
Creek (1)	2	0.01
Crow (2)	5	0.02
Iroquois	1	0.00
Kiowa (1)	2	0.01
Latin American Indians (16)	33	0.16
Navajo (14)	25	0.12
Ottawa	2	0.01
Paiute (3)	4	0.02
Pima (3)	3	0.01
Potawatomi	3	0.01
Pueblo (18)	25	0.12
Seminole	4	0.02
Shoshone (2)	2	0.01
Sioux (19)	25	0.12
Tohono O'Odham (2)	2	0.01
Yaqui (2)	6	0.03
All other tribes (25)	43	0.21
American Indian tribes, not spec.	33	0.16
Arab:	206	0.99
Arab/Arabic	15	0.07
Lebanese	30	0.14
Other Arab	161	0.78
Asian:	3,619	17.40
Bangladeshi (4)	4	0.02
Cambodian (23)	41	0.20
Chinese, ex. Taiwanese (990)	1,093	5.26
Filipino (1,179)	1,418	6.82
Hmong (14)	14	0.07
Indian (268)	315	1.51
Indonesian (15)	17	0.08
Japanese (115)	171	0.82
Korean (123)	147	0.71
Laotian (18)	22	0.11
Malaysian (3)	4	0.02
Pakistani (5)	8	0.04
Taiwanese (11)	17	0.08
Thai (12)	18	0.09
Vietnamese (227)	252	1.21
Other Asian, specified (7)	16	0.08
Other Asian, not specified (19)	62	0.30
Australian	11	0.05
Belgian	7	0.03
Brazilian	47	0.23
British	68	0.33
Canadian	23	0.11
Celtic	27	0.13
Croatian	40	0.19
Czechoslovakian	9	0.04
Danish	41	0.20
Dutch	55	0.26
English	581	2.80
Estonian	16	0.08
European	142	0.68
Finnish	10	0.05
French, except Basque	235	1.13
French Canadian	60	0.29
German	1,108	5.34
Greek	84	0.40
Hawaii Native/Pacific Islander:	476	2.29
Melanesian: (34)	45	0.22
Fijian (34)	45	0.22
Micronesian: (44)	73	0.35
Guamanian/Chamorro (35)	60	0.29
Other Micronesian (9)	13	0.06
Polynesian: (114)	255	1.23
Native Hawaiian (33)	143	0.69
Samoan (57)	76	0.37
Tongan (6)	15	0.07
Other Polynesian (18)	21	0.10
Other Pac. Isl., not spec. (39)	103	0.50
Hispanic or Latino:	6,753	32.48
Central American:	453	2.18
Costa Rican	11	0.05
Guatemalan	62	0.30
Honduran	27	0.13
Nicaraguan	150	0.72
Panamanian	3	0.01
Salvadoran	180	0.87
Other Central American	20	0.10
Cuban	29	0.14
Dominican Republic	5	0.02
Mexican	4,743	22.81

Notes: 1. Figures in the "Number" column do not add up to the total population due to: a) Ancestry/Race overlap — e.g. persons can report being both White and Irish, b) persons of Hispanic origin can report being any race, c) persons reporting two ancestries are counted in both categories. 2. Numbers in parentheses indicate the number of persons reporting this ancestry/race alone, not in combination with any other ancestry/race. 3. Refer to the Explanation of Data in the front of the book for more detailed information.

	Number	%
Puerto Rican	241	1.16
South American:	108	0.52
Bolivian	9	0.04
Chilean	8	0.04
Colombian	32	0.15
Ecuadorian	2	0.01
Peruvian	41	0.20
Uruguayan	2	0.01
Venezuelan	4	0.02
Other South American	10	0.05
Other Hispanic or Latino	1,174	5.65
Hungarian	21	0.10
Iranian	35	0.17
Irish	866	4.17
Italian	672	3.24
Latvian	7	0.03
Northern European	16	0.08
Norwegian	156	0.75
Pennsylvania German	4	0.02
Polish	71	0.34
Portuguese	607	2.92
Romanian	120	0.58
Russian	35	0.17
Scandinavian	24	0.12
Scotch-Irish	214	1.03
Scottish	200	0.96
Slavic	17	0.08
Swedish	103	0.50
Swiss	26	0.13
Ukrainian	10	0.05
United States or American	497	2.39
Welsh	60	0.29
West Indian, excl. Hispanic:	37	0.18
Barbadian	11	0.05
Jamaican	26	0.13
White:	9,248	44.48
Not Hispanic (5,583)	6,209	29.86
Hispanic (2,532)	3,039	14.62
Yugoslavian	20	0.10

Atascadero

Place Type: City
County: San Luis Obispo
Population: 26,411

Ancestry/Race	Number	%
African American/Black:	735	2.78
Not Hispanic (603)	697	2.64
Hispanic (20)	38	0.14
African, sub-Saharan:	9	0.03
African	9	0.03
Alaska Native tribes, specified:	4	0.02
Alaska Athabascan	1	0.00
Aleut	2	0.01
All other tribes (1)	1	0.00
Am. Ind. or Alaska Nat., not spec.	129	0.49
American Indian tribes, specified:	423	1.60
Apache (8)	23	0.09
Blackfeet (13)	30	0.11
Cherokee (35)	122	0.46
Cheyenne (1)	3	0.01
Chickasaw (3)	6	0.02
Chippewa (3)	4	0.02
Choctaw (13)	23	0.09
Comanche (1)	1	0.00
Creek	6	0.02
Iroquois	2	0.01
Latin American Indians (11)	21	0.08
Navajo (7)	11	0.04
Osage (3)	10	0.04
Ottawa	3	0.01
Paiute (1)	4	0.02
Pima	1	0.00
Potawatomi	2	0.01
Pueblo (4)	10	0.04
Seminole	2	0.01
Sioux (11)	18	0.07
Yakama (3)	3	0.01
Yaqui	6	0.02
All other tribes (56)	112	0.42
American Indian tribes, not spec.	33	0.12
Arab:	34	0.13
Iraqi	12	0.05
Syrian	22	0.08
Armenian	23	0.09
Asian:	536	2.03
Cambodian (1)	1	0.00
Chinese, ex. Taiwanese (58)	86	0.33
Filipino (129)	197	0.75
Indian (21)	27	0.10
Indonesian (4)	11	0.04
Japanese (39)	91	0.34
Korean (41)	58	0.22
Pakistani (1)	1	0.00
Sri Lankan (3)	4	0.02
Thai (2)	2	0.01
Vietnamese (24)	28	0.11
Other Asian, specified (1)	6	0.02
Other Asian, not specified (8)	24	0.09
Australian	9	0.03
Austrian	158	0.60
Basque	6	0.02
Belgian	25	0.09
Brazilian	13	0.05
British	117	0.44
Canadian	117	0.44
Celtic	5	0.02
Croatian	8	0.03
Czech	106	0.40
Czechoslovakian	71	0.27
Danish	418	1.58
Dutch	585	2.21
Eastern European	23	0.09
English	4,324	16.36
European	627	2.37
Finnish	103	0.39
French, except Basque	970	3.67
French Canadian	182	0.69
German	4,528	17.13
Greek	206	0.78
Hawaii Native/Pacific Islander:	86	0.33
Micronesian: (9)	18	0.07
Guamanian/Chamorro (7)	16	0.06
Other Micronesian (2)	2	0.01
Polynesian: (15)	51	0.19
Native Hawaiian (10)	40	0.15
Samoan (3)	9	0.03
Tongan (2)	2	0.01
Other Pac. Isl., not spec. (6)	17	0.06
Hispanic or Latino:	2,783	10.54
Central American:	54	0.20
Costa Rican	10	0.04
Guatemalan	16	0.06
Nicaraguan	8	0.03
Panamanian	8	0.03
Salvadoran	11	0.04
Other Central American	1	0.00
Cuban	19	0.07
Dominican Republic	3	0.01
Mexican	2,067	7.83
Puerto Rican	79	0.30
South American:	45	0.17
Argentinean	6	0.02
Bolivian	3	0.01
Colombian	9	0.03
Ecuadorian	8	0.03
Peruvian	5	0.02
Venezuelan	4	0.02
Other South American	10	0.04
Other Hispanic or Latino	516	1.95
Hungarian	127	0.48
Icelander	16	0.06
Iranian	17	0.06
Irish	3,752	14.20
Italian	1,763	6.67
Lithuanian	52	0.20
Northern European	42	0.16
Norwegian	664	2.51
Pennsylvania German	19	0.07
Polish	367	1.39
Portuguese	455	1.72
Romanian	23	0.09
Russian	286	1.08
Scandinavian	58	0.22
Scotch-Irish	606	2.29
Scottish	753	2.85
Serbian	8	0.03
Slavic	32	0.12
Slovak	14	0.05
Slovene	9	0.03
Swedish	651	2.46
Swiss	250	0.95
Turkish	8	0.03
Ukrainian	25	0.09
United States or American	1,578	5.97
Welsh	337	1.28
West Indian, excl. Hispanic:	13	0.05
Dutch West Indian	13	0.05
White:	24,266	91.88
Not Hispanic (21,850)	22,422	84.90
Hispanic (1,601)	1,844	6.98
Yugoslavian	50	0.19

Atwater

Place Type: City
County: Merced
Population: 23,113

Ancestry/Race	Number	%
African American/Black:	1,330	5.75
Not Hispanic (1,093)	1,221	5.28
Hispanic (60)	109	0.47
African, sub-Saharan:	84	0.37
African	77	0.34
Cape Verdean	7	0.03
Alaska Native tribes, specified:	5	0.02
Aleut	1	0.00
All other tribes	4	0.02
Alaska Native tribes, not specified	1	0.00
Am. Ind. or Alaska Nat., not spec.	187	0.81
American Indian tribes, specified:	359	1.55
Apache (10)	17	0.07
Blackfeet (3)	11	0.05
Cherokee (45)	107	0.46
Chickasaw (5)	7	0.03
Chippewa (6)	7	0.03
Choctaw (9)	28	0.12
Creek (8)	10	0.04
Delaware (2)	2	0.01
Iroquois (5)	13	0.06
Kiowa (4)	4	0.02
Latin American Indians (14)	40	0.17
Navajo (15)	16	0.07
Osage	1	0.00
Ottawa (3)	3	0.01
Paiute (3)	7	0.03
Potawatomi (2)	2	0.01
Puget Sound Salish (1)	7	0.03
Seminole	1	0.00
Sioux (4)	8	0.03
Yaqui (6)	6	0.03
All other tribes (32)	62	0.27
American Indian tribes, not spec.	32	0.14
Armenian	9	0.04
Asian:	1,676	7.25
Cambodian (17)	17	0.07
Chinese, ex. Taiwanese (80)	110	0.48
Filipino (197)	318	1.38
Hmong (462)	505	2.18
Indian (173)	212	0.92
Indonesian (3)	11	0.05
Japanese (70)	140	0.61
Korean (76)	105	0.45
Laotian (40)	60	0.26
Taiwanese (3)	3	0.01
Thai (49)	76	0.33
Vietnamese (38)	46	0.20
Other Asian, specified	2	0.01

Notes: 1. Figures in the "Number" column do not add up to the total population due to: a) Ancestry/Race overlap — e.g. persons can report being both White and Irish, b) persons of Hispanic origin can report being any race, c) persons reporting two ancestries are counted in both categories. 2. Numbers in parentheses indicate the number of persons reporting this ancestry/race alone, not in combination with any other ancestry/race. 3. Refer to the Explanation of Data in the front of the book for more detailed information.

Ancestry/Race	Number	%
Other Asian, not specified (27)	71	0.31
Assyrian/Chaldean/Syriac	8	0.03
Basque	16	0.07
British	41	0.18
Canadian	11	0.05
Croatian	81	0.35
Czech	41	0.18
Danish	58	0.25
Dutch	357	1.56
English	1,312	5.73
European	142	0.62
Finnish	8	0.03
French, except Basque	381	1.66
French Canadian	233	1.02
German	2,045	8.93
Greek	23	0.10
Hawaii Native/Pacific Islander:	183	0.79
Micronesian: (41)	56	0.24
Guamanian/Chamorro (40)	54	0.23
Other Micronesian (1)	2	0.01
Polynesian: (31)	83	0.36
Native Hawaiian (25)	72	0.31
Samoan (5)	9	0.04
Tongan (1)	1	0.00
Other Polynesian	1	0.00
Other Pac. Isl., not spec. (9)	44	0.19
Hispanic or Latino:	9,594	41.51
Central American:	59	0.26
Costa Rican	9	0.04
Guatemalan	6	0.03
Honduran	4	0.02
Nicaraguan	6	0.03
Panamanian	11	0.05
Salvadoran	15	0.06
Other Central American	8	0.03
Cuban	21	0.09
Mexican	8,333	36.05
Puerto Rican	96	0.42
South American:	19	0.08
Argentinean	1	0.00
Chilean	1	0.00
Colombian	7	0.03
Peruvian	10	0.04
Other Hispanic or Latino	1,066	4.61
Hungarian	44	0.19
Irish	1,663	7.26
Italian	466	2.04
Lithuanian	7	0.03
New Zealander	12	0.05
Northern European	8	0.03
Norwegian	307	1.34
Pennsylvania German	30	0.13
Polish	173	0.76
Portuguese	740	3.23
Romanian	12	0.05
Russian	9	0.04
Scandinavian	31	0.14
Scotch-Irish	162	0.71
Scottish	189	0.83
Slavic	11	0.05
Slovak	33	0.14
Swedish	192	0.84
Swiss	19	0.08
United States or American	1,223	5.34
Welsh	58	0.25
White:	14,428	62.42
Not Hispanic (10,245)	10,804	46.74
Hispanic (3,007)	3,624	15.68
Yugoslavian	10	0.04

Auburn

Place Type: City
County: Placer
Population: 12,462

Ancestry/Race	Number	%
African American/Black:	85	0.68
Not Hispanic (56)	84	0.67
Hispanic (1)	1	0.01
African, sub-Saharan:	10	0.08
South African	10	0.08
Alaska Native tribes, specified:	3	0.02
Alaska Athabascan	1	0.01
Tlingit-Haida	2	0.02
Am. Ind. or Alaska Nat., not spec.	49	0.39
Albanian	12	0.10
American Indian tribes, specified:	167	1.34
Apache (6)	12	0.10
Blackfeet (1)	2	0.02
Cherokee (16)	59	0.47
Cheyenne (1)	2	0.02
Chickasaw	2	0.02
Chippewa (5)	5	0.04
Choctaw (6)	10	0.08
Comanche	1	0.01
Creek (3)	7	0.06
Delaware	1	0.01
Latin American Indians (3)	5	0.04
Navajo (2)	2	0.02
Shoshone (1)	1	0.01
Sioux (2)	8	0.06
Ute (1)	1	0.01
Yaqui (1)	1	0.01
All other tribes (32)	48	0.39
American Indian tribes, not spec.	19	0.15
Arab:	8	0.06
Lebanese	8	0.06
Armenian	18	0.14
Asian:	258	2.07
Chinese, ex. Taiwanese (59)	92	0.74
Filipino (42)	58	0.47
Indian (2)	3	0.02
Indonesian (2)	3	0.02
Japanese (43)	70	0.56
Korean (10)	12	0.10
Vietnamese (1)	5	0.04
Other Asian, specified (1)	2	0.02
Other Asian, not specified (4)	13	0.10
Austrian	26	0.21
Basque	9	0.07
Belgian	24	0.19
British	186	1.49
Canadian	60	0.48
Celtic	22	0.18
Croatian	8	0.06
Czech	54	0.43
Czechoslovakian	55	0.44
Danish	123	0.99
Dutch	242	1.94
English	2,217	17.78
European	206	1.65
Finnish	85	0.68
French, except Basque	500	4.01
French Canadian	60	0.48
German	2,472	19.83
Greek	38	0.30
Hawaii Native/Pacific Islander:	43	0.35
Micronesian: (5)	6	0.05
Guamanian/Chamorro (5)	6	0.05
Polynesian: (7)	32	0.26
Native Hawaiian (5)	26	0.21
Samoan (1)	4	0.03
Tongan	1	0.01
Other Polynesian (1)	1	0.01
Other Pac. Isl., not spec.	5	0.04
Hispanic or Latino:	744	5.97
Central American:	20	0.16
Costa Rican	3	0.02
Guatemalan	5	0.04
Salvadoran	11	0.09
Other Central American	1	0.01
Cuban	13	0.10
Dominican Republic	1	0.01
Mexican	453	3.64
Puerto Rican	22	0.18
South American:	10	0.08
Argentinean	3	0.02
Chilean	4	0.03
Other South American	3	0.02
Other Hispanic or Latino	225	1.81
Hungarian	33	0.26
Irish	1,865	14.96
Italian	757	6.07
Latvian	8	0.06
Lithuanian	22	0.18
Maltese	10	0.08
Northern European	33	0.26
Norwegian	317	2.54
Pennsylvania German	6	0.05
Polish	170	1.36
Portuguese	356	2.86
Russian	117	0.94
Scandinavian	26	0.21
Scotch-Irish	472	3.79
Scottish	395	3.17
Swedish	359	2.88
Swiss	83	0.67
Turkish	7	0.06
Ukrainian	51	0.41
United States or American	472	3.79
Welsh	148	1.19
White:	11,913	95.59
Not Hispanic (11,155)	11,373	91.26
Hispanic (486)	540	4.33
Yugoslavian	49	0.39

Avenal

Place Type: City
County: Kings
Population: 14,674

Ancestry/Race	Number	%
African American/Black:	1,892	12.89
Not Hispanic (1,808)	1,828	12.46
Hispanic (42)	64	0.44
African, sub-Saharan:	8	0.05
African	8	0.05
Alaska Native tribes, specified:	4	0.03
Tlingit-Haida	4	0.03
Am. Ind. or Alaska Nat., not spec.	101	0.69
American Indian tribes, specified:	90	0.61
Cherokee (6)	21	0.14
Cheyenne	1	0.01
Chippewa (1)	1	0.01
Choctaw (2)	3	0.02
Creek	1	0.01
Iroquois (1)	1	0.01
Latin American Indians (27)	45	0.31
Osage	1	0.01
All other tribes (11)	16	0.11
American Indian tribes, not spec.	22	0.15
Asian:	107	0.73
Chinese, ex. Taiwanese (3)	3	0.02
Filipino (39)	51	0.35
Indian (5)	34	0.23
Japanese (2)	8	0.05
Korean (3)	3	0.02
Thai (1)	2	0.01
Vietnamese	2	0.01
Other Asian, not specified (4)	4	0.03
British	5	0.03
Danish	21	0.14
Dutch	7	0.05
English	100	0.68
European	4	0.03
French, except Basque	9	0.06
German	199	1.35
Greek	7	0.05
Hawaii Native/Pacific Islander:	25	0.17
Micronesian: (7)	7	0.05
Guamanian/Chamorro (7)	7	0.05
Polynesian: (1)	12	0.08
Native Hawaiian	3	0.02
Samoan (1)	9	0.06
Other Pac. Isl., not spec.	6	0.04
Hispanic or Latino:	9,667	65.88
Central American:	13	0.09
Guatemalan	7	0.05

Notes: 1. Figures in the "Number" column do not add up to the total population due to: a) Ancestry/Race overlap — e.g. persons can report being both White and Irish, b) persons of Hispanic origin can report being any race, c) persons reporting two ancestries are counted in both categories. 2. Numbers in parentheses indicate the number of persons reporting this ancestry/race alone, not in combination with any other ancestry/race. 3. Refer to the Explanation of Data in the front of the book for more detailed information.

Ancestry/Race	Number	%
Honduran	1	0.01
Salvadoran	3	0.02
Other Central American	2	0.01
Cuban	3	0.02
Mexican	8,780	59.83
Puerto Rican	15	0.10
South American:	7	0.05
Chilean	1	0.01
Colombian	6	0.04
Other Hispanic or Latino	849	5.79
Irish	200	1.36
Italian	34	0.23
Norwegian	3	0.02
Portuguese	61	0.41
Scotch-Irish	17	0.12
Scottish	5	0.03
Swiss	6	0.04
United States or American	220	1.50
White:	5,597	38.14
Not Hispanic (2,923)	3,026	20.62
Hispanic (2,336)	2,571	17.52
Yugoslavian	5	0.03

Avocado Heights

Place Type: Census Designated Place
County: Los Angeles
Population: 15,148

Ancestry/Race	Number	%
African American/Black:	271	1.79
Not Hispanic (87)	106	0.70
Hispanic (136)	165	1.09
African, sub-Saharan:	16	0.11
African	16	0.11
Am. Ind. or Alaska Nat., not spec.	113	0.75
American Indian tribes, specified:	123	0.81
Apache (1)	4	0.03
Cherokee (7)	13	0.09
Chickasaw (1)	1	0.01
Kiowa (7)	7	0.05
Latin American Indians (41)	52	0.34
Navajo (1)	5	0.03
Osage (1)	1	0.01
Pueblo (4)	5	0.03
Seminole	9	0.06
Tohono O'Odham	13	0.09
Yaqui (3)	7	0.05
All other tribes (2)	6	0.04
American Indian tribes, not spec.	13	0.09
Arab:	61	0.40
Arab/Arabic	53	0.35
Jordanian	8	0.05
Armenian	85	0.56
Asian:	1,521	10.04
Cambodian (18)	18	0.12
Chinese, ex. Taiwanese (347)	398	2.63
Filipino (337)	387	2.55
Indian (36)	40	0.26
Indonesian (2)	7	0.05
Japanese (222)	257	1.70
Korean (130)	137	0.90
Laotian (2)	2	0.01
Malaysian (3)	3	0.02
Taiwanese (10)	15	0.10
Thai (77)	88	0.58
Vietnamese (155)	161	1.06
Other Asian, not specified (5)	8	0.05
Austrian	27	0.18
Basque	4	0.03
Brazilian	13	0.09
British	5	0.03
Canadian	17	0.11
Czech	4	0.03
Czechoslovakian	24	0.16
Danish	38	0.25
Dutch	30	0.20
Eastern European	9	0.06
English	135	0.89
European	16	0.11
Finnish	5	0.03
French, except Basque	133	0.88
French Canadian	12	0.08
German	359	2.37
Greek	40	0.26
Hawaii Native/Pacific Islander:	28	0.18
Micronesian: (3)	3	0.02
Guamanian/Chamorro (3)	3	0.02
Polynesian: (12)	15	0.10
Native Hawaiian (10)	13	0.09
Samoan (2)	2	0.01
Other Pac. Isl., not spec. (1)	10	0.07
Hispanic or Latino:	11,776	77.74
Central American:	255	1.68
Costa Rican	10	0.07
Guatemalan	88	0.58
Honduran	7	0.05
Nicaraguan	24	0.16
Panamanian	5	0.03
Salvadoran	89	0.59
Other Central American	32	0.21
Cuban	61	0.40
Dominican Republic	1	0.01
Mexican	9,985	65.92
Puerto Rican	43	0.28
South American:	97	0.64
Argentinean	27	0.18
Bolivian	2	0.01
Chilean	12	0.08
Colombian	11	0.07
Ecuadorian	22	0.15
Peruvian	8	0.05
Venezuelan	1	0.01
Other South American	14	0.09
Other Hispanic or Latino	1,334	8.81
Irish	222	1.47
Italian	266	1.76
Norwegian	11	0.07
Pennsylvania German	6	0.04
Polish	45	0.30
Russian	49	0.32
Scotch-Irish	45	0.30
Scottish	28	0.18
Swedish	43	0.28
Swiss	45	0.30
Ukrainian	21	0.14
United States or American	318	2.10
Welsh	20	0.13
White:	8,267	54.57
Not Hispanic (1,757)	1,846	12.19
Hispanic (6,033)	6,421	42.39
Yugoslavian	13	0.09

Azusa

Place Type: City
County: Los Angeles
Population: 44,712

Ancestry/Race	Number	%
Afghan	36	0.08
African American/Black:	1,963	4.39
Not Hispanic (1,576)	1,749	3.91
Hispanic (112)	214	0.48
African, sub-Saharan:	155	0.35
African	100	0.23
Kenyan	36	0.08
Senegalese	6	0.01
Sierra Leonean	13	0.03
Alaska Native tribes, specified:	3	0.01
Alaska Athabascan (1)	2	0.00
Eskimo	1	0.00
Alaska Native tribes, not specified	1	0.00
Am. Ind. or Alaska Nat., not spec.	362	0.81
American Indian tribes, specified:	544	1.22
Apache (29)	54	0.12
Blackfeet (3)	8	0.02
Cherokee (27)	87	0.19
Cheyenne	1	0.00
Chickasaw (1)	1	0.00
Chippewa	7	0.02
Choctaw (1)	10	0.02
Colville (1)	1	0.00
Comanche (6)	7	0.02
Creek (3)	7	0.02
Iroquois (1)	6	0.01
Latin American Indians (123)	180	0.40
Lumbee (1)	1	0.00
Navajo (24)	35	0.08
Osage	1	0.00
Ottawa (1)	1	0.00
Paiute	1	0.00
Pima (5)	6	0.01
Pueblo (9)	9	0.02
Seminole	1	0.00
Sioux (8)	16	0.04
Ute	4	0.01
Yaqui (9)	12	0.03
Yuman (13)	14	0.03
All other tribes (45)	74	0.17
American Indian tribes, not spec.	55	0.12
Arab:	215	0.48
Arab/Arabic	43	0.10
Lebanese	105	0.24
Palestinian	25	0.06
Syrian	35	0.08
Other Arab	7	0.02
Armenian	111	0.25
Asian:	3,320	7.43
Bangladeshi	5	0.01
Cambodian (11)	14	0.03
Chinese, ex. Taiwanese (331)	448	1.00
Filipino (1,323)	1,545	3.46
Indian (179)	227	0.51
Indonesian (58)	94	0.21
Japanese (236)	335	0.75
Korean (163)	179	0.40
Malaysian (4)	4	0.01
Pakistani (18)	23	0.05
Sri Lankan (13)	13	0.03
Taiwanese (75)	81	0.18
Thai (67)	81	0.18
Vietnamese (143)	180	0.40
Other Asian, specified (5)	13	0.03
Other Asian, not specified (47)	78	0.17
Austrian	15	0.03
Basque	4	0.01
Belgian	20	0.05
Brazilian	10	0.02
British	95	0.21
Canadian	102	0.23
Croatian	7	0.02
Czech	29	0.07
Czechoslovakian	21	0.05
Danish	83	0.19
Dutch	246	0.55
Eastern European	21	0.05
English	1,854	4.18
European	123	0.28
Finnish	54	0.12
French, except Basque	630	1.42
French Canadian	145	0.33
German	2,623	5.91
Greek	129	0.29
Guyanese	37	0.08
Hawaii Native/Pacific Islander:	246	0.55
Melanesian: (5)	5	0.01
Fijian (5)	5	0.01
Micronesian: (6)	8	0.02
Guamanian/Chamorro (2)	3	0.01
Other Micronesian (4)	5	0.01
Polynesian: (40)	144	0.32
Native Hawaiian (17)	76	0.17
Samoan (22)	46	0.10
Tongan (1)	21	0.05
Other Polynesian	1	0.00
Other Pac. Isl., specified	7	0.02
Other Pac. Isl., not spec. (26)	82	0.18
Hispanic or Latino:	28,522	63.79
Central American:	842	1.88

Notes: 1. Figures in the "Number" column do not add up to the total population due to: a) Ancestry/Race overlap — e.g. persons can report being both White and Irish, b) persons of Hispanic origin can report being any race, c) persons reporting two ancestries are counted in both categories. 2. Numbers in parentheses indicate the number of persons reporting this ancestry/race alone, not in combination with any other ancestry/race. 3. Refer to the Explanation of Data in the front of the book for more detailed information.

Costa Rican	24	0.05
Guatemalan	230	0.51
Honduran	29	0.06
Nicaraguan	88	0.20
Panamanian	12	0.03
Salvadoran	361	0.81
Other Central American	98	0.22
Cuban	129	0.29
Dominican Republic	4	0.01
Mexican	23,836	53.31
Puerto Rican	208	0.47
South American:	276	0.62
Argentinean	51	0.11
Bolivian	3	0.01
Chilean	32	0.07
Colombian	60	0.13
Ecuadorian	32	0.07
Peruvian	64	0.14
Uruguayan	1	0.00
Venezuelan	7	0.02
Other South American	26	0.06
Other Hispanic or Latino	3,227	7.22
Hungarian	60	0.14
Icelander	21	0.05
Iranian	89	0.20
Irish	1,563	3.52
Israeli	9	0.02
Italian	966	2.18
Latvian	10	0.02
Lithuanian	6	0.01
Northern European	22	0.05
Norwegian	456	1.03
Pennsylvania German	13	0.03
Polish	357	0.80
Portuguese	100	0.23
Romanian	5	0.01
Russian	152	0.34
Scandinavian	98	0.22
Scotch-Irish	183	0.41
Scottish	278	0.63
Slavic	38	0.09
Swedish	269	0.61
Swiss	74	0.17
Turkish	15	0.03
Ukrainian	28	0.06
United States or American	1,276	2.88
Welsh	77	0.17
West Indian, excl. Hispanic:	80	0.18
Belizean	63	0.14
Haitian	12	0.03
West Indian	5	0.01
White:	25,553	57.15
Not Hispanic (10,824)	11,436	25.58
Hispanic (12,582)	14,117	31.57
Yugoslavian	37	0.08

Bakersfield

Place Type: City
County: Kern
Population: 247,057

Ancestry/Race	Number	%
African American/Black:	24,636	9.97
Not Hispanic (21,987)	23,481	9.50
Hispanic (654)	1,155	0.47
African, sub-Saharan:	1,722	0.70
African	1,378	0.56
Ethiopian	71	0.03
Nigerian	197	0.08
South African	10	0.00
Sudanese	66	0.03
Alaska Native tribes, specified:	27	0.01
Alaska Athabascan (6)	8	0.00
Aleut (2)	4	0.00
Eskimo (7)	11	0.00
Tlingit-Haida (3)	4	0.00
Alaska Native tribes, not specified	4	0.00
Am. Ind. or Alaska Nat., not spec.	1,988	0.80
Albanian	32	0.01
American Indian tribes, specified:	4,077	1.65
Apache (87)	176	0.07
Blackfeet (32)	115	0.05
Cherokee (472)	1,325	0.54
Cheyenne (9)	12	0.00
Chickasaw (42)	55	0.02
Chippewa (16)	32	0.01
Choctaw (204)	439	0.18
Colville (5)	5	0.00
Comanche (21)	41	0.02
Cree (3)	12	0.00
Creek (41)	121	0.05
Crow (4)	9	0.00
Delaware	2	0.00
Houma (1)	1	0.00
Iroquois (7)	26	0.01
Kiowa (7)	15	0.01
Latin American Indians (246)	364	0.15
Lumbee (3)	4	0.00
Navajo (55)	93	0.04
Osage (9)	19	0.01
Ottawa (1)	4	0.00
Paiute (139)	201	0.08
Pima (15)	20	0.01
Potawatomi (38)	63	0.03
Pueblo (25)	40	0.02
Puget Sound Salish (5)	7	0.00
Seminole (14)	29	0.01
Shoshone (19)	21	0.01
Sioux (25)	75	0.03
Tohono O'Odham (6)	11	0.00
Yakama (6)	6	0.00
Yaqui (53)	93	0.04
Yuman (3)	3	0.00
All other tribes (421)	638	0.26
American Indian tribes, not spec.	385	0.16
Arab:	1,161	0.47
Arab/Arabic	432	0.17
Egyptian	155	0.06
Iraqi	58	0.02
Jordanian	107	0.04
Lebanese	279	0.11
Palestinian	10	0.00
Syrian	90	0.04
Other Arab	30	0.01
Armenian	472	0.19
Asian:	13,405	5.43
Bangladeshi (18)	18	0.01
Cambodian (420)	548	0.22
Chinese, ex. Taiwanese (1,191)	1,593	0.64
Filipino (2,827)	3,767	1.52
Hmong (6)	8	0.00
Indian (3,204)	3,521	1.43
Indonesian (37)	74	0.03
Japanese (494)	841	0.34
Korean (1,070)	1,212	0.49
Laotian (149)	186	0.08
Malaysian (5)	13	0.01
Pakistani (75)	125	0.05
Sri Lankan (17)	22	0.01
Taiwanese (92)	114	0.05
Thai (113)	167	0.07
Vietnamese (500)	618	0.25
Other Asian, specified (96)	132	0.05
Other Asian, not specified (172)	446	0.18
Assyrian/Chaldean/Syriac	14	0.01
Australian	54	0.02
Austrian	274	0.11
Basque	562	0.23
Belgian	287	0.12
Brazilian	11	0.00
British	857	0.35
Canadian	503	0.20
Celtic	66	0.03
Croatian	124	0.05
Czech	268	0.11
Czechoslovakian	167	0.07
Danish	1,261	0.51
Dutch	3,070	1.24
Eastern European	53	0.02
English	17,663	7.14
European	1,761	0.71
Finnish	314	0.13
French, except Basque	5,147	2.08
French Canadian	898	0.36
German	25,541	10.32
Greek	716	0.29
Guyanese	7	0.00
Hawaii Native/Pacific Islander:	661	0.27
Melanesian: (1)	1	0.00
Fijian (1)	1	0.00
Micronesian: (94)	133	0.05
Guamanian/Chamorro (81)	116	0.05
Other Micronesian (13)	17	0.01
Polynesian: (157)	360	0.15
Native Hawaiian (96)	244	0.10
Samoan (54)	106	0.04
Tongan (5)	5	0.00
Other Polynesian (2)	5	0.00
Other Pac. Isl., specified	10	0.00
Other Pac. Isl., not spec. (43)	157	0.06
Hispanic or Latino:	80,170	32.45
Central American:	1,964	0.79
Costa Rican	54	0.02
Guatemalan	384	0.16
Honduran	126	0.05
Nicaraguan	49	0.02
Panamanian	17	0.01
Salvadoran	1,223	0.50
Other Central American	111	0.04
Cuban	189	0.08
Dominican Republic	19	0.01
Mexican	64,700	26.19
Puerto Rican	921	0.37
South American:	471	0.19
Argentinean	49	0.02
Bolivian	20	0.01
Chilean	31	0.01
Colombian	130	0.05
Ecuadorian	20	0.01
Peruvian	162	0.07
Uruguayan	5	0.00
Venezuelan	26	0.01
Other South American	28	0.01
Other Hispanic or Latino	11,906	4.82
Hungarian	313	0.13
Icelander	30	0.01
Iranian	212	0.09
Irish	19,049	7.70
Israeli	10	0.00
Italian	7,400	2.99
Latvian	23	0.01
Lithuanian	101	0.04
Luxemburger	5	0.00
Maltese	40	0.02
Northern European	53	0.02
Norwegian	2,294	0.93
Pennsylvania German	39	0.02
Polish	1,746	0.71
Portuguese	1,330	0.54
Romanian	109	0.04
Russian	729	0.29
Scandinavian	249	0.10
Scotch-Irish	2,809	1.14
Scottish	3,546	1.43
Serbian	15	0.01
Slavic	73	0.03
Slovak	46	0.02
Slovene	8	0.00
Swedish	2,679	1.08
Swiss	623	0.25
Turkish	66	0.03
Ukrainian	192	0.08
United States or American	13,935	5.63
Welsh	1,434	0.58
West Indian, excl. Hispanic:	120	0.05
Belizean	8	0.00
Dutch West Indian	40	0.02
Haitian	9	0.00
Jamaican	34	0.01

Notes: 1. Figures in the "Number" column do not add up to the total population due to: a) Ancestry/Race overlap — e.g. persons can report being both White and Irish, b) persons of Hispanic origin can report being any race, c) persons reporting two ancestries are counted in both categories. 2. Numbers in parentheses indicate the number of persons reporting this ancestry/race alone, not in combination with any other ancestry/race. 3. Refer to the Explanation of Data in the front of the book for more detailed information.

West Indian	29	0.01
White:	161,898	65.53
Not Hispanic (126,183)	131,024	53.03
Hispanic (26,666)	30,874	12.50
Yugoslavian	152	0.06

Baldwin Park

Place Type: City
County: Los Angeles
Population: 75,837

Ancestry/Race	Number	%
African American/Black:	1,442	1.90
Not Hispanic (1,071)	1,137	1.50
Hispanic (148)	305	0.40
African, sub-Saharan:	98	0.13
African	74	0.10
Nigerian	24	0.03
Alaska Native tribes, specified:	8	0.01
Eskimo (1)	1	0.00
Tlingit-Haida (1)	7	0.01
Alaska Native tribes, not specified	4	0.01
Am. Ind. or Alaska Nat., not spec.	697	0.92
American Indian tribes, specified:	683	0.90
Apache (38)	60	0.08
Blackfeet (1)	6	0.01
Cherokee (7)	62	0.08
Cheyenne (3)	3	0.00
Chickasaw	3	0.00
Chippewa (2)	5	0.01
Choctaw (5)	9	0.01
Colville	3	0.00
Comanche (6)	8	0.01
Creek (1)	1	0.00
Iroquois	1	0.00
Latin American Indians (220)	278	0.37
Lumbee (1)	1	0.00
Navajo (23)	30	0.04
Osage	5	0.01
Paiute (4)	4	0.01
Pima (3)	6	0.01
Potawatomi	11	0.01
Pueblo (20)	33	0.04
Puget Sound Salish (1)	1	0.00
Seminole (1)	6	0.01
Shoshone	6	0.01
Sioux (8)	18	0.02
Tohono O'Odham (2)	5	0.01
Yaqui (11)	23	0.03
Yuman (5)	9	0.01
All other tribes (65)	86	0.11
American Indian tribes, not spec.	157	0.21
Arab:	80	0.11
Arab/Arabic	19	0.03
Egyptian	18	0.02
Jordanian	7	0.01
Other Arab	36	0.05
Armenian	36	0.05
Asian:	9,670	12.75
Cambodian (137)	168	0.22
Chinese, ex. Taiwanese (2,961)	3,306	4.36
Filipino (3,337)	3,591	4.74
Indian (73)	134	0.18
Indonesian (34)	58	0.08
Japanese (141)	200	0.26
Korean (105)	117	0.15
Laotian (123)	134	0.18
Malaysian (7)	14	0.02
Pakistani (1)	1	0.00
Sri Lankan	1	0.00
Taiwanese (145)	195	0.26
Thai (143)	168	0.22
Vietnamese (1,229)	1,398	1.84
Other Asian, specified (36)	54	0.07
Other Asian, not specified (37)	131	0.17
Austrian	44	0.06
Basque	26	0.03
Belgian	38	0.05
Brazilian	19	0.03
British	27	0.04
Canadian	82	0.11
Czech	7	0.01
Czechoslovakian	6	0.01
Danish	54	0.07
Dutch	165	0.22
English	696	0.92
European	89	0.12
Finnish	12	0.02
French, except Basque	272	0.36
French Canadian	93	0.12
German	976	1.29
Greek	55	0.07
Guyanese	13	0.02
Hawaii Native/Pacific Islander:	207	0.27
Melanesian:	3	0.00
Fijian	3	0.00
Micronesian: (11)	14	0.02
Guamanian/Chamorro (10)	13	0.02
Other Micronesian (1)	1	0.00
Polynesian: (84)	125	0.16
Native Hawaiian (22)	46	0.06
Samoan (55)	61	0.08
Tongan (7)	10	0.01
Other Polynesian	8	0.01
Other Pac. Isl., specified	6	0.01
Other Pac. Isl., not spec. (15)	59	0.08
Hispanic or Latino:	59,660	78.67
Central American:	2,297	3.03
Costa Rican	52	0.07
Guatemalan	466	0.61
Honduran	93	0.12
Nicaraguan	258	0.34
Panamanian	14	0.02
Salvadoran	1,160	1.53
Other Central American	254	0.33
Cuban	211	0.28
Dominican Republic	2	0.00
Mexican	49,046	64.67
Puerto Rican	278	0.37
South American:	415	0.55
Argentinean	52	0.07
Bolivian	22	0.03
Chilean	25	0.03
Colombian	92	0.12
Ecuadorian	121	0.16
Paraguayan	4	0.01
Peruvian	61	0.08
Uruguayan	6	0.01
Venezuelan	5	0.01
Other South American	27	0.04
Other Hispanic or Latino	7,411	9.77
Hungarian	73	0.10
Irish	927	1.22
Italian	579	0.76
Lithuanian	18	0.02
Luxemburger	5	0.01
Norwegian	219	0.29
Pennsylvania German	12	0.02
Polish	141	0.19
Portuguese	17	0.02
Romanian	44	0.06
Russian	115	0.15
Scandinavian	53	0.07
Scotch-Irish	123	0.16
Scottish	246	0.32
Slavic	14	0.02
Swedish	162	0.21
Swiss	10	0.01
Ukrainian	14	0.02
United States or American	1,058	1.40
Welsh	41	0.05
West Indian, excl. Hispanic:	85	0.11
Barbadian	5	0.01
Belizean	53	0.07
West Indian	27	0.04
White:	33,319	43.94
Not Hispanic (5,508)	5,894	7.77
Hispanic (24,964)	27,425	36.16
Yugoslavian	37	0.05

Banning

Place Type: City
County: Riverside
Population: 23,562

Ancestry/Race	Number	%
African American/Black:	2,211	9.38
Not Hispanic (1,915)	2,055	8.72
Hispanic (99)	156	0.66
African, sub-Saharan:	100	0.43
African	92	0.39
Ghanian	8	0.03
Alaska Native tribes, specified:	2	0.01
Eskimo (1)	1	0.00
Tlingit-Haida (1)	1	0.00
Am. Ind. or Alaska Nat., not spec.	223	0.95
American Indian tribes, specified:	649	2.75
Apache (13)	34	0.14
Blackfeet (2)	14	0.06
Cherokee (13)	64	0.27
Cheyenne	1	0.00
Chickasaw (12)	14	0.06
Chippewa (1)	2	0.01
Choctaw (18)	37	0.16
Creek (1)	3	0.01
Iroquois (1)	5	0.02
Latin American Indians (22)	49	0.21
Navajo (4)	20	0.08
Osage (1)	2	0.01
Pima (1)	4	0.02
Pueblo (4)	7	0.03
Shoshone (1)	1	0.00
Sioux (6)	17	0.07
Tohono O'Odham (4)	4	0.02
Ute	5	0.02
Yaqui (5)	11	0.05
Yuman (2)	2	0.01
All other tribes (298)	353	1.50
American Indian tribes, not spec.	44	0.19
Arab:	68	0.29
Arab/Arabic	38	0.16
Egyptian	20	0.09
Other Arab	10	0.04
Armenian	17	0.07
Asian:	1,526	6.48
Cambodian (14)	15	0.06
Chinese, ex. Taiwanese (43)	62	0.26
Filipino (110)	144	0.61
Hmong (517)	595	2.53
Indian (51)	76	0.32
Indonesian (1)	5	0.02
Japanese (44)	51	0.22
Korean (34)	43	0.18
Laotian (297)	402	1.71
Pakistani (11)	13	0.06
Taiwanese (1)	5	0.02
Thai (23)	48	0.20
Vietnamese (24)	28	0.12
Other Asian, not specified (25)	39	0.17
Australian	13	0.06
Austrian	61	0.26
Belgian	9	0.04
British	184	0.78
Bulgarian	7	0.03
Canadian	51	0.22
Celtic	15	0.06
Croatian	18	0.08
Czech	26	0.11
Czechoslovakian	18	0.08
Danish	156	0.67
Dutch	459	1.96
English	2,157	9.20
European	92	0.39
French, except Basque	829	3.54
French Canadian	194	0.83
German	2,791	11.91
Greek	109	0.46
Hawaii Native/Pacific Islander:	69	0.29
Micronesian:	1	0.00

Notes: 1. Figures in the "Number" column do not add up to the total population due to: a) Ancestry/Race overlap — e.g. persons can report being both White and Irish, b) persons of Hispanic origin can report being any race, c) persons reporting two ancestries are counted in both categories. 2. Numbers in parentheses indicate the number of persons reporting this ancestry/race alone, not in combination with any other ancestry/race. 3. Refer to the Explanation of Data in the front of the book for more detailed information.

Guamanian/Chamorro	1	0.00
Polynesian: (25)	47	0.20
Native Hawaiian (6)	19	0.08
Samoan (19)	28	0.12
Other Pac. Isl., not spec. (5)	21	0.09
Hispanic or Latino:	7,119	30.21
Central American:	114	0.48
Costa Rican	5	0.02
Guatemalan	20	0.08
Honduran	28	0.12
Nicaraguan	24	0.10
Salvadoran	32	0.14
Other Central American	5	0.02
Cuban	27	0.11
Dominican Republic	2	0.01
Mexican	6,061	25.72
Puerto Rican	50	0.21
South American:	29	0.12
Argentinean	3	0.01
Bolivian	3	0.01
Chilean	4	0.02
Colombian	10	0.04
Peruvian	5	0.02
Venezuelan	1	0.00
Other South American	3	0.01
Other Hispanic or Latino	836	3.55
Hungarian	147	0.63
Iranian	10	0.04
Irish	2,164	9.23
Italian	742	3.17
Latvian	5	0.02
Lithuanian	30	0.13
Northern European	35	0.15
Norwegian	293	1.25
Pennsylvania German	15	0.06
Polish	201	0.86
Portuguese	67	0.29
Romanian	36	0.15
Russian	88	0.38
Scandinavian	31	0.13
Scotch-Irish	360	1.54
Scottish	381	1.63
Serbian	23	0.10
Slovak	24	0.10
Swedish	423	1.80
Swiss	78	0.33
Ukrainian	23	0.10
United States or American	885	3.78
Welsh	150	0.64
West Indian, excl. Hispanic:	5	0.02
Dutch West Indian	5	0.02
White:	15,929	67.60
Not Hispanic (12,354)	12,715	53.96
Hispanic (2,770)	3,214	13.64
Yugoslavian	14	0.06

Barstow

Place Type: City
County: San Bernardino
Population: 21,119

Ancestry/Race	Number	%
African American/Black:	2,777	13.15
Not Hispanic (2,349)	2,562	12.13
Hispanic (101)	215	1.02
African, sub-Saharan:	46	0.22
African	46	0.22
Alaska Native tribes, specified:	14	0.07
Eskimo (8)	14	0.07
Alaska Native tribes, not specified	3	0.01
Am. Ind. or Alaska Nat., not spec.	181	0.86
American Indian tribes, specified:	608	2.88
Apache (14)	26	0.12
Blackfeet (1)	6	0.03
Cherokee (24)	98	0.46
Cheyenne (2)	3	0.01
Chickasaw (3)	10	0.05
Chippewa (4)	4	0.02
Choctaw (5)	16	0.08
Comanche	2	0.01
Creek (1)	1	0.00
Crow (1)	1	0.00
Delaware	2	0.01
Iroquois (1)	2	0.01
Kiowa	1	0.00
Latin American Indians (18)	33	0.16
Navajo (89)	125	0.59
Osage	1	0.00
Ottawa (4)	4	0.02
Paiute (4)	6	0.03
Potawatomi (1)	1	0.00
Pueblo (131)	168	0.80
Puget Sound Salish (2)	3	0.01
Sioux (3)	11	0.05
Tohono O'Odham (3)	3	0.01
Ute (1)	3	0.01
Yaqui (1)	3	0.01
Yuman (3)	12	0.06
All other tribes (42)	63	0.30
American Indian tribes, not spec.	50	0.24
Arab:	151	0.72
Arab/Arabic	121	0.58
Lebanese	30	0.14
Armenian	24	0.11
Asian:	910	4.31
Cambodian (11)	11	0.05
Chinese, ex. Taiwanese (82)	101	0.48
Filipino (246)	327	1.55
Indian (64)	83	0.39
Japanese (68)	122	0.58
Korean (111)	161	0.76
Laotian (7)	7	0.03
Pakistani (1)	9	0.04
Taiwanese (8)	11	0.05
Thai (18)	18	0.09
Vietnamese (16)	19	0.09
Other Asian, specified (1)	3	0.01
Other Asian, not specified (8)	38	0.18
Austrian	33	0.16
Belgian	8	0.04
British	31	0.15
Canadian	62	0.30
Celtic	8	0.04
Czech	46	0.22
Czechoslovakian	6	0.03
Danish	53	0.25
Dutch	191	0.91
English	1,180	5.62
European	153	0.73
Finnish	25	0.12
French, except Basque	480	2.29
French Canadian	115	0.55
German	2,220	10.58
Greek	11	0.05
Guyanese	15	0.07
Hawaii Native/Pacific Islander:	297	1.41
Micronesian: (106)	128	0.61
Guamanian/Chamorro (104)	125	0.59
Other Micronesian (2)	3	0.01
Polynesian: (85)	129	0.61
Native Hawaiian (26)	58	0.27
Samoan (59)	69	0.33
Tongan	1	0.00
Other Polynesian	1	0.00
Other Pac. Isl., not spec. (8)	40	0.19
Hispanic or Latino:	7,708	36.50
Central American:	78	0.37
Costa Rican	1	0.00
Guatemalan	6	0.03
Honduran	7	0.03
Nicaraguan	6	0.03
Panamanian	18	0.09
Salvadoran	31	0.15
Other Central American	9	0.04
Cuban	30	0.14
Dominican Republic	4	0.02
Mexican	5,301	25.10
Puerto Rican	186	0.88
South American:	19	0.09
Argentinean	5	0.02
Bolivian	1	0.00
Chilean	6	0.03
Colombian	2	0.01
Peruvian	3	0.01
Other South American	2	0.01
Other Hispanic or Latino	2,090	9.90
Hungarian	38	0.18
Iranian	5	0.02
Irish	1,121	5.34
Israeli	6	0.03
Italian	352	1.68
Luxemburger	9	0.04
Maltese	25	0.12
Northern European	9	0.04
Norwegian	150	0.71
Pennsylvania German	12	0.06
Polish	180	0.86
Portuguese	11	0.05
Romanian	8	0.04
Russian	23	0.11
Scandinavian	9	0.04
Scotch-Irish	287	1.37
Scottish	206	0.98
Slovak	9	0.04
Swedish	287	1.37
Swiss	37	0.18
Ukrainian	32	0.15
United States or American	1,047	4.99
Welsh	145	0.69
West Indian, excl. Hispanic:	4	0.02
Other West Indian	4	0.02
White:	13,177	62.39
Not Hispanic (9,163)	9,707	45.96
Hispanic (2,896)	3,470	16.43

Bay Point

Place Type: Census Designated Place
County: Contra Costa
Population: 21,534

Ancestry/Race	Number	%
Afghan	106	0.49
African American/Black:	3,092	14.36
Not Hispanic (2,633)	2,914	13.53
Hispanic (103)	178	0.83
African, sub-Saharan:	246	1.15
African	83	0.39
Liberian	120	0.56
Nigerian	17	0.08
Other sub-Saharan African	26	0.12
Alaska Native tribes, specified:	9	0.04
Alaska Athabascan (1)	4	0.02
Aleut (2)	4	0.02
Eskimo	1	0.00
Alaska Native tribes, not specified	1	0.00
Am. Ind. or Alaska Nat., not spec.	184	0.85
American Indian tribes, specified:	395	1.83
Apache (12)	28	0.13
Blackfeet	25	0.12
Cherokee (35)	151	0.70
Cheyenne (3)	3	0.01
Chippewa (10)	15	0.07
Choctaw (17)	40	0.19
Creek	2	0.01
Iroquois (3)	3	0.01
Latin American Indians (38)	57	0.26
Menominee (1)	1	0.00
Navajo	5	0.02
Osage (1)	2	0.01
Pueblo (1)	3	0.01
Seminole (1)	2	0.01
Sioux (10)	15	0.07
Tohono O'Odham (1)	1	0.00
Ute	1	0.00
Yaqui	6	0.03
Yuman (4)	4	0.02
All other tribes (15)	32	0.15
American Indian tribes, not spec.	31	0.14

Notes: 1. Figures in the "Number" column do not add up to the total population due to: a) Ancestry/Race overlap — e.g. persons can report being both White and Irish, b) persons of Hispanic origin can report being any race, c) persons reporting two ancestries are counted in both categories. 2. Numbers in parentheses indicate the number of persons reporting this ancestry/race alone, not in combination with any other ancestry/race. 3. Refer to the Explanation of Data in the front of the book for more detailed information.

Ancestry/Race	Number	%
Arab:	70	0.33
Arab/Arabic	57	0.27
Lebanese	13	0.06
Armenian	13	0.06
Asian:	2,900	13.47
Bangladeshi	2	0.01
Cambodian (16)	19	0.09
Chinese, ex. Taiwanese (168)	237	1.10
Filipino (1,279)	1,525	7.08
Indian (231)	279	1.30
Indonesian (4)	5	0.02
Japanese (39)	90	0.42
Korean (18)	25	0.12
Laotian (27)	37	0.17
Pakistani (44)	47	0.22
Sri Lankan (3)	5	0.02
Taiwanese	1	0.00
Thai (11)	18	0.08
Vietnamese (480)	516	2.40
Other Asian, specified (23)	27	0.13
Other Asian, not specified (19)	67	0.31
Australian	16	0.07
Austrian	19	0.09
Basque	11	0.05
Belgian	9	0.04
British	33	0.15
Canadian	37	0.17
Celtic	10	0.05
Croatian	18	0.08
Czech	17	0.08
Czechoslovakian	17	0.08
Danish	136	0.64
Dutch	316	1.48
English	998	4.66
European	82	0.38
Finnish	58	0.27
French, except Basque	259	1.21
French Canadian	50	0.23
German	1,430	6.68
Greek	25	0.12
Guyanese	22	0.10
Hawaii Native/Pacific Islander:	316	1.47
Melanesian: (27)	28	0.13
Fijian (27)	28	0.13
Micronesian: (42)	66	0.31
Guamanian/Chamorro (42)	63	0.29
Other Micronesian	3	0.01
Polynesian: (97)	182	0.85
Native Hawaiian (17)	67	0.31
Samoan (18)	35	0.16
Tongan (62)	77	0.36
Other Polynesian	3	0.01
Other Pac. Isl., not spec. (11)	40	0.19
Hispanic or Latino:	8,321	38.64
Central American:	699	3.25
Costa Rican	3	0.01
Guatemalan	61	0.28
Honduran	10	0.05
Nicaraguan	136	0.63
Panamanian	16	0.07
Salvadoran	390	1.81
Other Central American	83	0.39
Cuban	31	0.14
Mexican	6,059	28.14
Puerto Rican	224	1.04
South American:	116	0.54
Argentinean	1	0.00
Bolivian	11	0.05
Chilean	3	0.01
Colombian	27	0.13
Ecuadorian	8	0.04
Peruvian	44	0.20
Uruguayan	1	0.00
Venezuelan	9	0.04
Other South American	12	0.06
Other Hispanic or Latino	1,192	5.54
Hungarian	37	0.17
Icelander	4	0.02
Irish	1,270	5.93
Israeli	9	0.04
Italian	682	3.18
Lithuanian	16	0.07
Norwegian	168	0.78
Polish	256	1.20
Portuguese	291	1.36
Romanian	11	0.05
Russian	36	0.17
Scandinavian	28	0.13
Scotch-Irish	195	0.91
Scottish	236	1.10
Slavic	11	0.05
Slovene	6	0.03
Swedish	242	1.13
Swiss	5	0.02
Ukrainian	10	0.05
United States or American	494	2.31
Welsh	231	1.08
West Indian, excl. Hispanic:	39	0.18
Jamaican	39	0.18
White:	11,332	52.62
Not Hispanic (6,946)	7,625	35.41
Hispanic (3,014)	3,707	17.21
Yugoslavian	15	0.07

Baywood-Los Osos

Place Type: Census Designated Place
County: San Luis Obispo
Population: 14,351

Ancestry/Race	Number	%
African American/Black:	163	1.14
Not Hispanic (87)	139	0.97
Hispanic (5)	24	0.17
African, sub-Saharan:	22	0.16
African	22	0.16
Alaska Native tribes, specified:	6	0.04
Eskimo (3)	5	0.03
Tlingit-Haida (1)	1	0.01
Am. Ind. or Alaska Nat., not spec.	74	0.52
Alsatian	13	0.09
American Indian tribes, specified:	196	1.37
Apache (2)	12	0.08
Blackfeet	6	0.04
Cherokee (19)	71	0.49
Cheyenne (3)	3	0.02
Chippewa (4)	11	0.08
Choctaw (1)	11	0.08
Cree	1	0.01
Delaware	1	0.01
Iroquois	6	0.04
Latin American Indians (6)	16	0.11
Navajo (1)	2	0.01
Osage (1)	4	0.03
Pima (1)	1	0.01
Potawatomi	1	0.01
Pueblo (4)	6	0.04
Sioux	8	0.06
Yaqui (1)	3	0.02
All other tribes (22)	33	0.23
American Indian tribes, not spec.	12	0.08
Arab:	72	0.51
Lebanese	9	0.06
Syrian	52	0.37
Other Arab	11	0.08
Armenian	111	0.78
Asian:	837	5.83
Cambodian (1)	1	0.01
Chinese, ex. Taiwanese (36)	57	0.40
Filipino (482)	551	3.84
Indian (5)	15	0.10
Indonesian (3)	5	0.03
Japanese (76)	128	0.89
Korean (23)	35	0.24
Laotian (4)	4	0.03
Thai (5)	5	0.03
Vietnamese (8)	11	0.08
Other Asian, specified (1)	3	0.02
Other Asian, not specified (5)	22	0.15
Australian	10	0.07
Austrian	62	0.44
Basque	48	0.34
Belgian	30	0.21
Brazilian	4	0.03
British	143	1.01
Canadian	61	0.43
Croatian	7	0.05
Czech	60	0.42
Czechoslovakian	37	0.26
Danish	205	1.45
Dutch	323	2.28
Eastern European	7	0.05
English	2,918	20.62
European	297	2.10
Finnish	32	0.23
French, except Basque	549	3.88
French Canadian	163	1.15
German	2,887	20.40
German Russian	12	0.08
Greek	19	0.13
Hawaii Native/Pacific Islander:	31	0.22
Micronesian: (2)	5	0.03
Guamanian/Chamorro (2)	5	0.03
Polynesian: (6)	21	0.15
Native Hawaiian (5)	19	0.13
Samoan (1)	2	0.01
Other Pac. Isl., not spec. (2)	5	0.03
Hispanic or Latino:	1,292	9.00
Central American:	21	0.15
Guatemalan	6	0.04
Nicaraguan	1	0.01
Panamanian	3	0.02
Salvadoran	10	0.07
Other Central American	1	0.01
Cuban	18	0.13
Mexican	1,002	6.98
Puerto Rican	25	0.17
South American:	25	0.17
Argentinean	5	0.03
Chilean	3	0.02
Colombian	8	0.06
Ecuadorian	5	0.03
Peruvian	4	0.03
Other Hispanic or Latino	201	1.40
Hungarian	125	0.88
Irish	1,955	13.81
Italian	887	6.27
Latvian	9	0.06
Lithuanian	58	0.41
Northern European	71	0.50
Norwegian	540	3.82
Polish	281	1.99
Portuguese	213	1.50
Romanian	24	0.17
Russian	243	1.72
Scandinavian	26	0.18
Scotch-Irish	416	2.94
Scottish	640	4.52
Slavic	25	0.18
Slovak	29	0.20
Slovene	9	0.06
Swedish	389	2.75
Swiss	92	0.65
Turkish	19	0.13
Ukrainian	28	0.20
United States or American	504	3.56
Welsh	187	1.32
West Indian, excl. Hispanic:	53	0.37
British West Indian	11	0.08
Jamaican	7	0.05
Trinidadian and Tobagonian	35	0.25
White:	13,086	91.19
Not Hispanic (11,871)	12,196	84.98
Hispanic (796)	890	6.20
Yugoslavian	46	0.32

Notes: 1. Figures in the "Number" column do not add up to the total population due to: a) Ancestry/Race overlap — e.g. persons can report being both White and Irish, b) persons of Hispanic origin can report being any race, c) persons reporting two ancestries are counted in both categories. 2. Numbers in parentheses indicate the number of persons reporting this ancestry/race alone, not in combination with any other ancestry/race. 3. Refer to the Explanation of Data in the front of the book for more detailed information.

Beaumont

Place Type: City
County: Riverside
Population: 11,384

Ancestry/Race	Number	%
African American/Black:	417	3.66
Not Hispanic (304)	375	3.29
Hispanic (27)	42	0.37
African, sub-Saharan:	29	0.26
African	29	0.26
Alaska Native tribes, specified:	4	0.04
Tlingit-Haida	4	0.04
Am. Ind. or Alaska Nat., not spec.	118	1.04
American Indian tribes, specified:	265	2.33
Apache (4)	15	0.13
Blackfeet (1)	8	0.07
Cherokee (15)	42	0.37
Chickasaw (4)	7	0.06
Chippewa	1	0.01
Choctaw (8)	11	0.10
Comanche	2	0.02
Creek (5)	7	0.06
Iroquois (1)	2	0.02
Latin American Indians (13)	23	0.20
Lumbee (1)	1	0.01
Navajo (9)	14	0.12
Osage	1	0.01
Pima (4)	4	0.04
Pueblo (8)	8	0.07
Sioux (5)	10	0.09
Tohono O'Odham (2)	6	0.05
Ute (1)	1	0.01
Yaqui (2)	4	0.04
Yuman (2)	4	0.04
All other tribes (81)	94	0.83
American Indian tribes, not spec.	25	0.22
Arab:	4	0.04
Egyptian	4	0.04
Asian:	252	2.21
Cambodian (6)	7	0.06
Chinese, ex. Taiwanese (18)	20	0.18
Filipino (73)	103	0.90
Hmong (3)	3	0.03
Indian (19)	27	0.24
Japanese (9)	18	0.16
Korean (11)	15	0.13
Laotian (18)	22	0.19
Pakistani (7)	8	0.07
Thai (15)	15	0.13
Vietnamese (5)	5	0.04
Other Asian, not specified (3)	9	0.08
Austrian	9	0.08
British	8	0.07
Bulgarian	17	0.15
Canadian	9	0.08
Celtic	7	0.06
Czech	10	0.09
Danish	51	0.45
Dutch	236	2.09
Eastern European	5	0.04
English	1,003	8.86
Estonian	6	0.05
European	104	0.92
Finnish	30	0.27
French, except Basque	326	2.88
French Canadian	31	0.27
German	1,165	10.30
Greek	18	0.16
Hawaii Native/Pacific Islander:	20	0.18
Micronesian: (5)	6	0.05
Guamanian/Chamorro (1)	2	0.02
Other Micronesian (4)	4	0.04
Polynesian: (2)	11	0.10
Native Hawaiian	8	0.07
Samoan (2)	3	0.03
Other Pac. Isl., not spec. (1)	3	0.03
Hispanic or Latino:	4,122	36.21
Central American:	52	0.46
Costa Rican	1	0.01
Guatemalan	25	0.22
Honduran	3	0.03
Nicaraguan	2	0.02
Panamanian	1	0.01
Salvadoran	14	0.12
Other Central American	6	0.05
Cuban	16	0.14
Mexican	3,504	30.78
Puerto Rican	22	0.19
South American:	21	0.18
Argentinean	8	0.07
Colombian	8	0.07
Ecuadorian	3	0.03
Peruvian	2	0.02
Other Hispanic or Latino	507	4.45
Hungarian	12	0.11
Iranian	12	0.11
Irish	1,318	11.65
Israeli	6	0.05
Italian	471	4.16
Norwegian	170	1.50
Polish	112	0.99
Portuguese	45	0.40
Romanian	9	0.08
Russian	7	0.06
Scandinavian	6	0.05
Scotch-Irish	171	1.51
Scottish	137	1.21
Swedish	125	1.10
Swiss	35	0.31
Ukrainian	12	0.11
United States or American	515	4.55
Welsh	76	0.67
West Indian, excl. Hispanic:	18	0.16
Jamaican	8	0.07
West Indian	10	0.09
White:	8,224	72.24
Not Hispanic (6,334)	6,548	57.52
Hispanic (1,417)	1,676	14.72
Yugoslavian	9	0.08

Bell Gardens

Place Type: City
County: Los Angeles
Population: 44,054

Ancestry/Race	Number	%
African American/Black:	505	1.15
Not Hispanic (251)	263	0.60
Hispanic (178)	242	0.55
African, sub-Saharan:	16	0.04
African	16	0.04
Am. Ind. or Alaska Nat., not spec.	441	1.00
American Indian tribes, specified:	423	0.96
Apache (13)	13	0.03
Blackfeet	4	0.01
Cherokee (7)	19	0.04
Chippewa (4)	10	0.02
Choctaw (15)	19	0.04
Comanche	1	0.00
Cree	4	0.01
Creek (1)	4	0.01
Delaware (1)	1	0.00
Kiowa (2)	2	0.00
Latin American Indians (166)	200	0.45
Menominee (3)	3	0.01
Navajo (36)	51	0.12
Ottawa (1)	1	0.00
Paiute (1)	1	0.00
Pima (6)	7	0.02
Potawatomi (1)	1	0.00
Pueblo (1)	2	0.00
Shoshone (3)	3	0.01
Sioux (15)	17	0.04
Tohono O'Odham (2)	2	0.00
Yaqui (7)	7	0.02
Yuman (3)	4	0.01
All other tribes (33)	47	0.11
American Indian tribes, not spec.	40	0.09
Arab:	27	0.06
Arab/Arabic	27	0.06
Asian:	375	0.85
Cambodian (35)	53	0.12
Chinese, ex. Taiwanese (19)	35	0.08
Filipino (60)	79	0.18
Hmong	1	0.00
Indian (44)	60	0.14
Indonesian (2)	2	0.00
Japanese (15)	27	0.06
Korean (13)	18	0.04
Pakistani (1)	1	0.00
Thai (7)	14	0.03
Vietnamese (58)	59	0.13
Other Asian, not specified (8)	26	0.06
Danish	19	0.04
Dutch	44	0.10
English	187	0.42
European	26	0.06
French, except Basque	160	0.36
French Canadian	32	0.07
German	329	0.75
Greek	7	0.02
Hawaii Native/Pacific Islander:	111	0.25
Micronesian: (1)	7	0.02
Guamanian/Chamorro (1)	7	0.02
Polynesian: (33)	58	0.13
Native Hawaiian (7)	25	0.06
Samoan (26)	33	0.07
Other Pac. Isl., not spec. (11)	46	0.10
Hispanic or Latino:	41,132	93.37
Central American:	2,429	5.51
Costa Rican	27	0.06
Guatemalan	547	1.24
Honduran	137	0.31
Nicaraguan	325	0.74
Panamanian	1	0.00
Salvadoran	1,124	2.55
Other Central American	268	0.61
Cuban	147	0.33
Dominican Republic	2	0.00
Mexican	32,875	74.62
Puerto Rican	110	0.25
South American:	175	0.40
Argentinean	15	0.03
Bolivian	2	0.00
Chilean	7	0.02
Colombian	38	0.09
Ecuadorian	33	0.07
Peruvian	58	0.13
Uruguayan	1	0.00
Venezuelan	1	0.00
Other South American	20	0.05
Other Hispanic or Latino	5,394	12.24
Iranian	33	0.07
Irish	259	0.59
Italian	141	0.32
Norwegian	20	0.05
Polish	8	0.02
Portuguese	9	0.02
Romanian	40	0.09
Russian	7	0.02
Scotch-Irish	60	0.14
Scottish	36	0.08
Swedish	10	0.02
Swiss	16	0.04
Ukrainian	6	0.01
United States or American	810	1.84
Welsh	9	0.02
West Indian, excl. Hispanic:	17	0.04
Belizean	17	0.04
White:	23,046	52.31
Not Hispanic (2,085)	2,191	4.97
Hispanic (19,095)	20,855	47.34
Yugoslavian	28	0.06

Notes: 1. Figures in the "Number" column do not add up to the total population due to: a) Ancestry/Race overlap — e.g. persons can report being both White and Irish, b) persons of Hispanic origin can report being any race, c) persons reporting two ancestries are counted in both categories. 2. Numbers in parentheses indicate the number of persons reporting this ancestry/race alone, not in combination with any other ancestry/race. 3. Refer to the Explanation of Data in the front of the book for more detailed information.

Bell

Place Type: City
County: Los Angeles
Population: 36,664

Ancestry/Race	Number	%
African American/Black:	537	1.46
Not Hispanic (307)	329	0.90
Hispanic (161)	208	0.57
African, sub-Saharan:	41	0.11
African	34	0.09
Nigerian	7	0.02
Alaska Native tribes, not specified	1	0.00
Am. Ind. or Alaska Nat., not spec.	317	0.86
American Indian tribes, specified:	247	0.67
Apache (2)	7	0.02
Cherokee (6)	10	0.03
Cheyenne	1	0.00
Choctaw (11)	11	0.03
Comanche (1)	2	0.01
Creek (1)	2	0.01
Kiowa (3)	3	0.01
Latin American Indians (91)	127	0.35
Navajo (26)	31	0.08
Osage	1	0.00
Ottawa (2)	2	0.01
Paiute (1)	1	0.00
Pima (7)	9	0.02
Potawatomi (1)	1	0.00
Pueblo (3)	7	0.02
Sioux (4)	4	0.01
Ute (1)	1	0.00
Yaqui (5)	5	0.01
Yuman (4)	9	0.02
All other tribes (9)	13	0.04
American Indian tribes, not spec.	45	0.12
Arab:	603	1.64
Arab/Arabic	158	0.43
Lebanese	378	1.03
Palestinian	53	0.14
Other Arab	14	0.04
Asian:	508	1.39
Chinese, ex. Taiwanese (38)	44	0.12
Filipino (111)	140	0.38
Indian (37)	52	0.14
Japanese (20)	29	0.08
Korean (128)	130	0.35
Laotian	1	0.00
Sri Lankan (1)	1	0.00
Thai (4)	5	0.01
Vietnamese (26)	29	0.08
Other Asian, not specified (22)	77	0.21
Brazilian	5	0.01
British	7	0.02
Canadian	23	0.06
Danish	14	0.04
Dutch	122	0.33
English	248	0.68
European	19	0.05
Finnish	7	0.02
French, except Basque	107	0.29
French Canadian	33	0.09
German	180	0.49
Greek	14	0.04
Hawaii Native/Pacific Islander:	38	0.10
Micronesian: (4)	5	0.01
Guamanian/Chamorro (4)	5	0.01
Polynesian: (12)	23	0.06
Native Hawaiian (9)	15	0.04
Samoan (3)	8	0.02
Other Pac. Isl., not spec. (6)	10	0.03
Hispanic or Latino:	33,328	90.90
Central American:	2,742	7.48
Costa Rican	28	0.08
Guatemalan	655	1.79
Honduran	154	0.42
Nicaraguan	247	0.67
Panamanian	11	0.03
Salvadoran	1,407	3.84
Other Central American	240	0.65
Cuban	939	2.56
Dominican Republic	2	0.01
Mexican	24,558	66.98
Puerto Rican	180	0.49
South American:	227	0.62
Argentinean	14	0.04
Bolivian	6	0.02
Chilean	10	0.03
Colombian	61	0.17
Ecuadorian	39	0.11
Peruvian	74	0.20
Uruguayan	1	0.00
Venezuelan	6	0.02
Other South American	16	0.04
Other Hispanic or Latino	4,680	12.76
Hungarian	10	0.03
Icelander	25	0.07
Irish	262	0.71
Italian	197	0.54
Norwegian	29	0.08
Polish	14	0.04
Romanian	31	0.08
Russian	50	0.14
Scotch-Irish	94	0.26
Scottish	9	0.02
Swedish	46	0.13
Turkish	8	0.02
United States or American	866	2.36
Welsh	17	0.05
White:	19,396	52.90
Not Hispanic (2,132)	2,447	6.67
Hispanic (15,632)	16,949	46.23

Bellflower

Place Type: City
County: Los Angeles
Population: 72,878

Ancestry/Race	Number	%
African American/Black:	10,311	14.15
Not Hispanic (9,239)	9,785	13.43
Hispanic (301)	526	0.72
African, sub-Saharan:	692	0.95
African	559	0.77
Ethiopian	21	0.03
Kenyan	24	0.03
Nigerian	81	0.11
South African	7	0.01
Alaska Native tribes, specified:	8	0.01
Alaska Athabascan (1)	1	0.00
Aleut (2)	6	0.01
Tlingit-Haida	1	0.00
Alaska Native tribes, not specified	1	0.00
Am. Ind. or Alaska Nat., not spec.	436	0.60
American Indian tribes, specified:	777	1.07
Apache (23)	49	0.07
Blackfeet (13)	42	0.06
Cherokee (33)	179	0.25
Cheyenne (2)	2	0.00
Chickasaw (4)	6	0.01
Chippewa (3)	7	0.01
Choctaw (19)	54	0.07
Comanche (8)	14	0.02
Cree (1)	1	0.00
Creek (1)	9	0.01
Iroquois (3)	11	0.02
Kiowa (1)	1	0.00
Latin American Indians (131)	180	0.25
Lumbee	3	0.00
Navajo (21)	32	0.04
Osage (2)	5	0.01
Ottawa (2)	2	0.00
Paiute (5)	6	0.01
Pima (3)	3	0.00
Potawatomi (2)	2	0.00
Pueblo (10)	22	0.03
Puget Sound Salish (1)	2	0.00
Seminole	1	0.00
Shoshone (5)	8	0.01
Sioux (24)	43	0.06
Tohono O'Odham (2)	2	0.00
Ute (1)	1	0.00
Yakama (1)	1	0.00
Yaqui (8)	13	0.02
Yuman	2	0.00
All other tribes (34)	74	0.10
American Indian tribes, not spec.	74	0.10
Arab:	771	1.06
Arab/Arabic	53	0.07
Egyptian	488	0.67
Jordanian	12	0.02
Lebanese	140	0.19
Palestinian	40	0.05
Syrian	38	0.05
Armenian	43	0.06
Asian:	8,141	11.17
Bangladeshi (24)	24	0.03
Cambodian (394)	521	0.71
Chinese, ex. Taiwanese (450)	683	0.94
Filipino (3,392)	3,787	5.20
Hmong (11)	11	0.02
Indian (419)	476	0.65
Indonesian (51)	96	0.13
Japanese (216)	360	0.49
Korean (991)	1,034	1.42
Laotian (15)	23	0.03
Malaysian (4)	9	0.01
Pakistani (17)	25	0.03
Sri Lankan (13)	15	0.02
Taiwanese (34)	41	0.06
Thai (380)	436	0.60
Vietnamese (417)	456	0.63
Other Asian, specified (11)	14	0.02
Other Asian, not specified (48)	130	0.18
Australian	8	0.01
Austrian	42	0.06
Basque	56	0.08
Belgian	89	0.12
Brazilian	17	0.02
British	93	0.13
Canadian	178	0.24
Croatian	33	0.05
Czech	114	0.16
Czechoslovakian	33	0.05
Danish	241	0.33
Dutch	2,410	3.31
English	3,200	4.39
Estonian	46	0.06
European	247	0.34
Finnish	37	0.05
French, except Basque	1,161	1.59
French Canadian	192	0.26
German	4,686	6.43
Greek	118	0.16
Hawaii Native/Pacific Islander:	792	1.09
Melanesian: (24)	33	0.05
Fijian (24)	33	0.05
Micronesian: (49)	91	0.12
Guamanian/Chamorro (47)	89	0.12
Other Micronesian (2)	2	0.00
Polynesian: (398)	547	0.75
Native Hawaiian (54)	149	0.20
Samoan (315)	358	0.49
Tongan (28)	37	0.05
Other Polynesian (1)	3	0.00
Other Pac. Isl., specified	3	0.00
Other Pac. Isl., not spec. (32)	118	0.16
Hispanic or Latino:	31,503	43.23
Central American:	1,549	2.13
Costa Rican	52	0.07
Guatemalan	370	0.51
Honduran	98	0.13
Nicaraguan	195	0.27
Panamanian	37	0.05
Salvadoran	674	0.92
Other Central American	123	0.17
Cuban	223	0.31
Dominican Republic	28	0.04

Notes: 1. Figures in the "Number" column do not add up to the total population due to: a) Ancestry/Race overlap — e.g. persons can report being both White and Irish, b) persons of Hispanic origin can report being any race, c) persons reporting two ancestries are counted in both categories. 2. Numbers in parentheses indicate the number of persons reporting this ancestry/race alone, not in combination with any other ancestry/race. 3. Refer to the Explanation of Data in the front of the book for more detailed information.

Mexican	24,433	33.53
Puerto Rican	485	0.67
South American:	522	0.72
Argentinean	49	0.07
Bolivian	10	0.01
Chilean	35	0.05
Colombian	127	0.17
Ecuadorian	87	0.12
Paraguayan	1	0.00
Peruvian	165	0.23
Uruguayan	5	0.01
Venezuelan	8	0.01
Other South American	35	0.05
Other Hispanic or Latino	4,263	5.85
Hungarian	227	0.31
Icelander	36	0.05
Iranian	75	0.10
Irish	3,583	4.92
Israeli	14	0.02
Italian	1,613	2.21
Latvian	18	0.02
Lithuanian	34	0.05
New Zealander	7	0.01
Northern European	10	0.01
Norwegian	591	0.81
Pennsylvania German	13	0.02
Polish	536	0.74
Portuguese	353	0.48
Romanian	68	0.09
Russian	254	0.35
Scandinavian	101	0.14
Scotch-Irish	538	0.74
Scottish	413	0.57
Slavic	19	0.03
Slovak	104	0.14
Swedish	273	0.37
Swiss	68	0.09
Ukrainian	17	0.02
United States or American	2,624	3.60
Welsh	222	0.30
West Indian, excl. Hispanic:	244	0.34
Barbadian	6	0.01
Belizean	140	0.19
British West Indian	29	0.04
Dutch West Indian	9	0.01
Jamaican	48	0.07
West Indian	12	0.02
White:	36,524	50.12
Not Hispanic (22,403)	23,704	32.53
Hispanic (11,190)	12,820	17.59
Yugoslavian	53	0.07

Belmont

Place Type: City
County: San Mateo
Population: 25,123

Ancestry/Race	Number	%
African American/Black:	514	2.05
Not Hispanic (389)	474	1.89
Hispanic (33)	40	0.16
African, sub-Saharan:	70	0.28
African	19	0.08
Cape Verdean	25	0.10
South African	14	0.06
Sudanese	6	0.02
Other sub-Saharan African	6	0.02
Alaska Native tribes, specified:	7	0.03
Aleut (1)	1	0.00
Eskimo	1	0.00
Tlingit-Haida (3)	4	0.02
All other tribes (1)	1	0.00
Alaska Native tribes, not specified	1	0.00
Am. Ind. or Alaska Nat., not spec.	57	0.23
Albanian	10	0.04
American Indian tribes, specified:	133	0.53
Apache (1)	8	0.03
Blackfeet (1)	8	0.03
Cherokee (11)	35	0.14
Cheyenne	1	0.00
Chickasaw (3)	4	0.02
Chippewa (3)	4	0.02
Choctaw (1)	3	0.01
Comanche	1	0.00
Creek	2	0.01
Delaware (1)	5	0.02
Iroquois	1	0.00
Latin American Indians (2)	7	0.03
Navajo (4)	6	0.02
Osage (1)	1	0.00
Potawatomi	1	0.00
Pueblo (5)	5	0.02
Puget Sound Salish	1	0.00
Seminole (2)	2	0.01
Shoshone (3)	3	0.01
Sioux	12	0.05
Yakama (2)	4	0.02
Yaqui	1	0.00
All other tribes (10)	18	0.07
American Indian tribes, not spec.	11	0.04
Arab:	332	1.32
Arab/Arabic	69	0.27
Egyptian	36	0.14
Iraqi	6	0.02
Jordanian	20	0.08
Lebanese	38	0.15
Moroccan	7	0.03
Palestinian	78	0.31
Syrian	17	0.07
Other Arab	61	0.24
Armenian	176	0.70
Asian:	4,568	18.18
Bangladeshi (2)	2	0.01
Cambodian (7)	7	0.03
Chinese, ex. Taiwanese (1,698)	1,966	7.83
Filipino (486)	642	2.56
Indian (810)	855	3.40
Indonesian (19)	35	0.14
Japanese (475)	667	2.65
Korean (116)	152	0.61
Pakistani (9)	15	0.06
Sri Lankan (3)	6	0.02
Taiwanese (35)	40	0.16
Thai (14)	21	0.08
Vietnamese (66)	86	0.34
Other Asian, specified (3)	7	0.03
Other Asian, not specified (21)	67	0.27
Assyrian/Chaldean/Syriac	8	0.03
Australian	67	0.27
Austrian	123	0.49
Basque	17	0.07
Belgian	66	0.26
Brazilian	45	0.18
British	280	1.11
Bulgarian	20	0.08
Canadian	127	0.51
Croatian	37	0.15
Czech	75	0.30
Czechoslovakian	55	0.22
Danish	288	1.15
Dutch	399	1.59
Eastern European	121	0.48
English	2,633	10.47
Estonian	21	0.08
European	428	1.70
Finnish	29	0.12
French, except Basque	921	3.66
French Canadian	97	0.39
German	3,839	15.27
Greek	281	1.12
Hawaii Native/Pacific Islander:	275	1.09
Melanesian: (7)	13	0.05
Fijian (7)	13	0.05
Micronesian: (20)	31	0.12
Guamanian/Chamorro (18)	29	0.12
Other Micronesian (2)	2	0.01
Polynesian: (83)	193	0.77
Native Hawaiian (30)	113	0.45
Samoan (4)	20	0.08
Tongan (46)	55	0.22
Other Polynesian (3)	5	0.02
Other Pac. Isl., specified	1	0.00
Other Pac. Isl., not spec. (18)	37	0.15
Hispanic or Latino:	2,090	8.32
Central American:	274	1.09
Costa Rican	22	0.09
Guatemalan	34	0.14
Nicaraguan	81	0.32
Panamanian	3	0.01
Salvadoran	112	0.45
Other Central American	22	0.09
Cuban	38	0.15
Dominican Republic	2	0.01
Mexican	936	3.73
Puerto Rican	95	0.38
South American:	204	0.81
Argentinean	15	0.06
Bolivian	9	0.04
Chilean	19	0.08
Colombian	32	0.13
Ecuadorian	6	0.02
Peruvian	98	0.39
Venezuelan	6	0.02
Other South American	19	0.08
Other Hispanic or Latino	541	2.15
Hungarian	215	0.86
Icelander	5	0.02
Iranian	529	2.10
Irish	3,591	14.29
Israeli	9	0.04
Italian	2,283	9.08
Latvian	27	0.11
Lithuanian	80	0.32
Luxemburger	6	0.02
Maltese	54	0.21
New Zealander	10	0.04
Northern European	4	0.02
Norwegian	390	1.55
Pennsylvania German	7	0.03
Polish	506	2.01
Portuguese	276	1.10
Romanian	90	0.36
Russian	690	2.74
Scandinavian	13	0.05
Scotch-Irish	444	1.77
Scottish	735	2.92
Serbian	5	0.02
Slavic	17	0.07
Slovak	37	0.15
Slovene	39	0.16
Soviet Union	26	0.10
Swedish	588	2.34
Swiss	184	0.73
Turkish	15	0.06
Ukrainian	166	0.66
United States or American	721	2.87
Welsh	219	0.87
White:	19,798	78.80
Not Hispanic (17,696)	18,399	73.24
Hispanic (1,193)	1,399	5.57
Yugoslavian	123	0.49

Benicia

Place Type: City
County: Solano
Population: 26,865

Ancestry/Race	Number	%
African American/Black:	1,556	5.79
Not Hispanic (1,253)	1,484	5.52
Hispanic (42)	72	0.27
African, sub-Saharan:	93	0.34
African	42	0.16
Ugandan	51	0.19
Alaska Native tribes, specified:	6	0.02
Alaska Athabascan	1	0.00
Eskimo (1)	5	0.02
Am. Ind. or Alaska Nat., not spec.	165	0.61

Notes: 1. Figures in the "Number" column do not add up to the total population due to: a) Ancestry/Race overlap — e.g. persons can report being both White and Irish, b) persons of Hispanic origin can report being any race, c) persons reporting two ancestries are counted in both categories. 2. Numbers in parentheses indicate the number of persons reporting this ancestry/race alone, not in combination with any other ancestry/race. 3. Refer to the Explanation of Data in the front of the book for more detailed information.

Alsatian	6	0.02
American Indian tribes, specified:	367	1.37
Apache (2)	15	0.06
Blackfeet (5)	31	0.12
Cherokee (12)	117	0.44
Chickasaw (2)	4	0.01
Chippewa (3)	12	0.04
Choctaw (7)	26	0.10
Comanche	1	0.00
Cree (1)	3	0.01
Creek (5)	9	0.03
Crow	2	0.01
Delaware (5)	9	0.03
Iroquois (4)	8	0.03
Kiowa	1	0.00
Latin American Indians (8)	17	0.06
Navajo	16	0.06
Osage (2)	7	0.03
Paiute	2	0.01
Pima (2)	2	0.01
Potawatomi	5	0.02
Pueblo (7)	13	0.05
Seminole	9	0.03
Sioux (6)	15	0.06
Yaqui (1)	7	0.03
All other tribes (20)	36	0.13
American Indian tribes, not spec.	30	0.11
Arab:	134	0.50
Arab/Arabic	27	0.10
Jordanian	23	0.09
Lebanese	56	0.21
Syrian	5	0.02
Other Arab	23	0.09
Armenian	64	0.24
Asian:	2,661	9.91
Bangladeshi (4)	4	0.01
Cambodian (4)	5	0.02
Chinese, ex. Taiwanese (429)	568	2.11
Filipino (1,031)	1,331	4.95
Hmong (5)	5	0.02
Indian (166)	193	0.72
Indonesian (4)	12	0.04
Japanese (143)	275	1.02
Korean (92)	114	0.42
Laotian (6)	6	0.02
Malaysian	2	0.01
Pakistani (9)	9	0.03
Taiwanese (4)	9	0.03
Thai (8)	15	0.06
Vietnamese (38)	48	0.18
Other Asian, specified (10)	22	0.08
Other Asian, not specified (21)	43	0.16
Australian	13	0.05
Austrian	77	0.29
Basque	45	0.17
Belgian	9	0.03
Brazilian	12	0.04
British	194	0.72
Canadian	133	0.49
Celtic	20	0.07
Croatian	17	0.06
Czech	116	0.43
Czechoslovakian	57	0.21
Danish	303	1.12
Dutch	352	1.31
Eastern European	19	0.07
English	3,836	14.22
European	933	3.46
Finnish	91	0.34
French, except Basque	967	3.59
French Canadian	288	1.07
German	4,743	17.59
Greek	222	0.82
Hawaii Native/Pacific Islander:	214	0.80
Micronesian: (40)	75	0.28
Guamanian/Chamorro (40)	73	0.27
Other Micronesian	2	0.01
Polynesian: (34)	120	0.45
Native Hawaiian (24)	99	0.37
Samoan (8)	17	0.06
Tongan (2)	4	0.01
Other Pac. Isl., specified	1	0.00
Other Pac. Isl., not spec. (1)	18	0.07
Hispanic or Latino:	2,424	9.02
Central American:	124	0.46
Costa Rican	8	0.03
Guatemalan	9	0.03
Honduran	1	0.00
Nicaraguan	15	0.06
Panamanian	5	0.02
Salvadoran	72	0.27
Other Central American	14	0.05
Cuban	36	0.13
Mexican	1,482	5.52
Puerto Rican	113	0.42
South American:	103	0.38
Argentinean	10	0.04
Chilean	16	0.06
Colombian	17	0.06
Ecuadorian	1	0.00
Paraguayan	1	0.00
Peruvian	36	0.13
Uruguayan	2	0.01
Venezuelan	14	0.05
Other South American	6	0.02
Other Hispanic or Latino	566	2.11
Hungarian	153	0.57
Icelander	35	0.13
Iranian	57	0.21
Irish	4,246	15.75
Israeli	14	0.05
Italian	2,211	8.20
Latvian	22	0.08
Lithuanian	78	0.29
Maltese	3	0.01
Northern European	40	0.15
Norwegian	791	2.93
Pennsylvania German	26	0.10
Polish	710	2.63
Portuguese	942	3.49
Romanian	68	0.25
Russian	408	1.51
Scandinavian	92	0.34
Scotch-Irish	699	2.59
Scottish	961	3.56
Slavic	37	0.14
Slovak	131	0.49
Swedish	735	2.73
Swiss	58	0.22
Ukrainian	6	0.02
United States or American	830	3.08
Welsh	207	0.77
West Indian, excl. Hispanic:	44	0.16
Barbadian	16	0.06
West Indian	28	0.10
White:	22,419	83.45
Not Hispanic (19,853)	20,802	77.43
Hispanic (1,342)	1,617	6.02
Yugoslavian	41	0.15

Berkeley

Place Type: City
County: Alameda
Population: 102,743

Ancestry/Race	Number	%
Acadian/Cajun	14	0.01
Afghan	44	0.04
African American/Black:	15,685	15.27
Not Hispanic (13,707)	15,125	14.72
Hispanic (300)	560	0.55
African, sub-Saharan:	1,667	1.62
African	1,226	1.19
Ethiopian	240	0.23
Ghanian	9	0.01
Liberian	6	0.01
Nigerian	85	0.08
South African	54	0.05
Sudanese	6	0.01
Zairian	6	0.01
Zimbabwean	2	0.00
Other sub-Saharan African	33	0.03
Alaska Native tribes, specified:	26	0.03
Alaska Athabascan (4)	8	0.01
Aleut (2)	4	0.00
Eskimo (2)	10	0.01
Tlingit-Haida (1)	4	0.00
Am. Ind. or Alaska Nat., not spec.	583	0.57
Albanian	24	0.02
Alsatian	20	0.02
American Indian tribes, specified:	1,040	1.01
Apache (10)	35	0.03
Blackfeet (10)	49	0.05
Cherokee (29)	293	0.29
Cheyenne (3)	5	0.00
Chickasaw	12	0.01
Chippewa (6)	23	0.02
Choctaw (15)	57	0.06
Comanche (1)	3	0.00
Cree (1)	8	0.01
Creek (2)	14	0.01
Delaware	1	0.00
Iroquois (11)	42	0.04
Kiowa	3	0.00
Latin American Indians (75)	162	0.16
Lumbee	1	0.00
Navajo (21)	35	0.03
Osage (1)	5	0.00
Ottawa (2)	2	0.00
Paiute	1	0.00
Pima (3)	6	0.01
Potawatomi (5)	7	0.01
Pueblo (6)	16	0.02
Seminole (1)	25	0.02
Shoshone (4)	6	0.01
Sioux (20)	48	0.05
Tohono O'Odham (1)	3	0.00
Ute	4	0.00
Yakama	1	0.00
Yaqui (7)	20	0.02
Yuman (4)	8	0.01
All other tribes (45)	145	0.14
American Indian tribes, not spec.	95	0.09
Arab:	760	0.74
Arab/Arabic	190	0.18
Egyptian	60	0.06
Iraqi	24	0.02
Jordanian	14	0.01
Lebanese	214	0.21
Moroccan	38	0.04
Palestinian	29	0.03
Syrian	39	0.04
Other Arab	152	0.15
Armenian	265	0.26
Asian:	19,911	19.38
Bangladeshi (12)	13	0.01
Cambodian (55)	81	0.08
Chinese, ex. Taiwanese (7,209)	8,255	8.03
Filipino (1,182)	1,677	1.63
Hmong (14)	14	0.01
Indian (1,736)	2,021	1.97
Indonesian (35)	80	0.08
Japanese (2,312)	3,084	3.00
Korean (1,916)	2,076	2.02
Laotian (104)	111	0.11
Malaysian (13)	21	0.02
Pakistani (151)	194	0.19
Sri Lankan (20)	35	0.03
Taiwanese (376)	469	0.46
Thai (191)	276	0.27
Vietnamese (868)	997	0.97
Other Asian, specified (29)	83	0.08
Other Asian, not specified (155)	424	0.41
Assyrian/Chaldean/Syriac	33	0.03
Australian	174	0.17
Austrian	555	0.54
Basque	78	0.08
Belgian	206	0.20
Brazilian	191	0.19

Notes: 1. Figures in the "Number" column do not add up to the total population due to: a) Ancestry/Race overlap — e.g. persons can report being both White and Irish, b) persons of Hispanic origin can report being any race, c) persons reporting two ancestries are counted in both categories. 2. Numbers in parentheses indicate the number of persons reporting this ancestry/race alone, not in combination with any other ancestry/race. 3. Refer to the Explanation of Data in the front of the book for more detailed information.

British	1,239	1.21
Bulgarian	57	0.06
Canadian	330	0.32
Celtic	156	0.15
Croatian	135	0.13
Cypriot	14	0.01
Czech	553	0.54
Czechoslovakian	140	0.14
Danish	710	0.69
Dutch	1,317	1.28
Eastern European	1,055	1.03
English	10,322	10.05
Estonian	41	0.04
European	2,593	2.52
Finnish	256	0.25
French, except Basque	2,734	2.66
French Canadian	514	0.50
German	11,402	11.10
Greek	587	0.57
Guyanese	14	0.01
Hawaii Native/Pacific Islander:	466	0.45
Melanesian: (3)	4	0.00
Fijian (2)	3	0.00
Other Melanesian (1)	1	0.00
Micronesian: (35)	60	0.06
Guamanian/Chamorro (27)	51	0.05
Other Micronesian (8)	9	0.01
Polynesian: (75)	248	0.24
Native Hawaiian (32)	172	0.17
Samoan (24)	49	0.05
Tongan (18)	19	0.02
Other Polynesian (1)	8	0.01
Other Pac. Isl., specified	26	0.03
Other Pac. Isl., not spec. (29)	128	0.12
Hispanic or Latino:	10,001	9.73
Central American:	585	0.57
Costa Rican	44	0.04
Guatemalan	141	0.14
Honduran	24	0.02
Nicaraguan	100	0.10
Panamanian	28	0.03
Salvadoran	191	0.19
Other Central American	57	0.06
Cuban	213	0.21
Dominican Republic	33	0.03
Mexican	6,448	6.28
Puerto Rican	379	0.37
South American:	774	0.75
Argentinean	146	0.14
Bolivian	19	0.02
Chilean	116	0.11
Colombian	105	0.10
Ecuadorian	53	0.05
Paraguayan	3	0.00
Peruvian	195	0.19
Uruguayan	17	0.02
Venezuelan	50	0.05
Other South American	70	0.07
Other Hispanic or Latino	1,569	1.53
Hungarian	683	0.66
Icelander	47	0.05
Iranian	799	0.78
Irish	9,137	8.89
Israeli	279	0.27
Italian	4,329	4.21
Latvian	179	0.17
Lithuanian	508	0.49
Luxemburger	13	0.01
Macedonian	13	0.01
Maltese	32	0.03
New Zealander	68	0.07
Northern European	299	0.29
Norwegian	1,492	1.45
Pennsylvania German	32	0.03
Polish	2,984	2.90
Portuguese	588	0.57
Romanian	314	0.31
Russian	4,359	4.24
Scandinavian	322	0.31
Scotch-Irish	1,654	1.61
Scottish	2,731	2.66
Serbian	123	0.12
Slavic	93	0.09
Slovak	127	0.12
Slovene	48	0.05
Swedish	1,795	1.75
Swiss	568	0.55
Turkish	94	0.09
Ukrainian	389	0.38
United States or American	1,379	1.34
Welsh	866	0.84
West Indian, excl. Hispanic:	342	0.33
Barbadian	39	0.04
Belizean	34	0.03
Bermudan	8	0.01
Haitian	44	0.04
Jamaican	166	0.16
Trinidadian and Tobagonian	7	0.01
West Indian	44	0.04
White:	65,422	63.68
Not Hispanic (56,691)	60,388	58.78
Hispanic (4,106)	5,034	4.90
Yugoslavian	86	0.08

Beverly Hills

Place Type: City
County: Los Angeles
Population: 33,784

Ancestry/Race	Number	%
African American/Black:	699	2.07
Not Hispanic (584)	678	2.01
Hispanic (13)	21	0.06
African, sub-Saharan:	227	0.67
African	92	0.27
Ethiopian	28	0.08
Nigerian	9	0.03
South African	98	0.29
Alaska Native tribes, specified:	2	0.01
Aleut	1	0.00
Eskimo (1)	1	0.00
Alaska Native tribes, not specified	2	0.01
Am. Ind. or Alaska Nat., not spec.	42	0.12
Alsatian	8	0.02
American Indian tribes, specified:	69	0.20
Apache (1)	4	0.01
Cherokee (4)	18	0.05
Chippewa (2)	4	0.01
Choctaw	4	0.01
Cree (1)	1	0.00
Creek (1)	2	0.01
Iroquois	2	0.01
Latin American Indians (5)	12	0.04
Osage	1	0.00
Pueblo (1)	1	0.00
Seminole	1	0.00
Sioux (2)	6	0.02
Yaqui (1)	3	0.01
All other tribes (2)	10	0.03
American Indian tribes, not spec.	10	0.03
Arab:	555	1.64
Arab/Arabic	42	0.12
Egyptian	73	0.22
Iraqi	86	0.25
Lebanese	144	0.43
Moroccan	20	0.06
Syrian	76	0.22
Other Arab	114	0.34
Armenian	204	0.60
Asian:	3,014	8.92
Bangladeshi (5)	8	0.02
Chinese, ex. Taiwanese (573)	658	1.95
Filipino (211)	278	0.82
Indian (111)	167	0.49
Indonesian (24)	46	0.14
Japanese (311)	353	1.04
Korean (824)	862	2.55
Laotian (1)	2	0.01
Malaysian (10)	14	0.04
Pakistani (3)	4	0.01
Sri Lankan (11)	15	0.04
Taiwanese (69)	75	0.22
Thai (47)	61	0.18
Vietnamese (71)	80	0.24
Other Asian, specified (6)	8	0.02
Other Asian, not specified (55)	383	1.13
Assyrian/Chaldean/Syriac	25	0.07
Australian	17	0.05
Austrian	275	0.81
Belgian	24	0.07
Brazilian	94	0.28
British	129	0.38
Bulgarian	18	0.05
Canadian	239	0.71
Celtic	10	0.03
Croatian	19	0.06
Czech	83	0.25
Czechoslovakian	166	0.49
Danish	70	0.21
Dutch	220	0.65
Eastern European	601	1.78
English	1,576	4.66
Estonian	39	0.12
European	376	1.11
Finnish	38	0.11
French, except Basque	903	2.67
French Canadian	72	0.21
German	1,806	5.34
Greek	180	0.53
Hawaii Native/Pacific Islander:	34	0.10
Melanesian: (2)	2	0.01
Fijian (2)	2	0.01
Micronesian:	2	0.01
Guamanian/Chamorro	2	0.01
Polynesian: (7)	16	0.05
Native Hawaiian (1)	10	0.03
Samoan (5)	5	0.01
Tongan (1)	1	0.00
Other Pac. Isl., specified	1	0.00
Other Pac. Isl., not spec. (1)	13	0.04
Hispanic or Latino:	1,565	4.63
Central American:	278	0.82
Costa Rican	9	0.03
Guatemalan	81	0.24
Honduran	10	0.03
Nicaraguan	18	0.05
Panamanian	10	0.03
Salvadoran	143	0.42
Other Central American	7	0.02
Cuban	54	0.16
Dominican Republic	3	0.01
Mexican	607	1.80
Puerto Rican	57	0.17
South American:	200	0.59
Argentinean	60	0.18
Bolivian	1	0.00
Chilean	21	0.06
Colombian	34	0.10
Ecuadorian	9	0.03
Peruvian	38	0.11
Uruguayan	6	0.02
Venezuelan	12	0.04
Other South American	19	0.06
Other Hispanic or Latino	366	1.08
Hungarian	557	1.65
Icelander	5	0.01
Iranian	6,260	18.50
Irish	1,521	4.50
Israeli	534	1.58
Italian	892	2.64
Latvian	14	0.04
Lithuanian	212	0.63
New Zealander	15	0.04
Northern European	37	0.11
Norwegian	373	1.10
Pennsylvania German	3	0.01
Polish	2,100	6.21
Portuguese	49	0.14
Romanian	328	0.97

Notes: 1. Figures in the "Number" column do not add up to the total population due to: a) Ancestry/Race overlap — e.g. persons can report being both White and Irish, b) persons of Hispanic origin can report being any race, c) persons reporting two ancestries are counted in both categories. 2. Numbers in parentheses indicate the number of persons reporting this ancestry/race alone, not in combination with any other ancestry/race. 3. Refer to the Explanation of Data in the front of the book for more detailed information.

Russian	3,184	9.41
Scandinavian	43	0.13
Scotch-Irish	266	0.79
Scottish	358	1.06
Serbian	39	0.12
Soviet Union	16	0.05
Swedish	283	0.84
Swiss	85	0.25
Turkish	40	0.12
Ukrainian	333	0.98
United States or American	2,098	6.20
Welsh	85	0.25
West Indian, excl. Hispanic:	31	0.09
Haitian	5	0.01
Jamaican	12	0.04
Trinidadian and Tobagonian	9	0.03
West Indian	5	0.01
White:	30,169	89.30
Not Hispanic (27,717)	29,058	86.01
Hispanic (1,019)	1,111	3.29
Yugoslavian	16	0.05

Blackhawk-Camino Tassajara

Place Type: Census Designated Place
County: Contra Costa
Population: 10,048

Ancestry/Race	Number	%
African American/Black:	261	2.60
Not Hispanic (226)	255	2.54
Hispanic (6)	6	0.06
African, sub-Saharan:	9	0.09
South African	9	0.09
Alaska Native tribes, specified:	1	0.01
Tlingit-Haida (1)	1	0.01
Am. Ind. or Alaska Nat., not spec.	14	0.14
American Indian tribes, specified:	23	0.23
Blackfeet (1)	2	0.02
Cherokee (3)	6	0.06
Chickasaw	1	0.01
Choctaw	3	0.03
Creek (3)	4	0.04
Crow (1)	1	0.01
All other tribes (5)	6	0.06
Arab:	51	0.51
Lebanese	26	0.26
Syrian	25	0.25
Armenian	56	0.56
Asian:	1,898	18.89
Chinese, ex. Taiwanese (740)	821	8.17
Filipino (185)	227	2.26
Indian (351)	371	3.69
Indonesian (7)	7	0.07
Japanese (69)	112	1.11
Korean (119)	132	1.31
Pakistani (55)	67	0.67
Taiwanese (51)	54	0.54
Thai (6)	6	0.06
Vietnamese (43)	49	0.49
Other Asian, specified (6)	8	0.08
Other Asian, not specified (15)	44	0.44
Australian	8	0.08
Austrian	37	0.37
Belgian	26	0.26
Brazilian	36	0.36
British	118	1.18
Bulgarian	9	0.09
Canadian	39	0.39
Croatian	19	0.19
Czech	22	0.22
Czechoslovakian	13	0.13
Danish	130	1.30
Dutch	213	2.14
Eastern European	9	0.09
English	1,268	12.72
European	158	1.59
Finnish	23	0.23
French, except Basque	278	2.79
French Canadian	57	0.57
German	1,567	15.72
Greek	92	0.92
Hawaii Native/Pacific Islander:	24	0.24
Melanesian: (1)	4	0.04
Fijian (1)	4	0.04
Micronesian: (2)	3	0.03
Guamanian/Chamorro (2)	3	0.03
Polynesian: (5)	10	0.10
Native Hawaiian (5)	10	0.10
Other Pac. Isl., not spec. (6)	7	0.07
Hispanic or Latino:	391	3.89
Central American:	20	0.20
Guatemalan	3	0.03
Nicaraguan	5	0.05
Panamanian	5	0.05
Salvadoran	7	0.07
Cuban	33	0.33
Dominican Republic	1	0.01
Mexican	164	1.63
Puerto Rican	9	0.09
South American:	32	0.32
Argentinean	2	0.02
Bolivian	4	0.04
Chilean	3	0.03
Colombian	13	0.13
Ecuadorian	1	0.01
Peruvian	4	0.04
Venezuelan	5	0.05
Other Hispanic or Latino	132	1.31
Hungarian	60	0.60
Icelander	13	0.13
Iranian	212	2.13
Irish	1,267	12.71
Israeli	19	0.19
Italian	828	8.31
Latvian	33	0.33
Maltese	8	0.08
Northern European	11	0.11
Norwegian	201	2.02
Polish	329	3.30
Portuguese	129	1.29
Romanian	13	0.13
Russian	278	2.79
Scandinavian	33	0.33
Scotch-Irish	147	1.48
Scottish	260	2.61
Slavic	19	0.19
Slovak	17	0.17
Slovene	42	0.42
Swedish	183	1.84
Swiss	60	0.60
Turkish	9	0.09
Ukrainian	25	0.25
United States or American	303	3.04
Welsh	129	1.29
White:	7,994	79.56
Not Hispanic (7,466)	7,673	76.36
Hispanic (281)	321	3.19
Yugoslavian	6	0.06

Bloomington

Place Type: Census Designated Place
County: San Bernardino
Population: 19,318

Ancestry/Race	Number	%
African American/Black:	885	4.58
Not Hispanic (736)	786	4.07
Hispanic (42)	99	0.51
African, sub-Saharan:	37	0.19
African	37	0.19
Am. Ind. or Alaska Nat., not spec.	190	0.98
American Indian tribes, specified:	278	1.44
Apache (9)	15	0.08
Blackfeet	13	0.07
Cherokee (22)	54	0.28
Chickasaw (1)	2	0.01
Chippewa (2)	4	0.02
Choctaw (9)	13	0.07
Delaware (1)	3	0.02
Iroquois (1)	1	0.01
Latin American Indians (66)	73	0.38
Navajo (5)	8	0.04
Ottawa (1)	5	0.03
Paiute (1)	1	0.01
Pueblo (9)	9	0.05
Seminole	3	0.02
Shoshone	1	0.01
Sioux (12)	14	0.07
Tohono O'Odham (2)	2	0.01
Yaqui (5)	6	0.03
Yuman (1)	10	0.05
All other tribes (26)	41	0.21
American Indian tribes, not spec.	27	0.14
Arab:	15	0.08
Arab/Arabic	7	0.04
Lebanese	8	0.04
Asian:	294	1.52
Cambodian (10)	10	0.05
Chinese, ex. Taiwanese (20)	26	0.13
Filipino (80)	100	0.52
Indian (26)	33	0.17
Indonesian (5)	11	0.06
Japanese (10)	36	0.19
Korean (3)	11	0.06
Taiwanese (16)	16	0.08
Thai (6)	7	0.04
Vietnamese (28)	28	0.14
Other Asian, not specified (9)	16	0.08
Austrian	21	0.11
Belgian	46	0.24
British	38	0.20
Canadian	18	0.09
Czech	20	0.10
Czechoslovakian	37	0.19
Danish	85	0.44
Dutch	95	0.49
English	644	3.35
European	85	0.44
French, except Basque	332	1.73
French Canadian	26	0.14
German	1,286	6.70
Greek	25	0.13
Hawaii Native/Pacific Islander:	61	0.32
Micronesian: (19)	22	0.11
Guamanian/Chamorro (19)	22	0.11
Polynesian: (15)	29	0.15
Native Hawaiian (3)	9	0.05
Samoan (11)	16	0.08
Tongan (1)	1	0.01
Other Polynesian	3	0.02
Other Pac. Isl., not spec. (4)	10	0.05
Hispanic or Latino:	12,436	64.38
Central American:	312	1.62
Costa Rican	15	0.08
Guatemalan	73	0.38
Honduran	14	0.07
Nicaraguan	29	0.15
Panamanian	2	0.01
Salvadoran	142	0.74
Other Central American	37	0.19
Cuban	32	0.17
Mexican	10,368	53.67
Puerto Rican	104	0.54
South American:	48	0.25
Argentinean	1	0.01
Chilean	5	0.03
Colombian	18	0.09
Ecuadorian	13	0.07
Peruvian	6	0.03
Venezuelan	1	0.01
Other South American	4	0.02
Other Hispanic or Latino	1,572	8.14
Hungarian	27	0.14
Irish	645	3.36
Italian	257	1.34
Norwegian	175	0.91
Polish	108	0.56

Notes: 1. Figures in the "Number" column do not add up to the total population due to: a) Ancestry/Race overlap — e.g. persons can report being both White and Irish, b) persons of Hispanic origin can report being any race, c) persons reporting two ancestries are counted in both categories. 2. Numbers in parentheses indicate the number of persons reporting this ancestry/race alone, not in combination with any other ancestry/race. 3. Refer to the Explanation of Data in the front of the book for more detailed information.

Ancestry/Race	Number	%
Portuguese	7	0.04
Romanian	36	0.19
Russian	18	0.09
Scotch-Irish	219	1.14
Scottish	227	1.18
Slavic	8	0.04
Swedish	151	0.79
Swiss	13	0.07
United States or American	508	2.65
Welsh	102	0.53
White:	11,168	57.81
Not Hispanic (5,581)	5,771	29.87
Hispanic (4,856)	5,397	27.94
Yugoslavian	13	0.07

Blythe

Place Type: City
County: Riverside
Population: 12,155

Ancestry/Race	Number	%
African American/Black:	1,152	9.48
Not Hispanic (972)	1,063	8.75
Hispanic (42)	89	0.73
Alaska Native tribes, specified:	2	0.02
Eskimo (1)	2	0.02
Am. Ind. or Alaska Nat., not spec.	91	0.75
American Indian tribes, specified:	156	1.28
Apache (7)	7	0.06
Blackfeet	3	0.02
Cherokee (12)	25	0.21
Chickasaw (1)	1	0.01
Chippewa (2)	2	0.02
Choctaw (7)	8	0.07
Comanche (1)	1	0.01
Creek	9	0.07
Delaware	1	0.01
Kiowa	3	0.02
Latin American Indians (16)	19	0.16
Lumbee (2)	2	0.02
Navajo (15)	17	0.14
Paiute (8)	8	0.07
Pima (1)	1	0.01
Potawatomi (1)	1	0.01
Pueblo (2)	2	0.02
Seminole (4)	9	0.07
Sioux (3)	3	0.02
Tohono O'Odham (1)	3	0.02
Yaqui (9)	11	0.09
Yuman (1)	1	0.01
All other tribes (11)	19	0.16
American Indian tribes, not spec.	11	0.09
Arab:	12	0.10
Arab/Arabic	12	0.10
Armenian	12	0.10
Asian:	221	1.82
Chinese, ex. Taiwanese (17)	22	0.18
Filipino (62)	82	0.67
Indian (41)	51	0.42
Japanese (13)	17	0.14
Korean (10)	13	0.11
Laotian (4)	4	0.03
Taiwanese (2)	7	0.06
Thai (8)	10	0.08
Vietnamese (9)	9	0.07
Other Asian, not specified (2)	6	0.05
Austrian	21	0.18
Basque	17	0.14
Belgian	10	0.08
British	24	0.20
Canadian	26	0.22
Czech	36	0.30
Czechoslovakian	17	0.14
Danish	34	0.29
Dutch	146	1.23
English	715	6.05
European	69	0.58
Finnish	10	0.08
French, except Basque	266	2.25
French Canadian	44	0.37
German	1,055	8.92
Greek	18	0.15
Hawaii Native/Pacific Islander:	37	0.30
Micronesian: (6)	6	0.05
Guamanian/Chamorro (2)	2	0.02
Other Micronesian (4)	4	0.03
Polynesian: (18)	31	0.26
Native Hawaiian (5)	9	0.07
Samoan (11)	20	0.16
Other Polynesian (2)	2	0.02
Hispanic or Latino:	5,571	45.83
Central American:	31	0.26
Costa Rican	3	0.02
Guatemalan	11	0.09
Nicaraguan	2	0.02
Salvadoran	14	0.12
Other Central American	1	0.01
Cuban	4	0.03
Mexican	4,800	39.49
Puerto Rican	25	0.21
South American:	7	0.06
Colombian	7	0.06
Other Hispanic or Latino	704	5.79
Hungarian	6	0.05
Irish	629	5.32
Italian	276	2.33
Norwegian	121	1.02
Polish	94	0.79
Portuguese	28	0.24
Russian	7	0.06
Scotch-Irish	65	0.55
Scottish	114	0.96
Slovak	10	0.08
Swedish	95	0.80
Swiss	35	0.30
Ukrainian	18	0.15
United States or American	540	4.57
Welsh	65	0.55
White:	7,206	59.28
Not Hispanic (5,105)	5,284	43.47
Hispanic (1,630)	1,922	15.81
Yugoslavian	7	0.06

Bonita

Place Type: Census Designated Place
County: San Diego
Population: 12,401

Ancestry/Race	Number	%
African American/Black:	447	3.60
Not Hispanic (370)	417	3.36
Hispanic (16)	30	0.24
African, sub-Saharan:	7	0.06
African	7	0.06
Alaska Native tribes, specified:	5	0.04
Alaska Athabascan (2)	2	0.02
Tlingit-Haida (3)	3	0.02
Am. Ind. or Alaska Nat., not spec.	56	0.45
American Indian tribes, specified:	94	0.76
Apache (3)	4	0.03
Blackfeet (1)	7	0.06
Cherokee (10)	21	0.17
Cheyenne	2	0.02
Chippewa (4)	4	0.03
Choctaw (3)	10	0.08
Comanche (4)	4	0.03
Creek	1	0.01
Kiowa (1)	1	0.01
Latin American Indians (3)	9	0.07
Navajo (1)	1	0.01
Osage	1	0.01
Pueblo (2)	2	0.02
Seminole	2	0.02
All other tribes (7)	25	0.20
American Indian tribes, not spec.	1	0.01
Arab:	74	0.62
Lebanese	54	0.45
Palestinian	10	0.08
Syrian	10	0.08
Asian:	1,345	10.85
Cambodian (6)	7	0.06
Chinese, ex. Taiwanese (87)	127	1.02
Filipino (621)	778	6.27
Indian (22)	31	0.25
Indonesian (3)	6	0.05
Japanese (158)	223	1.80
Korean (92)	107	0.86
Laotian (5)	5	0.04
Pakistani (2)	2	0.02
Thai (18)	18	0.15
Vietnamese (16)	20	0.16
Other Asian, specified (1)	1	0.01
Other Asian, not specified (8)	20	0.16
Australian	8	0.07
Austrian	7	0.06
Basque	7	0.06
British	56	0.47
Canadian	22	0.18
Czech	52	0.43
Czechoslovakian	18	0.15
Danish	97	0.81
Dutch	171	1.42
Eastern European	21	0.17
English	1,260	10.48
European	230	1.91
French, except Basque	397	3.30
French Canadian	76	0.63
German	1,444	12.02
Greek	35	0.29
Hawaii Native/Pacific Islander:	106	0.85
Micronesian: (26)	54	0.44
Guamanian/Chamorro (26)	53	0.43
Other Micronesian	1	0.01
Polynesian: (9)	33	0.27
Native Hawaiian (5)	23	0.19
Samoan (4)	10	0.08
Other Pac. Isl., not spec. (2)	19	0.15
Hispanic or Latino:	3,779	30.47
Central American:	35	0.28
Costa Rican	11	0.09
Guatemalan	2	0.02
Honduran	2	0.02
Panamanian	12	0.10
Salvadoran	8	0.06
Cuban	28	0.23
Dominican Republic	2	0.02
Mexican	3,148	25.39
Puerto Rican	76	0.61
South American:	92	0.74
Argentinean	9	0.07
Bolivian	3	0.02
Chilean	15	0.12
Colombian	22	0.18
Ecuadorian	1	0.01
Peruvian	29	0.23
Venezuelan	5	0.04
Other South American	8	0.06
Other Hispanic or Latino	398	3.21
Hungarian	9	0.07
Icelander	4	0.03
Iranian	13	0.11
Irish	1,252	10.42
Israeli	13	0.11
Italian	599	4.98
Lithuanian	16	0.13
Northern European	79	0.66
Norwegian	123	1.02
Polish	297	2.47
Portuguese	65	0.54
Russian	96	0.80
Scotch-Irish	126	1.05
Scottish	294	2.45
Slovak	9	0.07
Slovene	7	0.06
Swedish	148	1.23
Swiss	30	0.25
Turkish	28	0.23
Ukrainian	47	0.39

Notes: 1. Figures in the "Number" column do not add up to the total population due to: a) Ancestry/Race overlap — e.g. persons can report being both White and Irish, b) persons of Hispanic origin can report being any race, c) persons reporting two ancestries are counted in both categories. 2. Numbers in parentheses indicate the number of persons reporting this ancestry/race alone, not in combination with any other ancestry/race. 3. Refer to the Explanation of Data in the front of the book for more detailed information.

United States or American	290	2.41
Welsh	82	0.68
White:	9,436	76.09
Not Hispanic (6,763)	7,049	56.84
Hispanic (2,165)	2,387	19.25
Yugoslavian	85	0.71

Bostonia

Place Type: Census Designated Place
County: San Diego
Population: 15,169

Ancestry/Race	Number	%
Afghan	218	1.47
African American/Black:	741	4.88
Not Hispanic (574)	689	4.54
Hispanic (30)	52	0.34
African, sub-Saharan:	64	0.43
African	54	0.36
Ethiopian	10	0.07
Alaska Native tribes, specified:	6	0.04
Eskimo	3	0.02
Tlingit-Haida	3	0.02
Am. Ind. or Alaska Nat., not spec.	80	0.53
American Indian tribes, specified:	210	1.38
Apache (12)	15	0.10
Blackfeet	5	0.03
Cherokee (12)	62	0.41
Cheyenne	2	0.01
Chickasaw (12)	18	0.12
Chippewa (1)	6	0.04
Choctaw (4)	6	0.04
Comanche (1)	3	0.02
Creek (4)	6	0.04
Iroquois (1)	7	0.05
Latin American Indians (13)	18	0.12
Lumbee (1)	1	0.01
Navajo (10)	11	0.07
Pima	2	0.01
Potawatomi (2)	2	0.01
Pueblo (3)	7	0.05
Shoshone	2	0.01
Sioux (4)	6	0.04
Yaqui	5	0.03
All other tribes (13)	26	0.17
American Indian tribes, not spec.	19	0.13
Arab:	188	1.26
Iraqi	154	1.04
Lebanese	9	0.06
Other Arab	25	0.17
Armenian	8	0.05
Asian:	438	2.89
Chinese, ex. Taiwanese (28)	55	0.36
Filipino (116)	192	1.27
Hmong (1)	1	0.01
Indian (7)	18	0.12
Indonesian	1	0.01
Japanese (39)	83	0.55
Korean (10)	21	0.14
Laotian (1)	1	0.01
Pakistani	2	0.01
Taiwanese (1)	3	0.02
Thai (5)	6	0.04
Vietnamese (11)	16	0.11
Other Asian, not specified (2)	39	0.26
Assyrian/Chaldean/Syriac	474	3.19
Austrian	14	0.09
Belgian	4	0.03
Brazilian	22	0.15
British	54	0.36
Canadian	35	0.24
Croatian	6	0.04
Czech	26	0.17
Czechoslovakian	14	0.09
Danish	143	0.96
Dutch	225	1.51
English	1,479	9.95
European	82	0.55
Finnish	12	0.08
French, except Basque	553	3.72
French Canadian	96	0.65
German	2,330	15.67
Greek	136	0.91
Hawaii Native/Pacific Islander:	129	0.85
Melanesian: (4)	8	0.05
Fijian (4)	8	0.05
Micronesian: (32)	58	0.38
Guamanian/Chamorro (32)	58	0.38
Polynesian: (17)	45	0.30
Native Hawaiian (12)	38	0.25
Samoan (5)	7	0.05
Other Pac. Isl., not spec. (1)	18	0.12
Hispanic or Latino:	2,523	16.63
Central American:	44	0.29
Costa Rican	13	0.09
Guatemalan	6	0.04
Honduran	2	0.01
Nicaraguan	10	0.07
Panamanian	3	0.02
Salvadoran	6	0.04
Other Central American	4	0.03
Cuban	14	0.09
Dominican Republic	1	0.01
Mexican	1,981	13.06
Puerto Rican	68	0.45
South American:	32	0.21
Argentinean	2	0.01
Chilean	1	0.01
Colombian	13	0.09
Ecuadorian	2	0.01
Peruvian	5	0.03
Other South American	9	0.06
Other Hispanic or Latino	383	2.52
Hungarian	92	0.62
Irish	1,918	12.90
Italian	658	4.43
Latvian	6	0.04
Lithuanian	38	0.26
Luxemburger	15	0.10
Norwegian	225	1.51
Polish	266	1.79
Portuguese	70	0.47
Romanian	14	0.09
Russian	47	0.32
Scandinavian	8	0.05
Scotch-Irish	262	1.76
Scottish	274	1.84
Slovak	7	0.05
Slovene	39	0.26
Swedish	205	1.38
Swiss	42	0.28
Turkish	17	0.11
Ukrainian	14	0.09
United States or American	938	6.31
Welsh	50	0.34
West Indian, excl. Hispanic:	41	0.28
Barbadian	7	0.05
Belizean	6	0.04
Dutch West Indian	23	0.15
Jamaican	5	0.03
White:	12,874	84.87
Not Hispanic (11,103)	11,635	76.70
Hispanic (1,003)	1,239	8.17

Brawley

Place Type: City
County: Imperial
Population: 22,052

Ancestry/Race	Number	%
African American/Black:	613	2.78
Not Hispanic (464)	486	2.20
Hispanic (76)	127	0.58
African, sub-Saharan:	75	0.34
African	75	0.34
Am. Ind. or Alaska Nat., not spec.	150	0.68
Alsatian	10	0.05
American Indian tribes, specified:	156	0.71
Apache (1)	6	0.03
Cherokee (6)	25	0.11
Chippewa (6)	6	0.03
Choctaw (2)	8	0.04
Latin American Indians (44)	59	0.27
Navajo (6)	10	0.05
Osage (1)	3	0.01
Pima (1)	1	0.00
Pueblo	2	0.01
Shoshone (1)	1	0.00
Sioux (3)	5	0.02
Yaqui (20)	22	0.10
Yuman	2	0.01
All other tribes (5)	6	0.03
American Indian tribes, not spec.	43	0.19
Arab:	59	0.27
Arab/Arabic	25	0.11
Egyptian	14	0.06
Lebanese	6	0.03
Moroccan	6	0.03
Other Arab	8	0.04
Asian:	468	2.12
Cambodian (5)	5	0.02
Chinese, ex. Taiwanese (56)	79	0.36
Filipino (148)	260	1.18
Indian (36)	55	0.25
Japanese (19)	30	0.14
Korean (12)	19	0.09
Taiwanese (6)	6	0.03
Vietnamese (5)	8	0.04
Other Asian, not specified	6	0.03
Assyrian/Chaldean/Syriac	14	0.06
Austrian	25	0.11
Belgian	26	0.12
British	22	0.10
Canadian	21	0.10
Czech	16	0.07
Czechoslovakian	5	0.02
Danish	43	0.19
Dutch	44	0.20
English	542	2.45
European	30	0.14
French, except Basque	248	1.12
French Canadian	34	0.15
German	884	4.00
Hawaii Native/Pacific Islander:	55	0.25
Micronesian: (14)	14	0.06
Guamanian/Chamorro (14)	14	0.06
Polynesian: (17)	26	0.12
Native Hawaiian (12)	21	0.10
Samoan (5)	5	0.02
Other Pac. Isl., not spec. (10)	15	0.07
Hispanic or Latino:	16,280	73.83
Central American:	90	0.41
Costa Rican	1	0.00
Guatemalan	8	0.04
Honduran	5	0.02
Nicaraguan	6	0.03
Panamanian	2	0.01
Salvadoran	63	0.29
Other Central American	5	0.02
Cuban	9	0.04
Mexican	14,606	66.23
Puerto Rican	55	0.25
South American:	7	0.03
Peruvian	3	0.01
Other South American	4	0.02
Other Hispanic or Latino	1,513	6.86
Hungarian	5	0.02
Icelander	8	0.04
Irish	755	3.42
Italian	247	1.12
Lithuanian	3	0.01
Norwegian	111	0.50
Pennsylvania German	5	0.02
Polish	52	0.24
Portuguese	24	0.11
Romanian	10	0.05
Russian	55	0.25
Scandinavian	12	0.05

Notes: 1. Figures in the "Number" column do not add up to the total population due to: a) Ancestry/Race overlap — e.g. persons can report being both White and Irish, b) persons of Hispanic origin can report being any race, c) persons reporting two ancestries are counted in both categories. 2. Numbers in parentheses indicate the number of persons reporting this ancestry/race alone, not in combination with any other ancestry/race. 3. Refer to the Explanation of Data in the front of the book for more detailed information.

Ancestry/Race	Number	%
Scotch-Irish	126	0.57
Scottish	169	0.76
Swedish	30	0.14
Swiss	91	0.41
Ukrainian	13	0.06
United States or American	716	3.24
Welsh	38	0.17
White:	12,436	56.39
Not Hispanic (4,780)	4,947	22.43
Hispanic (6,858)	7,489	33.96
Yugoslavian	12	0.05

Brea

Place Type: City
County: Orange
Population: 35,410

Ancestry/Race	Number	%
African American/Black:	561	1.58
Not Hispanic (409)	504	1.42
Hispanic (38)	57	0.16
African, sub-Saharan:	68	0.19
African	44	0.13
Ethiopian	14	0.04
Sierra Leonean	10	0.03
Alaska Native tribes, specified:	3	0.01
Alaska Athabascan (2)	2	0.01
Tlingit-Haida (1)	1	0.00
Alaska Native tribes, not specified	1	0.00
Am. Ind. or Alaska Nat., not spec.	114	0.32
Albanian	15	0.04
American Indian tribes, specified:	295	0.83
Apache (4)	11	0.03
Blackfeet (4)	7	0.02
Cherokee (25)	84	0.24
Chickasaw (12)	12	0.03
Chippewa (5)	12	0.03
Choctaw (6)	22	0.06
Comanche	1	0.00
Cree	1	0.00
Creek	4	0.01
Crow	1	0.00
Delaware	9	0.03
Iroquois (3)	9	0.03
Kiowa (4)	4	0.01
Latin American Indians (21)	32	0.09
Navajo (11)	18	0.05
Osage (1)	1	0.00
Pima (1)	1	0.00
Potawatomi (3)	4	0.01
Pueblo (2)	9	0.03
Shoshone	5	0.01
Sioux (2)	6	0.02
Tohono O'Odham (2)	2	0.01
Yaqui (5)	7	0.02
All other tribes (17)	33	0.09
American Indian tribes, not spec.	17	0.05
Arab:	323	0.92
Arab/Arabic	101	0.29
Egyptian	40	0.11
Jordanian	64	0.18
Lebanese	99	0.28
Palestinian	10	0.03
Other Arab	9	0.03
Armenian	182	0.52
Asian:	3,738	10.56
Bangladeshi	3	0.01
Cambodian (4)	9	0.03
Chinese, ex. Taiwanese (657)	790	2.23
Filipino (503)	602	1.70
Indian (466)	504	1.42
Indonesian (17)	23	0.06
Japanese (368)	531	1.50
Korean (728)	772	2.18
Laotian	7	0.02
Malaysian (5)	12	0.03
Pakistani (34)	45	0.13
Sri Lankan (3)	4	0.01
Taiwanese (119)	146	0.41
Thai (25)	36	0.10
Vietnamese (183)	195	0.55
Other Asian, specified (5)	9	0.03
Other Asian, not specified (8)	50	0.14
Australian	25	0.07
Austrian	146	0.42
Basque	30	0.09
Belgian	59	0.17
Brazilian	23	0.07
British	250	0.71
Bulgarian	13	0.04
Canadian	78	0.22
Celtic	11	0.03
Croatian	55	0.16
Czech	86	0.24
Czechoslovakian	56	0.16
Danish	309	0.88
Dutch	608	1.73
Eastern European	30	0.09
English	4,492	12.79
European	376	1.07
Finnish	155	0.44
French, except Basque	1,273	3.62
French Canadian	158	0.45
German	5,961	16.97
Greek	256	0.73
Hawaii Native/Pacific Islander:	165	0.47
Melanesian: (4)	4	0.01
Fijian (4)	4	0.01
Micronesian: (28)	41	0.12
Guamanian/Chamorro (26)	37	0.10
Other Micronesian (2)	4	0.01
Polynesian: (36)	92	0.26
Native Hawaiian (17)	68	0.19
Samoan (17)	19	0.05
Tongan (2)	4	0.01
Other Polynesian	1	0.00
Other Pac. Isl., not spec. (8)	28	0.08
Hispanic or Latino:	7,205	20.35
Central American:	166	0.47
Costa Rican	21	0.06
Guatemalan	36	0.10
Honduran	31	0.09
Nicaraguan	22	0.06
Panamanian	16	0.05
Salvadoran	35	0.10
Other Central American	5	0.01
Cuban	71	0.20
Dominican Republic	6	0.02
Mexican	5,752	16.24
Puerto Rican	138	0.39
South American:	255	0.72
Argentinean	46	0.13
Bolivian	6	0.02
Chilean	10	0.03
Colombian	50	0.14
Ecuadorian	30	0.08
Peruvian	67	0.19
Venezuelan	4	0.01
Other South American	42	0.12
Other Hispanic or Latino	817	2.31
Hungarian	195	0.56
Iranian	346	0.99
Irish	3,915	11.15
Italian	2,544	7.24
Latvian	10	0.03
Lithuanian	55	0.16
New Zealander	6	0.02
Northern European	41	0.12
Norwegian	933	2.66
Pennsylvania German	36	0.10
Polish	783	2.23
Portuguese	120	0.34
Romanian	71	0.20
Russian	397	1.13
Scandinavian	145	0.41
Scotch-Irish	554	1.58
Scottish	917	2.61
Serbian	10	0.03
Slavic	8	0.02
Slovak	72	0.20
Slovene	49	0.14
Swedish	838	2.39
Swiss	149	0.42
Ukrainian	87	0.25
United States or American	1,129	3.21
Welsh	261	0.74
White:	28,586	80.73
Not Hispanic (23,541)	24,260	68.51
Hispanic (3,843)	4,326	12.22
Yugoslavian	60	0.17

Brentwood

Place Type: City
County: Contra Costa
Population: 23,302

Ancestry/Race	Number	%
African American/Black:	747	3.21
Not Hispanic (553)	694	2.98
Hispanic (26)	53	0.23
African, sub-Saharan:	92	0.40
African	62	0.27
Nigerian	30	0.13
Alaska Native tribes, specified:	1	0.00
Tlingit-Haida (1)	1	0.00
Am. Ind. or Alaska Nat., not spec.	94	0.40
American Indian tribes, specified:	240	1.03
Apache (3)	5	0.02
Blackfeet	6	0.03
Cherokee (28)	101	0.43
Chickasaw (2)	6	0.03
Chippewa (1)	3	0.01
Choctaw (7)	21	0.09
Comanche (1)	4	0.02
Creek (3)	5	0.02
Delaware (1)	2	0.01
Iroquois	1	0.00
Latin American Indians (20)	28	0.12
Menominee	1	0.00
Navajo (4)	5	0.02
Osage (1)	3	0.01
Potawatomi	1	0.00
Pueblo (3)	3	0.01
Seminole	1	0.00
Shoshone	1	0.00
Sioux (5)	5	0.02
Tohono O'Odham	2	0.01
Yaqui (2)	4	0.02
All other tribes (12)	32	0.14
American Indian tribes, not spec.	8	0.03
Arab:	63	0.27
Jordanian	9	0.04
Lebanese	32	0.14
Other Arab	22	0.09
Armenian	22	0.09
Asian:	1,021	4.38
Chinese, ex. Taiwanese (94)	138	0.59
Filipino (308)	497	2.13
Hmong (9)	9	0.04
Indian (49)	71	0.30
Indonesian	9	0.04
Japanese (98)	148	0.64
Korean (26)	43	0.18
Laotian (13)	22	0.09
Malaysian	3	0.01
Pakistani (5)	8	0.03
Thai (2)	3	0.01
Vietnamese (29)	38	0.16
Other Asian, specified (7)	9	0.04
Other Asian, not specified (11)	23	0.10
Australian	19	0.08
Austrian	9	0.04
Belgian	27	0.12
British	131	0.56
Canadian	149	0.64
Czech	20	0.09
Czechoslovakian	23	0.10
Danish	475	2.04

Notes: 1. Figures in the "Number" column do not add up to the total population due to: a) Ancestry/Race overlap — e.g. persons can report being both White and Irish, b) persons of Hispanic origin can report being any race, c) persons reporting two ancestries are counted in both categories. 2. Numbers in parentheses indicate the number of persons reporting this ancestry/race alone, not in combination with any other ancestry/race. 3. Refer to the Explanation of Data in the front of the book for more detailed information.

Dutch	403	1.73
Eastern European	11	0.05
English	2,161	9.28
European	261	1.12
Finnish	45	0.19
French, except Basque	784	3.37
French Canadian	60	0.26
German	3,625	15.57
Greek	75	0.32
Hawaii Native/Pacific Islander:	164	0.70
Melanesian: (8)	11	0.05
Fijian (8)	11	0.05
Micronesian: (18)	37	0.16
Guamanian/Chamorro (17)	32	0.14
Other Micronesian (1)	5	0.02
Polynesian: (39)	83	0.36
Native Hawaiian (30)	59	0.25
Samoan (9)	24	0.10
Other Pac. Isl., not spec. (8)	33	0.14
Hispanic or Latino:	6,565	28.17
Central American:	118	0.51
Guatemalan	23	0.10
Honduran	1	0.00
Nicaraguan	30	0.13
Panamanian	9	0.04
Salvadoran	42	0.18
Other Central American	13	0.06
Cuban	22	0.09
Dominican Republic	2	0.01
Mexican	5,266	22.60
Puerto Rican	204	0.88
South American:	58	0.25
Argentinean	8	0.03
Bolivian	2	0.01
Chilean	4	0.02
Colombian	14	0.06
Ecuadorian	2	0.01
Paraguayan	1	0.00
Peruvian	21	0.09
Venezuelan	5	0.02
Other South American	1	0.00
Other Hispanic or Latino	895	3.84
Hungarian	6	0.03
Irish	2,809	12.06
Italian	1,888	8.11
Lithuanian	11	0.05
Northern European	21	0.09
Norwegian	424	1.82
Pennsylvania German	9	0.04
Polish	264	1.13
Portuguese	838	3.60
Romanian	13	0.06
Russian	112	0.48
Scandinavian	85	0.37
Scotch-Irish	378	1.62
Scottish	503	2.16
Slavic	18	0.08
Slovene	9	0.04
Swedish	535	2.30
Swiss	184	0.79
Ukrainian	35	0.15
United States or American	1,095	4.70
Welsh	194	0.83
West Indian, excl. Hispanic:	44	0.19
Bermudan	44	0.19
White:	18,302	78.54
Not Hispanic (14,692)	15,269	65.53
Hispanic (2,509)	3,033	13.02
Yugoslavian	52	0.22

Buena Park

Place Type: City
County: Orange
Population: 78,282

Ancestry/Race	Number	%
Acadian/Cajun	15	0.02
Afghan	41	0.05
African American/Black:	3,503	4.47
Not Hispanic (2,826)	3,182	4.06
Hispanic (174)	321	0.41
African, sub-Saharan:	313	0.40
African	88	0.11
Ethiopian	180	0.23
Ghanian	10	0.01
Kenyan	18	0.02
Nigerian	11	0.01
Other sub-Saharan African	6	0.01
Alaska Native tribes, specified:	7	0.01
Tlingit-Haida (1)	1	0.00
All other tribes	6	0.01
Am. Ind. or Alaska Nat., not spec.	508	0.65
American Indian tribes, specified:	833	1.06
Apache (43)	90	0.11
Blackfeet (12)	39	0.05
Cherokee (58)	198	0.25
Chickasaw (2)	6	0.01
Chippewa (11)	17	0.02
Choctaw (8)	39	0.05
Comanche (1)	7	0.01
Cree	6	0.01
Creek (2)	11	0.01
Crow	4	0.01
Delaware (1)	2	0.00
Iroquois (7)	14	0.02
Kiowa (2)	5	0.01
Latin American Indians (105)	155	0.20
Menominee (1)	2	0.00
Navajo (18)	38	0.05
Osage (4)	5	0.01
Paiute	1	0.00
Pima (4)	6	0.01
Potawatomi (5)	5	0.01
Pueblo (9)	27	0.03
Seminole (1)	10	0.01
Shoshone (7)	9	0.01
Sioux (11)	34	0.04
Tohono O'Odham (4)	5	0.01
Yaqui (6)	12	0.02
Yuman (4)	7	0.01
All other tribes (49)	79	0.10
American Indian tribes, not spec.	73	0.09
Arab:	813	1.04
Arab/Arabic	220	0.28
Egyptian	124	0.16
Iraqi	5	0.01
Jordanian	173	0.22
Lebanese	92	0.12
Palestinian	32	0.04
Syrian	92	0.12
Other Arab	75	0.10
Armenian	150	0.19
Asian:	18,247	23.31
Bangladeshi (40)	47	0.06
Cambodian (194)	242	0.31
Chinese, ex. Taiwanese (1,180)	1,519	1.94
Filipino (4,985)	5,570	7.12
Hmong (10)	10	0.01
Indian (1,994)	2,162	2.76
Indonesian (50)	91	0.12
Japanese (768)	1,054	1.35
Korean (4,965)	5,115	6.53
Laotian (38)	44	0.06
Malaysian (10)	19	0.02
Pakistani (108)	151	0.19
Sri Lankan (33)	35	0.04
Taiwanese (271)	362	0.46
Thai (212)	237	0.30
Vietnamese (1,173)	1,284	1.64
Other Asian, specified (22)	25	0.03
Other Asian, not specified (82)	280	0.36
Assyrian/Chaldean/Syriac	55	0.07
Australian	42	0.05
Austrian	106	0.14
Belgian	25	0.03
Brazilian	94	0.12
British	154	0.20
Canadian	250	0.32
Croatian	60	0.08
Czech	110	0.14
Czechoslovakian	78	0.10
Danish	269	0.34
Dutch	1,005	1.28
English	4,527	5.78
European	555	0.71
Finnish	35	0.04
French, except Basque	1,370	1.75
French Canadian	249	0.32
German	6,214	7.93
Greek	196	0.25
Guyanese	12	0.02
Hawaii Native/Pacific Islander:	775	0.99
Melanesian: (13)	19	0.02
Fijian (13)	19	0.02
Micronesian: (77)	144	0.18
Guamanian/Chamorro (77)	142	0.18
Other Micronesian	2	0.00
Polynesian: (262)	479	0.61
Native Hawaiian (78)	194	0.25
Samoan (158)	222	0.28
Tongan (26)	49	0.06
Other Polynesian	14	0.02
Other Pac. Isl., specified	2	0.00
Other Pac. Isl., not spec. (25)	131	0.17
Hispanic or Latino:	26,221	33.50
Central American:	881	1.13
Costa Rican	53	0.07
Guatemalan	259	0.33
Honduran	43	0.05
Nicaraguan	132	0.17
Panamanian	32	0.04
Salvadoran	289	0.37
Other Central American	73	0.09
Cuban	294	0.38
Dominican Republic	12	0.02
Mexican	20,893	26.69
Puerto Rican	420	0.54
South American:	536	0.68
Argentinean	95	0.12
Bolivian	4	0.01
Chilean	29	0.04
Colombian	101	0.13
Ecuadorian	52	0.07
Paraguayan	1	0.00
Peruvian	182	0.23
Venezuelan	14	0.02
Other South American	58	0.07
Other Hispanic or Latino	3,185	4.07
Hungarian	198	0.25
Iranian	121	0.15
Irish	5,193	6.63
Italian	2,873	3.67
Latvian	10	0.01
Lithuanian	26	0.03
Northern European	12	0.02
Norwegian	735	0.94
Polish	1,169	1.49
Portuguese	291	0.37
Romanian	478	0.61
Russian	272	0.35
Scandinavian	53	0.07
Scotch-Irish	797	1.02
Scottish	868	1.11
Serbian	54	0.07
Slavic	13	0.02
Slovak	48	0.06
Slovene	15	0.02
Soviet Union	7	0.01
Swedish	981	1.25
Swiss	100	0.13
Turkish	9	0.01
Ukrainian	77	0.10
United States or American	2,741	3.50
Welsh	318	0.41
West Indian, excl. Hispanic:	173	0.22
Belizean	63	0.08
Dutch West Indian	6	0.01
Haitian	17	0.02
Jamaican	82	0.10

Notes: 1. Figures in the "Number" column do not add up to the total population due to: a) Ancestry/Race overlap — e.g. persons can report being both White and Irish, b) persons of Hispanic origin can report being any race, c) persons reporting two ancestries are counted in both categories. 2. Numbers in parentheses indicate the number of persons reporting this ancestry/race alone, not in combination with any other ancestry/race. 3. Refer to the Explanation of Data in the front of the book for more detailed information.

Trinidadian and Tobagonian	5	0.01
White:	44,961	57.43
Not Hispanic (29,885)	31,568	40.33
Hispanic (11,594)	13,393	17.11
Yugoslavian	170	0.22

Burbank

Place Type: City
County: Los Angeles
Population: 100,316

Ancestry/Race	Number	%
Acadian/Cajun	10	0.01
Afghan	50	0.05
African American/Black:	2,574	2.57
Not Hispanic (1,915)	2,308	2.30
Hispanic (151)	266	0.27
African, sub-Saharan:	170	0.17
African	142	0.14
Ethiopian	7	0.01
Nigerian	13	0.01
South African	8	0.01
Alaska Native tribes, specified:	6	0.01
Alaska Athabascan (1)	1	0.00
Aleut	1	0.00
Tlingit-Haida (3)	4	0.00
Am. Ind. or Alaska Nat., not spec.	328	0.33
American Indian tribes, specified:	876	0.87
Apache (39)	60	0.06
Blackfeet (4)	32	0.03
Cherokee (57)	248	0.25
Cheyenne	1	0.00
Chickasaw (3)	13	0.01
Chippewa (18)	20	0.02
Choctaw (11)	50	0.05
Comanche (5)	11	0.01
Cree (5)	6	0.01
Creek (3)	14	0.01
Delaware (2)	2	0.00
Iroquois (9)	23	0.02
Kiowa (1)	3	0.00
Latin American Indians (82)	139	0.14
Navajo (14)	26	0.03
Osage (4)	7	0.01
Ottawa	1	0.00
Paiute (1)	2	0.00
Pima (4)	4	0.00
Potawatomi (4)	8	0.01
Pueblo (21)	30	0.03
Puget Sound Salish	1	0.00
Seminole (1)	13	0.01
Shoshone (1)	1	0.00
Sioux (19)	50	0.05
Tohono O'Odham (6)	11	0.01
Ute (3)	3	0.00
Yakama (1)	1	0.00
Yaqui (5)	13	0.01
Yuman	1	0.00
All other tribes (46)	82	0.08
American Indian tribes, not spec.	55	0.05
Arab:	2,434	2.43
Arab/Arabic	322	0.32
Egyptian	454	0.45
Jordanian	92	0.09
Lebanese	580	0.58
Moroccan	12	0.01
Palestinian	24	0.02
Syrian	831	0.83
Other Arab	119	0.12
Armenian	8,312	8.29
Asian:	10,782	10.75
Bangladeshi (7)	12	0.01
Cambodian (12)	21	0.02
Chinese, ex. Taiwanese (837)	1,146	1.14
Filipino (3,341)	3,860	3.85
Indian (678)	828	0.83
Indonesian (33)	63	0.06
Japanese (758)	998	0.99
Korean (2,194)	2,295	2.29
Laotian (3)	4	0.00
Malaysian (7)	10	0.01
Pakistani (16)	38	0.04
Sri Lankan (75)	89	0.09
Taiwanese (33)	45	0.04
Thai (272)	340	0.34
Vietnamese (648)	706	0.70
Other Asian, specified (6)	10	0.01
Other Asian, not specified (73)	317	0.32
Assyrian/Chaldean/Syriac	167	0.17
Australian	74	0.07
Austrian	297	0.30
Basque	106	0.11
Belgian	87	0.09
Brazilian	62	0.06
British	497	0.50
Bulgarian	38	0.04
Canadian	311	0.31
Celtic	24	0.02
Croatian	183	0.18
Czech	308	0.31
Czechoslovakian	240	0.24
Danish	647	0.64
Dutch	1,195	1.19
Eastern European	56	0.06
English	8,893	8.86
Estonian	22	0.02
European	662	0.66
Finnish	147	0.15
French, except Basque	2,646	2.64
French Canadian	535	0.53
German	10,680	10.65
Greek	743	0.74
Hawaii Native/Pacific Islander:	348	0.35
Micronesian: (18)	40	0.04
Guamanian/Chamorro (17)	35	0.03
Other Micronesian (1)	5	0.00
Polynesian: (95)	208	0.21
Native Hawaiian (67)	163	0.16
Samoan (25)	39	0.04
Other Polynesian (3)	6	0.01
Other Pac. Isl., specified	2	0.00
Other Pac. Isl., not spec. (29)	98	0.10
Hispanic or Latino:	24,953	24.87
Central American:	2,833	2.82
Costa Rican	149	0.15
Guatemalan	792	0.79
Honduran	73	0.07
Nicaraguan	242	0.24
Panamanian	40	0.04
Salvadoran	1,262	1.26
Other Central American	275	0.27
Cuban	1,082	1.08
Dominican Republic	27	0.03
Mexican	14,216	14.17
Puerto Rican	506	0.50
South American:	1,835	1.83
Argentinean	215	0.21
Bolivian	159	0.16
Chilean	96	0.10
Colombian	502	0.50
Ecuadorian	274	0.27
Paraguayan	2	0.00
Peruvian	385	0.38
Uruguayan	7	0.01
Venezuelan	30	0.03
Other South American	166	0.17
Other Hispanic or Latino	4,454	4.44
Hungarian	717	0.71
Icelander	23	0.02
Iranian	892	0.89
Irish	10,005	9.97
Israeli	83	0.08
Italian	6,502	6.48
Latvian	8	0.01
Lithuanian	247	0.25
Macedonian	7	0.01
Maltese	11	0.01
New Zealander	18	0.02
Northern European	43	0.04
Norwegian	1,257	1.25
Pennsylvania German	46	0.05
Polish	1,785	1.78
Portuguese	329	0.33
Romanian	281	0.28
Russian	1,769	1.76
Scandinavian	183	0.18
Scotch-Irish	1,960	1.95
Scottish	1,854	1.85
Serbian	88	0.09
Slavic	33	0.03
Slovak	114	0.11
Slovene	53	0.05
Swedish	1,682	1.68
Swiss	252	0.25
Turkish	43	0.04
Ukrainian	327	0.33
United States or American	3,274	3.26
Welsh	796	0.79
West Indian, excl. Hispanic:	195	0.19
Belizean	14	0.01
British West Indian	7	0.01
Haitian	39	0.04
Jamaican	20	0.02
Trinidadian and Tobagonian	103	0.10
U.S. Virgin Islander	12	0.01
White:	77,906	77.66
Not Hispanic (59,590)	63,458	63.26
Hispanic (12,819)	14,448	14.40
Yugoslavian	231	0.23

Burlingame

Place Type: City
County: San Mateo
Population: 28,158

Ancestry/Race	Number	%
African American/Black:	393	1.40
Not Hispanic (266)	344	1.22
Hispanic (30)	49	0.17
African, sub-Saharan:	34	0.12
African	16	0.06
Nigerian	7	0.03
South African	11	0.04
Alaska Native tribes, specified:	2	0.01
Eskimo	1	0.00
Tlingit-Haida	1	0.00
Alaska Native tribes, not specified	3	0.01
Am. Ind. or Alaska Nat., not spec.	50	0.18
Alsatian	10	0.04
American Indian tribes, specified:	126	0.45
Apache (1)	6	0.02
Blackfeet (1)	5	0.02
Cherokee (3)	39	0.14
Chickasaw	1	0.00
Chippewa (1)	2	0.01
Choctaw (1)	8	0.03
Comanche	3	0.01
Crow (1)	1	0.00
Iroquois (1)	1	0.00
Latin American Indians (7)	20	0.07
Menominee (5)	5	0.02
Navajo (3)	5	0.02
Paiute	3	0.01
Potawatomi	1	0.00
Pueblo (1)	1	0.00
Seminole	1	0.00
Shoshone (1)	1	0.00
Sioux	3	0.01
All other tribes (14)	20	0.07
American Indian tribes, not spec.	17	0.06
Arab:	419	1.50
Arab/Arabic	106	0.38
Egyptian	35	0.13
Lebanese	74	0.26
Moroccan	7	0.03
Palestinian	87	0.31
Syrian	25	0.09
Other Arab	85	0.30

Notes: 1. Figures in the "Number" column do not add up to the total population due to: a) Ancestry/Race overlap — e.g. persons can report being both White and Irish, b) persons of Hispanic origin can report being any race, c) persons reporting two ancestries are counted in both categories. 2. Numbers in parentheses indicate the number of persons reporting this ancestry/race alone, not in combination with any other ancestry/race. 3. Refer to the Explanation of Data in the front of the book for more detailed information.

Ancestry/Race	Number	%
Armenian	125	0.45
Asian:	4,490	15.95
Bangladeshi (1)	1	0.00
Cambodian (6)	6	0.02
Chinese, ex. Taiwanese (1,635)	1,852	6.58
Filipino (692)	865	3.07
Indian (386)	428	1.52
Indonesian (10)	19	0.07
Japanese (574)	696	2.47
Korean (317)	373	1.32
Laotian (2)	2	0.01
Malaysian (1)	1	0.00
Pakistani (3)	5	0.02
Sri Lankan (1)	1	0.00
Taiwanese (65)	73	0.26
Thai (16)	19	0.07
Vietnamese (39)	56	0.20
Other Asian, specified (6)	8	0.03
Other Asian, not specified (31)	85	0.30
Assyrian/Chaldean/Syriac	6	0.02
Australian	32	0.11
Austrian	139	0.50
Basque	81	0.29
Belgian	32	0.11
Brazilian	19	0.07
British	213	0.76
Bulgarian	9	0.03
Canadian	164	0.59
Carpatho Rusyn	8	0.03
Celtic	17	0.06
Croatian	104	0.37
Czech	233	0.83
Czechoslovakian	69	0.25
Danish	173	0.62
Dutch	364	1.30
Eastern European	67	0.24
English	2,749	9.83
Estonian	33	0.12
European	377	1.35
Finnish	47	0.17
French, except Basque	1,235	4.41
French Canadian	190	0.68
German	3,829	13.69
Greek	402	1.44
Hawaii Native/Pacific Islander:	249	0.88
Melanesian: (19)	23	0.08
Fijian (19)	23	0.08
Micronesian: (6)	10	0.04
Guamanian/Chamorro (5)	9	0.03
Other Micronesian (1)	1	0.00
Polynesian: (84)	172	0.61
Native Hawaiian (18)	64	0.23
Samoan (25)	33	0.12
Tongan (37)	58	0.21
Other Polynesian (4)	17	0.06
Other Pac. Isl., not spec. (12)	44	0.16
Hispanic or Latino:	2,995	10.64
Central American:	501	1.78
Costa Rican	4	0.01
Guatemalan	79	0.28
Honduran	11	0.04
Nicaraguan	65	0.23
Panamanian	8	0.03
Salvadoran	267	0.95
Other Central American	67	0.24
Cuban	40	0.14
Dominican Republic	2	0.01
Mexican	1,265	4.49
Puerto Rican	91	0.32
South American:	338	1.20
Argentinean	51	0.18
Bolivian	9	0.03
Chilean	32	0.11
Colombian	60	0.21
Ecuadorian	6	0.02
Peruvian	113	0.40
Uruguayan	1	0.00
Venezuelan	7	0.02
Other South American	59	0.21
Other Hispanic or Latino	758	2.69
Hungarian	200	0.71
Icelander	12	0.04
Iranian	437	1.56
Irish	3,921	14.02
Israeli	29	0.10
Italian	3,294	11.77
Latvian	44	0.16
Lithuanian	71	0.25
Luxemburger	5	0.02
Macedonian	11	0.04
Maltese	97	0.35
New Zealander	7	0.03
Northern European	56	0.20
Norwegian	528	1.89
Pennsylvania German	8	0.03
Polish	641	2.29
Portuguese	334	1.19
Romanian	46	0.16
Russian	937	3.35
Scandinavian	64	0.23
Scotch-Irish	452	1.62
Scottish	616	2.20
Serbian	20	0.07
Slovak	14	0.05
Swedish	502	1.79
Swiss	197	0.70
Turkish	39	0.14
Ukrainian	131	0.47
United States or American	859	3.07
Welsh	197	0.70
West Indian, excl. Hispanic:	14	0.05
Jamaican	14	0.05
White:	22,619	80.33
Not Hispanic (20,063)	20,720	73.58
Hispanic (1,585)	1,899	6.74
Yugoslavian	65	0.23

Calabasas

Place Type: City
County: Los Angeles
Population: 20,033

Ancestry/Race	Number	%
African American/Black:	311	1.55
Not Hispanic (222)	292	1.46
Hispanic (14)	19	0.09
African, sub-Saharan:	88	0.44
African	18	0.09
Ghanian	6	0.03
South African	64	0.32
Alaska Native tribes, not specified	1	0.00
Am. Ind. or Alaska Nat., not spec.	29	0.14
American Indian tribes, specified:	66	0.33
Apache	4	0.02
Blackfeet	2	0.01
Cherokee (2)	22	0.11
Chippewa (1)	1	0.00
Choctaw	1	0.00
Comanche	1	0.00
Creek	1	0.00
Iroquois	1	0.00
Latin American Indians (1)	4	0.02
Navajo (2)	5	0.02
Potawatomi	1	0.00
Sioux	1	0.00
All other tribes (12)	22	0.11
American Indian tribes, not spec.	5	0.02
Arab:	263	1.31
Arab/Arabic	25	0.12
Egyptian	35	0.17
Iraqi	53	0.26
Lebanese	74	0.37
Moroccan	39	0.19
Syrian	37	0.18
Armenian	132	0.66
Asian:	1,867	9.32
Chinese, ex. Taiwanese (424)	505	2.52
Filipino (116)	169	0.84
Indian (263)	292	1.46
Indonesian (33)	38	0.19
Japanese (210)	279	1.39
Korean (352)	385	1.92
Malaysian	3	0.01
Pakistani (19)	37	0.18
Taiwanese (29)	30	0.15
Thai (11)	15	0.07
Vietnamese (48)	55	0.27
Other Asian, specified (3)	4	0.02
Other Asian, not specified (8)	55	0.27
Assyrian/Chaldean/Syriac	45	0.22
Australian	28	0.14
Austrian	267	1.33
Basque	50	0.25
Belgian	18	0.09
British	159	0.79
Bulgarian	16	0.08
Canadian	256	1.27
Croatian	15	0.07
Czech	97	0.48
Czechoslovakian	34	0.17
Danish	143	0.71
Dutch	167	0.83
Eastern European	261	1.30
English	2,067	10.28
Estonian	10	0.05
European	454	2.26
Finnish	15	0.07
French, except Basque	552	2.75
French Canadian	49	0.24
German	2,565	12.76
Greek	93	0.46
Hawaii Native/Pacific Islander:	28	0.14
Micronesian:	2	0.01
Guamanian/Chamorro	2	0.01
Polynesian: (2)	13	0.06
Native Hawaiian (2)	10	0.05
Other Polynesian	3	0.01
Other Pac. Isl., not spec. (7)	13	0.06
Hispanic or Latino:	949	4.74
Central American:	79	0.39
Costa Rican	5	0.02
Guatemalan	17	0.08
Honduran	3	0.01
Nicaraguan	12	0.06
Panamanian	9	0.04
Salvadoran	31	0.15
Other Central American	2	0.01
Cuban	39	0.19
Mexican	466	2.33
Puerto Rican	40	0.20
South American:	135	0.67
Argentinean	38	0.19
Bolivian	6	0.03
Chilean	16	0.08
Colombian	19	0.09
Ecuadorian	13	0.06
Paraguayan	1	0.00
Peruvian	22	0.11
Venezuelan	9	0.04
Other South American	11	0.05
Other Hispanic or Latino	190	0.95
Hungarian	347	1.73
Iranian	1,096	5.45
Irish	1,904	9.47
Israeli	178	0.89
Italian	1,089	5.42
Latvian	21	0.10
Lithuanian	101	0.50
New Zealander	23	0.11
Norwegian	304	1.51
Pennsylvania German	11	0.05
Polish	1,243	6.18
Portuguese	63	0.31
Romanian	180	0.90
Russian	2,259	11.24
Scandinavian	37	0.18
Scotch-Irish	317	1.58
Scottish	396	1.97
Serbian	13	0.06

Notes: 1. Figures in the "Number" column do not add up to the total population due to: a) Ancestry/Race overlap — e.g. persons can report being both White and Irish, b) persons of Hispanic origin can report being any race, c) persons reporting two ancestries are counted in both categories. 2. Numbers in parentheses indicate the number of persons reporting this ancestry/race alone, not in combination with any other ancestry/race. 3. Refer to the Explanation of Data in the front of the book for more detailed information.

Slavic	34	0.17
Swedish	354	1.76
Swiss	137	0.68
Turkish	69	0.34
Ukrainian	196	0.98
United States or American	1,335	6.64
Welsh	95	0.47
White:	17,922	89.46
Not Hispanic (16,789)	17,223	85.97
Hispanic (623)	699	3.49
Yugoslavian	75	0.37

Calexico

Place Type: City
County: Imperial
Population: 27,109

Ancestry/Race	Number	%
African American/Black:	162	0.60
Not Hispanic (37)	43	0.16
Hispanic (97)	119	0.44
African, sub-Saharan:	10	0.04
African	10	0.04
Am. Ind. or Alaska Nat., not spec.	112	0.41
Albanian	9	0.03
American Indian tribes, specified:	107	0.39
Apache	2	0.01
Cherokee (1)	1	0.00
Latin American Indians (47)	60	0.22
Navajo (2)	2	0.01
Paiute	2	0.01
Pueblo (3)	6	0.02
Tohono O'Odham (1)	9	0.03
Yaqui (15)	16	0.06
Yuman (2)	2	0.01
All other tribes (5)	7	0.03
American Indian tribes, not spec.	19	0.07
Arab:	48	0.18
Arab/Arabic	37	0.14
Lebanese	11	0.04
Asian:	653	2.41
Cambodian (1)	1	0.00
Chinese, ex. Taiwanese (354)	453	1.67
Filipino (25)	38	0.14
Indian (5)	11	0.04
Japanese (5)	26	0.10
Korean (54)	54	0.20
Taiwanese (13)	26	0.10
Thai	1	0.00
Vietnamese (5)	8	0.03
Other Asian, not specified (3)	35	0.13
Austrian	9	0.03
Basque	11	0.04
Belgian	23	0.09
Canadian	16	0.06
English	40	0.15
European	11	0.04
French, except Basque	86	0.32
German	105	0.39
Greek	29	0.11
Hawaii Native/Pacific Islander:	16	0.06
Micronesian: (1)	4	0.01
Guamanian/Chamorro (1)	4	0.01
Polynesian: (1)	5	0.02
Native Hawaiian	4	0.01
Samoan (1)	1	0.00
Other Pac. Isl., not spec. (4)	7	0.03
Hispanic or Latino:	25,832	95.29
Central American:	35	0.13
Guatemalan	6	0.02
Honduran	4	0.01
Panamanian	1	0.00
Salvadoran	20	0.07
Other Central American	4	0.01
Cuban	3	0.01
Dominican Republic	1	0.00
Mexican	23,781	87.72
Puerto Rican	35	0.13
South American:	17	0.06
Argentinean	8	0.03
Colombian	7	0.03
Ecuadorian	1	0.00
Other South American	1	0.00
Other Hispanic or Latino	1,960	7.23
Irish	60	0.22
Italian	137	0.51
Northern European	8	0.03
Polish	7	0.03
Portuguese	41	0.15
Scottish	12	0.04
Swedish	7	0.03
United States or American	248	0.92
West Indian, excl. Hispanic:	8	0.03
Dutch West Indian	8	0.03
White:	13,420	49.50
Not Hispanic (642)	699	2.58
Hispanic (11,979)	12,721	46.93

Camarillo

Place Type: City
County: Ventura
Population: 57,077

Ancestry/Race	Number	%
Acadian/Cajun	9	0.02
African American/Black:	1,110	1.94
Not Hispanic (802)	1,006	1.76
Hispanic (54)	104	0.18
African, sub-Saharan:	139	0.24
African	54	0.09
South African	55	0.10
Other sub-Saharan African	30	0.05
Alaska Native tribes, specified:	9	0.02
Alaska Athabascan (2)	2	0.00
Aleut (1)	1	0.00
Eskimo (3)	4	0.01
Tlingit-Haida (2)	2	0.00
Alaska Native tribes, not specified	1	0.00
Am. Ind. or Alaska Nat., not spec.	203	0.36
Albanian	17	0.03
American Indian tribes, specified:	487	0.85
Apache (14)	22	0.04
Blackfeet (4)	22	0.04
Cherokee (44)	184	0.32
Cheyenne	1	0.00
Chickasaw (1)	2	0.00
Chippewa (5)	7	0.01
Choctaw (9)	31	0.05
Colville	2	0.00
Comanche	1	0.00
Cree	4	0.01
Creek (3)	7	0.01
Delaware	1	0.00
Iroquois (8)	19	0.03
Kiowa (1)	2	0.00
Latin American Indians (12)	31	0.05
Navajo (7)	10	0.02
Osage (4)	6	0.01
Ottawa	1	0.00
Paiute (6)	9	0.02
Potawatomi (2)	3	0.01
Pueblo (7)	13	0.02
Puget Sound Salish (1)	1	0.00
Seminole	5	0.01
Sioux (6)	16	0.03
Ute (2)	3	0.01
Yakama	1	0.00
Yaqui (4)	5	0.01
All other tribes (42)	78	0.14
American Indian tribes, not spec.	15	0.03
Arab:	309	0.54
Arab/Arabic	59	0.10
Egyptian	39	0.07
Lebanese	65	0.11
Syrian	146	0.26
Armenian	95	0.17
Asian:	5,101	8.94
Cambodian (9)	26	0.05
Chinese, ex. Taiwanese (570)	762	1.34
Filipino (1,540)	1,864	3.27
Indian (293)	325	0.57
Indonesian (18)	37	0.06
Japanese (761)	1,031	1.81
Korean (349)	406	0.71
Laotian (9)	9	0.02
Malaysian (2)	10	0.02
Pakistani (19)	25	0.04
Sri Lankan (9)	11	0.02
Taiwanese (99)	115	0.20
Thai (31)	47	0.08
Vietnamese (310)	336	0.59
Other Asian, specified (2)	6	0.01
Other Asian, not specified (17)	91	0.16
Australian	15	0.03
Austrian	202	0.35
Basque	88	0.15
Belgian	31	0.05
Brazilian	42	0.07
British	257	0.45
Canadian	181	0.32
Celtic	17	0.03
Croatian	25	0.04
Czech	259	0.45
Czechoslovakian	116	0.20
Danish	676	1.18
Dutch	1,126	1.97
Eastern European	69	0.12
English	7,656	13.40
Estonian	29	0.05
European	748	1.31
Finnish	73	0.13
French, except Basque	1,951	3.42
French Canadian	449	0.79
German	10,548	18.47
Greek	298	0.52
Hawaii Native/Pacific Islander:	301	0.53
Melanesian: (1)	1	0.00
Fijian (1)	1	0.00
Micronesian: (39)	68	0.12
Guamanian/Chamorro (33)	59	0.10
Other Micronesian (6)	9	0.02
Polynesian: (58)	180	0.32
Native Hawaiian (29)	127	0.22
Samoan (25)	48	0.08
Other Polynesian (4)	5	0.01
Other Pac. Isl., specified	2	0.00
Other Pac. Isl., not spec. (14)	50	0.09
Hispanic or Latino:	8,869	15.54
Central American:	175	0.31
Costa Rican	6	0.01
Guatemalan	46	0.08
Honduran	6	0.01
Nicaraguan	22	0.04
Panamanian	7	0.01
Salvadoran	65	0.11
Other Central American	23	0.04
Cuban	75	0.13
Dominican Republic	17	0.03
Mexican	7,049	12.35
Puerto Rican	188	0.33
South American:	183	0.32
Argentinean	48	0.08
Bolivian	8	0.01
Chilean	12	0.02
Colombian	35	0.06
Ecuadorian	11	0.02
Paraguayan	2	0.00
Peruvian	34	0.06
Uruguayan	4	0.01
Venezuelan	15	0.03
Other South American	14	0.02
Other Hispanic or Latino	1,182	2.07
Hungarian	452	0.79
Iranian	64	0.11
Irish	7,018	12.29
Israeli	30	0.05
Italian	3,524	6.17
Latvian	44	0.08

Notes: 1. Figures in the "Number" column do not add up to the total population due to: a) Ancestry/Race overlap — e.g. persons can report being both White and Irish, b) persons of Hispanic origin can report being any race, c) persons reporting two ancestries are counted in both categories. 2. Numbers in parentheses indicate the number of persons reporting this ancestry/race alone, not in combination with any other ancestry/race. 3. Refer to the Explanation of Data in the front of the book for more detailed information.

Lithuanian	255	0.45
Macedonian	30	0.05
New Zealander	9	0.02
Northern European	86	0.15
Norwegian	1,243	2.18
Pennsylvania German	34	0.06
Polish	1,562	2.73
Portuguese	266	0.47
Romanian	124	0.22
Russian	1,182	2.07
Scandinavian	115	0.20
Scotch-Irish	1,258	2.20
Scottish	1,530	2.68
Slavic	32	0.06
Slovak	58	0.10
Slovene	23	0.04
Swedish	1,108	1.94
Swiss	288	0.50
Turkish	17	0.03
Ukrainian	134	0.23
United States or American	2,386	4.18
Welsh	618	1.08
West Indian, excl. Hispanic:	41	0.07
Belizean	6	0.01
Jamaican	6	0.01
U.S. Virgin Islander	6	0.01
West Indian	23	0.04
White:	47,838	83.81
Not Hispanic (41,543)	42,801	74.99
Hispanic (4,493)	5,037	8.82
Yugoslavian	57	0.10

Cameron Park

Place Type: Census Designated Place
County: El Dorado
Population: 14,549

Ancestry/Race	Number	%
African American/Black:	166	1.14
Not Hispanic (85)	146	1.00
Hispanic (7)	20	0.14
African, sub-Saharan:	30	0.21
South African	30	0.21
Am. Ind. or Alaska Nat., not spec.	69	0.47
American Indian tribes, specified:	205	1.41
Apache (6)	6	0.04
Blackfeet (2)	6	0.04
Cherokee (21)	61	0.42
Cheyenne	1	0.01
Chickasaw	1	0.01
Chippewa (5)	8	0.05
Choctaw (4)	19	0.13
Comanche	1	0.01
Crow	1	0.01
Delaware (3)	3	0.02
Latin American Indians	1	0.01
Navajo (1)	1	0.01
Osage	1	0.01
Ottawa	1	0.01
Paiute (4)	4	0.03
Potawatomi (2)	2	0.01
Pueblo (1)	1	0.01
Seminole	8	0.05
Shoshone (2)	2	0.01
Sioux (8)	13	0.09
Tohono O'Odham (1)	1	0.01
Yaqui (4)	4	0.03
Yuman (1)	5	0.03
All other tribes (32)	54	0.37
American Indian tribes, not spec.	11	0.08
Arab:	29	0.20
Arab/Arabic	9	0.06
Lebanese	8	0.05
Palestinian	12	0.08
Armenian	13	0.09
Asian:	348	2.39
Cambodian (1)	2	0.01
Chinese, ex. Taiwanese (42)	63	0.43
Filipino (62)	102	0.70
Indian (16)	16	0.11
Indonesian (2)	3	0.02
Japanese (38)	83	0.57
Korean (22)	36	0.25
Taiwanese	1	0.01
Vietnamese (12)	19	0.13
Other Asian, specified (1)	8	0.05
Other Asian, not specified (6)	15	0.10
Austrian	11	0.08
Basque	20	0.14
British	105	0.72
Bulgarian	8	0.05
Canadian	81	0.56
Celtic	44	0.30
Croatian	28	0.19
Czech	17	0.12
Czechoslovakian	26	0.18
Danish	315	2.16
Dutch	330	2.27
English	2,686	18.45
Estonian	10	0.07
European	237	1.63
Finnish	80	0.55
French, except Basque	755	5.19
French Canadian	88	0.60
German	3,031	20.82
Greek	126	0.87
Hawaii Native/Pacific Islander:	44	0.30
Melanesian: (1)	1	0.01
Fijian (1)	1	0.01
Micronesian: (3)	5	0.03
Guamanian/Chamorro (1)	3	0.02
Other Micronesian (2)	2	0.01
Polynesian: (13)	30	0.21
Native Hawaiian (7)	20	0.14
Samoan (1)	5	0.03
Tongan (4)	4	0.03
Other Polynesian (1)	1	0.01
Other Pac. Isl., specified	7	0.05
Other Pac. Isl., not spec. (1)	1	0.01
Hispanic or Latino:	975	6.70
Central American:	23	0.16
Costa Rican	1	0.01
Guatemalan	4	0.03
Honduran	2	0.01
Nicaraguan	4	0.03
Salvadoran	11	0.08
Other Central American	1	0.01
Cuban	10	0.07
Mexican	630	4.33
Puerto Rican	29	0.20
South American:	22	0.15
Argentinean	13	0.09
Colombian	5	0.03
Ecuadorian	2	0.01
Other South American	2	0.01
Other Hispanic or Latino	261	1.79
Hungarian	107	0.74
Iranian	7	0.05
Irish	2,347	16.12
Italian	1,208	8.30
Latvian	10	0.07
Maltese	44	0.30
Norwegian	449	3.08
Polish	239	1.64
Portuguese	154	1.06
Romanian	41	0.28
Russian	133	0.91
Scandinavian	14	0.10
Scotch-Irish	305	2.10
Scottish	392	2.69
Slavic	8	0.05
Swedish	425	2.92
Swiss	97	0.67
Ukrainian	10	0.07
United States or American	717	4.93
Welsh	234	1.61
West Indian, excl. Hispanic:	26	0.18
Jamaican	26	0.18
White:	13,805	94.89
Not Hispanic (12,847)	13,125	90.21
Hispanic (574)	680	4.67
Yugoslavian	25	0.17

Campbell

Place Type: City
County: Santa Clara
Population: 38,138

Ancestry/Race	Number	%
Afghan	30	0.08
African American/Black:	1,159	3.04
Not Hispanic (932)	1,088	2.85
Hispanic (32)	71	0.19
African, sub-Saharan:	221	0.58
African	48	0.13
Ethiopian	123	0.32
Ghanian	5	0.01
Kenyan	4	0.01
Nigerian	16	0.04
Somalian	20	0.05
South African	5	0.01
Alaska Native tribes, specified:	3	0.01
Aleut (2)	2	0.01
Tlingit-Haida (1)	1	0.00
Am. Ind. or Alaska Nat., not spec.	166	0.44
Albanian	5	0.01
American Indian tribes, specified:	359	0.94
Apache (14)	31	0.08
Blackfeet	16	0.04
Cherokee (34)	93	0.24
Cheyenne (1)	3	0.01
Chickasaw	3	0.01
Chippewa (4)	11	0.03
Choctaw (14)	27	0.07
Comanche	1	0.00
Creek (2)	15	0.04
Delaware	1	0.00
Iroquois (3)	11	0.03
Kiowa (2)	2	0.01
Latin American Indians (20)	33	0.09
Navajo (10)	16	0.04
Osage (2)	6	0.02
Paiute (2)	2	0.01
Pima	3	0.01
Pueblo (5)	10	0.03
Seminole	1	0.00
Sioux (3)	11	0.03
Ute (1)	1	0.00
Yaqui (5)	10	0.03
Yuman (1)	3	0.01
All other tribes (23)	49	0.13
American Indian tribes, not spec.	30	0.08
Arab:	128	0.34
Arab/Arabic	7	0.02
Egyptian	28	0.07
Lebanese	67	0.18
Syrian	19	0.05
Other Arab	7	0.02
Armenian	103	0.27
Asian:	6,271	16.44
Bangladeshi (3)	3	0.01
Cambodian (16)	27	0.07
Chinese, ex. Taiwanese (1,299)	1,526	4.00
Filipino (538)	776	2.03
Hmong (6)	8	0.02
Indian (673)	725	1.90
Indonesian (25)	35	0.09
Japanese (781)	1,004	2.63
Korean (862)	911	2.39
Laotian (9)	10	0.03
Malaysian (3)	4	0.01
Pakistani (33)	38	0.10
Sri Lankan (22)	22	0.06
Taiwanese (64)	73	0.19
Thai (29)	33	0.09
Vietnamese (905)	969	2.54
Other Asian, specified (2)	7	0.02
Other Asian, not specified (35)	100	0.26

Notes: 1. Figures in the "Number" column do not add up to the total population due to: a) Ancestry/Race overlap — e.g. persons can report being both White and Irish, b) persons of Hispanic origin can report being any race, c) persons reporting two ancestries are counted in both categories. 2. Numbers in parentheses indicate the number of persons reporting this ancestry/race alone, not in combination with any other ancestry/race. 3. Refer to the Explanation of Data in the front of the book for more detailed information.

Assyrian/Chaldean/Syriac	139	0.36
Australian	59	0.15
Austrian	159	0.42
Basque	49	0.13
Belgian	26	0.07
Brazilian	70	0.18
British	210	0.55
Bulgarian	40	0.10
Canadian	113	0.30
Celtic	14	0.04
Croatian	161	0.42
Czech	120	0.31
Czechoslovakian	45	0.12
Danish	338	0.89
Dutch	536	1.40
Eastern European	64	0.17
English	4,219	11.05
Estonian	5	0.01
European	351	0.92
Finnish	97	0.25
French, except Basque	1,070	2.80
French Canadian	236	0.62
German	4,771	12.49
Greek	268	0.70
Guyanese	15	0.04
Hawaii Native/Pacific Islander:	252	0.66
Melanesian: (5)	5	0.01
Fijian (5)	5	0.01
Micronesian: (20)	36	0.09
Guamanian/Chamorro (19)	35	0.09
Other Micronesian (1)	1	0.00
Polynesian: (55)	177	0.46
Native Hawaiian (39)	142	0.37
Samoan (10)	24	0.06
Tongan	3	0.01
Other Polynesian (6)	8	0.02
Other Pac. Isl., not spec. (7)	34	0.09
Hispanic or Latino:	5,083	13.33
Central American:	206	0.54
Costa Rican	13	0.03
Guatemalan	30	0.08
Honduran	13	0.03
Nicaraguan	41	0.11
Panamanian	12	0.03
Salvadoran	77	0.20
Other Central American	20	0.05
Cuban	48	0.13
Dominican Republic	9	0.02
Mexican	3,601	9.44
Puerto Rican	122	0.32
South American:	175	0.46
Argentinean	13	0.03
Bolivian	8	0.02
Chilean	24	0.06
Colombian	30	0.08
Ecuadorian	7	0.02
Peruvian	49	0.13
Uruguayan	1	0.00
Venezuelan	19	0.05
Other South American	24	0.06
Other Hispanic or Latino	922	2.42
Hungarian	195	0.51
Iranian	623	1.63
Irish	4,593	12.03
Israeli	43	0.11
Italian	3,589	9.40
Lithuanian	64	0.17
Luxemburger	10	0.03
Maltese	113	0.30
Northern European	17	0.04
Norwegian	800	2.09
Polish	773	2.02
Portuguese	808	2.12
Romanian	81	0.21
Russian	846	2.22
Scandinavian	102	0.27
Scotch-Irish	685	1.79
Scottish	992	2.60
Serbian	9	0.02
Slavic	14	0.04
Slovak	47	0.12
Slovene	9	0.02
Swedish	845	2.21
Swiss	190	0.50
Turkish	75	0.20
Ukrainian	88	0.23
United States or American	1,381	3.62
Welsh	312	0.82
West Indian, excl. Hispanic:	31	0.08
Belizean	25	0.07
Trinidadian and Tobagonian	6	0.02
White:	29,359	76.98
Not Hispanic (25,168)	26,337	69.06
Hispanic (2,590)	3,022	7.92
Yugoslavian	166	0.43

Capitola

Place Type: City
County: Santa Cruz
Population: 10,033

Ancestry/Race	Number	%
African American/Black:	166	1.65
Not Hispanic (109)	152	1.52
Hispanic (8)	14	0.14
African, sub-Saharan:	9	0.09
Ethiopian	9	0.09
Alaska Native tribes, specified:	4	0.04
Eskimo (2)	3	0.03
Tlingit-Haida (1)	1	0.01
Am. Ind. or Alaska Nat., not spec.	68	0.68
American Indian tribes, specified:	113	1.13
Apache (2)	3	0.03
Blackfeet (1)	8	0.08
Cherokee (8)	33	0.33
Chickasaw	2	0.02
Chippewa (2)	5	0.05
Choctaw (3)	6	0.06
Comanche	1	0.01
Creek (1)	5	0.05
Iroquois (1)	4	0.04
Latin American Indians (8)	9	0.09
Navajo (2)	2	0.02
Paiute	3	0.03
Pueblo	1	0.01
Puget Sound Salish (1)	1	0.01
Sioux (2)	2	0.02
Yaqui	4	0.04
All other tribes (10)	24	0.24
American Indian tribes, not spec.	12	0.12
Arab:	61	0.60
Arab/Arabic	39	0.38
Egyptian	9	0.09
Lebanese	6	0.06
Syrian	7	0.07
Armenian	13	0.13
Asian:	523	5.21
Cambodian (18)	18	0.18
Chinese, ex. Taiwanese (93)	109	1.09
Filipino (104)	140	1.40
Indian (41)	48	0.48
Indonesian (2)	3	0.03
Japanese (63)	93	0.93
Korean (28)	41	0.41
Malaysian	1	0.01
Sri Lankan (3)	3	0.03
Taiwanese (3)	3	0.03
Thai (11)	17	0.17
Vietnamese (29)	33	0.33
Other Asian, specified	1	0.01
Other Asian, not specified (2)	13	0.13
Australian	32	0.31
Austrian	100	0.98
Basque	8	0.08
Brazilian	15	0.15
British	106	1.04
Canadian	79	0.77
Croatian	36	0.35
Czech	8	0.08
Czechoslovakian	9	0.09
Danish	164	1.61
Dutch	138	1.35
Eastern European	29	0.28
English	1,350	13.23
Estonian	21	0.21
European	251	2.46
Finnish	30	0.29
French, except Basque	450	4.41
French Canadian	64	0.63
German	1,717	16.83
Greek	63	0.62
Hawaii Native/Pacific Islander:	45	0.45
Micronesian: (1)	3	0.03
Guamanian/Chamorro	1	0.01
Other Micronesian (1)	2	0.02
Polynesian: (15)	34	0.34
Native Hawaiian (6)	11	0.11
Samoan (9)	20	0.20
Other Polynesian	3	0.03
Other Pac. Isl., specified	1	0.01
Other Pac. Isl., not spec. (4)	7	0.07
Hispanic or Latino:	1,267	12.63
Central American:	21	0.21
Costa Rican	2	0.02
Guatemalan	5	0.05
Honduran	1	0.01
Nicaraguan	6	0.06
Panamanian	3	0.03
Salvadoran	4	0.04
Cuban	16	0.16
Mexican	949	9.46
Puerto Rican	35	0.35
South American:	33	0.33
Argentinean	7	0.07
Bolivian	1	0.01
Chilean	1	0.01
Colombian	5	0.05
Peruvian	11	0.11
Venezuelan	1	0.01
Other South American	7	0.07
Other Hispanic or Latino	213	2.12
Hungarian	89	0.87
Iranian	35	0.34
Irish	1,662	16.29
Italian	870	8.53
Latvian	14	0.14
Lithuanian	41	0.40
Northern European	18	0.18
Norwegian	263	2.58
Polish	387	3.79
Portuguese	176	1.72
Romanian	17	0.17
Russian	149	1.46
Scandinavian	36	0.35
Scotch-Irish	259	2.54
Scottish	330	3.23
Serbian	16	0.16
Slavic	23	0.23
Slovene	10	0.10
Swedish	138	1.35
Swiss	99	0.97
Turkish	7	0.07
Ukrainian	47	0.46
United States or American	316	3.10
Welsh	210	2.06
West Indian, excl. Hispanic:	10	0.10
Trinidadian and Tobagonian	10	0.10
White:	8,850	88.21
Not Hispanic (7,870)	8,168	81.41
Hispanic (542)	682	6.80
Yugoslavian	41	0.40

Carlsbad

Place Type: City
County: San Diego
Population: 78,247

Ancestry/Race	Number	%

Notes: 1. Figures in the "Number" column do not add up to the total population due to: a) Ancestry/Race overlap — e.g. persons can report being both White and Irish, b) persons of Hispanic origin can report being any race, c) persons reporting two ancestries are counted in both categories. 2. Numbers in parentheses indicate the number of persons reporting this ancestry/race alone, not in combination with any other ancestry/race. 3. Refer to the Explanation of Data in the front of the book for more detailed information.

Acadian/Cajun	8	0.01
Afghan	33	0.04
African American/Black:	1,006	1.29
Not Hispanic (691)	907	1.16
Hispanic (62)	99	0.13
African, sub-Saharan:	76	0.10
African	61	0.08
South African	7	0.01
Sudanese	8	0.01
Alaska Native tribes, specified:	8	0.01
Eskimo (3)	4	0.01
Tlingit-Haida (3)	4	0.01
Alaska Native tribes, not specified	1	0.00
Am. Ind. or Alaska Nat., not spec.	283	0.36
Albanian	7	0.01
Alsatian	19	0.02
American Indian tribes, specified:	516	0.66
Apache (13)	28	0.04
Blackfeet (2)	16	0.02
Cherokee (43)	146	0.19
Chickasaw (1)	4	0.01
Chippewa (8)	17	0.02
Choctaw (4)	17	0.02
Comanche (1)	1	0.00
Cree (1)	1	0.00
Creek	7	0.01
Crow (1)	2	0.00
Delaware	2	0.00
Iroquois (13)	31	0.04
Latin American Indians (48)	70	0.09
Lumbee (4)	4	0.01
Menominee (1)	1	0.00
Navajo (11)	19	0.02
Osage (6)	14	0.02
Paiute	1	0.00
Pima (1)	1	0.00
Potawatomi (6)	11	0.01
Pueblo (10)	14	0.02
Seminole (4)	4	0.01
Shoshone (2)	2	0.00
Sioux (7)	20	0.03
Tohono O'Odham (3)	4	0.01
Yakama	1	0.00
Yaqui (8)	11	0.01
Yuman	1	0.00
All other tribes (31)	66	0.08
American Indian tribes, not spec.	28	0.04
Arab:	393	0.50
Arab/Arabic	116	0.15
Egyptian	37	0.05
Jordanian	21	0.03
Lebanese	121	0.16
Moroccan	44	0.06
Palestinian	17	0.02
Syrian	25	0.03
Other Arab	12	0.02
Armenian	284	0.36
Asian:	4,494	5.74
Cambodian (15)	18	0.02
Chinese, ex. Taiwanese (817)	1,069	1.37
Filipino (485)	784	1.00
Indian (408)	471	0.60
Indonesian (15)	35	0.04
Japanese (677)	1,069	1.37
Korean (398)	471	0.60
Laotian (5)	7	0.01
Malaysian (10)	15	0.02
Pakistani (7)	15	0.02
Sri Lankan (2)	5	0.01
Taiwanese (83)	100	0.13
Thai (53)	74	0.09
Vietnamese (200)	237	0.30
Other Asian, specified (7)	19	0.02
Other Asian, not specified (36)	105	0.13
Assyrian/Chaldean/Syriac	108	0.14
Australian	90	0.12
Austrian	445	0.57
Basque	40	0.05
Belgian	227	0.29
Brazilian	50	0.06
British	760	0.97
Bulgarian	20	0.03
Canadian	503	0.64
Celtic	23	0.03
Croatian	98	0.13
Czech	415	0.53
Czechoslovakian	175	0.22
Danish	728	0.93
Dutch	1,329	1.70
Eastern European	95	0.12
English	10,981	14.08
European	930	1.19
Finnish	153	0.20
French, except Basque	2,959	3.79
French Canadian	645	0.83
German	14,022	17.98
Greek	665	0.85
Hawaii Native/Pacific Islander:	354	0.45
Melanesian: (6)	6	0.01
Fijian (4)	4	0.01
Other Melanesian (2)	2	0.00
Micronesian: (18)	36	0.05
Guamanian/Chamorro (17)	35	0.04
Other Micronesian (1)	1	0.00
Polynesian: (98)	242	0.31
Native Hawaiian (50)	158	0.20
Samoan (43)	70	0.09
Other Polynesian (5)	14	0.02
Other Pac. Isl., specified	2	0.00
Other Pac. Isl., not spec. (29)	68	0.09
Hispanic or Latino:	9,170	11.72
Central American:	186	0.24
Costa Rican	22	0.03
Guatemalan	26	0.03
Honduran	23	0.03
Nicaraguan	23	0.03
Panamanian	26	0.03
Salvadoran	48	0.06
Other Central American	18	0.02
Cuban	120	0.15
Dominican Republic	14	0.02
Mexican	7,107	9.08
Puerto Rican	213	0.27
South American:	299	0.38
Argentinean	47	0.06
Bolivian	11	0.01
Chilean	27	0.03
Colombian	75	0.10
Ecuadorian	14	0.02
Paraguayan	5	0.01
Peruvian	74	0.09
Uruguayan	2	0.00
Venezuelan	17	0.02
Other South American	27	0.03
Other Hispanic or Latino	1,231	1.57
Hungarian	812	1.04
Icelander	36	0.05
Iranian	370	0.47
Irish	11,394	14.61
Israeli	39	0.05
Italian	6,399	8.20
Latvian	42	0.05
Lithuanian	223	0.29
Luxemburger	14	0.02
Maltese	10	0.01
New Zealander	18	0.02
Northern European	96	0.12
Norwegian	2,055	2.63
Pennsylvania German	21	0.03
Polish	2,282	2.93
Portuguese	418	0.54
Romanian	277	0.36
Russian	1,517	1.94
Scandinavian	274	0.35
Scotch-Irish	1,532	1.96
Scottish	2,556	3.28
Serbian	161	0.21
Slovak	208	0.27
Slovene	21	0.03
Swedish	2,249	2.88
Swiss	429	0.55
Turkish	113	0.14
Ukrainian	238	0.31
United States or American	3,820	4.90
Welsh	798	1.02
West Indian, excl. Hispanic:	72	0.09
Haitian	8	0.01
Jamaican	48	0.06
West Indian	8	0.01
Other West Indian	8	0.01
White:	69,822	89.23
Not Hispanic (63,013)	64,511	82.45
Hispanic (4,710)	5,311	6.79
Yugoslavian	216	0.28

Carmichael

Place Type: Census Designated Place
County: Sacramento
Population: 49,742

Ancestry/Race	Number	%
Acadian/Cajun	6	0.01
African American/Black:	1,776	3.57
Not Hispanic (1,309)	1,695	3.41
Hispanic (29)	81	0.16
African, sub-Saharan:	248	0.50
African	190	0.38
Cape Verdean	16	0.03
Ethiopian	22	0.04
Other sub-Saharan African	20	0.04
Alaska Native tribes, specified:	19	0.04
Aleut (1)	5	0.01
Eskimo	2	0.00
Tlingit-Haida (10)	12	0.02
Am. Ind. or Alaska Nat., not spec.	257	0.52
Albanian	23	0.05
Alsatian	7	0.01
American Indian tribes, specified:	710	1.43
Apache (16)	40	0.08
Blackfeet (5)	30	0.06
Cherokee (78)	277	0.56
Cheyenne	2	0.00
Chickasaw (1)	5	0.01
Chippewa (12)	18	0.04
Choctaw (12)	52	0.10
Cree (1)	3	0.01
Creek (5)	11	0.02
Crow (1)	1	0.00
Delaware (1)	6	0.01
Iroquois (4)	16	0.03
Latin American Indians (6)	22	0.04
Menominee (1)	1	0.00
Navajo (9)	24	0.05
Osage (3)	4	0.01
Ottawa (2)	3	0.01
Paiute (1)	2	0.00
Pima (1)	1	0.00
Potawatomi (4)	9	0.02
Pueblo (8)	11	0.02
Puget Sound Salish (1)	2	0.00
Seminole	2	0.00
Shoshone (3)	4	0.01
Sioux (14)	32	0.06
Ute	2	0.00
Yakama (3)	5	0.01
Yaqui (3)	3	0.01
Yuman (4)	4	0.01
All other tribes (67)	118	0.24
American Indian tribes, not spec.	43	0.09
Arab:	171	0.34
Arab/Arabic	8	0.02
Egyptian	24	0.05
Jordanian	53	0.11
Lebanese	35	0.07
Palestinian	12	0.02
Syrian	39	0.08
Armenian	279	0.56
Asian:	2,411	4.85
Cambodian (9)	10	0.02

Notes: 1. Figures in the "Number" column do not add up to the total population due to: a) Ancestry/Race overlap — e.g. persons can report being both White and Irish, b) persons of Hispanic origin can report being any race, c) persons reporting two ancestries are counted in both categories. 2. Numbers in parentheses indicate the number of persons reporting this ancestry/race alone, not in combination with any other ancestry/race. 3. Refer to the Explanation of Data in the front of the book for more detailed information.

Chinese, ex. Taiwanese (367)	487	0.98
Filipino (270)	441	0.89
Hmong (4)	8	0.02
Indian (184)	233	0.47
Indonesian (10)	17	0.03
Japanese (333)	490	0.99
Korean (347)	383	0.77
Laotian (3)	3	0.01
Malaysian (6)	6	0.01
Pakistani (26)	37	0.07
Sri Lankan (7)	9	0.02
Taiwanese (8)	12	0.02
Thai (4)	18	0.04
Vietnamese (145)	167	0.34
Other Asian, specified (7)	10	0.02
Other Asian, not specified (26)	80	0.16
Australian	16	0.03
Austrian	145	0.29
Basque	63	0.13
Belgian	91	0.18
British	258	0.52
Bulgarian	6	0.01
Canadian	144	0.29
Celtic	88	0.18
Croatian	133	0.27
Czech	172	0.35
Czechoslovakian	98	0.20
Danish	409	0.82
Dutch	1,193	2.40
Eastern European	7	0.01
English	7,447	14.97
Estonian	6	0.01
European	979	1.97
Finnish	123	0.25
French, except Basque	2,244	4.51
French Canadian	297	0.60
German	9,515	19.13
Greek	425	0.85
Guyanese	18	0.04
Hawaii Native/Pacific Islander:	251	0.50
Melanesian: (22)	24	0.05
Fijian (22)	24	0.05
Micronesian: (33)	55	0.11
Guamanian/Chamorro (33)	55	0.11
Polynesian: (70)	132	0.27
Native Hawaiian (53)	102	0.21
Samoan (15)	19	0.04
Tongan (1)	6	0.01
Other Polynesian (1)	5	0.01
Other Pac. Isl., specified	2	0.00
Other Pac. Isl., not spec. (9)	38	0.08
Hispanic or Latino:	3,479	6.99
Central American:	137	0.28
Costa Rican	6	0.01
Guatemalan	19	0.04
Honduran	11	0.02
Nicaraguan	16	0.03
Panamanian	11	0.02
Salvadoran	58	0.12
Other Central American	16	0.03
Cuban	39	0.08
Dominican Republic	3	0.01
Mexican	2,182	4.39
Puerto Rican	135	0.27
South American:	88	0.18
Argentinean	16	0.03
Bolivian	3	0.01
Chilean	4	0.01
Colombian	21	0.04
Ecuadorian	4	0.01
Peruvian	18	0.04
Uruguayan	2	0.00
Venezuelan	7	0.01
Other South American	13	0.03
Other Hispanic or Latino	895	1.80
Hungarian	286	0.57
Icelander	39	0.08
Iranian	359	0.72
Irish	6,914	13.90
Israeli	67	0.13
Italian	3,370	6.77
Latvian	13	0.03
Lithuanian	109	0.22
Luxemburger	6	0.01
Maltese	24	0.05
Northern European	41	0.08
Norwegian	1,077	2.17
Pennsylvania German	21	0.04
Polish	887	1.78
Portuguese	818	1.64
Romanian	124	0.25
Russian	852	1.71
Scandinavian	250	0.50
Scotch-Irish	1,304	2.62
Scottish	1,520	3.06
Serbian	83	0.17
Slavic	65	0.13
Slovak	90	0.18
Slovene	37	0.07
Swedish	1,360	2.73
Swiss	278	0.56
Ukrainian	750	1.51
United States or American	2,282	4.59
Welsh	598	1.20
West Indian, excl. Hispanic:	60	0.12
Dutch West Indian	10	0.02
Jamaican	27	0.05
Trinidadian and Tobagonian	23	0.05
White:	44,844	90.15
Not Hispanic (41,081)	42,485	85.41
Hispanic (2,002)	2,359	4.74
Yugoslavian	183	0.37

Carpinteria

Place Type: City
County: Santa Barbara
Population: 14,194

Ancestry/Race	Number	%
African American/Black:	165	1.16
Not Hispanic (74)	121	0.85
Hispanic (10)	44	0.31
African, sub-Saharan:	37	0.26
African	11	0.08
Ethiopian	22	0.15
South African	4	0.03
Am. Ind. or Alaska Nat., not spec.	103	0.73
American Indian tribes, specified:	170	1.20
Apache (5)	8	0.06
Blackfeet	3	0.02
Cherokee (7)	23	0.16
Chickasaw (6)	7	0.05
Chippewa	10	0.07
Choctaw (2)	10	0.07
Comanche	2	0.01
Crow	2	0.01
Delaware	1	0.01
Iroquois	6	0.04
Latin American Indians (20)	25	0.18
Navajo (1)	4	0.03
Pima	1	0.01
Pueblo	2	0.01
Seminole (1)	2	0.01
Sioux (1)	5	0.04
Yaqui (1)	2	0.01
All other tribes (41)	58	0.41
American Indian tribes, not spec.	24	0.17
Arab:	58	0.40
Egyptian	8	0.06
Moroccan	5	0.03
Syrian	39	0.27
Other Arab	6	0.04
Armenian	13	0.09
Asian:	466	3.28
Chinese, ex. Taiwanese (38)	60	0.42
Filipino (51)	92	0.65
Indian (59)	66	0.46
Indonesian (4)	5	0.04
Japanese (93)	127	0.89
Korean (42)	56	0.39
Pakistani (1)	6	0.04
Taiwanese (4)	4	0.03
Thai (13)	13	0.09
Vietnamese (11)	14	0.10
Other Asian, specified	4	0.03
Other Asian, not specified (8)	19	0.13
Australian	9	0.06
Austrian	84	0.58
Basque	16	0.11
Belgian	4	0.03
Brazilian	6	0.04
British	82	0.57
Canadian	33	0.23
Croatian	45	0.31
Czech	16	0.11
Czechoslovakian	20	0.14
Danish	105	0.73
Dutch	190	1.32
English	1,561	10.86
European	140	0.97
Finnish	32	0.22
French, except Basque	269	1.87
French Canadian	99	0.69
German	1,628	11.32
Greek	34	0.24
Hawaii Native/Pacific Islander:	59	0.42
Micronesian: (14)	19	0.13
Guamanian/Chamorro (14)	19	0.13
Polynesian: (12)	31	0.22
Native Hawaiian (9)	27	0.19
Other Polynesian (3)	4	0.03
Other Pac. Isl., specified	4	0.03
Other Pac. Isl., not spec.	5	0.04
Hispanic or Latino:	6,175	43.50
Central American:	55	0.39
Costa Rican	12	0.08
Guatemalan	24	0.17
Nicaraguan	1	0.01
Salvadoran	15	0.11
Other Central American	3	0.02
Cuban	7	0.05
Dominican Republic	1	0.01
Mexican	5,476	38.58
Puerto Rican	21	0.15
South American:	33	0.23
Argentinean	8	0.06
Bolivian	8	0.06
Chilean	6	0.04
Colombian	2	0.01
Ecuadorian	1	0.01
Peruvian	6	0.04
Other South American	2	0.01
Other Hispanic or Latino	582	4.10
Hungarian	85	0.59
Icelander	21	0.15
Irish	1,220	8.49
Italian	758	5.27
Latvian	14	0.10
Lithuanian	28	0.19
New Zealander	11	0.08
Northern European	17	0.12
Norwegian	194	1.35
Pennsylvania German	38	0.26
Polish	242	1.68
Portuguese	45	0.31
Romanian	10	0.07
Russian	200	1.39
Scandinavian	38	0.26
Scotch-Irish	145	1.01
Scottish	321	2.23
Slavic	7	0.05
Slovene	8	0.06
Swedish	285	1.98
Swiss	18	0.13
Ukrainian	15	0.10
United States or American	436	3.03
Welsh	119	0.83
West Indian, excl. Hispanic:	8	0.06
Haitian	8	0.06

Notes: 1. Figures in the "Number" column do not add up to the total population due to: a) Ancestry/Race overlap — e.g. persons can report being both White and Irish, b) persons of Hispanic origin can report being any race, c) persons reporting two ancestries are counted in both categories. 2. Numbers in parentheses indicate the number of persons reporting this ancestry/race alone, not in combination with any other ancestry/race. 3. Refer to the Explanation of Data in the front of the book for more detailed information.

White:	10,965	77.25
Not Hispanic (7,266)	7,506	52.88
Hispanic (3,152)	3,459	24.37
Yugoslavian	16	0.11

Carson

Place Type: City
County: Los Angeles
Population: 89,730

Ancestry/Race	Number	%
Afghan	38	0.04
African American/Black:	23,838	26.57
Not Hispanic (22,485)	23,292	25.96
Hispanic (319)	546	0.61
African, sub-Saharan:	1,246	1.39
African	845	0.94
Ethiopian	111	0.12
Ghanian	11	0.01
Nigerian	244	0.27
Senegalese	10	0.01
Other sub-Saharan African	25	0.03
Alaska Native tribes, specified:	6	0.01
Eskimo (1)	3	0.00
Tlingit-Haida	3	0.00
Am. Ind. or Alaska Nat., not spec.	503	0.56
American Indian tribes, specified:	667	0.74
Apache (19)	37	0.04
Blackfeet (3)	37	0.04
Cherokee (20)	139	0.15
Cheyenne	4	0.00
Chickasaw (1)	7	0.01
Chippewa (5)	8	0.01
Choctaw (12)	43	0.05
Comanche (1)	3	0.00
Cree	2	0.00
Creek (2)	24	0.03
Crow	5	0.01
Delaware (1)	4	0.00
Iroquois (1)	10	0.01
Latin American Indians (74)	127	0.14
Navajo (34)	49	0.05
Osage	2	0.00
Paiute (1)	1	0.00
Pima (5)	6	0.01
Potawatomi (3)	3	0.00
Pueblo (2)	9	0.01
Seminole	4	0.00
Shoshone (3)	4	0.00
Sioux (15)	36	0.04
Tohono O'Odham (8)	14	0.02
Ute (3)	6	0.01
Yaqui (4)	12	0.01
All other tribes (41)	71	0.08
American Indian tribes, not spec.	70	0.08
Arab:	177	0.20
Arab/Arabic	74	0.08
Lebanese	69	0.08
Syrian	27	0.03
Other Arab	7	0.01
Armenian	66	0.07
Asian:	22,205	24.75
Cambodian (160)	190	0.21
Chinese, ex. Taiwanese (369)	690	0.77
Filipino (16,905)	18,223	20.31
Hmong (2)	2	0.00
Indian (287)	417	0.46
Indonesian (30)	67	0.07
Japanese (838)	1,154	1.29
Korean (559)	638	0.71
Laotian (6)	8	0.01
Malaysian (3)	24	0.03
Pakistani (50)	93	0.10
Sri Lankan (23)	27	0.03
Taiwanese (17)	23	0.03
Thai (60)	81	0.09
Vietnamese (328)	377	0.42
Other Asian, specified (13)	19	0.02
Other Asian, not specified (71)	172	0.19
Australian	8	0.01
Austrian	12	0.01
Belgian	8	0.01
Brazilian	28	0.03
British	39	0.04
Canadian	71	0.08
Celtic	12	0.01
Croatian	71	0.08
Czech	26	0.03
Czechoslovakian	22	0.02
Danish	137	0.15
Dutch	528	0.59
Eastern European	23	0.03
English	1,661	1.85
European	146	0.16
Finnish	18	0.02
French, except Basque	604	0.67
French Canadian	148	0.17
German	2,330	2.60
Greek	111	0.12
Guyanese	38	0.04
Hawaii Native/Pacific Islander:	3,541	3.95
Melanesian: (11)	20	0.02
Fijian (11)	20	0.02
Micronesian: (179)	270	0.30
Guamanian/Chamorro (175)	264	0.29
Other Micronesian (4)	6	0.01
Polynesian: (2,340)	3,025	3.37
Native Hawaiian (125)	393	0.44
Samoan (2,195)	2,575	2.87
Tongan (8)	10	0.01
Other Polynesian (12)	47	0.05
Other Pac. Isl., not spec. (55)	226	0.25
Hispanic or Latino:	31,332	34.92
Central American:	1,124	1.25
Costa Rican	51	0.06
Guatemalan	358	0.40
Honduran	66	0.07
Nicaraguan	74	0.08
Panamanian	38	0.04
Salvadoran	444	0.49
Other Central American	93	0.10
Cuban	226	0.25
Dominican Republic	18	0.02
Mexican	25,275	28.17
Puerto Rican	571	0.64
South American:	351	0.39
Argentinean	45	0.05
Bolivian	4	0.00
Chilean	20	0.02
Colombian	73	0.08
Ecuadorian	72	0.08
Peruvian	105	0.12
Venezuelan	3	0.00
Other South American	29	0.03
Other Hispanic or Latino	3,767	4.20
Hungarian	108	0.12
Iranian	12	0.01
Irish	1,701	1.90
Israeli	7	0.01
Italian	1,023	1.14
Lithuanian	69	0.08
Luxemburger	7	0.01
Norwegian	237	0.26
Pennsylvania German	15	0.02
Polish	218	0.24
Portuguese	124	0.14
Romanian	7	0.01
Russian	61	0.07
Scandinavian	36	0.04
Scotch-Irish	324	0.36
Scottish	324	0.36
Slavic	4	0.00
Slovak	28	0.03
Swedish	225	0.25
Swiss	21	0.02
Turkish	6	0.01
Ukrainian	36	0.04
United States or American	1,297	1.45
Welsh	113	0.13
West Indian, excl. Hispanic:	353	0.39
Barbadian	27	0.03
Belizean	42	0.05
Dutch West Indian	7	0.01
Haitian	6	0.01
Jamaican	252	0.28
Trinidadian and Tobagonian	19	0.02
White:	26,049	29.03
Not Hispanic (10,767)	12,157	13.55
Hispanic (12,282)	13,892	15.48
Yugoslavian	88	0.10

Casa de Oro-Mount Helix

Place Type: Census Designated Place
County: San Diego
Population: 18,874

Ancestry/Race	Number	%
Acadian/Cajun	12	0.06
Afghan	52	0.28
African American/Black:	1,107	5.87
Not Hispanic (930)	1,054	5.58
Hispanic (36)	53	0.28
African, sub-Saharan:	77	0.41
African	58	0.31
South African	19	0.10
Alaska Native tribes, specified:	9	0.05
Eskimo (1)	5	0.03
Tlingit-Haida (4)	4	0.02
Am. Ind. or Alaska Nat., not spec.	75	0.40
American Indian tribes, specified:	198	1.05
Apache (2)	12	0.06
Blackfeet	13	0.07
Cherokee (17)	67	0.35
Cheyenne (1)	4	0.02
Chickasaw (1)	3	0.02
Chippewa (1)	2	0.01
Choctaw (6)	18	0.10
Comanche	2	0.01
Creek (2)	2	0.01
Delaware (1)	3	0.02
Houma (3)	3	0.02
Iroquois (2)	11	0.06
Latin American Indians (4)	6	0.03
Navajo (4)	6	0.03
Pueblo (5)	5	0.03
Puget Sound Salish (1)	1	0.01
Seminole (2)	5	0.03
Sioux (5)	8	0.04
Yaqui (3)	3	0.02
Yuman (2)	2	0.01
All other tribes (15)	22	0.12
American Indian tribes, not spec.	6	0.03
Arab:	382	2.02
Arab/Arabic	62	0.33
Egyptian	2	0.01
Iraqi	178	0.94
Jordanian	9	0.05
Lebanese	93	0.49
Syrian	27	0.14
Other Arab	11	0.06
Armenian	66	0.35
Asian:	663	3.51
Chinese, ex. Taiwanese (60)	86	0.46
Filipino (131)	237	1.26
Indian (25)	40	0.21
Indonesian (3)	4	0.02
Japanese (79)	156	0.83
Korean (22)	26	0.14
Laotian (6)	6	0.03
Taiwanese (9)	10	0.05
Thai (5)	5	0.03
Vietnamese (44)	50	0.26
Other Asian, not specified (7)	43	0.23
Assyrian/Chaldean/Syriac	207	1.10
Australian	6	0.03
Austrian	75	0.40
Basque	13	0.07
Belgian	7	0.04

Notes: 1. Figures in the "Number" column do not add up to the total population due to: a) Ancestry/Race overlap — e.g. persons can report being both White and Irish, b) persons of Hispanic origin can report being any race, c) persons reporting two ancestries are counted in both categories. 2. Numbers in parentheses indicate the number of persons reporting this ancestry/race alone, not in combination with any other ancestry/race. 3. Refer to the Explanation of Data in the front of the book for more detailed information.

British	231	1.22
Bulgarian	35	0.19
Canadian	44	0.23
Croatian	13	0.07
Czech	104	0.55
Czechoslovakian	42	0.22
Danish	249	1.32
Dutch	236	1.25
Eastern European	30	0.16
English	2,700	14.31
European	417	2.21
Finnish	99	0.52
French, except Basque	866	4.59
French Canadian	126	0.67
German	3,398	18.01
German Russian	7	0.04
Greek	257	1.36
Hawaii Native/Pacific Islander:	127	0.67
Micronesian: (26)	52	0.28
Guamanian/Chamorro (26)	51	0.27
Other Micronesian	1	0.01
Polynesian: (30)	66	0.35
Native Hawaiian (23)	48	0.25
Samoan (6)	13	0.07
Other Polynesian (1)	5	0.03
Other Pac. Isl., not spec. (3)	9	0.05
Hispanic or Latino:	2,142	11.35
Central American:	38	0.20
Costa Rican	14	0.07
Guatemalan	8	0.04
Honduran	4	0.02
Nicaraguan	2	0.01
Panamanian	5	0.03
Salvadoran	3	0.02
Other Central American	2	0.01
Cuban	11	0.06
Dominican Republic	9	0.05
Mexican	1,615	8.56
Puerto Rican	73	0.39
South American:	54	0.29
Argentinean	3	0.02
Bolivian	3	0.02
Chilean	7	0.04
Colombian	18	0.10
Ecuadorian	5	0.03
Peruvian	5	0.03
Venezuelan	7	0.04
Other South American	6	0.03
Other Hispanic or Latino	342	1.81
Hungarian	110	0.58
Icelander	40	0.21
Iranian	25	0.13
Irish	2,212	11.72
Italian	1,206	6.39
Latvian	8	0.04
Lithuanian	45	0.24
Luxemburger	19	0.10
Macedonian	8	0.04
Northern European	33	0.17
Norwegian	621	3.29
Polish	505	2.68
Portuguese	57	0.30
Romanian	95	0.50
Russian	233	1.23
Scandinavian	99	0.52
Scotch-Irish	539	2.86
Scottish	524	2.78
Serbian	6	0.03
Slavic	28	0.15
Swedish	415	2.20
Swiss	117	0.62
Ukrainian	46	0.24
United States or American	974	5.16
Welsh	226	1.20
West Indian, excl. Hispanic:	3	0.02
Jamaican	3	0.02
White:	16,445	87.13
Not Hispanic (14,694)	15,170	80.38
Hispanic (1,106)	1,275	6.76
Yugoslavian	29	0.15

Castro Valley

Place Type: Census Designated Place
County: Alameda
Population: 57,292

Ancestry/Race	Number	%
Acadian/Cajun	14	0.02
Afghan	234	0.41
African American/Black:	3,397	5.93
Not Hispanic (2,868)	3,224	5.63
Hispanic (78)	173	0.30
African, sub-Saharan:	263	0.46
African	101	0.18
Cape Verdean	12	0.02
Ethiopian	24	0.04
Ghanian	7	0.01
Nigerian	23	0.04
Sudanese	72	0.13
Other sub-Saharan African	24	0.04
Alaska Native tribes, specified:	6	0.01
Aleut	1	0.00
Eskimo	1	0.00
Tlingit-Haida	4	0.01
Am. Ind. or Alaska Nat., not spec.	274	0.48
Albanian	6	0.01
Alsatian	7	0.01
American Indian tribes, specified:	713	1.24
Apache (27)	53	0.09
Blackfeet (2)	35	0.06
Cherokee (46)	222	0.39
Cheyenne (3)	16	0.03
Chickasaw	2	0.00
Chippewa (14)	21	0.04
Choctaw (13)	44	0.08
Comanche	9	0.02
Cree (2)	4	0.01
Creek (3)	12	0.02
Crow	2	0.00
Delaware (1)	2	0.00
Iroquois (6)	11	0.02
Latin American Indians (11)	52	0.09
Menominee	1	0.00
Navajo (11)	26	0.05
Osage	8	0.01
Paiute (1)	1	0.00
Pima (2)	4	0.01
Potawatomi (3)	4	0.01
Pueblo (8)	12	0.02
Seminole (1)	6	0.01
Shoshone	1	0.00
Sioux (9)	28	0.05
Tohono O'Odham	2	0.00
Ute	2	0.00
Yaqui (3)	7	0.01
All other tribes (57)	126	0.22
American Indian tribes, not spec.	44	0.08
Arab:	306	0.53
Arab/Arabic	63	0.11
Egyptian	44	0.08
Jordanian	21	0.04
Lebanese	114	0.20
Palestinian	49	0.09
Syrian	5	0.01
Other Arab	10	0.02
Armenian	71	0.12
Asian:	9,213	16.08
Bangladeshi (1)	1	0.00
Cambodian (52)	53	0.09
Chinese, ex. Taiwanese (3,763)	4,179	7.29
Filipino (1,212)	1,709	2.98
Indian (752)	862	1.50
Indonesian (26)	50	0.09
Japanese (504)	816	1.42
Korean (854)	931	1.63
Laotian (9)	11	0.02
Malaysian (1)	6	0.01
Pakistani (19)	25	0.04
Sri Lankan (2)	2	0.00
Taiwanese (70)	92	0.16
Thai (18)	28	0.05
Vietnamese (219)	260	0.45
Other Asian, specified (1)	2	0.00
Other Asian, not specified (69)	186	0.32
Australian	23	0.04
Austrian	301	0.52
Basque	47	0.08
Belgian	52	0.09
Brazilian	25	0.04
British	316	0.55
Bulgarian	20	0.03
Canadian	161	0.28
Celtic	44	0.08
Croatian	204	0.36
Cypriot	6	0.01
Czech	75	0.13
Czechoslovakian	44	0.08
Danish	682	1.19
Dutch	648	1.13
Eastern European	21	0.04
English	6,250	10.89
Estonian	11	0.02
European	1,125	1.96
Finnish	110	0.19
French, except Basque	1,519	2.65
French Canadian	230	0.40
German	7,286	12.69
Greek	402	0.70
Hawaii Native/Pacific Islander:	589	1.03
Melanesian: (56)	61	0.11
Fijian (56)	61	0.11
Micronesian: (35)	85	0.15
Guamanian/Chamorro (35)	83	0.14
Other Micronesian	2	0.00
Polynesian: (120)	316	0.55
Native Hawaiian (56)	222	0.39
Samoan (28)	50	0.09
Tongan (23)	27	0.05
Other Polynesian (13)	17	0.03
Other Pac. Isl., not spec. (38)	127	0.22
Hispanic or Latino:	6,984	12.19
Central American:	388	0.68
Costa Rican	13	0.02
Guatemalan	61	0.11
Honduran	4	0.01
Nicaraguan	124	0.22
Panamanian	28	0.05
Salvadoran	126	0.22
Other Central American	32	0.06
Cuban	56	0.10
Dominican Republic	5	0.01
Mexican	3,986	6.96
Puerto Rican	406	0.71
South American:	207	0.36
Argentinean	15	0.03
Bolivian	2	0.00
Chilean	29	0.05
Colombian	40	0.07
Ecuadorian	7	0.01
Peruvian	89	0.16
Venezuelan	8	0.01
Other South American	17	0.03
Other Hispanic or Latino	1,936	3.38
Hungarian	178	0.31
Icelander	32	0.06
Iranian	225	0.39
Irish	5,834	10.16
Israeli	21	0.04
Italian	4,855	8.46
Latvian	96	0.17
Lithuanian	101	0.18
Macedonian	7	0.01
New Zealander	53	0.09
Northern European	107	0.19
Norwegian	1,241	2.16
Pennsylvania German	15	0.03
Polish	771	1.34
Portuguese	3,268	5.69
Romanian	303	0.53
Russian	902	1.57

Notes: 1. Figures in the "Number" column do not add up to the total population due to: a) Ancestry/Race overlap — e.g. persons can report being both White and Irish, b) persons of Hispanic origin can report being any race, c) persons reporting two ancestries are counted in both categories. 2. Numbers in parentheses indicate the number of persons reporting this ancestry/race alone, not in combination with any other ancestry/race. 3. Refer to the Explanation of Data in the front of the book for more detailed information.

Ancestry/Race	Number	%
Scandinavian	185	0.32
Scotch-Irish	775	1.35
Scottish	1,382	2.41
Serbian	51	0.09
Slavic	22	0.04
Slovak	35	0.06
Slovene	94	0.16
Swedish	1,219	2.12
Swiss	192	0.33
Turkish	3	0.01
Ukrainian	262	0.46
United States or American	1,613	2.81
Welsh	397	0.69
West Indian, excl. Hispanic:	139	0.24
Dutch West Indian	23	0.04
Haitian	12	0.02
Jamaican	58	0.10
Trinidadian and Tobagonian	6	0.01
West Indian	40	0.07
White:	43,248	75.49
Not Hispanic (36,992)	38,908	67.91
Hispanic (3,595)	4,340	7.58
Yugoslavian	199	0.35

Cathedral City

Place Type: City
County: Riverside
Population: 42,647

Ancestry/Race	Number	%
Acadian/Cajun	2	0.00
African American/Black:	1,406	3.30
Not Hispanic (1,049)	1,216	2.85
Hispanic (120)	190	0.45
African, sub-Saharan:	39	0.09
African	32	0.07
Ethiopian	7	0.02
Am. Ind. or Alaska Nat., not spec.	250	0.59
Albanian	29	0.07
American Indian tribes, specified:	405	0.95
Apache (7)	13	0.03
Blackfeet (2)	6	0.01
Cherokee (20)	54	0.13
Chickasaw (2)	3	0.01
Chippewa (3)	4	0.01
Choctaw (5)	13	0.03
Comanche (3)	6	0.01
Creek (2)	3	0.01
Crow (2)	3	0.01
Houma	1	0.00
Iroquois (1)	5	0.01
Kiowa	3	0.01
Latin American Indians (67)	96	0.23
Navajo (5)	11	0.03
Osage (4)	6	0.01
Paiute (1)	1	0.00
Pima (2)	2	0.00
Potawatomi	1	0.00
Pueblo (5)	8	0.02
Seminole	1	0.00
Sioux (9)	11	0.03
Tohono O'Odham (1)	1	0.00
Ute (1)	1	0.00
Yakama	1	0.00
Yaqui (21)	30	0.07
Yuman	1	0.00
All other tribes (101)	120	0.28
American Indian tribes, not spec.	22	0.05
Arab:	34	0.08
Arab/Arabic	9	0.02
Lebanese	20	0.05
Syrian	5	0.01
Armenian	11	0.03
Asian:	1,948	4.57
Cambodian (16)	27	0.06
Chinese, ex. Taiwanese (125)	160	0.38
Filipino (1,018)	1,195	2.80
Indian (108)	124	0.29
Indonesian (1)	6	0.01
Japanese (84)	144	0.34
Korean (83)	98	0.23
Laotian (12)	18	0.04
Malaysian	2	0.00
Pakistani (4)	9	0.02
Sri Lankan (15)	16	0.04
Thai (21)	25	0.06
Vietnamese (39)	50	0.12
Other Asian, specified (4)	6	0.01
Other Asian, not specified (19)	68	0.16
Australian	8	0.02
Austrian	167	0.39
Basque	2	0.00
Belgian	11	0.03
British	132	0.31
Bulgarian	23	0.05
Canadian	173	0.40
Celtic	2	0.00
Croatian	22	0.05
Czech	49	0.11
Czechoslovakian	37	0.09
Danish	369	0.86
Dutch	544	1.27
English	2,811	6.55
European	169	0.39
Finnish	66	0.15
French, except Basque	1,168	2.72
French Canadian	199	0.46
German	3,994	9.31
Greek	105	0.24
Hawaii Native/Pacific Islander:	90	0.21
Micronesian: (7)	12	0.03
Guamanian/Chamorro (7)	11	0.03
Other Micronesian	1	0.00
Polynesian: (16)	38	0.09
Native Hawaiian (10)	27	0.06
Samoan (4)	8	0.02
Other Polynesian (2)	3	0.01
Other Pac. Isl., specified	2	0.00
Other Pac. Isl., not spec. (8)	38	0.09
Hispanic or Latino:	21,312	49.97
Central American:	740	1.74
Costa Rican	10	0.02
Guatemalan	339	0.79
Honduran	19	0.04
Nicaraguan	46	0.11
Panamanian	12	0.03
Salvadoran	266	0.62
Other Central American	48	0.11
Cuban	82	0.19
Mexican	17,791	41.72
Puerto Rican	177	0.42
South American:	152	0.36
Argentinean	20	0.05
Bolivian	1	0.00
Chilean	7	0.02
Colombian	31	0.07
Ecuadorian	14	0.03
Paraguayan	5	0.01
Peruvian	38	0.09
Uruguayan	13	0.03
Venezuelan	16	0.04
Other South American	7	0.02
Other Hispanic or Latino	2,370	5.56
Hungarian	139	0.32
Icelander	12	0.03
Iranian	18	0.04
Irish	2,991	6.97
Israeli	14	0.03
Italian	1,550	3.61
Latvian	4	0.01
Lithuanian	39	0.09
Luxemburger	9	0.02
Macedonian	3	0.01
Northern European	7	0.02
Norwegian	584	1.36
Pennsylvania German	6	0.01
Polish	759	1.77
Portuguese	54	0.13
Romanian	115	0.27
Russian	388	0.90
Scandinavian	22	0.05
Scotch-Irish	460	1.07
Scottish	447	1.04
Serbian	14	0.03
Slavic	4	0.01
Slovak	48	0.11
Slovene	10	0.02
Swedish	618	1.44
Swiss	84	0.20
Turkish	2	0.00
Ukrainian	35	0.08
United States or American	1,267	2.95
Welsh	359	0.84
West Indian, excl. Hispanic:	48	0.11
Belizean	10	0.02
Jamaican	20	0.05
West Indian	18	0.04
White:	29,370	68.87
Not Hispanic (17,908)	18,386	43.11
Hispanic (9,937)	10,984	25.76
Yugoslavian	136	0.32

Ceres

Place Type: City
County: Stanislaus
Population: 34,609

Ancestry/Race	Number	%
African American/Black:	1,130	3.27
Not Hispanic (889)	1,020	2.95
Hispanic (62)	110	0.32
African, sub-Saharan:	17	0.05
African	17	0.05
Alaska Native tribes, specified:	5	0.01
Aleut (1)	1	0.00
Tlingit-Haida	4	0.01
Am. Ind. or Alaska Nat., not spec.	251	0.73
American Indian tribes, specified:	704	2.03
Apache (6)	26	0.08
Blackfeet (6)	25	0.07
Cherokee (93)	256	0.74
Chickasaw (1)	19	0.05
Chippewa (8)	10	0.03
Choctaw (35)	95	0.27
Comanche (2)	3	0.01
Creek (19)	28	0.08
Delaware (3)	4	0.01
Iroquois (7)	9	0.03
Latin American Indians (44)	65	0.19
Lumbee (1)	1	0.00
Navajo (5)	10	0.03
Ottawa	1	0.00
Paiute (2)	5	0.01
Potawatomi (2)	2	0.01
Pueblo (11)	14	0.04
Seminole	1	0.00
Shoshone (1)	1	0.00
Sioux (8)	16	0.05
Tohono O'Odham (3)	5	0.01
Yaqui (9)	17	0.05
Yuman (1)	1	0.00
All other tribes (54)	90	0.26
American Indian tribes, not spec.	60	0.17
Arab:	52	0.15
Iraqi	27	0.08
Syrian	25	0.07
Armenian	17	0.05
Asian:	2,211	6.39
Cambodian (120)	153	0.44
Chinese, ex. Taiwanese (87)	123	0.36
Filipino (302)	442	1.28
Hmong (33)	33	0.10
Indian (900)	1,028	2.97
Indonesian (3)	11	0.03
Japanese (26)	87	0.25
Korean (32)	48	0.14
Laotian (165)	184	0.53
Malaysian (1)	1	0.00

Notes: 1. Figures in the "Number" column do not add up to the total population due to: a) Ancestry/Race overlap — e.g. persons can report being both White and Irish, b) persons of Hispanic origin can report being any race, c) persons reporting two ancestries are counted in both categories. 2. Numbers in parentheses indicate the number of persons reporting this ancestry/race alone, not in combination with any other ancestry/race. 3. Refer to the Explanation of Data in the front of the book for more detailed information.

Ancestry/Race	Number	%
Pakistani (9)	11	0.03
Thai (3)	3	0.01
Vietnamese (27)	27	0.08
Other Asian, specified	1	0.00
Other Asian, not specified (30)	59	0.17
Assyrian/Chaldean/Syriac	395	1.14
Austrian	8	0.02
Basque	5	0.01
Belgian	9	0.03
British	43	0.12
Canadian	21	0.06
Croatian	19	0.06
Czech	44	0.13
Czechoslovakian	55	0.16
Danish	137	0.40
Dutch	329	0.95
English	2,034	5.89
European	206	0.60
Finnish	66	0.19
French, except Basque	683	1.98
French Canadian	101	0.29
German	2,628	7.61
Greek	126	0.36
Hawaii Native/Pacific Islander:	264	0.76
Melanesian: (18)	18	0.05
Fijian (18)	18	0.05
Micronesian: (22)	40	0.12
Guamanian/Chamorro (18)	36	0.10
Other Micronesian (4)	4	0.01
Polynesian: (56)	115	0.33
Native Hawaiian (10)	55	0.16
Samoan (45)	57	0.16
Other Polynesian (1)	3	0.01
Other Pac. Isl., specified	1	0.00
Other Pac. Isl., not spec. (32)	90	0.26
Hispanic or Latino:	13,115	37.89
Central American:	150	0.43
Costa Rican	7	0.02
Guatemalan	18	0.05
Honduran	12	0.03
Nicaraguan	35	0.10
Panamanian	13	0.04
Salvadoran	52	0.15
Other Central American	13	0.04
Cuban	27	0.08
Mexican	11,185	32.32
Puerto Rican	168	0.49
South American:	79	0.23
Argentinean	7	0.02
Chilean	3	0.01
Colombian	28	0.08
Ecuadorian	4	0.01
Paraguayan	1	0.00
Peruvian	24	0.07
Venezuelan	3	0.01
Other South American	9	0.03
Other Hispanic or Latino	1,506	4.35
Hungarian	9	0.03
Iranian	28	0.08
Irish	2,479	7.18
Italian	868	2.51
Norwegian	241	0.70
Polish	264	0.76
Portuguese	1,425	4.13
Romanian	59	0.17
Russian	122	0.35
Scandinavian	66	0.19
Scotch-Irish	360	1.04
Scottish	433	1.25
Swedish	378	1.09
Swiss	116	0.34
Turkish	15	0.04
United States or American	2,153	6.23
Welsh	88	0.25
West Indian, excl. Hispanic:	27	0.08
Bahamian	8	0.02
Jamaican	19	0.06
White:	23,878	68.99
Not Hispanic (17,361)	18,142	52.42
Hispanic (4,963)	5,736	16.57

Cerritos

Place Type: City
County: Los Angeles
Population: 51,488

Ancestry/Race	Number	%
Afghan	69	0.13
African American/Black:	3,719	7.22
Not Hispanic (3,386)	3,614	7.02
Hispanic (46)	105	0.20
African, sub-Saharan:	409	0.79
African	250	0.49
Ethiopian	29	0.06
Nigerian	130	0.25
Am. Ind. or Alaska Nat., not spec.	153	0.30
American Indian tribes, specified:	240	0.47
Apache (1)	4	0.01
Blackfeet	4	0.01
Cherokee (24)	90	0.17
Cheyenne (1)	1	0.00
Chickasaw	1	0.00
Chippewa (2)	3	0.01
Choctaw (1)	11	0.02
Colville (1)	1	0.00
Comanche (4)	5	0.01
Cree	2	0.00
Creek (2)	8	0.02
Delaware	1	0.00
Iroquois (1)	2	0.00
Latin American Indians (17)	25	0.05
Navajo (8)	10	0.02
Paiute (2)	6	0.01
Potawatomi (1)	1	0.00
Pueblo (3)	6	0.01
Seminole (2)	9	0.02
Sioux (2)	9	0.02
Tohono O'Odham	1	0.00
Yaqui (3)	6	0.01
All other tribes (21)	34	0.07
American Indian tribes, not spec.	7	0.01
Arab:	501	0.97
Arab/Arabic	166	0.32
Egyptian	240	0.47
Iraqi	10	0.02
Lebanese	25	0.05
Palestinian	38	0.07
Syrian	22	0.04
Armenian	109	0.21
Asian:	32,023	62.20
Bangladeshi (16)	16	0.03
Cambodian (129)	140	0.27
Chinese, ex. Taiwanese (5,681)	6,378	12.39
Filipino (6,046)	6,560	12.74
Hmong (2)	2	0.00
Indian (2,891)	3,017	5.86
Indonesian (115)	203	0.39
Japanese (1,671)	2,044	3.97
Korean (8,938)	9,109	17.69
Laotian (18)	23	0.04
Malaysian (2)	7	0.01
Pakistani (135)	174	0.34
Sri Lankan (68)	82	0.16
Taiwanese (2,026)	2,333	4.53
Thai (631)	694	1.35
Vietnamese (940)	1,045	2.03
Other Asian, specified (23)	28	0.05
Other Asian, not specified (103)	168	0.33
Assyrian/Chaldean/Syriac	23	0.04
Australian	7	0.01
Austrian	88	0.17
Basque	13	0.03
Belgian	19	0.04
Brazilian	28	0.05
British	60	0.12
Bulgarian	4	0.01
Canadian	90	0.17
Croatian	43	0.08
Czech	52	0.10
Czechoslovakian	27	0.05
Danish	142	0.28
Dutch	610	1.18
English	1,780	3.46
European	191	0.37
Finnish	60	0.12
French, except Basque	426	0.83
French Canadian	134	0.26
German	2,440	4.74
Greek	97	0.19
Hawaii Native/Pacific Islander:	357	0.69
Melanesian: (1)	2	0.00
Fijian (1)	2	0.00
Micronesian: (38)	70	0.14
Guamanian/Chamorro (36)	65	0.13
Other Micronesian (2)	5	0.01
Polynesian: (50)	120	0.23
Native Hawaiian (36)	97	0.19
Samoan (13)	21	0.04
Other Polynesian (1)	2	0.00
Other Pac. Isl., specified	1	0.00
Other Pac. Isl., not spec. (6)	164	0.32
Hispanic or Latino:	5,349	10.39
Central American:	214	0.42
Costa Rican	26	0.05
Guatemalan	33	0.06
Honduran	7	0.01
Nicaraguan	42	0.08
Panamanian	16	0.03
Salvadoran	78	0.15
Other Central American	12	0.02
Cuban	169	0.33
Dominican Republic	13	0.03
Mexican	3,565	6.92
Puerto Rican	130	0.25
South American:	354	0.69
Argentinean	53	0.10
Bolivian	1	0.00
Chilean	26	0.05
Colombian	92	0.18
Ecuadorian	55	0.11
Peruvian	63	0.12
Uruguayan	4	0.01
Venezuelan	13	0.03
Other South American	47	0.09
Other Hispanic or Latino	904	1.76
Hungarian	99	0.19
Icelander	6	0.01
Iranian	242	0.47
Irish	1,913	3.71
Israeli	8	0.02
Italian	826	1.60
Latvian	27	0.05
Lithuanian	38	0.07
Northern European	16	0.03
Norwegian	219	0.43
Pennsylvania German	9	0.02
Polish	189	0.37
Portuguese	399	0.77
Romanian	11	0.02
Russian	166	0.32
Scandinavian	95	0.18
Scotch-Irish	483	0.94
Scottish	326	0.63
Slavic	12	0.02
Slovak	37	0.07
Slovene	7	0.01
Swedish	480	0.93
Swiss	104	0.20
Turkish	14	0.03
Ukrainian	22	0.04
United States or American	775	1.50
Welsh	103	0.20
West Indian, excl. Hispanic:	80	0.16
Jamaican	46	0.09
Trinidadian and Tobagonian	15	0.03
West Indian	19	0.04
White:	15,188	29.50
Not Hispanic (11,040)	12,008	23.32
Hispanic (2,811)	3,180	6.18
Yugoslavian	57	0.11

Notes: 1. Figures in the "Number" column do not add up to the total population due to: a) Ancestry/Race overlap — e.g. persons can report being both White and Irish, b) persons of Hispanic origin can report being any race, c) persons reporting two ancestries are counted in both categories. 2. Numbers in parentheses indicate the number of persons reporting this ancestry/race alone, not in combination with any other ancestry/race. 3. Refer to the Explanation of Data in the front of the book for more detailed information.

Cherryland

Place Type: Census Designated Place
County: Alameda
Population: 13,837

Ancestry/Race	Number	%
Afghan	35	0.25
African American/Black:	1,559	11.27
Not Hispanic (1,309)	1,456	10.52
Hispanic (51)	103	0.74
African, sub-Saharan:	142	1.03
African	54	0.39
Cape Verdean	22	0.16
Ethiopian	48	0.35
Sierra Leonean	18	0.13
Alaska Native tribes, specified:	3	0.02
Alaska Athabascan (1)	1	0.01
Tlingit-Haida (2)	2	0.01
Alaska Native tribes, not specified	1	0.01
Am. Ind. or Alaska Nat., not spec.	133	0.96
American Indian tribes, specified:	181	1.31
Apache (4)	7	0.05
Blackfeet (1)	5	0.04
Cherokee (11)	41	0.30
Cheyenne (1)	1	0.01
Chippewa (1)	1	0.01
Choctaw (4)	11	0.08
Comanche (2)	2	0.01
Cree	2	0.01
Creek	3	0.02
Iroquois (1)	3	0.02
Kiowa (6)	6	0.04
Latin American Indians (30)	41	0.30
Navajo (5)	8	0.06
Paiute (1)	7	0.05
Potawatomi	2	0.01
Seminole (1)	4	0.03
Shoshone	3	0.02
Sioux (2)	6	0.04
Tohono O'Odham (1)	5	0.04
Yaqui (1)	3	0.02
All other tribes (12)	20	0.14
American Indian tribes, not spec.	10	0.07
Arab:	62	0.45
Jordanian	5	0.04
Lebanese	10	0.07
Palestinian	26	0.19
Syrian	8	0.06
Other Arab	13	0.09
Armenian	11	0.08
Asian:	1,393	10.07
Cambodian (2)	2	0.01
Chinese, ex. Taiwanese (160)	202	1.46
Filipino (586)	707	5.11
Indian (103)	132	0.95
Indonesian (2)	5	0.04
Japanese (72)	95	0.69
Korean (50)	56	0.40
Laotian (2)	2	0.01
Pakistani (3)	3	0.02
Thai (8)	10	0.07
Vietnamese (136)	148	1.07
Other Asian, not specified (7)	31	0.22
Austrian	21	0.15
Brazilian	12	0.09
British	43	0.31
Bulgarian	13	0.09
Canadian	8	0.06
Celtic	15	0.11
Croatian	15	0.11
Czech	15	0.11
Czechoslovakian	27	0.20
Danish	36	0.26
Dutch	118	0.86
English	544	3.95
European	64	0.46
French, except Basque	213	1.55
French Canadian	100	0.73
German	738	5.35
Greek	59	0.43
Hawaii Native/Pacific Islander:	287	2.07
Melanesian: (30)	35	0.25
Fijian (30)	34	0.25
Other Melanesian	1	0.01
Micronesian: (15)	32	0.23
Guamanian/Chamorro (13)	28	0.20
Other Micronesian (2)	4	0.03
Polynesian: (106)	178	1.29
Native Hawaiian (31)	94	0.68
Samoan (37)	45	0.33
Tongan (38)	38	0.27
Other Polynesian	1	0.01
Other Pac. Isl., not spec. (24)	42	0.30
Hispanic or Latino:	5,774	41.73
Central American:	372	2.69
Costa Rican	9	0.07
Guatemalan	40	0.29
Honduran	3	0.02
Nicaraguan	112	0.81
Panamanian	11	0.08
Salvadoran	151	1.09
Other Central American	46	0.33
Cuban	30	0.22
Mexican	4,170	30.14
Puerto Rican	234	1.69
South American:	116	0.84
Argentinean	10	0.07
Bolivian	6	0.04
Chilean	19	0.14
Colombian	17	0.12
Ecuadorian	4	0.03
Paraguayan	1	0.01
Peruvian	54	0.39
Venezuelan	1	0.01
Other South American	4	0.03
Other Hispanic or Latino	852	6.16
Hungarian	15	0.11
Iranian	45	0.33
Irish	631	4.58
Italian	562	4.08
Latvian	12	0.09
Norwegian	106	0.77
Pennsylvania German	10	0.07
Polish	12	0.09
Portuguese	794	5.76
Romanian	12	0.09
Russian	39	0.28
Scandinavian	6	0.04
Scotch-Irish	77	0.56
Scottish	71	0.52
Slovak	4	0.03
Swedish	133	0.97
Swiss	17	0.12
United States or American	371	2.69
Welsh	38	0.28
West Indian, excl. Hispanic:	5	0.04
Belizean	5	0.04
White:	8,016	57.93
Not Hispanic (4,933)	5,284	38.19
Hispanic (2,386)	2,732	19.74
Yugoslavian	7	0.05

Chico

Place Type: City
County: Butte
Population: 59,954

Ancestry/Race	Number	%
Acadian/Cajun	9	0.02
African American/Black:	1,653	2.76
Not Hispanic (1,174)	1,546	2.58
Hispanic (41)	107	0.18
African, sub-Saharan:	100	0.17
African	76	0.13
Ghanian	17	0.03
Sierra Leonean	7	0.01
Alaska Native tribes, specified:	33	0.06
Alaska Athabascan (8)	9	0.02
Aleut (4)	9	0.02
Eskimo (6)	7	0.01
Tlingit-Haida (2)	6	0.01
All other tribes (2)	2	0.00
Alaska Native tribes, not specified	7	0.01
Am. Ind. or Alaska Nat., not spec.	402	0.67
American Indian tribes, specified:	1,102	1.84
Apache (19)	37	0.06
Blackfeet (11)	40	0.07
Cherokee (61)	254	0.42
Cheyenne	1	0.00
Chickasaw (3)	8	0.01
Chippewa (8)	10	0.02
Choctaw (33)	56	0.09
Comanche	9	0.02
Creek (4)	8	0.01
Delaware (3)	3	0.01
Iroquois (5)	9	0.02
Kiowa (1)	11	0.02
Latin American Indians (20)	46	0.08
Lumbee	2	0.00
Navajo (25)	44	0.07
Osage (1)	2	0.00
Paiute (8)	13	0.02
Pima	1	0.00
Potawatomi (3)	5	0.01
Pueblo (8)	17	0.03
Puget Sound Salish	1	0.00
Seminole (3)	6	0.01
Shoshone (2)	8	0.01
Sioux (19)	38	0.06
Tohono O'Odham	2	0.00
Yakama (1)	1	0.00
Yaqui (7)	11	0.02
All other tribes (297)	459	0.77
American Indian tribes, not spec.	59	0.10
Arab:	302	0.51
Arab/Arabic	60	0.10
Egyptian	7	0.01
Jordanian	26	0.04
Lebanese	78	0.13
Palestinian	18	0.03
Syrian	77	0.13
Other Arab	36	0.06
Armenian	73	0.12
Asian:	3,200	5.34
Cambodian (27)	32	0.05
Chinese, ex. Taiwanese (346)	465	0.78
Filipino (180)	337	0.56
Hmong (849)	921	1.54
Indian (175)	234	0.39
Indonesian (9)	13	0.02
Japanese (366)	500	0.83
Korean (81)	124	0.21
Laotian (177)	220	0.37
Malaysian (5)	7	0.01
Pakistani (11)	27	0.05
Sri Lankan (5)	7	0.01
Taiwanese (31)	40	0.07
Thai (39)	45	0.08
Vietnamese (101)	118	0.20
Other Asian, specified (3)	9	0.02
Other Asian, not specified (51)	101	0.17
Assyrian/Chaldean/Syriac	24	0.04
Australian	46	0.08
Austrian	156	0.26
Basque	93	0.16
Belgian	102	0.17
Brazilian	50	0.08
British	255	0.43
Bulgarian	16	0.03
Canadian	196	0.33
Celtic	16	0.03
Croatian	112	0.19
Cypriot	9	0.02
Czech	217	0.37
Czechoslovakian	139	0.23
Danish	578	0.97
Dutch	1,188	2.00
Eastern European	9	0.02

Notes: 1. Figures in the "Number" column do not add up to the total population due to: a) Ancestry/Race overlap — e.g. persons can report being both White and Irish, b) persons of Hispanic origin can report being any race, c) persons reporting two ancestries are counted in both categories. 2. Numbers in parentheses indicate the number of persons reporting this ancestry/race alone, not in combination with any other ancestry/race. 3. Refer to the Explanation of Data in the front of the book for more detailed information.

English	6,739	11.34
Estonian	22	0.04
European	1,029	1.73
Finnish	96	0.16
French, except Basque	2,012	3.38
French Canadian	225	0.38
German	9,842	16.56
Greek	150	0.25
Hawaii Native/Pacific Islander:	256	0.43
Melanesian: (4)	4	0.01
Fijian (4)	4	0.01
Micronesian: (40)	54	0.09
Guamanian/Chamorro (15)	26	0.04
Other Micronesian (25)	28	0.05
Polynesian: (53)	136	0.23
Native Hawaiian (34)	109	0.18
Samoan (19)	24	0.04
Tongan	2	0.00
Other Polynesian	1	0.00
Other Pac. Isl., specified	6	0.01
Other Pac. Isl., not spec. (16)	56	0.09
Hispanic or Latino:	7,351	12.26
Central American:	165	0.28
Costa Rican	22	0.04
Guatemalan	20	0.03
Honduran	8	0.01
Nicaraguan	30	0.05
Panamanian	13	0.02
Salvadoran	57	0.10
Other Central American	15	0.03
Cuban	34	0.06
Dominican Republic	7	0.01
Mexican	5,915	9.87
Puerto Rican	140	0.23
South American:	83	0.14
Argentinean	3	0.01
Bolivian	7	0.01
Chilean	8	0.01
Colombian	24	0.04
Ecuadorian	4	0.01
Paraguayan	1	0.00
Peruvian	17	0.03
Venezuelan	9	0.02
Other South American	6	0.01
Other Hispanic or Latino	1,007	1.68
Hungarian	368	0.62
Icelander	11	0.02
Iranian	28	0.05
Irish	7,437	12.51
Israeli	44	0.07
Italian	3,800	6.39
Latvian	36	0.06
Lithuanian	67	0.11
Maltese	10	0.02
Northern European	134	0.23
Norwegian	1,516	2.55
Pennsylvania German	7	0.01
Polish	913	1.54
Portuguese	918	1.54
Romanian	36	0.06
Russian	517	0.87
Scandinavian	207	0.35
Scotch-Irish	1,295	2.18
Scottish	1,803	3.03
Serbian	23	0.04
Slavic	23	0.04
Slovak	9	0.02
Slovene	8	0.01
Swedish	1,491	2.51
Swiss	250	0.42
Turkish	10	0.02
Ukrainian	119	0.20
United States or American	2,485	4.18
Welsh	663	1.12
West Indian, excl. Hispanic:	14	0.02
Jamaican	14	0.02
White:	51,627	86.11
Not Hispanic (46,258)	47,817	79.76
Hispanic (3,119)	3,810	6.35
Yugoslavian	117	0.20

Chino Hills

Place Type: City
County: San Bernardino
Population: 66,787

Ancestry/Race	Number	%
Acadian/Cajun	18	0.03
Afghan	51	0.08
African American/Black:	4,077	6.10
Not Hispanic (3,573)	3,870	5.79
Hispanic (124)	207	0.31
African, sub-Saharan:	519	0.78
African	216	0.32
Cape Verdean	6	0.01
Ethiopian	121	0.18
Ghanian	29	0.04
Kenyan	8	0.01
Nigerian	130	0.19
Other sub-Saharan African	9	0.01
Alaska Native tribes, specified:	2	0.00
Eskimo (1)	1	0.00
Tlingit-Haida (1)	1	0.00
Am. Ind. or Alaska Nat., not spec.	269	0.40
American Indian tribes, specified:	424	0.63
Apache (24)	51	0.08
Blackfeet (15)	31	0.05
Cherokee (32)	101	0.15
Cheyenne (1)	2	0.00
Chickasaw (6)	6	0.01
Chippewa (2)	4	0.01
Choctaw (8)	26	0.04
Comanche (1)	4	0.01
Cree (1)	1	0.00
Creek (1)	2	0.00
Delaware (1)	6	0.01
Iroquois (1)	4	0.01
Kiowa (1)	1	0.00
Latin American Indians (38)	48	0.07
Navajo (18)	26	0.04
Paiute (4)	6	0.01
Potawatomi (3)	5	0.01
Pueblo (12)	19	0.03
Seminole	2	0.00
Shoshone (5)	6	0.01
Sioux (2)	4	0.01
Tohono O'Odham (2)	2	0.00
Yakama (1)	1	0.00
Yaqui (9)	17	0.03
All other tribes (30)	49	0.07
American Indian tribes, not spec.	57	0.09
Arab:	432	0.65
Arab/Arabic	96	0.14
Egyptian	29	0.04
Jordanian	36	0.05
Lebanese	212	0.32
Palestinian	14	0.02
Syrian	7	0.01
Other Arab	38	0.06
Armenian	240	0.36
Asian:	16,655	24.94
Bangladeshi (4)	4	0.01
Cambodian (52)	88	0.13
Chinese, ex. Taiwanese (3,446)	4,007	6.00
Filipino (5,121)	5,738	8.59
Hmong (2)	3	0.00
Indian (1,320)	1,396	2.09
Indonesian (192)	277	0.41
Japanese (666)	1,039	1.56
Korean (1,515)	1,641	2.46
Laotian (29)	40	0.06
Malaysian (4)	15	0.02
Pakistani (169)	241	0.36
Sri Lankan (14)	15	0.02
Taiwanese (586)	693	1.04
Thai (241)	283	0.42
Vietnamese (799)	889	1.33
Other Asian, specified (28)	50	0.07
Other Asian, not specified (107)	236	0.35
Assyrian/Chaldean/Syriac	48	0.07
Australian	9	0.01
Austrian	192	0.29
Basque	68	0.10
Belgian	49	0.07
British	278	0.42
Canadian	131	0.20
Celtic	9	0.01
Croatian	92	0.14
Czech	263	0.39
Czechoslovakian	136	0.20
Danish	376	0.56
Dutch	1,179	1.77
Eastern European	18	0.03
English	5,061	7.59
Estonian	8	0.01
European	527	0.79
Finnish	26	0.04
French, except Basque	1,725	2.59
French Canadian	281	0.42
German	7,555	11.32
Greek	342	0.51
Guyanese	25	0.04
Hawaii Native/Pacific Islander:	251	0.38
Melanesian: (2)	4	0.01
Fijian (2)	4	0.01
Micronesian: (28)	40	0.06
Guamanian/Chamorro (28)	40	0.06
Polynesian: (43)	120	0.18
Native Hawaiian (19)	83	0.12
Samoan (14)	24	0.04
Tongan (8)	9	0.01
Other Polynesian (2)	4	0.01
Other Pac. Isl., specified	1	0.00
Other Pac. Isl., not spec. (11)	86	0.13
Hispanic or Latino:	17,151	25.68
Central American:	551	0.83
Costa Rican	36	0.05
Guatemalan	112	0.17
Honduran	29	0.04
Nicaraguan	92	0.14
Panamanian	9	0.01
Salvadoran	211	0.32
Other Central American	62	0.09
Cuban	308	0.46
Dominican Republic	19	0.03
Mexican	12,923	19.35
Puerto Rican	305	0.46
South American:	568	0.85
Argentinean	105	0.16
Bolivian	16	0.02
Chilean	56	0.08
Colombian	137	0.21
Ecuadorian	96	0.14
Paraguayan	3	0.00
Peruvian	63	0.09
Uruguayan	8	0.01
Venezuelan	17	0.03
Other South American	67	0.10
Other Hispanic or Latino	2,477	3.71
Hungarian	248	0.37
Iranian	173	0.26
Irish	5,598	8.39
Italian	3,210	4.81
Latvian	9	0.01
Lithuanian	98	0.15
Maltese	18	0.03
Northern European	49	0.07
Norwegian	1,062	1.59
Pennsylvania German	15	0.02
Polish	1,032	1.55
Portuguese	179	0.27
Romanian	94	0.14
Russian	725	1.09
Scandinavian	51	0.08
Scotch-Irish	656	0.98
Scottish	925	1.39
Serbian	12	0.02
Slavic	36	0.05
Slovak	58	0.09
Swedish	943	1.41

Notes: 1. Figures in the "Number" column do not add up to the total population due to: a) Ancestry/Race overlap — e.g. persons can report being both White and Irish, b) persons of Hispanic origin can report being any race, c) persons reporting two ancestries are counted in both categories. 2. Numbers in parentheses indicate the number of persons reporting this ancestry/race alone, not in combination with any other ancestry/race. 3. Refer to the Explanation of Data in the front of the book for more detailed information.

Swiss	175	0.26
Ukrainian	119	0.18
United States or American	2,129	3.19
Welsh	385	0.58
West Indian, excl. Hispanic:	111	0.17
Belizean	25	0.04
Haitian	28	0.04
Jamaican	58	0.09
White:	40,228	60.23
Not Hispanic (29,247)	30,668	45.92
Hispanic (8,409)	9,560	14.31
Yugoslavian	56	0.08

Chino

Place Type: City
County: San Bernardino
Population: 67,168

Ancestry/Race	Number	%
African American/Black:	5,575	8.30
Not Hispanic (5,100)	5,325	7.93
Hispanic (150)	250	0.37
African, sub-Saharan:	353	0.52
African	111	0.16
Cape Verdean	9	0.01
Ethiopian	39	0.06
Kenyan	23	0.03
Nigerian	143	0.21
Senegalese	8	0.01
South African	14	0.02
Other sub-Saharan African	6	0.01
Alaska Native tribes, specified:	13	0.02
Alaska Athabascan (1)	1	0.00
Aleut	3	0.00
Tlingit-Haida (4)	9	0.01
Am. Ind. or Alaska Nat., not spec.	452	0.67
Albanian	37	0.05
American Indian tribes, specified:	646	0.96
Apache (28)	53	0.08
Blackfeet (1)	17	0.03
Cherokee (23)	124	0.18
Cheyenne (2)	6	0.01
Chickasaw (3)	4	0.01
Chippewa (7)	13	0.02
Choctaw (11)	24	0.04
Comanche	3	0.00
Creek	7	0.01
Crow	6	0.01
Delaware (1)	2	0.00
Iroquois (1)	4	0.01
Kiowa	3	0.00
Latin American Indians (79)	138	0.21
Navajo (21)	36	0.05
Osage	2	0.00
Ottawa	2	0.00
Paiute	1	0.00
Pima (2)	9	0.01
Potawatomi (1)	1	0.00
Pueblo (8)	25	0.04
Shoshone (6)	11	0.02
Sioux (5)	15	0.02
Ute (1)	6	0.01
Yakama (1)	3	0.00
Yaqui (16)	27	0.04
Yuman (1)	2	0.00
All other tribes (79)	102	0.15
American Indian tribes, not spec.	69	0.10
Arab:	252	0.37
Arab/Arabic	89	0.13
Egyptian	24	0.04
Jordanian	10	0.01
Lebanese	129	0.19
Armenian	77	0.11
Asian:	4,127	6.14
Bangladeshi (4)	4	0.01
Cambodian (25)	29	0.04
Chinese, ex. Taiwanese (465)	641	0.95
Filipino (1,250)	1,532	2.28
Hmong (2)	2	0.00
Indian (326)	382	0.57
Indonesian (55)	99	0.15
Japanese (223)	360	0.54
Korean (234)	275	0.41
Laotian (15)	19	0.03
Malaysian (1)	1	0.00
Pakistani (16)	49	0.07
Sri Lankan (15)	26	0.04
Taiwanese (98)	122	0.18
Thai (56)	69	0.10
Vietnamese (352)	389	0.58
Other Asian, specified (7)	7	0.01
Other Asian, not specified (71)	121	0.18
Australian	46	0.07
Austrian	97	0.14
Basque	133	0.20
Belgian	28	0.04
Brazilian	6	0.01
British	182	0.27
Bulgarian	50	0.07
Canadian	271	0.40
Croatian	50	0.07
Czech	103	0.15
Czechoslovakian	71	0.11
Danish	149	0.22
Dutch	1,595	2.36
Eastern European	62	0.09
English	3,615	5.35
European	317	0.47
Finnish	22	0.03
French, except Basque	1,371	2.03
French Canadian	256	0.38
German	5,668	8.38
Greek	131	0.19
Hawaii Native/Pacific Islander:	315	0.47
Micronesian: (18)	23	0.03
Guamanian/Chamorro (18)	23	0.03
Polynesian: (95)	182	0.27
Native Hawaiian (33)	89	0.13
Samoan (52)	75	0.11
Tongan (8)	15	0.02
Other Polynesian (2)	3	0.00
Other Pac. Isl., not spec. (25)	110	0.16
Hispanic or Latino:	31,830	47.39
Central American:	727	1.08
Costa Rican	33	0.05
Guatemalan	190	0.28
Honduran	33	0.05
Nicaraguan	115	0.17
Panamanian	11	0.02
Salvadoran	276	0.41
Other Central American	69	0.10
Cuban	237	0.35
Dominican Republic	4	0.01
Mexican	26,232	39.05
Puerto Rican	247	0.37
South American:	465	0.69
Argentinean	150	0.22
Bolivian	8	0.01
Chilean	17	0.03
Colombian	119	0.18
Ecuadorian	51	0.08
Paraguayan	4	0.01
Peruvian	76	0.11
Uruguayan	1	0.00
Venezuelan	8	0.01
Other South American	31	0.05
Other Hispanic or Latino	3,918	5.83
Hungarian	185	0.27
Icelander	10	0.01
Iranian	8	0.01
Irish	3,835	5.67
Israeli	6	0.01
Italian	2,571	3.80
Lithuanian	99	0.15
Macedonian	25	0.04
Northern European	20	0.03
Norwegian	671	0.99
Pennsylvania German	13	0.02
Polish	874	1.29
Portuguese	895	1.32
Romanian	27	0.04
Russian	154	0.23
Scandinavian	97	0.14
Scotch-Irish	634	0.94
Scottish	713	1.05
Serbian	8	0.01
Slavic	21	0.03
Slovak	31	0.05
Swedish	700	1.04
Swiss	176	0.26
Ukrainian	82	0.12
United States or American	1,885	2.79
Welsh	230	0.34
West Indian, excl. Hispanic:	100	0.15
Belizean	28	0.04
British West Indian	12	0.02
Haitian	26	0.04
Jamaican	8	0.01
Trinidadian and Tobagonian	26	0.04
White:	40,185	59.83
Not Hispanic (25,267)	26,320	39.19
Hispanic (12,145)	13,865	20.64
Yugoslavian	49	0.07

Chowchilla

Place Type: City
County: Madera
Population: 11,127

Ancestry/Race	Number	%
African American/Black:	1,270	11.41
Not Hispanic (1,087)	1,184	10.64
Hispanic (55)	86	0.77
African, sub-Saharan:	138	1.24
African	131	1.17
Other sub-Saharan African	7	0.06
Alaska Native tribes, specified:	4	0.04
Aleut	3	0.03
Eskimo	1	0.01
Am. Ind. or Alaska Nat., not spec.	131	1.18
American Indian tribes, specified:	389	3.50
Apache (7)	23	0.21
Blackfeet (8)	22	0.20
Cherokee (55)	126	1.13
Cheyenne (1)	2	0.02
Chickasaw (1)	4	0.04
Chippewa (1)	3	0.03
Choctaw (17)	40	0.36
Comanche	1	0.01
Cree (1)	1	0.01
Creek (5)	8	0.07
Crow	1	0.01
Delaware (3)	6	0.05
Iroquois (3)	5	0.04
Latin American Indians (28)	36	0.32
Navajo (1)	1	0.01
Paiute (2)	3	0.03
Pima	1	0.01
Potawatomi (5)	9	0.08
Pueblo	1	0.01
Seminole	3	0.03
Shoshone (2)	2	0.02
Sioux (8)	10	0.09
Ute (1)	2	0.02
Yaqui (3)	8	0.07
Yuman (1)	2	0.02
All other tribes (48)	69	0.62
American Indian tribes, not spec.	39	0.35
Arab:	67	0.60
Arab/Arabic	43	0.39
Egyptian	6	0.05
Moroccan	5	0.04
Syrian	13	0.12
Armenian	15	0.13
Asian:	272	2.44
Cambodian (4)	4	0.04
Chinese, ex. Taiwanese (21)	33	0.30
Filipino (32)	89	0.80

Notes: 1. Figures in the "Number" column do not add up to the total population due to: a) Ancestry/Race overlap — e.g. persons can report being both White and Irish, b) persons of Hispanic origin can report being any race, c) persons reporting two ancestries are counted in both categories. 2. Numbers in parentheses indicate the number of persons reporting this ancestry/race alone, not in combination with any other ancestry/race. 3. Refer to the Explanation of Data in the front of the book for more detailed information.

Ancestry/Race	Number	%
Indian (58)	89	0.80
Japanese (6)	17	0.15
Korean (9)	11	0.10
Laotian (4)	4	0.04
Sri Lankan (1)	1	0.01
Thai	1	0.01
Vietnamese (6)	7	0.06
Other Asian, specified	1	0.01
Other Asian, not specified (1)	15	0.13
Austrian	6	0.05
Basque	5	0.04
Brazilian	14	0.13
British	31	0.28
Canadian	8	0.07
Celtic	14	0.13
Czechoslovakian	8	0.07
Danish	7	0.06
Dutch	136	1.22
English	729	6.53
European	11	0.10
French, except Basque	233	2.09
French Canadian	11	0.10
German	783	7.01
Greek	37	0.33
Hawaii Native/Pacific Islander:	89	0.80
Melanesian:	1	0.01
Fijian	1	0.01
Micronesian: (2)	5	0.04
Guamanian/Chamorro (2)	5	0.04
Polynesian: (21)	49	0.44
Native Hawaiian (11)	27	0.24
Samoan (10)	21	0.19
Tongan	1	0.01
Other Pac. Isl., not spec. (5)	34	0.31
Hispanic or Latino:	3,138	28.20
Central American:	22	0.20
Costa Rican	3	0.03
Guatemalan	2	0.02
Honduran	1	0.01
Nicaraguan	7	0.06
Panamanian	2	0.02
Salvadoran	6	0.05
Other Central American	1	0.01
Cuban	14	0.13
Mexican	2,558	22.99
Puerto Rican	80	0.72
South American:	11	0.10
Argentinean	1	0.01
Chilean	1	0.01
Colombian	6	0.05
Peruvian	2	0.02
Venezuelan	1	0.01
Other Hispanic or Latino	453	4.07
Hungarian	5	0.04
Irish	902	8.08
Italian	237	2.12
Norwegian	45	0.40
Polish	25	0.22
Portuguese	406	3.64
Romanian	16	0.14
Russian	17	0.15
Scandinavian	23	0.21
Scotch-Irish	42	0.38
Scottish	74	0.66
Swedish	68	0.61
Swiss	14	0.13
United States or American	697	6.24
Welsh	4	0.04
West Indian, excl. Hispanic:	28	0.25
Dutch West Indian	7	0.06
Haitian	7	0.06
Jamaican	7	0.06
Trinidadian and Tobagonian	7	0.06
White:	7,573	68.06
Not Hispanic (6,129)	6,423	57.72
Hispanic (932)	1,150	10.34

Chula Vista

Place Type: City
County: San Diego
Population: 173,556

Ancestry/Race	Number	%
Acadian/Cajun	26	0.01
Afghan	24	0.01
African American/Black:	9,457	5.45
Not Hispanic (7,517)	8,513	4.91
Hispanic (505)	944	0.54
African, sub-Saharan:	631	0.36
African	543	0.31
Cape Verdean	30	0.02
Nigerian	40	0.02
Somalian	4	0.00
Zimbabwean	6	0.00
Other sub-Saharan African	8	0.00
Alaska Native tribes, specified:	38	0.02
Alaska Athabascan (3)	9	0.01
Aleut (1)	7	0.00
Eskimo (7)	13	0.01
Tlingit-Haida (5)	8	0.00
All other tribes (1)	1	0.00
Alaska Native tribes, not specified	3	0.00
Am. Ind. or Alaska Nat., not spec.	879	0.51
Albanian	12	0.01
American Indian tribes, specified:	1,506	0.87
Apache (37)	80	0.05
Blackfeet (11)	56	0.03
Cherokee (89)	335	0.19
Cheyenne (3)	7	0.00
Chickasaw (14)	36	0.02
Chippewa (10)	23	0.01
Choctaw (31)	89	0.05
Comanche (1)	6	0.00
Cree (2)	5	0.00
Creek (5)	10	0.01
Crow (6)	7	0.00
Delaware (1)	4	0.00
Houma (1)	1	0.00
Iroquois (12)	37	0.02
Kiowa (1)	1	0.00
Latin American Indians (202)	310	0.18
Lumbee (4)	4	0.00
Navajo (55)	89	0.05
Osage (10)	18	0.01
Ottawa (3)	3	0.00
Paiute	2	0.00
Pima (3)	6	0.00
Potawatomi (1)	4	0.00
Pueblo (11)	21	0.01
Puget Sound Salish (3)	3	0.00
Seminole (5)	9	0.01
Shoshone (2)	5	0.00
Sioux (14)	50	0.03
Tohono O'Odham (4)	5	0.00
Ute (1)	5	0.00
Yakama (1)	1	0.00
Yaqui (35)	66	0.04
Yuman (7)	11	0.01
All other tribes (121)	197	0.11
American Indian tribes, not spec.	145	0.08
Arab:	1,180	0.68
Arab/Arabic	269	0.15
Egyptian	44	0.03
Iraqi	113	0.06
Jordanian	84	0.05
Lebanese	268	0.15
Moroccan	44	0.03
Palestinian	75	0.04
Syrian	131	0.08
Other Arab	152	0.09
Armenian	81	0.05
Asian:	23,250	13.40
Bangladeshi (13)	13	0.01
Cambodian (35)	42	0.02
Chinese, ex. Taiwanese (1,035)	1,526	0.88
Filipino (12,588)	15,001	8.64
Hmong (1)	3	0.00
Indian (340)	448	0.26
Indonesian (18)	40	0.02
Japanese (2,364)	3,252	1.87
Korean (1,544)	1,723	0.99
Laotian (39)	49	0.03
Malaysian (8)	38	0.02
Pakistani (45)	52	0.03
Sri Lankan (10)	12	0.01
Taiwanese (89)	111	0.06
Thai (49)	82	0.05
Vietnamese (457)	535	0.31
Other Asian, specified (13)	26	0.01
Other Asian, not specified (98)	297	0.17
Assyrian/Chaldean/Syriac	64	0.04
Australian	45	0.03
Austrian	195	0.11
Basque	80	0.05
Belgian	110	0.06
Brazilian	137	0.08
British	583	0.34
Canadian	314	0.18
Celtic	15	0.01
Croatian	113	0.06
Cypriot	20	0.01
Czech	178	0.10
Czechoslovakian	165	0.09
Danish	871	0.50
Dutch	1,580	0.91
Eastern European	32	0.02
English	8,910	5.12
European	1,435	0.83
Finnish	237	0.14
French, except Basque	3,460	1.99
French Canadian	696	0.40
German	12,545	7.22
German Russian	15	0.01
Greek	356	0.20
Guyanese	19	0.01
Hawaii Native/Pacific Islander:	1,872	1.08
Melanesian: (4)	7	0.00
Fijian (1)	4	0.00
Other Melanesian (3)	3	0.00
Micronesian: (546)	880	0.51
Guamanian/Chamorro (507)	838	0.48
Other Micronesian (39)	42	0.02
Polynesian: (376)	770	0.44
Native Hawaiian (179)	470	0.27
Samoan (160)	235	0.14
Tongan (34)	50	0.03
Other Polynesian (3)	15	0.01
Other Pac. Isl., specified	8	0.00
Other Pac. Isl., not spec. (63)	207	0.12
Hispanic or Latino:	86,073	49.59
Central American:	748	0.43
Costa Rican	75	0.04
Guatemalan	138	0.08
Honduran	59	0.03
Nicaraguan	80	0.05
Panamanian	121	0.07
Salvadoran	199	0.11
Other Central American	76	0.04
Cuban	306	0.18
Dominican Republic	51	0.03
Mexican	74,867	43.14
Puerto Rican	1,421	0.82
South American:	781	0.45
Argentinean	123	0.07
Bolivian	31	0.02
Chilean	64	0.04
Colombian	223	0.13
Ecuadorian	61	0.04
Peruvian	173	0.10
Uruguayan	8	0.00
Venezuelan	34	0.02
Other South American	64	0.04
Other Hispanic or Latino	7,899	4.55
Hungarian	451	0.26
Icelander	3	0.00
Iranian	293	0.17

Notes: 1. Figures in the "Number" column do not add up to the total population due to: a) Ancestry/Race overlap — e.g. persons can report being both White and Irish, b) persons of Hispanic origin can report being any race, c) persons reporting two ancestries are counted in both categories. 2. Numbers in parentheses indicate the number of persons reporting this ancestry/race alone, not in combination with any other ancestry/race. 3. Refer to the Explanation of Data in the front of the book for more detailed information.

Ancestry/Race	Number	%
Irish	10,266	5.90
Israeli	30	0.02
Italian	4,440	2.55
Latvian	22	0.01
Lithuanian	218	0.13
Luxemburger	13	0.01
Maltese	45	0.03
Northern European	15	0.01
Norwegian	2,004	1.15
Pennsylvania German	34	0.02
Polish	2,226	1.28
Portuguese	537	0.31
Romanian	100	0.06
Russian	667	0.38
Scandinavian	271	0.16
Scotch-Irish	1,588	0.91
Scottish	2,031	1.17
Serbian	80	0.05
Slavic	52	0.03
Slovak	109	0.06
Slovene	38	0.02
Swedish	1,635	0.94
Swiss	261	0.15
Turkish	155	0.09
Ukrainian	219	0.13
United States or American	4,840	2.78
Welsh	664	0.38
West Indian, excl. Hispanic:	313	0.18
Bahamian	4	0.00
Barbadian	9	0.01
Belizean	10	0.01
Dutch West Indian	11	0.01
Haitian	50	0.03
Jamaican	140	0.08
Trinidadian and Tobagonian	25	0.01
West Indian	64	0.04
White:	103,924	59.88
Not Hispanic (55,042)	58,878	33.92
Hispanic (40,511)	45,046	25.95
Yugoslavian	104	0.06

Citrus

Place Type: Census Designated Place
County: Los Angeles
Population: 10,581

Ancestry/Race	Number	%
African American/Black:	413	3.90
Not Hispanic (305)	344	3.25
Hispanic (38)	69	0.65
African, sub-Saharan:	18	0.17
African	18	0.17
Am. Ind. or Alaska Nat., not spec.	119	1.12
American Indian tribes, specified:	105	0.99
Apache (2)	7	0.07
Blackfeet (4)	5	0.05
Cherokee (13)	24	0.23
Chickasaw (1)	1	0.01
Chippewa (4)	6	0.06
Choctaw (1)	2	0.02
Delaware	1	0.01
Iroquois	5	0.05
Latin American Indians (17)	25	0.24
Navajo (2)	3	0.03
Pima	2	0.02
Pueblo	1	0.01
Sioux	4	0.04
Ute	2	0.02
Yaqui (6)	6	0.06
All other tribes (5)	11	0.10
American Indian tribes, not spec.	13	0.12
Arab:	27	0.25
Egyptian	27	0.25
Armenian	9	0.08
Asian:	865	8.18
Chinese, ex. Taiwanese (65)	101	0.95
Filipino (357)	414	3.91
Indian (55)	74	0.70
Indonesian (27)	37	0.35
Japanese (61)	83	0.78
Korean (13)	13	0.12
Laotian (1)	5	0.05
Pakistani (1)	1	0.01
Taiwanese (14)	21	0.20
Thai (27)	45	0.43
Vietnamese (49)	59	0.56
Other Asian, not specified (8)	12	0.11
Austrian	6	0.06
Belgian	9	0.08
Canadian	24	0.23
Czech	5	0.05
Danish	23	0.22
Dutch	21	0.20
English	352	3.31
European	32	0.30
Finnish	40	0.38
French, except Basque	160	1.50
French Canadian	63	0.59
German	564	5.30
Greek	24	0.23
Hawaii Native/Pacific Islander:	19	0.18
Polynesian: (2)	7	0.07
Native Hawaiian (1)	6	0.06
Samoan (1)	1	0.01
Other Pac. Isl., not spec. (3)	12	0.11
Hispanic or Latino:	6,861	64.84
Central American:	250	2.36
Costa Rican	17	0.16
Guatemalan	43	0.41
Honduran	10	0.09
Nicaraguan	37	0.35
Panamanian	5	0.05
Salvadoran	90	0.85
Other Central American	48	0.45
Cuban	37	0.35
Mexican	5,500	51.98
Puerto Rican	93	0.88
South American:	81	0.77
Argentinean	19	0.18
Chilean	5	0.05
Colombian	14	0.13
Ecuadorian	20	0.19
Peruvian	22	0.21
Other South American	1	0.01
Other Hispanic or Latino	900	8.51
Hungarian	67	0.63
Irish	488	4.58
Italian	220	2.07
Norwegian	24	0.23
Polish	53	0.50
Portuguese	13	0.12
Romanian	6	0.06
Russian	89	0.84
Scandinavian	24	0.23
Scotch-Irish	96	0.90
Scottish	216	2.03
Slavic	8	0.08
Slovene	6	0.06
Swedish	62	0.58
Swiss	6	0.06
United States or American	367	3.45
Welsh	54	0.51
West Indian, excl. Hispanic:	32	0.30
Barbadian	12	0.11
Jamaican	20	0.19
White:	5,969	56.41
Not Hispanic (2,515)	2,645	25.00
Hispanic (3,027)	3,324	31.41
Yugoslavian	12	0.11

Citrus Heights

Place Type: City
County: Sacramento
Population: 85,071

Ancestry/Race	Number	%
Afghan	9	0.01
African American/Black:	3,131	3.68
Not Hispanic (2,334)	2,916	3.43
Hispanic (108)	215	0.25
African, sub-Saharan:	353	0.41
African	267	0.31
Nigerian	32	0.04
Sierra Leonean	5	0.01
South African	49	0.06
Alaska Native tribes, specified:	20	0.02
Alaska Athabascan	1	0.00
Aleut (1)	1	0.00
Eskimo (6)	6	0.01
Tlingit-Haida (10)	12	0.01
Alaska Native tribes, not specified	1	0.00
Am. Ind. or Alaska Nat., not spec.	538	0.63
American Indian tribes, specified:	1,634	1.92
Apache (31)	81	0.10
Blackfeet (20)	79	0.09
Cherokee (151)	597	0.70
Cheyenne (3)	8	0.01
Chickasaw (9)	31	0.04
Chippewa (18)	43	0.05
Choctaw (29)	84	0.10
Comanche (1)	5	0.01
Cree (3)	9	0.01
Creek (7)	20	0.02
Crow (5)	9	0.01
Delaware (1)	2	0.00
Houma (3)	3	0.00
Iroquois (15)	35	0.04
Kiowa (1)	3	0.00
Latin American Indians (48)	90	0.11
Lumbee	1	0.00
Menominee (1)	1	0.00
Navajo (18)	35	0.04
Osage	8	0.01
Ottawa (1)	5	0.01
Paiute (7)	19	0.02
Pima	2	0.00
Potawatomi (4)	13	0.02
Pueblo (10)	18	0.02
Puget Sound Salish (5)	5	0.01
Seminole (1)	12	0.01
Shoshone (4)	11	0.01
Sioux (28)	60	0.07
Tohono O'Odham (2)	7	0.01
Yakama (1)	1	0.00
Yaqui (9)	24	0.03
Yuman	2	0.00
All other tribes (158)	311	0.37
American Indian tribes, not spec.	82	0.10
Arab:	274	0.32
Arab/Arabic	68	0.08
Lebanese	63	0.07
Moroccan	28	0.03
Palestinian	36	0.04
Syrian	40	0.05
Other Arab	39	0.05
Armenian	125	0.15
Asian:	3,709	4.36
Bangladeshi	3	0.00
Cambodian (19)	21	0.02
Chinese, ex. Taiwanese (278)	452	0.53
Filipino (696)	1,162	1.37
Hmong (19)	20	0.02
Indian (319)	420	0.49
Indonesian (5)	23	0.03
Japanese (343)	664	0.78
Korean (244)	329	0.39
Laotian (88)	96	0.11
Malaysian (1)	3	0.00
Pakistani (18)	20	0.02
Sri Lankan (7)	7	0.01
Taiwanese (10)	15	0.02
Thai (38)	63	0.07
Vietnamese (251)	300	0.35
Other Asian, specified (5)	10	0.01
Other Asian, not specified (41)	101	0.12
Australian	42	0.05
Austrian	214	0.25
Basque	26	0.03

Notes: 1. Figures in the "Number" column do not add up to the total population due to: a) Ancestry/Race overlap — e.g. persons can report being both White and Irish, b) persons of Hispanic origin can report being any race, c) persons reporting two ancestries are counted in both categories. 2. Numbers in parentheses indicate the number of persons reporting this ancestry/race alone, not in combination with any other ancestry/race. 3. Refer to the Explanation of Data in the front of the book for more detailed information.

Belgian	50	0.06
Brazilian	9	0.01
British	293	0.34
Canadian	478	0.56
Carpatho Rusyn	12	0.01
Celtic	19	0.02
Croatian	108	0.13
Czech	285	0.33
Czechoslovakian	145	0.17
Danish	909	1.07
Dutch	1,800	2.11
Eastern European	19	0.02
English	10,467	12.28
European	1,006	1.18
Finnish	203	0.24
French, except Basque	3,497	4.10
French Canadian	563	0.66
German	16,152	18.95
Greek	474	0.56
Hawaii Native/Pacific Islander:	621	0.73
Melanesian: (17)	19	0.02
Fijian (17)	19	0.02
Micronesian: (78)	130	0.15
Guamanian/Chamorro (74)	122	0.14
Other Micronesian (4)	8	0.01
Polynesian: (140)	319	0.37
Native Hawaiian (84)	238	0.28
Samoan (46)	70	0.08
Tongan (4)	5	0.01
Other Polynesian (6)	6	0.01
Other Pac. Isl., not spec. (46)	153	0.18
Hispanic or Latino:	8,539	10.04
Central American:	282	0.33
Costa Rican	8	0.01
Guatemalan	76	0.09
Honduran	26	0.03
Nicaraguan	33	0.04
Panamanian	36	0.04
Salvadoran	78	0.09
Other Central American	25	0.03
Cuban	67	0.08
Dominican Republic	2	0.00
Mexican	5,882	6.91
Puerto Rican	349	0.41
South American:	168	0.20
Argentinean	15	0.02
Bolivian	9	0.01
Chilean	24	0.03
Colombian	38	0.04
Ecuadorian	2	0.00
Peruvian	42	0.05
Uruguayan	5	0.01
Venezuelan	10	0.01
Other South American	23	0.03
Other Hispanic or Latino	1,789	2.10
Hungarian	493	0.58
Icelander	9	0.01
Iranian	394	0.46
Irish	11,262	13.21
Israeli	8	0.01
Italian	4,505	5.29
Latvian	28	0.03
Lithuanian	117	0.14
Luxemburger	8	0.01
Maltese	13	0.02
New Zealander	19	0.02
Northern European	73	0.09
Norwegian	1,887	2.21
Pennsylvania German	50	0.06
Polish	1,474	1.73
Portuguese	1,423	1.67
Romanian	662	0.78
Russian	1,094	1.28
Scandinavian	230	0.27
Scotch-Irish	2,086	2.45
Scottish	2,469	2.90
Serbian	41	0.05
Slavic	78	0.09
Slovak	68	0.08
Slovene	34	0.04
Swedish	1,887	2.21
Swiss	490	0.57
Turkish	17	0.02
Ukrainian	1,212	1.42
United States or American	5,346	6.27
Welsh	834	0.98
West Indian, excl. Hispanic:	61	0.07
Bahamian	6	0.01
Belizean	8	0.01
Bermudan	9	0.01
British West Indian	6	0.01
Jamaican	25	0.03
Trinidadian and Tobagonian	7	0.01
White:	75,634	88.91
Not Hispanic (67,809)	70,514	82.89
Hispanic (4,192)	5,120	6.02
Yugoslavian	246	0.29

Claremont

Place Type: City
County: Los Angeles
Population: 33,998

Ancestry/Race	Number	%
Afghan	37	0.11
African American/Black:	1,961	5.77
Not Hispanic (1,642)	1,882	5.54
Hispanic (50)	79	0.23
African, sub-Saharan:	212	0.62
African	141	0.41
Ethiopian	25	0.07
Kenyan	19	0.06
Nigerian	7	0.02
South African	15	0.04
Zimbabwean	5	0.01
Alaska Native tribes, specified:	1	0.00
Aleut	1	0.00
Alaska Native tribes, not specified	1	0.00
Am. Ind. or Alaska Nat., not spec.	143	0.42
American Indian tribes, specified:	283	0.83
Apache (6)	12	0.04
Blackfeet (1)	12	0.04
Cherokee (13)	66	0.19
Cheyenne	1	0.00
Chickasaw (2)	2	0.01
Chippewa (2)	10	0.03
Choctaw (5)	18	0.05
Colville (1)	1	0.00
Comanche (5)	6	0.02
Cree (7)	10	0.03
Creek	3	0.01
Iroquois (1)	8	0.02
Latin American Indians (17)	26	0.08
Menominee	1	0.00
Navajo (4)	8	0.02
Osage	4	0.01
Ottawa	5	0.01
Potawatomi	4	0.01
Pueblo (3)	8	0.02
Seminole	1	0.00
Sioux (2)	5	0.01
Tohono O'Odham	1	0.00
Ute (1)	3	0.01
Yakama (1)	1	0.00
Yuman (5)	5	0.01
All other tribes (45)	62	0.18
American Indian tribes, not spec.	29	0.09
Arab:	284	0.84
Arab/Arabic	62	0.18
Egyptian	66	0.19
Iraqi	16	0.05
Lebanese	23	0.07
Moroccan	10	0.03
Palestinian	16	0.05
Syrian	32	0.09
Other Arab	59	0.17
Armenian	103	0.30
Asian:	4,604	13.54
Bangladeshi (1)	1	0.00
Cambodian (2)	3	0.01
Chinese, ex. Taiwanese (1,205)	1,411	4.15
Filipino (305)	399	1.17
Indian (471)	535	1.57
Indonesian (40)	50	0.15
Japanese (328)	529	1.56
Korean (517)	570	1.68
Laotian (3)	4	0.01
Malaysian (4)	6	0.02
Pakistani (27)	30	0.09
Sri Lankan (23)	26	0.08
Taiwanese (295)	330	0.97
Thai (106)	129	0.38
Vietnamese (292)	315	0.93
Other Asian, specified (15)	30	0.09
Other Asian, not specified (159)	236	0.69
Assyrian/Chaldean/Syriac	17	0.05
Australian	21	0.06
Austrian	118	0.35
Basque	20	0.06
Belgian	55	0.16
Brazilian	8	0.02
British	399	1.17
Bulgarian	22	0.06
Canadian	217	0.64
Celtic	31	0.09
Croatian	54	0.16
Czech	91	0.27
Czechoslovakian	25	0.07
Danish	312	0.92
Dutch	615	1.81
Eastern European	58	0.17
English	4,488	13.21
Estonian	11	0.03
European	550	1.62
Finnish	75	0.22
French, except Basque	970	2.85
French Canadian	273	0.80
German	5,527	16.27
Greek	177	0.52
Hawaii Native/Pacific Islander:	159	0.47
Melanesian: (6)	6	0.02
Fijian (6)	6	0.02
Micronesian: (7)	16	0.05
Guamanian/Chamorro (6)	15	0.04
Other Micronesian (1)	1	0.00
Polynesian: (25)	86	0.25
Native Hawaiian (9)	41	0.12
Samoan (11)	34	0.10
Tongan (4)	9	0.03
Other Polynesian (1)	2	0.01
Other Pac. Isl., specified	5	0.01
Other Pac. Isl., not spec. (6)	46	0.14
Hispanic or Latino:	5,221	15.36
Central American:	204	0.60
Costa Rican	16	0.05
Guatemalan	41	0.12
Honduran	21	0.06
Nicaraguan	28	0.08
Panamanian	7	0.02
Salvadoran	73	0.21
Other Central American	18	0.05
Cuban	149	0.44
Dominican Republic	15	0.04
Mexican	3,624	10.66
Puerto Rican	140	0.41
South American:	234	0.69
Argentinean	59	0.17
Bolivian	3	0.01
Chilean	14	0.04
Colombian	62	0.18
Ecuadorian	21	0.06
Paraguayan	4	0.01
Peruvian	36	0.11
Uruguayan	1	0.00
Venezuelan	12	0.04
Other South American	22	0.06
Other Hispanic or Latino	855	2.51
Hungarian	182	0.54
Icelander	17	0.05

Notes: 1. Figures in the "Number" column do not add up to the total population due to: a) Ancestry/Race overlap — e.g. persons can report being both White and Irish, b) persons of Hispanic origin can report being any race, c) persons reporting two ancestries are counted in both categories. 2. Numbers in parentheses indicate the number of persons reporting this ancestry/race alone, not in combination with any other ancestry/race. 3. Refer to the Explanation of Data in the front of the book for more detailed information.

Ancestry/Race	Number	%
Iranian	205	0.60
Irish	3,024	8.90
Israeli	8	0.02
Italian	1,356	3.99
Latvian	16	0.05
Lithuanian	55	0.16
Luxemburger	37	0.11
Northern European	153	0.45
Norwegian	922	2.71
Pennsylvania German	14	0.04
Polish	837	2.46
Portuguese	204	0.60
Romanian	54	0.16
Russian	611	1.80
Scandinavian	88	0.26
Scotch-Irish	596	1.75
Scottish	1,023	3.01
Serbian	15	0.04
Slavic	7	0.02
Slovak	8	0.02
Slovene	48	0.14
Swedish	1,055	3.10
Swiss	170	0.50
Turkish	31	0.09
Ukrainian	136	0.40
United States or American	822	2.42
Welsh	359	1.06
West Indian, excl. Hispanic:	101	0.30
Belizean	32	0.09
Haitian	35	0.10
Jamaican	17	0.05
West Indian	17	0.05
White:	26,226	77.14
Not Hispanic (22,098)	22,948	67.50
Hispanic (2,885)	3,278	9.64
Yugoslavian	82	0.24

Clayton

Place Type: City
County: Contra Costa
Population: 10,762

Ancestry/Race	Number	%
Afghan	52	0.48
African American/Black:	155	1.44
Not Hispanic (113)	141	1.31
Hispanic (7)	14	0.13
Am. Ind. or Alaska Nat., not spec.	23	0.21
Albanian	8	0.07
American Indian tribes, specified:	68	0.63
Blackfeet	2	0.02
Cherokee (3)	24	0.22
Chickasaw (1)	1	0.01
Chippewa (1)	3	0.03
Choctaw	4	0.04
Creek (1)	1	0.01
Iroquois (1)	1	0.01
Latin American Indians (6)	6	0.06
Navajo (1)	1	0.01
Osage	1	0.01
Paiute (1)	1	0.01
Pueblo	10	0.09
Sioux	1	0.01
Yakama	1	0.01
Yaqui	2	0.02
All other tribes (3)	9	0.08
American Indian tribes, not spec.	3	0.03
Arab:	45	0.42
Egyptian	9	0.08
Lebanese	20	0.19
Syrian	9	0.08
Other Arab	7	0.06
Armenian	24	0.22
Asian:	825	7.67
Chinese, ex. Taiwanese (173)	229	2.13
Filipino (116)	180	1.67
Indian (95)	108	1.00
Indonesian (4)	7	0.07
Japanese (81)	153	1.42
Korean (44)	58	0.54
Laotian (2)	2	0.02
Malaysian	1	0.01
Pakistani (1)	5	0.05
Sri Lankan (4)	8	0.07
Taiwanese (6)	10	0.09
Thai (5)	7	0.07
Vietnamese (11)	13	0.12
Other Asian, specified (1)	7	0.07
Other Asian, not specified (4)	37	0.34
Austrian	57	0.53
Belgian	43	0.40
British	63	0.58
Canadian	63	0.58
Croatian	18	0.17
Czech	70	0.65
Czechoslovakian	25	0.23
Danish	143	1.33
Dutch	125	1.16
English	1,508	13.97
European	303	2.81
Finnish	39	0.36
French, except Basque	388	3.60
French Canadian	40	0.37
German	2,202	20.40
Greek	89	0.82
Hawaii Native/Pacific Islander:	35	0.33
Micronesian: (5)	10	0.09
Guamanian/Chamorro (5)	10	0.09
Polynesian: (5)	16	0.15
Native Hawaiian (4)	13	0.12
Samoan (1)	3	0.03
Other Pac. Isl., not spec. (1)	9	0.08
Hispanic or Latino:	681	6.33
Central American:	37	0.34
Guatemalan	8	0.07
Nicaraguan	11	0.10
Salvadoran	8	0.07
Other Central American	10	0.09
Cuban	15	0.14
Dominican Republic	4	0.04
Mexican	381	3.54
Puerto Rican	23	0.21
South American:	48	0.45
Argentinean	5	0.05
Bolivian	5	0.05
Chilean	8	0.07
Colombian	9	0.08
Ecuadorian	2	0.02
Peruvian	9	0.08
Venezuelan	3	0.03
Other South American	7	0.07
Other Hispanic or Latino	173	1.61
Hungarian	123	1.14
Icelander	21	0.19
Iranian	35	0.32
Irish	1,958	18.14
Italian	1,351	12.52
Latvian	6	0.06
Lithuanian	63	0.58
Maltese	20	0.19
Norwegian	331	3.07
Polish	440	4.08
Portuguese	161	1.49
Romanian	14	0.13
Russian	89	0.82
Scandinavian	12	0.11
Scotch-Irish	168	1.56
Scottish	287	2.66
Serbian	23	0.21
Slavic	13	0.12
Slovak	16	0.15
Slovene	6	0.06
Swedish	342	3.17
Swiss	99	0.92
Turkish	43	0.40
Ukrainian	74	0.69
United States or American	429	3.98
Welsh	150	1.39
White:	9,822	91.27
Not Hispanic (9,000)	9,302	86.43
Hispanic (465)	520	4.83
Yugoslavian	6	0.06

Clearlake

Place Type: City
County: Lake
Population: 13,142

Ancestry/Race	Number	%
Acadian/Cajun	7	0.05
African American/Black:	827	6.29
Not Hispanic (670)	790	6.01
Hispanic (14)	37	0.28
African, sub-Saharan:	32	0.24
African	32	0.24
Alaska Native tribes, specified:	25	0.19
Alaska Athabascan (1)	1	0.01
Aleut (4)	8	0.06
Eskimo (12)	14	0.11
Tlingit-Haida (2)	2	0.02
Alaska Native tribes, not specified	1	0.01
Am. Ind. or Alaska Nat., not spec.	153	1.16
American Indian tribes, specified:	505	3.84
Apache	17	0.13
Blackfeet (17)	39	0.30
Cherokee (52)	165	1.26
Cheyenne	1	0.01
Chickasaw (2)	5	0.04
Chippewa (11)	15	0.11
Choctaw (17)	45	0.34
Comanche	2	0.02
Creek (1)	1	0.01
Crow	1	0.01
Delaware (2)	3	0.02
Iroquois	4	0.03
Kiowa	2	0.02
Latin American Indians (10)	19	0.14
Navajo (2)	16	0.12
Osage (1)	1	0.01
Ottawa (1)	6	0.05
Paiute (1)	3	0.02
Pima (2)	3	0.02
Pueblo (2)	5	0.04
Seminole (1)	1	0.01
Shoshone (1)	1	0.01
Sioux (3)	10	0.08
Yaqui (7)	11	0.08
All other tribes (76)	129	0.98
American Indian tribes, not spec.	39	0.30
Armenian	7	0.05
Asian:	221	1.68
Cambodian (13)	13	0.10
Chinese, ex. Taiwanese (34)	41	0.31
Filipino (41)	72	0.55
Indian (24)	37	0.28
Japanese (27)	37	0.28
Korean (7)	8	0.06
Laotian (1)	6	0.05
Thai (1)	1	0.01
Vietnamese	1	0.01
Other Asian, specified	1	0.01
Other Asian, not specified	4	0.03
Australian	6	0.05
Belgian	12	0.09
Canadian	29	0.22
Croatian	6	0.05
Czech	68	0.52
Czechoslovakian	9	0.07
Danish	94	0.71
Dutch	196	1.49
English	1,333	10.12
European	137	1.04
Finnish	18	0.14
French, except Basque	468	3.55
French Canadian	106	0.80
German	1,976	15.00
Greek	15	0.11
Hawaii Native/Pacific Islander:	67	0.51

Notes: 1. Figures in the "Number" column do not add up to the total population due to: a) Ancestry/Race overlap — e.g. persons can report being both White and Irish, b) persons of Hispanic origin can report being any race, c) persons reporting two ancestries are counted in both categories. 2. Numbers in parentheses indicate the number of persons reporting this ancestry/race alone, not in combination with any other ancestry/race. 3. Refer to the Explanation of Data in the front of the book for more detailed information.

Micronesian: (2)	3	0.02
Guamanian/Chamorro (2)	3	0.02
Polynesian: (17)	55	0.42
Native Hawaiian (16)	48	0.37
Samoan (1)	4	0.03
Other Polynesian	3	0.02
Other Pac. Isl., specified	1	0.01
Other Pac. Isl., not spec. (2)	8	0.06
Hispanic or Latino:	1,449	11.03
Central American:	37	0.28
Costa Rican	2	0.02
Honduran	2	0.02
Nicaraguan	8	0.06
Salvadoran	22	0.17
Other Central American	3	0.02
Cuban	10	0.08
Mexican	1,080	8.22
Puerto Rican	32	0.24
South American:	5	0.04
Chilean	2	0.02
Peruvian	3	0.02
Other Hispanic or Latino	285	2.17
Hungarian	24	0.18
Iranian	10	0.08
Irish	1,775	13.47
Italian	745	5.66
Lithuanian	19	0.14
Norwegian	277	2.10
Polish	188	1.43
Portuguese	241	1.83
Russian	69	0.52
Scandinavian	40	0.30
Scotch-Irish	172	1.31
Scottish	166	1.26
Slavic	9	0.07
Slovak	8	0.06
Slovene	7	0.05
Swedish	330	2.51
Swiss	48	0.36
United States or American	935	7.10
Welsh	85	0.65
White:	11,348	86.35
Not Hispanic (10,086)	10,499	79.89
Hispanic (737)	849	6.46
Yugoslavian	24	0.18

Clovis

Place Type: City
County: Fresno
Population: 68,468

Ancestry/Race	Number	%
Acadian/Cajun	16	0.02
African American/Black:	1,659	2.42
Not Hispanic (1,207)	1,473	2.15
Hispanic (95)	186	0.27
African, sub-Saharan:	84	0.12
African	63	0.09
Nigerian	11	0.02
South African	10	0.01
Alaska Native tribes, specified:	3	0.00
Aleut (2)	3	0.00
Alaska Native tribes, not specified	5	0.01
Am. Ind. or Alaska Nat., not spec.	548	0.80
American Indian tribes, specified:	1,333	1.95
Apache (36)	79	0.12
Blackfeet (3)	22	0.03
Cherokee (163)	416	0.61
Cheyenne	6	0.01
Chickasaw (14)	28	0.04
Chippewa	2	0.00
Choctaw (31)	93	0.14
Comanche (2)	5	0.01
Cree (2)	2	0.00
Creek (13)	25	0.04
Crow (3)	3	0.00
Delaware (1)	1	0.00
Houma	3	0.00
Iroquois (7)	13	0.02
Kiowa (1)	2	0.00
Latin American Indians (51)	79	0.12
Lumbee	3	0.00
Menominee (1)	1	0.00
Navajo (8)	22	0.03
Osage	2	0.00
Paiute (1)	6	0.01
Pima (1)	5	0.01
Potawatomi (6)	13	0.02
Pueblo (5)	11	0.02
Seminole (7)	12	0.02
Shoshone	2	0.00
Sioux (10)	18	0.03
Tohono O'Odham (2)	2	0.00
Ute (1)	2	0.00
Yakama	7	0.01
Yaqui (10)	20	0.03
All other tribes (291)	428	0.63
American Indian tribes, not spec.	105	0.15
Arab:	196	0.29
Arab/Arabic	46	0.07
Lebanese	98	0.14
Palestinian	10	0.01
Syrian	11	0.02
Other Arab	31	0.05
Armenian	684	1.00
Asian:	5,416	7.91
Cambodian (42)	49	0.07
Chinese, ex. Taiwanese (385)	493	0.72
Filipino (598)	825	1.20
Hmong (1,573)	1,728	2.52
Indian (438)	530	0.77
Indonesian (19)	36	0.05
Japanese (513)	779	1.14
Korean (205)	238	0.35
Laotian (163)	195	0.28
Malaysian (1)	1	0.00
Pakistani (22)	25	0.04
Sri Lankan (6)	12	0.02
Taiwanese (8)	9	0.01
Thai (92)	111	0.16
Vietnamese (221)	242	0.35
Other Asian, specified	2	0.00
Other Asian, not specified (80)	141	0.21
Austrian	66	0.10
Basque	140	0.21
Belgian	62	0.09
Brazilian	21	0.03
British	411	0.60
Canadian	251	0.37
Celtic	38	0.06
Czech	146	0.21
Czechoslovakian	126	0.18
Danish	673	0.99
Dutch	1,449	2.12
Eastern European	43	0.06
English	7,008	10.28
European	650	0.95
Finnish	79	0.12
French, except Basque	1,880	2.76
French Canadian	390	0.57
German	10,955	16.06
Greek	207	0.30
Hawaii Native/Pacific Islander:	221	0.32
Melanesian: (6)	7	0.01
Fijian (6)	7	0.01
Micronesian: (24)	34	0.05
Guamanian/Chamorro (24)	34	0.05
Polynesian: (71)	126	0.18
Native Hawaiian (48)	100	0.15
Samoan (22)	25	0.04
Tongan (1)	1	0.00
Other Pac. Isl., specified	1	0.00
Other Pac. Isl., not spec. (7)	53	0.08
Hispanic or Latino:	13,876	20.27
Central American:	143	0.21
Costa Rican	22	0.03
Guatemalan	19	0.03
Honduran	5	0.01
Nicaraguan	14	0.02
Panamanian	11	0.02
Salvadoran	55	0.08
Other Central American	17	0.02
Cuban	39	0.06
Dominican Republic	4	0.01
Mexican	11,442	16.71
Puerto Rican	155	0.23
South American:	116	0.17
Argentinean	7	0.01
Bolivian	10	0.01
Chilean	18	0.03
Colombian	17	0.02
Ecuadorian	16	0.02
Paraguayan	3	0.00
Peruvian	24	0.04
Uruguayan	3	0.00
Venezuelan	9	0.01
Other South American	9	0.01
Other Hispanic or Latino	1,977	2.89
Hungarian	143	0.21
Icelander	6	0.01
Iranian	128	0.19
Irish	7,105	10.42
Italian	3,833	5.62
Lithuanian	24	0.04
Northern European	65	0.10
Norwegian	1,121	1.64
Pennsylvania German	16	0.02
Polish	771	1.13
Portuguese	1,078	1.58
Romanian	57	0.08
Russian	406	0.60
Scandinavian	166	0.24
Scotch-Irish	1,281	1.88
Scottish	1,545	2.27
Serbian	71	0.10
Slavic	18	0.03
Slovak	16	0.02
Slovene	16	0.02
Swedish	1,295	1.90
Swiss	250	0.37
Ukrainian	30	0.04
United States or American	4,041	5.93
Welsh	470	0.69
West Indian, excl. Hispanic:	9	0.01
Dutch West Indian	5	0.01
Haitian	4	0.01
White:	54,626	79.78
Not Hispanic (46,186)	47,870	69.92
Hispanic (5,728)	6,756	9.87
Yugoslavian	181	0.27

Coachella

Place Type: City
County: Riverside
Population: 22,724

Ancestry/Race	Number	%
African American/Black:	133	0.59
Not Hispanic (61)	72	0.32
Hispanic (42)	61	0.27
African, sub-Saharan:	14	0.06
African	4	0.02
Nigerian	10	0.04
Alaska Native tribes, specified:	2	0.01
Eskimo	2	0.01
Am. Ind. or Alaska Nat., not spec.	139	0.61
American Indian tribes, specified:	102	0.45
Cherokee (1)	6	0.03
Choctaw (6)	7	0.03
Houma (3)	3	0.01
Latin American Indians (52)	55	0.24
Paiute	1	0.00
Pima	4	0.02
Tohono O'Odham (1)	1	0.00
Yaqui	8	0.04
All other tribes (12)	17	0.07
American Indian tribes, not spec.	15	0.07
Arab:	23	0.10

Notes: 1. Figures in the "Number" column do not add up to the total population due to: a) Ancestry/Race overlap — e.g. persons can report being both White and Irish, b) persons of Hispanic origin can report being any race, c) persons reporting two ancestries are counted in both categories. 2. Numbers in parentheses indicate the number of persons reporting this ancestry/race alone, not in combination with any other ancestry/race. 3. Refer to the Explanation of Data in the front of the book for more detailed information.

Arab/Arabic	4	0.02
Lebanese	19	0.08
Asian:	141	0.62
Chinese, ex. Taiwanese (5)	6	0.03
Filipino (44)	79	0.35
Hmong (1)	1	0.00
Indian (6)	12	0.05
Indonesian	1	0.00
Japanese (3)	7	0.03
Laotian (7)	10	0.04
Other Asian, not specified (5)	25	0.11
Canadian	5	0.02
Dutch	11	0.05
English	36	0.16
German	40	0.18
Hawaii Native/Pacific Islander:	23	0.10
Micronesian: (1)	1	0.00
Guamanian/Chamorro (1)	1	0.00
Polynesian: (6)	12	0.05
Native Hawaiian (5)	10	0.04
Samoan (1)	2	0.01
Other Pac. Isl., not spec.	10	0.04
Hispanic or Latino:	22,132	97.39
Central American:	118	0.52
Guatemalan	13	0.06
Honduran	5	0.02
Nicaraguan	6	0.03
Salvadoran	89	0.39
Other Central American	5	0.02
Cuban	2	0.01
Mexican	19,824	87.24
Puerto Rican	13	0.06
South American:	2	0.01
Chilean	1	0.00
Colombian	1	0.00
Other Hispanic or Latino	2,173	9.56
Irish	14	0.06
Italian	33	0.15
Norwegian	24	0.11
Scotch-Irish	12	0.05
Swedish	5	0.02
United States or American	353	1.57
White:	9,398	41.36
Not Hispanic (363)	393	1.73
Hispanic (8,447)	9,005	39.63

Coalinga

Place Type: City
County: Fresno
Population: 11,668

Ancestry/Race	Number	%
African American/Black:	318	2.73
Not Hispanic (259)	277	2.37
Hispanic (17)	41	0.35
African, sub-Saharan:	49	0.42
Ghanian	49	0.42
Am. Ind. or Alaska Nat., not spec.	65	0.56
Albanian	6	0.05
American Indian tribes, specified:	222	1.90
Apache (6)	26	0.22
Blackfeet	1	0.01
Cherokee (46)	83	0.71
Chickasaw	1	0.01
Chippewa (1)	2	0.02
Choctaw (18)	28	0.24
Comanche	2	0.02
Cree	1	0.01
Creek (2)	4	0.03
Latin American Indians (11)	16	0.14
Navajo (3)	8	0.07
Osage (1)	3	0.03
Paiute (1)	1	0.01
Potawatomi (4)	6	0.05
Pueblo (2)	4	0.03
Puget Sound Salish (1)	1	0.01
Shoshone	1	0.01
Sioux (3)	5	0.04
Yaqui (13)	14	0.12
All other tribes (6)	15	0.13
American Indian tribes, not spec.	20	0.17
Armenian	5	0.04
Asian:	243	2.08
Cambodian (3)	4	0.03
Chinese, ex. Taiwanese (52)	61	0.52
Filipino (21)	34	0.29
Hmong (10)	10	0.09
Indian (14)	22	0.19
Indonesian (4)	5	0.04
Japanese (35)	41	0.35
Korean (10)	12	0.10
Laotian (1)	1	0.01
Pakistani (12)	12	0.10
Taiwanese (2)	3	0.03
Vietnamese (15)	16	0.14
Other Asian, not specified (12)	22	0.19
Australian	8	0.07
Basque	27	0.23
Belgian	6	0.05
British	17	0.14
Canadian	15	0.13
Celtic	5	0.04
Czech	12	0.10
Danish	45	0.38
Dutch	138	1.18
Eastern European	7	0.06
English	599	5.10
European	80	0.68
Finnish	17	0.14
French, except Basque	109	0.93
French Canadian	11	0.09
German	742	6.32
Greek	10	0.09
Hawaii Native/Pacific Islander:	46	0.39
Micronesian: (1)	2	0.02
Guamanian/Chamorro (1)	2	0.02
Polynesian: (27)	40	0.34
Native Hawaiian (17)	30	0.26
Samoan (10)	10	0.09
Other Pac. Isl., not spec.	4	0.03
Hispanic or Latino:	5,811	49.80
Central American:	71	0.61
Costa Rican	2	0.02
Guatemalan	5	0.04
Honduran	4	0.03
Nicaraguan	3	0.03
Panamanian	2	0.02
Salvadoran	50	0.43
Other Central American	5	0.04
Cuban	3	0.03
Mexican	5,015	42.98
Puerto Rican	23	0.20
South American:	12	0.10
Bolivian	1	0.01
Colombian	3	0.03
Ecuadorian	1	0.01
Paraguayan	1	0.01
Peruvian	6	0.05
Other Hispanic or Latino	687	5.89
Hungarian	15	0.13
Irish	644	5.48
Italian	182	1.55
Norwegian	119	1.01
Polish	64	0.55
Portuguese	132	1.12
Romanian	5	0.04
Russian	49	0.42
Scotch-Irish	124	1.06
Scottish	149	1.27
Swedish	160	1.36
Swiss	29	0.25
United States or American	582	4.96
Welsh	60	0.51
White:	7,174	61.48
Not Hispanic (5,056)	5,224	44.77
Hispanic (1,631)	1,950	16.71

Colton

Place Type: City
County: San Bernardino
Population: 47,662

Ancestry/Race	Number	%
African American/Black:	5,738	12.04
Not Hispanic (5,031)	5,374	11.28
Hispanic (215)	364	0.76
African, sub-Saharan:	419	0.87
African	320	0.67
Ghanian	12	0.02
Liberian	8	0.02
Nigerian	69	0.14
Other sub-Saharan African	10	0.02
Alaska Native tribes, specified:	3	0.01
Eskimo (3)	3	0.01
Am. Ind. or Alaska Nat., not spec.	356	0.75
Albanian	11	0.02
American Indian tribes, specified:	525	1.10
Apache (36)	50	0.10
Blackfeet (4)	21	0.04
Cherokee (39)	97	0.20
Cheyenne (4)	10	0.02
Chippewa (5)	11	0.02
Choctaw (7)	32	0.07
Comanche (2)	2	0.00
Cree	9	0.02
Creek (11)	14	0.03
Iroquois (4)	8	0.02
Kiowa	1	0.00
Latin American Indians (58)	79	0.17
Lumbee	1	0.00
Menominee (1)	1	0.00
Navajo (18)	23	0.05
Osage (1)	2	0.00
Ottawa	1	0.00
Paiute	5	0.01
Pima (15)	15	0.03
Potawatomi (7)	9	0.02
Pueblo (6)	13	0.03
Seminole (2)	2	0.00
Shoshone (1)	4	0.01
Sioux (3)	12	0.03
Tohono O'Odham (8)	9	0.02
Yaqui (7)	24	0.05
Yuman (1)	4	0.01
All other tribes (50)	66	0.14
American Indian tribes, not spec.	73	0.15
Arab:	556	1.16
Arab/Arabic	76	0.16
Egyptian	266	0.55
Jordanian	8	0.02
Lebanese	99	0.21
Palestinian	29	0.06
Syrian	40	0.08
Other Arab	38	0.08
Armenian	8	0.02
Asian:	3,076	6.45
Bangladeshi (7)	9	0.02
Cambodian (71)	96	0.20
Chinese, ex. Taiwanese (246)	364	0.76
Filipino (848)	1,011	2.12
Hmong (7)	7	0.01
Indian (274)	321	0.67
Indonesian (289)	347	0.73
Japanese (69)	120	0.25
Korean (228)	258	0.54
Laotian (11)	12	0.03
Malaysian	8	0.02
Pakistani (20)	26	0.05
Sri Lankan (1)	4	0.01
Taiwanese (15)	23	0.05
Thai (37)	49	0.10
Vietnamese (280)	311	0.65
Other Asian, specified (18)	21	0.04
Other Asian, not specified (37)	89	0.19
Australian	25	0.05
Austrian	33	0.07

Notes: 1. Figures in the "Number" column do not add up to the total population due to: a) Ancestry/Race overlap — e.g. persons can report being both White and Irish, b) persons of Hispanic origin can report being any race, c) persons reporting two ancestries are counted in both categories. 2. Numbers in parentheses indicate the number of persons reporting this ancestry/race alone, not in combination with any other ancestry/race. 3. Refer to the Explanation of Data in the front of the book for more detailed information.

Ancestry/Race	Number	%
Belgian	8	0.02
Brazilian	47	0.10
British	20	0.04
Bulgarian	10	0.02
Carpatho Rusyn	14	0.03
Croatian	9	0.02
Czech	45	0.09
Czechoslovakian	5	0.01
Danish	58	0.12
Dutch	352	0.73
English	1,521	3.17
Estonian	8	0.02
European	108	0.22
Finnish	37	0.08
French, except Basque	605	1.26
French Canadian	124	0.26
German	2,015	4.20
Greek	33	0.07
Guyanese	7	0.01
Hawaii Native/Pacific Islander:	225	0.47
Micronesian: (32)	43	0.09
Guamanian/Chamorro (32)	43	0.09
Polynesian: (64)	122	0.26
Native Hawaiian (29)	78	0.16
Samoan (23)	32	0.07
Tongan (12)	12	0.03
Other Pac. Isl., not spec. (12)	60	0.13
Hispanic or Latino:	28,934	60.71
Central American:	585	1.23
Costa Rican	19	0.04
Guatemalan	156	0.33
Honduran	34	0.07
Nicaraguan	72	0.15
Panamanian	15	0.03
Salvadoran	216	0.45
Other Central American	73	0.15
Cuban	100	0.21
Dominican Republic	6	0.01
Mexican	23,813	49.96
Puerto Rican	318	0.67
South American:	186	0.39
Argentinean	33	0.07
Bolivian	1	0.00
Chilean	15	0.03
Colombian	33	0.07
Ecuadorian	44	0.09
Paraguayan	4	0.01
Peruvian	37	0.08
Venezuelan	6	0.01
Other South American	13	0.03
Other Hispanic or Latino	3,926	8.24
Hungarian	110	0.23
Irish	1,490	3.10
Italian	869	1.81
Lithuanian	28	0.06
Norwegian	298	0.62
Polish	325	0.68
Portuguese	57	0.12
Romanian	38	0.08
Russian	108	0.22
Scotch-Irish	298	0.62
Scottish	315	0.66
Serbian	8	0.02
Slovak	8	0.02
Slovene	17	0.04
Swedish	237	0.49
Swiss	37	0.08
Ukrainian	38	0.08
United States or American	1,046	2.18
Welsh	108	0.22
West Indian, excl. Hispanic:	165	0.34
Bahamian	4	0.01
Belizean	51	0.11
Dutch West Indian	9	0.02
Haitian	4	0.01
Jamaican	26	0.05
Trinidadian and Tobagonian	35	0.07
U.S. Virgin Islander	6	0.01
West Indian	30	0.06
White:	22,237	46.66
Not Hispanic (9,911)	10,594	22.23
Hispanic (10,432)	11,643	24.43
Yugoslavian	24	0.05

Commerce

Place Type: City
County: Los Angeles
Population: 12,568

Ancestry/Race	Number	%
African American/Black:	118	0.94
Not Hispanic (63)	68	0.54
Hispanic (35)	50	0.40
Alaska Native tribes, specified:	2	0.02
Eskimo (1)	2	0.02
Am. Ind. or Alaska Nat., not spec.	103	0.82
American Indian tribes, specified:	133	1.06
Apache (5)	8	0.06
Blackfeet (2)	2	0.02
Cherokee (2)	10	0.08
Creek	2	0.02
Latin American Indians (34)	50	0.40
Navajo (9)	12	0.10
Pima (4)	4	0.03
Pueblo (7)	9	0.07
Seminole	2	0.02
Sioux (3)	6	0.05
Tohono O'Odham (8)	8	0.06
Yaqui (10)	15	0.12
All other tribes (5)	5	0.04
American Indian tribes, not spec.	16	0.13
Arab:	6	0.05
Arab/Arabic	6	0.05
Asian:	173	1.38
Cambodian	1	0.01
Chinese, ex. Taiwanese (27)	29	0.23
Filipino (30)	44	0.35
Indian (38)	45	0.36
Japanese (21)	22	0.18
Korean (8)	11	0.09
Laotian (4)	4	0.03
Thai (5)	5	0.04
Vietnamese	1	0.01
Other Asian, specified	6	0.05
Other Asian, not specified (1)	5	0.04
Dutch	8	0.06
English	48	0.38
European	19	0.15
French, except Basque	38	0.30
German	98	0.78
Greek	5	0.04
Hawaii Native/Pacific Islander:	20	0.16
Micronesian: (1)	1	0.01
Guamanian/Chamorro (1)	1	0.01
Polynesian: (4)	5	0.04
Native Hawaiian (4)	5	0.04
Other Pac. Isl., specified	6	0.05
Other Pac. Isl., not spec. (5)	8	0.06
Hispanic or Latino:	11,765	93.61
Central American:	419	3.33
Costa Rican	16	0.13
Guatemalan	80	0.64
Honduran	27	0.21
Nicaraguan	40	0.32
Panamanian	1	0.01
Salvadoran	210	1.67
Other Central American	45	0.36
Cuban	64	0.51
Dominican Republic	3	0.02
Mexican	9,941	79.10
Puerto Rican	37	0.29
South American:	54	0.43
Argentinean	6	0.05
Bolivian	1	0.01
Chilean	5	0.04
Colombian	13	0.10
Ecuadorian	7	0.06
Peruvian	12	0.10
Venezuelan	2	0.02
Other South American	8	0.06
Other Hispanic or Latino	1,247	9.92
Hungarian	55	0.44
Irish	100	0.79
Italian	42	0.33
Norwegian	11	0.09
Polish	30	0.24
Portuguese	8	0.06
Romanian	5	0.04
Russian	37	0.29
Scandinavian	5	0.04
Scotch-Irish	6	0.05
Swedish	6	0.05
United States or American	201	1.60
West Indian, excl. Hispanic:	12	0.10
Belizean	12	0.10
White:	6,167	49.07
Not Hispanic (519)	552	4.39
Hispanic (5,106)	5,615	44.68

Compton

Place Type: City
County: Los Angeles
Population: 93,493

Ancestry/Race	Number	%
African American/Black:	38,509	41.19
Not Hispanic (37,263)	37,816	40.45
Hispanic (427)	693	0.74
African, sub-Saharan:	1,535	1.65
African	1,467	1.57
Ethiopian	6	0.01
Nigerian	52	0.06
Other sub-Saharan African	10	0.01
Alaska Native tribes, specified:	5	0.01
Aleut	1	0.00
Eskimo (3)	4	0.00
Am. Ind. or Alaska Nat., not spec.	584	0.62
American Indian tribes, specified:	444	0.47
Apache (4)	10	0.01
Blackfeet (1)	34	0.04
Cherokee (10)	59	0.06
Cheyenne	1	0.00
Chickasaw	10	0.01
Chippewa (2)	2	0.00
Choctaw (3)	22	0.02
Creek (2)	10	0.01
Crow	2	0.00
Iroquois	2	0.00
Kiowa	2	0.00
Latin American Indians (126)	204	0.22
Lumbee (3)	3	0.00
Navajo (20)	23	0.02
Osage (1)	1	0.00
Pima	3	0.00
Pueblo (4)	8	0.01
Seminole	5	0.01
Shoshone	5	0.01
Sioux (8)	12	0.01
Tohono O'Odham	1	0.00
All other tribes (8)	25	0.03
American Indian tribes, not spec.	98	0.10
Arab:	31	0.03
Arab/Arabic	12	0.01
Lebanese	19	0.02
Armenian	39	0.04
Asian:	475	0.51
Cambodian (17)	21	0.02
Chinese, ex. Taiwanese (26)	65	0.07
Filipino (113)	203	0.22
Indian (24)	54	0.06
Japanese (14)	45	0.05
Korean (6)	12	0.01
Laotian (4)	4	0.00
Sri Lankan (3)	3	0.00
Thai (3)	9	0.01
Vietnamese (15)	18	0.02
Other Asian, specified	3	0.00
Other Asian, not specified (8)	38	0.04

Notes: 1. Figures in the "Number" column do not add up to the total population due to: a) Ancestry/Race overlap — e.g. persons can report being both White and Irish, b) persons of Hispanic origin can report being any race, c) persons reporting two ancestries are counted in both categories. 2. Numbers in parentheses indicate the number of persons reporting this ancestry/race alone, not in combination with any other ancestry/race. 3. Refer to the Explanation of Data in the front of the book for more detailed information.

Belgian	12	0.01
Canadian	50	0.05
Cypriot	4	0.00
Czechoslovakian	19	0.02
English	110	0.12
European	10	0.01
French, except Basque	158	0.17
French Canadian	29	0.03
German	139	0.15
Greek	21	0.02
Hawaii Native/Pacific Islander:	1,184	1.27
Micronesian: (14)	25	0.03
Guamanian/Chamorro (14)	25	0.03
Polynesian: (905)	1,046	1.12
Native Hawaiian (11)	25	0.03
Samoan (859)	959	1.03
Tongan (34)	55	0.06
Other Polynesian (1)	7	0.01
Other Pac. Isl., specified	3	0.00
Other Pac. Isl., not spec. (52)	110	0.12
Hispanic or Latino:	53,143	56.84
Central American:	2,191	2.34
Costa Rican	13	0.01
Guatemalan	617	0.66
Honduran	269	0.29
Nicaraguan	53	0.06
Panamanian	27	0.03
Salvadoran	1,024	1.10
Other Central American	188	0.20
Cuban	68	0.07
Dominican Republic	1	0.00
Mexican	43,839	46.89
Puerto Rican	161	0.17
South American:	104	0.11
Argentinean	8	0.01
Bolivian	7	0.01
Chilean	2	0.00
Colombian	22	0.02
Ecuadorian	23	0.02
Peruvian	27	0.03
Venezuelan	6	0.01
Other South American	9	0.01
Other Hispanic or Latino	6,779	7.25
Irish	198	0.21
Italian	69	0.07
Polish	3	0.00
Portuguese	24	0.03
Scandinavian	4	0.00
Scottish	20	0.02
Slavic	7	0.01
United States or American	869	0.93
West Indian, excl. Hispanic:	287	0.31
Barbadian	5	0.01
Belizean	151	0.16
British West Indian	6	0.01
Haitian	8	0.01
Jamaican	57	0.06
Trinidadian and Tobagonian	16	0.02
U.S. Virgin Islander	6	0.01
West Indian	38	0.04
White:	18,183	19.45
Not Hispanic (954)	1,266	1.35
Hispanic (14,671)	16,917	18.09

Concord

Place Type: City
County: Contra Costa
Population: 121,780

Ancestry/Race	Number	%
Acadian/Cajun	11	0.01
Afghan	1,863	1.53
African American/Black:	4,615	3.79
Not Hispanic (3,530)	4,212	3.46
Hispanic (176)	403	0.33
African, sub-Saharan:	467	0.38
African	276	0.23
Ghanian	8	0.01
Nigerian	36	0.03
South African	111	0.09
Sudanese	9	0.01
Zimbabwean	7	0.01
Other sub-Saharan African	20	0.02
Alaska Native tribes, specified:	16	0.01
Alaska Athabascan (2)	2	0.00
Aleut (2)	5	0.00
Eskimo (3)	3	0.00
Tlingit-Haida	6	0.00
Am. Ind. or Alaska Nat., not spec.	728	0.60
Albanian	25	0.02
American Indian tribes, specified:	1,475	1.21
Apache (37)	86	0.07
Blackfeet (16)	68	0.06
Cherokee (105)	458	0.38
Cheyenne (4)	11	0.01
Chickasaw (6)	19	0.02
Chippewa (21)	52	0.04
Choctaw (40)	108	0.09
Comanche	4	0.00
Cree (2)	8	0.01
Creek (8)	32	0.03
Crow	2	0.00
Delaware (7)	10	0.01
Iroquois (17)	28	0.02
Kiowa (2)	2	0.00
Latin American Indians (81)	158	0.13
Lumbee (1)	2	0.00
Menominee (2)	3	0.00
Navajo (15)	38	0.03
Osage (3)	9	0.01
Ottawa (1)	1	0.00
Paiute (6)	11	0.01
Pima (3)	3	0.00
Potawatomi (14)	18	0.01
Pueblo (10)	18	0.01
Seminole (2)	18	0.01
Shoshone (1)	2	0.00
Sioux (26)	65	0.05
Tohono O'Odham (2)	6	0.00
Ute (4)	9	0.01
Yakama (2)	2	0.00
Yaqui (5)	16	0.01
Yuman (3)	7	0.01
All other tribes (101)	201	0.17
American Indian tribes, not spec.	81	0.07
Arab:	730	0.60
Arab/Arabic	135	0.11
Egyptian	150	0.12
Iraqi	17	0.01
Jordanian	53	0.04
Lebanese	167	0.14
Moroccan	7	0.01
Palestinian	73	0.06
Syrian	7	0.01
Other Arab	121	0.10
Armenian	340	0.28
Asian:	14,482	11.89
Bangladeshi (3)	4	0.00
Cambodian (21)	29	0.02
Chinese, ex. Taiwanese (2,572)	3,188	2.62
Filipino (3,985)	5,016	4.12
Hmong (15)	15	0.01
Indian (1,634)	1,891	1.55
Indonesian (81)	138	0.11
Japanese (881)	1,306	1.07
Korean (690)	805	0.66
Laotian (66)	82	0.07
Malaysian (5)	16	0.01
Pakistani (87)	137	0.11
Sri Lankan (15)	18	0.01
Taiwanese (60)	62	0.05
Thai (85)	116	0.10
Vietnamese (792)	899	0.74
Other Asian, specified (48)	69	0.06
Other Asian, not specified (138)	691	0.57
Assyrian/Chaldean/Syriac	20	0.02
Australian	34	0.03
Austrian	389	0.32
Basque	57	0.05
Belgian	141	0.12
Brazilian	165	0.14
British	468	0.38
Bulgarian	144	0.12
Canadian	385	0.32
Celtic	108	0.09
Croatian	108	0.09
Cypriot	4	0.00
Czech	471	0.39
Czechoslovakian	198	0.16
Danish	960	0.79
Dutch	2,058	1.69
Eastern European	53	0.04
English	11,999	9.86
Estonian	18	0.01
European	1,729	1.42
Finnish	302	0.25
French, except Basque	3,569	2.93
French Canadian	798	0.66
German	15,586	12.81
Greek	586	0.48
Guyanese	115	0.09
Hawaii Native/Pacific Islander:	1,236	1.01
Melanesian: (27)	41	0.03
Fijian (25)	39	0.03
Other Melanesian (2)	2	0.00
Micronesian: (88)	150	0.12
Guamanian/Chamorro (69)	118	0.10
Other Micronesian (19)	32	0.03
Polynesian: (418)	832	0.68
Native Hawaiian (125)	363	0.30
Samoan (73)	141	0.12
Tongan (207)	287	0.24
Other Polynesian (13)	41	0.03
Other Pac. Isl., specified	7	0.01
Other Pac. Isl., not spec. (58)	206	0.17
Hispanic or Latino:	26,560	21.81
Central American:	2,543	2.09
Costa Rican	52	0.04
Guatemalan	292	0.24
Honduran	37	0.03
Nicaraguan	457	0.38
Panamanian	74	0.06
Salvadoran	1,431	1.18
Other Central American	200	0.16
Cuban	179	0.15
Dominican Republic	15	0.01
Mexican	17,446	14.33
Puerto Rican	666	0.55
South American:	1,027	0.84
Argentinean	44	0.04
Bolivian	39	0.03
Chilean	63	0.05
Colombian	122	0.10
Ecuadorian	64	0.05
Paraguayan	6	0.00
Peruvian	566	0.46
Venezuelan	28	0.02
Other South American	95	0.08
Other Hispanic or Latino	4,684	3.85
Hungarian	475	0.39
Icelander	16	0.01
Iranian	528	0.43
Irish	15,109	12.41
Israeli	15	0.01
Italian	8,540	7.02
Latvian	31	0.03
Lithuanian	160	0.13
Luxemburger	47	0.04
Maltese	118	0.10
New Zealander	17	0.01
Northern European	217	0.18
Norwegian	2,122	1.74
Pennsylvania German	6	0.00
Polish	2,447	2.01
Portuguese	2,374	1.95
Romanian	214	0.18
Russian	1,224	1.01
Scandinavian	240	0.20
Scotch-Irish	2,437	2.00

Notes: 1. Figures in the "Number" column do not add up to the total population due to: a) Ancestry/Race overlap — e.g. persons can report being both White and Irish, b) persons of Hispanic origin can report being any race, c) persons reporting two ancestries are counted in both categories. 2. Numbers in parentheses indicate the number of persons reporting this ancestry/race alone, not in combination with any other ancestry/race. 3. Refer to the Explanation of Data in the front of the book for more detailed information.

Scottish	2,729	2.24
Serbian	15	0.01
Slavic	36	0.03
Slovak	47	0.04
Slovene	88	0.07
Swedish	2,212	1.82
Swiss	582	0.48
Turkish	40	0.03
Ukrainian	324	0.27
United States or American	4,172	3.43
Welsh	1,149	0.94
West Indian, excl. Hispanic:	108	0.09
Belizean	17	0.01
Dutch West Indian	26	0.02
Haitian	37	0.03
Jamaican	15	0.01
Trinidadian and Tobagonian	3	0.00
U.S. Virgin Islander	10	0.01
White:	92,348	75.83
Not Hispanic (74,119)	78,325	64.32
Hispanic (11,995)	14,023	11.52
Yugoslavian	245	0.20

Corcoran

Place Type: City
County: Kings
Population: 14,458

Ancestry/Race	Number	%
African American/Black:	2,121	14.67
Not Hispanic (2,029)	2,070	14.32
Hispanic (25)	51	0.35
African, sub-Saharan:	8	0.06
African	8	0.06
Am. Ind. or Alaska Nat., not spec.	122	0.84
American Indian tribes, specified:	153	1.06
Apache (13)	21	0.15
Blackfeet	2	0.01
Cherokee (7)	28	0.19
Chickasaw	2	0.01
Choctaw (10)	14	0.10
Cree	3	0.02
Creek (6)	6	0.04
Delaware (1)	1	0.01
Iroquois	1	0.01
Latin American Indians (14)	20	0.14
Navajo (12)	17	0.12
Pima (1)	1	0.01
Potawatomi (13)	14	0.10
Pueblo (2)	2	0.01
Yakama (1)	1	0.01
Yaqui (2)	2	0.01
All other tribes (16)	18	0.12
American Indian tribes, not spec.	18	0.12
Asian:	126	0.87
Cambodian (1)	2	0.01
Chinese, ex. Taiwanese (38)	41	0.28
Filipino (21)	26	0.18
Hmong (8)	11	0.08
Indian (19)	20	0.14
Indonesian (1)	1	0.01
Japanese (1)	1	0.01
Laotian (1)	1	0.01
Thai	3	0.02
Vietnamese (4)	6	0.04
Other Asian, specified (2)	2	0.01
Other Asian, not specified (7)	12	0.08
Czech	7	0.05
Danish	27	0.19
Dutch	68	0.48
English	265	1.86
European	28	0.20
Finnish	6	0.04
French, except Basque	53	0.37
French Canadian	12	0.08
German	441	3.10
German Russian	8	0.06
Hawaii Native/Pacific Islander:	30	0.21
Micronesian: (3)	3	0.02
Guamanian/Chamorro (3)	3	0.02
Polynesian: (9)	21	0.15
Native Hawaiian (9)	21	0.15
Other Pac. Isl., not spec.	6	0.04
Hispanic or Latino:	8,618	59.61
Central American:	10	0.07
Guatemalan	2	0.01
Panamanian	1	0.01
Salvadoran	7	0.05
Cuban	10	0.07
Mexican	7,866	54.41
Puerto Rican	15	0.10
South American:	2	0.01
Argentinean	2	0.01
Other Hispanic or Latino	715	4.95
Hungarian	9	0.06
Irish	410	2.88
Italian	26	0.18
Norwegian	19	0.13
Pennsylvania German	22	0.15
Polish	25	0.18
Portuguese	43	0.30
Russian	8	0.06
Scotch-Irish	57	0.40
Scottish	12	0.08
Swedish	40	0.28
United States or American	217	1.52
White:	5,292	36.60
Not Hispanic (3,479)	3,589	24.82
Hispanic (1,448)	1,703	11.78

Corona

Place Type: City
County: Riverside
Population: 124,966

Ancestry/Race	Number	%
Acadian/Cajun	7	0.01
Afghan	11	0.01
African American/Black:	9,024	7.22
Not Hispanic (7,704)	8,420	6.74
Hispanic (327)	604	0.48
African, sub-Saharan:	754	0.60
African	513	0.41
Cape Verdean	9	0.01
Nigerian	169	0.14
South African	9	0.01
Zimbabwean	25	0.02
Other sub-Saharan African	29	0.02
Alaska Native tribes, specified:	12	0.01
Alaska Athabascan (2)	4	0.00
Eskimo	1	0.00
Tlingit-Haida (2)	6	0.00
All other tribes (1)	1	0.00
Am. Ind. or Alaska Nat., not spec.	709	0.57
Albanian	32	0.03
American Indian tribes, specified:	1,328	1.06
Apache (50)	95	0.08
Blackfeet (8)	58	0.05
Cherokee (62)	269	0.22
Cheyenne (3)	6	0.00
Chickasaw (4)	16	0.01
Chippewa (15)	32	0.03
Choctaw (26)	79	0.06
Colville (1)	3	0.00
Comanche	6	0.00
Cree (2)	3	0.00
Creek (9)	18	0.01
Delaware (2)	2	0.00
Iroquois (7)	17	0.01
Kiowa (1)	3	0.00
Latin American Indians (98)	171	0.14
Lumbee (2)	3	0.00
Menominee	1	0.00
Navajo (25)	53	0.04
Osage	5	0.00
Ottawa (1)	1	0.00
Paiute (6)	7	0.01
Pima (10)	12	0.01
Potawatomi (7)	13	0.01
Pueblo (25)	45	0.04
Puget Sound Salish (1)	1	0.00
Seminole	3	0.00
Shoshone (16)	20	0.02
Sioux (10)	43	0.03
Tohono O'Odham (5)	16	0.01
Ute (2)	10	0.01
Yakama	3	0.00
Yaqui (8)	34	0.03
Yuman (5)	8	0.01
All other tribes (181)	272	0.22
American Indian tribes, not spec.	98	0.08
Arab:	1,444	1.16
Arab/Arabic	216	0.17
Egyptian	309	0.25
Jordanian	129	0.10
Lebanese	367	0.29
Palestinian	54	0.04
Syrian	169	0.14
Other Arab	200	0.16
Armenian	143	0.11
Asian:	11,588	9.27
Bangladeshi (12)	13	0.01
Cambodian (192)	224	0.18
Chinese, ex. Taiwanese (742)	1,047	0.84
Filipino (3,331)	4,055	3.24
Hmong (2)	3	0.00
Indian (1,450)	1,620	1.30
Indonesian (65)	136	0.11
Japanese (431)	820	0.66
Korean (898)	1,022	0.82
Laotian (103)	132	0.11
Malaysian (6)	13	0.01
Pakistani (174)	257	0.21
Sri Lankan (34)	35	0.03
Taiwanese (72)	92	0.07
Thai (101)	139	0.11
Vietnamese (1,474)	1,604	1.28
Other Asian, specified (8)	28	0.02
Other Asian, not specified (112)	348	0.28
Assyrian/Chaldean/Syriac	97	0.08
Australian	25	0.02
Austrian	143	0.11
Basque	30	0.02
Belgian	60	0.05
Brazilian	18	0.01
British	304	0.24
Bulgarian	50	0.04
Canadian	509	0.41
Celtic	11	0.01
Croatian	39	0.03
Czech	300	0.24
Czechoslovakian	161	0.13
Danish	617	0.49
Dutch	1,971	1.58
Eastern European	33	0.03
English	9,140	7.32
European	1,164	0.93
Finnish	255	0.20
French, except Basque	3,131	2.51
French Canadian	711	0.57
German	14,680	11.75
Greek	332	0.27
Hawaii Native/Pacific Islander:	784	0.63
Melanesian: (19)	20	0.02
Fijian (19)	20	0.02
Micronesian: (97)	145	0.12
Guamanian/Chamorro (94)	136	0.11
Other Micronesian (3)	9	0.01
Polynesian: (217)	444	0.36
Native Hawaiian (83)	232	0.19
Samoan (120)	179	0.14
Tongan (11)	18	0.01
Other Polynesian (3)	15	0.01
Other Pac. Isl., specified	5	0.00
Other Pac. Isl., not spec. (44)	170	0.14
Hispanic or Latino:	44,569	35.66
Central American:	1,165	0.93
Costa Rican	78	0.06

Notes: 1. Figures in the "Number" column do not add up to the total population due to: a) Ancestry/Race overlap — e.g. persons can report being both White and Irish, b) persons of Hispanic origin can report being any race, c) persons reporting two ancestries are counted in both categories. 2. Numbers in parentheses indicate the number of persons reporting this ancestry/race alone, not in combination with any other ancestry/race. 3. Refer to the Explanation of Data in the front of the book for more detailed information.

Guatemalan	301	0.24
Honduran	106	0.08
Nicaraguan	92	0.07
Panamanian	82	0.07
Salvadoran	408	0.33
Other Central American	98	0.08
Cuban	446	0.36
Dominican Republic	21	0.02
Mexican	36,212	28.98
Puerto Rican	603	0.48
South American:	801	0.64
Argentinean	118	0.09
Bolivian	18	0.01
Chilean	69	0.06
Colombian	182	0.15
Ecuadorian	103	0.08
Peruvian	205	0.16
Uruguayan	9	0.01
Venezuelan	31	0.02
Other South American	66	0.05
Other Hispanic or Latino	5,321	4.26
Hungarian	460	0.37
Icelander	45	0.04
Iranian	406	0.32
Irish	9,241	7.40
Israeli	30	0.02
Italian	5,740	4.59
Latvian	41	0.03
Lithuanian	218	0.17
Maltese	9	0.01
New Zealander	5	0.00
Northern European	22	0.02
Norwegian	2,090	1.67
Pennsylvania German	32	0.03
Polish	2,078	1.66
Portuguese	401	0.32
Romanian	394	0.32
Russian	557	0.45
Scandinavian	214	0.17
Scotch-Irish	1,204	0.96
Scottish	1,880	1.50
Serbian	16	0.01
Slavic	79	0.06
Slovak	25	0.02
Slovene	127	0.10
Soviet Union	15	0.01
Swedish	1,741	1.39
Swiss	258	0.21
Turkish	46	0.04
Ukrainian	130	0.10
United States or American	5,553	4.44
Welsh	602	0.48
West Indian, excl. Hispanic:	333	0.27
Bahamian	31	0.02
Barbadian	23	0.02
Belizean	8	0.01
Dutch West Indian	16	0.01
Haitian	35	0.03
Jamaican	107	0.09
Trinidadian and Tobagonian	54	0.04
U.S. Virgin Islander	14	0.01
West Indian	45	0.04
White:	83,045	66.45
Not Hispanic (58,784)	61,649	49.33
Hispanic (18,730)	21,396	17.12
Yugoslavian	246	0.20

Coronado

Place Type: City
County: San Diego
Population: 24,100

Ancestry/Race	Number	%
Acadian/Cajun	12	0.05
African American/Black:	1,355	5.62
Not Hispanic (1,213)	1,320	5.48
Hispanic (28)	35	0.15
African, sub-Saharan:	131	0.54
African	63	0.26
Cape Verdean	14	0.06
Ethiopian	6	0.02
Ghanian	7	0.03
South African	27	0.11
Zimbabwean	7	0.03
Other sub-Saharan African	7	0.03
Alaska Native tribes, specified:	7	0.03
Alaska Athabascan	2	0.01
Aleut (1)	1	0.00
Eskimo	1	0.00
Tlingit-Haida (2)	2	0.01
All other tribes	1	0.00
Alaska Native tribes, not specified	1	0.00
Am. Ind. or Alaska Nat., not spec.	83	0.34
Alsatian	7	0.03
American Indian tribes, specified:	197	0.82
Apache (3)	11	0.05
Blackfeet (3)	7	0.03
Cherokee (30)	69	0.29
Cheyenne (1)	1	0.00
Chickasaw (1)	1	0.00
Chippewa (3)	4	0.02
Choctaw (4)	7	0.03
Cree (1)	3	0.01
Creek (2)	6	0.02
Crow	3	0.01
Iroquois (2)	5	0.02
Kiowa (2)	2	0.01
Latin American Indians (11)	14	0.06
Lumbee (3)	3	0.01
Menominee (2)	2	0.01
Navajo (20)	20	0.08
Paiute	2	0.01
Pima (1)	1	0.00
Potawatomi (1)	2	0.01
Pueblo (4)	7	0.03
Seminole	1	0.00
Sioux (1)	4	0.02
Tohono O'Odham (1)	3	0.01
Yaqui (1)	4	0.02
Yuman (1)	1	0.00
All other tribes (5)	14	0.06
American Indian tribes, not spec.	21	0.09
Arab:	192	0.79
Arab/Arabic	22	0.09
Egyptian	6	0.02
Lebanese	118	0.49
Moroccan	15	0.06
Syrian	15	0.06
Other Arab	16	0.07
Armenian	16	0.07
Asian:	1,215	5.04
Cambodian (3)	5	0.02
Chinese, ex. Taiwanese (66)	133	0.55
Filipino (487)	595	2.47
Hmong (5)	6	0.02
Indian (42)	54	0.22
Indonesian (2)	8	0.03
Japanese (80)	150	0.62
Korean (50)	72	0.30
Laotian (11)	11	0.05
Malaysian (1)	3	0.01
Pakistani (1)	1	0.00
Sri Lankan (1)	1	0.00
Taiwanese (1)	4	0.02
Thai (12)	14	0.06
Vietnamese (47)	61	0.25
Other Asian, specified (4)	6	0.02
Other Asian, not specified (60)	91	0.38
Australian	44	0.18
Austrian	150	0.62
Belgian	34	0.14
Brazilian	9	0.04
British	258	1.06
Canadian	96	0.40
Celtic	17	0.07
Croatian	42	0.17
Czech	136	0.56
Czechoslovakian	81	0.33
Danish	163	0.67
Dutch	344	1.42
Eastern European	6	0.02
English	3,317	13.69
European	301	1.24
Finnish	74	0.31
French, except Basque	919	3.79
French Canadian	220	0.91
German	4,294	17.72
Greek	150	0.62
Guyanese	6	0.02
Hawaii Native/Pacific Islander:	161	0.67
Melanesian: (2)	2	0.01
Fijian (2)	2	0.01
Micronesian: (28)	50	0.21
Guamanian/Chamorro (21)	37	0.15
Other Micronesian (7)	13	0.05
Polynesian: (31)	72	0.30
Native Hawaiian (23)	53	0.22
Samoan (7)	15	0.06
Other Polynesian (1)	4	0.02
Other Pac. Isl., specified	2	0.01
Other Pac. Isl., not spec. (9)	35	0.15
Hispanic or Latino:	2,369	9.83
Central American:	71	0.29
Costa Rican	3	0.01
Guatemalan	13	0.05
Honduran	5	0.02
Nicaraguan	5	0.02
Panamanian	19	0.08
Salvadoran	22	0.09
Other Central American	4	0.02
Cuban	29	0.12
Dominican Republic	12	0.05
Mexican	1,629	6.76
Puerto Rican	155	0.64
South American:	70	0.29
Argentinean	4	0.02
Bolivian	3	0.01
Chilean	10	0.04
Colombian	17	0.07
Ecuadorian	7	0.03
Peruvian	19	0.08
Uruguayan	4	0.02
Venezuelan	3	0.01
Other South American	3	0.01
Other Hispanic or Latino	403	1.67
Hungarian	55	0.23
Icelander	7	0.03
Iranian	33	0.14
Irish	3,905	16.12
Israeli	7	0.03
Italian	1,865	7.70
Latvian	6	0.02
Lithuanian	42	0.17
Northern European	62	0.26
Norwegian	441	1.82
Polish	571	2.36
Portuguese	103	0.43
Romanian	25	0.10
Russian	211	0.87
Scandinavian	137	0.57
Scotch-Irish	732	3.02
Scottish	992	4.09
Slavic	30	0.12
Slovak	19	0.08
Swedish	507	2.09
Swiss	112	0.46
Ukrainian	101	0.42
United States or American	1,061	4.38
Welsh	240	0.99
West Indian, excl. Hispanic:	116	0.48
Belizean	8	0.03
Dutch West Indian	19	0.08
Haitian	7	0.03
Jamaican	42	0.17
Trinidadian and Tobagonian	19	0.08
West Indian	21	0.09
White:	20,888	86.67
Not Hispanic (18,937)	19,349	80.29
Hispanic (1,404)	1,539	6.39

Notes: 1. Figures in the "Number" column do not add up to the total population due to: a) Ancestry/Race overlap — e.g. persons can report being both White and Irish, b) persons of Hispanic origin can report being any race, c) persons reporting two ancestries are counted in both categories. 2. Numbers in parentheses indicate the number of persons reporting this ancestry/race alone, not in combination with any other ancestry/race. 3. Refer to the Explanation of Data in the front of the book for more detailed information.

Yugoslavian	23	0.09

Costa Mesa

Place Type: City
County: Orange
Population: 108,724

Ancestry/Race	Number	%
Afghan	58	0.05
African American/Black:	1,964	1.81
Not Hispanic (1,313)	1,636	1.50
Hispanic (207)	328	0.30
African, sub-Saharan:	228	0.21
African	62	0.06
Ghanian	28	0.03
Nigerian	21	0.02
South African	55	0.05
Zairian	28	0.03
Other sub-Saharan African	34	0.03
Alaska Native tribes, specified:	5	0.00
Alaska Athabascan	1	0.00
Eskimo (1)	4	0.00
Am. Ind. or Alaska Nat., not spec.	589	0.54
Alsatian	30	0.03
American Indian tribes, specified:	924	0.85
Apache (22)	38	0.03
Blackfeet (12)	33	0.03
Cherokee (63)	231	0.21
Cheyenne (3)	6	0.01
Chickasaw (5)	7	0.01
Chippewa (17)	38	0.03
Choctaw (14)	40	0.04
Comanche (2)	3	0.00
Creek (5)	12	0.01
Crow (2)	7	0.01
Delaware (1)	1	0.00
Iroquois (2)	12	0.01
Kiowa	1	0.00
Latin American Indians (162)	243	0.22
Lumbee (6)	7	0.01
Menominee (1)	1	0.00
Navajo (20)	43	0.04
Osage (1)	4	0.00
Ottawa (2)	3	0.00
Paiute (3)	5	0.00
Pima (2)	3	0.00
Potawatomi (3)	4	0.00
Pueblo (11)	22	0.02
Puget Sound Salish	1	0.00
Seminole (1)	3	0.00
Shoshone (3)	7	0.01
Sioux (8)	28	0.03
Tohono O'Odham (2)	2	0.00
Ute	2	0.00
Yaqui (8)	17	0.02
Yuman	1	0.00
All other tribes (55)	99	0.09
American Indian tribes, not spec.	90	0.08
Arab:	799	0.73
Arab/Arabic	157	0.14
Egyptian	221	0.20
Jordanian	66	0.06
Lebanese	231	0.21
Moroccan	21	0.02
Palestinian	10	0.01
Syrian	37	0.03
Other Arab	56	0.05
Armenian	266	0.24
Asian:	8,966	8.25
Bangladeshi (9)	10	0.01
Cambodian (55)	75	0.07
Chinese, ex. Taiwanese (872)	1,147	1.05
Filipino (1,333)	1,715	1.58
Hmong (13)	15	0.01
Indian (588)	693	0.64
Indonesian (41)	104	0.10
Japanese (1,357)	1,671	1.54
Korean (516)	619	0.57
Laotian (39)	44	0.04
Malaysian (5)	6	0.01
Pakistani (34)	75	0.07
Sri Lankan (19)	21	0.02
Taiwanese (96)	121	0.11
Thai (91)	114	0.10
Vietnamese (2,180)	2,299	2.11
Other Asian, specified (24)	32	0.03
Other Asian, not specified (70)	205	0.19
Assyrian/Chaldean/Syriac	14	0.01
Australian	74	0.07
Austrian	411	0.38
Basque	77	0.07
Belgian	111	0.10
Brazilian	59	0.05
British	635	0.58
Bulgarian	55	0.05
Canadian	630	0.58
Celtic	43	0.04
Croatian	255	0.23
Czech	278	0.26
Czechoslovakian	159	0.15
Danish	714	0.66
Dutch	1,696	1.56
Eastern European	73	0.07
English	10,252	9.42
Estonian	12	0.01
European	1,240	1.14
Finnish	354	0.33
French, except Basque	3,289	3.02
French Canadian	510	0.47
German	13,468	12.38
Greek	444	0.41
Hawaii Native/Pacific Islander:	1,009	0.93
Melanesian: (21)	24	0.02
Fijian (21)	24	0.02
Micronesian: (338)	372	0.34
Guamanian/Chamorro (44)	71	0.07
Other Micronesian (294)	301	0.28
Polynesian: (235)	451	0.41
Native Hawaiian (143)	295	0.27
Samoan (68)	117	0.11
Tongan (12)	12	0.01
Other Polynesian (12)	27	0.02
Other Pac. Isl., specified	3	0.00
Other Pac. Isl., not spec. (56)	159	0.15
Hispanic or Latino:	34,523	31.75
Central American:	2,160	1.99
Costa Rican	41	0.04
Guatemalan	618	0.57
Honduran	105	0.10
Nicaraguan	65	0.06
Panamanian	25	0.02
Salvadoran	1,144	1.05
Other Central American	162	0.15
Cuban	174	0.16
Dominican Republic	31	0.03
Mexican	26,133	24.04
Puerto Rican	311	0.29
South American:	704	0.65
Argentinean	147	0.14
Bolivian	25	0.02
Chilean	39	0.04
Colombian	208	0.19
Ecuadorian	60	0.06
Paraguayan	4	0.00
Peruvian	129	0.12
Uruguayan	12	0.01
Venezuelan	22	0.02
Other South American	58	0.05
Other Hispanic or Latino	5,010	4.61
Hungarian	516	0.47
Icelander	12	0.01
Iranian	453	0.42
Irish	10,229	9.40
Israeli	13	0.01
Italian	5,436	5.00
Latvian	59	0.05
Lithuanian	262	0.24
Luxemburger	8	0.01
Macedonian	13	0.01
Maltese	6	0.01
New Zealander	33	0.03
Northern European	114	0.10
Norwegian	2,084	1.92
Pennsylvania German	21	0.02
Polish	1,984	1.82
Portuguese	398	0.37
Romanian	156	0.14
Russian	1,239	1.14
Scandinavian	262	0.24
Scotch-Irish	1,520	1.40
Scottish	2,876	2.64
Serbian	47	0.04
Slavic	46	0.04
Slovak	79	0.07
Slovene	47	0.04
Swedish	2,267	2.08
Swiss	354	0.33
Turkish	118	0.11
Ukrainian	178	0.16
United States or American	4,177	3.84
Welsh	788	0.72
West Indian, excl. Hispanic:	129	0.12
Bermudan	8	0.01
Dutch West Indian	6	0.01
Haitian	42	0.04
Jamaican	38	0.03
Trinidadian and Tobagonian	35	0.03
White:	79,618	73.23
Not Hispanic (61,778)	63,958	58.83
Hispanic (13,764)	15,660	14.40
Yugoslavian	88	0.08

Coto de Caza

Place Type: Census Designated Place
County: Orange
Population: 13,057

Ancestry/Race	Number	%
African American/Black:	136	1.04
Not Hispanic (92)	126	0.96
Hispanic (4)	10	0.08
African, sub-Saharan:	37	0.28
South African	37	0.28
Alaska Native tribes, specified:	1	0.01
Tlingit-Haida	1	0.01
Am. Ind. or Alaska Nat., not spec.	35	0.27
Albanian	15	0.11
American Indian tribes, specified:	56	0.43
Apache	2	0.02
Blackfeet	1	0.01
Cherokee (6)	34	0.26
Navajo	4	0.03
Ottawa (1)	1	0.01
Potawatomi (1)	1	0.01
Pueblo	3	0.02
Puget Sound Salish (3)	3	0.02
Sioux (2)	6	0.05
All other tribes	1	0.01
American Indian tribes, not spec.	1	0.01
Arab:	21	0.16
Lebanese	14	0.11
Syrian	7	0.05
Armenian	62	0.47
Asian:	875	6.70
Cambodian (11)	13	0.10
Chinese, ex. Taiwanese (129)	171	1.31
Filipino (154)	188	1.44
Indian (71)	89	0.68
Indonesian (6)	6	0.05
Japanese (104)	178	1.36
Korean (109)	126	0.96
Malaysian (1)	1	0.01
Pakistani (15)	21	0.16
Taiwanese (11)	12	0.09
Thai (2)	6	0.05
Vietnamese (43)	53	0.41
Other Asian, specified (1)	1	0.01
Other Asian, not specified	10	0.08

Notes: 1. Figures in the "Number" column do not add up to the total population due to: a) Ancestry/Race overlap — e.g. persons can report being both White and Irish, b) persons of Hispanic origin can report being any race, c) persons reporting two ancestries are counted in both categories. 2. Numbers in parentheses indicate the number of persons reporting this ancestry/race alone, not in combination with any other ancestry/race. 3. Refer to the Explanation of Data in the front of the book for more detailed information.

Ancestry/Race	Number	%
Australian	6	0.05
Austrian	66	0.51
Belgian	40	0.31
British	146	1.12
Bulgarian	11	0.08
Canadian	105	0.80
Croatian	66	0.51
Czech	110	0.84
Czechoslovakian	40	0.31
Danish	118	0.90
Dutch	366	2.80
Eastern European	19	0.15
English	2,420	18.53
European	78	0.60
Finnish	47	0.36
French, except Basque	487	3.73
French Canadian	94	0.72
German	3,135	24.01
Greek	129	0.99
Hawaii Native/Pacific Islander:	39	0.30
Micronesian: (9)	17	0.13
Guamanian/Chamorro (9)	17	0.13
Polynesian: (10)	20	0.15
Native Hawaiian (8)	17	0.13
Tongan	1	0.01
Other Polynesian (2)	2	0.02
Other Pac. Isl., not spec.	2	0.02
Hispanic or Latino:	868	6.65
Central American:	22	0.17
Costa Rican	7	0.05
Guatemalan	5	0.04
Nicaraguan	8	0.06
Salvadoran	2	0.02
Cuban	37	0.28
Mexican	531	4.07
Puerto Rican	26	0.20
South American:	67	0.51
Argentinean	18	0.14
Bolivian	5	0.04
Chilean	7	0.05
Colombian	13	0.10
Ecuadorian	2	0.02
Paraguayan	1	0.01
Peruvian	13	0.10
Venezuelan	2	0.02
Other South American	6	0.05
Other Hispanic or Latino	185	1.42
Hungarian	59	0.45
Icelander	21	0.16
Iranian	108	0.83
Irish	2,097	16.06
Italian	1,063	8.14
Latvian	10	0.08
Lithuanian	91	0.70
New Zealander	11	0.08
Northern European	12	0.09
Norwegian	322	2.47
Polish	672	5.15
Portuguese	18	0.14
Romanian	81	0.62
Russian	239	1.83
Scandinavian	78	0.60
Scotch-Irish	305	2.34
Scottish	474	3.63
Slavic	26	0.20
Slovak	6	0.05
Slovene	8	0.06
Swedish	284	2.18
Swiss	31	0.24
Turkish	42	0.32
Ukrainian	70	0.54
United States or American	749	5.74
Welsh	196	1.50
White:	12,001	91.91
Not Hispanic (11,098)	11,348	86.91
Hispanic (570)	653	5.00
Yugoslavian	93	0.71

Covina

Place Type: City
County: Los Angeles
Population: 46,837

Ancestry/Race	Number	%
Acadian/Cajun	14	0.03
African American/Black:	2,638	5.63
Not Hispanic (2,245)	2,442	5.21
Hispanic (109)	196	0.42
African, sub-Saharan:	173	0.37
African	98	0.21
Ethiopian	8	0.02
Ghanian	17	0.04
Liberian	16	0.03
Nigerian	34	0.07
Alaska Native tribes, specified:	2	0.00
Aleut (1)	1	0.00
Eskimo (1)	1	0.00
Am. Ind. or Alaska Nat., not spec.	296	0.63
American Indian tribes, specified:	486	1.04
Apache (24)	39	0.08
Blackfeet (7)	25	0.05
Cherokee (27)	117	0.25
Cheyenne (7)	13	0.03
Chickasaw (1)	1	0.00
Chippewa (2)	4	0.01
Choctaw (5)	9	0.02
Comanche	6	0.01
Cree (1)	1	0.00
Creek	7	0.01
Crow (1)	1	0.00
Delaware	7	0.01
Iroquois (3)	14	0.03
Latin American Indians (39)	66	0.14
Navajo (9)	29	0.06
Osage (1)	5	0.01
Ottawa	1	0.00
Paiute (5)	5	0.01
Pima (1)	3	0.01
Pueblo (6)	8	0.02
Shoshone (1)	2	0.00
Sioux (13)	29	0.06
Tohono O'Odham (8)	12	0.03
Yaqui (4)	15	0.03
Yuman (2)	4	0.01
All other tribes (37)	63	0.13
American Indian tribes, not spec.	58	0.12
Arab:	298	0.63
Arab/Arabic	104	0.22
Egyptian	141	0.30
Lebanese	35	0.07
Palestinian	11	0.02
Syrian	7	0.01
Armenian	75	0.16
Asian:	5,374	11.47
Bangladeshi (2)	2	0.00
Cambodian (31)	32	0.07
Chinese, ex. Taiwanese (1,169)	1,330	2.84
Filipino (1,440)	1,707	3.64
Hmong (7)	7	0.01
Indian (357)	398	0.85
Indonesian (130)	175	0.37
Japanese (420)	615	1.31
Korean (195)	223	0.48
Laotian (3)	4	0.01
Malaysian	2	0.00
Pakistani (38)	48	0.10
Sri Lankan (31)	37	0.08
Taiwanese (192)	224	0.48
Thai (113)	139	0.30
Vietnamese (294)	323	0.69
Other Asian, specified (34)	39	0.08
Other Asian, not specified (34)	69	0.15
Australian	13	0.03
Austrian	120	0.25
Basque	12	0.03
Belgian	63	0.13
Brazilian	7	0.01
British	189	0.40
Bulgarian	6	0.01
Canadian	121	0.26
Croatian	61	0.13
Czech	144	0.31
Czechoslovakian	34	0.07
Danish	138	0.29
Dutch	711	1.51
Eastern European	20	0.04
English	3,572	7.58
European	241	0.51
Finnish	32	0.07
French, except Basque	1,453	3.08
French Canadian	345	0.73
German	4,998	10.60
Greek	130	0.28
Hawaii Native/Pacific Islander:	252	0.54
Micronesian: (15)	22	0.05
Guamanian/Chamorro (15)	22	0.05
Polynesian: (64)	154	0.33
Native Hawaiian (35)	89	0.19
Samoan (28)	57	0.12
Other Polynesian (1)	8	0.02
Other Pac. Isl., specified	1	0.00
Other Pac. Isl., not spec. (15)	75	0.16
Hispanic or Latino:	18,871	40.29
Central American:	764	1.63
Costa Rican	36	0.08
Guatemalan	189	0.40
Honduran	21	0.04
Nicaraguan	126	0.27
Panamanian	17	0.04
Salvadoran	288	0.61
Other Central American	87	0.19
Cuban	236	0.50
Dominican Republic	12	0.03
Mexican	14,373	30.69
Puerto Rican	323	0.69
South American:	517	1.10
Argentinean	109	0.23
Bolivian	9	0.02
Chilean	32	0.07
Colombian	82	0.18
Ecuadorian	78	0.17
Paraguayan	1	0.00
Peruvian	143	0.31
Uruguayan	1	0.00
Venezuelan	8	0.02
Other South American	54	0.12
Other Hispanic or Latino	2,646	5.65
Hungarian	111	0.24
Icelander	5	0.01
Iranian	39	0.08
Irish	3,961	8.40
Italian	2,035	4.32
Lithuanian	57	0.12
Luxemburger	12	0.03
Maltese	6	0.01
Northern European	16	0.03
Norwegian	695	1.47
Pennsylvania German	20	0.04
Polish	506	1.07
Portuguese	82	0.17
Romanian	37	0.08
Russian	243	0.52
Scandinavian	69	0.15
Scotch-Irish	730	1.55
Scottish	687	1.46
Slavic	14	0.03
Slovak	58	0.12
Slovene	16	0.03
Swedish	792	1.68
Swiss	85	0.18
Turkish	4	0.01
Ukrainian	33	0.07
United States or American	1,483	3.15
Welsh	202	0.43
West Indian, excl. Hispanic:	57	0.12
Jamaican	12	0.03
Trinidadian and Tobagonian	24	0.05

Notes: 1. Figures in the "Number" column do not add up to the total population due to: a) Ancestry/Race overlap — e.g. persons can report being both White and Irish, b) persons of Hispanic origin can report being any race, c) persons reporting two ancestries are counted in both categories. 2. Numbers in parentheses indicate the number of persons reporting this ancestry/race alone, not in combination with any other ancestry/race. 3. Refer to the Explanation of Data in the front of the book for more detailed information.

West Indian	21	0.04
White:	31,001	66.19
Not Hispanic (19,801)	20,741	44.28
Hispanic (9,283)	10,260	21.91
Yugoslavian	70	0.15

Crestline

Place Type: Census Designated Place
County: San Bernardino
Population: 10,218

Ancestry/Race	Number	%
African American/Black:	115	1.13
Not Hispanic (77)	110	1.08
Hispanic (4)	5	0.05
African, sub-Saharan:	7	0.07
South African	7	0.07
Alaska Native tribes, specified:	4	0.04
Aleut	4	0.04
Am. Ind. or Alaska Nat., not spec.	71	0.69
American Indian tribes, specified:	196	1.92
Apache (5)	8	0.08
Blackfeet (5)	20	0.20
Cherokee (16)	60	0.59
Chickasaw (1)	1	0.01
Chippewa (1)	10	0.10
Choctaw (4)	7	0.07
Comanche	4	0.04
Cree	1	0.01
Crow (1)	4	0.04
Delaware (1)	1	0.01
Iroquois (4)	7	0.07
Latin American Indians	4	0.04
Navajo (1)	6	0.06
Osage (1)	2	0.02
Paiute (2)	2	0.02
Potawatomi (2)	2	0.02
Pueblo (5)	6	0.06
Seminole (1)	1	0.01
Shoshone (1)	4	0.04
Sioux (13)	19	0.19
Tohono O'Odham (3)	5	0.05
Yaqui (1)	5	0.05
All other tribes (9)	17	0.17
American Indian tribes, not spec.	19	0.19
Arab:	41	0.40
Arab/Arabic	9	0.09
Palestinian	32	0.31
Asian:	122	1.19
Bangladeshi	3	0.03
Chinese, ex. Taiwanese (6)	16	0.16
Filipino (27)	43	0.42
Indian (2)	5	0.05
Indonesian (1)	4	0.04
Japanese (11)	28	0.27
Korean (9)	11	0.11
Pakistani	2	0.02
Vietnamese (1)	5	0.05
Other Asian, not specified (1)	5	0.05
Australian	8	0.08
Austrian	75	0.73
Belgian	5	0.05
British	42	0.41
Canadian	68	0.67
Croatian	9	0.09
Czech	48	0.47
Czechoslovakian	17	0.17
Danish	82	0.80
Dutch	491	4.81
English	1,689	16.55
European	208	2.04
Finnish	10	0.10
French, except Basque	407	3.99
French Canadian	41	0.40
German	2,667	26.13
Greek	33	0.32
Hawaii Native/Pacific Islander:	32	0.31
Micronesian: (8)	8	0.08
Guamanian/Chamorro (8)	8	0.08
Polynesian: (9)	22	0.22
Native Hawaiian (8)	18	0.18
Samoan (1)	2	0.02
Tongan	1	0.01
Other Polynesian	1	0.01
Other Pac. Isl., not spec. (2)	2	0.02
Hispanic or Latino:	1,069	10.46
Central American:	40	0.39
Costa Rican	3	0.03
Guatemalan	26	0.25
Honduran	3	0.03
Panamanian	4	0.04
Salvadoran	1	0.01
Other Central American	3	0.03
Cuban	14	0.14
Mexican	783	7.66
Puerto Rican	37	0.36
South American:	6	0.06
Argentinean	1	0.01
Bolivian	1	0.01
Chilean	1	0.01
Colombian	2	0.02
Ecuadorian	1	0.01
Other Hispanic or Latino	189	1.85
Hungarian	106	1.04
Irish	1,461	14.32
Italian	433	4.24
Lithuanian	39	0.38
Northern European	13	0.13
Norwegian	315	3.09
Polish	254	2.49
Portuguese	59	0.58
Russian	53	0.52
Scandinavian	69	0.68
Scotch-Irish	483	4.73
Scottish	383	3.75
Slavic	26	0.25
Swedish	361	3.54
Swiss	105	1.03
United States or American	488	4.78
Welsh	88	0.86
West Indian, excl. Hispanic:	3	0.03
West Indian	3	0.03
White:	9,410	92.09
Not Hispanic (8,542)	8,861	86.72
Hispanic (454)	549	5.37
Yugoslavian	29	0.28

Cudahy

Place Type: City
County: Los Angeles
Population: 24,208

Ancestry/Race	Number	%
African American/Black:	363	1.50
Not Hispanic (184)	200	0.83
Hispanic (116)	163	0.67
Alaska Native tribes, specified:	1	0.00
Alaska Athabascan (1)	1	0.00
Am. Ind. or Alaska Nat., not spec.	184	0.76
American Indian tribes, specified:	228	0.94
Apache (22)	24	0.10
Cherokee (3)	22	0.09
Chickasaw (2)	2	0.01
Chippewa	1	0.00
Choctaw (4)	4	0.02
Creek (10)	10	0.04
Latin American Indians (81)	114	0.47
Navajo (7)	21	0.09
Ottawa (1)	1	0.00
Pima (1)	1	0.00
Pueblo	1	0.00
Puget Sound Salish (2)	2	0.01
Sioux (1)	5	0.02
Yaqui (1)	3	0.01
All other tribes (8)	17	0.07
American Indian tribes, not spec.	28	0.12
Arab:	15	0.06
Lebanese	5	0.02
Syrian	10	0.04
Armenian	38	0.16
Asian:	224	0.93
Cambodian (5)	5	0.02
Chinese, ex. Taiwanese (23)	39	0.16
Filipino (28)	34	0.14
Indian (33)	39	0.16
Japanese (10)	18	0.07
Korean (26)	26	0.11
Laotian (3)	7	0.03
Taiwanese (10)	10	0.04
Thai (9)	9	0.04
Vietnamese (21)	24	0.10
Other Asian, not specified (6)	13	0.05
Canadian	6	0.02
Celtic	9	0.04
Czech	17	0.07
Czechoslovakian	5	0.02
Danish	27	0.11
Dutch	76	0.31
English	69	0.29
European	31	0.13
French, except Basque	25	0.10
French Canadian	6	0.02
German	154	0.64
Hawaii Native/Pacific Islander:	102	0.42
Micronesian: (2)	2	0.01
Guamanian/Chamorro (2)	2	0.01
Polynesian: (25)	35	0.14
Native Hawaiian (10)	15	0.06
Samoan (15)	20	0.08
Other Pac. Isl., not spec. (14)	65	0.27
Hispanic or Latino:	22,790	94.14
Central American:	2,288	9.45
Costa Rican	39	0.16
Guatemalan	570	2.35
Honduran	136	0.56
Nicaraguan	236	0.97
Panamanian	1	0.00
Salvadoran	1,081	4.47
Other Central American	225	0.93
Cuban	235	0.97
Dominican Republic	10	0.04
Mexican	16,520	68.24
Puerto Rican	146	0.60
South American:	166	0.69
Argentinean	6	0.02
Chilean	6	0.02
Colombian	46	0.19
Ecuadorian	31	0.13
Peruvian	43	0.18
Uruguayan	2	0.01
Other South American	32	0.13
Other Hispanic or Latino	3,425	14.15
Hungarian	35	0.14
Iranian	10	0.04
Irish	125	0.52
Italian	97	0.40
Norwegian	25	0.10
Polish	14	0.06
Portuguese	6	0.02
Russian	4	0.02
Scotch-Irish	11	0.05
Scottish	10	0.04
Swedish	10	0.04
Turkish	9	0.04
United States or American	474	1.96
White:	11,588	47.87
Not Hispanic (872)	951	3.93
Hispanic (9,571)	10,637	43.94

Culver City

Place Type: City
County: Los Angeles
Population: 38,816

Ancestry/Race	Number	%
Afghan	42	0.11
African American/Black:	5,264	13.56

Notes: 1. Figures in the "Number" column do not add up to the total population due to: a) Ancestry/Race overlap — e.g. persons can report being both White and Irish, b) persons of Hispanic origin can report being any race, c) persons reporting two ancestries are counted in both categories. 2. Numbers in parentheses indicate the number of persons reporting this ancestry/race alone, not in combination with any other ancestry/race. 3. Refer to the Explanation of Data in the front of the book for more detailed information.

Not Hispanic (4,536)	5,067	13.05
Hispanic (108)	197	0.51
African, sub-Saharan:	590	1.52
African	244	0.63
Ethiopian	155	0.40
Ghanian	27	0.07
Nigerian	68	0.18
Somalian	20	0.05
South African	26	0.07
Sudanese	27	0.07
Other sub-Saharan African	23	0.06
Alaska Native tribes, specified:	1	0.00
Alaska Athabascan (1)	1	0.00
Am. Ind. or Alaska Nat., not spec.	202	0.52
Alsatian	8	0.02
American Indian tribes, specified:	460	1.19
Apache (8)	24	0.06
Blackfeet (3)	23	0.06
Cherokee (27)	125	0.32
Cheyenne	1	0.00
Chickasaw	7	0.02
Chippewa (2)	8	0.02
Choctaw	18	0.05
Colville (1)	2	0.01
Comanche	1	0.00
Cree	4	0.01
Creek (3)	17	0.04
Crow (1)	3	0.01
Delaware	1	0.00
Iroquois	2	0.01
Latin American Indians (60)	97	0.25
Navajo (18)	18	0.05
Paiute (1)	1	0.00
Pima (1)	2	0.01
Potawatomi (1)	1	0.00
Pueblo (17)	19	0.05
Seminole (2)	6	0.02
Shoshone	1	0.00
Sioux (1)	9	0.02
Ute	1	0.00
Yaqui (4)	8	0.02
Yuman	1	0.00
All other tribes (18)	60	0.15
American Indian tribes, not spec.	44	0.11
Arab:	481	1.24
Arab/Arabic	87	0.22
Egyptian	167	0.43
Iraqi	7	0.02
Jordanian	73	0.19
Lebanese	70	0.18
Moroccan	14	0.04
Palestinian	9	0.02
Syrian	38	0.10
Other Arab	16	0.04
Armenian	115	0.30
Asian:	5,569	14.35
Bangladeshi (2)	2	0.01
Cambodian (7)	7	0.02
Chinese, ex. Taiwanese (759)	928	2.39
Filipino (744)	940	2.42
Indian (725)	827	2.13
Indonesian (22)	35	0.09
Japanese (1,287)	1,604	4.13
Korean (565)	621	1.60
Laotian (1)	3	0.01
Malaysian (2)	3	0.01
Pakistani (114)	139	0.36
Sri Lankan (13)	13	0.03
Taiwanese (49)	60	0.15
Thai (63)	76	0.20
Vietnamese (145)	165	0.43
Other Asian, specified (25)	38	0.10
Other Asian, not specified (32)	108	0.28
Australian	20	0.05
Austrian	213	0.55
Basque	6	0.02
Belgian	60	0.15
Brazilian	76	0.20
British	351	0.90
Canadian	218	0.56
Celtic	13	0.03
Croatian	18	0.05
Czech	171	0.44
Czechoslovakian	45	0.12
Danish	152	0.39
Dutch	368	0.95
Eastern European	335	0.86
English	2,734	7.04
European	514	1.32
Finnish	42	0.11
French, except Basque	1,145	2.95
French Canadian	218	0.56
German	3,462	8.92
Greek	135	0.35
Hawaii Native/Pacific Islander:	222	0.57
Melanesian: (28)	33	0.09
Fijian (28)	33	0.09
Micronesian: (11)	12	0.03
Guamanian/Chamorro (11)	12	0.03
Polynesian: (36)	122	0.31
Native Hawaiian (15)	87	0.22
Samoan (15)	24	0.06
Tongan (6)	8	0.02
Other Polynesian	3	0.01
Other Pac. Isl., not spec. (3)	55	0.14
Hispanic or Latino:	9,199	23.70
Central American:	828	2.13
Costa Rican	41	0.11
Guatemalan	235	0.61
Honduran	58	0.15
Nicaraguan	45	0.12
Panamanian	23	0.06
Salvadoran	367	0.95
Other Central American	59	0.15
Cuban	444	1.14
Dominican Republic	5	0.01
Mexican	5,738	14.78
Puerto Rican	133	0.34
South American:	464	1.20
Argentinean	130	0.33
Bolivian	10	0.03
Chilean	43	0.11
Colombian	90	0.23
Ecuadorian	42	0.11
Paraguayan	5	0.01
Peruvian	80	0.21
Uruguayan	12	0.03
Venezuelan	4	0.01
Other South American	48	0.12
Other Hispanic or Latino	1,587	4.09
Hungarian	430	1.11
Icelander	9	0.02
Iranian	223	0.57
Irish	2,725	7.02
Israeli	96	0.25
Italian	1,715	4.42
Latvian	46	0.12
Lithuanian	136	0.35
New Zealander	16	0.04
Northern European	42	0.11
Norwegian	384	0.99
Pennsylvania German	26	0.07
Polish	1,355	3.49
Portuguese	140	0.36
Romanian	152	0.39
Russian	1,480	3.81
Scandinavian	78	0.20
Scotch-Irish	428	1.10
Scottish	675	1.74
Slovak	64	0.16
Swedish	522	1.34
Swiss	99	0.26
Turkish	46	0.12
Ukrainian	158	0.41
United States or American	1,462	3.77
Welsh	148	0.38
West Indian, excl. Hispanic:	367	0.95
Barbadian	26	0.07
Belizean	36	0.09
British West Indian	20	0.05
Dutch West Indian	6	0.02
Haitian	59	0.15
Jamaican	120	0.31
Trinidadian and Tobagonian	91	0.23
U.S. Virgin Islander	9	0.02
White:	24,746	63.75
Not Hispanic (18,675)	19,790	50.98
Hispanic (4,321)	4,956	12.77
Yugoslavian	48	0.12

Cupertino

Place Type: City
County: Santa Clara
Population: 50,546

Ancestry/Race	Number	%
Acadian/Cajun	6	0.01
African American/Black:	512	1.01
Not Hispanic (319)	439	0.87
Hispanic (28)	73	0.14
African, sub-Saharan:	49	0.10
African	11	0.02
Ethiopian	30	0.06
South African	8	0.02
Alaska Native tribes, specified:	1	0.00
Eskimo	1	0.00
Am. Ind. or Alaska Nat., not spec.	104	0.21
American Indian tribes, specified:	206	0.41
Apache (3)	5	0.01
Blackfeet (1)	9	0.02
Cherokee (18)	81	0.16
Chickasaw	4	0.01
Chippewa (2)	8	0.02
Choctaw (7)	13	0.03
Creek (1)	2	0.00
Iroquois (1)	10	0.02
Kiowa (1)	1	0.00
Latin American Indians (2)	14	0.03
Navajo (4)	7	0.01
Osage (2)	3	0.01
Pima (1)	1	0.00
Potawatomi (1)	1	0.00
Pueblo	1	0.00
Puget Sound Salish	1	0.00
Seminole	5	0.01
Sioux (4)	12	0.02
Tohono O'Odham (1)	1	0.00
Yakama (2)	2	0.00
Yaqui (1)	2	0.00
All other tribes (14)	23	0.05
American Indian tribes, not spec.	24	0.05
Arab:	583	1.15
Arab/Arabic	141	0.28
Egyptian	91	0.18
Jordanian	16	0.03
Lebanese	67	0.13
Moroccan	10	0.02
Syrian	74	0.15
Other Arab	184	0.36
Armenian	153	0.30
Asian:	23,808	47.10
Bangladeshi (15)	15	0.03
Cambodian (6)	12	0.02
Chinese, ex. Taiwanese (11,246)	11,867	23.48
Filipino (368)	509	1.01
Indian (4,408)	4,546	8.99
Indonesian (33)	52	0.10
Japanese (2,331)	2,660	5.26
Korean (2,100)	2,193	4.34
Laotian (1)	1	0.00
Malaysian (15)	19	0.04
Pakistani (111)	130	0.26
Sri Lankan (33)	34	0.07
Taiwanese (785)	910	1.80
Thai (36)	57	0.11
Vietnamese (523)	578	1.14
Other Asian, specified (28)	33	0.07
Other Asian, not specified (86)	192	0.38
Assyrian/Chaldean/Syriac	29	0.06

Notes: 1. Figures in the "Number" column do not add up to the total population due to: a) Ancestry/Race overlap — e.g. persons can report being both White and Irish, b) persons of Hispanic origin can report being any race, c) persons reporting two ancestries are counted in both categories. 2. Numbers in parentheses indicate the number of persons reporting this ancestry/race alone, not in combination with any other ancestry/race. 3. Refer to the Explanation of Data in the front of the book for more detailed information.

Australian	118	0.23
Austrian	149	0.29
Basque	6	0.01
Belgian	35	0.07
Brazilian	112	0.22
British	549	1.08
Bulgarian	53	0.10
Canadian	145	0.29
Croatian	152	0.30
Czech	104	0.21
Czechoslovakian	43	0.08
Danish	393	0.78
Dutch	514	1.01
Eastern European	46	0.09
English	4,047	7.99
Estonian	9	0.02
European	529	1.04
Finnish	159	0.31
French, except Basque	1,061	2.09
French Canadian	249	0.49
German	5,055	9.98
Greek	220	0.43
Hawaii Native/Pacific Islander:	174	0.34
Micronesian: (17)	24	0.05
Guamanian/Chamorro (17)	24	0.05
Polynesian: (35)	84	0.17
Native Hawaiian (17)	61	0.12
Samoan (9)	12	0.02
Tongan (3)	5	0.01
Other Polynesian (6)	6	0.01
Other Pac. Isl., specified	5	0.01
Other Pac. Isl., not spec. (15)	61	0.12
Hispanic or Latino:	2,010	3.98
Central American:	91	0.18
Costa Rican	6	0.01
Guatemalan	14	0.03
Honduran	2	0.00
Nicaraguan	22	0.04
Panamanian	3	0.01
Salvadoran	34	0.07
Other Central American	10	0.02
Cuban	35	0.07
Dominican Republic	5	0.01
Mexican	1,145	2.27
Puerto Rican	66	0.13
South American:	168	0.33
Argentinean	27	0.05
Bolivian	9	0.02
Chilean	22	0.04
Colombian	23	0.05
Ecuadorian	1	0.00
Peruvian	44	0.09
Venezuelan	14	0.03
Other South American	28	0.06
Other Hispanic or Latino	500	0.99
Hungarian	265	0.52
Icelander	7	0.01
Iranian	761	1.50
Irish	3,233	6.38
Israeli	518	1.02
Italian	2,070	4.09
Latvian	6	0.01
Lithuanian	107	0.21
Northern European	139	0.27
Norwegian	409	0.81
Pennsylvania German	9	0.02
Polish	926	1.83
Portuguese	414	0.82
Romanian	163	0.32
Russian	1,155	2.28
Scandinavian	69	0.14
Scotch-Irish	496	0.98
Scottish	836	1.65
Serbian	54	0.11
Slavic	43	0.08
Slovak	60	0.12
Slovene	37	0.07
Swedish	684	1.35
Swiss	218	0.43
Turkish	97	0.19
Ukrainian	167	0.33
United States or American	924	1.82
Welsh	231	0.46
West Indian, excl. Hispanic:	76	0.15
Haitian	13	0.03
Jamaican	39	0.08
Trinidadian and Tobagonian	24	0.05
White:	26,691	52.81
Not Hispanic (24,181)	25,338	50.13
Hispanic (1,161)	1,353	2.68
Yugoslavian	102	0.20

Cypress

Place Type: City
County: Orange
Population: 46,229

Ancestry/Race	Number	%
Afghan	5	0.01
African American/Black:	1,553	3.36
Not Hispanic (1,251)	1,475	3.19
Hispanic (29)	78	0.17
African, sub-Saharan:	155	0.33
African	59	0.13
Ethiopian	11	0.02
Nigerian	21	0.05
South African	10	0.02
Other sub-Saharan African	54	0.12
Alaska Native tribes, specified:	6	0.01
Eskimo	3	0.01
Tlingit-Haida (3)	3	0.01
Alaska Native tribes, not specified	1	0.00
Am. Ind. or Alaska Nat., not spec.	219	0.47
Alsatian	7	0.02
American Indian tribes, specified:	424	0.92
Apache (8)	26	0.06
Blackfeet (1)	30	0.06
Cherokee (43)	136	0.29
Cheyenne (3)	3	0.01
Chickasaw (1)	2	0.00
Chippewa (4)	11	0.02
Choctaw (7)	33	0.07
Comanche (1)	6	0.01
Creek (2)	5	0.01
Delaware	1	0.00
Iroquois (3)	12	0.03
Kiowa	5	0.01
Latin American Indians (16)	29	0.06
Navajo (8)	22	0.05
Osage (2)	3	0.01
Ottawa	2	0.00
Pima (1)	3	0.01
Potawatomi (1)	4	0.01
Pueblo (14)	18	0.04
Seminole	3	0.01
Shoshone	2	0.00
Sioux (7)	10	0.02
Yaqui (2)	3	0.01
All other tribes (28)	55	0.12
American Indian tribes, not spec.	25	0.05
Arab:	814	1.75
Arab/Arabic	151	0.32
Egyptian	124	0.27
Jordanian	33	0.07
Lebanese	314	0.67
Palestinian	55	0.12
Syrian	70	0.15
Other Arab	67	0.14
Armenian	278	0.60
Asian:	10,853	23.48
Bangladeshi (6)	6	0.01
Cambodian (86)	113	0.24
Chinese, ex. Taiwanese (1,410)	1,715	3.71
Filipino (2,049)	2,463	5.33
Hmong (13)	13	0.03
Indian (756)	805	1.74
Indonesian (42)	73	0.16
Japanese (1,214)	1,570	3.40
Korean (2,443)	2,548	5.51
Laotian (3)	3	0.01
Malaysian	10	0.02
Pakistani (107)	125	0.27
Sri Lankan (24)	25	0.05
Taiwanese (364)	409	0.88
Thai (132)	149	0.32
Vietnamese (665)	703	1.52
Other Asian, specified (3)	6	0.01
Other Asian, not specified (38)	117	0.25
Assyrian/Chaldean/Syriac	42	0.09
Australian	56	0.12
Austrian	104	0.22
Basque	99	0.21
Belgian	62	0.13
Brazilian	14	0.03
British	243	0.52
Bulgarian	10	0.02
Canadian	267	0.57
Croatian	33	0.07
Czech	174	0.37
Czechoslovakian	67	0.14
Danish	277	0.60
Dutch	1,162	2.50
Eastern European	31	0.07
English	4,251	9.14
European	457	0.98
Finnish	63	0.14
French, except Basque	1,564	3.36
French Canadian	302	0.65
German	5,673	12.19
German Russian	7	0.02
Greek	336	0.72
Hawaii Native/Pacific Islander:	336	0.73
Melanesian:	4	0.01
Fijian	4	0.01
Micronesian: (91)	119	0.26
Guamanian/Chamorro (90)	118	0.26
Other Micronesian (1)	1	0.00
Polynesian: (71)	134	0.29
Native Hawaiian (46)	88	0.19
Samoan (17)	36	0.08
Tongan (8)	9	0.02
Other Polynesian	1	0.00
Other Pac. Isl., not spec. (19)	79	0.17
Hispanic or Latino:	7,235	15.65
Central American:	198	0.43
Costa Rican	13	0.03
Guatemalan	46	0.10
Honduran	12	0.03
Nicaraguan	35	0.08
Panamanian	12	0.03
Salvadoran	59	0.13
Other Central American	21	0.05
Cuban	152	0.33
Dominican Republic	3	0.01
Mexican	5,321	11.51
Puerto Rican	163	0.35
South American:	278	0.60
Argentinean	49	0.11
Bolivian	2	0.00
Chilean	19	0.04
Colombian	60	0.13
Ecuadorian	24	0.05
Peruvian	78	0.17
Uruguayan	1	0.00
Venezuelan	10	0.02
Other South American	35	0.08
Other Hispanic or Latino	1,120	2.42
Hungarian	224	0.48
Icelander	31	0.07
Iranian	83	0.18
Irish	4,333	9.31
Israeli	12	0.03
Italian	2,408	5.17
Lithuanian	129	0.28
Luxemburger	8	0.02
Northern European	26	0.06
Norwegian	962	2.07
Pennsylvania German	7	0.02
Polish	945	2.03

Notes: 1. Figures in the "Number" column do not add up to the total population due to: a) Ancestry/Race overlap — e.g. persons can report being both White and Irish, b) persons of Hispanic origin can report being any race, c) persons reporting two ancestries are counted in both categories. 2. Numbers in parentheses indicate the number of persons reporting this ancestry/race alone, not in combination with any other ancestry/race. 3. Refer to the Explanation of Data in the front of the book for more detailed information.

Portuguese	358	0.77
Romanian	103	0.22
Russian	590	1.27
Scandinavian	93	0.20
Scotch-Irish	729	1.57
Scottish	763	1.64
Serbian	12	0.03
Slavic	28	0.06
Slovak	59	0.13
Slovene	17	0.04
Swedish	778	1.67
Swiss	131	0.28
Ukrainian	53	0.11
United States or American	2,194	4.71
Welsh	395	0.85
West Indian, excl. Hispanic:	76	0.16
Belizean	10	0.02
Jamaican	4	0.01
Trinidadian and Tobagonian	6	0.01
West Indian	56	0.12
White:	32,014	69.25
Not Hispanic (26,400)	27,486	59.46
Hispanic (3,932)	4,528	9.79
Yugoslavian	92	0.20

Daly City

Place Type: City
County: San Mateo
Population: 103,621

Ancestry/Race	Number	%
Afghan	14	0.01
African American/Black:	5,587	5.39
Not Hispanic (4,482)	5,163	4.98
Hispanic (238)	424	0.41
African, sub-Saharan:	515	0.50
African	445	0.43
Ethiopian	23	0.02
Ghanian	22	0.02
Nigerian	25	0.02
Alaska Native tribes, specified:	9	0.01
Aleut	2	0.00
Eskimo	1	0.00
Tlingit-Haida (2)	6	0.01
Am. Ind. or Alaska Nat., not spec.	450	0.43
Albanian	3	0.00
American Indian tribes, specified:	580	0.56
Apache (21)	45	0.04
Blackfeet (2)	23	0.02
Cherokee (27)	126	0.12
Cheyenne (1)	1	0.00
Chickasaw (1)	2	0.00
Chippewa (6)	11	0.01
Choctaw (7)	19	0.02
Comanche (3)	6	0.01
Creek (2)	8	0.01
Delaware	2	0.00
Iroquois (3)	18	0.02
Latin American Indians (63)	113	0.11
Lumbee (1)	4	0.00
Navajo (18)	35	0.03
Osage (1)	2	0.00
Paiute	6	0.01
Pima	3	0.00
Potawatomi (2)	4	0.00
Pueblo (11)	15	0.01
Seminole (1)	5	0.00
Shoshone (1)	8	0.01
Sioux (11)	26	0.03
Tohono O'Odham	1	0.00
Ute	3	0.00
Yaqui (1)	7	0.01
All other tribes (47)	87	0.08
American Indian tribes, not spec.	55	0.05
Arab:	1,794	1.73
Arab/Arabic	588	0.57
Egyptian	17	0.02
Iraqi	4	0.00
Jordanian	91	0.09
Lebanese	123	0.12
Palestinian	770	0.74
Syrian	23	0.02
Other Arab	178	0.17
Armenian	130	0.13
Asian:	56,690	54.71
Bangladeshi (12)	20	0.02
Cambodian (32)	61	0.06
Chinese, ex. Taiwanese (13,998)	15,185	14.65
Filipino (32,720)	35,099	33.87
Hmong (1)	2	0.00
Indian (1,073)	1,351	1.30
Indonesian (255)	340	0.33
Japanese (825)	1,188	1.15
Korean (789)	907	0.88
Laotian (20)	29	0.03
Malaysian (19)	49	0.05
Pakistani (133)	203	0.20
Sri Lankan (16)	23	0.02
Taiwanese (65)	71	0.07
Thai (197)	235	0.23
Vietnamese (720)	874	0.84
Other Asian, specified (514)	659	0.64
Other Asian, not specified (147)	394	0.38
Assyrian/Chaldean/Syriac	22	0.02
Australian	66	0.06
Austrian	112	0.11
Basque	22	0.02
Belgian	49	0.05
Brazilian	541	0.52
British	109	0.11
Bulgarian	13	0.01
Canadian	124	0.12
Carpatho Rusyn	10	0.01
Celtic	10	0.01
Croatian	99	0.10
Czech	86	0.08
Czechoslovakian	18	0.02
Danish	102	0.10
Dutch	192	0.19
Eastern European	34	0.03
English	1,928	1.86
European	461	0.45
Finnish	161	0.16
French, except Basque	877	0.85
French Canadian	122	0.12
German	3,054	2.95
Greek	426	0.41
Hawaii Native/Pacific Islander:	1,766	1.70
Melanesian: (77)	115	0.11
Fijian (77)	115	0.11
Micronesian: (56)	122	0.12
Guamanian/Chamorro (50)	111	0.11
Other Micronesian (6)	11	0.01
Polynesian: (709)	1,145	1.10
Native Hawaiian (92)	308	0.30
Samoan (570)	744	0.72
Tongan (43)	59	0.06
Other Polynesian (4)	34	0.03
Other Pac. Isl., specified	6	0.01
Other Pac. Isl., not spec. (63)	378	0.36
Hispanic or Latino:	23,072	22.27
Central American:	6,426	6.20
Costa Rican	49	0.05
Guatemalan	533	0.51
Honduran	103	0.10
Nicaraguan	2,052	1.98
Panamanian	48	0.05
Salvadoran	2,896	2.79
Other Central American	745	0.72
Cuban	116	0.11
Dominican Republic	25	0.02
Mexican	8,651	8.35
Puerto Rican	662	0.64
South American:	918	0.89
Argentinean	36	0.03
Bolivian	42	0.04
Chilean	43	0.04
Colombian	108	0.10
Ecuadorian	43	0.04
Peruvian	496	0.48
Uruguayan	1	0.00
Venezuelan	42	0.04
Other South American	107	0.10
Other Hispanic or Latino	6,274	6.05
Hungarian	118	0.11
Icelander	9	0.01
Iranian	115	0.11
Irish	3,823	3.69
Israeli	19	0.02
Italian	3,451	3.33
Lithuanian	91	0.09
Luxemburger	6	0.01
Maltese	41	0.04
New Zealander	8	0.01
Norwegian	499	0.48
Polish	593	0.57
Portuguese	378	0.37
Romanian	64	0.06
Russian	895	0.86
Scandinavian	86	0.08
Scotch-Irish	394	0.38
Scottish	483	0.47
Serbian	26	0.03
Slavic	36	0.03
Slovak	34	0.03
Slovene	46	0.04
Swedish	554	0.54
Swiss	151	0.15
Turkish	46	0.04
Ukrainian	162	0.16
United States or American	975	0.94
Welsh	148	0.14
West Indian, excl. Hispanic:	187	0.18
British West Indian	19	0.02
Jamaican	116	0.11
Trinidadian and Tobagonian	31	0.03
West Indian	21	0.02
White:	31,275	30.18
Not Hispanic (18,344)	20,914	20.18
Hispanic (8,492)	10,361	10.00
Yugoslavian	80	0.08

Dana Point

Place Type: City
County: Orange
Population: 35,110

Ancestry/Race	Number	%
African American/Black:	405	1.15
Not Hispanic (252)	348	0.99
Hispanic (36)	57	0.16
African, sub-Saharan:	41	0.12
African	31	0.09
South African	10	0.03
Alaska Native tribes, specified:	1	0.00
Tlingit-Haida (1)	1	0.00
Am. Ind. or Alaska Nat., not spec.	140	0.40
American Indian tribes, specified:	288	0.82
Apache (5)	9	0.03
Blackfeet	4	0.01
Cherokee (25)	76	0.22
Cheyenne (1)	1	0.00
Chickasaw (1)	1	0.00
Chippewa (2)	8	0.02
Choctaw (8)	23	0.07
Comanche (1)	2	0.01
Cree	5	0.01
Creek	7	0.02
Crow (2)	2	0.01
Delaware	3	0.01
Iroquois (3)	6	0.02
Latin American Indians (19)	26	0.07
Lumbee (2)	2	0.01
Navajo (2)	8	0.02
Osage (2)	4	0.01
Paiute	1	0.00
Potawatomi (2)	7	0.02
Pueblo (2)	5	0.01

Notes: 1. Figures in the "Number" column do not add up to the total population due to: a) Ancestry/Race overlap — e.g. persons can report being both White and Irish, b) persons of Hispanic origin can report being any race, c) persons reporting two ancestries are counted in both categories. 2. Numbers in parentheses indicate the number of persons reporting this ancestry/race alone, not in combination with any other ancestry/race. 3. Refer to the Explanation of Data in the front of the book for more detailed information.

Ancestry/Race	Number	%
Sioux (2)	7	0.02
Tohono O'Odham	1	0.00
Yaqui (2)	5	0.01
Yuman (5)	5	0.01
All other tribes (39)	70	0.20
American Indian tribes, not spec.	14	0.04
Arab:	402	1.15
Arab/Arabic	100	0.29
Egyptian	213	0.61
Lebanese	39	0.11
Palestinian	8	0.02
Syrian	35	0.10
Other Arab	7	0.02
Armenian	109	0.31
Asian:	1,270	3.62
Cambodian (12)	12	0.03
Chinese, ex. Taiwanese (188)	269	0.77
Filipino (170)	285	0.81
Indian (63)	78	0.22
Indonesian (13)	36	0.10
Japanese (210)	310	0.88
Korean (69)	89	0.25
Malaysian (1)	2	0.01
Pakistani (3)	7	0.02
Sri Lankan (1)	2	0.01
Taiwanese (19)	23	0.07
Thai (12)	23	0.07
Vietnamese (69)	81	0.23
Other Asian, specified (4)	11	0.03
Other Asian, not specified (12)	42	0.12
Assyrian/Chaldean/Syriac	15	0.04
Australian	5	0.01
Austrian	193	0.55
Basque	55	0.16
Belgian	27	0.08
Brazilian	37	0.11
British	356	1.02
Bulgarian	54	0.15
Canadian	86	0.25
Croatian	83	0.24
Czech	134	0.38
Czechoslovakian	59	0.17
Danish	389	1.12
Dutch	696	2.00
Eastern European	99	0.28
English	5,040	14.46
European	356	1.02
Finnish	178	0.51
French, except Basque	1,307	3.75
French Canadian	421	1.21
German	6,069	17.41
Greek	246	0.71
Hawaii Native/Pacific Islander:	150	0.43
Melanesian: (1)	1	0.00
Fijian (1)	1	0.00
Micronesian: (2)	8	0.02
Guamanian/Chamorro (1)	6	0.02
Other Micronesian (1)	2	0.01
Polynesian: (29)	100	0.28
Native Hawaiian (22)	82	0.23
Samoan (4)	7	0.02
Other Polynesian (3)	11	0.03
Other Pac. Isl., specified	2	0.01
Other Pac. Isl., not spec. (4)	39	0.11
Hispanic or Latino:	5,440	15.49
Central American:	123	0.35
Costa Rican	17	0.05
Guatemalan	53	0.15
Honduran	1	0.00
Nicaraguan	9	0.03
Panamanian	4	0.01
Salvadoran	31	0.09
Other Central American	8	0.02
Cuban	61	0.17
Mexican	4,316	12.29
Puerto Rican	70	0.20
South American:	146	0.42
Argentinean	42	0.12
Bolivian	9	0.03
Chilean	11	0.03
Colombian	24	0.07
Ecuadorian	4	0.01
Peruvian	28	0.08
Uruguayan	1	0.00
Venezuelan	15	0.04
Other South American	12	0.03
Other Hispanic or Latino	724	2.06
Hungarian	323	0.93
Iranian	167	0.48
Irish	4,565	13.10
Israeli	26	0.07
Italian	2,732	7.84
Lithuanian	61	0.18
Macedonian	7	0.02
Northern European	38	0.11
Norwegian	952	2.73
Polish	1,016	2.92
Portuguese	114	0.33
Romanian	53	0.15
Russian	850	2.44
Scandinavian	104	0.30
Scotch-Irish	764	2.19
Scottish	1,200	3.44
Serbian	8	0.02
Slavic	44	0.13
Slovak	53	0.15
Slovene	42	0.12
Swedish	767	2.20
Swiss	203	0.58
Turkish	54	0.15
Ukrainian	153	0.44
United States or American	1,536	4.41
Welsh	378	1.08
West Indian, excl. Hispanic:	37	0.11
Belizean	33	0.09
West Indian	4	0.01
White:	31,528	89.80
Not Hispanic (27,658)	28,254	80.47
Hispanic (2,975)	3,274	9.32
Yugoslavian	104	0.30

Danville

Place Type: Town
County: Contra Costa
Population: 41,715

Ancestry/Race	Number	%
African American/Black:	478	1.15
Not Hispanic (375)	462	1.11
Hispanic (7)	16	0.04
African, sub-Saharan:	58	0.14
African	39	0.09
Ethiopian	19	0.05
Alaska Native tribes, specified:	2	0.00
Alaska Athabascan	1	0.00
Tlingit-Haida (1)	1	0.00
Am. Ind. or Alaska Nat., not spec.	53	0.13
American Indian tribes, specified:	170	0.41
Apache (2)	4	0.01
Blackfeet (1)	4	0.01
Cherokee (12)	57	0.14
Chippewa (2)	12	0.03
Choctaw (8)	19	0.05
Comanche	1	0.00
Cree	1	0.00
Creek	1	0.00
Iroquois (1)	4	0.01
Latin American Indians (1)	7	0.02
Menominee	1	0.00
Navajo (3)	3	0.01
Osage (1)	2	0.00
Paiute	2	0.00
Pueblo (1)	7	0.02
Sioux	11	0.03
All other tribes (25)	34	0.08
American Indian tribes, not spec.	10	0.02
Arab:	345	0.82
Arab/Arabic	72	0.17
Egyptian	59	0.14
Lebanese	136	0.32
Palestinian	9	0.02
Syrian	57	0.14
Other Arab	12	0.03
Armenian	87	0.21
Asian:	4,525	10.85
Bangladeshi (2)	2	0.00
Cambodian (8)	8	0.02
Chinese, ex. Taiwanese (1,699)	1,988	4.77
Filipino (486)	684	1.64
Indian (577)	634	1.52
Indonesian (9)	22	0.05
Japanese (322)	541	1.30
Korean (200)	240	0.58
Laotian (2)	2	0.00
Malaysian (1)	3	0.01
Pakistani (30)	36	0.09
Sri Lankan (11)	13	0.03
Taiwanese (119)	129	0.31
Thai (8)	9	0.02
Vietnamese (101)	111	0.27
Other Asian, specified (8)	10	0.02
Other Asian, not specified (42)	93	0.22
Assyrian/Chaldean/Syriac	42	0.10
Australian	44	0.10
Austrian	255	0.61
Basque	66	0.16
Belgian	44	0.10
Brazilian	10	0.02
British	378	0.90
Bulgarian	40	0.09
Canadian	271	0.64
Celtic	10	0.02
Croatian	163	0.39
Czech	183	0.43
Czechoslovakian	86	0.20
Danish	551	1.31
Dutch	626	1.49
Eastern European	59	0.14
English	6,649	15.78
Estonian	7	0.02
European	1,008	2.39
Finnish	164	0.39
French, except Basque	1,509	3.58
French Canadian	238	0.56
German	7,704	18.29
Greek	538	1.28
Hawaii Native/Pacific Islander:	138	0.33
Melanesian: (5)	6	0.01
Fijian (2)	3	0.01
Other Melanesian (3)	3	0.01
Micronesian: (14)	24	0.06
Guamanian/Chamorro (11)	21	0.05
Other Micronesian (3)	3	0.01
Polynesian: (21)	68	0.16
Native Hawaiian (14)	56	0.13
Samoan (5)	5	0.01
Tongan (1)	1	0.00
Other Polynesian (1)	6	0.01
Other Pac. Isl., not spec. (8)	40	0.10
Hispanic or Latino:	1,945	4.66
Central American:	106	0.25
Costa Rican	10	0.02
Guatemalan	16	0.04
Honduran	3	0.01
Nicaraguan	20	0.05
Panamanian	4	0.01
Salvadoran	45	0.11
Other Central American	8	0.02
Cuban	52	0.12
Dominican Republic	6	0.01
Mexican	946	2.27
Puerto Rican	126	0.30
South American:	147	0.35
Argentinean	14	0.03
Chilean	26	0.06
Colombian	17	0.04
Ecuadorian	6	0.01
Peruvian	64	0.15
Uruguayan	4	0.01

Notes: 1. Figures in the "Number" column do not add up to the total population due to: a) Ancestry/Race overlap — e.g. persons can report being both White and Irish, b) persons of Hispanic origin can report being any race, c) persons reporting two ancestries are counted in both categories. 2. Numbers in parentheses indicate the number of persons reporting this ancestry/race alone, not in combination with any other ancestry/race. 3. Refer to the Explanation of Data in the front of the book for more detailed information.

Venezuelan	5	0.01
Other South American	11	0.03
Other Hispanic or Latino	562	1.35
Hungarian	377	0.89
Icelander	36	0.09
Iranian	493	1.17
Irish	6,908	16.40
Israeli	8	0.02
Italian	4,147	9.84
Latvian	17	0.04
Lithuanian	92	0.22
Luxemburger	15	0.04
Macedonian	9	0.02
Northern European	90	0.21
Norwegian	1,039	2.47
Pennsylvania German	24	0.06
Polish	1,205	2.86
Portuguese	1,077	2.56
Romanian	63	0.15
Russian	1,003	2.38
Scandinavian	174	0.41
Scotch-Irish	852	2.02
Scottish	1,440	3.42
Serbian	15	0.04
Slavic	33	0.08
Slovak	76	0.18
Slovene	19	0.05
Swedish	1,233	2.93
Swiss	296	0.70
Turkish	39	0.09
Ukrainian	166	0.39
United States or American	1,185	2.81
Welsh	358	0.85
West Indian, excl. Hispanic:	31	0.07
West Indian	31	0.07
White:	36,940	88.55
Not Hispanic (34,618)	35,394	84.85
Hispanic (1,382)	1,546	3.71
Yugoslavian	178	0.42

Davis

Place Type: City
County: Yolo
Population: 60,308

Ancestry/Race	Number	%
Acadian/Cajun	7	0.01
Afghan	98	0.16
African American/Black:	1,852	3.07
Not Hispanic (1,354)	1,708	2.83
Hispanic (63)	144	0.24
African, sub-Saharan:	506	0.84
African	206	0.34
Ethiopian	42	0.07
Nigerian	138	0.23
Senegalese	13	0.02
South African	10	0.02
Sudanese	35	0.06
Zimbabwean	11	0.02
Other sub-Saharan African	51	0.08
Alaska Native tribes, specified:	7	0.01
Aleut	1	0.00
Eskimo (2)	3	0.00
Tlingit-Haida (2)	2	0.00
All other tribes (1)	1	0.00
Am. Ind. or Alaska Nat., not spec.	265	0.44
Albanian	5	0.01
American Indian tribes, specified:	586	0.97
Apache (14)	28	0.05
Blackfeet	8	0.01
Cherokee (48)	181	0.30
Cheyenne (1)	4	0.01
Chickasaw (4)	7	0.01
Chippewa (6)	16	0.03
Choctaw (5)	31	0.05
Comanche (2)	6	0.01
Cree	3	0.00
Creek (7)	8	0.01
Crow (1)	1	0.00
Delaware (1)	1	0.00
Iroquois (6)	12	0.02
Latin American Indians (40)	83	0.14
Lumbee	1	0.00
Menominee (4)	4	0.01
Navajo (9)	20	0.03
Osage (3)	12	0.02
Paiute (3)	6	0.01
Pima (1)	3	0.00
Potawatomi (3)	6	0.01
Pueblo (9)	12	0.02
Puget Sound Salish	2	0.00
Seminole (7)	7	0.01
Shoshone	1	0.00
Sioux (13)	18	0.03
Tohono O'Odham	1	0.00
Ute (2)	2	0.00
Yaqui (9)	14	0.02
All other tribes (50)	88	0.15
American Indian tribes, not spec.	62	0.10
Arab:	363	0.60
Arab/Arabic	68	0.11
Egyptian	51	0.08
Iraqi	22	0.04
Jordanian	11	0.02
Lebanese	129	0.21
Moroccan	18	0.03
Palestinian	11	0.02
Syrian	17	0.03
Other Arab	36	0.06
Armenian	181	0.30
Asian:	12,327	20.44
Bangladeshi (8)	8	0.01
Cambodian (30)	43	0.07
Chinese, ex. Taiwanese (4,709)	5,270	8.74
Filipino (1,019)	1,368	2.27
Hmong (94)	98	0.16
Indian (962)	1,105	1.83
Indonesian (35)	48	0.08
Japanese (965)	1,439	2.39
Korean (867)	975	1.62
Laotian (47)	50	0.08
Malaysian (3)	13	0.02
Pakistani (79)	110	0.18
Sri Lankan (49)	52	0.09
Taiwanese (145)	182	0.30
Thai (84)	105	0.17
Vietnamese (1,061)	1,156	1.92
Other Asian, specified (67)	93	0.15
Other Asian, not specified (77)	212	0.35
Australian	104	0.17
Austrian	335	0.56
Basque	66	0.11
Belgian	65	0.11
Brazilian	43	0.07
British	703	1.17
Bulgarian	35	0.06
Canadian	249	0.41
Celtic	57	0.09
Croatian	168	0.28
Cypriot	11	0.02
Czech	336	0.56
Czechoslovakian	103	0.17
Danish	685	1.14
Dutch	898	1.49
Eastern European	169	0.28
English	7,184	11.91
European	2,104	3.49
Finnish	335	0.56
French, except Basque	1,736	2.88
French Canadian	345	0.57
German	9,286	15.39
Greek	261	0.43
Hawaii Native/Pacific Islander:	320	0.53
Melanesian: (65)	75	0.12
Fijian (65)	75	0.12
Micronesian: (12)	29	0.05
Guamanian/Chamorro (11)	27	0.04
Other Micronesian (1)	2	0.00
Polynesian: (39)	103	0.17
Native Hawaiian (15)	67	0.11
Samoan (17)	27	0.04
Tongan (7)	9	0.01
Other Pac. Isl., specified	6	0.01
Other Pac. Isl., not spec. (28)	107	0.18
Hispanic or Latino:	5,793	9.61
Central American:	349	0.58
Costa Rican	18	0.03
Guatemalan	66	0.11
Honduran	10	0.02
Nicaraguan	51	0.08
Panamanian	14	0.02
Salvadoran	139	0.23
Other Central American	51	0.08
Cuban	58	0.10
Dominican Republic	8	0.01
Mexican	3,966	6.58
Puerto Rican	170	0.28
South American:	343	0.57
Argentinean	54	0.09
Bolivian	20	0.03
Chilean	36	0.06
Colombian	62	0.10
Ecuadorian	13	0.02
Paraguayan	2	0.00
Peruvian	99	0.16
Uruguayan	6	0.01
Venezuelan	33	0.05
Other South American	18	0.03
Other Hispanic or Latino	899	1.49
Hungarian	308	0.51
Icelander	58	0.10
Iranian	440	0.73
Irish	6,954	11.52
Israeli	33	0.05
Italian	3,518	5.83
Latvian	28	0.05
Lithuanian	210	0.35
Macedonian	6	0.01
Maltese	27	0.04
New Zealander	58	0.10
Northern European	269	0.45
Norwegian	1,162	1.93
Pennsylvania German	17	0.03
Polish	1,509	2.50
Portuguese	860	1.43
Romanian	226	0.37
Russian	1,282	2.12
Scandinavian	144	0.24
Scotch-Irish	984	1.63
Scottish	1,831	3.03
Serbian	23	0.04
Slavic	73	0.12
Slovak	93	0.15
Slovene	13	0.02
Swedish	1,512	2.51
Swiss	444	0.74
Turkish	78	0.13
Ukrainian	294	0.49
United States or American	1,766	2.93
Welsh	747	1.24
West Indian, excl. Hispanic:	88	0.15
Bahamian	13	0.02
Belizean	5	0.01
Dutch West Indian	22	0.04
Haitian	6	0.01
Jamaican	25	0.04
West Indian	17	0.03
White:	44,742	74.19
Not Hispanic (39,714)	41,722	69.18
Hispanic (2,542)	3,020	5.01
Yugoslavian	114	0.19

Delano

Place Type: City
County: Kern
Population: 38,824

Ancestry/Race	Number	%

Notes: 1. Figures in the "Number" column do not add up to the total population due to: a) Ancestry/Race overlap — e.g. persons can report being both White and Irish, b) persons of Hispanic origin can report being any race, c) persons reporting two ancestries are counted in both categories. 2. Numbers in parentheses indicate the number of persons reporting this ancestry/race alone, not in combination with any other ancestry/race. 3. Refer to the Explanation of Data in the front of the book for more detailed information.

African American/Black:	2,256	5.81
Not Hispanic (1,997)	2,073	5.34
Hispanic (118)	183	0.47
African, sub-Saharan:	16	0.04
African	16	0.04
Alaska Native tribes, specified:	3	0.01
Alaska Athabascan	2	0.01
Tlingit-Haida (1)	1	0.00
Am. Ind. or Alaska Nat., not spec.	253	0.65
American Indian tribes, specified:	279	0.72
Apache (11)	22	0.06
Blackfeet (1)	5	0.01
Cherokee (12)	34	0.09
Chickasaw (2)	3	0.01
Choctaw (2)	9	0.02
Comanche	6	0.02
Creek	1	0.00
Latin American Indians (114)	141	0.36
Navajo (2)	7	0.02
Ottawa (2)	2	0.01
Paiute	2	0.01
Pima	6	0.02
Pueblo (1)	2	0.01
Yaqui (6)	7	0.02
All other tribes (17)	32	0.08
American Indian tribes, not spec.	33	0.08
Arab:	83	0.21
Arab/Arabic	28	0.07
Jordanian	18	0.05
Syrian	14	0.04
Other Arab	23	0.06
Armenian	11	0.03
Asian:	6,910	17.80
Cambodian (4)	4	0.01
Chinese, ex. Taiwanese (51)	97	0.25
Filipino (5,751)	6,372	16.41
Hmong	1	0.00
Indian (198)	239	0.62
Japanese (36)	48	0.12
Korean (32)	42	0.11
Malaysian (5)	11	0.03
Sri Lankan	3	0.01
Vietnamese (8)	10	0.03
Other Asian, not specified (38)	83	0.21
Croatian	55	0.14
Danish	52	0.13
Dutch	48	0.12
English	300	0.77
European	52	0.13
French, except Basque	90	0.23
French Canadian	17	0.04
German	287	0.74
Hawaii Native/Pacific Islander:	68	0.18
Micronesian: (10)	12	0.03
Guamanian/Chamorro (10)	12	0.03
Polynesian: (9)	33	0.08
Native Hawaiian (5)	19	0.05
Samoan (3)	3	0.01
Other Polynesian (1)	11	0.03
Other Pac. Isl., not spec. (3)	23	0.06
Hispanic or Latino:	26,584	68.47
Central American:	200	0.52
Costa Rican	6	0.02
Guatemalan	63	0.16
Honduran	6	0.02
Nicaraguan	4	0.01
Salvadoran	114	0.29
Other Central American	7	0.02
Cuban	3	0.01
Mexican	23,428	60.34
Puerto Rican	166	0.43
South American:	32	0.08
Argentinean	1	0.00
Chilean	8	0.02
Ecuadorian	4	0.01
Peruvian	10	0.03
Venezuelan	6	0.02
Other South American	3	0.01
Other Hispanic or Latino	2,755	7.10
Hungarian	28	0.07
Irish	440	1.13
Italian	125	0.32
Polish	28	0.07
Portuguese	49	0.13
Russian	37	0.09
Scotch-Irish	68	0.17
Scottish	151	0.39
Slavic	5	0.01
Slovene	14	0.04
Swedish	14	0.04
United States or American	497	1.27
Welsh	14	0.04
White:	11,336	29.20
Not Hispanic (3,556)	3,883	10.00
Hispanic (6,601)	7,453	19.20
Yugoslavian	9	0.02

Desert Hot Springs

Place Type: City
County: Riverside
Population: 16,582

Ancestry/Race	Number	%
Acadian/Cajun	5	0.03
African American/Black:	1,169	7.05
Not Hispanic (947)	1,072	6.46
Hispanic (67)	97	0.58
African, sub-Saharan:	106	0.64
African	106	0.64
Am. Ind. or Alaska Nat., not spec.	179	1.08
American Indian tribes, specified:	298	1.80
Apache (13)	23	0.14
Blackfeet	13	0.08
Cherokee (28)	96	0.58
Cheyenne	1	0.01
Chickasaw	3	0.02
Chippewa (4)	5	0.03
Choctaw (4)	9	0.05
Comanche	2	0.01
Creek (1)	5	0.03
Delaware (1)	1	0.01
Iroquois (1)	2	0.01
Kiowa (5)	5	0.03
Latin American Indians (16)	29	0.17
Navajo (10)	13	0.08
Osage (4)	5	0.03
Ottawa (5)	10	0.06
Pima (1)	1	0.01
Pueblo (1)	3	0.02
Seminole	2	0.01
Shoshone	1	0.01
Sioux (3)	9	0.05
Tohono O'Odham (3)	3	0.02
Ute	1	0.01
Yaqui (1)	4	0.02
All other tribes (30)	52	0.31
American Indian tribes, not spec.	16	0.10
Arab:	78	0.47
Arab/Arabic	39	0.24
Lebanese	26	0.16
Syrian	13	0.08
Armenian	23	0.14
Asian:	474	2.86
Cambodian (19)	28	0.17
Chinese, ex. Taiwanese (28)	43	0.26
Filipino (144)	203	1.22
Indian (36)	42	0.25
Indonesian	8	0.05
Japanese (18)	36	0.22
Korean (55)	57	0.34
Laotian (1)	1	0.01
Pakistani (3)	12	0.07
Sri Lankan (2)	3	0.02
Thai (2)	2	0.01
Vietnamese (7)	12	0.07
Other Asian, specified	6	0.04
Other Asian, not specified (3)	21	0.13
Austrian	60	0.36
Belgian	9	0.05
British	8	0.05
Bulgarian	30	0.18
Canadian	68	0.41
Czech	79	0.48
Czechoslovakian	84	0.51
Danish	69	0.42
Dutch	125	0.76
English	1,206	7.33
European	61	0.37
Finnish	43	0.26
French, except Basque	430	2.61
French Canadian	95	0.58
German	1,948	11.84
Greek	66	0.40
Hawaii Native/Pacific Islander:	53	0.32
Micronesian: (3)	5	0.03
Guamanian/Chamorro (3)	5	0.03
Polynesian: (7)	21	0.13
Native Hawaiian (3)	12	0.07
Samoan (4)	8	0.05
Other Polynesian	1	0.01
Other Pac. Isl., specified	6	0.04
Other Pac. Isl., not spec. (4)	21	0.13
Hispanic or Latino:	6,699	40.40
Central American:	209	1.26
Costa Rican	4	0.02
Guatemalan	69	0.42
Honduran	3	0.02
Nicaraguan	13	0.08
Panamanian	7	0.04
Salvadoran	99	0.60
Other Central American	14	0.08
Cuban	30	0.18
Dominican Republic	2	0.01
Mexican	5,536	33.39
Puerto Rican	58	0.35
South American:	35	0.21
Argentinean	8	0.05
Bolivian	2	0.01
Chilean	1	0.01
Colombian	11	0.07
Ecuadorian	7	0.04
Peruvian	5	0.03
Other South American	1	0.01
Other Hispanic or Latino	829	5.00
Hungarian	131	0.80
Irish	1,588	9.65
Israeli	10	0.06
Italian	585	3.55
Norwegian	113	0.69
Pennsylvania German	5	0.03
Polish	256	1.56
Portuguese	65	0.39
Romanian	90	0.55
Russian	119	0.72
Scandinavian	28	0.17
Scotch-Irish	223	1.35
Scottish	279	1.70
Slavic	10	0.06
Slovak	8	0.05
Swedish	197	1.20
Swiss	38	0.23
Ukrainian	7	0.04
United States or American	621	3.77
Welsh	81	0.49
West Indian, excl. Hispanic:	8	0.05
Jamaican	8	0.05
White:	12,172	73.40
Not Hispanic (8,040)	8,444	50.92
Hispanic (3,266)	3,728	22.48
Yugoslavian	28	0.17

Diamond Bar

Place Type: City
County: Los Angeles
Population: 56,287

Ancestry/Race	Number	%
African American/Black:	2,971	5.28

Notes: 1. Figures in the "Number" column do not add up to the total population due to: a) Ancestry/Race overlap — e.g. persons can report being both White and Irish, b) persons of Hispanic origin can report being any race, c) persons reporting two ancestries are counted in both categories. 2. Numbers in parentheses indicate the number of persons reporting this ancestry/race alone, not in combination with any other ancestry/race. 3. Refer to the Explanation of Data in the front of the book for more detailed information.

Not Hispanic (2,624)	2,855	5.07
Hispanic (56)	116	0.21
African, sub-Saharan:	456	0.81
African	122	0.22
Ethiopian	6	0.01
Ghanian	151	0.27
Nigerian	167	0.30
Other sub-Saharan African	10	0.02
Alaska Native tribes, specified:	2	0.00
Alaska Athabascan (1)	1	0.00
All other tribes	1	0.00
Am. Ind. or Alaska Nat., not spec.	207	0.37
Albanian	113	0.20
American Indian tribes, specified:	313	0.56
Apache (3)	11	0.02
Blackfeet	18	0.03
Cherokee (30)	83	0.15
Chickasaw (2)	8	0.01
Chippewa (1)	1	0.00
Choctaw (4)	24	0.04
Creek (3)	5	0.01
Delaware	4	0.01
Iroquois	5	0.01
Latin American Indians (13)	43	0.08
Lumbee	2	0.00
Navajo (12)	21	0.04
Osage	1	0.00
Ottawa (1)	1	0.00
Paiute (1)	1	0.00
Pima	1	0.00
Potawatomi	3	0.01
Pueblo	5	0.01
Seminole (2)	2	0.00
Shoshone (1)	1	0.00
Sioux (5)	8	0.01
Tohono O'Odham (1)	7	0.01
Ute	2	0.00
Yakama (2)	2	0.00
Yaqui (1)	8	0.01
Yuman (1)	2	0.00
All other tribes (18)	44	0.08
American Indian tribes, not spec.	16	0.03
Arab:	926	1.64
Arab/Arabic	84	0.15
Egyptian	278	0.49
Iraqi	23	0.04
Jordanian	61	0.11
Lebanese	242	0.43
Moroccan	25	0.04
Palestinian	54	0.10
Syrian	127	0.23
Other Arab	32	0.06
Armenian	278	0.49
Asian:	26,012	46.21
Bangladeshi (6)	7	0.01
Cambodian (37)	50	0.09
Chinese, ex. Taiwanese (7,941)	8,785	15.61
Filipino (3,010)	3,298	5.86
Indian (2,253)	2,403	4.27
Indonesian (244)	342	0.61
Japanese (955)	1,264	2.25
Korean (5,580)	5,742	10.20
Laotian (18)	37	0.07
Malaysian (15)	28	0.05
Pakistani (173)	227	0.40
Sri Lankan (20)	22	0.04
Taiwanese (2,150)	2,611	4.64
Thai (158)	189	0.34
Vietnamese (626)	700	1.24
Other Asian, specified (92)	125	0.22
Other Asian, not specified (73)	182	0.32
Australian	29	0.05
Austrian	30	0.05
Basque	44	0.08
British	133	0.24
Canadian	171	0.30
Celtic	6	0.01
Croatian	64	0.11
Czech	80	0.14
Czechoslovakian	33	0.06
Danish	134	0.24
Dutch	537	0.95
English	3,040	5.39
European	327	0.58
Finnish	71	0.13
French, except Basque	819	1.45
French Canadian	159	0.28
German	4,169	7.40
Greek	142	0.25
Hawaii Native/Pacific Islander:	262	0.47
Melanesian: (1)	1	0.00
Fijian (1)	1	0.00
Micronesian: (14)	20	0.04
Guamanian/Chamorro (14)	19	0.03
Other Micronesian	1	0.00
Polynesian: (37)	133	0.24
Native Hawaiian (17)	91	0.16
Samoan (10)	26	0.05
Tongan (7)	7	0.01
Other Polynesian (3)	9	0.02
Other Pac. Isl., specified	1	0.00
Other Pac. Isl., not spec. (15)	107	0.19
Hispanic or Latino:	10,393	18.46
Central American:	361	0.64
Costa Rican	38	0.07
Guatemalan	54	0.10
Honduran	17	0.03
Nicaraguan	70	0.12
Panamanian	17	0.03
Salvadoran	121	0.21
Other Central American	44	0.08
Cuban	228	0.41
Dominican Republic	3	0.01
Mexican	7,580	13.47
Puerto Rican	197	0.35
South American:	491	0.87
Argentinean	72	0.13
Bolivian	8	0.01
Chilean	29	0.05
Colombian	139	0.25
Ecuadorian	81	0.14
Paraguayan	1	0.00
Peruvian	91	0.16
Uruguayan	6	0.01
Venezuelan	10	0.02
Other South American	54	0.10
Other Hispanic or Latino	1,533	2.72
Hungarian	205	0.36
Iranian	365	0.65
Irish	3,338	5.92
Italian	1,940	3.44
Latvian	14	0.02
Lithuanian	27	0.05
Northern European	6	0.01
Norwegian	490	0.87
Pennsylvania German	7	0.01
Polish	897	1.59
Portuguese	112	0.20
Romanian	60	0.11
Russian	431	0.76
Scandinavian	18	0.03
Scotch-Irish	412	0.73
Scottish	634	1.13
Slavic	20	0.04
Swedish	515	0.91
Swiss	83	0.15
Ukrainian	90	0.16
United States or American	1,190	2.11
Welsh	220	0.39
West Indian, excl. Hispanic:	162	0.29
Belizean	44	0.08
Bermudan	5	0.01
Haitian	11	0.02
Jamaican	66	0.12
West Indian	36	0.06
White:	24,842	44.13
Not Hispanic (17,471)	18,607	33.06
Hispanic (5,632)	6,235	11.08
Yugoslavian	39	0.07

Dinuba

Place Type: City
County: Tulare
Population: 16,844

Ancestry/Race	Number	%
African American/Black:	83	0.49
Not Hispanic (30)	35	0.21
Hispanic (30)	48	0.28
African, sub-Saharan:	9	0.05
African	9	0.05
Am. Ind. or Alaska Nat., not spec.	139	0.83
American Indian tribes, specified:	172	1.02
Apache (17)	23	0.14
Blackfeet (1)	1	0.01
Cherokee (24)	52	0.31
Chippewa	2	0.01
Choctaw (4)	9	0.05
Comanche	4	0.02
Cree (1)	8	0.05
Creek (2)	2	0.01
Latin American Indians (22)	28	0.17
Navajo (1)	1	0.01
Pima (1)	1	0.01
Yaqui (1)	1	0.01
Yuman	2	0.01
All other tribes (32)	38	0.23
American Indian tribes, not spec.	25	0.15
Armenian	11	0.07
Asian:	576	3.42
Cambodian (6)	6	0.04
Chinese, ex. Taiwanese (82)	93	0.55
Filipino (179)	222	1.32
Indian (81)	89	0.53
Japanese (66)	87	0.52
Korean (12)	29	0.17
Laotian (10)	11	0.07
Pakistani	1	0.01
Other Asian, specified (1)	1	0.01
Other Asian, not specified	37	0.22
Australian	11	0.07
Croatian	6	0.04
Czech	4	0.02
Czechoslovakian	9	0.05
Dutch	127	0.75
Eastern European	8	0.05
English	613	3.63
European	45	0.27
French, except Basque	203	1.20
German	661	3.92
Greek	14	0.08
Hawaii Native/Pacific Islander:	44	0.26
Polynesian: (15)	31	0.18
Native Hawaiian (6)	15	0.09
Samoan (4)	7	0.04
Tongan (5)	5	0.03
Other Polynesian	4	0.02
Other Pac. Isl., not spec. (7)	13	0.08
Hispanic or Latino:	12,647	75.08
Central American:	49	0.29
Costa Rican	1	0.01
Guatemalan	14	0.08
Honduran	1	0.01
Nicaraguan	2	0.01
Salvadoran	24	0.14
Other Central American	7	0.04
Cuban	7	0.04
Mexican	11,052	65.61
Puerto Rican	21	0.12
South American:	9	0.05
Argentinean	1	0.01
Colombian	4	0.02
Venezuelan	4	0.02
Other Hispanic or Latino	1,509	8.96
Irish	440	2.61
Italian	20	0.12
Northern European	22	0.13
Norwegian	23	0.14
Polish	89	0.53

Notes: 1. Figures in the "Number" column do not add up to the total population due to: a) Ancestry/Race overlap — e.g. persons can report being both White and Irish, b) persons of Hispanic origin can report being any race, c) persons reporting two ancestries are counted in both categories. 2. Numbers in parentheses indicate the number of persons reporting this ancestry/race alone, not in combination with any other ancestry/race. 3. Refer to the Explanation of Data in the front of the book for more detailed information.

Portuguese	36	0.21
Russian	25	0.15
Scandinavian	8	0.05
Scotch-Irish	89	0.53
Scottish	16	0.09
Swedish	73	0.43
United States or American	452	2.68
Welsh	6	0.04
West Indian, excl. Hispanic:	12	0.07
Jamaican	12	0.07
White:	9,637	57.21
Not Hispanic (3,471)	3,636	21.59
Hispanic (5,345)	6,001	35.63

Dixon

Place Type: City
County: Solano
Population: 16,103

Ancestry/Race	Number	%
African American/Black:	409	2.54
Not Hispanic (292)	366	2.27
Hispanic (19)	43	0.27
African, sub-Saharan:	67	0.42
African	67	0.42
Alaska Native tribes, specified:	1	0.01
Aleut (1)	1	0.01
Am. Ind. or Alaska Nat., not spec.	86	0.53
American Indian tribes, specified:	218	1.35
Apache (4)	14	0.09
Blackfeet (5)	10	0.06
Cherokee (22)	56	0.35
Chickasaw (7)	9	0.06
Chippewa (1)	1	0.01
Choctaw (4)	9	0.06
Comanche	4	0.02
Creek (3)	3	0.02
Crow	1	0.01
Delaware (3)	4	0.02
Iroquois (4)	10	0.06
Latin American Indians (34)	36	0.22
Navajo (1)	4	0.02
Potawatomi	1	0.01
Pueblo (2)	3	0.02
Sioux (3)	12	0.07
Yaqui	1	0.01
Yuman (1)	1	0.01
All other tribes (22)	39	0.24
American Indian tribes, not spec.	20	0.12
Arab:	79	0.49
Arab/Arabic	17	0.11
Jordanian	7	0.04
Lebanese	45	0.28
Palestinian	10	0.06
Asian:	726	4.51
Chinese, ex. Taiwanese (81)	104	0.65
Filipino (222)	317	1.97
Indian (64)	76	0.47
Indonesian (1)	1	0.01
Japanese (61)	130	0.81
Korean (33)	46	0.29
Laotian (3)	5	0.03
Pakistani (2)	3	0.02
Taiwanese (5)	6	0.04
Thai (5)	11	0.07
Vietnamese (7)	9	0.06
Other Asian, specified	1	0.01
Other Asian, not specified (4)	17	0.11
Austrian	42	0.26
Basque	31	0.19
Belgian	7	0.04
British	38	0.24
Canadian	57	0.35
Czech	38	0.24
Czechoslovakian	35	0.22
Danish	112	0.70
Dutch	254	1.58
English	1,205	7.49
European	92	0.57
Finnish	35	0.22
French, except Basque	582	3.62
French Canadian	62	0.39
German	1,885	11.72
Greek	51	0.32
Hawaii Native/Pacific Islander:	105	0.65
Melanesian: (2)	2	0.01
Fijian (2)	2	0.01
Micronesian: (16)	30	0.19
Guamanian/Chamorro (16)	30	0.19
Polynesian: (24)	54	0.34
Native Hawaiian (8)	31	0.19
Samoan (15)	19	0.12
Tongan (1)	1	0.01
Other Polynesian	3	0.02
Other Pac. Isl., not spec. (6)	19	0.12
Hispanic or Latino:	5,414	33.62
Central American:	97	0.60
Guatemalan	43	0.27
Honduran	3	0.02
Nicaraguan	18	0.11
Panamanian	8	0.05
Salvadoran	18	0.11
Other Central American	7	0.04
Cuban	10	0.06
Dominican Republic	1	0.01
Mexican	4,606	28.60
Puerto Rican	62	0.39
South American:	12	0.07
Bolivian	6	0.04
Chilean	3	0.02
Peruvian	1	0.01
Other South American	2	0.01
Other Hispanic or Latino	626	3.89
Hungarian	24	0.15
Icelander	9	0.06
Iranian	61	0.38
Irish	1,470	9.14
Italian	616	3.83
Lithuanian	14	0.09
Luxemburger	9	0.06
Macedonian	18	0.11
Northern European	12	0.07
Norwegian	369	2.29
Pennsylvania German	9	0.06
Polish	198	1.23
Portuguese	365	2.27
Russian	27	0.17
Scandinavian	18	0.11
Scotch-Irish	198	1.23
Scottish	281	1.75
Serbian	8	0.05
Slovene	6	0.04
Swedish	235	1.46
Swiss	60	0.37
Ukrainian	10	0.06
United States or American	1,036	6.44
Welsh	125	0.78
White:	12,116	75.24
Not Hispanic (9,318)	9,720	60.36
Hispanic (2,036)	2,396	14.88
Yugoslavian	23	0.14

Downey

Place Type: City
County: Los Angeles
Population: 107,323

Ancestry/Race	Number	%
African American/Black:	4,502	4.19
Not Hispanic (3,717)	3,985	3.71
Hispanic (311)	517	0.48
African, sub-Saharan:	424	0.40
African	347	0.32
Ghanian	56	0.05
Kenyan	5	0.00
Ugandan	16	0.01
Alaska Native tribes, specified:	9	0.01
Alaska Athabascan	1	0.00
Aleut (1)	1	0.00
Eskimo (3)	3	0.00
Tlingit-Haida (2)	4	0.00
Alaska Native tribes, not specified	2	0.00
Am. Ind. or Alaska Nat., not spec.	621	0.58
Albanian	140	0.13
American Indian tribes, specified:	861	0.80
Apache (32)	71	0.07
Blackfeet (3)	28	0.03
Cherokee (39)	143	0.13
Cheyenne (2)	3	0.00
Chickasaw (3)	4	0.00
Chippewa (9)	16	0.01
Choctaw (31)	55	0.05
Colville	1	0.00
Comanche (2)	9	0.01
Cree	4	0.00
Creek (12)	18	0.02
Crow	1	0.00
Delaware (5)	5	0.00
Iroquois (1)	8	0.01
Kiowa (1)	1	0.00
Latin American Indians (147)	216	0.20
Lumbee (4)	4	0.00
Menominee	2	0.00
Navajo (40)	67	0.06
Paiute	1	0.00
Pima (1)	8	0.01
Potawatomi (3)	3	0.00
Pueblo (8)	25	0.02
Seminole (1)	4	0.00
Shoshone	1	0.00
Sioux (20)	27	0.03
Tohono O'Odham (5)	9	0.01
Ute (3)	4	0.00
Yaqui (13)	23	0.02
Yuman (9)	13	0.01
All other tribes (31)	87	0.08
American Indian tribes, not spec.	84	0.08
Arab:	1,724	1.61
Arab/Arabic	243	0.23
Egyptian	898	0.84
Iraqi	18	0.02
Jordanian	79	0.07
Lebanese	440	0.41
Moroccan	11	0.01
Syrian	26	0.02
Other Arab	9	0.01
Armenian	261	0.24
Asian:	9,360	8.72
Bangladeshi (13)	18	0.02
Cambodian (120)	157	0.15
Chinese, ex. Taiwanese (580)	752	0.70
Filipino (2,154)	2,407	2.24
Hmong (3)	4	0.00
Indian (659)	787	0.73
Indonesian (20)	40	0.04
Japanese (380)	543	0.51
Korean (3,255)	3,359	3.13
Laotian (12)	18	0.02
Malaysian (1)	4	0.00
Pakistani (61)	86	0.08
Sri Lankan (32)	39	0.04
Taiwanese (127)	138	0.13
Thai (248)	307	0.29
Vietnamese (432)	459	0.43
Other Asian, specified (15)	15	0.01
Other Asian, not specified (94)	227	0.21
Assyrian/Chaldean/Syriac	11	0.01
Australian	36	0.03
Austrian	173	0.16
Basque	51	0.05
Belgian	52	0.05
Brazilian	13	0.01
British	210	0.20
Bulgarian	14	0.01
Canadian	263	0.25
Celtic	9	0.01
Croatian	22	0.02
Czech	148	0.14

Notes: 1. Figures in the "Number" column do not add up to the total population due to: a) Ancestry/Race overlap — e.g. persons can report being both White and Irish, b) persons of Hispanic origin can report being any race, c) persons reporting two ancestries are counted in both categories. 2. Numbers in parentheses indicate the number of persons reporting this ancestry/race alone, not in combination with any other ancestry/race. 3. Refer to the Explanation of Data in the front of the book for more detailed information.

Czechoslovakian	71	0.07
Danish	308	0.29
Dutch	888	0.83
Eastern European	16	0.01
English	4,545	4.23
European	342	0.32
Finnish	24	0.02
French, except Basque	1,635	1.52
French Canadian	805	0.75
German	6,199	5.78
Greek	541	0.50
Hawaii Native/Pacific Islander:	458	0.43
Melanesian: (12)	20	0.02
Fijian (12)	19	0.02
Other Melanesian	1	0.00
Micronesian: (44)	58	0.05
Guamanian/Chamorro (44)	56	0.05
Other Micronesian	2	0.00
Polynesian: (131)	253	0.24
Native Hawaiian (45)	124	0.12
Samoan (78)	105	0.10
Tongan (3)	12	0.01
Other Polynesian (5)	12	0.01
Other Pac. Isl., not spec. (42)	127	0.12
Hispanic or Latino:	62,089	57.85
Central American:	4,276	3.98
Costa Rican	197	0.18
Guatemalan	1,007	0.94
Honduran	189	0.18
Nicaraguan	636	0.59
Panamanian	51	0.05
Salvadoran	1,834	1.71
Other Central American	362	0.34
Cuban	2,100	1.96
Dominican Republic	38	0.04
Mexican	43,241	40.29
Puerto Rican	661	0.62
South American:	2,478	2.31
Argentinean	350	0.33
Bolivian	75	0.07
Chilean	71	0.07
Colombian	472	0.44
Ecuadorian	362	0.34
Paraguayan	1	0.00
Peruvian	891	0.83
Uruguayan	18	0.02
Venezuelan	51	0.05
Other South American	187	0.17
Other Hispanic or Latino	9,295	8.66
Hungarian	325	0.30
Iranian	295	0.27
Irish	4,374	4.08
Italian	3,323	3.10
Lithuanian	23	0.02
Macedonian	20	0.02
Maltese	14	0.01
Northern European	22	0.02
Norwegian	739	0.69
Pennsylvania German	21	0.02
Polish	678	0.63
Portuguese	217	0.20
Romanian	184	0.17
Russian	703	0.66
Scandinavian	56	0.05
Scotch-Irish	1,038	0.97
Scottish	1,007	0.94
Serbian	11	0.01
Slavic	33	0.03
Slovak	52	0.05
Slovene	22	0.02
Swedish	678	0.63
Swiss	118	0.11
Turkish	3	0.00
Ukrainian	145	0.14
United States or American	2,869	2.67
Welsh	353	0.33
West Indian, excl. Hispanic:	98	0.09
Belizean	6	0.01
British West Indian	6	0.01
Haitian	49	0.05
West Indian	37	0.03
White:	61,853	57.63
Not Hispanic (30,851)	32,294	30.09
Hispanic (26,544)	29,559	27.54
Yugoslavian	173	0.16

Duarte

Place Type: City
County: Los Angeles
Population: 21,486

Ancestry/Race	Number	%
Acadian/Cajun	9	0.04
Afghan	15	0.07
African American/Black:	2,138	9.95
Not Hispanic (1,894)	2,027	9.43
Hispanic (58)	111	0.52
African, sub-Saharan:	192	0.89
African	167	0.78
Ghanian	16	0.07
South African	9	0.04
Am. Ind. or Alaska Nat., not spec.	127	0.59
Alsatian	7	0.03
American Indian tribes, specified:	236	1.10
Apache (4)	10	0.05
Blackfeet (6)	6	0.03
Cherokee (5)	29	0.13
Cheyenne	1	0.00
Chickasaw	1	0.00
Chippewa (3)	5	0.02
Choctaw	12	0.06
Creek	1	0.00
Crow	1	0.00
Iroquois (7)	8	0.04
Latin American Indians (32)	62	0.29
Navajo (13)	22	0.10
Osage	1	0.00
Ottawa (2)	2	0.01
Paiute (1)	1	0.00
Pima	1	0.00
Potawatomi	1	0.00
Pueblo	9	0.04
Sioux (2)	6	0.03
Tohono O'Odham (2)	2	0.01
Ute (2)	2	0.01
Yaqui (1)	8	0.04
All other tribes (34)	45	0.21
American Indian tribes, not spec.	15	0.07
Arab:	385	1.79
Arab/Arabic	20	0.09
Egyptian	117	0.54
Iraqi	36	0.17
Jordanian	58	0.27
Lebanese	70	0.33
Palestinian	61	0.28
Syrian	23	0.11
Armenian	431	2.01
Asian:	3,079	14.33
Cambodian (7)	7	0.03
Chinese, ex. Taiwanese (424)	526	2.45
Filipino (1,417)	1,530	7.12
Indian (289)	318	1.48
Indonesian (21)	54	0.25
Japanese (146)	202	0.94
Korean (83)	100	0.47
Laotian (3)	3	0.01
Malaysian	4	0.02
Pakistani (23)	31	0.14
Sri Lankan (8)	13	0.06
Taiwanese (25)	26	0.12
Thai (60)	77	0.36
Vietnamese (104)	116	0.54
Other Asian, specified (3)	5	0.02
Other Asian, not specified (21)	67	0.31
Australian	9	0.04
Austrian	29	0.13
Basque	12	0.06
Belgian	12	0.06
Brazilian	4	0.02
British	93	0.43
Canadian	41	0.19
Celtic	8	0.04
Croatian	26	0.12
Czech	16	0.07
Czechoslovakian	18	0.08
Danish	126	0.59
Dutch	245	1.14
Eastern European	9	0.04
English	1,188	5.53
Estonian	16	0.07
European	88	0.41
Finnish	18	0.08
French, except Basque	410	1.91
French Canadian	133	0.62
German	1,501	6.99
Greek	114	0.53
Guyanese	7	0.03
Hawaii Native/Pacific Islander:	82	0.38
Micronesian: (4)	7	0.03
Guamanian/Chamorro (4)	7	0.03
Polynesian: (11)	33	0.15
Native Hawaiian (6)	23	0.11
Samoan (3)	8	0.04
Other Polynesian (2)	2	0.01
Other Pac. Isl., not spec. (9)	42	0.20
Hispanic or Latino:	9,326	43.41
Central American:	355	1.65
Costa Rican	6	0.03
Guatemalan	72	0.34
Honduran	34	0.16
Nicaraguan	28	0.13
Panamanian	13	0.06
Salvadoran	171	0.80
Other Central American	31	0.14
Cuban	97	0.45
Mexican	7,321	34.07
Puerto Rican	80	0.37
South American:	237	1.10
Argentinean	51	0.24
Chilean	16	0.07
Colombian	42	0.20
Ecuadorian	45	0.21
Paraguayan	1	0.00
Peruvian	47	0.22
Uruguayan	2	0.01
Venezuelan	3	0.01
Other South American	30	0.14
Other Hispanic or Latino	1,236	5.75
Hungarian	59	0.27
Icelander	7	0.03
Iranian	37	0.17
Irish	1,075	5.00
Italian	800	3.72
Lithuanian	29	0.13
Northern European	23	0.11
Norwegian	151	0.70
Pennsylvania German	6	0.03
Polish	124	0.58
Portuguese	123	0.57
Russian	38	0.18
Scandinavian	8	0.04
Scotch-Irish	284	1.32
Scottish	327	1.52
Serbian	7	0.03
Slovak	21	0.10
Slovene	2	0.01
Swedish	261	1.21
Swiss	68	0.32
Ukrainian	65	0.30
United States or American	453	2.11
Welsh	76	0.35
West Indian, excl. Hispanic:	17	0.08
Dutch West Indian	7	0.03
Jamaican	10	0.05
White:	12,100	56.32
Not Hispanic (6,895)	7,321	34.07
Hispanic (4,283)	4,779	22.24
Yugoslavian	6	0.03

Notes: 1. Figures in the "Number" column do not add up to the total population due to: a) Ancestry/Race overlap — e.g. persons can report being both White and Irish, b) persons of Hispanic origin can report being any race, c) persons reporting two ancestries are counted in both categories. 2. Numbers in parentheses indicate the number of persons reporting this ancestry/race alone, not in combination with any other ancestry/race. 3. Refer to the Explanation of Data in the front of the book for more detailed information.

Dublin

Place Type: City
County: Alameda
Population: 29,973

Ancestry/Race	Number	%
Afghan	98	0.33
African American/Black:	3,161	10.55
Not Hispanic (2,995)	3,113	10.39
Hispanic (29)	48	0.16
African, sub-Saharan:	63	0.21
African	19	0.06
Ghanian	9	0.03
South African	8	0.03
Zimbabwean	27	0.09
Alaska Native tribes, specified:	4	0.01
Alaska Athabascan	1	0.00
Eskimo (2)	2	0.01
All other tribes	1	0.00
Alaska Native tribes, not specified	1	0.00
Am. Ind. or Alaska Nat., not spec.	157	0.52
American Indian tribes, specified:	257	0.86
Apache (2)	10	0.03
Blackfeet (1)	13	0.04
Cherokee (26)	73	0.24
Cheyenne (6)	6	0.02
Chickasaw	1	0.00
Chippewa	6	0.02
Choctaw (8)	25	0.08
Creek (1)	3	0.01
Delaware (1)	2	0.01
Iroquois (2)	3	0.01
Kiowa (1)	2	0.01
Latin American Indians (6)	19	0.06
Lumbee (1)	1	0.00
Navajo (5)	16	0.05
Osage (1)	1	0.00
Paiute (1)	1	0.00
Pueblo (10)	16	0.05
Seminole	1	0.00
Sioux (9)	9	0.03
Yaqui (3)	3	0.01
All other tribes (28)	46	0.15
American Indian tribes, not spec.	20	0.07
Arab:	199	0.66
Egyptian	16	0.05
Jordanian	9	0.03
Lebanese	102	0.34
Palestinian	18	0.06
Syrian	31	0.10
Other Arab	23	0.08
Armenian	80	0.27
Asian:	3,777	12.60
Bangladeshi (3)	3	0.01
Cambodian (9)	15	0.05
Chinese, ex. Taiwanese (808)	997	3.33
Filipino (770)	995	3.32
Indian (672)	716	2.39
Indonesian (22)	32	0.11
Japanese (194)	350	1.17
Korean (146)	187	0.62
Laotian (6)	6	0.02
Malaysian (1)	1	0.00
Pakistani (26)	36	0.12
Taiwanese (15)	18	0.06
Thai (22)	26	0.09
Vietnamese (170)	194	0.65
Other Asian, specified (4)	6	0.02
Other Asian, not specified (153)	195	0.65
Assyrian/Chaldean/Syriac	21	0.07
Australian	18	0.06
Austrian	114	0.38
Basque	29	0.10
Belgian	55	0.18
Brazilian	45	0.15
British	104	0.35
Bulgarian	19	0.06
Canadian	152	0.51
Celtic	6	0.02
Croatian	61	0.20
Czech	88	0.29
Czechoslovakian	24	0.08
Danish	296	0.99
Dutch	325	1.08
Eastern European	26	0.09
English	2,689	8.95
European	446	1.48
Finnish	14	0.05
French, except Basque	869	2.89
French Canadian	152	0.51
German	3,989	13.28
Greek	206	0.69
Hawaii Native/Pacific Islander:	233	0.78
Micronesian: (26)	52	0.17
Guamanian/Chamorro (25)	51	0.17
Other Micronesian (1)	1	0.00
Polynesian: (42)	130	0.43
Native Hawaiian (33)	116	0.39
Samoan (6)	9	0.03
Tongan (3)	5	0.02
Other Pac. Isl., not spec. (18)	51	0.17
Hispanic or Latino:	4,059	13.54
Central American:	127	0.42
Costa Rican	4	0.01
Guatemalan	8	0.03
Honduran	2	0.01
Nicaraguan	50	0.17
Panamanian	6	0.02
Salvadoran	48	0.16
Other Central American	9	0.03
Cuban	47	0.16
Dominican Republic	1	0.00
Mexican	1,878	6.27
Puerto Rican	89	0.30
South American:	119	0.40
Argentinean	24	0.08
Bolivian	7	0.02
Chilean	10	0.03
Colombian	20	0.07
Ecuadorian	3	0.01
Paraguayan	1	0.00
Peruvian	39	0.13
Uruguayan	1	0.00
Venezuelan	5	0.02
Other South American	9	0.03
Other Hispanic or Latino	1,798	6.00
Hungarian	166	0.55
Icelander	6	0.02
Iranian	291	0.97
Irish	3,592	11.96
Italian	2,320	7.72
Latvian	27	0.09
Lithuanian	58	0.19
New Zealander	7	0.02
Northern European	37	0.12
Norwegian	579	1.93
Polish	534	1.78
Portuguese	1,095	3.65
Romanian	2	0.01
Russian	319	1.06
Scandinavian	41	0.14
Scotch-Irish	354	1.18
Scottish	674	2.24
Serbian	4	0.01
Slavic	7	0.02
Slovak	75	0.25
Slovene	16	0.05
Swedish	564	1.88
Swiss	131	0.44
Ukrainian	82	0.27
United States or American	773	2.57
Welsh	164	0.55
West Indian, excl. Hispanic:	21	0.07
Jamaican	9	0.03
West Indian	12	0.04
White:	21,800	72.73
Not Hispanic (18,669)	19,447	64.88
Hispanic (2,124)	2,353	7.85
Yugoslavian	171	0.57

East Hemet

Place Type: Census Designated Place
County: Riverside
Population: 14,823

Ancestry/Race	Number	%
African American/Black:	294	1.98
Not Hispanic (202)	251	1.69
Hispanic (26)	43	0.29
African, sub-Saharan:	29	0.20
African	29	0.20
Alaska Native tribes, specified:	4	0.03
Alaska Athabascan (1)	1	0.01
Tlingit-Haida (3)	3	0.02
Am. Ind. or Alaska Nat., not spec.	88	0.59
American Indian tribes, specified:	307	2.07
Apache (2)	19	0.13
Blackfeet (2)	4	0.03
Cherokee (11)	65	0.44
Chickasaw (2)	2	0.01
Chippewa	5	0.03
Choctaw (10)	18	0.12
Comanche (1)	2	0.01
Cree (1)	2	0.01
Creek (2)	4	0.03
Crow	1	0.01
Iroquois	2	0.01
Kiowa (1)	1	0.01
Latin American Indians (20)	27	0.18
Lumbee	1	0.01
Navajo (5)	5	0.03
Osage (1)	2	0.01
Paiute	2	0.01
Potawatomi	2	0.01
Pueblo (2)	5	0.03
Puget Sound Salish	1	0.01
Sioux (4)	8	0.05
Yaqui (7)	12	0.08
All other tribes (86)	118	0.80
American Indian tribes, not spec.	13	0.09
Arab:	22	0.15
Lebanese	22	0.15
Asian:	225	1.52
Cambodian (6)	6	0.04
Chinese, ex. Taiwanese (20)	29	0.20
Filipino (44)	70	0.47
Indian (26)	33	0.22
Indonesian (1)	3	0.02
Japanese (8)	23	0.16
Korean (20)	27	0.18
Pakistani (9)	9	0.06
Taiwanese (5)	5	0.03
Thai (12)	12	0.08
Vietnamese (1)	3	0.02
Other Asian, not specified (1)	5	0.03
Australian	11	0.07
Belgian	27	0.18
British	90	0.61
Canadian	113	0.77
Celtic	11	0.07
Czech	20	0.14
Czechoslovakian	4	0.03
Danish	109	0.74
Dutch	283	1.92
English	1,736	11.80
European	64	0.43
Finnish	25	0.17
French, except Basque	696	4.73
French Canadian	83	0.56
German	2,718	18.47
Greek	18	0.12
Hawaii Native/Pacific Islander:	42	0.28
Micronesian: (3)	5	0.03
Guamanian/Chamorro (3)	5	0.03
Polynesian: (8)	29	0.20
Native Hawaiian (7)	25	0.17
Samoan	1	0.01
Tongan (1)	3	0.02
Other Pac. Isl., not spec. (2)	8	0.05

Notes: 1. Figures in the "Number" column do not add up to the total population due to: a) Ancestry/Race overlap — e.g. persons can report being both White and Irish, b) persons of Hispanic origin can report being any race, c) persons reporting two ancestries are counted in both categories. 2. Numbers in parentheses indicate the number of persons reporting this ancestry/race alone, not in combination with any other ancestry/race. 3. Refer to the Explanation of Data in the front of the book for more detailed information.

Hispanic or Latino:	3,692	24.91
Central American:	65	0.44
Costa Rican	10	0.07
Guatemalan	14	0.09
Honduran	4	0.03
Nicaraguan	10	0.07
Panamanian	8	0.05
Salvadoran	15	0.10
Other Central American	4	0.03
Cuban	28	0.19
Dominican Republic	1	0.01
Mexican	3,031	20.45
Puerto Rican	30	0.20
South American:	15	0.10
Argentinean	4	0.03
Chilean	8	0.05
Colombian	1	0.01
Ecuadorian	1	0.01
Other South American	1	0.01
Other Hispanic or Latino	522	3.52
Hungarian	120	0.82
Irish	1,880	12.77
Italian	751	5.10
Lithuanian	24	0.16
Northern European	26	0.18
Norwegian	226	1.54
Polish	298	2.02
Portuguese	61	0.41
Russian	144	0.98
Scandinavian	17	0.12
Scotch-Irish	278	1.89
Scottish	340	2.31
Slovak	17	0.12
Swedish	315	2.14
Swiss	20	0.14
Ukrainian	58	0.39
United States or American	799	5.43
Welsh	64	0.43
West Indian, excl. Hispanic:	6	0.04
U.S. Virgin Islander	6	0.04
White:	12,408	83.71
Not Hispanic (10,359)	10,612	71.59
Hispanic (1,505)	1,796	12.12
Yugoslavian	12	0.08

East Los Angeles

Place Type: Census Designated Place
County: Los Angeles
Population: 124,283

Ancestry/Race	Number	%
African American/Black:	728	0.59
Not Hispanic (192)	215	0.17
Hispanic (298)	513	0.41
African, sub-Saharan:	52	0.04
African	52	0.04
Alaska Native tribes, specified:	3	0.00
Eskimo (3)	3	0.00
Alaska Native tribes, not specified	1	0.00
Am. Ind. or Alaska Nat., not spec.	1,019	0.82
American Indian tribes, specified:	951	0.77
Apache (51)	88	0.07
Blackfeet (1)	2	0.00
Cherokee (20)	41	0.03
Cheyenne (1)	2	0.00
Chickasaw	1	0.00
Choctaw (1)	3	0.00
Comanche (1)	2	0.00
Creek (4)	4	0.00
Iroquois (1)	1	0.00
Latin American Indians (435)	579	0.47
Navajo (32)	60	0.05
Paiute (2)	2	0.00
Pima (2)	7	0.01
Potawatomi (1)	1	0.00
Pueblo (16)	20	0.02
Seminole (2)	2	0.00
Sioux (3)	9	0.01
Tohono O'Odham (7)	8	0.01
Yaqui (19)	32	0.03
Yuman (5)	5	0.00
All other tribes (53)	82	0.07
American Indian tribes, not spec.	160	0.13
Arab:	60	0.05
Arab/Arabic	60	0.05
Armenian	122	0.10
Asian:	1,243	1.00
Cambodian (4)	15	0.01
Chinese, ex. Taiwanese (222)	266	0.21
Filipino (146)	208	0.17
Hmong (3)	3	0.00
Indian (34)	77	0.06
Indonesian	4	0.00
Japanese (415)	493	0.40
Korean (42)	50	0.04
Laotian	1	0.00
Pakistani (2)	5	0.00
Taiwanese (2)	4	0.00
Thai (9)	11	0.01
Vietnamese (26)	32	0.03
Other Asian, specified (1)	7	0.01
Other Asian, not specified (19)	67	0.05
Austrian	16	0.01
Canadian	23	0.02
Croatian	17	0.01
Czech	22	0.02
Dutch	98	0.08
Eastern European	10	0.01
English	115	0.09
European	7	0.01
French, except Basque	238	0.19
French Canadian	6	0.00
German	280	0.23
Greek	25	0.02
Guyanese	36	0.03
Hawaii Native/Pacific Islander:	137	0.11
Micronesian: (12)	16	0.01
Guamanian/Chamorro (12)	15	0.01
Other Micronesian	1	0.00
Polynesian: (38)	52	0.04
Native Hawaiian (22)	31	0.02
Samoan (16)	21	0.02
Other Pac. Isl., specified	6	0.00
Other Pac. Isl., not spec. (20)	63	0.05
Hispanic or Latino:	120,307	96.80
Central American:	3,020	2.43
Costa Rican	19	0.02
Guatemalan	701	0.56
Honduran	212	0.17
Nicaraguan	140	0.11
Panamanian	12	0.01
Salvadoran	1,607	1.29
Other Central American	329	0.26
Cuban	140	0.11
Dominican Republic	4	0.00
Mexican	104,223	83.86
Puerto Rican	190	0.15
South American:	284	0.23
Argentinean	27	0.02
Bolivian	9	0.01
Chilean	8	0.01
Colombian	41	0.03
Ecuadorian	98	0.08
Peruvian	65	0.05
Uruguayan	2	0.00
Venezuelan	3	0.00
Other South American	31	0.02
Other Hispanic or Latino	12,446	10.01
Hungarian	13	0.01
Iranian	5	0.00
Irish	210	0.17
Italian	340	0.27
Latvian	5	0.00
Luxemburger	7	0.01
Norwegian	18	0.01
Pennsylvania German	7	0.01
Polish	45	0.04
Portuguese	47	0.04
Russian	128	0.10
Scotch-Irish	13	0.01
Scottish	28	0.02
Serbian	11	0.01
Slovak	5	0.00
Swedish	33	0.03
Ukrainian	21	0.02
United States or American	1,686	1.36
Welsh	9	0.01
West Indian, excl. Hispanic:	16	0.01
Haitian	7	0.01
West Indian	9	0.01
White:	53,443	43.00
Not Hispanic (2,275)	2,498	2.01
Hispanic (46,513)	50,945	40.99

East Palo Alto

Place Type: City
County: San Mateo
Population: 29,506

Ancestry/Race	Number	%
African American/Black:	7,147	24.22
Not Hispanic (6,641)	6,880	23.32
Hispanic (155)	267	0.90
African, sub-Saharan:	602	2.04
African	553	1.88
Ghanian	25	0.08
Nigerian	9	0.03
Other sub-Saharan African	15	0.05
Alaska Native tribes, specified:	1	0.00
Alaska Athabascan	1	0.00
Am. Ind. or Alaska Nat., not spec.	160	0.54
American Indian tribes, specified:	276	0.94
Apache (1)	4	0.01
Blackfeet (1)	12	0.04
Cherokee (5)	36	0.12
Cheyenne (1)	2	0.01
Chickasaw	1	0.00
Chippewa (1)	3	0.01
Choctaw (6)	23	0.08
Comanche	5	0.02
Cree	1	0.00
Creek (1)	1	0.00
Crow	1	0.00
Iroquois (2)	3	0.01
Latin American Indians (93)	130	0.44
Navajo (6)	13	0.04
Pueblo	1	0.00
Puget Sound Salish (1)	1	0.00
Seminole (1)	5	0.02
Shoshone	2	0.01
Sioux (1)	14	0.05
Ute	1	0.00
All other tribes (5)	17	0.06
American Indian tribes, not spec.	42	0.14
Arab:	33	0.11
Arab/Arabic	11	0.04
Syrian	22	0.07
Asian:	952	3.23
Cambodian (1)	6	0.02
Chinese, ex. Taiwanese (65)	85	0.29
Filipino (221)	275	0.93
Hmong (1)	1	0.00
Indian (160)	288	0.98
Indonesian (1)	4	0.01
Japanese (93)	124	0.42
Korean (14)	19	0.06
Laotian (26)	26	0.09
Malaysian (2)	2	0.01
Sri Lankan	1	0.00
Taiwanese (1)	2	0.01
Thai (3)	4	0.01
Vietnamese (40)	43	0.15
Other Asian, specified (7)	24	0.08
Other Asian, not specified (12)	48	0.16
Austrian	5	0.02
Basque	3	0.01
British	21	0.07
Croatian	19	0.06

Notes: 1. Figures in the "Number" column do not add up to the total population due to: a) Ancestry/Race overlap — e.g. persons can report being both White and Irish, b) persons of Hispanic origin can report being any race, c) persons reporting two ancestries are counted in both categories. 2. Numbers in parentheses indicate the number of persons reporting this ancestry/race alone, not in combination with any other ancestry/race. 3. Refer to the Explanation of Data in the front of the book for more detailed information.

Czech	21	0.07
Danish	32	0.11
Dutch	15	0.05
Eastern European	9	0.03
English	223	0.76
European	49	0.17
Finnish	5	0.02
French, except Basque	74	0.25
French Canadian	25	0.08
German	464	1.58
Greek	7	0.02
Hawaii Native/Pacific Islander:	2,599	8.81
Melanesian: (187)	203	0.69
Fijian (187)	203	0.69
Micronesian: (7)	11	0.04
Guamanian/Chamorro (2)	6	0.02
Other Micronesian (5)	5	0.02
Polynesian: (1,863)	2,086	7.07
Native Hawaiian (29)	51	0.17
Samoan (417)	479	1.62
Tongan (1,386)	1,497	5.07
Other Polynesian (31)	59	0.20
Other Pac. Isl., specified	16	0.05
Other Pac. Isl., not spec. (137)	283	0.96
Hispanic or Latino:	17,346	58.79
Central American:	1,037	3.51
Costa Rican	11	0.04
Guatemalan	185	0.63
Honduran	23	0.08
Nicaraguan	86	0.29
Panamanian	37	0.13
Salvadoran	643	2.18
Other Central American	52	0.18
Cuban	12	0.04
Dominican Republic	1	0.00
Mexican	14,550	49.31
Puerto Rican	70	0.24
South American:	89	0.30
Argentinean	6	0.02
Bolivian	16	0.05
Chilean	6	0.02
Colombian	7	0.02
Ecuadorian	6	0.02
Peruvian	40	0.14
Venezuelan	2	0.01
Other South American	6	0.02
Other Hispanic or Latino	1,587	5.38
Hungarian	10	0.03
Irish	263	0.89
Italian	148	0.50
Latvian	8	0.03
Maltese	10	0.03
New Zealander	29	0.10
Northern European	8	0.03
Norwegian	51	0.17
Pennsylvania German	7	0.02
Polish	28	0.10
Portuguese	66	0.22
Romanian	22	0.07
Russian	92	0.31
Scotch-Irish	20	0.07
Scottish	47	0.16
Swedish	45	0.15
Turkish	11	0.04
United States or American	351	1.19
Welsh	16	0.05
West Indian, excl. Hispanic:	64	0.22
Belizean	9	0.03
Haitian	5	0.02
Jamaican	45	0.15
West Indian	5	0.02
White:	8,845	29.98
Not Hispanic (1,930)	2,175	7.37
Hispanic (6,032)	6,670	22.61
Yugoslavian	10	0.03

East San Gabriel

Place Type: Census Designated Place
County: Los Angeles
Population: 14,512

Ancestry/Race	Number	%
African American/Black:	343	2.36
Not Hispanic (256)	310	2.14
Hispanic (13)	33	0.23
African, sub-Saharan:	14	0.10
African	4	0.03
Nigerian	10	0.07
Am. Ind. or Alaska Nat., not spec.	71	0.49
American Indian tribes, specified:	108	0.74
Apache (7)	10	0.07
Blackfeet	2	0.01
Cherokee (3)	13	0.09
Choctaw (1)	3	0.02
Comanche	1	0.01
Iroquois	1	0.01
Latin American Indians (25)	37	0.25
Navajo (2)	7	0.05
Paiute (3)	3	0.02
Seminole (1)	2	0.01
Shoshone (1)	1	0.01
Sioux (4)	4	0.03
Ute (3)	6	0.04
All other tribes (9)	18	0.12
American Indian tribes, not spec.	12	0.08
Arab:	194	1.33
Arab/Arabic	40	0.27
Egyptian	63	0.43
Lebanese	65	0.45
Palestinian	26	0.18
Armenian	88	0.60
Asian:	6,423	44.26
Cambodian (10)	18	0.12
Chinese, ex. Taiwanese (3,531)	3,829	26.39
Filipino (214)	269	1.85
Indian (216)	230	1.58
Indonesian (42)	61	0.42
Japanese (406)	477	3.29
Korean (272)	292	2.01
Laotian (4)	12	0.08
Malaysian (8)	15	0.10
Pakistani (16)	16	0.11
Sri Lankan (20)	20	0.14
Taiwanese (565)	708	4.88
Thai (52)	67	0.46
Vietnamese (235)	285	1.96
Other Asian, specified (8)	15	0.10
Other Asian, not specified (42)	109	0.75
Austrian	50	0.34
Belgian	13	0.09
British	39	0.27
Canadian	25	0.17
Celtic	6	0.04
Croatian	22	0.15
Czech	5	0.03
Czechoslovakian	10	0.07
Danish	58	0.40
Dutch	130	0.89
Eastern European	6	0.04
English	860	5.90
European	90	0.62
French, except Basque	227	1.56
French Canadian	40	0.27
German	920	6.31
Greek	31	0.21
Hawaii Native/Pacific Islander:	62	0.43
Micronesian: (1)	3	0.02
Guamanian/Chamorro (1)	3	0.02
Polynesian: (12)	26	0.18
Native Hawaiian (6)	13	0.09
Samoan (5)	10	0.07
Other Polynesian (1)	3	0.02
Other Pac. Isl., not spec.	33	0.23
Hispanic or Latino:	3,413	23.52
Central American:	157	1.08
Costa Rican	7	0.05
Guatemalan	39	0.27
Honduran	5	0.03
Nicaraguan	49	0.34
Panamanian	7	0.05
Salvadoran	41	0.28
Other Central American	9	0.06
Cuban	57	0.39
Mexican	2,565	17.68
Puerto Rican	34	0.23
South American:	142	0.98
Argentinean	31	0.21
Bolivian	1	0.01
Chilean	5	0.03
Colombian	21	0.14
Ecuadorian	16	0.11
Peruvian	52	0.36
Uruguayan	1	0.01
Venezuelan	10	0.07
Other South American	5	0.03
Other Hispanic or Latino	458	3.16
Hungarian	58	0.40
Icelander	14	0.10
Iranian	5	0.03
Irish	644	4.41
Italian	532	3.65
Lithuanian	29	0.20
New Zealander	8	0.05
Northern European	38	0.26
Norwegian	113	0.77
Polish	159	1.09
Portuguese	50	0.34
Romanian	11	0.08
Russian	36	0.25
Scandinavian	8	0.05
Scotch-Irish	187	1.28
Scottish	291	1.99
Serbian	12	0.08
Slavic	14	0.10
Slovak	19	0.13
Slovene	19	0.13
Swedish	121	0.83
Swiss	64	0.44
Ukrainian	52	0.36
United States or American	195	1.34
Welsh	47	0.32
West Indian, excl. Hispanic:	19	0.13
Jamaican	19	0.13
White:	6,636	45.73
Not Hispanic (4,511)	4,809	33.14
Hispanic (1,664)	1,827	12.59
Yugoslavian	34	0.23

El Cajon

Place Type: City
County: San Diego
Population: 94,869

Ancestry/Race	Number	%
Acadian/Cajun	15	0.02
Afghan	40	0.04
African American/Black:	6,149	6.48
Not Hispanic (4,828)	5,711	6.02
Hispanic (262)	438	0.46
African, sub-Saharan:	471	0.50
African	360	0.38
Ghanian	6	0.01
Liberian	86	0.09
South African	9	0.01
Other sub-Saharan African	10	0.01
Alaska Native tribes, specified:	26	0.03
Alaska Athabascan (1)	4	0.00
Aleut (4)	7	0.01
Eskimo (2)	6	0.01
Tlingit-Haida (6)	9	0.01
Alaska Native tribes, not specified	5	0.01
Am. Ind. or Alaska Nat., not spec.	527	0.56
Albanian	208	0.22
Alsatian	14	0.01

Notes: 1. Figures in the "Number" column do not add up to the total population due to: a) Ancestry/Race overlap — e.g. persons can report being both White and Irish, b) persons of Hispanic origin can report being any race, c) persons reporting two ancestries are counted in both categories. 2. Numbers in parentheses indicate the number of persons reporting this ancestry/race alone, not in combination with any other ancestry/race. 3. Refer to the Explanation of Data in the front of the book for more detailed information.

American Indian tribes, specified:	1,293	1.36
Apache (27)	62	0.07
Blackfeet (18)	67	0.07
Cherokee (104)	338	0.36
Cheyenne (4)	9	0.01
Chickasaw (8)	15	0.02
Chippewa (18)	32	0.03
Choctaw (34)	65	0.07
Comanche (2)	9	0.01
Cree	7	0.01
Creek (16)	26	0.03
Crow (2)	6	0.01
Delaware (1)	4	0.00
Houma (4)	4	0.00
Iroquois (9)	32	0.03
Latin American Indians (66)	116	0.12
Lumbee (8)	10	0.01
Menominee (1)	1	0.00
Navajo (38)	58	0.06
Osage (5)	14	0.01
Ottawa (1)	1	0.00
Paiute (5)	9	0.01
Pima (6)	11	0.01
Potawatomi (2)	9	0.01
Pueblo (12)	29	0.03
Puget Sound Salish	5	0.01
Seminole (1)	3	0.00
Sioux (24)	37	0.04
Tohono O'Odham (5)	6	0.01
Ute (1)	5	0.01
Yaqui (28)	42	0.04
Yuman (2)	9	0.01
All other tribes (161)	252	0.27
American Indian tribes, not spec.	89	0.09
Arab:	2,463	2.60
Arab/Arabic	568	0.60
Egyptian	86	0.09
Iraqi	1,237	1.30
Jordanian	104	0.11
Lebanese	62	0.07
Palestinian	16	0.02
Syrian	17	0.02
Other Arab	373	0.39
Armenian	77	0.08
Asian:	4,081	4.30
Bangladeshi (6)	6	0.01
Cambodian (71)	105	0.11
Chinese, ex. Taiwanese (322)	474	0.50
Filipino (1,189)	1,819	1.92
Hmong (10)	11	0.01
Indian (113)	157	0.17
Indonesian (20)	36	0.04
Japanese (242)	487	0.51
Korean (109)	157	0.17
Laotian (14)	21	0.02
Malaysian (1)	3	0.00
Pakistani (12)	32	0.03
Sri Lankan (1)	1	0.00
Taiwanese (13)	17	0.02
Thai (22)	44	0.05
Vietnamese (373)	429	0.45
Other Asian, specified	7	0.01
Other Asian, not specified (54)	275	0.29
Assyrian/Chaldean/Syriac	2,522	2.66
Australian	89	0.09
Austrian	181	0.19
Basque	42	0.04
Belgian	94	0.10
Brazilian	34	0.04
British	420	0.44
Bulgarian	25	0.03
Canadian	410	0.43
Celtic	10	0.01
Croatian	48	0.05
Czech	356	0.38
Czechoslovakian	153	0.16
Danish	482	0.51
Dutch	1,312	1.38
Eastern European	70	0.07
English	7,397	7.80
European	906	0.96
Finnish	73	0.08
French, except Basque	2,938	3.10
French Canadian	702	0.74
German	13,747	14.50
Greek	403	0.43
Hawaii Native/Pacific Islander:	697	0.73
Melanesian: (1)	1	0.00
Other Melanesian (1)	1	0.00
Micronesian: (177)	268	0.28
Guamanian/Chamorro (172)	259	0.27
Other Micronesian (5)	9	0.01
Polynesian: (150)	326	0.34
Native Hawaiian (81)	199	0.21
Samoan (63)	111	0.12
Tongan (3)	8	0.01
Other Polynesian (3)	8	0.01
Other Pac. Isl., specified	6	0.01
Other Pac. Isl., not spec. (20)	96	0.10
Hispanic or Latino:	21,313	22.47
Central American:	350	0.37
Costa Rican	45	0.05
Guatemalan	116	0.12
Honduran	30	0.03
Nicaraguan	22	0.02
Panamanian	49	0.05
Salvadoran	70	0.07
Other Central American	18	0.02
Cuban	88	0.09
Dominican Republic	19	0.02
Mexican	17,271	18.21
Puerto Rican	565	0.60
South American:	192	0.20
Argentinean	28	0.03
Bolivian	3	0.00
Chilean	13	0.01
Colombian	55	0.06
Ecuadorian	13	0.01
Peruvian	64	0.07
Uruguayan	2	0.00
Venezuelan	7	0.01
Other South American	8	0.01
Other Hispanic or Latino	2,828	2.98
Hungarian	386	0.41
Icelander	52	0.05
Iranian	148	0.16
Irish	9,324	9.83
Israeli	19	0.02
Italian	4,905	5.17
Lithuanian	98	0.10
Luxemburger	7	0.01
Maltese	18	0.02
New Zealander	29	0.03
Northern European	140	0.15
Norwegian	1,649	1.74
Pennsylvania German	56	0.06
Polish	1,947	2.05
Portuguese	514	0.54
Romanian	32	0.03
Russian	636	0.67
Scandinavian	159	0.17
Scotch-Irish	1,332	1.40
Scottish	1,540	1.62
Serbian	56	0.06
Slavic	27	0.03
Slovak	140	0.15
Slovene	30	0.03
Swedish	1,657	1.75
Swiss	213	0.22
Turkish	44	0.05
Ukrainian	211	0.22
United States or American	5,458	5.76
Welsh	455	0.48
West Indian, excl. Hispanic:	219	0.23
Bahamian	26	0.03
Belizean	11	0.01
Dutch West Indian	14	0.01
Haitian	26	0.03
Jamaican	36	0.04
U.S. Virgin Islander	10	0.01
West Indian	96	0.10
White:	75,249	79.32
Not Hispanic (61,188)	64,678	68.18
Hispanic (9,018)	10,571	11.14
Yugoslavian	133	0.14

El Centro

Place Type: City
County: Imperial
Population: 37,835

Ancestry/Race	Number	%
African American/Black:	1,339	3.54
Not Hispanic (1,042)	1,107	2.93
Hispanic (153)	232	0.61
African, sub-Saharan:	84	0.22
African	70	0.19
Other sub-Saharan African	14	0.04
Alaska Native tribes, specified:	1	0.00
Tlingit-Haida (1)	1	0.00
Am. Ind. or Alaska Nat., not spec.	299	0.79
American Indian tribes, specified:	262	0.69
Apache (5)	12	0.03
Blackfeet (1)	9	0.02
Cherokee (11)	51	0.13
Chickasaw (2)	3	0.01
Chippewa	3	0.01
Choctaw (14)	19	0.05
Comanche (1)	3	0.01
Creek	4	0.01
Kiowa	1	0.00
Latin American Indians (56)	80	0.21
Lumbee (1)	1	0.00
Navajo (8)	10	0.03
Osage	1	0.00
Paiute	1	0.00
Pima (6)	6	0.02
Pueblo (11)	14	0.04
Shoshone (1)	1	0.00
Sioux (3)	3	0.01
Tohono O'Odham (4)	6	0.02
Yaqui (1)	11	0.03
Yuman (4)	7	0.02
All other tribes (10)	16	0.04
American Indian tribes, not spec.	27	0.07
Armenian	7	0.02
Asian:	1,571	4.15
Cambodian (29)	34	0.09
Chinese, ex. Taiwanese (144)	184	0.49
Filipino (206)	314	0.83
Hmong	1	0.00
Indian (184)	232	0.61
Japanese (207)	223	0.59
Korean (418)	429	1.13
Laotian (18)	18	0.05
Malaysian (3)	5	0.01
Pakistani (1)	3	0.01
Sri Lankan (1)	1	0.00
Taiwanese (10)	11	0.03
Thai (12)	13	0.03
Vietnamese (71)	72	0.19
Other Asian, specified (2)	4	0.01
Other Asian, not specified (11)	27	0.07
Australian	6	0.02
Basque	31	0.08
Belgian	13	0.03
British	27	0.07
Canadian	32	0.08
Czech	31	0.08
Danish	102	0.27
Dutch	257	0.68
English	1,095	2.90
European	139	0.37
Finnish	28	0.07
French, except Basque	389	1.03
French Canadian	70	0.19
German	1,452	3.84
Greek	8	0.02
Hawaii Native/Pacific Islander:	56	0.15

Notes: 1. Figures in the "Number" column do not add up to the total population due to: a) Ancestry/Race overlap — e.g. persons can report being both White and Irish, b) persons of Hispanic origin can report being any race, c) persons reporting two ancestries are counted in both categories. 2. Numbers in parentheses indicate the number of persons reporting this ancestry/race alone, not in combination with any other ancestry/race. 3. Refer to the Explanation of Data in the front of the book for more detailed information.

Melanesian: (5)	5	0.01
Fijian (5)	5	0.01
Micronesian: (6)	10	0.03
Guamanian/Chamorro (6)	10	0.03
Polynesian: (23)	26	0.07
Native Hawaiian (8)	8	0.02
Samoan (12)	15	0.04
Tongan (2)	2	0.01
Other Polynesian (1)	1	0.00
Other Pac. Isl., not spec. (3)	15	0.04
Hispanic or Latino:	28,219	74.58
Central American:	165	0.44
Costa Rican	2	0.01
Guatemalan	30	0.08
Honduran	26	0.07
Nicaraguan	13	0.03
Panamanian	5	0.01
Salvadoran	82	0.22
Other Central American	7	0.02
Cuban	41	0.11
Dominican Republic	4	0.01
Mexican	25,251	66.74
Puerto Rican	79	0.21
South American:	32	0.08
Argentinean	3	0.01
Bolivian	2	0.01
Chilean	1	0.00
Colombian	10	0.03
Ecuadorian	4	0.01
Paraguayan	1	0.00
Peruvian	10	0.03
Other South American	1	0.00
Other Hispanic or Latino	2,647	7.00
Hungarian	34	0.09
Icelander	10	0.03
Iranian	18	0.05
Irish	1,337	3.54
Italian	426	1.13
Lithuanian	10	0.03
Northern European	11	0.03
Norwegian	144	0.38
Polish	157	0.42
Portuguese	16	0.04
Russian	63	0.17
Scandinavian	17	0.04
Scotch-Irish	197	0.52
Scottish	214	0.57
Swedish	118	0.31
Swiss	129	0.34
United States or American	884	2.34
Welsh	35	0.09
White:	18,907	49.97
Not Hispanic (6,837)	7,114	18.80
Hispanic (10,891)	11,793	31.17
Yugoslavian	16	0.04

El Cerrito

Place Type: City
County: Contra Costa
Population: 23,171

Ancestry/Race	Number	%
African American/Black:	2,274	9.81
Not Hispanic (1,931)	2,193	9.46
Hispanic (47)	81	0.35
African, sub-Saharan:	241	1.04
African	131	0.57
Cape Verdean	9	0.04
Ethiopian	23	0.10
Ghanian	36	0.16
Liberian	5	0.02
South African	4	0.02
Sudanese	25	0.11
Other sub-Saharan African	8	0.03
Alaska Native tribes, specified:	3	0.01
Eskimo (1)	2	0.01
All other tribes (1)	1	0.00
Am. Ind. or Alaska Nat., not spec.	90	0.39
Alsatian	8	0.03
American Indian tribes, specified:	208	0.90
Apache (1)	11	0.05
Blackfeet (1)	5	0.02
Cherokee (14)	63	0.27
Chickasaw	2	0.01
Chippewa (1)	9	0.04
Choctaw (3)	17	0.07
Comanche	3	0.01
Creek (3)	5	0.02
Delaware	1	0.00
Iroquois	2	0.01
Latin American Indians (11)	21	0.09
Navajo (3)	8	0.03
Osage	2	0.01
Paiute (1)	3	0.01
Pueblo (3)	6	0.03
Seminole	5	0.02
Shoshone	1	0.00
Sioux (8)	10	0.04
Tohono O'Odham (1)	1	0.00
Yaqui (1)	5	0.02
Yuman (1)	1	0.00
All other tribes (14)	27	0.12
American Indian tribes, not spec.	16	0.07
Arab:	172	0.74
Arab/Arabic	45	0.19
Egyptian	31	0.13
Lebanese	17	0.07
Moroccan	6	0.03
Palestinian	16	0.07
Syrian	15	0.06
Other Arab	42	0.18
Armenian	29	0.13
Asian:	6,415	27.69
Bangladeshi (4)	4	0.02
Cambodian (27)	33	0.14
Chinese, ex. Taiwanese (2,784)	3,050	13.16
Filipino (394)	559	2.41
Hmong (1)	1	0.00
Indian (366)	410	1.77
Indonesian (27)	36	0.16
Japanese (1,063)	1,288	5.56
Korean (271)	294	1.27
Laotian (57)	66	0.28
Malaysian (5)	7	0.03
Pakistani (40)	49	0.21
Sri Lankan (19)	21	0.09
Taiwanese (197)	216	0.93
Thai (53)	70	0.30
Vietnamese (156)	180	0.78
Other Asian, specified (17)	29	0.13
Other Asian, not specified (36)	102	0.44
Australian	10	0.04
Austrian	172	0.74
Belgian	39	0.17
Brazilian	60	0.26
British	204	0.88
Canadian	98	0.42
Celtic	34	0.15
Croatian	48	0.21
Czech	107	0.46
Czechoslovakian	42	0.18
Danish	134	0.58
Dutch	325	1.40
Eastern European	100	0.43
English	2,537	10.95
European	398	1.72
Finnish	102	0.44
French, except Basque	706	3.05
French Canadian	100	0.43
German	2,605	11.24
Greek	81	0.35
Guyanese	9	0.04
Hawaii Native/Pacific Islander:	162	0.70
Melanesian: (13)	21	0.09
Fijian (13)	21	0.09
Micronesian: (3)	9	0.04
Guamanian/Chamorro (2)	7	0.03
Other Micronesian (1)	2	0.01
Polynesian: (39)	100	0.43
Native Hawaiian (21)	70	0.30
Samoan (13)	23	0.10
Tongan (5)	5	0.02
Other Polynesian	2	0.01
Other Pac. Isl., not spec. (4)	32	0.14
Hispanic or Latino:	1,838	7.93
Central American:	121	0.52
Costa Rican	2	0.01
Guatemalan	25	0.11
Honduran	9	0.04
Nicaraguan	29	0.13
Panamanian	3	0.01
Salvadoran	42	0.18
Other Central American	11	0.05
Cuban	27	0.12
Dominican Republic	2	0.01
Mexican	953	4.11
Puerto Rican	59	0.25
South American:	239	1.03
Argentinean	35	0.15
Bolivian	8	0.03
Chilean	25	0.11
Colombian	12	0.05
Ecuadorian	15	0.06
Peruvian	92	0.40
Venezuelan	10	0.04
Other South American	42	0.18
Other Hispanic or Latino	437	1.89
Hungarian	103	0.44
Icelander	8	0.03
Iranian	317	1.37
Irish	1,955	8.43
Israeli	102	0.44
Italian	1,373	5.92
Latvian	20	0.09
Lithuanian	84	0.36
Luxemburger	14	0.06
Macedonian	5	0.02
Northern European	66	0.28
Norwegian	321	1.38
Polish	587	2.53
Portuguese	312	1.35
Romanian	18	0.08
Russian	448	1.93
Scandinavian	62	0.27
Scotch-Irish	450	1.94
Scottish	713	3.08
Slavic	39	0.17
Slovak	20	0.09
Slovene	46	0.20
Swedish	417	1.80
Swiss	240	1.04
Turkish	36	0.16
Ukrainian	64	0.28
United States or American	335	1.45
Welsh	230	0.99
West Indian, excl. Hispanic:	63	0.27
Belizean	23	0.10
Haitian	6	0.03
Jamaican	20	0.09
Trinidadian and Tobagonian	6	0.03
West Indian	8	0.03
White:	14,419	62.23
Not Hispanic (12,474)	13,330	57.53
Hispanic (917)	1,089	4.70
Yugoslavian	64	0.28

El Dorado Hills

Place Type: Census Designated Place
County: El Dorado
Population: 18,016

Ancestry/Race	Number	%
African American/Black:	172	0.95
Not Hispanic (137)	169	0.94
Hispanic (2)	3	0.02
African, sub-Saharan:	76	0.42
Ethiopian	13	0.07
Nigerian	31	0.17

Notes: 1. Figures in the "Number" column do not add up to the total population due to: a) Ancestry/Race overlap — e.g. persons can report being both White and Irish, b) persons of Hispanic origin can report being any race, c) persons reporting two ancestries are counted in both categories. 2. Numbers in parentheses indicate the number of persons reporting this ancestry/race alone, not in combination with any other ancestry/race. 3. Refer to the Explanation of Data in the front of the book for more detailed information.

Ancestry/Race	Number	%
South African	32	0.18
Am. Ind. or Alaska Nat., not spec.	54	0.30
American Indian tribes, specified:	128	0.71
Apache (2)	3	0.02
Blackfeet (1)	4	0.02
Cherokee (22)	56	0.31
Chickasaw (1)	1	0.01
Chippewa (1)	1	0.01
Choctaw (1)	10	0.06
Creek (1)	3	0.02
Delaware (1)	1	0.01
Latin American Indians (4)	5	0.03
Navajo (2)	8	0.04
Paiute (1)	2	0.01
Pueblo (3)	3	0.02
Seminole	2	0.01
Shoshone (2)	2	0.01
Sioux (1)	3	0.02
All other tribes (14)	24	0.13
American Indian tribes, not spec.	14	0.08
Arab:	88	0.49
Arab/Arabic	8	0.04
Lebanese	10	0.06
Palestinian	41	0.23
Syrian	29	0.16
Armenian	37	0.20
Asian:	1,057	5.87
Chinese, ex. Taiwanese (189)	285	1.58
Filipino (129)	200	1.11
Indian (169)	190	1.05
Indonesian (10)	14	0.08
Japanese (89)	178	0.99
Korean (62)	71	0.39
Pakistani (9)	13	0.07
Thai (7)	13	0.07
Vietnamese (49)	55	0.31
Other Asian, specified (2)	7	0.04
Other Asian, not specified (8)	31	0.17
Assyrian/Chaldean/Syriac	61	0.34
Australian	7	0.04
Austrian	42	0.23
Belgian	17	0.09
British	109	0.60
Canadian	104	0.58
Croatian	26	0.14
Czech	49	0.27
Czechoslovakian	18	0.10
Danish	345	1.91
Dutch	464	2.57
English	3,190	17.64
European	543	3.00
Finnish	64	0.35
French, except Basque	903	4.99
French Canadian	73	0.40
German	3,799	21.01
Greek	138	0.76
Hawaii Native/Pacific Islander:	67	0.37
Melanesian: (1)	1	0.01
Fijian (1)	1	0.01
Micronesian: (4)	6	0.03
Guamanian/Chamorro (4)	5	0.03
Other Micronesian	1	0.01
Polynesian: (22)	51	0.28
Native Hawaiian (13)	35	0.19
Samoan (9)	16	0.09
Other Pac. Isl., not spec. (3)	9	0.05
Hispanic or Latino:	896	4.97
Central American:	23	0.13
Costa Rican	3	0.02
Guatemalan	2	0.01
Honduran	1	0.01
Nicaraguan	11	0.06
Panamanian	3	0.02
Salvadoran	2	0.01
Other Central American	1	0.01
Cuban	13	0.07
Dominican Republic	3	0.02
Mexican	527	2.93
Puerto Rican	49	0.27
South American:	27	0.15
Argentinean	3	0.02
Bolivian	4	0.02
Colombian	2	0.01
Ecuadorian	1	0.01
Paraguayan	1	0.01
Peruvian	8	0.04
Venezuelan	6	0.03
Other South American	2	0.01
Other Hispanic or Latino	254	1.41
Hungarian	92	0.51
Iranian	106	0.59
Irish	2,802	15.50
Israeli	16	0.09
Italian	1,577	8.72
Lithuanian	46	0.25
Maltese	17	0.09
Northern European	31	0.17
Norwegian	587	3.25
Pennsylvania German	21	0.12
Polish	707	3.91
Portuguese	452	2.50
Romanian	70	0.39
Russian	177	0.98
Scandinavian	20	0.11
Scotch-Irish	422	2.33
Scottish	522	2.89
Slavic	19	0.11
Slovak	21	0.12
Swedish	669	3.70
Swiss	120	0.66
Turkish	9	0.05
Ukrainian	79	0.44
United States or American	745	4.12
Welsh	272	1.50
White:	16,740	92.92
Not Hispanic (15,665)	16,107	89.40
Hispanic (569)	633	3.51
Yugoslavian	45	0.25

El Monte

Place Type: City
County: Los Angeles
Population: 115,965

Ancestry/Race	Number	%
Afghan	3	0.00
African American/Black:	1,187	1.02
Not Hispanic (640)	755	0.65
Hispanic (249)	432	0.37
African, sub-Saharan:	102	0.09
African	79	0.07
Other sub-Saharan African	23	0.02
Alaska Native tribes, specified:	2	0.00
Aleut (2)	2	0.00
Am. Ind. or Alaska Nat., not spec.	1,169	1.01
Alsatian	5	0.00
American Indian tribes, specified:	940	0.81
Apache (55)	82	0.07
Blackfeet (1)	2	0.00
Cherokee (30)	82	0.07
Cheyenne (20)	22	0.02
Chippewa (8)	15	0.01
Choctaw (4)	15	0.01
Comanche (5)	10	0.01
Creek (2)	6	0.01
Crow	1	0.00
Iroquois	1	0.00
Latin American Indians (273)	404	0.35
Navajo (37)	49	0.04
Osage (1)	1	0.00
Ottawa (1)	1	0.00
Paiute (3)	5	0.00
Pima (1)	1	0.00
Potawatomi (1)	1	0.00
Pueblo (8)	14	0.01
Seminole	3	0.00
Shoshone (5)	7	0.01
Sioux (7)	10	0.01
Tohono O'Odham (6)	6	0.01
Ute (2)	2	0.00
Yaqui (12)	34	0.03
Yuman (4)	6	0.01
All other tribes (137)	160	0.14
American Indian tribes, not spec.	167	0.14
Arab:	85	0.07
Arab/Arabic	10	0.01
Egyptian	54	0.05
Lebanese	18	0.02
Syrian	3	0.00
Armenian	122	0.10
Asian:	23,258	20.06
Bangladeshi (2)	3	0.00
Cambodian (395)	520	0.45
Chinese, ex. Taiwanese (11,465)	12,506	10.78
Filipino (1,142)	1,321	1.14
Indian (155)	224	0.19
Indonesian (58)	77	0.07
Japanese (241)	350	0.30
Korean (201)	232	0.20
Laotian (43)	68	0.06
Malaysian (8)	32	0.03
Pakistani (8)	8	0.01
Sri Lankan	4	0.00
Taiwanese (507)	646	0.56
Thai (149)	187	0.16
Vietnamese (6,015)	6,766	5.83
Other Asian, specified (67)	87	0.08
Other Asian, not specified (118)	227	0.20
Austrian	56	0.05
Basque	6	0.01
Belgian	54	0.05
Brazilian	11	0.01
British	27	0.02
Canadian	60	0.05
Czech	18	0.02
Czechoslovakian	27	0.02
Danish	53	0.05
Dutch	212	0.18
English	1,317	1.13
European	97	0.08
Finnish	18	0.02
French, except Basque	482	0.41
French Canadian	81	0.07
German	1,772	1.52
Greek	89	0.08
Guyanese	9	0.01
Hawaii Native/Pacific Islander:	278	0.24
Melanesian: (4)	4	0.00
Fijian (4)	4	0.00
Micronesian: (17)	35	0.03
Guamanian/Chamorro (17)	35	0.03
Polynesian: (90)	127	0.11
Native Hawaiian (50)	71	0.06
Samoan (38)	50	0.04
Tongan (2)	6	0.01
Other Pac. Isl., not spec. (29)	112	0.10
Hispanic or Latino:	83,945	72.39
Central American:	3,030	2.61
Costa Rican	56	0.05
Guatemalan	667	0.58
Honduran	202	0.17
Nicaraguan	295	0.25
Panamanian	25	0.02
Salvadoran	1,504	1.30
Other Central American	281	0.24
Cuban	431	0.37
Dominican Republic	4	0.00
Mexican	69,880	60.26
Puerto Rican	283	0.24
South American:	418	0.36
Argentinean	105	0.09
Bolivian	4	0.00
Chilean	24	0.02
Colombian	65	0.06
Ecuadorian	68	0.06
Peruvian	119	0.10
Uruguayan	1	0.00
Venezuelan	2	0.00
Other South American	30	0.03

Notes: 1. Figures in the "Number" column do not add up to the total population due to: a) Ancestry/Race overlap — e.g. persons can report being both White and Irish, b) persons of Hispanic origin can report being any race, c) persons reporting two ancestries are counted in both categories. 2. Numbers in parentheses indicate the number of persons reporting this ancestry/race alone, not in combination with any other ancestry/race. 3. Refer to the Explanation of Data in the front of the book for more detailed information.

Other Hispanic or Latino	9,899	8.54
Hungarian	71	0.06
Iranian	16	0.01
Irish	1,479	1.27
Italian	766	0.66
Latvian	8	0.01
Lithuanian	72	0.06
Northern European	12	0.01
Norwegian	35	0.03
Polish	227	0.20
Portuguese	17	0.01
Russian	111	0.10
Scandinavian	7	0.01
Scotch-Irish	251	0.22
Scottish	261	0.22
Slovak	31	0.03
Swedish	200	0.17
Swiss	50	0.04
Turkish	6	0.01
Ukrainian	11	0.01
United States or American	1,786	1.54
Welsh	56	0.05
West Indian, excl. Hispanic:	25	0.02
Belizean	25	0.02
White:	45,481	39.22
Not Hispanic (8,542)	9,149	7.89
Hispanic (32,818)	36,332	31.33
Yugoslavian	28	0.02

El Paso de Robles

Place Type: City
County: San Luis Obispo
Population: 24,297

Ancestry/Race	Number	%
African American/Black:	1,005	4.14
Not Hispanic (751)	907	3.73
Hispanic (55)	98	0.40
African, sub-Saharan:	48	0.20
African	48	0.20
Alaska Native tribes, specified:	5	0.02
Alaska Athabascan (1)	1	0.00
Aleut (1)	3	0.01
Tlingit-Haida (1)	1	0.00
Alaska Native tribes, not specified	2	0.01
Am. Ind. or Alaska Nat., not spec.	209	0.86
American Indian tribes, specified:	387	1.59
Apache (12)	19	0.08
Blackfeet (7)	19	0.08
Cherokee (23)	84	0.35
Cheyenne	1	0.00
Chickasaw (3)	3	0.01
Chippewa (4)	11	0.05
Choctaw (13)	29	0.12
Comanche	4	0.02
Cree (1)	1	0.00
Creek (5)	8	0.03
Crow	2	0.01
Delaware	2	0.01
Iroquois	3	0.01
Latin American Indians (24)	33	0.14
Lumbee	2	0.01
Navajo (4)	12	0.05
Osage (1)	4	0.02
Ottawa	1	0.00
Paiute (5)	8	0.03
Pima (1)	1	0.00
Potawatomi (1)	3	0.01
Pueblo (5)	7	0.03
Puget Sound Salish	2	0.01
Seminole	1	0.00
Shoshone (1)	1	0.00
Sioux (5)	16	0.07
Tohono O'Odham (1)	1	0.00
Yaqui	5	0.02
Yuman (1)	1	0.00
All other tribes (58)	103	0.42
American Indian tribes, not spec.	18	0.07
Arab:	122	0.50
Arab/Arabic	68	0.28
Lebanese	47	0.19
Palestinian	7	0.03
Armenian	16	0.07
Asian:	653	2.69
Cambodian (18)	18	0.07
Chinese, ex. Taiwanese (43)	57	0.23
Filipino (120)	208	0.86
Hmong (7)	8	0.03
Indian (55)	69	0.28
Indonesian (5)	5	0.02
Japanese (46)	80	0.33
Korean (105)	123	0.51
Laotian (3)	3	0.01
Malaysian (1)	1	0.00
Sri Lankan (2)	2	0.01
Thai (10)	13	0.05
Vietnamese (36)	37	0.15
Other Asian, specified (1)	3	0.01
Other Asian, not specified (4)	26	0.11
Assyrian/Chaldean/Syriac	5	0.02
Austrian	150	0.62
Basque	7	0.03
Belgian	8	0.03
British	157	0.65
Canadian	67	0.28
Croatian	55	0.23
Czech	81	0.33
Czechoslovakian	27	0.11
Danish	201	0.83
Dutch	569	2.35
English	2,978	12.30
European	139	0.57
French, except Basque	814	3.36
French Canadian	109	0.45
German	3,427	14.15
Greek	62	0.26
Hawaii Native/Pacific Islander:	82	0.34
Micronesian: (16)	19	0.08
Guamanian/Chamorro (16)	19	0.08
Polynesian: (18)	46	0.19
Native Hawaiian (10)	35	0.14
Samoan (8)	11	0.05
Other Pac. Isl., specified	1	0.00
Other Pac. Isl., not spec.	16	0.07
Hispanic or Latino:	6,735	27.72
Central American:	117	0.48
Costa Rican	4	0.02
Guatemalan	14	0.06
Honduran	10	0.04
Nicaraguan	17	0.07
Panamanian	5	0.02
Salvadoran	54	0.22
Other Central American	13	0.05
Cuban	24	0.10
Mexican	5,712	23.51
Puerto Rican	87	0.36
South American:	32	0.13
Argentinean	4	0.02
Bolivian	2	0.01
Chilean	3	0.01
Colombian	13	0.05
Ecuadorian	3	0.01
Peruvian	6	0.02
Other South American	1	0.00
Other Hispanic or Latino	763	3.14
Hungarian	33	0.14
Icelander	11	0.05
Irish	2,823	11.66
Italian	1,062	4.39
Lithuanian	74	0.31
Macedonian	8	0.03
Maltese	8	0.03
Norwegian	541	2.23
Polish	425	1.76
Portuguese	257	1.06
Romanian	11	0.05
Russian	104	0.43
Scandinavian	85	0.35
Scotch-Irish	360	1.49
Scottish	429	1.77
Serbian	8	0.03
Slovak	17	0.07
Swedish	384	1.59
Swiss	217	0.90
Turkish	4	0.02
Ukrainian	25	0.10
United States or American	1,083	4.47
Welsh	188	0.78
West Indian, excl. Hispanic:	43	0.18
Belizean	31	0.13
Dutch West Indian	12	0.05
White:	19,242	79.19
Not Hispanic (15,600)	16,099	66.26
Hispanic (2,793)	3,143	12.94
Yugoslavian	76	0.31

El Segundo

Place Type: City
County: Los Angeles
Population: 16,033

Ancestry/Race	Number	%
Acadian/Cajun	21	0.13
Afghan	18	0.11
African American/Black:	287	1.79
Not Hispanic (181)	269	1.68
Hispanic (6)	18	0.11
African, sub-Saharan:	45	0.28
African	32	0.20
South African	13	0.08
Alaska Native tribes, specified:	1	0.01
Eskimo	1	0.01
Am. Ind. or Alaska Nat., not spec.	51	0.32
American Indian tribes, specified:	159	0.99
Apache (5)	18	0.11
Blackfeet	2	0.01
Cherokee (5)	42	0.26
Cheyenne (2)	2	0.01
Chickasaw	2	0.01
Chippewa (3)	4	0.02
Choctaw (2)	6	0.04
Comanche	1	0.01
Cree	1	0.01
Iroquois	8	0.05
Latin American Indians (4)	7	0.04
Navajo (10)	16	0.10
Osage (1)	4	0.02
Paiute	4	0.02
Pima (1)	2	0.01
Potawatomi	1	0.01
Pueblo	4	0.02
Seminole (1)	2	0.01
Shoshone (2)	2	0.01
Sioux (3)	8	0.05
Tohono O'Odham	1	0.01
Ute (1)	8	0.05
Yakama (1)	1	0.01
Yaqui (2)	2	0.01
All other tribes (6)	11	0.07
American Indian tribes, not spec.	6	0.04
Arab:	33	0.21
Egyptian	25	0.16
Lebanese	8	0.05
Armenian	92	0.58
Asian:	1,398	8.72
Cambodian (1)	1	0.01
Chinese, ex. Taiwanese (208)	274	1.71
Filipino (202)	306	1.91
Indian (186)	224	1.40
Indonesian (27)	36	0.22
Japanese (150)	262	1.63
Korean (70)	79	0.49
Laotian (5)	5	0.03
Malaysian (4)	6	0.04
Pakistani (22)	40	0.25
Sri Lankan (4)	4	0.02
Taiwanese (24)	24	0.15
Thai (22)	25	0.16

Notes: 1. Figures in the "Number" column do not add up to the total population due to: a) Ancestry/Race overlap — e.g. persons can report being both White and Irish, b) persons of Hispanic origin can report being any race, c) persons reporting two ancestries are counted in both categories. 2. Numbers in parentheses indicate the number of persons reporting this ancestry/race alone, not in combination with any other ancestry/race. 3. Refer to the Explanation of Data in the front of the book for more detailed information.

Ancestry/Race	Number	%
Vietnamese (61)	70	0.44
Other Asian, specified (1)	4	0.02
Other Asian, not specified (9)	38	0.24
Australian	7	0.04
Austrian	53	0.33
Basque	11	0.07
Belgian	21	0.13
British	156	0.98
Bulgarian	10	0.06
Canadian	102	0.64
Croatian	45	0.28
Czech	89	0.56
Czechoslovakian	88	0.55
Danish	104	0.65
Dutch	280	1.75
Eastern European	31	0.19
English	2,233	13.98
European	415	2.60
Finnish	13	0.08
French, except Basque	656	4.11
French Canadian	69	0.43
German	2,823	17.68
Greek	141	0.88
Hawaii Native/Pacific Islander:	100	0.62
Micronesian: (5)	6	0.04
Guamanian/Chamorro (5)	6	0.04
Polynesian: (38)	79	0.49
Native Hawaiian (24)	61	0.38
Samoan (12)	12	0.07
Tongan (2)	5	0.03
Other Polynesian	1	0.01
Other Pac. Isl., not spec. (4)	15	0.09
Hispanic or Latino:	1,765	11.01
Central American:	99	0.62
Costa Rican	12	0.07
Guatemalan	37	0.23
Honduran	12	0.07
Nicaraguan	9	0.06
Panamanian	3	0.02
Salvadoran	22	0.14
Other Central American	4	0.02
Cuban	50	0.31
Dominican Republic	1	0.01
Mexican	1,058	6.60
Puerto Rican	62	0.39
South American:	161	1.00
Argentinean	36	0.22
Bolivian	3	0.02
Chilean	21	0.13
Colombian	18	0.11
Ecuadorian	21	0.13
Peruvian	35	0.22
Venezuelan	8	0.05
Other South American	19	0.12
Other Hispanic or Latino	334	2.08
Hungarian	124	0.78
Iranian	107	0.67
Irish	2,604	16.31
Italian	1,064	6.66
Latvian	10	0.06
Lithuanian	67	0.42
Macedonian	17	0.11
New Zealander	19	0.12
Norwegian	354	2.22
Pennsylvania German	1	0.01
Polish	497	3.11
Portuguese	87	0.54
Romanian	17	0.11
Russian	181	1.13
Scandinavian	45	0.28
Scotch-Irish	442	2.77
Scottish	523	3.27
Slavic	14	0.09
Slovak	46	0.29
Slovene	25	0.16
Swedish	403	2.52
Swiss	81	0.51
Turkish	20	0.13
Ukrainian	45	0.28
United States or American	855	5.35
Welsh	114	0.71
West Indian, excl. Hispanic:	31	0.19
Belizean	12	0.08
Jamaican	19	0.12
White:	14,051	87.64
Not Hispanic (12,356)	12,828	80.01
Hispanic (1,049)	1,223	7.63
Yugoslavian	16	0.10

El Sobrante

Place Type: Census Designated Place
County: Contra Costa
Population: 12,260

Ancestry/Race	Number	%
Afghan	68	0.59
African American/Black:	1,681	13.71
Not Hispanic (1,473)	1,619	13.21
Hispanic (18)	62	0.51
African, sub-Saharan:	118	1.02
African	49	0.42
Ethiopian	29	0.25
Nigerian	22	0.19
Other sub-Saharan African	18	0.16
Am. Ind. or Alaska Nat., not spec.	84	0.69
Albanian	21	0.18
American Indian tribes, specified:	193	1.57
Apache (1)	3	0.02
Blackfeet (3)	16	0.13
Cherokee (20)	90	0.73
Cheyenne	1	0.01
Chickasaw (5)	7	0.06
Chippewa	2	0.02
Choctaw (1)	12	0.10
Comanche	1	0.01
Creek (1)	6	0.05
Latin American Indians (2)	7	0.06
Navajo	1	0.01
Osage	1	0.01
Pueblo (1)	2	0.02
Puget Sound Salish	1	0.01
Seminole	1	0.01
Shoshone (1)	3	0.02
Sioux (3)	6	0.05
Yaqui	2	0.02
All other tribes (6)	31	0.25
American Indian tribes, not spec.	29	0.24
Arab:	50	0.43
Arab/Arabic	5	0.04
Egyptian	5	0.04
Iraqi	8	0.07
Lebanese	17	0.15
Palestinian	15	0.13
Armenian	18	0.16
Asian:	1,882	15.35
Bangladeshi (4)	6	0.05
Cambodian (14)	14	0.11
Chinese, ex. Taiwanese (342)	419	3.42
Filipino (394)	508	4.14
Indian (394)	434	3.54
Indonesian (2)	6	0.05
Japanese (82)	129	1.05
Korean (42)	64	0.52
Laotian (38)	39	0.32
Malaysian (1)	1	0.01
Pakistani (58)	86	0.70
Taiwanese (9)	9	0.07
Thai (10)	10	0.08
Vietnamese (81)	90	0.73
Other Asian, specified (2)	9	0.07
Other Asian, not specified (22)	58	0.47
Assyrian/Chaldean/Syriac	42	0.36
Australian	11	0.09
Austrian	33	0.28
Belgian	10	0.09
Brazilian	7	0.06
British	17	0.15
Bulgarian	8	0.07
Celtic	8	0.07
Croatian	26	0.22
Czech	29	0.25
Czechoslovakian	24	0.21
Danish	95	0.82
Dutch	226	1.95
English	899	7.75
European	147	1.27
Finnish	83	0.72
French, except Basque	427	3.68
French Canadian	37	0.32
German	1,376	11.86
Greek	29	0.25
Hawaii Native/Pacific Islander:	93	0.76
Micronesian: (12)	20	0.16
Guamanian/Chamorro (12)	20	0.16
Polynesian: (14)	38	0.31
Native Hawaiian (10)	29	0.24
Samoan (4)	9	0.07
Other Pac. Isl., specified	3	0.02
Other Pac. Isl., not spec. (9)	32	0.26
Hispanic or Latino:	1,910	15.58
Central American:	213	1.74
Costa Rican	4	0.03
Guatemalan	11	0.09
Honduran	5	0.04
Nicaraguan	45	0.37
Panamanian	14	0.11
Salvadoran	112	0.91
Other Central American	22	0.18
Cuban	16	0.13
Mexican	1,066	8.69
Puerto Rican	73	0.60
South American:	67	0.55
Argentinean	15	0.12
Chilean	4	0.03
Colombian	6	0.05
Peruvian	28	0.23
Venezuelan	5	0.04
Other South American	9	0.07
Other Hispanic or Latino	475	3.87
Icelander	28	0.24
Iranian	18	0.16
Irish	1,254	10.81
Italian	779	6.71
Lithuanian	7	0.06
Northern European	21	0.18
Norwegian	249	2.15
Polish	112	0.97
Portuguese	209	1.80
Russian	146	1.26
Scandinavian	23	0.20
Scotch-Irish	171	1.47
Scottish	157	1.35
Slovak	16	0.14
Swedish	285	2.46
Swiss	60	0.52
Turkish	83	0.72
Ukrainian	33	0.28
United States or American	387	3.33
Welsh	33	0.28
West Indian, excl. Hispanic:	19	0.16
Jamaican	15	0.13
West Indian	4	0.03
White:	8,080	65.91
Not Hispanic (6,616)	7,079	57.74
Hispanic (783)	1,001	8.16
Yugoslavian	39	0.34

Elk Grove

Place Type: Census Designated Place
County: Sacramento
Population: 59,984

Ancestry/Race	Number	%
Afghan	31	0.05
African American/Black:	6,017	10.03
Not Hispanic (4,967)	5,717	9.53
Hispanic (143)	300	0.50
African, sub-Saharan:	585	0.97

Notes: 1. Figures in the "Number" column do not add up to the total population due to: a) Ancestry/Race overlap — e.g. persons can report being both White and Irish, b) persons of Hispanic origin can report being any race, c) persons reporting two ancestries are counted in both categories. 2. Numbers in parentheses indicate the number of persons reporting this ancestry/race alone, not in combination with any other ancestry/race. 3. Refer to the Explanation of Data in the front of the book for more detailed information.

African	389	0.65
Cape Verdean	25	0.04
Ethiopian	13	0.02
Nigerian	141	0.23
South African	9	0.01
Other sub-Saharan African	8	0.01
Alaska Native tribes, specified:	16	0.03
Alaska Athabascan (1)	1	0.00
Aleut (2)	7	0.01
Eskimo (1)	6	0.01
Tlingit-Haida	2	0.00
Am. Ind. or Alaska Nat., not spec.	414	0.69
American Indian tribes, specified:	924	1.54
Apache (12)	39	0.07
Blackfeet (7)	36	0.06
Cherokee (70)	277	0.46
Cheyenne (1)	2	0.00
Chickasaw (3)	7	0.01
Chippewa (9)	19	0.03
Choctaw (15)	46	0.08
Comanche (2)	4	0.01
Cree (4)	6	0.01
Creek (3)	12	0.02
Crow (5)	5	0.01
Delaware	5	0.01
Iroquois (7)	15	0.03
Kiowa (4)	4	0.01
Latin American Indians (31)	48	0.08
Lumbee (1)	3	0.01
Menominee	2	0.00
Navajo (10)	24	0.04
Osage	1	0.00
Ottawa (2)	2	0.00
Paiute (7)	15	0.03
Potawatomi (1)	5	0.01
Pueblo (4)	7	0.01
Seminole	11	0.02
Shoshone (4)	8	0.01
Sioux (12)	33	0.06
Tohono O'Odham (3)	4	0.01
Yakama (1)	4	0.01
Yaqui (1)	3	0.01
All other tribes (169)	277	0.46
American Indian tribes, not spec.	52	0.09
Arab:	134	0.22
Lebanese	75	0.12
Other Arab	59	0.10
Armenian	27	0.04
Asian:	12,461	20.77
Bangladeshi (1)	1	0.00
Cambodian (57)	77	0.13
Chinese, ex. Taiwanese (1,859)	2,208	3.68
Filipino (2,967)	3,661	6.10
Hmong (330)	343	0.57
Indian (1,372)	1,645	2.74
Indonesian (15)	29	0.05
Japanese (440)	809	1.35
Korean (283)	357	0.60
Laotian (265)	302	0.50
Malaysian (7)	15	0.03
Pakistani (89)	116	0.19
Sri Lankan (10)	11	0.02
Taiwanese (7)	10	0.02
Thai (42)	69	0.12
Vietnamese (2,494)	2,682	4.47
Other Asian, specified (9)	15	0.03
Other Asian, not specified (48)	111	0.19
Australian	9	0.01
Austrian	93	0.15
Basque	44	0.07
Belgian	44	0.07
Brazilian	17	0.03
British	187	0.31
Bulgarian	25	0.04
Canadian	113	0.19
Celtic	15	0.02
Croatian	110	0.18
Czech	155	0.26
Czechoslovakian	69	0.11
Danish	428	0.71
Dutch	809	1.34
Eastern European	11	0.02
English	4,612	7.65
Estonian	7	0.01
European	749	1.24
Finnish	130	0.22
French, except Basque	1,619	2.69
French Canadian	379	0.63
German	7,980	13.24
German Russian	7	0.01
Greek	335	0.56
Guyanese	8	0.01
Hawaii Native/Pacific Islander:	786	1.31
Melanesian: (93)	129	0.22
Fijian (93)	129	0.22
Micronesian: (113)	191	0.32
Guamanian/Chamorro (110)	186	0.31
Other Micronesian (3)	5	0.01
Polynesian: (78)	179	0.30
Native Hawaiian (22)	104	0.17
Samoan (28)	40	0.07
Tongan (28)	32	0.05
Other Polynesian	3	0.01
Other Pac. Isl., specified	1	0.00
Other Pac. Isl., not spec. (67)	286	0.48
Hispanic or Latino:	8,398	14.00
Central American:	272	0.45
Costa Rican	12	0.02
Guatemalan	24	0.04
Honduran	16	0.03
Nicaraguan	56	0.09
Panamanian	31	0.05
Salvadoran	96	0.16
Other Central American	37	0.06
Cuban	56	0.09
Dominican Republic	7	0.01
Mexican	6,300	10.50
Puerto Rican	236	0.39
South American:	97	0.16
Argentinean	8	0.01
Bolivian	7	0.01
Chilean	18	0.03
Colombian	9	0.02
Ecuadorian	14	0.02
Peruvian	34	0.06
Venezuelan	2	0.00
Other South American	5	0.01
Other Hispanic or Latino	1,430	2.38
Hungarian	268	0.44
Icelander	12	0.02
Iranian	91	0.15
Irish	5,772	9.58
Italian	3,262	5.41
Latvian	6	0.01
Lithuanian	37	0.06
Luxemburger	5	0.01
Macedonian	11	0.02
Maltese	50	0.08
Northern European	49	0.08
Norwegian	1,057	1.75
Pennsylvania German	17	0.03
Polish	783	1.30
Portuguese	1,342	2.23
Romanian	104	0.17
Russian	366	0.61
Scandinavian	76	0.13
Scotch-Irish	739	1.23
Scottish	849	1.41
Serbian	15	0.02
Slavic	21	0.03
Slovak	13	0.02
Slovene	18	0.03
Swedish	848	1.41
Swiss	299	0.50
Turkish	49	0.08
Ukrainian	249	0.41
United States or American	2,209	3.67
Welsh	406	0.67
West Indian, excl. Hispanic:	4	0.01
Jamaican	4	0.01
White:	38,601	64.35
Not Hispanic (32,252)	34,532	57.57
Hispanic (3,212)	4,069	6.78
Yugoslavian	103	0.17

Encinitas

Place Type: City
County: San Diego
Population: 58,014

Ancestry/Race	Number	%
African American/Black:	503	0.87
Not Hispanic (302)	442	0.76
Hispanic (38)	61	0.11
African, sub-Saharan:	49	0.08
African	34	0.06
South African	15	0.03
Alaska Native tribes, specified:	6	0.01
Alaska Athabascan (1)	2	0.00
Eskimo (2)	2	0.00
Tlingit-Haida (2)	2	0.00
Am. Ind. or Alaska Nat., not spec.	197	0.34
Alsatian	8	0.01
American Indian tribes, specified:	388	0.67
Apache (6)	17	0.03
Blackfeet	4	0.01
Cherokee (14)	94	0.16
Cheyenne	1	0.00
Chickasaw	3	0.01
Chippewa (10)	22	0.04
Choctaw (15)	22	0.04
Comanche (2)	3	0.01
Creek (5)	6	0.01
Houma (5)	5	0.01
Iroquois (2)	15	0.03
Latin American Indians (38)	75	0.13
Lumbee (3)	3	0.01
Menominee	1	0.00
Navajo (8)	13	0.02
Osage (3)	6	0.01
Paiute (1)	1	0.00
Pima	4	0.01
Potawatomi (1)	3	0.01
Pueblo (4)	4	0.01
Puget Sound Salish	1	0.00
Seminole	1	0.00
Shoshone	1	0.00
Sioux (8)	12	0.02
Tohono O'Odham (1)	1	0.00
Ute (1)	1	0.00
Yakama	1	0.00
Yaqui (4)	11	0.02
All other tribes (25)	57	0.10
American Indian tribes, not spec.	26	0.04
Arab:	272	0.47
Arab/Arabic	26	0.04
Iraqi	10	0.02
Lebanese	172	0.30
Moroccan	16	0.03
Palestinian	11	0.02
Syrian	37	0.06
Armenian	127	0.22
Asian:	2,509	4.32
Bangladeshi (5)	6	0.01
Cambodian (13)	13	0.02
Chinese, ex. Taiwanese (449)	565	0.97
Filipino (250)	404	0.70
Indian (232)	297	0.51
Indonesian (6)	26	0.04
Japanese (490)	753	1.30
Korean (143)	187	0.32
Laotian	1	0.00
Pakistani (13)	16	0.03
Taiwanese (40)	46	0.08
Thai (21)	27	0.05
Vietnamese (82)	103	0.18
Other Asian, specified (2)	5	0.01
Other Asian, not specified (27)	60	0.10
Assyrian/Chaldean/Syriac	10	0.02

Notes: 1. Figures in the "Number" column do not add up to the total population due to: a) Ancestry/Race overlap — e.g. persons can report being both White and Irish, b) persons of Hispanic origin can report being any race, c) persons reporting two ancestries are counted in both categories. 2. Numbers in parentheses indicate the number of persons reporting this ancestry/race alone, not in combination with any other ancestry/race. 3. Refer to the Explanation of Data in the front of the book for more detailed information.

Ancestry/Race	Number	%
Australian	62	0.11
Austrian	338	0.58
Basque	92	0.16
Belgian	51	0.09
Brazilian	75	0.13
British	527	0.91
Bulgarian	9	0.02
Canadian	326	0.56
Celtic	24	0.04
Croatian	115	0.20
Cypriot	9	0.02
Czech	264	0.45
Czechoslovakian	194	0.33
Danish	590	1.01
Dutch	1,144	1.97
Eastern European	85	0.15
English	7,862	13.51
European	1,085	1.86
Finnish	249	0.43
French, except Basque	2,468	4.24
French Canadian	484	0.83
German	11,041	18.97
Greek	433	0.74
Guyanese	6	0.01
Hawaii Native/Pacific Islander:	192	0.33
Melanesian: (2)	2	0.00
Fijian (1)	1	0.00
Other Melanesian (1)	1	0.00
Micronesian: (11)	36	0.06
Guamanian/Chamorro (10)	32	0.06
Other Micronesian (1)	4	0.01
Polynesian: (46)	118	0.20
Native Hawaiian (33)	95	0.16
Samoan (6)	12	0.02
Tongan (6)	7	0.01
Other Polynesian (1)	4	0.01
Other Pac. Isl., specified	3	0.01
Other Pac. Isl., not spec. (9)	33	0.06
Hispanic or Latino:	8,584	14.80
Central American:	211	0.36
Costa Rican	12	0.02
Guatemalan	99	0.17
Honduran	9	0.02
Nicaraguan	1	0.00
Panamanian	10	0.02
Salvadoran	59	0.10
Other Central American	21	0.04
Cuban	86	0.15
Dominican Republic	4	0.01
Mexican	6,919	11.93
Puerto Rican	130	0.22
South American:	188	0.32
Argentinean	31	0.05
Bolivian	6	0.01
Chilean	28	0.05
Colombian	42	0.07
Ecuadorian	6	0.01
Paraguayan	3	0.01
Peruvian	42	0.07
Venezuelan	15	0.03
Other South American	15	0.03
Other Hispanic or Latino	1,046	1.80
Hungarian	555	0.95
Icelander	34	0.06
Iranian	166	0.29
Irish	8,028	13.79
Israeli	27	0.05
Italian	3,871	6.65
Latvian	53	0.09
Lithuanian	152	0.26
Luxemburger	9	0.02
Macedonian	27	0.05
Maltese	10	0.02
New Zealander	44	0.08
Northern European	46	0.08
Norwegian	1,602	2.75
Pennsylvania German	18	0.03
Polish	2,129	3.66
Portuguese	287	0.49
Romanian	140	0.24
Russian	1,389	2.39
Scandinavian	272	0.47
Scotch-Irish	1,361	2.34
Scottish	1,859	3.19
Serbian	37	0.06
Slavic	30	0.05
Slovak	69	0.12
Slovene	33	0.06
Swedish	1,561	2.68
Swiss	370	0.64
Turkish	27	0.05
Ukrainian	217	0.37
United States or American	2,645	4.55
Welsh	659	1.13
West Indian, excl. Hispanic:	51	0.09
Jamaican	32	0.05
Trinidadian and Tobagonian	19	0.03
White:	51,781	89.26
Not Hispanic (45,852)	46,942	80.91
Hispanic (4,389)	4,839	8.34
Yugoslavian	121	0.21

Escondido

Place Type: City
County: San Diego
Population: 133,559

Ancestry/Race	Number	%
Acadian/Cajun	30	0.02
Afghan	17	0.01
African American/Black:	3,842	2.88
Not Hispanic (2,734)	3,327	2.49
Hispanic (275)	515	0.39
African, sub-Saharan:	379	0.28
African	333	0.25
Ethiopian	15	0.01
Nigerian	14	0.01
South African	9	0.01
Other sub-Saharan African	8	0.01
Alaska Native tribes, specified:	18	0.01
Aleut (5)	7	0.01
Eskimo (4)	4	0.00
Tlingit-Haida (1)	6	0.00
All other tribes	1	0.00
Alaska Native tribes, not specified	1	0.00
Am. Ind. or Alaska Nat., not spec.	1,230	0.92
Alsatian	7	0.01
American Indian tribes, specified:	1,712	1.28
Apache (41)	83	0.06
Blackfeet (11)	46	0.03
Cherokee (93)	307	0.23
Cheyenne	6	0.00
Chickasaw (2)	9	0.01
Chippewa (22)	45	0.03
Choctaw (22)	63	0.05
Comanche (3)	7	0.01
Cree	3	0.00
Creek (7)	9	0.01
Crow	1	0.00
Delaware (4)	10	0.01
Iroquois (16)	32	0.02
Kiowa (2)	2	0.00
Latin American Indians (244)	424	0.32
Lumbee (2)	2	0.00
Menominee (2)	5	0.00
Navajo (21)	48	0.04
Osage (3)	9	0.01
Ottawa (1)	3	0.00
Paiute	4	0.00
Pima (4)	11	0.01
Potawatomi (5)	10	0.01
Pueblo (13)	23	0.02
Seminole (1)	7	0.01
Shoshone (3)	8	0.01
Sioux (11)	28	0.02
Tohono O'Odham (6)	8	0.01
Ute (2)	5	0.00
Yakama (1)	1	0.00
Yaqui (14)	41	0.03
Yuman (7)	10	0.01
All other tribes (302)	442	0.33
American Indian tribes, not spec.	140	0.10
Arab:	601	0.45
Arab/Arabic	74	0.06
Egyptian	80	0.06
Iraqi	98	0.07
Lebanese	224	0.17
Moroccan	9	0.01
Palestinian	89	0.07
Syrian	18	0.01
Other Arab	9	0.01
Armenian	43	0.03
Asian:	7,462	5.59
Cambodian (44)	51	0.04
Chinese, ex. Taiwanese (493)	685	0.51
Filipino (2,417)	3,039	2.28
Hmong (31)	34	0.03
Indian (360)	439	0.33
Indonesian (20)	57	0.04
Japanese (352)	680	0.51
Korean (350)	441	0.33
Laotian (387)	429	0.32
Malaysian (3)	16	0.01
Pakistani (15)	18	0.01
Sri Lankan (8)	14	0.01
Taiwanese (43)	45	0.03
Thai (57)	75	0.06
Vietnamese (1,151)	1,221	0.91
Other Asian, specified (9)	17	0.01
Other Asian, not specified (97)	201	0.15
Assyrian/Chaldean/Syriac	83	0.06
Australian	71	0.05
Austrian	328	0.25
Basque	69	0.05
Belgian	113	0.08
Brazilian	10	0.01
British	565	0.42
Bulgarian	21	0.02
Canadian	553	0.41
Celtic	5	0.00
Croatian	110	0.08
Czech	272	0.20
Czechoslovakian	182	0.14
Danish	986	0.74
Dutch	2,100	1.57
Eastern European	19	0.01
English	11,407	8.54
Estonian	17	0.01
European	1,262	0.95
Finnish	231	0.17
French, except Basque	3,434	2.57
French Canadian	782	0.59
German	17,558	13.15
Greek	243	0.18
Guyanese	9	0.01
Hawaii Native/Pacific Islander:	683	0.51
Melanesian: (6)	7	0.01
Fijian (6)	7	0.01
Micronesian: (107)	180	0.13
Guamanian/Chamorro (102)	171	0.13
Other Micronesian (5)	9	0.01
Polynesian: (157)	384	0.29
Native Hawaiian (74)	246	0.18
Samoan (55)	99	0.07
Tongan (25)	28	0.02
Other Polynesian (3)	11	0.01
Other Pac. Isl., not spec. (30)	112	0.08
Hispanic or Latino:	51,693	38.70
Central American:	842	0.63
Costa Rican	29	0.02
Guatemalan	369	0.28
Honduran	65	0.05
Nicaraguan	35	0.03
Panamanian	21	0.02
Salvadoran	249	0.19
Other Central American	74	0.06
Cuban	118	0.09
Dominican Republic	12	0.01
Mexican	44,726	33.49

Notes: 1. Figures in the "Number" column do not add up to the total population due to: a) Ancestry/Race overlap — e.g. persons can report being both White and Irish, b) persons of Hispanic origin can report being any race, c) persons reporting two ancestries are counted in both categories. 2. Numbers in parentheses indicate the number of persons reporting this ancestry/race alone, not in combination with any other ancestry/race. 3. Refer to the Explanation of Data in the front of the book for more detailed information.

Ancestry/Race	Number	%
Puerto Rican	647	0.48
South American:	294	0.22
Argentinean	30	0.02
Bolivian	10	0.01
Chilean	19	0.01
Colombian	100	0.07
Ecuadorian	26	0.02
Paraguayan	4	0.00
Peruvian	51	0.04
Uruguayan	10	0.01
Venezuelan	11	0.01
Other South American	33	0.02
Other Hispanic or Latino	5,054	3.78
Hungarian	566	0.42
Icelander	25	0.02
Iranian	242	0.18
Irish	12,180	9.12
Israeli	6	0.00
Italian	5,736	4.30
Latvian	38	0.03
Lithuanian	272	0.20
Luxemburger	29	0.02
Macedonian	100	0.07
Maltese	9	0.01
New Zealander	31	0.02
Northern European	46	0.03
Norwegian	2,154	1.61
Pennsylvania German	28	0.02
Polish	2,128	1.59
Portuguese	374	0.28
Romanian	85	0.06
Russian	863	0.65
Scandinavian	359	0.27
Scotch-Irish	2,091	1.57
Scottish	2,015	1.51
Serbian	184	0.14
Slavic	62	0.05
Slovak	162	0.12
Slovene	32	0.02
Swedish	2,289	1.71
Swiss	341	0.26
Turkish	49	0.04
Ukrainian	162	0.12
United States or American	5,193	3.89
Welsh	760	0.57
West Indian, excl. Hispanic:	140	0.10
Bahamian	8	0.01
Barbadian	15	0.01
British West Indian	12	0.01
Haitian	20	0.01
Jamaican	47	0.04
West Indian	38	0.03
White:	96,192	72.02
Not Hispanic (69,305)	71,776	53.74
Hispanic (21,273)	24,416	18.28
Yugoslavian	309	0.23

Eureka

Place Type: City
County: Humboldt
Population: 26,128

Ancestry/Race	Number	%
Acadian/Cajun	10	0.04
African American/Black:	659	2.52
Not Hispanic (399)	602	2.30
Hispanic (28)	57	0.22
African, sub-Saharan:	40	0.15
African	22	0.08
South African	18	0.07
Alaska Native tribes, specified:	21	0.08
Alaska Athabascan (1)	1	0.00
Aleut (2)	5	0.02
Eskimo (1)	4	0.02
Tlingit-Haida (10)	11	0.04
Alaska Native tribes, not specified	1	0.00
Am. Ind. or Alaska Nat., not spec.	347	1.33
American Indian tribes, specified:	1,526	5.84
Apache (15)	35	0.13
Blackfeet (13)	45	0.17
Cherokee (95)	311	1.19
Cheyenne (1)	1	0.00
Chickasaw (5)	7	0.03
Chippewa (18)	33	0.13
Choctaw (12)	51	0.20
Comanche (2)	6	0.02
Cree	2	0.01
Creek (10)	12	0.05
Crow (1)	6	0.02
Delaware	1	0.00
Houma (1)	1	0.00
Iroquois (2)	17	0.07
Kiowa (1)	2	0.01
Latin American Indians (10)	26	0.10
Lumbee (1)	1	0.00
Navajo (8)	18	0.07
Osage (2)	2	0.01
Ottawa (1)	1	0.00
Paiute (3)	5	0.02
Potawatomi (5)	9	0.03
Pueblo (1)	4	0.02
Puget Sound Salish	3	0.01
Seminole	5	0.02
Shoshone (2)	9	0.03
Sioux (25)	40	0.15
Tohono O'Odham	1	0.00
Ute	1	0.00
Yakama (2)	2	0.01
Yaqui (5)	16	0.06
Yuman (1)	1	0.00
All other tribes (624)	852	3.26
American Indian tribes, not spec.	84	0.32
Arab:	40	0.15
Lebanese	25	0.10
Syrian	8	0.03
Other Arab	7	0.03
Armenian	20	0.08
Asian:	1,164	4.45
Cambodian (3)	5	0.02
Chinese, ex. Taiwanese (60)	83	0.32
Filipino (61)	123	0.47
Hmong (330)	352	1.35
Indian (84)	102	0.39
Indonesian	2	0.01
Japanese (50)	95	0.36
Korean (55)	69	0.26
Laotian (180)	220	0.84
Pakistani (5)	10	0.04
Sri Lankan (2)	4	0.02
Taiwanese (1)	1	0.00
Thai (11)	14	0.05
Vietnamese (37)	42	0.16
Other Asian, specified (1)	7	0.03
Other Asian, not specified (22)	35	0.13
Australian	59	0.23
Austrian	102	0.39
Belgian	27	0.10
British	98	0.38
Canadian	97	0.37
Celtic	57	0.22
Croatian	8	0.03
Czech	43	0.17
Czechoslovakian	40	0.15
Danish	397	1.53
Dutch	595	2.29
English	3,404	13.13
European	420	1.62
Finnish	156	0.60
French, except Basque	1,060	4.09
French Canadian	185	0.71
German	4,362	16.82
Greek	87	0.34
Hawaii Native/Pacific Islander:	173	0.66
Micronesian: (22)	30	0.11
Guamanian/Chamorro (3)	6	0.02
Other Micronesian (19)	24	0.09
Polynesian: (49)	104	0.40
Native Hawaiian (22)	57	0.22
Samoan (21)	37	0.14
Tongan (6)	8	0.03
Other Polynesian	2	0.01
Other Pac. Isl., specified	4	0.02
Other Pac. Isl., not spec. (15)	35	0.13
Hispanic or Latino:	2,031	7.77
Central American:	61	0.23
Costa Rican	4	0.02
Guatemalan	13	0.05
Honduran	7	0.03
Nicaraguan	4	0.02
Panamanian	5	0.02
Salvadoran	18	0.07
Other Central American	10	0.04
Cuban	22	0.08
Mexican	1,510	5.78
Puerto Rican	45	0.17
South American:	29	0.11
Argentinean	2	0.01
Bolivian	1	0.00
Chilean	8	0.03
Colombian	5	0.02
Peruvian	4	0.02
Other South American	9	0.03
Other Hispanic or Latino	364	1.39
Hungarian	55	0.21
Icelander	8	0.03
Iranian	8	0.03
Irish	3,829	14.77
Italian	1,459	5.63
Latvian	21	0.08
Lithuanian	8	0.03
Northern European	59	0.23
Norwegian	971	3.74
Pennsylvania German	11	0.04
Polish	505	1.95
Portuguese	506	1.95
Romanian	13	0.05
Russian	163	0.63
Scandinavian	131	0.51
Scotch-Irish	574	2.21
Scottish	686	2.65
Serbian	7	0.03
Slavic	21	0.08
Slovak	19	0.07
Slovene	8	0.03
Swedish	765	2.95
Swiss	258	1.00
Ukrainian	13	0.05
United States or American	1,395	5.38
Welsh	409	1.58
West Indian, excl. Hispanic:	36	0.14
Dutch West Indian	36	0.14
White:	22,718	86.95
Not Hispanic (20,548)	21,519	82.36
Hispanic (996)	1,199	4.59
Yugoslavian	150	0.58

Fair Oaks

Place Type: Census Designated Place
County: Sacramento
Population: 28,008

Ancestry/Race	Number	%
Afghan	101	0.36
African American/Black:	695	2.48
Not Hispanic (500)	643	2.30
Hispanic (14)	52	0.19
African, sub-Saharan:	100	0.36
African	40	0.14
Cape Verdean	41	0.15
Ethiopian	11	0.04
Other sub-Saharan African	8	0.03
Alaska Native tribes, specified:	3	0.01
Eskimo	1	0.00
Tlingit-Haida (2)	2	0.01
Am. Ind. or Alaska Nat., not spec.	94	0.34
American Indian tribes, specified:	303	1.08
Apache (7)	18	0.06
Blackfeet	3	0.01

Notes: 1. Figures in the "Number" column do not add up to the total population due to: a) Ancestry/Race overlap — e.g. persons can report being both White and Irish, b) persons of Hispanic origin can report being any race, c) persons reporting two ancestries are counted in both categories. 2. Numbers in parentheses indicate the number of persons reporting this ancestry/race alone, not in combination with any other ancestry/race. 3. Refer to the Explanation of Data in the front of the book for more detailed information.

Cherokee (50)	120	0.43
Cheyenne	2	0.01
Chickasaw (1)	9	0.03
Chippewa (3)	7	0.02
Choctaw (9)	31	0.11
Creek (1)	6	0.02
Delaware	1	0.00
Iroquois (2)	4	0.01
Latin American Indians	13	0.05
Lumbee	1	0.00
Navajo (2)	6	0.02
Osage (1)	2	0.01
Ottawa (1)	2	0.01
Potawatomi (3)	4	0.01
Pueblo (1)	5	0.02
Seminole (1)	2	0.01
Shoshone (3)	6	0.02
Sioux (2)	12	0.04
Ute	1	0.00
Yaqui (1)	2	0.01
All other tribes (21)	46	0.16
American Indian tribes, not spec.	16	0.06
Arab:	117	0.42
Arab/Arabic	26	0.09
Egyptian	15	0.05
Jordanian	15	0.05
Moroccan	7	0.02
Palestinian	10	0.04
Syrian	25	0.09
Other Arab	19	0.07
Armenian	107	0.38
Asian:	1,570	5.61
Bangladeshi (1)	1	0.00
Cambodian (14)	14	0.05
Chinese, ex. Taiwanese (234)	300	1.07
Filipino (172)	280	1.00
Hmong (8)	8	0.03
Indian (247)	268	0.96
Indonesian	2	0.01
Japanese (199)	322	1.15
Korean (162)	195	0.70
Laotian (1)	1	0.00
Malaysian (1)	1	0.00
Pakistani (33)	35	0.12
Taiwanese	1	0.00
Thai (13)	17	0.06
Vietnamese (58)	67	0.24
Other Asian, specified (4)	5	0.02
Other Asian, not specified (12)	53	0.19
Australian	23	0.08
Austrian	150	0.54
Basque	33	0.12
Belgian	11	0.04
Brazilian	16	0.06
British	149	0.53
Bulgarian	6	0.02
Canadian	133	0.47
Celtic	38	0.14
Croatian	51	0.18
Czech	99	0.35
Czechoslovakian	43	0.15
Danish	426	1.52
Dutch	479	1.71
English	4,504	16.08
Estonian	7	0.02
European	417	1.49
Finnish	129	0.46
French, except Basque	1,248	4.46
French Canadian	170	0.61
German	5,263	18.79
German Russian	7	0.02
Greek	128	0.46
Hawaii Native/Pacific Islander:	112	0.40
Melanesian: (4)	11	0.04
Fijian (4)	11	0.04
Micronesian: (12)	27	0.10
Guamanian/Chamorro (12)	24	0.09
Other Micronesian	3	0.01
Polynesian: (20)	50	0.18
Native Hawaiian (11)	35	0.12
Samoan (9)	10	0.04
Tongan	2	0.01
Other Polynesian	3	0.01
Other Pac. Isl., specified	1	0.00
Other Pac. Isl., not spec. (6)	23	0.08
Hispanic or Latino:	1,767	6.31
Central American:	48	0.17
Costa Rican	2	0.01
Guatemalan	5	0.02
Honduran	4	0.01
Nicaraguan	13	0.05
Panamanian	7	0.02
Salvadoran	12	0.04
Other Central American	5	0.02
Cuban	25	0.09
Mexican	1,127	4.02
Puerto Rican	77	0.27
South American:	66	0.24
Argentinean	13	0.05
Bolivian	1	0.00
Chilean	8	0.03
Colombian	17	0.06
Ecuadorian	3	0.01
Paraguayan	2	0.01
Peruvian	15	0.05
Uruguayan	1	0.00
Venezuelan	3	0.01
Other South American	3	0.01
Other Hispanic or Latino	424	1.51
Hungarian	156	0.56
Icelander	12	0.04
Iranian	189	0.67
Irish	3,909	13.96
Italian	1,941	6.93
Latvian	10	0.04
Lithuanian	75	0.27
Macedonian	6	0.02
New Zealander	9	0.03
Northern European	61	0.22
Norwegian	901	3.22
Pennsylvania German	20	0.07
Polish	621	2.22
Portuguese	330	1.18
Romanian	85	0.30
Russian	498	1.78
Scandinavian	141	0.50
Scotch-Irish	750	2.68
Scottish	1,020	3.64
Serbian	26	0.09
Slavic	50	0.18
Slovak	32	0.11
Slovene	36	0.13
Swedish	589	2.10
Swiss	181	0.65
Ukrainian	755	2.70
United States or American	1,286	4.59
Welsh	344	1.23
West Indian, excl. Hispanic:	20	0.07
Haitian	9	0.03
Jamaican	11	0.04
White:	25,515	91.10
Not Hispanic (23,559)	24,263	86.63
Hispanic (1,100)	1,252	4.47
Yugoslavian	70	0.25

Fairfield

Place Type: City
County: Solano
Population: 96,178

Ancestry/Race	Number	%
Acadian/Cajun	48	0.05
Afghan	26	0.03
African American/Black:	16,411	17.06
Not Hispanic (14,097)	15,732	16.36
Hispanic (349)	679	0.71
African, sub-Saharan:	1,026	1.07
African	923	0.96
Cape Verdean	34	0.04
Ethiopian	45	0.05
Nigerian	18	0.02
Other sub-Saharan African	6	0.01
Alaska Native tribes, specified:	14	0.01
Alaska Athabascan (1)	2	0.00
Aleut (1)	5	0.01
Eskimo	1	0.00
Tlingit-Haida (2)	5	0.01
All other tribes	1	0.00
Alaska Native tribes, not specified	4	0.00
Am. Ind. or Alaska Nat., not spec.	589	0.61
American Indian tribes, specified:	1,363	1.42
Apache (31)	80	0.08
Blackfeet (18)	105	0.11
Cherokee (113)	448	0.47
Cheyenne (2)	8	0.01
Chickasaw (7)	18	0.02
Chippewa (16)	37	0.04
Choctaw (28)	93	0.10
Colville	1	0.00
Comanche (1)	12	0.01
Cree	2	0.00
Creek (14)	36	0.04
Crow (1)	1	0.00
Delaware (3)	4	0.00
Iroquois (8)	27	0.03
Kiowa (6)	6	0.01
Latin American Indians (43)	75	0.08
Lumbee	1	0.00
Menominee (1)	2	0.00
Navajo (30)	58	0.06
Osage (7)	16	0.02
Ottawa (1)	1	0.00
Paiute (3)	14	0.01
Potawatomi (5)	9	0.01
Pueblo (22)	33	0.03
Puget Sound Salish (5)	7	0.01
Seminole (3)	13	0.01
Shoshone (12)	14	0.01
Sioux (23)	48	0.05
Tohono O'Odham (1)	1	0.00
Ute	1	0.00
Yaqui (6)	11	0.01
All other tribes (82)	181	0.19
American Indian tribes, not spec.	98	0.10
Arab:	450	0.47
Arab/Arabic	115	0.12
Egyptian	8	0.01
Jordanian	111	0.12
Lebanese	20	0.02
Palestinian	130	0.14
Syrian	11	0.01
Other Arab	55	0.06
Armenian	61	0.06
Asian:	13,967	14.52
Bangladeshi (1)	1	0.00
Cambodian (25)	32	0.03
Chinese, ex. Taiwanese (896)	1,340	1.39
Filipino (5,929)	7,534	7.83
Hmong (63)	65	0.07
Indian (940)	1,157	1.20
Indonesian (5)	25	0.03
Japanese (762)	1,483	1.54
Korean (449)	681	0.71
Laotian (312)	359	0.37
Malaysian (1)	13	0.01
Pakistani (28)	63	0.07
Sri Lankan (9)	12	0.01
Taiwanese (23)	41	0.04
Thai (169)	297	0.31
Vietnamese (495)	588	0.61
Other Asian, specified (7)	17	0.02
Other Asian, not specified (118)	259	0.27
Assyrian/Chaldean/Syriac	41	0.04
Australian	25	0.03
Austrian	136	0.14
Basque	89	0.09
Belgian	43	0.04
British	394	0.41
Canadian	365	0.38

Notes: 1. Figures in the "Number" column do not add up to the total population due to: a) Ancestry/Race overlap — e.g. persons can report being both White and Irish, b) persons of Hispanic origin can report being any race, c) persons reporting two ancestries are counted in both categories. 2. Numbers in parentheses indicate the number of persons reporting this ancestry/race alone, not in combination with any other ancestry/race. 3. Refer to the Explanation of Data in the front of the book for more detailed information.

Celtic	36	0.04
Croatian	64	0.07
Czech	270	0.28
Czechoslovakian	184	0.19
Danish	383	0.40
Dutch	1,190	1.24
Eastern European	7	0.01
English	6,996	7.27
Estonian	41	0.04
European	930	0.97
Finnish	199	0.21
French, except Basque	2,953	3.07
French Canadian	794	0.83
German	10,368	10.78
German Russian	38	0.04
Greek	361	0.38
Guyanese	6	0.01
Hawaii Native/Pacific Islander:	1,740	1.81
Melanesian: (47)	70	0.07
Fijian (47)	70	0.07
Micronesian: (471)	742	0.77
Guamanian/Chamorro (462)	731	0.76
Other Micronesian (9)	11	0.01
Polynesian: (318)	707	0.74
Native Hawaiian (168)	514	0.53
Samoan (134)	168	0.17
Tongan (9)	14	0.01
Other Polynesian (7)	11	0.01
Other Pac. Isl., specified	6	0.01
Other Pac. Isl., not spec. (57)	215	0.22
Hispanic or Latino:	18,050	18.77
Central American:	858	0.89
Costa Rican	24	0.02
Guatemalan	118	0.12
Honduran	32	0.03
Nicaraguan	186	0.19
Panamanian	91	0.09
Salvadoran	349	0.36
Other Central American	58	0.06
Cuban	116	0.12
Dominican Republic	30	0.03
Mexican	12,894	13.41
Puerto Rican	850	0.88
South American:	281	0.29
Argentinean	13	0.01
Bolivian	4	0.00
Chilean	31	0.03
Colombian	65	0.07
Ecuadorian	33	0.03
Peruvian	95	0.10
Uruguayan	5	0.01
Venezuelan	15	0.02
Other South American	20	0.02
Other Hispanic or Latino	3,021	3.14
Hungarian	250	0.26
Icelander	6	0.01
Iranian	89	0.09
Irish	8,671	9.02
Israeli	18	0.02
Italian	4,748	4.94
Latvian	19	0.02
Lithuanian	173	0.18
Luxemburger	15	0.02
Maltese	13	0.01
Northern European	53	0.06
Norwegian	1,670	1.74
Pennsylvania German	45	0.05
Polish	1,163	1.21
Portuguese	1,199	1.25
Romanian	49	0.05
Russian	448	0.47
Scandinavian	132	0.14
Scotch-Irish	1,323	1.38
Scottish	1,691	1.76
Serbian	32	0.03
Slavic	19	0.02
Slovak	45	0.05
Slovene	36	0.04
Swedish	1,156	1.20
Swiss	102	0.11
Turkish	52	0.05
Ukrainian	200	0.21
United States or American	3,864	4.02
Welsh	589	0.61
West Indian, excl. Hispanic:	252	0.26
Haitian	40	0.04
Jamaican	109	0.11
Trinidadian and Tobagonian	16	0.02
West Indian	87	0.09
White:	59,562	61.93
Not Hispanic (47,094)	50,935	52.96
Hispanic (6,969)	8,627	8.97
Yugoslavian	104	0.11

Fallbrook

Place Type: Census Designated Place
County: San Diego
Population: 29,100

Ancestry/Race	Number	%
African American/Black:	516	1.77
Not Hispanic (362)	428	1.47
Hispanic (53)	88	0.30
African, sub-Saharan:	53	0.18
African	53	0.18
Alaska Native tribes, not specified	1	0.00
Am. Ind. or Alaska Nat., not spec.	163	0.56
American Indian tribes, specified:	316	1.09
Apache (4)	12	0.04
Blackfeet	3	0.01
Cherokee (23)	70	0.24
Chickasaw (4)	4	0.01
Chippewa (5)	10	0.03
Choctaw (2)	14	0.05
Comanche (2)	3	0.01
Cree	2	0.01
Creek (1)	1	0.00
Delaware	3	0.01
Iroquois (5)	6	0.02
Kiowa (1)	1	0.00
Latin American Indians (54)	91	0.31
Menominee	1	0.00
Navajo (11)	16	0.05
Osage (2)	8	0.03
Paiute (3)	3	0.01
Pima (1)	3	0.01
Potawatomi (2)	4	0.01
Pueblo (2)	5	0.02
Puget Sound Salish (1)	1	0.00
Seminole (1)	2	0.01
Shoshone (1)	1	0.00
Sioux (1)	3	0.01
Yaqui	2	0.01
All other tribes (34)	47	0.16
American Indian tribes, not spec.	40	0.14
Arab:	111	0.38
Arab/Arabic	20	0.07
Lebanese	84	0.29
Syrian	7	0.02
Armenian	10	0.03
Asian:	772	2.65
Cambodian (7)	13	0.04
Chinese, ex. Taiwanese (30)	70	0.24
Filipino (208)	323	1.11
Indian (16)	26	0.09
Indonesian	11	0.04
Japanese (96)	187	0.64
Korean (46)	70	0.24
Laotian (1)	2	0.01
Malaysian (1)	1	0.00
Sri Lankan	1	0.00
Taiwanese	5	0.02
Thai (2)	4	0.01
Vietnamese (18)	33	0.11
Other Asian, specified (2)	11	0.04
Other Asian, not specified (3)	15	0.05
Austrian	43	0.15
Belgian	39	0.13
British	126	0.43
Canadian	95	0.33
Croatian	22	0.08
Czech	161	0.55
Czechoslovakian	85	0.29
Danish	173	0.59
Dutch	522	1.79
English	3,157	10.81
European	216	0.74
Finnish	73	0.25
French, except Basque	668	2.29
French Canadian	180	0.62
German	4,602	15.76
Greek	45	0.15
Hawaii Native/Pacific Islander:	179	0.62
Micronesian: (26)	37	0.13
Guamanian/Chamorro (26)	37	0.13
Polynesian: (57)	118	0.41
Native Hawaiian (23)	66	0.23
Samoan (9)	22	0.08
Tongan (23)	24	0.08
Other Polynesian (2)	6	0.02
Other Pac. Isl., not spec. (3)	24	0.08
Hispanic or Latino:	10,853	37.30
Central American:	400	1.37
Costa Rican	7	0.02
Guatemalan	339	1.16
Honduran	4	0.01
Nicaraguan	7	0.02
Panamanian	6	0.02
Salvadoran	22	0.08
Other Central American	15	0.05
Cuban	33	0.11
Dominican Republic	4	0.01
Mexican	9,181	31.55
Puerto Rican	110	0.38
South American:	57	0.20
Argentinean	12	0.04
Bolivian	1	0.00
Chilean	5	0.02
Colombian	5	0.02
Ecuadorian	11	0.04
Peruvian	9	0.03
Uruguayan	1	0.00
Venezuelan	6	0.02
Other South American	7	0.02
Other Hispanic or Latino	1,068	3.67
Hungarian	99	0.34
Irish	3,328	11.40
Israeli	8	0.03
Italian	1,055	3.61
Lithuanian	115	0.39
Northern European	23	0.08
Norwegian	707	2.42
Polish	426	1.46
Portuguese	138	0.47
Romanian	29	0.10
Russian	255	0.87
Scandinavian	70	0.24
Scotch-Irish	558	1.91
Scottish	529	1.81
Serbian	18	0.06
Slavic	12	0.04
Slovak	6	0.02
Slovene	12	0.04
Swedish	502	1.72
Swiss	59	0.20
Ukrainian	115	0.39
United States or American	1,136	3.89
Welsh	227	0.78
West Indian, excl. Hispanic:	15	0.05
Haitian	6	0.02
Jamaican	9	0.03
White:	21,836	75.04
Not Hispanic (16,687)	17,133	58.88
Hispanic (4,201)	4,703	16.16
Yugoslavian	32	0.11

Notes: 1. Figures in the "Number" column do not add up to the total population due to: a) Ancestry/Race overlap — e.g. persons can report being both White and Irish, b) persons of Hispanic origin can report being any race, c) persons reporting two ancestries are counted in both categories. 2. Numbers in parentheses indicate the number of persons reporting this ancestry/race alone, not in combination with any other ancestry/race. 3. Refer to the Explanation of Data in the front of the book for more detailed information.

Fillmore

Place Type: City
County: Ventura
Population: 13,643

Ancestry/Race	Number	%
African American/Black:	70	0.51
Not Hispanic (26)	38	0.28
Hispanic (18)	32	0.23
African, sub-Saharan:	25	0.19
African	25	0.19
Am. Ind. or Alaska Nat., not spec.	83	0.61
American Indian tribes, specified:	193	1.41
Apache (7)	16	0.12
Blackfeet (2)	6	0.04
Cherokee (10)	38	0.28
Chippewa (1)	3	0.02
Choctaw (4)	13	0.10
Delaware (3)	3	0.02
Iroquois	1	0.01
Latin American Indians (43)	45	0.33
Navajo (2)	6	0.04
Paiute (4)	5	0.04
Pueblo (1)	3	0.02
Sioux (3)	5	0.04
Yaqui (10)	13	0.10
All other tribes (22)	36	0.26
American Indian tribes, not spec.	15	0.11
Arab:	65	0.48
Egyptian	34	0.25
Syrian	31	0.23
Armenian	7	0.05
Asian:	217	1.59
Cambodian (10)	10	0.07
Chinese, ex. Taiwanese (25)	34	0.25
Filipino (38)	75	0.55
Indian (18)	23	0.17
Indonesian	2	0.01
Japanese (12)	27	0.20
Korean (16)	18	0.13
Thai (2)	5	0.04
Vietnamese (4)	6	0.04
Other Asian, specified (1)	3	0.02
Other Asian, not specified (3)	14	0.10
Austrian	67	0.50
Basque	14	0.10
Belgian	10	0.07
British	17	0.13
Canadian	29	0.22
Czech	15	0.11
Danish	18	0.13
Dutch	137	1.02
Eastern European	16	0.12
English	718	5.33
European	128	0.95
Finnish	8	0.06
French, except Basque	258	1.91
French Canadian	52	0.39
German	902	6.69
Hawaii Native/Pacific Islander:	42	0.31
Melanesian: (3)	3	0.02
Fijian (3)	3	0.02
Micronesian: (1)	3	0.02
Guamanian/Chamorro (1)	3	0.02
Polynesian: (3)	23	0.17
Native Hawaiian (1)	16	0.12
Samoan (2)	7	0.05
Other Pac. Isl., not spec. (7)	13	0.10
Hispanic or Latino:	9,090	66.63
Central American:	38	0.28
Costa Rican	1	0.01
Guatemalan	15	0.11
Honduran	1	0.01
Nicaraguan	1	0.01
Salvadoran	20	0.15
Cuban	11	0.08
Dominican Republic	1	0.01
Mexican	8,134	59.62
Puerto Rican	20	0.15
South American:	14	0.10
Argentinean	1	0.01
Chilean	3	0.02
Colombian	3	0.02
Ecuadorian	4	0.03
Peruvian	2	0.01
Uruguayan	1	0.01
Other Hispanic or Latino	872	6.39
Hungarian	27	0.20
Irish	759	5.63
Italian	258	1.91
Lithuanian	46	0.34
Norwegian	72	0.53
Pennsylvania German	7	0.05
Polish	72	0.53
Romanian	7	0.05
Russian	61	0.45
Scotch-Irish	156	1.16
Scottish	261	1.94
Swedish	71	0.53
Swiss	8	0.06
United States or American	321	2.38
Welsh	28	0.21
White:	7,816	57.29
Not Hispanic (4,178)	4,318	31.65
Hispanic (3,126)	3,498	25.64

Florence-Graham

Place Type: Census Designated Place
County: Los Angeles
Population: 60,197

Ancestry/Race	Number	%
African American/Black:	8,093	13.44
Not Hispanic (7,624)	7,710	12.81
Hispanic (284)	383	0.64
African, sub-Saharan:	323	0.54
African	323	0.54
Am. Ind. or Alaska Nat., not spec.	386	0.64
American Indian tribes, specified:	315	0.52
Apache (3)	5	0.01
Blackfeet	1	0.00
Cherokee (4)	17	0.03
Chickasaw (2)	2	0.00
Choctaw	4	0.01
Cree	3	0.00
Creek (2)	4	0.01
Latin American Indians (195)	240	0.40
Navajo (4)	4	0.01
Osage	1	0.00
Paiute (1)	1	0.00
Pueblo	2	0.00
Seminole	1	0.00
Tohono O'Odham (9)	9	0.01
Yaqui (1)	2	0.00
All other tribes (15)	19	0.03
American Indian tribes, not spec.	68	0.11
Arab:	9	0.01
Egyptian	9	0.01
Asian:	177	0.29
Chinese, ex. Taiwanese (10)	19	0.03
Filipino (10)	19	0.03
Hmong	1	0.00
Indian (26)	45	0.07
Indonesian (1)	6	0.01
Japanese (13)	22	0.04
Korean (5)	14	0.02
Vietnamese	1	0.00
Other Asian, not specified (5)	50	0.08
Canadian	7	0.01
English	39	0.06
French, except Basque	63	0.10
German	77	0.13
Hawaii Native/Pacific Islander:	110	0.18
Micronesian: (23)	31	0.05
Guamanian/Chamorro (23)	31	0.05
Polynesian: (20)	26	0.04
Native Hawaiian (5)	8	0.01
Samoan (15)	18	0.03
Other Pac. Isl., not spec. (12)	53	0.09
Hispanic or Latino:	51,712	85.90
Central American:	2,345	3.90
Costa Rican	6	0.01
Guatemalan	493	0.82
Honduran	135	0.22
Nicaraguan	117	0.19
Panamanian	11	0.02
Salvadoran	1,335	2.22
Other Central American	248	0.41
Cuban	43	0.07
Dominican Republic	2	0.00
Mexican	41,897	69.60
Puerto Rican	162	0.27
South American:	57	0.09
Argentinean	2	0.00
Chilean	8	0.01
Colombian	7	0.01
Ecuadorian	26	0.04
Peruvian	8	0.01
Other South American	6	0.01
Other Hispanic or Latino	7,206	11.97
Irish	55	0.09
Italian	79	0.13
Latvian	9	0.01
Lithuanian	6	0.01
Scotch-Irish	8	0.01
Swedish	7	0.01
United States or American	837	1.39
West Indian, excl. Hispanic:	65	0.11
Belizean	4	0.01
British West Indian	6	0.01
Haitian	6	0.01
Jamaican	49	0.08
White:	17,305	28.75
Not Hispanic (587)	655	1.09
Hispanic (14,191)	16,650	27.66

Florin

Place Type: Census Designated Place
County: Sacramento
Population: 27,653

Ancestry/Race	Number	%
African American/Black:	5,719	20.68
Not Hispanic (5,026)	5,453	19.72
Hispanic (159)	266	0.96
African, sub-Saharan:	285	1.03
African	262	0.95
Cape Verdean	12	0.04
Ethiopian	5	0.02
Nigerian	6	0.02
Alaska Native tribes, specified:	5	0.02
Aleut (1)	1	0.00
Eskimo (1)	1	0.00
Tlingit-Haida	3	0.01
Am. Ind. or Alaska Nat., not spec.	236	0.85
Alsatian	6	0.02
American Indian tribes, specified:	563	2.04
Apache (9)	31	0.11
Blackfeet (9)	31	0.11
Cherokee (44)	159	0.57
Cheyenne (1)	1	0.00
Chickasaw (9)	20	0.07
Chippewa (4)	11	0.04
Choctaw (5)	31	0.11
Cree	5	0.02
Creek (4)	7	0.03
Crow	7	0.03
Iroquois (1)	4	0.01
Latin American Indians (17)	33	0.12
Menominee (2)	4	0.01
Navajo (11)	17	0.06
Osage (1)	1	0.00
Ottawa	1	0.00
Paiute (2)	8	0.03
Pima (1)	1	0.00
Potawatomi (1)	3	0.01
Pueblo (1)	4	0.01

Notes: 1. Figures in the "Number" column do not add up to the total population due to: a) Ancestry/Race overlap — e.g. persons can report being both White and Irish, b) persons of Hispanic origin can report being any race, c) persons reporting two ancestries are counted in both categories. 2. Numbers in parentheses indicate the number of persons reporting this ancestry/race alone, not in combination with any other ancestry/race. 3. Refer to the Explanation of Data in the front of the book for more detailed information.

Puget Sound Salish (1)	1	0.00
Seminole	2	0.01
Shoshone (2)	2	0.01
Sioux (2)	30	0.11
Yaqui (2)	6	0.02
Yuman (3)	3	0.01
All other tribes (88)	140	0.51
American Indian tribes, not spec.	27	0.10
Arab:	28	0.10
Jordanian	11	0.04
Syrian	17	0.06
Armenian	34	0.12
Asian:	6,281	22.71
Cambodian (194)	215	0.78
Chinese, ex. Taiwanese (646)	778	2.81
Filipino (1,125)	1,390	5.03
Hmong (851)	950	3.44
Indian (336)	483	1.75
Indonesian (1)	1	0.00
Japanese (181)	270	0.98
Korean (78)	96	0.35
Laotian (340)	407	1.47
Malaysian	1	0.00
Pakistani (41)	46	0.17
Taiwanese (5)	9	0.03
Thai (12)	29	0.10
Vietnamese (1,378)	1,491	5.39
Other Asian, specified	2	0.01
Other Asian, not specified (64)	113	0.41
Austrian	31	0.11
Basque	6	0.02
Belgian	7	0.03
Brazilian	9	0.03
British	68	0.25
Canadian	11	0.04
Croatian	18	0.07
Czech	5	0.02
Czechoslovakian	24	0.09
Danish	71	0.26
Dutch	338	1.23
English	1,303	4.72
European	147	0.53
Finnish	26	0.09
French, except Basque	373	1.35
French Canadian	129	0.47
German	1,809	6.56
Greek	47	0.17
Hawaii Native/Pacific Islander:	473	1.71
Melanesian: (94)	114	0.41
Fijian (94)	114	0.41
Micronesian: (25)	50	0.18
Guamanian/Chamorro (17)	41	0.15
Other Micronesian (8)	9	0.03
Polynesian: (92)	172	0.62
Native Hawaiian (25)	71	0.26
Samoan (19)	26	0.09
Tongan (48)	68	0.25
Other Polynesian	7	0.03
Other Pac. Isl., specified	1	0.00
Other Pac. Isl., not spec. (23)	136	0.49
Hispanic or Latino:	5,760	20.83
Central American:	128	0.46
Costa Rican	8	0.03
Guatemalan	16	0.06
Honduran	4	0.01
Nicaraguan	23	0.08
Panamanian	15	0.05
Salvadoran	56	0.20
Other Central American	6	0.02
Cuban	31	0.11
Dominican Republic	5	0.02
Mexican	4,461	16.13
Puerto Rican	173	0.63
South American:	48	0.17
Argentinean	7	0.03
Chilean	14	0.05
Colombian	5	0.02
Peruvian	17	0.06
Venezuelan	2	0.01
Other South American	3	0.01
Other Hispanic or Latino	914	3.31
Hungarian	31	0.11
Iranian	17	0.06
Irish	1,712	6.21
Italian	909	3.30
Lithuanian	7	0.03
Luxemburger	9	0.03
Norwegian	299	1.08
Pennsylvania German	6	0.02
Polish	131	0.48
Portuguese	214	0.78
Romanian	186	0.67
Russian	251	0.91
Scandinavian	40	0.15
Scotch-Irish	201	0.73
Scottish	254	0.92
Slovak	10	0.04
Swedish	145	0.53
Swiss	55	0.20
Ukrainian	158	0.57
United States or American	1,056	3.83
Welsh	79	0.29
West Indian, excl. Hispanic:	31	0.11
Jamaican	15	0.05
West Indian	7	0.03
Other West Indian	9	0.03
White:	12,831	46.40
Not Hispanic (9,675)	10,559	38.18
Hispanic (1,827)	2,272	8.22
Yugoslavian	7	0.03

Folsom

Place Type: City
County: Sacramento
Population: 51,884

Ancestry/Race	Number	%
African American/Black:	3,309	6.38
Not Hispanic (3,086)	3,258	6.28
Hispanic (23)	51	0.10
African, sub-Saharan:	182	0.35
African	155	0.30
South African	14	0.03
Other sub-Saharan African	13	0.03
Alaska Native tribes, specified:	7	0.01
Aleut (1)	1	0.00
Eskimo (1)	1	0.00
Tlingit-Haida (1)	5	0.01
Alaska Native tribes, not specified	2	0.00
Am. Ind. or Alaska Nat., not spec.	183	0.35
American Indian tribes, specified:	445	0.86
Apache (9)	18	0.03
Blackfeet (2)	13	0.03
Cherokee (43)	147	0.28
Cheyenne (1)	1	0.00
Chickasaw	8	0.02
Chippewa (5)	12	0.02
Choctaw (5)	26	0.05
Comanche (1)	2	0.00
Cree (4)	6	0.01
Creek (1)	10	0.02
Crow	3	0.01
Delaware	3	0.01
Iroquois (2)	5	0.01
Kiowa (1)	1	0.00
Latin American Indians (12)	22	0.04
Lumbee (4)	4	0.01
Menominee (1)	1	0.00
Navajo (9)	21	0.04
Osage	4	0.01
Paiute (6)	7	0.01
Potawatomi (2)	4	0.01
Pueblo (3)	11	0.02
Puget Sound Salish (1)	2	0.00
Seminole (1)	2	0.00
Shoshone (4)	5	0.01
Sioux (2)	12	0.02
Yakama	3	0.01
Yaqui (4)	8	0.02
Yuman (3)	5	0.01
All other tribes (53)	82	0.16
American Indian tribes, not spec.	45	0.09
Arab:	191	0.37
Arab/Arabic	43	0.08
Iraqi	15	0.03
Jordanian	30	0.06
Lebanese	85	0.16
Palestinian	9	0.02
Syrian	9	0.02
Armenian	120	0.23
Asian:	4,584	8.84
Bangladeshi (8)	9	0.02
Cambodian (4)	4	0.01
Chinese, ex. Taiwanese (710)	917	1.77
Filipino (710)	933	1.80
Hmong (2)	2	0.00
Indian (1,153)	1,281	2.47
Indonesian (24)	34	0.07
Japanese (297)	494	0.95
Korean (281)	321	0.62
Laotian (6)	12	0.02
Malaysian (14)	20	0.04
Pakistani (32)	46	0.09
Sri Lankan (22)	22	0.04
Taiwanese (20)	21	0.04
Thai (18)	24	0.05
Vietnamese (278)	303	0.58
Other Asian, specified (5)	7	0.01
Other Asian, not specified (71)	134	0.26
Assyrian/Chaldean/Syriac	30	0.06
Australian	51	0.10
Austrian	115	0.22
Basque	28	0.05
Belgian	63	0.12
British	319	0.61
Canadian	118	0.23
Croatian	163	0.31
Czech	215	0.41
Czechoslovakian	128	0.25
Danish	608	1.17
Dutch	948	1.83
Eastern European	28	0.05
English	6,565	12.65
European	646	1.24
Finnish	202	0.39
French, except Basque	1,624	3.13
French Canadian	323	0.62
German	9,356	18.02
Greek	210	0.40
Hawaii Native/Pacific Islander:	273	0.53
Melanesian: (26)	33	0.06
Fijian (26)	30	0.06
Other Melanesian	3	0.01
Micronesian: (22)	32	0.06
Guamanian/Chamorro (22)	32	0.06
Polynesian: (36)	129	0.25
Native Hawaiian (30)	122	0.24
Samoan (5)	6	0.01
Tongan (1)	1	0.00
Other Pac. Isl., specified	2	0.00
Other Pac. Isl., not spec. (15)	77	0.15
Hispanic or Latino:	4,914	9.47
Central American:	107	0.21
Costa Rican	10	0.02
Guatemalan	9	0.02
Honduran	9	0.02
Nicaraguan	19	0.04
Panamanian	12	0.02
Salvadoran	38	0.07
Other Central American	10	0.02
Cuban	50	0.10
Dominican Republic	1	0.00
Mexican	3,727	7.18
Puerto Rican	167	0.32
South American:	109	0.21
Argentinean	16	0.03
Chilean	11	0.02
Colombian	35	0.07
Ecuadorian	9	0.02

Notes: 1. Figures in the "Number" column do not add up to the total population due to: a) Ancestry/Race overlap — e.g. persons can report being both White and Irish, b) persons of Hispanic origin can report being any race, c) persons reporting two ancestries are counted in both categories. 2. Numbers in parentheses indicate the number of persons reporting this ancestry/race alone, not in combination with any other ancestry/race. 3. Refer to the Explanation of Data in the front of the book for more detailed information.

Peruvian	11	0.02
Uruguayan	2	0.00
Venezuelan	16	0.03
Other South American	9	0.02
Other Hispanic or Latino	753	1.45
Hungarian	173	0.33
Iranian	554	1.07
Irish	6,171	11.89
Italian	3,597	6.93
Lithuanian	73	0.14
Luxemburger	4	0.01
Maltese	53	0.10
New Zealander	8	0.02
Northern European	58	0.11
Norwegian	1,333	2.57
Pennsylvania German	7	0.01
Polish	1,179	2.27
Portuguese	651	1.25
Romanian	35	0.07
Russian	415	0.80
Scandinavian	108	0.21
Scotch-Irish	970	1.87
Scottish	1,287	2.48
Serbian	20	0.04
Slavic	9	0.02
Slovak	70	0.13
Slovene	19	0.04
Swedish	1,423	2.74
Swiss	235	0.45
Turkish	16	0.03
Ukrainian	68	0.13
United States or American	2,124	4.09
Welsh	563	1.08
West Indian, excl. Hispanic:	86	0.17
Barbadian	11	0.02
Dutch West Indian	22	0.04
Jamaican	53	0.10
White:	41,958	80.87
Not Hispanic (38,500)	39,559	76.25
Hispanic (1,915)	2,399	4.62
Yugoslavian	211	0.41

Fontana

Place Type: City
County: San Bernardino
Population: 128,929

Ancestry/Race	Number	%
Afghan	21	0.02
African American/Black:	16,652	12.92
Not Hispanic (14,629)	15,604	12.10
Hispanic (626)	1,048	0.81
African, sub-Saharan:	1,322	1.03
African	1,089	0.85
Ethiopian	30	0.02
Ghanian	22	0.02
Liberian	11	0.01
Nigerian	118	0.09
South African	37	0.03
Other sub-Saharan African	15	0.01
Alaska Native tribes, specified:	19	0.01
Alaska Athabascan (1)	1	0.00
Aleut	1	0.00
Eskimo (5)	8	0.01
Tlingit-Haida (1)	5	0.00
All other tribes	4	0.00
Am. Ind. or Alaska Nat., not spec.	956	0.74
American Indian tribes, specified:	1,557	1.21
Apache (79)	151	0.12
Blackfeet (14)	86	0.07
Cherokee (78)	282	0.22
Cheyenne (7)	14	0.01
Chickasaw (2)	4	0.00
Chippewa (8)	17	0.01
Choctaw (17)	49	0.04
Comanche (3)	7	0.01
Creek (1)	18	0.01
Crow	1	0.00
Houma	3	0.00
Iroquois (3)	16	0.01
Kiowa (2)	5	0.00
Latin American Indians (248)	334	0.26
Lumbee (5)	5	0.00
Navajo (28)	72	0.06
Osage (15)	19	0.01
Ottawa	1	0.00
Paiute	3	0.00
Pima (16)	28	0.02
Potawatomi (3)	10	0.01
Pueblo (32)	63	0.05
Puget Sound Salish	1	0.00
Seminole (1)	8	0.01
Shoshone (1)	13	0.01
Sioux (32)	47	0.04
Tohono O'Odham (9)	18	0.01
Ute (1)	4	0.00
Yakama	2	0.00
Yaqui (38)	77	0.06
Yuman (7)	12	0.01
All other tribes (99)	187	0.15
American Indian tribes, not spec.	151	0.12
Arab:	551	0.43
Arab/Arabic	229	0.18
Egyptian	64	0.05
Jordanian	46	0.04
Lebanese	20	0.02
Moroccan	21	0.02
Palestinian	22	0.02
Syrian	50	0.04
Other Arab	99	0.08
Armenian	38	0.03
Asian:	6,977	5.41
Bangladeshi (12)	18	0.01
Cambodian (176)	232	0.18
Chinese, ex. Taiwanese (507)	787	0.61
Filipino (2,892)	3,381	2.62
Hmong	1	0.00
Indian (466)	551	0.43
Indonesian (160)	239	0.19
Japanese (170)	379	0.29
Korean (283)	356	0.28
Laotian (65)	71	0.06
Malaysian	7	0.01
Pakistani (51)	60	0.05
Sri Lankan (12)	12	0.01
Taiwanese (52)	71	0.06
Thai (79)	119	0.09
Vietnamese (433)	497	0.39
Other Asian, specified (11)	15	0.01
Other Asian, not specified (86)	181	0.14
Assyrian/Chaldean/Syriac	22	0.02
Austrian	104	0.08
Belgian	27	0.02
Brazilian	63	0.05
British	149	0.12
Bulgarian	9	0.01
Canadian	294	0.23
Celtic	36	0.03
Croatian	93	0.07
Czech	102	0.08
Czechoslovakian	101	0.08
Danish	286	0.22
Dutch	1,063	0.83
Eastern European	9	0.01
English	4,778	3.73
European	591	0.46
Finnish	102	0.08
French, except Basque	1,795	1.40
French Canadian	232	0.18
German	6,900	5.38
German Russian	7	0.01
Greek	223	0.17
Hawaii Native/Pacific Islander:	808	0.63
Melanesian: (4)	11	0.01
Fijian (4)	6	0.00
Other Melanesian	5	0.00
Micronesian: (39)	73	0.06
Guamanian/Chamorro (39)	72	0.06
Other Micronesian	1	0.00
Polynesian: (309)	548	0.43
Native Hawaiian (65)	191	0.15
Samoan (96)	160	0.12
Tongan (139)	180	0.14
Other Polynesian (9)	17	0.01
Other Pac. Isl., specified	1	0.00
Other Pac. Isl., not spec. (61)	175	0.14
Hispanic or Latino:	74,424	57.72
Central American:	3,141	2.44
Costa Rican	83	0.06
Guatemalan	638	0.49
Honduran	195	0.15
Nicaraguan	436	0.34
Panamanian	97	0.08
Salvadoran	1,310	1.02
Other Central American	382	0.30
Cuban	315	0.24
Dominican Republic	26	0.02
Mexican	59,386	46.06
Puerto Rican	855	0.66
South American:	905	0.70
Argentinean	166	0.13
Bolivian	44	0.03
Chilean	62	0.05
Colombian	186	0.14
Ecuadorian	117	0.09
Paraguayan	2	0.00
Peruvian	203	0.16
Uruguayan	17	0.01
Venezuelan	28	0.02
Other South American	80	0.06
Other Hispanic or Latino	9,796	7.60
Hungarian	211	0.16
Icelander	17	0.01
Iranian	52	0.04
Irish	5,116	3.99
Italian	3,495	2.73
Latvian	40	0.03
Lithuanian	69	0.05
Luxemburger	6	0.00
Northern European	7	0.01
Norwegian	560	0.44
Pennsylvania German	23	0.02
Polish	672	0.52
Portuguese	278	0.22
Romanian	61	0.05
Russian	386	0.30
Scandinavian	24	0.02
Scotch-Irish	459	0.36
Scottish	742	0.58
Serbian	6	0.00
Slavic	7	0.01
Slovak	158	0.12
Slovene	89	0.07
Swedish	734	0.57
Swiss	130	0.10
Turkish	15	0.01
Ukrainian	46	0.04
United States or American	2,943	2.30
Welsh	215	0.17
West Indian, excl. Hispanic:	424	0.33
Barbadian	14	0.01
Belizean	179	0.14
Haitian	29	0.02
Jamaican	103	0.08
Trinidadian and Tobagonian	37	0.03
West Indian	62	0.05
White:	63,611	49.34
Not Hispanic (30,865)	32,763	25.41
Hispanic (27,141)	30,848	23.93
Yugoslavian	63	0.05

Foothill Farms

Place Type: Census Designated Place
County: Sacramento
Population: 17,426

Ancestry/Race	Number	%
African American/Black:	2,515	14.43

Notes: 1. Figures in the "Number" column do not add up to the total population due to: a) Ancestry/Race overlap — e.g. persons can report being both White and Irish, b) persons of Hispanic origin can report being any race, c) persons reporting two ancestries are counted in both categories. 2. Numbers in parentheses indicate the number of persons reporting this ancestry/race alone, not in combination with any other ancestry/race. 3. Refer to the Explanation of Data in the front of the book for more detailed information.

Not Hispanic (2,092)	2,388	13.70
Hispanic (63)	127	0.73
African, sub-Saharan:	169	0.97
African	129	0.74
Liberian	40	0.23
Alaska Native tribes, specified:	8	0.05
Aleut (2)	4	0.02
Tlingit-Haida (2)	4	0.02
Alaska Native tribes, not specified	1	0.01
Am. Ind. or Alaska Nat., not spec.	131	0.75
American Indian tribes, specified:	328	1.88
Apache (5)	11	0.06
Blackfeet (12)	31	0.18
Cherokee (38)	110	0.63
Cheyenne	1	0.01
Chickasaw	5	0.03
Chippewa (3)	6	0.03
Choctaw (6)	25	0.14
Colville	3	0.02
Crow	2	0.01
Kiowa (1)	1	0.01
Latin American Indians (7)	10	0.06
Lumbee (1)	1	0.01
Navajo (3)	4	0.02
Osage	2	0.01
Paiute (8)	10	0.06
Potawatomi	3	0.02
Pueblo	1	0.01
Puget Sound Salish	3	0.02
Seminole (1)	6	0.03
Shoshone (2)	3	0.02
Sioux (8)	10	0.06
Yaqui (1)	2	0.01
All other tribes (45)	78	0.45
American Indian tribes, not spec.	19	0.11
Arab:	44	0.25
Jordanian	31	0.18
Lebanese	6	0.03
Syrian	7	0.04
Armenian	19	0.11
Asian:	1,079	6.19
Chinese, ex. Taiwanese (60)	92	0.53
Filipino (227)	359	2.06
Hmong (9)	9	0.05
Indian (120)	134	0.77
Indonesian (5)	11	0.06
Japanese (80)	151	0.87
Korean (31)	49	0.28
Laotian (38)	42	0.24
Pakistani (10)	12	0.07
Sri Lankan (3)	3	0.02
Taiwanese (1)	1	0.01
Thai (30)	46	0.26
Vietnamese (125)	139	0.80
Other Asian, not specified (5)	31	0.18
Austrian	16	0.09
Belgian	22	0.13
British	79	0.45
Canadian	22	0.13
Czech	55	0.32
Czechoslovakian	36	0.21
Danish	133	0.76
Dutch	319	1.83
English	1,763	10.14
European	109	0.63
Finnish	55	0.32
French, except Basque	492	2.83
French Canadian	140	0.80
German	2,751	15.82
Greek	48	0.28
Hawaii Native/Pacific Islander:	156	0.90
Melanesian: (6)	6	0.03
Fijian (6)	6	0.03
Micronesian: (18)	30	0.17
Guamanian/Chamorro (15)	25	0.14
Other Micronesian (3)	5	0.03
Polynesian: (62)	100	0.57
Native Hawaiian (11)	35	0.20
Samoan (41)	54	0.31
Tongan (9)	9	0.05
Other Polynesian (1)	2	0.01
Other Pac. Isl., not spec. (6)	20	0.11
Hispanic or Latino:	2,523	14.48
Central American:	86	0.49
Costa Rican	8	0.05
Guatemalan	2	0.01
Honduran	3	0.02
Nicaraguan	5	0.03
Panamanian	13	0.07
Salvadoran	45	0.26
Other Central American	10	0.06
Cuban	44	0.25
Mexican	1,761	10.11
Puerto Rican	77	0.44
South American:	46	0.26
Argentinean	1	0.01
Chilean	17	0.10
Colombian	6	0.03
Ecuadorian	3	0.02
Peruvian	13	0.07
Venezuelan	1	0.01
Other South American	5	0.03
Other Hispanic or Latino	509	2.92
Hungarian	25	0.14
Iranian	25	0.14
Irish	1,879	10.80
Italian	877	5.04
Lithuanian	13	0.07
Macedonian	7	0.04
Norwegian	261	1.50
Pennsylvania German	9	0.05
Polish	139	0.80
Portuguese	292	1.68
Romanian	50	0.29
Russian	335	1.93
Scandinavian	10	0.06
Scotch-Irish	77	0.44
Scottish	320	1.84
Serbian	8	0.05
Slovak	8	0.05
Soviet Union	10	0.06
Swedish	354	2.04
Swiss	55	0.32
Turkish	8	0.05
Ukrainian	229	1.32
United States or American	867	4.98
Welsh	120	0.69
West Indian, excl. Hispanic:	19	0.11
Dutch West Indian	10	0.06
West Indian	9	0.05
White:	12,989	74.54
Not Hispanic (11,058)	11,655	66.88
Hispanic (1,104)	1,334	7.66
Yugoslavian	248	1.43

Foothill Ranch

Place Type: Census Designated Place
County: Orange
Population: 10,899

Ancestry/Race	Number	%
African American/Black:	275	2.52
Not Hispanic (199)	256	2.35
Hispanic (10)	19	0.17
African, sub-Saharan:	19	0.17
South African	19	0.17
Am. Ind. or Alaska Nat., not spec.	44	0.40
American Indian tribes, specified:	67	0.61
Apache	1	0.01
Blackfeet (1)	10	0.09
Cherokee (5)	21	0.19
Choctaw (3)	6	0.06
Iroquois	2	0.02
Latin American Indians (3)	4	0.04
Navajo (3)	6	0.06
Pueblo (1)	2	0.02
Sioux (2)	2	0.02
All other tribes (6)	13	0.12
American Indian tribes, not spec.	3	0.03
Arab:	221	2.03
Iraqi	63	0.58
Lebanese	93	0.85
Palestinian	29	0.27
Syrian	19	0.17
Other Arab	17	0.16
Armenian	62	0.57
Asian:	1,911	17.53
Cambodian (11)	11	0.10
Chinese, ex. Taiwanese (339)	403	3.70
Filipino (413)	487	4.47
Indian (212)	223	2.05
Indonesian (5)	6	0.06
Japanese (136)	228	2.09
Korean (144)	151	1.39
Laotian (11)	12	0.11
Malaysian (2)	3	0.03
Pakistani (5)	6	0.06
Sri Lankan (3)	3	0.03
Taiwanese (52)	52	0.48
Thai (4)	5	0.05
Vietnamese (257)	284	2.61
Other Asian, not specified (12)	37	0.34
Austrian	66	0.61
Basque	15	0.14
Belgian	7	0.06
Brazilian	9	0.08
British	73	0.67
Canadian	96	0.88
Czech	20	0.18
Czechoslovakian	8	0.07
Danish	64	0.59
Dutch	206	1.89
English	1,532	14.05
European	195	1.79
Finnish	21	0.19
French, except Basque	528	4.84
French Canadian	23	0.21
German	1,883	17.26
Greek	86	0.79
Hawaii Native/Pacific Islander:	75	0.69
Micronesian: (6)	15	0.14
Guamanian/Chamorro (6)	15	0.14
Polynesian: (18)	40	0.37
Native Hawaiian (15)	34	0.31
Samoan (3)	6	0.06
Other Pac. Isl., not spec. (7)	20	0.18
Hispanic or Latino:	1,183	10.85
Central American:	37	0.34
Costa Rican	9	0.08
Honduran	2	0.02
Nicaraguan	9	0.08
Panamanian	1	0.01
Salvadoran	13	0.12
Other Central American	3	0.03
Cuban	33	0.30
Mexican	764	7.01
Puerto Rican	54	0.50
South American:	91	0.83
Argentinean	14	0.13
Bolivian	3	0.03
Chilean	1	0.01
Colombian	27	0.25
Ecuadorian	8	0.07
Peruvian	18	0.17
Venezuelan	12	0.11
Other South American	8	0.07
Other Hispanic or Latino	204	1.87
Hungarian	41	0.38
Iranian	112	1.03
Irish	1,380	12.65
Italian	866	7.94
Lithuanian	99	0.91
Northern European	10	0.09
Norwegian	241	2.21
Pennsylvania German	8	0.07
Polish	268	2.46
Portuguese	28	0.26
Romanian	20	0.18
Russian	212	1.94

Notes: 1. Figures in the "Number" column do not add up to the total population due to: a) Ancestry/Race overlap — e.g. persons can report being both White and Irish, b) persons of Hispanic origin can report being any race, c) persons reporting two ancestries are counted in both categories. 2. Numbers in parentheses indicate the number of persons reporting this ancestry/race alone, not in combination with any other ancestry/race. 3. Refer to the Explanation of Data in the front of the book for more detailed information.

Scandinavian	25	0.23
Scotch-Irish	212	1.94
Scottish	175	1.60
Slavic	25	0.23
Slovene	9	0.08
Swedish	370	3.39
Swiss	49	0.45
Turkish	7	0.06
Ukrainian	21	0.19
United States or American	347	3.18
Welsh	70	0.64
White:	8,568	78.61
Not Hispanic (7,443)	7,795	71.52
Hispanic (664)	773	7.09
Yugoslavian	48	0.44

Fortuna

Place Type: City
County: Humboldt
Population: 10,497

Ancestry/Race	Number	%
African American/Black:	73	0.70
Not Hispanic (41)	63	0.60
Hispanic (6)	10	0.10
Alaska Native tribes, specified:	3	0.03
Aleut (3)	3	0.03
Am. Ind. or Alaska Nat., not spec.	112	1.07
American Indian tribes, specified:	384	3.66
Apache	4	0.04
Blackfeet	8	0.08
Cherokee (34)	82	0.78
Chickasaw (6)	9	0.09
Chippewa (1)	2	0.02
Choctaw (15)	26	0.25
Cree (2)	3	0.03
Creek (1)	1	0.01
Delaware	1	0.01
Iroquois (5)	11	0.10
Latin American Indians	7	0.07
Navajo (5)	7	0.07
Osage (4)	4	0.04
Ottawa (1)	4	0.04
Paiute (3)	4	0.04
Potawatomi	3	0.03
Pueblo (3)	4	0.04
Shoshone	2	0.02
Sioux (2)	2	0.02
Ute (1)	1	0.01
Yaqui (1)	1	0.01
All other tribes (152)	198	1.89
American Indian tribes, not spec.	16	0.15
Arab:	24	0.23
Lebanese	12	0.12
Palestinian	12	0.12
Armenian	64	0.62
Asian:	148	1.41
Chinese, ex. Taiwanese (15)	23	0.22
Filipino (18)	35	0.33
Hmong (1)	1	0.01
Indian (28)	30	0.29
Japanese (7)	18	0.17
Korean (13)	18	0.17
Laotian (8)	8	0.08
Vietnamese (3)	5	0.05
Other Asian, specified	1	0.01
Other Asian, not specified (7)	9	0.09
Austrian	13	0.13
Basque	27	0.26
British	72	0.69
Canadian	6	0.06
Croatian	9	0.09
Czech	24	0.23
Czechoslovakian	27	0.26
Danish	179	1.73
Dutch	273	2.63
Eastern European	3	0.03
English	1,363	13.15
European	52	0.50
Finnish	22	0.21
French, except Basque	396	3.82
French Canadian	67	0.65
German	1,799	17.36
Greek	32	0.31
Hawaii Native/Pacific Islander:	34	0.32
Melanesian:	1	0.01
Fijian	1	0.01
Micronesian: (1)	3	0.03
Guamanian/Chamorro (1)	3	0.03
Polynesian: (16)	24	0.23
Native Hawaiian (12)	19	0.18
Samoan (1)	2	0.02
Tongan (3)	3	0.03
Other Pac. Isl., specified	1	0.01
Other Pac. Isl., not spec. (1)	5	0.05
Hispanic or Latino:	1,097	10.45
Central American:	17	0.16
Costa Rican	2	0.02
Guatemalan	7	0.07
Honduran	3	0.03
Nicaraguan	1	0.01
Salvadoran	3	0.03
Other Central American	1	0.01
Cuban	13	0.12
Mexican	931	8.87
Puerto Rican	14	0.13
South American:	10	0.10
Peruvian	5	0.05
Other South American	5	0.05
Other Hispanic or Latino	112	1.07
Hungarian	14	0.14
Irish	1,112	10.73
Israeli	5	0.05
Italian	804	7.76
Macedonian	6	0.06
Northern European	8	0.08
Norwegian	294	2.84
Pennsylvania German	7	0.07
Polish	170	1.64
Portuguese	335	3.23
Romanian	20	0.19
Russian	64	0.62
Scandinavian	36	0.35
Scotch-Irish	169	1.63
Scottish	259	2.50
Swedish	355	3.43
Swiss	182	1.76
Ukrainian	6	0.06
United States or American	807	7.79
Welsh	112	1.08
West Indian, excl. Hispanic:	4	0.04
Dutch West Indian	4	0.04
White:	9,601	91.46
Not Hispanic (8,704)	8,957	85.33
Hispanic (574)	644	6.14
Yugoslavian	12	0.12

Foster City

Place Type: City
County: San Mateo
Population: 28,803

Ancestry/Race	Number	%
African American/Black:	733	2.54
Not Hispanic (595)	708	2.46
Hispanic (7)	25	0.09
African, sub-Saharan:	168	0.58
African	62	0.22
Cape Verdean	5	0.02
Ethiopian	5	0.02
Nigerian	9	0.03
South African	87	0.30
Alaska Native tribes, specified:	3	0.01
Aleut	2	0.01
Tlingit-Haida (1)	1	0.00
Am. Ind. or Alaska Nat., not spec.	63	0.22
American Indian tribes, specified:	97	0.34
Blackfeet	8	0.03
Cherokee (8)	32	0.11
Chippewa (1)	1	0.00
Choctaw (1)	6	0.02
Creek (1)	3	0.01
Delaware (1)	3	0.01
Houma	2	0.01
Iroquois	2	0.01
Latin American Indians (1)	10	0.03
Navajo (1)	1	0.00
Osage	2	0.01
Pueblo (1)	4	0.01
Seminole (1)	2	0.01
Sioux	6	0.02
Yaqui	4	0.01
Yuman (1)	1	0.00
All other tribes (5)	10	0.03
American Indian tribes, not spec.	3	0.01
Arab:	485	1.68
Arab/Arabic	52	0.18
Egyptian	47	0.16
Iraqi	4	0.01
Jordanian	15	0.05
Lebanese	85	0.30
Moroccan	10	0.03
Palestinian	106	0.37
Syrian	74	0.26
Other Arab	92	0.32
Armenian	153	0.53
Asian:	10,258	35.61
Bangladeshi (6)	6	0.02
Cambodian (1)	3	0.01
Chinese, ex. Taiwanese (4,601)	4,921	17.09
Filipino (955)	1,208	4.19
Indian (1,636)	1,720	5.97
Indonesian (17)	31	0.11
Japanese (1,317)	1,555	5.40
Korean (342)	392	1.36
Laotian (2)	2	0.01
Malaysian (7)	15	0.05
Pakistani (25)	32	0.11
Sri Lankan (3)	3	0.01
Taiwanese (105)	134	0.47
Thai (36)	43	0.15
Vietnamese (99)	113	0.39
Other Asian, specified (10)	12	0.04
Other Asian, not specified (19)	68	0.24
Assyrian/Chaldean/Syriac	28	0.10
Australian	114	0.40
Austrian	151	0.52
Basque	11	0.04
Belgian	17	0.06
Brazilian	39	0.14
British	187	0.65
Canadian	119	0.41
Croatian	72	0.25
Czech	80	0.28
Czechoslovakian	67	0.23
Danish	188	0.65
Dutch	385	1.34
Eastern European	71	0.25
English	2,480	8.61
European	285	0.99
Finnish	29	0.10
French, except Basque	978	3.40
French Canadian	127	0.44
German	3,167	11.00
Greek	289	1.00
Guyanese	8	0.03
Hawaii Native/Pacific Islander:	306	1.06
Melanesian: (28)	38	0.13
Fijian (28)	38	0.13
Micronesian: (36)	48	0.17
Guamanian/Chamorro (35)	47	0.16
Other Micronesian (1)	1	0.00
Polynesian: (82)	146	0.51
Native Hawaiian (27)	74	0.26
Samoan (16)	22	0.08
Tongan (37)	43	0.15
Other Polynesian (2)	7	0.02
Other Pac. Isl., not spec. (20)	74	0.26

Notes: 1. Figures in the "Number" column do not add up to the total population due to: a) Ancestry/Race overlap — e.g. persons can report being both White and Irish, b) persons of Hispanic origin can report being any race, c) persons reporting two ancestries are counted in both categories. 2. Numbers in parentheses indicate the number of persons reporting this ancestry/race alone, not in combination with any other ancestry/race. 3. Refer to the Explanation of Data in the front of the book for more detailed information.

Hispanic or Latino:	1,531	5.32
Central American:	170	0.59
Costa Rican	4	0.01
Guatemalan	7	0.02
Honduran	4	0.01
Nicaraguan	45	0.16
Panamanian	6	0.02
Salvadoran	64	0.22
Other Central American	40	0.14
Cuban	37	0.13
Dominican Republic	3	0.01
Mexican	626	2.17
Puerto Rican	61	0.21
South American:	209	0.73
Argentinean	15	0.05
Bolivian	10	0.03
Chilean	28	0.10
Colombian	46	0.16
Ecuadorian	10	0.03
Paraguayan	1	0.00
Peruvian	69	0.24
Uruguayan	2	0.01
Venezuelan	6	0.02
Other South American	22	0.08
Other Hispanic or Latino	425	1.48
Hungarian	189	0.66
Icelander	7	0.02
Iranian	314	1.09
Irish	2,329	8.09
Israeli	88	0.31
Italian	1,857	6.45
Latvian	24	0.08
Lithuanian	31	0.11
Maltese	22	0.08
New Zealander	5	0.02
Northern European	9	0.03
Norwegian	324	1.12
Pennsylvania German	6	0.02
Polish	771	2.68
Portuguese	206	0.72
Romanian	28	0.10
Russian	1,041	3.61
Scandinavian	71	0.25
Scotch-Irish	246	0.85
Scottish	630	2.19
Serbian	13	0.05
Slovak	55	0.19
Slovene	23	0.08
Swedish	510	1.77
Swiss	159	0.55
Turkish	200	0.69
Ukrainian	203	0.70
United States or American	686	2.38
Welsh	150	0.52
West Indian, excl. Hispanic:	30	0.10
Jamaican	30	0.10
White:	18,083	62.78
Not Hispanic (16,090)	16,922	58.75
Hispanic (997)	1,161	4.03
Yugoslavian	20	0.07

Fountain Valley

Place Type: City
County: Orange
Population: 54,978

Ancestry/Race	Number	%
Acadian/Cajun	14	0.03
Afghan	12	0.02
African American/Black:	819	1.49
Not Hispanic (584)	744	1.35
Hispanic (27)	75	0.14
African, sub-Saharan:	73	0.13
African	23	0.04
Ethiopian	6	0.01
Somalian	15	0.03
South African	19	0.03
Sudanese	10	0.02
Alaska Native tribes, specified:	4	0.01
Alaska Athabascan (2)	2	0.00
Tlingit-Haida (2)	2	0.00
Am. Ind. or Alaska Nat., not spec.	213	0.39
Albanian	8	0.01
American Indian tribes, specified:	444	0.81
Apache (4)	15	0.03
Blackfeet (2)	15	0.03
Cherokee (24)	148	0.27
Cheyenne (4)	4	0.01
Chickasaw (6)	11	0.02
Chippewa (10)	10	0.02
Choctaw (14)	35	0.06
Colville	1	0.00
Cree (5)	6	0.01
Creek (4)	12	0.02
Delaware	4	0.01
Iroquois (2)	6	0.01
Latin American Indians (18)	39	0.07
Lumbee (9)	11	0.02
Navajo (7)	13	0.02
Osage (1)	2	0.00
Paiute (1)	1	0.00
Potawatomi (1)	3	0.01
Pueblo (4)	11	0.02
Puget Sound Salish	3	0.01
Seminole (1)	6	0.01
Shoshone	2	0.00
Sioux (5)	11	0.02
Ute	1	0.00
Yakama (1)	1	0.00
Yaqui (1)	4	0.01
All other tribes (36)	69	0.13
American Indian tribes, not spec.	15	0.03
Arab:	1,039	1.89
Arab/Arabic	193	0.35
Egyptian	191	0.35
Jordanian	109	0.20
Lebanese	359	0.65
Palestinian	73	0.13
Syrian	101	0.18
Other Arab	13	0.02
Armenian	334	0.61
Asian:	15,675	28.51
Bangladeshi (2)	2	0.00
Cambodian (62)	86	0.16
Chinese, ex. Taiwanese (2,016)	2,460	4.47
Filipino (585)	830	1.51
Hmong (36)	39	0.07
Indian (531)	590	1.07
Indonesian (42)	80	0.15
Japanese (1,421)	1,809	3.29
Korean (1,120)	1,221	2.22
Laotian (79)	102	0.19
Malaysian	2	0.00
Pakistani (42)	75	0.14
Sri Lankan (5)	5	0.01
Taiwanese (564)	667	1.21
Thai (85)	114	0.21
Vietnamese (7,088)	7,358	13.38
Other Asian, specified (45)	51	0.09
Other Asian, not specified (60)	184	0.33
Assyrian/Chaldean/Syriac	36	0.07
Australian	52	0.09
Austrian	151	0.27
Basque	12	0.02
Belgian	76	0.14
Brazilian	57	0.10
British	302	0.55
Bulgarian	19	0.03
Canadian	413	0.75
Croatian	49	0.09
Cypriot	15	0.03
Czech	146	0.27
Czechoslovakian	82	0.15
Danish	330	0.60
Dutch	915	1.66
Eastern European	28	0.05
English	5,817	10.58
European	675	1.23
Finnish	112	0.20
French, except Basque	1,574	2.86
French Canadian	433	0.79
German	7,568	13.76
Greek	229	0.42
Guyanese	7	0.01
Hawaii Native/Pacific Islander:	457	0.83
Melanesian: (2)	2	0.00
Other Melanesian (2)	2	0.00
Micronesian: (49)	78	0.14
Guamanian/Chamorro (31)	58	0.11
Other Micronesian (18)	20	0.04
Polynesian: (136)	274	0.50
Native Hawaiian (60)	143	0.26
Samoan (57)	82	0.15
Tongan (10)	23	0.04
Other Polynesian (9)	26	0.05
Other Pac. Isl., not spec. (33)	103	0.19
Hispanic or Latino:	5,870	10.68
Central American:	226	0.41
Costa Rican	33	0.06
Guatemalan	37	0.07
Honduran	9	0.02
Nicaraguan	46	0.08
Panamanian	13	0.02
Salvadoran	55	0.10
Other Central American	33	0.06
Cuban	128	0.23
Dominican Republic	13	0.02
Mexican	4,176	7.60
Puerto Rican	140	0.25
South American:	301	0.55
Argentinean	80	0.15
Bolivian	24	0.04
Chilean	29	0.05
Colombian	52	0.09
Ecuadorian	23	0.04
Peruvian	52	0.09
Uruguayan	3	0.01
Venezuelan	5	0.01
Other South American	33	0.06
Other Hispanic or Latino	886	1.61
Hungarian	318	0.58
Icelander	11	0.02
Iranian	289	0.53
Irish	5,261	9.57
Israeli	27	0.05
Italian	2,954	5.37
Latvian	26	0.05
Lithuanian	55	0.10
Macedonian	17	0.03
Northern European	89	0.16
Norwegian	956	1.74
Pennsylvania German	8	0.01
Polish	870	1.58
Portuguese	236	0.43
Romanian	167	0.30
Russian	536	0.97
Scandinavian	111	0.20
Scotch-Irish	803	1.46
Scottish	1,213	2.21
Serbian	15	0.03
Slavic	17	0.03
Slovak	135	0.25
Slovene	4	0.01
Swedish	840	1.53
Swiss	135	0.25
Turkish	59	0.11
Ukrainian	82	0.15
United States or American	2,498	4.54
Welsh	373	0.68
West Indian, excl. Hispanic:	17	0.03
Dutch West Indian	10	0.02
West Indian	7	0.01
White:	37,274	67.80
Not Hispanic (32,144)	33,698	61.29
Hispanic (3,052)	3,576	6.50
Yugoslavian	115	0.21

Notes: 1. Figures in the "Number" column do not add up to the total population due to: a) Ancestry/Race overlap — e.g. persons can report being both White and Irish, b) persons of Hispanic origin can report being any race, c) persons reporting two ancestries are counted in both categories. 2. Numbers in parentheses indicate the number of persons reporting this ancestry/race alone, not in combination with any other ancestry/race. 3. Refer to the Explanation of Data in the front of the book for more detailed information.

Fremont

Place Type: City
County: Alameda
Population: 203,413

Ancestry/Race	Number	%
Acadian/Cajun	7	0.00
Afghan	3,421	1.68
African American/Black:	7,697	3.78
Not Hispanic (6,084)	7,210	3.54
Hispanic (226)	487	0.24
African, sub-Saharan:	855	0.42
African	444	0.22
Ethiopian	136	0.07
Ghanian	34	0.02
Nigerian	189	0.09
South African	44	0.02
Other sub-Saharan African	8	0.00
Alaska Native tribes, specified:	43	0.02
Alaska Athabascan	6	0.00
Aleut (2)	5	0.00
Eskimo (7)	9	0.00
Tlingit-Haida (15)	22	0.01
All other tribes (1)	1	0.00
Am. Ind. or Alaska Nat., not spec.	912	0.45
American Indian tribes, specified:	1,674	0.82
Apache (47)	103	0.05
Blackfeet (21)	80	0.04
Cherokee (120)	530	0.26
Cheyenne (1)	10	0.00
Chickasaw (17)	30	0.01
Chippewa (27)	44	0.02
Choctaw (30)	116	0.06
Comanche (4)	17	0.01
Cree	6	0.00
Creek (8)	23	0.01
Crow	1	0.00
Delaware (1)	15	0.01
Iroquois (9)	32	0.02
Kiowa (8)	8	0.00
Latin American Indians (70)	135	0.07
Menominee	1	0.00
Navajo (29)	75	0.04
Osage (5)	11	0.01
Ottawa (2)	3	0.00
Paiute (3)	9	0.00
Pima	2	0.00
Potawatomi (5)	11	0.01
Pueblo (22)	38	0.02
Puget Sound Salish	3	0.00
Seminole (7)	23	0.01
Shoshone (1)	9	0.00
Sioux (35)	70	0.03
Tohono O'Odham (3)	12	0.01
Ute (4)	15	0.01
Yaqui (17)	22	0.01
Yuman (5)	6	0.00
All other tribes (108)	214	0.11
American Indian tribes, not spec.	130	0.06
Arab:	1,519	0.75
Arab/Arabic	368	0.18
Egyptian	162	0.08
Iraqi	83	0.04
Jordanian	50	0.02
Lebanese	405	0.20
Moroccan	6	0.00
Palestinian	254	0.12
Syrian	71	0.03
Other Arab	120	0.06
Armenian	306	0.15
Asian:	82,664	40.64
Bangladeshi (97)	112	0.06
Cambodian (115)	143	0.07
Chinese, ex. Taiwanese (27,271)	29,145	14.33
Filipino (11,782)	13,863	6.82
Hmong (93)	95	0.05
Indian (20,742)	21,618	10.63
Indonesian (191)	284	0.14
Japanese (2,044)	3,002	1.48
Korean (3,168)	3,464	1.70
Laotian (106)	128	0.06
Malaysian (30)	85	0.04
Pakistani (1,049)	1,294	0.64
Sri Lankan (70)	86	0.04
Taiwanese (1,969)	2,372	1.17
Thai (218)	291	0.14
Vietnamese (4,135)	4,459	2.19
Other Asian, specified (419)	510	0.25
Other Asian, not specified (361)	1,713	0.84
Assyrian/Chaldean/Syriac	234	0.12
Australian	99	0.05
Austrian	212	0.10
Basque	57	0.03
Belgian	188	0.09
Brazilian	81	0.04
British	828	0.41
Bulgarian	8	0.00
Canadian	649	0.32
Celtic	70	0.03
Croatian	210	0.10
Czech	307	0.15
Czechoslovakian	270	0.13
Danish	1,384	0.68
Dutch	2,229	1.10
Eastern European	91	0.04
English	13,514	6.64
Estonian	16	0.01
European	2,147	1.06
Finnish	435	0.21
French, except Basque	4,131	2.03
French Canadian	764	0.38
German	18,950	9.32
German Russian	12	0.01
Greek	669	0.33
Guyanese	39	0.02
Hawaii Native/Pacific Islander:	2,039	1.00
Melanesian: (105)	121	0.06
Fijian (105)	120	0.06
Other Melanesian	1	0.00
Micronesian: (230)	382	0.19
Guamanian/Chamorro (223)	373	0.18
Other Micronesian (7)	9	0.00
Polynesian: (393)	995	0.49
Native Hawaiian (256)	792	0.39
Samoan (81)	134	0.07
Tongan (51)	58	0.03
Other Polynesian (5)	11	0.01
Other Pac. Isl., specified	10	0.00
Other Pac. Isl., not spec. (85)	531	0.26
Hispanic or Latino:	27,409	13.47
Central American:	1,279	0.63
Costa Rican	49	0.02
Guatemalan	149	0.07
Honduran	21	0.01
Nicaraguan	315	0.15
Panamanian	75	0.04
Salvadoran	547	0.27
Other Central American	123	0.06
Cuban	172	0.08
Dominican Republic	14	0.01
Mexican	18,848	9.27
Puerto Rican	1,233	0.61
South American:	844	0.41
Argentinean	64	0.03
Bolivian	40	0.02
Chilean	101	0.05
Colombian	148	0.07
Ecuadorian	40	0.02
Paraguayan	3	0.00
Peruvian	293	0.14
Uruguayan	12	0.01
Venezuelan	43	0.02
Other South American	100	0.05
Other Hispanic or Latino	5,019	2.47
Hungarian	662	0.33
Icelander	15	0.01
Iranian	1,485	0.73
Irish	14,578	7.17
Israeli	73	0.04
Italian	8,513	4.19
Latvian	15	0.01
Lithuanian	289	0.14
Luxemburger	10	0.00
Macedonian	9	0.00
Maltese	59	0.03
Northern European	177	0.09
Norwegian	2,791	1.37
Pennsylvania German	26	0.01
Polish	2,197	1.08
Portuguese	6,475	3.18
Romanian	321	0.16
Russian	1,688	0.83
Scandinavian	409	0.20
Scotch-Irish	1,885	0.93
Scottish	2,555	1.26
Serbian	114	0.06
Slavic	47	0.02
Slovak	211	0.10
Slovene	29	0.01
Swedish	2,981	1.47
Swiss	746	0.37
Turkish	32	0.02
Ukrainian	334	0.16
United States or American	4,790	2.35
Welsh	916	0.45
West Indian, excl. Hispanic:	233	0.11
Dutch West Indian	13	0.01
Haitian	74	0.04
Jamaican	76	0.04
Trinidadian and Tobagonian	58	0.03
West Indian	7	0.00
Other West Indian	5	0.00
White:	106,512	52.36
Not Hispanic (84,149)	91,403	44.93
Hispanic (12,819)	15,109	7.43
Yugoslavian	213	0.10

Fresno

Place Type: City
County: Fresno
Population: 427,652

Ancestry/Race	Number	%
Acadian/Cajun	44	0.01
Afghan	87	0.02
African American/Black:	39,362	9.20
Not Hispanic (34,357)	36,800	8.61
Hispanic (1,406)	2,562	0.60
African, sub-Saharan:	3,081	0.72
African	2,276	0.53
Cape Verdean	7	0.00
Ethiopian	293	0.07
Ghanian	38	0.01
Nigerian	367	0.09
Somalian	20	0.00
South African	14	0.00
Sudanese	20	0.00
Ugandan	23	0.01
Other sub-Saharan African	23	0.01
Alaska Native tribes, specified:	40	0.01
Alaska Athabascan (1)	4	0.00
Aleut (1)	2	0.00
Eskimo (14)	20	0.00
Tlingit-Haida (3)	11	0.00
All other tribes (1)	3	0.00
Alaska Native tribes, not specified	5	0.00
Am. Ind. or Alaska Nat., not spec.	4,140	0.97
Albanian	10	0.00
Alsatian	5	0.00
American Indian tribes, specified:	6,764	1.58
Apache (261)	434	0.10
Blackfeet (51)	173	0.04
Cherokee (490)	1,502	0.35
Cheyenne (4)	17	0.00
Chickasaw (26)	66	0.02
Chippewa (47)	76	0.02
Choctaw (130)	353	0.08
Colville (3)	3	0.00

Notes: 1. Figures in the "Number" column do not add up to the total population due to: a) Ancestry/Race overlap — e.g. persons can report being both White and Irish, b) persons of Hispanic origin can report being any race, c) persons reporting two ancestries are counted in both categories. 2. Numbers in parentheses indicate the number of persons reporting this ancestry/race alone, not in combination with any other ancestry/race. 3. Refer to the Explanation of Data in the front of the book for more detailed information.

Comanche (43)	63	0.01
Cree (3)	15	0.00
Creek (70)	149	0.03
Crow (8)	21	0.00
Delaware (4)	16	0.00
Iroquois (23)	73	0.02
Kiowa (9)	13	0.00
Latin American Indians (868)	1,174	0.27
Lumbee (11)	13	0.00
Navajo (103)	193	0.05
Osage (14)	42	0.01
Ottawa (6)	7	0.00
Paiute (45)	81	0.02
Pima (27)	32	0.01
Potawatomi (38)	53	0.01
Pueblo (32)	48	0.01
Puget Sound Salish (4)	15	0.00
Seminole (24)	33	0.01
Shoshone (6)	20	0.00
Sioux (63)	145	0.03
Tohono O'Odham (48)	68	0.02
Ute (3)	3	0.00
Yakama (2)	3	0.00
Yaqui (172)	260	0.06
Yuman (15)	23	0.01
All other tribes (1,123)	1,577	0.37
American Indian tribes, not spec.	644	0.15
Arab:	1,574	0.37
Arab/Arabic	546	0.13
Egyptian	179	0.04
Jordanian	57	0.01
Lebanese	337	0.08
Moroccan	32	0.01
Palestinian	199	0.05
Syrian	157	0.04
Other Arab	67	0.02
Armenian	6,024	1.41
Asian:	55,436	12.96
Bangladeshi (6)	8	0.00
Cambodian (3,896)	4,522	1.06
Chinese, ex. Taiwanese (3,345)	4,181	0.98
Filipino (3,876)	5,264	1.23
Hmong (18,780)	20,390	4.77
Indian (4,123)	4,993	1.17
Indonesian (133)	204	0.05
Japanese (2,693)	3,629	0.85
Korean (935)	1,155	0.27
Laotian (5,660)	6,575	1.54
Malaysian (25)	58	0.01
Pakistani (110)	170	0.04
Sri Lankan (22)	32	0.01
Taiwanese (91)	105	0.02
Thai (218)	314	0.07
Vietnamese (1,953)	2,175	0.51
Other Asian, specified (34)	72	0.02
Other Asian, not specified (1,066)	1,589	0.37
Assyrian/Chaldean/Syriac	53	0.01
Australian	64	0.01
Austrian	433	0.10
Basque	457	0.11
Belgian	122	0.03
Brazilian	56	0.01
British	667	0.16
Bulgarian	43	0.01
Canadian	592	0.14
Celtic	81	0.02
Croatian	102	0.02
Czech	673	0.16
Czechoslovakian	351	0.08
Danish	2,763	0.65
Dutch	3,595	0.84
Eastern European	48	0.01
English	23,236	5.44
Estonian	10	0.00
European	2,727	0.64
Finnish	311	0.07
French, except Basque	7,321	1.71
French Canadian	1,104	0.26
German	36,751	8.60
German Russian	40	0.01
Greek	901	0.21
Guyanese	93	0.02
Hawaii Native/Pacific Islander:	1,635	0.38
Melanesian: (22)	27	0.01
Fijian (22)	25	0.01
Other Melanesian	2	0.00
Micronesian: (101)	199	0.05
Guamanian/Chamorro (93)	180	0.04
Other Micronesian (8)	19	0.00
Polynesian: (341)	701	0.16
Native Hawaiian (140)	398	0.09
Samoan (179)	271	0.06
Tongan (11)	14	0.00
Other Polynesian (11)	18	0.00
Other Pac. Isl., specified	28	0.01
Other Pac. Isl., not spec. (111)	680	0.16
Hispanic or Latino:	170,520	39.87
Central American:	1,571	0.37
Costa Rican	62	0.01
Guatemalan	224	0.05
Honduran	104	0.02
Nicaraguan	172	0.04
Panamanian	56	0.01
Salvadoran	799	0.19
Other Central American	154	0.04
Cuban	288	0.07
Dominican Republic	29	0.01
Mexican	144,772	33.85
Puerto Rican	1,105	0.26
South American:	546	0.13
Argentinean	79	0.02
Bolivian	16	0.00
Chilean	65	0.02
Colombian	133	0.03
Ecuadorian	51	0.01
Paraguayan	7	0.00
Peruvian	107	0.03
Uruguayan	3	0.00
Venezuelan	39	0.01
Other South American	46	0.01
Other Hispanic or Latino	22,209	5.19
Hungarian	488	0.11
Icelander	43	0.01
Iranian	833	0.19
Irish	22,970	5.38
Israeli	64	0.01
Italian	13,914	3.26
Latvian	75	0.02
Lithuanian	279	0.07
Luxemburger	19	0.00
Macedonian	6	0.00
New Zealander	47	0.01
Northern European	227	0.05
Norwegian	3,151	0.74
Pennsylvania German	153	0.04
Polish	2,426	0.57
Portuguese	4,337	1.02
Romanian	200	0.05
Russian	2,206	0.52
Scandinavian	336	0.08
Scotch-Irish	3,986	0.93
Scottish	4,909	1.15
Serbian	54	0.01
Slavic	95	0.02
Slovak	105	0.02
Slovene	50	0.01
Swedish	4,032	0.94
Swiss	798	0.19
Turkish	70	0.02
Ukrainian	643	0.15
United States or American	11,686	2.74
Welsh	1,489	0.35
West Indian, excl. Hispanic:	199	0.05
Belizean	5	0.00
Dutch West Indian	55	0.01
Haitian	59	0.01
Jamaican	60	0.01
U.S. Virgin Islander	9	0.00
West Indian	11	0.00
White:	230,797	53.97
Not Hispanic (159,473)	167,387	39.14
Hispanic (55,083)	63,410	14.83
Yugoslavian	379	0.09

Fullerton

Place Type: City
County: Orange
Population: 126,003

Ancestry/Race	Number	%
Afghan	9	0.01
African American/Black:	3,390	2.69
Not Hispanic (2,675)	3,051	2.42
Hispanic (186)	339	0.27
African, sub-Saharan:	462	0.37
African	244	0.19
Cape Verdean	8	0.01
Ghanian	39	0.03
Kenyan	29	0.02
Nigerian	117	0.09
South African	19	0.02
Other sub-Saharan African	6	0.00
Alaska Native tribes, specified:	3	0.00
Aleut	1	0.00
Eskimo (1)	1	0.00
Tlingit-Haida (1)	1	0.00
Am. Ind. or Alaska Nat., not spec.	649	0.52
Albanian	10	0.01
Alsatian	8	0.01
American Indian tribes, specified:	1,045	0.83
Apache (35)	79	0.06
Blackfeet (1)	33	0.03
Cherokee (74)	282	0.22
Cheyenne (2)	5	0.00
Chickasaw (4)	7	0.01
Chippewa (10)	20	0.02
Choctaw (29)	66	0.05
Colville (5)	5	0.00
Comanche (4)	11	0.01
Cree (4)	4	0.00
Creek (8)	23	0.02
Crow (1)	2	0.00
Delaware (1)	1	0.00
Iroquois (7)	16	0.01
Kiowa	1	0.00
Latin American Indians (97)	160	0.13
Lumbee	2	0.00
Menominee (1)	2	0.00
Navajo (35)	54	0.04
Osage (8)	11	0.01
Ottawa (1)	2	0.00
Paiute (2)	3	0.00
Pima (1)	3	0.00
Potawatomi (7)	16	0.01
Pueblo (8)	18	0.01
Puget Sound Salish (1)	2	0.00
Seminole (1)	19	0.02
Shoshone (3)	7	0.01
Sioux (6)	16	0.01
Tohono O'Odham (6)	6	0.00
Ute (1)	6	0.00
Yaqui (13)	27	0.02
Yuman (4)	4	0.00
All other tribes (71)	132	0.10
American Indian tribes, not spec.	112	0.09
Arab:	1,170	0.93
Arab/Arabic	225	0.18
Egyptian	207	0.16
Iraqi	30	0.02
Jordanian	137	0.11
Lebanese	325	0.26
Moroccan	8	0.01
Palestinian	10	0.01
Syrian	177	0.14
Other Arab	51	0.04
Armenian	205	0.16
Asian:	22,406	17.78
Bangladeshi (30)	39	0.03
Cambodian (135)	176	0.14

Notes: 1. Figures in the "Number" column do not add up to the total population due to: a) Ancestry/Race overlap — e.g. persons can report being both White and Irish, b) persons of Hispanic origin can report being any race, c) persons reporting two ancestries are counted in both categories. 2. Numbers in parentheses indicate the number of persons reporting this ancestry/race alone, not in combination with any other ancestry/race. 3. Refer to the Explanation of Data in the front of the book for more detailed information.

Chinese, ex. Taiwanese (2,622)	3,153	2.50
Filipino (1,736)	2,157	1.71
Hmong (22)	34	0.03
Indian (1,720)	1,903	1.51
Indonesian (201)	317	0.25
Japanese (1,225)	1,635	1.30
Korean (9,093)	9,301	7.38
Laotian (135)	173	0.14
Malaysian (7)	13	0.01
Pakistani (154)	219	0.17
Sri Lankan (16)	19	0.02
Taiwanese (500)	612	0.49
Thai (166)	220	0.17
Vietnamese (1,911)	2,060	1.63
Other Asian, specified (37)	48	0.04
Other Asian, not specified (122)	327	0.26
Assyrian/Chaldean/Syriac	91	0.07
Australian	44	0.03
Austrian	345	0.27
Basque	77	0.06
Belgian	133	0.11
Brazilian	104	0.08
British	490	0.39
Bulgarian	11	0.01
Canadian	334	0.26
Celtic	6	0.00
Croatian	102	0.08
Czech	383	0.30
Czechoslovakian	190	0.15
Danish	849	0.67
Dutch	1,939	1.54
Eastern European	12	0.01
English	11,393	9.02
Estonian	13	0.01
European	1,428	1.13
Finnish	219	0.17
French, except Basque	2,923	2.32
French Canadian	623	0.49
German	14,710	11.65
Greek	451	0.36
Guyanese	9	0.01
Hawaii Native/Pacific Islander:	613	0.49
Melanesian: (2)	3	0.00
Fijian (2)	3	0.00
Micronesian: (40)	81	0.06
Guamanian/Chamorro (39)	76	0.06
Other Micronesian (1)	5	0.00
Polynesian: (195)	349	0.28
Native Hawaiian (97)	207	0.16
Samoan (87)	120	0.10
Tongan (10)	14	0.01
Other Polynesian (1)	8	0.01
Other Pac. Isl., specified	2	0.00
Other Pac. Isl., not spec. (56)	178	0.14
Hispanic or Latino:	38,014	30.17
Central American:	955	0.76
Costa Rican	70	0.06
Guatemalan	255	0.20
Honduran	67	0.05
Nicaraguan	135	0.11
Panamanian	38	0.03
Salvadoran	327	0.26
Other Central American	63	0.05
Cuban	349	0.28
Dominican Republic	14	0.01
Mexican	31,252	24.80
Puerto Rican	422	0.33
South American:	741	0.59
Argentinean	116	0.09
Bolivian	25	0.02
Chilean	33	0.03
Colombian	158	0.13
Ecuadorian	80	0.06
Paraguayan	1	0.00
Peruvian	217	0.17
Uruguayan	9	0.01
Venezuelan	26	0.02
Other South American	76	0.06
Other Hispanic or Latino	4,281	3.40
Hungarian	550	0.44
Icelander	6	0.00
Iranian	691	0.55
Irish	10,507	8.32
Israeli	8	0.01
Italian	4,980	3.94
Latvian	35	0.03
Lithuanian	122	0.10
Luxemburger	19	0.02
New Zealander	7	0.01
Northern European	95	0.08
Norwegian	1,650	1.31
Pennsylvania German	18	0.01
Polish	2,241	1.78
Portuguese	265	0.21
Romanian	593	0.47
Russian	1,110	0.88
Scandinavian	220	0.17
Scotch-Irish	1,639	1.30
Scottish	2,294	1.82
Serbian	84	0.07
Slavic	75	0.06
Slovak	120	0.10
Slovene	52	0.04
Swedish	1,786	1.41
Swiss	517	0.41
Turkish	32	0.03
Ukrainian	247	0.20
United States or American	4,309	3.41
Welsh	892	0.71
West Indian, excl. Hispanic:	172	0.14
Belizean	46	0.04
British West Indian	7	0.01
Haitian	7	0.01
Jamaican	69	0.05
Trinidadian and Tobagonian	23	0.02
West Indian	20	0.02
White:	82,132	65.18
Not Hispanic (61,420)	63,688	50.54
Hispanic (16,557)	18,444	14.64
Yugoslavian	188	0.15

Galt

Place Type: City
County: Sacramento
Population: 19,472

Ancestry/Race	Number	%
African American/Black:	340	1.75
Not Hispanic (186)	267	1.37
Hispanic (39)	73	0.37
African, sub-Saharan:	82	0.42
African	82	0.42
Alaska Native tribes, specified:	2	0.01
Aleut	1	0.01
Tlingit-Haida (1)	1	0.01
Am. Ind. or Alaska Nat., not spec.	135	0.69
American Indian tribes, specified:	317	1.63
Apache (3)	14	0.07
Blackfeet	17	0.09
Cherokee (35)	126	0.65
Cheyenne	2	0.01
Chickasaw	1	0.01
Choctaw (7)	24	0.12
Comanche (2)	3	0.02
Creek (6)	10	0.05
Iroquois (1)	3	0.02
Latin American Indians (11)	17	0.09
Lumbee	1	0.01
Navajo (2)	2	0.01
Paiute (1)	1	0.01
Potawatomi (1)	1	0.01
Pueblo (6)	12	0.06
Seminole	5	0.03
Shoshone (2)	3	0.02
Sioux (6)	9	0.05
Tohono O'Odham	1	0.01
Ute (1)	4	0.02
Yaqui	1	0.01
All other tribes (45)	60	0.31
American Indian tribes, not spec.	8	0.04
Arab:	11	0.06
Syrian	11	0.06
Asian:	880	4.52
Cambodian (1)	1	0.01
Chinese, ex. Taiwanese (58)	95	0.49
Filipino (275)	448	2.30
Hmong (11)	11	0.06
Indian (50)	69	0.35
Indonesian	4	0.02
Japanese (54)	114	0.59
Korean (18)	21	0.11
Laotian (17)	18	0.09
Malaysian	1	0.01
Pakistani (17)	20	0.10
Taiwanese (1)	2	0.01
Thai (4)	7	0.04
Vietnamese (19)	33	0.17
Other Asian, not specified (16)	36	0.18
Assyrian/Chaldean/Syriac	13	0.07
Austrian	11	0.06
Basque	23	0.12
British	41	0.21
Canadian	40	0.20
Czech	16	0.08
Czechoslovakian	11	0.06
Danish	124	0.64
Dutch	277	1.42
English	1,630	8.35
European	56	0.29
French, except Basque	606	3.10
French Canadian	123	0.63
German	3,241	16.60
Greek	42	0.22
Hawaii Native/Pacific Islander:	101	0.52
Melanesian: (9)	18	0.09
Fijian (9)	18	0.09
Micronesian: (9)	23	0.12
Guamanian/Chamorro (9)	23	0.12
Polynesian: (8)	36	0.18
Native Hawaiian (6)	25	0.13
Samoan (2)	11	0.06
Other Pac. Isl., not spec. (5)	24	0.12
Hispanic or Latino:	6,465	33.20
Central American:	46	0.24
Guatemalan	6	0.03
Honduran	7	0.04
Nicaraguan	5	0.03
Panamanian	5	0.03
Salvadoran	23	0.12
Cuban	11	0.06
Dominican Republic	2	0.01
Mexican	5,649	29.01
Puerto Rican	60	0.31
South American:	17	0.09
Colombian	4	0.02
Ecuadorian	8	0.04
Peruvian	5	0.03
Other Hispanic or Latino	680	3.49
Hungarian	36	0.18
Icelander	10	0.05
Irish	1,720	8.81
Italian	672	3.44
Lithuanian	15	0.08
Norwegian	330	1.69
Polish	203	1.04
Portuguese	668	3.42
Russian	133	0.68
Scandinavian	34	0.17
Scotch-Irish	193	0.99
Scottish	312	1.60
Slovak	46	0.24
Swedish	493	2.52
Swiss	100	0.51
Ukrainian	40	0.20
United States or American	734	3.76
Welsh	97	0.50
White:	14,691	75.45
Not Hispanic (11,529)	12,059	61.93
Hispanic (2,197)	2,632	13.52

Notes: 1. Figures in the "Number" column do not add up to the total population due to: a) Ancestry/Race overlap — e.g. persons can report being both White and Irish, b) persons of Hispanic origin can report being any race, c) persons reporting two ancestries are counted in both categories. 2. Numbers in parentheses indicate the number of persons reporting this ancestry/race alone, not in combination with any other ancestry/race. 3. Refer to the Explanation of Data in the front of the book for more detailed information.

Garden Grove

Place Type: City
County: Orange
Population: 165,196

Ancestry/Race	Number	%
Acadian/Cajun	20	0.01
Afghan	200	0.12
African American/Black:	2,895	1.75
Not Hispanic (1,873)	2,367	1.43
Hispanic (295)	528	0.32
African, sub-Saharan:	242	0.15
African	148	0.09
Cape Verdean	31	0.02
Ethiopian	50	0.03
Nigerian	13	0.01
Alaska Native tribes, specified:	11	0.01
Eskimo (1)	1	0.00
Tlingit-Haida (2)	6	0.00
All other tribes	4	0.00
Alaska Native tribes, not specified	1	0.00
Am. Ind. or Alaska Nat., not spec.	982	0.59
Albanian	7	0.00
American Indian tribes, specified:	1,197	0.72
Apache (50)	91	0.06
Blackfeet (3)	18	0.01
Cherokee (86)	273	0.17
Cheyenne (1)	2	0.00
Chickasaw (8)	19	0.01
Chippewa (4)	18	0.01
Choctaw (28)	51	0.03
Comanche (1)	17	0.01
Cree (3)	6	0.00
Creek (6)	18	0.01
Crow (2)	3	0.00
Delaware (2)	6	0.00
Iroquois (16)	36	0.02
Kiowa	1	0.00
Latin American Indians (161)	223	0.13
Navajo (30)	60	0.04
Osage	1	0.00
Ottawa (1)	1	0.00
Paiute (2)	14	0.01
Pima (3)	3	0.00
Potawatomi (1)	5	0.00
Pueblo (22)	41	0.02
Puget Sound Salish (1)	2	0.00
Seminole (5)	19	0.01
Shoshone	1	0.00
Sioux (20)	36	0.02
Tohono O'Odham (5)	10	0.01
Ute (1)	3	0.00
Yakama (1)	1	0.00
Yaqui (11)	28	0.02
Yuman (4)	4	0.00
All other tribes (116)	186	0.11
American Indian tribes, not spec.	123	0.07
Arab:	749	0.45
Arab/Arabic	296	0.18
Egyptian	74	0.04
Iraqi	3	0.00
Jordanian	57	0.03
Lebanese	146	0.09
Moroccan	13	0.01
Palestinian	47	0.03
Syrian	44	0.03
Other Arab	69	0.04
Armenian	289	0.17
Asian:	54,134	32.77
Bangladeshi (8)	12	0.01
Cambodian (469)	546	0.33
Chinese, ex. Taiwanese (2,129)	2,827	1.71
Filipino (2,767)	3,349	2.03
Hmong (164)	188	0.11
Indian (793)	965	0.58
Indonesian (124)	181	0.11
Japanese (1,084)	1,447	0.88
Korean (6,240)	6,439	3.90
Laotian (321)	372	0.23
Malaysian (4)	13	0.01
Pakistani (265)	348	0.21
Sri Lankan (35)	40	0.02
Taiwanese (87)	105	0.06
Thai (143)	170	0.10
Vietnamese (35,406)	36,532	22.11
Other Asian, specified (29)	45	0.03
Other Asian, not specified (238)	555	0.34
Australian	65	0.04
Austrian	186	0.11
Basque	7	0.00
Belgian	110	0.07
Brazilian	77	0.05
British	311	0.19
Bulgarian	27	0.02
Canadian	395	0.24
Carpatho Rusyn	6	0.00
Celtic	20	0.01
Croatian	69	0.04
Czech	335	0.20
Czechoslovakian	195	0.12
Danish	631	0.38
Dutch	1,586	0.96
Eastern European	45	0.03
English	9,159	5.53
Estonian	30	0.02
European	994	0.60
Finnish	89	0.05
French, except Basque	2,647	1.60
French Canadian	719	0.43
German	12,105	7.30
German Russian	8	0.00
Greek	403	0.24
Guyanese	7	0.00
Hawaii Native/Pacific Islander:	1,671	1.01
Melanesian:	1	0.00
Other Melanesian	1	0.00
Micronesian: (156)	231	0.14
Guamanian/Chamorro (150)	222	0.13
Other Micronesian (6)	9	0.01
Polynesian: (850)	1,221	0.74
Native Hawaiian (135)	350	0.21
Samoan (680)	810	0.49
Tongan (28)	39	0.02
Other Polynesian (7)	22	0.01
Other Pac. Isl., not spec. (58)	218	0.13
Hispanic or Latino:	53,608	32.45
Central American:	2,014	1.22
Costa Rican	69	0.04
Guatemalan	488	0.30
Honduran	124	0.08
Nicaraguan	82	0.05
Panamanian	30	0.02
Salvadoran	1,011	0.61
Other Central American	210	0.13
Cuban	360	0.22
Dominican Republic	39	0.02
Mexican	43,576	26.38
Puerto Rican	578	0.35
South American:	989	0.60
Argentinean	112	0.07
Bolivian	59	0.04
Chilean	56	0.03
Colombian	226	0.14
Ecuadorian	65	0.04
Paraguayan	1	0.00
Peruvian	362	0.22
Uruguayan	10	0.01
Venezuelan	20	0.01
Other South American	78	0.05
Other Hispanic or Latino	6,052	3.66
Hungarian	307	0.19
Icelander	16	0.01
Iranian	198	0.12
Irish	8,907	5.38
Israeli	92	0.06
Italian	4,226	2.55
Latvian	54	0.03
Lithuanian	190	0.11
Luxemburger	5	0.00
Maltese	15	0.01
Northern European	47	0.03
Norwegian	1,377	0.83
Pennsylvania German	20	0.01
Polish	1,716	1.04
Portuguese	291	0.18
Romanian	377	0.23
Russian	548	0.33
Scandinavian	260	0.16
Scotch-Irish	1,326	0.80
Scottish	1,901	1.15
Serbian	49	0.03
Slavic	40	0.02
Slovak	109	0.07
Slovene	15	0.01
Swedish	1,465	0.88
Swiss	211	0.13
Turkish	59	0.04
Ukrainian	112	0.07
United States or American	5,176	3.12
Welsh	700	0.42
West Indian, excl. Hispanic:	217	0.13
Belizean	28	0.02
Dutch West Indian	17	0.01
Haitian	12	0.01
Jamaican	51	0.03
Trinidadian and Tobagonian	57	0.03
West Indian	52	0.03
White:	83,127	50.32
Not Hispanic (53,735)	56,501	34.20
Hispanic (23,708)	26,626	16.12
Yugoslavian	109	0.07

Gardena

Place Type: City
County: Los Angeles
Population: 57,746

Ancestry/Race	Number	%
Afghan	44	0.08
African American/Black:	15,684	27.16
Not Hispanic (14,701)	15,207	26.33
Hispanic (309)	477	0.83
African, sub-Saharan:	961	1.66
African	591	1.02
Cape Verdean	9	0.02
Ethiopian	22	0.04
Nigerian	327	0.57
Other sub-Saharan African	12	0.02
Alaska Native tribes, specified:	1	0.00
Tlingit-Haida	1	0.00
Am. Ind. or Alaska Nat., not spec.	299	0.52
Alsatian	6	0.01
American Indian tribes, specified:	401	0.69
Apache (11)	24	0.04
Blackfeet (3)	30	0.05
Cherokee (8)	93	0.16
Cheyenne (1)	1	0.00
Chickasaw (2)	3	0.01
Chippewa (4)	7	0.01
Choctaw (7)	24	0.04
Comanche	5	0.01
Cree	2	0.00
Creek	2	0.00
Delaware (1)	1	0.00
Iroquois	1	0.00
Latin American Indians (74)	87	0.15
Navajo (17)	20	0.03
Paiute (3)	5	0.01
Potawatomi (3)	8	0.01
Pueblo (19)	27	0.05
Seminole	2	0.00
Shoshone (1)	2	0.00
Sioux (4)	12	0.02
Tohono O'Odham (3)	3	0.01
Yaqui (1)	4	0.01
Yuman (1)	1	0.00
All other tribes (23)	37	0.06
American Indian tribes, not spec.	40	0.07

Notes: 1. Figures in the "Number" column do not add up to the total population due to: a) Ancestry/Race overlap — e.g. persons can report being both White and Irish, b) persons of Hispanic origin can report being any race, c) persons reporting two ancestries are counted in both categories. 2. Numbers in parentheses indicate the number of persons reporting this ancestry/race alone, not in combination with any other ancestry/race. 3. Refer to the Explanation of Data in the front of the book for more detailed information.

Arab:	175	0.30
Arab/Arabic	33	0.06
Egyptian	58	0.10
Lebanese	84	0.15
Armenian	144	0.25
Asian:	17,122	29.65
Bangladeshi (1)	1	0.00
Cambodian (67)	81	0.14
Chinese, ex. Taiwanese (883)	1,265	2.19
Filipino (1,916)	2,320	4.02
Hmong (1)	1	0.00
Indian (192)	260	0.45
Indonesian (44)	57	0.10
Japanese (6,712)	7,445	12.89
Korean (3,588)	3,748	6.49
Laotian (4)	4	0.01
Malaysian (2)	10	0.02
Pakistani (24)	33	0.06
Sri Lankan (34)	38	0.07
Taiwanese (58)	71	0.12
Thai (124)	146	0.25
Vietnamese (1,401)	1,469	2.54
Other Asian, specified (25)	41	0.07
Other Asian, not specified (51)	132	0.23
Austrian	43	0.07
Basque	5	0.01
Brazilian	29	0.05
British	50	0.09
Canadian	72	0.12
Croatian	11	0.02
Czech	92	0.16
Czechoslovakian	14	0.02
Danish	152	0.26
Dutch	257	0.44
English	940	1.63
Estonian	19	0.03
European	175	0.30
Finnish	17	0.03
French, except Basque	528	0.91
French Canadian	113	0.20
German	1,617	2.80
Greek	46	0.08
Guyanese	6	0.01
Hawaii Native/Pacific Islander:	791	1.37
Melanesian: (11)	14	0.02
Fijian (11)	14	0.02
Micronesian: (24)	45	0.08
Guamanian/Chamorro (21)	40	0.07
Other Micronesian (3)	5	0.01
Polynesian: (358)	658	1.14
Native Hawaiian (143)	358	0.62
Samoan (209)	277	0.48
Tongan (3)	11	0.02
Other Polynesian (3)	12	0.02
Other Pac. Isl., specified	1	0.00
Other Pac. Isl., not spec. (10)	73	0.13
Hispanic or Latino:	18,372	31.82
Central American:	1,330	2.30
Costa Rican	57	0.10
Guatemalan	388	0.67
Honduran	59	0.10
Nicaraguan	107	0.19
Panamanian	27	0.05
Salvadoran	565	0.98
Other Central American	127	0.22
Cuban	196	0.34
Dominican Republic	21	0.04
Mexican	13,133	22.74
Puerto Rican	401	0.69
South American:	458	0.79
Argentinean	40	0.07
Bolivian	4	0.01
Chilean	22	0.04
Colombian	53	0.09
Ecuadorian	101	0.17
Peruvian	189	0.33
Uruguayan	3	0.01
Venezuelan	13	0.02
Other South American	33	0.06
Other Hispanic or Latino	2,833	4.91
Hungarian	141	0.24
Iranian	32	0.06
Irish	1,116	1.93
Italian	627	1.08
Northern European	3	0.01
Norwegian	188	0.33
Pennsylvania German	13	0.02
Polish	172	0.30
Portuguese	184	0.32
Romanian	9	0.02
Russian	97	0.17
Scandinavian	14	0.02
Scotch-Irish	190	0.33
Scottish	149	0.26
Slavic	15	0.03
Slovak	5	0.01
Slovene	7	0.01
Swedish	322	0.56
Swiss	60	0.10
Turkish	15	0.03
Ukrainian	15	0.03
United States or American	769	1.33
Welsh	99	0.17
West Indian, excl. Hispanic:	453	0.78
Barbadian	9	0.02
Belizean	276	0.48
British West Indian	11	0.02
Haitian	8	0.01
Jamaican	110	0.19
Trinidadian and Tobagonian	15	0.03
West Indian	24	0.04
White:	15,893	27.52
Not Hispanic (7,064)	8,125	14.07
Hispanic (6,691)	7,768	13.45
Yugoslavian	15	0.03

Gilroy

Place Type: City
County: Santa Clara
Population: 41,464

Ancestry/Race	Number	%
African American/Black:	942	2.27
Not Hispanic (615)	742	1.79
Hispanic (130)	200	0.48
African, sub-Saharan:	147	0.35
African	44	0.11
Ethiopian	103	0.25
Alaska Native tribes, specified:	7	0.02
Alaska Athabascan (1)	1	0.00
Eskimo	5	0.01
Tlingit-Haida	1	0.00
Alaska Native tribes, not specified	0	0.00
Am. Ind. or Alaska Nat., not spec.	370	0.89
American Indian tribes, specified:	591	1.43
Apache (37)	71	0.17
Blackfeet (6)	16	0.04
Cherokee (32)	86	0.21
Cheyenne	3	0.01
Chickasaw	4	0.01
Chippewa (9)	13	0.03
Choctaw (1)	4	0.01
Colville	1	0.00
Comanche (3)	11	0.03
Cree	1	0.00
Creek (1)	5	0.01
Iroquois	1	0.00
Latin American Indians (153)	193	0.47
Navajo (16)	29	0.07
Paiute (1)	1	0.00
Pima (1)	2	0.00
Pueblo (16)	18	0.04
Puget Sound Salish (2)	3	0.01
Seminole	3	0.01
Shoshone (11)	12	0.03
Sioux (11)	17	0.04
Tohono O'Odham (1)	1	0.00
Yaqui (4)	12	0.03
Yuman (5)	5	0.01
All other tribes (42)	79	0.19
American Indian tribes, not spec.	67	0.16
Arab:	104	0.25
Arab/Arabic	23	0.06
Jordanian	7	0.02
Lebanese	17	0.04
Moroccan	8	0.02
Syrian	8	0.02
Other Arab	41	0.10
Armenian	50	0.12
Asian:	2,461	5.94
Cambodian (20)	20	0.05
Chinese, ex. Taiwanese (256)	352	0.85
Filipino (671)	956	2.31
Indian (129)	158	0.38
Indonesian (6)	9	0.02
Japanese (328)	509	1.23
Korean (86)	108	0.26
Laotian (7)	7	0.02
Malaysian	1	0.00
Pakistani (6)	12	0.03
Sri Lankan	10	0.02
Taiwanese (4)	4	0.01
Thai (6)	14	0.03
Vietnamese (219)	236	0.57
Other Asian, specified (2)	10	0.02
Other Asian, not specified (24)	55	0.13
Assyrian/Chaldean/Syriac	7	0.02
Australian	4	0.01
Austrian	49	0.12
Basque	40	0.10
Belgian	18	0.04
British	140	0.34
Canadian	112	0.27
Celtic	33	0.08
Croatian	20	0.05
Czech	80	0.19
Czechoslovakian	42	0.10
Danish	280	0.67
Dutch	483	1.16
English	2,559	6.15
European	346	0.83
Finnish	27	0.06
French, except Basque	836	2.01
French Canadian	186	0.45
German	3,614	8.69
Greek	60	0.14
Hawaii Native/Pacific Islander:	236	0.57
Micronesian: (37)	65	0.16
Guamanian/Chamorro (37)	65	0.16
Polynesian: (60)	129	0.31
Native Hawaiian (39)	105	0.25
Samoan (13)	16	0.04
Tongan (7)	7	0.02
Other Polynesian (1)	1	0.00
Other Pac. Isl., specified	4	0.01
Other Pac. Isl., not spec. (8)	38	0.09
Hispanic or Latino:	22,298	53.78
Central American:	240	0.58
Costa Rican	8	0.02
Guatemalan	76	0.18
Honduran	26	0.06
Nicaraguan	16	0.04
Panamanian	5	0.01
Salvadoran	95	0.23
Other Central American	14	0.03
Cuban	32	0.08
Dominican Republic	10	0.02
Mexican	19,226	46.37
Puerto Rican	175	0.42
South American:	106	0.26
Argentinean	9	0.02
Bolivian	4	0.01
Chilean	5	0.01
Colombian	28	0.07
Ecuadorian	9	0.02
Peruvian	37	0.09
Venezuelan	2	0.00
Other South American	12	0.03
Other Hispanic or Latino	2,509	6.05

Notes: 1. Figures in the "Number" column do not add up to the total population due to: a) Ancestry/Race overlap — e.g. persons can report being both White and Irish, b) persons of Hispanic origin can report being any race, c) persons reporting two ancestries are counted in both categories. 2. Numbers in parentheses indicate the number of persons reporting this ancestry/race alone, not in combination with any other ancestry/race. 3. Refer to the Explanation of Data in the front of the book for more detailed information.

Ancestry/Race	Number	%
Hungarian	28	0.07
Iranian	9	0.02
Irish	2,947	7.09
Italian	2,840	6.83
Lithuanian	20	0.05
Luxemburger	10	0.02
Northern European	49	0.12
Norwegian	421	1.01
Polish	594	1.43
Portuguese	1,080	2.60
Russian	164	0.39
Scandinavian	51	0.12
Scotch-Irish	395	0.95
Scottish	480	1.15
Slavic	15	0.04
Slovak	7	0.02
Swedish	539	1.30
Swiss	165	0.40
Ukrainian	81	0.19
United States or American	903	2.17
Welsh	163	0.39
West Indian, excl. Hispanic:	35	0.08
Belizean	10	0.02
Dutch West Indian	7	0.02
Jamaican	18	0.04
White:	26,364	63.58
Not Hispanic (15,767)	16,469	39.72
Hispanic (8,659)	9,895	23.86
Yugoslavian	114	0.27

Glen Avon

Place Type: Census Designated Place
County: Riverside
Population: 14,853

Ancestry/Race	Number	%
African American/Black:	629	4.23
Not Hispanic (542)	583	3.93
Hispanic (24)	46	0.31
African, sub-Saharan:	15	0.10
African	6	0.04
Sudanese	9	0.06
Alaska Native tribes, specified:	1	0.01
Tlingit-Haida (1)	1	0.01
Alaska Native tribes, not specified	2	0.01
Am. Ind. or Alaska Nat., not spec.	133	0.90
American Indian tribes, specified:	192	1.29
Apache (12)	21	0.14
Blackfeet (6)	9	0.06
Cherokee (14)	41	0.28
Cheyenne (1)	1	0.01
Chickasaw (5)	6	0.04
Chippewa (1)	2	0.01
Choctaw (7)	11	0.07
Comanche (10)	10	0.07
Creek (1)	3	0.02
Iroquois	5	0.03
Latin American Indians (27)	29	0.20
Navajo (9)	17	0.11
Osage (1)	1	0.01
Paiute	2	0.01
Pima	2	0.01
Potawatomi (4)	5	0.03
Pueblo (5)	11	0.07
Seminole	1	0.01
Shoshone (2)	2	0.01
Sioux	3	0.02
Tohono O'Odham (1)	1	0.01
Yuman	1	0.01
All other tribes (5)	8	0.05
American Indian tribes, not spec.	26	0.18
Arab:	35	0.24
Arab/Arabic	15	0.10
Egyptian	20	0.13
Armenian	16	0.11
Asian:	465	3.13
Cambodian (16)	16	0.11
Chinese, ex. Taiwanese (23)	45	0.30
Filipino (104)	138	0.93
Indian (26)	36	0.24
Indonesian (8)	15	0.10
Japanese (52)	77	0.52
Korean (45)	51	0.34
Laotian (9)	10	0.07
Taiwanese (5)	7	0.05
Thai (5)	5	0.03
Vietnamese (33)	38	0.26
Other Asian, not specified (3)	27	0.18
Australian	15	0.10
Austrian	75	0.51
British	6	0.04
Canadian	50	0.34
Czech	8	0.05
Danish	32	0.22
Dutch	145	0.98
English	911	6.14
European	22	0.15
Finnish	7	0.05
French, except Basque	329	2.22
French Canadian	81	0.55
German	1,267	8.54
Greek	19	0.13
Hawaii Native/Pacific Islander:	63	0.42
Melanesian: (1)	1	0.01
Fijian (1)	1	0.01
Micronesian: (4)	8	0.05
Guamanian/Chamorro (4)	8	0.05
Polynesian: (22)	45	0.30
Native Hawaiian (6)	23	0.15
Samoan (12)	16	0.11
Tongan (3)	5	0.03
Other Polynesian (1)	1	0.01
Other Pac. Isl., not spec. (2)	9	0.06
Hispanic or Latino:	7,006	47.17
Central American:	139	0.94
Costa Rican	4	0.03
Guatemalan	24	0.16
Honduran	12	0.08
Nicaraguan	22	0.15
Panamanian	2	0.01
Salvadoran	55	0.37
Other Central American	20	0.13
Cuban	39	0.26
Dominican Republic	2	0.01
Mexican	5,785	38.95
Puerto Rican	87	0.59
South American:	63	0.42
Argentinean	14	0.09
Bolivian	8	0.05
Colombian	17	0.11
Ecuadorian	7	0.05
Peruvian	12	0.08
Other South American	5	0.03
Other Hispanic or Latino	891	6.00
Hungarian	22	0.15
Iranian	15	0.10
Irish	939	6.33
Italian	275	1.85
Latvian	10	0.07
Lithuanian	8	0.05
Norwegian	207	1.39
Polish	105	0.71
Portuguese	58	0.39
Romanian	55	0.37
Russian	47	0.32
Scandinavian	30	0.20
Scotch-Irish	132	0.89
Scottish	125	0.84
Slavic	7	0.05
Slovak	10	0.07
Slovene	16	0.11
Swedish	75	0.51
Swiss	46	0.31
Ukrainian	8	0.05
United States or American	961	6.47
Welsh	57	0.38
White:	9,588	64.55
Not Hispanic (6,592)	6,816	45.89
Hispanic (2,437)	2,772	18.66

Glendale

Place Type: City
County: Los Angeles
Population: 194,973

Ancestry/Race	Number	%
Afghan	138	0.07
African American/Black:	3,100	1.59
Not Hispanic (2,230)	2,687	1.38
Hispanic (238)	413	0.21
African, sub-Saharan:	199	0.10
African	110	0.06
Ethiopian	18	0.01
Kenyan	10	0.01
Nigerian	38	0.02
South African	23	0.01
Alaska Native tribes, specified:	9	0.00
Alaska Athabascan (1)	3	0.00
Eskimo (2)	2	0.00
Tlingit-Haida (2)	4	0.00
Alaska Native tribes, not specified	1	0.00
Am. Ind. or Alaska Nat., not spec.	491	0.25
Albanian	4	0.00
American Indian tribes, specified:	773	0.40
Apache (17)	38	0.02
Blackfeet (8)	39	0.02
Cherokee (43)	190	0.10
Cheyenne (1)	1	0.00
Chickasaw (2)	10	0.01
Chippewa (10)	17	0.01
Choctaw (5)	26	0.01
Comanche (8)	9	0.00
Cree	1	0.00
Creek (5)	12	0.01
Crow	1	0.00
Delaware (1)	1	0.00
Iroquois (14)	24	0.01
Latin American Indians (104)	172	0.09
Lumbee (1)	1	0.00
Navajo (29)	33	0.02
Osage (2)	5	0.00
Ottawa (1)	2	0.00
Paiute (1)	2	0.00
Potawatomi (1)	1	0.00
Pueblo (18)	34	0.02
Puget Sound Salish	3	0.00
Seminole (6)	9	0.00
Shoshone (3)	7	0.00
Sioux (18)	33	0.02
Tohono O'Odham (13)	15	0.01
Ute	5	0.00
Yakama	4	0.00
Yaqui (10)	16	0.01
Yuman (1)	2	0.00
All other tribes (34)	60	0.03
American Indian tribes, not spec.	52	0.03
Arab:	4,054	2.08
Arab/Arabic	294	0.15
Egyptian	467	0.24
Iraqi	453	0.23
Jordanian	96	0.05
Lebanese	1,849	0.95
Moroccan	55	0.03
Palestinian	70	0.04
Syrian	598	0.31
Other Arab	172	0.09
Armenian	53,840	27.60
Asian:	34,903	17.90
Bangladeshi (66)	118	0.06
Cambodian (13)	19	0.01
Chinese, ex. Taiwanese (2,520)	3,114	1.60
Filipino (11,083)	12,099	6.21
Hmong (1)	1	0.00
Indian (1,277)	1,591	0.82
Indonesian (93)	139	0.07
Japanese (1,465)	1,920	0.98
Korean (12,504)	12,800	6.57
Laotian (11)	17	0.01
Malaysian (9)	21	0.01

Notes: 1. Figures in the "Number" column do not add up to the total population due to: a) Ancestry/Race overlap — e.g. persons can report being both White and Irish, b) persons of Hispanic origin can report being any race, c) persons reporting two ancestries are counted in both categories. 2. Numbers in parentheses indicate the number of persons reporting this ancestry/race alone, not in combination with any other ancestry/race. 3. Refer to the Explanation of Data in the front of the book for more detailed information.

Pakistani (94)	147	0.08
Sri Lankan (42)	50	0.03
Taiwanese (75)	95	0.05
Thai (568)	669	0.34
Vietnamese (887)	993	0.51
Other Asian, specified (29)	39	0.02
Other Asian, not specified (158)	1,071	0.55
Assyrian/Chaldean/Syriac	352	0.18
Australian	158	0.08
Austrian	356	0.18
Basque	30	0.02
Belgian	101	0.05
Brazilian	130	0.07
British	889	0.46
Bulgarian	262	0.13
Canadian	540	0.28
Celtic	27	0.01
Croatian	396	0.20
Czech	326	0.17
Czechoslovakian	175	0.09
Danish	713	0.37
Dutch	1,485	0.76
Eastern European	125	0.06
English	10,141	5.20
Estonian	17	0.01
European	835	0.43
Finnish	231	0.12
French, except Basque	2,849	1.46
French Canadian	381	0.20
German	11,359	5.82
Greek	620	0.32
Guyanese	48	0.02
Hawaii Native/Pacific Islander:	533	0.27
Melanesian: (1)	1	0.00
Fijian (1)	1	0.00
Micronesian: (25)	46	0.02
Guamanian/Chamorro (25)	44	0.02
Other Micronesian	2	0.00
Polynesian: (88)	249	0.13
Native Hawaiian (68)	198	0.10
Samoan (18)	44	0.02
Tongan (1)	1	0.00
Other Polynesian (1)	6	0.00
Other Pac. Isl., specified	1	0.00
Other Pac. Isl., not spec. (48)	236	0.12
Hispanic or Latino:	38,452	19.72
Central American:	5,056	2.59
Costa Rican	140	0.07
Guatemalan	1,142	0.59
Honduran	259	0.13
Nicaraguan	383	0.20
Panamanian	56	0.03
Salvadoran	2,564	1.32
Other Central American	512	0.26
Cuban	1,838	0.94
Dominican Republic	45	0.02
Mexican	20,810	10.67
Puerto Rican	624	0.32
South American:	2,691	1.38
Argentinean	408	0.21
Bolivian	70	0.04
Chilean	165	0.08
Colombian	632	0.32
Ecuadorian	411	0.21
Paraguayan	11	0.01
Peruvian	630	0.32
Uruguayan	25	0.01
Venezuelan	61	0.03
Other South American	278	0.14
Other Hispanic or Latino	7,388	3.79
Hungarian	706	0.36
Icelander	25	0.01
Iranian	5,612	2.88
Irish	9,286	4.76
Israeli	86	0.04
Italian	5,525	2.83
Latvian	43	0.02
Lithuanian	216	0.11
Luxemburger	22	0.01
Macedonian	3	0.00
Maltese	8	0.00
New Zealander	39	0.02
Northern European	142	0.07
Norwegian	1,347	0.69
Pennsylvania German	17	0.01
Polish	1,883	0.97
Portuguese	369	0.19
Romanian	632	0.32
Russian	2,111	1.08
Scandinavian	156	0.08
Scotch-Irish	1,700	0.87
Scottish	2,201	1.13
Serbian	87	0.04
Slavic	90	0.05
Slovak	73	0.04
Slovene	20	0.01
Swedish	1,825	0.94
Swiss	429	0.22
Turkish	182	0.09
Ukrainian	403	0.21
United States or American	3,742	1.92
Welsh	705	0.36
West Indian, excl. Hispanic:	339	0.17
Belizean	92	0.05
Dutch West Indian	19	0.01
Haitian	85	0.04
Jamaican	121	0.06
Trinidadian and Tobagonian	5	0.00
U.S. Virgin Islander	8	0.00
West Indian	9	0.00
White:	142,615	73.15
Not Hispanic (105,597)	121,608	62.37
Hispanic (18,363)	21,007	10.77
Yugoslavian	204	0.10

Glendora

Place Type: City
County: Los Angeles
Population: 49,415

Ancestry/Race	Number	%
African American/Black:	889	1.80
Not Hispanic (704)	820	1.66
Hispanic (36)	69	0.14
African, sub-Saharan:	124	0.25
African	103	0.21
Kenyan	14	0.03
Nigerian	7	0.01
Alaska Native tribes, specified:	3	0.01
Tlingit-Haida (1)	3	0.01
Alaska Native tribes, not specified	1	0.00
Am. Ind. or Alaska Nat., not spec.	162	0.33
American Indian tribes, specified:	452	0.91
Apache (11)	38	0.08
Blackfeet (2)	8	0.02
Cherokee (29)	118	0.24
Cheyenne (4)	5	0.01
Chickasaw	2	0.00
Chippewa (12)	15	0.03
Choctaw (1)	18	0.04
Comanche (5)	9	0.02
Creek (2)	11	0.02
Delaware	1	0.00
Iroquois (9)	14	0.03
Kiowa (4)	4	0.01
Latin American Indians (43)	58	0.12
Lumbee	1	0.00
Navajo (20)	28	0.06
Osage	2	0.00
Ottawa (1)	3	0.01
Paiute (1)	1	0.00
Pima (1)	3	0.01
Potawatomi	2	0.00
Pueblo (4)	14	0.03
Puget Sound Salish (1)	1	0.00
Seminole	3	0.01
Shoshone (1)	1	0.00
Sioux (3)	13	0.03
Tohono O'Odham (9)	12	0.02
Ute	1	0.00
Yakama (2)	2	0.00
Yaqui (8)	14	0.03
Yuman (4)	4	0.01
All other tribes (32)	46	0.09
American Indian tribes, not spec.	26	0.05
Arab:	1,456	2.93
Arab/Arabic	181	0.36
Egyptian	163	0.33
Jordanian	70	0.14
Lebanese	488	0.98
Palestinian	101	0.20
Syrian	442	0.89
Other Arab	11	0.02
Armenian	261	0.52
Asian:	3,791	7.67
Cambodian (1)	8	0.02
Chinese, ex. Taiwanese (656)	813	1.65
Filipino (1,049)	1,247	2.52
Indian (322)	353	0.71
Indonesian (45)	117	0.24
Japanese (340)	497	1.01
Korean (165)	200	0.40
Laotian (2)	2	0.00
Pakistani (10)	21	0.04
Sri Lankan (15)	18	0.04
Taiwanese (115)	144	0.29
Thai (76)	80	0.16
Vietnamese (158)	192	0.39
Other Asian, specified (4)	4	0.01
Other Asian, not specified (23)	95	0.19
Assyrian/Chaldean/Syriac	15	0.03
Australian	6	0.01
Austrian	144	0.29
Basque	19	0.04
Belgian	72	0.14
Brazilian	9	0.02
British	266	0.54
Canadian	150	0.30
Carpatho Rusyn	7	0.01
Croatian	121	0.24
Czech	215	0.43
Czechoslovakian	67	0.13
Danish	632	1.27
Dutch	1,203	2.42
English	6,140	12.35
European	598	1.20
Finnish	98	0.20
French, except Basque	1,753	3.53
French Canadian	468	0.94
German	7,764	15.62
Greek	175	0.35
Guyanese	15	0.03
Hawaii Native/Pacific Islander:	178	0.36
Micronesian: (5)	11	0.02
Guamanian/Chamorro (5)	11	0.02
Polynesian: (24)	82	0.17
Native Hawaiian (16)	55	0.11
Samoan (7)	22	0.04
Tongan (1)	4	0.01
Other Polynesian	1	0.00
Other Pac. Isl., not spec. (8)	85	0.17
Hispanic or Latino:	10,740	21.73
Central American:	355	0.72
Costa Rican	18	0.04
Guatemalan	71	0.14
Honduran	10	0.02
Nicaraguan	80	0.16
Panamanian	9	0.02
Salvadoran	125	0.25
Other Central American	42	0.08
Cuban	199	0.40
Dominican Republic	12	0.02
Mexican	7,871	15.93
Puerto Rican	173	0.35
South American:	375	0.76
Argentinean	100	0.20
Bolivian	21	0.04
Chilean	23	0.05
Colombian	84	0.17

Notes: 1. Figures in the "Number" column do not add up to the total population due to: a) Ancestry/Race overlap — e.g. persons can report being both White and Irish, b) persons of Hispanic origin can report being any race, c) persons reporting two ancestries are counted in both categories. 2. Numbers in parentheses indicate the number of persons reporting this ancestry/race alone, not in combination with any other ancestry/race. 3. Refer to the Explanation of Data in the front of the book for more detailed information.

Ecuadorian	30	0.06
Paraguayan	3	0.01
Peruvian	83	0.17
Venezuelan	8	0.02
Other South American	23	0.05
Other Hispanic or Latino	1,755	3.55
Hungarian	349	0.70
Icelander	12	0.02
Iranian	123	0.25
Irish	5,926	11.92
Israeli	21	0.04
Italian	3,499	7.04
Latvian	55	0.11
Lithuanian	51	0.10
Luxemburger	11	0.02
Macedonian	7	0.01
Maltese	4	0.01
Northern European	10	0.02
Norwegian	1,088	2.19
Pennsylvania German	14	0.03
Polish	1,071	2.15
Portuguese	133	0.27
Romanian	117	0.24
Russian	307	0.62
Scandinavian	316	0.64
Scotch-Irish	1,018	2.05
Scottish	1,399	2.81
Slavic	10	0.02
Slovak	43	0.09
Slovene	26	0.05
Swedish	1,095	2.20
Swiss	129	0.26
Turkish	44	0.09
Ukrainian	124	0.25
United States or American	1,855	3.73
Welsh	348	0.70
West Indian, excl. Hispanic:	46	0.09
Dutch West Indian	2	0.00
Jamaican	39	0.08
Trinidadian and Tobagonian	5	0.01
White:	41,473	83.93
Not Hispanic (33,564)	34,569	69.96
Hispanic (6,117)	6,904	13.97
Yugoslavian	81	0.16

Goleta

Place Type: Census Designated Place
County: Santa Barbara
Population: 55,204

Ancestry/Race	Number	%
Acadian/Cajun	5	0.01
Afghan	10	0.02
African American/Black:	951	1.72
Not Hispanic (630)	834	1.51
Hispanic (73)	117	0.21
African, sub-Saharan:	118	0.21
African	61	0.11
Ethiopian	11	0.02
South African	29	0.05
Other sub-Saharan African	17	0.03
Alaska Native tribes, specified:	9	0.02
Alaska Athabascan	4	0.01
Eskimo (1)	2	0.00
Tlingit-Haida (3)	3	0.01
Alaska Native tribes, not specified	1	0.00
Am. Ind. or Alaska Nat., not spec.	242	0.44
Alsatian	6	0.01
American Indian tribes, specified:	617	1.12
Apache (14)	39	0.07
Blackfeet (3)	10	0.02
Cherokee (21)	96	0.17
Cheyenne (1)	11	0.02
Chickasaw	5	0.01
Chippewa (4)	11	0.02
Choctaw (8)	21	0.04
Comanche (7)	12	0.02
Creek (6)	10	0.02
Crow	2	0.00
Delaware (1)	2	0.00
Iroquois (4)	12	0.02
Kiowa	1	0.00
Latin American Indians (48)	66	0.12
Menominee	1	0.00
Navajo (9)	12	0.02
Osage	3	0.01
Paiute (3)	4	0.01
Pima (4)	6	0.01
Potawatomi (1)	2	0.00
Pueblo (5)	6	0.01
Puget Sound Salish	1	0.00
Seminole (1)	6	0.01
Shoshone	1	0.00
Sioux (6)	17	0.03
Tohono O'Odham	1	0.00
Ute	1	0.00
Yaqui (6)	9	0.02
All other tribes (149)	249	0.45
American Indian tribes, not spec.	36	0.07
Arab:	192	0.35
Arab/Arabic	34	0.06
Egyptian	11	0.02
Jordanian	6	0.01
Lebanese	74	0.13
Moroccan	13	0.02
Palestinian	8	0.01
Syrian	46	0.08
Armenian	186	0.34
Asian:	4,296	7.78
Bangladeshi	3	0.01
Cambodian (27)	31	0.06
Chinese, ex. Taiwanese (944)	1,150	2.08
Filipino (605)	755	1.37
Hmong (100)	104	0.19
Indian (298)	356	0.64
Indonesian (17)	34	0.06
Japanese (449)	629	1.14
Korean (368)	409	0.74
Laotian (82)	97	0.18
Malaysian (6)	7	0.01
Pakistani (4)	9	0.02
Sri Lankan (15)	20	0.04
Taiwanese (50)	72	0.13
Thai (47)	67	0.12
Vietnamese (412)	462	0.84
Other Asian, specified (7)	12	0.02
Other Asian, not specified (31)	79	0.14
Assyrian/Chaldean/Syriac	9	0.02
Australian	51	0.09
Austrian	242	0.44
Basque	79	0.14
Belgian	79	0.14
Brazilian	33	0.06
British	336	0.61
Bulgarian	5	0.01
Canadian	266	0.48
Carpatho Rusyn	7	0.01
Celtic	16	0.03
Croatian	50	0.09
Czech	303	0.55
Czechoslovakian	128	0.23
Danish	814	1.47
Dutch	1,142	2.06
Eastern European	100	0.18
English	7,480	13.51
Estonian	13	0.02
European	1,024	1.85
Finnish	108	0.20
French, except Basque	2,098	3.79
French Canadian	410	0.74
German	8,446	15.25
Greek	240	0.43
Hawaii Native/Pacific Islander:	164	0.30
Melanesian: (2)	2	0.00
Fijian (2)	2	0.00
Micronesian: (6)	17	0.03
Guamanian/Chamorro (5)	16	0.03
Other Micronesian (1)	1	0.00
Polynesian: (42)	100	0.18
Native Hawaiian (36)	84	0.15
Samoan (6)	15	0.03
Other Polynesian	1	0.00
Other Pac. Isl., not spec. (8)	45	0.08
Hispanic or Latino:	12,326	22.33
Central American:	266	0.48
Costa Rican	5	0.01
Guatemalan	141	0.26
Honduran	22	0.04
Nicaraguan	6	0.01
Panamanian	14	0.03
Salvadoran	47	0.09
Other Central American	31	0.06
Cuban	54	0.10
Dominican Republic	3	0.01
Mexican	10,351	18.75
Puerto Rican	118	0.21
South American:	193	0.35
Argentinean	26	0.05
Bolivian	4	0.01
Chilean	40	0.07
Colombian	40	0.07
Ecuadorian	7	0.01
Paraguayan	2	0.00
Peruvian	44	0.08
Uruguayan	1	0.00
Venezuelan	12	0.02
Other South American	17	0.03
Other Hispanic or Latino	1,341	2.43
Hungarian	324	0.59
Iranian	295	0.53
Irish	5,778	10.44
Israeli	98	0.18
Italian	3,494	6.31
Latvian	18	0.03
Lithuanian	165	0.30
Luxemburger	17	0.03
Macedonian	14	0.03
New Zealander	6	0.01
Northern European	128	0.23
Norwegian	1,374	2.48
Pennsylvania German	24	0.04
Polish	1,143	2.06
Portuguese	310	0.56
Romanian	56	0.10
Russian	995	1.80
Scandinavian	235	0.42
Scotch-Irish	1,035	1.87
Scottish	1,573	2.84
Serbian	58	0.10
Slavic	64	0.12
Slovak	39	0.07
Slovene	12	0.02
Swedish	1,330	2.40
Swiss	485	0.88
Turkish	76	0.14
Ukrainian	289	0.52
United States or American	1,813	3.27
Welsh	527	0.95
West Indian, excl. Hispanic:	45	0.08
Jamaican	32	0.06
West Indian	13	0.02
White:	45,133	81.76
Not Hispanic (37,230)	38,251	69.29
Hispanic (6,167)	6,882	12.47
Yugoslavian	145	0.26

Grand Terrace

Place Type: City
County: San Bernardino
Population: 11,626

Ancestry/Race	Number	%
African American/Black:	643	5.53
Not Hispanic (529)	614	5.28
Hispanic (8)	29	0.25
African, sub-Saharan:	78	0.66
African	41	0.35
Nigerian	37	0.31

Notes: 1. Figures in the "Number" column do not add up to the total population due to: a) Ancestry/Race overlap — e.g. persons can report being both White and Irish, b) persons of Hispanic origin can report being any race, c) persons reporting two ancestries are counted in both categories. 2. Numbers in parentheses indicate the number of persons reporting this ancestry/race alone, not in combination with any other ancestry/race. 3. Refer to the Explanation of Data in the front of the book for more detailed information.

Alaska Native tribes, specified:	8	0.07
Aleut (1)	1	0.01
Eskimo	3	0.03
All other tribes	4	0.03
Am. Ind. or Alaska Nat., not spec.	54	0.46
American Indian tribes, specified:	124	1.07
Apache (1)	8	0.07
Blackfeet (1)	1	0.01
Cherokee (16)	46	0.40
Chippewa	2	0.02
Choctaw	3	0.03
Comanche (2)	2	0.02
Creek (1)	2	0.02
Iroquois	1	0.01
Latin American Indians (4)	5	0.04
Navajo (6)	7	0.06
Osage (4)	4	0.03
Pima (5)	5	0.04
Pueblo	1	0.01
Sioux (5)	11	0.09
Ute	2	0.02
Yaqui (3)	4	0.03
All other tribes (12)	20	0.17
American Indian tribes, not spec.	1	0.01
Arab:	170	1.44
Egyptian	40	0.34
Lebanese	66	0.56
Palestinian	64	0.54
Armenian	15	0.13
Asian:	830	7.14
Bangladeshi (1)	1	0.01
Cambodian (2)	3	0.03
Chinese, ex. Taiwanese (74)	115	0.99
Filipino (183)	237	2.04
Indian (90)	102	0.88
Indonesian (52)	63	0.54
Japanese (51)	94	0.81
Korean (105)	118	1.01
Malaysian (3)	3	0.03
Pakistani (3)	9	0.08
Taiwanese	2	0.02
Thai (30)	33	0.28
Vietnamese (19)	23	0.20
Other Asian, specified (5)	6	0.05
Other Asian, not specified (13)	21	0.18
Austrian	34	0.29
Basque	11	0.09
Belgian	13	0.11
British	69	0.59
Canadian	12	0.10
Czech	16	0.14
Czechoslovakian	23	0.20
Danish	134	1.14
Dutch	177	1.50
English	1,268	10.75
European	102	0.86
Finnish	16	0.14
French, except Basque	551	4.67
French Canadian	26	0.22
German	1,566	13.28
Greek	87	0.74
Guyanese	56	0.47
Hawaii Native/Pacific Islander:	64	0.55
Micronesian: (8)	12	0.10
Guamanian/Chamorro (8)	9	0.08
Other Micronesian	3	0.03
Polynesian: (20)	34	0.29
Native Hawaiian (3)	16	0.14
Samoan (14)	15	0.13
Other Polynesian (3)	3	0.03
Other Pac. Isl., not spec. (8)	18	0.15
Hispanic or Latino:	2,954	25.41
Central American:	67	0.58
Costa Rican	4	0.03
Guatemalan	9	0.08
Honduran	2	0.02
Nicaraguan	20	0.17
Panamanian	1	0.01
Salvadoran	19	0.16
Other Central American	12	0.10
Cuban	18	0.15
Mexican	2,318	19.94
Puerto Rican	58	0.50
South American:	55	0.47
Argentinean	13	0.11
Chilean	3	0.03
Colombian	21	0.18
Ecuadorian	2	0.02
Peruvian	10	0.09
Other South American	6	0.05
Other Hispanic or Latino	438	3.77
Hungarian	77	0.65
Iranian	59	0.50
Irish	1,225	10.39
Italian	558	4.73
Lithuanian	27	0.23
Northern European	7	0.06
Norwegian	189	1.60
Pennsylvania German	6	0.05
Polish	284	2.41
Portuguese	32	0.27
Romanian	87	0.74
Russian	55	0.47
Scandinavian	19	0.16
Scotch-Irish	101	0.86
Scottish	334	2.83
Serbian	24	0.20
Slovak	22	0.19
Swedish	244	2.07
Ukrainian	8	0.07
United States or American	567	4.81
Welsh	62	0.53
West Indian, excl. Hispanic:	103	0.87
Barbadian	6	0.05
Haitian	26	0.22
Jamaican	42	0.36
Trinidadian and Tobagonian	8	0.07
West Indian	21	0.18
White:	9,095	78.23
Not Hispanic (7,071)	7,349	63.21
Hispanic (1,504)	1,746	15.02
Yugoslavian	10	0.08

Granite Bay

Place Type: Census Designated Place
County: Placer
Population: 19,388

Ancestry/Race	Number	%
African American/Black:	179	0.92
Not Hispanic (125)	167	0.86
Hispanic (6)	12	0.06
African, sub-Saharan:	19	0.10
Cape Verdean	10	0.05
Nigerian	9	0.05
Alaska Native tribes, specified:	4	0.02
Aleut (1)	1	0.01
Tlingit-Haida (3)	3	0.02
Am. Ind. or Alaska Nat., not spec.	59	0.30
American Indian tribes, specified:	192	0.99
Apache (8)	12	0.06
Blackfeet (4)	10	0.05
Cherokee (22)	73	0.38
Cheyenne	2	0.01
Chickasaw (2)	5	0.03
Chippewa (2)	4	0.02
Choctaw (8)	23	0.12
Creek (1)	2	0.01
Crow	1	0.01
Iroquois (3)	7	0.04
Latin American Indians (3)	3	0.02
Navajo (1)	2	0.01
Osage	1	0.01
Potawatomi (3)	3	0.02
Pueblo (4)	4	0.02
Shoshone	1	0.01
Sioux (6)	9	0.05
Yaqui (1)	1	0.01
All other tribes (17)	29	0.15
American Indian tribes, not spec.	4	0.02
Arab:	50	0.26
Egyptian	11	0.06
Lebanese	6	0.03
Syrian	25	0.13
Other Arab	8	0.04
Armenian	76	0.39
Asian:	923	4.76
Chinese, ex. Taiwanese (181)	239	1.23
Filipino (83)	131	0.68
Indian (134)	153	0.79
Indonesian (2)	14	0.07
Japanese (153)	229	1.18
Korean (53)	70	0.36
Pakistani (15)	15	0.08
Sri Lankan (2)	2	0.01
Thai (6)	7	0.04
Vietnamese (24)	27	0.14
Other Asian, specified	6	0.03
Other Asian, not specified (4)	30	0.15
Assyrian/Chaldean/Syriac	6	0.03
Austrian	82	0.42
Belgian	40	0.21
Brazilian	8	0.04
British	121	0.62
Canadian	93	0.48
Croatian	19	0.10
Czech	97	0.50
Czechoslovakian	36	0.19
Danish	244	1.26
Dutch	334	1.72
English	3,428	17.63
European	223	1.15
Finnish	78	0.40
French, except Basque	885	4.55
French Canadian	82	0.42
German	4,202	21.61
Greek	118	0.61
Hawaii Native/Pacific Islander:	61	0.31
Micronesian: (3)	6	0.03
Guamanian/Chamorro (3)	6	0.03
Polynesian: (6)	29	0.15
Native Hawaiian (3)	22	0.11
Samoan (2)	6	0.03
Other Polynesian (1)	1	0.01
Other Pac. Isl., specified	2	0.01
Other Pac. Isl., not spec. (7)	24	0.12
Hispanic or Latino:	910	4.69
Central American:	18	0.09
Costa Rican	1	0.01
Guatemalan	4	0.02
Nicaraguan	2	0.01
Panamanian	3	0.02
Salvadoran	7	0.04
Other Central American	1	0.01
Cuban	26	0.13
Mexican	583	3.01
Puerto Rican	55	0.28
South American:	20	0.10
Argentinean	7	0.04
Chilean	3	0.02
Colombian	4	0.02
Paraguayan	1	0.01
Peruvian	3	0.02
Other South American	2	0.01
Other Hispanic or Latino	208	1.07
Hungarian	191	0.98
Icelander	7	0.04
Iranian	115	0.59
Irish	3,136	16.13
Israeli	38	0.20
Italian	1,767	9.09
Latvian	10	0.05
Lithuanian	59	0.30
Northern European	54	0.28
Norwegian	689	3.54
Pennsylvania German	6	0.03
Polish	575	2.96
Portuguese	211	1.09
Romanian	142	0.73

Notes: 1. Figures in the "Number" column do not add up to the total population due to: a) Ancestry/Race overlap — e.g. persons can report being both White and Irish, b) persons of Hispanic origin can report being any race, c) persons reporting two ancestries are counted in both categories. 2. Numbers in parentheses indicate the number of persons reporting this ancestry/race alone, not in combination with any other ancestry/race. 3. Refer to the Explanation of Data in the front of the book for more detailed information.

Russian	324	1.67
Scandinavian	65	0.33
Scotch-Irish	364	1.87
Scottish	564	2.90
Serbian	7	0.04
Slavic	25	0.13
Slovene	15	0.08
Swedish	518	2.66
Swiss	172	0.88
Ukrainian	76	0.39
United States or American	1,089	5.60
Welsh	294	1.51
West Indian, excl. Hispanic:	39	0.20
Jamaican	39	0.20
White:	18,196	93.85
Not Hispanic (17,140)	17,521	90.37
Hispanic (580)	675	3.48
Yugoslavian	60	0.31

Grass Valley

Place Type: City
County: Nevada
Population: 10,922

Ancestry/Race	Number	%
African American/Black:	77	0.70
Not Hispanic (29)	67	0.61
Hispanic	10	0.09
African, sub-Saharan:	16	0.14
African	16	0.14
Alaska Native tribes, specified:	2	0.02
Tlingit-Haida (2)	2	0.02
Am. Ind. or Alaska Nat., not spec.	65	0.60
American Indian tribes, specified:	280	2.56
Apache (1)	3	0.03
Blackfeet (2)	10	0.09
Cherokee (25)	99	0.91
Cheyenne (1)	2	0.02
Chickasaw (1)	4	0.04
Chippewa (1)	1	0.01
Choctaw (2)	16	0.15
Comanche (3)	5	0.05
Creek (1)	1	0.01
Crow	2	0.02
Iroquois	1	0.01
Kiowa	2	0.02
Latin American Indians (9)	11	0.10
Navajo (4)	10	0.09
Paiute (3)	6	0.05
Potawatomi (1)	9	0.08
Pueblo (1)	1	0.01
Seminole	1	0.01
Sioux (13)	19	0.17
Ute (2)	2	0.02
Yakama	1	0.01
All other tribes (42)	74	0.68
American Indian tribes, not spec.	11	0.10
Arab:	7	0.06
Lebanese	7	0.06
Asian:	193	1.77
Cambodian (6)	6	0.05
Chinese, ex. Taiwanese (33)	51	0.47
Filipino (16)	44	0.40
Indian (21)	22	0.20
Japanese (14)	35	0.32
Korean (5)	13	0.12
Laotian (3)	3	0.03
Thai (1)	1	0.01
Vietnamese (13)	13	0.12
Other Asian, specified	1	0.01
Other Asian, not specified (2)	4	0.04
Basque	8	0.07
Belgian	8	0.07
British	91	0.82
Bulgarian	6	0.05
Canadian	42	0.38
Croatian	7	0.06
Czech	19	0.17
Danish	138	1.24
Dutch	212	1.90
English	2,045	18.32
European	106	0.95
Finnish	22	0.20
French, except Basque	515	4.61
French Canadian	107	0.96
German	1,962	17.58
Greek	22	0.20
Hawaii Native/Pacific Islander:	32	0.29
Melanesian:	1	0.01
Fijian	1	0.01
Micronesian: (3)	6	0.05
Guamanian/Chamorro (3)	6	0.05
Polynesian: (4)	19	0.17
Native Hawaiian (1)	14	0.13
Samoan (1)	2	0.02
Tongan (2)	3	0.03
Other Pac. Isl., specified	1	0.01
Other Pac. Isl., not spec. (1)	5	0.05
Hispanic or Latino:	717	6.56
Central American:	22	0.20
Guatemalan	2	0.02
Honduran	3	0.03
Nicaraguan	14	0.13
Salvadoran	2	0.02
Other Central American	1	0.01
Cuban	10	0.09
Dominican Republic	5	0.05
Mexican	506	4.63
Puerto Rican	38	0.35
South American:	8	0.07
Argentinean	1	0.01
Colombian	3	0.03
Peruvian	3	0.03
Venezuelan	1	0.01
Other Hispanic or Latino	128	1.17
Hungarian	44	0.39
Icelander	9	0.08
Irish	1,967	17.62
Italian	1,151	10.31
Lithuanian	8	0.07
New Zealander	9	0.08
Norwegian	411	3.68
Pennsylvania German	9	0.08
Polish	117	1.05
Portuguese	337	3.02
Romanian	10	0.09
Russian	60	0.54
Scandinavian	60	0.54
Scotch-Irish	448	4.01
Scottish	312	2.80
Slavic	7	0.06
Swedish	335	3.00
Swiss	31	0.28
Ukrainian	64	0.57
United States or American	538	4.82
Welsh	150	1.34
West Indian, excl. Hispanic:	19	0.17
Haitian	19	0.17
White:	10,421	95.41
Not Hispanic (9,628)	9,926	90.88
Hispanic (410)	495	4.53
Yugoslavian	9	0.08

Greenfield

Place Type: City
County: Monterey
Population: 12,583

Ancestry/Race	Number	%
African American/Black:	172	1.37
Not Hispanic (113)	120	0.95
Hispanic (35)	52	0.41
African, sub-Saharan:	21	0.17
African	21	0.17
Am. Ind. or Alaska Nat., not spec.	139	1.10
American Indian tribes, specified:	91	0.72
Apache (1)	4	0.03
Blackfeet	1	0.01
Cherokee (5)	11	0.09
Chickasaw (3)	3	0.02
Chippewa (1)	1	0.01
Creek (1)	1	0.01
Iroquois	1	0.01
Latin American Indians (27)	39	0.31
Navajo (1)	4	0.03
Potawatomi (1)	1	0.01
Shoshone	3	0.02
Sioux	1	0.01
Yaqui (1)	1	0.01
All other tribes (10)	20	0.16
American Indian tribes, not spec.	17	0.14
Asian:	157	1.25
Chinese, ex. Taiwanese (9)	11	0.09
Filipino (57)	102	0.81
Indian (9)	12	0.10
Japanese (5)	8	0.06
Korean (12)	16	0.13
Vietnamese (3)	3	0.02
Other Asian, not specified (1)	5	0.04
British	15	0.12
Danish	32	0.25
Dutch	43	0.34
English	144	1.14
European	9	0.07
French, except Basque	38	0.30
French Canadian	10	0.08
German	140	1.11
Hawaii Native/Pacific Islander:	32	0.25
Micronesian: (4)	11	0.09
Guamanian/Chamorro (4)	11	0.09
Polynesian: (14)	20	0.16
Native Hawaiian (5)	6	0.05
Samoan (9)	14	0.11
Other Pac. Isl., not spec. (1)	1	0.01
Hispanic or Latino:	11,055	87.86
Central American:	33	0.26
Costa Rican	1	0.01
Guatemalan	3	0.02
Honduran	3	0.02
Salvadoran	25	0.20
Other Central American	1	0.01
Cuban	2	0.02
Mexican	9,814	77.99
Puerto Rican	16	0.13
South American:	2	0.02
Chilean	1	0.01
Ecuadorian	1	0.01
Other Hispanic or Latino	1,188	9.44
Irish	90	0.71
Italian	86	0.68
Lithuanian	8	0.06
Polish	9	0.07
Portuguese	41	0.32
Romanian	33	0.26
Scotch-Irish	66	0.52
Scottish	17	0.13
Swedish	36	0.29
Swiss	102	0.81
United States or American	190	1.50
Welsh	27	0.21
White:	5,552	44.12
Not Hispanic (1,188)	1,262	10.03
Hispanic (3,801)	4,290	34.09

Grover Beach

Place Type: City
County: San Luis Obispo
Population: 13,067

Ancestry/Race	Number	%
African American/Black:	190	1.45
Not Hispanic (99)	140	1.07
Hispanic (36)	50	0.38
African, sub-Saharan:	7	0.05
African	7	0.05
Alaska Native tribes, specified:	1	0.01
Tlingit-Haida (1)	1	0.01

Notes: 1. Figures in the "Number" column do not add up to the total population due to: a) Ancestry/Race overlap — e.g. persons can report being both White and Irish, b) persons of Hispanic origin can report being any race, c) persons reporting two ancestries are counted in both categories. 2. Numbers in parentheses indicate the number of persons reporting this ancestry/race alone, not in combination with any other ancestry/race. 3. Refer to the Explanation of Data in the front of the book for more detailed information.

Am. Ind. or Alaska Nat., not spec.	123	0.94
American Indian tribes, specified:	257	1.97
Apache (12)	13	0.10
Blackfeet (3)	12	0.09
Cherokee (18)	66	0.51
Cheyenne (1)	2	0.02
Chippewa	1	0.01
Choctaw (2)	4	0.03
Creek (1)	4	0.03
Iroquois (4)	9	0.07
Latin American Indians (20)	35	0.27
Navajo (4)	8	0.06
Osage	6	0.05
Paiute (4)	5	0.04
Potawatomi (2)	10	0.08
Pueblo (5)	5	0.04
Puget Sound Salish (3)	3	0.02
Seminole	2	0.02
Shoshone (4)	4	0.03
Sioux (4)	5	0.04
Tohono O'Odham (4)	4	0.03
Yakama (1)	1	0.01
Yaqui (5)	8	0.06
All other tribes (28)	50	0.38
American Indian tribes, not spec.	13	0.10
Arab:	32	0.25
Lebanese	8	0.06
Moroccan	24	0.18
Armenian	23	0.18
Asian:	690	5.28
Bangladeshi (4)	4	0.03
Cambodian (2)	3	0.02
Chinese, ex. Taiwanese (63)	74	0.57
Filipino (275)	398	3.05
Indian (15)	17	0.13
Indonesian	5	0.04
Japanese (56)	92	0.70
Korean (36)	39	0.30
Pakistani (5)	6	0.05
Thai (2)	3	0.02
Vietnamese (19)	25	0.19
Other Asian, specified	7	0.05
Other Asian, not specified (8)	17	0.13
Austrian	38	0.29
Basque	3	0.02
Belgian	10	0.08
British	53	0.41
Canadian	90	0.69
Croatian	6	0.05
Czech	29	0.22
Danish	133	1.02
Dutch	146	1.12
English	1,654	12.72
European	138	1.06
Finnish	38	0.29
French, except Basque	494	3.80
French Canadian	68	0.52
German	2,225	17.11
German Russian	8	0.06
Greek	17	0.13
Hawaii Native/Pacific Islander:	76	0.58
Micronesian: (6)	6	0.05
Guamanian/Chamorro (6)	6	0.05
Polynesian: (31)	57	0.44
Native Hawaiian (15)	35	0.27
Samoan (11)	17	0.13
Tongan (5)	5	0.04
Other Pac. Isl., specified	5	0.04
Other Pac. Isl., not spec. (2)	8	0.06
Hispanic or Latino:	2,941	22.51
Central American:	21	0.16
Costa Rican	4	0.03
Guatemalan	5	0.04
Honduran	1	0.01
Panamanian	1	0.01
Salvadoran	10	0.08
Cuban	14	0.11
Mexican	2,432	18.61
Puerto Rican	35	0.27
South American:	39	0.30
Argentinean	2	0.02
Bolivian	1	0.01
Chilean	5	0.04
Colombian	9	0.07
Ecuadorian	2	0.02
Peruvian	20	0.15
Other Hispanic or Latino	400	3.06
Hungarian	32	0.25
Irish	1,734	13.33
Israeli	6	0.05
Italian	688	5.29
Lithuanian	13	0.10
Maltese	17	0.13
Northern European	31	0.24
Norwegian	323	2.48
Pennsylvania German	7	0.05
Polish	127	0.98
Portuguese	245	1.88
Russian	93	0.72
Scandinavian	9	0.07
Scotch-Irish	228	1.75
Scottish	340	2.61
Slovene	9	0.07
Swedish	206	1.58
Swiss	94	0.72
Ukrainian	26	0.20
United States or American	466	3.58
Welsh	113	0.87
West Indian, excl. Hispanic:	32	0.25
Dutch West Indian	25	0.19
Jamaican	7	0.05
White:	10,911	83.50
Not Hispanic (9,023)	9,346	71.52
Hispanic (1,398)	1,565	11.98
Yugoslavian	17	0.13

Hacienda Heights

Place Type: Census Designated Place
County: Los Angeles
Population: 53,122

Ancestry/Race	Number	%
African American/Black:	994	1.87
Not Hispanic (750)	858	1.62
Hispanic (75)	136	0.26
African, sub-Saharan:	79	0.15
African	51	0.10
Nigerian	22	0.04
Other sub-Saharan African	6	0.01
Alaska Native tribes, specified:	5	0.01
Alaska Athabascan (3)	3	0.01
Aleut (1)	1	0.00
Tlingit-Haida (1)	1	0.00
Am. Ind. or Alaska Nat., not spec.	251	0.47
Alsatian	5	0.01
American Indian tribes, specified:	358	0.67
Apache (12)	28	0.05
Blackfeet (3)	10	0.02
Cherokee (18)	57	0.11
Cheyenne	1	0.00
Chickasaw	2	0.00
Chippewa	2	0.00
Choctaw (4)	10	0.02
Colville	2	0.00
Comanche	4	0.01
Creek (1)	5	0.01
Iroquois (7)	9	0.02
Kiowa	3	0.01
Latin American Indians (50)	97	0.18
Navajo (16)	22	0.04
Paiute (2)	2	0.00
Pima	4	0.01
Pueblo (11)	15	0.03
Seminole	2	0.00
Shoshone	4	0.01
Sioux (14)	18	0.03
Tohono O'Odham (5)	11	0.02
Yaqui	3	0.01
All other tribes (23)	47	0.09
American Indian tribes, not spec.	66	0.12
Arab:	423	0.80
Arab/Arabic	64	0.12
Jordanian	62	0.12
Lebanese	175	0.33
Palestinian	18	0.03
Syrian	104	0.20
Armenian	289	0.54
Asian:	20,921	39.38
Cambodian (37)	61	0.11
Chinese, ex. Taiwanese (9,396)	10,394	19.57
Filipino (1,088)	1,308	2.46
Indian (346)	420	0.79
Indonesian (107)	151	0.28
Japanese (1,346)	1,606	3.02
Korean (2,951)	3,055	5.75
Laotian (37)	39	0.07
Malaysian (7)	17	0.03
Pakistani (15)	22	0.04
Sri Lankan (1)	2	0.00
Taiwanese (2,525)	3,157	5.94
Thai (160)	202	0.38
Vietnamese (255)	308	0.58
Other Asian, specified (13)	19	0.04
Other Asian, not specified (55)	160	0.30
Austrian	67	0.13
Basque	10	0.02
Belgian	42	0.08
Brazilian	49	0.09
British	82	0.15
Bulgarian	5	0.01
Canadian	121	0.23
Croatian	46	0.09
Czech	46	0.09
Czechoslovakian	21	0.04
Danish	258	0.49
Dutch	401	0.76
Eastern European	28	0.05
English	2,314	4.36
European	141	0.27
Finnish	25	0.05
French, except Basque	629	1.18
French Canadian	148	0.28
German	2,578	4.85
Greek	103	0.19
Guyanese	46	0.09
Hawaii Native/Pacific Islander:	254	0.48
Melanesian: (1)	4	0.01
Fijian (1)	4	0.01
Micronesian: (9)	12	0.02
Guamanian/Chamorro (9)	12	0.02
Polynesian: (52)	119	0.22
Native Hawaiian (20)	74	0.14
Samoan (30)	40	0.08
Tongan (1)	3	0.01
Other Polynesian (1)	2	0.00
Other Pac. Isl., not spec. (1)	119	0.22
Hispanic or Latino:	20,320	38.25
Central American:	664	1.25
Costa Rican	46	0.09
Guatemalan	143	0.27
Honduran	16	0.03
Nicaraguan	94	0.18
Panamanian	14	0.03
Salvadoran	287	0.54
Other Central American	64	0.12
Cuban	134	0.25
Dominican Republic	3	0.01
Mexican	16,375	30.83
Puerto Rican	172	0.32
South American:	392	0.74
Argentinean	60	0.11
Bolivian	15	0.03
Chilean	19	0.04
Colombian	66	0.12
Ecuadorian	84	0.16
Peruvian	102	0.19
Uruguayan	2	0.00
Venezuelan	18	0.03
Other South American	26	0.05

Notes: 1. Figures in the "Number" column do not add up to the total population due to: a) Ancestry/Race overlap — e.g. persons can report being both White and Irish, b) persons of Hispanic origin can report being any race, c) persons reporting two ancestries are counted in both categories. 2. Numbers in parentheses indicate the number of persons reporting this ancestry/race alone, not in combination with any other ancestry/race. 3. Refer to the Explanation of Data in the front of the book for more detailed information.

Other Hispanic or Latino	2,580	4.86
Hungarian	97	0.18
Icelander	12	0.02
Iranian	91	0.17
Irish	1,629	3.07
Italian	1,414	2.66
Latvian	30	0.06
Lithuanian	58	0.11
Luxemburger	6	0.01
Northern European	17	0.03
Norwegian	274	0.52
Polish	322	0.61
Portuguese	66	0.12
Romanian	19	0.04
Russian	392	0.74
Scandinavian	74	0.14
Scotch-Irish	347	0.65
Scottish	502	0.95
Serbian	18	0.03
Slovak	45	0.08
Slovene	19	0.04
Swedish	317	0.60
Swiss	86	0.16
Ukrainian	50	0.09
United States or American	738	1.39
Welsh	163	0.31
West Indian, excl. Hispanic:	102	0.19
Belizean	5	0.01
Haitian	28	0.05
Jamaican	62	0.12
Trinidadian and Tobagonian	7	0.01
White:	23,348	43.95
Not Hispanic (11,754)	12,436	23.41
Hispanic (10,043)	10,912	20.54
Yugoslavian	68	0.13

Half Moon Bay

Place Type: City
County: San Mateo
Population: 11,842

Ancestry/Race	Number	%
African American/Black:	520	4.39
Not Hispanic (448)	497	4.20
Hispanic (15)	23	0.19
African, sub-Saharan:	41	0.34
African	41	0.34
Alaska Native tribes, specified:	3	0.03
Aleut (1)	1	0.01
Eskimo (2)	2	0.02
Am. Ind. or Alaska Nat., not spec.	50	0.42
American Indian tribes, specified:	97	0.82
Apache	1	0.01
Blackfeet (1)	5	0.04
Cherokee (3)	33	0.28
Chippewa (1)	5	0.04
Choctaw	4	0.03
Comanche	1	0.01
Creek	1	0.01
Iroquois	2	0.02
Latin American Indians (18)	19	0.16
Pueblo (1)	2	0.02
Seminole (1)	3	0.03
Shoshone	2	0.02
Sioux (2)	10	0.08
All other tribes (3)	9	0.08
American Indian tribes, not spec.	7	0.06
Arab:	44	0.37
Egyptian	6	0.05
Lebanese	28	0.23
Moroccan	10	0.08
Armenian	10	0.08
Asian:	546	4.61
Cambodian (1)	1	0.01
Chinese, ex. Taiwanese (92)	130	1.10
Filipino (144)	194	1.64
Indian (9)	16	0.14
Indonesian (1)	4	0.03
Japanese (91)	135	1.14
Korean (22)	30	0.25
Laotian (2)	2	0.02
Sri Lankan (1)	1	0.01
Thai (8)	8	0.07
Vietnamese (6)	9	0.08
Other Asian, specified (1)	1	0.01
Other Asian, not specified (5)	15	0.13
Australian	6	0.05
Austrian	60	0.50
Belgian	36	0.30
Brazilian	39	0.33
British	211	1.76
Canadian	148	1.24
Celtic	56	0.47
Croatian	9	0.08
Czech	35	0.29
Czechoslovakian	9	0.08
Danish	58	0.48
Dutch	256	2.14
Eastern European	10	0.08
English	1,240	10.35
Estonian	24	0.20
European	203	1.70
Finnish	28	0.23
French, except Basque	323	2.70
French Canadian	28	0.23
German	1,690	14.11
Greek	65	0.54
Hawaii Native/Pacific Islander:	40	0.34
Melanesian: (1)	1	0.01
Fijian (1)	1	0.01
Micronesian:	1	0.01
Guamanian/Chamorro	1	0.01
Polynesian: (10)	24	0.20
Native Hawaiian (3)	13	0.11
Samoan (6)	9	0.08
Other Polynesian (1)	2	0.02
Other Pac. Isl., not spec. (3)	14	0.12
Hispanic or Latino:	2,751	23.23
Central American:	67	0.57
Costa Rican	4	0.03
Guatemalan	12	0.10
Honduran	13	0.11
Nicaraguan	8	0.07
Panamanian	1	0.01
Salvadoran	25	0.21
Other Central American	4	0.03
Cuban	18	0.15
Dominican Republic	1	0.01
Mexican	2,359	19.92
Puerto Rican	39	0.33
South American:	31	0.26
Argentinean	6	0.05
Bolivian	2	0.02
Chilean	7	0.06
Colombian	1	0.01
Peruvian	12	0.10
Other South American	3	0.03
Other Hispanic or Latino	236	1.99
Hungarian	7	0.06
Iranian	62	0.52
Irish	1,547	12.92
Israeli	17	0.14
Italian	1,080	9.02
Lithuanian	27	0.23
Northern European	45	0.38
Norwegian	386	3.22
Polish	184	1.54
Portuguese	656	5.48
Romanian	4	0.03
Russian	171	1.43
Scandinavian	50	0.42
Scotch-Irish	239	2.00
Scottish	475	3.97
Slavic	8	0.07
Slovene	9	0.08
Swedish	183	1.53
Swiss	92	0.77
Ukrainian	30	0.25
United States or American	222	1.85
Welsh	126	1.05
White:	9,567	80.79
Not Hispanic (7,882)	8,166	68.96
Hispanic (1,268)	1,401	11.83
Yugoslavian	30	0.25

Hanford

Place Type: City
County: Kings
Population: 41,686

Ancestry/Race	Number	%
African American/Black:	2,324	5.58
Not Hispanic (1,989)	2,145	5.15
Hispanic (101)	179	0.43
African, sub-Saharan:	151	0.36
African	115	0.28
Ethiopian	34	0.08
Nigerian	2	0.00
Alaska Native tribes, not specified	1	0.00
Am. Ind. or Alaska Nat., not spec.	345	0.83
American Indian tribes, specified:	591	1.42
Apache (10)	23	0.06
Blackfeet (6)	15	0.04
Cherokee (54)	183	0.44
Cheyenne (1)	1	0.00
Chickasaw (6)	12	0.03
Chippewa (1)	2	0.00
Choctaw (18)	39	0.09
Comanche (1)	1	0.00
Cree (1)	1	0.00
Creek (2)	12	0.03
Crow (1)	1	0.00
Iroquois	5	0.01
Latin American Indians (37)	48	0.12
Navajo (13)	18	0.04
Osage	5	0.01
Paiute	1	0.00
Pima (10)	10	0.02
Potawatomi (2)	8	0.02
Pueblo (6)	7	0.02
Shoshone (1)	1	0.00
Sioux (8)	22	0.05
Tohono O'Odham (3)	8	0.02
Yakama (1)	1	0.00
Yaqui (8)	13	0.03
All other tribes (126)	154	0.37
American Indian tribes, not spec.	54	0.13
Arab:	93	0.22
Arab/Arabic	62	0.15
Lebanese	24	0.06
Syrian	7	0.02
Armenian	120	0.29
Asian:	1,688	4.05
Cambodian (27)	27	0.06
Chinese, ex. Taiwanese (195)	252	0.60
Filipino (606)	835	2.00
Hmong (48)	64	0.15
Indian (81)	113	0.27
Indonesian (1)	1	0.00
Japanese (128)	203	0.49
Korean (28)	45	0.11
Laotian (2)	19	0.05
Malaysian	1	0.00
Pakistani	1	0.00
Sri Lankan (4)	4	0.01
Taiwanese (2)	3	0.01
Thai (5)	15	0.04
Vietnamese (22)	33	0.08
Other Asian, specified (1)	3	0.01
Other Asian, not specified (9)	68	0.16
Austrian	50	0.12
Basque	10	0.02
Belgian	9	0.02
Brazilian	18	0.04
British	49	0.12
Canadian	21	0.05
Celtic	10	0.02
Croatian	7	0.02

Notes: 1. Figures in the "Number" column do not add up to the total population due to: a) Ancestry/Race overlap — e.g. persons can report being both White and Irish, b) persons of Hispanic origin can report being any race, c) persons reporting two ancestries are counted in both categories. 2. Numbers in parentheses indicate the number of persons reporting this ancestry/race alone, not in combination with any other ancestry/race. 3. Refer to the Explanation of Data in the front of the book for more detailed information.

Czech	56	0.13
Czechoslovakian	10	0.02
Danish	292	0.70
Dutch	953	2.28
English	2,723	6.53
European	176	0.42
Finnish	55	0.13
French, except Basque	980	2.35
French Canadian	116	0.28
German	3,528	8.45
Greek	72	0.17
Hawaii Native/Pacific Islander:	174	0.42
Melanesian: (6)	6	0.01
Fijian (6)	6	0.01
Micronesian: (17)	33	0.08
Guamanian/Chamorro (17)	33	0.08
Polynesian: (39)	92	0.22
Native Hawaiian (27)	69	0.17
Samoan (10)	19	0.05
Other Polynesian (2)	4	0.01
Other Pac. Isl., not spec. (8)	43	0.10
Hispanic or Latino:	16,116	38.66
Central American:	91	0.22
Costa Rican	4	0.01
Guatemalan	11	0.03
Honduran	23	0.06
Nicaraguan	7	0.02
Panamanian	14	0.03
Salvadoran	21	0.05
Other Central American	11	0.03
Cuban	22	0.05
Dominican Republic	4	0.01
Mexican	13,921	33.39
Puerto Rican	109	0.26
South American:	36	0.09
Argentinean	2	0.00
Bolivian	5	0.01
Chilean	14	0.03
Colombian	6	0.01
Peruvian	6	0.01
Venezuelan	2	0.00
Other South American	1	0.00
Other Hispanic or Latino	1,933	4.64
Hungarian	49	0.12
Icelander	8	0.02
Iranian	15	0.04
Irish	3,075	7.37
Italian	1,208	2.89
Lithuanian	27	0.06
Northern European	95	0.23
Norwegian	299	0.72
Pennsylvania German	13	0.03
Polish	239	0.57
Portuguese	3,123	7.48
Romanian	3	0.01
Russian	111	0.27
Scandinavian	63	0.15
Scotch-Irish	431	1.03
Scottish	640	1.53
Slovak	9	0.02
Swedish	419	1.00
Swiss	95	0.23
Ukrainian	16	0.04
United States or American	1,903	4.56
Welsh	197	0.47
West Indian, excl. Hispanic:	65	0.16
Bermudan	31	0.07
Dutch West Indian	25	0.06
Jamaican	9	0.02
White:	28,862	69.24
Not Hispanic (20,794)	21,909	52.56
Hispanic (5,910)	6,953	16.68
Yugoslavian	49	0.12

Hawaiian Gardens

Place Type: City
County: Los Angeles
Population: 14,779

Ancestry/Race	Number	%
African American/Black:	726	4.91
Not Hispanic (621)	664	4.49
Hispanic (36)	62	0.42
African, sub-Saharan:	40	0.27
African	23	0.15
Ethiopian	17	0.11
Alaska Native tribes, specified:	1	0.01
Alaska Athabascan (1)	1	0.01
Am. Ind. or Alaska Nat., not spec.	118	0.80
American Indian tribes, specified:	165	1.12
Apache (12)	16	0.11
Blackfeet (1)	1	0.01
Cherokee (2)	11	0.07
Chickasaw (3)	3	0.02
Crow (3)	3	0.02
Latin American Indians (45)	64	0.43
Navajo (11)	17	0.12
Paiute (6)	6	0.04
Sioux (8)	9	0.06
Yaqui (2)	2	0.01
All other tribes (18)	33	0.22
American Indian tribes, not spec.	7	0.05
Arab:	22	0.15
Lebanese	22	0.15
Asian:	1,505	10.18
Bangladeshi (4)	6	0.04
Cambodian (61)	82	0.55
Chinese, ex. Taiwanese (135)	155	1.05
Filipino (232)	288	1.95
Indian (31)	67	0.45
Indonesian	1	0.01
Japanese (16)	28	0.19
Korean (732)	761	5.15
Malaysian	4	0.03
Taiwanese (20)	27	0.18
Thai (11)	12	0.08
Vietnamese (37)	50	0.34
Other Asian, not specified (6)	24	0.16
British	18	0.12
Canadian	22	0.15
Danish	15	0.10
Dutch	82	0.55
English	271	1.82
European	29	0.19
French, except Basque	104	0.70
French Canadian	11	0.07
German	219	1.47
Greek	48	0.32
Hawaii Native/Pacific Islander:	166	1.12
Melanesian:	1	0.01
Fijian	1	0.01
Micronesian: (4)	9	0.06
Guamanian/Chamorro (4)	9	0.06
Polynesian: (89)	120	0.81
Native Hawaiian (12)	29	0.20
Samoan (63)	68	0.46
Tongan (14)	23	0.16
Other Pac. Isl., not spec. (14)	36	0.24
Hispanic or Latino:	10,869	73.54
Central American:	273	1.85
Costa Rican	7	0.05
Guatemalan	94	0.64
Honduran	21	0.14
Nicaraguan	22	0.15
Panamanian	2	0.01
Salvadoran	103	0.70
Other Central American	24	0.16
Cuban	27	0.18
Mexican	9,577	64.80
Puerto Rican	39	0.26
South American:	58	0.39
Argentinean	3	0.02
Chilean	9	0.06
Colombian	10	0.07
Ecuadorian	17	0.12
Peruvian	11	0.07
Other South American	8	0.05
Other Hispanic or Latino	895	6.06
Hungarian	5	0.03
Iranian	20	0.13
Irish	204	1.37
Italian	94	0.63
Norwegian	12	0.08
Polish	58	0.39
Portuguese	14	0.09
Scotch-Irish	74	0.50
Scottish	52	0.35
Swedish	28	0.19
United States or American	285	1.91
Welsh	38	0.25
West Indian, excl. Hispanic:	12	0.08
Belizean	6	0.04
Jamaican	6	0.04
White:	6,202	41.96
Not Hispanic (1,595)	1,739	11.77
Hispanic (4,056)	4,463	30.20

Hawthorne

Place Type: City
County: Los Angeles
Population: 84,112

Ancestry/Race	Number	%
Acadian/Cajun	5	0.01
Afghan	28	0.03
African American/Black:	28,945	34.41
Not Hispanic (27,208)	28,042	33.34
Hispanic (567)	903	1.07
African, sub-Saharan:	2,022	2.41
African	1,173	1.40
Ethiopian	117	0.14
Ghanian	48	0.06
Nigerian	590	0.70
Senegalese	27	0.03
Sierra Leonean	13	0.02
Somalian	10	0.01
Sudanese	17	0.02
Other sub-Saharan African	27	0.03
Alaska Native tribes, specified:	4	0.00
Alaska Athabascan (1)	3	0.00
Tlingit-Haida	1	0.00
Am. Ind. or Alaska Nat., not spec.	532	0.63
Albanian	32	0.04
American Indian tribes, specified:	634	0.75
Apache (10)	27	0.03
Blackfeet (3)	25	0.03
Cherokee (30)	140	0.17
Cheyenne	2	0.00
Chippewa (6)	17	0.02
Choctaw (3)	16	0.02
Colville	1	0.00
Comanche (5)	10	0.01
Cree	3	0.00
Creek (6)	12	0.01
Crow	1	0.00
Delaware (3)	4	0.00
Iroquois (2)	4	0.00
Latin American Indians (162)	226	0.27
Navajo (5)	13	0.02
Osage	4	0.00
Paiute (1)	2	0.00
Pima (5)	6	0.01
Potawatomi	1	0.00
Pueblo (6)	14	0.02
Seminole (1)	18	0.02
Shoshone (1)	3	0.00
Sioux (3)	17	0.02
Tohono O'Odham	3	0.00
Ute	5	0.01
Yaqui (2)	8	0.01
All other tribes (23)	52	0.06
American Indian tribes, not spec.	61	0.07

Notes: 1. Figures in the "Number" column do not add up to the total population due to: a) Ancestry/Race overlap — e.g. persons can report being both White and Irish, b) persons of Hispanic origin can report being any race, c) persons reporting two ancestries are counted in both categories. 2. Numbers in parentheses indicate the number of persons reporting this ancestry/race alone, not in combination with any other ancestry/race. 3. Refer to the Explanation of Data in the front of the book for more detailed information.

Ancestry/Race	Number	%
Arab:	440	0.52
Arab/Arabic	73	0.09
Egyptian	159	0.19
Jordanian	14	0.02
Lebanese	55	0.07
Moroccan	26	0.03
Palestinian	100	0.12
Syrian	13	0.02
Armenian	86	0.10
Asian:	6,688	7.95
Bangladeshi (20)	32	0.04
Cambodian (5)	9	0.01
Chinese, ex. Taiwanese (440)	611	0.73
Filipino (2,079)	2,373	2.82
Hmong	2	0.00
Indian (517)	629	0.75
Indonesian (21)	58	0.07
Japanese (353)	513	0.61
Korean (307)	354	0.42
Laotian (5)	5	0.01
Malaysian (1)	11	0.01
Pakistani (146)	238	0.28
Sri Lankan (29)	38	0.05
Taiwanese (5)	8	0.01
Thai (53)	78	0.09
Vietnamese (1,487)	1,569	1.87
Other Asian, specified (9)	13	0.02
Other Asian, not specified (48)	147	0.17
Assyrian/Chaldean/Syriac	6	0.01
Australian	10	0.01
Austrian	83	0.10
Basque	9	0.01
Belgian	9	0.01
Brazilian	54	0.06
British	62	0.07
Canadian	45	0.05
Croatian	62	0.07
Cypriot	5	0.01
Czech	42	0.05
Czechoslovakian	33	0.04
Danish	107	0.13
Dutch	265	0.32
Eastern European	22	0.03
English	1,888	2.25
European	137	0.16
Finnish	13	0.02
French, except Basque	587	0.70
French Canadian	125	0.15
German	2,407	2.87
Greek	130	0.15
Guyanese	87	0.10
Hawaii Native/Pacific Islander:	1,044	1.24
Melanesian: (36)	49	0.06
Fijian (36)	49	0.06
Micronesian: (42)	51	0.06
Guamanian/Chamorro (40)	49	0.06
Other Micronesian (2)	2	0.00
Polynesian: (582)	809	0.96
Native Hawaiian (51)	150	0.18
Samoan (96)	146	0.17
Tongan (395)	448	0.53
Other Polynesian (40)	65	0.08
Other Pac. Isl., not spec. (31)	135	0.16
Hispanic or Latino:	37,227	44.26
Central American:	4,681	5.57
Costa Rican	106	0.13
Guatemalan	1,879	2.23
Honduran	170	0.20
Nicaraguan	349	0.41
Panamanian	73	0.09
Salvadoran	1,673	1.99
Other Central American	431	0.51
Cuban	954	1.13
Dominican Republic	54	0.06
Mexican	22,385	26.61
Puerto Rican	687	0.82
South American:	1,230	1.46
Argentinean	94	0.11
Bolivian	13	0.02
Chilean	60	0.07
Colombian	295	0.35
Ecuadorian	188	0.22
Paraguayan	2	0.00
Peruvian	447	0.53
Uruguayan	15	0.02
Venezuelan	20	0.02
Other South American	96	0.11
Other Hispanic or Latino	7,236	8.60
Hungarian	161	0.19
Iranian	122	0.15
Irish	1,972	2.35
Italian	1,004	1.20
Lithuanian	16	0.02
Northern European	19	0.02
Norwegian	353	0.42
Pennsylvania German	22	0.03
Polish	295	0.35
Portuguese	40	0.05
Romanian	50	0.06
Russian	182	0.22
Scandinavian	14	0.02
Scotch-Irish	285	0.34
Scottish	327	0.39
Slovak	20	0.02
Swedish	283	0.34
Swiss	35	0.04
Ukrainian	6	0.01
United States or American	1,809	2.15
Welsh	80	0.10
West Indian, excl. Hispanic:	756	0.90
Bahamian	5	0.01
Belizean	435	0.52
British West Indian	31	0.04
Dutch West Indian	10	0.01
Haitian	23	0.03
Jamaican	199	0.24
Trinidadian and Tobagonian	18	0.02
U.S. Virgin Islander	27	0.03
West Indian	8	0.01
White:	27,726	32.96
Not Hispanic (10,937)	12,131	14.42
Hispanic (13,681)	15,595	18.54
Yugoslavian	48	0.06

Hayward

Place Type: City
County: Alameda
Population: 140,030

Ancestry/Race	Number	%
Acadian/Cajun	24	0.02
Afghan	1,171	0.84
African American/Black:	17,181	12.27
Not Hispanic (14,846)	16,240	11.60
Hispanic (528)	941	0.67
African, sub-Saharan:	1,707	1.22
African	1,029	0.74
Cape Verdean	50	0.04
Ethiopian	121	0.09
Ghanian	9	0.01
Kenyan	30	0.02
Nigerian	349	0.25
Sierra Leonean	11	0.01
Somalian	18	0.01
South African	16	0.01
Sudanese	52	0.04
Other sub-Saharan African	22	0.02
Alaska Native tribes, specified:	22	0.02
Alaska Athabascan	1	0.00
Aleut (4)	4	0.00
Eskimo (1)	6	0.00
Tlingit-Haida (2)	8	0.01
All other tribes (1)	3	0.00
Alaska Native tribes, not specified	3	0.00
Am. Ind. or Alaska Nat., not spec.	965	0.69
Alsatian	13	0.01
American Indian tribes, specified:	1,616	1.15
Apache (30)	77	0.05
Blackfeet (6)	83	0.06
Cherokee (94)	472	0.34
Cheyenne (3)	13	0.01
Chickasaw (1)	4	0.00
Chippewa (14)	22	0.02
Choctaw (22)	73	0.05
Comanche (2)	18	0.01
Cree (4)	9	0.01
Creek (9)	27	0.02
Crow	4	0.00
Iroquois (8)	25	0.02
Kiowa (1)	9	0.01
Latin American Indians (136)	247	0.18
Lumbee (1)	3	0.00
Navajo (35)	67	0.05
Osage (1)	4	0.00
Ottawa	1	0.00
Paiute (17)	38	0.03
Pima (1)	3	0.00
Potawatomi (3)	4	0.00
Pueblo (33)	43	0.03
Puget Sound Salish (1)	1	0.00
Seminole (4)	16	0.01
Shoshone (3)	4	0.00
Sioux (27)	64	0.05
Ute (2)	5	0.00
Yaqui (16)	34	0.02
Yuman (4)	5	0.00
All other tribes (134)	241	0.17
American Indian tribes, not spec.	155	0.11
Arab:	599	0.43
Arab/Arabic	206	0.15
Egyptian	32	0.02
Iraqi	21	0.02
Jordanian	31	0.02
Lebanese	93	0.07
Moroccan	7	0.01
Palestinian	9	0.01
Syrian	44	0.03
Other Arab	156	0.11
Armenian	208	0.15
Asian:	31,255	22.32
Bangladeshi (3)	7	0.00
Cambodian (133)	167	0.12
Chinese, ex. Taiwanese (3,926)	4,674	3.34
Filipino (12,755)	14,443	10.31
Hmong (14)	15	0.01
Indian (4,086)	5,141	3.67
Indonesian (114)	181	0.13
Japanese (1,006)	1,431	1.02
Korean (780)	932	0.67
Laotian (50)	61	0.04
Malaysian (7)	23	0.02
Pakistani (121)	184	0.13
Sri Lankan (21)	25	0.02
Taiwanese (72)	79	0.06
Thai (113)	148	0.11
Vietnamese (2,783)	2,979	2.13
Other Asian, specified (24)	46	0.03
Other Asian, not specified (141)	719	0.51
Assyrian/Chaldean/Syriac	7	0.01
Australian	77	0.06
Austrian	128	0.09
Basque	40	0.03
Belgian	100	0.07
Brazilian	64	0.05
British	195	0.14
Bulgarian	23	0.02
Canadian	238	0.17
Celtic	61	0.04
Croatian	176	0.13
Czech	219	0.16
Czechoslovakian	122	0.09
Danish	448	0.32
Dutch	1,018	0.73
Eastern European	23	0.02
English	5,387	3.85
Estonian	15	0.01
European	710	0.51
Finnish	155	0.11
French, except Basque	2,142	1.53

Notes: 1. Figures in the "Number" column do not add up to the total population due to: a) Ancestry/Race overlap — e.g. persons can report being both White and Irish, b) persons of Hispanic origin can report being any race, c) persons reporting two ancestries are counted in both categories. 2. Numbers in parentheses indicate the number of persons reporting this ancestry/race alone, not in combination with any other ancestry/race. 3. Refer to the Explanation of Data in the front of the book for more detailed information.

Ancestry/Race	Number	%
French Canadian	452	0.32
German	8,000	5.72
Greek	597	0.43
Guyanese	47	0.03
Hawaii Native/Pacific Islander:	4,814	3.44
Melanesian: (919)	1,149	0.82
Fijian (919)	1,149	0.82
Micronesian: (381)	577	0.41
Guamanian/Chamorro (347)	530	0.38
Other Micronesian (34)	47	0.03
Polynesian: (975)	1,779	1.27
Native Hawaiian (299)	847	0.60
Samoan (395)	556	0.40
Tongan (258)	335	0.24
Other Polynesian (23)	41	0.03
Other Pac. Isl., specified	4	0.00
Other Pac. Isl., not spec. (348)	1,305	0.93
Hispanic or Latino:	47,850	34.17
Central American:	3,401	2.43
Costa Rican	68	0.05
Guatemalan	486	0.35
Honduran	93	0.07
Nicaraguan	1,045	0.75
Panamanian	79	0.06
Salvadoran	1,349	0.96
Other Central American	281	0.20
Cuban	213	0.15
Dominican Republic	15	0.01
Mexican	34,035	24.31
Puerto Rican	2,177	1.55
South American:	882	0.63
Argentinean	45	0.03
Bolivian	49	0.03
Chilean	78	0.06
Colombian	116	0.08
Ecuadorian	38	0.03
Paraguayan	4	0.00
Peruvian	421	0.30
Uruguayan	4	0.00
Venezuelan	27	0.02
Other South American	100	0.07
Other Hispanic or Latino	7,127	5.09
Hungarian	213	0.15
Icelander	25	0.02
Iranian	211	0.15
Irish	7,244	5.18
Israeli	7	0.01
Italian	4,301	3.07
Latvian	49	0.04
Lithuanian	127	0.09
Luxemburger	11	0.01
New Zealander	8	0.01
Northern European	15	0.01
Norwegian	1,107	0.79
Pennsylvania German	19	0.01
Polish	1,144	0.82
Portuguese	4,751	3.40
Romanian	195	0.14
Russian	606	0.43
Scandinavian	112	0.08
Scotch-Irish	1,191	0.85
Scottish	1,045	0.75
Serbian	32	0.02
Slavic	57	0.04
Slovak	86	0.06
Swedish	1,281	0.92
Swiss	159	0.11
Turkish	36	0.03
Ukrainian	103	0.07
United States or American	2,662	1.90
Welsh	482	0.34
West Indian, excl. Hispanic:	352	0.25
Barbadian	11	0.01
Belizean	11	0.01
British West Indian	25	0.02
Haitian	6	0.00
Jamaican	179	0.13
Trinidadian and Tobagonian	43	0.03
U.S. Virgin Islander	8	0.01
West Indian	69	0.05
White:	67,535	48.23
Not Hispanic (40,896)	44,984	32.12
Hispanic (19,250)	22,551	16.10
Yugoslavian	118	0.08

Healdsburg

Place Type: City
County: Sonoma
Population: 10,722

Ancestry/Race	Number	%
African American/Black:	71	0.66
Not Hispanic (35)	47	0.44
Hispanic (19)	24	0.22
African, sub-Saharan:	22	0.21
African	22	0.21
Alaska Native tribes, specified:	2	0.02
Aleut	2	0.02
Alaska Native tribes, not specified	1	0.01
Am. Ind. or Alaska Nat., not spec.	95	0.89
American Indian tribes, specified:	200	1.87
Apache	4	0.04
Blackfeet	3	0.03
Cherokee (9)	23	0.21
Chippewa (2)	6	0.06
Choctaw (1)	4	0.04
Houma (1)	1	0.01
Latin American Indians (29)	45	0.42
Navajo (2)	4	0.04
Pima	1	0.01
Pueblo (1)	1	0.01
Sioux	2	0.02
Yaqui (3)	4	0.04
All other tribes (74)	102	0.95
American Indian tribes, not spec.	20	0.19
Armenian	7	0.07
Asian:	158	1.47
Chinese, ex. Taiwanese (23)	38	0.35
Filipino (5)	21	0.20
Indian (14)	24	0.22
Indonesian (1)	1	0.01
Japanese (31)	69	0.64
Korean (2)	2	0.02
Thai (1)	1	0.01
Other Asian, not specified (1)	2	0.02
Australian	9	0.08
Austrian	35	0.33
Basque	40	0.38
Belgian	27	0.25
British	34	0.32
Canadian	122	1.15
Celtic	11	0.10
Czech	12	0.11
Czechoslovakian	63	0.59
Danish	108	1.01
Dutch	170	1.60
Eastern European	11	0.10
English	1,466	13.77
European	114	1.07
Finnish	23	0.22
French, except Basque	233	2.19
French Canadian	80	0.75
German	1,493	14.02
Greek	69	0.65
Hawaii Native/Pacific Islander:	15	0.14
Micronesian: (1)	1	0.01
Guamanian/Chamorro (1)	1	0.01
Polynesian: (4)	13	0.12
Native Hawaiian (3)	11	0.10
Other Polynesian (1)	2	0.02
Other Pac. Isl., not spec. (1)	1	0.01
Hispanic or Latino:	3,090	28.82
Central American:	26	0.24
Costa Rican	2	0.02
Guatemalan	11	0.10
Nicaraguan	4	0.04
Salvadoran	9	0.08
Cuban	26	0.24
Mexican	2,753	25.68
Puerto Rican	15	0.14
South American:	7	0.07
Argentinean	1	0.01
Bolivian	1	0.01
Chilean	1	0.01
Colombian	2	0.02
Ecuadorian	1	0.01
Other South American	1	0.01
Other Hispanic or Latino	263	2.45
Hungarian	12	0.11
Iranian	6	0.06
Irish	1,314	12.34
Italian	1,062	9.97
Latvian	14	0.13
Lithuanian	9	0.08
Macedonian	20	0.19
New Zealander	16	0.15
Northern European	50	0.47
Norwegian	125	1.17
Pennsylvania German	6	0.06
Polish	207	1.94
Portuguese	168	1.58
Russian	183	1.72
Scandinavian	42	0.39
Scotch-Irish	257	2.41
Scottish	239	2.24
Slovak	6	0.06
Swedish	321	3.01
Swiss	94	0.88
United States or American	486	4.56
Welsh	173	1.62
White:	8,919	83.18
Not Hispanic (7,265)	7,419	69.19
Hispanic (1,301)	1,500	13.99
Yugoslavian	9	0.08

Hemet

Place Type: City
County: Riverside
Population: 58,812

Ancestry/Race	Number	%
Acadian/Cajun	32	0.05
African American/Black:	1,901	3.23
Not Hispanic (1,407)	1,655	2.81
Hispanic (120)	246	0.42
African, sub-Saharan:	157	0.27
African	139	0.24
Ethiopian	9	0.02
South African	9	0.02
Alaska Native tribes, specified:	13	0.02
Alaska Athabascan (5)	6	0.01
Aleut (2)	2	0.00
Eskimo (1)	2	0.00
Tlingit-Haida (2)	2	0.00
All other tribes (1)	1	0.00
Am. Ind. or Alaska Nat., not spec.	359	0.61
American Indian tribes, specified:	863	1.47
Apache (22)	44	0.07
Blackfeet (5)	27	0.05
Cherokee (66)	205	0.35
Chickasaw (10)	13	0.02
Chippewa (6)	17	0.03
Choctaw (18)	50	0.09
Colville (3)	3	0.01
Comanche (2)	6	0.01
Cree (1)	3	0.01
Creek (6)	7	0.01
Crow	2	0.00
Delaware (1)	1	0.00
Iroquois (3)	15	0.03
Kiowa (2)	2	0.00
Latin American Indians (37)	75	0.13
Navajo (31)	47	0.08
Osage	1	0.00
Ottawa (1)	1	0.00
Paiute (3)	3	0.01
Pima	3	0.01
Potawatomi	8	0.01

Notes: 1. Figures in the "Number" column do not add up to the total population due to: a) Ancestry/Race overlap — e.g. persons can report being both White and Irish, b) persons of Hispanic origin can report being any race, c) persons reporting two ancestries are counted in both categories. 2. Numbers in parentheses indicate the number of persons reporting this ancestry/race alone, not in combination with any other ancestry/race. 3. Refer to the Explanation of Data in the front of the book for more detailed information.

Ancestry/Race	Number	%
Pueblo (7)	10	0.02
Seminole (3)	9	0.02
Shoshone (3)	4	0.01
Sioux (11)	29	0.05
Tohono O'Odham (1)	7	0.01
Ute	4	0.01
Yaqui (3)	12	0.02
All other tribes (209)	255	0.43
American Indian tribes, not spec.	36	0.06
Arab:	227	0.39
Arab/Arabic	27	0.05
Iraqi	12	0.02
Jordanian	85	0.14
Lebanese	20	0.03
Syrian	83	0.14
Armenian	37	0.06
Asian:	1,232	2.09
Cambodian (11)	16	0.03
Chinese, ex. Taiwanese (112)	163	0.28
Filipino (309)	430	0.73
Indian (120)	132	0.22
Indonesian (9)	16	0.03
Japanese (85)	173	0.29
Korean (47)	70	0.12
Laotian (41)	42	0.07
Malaysian (3)	3	0.01
Pakistani (25)	28	0.05
Sri Lankan (2)	2	0.00
Taiwanese (1)	4	0.01
Thai (29)	42	0.07
Vietnamese (52)	68	0.12
Other Asian, specified (5)	7	0.01
Other Asian, not specified (8)	36	0.06
Australian	23	0.04
Austrian	224	0.38
Basque	18	0.03
Belgian	80	0.14
British	197	0.34
Bulgarian	29	0.05
Canadian	322	0.55
Celtic	22	0.04
Croatian	46	0.08
Czech	196	0.33
Czechoslovakian	133	0.23
Danish	387	0.66
Dutch	1,323	2.25
Eastern European	11	0.02
English	7,793	13.26
European	402	0.68
Finnish	66	0.11
French, except Basque	2,188	3.72
French Canadian	455	0.77
German	8,789	14.95
Greek	189	0.32
Hawaii Native/Pacific Islander:	201	0.34
Micronesian: (11)	32	0.05
Guamanian/Chamorro (11)	32	0.05
Polynesian: (59)	142	0.24
Native Hawaiian (29)	96	0.16
Samoan (18)	33	0.06
Tongan (10)	11	0.02
Other Polynesian (2)	2	0.00
Other Pac. Isl., not spec. (7)	27	0.05
Hispanic or Latino:	13,585	23.10
Central American:	224	0.38
Costa Rican	5	0.01
Guatemalan	95	0.16
Honduran	7	0.01
Nicaraguan	18	0.03
Panamanian	13	0.02
Salvadoran	68	0.12
Other Central American	18	0.03
Cuban	68	0.12
Mexican	10,963	18.64
Puerto Rican	272	0.46
South American:	105	0.18
Argentinean	17	0.03
Bolivian	5	0.01
Chilean	12	0.02
Colombian	17	0.03
Ecuadorian	10	0.02
Paraguayan	3	0.01
Peruvian	19	0.03
Uruguayan	1	0.00
Venezuelan	9	0.02
Other South American	12	0.02
Other Hispanic or Latino	1,953	3.32
Hungarian	312	0.53
Icelander	9	0.02
Iranian	35	0.06
Irish	6,238	10.61
Israeli	20	0.03
Italian	2,570	4.37
Latvian	6	0.01
Lithuanian	56	0.10
Luxemburger	16	0.03
Northern European	45	0.08
Norwegian	941	1.60
Pennsylvania German	60	0.10
Polish	1,052	1.79
Portuguese	221	0.38
Romanian	47	0.08
Russian	344	0.59
Scandinavian	143	0.24
Scotch-Irish	1,306	2.22
Scottish	1,218	2.07
Serbian	13	0.02
Slavic	21	0.04
Slovak	40	0.07
Slovene	7	0.01
Swedish	1,197	2.04
Swiss	182	0.31
Turkish	21	0.04
Ukrainian	121	0.21
United States or American	3,275	5.57
Welsh	505	0.86
West Indian, excl. Hispanic:	171	0.29
Belizean	20	0.03
Haitian	7	0.01
Jamaican	112	0.19
Trinidadian and Tobagonian	8	0.01
West Indian	24	0.04
White:	49,158	83.58
Not Hispanic (41,345)	42,325	71.97
Hispanic (5,990)	6,833	11.62
Yugoslavian	107	0.18

Hercules

Place Type: City
County: Contra Costa
Population: 19,488

Ancestry/Race	Number	%
Afghan	44	0.23
African American/Black:	3,928	20.16
Not Hispanic (3,571)	3,802	19.51
Hispanic (88)	126	0.65
African, sub-Saharan:	472	2.45
African	335	1.74
Ethiopian	14	0.07
Ghanian	31	0.16
Nigerian	48	0.25
Somalian	44	0.23
Alaska Native tribes, specified:	4	0.02
Eskimo	2	0.01
All other tribes	2	0.01
Am. Ind. or Alaska Nat., not spec.	70	0.36
Alsatian	8	0.04
American Indian tribes, specified:	114	0.58
Apache	1	0.01
Blackfeet (1)	9	0.05
Cherokee (11)	45	0.23
Cheyenne	1	0.01
Chippewa	3	0.02
Choctaw (1)	10	0.05
Comanche	1	0.01
Cree	1	0.01
Creek (1)	1	0.01
Delaware (1)	1	0.01
Iroquois	4	0.02
Latin American Indians (7)	12	0.06
Navajo (1)	1	0.01
Potawatomi (1)	1	0.01
Pueblo (2)	2	0.01
Seminole	2	0.01
Shoshone	1	0.01
Sioux (1)	5	0.03
All other tribes (3)	13	0.07
American Indian tribes, not spec.	7	0.04
Arab:	144	0.75
Arab/Arabic	51	0.26
Iraqi	23	0.12
Lebanese	10	0.05
Palestinian	37	0.19
Syrian	6	0.03
Other Arab	17	0.09
Asian:	9,005	46.21
Cambodian (52)	66	0.34
Chinese, ex. Taiwanese (1,769)	1,946	9.99
Filipino (4,877)	5,246	26.92
Hmong (6)	6	0.03
Indian (717)	742	3.81
Indonesian (12)	17	0.09
Japanese (209)	308	1.58
Korean (153)	175	0.90
Laotian (86)	102	0.52
Malaysian (9)	10	0.05
Pakistani (37)	55	0.28
Sri Lankan (1)	1	0.01
Taiwanese (20)	22	0.11
Thai (13)	19	0.10
Vietnamese (209)	216	1.11
Other Asian, specified (4)	4	0.02
Other Asian, not specified (20)	70	0.36
Assyrian/Chaldean/Syriac	9	0.05
Basque	8	0.04
Brazilian	35	0.18
British	34	0.18
Canadian	23	0.12
Croatian	12	0.06
Czech	18	0.09
Czechoslovakian	3	0.02
Danish	94	0.49
Dutch	143	0.74
Eastern European	8	0.04
English	834	4.32
European	114	0.59
Finnish	56	0.29
French, except Basque	226	1.17
French Canadian	30	0.16
German	942	4.88
Greek	57	0.30
Hawaii Native/Pacific Islander:	193	0.99
Melanesian: (21)	28	0.14
Fijian (21)	28	0.14
Micronesian: (7)	22	0.11
Guamanian/Chamorro (7)	22	0.11
Polynesian: (44)	96	0.49
Native Hawaiian (22)	63	0.32
Samoan (12)	21	0.11
Tongan (10)	12	0.06
Other Pac. Isl., not spec. (12)	47	0.24
Hispanic or Latino:	2,106	10.81
Central American:	243	1.25
Costa Rican	8	0.04
Guatemalan	31	0.16
Honduran	8	0.04
Nicaraguan	61	0.31
Panamanian	14	0.07
Salvadoran	87	0.45
Other Central American	34	0.17
Cuban	28	0.14
Dominican Republic	5	0.03
Mexican	1,154	5.92
Puerto Rican	92	0.47
South American:	99	0.51
Argentinean	6	0.03
Chilean	12	0.06
Colombian	11	0.06

Notes: 1. Figures in the "Number" column do not add up to the total population due to: a) Ancestry/Race overlap — e.g. persons can report being both White and Irish, b) persons of Hispanic origin can report being any race, c) persons reporting two ancestries are counted in both categories. 2. Numbers in parentheses indicate the number of persons reporting this ancestry/race alone, not in combination with any other ancestry/race. 3. Refer to the Explanation of Data in the front of the book for more detailed information.

Ancestry/Race	Number	%
Ecuadorian	1	0.01
Peruvian	49	0.25
Venezuelan	1	0.01
Other South American	19	0.10
Other Hispanic or Latino	485	2.49
Iranian	57	0.30
Irish	1,052	5.45
Italian	615	3.19
Latvian	9	0.05
Lithuanian	6	0.03
Norwegian	221	1.15
Polish	119	0.62
Portuguese	120	0.62
Russian	93	0.48
Scandinavian	66	0.34
Scotch-Irish	112	0.58
Scottish	132	0.68
Slovak	9	0.05
Swedish	189	0.98
Swiss	17	0.09
Ukrainian	10	0.05
United States or American	343	1.78
Welsh	18	0.09
West Indian, excl. Hispanic:	27	0.14
British West Indian	10	0.05
Haitian	10	0.05
Jamaican	7	0.04
White:	6,193	31.78
Not Hispanic (4,624)	5,140	26.38
Hispanic (829)	1,053	5.40
Yugoslavian	10	0.05

Hermosa Beach

Place Type: City
County: Los Angeles
Population: 18,566

Ancestry/Race	Number	%
African American/Black:	233	1.25
Not Hispanic (141)	212	1.14
Hispanic (9)	21	0.11
African, sub-Saharan:	68	0.37
African	37	0.20
South African	27	0.15
Other sub-Saharan African	4	0.02
Alaska Native tribes, specified:	1	0.01
Eskimo (1)	1	0.01
Am. Ind. or Alaska Nat., not spec.	44	0.24
American Indian tribes, specified:	117	0.63
Apache (4)	13	0.07
Blackfeet (6)	7	0.04
Cherokee (9)	35	0.19
Cheyenne (1)	1	0.01
Chickasaw (1)	1	0.01
Chippewa	5	0.03
Choctaw (2)	4	0.02
Cree	1	0.01
Creek (1)	1	0.01
Iroquois (2)	5	0.03
Latin American Indians (3)	10	0.05
Lumbee (1)	1	0.01
Navajo (1)	3	0.02
Pima (1)	1	0.01
Potawatomi (1)	1	0.01
Pueblo (6)	12	0.06
Seminole	1	0.01
Sioux (2)	3	0.02
Yakama	1	0.01
All other tribes (7)	11	0.06
American Indian tribes, not spec.	4	0.02
Arab:	115	0.62
Arab/Arabic	50	0.27
Egyptian	25	0.14
Jordanian	7	0.04
Lebanese	13	0.07
Palestinian	15	0.08
Syrian	5	0.03
Armenian	61	0.33
Asian:	1,107	5.96
Chinese, ex. Taiwanese (202)	279	1.50
Filipino (119)	177	0.95
Hmong	1	0.01
Indian (45)	60	0.32
Indonesian (3)	11	0.06
Japanese (250)	359	1.93
Korean (98)	123	0.66
Laotian (1)	1	0.01
Pakistani (2)	4	0.02
Taiwanese (13)	14	0.08
Thai (7)	11	0.06
Vietnamese (39)	47	0.25
Other Asian, specified	1	0.01
Other Asian, not specified (7)	19	0.10
Assyrian/Chaldean/Syriac	17	0.09
Australian	23	0.12
Austrian	138	0.75
Basque	7	0.04
Belgian	73	0.40
Brazilian	34	0.18
British	179	0.97
Bulgarian	16	0.09
Canadian	102	0.55
Croatian	29	0.16
Czech	154	0.84
Czechoslovakian	25	0.14
Danish	125	0.68
Dutch	467	2.53
Eastern European	53	0.29
English	2,627	14.24
Estonian	6	0.03
European	305	1.65
Finnish	29	0.16
French, except Basque	1,039	5.63
French Canadian	90	0.49
German	3,543	19.21
Greek	179	0.97
Hawaii Native/Pacific Islander:	80	0.43
Melanesian: (1)	1	0.01
Fijian (1)	1	0.01
Micronesian: (5)	7	0.04
Guamanian/Chamorro (5)	7	0.04
Polynesian: (24)	48	0.26
Native Hawaiian (18)	38	0.20
Samoan (6)	9	0.05
Other Polynesian	1	0.01
Other Pac. Isl., not spec. (10)	24	0.13
Hispanic or Latino:	1,253	6.75
Central American:	58	0.31
Costa Rican	18	0.10
Guatemalan	12	0.06
Honduran	3	0.02
Nicaraguan	11	0.06
Panamanian	2	0.01
Salvadoran	6	0.03
Other Central American	6	0.03
Cuban	47	0.25
Dominican Republic	1	0.01
Mexican	714	3.85
Puerto Rican	74	0.40
South American:	115	0.62
Argentinean	23	0.12
Bolivian	3	0.02
Chilean	9	0.05
Colombian	26	0.14
Ecuadorian	12	0.06
Peruvian	23	0.12
Uruguayan	3	0.02
Venezuelan	5	0.03
Other South American	11	0.06
Other Hispanic or Latino	244	1.31
Hungarian	240	1.30
Icelander	8	0.04
Iranian	71	0.38
Irish	2,785	15.10
Israeli	14	0.08
Italian	1,570	8.51
Latvian	7	0.04
Lithuanian	93	0.50
Maltese	6	0.03
Northern European	47	0.25
Norwegian	548	2.97
Pennsylvania German	15	0.08
Polish	671	3.64
Portuguese	99	0.54
Romanian	60	0.33
Russian	708	3.84
Scandinavian	82	0.44
Scotch-Irish	393	2.13
Scottish	561	3.04
Serbian	28	0.15
Slovak	37	0.20
Slovene	15	0.08
Swedish	493	2.67
Swiss	85	0.46
Turkish	5	0.03
Ukrainian	181	0.98
United States or American	505	2.74
Welsh	175	0.95
West Indian, excl. Hispanic:	20	0.11
Jamaican	20	0.11
White:	17,114	92.18
Not Hispanic (15,822)	16,193	87.22
Hispanic (810)	921	4.96
Yugoslavian	100	0.54

Hesperia

Place Type: City
County: San Bernardino
Population: 62,582

Ancestry/Race	Number	%
Acadian/Cajun	31	0.05
African American/Black:	2,958	4.73
Not Hispanic (2,388)	2,733	4.37
Hispanic (134)	225	0.36
African, sub-Saharan:	157	0.25
African	135	0.22
Nigerian	15	0.02
Somalian	7	0.01
Alaska Native tribes, specified:	4	0.01
Eskimo	3	0.00
Tlingit-Haida (1)	1	0.00
Am. Ind. or Alaska Nat., not spec.	502	0.80
American Indian tribes, specified:	1,009	1.61
Apache (40)	72	0.12
Blackfeet (15)	43	0.07
Cherokee (82)	292	0.47
Cheyenne (5)	7	0.01
Chickasaw (1)	5	0.01
Chippewa (11)	19	0.03
Choctaw (16)	58	0.09
Comanche (4)	13	0.02
Cree (1)	2	0.00
Creek (2)	4	0.01
Crow	6	0.01
Delaware	2	0.00
Iroquois (7)	19	0.03
Latin American Indians (58)	97	0.15
Navajo (33)	62	0.10
Osage (4)	8	0.01
Ottawa (3)	3	0.00
Paiute (7)	11	0.02
Pima (9)	12	0.02
Potawatomi (5)	8	0.01
Pueblo (19)	46	0.07
Seminole (1)	5	0.01
Shoshone (1)	5	0.01
Sioux (12)	29	0.05
Tohono O'Odham (2)	5	0.01
Ute	1	0.00
Yakama (1)	1	0.00
Yaqui (9)	18	0.03
Yuman	3	0.00
All other tribes (110)	153	0.24
American Indian tribes, not spec.	98	0.16
Arab:	138	0.22
Arab/Arabic	10	0.02
Lebanese	54	0.09

Notes: 1. Figures in the "Number" column do not add up to the total population due to: a) Ancestry/Race overlap — e.g. persons can report being both White and Irish, b) persons of Hispanic origin can report being any race, c) persons reporting two ancestries are counted in both categories. 2. Numbers in parentheses indicate the number of persons reporting this ancestry/race alone, not in combination with any other ancestry/race. 3. Refer to the Explanation of Data in the front of the book for more detailed information.

Ancestry/Race	Number	%
Syrian	74	0.12
Armenian	65	0.10
Asian:	1,148	1.83
Cambodian (17)	23	0.04
Chinese, ex. Taiwanese (42)	87	0.14
Filipino (259)	458	0.73
Indian (63)	77	0.12
Indonesian (19)	38	0.06
Japanese (88)	178	0.28
Korean (63)	105	0.17
Laotian (1)	1	0.00
Malaysian	4	0.01
Sri Lankan (1)	2	0.00
Taiwanese (6)	6	0.01
Thai (27)	41	0.07
Vietnamese (57)	67	0.11
Other Asian, specified	2	0.00
Other Asian, not specified (18)	59	0.09
Australian	31	0.05
Austrian	66	0.11
Basque	65	0.10
Belgian	22	0.04
British	59	0.09
Bulgarian	20	0.03
Canadian	261	0.42
Celtic	21	0.03
Croatian	6	0.01
Czech	216	0.35
Czechoslovakian	70	0.11
Danish	403	0.64
Dutch	1,033	1.65
English	5,869	9.38
European	719	1.15
Finnish	124	0.20
French, except Basque	2,228	3.56
French Canadian	402	0.64
German	9,052	14.47
Greek	108	0.17
Hawaii Native/Pacific Islander:	268	0.43
Micronesian: (25)	41	0.07
Guamanian/Chamorro (25)	40	0.06
Other Micronesian	1	0.00
Polynesian: (82)	189	0.30
Native Hawaiian (35)	100	0.16
Samoan (36)	72	0.12
Tongan	1	0.00
Other Polynesian (11)	16	0.03
Other Pac. Isl., not spec. (14)	38	0.06
Hispanic or Latino:	18,400	29.40
Central American:	515	0.82
Costa Rican	23	0.04
Guatemalan	183	0.29
Honduran	15	0.02
Nicaraguan	45	0.07
Panamanian	16	0.03
Salvadoran	175	0.28
Other Central American	58	0.09
Cuban	189	0.30
Dominican Republic	15	0.02
Mexican	14,184	22.66
Puerto Rican	345	0.55
South American:	119	0.19
Argentinean	22	0.04
Bolivian	3	0.00
Chilean	5	0.01
Colombian	42	0.07
Ecuadorian	18	0.03
Peruvian	19	0.03
Venezuelan	1	0.00
Other South American	9	0.01
Other Hispanic or Latino	3,033	4.85
Hungarian	161	0.26
Iranian	41	0.07
Irish	6,136	9.81
Italian	2,550	4.07
Latvian	8	0.01
Lithuanian	96	0.15
Luxemburger	9	0.01
Northern European	14	0.02
Norwegian	660	1.05
Pennsylvania German	23	0.04
Polish	1,135	1.81
Portuguese	154	0.25
Romanian	30	0.05
Russian	249	0.40
Scandinavian	118	0.19
Scotch-Irish	1,090	1.74
Scottish	812	1.30
Slavic	36	0.06
Slovak	56	0.09
Swedish	1,039	1.66
Swiss	121	0.19
Ukrainian	22	0.04
United States or American	3,937	6.29
Welsh	394	0.63
West Indian, excl. Hispanic:	96	0.15
Barbadian	2	0.00
Belizean	10	0.02
Dutch West Indian	10	0.02
Haitian	9	0.01
Jamaican	46	0.07
Trinidadian and Tobagonian	19	0.03
White:	49,113	78.48
Not Hispanic (39,057)	40,355	64.48
Hispanic (7,428)	8,758	13.99
Yugoslavian	58	0.09

Highland

Place Type: City
County: San Bernardino
Population: 44,605

Ancestry/Race	Number	%
African American/Black:	5,944	13.33
Not Hispanic (5,226)	5,640	12.64
Hispanic (177)	304	0.68
African, sub-Saharan:	335	0.75
African	233	0.52
Nigerian	102	0.23
Alaska Native tribes, specified:	15	0.03
Aleut (2)	3	0.01
Eskimo (1)	4	0.01
Tlingit-Haida (4)	8	0.02
Am. Ind. or Alaska Nat., not spec.	386	0.87
American Indian tribes, specified:	678	1.52
Apache (15)	50	0.11
Blackfeet (4)	32	0.07
Cherokee (73)	200	0.45
Cheyenne	2	0.00
Chickasaw (2)	5	0.01
Chippewa (5)	10	0.02
Choctaw (10)	31	0.07
Comanche (1)	6	0.01
Creek (6)	12	0.03
Iroquois (5)	12	0.03
Latin American Indians (47)	79	0.18
Lumbee	3	0.01
Menominee	2	0.00
Navajo (28)	40	0.09
Osage	2	0.00
Ottawa (1)	1	0.00
Paiute (1)	2	0.00
Pima (1)	3	0.01
Potawatomi (2)	3	0.01
Pueblo (13)	14	0.03
Seminole (1)	2	0.00
Shoshone (1)	9	0.02
Sioux (15)	23	0.05
Tohono O'Odham (3)	5	0.01
Yaqui (10)	17	0.04
Yuman	3	0.01
All other tribes (65)	110	0.25
American Indian tribes, not spec.	45	0.10
Arab:	156	0.35
Arab/Arabic	48	0.11
Egyptian	25	0.06
Jordanian	28	0.06
Lebanese	33	0.07
Palestinian	22	0.05
Armenian	64	0.14
Asian:	3,357	7.53
Bangladeshi (3)	8	0.02
Cambodian (121)	146	0.33
Chinese, ex. Taiwanese (162)	258	0.58
Filipino (784)	944	2.12
Hmong	1	0.00
Indian (131)	180	0.40
Indonesian (49)	80	0.18
Japanese (125)	248	0.56
Korean (181)	206	0.46
Laotian (17)	26	0.06
Malaysian (3)	3	0.01
Pakistani (19)	28	0.06
Sri Lankan (8)	8	0.02
Taiwanese (11)	16	0.04
Thai (95)	127	0.28
Vietnamese (900)	966	2.17
Other Asian, specified (3)	8	0.02
Other Asian, not specified (45)	104	0.23
Australian	39	0.09
Austrian	18	0.04
Basque	39	0.09
Belgian	57	0.13
British	142	0.32
Canadian	116	0.26
Celtic	18	0.04
Czech	136	0.30
Czechoslovakian	97	0.22
Danish	335	0.75
Dutch	449	1.01
Eastern European	21	0.05
English	2,852	6.39
European	204	0.46
Finnish	45	0.10
French, except Basque	1,108	2.48
French Canadian	138	0.31
German	4,431	9.93
Greek	152	0.34
Hawaii Native/Pacific Islander:	268	0.60
Melanesian: (4)	7	0.02
Fijian (4)	7	0.02
Micronesian: (38)	44	0.10
Guamanian/Chamorro (21)	27	0.06
Other Micronesian (17)	17	0.04
Polynesian: (96)	162	0.36
Native Hawaiian (23)	64	0.14
Samoan (62)	80	0.18
Tongan (11)	17	0.04
Other Polynesian	1	0.00
Other Pac. Isl., specified	5	0.01
Other Pac. Isl., not spec. (13)	50	0.11
Hispanic or Latino:	16,342	36.64
Central American:	318	0.71
Costa Rican	15	0.03
Guatemalan	47	0.11
Honduran	29	0.07
Nicaraguan	66	0.15
Panamanian	26	0.06
Salvadoran	108	0.24
Other Central American	27	0.06
Cuban	68	0.15
Dominican Republic	11	0.02
Mexican	13,397	30.03
Puerto Rican	245	0.55
South American:	94	0.21
Argentinean	12	0.03
Bolivian	4	0.01
Chilean	9	0.02
Colombian	15	0.03
Ecuadorian	12	0.03
Peruvian	25	0.06
Uruguayan	1	0.00
Venezuelan	6	0.01
Other South American	10	0.02
Other Hispanic or Latino	2,209	4.95
Hungarian	155	0.35
Iranian	40	0.09
Irish	3,449	7.73
Italian	1,410	3.16

Notes: 1. Figures in the "Number" column do not add up to the total population due to: a) Ancestry/Race overlap — e.g. persons can report being both White and Irish, b) persons of Hispanic origin can report being any race, c) persons reporting two ancestries are counted in both categories. 2. Numbers in parentheses indicate the number of persons reporting this ancestry/race alone, not in combination with any other ancestry/race. 3. Refer to the Explanation of Data in the front of the book for more detailed information.

Lithuanian	20	0.04
New Zealander	7	0.02
Norwegian	467	1.05
Polish	678	1.52
Portuguese	70	0.16
Romanian	47	0.11
Russian	132	0.30
Scandinavian	9	0.02
Scotch-Irish	402	0.90
Scottish	414	0.93
Serbian	12	0.03
Slovak	10	0.02
Slovene	34	0.08
Swedish	513	1.15
Swiss	45	0.10
Ukrainian	81	0.18
United States or American	1,476	3.31
Welsh	156	0.35
West Indian, excl. Hispanic:	59	0.13
Haitian	38	0.09
Jamaican	17	0.04
West Indian	4	0.01
White:	27,008	60.55
Not Hispanic (18,619)	19,617	43.98
Hispanic (6,470)	7,391	16.57
Yugoslavian	53	0.12

Hillsborough

Place Type: Town
County: San Mateo
Population: 10,825

Ancestry/Race	Number	%
African American/Black:	69	0.64
Not Hispanic (54)	69	0.64
African, sub-Saharan:	8	0.07
South African	8	0.07
Am. Ind. or Alaska Nat., not spec.	8	0.07
American Indian tribes, specified:	15	0.14
Cherokee	4	0.04
Choctaw	2	0.02
Latin American Indians	3	0.03
Lumbee	3	0.03
Potawatomi (1)	1	0.01
Sioux	1	0.01
All other tribes	1	0.01
American Indian tribes, not spec.	8	0.07
Arab:	56	0.52
Arab/Arabic	11	0.10
Egyptian	29	0.27
Iraqi	9	0.08
Lebanese	7	0.06
Armenian	95	0.88
Asian:	2,881	26.61
Chinese, ex. Taiwanese (1,860)	2,000	18.48
Filipino (183)	243	2.24
Indian (119)	137	1.27
Indonesian (8)	13	0.12
Japanese (157)	238	2.20
Korean (53)	69	0.64
Pakistani (6)	8	0.07
Taiwanese (113)	122	1.13
Thai (9)	11	0.10
Vietnamese (3)	3	0.03
Other Asian, specified (2)	3	0.03
Other Asian, not specified (13)	34	0.31
Austrian	70	0.65
Basque	9	0.08
Belgian	7	0.06
British	94	0.87
Canadian	17	0.16
Croatian	17	0.16
Czech	98	0.91
Czechoslovakian	17	0.16
Danish	93	0.86
Dutch	126	1.16
Eastern European	6	0.06
English	1,206	11.14
Estonian	44	0.41
European	144	1.33
Finnish	51	0.47
French, except Basque	271	2.50
French Canadian	17	0.16
German	1,750	16.17
Greek	324	2.99
Hawaii Native/Pacific Islander:	38	0.35
Melanesian: (2)	3	0.03
Fijian (2)	3	0.03
Micronesian: (3)	3	0.03
Guamanian/Chamorro (3)	3	0.03
Polynesian: (17)	25	0.23
Native Hawaiian (1)	6	0.06
Tongan (14)	16	0.15
Other Polynesian (2)	3	0.03
Other Pac. Isl., not spec. (1)	7	0.06
Hispanic or Latino:	304	2.81
Central American:	41	0.38
Costa Rican	1	0.01
Guatemalan	12	0.11
Honduran	1	0.01
Nicaraguan	2	0.02
Salvadoran	21	0.19
Other Central American	4	0.04
Cuban	17	0.16
Dominican Republic	1	0.01
Mexican	120	1.11
Puerto Rican	9	0.08
South American:	32	0.30
Argentinean	14	0.13
Bolivian	2	0.02
Colombian	2	0.02
Ecuadorian	1	0.01
Peruvian	11	0.10
Other South American	2	0.02
Other Hispanic or Latino	84	0.78
Hungarian	73	0.67
Iranian	173	1.60
Irish	1,396	12.90
Italian	1,178	10.88
Latvian	6	0.06
Lithuanian	14	0.13
Maltese	16	0.15
Northern European	68	0.63
Norwegian	161	1.49
Polish	285	2.63
Portuguese	42	0.39
Romanian	80	0.74
Russian	368	3.40
Scotch-Irish	172	1.59
Scottish	260	2.40
Serbian	6	0.06
Swedish	306	2.83
Swiss	148	1.37
Turkish	18	0.17
Ukrainian	29	0.27
United States or American	322	2.98
Welsh	58	0.54
West Indian, excl. Hispanic:	14	0.13
Jamaican	14	0.13
White:	8,028	74.16
Not Hispanic (7,541)	7,783	71.90
Hispanic (231)	245	2.26
Yugoslavian	16	0.15

Hollister

Place Type: City
County: San Benito
Population: 34,413

Ancestry/Race	Number	%
African American/Black:	609	1.77
Not Hispanic (387)	475	1.38
Hispanic (82)	134	0.39
African, sub-Saharan:	44	0.13
African	44	0.13
Alaska Native tribes, specified:	3	0.01
Alaska Athabascan (1)	1	0.00
Tlingit-Haida	2	0.01
Am. Ind. or Alaska Nat., not spec.	250	0.73
Alsatian	3	0.01
American Indian tribes, specified:	526	1.53
Apache (20)	31	0.09
Blackfeet (14)	33	0.10
Cherokee (19)	105	0.31
Cheyenne	1	0.00
Chickasaw (1)	7	0.02
Chippewa (2)	8	0.02
Choctaw (5)	26	0.08
Cree (1)	3	0.01
Creek (1)	5	0.01
Crow	5	0.01
Delaware	1	0.00
Iroquois (2)	6	0.02
Kiowa (1)	1	0.00
Latin American Indians (57)	103	0.30
Lumbee (1)	1	0.00
Navajo (8)	12	0.03
Osage (1)	5	0.01
Ottawa (1)	1	0.00
Paiute	5	0.01
Pima (1)	3	0.01
Potawatomi (7)	15	0.04
Pueblo (4)	4	0.01
Puget Sound Salish	1	0.00
Seminole	3	0.01
Shoshone	2	0.01
Sioux (4)	7	0.02
Tohono O'Odham	1	0.00
Ute	4	0.01
Yakama	3	0.01
Yaqui (4)	15	0.04
Yuman (3)	4	0.01
All other tribes (63)	105	0.31
American Indian tribes, not spec.	29	0.08
Arab:	66	0.19
Syrian	9	0.03
Other Arab	57	0.16
Asian:	1,512	4.39
Cambodian (15)	15	0.04
Chinese, ex. Taiwanese (98)	171	0.50
Filipino (521)	794	2.31
Hmong (11)	18	0.05
Indian (54)	74	0.22
Indonesian (2)	15	0.04
Japanese (114)	232	0.67
Korean (55)	73	0.21
Laotian (7)	8	0.02
Pakistani (6)	6	0.02
Taiwanese (1)	4	0.01
Thai (3)	4	0.01
Vietnamese (43)	58	0.17
Other Asian, specified	2	0.01
Other Asian, not specified (9)	38	0.11
Australian	5	0.01
Austrian	40	0.12
Basque	9	0.03
Belgian	7	0.02
British	64	0.18
Canadian	88	0.25
Celtic	9	0.03
Croatian	79	0.23
Czech	74	0.21
Czechoslovakian	31	0.09
Danish	199	0.57
Dutch	249	0.72
English	1,547	4.47
European	162	0.47
Finnish	10	0.03
French, except Basque	493	1.42
French Canadian	34	0.10
German	3,003	8.68
Hawaii Native/Pacific Islander:	176	0.51
Melanesian: (3)	3	0.01
Fijian (3)	3	0.01
Micronesian: (10)	31	0.09
Guamanian/Chamorro (10)	31	0.09
Polynesian: (32)	96	0.28
Native Hawaiian (12)	60	0.17

Notes: 1. Figures in the "Number" column do not add up to the total population due to: a) Ancestry/Race overlap — e.g. persons can report being both White and Irish, b) persons of Hispanic origin can report being any race, c) persons reporting two ancestries are counted in both categories. 2. Numbers in parentheses indicate the number of persons reporting this ancestry/race alone, not in combination with any other ancestry/race. 3. Refer to the Explanation of Data in the front of the book for more detailed information.

Samoan (17)	28	0.08
Tongan (1)	2	0.01
Other Polynesian (2)	6	0.02
Other Pac. Isl., not spec. (17)	46	0.13
Hispanic or Latino:	18,949	55.06
Central American:	158	0.46
Costa Rican	1	0.00
Guatemalan	39	0.11
Honduran	14	0.04
Nicaraguan	26	0.08
Panamanian	6	0.02
Salvadoran	57	0.17
Other Central American	15	0.04
Cuban	21	0.06
Dominican Republic	4	0.01
Mexican	16,381	47.60
Puerto Rican	121	0.35
South American:	63	0.18
Argentinean	9	0.03
Bolivian	3	0.01
Chilean	10	0.03
Colombian	15	0.04
Ecuadorian	4	0.01
Peruvian	9	0.03
Uruguayan	2	0.01
Venezuelan	5	0.01
Other South American	6	0.02
Other Hispanic or Latino	2,201	6.40
Hungarian	80	0.23
Icelander	9	0.03
Iranian	72	0.21
Irish	2,611	7.54
Italian	1,681	4.86
Maltese	9	0.03
Northern European	8	0.02
Norwegian	409	1.18
Pennsylvania German	5	0.01
Polish	207	0.60
Portuguese	1,010	2.92
Romanian	28	0.08
Russian	128	0.37
Scandinavian	89	0.26
Scotch-Irish	304	0.88
Scottish	535	1.55
Slovene	12	0.03
Swedish	419	1.21
Swiss	169	0.49
United States or American	1,204	3.48
Welsh	174	0.50
West Indian, excl. Hispanic:	23	0.07
Bahamian	7	0.02
Trinidadian and Tobagonian	16	0.05
White:	21,944	63.77
Not Hispanic (13,246)	13,853	40.26
Hispanic (7,095)	8,091	23.51
Yugoslavian	39	0.11

Huntington Beach

Place Type: City
County: Orange
Population: 189,594

Ancestry/Race	Number	%
Acadian/Cajun	8	0.00
Afghan	97	0.05
African American/Black:	2,179	1.15
Not Hispanic (1,383)	1,903	1.00
Hispanic (144)	276	0.15
African, sub-Saharan:	360	0.19
African	84	0.04
Ethiopian	23	0.01
Liberian	23	0.01
Nigerian	42	0.02
South African	156	0.08
Ugandan	16	0.01
Other sub-Saharan African	16	0.01
Alaska Native tribes, specified:	17	0.01
Alaska Athabascan (1)	3	0.00
Aleut (4)	7	0.00
Eskimo (3)	3	0.00
Tlingit-Haida (2)	4	0.00
Alaska Native tribes, not specified	3	0.00
Am. Ind. or Alaska Nat., not spec.	806	0.43
Albanian	42	0.02
Alsatian	29	0.02
American Indian tribes, specified:	2,049	1.08
Apache (56)	137	0.07
Blackfeet (15)	91	0.05
Cherokee (185)	689	0.36
Cheyenne (3)	8	0.00
Chickasaw (17)	31	0.02
Chippewa (41)	69	0.04
Choctaw (54)	156	0.08
Colville (3)	3	0.00
Comanche (5)	14	0.01
Cree (4)	10	0.01
Creek (23)	31	0.02
Crow (1)	2	0.00
Delaware (8)	13	0.01
Iroquois (12)	36	0.02
Kiowa	2	0.00
Latin American Indians (80)	155	0.08
Lumbee (4)	12	0.01
Menominee (1)	2	0.00
Navajo (24)	53	0.03
Osage (5)	19	0.01
Ottawa (4)	8	0.00
Paiute (12)	19	0.01
Pima (3)	5	0.00
Potawatomi (12)	29	0.02
Pueblo (21)	40	0.02
Puget Sound Salish (3)	4	0.00
Seminole (6)	16	0.01
Shoshone (7)	12	0.01
Sioux (28)	75	0.04
Tohono O'Odham (6)	6	0.00
Ute	2	0.00
Yaqui (20)	36	0.02
Yuman (2)	5	0.00
All other tribes (123)	259	0.14
American Indian tribes, not spec.	84	0.04
Arab:	1,966	1.04
Arab/Arabic	151	0.08
Egyptian	693	0.36
Iraqi	45	0.02
Jordanian	31	0.02
Lebanese	489	0.26
Moroccan	64	0.03
Palestinian	106	0.06
Syrian	269	0.14
Other Arab	118	0.06
Armenian	693	0.36
Asian:	21,200	11.18
Bangladeshi (10)	12	0.01
Cambodian (68)	87	0.05
Chinese, ex. Taiwanese (3,042)	3,785	2.00
Filipino (1,825)	2,717	1.43
Hmong (28)	28	0.01
Indian (1,005)	1,162	0.61
Indonesian (110)	243	0.13
Japanese (3,110)	4,174	2.20
Korean (1,637)	1,822	0.96
Laotian (78)	89	0.05
Malaysian (4)	13	0.01
Pakistani (83)	113	0.06
Sri Lankan (32)	36	0.02
Taiwanese (477)	571	0.30
Thai (184)	242	0.13
Vietnamese (5,422)	5,706	3.01
Other Asian, specified (30)	39	0.02
Other Asian, not specified (119)	361	0.19
Assyrian/Chaldean/Syriac	82	0.04
Australian	147	0.08
Austrian	873	0.46
Basque	145	0.08
Belgian	297	0.16
Brazilian	143	0.08
British	1,186	0.62
Bulgarian	15	0.01
Canadian	1,141	0.60
Celtic	44	0.02
Croatian	466	0.25
Cypriot	25	0.01
Czech	605	0.32
Czechoslovakian	313	0.16
Danish	1,770	0.93
Dutch	3,898	2.05
Eastern European	133	0.07
English	22,467	11.83
European	2,127	1.12
Finnish	547	0.29
French, except Basque	7,021	3.70
French Canadian	1,754	0.92
German	31,677	16.68
German Russian	13	0.01
Greek	1,197	0.63
Guyanese	22	0.01
Hawaii Native/Pacific Islander:	1,114	0.59
Micronesian: (117)	174	0.09
Guamanian/Chamorro (86)	141	0.07
Other Micronesian (31)	33	0.02
Polynesian: (300)	692	0.36
Native Hawaiian (188)	514	0.27
Samoan (84)	121	0.06
Tongan (21)	30	0.02
Other Polynesian (7)	27	0.01
Other Pac. Isl., specified	3	0.00
Other Pac. Isl., not spec. (30)	245	0.13
Hispanic or Latino:	27,798	14.66
Central American:	641	0.34
Costa Rican	69	0.04
Guatemalan	184	0.10
Honduran	39	0.02
Nicaraguan	60	0.03
Panamanian	48	0.03
Salvadoran	152	0.08
Other Central American	89	0.05
Cuban	485	0.26
Dominican Republic	14	0.01
Mexican	20,894	11.02
Puerto Rican	629	0.33
South American:	1,062	0.56
Argentinean	222	0.12
Bolivian	37	0.02
Chilean	92	0.05
Colombian	201	0.11
Ecuadorian	87	0.05
Paraguayan	3	0.00
Peruvian	242	0.13
Uruguayan	30	0.02
Venezuelan	23	0.01
Other South American	125	0.07
Other Hispanic or Latino	4,073	2.15
Hungarian	1,305	0.69
Iranian	1,192	0.63
Irish	25,309	13.32
Israeli	215	0.11
Italian	13,455	7.08
Latvian	47	0.02
Lithuanian	726	0.38
Luxemburger	30	0.02
Macedonian	7	0.00
Maltese	81	0.04
New Zealander	59	0.03
Northern European	239	0.13
Norwegian	3,874	2.04
Pennsylvania German	49	0.03
Polish	4,812	2.53
Portuguese	993	0.52
Romanian	522	0.27
Russian	2,925	1.54
Scandinavian	498	0.26
Scotch-Irish	3,781	1.99
Scottish	4,900	2.58
Serbian	118	0.06
Slavic	89	0.05
Slovak	302	0.16
Slovene	114	0.06
Swedish	4,466	2.35

Notes: 1. Figures in the "Number" column do not add up to the total population due to: a) Ancestry/Race overlap — e.g. persons can report being both White and Irish, b) persons of Hispanic origin can report being any race, c) persons reporting two ancestries are counted in both categories. 2. Numbers in parentheses indicate the number of persons reporting this ancestry/race alone, not in combination with any other ancestry/race. 3. Refer to the Explanation of Data in the front of the book for more detailed information.

Ancestry/Race	Number	%
Swiss	697	0.37
Turkish	306	0.16
Ukrainian	533	0.28
United States or American	8,322	4.38
Welsh	1,795	0.95
West Indian, excl. Hispanic:	98	0.05
Belizean	14	0.01
Bermudan	18	0.01
Dutch West Indian	7	0.00
Haitian	15	0.01
Jamaican	19	0.01
Trinidadian and Tobagonian	4	0.00
West Indian	21	0.01
White:	156,886	82.75
Not Hispanic (136,237)	140,797	74.26
Hispanic (13,957)	16,089	8.49
Yugoslavian	510	0.27

Huntington Park

Place Type: City
County: Los Angeles
Population: 61,348

Ancestry/Race	Number	%
African American/Black:	612	1.00
Not Hispanic (304)	328	0.53
Hispanic (174)	284	0.46
African, sub-Saharan:	33	0.05
African	33	0.05
Am. Ind. or Alaska Nat., not spec.	448	0.73
Albanian	8	0.01
American Indian tribes, specified:	330	0.54
Apache (4)	11	0.02
Blackfeet (2)	4	0.01
Cherokee (4)	10	0.02
Chippewa (2)	2	0.00
Choctaw	7	0.01
Comanche (1)	5	0.01
Creek (1)	5	0.01
Crow (1)	1	0.00
Latin American Indians (176)	218	0.36
Navajo (20)	24	0.04
Pueblo (4)	7	0.01
Seminole	1	0.00
Shoshone	7	0.01
Sioux (1)	1	0.00
Tohono O'Odham (1)	1	0.00
Yaqui (11)	13	0.02
All other tribes (10)	13	0.02
American Indian tribes, not spec.	47	0.08
Arab:	94	0.15
Arab/Arabic	56	0.09
Lebanese	38	0.06
Asian:	636	1.04
Bangladeshi (1)	1	0.00
Chinese, ex. Taiwanese (47)	66	0.11
Filipino (243)	265	0.43
Indian (38)	75	0.12
Indonesian (2)	2	0.00
Japanese (31)	51	0.08
Korean (10)	12	0.02
Laotian (8)	9	0.01
Pakistani	2	0.00
Sri Lankan	1	0.00
Taiwanese (6)	10	0.02
Thai (6)	10	0.02
Vietnamese (78)	85	0.14
Other Asian, not specified (8)	47	0.08
Canadian	12	0.02
Celtic	12	0.02
Czech	9	0.01
Czechoslovakian	18	0.03
Dutch	30	0.05
English	162	0.26
Estonian	9	0.01
European	15	0.02
French, except Basque	62	0.10
French Canadian	11	0.02
German	288	0.47
Hawaii Native/Pacific Islander:	91	0.15
Micronesian: (8)	16	0.03
Guamanian/Chamorro (8)	15	0.02
Other Micronesian	1	0.00
Polynesian: (11)	28	0.05
Native Hawaiian (5)	21	0.03
Samoan (6)	7	0.01
Other Pac. Isl., not spec. (19)	47	0.08
Hispanic or Latino:	58,636	95.58
Central American:	4,334	7.06
Costa Rican	58	0.09
Guatemalan	995	1.62
Honduran	230	0.37
Nicaraguan	334	0.54
Panamanian	23	0.04
Salvadoran	2,258	3.68
Other Central American	436	0.71
Cuban	689	1.12
Dominican Republic	20	0.03
Mexican	44,948	73.27
Puerto Rican	234	0.38
South American:	419	0.68
Argentinean	32	0.05
Bolivian	11	0.02
Chilean	8	0.01
Colombian	115	0.19
Ecuadorian	119	0.19
Paraguayan	1	0.00
Peruvian	85	0.14
Venezuelan	12	0.02
Other South American	36	0.06
Other Hispanic or Latino	7,992	13.03
Hungarian	31	0.05
Irish	233	0.38
Israeli	7	0.01
Italian	169	0.28
Latvian	11	0.02
Polish	58	0.09
Portuguese	6	0.01
Romanian	44	0.07
Russian	27	0.04
Scotch-Irish	32	0.05
Scottish	34	0.06
Slavic	8	0.01
Slovak	20	0.03
Swedish	5	0.01
Swiss	8	0.01
Turkish	4	0.01
Ukrainian	9	0.01
United States or American	978	1.59
Welsh	20	0.03
West Indian, excl. Hispanic:	110	0.18
Belizean	59	0.10
Haitian	20	0.03
Jamaican	31	0.05
White:	28,136	45.86
Not Hispanic (1,657)	1,771	2.89
Hispanic (23,755)	26,365	42.98
Yugoslavian	7	0.01

Imperial Beach

Place Type: City
County: San Diego
Population: 26,992

Ancestry/Race	Number	%
Acadian/Cajun	14	0.05
African American/Black:	1,723	6.38
Not Hispanic (1,343)	1,575	5.84
Hispanic (78)	148	0.55
African, sub-Saharan:	38	0.14
African	20	0.07
Cape Verdean	18	0.07
Alaska Native tribes, specified:	20	0.07
Alaska Athabascan (5)	9	0.03
Aleut (2)	2	0.01
Eskimo (1)	5	0.02
Tlingit-Haida (2)	4	0.01
Alaska Native tribes, not specified	1	0.00
Am. Ind. or Alaska Nat., not spec.	175	0.65
American Indian tribes, specified:	381	1.41
Apache (11)	17	0.06
Blackfeet (8)	17	0.06
Cherokee (25)	107	0.40
Chickasaw (6)	8	0.03
Chippewa (9)	12	0.04
Choctaw (8)	12	0.04
Colville (1)	1	0.00
Comanche (2)	6	0.02
Creek (2)	5	0.02
Crow	3	0.01
Delaware (3)	4	0.01
Iroquois (10)	11	0.04
Latin American Indians (38)	54	0.20
Lumbee (4)	4	0.01
Navajo (20)	33	0.12
Osage	7	0.03
Paiute (1)	2	0.01
Pueblo (7)	9	0.03
Puget Sound Salish (1)	3	0.01
Sioux (1)	7	0.03
Tohono O'Odham	1	0.00
Yaqui (8)	8	0.03
Yuman (1)	2	0.01
All other tribes (30)	48	0.18
American Indian tribes, not spec.	20	0.07
Arab:	118	0.44
Arab/Arabic	66	0.24
Iraqi	28	0.10
Lebanese	20	0.07
Other Arab	4	0.01
Asian:	2,569	9.52
Cambodian (3)	8	0.03
Chinese, ex. Taiwanese (47)	120	0.44
Filipino (1,418)	1,910	7.08
Hmong (2)	2	0.01
Indian (9)	23	0.09
Indonesian (1)	9	0.03
Japanese (138)	288	1.07
Korean (37)	48	0.18
Laotian (4)	6	0.02
Malaysian	2	0.01
Pakistani (2)	2	0.01
Sri Lankan (1)	1	0.00
Taiwanese (5)	7	0.03
Thai (19)	30	0.11
Vietnamese (43)	71	0.26
Other Asian, specified (1)	3	0.01
Other Asian, not specified (9)	39	0.14
Australian	32	0.12
Austrian	5	0.02
Belgian	22	0.08
British	77	0.29
Bulgarian	11	0.04
Canadian	127	0.47
Croatian	16	0.06
Czech	49	0.18
Czechoslovakian	20	0.07
Danish	201	0.74
Dutch	342	1.27
English	1,711	6.34
European	261	0.97
Finnish	49	0.18
French, except Basque	631	2.34
French Canadian	154	0.57
German	2,943	10.91
Greek	97	0.36
Hawaii Native/Pacific Islander:	370	1.37
Melanesian: (4)	8	0.03
Fijian (3)	7	0.03
Other Melanesian (1)	1	0.00
Micronesian: (56)	104	0.39
Guamanian/Chamorro (51)	99	0.37
Other Micronesian (5)	5	0.02
Polynesian: (74)	187	0.69
Native Hawaiian (29)	100	0.37
Samoan (34)	71	0.26
Tongan (1)	3	0.01
Other Polynesian (10)	13	0.05

Notes: 1. Figures in the "Number" column do not add up to the total population due to: a) Ancestry/Race overlap — e.g. persons can report being both White and Irish, b) persons of Hispanic origin can report being any race, c) persons reporting two ancestries are counted in both categories. 2. Numbers in parentheses indicate the number of persons reporting this ancestry/race alone, not in combination with any other ancestry/race. 3. Refer to the Explanation of Data in the front of the book for more detailed information.

Ancestry/Race	Number	%
Other Pac. Isl., specified	2	0.01
Other Pac. Isl., not spec. (22)	69	0.26
Hispanic or Latino:	10,818	40.08
Central American:	67	0.25
Costa Rican	2	0.01
Guatemalan	14	0.05
Honduran	11	0.04
Nicaraguan	6	0.02
Panamanian	9	0.03
Salvadoran	21	0.08
Other Central American	4	0.01
Cuban	41	0.15
Dominican Republic	6	0.02
Mexican	9,081	33.64
Puerto Rican	245	0.91
South American:	59	0.22
Argentinean	13	0.05
Chilean	4	0.01
Colombian	11	0.04
Ecuadorian	7	0.03
Peruvian	19	0.07
Venezuelan	2	0.01
Other South American	3	0.01
Other Hispanic or Latino	1,319	4.89
Hungarian	92	0.34
Iranian	7	0.03
Irish	1,803	6.68
Italian	1,088	4.03
Latvian	15	0.06
Lithuanian	14	0.05
Luxemburger	6	0.02
Northern European	19	0.07
Norwegian	313	1.16
Pennsylvania German	8	0.03
Polish	266	0.99
Portuguese	179	0.66
Romanian	53	0.20
Russian	111	0.41
Scandinavian	40	0.15
Scotch-Irish	470	1.74
Scottish	422	1.56
Serbian	8	0.03
Swedish	283	1.05
Swiss	47	0.17
Ukrainian	59	0.22
United States or American	1,050	3.89
Welsh	160	0.59
West Indian, excl. Hispanic:	77	0.29
Belizean	10	0.04
Jamaican	44	0.16
Trinidadian and Tobagonian	10	0.04
West Indian	13	0.05
White:	18,220	67.50
Not Hispanic (11,737)	12,581	46.61
Hispanic (5,068)	5,639	20.89

Indio

Place Type: City
County: Riverside
Population: 49,116

Ancestry/Race	Number	%
Acadian/Cajun	24	0.05
African American/Black:	1,542	3.14
Not Hispanic (1,199)	1,283	2.61
Hispanic (162)	259	0.53
African, sub-Saharan:	46	0.09
African	40	0.08
Nigerian	6	0.01
Alaska Native tribes, specified:	2	0.00
Alaska Athabascan (1)	1	0.00
Eskimo	1	0.00
Am. Ind. or Alaska Nat., not spec.	308	0.63
American Indian tribes, specified:	398	0.81
Apache (35)	43	0.09
Blackfeet (6)	11	0.02
Cherokee (13)	83	0.17
Chippewa	2	0.00
Choctaw (6)	10	0.02
Comanche	1	0.00
Cree	1	0.00
Creek (1)	4	0.01
Iroquois (6)	10	0.02
Latin American Indians (70)	95	0.19
Lumbee	2	0.00
Navajo (12)	14	0.03
Osage (3)	5	0.01
Paiute (1)	1	0.00
Pima (6)	6	0.01
Pueblo (3)	4	0.01
Puget Sound Salish (3)	3	0.01
Sioux (8)	13	0.03
Tohono O'Odham (2)	3	0.01
Yakama (1)	1	0.00
Yaqui (12)	19	0.04
Yuman (1)	1	0.00
All other tribes (54)	66	0.13
American Indian tribes, not spec.	42	0.09
Arab:	47	0.10
Arab/Arabic	8	0.02
Jordanian	7	0.01
Lebanese	27	0.05
Palestinian	5	0.01
Armenian	77	0.16
Asian:	982	2.00
Cambodian (4)	15	0.03
Chinese, ex. Taiwanese (78)	109	0.22
Filipino (305)	415	0.84
Indian (124)	140	0.29
Indonesian	1	0.00
Japanese (103)	147	0.30
Korean (21)	32	0.07
Pakistani (8)	8	0.02
Sri Lankan (5)	5	0.01
Thai (6)	12	0.02
Vietnamese (61)	64	0.13
Other Asian, specified (2)	3	0.01
Other Asian, not specified (19)	31	0.06
Australian	8	0.02
Austrian	16	0.03
Basque	17	0.03
Belgian	14	0.03
British	84	0.17
Canadian	216	0.44
Czech	42	0.09
Czechoslovakian	6	0.01
Danish	123	0.25
Dutch	319	0.65
English	1,492	3.04
European	119	0.24
Finnish	18	0.04
French, except Basque	556	1.13
French Canadian	96	0.20
German	1,872	3.81
Greek	27	0.05
Hawaii Native/Pacific Islander:	88	0.18
Micronesian: (12)	12	0.02
Guamanian/Chamorro (12)	12	0.02
Polynesian: (19)	47	0.10
Native Hawaiian (12)	34	0.07
Samoan (7)	9	0.02
Other Polynesian	4	0.01
Other Pac. Isl., not spec. (17)	29	0.06
Hispanic or Latino:	37,028	75.39
Central American:	326	0.66
Costa Rican	2	0.00
Guatemalan	50	0.10
Honduran	12	0.02
Nicaraguan	25	0.05
Panamanian	13	0.03
Salvadoran	198	0.40
Other Central American	26	0.05
Cuban	31	0.06
Dominican Republic	1	0.00
Mexican	32,985	67.16
Puerto Rican	93	0.19
South American:	33	0.07
Argentinean	15	0.03
Chilean	4	0.01
Colombian	3	0.01
Ecuadorian	1	0.00
Peruvian	8	0.02
Other South American	2	0.00
Other Hispanic or Latino	3,559	7.25
Hungarian	45	0.09
Icelander	9	0.02
Iranian	30	0.06
Irish	1,302	2.65
Italian	548	1.11
Lithuanian	9	0.02
Northern European	26	0.05
Norwegian	217	0.44
Pennsylvania German	27	0.05
Polish	213	0.43
Portuguese	62	0.13
Romanian	9	0.02
Russian	108	0.22
Scandinavian	14	0.03
Scotch-Irish	204	0.41
Scottish	434	0.88
Serbian	12	0.02
Slovak	55	0.11
Swedish	277	0.56
Swiss	66	0.13
Ukrainian	13	0.03
United States or American	909	1.85
Welsh	29	0.06
West Indian, excl. Hispanic:	4	0.01
Jamaican	4	0.01
White:	25,565	52.05
Not Hispanic (9,586)	9,926	20.21
Hispanic (14,317)	15,639	31.84
Yugoslavian	33	0.07

Inglewood

Place Type: City
County: Los Angeles
Population: 112,580

Ancestry/Race	Number	%
Afghan	59	0.05
African American/Black:	54,823	48.70
Not Hispanic (52,260)	53,648	47.65
Hispanic (800)	1,175	1.04
African, sub-Saharan:	2,483	2.21
African	1,894	1.68
Ethiopian	166	0.15
Kenyan	12	0.01
Liberian	17	0.02
Nigerian	308	0.27
Sierra Leonean	65	0.06
Other sub-Saharan African	21	0.02
Alaska Native tribes, specified:	6	0.01
Alaska Athabascan (1)	2	0.00
Tlingit-Haida (1)	4	0.00
Am. Ind. or Alaska Nat., not spec.	749	0.67
American Indian tribes, specified:	784	0.70
Apache (7)	26	0.02
Blackfeet (2)	62	0.06
Cherokee (21)	138	0.12
Cheyenne	3	0.00
Chickasaw	6	0.01
Chippewa	2	0.00
Choctaw (7)	75	0.07
Colville (1)	1	0.00
Comanche (1)	4	0.00
Cree	2	0.00
Creek (5)	37	0.03
Iroquois (1)	4	0.00
Kiowa	1	0.00
Latin American Indians (195)	261	0.23
Navajo (23)	34	0.03
Osage	2	0.00
Paiute (1)	2	0.00
Potawatomi (1)	1	0.00
Pueblo (11)	18	0.02
Puget Sound Salish	1	0.00
Seminole (4)	14	0.01

Notes: 1. Figures in the "Number" column do not add up to the total population due to: a) Ancestry/Race overlap — e.g. persons can report being both White and Irish, b) persons of Hispanic origin can report being any race, c) persons reporting two ancestries are counted in both categories. 2. Numbers in parentheses indicate the number of persons reporting this ancestry/race alone, not in combination with any other ancestry/race. 3. Refer to the Explanation of Data in the front of the book for more detailed information.

Shoshone (8)	12	0.01
Sioux (2)	8	0.01
Tohono O'Odham (6)	6	0.01
Yaqui (1)	8	0.01
Yuman	2	0.00
All other tribes (23)	54	0.05
American Indian tribes, not spec.	76	0.07
Arab:	139	0.12
Arab/Arabic	20	0.02
Egyptian	50	0.04
Lebanese	16	0.01
Syrian	9	0.01
Other Arab	44	0.04
Armenian	61	0.05
Asian:	1,797	1.60
Bangladeshi (6)	8	0.01
Cambodian (2)	2	0.00
Chinese, ex. Taiwanese (97)	159	0.14
Filipino (479)	617	0.55
Hmong (9)	12	0.01
Indian (258)	363	0.32
Indonesian (16)	33	0.03
Japanese (153)	212	0.19
Korean (56)	85	0.08
Laotian	1	0.00
Pakistani (18)	28	0.02
Sri Lankan (9)	19	0.02
Taiwanese (11)	12	0.01
Thai (23)	30	0.03
Vietnamese (66)	89	0.08
Other Asian, specified (14)	19	0.02
Other Asian, not specified (31)	108	0.10
Austrian	7	0.01
Basque	7	0.01
Belgian	16	0.01
British	90	0.08
Canadian	130	0.12
Croatian	23	0.02
Czech	15	0.01
Czechoslovakian	31	0.03
Danish	36	0.03
Dutch	118	0.10
English	557	0.50
European	53	0.05
Finnish	7	0.01
French, except Basque	575	0.51
French Canadian	93	0.08
German	747	0.66
German Russian	29	0.03
Greek	40	0.04
Guyanese	68	0.06
Hawaii Native/Pacific Islander:	629	0.56
Melanesian: (32)	55	0.05
Fijian (32)	55	0.05
Micronesian: (34)	45	0.04
Guamanian/Chamorro (32)	43	0.04
Other Micronesian (2)	2	0.00
Polynesian: (300)	406	0.36
Native Hawaiian (26)	60	0.05
Samoan (48)	83	0.07
Tongan (215)	247	0.22
Other Polynesian (11)	16	0.01
Other Pac. Isl., specified	4	0.00
Other Pac. Isl., not spec. (37)	119	0.11
Hispanic or Latino:	51,829	46.04
Central American:	5,083	4.52
Costa Rican	70	0.06
Guatemalan	1,806	1.60
Honduran	307	0.27
Nicaraguan	221	0.20
Panamanian	100	0.09
Salvadoran	2,091	1.86
Other Central American	488	0.43
Cuban	426	0.38
Dominican Republic	24	0.02
Mexican	37,272	33.11
Puerto Rican	454	0.40
South American:	377	0.33
Argentinean	47	0.04
Bolivian	6	0.01
Chilean	12	0.01
Colombian	101	0.09
Ecuadorian	77	0.07
Paraguayan	1	0.00
Peruvian	88	0.08
Venezuelan	9	0.01
Other South American	36	0.03
Other Hispanic or Latino	8,193	7.28
Hungarian	37	0.03
Icelander	5	0.00
Iranian	31	0.03
Irish	682	0.61
Israeli	14	0.01
Italian	343	0.30
Latvian	27	0.02
Lithuanian	30	0.03
New Zealander	5	0.00
Norwegian	141	0.13
Polish	217	0.19
Portuguese	68	0.06
Romanian	41	0.04
Russian	90	0.08
Scandinavian	13	0.01
Scotch-Irish	151	0.13
Scottish	116	0.10
Serbian	15	0.01
Swedish	109	0.10
Swiss	30	0.03
Ukrainian	40	0.04
United States or American	1,475	1.31
Welsh	61	0.05
West Indian, excl. Hispanic:	1,580	1.40
Barbadian	15	0.01
Belizean	581	0.52
British West Indian	50	0.04
Haitian	68	0.06
Jamaican	630	0.56
Trinidadian and Tobagonian	152	0.14
U.S. Virgin Islander	44	0.04
West Indian	40	0.04
White:	24,696	21.94
Not Hispanic (4,628)	5,429	4.82
Hispanic (16,877)	19,267	17.11
Yugoslavian	18	0.02

Irvine

Place Type: City
County: Orange
Population: 143,072

Ancestry/Race	Number	%
Afghan	1,231	0.86
African American/Black:	2,640	1.85
Not Hispanic (1,977)	2,465	1.72
Hispanic (91)	175	0.12
African, sub-Saharan:	1,019	0.71
African	146	0.10
Cape Verdean	13	0.01
Ethiopian	37	0.03
Ghanian	31	0.02
Kenyan	6	0.00
Nigerian	3	0.00
Somalian	11	0.01
South African	751	0.53
Other sub-Saharan African	21	0.01
Alaska Native tribes, specified:	6	0.00
Alaska Athabascan (1)	1	0.00
Aleut	3	0.00
Eskimo (1)	2	0.00
Am. Ind. or Alaska Nat., not spec.	254	0.18
American Indian tribes, specified:	625	0.44
Apache (12)	37	0.03
Blackfeet (2)	29	0.02
Cherokee (33)	199	0.14
Cheyenne (2)	2	0.00
Chickasaw	11	0.01
Chippewa (6)	20	0.01
Choctaw (9)	35	0.02
Comanche (2)	2	0.00
Cree (1)	2	0.00
Creek (5)	13	0.01
Delaware	1	0.00
Houma (1)	1	0.00
Iroquois (2)	21	0.01
Kiowa	1	0.00
Latin American Indians (36)	68	0.05
Navajo (5)	19	0.01
Osage (3)	13	0.01
Ottawa	2	0.00
Paiute (5)	8	0.01
Potawatomi (1)	3	0.00
Pueblo (8)	18	0.01
Seminole	1	0.00
Shoshone	3	0.00
Sioux (9)	31	0.02
Tohono O'Odham (1)	2	0.00
Ute	1	0.00
Yaqui (5)	12	0.01
Yuman (1)	3	0.00
All other tribes (29)	67	0.05
American Indian tribes, not spec.	36	0.03
Arab:	1,714	1.20
Arab/Arabic	527	0.37
Egyptian	303	0.21
Iraqi	11	0.01
Jordanian	19	0.01
Lebanese	379	0.26
Moroccan	73	0.05
Palestinian	86	0.06
Syrian	112	0.08
Other Arab	204	0.14
Armenian	757	0.53
Asian:	47,527	33.22
Bangladeshi (21)	22	0.02
Cambodian (147)	183	0.13
Chinese, ex. Taiwanese (12,175)	13,620	9.52
Filipino (3,474)	4,223	2.95
Hmong (41)	41	0.03
Indian (4,450)	4,762	3.33
Indonesian (144)	251	0.18
Japanese (5,088)	6,075	4.25
Korean (7,593)	7,913	5.53
Laotian (49)	60	0.04
Malaysian (17)	31	0.02
Pakistani (467)	581	0.41
Sri Lankan (90)	112	0.08
Taiwanese (2,798)	3,341	2.34
Thai (403)	493	0.34
Vietnamese (4,414)	4,734	3.31
Other Asian, specified (40)	68	0.05
Other Asian, not specified (209)	1,017	0.71
Assyrian/Chaldean/Syriac	25	0.02
Australian	172	0.12
Austrian	518	0.36
Basque	95	0.07
Belgian	99	0.07
Brazilian	197	0.14
British	1,126	0.79
Bulgarian	150	0.10
Canadian	795	0.56
Celtic	27	0.02
Croatian	180	0.13
Czech	548	0.38
Czechoslovakian	215	0.15
Danish	1,109	0.78
Dutch	1,909	1.33
Eastern European	452	0.32
English	14,694	10.27
Estonian	37	0.03
European	2,029	1.42
Finnish	452	0.32
French, except Basque	3,449	2.41
French Canadian	591	0.41
German	16,574	11.59
Greek	690	0.48
Hawaii Native/Pacific Islander:	660	0.46
Melanesian:	7	0.00
Fijian	7	0.00
Micronesian: (37)	81	0.06

Notes: 1. Figures in the "Number" column do not add up to the total population due to: a) Ancestry/Race overlap — e.g. persons can report being both White and Irish, b) persons of Hispanic origin can report being any race, c) persons reporting two ancestries are counted in both categories. 2. Numbers in parentheses indicate the number of persons reporting this ancestry/race alone, not in combination with any other ancestry/race. 3. Refer to the Explanation of Data in the front of the book for more detailed information.

Guamanian/Chamorro (36)	79	0.06
Other Micronesian (1)	2	0.00
Polynesian: (133)	313	0.22
Native Hawaiian (72)	214	0.15
Samoan (54)	78	0.05
Tongan (5)	5	0.00
Other Polynesian (2)	16	0.01
Other Pac. Isl., specified	2	0.00
Other Pac. Isl., not spec. (24)	257	0.18
Hispanic or Latino:	10,539	7.37
Central American:	474	0.33
Costa Rican	61	0.04
Guatemalan	114	0.08
Honduran	23	0.02
Nicaraguan	59	0.04
Panamanian	30	0.02
Salvadoran	150	0.10
Other Central American	37	0.03
Cuban	319	0.22
Dominican Republic	41	0.03
Mexican	6,409	4.48
Puerto Rican	351	0.25
South American:	1,062	0.74
Argentinean	189	0.13
Bolivian	37	0.03
Chilean	86	0.06
Colombian	229	0.16
Ecuadorian	81	0.06
Paraguayan	3	0.00
Peruvian	267	0.19
Uruguayan	8	0.01
Venezuelan	61	0.04
Other South American	101	0.07
Other Hispanic or Latino	1,883	1.32
Hungarian	879	0.61
Icelander	53	0.04
Iranian	5,307	3.71
Irish	11,656	8.15
Israeli	187	0.13
Italian	6,766	4.73
Latvian	85	0.06
Lithuanian	378	0.26
Luxemburger	6	0.00
Macedonian	7	0.00
New Zealander	81	0.06
Northern European	42	0.03
Norwegian	2,366	1.65
Pennsylvania German	9	0.01
Polish	3,417	2.39
Portuguese	486	0.34
Romanian	391	0.27
Russian	2,703	1.89
Scandinavian	346	0.24
Scotch-Irish	1,923	1.34
Scottish	2,933	2.05
Serbian	145	0.10
Slavic	183	0.13
Slovak	177	0.12
Slovene	116	0.08
Swedish	2,773	1.94
Swiss	619	0.43
Turkish	211	0.15
Ukrainian	455	0.32
United States or American	4,601	3.22
Welsh	1,034	0.72
West Indian, excl. Hispanic:	101	0.07
Belizean	14	0.01
Haitian	6	0.00
Jamaican	61	0.04
Trinidadian and Tobagonian	20	0.01
White:	93,217	65.15
Not Hispanic (81,613)	86,475	60.44
Hispanic (5,741)	6,742	4.71
Yugoslavian	265	0.19

Isla Vista

Place Type: Census Designated Place
County: Santa Barbara
Population: 18,344

Ancestry/Race	Number	%
African American/Black:	527	2.87
Not Hispanic (341)	456	2.49
Hispanic (44)	71	0.39
African, sub-Saharan:	53	0.29
African	34	0.18
Ethiopian	7	0.04
Nigerian	7	0.04
South African	5	0.03
Alaska Native tribes, specified:	1	0.01
Aleut	1	0.01
Am. Ind. or Alaska Nat., not spec.	105	0.57
American Indian tribes, specified:	155	0.84
Apache (3)	6	0.03
Blackfeet	3	0.02
Cherokee (14)	48	0.26
Chickasaw	2	0.01
Chippewa (1)	2	0.01
Choctaw (2)	7	0.04
Comanche	1	0.01
Creek	1	0.01
Iroquois	2	0.01
Latin American Indians (8)	19	0.10
Navajo (3)	6	0.03
Osage (1)	2	0.01
Paiute (1)	4	0.02
Potawatomi (1)	1	0.01
Pueblo	1	0.01
Seminole	2	0.01
Shoshone (1)	1	0.01
Sioux (1)	4	0.02
Ute	1	0.01
Yaqui (4)	8	0.04
Yuman	1	0.01
All other tribes (14)	33	0.18
American Indian tribes, not spec.	37	0.20
Arab:	221	1.20
Arab/Arabic	29	0.16
Egyptian	82	0.45
Iraqi	5	0.03
Jordanian	6	0.03
Lebanese	43	0.23
Moroccan	6	0.03
Palestinian	33	0.18
Syrian	7	0.04
Other Arab	10	0.05
Armenian	39	0.21
Asian:	2,620	14.28
Bangladeshi (1)	1	0.01
Cambodian (14)	20	0.11
Chinese, ex. Taiwanese (712)	853	4.65
Filipino (250)	360	1.96
Hmong (15)	17	0.09
Indian (189)	218	1.19
Indonesian (1)	9	0.05
Japanese (210)	344	1.88
Korean (325)	355	1.94
Laotian (25)	29	0.16
Malaysian	6	0.03
Pakistani (6)	8	0.04
Sri Lankan (6)	6	0.03
Taiwanese (43)	50	0.27
Thai (27)	39	0.21
Vietnamese (190)	208	1.13
Other Asian, specified (2)	5	0.03
Other Asian, not specified (48)	92	0.50
Australian	27	0.15
Austrian	124	0.67
Basque	14	0.08
Belgian	17	0.09
Brazilian	21	0.11
British	95	0.52
Canadian	85	0.46
Celtic	10	0.05
Croatian	11	0.06
Czech	61	0.33
Czechoslovakian	43	0.23
Danish	81	0.44
Dutch	181	0.98
Eastern European	17	0.09
English	1,075	5.85
European	297	1.62
Finnish	31	0.17
French, except Basque	330	1.80
French Canadian	91	0.50
German	1,856	10.10
Greek	87	0.47
Hawaii Native/Pacific Islander:	112	0.61
Melanesian: (3)	4	0.02
Fijian	1	0.01
Other Melanesian (3)	3	0.02
Micronesian: (10)	16	0.09
Guamanian/Chamorro (10)	15	0.08
Other Micronesian	1	0.01
Polynesian: (25)	55	0.30
Native Hawaiian (14)	37	0.20
Samoan (10)	16	0.09
Tongan (1)	1	0.01
Other Polynesian	1	0.01
Other Pac. Isl., not spec. (4)	37	0.20
Hispanic or Latino:	3,671	20.01
Central American:	137	0.75
Costa Rican	6	0.03
Guatemalan	59	0.32
Honduran	5	0.03
Nicaraguan	12	0.07
Panamanian	4	0.02
Salvadoran	40	0.22
Other Central American	11	0.06
Cuban	33	0.18
Mexican	2,936	16.01
Puerto Rican	43	0.23
South American:	96	0.52
Argentinean	21	0.11
Bolivian	2	0.01
Chilean	18	0.10
Colombian	15	0.08
Ecuadorian	5	0.03
Peruvian	30	0.16
Uruguayan	1	0.01
Other South American	4	0.02
Other Hispanic or Latino	426	2.32
Hungarian	93	0.51
Icelander	6	0.03
Iranian	142	0.77
Irish	1,668	9.07
Israeli	20	0.11
Italian	1,028	5.59
Latvian	18	0.10
Lithuanian	31	0.17
Northern European	9	0.05
Norwegian	296	1.61
Polish	458	2.49
Portuguese	99	0.54
Romanian	57	0.31
Russian	390	2.12
Scandinavian	53	0.29
Scotch-Irish	239	1.30
Scottish	264	1.44
Serbian	20	0.11
Slavic	12	0.07
Slovak	6	0.03
Swedish	249	1.35
Swiss	65	0.35
Turkish	29	0.16
Ukrainian	17	0.09
United States or American	177	0.96
Welsh	87	0.47
West Indian, excl. Hispanic:	16	0.09
Jamaican	12	0.07
West Indian	4	0.02
White:	13,684	74.60
Not Hispanic (11,326)	12,012	65.48
Hispanic (1,422)	1,672	9.11

Notes: 1. Figures in the "Number" column do not add up to the total population due to: a) Ancestry/Race overlap — e.g. persons can report being both White and Irish, b) persons of Hispanic origin can report being any race, c) persons reporting two ancestries are counted in both categories. 2. Numbers in parentheses indicate the number of persons reporting this ancestry/race alone, not in combination with any other ancestry/race. 3. Refer to the Explanation of Data in the front of the book for more detailed information.

Yugoslavian	11	0.06

King City

Place Type: City
County: Monterey
Population: 11,094

Ancestry/Race	Number	%
African American/Black:	87	0.78
Not Hispanic (17)	24	0.22
Hispanic (48)	63	0.57
African, sub-Saharan:	16	0.14
African	16	0.14
Am. Ind. or Alaska Nat., not spec.	83	0.75
American Indian tribes, specified:	83	0.75
Blackfeet (1)	1	0.01
Cherokee (1)	8	0.07
Chickasaw	3	0.03
Choctaw (1)	1	0.01
Comanche	1	0.01
Creek (1)	1	0.01
Latin American Indians (15)	20	0.18
Navajo (1)	2	0.02
Potawatomi (3)	3	0.03
Pueblo	1	0.01
Sioux	1	0.01
Yaqui (1)	1	0.01
All other tribes (29)	40	0.36
American Indian tribes, not spec.	3	0.03
Arab:	8	0.07
Lebanese	8	0.07
Asian:	197	1.78
Chinese, ex. Taiwanese (7)	8	0.07
Filipino (78)	124	1.12
Indian (22)	27	0.24
Indonesian	1	0.01
Japanese (11)	13	0.12
Korean (16)	18	0.16
Other Asian, specified (1)	1	0.01
Other Asian, not specified	5	0.05
Austrian	7	0.06
Canadian	9	0.08
Celtic	34	0.30
Czech	9	0.08
Danish	12	0.11
Dutch	111	0.99
English	291	2.59
European	24	0.21
Finnish	8	0.07
French, except Basque	77	0.69
French Canadian	6	0.05
German	526	4.68
Hawaii Native/Pacific Islander:	38	0.34
Micronesian: (8)	9	0.08
Guamanian/Chamorro (6)	7	0.06
Other Micronesian (2)	2	0.02
Polynesian: (7)	17	0.15
Native Hawaiian (3)	13	0.12
Samoan (4)	4	0.04
Other Pac. Isl., not spec.	12	0.11
Hispanic or Latino:	8,922	80.42
Central American:	115	1.04
Costa Rican	1	0.01
Guatemalan	6	0.05
Honduran	22	0.20
Panamanian	1	0.01
Salvadoran	72	0.65
Other Central American	13	0.12
Cuban	3	0.03
Dominican Republic	1	0.01
Mexican	7,828	70.56
Puerto Rican	20	0.18
South American:	4	0.04
Bolivian	2	0.02
Colombian	1	0.01
Venezuelan	1	0.01
Other Hispanic or Latino	951	8.57
Hungarian	41	0.36
Irish	336	2.99
Italian	141	1.26
Norwegian	30	0.27
Polish	34	0.30
Portuguese	131	1.17
Russian	3	0.03
Scotch-Irish	38	0.34
Scottish	27	0.24
Swedish	21	0.19
Swiss	110	0.98
United States or American	210	1.87
White:	5,116	46.12
Not Hispanic (1,892)	1,963	17.69
Hispanic (2,777)	3,153	28.42

La Canada Flintridge

Place Type: City
County: Los Angeles
Population: 20,318

Ancestry/Race	Number	%
Afghan	23	0.11
African American/Black:	112	0.55
Not Hispanic (70)	108	0.53
Hispanic (3)	4	0.02
African, sub-Saharan:	26	0.13
African	17	0.08
South African	9	0.04
Am. Ind. or Alaska Nat., not spec.	37	0.18
Albanian	6	0.03
American Indian tribes, specified:	79	0.39
Apache	4	0.02
Blackfeet	4	0.02
Cherokee (9)	33	0.16
Cheyenne	2	0.01
Chippewa (5)	8	0.04
Choctaw	4	0.02
Iroquois (7)	7	0.03
Latin American Indians	3	0.01
Navajo (1)	2	0.01
Osage (4)	4	0.02
Seminole	2	0.01
Sioux (1)	1	0.00
Yaqui (1)	3	0.01
Yuman	2	0.01
American Indian tribes, not spec.	8	0.04
Arab:	194	0.95
Arab/Arabic	6	0.03
Egyptian	56	0.27
Iraqi	43	0.21
Lebanese	81	0.40
Syrian	8	0.04
Armenian	656	3.22
Asian:	4,681	23.04
Chinese, ex. Taiwanese (905)	1,087	5.35
Filipino (150)	192	0.94
Indian (264)	302	1.49
Indonesian (15)	24	0.12
Japanese (373)	545	2.68
Korean (2,226)	2,297	11.31
Malaysian	1	0.00
Pakistani	10	0.05
Sri Lankan (14)	18	0.09
Taiwanese (68)	86	0.42
Thai (29)	41	0.20
Vietnamese (23)	27	0.13
Other Asian, specified (4)	6	0.03
Other Asian, not specified (12)	45	0.22
Australian	61	0.30
Austrian	99	0.49
Belgian	16	0.08
Brazilian	5	0.02
British	167	0.82
Canadian	90	0.44
Celtic	37	0.18
Croatian	15	0.07
Czech	158	0.78
Czechoslovakian	124	0.61
Danish	226	1.11
Dutch	382	1.87
Eastern European	117	0.57
English	3,377	16.57
Estonian	25	0.12
European	452	2.22
Finnish	62	0.30
French, except Basque	393	1.93
French Canadian	98	0.48
German	3,020	14.82
Greek	23	0.11
Hawaii Native/Pacific Islander:	26	0.13
Micronesian: (5)	8	0.04
Guamanian/Chamorro (5)	8	0.04
Polynesian: (4)	9	0.04
Native Hawaiian (3)	8	0.04
Samoan (1)	1	0.00
Other Pac. Isl., not spec.	9	0.04
Hispanic or Latino:	976	4.80
Central American:	62	0.31
Costa Rican	3	0.01
Guatemalan	19	0.09
Honduran	10	0.05
Nicaraguan	5	0.02
Panamanian	1	0.00
Salvadoran	22	0.11
Other Central American	2	0.01
Cuban	106	0.52
Dominican Republic	2	0.01
Mexican	502	2.47
Puerto Rican	20	0.10
South American:	76	0.37
Argentinean	24	0.12
Chilean	12	0.06
Colombian	7	0.03
Ecuadorian	4	0.02
Peruvian	9	0.04
Venezuelan	4	0.02
Other South American	16	0.08
Other Hispanic or Latino	208	1.02
Hungarian	152	0.75
Iranian	246	1.21
Irish	2,261	11.09
Israeli	5	0.02
Italian	1,266	6.21
Latvian	8	0.04
Lithuanian	146	0.72
New Zealander	14	0.07
Northern European	50	0.25
Norwegian	493	2.42
Polish	390	1.91
Portuguese	59	0.29
Romanian	82	0.40
Russian	374	1.84
Scandinavian	65	0.32
Scotch-Irish	547	2.68
Scottish	702	3.44
Slavic	19	0.09
Slovak	35	0.17
Swedish	452	2.22
Swiss	195	0.96
Turkish	8	0.04
Ukrainian	98	0.48
United States or American	741	3.64
Welsh	223	1.09
West Indian, excl. Hispanic:	24	0.12
British West Indian	14	0.07
Jamaican	10	0.05
White:	15,752	77.53
Not Hispanic (14,443)	14,980	73.73
Hispanic (699)	772	3.80
Yugoslavian	7	0.03

La Crescenta-Montrose

Place Type: Census Designated Place
County: Los Angeles
Population: 18,532

Ancestry/Race	Number	%
African American/Black:	146	0.79
Not Hispanic (83)	122	0.66

Notes: 1. Figures in the "Number" column do not add up to the total population due to: a) Ancestry/Race overlap — e.g. persons can report being both White and Irish, b) persons of Hispanic origin can report being any race, c) persons reporting two ancestries are counted in both categories. 2. Numbers in parentheses indicate the number of persons reporting this ancestry/race alone, not in combination with any other ancestry/race. 3. Refer to the Explanation of Data in the front of the book for more detailed information.

Hispanic (13)	24	0.13
African, sub-Saharan:	19	0.10
African	19	0.10
Alaska Native tribes, specified:	4	0.02
Tlingit-Haida (4)	4	0.02
Am. Ind. or Alaska Nat., not spec.	50	0.27
American Indian tribes, specified:	114	0.62
Apache (4)	10	0.05
Blackfeet	5	0.03
Cherokee (12)	44	0.24
Chippewa	1	0.01
Choctaw (4)	11	0.06
Creek (5)	5	0.03
Iroquois	1	0.01
Latin American Indians (2)	9	0.05
Navajo	3	0.02
Osage	1	0.01
Potawatomi	2	0.01
Seminole	1	0.01
Sioux (1)	2	0.01
Tohono O'Odham (2)	2	0.01
Ute (1)	1	0.01
Yaqui (2)	2	0.01
All other tribes (10)	14	0.08
American Indian tribes, not spec.	8	0.04
Arab:	204	1.11
Arab/Arabic	15	0.08
Lebanese	98	0.53
Palestinian	8	0.04
Syrian	83	0.45
Armenian	1,382	7.51
Asian:	3,803	20.52
Bangladeshi (4)	4	0.02
Chinese, ex. Taiwanese (182)	245	1.32
Filipino (327)	404	2.18
Indian (76)	87	0.47
Indonesian (6)	28	0.15
Japanese (192)	296	1.60
Korean (2,538)	2,596	14.01
Laotian (1)	1	0.01
Malaysian (1)	1	0.01
Pakistani (3)	3	0.02
Sri Lankan (6)	9	0.05
Taiwanese (1)	1	0.01
Thai (27)	31	0.17
Vietnamese (42)	51	0.28
Other Asian, specified (1)	2	0.01
Other Asian, not specified (5)	44	0.24
Australian	13	0.07
Austrian	47	0.26
Belgian	5	0.03
Brazilian	35	0.19
British	74	0.40
Bulgarian	56	0.30
Canadian	48	0.26
Celtic	24	0.13
Croatian	59	0.32
Czech	95	0.52
Czechoslovakian	42	0.23
Danish	181	0.98
Dutch	271	1.47
Eastern European	7	0.04
English	1,997	10.85
European	321	1.74
Finnish	53	0.29
French, except Basque	562	3.05
French Canadian	155	0.84
German	2,403	13.05
Greek	156	0.85
Hawaii Native/Pacific Islander:	40	0.22
Micronesian: (1)	3	0.02
Guamanian/Chamorro (1)	3	0.02
Polynesian: (7)	21	0.11
Native Hawaiian (2)	11	0.06
Samoan (4)	7	0.04
Tongan (1)	3	0.02
Other Pac. Isl., specified	1	0.01
Other Pac. Isl., not spec.	15	0.08
Hispanic or Latino:	1,837	9.91
Central American:	163	0.88
Costa Rican	17	0.09
Guatemalan	56	0.30
Honduran	2	0.01
Nicaraguan	14	0.08
Panamanian	2	0.01
Salvadoran	59	0.32
Other Central American	13	0.07
Cuban	100	0.54
Mexican	985	5.32
Puerto Rican	56	0.30
South American:	158	0.85
Argentinean	18	0.10
Bolivian	8	0.04
Chilean	14	0.08
Colombian	41	0.22
Ecuadorian	26	0.14
Peruvian	41	0.22
Uruguayan	1	0.01
Venezuelan	4	0.02
Other South American	5	0.03
Other Hispanic or Latino	375	2.02
Hungarian	125	0.68
Icelander	10	0.05
Iranian	126	0.68
Irish	1,585	8.61
Italian	1,299	7.06
Lithuanian	58	0.32
Luxemburger	5	0.03
Maltese	5	0.03
Northern European	36	0.20
Norwegian	324	1.76
Pennsylvania German	16	0.09
Polish	451	2.45
Portuguese	46	0.25
Romanian	74	0.40
Russian	187	1.02
Scandinavian	16	0.09
Scotch-Irish	302	1.64
Scottish	587	3.19
Serbian	20	0.11
Slavic	15	0.08
Slovak	6	0.03
Swedish	383	2.08
Swiss	84	0.46
Turkish	42	0.23
Ukrainian	56	0.30
United States or American	793	4.31
Welsh	164	0.89
West Indian, excl. Hispanic:	49	0.27
Belizean	19	0.10
Haitian	4	0.02
Jamaican	7	0.04
West Indian	19	0.10
White:	14,317	77.26
Not Hispanic (12,417)	13,044	70.39
Hispanic (1,099)	1,273	6.87
Yugoslavian	12	0.07

La Habra

Place Type: City
County: Orange
Population: 58,974

Ancestry/Race	Number	%
Acadian/Cajun	5	0.01
Afghan	11	0.02
African American/Black:	1,200	2.03
Not Hispanic (808)	969	1.64
Hispanic (118)	231	0.39
African, sub-Saharan:	174	0.29
African	117	0.20
Ethiopian	24	0.04
Kenyan	27	0.05
South African	6	0.01
Alaska Native tribes, specified:	1	0.00
Tlingit-Haida (1)	1	0.00
Am. Ind. or Alaska Nat., not spec.	385	0.65
American Indian tribes, specified:	565	0.96
Apache (27)	41	0.07
Blackfeet (3)	16	0.03
Cherokee (19)	107	0.18
Chickasaw (7)	10	0.02
Chippewa (5)	8	0.01
Choctaw (6)	21	0.04
Comanche	6	0.01
Cree	1	0.00
Creek (7)	8	0.01
Crow (1)	2	0.00
Delaware (2)	4	0.01
Iroquois (5)	10	0.02
Kiowa (1)	2	0.00
Latin American Indians (77)	122	0.21
Lumbee (6)	6	0.01
Navajo (32)	52	0.09
Osage	5	0.01
Paiute (1)	1	0.00
Pima	5	0.01
Potawatomi (2)	6	0.01
Pueblo (8)	15	0.03
Shoshone (1)	1	0.00
Sioux (5)	20	0.03
Tohono O'Odham (7)	10	0.02
Ute (3)	4	0.01
Yaqui (12)	17	0.03
All other tribes (43)	65	0.11
American Indian tribes, not spec.	34	0.06
Arab:	467	0.79
Arab/Arabic	91	0.15
Egyptian	43	0.07
Jordanian	33	0.06
Lebanese	223	0.38
Palestinian	32	0.05
Syrian	45	0.08
Armenian	138	0.23
Asian:	4,210	7.14
Cambodian (26)	49	0.08
Chinese, ex. Taiwanese (565)	724	1.23
Filipino (740)	955	1.62
Indian (358)	398	0.67
Indonesian (57)	76	0.13
Japanese (321)	454	0.77
Korean (948)	992	1.68
Laotian (14)	14	0.02
Pakistani (23)	41	0.07
Sri Lankan (8)	12	0.02
Taiwanese (92)	123	0.21
Thai (68)	89	0.15
Vietnamese (147)	177	0.30
Other Asian, specified (6)	17	0.03
Other Asian, not specified (17)	89	0.15
Assyrian/Chaldean/Syriac	24	0.04
Australian	12	0.02
Austrian	142	0.24
Basque	43	0.07
Belgian	19	0.03
Brazilian	21	0.04
British	325	0.55
Canadian	163	0.28
Celtic	20	0.03
Croatian	28	0.05
Czech	92	0.16
Czechoslovakian	13	0.02
Danish	282	0.48
Dutch	694	1.17
Eastern European	5	0.01
English	4,027	6.80
Estonian	10	0.02
European	327	0.55
Finnish	81	0.14
French, except Basque	1,424	2.41
French Canadian	237	0.40
German	5,698	9.63
Greek	155	0.26
Hawaii Native/Pacific Islander:	286	0.48
Melanesian: (1)	1	0.00
Fijian (1)	1	0.00
Micronesian: (46)	57	0.10
Guamanian/Chamorro (46)	57	0.10
Polynesian: (67)	166	0.28

Notes: 1. Figures in the "Number" column do not add up to the total population due to: a) Ancestry/Race overlap — e.g. persons can report being both White and Irish, b) persons of Hispanic origin can report being any race, c) persons reporting two ancestries are counted in both categories. 2. Numbers in parentheses indicate the number of persons reporting this ancestry/race alone, not in combination with any other ancestry/race. 3. Refer to the Explanation of Data in the front of the book for more detailed information.

Native Hawaiian (47)	136	0.23
Samoan (18)	26	0.04
Tongan	2	0.00
Other Polynesian (2)	2	0.00
Other Pac. Isl., specified	5	0.01
Other Pac. Isl., not spec. (11)	57	0.10
Hispanic or Latino:	28,922	49.04
Central American:	595	1.01
Costa Rican	24	0.04
Guatemalan	180	0.31
Honduran	36	0.06
Nicaraguan	41	0.07
Panamanian	9	0.02
Salvadoran	243	0.41
Other Central American	62	0.11
Cuban	181	0.31
Dominican Republic	14	0.02
Mexican	24,195	41.03
Puerto Rican	281	0.48
South American:	371	0.63
Argentinean	79	0.13
Bolivian	22	0.04
Chilean	13	0.02
Colombian	78	0.13
Ecuadorian	60	0.10
Paraguayan	1	0.00
Peruvian	81	0.14
Uruguayan	6	0.01
Venezuelan	2	0.00
Other South American	29	0.05
Other Hispanic or Latino	3,285	5.57
Hungarian	305	0.52
Icelander	13	0.02
Iranian	188	0.32
Irish	4,302	7.27
Italian	2,654	4.48
Latvian	6	0.01
Lithuanian	139	0.23
Northern European	47	0.08
Norwegian	856	1.45
Pennsylvania German	13	0.02
Polish	905	1.53
Portuguese	78	0.13
Romanian	221	0.37
Russian	583	0.98
Scandinavian	97	0.16
Scotch-Irish	432	0.73
Scottish	912	1.54
Serbian	23	0.04
Slavic	27	0.05
Slovak	44	0.07
Slovene	6	0.01
Swedish	847	1.43
Swiss	154	0.26
Turkish	42	0.07
Ukrainian	94	0.16
United States or American	1,782	3.01
Welsh	293	0.50
West Indian, excl. Hispanic:	43	0.07
Belizean	16	0.03
Jamaican	13	0.02
West Indian	14	0.02
White:	39,558	67.08
Not Hispanic (24,399)	25,269	42.85
Hispanic (12,754)	14,289	24.23
Yugoslavian	67	0.11

La Mesa

Place Type: City
County: San Diego
Population: 54,749

Ancestry/Race	Number	%
Afghan	139	0.25
African American/Black:	3,152	5.76
Not Hispanic (2,561)	2,978	5.44
Hispanic (99)	174	0.32
African, sub-Saharan:	249	0.45
African	198	0.36
Ethiopian	28	0.05
Kenyan	6	0.01
Nigerian	7	0.01
Ugandan	10	0.02
Alaska Native tribes, specified:	5	0.01
Alaska Athabascan	1	0.00
Aleut (1)	1	0.00
Tlingit-Haida (3)	3	0.01
Am. Ind. or Alaska Nat., not spec.	275	0.50
American Indian tribes, specified:	521	0.95
Apache (10)	21	0.04
Blackfeet (4)	15	0.03
Cherokee (42)	152	0.28
Chickasaw	2	0.00
Chippewa (11)	23	0.04
Choctaw (13)	22	0.04
Comanche (1)	6	0.01
Cree	2	0.00
Creek (4)	18	0.03
Crow (1)	1	0.00
Delaware (1)	3	0.01
Iroquois (8)	19	0.03
Kiowa (2)	2	0.00
Latin American Indians (21)	36	0.07
Lumbee (1)	2	0.00
Menominee (1)	1	0.00
Navajo (12)	22	0.04
Osage (1)	4	0.01
Ottawa (1)	1	0.00
Paiute (5)	5	0.01
Pima (2)	5	0.01
Pueblo (6)	13	0.02
Puget Sound Salish (1)	2	0.00
Seminole (1)	3	0.01
Sioux (25)	35	0.06
Tohono O'Odham (5)	8	0.01
Ute	1	0.00
Yaqui (4)	13	0.02
All other tribes (45)	84	0.15
American Indian tribes, not spec.	42	0.08
Arab:	528	0.96
Arab/Arabic	40	0.07
Egyptian	17	0.03
Iraqi	164	0.30
Jordanian	10	0.02
Lebanese	87	0.16
Moroccan	12	0.02
Palestinian	20	0.04
Syrian	60	0.11
Other Arab	118	0.22
Armenian	180	0.33
Asian:	3,051	5.57
Cambodian (39)	42	0.08
Chinese, ex. Taiwanese (411)	506	0.92
Filipino (602)	929	1.70
Hmong	4	0.01
Indian (88)	113	0.21
Indonesian (44)	61	0.11
Japanese (323)	500	0.91
Korean (135)	177	0.32
Laotian (21)	31	0.06
Malaysian (2)	3	0.01
Pakistani (14)	19	0.03
Taiwanese (30)	40	0.07
Thai (53)	71	0.13
Vietnamese (365)	400	0.73
Other Asian, specified (10)	12	0.02
Other Asian, not specified (52)	143	0.26
Assyrian/Chaldean/Syriac	92	0.17
Australian	33	0.06
Austrian	245	0.45
Basque	19	0.03
Belgian	16	0.03
Brazilian	102	0.19
British	447	0.82
Bulgarian	75	0.14
Canadian	264	0.48
Celtic	31	0.06
Croatian	51	0.09
Czech	255	0.47
Czechoslovakian	90	0.16
Danish	409	0.75
Dutch	720	1.32
Eastern European	44	0.08
English	6,507	11.88
European	1,074	1.96
Finnish	192	0.35
French, except Basque	2,233	4.08
French Canadian	429	0.78
German	9,086	16.60
German Russian	14	0.03
Greek	302	0.55
Hawaii Native/Pacific Islander:	398	0.73
Melanesian: (2)	4	0.01
Fijian (2)	4	0.01
Micronesian: (126)	168	0.31
Guamanian/Chamorro (126)	168	0.31
Polynesian: (74)	183	0.33
Native Hawaiian (33)	98	0.18
Samoan (40)	74	0.14
Tongan	6	0.01
Other Polynesian (1)	5	0.01
Other Pac. Isl., not spec. (14)	43	0.08
Hispanic or Latino:	7,402	13.52
Central American:	147	0.27
Costa Rican	16	0.03
Guatemalan	16	0.03
Honduran	11	0.02
Nicaraguan	25	0.05
Panamanian	45	0.08
Salvadoran	23	0.04
Other Central American	11	0.02
Cuban	69	0.13
Dominican Republic	15	0.03
Mexican	5,636	10.29
Puerto Rican	266	0.49
South American:	185	0.34
Argentinean	19	0.03
Bolivian	8	0.01
Chilean	21	0.04
Colombian	48	0.09
Ecuadorian	15	0.03
Peruvian	33	0.06
Uruguayan	4	0.01
Venezuelan	19	0.03
Other South American	18	0.03
Other Hispanic or Latino	1,084	1.98
Hungarian	371	0.68
Iranian	221	0.40
Irish	7,258	13.26
Israeli	22	0.04
Italian	2,905	5.31
Latvian	31	0.06
Lithuanian	177	0.32
Macedonian	7	0.01
Maltese	13	0.02
Northern European	46	0.08
Norwegian	1,124	2.05
Pennsylvania German	23	0.04
Polish	1,320	2.41
Portuguese	371	0.68
Romanian	93	0.17
Russian	860	1.57
Scandinavian	178	0.33
Scotch-Irish	1,317	2.41
Scottish	1,564	2.86
Serbian	32	0.06
Slavic	19	0.03
Slovak	107	0.20
Slovene	35	0.06
Soviet Union	5	0.01
Swedish	1,380	2.52
Swiss	317	0.58
Turkish	24	0.04
Ukrainian	283	0.52
United States or American	2,440	4.46
Welsh	473	0.86
West Indian, excl. Hispanic:	166	0.30
Belizean	78	0.14
Haitian	12	0.02

Notes: 1. Figures in the "Number" column do not add up to the total population due to: a) Ancestry/Race overlap — e.g. persons can report being both White and Irish, b) persons of Hispanic origin can report being any race, c) persons reporting two ancestries are counted in both categories. 2. Numbers in parentheses indicate the number of persons reporting this ancestry/race alone, not in combination with any other ancestry/race. 3. Refer to the Explanation of Data in the front of the book for more detailed information.

Jamaican	37	0.07
Trinidadian and Tobagonian	12	0.02
West Indian	27	0.05
White:	46,194	84.37
Not Hispanic (40,371)	41,853	76.45
Hispanic (3,777)	4,341	7.93
Yugoslavian	47	0.09

La Mirada

Place Type: City
County: Los Angeles
Population: 46,783

Ancestry/Race	Number	%
Acadian/Cajun	21	0.04
African American/Black:	1,070	2.29
Not Hispanic (851)	971	2.08
Hispanic (52)	99	0.21
African, sub-Saharan:	136	0.29
African	49	0.10
Cape Verdean	7	0.01
Ethiopian	17	0.04
Kenyan	63	0.13
Alaska Native tribes, specified:	7	0.01
Eskimo	1	0.00
Tlingit-Haida (2)	6	0.01
Am. Ind. or Alaska Nat., not spec.	235	0.50
American Indian tribes, specified:	433	0.93
Apache (12)	33	0.07
Blackfeet (8)	19	0.04
Cherokee (22)	110	0.24
Cheyenne	1	0.00
Chickasaw (3)	8	0.02
Chippewa (5)	8	0.02
Choctaw (3)	24	0.05
Comanche (1)	3	0.01
Creek	8	0.02
Delaware (1)	2	0.00
Iroquois (9)	16	0.03
Kiowa (2)	2	0.00
Latin American Indians (23)	41	0.09
Menominee	1	0.00
Navajo (13)	21	0.04
Osage (7)	7	0.01
Paiute (1)	1	0.00
Pima (5)	5	0.01
Potawatomi (6)	7	0.01
Pueblo (15)	27	0.06
Puget Sound Salish (1)	1	0.00
Seminole	10	0.02
Shoshone (1)	2	0.00
Sioux (8)	11	0.02
Tohono O'Odham	2	0.00
Yaqui (8)	9	0.02
Yuman (2)	2	0.00
All other tribes (33)	52	0.11
American Indian tribes, not spec.	27	0.06
Arab:	311	0.66
Arab/Arabic	41	0.09
Egyptian	179	0.38
Jordanian	12	0.03
Lebanese	74	0.16
Syrian	5	0.01
Armenian	101	0.22
Asian:	7,652	16.36
Bangladeshi (12)	12	0.03
Cambodian (49)	59	0.13
Chinese, ex. Taiwanese (753)	889	1.90
Filipino (2,027)	2,281	4.88
Hmong (4)	7	0.01
Indian (562)	612	1.31
Indonesian (26)	56	0.12
Japanese (450)	602	1.29
Korean (2,306)	2,365	5.06
Laotian (31)	31	0.07
Malaysian (6)	6	0.01
Pakistani (13)	13	0.03
Sri Lankan (6)	8	0.02
Taiwanese (105)	114	0.24
Thai (72)	94	0.20
Vietnamese (353)	373	0.80
Other Asian, specified (3)	11	0.02
Other Asian, not specified (62)	119	0.25
Assyrian/Chaldean/Syriac	8	0.02
Austrian	110	0.24
Basque	23	0.05
Belgian	39	0.08
Brazilian	34	0.07
British	206	0.44
Bulgarian	47	0.10
Canadian	207	0.44
Celtic	6	0.01
Croatian	28	0.06
Czech	90	0.19
Czechoslovakian	49	0.10
Danish	196	0.42
Dutch	895	1.91
Eastern European	4	0.01
English	3,822	8.17
European	330	0.71
Finnish	61	0.13
French, except Basque	909	1.94
French Canadian	237	0.51
German	5,307	11.34
Greek	181	0.39
Hawaii Native/Pacific Islander:	259	0.55
Melanesian:	1	0.00
Fijian	1	0.00
Micronesian: (20)	34	0.07
Guamanian/Chamorro (20)	34	0.07
Polynesian: (72)	139	0.30
Native Hawaiian (31)	80	0.17
Samoan (34)	50	0.11
Tongan	2	0.00
Other Polynesian (7)	7	0.01
Other Pac. Isl., not spec. (31)	85	0.18
Hispanic or Latino:	15,657	33.47
Central American:	534	1.14
Costa Rican	31	0.07
Guatemalan	147	0.31
Honduran	18	0.04
Nicaraguan	56	0.12
Panamanian	15	0.03
Salvadoran	211	0.45
Other Central American	56	0.12
Cuban	277	0.59
Dominican Republic	6	0.01
Mexican	11,950	25.54
Puerto Rican	223	0.48
South American:	412	0.88
Argentinean	69	0.15
Bolivian	4	0.01
Chilean	18	0.04
Colombian	88	0.19
Ecuadorian	58	0.12
Peruvian	128	0.27
Uruguayan	11	0.02
Venezuelan	7	0.01
Other South American	29	0.06
Other Hispanic or Latino	2,255	4.82
Hungarian	157	0.34
Iranian	77	0.16
Irish	3,341	7.14
Italian	1,880	4.02
Latvian	7	0.01
Lithuanian	76	0.16
Macedonian	6	0.01
Northern European	13	0.03
Norwegian	720	1.54
Pennsylvania German	7	0.01
Polish	637	1.36
Portuguese	176	0.38
Romanian	237	0.51
Russian	285	0.61
Scandinavian	40	0.09
Scotch-Irish	655	1.40
Scottish	897	1.92
Serbian	14	0.03
Slavic	5	0.01
Slovak	44	0.09
Swedish	674	1.44
Swiss	81	0.17
Ukrainian	98	0.21
United States or American	1,913	4.09
Welsh	247	0.53
West Indian, excl. Hispanic:	59	0.13
Belizean	22	0.05
Jamaican	23	0.05
U.S. Virgin Islander	9	0.02
West Indian	5	0.01
White:	31,784	67.94
Not Hispanic (22,058)	22,850	48.84
Hispanic (8,097)	8,934	19.10
Yugoslavian	45	0.10

La Palma

Place Type: City
County: Orange
Population: 15,408

Ancestry/Race	Number	%
Afghan	24	0.16
African American/Black:	773	5.02
Not Hispanic (696)	747	4.85
Hispanic (14)	26	0.17
African, sub-Saharan:	53	0.35
African	7	0.05
Nigerian	15	0.10
Somalian	5	0.03
Other sub-Saharan African	26	0.17
Alaska Native tribes, specified:	1	0.01
Tlingit-Haida (1)	1	0.01
Am. Ind. or Alaska Nat., not spec.	60	0.39
American Indian tribes, specified:	81	0.53
Apache (6)	8	0.05
Blackfeet (4)	4	0.03
Cherokee (3)	17	0.11
Chickasaw (2)	3	0.02
Chippewa (1)	9	0.06
Choctaw (1)	10	0.06
Creek (3)	3	0.02
Delaware	1	0.01
Iroquois (2)	2	0.01
Latin American Indians (2)	5	0.03
Navajo	5	0.03
Potawatomi (1)	1	0.01
Seminole (1)	2	0.01
Sioux	1	0.01
All other tribes (5)	10	0.06
American Indian tribes, not spec.	8	0.05
Arab:	81	0.54
Lebanese	17	0.11
Palestinian	32	0.21
Syrian	32	0.21
Armenian	24	0.16
Asian:	7,377	47.88
Bangladeshi (4)	4	0.03
Cambodian (44)	53	0.34
Chinese, ex. Taiwanese (1,017)	1,142	7.41
Filipino (1,086)	1,220	7.92
Indian (580)	611	3.97
Indonesian (11)	19	0.12
Japanese (740)	847	5.50
Korean (2,630)	2,685	17.43
Laotian (9)	9	0.06
Malaysian (1)	1	0.01
Pakistani (30)	32	0.21
Sri Lankan (3)	10	0.06
Taiwanese (265)	315	2.04
Thai (73)	100	0.65
Vietnamese (227)	256	1.66
Other Asian, specified (3)	7	0.05
Other Asian, not specified (21)	66	0.43
Assyrian/Chaldean/Syriac	28	0.19
Australian	6	0.04
Austrian	30	0.20
Belgian	7	0.05
Brazilian	5	0.03

Notes: 1. Figures in the "Number" column do not add up to the total population due to: a) Ancestry/Race overlap — e.g. persons can report being both White and Irish, b) persons of Hispanic origin can report being any race, c) persons reporting two ancestries are counted in both categories. 2. Numbers in parentheses indicate the number of persons reporting this ancestry/race alone, not in combination with any other ancestry/race. 3. Refer to the Explanation of Data in the front of the book for more detailed information.

British	29	0.19
Canadian	36	0.24
Czech	16	0.11
Danish	69	0.46
Dutch	254	1.68
English	958	6.33
European	102	0.67
Finnish	45	0.30
French, except Basque	282	1.86
French Canadian	106	0.70
German	1,337	8.84
Greek	118	0.78
Hawaii Native/Pacific Islander:	115	0.75
Melanesian: (2)	5	0.03
Fijian (2)	5	0.03
Micronesian: (10)	15	0.10
Guamanian/Chamorro (10)	15	0.10
Polynesian: (29)	50	0.32
Native Hawaiian (4)	19	0.12
Samoan (24)	30	0.19
Tongan (1)	1	0.01
Other Pac. Isl., not spec. (4)	45	0.29
Hispanic or Latino:	1,736	11.27
Central American:	53	0.34
Costa Rican	6	0.04
Guatemalan	9	0.06
Honduran	5	0.03
Nicaraguan	15	0.10
Panamanian	4	0.03
Salvadoran	6	0.04
Other Central American	8	0.05
Cuban	52	0.34
Dominican Republic	11	0.07
Mexican	1,113	7.22
Puerto Rican	62	0.40
South American:	147	0.95
Argentinean	35	0.23
Bolivian	9	0.06
Chilean	4	0.03
Colombian	43	0.28
Ecuadorian	18	0.12
Peruvian	19	0.12
Venezuelan	2	0.01
Other South American	17	0.11
Other Hispanic or Latino	298	1.93
Hungarian	39	0.26
Iranian	75	0.50
Irish	1,110	7.34
Italian	680	4.49
Lithuanian	13	0.09
Luxemburger	13	0.09
Norwegian	126	0.83
Polish	200	1.32
Portuguese	61	0.40
Romanian	11	0.07
Russian	64	0.42
Scandinavian	17	0.11
Scotch-Irish	110	0.73
Scottish	196	1.30
Serbian	4	0.03
Slovak	48	0.32
Slovene	5	0.03
Swedish	108	0.71
Swiss	30	0.20
Ukrainian	28	0.19
United States or American	138	0.91
Welsh	68	0.45
West Indian, excl. Hispanic:	12	0.08
Jamaican	4	0.03
West Indian	8	0.05
White:	7,018	45.55
Not Hispanic (5,592)	5,863	38.05
Hispanic (1,040)	1,155	7.50
Yugoslavian	7	0.05

La Presa

Place Type: Census Designated Place
County: San Diego
Population: 32,721

Ancestry/Race	Number	%
Afghan	41	0.12
African American/Black:	5,334	16.30
Not Hispanic (4,563)	5,012	15.32
Hispanic (176)	322	0.98
African, sub-Saharan:	388	1.18
African	388	1.18
Alaska Native tribes, specified:	6	0.02
Aleut (1)	1	0.00
Eskimo (1)	1	0.00
Tlingit-Haida (2)	4	0.01
Am. Ind. or Alaska Nat., not spec.	183	0.56
American Indian tribes, specified:	485	1.48
Apache (18)	54	0.17
Blackfeet (9)	23	0.07
Cherokee (28)	124	0.38
Cheyenne (2)	9	0.03
Chickasaw	3	0.01
Chippewa (2)	8	0.02
Choctaw (7)	11	0.03
Comanche (5)	12	0.04
Creek (2)	4	0.01
Crow (2)	3	0.01
Delaware (1)	1	0.00
Iroquois (1)	3	0.01
Kiowa	2	0.01
Latin American Indians (25)	48	0.15
Navajo (11)	19	0.06
Osage (2)	5	0.02
Ottawa (1)	1	0.00
Paiute (1)	1	0.00
Pima (2)	5	0.02
Potawatomi	4	0.01
Pueblo (9)	14	0.04
Seminole (1)	7	0.02
Shoshone (1)	4	0.01
Sioux (12)	26	0.08
Tohono O'Odham	3	0.01
Ute	3	0.01
Yaqui (2)	9	0.03
Yuman (1)	1	0.00
All other tribes (41)	78	0.24
American Indian tribes, not spec.	24	0.07
Arab:	155	0.47
Arab/Arabic	84	0.26
Egyptian	10	0.03
Iraqi	16	0.05
Lebanese	5	0.02
Syrian	15	0.05
Other Arab	25	0.08
Armenian	27	0.08
Asian:	4,268	13.04
Cambodian (19)	20	0.06
Chinese, ex. Taiwanese (50)	163	0.50
Filipino (2,701)	3,404	10.40
Hmong (1)	1	0.00
Indian (13)	31	0.09
Indonesian	4	0.01
Japanese (157)	306	0.94
Korean (55)	78	0.24
Laotian (10)	26	0.08
Malaysian (3)	10	0.03
Pakistani (4)	4	0.01
Taiwanese (3)	5	0.02
Thai (16)	32	0.10
Vietnamese (97)	118	0.36
Other Asian, specified	10	0.03
Other Asian, not specified (25)	56	0.17
Assyrian/Chaldean/Syriac	35	0.11
Australian	18	0.05
Austrian	47	0.14
Brazilian	46	0.14
British	101	0.31
Canadian	54	0.16
Celtic	18	0.05
Croatian	43	0.13
Czech	44	0.13
Czechoslovakian	39	0.12
Danish	67	0.20
Dutch	330	1.00
English	1,771	5.39
European	307	0.93
Finnish	19	0.06
French, except Basque	704	2.14
French Canadian	181	0.55
German	2,410	7.34
Greek	82	0.25
Hawaii Native/Pacific Islander:	647	1.98
Micronesian: (176)	269	0.82
Guamanian/Chamorro (176)	263	0.80
Other Micronesian	6	0.02
Polynesian: (184)	321	0.98
Native Hawaiian (48)	137	0.42
Samoan (132)	175	0.53
Other Polynesian (4)	9	0.03
Other Pac. Isl., specified	10	0.03
Other Pac. Isl., not spec. (7)	47	0.14
Hispanic or Latino:	10,813	33.05
Central American:	131	0.40
Costa Rican	14	0.04
Guatemalan	20	0.06
Honduran	8	0.02
Nicaraguan	13	0.04
Panamanian	44	0.13
Salvadoran	27	0.08
Other Central American	5	0.02
Cuban	41	0.13
Dominican Republic	8	0.02
Mexican	9,130	27.90
Puerto Rican	282	0.86
South American:	73	0.22
Argentinean	6	0.02
Bolivian	3	0.01
Chilean	3	0.01
Colombian	32	0.10
Ecuadorian	5	0.02
Peruvian	20	0.06
Other South American	4	0.01
Other Hispanic or Latino	1,148	3.51
Hungarian	118	0.36
Icelander	11	0.03
Iranian	7	0.02
Irish	2,145	6.53
Israeli	13	0.04
Italian	688	2.09
Lithuanian	42	0.13
Luxemburger	11	0.03
Northern European	9	0.03
Norwegian	358	1.09
Pennsylvania German	34	0.10
Polish	397	1.21
Portuguese	59	0.18
Romanian	8	0.02
Russian	35	0.11
Scandinavian	104	0.32
Scotch-Irish	447	1.36
Scottish	320	0.97
Serbian	8	0.02
Slavic	39	0.12
Slovak	13	0.04
Swedish	198	0.60
Swiss	39	0.12
Turkish	5	0.02
Ukrainian	101	0.31
United States or American	1,080	3.29
Welsh	229	0.70
West Indian, excl. Hispanic:	110	0.33
Belizean	45	0.14
British West Indian	13	0.04
Jamaican	38	0.12
West Indian	14	0.04
White:	18,172	55.54
Not Hispanic (12,238)	13,311	40.68
Hispanic (4,190)	4,861	14.86

Notes: 1. Figures in the "Number" column do not add up to the total population due to: a) Ancestry/Race overlap — e.g. persons can report being both White and Irish, b) persons of Hispanic origin can report being any race, c) persons reporting two ancestries are counted in both categories. 2. Numbers in parentheses indicate the number of persons reporting this ancestry/race alone, not in combination with any other ancestry/race. 3. Refer to the Explanation of Data in the front of the book for more detailed information.

La Puente

Place Type: City
County: Los Angeles
Population: 41,063

Ancestry/Race	Number	%
African American/Black:	999	2.43
Not Hispanic (688)	783	1.91
Hispanic (116)	216	0.53
African, sub-Saharan:	18	0.04
African	8	0.02
Nigerian	10	0.02
Am. Ind. or Alaska Nat., not spec.	373	0.91
American Indian tribes, specified:	390	0.95
Apache (17)	31	0.08
Blackfeet (1)	3	0.01
Cherokee (2)	42	0.10
Chickasaw	2	0.00
Chippewa (2)	5	0.01
Choctaw (5)	12	0.03
Comanche (1)	5	0.01
Crow (4)	8	0.02
Delaware	1	0.00
Iroquois	4	0.01
Kiowa	4	0.01
Latin American Indians (89)	144	0.35
Navajo (7)	9	0.02
Osage	5	0.01
Pima (2)	5	0.01
Pueblo (15)	23	0.06
Shoshone (1)	1	0.00
Sioux	6	0.01
Tohono O'Odham (4)	5	0.01
Ute (4)	4	0.01
Yaqui (19)	24	0.06
All other tribes (25)	47	0.11
American Indian tribes, not spec.	55	0.13
Arab:	7	0.02
Lebanese	7	0.02
Asian:	3,315	8.07
Bangladeshi	1	0.00
Cambodian (28)	30	0.07
Chinese, ex. Taiwanese (771)	845	2.06
Filipino (1,139)	1,257	3.06
Hmong (1)	1	0.00
Indian (62)	82	0.20
Indonesian (18)	41	0.10
Japanese (95)	146	0.36
Korean (212)	244	0.59
Laotian (9)	22	0.05
Malaysian (3)	4	0.01
Pakistani (2)	3	0.01
Sri Lankan (2)	2	0.00
Taiwanese (73)	86	0.21
Thai (53)	65	0.16
Vietnamese (394)	432	1.05
Other Asian, specified (5)	11	0.03
Other Asian, not specified (20)	43	0.10
Basque	6	0.01
Belgian	14	0.03
British	10	0.02
Canadian	14	0.03
Czech	7	0.02
Czechoslovakian	8	0.02
Danish	39	0.10
Dutch	122	0.30
English	396	0.97
European	26	0.06
French, except Basque	279	0.68
French Canadian	38	0.09
German	638	1.56
Greek	22	0.05
Guyanese	18	0.04
Hawaii Native/Pacific Islander:	147	0.36
Micronesian: (19)	24	0.06
Guamanian/Chamorro (19)	24	0.06
Polynesian: (34)	70	0.17
Native Hawaiian (9)	39	0.09
Samoan (25)	31	0.08
Other Pac. Isl., specified	1	0.00
Other Pac. Isl., not spec. (15)	52	0.13
Hispanic or Latino:	34,122	83.10
Central American:	1,466	3.57
Costa Rican	25	0.06
Guatemalan	278	0.68
Honduran	59	0.14
Nicaraguan	156	0.38
Panamanian	12	0.03
Salvadoran	790	1.92
Other Central American	146	0.36
Cuban	81	0.20
Dominican Republic	6	0.01
Mexican	28,108	68.45
Puerto Rican	217	0.53
South American:	244	0.59
Argentinean	31	0.08
Bolivian	11	0.03
Chilean	8	0.02
Colombian	59	0.14
Ecuadorian	77	0.19
Peruvian	53	0.13
Other South American	5	0.01
Other Hispanic or Latino	4,000	9.74
Hungarian	52	0.13
Iranian	25	0.06
Irish	326	0.79
Italian	372	0.91
Latvian	11	0.03
Lithuanian	6	0.01
Norwegian	43	0.10
Polish	80	0.20
Portuguese	56	0.14
Russian	64	0.16
Scandinavian	4	0.01
Scotch-Irish	42	0.10
Scottish	115	0.28
Serbian	8	0.02
Swedish	45	0.11
Swiss	14	0.03
United States or American	644	1.57
West Indian, excl. Hispanic:	18	0.04
West Indian	18	0.04
White:	17,824	43.41
Not Hispanic (2,749)	3,007	7.32
Hispanic (13,311)	14,817	36.08
Yugoslavian	6	0.01

La Quinta

Place Type: City
County: Riverside
Population: 23,694

Ancestry/Race	Number	%
African American/Black:	423	1.79
Not Hispanic (296)	358	1.51
Hispanic (40)	65	0.27
Alaska Native tribes, specified:	4	0.02
Alaska Athabascan (1)	1	0.00
Eskimo (3)	3	0.01
Am. Ind. or Alaska Nat., not spec.	130	0.55
Alsatian	7	0.03
American Indian tribes, specified:	220	0.93
Apache (6)	16	0.07
Blackfeet (1)	4	0.02
Cherokee (7)	58	0.24
Chickasaw	6	0.03
Chippewa (1)	4	0.02
Choctaw (10)	16	0.07
Comanche (1)	2	0.01
Creek	4	0.02
Delaware (4)	5	0.02
Iroquois (2)	2	0.01
Latin American Indians (20)	35	0.15
Menominee	3	0.01
Navajo (10)	14	0.06
Osage	1	0.00
Potawatomi	1	0.00
Pueblo (1)	1	0.00
Tohono O'Odham (13)	13	0.05
Yaqui (3)	15	0.06
All other tribes (12)	20	0.08
American Indian tribes, not spec.	3	0.01
Arab:	35	0.15
Arab/Arabic	9	0.04
Lebanese	18	0.08
Syrian	8	0.03
Armenian	100	0.42
Asian:	623	2.63
Cambodian	1	0.00
Chinese, ex. Taiwanese (61)	100	0.42
Filipino (137)	188	0.79
Indian (41)	47	0.20
Indonesian (3)	4	0.02
Japanese (87)	144	0.61
Korean (62)	73	0.31
Pakistani	1	0.00
Taiwanese (11)	11	0.05
Thai (9)	17	0.07
Vietnamese (15)	24	0.10
Other Asian, not specified (1)	13	0.05
Australian	24	0.10
Austrian	82	0.35
Basque	20	0.08
Belgian	19	0.08
Brazilian	38	0.16
British	133	0.56
Canadian	84	0.36
Croatian	8	0.03
Czech	102	0.43
Czechoslovakian	42	0.18
Danish	140	0.59
Dutch	379	1.60
English	2,845	12.03
European	141	0.60
Finnish	54	0.23
French, except Basque	861	3.64
French Canadian	186	0.79
German	3,397	14.36
Greek	151	0.64
Hawaii Native/Pacific Islander:	62	0.26
Micronesian: (5)	11	0.05
Guamanian/Chamorro (5)	10	0.04
Other Micronesian	1	0.00
Polynesian: (16)	41	0.17
Native Hawaiian (12)	33	0.14
Samoan (4)	5	0.02
Other Polynesian	3	0.01
Other Pac. Isl., not spec.	10	0.04
Hispanic or Latino:	7,584	32.01
Central American:	81	0.34
Costa Rican	2	0.01
Guatemalan	20	0.08
Honduran	2	0.01
Nicaraguan	5	0.02
Panamanian	6	0.03
Salvadoran	43	0.18
Other Central American	3	0.01
Cuban	37	0.16
Dominican Republic	2	0.01
Mexican	6,474	27.32
Puerto Rican	57	0.24
South American:	39	0.16
Argentinean	9	0.04
Chilean	1	0.00
Colombian	16	0.07
Ecuadorian	5	0.02
Peruvian	3	0.01
Uruguayan	1	0.00
Other South American	4	0.02
Other Hispanic or Latino	894	3.77
Hungarian	95	0.40
Icelander	10	0.04
Iranian	8	0.03
Irish	2,591	10.95
Italian	1,445	6.11
Lithuanian	66	0.28
Northern European	17	0.07
Norwegian	540	2.28

Notes: 1. Figures in the "Number" column do not add up to the total population due to: a) Ancestry/Race overlap — e.g. persons can report being both White and Irish, b) persons of Hispanic origin can report being any race, c) persons reporting two ancestries are counted in both categories. 2. Numbers in parentheses indicate the number of persons reporting this ancestry/race alone, not in combination with any other ancestry/race. 3. Refer to the Explanation of Data in the front of the book for more detailed information.

Pennsylvania German	7	0.03
Polish	434	1.83
Portuguese	98	0.41
Romanian	79	0.33
Russian	213	0.90
Scandinavian	108	0.46
Scotch-Irish	471	1.99
Scottish	610	2.58
Serbian	8	0.03
Slovak	28	0.12
Slovene	8	0.03
Swedish	524	2.22
Swiss	136	0.57
Turkish	6	0.03
Ukrainian	30	0.13
United States or American	1,038	4.39
Welsh	176	0.74
White:	19,356	81.69
Not Hispanic (14,893)	15,256	64.39
Hispanic (3,709)	4,100	17.30
Yugoslavian	67	0.28

La Riviera

Place Type: Census Designated Place
County: Sacramento
Population: 10,273

Ancestry/Race	Number	%
Afghan	31	0.30
African American/Black:	1,015	9.88
Not Hispanic (839)	957	9.32
Hispanic (33)	58	0.56
African, sub-Saharan:	124	1.21
African	95	0.92
Cape Verdean	23	0.22
Nigerian	6	0.06
Alaska Native tribes, specified:	3	0.03
Eskimo	1	0.01
Tlingit-Haida (2)	2	0.02
Am. Ind. or Alaska Nat., not spec.	44	0.43
American Indian tribes, specified:	143	1.39
Apache (1)	2	0.02
Blackfeet	3	0.03
Cherokee (13)	48	0.47
Cheyenne	2	0.02
Chickasaw	2	0.02
Choctaw (3)	22	0.21
Creek	1	0.01
Delaware (1)	1	0.01
Iroquois (1)	3	0.03
Latin American Indians (5)	6	0.06
Menominee	1	0.01
Navajo (1)	3	0.03
Osage (1)	2	0.02
Ottawa (1)	1	0.01
Paiute	1	0.01
Potawatomi (1)	1	0.01
Pueblo	1	0.01
Seminole	1	0.01
Sioux (4)	8	0.08
Yuman (1)	1	0.01
All other tribes (11)	33	0.32
American Indian tribes, not spec.	12	0.12
Armenian	8	0.08
Asian:	1,065	10.37
Bangladeshi (2)	2	0.02
Cambodian (2)	2	0.02
Chinese, ex. Taiwanese (175)	229	2.23
Filipino (169)	240	2.34
Hmong (8)	8	0.08
Indian (52)	63	0.61
Indonesian	6	0.06
Japanese (138)	195	1.90
Korean (104)	127	1.24
Laotian (16)	19	0.18
Malaysian	1	0.01
Pakistani (1)	7	0.07
Sri Lankan (2)	2	0.02
Taiwanese (18)	22	0.21
Thai (5)	8	0.08
Vietnamese (90)	106	1.03
Other Asian, specified	3	0.03
Other Asian, not specified (10)	25	0.24
Assyrian/Chaldean/Syriac	75	0.73
Australian	17	0.17
Austrian	19	0.18
Basque	23	0.22
Belgian	16	0.16
British	53	0.52
Canadian	6	0.06
Croatian	8	0.08
Czech	28	0.27
Danish	121	1.18
Dutch	104	1.01
English	1,130	11.00
European	90	0.88
Finnish	31	0.30
French, except Basque	333	3.24
French Canadian	56	0.55
German	1,545	15.04
Greek	42	0.41
Hawaii Native/Pacific Islander:	99	0.96
Melanesian: (6)	6	0.06
Fijian (6)	6	0.06
Micronesian: (17)	18	0.18
Guamanian/Chamorro (11)	12	0.12
Other Micronesian (6)	6	0.06
Polynesian: (23)	48	0.47
Native Hawaiian (11)	35	0.34
Samoan (11)	12	0.12
Tongan (1)	1	0.01
Other Pac. Isl., not spec. (13)	27	0.26
Hispanic or Latino:	1,165	11.34
Central American:	43	0.42
Costa Rican	4	0.04
Guatemalan	6	0.06
Nicaraguan	5	0.05
Panamanian	10	0.10
Salvadoran	14	0.14
Other Central American	4	0.04
Cuban	8	0.08
Mexican	781	7.60
Puerto Rican	69	0.67
South American:	27	0.26
Bolivian	2	0.02
Chilean	1	0.01
Colombian	5	0.05
Ecuadorian	1	0.01
Paraguayan	1	0.01
Peruvian	2	0.02
Uruguayan	3	0.03
Venezuelan	5	0.05
Other South American	7	0.07
Other Hispanic or Latino	237	2.31
Hungarian	37	0.36
Iranian	22	0.21
Irish	1,221	11.89
Italian	649	6.32
Latvian	6	0.06
Lithuanian	12	0.12
Northern European	9	0.09
Norwegian	224	2.18
Polish	120	1.17
Portuguese	249	2.42
Romanian	20	0.19
Russian	67	0.65
Scandinavian	15	0.15
Scotch-Irish	210	2.04
Scottish	267	2.60
Serbian	21	0.20
Slovak	10	0.10
Swedish	163	1.59
Swiss	62	0.60
Turkish	16	0.16
Ukrainian	25	0.24
United States or American	423	4.12
Welsh	71	0.69
West Indian, excl. Hispanic:	19	0.18
Jamaican	9	0.09
West Indian	10	0.10
White:	7,938	77.27
Not Hispanic (6,903)	7,268	70.75
Hispanic (541)	670	6.52
Yugoslavian	12	0.12

La Verne

Place Type: City
County: Los Angeles
Population: 31,638

Ancestry/Race	Number	%
African American/Black:	1,174	3.71
Not Hispanic (975)	1,088	3.44
Hispanic (41)	86	0.27
African, sub-Saharan:	116	0.36
African	76	0.24
Nigerian	34	0.11
South African	6	0.02
Alaska Native tribes, specified:	5	0.02
Aleut (5)	5	0.02
Am. Ind. or Alaska Nat., not spec.	125	0.40
American Indian tribes, specified:	268	0.85
Apache (6)	23	0.07
Blackfeet (3)	15	0.05
Cherokee (11)	55	0.17
Chickasaw (2)	9	0.03
Chippewa (6)	10	0.03
Choctaw (12)	18	0.06
Comanche (1)	5	0.02
Cree	4	0.01
Creek (1)	4	0.01
Crow	5	0.02
Iroquois (1)	1	0.00
Latin American Indians (16)	34	0.11
Lumbee (1)	1	0.00
Navajo (13)	18	0.06
Ottawa (2)	3	0.01
Pima (3)	3	0.01
Potawatomi (1)	6	0.02
Pueblo (2)	2	0.01
Sioux	3	0.01
Ute	1	0.00
Yaqui (1)	3	0.01
Yuman (2)	3	0.01
All other tribes (20)	42	0.13
American Indian tribes, not spec.	13	0.04
Arab:	517	1.62
Arab/Arabic	61	0.19
Egyptian	122	0.38
Iraqi	6	0.02
Jordanian	37	0.12
Lebanese	106	0.33
Syrian	173	0.54
Other Arab	12	0.04
Armenian	421	1.32
Asian:	2,741	8.66
Cambodian (22)	34	0.11
Chinese, ex. Taiwanese (497)	620	1.96
Filipino (615)	729	2.30
Hmong (2)	2	0.01
Indian (345)	373	1.18
Indonesian (36)	71	0.22
Japanese (211)	313	0.99
Korean (219)	245	0.77
Laotian (2)	2	0.01
Malaysian	2	0.01
Pakistani (18)	21	0.07
Sri Lankan (14)	18	0.06
Taiwanese (59)	75	0.24
Thai (31)	37	0.12
Vietnamese (120)	132	0.42
Other Asian, specified (5)	5	0.02
Other Asian, not specified (23)	62	0.20
Australian	16	0.05
Austrian	23	0.07
Basque	31	0.10
Belgian	49	0.15
Brazilian	18	0.06

Notes: 1. Figures in the "Number" column do not add up to the total population due to: a) Ancestry/Race overlap — e.g. persons can report being both White and Irish, b) persons of Hispanic origin can report being any race, c) persons reporting two ancestries are counted in both categories. 2. Numbers in parentheses indicate the number of persons reporting this ancestry/race alone, not in combination with any other ancestry/race. 3. Refer to the Explanation of Data in the front of the book for more detailed information.

British	220	0.69
Canadian	168	0.53
Celtic	18	0.06
Croatian	41	0.13
Czech	67	0.21
Czechoslovakian	27	0.08
Danish	236	0.74
Dutch	593	1.86
Eastern European	10	0.03
English	3,478	10.92
European	431	1.35
Finnish	78	0.24
French, except Basque	1,145	3.60
French Canadian	250	0.79
German	4,959	15.57
Greek	153	0.48
Hawaii Native/Pacific Islander:	136	0.43
Micronesian: (14)	15	0.05
Guamanian/Chamorro (14)	15	0.05
Polynesian: (24)	74	0.23
Native Hawaiian (16)	54	0.17
Samoan (4)	14	0.04
Other Polynesian (4)	6	0.02
Other Pac. Isl., not spec. (16)	47	0.15
Hispanic or Latino:	7,315	23.12
Central American:	187	0.59
Costa Rican	17	0.05
Guatemalan	43	0.14
Honduran	10	0.03
Nicaraguan	43	0.14
Panamanian	3	0.01
Salvadoran	52	0.16
Other Central American	19	0.06
Cuban	145	0.46
Dominican Republic	12	0.04
Mexican	5,553	17.55
Puerto Rican	118	0.37
South American:	241	0.76
Argentinean	70	0.22
Bolivian	21	0.07
Chilean	21	0.07
Colombian	55	0.17
Ecuadorian	32	0.10
Paraguayan	1	0.00
Peruvian	27	0.09
Venezuelan	1	0.00
Other South American	13	0.04
Other Hispanic or Latino	1,059	3.35
Hungarian	178	0.56
Iranian	257	0.81
Irish	3,448	10.83
Italian	2,038	6.40
Latvian	7	0.02
Lithuanian	42	0.13
Maltese	12	0.04
New Zealander	8	0.03
Northern European	81	0.25
Norwegian	685	2.15
Pennsylvania German	6	0.02
Polish	674	2.12
Portuguese	109	0.34
Romanian	31	0.10
Russian	411	1.29
Scandinavian	57	0.18
Scotch-Irish	584	1.83
Scottish	870	2.73
Slavic	10	0.03
Slovak	46	0.14
Slovene	53	0.17
Swedish	584	1.83
Swiss	89	0.28
Ukrainian	76	0.24
United States or American	1,192	3.74
Welsh	278	0.87
West Indian, excl. Hispanic:	38	0.12
Haitian	38	0.12
White:	25,583	80.86
Not Hispanic (20,129)	20,830	65.84
Hispanic (4,250)	4,753	15.02
Yugoslavian	49	0.15

Lafayette

Place Type: City
County: Contra Costa
Population: 23,908

Ancestry/Race	Number	%
Acadian/Cajun	9	0.04
African American/Black:	209	0.87
Not Hispanic (129)	201	0.84
Hispanic (2)	8	0.03
African, sub-Saharan:	26	0.11
South African	19	0.08
Other sub-Saharan African	7	0.03
Alaska Native tribes, specified:	5	0.02
Aleut (1)	3	0.01
Tlingit-Haida (1)	2	0.01
Am. Ind. or Alaska Nat., not spec.	60	0.25
American Indian tribes, specified:	108	0.45
Apache (1)	2	0.01
Blackfeet (1)	2	0.01
Cherokee (4)	43	0.18
Chickasaw	1	0.00
Chippewa (1)	3	0.01
Choctaw	4	0.02
Cree (1)	1	0.00
Creek (1)	5	0.02
Crow (1)	2	0.01
Houma (2)	2	0.01
Iroquois	7	0.03
Latin American Indians (1)	3	0.01
Navajo (3)	5	0.02
Paiute (1)	1	0.00
Pueblo (1)	4	0.02
Puget Sound Salish (1)	1	0.00
Sioux (1)	2	0.01
Yaqui	7	0.03
All other tribes (12)	13	0.05
American Indian tribes, not spec.	5	0.02
Arab:	113	0.48
Jordanian	17	0.07
Lebanese	63	0.27
Moroccan	5	0.02
Palestinian	16	0.07
Syrian	5	0.02
Other Arab	7	0.03
Armenian	152	0.65
Asian:	2,505	10.48
Cambodian	1	0.00
Chinese, ex. Taiwanese (900)	1,115	4.66
Filipino (154)	236	0.99
Hmong (2)	3	0.01
Indian (187)	233	0.97
Indonesian (8)	25	0.10
Japanese (277)	444	1.86
Korean (268)	295	1.23
Laotian (1)	5	0.02
Malaysian	1	0.00
Pakistani (7)	9	0.04
Sri Lankan (6)	6	0.03
Taiwanese (34)	37	0.15
Thai (7)	16	0.07
Vietnamese (32)	40	0.17
Other Asian, specified (2)	2	0.01
Other Asian, not specified (13)	37	0.15
Australian	11	0.05
Austrian	149	0.64
Basque	16	0.07
Belgian	46	0.20
Brazilian	11	0.05
British	333	1.42
Bulgarian	6	0.03
Canadian	108	0.46
Croatian	174	0.74
Czech	99	0.42
Czechoslovakian	34	0.14
Danish	380	1.62
Dutch	461	1.96
Eastern European	136	0.58
English	4,640	19.78
Estonian	6	0.03
European	486	2.07
Finnish	117	0.50
French, except Basque	1,013	4.32
French Canadian	156	0.66
German	4,242	18.08
Greek	180	0.77
Hawaii Native/Pacific Islander:	79	0.33
Micronesian: (2)	4	0.02
Guamanian/Chamorro (1)	3	0.01
Other Micronesian (1)	1	0.00
Polynesian: (18)	59	0.25
Native Hawaiian (12)	47	0.20
Samoan (1)	3	0.01
Tongan (1)	1	0.00
Other Polynesian (4)	8	0.03
Other Pac. Isl., not spec. (1)	16	0.07
Hispanic or Latino:	945	3.95
Central American:	69	0.29
Costa Rican	4	0.02
Guatemalan	14	0.06
Honduran	3	0.01
Nicaraguan	19	0.08
Panamanian	3	0.01
Salvadoran	19	0.08
Other Central American	7	0.03
Cuban	14	0.06
Mexican	474	1.98
Puerto Rican	34	0.14
South American:	79	0.33
Argentinean	4	0.02
Bolivian	5	0.02
Chilean	6	0.03
Colombian	9	0.04
Ecuadorian	1	0.00
Peruvian	31	0.13
Uruguayan	1	0.00
Venezuelan	16	0.07
Other South American	6	0.03
Other Hispanic or Latino	275	1.15
Hungarian	208	0.89
Icelander	7	0.03
Iranian	136	0.58
Irish	3,656	15.58
Israeli	18	0.08
Italian	1,815	7.74
Latvian	31	0.13
Lithuanian	73	0.31
Luxemburger	8	0.03
Northern European	113	0.48
Norwegian	704	3.00
Pennsylvania German	28	0.12
Polish	598	2.55
Portuguese	237	1.01
Romanian	79	0.34
Russian	646	2.75
Scandinavian	112	0.48
Scotch-Irish	588	2.51
Scottish	1,075	4.58
Serbian	43	0.18
Slavic	12	0.05
Slovak	21	0.09
Slovene	19	0.08
Swedish	874	3.73
Swiss	301	1.28
Turkish	50	0.21
Ukrainian	49	0.21
United States or American	933	3.98
Welsh	311	1.33
West Indian, excl. Hispanic:	12	0.05
Haitian	2	0.01
Jamaican	5	0.02
West Indian	5	0.02
White:	21,485	89.87
Not Hispanic (20,123)	20,742	86.76
Hispanic (631)	743	3.11
Yugoslavian	22	0.09

Notes: 1. Figures in the "Number" column do not add up to the total population due to: a) Ancestry/Race overlap — e.g. persons can report being both White and Irish, b) persons of Hispanic origin can report being any race, c) persons reporting two ancestries are counted in both categories. 2. Numbers in parentheses indicate the number of persons reporting this ancestry/race alone, not in combination with any other ancestry/race. 3. Refer to the Explanation of Data in the front of the book for more detailed information.

Laguna Beach

Place Type: City
County: Orange
Population: 23,727

Ancestry/Race	Number	%
Afghan	11	0.05
African American/Black:	267	1.13
Not Hispanic (183)	247	1.04
Hispanic (7)	20	0.08
African, sub-Saharan:	31	0.13
African	19	0.08
South African	12	0.05
Alaska Native tribes, specified:	4	0.02
Alaska Athabascan	1	0.00
Aleut (1)	2	0.01
Eskimo (1)	1	0.00
Am. Ind. or Alaska Nat., not spec.	43	0.18
Alsatian	7	0.03
American Indian tribes, specified:	169	0.71
Apache (5)	7	0.03
Blackfeet (1)	4	0.02
Cherokee (10)	60	0.25
Chickasaw	1	0.00
Chippewa (6)	12	0.05
Choctaw (1)	6	0.03
Comanche (1)	1	0.00
Creek	3	0.01
Iroquois (2)	2	0.01
Latin American Indians (3)	10	0.04
Lumbee	1	0.00
Navajo (5)	7	0.03
Osage (7)	7	0.03
Paiute (1)	1	0.00
Pima (1)	3	0.01
Potawatomi (1)	3	0.01
Pueblo (1)	1	0.00
Puget Sound Salish (1)	1	0.00
Shoshone	1	0.00
Sioux	6	0.03
Ute (1)	2	0.01
Yaqui (2)	5	0.02
All other tribes (11)	25	0.11
American Indian tribes, not spec.	12	0.05
Arab:	161	0.69
Arab/Arabic	27	0.12
Egyptian	25	0.11
Lebanese	64	0.27
Palestinian	36	0.15
Syrian	9	0.04
Armenian	100	0.43
Asian:	747	3.15
Cambodian (5)	6	0.03
Chinese, ex. Taiwanese (106)	155	0.65
Filipino (83)	144	0.61
Hmong (1)	1	0.00
Indian (72)	96	0.40
Indonesian (1)	5	0.02
Japanese (102)	166	0.70
Korean (61)	71	0.30
Malaysian (1)	1	0.00
Pakistani (1)	6	0.03
Taiwanese (4)	10	0.04
Thai (5)	5	0.02
Vietnamese (36)	41	0.17
Other Asian, specified	2	0.01
Other Asian, not specified (2)	38	0.16
Assyrian/Chaldean/Syriac	7	0.03
Australian	44	0.19
Austrian	176	0.75
Basque	46	0.20
Belgian	84	0.36
Brazilian	19	0.08
British	461	1.98
Bulgarian	25	0.11
Canadian	275	1.18
Celtic	17	0.07
Croatian	28	0.12
Czech	146	0.63
Czechoslovakian	46	0.20
Danish	282	1.21
Dutch	525	2.25
Eastern European	120	0.51
English	3,997	17.14
Estonian	32	0.14
European	592	2.54
Finnish	54	0.23
French, except Basque	1,045	4.48
French Canadian	133	0.57
German	4,201	18.02
Greek	95	0.41
Hawaii Native/Pacific Islander:	59	0.25
Micronesian: (4)	7	0.03
Guamanian/Chamorro (1)	3	0.01
Other Micronesian (3)	4	0.02
Polynesian: (13)	43	0.18
Native Hawaiian (6)	32	0.13
Samoan (4)	4	0.02
Tongan (3)	5	0.02
Other Polynesian	2	0.01
Other Pac. Isl., not spec. (3)	9	0.04
Hispanic or Latino:	1,570	6.62
Central American:	30	0.13
Costa Rican	5	0.02
Guatemalan	3	0.01
Honduran	3	0.01
Nicaraguan	1	0.00
Panamanian	9	0.04
Salvadoran	8	0.03
Other Central American	1	0.00
Cuban	37	0.16
Dominican Republic	3	0.01
Mexican	1,100	4.64
Puerto Rican	38	0.16
South American:	90	0.38
Argentinean	16	0.07
Bolivian	2	0.01
Chilean	9	0.04
Colombian	19	0.08
Ecuadorian	7	0.03
Peruvian	12	0.05
Uruguayan	1	0.00
Venezuelan	8	0.03
Other South American	16	0.07
Other Hispanic or Latino	272	1.15
Hungarian	204	0.87
Icelander	20	0.09
Iranian	243	1.04
Irish	3,205	13.75
Israeli	7	0.03
Italian	1,700	7.29
Latvian	87	0.37
Lithuanian	81	0.35
Maltese	8	0.03
New Zealander	14	0.06
Northern European	92	0.39
Norwegian	595	2.55
Pennsylvania German	16	0.07
Polish	696	2.98
Portuguese	140	0.60
Romanian	82	0.35
Russian	775	3.32
Scandinavian	134	0.57
Scotch-Irish	573	2.46
Scottish	975	4.18
Serbian	41	0.18
Slavic	5	0.02
Slovak	15	0.06
Slovene	6	0.03
Swedish	774	3.32
Swiss	286	1.23
Turkish	73	0.31
Ukrainian	158	0.68
United States or American	895	3.84
Welsh	281	1.21
West Indian, excl. Hispanic:	29	0.12
Jamaican	24	0.10
West Indian	5	0.02
White:	22,341	94.16
Not Hispanic (20,921)	21,318	89.85
Hispanic (905)	1,023	4.31
Yugoslavian	56	0.24

Laguna

Place Type: Census Designated Place
County: Sacramento
Population: 34,309

Ancestry/Race	Number	%
Afghan	89	0.26
African American/Black:	3,889	11.34
Not Hispanic (3,258)	3,729	10.87
Hispanic (71)	160	0.47
African, sub-Saharan:	509	1.48
African	174	0.51
Cape Verdean	96	0.28
Ethiopian	50	0.15
Kenyan	13	0.04
Nigerian	176	0.51
Alaska Native tribes, specified:	5	0.01
Aleut (1)	1	0.00
Tlingit-Haida (4)	4	0.01
Alaska Native tribes, not specified	1	0.00
Am. Ind. or Alaska Nat., not spec.	152	0.44
Albanian	15	0.04
American Indian tribes, specified:	430	1.25
Apache (5)	22	0.06
Blackfeet (1)	13	0.04
Cherokee (39)	143	0.42
Cheyenne (1)	2	0.01
Chickasaw (2)	2	0.01
Chippewa (12)	15	0.04
Choctaw (5)	22	0.06
Comanche (1)	3	0.01
Cree	2	0.01
Creek	7	0.02
Delaware	2	0.01
Iroquois (2)	5	0.01
Latin American Indians (10)	27	0.08
Lumbee (1)	2	0.01
Menominee	3	0.01
Navajo (7)	14	0.04
Osage	2	0.01
Paiute (2)	2	0.01
Potawatomi (7)	14	0.04
Pueblo (2)	2	0.01
Seminole	3	0.01
Sioux (12)	21	0.06
Tohono O'Odham	1	0.00
Ute	1	0.00
Yaqui (1)	13	0.04
All other tribes (49)	87	0.25
American Indian tribes, not spec.	20	0.06
Arab:	326	0.95
Arab/Arabic	95	0.28
Egyptian	55	0.16
Lebanese	16	0.05
Palestinian	116	0.34
Syrian	8	0.02
Other Arab	36	0.10
Armenian	34	0.10
Asian:	7,558	22.03
Cambodian (36)	49	0.14
Chinese, ex. Taiwanese (1,966)	2,299	6.70
Filipino (1,869)	2,402	7.00
Hmong (27)	28	0.08
Indian (530)	653	1.90
Indonesian (6)	22	0.06
Japanese (507)	842	2.45
Korean (181)	240	0.70
Laotian (41)	52	0.15
Malaysian (1)	1	0.00
Pakistani (63)	75	0.22
Sri Lankan (4)	4	0.01
Taiwanese (7)	10	0.03
Thai (15)	20	0.06
Vietnamese (678)	756	2.20
Other Asian, specified (6)	9	0.03

Notes: 1. Figures in the "Number" column do not add up to the total population due to: a) Ancestry/Race overlap — e.g. persons can report being both White and Irish, b) persons of Hispanic origin can report being any race, c) persons reporting two ancestries are counted in both categories. 2. Numbers in parentheses indicate the number of persons reporting this ancestry/race alone, not in combination with any other ancestry/race. 3. Refer to the Explanation of Data in the front of the book for more detailed information.

Other Asian, not specified (42)	96	0.28
Australian	17	0.05
Austrian	83	0.24
Basque	17	0.05
Belgian	21	0.06
British	57	0.17
Canadian	27	0.08
Celtic	14	0.04
Croatian	74	0.22
Czech	59	0.17
Czechoslovakian	95	0.28
Danish	238	0.69
Dutch	450	1.31
Eastern European	14	0.04
English	2,648	7.70
European	394	1.15
Finnish	105	0.31
French, except Basque	845	2.46
French Canadian	254	0.74
German	4,871	14.16
German Russian	8	0.02
Greek	334	0.97
Hawaii Native/Pacific Islander:	355	1.03
Melanesian: (32)	41	0.12
Fijian (32)	41	0.12
Micronesian: (32)	72	0.21
Guamanian/Chamorro (25)	58	0.17
Other Micronesian (7)	14	0.04
Polynesian: (32)	123	0.36
Native Hawaiian (21)	105	0.31
Samoan (1)	6	0.02
Tongan (9)	11	0.03
Other Polynesian (1)	1	0.00
Other Pac. Isl., not spec. (23)	119	0.35
Hispanic or Latino:	4,984	14.53
Central American:	140	0.41
Costa Rican	7	0.02
Guatemalan	18	0.05
Honduran	7	0.02
Nicaraguan	37	0.11
Panamanian	23	0.07
Salvadoran	40	0.12
Other Central American	8	0.02
Cuban	50	0.15
Dominican Republic	8	0.02
Mexican	3,729	10.87
Puerto Rican	182	0.53
South American:	98	0.29
Argentinean	4	0.01
Bolivian	2	0.01
Chilean	23	0.07
Colombian	20	0.06
Ecuadorian	13	0.04
Peruvian	27	0.08
Venezuelan	2	0.01
Other South American	7	0.02
Other Hispanic or Latino	777	2.26
Hungarian	75	0.22
Icelander	18	0.05
Iranian	148	0.43
Irish	3,506	10.19
Israeli	16	0.05
Italian	2,181	6.34
Lithuanian	30	0.09
Maltese	33	0.10
Northern European	27	0.08
Norwegian	724	2.10
Polish	456	1.33
Portuguese	613	1.78
Romanian	35	0.10
Russian	226	0.66
Scandinavian	126	0.37
Scotch-Irish	483	1.40
Scottish	698	2.03
Slavic	17	0.05
Slovak	46	0.13
Slovene	29	0.08
Swedish	631	1.83
Swiss	300	0.87
Ukrainian	20	0.06
United States or American	1,038	3.02
Welsh	326	0.95
West Indian, excl. Hispanic:	59	0.17
Jamaican	50	0.15
West Indian	9	0.03
White:	22,060	64.30
Not Hispanic (18,035)	19,312	56.29
Hispanic (2,240)	2,748	8.01
Yugoslavian	48	0.14

Laguna Hills

Place Type: City
County: Orange
Population: 31,178

Ancestry/Race	Number	%
Afghan	24	0.08
African American/Black:	552	1.77
Not Hispanic (404)	518	1.66
Hispanic (25)	34	0.11
African, sub-Saharan:	30	0.10
African	15	0.05
South African	15	0.05
Am. Ind. or Alaska Nat., not spec.	101	0.32
Alsatian	8	0.03
American Indian tribes, specified:	177	0.57
Apache (9)	13	0.04
Blackfeet	3	0.01
Cherokee (29)	67	0.21
Chippewa (2)	4	0.01
Choctaw (7)	10	0.03
Cree (1)	1	0.00
Creek (2)	8	0.03
Delaware (2)	3	0.01
Iroquois (3)	6	0.02
Latin American Indians (7)	9	0.03
Navajo (3)	6	0.02
Osage	5	0.02
Ottawa	1	0.00
Pueblo	2	0.01
Puget Sound Salish	1	0.00
Seminole (5)	6	0.02
Sioux (1)	1	0.00
All other tribes (14)	31	0.10
American Indian tribes, not spec.	6	0.02
Arab:	450	1.44
Arab/Arabic	28	0.09
Egyptian	108	0.35
Jordanian	8	0.03
Lebanese	216	0.69
Palestinian	34	0.11
Syrian	48	0.15
Other Arab	8	0.03
Armenian	147	0.47
Asian:	3,757	12.05
Bangladeshi (6)	8	0.03
Cambodian (18)	19	0.06
Chinese, ex. Taiwanese (573)	685	2.20
Filipino (641)	774	2.48
Indian (326)	374	1.20
Indonesian (34)	59	0.19
Japanese (312)	431	1.38
Korean (509)	539	1.73
Laotian (4)	4	0.01
Malaysian (2)	3	0.01
Pakistani (12)	31	0.10
Sri Lankan (4)	4	0.01
Taiwanese (163)	187	0.60
Thai (39)	52	0.17
Vietnamese (420)	447	1.43
Other Asian, specified (7)	9	0.03
Other Asian, not specified (40)	131	0.42
Assyrian/Chaldean/Syriac	21	0.07
Australian	42	0.13
Austrian	141	0.45
Basque	9	0.03
Belgian	53	0.17
Brazilian	8	0.03
British	194	0.62
Bulgarian	8	0.03
Canadian	175	0.56
Croatian	46	0.15
Czech	127	0.41
Czechoslovakian	81	0.26
Danish	402	1.29
Dutch	628	2.01
Eastern European	16	0.05
English	3,898	12.46
European	289	0.92
Finnish	54	0.17
French, except Basque	776	2.48
French Canadian	239	0.76
German	4,789	15.31
German Russian	4	0.01
Greek	306	0.98
Hawaii Native/Pacific Islander:	120	0.38
Micronesian: (5)	7	0.02
Guamanian/Chamorro (5)	7	0.02
Polynesian: (31)	75	0.24
Native Hawaiian (13)	47	0.15
Samoan (10)	12	0.04
Tongan (7)	9	0.03
Other Polynesian (1)	7	0.02
Other Pac. Isl., specified	1	0.00
Other Pac. Isl., not spec. (8)	37	0.12
Hispanic or Latino:	5,113	16.40
Central American:	193	0.62
Costa Rican	19	0.06
Guatemalan	66	0.21
Honduran	5	0.02
Nicaraguan	8	0.03
Panamanian	9	0.03
Salvadoran	74	0.24
Other Central American	12	0.04
Cuban	65	0.21
Dominican Republic	3	0.01
Mexican	3,693	11.84
Puerto Rican	95	0.30
South American:	281	0.90
Argentinean	65	0.21
Bolivian	27	0.09
Chilean	23	0.07
Colombian	82	0.26
Ecuadorian	17	0.05
Paraguayan	2	0.01
Peruvian	41	0.13
Venezuelan	4	0.01
Other South American	20	0.06
Other Hispanic or Latino	783	2.51
Hungarian	278	0.89
Iranian	610	1.95
Irish	3,529	11.28
Italian	1,817	5.81
Latvian	18	0.06
Lithuanian	106	0.34
Macedonian	8	0.03
Maltese	21	0.07
Northern European	5	0.02
Norwegian	665	2.13
Polish	918	2.94
Portuguese	102	0.33
Romanian	30	0.10
Russian	803	2.57
Scandinavian	89	0.28
Scotch-Irish	469	1.50
Scottish	758	2.42
Serbian	34	0.11
Slavic	13	0.04
Slovak	94	0.30
Slovene	26	0.08
Swedish	680	2.17
Swiss	82	0.26
Ukrainian	117	0.37
United States or American	1,288	4.12
Welsh	290	0.93
West Indian, excl. Hispanic:	20	0.06
Jamaican	20	0.06
White:	24,983	80.13
Not Hispanic (21,471)	22,194	71.18

Notes: 1. Figures in the "Number" column do not add up to the total population due to: a) Ancestry/Race overlap — e.g. persons can report being both White and Irish, b) persons of Hispanic origin can report being any race, c) persons reporting two ancestries are counted in both categories. 2. Numbers in parentheses indicate the number of persons reporting this ancestry/race alone, not in combination with any other ancestry/race. 3. Refer to the Explanation of Data in the front of the book for more detailed information.

Hispanic (2,483)	2,789	8.95
Yugoslavian	17	0.05

Laguna Niguel

Place Type: City
County: Orange
Population: 61,891

Ancestry/Race	Number	%
Afghan	178	0.29
African American/Black:	996	1.61
Not Hispanic (723)	907	1.47
Hispanic (53)	89	0.14
African, sub-Saharan:	151	0.24
African	8	0.01
Nigerian	19	0.03
South African	69	0.11
Ugandan	55	0.09
Alaska Native tribes, specified:	4	0.01
Aleut	2	0.00
Eskimo (1)	1	0.00
Tlingit-Haida (1)	1	0.00
Am. Ind. or Alaska Nat., not spec.	160	0.26
Alsatian	7	0.01
American Indian tribes, specified:	330	0.53
Apache (3)	24	0.04
Blackfeet (1)	6	0.01
Cherokee (22)	100	0.16
Chickasaw (4)	7	0.01
Chippewa (1)	3	0.00
Choctaw (10)	30	0.05
Comanche	6	0.01
Creek	2	0.00
Crow	1	0.00
Delaware	2	0.00
Iroquois (1)	5	0.01
Latin American Indians (5)	28	0.05
Navajo (8)	9	0.01
Osage (3)	5	0.01
Pima	1	0.00
Potawatomi (2)	2	0.00
Pueblo (2)	12	0.02
Seminole (1)	5	0.01
Sioux (9)	16	0.03
Ute	1	0.00
All other tribes (28)	65	0.11
American Indian tribes, not spec.	17	0.03
Arab:	874	1.41
Arab/Arabic	49	0.08
Egyptian	202	0.33
Iraqi	14	0.02
Jordanian	9	0.01
Lebanese	385	0.62
Palestinian	38	0.06
Syrian	130	0.21
Other Arab	47	0.08
Armenian	366	0.59
Asian:	5,846	9.45
Cambodian (25)	36	0.06
Chinese, ex. Taiwanese (1,109)	1,319	2.13
Filipino (895)	1,104	1.78
Indian (465)	517	0.84
Indonesian (69)	99	0.16
Japanese (762)	1,068	1.73
Korean (468)	553	0.89
Laotian (2)	8	0.01
Malaysian (2)	3	0.00
Pakistani (32)	35	0.06
Sri Lankan (5)	5	0.01
Taiwanese (196)	226	0.37
Thai (78)	89	0.14
Vietnamese (491)	534	0.86
Other Asian, specified (8)	10	0.02
Other Asian, not specified (58)	240	0.39
Assyrian/Chaldean/Syriac	42	0.07
Australian	21	0.03
Austrian	376	0.61
Basque	66	0.11
Belgian	116	0.19
Brazilian	40	0.06
British	448	0.72
Bulgarian	43	0.07
Canadian	302	0.49
Celtic	33	0.05
Croatian	193	0.31
Czech	331	0.53
Czechoslovakian	119	0.19
Danish	579	0.93
Dutch	1,141	1.84
Eastern European	66	0.11
English	8,534	13.77
Estonian	23	0.04
European	1,104	1.78
Finnish	118	0.19
French, except Basque	2,239	3.61
French Canadian	379	0.61
German	10,404	16.79
Greek	524	0.85
Hawaii Native/Pacific Islander:	181	0.29
Melanesian: (1)	1	0.00
Fijian (1)	1	0.00
Micronesian: (16)	27	0.04
Guamanian/Chamorro (16)	27	0.04
Polynesian: (45)	89	0.14
Native Hawaiian (30)	61	0.10
Samoan (12)	22	0.04
Tongan (2)	4	0.01
Other Polynesian (1)	2	0.00
Other Pac. Isl., not spec. (11)	64	0.10
Hispanic or Latino:	6,425	10.38
Central American:	275	0.44
Costa Rican	28	0.05
Guatemalan	97	0.16
Honduran	8	0.01
Nicaraguan	27	0.04
Panamanian	22	0.04
Salvadoran	63	0.10
Other Central American	30	0.05
Cuban	167	0.27
Dominican Republic	7	0.01
Mexican	4,346	7.02
Puerto Rican	180	0.29
South American:	453	0.73
Argentinean	95	0.15
Bolivian	10	0.02
Chilean	15	0.02
Colombian	143	0.23
Ecuadorian	23	0.04
Peruvian	93	0.15
Uruguayan	1	0.00
Venezuelan	28	0.05
Other South American	45	0.07
Other Hispanic or Latino	997	1.61
Hungarian	606	0.98
Icelander	45	0.07
Iranian	2,276	3.67
Irish	7,982	12.88
Israeli	22	0.04
Italian	5,243	8.46
Latvian	14	0.02
Lithuanian	255	0.41
Macedonian	7	0.01
Maltese	19	0.03
Northern European	112	0.18
Norwegian	1,382	2.23
Pennsylvania German	10	0.02
Polish	1,881	3.04
Portuguese	257	0.41
Romanian	187	0.30
Russian	1,293	2.09
Scandinavian	323	0.52
Scotch-Irish	912	1.47
Scottish	1,621	2.62
Serbian	64	0.10
Slavic	57	0.09
Slovak	88	0.14
Slovene	88	0.14
Swedish	1,710	2.76
Swiss	360	0.58
Turkish	58	0.09
Ukrainian	295	0.48
United States or American	2,929	4.73
Welsh	591	0.95
West Indian, excl. Hispanic:	23	0.04
Trinidadian and Tobagonian	8	0.01
West Indian	15	0.02
White:	53,709	86.78
Not Hispanic (47,916)	49,523	80.02
Hispanic (3,766)	4,186	6.76
Yugoslavian	213	0.34

Laguna Woods

Place Type: City
County: Orange
Population: 16,507

Ancestry/Race	Number	%
African American/Black:	51	0.31
Not Hispanic (41)	51	0.31
African, sub-Saharan:	12	0.07
African	3	0.02
South African	9	0.06
Am. Ind. or Alaska Nat., not spec.	12	0.07
American Indian tribes, specified:	37	0.22
Blackfeet	2	0.01
Cherokee (4)	14	0.08
Chickasaw	1	0.01
Chippewa (2)	2	0.01
Choctaw	1	0.01
Comanche (1)	2	0.01
Creek	2	0.01
Delaware	1	0.01
Iroquois (1)	1	0.01
Navajo (1)	1	0.01
Osage	1	0.01
Ottawa (1)	1	0.01
Potawatomi	1	0.01
Pueblo	1	0.01
Sioux (1)	1	0.01
All other tribes (3)	5	0.03
American Indian tribes, not spec.	5	0.03
Arab:	95	0.58
Egyptian	16	0.10
Lebanese	44	0.27
Palestinian	27	0.17
Syrian	8	0.05
Armenian	25	0.15
Asian:	475	2.88
Cambodian (2)	2	0.01
Chinese, ex. Taiwanese (106)	111	0.67
Filipino (103)	123	0.75
Indian (18)	26	0.16
Indonesian (6)	11	0.07
Japanese (89)	106	0.64
Korean (58)	62	0.38
Taiwanese (5)	7	0.04
Thai (3)	3	0.02
Vietnamese (16)	16	0.10
Other Asian, specified	1	0.01
Other Asian, not specified (1)	7	0.04
Assyrian/Chaldean/Syriac	8	0.05
Australian	13	0.08
Austrian	251	1.54
Basque	12	0.07
Belgian	16	0.10
British	171	1.05
Bulgarian	22	0.14
Canadian	135	0.83
Celtic	7	0.04
Czech	77	0.47
Czechoslovakian	70	0.43
Danish	132	0.81
Dutch	332	2.04
Eastern European	14	0.09
English	2,728	16.79
Estonian	7	0.04
European	121	0.74
Finnish	35	0.22

Notes: 1. Figures in the "Number" column do not add up to the total population due to: a) Ancestry/Race overlap — e.g. persons can report being both White and Irish, b) persons of Hispanic origin can report being any race, c) persons reporting two ancestries are counted in both categories. 2. Numbers in parentheses indicate the number of persons reporting this ancestry/race alone, not in combination with any other ancestry/race. 3. Refer to the Explanation of Data in the front of the book for more detailed information.

French, except Basque	493	3.03
French Canadian	113	0.70
German	2,532	15.58
Greek	57	0.35
Hawaii Native/Pacific Islander:	19	0.12
Polynesian: (6)	10	0.06
Native Hawaiian (6)	9	0.05
Other Polynesian	1	0.01
Other Pac. Isl., specified	1	0.01
Other Pac. Isl., not spec. (3)	8	0.05
Hispanic or Latino:	340	2.06
Central American:	12	0.07
Costa Rican	1	0.01
Guatemalan	3	0.02
Nicaraguan	3	0.02
Panamanian	2	0.01
Salvadoran	3	0.02
Cuban	16	0.10
Mexican	181	1.10
Puerto Rican	19	0.12
South American:	33	0.20
Argentinean	5	0.03
Bolivian	4	0.02
Chilean	5	0.03
Colombian	5	0.03
Ecuadorian	5	0.03
Peruvian	1	0.01
Uruguayan	2	0.01
Other South American	6	0.04
Other Hispanic or Latino	79	0.48
Hungarian	312	1.92
Iranian	14	0.09
Irish	1,491	9.17
Israeli	25	0.15
Italian	601	3.70
Latvian	42	0.26
Lithuanian	94	0.58
Luxemburger	16	0.10
Northern European	6	0.04
Norwegian	396	2.44
Pennsylvania German	16	0.10
Polish	873	5.37
Portuguese	82	0.50
Romanian	97	0.60
Russian	1,137	7.00
Scandinavian	47	0.29
Scotch-Irish	577	3.55
Scottish	576	3.54
Serbian	13	0.08
Slovak	38	0.23
Slovene	7	0.04
Swedish	460	2.83
Swiss	137	0.84
Turkish	22	0.14
Ukrainian	140	0.86
United States or American	963	5.93
Welsh	138	0.85
West Indian, excl. Hispanic:	8	0.05
Bahamian	8	0.05
White:	15,982	96.82
Not Hispanic (15,580)	15,674	94.95
Hispanic (286)	308	1.87
Yugoslavian	85	0.52

Lake Elsinore

Place Type: City
County: Riverside
Population: 28,928

Ancestry/Race	Number	%
African American/Black:	1,792	6.19
Not Hispanic (1,434)	1,651	5.71
Hispanic (67)	141	0.49
African, sub-Saharan:	56	0.19
African	56	0.19
Alaska Native tribes, specified:	1	0.00
Aleut	1	0.00
Am. Ind. or Alaska Nat., not spec.	210	0.73
American Indian tribes, specified:	506	1.75
Apache (10)	32	0.11
Blackfeet (4)	21	0.07
Cherokee (46)	128	0.44
Cheyenne (1)	4	0.01
Chippewa (8)	24	0.08
Choctaw (7)	18	0.06
Cree	1	0.00
Creek (2)	5	0.02
Delaware (4)	7	0.02
Iroquois (4)	5	0.02
Latin American Indians (29)	48	0.17
Lumbee	3	0.01
Navajo (4)	13	0.04
Osage	2	0.01
Pima (1)	1	0.00
Pueblo (13)	22	0.08
Seminole (1)	5	0.02
Shoshone	3	0.01
Sioux (3)	17	0.06
Tohono O'Odham (2)	4	0.01
Yaqui (24)	28	0.10
Yuman (1)	3	0.01
All other tribes (70)	112	0.39
American Indian tribes, not spec.	37	0.13
Arab:	38	0.13
Egyptian	9	0.03
Jordanian	12	0.04
Lebanese	7	0.02
Syrian	10	0.03
Armenian	8	0.03
Asian:	947	3.27
Cambodian (83)	112	0.39
Chinese, ex. Taiwanese (56)	125	0.43
Filipino (182)	312	1.08
Indian (36)	50	0.17
Indonesian (2)	20	0.07
Japanese (56)	112	0.39
Korean (80)	92	0.32
Laotian (11)	11	0.04
Malaysian (3)	3	0.01
Sri Lankan (4)	4	0.01
Thai (8)	13	0.04
Vietnamese (43)	60	0.21
Other Asian, specified	4	0.01
Other Asian, not specified (7)	29	0.10
Assyrian/Chaldean/Syriac	56	0.19
Austrian	52	0.18
Basque	16	0.05
Belgian	17	0.06
Brazilian	24	0.08
British	85	0.29
Canadian	76	0.26
Croatian	12	0.04
Czech	75	0.26
Czechoslovakian	24	0.08
Danish	188	0.64
Dutch	422	1.44
English	2,392	8.17
European	312	1.07
Finnish	20	0.07
French, except Basque	541	1.85
French Canadian	205	0.70
German	3,144	10.73
Greek	79	0.27
Guyanese	10	0.03
Hawaii Native/Pacific Islander:	186	0.64
Micronesian: (14)	21	0.07
Guamanian/Chamorro (14)	19	0.07
Other Micronesian	2	0.01
Polynesian: (69)	138	0.48
Native Hawaiian (20)	53	0.18
Samoan (49)	80	0.28
Tongan	5	0.02
Other Pac. Isl., not spec. (3)	27	0.09
Hispanic or Latino:	11,007	38.05
Central American:	443	1.53
Costa Rican	13	0.04
Guatemalan	246	0.85
Honduran	13	0.04
Nicaraguan	33	0.11
Panamanian	10	0.03
Salvadoran	95	0.33
Other Central American	33	0.11
Cuban	69	0.24
Dominican Republic	7	0.02
Mexican	8,585	29.68
Puerto Rican	184	0.64
South American:	112	0.39
Argentinean	29	0.10
Bolivian	5	0.02
Chilean	9	0.03
Colombian	20	0.07
Ecuadorian	7	0.02
Peruvian	26	0.09
Venezuelan	7	0.02
Other South American	9	0.03
Other Hispanic or Latino	1,607	5.56
Hungarian	94	0.32
Icelander	23	0.08
Iranian	37	0.13
Irish	2,499	8.53
Italian	1,106	3.78
Lithuanian	65	0.22
Northern European	22	0.08
Norwegian	510	1.74
Pennsylvania German	8	0.03
Polish	423	1.44
Portuguese	141	0.48
Romanian	20	0.07
Russian	82	0.28
Scandinavian	85	0.29
Scotch-Irish	368	1.26
Scottish	365	1.25
Serbian	32	0.11
Slovak	13	0.04
Swedish	533	1.82
Swiss	25	0.09
Ukrainian	51	0.17
United States or American	1,695	5.79
Welsh	206	0.70
West Indian, excl. Hispanic:	24	0.08
Trinidadian and Tobagonian	9	0.03
West Indian	15	0.05
White:	20,206	69.85
Not Hispanic (14,877)	15,451	53.41
Hispanic (4,104)	4,755	16.44
Yugoslavian	28	0.10

Lake Forest

Place Type: City
County: Orange
Population: 58,707

Ancestry/Race	Number	%
Afghan	153	0.26
African American/Black:	1,373	2.34
Not Hispanic (998)	1,243	2.12
Hispanic (75)	130	0.22
African, sub-Saharan:	136	0.23
African	112	0.19
Senegalese	8	0.01
South African	16	0.03
Alaska Native tribes, specified:	4	0.01
Eskimo (1)	1	0.00
Tlingit-Haida (3)	3	0.01
Am. Ind. or Alaska Nat., not spec.	222	0.38
American Indian tribes, specified:	461	0.79
Apache (9)	13	0.02
Blackfeet (5)	21	0.04
Cherokee (23)	117	0.20
Cheyenne (1)	4	0.01
Chickasaw (1)	11	0.02
Chippewa (1)	3	0.01
Choctaw (12)	29	0.05
Comanche (3)	6	0.01
Cree	1	0.00
Creek (1)	3	0.01
Crow (1)	2	0.00
Delaware (1)	1	0.00

Notes: 1. Figures in the "Number" column do not add up to the total population due to: a) Ancestry/Race overlap — e.g. persons can report being both White and Irish, b) persons of Hispanic origin can report being any race, c) persons reporting two ancestries are counted in both categories. 2. Numbers in parentheses indicate the number of persons reporting this ancestry/race alone, not in combination with any other ancestry/race. 3. Refer to the Explanation of Data in the front of the book for more detailed information.

Houma (1)	1	0.00
Iroquois (6)	10	0.02
Latin American Indians (62)	90	0.15
Menominee (1)	1	0.00
Navajo (3)	17	0.03
Osage (4)	6	0.01
Pima	1	0.00
Potawatomi (1)	4	0.01
Pueblo (5)	11	0.02
Shoshone (2)	2	0.00
Sioux (11)	22	0.04
Yaqui (4)	10	0.02
Yuman (1)	1	0.00
All other tribes (40)	74	0.13
American Indian tribes, not spec.	26	0.04
Arab:	251	0.43
Arab/Arabic	24	0.04
Egyptian	90	0.15
Lebanese	82	0.14
Moroccan	3	0.01
Palestinian	32	0.05
Syrian	20	0.03
Armenian	101	0.17
Asian:	6,838	11.65
Bangladeshi (9)	13	0.02
Cambodian (9)	12	0.02
Chinese, ex. Taiwanese (598)	824	1.40
Filipino (1,301)	1,620	2.76
Hmong (1)	1	0.00
Indian (623)	690	1.18
Indonesian (54)	79	0.13
Japanese (586)	842	1.43
Korean (641)	699	1.19
Laotian (52)	55	0.09
Malaysian (11)	14	0.02
Pakistani (49)	81	0.14
Sri Lankan (43)	46	0.08
Taiwanese (85)	109	0.19
Thai (44)	69	0.12
Vietnamese (1,402)	1,498	2.55
Other Asian, specified (8)	21	0.04
Other Asian, not specified (48)	165	0.28
Australian	31	0.05
Austrian	164	0.28
Basque	35	0.06
Belgian	83	0.14
Brazilian	24	0.04
British	426	0.72
Bulgarian	28	0.05
Canadian	331	0.56
Croatian	55	0.09
Czech	162	0.28
Czechoslovakian	69	0.12
Danish	334	0.57
Dutch	1,147	1.95
Eastern European	66	0.11
English	7,214	12.27
Estonian	6	0.01
European	499	0.85
Finnish	164	0.28
French, except Basque	2,072	3.52
French Canadian	340	0.58
German	10,312	17.54
German Russian	7	0.01
Greek	190	0.32
Hawaii Native/Pacific Islander:	301	0.51
Melanesian: (2)	2	0.00
Fijian (2)	2	0.00
Micronesian: (41)	59	0.10
Guamanian/Chamorro (30)	44	0.07
Other Micronesian (11)	15	0.03
Polynesian: (68)	182	0.31
Native Hawaiian (35)	130	0.22
Samoan (32)	46	0.08
Tongan	1	0.00
Other Polynesian (1)	5	0.01
Other Pac. Isl., not spec. (8)	58	0.10
Hispanic or Latino:	10,913	18.59
Central American:	536	0.91
Costa Rican	28	0.05
Guatemalan	231	0.39
Honduran	20	0.03
Nicaraguan	28	0.05
Panamanian	8	0.01
Salvadoran	178	0.30
Other Central American	43	0.07
Cuban	148	0.25
Dominican Republic	17	0.03
Mexican	7,789	13.27
Puerto Rican	208	0.35
South American:	616	1.05
Argentinean	97	0.17
Bolivian	46	0.08
Chilean	41	0.07
Colombian	212	0.36
Ecuadorian	61	0.10
Paraguayan	1	0.00
Peruvian	91	0.16
Uruguayan	7	0.01
Venezuelan	6	0.01
Other South American	54	0.09
Other Hispanic or Latino	1,599	2.72
Hungarian	402	0.68
Icelander	14	0.02
Iranian	1,170	1.99
Irish	6,605	11.23
Israeli	44	0.07
Italian	4,473	7.61
Lithuanian	77	0.13
Luxemburger	6	0.01
Maltese	6	0.01
New Zealander	17	0.03
Northern European	36	0.06
Norwegian	1,218	2.07
Pennsylvania German	6	0.01
Polish	1,488	2.53
Portuguese	165	0.28
Romanian	130	0.22
Russian	750	1.28
Scandinavian	166	0.28
Scotch-Irish	816	1.39
Scottish	1,568	2.67
Serbian	45	0.08
Slavic	15	0.03
Slovak	127	0.22
Slovene	27	0.05
Swedish	1,290	2.19
Swiss	198	0.34
Turkish	45	0.08
Ukrainian	295	0.50
United States or American	2,170	3.69
Welsh	386	0.66
West Indian, excl. Hispanic:	55	0.09
Haitian	23	0.04
Jamaican	8	0.01
Trinidadian and Tobagonian	24	0.04
White:	46,866	79.83
Not Hispanic (39,161)	40,619	69.19
Hispanic (5,468)	6,247	10.64
Yugoslavian	122	0.21

Lake Los Angeles

Place Type: Census Designated Place
County: Los Angeles
Population: 11,523

Ancestry/Race	Number	%
African American/Black:	1,579	13.70
Not Hispanic (1,363)	1,521	13.20
Hispanic (33)	58	0.50
African, sub-Saharan:	48	0.41
African	48	0.41
Am. Ind. or Alaska Nat., not spec.	127	1.10
Alsatian	3	0.03
American Indian tribes, specified:	254	2.20
Apache (12)	26	0.23
Blackfeet (6)	23	0.20
Cherokee (26)	84	0.73
Cheyenne (2)	2	0.02
Chippewa (3)	10	0.09
Choctaw (3)	18	0.16
Comanche	2	0.02
Creek	4	0.03
Crow	1	0.01
Iroquois (2)	8	0.07
Kiowa (1)	1	0.01
Latin American Indians (17)	22	0.19
Navajo (4)	6	0.05
Osage	1	0.01
Paiute	5	0.04
Pima (4)	4	0.03
Pueblo (1)	2	0.02
Seminole	3	0.03
Shoshone (3)	3	0.03
Sioux (2)	9	0.08
Ute (1)	1	0.01
Yaqui	1	0.01
All other tribes (15)	18	0.16
American Indian tribes, not spec.	13	0.11
Arab:	41	0.35
Arab/Arabic	30	0.25
Syrian	11	0.09
Asian:	231	2.00
Cambodian (3)	3	0.03
Chinese, ex. Taiwanese (6)	25	0.22
Filipino (52)	92	0.80
Indian (6)	12	0.10
Indonesian (1)	6	0.05
Japanese (13)	28	0.24
Korean (7)	13	0.11
Taiwanese (1)	1	0.01
Thai (16)	16	0.14
Vietnamese (8)	13	0.11
Other Asian, specified	4	0.03
Other Asian, not specified (1)	18	0.16
Belgian	8	0.07
Canadian	45	0.38
Croatian	6	0.05
Czech	42	0.36
Czechoslovakian	8	0.07
Danish	6	0.05
Dutch	279	2.37
English	628	5.33
European	152	1.29
French, except Basque	300	2.55
French Canadian	55	0.47
German	1,608	13.65
Greek	11	0.09
Hawaii Native/Pacific Islander:	52	0.45
Micronesian: (1)	2	0.02
Guamanian/Chamorro	1	0.01
Other Micronesian (1)	1	0.01
Polynesian: (16)	40	0.35
Native Hawaiian (6)	24	0.21
Samoan (10)	16	0.14
Other Pac. Isl., not spec. (2)	10	0.09
Hispanic or Latino:	3,869	33.58
Central American:	252	2.19
Costa Rican	6	0.05
Guatemalan	49	0.43
Honduran	22	0.19
Nicaraguan	8	0.07
Panamanian	8	0.07
Salvadoran	140	1.21
Other Central American	19	0.16
Cuban	37	0.32
Dominican Republic	1	0.01
Mexican	2,843	24.67
Puerto Rican	81	0.70
South American:	39	0.34
Argentinean	13	0.11
Chilean	3	0.03
Colombian	8	0.07
Ecuadorian	5	0.04
Peruvian	2	0.02
Venezuelan	5	0.04
Other South American	3	0.03
Other Hispanic or Latino	616	5.35
Hungarian	24	0.20

Notes: 1. Figures in the "Number" column do not add up to the total population due to: a) Ancestry/Race overlap — e.g. persons can report being both White and Irish, b) persons of Hispanic origin can report being any race, c) persons reporting two ancestries are counted in both categories. 2. Numbers in parentheses indicate the number of persons reporting this ancestry/race alone, not in combination with any other ancestry/race. 3. Refer to the Explanation of Data in the front of the book for more detailed information.

Ancestry/Race	Number	%
Iranian	9	0.08
Irish	885	7.51
Italian	531	4.51
Lithuanian	12	0.10
Norwegian	212	1.80
Polish	169	1.43
Portuguese	19	0.16
Russian	77	0.65
Scandinavian	8	0.07
Scotch-Irish	130	1.10
Scottish	62	0.53
Swedish	133	1.13
Swiss	17	0.14
Turkish	25	0.21
United States or American	467	3.96
Welsh	98	0.83
West Indian, excl. Hispanic:	139	1.18
Haitian	70	0.59
West Indian	69	0.59
White:	7,541	65.44
Not Hispanic (5,694)	5,957	51.70
Hispanic (1,336)	1,584	13.75
Yugoslavian	8	0.07

Lakeside

Place Type: Census Designated Place
County: San Diego
Population: 19,560

Ancestry/Race	Number	%
Afghan	59	0.30
African American/Black:	215	1.10
Not Hispanic (141)	201	1.03
Hispanic (5)	14	0.07
African, sub-Saharan:	37	0.19
African	37	0.19
Alaska Native tribes, specified:	9	0.05
Alaska Athabascan (1)	1	0.01
Aleut (2)	2	0.01
Eskimo (3)	6	0.03
Am. Ind. or Alaska Nat., not spec.	130	0.66
American Indian tribes, specified:	267	1.37
Apache (6)	10	0.05
Blackfeet (3)	14	0.07
Cherokee (18)	67	0.34
Chickasaw (2)	2	0.01
Chippewa (5)	9	0.05
Choctaw (2)	6	0.03
Comanche (2)	8	0.04
Cree	1	0.01
Creek (4)	4	0.02
Crow	1	0.01
Iroquois (1)	1	0.01
Latin American Indians (8)	23	0.12
Navajo (1)	7	0.04
Osage (1)	1	0.01
Pima (1)	1	0.01
Potawatomi	1	0.01
Puget Sound Salish	1	0.01
Shoshone (3)	3	0.02
Sioux (21)	30	0.15
Ute (1)	3	0.02
Yaqui (2)	7	0.04
All other tribes (44)	67	0.34
American Indian tribes, not spec.	25	0.13
Arab:	151	0.77
Arab/Arabic	7	0.04
Jordanian	31	0.16
Lebanese	39	0.20
Palestinian	28	0.14
Syrian	46	0.24
Armenian	33	0.17
Asian:	488	2.49
Chinese, ex. Taiwanese (15)	50	0.26
Filipino (136)	250	1.28
Indian (3)	15	0.08
Indonesian (3)	9	0.05
Japanese (39)	87	0.44
Korean (11)	19	0.10
Laotian (2)	2	0.01
Taiwanese (2)	4	0.02
Thai (2)	5	0.03
Vietnamese (22)	30	0.15
Other Asian, specified	3	0.02
Other Asian, not specified (5)	14	0.07
Assyrian/Chaldean/Syriac	10	0.05
Australian	15	0.08
Austrian	123	0.63
Belgian	35	0.18
British	51	0.26
Canadian	46	0.24
Celtic	7	0.04
Croatian	32	0.16
Czech	102	0.52
Czechoslovakian	119	0.61
Danish	192	0.98
Dutch	319	1.63
English	2,543	13.02
European	280	1.43
Finnish	39	0.20
French, except Basque	780	3.99
French Canadian	110	0.56
German	3,503	17.94
Greek	123	0.63
Hawaii Native/Pacific Islander:	131	0.67
Micronesian: (18)	35	0.18
Guamanian/Chamorro (18)	35	0.18
Polynesian: (37)	72	0.37
Native Hawaiian (24)	49	0.25
Samoan (13)	23	0.12
Other Pac. Isl., specified	3	0.02
Other Pac. Isl., not spec.	21	0.11
Hispanic or Latino:	2,254	11.52
Central American:	26	0.13
Costa Rican	8	0.04
Guatemalan	3	0.02
Honduran	3	0.02
Panamanian	5	0.03
Salvadoran	6	0.03
Other Central American	1	0.01
Cuban	20	0.10
Mexican	1,733	8.86
Puerto Rican	66	0.34
South American:	12	0.06
Chilean	3	0.02
Colombian	4	0.02
Peruvian	4	0.02
Venezuelan	1	0.01
Other Hispanic or Latino	397	2.03
Hungarian	120	0.61
Icelander	28	0.14
Irish	2,654	13.59
Italian	1,320	6.76
Lithuanian	32	0.16
Norwegian	567	2.90
Polish	735	3.76
Portuguese	285	1.46
Romanian	17	0.09
Russian	47	0.24
Scandinavian	16	0.08
Scotch-Irish	423	2.17
Scottish	454	2.32
Slavic	5	0.03
Slovak	54	0.28
Slovene	9	0.05
Swedish	447	2.29
Swiss	118	0.60
Turkish	12	0.06
Ukrainian	36	0.18
United States or American	1,314	6.73
Welsh	245	1.25
West Indian, excl. Hispanic:	25	0.13
Barbadian	25	0.13
White:	18,194	93.02
Not Hispanic (16,245)	16,649	85.12
Hispanic (1,326)	1,545	7.90

Lakewood

Place Type: City
County: Los Angeles
Population: 79,345

Ancestry/Race	Number	%
Acadian/Cajun	8	0.01
Afghan	78	0.10
African American/Black:	6,458	8.14
Not Hispanic (5,663)	6,184	7.79
Hispanic (162)	274	0.35
African, sub-Saharan:	456	0.57
African	281	0.35
Ethiopian	47	0.06
Nigerian	83	0.10
South African	8	0.01
Ugandan	29	0.04
Other sub-Saharan African	8	0.01
Alaska Native tribes, specified:	7	0.01
Alaska Athabascan	2	0.00
Eskimo (1)	1	0.00
Tlingit-Haida (3)	4	0.01
Am. Ind. or Alaska Nat., not spec.	408	0.51
Albanian	13	0.02
Alsatian	6	0.01
American Indian tribes, specified:	851	1.07
Apache (41)	70	0.09
Blackfeet (2)	51	0.06
Cherokee (59)	257	0.32
Cheyenne (5)	5	0.01
Chickasaw (9)	20	0.03
Chippewa (10)	21	0.03
Choctaw (17)	47	0.06
Colville (1)	1	0.00
Comanche (2)	4	0.01
Cree	2	0.00
Creek (7)	13	0.02
Delaware (3)	5	0.01
Iroquois (3)	12	0.02
Kiowa	1	0.00
Latin American Indians (25)	68	0.09
Menominee	3	0.00
Navajo (38)	56	0.07
Osage (3)	7	0.01
Ottawa (1)	1	0.00
Paiute (5)	8	0.01
Pima (2)	6	0.01
Potawatomi	8	0.01
Pueblo (14)	32	0.04
Puget Sound Salish (1)	1	0.00
Seminole (2)	6	0.01
Shoshone	5	0.01
Sioux (16)	32	0.04
Ute (1)	5	0.01
Yaqui (7)	17	0.02
Yuman	3	0.00
All other tribes (28)	84	0.11
American Indian tribes, not spec.	51	0.06
Arab:	469	0.59
Arab/Arabic	176	0.22
Egyptian	79	0.10
Iraqi	6	0.01
Lebanese	139	0.18
Palestinian	11	0.01
Syrian	6	0.01
Other Arab	52	0.07
Armenian	130	0.16
Asian:	12,751	16.07
Bangladeshi (11)	22	0.03
Cambodian (670)	820	1.03
Chinese, ex. Taiwanese (974)	1,387	1.75
Filipino (4,541)	5,372	6.77
Hmong (1)	1	0.00
Indian (404)	444	0.56
Indonesian (64)	163	0.21
Japanese (681)	1,066	1.34
Korean (1,594)	1,677	2.11
Laotian (28)	31	0.04
Malaysian (2)	14	0.02

Notes: 1. Figures in the "Number" column do not add up to the total population due to: a) Ancestry/Race overlap — e.g. persons can report being both White and Irish, b) persons of Hispanic origin can report being any race, c) persons reporting two ancestries are counted in both categories. 2. Numbers in parentheses indicate the number of persons reporting this ancestry/race alone, not in combination with any other ancestry/race. 3. Refer to the Explanation of Data in the front of the book for more detailed information.

Pakistani (45)	64	0.08
Sri Lankan (31)	39	0.05
Taiwanese (103)	140	0.18
Thai (285)	329	0.41
Vietnamese (883)	978	1.23
Other Asian, specified (7)	20	0.03
Other Asian, not specified (104)	184	0.23
Assyrian/Chaldean/Syriac	6	0.01
Australian	16	0.02
Austrian	208	0.26
Basque	14	0.02
Belgian	38	0.05
Brazilian	13	0.02
British	354	0.45
Bulgarian	7	0.01
Canadian	393	0.49
Celtic	7	0.01
Croatian	80	0.10
Cypriot	7	0.01
Czech	189	0.24
Czechoslovakian	119	0.15
Danish	647	0.81
Dutch	2,088	2.63
Eastern European	86	0.11
English	7,055	8.88
European	830	1.05
Finnish	88	0.11
French, except Basque	2,368	2.98
French Canadian	529	0.67
German	10,244	12.90
German Russian	16	0.02
Greek	289	0.36
Guyanese	66	0.08
Hawaii Native/Pacific Islander:	949	1.20
Melanesian: (1)	1	0.00
Fijian (1)	1	0.00
Micronesian: (129)	234	0.29
Guamanian/Chamorro (127)	228	0.29
Other Micronesian (2)	6	0.01
Polynesian: (328)	528	0.67
Native Hawaiian (98)	227	0.29
Samoan (209)	268	0.34
Tongan (14)	17	0.02
Other Polynesian (7)	16	0.02
Other Pac. Isl., specified	4	0.01
Other Pac. Isl., not spec. (23)	182	0.23
Hispanic or Latino:	18,071	22.78
Central American:	637	0.80
Costa Rican	81	0.10
Guatemalan	135	0.17
Honduran	31	0.04
Nicaraguan	65	0.08
Panamanian	48	0.06
Salvadoran	211	0.27
Other Central American	66	0.08
Cuban	311	0.39
Dominican Republic	37	0.05
Mexican	13,506	17.02
Puerto Rican	466	0.59
South American:	485	0.61
Argentinean	73	0.09
Bolivian	3	0.00
Chilean	24	0.03
Colombian	103	0.13
Ecuadorian	58	0.07
Peruvian	139	0.18
Uruguayan	10	0.01
Venezuelan	4	0.01
Other South American	71	0.09
Other Hispanic or Latino	2,629	3.31
Hungarian	441	0.56
Icelander	7	0.01
Iranian	132	0.17
Irish	8,466	10.66
Israeli	23	0.03
Italian	3,455	4.35
Latvian	14	0.02
Lithuanian	126	0.16
Luxemburger	18	0.02
Macedonian	4	0.01
Maltese	7	0.01
Northern European	45	0.06
Norwegian	1,312	1.65
Pennsylvania German	20	0.03
Polish	1,031	1.30
Portuguese	443	0.56
Romanian	151	0.19
Russian	588	0.74
Scandinavian	191	0.24
Scotch-Irish	1,287	1.62
Scottish	1,191	1.50
Serbian	6	0.01
Slavic	64	0.08
Slovak	52	0.07
Slovene	12	0.02
Swedish	1,277	1.61
Swiss	208	0.26
Turkish	27	0.03
Ukrainian	26	0.03
United States or American	3,076	3.87
Welsh	650	0.82
West Indian, excl. Hispanic:	142	0.18
Belizean	77	0.10
British West Indian	5	0.01
Haitian	10	0.01
Jamaican	28	0.04
West Indian	22	0.03
White:	52,963	66.75
Not Hispanic (41,577)	43,555	54.89
Hispanic (8,147)	9,408	11.86
Yugoslavian	82	0.10

Lamont

Place Type: Census Designated Place
County: Kern
Population: 13,296

Ancestry/Race	Number	%
African American/Black:	405	3.05
Not Hispanic (33)	35	0.26
Hispanic (338)	370	2.78
Am. Ind. or Alaska Nat., not spec.	98	0.74
American Indian tribes, specified:	159	1.20
Apache (2)	3	0.02
Cherokee (6)	25	0.19
Cheyenne	1	0.01
Chickasaw (1)	5	0.04
Choctaw (2)	8	0.06
Latin American Indians (94)	98	0.74
Navajo (2)	3	0.02
Paiute (2)	5	0.04
Potawatomi	1	0.01
Tohono O'Odham (1)	1	0.01
Yaqui (1)	2	0.02
All other tribes (3)	7	0.05
American Indian tribes, not spec.	17	0.13
Arab:	10	0.08
Other Arab	10	0.08
Asian:	186	1.40
Cambodian	9	0.07
Chinese, ex. Taiwanese (6)	12	0.09
Filipino (92)	118	0.89
Indian (27)	31	0.23
Japanese	1	0.01
Korean (5)	6	0.05
Other Asian, not specified (8)	9	0.07
Dutch	15	0.11
English	98	0.74
European	21	0.16
French, except Basque	19	0.14
German	75	0.57
Greek	9	0.07
Hawaii Native/Pacific Islander:	25	0.19
Micronesian: (3)	3	0.02
Guamanian/Chamorro (3)	3	0.02
Polynesian: (3)	5	0.04
Native Hawaiian (3)	4	0.03
Samoan	1	0.01
Other Pac. Isl., not spec. (5)	17	0.13
Hispanic or Latino:	11,814	88.85
Central American:	272	2.05
Guatemalan	131	0.99
Honduran	16	0.12
Nicaraguan	12	0.09
Salvadoran	85	0.64
Other Central American	28	0.21
Cuban	8	0.06
Mexican	9,964	74.94
Puerto Rican	284	2.14
South American:	6	0.05
Argentinean	6	0.05
Other Hispanic or Latino	1,280	9.63
Irish	139	1.05
Italian	21	0.16
Norwegian	13	0.10
Scotch-Irish	19	0.14
Scottish	5	0.04
United States or American	225	1.70
West Indian, excl. Hispanic:	21	0.16
West Indian	21	0.16
White:	6,377	47.96
Not Hispanic (1,221)	1,295	9.74
Hispanic (4,696)	5,082	38.22

Lancaster

Place Type: City
County: Los Angeles
Population: 118,718

Ancestry/Race	Number	%
Acadian/Cajun	29	0.02
Afghan	30	0.03
African American/Black:	20,753	17.48
Not Hispanic (18,548)	19,902	16.76
Hispanic (461)	851	0.72
African, sub-Saharan:	899	0.76
African	771	0.65
Cape Verdean	13	0.01
Ethiopian	16	0.01
Ghanian	10	0.01
Nigerian	47	0.04
Other sub-Saharan African	42	0.04
Alaska Native tribes, specified:	18	0.02
Alaska Athabascan (1)	3	0.00
Aleut (1)	3	0.00
Eskimo (9)	9	0.01
Tlingit-Haida (3)	3	0.00
Alaska Native tribes, not specified	4	0.00
Am. Ind. or Alaska Nat., not spec.	851	0.72
Albanian	11	0.01
American Indian tribes, specified:	1,815	1.53
Apache (51)	140	0.12
Blackfeet (22)	108	0.09
Cherokee (156)	574	0.48
Cheyenne (2)	10	0.01
Chickasaw (1)	13	0.01
Chippewa (25)	51	0.04
Choctaw (32)	116	0.10
Colville (1)	1	0.00
Comanche (6)	22	0.02
Cree (1)	5	0.00
Creek (13)	37	0.03
Crow (5)	9	0.01
Delaware (3)	9	0.01
Iroquois (18)	36	0.03
Kiowa (4)	4	0.00
Latin American Indians (86)	138	0.12
Lumbee (2)	2	0.00
Navajo (33)	62	0.05
Osage (6)	18	0.02
Ottawa (10)	18	0.02
Paiute (5)	16	0.01
Pima (1)	1	0.00
Potawatomi (3)	6	0.01
Pueblo (27)	49	0.04
Puget Sound Salish (5)	5	0.00
Seminole (10)	38	0.03
Shoshone (3)	16	0.01

Notes: 1. Figures in the "Number" column do not add up to the total population due to: a) Ancestry/Race overlap — e.g. persons can report being both White and Irish, b) persons of Hispanic origin can report being any race, c) persons reporting two ancestries are counted in both categories. 2. Numbers in parentheses indicate the number of persons reporting this ancestry/race alone, not in combination with any other ancestry/race. 3. Refer to the Explanation of Data in the front of the book for more detailed information.

Sioux (20)	63	0.05
Tohono O'Odham (13)	16	0.01
Ute (10)	14	0.01
Yaqui (18)	28	0.02
Yuman (8)	11	0.01
All other tribes (75)	179	0.15
American Indian tribes, not spec.	108	0.09
Arab:	841	0.71
Arab/Arabic	254	0.21
Egyptian	109	0.09
Jordanian	25	0.02
Lebanese	115	0.10
Palestinian	23	0.02
Syrian	234	0.20
Other Arab	81	0.07
Armenian	164	0.14
Asian:	5,954	5.02
Cambodian (56)	63	0.05
Chinese, ex. Taiwanese (410)	595	0.50
Filipino (2,039)	2,556	2.15
Hmong (8)	9	0.01
Indian (460)	567	0.48
Indonesian (26)	52	0.04
Japanese (321)	596	0.50
Korean (314)	434	0.37
Laotian (6)	8	0.01
Malaysian (1)	5	0.00
Pakistani (11)	19	0.02
Sri Lankan (58)	78	0.07
Taiwanese (39)	46	0.04
Thai (86)	150	0.13
Vietnamese (374)	439	0.37
Other Asian, specified (11)	20	0.02
Other Asian, not specified (213)	317	0.27
Australian	60	0.05
Austrian	137	0.12
Basque	59	0.05
Belgian	30	0.03
British	448	0.38
Bulgarian	20	0.02
Canadian	320	0.27
Carpatho Rusyn	7	0.01
Celtic	42	0.04
Croatian	68	0.06
Czech	287	0.24
Czechoslovakian	135	0.11
Danish	703	0.59
Dutch	1,825	1.54
Eastern European	36	0.03
English	9,243	7.78
European	1,186	1.00
Finnish	164	0.14
French, except Basque	3,087	2.60
French Canadian	757	0.64
German	15,432	12.99
German Russian	7	0.01
Greek	328	0.28
Guyanese	9	0.01
Hawaii Native/Pacific Islander:	552	0.46
Melanesian: (8)	8	0.01
Fijian (8)	8	0.01
Micronesian: (70)	100	0.08
Guamanian/Chamorro (70)	100	0.08
Polynesian: (155)	319	0.27
Native Hawaiian (89)	222	0.19
Samoan (60)	87	0.07
Tongan (5)	6	0.01
Other Polynesian (1)	4	0.00
Other Pac. Isl., specified	5	0.00
Other Pac. Isl., not spec. (40)	120	0.10
Hispanic or Latino:	28,644	24.13
Central American:	1,545	1.30
Costa Rican	70	0.06
Guatemalan	340	0.29
Honduran	78	0.07
Nicaraguan	97	0.08
Panamanian	70	0.06
Salvadoran	742	0.63
Other Central American	148	0.12
Cuban	263	0.22
Dominican Republic	27	0.02
Mexican	20,120	16.95
Puerto Rican	718	0.60
South American:	629	0.53
Argentinean	60	0.05
Bolivian	8	0.01
Chilean	144	0.12
Colombian	112	0.09
Ecuadorian	49	0.04
Paraguayan	4	0.00
Peruvian	191	0.16
Uruguayan	8	0.01
Venezuelan	8	0.01
Other South American	45	0.04
Other Hispanic or Latino	5,342	4.50
Hungarian	505	0.43
Icelander	30	0.03
Iranian	51	0.04
Irish	11,029	9.28
Israeli	45	0.04
Italian	4,985	4.20
Latvian	15	0.01
Lithuanian	130	0.11
Luxemburger	5	0.00
Northern European	16	0.01
Norwegian	1,773	1.49
Pennsylvania German	27	0.02
Polish	1,929	1.62
Portuguese	316	0.27
Romanian	117	0.10
Russian	662	0.56
Scandinavian	265	0.22
Scotch-Irish	1,885	1.59
Scottish	1,916	1.61
Serbian	42	0.04
Slavic	86	0.07
Slovak	128	0.11
Slovene	28	0.02
Swedish	1,470	1.24
Swiss	155	0.13
Turkish	37	0.03
Ukrainian	122	0.10
United States or American	6,178	5.20
Welsh	542	0.46
West Indian, excl. Hispanic:	459	0.39
Bahamian	9	0.01
Belizean	133	0.11
Dutch West Indian	24	0.02
Jamaican	240	0.20
U.S. Virgin Islander	6	0.01
West Indian	47	0.04
White:	79,538	67.00
Not Hispanic (62,256)	65,217	54.93
Hispanic (12,317)	14,321	12.06
Yugoslavian	133	0.11

Larkspur

Place Type: City
County: Marin
Population: 12,014

Ancestry/Race	Number	%
African American/Black:	143	1.19
Not Hispanic (91)	134	1.12
Hispanic (5)	9	0.07
African, sub-Saharan:	24	0.20
Cape Verdean	15	0.12
South African	9	0.07
Am. Ind. or Alaska Nat., not spec.	31	0.26
American Indian tribes, specified:	68	0.57
Blackfeet (1)	4	0.03
Cherokee (4)	26	0.22
Chickasaw	1	0.01
Chippewa (1)	4	0.03
Choctaw	1	0.01
Comanche	1	0.01
Cree	1	0.01
Crow	1	0.01
Delaware (3)	3	0.02
Iroquois	1	0.01
Latin American Indians (5)	10	0.08
Potawatomi	2	0.02
Pueblo	1	0.01
Puget Sound Salish	1	0.01
Sioux	3	0.02
Yakama (1)	1	0.01
All other tribes (4)	7	0.06
Arab:	44	0.37
Lebanese	29	0.24
Moroccan	6	0.05
Syrian	9	0.07
Armenian	67	0.56
Asian:	644	5.36
Cambodian (3)	3	0.02
Chinese, ex. Taiwanese (168)	239	1.99
Filipino (64)	85	0.71
Indian (32)	38	0.32
Indonesian (1)	2	0.02
Japanese (115)	166	1.38
Korean (36)	54	0.45
Malaysian (1)	1	0.01
Pakistani (4)	10	0.08
Sri Lankan (3)	4	0.03
Taiwanese (5)	5	0.04
Thai (6)	8	0.07
Vietnamese (6)	11	0.09
Other Asian, not specified (5)	18	0.15
Assyrian/Chaldean/Syriac	8	0.07
Australian	49	0.41
Austrian	140	1.17
Basque	46	0.38
Belgian	17	0.14
Brazilian	75	0.62
British	207	1.72
Canadian	35	0.29
Croatian	57	0.47
Czech	77	0.64
Czechoslovakian	16	0.13
Danish	199	1.66
Dutch	275	2.29
Eastern European	69	0.57
English	2,118	17.65
European	280	2.33
Finnish	71	0.59
French, except Basque	584	4.87
French Canadian	103	0.86
German	1,989	16.57
Greek	67	0.56
Hawaii Native/Pacific Islander:	39	0.32
Melanesian: (2)	2	0.02
Other Melanesian (2)	2	0.02
Micronesian: (1)	5	0.04
Guamanian/Chamorro (1)	5	0.04
Polynesian: (11)	28	0.23
Native Hawaiian (5)	18	0.15
Samoan (2)	6	0.05
Tongan (2)	2	0.02
Other Polynesian (2)	2	0.02
Other Pac. Isl., not spec. (1)	4	0.03
Hispanic or Latino:	515	4.29
Central American:	55	0.46
Costa Rican	5	0.04
Guatemalan	9	0.07
Honduran	2	0.02
Nicaraguan	10	0.08
Panamanian	9	0.07
Salvadoran	19	0.16
Other Central American	1	0.01
Cuban	18	0.15
Dominican Republic	1	0.01
Mexican	229	1.91
Puerto Rican	28	0.23
South American:	61	0.51
Argentinean	7	0.06
Bolivian	5	0.04
Chilean	5	0.04
Colombian	15	0.12
Ecuadorian	3	0.02
Paraguayan	1	0.01

Notes: 1. Figures in the "Number" column do not add up to the total population due to: a) Ancestry/Race overlap — e.g. persons can report being both White and Irish, b) persons of Hispanic origin can report being any race, c) persons reporting two ancestries are counted in both categories. 2. Numbers in parentheses indicate the number of persons reporting this ancestry/race alone, not in combination with any other ancestry/race. 3. Refer to the Explanation of Data in the front of the book for more detailed information.

Peruvian	15	0.12
Uruguayan	1	0.01
Other South American	9	0.07
Other Hispanic or Latino	123	1.02
Hungarian	117	0.97
Iranian	149	1.24
Irish	1,966	16.38
Israeli	31	0.26
Italian	1,138	9.48
Lithuanian	93	0.77
Luxemburger	10	0.08
Maltese	8	0.07
Northern European	58	0.48
Norwegian	390	3.25
Pennsylvania German	6	0.05
Polish	493	4.11
Portuguese	79	0.66
Romanian	16	0.13
Russian	607	5.06
Scandinavian	29	0.24
Scotch-Irish	317	2.64
Scottish	454	3.78
Serbian	20	0.17
Slavic	12	0.10
Slovak	26	0.22
Swedish	311	2.59
Swiss	105	0.87
Turkish	47	0.39
Ukrainian	43	0.36
United States or American	392	3.27
Welsh	280	2.33
West Indian, excl. Hispanic:	36	0.30
Belizean	24	0.20
Jamaican	12	0.10
White:	11,255	93.68
Not Hispanic (10,623)	10,869	90.47
Hispanic (340)	386	3.21
Yugoslavian	58	0.48

Lathrop

Place Type: City
County: San Joaquin
Population: 10,445

Ancestry/Race	Number	%
African American/Black:	575	5.51
Not Hispanic (456)	543	5.20
Hispanic (13)	32	0.31
African, sub-Saharan:	3	0.03
African	3	0.03
Alaska Native tribes, specified:	2	0.02
Aleut (1)	1	0.01
Eskimo	1	0.01
Am. Ind. or Alaska Nat., not spec.	112	1.07
American Indian tribes, specified:	165	1.58
Apache (5)	10	0.10
Blackfeet (1)	6	0.06
Cherokee (12)	59	0.56
Cheyenne (1)	1	0.01
Chippewa	1	0.01
Choctaw (2)	9	0.09
Cree (1)	1	0.01
Creek (3)	3	0.03
Houma	1	0.01
Iroquois (2)	5	0.05
Latin American Indians (2)	7	0.07
Lumbee (1)	1	0.01
Navajo	7	0.07
Paiute (7)	10	0.10
Pima	1	0.01
Potawatomi (1)	1	0.01
Shoshone (2)	5	0.05
Sioux (2)	10	0.10
Yaqui (1)	2	0.02
All other tribes (11)	25	0.24
American Indian tribes, not spec.	37	0.35
Asian:	1,750	16.75
Cambodian (6)	6	0.06
Chinese, ex. Taiwanese (27)	58	0.56
Filipino (1,032)	1,251	11.98
Hmong (22)	22	0.21
Indian (166)	199	1.91
Indonesian (2)	3	0.03
Japanese (28)	47	0.45
Korean (6)	10	0.10
Laotian (35)	43	0.41
Malaysian	1	0.01
Pakistani (10)	16	0.15
Thai (5)	7	0.07
Vietnamese (23)	25	0.24
Other Asian, not specified (9)	62	0.59
Australian	22	0.21
Basque	24	0.23
Canadian	20	0.19
Czech	26	0.25
Czechoslovakian	8	0.08
Danish	9	0.09
Dutch	69	0.67
English	488	4.72
European	66	0.64
French, except Basque	265	2.56
French Canadian	7	0.07
German	912	8.83
Hawaii Native/Pacific Islander:	135	1.29
Melanesian: (5)	7	0.07
Fijian (5)	7	0.07
Micronesian: (24)	29	0.28
Guamanian/Chamorro (24)	29	0.28
Polynesian: (25)	60	0.57
Native Hawaiian (14)	41	0.39
Samoan (9)	13	0.12
Tongan (2)	2	0.02
Other Polynesian	4	0.04
Other Pac. Isl., not spec.	39	0.37
Hispanic or Latino:	4,031	38.59
Central American:	48	0.46
Guatemalan	10	0.10
Honduran	4	0.04
Nicaraguan	2	0.02
Panamanian	5	0.05
Salvadoran	21	0.20
Other Central American	6	0.06
Cuban	5	0.05
Dominican Republic	2	0.02
Mexican	3,307	31.66
Puerto Rican	109	1.04
South American:	43	0.41
Chilean	8	0.08
Colombian	6	0.06
Peruvian	27	0.26
Other South American	2	0.02
Other Hispanic or Latino	517	4.95
Irish	630	6.10
Italian	468	4.53
Maltese	14	0.14
Norwegian	54	0.52
Polish	47	0.45
Portuguese	520	5.03
Russian	11	0.11
Scandinavian	28	0.27
Scotch-Irish	100	0.97
Scottish	116	1.12
Slavic	10	0.10
Swedish	118	1.14
Swiss	38	0.37
United States or American	216	2.09
Welsh	63	0.61
White:	5,996	57.41
Not Hispanic (3,989)	4,409	42.21
Hispanic (1,330)	1,587	15.19

Lawndale

Place Type: City
County: Los Angeles
Population: 31,711

Ancestry/Race	Number	%
Afghan	25	0.08
African American/Black:	4,325	13.64
Not Hispanic (3,852)	4,094	12.91
Hispanic (146)	231	0.73
African, sub-Saharan:	502	1.58
African	301	0.95
Cape Verdean	37	0.12
Nigerian	111	0.35
Somalian	10	0.03
Other sub-Saharan African	43	0.14
Alaska Native tribes, specified:	3	0.01
Alaska Athabascan	1	0.00
Eskimo	1	0.00
Tlingit-Haida (1)	1	0.00
Am. Ind. or Alaska Nat., not spec.	199	0.63
American Indian tribes, specified:	334	1.05
Apache (9)	20	0.06
Blackfeet (4)	18	0.06
Cherokee (10)	40	0.13
Cheyenne	7	0.02
Chippewa (2)	7	0.02
Choctaw	3	0.01
Comanche (1)	2	0.01
Creek (3)	3	0.01
Crow	1	0.00
Delaware (4)	8	0.03
Iroquois (2)	3	0.01
Latin American Indians (69)	110	0.35
Navajo (17)	24	0.08
Osage	1	0.00
Paiute (1)	6	0.02
Pima (2)	4	0.01
Potawatomi (1)	2	0.01
Pueblo (8)	12	0.04
Seminole	2	0.01
Shoshone (1)	2	0.01
Sioux (5)	13	0.04
Tohono O'Odham	4	0.01
Ute (1)	1	0.00
Yaqui (8)	14	0.04
Yuman (1)	3	0.01
All other tribes (13)	24	0.08
American Indian tribes, not spec.	43	0.14
Arab:	396	1.25
Arab/Arabic	73	0.23
Egyptian	136	0.43
Iraqi	15	0.05
Jordanian	41	0.13
Lebanese	8	0.03
Palestinian	51	0.16
Other Arab	72	0.23
Armenian	39	0.12
Asian:	3,631	11.45
Bangladeshi (5)	5	0.02
Cambodian (10)	13	0.04
Chinese, ex. Taiwanese (189)	285	0.90
Filipino (664)	805	2.54
Indian (206)	256	0.81
Indonesian (37)	62	0.20
Japanese (183)	260	0.82
Korean (116)	141	0.44
Laotian (1)	1	0.00
Malaysian (5)	5	0.02
Pakistani (69)	127	0.40
Sri Lankan (3)	16	0.05
Taiwanese (9)	15	0.05
Thai (28)	43	0.14
Vietnamese (1,436)	1,500	4.73
Other Asian, specified (1)	1	0.00
Other Asian, not specified (21)	96	0.30
Australian	7	0.02
Austrian	35	0.11
Belgian	18	0.06
Brazilian	21	0.07
British	24	0.08
Canadian	12	0.04
Croatian	30	0.09
Czech	74	0.23
Czechoslovakian	66	0.21
Danish	86	0.27
Dutch	199	0.63

Notes: 1. Figures in the "Number" column do not add up to the total population due to: a) Ancestry/Race overlap — e.g. persons can report being both White and Irish, b) persons of Hispanic origin can report being any race, c) persons reporting two ancestries are counted in both categories. 2. Numbers in parentheses indicate the number of persons reporting this ancestry/race alone, not in combination with any other ancestry/race. 3. Refer to the Explanation of Data in the front of the book for more detailed information.

Ancestry/Race	Number	%
Eastern European	8	0.03
English	791	2.49
European	124	0.39
Finnish	7	0.02
French, except Basque	317	1.00
French Canadian	147	0.46
German	1,093	3.44
German Russian	6	0.02
Greek	55	0.17
Hawaii Native/Pacific Islander:	393	1.24
Melanesian: (1)	2	0.01
Fijian (1)	2	0.01
Micronesian: (22)	29	0.09
Guamanian/Chamorro (22)	29	0.09
Polynesian: (222)	301	0.95
Native Hawaiian (43)	86	0.27
Samoan (106)	132	0.42
Tongan (69)	79	0.25
Other Polynesian (4)	4	0.01
Other Pac. Isl., not spec. (32)	61	0.19
Hispanic or Latino:	16,515	52.08
Central American:	1,785	5.63
Costa Rican	52	0.16
Guatemalan	791	2.49
Honduran	81	0.26
Nicaraguan	164	0.52
Panamanian	20	0.06
Salvadoran	527	1.66
Other Central American	150	0.47
Cuban	352	1.11
Dominican Republic	25	0.08
Mexican	10,423	32.87
Puerto Rican	341	1.08
South American:	580	1.83
Argentinean	32	0.10
Bolivian	9	0.03
Chilean	23	0.07
Colombian	148	0.47
Ecuadorian	92	0.29
Paraguayan	3	0.01
Peruvian	236	0.74
Uruguayan	2	0.01
Venezuelan	6	0.02
Other South American	29	0.09
Other Hispanic or Latino	3,009	9.49
Hungarian	64	0.20
Iranian	33	0.10
Irish	1,135	3.58
Israeli	6	0.02
Italian	631	1.99
Lithuanian	66	0.21
Macedonian	8	0.03
Northern European	6	0.02
Norwegian	165	0.52
Polish	159	0.50
Portuguese	63	0.20
Romanian	24	0.08
Russian	113	0.36
Scandinavian	27	0.09
Scotch-Irish	277	0.87
Scottish	190	0.60
Slavic	10	0.03
Slovak	37	0.12
Swedish	114	0.36
Swiss	6	0.02
Turkish	18	0.06
Ukrainian	9	0.03
United States or American	800	2.52
Welsh	68	0.21
West Indian, excl. Hispanic:	172	0.54
Barbadian	7	0.02
Belizean	119	0.38
British West Indian	20	0.06
Jamaican	26	0.08
White:	15,073	47.53
Not Hispanic (6,946)	7,656	24.14
Hispanic (6,448)	7,417	23.39
Yugoslavian	25	0.08

Lemon Grove

Place Type: City
County: San Diego
Population: 24,918

Ancestry/Race	Number	%
Afghan	101	0.40
African American/Black:	3,473	13.94
Not Hispanic (2,874)	3,224	12.94
Hispanic (136)	249	1.00
African, sub-Saharan:	196	0.79
African	176	0.71
Cape Verdean	5	0.02
Other sub-Saharan African	15	0.06
Alaska Native tribes, specified:	5	0.02
Aleut (1)	1	0.00
Eskimo (2)	2	0.01
Tlingit-Haida (2)	2	0.01
Alaska Native tribes, not specified	1	0.00
Am. Ind. or Alaska Nat., not spec.	180	0.72
Albanian	57	0.23
American Indian tribes, specified:	360	1.44
Apache (9)	18	0.07
Blackfeet (5)	16	0.06
Cherokee (27)	92	0.37
Chickasaw	3	0.01
Chippewa (4)	5	0.02
Choctaw (7)	17	0.07
Comanche (2)	3	0.01
Cree	1	0.00
Creek (2)	3	0.01
Crow (1)	1	0.00
Delaware (2)	2	0.01
Iroquois (7)	18	0.07
Latin American Indians (26)	39	0.16
Navajo (8)	9	0.04
Osage (1)	1	0.00
Paiute (3)	3	0.01
Pima (3)	4	0.02
Potawatomi (5)	5	0.02
Pueblo (11)	16	0.06
Seminole	1	0.00
Sioux (6)	12	0.05
Tohono O'Odham (4)	4	0.02
Ute (2)	2	0.01
Yaqui (3)	13	0.05
All other tribes (49)	72	0.29
American Indian tribes, not spec.	23	0.09
Arab:	171	0.69
Arab/Arabic	17	0.07
Iraqi	42	0.17
Jordanian	5	0.02
Lebanese	28	0.11
Moroccan	8	0.03
Palestinian	6	0.02
Syrian	5	0.02
Other Arab	60	0.24
Armenian	23	0.09
Asian:	2,052	8.24
Cambodian (10)	10	0.04
Chinese, ex. Taiwanese (94)	169	0.68
Filipino (719)	1,044	4.19
Hmong (4)	4	0.02
Indian (33)	55	0.22
Indonesian (2)	4	0.02
Japanese (147)	256	1.03
Korean (30)	42	0.17
Laotian (53)	57	0.23
Malaysian (1)	3	0.01
Pakistani (5)	9	0.04
Thai (9)	12	0.05
Vietnamese (290)	314	1.26
Other Asian, specified	5	0.02
Other Asian, not specified (10)	68	0.27
Australian	11	0.04
Austrian	74	0.30
Belgian	4	0.02
Brazilian	7	0.03
British	115	0.46
Bulgarian	15	0.06
Canadian	46	0.18
Celtic	12	0.05
Czech	112	0.45
Czechoslovakian	92	0.37
Danish	66	0.26
Dutch	331	1.33
Eastern European	6	0.02
English	1,778	7.13
European	318	1.27
Finnish	23	0.09
French, except Basque	592	2.37
French Canadian	136	0.55
German	2,712	10.87
Greek	41	0.16
Guyanese	13	0.05
Hawaii Native/Pacific Islander:	390	1.57
Micronesian: (99)	158	0.63
Guamanian/Chamorro (99)	158	0.63
Polynesian: (104)	200	0.80
Native Hawaiian (23)	87	0.35
Samoan (81)	113	0.45
Other Pac. Isl., not spec. (3)	32	0.13
Hispanic or Latino:	7,107	28.52
Central American:	98	0.39
Costa Rican	17	0.07
Guatemalan	6	0.02
Honduran	9	0.04
Nicaraguan	12	0.05
Panamanian	30	0.12
Salvadoran	17	0.07
Other Central American	7	0.03
Cuban	42	0.17
Dominican Republic	13	0.05
Mexican	5,733	23.01
Puerto Rican	187	0.75
South American:	90	0.36
Argentinean	3	0.01
Bolivian	8	0.03
Chilean	8	0.03
Colombian	37	0.15
Ecuadorian	9	0.04
Peruvian	14	0.06
Venezuelan	9	0.04
Other South American	2	0.01
Other Hispanic or Latino	944	3.79
Hungarian	86	0.34
Icelander	22	0.09
Iranian	17	0.07
Irish	2,157	8.64
Italian	749	3.00
Lithuanian	55	0.22
New Zealander	12	0.05
Northern European	11	0.04
Norwegian	448	1.80
Pennsylvania German	14	0.06
Polish	371	1.49
Portuguese	115	0.46
Romanian	20	0.08
Russian	107	0.43
Scandinavian	29	0.12
Scotch-Irish	299	1.20
Scottish	379	1.52
Slavic	17	0.07
Slovak	38	0.15
Slovene	17	0.07
Swedish	445	1.78
Swiss	98	0.39
Turkish	19	0.08
Ukrainian	34	0.14
United States or American	934	3.74
Welsh	108	0.43
West Indian, excl. Hispanic:	32	0.13
Barbadian	4	0.02
Haitian	10	0.04
Jamaican	13	0.05
West Indian	5	0.02
White:	16,269	65.29
Not Hispanic (12,017)	12,905	51.79
Hispanic (2,842)	3,364	13.50

Notes: 1. Figures in the "Number" column do not add up to the total population due to: a) Ancestry/Race overlap — e.g. persons can report being both White and Irish, b) persons of Hispanic origin can report being any race, c) persons reporting two ancestries are counted in both categories. 2. Numbers in parentheses indicate the number of persons reporting this ancestry/race alone, not in combination with any other ancestry/race. 3. Refer to the Explanation of Data in the front of the book for more detailed information.

Ancestry/Race	Number	%
Yugoslavian	32	0.13

Lemoore

Place Type: City
County: Kings
Population: 19,712

Ancestry/Race	Number	%
African American/Black:	1,651	8.38
Not Hispanic (1,373)	1,551	7.87
Hispanic (62)	100	0.51
African, sub-Saharan:	123	0.63
African	107	0.55
Nigerian	16	0.08
Alaska Native tribes, specified:	3	0.02
Aleut (2)	2	0.01
Tlingit-Haida (1)	1	0.01
Am. Ind. or Alaska Nat., not spec.	154	0.78
American Indian tribes, specified:	326	1.65
Apache (2)	11	0.06
Blackfeet (2)	8	0.04
Cherokee (30)	58	0.29
Cheyenne (1)	1	0.01
Chippewa	1	0.01
Choctaw (12)	28	0.14
Creek (2)	2	0.01
Crow	5	0.03
Iroquois (3)	6	0.03
Latin American Indians (13)	26	0.13
Lumbee (1)	1	0.01
Navajo (7)	14	0.07
Ottawa (1)	1	0.01
Paiute (5)	5	0.03
Pima	1	0.01
Pueblo (2)	3	0.02
Puget Sound Salish	1	0.01
Shoshone	1	0.01
Sioux (7)	13	0.07
Yaqui (4)	12	0.06
All other tribes (97)	128	0.65
American Indian tribes, not spec.	25	0.13
Arab:	107	0.55
Arab/Arabic	20	0.10
Lebanese	18	0.09
Palestinian	6	0.03
Syrian	51	0.26
Other Arab	12	0.06
Armenian	89	0.46
Asian:	2,058	10.44
Cambodian (1)	6	0.03
Chinese, ex. Taiwanese (72)	99	0.50
Filipino (1,345)	1,635	8.29
Hmong (1)	1	0.01
Indian (43)	47	0.24
Japanese (75)	120	0.61
Korean (50)	72	0.37
Laotian (1)	6	0.03
Malaysian (2)	5	0.03
Pakistani (10)	12	0.06
Sri Lankan (1)	1	0.01
Taiwanese (1)	2	0.01
Thai (3)	4	0.02
Vietnamese (19)	20	0.10
Other Asian, specified	1	0.01
Other Asian, not specified (11)	27	0.14
Austrian	6	0.03
Canadian	24	0.12
Celtic	8	0.04
Czech	71	0.36
Danish	63	0.32
Dutch	246	1.26
English	1,353	6.93
European	129	0.66
Finnish	5	0.03
French, except Basque	375	1.92
French Canadian	66	0.34
German	1,902	9.74
German Russian	7	0.04
Greek	32	0.16
Hawaii Native/Pacific Islander:	119	0.60
Melanesian: (1)	1	0.01
Other Melanesian (1)	1	0.01
Micronesian: (29)	31	0.16
Guamanian/Chamorro (27)	29	0.15
Other Micronesian (2)	2	0.01
Polynesian: (25)	57	0.29
Native Hawaiian (14)	42	0.21
Samoan (7)	10	0.05
Tongan (4)	4	0.02
Other Polynesian	1	0.01
Other Pac. Isl., not spec. (9)	30	0.15
Hispanic or Latino:	6,013	30.50
Central American:	46	0.23
Guatemalan	1	0.01
Honduran	21	0.11
Nicaraguan	2	0.01
Panamanian	1	0.01
Salvadoran	15	0.08
Other Central American	6	0.03
Cuban	12	0.06
Dominican Republic	2	0.01
Mexican	5,068	25.71
Puerto Rican	91	0.46
South American:	7	0.04
Argentinean	1	0.01
Bolivian	1	0.01
Chilean	3	0.02
Colombian	1	0.01
Ecuadorian	1	0.01
Other Hispanic or Latino	787	3.99
Hungarian	16	0.08
Icelander	22	0.11
Iranian	8	0.04
Irish	1,797	9.20
Italian	688	3.52
Lithuanian	15	0.08
Luxemburger	11	0.06
Norwegian	173	0.89
Polish	175	0.90
Portuguese	964	4.94
Russian	42	0.22
Scandinavian	18	0.09
Scotch-Irish	212	1.09
Scottish	153	0.78
Serbian	6	0.03
Slovak	20	0.10
Slovene	5	0.03
Swedish	193	0.99
Swiss	113	0.58
United States or American	891	4.56
Welsh	98	0.50
West Indian, excl. Hispanic:	24	0.12
Dutch West Indian	15	0.08
Jamaican	9	0.05
White:	12,644	64.14
Not Hispanic (9,674)	10,298	52.24
Hispanic (2,013)	2,346	11.90
Yugoslavian	10	0.05

Lennox

Place Type: Census Designated Place
County: Los Angeles
Population: 22,950

Ancestry/Race	Number	%
African American/Black:	1,012	4.41
Not Hispanic (879)	903	3.93
Hispanic (73)	109	0.47
African, sub-Saharan:	21	0.09
African	21	0.09
Alaska Native tribes, not specified	2	0.01
Am. Ind. or Alaska Nat., not spec.	145	0.63
American Indian tribes, specified:	147	0.64
Apache (1)	2	0.01
Blackfeet (5)	6	0.03
Cherokee	7	0.03
Chippewa	1	0.00
Choctaw (1)	2	0.01
Comanche	2	0.01
Creek	2	0.01
Delaware (1)	2	0.01
Iroquois (1)	1	0.00
Latin American Indians (82)	111	0.48
Navajo (5)	5	0.02
Pueblo (3)	3	0.01
Yaqui (1)	1	0.00
All other tribes (2)	2	0.01
American Indian tribes, not spec.	17	0.07
Arab:	58	0.25
Arab/Arabic	58	0.25
Armenian	26	0.11
Asian:	218	0.95
Chinese, ex. Taiwanese (7)	11	0.05
Filipino (118)	124	0.54
Indian (20)	25	0.11
Indonesian (2)	2	0.01
Japanese (11)	16	0.07
Korean	2	0.01
Thai (2)	2	0.01
Vietnamese (24)	24	0.10
Other Asian, not specified (4)	12	0.05
Brazilian	34	0.15
Danish	6	0.03
Dutch	22	0.09
English	54	0.23
European	9	0.04
French, except Basque	80	0.34
German	85	0.37
Hawaii Native/Pacific Islander:	394	1.72
Micronesian:	3	0.01
Guamanian/Chamorro	3	0.01
Polynesian: (274)	355	1.55
Native Hawaiian (8)	14	0.06
Samoan (24)	29	0.13
Tongan (228)	273	1.19
Other Polynesian (14)	39	0.17
Other Pac. Isl., not spec. (19)	36	0.16
Hispanic or Latino:	20,602	89.77
Central American:	1,980	8.63
Costa Rican	18	0.08
Guatemalan	811	3.53
Honduran	106	0.46
Nicaraguan	123	0.54
Panamanian	6	0.03
Salvadoran	751	3.27
Other Central American	165	0.72
Cuban	242	1.05
Mexican	15,080	65.71
Puerto Rican	82	0.36
South American:	124	0.54
Argentinean	13	0.06
Bolivian	1	0.00
Chilean	11	0.05
Colombian	12	0.05
Ecuadorian	25	0.11
Peruvian	51	0.22
Uruguayan	2	0.01
Venezuelan	1	0.00
Other South American	8	0.03
Other Hispanic or Latino	3,094	13.48
Hungarian	15	0.06
Irish	139	0.60
Italian	69	0.30
Norwegian	9	0.04
Portuguese	8	0.03
Russian	4	0.02
Scottish	14	0.06
United States or American	422	1.82
West Indian, excl. Hispanic:	33	0.14
Trinidadian and Tobagonian	33	0.14
White:	8,210	35.77
Not Hispanic (810)	875	3.81
Hispanic (6,465)	7,335	31.96

Notes: 1. Figures in the "Number" column do not add up to the total population due to: a) Ancestry/Race overlap — e.g. persons can report being both White and Irish, b) persons of Hispanic origin can report being any race, c) persons reporting two ancestries are counted in both categories. 2. Numbers in parentheses indicate the number of persons reporting this ancestry/race alone, not in combination with any other ancestry/race. 3. Refer to the Explanation of Data in the front of the book for more detailed information.

Lincoln

Place Type: City
County: Placer
Population: 11,205

Ancestry/Race	Number	%
African American/Black:	73	0.65
Not Hispanic (42)	60	0.54
Hispanic (7)	13	0.12
Alaska Native tribes, specified:	8	0.07
Aleut (3)	7	0.06
Tlingit-Haida	1	0.01
Am. Ind. or Alaska Nat., not spec.	56	0.50
American Indian tribes, specified:	220	1.96
Apache (6)	11	0.10
Blackfeet	1	0.01
Cherokee (26)	86	0.77
Chippewa	7	0.06
Choctaw (7)	12	0.11
Colville	2	0.02
Creek	4	0.04
Delaware (1)	1	0.01
Iroquois	1	0.01
Latin American Indians (27)	32	0.29
Navajo (1)	3	0.03
Pima	1	0.01
Pueblo	2	0.02
Seminole	1	0.01
Shoshone (1)	2	0.02
Sioux (1)	4	0.04
Yaqui (3)	3	0.03
All other tribes (27)	47	0.42
American Indian tribes, not spec.	15	0.13
Arab:	56	0.51
Lebanese	49	0.45
Moroccan	7	0.06
Armenian	6	0.05
Asian:	187	1.67
Chinese, ex. Taiwanese (5)	9	0.08
Filipino (48)	69	0.62
Indian (15)	28	0.25
Japanese (34)	53	0.47
Korean (7)	11	0.10
Laotian (1)	2	0.02
Thai (3)	6	0.05
Vietnamese (2)	2	0.02
Other Asian, specified	1	0.01
Other Asian, not specified (3)	6	0.05
Austrian	31	0.28
British	6	0.05
Bulgarian	10	0.09
Celtic	9	0.08
Croatian	24	0.22
Czech	41	0.37
Czechoslovakian	12	0.11
Danish	55	0.50
Dutch	209	1.91
English	1,122	10.26
European	108	0.99
Finnish	29	0.27
French, except Basque	384	3.51
French Canadian	73	0.67
German	1,626	14.86
Greek	69	0.63
Hawaii Native/Pacific Islander:	39	0.35
Melanesian: (4)	4	0.04
Fijian (4)	4	0.04
Micronesian: (3)	3	0.03
Guamanian/Chamorro (3)	3	0.03
Polynesian: (6)	20	0.18
Native Hawaiian (5)	13	0.12
Samoan (1)	7	0.06
Other Pac. Isl., not spec. (3)	12	0.11
Hispanic or Latino:	2,911	25.98
Central American:	31	0.28
Guatemalan	3	0.03
Honduran	1	0.01
Panamanian	1	0.01
Salvadoran	21	0.19
Other Central American	5	0.04
Cuban	7	0.06
Mexican	2,507	22.37
Puerto Rican	45	0.40
South American:	11	0.10
Chilean	6	0.05
Peruvian	4	0.04
Venezuelan	1	0.01
Other Hispanic or Latino	310	2.77
Hungarian	25	0.23
Icelander	15	0.14
Irish	869	7.94
Italian	429	3.92
Latvian	8	0.07
Lithuanian	32	0.29
New Zealander	17	0.16
Northern European	25	0.23
Norwegian	202	1.85
Pennsylvania German	19	0.17
Polish	122	1.12
Portuguese	338	3.09
Romanian	15	0.14
Russian	74	0.68
Scandinavian	84	0.77
Scotch-Irish	168	1.54
Scottish	192	1.76
Slavic	7	0.06
Slovak	9	0.08
Swedish	216	1.97
Swiss	68	0.62
Ukrainian	121	1.11
United States or American	856	7.83
Welsh	122	1.12
White:	9,338	83.34
Not Hispanic (7,792)	8,003	71.42
Hispanic (1,132)	1,335	11.91
Yugoslavian	9	0.08

Linda

Place Type: Census Designated Place
County: Yuba
Population: 13,474

Ancestry/Race	Number	%
African American/Black:	589	4.37
Not Hispanic (404)	535	3.97
Hispanic (19)	54	0.40
African, sub-Saharan:	29	0.22
African	19	0.14
Somalian	10	0.07
Alaska Native tribes, specified:	5	0.04
Alaska Athabascan (1)	1	0.01
Eskimo	1	0.01
Tlingit-Haida (1)	1	0.01
All other tribes	2	0.01
Am. Ind. or Alaska Nat., not spec.	229	1.70
American Indian tribes, specified:	481	3.57
Apache (5)	14	0.10
Blackfeet (7)	12	0.09
Cherokee (97)	216	1.60
Chickasaw (3)	5	0.04
Chippewa (9)	15	0.11
Choctaw (17)	35	0.26
Colville (4)	4	0.03
Cree (1)	1	0.01
Creek	1	0.01
Crow (1)	1	0.01
Delaware	2	0.01
Iroquois (1)	2	0.01
Kiowa	2	0.01
Latin American Indians (24)	34	0.25
Navajo (5)	5	0.04
Osage (1)	2	0.01
Paiute (3)	4	0.03
Pima	1	0.01
Potawatomi (1)	1	0.01
Pueblo (2)	4	0.03
Seminole (2)	3	0.02
Sioux (2)	4	0.03
Yakama (3)	3	0.02
Yaqui (1)	2	0.01
All other tribes (78)	108	0.80
American Indian tribes, not spec.	42	0.31
Asian:	2,820	20.93
Cambodian (27)	27	0.20
Chinese, ex. Taiwanese (13)	25	0.19
Filipino (70)	118	0.88
Hmong (1,976)	2,174	16.13
Indian (82)	109	0.81
Indonesian (1)	4	0.03
Japanese (25)	45	0.33
Korean (19)	30	0.22
Laotian (129)	183	1.36
Pakistani	3	0.02
Thai (25)	43	0.32
Vietnamese (1)	4	0.03
Other Asian, specified	2	0.01
Other Asian, not specified (27)	53	0.39
British	31	0.23
Canadian	31	0.23
Czech	8	0.06
Czechoslovakian	10	0.07
Danish	27	0.20
Dutch	189	1.41
English	729	5.43
European	49	0.37
French, except Basque	183	1.36
French Canadian	16	0.12
German	881	6.57
Greek	8	0.06
Hawaii Native/Pacific Islander:	76	0.56
Melanesian: (5)	5	0.04
Fijian (5)	5	0.04
Micronesian: (9)	14	0.10
Guamanian/Chamorro (9)	14	0.10
Polynesian: (7)	21	0.16
Native Hawaiian (3)	11	0.08
Samoan (4)	7	0.05
Tongan	3	0.02
Other Pac. Isl., specified	1	0.01
Other Pac. Isl., not spec. (7)	35	0.26
Hispanic or Latino:	2,984	22.15
Central American:	30	0.22
Guatemalan	7	0.05
Nicaraguan	6	0.04
Panamanian	2	0.01
Salvadoran	13	0.10
Other Central American	2	0.01
Cuban	10	0.07
Mexican	2,526	18.75
Puerto Rican	37	0.27
South American:	13	0.10
Chilean	5	0.04
Peruvian	8	0.06
Other Hispanic or Latino	368	2.73
Hungarian	32	0.24
Irish	729	5.43
Italian	234	1.74
Lithuanian	9	0.07
Northern European	22	0.16
Norwegian	62	0.46
Polish	153	1.14
Portuguese	38	0.28
Romanian	12	0.09
Russian	42	0.31
Scotch-Irish	113	0.84
Scottish	253	1.89
Swedish	77	0.57
Swiss	42	0.31
United States or American	882	6.57
Welsh	40	0.30
West Indian, excl. Hispanic:	11	0.08
Dutch West Indian	7	0.05
Jamaican	4	0.03
White:	8,104	60.15
Not Hispanic (6,670)	7,120	52.84
Hispanic (723)	984	7.30

Notes: 1. Figures in the "Number" column do not add up to the total population due to: a) Ancestry/Race overlap — e.g. persons can report being both White and Irish, b) persons of Hispanic origin can report being any race, c) persons reporting two ancestries are counted in both categories. 2. Numbers in parentheses indicate the number of persons reporting this ancestry/race alone, not in combination with any other ancestry/race. 3. Refer to the Explanation of Data in the front of the book for more detailed information.

Lindsay

Place Type: City
County: Tulare
Population: 10,297

Ancestry/Race	Number	%
African American/Black:	84	0.82
Not Hispanic (31)	46	0.45
Hispanic (28)	38	0.37
Am. Ind. or Alaska Nat., not spec.	91	0.88
American Indian tribes, specified:	105	1.02
Apache (2)	2	0.02
Blackfeet	1	0.01
Cherokee (13)	25	0.24
Choctaw (3)	10	0.10
Cree	1	0.01
Latin American Indians (33)	33	0.32
Navajo (2)	2	0.02
Pueblo (1)	3	0.03
Shoshone (1)	2	0.02
Yaqui (1)	1	0.01
All other tribes (24)	25	0.24
American Indian tribes, not spec.	19	0.18
Asian:	152	1.48
Chinese, ex. Taiwanese (17)	26	0.25
Filipino (11)	12	0.12
Hmong (7)	7	0.07
Indian (41)	53	0.51
Indonesian (1)	2	0.02
Japanese (12)	19	0.18
Korean (2)	3	0.03
Pakistani (6)	10	0.10
Vietnamese (10)	15	0.15
Other Asian, not specified (2)	5	0.05
Danish	8	0.08
Dutch	21	0.20
English	360	3.50
French, except Basque	56	0.54
French Canadian	14	0.14
German	225	2.18
Hawaii Native/Pacific Islander:	16	0.16
Micronesian: (3)	3	0.03
Guamanian/Chamorro (3)	3	0.03
Polynesian: (12)	13	0.13
Native Hawaiian (7)	8	0.08
Samoan (5)	5	0.05
Hispanic or Latino:	8,029	77.97
Central American:	40	0.39
Guatemalan	2	0.02
Honduran	8	0.08
Panamanian	5	0.05
Salvadoran	23	0.22
Other Central American	2	0.02
Mexican	7,140	69.34
Puerto Rican	40	0.39
South American:	3	0.03
Colombian	2	0.02
Other South American	1	0.01
Other Hispanic or Latino	806	7.83
Irish	335	3.25
Italian	41	0.40
Norwegian	28	0.27
Polish	41	0.40
Portuguese	12	0.12
Scotch-Irish	43	0.42
Scottish	45	0.44
Swedish	48	0.47
Swiss	10	0.10
Ukrainian	5	0.05
United States or American	301	2.92
Welsh	17	0.17
White:	4,944	48.01
Not Hispanic (1,956)	2,052	19.93
Hispanic (2,660)	2,892	28.09

Live Oak

Place Type: Census Designated Place
County: Santa Cruz
Population: 16,628

Ancestry/Race	Number	%
African American/Black:	383	2.30
Not Hispanic (204)	331	1.99
Hispanic (23)	52	0.31
African, sub-Saharan:	89	0.54
African	64	0.39
Ethiopian	11	0.07
Nigerian	14	0.08
Alaska Native tribes, specified:	4	0.02
Aleut (3)	3	0.02
Eskimo	1	0.01
Alaska Native tribes, not specified	1	0.01
Am. Ind. or Alaska Nat., not spec.	140	0.84
American Indian tribes, specified:	275	1.65
Apache (11)	17	0.10
Blackfeet (1)	16	0.10
Cherokee (11)	69	0.41
Chickasaw (2)	2	0.01
Chippewa (5)	8	0.05
Choctaw (7)	15	0.09
Comanche (2)	6	0.04
Cree (1)	2	0.01
Creek (2)	3	0.02
Iroquois (1)	9	0.05
Kiowa	1	0.01
Latin American Indians (33)	39	0.23
Navajo (9)	18	0.11
Osage	2	0.01
Ottawa (2)	2	0.01
Pueblo (3)	8	0.05
Seminole	2	0.01
Shoshone	1	0.01
Sioux (3)	7	0.04
Yakama	3	0.02
Yaqui (1)	2	0.01
All other tribes (19)	43	0.26
American Indian tribes, not spec.	21	0.13
Armenian	48	0.29
Asian:	856	5.15
Cambodian (38)	43	0.26
Chinese, ex. Taiwanese (137)	170	1.02
Filipino (172)	254	1.53
Indian (32)	40	0.24
Indonesian (6)	11	0.07
Japanese (98)	141	0.85
Korean (66)	77	0.46
Laotian (1)	1	0.01
Malaysian	1	0.01
Pakistani (3)	6	0.04
Taiwanese	2	0.01
Thai (9)	12	0.07
Vietnamese (54)	63	0.38
Other Asian, specified	4	0.02
Other Asian, not specified (8)	31	0.19
Australian	31	0.19
Austrian	35	0.21
Belgian	7	0.04
Brazilian	52	0.32
British	100	0.61
Canadian	42	0.25
Celtic	8	0.05
Croatian	13	0.08
Czech	43	0.26
Czechoslovakian	29	0.18
Danish	149	0.90
Dutch	227	1.38
Eastern European	5	0.03
English	2,016	12.22
Estonian	6	0.04
European	316	1.92
Finnish	49	0.30
French, except Basque	687	4.16
French Canadian	122	0.74
German	2,401	14.55
Greek	125	0.76
Hawaii Native/Pacific Islander:	77	0.46
Micronesian: (2)	11	0.07
Guamanian/Chamorro (2)	9	0.05
Other Micronesian	2	0.01
Polynesian: (14)	47	0.28
Native Hawaiian (4)	32	0.19
Samoan (9)	12	0.07
Tongan (1)	2	0.01
Other Polynesian	1	0.01
Other Pac. Isl., specified	4	0.02
Other Pac. Isl., not spec. (2)	15	0.09
Hispanic or Latino:	3,655	21.98
Central American:	87	0.52
Costa Rican	3	0.02
Guatemalan	10	0.06
Honduran	4	0.02
Nicaraguan	8	0.05
Panamanian	3	0.02
Salvadoran	51	0.31
Other Central American	8	0.05
Cuban	17	0.10
Dominican Republic	2	0.01
Mexican	2,947	17.72
Puerto Rican	67	0.40
South American:	38	0.23
Argentinean	9	0.05
Bolivian	1	0.01
Chilean	5	0.03
Colombian	9	0.05
Ecuadorian	1	0.01
Peruvian	7	0.04
Uruguayan	1	0.01
Venezuelan	3	0.02
Other South American	2	0.01
Other Hispanic or Latino	497	2.99
Hungarian	62	0.38
Iranian	6	0.04
Irish	1,842	11.16
Italian	1,389	8.42
Latvian	8	0.05
Lithuanian	76	0.46
Maltese	11	0.07
Norwegian	373	2.26
Pennsylvania German	11	0.07
Polish	430	2.61
Portuguese	375	2.27
Romanian	5	0.03
Russian	233	1.41
Scandinavian	79	0.48
Scotch-Irish	273	1.65
Scottish	471	2.85
Serbian	17	0.10
Slavic	29	0.18
Slovak	21	0.13
Slovene	14	0.08
Swedish	281	1.70
Swiss	123	0.75
Ukrainian	63	0.38
United States or American	568	3.44
Welsh	209	1.27
West Indian, excl. Hispanic:	8	0.05
Jamaican	8	0.05
White:	13,637	82.01
Not Hispanic (11,468)	11,926	71.72
Hispanic (1,437)	1,711	10.29
Yugoslavian	37	0.22

Livermore

Place Type: City
County: Alameda
Population: 73,345

Ancestry/Race	Number	%
Afghan	336	0.46
African American/Black:	1,521	2.07
Not Hispanic (1,094)	1,403	1.91
Hispanic (54)	118	0.16
African, sub-Saharan:	211	0.29

Notes: 1. Figures in the "Number" column do not add up to the total population due to: a) Ancestry/Race overlap — e.g. persons can report being both White and Irish, b) persons of Hispanic origin can report being any race, c) persons reporting two ancestries are counted in both categories. 2. Numbers in parentheses indicate the number of persons reporting this ancestry/race alone, not in combination with any other ancestry/race. 3. Refer to the Explanation of Data in the front of the book for more detailed information.

Ancestry/Race	Number	%
African	136	0.19
Nigerian	60	0.08
South African	15	0.02
Alaska Native tribes, specified:	17	0.02
Alaska Athabascan (1)	2	0.00
Aleut (2)	2	0.00
Eskimo	3	0.00
Tlingit-Haida (4)	10	0.01
Alaska Native tribes, not specified	2	0.00
Am. Ind. or Alaska Nat., not spec.	357	0.49
Albanian	8	0.01
Alsatian	9	0.01
American Indian tribes, specified:	795	1.08
Apache (28)	59	0.08
Blackfeet (13)	43	0.06
Cherokee (67)	243	0.33
Cheyenne	8	0.01
Chickasaw (5)	8	0.01
Chippewa (9)	15	0.02
Choctaw (20)	58	0.08
Comanche	4	0.01
Cree (1)	2	0.00
Creek	7	0.01
Crow	1	0.00
Delaware (4)	5	0.01
Iroquois (2)	13	0.02
Kiowa (3)	8	0.01
Latin American Indians (21)	34	0.05
Lumbee	1	0.00
Navajo (10)	30	0.04
Osage (3)	10	0.01
Paiute (4)	8	0.01
Pima	5	0.01
Potawatomi (2)	9	0.01
Pueblo (10)	20	0.03
Puget Sound Salish (2)	4	0.01
Seminole (5)	7	0.01
Shoshone (4)	5	0.01
Sioux (15)	36	0.05
Tohono O'Odham (1)	1	0.00
Ute (1)	4	0.01
Yakama	1	0.00
Yaqui (6)	12	0.02
Yuman	2	0.00
All other tribes (36)	132	0.18
American Indian tribes, not spec.	64	0.09
Arab:	129	0.18
Arab/Arabic	8	0.01
Egyptian	8	0.01
Lebanese	43	0.06
Moroccan	6	0.01
Palestinian	9	0.01
Syrian	55	0.07
Armenian	96	0.13
Asian:	5,711	7.79
Cambodian (11)	20	0.03
Chinese, ex. Taiwanese (722)	1,036	1.41
Filipino (1,591)	2,167	2.95
Hmong (5)	5	0.01
Indian (712)	797	1.09
Indonesian (22)	34	0.05
Japanese (327)	612	0.83
Korean (261)	320	0.44
Laotian (1)	4	0.01
Malaysian (1)	1	0.00
Pakistani (40)	43	0.06
Sri Lankan (9)	16	0.02
Taiwanese (36)	43	0.06
Thai (25)	46	0.06
Vietnamese (324)	390	0.53
Other Asian, specified (4)	7	0.01
Other Asian, not specified (73)	170	0.23
Assyrian/Chaldean/Syriac	7	0.01
Australian	36	0.05
Austrian	157	0.21
Basque	23	0.03
Belgian	52	0.07
Brazilian	47	0.06
British	628	0.86
Bulgarian	18	0.02
Canadian	223	0.30
Celtic	56	0.08
Croatian	72	0.10
Czech	310	0.42
Czechoslovakian	111	0.15
Danish	1,124	1.53
Dutch	1,405	1.91
Eastern European	35	0.05
English	8,672	11.81
European	1,558	2.12
Finnish	239	0.33
French, except Basque	2,675	3.64
French Canadian	514	0.70
German	13,619	18.55
Greek	438	0.60
Hawaii Native/Pacific Islander:	492	0.67
Melanesian: (12)	12	0.02
Fijian (12)	12	0.02
Micronesian: (52)	97	0.13
Guamanian/Chamorro (51)	92	0.13
Other Micronesian (1)	5	0.01
Polynesian: (104)	286	0.39
Native Hawaiian (63)	224	0.31
Samoan (25)	43	0.06
Tongan (16)	18	0.02
Other Polynesian	1	0.00
Other Pac. Isl., specified	2	0.00
Other Pac. Isl., not spec. (39)	95	0.13
Hispanic or Latino:	10,541	14.37
Central American:	269	0.37
Costa Rican	14	0.02
Guatemalan	25	0.03
Honduran	16	0.02
Nicaraguan	47	0.06
Panamanian	14	0.02
Salvadoran	113	0.15
Other Central American	40	0.05
Cuban	63	0.09
Dominican Republic	3	0.00
Mexican	7,573	10.33
Puerto Rican	386	0.53
South American:	217	0.30
Argentinean	34	0.05
Bolivian	15	0.02
Chilean	24	0.03
Colombian	40	0.05
Ecuadorian	7	0.01
Paraguayan	3	0.00
Peruvian	62	0.08
Uruguayan	1	0.00
Venezuelan	6	0.01
Other South American	25	0.03
Other Hispanic or Latino	2,030	2.77
Hungarian	385	0.52
Iranian	94	0.13
Irish	10,449	14.23
Israeli	16	0.02
Italian	5,798	7.90
Latvian	66	0.09
Lithuanian	215	0.29
Luxemburger	49	0.07
Maltese	48	0.07
New Zealander	25	0.03
Northern European	156	0.21
Norwegian	1,792	2.44
Pennsylvania German	20	0.03
Polish	1,685	2.29
Portuguese	2,947	4.01
Romanian	166	0.23
Russian	791	1.08
Scandinavian	281	0.38
Scotch-Irish	1,437	1.96
Scottish	1,845	2.51
Serbian	61	0.08
Slavic	61	0.08
Slovak	133	0.18
Slovene	34	0.05
Swedish	1,902	2.59
Swiss	425	0.58
Turkish	27	0.04
Ukrainian	194	0.26
United States or American	2,853	3.89
Welsh	891	1.21
West Indian, excl. Hispanic:	93	0.13
Jamaican	78	0.11
Trinidadian and Tobagonian	15	0.02
White:	63,030	85.94
Not Hispanic (54,587)	56,623	77.20
Hispanic (5,483)	6,407	8.74
Yugoslavian	150	0.20

Livingston

Place Type: City
County: Merced
Population: 10,473

Ancestry/Race	Number	%
African American/Black:	115	1.10
Not Hispanic (62)	84	0.80
Hispanic (15)	31	0.30
African, sub-Saharan:	10	0.10
African	10	0.10
Alaska Native tribes, not specified	1	0.01
Am. Ind. or Alaska Nat., not spec.	93	0.89
American Indian tribes, specified:	76	0.73
Apache (3)	3	0.03
Blackfeet	2	0.02
Cherokee (1)	7	0.07
Choctaw	1	0.01
Comanche (1)	1	0.01
Iroquois	2	0.02
Latin American Indians (25)	29	0.28
Pima	1	0.01
Pueblo	3	0.03
Seminole	3	0.03
Sioux (2)	2	0.02
Yaqui (2)	2	0.02
All other tribes (16)	20	0.19
American Indian tribes, not spec.	5	0.05
Asian:	1,718	16.40
Chinese, ex. Taiwanese (20)	28	0.27
Filipino (117)	153	1.46
Hmong (72)	72	0.69
Indian (1,221)	1,366	13.04
Japanese (26)	39	0.37
Korean (3)	4	0.04
Laotian (2)	2	0.02
Pakistani (17)	18	0.17
Vietnamese (14)	17	0.16
Other Asian, not specified (14)	19	0.18
Austrian	29	0.28
Dutch	50	0.48
English	43	0.42
French, except Basque	38	0.37
German	174	1.68
Greek	26	0.25
Hawaii Native/Pacific Islander:	31	0.30
Micronesian: (1)	6	0.06
Guamanian/Chamorro (1)	6	0.06
Polynesian: (4)	8	0.08
Native Hawaiian (3)	7	0.07
Samoan (1)	1	0.01
Other Pac. Isl., not spec. (3)	17	0.16
Hispanic or Latino:	7,521	71.81
Central American:	25	0.24
Guatemalan	6	0.06
Honduran	1	0.01
Nicaraguan	1	0.01
Panamanian	3	0.03
Salvadoran	14	0.13
Mexican	6,852	65.43
Puerto Rican	10	0.10
Other Hispanic or Latino	634	6.05
Irish	68	0.66
Italian	53	0.51
Maltese	7	0.07
Norwegian	14	0.14
Polish	9	0.09
Portuguese	308	2.98

Notes: 1. Figures in the "Number" column do not add up to the total population due to: a) Ancestry/Race overlap — e.g. persons can report being both White and Irish, b) persons of Hispanic origin can report being any race, c) persons reporting two ancestries are counted in both categories. 2. Numbers in parentheses indicate the number of persons reporting this ancestry/race alone, not in combination with any other ancestry/race. 3. Refer to the Explanation of Data in the front of the book for more detailed information.

Scotch-Irish	7	0.07
Swedish	31	0.30
Swiss	10	0.10
United States or American	155	1.50
White:	4,242	40.50
Not Hispanic (1,065)	1,167	11.14
Hispanic (2,760)	3,075	29.36

Lodi

Place Type: City
County: San Joaquin
Population: 56,999

Ancestry/Race	Number	%
Acadian/Cajun	14	0.02
Afghan	76	0.13
African American/Black:	521	0.91
Not Hispanic (260)	382	0.67
Hispanic (84)	139	0.24
African, sub-Saharan:	60	0.11
African	60	0.11
Alaska Native tribes, specified:	12	0.02
Alaska Athabascan	1	0.00
Aleut (1)	5	0.01
Eskimo (2)	3	0.01
Tlingit-Haida	3	0.01
Alaska Native tribes, not specified	2	0.00
Am. Ind. or Alaska Nat., not spec.	324	0.57
Alsatian	6	0.01
American Indian tribes, specified:	707	1.24
Apache (10)	28	0.05
Blackfeet (5)	20	0.04
Cherokee (62)	234	0.41
Cheyenne (1)	1	0.00
Chickasaw (6)	13	0.02
Chippewa (11)	20	0.04
Choctaw (11)	47	0.08
Colville	1	0.00
Comanche (2)	7	0.01
Creek (9)	26	0.05
Crow	2	0.00
Iroquois (1)	3	0.01
Kiowa (2)	6	0.01
Latin American Indians (66)	114	0.20
Lumbee	1	0.00
Navajo (10)	21	0.04
Osage (1)	4	0.01
Paiute (2)	2	0.00
Potawatomi (3)	5	0.01
Pueblo (2)	15	0.03
Seminole	4	0.01
Shoshone (7)	8	0.01
Sioux (14)	17	0.03
Ute (6)	7	0.01
Yakama (2)	2	0.00
Yaqui (3)	8	0.01
Yuman (2)	2	0.00
All other tribes (50)	89	0.16
American Indian tribes, not spec.	44	0.08
Arab:	396	0.69
Arab/Arabic	143	0.25
Lebanese	60	0.11
Palestinian	101	0.18
Syrian	66	0.12
Other Arab	26	0.05
Armenian	15	0.03
Asian:	3,887	6.82
Cambodian (9)	18	0.03
Chinese, ex. Taiwanese (221)	299	0.52
Filipino (541)	850	1.49
Hmong (8)	9	0.02
Indian (715)	856	1.50
Indonesian (3)	12	0.02
Japanese (581)	724	1.27
Korean (71)	96	0.17
Laotian (57)	71	0.12
Malaysian	3	0.01
Pakistani (470)	707	1.24
Taiwanese (9)	9	0.02
Thai (9)	16	0.03
Vietnamese (47)	53	0.09
Other Asian, specified (1)	3	0.01
Other Asian, not specified (81)	161	0.28
Assyrian/Chaldean/Syriac	16	0.03
Australian	46	0.08
Austrian	66	0.12
Basque	51	0.09
Belgian	73	0.13
Brazilian	6	0.01
British	204	0.36
Canadian	115	0.20
Celtic	25	0.04
Croatian	57	0.10
Czech	116	0.20
Czechoslovakian	67	0.12
Danish	446	0.78
Dutch	809	1.42
Eastern European	6	0.01
English	4,767	8.36
European	455	0.80
Finnish	115	0.20
French, except Basque	1,251	2.19
French Canadian	199	0.35
German	11,706	20.52
German Russian	24	0.04
Greek	341	0.60
Hawaii Native/Pacific Islander:	223	0.39
Melanesian: (7)	17	0.03
Fijian (7)	17	0.03
Micronesian: (7)	32	0.06
Guamanian/Chamorro (7)	32	0.06
Polynesian: (37)	107	0.19
Native Hawaiian (28)	89	0.16
Samoan (7)	15	0.03
Tongan (1)	2	0.00
Other Polynesian (1)	1	0.00
Other Pac. Isl., not spec. (17)	67	0.12
Hispanic or Latino:	15,464	27.13
Central American:	172	0.30
Costa Rican	13	0.02
Guatemalan	45	0.08
Honduran	9	0.02
Nicaraguan	10	0.02
Panamanian	10	0.02
Salvadoran	54	0.09
Other Central American	31	0.05
Cuban	30	0.05
Mexican	13,215	23.18
Puerto Rican	176	0.31
South American:	34	0.06
Argentinean	5	0.01
Chilean	4	0.01
Colombian	9	0.02
Ecuadorian	2	0.00
Peruvian	10	0.02
Venezuelan	1	0.00
Other South American	3	0.01
Other Hispanic or Latino	1,837	3.22
Hungarian	154	0.27
Irish	4,744	8.32
Israeli	6	0.01
Italian	3,086	5.41
Lithuanian	31	0.05
Luxemburger	6	0.01
New Zealander	8	0.01
Northern European	46	0.08
Norwegian	1,060	1.86
Pennsylvania German	12	0.02
Polish	383	0.67
Portuguese	984	1.73
Romanian	67	0.12
Russian	495	0.87
Scandinavian	92	0.16
Scotch-Irish	694	1.22
Scottish	1,044	1.83
Serbian	39	0.07
Slavic	6	0.01
Slovak	46	0.08
Slovene	8	0.01
Swedish	966	1.69
Swiss	224	0.39
Turkish	8	0.01
Ukrainian	142	0.25
United States or American	2,600	4.56
Welsh	171	0.30
White:	44,715	78.45
Not Hispanic (36,200)	37,550	65.88
Hispanic (6,221)	7,165	12.57
Yugoslavian	53	0.09

Loma Linda

Place Type: City
County: San Bernardino
Population: 18,681

Ancestry/Race	Number	%
Acadian/Cajun	10	0.05
African American/Black:	1,553	8.31
Not Hispanic (1,300)	1,459	7.81
Hispanic (47)	94	0.50
African, sub-Saharan:	292	1.57
African	143	0.77
Ethiopian	45	0.24
Nigerian	10	0.05
Other sub-Saharan African	94	0.51
Alaska Native tribes, specified:	2	0.01
Eskimo	2	0.01
Am. Ind. or Alaska Nat., not spec.	79	0.42
American Indian tribes, specified:	123	0.66
Apache (5)	10	0.05
Blackfeet (1)	2	0.01
Cherokee (16)	39	0.21
Cheyenne	2	0.01
Chickasaw	1	0.01
Choctaw (1)	5	0.03
Delaware	1	0.01
Iroquois (2)	3	0.02
Latin American Indians (13)	24	0.13
Navajo (6)	9	0.05
Ottawa	1	0.01
Potawatomi	1	0.01
Seminole	2	0.01
Sioux	2	0.01
Yaqui (1)	1	0.01
Yuman (2)	2	0.01
All other tribes (10)	18	0.10
American Indian tribes, not spec.	19	0.10
Arab:	214	1.15
Arab/Arabic	51	0.27
Egyptian	45	0.24
Iraqi	26	0.14
Lebanese	92	0.50
Armenian	151	0.81
Asian:	5,215	27.92
Bangladeshi (15)	35	0.19
Cambodian (62)	80	0.43
Chinese, ex. Taiwanese (612)	744	3.98
Filipino (1,414)	1,574	8.43
Hmong (7)	8	0.04
Indian (388)	453	2.42
Indonesian (578)	728	3.90
Japanese (191)	247	1.32
Korean (561)	594	3.18
Laotian (5)	6	0.03
Malaysian (7)	19	0.10
Pakistani (80)	92	0.49
Sri Lankan (7)	7	0.04
Taiwanese (44)	67	0.36
Thai (141)	153	0.82
Vietnamese (272)	304	1.63
Other Asian, specified (17)	24	0.13
Other Asian, not specified (32)	80	0.43
Australian	21	0.11
Austrian	43	0.23
Basque	14	0.08
Brazilian	9	0.05
British	105	0.57
Bulgarian	7	0.04

Notes: 1. Figures in the "Number" column do not add up to the total population due to: a) Ancestry/Race overlap — e.g. persons can report being both White and Irish, b) persons of Hispanic origin can report being any race, c) persons reporting two ancestries are counted in both categories. 2. Numbers in parentheses indicate the number of persons reporting this ancestry/race alone, not in combination with any other ancestry/race. 3. Refer to the Explanation of Data in the front of the book for more detailed information.

Canadian	86	0.46
Croatian	16	0.09
Czech	34	0.18
Czechoslovakian	16	0.09
Danish	232	1.25
Dutch	254	1.37
Eastern European	5	0.03
English	1,437	7.73
European	215	1.16
Finnish	10	0.05
French, except Basque	404	2.17
French Canadian	67	0.36
German	2,322	12.50
Greek	56	0.30
Hawaii Native/Pacific Islander:	170	0.91
Melanesian:	1	0.01
Other Melanesian	1	0.01
Micronesian: (13)	25	0.13
Guamanian/Chamorro (10)	18	0.10
Other Micronesian (3)	7	0.04
Polynesian: (18)	78	0.42
Native Hawaiian (13)	57	0.31
Samoan (4)	6	0.03
Tongan	8	0.04
Other Polynesian (1)	7	0.04
Other Pac. Isl., not spec. (1)	66	0.35
Hispanic or Latino:	3,050	16.33
Central American:	107	0.57
Costa Rican	8	0.04
Guatemalan	8	0.04
Honduran	18	0.10
Nicaraguan	10	0.05
Panamanian	23	0.12
Salvadoran	34	0.18
Other Central American	6	0.03
Cuban	50	0.27
Dominican Republic	11	0.06
Mexican	1,959	10.49
Puerto Rican	162	0.87
South American:	152	0.81
Argentinean	32	0.17
Bolivian	5	0.03
Chilean	5	0.03
Colombian	18	0.10
Ecuadorian	14	0.07
Peruvian	49	0.26
Uruguayan	3	0.02
Venezuelan	3	0.02
Other South American	23	0.12
Other Hispanic or Latino	609	3.26
Hungarian	103	0.55
Icelander	12	0.06
Iranian	19	0.10
Irish	887	4.77
Israeli	6	0.03
Italian	424	2.28
Lithuanian	6	0.03
New Zealander	13	0.07
Northern European	41	0.22
Norwegian	347	1.87
Polish	216	1.16
Portuguese	66	0.36
Romanian	351	1.89
Russian	80	0.43
Scandinavian	64	0.34
Scotch-Irish	223	1.20
Scottish	306	1.65
Slavic	6	0.03
Slovak	8	0.04
Swedish	300	1.61
Swiss	38	0.20
Ukrainian	44	0.24
United States or American	580	3.12
Welsh	59	0.32
West Indian, excl. Hispanic:	223	1.20
Barbadian	27	0.15
Belizean	19	0.10
British West Indian	10	0.05
Dutch West Indian	32	0.17
Jamaican	116	0.62
West Indian	12	0.06
Other West Indian	7	0.04
White:	10,869	58.18
Not Hispanic (8,799)	9,343	50.01
Hispanic (1,322)	1,526	8.17

Lomita

Place Type: City
County: Los Angeles
Population: 20,046

Ancestry/Race	Number	%
Afghan	12	0.06
African American/Black:	1,005	5.01
Not Hispanic (821)	948	4.73
Hispanic (17)	57	0.28
African, sub-Saharan:	13	0.07
African	8	0.04
Sudanese	5	0.03
Alaska Native tribes, specified:	9	0.04
Alaska Athabascan (2)	2	0.01
Aleut (1)	1	0.00
Eskimo (3)	6	0.03
Am. Ind. or Alaska Nat., not spec.	104	0.52
Alsatian	13	0.07
American Indian tribes, specified:	214	1.07
Apache (7)	17	0.08
Blackfeet (2)	10	0.05
Cherokee (15)	54	0.27
Cheyenne	1	0.00
Chippewa (4)	7	0.03
Choctaw (5)	16	0.08
Creek	2	0.01
Delaware	6	0.03
Iroquois (1)	3	0.01
Latin American Indians (4)	8	0.04
Navajo (3)	7	0.03
Paiute	1	0.00
Potawatomi	1	0.00
Pueblo (12)	18	0.09
Puget Sound Salish (1)	1	0.00
Seminole (1)	2	0.01
Sioux (16)	28	0.14
All other tribes (17)	32	0.16
American Indian tribes, not spec.	10	0.05
Arab:	181	0.91
Arab/Arabic	18	0.09
Egyptian	31	0.16
Lebanese	35	0.18
Moroccan	10	0.05
Syrian	56	0.28
Other Arab	31	0.16
Armenian	54	0.27
Asian:	2,850	14.22
Bangladeshi (1)	1	0.00
Cambodian (8)	9	0.04
Chinese, ex. Taiwanese (278)	386	1.93
Filipino (492)	677	3.38
Hmong	1	0.00
Indian (204)	226	1.13
Indonesian (10)	27	0.13
Japanese (542)	699	3.49
Korean (410)	456	2.27
Malaysian (2)	2	0.01
Pakistani (66)	83	0.41
Sri Lankan (28)	28	0.14
Taiwanese (62)	66	0.33
Thai (18)	26	0.13
Vietnamese (87)	93	0.46
Other Asian, specified (11)	13	0.06
Other Asian, not specified (20)	57	0.28
Australian	19	0.10
Austrian	69	0.35
Belgian	7	0.04
British	99	0.50
Bulgarian	25	0.13
Canadian	50	0.25
Croatian	33	0.17
Czech	67	0.34
Czechoslovakian	113	0.57
Danish	96	0.48
Dutch	267	1.34
English	1,746	8.74
Estonian	37	0.19
European	230	1.15
Finnish	42	0.21
French, except Basque	678	3.39
French Canadian	165	0.83
German	2,706	13.54
Greek	94	0.47
Hawaii Native/Pacific Islander:	221	1.10
Micronesian: (20)	36	0.18
Guamanian/Chamorro (18)	34	0.17
Other Micronesian (2)	2	0.01
Polynesian: (79)	165	0.82
Native Hawaiian (21)	79	0.39
Samoan (58)	80	0.40
Tongan	2	0.01
Other Polynesian	4	0.02
Other Pac. Isl., not spec.	20	0.10
Hispanic or Latino:	5,252	26.20
Central American:	233	1.16
Costa Rican	25	0.12
Guatemalan	110	0.55
Honduran	3	0.01
Nicaraguan	31	0.15
Panamanian	2	0.01
Salvadoran	50	0.25
Other Central American	12	0.06
Cuban	146	0.73
Dominican Republic	2	0.01
Mexican	3,665	18.28
Puerto Rican	120	0.60
South American:	252	1.26
Argentinean	57	0.28
Bolivian	2	0.01
Chilean	15	0.07
Colombian	58	0.29
Ecuadorian	19	0.09
Peruvian	78	0.39
Uruguayan	4	0.02
Venezuelan	5	0.02
Other South American	14	0.07
Other Hispanic or Latino	834	4.16
Hungarian	163	0.82
Iranian	157	0.79
Irish	2,207	11.04
Italian	1,116	5.58
Lithuanian	52	0.26
Luxemburger	8	0.04
Northern European	60	0.30
Norwegian	322	1.61
Polish	275	1.38
Portuguese	58	0.29
Romanian	20	0.10
Russian	191	0.96
Scandinavian	86	0.43
Scotch-Irish	200	1.00
Scottish	454	2.27
Serbian	27	0.14
Slavic	7	0.04
Slovak	10	0.05
Slovene	5	0.03
Swedish	278	1.39
Swiss	46	0.23
Ukrainian	33	0.17
United States or American	561	2.81
Welsh	107	0.54
West Indian, excl. Hispanic:	57	0.29
Belizean	57	0.29
White:	14,333	71.50
Not Hispanic (10,735)	11,379	56.76
Hispanic (2,528)	2,954	14.74
Yugoslavian	67	0.34

Notes: 1. Figures in the "Number" column do not add up to the total population due to: a) Ancestry/Race overlap — e.g. persons can report being both White and Irish, b) persons of Hispanic origin can report being any race, c) persons reporting two ancestries are counted in both categories. 2. Numbers in parentheses indicate the number of persons reporting this ancestry/race alone, not in combination with any other ancestry/race. 3. Refer to the Explanation of Data in the front of the book for more detailed information.

Lompoc

Place Type: City
County: Santa Barbara
Population: 41,103

Ancestry/Race	Number	%
Acadian/Cajun	44	0.11
African American/Black:	3,449	8.39
Not Hispanic (2,887)	3,187	7.75
Hispanic (130)	262	0.64
African, sub-Saharan:	162	0.39
African	143	0.35
Ethiopian	19	0.05
Alaska Native tribes, specified:	7	0.02
Eskimo (2)	4	0.01
Tlingit-Haida (1)	3	0.01
Alaska Native tribes, not specified	1	0.00
Am. Ind. or Alaska Nat., not spec.	485	1.18
Albanian	6	0.01
American Indian tribes, specified:	748	1.82
Apache (17)	58	0.14
Blackfeet (7)	32	0.08
Cherokee (51)	140	0.34
Cheyenne (1)	2	0.00
Chickasaw (2)	11	0.03
Chippewa (1)	5	0.01
Choctaw (19)	42	0.10
Comanche (1)	5	0.01
Cree (1)	1	0.00
Creek (14)	15	0.04
Crow	1	0.00
Iroquois (3)	13	0.03
Latin American Indians (48)	91	0.22
Lumbee	1	0.00
Navajo (6)	14	0.03
Osage (5)	6	0.01
Paiute	1	0.00
Pima (1)	2	0.00
Potawatomi (2)	6	0.01
Pueblo (13)	18	0.04
Seminole (1)	3	0.01
Shoshone	1	0.00
Sioux (11)	31	0.08
Tohono O'Odham (2)	6	0.01
Ute (1)	3	0.01
Yaqui (8)	15	0.04
Yuman (1)	1	0.00
All other tribes (132)	224	0.54
American Indian tribes, not spec.	51	0.12
Arab:	11	0.03
Lebanese	11	0.03
Armenian	53	0.13
Asian:	2,276	5.54
Cambodian (7)	11	0.03
Chinese, ex. Taiwanese (79)	152	0.37
Filipino (431)	705	1.72
Hmong (405)	445	1.08
Indian (85)	108	0.26
Indonesian (6)	11	0.03
Japanese (128)	270	0.66
Korean (86)	130	0.32
Laotian (100)	117	0.28
Malaysian (1)	2	0.00
Pakistani (9)	10	0.02
Sri Lankan (6)	8	0.02
Taiwanese (5)	5	0.01
Thai (31)	52	0.13
Vietnamese (122)	146	0.36
Other Asian, specified	3	0.01
Other Asian, not specified (58)	101	0.25
Australian	17	0.04
Austrian	35	0.09
Basque	80	0.19
Belgian	50	0.12
British	126	0.31
Bulgarian	6	0.01
Canadian	79	0.19
Celtic	7	0.02
Croatian	47	0.11
Czech	69	0.17
Czechoslovakian	5	0.01
Danish	257	0.63
Dutch	354	0.86
English	3,080	7.50
European	233	0.57
Finnish	126	0.31
French, except Basque	933	2.27
French Canadian	227	0.55
German	4,091	9.96
Greek	130	0.32
Guyanese	12	0.03
Hawaii Native/Pacific Islander:	285	0.69
Micronesian: (70)	97	0.24
Guamanian/Chamorro (67)	94	0.23
Other Micronesian (3)	3	0.01
Polynesian: (58)	144	0.35
Native Hawaiian (35)	110	0.27
Samoan (19)	29	0.07
Tongan (4)	5	0.01
Other Pac. Isl., specified	3	0.01
Other Pac. Isl., not spec. (5)	41	0.10
Hispanic or Latino:	15,337	37.31
Central American:	235	0.57
Costa Rican	19	0.05
Guatemalan	82	0.20
Honduran	26	0.06
Nicaraguan	10	0.02
Panamanian	6	0.01
Salvadoran	79	0.19
Other Central American	13	0.03
Cuban	69	0.17
Dominican Republic	8	0.02
Mexican	12,978	31.57
Puerto Rican	174	0.42
South American:	89	0.22
Argentinean	6	0.01
Bolivian	2	0.00
Chilean	5	0.01
Colombian	51	0.12
Ecuadorian	7	0.02
Peruvian	11	0.03
Venezuelan	4	0.01
Other South American	3	0.01
Other Hispanic or Latino	1,784	4.34
Hungarian	86	0.21
Irish	2,814	6.85
Italian	1,308	3.18
Latvian	6	0.01
Lithuanian	82	0.20
Macedonian	7	0.02
Maltese	7	0.02
Northern European	29	0.07
Norwegian	576	1.40
Pennsylvania German	25	0.06
Polish	310	0.75
Portuguese	378	0.92
Russian	173	0.42
Scandinavian	56	0.14
Scotch-Irish	498	1.21
Scottish	581	1.41
Slavic	12	0.03
Slovak	14	0.03
Slovene	21	0.05
Swedish	538	1.31
Swiss	264	0.64
Ukrainian	32	0.08
United States or American	1,768	4.30
Welsh	273	0.66
West Indian, excl. Hispanic:	59	0.14
Belizean	5	0.01
Jamaican	13	0.03
Other West Indian	41	0.10
White:	28,878	70.26
Not Hispanic (19,696)	20,630	50.19
Hispanic (7,354)	8,248	20.07
Yugoslavian	25	0.06

Long Beach

Place Type: City
County: Los Angeles
Population: 461,522

Ancestry/Race	Number	%
Acadian/Cajun	10	0.00
Afghan	67	0.01
African American/Black:	73,911	16.01
Not Hispanic (66,836)	70,935	15.37
Hispanic (1,782)	2,976	0.64
African, sub-Saharan:	3,505	0.76
African	2,934	0.64
Cape Verdean	16	0.00
Ethiopian	205	0.04
Ghanian	8	0.00
Kenyan	56	0.01
Nigerian	179	0.04
Somalian	7	0.00
South African	31	0.01
Sudanese	35	0.01
Ugandan	9	0.00
Zimbabwean	16	0.00
Other sub-Saharan African	9	0.00
Alaska Native tribes, specified:	52	0.01
Alaska Athabascan (9)	9	0.00
Aleut (3)	6	0.00
Eskimo (15)	18	0.00
Tlingit-Haida (9)	14	0.00
All other tribes	5	0.00
Alaska Native tribes, not specified	8	0.00
Am. Ind. or Alaska Nat., not spec.	2,971	0.64
Albanian	35	0.01
Alsatian	28	0.01
American Indian tribes, specified:	4,615	1.00
Apache (113)	298	0.06
Blackfeet (30)	243	0.05
Cherokee (247)	1,109	0.24
Cheyenne (10)	26	0.01
Chickasaw (19)	54	0.01
Chippewa (55)	113	0.02
Choctaw (69)	232	0.05
Colville (6)	9	0.00
Comanche (13)	42	0.01
Cree (5)	20	0.00
Creek (46)	100	0.02
Crow (4)	19	0.00
Delaware (5)	19	0.00
Iroquois (33)	96	0.02
Kiowa (6)	15	0.00
Latin American Indians (571)	969	0.21
Lumbee (11)	19	0.00
Navajo (158)	248	0.05
Osage (11)	30	0.01
Ottawa (2)	9	0.00
Paiute (18)	30	0.01
Pima (16)	22	0.00
Potawatomi (12)	31	0.01
Pueblo (71)	122	0.03
Puget Sound Salish (3)	5	0.00
Seminole (8)	41	0.01
Shoshone (5)	14	0.00
Sioux (58)	144	0.03
Tohono O'Odham (16)	21	0.00
Ute (4)	15	0.00
Yakama (2)	4	0.00
Yaqui (38)	76	0.02
Yuman (34)	42	0.01
All other tribes (189)	378	0.08
American Indian tribes, not spec.	465	0.10
Arab:	1,624	0.35
Arab/Arabic	283	0.06
Egyptian	200	0.04
Iraqi	35	0.01
Jordanian	72	0.02
Lebanese	526	0.11
Moroccan	71	0.02
Palestinian	153	0.03
Syrian	97	0.02

Notes: 1. Figures in the "Number" column do not add up to the total population due to: a) Ancestry/Race overlap — e.g. persons can report being both White and Irish, b) persons of Hispanic origin can report being any race, c) persons reporting two ancestries are counted in both categories. 2. Numbers in parentheses indicate the number of persons reporting this ancestry/race alone, not in combination with any other ancestry/race. 3. Refer to the Explanation of Data in the front of the book for more detailed information.

Ancestry/Race	Number	%
Other Arab	187	0.04
Armenian	597	0.13
Asian:	65,538	14.20
Bangladeshi (61)	102	0.02
Cambodian (17,396)	20,262	4.39
Chinese, ex. Taiwanese (3,360)	5,076	1.10
Filipino (18,608)	21,502	4.66
Hmong (375)	416	0.09
Indian (1,338)	1,897	0.41
Indonesian (114)	256	0.06
Japanese (3,147)	4,363	0.95
Korean (1,608)	1,911	0.41
Laotian (643)	916	0.20
Malaysian (36)	67	0.01
Pakistani (83)	128	0.03
Sri Lankan (79)	112	0.02
Taiwanese (190)	251	0.05
Thai (656)	967	0.21
Vietnamese (5,074)	5,697	1.23
Other Asian, specified (95)	135	0.03
Other Asian, not specified (850)	1,480	0.32
Assyrian/Chaldean/Syriac	153	0.03
Australian	118	0.03
Austrian	838	0.18
Basque	193	0.04
Belgian	229	0.05
Brazilian	185	0.04
British	1,464	0.32
Bulgarian	86	0.02
Canadian	1,036	0.22
Carpatho Rusyn	6	0.00
Celtic	69	0.01
Croatian	524	0.11
Cypriot	7	0.00
Czech	814	0.18
Czechoslovakian	460	0.10
Danish	2,042	0.44
Dutch	4,420	0.96
Eastern European	357	0.08
English	25,747	5.58
Estonian	29	0.01
European	3,799	0.82
Finnish	601	0.13
French, except Basque	8,562	1.86
French Canadian	1,612	0.35
German	33,634	7.29
German Russian	8	0.00
Greek	1,667	0.36
Guyanese	79	0.02
Hawaii Native/Pacific Islander:	8,022	1.74
Melanesian: (5)	13	0.00
Fijian (5)	11	0.00
Other Melanesian	2	0.00
Micronesian: (597)	863	0.19
Guamanian/Chamorro (578)	833	0.18
Other Micronesian (19)	30	0.01
Polynesian: (4,660)	6,016	1.30
Native Hawaiian (306)	876	0.19
Samoan (3,951)	4,617	1.00
Tongan (317)	373	0.08
Other Polynesian (86)	150	0.03
Other Pac. Isl., specified	13	0.00
Other Pac. Isl., not spec. (234)	1,117	0.24
Hispanic or Latino:	165,092	35.77
Central American:	8,924	1.93
Costa Rican	278	0.06
Guatemalan	2,443	0.53
Honduran	1,230	0.27
Nicaraguan	509	0.11
Panamanian	221	0.05
Salvadoran	3,418	0.74
Other Central American	825	0.18
Cuban	1,067	0.23
Dominican Republic	82	0.02
Mexican	127,129	27.55
Puerto Rican	2,339	0.51
South American:	2,228	0.48
Argentinean	275	0.06
Bolivian	43	0.01
Chilean	182	0.04
Colombian	594	0.13
Ecuadorian	339	0.07
Paraguayan	10	0.00
Peruvian	556	0.12
Uruguayan	8	0.00
Venezuelan	58	0.01
Other South American	163	0.04
Other Hispanic or Latino	23,323	5.05
Hungarian	1,491	0.32
Icelander	120	0.03
Iranian	1,043	0.23
Irish	27,575	5.98
Israeli	260	0.06
Italian	13,576	2.94
Latvian	172	0.04
Lithuanian	436	0.09
Luxemburger	25	0.01
Macedonian	49	0.01
Maltese	29	0.01
New Zealander	45	0.01
Northern European	206	0.04
Norwegian	5,217	1.13
Pennsylvania German	155	0.03
Polish	5,192	1.13
Portuguese	1,188	0.26
Romanian	730	0.16
Russian	3,626	0.79
Scandinavian	558	0.12
Scotch-Irish	4,500	0.98
Scottish	5,359	1.16
Serbian	143	0.03
Slavic	233	0.05
Slovak	289	0.06
Slovene	73	0.02
Swedish	4,658	1.01
Swiss	901	0.20
Turkish	220	0.05
Ukrainian	570	0.12
United States or American	10,639	2.31
Welsh	1,984	0.43
West Indian, excl. Hispanic:	1,691	0.37
Bahamian	23	0.00
Barbadian	57	0.01
Belizean	254	0.06
British West Indian	166	0.04
Haitian	115	0.02
Jamaican	511	0.11
Trinidadian and Tobagonian	329	0.07
U.S. Virgin Islander	11	0.00
West Indian	218	0.05
Other West Indian	7	0.00
White:	225,899	48.95
Not Hispanic (152,899)	161,584	35.01
Hispanic (55,511)	64,315	13.94
Yugoslavian	504	0.11

Los Alamitos

Place Type: City
County: Orange
Population: 11,536

Ancestry/Race	Number	%
African American/Black:	423	3.67
Not Hispanic (358)	406	3.52
Hispanic (11)	17	0.15
African, sub-Saharan:	64	0.57
African	18	0.16
Nigerian	46	0.41
Alaska Native tribes, specified:	3	0.03
Eskimo (1)	1	0.01
Tlingit-Haida	1	0.01
All other tribes	1	0.01
Alaska Native tribes, not specified	1	0.01
Am. Ind. or Alaska Nat., not spec.	50	0.43
Albanian	7	0.06
American Indian tribes, specified:	119	1.03
Apache (4)	17	0.15
Blackfeet (1)	5	0.04
Cherokee (5)	39	0.34
Chippewa	1	0.01
Choctaw	2	0.02
Creek (4)	4	0.03
Iroquois (1)	4	0.03
Latin American Indians (13)	15	0.13
Navajo (4)	5	0.04
Potawatomi (2)	2	0.02
Pueblo (1)	8	0.07
Sioux (2)	4	0.03
Tohono O'Odham	1	0.01
All other tribes (5)	12	0.10
American Indian tribes, not spec.	6	0.05
Arab:	207	1.84
Arab/Arabic	107	0.95
Egyptian	29	0.26
Jordanian	34	0.30
Lebanese	6	0.05
Palestinian	19	0.17
Syrian	12	0.11
Armenian	5	0.04
Asian:	1,334	11.56
Bangladeshi	1	0.01
Cambodian (12)	18	0.16
Chinese, ex. Taiwanese (142)	183	1.59
Filipino (213)	304	2.64
Hmong (1)	1	0.01
Indian (48)	59	0.51
Indonesian (1)	5	0.04
Japanese (121)	191	1.66
Korean (371)	390	3.38
Laotian (2)	4	0.03
Pakistani (5)	5	0.04
Sri Lankan (9)	15	0.13
Taiwanese (29)	31	0.27
Thai (19)	27	0.23
Vietnamese (80)	82	0.71
Other Asian, specified (2)	2	0.02
Other Asian, not specified (9)	16	0.14
Assyrian/Chaldean/Syriac	16	0.14
Australian	22	0.20
Austrian	33	0.29
Basque	4	0.04
British	87	0.77
Canadian	81	0.72
Croatian	37	0.33
Czech	20	0.18
Czechoslovakian	16	0.14
Danish	58	0.52
Dutch	245	2.18
English	1,225	10.88
European	141	1.25
Finnish	48	0.43
French, except Basque	437	3.88
French Canadian	139	1.23
German	1,788	15.88
Greek	76	0.67
Hawaii Native/Pacific Islander:	85	0.74
Melanesian: (2)	2	0.02
Fijian (2)	2	0.02
Micronesian: (19)	28	0.24
Guamanian/Chamorro (19)	28	0.24
Polynesian: (16)	45	0.39
Native Hawaiian (3)	27	0.23
Samoan (12)	17	0.15
Tongan (1)	1	0.01
Other Pac. Isl., not spec. (1)	10	0.09
Hispanic or Latino:	1,848	16.02
Central American:	79	0.68
Costa Rican	4	0.03
Guatemalan	34	0.29
Nicaraguan	8	0.07
Panamanian	2	0.02
Salvadoran	25	0.22
Other Central American	6	0.05
Cuban	35	0.30
Dominican Republic	2	0.02
Mexican	1,314	11.39
Puerto Rican	50	0.43
South American:	68	0.59
Argentinean	17	0.15

Notes: 1. Figures in the "Number" column do not add up to the total population due to: a) Ancestry/Race overlap — e.g. persons can report being both White and Irish, b) persons of Hispanic origin can report being any race, c) persons reporting two ancestries are counted in both categories. 2. Numbers in parentheses indicate the number of persons reporting this ancestry/race alone, not in combination with any other ancestry/race. 3. Refer to the Explanation of Data in the front of the book for more detailed information.

Bolivian	1	0.01
Chilean	2	0.02
Colombian	9	0.08
Ecuadorian	5	0.04
Paraguayan	1	0.01
Peruvian	24	0.21
Venezuelan	2	0.02
Other South American	7	0.06
Other Hispanic or Latino	300	2.60
Hungarian	104	0.92
Iranian	50	0.44
Irish	1,234	10.96
Israeli	8	0.07
Italian	662	5.88
Lithuanian	30	0.27
Norwegian	210	1.87
Pennsylvania German	9	0.08
Polish	220	1.95
Portuguese	101	0.90
Romanian	25	0.22
Russian	167	1.48
Scandinavian	13	0.12
Scotch-Irish	227	2.02
Scottish	355	3.15
Slavic	11	0.10
Slovak	6	0.05
Slovene	7	0.06
Swedish	238	2.11
Swiss	82	0.73
Ukrainian	33	0.29
United States or American	349	3.10
Welsh	83	0.74
West Indian, excl. Hispanic:	21	0.19
West Indian	21	0.19
White:	9,285	80.49
Not Hispanic (7,836)	8,117	70.36
Hispanic (1,043)	1,168	10.12
Yugoslavian	17	0.15

Los Altos

Place Type: City
County: Santa Clara
Population: 27,693

Ancestry/Race	Number	%
African American/Black:	178	0.64
Not Hispanic (127)	167	0.60
Hispanic (3)	11	0.04
African, sub-Saharan:	32	0.12
African	9	0.03
South African	23	0.08
Alaska Native tribes, specified:	3	0.01
Eskimo	1	0.00
Tlingit-Haida (1)	2	0.01
Am. Ind. or Alaska Nat., not spec.	51	0.18
American Indian tribes, specified:	70	0.25
Apache (1)	2	0.01
Blackfeet	1	0.00
Cherokee (6)	28	0.10
Chickasaw (3)	4	0.01
Choctaw (3)	4	0.01
Iroquois (1)	1	0.00
Latin American Indians (6)	9	0.03
Potawatomi	3	0.01
Puget Sound Salish (1)	1	0.00
Sioux (3)	4	0.01
Yuman	1	0.00
All other tribes (3)	12	0.04
American Indian tribes, not spec.	3	0.01
Arab:	126	0.46
Arab/Arabic	22	0.08
Egyptian	18	0.07
Iraqi	12	0.04
Lebanese	42	0.15
Palestinian	12	0.04
Syrian	20	0.07
Armenian	80	0.29
Asian:	4,887	17.65
Bangladeshi (2)	2	0.01
Chinese, ex. Taiwanese (2,106)	2,367	8.55
Filipino (110)	167	0.60
Indian (710)	756	2.73
Indonesian (2)	3	0.01
Japanese (717)	920	3.32
Korean (264)	305	1.10
Laotian	1	0.00
Malaysian (2)	4	0.01
Pakistani (19)	20	0.07
Sri Lankan (8)	9	0.03
Taiwanese (138)	168	0.61
Thai (10)	20	0.07
Vietnamese (72)	89	0.32
Other Asian, specified (6)	6	0.02
Other Asian, not specified (18)	50	0.18
Assyrian/Chaldean/Syriac	35	0.13
Australian	6	0.02
Austrian	177	0.64
Basque	20	0.07
Belgian	72	0.26
Brazilian	16	0.06
British	330	1.20
Canadian	193	0.70
Croatian	76	0.28
Czech	171	0.62
Czechoslovakian	57	0.21
Danish	372	1.35
Dutch	551	2.00
Eastern European	185	0.67
English	4,134	14.99
Estonian	10	0.04
European	601	2.18
Finnish	73	0.26
French, except Basque	991	3.59
French Canadian	150	0.54
German	4,541	16.46
Greek	100	0.36
Hawaii Native/Pacific Islander:	81	0.29
Melanesian: (6)	6	0.02
Fijian (6)	6	0.02
Micronesian: (6)	19	0.07
Guamanian/Chamorro (6)	18	0.06
Other Micronesian	1	0.00
Polynesian: (20)	31	0.11
Native Hawaiian (8)	16	0.06
Samoan (2)	3	0.01
Tongan (7)	9	0.03
Other Polynesian (3)	3	0.01
Other Pac. Isl., not spec. (12)	25	0.09
Hispanic or Latino:	822	2.97
Central American:	35	0.13
Costa Rican	1	0.00
Guatemalan	7	0.03
Nicaraguan	5	0.02
Panamanian	1	0.00
Salvadoran	12	0.04
Other Central American	9	0.03
Cuban	20	0.07
Dominican Republic	5	0.02
Mexican	439	1.59
Puerto Rican	37	0.13
South American:	89	0.32
Argentinean	9	0.03
Bolivian	3	0.01
Chilean	20	0.07
Colombian	17	0.06
Ecuadorian	6	0.02
Peruvian	12	0.04
Uruguayan	1	0.00
Venezuelan	4	0.01
Other South American	17	0.06
Other Hispanic or Latino	197	0.71
Hungarian	190	0.69
Icelander	19	0.07
Iranian	395	1.43
Irish	3,045	11.04
Israeli	89	0.32
Italian	1,866	6.76
Latvian	48	0.17
Lithuanian	97	0.35
Macedonian	6	0.02
Northern European	95	0.34
Norwegian	650	2.36
Pennsylvania German	7	0.03
Polish	808	2.93
Portuguese	209	0.76
Romanian	94	0.34
Russian	790	2.86
Scandinavian	43	0.16
Scotch-Irish	597	2.16
Scottish	882	3.20
Slavic	10	0.04
Slovak	66	0.24
Slovene	19	0.07
Swedish	769	2.79
Swiss	341	1.24
Turkish	44	0.16
Ukrainian	113	0.41
United States or American	1,119	4.06
Welsh	295	1.07
White:	22,951	82.88
Not Hispanic (21,656)	22,297	80.51
Hispanic (594)	654	2.36
Yugoslavian	29	0.11

Los Angeles

Place Type: City
County: Los Angeles
Population: 3,694,820

Ancestry/Race	Number	%
Acadian/Cajun	238	0.01
Afghan	2,335	0.06
African American/Black:	444,635	12.03
Not Hispanic (401,986)	422,819	11.44
Hispanic (13,209)	21,816	0.59
African, sub-Saharan:	29,946	0.81
African	19,718	0.53
Cape Verdean	325	0.01
Ethiopian	2,991	0.08
Ghanian	530	0.01
Kenyan	247	0.01
Liberian	41	0.00
Nigerian	2,803	0.08
Senegalese	125	0.00
Sierra Leonean	45	0.00
Somalian	68	0.00
South African	1,982	0.05
Sudanese	65	0.00
Ugandan	202	0.01
Zairian	59	0.00
Zimbabwean	58	0.00
Other sub-Saharan African	687	0.02
Alaska Native tribes, specified:	223	0.01
Alaska Athabascan (21)	44	0.00
Aleut (17)	41	0.00
Eskimo (18)	45	0.00
Tlingit-Haida (29)	78	0.00
All other tribes (2)	15	0.00
Alaska Native tribes, not specified	42	0.00
Am. Ind. or Alaska Nat., not spec.	22,100	0.60
Albanian	443	0.01
Alsatian	131	0.00
American Indian tribes, specified:	28,656	0.78
Apache (686)	1,495	0.04
Blackfeet (172)	1,037	0.03
Cherokee (1,057)	5,126	0.14
Cheyenne (39)	96	0.00
Chickasaw (52)	191	0.01
Chippewa (184)	372	0.01
Choctaw (245)	1,003	0.03
Colville (12)	22	0.00
Comanche (54)	148	0.00
Cree (30)	87	0.00
Creek (129)	349	0.01
Crow (15)	52	0.00
Delaware (20)	86	0.00
Houma (5)	11	0.00
Iroquois (145)	417	0.01

Notes: 1. Figures in the "Number" column do not add up to the total population due to: a) Ancestry/Race overlap — e.g. persons can report being both White and Irish, b) persons of Hispanic origin can report being any race, c) persons reporting two ancestries are counted in both categories. 2. Numbers in parentheses indicate the number of persons reporting this ancestry/race alone, not in combination with any other ancestry/race. 3. Refer to the Explanation of Data in the front of the book for more detailed information.

Kiowa (26)	47	0.00
Latin American Indians (7,296)	11,226	0.30
Lumbee (22)	52	0.00
Menominee (17)	35	0.00
Navajo (661)	1,089	0.03
Osage (42)	118	0.00
Ottawa (14)	32	0.00
Paiute (73)	104	0.00
Pima (81)	165	0.00
Potawatomi (33)	104	0.00
Pueblo (398)	668	0.02
Puget Sound Salish (9)	33	0.00
Seminole (69)	259	0.01
Shoshone (69)	128	0.00
Sioux (370)	817	0.02
Tohono O'Odham (139)	201	0.01
Ute (23)	56	0.00
Yakama (8)	19	0.00
Yaqui (242)	480	0.01
Yuman (57)	100	0.00
All other tribes (1,251)	2,431	0.07
American Indian tribes, not spec.	3,258	0.09
Arab:	25,937	0.70
Arab/Arabic	3,002	0.08
Egyptian	5,792	0.16
Iraqi	812	0.02
Jordanian	836	0.02
Lebanese	7,769	0.21
Moroccan	1,412	0.04
Palestinian	1,009	0.03
Syrian	2,995	0.08
Other Arab	2,310	0.06
Armenian	64,997	1.76
Asian:	417,435	11.30
Bangladeshi (1,198)	1,629	0.04
Cambodian (3,429)	4,364	0.12
Chinese, ex. Taiwanese (59,604)	69,668	1.89
Filipino (101,062)	113,793	3.08
Hmong (79)	100	0.00
Indian (24,739)	29,604	0.80
Indonesian (2,111)	3,258	0.09
Japanese (36,992)	45,176	1.22
Korean (91,595)	95,106	2.57
Laotian (657)	812	0.02
Malaysian (178)	355	0.01
Pakistani (1,760)	2,423	0.07
Sri Lankan (1,460)	1,800	0.05
Taiwanese (3,471)	4,200	0.11
Thai (9,604)	11,398	0.31
Vietnamese (19,747)	22,156	0.60
Other Asian, specified (695)	1,095	0.03
Other Asian, not specified (3,198)	10,498	0.28
Assyrian/Chaldean/Syriac	2,031	0.05
Australian	1,515	0.04
Austrian	11,430	0.31
Basque	1,197	0.03
Belgian	2,151	0.06
Brazilian	2,758	0.07
British	11,653	0.32
Bulgarian	1,479	0.04
Canadian	8,181	0.22
Carpatho Rusyn	44	0.00
Celtic	809	0.02
Croatian	5,425	0.15
Cypriot	63	0.00
Czech	5,900	0.16
Czechoslovakian	3,493	0.09
Danish	10,270	0.28
Dutch	18,200	0.49
Eastern European	8,891	0.24
English	127,632	3.45
Estonian	492	0.01
European	22,598	0.61
Finnish	3,079	0.08
French, except Basque	49,284	1.33
French Canadian	7,940	0.21
German	167,160	4.52
German Russian	134	0.00
Greek	11,016	0.30
Guyanese	549	0.01
Hawaii Native/Pacific Islander:	13,390	0.36
Melanesian: (239)	327	0.01
Fijian (235)	320	0.01
Other Melanesian (4)	7	0.00
Micronesian: (978)	1,604	0.04
Guamanian/Chamorro (955)	1,563	0.04
Other Micronesian (23)	41	0.00
Polynesian: (3,528)	6,994	0.19
Native Hawaiian (1,379)	3,788	0.10
Samoan (1,641)	2,404	0.07
Tongan (411)	541	0.01
Other Polynesian (97)	261	0.01
Other Pac. Isl., specified	157	0.00
Other Pac. Isl., not spec. (1,057)	4,308	0.12
Hispanic or Latino:	1,719,073	46.53
Central American:	238,191	6.45
Costa Rican	2,125	0.06
Guatemalan	65,922	1.78
Honduran	12,030	0.33
Nicaraguan	8,792	0.24
Panamanian	1,415	0.04
Salvadoran	126,197	3.42
Other Central American	21,710	0.59
Cuban	12,431	0.34
Dominican Republic	706	0.02
Mexican	1,091,686	29.55
Puerto Rican	13,427	0.36
South American:	31,518	0.85
Argentinean	5,126	0.14
Bolivian	1,301	0.04
Chilean	2,736	0.07
Colombian	5,819	0.16
Ecuadorian	4,692	0.13
Paraguayan	105	0.00
Peruvian	7,565	0.20
Uruguayan	320	0.01
Venezuelan	790	0.02
Other South American	3,064	0.08
Other Hispanic or Latino	331,114	8.96
Hungarian	19,612	0.53
Icelander	405	0.01
Iranian	44,521	1.20
Irish	138,379	3.75
Israeli	11,480	0.31
Italian	95,263	2.58
Latvian	1,687	0.05
Lithuanian	6,800	0.18
Luxemburger	163	0.00
Macedonian	341	0.01
Maltese	161	0.00
New Zealander	476	0.01
Northern European	1,389	0.04
Norwegian	21,111	0.57
Pennsylvania German	505	0.01
Polish	56,670	1.53
Portuguese	5,228	0.14
Romanian	10,274	0.28
Russian	87,419	2.37
Scandinavian	2,919	0.08
Scotch-Irish	22,037	0.60
Scottish	29,048	0.79
Serbian	1,214	0.03
Slavic	962	0.03
Slovak	1,792	0.05
Slovene	699	0.02
Soviet Union	25	0.00
Swedish	23,026	0.62
Swiss	6,169	0.17
Turkish	2,587	0.07
Ukrainian	12,292	0.33
United States or American	94,294	2.55
Welsh	10,233	0.28
West Indian, excl. Hispanic:	17,241	0.47
Bahamian	180	0.00
Barbadian	257	0.01
Belizean	7,742	0.21
Bermudan	72	0.00
British West Indian	383	0.01
Dutch West Indian	40	0.00
Haitian	980	0.03
Jamaican	5,537	0.15
Trinidadian and Tobagonian	800	0.02
U.S. Virgin Islander	94	0.00
West Indian	1,121	0.03
Other West Indian	35	0.00
White:	1,891,358	51.19
Not Hispanic (1,099,188)	1,167,030	31.59
Hispanic (634,848)	724,328	19.60
Yugoslavian	3,995	0.11

Los Banos

Place Type: City
County: Merced
Population: 25,869

Ancestry/Race	Number	%
Afghan	20	0.08
African American/Black:	1,307	5.05
Not Hispanic (1,007)	1,134	4.38
Hispanic (93)	173	0.67
African, sub-Saharan:	58	0.22
African	42	0.16
Cape Verdean	16	0.06
Alaska Native tribes, specified:	4	0.02
Aleut	1	0.00
Eskimo (1)	1	0.00
Tlingit-Haida	2	0.01
Am. Ind. or Alaska Nat., not spec.	229	0.89
American Indian tribes, specified:	403	1.56
Apache (19)	44	0.17
Blackfeet (7)	15	0.06
Cherokee (30)	107	0.41
Cheyenne	3	0.01
Chickasaw	4	0.02
Chippewa (3)	9	0.03
Choctaw (6)	20	0.08
Comanche (3)	10	0.04
Creek	4	0.02
Delaware (1)	2	0.01
Iroquois (1)	4	0.02
Kiowa	1	0.00
Latin American Indians (74)	94	0.36
Lumbee (1)	1	0.00
Navajo (5)	8	0.03
Osage (1)	3	0.01
Ottawa (1)	1	0.00
Paiute (3)	3	0.01
Pima	1	0.00
Potawatomi (7)	9	0.03
Pueblo (3)	3	0.01
Puget Sound Salish (1)	1	0.00
Seminole (1)	4	0.02
Sioux	2	0.01
Tohono O'Odham (5)	11	0.04
Yaqui (9)	9	0.03
All other tribes (15)	30	0.12
American Indian tribes, not spec.	45	0.17
Arab:	25	0.10
Arab/Arabic	25	0.10
Armenian	35	0.14
Asian:	983	3.80
Cambodian (9)	17	0.07
Chinese, ex. Taiwanese (72)	109	0.42
Filipino (319)	497	1.92
Indian (99)	147	0.57
Indonesian (6)	12	0.05
Japanese (28)	73	0.28
Korean (28)	47	0.18
Laotian (4)	6	0.02
Pakistani	1	0.00
Thai	3	0.01
Vietnamese (28)	33	0.13
Other Asian, not specified (2)	38	0.15
Austrian	17	0.07
Basque	127	0.49
Canadian	25	0.10
Czech	25	0.10
Czechoslovakian	7	0.03
Danish	246	0.95

Notes: 1. Figures in the "Number" column do not add up to the total population due to: a) Ancestry/Race overlap — e.g. persons can report being both White and Irish, b) persons of Hispanic origin can report being any race, c) persons reporting two ancestries are counted in both categories. 2. Numbers in parentheses indicate the number of persons reporting this ancestry/race alone, not in combination with any other ancestry/race. 3. Refer to the Explanation of Data in the front of the book for more detailed information.

Ancestry/Race	Number	%
Dutch	171	0.66
English	1,257	4.86
European	55	0.21
Finnish	18	0.07
French, except Basque	425	1.64
French Canadian	64	0.25
German	2,290	8.85
Hawaii Native/Pacific Islander:	183	0.71
Melanesian: (4)	4	0.02
Fijian (4)	4	0.02
Micronesian: (42)	61	0.24
Guamanian/Chamorro (39)	58	0.22
Other Micronesian (3)	3	0.01
Polynesian: (32)	86	0.33
Native Hawaiian (15)	54	0.21
Samoan (15)	25	0.10
Tongan (2)	5	0.02
Other Polynesian	2	0.01
Other Pac. Isl., not spec. (3)	32	0.12
Hispanic or Latino:	13,048	50.44
Central American:	207	0.80
Costa Rican	3	0.01
Guatemalan	34	0.13
Honduran	10	0.04
Nicaraguan	36	0.14
Panamanian	8	0.03
Salvadoran	97	0.37
Other Central American	19	0.07
Cuban	15	0.06
Dominican Republic	2	0.01
Mexican	10,753	41.57
Puerto Rican	142	0.55
South American:	50	0.19
Argentinean	7	0.03
Bolivian	1	0.00
Chilean	2	0.01
Colombian	2	0.01
Ecuadorian	4	0.02
Peruvian	26	0.10
Uruguayan	5	0.02
Other South American	3	0.01
Other Hispanic or Latino	1,879	7.26
Hungarian	20	0.08
Irish	1,709	6.60
Italian	1,739	6.72
Latvian	6	0.02
Lithuanian	6	0.02
Northern European	9	0.03
Norwegian	238	0.92
Polish	91	0.35
Portuguese	1,798	6.95
Russian	38	0.15
Scandinavian	25	0.10
Scotch-Irish	176	0.68
Scottish	243	0.94
Swedish	225	0.87
Swiss	41	0.16
Ukrainian	12	0.05
United States or American	842	3.25
Welsh	78	0.30
White:	16,481	63.71
Not Hispanic (10,290)	10,865	42.00
Hispanic (4,871)	5,616	21.71
Yugoslavian	11	0.04

Los Gatos

Place Type: Town
County: Santa Clara
Population: 28,592

Ancestry/Race	Number	%
Acadian/Cajun	32	0.11
African American/Black:	309	1.08
Not Hispanic (217)	292	1.02
Hispanic (9)	17	0.06
African, sub-Saharan:	67	0.23
African	13	0.05
Ethiopian	11	0.04
South African	43	0.15
Alaska Native tribes, specified:	5	0.02
Aleut (1)	4	0.01
Eskimo (1)	1	0.00
Alaska Native tribes, not specified	2	0.01
Am. Ind. or Alaska Nat., not spec.	61	0.21
Albanian	13	0.05
Alsatian	4	0.01
American Indian tribes, specified:	162	0.57
Apache (4)	5	0.02
Blackfeet	5	0.02
Cherokee (9)	60	0.21
Chickasaw (2)	6	0.02
Chippewa (1)	6	0.02
Choctaw (2)	14	0.05
Creek (2)	4	0.01
Crow	1	0.00
Iroquois (6)	7	0.02
Latin American Indians (10)	14	0.05
Navajo (3)	6	0.02
Osage (1)	2	0.01
Pima (1)	1	0.00
Potawatomi (1)	1	0.00
Pueblo	1	0.00
Seminole	2	0.01
Shoshone	1	0.00
Sioux (3)	7	0.02
Ute	1	0.00
Yaqui (4)	5	0.02
All other tribes (4)	13	0.05
American Indian tribes, not spec.	15	0.05
Arab:	185	0.64
Egyptian	61	0.21
Lebanese	45	0.16
Palestinian	42	0.15
Other Arab	37	0.13
Armenian	62	0.22
Asian:	2,704	9.46
Bangladeshi (10)	10	0.03
Cambodian (3)	7	0.02
Chinese, ex. Taiwanese (706)	872	3.05
Filipino (168)	282	0.99
Indian (308)	340	1.19
Indonesian (9)	11	0.04
Japanese (441)	576	2.01
Korean (165)	184	0.64
Laotian (2)	3	0.01
Malaysian	1	0.00
Pakistani (15)	18	0.06
Sri Lankan (9)	10	0.03
Taiwanese (26)	39	0.14
Thai (2)	5	0.02
Vietnamese (235)	257	0.90
Other Asian, specified (1)	5	0.02
Other Asian, not specified (17)	84	0.29
Assyrian/Chaldean/Syriac	34	0.12
Australian	48	0.17
Austrian	159	0.55
Basque	33	0.12
Belgian	30	0.10
Brazilian	19	0.07
British	487	1.70
Canadian	242	0.84
Celtic	17	0.06
Croatian	56	0.20
Czech	208	0.73
Czechoslovakian	96	0.33
Danish	383	1.34
Dutch	529	1.84
Eastern European	120	0.42
English	4,223	14.72
European	787	2.74
Finnish	173	0.60
French, except Basque	1,307	4.56
French Canadian	138	0.48
German	5,217	18.19
German Russian	7	0.02
Greek	333	1.16
Hawaii Native/Pacific Islander:	85	0.30
Melanesian: (2)	2	0.01
Fijian (2)	2	0.01
Micronesian: (4)	8	0.03
Guamanian/Chamorro (4)	8	0.03
Polynesian: (10)	52	0.18
Native Hawaiian (9)	50	0.17
Samoan (1)	2	0.01
Other Pac. Isl., specified	1	0.00
Other Pac. Isl., not spec. (4)	22	0.08
Hispanic or Latino:	1,491	5.21
Central American:	74	0.26
Costa Rican	8	0.03
Guatemalan	11	0.04
Honduran	4	0.01
Nicaraguan	23	0.08
Panamanian	2	0.01
Salvadoran	18	0.06
Other Central American	8	0.03
Cuban	22	0.08
Dominican Republic	1	0.00
Mexican	873	3.05
Puerto Rican	60	0.21
South American:	88	0.31
Argentinean	15	0.05
Chilean	19	0.07
Colombian	11	0.04
Ecuadorian	3	0.01
Paraguayan	1	0.00
Peruvian	17	0.06
Uruguayan	5	0.02
Venezuelan	5	0.02
Other South American	12	0.04
Other Hispanic or Latino	373	1.30
Hungarian	126	0.44
Icelander	20	0.07
Iranian	614	2.14
Irish	4,198	14.64
Israeli	90	0.31
Italian	2,423	8.45
Latvian	21	0.07
Lithuanian	107	0.37
Luxemburger	6	0.02
Maltese	4	0.01
Northern European	184	0.64
Norwegian	561	1.96
Pennsylvania German	8	0.03
Polish	865	3.02
Portuguese	461	1.61
Romanian	50	0.17
Russian	592	2.06
Scandinavian	31	0.11
Scotch-Irish	534	1.86
Scottish	1,046	3.65
Slavic	39	0.14
Slovak	32	0.11
Slovene	17	0.06
Swedish	736	2.57
Swiss	253	0.88
Turkish	34	0.12
Ukrainian	139	0.48
United States or American	975	3.40
Welsh	335	1.17
White:	25,640	89.68
Not Hispanic (23,821)	24,539	85.82
Hispanic (963)	1,101	3.85
Yugoslavian	102	0.36

Lynwood

Place Type: City
County: Los Angeles
Population: 69,845

Ancestry/Race	Number	%
Acadian/Cajun	4	0.01
African American/Black:	9,752	13.96
Not Hispanic (9,118)	9,281	13.29
Hispanic (333)	471	0.67
African, sub-Saharan:	437	0.63
African	437	0.63
Alaska Native tribes, specified:	1	0.00
Eskimo	1	0.00

Notes: 1. Figures in the "Number" column do not add up to the total population due to: a) Ancestry/Race overlap — e.g. persons can report being both White and Irish, b) persons of Hispanic origin can report being any race, c) persons reporting two ancestries are counted in both categories. 2. Numbers in parentheses indicate the number of persons reporting this ancestry/race alone, not in combination with any other ancestry/race. 3. Refer to the Explanation of Data in the front of the book for more detailed information.

Am. Ind. or Alaska Nat., not spec.	609	0.87
American Indian tribes, specified:	473	0.68
Apache (5)	6	0.01
Blackfeet	11	0.02
Cherokee (11)	42	0.06
Chickasaw	3	0.00
Chippewa	1	0.00
Choctaw (4)	16	0.02
Crow	1	0.00
Delaware (3)	3	0.00
Houma	1	0.00
Iroquois	3	0.00
Kiowa (3)	3	0.00
Latin American Indians (233)	286	0.41
Navajo (7)	18	0.03
Pueblo (12)	19	0.03
Sioux (2)	3	0.00
Yakama (1)	1	0.00
Yaqui (10)	15	0.02
All other tribes (18)	41	0.06
American Indian tribes, not spec.	83	0.12
Arab:	11	0.02
Egyptian	11	0.02
Asian:	728	1.04
Cambodian (23)	26	0.04
Chinese, ex. Taiwanese (22)	39	0.06
Filipino (161)	223	0.32
Indian (108)	139	0.20
Indonesian (7)	18	0.03
Japanese (24)	43	0.06
Korean (14)	17	0.02
Laotian (81)	86	0.12
Malaysian	1	0.00
Thai (63)	79	0.11
Vietnamese (8)	9	0.01
Other Asian, specified (1)	5	0.01
Other Asian, not specified (10)	43	0.06
Australian	22	0.03
Austrian	4	0.01
British	25	0.04
Canadian	13	0.02
Danish	28	0.04
Dutch	72	0.10
English	215	0.31
European	26	0.04
French, except Basque	91	0.13
French Canadian	29	0.04
German	181	0.26
Greek	10	0.01
Hawaii Native/Pacific Islander:	349	0.50
Micronesian: (17)	37	0.05
Guamanian/Chamorro (17)	36	0.05
Other Micronesian	1	0.00
Polynesian: (230)	273	0.39
Native Hawaiian (2)	17	0.02
Samoan (223)	241	0.35
Tongan (5)	8	0.01
Other Polynesian	7	0.01
Other Pac. Isl., not spec. (20)	39	0.06
Hispanic or Latino:	57,503	82.33
Central American:	3,441	4.93
Costa Rican	33	0.05
Guatemalan	959	1.37
Honduran	189	0.27
Nicaraguan	175	0.25
Panamanian	19	0.03
Salvadoran	1,775	2.54
Other Central American	291	0.42
Cuban	94	0.13
Dominican Republic	11	0.02
Mexican	46,491	66.56
Puerto Rican	173	0.25
South American:	231	0.33
Argentinean	13	0.02
Bolivian	6	0.01
Chilean	8	0.01
Colombian	35	0.05
Ecuadorian	81	0.12
Peruvian	61	0.09
Uruguayan	5	0.01
Venezuelan	1	0.00
Other South American	21	0.03
Other Hispanic or Latino	7,062	10.11
Hungarian	15	0.02
Icelander	13	0.02
Iranian	5	0.01
Irish	281	0.40
Italian	137	0.20
Norwegian	30	0.04
Polish	25	0.04
Portuguese	9	0.01
Romanian	24	0.03
Russian	22	0.03
Scotch-Irish	29	0.04
Scottish	26	0.04
Serbian	8	0.01
Swedish	27	0.04
Swiss	9	0.01
Turkish	8	0.01
United States or American	937	1.34
Welsh	9	0.01
West Indian, excl. Hispanic:	96	0.14
Barbadian	8	0.01
Belizean	23	0.03
British West Indian	15	0.02
Jamaican	36	0.05
West Indian	14	0.02
White:	26,084	37.35
Not Hispanic (2,044)	2,207	3.16
Hispanic (21,437)	23,877	34.19
Yugoslavian	6	0.01

Madera

Place Type: City
County: Madera
Population: 43,207

Ancestry/Race	Number	%
African American/Black:	1,886	4.37
Not Hispanic (1,426)	1,537	3.56
Hispanic (239)	349	0.81
African, sub-Saharan:	35	0.08
African	35	0.08
Alaska Native tribes, specified:	1	0.00
Eskimo	1	0.00
Am. Ind. or Alaska Nat., not spec.	517	1.20
American Indian tribes, specified:	1,104	2.56
Apache (7)	24	0.06
Blackfeet (5)	14	0.03
Cherokee (44)	102	0.24
Cheyenne	1	0.00
Chickasaw	6	0.01
Chippewa (5)	14	0.03
Choctaw (10)	32	0.07
Colville	2	0.00
Comanche (3)	6	0.01
Creek (5)	7	0.02
Crow	1	0.00
Delaware (2)	2	0.00
Iroquois	3	0.01
Latin American Indians (557)	677	1.57
Lumbee	2	0.00
Navajo (7)	11	0.03
Paiute (3)	5	0.01
Pima (2)	2	0.00
Pueblo (13)	20	0.05
Seminole (3)	5	0.01
Shoshone	3	0.01
Sioux (2)	6	0.01
Yakama (1)	4	0.01
Yaqui (18)	24	0.06
All other tribes (83)	131	0.30
American Indian tribes, not spec.	90	0.21
Arab:	74	0.17
Arab/Arabic	23	0.05
Iraqi	9	0.02
Jordanian	15	0.03
Lebanese	16	0.04
Palestinian	4	0.01
Other Arab	7	0.02
Armenian	56	0.13
Asian:	930	2.15
Chinese, ex. Taiwanese (72)	95	0.22
Filipino (162)	293	0.68
Hmong (42)	44	0.10
Indian (229)	302	0.70
Indonesian (2)	6	0.01
Japanese (40)	77	0.18
Korean (15)	22	0.05
Pakistani (28)	33	0.08
Taiwanese (1)	4	0.01
Thai (3)	3	0.01
Vietnamese (4)	4	0.01
Other Asian, specified	4	0.01
Other Asian, not specified (9)	43	0.10
Austrian	29	0.07
Basque	38	0.09
Brazilian	23	0.05
British	42	0.10
Canadian	79	0.18
Celtic	11	0.03
Czech	10	0.02
Czechoslovakian	7	0.02
Danish	114	0.26
Dutch	196	0.45
English	1,414	3.26
European	80	0.18
Finnish	27	0.06
French, except Basque	557	1.28
French Canadian	53	0.12
German	1,968	4.54
Greek	58	0.13
Hawaii Native/Pacific Islander:	97	0.22
Melanesian:	1	0.00
Fijian	1	0.00
Micronesian: (1)	8	0.02
Guamanian/Chamorro (1)	8	0.02
Polynesian: (30)	56	0.13
Native Hawaiian (7)	20	0.05
Samoan (18)	31	0.07
Tongan (5)	5	0.01
Other Pac. Isl., specified	1	0.00
Other Pac. Isl., not spec. (13)	31	0.07
Hispanic or Latino:	29,274	67.75
Central American:	197	0.46
Guatemalan	57	0.13
Honduran	27	0.06
Nicaraguan	9	0.02
Panamanian	2	0.00
Salvadoran	79	0.18
Other Central American	23	0.05
Cuban	21	0.05
Mexican	25,562	59.16
Puerto Rican	107	0.25
South American:	66	0.15
Argentinean	16	0.04
Bolivian	9	0.02
Chilean	1	0.00
Colombian	7	0.02
Ecuadorian	1	0.00
Peruvian	31	0.07
Other South American	1	0.00
Other Hispanic or Latino	3,321	7.69
Hungarian	33	0.08
Irish	1,527	3.52
Italian	1,222	2.82
Lithuanian	10	0.02
Norwegian	221	0.51
Pennsylvania German	10	0.02
Polish	142	0.33
Portuguese	467	1.08
Romanian	6	0.01
Russian	70	0.16
Scandinavian	45	0.10
Scotch-Irish	123	0.28
Scottish	228	0.53
Slovak	21	0.05
Swedish	242	0.56
Swiss	25	0.06

Notes: 1. Figures in the "Number" column do not add up to the total population due to: a) Ancestry/Race overlap — e.g. persons can report being both White and Irish, b) persons of Hispanic origin can report being any race, c) persons reporting two ancestries are counted in both categories. 2. Numbers in parentheses indicate the number of persons reporting this ancestry/race alone, not in combination with any other ancestry/race. 3. Refer to the Explanation of Data in the front of the book for more detailed information.

Ancestry/Race	Number	%
Ukrainian	29	0.07
United States or American	1,091	2.52
Welsh	42	0.10
West Indian, excl. Hispanic:	3	0.01
Belizean	3	0.01
White:	22,850	52.88
Not Hispanic (10,859)	11,389	26.36
Hispanic (9,945)	11,461	26.53

Magalia

Place Type: Census Designated Place
County: Butte
Population: 10,569

Ancestry/Race	Number	%
African American/Black:	64	0.61
Not Hispanic (39)	58	0.55
Hispanic (4)	6	0.06
Alaska Native tribes, specified:	1	0.01
Eskimo	1	0.01
Am. Ind. or Alaska Nat., not spec.	79	0.75
American Indian tribes, specified:	185	1.75
Apache (11)	12	0.11
Blackfeet (1)	7	0.07
Cherokee (15)	72	0.68
Cheyenne	2	0.02
Chickasaw	1	0.01
Chippewa (2)	2	0.02
Choctaw (3)	8	0.08
Comanche	1	0.01
Cree	4	0.04
Creek (2)	2	0.02
Delaware (1)	1	0.01
Iroquois (1)	6	0.06
Latin American Indians (12)	13	0.12
Navajo (1)	1	0.01
Osage	1	0.01
Paiute	2	0.02
Pima (1)	1	0.01
Pueblo	2	0.02
Shoshone	1	0.01
Sioux (6)	9	0.09
Tohono O'Odham (1)	1	0.01
Yaqui (7)	7	0.07
All other tribes (9)	29	0.27
American Indian tribes, not spec.	8	0.08
Arab:	7	0.07
Lebanese	7	0.07
Armenian	5	0.05
Asian:	99	0.94
Chinese, ex. Taiwanese (2)	8	0.08
Filipino (13)	24	0.23
Indian (6)	6	0.06
Indonesian (4)	6	0.06
Japanese (21)	27	0.26
Korean (10)	12	0.11
Thai	1	0.01
Vietnamese (3)	5	0.05
Other Asian, not specified (2)	10	0.09
Australian	34	0.32
Austrian	8	0.08
Basque	6	0.06
Belgian	27	0.26
British	81	0.77
Canadian	36	0.34
Celtic	8	0.08
Croatian	29	0.28
Czech	20	0.19
Danish	81	0.77
Dutch	335	3.18
English	1,835	17.40
European	125	1.19
Finnish	53	0.50
French, except Basque	742	7.04
French Canadian	50	0.47
German	2,238	21.22
Greek	49	0.46
Hawaii Native/Pacific Islander:	30	0.28
Polynesian: (8)	24	0.23
Native Hawaiian (5)	15	0.14
Samoan (3)	4	0.04
Other Polynesian	5	0.05
Other Pac. Isl., not spec. (2)	6	0.06
Hispanic or Latino:	516	4.88
Central American:	9	0.09
Costa Rican	1	0.01
Guatemalan	3	0.03
Nicaraguan	2	0.02
Panamanian	1	0.01
Other Central American	2	0.02
Cuban	5	0.05
Dominican Republic	1	0.01
Mexican	342	3.24
Puerto Rican	16	0.15
South American:	10	0.09
Bolivian	2	0.02
Chilean	3	0.03
Colombian	1	0.01
Peruvian	3	0.03
Other South American	1	0.01
Other Hispanic or Latino	133	1.26
Hungarian	53	0.50
Irish	1,559	14.78
Italian	594	5.63
Lithuanian	18	0.17
Norwegian	313	2.97
Polish	180	1.71
Portuguese	92	0.87
Romanian	31	0.29
Russian	126	1.19
Scandinavian	47	0.45
Scotch-Irish	350	3.32
Scottish	361	3.42
Slovak	18	0.17
Swedish	323	3.06
Swiss	17	0.16
Ukrainian	18	0.17
United States or American	778	7.38
Welsh	99	0.94
White:	10,205	96.56
Not Hispanic (9,611)	9,818	92.89
Hispanic (333)	387	3.66
Yugoslavian	8	0.08

Malibu

Place Type: City
County: Los Angeles
Population: 12,575

Ancestry/Race	Number	%
African American/Black:	148	1.18
Not Hispanic (109)	139	1.11
Hispanic (4)	9	0.07
African, sub-Saharan:	76	0.61
African	35	0.28
South African	41	0.33
Alaska Native tribes, not specified	1	0.01
Am. Ind. or Alaska Nat., not spec.	24	0.19
American Indian tribes, specified:	75	0.60
Apache (1)	4	0.03
Blackfeet	1	0.01
Cherokee (3)	23	0.18
Chickasaw	1	0.01
Chippewa	1	0.01
Choctaw (2)	3	0.02
Comanche (1)	1	0.01
Creek	1	0.01
Crow	2	0.02
Iroquois	2	0.02
Latin American Indians (3)	6	0.05
Navajo	4	0.03
Osage	2	0.02
Paiute (1)	1	0.01
Pima	4	0.03
Pueblo	3	0.02
Seminole	1	0.01
Sioux (1)	4	0.03
Yaqui (1)	1	0.01
All other tribes (5)	10	0.08
American Indian tribes, not spec.	11	0.09
Arab:	61	0.49
Arab/Arabic	11	0.09
Egyptian	37	0.30
Iraqi	7	0.06
Syrian	6	0.05
Armenian	57	0.46
Asian:	479	3.81
Cambodian (4)	5	0.04
Chinese, ex. Taiwanese (78)	120	0.95
Filipino (41)	82	0.65
Indian (30)	38	0.30
Indonesian (4)	9	0.07
Japanese (70)	109	0.87
Korean (40)	51	0.41
Laotian (1)	3	0.02
Malaysian (2)	3	0.02
Pakistani (1)	1	0.01
Sri Lankan	2	0.02
Taiwanese (7)	10	0.08
Thai (2)	2	0.02
Vietnamese (12)	16	0.13
Other Asian, specified (1)	1	0.01
Other Asian, not specified (8)	27	0.21
Australian	73	0.58
Austrian	169	1.35
Basque	7	0.06
Brazilian	14	0.11
British	161	1.29
Bulgarian	7	0.06
Canadian	100	0.80
Celtic	39	0.31
Czech	60	0.48
Czechoslovakian	26	0.21
Danish	93	0.74
Dutch	247	1.97
Eastern European	45	0.36
English	1,696	13.55
European	242	1.93
Finnish	89	0.71
French, except Basque	393	3.14
French Canadian	18	0.14
German	1,918	15.33
Greek	145	1.16
Hawaii Native/Pacific Islander:	40	0.32
Melanesian:	1	0.01
Fijian	1	0.01
Micronesian: (2)	4	0.03
Guamanian/Chamorro (2)	4	0.03
Polynesian: (9)	27	0.21
Native Hawaiian (6)	19	0.15
Samoan (2)	7	0.06
Other Polynesian (1)	1	0.01
Other Pac. Isl., not spec. (1)	8	0.06
Hispanic or Latino:	689	5.48
Central American:	81	0.64
Costa Rican	2	0.02
Guatemalan	25	0.20
Honduran	3	0.02
Nicaraguan	1	0.01
Salvadoran	44	0.35
Other Central American	6	0.05
Cuban	16	0.13
Dominican Republic	2	0.02
Mexican	375	2.98
Puerto Rican	29	0.23
South American:	34	0.27
Argentinean	9	0.07
Chilean	5	0.04
Colombian	6	0.05
Peruvian	8	0.06
Venezuelan	4	0.03
Other South American	2	0.02
Other Hispanic or Latino	152	1.21
Hungarian	152	1.21
Iranian	180	1.44
Irish	1,767	14.12
Israeli	19	0.15
Italian	967	7.73

Notes: 1. Figures in the "Number" column do not add up to the total population due to: a) Ancestry/Race overlap — e.g. persons can report being both White and Irish, b) persons of Hispanic origin can report being any race, c) persons reporting two ancestries are counted in both categories. 2. Numbers in parentheses indicate the number of persons reporting this ancestry/race alone, not in combination with any other ancestry/race. 3. Refer to the Explanation of Data in the front of the book for more detailed information.

Lithuanian	51	0.41
New Zealander	26	0.21
Northern European	43	0.34
Norwegian	176	1.41
Polish	616	4.92
Portuguese	14	0.11
Romanian	74	0.59
Russian	856	6.84
Scandinavian	37	0.30
Scotch-Irish	277	2.21
Scottish	430	3.44
Slavic	16	0.13
Soviet Union	8	0.06
Swedish	302	2.41
Swiss	45	0.36
Turkish	9	0.07
United States or American	618	4.94
Welsh	114	0.91
White:	11,876	94.44
Not Hispanic (11,134)	11,387	90.55
Hispanic (424)	489	3.89
Yugoslavian	90	0.72

Manhattan Beach

Place Type: City
County: Los Angeles
Population: 33,852

Ancestry/Race	Number	%
Afghan	14	0.04
African American/Black:	321	0.95
Not Hispanic (206)	310	0.92
Hispanic (2)	11	0.03
African, sub-Saharan:	67	0.20
African	16	0.05
South African	7	0.02
Ugandan	8	0.02
Other sub-Saharan African	36	0.11
Alaska Native tribes, specified:	4	0.01
Alaska Athabascan (1)	1	0.00
Tlingit-Haida (1)	1	0.00
All other tribes (1)	2	0.01
Alaska Native tribes, not specified	1	0.00
Am. Ind. or Alaska Nat., not spec.	60	0.18
Albanian	14	0.04
Alsatian	10	0.03
American Indian tribes, specified:	155	0.46
Apache (3)	7	0.02
Blackfeet (1)	6	0.02
Cherokee (12)	65	0.19
Chickasaw	2	0.01
Chippewa (2)	3	0.01
Choctaw (3)	9	0.03
Comanche	5	0.01
Cree (1)	2	0.01
Creek	1	0.00
Crow	2	0.01
Delaware (1)	3	0.01
Iroquois (1)	3	0.01
Latin American Indians (3)	10	0.03
Navajo (2)	3	0.01
Osage	1	0.00
Ottawa	1	0.00
Paiute (3)	3	0.01
Potawatomi	1	0.00
Pueblo (1)	4	0.01
Shoshone (1)	1	0.00
Sioux (5)	10	0.03
Yaqui	1	0.00
All other tribes (10)	12	0.04
American Indian tribes, not spec.	3	0.01
Arab:	243	0.71
Arab/Arabic	18	0.05
Egyptian	100	0.29
Iraqi	6	0.02
Lebanese	69	0.20
Syrian	50	0.15
Armenian	114	0.33
Asian:	2,695	7.96
Cambodian (3)	3	0.01
Chinese, ex. Taiwanese (555)	750	2.22
Filipino (161)	261	0.77
Indian (184)	206	0.61
Indonesian (8)	18	0.05
Japanese (611)	879	2.60
Korean (218)	288	0.85
Laotian (1)	3	0.01
Pakistani (10)	14	0.04
Taiwanese (47)	53	0.16
Thai (33)	42	0.12
Vietnamese (107)	116	0.34
Other Asian, specified (7)	11	0.03
Other Asian, not specified (21)	51	0.15
Australian	24	0.07
Austrian	318	0.93
Basque	16	0.05
Belgian	74	0.22
Brazilian	74	0.22
British	285	0.84
Canadian	184	0.54
Croatian	114	0.33
Czech	156	0.46
Czechoslovakian	126	0.37
Danish	346	1.02
Dutch	521	1.53
Eastern European	188	0.55
English	4,911	14.43
Estonian	25	0.07
European	652	1.92
Finnish	166	0.49
French, except Basque	1,386	4.07
French Canadian	243	0.71
German	6,707	19.70
Greek	365	1.07
Hawaii Native/Pacific Islander:	111	0.33
Micronesian: (12)	15	0.04
Guamanian/Chamorro (12)	15	0.04
Polynesian: (23)	71	0.21
Native Hawaiian (21)	63	0.19
Samoan (2)	4	0.01
Tongan	1	0.00
Other Polynesian	3	0.01
Other Pac. Isl., not spec. (2)	25	0.07
Hispanic or Latino:	1,756	5.19
Central American:	84	0.25
Costa Rican	16	0.05
Guatemalan	11	0.03
Honduran	7	0.02
Nicaraguan	14	0.04
Panamanian	1	0.00
Salvadoran	31	0.09
Other Central American	4	0.01
Cuban	91	0.27
Dominican Republic	6	0.02
Mexican	955	2.82
Puerto Rican	75	0.22
South American:	148	0.44
Argentinean	37	0.11
Bolivian	1	0.00
Chilean	14	0.04
Colombian	27	0.08
Ecuadorian	15	0.04
Peruvian	34	0.10
Venezuelan	1	0.00
Other South American	19	0.06
Other Hispanic or Latino	397	1.17
Hungarian	352	1.03
Iranian	272	0.80
Irish	4,737	13.92
Israeli	59	0.17
Italian	2,688	7.90
Latvian	101	0.30
Lithuanian	95	0.28
Macedonian	24	0.07
Maltese	7	0.02
Northern European	86	0.25
Norwegian	889	2.61
Polish	1,216	3.57
Portuguese	189	0.56
Romanian	99	0.29
Russian	1,558	4.58
Scandinavian	105	0.31
Scotch-Irish	942	2.77
Scottish	1,192	3.50
Serbian	75	0.22
Slavic	28	0.08
Slovak	110	0.32
Slovene	7	0.02
Swedish	1,108	3.26
Swiss	289	0.85
Turkish	42	0.12
Ukrainian	167	0.49
United States or American	1,566	4.60
Welsh	337	0.99
West Indian, excl. Hispanic:	68	0.20
Belizean	8	0.02
Haitian	10	0.03
Jamaican	27	0.08
Trinidadian and Tobagonian	14	0.04
U.S. Virgin Islander	9	0.03
White:	31,004	91.59
Not Hispanic (28,913)	29,635	87.54
Hispanic (1,211)	1,369	4.04
Yugoslavian	121	0.36

Manteca

Place Type: City
County: San Joaquin
Population: 49,258

Ancestry/Race	Number	%
Afghan	42	0.09
African American/Black:	1,746	3.54
Not Hispanic (1,336)	1,582	3.21
Hispanic (70)	164	0.33
African, sub-Saharan:	132	0.27
African	72	0.15
Sudanese	28	0.06
Zimbabwean	32	0.07
Alaska Native tribes, specified:	8	0.02
Aleut (4)	8	0.02
Am. Ind. or Alaska Nat., not spec.	374	0.76
Albanian	6	0.01
Alsatian	8	0.02
American Indian tribes, specified:	949	1.93
Apache (15)	42	0.09
Blackfeet (13)	31	0.06
Cherokee (93)	320	0.65
Cheyenne	3	0.01
Chickasaw (5)	8	0.02
Chippewa (17)	26	0.05
Choctaw (23)	74	0.15
Colville (3)	4	0.01
Comanche (5)	12	0.02
Cree	5	0.01
Creek (5)	8	0.02
Crow (1)	1	0.00
Delaware (1)	3	0.01
Iroquois	1	0.00
Kiowa (3)	6	0.01
Latin American Indians (40)	76	0.15
Lumbee (1)	1	0.00
Navajo (36)	56	0.11
Osage (1)	5	0.01
Ottawa (5)	9	0.02
Paiute (13)	21	0.04
Pima	1	0.00
Potawatomi (6)	8	0.02
Pueblo (2)	4	0.01
Puget Sound Salish (3)	6	0.01
Seminole (1)	9	0.02
Shoshone (4)	6	0.01
Sioux (23)	40	0.08
Tohono O'Odham (4)	4	0.01
Ute (2)	6	0.01
Yakama (2)	7	0.01
Yaqui (8)	11	0.02
Yuman (8)	8	0.02

Notes: 1. Figures in the "Number" column do not add up to the total population due to: a) Ancestry/Race overlap — e.g. persons can report being both White and Irish, b) persons of Hispanic origin can report being any race, c) persons reporting two ancestries are counted in both categories. 2. Numbers in parentheses indicate the number of persons reporting this ancestry/race alone, not in combination with any other ancestry/race. 3. Refer to the Explanation of Data in the front of the book for more detailed information.

Ancestry/Race	Number	%
All other tribes (87)	127	0.26
American Indian tribes, not spec.	107	0.22
Arab:	226	0.46
Arab/Arabic	120	0.24
Egyptian	47	0.10
Lebanese	23	0.05
Syrian	13	0.03
Other Arab	23	0.05
Armenian	108	0.22
Asian:	2,569	5.22
Cambodian (14)	15	0.03
Chinese, ex. Taiwanese (204)	323	0.66
Filipino (766)	1,176	2.39
Hmong (8)	9	0.02
Indian (392)	442	0.90
Indonesian (15)	34	0.07
Japanese (112)	223	0.45
Korean (78)	119	0.24
Laotian (23)	23	0.05
Malaysian	1	0.00
Pakistani (15)	16	0.03
Sri Lankan (3)	3	0.01
Taiwanese (3)	4	0.01
Thai (3)	7	0.01
Vietnamese (44)	53	0.11
Other Asian, specified (5)	5	0.01
Other Asian, not specified (23)	116	0.24
Assyrian/Chaldean/Syriac	18	0.04
Australian	18	0.04
Austrian	107	0.22
Basque	36	0.07
Belgian	48	0.10
Brazilian	13	0.03
British	116	0.24
Canadian	55	0.11
Carpatho Rusyn	7	0.01
Czech	69	0.14
Czechoslovakian	80	0.16
Danish	396	0.80
Dutch	1,140	2.32
English	4,032	8.19
Estonian	9	0.02
European	331	0.67
Finnish	62	0.13
French, except Basque	1,306	2.65
French Canadian	291	0.59
German	6,205	12.61
German Russian	7	0.01
Greek	167	0.34
Hawaii Native/Pacific Islander:	444	0.90
Melanesian: (15)	18	0.04
Fijian (15)	18	0.04
Micronesian: (52)	86	0.17
Guamanian/Chamorro (52)	85	0.17
Other Micronesian	1	0.00
Polynesian: (88)	263	0.53
Native Hawaiian (66)	222	0.45
Samoan (16)	33	0.07
Tongan (6)	6	0.01
Other Polynesian	2	0.00
Other Pac. Isl., not spec. (18)	77	0.16
Hispanic or Latino:	12,363	25.10
Central American:	121	0.25
Costa Rican	4	0.01
Guatemalan	4	0.01
Honduran	14	0.03
Nicaraguan	34	0.07
Panamanian	8	0.02
Salvadoran	37	0.08
Other Central American	20	0.04
Cuban	55	0.11
Mexican	9,732	19.76
Puerto Rican	451	0.92
South American:	76	0.15
Argentinean	7	0.01
Chilean	11	0.02
Colombian	21	0.04
Ecuadorian	2	0.00
Peruvian	32	0.06
Uruguayan	2	0.00
Venezuelan	1	0.00
Other Hispanic or Latino	1,928	3.91
Hungarian	192	0.39
Icelander	12	0.02
Iranian	31	0.06
Irish	4,911	9.98
Israeli	17	0.03
Italian	2,615	5.31
Latvian	14	0.03
Maltese	6	0.01
New Zealander	45	0.09
Norwegian	891	1.81
Pennsylvania German	26	0.05
Polish	506	1.03
Portuguese	2,852	5.80
Russian	131	0.27
Scandinavian	100	0.20
Scotch-Irish	838	1.70
Scottish	666	1.35
Slavic	8	0.02
Slovak	8	0.02
Slovene	17	0.03
Swedish	722	1.47
Swiss	320	0.65
United States or American	2,924	5.94
Welsh	324	0.66
West Indian, excl. Hispanic:	95	0.19
Belizean	10	0.02
Dutch West Indian	37	0.08
Jamaican	48	0.10
White:	39,229	79.64
Not Hispanic (31,556)	33,141	67.28
Hispanic (4,978)	6,088	12.36
Yugoslavian	93	0.19

Marina

Place Type: City
County: Monterey
Population: 25,101

Ancestry/Race	Number	%
African American/Black:	4,104	16.35
Not Hispanic (3,494)	3,917	15.60
Hispanic (106)	187	0.74
African, sub-Saharan:	200	0.80
African	125	0.50
Nigerian	75	0.30
Alaska Native tribes, specified:	10	0.04
Eskimo (1)	8	0.03
Tlingit-Haida	2	0.01
Am. Ind. or Alaska Nat., not spec.	202	0.80
American Indian tribes, specified:	358	1.43
Apache (11)	28	0.11
Blackfeet (3)	14	0.06
Cherokee (18)	97	0.39
Cheyenne (2)	6	0.02
Chickasaw (1)	3	0.01
Chippewa	7	0.03
Choctaw (1)	8	0.03
Comanche	3	0.01
Creek (2)	4	0.02
Crow (1)	1	0.00
Delaware	1	0.00
Iroquois	4	0.02
Latin American Indians (26)	117	0.47
Navajo	10	0.04
Osage (2)	2	0.01
Seminole	2	0.01
Shoshone	1	0.00
Sioux (5)	11	0.04
Ute	1	0.00
Yaqui (1)	1	0.00
All other tribes (19)	37	0.15
American Indian tribes, not spec.	11	0.04
Arab:	121	0.48
Egyptian	28	0.11
Iraqi	5	0.02
Lebanese	88	0.35
Armenian	5	0.02
Asian:	5,348	21.31
Cambodian (5)	5	0.02
Chinese, ex. Taiwanese (209)	297	1.18
Filipino (1,375)	1,831	7.29
Hmong (2)	2	0.01
Indian (119)	197	0.78
Indonesian (4)	8	0.03
Japanese (402)	744	2.96
Korean (1,058)	1,313	5.23
Malaysian (1)	2	0.01
Pakistani (6)	6	0.02
Sri Lankan (1)	1	0.00
Taiwanese (2)	3	0.01
Thai (64)	82	0.33
Vietnamese (687)	761	3.03
Other Asian, specified (1)	3	0.01
Other Asian, not specified (39)	93	0.37
Austrian	33	0.13
Basque	4	0.02
Belgian	24	0.10
Brazilian	10	0.04
British	67	0.27
Canadian	37	0.15
Celtic	10	0.04
Croatian	25	0.10
Czech	54	0.22
Czechoslovakian	44	0.18
Danish	48	0.19
Dutch	184	0.73
English	1,256	5.01
European	198	0.79
Finnish	31	0.12
French, except Basque	365	1.46
French Canadian	61	0.24
German	2,064	8.24
Greek	33	0.13
Guyanese	6	0.02
Hawaii Native/Pacific Islander:	911	3.63
Melanesian: (28)	46	0.18
Fijian (28)	46	0.18
Micronesian: (188)	312	1.24
Guamanian/Chamorro (169)	289	1.15
Other Micronesian (19)	23	0.09
Polynesian: (265)	456	1.82
Native Hawaiian (73)	208	0.83
Samoan (180)	231	0.92
Tongan (11)	13	0.05
Other Polynesian (1)	4	0.02
Other Pac. Isl., not spec. (23)	97	0.39
Hispanic or Latino:	5,822	23.19
Central American:	183	0.73
Costa Rican	3	0.01
Guatemalan	20	0.08
Honduran	10	0.04
Nicaraguan	8	0.03
Panamanian	27	0.11
Salvadoran	107	0.43
Other Central American	8	0.03
Cuban	20	0.08
Dominican Republic	2	0.01
Mexican	4,752	18.93
Puerto Rican	284	1.13
South American:	72	0.29
Chilean	21	0.08
Colombian	17	0.07
Ecuadorian	4	0.02
Paraguayan	2	0.01
Peruvian	13	0.05
Venezuelan	3	0.01
Other South American	12	0.05
Other Hispanic or Latino	509	2.03
Hungarian	53	0.21
Iranian	12	0.05
Irish	1,257	5.02
Italian	972	3.88
Lithuanian	14	0.06
Luxemburger	4	0.02
Northern European	6	0.02
Norwegian	167	0.67
Pennsylvania German	4	0.02

Notes: 1. Figures in the "Number" column do not add up to the total population due to: a) Ancestry/Race overlap — e.g. persons can report being both White and Irish, b) persons of Hispanic origin can report being any race, c) persons reporting two ancestries are counted in both categories. 2. Numbers in parentheses indicate the number of persons reporting this ancestry/race alone, not in combination with any other ancestry/race. 3. Refer to the Explanation of Data in the front of the book for more detailed information.

Polish	188	0.75
Portuguese	221	0.88
Romanian	7	0.03
Russian	104	0.42
Scandinavian	27	0.11
Scotch-Irish	166	0.66
Scottish	242	0.97
Slavic	11	0.04
Slovak	42	0.17
Slovene	11	0.04
Swedish	208	0.83
Swiss	51	0.20
Turkish	10	0.04
Ukrainian	31	0.12
United States or American	495	1.98
Welsh	89	0.36
West Indian, excl. Hispanic:	16	0.06
Belizean	16	0.06
White:	12,402	49.41
Not Hispanic (9,500)	10,535	41.97
Hispanic (1,479)	1,867	7.44
Yugoslavian	37	0.15

Martinez

Place Type: City
County: Contra Costa
Population: 35,866

Ancestry/Race	Number	%
Afghan	113	0.31
African American/Black:	1,423	3.97
Not Hispanic (1,181)	1,375	3.83
Hispanic (20)	48	0.13
African, sub-Saharan:	41	0.11
African	41	0.11
Alaska Native tribes, specified:	7	0.02
Alaska Athabascan (1)	1	0.00
Eskimo (2)	3	0.01
Tlingit-Haida	3	0.01
Am. Ind. or Alaska Nat., not spec.	159	0.44
Alsatian	7	0.02
American Indian tribes, specified:	556	1.55
Apache (16)	25	0.07
Blackfeet (3)	31	0.09
Cherokee (35)	190	0.53
Cheyenne (1)	2	0.01
Chickasaw (4)	13	0.04
Chippewa (8)	10	0.03
Choctaw (17)	49	0.14
Comanche (3)	5	0.01
Creek (4)	17	0.05
Crow	1	0.00
Delaware	2	0.01
Iroquois (2)	13	0.04
Kiowa	2	0.01
Latin American Indians (11)	18	0.05
Navajo (15)	21	0.06
Osage	1	0.00
Paiute	4	0.01
Potawatomi (5)	10	0.03
Pueblo (6)	7	0.02
Puget Sound Salish (1)	4	0.01
Seminole (1)	8	0.02
Shoshone	1	0.00
Sioux (12)	29	0.08
Ute (4)	6	0.02
Yakama	4	0.01
Yaqui (1)	5	0.01
Yuman	1	0.00
All other tribes (33)	77	0.21
American Indian tribes, not spec.	33	0.09
Arab:	85	0.24
Arab/Arabic	8	0.02
Egyptian	40	0.11
Iraqi	4	0.01
Jordanian	9	0.02
Lebanese	6	0.02
Other Arab	18	0.05
Armenian	61	0.17
Asian:	3,122	8.70
Cambodian (4)	4	0.01
Chinese, ex. Taiwanese (531)	728	2.03
Filipino (784)	1,043	2.91
Hmong (16)	16	0.04
Indian (251)	332	0.93
Indonesian (15)	29	0.08
Japanese (267)	410	1.14
Korean (231)	255	0.71
Laotian (13)	14	0.04
Pakistani (16)	27	0.08
Sri Lankan (12)	12	0.03
Taiwanese (6)	6	0.02
Thai (20)	32	0.09
Vietnamese (87)	104	0.29
Other Asian, specified (8)	10	0.03
Other Asian, not specified (41)	100	0.28
Assyrian/Chaldean/Syriac	14	0.04
Australian	15	0.04
Austrian	103	0.28
Basque	44	0.12
Belgian	30	0.08
Brazilian	13	0.04
British	265	0.73
Bulgarian	7	0.02
Canadian	170	0.47
Celtic	45	0.12
Croatian	74	0.20
Czech	139	0.38
Czechoslovakian	50	0.14
Danish	434	1.20
Dutch	837	2.31
Eastern European	6	0.02
English	4,536	12.54
European	654	1.81
Finnish	239	0.66
French, except Basque	1,198	3.31
French Canadian	191	0.53
German	5,647	15.61
Greek	343	0.95
Hawaii Native/Pacific Islander:	223	0.62
Melanesian:	1	0.00
Fijian	1	0.00
Micronesian: (20)	49	0.14
Guamanian/Chamorro (17)	44	0.12
Other Micronesian (3)	5	0.01
Polynesian: (50)	116	0.32
Native Hawaiian (31)	84	0.23
Samoan (14)	24	0.07
Tongan (2)	2	0.01
Other Polynesian (3)	6	0.02
Other Pac. Isl., specified	1	0.00
Other Pac. Isl., not spec. (13)	56	0.16
Hispanic or Latino:	3,660	10.20
Central American:	238	0.66
Costa Rican	18	0.05
Guatemalan	16	0.04
Honduran	3	0.01
Nicaraguan	66	0.18
Panamanian	11	0.03
Salvadoran	99	0.28
Other Central American	25	0.07
Cuban	37	0.10
Dominican Republic	13	0.04
Mexican	2,096	5.84
Puerto Rican	135	0.38
South American:	169	0.47
Argentinean	25	0.07
Bolivian	3	0.01
Chilean	17	0.05
Colombian	22	0.06
Ecuadorian	5	0.01
Paraguayan	3	0.01
Peruvian	61	0.17
Uruguayan	1	0.00
Venezuelan	6	0.02
Other South American	26	0.07
Other Hispanic or Latino	972	2.71
Hungarian	124	0.34
Icelander	15	0.04
Iranian	66	0.18
Irish	5,318	14.70
Israeli	21	0.06
Italian	3,771	10.43
Lithuanian	46	0.13
Maltese	53	0.15
Northern European	81	0.22
Norwegian	922	2.55
Pennsylvania German	12	0.03
Polish	688	1.90
Portuguese	1,093	3.02
Romanian	22	0.06
Russian	423	1.17
Scandinavian	99	0.27
Scotch-Irish	659	1.82
Scottish	937	2.59
Serbian	14	0.04
Slavic	187	0.52
Slovak	12	0.03
Swedish	1,026	2.84
Swiss	193	0.53
Turkish	10	0.03
Ukrainian	127	0.35
United States or American	1,661	4.59
Welsh	558	1.54
West Indian, excl. Hispanic:	58	0.16
Jamaican	39	0.11
Trinidadian and Tobagonian	10	0.03
West Indian	9	0.02
White:	30,572	85.24
Not Hispanic (27,096)	28,188	78.59
Hispanic (1,968)	2,384	6.65
Yugoslavian	131	0.36

Marysville

Place Type: City
County: Yuba
Population: 12,268

Ancestry/Race	Number	%
Acadian/Cajun	16	0.13
African American/Black:	722	5.89
Not Hispanic (548)	669	5.45
Hispanic (41)	53	0.43
African, sub-Saharan:	50	0.41
African	50	0.41
Alaska Native tribes, specified:	2	0.02
Tlingit-Haida	2	0.02
Am. Ind. or Alaska Nat., not spec.	162	1.32
American Indian tribes, specified:	427	3.48
Apache (6)	17	0.14
Blackfeet (3)	24	0.20
Cherokee (80)	197	1.61
Cheyenne (2)	3	0.02
Chickasaw (3)	7	0.06
Chippewa (4)	10	0.08
Choctaw (4)	18	0.15
Cree (1)	2	0.02
Creek	5	0.04
Delaware (3)	3	0.02
Iroquois	3	0.02
Latin American Indians (8)	8	0.07
Menominee (2)	2	0.02
Navajo (2)	5	0.04
Osage	1	0.01
Pima (1)	1	0.01
Potawatomi (2)	6	0.05
Pueblo (1)	3	0.02
Puget Sound Salish	2	0.02
Seminole (1)	3	0.02
Shoshone (1)	3	0.02
Sioux (4)	6	0.05
Tohono O'Odham	2	0.02
Yakama	1	0.01
Yaqui (1)	6	0.05
Yuman	1	0.01
All other tribes (65)	88	0.72
American Indian tribes, not spec.	21	0.17
Arab:	7	0.06

Notes: 1. Figures in the "Number" column do not add up to the total population due to: a) Ancestry/Race overlap — e.g. persons can report being both White and Irish, b) persons of Hispanic origin can report being any race, c) persons reporting two ancestries are counted in both categories. 2. Numbers in parentheses indicate the number of persons reporting this ancestry/race alone, not in combination with any other ancestry/race. 3. Refer to the Explanation of Data in the front of the book for more detailed information.

Palestinian	7	0.06
Armenian	15	0.12
Asian:	892	7.27
Cambodian (23)	29	0.24
Chinese, ex. Taiwanese (116)	132	1.08
Filipino (116)	156	1.27
Hmong (227)	240	1.96
Indian (59)	79	0.64
Indonesian (4)	4	0.03
Japanese (65)	96	0.78
Korean (21)	35	0.29
Laotian (22)	27	0.22
Sri Lankan (2)	2	0.02
Thai (7)	16	0.13
Vietnamese (53)	53	0.43
Other Asian, not specified (15)	23	0.19
Australian	6	0.05
Austrian	17	0.14
Basque	30	0.24
Belgian	14	0.11
British	19	0.15
Canadian	21	0.17
Czech	22	0.18
Czechoslovakian	27	0.22
Danish	100	0.81
Dutch	261	2.12
English	1,115	9.07
European	179	1.46
French, except Basque	311	2.53
French Canadian	93	0.76
German	1,854	15.08
Greek	64	0.52
Hawaii Native/Pacific Islander:	60	0.49
Melanesian:	4	0.03
Fijian	4	0.03
Micronesian: (8)	19	0.15
Guamanian/Chamorro (8)	19	0.15
Polynesian: (8)	14	0.11
Native Hawaiian (7)	13	0.11
Samoan (1)	1	0.01
Other Pac. Isl., not spec. (5)	23	0.19
Hispanic or Latino:	2,152	17.54
Central American:	10	0.08
Guatemalan	1	0.01
Panamanian	4	0.03
Salvadoran	5	0.04
Cuban	11	0.09
Mexican	1,745	14.22
Puerto Rican	56	0.46
South American:	12	0.10
Colombian	6	0.05
Peruvian	6	0.05
Other Hispanic or Latino	318	2.59
Hungarian	32	0.26
Irish	1,197	9.73
Italian	532	4.33
Lithuanian	16	0.13
Northern European	14	0.11
Norwegian	99	0.81
Polish	190	1.54
Portuguese	93	0.76
Russian	36	0.29
Scandinavian	4	0.03
Scotch-Irish	114	0.93
Scottish	274	2.23
Slavic	4	0.03
Swedish	170	1.38
Swiss	22	0.18
United States or American	851	6.92
Welsh	34	0.28
West Indian, excl. Hispanic:	11	0.09
British West Indian	11	0.09
White:	9,281	75.65
Not Hispanic (8,069)	8,478	69.11
Hispanic (635)	803	6.55

Maywood

Place Type: City
County: Los Angeles
Population: 28,083

Ancestry/Race	Number	%
African American/Black:	147	0.52
Not Hispanic (43)	46	0.16
Hispanic (59)	101	0.36
African, sub-Saharan:	23	0.08
African	23	0.08
Am. Ind. or Alaska Nat., not spec.	201	0.72
American Indian tribes, specified:	160	0.57
Apache (6)	7	0.02
Chickasaw (1)	1	0.00
Choctaw (2)	6	0.02
Comanche (1)	1	0.00
Iroquois	2	0.01
Latin American Indians (93)	110	0.39
Navajo (5)	6	0.02
Pima	2	0.01
Pueblo (4)	7	0.02
Sioux	3	0.01
Tohono O'Odham (6)	6	0.02
Yaqui (4)	4	0.01
Yuman (1)	1	0.00
All other tribes (4)	4	0.01
American Indian tribes, not spec.	27	0.10
Asian:	143	0.51
Cambodian	1	0.00
Chinese, ex. Taiwanese (6)	7	0.02
Filipino (25)	35	0.12
Indian (17)	22	0.08
Japanese (10)	20	0.07
Korean (23)	25	0.09
Laotian (1)	1	0.00
Malaysian (1)	1	0.00
Thai (5)	5	0.02
Vietnamese (6)	7	0.02
Other Asian, specified	2	0.01
Other Asian, not specified (5)	17	0.06
Canadian	12	0.04
Czech	4	0.01
Dutch	34	0.12
English	43	0.15
French, except Basque	56	0.20
German	87	0.31
Greek	9	0.03
Hawaii Native/Pacific Islander:	53	0.19
Melanesian: (3)	4	0.01
Fijian (3)	4	0.01
Micronesian: (1)	2	0.01
Guamanian/Chamorro (1)	2	0.01
Polynesian: (31)	32	0.11
Native Hawaiian (6)	6	0.02
Samoan (22)	22	0.08
Tongan (3)	4	0.01
Other Pac. Isl., specified	2	0.01
Other Pac. Isl., not spec. (1)	13	0.05
Hispanic or Latino:	27,051	96.33
Central American:	1,517	5.40
Costa Rican	3	0.01
Guatemalan	309	1.10
Honduran	86	0.31
Nicaraguan	195	0.69
Panamanian	4	0.01
Salvadoran	768	2.73
Other Central American	152	0.54
Cuban	209	0.74
Mexican	21,556	76.76
Puerto Rican	51	0.18
South American:	130	0.46
Argentinean	5	0.02
Chilean	5	0.02
Colombian	22	0.08
Ecuadorian	36	0.13
Peruvian	43	0.15
Other South American	19	0.07
Other Hispanic or Latino	3,588	12.78
Irish	76	0.27
Italian	89	0.32
Lithuanian	3	0.01
Norwegian	6	0.02
Polish	26	0.09
Portuguese	6	0.02
Russian	16	0.06
Scotch-Irish	20	0.07
Swiss	6	0.02
United States or American	416	1.48
West Indian, excl. Hispanic:	7	0.02
West Indian	7	0.02
White:	13,267	47.24
Not Hispanic (739)	793	2.82
Hispanic (11,334)	12,474	44.42

McKinleyville

Place Type: Census Designated Place
County: Humboldt
Population: 13,599

Ancestry/Race	Number	%
African American/Black:	92	0.68
Not Hispanic (48)	84	0.62
Hispanic (4)	8	0.06
African, sub-Saharan:	20	0.15
African	19	0.14
Nigerian	1	0.01
Alaska Native tribes, specified:	20	0.15
Aleut (2)	6	0.04
Eskimo (3)	7	0.05
Tlingit-Haida (6)	7	0.05
Alaska Native tribes, not specified	1	0.01
Am. Ind. or Alaska Nat., not spec.	150	1.10
Alsatian	6	0.04
American Indian tribes, specified:	840	6.18
Apache (5)	10	0.07
Blackfeet (6)	30	0.22
Cherokee (30)	155	1.14
Chickasaw (7)	11	0.08
Chippewa (5)	7	0.05
Choctaw (19)	36	0.26
Cree	1	0.01
Creek	3	0.02
Crow	5	0.04
Delaware (1)	1	0.01
Iroquois (8)	17	0.13
Latin American Indians (6)	12	0.09
Navajo (3)	7	0.05
Osage (6)	7	0.05
Ottawa (1)	1	0.01
Potawatomi (1)	2	0.01
Pueblo (1)	1	0.01
Puget Sound Salish (7)	7	0.05
Seminole (1)	2	0.01
Shoshone	1	0.01
Sioux (11)	24	0.18
Tohono O'Odham	1	0.01
Ute	1	0.01
All other tribes (372)	498	3.66
American Indian tribes, not spec.	47	0.35
Arab:	6	0.04
Arab/Arabic	6	0.04
Armenian	27	0.20
Asian:	223	1.64
Cambodian (3)	4	0.03
Chinese, ex. Taiwanese (31)	38	0.28
Filipino (19)	41	0.30
Hmong	1	0.01
Indian (20)	26	0.19
Indonesian (1)	3	0.02
Japanese (38)	53	0.39
Korean (14)	24	0.18
Laotian (2)	4	0.03
Malaysian (1)	1	0.01
Pakistani (1)	1	0.01
Thai (5)	7	0.05
Vietnamese (2)	5	0.04
Other Asian, specified (5)	6	0.04

Notes: 1. Figures in the "Number" column do not add up to the total population due to: a) Ancestry/Race overlap — e.g. persons can report being both White and Irish, b) persons of Hispanic origin can report being any race, c) persons reporting two ancestries are counted in both categories. 2. Numbers in parentheses indicate the number of persons reporting this ancestry/race alone, not in combination with any other ancestry/race. 3. Refer to the Explanation of Data in the front of the book for more detailed information.

Other Asian, not specified (1)	9	0.07
Australian	7	0.05
Austrian	57	0.42
Basque	35	0.26
Belgian	18	0.13
Brazilian	24	0.18
British	180	1.32
Canadian	25	0.18
Celtic	41	0.30
Croatian	7	0.05
Czech	26	0.19
Czechoslovakian	45	0.33
Danish	245	1.80
Dutch	436	3.21
Eastern European	7	0.05
English	1,583	11.64
Estonian	12	0.09
European	384	2.82
Finnish	119	0.87
French, except Basque	758	5.57
French Canadian	87	0.64
German	2,302	16.93
Greek	28	0.21
Hawaii Native/Pacific Islander:	29	0.21
Micronesian:	2	0.01
Guamanian/Chamorro	2	0.01
Polynesian: (6)	22	0.16
Native Hawaiian (4)	17	0.13
Samoan (2)	3	0.02
Tongan	1	0.01
Other Polynesian	1	0.01
Other Pac. Isl., specified	1	0.01
Other Pac. Isl., not spec. (2)	4	0.03
Hispanic or Latino:	589	4.33
Central American:	13	0.10
Guatemalan	1	0.01
Honduran	7	0.05
Panamanian	3	0.02
Salvadoran	1	0.01
Other Central American	1	0.01
Cuban	10	0.07
Dominican Republic	1	0.01
Mexican	400	2.94
Puerto Rican	19	0.14
South American:	18	0.13
Bolivian	4	0.03
Chilean	3	0.02
Ecuadorian	5	0.04
Peruvian	5	0.04
Other South American	1	0.01
Other Hispanic or Latino	128	0.94
Hungarian	32	0.24
Irish	2,119	15.58
Italian	617	4.54
Lithuanian	33	0.24
Northern European	167	1.23
Norwegian	410	3.01
Pennsylvania German	6	0.04
Polish	141	1.04
Portuguese	431	3.17
Romanian	2	0.01
Russian	177	1.30
Scandinavian	34	0.25
Scotch-Irish	250	1.84
Scottish	412	3.03
Slavic	5	0.04
Slovak	9	0.07
Slovene	9	0.07
Swedish	436	3.21
Swiss	117	0.86
Turkish	11	0.08
Ukrainian	20	0.15
United States or American	1,036	7.62
Welsh	122	0.90
White:	12,519	92.06
Not Hispanic (11,649)	12,181	89.57
Hispanic (269)	338	2.49
Yugoslavian	35	0.26

Menlo Park

Place Type: City
County: San Mateo
Population: 30,785

Ancestry/Race	Number	%
African American/Black:	2,333	7.58
Not Hispanic (2,124)	2,266	7.36
Hispanic (39)	67	0.22
African, sub-Saharan:	111	0.36
African	79	0.26
South African	32	0.10
Alaska Native tribes, specified:	6	0.02
Alaska Athabascan	1	0.00
Aleut	2	0.01
Eskimo (1)	1	0.00
Tlingit-Haida (2)	2	0.01
Am. Ind. or Alaska Nat., not spec.	145	0.47
American Indian tribes, specified:	148	0.48
Apache (4)	7	0.02
Blackfeet (1)	3	0.01
Cherokee (5)	33	0.11
Cheyenne (1)	1	0.00
Chickasaw	1	0.00
Chippewa (1)	5	0.02
Choctaw	2	0.01
Cree	2	0.01
Creek	3	0.01
Iroquois (1)	3	0.01
Latin American Indians (18)	44	0.14
Navajo (1)	6	0.02
Osage	2	0.01
Potawatomi (1)	1	0.00
Pueblo (2)	5	0.02
Seminole	3	0.01
Shoshone (1)	1	0.00
Sioux (4)	7	0.02
Yaqui (1)	1	0.00
All other tribes (6)	18	0.06
American Indian tribes, not spec.	4	0.01
Arab:	143	0.46
Iraqi	9	0.03
Jordanian	37	0.12
Lebanese	27	0.09
Moroccan	19	0.06
Syrian	51	0.17
Armenian	61	0.20
Asian:	2,690	8.74
Cambodian (2)	2	0.01
Chinese, ex. Taiwanese (863)	996	3.24
Filipino (219)	302	0.98
Indian (333)	394	1.28
Indonesian (11)	20	0.06
Japanese (449)	591	1.92
Korean (146)	171	0.56
Laotian (6)	6	0.02
Malaysian (1)	7	0.02
Pakistani (5)	6	0.02
Sri Lankan (6)	7	0.02
Taiwanese (22)	24	0.08
Thai (22)	33	0.11
Vietnamese (50)	67	0.22
Other Asian, specified (4)	9	0.03
Other Asian, not specified (19)	55	0.18
Assyrian/Chaldean/Syriac	48	0.16
Australian	55	0.18
Austrian	192	0.62
Basque	16	0.05
Belgian	60	0.19
Brazilian	39	0.13
British	327	1.06
Bulgarian	11	0.04
Canadian	190	0.62
Celtic	27	0.09
Croatian	40	0.13
Czech	116	0.38
Czechoslovakian	75	0.24
Danish	309	1.00
Dutch	402	1.31
Eastern European	58	0.19
English	4,298	13.96
Estonian	13	0.04
European	361	1.17
Finnish	129	0.42
French, except Basque	1,059	3.44
French Canadian	218	0.71
German	4,285	13.92
Greek	171	0.56
Hawaii Native/Pacific Islander:	517	1.68
Melanesian: (21)	40	0.13
Fijian (21)	40	0.13
Micronesian: (5)	11	0.04
Guamanian/Chamorro (3)	5	0.02
Other Micronesian (2)	6	0.02
Polynesian: (325)	409	1.33
Native Hawaiian (13)	36	0.12
Samoan (60)	73	0.24
Tongan (251)	290	0.94
Other Polynesian (1)	10	0.03
Other Pac. Isl., specified	2	0.01
Other Pac. Isl., not spec. (29)	55	0.18
Hispanic or Latino:	4,803	15.60
Central American:	390	1.27
Costa Rican	8	0.03
Guatemalan	41	0.13
Honduran	12	0.04
Nicaraguan	57	0.19
Panamanian	6	0.02
Salvadoran	234	0.76
Other Central American	32	0.10
Cuban	31	0.10
Dominican Republic	6	0.02
Mexican	3,502	11.38
Puerto Rican	46	0.15
South American:	152	0.49
Argentinean	18	0.06
Bolivian	23	0.07
Chilean	15	0.05
Colombian	25	0.08
Peruvian	49	0.16
Uruguayan	1	0.00
Venezuelan	5	0.02
Other South American	16	0.05
Other Hispanic or Latino	676	2.20
Hungarian	183	0.59
Icelander	7	0.02
Iranian	217	0.70
Irish	3,214	10.44
Israeli	26	0.08
Italian	2,035	6.61
Latvian	26	0.08
Lithuanian	81	0.26
Luxemburger	29	0.09
Macedonian	9	0.03
Maltese	27	0.09
New Zealander	59	0.19
Northern European	145	0.47
Norwegian	788	2.56
Pennsylvania German	13	0.04
Polish	605	1.97
Portuguese	177	0.57
Romanian	37	0.12
Russian	1,003	3.26
Scandinavian	161	0.52
Scotch-Irish	551	1.79
Scottish	956	3.11
Serbian	19	0.06
Slavic	36	0.12
Slovak	49	0.16
Swedish	591	1.92
Swiss	242	0.79
Turkish	54	0.18
Ukrainian	111	0.36
United States or American	753	2.45
Welsh	230	0.75
West Indian, excl. Hispanic:	65	0.21
Haitian	26	0.08
Jamaican	19	0.06
West Indian	20	0.06

Notes: 1. Figures in the "Number" column do not add up to the total population due to: a) Ancestry/Race overlap — e.g. persons can report being both White and Irish, b) persons of Hispanic origin can report being any race, c) persons reporting two ancestries are counted in both categories. 2. Numbers in parentheses indicate the number of persons reporting this ancestry/race alone, not in combination with any other ancestry/race. 3. Refer to the Explanation of Data in the front of the book for more detailed information.

White:	23,043	74.85
Not Hispanic (20,452)	20,998	68.21
Hispanic (1,822)	2,045	6.64
Yugoslavian	28	0.09

Merced

Place Type: City
County: Merced
Population: 63,893

Ancestry/Race	Number	%
Acadian/Cajun	10	0.02
African American/Black:	4,656	7.29
Not Hispanic (3,864)	4,253	6.66
Hispanic (180)	403	0.63
African, sub-Saharan:	264	0.41
African	225	0.35
Ethiopian	7	0.01
South African	32	0.05
Alaska Native tribes, specified:	4	0.01
Aleut (1)	1	0.00
Eskimo	2	0.00
Tlingit-Haida (1)	1	0.00
Am. Ind. or Alaska Nat., not spec.	601	0.94
Albanian	10	0.02
American Indian tribes, specified:	940	1.47
Apache (27)	65	0.10
Blackfeet (2)	14	0.02
Cherokee (89)	265	0.41
Cheyenne (1)	6	0.01
Chickasaw (3)	6	0.01
Chippewa (11)	22	0.03
Choctaw (23)	65	0.10
Comanche (2)	5	0.01
Creek	7	0.01
Crow	1	0.00
Delaware (1)	5	0.01
Iroquois (4)	11	0.02
Latin American Indians (129)	169	0.26
Navajo (5)	20	0.03
Osage (6)	9	0.01
Paiute (1)	17	0.03
Pima (5)	5	0.01
Potawatomi (1)	2	0.00
Pueblo (1)	9	0.01
Puget Sound Salish (2)	2	0.00
Seminole (4)	17	0.03
Shoshone	2	0.00
Sioux (15)	41	0.06
Tohono O'Odham (3)	3	0.00
Yaqui (15)	28	0.04
Yuman (2)	2	0.00
All other tribes (85)	142	0.22
American Indian tribes, not spec.	112	0.18
Arab:	147	0.23
Arab/Arabic	19	0.03
Jordanian	38	0.06
Lebanese	40	0.06
Syrian	9	0.01
Other Arab	41	0.06
Armenian	53	0.08
Asian:	8,366	13.09
Bangladeshi (1)	2	0.00
Cambodian (24)	37	0.06
Chinese, ex. Taiwanese (168)	255	0.40
Filipino (383)	579	0.91
Hmong (4,096)	4,464	6.99
Indian (284)	380	0.59
Indonesian (1)	5	0.01
Japanese (143)	262	0.41
Korean (50)	75	0.12
Laotian (1,570)	1,846	2.89
Pakistani (8)	14	0.02
Sri Lankan (1)	1	0.00
Thai (47)	85	0.13
Vietnamese (75)	79	0.12
Other Asian, specified (1)	1	0.00
Other Asian, not specified (211)	281	0.44
Assyrian/Chaldean/Syriac	17	0.03
Austrian	72	0.11
Basque	13	0.02
Belgian	43	0.07
Brazilian	13	0.02
British	301	0.47
Canadian	94	0.15
Celtic	8	0.01
Croatian	24	0.04
Czech	134	0.21
Czechoslovakian	13	0.02
Danish	167	0.26
Dutch	660	1.03
English	3,400	5.31
Estonian	6	0.01
European	359	0.56
Finnish	56	0.09
French, except Basque	1,005	1.57
French Canadian	121	0.19
German	5,231	8.17
Greek	164	0.26
Hawaii Native/Pacific Islander:	349	0.55
Melanesian: (2)	4	0.01
Fijian (2)	4	0.01
Micronesian: (29)	45	0.07
Guamanian/Chamorro (21)	37	0.06
Other Micronesian (8)	8	0.01
Polynesian: (65)	134	0.21
Native Hawaiian (44)	103	0.16
Samoan (18)	28	0.04
Tongan (2)	2	0.00
Other Polynesian (1)	1	0.00
Other Pac. Isl., not spec. (37)	166	0.26
Hispanic or Latino:	26,425	41.36
Central American:	216	0.34
Costa Rican	8	0.01
Guatemalan	31	0.05
Honduran	24	0.04
Nicaraguan	56	0.09
Panamanian	10	0.02
Salvadoran	48	0.08
Other Central American	39	0.06
Cuban	44	0.07
Dominican Republic	3	0.00
Mexican	22,616	35.40
Puerto Rican	200	0.31
South American:	68	0.11
Argentinean	4	0.01
Bolivian	4	0.01
Chilean	8	0.01
Colombian	13	0.02
Ecuadorian	8	0.01
Peruvian	9	0.01
Uruguayan	7	0.01
Venezuelan	2	0.00
Other South American	13	0.02
Other Hispanic or Latino	3,278	5.13
Hungarian	124	0.19
Iranian	12	0.02
Irish	4,325	6.76
Italian	1,892	2.96
Latvian	19	0.03
Lithuanian	33	0.05
Maltese	30	0.05
Northern European	16	0.03
Norwegian	419	0.65
Pennsylvania German	19	0.03
Polish	299	0.47
Portuguese	1,339	2.09
Romanian	22	0.03
Russian	92	0.14
Scandinavian	38	0.06
Scotch-Irish	538	0.84
Scottish	771	1.20
Serbian	8	0.01
Slavic	8	0.01
Slovak	31	0.05
Swedish	518	0.81
Swiss	157	0.25
Ukrainian	83	0.13
United States or American	2,126	3.32
Welsh	162	0.25
West Indian, excl. Hispanic:	78	0.12
Bahamian	5	0.01
Dutch West Indian	14	0.02
Jamaican	33	0.05
West Indian	26	0.04
White:	35,955	56.27
Not Hispanic (24,121)	25,298	39.59
Hispanic (9,360)	10,657	16.68
Yugoslavian	72	0.11

Mill Valley

Place Type: City
County: Marin
Population: 13,600

Ancestry/Race	Number	%
African American/Black:	184	1.35
Not Hispanic (132)	178	1.31
Hispanic (3)	6	0.04
African, sub-Saharan:	42	0.31
African	21	0.15
South African	21	0.15
Alaska Native tribes, specified:	3	0.02
Aleut	1	0.01
Tlingit-Haida (2)	2	0.01
Am. Ind. or Alaska Nat., not spec.	32	0.24
American Indian tribes, specified:	64	0.47
Apache (2)	6	0.04
Cherokee (6)	24	0.18
Cheyenne (1)	3	0.02
Chickasaw (1)	1	0.01
Chippewa (1)	3	0.02
Cree	2	0.01
Crow (1)	1	0.01
Iroquois	1	0.01
Latin American Indians (3)	5	0.04
Ottawa	1	0.01
Pueblo (1)	2	0.01
Seminole	3	0.02
Sioux	4	0.03
Tohono O'Odham	1	0.01
Yuman	1	0.01
All other tribes (1)	6	0.04
American Indian tribes, not spec.	5	0.04
Arab:	43	0.32
Arab/Arabic	8	0.06
Egyptian	15	0.11
Lebanese	12	0.09
Syrian	8	0.06
Armenian	18	0.13
Asian:	785	5.77
Cambodian (6)	6	0.04
Chinese, ex. Taiwanese (158)	230	1.69
Filipino (35)	65	0.48
Indian (144)	165	1.21
Indonesian (1)	2	0.01
Japanese (119)	190	1.40
Korean (47)	71	0.52
Pakistani	1	0.01
Taiwanese (1)	1	0.01
Thai (16)	18	0.13
Vietnamese (13)	18	0.13
Other Asian, specified (1)	6	0.04
Other Asian, not specified (2)	12	0.09
Australian	24	0.18
Austrian	151	1.11
Basque	34	0.25
Brazilian	38	0.28
British	175	1.29
Bulgarian	17	0.13
Canadian	139	1.03
Celtic	26	0.19
Croatian	39	0.29
Czech	118	0.87
Czechoslovakian	38	0.28
Danish	154	1.14
Dutch	331	2.44
Eastern European	83	0.61

Notes: 1. Figures in the "Number" column do not add up to the total population due to: a) Ancestry/Race overlap — e.g. persons can report being both White and Irish, b) persons of Hispanic origin can report being any race, c) persons reporting two ancestries are counted in both categories. 2. Numbers in parentheses indicate the number of persons reporting this ancestry/race alone, not in combination with any other ancestry/race. 3. Refer to the Explanation of Data in the front of the book for more detailed information.

Ancestry/Race	Number	%
English	2,589	19.09
European	312	2.30
Finnish	36	0.27
French, except Basque	443	3.27
French Canadian	143	1.05
German	2,147	15.83
Greek	133	0.98
Hawaii Native/Pacific Islander:	50	0.37
Melanesian: (7)	9	0.07
Fijian (6)	6	0.04
Other Melanesian (1)	3	0.02
Micronesian:	3	0.02
Guamanian/Chamorro	3	0.02
Polynesian: (13)	24	0.18
Native Hawaiian (11)	22	0.16
Samoan (1)	1	0.01
Other Polynesian (1)	1	0.01
Other Pac. Isl., specified	3	0.02
Other Pac. Isl., not spec. (8)	11	0.08
Hispanic or Latino:	472	3.47
Central American:	52	0.38
Costa Rican	1	0.01
Guatemalan	23	0.17
Honduran	2	0.01
Nicaraguan	7	0.05
Panamanian	2	0.01
Salvadoran	15	0.11
Other Central American	2	0.01
Cuban	17	0.13
Dominican Republic	4	0.03
Mexican	206	1.51
Puerto Rican	29	0.21
South American:	52	0.38
Argentinean	8	0.06
Bolivian	2	0.01
Chilean	9	0.07
Colombian	12	0.09
Ecuadorian	3	0.02
Peruvian	4	0.03
Venezuelan	4	0.03
Other South American	10	0.07
Other Hispanic or Latino	112	0.82
Hungarian	140	1.03
Iranian	37	0.27
Irish	2,234	16.47
Israeli	40	0.29
Italian	985	7.26
Latvian	6	0.04
Lithuanian	95	0.70
Luxemburger	9	0.07
Macedonian	6	0.04
New Zealander	7	0.05
Northern European	53	0.39
Norwegian	372	2.74
Polish	491	3.62
Portuguese	69	0.51
Romanian	76	0.56
Russian	795	5.86
Scandinavian	72	0.53
Scotch-Irish	406	2.99
Scottish	742	5.47
Serbian	8	0.06
Slavic	14	0.10
Slovak	17	0.13
Swedish	372	2.74
Swiss	213	1.57
Turkish	7	0.05
Ukrainian	108	0.80
United States or American	441	3.25
Welsh	200	1.47
White:	12,724	93.56
Not Hispanic (12,118)	12,357	90.86
Hispanic (317)	367	2.70
Yugoslavian	14	0.10

Millbrae

Place Type: City
County: San Mateo
Population: 20,718

Ancestry/Race	Number	%
African American/Black:	234	1.13
Not Hispanic (154)	212	1.02
Hispanic (11)	22	0.11
African, sub-Saharan:	15	0.07
African	15	0.07
Am. Ind. or Alaska Nat., not spec.	46	0.22
Alsatian	17	0.08
American Indian tribes, specified:	64	0.31
Apache (1)	4	0.02
Blackfeet (1)	2	0.01
Cherokee (7)	20	0.10
Chippewa	1	0.00
Choctaw (4)	5	0.02
Colville (1)	1	0.00
Cree (1)	3	0.01
Delaware (2)	2	0.01
Iroquois	2	0.01
Latin American Indians (4)	8	0.04
Navajo (2)	6	0.03
Potawatomi	1	0.00
Sioux (1)	1	0.00
Yaqui	1	0.00
All other tribes (1)	7	0.03
American Indian tribes, not spec.	4	0.02
Arab:	705	3.40
Arab/Arabic	143	0.69
Iraqi	35	0.17
Jordanian	40	0.19
Lebanese	126	0.61
Palestinian	294	1.42
Syrian	31	0.15
Other Arab	36	0.17
Armenian	111	0.54
Asian:	6,190	29.88
Chinese, ex. Taiwanese (3,334)	3,558	17.17
Filipino (750)	913	4.41
Indian (222)	257	1.24
Indonesian (7)	13	0.06
Japanese (492)	600	2.90
Korean (513)	541	2.61
Laotian (1)	2	0.01
Malaysian (1)	4	0.02
Pakistani (5)	5	0.02
Sri Lankan (15)	15	0.07
Taiwanese (93)	118	0.57
Thai (34)	42	0.20
Vietnamese (46)	57	0.28
Other Asian, specified (4)	6	0.03
Other Asian, not specified (7)	59	0.28
Assyrian/Chaldean/Syriac	44	0.21
Australian	18	0.09
Austrian	91	0.44
Basque	23	0.11
Belgian	12	0.06
Brazilian	6	0.03
British	149	0.72
Bulgarian	29	0.14
Canadian	34	0.16
Croatian	45	0.22
Czech	45	0.22
Czechoslovakian	95	0.46
Danish	93	0.45
Dutch	87	0.42
Eastern European	7	0.03
English	1,223	5.90
Estonian	6	0.03
European	176	0.85
Finnish	41	0.20
French, except Basque	465	2.24
French Canadian	66	0.32
German	1,784	8.61
Greek	476	2.30
Hawaii Native/Pacific Islander:	354	1.71
Melanesian: (45)	46	0.22
Fijian (45)	46	0.22
Micronesian: (8)	12	0.06
Guamanian/Chamorro (7)	11	0.05
Other Micronesian (1)	1	0.00
Polynesian: (161)	237	1.14
Native Hawaiian (24)	52	0.25
Samoan (25)	39	0.19
Tongan (112)	134	0.65
Other Polynesian	12	0.06
Other Pac. Isl., specified	1	0.00
Other Pac. Isl., not spec. (18)	58	0.28
Hispanic or Latino:	2,376	11.47
Central American:	377	1.82
Costa Rican	16	0.08
Guatemalan	30	0.14
Honduran	5	0.02
Nicaraguan	115	0.56
Panamanian	8	0.04
Salvadoran	167	0.81
Other Central American	36	0.17
Cuban	11	0.05
Dominican Republic	1	0.00
Mexican	1,090	5.26
Puerto Rican	117	0.56
South American:	149	0.72
Argentinean	8	0.04
Bolivian	6	0.03
Chilean	7	0.03
Colombian	27	0.13
Ecuadorian	3	0.01
Peruvian	73	0.35
Venezuelan	4	0.02
Other South American	21	0.10
Other Hispanic or Latino	631	3.05
Hungarian	50	0.24
Iranian	164	0.79
Irish	2,334	11.26
Italian	2,623	12.65
Latvian	19	0.09
Lithuanian	12	0.06
Maltese	212	1.02
Northern European	7	0.03
Norwegian	201	0.97
Polish	240	1.16
Portuguese	67	0.32
Romanian	7	0.03
Russian	274	1.32
Scandinavian	56	0.27
Scotch-Irish	256	1.24
Scottish	353	1.70
Serbian	30	0.14
Slavic	22	0.11
Slovak	20	0.10
Slovene	6	0.03
Soviet Union	11	0.05
Swedish	244	1.18
Swiss	117	0.56
Turkish	49	0.24
Ukrainian	45	0.22
United States or American	365	1.76
Welsh	87	0.42
West Indian, excl. Hispanic:	6	0.03
Other West Indian	6	0.03
White:	13,767	66.45
Not Hispanic (11,674)	12,173	58.76
Hispanic (1,387)	1,594	7.69
Yugoslavian	40	0.19

Milpitas

Place Type: City
County: Santa Clara
Population: 62,698

Ancestry/Race	Number	%
Afghan	104	0.17
African American/Black:	2,746	4.38
Not Hispanic (2,187)	2,548	4.06
Hispanic (108)	198	0.32

Notes: 1. Figures in the "Number" column do not add up to the total population due to: a) Ancestry/Race overlap — e.g. persons can report being both White and Irish, b) persons of Hispanic origin can report being any race, c) persons reporting two ancestries are counted in both categories. 2. Numbers in parentheses indicate the number of persons reporting this ancestry/race alone, not in combination with any other ancestry/race. 3. Refer to the Explanation of Data in the front of the book for more detailed information.

African, sub-Saharan:	221	0.35
African	214	0.34
South African	7	0.01
Alaska Native tribes, specified:	13	0.02
Alaska Athabascan	1	0.00
Aleut (2)	2	0.00
Eskimo	3	0.00
Tlingit-Haida	7	0.01
Alaska Native tribes, not specified	1	0.00
Am. Ind. or Alaska Nat., not spec.	281	0.45
American Indian tribes, specified:	536	0.85
Apache (12)	36	0.06
Blackfeet (3)	15	0.02
Cherokee (26)	117	0.19
Chickasaw	6	0.01
Chippewa (26)	38	0.06
Choctaw (11)	21	0.03
Comanche (9)	10	0.02
Creek (3)	11	0.02
Crow	1	0.00
Iroquois (6)	16	0.03
Kiowa (3)	7	0.01
Latin American Indians (40)	61	0.10
Lumbee	3	0.00
Navajo (27)	40	0.06
Osage (2)	2	0.00
Ottawa	1	0.00
Paiute (4)	5	0.01
Pima (1)	2	0.00
Potawatomi (4)	4	0.01
Pueblo (6)	16	0.03
Puget Sound Salish (1)	3	0.00
Seminole (8)	8	0.01
Shoshone (2)	2	0.00
Sioux (21)	29	0.05
Tohono O'Odham (1)	3	0.00
Yakama (1)	1	0.00
Yaqui (5)	12	0.02
Yuman (4)	4	0.01
All other tribes (29)	62	0.10
American Indian tribes, not spec.	45	0.07
Arab:	210	0.33
Arab/Arabic	84	0.13
Iraqi	56	0.09
Lebanese	38	0.06
Palestinian	17	0.03
Syrian	15	0.02
Armenian	41	0.07
Asian:	34,713	55.37
Bangladeshi (22)	22	0.04
Cambodian (135)	161	0.26
Chinese, ex. Taiwanese (7,826)	8,446	13.47
Filipino (9,381)	10,265	16.37
Hmong (10)	26	0.04
Indian (4,295)	4,495	7.17
Indonesian (58)	92	0.15
Japanese (523)	745	1.19
Korean (723)	792	1.26
Laotian (120)	139	0.22
Malaysian (16)	45	0.07
Pakistani (151)	202	0.32
Sri Lankan (11)	13	0.02
Taiwanese (272)	342	0.55
Thai (59)	74	0.12
Vietnamese (8,175)	8,566	13.66
Other Asian, specified (50)	62	0.10
Other Asian, not specified (118)	226	0.36
Assyrian/Chaldean/Syriac	16	0.03
Australian	32	0.05
Austrian	50	0.08
Belgian	64	0.10
Brazilian	7	0.01
British	238	0.38
Bulgarian	23	0.04
Canadian	95	0.15
Croatian	24	0.04
Czech	43	0.07
Czechoslovakian	13	0.02
Danish	146	0.23
Dutch	305	0.49
Eastern European	20	0.03
English	2,113	3.37
Estonian	7	0.01
European	276	0.44
Finnish	48	0.08
French, except Basque	850	1.36
French Canadian	175	0.28
German	3,412	5.44
Greek	74	0.12
Hawaii Native/Pacific Islander:	759	1.21
Melanesian: (21)	27	0.04
Fijian (21)	27	0.04
Micronesian: (159)	230	0.37
Guamanian/Chamorro (157)	228	0.36
Other Micronesian (2)	2	0.00
Polynesian: (155)	301	0.48
Native Hawaiian (48)	148	0.24
Samoan (96)	124	0.20
Tongan (11)	23	0.04
Other Polynesian	6	0.01
Other Pac. Isl., specified	1	0.00
Other Pac. Isl., not spec. (49)	200	0.32
Hispanic or Latino:	10,417	16.61
Central American:	382	0.61
Costa Rican	24	0.04
Guatemalan	29	0.05
Honduran	9	0.01
Nicaraguan	159	0.25
Panamanian	15	0.02
Salvadoran	120	0.19
Other Central American	26	0.04
Cuban	53	0.08
Dominican Republic	3	0.00
Mexican	8,132	12.97
Puerto Rican	221	0.35
South American:	231	0.37
Argentinean	31	0.05
Bolivian	13	0.02
Chilean	21	0.03
Colombian	26	0.04
Ecuadorian	11	0.02
Paraguayan	2	0.00
Peruvian	106	0.17
Uruguayan	3	0.00
Venezuelan	4	0.01
Other South American	14	0.02
Other Hispanic or Latino	1,395	2.22
Hungarian	97	0.15
Icelander	9	0.01
Iranian	148	0.24
Irish	2,310	3.68
Israeli	11	0.02
Italian	1,545	2.46
Latvian	8	0.01
Lithuanian	8	0.01
Maltese	9	0.01
Northern European	77	0.12
Norwegian	356	0.57
Polish	544	0.87
Portuguese	740	1.18
Romanian	50	0.08
Russian	171	0.27
Scandinavian	40	0.06
Scotch-Irish	549	0.88
Scottish	553	0.88
Serbian	9	0.01
Slavic	10	0.02
Slovak	5	0.01
Swedish	645	1.03
Swiss	80	0.13
Ukrainian	44	0.07
United States or American	1,040	1.66
Welsh	127	0.20
West Indian, excl. Hispanic:	38	0.06
Jamaican	38	0.06
White:	21,555	34.38
Not Hispanic (14,917)	16,399	26.16
Hispanic (4,436)	5,156	8.22
Yugoslavian	125	0.20

Mira Loma

Place Type: Census Designated Place
County: Riverside
Population: 17,617

Ancestry/Race	Number	%
Acadian/Cajun	8	0.04
African American/Black:	292	1.66
Not Hispanic (213)	255	1.45
Hispanic (20)	37	0.21
African, sub-Saharan:	9	0.05
African	9	0.05
Alaska Native tribes, specified:	3	0.02
Alaska Athabascan (1)	1	0.01
Tlingit-Haida (2)	2	0.01
Am. Ind. or Alaska Nat., not spec.	149	0.85
American Indian tribes, specified:	246	1.40
Apache (5)	15	0.09
Blackfeet (4)	8	0.05
Cherokee (20)	61	0.35
Cheyenne (1)	3	0.02
Chickasaw (5)	9	0.05
Chippewa (2)	3	0.02
Choctaw (16)	26	0.15
Comanche	2	0.01
Creek (1)	2	0.01
Crow	1	0.01
Iroquois	1	0.01
Latin American Indians (28)	38	0.22
Navajo (2)	8	0.05
Pima (1)	1	0.01
Pueblo (1)	8	0.05
Puget Sound Salish	1	0.01
Seminole (1)	1	0.01
Sioux (2)	6	0.03
Ute (1)	1	0.01
Yaqui	7	0.04
All other tribes (23)	44	0.25
American Indian tribes, not spec.	20	0.11
Arab:	54	0.30
Arab/Arabic	9	0.05
Lebanese	45	0.25
Armenian	6	0.03
Asian:	297	1.69
Chinese, ex. Taiwanese (22)	42	0.24
Filipino (62)	103	0.58
Indian (7)	23	0.13
Indonesian (1)	7	0.04
Japanese (17)	39	0.22
Korean (24)	31	0.18
Pakistani (5)	10	0.06
Thai (2)	4	0.02
Vietnamese (10)	15	0.09
Other Asian, specified	4	0.02
Other Asian, not specified (5)	19	0.11
Basque	56	0.31
British	9	0.05
Canadian	59	0.33
Croatian	22	0.12
Czech	7	0.04
Czechoslovakian	26	0.15
Danish	107	0.60
Dutch	375	2.10
English	1,105	6.20
European	54	0.30
Finnish	23	0.13
French, except Basque	559	3.13
French Canadian	186	1.04
German	1,816	10.18
Greek	6	0.03
Hawaii Native/Pacific Islander:	91	0.52
Micronesian: (5)	7	0.04
Guamanian/Chamorro (5)	7	0.04
Polynesian: (32)	73	0.41
Native Hawaiian (13)	40	0.23
Samoan (14)	27	0.15
Tongan (1)	1	0.01
Other Polynesian (4)	5	0.03
Other Pac. Isl., specified	3	0.02

Notes: 1. Figures in the "Number" column do not add up to the total population due to: a) Ancestry/Race overlap — e.g. persons can report being both White and Irish, b) persons of Hispanic origin can report being any race, c) persons reporting two ancestries are counted in both categories. 2. Numbers in parentheses indicate the number of persons reporting this ancestry/race alone, not in combination with any other ancestry/race. 3. Refer to the Explanation of Data in the front of the book for more detailed information.

Other Pac. Isl., not spec. (3)	8	0.05
Hispanic or Latino:	8,513	48.32
Central American:	68	0.39
Costa Rican	6	0.03
Guatemalan	20	0.11
Honduran	1	0.01
Nicaraguan	7	0.04
Panamanian	1	0.01
Salvadoran	28	0.16
Other Central American	5	0.03
Cuban	44	0.25
Dominican Republic	4	0.02
Mexican	7,281	41.33
Puerto Rican	68	0.39
South American:	45	0.26
Argentinean	1	0.01
Bolivian	6	0.03
Chilean	8	0.05
Colombian	16	0.09
Ecuadorian	7	0.04
Peruvian	7	0.04
Other Hispanic or Latino	1,003	5.69
Hungarian	35	0.20
Irish	1,438	8.06
Italian	471	2.64
Lithuanian	33	0.19
New Zealander	8	0.04
Norwegian	160	0.90
Polish	233	1.31
Portuguese	93	0.52
Russian	63	0.35
Scandinavian	51	0.29
Scotch-Irish	264	1.48
Scottish	249	1.40
Slovak	7	0.04
Swedish	163	0.91
Swiss	37	0.21
Ukrainian	9	0.05
United States or American	644	3.61
Welsh	27	0.15
West Indian, excl. Hispanic:	3	0.02
Bahamian	3	0.02
White:	11,888	67.48
Not Hispanic (8,321)	8,575	48.67
Hispanic (2,960)	3,313	18.81

Mission Viejo

Place Type: City
County: Orange
Population: 93,102

Ancestry/Race	Number	%
Afghan	275	0.30
African American/Black:	1,452	1.56
Not Hispanic (1,032)	1,358	1.46
Hispanic (35)	94	0.10
African, sub-Saharan:	169	0.18
African	30	0.03
Nigerian	11	0.01
South African	100	0.11
Other sub-Saharan African	28	0.03
Alaska Native tribes, specified:	5	0.01
Aleut	1	0.00
Eskimo (1)	1	0.00
Tlingit-Haida (1)	3	0.00
Alaska Native tribes, not specified	1	0.00
Am. Ind. or Alaska Nat., not spec.	267	0.29
American Indian tribes, specified:	540	0.58
Apache (9)	30	0.03
Blackfeet (4)	13	0.01
Cherokee (50)	177	0.19
Cheyenne	2	0.00
Chickasaw (10)	22	0.02
Chippewa (5)	14	0.02
Choctaw (8)	22	0.02
Comanche (4)	12	0.01
Creek (7)	20	0.02
Delaware	1	0.00
Iroquois (14)	25	0.03
Kiowa (1)	4	0.00
Latin American Indians (12)	45	0.05
Lumbee (5)	5	0.01
Navajo (11)	22	0.02
Osage	5	0.01
Paiute (2)	2	0.00
Potawatomi	4	0.00
Pueblo (8)	10	0.01
Puget Sound Salish	1	0.00
Seminole (1)	2	0.00
Sioux (6)	11	0.01
Yaqui (1)	2	0.00
All other tribes (52)	89	0.10
American Indian tribes, not spec.	39	0.04
Arab:	1,189	1.28
Arab/Arabic	141	0.15
Egyptian	266	0.29
Iraqi	29	0.03
Jordanian	34	0.04
Lebanese	317	0.34
Moroccan	15	0.02
Palestinian	171	0.18
Syrian	146	0.16
Other Arab	70	0.08
Armenian	247	0.27
Asian:	8,865	9.52
Cambodian (28)	36	0.04
Chinese, ex. Taiwanese (1,306)	1,615	1.73
Filipino (1,536)	1,943	2.09
Hmong (5)	6	0.01
Indian (798)	894	0.96
Indonesian (67)	111	0.12
Japanese (1,001)	1,528	1.64
Korean (718)	843	0.91
Laotian (7)	7	0.01
Malaysian (2)	3	0.00
Pakistani (71)	99	0.11
Sri Lankan (20)	29	0.03
Taiwanese (185)	209	0.22
Thai (71)	96	0.10
Vietnamese (1,103)	1,176	1.26
Other Asian, specified (34)	39	0.04
Other Asian, not specified (66)	231	0.25
Assyrian/Chaldean/Syriac	36	0.04
Australian	58	0.06
Austrian	424	0.46
Basque	121	0.13
Belgian	166	0.18
Brazilian	66	0.07
British	814	0.88
Bulgarian	20	0.02
Canadian	495	0.53
Croatian	183	0.20
Cypriot	19	0.02
Czech	430	0.46
Czechoslovakian	180	0.19
Danish	953	1.03
Dutch	2,008	2.16
Eastern European	68	0.07
English	12,595	13.58
Estonian	25	0.03
European	1,399	1.51
Finnish	282	0.30
French, except Basque	3,463	3.73
French Canadian	698	0.75
German	16,656	17.95
Greek	568	0.61
Guyanese	12	0.01
Hawaii Native/Pacific Islander:	421	0.45
Micronesian: (53)	78	0.08
Guamanian/Chamorro (45)	69	0.07
Other Micronesian (8)	9	0.01
Polynesian: (97)	242	0.26
Native Hawaiian (55)	172	0.18
Samoan (34)	58	0.06
Tongan (1)	3	0.00
Other Polynesian (7)	9	0.01
Other Pac. Isl., specified	1	0.00
Other Pac. Isl., not spec. (22)	100	0.11
Hispanic or Latino:	11,266	12.10
Central American:	423	0.45
Costa Rican	55	0.06
Guatemalan	137	0.15
Honduran	12	0.01
Nicaraguan	66	0.07
Panamanian	19	0.02
Salvadoran	104	0.11
Other Central American	30	0.03
Cuban	245	0.26
Dominican Republic	10	0.01
Mexican	7,400	7.95
Puerto Rican	301	0.32
South American:	948	1.02
Argentinean	181	0.19
Bolivian	47	0.05
Chilean	54	0.06
Colombian	299	0.32
Ecuadorian	68	0.07
Peruvian	170	0.18
Uruguayan	6	0.01
Venezuelan	29	0.03
Other South American	94	0.10
Other Hispanic or Latino	1,939	2.08
Hungarian	609	0.66
Iranian	2,033	2.19
Irish	11,577	12.48
Israeli	100	0.11
Italian	6,809	7.34
Latvian	49	0.05
Lithuanian	456	0.49
Luxemburger	8	0.01
New Zealander	5	0.01
Northern European	151	0.16
Norwegian	2,528	2.72
Pennsylvania German	40	0.04
Polish	2,908	3.13
Portuguese	308	0.33
Romanian	228	0.25
Russian	1,605	1.73
Scandinavian	247	0.27
Scotch-Irish	1,661	1.79
Scottish	2,673	2.88
Serbian	18	0.02
Slavic	86	0.09
Slovak	89	0.10
Slovene	60	0.06
Swedish	2,585	2.79
Swiss	529	0.57
Turkish	75	0.08
Ukrainian	398	0.43
United States or American	3,744	4.04
Welsh	1,040	1.12
West Indian, excl. Hispanic:	133	0.14
Bermudan	11	0.01
Haitian	7	0.01
Jamaican	45	0.05
Trinidadian and Tobagonian	14	0.02
West Indian	56	0.06
White:	80,410	86.37
Not Hispanic (70,735)	72,959	78.36
Hispanic (6,683)	7,451	8.00
Yugoslavian	313	0.34

Modesto

Place Type: City
County: Stanislaus
Population: 188,856

Ancestry/Race	Number	%
Acadian/Cajun	20	0.01
Afghan	23	0.01
African American/Black:	9,114	4.83
Not Hispanic (7,013)	8,181	4.33
Hispanic (486)	933	0.49
African, sub-Saharan:	625	0.33
African	560	0.30
Cape Verdean	7	0.00
Ethiopian	9	0.00
Kenyan	8	0.00

Notes: 1. Figures in the "Number" column do not add up to the total population due to: a) Ancestry/Race overlap — e.g. persons can report being both White and Irish, b) persons of Hispanic origin can report being any race, c) persons reporting two ancestries are counted in both categories. 2. Numbers in parentheses indicate the number of persons reporting this ancestry/race alone, not in combination with any other ancestry/race. 3. Refer to the Explanation of Data in the front of the book for more detailed information.

Ancestry/Race	Number	%
Nigerian	41	0.02
Alaska Native tribes, specified:	31	0.02
Alaska Athabascan (3)	6	0.00
Aleut (8)	8	0.00
Eskimo (10)	12	0.01
Tlingit-Haida (2)	3	0.00
All other tribes (2)	2	0.00
Am. Ind. or Alaska Nat., not spec.	1,411	0.75
Albanian	15	0.01
Alsatian	6	0.00
American Indian tribes, specified:	3,376	1.79
Apache (77)	243	0.13
Blackfeet (19)	91	0.05
Cherokee (338)	1,174	0.62
Cheyenne (4)	15	0.01
Chickasaw (32)	73	0.04
Chippewa (30)	49	0.03
Choctaw (154)	383	0.20
Colville (5)	5	0.00
Comanche (9)	34	0.02
Cree	1	0.00
Creek (34)	73	0.04
Crow (7)	10	0.01
Delaware (1)	4	0.00
Houma	1	0.00
Iroquois (17)	30	0.02
Kiowa (1)	7	0.00
Latin American Indians (217)	320	0.17
Lumbee (4)	4	0.00
Navajo (53)	105	0.06
Osage (8)	14	0.01
Ottawa (1)	9	0.00
Paiute (53)	73	0.04
Pima (18)	27	0.01
Potawatomi (8)	13	0.01
Pueblo (33)	51	0.03
Seminole (12)	28	0.01
Shoshone (5)	8	0.00
Sioux (35)	113	0.06
Tohono O'Odham (9)	18	0.01
Ute (6)	10	0.01
Yakama (7)	8	0.00
Yaqui (24)	42	0.02
Yuman (4)	7	0.00
All other tribes (171)	333	0.18
American Indian tribes, not spec.	252	0.13
Arab:	872	0.46
Arab/Arabic	310	0.16
Egyptian	72	0.04
Iraqi	106	0.06
Lebanese	66	0.03
Moroccan	7	0.00
Palestinian	106	0.06
Syrian	102	0.05
Other Arab	103	0.05
Armenian	335	0.18
Asian:	15,041	7.96
Cambodian (2,429)	2,880	1.52
Chinese, ex. Taiwanese (1,156)	1,554	0.82
Filipino (1,740)	2,695	1.43
Hmong (483)	513	0.27
Indian (2,019)	2,982	1.58
Indonesian (20)	49	0.03
Japanese (374)	762	0.40
Korean (309)	397	0.21
Laotian (1,185)	1,369	0.72
Malaysian	5	0.00
Pakistani (38)	69	0.04
Sri Lankan (3)	6	0.00
Taiwanese (18)	24	0.01
Thai (43)	73	0.04
Vietnamese (1,016)	1,169	0.62
Other Asian, specified (8)	25	0.01
Other Asian, not specified (222)	469	0.25
Assyrian/Chaldean/Syriac	2,967	1.57
Australian	68	0.04
Austrian	239	0.13
Basque	124	0.07
Belgian	192	0.10
Brazilian	60	0.03
British	687	0.36
Bulgarian	145	0.08
Canadian	410	0.22
Celtic	33	0.02
Croatian	106	0.06
Czech	345	0.18
Czechoslovakian	212	0.11
Danish	1,165	0.61
Dutch	4,194	2.21
Eastern European	49	0.03
English	15,931	8.41
European	1,783	0.94
Finnish	286	0.15
French, except Basque	4,901	2.59
French Canadian	665	0.35
German	21,750	11.48
German Russian	34	0.02
Greek	909	0.48
Hawaii Native/Pacific Islander:	2,281	1.21
Melanesian: (368)	454	0.24
Fijian (368)	454	0.24
Micronesian: (97)	208	0.11
Guamanian/Chamorro (89)	200	0.11
Other Micronesian (8)	8	0.00
Polynesian: (250)	654	0.35
Native Hawaiian (116)	396	0.21
Samoan (128)	235	0.12
Tongan (2)	3	0.00
Other Polynesian (4)	20	0.01
Other Pac. Isl., specified	13	0.01
Other Pac. Isl., not spec. (202)	952	0.50
Hispanic or Latino:	48,310	25.58
Central American:	900	0.48
Costa Rican	24	0.01
Guatemalan	150	0.08
Honduran	48	0.03
Nicaraguan	246	0.13
Panamanian	46	0.02
Salvadoran	279	0.15
Other Central American	107	0.06
Cuban	153	0.08
Dominican Republic	22	0.01
Mexican	38,819	20.55
Puerto Rican	1,049	0.56
South American:	296	0.16
Argentinean	22	0.01
Bolivian	13	0.01
Chilean	37	0.02
Colombian	80	0.04
Ecuadorian	12	0.01
Paraguayan	10	0.01
Peruvian	60	0.03
Uruguayan	7	0.00
Venezuelan	20	0.01
Other South American	35	0.02
Other Hispanic or Latino	7,071	3.74
Hungarian	317	0.17
Icelander	42	0.02
Iranian	264	0.14
Irish	16,588	8.76
Israeli	17	0.01
Italian	8,422	4.45
Latvian	28	0.01
Lithuanian	88	0.05
Luxemburger	6	0.00
Maltese	80	0.04
New Zealander	26	0.01
Northern European	158	0.08
Norwegian	3,072	1.62
Pennsylvania German	41	0.02
Polish	1,749	0.92
Portuguese	6,477	3.42
Romanian	319	0.17
Russian	604	0.32
Scandinavian	239	0.13
Scotch-Irish	2,332	1.23
Scottish	2,681	1.42
Serbian	53	0.03
Slavic	62	0.03
Slovak	71	0.04
Slovene	18	0.01
Swedish	3,276	1.73
Swiss	1,037	0.55
Turkish	29	0.02
Ukrainian	608	0.32
United States or American	8,806	4.65
Welsh	1,293	0.68
West Indian, excl. Hispanic:	92	0.05
Dutch West Indian	61	0.03
Jamaican	31	0.02
White:	140,170	74.22
Not Hispanic (112,466)	117,806	62.38
Hispanic (18,948)	22,364	11.84
Yugoslavian	262	0.14

Monrovia

Place Type: City
County: Los Angeles
Population: 36,929

Ancestry/Race	Number	%
African American/Black:	3,526	9.55
Not Hispanic (3,074)	3,297	8.93
Hispanic (128)	229	0.62
African, sub-Saharan:	80	0.22
African	80	0.22
Alaska Native tribes, specified:	1	0.00
Tlingit-Haida	1	0.00
Alaska Native tribes, not specified	3	0.01
Am. Ind. or Alaska Nat., not spec.	261	0.71
Albanian	7	0.02
American Indian tribes, specified:	378	1.02
Apache (14)	34	0.09
Blackfeet (2)	16	0.04
Cherokee (28)	91	0.25
Cheyenne	2	0.01
Chickasaw	1	0.00
Chippewa (2)	3	0.01
Choctaw (4)	19	0.05
Comanche (3)	3	0.01
Cree	4	0.01
Creek	10	0.03
Iroquois (3)	7	0.02
Latin American Indians (33)	53	0.14
Navajo (10)	15	0.04
Osage (1)	3	0.01
Ottawa (5)	5	0.01
Paiute (2)	8	0.02
Pima (4)	4	0.01
Potawatomi (2)	3	0.01
Pueblo (4)	7	0.02
Seminole	1	0.00
Shoshone	4	0.01
Sioux (3)	13	0.04
Yaqui (5)	8	0.02
All other tribes (35)	64	0.17
American Indian tribes, not spec.	27	0.07
Arab:	259	0.70
Egyptian	28	0.08
Lebanese	206	0.56
Syrian	25	0.07
Armenian	204	0.55
Asian:	3,150	8.53
Bangladeshi (4)	13	0.04
Cambodian (11)	12	0.03
Chinese, ex. Taiwanese (755)	896	2.43
Filipino (881)	1,023	2.77
Indian (172)	207	0.56
Indonesian (49)	88	0.24
Japanese (240)	334	0.90
Korean (100)	125	0.34
Malaysian (4)	6	0.02
Pakistani (15)	21	0.06
Sri Lankan (17)	22	0.06
Taiwanese (91)	121	0.33
Thai (59)	86	0.23
Vietnamese (106)	127	0.34
Other Asian, specified (9)	14	0.04
Other Asian, not specified (9)	55	0.15

Notes: 1. Figures in the "Number" column do not add up to the total population due to: a) Ancestry/Race overlap — e.g. persons can report being both White and Irish, b) persons of Hispanic origin can report being any race, c) persons reporting two ancestries are counted in both categories. 2. Numbers in parentheses indicate the number of persons reporting this ancestry/race alone, not in combination with any other ancestry/race. 3. Refer to the Explanation of Data in the front of the book for more detailed information.

Assyrian/Chaldean/Syriac	9	0.02
Australian	10	0.03
Austrian	82	0.22
Basque	9	0.02
Belgian	24	0.07
Brazilian	5	0.01
British	304	0.83
Bulgarian	8	0.02
Canadian	164	0.45
Celtic	30	0.08
Croatian	98	0.27
Czech	85	0.23
Czechoslovakian	42	0.11
Danish	166	0.45
Dutch	509	1.38
Eastern European	7	0.02
English	3,407	9.25
Estonian	7	0.02
European	526	1.43
Finnish	20	0.05
French, except Basque	788	2.14
French Canadian	221	0.60
German	4,112	11.17
Greek	129	0.35
Hawaii Native/Pacific Islander:	167	0.45
Micronesian: (12)	21	0.06
Guamanian/Chamorro (10)	19	0.05
Other Micronesian (2)	2	0.01
Polynesian: (26)	100	0.27
Native Hawaiian (10)	66	0.18
Samoan (15)	27	0.07
Tongan (1)	5	0.01
Other Polynesian	2	0.01
Other Pac. Isl., specified	2	0.01
Other Pac. Isl., not spec. (9)	44	0.12
Hispanic or Latino:	13,012	35.24
Central American:	551	1.49
Costa Rican	21	0.06
Guatemalan	97	0.26
Honduran	46	0.12
Nicaraguan	87	0.24
Panamanian	20	0.05
Salvadoran	220	0.60
Other Central American	60	0.16
Cuban	205	0.56
Dominican Republic	7	0.02
Mexican	9,854	26.68
Puerto Rican	233	0.63
South American:	345	0.93
Argentinean	85	0.23
Bolivian	7	0.02
Chilean	22	0.06
Colombian	82	0.22
Ecuadorian	32	0.09
Paraguayan	1	0.00
Peruvian	88	0.24
Venezuelan	4	0.01
Other South American	24	0.06
Other Hispanic or Latino	1,817	4.92
Hungarian	270	0.73
Icelander	12	0.03
Iranian	49	0.13
Irish	2,808	7.63
Israeli	11	0.03
Italian	1,389	3.77
Latvian	14	0.04
Lithuanian	9	0.02
Northern European	64	0.17
Norwegian	735	2.00
Pennsylvania German	27	0.07
Polish	596	1.62
Portuguese	123	0.33
Romanian	78	0.21
Russian	323	0.88
Scandinavian	36	0.10
Scotch-Irish	683	1.86
Scottish	614	1.67
Serbian	73	0.20
Slavic	6	0.02
Slovak	55	0.15
Slovene	14	0.04
Swedish	406	1.10
Swiss	57	0.15
Ukrainian	52	0.14
United States or American	1,410	3.83
Welsh	188	0.51
West Indian, excl. Hispanic:	61	0.17
Belizean	39	0.11
British West Indian	6	0.02
Haitian	16	0.04
White:	24,706	66.90
Not Hispanic (17,211)	17,912	48.50
Hispanic (6,026)	6,794	18.40
Yugoslavian	40	0.11

Montclair

Place Type: City
County: San Bernardino
Population: 33,049

Ancestry/Race	Number	%
African American/Black:	2,270	6.87
Not Hispanic (1,986)	2,093	6.33
Hispanic (126)	177	0.54
African, sub-Saharan:	187	0.56
African	130	0.39
Cape Verdean	6	0.02
Ethiopian	13	0.04
Ghanian	14	0.04
Nigerian	24	0.07
Alaska Native tribes, specified:	2	0.01
Eskimo (1)	2	0.01
Am. Ind. or Alaska Nat., not spec.	265	0.80
American Indian tribes, specified:	293	0.89
Apache (7)	22	0.07
Blackfeet (4)	14	0.04
Cherokee (13)	70	0.21
Cheyenne (3)	5	0.02
Chickasaw	2	0.01
Chippewa (5)	9	0.03
Choctaw (3)	16	0.05
Comanche (1)	3	0.01
Creek (2)	7	0.02
Delaware (1)	2	0.01
Iroquois	2	0.01
Latin American Indians (18)	39	0.12
Lumbee (1)	4	0.01
Navajo (9)	9	0.03
Paiute (1)	1	0.00
Pima (1)	1	0.00
Potawatomi (1)	1	0.00
Pueblo (12)	17	0.05
Seminole	2	0.01
Sioux (4)	12	0.04
Tohono O'Odham (12)	16	0.05
Ute	1	0.00
Yakama (1)	1	0.00
Yaqui	1	0.00
Yuman	2	0.01
All other tribes (25)	34	0.10
American Indian tribes, not spec.	28	0.08
Arab:	106	0.32
Arab/Arabic	71	0.21
Lebanese	31	0.09
Syrian	4	0.01
Asian:	3,113	9.42
Cambodian (43)	57	0.17
Chinese, ex. Taiwanese (293)	370	1.12
Filipino (460)	560	1.69
Hmong (20)	30	0.09
Indian (80)	127	0.38
Indonesian (237)	288	0.87
Japanese (56)	94	0.28
Korean (47)	58	0.18
Laotian (53)	67	0.20
Malaysian (1)	1	0.00
Pakistani (14)	25	0.08
Taiwanese (17)	21	0.06
Thai (72)	80	0.24
Vietnamese (1,186)	1,269	3.84
Other Asian, specified (1)	10	0.03
Other Asian, not specified (21)	56	0.17
Australian	21	0.06
Austrian	13	0.04
Brazilian	13	0.04
British	43	0.13
Canadian	23	0.07
Czech	10	0.03
Czechoslovakian	8	0.02
Danish	60	0.18
Dutch	158	0.48
English	1,193	3.60
European	232	0.70
Finnish	10	0.03
French, except Basque	519	1.57
French Canadian	189	0.57
German	1,772	5.35
Greek	13	0.04
Hawaii Native/Pacific Islander:	164	0.50
Melanesian: (2)	2	0.01
Fijian (2)	2	0.01
Micronesian: (5)	8	0.02
Guamanian/Chamorro (5)	8	0.02
Polynesian: (74)	103	0.31
Native Hawaiian (9)	29	0.09
Samoan (22)	26	0.08
Tongan (34)	36	0.11
Other Polynesian (9)	12	0.04
Other Pac. Isl., not spec. (20)	51	0.15
Hispanic or Latino:	19,823	59.98
Central American:	929	2.81
Costa Rican	48	0.15
Guatemalan	199	0.60
Honduran	42	0.13
Nicaraguan	142	0.43
Panamanian	22	0.07
Salvadoran	389	1.18
Other Central American	87	0.26
Cuban	153	0.46
Dominican Republic	2	0.01
Mexican	15,851	47.96
Puerto Rican	145	0.44
South American:	193	0.58
Argentinean	34	0.10
Bolivian	5	0.02
Chilean	8	0.02
Colombian	51	0.15
Ecuadorian	33	0.10
Peruvian	31	0.09
Venezuelan	4	0.01
Other South American	27	0.08
Other Hispanic or Latino	2,550	7.72
Hungarian	46	0.14
Iranian	77	0.23
Irish	1,561	4.71
Italian	787	2.38
Lithuanian	40	0.12
Northern European	17	0.05
Norwegian	90	0.27
Polish	213	0.64
Portuguese	12	0.04
Romanian	6	0.02
Russian	96	0.29
Scandinavian	12	0.04
Scotch-Irish	215	0.65
Scottish	302	0.91
Slavic	7	0.02
Swedish	186	0.56
Swiss	26	0.08
Ukrainian	60	0.18
United States or American	841	2.54
Welsh	99	0.30
West Indian, excl. Hispanic:	54	0.16
Barbadian	6	0.02
Jamaican	48	0.14
White:	16,094	48.70
Not Hispanic (7,784)	8,180	24.75
Hispanic (7,012)	7,914	23.95

Notes: 1. Figures in the "Number" column do not add up to the total population due to: a) Ancestry/Race overlap — e.g. persons can report being both White and Irish, b) persons of Hispanic origin can report being any race, c) persons reporting two ancestries are counted in both categories. 2. Numbers in parentheses indicate the number of persons reporting this ancestry/race alone, not in combination with any other ancestry/race. 3. Refer to the Explanation of Data in the front of the book for more detailed information.

Montebello

Place Type: City
County: Los Angeles
Population: 62,150

Ancestry/Race	Number	%
African American/Black:	699	1.12
Not Hispanic (395)	436	0.70
Hispanic (164)	263	0.42
African, sub-Saharan:	57	0.09
African	57	0.09
Am. Ind. or Alaska Nat., not spec.	571	0.92
American Indian tribes, specified:	483	0.78
Apache (36)	56	0.09
Blackfeet (8)	12	0.02
Cherokee (18)	34	0.05
Cheyenne (1)	1	0.00
Chippewa	1	0.00
Choctaw	3	0.00
Cree	1	0.00
Creek (2)	2	0.00
Delaware (3)	3	0.00
Iroquois	3	0.00
Kiowa (1)	1	0.00
Latin American Indians (126)	200	0.32
Navajo (12)	21	0.03
Osage	1	0.00
Paiute	3	0.00
Pima	2	0.00
Pueblo (7)	15	0.02
Seminole	5	0.01
Shoshone (3)	3	0.00
Sioux (8)	9	0.01
Tohono O'Odham (9)	20	0.03
Yaqui (22)	40	0.06
Yuman (1)	1	0.00
All other tribes (35)	46	0.07
American Indian tribes, not spec.	68	0.11
Arab:	291	0.47
Egyptian	37	0.06
Jordanian	14	0.02
Lebanese	159	0.26
Palestinian	7	0.01
Syrian	67	0.11
Other Arab	7	0.01
Armenian	2,736	4.42
Asian:	7,992	12.86
Bangladeshi (9)	10	0.02
Cambodian (30)	59	0.09
Chinese, ex. Taiwanese (2,614)	2,905	4.67
Filipino (913)	1,075	1.73
Indian (318)	360	0.58
Indonesian (11)	18	0.03
Japanese (1,883)	2,095	3.37
Korean (749)	798	1.28
Laotian (5)	5	0.01
Malaysian (2)	5	0.01
Pakistani (7)	11	0.02
Taiwanese (108)	125	0.20
Thai (94)	122	0.20
Vietnamese (239)	270	0.43
Other Asian, specified (13)	21	0.03
Other Asian, not specified (24)	113	0.18
Austrian	26	0.04
Basque	32	0.05
Brazilian	7	0.01
British	46	0.07
Bulgarian	8	0.01
Canadian	16	0.03
Croatian	19	0.03
Czech	25	0.04
Danish	38	0.06
Dutch	51	0.08
Eastern European	22	0.04
English	376	0.61
European	110	0.18
French, except Basque	401	0.65
German	928	1.50
Greek	108	0.17
Hawaii Native/Pacific Islander:	147	0.24
Melanesian: (1)	2	0.00
Fijian (1)	2	0.00
Micronesian: (11)	15	0.02
Guamanian/Chamorro (11)	15	0.02
Polynesian: (34)	87	0.14
Native Hawaiian (10)	61	0.10
Samoan (24)	26	0.04
Other Pac. Isl., specified	1	0.00
Other Pac. Isl., not spec. (5)	42	0.07
Hispanic or Latino:	46,347	74.57
Central American:	1,715	2.76
Costa Rican	39	0.06
Guatemalan	346	0.56
Honduran	82	0.13
Nicaraguan	178	0.29
Panamanian	15	0.02
Salvadoran	864	1.39
Other Central American	191	0.31
Cuban	136	0.22
Dominican Republic	13	0.02
Mexican	38,881	62.56
Puerto Rican	230	0.37
South American:	484	0.78
Argentinean	68	0.11
Bolivian	17	0.03
Chilean	17	0.03
Colombian	123	0.20
Ecuadorian	77	0.12
Paraguayan	5	0.01
Peruvian	128	0.21
Uruguayan	9	0.01
Venezuelan	6	0.01
Other South American	34	0.05
Other Hispanic or Latino	4,888	7.86
Hungarian	11	0.02
Iranian	73	0.12
Irish	679	1.10
Italian	799	1.29
Lithuanian	12	0.02
Norwegian	46	0.07
Polish	143	0.23
Portuguese	74	0.12
Romanian	7	0.01
Russian	457	0.74
Scotch-Irish	116	0.19
Scottish	78	0.13
Slavic	6	0.01
Slovene	11	0.02
Swedish	30	0.05
Turkish	5	0.01
Ukrainian	154	0.25
United States or American	831	1.34
Welsh	36	0.06
West Indian, excl. Hispanic:	55	0.09
Belizean	24	0.04
Jamaican	31	0.05
White:	32,010	51.50
Not Hispanic (6,911)	7,909	12.73
Hispanic (22,187)	24,101	38.78
Yugoslavian	23	0.04

Montecito

Place Type: Census Designated Place
County: Santa Barbara
Population: 10,000

Ancestry/Race	Number	%
African American/Black:	65	0.65
Not Hispanic (44)	61	0.61
Hispanic (4)	4	0.04
African, sub-Saharan:	21	0.21
African	12	0.12
Kenyan	9	0.09
Am. Ind. or Alaska Nat., not spec.	29	0.29
Alsatian	14	0.14
American Indian tribes, specified:	47	0.47
Apache	1	0.01
Blackfeet	3	0.03
Cherokee (7)	20	0.20
Delaware (1)	1	0.01
Latin American Indians	1	0.01
Osage (4)	6	0.06
Sioux (1)	2	0.02
Ute	1	0.01
Yaqui	2	0.02
All other tribes (6)	10	0.10
American Indian tribes, not spec.	1	0.01
Arab:	25	0.25
Lebanese	25	0.25
Armenian	39	0.39
Asian:	221	2.21
Cambodian (1)	1	0.01
Chinese, ex. Taiwanese (26)	52	0.52
Filipino (23)	42	0.42
Indian (10)	12	0.12
Japanese (20)	34	0.34
Korean (14)	26	0.26
Sri Lankan (5)	5	0.05
Taiwanese (1)	2	0.02
Vietnamese (11)	17	0.17
Other Asian, specified (3)	3	0.03
Other Asian, not specified (7)	27	0.27
Australian	19	0.19
Austrian	144	1.43
Belgian	43	0.43
Brazilian	5	0.05
British	168	1.67
Canadian	89	0.88
Croatian	17	0.17
Czech	14	0.14
Czechoslovakian	14	0.14
Danish	86	0.85
Dutch	191	1.89
Eastern European	21	0.21
English	2,166	21.47
European	308	3.05
Finnish	25	0.25
French, except Basque	521	5.16
French Canadian	21	0.21
German	1,558	15.44
Greek	79	0.78
Hawaii Native/Pacific Islander:	47	0.47
Melanesian:	1	0.01
Fijian	1	0.01
Micronesian:	2	0.02
Guamanian/Chamorro	2	0.02
Polynesian: (13)	25	0.25
Native Hawaiian (2)	4	0.04
Tongan (11)	16	0.16
Other Polynesian	5	0.05
Other Pac. Isl., not spec. (3)	19	0.19
Hispanic or Latino:	519	5.19
Central American:	23	0.23
Costa Rican	3	0.03
Guatemalan	2	0.02
Honduran	3	0.03
Panamanian	1	0.01
Salvadoran	14	0.14
Cuban	9	0.09
Mexican	339	3.39
South American:	21	0.21
Argentinean	4	0.04
Chilean	7	0.07
Colombian	3	0.03
Ecuadorian	2	0.02
Peruvian	4	0.04
Venezuelan	1	0.01
Other Hispanic or Latino	127	1.27
Hungarian	154	1.53
Iranian	50	0.50
Irish	1,222	12.11
Italian	404	4.00
Lithuanian	104	1.03
Northern European	64	0.63
Norwegian	351	3.48
Polish	222	2.20
Portuguese	72	0.71
Romanian	38	0.38

Notes: 1. Figures in the "Number" column do not add up to the total population due to: a) Ancestry/Race overlap — e.g. persons can report being both White and Irish, b) persons of Hispanic origin can report being any race, c) persons reporting two ancestries are counted in both categories. 2. Numbers in parentheses indicate the number of persons reporting this ancestry/race alone, not in combination with any other ancestry/race. 3. Refer to the Explanation of Data in the front of the book for more detailed information.

Ancestry/Race	Number	%
Russian	383	3.80
Scandinavian	28	0.28
Scotch-Irish	200	1.98
Scottish	530	5.25
Slavic	7	0.07
Slovak	11	0.11
Swedish	270	2.68
Swiss	89	0.88
Ukrainian	62	0.61
United States or American	428	4.24
Welsh	123	1.22
West Indian, excl. Hispanic:	10	0.10
Barbadian	10	0.10
White:	9,534	95.34
Not Hispanic (9,125)	9,235	92.35
Hispanic (278)	299	2.99
Yugoslavian	43	0.43

Monterey Park

Place Type: City
County: Los Angeles
Population: 60,051

Ancestry/Race	Number	%
African American/Black:	405	0.67
Not Hispanic (182)	291	0.48
Hispanic (44)	114	0.19
African, sub-Saharan:	16	0.03
African	11	0.02
Cape Verdean	5	0.01
Alaska Native tribes, specified:	6	0.01
Eskimo (4)	6	0.01
Am. Ind. or Alaska Nat., not spec.	243	0.40
American Indian tribes, specified:	346	0.58
Apache (16)	42	0.07
Blackfeet (3)	5	0.01
Cherokee (8)	35	0.06
Cheyenne (2)	4	0.01
Choctaw	3	0.00
Colville (1)	1	0.00
Comanche (1)	5	0.01
Creek (1)	1	0.00
Crow	1	0.00
Delaware (1)	1	0.00
Iroquois (1)	4	0.01
Latin American Indians (86)	107	0.18
Navajo (25)	27	0.04
Pima (7)	9	0.01
Potawatomi (2)	2	0.00
Pueblo (6)	10	0.02
Seminole (1)	1	0.00
Shoshone (1)	1	0.00
Sioux (3)	3	0.00
Tohono O'Odham (4)	5	0.01
Ute (1)	1	0.00
Yaqui (5)	13	0.02
Yuman (2)	6	0.01
All other tribes (42)	59	0.10
American Indian tribes, not spec.	43	0.07
Arab:	338	0.56
Arab/Arabic	110	0.18
Egyptian	95	0.16
Lebanese	116	0.19
Syrian	17	0.03
Armenian	97	0.16
Asian:	39,783	66.25
Cambodian (465)	597	0.99
Chinese, ex. Taiwanese (23,642)	25,411	42.32
Filipino (871)	1,092	1.82
Hmong (1)	1	0.00
Indian (161)	225	0.37
Indonesian (200)	283	0.47
Japanese (4,433)	4,856	8.09
Korean (862)	960	1.60
Laotian (51)	58	0.10
Malaysian (31)	51	0.08
Pakistani (7)	7	0.01
Sri Lankan (5)	5	0.01
Taiwanese (1,116)	1,399	2.33
Thai (402)	470	0.78
Vietnamese (3,101)	3,850	6.41
Other Asian, specified (130)	146	0.24
Other Asian, not specified (167)	372	0.62
Austrian	44	0.07
Basque	6	0.01
Brazilian	55	0.09
British	22	0.04
Canadian	37	0.06
Czech	45	0.08
Czechoslovakian	23	0.04
Danish	54	0.09
Dutch	127	0.21
Eastern European	7	0.01
English	656	1.09
European	57	0.10
Finnish	7	0.01
French, except Basque	371	0.62
French Canadian	32	0.05
German	1,173	1.96
Greek	79	0.13
Hawaii Native/Pacific Islander:	167	0.28
Micronesian: (3)	11	0.02
Guamanian/Chamorro (3)	10	0.02
Other Micronesian	1	0.00
Polynesian: (21)	74	0.12
Native Hawaiian (17)	65	0.11
Samoan (4)	7	0.01
Other Polynesian	2	0.00
Other Pac. Isl., not spec. (13)	82	0.14
Hispanic or Latino:	17,359	28.91
Central American:	696	1.16
Costa Rican	27	0.04
Guatemalan	144	0.24
Honduran	42	0.07
Nicaraguan	106	0.18
Panamanian	9	0.01
Salvadoran	289	0.48
Other Central American	79	0.13
Cuban	122	0.20
Dominican Republic	1	0.00
Mexican	14,123	23.52
Puerto Rican	152	0.25
South American:	242	0.40
Argentinean	33	0.05
Bolivian	6	0.01
Chilean	7	0.01
Colombian	55	0.09
Ecuadorian	26	0.04
Peruvian	97	0.16
Venezuelan	7	0.01
Other South American	11	0.02
Other Hispanic or Latino	2,023	3.37
Hungarian	88	0.15
Iranian	70	0.12
Irish	688	1.15
Italian	805	1.34
Latvian	8	0.01
Northern European	20	0.03
Norwegian	79	0.13
Polish	178	0.30
Portuguese	82	0.14
Romanian	71	0.12
Russian	151	0.25
Scotch-Irish	75	0.13
Scottish	86	0.14
Slavic	13	0.02
Swedish	115	0.19
Ukrainian	82	0.14
United States or American	502	0.84
Welsh	65	0.11
West Indian, excl. Hispanic:	14	0.02
Belizean	10	0.02
Jamaican	4	0.01
White:	14,207	23.66
Not Hispanic (4,362)	5,027	8.37
Hispanic (8,424)	9,180	15.29
Yugoslavian	14	0.02

Monterey

Place Type: City
County: Monterey
Population: 29,674

Ancestry/Race	Number	%
Afghan	18	0.06
African American/Black:	959	3.23
Not Hispanic (716)	893	3.01
Hispanic (33)	66	0.22
African, sub-Saharan:	174	0.58
African	82	0.28
Cape Verdean	10	0.03
Ethiopian	16	0.05
Kenyan	11	0.04
South African	20	0.07
Other sub-Saharan African	35	0.12
Alaska Native tribes, specified:	5	0.02
Alaska Athabascan (1)	1	0.00
Aleut (1)	2	0.01
Eskimo	2	0.01
Am. Ind. or Alaska Nat., not spec.	125	0.42
Albanian	6	0.02
American Indian tribes, specified:	284	0.96
Apache (10)	19	0.06
Blackfeet (5)	18	0.06
Cherokee (18)	76	0.26
Chickasaw (2)	6	0.02
Chippewa (7)	9	0.03
Choctaw (1)	18	0.06
Colville	1	0.00
Comanche (2)	2	0.01
Creek (3)	10	0.03
Crow (1)	1	0.00
Delaware (2)	4	0.01
Iroquois (4)	15	0.05
Latin American Indians (3)	12	0.04
Navajo (1)	1	0.00
Osage (1)	2	0.01
Paiute (3)	3	0.01
Potawatomi	1	0.00
Pueblo (1)	2	0.01
Puget Sound Salish	3	0.01
Seminole	1	0.00
Shoshone (1)	2	0.01
Sioux (2)	13	0.04
Yaqui	2	0.01
All other tribes (36)	63	0.21
American Indian tribes, not spec.	37	0.12
Arab:	384	1.29
Arab/Arabic	53	0.18
Egyptian	113	0.38
Iraqi	8	0.03
Jordanian	29	0.10
Lebanese	115	0.39
Moroccan	21	0.07
Palestinian	19	0.06
Syrian	11	0.04
Other Arab	15	0.05
Armenian	105	0.35
Asian:	2,853	9.61
Cambodian (3)	3	0.01
Chinese, ex. Taiwanese (352)	455	1.53
Filipino (402)	586	1.97
Indian (208)	247	0.83
Indonesian (38)	46	0.16
Japanese (603)	802	2.70
Korean (341)	396	1.33
Laotian (2)	2	0.01
Malaysian (3)	5	0.02
Pakistani (1)	1	0.00
Sri Lankan (3)	3	0.01
Taiwanese (18)	23	0.08
Thai (48)	61	0.21
Vietnamese (87)	104	0.35
Other Asian, specified (22)	29	0.10
Other Asian, not specified (24)	90	0.30
Assyrian/Chaldean/Syriac	20	0.07
Australian	13	0.04

Notes: 1. Figures in the "Number" column do not add up to the total population due to: a) Ancestry/Race overlap — e.g. persons can report being both White and Irish, b) persons of Hispanic origin can report being any race, c) persons reporting two ancestries are counted in both categories. 2. Numbers in parentheses indicate the number of persons reporting this ancestry/race alone, not in combination with any other ancestry/race. 3. Refer to the Explanation of Data in the front of the book for more detailed information.

Ancestry/Race	Number	%
Austrian	130	0.44
Basque	40	0.13
Belgian	39	0.13
Brazilian	41	0.14
British	263	0.88
Bulgarian	51	0.17
Canadian	93	0.31
Celtic	29	0.10
Croatian	61	0.20
Czech	206	0.69
Czechoslovakian	104	0.35
Danish	354	1.19
Dutch	459	1.54
Eastern European	27	0.09
English	3,768	12.66
Estonian	2	0.01
European	473	1.59
Finnish	57	0.19
French, except Basque	885	2.97
French Canadian	229	0.77
German	5,100	17.13
Greek	189	0.63
Hawaii Native/Pacific Islander:	180	0.61
Melanesian: (8)	12	0.04
Fijian (8)	12	0.04
Micronesian: (39)	59	0.20
Guamanian/Chamorro (22)	38	0.13
Other Micronesian (17)	21	0.07
Polynesian: (29)	72	0.24
Native Hawaiian (26)	65	0.22
Samoan (2)	4	0.01
Tongan (1)	3	0.01
Other Pac. Isl., not spec. (10)	37	0.12
Hispanic or Latino:	3,222	10.86
Central American:	258	0.87
Costa Rican	7	0.02
Guatemalan	13	0.04
Honduran	5	0.02
Nicaraguan	10	0.03
Panamanian	30	0.10
Salvadoran	170	0.57
Other Central American	23	0.08
Cuban	43	0.14
Dominican Republic	10	0.03
Mexican	1,960	6.61
Puerto Rican	163	0.55
South American:	162	0.55
Argentinean	12	0.04
Bolivian	2	0.01
Chilean	25	0.08
Colombian	39	0.13
Ecuadorian	12	0.04
Paraguayan	9	0.03
Peruvian	23	0.08
Uruguayan	2	0.01
Venezuelan	23	0.08
Other South American	15	0.05
Other Hispanic or Latino	626	2.11
Hungarian	249	0.84
Icelander	8	0.03
Iranian	47	0.16
Irish	3,569	11.99
Israeli	24	0.08
Italian	3,203	10.76
Latvian	6	0.02
Lithuanian	89	0.30
Macedonian	22	0.07
New Zealander	16	0.05
Northern European	47	0.16
Norwegian	522	1.75
Pennsylvania German	65	0.22
Polish	848	2.85
Portuguese	377	1.27
Romanian	67	0.23
Russian	483	1.62
Scandinavian	107	0.36
Scotch-Irish	613	2.06
Scottish	1,202	4.04
Serbian	11	0.04
Slavic	16	0.05
Slovak	40	0.13
Slovene	37	0.12
Swedish	595	2.00
Swiss	204	0.69
Turkish	200	0.67
Ukrainian	100	0.34
United States or American	895	3.01
Welsh	301	1.01
West Indian, excl. Hispanic:	49	0.16
Barbadian	4	0.01
British West Indian	7	0.02
Dutch West Indian	8	0.03
Haitian	22	0.07
Trinidadian and Tobagonian	7	0.02
West Indian	1	0.00
White:	25,157	84.78
Not Hispanic (22,246)	23,171	78.09
Hispanic (1,739)	1,986	6.69
Yugoslavian	77	0.26

Moorpark

Place Type: City
County: Ventura
Population: 31,415

Ancestry/Race	Number	%
Afghan	16	0.05
African American/Black:	598	1.90
Not Hispanic (435)	527	1.68
Hispanic (41)	71	0.23
African, sub-Saharan:	106	0.34
African	88	0.28
Ethiopian	7	0.02
Nigerian	11	0.04
Alaska Native tribes, specified:	4	0.01
Tlingit-Haida (4)	4	0.01
Alaska Native tribes, not specified	1	0.00
Am. Ind. or Alaska Nat., not spec.	117	0.37
American Indian tribes, specified:	251	0.80
Apache (8)	15	0.05
Blackfeet	17	0.05
Cherokee (15)	89	0.28
Chickasaw (1)	2	0.01
Chippewa (3)	12	0.04
Choctaw (6)	11	0.04
Comanche (1)	3	0.01
Cree (1)	10	0.03
Creek (2)	6	0.02
Delaware (1)	1	0.00
Iroquois	2	0.01
Latin American Indians (3)	23	0.07
Menominee	2	0.01
Navajo (13)	15	0.05
Osage (1)	1	0.00
Paiute (1)	1	0.00
Potawatomi	1	0.00
Pueblo (11)	14	0.04
Seminole	1	0.00
Sioux (1)	2	0.01
Tohono O'Odham (1)	1	0.00
All other tribes (8)	22	0.07
American Indian tribes, not spec.	15	0.05
Arab:	435	1.39
Arab/Arabic	32	0.10
Egyptian	195	0.62
Lebanese	81	0.26
Palestinian	40	0.13
Syrian	87	0.28
Armenian	117	0.37
Asian:	2,200	7.00
Bangladeshi (2)	2	0.01
Cambodian (23)	30	0.10
Chinese, ex. Taiwanese (249)	340	1.08
Filipino (386)	492	1.57
Indian (352)	376	1.20
Indonesian (20)	34	0.11
Japanese (253)	382	1.22
Korean (126)	145	0.46
Laotian (1)	1	0.00
Malaysian (8)	8	0.03
Pakistani (17)	20	0.06
Sri Lankan (13)	15	0.05
Taiwanese (21)	25	0.08
Thai (31)	38	0.12
Vietnamese (211)	232	0.74
Other Asian, specified (4)	11	0.04
Other Asian, not specified (17)	49	0.16
Austrian	142	0.45
Basque	9	0.03
Belgian	17	0.05
British	94	0.30
Canadian	101	0.32
Croatian	36	0.12
Czech	92	0.29
Czechoslovakian	56	0.18
Danish	205	0.66
Dutch	730	2.33
Eastern European	38	0.12
English	2,825	9.03
European	505	1.61
Finnish	7	0.02
French, except Basque	772	2.47
French Canadian	208	0.67
German	4,572	14.62
Greek	129	0.41
Hawaii Native/Pacific Islander:	119	0.38
Micronesian: (6)	8	0.03
Guamanian/Chamorro (6)	8	0.03
Polynesian: (31)	81	0.26
Native Hawaiian (20)	60	0.19
Samoan (5)	10	0.03
Tongan (1)	2	0.01
Other Polynesian (5)	9	0.03
Other Pac. Isl., specified	1	0.00
Other Pac. Isl., not spec. (9)	29	0.09
Hispanic or Latino:	8,735	27.81
Central American:	195	0.62
Costa Rican	15	0.05
Guatemalan	73	0.23
Honduran	17	0.05
Nicaraguan	4	0.01
Panamanian	3	0.01
Salvadoran	73	0.23
Other Central American	10	0.03
Cuban	70	0.22
Dominican Republic	8	0.03
Mexican	7,255	23.09
Puerto Rican	107	0.34
South American:	164	0.52
Argentinean	22	0.07
Bolivian	5	0.02
Chilean	11	0.04
Colombian	50	0.16
Ecuadorian	20	0.06
Paraguayan	1	0.00
Peruvian	25	0.08
Uruguayan	8	0.03
Venezuelan	1	0.00
Other South American	21	0.07
Other Hispanic or Latino	936	2.98
Hungarian	150	0.48
Iranian	208	0.67
Irish	3,302	10.56
Italian	2,661	8.51
Latvian	6	0.02
Lithuanian	33	0.11
New Zealander	6	0.02
Northern European	70	0.22
Norwegian	818	2.62
Polish	881	2.82
Portuguese	138	0.44
Romanian	73	0.23
Russian	619	1.98
Scandinavian	58	0.19
Scotch-Irish	440	1.41
Scottish	697	2.23
Serbian	7	0.02
Slavic	11	0.04
Slovak	31	0.10

Notes: 1. Figures in the "Number" column do not add up to the total population due to: a) Ancestry/Race overlap — e.g. persons can report being both White and Irish, b) persons of Hispanic origin can report being any race, c) persons reporting two ancestries are counted in both categories. 2. Numbers in parentheses indicate the number of persons reporting this ancestry/race alone, not in combination with any other ancestry/race. 3. Refer to the Explanation of Data in the front of the book for more detailed information.

Slovene	25	0.08
Swedish	397	1.27
Swiss	127	0.41
Turkish	7	0.02
Ukrainian	71	0.23
United States or American	1,648	5.27
Welsh	190	0.61
West Indian, excl. Hispanic:	21	0.07
Jamaican	11	0.04
West Indian	10	0.03
White:	24,449	77.83
Not Hispanic (19,611)	20,249	64.46
Hispanic (3,767)	4,200	13.37
Yugoslavian	49	0.16

Moraga

Place Type: Town
County: Contra Costa
Population: 16,290

Ancestry/Race	Number	%
Afghan	32	0.19
African American/Black:	205	1.26
Not Hispanic (161)	200	1.23
Hispanic (4)	5	0.03
African, sub-Saharan:	88	0.53
African	53	0.32
Ethiopian	7	0.04
Nigerian	6	0.04
South African	22	0.13
Alaska Native tribes, specified:	1	0.01
Aleut	1	0.01
Am. Ind. or Alaska Nat., not spec.	14	0.09
Albanian	5	0.03
Alsatian	7	0.04
American Indian tribes, specified:	81	0.50
Apache	1	0.01
Blackfeet	4	0.02
Cherokee (3)	24	0.15
Chickasaw	1	0.01
Chippewa	6	0.04
Choctaw (1)	8	0.05
Creek	2	0.01
Iroquois (1)	2	0.01
Latin American Indians (5)	9	0.06
Navajo (2)	4	0.02
Seminole	1	0.01
Sioux (1)	4	0.02
Yaqui	1	0.01
All other tribes (9)	14	0.09
American Indian tribes, not spec.	3	0.02
Arab:	135	0.81
Arab/Arabic	21	0.13
Egyptian	11	0.07
Jordanian	19	0.11
Lebanese	52	0.31
Palestinian	26	0.16
Other Arab	6	0.04
Armenian	178	1.07
Asian:	2,520	15.47
Chinese, ex. Taiwanese (1,069)	1,268	7.78
Filipino (126)	218	1.34
Hmong (1)	1	0.01
Indian (123)	158	0.97
Indonesian	3	0.02
Japanese (262)	398	2.44
Korean (211)	240	1.47
Laotian (1)	1	0.01
Malaysian (2)	9	0.06
Pakistani (8)	12	0.07
Sri Lankan	1	0.01
Taiwanese (70)	86	0.53
Thai (6)	9	0.06
Vietnamese (37)	52	0.32
Other Asian, specified (1)	2	0.01
Other Asian, not specified (19)	62	0.38
Australian	19	0.11
Austrian	252	1.51
Belgian	50	0.30
British	222	1.33
Bulgarian	16	0.10
Canadian	66	0.40
Celtic	26	0.16
Croatian	63	0.38
Czech	66	0.40
Czechoslovakian	39	0.23
Danish	220	1.32
Dutch	270	1.62
Eastern European	91	0.55
English	2,624	15.77
Estonian	13	0.08
European	440	2.64
Finnish	173	1.04
French, except Basque	689	4.14
French Canadian	140	0.84
German	2,817	16.93
Greek	193	1.16
Hawaii Native/Pacific Islander:	60	0.37
Micronesian: (8)	9	0.06
Guamanian/Chamorro (8)	9	0.06
Polynesian: (5)	38	0.23
Native Hawaiian (3)	30	0.18
Samoan	5	0.03
Tongan (2)	2	0.01
Other Polynesian	1	0.01
Other Pac. Isl., not spec. (1)	13	0.08
Hispanic or Latino:	775	4.76
Central American:	49	0.30
Costa Rican	11	0.07
Guatemalan	4	0.02
Nicaraguan	3	0.02
Panamanian	4	0.02
Salvadoran	24	0.15
Other Central American	3	0.02
Cuban	13	0.08
Mexican	404	2.48
Puerto Rican	27	0.17
South American:	94	0.58
Argentinean	8	0.05
Bolivian	2	0.01
Chilean	19	0.12
Colombian	26	0.16
Ecuadorian	7	0.04
Peruvian	18	0.11
Venezuelan	6	0.04
Other South American	8	0.05
Other Hispanic or Latino	188	1.15
Hungarian	114	0.69
Icelander	8	0.05
Iranian	210	1.26
Irish	2,529	15.20
Israeli	22	0.13
Italian	1,455	8.74
Latvian	33	0.20
Lithuanian	92	0.55
Northern European	62	0.37
Norwegian	266	1.60
Polish	523	3.14
Portuguese	174	1.05
Romanian	2	0.01
Russian	448	2.69
Scandinavian	123	0.74
Scotch-Irish	344	2.07
Scottish	667	4.01
Slovak	22	0.13
Slovene	48	0.29
Swedish	509	3.06
Swiss	123	0.74
Turkish	19	0.11
Ukrainian	26	0.16
United States or American	487	2.93
Welsh	125	0.75
West Indian, excl. Hispanic:	6	0.04
Haitian	6	0.04
White:	13,772	84.54
Not Hispanic (12,760)	13,242	81.29
Hispanic (452)	530	3.25
Yugoslavian	29	0.17

Moreno Valley

Place Type: City
County: Riverside
Population: 142,381

Ancestry/Race	Number	%
Acadian/Cajun	28	0.02
Afghan	141	0.10
African American/Black:	30,752	21.60
Not Hispanic (27,536)	29,445	20.68
Hispanic (774)	1,307	0.92
African, sub-Saharan:	1,486	1.04
African	1,231	0.86
Cape Verdean	9	0.01
Ethiopian	20	0.01
Ghanian	21	0.01
Kenyan	47	0.03
Nigerian	102	0.07
Sierra Leonean	22	0.02
Somalian	8	0.01
Zimbabwean	10	0.01
Other sub-Saharan African	16	0.01
Alaska Native tribes, specified:	13	0.01
Alaska Athabascan (1)	2	0.00
Aleut	1	0.00
Eskimo (2)	3	0.00
Tlingit-Haida (1)	7	0.00
Alaska Native tribes, not specified	1	0.00
Am. Ind. or Alaska Nat., not spec.	1,065	0.75
Albanian	28	0.02
American Indian tribes, specified:	1,622	1.14
Apache (58)	135	0.09
Blackfeet (13)	87	0.06
Cherokee (86)	449	0.32
Cheyenne (2)	10	0.01
Chickasaw	9	0.01
Chippewa (23)	38	0.03
Choctaw (39)	97	0.07
Colville (1)	1	0.00
Comanche (3)	10	0.01
Cree (1)	5	0.00
Creek (4)	18	0.01
Delaware	6	0.00
Houma	3	0.00
Iroquois (13)	22	0.02
Latin American Indians (178)	262	0.18
Lumbee (1)	1	0.00
Menominee	2	0.00
Navajo (53)	85	0.06
Osage (3)	11	0.01
Ottawa	4	0.00
Paiute (5)	10	0.01
Pima (6)	9	0.01
Potawatomi (2)	4	0.00
Pueblo (16)	26	0.02
Puget Sound Salish (4)	9	0.01
Seminole (5)	13	0.01
Shoshone (1)	5	0.00
Sioux (9)	33	0.02
Tohono O'Odham (6)	10	0.01
Ute	2	0.00
Yakama	1	0.00
Yaqui (6)	24	0.02
Yuman (10)	11	0.01
All other tribes (98)	210	0.15
American Indian tribes, not spec.	144	0.10
Arab:	959	0.67
Arab/Arabic	425	0.30
Egyptian	143	0.10
Iraqi	68	0.05
Jordanian	48	0.03
Lebanese	217	0.15
Palestinian	50	0.04
Syrian	8	0.01
Armenian	153	0.11
Asian:	10,911	7.66
Bangladeshi (8)	12	0.01
Cambodian (300)	386	0.27
Chinese, ex. Taiwanese (490)	822	0.58

Notes: 1. Figures in the "Number" column do not add up to the total population due to: a) Ancestry/Race overlap — e.g. persons can report being both White and Irish, b) persons of Hispanic origin can report being any race, c) persons reporting two ancestries are counted in both categories. 2. Numbers in parentheses indicate the number of persons reporting this ancestry/race alone, not in combination with any other ancestry/race. 3. Refer to the Explanation of Data in the front of the book for more detailed information.

Ancestry/Race	Number	%
Filipino (3,968)	4,970	3.49
Hmong (90)	92	0.06
Indian (514)	652	0.46
Indonesian (67)	132	0.09
Japanese (443)	870	0.61
Korean (629)	794	0.56
Laotian (309)	393	0.28
Malaysian (3)	12	0.01
Pakistani (52)	94	0.07
Sri Lankan (7)	8	0.01
Taiwanese (65)	98	0.07
Thai (226)	351	0.25
Vietnamese (844)	943	0.66
Other Asian, specified (3)	12	0.01
Other Asian, not specified (126)	270	0.19
Australian	8	0.01
Austrian	65	0.05
Basque	96	0.07
Belgian	12	0.01
Brazilian	25	0.02
British	358	0.25
Bulgarian	19	0.01
Canadian	366	0.26
Celtic	12	0.01
Croatian	56	0.04
Czech	117	0.08
Czechoslovakian	187	0.13
Danish	574	0.40
Dutch	1,715	1.20
English	7,170	5.03
European	902	0.63
Finnish	98	0.07
French, except Basque	2,545	1.79
French Canadian	577	0.40
German	11,124	7.80
German Russian	12	0.01
Greek	265	0.19
Hawaii Native/Pacific Islander:	1,351	0.95
Melanesian: (1)	11	0.01
Fijian (1)	11	0.01
Micronesian: (208)	302	0.21
Guamanian/Chamorro (189)	282	0.20
Other Micronesian (19)	20	0.01
Polynesian: (455)	847	0.59
Native Hawaiian (107)	371	0.26
Samoan (292)	393	0.28
Tongan (55)	69	0.05
Other Polynesian (1)	14	0.01
Other Pac. Isl., specified	3	0.00
Other Pac. Isl., not spec. (42)	188	0.13
Hispanic or Latino:	54,689	38.41
Central American:	1,586	1.11
Costa Rican	113	0.08
Guatemalan	319	0.22
Honduran	86	0.06
Nicaraguan	198	0.14
Panamanian	76	0.05
Salvadoran	628	0.44
Other Central American	166	0.12
Cuban	417	0.29
Dominican Republic	15	0.01
Mexican	43,485	30.54
Puerto Rican	1,177	0.83
South American:	727	0.51
Argentinean	94	0.07
Bolivian	27	0.02
Chilean	21	0.01
Colombian	139	0.10
Ecuadorian	143	0.10
Peruvian	194	0.14
Uruguayan	9	0.01
Venezuelan	34	0.02
Other South American	66	0.05
Other Hispanic or Latino	7,282	5.11
Hungarian	367	0.26
Icelander	79	0.06
Iranian	177	0.12
Irish	8,735	6.13
Israeli	14	0.01
Italian	4,383	3.07
Latvian	5	0.00
Lithuanian	191	0.13
Maltese	15	0.01
New Zealander	3	0.00
Northern European	36	0.03
Norwegian	1,209	0.85
Pennsylvania German	68	0.05
Polish	1,893	1.33
Portuguese	375	0.26
Romanian	177	0.12
Russian	355	0.25
Scandinavian	99	0.07
Scotch-Irish	1,220	0.86
Scottish	1,399	0.98
Slavic	15	0.01
Slovak	85	0.06
Slovene	36	0.03
Swedish	1,619	1.14
Swiss	118	0.08
Turkish	12	0.01
Ukrainian	37	0.03
United States or American	4,135	2.90
Welsh	689	0.48
West Indian, excl. Hispanic:	908	0.64
Barbadian	11	0.01
Belizean	209	0.15
Bermudan	9	0.01
British West Indian	43	0.03
Dutch West Indian	12	0.01
Haitian	64	0.04
Jamaican	470	0.33
Trinidadian and Tobagonian	80	0.06
West Indian	10	0.01
White:	73,173	51.39
Not Hispanic (45,881)	49,273	34.61
Hispanic (20,808)	23,900	16.79
Yugoslavian	68	0.05

Morgan Hill

Place Type: City
County: Santa Clara
Population: 33,556

Ancestry/Race	Number	%
African American/Black:	739	2.20
Not Hispanic (537)	661	1.97
Hispanic (36)	78	0.23
African, sub-Saharan:	84	0.25
African	66	0.20
Ethiopian	14	0.04
South African	4	0.01
Alaska Native tribes, specified:	7	0.02
Aleut	1	0.00
Eskimo (1)	3	0.01
Tlingit-Haida	1	0.00
All other tribes (1)	2	0.01
Am. Ind. or Alaska Nat., not spec.	203	0.60
American Indian tribes, specified:	413	1.23
Apache (24)	45	0.13
Blackfeet	2	0.01
Cherokee (25)	116	0.35
Cheyenne (7)	7	0.02
Chickasaw (1)	1	0.00
Chippewa	2	0.01
Choctaw (2)	16	0.05
Comanche (3)	5	0.01
Cree (2)	6	0.02
Delaware	1	0.00
Iroquois	3	0.01
Kiowa	6	0.02
Latin American Indians (12)	51	0.15
Navajo (20)	27	0.08
Osage (3)	3	0.01
Ottawa	1	0.00
Potawatomi (2)	2	0.01
Pueblo (1)	4	0.01
Shoshone (3)	3	0.01
Sioux (14)	27	0.08
Yaqui (15)	27	0.08
All other tribes (31)	58	0.17
American Indian tribes, not spec.	108	0.32
Arab:	184	0.55
Arab/Arabic	72	0.21
Egyptian	46	0.14
Lebanese	11	0.03
Moroccan	13	0.04
Syrian	34	0.10
Other Arab	8	0.02
Armenian	43	0.13
Asian:	2,733	8.14
Cambodian (19)	24	0.07
Chinese, ex. Taiwanese (451)	634	1.89
Filipino (383)	625	1.86
Indian (351)	401	1.20
Indonesian (7)	13	0.04
Japanese (357)	523	1.56
Korean (110)	143	0.43
Malaysian (2)	3	0.01
Pakistani (8)	11	0.03
Taiwanese (13)	15	0.04
Thai (14)	23	0.07
Vietnamese (239)	257	0.77
Other Asian, specified	3	0.01
Other Asian, not specified (16)	58	0.17
Assyrian/Chaldean/Syriac	11	0.03
Australian	5	0.01
Austrian	104	0.31
Belgian	9	0.03
British	208	0.62
Canadian	123	0.37
Celtic	35	0.10
Croatian	95	0.28
Czech	60	0.18
Czechoslovakian	64	0.19
Danish	457	1.36
Dutch	454	1.35
Eastern European	12	0.04
English	3,293	9.79
Estonian	6	0.02
European	304	0.90
Finnish	78	0.23
French, except Basque	1,027	3.05
French Canadian	215	0.64
German	5,165	15.36
Greek	268	0.80
Hawaii Native/Pacific Islander:	249	0.74
Micronesian: (19)	51	0.15
Guamanian/Chamorro (19)	51	0.15
Polynesian: (44)	155	0.46
Native Hawaiian (28)	127	0.38
Samoan (10)	16	0.05
Tongan (6)	9	0.03
Other Polynesian	3	0.01
Other Pac. Isl., specified	2	0.01
Other Pac. Isl., not spec. (14)	41	0.12
Hispanic or Latino:	9,229	27.50
Central American:	157	0.47
Costa Rican	6	0.02
Guatemalan	53	0.16
Honduran	4	0.01
Nicaraguan	24	0.07
Panamanian	2	0.01
Salvadoran	56	0.17
Other Central American	12	0.04
Cuban	36	0.11
Dominican Republic	1	0.00
Mexican	7,501	22.35
Puerto Rican	108	0.32
South American:	109	0.32
Argentinean	10	0.03
Bolivian	9	0.03
Chilean	21	0.06
Colombian	23	0.07
Ecuadorian	3	0.01
Peruvian	18	0.05
Uruguayan	1	0.00
Venezuelan	11	0.03
Other South American	13	0.04
Other Hispanic or Latino	1,317	3.92

Notes: 1. Figures in the "Number" column do not add up to the total population due to: a) Ancestry/Race overlap — e.g. persons can report being both White and Irish, b) persons of Hispanic origin can report being any race, c) persons reporting two ancestries are counted in both categories. 2. Numbers in parentheses indicate the number of persons reporting this ancestry/race alone, not in combination with any other ancestry/race. 3. Refer to the Explanation of Data in the front of the book for more detailed information.

Hungarian	125	0.37
Icelander	16	0.05
Iranian	147	0.44
Irish	3,422	10.17
Israeli	17	0.05
Italian	3,083	9.17
Latvian	66	0.20
Lithuanian	96	0.29
New Zealander	12	0.04
Northern European	42	0.12
Norwegian	572	1.70
Pennsylvania German	17	0.05
Polish	607	1.80
Portuguese	761	2.26
Romanian	9	0.03
Russian	346	1.03
Scandinavian	113	0.34
Scotch-Irish	513	1.53
Scottish	639	1.90
Slovak	34	0.10
Slovene	38	0.11
Swedish	631	1.88
Swiss	268	0.80
Ukrainian	46	0.14
United States or American	1,415	4.21
Welsh	266	0.79
West Indian, excl. Hispanic:	24	0.07
Bermudan	15	0.04
Jamaican	9	0.03
White:	25,739	76.70
Not Hispanic (20,583)	21,410	63.80
Hispanic (3,713)	4,329	12.90
Yugoslavian	90	0.27

Morro Bay

Place Type: City
County: San Luis Obispo
Population: 10,350

Ancestry/Race	Number	%
African American/Black:	106	1.02
Not Hispanic (59)	82	0.79
Hispanic (11)	24	0.23
Alaska Native tribes, specified:	2	0.02
Aleut	1	0.01
Eskimo	1	0.01
Am. Ind. or Alaska Nat., not spec.	56	0.54
American Indian tribes, specified:	137	1.32
Apache (2)	6	0.06
Blackfeet (1)	3	0.03
Cherokee (14)	40	0.39
Chickasaw (2)	3	0.03
Chippewa (2)	3	0.03
Choctaw (6)	17	0.16
Latin American Indians (2)	7	0.07
Navajo	4	0.04
Seminole	1	0.01
Sioux (8)	8	0.08
Yaqui (4)	4	0.04
All other tribes (30)	41	0.40
American Indian tribes, not spec.	7	0.07
Arab:	78	0.76
Egyptian	9	0.09
Lebanese	30	0.29
Syrian	39	0.38
Armenian	26	0.25
Asian:	275	2.66
Cambodian	1	0.01
Chinese, ex. Taiwanese (31)	42	0.41
Filipino (30)	72	0.70
Indian (20)	31	0.30
Indonesian (1)	4	0.04
Japanese (43)	55	0.53
Korean (33)	36	0.35
Pakistani (2)	2	0.02
Taiwanese (8)	8	0.08
Thai (5)	5	0.05
Vietnamese (9)	9	0.09
Other Asian, specified (1)	5	0.05
Other Asian, not specified (2)	5	0.05
Austrian	17	0.16
Basque	9	0.09
Belgian	8	0.08
British	72	0.70
Canadian	45	0.44
Celtic	35	0.34
Czech	50	0.49
Czechoslovakian	17	0.16
Danish	155	1.50
Dutch	257	2.49
Eastern European	21	0.20
English	1,672	16.22
European	353	3.42
Finnish	62	0.60
French, except Basque	337	3.27
French Canadian	100	0.97
German	1,833	17.78
Greek	25	0.24
Hawaii Native/Pacific Islander:	23	0.22
Melanesian:	1	0.01
Fijian	1	0.01
Polynesian: (9)	17	0.16
Native Hawaiian (7)	14	0.14
Samoan (2)	3	0.03
Other Pac. Isl., not spec.	5	0.05
Hispanic or Latino:	1,183	11.43
Central American:	17	0.16
Guatemalan	7	0.07
Honduran	1	0.01
Nicaraguan	3	0.03
Salvadoran	4	0.04
Other Central American	2	0.02
Cuban	2	0.02
Mexican	949	9.17
Puerto Rican	18	0.17
South American:	13	0.13
Argentinean	2	0.02
Chilean	4	0.04
Colombian	1	0.01
Ecuadorian	2	0.02
Venezuelan	1	0.01
Other South American	3	0.03
Other Hispanic or Latino	184	1.78
Hungarian	24	0.23
Iranian	32	0.31
Irish	1,628	15.79
Italian	447	4.34
Lithuanian	10	0.10
Northern European	30	0.29
Norwegian	223	2.16
Pennsylvania German	15	0.15
Polish	117	1.14
Portuguese	177	1.72
Romanian	21	0.20
Russian	82	0.80
Scandinavian	42	0.41
Scotch-Irish	283	2.75
Scottish	424	4.11
Serbian	11	0.11
Slavic	7	0.07
Swedish	273	2.65
Swiss	82	0.80
Ukrainian	7	0.07
United States or American	507	4.92
Welsh	172	1.67
White:	9,530	92.08
Not Hispanic (8,630)	8,813	85.15
Hispanic (627)	717	6.93
Yugoslavian	8	0.08

Mountain View

Place Type: City
County: Santa Clara
Population: 70,708

Ancestry/Race	Number	%
African American/Black:	2,201	3.11
Not Hispanic (1,674)	2,004	2.83
Hispanic (115)	197	0.28
African, sub-Saharan:	209	0.30
African	102	0.14
Cape Verdean	8	0.01
Ethiopian	30	0.04
Kenyan	4	0.01
Nigerian	10	0.01
Senegalese	7	0.01
South African	16	0.02
Other sub-Saharan African	32	0.05
Alaska Native tribes, specified:	15	0.02
Alaska Athabascan (2)	3	0.00
Aleut (1)	3	0.00
Eskimo	1	0.00
Tlingit-Haida (5)	7	0.01
All other tribes (1)	1	0.00
Am. Ind. or Alaska Nat., not spec.	233	0.33
Alsatian	20	0.03
American Indian tribes, specified:	409	0.58
Apache (11)	20	0.03
Blackfeet (1)	7	0.01
Cherokee (30)	125	0.18
Chickasaw (4)	4	0.01
Chippewa (2)	4	0.01
Choctaw (4)	13	0.02
Comanche	5	0.01
Cree	2	0.00
Creek (3)	13	0.02
Crow (1)	1	0.00
Delaware (2)	2	0.00
Iroquois (8)	17	0.02
Kiowa (2)	2	0.00
Latin American Indians (33)	65	0.09
Lumbee	1	0.00
Navajo (14)	23	0.03
Osage (1)	4	0.01
Paiute (1)	3	0.00
Pima (5)	7	0.01
Potawatomi (2)	4	0.01
Pueblo (1)	4	0.01
Puget Sound Salish (1)	3	0.00
Seminole (1)	6	0.01
Shoshone (1)	1	0.00
Sioux (7)	14	0.02
Tohono O'Odham (1)	1	0.00
Yaqui (5)	6	0.01
All other tribes (20)	52	0.07
American Indian tribes, not spec.	18	0.03
Arab:	498	0.71
Arab/Arabic	112	0.16
Egyptian	56	0.08
Iraqi	21	0.03
Lebanese	135	0.19
Palestinian	53	0.08
Syrian	41	0.06
Other Arab	80	0.11
Armenian	239	0.34
Asian:	16,219	22.94
Bangladeshi (4)	4	0.01
Cambodian (27)	29	0.04
Chinese, ex. Taiwanese (5,440)	5,931	8.39
Filipino (2,224)	2,638	3.73
Hmong (7)	8	0.01
Indian (3,072)	3,206	4.53
Indonesian (52)	81	0.11
Japanese (1,658)	2,040	2.89
Korean (682)	773	1.09
Laotian (7)	9	0.01
Malaysian (14)	20	0.03
Pakistani (86)	117	0.17
Sri Lankan (44)	52	0.07
Taiwanese (144)	176	0.25
Thai (56)	64	0.09
Vietnamese (694)	740	1.05
Other Asian, specified (59)	81	0.11
Other Asian, not specified (112)	250	0.35
Assyrian/Chaldean/Syriac	15	0.02
Australian	65	0.09
Austrian	278	0.39
Basque	25	0.04

Notes: 1. Figures in the "Number" column do not add up to the total population due to: a) Ancestry/Race overlap — e.g. persons can report being both White and Irish, b) persons of Hispanic origin can report being any race, c) persons reporting two ancestries are counted in both categories. 2. Numbers in parentheses indicate the number of persons reporting this ancestry/race alone, not in combination with any other ancestry/race. 3. Refer to the Explanation of Data in the front of the book for more detailed information.

Belgian	90	0.13
Brazilian	34	0.05
British	603	0.86
Bulgarian	37	0.05
Canadian	295	0.42
Celtic	49	0.07
Croatian	265	0.38
Czech	282	0.40
Czechoslovakian	129	0.18
Danish	331	0.47
Dutch	862	1.22
Eastern European	233	0.33
English	6,411	9.10
Estonian	14	0.02
European	859	1.22
Finnish	189	0.27
French, except Basque	1,979	2.81
French Canadian	352	0.50
German	8,065	11.45
Greek	316	0.45
Guyanese	9	0.01
Hawaii Native/Pacific Islander:	412	0.58
Melanesian: (28)	30	0.04
Fijian (28)	30	0.04
Micronesian: (40)	79	0.11
Guamanian/Chamorro (39)	77	0.11
Other Micronesian (1)	2	0.00
Polynesian: (75)	190	0.27
Native Hawaiian (28)	113	0.16
Samoan (23)	35	0.05
Tongan (22)	36	0.05
Other Polynesian (2)	6	0.01
Other Pac. Isl., specified	3	0.00
Other Pac. Isl., not spec. (37)	110	0.16
Hispanic or Latino:	12,911	18.26
Central American:	956	1.35
Costa Rican	19	0.03
Guatemalan	215	0.30
Honduran	33	0.05
Nicaraguan	52	0.07
Panamanian	27	0.04
Salvadoran	521	0.74
Other Central American	89	0.13
Cuban	88	0.12
Dominican Republic	16	0.02
Mexican	9,243	13.07
Puerto Rican	282	0.40
South American:	445	0.63
Argentinean	51	0.07
Bolivian	49	0.07
Chilean	30	0.04
Colombian	67	0.09
Ecuadorian	18	0.03
Paraguayan	3	0.00
Peruvian	142	0.20
Uruguayan	5	0.01
Venezuelan	26	0.04
Other South American	54	0.08
Other Hispanic or Latino	1,881	2.66
Hungarian	466	0.66
Iranian	620	0.88
Irish	5,746	8.15
Israeli	160	0.23
Italian	3,080	4.37
Latvian	62	0.09
Lithuanian	153	0.22
Luxemburger	3	0.00
Maltese	33	0.05
New Zealander	65	0.09
Northern European	134	0.19
Norwegian	981	1.39
Pennsylvania German	15	0.02
Polish	1,579	2.24
Portuguese	556	0.79
Romanian	158	0.22
Russian	2,142	3.04
Scandinavian	127	0.18
Scotch-Irish	908	1.29
Scottish	1,758	2.49
Serbian	85	0.12
Slavic	85	0.12
Slovak	127	0.18
Slovene	27	0.04
Swedish	1,431	2.03
Swiss	516	0.73
Turkish	93	0.13
Ukrainian	599	0.85
United States or American	1,709	2.43
Welsh	471	0.67
West Indian, excl. Hispanic:	56	0.08
Jamaican	50	0.07
Trinidadian and Tobagonian	6	0.01
White:	47,505	67.18
Not Hispanic (39,029)	40,707	57.57
Hispanic (6,061)	6,798	9.61
Yugoslavian	160	0.23

Murrieta

Place Type: City
County: Riverside
Population: 44,282

Ancestry/Race	Number	%
Acadian/Cajun	9	0.02
Afghan	23	0.05
African American/Black:	1,811	4.09
Not Hispanic (1,401)	1,662	3.75
Hispanic (99)	149	0.34
African, sub-Saharan:	53	0.12
African	44	0.10
South African	9	0.02
Alaska Native tribes, specified:	19	0.04
Alaska Athabascan (1)	3	0.01
Aleut (2)	6	0.01
Eskimo (2)	4	0.01
Tlingit-Haida (6)	6	0.01
Alaska Native tribes, not specified	1	0.00
Am. Ind. or Alaska Nat., not spec.	187	0.42
Albanian	10	0.02
Alsatian	7	0.02
American Indian tribes, specified:	507	1.14
Apache (11)	17	0.04
Blackfeet (1)	9	0.02
Cherokee (37)	183	0.41
Cheyenne	6	0.01
Chippewa (2)	7	0.02
Choctaw (7)	17	0.04
Colville (4)	4	0.01
Comanche (2)	5	0.01
Cree (1)	3	0.01
Creek (1)	4	0.01
Crow	4	0.01
Delaware	5	0.01
Iroquois (1)	17	0.04
Kiowa (2)	5	0.01
Latin American Indians (9)	19	0.04
Navajo (4)	12	0.03
Ottawa (2)	2	0.00
Paiute (2)	10	0.02
Potawatomi (2)	7	0.02
Pueblo (6)	13	0.03
Seminole (1)	6	0.01
Shoshone (2)	3	0.01
Sioux (2)	6	0.01
Ute	4	0.01
Yaqui (4)	10	0.02
All other tribes (74)	129	0.29
American Indian tribes, not spec.	22	0.05
Arab:	191	0.43
Arab/Arabic	27	0.06
Egyptian	26	0.06
Lebanese	89	0.20
Moroccan	4	0.01
Palestinian	36	0.08
Syrian	9	0.02
Armenian	180	0.41
Asian:	2,526	5.70
Cambodian (14)	21	0.05
Chinese, ex. Taiwanese (134)	261	0.59
Filipino (972)	1,237	2.79
Hmong (3)	3	0.01
Indian (69)	98	0.22
Indonesian (11)	43	0.10
Japanese (162)	347	0.78
Korean (125)	168	0.38
Laotian (32)	46	0.10
Malaysian	2	0.00
Pakistani (12)	12	0.03
Taiwanese (4)	9	0.02
Thai (24)	42	0.09
Vietnamese (148)	175	0.40
Other Asian, specified	8	0.02
Other Asian, not specified (25)	54	0.12
Assyrian/Chaldean/Syriac	48	0.11
Australian	15	0.03
Austrian	121	0.27
Basque	28	0.06
Belgian	41	0.09
Brazilian	18	0.04
British	160	0.36
Bulgarian	7	0.02
Canadian	277	0.62
Celtic	70	0.16
Croatian	45	0.10
Czech	140	0.32
Czechoslovakian	112	0.25
Danish	360	0.81
Dutch	1,014	2.29
English	5,227	11.79
European	642	1.45
Finnish	149	0.34
French, except Basque	2,087	4.71
French Canadian	387	0.87
German	7,834	17.66
Greek	168	0.38
Hawaii Native/Pacific Islander:	260	0.59
Melanesian: (1)	1	0.00
Fijian (1)	1	0.00
Micronesian: (39)	57	0.13
Guamanian/Chamorro (39)	57	0.13
Polynesian: (49)	154	0.35
Native Hawaiian (22)	89	0.20
Samoan (25)	57	0.13
Other Polynesian (2)	8	0.02
Other Pac. Isl., specified	5	0.01
Other Pac. Isl., not spec. (7)	43	0.10
Hispanic or Latino:	7,739	17.48
Central American:	218	0.49
Costa Rican	15	0.03
Guatemalan	55	0.12
Honduran	15	0.03
Nicaraguan	20	0.05
Panamanian	30	0.07
Salvadoran	70	0.16
Other Central American	13	0.03
Cuban	128	0.29
Dominican Republic	6	0.01
Mexican	5,790	13.08
Puerto Rican	252	0.57
South American:	188	0.42
Argentinean	53	0.12
Bolivian	7	0.02
Chilean	17	0.04
Colombian	51	0.12
Ecuadorian	9	0.02
Peruvian	32	0.07
Uruguayan	2	0.00
Venezuelan	10	0.02
Other South American	7	0.02
Other Hispanic or Latino	1,157	2.61
Hungarian	257	0.58
Iranian	58	0.13
Irish	6,157	13.88
Italian	3,356	7.57
Lithuanian	137	0.31
Maltese	8	0.02
Northern European	16	0.04
Norwegian	824	1.86
Polish	1,314	2.96

Notes: 1. Figures in the "Number" column do not add up to the total population due to: a) Ancestry/Race overlap — e.g. persons can report being both White and Irish, b) persons of Hispanic origin can report being any race, c) persons reporting two ancestries are counted in both categories. 2. Numbers in parentheses indicate the number of persons reporting this ancestry/race alone, not in combination with any other ancestry/race. 3. Refer to the Explanation of Data in the front of the book for more detailed information.

Ancestry/Race	Number	%
Portuguese	100	0.23
Romanian	57	0.13
Russian	361	0.81
Scandinavian	165	0.37
Scotch-Irish	845	1.91
Scottish	1,128	2.54
Serbian	23	0.05
Slavic	36	0.08
Slovak	40	0.09
Slovene	41	0.09
Swedish	1,106	2.49
Swiss	201	0.45
Turkish	45	0.10
Ukrainian	86	0.19
United States or American	2,225	5.02
Welsh	354	0.80
West Indian, excl. Hispanic:	129	0.29
Belizean	17	0.04
Jamaican	65	0.15
West Indian	47	0.11
White:	37,828	85.43
Not Hispanic (31,811)	32,925	74.35
Hispanic (4,341)	4,903	11.07
Yugoslavian	171	0.39

Napa

Place Type: City
County: Napa
Population: 72,585

Ancestry/Race	Number	%
African American/Black:	561	0.77
Not Hispanic (304)	445	0.61
Hispanic (77)	116	0.16
African, sub-Saharan:	55	0.08
African	28	0.04
South African	27	0.04
Alaska Native tribes, specified:	2	0.00
Aleut	1	0.00
Eskimo	1	0.00
Alaska Native tribes, not specified	1	0.00
Am. Ind. or Alaska Nat., not spec.	454	0.63
American Indian tribes, specified:	980	1.35
Apache (20)	41	0.06
Blackfeet (8)	33	0.05
Cherokee (97)	314	0.43
Cheyenne	3	0.00
Chickasaw	7	0.01
Chippewa (10)	26	0.04
Choctaw (13)	53	0.07
Colville	1	0.00
Comanche (3)	6	0.01
Cree	1	0.00
Creek (4)	13	0.02
Crow (3)	9	0.01
Delaware (8)	13	0.02
Iroquois (12)	29	0.04
Kiowa	3	0.00
Latin American Indians (73)	115	0.16
Menominee (1)	1	0.00
Navajo (12)	23	0.03
Osage (6)	16	0.02
Ottawa (1)	1	0.00
Paiute	1	0.00
Pima (1)	1	0.00
Potawatomi (10)	19	0.03
Pueblo (10)	16	0.02
Puget Sound Salish (1)	3	0.00
Seminole (2)	7	0.01
Shoshone (2)	3	0.00
Sioux (23)	46	0.06
Tohono O'Odham (1)	1	0.00
Yaqui (2)	5	0.01
Yuman (1)	1	0.00
All other tribes (93)	169	0.23
American Indian tribes, not spec.	71	0.10
Arab:	135	0.19
Arab/Arabic	29	0.04
Jordanian	9	0.01
Lebanese	35	0.05
Moroccan	15	0.02
Palestinian	47	0.06
Armenian	29	0.04
Asian:	1,855	2.56
Cambodian (6)	8	0.01
Chinese, ex. Taiwanese (267)	381	0.52
Filipino (296)	503	0.69
Indian (127)	165	0.23
Indonesian (15)	35	0.05
Japanese (254)	395	0.54
Korean (136)	161	0.22
Laotian (1)	1	0.00
Malaysian	2	0.00
Pakistani (20)	24	0.03
Sri Lankan (3)	3	0.00
Taiwanese (2)	3	0.00
Thai (13)	28	0.04
Vietnamese (67)	83	0.11
Other Asian, specified (4)	10	0.01
Other Asian, not specified (8)	53	0.07
Australian	48	0.07
Austrian	277	0.38
Basque	28	0.04
Belgian	69	0.09
Brazilian	42	0.06
British	405	0.56
Bulgarian	6	0.01
Canadian	237	0.33
Carpatho Rusyn	8	0.01
Celtic	8	0.01
Croatian	95	0.13
Czech	262	0.36
Czechoslovakian	170	0.23
Danish	1,033	1.42
Dutch	1,341	1.84
Eastern European	96	0.13
English	9,022	12.40
European	509	0.70
Finnish	243	0.33
French, except Basque	2,425	3.33
French Canadian	430	0.59
German	10,661	14.65
Greek	465	0.64
Hawaii Native/Pacific Islander:	277	0.38
Melanesian: (1)	1	0.00
Fijian (1)	1	0.00
Micronesian: (31)	70	0.10
Guamanian/Chamorro (28)	67	0.09
Other Micronesian (3)	3	0.00
Polynesian: (69)	161	0.22
Native Hawaiian (41)	118	0.16
Samoan (19)	29	0.04
Tongan (8)	10	0.01
Other Polynesian (1)	4	0.01
Other Pac. Isl., specified	5	0.01
Other Pac. Isl., not spec. (12)	40	0.06
Hispanic or Latino:	19,475	26.83
Central American:	312	0.43
Costa Rican	30	0.04
Guatemalan	113	0.16
Honduran	18	0.02
Nicaraguan	34	0.05
Panamanian	7	0.01
Salvadoran	88	0.12
Other Central American	22	0.03
Cuban	52	0.07
Dominican Republic	3	0.00
Mexican	16,889	23.27
Puerto Rican	177	0.24
South American:	119	0.16
Argentinean	23	0.03
Bolivian	4	0.01
Chilean	12	0.02
Colombian	40	0.06
Ecuadorian	7	0.01
Peruvian	24	0.03
Uruguayan	1	0.00
Venezuelan	4	0.01
Other South American	4	0.01
Other Hispanic or Latino	1,923	2.65
Hungarian	418	0.57
Icelander	16	0.02
Iranian	63	0.09
Irish	9,242	12.70
Italian	5,291	7.27
Latvian	65	0.09
Lithuanian	142	0.20
Luxemburger	35	0.05
Macedonian	7	0.01
Maltese	18	0.02
Northern European	82	0.11
Norwegian	1,790	2.46
Pennsylvania German	30	0.04
Polish	1,342	1.84
Portuguese	1,295	1.78
Romanian	102	0.14
Russian	656	0.90
Scandinavian	238	0.33
Scotch-Irish	1,417	1.95
Scottish	1,677	2.30
Serbian	38	0.05
Slavic	56	0.08
Slovak	66	0.09
Slovene	43	0.06
Swedish	1,495	2.05
Swiss	333	0.46
Turkish	6	0.01
Ukrainian	109	0.15
United States or American	2,940	4.04
Welsh	726	1.00
West Indian, excl. Hispanic:	8	0.01
Bahamian	8	0.01
White:	60,796	83.76
Not Hispanic (49,536)	50,914	70.14
Hispanic (8,766)	9,882	13.61
Yugoslavian	216	0.30

National City

Place Type: City
County: San Diego
Population: 54,260

Ancestry/Race	Number	%
African American/Black:	3,568	6.58
Not Hispanic (2,823)	3,206	5.91
Hispanic (203)	362	0.67
African, sub-Saharan:	275	0.51
African	179	0.33
Cape Verdean	7	0.01
Ethiopian	50	0.09
Liberian	15	0.03
Nigerian	18	0.03
Sudanese	6	0.01
Alaska Native tribes, specified:	8	0.01
Aleut (2)	3	0.01
Eskimo (1)	3	0.01
Tlingit-Haida	1	0.00
All other tribes (1)	1	0.00
Alaska Native tribes, not specified	2	0.00
Am. Ind. or Alaska Nat., not spec.	324	0.60
Albanian	6	0.01
American Indian tribes, specified:	460	0.85
Apache (20)	31	0.06
Blackfeet (4)	21	0.04
Cherokee (32)	79	0.15
Cheyenne (2)	3	0.01
Chippewa (6)	11	0.02
Choctaw (5)	6	0.01
Colville	1	0.00
Comanche (1)	1	0.00
Cree	1	0.00
Creek (1)	3	0.01
Crow (1)	4	0.01
Houma (1)	1	0.00
Iroquois (4)	4	0.01
Latin American Indians (70)	95	0.18
Navajo (28)	35	0.06
Ottawa	1	0.00

Notes: 1. Figures in the "Number" column do not add up to the total population due to: a) Ancestry/Race overlap — e.g. persons can report being both White and Irish, b) persons of Hispanic origin can report being any race, c) persons reporting two ancestries are counted in both categories. 2. Numbers in parentheses indicate the number of persons reporting this ancestry/race alone, not in combination with any other ancestry/race. 3. Refer to the Explanation of Data in the front of the book for more detailed information.

Ancestry/Race	Number	%
Paiute (4)	7	0.01
Potawatomi (1)	1	0.00
Pueblo (18)	25	0.05
Seminole	9	0.02
Shoshone	3	0.01
Sioux (3)	7	0.01
Tohono O'Odham (4)	4	0.01
Yakama	1	0.00
Yaqui (14)	26	0.05
All other tribes (63)	80	0.15
American Indian tribes, not spec.	72	0.13
Arab:	54	0.10
Arab/Arabic	9	0.02
Lebanese	45	0.08
Asian:	11,161	20.57
Cambodian (17)	20	0.04
Chinese, ex. Taiwanese (75)	133	0.25
Filipino (9,363)	10,207	18.81
Hmong (12)	12	0.02
Indian (54)	74	0.14
Indonesian (3)	7	0.01
Japanese (167)	289	0.53
Korean (78)	90	0.17
Laotian (102)	129	0.24
Malaysian	14	0.03
Pakistani (3)	3	0.01
Taiwanese (2)	3	0.01
Thai (8)	18	0.03
Vietnamese (68)	86	0.16
Other Asian, specified (1)	2	0.00
Other Asian, not specified (44)	74	0.14
Austrian	20	0.04
Basque	14	0.03
Brazilian	26	0.05
British	16	0.03
Bulgarian	8	0.01
Canadian	48	0.09
Croatian	7	0.01
Czech	47	0.09
Czechoslovakian	39	0.07
Danish	41	0.08
Dutch	210	0.39
English	1,012	1.86
European	107	0.20
Finnish	43	0.08
French, except Basque	406	0.75
French Canadian	117	0.22
German	2,006	3.69
Greek	15	0.03
Guyanese	7	0.01
Hawaii Native/Pacific Islander:	691	1.27
Melanesian: (3)	3	0.01
Fijian (3)	3	0.01
Micronesian: (270)	356	0.66
Guamanian/Chamorro (265)	351	0.65
Other Micronesian (5)	5	0.01
Polynesian: (178)	249	0.46
Native Hawaiian (47)	85	0.16
Samoan (128)	157	0.29
Tongan (3)	5	0.01
Other Polynesian	2	0.00
Other Pac. Isl., specified	1	0.00
Other Pac. Isl., not spec. (24)	82	0.15
Hispanic or Latino:	32,053	59.07
Central American:	272	0.50
Costa Rican	33	0.06
Guatemalan	43	0.08
Honduran	43	0.08
Nicaraguan	23	0.04
Panamanian	36	0.07
Salvadoran	66	0.12
Other Central American	28	0.05
Cuban	52	0.10
Dominican Republic	26	0.05
Mexican	28,544	52.61
Puerto Rican	358	0.66
South American:	135	0.25
Argentinean	23	0.04
Bolivian	20	0.04
Chilean	6	0.01
Colombian	37	0.07
Ecuadorian	12	0.02
Peruvian	22	0.04
Uruguayan	1	0.00
Venezuelan	8	0.01
Other South American	6	0.01
Other Hispanic or Latino	2,666	4.91
Hungarian	35	0.06
Iranian	5	0.01
Irish	1,267	2.33
Italian	645	1.19
Lithuanian	17	0.03
Norwegian	185	0.34
Polish	274	0.50
Portuguese	124	0.23
Romanian	8	0.01
Russian	10	0.02
Scandinavian	15	0.03
Scotch-Irish	279	0.51
Scottish	223	0.41
Serbian	5	0.01
Slovene	43	0.08
Swedish	184	0.34
Swiss	23	0.04
Turkish	10	0.02
Ukrainian	30	0.06
United States or American	949	1.74
Welsh	76	0.14
West Indian, excl. Hispanic:	60	0.11
Jamaican	54	0.10
Other West Indian	6	0.01
White:	21,194	39.06
Not Hispanic (7,653)	8,358	15.40
Hispanic (11,417)	12,836	23.66
Yugoslavian	5	0.01

Newark

Place Type: City
County: Alameda
Population: 42,471

Ancestry/Race	Number	%
Afghan	596	1.40
African American/Black:	2,017	4.75
Not Hispanic (1,639)	1,875	4.41
Hispanic (66)	142	0.33
African, sub-Saharan:	157	0.37
African	103	0.24
Ethiopian	25	0.06
Ghanian	8	0.02
Kenyan	8	0.02
Nigerian	13	0.03
Alaska Native tribes, specified:	6	0.01
Alaska Athabascan (1)	1	0.00
Aleut (1)	1	0.00
Tlingit-Haida	3	0.01
All other tribes	1	0.00
Am. Ind. or Alaska Nat., not spec.	238	0.56
American Indian tribes, specified:	428	1.01
Apache (3)	28	0.07
Blackfeet (5)	12	0.03
Cherokee (36)	131	0.31
Cheyenne	3	0.01
Chippewa (7)	11	0.03
Choctaw (2)	12	0.03
Comanche (5)	6	0.01
Creek (1)	8	0.02
Crow	5	0.01
Delaware (1)	3	0.01
Iroquois	5	0.01
Kiowa (7)	9	0.02
Latin American Indians (32)	68	0.16
Navajo (21)	31	0.07
Osage	3	0.01
Paiute	1	0.00
Pima (2)	5	0.01
Potawatomi (1)	1	0.00
Pueblo (10)	11	0.03
Puget Sound Salish	1	0.00
Seminole	2	0.00
Shoshone (1)	3	0.01
Sioux (10)	13	0.03
Yakama (1)	1	0.00
Yaqui (5)	7	0.02
All other tribes (25)	48	0.11
American Indian tribes, not spec.	19	0.04
Arab:	79	0.19
Arab/Arabic	7	0.02
Egyptian	38	0.09
Lebanese	26	0.06
Palestinian	8	0.02
Armenian	53	0.12
Asian:	10,583	24.92
Bangladeshi (3)	11	0.03
Cambodian (34)	41	0.10
Chinese, ex. Taiwanese (1,730)	2,017	4.75
Filipino (3,526)	4,078	9.60
Hmong (15)	15	0.04
Indian (1,658)	1,875	4.41
Indonesian (37)	61	0.14
Japanese (271)	419	0.99
Korean (330)	384	0.90
Laotian (136)	147	0.35
Malaysian (13)	25	0.06
Pakistani (109)	137	0.32
Sri Lankan (4)	7	0.02
Taiwanese (50)	63	0.15
Thai (54)	59	0.14
Vietnamese (843)	887	2.09
Other Asian, specified (25)	44	0.10
Other Asian, not specified (56)	313	0.74
Assyrian/Chaldean/Syriac	8	0.02
Australian	33	0.08
Austrian	59	0.14
Belgian	18	0.04
Brazilian	56	0.13
British	103	0.24
Canadian	42	0.10
Croatian	56	0.13
Czech	62	0.15
Czechoslovakian	65	0.15
Danish	258	0.61
Dutch	480	1.13
Eastern European	34	0.08
English	2,367	5.57
European	315	0.74
Finnish	50	0.12
French, except Basque	829	1.95
French Canadian	135	0.32
German	3,753	8.84
Greek	116	0.27
Hawaii Native/Pacific Islander:	857	2.02
Melanesian: (100)	144	0.34
Fijian (100)	144	0.34
Micronesian: (80)	148	0.35
Guamanian/Chamorro (77)	140	0.33
Other Micronesian (3)	8	0.02
Polynesian: (185)	359	0.85
Native Hawaiian (64)	189	0.45
Samoan (72)	108	0.25
Tongan (47)	57	0.13
Other Polynesian (2)	5	0.01
Other Pac. Isl., specified	9	0.02
Other Pac. Isl., not spec. (51)	197	0.46
Hispanic or Latino:	12,145	28.60
Central American:	510	1.20
Costa Rican	8	0.02
Guatemalan	96	0.23
Honduran	9	0.02
Nicaraguan	153	0.36
Panamanian	16	0.04
Salvadoran	174	0.41
Other Central American	54	0.13
Cuban	71	0.17
Dominican Republic	9	0.02
Mexican	9,240	21.76
Puerto Rican	373	0.88
South American:	227	0.53
Argentinean	9	0.02

Notes: 1. Figures in the "Number" column do not add up to the total population due to: a) Ancestry/Race overlap — e.g. persons can report being both White and Irish, b) persons of Hispanic origin can report being any race, c) persons reporting two ancestries are counted in both categories. 2. Numbers in parentheses indicate the number of persons reporting this ancestry/race alone, not in combination with any other ancestry/race. 3. Refer to the Explanation of Data in the front of the book for more detailed information.

Bolivian	34	0.08
Chilean	19	0.04
Colombian	29	0.07
Ecuadorian	6	0.01
Paraguayan	2	0.00
Peruvian	74	0.17
Uruguayan	4	0.01
Venezuelan	17	0.04
Other South American	33	0.08
Other Hispanic or Latino	1,715	4.04
Hungarian	110	0.26
Icelander	8	0.02
Iranian	194	0.46
Irish	3,202	7.54
Israeli	9	0.02
Italian	1,660	3.91
Latvian	13	0.03
Lithuanian	33	0.08
Luxemburger	7	0.02
Maltese	31	0.07
Northern European	41	0.10
Norwegian	505	1.19
Pennsylvania German	20	0.05
Polish	430	1.01
Portuguese	2,008	4.73
Romanian	68	0.16
Russian	221	0.52
Scandinavian	12	0.03
Scotch-Irish	373	0.88
Scottish	710	1.67
Slavic	11	0.03
Slovak	5	0.01
Swedish	515	1.21
Swiss	183	0.43
Turkish	13	0.03
Ukrainian	77	0.18
United States or American	1,151	2.71
Welsh	182	0.43
West Indian, excl. Hispanic:	19	0.04
Dutch West Indian	8	0.02
Jamaican	6	0.01
West Indian	5	0.01
White:	24,550	57.80
Not Hispanic (17,103)	18,604	43.80
Hispanic (5,076)	5,946	14.00
Yugoslavian	37	0.09

Newport Beach

Place Type: City
County: Orange
Population: 70,032

Ancestry/Race	Number	%
Afghan	10	0.01
African American/Black:	456	0.65
Not Hispanic (354)	426	0.61
Hispanic (17)	30	0.04
African, sub-Saharan:	161	0.23
African	47	0.07
Ethiopian	16	0.02
South African	98	0.14
Alaska Native tribes, specified:	2	0.00
Alaska Athabascan	1	0.00
Aleut	1	0.00
Alaska Native tribes, not specified	1	0.00
Am. Ind. or Alaska Nat., not spec.	107	0.15
Albanian	19	0.03
Alsatian	9	0.01
American Indian tribes, specified:	279	0.40
Apache (14)	24	0.03
Blackfeet (5)	13	0.02
Cherokee (35)	88	0.13
Chickasaw	4	0.01
Chippewa (5)	13	0.02
Choctaw (10)	24	0.03
Creek (1)	2	0.00
Crow (1)	1	0.00
Delaware (2)	2	0.00
Iroquois (1)	2	0.00
Kiowa	1	0.00
Latin American Indians (4)	11	0.02
Menominee (1)	1	0.00
Navajo (6)	21	0.03
Osage (4)	4	0.01
Ottawa (2)	2	0.00
Potawatomi (1)	3	0.00
Pueblo (2)	2	0.00
Puget Sound Salish	1	0.00
Seminole	4	0.01
Shoshone	4	0.01
Sioux (7)	9	0.01
Ute (1)	1	0.00
Yaqui (2)	5	0.01
All other tribes (21)	37	0.05
American Indian tribes, not spec.	25	0.04
Arab:	771	1.10
Arab/Arabic	81	0.12
Egyptian	92	0.13
Iraqi	92	0.13
Jordanian	23	0.03
Lebanese	367	0.52
Syrian	87	0.12
Other Arab	29	0.04
Armenian	439	0.63
Asian:	3,504	5.00
Cambodian (3)	5	0.01
Chinese, ex. Taiwanese (713)	907	1.30
Filipino (262)	419	0.60
Hmong (4)	4	0.01
Indian (381)	433	0.62
Indonesian (12)	17	0.02
Japanese (615)	808	1.15
Korean (323)	381	0.54
Laotian (1)	2	0.00
Malaysian (2)	2	0.00
Pakistani (7)	14	0.02
Sri Lankan (10)	11	0.02
Taiwanese (120)	142	0.20
Thai (29)	37	0.05
Vietnamese (171)	203	0.29
Other Asian, specified (12)	17	0.02
Other Asian, not specified (35)	102	0.15
Australian	150	0.21
Austrian	391	0.56
Basque	58	0.08
Belgian	135	0.19
Brazilian	36	0.05
British	843	1.20
Bulgarian	71	0.10
Canadian	320	0.46
Croatian	189	0.27
Czech	261	0.37
Czechoslovakian	212	0.30
Danish	798	1.14
Dutch	1,444	2.06
Eastern European	211	0.30
English	12,707	18.15
Estonian	33	0.05
European	1,255	1.79
Finnish	112	0.16
French, except Basque	3,204	4.58
French Canadian	467	0.67
German	12,308	17.58
Greek	641	0.92
Hawaii Native/Pacific Islander:	205	0.29
Micronesian: (13)	23	0.03
Guamanian/Chamorro (13)	19	0.03
Other Micronesian	4	0.01
Polynesian: (58)	139	0.20
Native Hawaiian (35)	100	0.14
Samoan (22)	35	0.05
Other Polynesian (1)	4	0.01
Other Pac. Isl., not spec. (12)	43	0.06
Hispanic or Latino:	3,301	4.71
Central American:	147	0.21
Costa Rican	37	0.05
Guatemalan	26	0.04
Honduran	9	0.01
Nicaraguan	12	0.02
Panamanian	8	0.01
Salvadoran	40	0.06
Other Central American	15	0.02
Cuban	108	0.15
Dominican Republic	5	0.01
Mexican	2,016	2.88
Puerto Rican	120	0.17
South American:	245	0.35
Argentinean	63	0.09
Bolivian	8	0.01
Chilean	29	0.04
Colombian	61	0.09
Ecuadorian	17	0.02
Peruvian	39	0.06
Uruguayan	5	0.01
Venezuelan	4	0.01
Other South American	19	0.03
Other Hispanic or Latino	660	0.94
Hungarian	551	0.79
Iranian	1,128	1.61
Irish	10,786	15.40
Israeli	15	0.02
Italian	5,588	7.98
Latvian	49	0.07
Lithuanian	224	0.32
Luxemburger	21	0.03
New Zealander	8	0.01
Northern European	141	0.20
Norwegian	1,644	2.35
Pennsylvania German	33	0.05
Polish	2,040	2.91
Portuguese	232	0.33
Romanian	162	0.23
Russian	1,793	2.56
Scandinavian	289	0.41
Scotch-Irish	1,909	2.73
Scottish	2,661	3.80
Serbian	43	0.06
Slavic	47	0.07
Slovak	109	0.16
Slovene	63	0.09
Swedish	2,262	3.23
Swiss	656	0.94
Turkish	70	0.10
Ukrainian	238	0.34
United States or American	3,191	4.56
Welsh	681	0.97
White:	65,707	93.82
Not Hispanic (62,342)	63,228	90.28
Hispanic (2,241)	2,479	3.54
Yugoslavian	143	0.20

Nipomo

Place Type: Census Designated Place
County: San Luis Obispo
Population: 12,626

Ancestry/Race	Number	%
African American/Black:	116	0.92
Not Hispanic (64)	92	0.73
Hispanic (12)	24	0.19
African, sub-Saharan:	11	0.09
South African	11	0.09
Alaska Native tribes, specified:	8	0.06
Aleut (1)	2	0.02
Tlingit-Haida (5)	6	0.05
Am. Ind. or Alaska Nat., not spec.	89	0.70
American Indian tribes, specified:	232	1.84
Apache (2)	5	0.04
Blackfeet (1)	3	0.02
Cherokee (22)	57	0.45
Chickasaw	2	0.02
Choctaw (5)	9	0.07
Comanche	1	0.01
Cree (1)	2	0.02
Creek	4	0.03
Iroquois (2)	4	0.03
Kiowa	1	0.01
Latin American Indians (23)	71	0.56

Notes: 1. Figures in the "Number" column do not add up to the total population due to: a) Ancestry/Race overlap — e.g. persons can report being both White and Irish, b) persons of Hispanic origin can report being any race, c) persons reporting two ancestries are counted in both categories. 2. Numbers in parentheses indicate the number of persons reporting this ancestry/race alone, not in combination with any other ancestry/race. 3. Refer to the Explanation of Data in the front of the book for more detailed information.

Navajo (12)	15	0.12
Osage (1)	1	0.01
Ottawa (2)	2	0.02
Potawatomi (1)	2	0.02
Pueblo	3	0.02
Seminole (1)	4	0.03
Sioux (1)	2	0.02
Yaqui (2)	6	0.05
All other tribes (22)	38	0.30
American Indian tribes, not spec.	15	0.12
Arab:	9	0.07
Lebanese	9	0.07
Asian:	347	2.75
Cambodian (1)	2	0.02
Chinese, ex. Taiwanese (19)	33	0.26
Filipino (95)	190	1.50
Indian (4)	18	0.14
Indonesian	3	0.02
Japanese (30)	52	0.41
Korean (18)	26	0.21
Laotian (7)	7	0.06
Pakistani	1	0.01
Thai (1)	4	0.03
Vietnamese (4)	5	0.04
Other Asian, not specified (1)	6	0.05
Austrian	6	0.05
Basque	40	0.32
Belgian	9	0.07
British	23	0.18
Croatian	8	0.06
Czech	26	0.21
Czechoslovakian	27	0.21
Danish	210	1.67
Dutch	272	2.16
English	1,190	9.44
European	56	0.44
French, except Basque	258	2.05
French Canadian	80	0.63
German	1,630	12.94
Greek	47	0.37
Hawaii Native/Pacific Islander:	53	0.42
Micronesian:	9	0.07
Guamanian/Chamorro	9	0.07
Polynesian: (3)	40	0.32
Native Hawaiian (3)	33	0.26
Samoan	7	0.06
Other Pac. Isl., not spec. (1)	4	0.03
Hispanic or Latino:	4,362	34.55
Central American:	33	0.26
Costa Rican	6	0.05
Guatemalan	2	0.02
Honduran	2	0.02
Nicaraguan	5	0.04
Panamanian	2	0.02
Salvadoran	12	0.10
Other Central American	4	0.03
Cuban	10	0.08
Dominican Republic	1	0.01
Mexican	3,772	29.87
Puerto Rican	25	0.20
South American:	10	0.08
Bolivian	2	0.02
Chilean	1	0.01
Colombian	4	0.03
Ecuadorian	1	0.01
Peruvian	2	0.02
Other Hispanic or Latino	511	4.05
Hungarian	61	0.48
Iranian	17	0.13
Irish	1,454	11.54
Italian	689	5.47
Lithuanian	9	0.07
Luxemburger	14	0.11
Northern European	21	0.17
Norwegian	150	1.19
Pennsylvania German	7	0.06
Polish	175	1.39
Portuguese	254	2.02
Russian	40	0.32
Scandinavian	64	0.51
Scotch-Irish	176	1.40
Scottish	301	2.39
Serbian	18	0.14
Swedish	67	0.53
Swiss	123	0.98
Ukrainian	9	0.07
United States or American	767	6.09
Welsh	31	0.25
West Indian, excl. Hispanic:	14	0.11
Jamaican	14	0.11
White:	10,091	79.92
Not Hispanic (7,653)	7,907	62.62
Hispanic (1,929)	2,184	17.30

Norco

Place Type: City
County: Riverside
Population: 24,157

Ancestry/Race	Number	%
Acadian/Cajun	22	0.09
African American/Black:	1,537	6.36
Not Hispanic (1,468)	1,514	6.27
Hispanic (13)	23	0.10
African, sub-Saharan:	18	0.08
African	7	0.03
Ghanian	11	0.05
Alaska Native tribes, specified:	4	0.02
Aleut	2	0.01
Tlingit-Haida (1)	2	0.01
Am. Ind. or Alaska Nat., not spec.	129	0.53
American Indian tribes, specified:	257	1.06
Apache (12)	17	0.07
Blackfeet (9)	14	0.06
Cherokee (29)	81	0.34
Chickasaw	4	0.02
Chippewa	3	0.01
Choctaw (6)	15	0.06
Comanche (1)	2	0.01
Cree (1)	2	0.01
Creek (1)	6	0.02
Crow (4)	4	0.02
Delaware (3)	10	0.04
Iroquois (6)	6	0.02
Latin American Indians (11)	12	0.05
Navajo (3)	6	0.02
Paiute (1)	1	0.00
Pima (1)	2	0.01
Pueblo (3)	5	0.02
Shoshone (6)	6	0.02
Sioux (7)	15	0.06
Yaqui	6	0.02
All other tribes (15)	40	0.17
American Indian tribes, not spec.	11	0.05
Arab:	47	0.20
Iraqi	24	0.10
Lebanese	23	0.10
Asian:	424	1.76
Chinese, ex. Taiwanese (35)	49	0.20
Filipino (78)	131	0.54
Indian (27)	38	0.16
Indonesian (5)	13	0.05
Japanese (49)	91	0.38
Korean (34)	44	0.18
Laotian (10)	10	0.04
Pakistani	2	0.01
Sri Lankan (2)	6	0.02
Taiwanese (12)	12	0.05
Thai (2)	2	0.01
Vietnamese (17)	19	0.08
Other Asian, not specified (2)	7	0.03
Australian	10	0.04
Austrian	15	0.06
Basque	5	0.02
Belgian	18	0.08
British	69	0.29
Canadian	50	0.21
Croatian	19	0.08
Czech	139	0.58
Czechoslovakian	6	0.03
Danish	255	1.07
Dutch	681	2.86
Eastern European	8	0.03
English	2,375	9.98
European	183	0.77
Finnish	40	0.17
French, except Basque	810	3.40
French Canadian	202	0.85
German	3,602	15.14
Greek	99	0.42
Hawaii Native/Pacific Islander:	70	0.29
Melanesian: (5)	5	0.02
Fijian (5)	5	0.02
Micronesian: (3)	7	0.03
Guamanian/Chamorro (3)	7	0.03
Polynesian: (22)	48	0.20
Native Hawaiian (16)	39	0.16
Samoan (6)	9	0.04
Other Pac. Isl., not spec. (3)	10	0.04
Hispanic or Latino:	5,504	22.78
Central American:	63	0.26
Costa Rican	5	0.02
Guatemalan	22	0.09
Honduran	1	0.00
Nicaraguan	4	0.02
Panamanian	1	0.00
Salvadoran	25	0.10
Other Central American	5	0.02
Cuban	59	0.24
Dominican Republic	2	0.01
Mexican	4,829	19.99
Puerto Rican	60	0.25
South American:	43	0.18
Argentinean	9	0.04
Bolivian	5	0.02
Chilean	5	0.02
Colombian	6	0.02
Ecuadorian	9	0.04
Peruvian	5	0.02
Uruguayan	1	0.00
Venezuelan	3	0.01
Other Hispanic or Latino	448	1.85
Hungarian	86	0.36
Irish	2,270	9.54
Italian	1,109	4.66
Lithuanian	23	0.10
Luxemburger	8	0.03
Maltese	12	0.05
Northern European	24	0.10
Norwegian	487	2.05
Polish	484	2.03
Portuguese	208	0.87
Romanian	28	0.12
Russian	62	0.26
Scandinavian	23	0.10
Scotch-Irish	335	1.41
Scottish	456	1.92
Serbian	8	0.03
Slavic	17	0.07
Slovene	8	0.03
Swedish	302	1.27
Swiss	44	0.18
Turkish	12	0.05
United States or American	1,307	5.49
Welsh	148	0.62
White:	20,600	85.28
Not Hispanic (16,334)	16,729	69.25
Hispanic (3,581)	3,871	16.02
Yugoslavian	30	0.13

North Auburn

Place Type: Census Designated Place
County: Placer
Population: 11,847

Ancestry/Race	Number	%
African American/Black:	130	1.10
Not Hispanic (70)	114	0.96

Notes: 1. Figures in the "Number" column do not add up to the total population due to: a) Ancestry/Race overlap — e.g. persons can report being both White and Irish, b) persons of Hispanic origin can report being any race, c) persons reporting two ancestries are counted in both categories. 2. Numbers in parentheses indicate the number of persons reporting this ancestry/race alone, not in combination with any other ancestry/race. 3. Refer to the Explanation of Data in the front of the book for more detailed information.

Ancestry/Race	Number	%
Hispanic (14)	16	0.14
Alaska Native tribes, specified:	3	0.03
Aleut	1	0.01
Eskimo	1	0.01
Tlingit-Haida (1)	1	0.01
Am. Ind. or Alaska Nat., not spec.	53	0.45
American Indian tribes, specified:	196	1.65
Apache (1)	5	0.04
Blackfeet	8	0.07
Cherokee (14)	51	0.43
Cheyenne	3	0.03
Chickasaw (1)	3	0.03
Chippewa	1	0.01
Choctaw (4)	7	0.06
Comanche	1	0.01
Creek	1	0.01
Latin American Indians (13)	18	0.15
Osage (1)	2	0.02
Paiute (4)	5	0.04
Potawatomi	2	0.02
Pueblo (1)	1	0.01
Seminole (1)	1	0.01
Shoshone	4	0.03
Sioux (4)	9	0.08
Tohono O'Odham	2	0.02
Yaqui (2)	2	0.02
All other tribes (52)	70	0.59
American Indian tribes, not spec.	22	0.19
Arab:	60	0.51
Jordanian	43	0.36
Lebanese	12	0.10
Moroccan	5	0.04
Asian:	296	2.50
Cambodian (4)	5	0.04
Chinese, ex. Taiwanese (31)	42	0.35
Filipino (70)	97	0.82
Indian (28)	30	0.25
Indonesian (5)	8	0.07
Japanese (51)	74	0.62
Korean (15)	17	0.14
Malaysian (1)	1	0.01
Thai	4	0.03
Vietnamese (4)	5	0.04
Other Asian, not specified (2)	13	0.11
Australian	11	0.09
Austrian	39	0.33
British	71	0.60
Canadian	29	0.25
Celtic	7	0.06
Czech	23	0.20
Czechoslovakian	9	0.08
Danish	136	1.15
Dutch	258	2.19
English	1,883	15.98
European	78	0.66
Finnish	15	0.13
French, except Basque	610	5.18
French Canadian	70	0.59
German	2,250	19.10
Greek	31	0.26
Hawaii Native/Pacific Islander:	29	0.24
Micronesian: (3)	5	0.04
Guamanian/Chamorro (3)	5	0.04
Polynesian: (7)	22	0.19
Native Hawaiian (5)	18	0.15
Samoan (2)	4	0.03
Other Pac. Isl., not spec.	2	0.02
Hispanic or Latino:	1,091	9.21
Central American:	64	0.54
Costa Rican	1	0.01
Guatemalan	19	0.16
Panamanian	1	0.01
Salvadoran	37	0.31
Other Central American	6	0.05
Cuban	10	0.08
Mexican	779	6.58
Puerto Rican	23	0.19
South American:	16	0.14
Chilean	4	0.03
Colombian	5	0.04
Ecuadorian	3	0.03
Peruvian	3	0.03
Other South American	1	0.01
Other Hispanic or Latino	199	1.68
Hungarian	43	0.36
Iranian	22	0.19
Irish	1,621	13.76
Italian	753	6.39
Lithuanian	16	0.14
Northern European	5	0.04
Norwegian	330	2.80
Pennsylvania German	7	0.06
Polish	221	1.88
Portuguese	240	2.04
Russian	71	0.60
Scandinavian	15	0.13
Scotch-Irish	288	2.44
Scottish	428	3.63
Slavic	8	0.07
Slovene	7	0.06
Swedish	347	2.95
Swiss	46	0.39
Turkish	6	0.05
United States or American	725	6.15
Welsh	90	0.76
West Indian, excl. Hispanic:	6	0.05
Jamaican	6	0.05
White:	10,923	92.20
Not Hispanic (10,106)	10,325	87.15
Hispanic (526)	598	5.05
Yugoslavian	30	0.25

North Fair Oaks

Place Type: Census Designated Place
County: San Mateo
Population: 15,440

Ancestry/Race	Number	%
African American/Black:	354	2.29
Not Hispanic (262)	291	1.88
Hispanic (34)	63	0.41
African, sub-Saharan:	83	0.54
African	41	0.27
Nigerian	29	0.19
Other sub-Saharan African	13	0.08
Am. Ind. or Alaska Nat., not spec.	88	0.57
Alsatian	8	0.05
American Indian tribes, specified:	115	0.74
Apache (4)	5	0.03
Blackfeet (3)	6	0.04
Cherokee (6)	22	0.14
Chickasaw	1	0.01
Chippewa	1	0.01
Choctaw (3)	5	0.03
Comanche (1)	1	0.01
Creek	2	0.01
Iroquois	3	0.02
Latin American Indians (25)	36	0.23
Navajo (15)	16	0.10
Paiute	1	0.01
Sioux	1	0.01
Ute (1)	1	0.01
Yaqui	1	0.01
All other tribes (7)	13	0.08
American Indian tribes, not spec.	6	0.04
Arab:	12	0.08
Lebanese	12	0.08
Asian:	589	3.81
Cambodian (1)	1	0.01
Chinese, ex. Taiwanese (87)	108	0.70
Filipino (134)	164	1.06
Indian (87)	121	0.78
Japanese (37)	55	0.36
Korean (24)	26	0.17
Laotian (36)	53	0.34
Malaysian	1	0.01
Taiwanese (6)	6	0.04
Thai (2)	5	0.03
Vietnamese (20)	26	0.17
Other Asian, specified (1)	2	0.01
Other Asian, not specified (11)	21	0.14
Austrian	8	0.05
Brazilian	6	0.04
British	18	0.12
Canadian	4	0.03
Celtic	4	0.03
Czech	22	0.14
Czechoslovakian	22	0.14
Danish	38	0.25
Dutch	87	0.56
Eastern European	35	0.23
English	480	3.11
European	104	0.67
Finnish	15	0.10
French, except Basque	245	1.59
French Canadian	13	0.08
German	720	4.66
Greek	68	0.44
Hawaii Native/Pacific Islander:	248	1.61
Melanesian: (15)	19	0.12
Fijian (15)	19	0.12
Micronesian: (5)	5	0.03
Guamanian/Chamorro (5)	5	0.03
Polynesian: (167)	190	1.23
Native Hawaiian (4)	16	0.10
Samoan (4)	9	0.06
Tongan (158)	164	1.06
Other Polynesian (1)	1	0.01
Other Pac. Isl., not spec. (10)	34	0.22
Hispanic or Latino:	10,741	69.57
Central American:	785	5.08
Guatemalan	218	1.41
Honduran	15	0.10
Nicaraguan	61	0.40
Salvadoran	406	2.63
Other Central American	85	0.55
Cuban	19	0.12
Dominican Republic	2	0.01
Mexican	8,569	55.50
Puerto Rican	57	0.37
South American:	97	0.63
Argentinean	11	0.07
Bolivian	11	0.07
Chilean	13	0.08
Colombian	7	0.05
Ecuadorian	6	0.04
Peruvian	22	0.14
Venezuelan	4	0.03
Other South American	23	0.15
Other Hispanic or Latino	1,212	7.85
Hungarian	68	0.44
Icelander	7	0.05
Iranian	44	0.28
Irish	609	3.94
Israeli	33	0.21
Italian	471	3.05
Latvian	5	0.03
Northern European	25	0.16
Norwegian	112	0.72
Polish	78	0.50
Portuguese	24	0.16
Romanian	9	0.06
Russian	94	0.61
Scotch-Irish	130	0.84
Scottish	188	1.22
Swedish	103	0.67
Swiss	35	0.23
Turkish	17	0.11
Ukrainian	7	0.05
United States or American	202	1.31
Welsh	26	0.17
West Indian, excl. Hispanic:	24	0.16
Bermudan	24	0.16
White:	8,396	54.38
Not Hispanic (3,575)	3,698	23.95
Hispanic (4,238)	4,698	30.43
Yugoslavian	6	0.04

Notes: 1. Figures in the "Number" column do not add up to the total population due to: a) Ancestry/Race overlap — e.g. persons can report being both White and Irish, b) persons of Hispanic origin can report being any race, c) persons reporting two ancestries are counted in both categories. 2. Numbers in parentheses indicate the number of persons reporting this ancestry/race alone, not in combination with any other ancestry/race. 3. Refer to the Explanation of Data in the front of the book for more detailed information.

North Highlands

Place Type: Census Designated Place
County: Sacramento
Population: 44,187

Ancestry/Race	Number	%
African American/Black:	5,949	13.46
Not Hispanic (4,772)	5,649	12.78
Hispanic (148)	300	0.68
African, sub-Saharan:	284	0.64
African	229	0.52
Cape Verdean	13	0.03
Ethiopian	23	0.05
Somalian	19	0.04
Alaska Native tribes, specified:	15	0.03
Alaska Athabascan (2)	2	0.00
Eskimo (4)	9	0.02
Tlingit-Haida	4	0.01
Am. Ind. or Alaska Nat., not spec.	418	0.95
Albanian	9	0.02
American Indian tribes, specified:	1,167	2.64
Apache (40)	68	0.15
Blackfeet (14)	90	0.20
Cherokee (115)	435	0.98
Cheyenne (4)	6	0.01
Chickasaw (3)	7	0.02
Chippewa (2)	15	0.03
Choctaw (10)	49	0.11
Colville (1)	1	0.00
Comanche (2)	4	0.01
Cree	4	0.01
Creek (3)	19	0.04
Crow (2)	6	0.01
Delaware	1	0.00
Houma (3)	3	0.01
Iroquois (6)	11	0.02
Kiowa	1	0.00
Latin American Indians (65)	110	0.25
Menominee (1)	1	0.00
Navajo (3)	13	0.03
Osage (4)	8	0.02
Ottawa (2)	3	0.01
Paiute (22)	28	0.06
Potawatomi (5)	7	0.02
Pueblo (17)	30	0.07
Puget Sound Salish (1)	1	0.00
Seminole (5)	26	0.06
Shoshone (6)	12	0.03
Sioux (12)	30	0.07
Tohono O'Odham (1)	1	0.00
Yaqui (5)	11	0.02
Yuman (2)	2	0.00
All other tribes (95)	164	0.37
American Indian tribes, not spec.	60	0.14
Arab:	70	0.16
Arab/Arabic	24	0.05
Lebanese	46	0.10
Armenian	154	0.35
Asian:	3,351	7.58
Cambodian (14)	20	0.05
Chinese, ex. Taiwanese (79)	146	0.33
Filipino (591)	912	2.06
Hmong (193)	232	0.53
Indian (148)	207	0.47
Indonesian (12)	20	0.05
Japanese (182)	328	0.74
Korean (131)	184	0.42
Laotian (444)	464	1.05
Pakistani (5)	13	0.03
Taiwanese (3)	8	0.02
Thai (80)	111	0.25
Vietnamese (544)	572	1.29
Other Asian, specified	5	0.01
Other Asian, not specified (39)	129	0.29
Australian	24	0.05
Austrian	76	0.17
Belgian	5	0.01
Brazilian	32	0.07
British	85	0.19
Canadian	78	0.18
Croatian	30	0.07
Czech	37	0.08
Czechoslovakian	15	0.03
Danish	337	0.76
Dutch	613	1.39
Eastern European	7	0.02
English	3,395	7.70
European	656	1.49
Finnish	20	0.05
French, except Basque	1,423	3.23
French Canadian	211	0.48
German	5,120	11.62
German Russian	8	0.02
Greek	106	0.24
Hawaii Native/Pacific Islander:	475	1.07
Melanesian: (60)	83	0.19
Fijian (60)	83	0.19
Micronesian: (45)	72	0.16
Guamanian/Chamorro (43)	68	0.15
Other Micronesian (2)	4	0.01
Polynesian: (98)	232	0.53
Native Hawaiian (29)	128	0.29
Samoan (53)	74	0.17
Tongan (15)	27	0.06
Other Polynesian (1)	3	0.01
Other Pac. Isl., not spec. (26)	88	0.20
Hispanic or Latino:	6,695	15.15
Central American:	155	0.35
Costa Rican	4	0.01
Guatemalan	30	0.07
Honduran	14	0.03
Nicaraguan	28	0.06
Panamanian	6	0.01
Salvadoran	62	0.14
Other Central American	11	0.02
Cuban	45	0.10
Dominican Republic	5	0.01
Mexican	5,012	11.34
Puerto Rican	242	0.55
South American:	54	0.12
Argentinean	1	0.00
Bolivian	7	0.02
Chilean	12	0.03
Colombian	7	0.02
Ecuadorian	4	0.01
Peruvian	17	0.04
Venezuelan	3	0.01
Other South American	1	0.00
Other Hispanic or Latino	1,182	2.67
Hungarian	30	0.07
Icelander	8	0.02
Iranian	33	0.07
Irish	3,701	8.40
Italian	1,552	3.52
Lithuanian	46	0.10
Northern European	23	0.05
Norwegian	597	1.35
Pennsylvania German	17	0.04
Polish	396	0.90
Portuguese	682	1.55
Romanian	179	0.41
Russian	1,390	3.15
Scandinavian	78	0.18
Scotch-Irish	664	1.51
Scottish	724	1.64
Slavic	75	0.17
Slovak	19	0.04
Soviet Union	7	0.02
Swedish	523	1.19
Swiss	123	0.28
Turkish	21	0.05
Ukrainian	1,536	3.48
United States or American	2,614	5.93
Welsh	262	0.59
West Indian, excl. Hispanic:	16	0.04
Dutch West Indian	6	0.01
Jamaican	10	0.02
White:	32,647	73.88
Not Hispanic (27,177)	29,118	65.90
Hispanic (2,829)	3,529	7.99
Yugoslavian	44	0.10

Norwalk

Place Type: City
County: Los Angeles
Population: 103,298

Ancestry/Race	Number	%
Acadian/Cajun	28	0.03
Afghan	6	0.01
African American/Black:	5,267	5.10
Not Hispanic (4,529)	4,810	4.66
Hispanic (245)	457	0.44
African, sub-Saharan:	270	0.26
African	218	0.21
Ethiopian	28	0.03
Nigerian	17	0.02
Sierra Leonean	7	0.01
Alaska Native tribes, specified:	2	0.00
Eskimo (1)	2	0.00
Am. Ind. or Alaska Nat., not spec.	715	0.69
Albanian	5	0.00
American Indian tribes, specified:	1,068	1.03
Apache (48)	97	0.09
Blackfeet (21)	42	0.04
Cherokee (33)	163	0.16
Cheyenne (9)	10	0.01
Chickasaw (4)	7	0.01
Chippewa (33)	40	0.04
Choctaw (17)	38	0.04
Colville (1)	3	0.00
Comanche	7	0.01
Cree (2)	6	0.01
Creek (14)	21	0.02
Crow	1	0.00
Delaware (2)	5	0.00
Iroquois (8)	13	0.01
Latin American Indians (130)	188	0.18
Menominee (4)	6	0.01
Navajo (49)	92	0.09
Osage	1	0.00
Paiute (11)	13	0.01
Pima (17)	25	0.02
Potawatomi (4)	9	0.01
Pueblo (42)	54	0.05
Seminole (9)	15	0.01
Shoshone (10)	17	0.02
Sioux (13)	16	0.02
Tohono O'Odham (5)	9	0.01
Ute (1)	1	0.00
Yakama (4)	4	0.00
Yaqui (5)	21	0.02
Yuman (10)	15	0.01
All other tribes (72)	129	0.12
American Indian tribes, not spec.	130	0.13
Arab:	220	0.21
Arab/Arabic	35	0.03
Egyptian	105	0.10
Jordanian	28	0.03
Lebanese	37	0.04
Palestinian	10	0.01
Syrian	5	0.00
Armenian	49	0.05
Asian:	13,194	12.77
Bangladeshi (18)	23	0.02
Cambodian (500)	623	0.60
Chinese, ex. Taiwanese (824)	1,036	1.00
Filipino (4,552)	5,019	4.86
Hmong (6)	14	0.01
Indian (1,038)	1,135	1.10
Indonesian (51)	87	0.08
Japanese (344)	499	0.48
Korean (2,753)	2,831	2.74
Laotian (27)	41	0.04
Malaysian	8	0.01
Pakistani (64)	103	0.10
Sri Lankan (12)	13	0.01
Taiwanese (103)	123	0.12

Notes: 1. Figures in the "Number" column do not add up to the total population due to: a) Ancestry/Race overlap — e.g. persons can report being both White and Irish, b) persons of Hispanic origin can report being any race, c) persons reporting two ancestries are counted in both categories. 2. Numbers in parentheses indicate the number of persons reporting this ancestry/race alone, not in combination with any other ancestry/race. 3. Refer to the Explanation of Data in the front of the book for more detailed information.

Ancestry/Race	Number	%
Thai (273)	313	0.30
Vietnamese (1,069)	1,145	1.11
Other Asian, specified (9)	13	0.01
Other Asian, not specified (89)	168	0.16
Australian	8	0.01
Austrian	63	0.06
Basque	9	0.01
Belgian	22	0.02
Brazilian	15	0.01
British	128	0.12
Bulgarian	8	0.01
Canadian	183	0.18
Celtic	13	0.01
Croatian	24	0.02
Czech	109	0.11
Czechoslovakian	69	0.07
Danish	304	0.29
Dutch	793	0.77
Eastern European	6	0.01
English	3,208	3.11
European	184	0.18
Finnish	69	0.07
French, except Basque	1,178	1.14
French Canadian	207	0.20
German	4,496	4.36
German Russian	4	0.00
Greek	177	0.17
Guyanese	9	0.01
Hawaii Native/Pacific Islander:	675	0.65
Melanesian: (8)	10	0.01
Fijian (8)	10	0.01
Micronesian: (83)	110	0.11
Guamanian/Chamorro (79)	104	0.10
Other Micronesian (4)	6	0.01
Polynesian: (266)	414	0.40
Native Hawaiian (75)	165	0.16
Samoan (140)	183	0.18
Tongan (44)	51	0.05
Other Polynesian (7)	15	0.01
Other Pac. Isl., specified	2	0.00
Other Pac. Isl., not spec. (35)	139	0.13
Hispanic or Latino:	64,965	62.89
Central American:	2,728	2.64
Costa Rican	130	0.13
Guatemalan	555	0.54
Honduran	102	0.10
Nicaraguan	314	0.30
Panamanian	32	0.03
Salvadoran	1,346	1.30
Other Central American	249	0.24
Cuban	332	0.32
Dominican Republic	18	0.02
Mexican	52,652	50.97
Puerto Rican	480	0.46
South American:	722	0.70
Argentinean	59	0.06
Bolivian	9	0.01
Chilean	23	0.02
Colombian	169	0.16
Ecuadorian	175	0.17
Peruvian	227	0.22
Uruguayan	4	0.00
Venezuelan	11	0.01
Other South American	45	0.04
Other Hispanic or Latino	8,033	7.78
Hungarian	215	0.21
Iranian	87	0.08
Irish	3,050	2.95
Italian	1,587	1.54
Lithuanian	47	0.05
Maltese	6	0.01
New Zealander	13	0.01
Northern European	6	0.01
Norwegian	540	0.52
Pennsylvania German	8	0.01
Polish	728	0.71
Portuguese	367	0.36
Romanian	53	0.05
Russian	201	0.19
Scandinavian	11	0.01
Scotch-Irish	612	0.59
Scottish	465	0.45
Serbian	14	0.01
Slovak	13	0.01
Swedish	408	0.40
Swiss	56	0.05
Turkish	10	0.01
Ukrainian	26	0.03
United States or American	2,312	2.24
Welsh	194	0.19
West Indian, excl. Hispanic:	156	0.15
Belizean	42	0.04
Jamaican	114	0.11
White:	50,235	48.63
Not Hispanic (19,574)	20,672	20.01
Hispanic (26,729)	29,563	28.62
Yugoslavian	58	0.06

Novato

Place Type: City
County: Marin
Population: 47,630

Ancestry/Race	Number	%
Afghan	113	0.24
African American/Black:	1,277	2.68
Not Hispanic (893)	1,177	2.47
Hispanic (55)	100	0.21
African, sub-Saharan:	198	0.41
African	62	0.13
Ethiopian	48	0.10
Kenyan	56	0.12
South African	11	0.02
Other sub-Saharan African	21	0.04
Alaska Native tribes, specified:	22	0.05
Alaska Athabascan	1	0.00
Aleut	6	0.01
Eskimo (1)	6	0.01
Tlingit-Haida (7)	8	0.02
All other tribes (1)	1	0.00
Alaska Native tribes, not specified	2	0.00
Am. Ind. or Alaska Nat., not spec.	196	0.41
American Indian tribes, specified:	407	0.85
Apache (4)	12	0.03
Blackfeet (1)	20	0.04
Cherokee (28)	114	0.24
Cheyenne	1	0.00
Chickasaw (1)	4	0.01
Chippewa (6)	9	0.02
Choctaw (4)	25	0.05
Comanche (2)	3	0.01
Cree	4	0.01
Creek	5	0.01
Crow (1)	1	0.00
Iroquois (1)	12	0.03
Latin American Indians (16)	44	0.09
Lumbee	1	0.00
Menominee (1)	1	0.00
Navajo (13)	23	0.05
Osage	4	0.01
Paiute	1	0.00
Potawatomi (1)	7	0.01
Pueblo (4)	7	0.01
Seminole	9	0.02
Shoshone	3	0.01
Sioux (3)	15	0.03
Ute (1)	1	0.00
Yakama	1	0.00
Yaqui (1)	5	0.01
Yuman (2)	5	0.01
All other tribes (35)	70	0.15
American Indian tribes, not spec.	23	0.05
Arab:	209	0.44
Arab/Arabic	45	0.09
Egyptian	14	0.03
Iraqi	31	0.06
Lebanese	55	0.12
Moroccan	37	0.08
Syrian	6	0.01
Other Arab	21	0.04
Armenian	170	0.36
Asian:	3,318	6.97
Bangladeshi (1)	1	0.00
Cambodian (72)	83	0.17
Chinese, ex. Taiwanese (816)	1,050	2.20
Filipino (513)	733	1.54
Indian (237)	280	0.59
Indonesian (7)	20	0.04
Japanese (252)	433	0.91
Korean (217)	257	0.54
Laotian (17)	32	0.07
Malaysian (2)	5	0.01
Pakistani (19)	22	0.05
Sri Lankan (1)	2	0.00
Taiwanese (19)	27	0.06
Thai (16)	46	0.10
Vietnamese (191)	220	0.46
Other Asian, specified (6)	10	0.02
Other Asian, not specified (20)	97	0.20
Australian	16	0.03
Austrian	214	0.45
Basque	89	0.19
Belgian	58	0.12
Brazilian	143	0.30
British	314	0.66
Canadian	160	0.33
Croatian	124	0.26
Czech	148	0.31
Czechoslovakian	95	0.20
Danish	686	1.44
Dutch	714	1.49
Eastern European	64	0.13
English	5,847	12.23
Estonian	32	0.07
European	607	1.27
Finnish	157	0.33
French, except Basque	2,017	4.22
French Canadian	399	0.83
German	7,296	15.27
Greek	425	0.89
Hawaii Native/Pacific Islander:	215	0.45
Melanesian: (9)	13	0.03
Fijian (9)	11	0.02
Other Melanesian	2	0.00
Micronesian: (20)	24	0.05
Guamanian/Chamorro (15)	19	0.04
Other Micronesian (5)	5	0.01
Polynesian: (38)	141	0.30
Native Hawaiian (22)	108	0.23
Samoan (14)	23	0.05
Tongan	2	0.00
Other Polynesian (2)	8	0.02
Other Pac. Isl., specified	1	0.00
Other Pac. Isl., not spec. (13)	36	0.08
Hispanic or Latino:	6,229	13.08
Central American:	817	1.72
Costa Rican	25	0.05
Guatemalan	307	0.64
Honduran	16	0.03
Nicaraguan	85	0.18
Panamanian	7	0.01
Salvadoran	316	0.66
Other Central American	61	0.13
Cuban	43	0.09
Dominican Republic	13	0.03
Mexican	3,620	7.60
Puerto Rican	112	0.24
South American:	410	0.86
Argentinean	44	0.09
Bolivian	29	0.06
Chilean	30	0.06
Colombian	44	0.09
Ecuadorian	26	0.05
Paraguayan	1	0.00
Peruvian	190	0.40
Uruguayan	1	0.00
Venezuelan	11	0.02
Other South American	34	0.07
Other Hispanic or Latino	1,214	2.55

Notes: 1. Figures in the "Number" column do not add up to the total population due to: a) Ancestry/Race overlap — e.g. persons can report being both White and Irish, b) persons of Hispanic origin can report being any race, c) persons reporting two ancestries are counted in both categories. 2. Numbers in parentheses indicate the number of persons reporting this ancestry/race alone, not in combination with any other ancestry/race. 3. Refer to the Explanation of Data in the front of the book for more detailed information.

Ancestry/Race	Number	%
Hungarian	276	0.58
Iranian	228	0.48
Irish	7,364	15.41
Israeli	60	0.13
Italian	5,121	10.71
Lithuanian	118	0.25
Luxemburger	8	0.02
Maltese	56	0.12
New Zealander	19	0.04
Northern European	182	0.38
Norwegian	1,175	2.46
Pennsylvania German	26	0.05
Polish	1,149	2.40
Portuguese	735	1.54
Romanian	113	0.24
Russian	1,306	2.73
Scandinavian	302	0.63
Scotch-Irish	1,073	2.25
Scottish	1,285	2.69
Serbian	28	0.06
Slavic	20	0.04
Slovak	97	0.20
Slovene	8	0.02
Swedish	1,356	2.84
Swiss	633	1.32
Ukrainian	167	0.35
United States or American	1,573	3.29
Welsh	577	1.21
West Indian, excl. Hispanic:	154	0.32
Haitian	122	0.26
Jamaican	32	0.07
White:	41,056	86.20
Not Hispanic (36,336)	37,582	78.90
Hispanic (3,078)	3,474	7.29
Yugoslavian	252	0.53

Oakdale

Place Type: City
County: Stanislaus
Population: 15,503

Ancestry/Race	Number	%
African American/Black:	120	0.77
Not Hispanic (62)	93	0.60
Hispanic (12)	27	0.17
African, sub-Saharan:	4	0.03
African	4	0.03
Alaska Native tribes, specified:	1	0.01
Eskimo (1)	1	0.01
Am. Ind. or Alaska Nat., not spec.	84	0.54
American Indian tribes, specified:	294	1.90
Apache (4)	18	0.12
Blackfeet (1)	6	0.04
Cherokee (46)	142	0.92
Chickasaw (3)	4	0.03
Chippewa (4)	7	0.05
Choctaw (13)	25	0.16
Colville	1	0.01
Cree (1)	7	0.05
Creek (1)	3	0.02
Iroquois (4)	9	0.06
Kiowa	1	0.01
Latin American Indians (2)	9	0.06
Navajo (1)	4	0.03
Paiute (2)	2	0.01
Pima (1)	1	0.01
Pueblo (2)	4	0.03
Seminole	1	0.01
Sioux (3)	8	0.05
Yaqui (2)	2	0.01
All other tribes (24)	40	0.26
American Indian tribes, not spec.	11	0.07
Arab:	10	0.06
Arab/Arabic	10	0.06
Armenian	11	0.07
Asian:	294	1.90
Cambodian (10)	12	0.08
Chinese, ex. Taiwanese (31)	41	0.26
Filipino (63)	110	0.71
Indian (60)	63	0.41
Indonesian	3	0.02
Japanese (11)	38	0.25
Korean (1)	3	0.02
Laotian	1	0.01
Vietnamese (4)	7	0.05
Other Asian, specified	1	0.01
Other Asian, not specified (1)	15	0.10
Australian	13	0.08
Austrian	40	0.26
Belgian	10	0.06
British	57	0.36
Bulgarian	12	0.08
Canadian	35	0.22
Croatian	8	0.05
Czech	29	0.19
Czechoslovakian	6	0.04
Danish	124	0.79
Dutch	258	1.65
English	1,780	11.37
European	89	0.57
Finnish	17	0.11
French, except Basque	408	2.61
French Canadian	63	0.40
German	2,111	13.49
Greek	35	0.22
Hawaii Native/Pacific Islander:	43	0.28
Melanesian: (2)	2	0.01
Fijian (2)	2	0.01
Micronesian: (1)	2	0.01
Guamanian/Chamorro (1)	2	0.01
Polynesian: (11)	22	0.14
Native Hawaiian (11)	18	0.12
Samoan	2	0.01
Other Polynesian	2	0.01
Other Pac. Isl., not spec. (4)	17	0.11
Hispanic or Latino:	3,109	20.05
Central American:	18	0.12
Costa Rican	7	0.05
Guatemalan	1	0.01
Nicaraguan	1	0.01
Salvadoran	5	0.03
Other Central American	4	0.03
Cuban	5	0.03
Mexican	2,521	16.26
Puerto Rican	47	0.30
South American:	21	0.14
Chilean	7	0.05
Colombian	7	0.05
Ecuadorian	2	0.01
Peruvian	6	0.04
Other Hispanic or Latino	497	3.21
Hungarian	36	0.23
Irish	1,488	9.51
Italian	833	5.32
Latvian	13	0.08
Luxemburger	5	0.03
Northern European	26	0.17
Norwegian	319	2.04
Polish	117	0.75
Portuguese	836	5.34
Russian	40	0.26
Scandinavian	43	0.27
Scotch-Irish	241	1.54
Scottish	165	1.05
Slovene	8	0.05
Swedish	295	1.88
Swiss	94	0.60
United States or American	1,538	9.83
Welsh	63	0.40
West Indian, excl. Hispanic:	7	0.04
Dutch West Indian	7	0.04
White:	13,579	87.59
Not Hispanic (11,651)	12,007	77.45
Hispanic (1,344)	1,572	10.14
Yugoslavian	6	0.04

Oakland

Place Type: City
County: Alameda
Population: 399,484

Ancestry/Race	Number	%
Acadian/Cajun	42	0.01
Afghan	159	0.04
African American/Black:	150,139	37.58
Not Hispanic (140,139)	146,510	36.67
Hispanic (2,321)	3,629	0.91
African, sub-Saharan:	10,683	2.67
African	7,521	1.88
Cape Verdean	227	0.06
Ethiopian	1,195	0.30
Ghanian	114	0.03
Kenyan	127	0.03
Liberian	144	0.04
Nigerian	801	0.20
Senegalese	59	0.01
Sierra Leonean	27	0.01
Somalian	48	0.01
South African	73	0.02
Sudanese	19	0.00
Ugandan	13	0.00
Zimbabwean	32	0.01
Other sub-Saharan African	283	0.07
Alaska Native tribes, specified:	57	0.01
Alaska Athabascan (5)	8	0.00
Aleut (3)	6	0.00
Eskimo (4)	16	0.00
Tlingit-Haida (7)	10	0.00
All other tribes (2)	17	0.00
Alaska Native tribes, not specified	5	0.00
Am. Ind. or Alaska Nat., not spec.	2,672	0.67
Albanian	38	0.01
Alsatian	10	0.00
American Indian tribes, specified:	3,922	0.98
Apache (55)	164	0.04
Blackfeet (24)	254	0.06
Cherokee (123)	903	0.23
Cheyenne (3)	16	0.00
Chickasaw (10)	39	0.01
Chippewa (43)	80	0.02
Choctaw (50)	260	0.07
Colville (2)	3	0.00
Comanche (4)	38	0.01
Cree (5)	22	0.01
Creek (19)	66	0.02
Crow (11)	17	0.00
Delaware (2)	7	0.00
Houma (1)	2	0.00
Iroquois (34)	83	0.02
Kiowa	5	0.00
Latin American Indians (371)	674	0.17
Lumbee (4)	4	0.00
Menominee	5	0.00
Navajo (116)	198	0.05
Osage (3)	10	0.00
Ottawa (2)	3	0.00
Paiute (25)	47	0.01
Pima (19)	31	0.01
Potawatomi (8)	14	0.00
Pueblo (65)	97	0.02
Puget Sound Salish	10	0.00
Seminole (9)	55	0.01
Shoshone (14)	25	0.01
Sioux (98)	188	0.05
Tohono O'Odham (11)	19	0.00
Ute (4)	11	0.00
Yakama (2)	3	0.00
Yaqui (28)	61	0.02
Yuman (6)	12	0.00
All other tribes (244)	496	0.12
American Indian tribes, not spec.	361	0.09
Arab:	1,031	0.26
Arab/Arabic	495	0.12
Egyptian	134	0.03
Iraqi	5	0.00

Notes: 1. Figures in the "Number" column do not add up to the total population due to: a) Ancestry/Race overlap — e.g. persons can report being both White and Irish, b) persons of Hispanic origin can report being any race, c) persons reporting two ancestries are counted in both categories. 2. Numbers in parentheses indicate the number of persons reporting this ancestry/race alone, not in combination with any other ancestry/race. 3. Refer to the Explanation of Data in the front of the book for more detailed information.

Jordanian	9	0.00
Lebanese	159	0.04
Moroccan	66	0.02
Palestinian	9	0.00
Syrian	34	0.01
Other Arab	120	0.03
Armenian	395	0.10
Asian:	68,311	17.10
Bangladeshi (3)	4	0.00
Cambodian (2,716)	3,237	0.81
Chinese, ex. Taiwanese (31,742)	34,139	8.55
Filipino (6,407)	8,191	2.05
Hmong (6)	7	0.00
Indian (1,753)	2,321	0.58
Indonesian (104)	171	0.04
Japanese (2,128)	3,162	0.79
Korean (1,780)	2,131	0.53
Laotian (2,850)	3,206	0.80
Malaysian (21)	50	0.01
Pakistani (75)	120	0.03
Sri Lankan (32)	40	0.01
Taiwanese (92)	114	0.03
Thai (199)	285	0.07
Vietnamese (8,657)	9,658	2.42
Other Asian, specified (62)	116	0.03
Other Asian, not specified (700)	1,359	0.34
Assyrian/Chaldean/Syriac	67	0.02
Australian	110	0.03
Austrian	907	0.23
Basque	33	0.01
Belgian	244	0.06
Brazilian	301	0.08
British	1,416	0.35
Bulgarian	49	0.01
Canadian	639	0.16
Celtic	151	0.04
Croatian	380	0.10
Czech	805	0.20
Czechoslovakian	298	0.07
Danish	1,453	0.36
Dutch	2,145	0.54
Eastern European	820	0.21
English	15,991	4.00
Estonian	35	0.01
European	3,490	0.87
Finnish	421	0.11
French, except Basque	5,302	1.33
French Canadian	796	0.20
German	19,451	4.87
German Russian	3	0.00
Greek	1,122	0.28
Guyanese	43	0.01
Hawaii Native/Pacific Islander:	3,339	0.84
Melanesian: (81)	111	0.03
Fijian (80)	105	0.03
Other Melanesian (1)	6	0.00
Micronesian: (125)	223	0.06
Guamanian/Chamorro (115)	212	0.05
Other Micronesian (10)	11	0.00
Polynesian: (1,459)	2,294	0.57
Native Hawaiian (187)	547	0.14
Samoan (363)	514	0.13
Tongan (886)	1,129	0.28
Other Polynesian (23)	104	0.03
Other Pac. Isl., specified	32	0.01
Other Pac. Isl., not spec. (258)	679	0.17
Hispanic or Latino:	87,467	21.89
Central American:	6,759	1.69
Costa Rican	66	0.02
Guatemalan	1,549	0.39
Honduran	459	0.11
Nicaraguan	652	0.16
Panamanian	153	0.04
Salvadoran	3,207	0.80
Other Central American	673	0.17
Cuban	581	0.15
Dominican Republic	64	0.02
Mexican	65,094	16.29
Puerto Rican	2,325	0.58
South American:	1,178	0.29
Argentinean	147	0.04
Bolivian	51	0.01
Chilean	141	0.04
Colombian	213	0.05
Ecuadorian	64	0.02
Paraguayan	6	0.00
Peruvian	351	0.09
Uruguayan	10	0.00
Venezuelan	90	0.02
Other South American	105	0.03
Other Hispanic or Latino	11,466	2.87
Hungarian	1,137	0.28
Icelander	54	0.01
Iranian	642	0.16
Irish	17,021	4.26
Israeli	156	0.04
Italian	8,835	2.21
Latvian	122	0.03
Lithuanian	685	0.17
Luxemburger	51	0.01
Macedonian	14	0.00
Maltese	12	0.00
New Zealander	79	0.02
Northern European	560	0.14
Norwegian	2,655	0.66
Pennsylvania German	64	0.02
Polish	4,112	1.03
Portuguese	2,489	0.62
Romanian	519	0.13
Russian	4,760	1.19
Scandinavian	384	0.10
Scotch-Irish	2,689	0.67
Scottish	4,547	1.14
Serbian	120	0.03
Slavic	128	0.03
Slovak	275	0.07
Slovene	85	0.02
Swedish	3,117	0.78
Swiss	899	0.23
Turkish	112	0.03
Ukrainian	649	0.16
United States or American	5,073	1.27
Welsh	1,579	0.40
West Indian, excl. Hispanic:	1,670	0.42
Bahamian	5	0.00
Barbadian	68	0.02
Belizean	244	0.06
Bermudan	26	0.01
British West Indian	37	0.01
Dutch West Indian	5	0.00
Haitian	157	0.04
Jamaican	795	0.20
Trinidadian and Tobagonian	160	0.04
U.S. Virgin Islander	30	0.01
West Indian	134	0.03
Other West Indian	9	0.00
White:	138,593	34.69
Not Hispanic (93,953)	101,996	25.53
Hispanic (31,060)	36,597	9.16
Yugoslavian	916	0.23

Oakley

Place Type: City
County: Contra Costa
Population: 25,619

Ancestry/Race	Number	%
African American/Black:	1,047	4.09
Not Hispanic (832)	967	3.77
Hispanic (44)	80	0.31
African, sub-Saharan:	14	0.05
African	14	0.05
Alaska Native tribes, specified:	6	0.02
Aleut (3)	4	0.02
Tlingit-Haida	2	0.01
Alaska Native tribes, not specified	1	0.00
Am. Ind. or Alaska Nat., not spec.	187	0.73
Albanian	20	0.08
American Indian tribes, specified:	432	1.69
Apache (5)	26	0.10
Blackfeet (4)	27	0.11
Cherokee (38)	146	0.57
Cheyenne	3	0.01
Chickasaw (5)	7	0.03
Chippewa (1)	2	0.01
Choctaw (16)	42	0.16
Comanche (2)	4	0.02
Cree	1	0.00
Creek (3)	3	0.01
Crow	4	0.02
Houma (5)	5	0.02
Iroquois (1)	2	0.01
Kiowa (4)	11	0.04
Latin American Indians (8)	32	0.12
Navajo (7)	26	0.10
Osage (1)	8	0.03
Paiute (3)	7	0.03
Potawatomi (3)	3	0.01
Pueblo (3)	6	0.02
Puget Sound Salish	2	0.01
Shoshone	2	0.01
Sioux (13)	21	0.08
Ute	3	0.01
Yaqui (3)	3	0.01
All other tribes (19)	36	0.14
American Indian tribes, not spec.	23	0.09
Arab:	50	0.20
Lebanese	50	0.20
Armenian	7	0.03
Asian:	1,324	5.17
Cambodian (9)	9	0.04
Chinese, ex. Taiwanese (130)	233	0.91
Filipino (409)	701	2.74
Indian (32)	50	0.20
Indonesian (2)	8	0.03
Japanese (58)	182	0.71
Korean (23)	45	0.18
Laotian (6)	6	0.02
Malaysian	5	0.02
Pakistani (1)	3	0.01
Taiwanese (1)	1	0.00
Thai (1)	2	0.01
Vietnamese (33)	42	0.16
Other Asian, specified (2)	3	0.01
Other Asian, not specified (4)	34	0.13
Australian	20	0.08
Austrian	24	0.09
Basque	9	0.04
Belgian	7	0.03
British	12	0.05
Bulgarian	49	0.19
Canadian	106	0.42
Croatian	13	0.05
Cypriot	59	0.23
Czech	62	0.24
Czechoslovakian	9	0.04
Danish	205	0.81
Dutch	355	1.39
English	2,172	8.53
European	144	0.57
Finnish	56	0.22
French, except Basque	1,044	4.10
French Canadian	176	0.69
German	3,312	13.01
Greek	56	0.22
Hawaii Native/Pacific Islander:	249	0.97
Melanesian: (3)	7	0.03
Fijian (3)	7	0.03
Micronesian: (23)	51	0.20
Guamanian/Chamorro (21)	48	0.19
Other Micronesian (2)	3	0.01
Polynesian: (37)	155	0.61
Native Hawaiian (15)	111	0.43
Samoan (14)	29	0.11
Tongan (5)	10	0.04
Other Polynesian (3)	5	0.02
Other Pac. Isl., not spec. (9)	36	0.14
Hispanic or Latino:	6,399	24.98
Central American:	202	0.79

Notes: 1. Figures in the "Number" column do not add up to the total population due to: a) Ancestry/Race overlap — e.g. persons can report being both White and Irish, b) persons of Hispanic origin can report being any race, c) persons reporting two ancestries are counted in both categories. 2. Numbers in parentheses indicate the number of persons reporting this ancestry/race alone, not in combination with any other ancestry/race. 3. Refer to the Explanation of Data in the front of the book for more detailed information.

Costa Rican	3	0.01
Guatemalan	17	0.07
Honduran	1	0.00
Nicaraguan	80	0.31
Panamanian	11	0.04
Salvadoran	70	0.27
Other Central American	20	0.08
Cuban	27	0.11
Dominican Republic	2	0.01
Mexican	4,753	18.55
Puerto Rican	226	0.88
South American:	54	0.21
Argentinean	2	0.01
Bolivian	1	0.00
Chilean	6	0.02
Colombian	18	0.07
Ecuadorian	1	0.00
Peruvian	24	0.09
Venezuelan	2	0.01
Other Hispanic or Latino	1,135	4.43
Hungarian	32	0.13
Icelander	27	0.11
Iranian	39	0.15
Irish	3,109	12.21
Italian	2,469	9.70
Latvian	9	0.04
Lithuanian	15	0.06
Maltese	48	0.19
Northern European	14	0.05
Norwegian	587	2.31
Polish	236	0.93
Portuguese	1,352	5.31
Romanian	13	0.05
Russian	203	0.80
Scandinavian	23	0.09
Scotch-Irish	520	2.04
Scottish	394	1.55
Slavic	25	0.10
Slovak	24	0.09
Swedish	406	1.59
Swiss	200	0.79
Ukrainian	24	0.09
United States or American	1,407	5.53
Welsh	244	0.96
West Indian, excl. Hispanic:	18	0.07
Bermudan	8	0.03
West Indian	10	0.04
White:	20,821	81.27
Not Hispanic (16,469)	17,321	67.61
Hispanic (2,873)	3,500	13.66
Yugoslavian	48	0.19

Oceanside

Place Type: City
County: San Diego
Population: 161,029

Ancestry/Race	Number	%
Afghan	114	0.07
African American/Black:	11,973	7.44
Not Hispanic (9,504)	10,914	6.78
Hispanic (685)	1,059	0.66
African, sub-Saharan:	756	0.47
African	667	0.41
Cape Verdean	17	0.01
Ethiopian	38	0.02
Nigerian	10	0.01
South African	24	0.01
Alaska Native tribes, specified:	14	0.01
Alaska Athabascan	2	0.00
Aleut (3)	4	0.00
Eskimo	2	0.00
Tlingit-Haida (5)	6	0.00
Alaska Native tribes, not specified	5	0.00
Am. Ind. or Alaska Nat., not spec.	968	0.60
Albanian	33	0.02
Alsatian	8	0.00
American Indian tribes, specified:	1,708	1.06
Apache (74)	119	0.07
Blackfeet (17)	68	0.04
Cherokee (88)	388	0.24
Cheyenne (3)	5	0.00
Chickasaw (4)	13	0.01
Chippewa (14)	32	0.02
Choctaw (29)	91	0.06
Colville (3)	3	0.00
Comanche (4)	8	0.00
Cree	7	0.00
Creek (14)	22	0.01
Crow	2	0.00
Delaware (3)	7	0.00
Iroquois (9)	24	0.01
Kiowa (4)	6	0.00
Latin American Indians (263)	342	0.21
Lumbee (5)	6	0.00
Menominee	1	0.00
Navajo (59)	84	0.05
Osage (8)	16	0.01
Paiute (3)	5	0.00
Pima (1)	4	0.00
Potawatomi (2)	6	0.00
Pueblo (22)	30	0.02
Puget Sound Salish (3)	3	0.00
Seminole (5)	23	0.01
Shoshone (6)	15	0.01
Sioux (19)	60	0.04
Ute (3)	6	0.00
Yakama (1)	1	0.00
Yaqui (5)	16	0.01
Yuman (7)	9	0.01
All other tribes (169)	286	0.18
American Indian tribes, not spec.	138	0.09
Arab:	641	0.40
Arab/Arabic	130	0.08
Egyptian	91	0.06
Iraqi	69	0.04
Jordanian	46	0.03
Lebanese	190	0.12
Moroccan	36	0.02
Palestinian	9	0.01
Syrian	33	0.02
Other Arab	37	0.02
Armenian	101	0.06
Asian:	12,242	7.60
Bangladeshi (5)	7	0.00
Cambodian (69)	79	0.05
Chinese, ex. Taiwanese (662)	1,089	0.68
Filipino (4,835)	6,390	3.97
Hmong (4)	4	0.00
Indian (281)	403	0.25
Indonesian (35)	86	0.05
Japanese (1,231)	2,079	1.29
Korean (461)	620	0.39
Laotian (23)	33	0.02
Malaysian (10)	30	0.02
Pakistani (17)	20	0.01
Sri Lankan (5)	5	0.00
Taiwanese (49)	63	0.04
Thai (114)	144	0.09
Vietnamese (777)	879	0.55
Other Asian, specified (27)	63	0.04
Other Asian, not specified (99)	248	0.15
Assyrian/Chaldean/Syriac	22	0.01
Australian	89	0.06
Austrian	392	0.24
Basque	51	0.03
Belgian	184	0.11
Brazilian	92	0.06
British	839	0.52
Canadian	537	0.33
Celtic	80	0.05
Croatian	164	0.10
Czech	624	0.39
Czechoslovakian	310	0.19
Danish	1,179	0.73
Dutch	2,006	1.25
Eastern European	88	0.05
English	15,479	9.62
Estonian	20	0.01
European	1,353	0.84
Finnish	435	0.27
French, except Basque	5,050	3.14
French Canadian	1,130	0.70
German	19,685	12.23
Greek	686	0.43
Hawaii Native/Pacific Islander:	3,152	1.96
Melanesian: (3)	5	0.00
Fijian (3)	5	0.00
Micronesian: (304)	457	0.28
Guamanian/Chamorro (287)	426	0.26
Other Micronesian (17)	31	0.02
Polynesian: (1,629)	2,450	1.52
Native Hawaiian (219)	668	0.41
Samoan (1,382)	1,720	1.07
Tongan (15)	29	0.02
Other Polynesian (13)	33	0.02
Other Pac. Isl., specified	8	0.00
Other Pac. Isl., not spec. (53)	232	0.14
Hispanic or Latino:	48,691	30.24
Central American:	832	0.52
Costa Rican	58	0.04
Guatemalan	166	0.10
Honduran	69	0.04
Nicaraguan	59	0.04
Panamanian	150	0.09
Salvadoran	260	0.16
Other Central American	70	0.04
Cuban	206	0.13
Dominican Republic	87	0.05
Mexican	40,729	25.29
Puerto Rican	1,306	0.81
South American:	473	0.29
Argentinean	42	0.03
Bolivian	17	0.01
Chilean	40	0.02
Colombian	124	0.08
Ecuadorian	51	0.03
Paraguayan	2	0.00
Peruvian	111	0.07
Uruguayan	9	0.01
Venezuelan	41	0.03
Other South American	36	0.02
Other Hispanic or Latino	5,058	3.14
Hungarian	836	0.52
Icelander	6	0.00
Iranian	210	0.13
Irish	15,506	9.64
Israeli	17	0.01
Italian	7,887	4.90
Latvian	75	0.05
Lithuanian	290	0.18
Luxemburger	21	0.01
Macedonian	30	0.02
New Zealander	20	0.01
Northern European	145	0.09
Norwegian	2,674	1.66
Pennsylvania German	76	0.05
Polish	3,234	2.01
Portuguese	780	0.48
Romanian	220	0.14
Russian	1,479	0.92
Scandinavian	408	0.25
Scotch-Irish	2,682	1.67
Scottish	3,353	2.08
Serbian	60	0.04
Slavic	61	0.04
Slovak	185	0.11
Slovene	17	0.01
Swedish	2,603	1.62
Swiss	533	0.33
Turkish	92	0.06
Ukrainian	260	0.16
United States or American	5,733	3.56
Welsh	1,228	0.76
West Indian, excl. Hispanic:	459	0.29
Barbadian	29	0.02
Belizean	41	0.03
British West Indian	21	0.01
Dutch West Indian	11	0.01

Notes: 1. Figures in the "Number" column do not add up to the total population due to: a) Ancestry/Race overlap — e.g. persons can report being both White and Irish, b) persons of Hispanic origin can report being any race, c) persons reporting two ancestries are counted in both categories. 2. Numbers in parentheses indicate the number of persons reporting this ancestry/race alone, not in combination with any other ancestry/race. 3. Refer to the Explanation of Data in the front of the book for more detailed information.

Haitian	23	0.01
Jamaican	232	0.14
Trinidadian and Tobagonian	8	0.00
West Indian	87	0.05
Other West Indian	7	0.00
White:	113,622	70.56
Not Hispanic (86,310)	90,451	56.17
Hispanic (20,556)	23,171	14.39
Yugoslavian	201	0.12

Oildale

Place Type: Census Designated Place
County: Kern
Population: 27,885

Ancestry/Race	Number	%
African American/Black:	145	0.52
Not Hispanic (83)	128	0.46
Hispanic (12)	17	0.06
Alaska Native tribes, specified:	2	0.01
Eskimo	1	0.00
Tlingit-Haida (1)	1	0.00
Am. Ind. or Alaska Nat., not spec.	218	0.78
American Indian tribes, specified:	855	3.07
Apache (9)	20	0.07
Blackfeet (9)	39	0.14
Cherokee (153)	356	1.28
Cheyenne (2)	6	0.02
Chickasaw (11)	23	0.08
Chippewa (2)	7	0.03
Choctaw (48)	86	0.31
Comanche (1)	3	0.01
Cree	2	0.01
Creek (16)	25	0.09
Crow	1	0.00
Delaware	5	0.02
Iroquois (1)	4	0.01
Latin American Indians (17)	22	0.08
Lumbee (16)	17	0.06
Navajo (49)	61	0.22
Osage	3	0.01
Paiute (38)	59	0.21
Pima (1)	1	0.00
Potawatomi (5)	10	0.04
Pueblo (9)	10	0.04
Seminole (1)	1	0.00
Shoshone (1)	3	0.01
Sioux (1)	3	0.01
Tohono O'Odham	1	0.00
Ute (1)	1	0.00
Yakama	4	0.01
Yaqui (4)	4	0.01
Yuman	2	0.01
All other tribes (49)	76	0.27
American Indian tribes, not spec.	73	0.26
Arab:	31	0.11
Arab/Arabic	8	0.03
Lebanese	17	0.06
Syrian	6	0.02
Armenian	12	0.04
Asian:	175	0.63
Chinese, ex. Taiwanese (4)	12	0.04
Filipino (52)	93	0.33
Indian (9)	13	0.05
Indonesian	2	0.01
Japanese (9)	17	0.06
Korean (16)	24	0.09
Laotian	1	0.00
Pakistani	2	0.01
Vietnamese (2)	5	0.02
Other Asian, not specified	6	0.02
Austrian	65	0.23
Basque	181	0.65
Belgian	6	0.02
British	88	0.32
Canadian	88	0.32
Celtic	10	0.04
Czech	10	0.04
Danish	143	0.51
Dutch	435	1.56
English	2,655	9.52
European	208	0.75
Finnish	15	0.05
French, except Basque	865	3.10
French Canadian	153	0.55
German	3,532	12.67
Greek	93	0.33
Hawaii Native/Pacific Islander:	38	0.14
Micronesian: (2)	3	0.01
Guamanian/Chamorro (2)	3	0.01
Polynesian: (12)	23	0.08
Native Hawaiian (4)	15	0.05
Tongan (7)	7	0.03
Other Polynesian (1)	1	0.00
Other Pac. Isl., not spec. (4)	12	0.04
Hispanic or Latino:	2,828	10.14
Central American:	37	0.13
Guatemalan	4	0.01
Honduran	6	0.02
Nicaraguan	2	0.01
Panamanian	1	0.00
Salvadoran	20	0.07
Other Central American	4	0.01
Cuban	24	0.09
Mexican	2,278	8.17
Puerto Rican	55	0.20
South American:	23	0.08
Chilean	2	0.01
Colombian	1	0.00
Ecuadorian	1	0.00
Peruvian	16	0.06
Venezuelan	1	0.00
Other South American	2	0.01
Other Hispanic or Latino	411	1.47
Hungarian	25	0.09
Irish	3,736	13.40
Italian	736	2.64
Lithuanian	16	0.06
Northern European	14	0.05
Norwegian	265	0.95
Polish	202	0.72
Portuguese	75	0.27
Romanian	14	0.05
Russian	118	0.42
Scandinavian	28	0.10
Scotch-Irish	401	1.44
Scottish	470	1.69
Slovak	6	0.02
Swedish	194	0.70
Swiss	48	0.17
Turkish	8	0.03
Ukrainian	13	0.05
United States or American	2,928	10.50
Welsh	216	0.77
West Indian, excl. Hispanic:	59	0.21
Dutch West Indian	59	0.21
White:	25,665	92.04
Not Hispanic (23,664)	24,281	87.08
Hispanic (1,150)	1,384	4.96
Yugoslavian	12	0.04

Olivehurst

Place Type: Census Designated Place
County: Yuba
Population: 11,061

Ancestry/Race	Number	%
African American/Black:	244	2.21
Not Hispanic (174)	220	1.99
Hispanic (9)	24	0.22
Alaska Native tribes, specified:	1	0.01
Eskimo (1)	1	0.01
Alaska Native tribes, not specified	1	0.01
Am. Ind. or Alaska Nat., not spec.	176	1.59
American Indian tribes, specified:	619	5.60
Apache (7)	23	0.21
Blackfeet (3)	26	0.24
Cherokee (155)	322	2.91
Cheyenne	1	0.01
Chippewa (8)	15	0.14
Choctaw (46)	76	0.69
Comanche (5)	7	0.06
Creek (1)	2	0.02
Iroquois (2)	9	0.08
Latin American Indians (17)	26	0.24
Navajo (3)	7	0.06
Osage (1)	3	0.03
Potawatomi (4)	5	0.05
Seminole	4	0.04
Sioux (3)	6	0.05
Tohono O'Odham	1	0.01
Ute (1)	1	0.01
Yaqui (1)	2	0.02
All other tribes (50)	83	0.75
American Indian tribes, not spec.	30	0.27
Asian:	708	6.40
Cambodian (2)	2	0.02
Chinese, ex. Taiwanese (11)	18	0.16
Filipino (43)	75	0.68
Hmong (371)	416	3.76
Indian (53)	78	0.71
Indonesian (1)	4	0.04
Japanese (17)	40	0.36
Korean (9)	16	0.14
Laotian (15)	37	0.33
Thai (6)	11	0.10
Other Asian, not specified (3)	11	0.10
British	41	0.37
Canadian	13	0.12
Czech	2	0.02
Danish	44	0.40
Dutch	135	1.22
English	574	5.17
European	40	0.36
French, except Basque	380	3.43
French Canadian	50	0.45
German	1,171	10.56
Greek	6	0.05
Hawaii Native/Pacific Islander:	47	0.42
Micronesian:	1	0.01
Guamanian/Chamorro	1	0.01
Polynesian: (12)	31	0.28
Native Hawaiian (12)	26	0.24
Samoan	2	0.02
Tongan	2	0.02
Other Polynesian	1	0.01
Other Pac. Isl., not spec. (6)	15	0.14
Hispanic or Latino:	2,760	24.95
Central American:	20	0.18
Guatemalan	7	0.06
Honduran	3	0.03
Nicaraguan	1	0.01
Panamanian	1	0.01
Salvadoran	2	0.02
Other Central American	6	0.05
Cuban	4	0.04
Dominican Republic	3	0.03
Mexican	2,365	21.38
Puerto Rican	23	0.21
South American:	9	0.08
Argentinean	1	0.01
Colombian	6	0.05
Ecuadorian	2	0.02
Other Hispanic or Latino	336	3.04
Hungarian	7	0.06
Irish	900	8.11
Italian	304	2.74
Lithuanian	11	0.10
Norwegian	52	0.47
Polish	90	0.81
Portuguese	199	1.79
Romanian	49	0.44
Russian	45	0.41
Scandinavian	3	0.03
Scotch-Irish	108	0.97
Scottish	168	1.51
Slovak	7	0.06
Swedish	57	0.51

Notes: 1. Figures in the "Number" column do not add up to the total population due to: a) Ancestry/Race overlap — e.g. persons can report being both White and Irish, b) persons of Hispanic origin can report being any race, c) persons reporting two ancestries are counted in both categories. 2. Numbers in parentheses indicate the number of persons reporting this ancestry/race alone, not in combination with any other ancestry/race. 3. Refer to the Explanation of Data in the front of the book for more detailed information.

	Number	%
Swiss	9	0.08
Ukrainian	5	0.05
United States or American	1,362	12.28
Welsh	31	0.28
West Indian, excl. Hispanic:	19	0.17
Dutch West Indian	19	0.17
White:	8,098	73.21
Not Hispanic (6,661)	7,148	64.62
Hispanic (782)	950	8.59

Ontario

Place Type: City
County: San Bernardino
Population: 158,007

Ancestry/Race	Number	%
Acadian/Cajun	9	0.01
Afghan	58	0.04
African American/Black:	13,069	8.27
Not Hispanic (11,317)	12,107	7.66
Hispanic (547)	962	0.61
African, sub-Saharan:	781	0.50
African	594	0.38
Cape Verdean	30	0.02
Ethiopian	16	0.01
Ghanian	25	0.02
Liberian	15	0.01
Nigerian	20	0.01
South African	15	0.01
Other sub-Saharan African	66	0.04
Alaska Native tribes, specified:	12	0.01
Alaska Athabascan (1)	4	0.00
Aleut (1)	2	0.00
Eskimo (3)	3	0.00
Tlingit-Haida (2)	3	0.00
Alaska Native tribes, not specified	1	0.00
Am. Ind. or Alaska Nat., not spec.	1,219	0.77
American Indian tribes, specified:	1,603	1.01
Apache (50)	105	0.07
Blackfeet (5)	70	0.04
Cherokee (89)	347	0.22
Cheyenne (3)	3	0.00
Chickasaw (8)	16	0.01
Chippewa (13)	21	0.01
Choctaw (31)	53	0.03
Colville (1)	1	0.00
Comanche (8)	17	0.01
Cree (4)	5	0.00
Creek (2)	15	0.01
Delaware (3)	3	0.00
Iroquois (2)	23	0.01
Kiowa (1)	8	0.01
Latin American Indians (345)	470	0.30
Navajo (19)	61	0.04
Osage (1)	6	0.00
Paiute (5)	6	0.00
Pima (5)	7	0.00
Potawatomi (2)	5	0.00
Pueblo (25)	54	0.03
Seminole (9)	14	0.01
Shoshone (2)	4	0.00
Sioux (15)	44	0.03
Tohono O'Odham (4)	8	0.01
Yaqui (25)	66	0.04
Yuman	1	0.00
All other tribes (93)	170	0.11
American Indian tribes, not spec.	155	0.10
Arab:	293	0.19
Arab/Arabic	73	0.05
Egyptian	97	0.06
Lebanese	27	0.02
Syrian	53	0.03
Other Arab	43	0.03
Armenian	105	0.07
Asian:	7,773	4.92
Bangladeshi (8)	33	0.02
Cambodian (196)	227	0.14
Chinese, ex. Taiwanese (558)	797	0.50
Filipino (2,129)	2,662	1.68
Hmong (36)	49	0.03
Indian (514)	643	0.41
Indonesian (223)	332	0.21
Japanese (277)	542	0.34
Korean (388)	514	0.33
Laotian (28)	57	0.04
Pakistani (60)	97	0.06
Sri Lankan (13)	16	0.01
Taiwanese (64)	92	0.06
Thai (77)	109	0.07
Vietnamese (1,272)	1,353	0.86
Other Asian, specified (8)	23	0.01
Other Asian, not specified (93)	227	0.14
Australian	6	0.00
Austrian	169	0.11
Basque	102	0.06
Belgian	132	0.08
Brazilian	5	0.00
British	256	0.16
Canadian	337	0.21
Celtic	13	0.01
Croatian	73	0.05
Czech	172	0.11
Czechoslovakian	85	0.05
Danish	375	0.24
Dutch	2,436	1.55
Eastern European	32	0.02
English	6,167	3.92
Estonian	25	0.02
European	627	0.40
Finnish	86	0.05
French, except Basque	2,257	1.43
French Canadian	437	0.28
German	9,321	5.92
Greek	268	0.17
Guyanese	24	0.02
Hawaii Native/Pacific Islander:	929	0.59
Melanesian: (8)	10	0.01
Fijian (8)	8	0.01
Other Melanesian	2	0.00
Micronesian: (48)	82	0.05
Guamanian/Chamorro (45)	78	0.05
Other Micronesian (3)	4	0.00
Polynesian: (478)	676	0.43
Native Hawaiian (63)	181	0.11
Samoan (122)	167	0.11
Tongan (278)	308	0.19
Other Polynesian (15)	20	0.01
Other Pac. Isl., specified	1	0.00
Other Pac. Isl., not spec. (41)	160	0.10
Hispanic or Latino:	94,610	59.88
Central American:	2,958	1.87
Costa Rican	121	0.08
Guatemalan	743	0.47
Honduran	291	0.18
Nicaraguan	315	0.20
Panamanian	49	0.03
Salvadoran	1,104	0.70
Other Central American	335	0.21
Cuban	401	0.25
Dominican Republic	19	0.01
Mexican	77,476	49.03
Puerto Rican	717	0.45
South American:	949	0.60
Argentinean	158	0.10
Bolivian	28	0.02
Chilean	44	0.03
Colombian	253	0.16
Ecuadorian	136	0.09
Peruvian	210	0.13
Uruguayan	6	0.00
Venezuelan	14	0.01
Other South American	100	0.06
Other Hispanic or Latino	12,090	7.65
Hungarian	416	0.26
Icelander	8	0.01
Iranian	91	0.06
Irish	6,849	4.35
Italian	3,729	2.37
Latvian	14	0.01
Lithuanian	94	0.06
Northern European	14	0.01
Norwegian	796	0.51
Pennsylvania German	14	0.01
Polish	1,099	0.70
Portuguese	926	0.59
Romanian	82	0.05
Russian	432	0.27
Scandinavian	285	0.18
Scotch-Irish	1,084	0.69
Scottish	918	0.58
Serbian	6	0.00
Slavic	8	0.01
Slovak	31	0.02
Slovene	14	0.01
Swedish	1,169	0.74
Swiss	209	0.13
Turkish	16	0.01
Ukrainian	80	0.05
United States or American	4,501	2.86
Welsh	362	0.23
West Indian, excl. Hispanic:	389	0.25
Barbadian	7	0.00
Belizean	79	0.05
Bermudan	8	0.01
British West Indian	6	0.00
Dutch West Indian	6	0.00
Haitian	50	0.03
Jamaican	179	0.11
Trinidadian and Tobagonian	30	0.02
U.S. Virgin Islander	9	0.01
West Indian	15	0.01
White:	82,485	52.20
Not Hispanic (42,048)	44,183	27.96
Hispanic (33,527)	38,302	24.24
Yugoslavian	73	0.05

Orange

Place Type: City
County: Orange
Population: 128,821

Ancestry/Race	Number	%
Acadian/Cajun	15	0.01
Afghan	218	0.17
African American/Black:	2,608	2.02
Not Hispanic (1,798)	2,216	1.72
Hispanic (258)	392	0.30
African, sub-Saharan:	138	0.11
African	109	0.08
Ethiopian	13	0.01
South African	11	0.01
Zimbabwean	5	0.00
Alaska Native tribes, specified:	8	0.01
Alaska Athabascan	2	0.00
Aleut (1)	1	0.00
Eskimo (2)	2	0.00
Tlingit-Haida (1)	3	0.00
Am. Ind. or Alaska Nat., not spec.	670	0.52
Alsatian	5	0.00
American Indian tribes, specified:	1,057	0.82
Apache (49)	93	0.07
Blackfeet (10)	28	0.02
Cherokee (72)	232	0.18
Cheyenne (3)	6	0.00
Chickasaw	8	0.01
Chippewa (15)	27	0.02
Choctaw (22)	40	0.03
Comanche (3)	9	0.01
Cree	6	0.00
Creek (7)	13	0.01
Delaware (2)	2	0.00
Iroquois (6)	27	0.02
Kiowa (1)	1	0.00
Latin American Indians (182)	232	0.18
Menominee (1)	1	0.00
Navajo (16)	25	0.02
Osage	2	0.00
Paiute (1)	3	0.00

Notes: 1. Figures in the "Number" column do not add up to the total population due to: a) Ancestry/Race overlap — e.g. persons can report being both White and Irish, b) persons of Hispanic origin can report being any race, c) persons reporting two ancestries are counted in both categories. 2. Numbers in parentheses indicate the number of persons reporting this ancestry/race alone, not in combination with any other ancestry/race. 3. Refer to the Explanation of Data in the front of the book for more detailed information.

Ancestry/Race	Number	%
Pima (1)	5	0.00
Potawatomi	1	0.00
Pueblo (7)	12	0.01
Puget Sound Salish (2)	2	0.00
Seminole (3)	9	0.01
Shoshone (3)	6	0.00
Sioux (9)	34	0.03
Tohono O'Odham (4)	11	0.01
Ute	2	0.00
Yaqui (7)	27	0.02
Yuman (2)	2	0.00
All other tribes (139)	191	0.15
American Indian tribes, not spec.	94	0.07
Arab:	1,163	0.91
Arab/Arabic	103	0.08
Egyptian	181	0.14
Iraqi	67	0.05
Jordanian	77	0.06
Lebanese	422	0.33
Palestinian	130	0.10
Syrian	169	0.13
Other Arab	14	0.01
Armenian	220	0.17
Asian:	13,719	10.65
Bangladeshi (16)	29	0.02
Cambodian (230)	241	0.19
Chinese, ex. Taiwanese (1,566)	1,939	1.51
Filipino (1,905)	2,311	1.79
Hmong (9)	9	0.01
Indian (1,021)	1,146	0.89
Indonesian (81)	134	0.10
Japanese (1,136)	1,553	1.21
Korean (1,343)	1,451	1.13
Laotian (34)	36	0.03
Malaysian (8)	10	0.01
Pakistani (75)	90	0.07
Sri Lankan (14)	15	0.01
Taiwanese (377)	431	0.33
Thai (79)	100	0.08
Vietnamese (3,743)	3,940	3.06
Other Asian, specified (14)	27	0.02
Other Asian, not specified (99)	257	0.20
Assyrian/Chaldean/Syriac	115	0.09
Australian	20	0.02
Austrian	340	0.26
Basque	117	0.09
Belgian	112	0.09
Brazilian	69	0.05
British	503	0.39
Canadian	513	0.40
Celtic	37	0.03
Croatian	198	0.15
Czech	344	0.27
Czechoslovakian	265	0.21
Danish	840	0.65
Dutch	2,006	1.56
Eastern European	61	0.05
English	12,032	9.37
Estonian	10	0.01
European	1,242	0.97
Finnish	197	0.15
French, except Basque	4,183	3.26
French Canadian	732	0.57
German	17,559	13.67
Greek	484	0.38
Hawaii Native/Pacific Islander:	645	0.50
Melanesian: (2)	2	0.00
Fijian (2)	2	0.00
Micronesian: (48)	80	0.06
Guamanian/Chamorro (48)	80	0.06
Polynesian: (207)	405	0.31
Native Hawaiian (98)	247	0.19
Samoan (76)	111	0.09
Tongan (33)	40	0.03
Other Polynesian	7	0.01
Other Pac. Isl., specified	5	0.00
Other Pac. Isl., not spec. (36)	153	0.12
Hispanic or Latino:	41,434	32.16
Central American:	1,194	0.93
Costa Rican	41	0.03
Guatemalan	386	0.30
Honduran	85	0.07
Nicaraguan	80	0.06
Panamanian	11	0.01
Salvadoran	425	0.33
Other Central American	166	0.13
Cuban	272	0.21
Dominican Republic	26	0.02
Mexican	34,329	26.65
Puerto Rican	338	0.26
South American:	655	0.51
Argentinean	116	0.09
Bolivian	35	0.03
Chilean	33	0.03
Colombian	108	0.08
Ecuadorian	46	0.04
Paraguayan	1	0.00
Peruvian	204	0.16
Uruguayan	3	0.00
Venezuelan	20	0.02
Other South American	89	0.07
Other Hispanic or Latino	4,620	3.59
Hungarian	525	0.41
Icelander	13	0.01
Iranian	688	0.54
Irish	11,674	9.09
Israeli	86	0.07
Italian	6,174	4.81
Latvian	77	0.06
Lithuanian	122	0.09
Maltese	31	0.02
New Zealander	25	0.02
Northern European	66	0.05
Norwegian	2,082	1.62
Pennsylvania German	24	0.02
Polish	2,293	1.79
Portuguese	533	0.41
Romanian	226	0.18
Russian	1,203	0.94
Scandinavian	304	0.24
Scotch-Irish	1,647	1.28
Scottish	2,457	1.91
Serbian	61	0.05
Slavic	64	0.05
Slovak	127	0.10
Slovene	53	0.04
Swedish	2,131	1.66
Swiss	380	0.30
Turkish	37	0.03
Ukrainian	290	0.23
United States or American	5,149	4.01
Welsh	833	0.65
West Indian, excl. Hispanic:	164	0.13
Belizean	13	0.01
British West Indian	7	0.01
Dutch West Indian	7	0.01
Haitian	10	0.01
Jamaican	113	0.09
Trinidadian and Tobagonian	6	0.00
West Indian	4	0.00
Other West Indian	4	0.00
White:	95,000	73.75
Not Hispanic (70,292)	72,481	56.26
Hispanic (20,530)	22,519	17.48
Yugoslavian	155	0.12

Orangevale

Place Type: Census Designated Place
County: Sacramento
Population: 26,705

Ancestry/Race	Number	%
African American/Black:	465	1.74
Not Hispanic (288)	424	1.59
Hispanic (13)	41	0.15
African, sub-Saharan:	30	0.11
African	17	0.06
Other sub-Saharan African	13	0.05
Alaska Native tribes, specified:	11	0.04
Aleut (4)	4	0.01
Eskimo (6)	7	0.03
Alaska Native tribes, not specified	1	0.00
Am. Ind. or Alaska Nat., not spec.	156	0.58
American Indian tribes, specified:	482	1.80
Apache (5)	10	0.04
Blackfeet (5)	37	0.14
Cherokee (47)	178	0.67
Cheyenne	3	0.01
Chickasaw (3)	7	0.03
Chippewa (4)	11	0.04
Choctaw (15)	28	0.10
Comanche (2)	2	0.01
Cree (6)	6	0.02
Crow (1)	1	0.00
Iroquois (5)	10	0.04
Latin American Indians (4)	15	0.06
Navajo (5)	7	0.03
Osage	4	0.01
Ottawa (1)	1	0.00
Paiute (1)	7	0.03
Pima	1	0.00
Potawatomi	3	0.01
Pueblo (5)	8	0.03
Seminole (1)	6	0.02
Shoshone (5)	6	0.02
Sioux (25)	37	0.14
Tohono O'Odham (1)	1	0.00
All other tribes (46)	93	0.35
American Indian tribes, not spec.	38	0.14
Arab:	82	0.31
Arab/Arabic	16	0.06
Egyptian	22	0.08
Lebanese	15	0.06
Syrian	16	0.06
Other Arab	13	0.05
Armenian	66	0.25
Asian:	1,073	4.02
Chinese, ex. Taiwanese (115)	187	0.70
Filipino (119)	254	0.95
Hmong (1)	1	0.00
Indian (181)	221	0.83
Indonesian (4)	7	0.03
Japanese (99)	210	0.79
Korean (48)	71	0.27
Malaysian (1)	1	0.00
Pakistani (3)	5	0.02
Sri Lankan (4)	6	0.02
Taiwanese (3)	4	0.01
Thai (7)	13	0.05
Vietnamese (44)	55	0.21
Other Asian, specified (4)	10	0.04
Other Asian, not specified (6)	28	0.10
Assyrian/Chaldean/Syriac	7	0.03
Australian	37	0.14
Austrian	81	0.30
Basque	44	0.16
Belgian	20	0.07
Brazilian	16	0.06
British	78	0.29
Canadian	57	0.21
Celtic	9	0.03
Croatian	53	0.20
Czech	110	0.41
Czechoslovakian	89	0.33
Danish	269	1.01
Dutch	557	2.08
English	3,991	14.92
European	327	1.22
Finnish	86	0.32
French, except Basque	1,438	5.38
French Canadian	193	0.72
German	5,674	21.22
German Russian	53	0.20
Greek	176	0.66
Hawaii Native/Pacific Islander:	125	0.47
Melanesian: (7)	10	0.04
Fijian (7)	10	0.04
Micronesian: (8)	21	0.08
Guamanian/Chamorro (7)	20	0.07

Notes: 1. Figures in the "Number" column do not add up to the total population due to: a) Ancestry/Race overlap — e.g. persons can report being both White and Irish, b) persons of Hispanic origin can report being any race, c) persons reporting two ancestries are counted in both categories. 2. Numbers in parentheses indicate the number of persons reporting this ancestry/race alone, not in combination with any other ancestry/race. 3. Refer to the Explanation of Data in the front of the book for more detailed information.

Ancestry/Race	Number	%
Other Micronesian (1)	1	0.00
Polynesian: (22)	56	0.21
Native Hawaiian (20)	47	0.18
Samoan (2)	7	0.03
Tongan	1	0.00
Other Polynesian	1	0.00
Other Pac. Isl., specified	1	0.00
Other Pac. Isl., not spec. (12)	37	0.14
Hispanic or Latino:	1,816	6.80
Central American:	30	0.11
Costa Rican	5	0.02
Guatemalan	17	0.06
Honduran	3	0.01
Salvadoran	5	0.02
Cuban	29	0.11
Mexican	1,219	4.56
Puerto Rican	69	0.26
South American:	50	0.19
Argentinean	5	0.02
Chilean	10	0.04
Colombian	14	0.05
Ecuadorian	3	0.01
Peruvian	9	0.03
Venezuelan	5	0.02
Other South American	4	0.01
Other Hispanic or Latino	419	1.57
Hungarian	183	0.68
Iranian	196	0.73
Irish	3,916	14.64
Israeli	7	0.03
Italian	1,811	6.77
Lithuanian	40	0.15
Maltese	22	0.08
Northern European	107	0.40
Norwegian	744	2.78
Pennsylvania German	39	0.15
Polish	638	2.39
Portuguese	318	1.19
Romanian	32	0.12
Russian	321	1.20
Scandinavian	114	0.43
Scotch-Irish	611	2.28
Scottish	765	2.86
Serbian	29	0.11
Slavic	14	0.05
Slovak	27	0.10
Swedish	604	2.26
Swiss	114	0.43
Turkish	25	0.09
Ukrainian	146	0.55
United States or American	1,535	5.74
Welsh	200	0.75
West Indian, excl. Hispanic:	14	0.05
Dutch West Indian	6	0.02
Jamaican	8	0.03
White:	24,862	93.10
Not Hispanic (22,759)	23,540	88.15
Hispanic (1,147)	1,322	4.95
Yugoslavian	97	0.36

Orcutt

Place Type: Census Designated Place
County: Santa Barbara
Population: 28,830

Ancestry/Race	Number	%
African American/Black:	539	1.87
Not Hispanic (390)	498	1.73
Hispanic (13)	41	0.14
African, sub-Saharan:	98	0.34
African	48	0.17
Ethiopian	13	0.05
Nigerian	28	0.10
Zimbabwean	9	0.03
Alaska Native tribes, specified:	5	0.02
Eskimo (4)	4	0.01
Tlingit-Haida	1	0.00
Am. Ind. or Alaska Nat., not spec.	132	0.46
American Indian tribes, specified:	423	1.47
Apache (21)	27	0.09
Blackfeet (3)	12	0.04
Cherokee (22)	110	0.38
Cheyenne (2)	5	0.02
Chickasaw	5	0.02
Chippewa (4)	8	0.03
Choctaw (27)	43	0.15
Comanche (1)	1	0.00
Creek (1)	1	0.00
Iroquois (3)	3	0.01
Kiowa	2	0.01
Latin American Indians (21)	46	0.16
Menominee	1	0.00
Navajo (1)	2	0.01
Osage (1)	1	0.00
Paiute (1)	1	0.00
Pima	1	0.00
Potawatomi (2)	4	0.01
Pueblo (2)	4	0.01
Seminole (1)	4	0.01
Shoshone (1)	1	0.00
Sioux (4)	5	0.02
Tohono O'Odham (1)	4	0.01
Yaqui (2)	4	0.01
All other tribes (75)	128	0.44
American Indian tribes, not spec.	10	0.03
Arab:	38	0.13
Egyptian	7	0.02
Lebanese	27	0.09
Other Arab	4	0.01
Armenian	29	0.10
Asian:	1,394	4.84
Cambodian (6)	6	0.02
Chinese, ex. Taiwanese (108)	165	0.57
Filipino (293)	498	1.73
Indian (77)	97	0.34
Indonesian (4)	15	0.05
Japanese (207)	333	1.16
Korean (132)	169	0.59
Pakistani (11)	14	0.05
Sri Lankan (9)	9	0.03
Taiwanese (2)	2	0.01
Thai (10)	21	0.07
Vietnamese (28)	39	0.14
Other Asian, specified (1)	1	0.00
Other Asian, not specified (11)	25	0.09
Australian	22	0.08
Austrian	109	0.38
Basque	14	0.05
Belgian	53	0.18
British	215	0.75
Canadian	220	0.76
Celtic	8	0.03
Croatian	35	0.12
Czech	108	0.37
Czechoslovakian	45	0.16
Danish	312	1.08
Dutch	653	2.26
Eastern European	6	0.02
English	4,330	15.01
European	362	1.25
Finnish	94	0.33
French, except Basque	1,204	4.17
French Canadian	230	0.80
German	5,237	18.16
Greek	110	0.38
Hawaii Native/Pacific Islander:	86	0.30
Micronesian: (12)	19	0.07
Guamanian/Chamorro (10)	17	0.06
Other Micronesian (2)	2	0.01
Polynesian: (12)	44	0.15
Native Hawaiian (10)	38	0.13
Samoan (2)	6	0.02
Other Pac. Isl., not spec.	23	0.08
Hispanic or Latino:	4,165	14.45
Central American:	49	0.17
Costa Rican	6	0.02
Guatemalan	10	0.03
Honduran	5	0.02
Nicaraguan	10	0.03
Panamanian	5	0.02
Salvadoran	10	0.03
Other Central American	3	0.01
Cuban	10	0.03
Mexican	3,394	11.77
Puerto Rican	79	0.27
South American:	43	0.15
Argentinean	5	0.02
Chilean	11	0.04
Colombian	13	0.05
Paraguayan	1	0.00
Peruvian	5	0.02
Venezuelan	4	0.01
Other South American	4	0.01
Other Hispanic or Latino	590	2.05
Hungarian	110	0.38
Icelander	44	0.15
Iranian	24	0.08
Irish	3,514	12.18
Israeli	4	0.01
Italian	1,713	5.94
Lithuanian	31	0.11
Luxemburger	23	0.08
New Zealander	7	0.02
Northern European	21	0.07
Norwegian	868	3.01
Pennsylvania German	17	0.06
Polish	525	1.82
Portuguese	470	1.63
Romanian	11	0.04
Russian	151	0.52
Scandinavian	96	0.33
Scotch-Irish	685	2.37
Scottish	727	2.52
Slavic	14	0.05
Slovak	38	0.13
Slovene	34	0.12
Swedish	683	2.37
Swiss	300	1.04
Ukrainian	72	0.25
United States or American	1,710	5.93
Welsh	363	1.26
West Indian, excl. Hispanic:	27	0.09
Trinidadian and Tobagonian	12	0.04
West Indian	15	0.05
White:	25,957	90.03
Not Hispanic (22,479)	23,105	80.14
Hispanic (2,511)	2,852	9.89
Yugoslavian	23	0.08

Orinda

Place Type: City
County: Contra Costa
Population: 17,599

Ancestry/Race	Number	%
African American/Black:	145	0.82
Not Hispanic (79)	135	0.77
Hispanic (3)	10	0.06
African, sub-Saharan:	97	0.56
South African	88	0.50
Zimbabwean	2	0.01
Other sub-Saharan African	7	0.04
Alaska Native tribes, specified:	7	0.04
Aleut (1)	4	0.02
Eskimo (2)	2	0.01
Tlingit-Haida	1	0.01
Am. Ind. or Alaska Nat., not spec.	29	0.16
Alsatian	6	0.03
American Indian tribes, specified:	76	0.43
Apache (1)	2	0.01
Cherokee (7)	33	0.19
Chickasaw	7	0.04
Chippewa	1	0.01
Choctaw	9	0.05
Cree	1	0.01
Creek	4	0.02
Latin American Indians (3)	3	0.02
Paiute	1	0.01

Notes: 1. Figures in the "Number" column do not add up to the total population due to: a) Ancestry/Race overlap — e.g. persons can report being both White and Irish, b) persons of Hispanic origin can report being any race, c) persons reporting two ancestries are counted in both categories. 2. Numbers in parentheses indicate the number of persons reporting this ancestry/race alone, not in combination with any other ancestry/race. 3. Refer to the Explanation of Data in the front of the book for more detailed information.

Pueblo (1)	1	0.01
Yuman (1)	1	0.01
All other tribes (9)	13	0.07
American Indian tribes, not spec.	8	0.05
Arab:	116	0.66
Arab/Arabic	2	0.01
Lebanese	38	0.22
Palestinian	65	0.37
Syrian	7	0.04
Other Arab	4	0.02
Armenian	40	0.23
Asian:	2,010	11.42
Bangladeshi (1)	1	0.01
Chinese, ex. Taiwanese (902)	1,094	6.22
Filipino (93)	153	0.87
Indian (152)	182	1.03
Indonesian	6	0.03
Japanese (195)	298	1.69
Korean (89)	115	0.65
Pakistani (22)	25	0.14
Taiwanese (38)	38	0.22
Thai (3)	3	0.02
Vietnamese (49)	60	0.34
Other Asian, specified	6	0.03
Other Asian, not specified (14)	29	0.16
Assyrian/Chaldean/Syriac	7	0.04
Australian	100	0.57
Austrian	155	0.89
Basque	4	0.02
Belgian	22	0.13
Brazilian	15	0.09
British	272	1.56
Bulgarian	11	0.06
Canadian	91	0.52
Croatian	41	0.24
Czech	54	0.31
Czechoslovakian	34	0.19
Danish	327	1.87
Dutch	342	1.96
Eastern European	124	0.71
English	3,124	17.91
Estonian	13	0.07
European	528	3.03
Finnish	81	0.46
French, except Basque	760	4.36
French Canadian	69	0.40
German	2,919	16.73
Greek	249	1.43
Hawaii Native/Pacific Islander:	36	0.20
Polynesian: (7)	30	0.17
Native Hawaiian (1)	20	0.11
Samoan (4)	8	0.05
Tongan (2)	2	0.01
Other Pac. Isl., specified	4	0.02
Other Pac. Isl., not spec.	2	0.01
Hispanic or Latino:	560	3.18
Central American:	56	0.32
Costa Rican	14	0.08
Guatemalan	7	0.04
Nicaraguan	13	0.07
Salvadoran	18	0.10
Other Central American	4	0.02
Cuban	8	0.05
Mexican	256	1.45
Puerto Rican	28	0.16
South American:	60	0.34
Argentinean	12	0.07
Chilean	13	0.07
Colombian	12	0.07
Ecuadorian	1	0.01
Paraguayan	2	0.01
Peruvian	9	0.05
Venezuelan	7	0.04
Other South American	4	0.02
Other Hispanic or Latino	152	0.86
Hungarian	109	0.62
Icelander	20	0.11
Iranian	353	2.02
Irish	2,608	14.95
Israeli	7	0.04
Italian	1,353	7.76
Latvian	22	0.13
Lithuanian	83	0.48
Maltese	16	0.09
Northern European	81	0.46
Norwegian	464	2.66
Pennsylvania German	22	0.13
Polish	451	2.59
Portuguese	155	0.89
Romanian	66	0.38
Russian	466	2.67
Scandinavian	40	0.23
Scotch-Irish	350	2.01
Scottish	712	4.08
Slovak	52	0.30
Slovene	6	0.03
Swedish	632	3.62
Swiss	203	1.16
Turkish	11	0.06
Ukrainian	52	0.30
United States or American	602	3.45
Welsh	286	1.64
White:	15,703	89.23
Not Hispanic (14,857)	15,242	86.61
Hispanic (389)	461	2.62
Yugoslavian	51	0.29

Oroville

Place Type: City
County: Butte
Population: 13,004

Ancestry/Race	Number	%
African American/Black:	661	5.08
Not Hispanic (504)	618	4.75
Hispanic (20)	43	0.33
African, sub-Saharan:	60	0.46
African	53	0.41
Nigerian	7	0.05
Alaska Native tribes, specified:	9	0.07
Aleut (1)	2	0.02
Eskimo (1)	1	0.01
Tlingit-Haida (5)	6	0.05
Am. Ind. or Alaska Nat., not spec.	226	1.74
American Indian tribes, specified:	618	4.75
Apache (8)	25	0.19
Blackfeet (5)	12	0.09
Cherokee (58)	157	1.21
Cheyenne	2	0.02
Chippewa (5)	8	0.06
Choctaw (14)	35	0.27
Comanche	5	0.04
Creek	2	0.02
Crow	2	0.02
Iroquois	4	0.03
Latin American Indians (5)	13	0.10
Navajo (2)	8	0.06
Osage	1	0.01
Paiute (1)	7	0.05
Potawatomi	7	0.05
Pueblo (2)	5	0.04
Puget Sound Salish (3)	3	0.02
Seminole (3)	7	0.05
Shoshone (3)	3	0.02
Sioux (12)	18	0.14
Ute (1)	1	0.01
Yaqui	3	0.02
Yuman	1	0.01
All other tribes (225)	289	2.22
American Indian tribes, not spec.	57	0.44
Arab:	60	0.46
Arab/Arabic	6	0.05
Syrian	54	0.42
Asian:	991	7.62
Cambodian	3	0.02
Chinese, ex. Taiwanese (20)	39	0.30
Filipino (30)	64	0.49
Hmong (531)	574	4.41
Indian (40)	56	0.43
Indonesian (3)	4	0.03
Japanese (11)	19	0.15
Korean (1)	4	0.03
Laotian (143)	173	1.33
Pakistani (2)	8	0.06
Thai (1)	5	0.04
Vietnamese (18)	19	0.15
Other Asian, not specified (13)	23	0.18
Australian	9	0.07
Austrian	6	0.05
Belgian	13	0.10
British	33	0.25
Czech	38	0.29
Czechoslovakian	5	0.04
Danish	93	0.72
Dutch	231	1.78
Eastern European	6	0.05
English	1,322	10.19
European	127	0.98
Finnish	28	0.22
French, except Basque	311	2.40
French Canadian	82	0.63
German	1,891	14.58
Greek	86	0.66
Hawaii Native/Pacific Islander:	85	0.65
Micronesian: (2)	3	0.02
Guamanian/Chamorro (2)	2	0.02
Other Micronesian	1	0.01
Polynesian: (29)	51	0.39
Native Hawaiian (18)	36	0.28
Samoan (11)	15	0.12
Other Pac. Isl., not spec. (3)	31	0.24
Hispanic or Latino:	1,073	8.25
Central American:	26	0.20
Guatemalan	7	0.05
Honduran	1	0.01
Nicaraguan	1	0.01
Panamanian	1	0.01
Salvadoran	15	0.12
Other Central American	1	0.01
Cuban	25	0.19
Mexican	763	5.87
Puerto Rican	49	0.38
South American:	6	0.05
Argentinean	2	0.02
Colombian	1	0.01
Peruvian	3	0.02
Other Hispanic or Latino	204	1.57
Hungarian	52	0.40
Irish	1,313	10.12
Italian	537	4.14
Lithuanian	12	0.09
Maltese	6	0.05
Northern European	13	0.10
Norwegian	178	1.37
Pennsylvania German	13	0.10
Polish	77	0.59
Portuguese	204	1.57
Romanian	124	0.96
Russian	53	0.41
Scandinavian	7	0.05
Scotch-Irish	184	1.42
Scottish	208	1.60
Slovak	8	0.06
Swedish	185	1.43
Swiss	27	0.21
Ukrainian	16	0.12
United States or American	798	6.15
Welsh	61	0.47
West Indian, excl. Hispanic:	5	0.04
British West Indian	5	0.04
White:	10,629	81.74
Not Hispanic (9,560)	10,013	77.00
Hispanic (483)	616	4.74

Notes: 1. Figures in the "Number" column do not add up to the total population due to: a) Ancestry/Race overlap — e.g. persons can report being both White and Irish, b) persons of Hispanic origin can report being any race, c) persons reporting two ancestries are counted in both categories. 2. Numbers in parentheses indicate the number of persons reporting this ancestry/race alone, not in combination with any other ancestry/race. 3. Refer to the Explanation of Data in the front of the book for more detailed information.

Oxnard

Place Type: City
County: Ventura
Population: 170,358

Ancestry/Race	Number	%
Acadian/Cajun	29	0.02
African American/Black:	7,476	4.39
Not Hispanic (5,923)	6,541	3.84
Hispanic (523)	935	0.55
African, sub-Saharan:	367	0.22
African	320	0.19
Nigerian	34	0.02
South African	9	0.01
Other sub-Saharan African	4	0.00
Alaska Native tribes, specified:	17	0.01
Alaska Athabascan (1)	2	0.00
Aleut (3)	4	0.00
Eskimo (7)	9	0.01
Tlingit-Haida	2	0.00
Am. Ind. or Alaska Nat., not spec.	1,239	0.73
Albanian	39	0.02
Alsatian	9	0.01
American Indian tribes, specified:	2,103	1.23
Apache (65)	132	0.08
Blackfeet (6)	46	0.03
Cherokee (98)	370	0.22
Cheyenne (1)	13	0.01
Chickasaw (5)	14	0.01
Chippewa (10)	15	0.01
Choctaw (15)	63	0.04
Comanche (3)	19	0.01
Cree (3)	3	0.00
Creek (5)	8	0.00
Crow	3	0.00
Delaware	5	0.00
Iroquois (4)	19	0.01
Kiowa (3)	7	0.00
Latin American Indians (503)	652	0.38
Lumbee	5	0.00
Navajo (34)	73	0.04
Osage (3)	13	0.01
Paiute (1)	9	0.01
Pima (9)	13	0.01
Potawatomi (6)	8	0.00
Pueblo (17)	30	0.02
Puget Sound Salish (2)	5	0.00
Seminole	8	0.00
Shoshone (1)	2	0.00
Sioux (23)	38	0.02
Tohono O'Odham (4)	8	0.00
Ute	8	0.00
Yakama	1	0.00
Yaqui (47)	75	0.04
Yuman (2)	3	0.00
All other tribes (291)	435	0.26
American Indian tribes, not spec.	172	0.10
Arab:	337	0.20
Arab/Arabic	211	0.12
Egyptian	24	0.01
Lebanese	86	0.05
Syrian	9	0.01
Other Arab	7	0.00
Armenian	94	0.06
Asian:	14,898	8.75
Bangladeshi (15)	15	0.01
Cambodian (49)	70	0.04
Chinese, ex. Taiwanese (440)	667	0.39
Filipino (8,707)	9,907	5.82
Hmong	1	0.00
Indian (394)	487	0.29
Indonesian (29)	45	0.03
Japanese (1,019)	1,551	0.91
Korean (527)	604	0.35
Laotian (54)	57	0.03
Malaysian (12)	41	0.02
Pakistani (18)	19	0.01
Sri Lankan (2)	9	0.01
Taiwanese (44)	49	0.03
Thai (54)	84	0.05
Vietnamese (954)	1,034	0.61
Other Asian, specified (11)	32	0.02
Other Asian, not specified (107)	226	0.13
Assyrian/Chaldean/Syriac	4	0.00
Australian	65	0.04
Austrian	221	0.13
Basque	82	0.05
Belgian	123	0.07
Brazilian	74	0.04
British	196	0.11
Canadian	246	0.14
Carpatho Rusyn	8	0.00
Celtic	36	0.02
Croatian	44	0.03
Cypriot	5	0.00
Czech	62	0.04
Czechoslovakian	108	0.06
Danish	387	0.23
Dutch	1,006	0.59
Eastern European	19	0.01
English	6,024	3.53
European	443	0.26
Finnish	93	0.05
French, except Basque	1,878	1.10
French Canadian	283	0.17
German	7,682	4.50
Greek	179	0.10
Hawaii Native/Pacific Islander:	1,260	0.74
Micronesian: (139)	226	0.13
Guamanian/Chamorro (137)	219	0.13
Other Micronesian (2)	7	0.00
Polynesian: (489)	796	0.47
Native Hawaiian (107)	271	0.16
Samoan (374)	498	0.29
Tongan (4)	6	0.00
Other Polynesian (4)	21	0.01
Other Pac. Isl., specified	20	0.01
Other Pac. Isl., not spec. (56)	218	0.13
Hispanic or Latino:	112,807	66.22
Central American:	963	0.57
Costa Rican	27	0.02
Guatemalan	219	0.13
Honduran	79	0.05
Nicaraguan	64	0.04
Panamanian	63	0.04
Salvadoran	401	0.24
Other Central American	110	0.06
Cuban	125	0.07
Dominican Republic	24	0.01
Mexican	101,264	59.44
Puerto Rican	529	0.31
South American:	425	0.25
Argentinean	64	0.04
Bolivian	24	0.01
Chilean	41	0.02
Colombian	104	0.06
Ecuadorian	45	0.03
Peruvian	79	0.05
Uruguayan	11	0.01
Venezuelan	18	0.01
Other South American	39	0.02
Other Hispanic or Latino	9,477	5.56
Hungarian	225	0.13
Iranian	177	0.10
Irish	6,137	3.60
Israeli	9	0.01
Italian	2,662	1.56
Latvian	34	0.02
Lithuanian	104	0.06
Maltese	7	0.00
New Zealander	18	0.01
Northern European	29	0.02
Norwegian	841	0.49
Pennsylvania German	48	0.03
Polish	1,001	0.59
Portuguese	351	0.21
Romanian	49	0.03
Russian	675	0.40
Scandinavian	102	0.06
Scotch-Irish	973	0.57
Scottish	1,197	0.70
Slavic	100	0.06
Slovak	67	0.04
Slovene	10	0.01
Swedish	1,152	0.68
Swiss	161	0.09
Turkish	45	0.03
Ukrainian	109	0.06
United States or American	4,059	2.38
Welsh	342	0.20
West Indian, excl. Hispanic:	80	0.05
Dutch West Indian	13	0.01
Jamaican	28	0.02
Trinidadian and Tobagonian	11	0.01
West Indian	28	0.02
White:	78,236	45.92
Not Hispanic (35,049)	37,354	21.93
Hispanic (36,639)	40,882	24.00
Yugoslavian	119	0.07

Pacific Grove

Place Type: City
County: Monterey
Population: 15,522

Ancestry/Race	Number	%
Acadian/Cajun	8	0.05
African American/Black:	254	1.64
Not Hispanic (170)	234	1.51
Hispanic (7)	20	0.13
African, sub-Saharan:	39	0.25
African	31	0.20
Other sub-Saharan African	8	0.05
Alaska Native tribes, specified:	1	0.01
Tlingit-Haida (1)	1	0.01
Am. Ind. or Alaska Nat., not spec.	52	0.34
American Indian tribes, specified:	164	1.06
Apache (2)	8	0.05
Blackfeet (2)	7	0.05
Cherokee (14)	42	0.27
Chippewa (1)	1	0.01
Choctaw (3)	6	0.04
Colville	1	0.01
Creek	1	0.01
Crow (1)	3	0.02
Iroquois (2)	9	0.06
Latin American Indians (7)	10	0.06
Navajo (2)	6	0.04
Ottawa	1	0.01
Paiute	3	0.02
Potawatomi (4)	4	0.03
Pueblo (3)	3	0.02
Seminole	1	0.01
Shoshone	3	0.02
Sioux	6	0.04
Ute (1)	1	0.01
Yaqui (1)	4	0.03
All other tribes (23)	44	0.28
American Indian tribes, not spec.	10	0.06
Arab:	119	0.77
Arab/Arabic	36	0.23
Egyptian	29	0.19
Iraqi	8	0.05
Jordanian	13	0.08
Lebanese	5	0.03
Syrian	7	0.05
Other Arab	21	0.14
Armenian	57	0.37
Asian:	960	6.18
Cambodian (1)	1	0.01
Chinese, ex. Taiwanese (143)	187	1.20
Filipino (106)	182	1.17
Indian (30)	34	0.22
Indonesian (28)	37	0.24
Japanese (180)	285	1.84
Korean (138)	161	1.04
Laotian (1)	1	0.01
Sri Lankan (1)	3	0.02

Notes: 1. Figures in the "Number" column do not add up to the total population due to: a) Ancestry/Race overlap — e.g. persons can report being both White and Irish, b) persons of Hispanic origin can report being any race, c) persons reporting two ancestries are counted in both categories. 2. Numbers in parentheses indicate the number of persons reporting this ancestry/race alone, not in combination with any other ancestry/race. 3. Refer to the Explanation of Data in the front of the book for more detailed information.

Taiwanese (1)	1	0.01
Thai (9)	13	0.08
Vietnamese (27)	35	0.23
Other Asian, specified (4)	5	0.03
Other Asian, not specified (9)	15	0.10
Assyrian/Chaldean/Syriac	3	0.02
Australian	25	0.16
Austrian	23	0.15
Basque	31	0.20
Belgian	44	0.28
Brazilian	21	0.14
British	239	1.55
Bulgarian	19	0.12
Canadian	60	0.39
Croatian	32	0.21
Czech	91	0.59
Czechoslovakian	40	0.26
Danish	245	1.58
Dutch	272	1.76
Eastern European	15	0.10
English	2,527	16.35
European	324	2.10
Finnish	42	0.27
French, except Basque	655	4.24
French Canadian	165	1.07
German	2,571	16.63
Greek	140	0.91
Hawaii Native/Pacific Islander:	84	0.54
Melanesian: (3)	4	0.03
Fijian (3)	4	0.03
Micronesian: (17)	24	0.15
Guamanian/Chamorro (16)	23	0.15
Other Micronesian (1)	1	0.01
Polynesian: (19)	36	0.23
Native Hawaiian (4)	19	0.12
Samoan (1)	2	0.01
Tongan (13)	13	0.08
Other Polynesian (1)	2	0.01
Other Pac. Isl., not spec. (2)	20	0.13
Hispanic or Latino:	1,108	7.14
Central American:	45	0.29
Guatemalan	5	0.03
Nicaraguan	3	0.02
Panamanian	2	0.01
Salvadoran	32	0.21
Other Central American	3	0.02
Cuban	16	0.10
Mexican	656	4.23
Puerto Rican	34	0.22
South American:	71	0.46
Argentinean	6	0.04
Bolivian	4	0.03
Chilean	5	0.03
Colombian	8	0.05
Ecuadorian	4	0.03
Paraguayan	7	0.05
Peruvian	27	0.17
Uruguayan	1	0.01
Venezuelan	2	0.01
Other South American	7	0.05
Other Hispanic or Latino	286	1.84
Hungarian	190	1.23
Icelander	7	0.05
Iranian	37	0.24
Irish	2,233	14.44
Israeli	12	0.08
Italian	1,259	8.14
Lithuanian	35	0.23
New Zealander	16	0.10
Northern European	35	0.23
Norwegian	446	2.89
Pennsylvania German	5	0.03
Polish	281	1.82
Portuguese	393	2.54
Romanian	13	0.08
Russian	195	1.26
Scandinavian	71	0.46
Scotch-Irish	538	3.48
Scottish	603	3.90
Serbian	6	0.04
Slovak	37	0.24
Slovene	14	0.09
Swedish	405	2.62
Swiss	154	1.00
Turkish	13	0.08
Ukrainian	86	0.56
United States or American	575	3.72
Welsh	319	2.06
West Indian, excl. Hispanic:	7	0.05
Jamaican	7	0.05
White:	14,196	91.46
Not Hispanic (12,957)	13,379	86.19
Hispanic (708)	817	5.26
Yugoslavian	33	0.21

Pacifica

Place Type: City
County: San Mateo
Population: 38,390

Ancestry/Race	Number	%
African American/Black:	1,595	4.15
Not Hispanic (1,219)	1,504	3.92
Hispanic (35)	91	0.24
African, sub-Saharan:	106	0.28
African	106	0.28
Alaska Native tribes, specified:	10	0.03
Aleut (3)	4	0.01
Eskimo	3	0.01
Tlingit-Haida (1)	3	0.01
Am. Ind. or Alaska Nat., not spec.	183	0.48
Albanian	7	0.02
American Indian tribes, specified:	417	1.09
Apache (9)	24	0.06
Blackfeet (3)	24	0.06
Cherokee (27)	135	0.35
Chickasaw (3)	4	0.01
Chippewa (10)	14	0.04
Choctaw (10)	24	0.06
Comanche (3)	8	0.02
Creek (8)	12	0.03
Crow (1)	1	0.00
Iroquois (2)	15	0.04
Kiowa	3	0.01
Latin American Indians (6)	22	0.06
Navajo (6)	9	0.02
Osage	2	0.01
Ottawa (1)	1	0.00
Paiute	1	0.00
Pima	2	0.01
Potawatomi	1	0.00
Pueblo	6	0.02
Puget Sound Salish (1)	1	0.00
Seminole (2)	10	0.03
Shoshone	3	0.01
Sioux (4)	12	0.03
Ute (1)	2	0.01
Yaqui (8)	11	0.03
Yuman (1)	2	0.01
All other tribes (32)	68	0.18
American Indian tribes, not spec.	25	0.07
Arab:	382	0.99
Arab/Arabic	80	0.21
Egyptian	71	0.18
Jordanian	55	0.14
Lebanese	70	0.18
Moroccan	13	0.03
Palestinian	59	0.15
Other Arab	34	0.09
Armenian	42	0.11
Asian:	7,416	19.32
Cambodian (5)	17	0.04
Chinese, ex. Taiwanese (1,491)	1,926	5.02
Filipino (3,215)	3,925	10.22
Hmong (1)	3	0.01
Indian (227)	291	0.76
Indonesian (23)	51	0.13
Japanese (324)	604	1.57
Korean (177)	209	0.54
Laotian	1	0.00
Malaysian (4)	11	0.03
Pakistani (11)	26	0.07
Sri Lankan (4)	5	0.01
Taiwanese (13)	26	0.07
Thai (30)	41	0.11
Vietnamese (120)	145	0.38
Other Asian, specified (22)	31	0.08
Other Asian, not specified (39)	104	0.27
Australian	27	0.07
Austrian	145	0.38
Basque	116	0.30
Belgian	49	0.13
Brazilian	42	0.11
British	226	0.59
Canadian	110	0.29
Celtic	45	0.12
Croatian	28	0.07
Czech	124	0.32
Czechoslovakian	103	0.27
Danish	463	1.21
Dutch	539	1.40
Eastern European	43	0.11
English	3,918	10.20
Estonian	7	0.02
European	478	1.24
Finnish	85	0.22
French, except Basque	1,345	3.50
French Canadian	190	0.49
German	5,225	13.60
German Russian	4	0.01
Greek	358	0.93
Hawaii Native/Pacific Islander:	593	1.54
Melanesian: (24)	29	0.08
Fijian (24)	29	0.08
Micronesian: (45)	69	0.18
Guamanian/Chamorro (44)	68	0.18
Other Micronesian (1)	1	0.00
Polynesian: (169)	368	0.96
Native Hawaiian (45)	191	0.50
Samoan (83)	130	0.34
Tongan (41)	44	0.11
Other Polynesian	3	0.01
Other Pac. Isl., specified	1	0.00
Other Pac. Isl., not spec. (18)	126	0.33
Hispanic or Latino:	5,609	14.61
Central American:	880	2.29
Costa Rican	11	0.03
Guatemalan	99	0.26
Honduran	14	0.04
Nicaraguan	253	0.66
Panamanian	17	0.04
Salvadoran	414	1.08
Other Central American	72	0.19
Cuban	70	0.18
Dominican Republic	11	0.03
Mexican	2,483	6.47
Puerto Rican	298	0.78
South American:	214	0.56
Argentinean	21	0.05
Bolivian	11	0.03
Chilean	36	0.09
Colombian	22	0.06
Ecuadorian	15	0.04
Paraguayan	2	0.01
Peruvian	67	0.17
Uruguayan	6	0.02
Venezuelan	7	0.02
Other South American	27	0.07
Other Hispanic or Latino	1,653	4.31
Hungarian	214	0.56
Iranian	23	0.06
Irish	6,095	15.87
Italian	4,264	11.10
Latvian	60	0.16
Lithuanian	126	0.33
Maltese	100	0.26
Northern European	57	0.15
Norwegian	756	1.97
Pennsylvania German	7	0.02

Notes: 1. Figures in the "Number" column do not add up to the total population due to: a) Ancestry/Race overlap — e.g. persons can report being both White and Irish, b) persons of Hispanic origin can report being any race, c) persons reporting two ancestries are counted in both categories. 2. Numbers in parentheses indicate the number of persons reporting this ancestry/race alone, not in combination with any other ancestry/race. 3. Refer to the Explanation of Data in the front of the book for more detailed information.

Polish	664	1.73
Portuguese	524	1.36
Romanian	94	0.24
Russian	887	2.31
Scandinavian	30	0.08
Scotch-Irish	871	2.27
Scottish	927	2.41
Serbian	16	0.04
Slavic	8	0.02
Slovak	64	0.17
Slovene	12	0.03
Swedish	795	2.07
Swiss	268	0.70
Ukrainian	204	0.53
United States or American	986	2.57
Welsh	336	0.87
West Indian, excl. Hispanic:	59	0.15
Belizean	47	0.12
Jamaican	7	0.02
West Indian	5	0.01
White:	28,790	74.99
Not Hispanic (23,549)	24,998	65.12
Hispanic (3,135)	3,792	9.88
Yugoslavian	50	0.13

Palm Desert

Place Type: City
County: Riverside
Population: 41,155

Ancestry/Race	Number	%
African American/Black:	638	1.55
Not Hispanic (446)	538	1.31
Hispanic (49)	100	0.24
African, sub-Saharan:	131	0.32
African	114	0.28
South African	17	0.04
Alaska Native tribes, specified:	2	0.00
Eskimo	1	0.00
Tlingit-Haida (1)	1	0.00
Am. Ind. or Alaska Nat., not spec.	140	0.34
Albanian	50	0.12
American Indian tribes, specified:	230	0.56
Apache (2)	9	0.02
Blackfeet (5)	7	0.02
Cherokee (26)	68	0.17
Chickasaw (1)	6	0.01
Chippewa	5	0.01
Choctaw (6)	14	0.03
Colville (1)	1	0.00
Comanche (1)	1	0.00
Creek (6)	10	0.02
Delaware	1	0.00
Iroquois	2	0.00
Kiowa (1)	1	0.00
Latin American Indians (10)	30	0.07
Navajo (2)	3	0.01
Osage (2)	2	0.00
Pima (4)	6	0.01
Potawatomi (1)	1	0.00
Pueblo (2)	2	0.00
Puget Sound Salish (3)	3	0.01
Seminole (1)	1	0.00
Shoshone (1)	1	0.00
Sioux (3)	9	0.02
Tohono O'Odham (1)	1	0.00
Yaqui (3)	6	0.01
All other tribes (25)	40	0.10
American Indian tribes, not spec.	13	0.03
Arab:	201	0.49
Arab/Arabic	2	0.00
Lebanese	150	0.36
Moroccan	2	0.00
Palestinian	14	0.03
Syrian	33	0.08
Armenian	55	0.13
Asian:	1,338	3.25
Cambodian (4)	4	0.01
Chinese, ex. Taiwanese (218)	274	0.67
Filipino (190)	278	0.68
Indian (66)	94	0.23
Indonesian (6)	9	0.02
Japanese (208)	274	0.67
Korean (122)	138	0.34
Malaysian (1)	1	0.00
Pakistani (10)	10	0.02
Sri Lankan (9)	17	0.04
Taiwanese (31)	39	0.09
Thai (14)	15	0.04
Vietnamese (115)	130	0.32
Other Asian, specified (2)	3	0.01
Other Asian, not specified (30)	52	0.13
Australian	29	0.07
Austrian	275	0.67
Basque	6	0.01
Belgian	43	0.10
Brazilian	61	0.15
British	291	0.70
Canadian	406	0.98
Celtic	22	0.05
Croatian	85	0.21
Czech	211	0.51
Czechoslovakian	97	0.23
Danish	315	0.76
Dutch	647	1.57
Eastern European	18	0.04
English	5,888	14.26
Estonian	25	0.06
European	249	0.60
Finnish	59	0.14
French, except Basque	1,610	3.90
French Canadian	319	0.77
German	6,782	16.43
Greek	165	0.40
Hawaii Native/Pacific Islander:	82	0.20
Micronesian: (7)	11	0.03
Guamanian/Chamorro (6)	10	0.02
Other Micronesian (1)	1	0.00
Polynesian: (26)	50	0.12
Native Hawaiian (15)	38	0.09
Samoan (6)	6	0.01
Other Polynesian (5)	6	0.01
Other Pac. Isl., not spec. (7)	21	0.05
Hispanic or Latino:	7,031	17.08
Central American:	186	0.45
Costa Rican	3	0.01
Guatemalan	24	0.06
Honduran	11	0.03
Nicaraguan	22	0.05
Panamanian	8	0.02
Salvadoran	96	0.23
Other Central American	22	0.05
Cuban	65	0.16
Dominican Republic	5	0.01
Mexican	5,532	13.44
Puerto Rican	104	0.25
South American:	148	0.36
Argentinean	17	0.04
Chilean	16	0.04
Colombian	48	0.12
Ecuadorian	12	0.03
Peruvian	31	0.08
Venezuelan	9	0.02
Other South American	15	0.04
Other Hispanic or Latino	991	2.41
Hungarian	339	0.82
Icelander	14	0.03
Iranian	82	0.20
Irish	5,035	12.20
Israeli	7	0.02
Italian	2,110	5.11
Latvian	26	0.06
Lithuanian	129	0.31
Northern European	17	0.04
Norwegian	1,278	3.10
Polish	1,072	2.60
Portuguese	196	0.47
Romanian	196	0.47
Russian	1,206	2.92
Scandinavian	130	0.31
Scotch-Irish	912	2.21
Scottish	1,304	3.16
Serbian	24	0.06
Slavic	14	0.03
Slovak	39	0.09
Slovene	15	0.04
Swedish	1,150	2.79
Swiss	199	0.48
Turkish	24	0.06
Ukrainian	122	0.30
United States or American	1,973	4.78
Welsh	462	1.12
West Indian, excl. Hispanic:	58	0.14
Haitian	31	0.08
Jamaican	27	0.07
White:	36,576	88.87
Not Hispanic (31,919)	32,392	78.71
Hispanic (3,820)	4,184	10.17
Yugoslavian	235	0.57

Palm Springs

Place Type: City
County: Riverside
Population: 42,807

Ancestry/Race	Number	%
Afghan	2	0.00
African American/Black:	1,873	4.38
Not Hispanic (1,621)	1,769	4.13
Hispanic (60)	104	0.24
African, sub-Saharan:	73	0.17
African	65	0.15
Liberian	2	0.00
South African	4	0.01
Other sub-Saharan African	2	0.00
Alaska Native tribes, specified:	5	0.01
Alaska Athabascan (2)	2	0.00
Eskimo (1)	1	0.00
Tlingit-Haida (1)	1	0.00
All other tribes (1)	1	0.00
Alaska Native tribes, not specified	1	0.00
Am. Ind. or Alaska Nat., not spec.	209	0.49
Albanian	3	0.01
American Indian tribes, specified:	467	1.09
Apache (9)	13	0.03
Blackfeet (5)	13	0.03
Cherokee (33)	100	0.23
Cheyenne	2	0.00
Chickasaw	1	0.00
Chippewa (3)	5	0.01
Choctaw (5)	19	0.04
Comanche (6)	10	0.02
Cree	1	0.00
Creek (5)	8	0.02
Crow (1)	1	0.00
Delaware	2	0.00
Iroquois (4)	8	0.02
Kiowa	3	0.01
Latin American Indians (17)	40	0.09
Navajo (5)	16	0.04
Osage (4)	4	0.01
Pima	3	0.01
Potawatomi (6)	9	0.02
Pueblo (3)	8	0.02
Seminole (1)	1	0.00
Shoshone (2)	4	0.01
Sioux (10)	19	0.04
Tohono O'Odham	3	0.01
Ute (1)	1	0.00
Yakama	1	0.00
Yaqui (5)	5	0.01
Yuman (2)	2	0.00
All other tribes (128)	165	0.39
American Indian tribes, not spec.	42	0.10
Arab:	174	0.41
Arab/Arabic	43	0.10
Egyptian	19	0.04
Iraqi	4	0.01

Notes: 1. Figures in the "Number" column do not add up to the total population due to: a) Ancestry/Race overlap — e.g. persons can report being both White and Irish, b) persons of Hispanic origin can report being any race, c) persons reporting two ancestries are counted in both categories. 2. Numbers in parentheses indicate the number of persons reporting this ancestry/race alone, not in combination with any other ancestry/race. 3. Refer to the Explanation of Data in the front of the book for more detailed information.

Jordanian	7	0.02
Lebanese	57	0.13
Syrian	42	0.10
Other Arab	2	0.00
Armenian	93	0.22
Asian:	1,938	4.53
Cambodian	1	0.00
Chinese, ex. Taiwanese (112)	168	0.39
Filipino (1,086)	1,215	2.84
Hmong (3)	3	0.01
Indian (100)	133	0.31
Indonesian (7)	10	0.02
Japanese (109)	150	0.35
Korean (81)	94	0.22
Laotian (1)	2	0.00
Malaysian (1)	1	0.00
Pakistani (16)	18	0.04
Sri Lankan (31)	44	0.10
Taiwanese (5)	5	0.01
Thai (17)	21	0.05
Vietnamese (23)	36	0.08
Other Asian, not specified (21)	37	0.09
Assyrian/Chaldean/Syriac	17	0.04
Australian	39	0.09
Austrian	252	0.59
Basque	17	0.04
Belgian	67	0.16
Brazilian	6	0.01
British	209	0.49
Bulgarian	58	0.14
Canadian	307	0.72
Celtic	48	0.11
Croatian	86	0.20
Czech	141	0.33
Czechoslovakian	96	0.22
Danish	299	0.70
Dutch	674	1.57
Eastern European	43	0.10
English	5,236	12.22
European	291	0.68
Finnish	49	0.11
French, except Basque	1,548	3.61
French Canadian	267	0.62
German	5,626	13.13
Greek	247	0.58
Guyanese	17	0.04
Hawaii Native/Pacific Islander:	121	0.28
Micronesian: (19)	30	0.07
Guamanian/Chamorro (19)	30	0.07
Polynesian: (33)	69	0.16
Native Hawaiian (21)	51	0.12
Samoan (9)	15	0.04
Tongan (2)	2	0.00
Other Polynesian (1)	1	0.00
Other Pac. Isl., not spec. (3)	22	0.05
Hispanic or Latino:	10,155	23.72
Central American:	414	0.97
Costa Rican	17	0.04
Guatemalan	191	0.45
Honduran	12	0.03
Nicaraguan	31	0.07
Panamanian	9	0.02
Salvadoran	82	0.19
Other Central American	72	0.17
Cuban	85	0.20
Dominican Republic	6	0.01
Mexican	7,910	18.48
Puerto Rican	105	0.25
South American:	188	0.44
Argentinean	16	0.04
Bolivian	6	0.01
Chilean	10	0.02
Colombian	35	0.08
Ecuadorian	11	0.03
Paraguayan	1	0.00
Peruvian	87	0.20
Uruguayan	16	0.04
Venezuelan	2	0.00
Other South American	4	0.01
Other Hispanic or Latino	1,447	3.38
Hungarian	362	0.84
Icelander	32	0.07
Iranian	79	0.18
Irish	4,223	9.86
Israeli	23	0.05
Italian	1,915	4.47
Latvian	14	0.03
Lithuanian	164	0.38
Luxemburger	10	0.02
Maltese	8	0.02
New Zealander	2	0.00
Northern European	27	0.06
Norwegian	810	1.89
Pennsylvania German	24	0.06
Polish	1,128	2.63
Portuguese	159	0.37
Romanian	150	0.35
Russian	1,020	2.38
Scandinavian	89	0.21
Scotch-Irish	801	1.87
Scottish	1,004	2.34
Serbian	56	0.13
Slavic	9	0.02
Slovak	49	0.11
Slovene	2	0.00
Swedish	836	1.95
Swiss	195	0.46
Turkish	15	0.04
Ukrainian	113	0.26
United States or American	1,761	4.11
Welsh	372	0.87
West Indian, excl. Hispanic:	62	0.14
Jamaican	57	0.13
West Indian	5	0.01
White:	34,666	80.98
Not Hispanic (28,474)	29,003	67.75
Hispanic (5,057)	5,663	13.23
Yugoslavian	101	0.24

Palmdale

Place Type: City
County: Los Angeles
Population: 116,670

Ancestry/Race	Number	%
African American/Black:	18,443	15.81
Not Hispanic (16,447)	17,563	15.05
Hispanic (466)	880	0.75
African, sub-Saharan:	1,045	0.90
African	700	0.60
Ethiopian	40	0.03
Nigerian	208	0.18
Sierra Leonean	47	0.04
South African	42	0.04
Other sub-Saharan African	8	0.01
Alaska Native tribes, specified:	11	0.01
Alaska Athabascan	1	0.00
Eskimo (4)	10	0.01
Am. Ind. or Alaska Nat., not spec.	770	0.66
Albanian	12	0.01
American Indian tribes, specified:	1,408	1.21
Apache (49)	96	0.08
Blackfeet (9)	64	0.05
Cherokee (101)	356	0.31
Cheyenne (3)	14	0.01
Chickasaw (2)	4	0.00
Chippewa (11)	19	0.02
Choctaw (28)	73	0.06
Colville (1)	1	0.00
Comanche (7)	12	0.01
Cree (1)	2	0.00
Creek (5)	14	0.01
Crow (1)	2	0.00
Delaware (2)	6	0.01
Iroquois (5)	30	0.03
Kiowa (1)	1	0.00
Latin American Indians (165)	224	0.19
Navajo (46)	73	0.06
Osage (2)	5	0.00
Ottawa (2)	7	0.01
Paiute (7)	14	0.01
Pima (1)	2	0.00
Potawatomi (11)	16	0.01
Pueblo (30)	38	0.03
Puget Sound Salish	1	0.00
Seminole (2)	18	0.02
Shoshone (6)	13	0.01
Sioux (28)	57	0.05
Tohono O'Odham (7)	10	0.01
Ute (4)	8	0.01
Yaqui (10)	23	0.02
Yuman (5)	6	0.01
All other tribes (134)	199	0.17
American Indian tribes, not spec.	138	0.12
Arab:	597	0.51
Arab/Arabic	104	0.09
Egyptian	217	0.19
Iraqi	45	0.04
Jordanian	7	0.01
Lebanese	133	0.11
Syrian	52	0.04
Other Arab	39	0.03
Armenian	475	0.41
Asian:	5,939	5.09
Bangladeshi (2)	7	0.01
Cambodian (40)	49	0.04
Chinese, ex. Taiwanese (331)	522	0.45
Filipino (2,465)	3,094	2.65
Hmong (5)	5	0.00
Indian (390)	495	0.42
Indonesian (51)	100	0.09
Japanese (283)	531	0.46
Korean (256)	354	0.30
Laotian (7)	9	0.01
Malaysian (4)	5	0.00
Pakistani (30)	55	0.05
Sri Lankan (38)	49	0.04
Taiwanese (10)	19	0.02
Thai (93)	123	0.11
Vietnamese (277)	318	0.27
Other Asian, specified (7)	12	0.01
Other Asian, not specified (74)	192	0.16
Assyrian/Chaldean/Syriac	86	0.07
Australian	165	0.14
Austrian	187	0.16
Basque	59	0.05
Belgian	113	0.10
Brazilian	25	0.02
British	345	0.30
Bulgarian	69	0.06
Canadian	265	0.23
Croatian	122	0.10
Czech	314	0.27
Czechoslovakian	184	0.16
Danish	850	0.73
Dutch	1,069	0.92
Eastern European	17	0.01
English	7,465	6.40
European	869	0.75
Finnish	128	0.11
French, except Basque	2,577	2.21
French Canadian	420	0.36
German	10,406	8.93
Greek	556	0.48
Guyanese	120	0.10
Hawaii Native/Pacific Islander:	470	0.40
Melanesian: (3)	4	0.00
Fijian (3)	4	0.00
Micronesian: (51)	69	0.06
Guamanian/Chamorro (49)	66	0.06
Other Micronesian (2)	3	0.00
Polynesian: (112)	252	0.22
Native Hawaiian (59)	160	0.14
Samoan (52)	79	0.07
Tongan	8	0.01
Other Polynesian (1)	5	0.00
Other Pac. Isl., not spec. (56)	145	0.12
Hispanic or Latino:	43,991	37.71
Central American:	3,579	3.07

Notes: 1. Figures in the "Number" column do not add up to the total population due to: a) Ancestry/Race overlap — e.g. persons can report being both White and Irish, b) persons of Hispanic origin can report being any race, c) persons reporting two ancestries are counted in both categories. 2. Numbers in parentheses indicate the number of persons reporting this ancestry/race alone, not in combination with any other ancestry/race. 3. Refer to the Explanation of Data in the front of the book for more detailed information.

Ancestry/Race	Number	%
Costa Rican	73	0.06
Guatemalan	767	0.66
Honduran	85	0.07
Nicaraguan	213	0.18
Panamanian	63	0.05
Salvadoran	2,067	1.77
Other Central American	311	0.27
Cuban	586	0.50
Dominican Republic	31	0.03
Mexican	30,117	25.81
Puerto Rican	858	0.74
South American:	790	0.68
Argentinean	160	0.14
Bolivian	32	0.03
Chilean	62	0.05
Colombian	150	0.13
Ecuadorian	102	0.09
Paraguayan	4	0.00
Peruvian	160	0.14
Uruguayan	4	0.00
Venezuelan	28	0.02
Other South American	88	0.08
Other Hispanic or Latino	8,030	6.88
Hungarian	527	0.45
Icelander	20	0.02
Iranian	293	0.25
Irish	8,072	6.92
Israeli	8	0.01
Italian	5,145	4.41
Latvian	23	0.02
Lithuanian	93	0.08
Macedonian	8	0.01
Maltese	9	0.01
New Zealander	8	0.01
Northern European	70	0.06
Norwegian	1,209	1.04
Pennsylvania German	8	0.01
Polish	1,586	1.36
Portuguese	151	0.13
Romanian	88	0.08
Russian	924	0.79
Scandinavian	170	0.15
Scotch-Irish	1,087	0.93
Scottish	1,498	1.29
Serbian	30	0.03
Slavic	9	0.01
Slovak	41	0.04
Swedish	1,228	1.05
Swiss	112	0.10
Turkish	73	0.06
Ukrainian	75	0.06
United States or American	4,330	3.71
Welsh	437	0.37
West Indian, excl. Hispanic:	386	0.33
Belizean	79	0.07
British West Indian	8	0.01
Dutch West Indian	24	0.02
Haitian	76	0.07
Jamaican	93	0.08
Trinidadian and Tobagonian	7	0.01
West Indian	99	0.08
White:	68,935	59.09
Not Hispanic (47,831)	50,250	43.07
Hispanic (16,074)	18,685	16.02
Yugoslavian	136	0.12

Palo Alto

Place Type: City
County: Santa Clara
Population: 58,598

Ancestry/Race	Number	%
African American/Black:	1,488	2.54
Not Hispanic (1,166)	1,435	2.45
Hispanic (18)	53	0.09
African, sub-Saharan:	257	0.44
African	87	0.15
Ethiopian	47	0.08
Ghanian	11	0.02
Liberian	7	0.01
Nigerian	4	0.01
South African	77	0.13
Zimbabwean	6	0.01
Other sub-Saharan African	18	0.03
Alaska Native tribes, specified:	7	0.01
Alaska Athabascan	2	0.00
Aleut	1	0.00
Eskimo (1)	1	0.00
Tlingit-Haida (1)	3	0.01
Am. Ind. or Alaska Nat., not spec.	144	0.25
American Indian tribes, specified:	274	0.47
Apache (5)	13	0.02
Blackfeet (2)	11	0.02
Cherokee (9)	72	0.12
Cheyenne	1	0.00
Chickasaw (3)	11	0.02
Chippewa (2)	5	0.01
Choctaw (1)	11	0.02
Comanche	1	0.00
Creek (2)	3	0.01
Iroquois (4)	9	0.02
Latin American Indians (23)	35	0.06
Navajo (15)	25	0.04
Osage (1)	1	0.00
Paiute (1)	2	0.00
Potawatomi (4)	4	0.01
Pueblo (2)	3	0.01
Seminole	3	0.01
Shoshone	2	0.00
Sioux (4)	15	0.03
Tohono O'Odham	1	0.00
Ute	1	0.00
Yakama (1)	1	0.00
Yaqui (1)	2	0.00
Yuman	1	0.00
All other tribes (13)	41	0.07
American Indian tribes, not spec.	17	0.03
Arab:	260	0.44
Arab/Arabic	19	0.03
Egyptian	34	0.06
Iraqi	5	0.01
Lebanese	128	0.22
Palestinian	24	0.04
Syrian	27	0.05
Other Arab	23	0.04
Armenian	111	0.19
Asian:	11,454	19.55
Bangladeshi (1)	2	0.00
Cambodian (2)	2	0.00
Chinese, ex. Taiwanese (5,193)	5,740	9.80
Filipino (385)	568	0.97
Hmong (2)	2	0.00
Indian (1,251)	1,394	2.38
Indonesian (12)	30	0.05
Japanese (1,368)	1,703	2.91
Korean (961)	1,052	1.80
Laotian (2)	3	0.01
Malaysian (10)	17	0.03
Pakistani (73)	80	0.14
Sri Lankan (22)	26	0.04
Taiwanese (257)	308	0.53
Thai (37)	51	0.09
Vietnamese (224)	262	0.45
Other Asian, specified (12)	31	0.05
Other Asian, not specified (82)	183	0.31
Assyrian/Chaldean/Syriac	13	0.02
Australian	162	0.28
Austrian	554	0.94
Basque	6	0.01
Belgian	130	0.22
Brazilian	92	0.16
British	1,035	1.76
Bulgarian	48	0.08
Canadian	354	0.60
Celtic	93	0.16
Croatian	232	0.39
Czech	253	0.43
Czechoslovakian	161	0.27
Danish	766	1.30
Dutch	776	1.32
Eastern European	491	0.84
English	8,084	13.75
Estonian	87	0.15
European	1,255	2.13
Finnish	187	0.32
French, except Basque	2,198	3.74
French Canadian	181	0.31
German	8,281	14.09
Greek	409	0.70
Hawaii Native/Pacific Islander:	205	0.35
Melanesian: (5)	5	0.01
Fijian (4)	4	0.01
Other Melanesian (1)	1	0.00
Micronesian: (11)	22	0.04
Guamanian/Chamorro (10)	17	0.03
Other Micronesian (1)	5	0.01
Polynesian: (56)	126	0.22
Native Hawaiian (14)	67	0.11
Samoan (9)	15	0.03
Tongan (33)	44	0.08
Other Pac. Isl., specified	8	0.01
Other Pac. Isl., not spec. (10)	44	0.08
Hispanic or Latino:	2,722	4.65
Central American:	179	0.31
Costa Rican	7	0.01
Guatemalan	46	0.08
Honduran	14	0.02
Nicaraguan	17	0.03
Panamanian	9	0.02
Salvadoran	69	0.12
Other Central American	17	0.03
Cuban	75	0.13
Dominican Republic	5	0.01
Mexican	1,543	2.63
Puerto Rican	72	0.12
South American:	310	0.53
Argentinean	62	0.11
Bolivian	11	0.02
Chilean	52	0.09
Colombian	58	0.10
Ecuadorian	10	0.02
Paraguayan	2	0.00
Peruvian	71	0.12
Uruguayan	5	0.01
Venezuelan	12	0.02
Other South American	27	0.05
Other Hispanic or Latino	538	0.92
Hungarian	555	0.94
Icelander	13	0.02
Iranian	505	0.86
Irish	5,528	9.40
Israeli	298	0.51
Italian	2,532	4.31
Latvian	62	0.11
Lithuanian	250	0.43
Luxemburger	7	0.01
Macedonian	3	0.01
Maltese	6	0.01
New Zealander	6	0.01
Northern European	178	0.30
Norwegian	1,165	1.98
Pennsylvania German	20	0.03
Polish	1,965	3.34
Portuguese	316	0.54
Romanian	217	0.37
Russian	2,646	4.50
Scandinavian	304	0.52
Scotch-Irish	1,091	1.86
Scottish	1,903	3.24
Serbian	47	0.08
Slavic	71	0.12
Slovak	82	0.14
Slovene	35	0.06
Swedish	1,676	2.85
Swiss	543	0.92
Turkish	48	0.08
Ukrainian	362	0.62
United States or American	1,649	2.81
Welsh	588	1.00

Notes: 1. Figures in the "Number" column do not add up to the total population due to: a) Ancestry/Race overlap — e.g. persons can report being both White and Irish, b) persons of Hispanic origin can report being any race, c) persons reporting two ancestries are counted in both categories. 2. Numbers in parentheses indicate the number of persons reporting this ancestry/race alone, not in combination with any other ancestry/race. 3. Refer to the Explanation of Data in the front of the book for more detailed information.

West Indian, excl. Hispanic:	42	0.07
Haitian	5	0.01
Jamaican	9	0.02
Trinidadian and Tobagonian	6	0.01
West Indian	22	0.04
White:	46,051	78.59
Not Hispanic (42,682)	44,110	75.28
Hispanic (1,709)	1,941	3.31
Yugoslavian	184	0.31

Palos Verdes Estates

Place Type: City
County: Los Angeles
Population: 13,340

Ancestry/Race	Number	%
African American/Black:	159	1.19
Not Hispanic (130)	157	1.18
Hispanic (2)	2	0.01
African, sub-Saharan:	23	0.17
African	5	0.04
South African	9	0.07
Zairian	3	0.02
Other sub-Saharan African	6	0.04
Am. Ind. or Alaska Nat., not spec.	25	0.19
Albanian	13	0.10
American Indian tribes, specified:	34	0.25
Apache	3	0.02
Blackfeet	1	0.01
Cherokee (7)	10	0.07
Chickasaw	1	0.01
Chippewa	3	0.02
Creek	1	0.01
Iroquois (1)	1	0.01
Latin American Indians (1)	3	0.02
Pueblo (1)	1	0.01
Puget Sound Salish (1)	1	0.01
Seminole	1	0.01
All other tribes (6)	8	0.06
American Indian tribes, not spec.	2	0.01
Arab:	77	0.58
Arab/Arabic	7	0.05
Iraqi	16	0.12
Lebanese	30	0.22
Other Arab	24	0.18
Armenian	116	0.87
Asian:	2,622	19.66
Cambodian (1)	1	0.01
Chinese, ex. Taiwanese (689)	790	5.92
Filipino (97)	132	0.99
Indian (207)	251	1.88
Indonesian (1)	4	0.03
Japanese (588)	681	5.10
Korean (317)	358	2.68
Laotian (1)	1	0.01
Malaysian (1)	3	0.02
Pakistani (8)	12	0.09
Sri Lankan (2)	3	0.02
Taiwanese (261)	300	2.25
Thai (8)	12	0.09
Vietnamese (23)	29	0.22
Other Asian, specified (1)	5	0.04
Other Asian, not specified (20)	40	0.30
Australian	56	0.42
Austrian	114	0.85
Belgian	14	0.10
Brazilian	2	0.01
British	281	2.11
Canadian	75	0.56
Celtic	13	0.10
Croatian	51	0.38
Czech	103	0.77
Czechoslovakian	16	0.12
Danish	141	1.06
Dutch	137	1.03
Eastern European	24	0.18
English	2,708	20.30
European	103	0.77
Finnish	41	0.31
French, except Basque	401	3.01
French Canadian	86	0.64
German	2,093	15.69
Greek	90	0.67
Hawaii Native/Pacific Islander:	44	0.33
Melanesian: (1)	1	0.01
Fijian (1)	1	0.01
Micronesian: (5)	6	0.04
Guamanian/Chamorro (5)	6	0.04
Polynesian: (8)	32	0.24
Native Hawaiian	23	0.17
Samoan (6)	7	0.05
Other Polynesian (2)	2	0.01
Other Pac. Isl., not spec. (1)	5	0.04
Hispanic or Latino:	378	2.83
Central American:	34	0.25
Costa Rican	2	0.01
Guatemalan	19	0.14
Nicaraguan	4	0.03
Panamanian	1	0.01
Salvadoran	7	0.05
Other Central American	1	0.01
Cuban	11	0.08
Dominican Republic	2	0.01
Mexican	190	1.42
Puerto Rican	18	0.13
South American:	49	0.37
Argentinean	8	0.06
Bolivian	1	0.01
Chilean	4	0.03
Colombian	11	0.08
Ecuadorian	7	0.05
Peruvian	9	0.07
Uruguayan	1	0.01
Venezuelan	2	0.01
Other South American	6	0.04
Other Hispanic or Latino	74	0.55
Hungarian	85	0.64
Iranian	275	2.06
Irish	1,560	11.69
Israeli	58	0.43
Italian	920	6.90
Latvian	12	0.09
Lithuanian	86	0.64
Luxemburger	9	0.07
Macedonian	10	0.07
Northern European	83	0.62
Norwegian	267	2.00
Polish	372	2.79
Portuguese	19	0.14
Romanian	33	0.25
Russian	469	3.52
Scandinavian	15	0.11
Scotch-Irish	291	2.18
Scottish	527	3.95
Slavic	32	0.24
Slovak	50	0.37
Swedish	296	2.22
Swiss	95	0.71
Turkish	5	0.04
Ukrainian	30	0.22
United States or American	587	4.40
Welsh	132	0.99
West Indian, excl. Hispanic:	21	0.16
Haitian	5	0.04
Jamaican	16	0.12
White:	10,750	80.58
Not Hispanic (10,155)	10,436	78.23
Hispanic (293)	314	2.35
Yugoslavian	54	0.40

Paradise

Place Type: Town
County: Butte
Population: 26,408

Ancestry/Race	Number	%
Acadian/Cajun	11	0.04
African American/Black:	114	0.43
Not Hispanic (50)	108	0.41
Hispanic (1)	6	0.02
Alaska Native tribes, specified:	13	0.05
Alaska Athabascan (2)	2	0.01
Aleut (7)	8	0.03
Eskimo	1	0.00
Tlingit-Haida (1)	2	0.01
Am. Ind. or Alaska Nat., not spec.	155	0.59
American Indian tribes, specified:	444	1.68
Apache (14)	24	0.09
Blackfeet (6)	26	0.10
Cherokee (45)	143	0.54
Chickasaw	2	0.01
Chippewa (3)	10	0.04
Choctaw (16)	42	0.16
Comanche (1)	2	0.01
Cree (2)	2	0.01
Creek	3	0.01
Crow (2)	3	0.01
Delaware (4)	7	0.03
Iroquois (4)	9	0.03
Latin American Indians (13)	21	0.08
Lumbee (2)	2	0.01
Navajo (2)	5	0.02
Osage (1)	2	0.01
Potawatomi	3	0.01
Pueblo	1	0.00
Puget Sound Salish (1)	1	0.00
Seminole (3)	3	0.01
Shoshone (1)	2	0.01
Sioux (14)	24	0.09
Ute	1	0.00
Yakama (1)	1	0.00
All other tribes (67)	105	0.40
American Indian tribes, not spec.	21	0.08
Arab:	90	0.34
Egyptian	14	0.05
Lebanese	59	0.22
Palestinian	17	0.06
Armenian	15	0.06
Asian:	444	1.68
Cambodian (6)	7	0.03
Chinese, ex. Taiwanese (43)	61	0.23
Filipino (101)	141	0.53
Hmong (16)	26	0.10
Indian (15)	42	0.16
Indonesian (3)	13	0.05
Japanese (35)	74	0.28
Korean (35)	41	0.16
Malaysian (1)	2	0.01
Pakistani (1)	1	0.00
Thai (2)	2	0.01
Vietnamese (13)	17	0.06
Other Asian, specified	3	0.01
Other Asian, not specified (1)	14	0.05
Assyrian/Chaldean/Syriac	17	0.06
Austrian	96	0.36
Basque	29	0.11
Belgian	8	0.03
British	166	0.63
Canadian	104	0.39
Croatian	36	0.14
Czech	139	0.53
Czechoslovakian	41	0.16
Danish	438	1.66
Dutch	792	2.99
English	4,450	16.82
European	268	1.01
Finnish	63	0.24
French, except Basque	1,165	4.40
French Canadian	198	0.75
German	5,113	19.33
Greek	118	0.45
Hawaii Native/Pacific Islander:	79	0.30
Micronesian: (9)	17	0.06
Guamanian/Chamorro (6)	11	0.04
Other Micronesian (3)	6	0.02
Polynesian: (15)	45	0.17
Native Hawaiian (12)	35	0.13
Samoan (2)	8	0.03

Notes: 1. Figures in the "Number" column do not add up to the total population due to: a) Ancestry/Race overlap — e.g. persons can report being both White and Irish, b) persons of Hispanic origin can report being any race, c) persons reporting two ancestries are counted in both categories. 2. Numbers in parentheses indicate the number of persons reporting this ancestry/race alone, not in combination with any other ancestry/race. 3. Refer to the Explanation of Data in the front of the book for more detailed information.

Tongan	1	0.00
Other Polynesian (1)	1	0.00
Other Pac. Isl., specified	3	0.01
Other Pac. Isl., not spec. (7)	14	0.05
Hispanic or Latino:	1,127	4.27
Central American:	21	0.08
Costa Rican	4	0.02
Guatemalan	1	0.00
Honduran	1	0.00
Nicaraguan	5	0.02
Salvadoran	7	0.03
Other Central American	3	0.01
Cuban	9	0.03
Mexican	786	2.98
Puerto Rican	42	0.16
South American:	12	0.05
Argentinean	2	0.01
Chilean	1	0.00
Colombian	6	0.02
Peruvian	2	0.01
Venezuelan	1	0.00
Other Hispanic or Latino	257	0.97
Hungarian	306	1.16
Icelander	15	0.06
Irish	3,256	12.31
Italian	1,545	5.84
Latvian	7	0.03
Lithuanian	15	0.06
Luxemburger	6	0.02
Maltese	5	0.02
Northern European	70	0.26
Norwegian	965	3.65
Pennsylvania German	17	0.06
Polish	472	1.78
Portuguese	472	1.78
Romanian	49	0.19
Russian	298	1.13
Scandinavian	77	0.29
Scotch-Irish	876	3.31
Scottish	958	3.62
Slavic	15	0.06
Slovak	21	0.08
Slovene	9	0.03
Swedish	974	3.68
Swiss	183	0.69
Ukrainian	7	0.03
United States or American	2,010	7.60
Welsh	461	1.74
White:	25,414	96.24
Not Hispanic (24,080)	24,630	93.27
Hispanic (671)	784	2.97
Yugoslavian	43	0.16

Paramount

Place Type: City
County: Los Angeles
Population: 55,266

Ancestry/Race	Number	%
African American/Black:	7,923	14.34
Not Hispanic (7,184)	7,449	13.48
Hispanic (324)	474	0.86
African, sub-Saharan:	428	0.77
African	272	0.49
Nigerian	145	0.26
Other sub-Saharan African	11	0.02
Alaska Native tribes, specified:	4	0.01
Aleut	3	0.01
Tlingit-Haida (1)	1	0.00
Am. Ind. or Alaska Nat., not spec.	468	0.85
American Indian tribes, specified:	405	0.73
Apache (5)	20	0.04
Blackfeet (2)	9	0.02
Cherokee (7)	52	0.09
Cheyenne	1	0.00
Chickasaw	1	0.00
Chippewa	1	0.00
Choctaw (6)	15	0.03
Colville (4)	4	0.01
Cree (3)	3	0.01
Creek	7	0.01
Houma	1	0.00
Iroquois (4)	5	0.01
Kiowa (1)	1	0.00
Latin American Indians (113)	171	0.31
Navajo (5)	20	0.04
Paiute	1	0.00
Pima (1)	1	0.00
Potawatomi	1	0.00
Pueblo (5)	9	0.02
Seminole (1)	4	0.01
Sioux (6)	11	0.02
Tohono O'Odham (2)	2	0.00
Ute	2	0.00
Yakama (3)	3	0.01
Yaqui (8)	12	0.02
Yuman	2	0.00
All other tribes (25)	46	0.08
American Indian tribes, not spec.	62	0.11
Arab:	57	0.10
Egyptian	15	0.03
Lebanese	35	0.06
Moroccan	7	0.01
Armenian	6	0.01
Asian:	2,247	4.07
Bangladeshi (3)	3	0.01
Cambodian (273)	321	0.58
Chinese, ex. Taiwanese (109)	173	0.31
Filipino (829)	950	1.72
Hmong (7)	7	0.01
Indian (79)	115	0.21
Indonesian (4)	8	0.01
Japanese (77)	117	0.21
Korean (196)	205	0.37
Laotian (3)	7	0.01
Pakistani (16)	38	0.07
Sri Lankan (3)	6	0.01
Taiwanese (2)	3	0.01
Thai (122)	138	0.25
Vietnamese (80)	94	0.17
Other Asian, specified	7	0.01
Other Asian, not specified (19)	55	0.10
Austrian	13	0.02
Belgian	6	0.01
Brazilian	11	0.02
British	26	0.05
Canadian	23	0.04
Celtic	24	0.04
Croatian	32	0.06
Czech	34	0.06
Czechoslovakian	8	0.01
Danish	25	0.05
Dutch	275	0.50
English	564	1.02
European	226	0.41
French, except Basque	250	0.45
French Canadian	50	0.09
German	1,126	2.04
Greek	45	0.08
Hawaii Native/Pacific Islander:	585	1.06
Micronesian: (21)	52	0.09
Guamanian/Chamorro (21)	52	0.09
Polynesian: (402)	467	0.85
Native Hawaiian (19)	35	0.06
Samoan (354)	392	0.71
Tongan (25)	29	0.05
Other Polynesian (4)	11	0.02
Other Pac. Isl., specified	2	0.00
Other Pac. Isl., not spec. (32)	64	0.12
Hispanic or Latino:	39,945	72.28
Central American:	1,665	3.01
Costa Rican	34	0.06
Guatemalan	497	0.90
Honduran	102	0.18
Nicaraguan	128	0.23
Panamanian	33	0.06
Salvadoran	725	1.31
Other Central American	146	0.26
Cuban	125	0.23
Dominican Republic	9	0.02
Mexican	33,129	59.94
Puerto Rican	212	0.38
South American:	246	0.45
Argentinean	16	0.03
Bolivian	2	0.00
Chilean	48	0.09
Colombian	40	0.07
Ecuadorian	44	0.08
Peruvian	74	0.13
Uruguayan	2	0.00
Venezuelan	1	0.00
Other South American	19	0.03
Other Hispanic or Latino	4,559	8.25
Iranian	101	0.18
Irish	893	1.61
Israeli	9	0.02
Italian	320	0.58
Latvian	6	0.01
Norwegian	180	0.33
Polish	107	0.19
Portuguese	21	0.04
Romanian	17	0.03
Russian	27	0.05
Scotch-Irish	112	0.20
Scottish	131	0.24
Swedish	142	0.26
United States or American	989	1.79
Welsh	54	0.10
West Indian, excl. Hispanic:	247	0.45
Bahamian	20	0.04
Barbadian	7	0.01
Belizean	37	0.07
Haitian	24	0.04
Jamaican	159	0.29
White:	21,272	38.49
Not Hispanic (4,982)	5,395	9.76
Hispanic (14,195)	15,877	28.73

Parkway-South Sacramento

Place Type: Census Designated Place
County: Sacramento
Population: 36,468

Ancestry/Race	Number	%
Afghan	25	0.07
African American/Black:	6,831	18.73
Not Hispanic (5,827)	6,395	17.54
Hispanic (240)	436	1.20
African, sub-Saharan:	344	0.94
African	311	0.85
Cape Verdean	5	0.01
Nigerian	9	0.02
Other sub-Saharan African	19	0.05
Alaska Native tribes, specified:	16	0.04
Aleut	7	0.02
Eskimo (1)	6	0.02
Tlingit-Haida (1)	3	0.01
Am. Ind. or Alaska Nat., not spec.	403	1.11
American Indian tribes, specified:	795	2.18
Apache (24)	51	0.14
Blackfeet (6)	47	0.13
Cherokee (32)	167	0.46
Cheyenne	4	0.01
Chickasaw	2	0.01
Chippewa (7)	8	0.02
Choctaw (4)	15	0.04
Comanche (4)	8	0.02
Creek (1)	6	0.02
Iroquois (2)	6	0.02
Kiowa	1	0.00
Latin American Indians (67)	113	0.31
Lumbee (1)	3	0.01
Navajo (12)	28	0.08
Osage	1	0.00
Ottawa	1	0.00
Paiute (7)	9	0.02
Pima (1)	2	0.01

Notes: 1. Figures in the "Number" column do not add up to the total population due to: a) Ancestry/Race overlap — e.g. persons can report being both White and Irish, b) persons of Hispanic origin can report being any race, c) persons reporting two ancestries are counted in both categories. 2. Numbers in parentheses indicate the number of persons reporting this ancestry/race alone, not in combination with any other ancestry/race. 3. Refer to the Explanation of Data in the front of the book for more detailed information.

Ancestry/Race	Number	%
Potawatomi (3)	3	0.01
Pueblo (6)	9	0.02
Puget Sound Salish (1)	1	0.00
Seminole	7	0.02
Shoshone (3)	5	0.01
Sioux (5)	18	0.05
Tohono O'Odham (3)	5	0.01
Ute	1	0.00
Yakama (1)	1	0.00
Yaqui (5)	18	0.05
All other tribes (162)	255	0.70
American Indian tribes, not spec.	62	0.17
Arab:	18	0.05
Arab/Arabic	7	0.02
Lebanese	11	0.03
Armenian	18	0.05
Asian:	7,461	20.46
Bangladeshi (1)	1	0.00
Cambodian (202)	258	0.71
Chinese, ex. Taiwanese (612)	712	1.95
Filipino (418)	683	1.87
Hmong (2,273)	2,553	7.00
Indian (187)	342	0.94
Indonesian (2)	5	0.01
Japanese (195)	266	0.73
Korean (30)	63	0.17
Laotian (1,197)	1,401	3.84
Pakistani (13)	20	0.05
Taiwanese	4	0.01
Thai (20)	30	0.08
Vietnamese (902)	984	2.70
Other Asian, specified	2	0.01
Other Asian, not specified (94)	137	0.38
Australian	13	0.04
Austrian	12	0.03
Belgian	39	0.11
Brazilian	12	0.03
British	71	0.19
Canadian	35	0.10
Croatian	48	0.13
Czech	35	0.10
Czechoslovakian	16	0.04
Danish	70	0.19
Dutch	206	0.56
English	1,390	3.81
European	210	0.58
Finnish	23	0.06
French, except Basque	643	1.76
French Canadian	76	0.21
German	2,630	7.21
Greek	125	0.34
Hawaii Native/Pacific Islander:	561	1.54
Melanesian: (77)	115	0.32
Fijian (77)	115	0.32
Micronesian: (25)	44	0.12
Guamanian/Chamorro (17)	32	0.09
Other Micronesian (8)	12	0.03
Polynesian: (86)	188	0.52
Native Hawaiian (24)	95	0.26
Samoan (21)	41	0.11
Tongan (38)	46	0.13
Other Polynesian (3)	6	0.02
Other Pac. Isl., specified	1	0.00
Other Pac. Isl., not spec. (40)	213	0.58
Hispanic or Latino:	12,402	34.01
Central American:	198	0.54
Costa Rican	5	0.01
Guatemalan	48	0.13
Honduran	11	0.03
Nicaraguan	28	0.08
Panamanian	7	0.02
Salvadoran	87	0.24
Other Central American	12	0.03
Cuban	33	0.09
Dominican Republic	2	0.01
Mexican	10,299	28.24
Puerto Rican	254	0.70
South American:	45	0.12
Argentinean	2	0.01
Bolivian	1	0.00
Chilean	4	0.01
Colombian	7	0.02
Ecuadorian	2	0.01
Peruvian	21	0.06
Venezuelan	5	0.01
Other South American	3	0.01
Other Hispanic or Latino	1,571	4.31
Hungarian	5	0.01
Iranian	6	0.02
Irish	1,612	4.42
Israeli	14	0.04
Italian	902	2.47
Lithuanian	15	0.04
Norwegian	234	0.64
Polish	126	0.35
Portuguese	400	1.10
Romanian	86	0.24
Russian	229	0.63
Scandinavian	17	0.05
Scotch-Irish	227	0.62
Scottish	209	0.57
Slavic	15	0.04
Swedish	249	0.68
Swiss	104	0.29
Turkish	19	0.05
Ukrainian	303	0.83
United States or American	797	2.18
Welsh	82	0.22
West Indian, excl. Hispanic:	57	0.16
British West Indian	9	0.02
Dutch West Indian	12	0.03
Haitian	5	0.01
Jamaican	8	0.02
West Indian	23	0.06
White:	15,686	43.01
Not Hispanic (9,738)	10,694	29.32
Hispanic (4,157)	4,992	13.69
Yugoslavian	34	0.09

Parlier

Place Type: City
County: Fresno
Population: 11,145

Ancestry/Race	Number	%
African American/Black:	103	0.92
Not Hispanic (9)	12	0.11
Hispanic (56)	91	0.82
African, sub-Saharan:	9	0.08
African	9	0.08
Am. Ind. or Alaska Nat., not spec.	60	0.54
American Indian tribes, specified:	200	1.79
Blackfeet	1	0.01
Cherokee	1	0.01
Chickasaw	1	0.01
Creek (1)	1	0.01
Latin American Indians (173)	191	1.71
Navajo (1)	3	0.03
Paiute	2	0.02
American Indian tribes, not spec.	11	0.10
Armenian	43	0.39
Asian:	125	1.12
Chinese, ex. Taiwanese (21)	21	0.19
Filipino (15)	29	0.26
Indian (26)	34	0.31
Japanese (25)	30	0.27
Other Asian, specified	6	0.05
Other Asian, not specified (4)	5	0.04
Danish	9	0.08
English	18	0.16
French, except Basque	5	0.05
German	34	0.31
Hawaii Native/Pacific Islander:	21	0.19
Polynesian: (5)	11	0.10
Native Hawaiian (1)	2	0.02
Samoan	5	0.04
Tongan (4)	4	0.04
Other Pac. Isl., specified	6	0.05
Other Pac. Isl., not spec.	4	0.04
Hispanic or Latino:	10,807	96.97
Central American:	17	0.15
Guatemalan	8	0.07
Honduran	2	0.02
Nicaraguan	1	0.01
Salvadoran	4	0.04
Other Central American	2	0.02
Cuban	2	0.02
Mexican	9,631	86.42
Puerto Rican	6	0.05
South American:	1	0.01
Colombian	1	0.01
Other Hispanic or Latino	1,150	10.32
Irish	13	0.12
Portuguese	5	0.05
United States or American	38	0.34
White:	4,069	36.51
Not Hispanic (190)	230	2.06
Hispanic (3,558)	3,839	34.45

Pasadena

Place Type: City
County: Los Angeles
Population: 133,936

Ancestry/Race	Number	%
African American/Black:	20,941	15.64
Not Hispanic (18,711)	19,954	14.90
Hispanic (608)	987	0.74
African, sub-Saharan:	2,074	1.55
African	1,517	1.13
Cape Verdean	9	0.01
Ethiopian	203	0.15
Ghanian	18	0.01
Kenyan	66	0.05
Nigerian	145	0.11
Senegalese	8	0.01
South African	36	0.03
Zimbabwean	9	0.01
Other sub-Saharan African	63	0.05
Alaska Native tribes, specified:	21	0.02
Alaska Athabascan (6)	6	0.00
Eskimo	2	0.00
Tlingit-Haida (6)	13	0.01
Am. Ind. or Alaska Nat., not spec.	787	0.59
Albanian	11	0.01
American Indian tribes, specified:	1,137	0.85
Apache (26)	52	0.04
Blackfeet (7)	71	0.05
Cherokee (53)	221	0.17
Cheyenne (1)	5	0.00
Chickasaw (9)	16	0.01
Chippewa (6)	14	0.01
Choctaw (6)	43	0.03
Colville (2)	3	0.00
Comanche (5)	9	0.01
Cree (1)	9	0.01
Creek (3)	14	0.01
Crow	1	0.00
Delaware (1)	1	0.00
Houma	2	0.00
Iroquois (1)	17	0.01
Kiowa (2)	2	0.00
Latin American Indians (259)	383	0.29
Lumbee (2)	2	0.00
Navajo (24)	46	0.03
Osage (2)	7	0.01
Paiute (3)	8	0.01
Pima (1)	6	0.00
Potawatomi	9	0.01
Pueblo (6)	15	0.01
Puget Sound Salish	1	0.00
Seminole	17	0.01
Shoshone (1)	2	0.00
Sioux (18)	40	0.03
Tohono O'Odham (6)	8	0.01
Ute (2)	4	0.00
Yakama (1)	1	0.00
Yaqui (10)	23	0.02

Notes: 1. Figures in the "Number" column do not add up to the total population due to: a) Ancestry/Race overlap — e.g. persons can report being both White and Irish, b) persons of Hispanic origin can report being any race, c) persons reporting two ancestries are counted in both categories. 2. Numbers in parentheses indicate the number of persons reporting this ancestry/race alone, not in combination with any other ancestry/race. 3. Refer to the Explanation of Data in the front of the book for more detailed information.

Ancestry/Race	Number	%
Yuman (2)	3	0.00
All other tribes (34)	82	0.06
American Indian tribes, not spec.	96	0.07
Arab:	1,384	1.03
Arab/Arabic	240	0.18
Egyptian	231	0.17
Iraqi	7	0.01
Jordanian	119	0.09
Lebanese	543	0.41
Moroccan	9	0.01
Palestinian	117	0.09
Syrian	58	0.04
Other Arab	60	0.04
Armenian	4,400	3.29
Asian:	15,648	11.68
Bangladeshi (12)	17	0.01
Cambodian (17)	22	0.02
Chinese, ex. Taiwanese (4,014)	4,686	3.50
Filipino (2,855)	3,367	2.51
Indian (968)	1,179	0.88
Indonesian (171)	284	0.21
Japanese (2,168)	2,670	1.99
Korean (1,307)	1,435	1.07
Laotian (5)	9	0.01
Malaysian (16)	34	0.03
Pakistani (32)	42	0.03
Sri Lankan (89)	121	0.09
Taiwanese (379)	475	0.35
Thai (163)	204	0.15
Vietnamese (628)	696	0.52
Other Asian, specified (52)	73	0.05
Other Asian, not specified (118)	334	0.25
Assyrian/Chaldean/Syriac	7	0.01
Australian	75	0.06
Austrian	344	0.26
Basque	46	0.03
Belgian	161	0.12
Brazilian	131	0.10
British	608	0.45
Bulgarian	11	0.01
Canadian	586	0.44
Celtic	69	0.05
Croatian	112	0.08
Cypriot	7	0.01
Czech	253	0.19
Czechoslovakian	112	0.08
Danish	749	0.56
Dutch	1,328	0.99
Eastern European	156	0.12
English	9,537	7.12
Estonian	31	0.02
European	1,203	0.90
Finnish	206	0.15
French, except Basque	2,606	1.95
French Canadian	405	0.30
German	9,972	7.45
German Russian	4	0.00
Greek	670	0.50
Guyanese	21	0.02
Hawaii Native/Pacific Islander:	436	0.33
Melanesian: (9)	9	0.01
Fijian (8)	8	0.01
Other Melanesian (1)	1	0.00
Micronesian: (24)	47	0.04
Guamanian/Chamorro (12)	32	0.02
Other Micronesian (12)	15	0.01
Polynesian: (66)	216	0.16
Native Hawaiian (42)	162	0.12
Samoan (23)	47	0.04
Tongan (1)	4	0.00
Other Polynesian	3	0.00
Other Pac. Isl., specified	4	0.00
Other Pac. Isl., not spec. (28)	160	0.12
Hispanic or Latino:	44,734	33.40
Central American:	3,687	2.75
Costa Rican	119	0.09
Guatemalan	712	0.53
Honduran	463	0.35
Nicaraguan	187	0.14
Panamanian	110	0.08
Salvadoran	1,686	1.26
Other Central American	410	0.31
Cuban	504	0.38
Dominican Republic	36	0.03
Mexican	32,276	24.10
Puerto Rican	429	0.32
South American:	1,474	1.10
Argentinean	267	0.20
Bolivian	46	0.03
Chilean	106	0.08
Colombian	362	0.27
Ecuadorian	147	0.11
Paraguayan	4	0.00
Peruvian	340	0.25
Uruguayan	7	0.01
Venezuelan	39	0.03
Other South American	156	0.12
Other Hispanic or Latino	6,328	4.72
Hungarian	574	0.43
Icelander	75	0.06
Iranian	671	0.50
Irish	8,141	6.08
Israeli	55	0.04
Italian	4,562	3.41
Latvian	30	0.02
Lithuanian	188	0.14
Luxemburger	19	0.01
Macedonian	8	0.01
New Zealander	26	0.02
Northern European	189	0.14
Norwegian	1,420	1.06
Pennsylvania German	39	0.03
Polish	1,533	1.15
Portuguese	305	0.23
Romanian	323	0.24
Russian	1,341	1.00
Scandinavian	193	0.14
Scotch-Irish	1,539	1.15
Scottish	2,418	1.81
Serbian	67	0.05
Slavic	51	0.04
Slovak	80	0.06
Slovene	64	0.05
Swedish	1,732	1.29
Swiss	592	0.44
Turkish	106	0.08
Ukrainian	201	0.15
United States or American	2,919	2.18
Welsh	678	0.51
West Indian, excl. Hispanic:	597	0.45
Bahamian	5	0.00
Barbadian	17	0.01
Belizean	39	0.03
Bermudan	6	0.00
British West Indian	14	0.01
Haitian	30	0.02
Jamaican	347	0.26
Trinidadian and Tobagonian	66	0.05
West Indian	73	0.05
White:	77,304	57.72
Not Hispanic (52,381)	55,646	41.55
Hispanic (19,088)	21,658	16.17
Yugoslavian	199	0.15

Patterson

Place Type: City
County: Stanislaus
Population: 11,606

Ancestry/Race	Number	%
African American/Black:	287	2.47
Not Hispanic (188)	227	1.96
Hispanic (31)	60	0.52
African, sub-Saharan:	20	0.18
African	20	0.18
Am. Ind. or Alaska Nat., not spec.	111	0.96
American Indian tribes, specified:	176	1.52
Blackfeet (1)	11	0.09
Cherokee (17)	49	0.42
Cheyenne	9	0.08
Chickasaw (2)	2	0.02
Chippewa (7)	7	0.06
Choctaw (10)	15	0.13
Comanche (1)	1	0.01
Cree (3)	4	0.03
Creek (1)	4	0.03
Iroquois (2)	2	0.02
Latin American Indians (23)	30	0.26
Lumbee	1	0.01
Navajo (7)	7	0.06
Paiute	1	0.01
Pueblo (1)	2	0.02
Seminole	1	0.01
Sioux (6)	10	0.09
Tohono O'Odham (3)	4	0.03
Yaqui (2)	2	0.02
All other tribes (6)	14	0.12
American Indian tribes, not spec.	9	0.08
Asian:	348	3.00
Cambodian (14)	14	0.12
Chinese, ex. Taiwanese (59)	62	0.53
Filipino (82)	134	1.15
Hmong (14)	14	0.12
Indian (27)	29	0.25
Indonesian (1)	2	0.02
Japanese (12)	38	0.33
Korean (8)	14	0.12
Laotian (4)	5	0.04
Malaysian (2)	2	0.02
Pakistani (10)	14	0.12
Thai (4)	5	0.04
Vietnamese (3)	4	0.03
Other Asian, not specified (3)	11	0.09
Austrian	8	0.07
Basque	4	0.04
British	8	0.07
Canadian	18	0.16
Croatian	23	0.20
Dutch	162	1.42
English	555	4.87
European	40	0.35
Finnish	25	0.22
French, except Basque	184	1.61
French Canadian	22	0.19
German	936	8.21
Greek	5	0.04
Hawaii Native/Pacific Islander:	82	0.71
Melanesian: (5)	5	0.04
Fijian (5)	5	0.04
Micronesian: (3)	14	0.12
Guamanian/Chamorro (3)	14	0.12
Polynesian: (33)	50	0.43
Native Hawaiian (31)	44	0.38
Samoan (2)	6	0.05
Other Pac. Isl., not spec. (6)	13	0.11
Hispanic or Latino:	6,611	56.96
Central American:	178	1.53
Guatemalan	25	0.22
Honduran	8	0.07
Nicaraguan	20	0.17
Salvadoran	112	0.97
Other Central American	13	0.11
Cuban	5	0.04
Mexican	5,577	48.05
Puerto Rican	95	0.82
South American:	2	0.02
Ecuadorian	1	0.01
Venezuelan	1	0.01
Other Hispanic or Latino	754	6.50
Irish	572	5.02
Italian	250	2.19
Norwegian	141	1.24
Polish	71	0.62
Portuguese	375	3.29
Russian	37	0.32
Scandinavian	16	0.14
Scotch-Irish	66	0.58
Scottish	79	0.69
Swedish	141	1.24

Notes: 1. Figures in the "Number" column do not add up to the total population due to: a) Ancestry/Race overlap — e.g. persons can report being both White and Irish, b) persons of Hispanic origin can report being any race, c) persons reporting two ancestries are counted in both categories. 2. Numbers in parentheses indicate the number of persons reporting this ancestry/race alone, not in combination with any other ancestry/race. 3. Refer to the Explanation of Data in the front of the book for more detailed information.

Swiss	64	0.56
Ukrainian	41	0.36
United States or American	332	2.91
Welsh	31	0.27
White:	7,184	61.90
Not Hispanic (4,189)	4,398	37.89
Hispanic (2,270)	2,786	24.00

Pedley

Place Type: Census Designated Place
County: Riverside
Population: 11,207

Ancestry/Race	Number	%
African American/Black:	587	5.24
Not Hispanic (493)	548	4.89
Hispanic (24)	39	0.35
African, sub-Saharan:	10	0.09
African	10	0.09
Am. Ind. or Alaska Nat., not spec.	67	0.60
American Indian tribes, specified:	149	1.33
Apache (2)	7	0.06
Blackfeet	4	0.04
Cherokee (25)	66	0.59
Chippewa (1)	7	0.06
Choctaw (1)	1	0.01
Comanche (6)	6	0.05
Creek	5	0.04
Crow (1)	1	0.01
Iroquois (1)	1	0.01
Kiowa (1)	1	0.01
Latin American Indians (12)	14	0.12
Navajo (5)	5	0.04
Osage	3	0.03
Potawatomi (3)	3	0.03
Shoshone	2	0.02
Sioux (2)	4	0.04
Yaqui (1)	1	0.01
All other tribes (10)	18	0.16
American Indian tribes, not spec.	8	0.07
Arab:	114	1.03
Arab/Arabic	16	0.14
Jordanian	73	0.66
Lebanese	7	0.06
Other Arab	18	0.16
Armenian	7	0.06
Asian:	561	5.01
Cambodian (12)	20	0.18
Chinese, ex. Taiwanese (28)	51	0.46
Filipino (119)	142	1.27
Indian (65)	72	0.64
Indonesian (5)	7	0.06
Japanese (18)	49	0.44
Korean (34)	44	0.39
Malaysian (1)	3	0.03
Pakistani (4)	12	0.11
Sri Lankan (14)	15	0.13
Taiwanese	2	0.02
Thai (9)	11	0.10
Vietnamese (92)	92	0.82
Other Asian, not specified (10)	41	0.37
Austrian	20	0.18
Belgian	27	0.24
Brazilian	11	0.10
British	63	0.57
Canadian	61	0.55
Czech	29	0.26
Czechoslovakian	8	0.07
Danish	31	0.28
Dutch	199	1.80
English	988	8.92
European	71	0.64
Finnish	42	0.38
French, except Basque	376	3.39
French Canadian	26	0.23
German	1,516	13.69
Greek	25	0.23
Hawaii Native/Pacific Islander:	48	0.43
Micronesian: (12)	13	0.12
Guamanian/Chamorro (12)	13	0.12
Polynesian: (9)	20	0.18
Native Hawaiian (4)	14	0.12
Samoan (5)	6	0.05
Other Pac. Isl., not spec. (4)	15	0.13
Hispanic or Latino:	3,840	34.26
Central American:	69	0.62
Costa Rican	10	0.09
Guatemalan	15	0.13
Honduran	6	0.05
Nicaraguan	7	0.06
Panamanian	5	0.04
Salvadoran	21	0.19
Other Central American	5	0.04
Cuban	26	0.23
Mexican	3,110	27.75
Puerto Rican	56	0.50
South American:	29	0.26
Argentinean	9	0.08
Bolivian	2	0.02
Chilean	4	0.04
Colombian	5	0.04
Ecuadorian	3	0.03
Peruvian	3	0.03
Uruguayan	2	0.02
Venezuelan	1	0.01
Other Hispanic or Latino	550	4.91
Hungarian	15	0.14
Irish	1,156	10.44
Italian	599	5.41
Lithuanian	35	0.32
Northern European	20	0.18
Norwegian	126	1.14
Polish	217	1.96
Portuguese	99	0.89
Russian	106	0.96
Scandinavian	58	0.52
Scotch-Irish	150	1.35
Scottish	152	1.37
Slovak	14	0.13
Swedish	84	0.76
Swiss	10	0.09
United States or American	447	4.04
Welsh	119	1.07
White:	7,992	71.31
Not Hispanic (6,036)	6,317	56.37
Hispanic (1,456)	1,675	14.95
Yugoslavian	20	0.18

Perris

Place Type: City
County: Riverside
Population: 36,189

Ancestry/Race	Number	%
African American/Black:	6,264	17.31
Not Hispanic (5,574)	5,933	16.39
Hispanic (174)	331	0.91
African, sub-Saharan:	373	1.03
African	307	0.85
Ethiopian	10	0.03
Ghanian	6	0.02
Nigerian	50	0.14
Alaska Native tribes, specified:	3	0.01
Alaska Athabascan	3	0.01
Eskimo	1	0.00
Am. Ind. or Alaska Nat., not spec.	313	0.86
American Indian tribes, specified:	553	1.53
Apache (31)	46	0.13
Blackfeet (1)	24	0.07
Cherokee (22)	104	0.29
Cheyenne (1)	3	0.01
Chickasaw (1)	3	0.01
Chippewa (3)	16	0.04
Choctaw (8)	34	0.09
Colville	3	0.01
Comanche	1	0.00
Cree (1)	2	0.01
Creek (2)	7	0.02
Iroquois	1	0.00
Latin American Indians (93)	117	0.32
Navajo (20)	35	0.10
Paiute (9)	9	0.02
Pima (1)	1	0.00
Pueblo (17)	20	0.06
Seminole	2	0.01
Sioux (3)	10	0.03
Ute (2)	2	0.01
Yakama (1)	1	0.00
Yaqui (3)	6	0.02
Yuman (1)	2	0.01
All other tribes (76)	104	0.29
American Indian tribes, not spec.	57	0.16
Arab:	62	0.17
Arab/Arabic	34	0.09
Lebanese	20	0.06
Syrian	8	0.02
Asian:	1,383	3.82
Cambodian (31)	34	0.09
Chinese, ex. Taiwanese (54)	109	0.30
Filipino (536)	676	1.87
Indian (127)	174	0.48
Indonesian (7)	13	0.04
Japanese (57)	135	0.37
Korean (31)	56	0.15
Laotian (33)	43	0.12
Malaysian (1)	1	0.00
Pakistani (12)	12	0.03
Taiwanese (1)	1	0.00
Thai (16)	30	0.08
Vietnamese (44)	51	0.14
Other Asian, specified	3	0.01
Other Asian, not specified (17)	45	0.12
Assyrian/Chaldean/Syriac	51	0.14
Austrian	17	0.05
Basque	3	0.01
Belgian	23	0.06
British	18	0.05
Canadian	28	0.08
Croatian	11	0.03
Czech	28	0.08
Czechoslovakian	28	0.08
Danish	79	0.22
Dutch	189	0.52
English	840	2.32
European	183	0.51
Finnish	59	0.16
French, except Basque	325	0.90
French Canadian	51	0.14
German	1,617	4.47
Greek	49	0.14
Guyanese	24	0.07
Hawaii Native/Pacific Islander:	213	0.59
Melanesian: (9)	9	0.02
Fijian (9)	9	0.02
Micronesian: (31)	45	0.12
Guamanian/Chamorro (25)	39	0.11
Other Micronesian (6)	6	0.02
Polynesian: (64)	112	0.31
Native Hawaiian (26)	62	0.17
Samoan (38)	50	0.14
Other Pac. Isl., specified	2	0.01
Other Pac. Isl., not spec. (13)	45	0.12
Hispanic or Latino:	20,322	56.16
Central American:	473	1.31
Costa Rican	30	0.08
Guatemalan	116	0.32
Honduran	7	0.02
Nicaraguan	39	0.11
Panamanian	9	0.02
Salvadoran	223	0.62
Other Central American	49	0.14
Cuban	109	0.30
Dominican Republic	2	0.01
Mexican	16,783	46.38
Puerto Rican	251	0.69
South American:	128	0.35
Argentinean	15	0.04
Bolivian	2	0.01

Notes: 1. Figures in the "Number" column do not add up to the total population due to: a) Ancestry/Race overlap — e.g. persons can report being both White and Irish, b) persons of Hispanic origin can report being any race, c) persons reporting two ancestries are counted in both categories. 2. Numbers in parentheses indicate the number of persons reporting this ancestry/race alone, not in combination with any other ancestry/race. 3. Refer to the Explanation of Data in the front of the book for more detailed information.

Ancestry/Race	Number	%
Chilean	5	0.01
Colombian	45	0.12
Ecuadorian	13	0.04
Peruvian	36	0.10
Uruguayan	1	0.00
Venezuelan	1	0.00
Other South American	10	0.03
Other Hispanic or Latino	2,576	7.12
Hungarian	92	0.25
Irish	1,437	3.97
Israeli	15	0.04
Italian	643	1.78
Luxemburger	13	0.04
Northern European	7	0.02
Norwegian	165	0.46
Pennsylvania German	6	0.02
Polish	147	0.41
Portuguese	110	0.30
Romanian	5	0.01
Russian	170	0.47
Scandinavian	56	0.15
Scotch-Irish	169	0.47
Scottish	159	0.44
Slovak	7	0.02
Swedish	136	0.38
Swiss	28	0.08
Turkish	4	0.01
Ukrainian	32	0.09
United States or American	1,123	3.10
Welsh	98	0.27
West Indian, excl. Hispanic:	179	0.49
Belizean	113	0.31
Dutch West Indian	11	0.03
Jamaican	27	0.07
Trinidadian and Tobagonian	23	0.06
West Indian	5	0.01
White:	16,588	45.84
Not Hispanic (8,243)	8,834	24.41
Hispanic (6,666)	7,754	21.43
Yugoslavian	6	0.02

Petaluma

Place Type: City
County: Sonoma
Population: 54,548

Ancestry/Race	Number	%
African American/Black:	936	1.72
Not Hispanic (581)	837	1.53
Hispanic (51)	99	0.18
African, sub-Saharan:	106	0.19
African	54	0.10
Ghanian	31	0.06
South African	9	0.02
Other sub-Saharan African	12	0.02
Alaska Native tribes, specified:	5	0.01
Alaska Athabascan	1	0.00
Aleut	2	0.00
Eskimo	1	0.00
Tlingit-Haida (1)	1	0.00
Alaska Native tribes, not specified	1	0.00
Am. Ind. or Alaska Nat., not spec.	249	0.46
Albanian	8	0.01
American Indian tribes, specified:	567	1.04
Apache (3)	19	0.03
Blackfeet (3)	26	0.05
Cherokee (34)	170	0.31
Chickasaw	7	0.01
Chippewa (4)	15	0.03
Choctaw (12)	24	0.04
Comanche (2)	2	0.00
Crow	5	0.01
Delaware (5)	9	0.02
Iroquois (5)	15	0.03
Latin American Indians (44)	87	0.16
Navajo (10)	16	0.03
Osage	3	0.01
Pima (1)	1	0.00
Potawatomi (2)	12	0.02
Pueblo (1)	6	0.01
Puget Sound Salish (1)	3	0.01
Seminole (1)	5	0.01
Shoshone (2)	6	0.01
Sioux (4)	12	0.02
Ute	1	0.00
Yakama (1)	1	0.00
Yaqui (2)	5	0.01
Yuman (1)	1	0.00
All other tribes (48)	116	0.21
American Indian tribes, not spec.	31	0.06
Arab:	194	0.36
Arab/Arabic	24	0.04
Egyptian	9	0.02
Jordanian	2	0.00
Lebanese	23	0.04
Moroccan	12	0.02
Palestinian	90	0.17
Syrian	25	0.05
Other Arab	9	0.02
Armenian	57	0.10
Asian:	2,909	5.33
Cambodian (19)	24	0.04
Chinese, ex. Taiwanese (659)	795	1.46
Filipino (416)	645	1.18
Hmong (15)	17	0.03
Indian (268)	328	0.60
Indonesian (13)	26	0.05
Japanese (224)	422	0.77
Korean (144)	195	0.36
Laotian (50)	61	0.11
Malaysian (2)	8	0.01
Pakistani (63)	71	0.13
Sri Lankan (1)	1	0.00
Taiwanese (11)	14	0.03
Thai (40)	57	0.10
Vietnamese (136)	162	0.30
Other Asian, specified (6)	13	0.02
Other Asian, not specified (25)	70	0.13
Assyrian/Chaldean/Syriac	53	0.10
Australian	115	0.21
Austrian	179	0.33
Basque	59	0.11
Belgian	41	0.08
Brazilian	18	0.03
British	240	0.44
Bulgarian	15	0.03
Canadian	179	0.33
Celtic	48	0.09
Croatian	87	0.16
Czech	181	0.33
Czechoslovakian	102	0.19
Danish	976	1.79
Dutch	737	1.35
Eastern European	29	0.05
English	7,331	13.44
Estonian	15	0.03
European	931	1.71
Finnish	287	0.53
French, except Basque	2,330	4.27
French Canadian	352	0.65
German	8,836	16.20
Greek	403	0.74
Hawaii Native/Pacific Islander:	256	0.47
Melanesian: (10)	11	0.02
Fijian (10)	10	0.02
Other Melanesian	1	0.00
Micronesian: (15)	27	0.05
Guamanian/Chamorro (11)	23	0.04
Other Micronesian (4)	4	0.01
Polynesian: (53)	167	0.31
Native Hawaiian (36)	136	0.25
Samoan (15)	23	0.04
Tongan (1)	2	0.00
Other Polynesian (1)	6	0.01
Other Pac. Isl., specified	5	0.01
Other Pac. Isl., not spec. (14)	46	0.08
Hispanic or Latino:	7,985	14.64
Central American:	573	1.05
Costa Rican	15	0.03
Guatemalan	103	0.19
Honduran	21	0.04
Nicaraguan	89	0.16
Panamanian	12	0.02
Salvadoran	268	0.49
Other Central American	65	0.12
Cuban	45	0.08
Dominican Republic	13	0.02
Mexican	5,546	10.17
Puerto Rican	152	0.28
South American:	234	0.43
Argentinean	16	0.03
Bolivian	7	0.01
Chilean	22	0.04
Colombian	43	0.08
Ecuadorian	9	0.02
Paraguayan	1	0.00
Peruvian	119	0.22
Venezuelan	6	0.01
Other South American	11	0.02
Other Hispanic or Latino	1,422	2.61
Hungarian	330	0.61
Icelander	15	0.03
Iranian	100	0.18
Irish	10,063	18.45
Israeli	21	0.04
Italian	6,055	11.10
Latvian	27	0.05
Lithuanian	139	0.25
Luxemburger	12	0.02
Macedonian	40	0.07
Maltese	153	0.28
New Zealander	42	0.08
Northern European	164	0.30
Norwegian	1,196	2.19
Pennsylvania German	17	0.03
Polish	1,261	2.31
Portuguese	1,279	2.35
Romanian	145	0.27
Russian	813	1.49
Scandinavian	166	0.30
Scotch-Irish	1,096	2.01
Scottish	1,929	3.54
Serbian	29	0.05
Slavic	27	0.05
Slovak	35	0.06
Slovene	36	0.07
Swedish	1,269	2.33
Swiss	573	1.05
Turkish	9	0.02
Ukrainian	117	0.21
United States or American	1,828	3.35
Welsh	487	0.89
West Indian, excl. Hispanic:	40	0.07
Haitian	40	0.07
White:	47,874	87.76
Not Hispanic (41,996)	43,412	79.58
Hispanic (3,910)	4,462	8.18
Yugoslavian	163	0.30

Pico Rivera

Place Type: City
County: Los Angeles
Population: 63,428

Ancestry/Race	Number	%
African American/Black:	602	0.95
Not Hispanic (313)	366	0.58
Hispanic (137)	236	0.37
African, sub-Saharan:	34	0.05
African	34	0.05
Alaska Native tribes, specified:	5	0.01
Eskimo	1	0.00
Tlingit-Haida	4	0.01
Am. Ind. or Alaska Nat., not spec.	554	0.87
American Indian tribes, specified:	617	0.97
Apache (47)	80	0.13
Blackfeet (7)	10	0.02
Cherokee (12)	51	0.08

Notes: 1. Figures in the "Number" column do not add up to the total population due to: a) Ancestry/Race overlap — e.g. persons can report being both White and Irish, b) persons of Hispanic origin can report being any race, c) persons reporting two ancestries are counted in both categories. 2. Numbers in parentheses indicate the number of persons reporting this ancestry/race alone, not in combination with any other ancestry/race. 3. Refer to the Explanation of Data in the front of the book for more detailed information.

Cheyenne	1	0.00
Chickasaw (2)	3	0.00
Chippewa (8)	16	0.03
Choctaw (3)	8	0.01
Comanche (4)	5	0.01
Crow	1	0.00
Iroquois (1)	2	0.00
Kiowa (7)	9	0.01
Latin American Indians (125)	188	0.30
Navajo (32)	45	0.07
Osage (1)	1	0.00
Paiute	4	0.01
Pima (12)	13	0.02
Pueblo (11)	22	0.03
Seminole (5)	6	0.01
Sioux (7)	20	0.03
Tohono O'Odham (1)	6	0.01
Ute	3	0.00
Yaqui (13)	27	0.04
Yuman (7)	13	0.02
All other tribes (50)	83	0.13
American Indian tribes, not spec.	88	0.14
Arab:	188	0.30
Arab/Arabic	30	0.05
Egyptian	154	0.24
Lebanese	4	0.01
Armenian	190	0.30
Asian:	2,039	3.21
Cambodian (82)	93	0.15
Chinese, ex. Taiwanese (176)	253	0.40
Filipino (769)	896	1.41
Indian (99)	120	0.19
Indonesian (5)	14	0.02
Japanese (171)	245	0.39
Korean (76)	83	0.13
Laotian	1	0.00
Pakistani (5)	13	0.02
Sri Lankan (1)	2	0.00
Taiwanese (9)	11	0.02
Thai (70)	75	0.12
Vietnamese (144)	171	0.27
Other Asian, specified (19)	28	0.04
Other Asian, not specified (19)	34	0.05
Austrian	49	0.08
Basque	21	0.03
Brazilian	11	0.02
British	9	0.01
Canadian	93	0.15
Croatian	11	0.02
Czech	20	0.03
Czechoslovakian	9	0.01
Danish	56	0.09
Dutch	97	0.15
English	646	1.02
European	98	0.16
French, except Basque	396	0.63
French Canadian	40	0.06
German	951	1.51
Hawaii Native/Pacific Islander:	166	0.26
Micronesian: (10)	24	0.04
Guamanian/Chamorro (10)	24	0.04
Polynesian: (48)	102	0.16
Native Hawaiian (15)	57	0.09
Samoan (33)	44	0.07
Other Polynesian	1	0.00
Other Pac. Isl., specified	4	0.01
Other Pac. Isl., not spec. (19)	36	0.06
Hispanic or Latino:	56,000	88.29
Central American:	1,558	2.46
Costa Rican	48	0.08
Guatemalan	313	0.49
Honduran	48	0.08
Nicaraguan	153	0.24
Panamanian	6	0.01
Salvadoran	824	1.30
Other Central American	166	0.26
Cuban	134	0.21
Dominican Republic	11	0.02
Mexican	48,033	75.73
Puerto Rican	236	0.37
South American:	366	0.58
Argentinean	43	0.07
Bolivian	8	0.01
Chilean	18	0.03
Colombian	87	0.14
Ecuadorian	71	0.11
Paraguayan	1	0.00
Peruvian	87	0.14
Uruguayan	1	0.00
Venezuelan	10	0.02
Other South American	40	0.06
Other Hispanic or Latino	5,662	8.93
Hungarian	28	0.04
Iranian	24	0.04
Irish	859	1.36
Italian	569	0.90
Northern European	6	0.01
Norwegian	64	0.10
Polish	140	0.22
Portuguese	18	0.03
Romanian	74	0.12
Russian	62	0.10
Scandinavian	16	0.03
Scotch-Irish	112	0.18
Scottish	72	0.11
Serbian	11	0.02
Swedish	95	0.15
Turkish	8	0.01
United States or American	863	1.37
West Indian, excl. Hispanic:	7	0.01
Jamaican	7	0.01
White:	34,411	54.25
Not Hispanic (4,914)	5,199	8.20
Hispanic (26,446)	29,212	46.06

Piedmont

Place Type: City
County: Alameda
Population: 10,952

Ancestry/Race	Number	%
African American/Black:	197	1.80
Not Hispanic (134)	187	1.71
Hispanic (2)	10	0.09
Am. Ind. or Alaska Nat., not spec.	23	0.21
American Indian tribes, specified:	38	0.35
Apache	4	0.04
Blackfeet	1	0.01
Cherokee (1)	7	0.06
Choctaw	11	0.10
Comanche	1	0.01
Delaware	1	0.01
Latin American Indians (2)	6	0.05
Sioux (5)	5	0.05
All other tribes	2	0.02
American Indian tribes, not spec.	2	0.02
Arab:	85	0.78
Iraqi	20	0.18
Lebanese	36	0.33
Syrian	29	0.26
Armenian	73	0.67
Asian:	2,077	18.96
Chinese, ex. Taiwanese (1,223)	1,378	12.58
Filipino (55)	87	0.79
Indian (67)	95	0.87
Indonesian (1)	5	0.05
Japanese (145)	253	2.31
Korean (139)	171	1.56
Laotian (2)	2	0.02
Pakistani (11)	11	0.10
Taiwanese (19)	19	0.17
Thai (2)	4	0.04
Vietnamese (33)	37	0.34
Other Asian, not specified (11)	15	0.14
Assyrian/Chaldean/Syriac	23	0.21
Australian	7	0.06
Austrian	115	1.05
Basque	42	0.38
Belgian	8	0.07
Brazilian	7	0.06
British	91	0.83
Canadian	39	0.36
Croatian	64	0.58
Czech	66	0.60
Czechoslovakian	25	0.23
Danish	92	0.84
Dutch	210	1.92
Eastern European	83	0.76
English	2,170	19.81
European	286	2.61
Finnish	72	0.66
French, except Basque	401	3.66
French Canadian	65	0.59
German	1,500	13.70
German Russian	6	0.05
Greek	110	1.00
Hawaii Native/Pacific Islander:	33	0.30
Polynesian: (4)	29	0.26
Native Hawaiian (2)	22	0.20
Samoan (1)	4	0.04
Tongan (1)	1	0.01
Other Polynesian	2	0.02
Other Pac. Isl., not spec.	4	0.04
Hispanic or Latino:	325	2.97
Central American:	35	0.32
Guatemalan	5	0.05
Honduran	1	0.01
Nicaraguan	5	0.05
Salvadoran	22	0.20
Other Central American	2	0.02
Cuban	7	0.06
Dominican Republic	7	0.06
Mexican	153	1.40
Puerto Rican	5	0.05
South American:	34	0.31
Argentinean	4	0.04
Chilean	5	0.05
Colombian	3	0.03
Ecuadorian	2	0.02
Peruvian	13	0.12
Venezuelan	4	0.04
Other South American	3	0.03
Other Hispanic or Latino	84	0.77
Hungarian	126	1.15
Iranian	74	0.68
Irish	1,281	11.70
Italian	349	3.19
Latvian	54	0.49
Lithuanian	60	0.55
Maltese	29	0.26
Northern European	46	0.42
Norwegian	163	1.49
Polish	316	2.89
Portuguese	97	0.89
Romanian	30	0.27
Russian	478	4.36
Scandinavian	49	0.45
Scotch-Irish	288	2.63
Scottish	403	3.68
Serbian	15	0.14
Slavic	19	0.17
Slovene	30	0.27
Swedish	245	2.24
Swiss	106	0.97
Turkish	32	0.29
Ukrainian	34	0.31
United States or American	408	3.73
Welsh	137	1.25
White:	8,938	81.61
Not Hispanic (8,408)	8,691	79.36
Hispanic (199)	247	2.26
Yugoslavian	24	0.22

Notes: 1. Figures in the "Number" column do not add up to the total population due to: a) Ancestry/Race overlap — e.g. persons can report being both White and Irish, b) persons of Hispanic origin can report being any race, c) persons reporting two ancestries are counted in both categories. 2. Numbers in parentheses indicate the number of persons reporting this ancestry/race alone, not in combination with any other ancestry/race. 3. Refer to the Explanation of Data in the front of the book for more detailed information.

Pinole

Place Type: City
County: Contra Costa
Population: 19,039

Ancestry/Race	Number	%
Afghan	57	0.29
African American/Black:	2,386	12.53
Not Hispanic (2,079)	2,312	12.14
Hispanic (36)	74	0.39
African, sub-Saharan:	129	0.67
African	70	0.36
Cape Verdean	7	0.04
Kenyan	5	0.03
Nigerian	6	0.03
Somalian	33	0.17
South African	8	0.04
Alaska Native tribes, specified:	5	0.03
Aleut (1)	5	0.03
Am. Ind. or Alaska Nat., not spec.	80	0.42
American Indian tribes, specified:	263	1.38
Apache (3)	12	0.06
Blackfeet (2)	9	0.05
Cherokee (16)	88	0.46
Chickasaw (1)	8	0.04
Chippewa (3)	6	0.03
Choctaw (6)	27	0.14
Comanche (1)	4	0.02
Cree	1	0.01
Creek (1)	8	0.04
Delaware	2	0.01
Iroquois	3	0.02
Latin American Indians (16)	37	0.19
Navajo (1)	1	0.01
Ottawa	1	0.01
Pima	1	0.01
Potawatomi (1)	1	0.01
Pueblo (4)	7	0.04
Seminole	2	0.01
Sioux (5)	15	0.08
All other tribes (9)	30	0.16
American Indian tribes, not spec.	14	0.07
Arab:	78	0.40
Arab/Arabic	23	0.12
Egyptian	21	0.11
Lebanese	10	0.05
Syrian	9	0.05
Other Arab	15	0.08
Armenian	39	0.20
Asian:	4,770	25.05
Bangladeshi (1)	5	0.03
Cambodian (9)	12	0.06
Chinese, ex. Taiwanese (974)	1,138	5.98
Filipino (1,853)	2,144	11.26
Indian (352)	414	2.17
Indonesian (18)	27	0.14
Japanese (199)	316	1.66
Korean (227)	257	1.35
Laotian (49)	53	0.28
Malaysian	3	0.02
Pakistani (31)	33	0.17
Sri Lankan (2)	4	0.02
Taiwanese	8	0.04
Thai (28)	39	0.20
Vietnamese (205)	222	1.17
Other Asian, specified (16)	19	0.10
Other Asian, not specified (21)	76	0.40
Assyrian/Chaldean/Syriac	16	0.08
Australian	4	0.02
Austrian	23	0.12
Basque	8	0.04
Belgian	25	0.13
Brazilian	30	0.15
British	121	0.62
Canadian	31	0.16
Croatian	21	0.11
Danish	168	0.87
Dutch	235	1.21
Eastern European	7	0.04
English	1,639	8.45
European	176	0.91
Finnish	47	0.24
French, except Basque	559	2.88
French Canadian	29	0.15
German	2,143	11.05
Greek	75	0.39
Hawaii Native/Pacific Islander:	180	0.95
Melanesian: (6)	7	0.04
Fijian (6)	7	0.04
Micronesian: (5)	12	0.06
Guamanian/Chamorro (5)	12	0.06
Polynesian: (38)	90	0.47
Native Hawaiian (18)	61	0.32
Samoan (14)	16	0.08
Tongan (2)	8	0.04
Other Polynesian (4)	5	0.03
Other Pac. Isl., not spec. (19)	71	0.37
Hispanic or Latino:	2,618	13.75
Central American:	259	1.36
Costa Rican	1	0.01
Guatemalan	21	0.11
Honduran	6	0.03
Nicaraguan	67	0.35
Panamanian	4	0.02
Salvadoran	118	0.62
Other Central American	42	0.22
Cuban	26	0.14
Dominican Republic	4	0.02
Mexican	1,505	7.90
Puerto Rican	90	0.47
South American:	97	0.51
Argentinean	9	0.05
Bolivian	2	0.01
Chilean	9	0.05
Colombian	14	0.07
Ecuadorian	3	0.02
Peruvian	48	0.25
Venezuelan	3	0.02
Other South American	9	0.05
Other Hispanic or Latino	637	3.35
Hungarian	23	0.12
Iranian	113	0.58
Irish	1,801	9.29
Israeli	24	0.12
Italian	1,042	5.37
Lithuanian	21	0.11
Maltese	7	0.04
Northern European	6	0.03
Norwegian	234	1.21
Polish	362	1.87
Portuguese	549	2.83
Romanian	25	0.13
Russian	181	0.93
Scandinavian	38	0.20
Scotch-Irish	236	1.22
Scottish	197	1.02
Slavic	38	0.20
Slovak	15	0.08
Swedish	202	1.04
Swiss	118	0.61
Turkish	7	0.04
Ukrainian	36	0.19
United States or American	412	2.12
Welsh	98	0.51
West Indian, excl. Hispanic:	31	0.16
British West Indian	23	0.12
Dutch West Indian	2	0.01
Haitian	6	0.03
White:	11,221	58.94
Not Hispanic (9,219)	9,835	51.66
Hispanic (1,137)	1,386	7.28
Yugoslavian	22	0.11

Pittsburg

Place Type: City
County: Contra Costa
Population: 56,769

Ancestry/Race	Number	%
Afghan	68	0.12
African American/Black:	11,776	20.74
Not Hispanic (10,457)	11,255	19.83
Hispanic (267)	521	0.92
African, sub-Saharan:	843	1.48
African	813	1.43
Cape Verdean	6	0.01
Ethiopian	10	0.02
Nigerian	6	0.01
South African	8	0.01
Alaska Native tribes, specified:	6	0.01
Aleut	2	0.00
Eskimo	1	0.00
Tlingit-Haida (2)	3	0.01
Am. Ind. or Alaska Nat., not spec.	380	0.67
Alsatian	9	0.02
American Indian tribes, specified:	694	1.22
Apache (5)	29	0.05
Blackfeet (10)	54	0.10
Cherokee (36)	201	0.35
Cheyenne	2	0.00
Chickasaw (2)	7	0.01
Chippewa (3)	5	0.01
Choctaw (9)	52	0.09
Comanche	4	0.01
Cree (2)	3	0.01
Creek (13)	23	0.04
Crow	3	0.01
Iroquois (4)	8	0.01
Latin American Indians (64)	111	0.20
Navajo (2)	16	0.03
Ottawa	3	0.01
Paiute (1)	3	0.01
Pima	1	0.00
Potawatomi (3)	4	0.01
Pueblo (2)	8	0.01
Seminole (1)	22	0.04
Sioux (9)	37	0.07
Tohono O'Odham (3)	4	0.01
Ute	4	0.01
Yaqui (9)	12	0.02
Yuman (3)	5	0.01
All other tribes (35)	73	0.13
American Indian tribes, not spec.	58	0.10
Arab:	137	0.24
Arab/Arabic	42	0.07
Egyptian	50	0.09
Lebanese	32	0.06
Palestinian	13	0.02
Armenian	10	0.02
Asian:	8,665	15.26
Bangladeshi (6)	15	0.03
Cambodian (53)	55	0.10
Chinese, ex. Taiwanese (399)	597	1.05
Filipino (4,967)	5,764	10.15
Hmong (1)	2	0.00
Indian (754)	934	1.65
Indonesian (24)	43	0.08
Japanese (159)	288	0.51
Korean (81)	116	0.20
Laotian (62)	88	0.16
Malaysian (8)	8	0.01
Pakistani (36)	65	0.11
Sri Lankan (4)	8	0.01
Taiwanese (2)	3	0.01
Thai (36)	59	0.10
Vietnamese (422)	462	0.81
Other Asian, specified (4)	13	0.02
Other Asian, not specified (51)	145	0.26
Australian	8	0.01
Austrian	41	0.07
Basque	9	0.02
Belgian	48	0.08

Notes: 1. Figures in the "Number" column do not add up to the total population due to: a) Ancestry/Race overlap — e.g. persons can report being both White and Irish, b) persons of Hispanic origin can report being any race, c) persons reporting two ancestries are counted in both categories. 2. Numbers in parentheses indicate the number of persons reporting this ancestry/race alone, not in combination with any other ancestry/race. 3. Refer to the Explanation of Data in the front of the book for more detailed information.

Brazilian	36	0.06
British	54	0.10
Bulgarian	9	0.02
Canadian	98	0.17
Celtic	7	0.01
Croatian	51	0.09
Czech	28	0.05
Czechoslovakian	22	0.04
Danish	326	0.57
Dutch	455	0.80
English	2,169	3.82
European	481	0.85
Finnish	72	0.13
French, except Basque	934	1.64
French Canadian	177	0.31
German	3,555	6.26
German Russian	5	0.01
Greek	194	0.34
Guyanese	41	0.07
Hawaii Native/Pacific Islander:	880	1.55
Melanesian: (59)	76	0.13
Fijian (59)	76	0.13
Micronesian: (52)	107	0.19
Guamanian/Chamorro (52)	107	0.19
Polynesian: (309)	495	0.87
Native Hawaiian (55)	163	0.29
Samoan (70)	119	0.21
Tongan (166)	189	0.33
Other Polynesian (18)	24	0.04
Other Pac. Isl., not spec. (56)	202	0.36
Hispanic or Latino:	18,287	32.21
Central American:	1,487	2.62
Costa Rican	30	0.05
Guatemalan	127	0.22
Honduran	27	0.05
Nicaraguan	381	0.67
Panamanian	39	0.07
Salvadoran	758	1.34
Other Central American	125	0.22
Cuban	78	0.14
Dominican Republic	3	0.01
Mexican	13,087	23.05
Puerto Rican	703	1.24
South American:	315	0.55
Argentinean	19	0.03
Bolivian	8	0.01
Chilean	30	0.05
Colombian	45	0.08
Ecuadorian	19	0.03
Paraguayan	2	0.00
Peruvian	163	0.29
Venezuelan	10	0.02
Other South American	19	0.03
Other Hispanic or Latino	2,614	4.60
Hungarian	113	0.20
Iranian	111	0.20
Irish	3,338	5.87
Italian	3,481	6.13
Latvian	5	0.01
Lithuanian	12	0.02
Maltese	23	0.04
Northern European	23	0.04
Norwegian	450	0.79
Pennsylvania German	8	0.01
Polish	512	0.90
Portuguese	587	1.03
Romanian	65	0.11
Russian	197	0.35
Scandinavian	66	0.12
Scotch-Irish	459	0.81
Scottish	625	1.10
Slavic	8	0.01
Swedish	505	0.89
Swiss	76	0.13
Ukrainian	40	0.07
United States or American	1,271	2.24
Welsh	219	0.39
West Indian, excl. Hispanic:	28	0.05
British West Indian	8	0.01
Jamaican	20	0.04
White:	27,773	48.92
Not Hispanic (17,697)	19,440	34.24
Hispanic (7,015)	8,333	14.68
Yugoslavian	64	0.11

Placentia

Place Type: City
County: Orange
Population: 46,488

Ancestry/Race	Number	%
African American/Black:	983	2.11
Not Hispanic (746)	868	1.87
Hispanic (75)	115	0.25
African, sub-Saharan:	64	0.14
African	42	0.09
Kenyan	14	0.03
South African	8	0.02
Am. Ind. or Alaska Nat., not spec.	222	0.48
American Indian tribes, specified:	440	0.95
Apache (22)	41	0.09
Blackfeet	10	0.02
Cherokee (27)	88	0.19
Chickasaw (1)	1	0.00
Chippewa (5)	9	0.02
Choctaw (6)	22	0.05
Comanche (5)	8	0.02
Cree (6)	8	0.02
Creek (1)	11	0.02
Iroquois (2)	4	0.01
Latin American Indians (69)	82	0.18
Navajo (10)	16	0.03
Osage (1)	1	0.00
Pima	1	0.00
Potawatomi (3)	3	0.01
Pueblo (9)	11	0.02
Seminole	1	0.00
Shoshone	3	0.01
Sioux (10)	23	0.05
Ute (4)	5	0.01
Yaqui (3)	8	0.02
All other tribes (60)	84	0.18
American Indian tribes, not spec.	34	0.07
Arab:	252	0.54
Arab/Arabic	18	0.04
Egyptian	24	0.05
Iraqi	13	0.03
Jordanian	10	0.02
Lebanese	113	0.24
Palestinian	25	0.05
Syrian	36	0.08
Other Arab	13	0.03
Armenian	211	0.45
Asian:	5,842	12.57
Bangladeshi (2)	2	0.00
Cambodian (46)	55	0.12
Chinese, ex. Taiwanese (1,007)	1,152	2.48
Filipino (743)	897	1.93
Hmong (22)	26	0.06
Indian (624)	677	1.46
Indonesian (41)	72	0.15
Japanese (490)	673	1.45
Korean (569)	614	1.32
Laotian (23)	32	0.07
Malaysian (10)	10	0.02
Pakistani (65)	81	0.17
Sri Lankan (10)	10	0.02
Taiwanese (284)	321	0.69
Thai (52)	53	0.11
Vietnamese (1,009)	1,053	2.27
Other Asian, specified (16)	20	0.04
Other Asian, not specified (42)	94	0.20
Assyrian/Chaldean/Syriac	49	0.10
Australian	28	0.06
Austrian	141	0.30
Basque	13	0.03
Belgian	15	0.03
Brazilian	9	0.02
British	173	0.37
Canadian	292	0.62
Croatian	63	0.13
Czech	179	0.38
Czechoslovakian	100	0.21
Danish	377	0.80
Dutch	620	1.32
Eastern European	18	0.04
English	5,184	11.01
European	501	1.06
Finnish	61	0.13
French, except Basque	1,229	2.61
French Canadian	279	0.59
German	6,728	14.28
Greek	112	0.24
Hawaii Native/Pacific Islander:	170	0.37
Melanesian: (1)	1	0.00
Fijian (1)	1	0.00
Micronesian: (12)	20	0.04
Guamanian/Chamorro (12)	20	0.04
Polynesian: (49)	100	0.22
Native Hawaiian (20)	62	0.13
Samoan (23)	30	0.06
Tongan (5)	6	0.01
Other Polynesian (1)	2	0.00
Other Pac. Isl., not spec. (20)	49	0.11
Hispanic or Latino:	14,460	31.10
Central American:	394	0.85
Costa Rican	23	0.05
Guatemalan	202	0.43
Honduran	18	0.04
Nicaraguan	18	0.04
Panamanian	4	0.01
Salvadoran	94	0.20
Other Central American	35	0.08
Cuban	135	0.29
Dominican Republic	2	0.00
Mexican	12,024	25.86
Puerto Rican	92	0.20
South American:	247	0.53
Argentinean	38	0.08
Bolivian	5	0.01
Chilean	24	0.05
Colombian	60	0.13
Ecuadorian	29	0.06
Paraguayan	2	0.00
Peruvian	52	0.11
Uruguayan	1	0.00
Venezuelan	10	0.02
Other South American	26	0.06
Other Hispanic or Latino	1,566	3.37
Hungarian	170	0.36
Iranian	201	0.43
Irish	4,510	9.58
Italian	2,184	4.64
Latvian	23	0.05
Lithuanian	132	0.28
Luxemburger	8	0.02
Maltese	25	0.05
Northern European	21	0.04
Norwegian	849	1.80
Pennsylvania German	37	0.08
Polish	988	2.10
Portuguese	218	0.46
Romanian	184	0.39
Russian	396	0.84
Scandinavian	131	0.28
Scotch-Irish	608	1.29
Scottish	800	1.70
Serbian	20	0.04
Slavic	6	0.01
Slovak	97	0.21
Swedish	888	1.89
Swiss	107	0.23
Turkish	9	0.02
Ukrainian	99	0.21
United States or American	1,407	2.99
Welsh	178	0.38
West Indian, excl. Hispanic:	34	0.07
Jamaican	34	0.07
White:	32,914	70.80

Notes: 1. Figures in the "Number" column do not add up to the total population due to: a) Ancestry/Race overlap — e.g. persons can report being both White and Irish, b) persons of Hispanic origin can report being any race, c) persons reporting two ancestries are counted in both categories. 2. Numbers in parentheses indicate the number of persons reporting this ancestry/race alone, not in combination with any other ancestry/race. 3. Refer to the Explanation of Data in the front of the book for more detailed information.

Not Hispanic (24,967)	25,719	55.32
Hispanic (6,533)	7,195	15.48
Yugoslavian	15	0.03

Pleasant Hill

Place Type: City
County: Contra Costa
Population: 32,837

Ancestry/Race	Number	%
Afghan	7	0.02
African American/Black:	682	2.08
Not Hispanic (493)	659	2.01
Hispanic (11)	23	0.07
African, sub-Saharan:	122	0.37
African	84	0.26
Ethiopian	9	0.03
Nigerian	29	0.09
Alaska Native tribes, specified:	8	0.02
Aleut	2	0.01
Eskimo	2	0.01
Tlingit-Haida (2)	3	0.01
All other tribes (1)	1	0.00
Am. Ind. or Alaska Nat., not spec.	121	0.37
American Indian tribes, specified:	290	0.88
Apache (10)	18	0.05
Blackfeet (3)	19	0.06
Cherokee (30)	96	0.29
Cheyenne (1)	2	0.01
Chickasaw	6	0.02
Chippewa (4)	8	0.02
Choctaw (7)	13	0.04
Cree (2)	2	0.01
Creek (2)	6	0.02
Iroquois (4)	8	0.02
Latin American Indians (8)	16	0.05
Navajo (3)	4	0.01
Osage (2)	3	0.01
Paiute (1)	6	0.02
Potawatomi	2	0.01
Pueblo (1)	7	0.02
Puget Sound Salish (2)	2	0.01
Seminole	5	0.02
Shoshone (1)	4	0.01
Sioux (9)	14	0.04
Ute	3	0.01
Yaqui (1)	4	0.01
Yuman (1)	1	0.00
All other tribes (17)	41	0.12
American Indian tribes, not spec.	18	0.05
Arab:	269	0.82
Arab/Arabic	52	0.16
Egyptian	18	0.05
Iraqi	40	0.12
Jordanian	27	0.08
Lebanese	65	0.20
Palestinian	42	0.13
Other Arab	25	0.08
Armenian	144	0.44
Asian:	3,843	11.70
Bangladeshi (4)	4	0.01
Cambodian (20)	20	0.06
Chinese, ex. Taiwanese (969)	1,145	3.49
Filipino (669)	892	2.72
Indian (268)	309	0.94
Indonesian (28)	72	0.22
Japanese (417)	582	1.77
Korean (341)	386	1.18
Laotian (5)	6	0.02
Malaysian (4)	4	0.01
Pakistani (26)	32	0.10
Sri Lankan (15)	18	0.05
Taiwanese (30)	36	0.11
Thai (25)	33	0.10
Vietnamese (161)	184	0.56
Other Asian, specified (19)	27	0.08
Other Asian, not specified (12)	93	0.28
Assyrian/Chaldean/Syriac	7	0.02
Australian	7	0.02
Austrian	174	0.53
Basque	24	0.07
Belgian	13	0.04
Brazilian	23	0.07
British	313	0.95
Canadian	99	0.30
Celtic	5	0.02
Croatian	90	0.27
Czech	150	0.46
Czechoslovakian	51	0.16
Danish	404	1.23
Dutch	604	1.84
Eastern European	82	0.25
English	4,483	13.65
Estonian	8	0.02
European	639	1.95
Finnish	216	0.66
French, except Basque	1,145	3.49
French Canadian	290	0.88
German	5,106	15.54
Greek	328	1.00
Hawaii Native/Pacific Islander:	209	0.64
Melanesian: (5)	10	0.03
Fijian (5)	10	0.03
Micronesian: (13)	31	0.09
Guamanian/Chamorro (13)	31	0.09
Polynesian: (64)	108	0.33
Native Hawaiian (30)	70	0.21
Samoan (16)	19	0.06
Tongan (15)	15	0.05
Other Polynesian (3)	4	0.01
Other Pac. Isl., specified	2	0.01
Other Pac. Isl., not spec. (8)	58	0.18
Hispanic or Latino:	2,767	8.43
Central American:	225	0.69
Costa Rican	19	0.06
Guatemalan	16	0.05
Honduran	10	0.03
Nicaraguan	63	0.19
Panamanian	7	0.02
Salvadoran	77	0.23
Other Central American	33	0.10
Cuban	47	0.14
Dominican Republic	5	0.02
Mexican	1,471	4.48
Puerto Rican	150	0.46
South American:	217	0.66
Argentinean	14	0.04
Bolivian	3	0.01
Chilean	19	0.06
Colombian	22	0.07
Ecuadorian	4	0.01
Peruvian	124	0.38
Uruguayan	4	0.01
Venezuelan	10	0.03
Other South American	17	0.05
Other Hispanic or Latino	652	1.99
Hungarian	145	0.44
Iranian	120	0.37
Irish	4,865	14.81
Israeli	32	0.10
Italian	3,123	9.51
Latvian	32	0.10
Lithuanian	93	0.28
Luxemburger	10	0.03
Maltese	61	0.19
New Zealander	36	0.11
Northern European	75	0.23
Norwegian	877	2.67
Pennsylvania German	36	0.11
Polish	815	2.48
Portuguese	868	2.64
Romanian	80	0.24
Russian	643	1.96
Scandinavian	67	0.20
Scotch-Irish	704	2.14
Scottish	1,193	3.63
Serbian	33	0.10
Slavic	12	0.04
Slovak	64	0.19
Slovene	19	0.06
Swedish	1,121	3.41
Swiss	141	0.43
Turkish	16	0.05
Ukrainian	137	0.42
United States or American	1,292	3.93
Welsh	420	1.28
West Indian, excl. Hispanic:	13	0.04
Jamaican	7	0.02
West Indian	6	0.02
White:	28,038	85.39
Not Hispanic (25,139)	26,111	79.52
Hispanic (1,713)	1,927	5.87
Yugoslavian	81	0.25

Pleasanton

Place Type: City
County: Alameda
Population: 63,654

Ancestry/Race	Number	%
Acadian/Cajun	7	0.01
Afghan	57	0.09
African American/Black:	1,084	1.70
Not Hispanic (845)	1,006	1.58
Hispanic (31)	78	0.12
African, sub-Saharan:	82	0.13
African	22	0.03
Ghanian	7	0.01
Nigerian	7	0.01
South African	46	0.07
Alaska Native tribes, specified:	12	0.02
Alaska Athabascan	2	0.00
Aleut (1)	3	0.00
Tlingit-Haida (5)	5	0.01
All other tribes (2)	2	0.00
Am. Ind. or Alaska Nat., not spec.	153	0.24
Albanian	37	0.06
American Indian tribes, specified:	398	0.63
Apache (3)	19	0.03
Blackfeet (3)	19	0.03
Cherokee (29)	134	0.21
Cheyenne	2	0.00
Chickasaw (2)	6	0.01
Chippewa (3)	8	0.01
Choctaw (16)	40	0.06
Comanche (2)	2	0.00
Creek (1)	4	0.01
Crow (1)	2	0.00
Iroquois	7	0.01
Kiowa (1)	1	0.00
Latin American Indians (10)	20	0.03
Lumbee	1	0.00
Navajo (2)	11	0.02
Osage (4)	7	0.01
Ottawa	1	0.00
Paiute (1)	3	0.00
Potawatomi (8)	8	0.01
Pueblo (4)	9	0.01
Seminole (3)	6	0.01
Shoshone	2	0.00
Sioux (4)	20	0.03
Ute (2)	2	0.00
Yakama (1)	1	0.00
Yaqui (2)	2	0.00
All other tribes (20)	61	0.10
American Indian tribes, not spec.	23	0.04
Arab:	388	0.61
Egyptian	39	0.06
Iraqi	14	0.02
Lebanese	149	0.23
Moroccan	27	0.04
Palestinian	59	0.09
Syrian	62	0.10
Other Arab	38	0.06
Armenian	53	0.08
Asian:	8,867	13.93
Bangladeshi (14)	19	0.03
Cambodian (6)	11	0.02

Notes: 1. Figures in the "Number" column do not add up to the total population due to: a) Ancestry/Race overlap — e.g. persons can report being both White and Irish, b) persons of Hispanic origin can report being any race, c) persons reporting two ancestries are counted in both categories. 2. Numbers in parentheses indicate the number of persons reporting this ancestry/race alone, not in combination with any other ancestry/race. 3. Refer to the Explanation of Data in the front of the book for more detailed information.

Chinese, ex. Taiwanese (2,772)	3,132	4.92
Filipino (996)	1,389	2.18
Indian (1,754)	1,894	2.98
Indonesian (29)	58	0.09
Japanese (521)	889	1.40
Korean (636)	708	1.11
Laotian (13)	13	0.02
Malaysian (2)	2	0.00
Pakistani (118)	158	0.25
Sri Lankan (3)	10	0.02
Taiwanese (94)	103	0.16
Thai (41)	50	0.08
Vietnamese (225)	273	0.43
Other Asian, specified (34)	51	0.08
Other Asian, not specified (31)	107	0.17
Assyrian/Chaldean/Syriac	14	0.02
Australian	22	0.03
Austrian	168	0.26
Belgian	204	0.32
Brazilian	102	0.16
British	656	1.03
Bulgarian	33	0.05
Canadian	312	0.49
Carpatho Rusyn	4	0.01
Celtic	33	0.05
Croatian	165	0.26
Czech	250	0.39
Czechoslovakian	118	0.19
Danish	1,099	1.73
Dutch	1,294	2.04
Eastern European	72	0.11
English	7,799	12.27
Estonian	7	0.01
European	1,335	2.10
Finnish	194	0.31
French, except Basque	2,240	3.52
French Canadian	516	0.81
German	11,145	17.53
Greek	715	1.12
Hawaii Native/Pacific Islander:	300	0.47
Melanesian:	3	0.00
Fijian	3	0.00
Micronesian: (21)	31	0.05
Guamanian/Chamorro (21)	31	0.05
Polynesian: (48)	201	0.32
Native Hawaiian (38)	172	0.27
Samoan (10)	29	0.05
Other Pac. Isl., not spec. (13)	65	0.10
Hispanic or Latino:	5,011	7.87
Central American:	174	0.27
Costa Rican	21	0.03
Guatemalan	23	0.04
Honduran	6	0.01
Nicaraguan	32	0.05
Panamanian	12	0.02
Salvadoran	56	0.09
Other Central American	24	0.04
Cuban	76	0.12
Dominican Republic	4	0.01
Mexican	3,218	5.06
Puerto Rican	179	0.28
South American:	215	0.34
Argentinean	15	0.02
Bolivian	19	0.03
Chilean	33	0.05
Colombian	57	0.09
Ecuadorian	5	0.01
Paraguayan	5	0.01
Peruvian	41	0.06
Venezuelan	16	0.03
Other South American	24	0.04
Other Hispanic or Latino	1,145	1.80
Hungarian	395	0.62
Icelander	5	0.01
Iranian	522	0.82
Irish	9,000	14.16
Israeli	18	0.03
Italian	5,964	9.38
Latvian	7	0.01
Lithuanian	102	0.16
Luxemburger	10	0.02
Maltese	21	0.03
New Zealander	15	0.02
Northern European	155	0.24
Norwegian	1,537	2.42
Polish	1,582	2.49
Portuguese	2,335	3.67
Romanian	113	0.18
Russian	732	1.15
Scandinavian	152	0.24
Scotch-Irish	1,156	1.82
Scottish	1,750	2.75
Serbian	40	0.06
Slavic	26	0.04
Slovak	127	0.20
Slovene	6	0.01
Swedish	1,918	3.02
Swiss	544	0.86
Turkish	32	0.05
Ukrainian	207	0.33
United States or American	2,296	3.61
Welsh	650	1.02
West Indian, excl. Hispanic:	56	0.09
Bahamian	5	0.01
Belizean	6	0.01
British West Indian	9	0.01
Jamaican	29	0.05
U.S. Virgin Islander	7	0.01
White:	53,235	83.63
Not Hispanic (48,253)	49,818	78.26
Hispanic (2,950)	3,417	5.37
Yugoslavian	266	0.42

Pomona

Place Type: City
County: Los Angeles
Population: 149,473

Ancestry/Race	Number	%
Afghan	6	0.00
African American/Black:	15,606	10.44
Not Hispanic (13,834)	14,691	9.83
Hispanic (564)	915	0.61
African, sub-Saharan:	1,282	0.86
African	1,016	0.68
Cape Verdean	12	0.01
Ethiopian	125	0.08
Ghanian	0	0.00
Kenyan	67	0.04
Nigerian	31	0.02
South African	0	0.00
Zimbabwean	14	0.01
Other sub-Saharan African	3	0.00
Alaska Native tribes, specified:	4	0.00
Aleut (1)	0	0.00
Eskimo (1)	3	0.00
Am. Ind. or Alaska Nat., not spec.	1,358	0.91
Albanian	55	0.04
American Indian tribes, specified:	1,460	0.98
Apache (63)	111	0.07
Blackfeet (5)	55	0.04
Cherokee (63)	240	0.16
Cheyenne (2)	12	0.01
Chickasaw (2)	1	0.01
Chippewa (10)	21	0.01
Choctaw (18)	65	0.04
Comanche (9)	12	0.01
Cree	3	0.00
Creek (3)	12	0.01
Crow (1)	2	0.00
Delaware (1)	1	0.00
Iroquois (7)	21	0.01
Latin American Indians (375)	485	0.32
Lumbee	3	0.00
Navajo (44)	86	0.06
Osage	3	0.00
Ottawa (1)	2	0.00
Paiute (6)	9	0.01
Pima (1)	6	0.00
Potawatomi (1)	1	0.00
Pueblo (23)	34	0.02
Puget Sound Salish (1)	1	0.00
Seminole (8)	16	0.01
Shoshone (4)	6	0.00
Sioux (12)	17	0.01
Tohono O'Odham (7)	11	0.01
Ute	3	0.00
Yaqui (15)	37	0.02
Yuman (5)	5	0.00
All other tribes (110)	171	0.11
American Indian tribes, not spec.	203	0.14
Arab:	442	0.30
Arab/Arabic	88	0.06
Egyptian	9	0.01
Iraqi	17	0.01
Jordanian	32	0.02
Lebanese	228	0.15
Moroccan	6	0.00
Palestinian	16	0.01
Syrian	30	0.02
Other Arab	16	0.01
Armenian	183	0.12
Asian:	12,603	8.43
Bangladeshi (20)	20	0.01
Cambodian (923)	1,100	0.74
Chinese, ex. Taiwanese (2,072)	2,446	1.64
Filipino (2,938)	3,335	2.23
Hmong (54)	58	0.04
Indian (729)	873	0.58
Indonesian (140)	232	0.16
Japanese (443)	667	0.45
Korean (633)	688	0.46
Laotian (257)	333	0.22
Malaysian (5)	5	0.00
Pakistani (69)	90	0.06
Sri Lankan (18)	19	0.01
Taiwanese (145)	178	0.12
Thai (190)	240	0.16
Vietnamese (1,643)	1,782	1.19
Other Asian, specified (7)	30	0.02
Other Asian, not specified (182)	507	0.34
Australian	7	0.00
Austrian	139	0.09
Basque	85	0.06
Belgian	44	0.03
Brazilian	10	0.01
British	219	0.15
Canadian	177	0.12
Croatian	27	0.02
Czech	103	0.07
Czechoslovakian	26	0.02
Danish	258	0.17
Dutch	743	0.50
Eastern European	6	0.00
English	3,445	2.30
European	387	0.26
Finnish	25	0.02
French, except Basque	1,678	1.12
French Canadian	208	0.14
German	5,909	3.95
Greek	77	0.05
Guyanese	26	0.02
Hawaii Native/Pacific Islander:	684	0.46
Melanesian: (1)	4	0.00
Fijian (1)	4	0.00
Micronesian: (57)	96	0.06
Guamanian/Chamorro (51)	87	0.06
Other Micronesian (6)	9	0.01
Polynesian: (210)	390	0.26
Native Hawaiian (56)	154	0.10
Samoan (141)	198	0.13
Tongan (6)	13	0.01
Other Polynesian (7)	25	0.02
Other Pac. Isl., specified	2	0.00
Other Pac. Isl., not spec. (38)	192	0.13
Hispanic or Latino:	96,370	64.47
Central American:	3,823	2.56
Costa Rican	71	0.05
Guatemalan	883	0.59

Notes: 1. Figures in the "Number" column do not add up to the total population due to: a) Ancestry/Race overlap — e.g. persons can report being both White and Irish, b) persons of Hispanic origin can report being any race, c) persons reporting two ancestries are counted in both categories. 2. Numbers in parentheses indicate the number of persons reporting this ancestry/race alone, not in combination with any other ancestry/race. 3. Refer to the Explanation of Data in the front of the book for more detailed information.

Ancestry/Race	Number	%
Honduran	342	0.23
Nicaraguan	360	0.24
Panamanian	53	0.04
Salvadoran	1,688	1.13
Other Central American	426	0.29
Cuban	370	0.25
Dominican Republic	16	0.01
Mexican	79,757	53.36
Puerto Rican	602	0.40
South American:	734	0.49
Argentinean	89	0.06
Bolivian	16	0.01
Chilean	44	0.03
Colombian	177	0.12
Ecuadorian	119	0.08
Paraguayan	5	0.00
Peruvian	194	0.13
Uruguayan	9	0.01
Venezuelan	10	0.01
Other South American	71	0.05
Other Hispanic or Latino	11,068	7.40
Hungarian	269	0.18
Icelander	12	0.01
Iranian	137	0.09
Irish	3,990	2.67
Israeli	7	0.00
Italian	2,144	1.43
Lithuanian	73	0.05
Northern European	36	0.02
Norwegian	700	0.47
Pennsylvania German	28	0.02
Polish	683	0.46
Portuguese	147	0.10
Romanian	57	0.04
Russian	345	0.23
Scandinavian	64	0.04
Scotch-Irish	696	0.47
Scottish	696	0.47
Serbian	6	0.00
Slavic	12	0.01
Slovak	60	0.04
Slovene	27	0.02
Swedish	727	0.49
Swiss	107	0.07
Turkish	21	0.01
Ukrainian	79	0.05
United States or American	3,324	2.22
Welsh	326	0.22
West Indian, excl. Hispanic:	210	0.14
Barbadian	14	0.01
Belizean	55	0.04
Haitian	15	0.01
Jamaican	122	0.08
West Indian	4	0.00
White:	68,223	45.64
Not Hispanic (25,348)	26,982	18.05
Hispanic (37,071)	41,241	27.59
Yugoslavian	82	0.05

Port Hueneme

Place Type: City
County: Ventura
Population: 21,845

Ancestry/Race	Number	%
African American/Black:	1,594	7.30
Not Hispanic (1,216)	1,412	6.46
Hispanic (108)	182	0.83
African, sub-Saharan:	210	0.96
African	183	0.84
Nigerian	27	0.12
Am. Ind. or Alaska Nat., not spec.	257	1.18
Albanian	10	0.05
American Indian tribes, specified:	373	1.71
Apache (11)	24	0.11
Blackfeet (2)	13	0.06
Cherokee (25)	89	0.41
Cheyenne	1	0.00
Chickasaw (1)	2	0.01
Chippewa (4)	10	0.05
Choctaw (10)	17	0.08
Comanche (11)	13	0.06
Cree	2	0.01
Creek (1)	5	0.02
Iroquois (1)	3	0.01
Latin American Indians (28)	36	0.16
Navajo (7)	10	0.05
Osage (1)	4	0.02
Ottawa	1	0.00
Paiute (1)	3	0.01
Pima	3	0.01
Potawatomi (1)	3	0.01
Pueblo (4)	6	0.03
Sioux (11)	17	0.08
Tohono O'Odham (4)	8	0.04
Ute (1)	1	0.00
Yaqui (9)	12	0.05
All other tribes (64)	90	0.41
American Indian tribes, not spec.	33	0.15
Arab:	57	0.26
Arab/Arabic	18	0.08
Lebanese	17	0.08
Syrian	22	0.10
Asian:	1,865	8.54
Bangladeshi (5)	5	0.02
Cambodian (5)	13	0.06
Chinese, ex. Taiwanese (44)	86	0.39
Filipino (953)	1,200	5.49
Indian (47)	60	0.27
Indonesian	3	0.01
Japanese (157)	269	1.23
Korean (47)	68	0.31
Laotian (1)	1	0.00
Pakistani (3)	6	0.03
Sri Lankan (1)	1	0.00
Taiwanese (2)	2	0.01
Thai (11)	24	0.11
Vietnamese (78)	83	0.38
Other Asian, specified	7	0.03
Other Asian, not specified (12)	37	0.17
Assyrian/Chaldean/Syriac	12	0.05
Austrian	40	0.18
Basque	21	0.10
Belgian	10	0.05
Brazilian	16	0.07
British	81	0.37
Canadian	55	0.25
Croatian	30	0.14
Czech	92	0.42
Czechoslovakian	6	0.03
Danish	229	1.05
Dutch	326	1.49
Eastern European	36	0.16
English	1,285	5.88
European	150	0.69
Finnish	13	0.06
French, except Basque	413	1.89
French Canadian	61	0.28
German	2,079	9.52
Greek	41	0.19
Hawaii Native/Pacific Islander:	200	0.92
Micronesian: (42)	54	0.25
Guamanian/Chamorro (35)	46	0.21
Other Micronesian (7)	8	0.04
Polynesian: (55)	117	0.54
Native Hawaiian (14)	67	0.31
Samoan (37)	46	0.21
Tongan (4)	4	0.02
Other Pac. Isl., not spec. (12)	29	0.13
Hispanic or Latino:	8,960	41.02
Central American:	125	0.57
Costa Rican	8	0.04
Guatemalan	20	0.09
Honduran	10	0.05
Nicaraguan	9	0.04
Panamanian	15	0.07
Salvadoran	42	0.19
Other Central American	21	0.10
Cuban	23	0.11
Dominican Republic	7	0.03
Mexican	7,520	34.42
Puerto Rican	129	0.59
South American:	59	0.27
Argentinean	5	0.02
Bolivian	2	0.01
Chilean	7	0.03
Colombian	10	0.05
Ecuadorian	2	0.01
Peruvian	14	0.06
Venezuelan	3	0.01
Other South American	16	0.07
Other Hispanic or Latino	1,097	5.02
Hungarian	84	0.38
Iranian	23	0.11
Irish	1,593	7.29
Italian	701	3.21
Lithuanian	47	0.22
Northern European	12	0.05
Norwegian	327	1.50
Polish	270	1.24
Portuguese	96	0.44
Romanian	37	0.17
Russian	93	0.43
Scandinavian	43	0.20
Scotch-Irish	274	1.25
Scottish	432	1.98
Swedish	244	1.12
Swiss	47	0.22
Turkish	12	0.05
United States or American	849	3.89
Welsh	125	0.57
West Indian, excl. Hispanic:	40	0.18
Jamaican	34	0.16
West Indian	6	0.03
White:	13,629	62.39
Not Hispanic (9,321)	9,902	45.33
Hispanic (3,189)	3,727	17.06
Yugoslavian	30	0.14

Porterville

Place Type: City
County: Tulare
Population: 39,615

Ancestry/Race	Number	%
Acadian/Cajun	8	0.02
African American/Black:	658	1.66
Not Hispanic (406)	495	1.25
Hispanic (100)	163	0.41
African, sub-Saharan:	34	0.08
African	34	0.08
Alaska Native tribes, specified:	9	0.02
Eskimo (2)	6	0.02
Tlingit-Haida	3	0.01
Alaska Native tribes, not specified	3	0.01
Am. Ind. or Alaska Nat., not spec.	343	0.87
American Indian tribes, specified:	747	1.89
Apache (20)	30	0.08
Blackfeet (3)	10	0.03
Cherokee (53)	138	0.35
Chickasaw (1)	6	0.02
Chippewa (1)	7	0.02
Choctaw (10)	34	0.09
Colville (2)	2	0.01
Comanche (1)	2	0.01
Creek (2)	6	0.02
Delaware (2)	2	0.01
Kiowa (4)	6	0.02
Latin American Indians (54)	104	0.26
Menominee (1)	7	0.02
Navajo (3)	6	0.02
Osage (1)	5	0.01
Paiute (2)	2	0.01
Pima (1)	1	0.00
Potawatomi (1)	6	0.02
Pueblo (15)	17	0.04
Seminole	1	0.00
Shoshone (1)	7	0.02

Notes: 1. Figures in the "Number" column do not add up to the total population due to: a) Ancestry/Race overlap — e.g. persons can report being both White and Irish, b) persons of Hispanic origin can report being any race, c) persons reporting two ancestries are counted in both categories. 2. Numbers in parentheses indicate the number of persons reporting this ancestry/race alone, not in combination with any other ancestry/race. 3. Refer to the Explanation of Data in the front of the book for more detailed information.

Ancestry/Race	Number	%
Sioux (17)	27	0.07
Tohono O'Odham (4)	5	0.01
Ute	1	0.00
Yakama	1	0.00
Yaqui (8)	15	0.04
All other tribes (231)	299	0.75
American Indian tribes, not spec.	62	0.16
Arab:	112	0.28
Arab/Arabic	88	0.22
Egyptian	7	0.02
Lebanese	7	0.02
Other Arab	10	0.02
Armenian	21	0.05
Asian:	2,254	5.69
Cambodian (12)	21	0.05
Chinese, ex. Taiwanese (125)	160	0.40
Filipino (880)	1,075	2.71
Hmong (195)	216	0.55
Indian (172)	206	0.52
Indonesian (2)	11	0.03
Japanese (49)	80	0.20
Korean (24)	33	0.08
Laotian (238)	289	0.73
Malaysian (1)	1	0.00
Pakistani (34)	47	0.12
Taiwanese (3)	5	0.01
Thai (10)	19	0.05
Vietnamese (16)	18	0.05
Other Asian, specified	1	0.00
Other Asian, not specified (44)	72	0.18
Australian	10	0.02
Austrian	30	0.07
Basque	22	0.05
Belgian	10	0.02
Brazilian	27	0.07
British	13	0.03
Canadian	24	0.06
Celtic	15	0.04
Czech	7	0.02
Danish	102	0.25
Dutch	363	0.91
English	2,302	5.75
European	246	0.61
Finnish	7	0.02
French, except Basque	602	1.50
French Canadian	54	0.13
German	2,092	5.23
Greek	24	0.06
Hawaii Native/Pacific Islander:	143	0.36
Melanesian:	1	0.00
Fijian	1	0.00
Micronesian: (15)	21	0.05
Guamanian/Chamorro (3)	9	0.02
Other Micronesian (12)	12	0.03
Polynesian: (23)	71	0.18
Native Hawaiian (12)	43	0.11
Samoan (10)	24	0.06
Tongan (1)	2	0.01
Other Polynesian	2	0.01
Other Pac. Isl., not spec. (20)	50	0.13
Hispanic or Latino:	19,589	49.45
Central American:	74	0.19
Costa Rican	3	0.01
Guatemalan	19	0.05
Honduran	7	0.02
Nicaraguan	4	0.01
Panamanian	5	0.01
Salvadoran	26	0.07
Other Central American	11	0.03
Cuban	6	0.02
Dominican Republic	1	0.00
Mexican	17,148	43.29
Puerto Rican	78	0.20
South American:	20	0.05
Argentinean	2	0.01
Bolivian	6	0.02
Chilean	2	0.01
Colombian	3	0.01
Ecuadorian	2	0.01
Peruvian	3	0.01
Other South American	2	0.01
Other Hispanic or Latino	2,262	5.71
Hungarian	2	0.00
Icelander	16	0.04
Irish	2,023	5.05
Italian	625	1.56
Lithuanian	11	0.03
Northern European	26	0.06
Norwegian	347	0.87
Pennsylvania German	12	0.03
Polish	147	0.37
Portuguese	196	0.49
Romanian	68	0.17
Russian	57	0.14
Scandinavian	13	0.03
Scotch-Irish	283	0.71
Scottish	257	0.64
Serbian	11	0.03
Swedish	409	1.02
Swiss	95	0.24
Turkish	6	0.01
Ukrainian	25	0.06
United States or American	2,631	6.57
Welsh	29	0.07
West Indian, excl. Hispanic:	13	0.03
Dutch West Indian	7	0.02
Jamaican	6	0.01
White:	23,220	58.61
Not Hispanic (16,649)	17,250	43.54
Hispanic (5,041)	5,970	15.07
Yugoslavian	14	0.03

Poway

Place Type: City
County: San Diego
Population: 48,044

Ancestry/Race	Number	%
Acadian/Cajun	22	0.05
Afghan	40	0.08
African American/Black:	992	2.06
Not Hispanic (752)	903	1.88
Hispanic (48)	89	0.19
African, sub-Saharan:	132	0.27
African	61	0.13
South African	62	0.13
Ugandan	9	0.02
Alaska Native tribes, specified:	6	0.01
Eskimo	5	0.01
Tlingit-Haida	1	0.00
Am. Ind. or Alaska Nat., not spec.	168	0.35
Albanian	12	0.02
American Indian tribes, specified:	385	0.80
Apache (6)	19	0.04
Blackfeet (2)	14	0.03
Cherokee (44)	140	0.29
Cheyenne	2	0.00
Chickasaw (5)	6	0.01
Chippewa (4)	15	0.03
Choctaw (13)	24	0.05
Comanche	1	0.00
Cree	5	0.01
Creek	1	0.00
Delaware (1)	5	0.01
Iroquois (1)	5	0.01
Kiowa	1	0.00
Latin American Indians (17)	24	0.05
Lumbee (1)	2	0.00
Menominee (2)	3	0.01
Navajo (1)	9	0.02
Osage	1	0.00
Paiute	3	0.01
Potawatomi (7)	7	0.01
Pueblo	3	0.01
Puget Sound Salish (1)	2	0.00
Seminole (1)	4	0.01
Shoshone	3	0.01
Sioux (12)	26	0.05
Yaqui (1)	5	0.01
Yuman (1)	2	0.00
All other tribes (30)	53	0.11
American Indian tribes, not spec.	38	0.08
Arab:	175	0.36
Arab/Arabic	24	0.05
Egyptian	40	0.08
Iraqi	17	0.04
Jordanian	6	0.01
Lebanese	63	0.13
Moroccan	18	0.04
Palestinian	7	0.01
Armenian	100	0.21
Asian:	4,485	9.34
Cambodian (13)	15	0.03
Chinese, ex. Taiwanese (638)	782	1.63
Filipino (1,509)	1,858	3.87
Indian (277)	336	0.70
Indonesian (8)	22	0.05
Japanese (302)	528	1.10
Korean (225)	274	0.57
Laotian (21)	33	0.07
Malaysian	1	0.00
Pakistani (27)	30	0.06
Sri Lankan (2)	4	0.01
Taiwanese (128)	149	0.31
Thai (13)	27	0.06
Vietnamese (305)	328	0.68
Other Asian, specified (6)	13	0.03
Other Asian, not specified (30)	85	0.18
Australian	58	0.12
Austrian	239	0.49
Basque	26	0.05
Belgian	173	0.36
Brazilian	17	0.04
British	267	0.55
Bulgarian	34	0.07
Canadian	130	0.27
Celtic	9	0.02
Croatian	49	0.10
Czech	230	0.48
Czechoslovakian	97	0.20
Danish	543	1.12
Dutch	904	1.87
Eastern European	67	0.14
English	5,866	12.15
Estonian	26	0.05
European	1,285	2.66
Finnish	185	0.38
French, except Basque	2,226	4.61
French Canadian	458	0.95
German	8,812	18.25
German Russian	10	0.02
Greek	224	0.46
Guyanese	52	0.11
Hawaii Native/Pacific Islander:	309	0.64
Micronesian: (57)	103	0.21
Guamanian/Chamorro (54)	97	0.20
Other Micronesian (3)	6	0.01
Polynesian: (64)	166	0.35
Native Hawaiian (46)	139	0.29
Samoan (18)	26	0.05
Other Polynesian	1	0.00
Other Pac. Isl., not spec. (12)	40	0.08
Hispanic or Latino:	4,974	10.35
Central American:	119	0.25
Costa Rican	25	0.05
Guatemalan	25	0.05
Honduran	8	0.02
Nicaraguan	23	0.05
Panamanian	15	0.03
Salvadoran	22	0.05
Other Central American	1	0.00
Cuban	48	0.10
Dominican Republic	11	0.02
Mexican	3,655	7.61
Puerto Rican	228	0.47
South American:	133	0.28
Argentinean	3	0.01
Bolivian	4	0.01
Chilean	13	0.03

Notes: 1. Figures in the "Number" column do not add up to the total population due to: a) Ancestry/Race overlap — e.g. persons can report being both White and Irish, b) persons of Hispanic origin can report being any race, c) persons reporting two ancestries are counted in both categories. 2. Numbers in parentheses indicate the number of persons reporting this ancestry/race alone, not in combination with any other ancestry/race. 3. Refer to the Explanation of Data in the front of the book for more detailed information.

Colombian	37	0.08
Ecuadorian	14	0.03
Peruvian	39	0.08
Venezuelan	11	0.02
Other South American	12	0.02
Other Hispanic or Latino	780	1.62
Hungarian	438	0.91
Icelander	33	0.07
Iranian	176	0.36
Irish	6,363	13.18
Israeli	37	0.08
Italian	3,310	6.85
Latvian	60	0.12
Lithuanian	189	0.39
Luxemburger	6	0.01
Maltese	34	0.07
Northern European	67	0.14
Norwegian	1,036	2.15
Pennsylvania German	22	0.05
Polish	1,673	3.46
Portuguese	213	0.44
Romanian	58	0.12
Russian	753	1.56
Scandinavian	48	0.10
Scotch-Irish	924	1.91
Scottish	1,284	2.66
Slavic	13	0.03
Slovak	98	0.20
Slovene	16	0.03
Swedish	1,018	2.11
Swiss	237	0.49
Turkish	28	0.06
Ukrainian	181	0.37
United States or American	2,763	5.72
Welsh	474	0.98
West Indian, excl. Hispanic:	20	0.04
Belizean	6	0.01
Jamaican	14	0.03
White:	41,548	86.48
Not Hispanic (37,092)	38,286	79.69
Hispanic (2,715)	3,262	6.79
Yugoslavian	46	0.10

Prunedale

Place Type: Census Designated Place
County: Monterey
Population: 16,432

Ancestry/Race	Number	%
African American/Black:	298	1.81
Not Hispanic (201)	281	1.71
Hispanic (8)	17	0.10
African, sub-Saharan:	2	0.01
African	2	0.01
Am. Ind. or Alaska Nat., not spec.	150	0.91
American Indian tribes, specified:	258	1.57
Apache (4)	18	0.11
Blackfeet (2)	8	0.05
Cherokee (24)	90	0.55
Chickasaw (2)	5	0.03
Chippewa	2	0.01
Choctaw (4)	15	0.09
Creek (5)	5	0.03
Delaware	3	0.02
Iroquois (1)	2	0.01
Latin American Indians (16)	34	0.21
Navajo (4)	7	0.04
Osage	3	0.02
Paiute	1	0.01
Pima	1	0.01
Potawatomi (1)	5	0.03
Pueblo (2)	5	0.03
Shoshone (2)	5	0.03
Sioux (5)	11	0.07
Yaqui (2)	5	0.03
All other tribes (15)	33	0.20
American Indian tribes, not spec.	12	0.07
Arab:	20	0.12
Arab/Arabic	7	0.04
Egyptian	13	0.08
Armenian	8	0.05
Asian:	923	5.62
Cambodian (6)	6	0.04
Chinese, ex. Taiwanese (46)	72	0.44
Filipino (254)	397	2.42
Indian (41)	58	0.35
Indonesian	2	0.01
Japanese (120)	230	1.40
Korean (75)	100	0.61
Sri Lankan (1)	1	0.01
Taiwanese (1)	4	0.02
Vietnamese (31)	36	0.22
Other Asian, specified (2)	2	0.01
Other Asian, not specified (8)	15	0.09
Austrian	100	0.60
Belgian	19	0.11
Brazilian	11	0.07
British	179	1.08
Bulgarian	7	0.04
Canadian	29	0.17
Celtic	10	0.06
Croatian	27	0.16
Czech	49	0.29
Czechoslovakian	15	0.09
Danish	244	1.47
Dutch	222	1.33
Eastern European	11	0.07
English	1,947	11.70
European	148	0.89
Finnish	31	0.19
French, except Basque	553	3.32
French Canadian	85	0.51
German	2,306	13.86
Greek	69	0.41
Hawaii Native/Pacific Islander:	100	0.61
Micronesian: (9)	21	0.13
Guamanian/Chamorro (8)	20	0.12
Other Micronesian (1)	1	0.01
Polynesian: (15)	63	0.38
Native Hawaiian (13)	47	0.29
Samoan (2)	11	0.07
Tongan	5	0.03
Other Pac. Isl., not spec. (4)	16	0.10
Hispanic or Latino:	3,781	23.01
Central American:	39	0.24
Costa Rican	2	0.01
Guatemalan	8	0.05
Honduran	3	0.02
Nicaraguan	2	0.01
Panamanian	10	0.06
Salvadoran	14	0.09
Cuban	19	0.12
Mexican	3,236	19.69
Puerto Rican	46	0.28
South American:	26	0.16
Argentinean	2	0.01
Chilean	3	0.02
Colombian	10	0.06
Peruvian	8	0.05
Venezuelan	2	0.01
Other South American	1	0.01
Other Hispanic or Latino	415	2.53
Hungarian	84	0.50
Iranian	52	0.31
Irish	1,737	10.44
Italian	971	5.83
Lithuanian	17	0.10
Maltese	5	0.03
Northern European	25	0.15
Norwegian	272	1.63
Polish	210	1.26
Portuguese	613	3.68
Romanian	22	0.13
Russian	129	0.78
Scandinavian	51	0.31
Scotch-Irish	385	2.31
Scottish	253	1.52
Slavic	18	0.11
Slovak	10	0.06
Slovene	49	0.29
Swedish	265	1.59
Swiss	159	0.96
Ukrainian	7	0.04
United States or American	1,289	7.75
Welsh	96	0.58
West Indian, excl. Hispanic:	9	0.05
Haitian	9	0.05
White:	13,448	81.84
Not Hispanic (11,168)	11,695	71.17
Hispanic (1,480)	1,753	10.67
Yugoslavian	30	0.18

Ramona

Place Type: Census Designated Place
County: San Diego
Population: 15,691

Ancestry/Race	Number	%
African American/Black:	171	1.09
Not Hispanic (117)	154	0.98
Hispanic (5)	17	0.11
Alaska Native tribes, specified:	1	0.01
Tlingit-Haida	1	0.01
Am. Ind. or Alaska Nat., not spec.	97	0.62
American Indian tribes, specified:	283	1.80
Apache (6)	15	0.10
Blackfeet (1)	4	0.03
Cherokee (15)	73	0.47
Cheyenne	6	0.04
Chickasaw (10)	10	0.06
Chippewa	5	0.03
Choctaw (4)	10	0.06
Comanche (5)	5	0.03
Cree (1)	2	0.01
Creek (1)	9	0.06
Crow (1)	2	0.01
Iroquois (3)	4	0.03
Latin American Indians (12)	19	0.12
Menominee	1	0.01
Navajo (9)	16	0.10
Paiute	1	0.01
Pima	2	0.01
Potawatomi (6)	6	0.04
Pueblo (3)	6	0.04
Seminole (1)	2	0.01
Shoshone	1	0.01
Sioux (1)	10	0.06
Ute (1)	1	0.01
Yaqui (1)	1	0.01
All other tribes (54)	72	0.46
American Indian tribes, not spec.	16	0.10
Arab:	13	0.08
Iraqi	8	0.05
Other Arab	5	0.03
Asian:	215	1.37
Cambodian (1)	5	0.03
Chinese, ex. Taiwanese (18)	32	0.20
Filipino (47)	78	0.50
Indian	3	0.02
Japanese (22)	58	0.37
Korean (5)	5	0.03
Laotian (2)	2	0.01
Pakistani	1	0.01
Taiwanese (3)	3	0.02
Thai (2)	3	0.02
Vietnamese (11)	12	0.08
Other Asian, specified	3	0.02
Other Asian, not specified (5)	10	0.06
Australian	9	0.06
Austrian	8	0.05
British	38	0.24
Canadian	50	0.32
Celtic	8	0.05
Croatian	38	0.24
Czech	15	0.10
Czechoslovakian	81	0.52
Danish	197	1.25
Dutch	285	1.81

Notes: 1. Figures in the "Number" column do not add up to the total population due to: a) Ancestry/Race overlap — e.g. persons can report being both White and Irish, b) persons of Hispanic origin can report being any race, c) persons reporting two ancestries are counted in both categories. 2. Numbers in parentheses indicate the number of persons reporting this ancestry/race alone, not in combination with any other ancestry/race. 3. Refer to the Explanation of Data in the front of the book for more detailed information.

Ancestry/Race	Number	%
English	1,133	7.21
European	190	1.21
Finnish	48	0.31
French, except Basque	663	4.22
French Canadian	140	0.89
German	2,646	16.84
Greek	84	0.53
Hawaii Native/Pacific Islander:	71	0.45
Micronesian: (10)	14	0.09
Guamanian/Chamorro (10)	14	0.09
Polynesian: (29)	46	0.29
Native Hawaiian (22)	37	0.24
Samoan (7)	7	0.04
Tongan	2	0.01
Other Pac. Isl., specified	3	0.02
Other Pac. Isl., not spec. (4)	8	0.05
Hispanic or Latino:	3,921	24.99
Central American:	45	0.29
Guatemalan	14	0.09
Honduran	8	0.05
Nicaraguan	7	0.04
Panamanian	1	0.01
Salvadoran	12	0.08
Other Central American	3	0.02
Cuban	20	0.13
Dominican Republic	1	0.01
Mexican	3,291	20.97
Puerto Rican	30	0.19
South American:	15	0.10
Argentinean	1	0.01
Chilean	1	0.01
Colombian	4	0.03
Peruvian	8	0.05
Venezuelan	1	0.01
Other Hispanic or Latino	519	3.31
Hungarian	37	0.24
Iranian	32	0.20
Irish	1,605	10.22
Israeli	5	0.03
Italian	799	5.09
Lithuanian	18	0.11
Norwegian	367	2.34
Polish	262	1.67
Portuguese	130	0.83
Russian	124	0.79
Scandinavian	20	0.13
Scotch-Irish	338	2.15
Scottish	376	2.39
Serbian	102	0.65
Slavic	8	0.05
Slovak	10	0.06
Swedish	381	2.43
Swiss	70	0.45
Ukrainian	7	0.04
United States or American	903	5.75
Welsh	47	0.30
West Indian, excl. Hispanic:	9	0.06
Jamaican	9	0.06
White:	13,203	84.14
Not Hispanic (11,013)	11,291	71.96
Hispanic (1,634)	1,912	12.19
Yugoslavian	18	0.11

Rancho Cordova

Place Type: Census Designated Place
County: Sacramento
Population: 55,060

Ancestry/Race	Number	%
Acadian/Cajun	13	0.02
Afghan	36	0.07
African American/Black:	7,251	13.17
Not Hispanic (6,075)	6,930	12.59
Hispanic (170)	321	0.58
African, sub-Saharan:	431	0.79
African	316	0.58
Ghanian	19	0.03
Nigerian	96	0.18
Alaska Native tribes, specified:	6	0.01
Aleut (3)	3	0.01
Eskimo	2	0.00
Tlingit-Haida (1)	1	0.00
Alaska Native tribes, not specified	1	0.00
Am. Ind. or Alaska Nat., not spec.	367	0.67
Alsatian	9	0.02
American Indian tribes, specified:	909	1.65
Apache (18)	51	0.09
Blackfeet (6)	50	0.09
Cherokee (79)	317	0.58
Cheyenne (1)	2	0.00
Chickasaw (5)	11	0.02
Chippewa (7)	17	0.03
Choctaw (37)	75	0.14
Comanche (6)	10	0.02
Cree (3)	6	0.01
Creek (4)	11	0.02
Crow	1	0.00
Delaware	4	0.01
Iroquois (9)	18	0.03
Kiowa (1)	4	0.01
Latin American Indians (13)	35	0.06
Menominee (1)	2	0.00
Navajo (11)	25	0.05
Osage (2)	7	0.01
Ottawa (1)	1	0.00
Paiute (6)	12	0.02
Pima (4)	4	0.01
Potawatomi (9)	14	0.03
Pueblo (10)	14	0.03
Puget Sound Salish	2	0.00
Seminole (5)	9	0.02
Shoshone (2)	10	0.02
Sioux (14)	30	0.05
Ute	1	0.00
Yakama (3)	3	0.01
Yaqui (2)	8	0.01
Yuman (1)	5	0.01
All other tribes (86)	150	0.27
American Indian tribes, not spec.	37	0.07
Arab:	166	0.30
Egyptian	30	0.05
Iraqi	7	0.01
Lebanese	70	0.13
Moroccan	17	0.03
Palestinian	5	0.01
Syrian	25	0.05
Other Arab	12	0.02
Armenian	957	1.75
Asian:	5,888	10.69
Bangladeshi (4)	7	0.01
Cambodian (17)	29	0.05
Chinese, ex. Taiwanese (438)	598	1.09
Filipino (1,170)	1,647	2.99
Hmong (297)	326	0.59
Indian (683)	848	1.54
Indonesian (11)	16	0.03
Japanese (344)	611	1.11
Korean (499)	579	1.05
Laotian (80)	118	0.21
Malaysian (8)	10	0.02
Pakistani (48)	55	0.10
Sri Lankan (10)	11	0.02
Taiwanese (12)	17	0.03
Thai (53)	89	0.16
Vietnamese (724)	781	1.42
Other Asian, specified (1)	11	0.02
Other Asian, not specified (39)	135	0.25
Assyrian/Chaldean/Syriac	7	0.01
Australian	27	0.05
Austrian	63	0.12
Basque	48	0.09
Belgian	65	0.12
British	225	0.41
Bulgarian	6	0.01
Canadian	85	0.16
Celtic	45	0.08
Croatian	61	0.11
Czech	119	0.22
Czechoslovakian	28	0.05
Danish	355	0.65
Dutch	725	1.33
English	4,613	8.45
European	290	0.53
Finnish	141	0.26
French, except Basque	1,700	3.11
French Canadian	352	0.64
German	7,228	13.24
Greek	128	0.23
Hawaii Native/Pacific Islander:	669	1.22
Melanesian: (73)	151	0.27
Fijian (73)	151	0.27
Micronesian: (32)	55	0.10
Guamanian/Chamorro (31)	54	0.10
Other Micronesian (1)	1	0.00
Polynesian: (153)	334	0.61
Native Hawaiian (46)	182	0.33
Samoan (81)	107	0.19
Tongan (26)	45	0.08
Other Pac. Isl., specified	1	0.00
Other Pac. Isl., not spec. (30)	128	0.23
Hispanic or Latino:	7,100	12.90
Central American:	337	0.61
Costa Rican	4	0.01
Guatemalan	51	0.09
Honduran	25	0.05
Nicaraguan	61	0.11
Panamanian	13	0.02
Salvadoran	150	0.27
Other Central American	33	0.06
Cuban	51	0.09
Dominican Republic	12	0.02
Mexican	4,969	9.02
Puerto Rican	359	0.65
South American:	132	0.24
Argentinean	5	0.01
Bolivian	6	0.01
Chilean	16	0.03
Colombian	24	0.04
Ecuadorian	7	0.01
Paraguayan	1	0.00
Peruvian	50	0.09
Uruguayan	1	0.00
Venezuelan	3	0.01
Other South American	19	0.03
Other Hispanic or Latino	1,240	2.25
Hungarian	186	0.34
Iranian	65	0.12
Irish	5,447	9.98
Israeli	21	0.04
Italian	2,177	3.99
Latvian	37	0.07
Lithuanian	64	0.12
Maltese	64	0.12
New Zealander	14	0.03
Northern European	68	0.12
Norwegian	1,006	1.84
Pennsylvania German	10	0.02
Polish	779	1.43
Portuguese	569	1.04
Romanian	242	0.44
Russian	1,222	2.24
Scandinavian	157	0.29
Scotch-Irish	823	1.51
Scottish	885	1.62
Serbian	18	0.03
Slavic	46	0.08
Slovak	27	0.05
Slovene	35	0.06
Swedish	990	1.81
Swiss	175	0.32
Turkish	69	0.13
Ukrainian	2,083	3.82
United States or American	2,585	4.74
Welsh	403	0.74
West Indian, excl. Hispanic:	134	0.25
Belizean	15	0.03
Haitian	21	0.04
Jamaican	45	0.08
West Indian	53	0.10

Notes: 1. Figures in the "Number" column do not add up to the total population due to: a) Ancestry/Race overlap — e.g. persons can report being both White and Irish, b) persons of Hispanic origin can report being any race, c) persons reporting two ancestries are counted in both categories. 2. Numbers in parentheses indicate the number of persons reporting this ancestry/race alone, not in combination with any other ancestry/race. 3. Refer to the Explanation of Data in the front of the book for more detailed information.

Ancestry/Race	Number	%
White:	39,561	71.85
Not Hispanic (33,790)	36,028	65.43
Hispanic (2,914)	3,533	6.42
Yugoslavian	108	0.20

Rancho Cucamonga

Place Type: City
County: San Bernardino
Population: 127,743

Ancestry/Race	Number	%
Acadian/Cajun	25	0.02
Afghan	159	0.12
African American/Black:	11,325	8.87
Not Hispanic (9,789)	10,784	8.44
Hispanic (270)	541	0.42
African, sub-Saharan:	613	0.48
African	472	0.37
Ethiopian	33	0.03
Ghanian	27	0.02
Nigerian	29	0.02
South African	36	0.03
Other sub-Saharan African	16	0.01
Alaska Native tribes, specified:	10	0.01
Alaska Athabascan (1)	5	0.00
Eskimo (1)	3	0.00
Tlingit-Haida (2)	2	0.00
Alaska Native tribes, not specified	4	0.00
Am. Ind. or Alaska Nat., not spec.	664	0.52
Albanian	17	0.01
Alsatian	16	0.01
American Indian tribes, specified:	1,385	1.08
Apache (41)	91	0.07
Blackfeet (13)	81	0.06
Cherokee (71)	366	0.29
Cheyenne	1	0.00
Chickasaw (2)	8	0.01
Chippewa (5)	27	0.02
Choctaw (26)	83	0.06
Colville (3)	7	0.01
Comanche (9)	15	0.01
Cree	7	0.01
Creek (10)	33	0.03
Crow (1)	2	0.00
Delaware (1)	1	0.00
Iroquois (6)	16	0.01
Kiowa	2	0.00
Latin American Indians (101)	166	0.13
Lumbee (4)	8	0.01
Navajo (46)	106	0.08
Osage (1)	7	0.01
Ottawa (1)	1	0.00
Paiute (5)	13	0.01
Pima (9)	13	0.01
Potawatomi (4)	7	0.01
Pueblo (23)	41	0.03
Seminole (4)	12	0.01
Shoshone (8)	15	0.01
Sioux (23)	58	0.05
Tohono O'Odham (1)	3	0.00
Ute (5)	8	0.01
Yakama (1)	4	0.00
Yaqui (17)	49	0.04
Yuman (6)	11	0.01
All other tribes (68)	123	0.10
American Indian tribes, not spec.	79	0.06
Arab:	1,866	1.46
Arab/Arabic	853	0.67
Egyptian	285	0.22
Iraqi	41	0.03
Jordanian	84	0.07
Lebanese	243	0.19
Moroccan	10	0.01
Palestinian	51	0.04
Syrian	259	0.20
Other Arab	40	0.03
Armenian	164	0.13
Asian:	9,645	7.55
Bangladeshi (19)	20	0.02
Cambodian (63)	77	0.06
Chinese, ex. Taiwanese (1,145)	1,470	1.15
Filipino (2,440)	3,050	2.39
Hmong (11)	11	0.01
Indian (883)	1,005	0.79
Indonesian (233)	380	0.30
Japanese (480)	873	0.68
Korean (887)	976	0.76
Laotian (15)	19	0.01
Malaysian (4)	9	0.01
Pakistani (160)	196	0.15
Sri Lankan (28)	37	0.03
Taiwanese (183)	223	0.17
Thai (207)	256	0.20
Vietnamese (570)	622	0.49
Other Asian, specified (22)	39	0.03
Other Asian, not specified (135)	382	0.30
Assyrian/Chaldean/Syriac	91	0.07
Australian	87	0.07
Austrian	123	0.10
Basque	209	0.16
Belgian	151	0.12
Brazilian	75	0.06
British	523	0.41
Bulgarian	91	0.07
Canadian	457	0.36
Celtic	23	0.02
Croatian	85	0.07
Czech	264	0.21
Czechoslovakian	265	0.21
Danish	894	0.70
Dutch	2,242	1.75
Eastern European	7	0.01
English	10,592	8.26
Estonian	9	0.01
European	1,610	1.26
Finnish	82	0.06
French, except Basque	3,870	3.02
French Canadian	954	0.74
German	16,525	12.89
German Russian	16	0.01
Greek	457	0.36
Guyanese	59	0.05
Hawaii Native/Pacific Islander:	748	0.59
Melanesian:	2	0.00
Other Melanesian	2	0.00
Micronesian: (32)	62	0.05
Guamanian/Chamorro (30)	56	0.04
Other Micronesian (2)	6	0.00
Polynesian: (278)	544	0.43
Native Hawaiian (60)	205	0.16
Samoan (75)	116	0.09
Tongan (106)	160	0.13
Other Polynesian (37)	63	0.05
Other Pac. Isl., not spec. (16)	140	0.11
Hispanic or Latino:	35,491	27.78
Central American:	1,217	0.95
Costa Rican	105	0.08
Guatemalan	322	0.25
Honduran	50	0.04
Nicaraguan	179	0.14
Panamanian	44	0.03
Salvadoran	361	0.28
Other Central American	156	0.12
Cuban	457	0.36
Dominican Republic	30	0.02
Mexican	26,537	20.77
Puerto Rican	841	0.66
South American:	1,150	0.90
Argentinean	250	0.20
Bolivian	32	0.03
Chilean	83	0.06
Colombian	248	0.19
Ecuadorian	132	0.10
Paraguayan	4	0.00
Peruvian	284	0.22
Uruguayan	1	0.00
Venezuelan	27	0.02
Other South American	89	0.07
Other Hispanic or Latino	5,259	4.12
Hungarian	724	0.56
Icelander	11	0.01
Iranian	383	0.30
Irish	11,717	9.14
Israeli	32	0.02
Italian	7,878	6.15
Latvian	22	0.02
Lithuanian	199	0.16
Luxemburger	6	0.00
Maltese	8	0.01
New Zealander	8	0.01
Northern European	92	0.07
Norwegian	1,811	1.41
Pennsylvania German	21	0.02
Polish	2,442	1.91
Portuguese	480	0.37
Romanian	214	0.17
Russian	1,118	0.87
Scandinavian	177	0.14
Scotch-Irish	1,931	1.51
Scottish	2,279	1.78
Serbian	40	0.03
Slavic	58	0.05
Slovak	111	0.09
Slovene	70	0.05
Soviet Union	11	0.01
Swedish	2,076	1.62
Swiss	455	0.36
Turkish	87	0.07
Ukrainian	203	0.16
United States or American	5,867	4.58
Welsh	801	0.62
West Indian, excl. Hispanic:	404	0.32
British West Indian	8	0.01
Haitian	83	0.06
Jamaican	197	0.15
Trinidadian and Tobagonian	49	0.04
U.S. Virgin Islander	14	0.01
West Indian	53	0.04
White:	90,760	71.05
Not Hispanic (70,028)	73,288	57.37
Hispanic (14,959)	17,472	13.68
Yugoslavian	269	0.21

Rancho Mirage

Place Type: City
County: Riverside
Population: 13,249

Ancestry/Race	Number	%
African American/Black:	166	1.25
Not Hispanic (115)	161	1.22
Hispanic (3)	5	0.04
Am. Ind. or Alaska Nat., not spec.	26	0.20
Albanian	10	0.08
Alsatian	9	0.07
American Indian tribes, specified:	45	0.34
Apache	2	0.02
Blackfeet	1	0.01
Cherokee (5)	17	0.13
Chickasaw (1)	1	0.01
Choctaw	1	0.01
Cree	1	0.01
Delaware	1	0.01
Iroquois	3	0.02
Latin American Indians (4)	6	0.05
Osage (1)	1	0.01
Pueblo (4)	4	0.03
Shoshone (1)	1	0.01
Sioux (1)	2	0.02
Yaqui	1	0.01
All other tribes (2)	3	0.02
American Indian tribes, not spec.	10	0.08
Arab:	38	0.29
Egyptian	8	0.06
Lebanese	10	0.08
Moroccan	7	0.05
Syrian	13	0.10
Armenian	63	0.49

Notes: 1. Figures in the "Number" column do not add up to the total population due to: a) Ancestry/Race overlap — e.g. persons can report being both White and Irish, b) persons of Hispanic origin can report being any race, c) persons reporting two ancestries are counted in both categories. 2. Numbers in parentheses indicate the number of persons reporting this ancestry/race alone, not in combination with any other ancestry/race. 3. Refer to the Explanation of Data in the front of the book for more detailed information.

Ancestry/Race	Number	%
Asian:	203	1.53
Chinese, ex. Taiwanese (21)	28	0.21
Filipino (47)	61	0.46
Indian (34)	35	0.26
Japanese (34)	37	0.28
Korean (5)	7	0.05
Taiwanese (5)	7	0.05
Thai (7)	7	0.05
Vietnamese (9)	11	0.08
Other Asian, specified (1)	1	0.01
Other Asian, not specified	9	0.07
Australian	13	0.10
Austrian	153	1.18
Belgian	9	0.07
Brazilian	38	0.29
British	139	1.07
Bulgarian	59	0.45
Canadian	197	1.52
Croatian	17	0.13
Czech	110	0.85
Czechoslovakian	24	0.18
Danish	196	1.51
Dutch	214	1.65
Eastern European	17	0.13
English	2,257	17.40
European	74	0.57
Finnish	14	0.11
French, except Basque	634	4.89
French Canadian	135	1.04
German	2,019	15.56
Greek	113	0.87
Hawaii Native/Pacific Islander:	24	0.18
Micronesian: (4)	7	0.05
Guamanian/Chamorro (3)	6	0.05
Other Micronesian (1)	1	0.01
Polynesian: (10)	16	0.12
Native Hawaiian (3)	6	0.05
Samoan (6)	6	0.05
Tongan	1	0.01
Other Polynesian (1)	3	0.02
Other Pac. Isl., not spec.	1	0.01
Hispanic or Latino:	1,251	9.44
Central American:	59	0.45
Costa Rican	3	0.02
Guatemalan	11	0.08
Honduran	10	0.08
Nicaraguan	10	0.08
Panamanian	3	0.02
Salvadoran	15	0.11
Other Central American	7	0.05
Cuban	16	0.12
Mexican	959	7.24
Puerto Rican	25	0.19
South American:	28	0.21
Argentinean	6	0.05
Bolivian	1	0.01
Chilean	6	0.05
Colombian	10	0.08
Paraguayan	1	0.01
Peruvian	2	0.02
Venezuelan	1	0.01
Other South American	1	0.01
Other Hispanic or Latino	164	1.24
Hungarian	211	1.63
Icelander	22	0.17
Iranian	31	0.24
Irish	1,529	11.79
Israeli	22	0.17
Italian	703	5.42
Latvian	3	0.02
Lithuanian	82	0.63
Norwegian	312	2.40
Polish	326	2.51
Portuguese	28	0.22
Romanian	96	0.74
Russian	682	5.26
Scandinavian	63	0.49
Scotch-Irish	326	2.51
Scottish	367	2.83
Slovak	8	0.06
Slovene	9	0.07
Swedish	321	2.47
Swiss	50	0.39
Ukrainian	34	0.26
United States or American	591	4.56
Welsh	161	1.24
White:	12,410	93.67
Not Hispanic (11,559)	11,646	87.90
Hispanic (721)	764	5.77
Yugoslavian	11	0.08

Rancho Palos Verdes

Place Type: City
County: Los Angeles
Population: 41,145

Ancestry/Race	Number	%
African American/Black:	998	2.43
Not Hispanic (803)	967	2.35
Hispanic (12)	31	0.08
African, sub-Saharan:	167	0.40
African	52	0.13
Kenyan	21	0.05
Nigerian	87	0.21
South African	7	0.02
Alaska Native tribes, specified:	4	0.01
Alaska Athabascan (1)	2	0.00
Eskimo (1)	1	0.00
Tlingit-Haida (1)	1	0.00
Alaska Native tribes, not specified	1	0.00
Am. Ind. or Alaska Nat., not spec.	75	0.18
Albanian	30	0.07
Alsatian	9	0.02
American Indian tribes, specified:	151	0.37
Apache (6)	13	0.03
Blackfeet	11	0.03
Cherokee (9)	42	0.10
Chickasaw (1)	3	0.01
Chippewa (3)	3	0.01
Choctaw (2)	10	0.02
Cree	2	0.00
Delaware (1)	1	0.00
Iroquois (1)	2	0.00
Latin American Indians (4)	25	0.06
Lumbee (3)	3	0.01
Navajo (1)	4	0.01
Osage	1	0.00
Potawatomi	1	0.00
Pueblo	1	0.00
Seminole	2	0.00
Sioux (2)	8	0.02
Yaqui (1)	1	0.00
All other tribes (5)	18	0.04
American Indian tribes, not spec.	15	0.04
Arab:	382	0.92
Arab/Arabic	29	0.07
Egyptian	109	0.26
Jordanian	45	0.11
Lebanese	94	0.23
Palestinian	6	0.01
Syrian	47	0.11
Other Arab	52	0.13
Armenian	292	0.71
Asian:	11,817	28.72
Bangladeshi (3)	3	0.01
Cambodian (3)	12	0.03
Chinese, ex. Taiwanese (2,783)	3,166	7.69
Filipino (633)	820	1.99
Indian (672)	765	1.86
Indonesian (14)	27	0.07
Japanese (3,268)	3,679	8.94
Korean (2,045)	2,130	5.18
Malaysian (10)	14	0.03
Pakistani (70)	92	0.22
Sri Lankan (13)	13	0.03
Taiwanese (695)	813	1.98
Thai (18)	26	0.06
Vietnamese (95)	111	0.27
Other Asian, specified (19)	28	0.07
Other Asian, not specified (36)	118	0.29
Assyrian/Chaldean/Syriac	16	0.04
Australian	32	0.08
Austrian	326	0.79
Basque	20	0.05
Belgian	40	0.10
Brazilian	56	0.14
British	316	0.77
Canadian	227	0.55
Croatian	579	1.40
Czech	141	0.34
Czechoslovakian	118	0.29
Danish	399	0.97
Dutch	634	1.54
Eastern European	99	0.24
English	4,963	12.02
Estonian	23	0.06
European	641	1.55
Finnish	94	0.23
French, except Basque	1,129	2.73
French Canadian	166	0.40
German	4,774	11.56
Greek	325	0.79
Hawaii Native/Pacific Islander:	113	0.27
Melanesian: (1)	1	0.00
Fijian (1)	1	0.00
Micronesian: (7)	12	0.03
Guamanian/Chamorro (7)	11	0.03
Other Micronesian	1	0.00
Polynesian: (25)	61	0.15
Native Hawaiian (17)	50	0.12
Samoan (8)	11	0.03
Other Pac. Isl., specified	1	0.00
Other Pac. Isl., not spec. (6)	38	0.09
Hispanic or Latino:	2,339	5.68
Central American:	109	0.26
Costa Rican	18	0.04
Guatemalan	30	0.07
Honduran	10	0.02
Nicaraguan	12	0.03
Panamanian	4	0.01
Salvadoran	35	0.09
Cuban	74	0.18
Dominican Republic	6	0.01
Mexican	1,340	3.26
Puerto Rican	86	0.21
South American:	252	0.61
Argentinean	42	0.10
Bolivian	1	0.00
Chilean	35	0.09
Colombian	58	0.14
Ecuadorian	33	0.08
Peruvian	52	0.13
Uruguayan	1	0.00
Venezuelan	10	0.02
Other South American	20	0.05
Other Hispanic or Latino	472	1.15
Hungarian	397	0.96
Icelander	14	0.03
Iranian	1,004	2.43
Irish	3,782	9.16
Israeli	22	0.05
Italian	2,786	6.75
Latvian	10	0.02
Lithuanian	157	0.38
Macedonian	25	0.06
New Zealander	31	0.08
Northern European	78	0.19
Norwegian	866	2.10
Pennsylvania German	28	0.07
Polish	1,079	2.61
Portuguese	107	0.26
Romanian	152	0.37
Russian	946	2.29
Scandinavian	51	0.12
Scotch-Irish	751	1.82
Scottish	881	2.13
Serbian	6	0.01
Slavic	55	0.13
Slovak	84	0.20

Notes: 1. Figures in the "Number" column do not add up to the total population due to: a) Ancestry/Race overlap — e.g. persons can report being both White and Irish, b) persons of Hispanic origin can report being any race, c) persons reporting two ancestries are counted in both categories. 2. Numbers in parentheses indicate the number of persons reporting this ancestry/race alone, not in combination with any other ancestry/race. 3. Refer to the Explanation of Data in the front of the book for more detailed information.

Ancestry/Race	Number	%
Slovene	15	0.04
Swedish	850	2.06
Swiss	298	0.72
Turkish	83	0.20
Ukrainian	134	0.32
United States or American	1,784	4.32
Welsh	390	0.94
West Indian, excl. Hispanic:	58	0.14
Jamaican	42	0.10
West Indian	16	0.04
White:	28,846	70.11
Not Hispanic (25,979)	27,017	65.66
Hispanic (1,681)	1,829	4.45
Yugoslavian	381	0.92

Rancho San Diego

Place Type: Census Designated Place
County: San Diego
Population: 20,155

Ancestry/Race	Number	%
African American/Black:	768	3.81
Not Hispanic (635)	729	3.62
Hispanic (21)	39	0.19
African, sub-Saharan:	83	0.41
African	70	0.35
Other sub-Saharan African	13	0.06
Am. Ind. or Alaska Nat., not spec.	61	0.30
American Indian tribes, specified:	144	0.71
Apache (2)	13	0.06
Blackfeet (2)	5	0.02
Cherokee (15)	30	0.15
Chippewa (1)	3	0.01
Choctaw (2)	4	0.02
Cree	1	0.00
Creek (3)	4	0.02
Crow (1)	1	0.00
Iroquois (1)	1	0.00
Latin American Indians (16)	21	0.10
Lumbee	4	0.02
Navajo	2	0.01
Potawatomi	2	0.01
Pueblo	4	0.02
Puget Sound Salish (1)	2	0.01
Sioux (7)	9	0.04
Yaqui (3)	10	0.05
Yuman (1)	1	0.00
All other tribes (22)	27	0.13
American Indian tribes, not spec.	12	0.06
Arab:	942	4.70
Arab/Arabic	358	1.79
Egyptian	8	0.04
Iraqi	448	2.24
Jordanian	79	0.39
Lebanese	16	0.08
Palestinian	3	0.01
Other Arab	30	0.15
Armenian	43	0.21
Asian:	1,222	6.06
Cambodian (10)	12	0.06
Chinese, ex. Taiwanese (116)	161	0.80
Filipino (382)	531	2.63
Indian (69)	89	0.44
Indonesian (2)	8	0.04
Japanese (92)	173	0.86
Korean (52)	81	0.40
Laotian (6)	6	0.03
Pakistani	4	0.02
Sri Lankan	1	0.00
Taiwanese (1)	1	0.00
Thai (11)	20	0.10
Vietnamese (61)	65	0.32
Other Asian, specified (1)	2	0.01
Other Asian, not specified (14)	68	0.34
Assyrian/Chaldean/Syriac	686	3.42
Australian	4	0.02
Austrian	17	0.08
Belgian	28	0.14
Brazilian	9	0.04
British	302	1.51
Bulgarian	5	0.02
Canadian	103	0.51
Croatian	27	0.13
Czech	84	0.42
Czechoslovakian	36	0.18
Danish	188	0.94
Dutch	257	1.28
English	2,852	14.23
European	319	1.59
Finnish	39	0.19
French, except Basque	812	4.05
French Canadian	177	0.88
German	4,161	20.76
Greek	83	0.41
Hawaii Native/Pacific Islander:	121	0.60
Micronesian: (26)	38	0.19
Guamanian/Chamorro (26)	38	0.19
Polynesian: (28)	70	0.35
Native Hawaiian (10)	44	0.22
Samoan (18)	24	0.12
Other Polynesian	2	0.01
Other Pac. Isl., not spec. (2)	13	0.06
Hispanic or Latino:	2,177	10.80
Central American:	23	0.11
Costa Rican	5	0.02
Guatemalan	1	0.00
Honduran	8	0.04
Nicaraguan	2	0.01
Panamanian	2	0.01
Salvadoran	4	0.02
Other Central American	1	0.00
Cuban	26	0.13
Dominican Republic	12	0.06
Mexican	1,658	8.23
Puerto Rican	88	0.44
South American:	39	0.19
Argentinean	3	0.01
Chilean	1	0.00
Colombian	15	0.07
Ecuadorian	2	0.01
Peruvian	9	0.04
Other South American	9	0.04
Other Hispanic or Latino	331	1.64
Hungarian	134	0.67
Icelander	11	0.05
Iranian	72	0.36
Irish	2,494	12.44
Israeli	31	0.15
Italian	1,578	7.87
Latvian	12	0.06
Lithuanian	64	0.32
Luxemburger	5	0.02
Northern European	31	0.15
Norwegian	307	1.53
Pennsylvania German	4	0.02
Polish	504	2.51
Portuguese	140	0.70
Romanian	70	0.35
Russian	249	1.24
Scandinavian	110	0.55
Scotch-Irish	245	1.22
Scottish	352	1.76
Slovak	59	0.29
Slovene	10	0.05
Swedish	426	2.13
Swiss	86	0.43
Turkish	22	0.11
Ukrainian	83	0.41
United States or American	807	4.03
Welsh	165	0.82
West Indian, excl. Hispanic:	21	0.10
West Indian	21	0.10
White:	17,744	88.04
Not Hispanic (15,583)	16,292	80.83
Hispanic (1,274)	1,452	7.20
Yugoslavian	64	0.32

Rancho Santa Margarita

Place Type: City
County: Orange
Population: 47,214

Ancestry/Race	Number	%
Afghan	78	0.16
African American/Black:	1,084	2.30
Not Hispanic (787)	1,012	2.14
Hispanic (39)	72	0.15
African, sub-Saharan:	97	0.20
African	50	0.10
South African	37	0.08
Zimbabwean	10	0.02
Alaska Native tribes, specified:	6	0.01
Aleut (3)	3	0.01
Eskimo	1	0.00
Tlingit-Haida (2)	2	0.00
Am. Ind. or Alaska Nat., not spec.	134	0.28
Albanian	21	0.04
American Indian tribes, specified:	337	0.71
Apache (4)	16	0.03
Blackfeet (2)	15	0.03
Cherokee (30)	121	0.26
Cheyenne (1)	2	0.00
Chickasaw (1)	4	0.01
Chippewa (1)	2	0.00
Choctaw (9)	19	0.04
Comanche (1)	1	0.00
Cree	2	0.00
Creek	4	0.01
Crow	1	0.00
Delaware (2)	3	0.01
Iroquois (5)	12	0.03
Kiowa	2	0.00
Latin American Indians (4)	25	0.05
Lumbee (4)	5	0.01
Navajo (5)	7	0.01
Osage (1)	4	0.01
Ottawa	1	0.00
Potawatomi (4)	5	0.01
Pueblo (6)	8	0.02
Puget Sound Salish (2)	2	0.00
Seminole	3	0.01
Shoshone	3	0.01
Sioux (10)	14	0.03
Tohono O'Odham	1	0.00
Ute	1	0.00
Yaqui (4)	5	0.01
All other tribes (26)	49	0.10
American Indian tribes, not spec.	31	0.07
Arab:	348	0.73
Arab/Arabic	20	0.04
Egyptian	44	0.09
Iraqi	51	0.11
Lebanese	155	0.32
Palestinian	29	0.06
Syrian	49	0.10
Armenian	252	0.53
Asian:	4,584	9.71
Cambodian (13)	20	0.04
Chinese, ex. Taiwanese (543)	784	1.66
Filipino (1,135)	1,462	3.10
Indian (288)	358	0.76
Indonesian (22)	57	0.12
Japanese (436)	698	1.48
Korean (266)	340	0.72
Laotian (10)	17	0.04
Malaysian (1)	2	0.00
Pakistani (23)	32	0.07
Sri Lankan (12)	15	0.03
Taiwanese (55)	65	0.14
Thai (31)	50	0.11
Vietnamese (503)	558	1.18
Other Asian, specified (1)	6	0.01
Other Asian, not specified (43)	120	0.25
Australian	45	0.09
Austrian	122	0.26
Basque	7	0.01

Notes: 1. Figures in the "Number" column do not add up to the total population due to: a) Ancestry/Race overlap — e.g. persons can report being both White and Irish, b) persons of Hispanic origin can report being any race, c) persons reporting two ancestries are counted in both categories. 2. Numbers in parentheses indicate the number of persons reporting this ancestry/race alone, not in combination with any other ancestry/race. 3. Refer to the Explanation of Data in the front of the book for more detailed information.

Belgian	50	0.10
Brazilian	54	0.11
British	366	0.77
Canadian	298	0.62
Celtic	6	0.01
Croatian	121	0.25
Czech	147	0.31
Czechoslovakian	101	0.21
Danish	528	1.11
Dutch	770	1.61
Eastern European	41	0.09
English	5,717	11.98
Estonian	7	0.01
European	764	1.60
Finnish	139	0.29
French, except Basque	1,985	4.16
French Canadian	540	1.13
German	8,521	17.86
Greek	304	0.64
Hawaii Native/Pacific Islander:	233	0.49
Melanesian: (5)	5	0.01
Fijian (5)	5	0.01
Micronesian: (11)	31	0.07
Guamanian/Chamorro (11)	31	0.07
Polynesian: (67)	136	0.29
Native Hawaiian (42)	100	0.21
Samoan (15)	25	0.05
Tongan (9)	9	0.02
Other Polynesian (1)	2	0.00
Other Pac. Isl., not spec. (14)	61	0.13
Hispanic or Latino:	6,139	13.00
Central American:	205	0.43
Costa Rican	16	0.03
Guatemalan	48	0.10
Honduran	17	0.04
Nicaraguan	33	0.07
Panamanian	14	0.03
Salvadoran	56	0.12
Other Central American	21	0.04
Cuban	160	0.34
Dominican Republic	8	0.02
Mexican	4,127	8.74
Puerto Rican	180	0.38
South American:	440	0.93
Argentinean	90	0.19
Bolivian	23	0.05
Chilean	13	0.03
Colombian	135	0.29
Ecuadorian	26	0.06
Paraguayan	1	0.00
Peruvian	84	0.18
Uruguayan	2	0.00
Venezuelan	32	0.07
Other South American	34	0.07
Other Hispanic or Latino	1,019	2.16
Hungarian	322	0.67
Icelander	23	0.05
Iranian	672	1.41
Irish	6,796	14.24
Israeli	12	0.03
Italian	4,112	8.62
Latvian	31	0.06
Lithuanian	140	0.29
Macedonian	30	0.06
New Zealander	9	0.02
Northern European	97	0.20
Norwegian	930	1.95
Pennsylvania German	7	0.01
Polish	1,805	3.78
Portuguese	271	0.57
Romanian	57	0.12
Russian	599	1.26
Scandinavian	112	0.23
Scotch-Irish	772	1.62
Scottish	1,562	3.27
Serbian	17	0.04
Slavic	31	0.06
Slovak	63	0.13
Slovene	7	0.01
Swedish	1,397	2.93
Swiss	182	0.38
Turkish	26	0.05
Ukrainian	144	0.30
United States or American	2,092	4.38
Welsh	460	0.96
West Indian, excl. Hispanic:	36	0.08
Jamaican	36	0.08
White:	40,266	85.28
Not Hispanic (35,132)	36,379	77.05
Hispanic (3,391)	3,887	8.23
Yugoslavian	135	0.28

Red Bluff

Place Type: City
County: Tehama
Population: 13,147

Ancestry/Race	Number	%
African American/Black:	139	1.06
Not Hispanic (74)	128	0.97
Hispanic (7)	11	0.08
African, sub-Saharan:	9	0.07
African	9	0.07
Alaska Native tribes, specified:	15	0.11
Alaska Athabascan (2)	2	0.02
Aleut (4)	6	0.05
Tlingit-Haida (7)	7	0.05
Alaska Native tribes, not specified	1	0.01
Am. Ind. or Alaska Nat., not spec.	113	0.86
American Indian tribes, specified:	347	2.64
Apache (1)	6	0.05
Blackfeet (2)	9	0.07
Cherokee (33)	82	0.62
Chickasaw (2)	2	0.02
Chippewa (2)	10	0.08
Choctaw (10)	26	0.20
Colville (3)	3	0.02
Creek (9)	9	0.07
Crow	1	0.01
Delaware (1)	1	0.01
Iroquois (6)	8	0.06
Kiowa	1	0.01
Latin American Indians (6)	10	0.08
Navajo (5)	6	0.05
Osage	1	0.01
Ottawa (1)	1	0.01
Paiute (7)	7	0.05
Pima	1	0.01
Potawatomi (1)	2	0.02
Seminole	4	0.03
Sioux (4)	9	0.07
Yakama	2	0.02
Yaqui (1)	1	0.01
All other tribes (101)	144	1.10
American Indian tribes, not spec.	4	0.03
Armenian	6	0.05
Asian:	281	2.14
Chinese, ex. Taiwanese (35)	39	0.30
Filipino (41)	71	0.54
Indian (79)	84	0.64
Indonesian (1)	1	0.01
Japanese (15)	35	0.27
Korean (12)	19	0.14
Laotian (3)	4	0.03
Pakistani (5)	5	0.04
Taiwanese (2)	2	0.02
Vietnamese (11)	11	0.08
Other Asian, not specified (7)	10	0.08
Austrian	6	0.05
Basque	13	0.10
British	55	0.42
Canadian	38	0.29
Celtic	11	0.08
Croatian	7	0.05
Czech	63	0.48
Czechoslovakian	8	0.06
Danish	33	0.25
Dutch	276	2.09
English	1,362	10.32
European	75	0.57
Finnish	42	0.32
French, except Basque	380	2.88
French Canadian	65	0.49
German	2,112	16.00
Greek	82	0.62
Hawaii Native/Pacific Islander:	19	0.14
Micronesian: (2)	2	0.02
Guamanian/Chamorro (2)	2	0.02
Polynesian: (6)	13	0.10
Native Hawaiian (5)	9	0.07
Tongan (1)	2	0.02
Other Polynesian	2	0.02
Other Pac. Isl., not spec. (1)	4	0.03
Hispanic or Latino:	1,799	13.68
Central American:	32	0.24
Guatemalan	5	0.04
Honduran	7	0.05
Nicaraguan	1	0.01
Salvadoran	17	0.13
Other Central American	2	0.02
Cuban	10	0.08
Dominican Republic	1	0.01
Mexican	1,458	11.09
Puerto Rican	35	0.27
South American:	2	0.02
Peruvian	2	0.02
Other Hispanic or Latino	261	1.99
Hungarian	18	0.14
Irish	1,797	13.61
Italian	421	3.19
Luxemburger	13	0.10
Norwegian	282	2.14
Pennsylvania German	7	0.05
Polish	173	1.31
Portuguese	278	2.11
Russian	29	0.22
Scandinavian	41	0.31
Scotch-Irish	311	2.36
Scottish	234	1.77
Slovene	9	0.07
Swedish	211	1.60
Swiss	57	0.43
Ukrainian	28	0.21
United States or American	883	6.69
Welsh	87	0.66
West Indian, excl. Hispanic:	8	0.06
Jamaican	8	0.06
White:	11,775	89.56
Not Hispanic (10,538)	10,802	82.16
Hispanic (859)	973	7.40

Redding

Place Type: City
County: Shasta
Population: 80,865

Ancestry/Race	Number	%
Afghan	7	0.01
African American/Black:	1,234	1.53
Not Hispanic (828)	1,159	1.43
Hispanic (23)	75	0.09
African, sub-Saharan:	18	0.02
African	18	0.02
Alaska Native tribes, specified:	40	0.05
Alaska Athabascan (2)	5	0.01
Aleut (2)	4	0.00
Eskimo (17)	25	0.03
Tlingit-Haida (4)	5	0.01
All other tribes	1	0.00
Alaska Native tribes, not specified	6	0.01
Am. Ind. or Alaska Nat., not spec.	611	0.76
Albanian	8	0.01
American Indian tribes, specified:	2,515	3.11
Apache (17)	43	0.05
Blackfeet (27)	81	0.10
Cherokee (191)	582	0.72
Cheyenne (4)	12	0.01
Chickasaw (3)	14	0.02

Notes: 1. Figures in the "Number" column do not add up to the total population due to: a) Ancestry/Race overlap — e.g. persons can report being both White and Irish, b) persons of Hispanic origin can report being any race, c) persons reporting two ancestries are counted in both categories. 2. Numbers in parentheses indicate the number of persons reporting this ancestry/race alone, not in combination with any other ancestry/race. 3. Refer to the Explanation of Data in the front of the book for more detailed information.

Ancestry/Race	Number	%
Chippewa (24)	59	0.07
Choctaw (41)	134	0.17
Colville (2)	3	0.00
Comanche (2)	7	0.01
Cree (3)	7	0.01
Creek (9)	23	0.03
Crow	3	0.00
Delaware (8)	8	0.01
Iroquois (15)	30	0.04
Kiowa (1)	1	0.00
Latin American Indians (13)	42	0.05
Lumbee (7)	10	0.01
Navajo (7)	15	0.02
Osage (2)	6	0.01
Ottawa (2)	5	0.01
Paiute (13)	24	0.03
Pima	2	0.00
Potawatomi (2)	14	0.02
Pueblo (5)	7	0.01
Puget Sound Salish (1)	1	0.00
Seminole (4)	12	0.01
Shoshone (8)	20	0.02
Sioux (49)	108	0.13
Tohono O'Odham (8)	8	0.01
Ute (6)	12	0.01
Yakama (1)	2	0.00
Yaqui (7)	9	0.01
Yuman (2)	10	0.01
All other tribes (856)	1,201	1.49
American Indian tribes, not spec.	89	0.11
Arab:	223	0.27
Iraqi	6	0.01
Lebanese	105	0.13
Moroccan	26	0.03
Palestinian	38	0.05
Syrian	48	0.06
Armenian	90	0.11
Asian:	3,017	3.73
Bangladeshi (3)	4	0.00
Cambodian (14)	18	0.02
Chinese, ex. Taiwanese (232)	317	0.39
Filipino (188)	357	0.44
Hmong (52)	55	0.07
Indian (176)	221	0.27
Indonesian (4)	9	0.01
Japanese (115)	253	0.31
Korean (76)	126	0.16
Laotian (1,338)	1,437	1.78
Malaysian (1)	7	0.01
Pakistani (4)	8	0.01
Taiwanese (3)	4	0.00
Thai (12)	14	0.02
Vietnamese (73)	81	0.10
Other Asian, specified (6)	8	0.01
Other Asian, not specified (60)	99	0.12
Australian	39	0.05
Austrian	331	0.41
Basque	40	0.05
Belgian	58	0.07
Brazilian	18	0.02
British	409	0.50
Bulgarian	34	0.04
Canadian	384	0.47
Celtic	45	0.06
Croatian	83	0.10
Czech	338	0.42
Czechoslovakian	319	0.39
Danish	943	1.16
Dutch	1,785	2.20
Eastern European	8	0.01
English	11,403	14.04
Estonian	11	0.01
European	995	1.23
Finnish	362	0.45
French, except Basque	3,395	4.18
French Canadian	705	0.87
German	14,261	17.56
Greek	257	0.32
Hawaii Native/Pacific Islander:	263	0.33
Melanesian: (1)	1	0.00
Fijian (1)	1	0.00
Micronesian: (26)	57	0.07
Guamanian/Chamorro (23)	51	0.06
Other Micronesian (3)	6	0.01
Polynesian: (55)	136	0.17
Native Hawaiian (40)	109	0.13
Samoan (15)	24	0.03
Other Polynesian	3	0.00
Other Pac. Isl., specified	2	0.00
Other Pac. Isl., not spec. (11)	67	0.08
Hispanic or Latino:	4,393	5.43
Central American:	100	0.12
Costa Rican	19	0.02
Guatemalan	4	0.00
Honduran	3	0.00
Nicaraguan	23	0.03
Panamanian	5	0.01
Salvadoran	40	0.05
Other Central American	6	0.01
Cuban	35	0.04
Mexican	3,141	3.88
Puerto Rican	161	0.20
South American:	54	0.07
Argentinean	4	0.00
Bolivian	2	0.00
Chilean	7	0.01
Colombian	18	0.02
Ecuadorian	10	0.01
Peruvian	6	0.01
Venezuelan	2	0.00
Other South American	5	0.01
Other Hispanic or Latino	902	1.12
Hungarian	282	0.35
Icelander	6	0.01
Iranian	93	0.11
Irish	11,063	13.62
Italian	4,188	5.16
Lithuanian	153	0.19
Maltese	23	0.03
Northern European	59	0.07
Norwegian	1,884	2.32
Pennsylvania German	39	0.05
Polish	1,119	1.38
Portuguese	1,451	1.79
Romanian	21	0.03
Russian	458	0.56
Scandinavian	223	0.27
Scotch-Irish	1,702	2.10
Scottish	2,079	2.56
Serbian	15	0.02
Slavic	76	0.09
Slovak	78	0.10
Slovene	35	0.04
Swedish	1,996	2.46
Swiss	296	0.36
Turkish	47	0.06
Ukrainian	98	0.12
United States or American	5,626	6.93
Welsh	939	1.16
West Indian, excl. Hispanic:	31	0.04
Dutch West Indian	8	0.01
Jamaican	15	0.02
West Indian	8	0.01
White:	74,153	91.70
Not Hispanic (69,293)	71,234	88.09
Hispanic (2,434)	2,919	3.61
Yugoslavian	174	0.21

Redlands

Place Type: City
County: San Bernardino
Population: 63,591

Ancestry/Race	Number	%
Afghan	39	0.06
African American/Black:	3,263	5.13
Not Hispanic (2,625)	3,038	4.78
Hispanic (114)	225	0.35
African, sub-Saharan:	301	0.47
African	226	0.35
Ethiopian	20	0.03
Kenyan	11	0.02
Nigerian	13	0.02
South African	13	0.02
Other sub-Saharan African	18	0.03
Alaska Native tribes, specified:	16	0.03
Alaska Athabascan	2	0.00
Aleut (2)	7	0.01
Eskimo	1	0.00
Tlingit-Haida (6)	6	0.01
Alaska Native tribes, not specified	3	0.00
Am. Ind. or Alaska Nat., not spec.	387	0.61
Albanian	10	0.02
American Indian tribes, specified:	763	1.20
Apache (34)	61	0.10
Blackfeet (3)	30	0.05
Cherokee (53)	207	0.33
Cheyenne	4	0.01
Chickasaw (4)	8	0.01
Chippewa (6)	12	0.02
Choctaw (19)	41	0.06
Comanche	10	0.02
Creek (1)	7	0.01
Crow	1	0.00
Delaware (4)	5	0.01
Iroquois (12)	20	0.03
Latin American Indians (44)	82	0.13
Navajo (28)	47	0.07
Osage (4)	4	0.01
Ottawa (5)	6	0.01
Paiute (1)	1	0.00
Pima (1)	1	0.00
Potawatomi (8)	8	0.01
Pueblo (8)	16	0.03
Seminole	4	0.01
Shoshone (3)	4	0.01
Sioux (6)	18	0.03
Tohono O'Odham (5)	8	0.01
Yakama (1)	1	0.00
Yaqui (13)	30	0.05
Yuman (1)	2	0.00
All other tribes (93)	125	0.20
American Indian tribes, not spec.	49	0.08
Arab:	494	0.78
Arab/Arabic	106	0.17
Egyptian	71	0.11
Iraqi	20	0.03
Lebanese	120	0.19
Palestinian	50	0.08
Syrian	110	0.17
Other Arab	17	0.03
Armenian	69	0.11
Asian:	4,159	6.54
Bangladeshi (3)	3	0.00
Cambodian (15)	23	0.04
Chinese, ex. Taiwanese (557)	728	1.14
Filipino (646)	874	1.37
Indian (467)	534	0.84
Indonesian (238)	306	0.48
Japanese (241)	451	0.71
Korean (472)	553	0.87
Laotian (2)	2	0.00
Malaysian (3)	6	0.01
Pakistani (35)	50	0.08
Sri Lankan (13)	14	0.02
Taiwanese (62)	78	0.12
Thai (99)	139	0.22
Vietnamese (271)	300	0.47
Other Asian, specified (4)	15	0.02
Other Asian, not specified (39)	83	0.13
Assyrian/Chaldean/Syriac	10	0.02
Australian	62	0.10
Austrian	212	0.33
Basque	11	0.02
Belgian	32	0.05
Brazilian	18	0.03
British	362	0.57
Bulgarian	11	0.02
Canadian	253	0.40

Notes: 1. Figures in the "Number" column do not add up to the total population due to: a) Ancestry/Race overlap — e.g. persons can report being both White and Irish, b) persons of Hispanic origin can report being any race, c) persons reporting two ancestries are counted in both categories. 2. Numbers in parentheses indicate the number of persons reporting this ancestry/race alone, not in combination with any other ancestry/race. 3. Refer to the Explanation of Data in the front of the book for more detailed information.

Celtic	38	0.06
Croatian	79	0.12
Czech	109	0.17
Czechoslovakian	77	0.12
Danish	659	1.03
Dutch	2,260	3.55
Eastern European	49	0.08
English	8,451	13.27
Estonian	5	0.01
European	741	1.16
Finnish	101	0.16
French, except Basque	2,385	3.75
French Canadian	297	0.47
German	9,503	14.92
Greek	267	0.42
Hawaii Native/Pacific Islander:	343	0.54
Melanesian: (1)	2	0.00
Fijian (1)	2	0.00
Micronesian: (34)	64	0.10
Guamanian/Chamorro (26)	51	0.08
Other Micronesian (8)	13	0.02
Polynesian: (84)	198	0.31
Native Hawaiian (35)	117	0.18
Samoan (46)	63	0.10
Tongan (2)	11	0.02
Other Polynesian (1)	7	0.01
Other Pac. Isl., specified	4	0.01
Other Pac. Isl., not spec. (26)	75	0.12
Hispanic or Latino:	15,304	24.07
Central American:	210	0.33
Costa Rican	35	0.06
Guatemalan	30	0.05
Honduran	4	0.01
Nicaraguan	20	0.03
Panamanian	17	0.03
Salvadoran	71	0.11
Other Central American	33	0.05
Cuban	120	0.19
Dominican Republic	3	0.00
Mexican	12,196	19.18
Puerto Rican	285	0.45
South American:	204	0.32
Argentinean	25	0.04
Bolivian	4	0.01
Chilean	21	0.03
Colombian	46	0.07
Ecuadorian	12	0.02
Paraguayan	1	0.00
Peruvian	60	0.09
Uruguayan	12	0.02
Venezuelan	14	0.02
Other South American	9	0.01
Other Hispanic or Latino	2,286	3.59
Hungarian	273	0.43
Icelander	79	0.12
Iranian	134	0.21
Irish	6,699	10.52
Israeli	15	0.02
Italian	2,429	3.81
Latvian	14	0.02
Lithuanian	133	0.21
Macedonian	8	0.01
New Zealander	7	0.01
Northern European	58	0.09
Norwegian	1,176	1.85
Pennsylvania German	22	0.03
Polish	1,222	1.92
Portuguese	265	0.42
Romanian	236	0.37
Russian	541	0.85
Scandinavian	83	0.13
Scotch-Irish	1,415	2.22
Scottish	1,422	2.23
Serbian	113	0.18
Slavic	28	0.04
Slovak	87	0.14
Slovene	39	0.06
Swedish	1,254	1.97
Swiss	369	0.58
Turkish	50	0.08
Ukrainian	150	0.24
United States or American	2,704	4.25
Welsh	478	0.75
West Indian, excl. Hispanic:	60	0.09
Belizean	6	0.01
Bermudan	10	0.02
Dutch West Indian	15	0.02
Jamaican	9	0.01
U.S. Virgin Islander	12	0.02
West Indian	8	0.01
White:	49,214	77.39
Not Hispanic (40,265)	41,631	65.47
Hispanic (6,593)	7,583	11.92
Yugoslavian	138	0.22

Redondo Beach

Place Type: City
County: Los Angeles
Population: 63,261

Ancestry/Race	Number	%
Acadian/Cajun	4	0.01
Afghan	140	0.22
African American/Black:	1,969	3.11
Not Hispanic (1,531)	1,840	2.91
Hispanic (61)	129	0.20
African, sub-Saharan:	251	0.40
African	116	0.18
Ethiopian	83	0.13
Nigerian	37	0.06
South African	15	0.02
Alaska Native tribes, specified:	12	0.02
Aleut (2)	2	0.00
Eskimo (1)	2	0.00
Tlingit-Haida	6	0.01
All other tribes	2	0.00
Alaska Native tribes, not specified	1	0.00
Am. Ind. or Alaska Nat., not spec.	213	0.34
Albanian	9	0.01
American Indian tribes, specified:	514	0.81
Apache (20)	46	0.07
Blackfeet (9)	20	0.03
Cherokee (36)	144	0.23
Cheyenne (2)	4	0.01
Chickasaw (2)	9	0.01
Chippewa (6)	15	0.02
Choctaw (14)	28	0.04
Colville (2)	3	0.00
Comanche	1	0.00
Cree (1)	4	0.01
Creek (2)	3	0.00
Crow (1)	1	0.00
Delaware	1	0.00
Iroquois (8)	16	0.03
Kiowa (1)	1	0.00
Latin American Indians (25)	50	0.08
Lumbee (2)	3	0.00
Navajo (19)	36	0.06
Osage	11	0.02
Potawatomi (2)	3	0.00
Pueblo (4)	8	0.01
Puget Sound Salish	3	0.00
Shoshone	3	0.00
Sioux (16)	25	0.04
Tohono O'Odham (2)	3	0.00
Ute	1	0.00
Yaqui (5)	21	0.03
Yuman (1)	1	0.00
All other tribes (24)	50	0.08
American Indian tribes, not spec.	22	0.03
Arab:	561	0.89
Arab/Arabic	61	0.10
Egyptian	86	0.14
Iraqi	21	0.03
Jordanian	75	0.12
Lebanese	119	0.19
Moroccan	46	0.07
Palestinian	7	0.01
Syrian	67	0.11
Other Arab	79	0.12
Armenian	403	0.64
Asian:	7,368	11.65
Bangladeshi (3)	3	0.00
Cambodian (15)	17	0.03
Chinese, ex. Taiwanese (1,147)	1,537	2.43
Filipino (839)	1,224	1.93
Indian (426)	513	0.81
Indonesian (38)	92	0.15
Japanese (1,618)	2,125	3.36
Korean (691)	811	1.28
Laotian (4)	9	0.01
Malaysian (7)	9	0.01
Pakistani (57)	86	0.14
Sri Lankan (16)	19	0.03
Taiwanese (101)	129	0.20
Thai (94)	125	0.20
Vietnamese (402)	457	0.72
Other Asian, specified (22)	42	0.07
Other Asian, not specified (52)	170	0.27
Assyrian/Chaldean/Syriac	9	0.01
Australian	60	0.09
Austrian	262	0.41
Basque	57	0.09
Belgian	94	0.15
Brazilian	249	0.39
British	440	0.70
Bulgarian	8	0.01
Canadian	306	0.48
Celtic	35	0.06
Croatian	199	0.31
Czech	409	0.65
Czechoslovakian	159	0.25
Danish	605	0.96
Dutch	896	1.42
Eastern European	179	0.28
English	7,353	11.62
European	1,083	1.71
Finnish	183	0.29
French, except Basque	2,235	3.53
French Canadian	563	0.89
German	9,468	14.97
German Russian	9	0.01
Greek	506	0.80
Hawaii Native/Pacific Islander:	482	0.76
Melanesian: (3)	4	0.01
Fijian (3)	4	0.01
Micronesian: (29)	52	0.08
Guamanian/Chamorro (29)	51	0.08
Other Micronesian	1	0.00
Polynesian: (155)	337	0.53
Native Hawaiian (81)	207	0.33
Samoan (46)	83	0.13
Tongan (17)	29	0.05
Other Polynesian (11)	18	0.03
Other Pac. Isl., specified	3	0.00
Other Pac. Isl., not spec. (29)	86	0.14
Hispanic or Latino:	8,524	13.47
Central American:	425	0.67
Costa Rican	47	0.07
Guatemalan	146	0.23
Honduran	20	0.03
Nicaraguan	48	0.08
Panamanian	20	0.03
Salvadoran	110	0.17
Other Central American	34	0.05
Cuban	295	0.47
Dominican Republic	12	0.02
Mexican	5,158	8.15
Puerto Rican	305	0.48
South American:	790	1.25
Argentinean	156	0.25
Bolivian	15	0.02
Chilean	93	0.15
Colombian	160	0.25
Ecuadorian	44	0.07
Paraguayan	1	0.00
Peruvian	223	0.35
Uruguayan	12	0.02
Venezuelan	27	0.04

Notes: 1. Figures in the "Number" column do not add up to the total population due to: a) Ancestry/Race overlap — e.g. persons can report being both White and Irish, b) persons of Hispanic origin can report being any race, c) persons reporting two ancestries are counted in both categories. 2. Numbers in parentheses indicate the number of persons reporting this ancestry/race alone, not in combination with any other ancestry/race. 3. Refer to the Explanation of Data in the front of the book for more detailed information.

Other South American	59	0.09
Other Hispanic or Latino	1,539	2.43
Hungarian	610	0.96
Iranian	561	0.89
Irish	8,149	12.88
Israeli	70	0.11
Italian	4,955	7.83
Latvian	83	0.13
Lithuanian	291	0.46
Luxemburger	24	0.04
Macedonian	19	0.03
Maltese	15	0.02
New Zealander	16	0.03
Northern European	74	0.12
Norwegian	1,458	2.30
Pennsylvania German	11	0.02
Polish	1,887	2.98
Portuguese	303	0.48
Romanian	269	0.43
Russian	1,378	2.18
Scandinavian	257	0.41
Scotch-Irish	817	1.29
Scottish	1,716	2.71
Serbian	44	0.07
Slavic	30	0.05
Slovak	136	0.21
Slovene	16	0.03
Swedish	1,283	2.03
Swiss	324	0.51
Turkish	72	0.11
Ukrainian	328	0.52
United States or American	2,575	4.07
Welsh	570	0.90
West Indian, excl. Hispanic:	74	0.12
Dutch West Indian	9	0.01
Haitian	4	0.01
Jamaican	45	0.07
Trinidadian and Tobagonian	5	0.01
West Indian	11	0.02
White:	52,293	82.66
Not Hispanic (44,819)	46,695	73.81
Hispanic (4,916)	5,598	8.85
Yugoslavian	161	0.25

Redwood City

Place Type: City
County: San Mateo
Population: 75,402

Ancestry/Race	Number	%
Acadian/Cajun	11	0.01
African American/Black:	2,298	3.05
Not Hispanic (1,791)	2,093	2.78
Hispanic (125)	205	0.27
African, sub-Saharan:	184	0.24
African	130	0.17
Cape Verdean	7	0.01
Ethiopian	13	0.02
Kenyan	25	0.03
South African	9	0.01
Alaska Native tribes, specified:	8	0.01
Aleut (1)	1	0.00
Tlingit-Haida (4)	6	0.01
All other tribes (1)	1	0.00
Alaska Native tribes, not specified	3	0.00
Am. Ind. or Alaska Nat., not spec.	264	0.35
Albanian	35	0.05
Alsatian	20	0.03
American Indian tribes, specified:	584	0.77
Apache (9)	35	0.05
Blackfeet (6)	15	0.02
Cherokee (31)	156	0.21
Cheyenne (1)	1	0.00
Chickasaw (4)	9	0.01
Chippewa (10)	25	0.03
Choctaw (2)	24	0.03
Cree (2)	5	0.01
Creek (1)	7	0.01
Iroquois (1)	12	0.02
Kiowa	1	0.00
Latin American Indians (74)	130	0.17
Lumbee (1)	3	0.00
Menominee	2	0.00
Navajo (13)	37	0.05
Osage (2)	2	0.00
Ottawa (1)	2	0.00
Paiute (2)	3	0.00
Potawatomi	3	0.00
Pueblo (5)	7	0.01
Puget Sound Salish (1)	1	0.00
Seminole	2	0.00
Shoshone (1)	2	0.00
Sioux (4)	14	0.02
Tohono O'Odham	2	0.00
Ute (1)	4	0.01
Yaqui (1)	3	0.00
Yuman (6)	8	0.01
All other tribes (38)	69	0.09
American Indian tribes, not spec.	38	0.05
Arab:	557	0.74
Arab/Arabic	35	0.05
Egyptian	50	0.07
Iraqi	23	0.03
Jordanian	33	0.04
Lebanese	239	0.32
Moroccan	44	0.06
Palestinian	54	0.07
Syrian	28	0.04
Other Arab	51	0.07
Armenian	231	0.31
Asian:	7,991	10.60
Bangladeshi (4)	4	0.01
Cambodian (13)	18	0.02
Chinese, ex. Taiwanese (2,617)	3,004	3.98
Filipino (1,187)	1,555	2.06
Indian (1,145)	1,250	1.66
Indonesian (48)	83	0.11
Japanese (644)	960	1.27
Korean (314)	403	0.53
Laotian (35)	39	0.05
Malaysian (3)	9	0.01
Pakistani (21)	26	0.03
Sri Lankan (11)	14	0.02
Taiwanese (45)	54	0.07
Thai (62)	72	0.10
Vietnamese (304)	340	0.45
Other Asian, specified (19)	22	0.03
Other Asian, not specified (57)	138	0.18
Assyrian/Chaldean/Syriac	67	0.09
Australian	56	0.07
Austrian	230	0.30
Basque	85	0.11
Belgian	51	0.07
Brazilian	37	0.05
British	393	0.52
Bulgarian	6	0.01
Canadian	283	0.38
Celtic	13	0.02
Croatian	209	0.28
Czech	143	0.19
Czechoslovakian	100	0.13
Danish	672	0.89
Dutch	810	1.07
Eastern European	131	0.17
English	5,996	7.95
Estonian	43	0.06
European	908	1.20
Finnish	209	0.28
French, except Basque	2,416	3.20
French Canadian	308	0.41
German	8,853	11.73
Greek	571	0.76
Hawaii Native/Pacific Islander:	992	1.32
Melanesian: (70)	87	0.12
Fijian (69)	86	0.11
Other Melanesian (1)	1	0.00
Micronesian: (32)	47	0.06
Guamanian/Chamorro (32)	47	0.06
Polynesian: (489)	716	0.95
Native Hawaiian (76)	175	0.23
Samoan (77)	114	0.15
Tongan (309)	384	0.51
Other Polynesian (27)	43	0.06
Other Pac. Isl., not spec. (46)	142	0.19
Hispanic or Latino:	23,557	31.24
Central American:	2,381	3.16
Costa Rican	43	0.06
Guatemalan	508	0.67
Honduran	35	0.05
Nicaraguan	285	0.38
Panamanian	19	0.03
Salvadoran	1,260	1.67
Other Central American	231	0.31
Cuban	157	0.21
Dominican Republic	10	0.01
Mexican	16,450	21.82
Puerto Rican	264	0.35
South American:	756	1.00
Argentinean	81	0.11
Bolivian	47	0.06
Chilean	80	0.11
Colombian	92	0.12
Ecuadorian	25	0.03
Paraguayan	1	0.00
Peruvian	325	0.43
Uruguayan	12	0.02
Venezuelan	17	0.02
Other South American	76	0.10
Other Hispanic or Latino	3,539	4.69
Hungarian	319	0.42
Iranian	255	0.34
Irish	7,854	10.41
Israeli	22	0.03
Italian	6,450	8.55
Latvian	77	0.10
Lithuanian	138	0.18
Luxemburger	21	0.03
Macedonian	16	0.02
Maltese	95	0.13
New Zealander	25	0.03
Northern European	92	0.12
Norwegian	1,230	1.63
Pennsylvania German	18	0.02
Polish	1,358	1.80
Portuguese	889	1.18
Romanian	98	0.13
Russian	1,140	1.51
Scandinavian	194	0.26
Scotch-Irish	1,206	1.60
Scottish	1,411	1.87
Serbian	21	0.03
Slavic	54	0.07
Slovak	64	0.08
Slovene	20	0.03
Swedish	1,275	1.69
Swiss	499	0.66
Turkish	28	0.04
Ukrainian	177	0.23
United States or American	1,884	2.50
Welsh	388	0.51
West Indian, excl. Hispanic:	98	0.13
Belizean	6	0.01
Haitian	13	0.02
Jamaican	50	0.07
Trinidadian and Tobagonian	12	0.02
West Indian	17	0.02
White:	54,749	72.61
Not Hispanic (40,656)	42,206	55.97
Hispanic (11,352)	12,543	16.63
Yugoslavian	281	0.37

Reedley

Place Type: City
County: Fresno
Population: 20,756

Ancestry/Race	Number	%
African American/Black:	148	0.71

Notes: 1. Figures in the "Number" column do not add up to the total population due to: a) Ancestry/Race overlap — e.g. persons can report being both White and Irish, b) persons of Hispanic origin can report being any race, c) persons reporting two ancestries are counted in both categories. 2. Numbers in parentheses indicate the number of persons reporting this ancestry/race alone, not in combination with any other ancestry/race. 3. Refer to the Explanation of Data in the front of the book for more detailed information.

Ancestry/Race	Number	%
Not Hispanic (42)	68	0.33
Hispanic (47)	80	0.39
Am. Ind. or Alaska Nat., not spec.	150	0.72
American Indian tribes, specified:	207	1.00
Apache (3)	7	0.03
Blackfeet	4	0.02
Cherokee (8)	40	0.19
Chickasaw	1	0.00
Choctaw (4)	8	0.04
Creek (1)	3	0.01
Crow	1	0.00
Delaware (1)	1	0.00
Latin American Indians (53)	80	0.39
Navajo (2)	3	0.01
Potawatomi (3)	4	0.02
Pueblo	1	0.00
Seminole	1	0.00
Sioux	2	0.01
Tohono O'Odham (4)	4	0.02
All other tribes (44)	47	0.23
American Indian tribes, not spec.	24	0.12
Arab:	36	0.17
Arab/Arabic	7	0.03
Lebanese	29	0.14
Armenian	49	0.24
Asian:	1,127	5.43
Cambodian (3)	3	0.01
Chinese, ex. Taiwanese (73)	93	0.45
Filipino (329)	423	2.04
Indian (35)	40	0.19
Japanese (393)	481	2.32
Korean (17)	22	0.11
Laotian (1)	1	0.00
Pakistani (3)	3	0.01
Sri Lankan (4)	4	0.02
Thai (1)	1	0.00
Vietnamese (15)	16	0.08
Other Asian, specified (1)	6	0.03
Other Asian, not specified (17)	34	0.16
Austrian	11	0.05
Belgian	5	0.02
British	47	0.23
Canadian	42	0.20
Czech	58	0.28
Danish	113	0.54
Dutch	304	1.46
English	594	2.86
European	108	0.52
Finnish	54	0.26
French, except Basque	132	0.64
French Canadian	31	0.15
German	1,821	8.76
Hawaii Native/Pacific Islander:	42	0.20
Micronesian: (1)	1	0.00
Guamanian/Chamorro (1)	1	0.00
Polynesian: (10)	32	0.15
Native Hawaiian (3)	17	0.08
Samoan (7)	15	0.07
Other Pac. Isl., specified	2	0.01
Other Pac. Isl., not spec. (4)	7	0.03
Hispanic or Latino:	14,028	67.59
Central American:	126	0.61
Guatemalan	7	0.03
Honduran	5	0.02
Nicaraguan	5	0.02
Salvadoran	99	0.48
Other Central American	10	0.05
Cuban	3	0.01
Mexican	12,379	59.64
Puerto Rican	38	0.18
South American:	9	0.04
Colombian	1	0.00
Paraguayan	1	0.00
Venezuelan	1	0.00
Other South American	6	0.03
Other Hispanic or Latino	1,473	7.10
Hungarian	25	0.12
Irish	519	2.50
Israeli	5	0.02
Italian	150	0.72
Northern European	25	0.12
Norwegian	101	0.49
Pennsylvania German	5	0.02
Polish	72	0.35
Portuguese	56	0.27
Romanian	23	0.11
Russian	57	0.27
Scandinavian	15	0.07
Scotch-Irish	92	0.44
Scottish	107	0.52
Slovene	5	0.02
Swedish	217	1.04
Swiss	31	0.15
Ukrainian	14	0.07
United States or American	559	2.69
Welsh	86	0.41
West Indian, excl. Hispanic:	3	0.01
Dutch West Indian	3	0.01
White:	11,559	55.69
Not Hispanic (5,453)	5,676	27.35
Hispanic (5,290)	5,883	28.34
Yugoslavian	18	0.09

Rialto

Place Type: City
County: San Bernardino
Population: 91,873

Ancestry/Race	Number	%
Afghan	69	0.08
African American/Black:	21,801	23.73
Not Hispanic (19,954)	20,953	22.81
Hispanic (510)	848	0.92
African, sub-Saharan:	1,169	1.27
African	779	0.85
Ethiopian	16	0.02
Ghanian	93	0.10
Liberian	7	0.01
Nigerian	261	0.28
Sudanese	5	0.01
Other sub-Saharan African	8	0.01
Alaska Native tribes, specified:	5	0.01
Alaska Athabascan (1)	1	0.00
Aleut	2	0.00
Eskimo	2	0.00
Am. Ind. or Alaska Nat., not spec.	645	0.70
Albanian	14	0.02
American Indian tribes, specified:	1,238	1.35
Apache (31)	86	0.09
Blackfeet (4)	73	0.08
Cherokee (71)	322	0.35
Cheyenne (1)	5	0.01
Chickasaw (1)	13	0.01
Chippewa (3)	18	0.02
Choctaw (11)	48	0.05
Comanche (1)	4	0.00
Cree	1	0.00
Creek (2)	10	0.01
Crow (1)	3	0.00
Delaware (1)	5	0.01
Iroquois (2)	20	0.02
Latin American Indians (132)	211	0.23
Lumbee (5)	6	0.01
Navajo (36)	64	0.07
Osage (3)	8	0.01
Paiute (6)	7	0.01
Pima (8)	9	0.01
Potawatomi (5)	11	0.01
Pueblo (36)	59	0.06
Seminole (2)	17	0.02
Shoshone (4)	6	0.01
Sioux (11)	27	0.03
Tohono O'Odham (2)	3	0.00
Ute (5)	8	0.01
Yaqui (35)	53	0.06
Yuman (2)	9	0.01
All other tribes (76)	132	0.14
American Indian tribes, not spec.	119	0.13
Arab:	445	0.49
Arab/Arabic	71	0.08
Egyptian	122	0.13
Jordanian	7	0.01
Lebanese	160	0.17
Palestinian	65	0.07
Syrian	20	0.02
Armenian	14	0.02
Asian:	3,113	3.39
Cambodian (227)	270	0.29
Chinese, ex. Taiwanese (152)	267	0.29
Filipino (811)	1,063	1.16
Indian (236)	323	0.35
Indonesian (47)	89	0.10
Japanese (119)	251	0.27
Korean (106)	147	0.16
Laotian (40)	44	0.05
Malaysian (2)	3	0.00
Pakistani (49)	84	0.09
Sri Lankan	3	0.00
Taiwanese (6)	13	0.01
Thai (62)	83	0.09
Vietnamese (319)	355	0.39
Other Asian, specified (11)	11	0.01
Other Asian, not specified (36)	107	0.12
Australian	16	0.02
Austrian	9	0.01
Basque	56	0.06
Belgian	6	0.01
Brazilian	31	0.03
British	78	0.09
Canadian	63	0.07
Celtic	10	0.01
Croatian	34	0.04
Czech	54	0.06
Czechoslovakian	25	0.03
Danish	132	0.14
Dutch	603	0.66
English	2,774	3.02
European	315	0.34
Finnish	14	0.02
French, except Basque	1,393	1.52
French Canadian	247	0.27
German	4,260	4.65
Greek	67	0.07
Guyanese	19	0.02
Hawaii Native/Pacific Islander:	644	0.70
Melanesian: (14)	16	0.02
Fijian (14)	16	0.02
Micronesian: (28)	44	0.05
Guamanian/Chamorro (25)	41	0.04
Other Micronesian (3)	3	0.00
Polynesian: (311)	473	0.51
Native Hawaiian (47)	120	0.13
Samoan (234)	294	0.32
Tongan (29)	50	0.05
Other Polynesian (1)	9	0.01
Other Pac. Isl., not spec. (30)	111	0.12
Hispanic or Latino:	47,050	51.21
Central American:	1,835	2.00
Costa Rican	72	0.08
Guatemalan	387	0.42
Honduran	89	0.10
Nicaraguan	247	0.27
Panamanian	58	0.06
Salvadoran	781	0.85
Other Central American	201	0.22
Cuban	258	0.28
Dominican Republic	35	0.04
Mexican	37,589	40.91
Puerto Rican	677	0.74
South American:	368	0.40
Argentinean	58	0.06
Bolivian	10	0.01
Chilean	14	0.02
Colombian	77	0.08
Ecuadorian	77	0.08
Peruvian	86	0.09
Uruguayan	4	0.00
Venezuelan	11	0.01
Other South American	31	0.03

Notes: 1. Figures in the "Number" column do not add up to the total population due to: a) Ancestry/Race overlap — e.g. persons can report being both White and Irish, b) persons of Hispanic origin can report being any race, c) persons reporting two ancestries are counted in both categories. 2. Numbers in parentheses indicate the number of persons reporting this ancestry/race alone, not in combination with any other ancestry/race. 3. Refer to the Explanation of Data in the front of the book for more detailed information.

Other Hispanic or Latino	6,288	6.84
Hungarian	160	0.17
Iranian	23	0.03
Irish	3,814	4.16
Israeli	6	0.01
Italian	1,482	1.62
Lithuanian	75	0.08
Northern European	15	0.02
Norwegian	374	0.41
Polish	687	0.75
Portuguese	155	0.17
Romanian	69	0.08
Russian	214	0.23
Scandinavian	93	0.10
Scotch-Irish	597	0.65
Scottish	532	0.58
Serbian	33	0.04
Slavic	83	0.09
Slovak	38	0.04
Slovene	9	0.01
Swedish	545	0.59
Swiss	82	0.09
Ukrainian	26	0.03
United States or American	2,663	2.90
Welsh	238	0.26
West Indian, excl. Hispanic:	346	0.38
Belizean	113	0.12
British West Indian	8	0.01
Haitian	15	0.02
Jamaican	110	0.12
Trinidadian and Tobagonian	28	0.03
U.S. Virgin Islander	6	0.01
West Indian	66	0.07
White:	39,820	43.34
Not Hispanic (19,713)	21,124	22.99
Hispanic (16,455)	18,696	20.35
Yugoslavian	22	0.02

Richmond

Place Type: City
County: Contra Costa
Population: 99,216

Ancestry/Race	Number	%
Afghan	59	0.06
African American/Black:	37,543	37.84
Not Hispanic (35,279)	36,682	36.97
Hispanic (498)	861	0.87
African, sub-Saharan:	2,217	2.22
African	1,863	1.87
Ethiopian	82	0.08
Kenyan	56	0.06
Nigerian	201	0.20
Senegalese	6	0.01
Sierra Leonean	4	0.00
Other sub-Saharan African	5	0.01
Alaska Native tribes, specified:	9	0.01
Alaska Athabascan (1)	1	0.00
Aleut (1)	5	0.01
Eskimo (1)	2	0.00
Tlingit-Haida	1	0.00
Alaska Native tribes, not specified	2	0.00
Am. Ind. or Alaska Nat., not spec.	601	0.61
American Indian tribes, specified:	974	0.98
Apache (18)	51	0.05
Blackfeet (9)	63	0.06
Cherokee (44)	225	0.23
Cheyenne (1)	4	0.00
Chickasaw (2)	11	0.01
Chippewa (9)	17	0.02
Choctaw (10)	64	0.06
Colville	1	0.00
Comanche	1	0.00
Cree (3)	9	0.01
Creek (3)	17	0.02
Crow (1)	2	0.00
Delaware (1)	4	0.00
Houma	1	0.00
Iroquois (3)	12	0.01
Latin American Indians (130)	190	0.19
Menominee	4	0.00
Navajo (20)	36	0.04
Osage	4	0.00
Paiute (8)	14	0.01
Pima (4)	5	0.01
Potawatomi (1)	3	0.00
Pueblo (13)	21	0.02
Seminole (4)	19	0.02
Shoshone (1)	2	0.00
Sioux (22)	48	0.05
Ute	1	0.00
Yakama	1	0.00
Yaqui (1)	10	0.01
Yuman (2)	2	0.00
All other tribes (59)	132	0.13
American Indian tribes, not spec.	46	0.05
Arab:	452	0.45
Arab/Arabic	189	0.19
Egyptian	9	0.01
Lebanese	64	0.06
Moroccan	26	0.03
Palestinian	95	0.10
Syrian	39	0.04
Other Arab	30	0.03
Armenian	56	0.06
Asian:	14,183	14.30
Bangladeshi (5)	5	0.01
Cambodian (70)	130	0.13
Chinese, ex. Taiwanese (3,152)	3,586	3.61
Filipino (3,105)	3,705	3.73
Hmong (36)	49	0.05
Indian (1,148)	1,322	1.33
Indonesian (54)	89	0.09
Japanese (847)	1,193	1.20
Korean (526)	607	0.61
Laotian (1,849)	2,108	2.12
Malaysian (20)	40	0.04
Pakistani (79)	97	0.10
Sri Lankan (18)	20	0.02
Taiwanese (92)	111	0.11
Thai (129)	181	0.18
Vietnamese (500)	571	0.58
Other Asian, specified (17)	40	0.04
Other Asian, not specified (178)	329	0.33
Australian	18	0.02
Austrian	172	0.17
Basque	22	0.02
Belgian	90	0.09
Brazilian	175	0.18
British	267	0.27
Bulgarian	7	0.01
Canadian	94	0.09
Celtic	55	0.06
Croatian	71	0.07
Czech	246	0.25
Czechoslovakian	41	0.04
Danish	353	0.35
Dutch	676	0.68
Eastern European	65	0.07
English	3,553	3.56
European	566	0.57
Finnish	192	0.19
French, except Basque	1,277	1.28
French Canadian	159	0.16
German	4,534	4.55
Greek	172	0.17
Guyanese	10	0.01
Hawaii Native/Pacific Islander:	870	0.88
Melanesian: (58)	64	0.06
Fijian (58)	64	0.06
Micronesian: (42)	78	0.08
Guamanian/Chamorro (34)	69	0.07
Other Micronesian (8)	9	0.01
Polynesian: (331)	532	0.54
Native Hawaiian (69)	210	0.21
Samoan (189)	222	0.22
Tongan (64)	78	0.08
Other Polynesian (9)	22	0.02
Other Pac. Isl., specified	15	0.02
Other Pac. Isl., not spec. (55)	181	0.18
Hispanic or Latino:	26,319	26.53
Central American:	2,528	2.55
Costa Rican	17	0.02
Guatemalan	368	0.37
Honduran	76	0.08
Nicaraguan	416	0.42
Panamanian	55	0.06
Salvadoran	1,340	1.35
Other Central American	256	0.26
Cuban	119	0.12
Dominican Republic	7	0.01
Mexican	18,396	18.54
Puerto Rican	458	0.46
South American:	482	0.49
Argentinean	20	0.02
Bolivian	8	0.01
Chilean	71	0.07
Colombian	42	0.04
Ecuadorian	27	0.03
Paraguayan	1	0.00
Peruvian	250	0.25
Uruguayan	1	0.00
Venezuelan	12	0.01
Other South American	50	0.05
Other Hispanic or Latino	4,329	4.36
Hungarian	183	0.18
Iranian	243	0.24
Irish	3,619	3.63
Israeli	23	0.02
Italian	2,340	2.35
Latvian	31	0.03
Lithuanian	120	0.12
Macedonian	6	0.01
Maltese	7	0.01
Northern European	64	0.06
Norwegian	737	0.74
Polish	610	0.61
Portuguese	627	0.63
Romanian	101	0.10
Russian	615	0.62
Scandinavian	54	0.05
Scotch-Irish	588	0.59
Scottish	832	0.83
Serbian	16	0.02
Slavic	26	0.03
Slovak	6	0.01
Swedish	760	0.76
Swiss	177	0.18
Turkish	68	0.07
Ukrainian	145	0.15
United States or American	1,383	1.39
Welsh	293	0.29
West Indian, excl. Hispanic:	357	0.36
Barbadian	16	0.02
Belizean	52	0.05
British West Indian	39	0.04
Dutch West Indian	7	0.01
Haitian	14	0.01
Jamaican	185	0.19
Trinidadian and Tobagonian	30	0.03
West Indian	14	0.01
White:	34,723	35.00
Not Hispanic (21,081)	23,074	23.26
Hispanic (10,036)	11,649	11.74
Yugoslavian	138	0.14

Ridgecrest

Place Type: City
County: Kern
Population: 24,927

Ancestry/Race	Number	%
Acadian/Cajun	11	0.04
African American/Black:	1,066	4.28
Not Hispanic (846)	996	4.00
Hispanic (33)	70	0.28
African, sub-Saharan:	53	0.21
African	53	0.21

Notes: 1. Figures in the "Number" column do not add up to the total population due to: a) Ancestry/Race overlap — e.g. persons can report being both White and Irish, b) persons of Hispanic origin can report being any race, c) persons reporting two ancestries are counted in both categories. 2. Numbers in parentheses indicate the number of persons reporting this ancestry/race alone, not in combination with any other ancestry/race. 3. Refer to the Explanation of Data in the front of the book for more detailed information.

Alaska Native tribes, specified:	11	0.04
Aleut (2)	3	0.01
Tlingit-Haida (5)	8	0.03
Alaska Native tribes, not specified	1	0.00
Am. Ind. or Alaska Nat., not spec.	143	0.57
Albanian	8	0.03
American Indian tribes, specified:	416	1.67
Apache (16)	39	0.16
Blackfeet (4)	17	0.07
Cherokee (38)	147	0.59
Cheyenne (1)	2	0.01
Chickasaw (3)	5	0.02
Chippewa (9)	14	0.06
Choctaw (14)	32	0.13
Comanche (1)	3	0.01
Cree	1	0.00
Creek (1)	6	0.02
Crow	2	0.01
Delaware (2)	2	0.01
Houma (2)	2	0.01
Iroquois	6	0.02
Latin American Indians (11)	19	0.08
Lumbee (1)	1	0.00
Navajo (5)	8	0.03
Osage (1)	6	0.02
Paiute (22)	30	0.12
Potawatomi (2)	4	0.02
Shoshone (3)	3	0.01
Sioux (7)	16	0.06
Yaqui (3)	3	0.01
All other tribes (34)	48	0.19
American Indian tribes, not spec.	35	0.14
Arab:	35	0.14
Egyptian	11	0.04
Lebanese	12	0.05
Syrian	12	0.05
Armenian	6	0.02
Asian:	1,318	5.29
Cambodian (7)	11	0.04
Chinese, ex. Taiwanese (111)	159	0.64
Filipino (408)	559	2.24
Hmong (1)	1	0.00
Indian (72)	78	0.31
Indonesian (12)	21	0.08
Japanese (92)	173	0.69
Korean (69)	94	0.38
Malaysian (2)	2	0.01
Pakistani (7)	12	0.05
Sri Lankan (3)	4	0.02
Taiwanese (6)	8	0.03
Thai (16)	21	0.08
Vietnamese (116)	122	0.49
Other Asian, specified	5	0.02
Other Asian, not specified (31)	48	0.19
Australian	5	0.02
Austrian	69	0.27
Belgian	61	0.24
British	140	0.56
Canadian	50	0.20
Celtic	25	0.10
Croatian	8	0.03
Czech	31	0.12
Czechoslovakian	49	0.19
Danish	309	1.23
Dutch	732	2.91
English	3,595	14.27
Estonian	7	0.03
European	388	1.54
Finnish	25	0.10
French, except Basque	894	3.55
French Canadian	231	0.92
German	4,437	17.61
Greek	98	0.39
Hawaii Native/Pacific Islander:	216	0.87
Melanesian: (1)	1	0.00
Fijian (1)	1	0.00
Micronesian: (78)	95	0.38
Guamanian/Chamorro (74)	87	0.35
Other Micronesian (4)	8	0.03
Polynesian: (62)	99	0.40
Native Hawaiian (11)	36	0.14
Samoan (51)	63	0.25
Other Pac. Isl., specified	2	0.01
Other Pac. Isl., not spec. (1)	19	0.08
Hispanic or Latino:	3,001	12.04
Central American:	76	0.30
Costa Rican	3	0.01
Guatemalan	8	0.03
Honduran	14	0.06
Nicaraguan	13	0.05
Panamanian	7	0.03
Salvadoran	29	0.12
Other Central American	2	0.01
Cuban	19	0.08
Dominican Republic	7	0.03
Mexican	2,288	9.18
Puerto Rican	107	0.43
South American:	35	0.14
Argentinean	5	0.02
Bolivian	1	0.00
Chilean	3	0.01
Colombian	11	0.04
Peruvian	12	0.05
Uruguayan	2	0.01
Other South American	1	0.00
Other Hispanic or Latino	469	1.88
Hungarian	50	0.20
Icelander	7	0.03
Iranian	4	0.02
Irish	2,841	11.28
Italian	939	3.73
Lithuanian	14	0.06
Northern European	8	0.03
Norwegian	800	3.18
Pennsylvania German	8	0.03
Polish	419	1.66
Portuguese	140	0.56
Romanian	27	0.11
Russian	99	0.39
Scandinavian	49	0.19
Scotch-Irish	455	1.81
Scottish	543	2.16
Serbian	11	0.04
Slavic	26	0.10
Slovak	14	0.06
Slovene	12	0.05
Swedish	467	1.85
Swiss	53	0.21
Ukrainian	38	0.15
United States or American	1,815	7.20
Welsh	245	0.97
West Indian, excl. Hispanic:	37	0.15
Belizean	18	0.07
Dutch West Indian	19	0.08
White:	21,327	85.56
Not Hispanic (19,067)	19,689	78.99
Hispanic (1,379)	1,638	6.57
Yugoslavian	6	0.02

Rio Linda

Place Type: Census Designated Place
County: Sacramento
Population: 10,466

Ancestry/Race	Number	%
African American/Black:	297	2.84
Not Hispanic (209)	255	2.44
Hispanic (24)	42	0.40
Alaska Native tribes, specified:	1	0.01
Eskimo (1)	1	0.01
Alaska Native tribes, not specified	2	0.02
Am. Ind. or Alaska Nat., not spec.	113	1.08
American Indian tribes, specified:	286	2.73
Apache (5)	14	0.13
Blackfeet (2)	14	0.13
Cherokee (51)	140	1.34
Cheyenne	2	0.02
Chickasaw	1	0.01
Chippewa (3)	6	0.06
Choctaw (6)	21	0.20
Comanche	2	0.02
Cree	1	0.01
Creek	2	0.02
Crow (1)	1	0.01
Iroquois (2)	3	0.03
Latin American Indians (3)	10	0.10
Menominee (1)	1	0.01
Navajo (5)	7	0.07
Osage (1)	2	0.02
Ottawa (4)	5	0.05
Paiute (1)	2	0.02
Potawatomi (5)	5	0.05
Shoshone	1	0.01
Sioux (1)	3	0.03
Yaqui (1)	1	0.01
All other tribes (16)	42	0.40
American Indian tribes, not spec.	13	0.12
Arab:	9	0.09
Lebanese	9	0.09
Armenian	9	0.09
Asian:	413	3.95
Chinese, ex. Taiwanese (30)	45	0.43
Filipino (71)	121	1.16
Hmong (63)	69	0.66
Indian (19)	29	0.28
Indonesian	3	0.03
Japanese (23)	51	0.49
Korean (6)	13	0.12
Laotian (40)	43	0.41
Pakistani (1)	2	0.02
Taiwanese (1)	1	0.01
Thai (6)	11	0.11
Vietnamese (20)	21	0.20
Other Asian, not specified (1)	4	0.04
Australian	14	0.13
Brazilian	9	0.09
British	16	0.15
Croatian	9	0.09
Czech	69	0.66
Czechoslovakian	7	0.07
Danish	46	0.44
Dutch	124	1.19
English	742	7.10
European	93	0.89
Finnish	24	0.23
French, except Basque	298	2.85
French Canadian	33	0.32
German	1,087	10.40
Greek	10	0.10
Hawaii Native/Pacific Islander:	95	0.91
Melanesian: (2)	3	0.03
Fijian (2)	3	0.03
Micronesian: (24)	32	0.31
Guamanian/Chamorro (24)	32	0.31
Polynesian: (12)	40	0.38
Native Hawaiian (6)	20	0.19
Samoan (6)	8	0.08
Tongan	6	0.06
Other Polynesian	6	0.06
Other Pac. Isl., not spec. (6)	20	0.19
Hispanic or Latino:	1,162	11.10
Central American:	10	0.10
Nicaraguan	2	0.02
Panamanian	3	0.03
Salvadoran	5	0.05
Cuban	4	0.04
Dominican Republic	1	0.01
Mexican	912	8.71
Puerto Rican	25	0.24
South American:	1	0.01
Peruvian	1	0.01
Other Hispanic or Latino	209	2.00
Hungarian	18	0.17
Irish	1,218	11.66
Italian	422	4.04
Northern European	18	0.17
Norwegian	156	1.49
Polish	75	0.72
Portuguese	102	0.98

Notes: 1. Figures in the "Number" column do not add up to the total population due to: a) Ancestry/Race overlap — e.g. persons can report being both White and Irish, b) persons of Hispanic origin can report being any race, c) persons reporting two ancestries are counted in both categories. 2. Numbers in parentheses indicate the number of persons reporting this ancestry/race alone, not in combination with any other ancestry/race. 3. Refer to the Explanation of Data in the front of the book for more detailed information.

Ancestry/Race	Number	%
Romanian	189	1.81
Russian	7	0.07
Scandinavian	19	0.18
Scotch-Irish	200	1.91
Scottish	170	1.63
Slavic	7	0.07
Swedish	136	1.30
Swiss	15	0.14
United States or American	1,307	12.51
Welsh	60	0.57
White:	9,177	87.68
Not Hispanic (8,210)	8,579	81.97
Hispanic (481)	598	5.71
Yugoslavian	13	0.12

Ripon

Place Type: City
County: San Joaquin
Population: 10,146

Ancestry/Race	Number	%
African American/Black:	55	0.54
Not Hispanic (25)	41	0.40
Hispanic (10)	14	0.14
African, sub-Saharan:	16	0.16
African	16	0.16
Alaska Native tribes, specified:	2	0.02
Eskimo (2)	2	0.02
Am. Ind. or Alaska Nat., not spec.	52	0.51
American Indian tribes, specified:	120	1.18
Apache	1	0.01
Blackfeet (4)	5	0.05
Cherokee (10)	53	0.52
Chickasaw	2	0.02
Chippewa (8)	8	0.08
Choctaw (4)	16	0.16
Comanche	1	0.01
Creek (1)	1	0.01
Latin American Indians (5)	6	0.06
Navajo (1)	1	0.01
Paiute (3)	3	0.03
Pima	3	0.03
Potawatomi	2	0.02
Pueblo (1)	2	0.02
Sioux	1	0.01
Yakama	1	0.01
Yaqui (1)	1	0.01
All other tribes (2)	13	0.13
American Indian tribes, not spec.	6	0.06
Arab:	9	0.09
Lebanese	9	0.09
Armenian	8	0.08
Asian:	266	2.62
Chinese, ex. Taiwanese (30)	55	0.54
Filipino (48)	99	0.98
Indian (29)	30	0.30
Indonesian (1)	1	0.01
Japanese (10)	25	0.25
Korean (22)	30	0.30
Pakistani	1	0.01
Taiwanese (1)	1	0.01
Thai (1)	1	0.01
Vietnamese (1)	1	0.01
Other Asian, not specified	22	0.22
Austrian	28	0.28
British	57	0.56
Canadian	18	0.18
Czech	10	0.10
Czechoslovakian	5	0.05
Danish	11	0.11
Dutch	1,260	12.43
English	860	8.49
European	69	0.68
Finnish	37	0.37
French, except Basque	314	3.10
French Canadian	72	0.71
German	1,598	15.77
Greek	92	0.91
Hawaii Native/Pacific Islander:	53	0.52
Micronesian: (5)	9	0.09
Guamanian/Chamorro (5)	9	0.09
Polynesian: (21)	37	0.36
Native Hawaiian (6)	20	0.20
Samoan (14)	14	0.14
Other Polynesian (1)	3	0.03
Other Pac. Isl., not spec. (2)	7	0.07
Hispanic or Latino:	1,843	18.16
Central American:	9	0.09
Costa Rican	1	0.01
Nicaraguan	2	0.02
Salvadoran	6	0.06
Cuban	5	0.05
Mexican	1,525	15.03
Puerto Rican	43	0.42
South American:	11	0.11
Argentinean	2	0.02
Colombian	2	0.02
Peruvian	4	0.04
Venezuelan	2	0.02
Other South American	1	0.01
Other Hispanic or Latino	250	2.46
Hungarian	17	0.17
Irish	1,149	11.34
Italian	727	7.17
Northern European	80	0.79
Norwegian	260	2.57
Polish	76	0.75
Portuguese	540	5.33
Russian	27	0.27
Scandinavian	7	0.07
Scotch-Irish	147	1.45
Scottish	310	3.06
Swedish	178	1.76
Swiss	138	1.36
Ukrainian	5	0.05
United States or American	603	5.95
Welsh	21	0.21
White:	8,923	87.95
Not Hispanic (7,844)	8,052	79.36
Hispanic (731)	871	8.58
Yugoslavian	11	0.11

Riverbank

Place Type: City
County: Stanislaus
Population: 15,826

Ancestry/Race	Number	%
African American/Black:	333	2.10
Not Hispanic (200)	266	1.68
Hispanic (42)	67	0.42
Alaska Native tribes, specified:	3	0.02
Tlingit-Haida (1)	3	0.02
Alaska Native tribes, not specified	1	0.01
Am. Ind. or Alaska Nat., not spec.	104	0.66
American Indian tribes, specified:	321	2.03
Apache (9)	17	0.11
Blackfeet	5	0.03
Cherokee (31)	130	0.82
Chickasaw (7)	9	0.06
Choctaw (11)	33	0.21
Colville (1)	1	0.01
Cree	3	0.02
Creek (3)	3	0.02
Iroquois	1	0.01
Latin American Indians (15)	26	0.16
Navajo (19)	21	0.13
Ottawa	4	0.03
Paiute (6)	12	0.08
Potawatomi (1)	1	0.01
Pueblo (2)	3	0.02
Seminole (1)	3	0.02
Sioux (1)	1	0.01
Ute (1)	1	0.01
Yaqui (1)	2	0.01
All other tribes (28)	45	0.28
American Indian tribes, not spec.	17	0.11
Asian:	324	2.05
Cambodian (20)	22	0.14
Chinese, ex. Taiwanese (40)	64	0.40
Filipino (67)	115	0.73
Indian (22)	37	0.23
Indonesian (5)	6	0.04
Japanese (18)	26	0.16
Korean (9)	21	0.13
Laotian (1)	1	0.01
Pakistani	2	0.01
Sri Lankan (1)	1	0.01
Vietnamese (7)	10	0.06
Other Asian, specified	4	0.03
Other Asian, not specified (11)	15	0.09
Assyrian/Chaldean/Syriac	49	0.31
Austrian	41	0.26
Basque	16	0.10
British	7	0.04
Czechoslovakian	8	0.05
Danish	29	0.18
Dutch	356	2.25
English	699	4.41
European	70	0.44
French, except Basque	293	1.85
French Canadian	50	0.32
German	1,557	9.82
Greek	48	0.30
Hawaii Native/Pacific Islander:	73	0.46
Melanesian: (1)	5	0.03
Fijian (1)	5	0.03
Micronesian: (6)	9	0.06
Guamanian/Chamorro (6)	9	0.06
Polynesian: (13)	33	0.21
Native Hawaiian (9)	22	0.14
Samoan (3)	6	0.04
Tongan (1)	3	0.02
Other Polynesian	2	0.01
Other Pac. Isl., specified	4	0.03
Other Pac. Isl., not spec.	22	0.14
Hispanic or Latino:	7,266	45.91
Central American:	32	0.20
Guatemalan	8	0.05
Honduran	11	0.07
Nicaraguan	1	0.01
Salvadoran	10	0.06
Other Central American	2	0.01
Cuban	8	0.05
Mexican	6,334	40.02
Puerto Rican	72	0.45
South American:	26	0.16
Argentinean	4	0.03
Chilean	3	0.02
Colombian	10	0.06
Ecuadorian	4	0.03
Peruvian	3	0.02
Venezuelan	1	0.01
Other South American	1	0.01
Other Hispanic or Latino	794	5.02
Hungarian	45	0.28
Irish	918	5.79
Italian	603	3.80
Norwegian	125	0.79
Polish	94	0.59
Portuguese	505	3.18
Romanian	33	0.21
Russian	37	0.23
Scotch-Irish	98	0.62
Scottish	166	1.05
Slavic	6	0.04
Swedish	134	0.85
Swiss	45	0.28
Ukrainian	13	0.08
United States or American	907	5.72
Welsh	20	0.13
West Indian, excl. Hispanic:	8	0.05
Haitian	8	0.05
White:	11,234	70.98
Not Hispanic (7,612)	7,963	50.32
Hispanic (2,967)	3,271	20.67
Yugoslavian	14	0.09

Notes: 1. Figures in the "Number" column do not add up to the total population due to: a) Ancestry/Race overlap — e.g. persons can report being both White and Irish, b) persons of Hispanic origin can report being any race, c) persons reporting two ancestries are counted in both categories. 2. Numbers in parentheses indicate the number of persons reporting this ancestry/race alone, not in combination with any other ancestry/race. 3. Refer to the Explanation of Data in the front of the book for more detailed information.

Riverside

Place Type: City
County: Riverside
Population: 255,166

Ancestry/Race	Number	%
Acadian/Cajun	20	0.01
African American/Black:	21,495	8.42
Not Hispanic (18,051)	19,993	7.84
Hispanic (855)	1,502	0.59
African, sub-Saharan:	1,256	0.49
African	1,121	0.44
Ethiopian	31	0.01
Nigerian	57	0.02
Somalian	16	0.01
South African	17	0.01
Other sub-Saharan African	14	0.01
Alaska Native tribes, specified:	24	0.01
Alaska Athabascan (4)	6	0.00
Aleut (2)	2	0.00
Eskimo (9)	13	0.01
Tlingit-Haida (1)	3	0.00
Alaska Native tribes, not specified	3	0.00
Am. Ind. or Alaska Nat., not spec.	1,706	0.67
Albanian	45	0.02
American Indian tribes, specified:	3,513	1.38
Apache (108)	235	0.09
Blackfeet (22)	101	0.04
Cherokee (216)	819	0.32
Cheyenne (1)	6	0.00
Chickasaw (19)	43	0.02
Chippewa (35)	82	0.03
Choctaw (50)	133	0.05
Colville (2)	2	0.00
Comanche (17)	55	0.02
Cree (1)	9	0.00
Creek (11)	48	0.02
Crow	8	0.00
Delaware (8)	9	0.00
Iroquois (8)	46	0.02
Kiowa (10)	15	0.01
Latin American Indians (325)	517	0.20
Lumbee (9)	12	0.00
Menominee (3)	4	0.00
Navajo (108)	167	0.07
Osage (22)	36	0.01
Ottawa (3)	6	0.00
Paiute (20)	31	0.01
Pima (21)	42	0.02
Potawatomi (4)	10	0.00
Pueblo (81)	122	0.05
Puget Sound Salish (2)	3	0.00
Seminole (14)	25	0.01
Shoshone (10)	21	0.01
Sioux (39)	106	0.04
Tohono O'Odham (23)	35	0.01
Ute (9)	19	0.01
Yaqui (33)	86	0.03
Yuman (27)	49	0.02
All other tribes (398)	611	0.24
American Indian tribes, not spec.	267	0.10
Arab:	1,556	0.61
Arab/Arabic	280	0.11
Egyptian	293	0.11
Iraqi	52	0.02
Jordanian	215	0.08
Lebanese	357	0.14
Moroccan	37	0.01
Palestinian	142	0.06
Syrian	113	0.04
Other Arab	67	0.03
Armenian	454	0.18
Asian:	17,596	6.90
Bangladeshi (25)	30	0.01
Cambodian (190)	285	0.11
Chinese, ex. Taiwanese (2,482)	3,083	1.21
Filipino (3,039)	3,952	1.55
Hmong (26)	27	0.01
Indian (1,541)	1,739	0.68
Indonesian (107)	224	0.09
Japanese (878)	1,460	0.57
Korean (1,847)	2,008	0.79
Laotian (377)	408	0.16
Malaysian (12)	22	0.01
Pakistani (115)	179	0.07
Sri Lankan (53)	69	0.03
Taiwanese (345)	414	0.16
Thai (223)	308	0.12
Vietnamese (2,586)	2,830	1.11
Other Asian, specified (37)	69	0.03
Other Asian, not specified (219)	489	0.19
Assyrian/Chaldean/Syriac	93	0.04
Australian	59	0.02
Austrian	379	0.15
Basque	143	0.06
Belgian	170	0.07
Brazilian	212	0.08
British	1,037	0.41
Bulgarian	47	0.02
Canadian	757	0.30
Carpatho Rusyn	8	0.00
Celtic	52	0.02
Croatian	147	0.06
Czech	493	0.19
Czechoslovakian	256	0.10
Danish	977	0.38
Dutch	3,564	1.40
Eastern European	56	0.02
English	19,858	7.78
Estonian	14	0.01
European	1,812	0.71
Finnish	243	0.10
French, except Basque	6,069	2.38
French Canadian	1,256	0.49
German	26,216	10.28
German Russian	39	0.02
Greek	617	0.24
Guyanese	29	0.01
Hawaii Native/Pacific Islander:	1,813	0.71
Melanesian: (14)	29	0.01
Fijian (14)	29	0.01
Micronesian: (189)	285	0.11
Guamanian/Chamorro (187)	283	0.11
Other Micronesian (2)	2	0.00
Polynesian: (698)	1,157	0.45
Native Hawaiian (172)	425	0.17
Samoan (350)	487	0.19
Tongan (158)	208	0.08
Other Polynesian (18)	37	0.01
Other Pac. Isl., specified	6	0.00
Other Pac. Isl., not spec. (68)	336	0.13
Hispanic or Latino:	97,315	38.14
Central American:	2,438	0.96
Costa Rican	142	0.06
Guatemalan	978	0.38
Honduran	74	0.03
Nicaraguan	184	0.07
Panamanian	120	0.05
Salvadoran	763	0.30
Other Central American	177	0.07
Cuban	608	0.24
Dominican Republic	34	0.01
Mexican	79,041	30.98
Puerto Rican	1,562	0.61
South American:	1,117	0.44
Argentinean	169	0.07
Bolivian	85	0.03
Chilean	80	0.03
Colombian	278	0.11
Ecuadorian	123	0.05
Paraguayan	2	0.00
Peruvian	272	0.11
Uruguayan	7	0.00
Venezuelan	35	0.01
Other South American	66	0.03
Other Hispanic or Latino	12,515	4.90
Hungarian	868	0.34
Icelander	37	0.01
Iranian	282	0.11
Irish	20,181	7.91
Israeli	64	0.03
Italian	9,289	3.64
Latvian	24	0.01
Lithuanian	259	0.10
Luxemburger	5	0.00
Maltese	14	0.01
New Zealander	28	0.01
Northern European	170	0.07
Norwegian	2,863	1.12
Pennsylvania German	123	0.05
Polish	3,747	1.47
Portuguese	875	0.34
Romanian	771	0.30
Russian	1,276	0.50
Scandinavian	395	0.15
Scotch-Irish	2,890	1.13
Scottish	3,904	1.53
Serbian	59	0.02
Slavic	58	0.02
Slovak	227	0.09
Slovene	21	0.01
Swedish	2,904	1.14
Swiss	563	0.22
Turkish	61	0.02
Ukrainian	360	0.14
United States or American	9,981	3.91
Welsh	1,617	0.63
West Indian, excl. Hispanic:	661	0.26
Barbadian	5	0.00
Belizean	103	0.04
British West Indian	46	0.02
Haitian	24	0.01
Jamaican	275	0.11
Trinidadian and Tobagonian	72	0.03
West Indian	114	0.04
Other West Indian	22	0.01
White:	162,256	63.59
Not Hispanic (116,254)	121,595	47.65
Hispanic (35,123)	40,661	15.94
Yugoslavian	68	0.03

Rocklin

Place Type: City
County: Placer
Population: 36,330

Ancestry/Race	Number	%
African American/Black:	466	1.28
Not Hispanic (317)	429	1.18
Hispanic (13)	37	0.10
African, sub-Saharan:	59	0.16
African	44	0.12
Kenyan	7	0.02
South African	8	0.02
Alaska Native tribes, specified:	6	0.02
Alaska Athabascan	1	0.00
Eskimo (1)	1	0.00
Tlingit-Haida (1)	4	0.01
Am. Ind. or Alaska Nat., not spec.	192	0.53
American Indian tribes, specified:	436	1.20
Apache (5)	18	0.05
Blackfeet (2)	18	0.05
Cherokee (48)	141	0.39
Cheyenne (1)	5	0.01
Chippewa (11)	18	0.05
Choctaw (10)	25	0.07
Comanche (1)	2	0.01
Creek (2)	10	0.03
Crow	4	0.01
Delaware (1)	2	0.01
Iroquois (1)	3	0.01
Latin American Indians (4)	25	0.07
Lumbee (1)	3	0.01
Navajo (2)	5	0.01
Paiute (1)	3	0.01
Potawatomi (2)	6	0.02
Pueblo (1)	8	0.02
Puget Sound Salish (2)	2	0.01

Notes: 1. Figures in the "Number" column do not add up to the total population due to: a) Ancestry/Race overlap — e.g. persons can report being both White and Irish, b) persons of Hispanic origin can report being any race, c) persons reporting two ancestries are counted in both categories. 2. Numbers in parentheses indicate the number of persons reporting this ancestry/race alone, not in combination with any other ancestry/race. 3. Refer to the Explanation of Data in the front of the book for more detailed information.

Seminole (3)	5	0.01
Shoshone	1	0.00
Sioux (24)	39	0.11
Ute	4	0.01
Yakama	3	0.01
Yaqui (1)	1	0.00
Yuman	1	0.00
All other tribes (55)	84	0.23
American Indian tribes, not spec.	39	0.11
Arab:	91	0.25
Arab/Arabic	11	0.03
Egyptian	23	0.06
Jordanian	6	0.02
Lebanese	30	0.08
Syrian	21	0.06
Armenian	27	0.07
Asian:	2,177	5.99
Bangladeshi (5)	5	0.01
Cambodian (11)	19	0.05
Chinese, ex. Taiwanese (306)	454	1.25
Filipino (296)	491	1.35
Hmong (2)	3	0.01
Indian (208)	248	0.68
Indonesian (5)	9	0.02
Japanese (330)	526	1.45
Korean (136)	168	0.46
Laotian (5)	5	0.01
Malaysian (7)	13	0.04
Pakistani (4)	11	0.03
Sri Lankan (6)	7	0.02
Taiwanese (8)	14	0.04
Thai (15)	23	0.06
Vietnamese (85)	107	0.29
Other Asian, specified	5	0.01
Other Asian, not specified (27)	69	0.19
Assyrian/Chaldean/Syriac	9	0.02
Australian	36	0.10
Austrian	108	0.30
Basque	27	0.07
Belgian	23	0.06
Brazilian	24	0.07
British	255	0.70
Canadian	61	0.17
Croatian	50	0.14
Czech	157	0.43
Czechoslovakian	47	0.13
Danish	457	1.25
Dutch	848	2.32
Eastern European	30	0.08
English	5,275	14.43
Estonian	10	0.03
European	869	2.38
Finnish	80	0.22
French, except Basque	1,629	4.46
French Canadian	265	0.72
German	7,678	21.00
Greek	232	0.63
Hawaii Native/Pacific Islander:	176	0.48
Melanesian: (2)	2	0.01
Fijian (2)	2	0.01
Micronesian: (9)	18	0.05
Guamanian/Chamorro (7)	14	0.04
Other Micronesian (2)	4	0.01
Polynesian: (45)	111	0.31
Native Hawaiian (31)	82	0.23
Samoan (11)	21	0.06
Tongan (2)	3	0.01
Other Polynesian (1)	5	0.01
Other Pac. Isl., specified	4	0.01
Other Pac. Isl., not spec. (14)	41	0.11
Hispanic or Latino:	2,874	7.91
Central American:	88	0.24
Costa Rican	10	0.03
Guatemalan	7	0.02
Honduran	10	0.03
Nicaraguan	20	0.06
Panamanian	10	0.03
Salvadoran	18	0.05
Other Central American	13	0.04
Cuban	41	0.11
Dominican Republic	1	0.00
Mexican	1,855	5.11
Puerto Rican	108	0.30
South American:	78	0.21
Argentinean	11	0.03
Bolivian	6	0.02
Chilean	9	0.02
Colombian	26	0.07
Ecuadorian	7	0.02
Peruvian	14	0.04
Venezuelan	1	0.00
Other South American	4	0.01
Other Hispanic or Latino	703	1.94
Hungarian	145	0.40
Iranian	90	0.25
Irish	5,487	15.01
Italian	3,255	8.90
Latvian	13	0.04
Lithuanian	53	0.14
Macedonian	25	0.07
Maltese	14	0.04
Northern European	32	0.09
Norwegian	1,046	2.86
Pennsylvania German	20	0.05
Polish	783	2.14
Portuguese	941	2.57
Romanian	29	0.08
Russian	307	0.84
Scandinavian	131	0.36
Scotch-Irish	814	2.23
Scottish	1,081	2.96
Slavic	5	0.01
Slovak	18	0.05
Slovene	6	0.02
Swedish	1,145	3.13
Swiss	166	0.45
Turkish	9	0.02
Ukrainian	113	0.31
United States or American	2,016	5.51
Welsh	305	0.83
West Indian, excl. Hispanic:	32	0.09
Jamaican	32	0.09
White:	33,321	91.72
Not Hispanic (30,315)	31,246	86.01
Hispanic (1,771)	2,075	5.71
Yugoslavian	85	0.23

Rohnert Park

Place Type: City
County: Sonoma
Population: 42,236

Ancestry/Race	Number	%
Afghan	20	0.05
African American/Black:	1,224	2.90
Not Hispanic (799)	1,141	2.70
Hispanic (34)	83	0.20
African, sub-Saharan:	221	0.52
African	126	0.30
Cape Verdean	9	0.02
Kenyan	49	0.12
Sudanese	37	0.09
Alaska Native tribes, specified:	12	0.03
Alaska Athabascan (1)	1	0.00
Aleut (1)	4	0.01
Eskimo	1	0.00
Tlingit-Haida (3)	6	0.01
Alaska Native tribes, not specified	3	0.01
Am. Ind. or Alaska Nat., not spec.	230	0.54
American Indian tribes, specified:	628	1.49
Apache (8)	23	0.05
Blackfeet (2)	31	0.07
Cherokee (24)	135	0.32
Cheyenne	4	0.01
Chickasaw	7	0.02
Chippewa (7)	22	0.05
Choctaw (10)	53	0.13
Colville	2	0.00
Comanche (4)	4	0.01
Creek	5	0.01
Crow (2)	3	0.01
Delaware (2)	4	0.01
Iroquois (9)	22	0.05
Latin American Indians (27)	42	0.10
Navajo (3)	16	0.04
Osage (1)	3	0.01
Ottawa (2)	2	0.00
Paiute (3)	7	0.02
Potawatomi (2)	2	0.00
Pueblo (2)	4	0.01
Puget Sound Salish (1)	1	0.00
Seminole	8	0.02
Shoshone	3	0.01
Sioux (10)	31	0.07
Tohono O'Odham	2	0.00
Ute (1)	5	0.01
Yaqui (7)	11	0.03
All other tribes (93)	176	0.42
American Indian tribes, not spec.	43	0.10
Arab:	444	1.05
Arab/Arabic	228	0.54
Egyptian	66	0.16
Jordanian	43	0.10
Lebanese	80	0.19
Moroccan	15	0.04
Other Arab	12	0.03
Armenian	91	0.21
Asian:	3,202	7.58
Bangladeshi (2)	2	0.00
Cambodian (35)	52	0.12
Chinese, ex. Taiwanese (448)	604	1.43
Filipino (533)	827	1.96
Hmong (11)	12	0.03
Indian (393)	441	1.04
Indonesian (28)	43	0.10
Japanese (217)	408	0.97
Korean (208)	243	0.58
Laotian (96)	107	0.25
Malaysian (6)	8	0.02
Pakistani (7)	13	0.03
Sri Lankan (4)	5	0.01
Taiwanese (13)	17	0.04
Thai (37)	46	0.11
Vietnamese (241)	273	0.65
Other Asian, specified (13)	21	0.05
Other Asian, not specified (16)	80	0.19
Australian	35	0.08
Austrian	122	0.29
Basque	39	0.09
Belgian	45	0.11
Brazilian	11	0.03
British	350	0.83
Canadian	184	0.43
Celtic	25	0.06
Croatian	74	0.17
Czech	136	0.32
Czechoslovakian	64	0.15
Danish	535	1.26
Dutch	707	1.67
Eastern European	17	0.04
English	4,555	10.75
European	762	1.80
Finnish	159	0.38
French, except Basque	1,754	4.14
French Canadian	243	0.57
German	7,301	17.22
Greek	195	0.46
Hawaii Native/Pacific Islander:	433	1.03
Melanesian: (20)	30	0.07
Fijian (20)	30	0.07
Micronesian: (20)	45	0.11
Guamanian/Chamorro (20)	45	0.11
Polynesian: (101)	257	0.61
Native Hawaiian (49)	136	0.32
Samoan (37)	97	0.23
Tongan (10)	13	0.03
Other Polynesian (5)	11	0.03
Other Pac. Isl., specified	3	0.01
Other Pac. Isl., not spec. (28)	98	0.23

Notes: 1. Figures in the "Number" column do not add up to the total population due to: a) Ancestry/Race overlap — e.g. persons can report being both White and Irish, b) persons of Hispanic origin can report being any race, c) persons reporting two ancestries are counted in both categories. 2. Numbers in parentheses indicate the number of persons reporting this ancestry/race alone, not in combination with any other ancestry/race. 3. Refer to the Explanation of Data in the front of the book for more detailed information.

Hispanic or Latino:	5,731	13.57
Central American:	385	0.91
Costa Rican	11	0.03
Guatemalan	55	0.13
Honduran	6	0.01
Nicaraguan	59	0.14
Panamanian	13	0.03
Salvadoran	209	0.49
Other Central American	32	0.08
Cuban	41	0.10
Dominican Republic	5	0.01
Mexican	4,009	9.49
Puerto Rican	190	0.45
South American:	138	0.33
Argentinean	9	0.02
Bolivian	6	0.01
Chilean	9	0.02
Colombian	49	0.12
Ecuadorian	6	0.01
Peruvian	36	0.09
Venezuelan	12	0.03
Other South American	11	0.03
Other Hispanic or Latino	963	2.28
Hungarian	153	0.36
Icelander	24	0.06
Iranian	143	0.34
Irish	6,590	15.55
Italian	4,420	10.43
Latvian	27	0.06
Lithuanian	50	0.12
Macedonian	6	0.01
Maltese	57	0.13
New Zealander	13	0.03
Northern European	42	0.10
Norwegian	1,065	2.51
Pennsylvania German	8	0.02
Polish	887	2.09
Portuguese	1,238	2.92
Romanian	29	0.07
Russian	586	1.38
Scandinavian	88	0.21
Scotch-Irish	673	1.59
Scottish	1,234	2.91
Slavic	46	0.11
Slovak	52	0.12
Slovene	17	0.04
Swedish	982	2.32
Swiss	289	0.68
Turkish	7	0.02
Ukrainian	73	0.17
United States or American	1,718	4.05
Welsh	450	1.06
West Indian, excl. Hispanic:	38	0.09
Belizean	16	0.04
Haitian	5	0.01
Jamaican	17	0.04
White:	35,844	84.87
Not Hispanic (31,266)	32,692	77.40
Hispanic (2,641)	3,152	7.46
Yugoslavian	133	0.31

Rosamond

Place Type: Census Designated Place
County: Kern
Population: 14,349

Ancestry/Race	Number	%
African American/Black:	1,103	7.69
Not Hispanic (924)	1,054	7.35
Hispanic (26)	49	0.34
African, sub-Saharan:	8	0.06
African	8	0.06
Am. Ind. or Alaska Nat., not spec.	125	0.87
American Indian tribes, specified:	242	1.69
Apache (11)	26	0.18
Blackfeet	9	0.06
Cherokee (22)	69	0.48
Chickasaw	2	0.01
Chippewa (3)	8	0.06
Choctaw (14)	25	0.17
Comanche	2	0.01
Creek (2)	5	0.03
Delaware (1)	1	0.01
Iroquois (2)	4	0.03
Kiowa	4	0.03
Latin American Indians (12)	20	0.14
Navajo (4)	5	0.03
Osage	5	0.03
Ottawa (4)	4	0.03
Paiute (8)	10	0.07
Pima (1)	3	0.02
Pueblo	2	0.01
Seminole (1)	4	0.03
Shoshone (2)	2	0.01
Sioux (1)	5	0.03
Tohono O'Odham (1)	1	0.01
Ute (1)	1	0.01
All other tribes (18)	25	0.17
American Indian tribes, not spec.	17	0.12
Arab:	8	0.06
Lebanese	8	0.06
Armenian	20	0.14
Asian:	653	4.55
Chinese, ex. Taiwanese (14)	32	0.22
Filipino (220)	313	2.18
Indian (33)	39	0.27
Indonesian (1)	4	0.03
Japanese (53)	99	0.69
Korean (44)	77	0.54
Thai (38)	53	0.37
Vietnamese (15)	16	0.11
Other Asian, not specified (11)	20	0.14
Assyrian/Chaldean/Syriac	26	0.18
Austrian	56	0.39
Basque	9	0.06
Belgian	8	0.06
British	45	0.31
Canadian	26	0.18
Czech	25	0.17
Czechoslovakian	29	0.20
Danish	146	1.01
Dutch	214	1.48
Eastern European	20	0.14
English	1,083	7.49
European	255	1.76
Finnish	20	0.14
French, except Basque	565	3.91
French Canadian	192	1.33
German	1,848	12.78
German Russian	21	0.15
Greek	13	0.09
Hawaii Native/Pacific Islander:	67	0.47
Micronesian: (16)	24	0.17
Guamanian/Chamorro (14)	21	0.15
Other Micronesian (2)	3	0.02
Polynesian: (11)	29	0.20
Native Hawaiian (8)	21	0.15
Samoan	4	0.03
Tongan	1	0.01
Other Polynesian (3)	3	0.02
Other Pac. Isl., not spec. (2)	14	0.10
Hispanic or Latino:	3,684	25.67
Central American:	171	1.19
Costa Rican	2	0.01
Guatemalan	55	0.38
Honduran	13	0.09
Nicaraguan	10	0.07
Panamanian	8	0.06
Salvadoran	71	0.49
Other Central American	12	0.08
Cuban	27	0.19
Dominican Republic	1	0.01
Mexican	2,580	17.98
Puerto Rican	82	0.57
South American:	41	0.29
Argentinean	1	0.01
Bolivian	3	0.02
Chilean	6	0.04
Colombian	13	0.09
Ecuadorian	11	0.08
Peruvian	5	0.03
Uruguayan	1	0.01
Other South American	1	0.01
Other Hispanic or Latino	782	5.45
Hungarian	49	0.34
Irish	1,456	10.07
Italian	587	4.06
Lithuanian	50	0.35
Northern European	9	0.06
Norwegian	294	2.03
Pennsylvania German	18	0.12
Polish	190	1.31
Portuguese	5	0.03
Romanian	40	0.28
Russian	34	0.24
Scandinavian	19	0.13
Scotch-Irish	136	0.94
Scottish	336	2.32
Slavic	9	0.06
Swedish	199	1.38
Swiss	28	0.19
Ukrainian	7	0.05
United States or American	973	6.73
Welsh	88	0.61
West Indian, excl. Hispanic:	15	0.10
Jamaican	15	0.10
White:	10,968	76.44
Not Hispanic (8,695)	9,065	63.18
Hispanic (1,638)	1,903	13.26

Rosemead

Place Type: City
County: Los Angeles
Population: 53,505

Ancestry/Race	Number	%
Afghan	104	0.20
African American/Black:	490	0.92
Not Hispanic (262)	335	0.63
Hispanic (101)	155	0.29
African, sub-Saharan:	45	0.08
African	34	0.06
Ghanian	5	0.01
Nigerian	6	0.01
Am. Ind. or Alaska Nat., not spec.	343	0.64
American Indian tribes, specified:	358	0.67
Apache (14)	30	0.06
Blackfeet (3)	4	0.01
Cherokee (11)	29	0.05
Cheyenne	1	0.00
Chickasaw (5)	5	0.01
Chippewa (6)	9	0.02
Choctaw (2)	11	0.02
Iroquois (1)	3	0.01
Latin American Indians (97)	150	0.28
Lumbee (1)	1	0.00
Navajo (7)	24	0.04
Pima	1	0.00
Pueblo (1)	6	0.01
Sioux (15)	22	0.04
Tohono O'Odham	6	0.01
Ute	3	0.01
Yaqui (7)	12	0.02
Yuman (8)	8	0.01
All other tribes (26)	33	0.06
American Indian tribes, not spec.	50	0.09
Arab:	225	0.42
Arab/Arabic	13	0.02
Egyptian	67	0.13
Lebanese	37	0.07
Syrian	88	0.17
Other Arab	20	0.04
Armenian	36	0.07
Asian:	28,376	53.03
Bangladeshi (1)	2	0.00
Cambodian (492)	720	1.35
Chinese, ex. Taiwanese (15,322)	16,995	31.76
Filipino (744)	876	1.64

Notes: 1. Figures in the "Number" column do not add up to the total population due to: a) Ancestry/Race overlap — e.g. persons can report being both White and Irish, b) persons of Hispanic origin can report being any race, c) persons reporting two ancestries are counted in both categories. 2. Numbers in parentheses indicate the number of persons reporting this ancestry/race alone, not in combination with any other ancestry/race. 3. Refer to the Explanation of Data in the front of the book for more detailed information.

Hmong (1)	1	0.00
Indian (169)	218	0.41
Indonesian (47)	70	0.13
Japanese (786)	887	1.66
Korean (244)	270	0.50
Laotian (35)	42	0.08
Malaysian (4)	18	0.03
Pakistani (6)	7	0.01
Sri Lankan (6)	14	0.03
Taiwanese (356)	446	0.83
Thai (159)	188	0.35
Vietnamese (5,931)	7,175	13.41
Other Asian, specified (134)	168	0.31
Other Asian, not specified (149)	279	0.52
Austrian	21	0.04
Basque	47	0.09
Belgian	6	0.01
Brazilian	13	0.02
British	41	0.08
Canadian	45	0.08
Celtic	11	0.02
Czech	26	0.05
Czechoslovakian	9	0.02
Danish	50	0.09
Dutch	55	0.10
English	633	1.19
Estonian	5	0.01
European	18	0.03
Finnish	5	0.01
French, except Basque	176	0.33
French Canadian	108	0.20
German	663	1.24
Greek	6	0.01
Hawaii Native/Pacific Islander:	142	0.27
Micronesian: (7)	8	0.01
Guamanian/Chamorro (7)	8	0.01
Polynesian: (19)	47	0.09
Native Hawaiian (15)	36	0.07
Samoan (4)	10	0.02
Other Polynesian	1	0.00
Other Pac. Isl., not spec. (7)	87	0.16
Hispanic or Latino:	22,097	41.30
Central American:	863	1.61
Costa Rican	16	0.03
Guatemalan	180	0.34
Honduran	34	0.06
Nicaraguan	130	0.24
Panamanian	3	0.01
Salvadoran	404	0.76
Other Central American	96	0.18
Cuban	193	0.36
Dominican Republic	2	0.00
Mexican	17,853	33.37
Puerto Rican	124	0.23
South American:	207	0.39
Argentinean	24	0.04
Bolivian	10	0.02
Chilean	18	0.03
Colombian	37	0.07
Ecuadorian	40	0.07
Peruvian	51	0.10
Uruguayan	5	0.01
Venezuelan	3	0.01
Other South American	19	0.04
Other Hispanic or Latino	2,855	5.34
Hungarian	17	0.03
Iranian	7	0.01
Irish	579	1.09
Italian	723	1.36
Lithuanian	22	0.04
Northern European	9	0.02
Norwegian	59	0.11
Pennsylvania German	9	0.02
Polish	102	0.19
Portuguese	8	0.02
Romanian	6	0.01
Russian	56	0.11
Scandinavian	10	0.02
Scotch-Irish	132	0.25
Scottish	189	0.35
Slovak	13	0.02
Swedish	69	0.13
Swiss	7	0.01
Turkish	9	0.02
Ukrainian	17	0.03
United States or American	636	1.19
Welsh	104	0.20
West Indian, excl. Hispanic:	40	0.08
Belizean	36	0.07
Jamaican	4	0.01
White:	15,513	28.99
Not Hispanic (4,295)	4,668	8.72
Hispanic (9,922)	10,845	20.27
Yugoslavian	13	0.02

Rosemont

Place Type: Census Designated Place
County: Sacramento
Population: 22,904

Ancestry/Race	Number	%
Afghan	79	0.35
African American/Black:	2,924	12.77
Not Hispanic (2,373)	2,728	11.91
Hispanic (123)	196	0.86
African, sub-Saharan:	68	0.30
African	61	0.27
Other sub-Saharan African	7	0.03
Alaska Native tribes, specified:	1	0.00
Tlingit-Haida	1	0.00
Am. Ind. or Alaska Nat., not spec.	206	0.90
American Indian tribes, specified:	421	1.84
Apache (9)	18	0.08
Blackfeet (2)	31	0.14
Cherokee (44)	147	0.64
Chickasaw (1)	2	0.01
Chippewa (7)	9	0.04
Choctaw (12)	24	0.10
Comanche (1)	1	0.00
Creek (1)	2	0.01
Delaware	1	0.00
Iroquois (5)	7	0.03
Latin American Indians (7)	24	0.10
Navajo (3)	9	0.04
Ottawa	1	0.00
Paiute (3)	5	0.02
Potawatomi (3)	4	0.02
Pueblo (5)	9	0.04
Seminole (1)	1	0.00
Shoshone (1)	5	0.02
Sioux (8)	16	0.07
Tohono O'Odham	4	0.02
Yakama	1	0.00
Yaqui (4)	5	0.02
All other tribes (59)	95	0.41
American Indian tribes, not spec.	10	0.04
Arab:	501	2.19
Arab/Arabic	88	0.39
Jordanian	45	0.20
Lebanese	154	0.67
Moroccan	13	0.06
Palestinian	24	0.11
Syrian	48	0.21
Other Arab	129	0.57
Armenian	481	2.11
Asian:	3,157	13.78
Cambodian (17)	21	0.09
Chinese, ex. Taiwanese (346)	438	1.91
Filipino (551)	732	3.20
Hmong (33)	59	0.26
Indian (225)	278	1.21
Indonesian (15)	20	0.09
Japanese (242)	372	1.62
Korean (423)	470	2.05
Laotian (46)	51	0.22
Malaysian (8)	8	0.03
Pakistani (38)	50	0.22
Sri Lankan (4)	4	0.02
Taiwanese (4)	7	0.03
Thai (16)	24	0.10
Vietnamese (500)	544	2.38
Other Asian, specified (4)	12	0.05
Other Asian, not specified (36)	67	0.29
Austrian	67	0.29
Basque	23	0.10
Brazilian	9	0.04
British	94	0.41
Canadian	89	0.39
Celtic	19	0.08
Croatian	13	0.06
Czech	11	0.05
Czechoslovakian	29	0.13
Danish	202	0.88
Dutch	257	1.13
English	1,964	8.60
European	259	1.13
Finnish	36	0.16
French, except Basque	617	2.70
French Canadian	136	0.60
German	2,755	12.07
Greek	184	0.81
Hawaii Native/Pacific Islander:	228	1.00
Melanesian: (23)	26	0.11
Fijian (23)	26	0.11
Micronesian: (18)	40	0.17
Guamanian/Chamorro (18)	37	0.16
Other Micronesian	3	0.01
Polynesian: (43)	84	0.37
Native Hawaiian (16)	48	0.21
Samoan (25)	30	0.13
Tongan (2)	6	0.03
Other Pac. Isl., specified	5	0.02
Other Pac. Isl., not spec. (9)	73	0.32
Hispanic or Latino:	3,023	13.20
Central American:	84	0.37
Costa Rican	3	0.01
Guatemalan	18	0.08
Honduran	2	0.01
Nicaraguan	11	0.05
Panamanian	13	0.06
Salvadoran	26	0.11
Other Central American	11	0.05
Cuban	33	0.14
Dominican Republic	3	0.01
Mexican	2,108	9.20
Puerto Rican	154	0.67
South American:	53	0.23
Argentinean	7	0.03
Bolivian	3	0.01
Chilean	7	0.03
Colombian	12	0.05
Ecuadorian	1	0.00
Peruvian	19	0.08
Venezuelan	1	0.00
Other South American	3	0.01
Other Hispanic or Latino	588	2.57
Hungarian	73	0.32
Icelander	8	0.04
Iranian	27	0.12
Irish	2,123	9.30
Israeli	9	0.04
Italian	1,222	5.35
Lithuanian	21	0.09
Maltese	10	0.04
Norwegian	333	1.46
Polish	278	1.22
Portuguese	355	1.55
Romanian	21	0.09
Russian	227	0.99
Scandinavian	33	0.14
Scotch-Irish	355	1.55
Scottish	458	2.01
Serbian	18	0.08
Slavic	14	0.06
Slovak	43	0.19
Slovene	17	0.07
Swedish	299	1.31
Swiss	60	0.26
Ukrainian	205	0.90

Notes: 1. Figures in the "Number" column do not add up to the total population due to: a) Ancestry/Race overlap — e.g. persons can report being both White and Irish, b) persons of Hispanic origin can report being any race, c) persons reporting two ancestries are counted in both categories. 2. Numbers in parentheses indicate the number of persons reporting this ancestry/race alone, not in combination with any other ancestry/race. 3. Refer to the Explanation of Data in the front of the book for more detailed information.

Ancestry/Race	Number	%
United States or American	1,210	5.30
Welsh	154	0.67
West Indian, excl. Hispanic:	25	0.11
Haitian	9	0.04
Jamaican	9	0.04
Other West Indian	7	0.03
White:	15,998	69.85
Not Hispanic (13,531)	14,480	63.22
Hispanic (1,240)	1,518	6.63
Yugoslavian	68	0.30

Roseville

Place Type: City
County: Placer
Population: 79,921

Ancestry/Race	Number	%
Acadian/Cajun	23	0.03
African American/Black:	1,394	1.74
Not Hispanic (992)	1,287	1.61
Hispanic (55)	107	0.13
African, sub-Saharan:	105	0.13
African	79	0.10
Cape Verdean	26	0.03
Alaska Native tribes, specified:	9	0.01
Alaska Athabascan (1)	1	0.00
Aleut (1)	1	0.00
Eskimo	3	0.00
Tlingit-Haida (2)	4	0.01
Alaska Native tribes, not specified	2	0.00
Am. Ind. or Alaska Nat., not spec.	354	0.44
American Indian tribes, specified:	895	1.12
Apache (8)	37	0.05
Blackfeet (13)	38	0.05
Cherokee (118)	353	0.44
Chickasaw (4)	7	0.01
Chippewa (14)	29	0.04
Choctaw (28)	59	0.07
Comanche (2)	7	0.01
Cree	3	0.00
Creek (11)	23	0.03
Crow (4)	6	0.01
Delaware (1)	3	0.00
Iroquois (5)	18	0.02
Kiowa (2)	2	0.00
Latin American Indians (33)	52	0.07
Lumbee (1)	2	0.00
Menominee	1	0.00
Navajo (15)	22	0.03
Osage (4)	5	0.01
Paiute (9)	17	0.02
Pima (1)	1	0.00
Potawatomi (3)	11	0.01
Pueblo (6)	7	0.01
Puget Sound Salish	1	0.00
Seminole (1)	9	0.01
Shoshone (2)	3	0.00
Sioux (12)	32	0.04
Yakama	1	0.00
Yaqui (7)	11	0.01
Yuman (1)	1	0.00
All other tribes (80)	134	0.17
American Indian tribes, not spec.	67	0.08
Arab:	378	0.47
Arab/Arabic	81	0.10
Egyptian	64	0.08
Lebanese	71	0.09
Palestinian	18	0.02
Syrian	126	0.16
Other Arab	18	0.02
Armenian	185	0.23
Asian:	4,564	5.71
Bangladeshi	3	0.00
Cambodian (17)	27	0.03
Chinese, ex. Taiwanese (561)	776	0.97
Filipino (831)	1,178	1.47
Hmong (12)	16	0.02
Indian (758)	846	1.06
Indonesian (13)	27	0.03
Japanese (538)	852	1.07
Korean (263)	341	0.43
Laotian (6)	10	0.01
Malaysian	2	0.00
Pakistani (36)	49	0.06
Sri Lankan (10)	10	0.01
Taiwanese (15)	28	0.04
Thai (35)	63	0.08
Vietnamese (217)	245	0.31
Other Asian, specified (5)	9	0.01
Other Asian, not specified (20)	82	0.10
Assyrian/Chaldean/Syriac	38	0.05
Australian	21	0.03
Austrian	247	0.31
Basque	52	0.06
Belgian	20	0.02
Brazilian	23	0.03
British	346	0.43
Bulgarian	25	0.03
Canadian	237	0.30
Celtic	23	0.03
Croatian	136	0.17
Czech	296	0.37
Czechoslovakian	176	0.22
Danish	995	1.24
Dutch	1,616	2.02
Eastern European	7	0.01
English	11,165	13.94
Estonian	16	0.02
European	1,105	1.38
Finnish	348	0.43
French, except Basque	3,005	3.75
French Canadian	534	0.67
German	14,026	17.51
Greek	352	0.44
Hawaii Native/Pacific Islander:	395	0.49
Melanesian: (6)	8	0.01
Fijian (6)	8	0.01
Micronesian: (44)	93	0.12
Guamanian/Chamorro (40)	89	0.11
Other Micronesian (4)	4	0.01
Polynesian: (85)	212	0.27
Native Hawaiian (37)	136	0.17
Samoan (45)	71	0.09
Tongan (2)	4	0.01
Other Polynesian (1)	1	0.00
Other Pac. Isl., specified	4	0.01
Other Pac. Isl., not spec. (19)	78	0.10
Hispanic or Latino:	9,225	11.54
Central American:	147	0.18
Costa Rican	10	0.01
Guatemalan	26	0.03
Honduran	7	0.01
Nicaraguan	33	0.04
Panamanian	18	0.02
Salvadoran	44	0.06
Other Central American	9	0.01
Cuban	81	0.10
Dominican Republic	2	0.00
Mexican	6,861	8.58
Puerto Rican	283	0.35
South American:	137	0.17
Argentinean	15	0.02
Bolivian	2	0.00
Chilean	22	0.03
Colombian	40	0.05
Ecuadorian	7	0.01
Peruvian	32	0.04
Uruguayan	5	0.01
Venezuelan	1	0.00
Other South American	13	0.02
Other Hispanic or Latino	1,714	2.14
Hungarian	569	0.71
Icelander	9	0.01
Iranian	238	0.30
Irish	11,339	14.16
Israeli	41	0.05
Italian	6,366	7.95
Latvian	21	0.03
Lithuanian	166	0.21
Luxemburger	8	0.01
Maltese	33	0.04
Northern European	185	0.23
Norwegian	1,858	2.32
Pennsylvania German	48	0.06
Polish	1,417	1.77
Portuguese	1,532	1.91
Romanian	141	0.18
Russian	837	1.05
Scandinavian	209	0.26
Scotch-Irish	1,411	1.76
Scottish	2,018	2.52
Serbian	123	0.15
Slavic	43	0.05
Slovak	41	0.05
Slovene	25	0.03
Soviet Union	15	0.02
Swedish	2,207	2.76
Swiss	392	0.49
Turkish	23	0.03
Ukrainian	445	0.56
United States or American	4,086	5.10
Welsh	740	0.92
West Indian, excl. Hispanic:	102	0.13
British West Indian	28	0.03
Jamaican	74	0.09
White:	71,322	89.24
Not Hispanic (63,737)	65,513	81.97
Hispanic (5,019)	5,809	7.27
Yugoslavian	186	0.23

Rossmoor

Place Type: Census Designated Place
County: Orange
Population: 10,298

Ancestry/Race	Number	%
African American/Black:	106	1.03
Not Hispanic (77)	103	1.00
Hispanic (3)	3	0.03
Alaska Native tribes, specified:	1	0.01
Aleut (1)	1	0.01
Am. Ind. or Alaska Nat., not spec.	24	0.23
American Indian tribes, specified:	83	0.81
Apache (3)	3	0.03
Cherokee (4)	39	0.38
Chippewa (2)	3	0.03
Choctaw (3)	7	0.07
Comanche (1)	1	0.01
Creek (4)	4	0.04
Iroquois	8	0.08
Latin American Indians (2)	2	0.02
Lumbee (1)	1	0.01
Navajo (1)	6	0.06
Osage	1	0.01
Sioux (2)	3	0.03
All other tribes (2)	5	0.05
American Indian tribes, not spec.	2	0.02
Arab:	46	0.45
Arab/Arabic	27	0.26
Lebanese	15	0.15
Syrian	4	0.04
Armenian	57	0.56
Asian:	764	7.42
Cambodian	1	0.01
Chinese, ex. Taiwanese (123)	172	1.67
Filipino (97)	136	1.32
Indian (41)	42	0.41
Indonesian (2)	4	0.04
Japanese (160)	237	2.30
Korean (65)	73	0.71
Malaysian	5	0.05
Pakistani (1)	1	0.01
Sri Lankan (6)	7	0.07
Taiwanese (59)	66	0.64
Thai (2)	2	0.02
Vietnamese (7)	8	0.08
Other Asian, not specified (1)	10	0.10
Australian	7	0.07

Notes: 1. Figures in the "Number" column do not add up to the total population due to: a) Ancestry/Race overlap — e.g. persons can report being both White and Irish, b) persons of Hispanic origin can report being any race, c) persons reporting two ancestries are counted in both categories. 2. Numbers in parentheses indicate the number of persons reporting this ancestry/race alone, not in combination with any other ancestry/race. 3. Refer to the Explanation of Data in the front of the book for more detailed information.

Ancestry/Race	Number	%
Austrian	38	0.37
Brazilian	13	0.13
British	108	1.05
Canadian	17	0.17
Celtic	21	0.20
Croatian	70	0.68
Czech	69	0.67
Czechoslovakian	25	0.24
Danish	231	2.25
Dutch	234	2.28
Eastern European	28	0.27
English	1,792	17.48
European	188	1.83
Finnish	41	0.40
French, except Basque	437	4.26
French Canadian	88	0.86
German	1,789	17.45
Greek	145	1.41
Hawaii Native/Pacific Islander:	42	0.41
Melanesian: (1)	4	0.04
Fijian (1)	4	0.04
Micronesian: (6)	8	0.08
Guamanian/Chamorro (6)	8	0.08
Polynesian: (3)	26	0.25
Native Hawaiian (2)	19	0.18
Samoan (1)	7	0.07
Other Pac. Isl., not spec.	4	0.04
Hispanic or Latino:	687	6.67
Central American:	29	0.28
Costa Rican	1	0.01
Guatemalan	8	0.08
Honduran	6	0.06
Nicaraguan	6	0.06
Panamanian	1	0.01
Salvadoran	3	0.03
Other Central American	4	0.04
Cuban	34	0.33
Dominican Republic	1	0.01
Mexican	445	4.32
Puerto Rican	19	0.18
South American:	31	0.30
Argentinean	3	0.03
Bolivian	1	0.01
Chilean	2	0.02
Colombian	2	0.02
Ecuadorian	7	0.07
Peruvian	11	0.11
Venezuelan	1	0.01
Other South American	4	0.04
Other Hispanic or Latino	128	1.24
Hungarian	94	0.92
Icelander	6	0.06
Iranian	32	0.31
Irish	1,537	14.99
Italian	849	8.28
Lithuanian	33	0.32
Northern European	12	0.12
Norwegian	299	2.92
Pennsylvania German	14	0.14
Polish	309	3.01
Portuguese	38	0.37
Romanian	31	0.30
Russian	220	2.15
Scandinavian	6	0.06
Scotch-Irish	242	2.36
Scottish	363	3.54
Serbian	11	0.11
Slavic	20	0.20
Slovak	10	0.10
Swedish	269	2.62
Swiss	71	0.69
Turkish	20	0.20
Ukrainian	38	0.37
United States or American	523	5.10
Welsh	193	1.88
White:	9,419	91.46
Not Hispanic (8,662)	8,869	86.12
Hispanic (491)	550	5.34
Yugoslavian	35	0.34

Rowland Heights

Place Type: Census Designated Place
County: Los Angeles
Population: 48,553

Ancestry/Race	Number	%
Acadian/Cajun	19	0.04
African American/Black:	1,498	3.09
Not Hispanic (1,163)	1,313	2.70
Hispanic (105)	185	0.38
African, sub-Saharan:	161	0.33
African	134	0.28
Ethiopian	19	0.04
Kenyan	8	0.02
Alaska Native tribes, specified:	4	0.01
Tlingit-Haida	4	0.01
Am. Ind. or Alaska Nat., not spec.	221	0.46
American Indian tribes, specified:	250	0.51
Apache (22)	48	0.10
Blackfeet	4	0.01
Cherokee (5)	33	0.07
Chickasaw	3	0.01
Chippewa (1)	2	0.00
Choctaw (2)	8	0.02
Comanche (6)	8	0.02
Cree	4	0.01
Creek	1	0.00
Delaware (1)	2	0.00
Houma	4	0.01
Iroquois	7	0.01
Latin American Indians (20)	49	0.10
Navajo (12)	22	0.05
Pima (2)	3	0.01
Pueblo (5)	11	0.02
Seminole (1)	1	0.00
Sioux (2)	5	0.01
Tohono O'Odham	4	0.01
Ute	2	0.00
Yakama (1)	1	0.00
Yaqui (5)	9	0.02
Yuman (1)	4	0.01
All other tribes (5)	15	0.03
American Indian tribes, not spec.	45	0.09
Arab:	357	0.74
Arab/Arabic	101	0.21
Egyptian	204	0.42
Lebanese	23	0.05
Palestinian	19	0.04
Syrian	10	0.02
Armenian	142	0.29
Asian:	26,380	54.33
Bangladeshi (11)	11	0.02
Cambodian (76)	115	0.24
Chinese, ex. Taiwanese (11,398)	12,445	25.63
Filipino (3,112)	3,425	7.05
Hmong (2)	2	0.00
Indian (635)	696	1.43
Indonesian (181)	305	0.63
Japanese (739)	937	1.93
Korean (3,730)	3,821	7.87
Laotian (40)	51	0.11
Malaysian (16)	31	0.06
Pakistani (51)	80	0.16
Sri Lankan (4)	8	0.02
Taiwanese (2,659)	3,295	6.79
Thai (201)	242	0.50
Vietnamese (527)	636	1.31
Other Asian, specified (84)	87	0.18
Other Asian, not specified (72)	193	0.40
Austrian	100	0.21
Basque	19	0.04
Brazilian	13	0.03
British	62	0.13
Bulgarian	30	0.06
Canadian	63	0.13
Croatian	27	0.06
Czech	42	0.09
Czechoslovakian	13	0.03
Danish	149	0.31
Dutch	209	0.43
English	1,520	3.15
European	91	0.19
French, except Basque	458	0.95
French Canadian	55	0.11
German	1,669	3.45
Greek	12	0.02
Hawaii Native/Pacific Islander:	379	0.78
Melanesian: (1)	2	0.00
Fijian (1)	2	0.00
Micronesian: (6)	11	0.02
Guamanian/Chamorro (6)	11	0.02
Polynesian: (133)	201	0.41
Native Hawaiian (26)	73	0.15
Samoan (83)	102	0.21
Tongan (24)	24	0.05
Other Polynesian	2	0.00
Other Pac. Isl., not spec. (9)	165	0.34
Hispanic or Latino:	13,748	28.32
Central American:	531	1.09
Costa Rican	19	0.04
Guatemalan	144	0.30
Honduran	17	0.04
Nicaraguan	79	0.16
Panamanian	10	0.02
Salvadoran	225	0.46
Other Central American	37	0.08
Cuban	93	0.19
Dominican Republic	4	0.01
Mexican	10,752	22.14
Puerto Rican	140	0.29
South American:	392	0.81
Argentinean	55	0.11
Bolivian	13	0.03
Chilean	17	0.04
Colombian	88	0.18
Ecuadorian	76	0.16
Paraguayan	3	0.01
Peruvian	76	0.16
Uruguayan	3	0.01
Venezuelan	12	0.02
Other South American	49	0.10
Other Hispanic or Latino	1,836	3.78
Hungarian	63	0.13
Iranian	35	0.07
Irish	1,646	3.41
Italian	949	1.96
Lithuanian	9	0.02
Norwegian	281	0.58
Pennsylvania German	8	0.02
Polish	219	0.45
Portuguese	62	0.13
Romanian	98	0.20
Russian	264	0.55
Scandinavian	8	0.02
Scotch-Irish	153	0.32
Scottish	235	0.49
Slavic	6	0.01
Slovak	7	0.01
Slovene	8	0.02
Swedish	137	0.28
Swiss	75	0.16
Ukrainian	48	0.10
United States or American	614	1.27
Welsh	24	0.05
West Indian, excl. Hispanic:	20	0.04
Barbadian	6	0.01
West Indian	14	0.03
White:	15,541	32.01
Not Hispanic (7,899)	8,557	17.62
Hispanic (6,307)	6,984	14.38
Yugoslavian	109	0.23

Rubidoux

Place Type: Census Designated Place
County: Riverside
Population: 29,180

Ancestry/Race	Number	%

Notes: 1. Figures in the "Number" column do not add up to the total population due to: a) Ancestry/Race overlap — e.g. persons can report being both White and Irish, b) persons of Hispanic origin can report being any race, c) persons reporting two ancestries are counted in both categories. 2. Numbers in parentheses indicate the number of persons reporting this ancestry/race alone, not in combination with any other ancestry/race. 3. Refer to the Explanation of Data in the front of the book for more detailed information.

African American/Black:	2,378	8.15
Not Hispanic (2,031)	2,193	7.52
Hispanic (106)	185	0.63
African, sub-Saharan:	70	0.24
African	64	0.22
South African	6	0.02
Alaska Native tribes, specified:	2	0.01
Tlingit-Haida (2)	2	0.01
Am. Ind. or Alaska Nat., not spec.	254	0.87
American Indian tribes, specified:	405	1.39
Apache (6)	36	0.12
Blackfeet	4	0.01
Cherokee (24)	80	0.27
Cheyenne (5)	5	0.02
Chickasaw	1	0.00
Chippewa (7)	9	0.03
Choctaw (7)	16	0.05
Comanche	1	0.00
Creek (2)	3	0.01
Crow (1)	1	0.00
Delaware	1	0.00
Iroquois (5)	6	0.02
Latin American Indians (56)	72	0.25
Navajo (17)	21	0.07
Osage (5)	6	0.02
Paiute (2)	2	0.01
Pima (3)	4	0.01
Potawatomi (5)	6	0.02
Pueblo (7)	17	0.06
Seminole (1)	1	0.00
Shoshone	1	0.00
Sioux (1)	6	0.02
Tohono O'Odham	3	0.01
Yakama	3	0.01
Yaqui	11	0.04
Yuman (1)	3	0.01
All other tribes (75)	86	0.29
American Indian tribes, not spec.	24	0.08
Arab:	158	0.54
Lebanese	60	0.20
Syrian	91	0.31
Other Arab	7	0.02
Armenian	70	0.24
Asian:	889	3.05
Cambodian (21)	23	0.08
Chinese, ex. Taiwanese (41)	58	0.20
Filipino (243)	338	1.16
Indian (58)	88	0.30
Indonesian (5)	7	0.02
Japanese (49)	87	0.30
Korean (58)	81	0.28
Laotian (10)	10	0.03
Pakistani (6)	12	0.04
Sri Lankan (8)	8	0.03
Taiwanese (12)	13	0.04
Thai (8)	9	0.03
Vietnamese (114)	125	0.43
Other Asian, not specified (6)	30	0.10
Australian	14	0.05
Austrian	32	0.11
Belgian	35	0.12
British	18	0.06
Canadian	83	0.28
Croatian	39	0.13
Czech	9	0.03
Czechoslovakian	16	0.05
Danish	96	0.33
Dutch	187	0.64
English	1,422	4.85
European	202	0.69
French, except Basque	515	1.76
French Canadian	161	0.55
German	1,975	6.74
Greek	120	0.41
Hawaii Native/Pacific Islander:	156	0.53
Micronesian: (18)	30	0.10
Guamanian/Chamorro (16)	28	0.10
Other Micronesian (2)	2	0.01
Polynesian: (59)	101	0.35
Native Hawaiian (10)	43	0.15
Samoan (27)	32	0.11
Tongan (22)	26	0.09
Other Pac. Isl., not spec. (5)	25	0.09
Hispanic or Latino:	15,843	54.29
Central American:	313	1.07
Costa Rican	7	0.02
Guatemalan	110	0.38
Honduran	23	0.08
Nicaraguan	13	0.04
Panamanian	10	0.03
Salvadoran	120	0.41
Other Central American	30	0.10
Cuban	28	0.10
Dominican Republic	1	0.00
Mexican	13,271	45.48
Puerto Rican	176	0.60
South American:	72	0.25
Argentinean	13	0.04
Bolivian	1	0.00
Chilean	5	0.02
Colombian	8	0.03
Ecuadorian	8	0.03
Peruvian	28	0.10
Uruguayan	1	0.00
Venezuelan	1	0.00
Other South American	7	0.02
Other Hispanic or Latino	1,982	6.79
Hungarian	36	0.12
Iranian	18	0.06
Irish	1,835	6.26
Italian	905	3.09
Lithuanian	10	0.03
Northern European	6	0.02
Norwegian	180	0.61
Pennsylvania German	26	0.09
Polish	109	0.37
Portuguese	223	0.76
Romanian	25	0.09
Russian	87	0.30
Scandinavian	22	0.08
Scotch-Irish	407	1.39
Scottish	439	1.50
Serbian	9	0.03
Slavic	7	0.02
Slovak	44	0.15
Swedish	106	0.36
Swiss	15	0.05
Ukrainian	36	0.12
United States or American	862	2.94
Welsh	56	0.19
West Indian, excl. Hispanic:	27	0.09
Jamaican	11	0.04
U.S. Virgin Islander	8	0.03
West Indian	8	0.03
White:	16,279	55.79
Not Hispanic (9,850)	10,272	35.20
Hispanic (5,257)	6,007	20.59
Yugoslavian	42	0.14

Sacramento

Place Type: City
County: Sacramento
Population: 407,018

Ancestry/Race	Number	%
Acadian/Cajun	32	0.01
Afghan	269	0.07
African American/Black:	70,218	17.25
Not Hispanic (61,136)	66,927	16.44
Hispanic (1,832)	3,291	0.81
African, sub-Saharan:	4,494	1.10
African	3,647	0.90
Cape Verdean	337	0.08
Ethiopian	147	0.04
Ghanian	24	0.01
Kenyan	16	0.00
Nigerian	176	0.04
Senegalese	6	0.00
Somalian	7	0.00
South African	87	0.02
Ugandan	36	0.01
Other sub-Saharan African	11	0.00
Alaska Native tribes, specified:	106	0.03
Alaska Athabascan (3)	7	0.00
Aleut (14)	29	0.01
Eskimo (17)	35	0.01
Tlingit-Haida (13)	20	0.00
All other tribes (5)	15	0.00
Alaska Native tribes, not specified	8	0.00
Am. Ind. or Alaska Nat., not spec.	3,551	0.87
Albanian	32	0.01
American Indian tribes, specified:	7,639	1.88
Apache (207)	449	0.11
Blackfeet (77)	428	0.11
Cherokee (544)	2,028	0.50
Cheyenne (13)	36	0.01
Chickasaw (23)	76	0.02
Chippewa (131)	203	0.05
Choctaw (76)	373	0.09
Colville (1)	2	0.00
Comanche (15)	39	0.01
Cree (6)	24	0.01
Creek (31)	131	0.03
Crow (17)	38	0.01
Delaware (7)	12	0.00
Houma (3)	8	0.00
Iroquois (53)	120	0.03
Kiowa (5)	19	0.00
Latin American Indians (469)	753	0.19
Lumbee (10)	18	0.00
Menominee (2)	5	0.00
Navajo (136)	266	0.07
Osage (10)	37	0.01
Ottawa (4)	7	0.00
Paiute (34)	75	0.02
Pima (14)	20	0.00
Potawatomi (21)	45	0.01
Pueblo (46)	86	0.02
Puget Sound Salish (11)	11	0.00
Seminole (13)	52	0.01
Shoshone (43)	74	0.02
Sioux (146)	295	0.07
Tohono O'Odham (6)	14	0.00
Ute (6)	18	0.00
Yakama (6)	14	0.00
Yaqui (112)	173	0.04
Yuman (14)	19	0.00
All other tribes (1,012)	1,671	0.41
American Indian tribes, not spec.	502	0.12
Arab:	1,372	0.34
Arab/Arabic	236	0.06
Egyptian	181	0.04
Iraqi	24	0.01
Jordanian	98	0.02
Lebanese	527	0.13
Moroccan	20	0.00
Palestinian	69	0.02
Syrian	140	0.03
Other Arab	77	0.02
Armenian	472	0.12
Asian:	79,286	19.48
Bangladeshi (6)	6	0.00
Cambodian (390)	511	0.13
Chinese, ex. Taiwanese (19,287)	21,450	5.27
Filipino (8,515)	11,156	2.74
Hmong (11,295)	12,610	3.10
Indian (4,944)	6,838	1.68
Indonesian (126)	262	0.06
Japanese (6,642)	8,710	2.14
Korean (815)	1,140	0.28
Laotian (5,924)	6,876	1.69
Malaysian (18)	35	0.01
Pakistani (724)	1,004	0.25
Sri Lankan (28)	32	0.01
Taiwanese (138)	168	0.04
Thai (202)	362	0.09
Vietnamese (6,171)	6,753	1.66
Other Asian, specified (22)	63	0.02
Other Asian, not specified (629)	1,310	0.32

Notes: 1. Figures in the "Number" column do not add up to the total population due to: a) Ancestry/Race overlap — e.g. persons can report being both White and Irish, b) persons of Hispanic origin can report being any race, c) persons reporting two ancestries are counted in both categories. 2. Numbers in parentheses indicate the number of persons reporting this ancestry/race alone, not in combination with any other ancestry/race. 3. Refer to the Explanation of Data in the front of the book for more detailed information.

Ancestry/Race	Number	%
Assyrian/Chaldean/Syriac	45	0.01
Australian	89	0.02
Austrian	648	0.16
Basque	258	0.06
Belgian	223	0.05
Brazilian	54	0.01
British	1,426	0.35
Bulgarian	42	0.01
Canadian	717	0.18
Carpatho Rusyn	7	0.00
Celtic	196	0.05
Croatian	584	0.14
Cypriot	6	0.00
Czech	720	0.18
Czechoslovakian	385	0.09
Danish	2,069	0.51
Dutch	3,823	0.94
Eastern European	149	0.04
English	25,698	6.31
European	3,453	0.85
Finnish	539	0.13
French, except Basque	8,389	2.06
French Canadian	1,198	0.29
German	34,198	8.40
German Russian	6	0.00
Greek	2,203	0.54
Hawaii Native/Pacific Islander:	6,961	1.71
Melanesian: (929)	1,254	0.31
Fijian (929)	1,253	0.31
Other Melanesian	1	0.00
Micronesian: (352)	523	0.13
Guamanian/Chamorro (276)	438	0.11
Other Micronesian (76)	85	0.02
Polynesian: (1,921)	2,894	0.71
Native Hawaiian (312)	877	0.22
Samoan (771)	937	0.23
Tongan (797)	970	0.24
Other Polynesian (41)	110	0.03
Other Pac. Isl., specified	8	0.00
Other Pac. Isl., not spec. (582)	2,282	0.56
Hispanic or Latino:	87,974	21.61
Central American:	1,891	0.46
Costa Rican	95	0.02
Guatemalan	342	0.08
Honduran	63	0.02
Nicaraguan	321	0.08
Panamanian	153	0.04
Salvadoran	762	0.19
Other Central American	155	0.04
Cuban	474	0.12
Dominican Republic	68	0.02
Mexican	70,758	17.38
Puerto Rican	2,053	0.50
South American:	680	0.17
Argentinean	51	0.01
Bolivian	28	0.01
Chilean	105	0.03
Colombian	157	0.04
Ecuadorian	35	0.01
Paraguayan	3	0.00
Peruvian	194	0.05
Uruguayan	12	0.00
Venezuelan	30	0.01
Other South American	65	0.02
Other Hispanic or Latino	12,050	2.96
Hungarian	985	0.24
Icelander	47	0.01
Iranian	511	0.13
Irish	27,663	6.80
Israeli	60	0.01
Italian	15,643	3.84
Latvian	114	0.03
Lithuanian	430	0.11
Luxemburger	41	0.01
Maltese	64	0.02
New Zealander	53	0.01
Northern European	550	0.14
Norwegian	4,601	1.13
Pennsylvania German	107	0.03
Polish	3,313	0.81
Portuguese	5,414	1.33
Romanian	876	0.22
Russian	4,140	1.02
Scandinavian	534	0.13
Scotch-Irish	4,605	1.13
Scottish	5,248	1.29
Serbian	171	0.04
Slavic	94	0.02
Slovak	193	0.05
Slovene	50	0.01
Swedish	4,317	1.06
Swiss	1,375	0.34
Turkish	222	0.05
Ukrainian	2,287	0.56
United States or American	12,801	3.14
Welsh	2,080	0.51
West Indian, excl. Hispanic:	682	0.17
Belizean	33	0.01
British West Indian	15	0.00
Dutch West Indian	28	0.01
Haitian	21	0.01
Jamaican	405	0.10
Trinidadian and Tobagonian	72	0.02
West Indian	108	0.03
White:	214,140	52.61
Not Hispanic (164,974)	176,446	43.35
Hispanic (31,575)	37,694	9.26
Yugoslavian	743	0.18

Salida

Place Type: Census Designated Place
County: Stanislaus
Population: 12,560

Ancestry/Race	Number	%
African American/Black:	494	3.93
Not Hispanic (410)	466	3.71
Hispanic (14)	28	0.22
African, sub-Saharan:	68	0.54
African	19	0.15
Nigerian	49	0.39
Alaska Native tribes, specified:	5	0.04
Aleut	2	0.02
Eskimo	3	0.02
Am. Ind. or Alaska Nat., not spec.	87	0.69
American Indian tribes, specified:	217	1.73
Apache (2)	11	0.09
Blackfeet (4)	19	0.15
Cherokee (20)	63	0.50
Cheyenne	2	0.02
Chickasaw (1)	1	0.01
Choctaw (13)	18	0.14
Houma (1)	1	0.01
Iroquois (1)	1	0.01
Kiowa	1	0.01
Latin American Indians (23)	26	0.21
Navajo (4)	5	0.04
Paiute (3)	9	0.07
Pima	1	0.01
Pueblo (1)	3	0.02
Sioux (10)	12	0.10
Yaqui (1)	5	0.04
Yuman	1	0.01
All other tribes (23)	38	0.30
American Indian tribes, not spec.	6	0.05
Arab:	12	0.10
Arab/Arabic	12	0.10
Armenian	71	0.57
Asian:	865	6.89
Cambodian (40)	60	0.48
Chinese, ex. Taiwanese (40)	74	0.59
Filipino (274)	400	3.18
Hmong (18)	24	0.19
Indian (93)	115	0.92
Indonesian (1)	3	0.02
Japanese (31)	67	0.53
Korean (4)	11	0.09
Laotian (7)	7	0.06
Malaysian	1	0.01
Pakistani (22)	22	0.18
Taiwanese (3)	3	0.02
Thai (8)	8	0.06
Vietnamese (40)	56	0.45
Other Asian, not specified (1)	14	0.11
Assyrian/Chaldean/Syriac	31	0.25
Basque	11	0.09
Belgian	24	0.19
British	9	0.07
Canadian	25	0.20
Celtic	8	0.06
Czech	14	0.11
Czechoslovakian	33	0.26
Danish	93	0.74
Dutch	308	2.45
English	801	6.38
European	43	0.34
Finnish	5	0.04
French, except Basque	220	1.75
French Canadian	56	0.45
German	1,405	11.19
Greek	46	0.37
Hawaii Native/Pacific Islander:	90	0.72
Melanesian: (1)	4	0.03
Fijian (1)	4	0.03
Micronesian: (8)	9	0.07
Guamanian/Chamorro (8)	9	0.07
Polynesian: (14)	44	0.35
Native Hawaiian (7)	32	0.25
Samoan (7)	11	0.09
Tongan	1	0.01
Other Pac. Isl., not spec. (6)	33	0.26
Hispanic or Latino:	3,902	31.07
Central American:	63	0.50
Costa Rican	7	0.06
Guatemalan	7	0.06
Honduran	5	0.04
Nicaraguan	5	0.04
Panamanian	1	0.01
Salvadoran	38	0.30
Cuban	1	0.01
Mexican	3,124	24.87
Puerto Rican	81	0.64
South American:	21	0.17
Argentinean	4	0.03
Bolivian	1	0.01
Chilean	3	0.02
Colombian	3	0.02
Peruvian	7	0.06
Venezuelan	2	0.02
Other South American	1	0.01
Other Hispanic or Latino	612	4.87
Hungarian	45	0.36
Iranian	14	0.11
Irish	871	6.93
Italian	648	5.16
Norwegian	92	0.73
Polish	178	1.42
Portuguese	675	5.37
Russian	100	0.80
Scotch-Irish	199	1.58
Scottish	119	0.95
Serbian	4	0.03
Slavic	18	0.14
Swedish	177	1.41
Swiss	18	0.14
Turkish	22	0.18
United States or American	658	5.24
Welsh	78	0.62
West Indian, excl. Hispanic:	21	0.17
Jamaican	21	0.17
White:	9,255	73.69
Not Hispanic (7,095)	7,444	59.27
Hispanic (1,533)	1,811	14.42
Yugoslavian	48	0.38

Notes: 1. Figures in the "Number" column do not add up to the total population due to: a) Ancestry/Race overlap — e.g. persons can report being both White and Irish, b) persons of Hispanic origin can report being any race, c) persons reporting two ancestries are counted in both categories. 2. Numbers in parentheses indicate the number of persons reporting this ancestry/race alone, not in combination with any other ancestry/race. 3. Refer to the Explanation of Data in the front of the book for more detailed information.

Salinas

Place Type: City
County: Monterey
Population: 151,060

Ancestry/Race	Number	%
African American/Black:	5,819	3.85
Not Hispanic (4,569)	5,091	3.37
Hispanic (374)	728	0.48
African, sub-Saharan:	470	0.31
African	381	0.25
Cape Verdean	24	0.02
Kenyan	18	0.01
Nigerian	4	0.00
South African	36	0.02
Sudanese	7	0.00
Alaska Native tribes, specified:	18	0.01
Aleut	2	0.00
Eskimo (4)	7	0.00
Tlingit-Haida (5)	8	0.01
All other tribes (1)	1	0.00
Alaska Native tribes, not specified	1	0.00
Am. Ind. or Alaska Nat., not spec.	1,292	0.86
Alsatian	12	0.01
American Indian tribes, specified:	1,684	1.11
Apache (57)	101	0.07
Blackfeet (10)	51	0.03
Cherokee (84)	316	0.21
Cheyenne	4	0.00
Chickasaw (16)	32	0.02
Chippewa (4)	13	0.01
Choctaw (27)	67	0.04
Colville	4	0.00
Comanche (7)	21	0.01
Cree (1)	1	0.00
Creek (6)	14	0.01
Crow	2	0.00
Delaware (2)	2	0.00
Houma (1)	1	0.00
Iroquois (2)	10	0.01
Kiowa (3)	4	0.00
Latin American Indians (417)	567	0.38
Menominee	1	0.00
Navajo (15)	38	0.03
Osage	3	0.00
Paiute (4)	10	0.01
Pima (1)	7	0.00
Potawatomi (8)	13	0.01
Pueblo (6)	19	0.01
Puget Sound Salish (2)	3	0.00
Seminole (2)	13	0.01
Shoshone (2)	6	0.00
Sioux (23)	28	0.02
Tohono O'Odham (1)	6	0.00
Ute (2)	2	0.00
Yaqui (34)	51	0.03
Yuman (3)	3	0.00
All other tribes (144)	271	0.18
American Indian tribes, not spec.	173	0.11
Arab:	209	0.14
Arab/Arabic	87	0.06
Egyptian	67	0.04
Lebanese	17	0.01
Moroccan	5	0.00
Syrian	7	0.00
Other Arab	26	0.02
Armenian	89	0.06
Asian:	11,887	7.87
Cambodian (17)	22	0.01
Chinese, ex. Taiwanese (856)	1,066	0.71
Filipino (5,863)	7,345	4.86
Hmong (17)	17	0.01
Indian (499)	615	0.41
Indonesian (13)	16	0.01
Japanese (787)	1,245	0.82
Korean (603)	778	0.52
Laotian (4)	7	0.00
Malaysian (1)	5	0.00
Pakistani (3)	6	0.00
Sri Lankan (9)	10	0.01
Taiwanese (3)	6	0.00
Thai (25)	42	0.03
Vietnamese (419)	482	0.32
Other Asian, specified (3)	6	0.00
Other Asian, not specified (100)	219	0.14
Assyrian/Chaldean/Syriac	9	0.01
Australian	27	0.02
Austrian	109	0.07
Basque	8	0.01
Belgian	44	0.03
Brazilian	7	0.00
British	223	0.15
Bulgarian	9	0.01
Canadian	197	0.13
Celtic	105	0.07
Croatian	78	0.05
Czech	85	0.06
Czechoslovakian	116	0.08
Danish	714	0.47
Dutch	851	0.56
English	5,020	3.33
Estonian	8	0.01
European	728	0.48
Finnish	116	0.08
French, except Basque	1,598	1.06
French Canadian	230	0.15
German	7,159	4.75
German Russian	23	0.02
Greek	195	0.13
Hawaii Native/Pacific Islander:	888	0.59
Melanesian: (5)	6	0.00
Fijian (5)	5	0.00
Other Melanesian	1	0.00
Micronesian: (162)	254	0.17
Guamanian/Chamorro (159)	250	0.17
Other Micronesian (3)	4	0.00
Polynesian: (141)	391	0.26
Native Hawaiian (74)	294	0.19
Samoan (61)	81	0.05
Tongan (5)	10	0.01
Other Polynesian (1)	6	0.00
Other Pac. Isl., specified	2	0.00
Other Pac. Isl., not spec. (89)	235	0.16
Hispanic or Latino:	96,880	64.13
Central American:	661	0.44
Costa Rican	17	0.01
Guatemalan	116	0.08
Honduran	41	0.03
Nicaraguan	30	0.02
Panamanian	52	0.03
Salvadoran	373	0.25
Other Central American	32	0.02
Cuban	86	0.06
Dominican Republic	15	0.01
Mexican	84,815	56.15
Puerto Rican	583	0.39
South American:	275	0.18
Argentinean	18	0.01
Bolivian	4	0.00
Chilean	37	0.02
Colombian	45	0.03
Ecuadorian	12	0.01
Paraguayan	4	0.00
Peruvian	121	0.08
Uruguayan	1	0.00
Venezuelan	11	0.01
Other South American	22	0.01
Other Hispanic or Latino	10,445	6.91
Hungarian	101	0.07
Icelander	8	0.01
Iranian	41	0.03
Irish	5,623	3.73
Italian	3,250	2.16
Lithuanian	49	0.03
Luxemburger	15	0.01
Macedonian	16	0.01
Maltese	46	0.03
New Zealander	7	0.00
Northern European	37	0.02
Norwegian	1,059	0.70
Pennsylvania German	16	0.01
Polish	858	0.57
Portuguese	1,247	0.83
Romanian	36	0.02
Russian	282	0.19
Scandinavian	98	0.07
Scotch-Irish	864	0.57
Scottish	1,333	0.88
Serbian	10	0.01
Slavic	3	0.00
Slovak	38	0.03
Swedish	930	0.62
Swiss	757	0.50
Turkish	39	0.03
Ukrainian	89	0.06
United States or American	3,682	2.44
Welsh	345	0.23
West Indian, excl. Hispanic:	92	0.06
Bermudan	16	0.01
Dutch West Indian	17	0.01
Jamaican	10	0.01
Trinidadian and Tobagonian	16	0.01
West Indian	33	0.02
White:	74,572	49.37
Not Hispanic (36,535)	38,814	25.69
Hispanic (31,683)	35,758	23.67
Yugoslavian	95	0.06

San Anselmo

Place Type: Town
County: Marin
Population: 12,378

Ancestry/Race	Number	%
Acadian/Cajun	38	0.30
African American/Black:	194	1.57
Not Hispanic (128)	192	1.55
Hispanic (2)	2	0.02
African, sub-Saharan:	64	0.51
African	44	0.35
Ethiopian	5	0.04
Ghanian	15	0.12
Alaska Native tribes, specified:	6	0.05
Alaska Athabascan (3)	4	0.03
Aleut (1)	1	0.01
Eskimo	1	0.01
Am. Ind. or Alaska Nat., not spec.	48	0.39
American Indian tribes, specified:	108	0.87
Apache (1)	7	0.06
Blackfeet	6	0.05
Cherokee (6)	27	0.22
Chickasaw	3	0.02
Chippewa	1	0.01
Choctaw (1)	8	0.06
Comanche (1)	4	0.03
Creek (1)	5	0.04
Iroquois (1)	2	0.02
Kiowa	1	0.01
Latin American Indians (9)	13	0.11
Navajo (2)	7	0.06
Paiute (3)	3	0.02
Potawatomi (1)	1	0.01
Shoshone (1)	2	0.02
Sioux (2)	3	0.02
Tohono O'Odham (1)	1	0.01
All other tribes (5)	14	0.11
American Indian tribes, not spec.	2	0.02
Arab:	76	0.61
Lebanese	33	0.26
Moroccan	11	0.09
Syrian	12	0.10
Other Arab	20	0.16
Armenian	8	0.06
Asian:	529	4.27
Cambodian (1)	1	0.01
Chinese, ex. Taiwanese (107)	156	1.26
Filipino (32)	66	0.53
Indian (21)	32	0.26

Notes: 1. Figures in the "Number" column do not add up to the total population due to: a) Ancestry/Race overlap — e.g. persons can report being both White and Irish, b) persons of Hispanic origin can report being any race, c) persons reporting two ancestries are counted in both categories. 2. Numbers in parentheses indicate the number of persons reporting this ancestry/race alone, not in combination with any other ancestry/race. 3. Refer to the Explanation of Data in the front of the book for more detailed information.

Ancestry/Race	Number	%
Indonesian	2	0.02
Japanese (68)	122	0.99
Korean (103)	112	0.90
Laotian (1)	1	0.01
Malaysian (1)	1	0.01
Sri Lankan	1	0.01
Taiwanese (3)	3	0.02
Thai (5)	12	0.10
Vietnamese (4)	10	0.08
Other Asian, specified (1)	1	0.01
Other Asian, not specified (1)	9	0.07
Australian	28	0.22
Austrian	92	0.73
Basque	6	0.05
Belgian	39	0.31
Brazilian	27	0.22
British	219	1.75
Canadian	47	0.38
Celtic	44	0.35
Croatian	8	0.06
Czech	45	0.36
Czechoslovakian	6	0.05
Danish	178	1.42
Dutch	297	2.37
Eastern European	63	0.50
English	2,117	16.91
Estonian	7	0.06
European	255	2.04
Finnish	37	0.30
French, except Basque	634	5.06
French Canadian	106	0.85
German	2,188	17.47
Greek	61	0.49
Hawaii Native/Pacific Islander:	40	0.32
Micronesian: (2)	3	0.02
Guamanian/Chamorro (2)	3	0.02
Polynesian: (11)	30	0.24
Native Hawaiian (6)	24	0.19
Samoan (5)	6	0.05
Other Pac. Isl., not spec. (1)	7	0.06
Hispanic or Latino:	513	4.14
Central American:	67	0.54
Guatemalan	27	0.22
Honduran	5	0.04
Nicaraguan	7	0.06
Salvadoran	27	0.22
Other Central American	1	0.01
Cuban	29	0.23
Dominican Republic	3	0.02
Mexican	209	1.69
Puerto Rican	16	0.13
South American:	46	0.37
Argentinean	5	0.04
Bolivian	10	0.08
Chilean	7	0.06
Colombian	7	0.06
Ecuadorian	1	0.01
Paraguayan	1	0.01
Peruvian	9	0.07
Venezuelan	1	0.01
Other South American	5	0.04
Other Hispanic or Latino	143	1.16
Hungarian	59	0.47
Iranian	24	0.19
Irish	2,151	17.18
Israeli	9	0.07
Italian	1,413	11.29
Latvian	27	0.22
Lithuanian	84	0.67
Luxemburger	9	0.07
New Zealander	34	0.27
Northern European	97	0.77
Norwegian	226	1.80
Pennsylvania German	5	0.04
Polish	485	3.87
Portuguese	127	1.01
Romanian	13	0.10
Russian	733	5.85
Scandinavian	58	0.46
Scotch-Irish	396	3.16
Scottish	623	4.98
Serbian	5	0.04
Slavic	8	0.06
Slovak	29	0.23
Swedish	384	3.07
Swiss	95	0.76
Turkish	17	0.14
Ukrainian	120	0.96
United States or American	365	2.92
Welsh	259	2.07
West Indian, excl. Hispanic:	29	0.23
Jamaican	29	0.23
White:	11,679	94.35
Not Hispanic (11,011)	11,289	91.20
Hispanic (330)	390	3.15
Yugoslavian	22	0.18

San Bernardino

Place Type: City
County: San Bernardino
Population: 185,401

Ancestry/Race	Number	%
African American/Black:	32,946	17.77
Not Hispanic (29,654)	31,452	16.96
Hispanic (771)	1,494	0.81
African, sub-Saharan:	1,686	0.91
African	1,335	0.72
Cape Verdean	15	0.01
Ethiopian	111	0.06
Ghanian	21	0.01
Nigerian	133	0.07
Sierra Leonean	59	0.03
South African	12	0.01
Alaska Native tribes, specified:	22	0.01
Alaska Athabascan (5)	5	0.00
Aleut (2)	2	0.00
Eskimo (5)	11	0.01
Tlingit-Haida (2)	4	0.00
Alaska Native tribes, not specified	2	0.00
Am. Ind. or Alaska Nat., not spec.	1,817	0.98
Albanian	7	0.00
American Indian tribes, specified:	2,610	1.41
Apache (95)	184	0.10
Blackfeet (18)	102	0.06
Cherokee (197)	623	0.34
Cheyenne (6)	11	0.01
Chickasaw (10)	24	0.01
Chippewa (14)	30	0.02
Choctaw (43)	145	0.08
Comanche (3)	18	0.01
Cree (2)	8	0.00
Creek (25)	57	0.03
Delaware (4)	6	0.00
Houma	1	0.00
Iroquois (35)	57	0.03
Kiowa (5)	5	0.00
Latin American Indians (276)	443	0.24
Lumbee (13)	13	0.01
Menominee	3	0.00
Navajo (54)	125	0.07
Osage (1)	13	0.01
Ottawa (2)	3	0.00
Paiute (3)	9	0.00
Pima (10)	28	0.02
Potawatomi (5)	9	0.00
Pueblo (56)	71	0.04
Puget Sound Salish (1)	2	0.00
Seminole (5)	10	0.01
Shoshone (10)	12	0.01
Sioux (41)	84	0.05
Tohono O'Odham (4)	11	0.01
Ute (3)	6	0.00
Yakama	1	0.00
Yaqui (44)	71	0.04
Yuman (8)	17	0.01
All other tribes (279)	408	0.22
American Indian tribes, not spec.	277	0.15
Arab:	1,068	0.58
Arab/Arabic	357	0.19
Egyptian	104	0.06
Iraqi	10	0.01
Jordanian	252	0.14
Lebanese	214	0.12
Moroccan	9	0.00
Syrian	69	0.04
Other Arab	53	0.03
Armenian	69	0.04
Asian:	9,727	5.25
Bangladeshi (21)	25	0.01
Cambodian (869)	1,070	0.58
Chinese, ex. Taiwanese (501)	745	0.40
Filipino (1,898)	2,416	1.30
Hmong (67)	72	0.04
Indian (459)	614	0.33
Indonesian (477)	597	0.32
Japanese (347)	636	0.34
Korean (496)	584	0.31
Laotian (104)	177	0.10
Malaysian (2)	7	0.00
Pakistani (68)	90	0.05
Sri Lankan (22)	28	0.02
Taiwanese (84)	100	0.05
Thai (198)	297	0.16
Vietnamese (1,753)	1,881	1.01
Other Asian, specified (9)	21	0.01
Other Asian, not specified (177)	367	0.20
Australian	43	0.02
Austrian	74	0.04
Basque	31	0.02
Belgian	38	0.02
Brazilian	72	0.04
British	362	0.20
Canadian	282	0.15
Celtic	46	0.02
Croatian	98	0.05
Cypriot	7	0.00
Czech	264	0.14
Czechoslovakian	105	0.06
Danish	551	0.30
Dutch	1,606	0.87
Eastern European	19	0.01
English	7,909	4.27
European	882	0.48
Finnish	201	0.11
French, except Basque	3,028	1.63
French Canadian	663	0.36
German	12,247	6.61
Greek	422	0.23
Hawaii Native/Pacific Islander:	1,103	0.59
Melanesian: (10)	15	0.01
Fijian (10)	15	0.01
Micronesian: (133)	167	0.09
Guamanian/Chamorro (89)	120	0.06
Other Micronesian (44)	47	0.03
Polynesian: (446)	718	0.39
Native Hawaiian (77)	225	0.12
Samoan (294)	360	0.19
Tongan (65)	104	0.06
Other Polynesian (10)	29	0.02
Other Pac. Isl., specified	4	0.00
Other Pac. Isl., not spec. (71)	199	0.11
Hispanic or Latino:	88,022	47.48
Central American:	1,832	0.99
Costa Rican	73	0.04
Guatemalan	430	0.23
Honduran	157	0.08
Nicaraguan	192	0.10
Panamanian	91	0.05
Salvadoran	700	0.38
Other Central American	189	0.10
Cuban	251	0.14
Dominican Republic	21	0.01
Mexican	71,891	38.78
Puerto Rican	1,077	0.58
South American:	428	0.23
Argentinean	43	0.02
Bolivian	7	0.00
Chilean	31	0.02

Notes: 1. Figures in the "Number" column do not add up to the total population due to: a) Ancestry/Race overlap — e.g. persons can report being both White and Irish, b) persons of Hispanic origin can report being any race, c) persons reporting two ancestries are counted in both categories. 2. Numbers in parentheses indicate the number of persons reporting this ancestry/race alone, not in combination with any other ancestry/race. 3. Refer to the Explanation of Data in the front of the book for more detailed information.

Colombian	126	0.07
Ecuadorian	51	0.03
Paraguayan	1	0.00
Peruvian	93	0.05
Uruguayan	7	0.00
Venezuelan	23	0.01
Other South American	46	0.02
Other Hispanic or Latino	12,522	6.75
Hungarian	544	0.29
Icelander	51	0.03
Iranian	71	0.04
Irish	8,285	4.47
Israeli	17	0.01
Italian	4,695	2.53
Latvian	9	0.00
Lithuanian	55	0.03
Macedonian	9	0.00
Northern European	71	0.04
Norwegian	1,258	0.68
Pennsylvania German	28	0.02
Polish	1,395	0.75
Portuguese	352	0.19
Romanian	392	0.21
Russian	469	0.25
Scandinavian	97	0.05
Scotch-Irish	1,784	0.96
Scottish	1,490	0.80
Serbian	19	0.01
Slavic	9	0.00
Slovak	53	0.03
Swedish	1,288	0.69
Swiss	100	0.05
Turkish	10	0.01
Ukrainian	51	0.03
United States or American	5,701	3.08
Welsh	533	0.29
West Indian, excl. Hispanic:	435	0.23
Belizean	72	0.04
Dutch West Indian	7	0.00
Jamaican	246	0.13
Trinidadian and Tobagonian	22	0.01
West Indian	76	0.04
Other West Indian	12	0.01
White:	91,523	49.36
Not Hispanic (53,630)	56,878	30.68
Hispanic (30,219)	34,645	18.69
Yugoslavian	33	0.02

San Bruno

Place Type: City
County: San Mateo
Population: 40,165

Ancestry/Race	Number	%
Acadian/Cajun	10	0.02
African American/Black:	1,059	2.64
Not Hispanic (753)	943	2.35
Hispanic (54)	116	0.29
African, sub-Saharan:	66	0.16
African	56	0.14
Other sub-Saharan African	10	0.02
Alaska Native tribes, specified:	3	0.01
Aleut (1)	1	0.00
Eskimo (1)	2	0.00
Am. Ind. or Alaska Nat., not spec.	181	0.45
American Indian tribes, specified:	270	0.67
Apache (9)	22	0.05
Blackfeet (2)	15	0.04
Cherokee (14)	63	0.16
Cheyenne	1	0.00
Chickasaw (1)	1	0.00
Chippewa (2)	8	0.02
Choctaw (5)	19	0.05
Comanche (1)	3	0.01
Cree (1)	1	0.00
Creek (1)	4	0.01
Delaware	3	0.01
Iroquois (1)	3	0.01
Latin American Indians (22)	46	0.11
Navajo (4)	11	0.03
Osage	2	0.00
Paiute (1)	1	0.00
Potawatomi	2	0.00
Pueblo	2	0.00
Seminole (2)	6	0.01
Sioux (1)	8	0.02
Ute (1)	1	0.00
Yaqui (2)	2	0.00
All other tribes (17)	46	0.11
American Indian tribes, not spec.	52	0.13
Arab:	786	1.96
Arab/Arabic	258	0.64
Iraqi	6	0.01
Lebanese	43	0.11
Palestinian	479	1.19
Armenian	104	0.26
Asian:	9,056	22.55
Cambodian (5)	5	0.01
Chinese, ex. Taiwanese (2,171)	2,501	6.23
Filipino (3,075)	3,634	9.05
Indian (877)	1,228	3.06
Indonesian (29)	69	0.17
Japanese (480)	725	1.81
Korean (478)	537	1.34
Laotian	3	0.01
Malaysian (1)	4	0.01
Pakistani (17)	42	0.10
Sri Lankan (2)	3	0.01
Taiwanese (15)	16	0.04
Thai (26)	38	0.09
Vietnamese (99)	116	0.29
Other Asian, specified (8)	22	0.05
Other Asian, not specified (31)	113	0.28
Assyrian/Chaldean/Syriac	10	0.02
Austrian	69	0.17
Basque	35	0.09
Belgian	70	0.17
Brazilian	64	0.16
British	110	0.27
Bulgarian	34	0.08
Canadian	122	0.30
Celtic	12	0.03
Croatian	97	0.24
Czech	65	0.16
Czechoslovakian	33	0.08
Danish	284	0.71
Dutch	323	0.80
Eastern European	6	0.01
English	2,175	5.42
Estonian	19	0.05
European	320	0.80
Finnish	86	0.21
French, except Basque	1,034	2.57
French Canadian	138	0.34
German	3,638	9.06
Greek	551	1.37
Hawaii Native/Pacific Islander:	1,832	4.56
Melanesian: (262)	353	0.88
Fijian (261)	352	0.88
Other Melanesian (1)	1	0.00
Micronesian: (34)	64	0.16
Guamanian/Chamorro (30)	59	0.15
Other Micronesian (4)	5	0.01
Polynesian: (699)	968	2.41
Native Hawaiian (61)	163	0.41
Samoan (186)	253	0.63
Tongan (430)	513	1.28
Other Polynesian (22)	39	0.10
Other Pac. Isl., not spec. (120)	447	1.11
Hispanic or Latino:	9,686	24.12
Central American:	1,562	3.89
Costa Rican	14	0.03
Guatemalan	166	0.41
Honduran	41	0.10
Nicaraguan	508	1.26
Panamanian	27	0.07
Salvadoran	639	1.59
Other Central American	167	0.42
Cuban	64	0.16
Dominican Republic	8	0.02
Mexican	5,050	12.57
Puerto Rican	302	0.75
South American:	369	0.92
Argentinean	25	0.06
Bolivian	20	0.05
Chilean	33	0.08
Colombian	32	0.08
Ecuadorian	16	0.04
Paraguayan	2	0.00
Peruvian	204	0.51
Uruguayan	3	0.01
Venezuelan	7	0.02
Other South American	27	0.07
Other Hispanic or Latino	2,331	5.80
Hungarian	97	0.24
Iranian	46	0.11
Irish	4,745	11.81
Israeli	10	0.02
Italian	4,350	10.83
Lithuanian	63	0.16
Maltese	285	0.71
Northern European	22	0.05
Norwegian	501	1.25
Pennsylvania German	30	0.07
Polish	552	1.37
Portuguese	298	0.74
Romanian	22	0.05
Russian	795	1.98
Scandinavian	17	0.04
Scotch-Irish	579	1.44
Scottish	484	1.21
Serbian	5	0.01
Slavic	14	0.03
Slovene	48	0.12
Swedish	478	1.19
Swiss	207	0.52
Turkish	11	0.03
Ukrainian	135	0.34
United States or American	865	2.15
Welsh	136	0.34
West Indian, excl. Hispanic:	54	0.13
Belizean	4	0.01
Jamaican	16	0.04
Trinidadian and Tobagonian	21	0.05
West Indian	13	0.03
White:	25,343	63.10
Not Hispanic (18,822)	20,222	50.35
Hispanic (4,334)	5,121	12.75
Yugoslavian	56	0.14

San Buenaventura

Place Type: City
County: Ventura
Population: 100,916

Ancestry/Race	Number	%
Acadian/Cajun	22	0.02
African American/Black:	2,029	2.01
Not Hispanic (1,284)	1,758	1.74
Hispanic (137)	271	0.27
African, sub-Saharan:	229	0.23
African	137	0.14
Ethiopian	16	0.02
Nigerian	12	0.01
South African	10	0.01
Other sub-Saharan African	54	0.05
Alaska Native tribes, specified:	13	0.01
Aleut (6)	6	0.01
Eskimo	2	0.00
Tlingit-Haida (3)	5	0.00
Alaska Native tribes, not specified	1	0.00
Am. Ind. or Alaska Nat., not spec.	566	0.56
Albanian	23	0.02
Alsatian	5	0.00
American Indian tribes, specified:	1,947	1.93
Apache (45)	104	0.10
Blackfeet (16)	76	0.08
Cherokee (164)	580	0.57

Notes: 1. Figures in the "Number" column do not add up to the total population due to: a) Ancestry/Race overlap — e.g. persons can report being both White and Irish, b) persons of Hispanic origin can report being any race, c) persons reporting two ancestries are counted in both categories. 2. Numbers in parentheses indicate the number of persons reporting this ancestry/race alone, not in combination with any other ancestry/race. 3. Refer to the Explanation of Data in the front of the book for more detailed information.

Ancestry/Race	Number	%
Cheyenne	3	0.00
Chickasaw (8)	18	0.02
Chippewa (14)	36	0.04
Choctaw (51)	149	0.15
Comanche (13)	30	0.03
Cree	1	0.00
Creek (10)	23	0.02
Crow (2)	6	0.01
Delaware (5)	10	0.01
Iroquois (4)	29	0.03
Kiowa	1	0.00
Latin American Indians (103)	155	0.15
Menominee	4	0.00
Navajo (12)	42	0.04
Osage (7)	17	0.02
Paiute (2)	10	0.01
Pima (4)	9	0.01
Potawatomi (8)	11	0.01
Pueblo (11)	30	0.03
Puget Sound Salish (1)	1	0.00
Seminole	11	0.01
Shoshone (1)	1	0.00
Sioux (16)	67	0.07
Tohono O'Odham (16)	26	0.03
Ute (1)	7	0.01
Yaqui (31)	63	0.06
Yuman (3)	4	0.00
All other tribes (239)	423	0.42
American Indian tribes, not spec.	91	0.09
Arab:	561	0.55
Arab/Arabic	49	0.05
Egyptian	23	0.02
Lebanese	220	0.22
Moroccan	13	0.01
Syrian	214	0.21
Other Arab	42	0.04
Armenian	126	0.12
Asian:	4,238	4.20
Bangladeshi (14)	18	0.02
Cambodian (43)	46	0.05
Chinese, ex. Taiwanese (470)	679	0.67
Filipino (611)	999	0.99
Hmong (2)	2	0.00
Indian (376)	432	0.43
Indonesian (39)	63	0.06
Japanese (429)	765	0.76
Korean (416)	491	0.49
Laotian (78)	90	0.09
Malaysian (4)	5	0.00
Pakistani (9)	11	0.01
Sri Lankan (22)	36	0.04
Taiwanese (29)	38	0.04
Thai (65)	87	0.09
Vietnamese (301)	343	0.34
Other Asian, specified (2)	11	0.01
Other Asian, not specified (53)	122	0.12
Assyrian/Chaldean/Syriac	25	0.02
Australian	39	0.04
Austrian	380	0.38
Basque	141	0.14
Belgian	144	0.14
Brazilian	10	0.01
British	616	0.61
Bulgarian	8	0.01
Canadian	424	0.42
Celtic	76	0.08
Croatian	60	0.06
Cypriot	22	0.02
Czech	501	0.50
Czechoslovakian	146	0.14
Danish	980	0.97
Dutch	1,753	1.73
Eastern European	74	0.07
English	13,417	13.26
Estonian	15	0.01
European	2,003	1.98
Finnish	304	0.30
French, except Basque	3,907	3.86
French Canadian	779	0.77
German	16,176	15.99
German Russian	2	0.00
Greek	469	0.46
Guyanese	25	0.02
Hawaii Native/Pacific Islander:	408	0.40
Melanesian: (8)	8	0.01
Fijian (8)	8	0.01
Micronesian: (27)	62	0.06
Guamanian/Chamorro (25)	58	0.06
Other Micronesian (2)	4	0.00
Polynesian: (104)	247	0.24
Native Hawaiian (72)	188	0.19
Samoan (30)	49	0.05
Tongan (2)	10	0.01
Other Pac. Isl., specified	1	0.00
Other Pac. Isl., not spec. (31)	90	0.09
Hispanic or Latino:	24,573	24.35
Central American:	325	0.32
Costa Rican	24	0.02
Guatemalan	97	0.10
Honduran	27	0.03
Nicaraguan	41	0.04
Panamanian	20	0.02
Salvadoran	97	0.10
Other Central American	19	0.02
Cuban	100	0.10
Dominican Republic	7	0.01
Mexican	19,968	19.79
Puerto Rican	294	0.29
South American:	345	0.34
Argentinean	59	0.06
Bolivian	9	0.01
Chilean	42	0.04
Colombian	67	0.07
Ecuadorian	23	0.02
Paraguayan	1	0.00
Peruvian	100	0.10
Uruguayan	6	0.01
Venezuelan	20	0.02
Other South American	18	0.02
Other Hispanic or Latino	3,534	3.50
Hungarian	557	0.55
Icelander	46	0.05
Iranian	238	0.24
Irish	12,879	12.73
Israeli	38	0.04
Italian	4,719	4.67
Latvian	13	0.01
Lithuanian	262	0.26
Luxemburger	15	0.01
New Zealander	27	0.03
Northern European	164	0.16
Norwegian	2,226	2.20
Pennsylvania German	11	0.01
Polish	2,351	2.32
Portuguese	428	0.42
Romanian	126	0.12
Russian	1,238	1.22
Scandinavian	280	0.28
Scotch-Irish	2,309	2.28
Scottish	2,706	2.68
Serbian	13	0.01
Slavic	43	0.04
Slovak	82	0.08
Slovene	35	0.03
Swedish	2,353	2.33
Swiss	347	0.34
Turkish	54	0.05
Ukrainian	338	0.33
United States or American	4,211	4.16
Welsh	1,247	1.23
West Indian, excl. Hispanic:	73	0.07
Dutch West Indian	4	0.00
Jamaican	46	0.05
Trinidadian and Tobagonian	17	0.02
West Indian	6	0.01
White:	83,444	82.69
Not Hispanic (68,710)	71,019	70.37
Hispanic (10,801)	12,425	12.31
Yugoslavian	97	0.10

San Carlos

Place Type: City
County: San Mateo
Population: 27,718

Ancestry/Race	Number	%
African American/Black:	280	1.01
Not Hispanic (193)	256	0.92
Hispanic (16)	24	0.09
African, sub-Saharan:	124	0.45
African	80	0.29
Cape Verdean	8	0.03
Ethiopian	11	0.04
Ghanian	4	0.01
South African	21	0.08
Alaska Native tribes, specified:	4	0.01
Alaska Athabascan (1)	4	0.01
Alaska Native tribes, not specified	2	0.01
Am. Ind. or Alaska Nat., not spec.	54	0.19
Albanian	21	0.08
American Indian tribes, specified:	126	0.45
Apache (3)	4	0.01
Blackfeet	4	0.01
Cherokee (4)	42	0.15
Chippewa (1)	4	0.01
Choctaw (4)	11	0.04
Cree	1	0.00
Creek (2)	6	0.02
Iroquois (1)	2	0.01
Latin American Indians (6)	12	0.04
Navajo (1)	1	0.00
Pima (1)	1	0.00
Pueblo (1)	3	0.01
Seminole	1	0.00
Sioux (2)	8	0.03
Yaqui	1	0.00
Yuman	2	0.01
All other tribes (11)	23	0.08
American Indian tribes, not spec.	8	0.03
Arab:	271	0.98
Arab/Arabic	52	0.19
Egyptian	27	0.10
Jordanian	28	0.10
Lebanese	90	0.32
Palestinian	11	0.04
Syrian	45	0.16
Other Arab	18	0.06
Armenian	138	0.50
Asian:	2,768	9.99
Cambodian (1)	6	0.02
Chinese, ex. Taiwanese (925)	1,143	4.12
Filipino (329)	472	1.70
Hmong (1)	1	0.00
Indian (283)	318	1.15
Indonesian (5)	9	0.03
Japanese (301)	434	1.57
Korean (104)	140	0.51
Laotian (2)	2	0.01
Malaysian	2	0.01
Pakistani (18)	19	0.07
Taiwanese (43)	50	0.18
Thai (17)	25	0.09
Vietnamese (60)	72	0.26
Other Asian, specified (3)	11	0.04
Other Asian, not specified (20)	64	0.23
Assyrian/Chaldean/Syriac	22	0.08
Australian	4	0.01
Austrian	226	0.82
Basque	79	0.29
Belgian	25	0.09
Brazilian	9	0.03
British	261	0.94
Canadian	120	0.43
Celtic	14	0.05
Croatian	110	0.40
Czech	134	0.48
Czechoslovakian	91	0.33
Danish	360	1.30
Dutch	460	1.66

Notes: 1. Figures in the "Number" column do not add up to the total population due to: a) Ancestry/Race overlap — e.g. persons can report being both White and Irish, b) persons of Hispanic origin can report being any race, c) persons reporting two ancestries are counted in both categories. 2. Numbers in parentheses indicate the number of persons reporting this ancestry/race alone, not in combination with any other ancestry/race. 3. Refer to the Explanation of Data in the front of the book for more detailed information.

Eastern European	74	0.27
English	3,865	13.95
European	454	1.64
Finnish	108	0.39
French, except Basque	997	3.60
French Canadian	215	0.78
German	5,102	18.42
Greek	294	1.06
Guyanese	6	0.02
Hawaii Native/Pacific Islander:	189	0.68
Melanesian: (17)	19	0.07
Fijian (17)	19	0.07
Micronesian: (6)	15	0.05
Guamanian/Chamorro (4)	13	0.05
Other Micronesian (2)	2	0.01
Polynesian: (70)	122	0.44
Native Hawaiian (11)	52	0.19
Samoan (10)	12	0.04
Tongan (48)	56	0.20
Other Polynesian (1)	2	0.01
Other Pac. Isl., specified	3	0.01
Other Pac. Isl., not spec. (16)	30	0.11
Hispanic or Latino:	2,133	7.70
Central American:	222	0.80
Costa Rican	8	0.03
Guatemalan	23	0.08
Honduran	5	0.02
Nicaraguan	50	0.18
Panamanian	10	0.04
Salvadoran	102	0.37
Other Central American	24	0.09
Cuban	32	0.12
Dominican Republic	1	0.00
Mexican	1,003	3.62
Puerto Rican	89	0.32
South American:	191	0.69
Argentinean	41	0.15
Bolivian	7	0.03
Chilean	18	0.06
Colombian	28	0.10
Ecuadorian	9	0.03
Paraguayan	1	0.00
Peruvian	58	0.21
Uruguayan	3	0.01
Venezuelan	6	0.02
Other South American	20	0.07
Other Hispanic or Latino	595	2.15
Hungarian	217	0.78
Icelander	10	0.04
Iranian	291	1.05
Irish	4,130	14.91
Israeli	5	0.02
Italian	3,326	12.01
Lithuanian	174	0.63
Luxemburger	17	0.06
Maltese	89	0.32
New Zealander	6	0.02
Norwegian	712	2.57
Polish	826	2.98
Portuguese	312	1.13
Romanian	36	0.13
Russian	639	2.31
Scandinavian	114	0.41
Scotch-Irish	451	1.63
Scottish	930	3.36
Serbian	18	0.06
Slavic	13	0.05
Slovak	41	0.15
Slovene	43	0.16
Swedish	770	2.78
Swiss	269	0.97
Turkish	32	0.12
Ukrainian	174	0.63
United States or American	796	2.87
Welsh	209	0.75
West Indian, excl. Hispanic:	66	0.24
Belizean	10	0.04
Haitian	4	0.01
Jamaican	19	0.07
Trinidadian and Tobagonian	33	0.12
White:	24,423	88.11
Not Hispanic (22,234)	22,984	82.92
Hispanic (1,200)	1,439	5.19
Yugoslavian	101	0.36

San Clemente

Place Type: City
County: Orange
Population: 49,936

Ancestry/Race	Number	%
African American/Black:	538	1.08
Not Hispanic (320)	433	0.87
Hispanic (65)	105	0.21
African, sub-Saharan:	60	0.12
African	39	0.08
South African	15	0.03
Sudanese	6	0.01
Alaska Native tribes, specified:	1	0.00
Tlingit-Haida	1	0.00
Am. Ind. or Alaska Nat., not spec.	235	0.47
Albanian	10	0.02
Alsatian	7	0.01
American Indian tribes, specified:	428	0.86
Apache (12)	30	0.06
Blackfeet (1)	12	0.02
Cherokee (23)	106	0.21
Chickasaw	5	0.01
Chippewa (4)	12	0.02
Choctaw (13)	17	0.03
Comanche (3)	6	0.01
Creek (1)	4	0.01
Delaware (2)	4	0.01
Iroquois (3)	9	0.02
Kiowa (4)	5	0.01
Latin American Indians (30)	51	0.10
Navajo (4)	9	0.02
Osage (3)	9	0.02
Ottawa (2)	6	0.01
Paiute (1)	3	0.01
Potawatomi (1)	4	0.01
Pueblo (2)	11	0.02
Seminole (1)	7	0.01
Shoshone	5	0.01
Sioux (4)	12	0.02
Yaqui (3)	7	0.01
All other tribes (50)	94	0.19
American Indian tribes, not spec.	16	0.03
Arab:	319	0.64
Arab/Arabic	22	0.04
Egyptian	95	0.19
Jordanian	8	0.02
Lebanese	129	0.26
Syrian	51	0.10
Other Arab	14	0.03
Armenian	152	0.30
Asian:	1,878	3.76
Bangladeshi (15)	23	0.05
Cambodian (5)	17	0.03
Chinese, ex. Taiwanese (222)	319	0.64
Filipino (289)	418	0.84
Hmong (3)	3	0.01
Indian (196)	238	0.48
Indonesian (9)	27	0.05
Japanese (251)	416	0.83
Korean (125)	150	0.30
Malaysian (1)	2	0.00
Pakistani (1)	10	0.02
Sri Lankan (1)	1	0.00
Taiwanese (24)	30	0.06
Thai (27)	42	0.08
Vietnamese (87)	105	0.21
Other Asian, specified (2)	9	0.02
Other Asian, not specified (17)	68	0.14
Assyrian/Chaldean/Syriac	23	0.05
Australian	40	0.08
Austrian	161	0.32
Basque	64	0.13
Belgian	146	0.29
Brazilian	27	0.05
British	401	0.80
Bulgarian	6	0.01
Canadian	249	0.50
Celtic	81	0.16
Croatian	138	0.28
Czech	160	0.32
Czechoslovakian	90	0.18
Danish	679	1.36
Dutch	1,044	2.09
Eastern European	25	0.05
English	7,327	14.69
European	658	1.32
Finnish	112	0.22
French, except Basque	2,018	4.05
French Canadian	403	0.81
German	9,084	18.22
Greek	259	0.52
Guyanese	53	0.11
Hawaii Native/Pacific Islander:	216	0.43
Melanesian: (1)	5	0.01
Fijian (1)	5	0.01
Micronesian: (17)	28	0.06
Guamanian/Chamorro (10)	20	0.04
Other Micronesian (7)	8	0.02
Polynesian: (46)	128	0.26
Native Hawaiian (39)	105	0.21
Samoan (6)	19	0.04
Tongan (1)	2	0.00
Other Polynesian	2	0.00
Other Pac. Isl., specified	6	0.01
Other Pac. Isl., not spec. (4)	49	0.10
Hispanic or Latino:	7,933	15.89
Central American:	163	0.33
Costa Rican	20	0.04
Guatemalan	35	0.07
Honduran	9	0.02
Nicaraguan	6	0.01
Panamanian	16	0.03
Salvadoran	70	0.14
Other Central American	7	0.01
Cuban	58	0.12
Dominican Republic	5	0.01
Mexican	6,317	12.65
Puerto Rican	132	0.26
South American:	226	0.45
Argentinean	57	0.11
Bolivian	8	0.02
Chilean	13	0.03
Colombian	48	0.10
Ecuadorian	24	0.05
Peruvian	37	0.07
Venezuelan	24	0.05
Other South American	15	0.03
Other Hispanic or Latino	1,032	2.07
Hungarian	301	0.60
Iranian	223	0.45
Irish	6,711	13.46
Israeli	11	0.02
Italian	3,507	7.03
Latvian	7	0.01
Lithuanian	91	0.18
Macedonian	34	0.07
Maltese	9	0.02
Northern European	5	0.01
Norwegian	1,454	2.92
Pennsylvania German	33	0.07
Polish	1,264	2.54
Portuguese	193	0.39
Romanian	28	0.06
Russian	681	1.37
Scandinavian	173	0.35
Scotch-Irish	1,145	2.30
Scottish	1,551	3.11
Serbian	55	0.11
Slavic	28	0.06
Slovak	83	0.17
Slovene	14	0.03
Swedish	1,310	2.63
Swiss	219	0.44

Notes: 1. Figures in the "Number" column do not add up to the total population due to: a) Ancestry/Race overlap — e.g. persons can report being both White and Irish, b) persons of Hispanic origin can report being any race, c) persons reporting two ancestries are counted in both categories. 2. Numbers in parentheses indicate the number of persons reporting this ancestry/race alone, not in combination with any other ancestry/race. 3. Refer to the Explanation of Data in the front of the book for more detailed information.

Ancestry/Race	Number	%
Turkish	42	0.08
Ukrainian	110	0.22
United States or American	2,566	5.15
Welsh	538	1.08
West Indian, excl. Hispanic:	26	0.05
Dutch West Indian	7	0.01
Jamaican	19	0.04
White:	45,140	90.40
Not Hispanic (39,155)	39,988	80.08
Hispanic (4,750)	5,152	10.32
Yugoslavian	114	0.23

San Diego

Place Type: City
County: San Diego
Population: 1,223,400

Ancestry/Race	Number	%
Acadian/Cajun	178	0.01
Afghan	1,773	0.14
African American/Black:	109,470	8.95
Not Hispanic (92,830)	103,508	8.46
Hispanic (3,386)	5,962	0.49
African, sub-Saharan:	13,364	1.09
African	6,333	0.52
Cape Verdean	151	0.01
Ethiopian	1,707	0.14
Ghanian	68	0.01
Kenyan	43	0.00
Liberian	35	0.00
Nigerian	496	0.04
Senegalese	12	0.00
Sierra Leonean	18	0.00
Somalian	2,538	0.21
South African	1,250	0.10
Sudanese	346	0.03
Ugandan	130	0.01
Zimbabwean	16	0.00
Other sub-Saharan African	221	0.02
Alaska Native tribes, specified:	173	0.01
Alaska Athabascan (10)	11	0.00
Aleut (37)	52	0.00
Eskimo (16)	42	0.00
Tlingit-Haida (45)	63	0.01
All other tribes (3)	5	0.00
Alaska Native tribes, not specified	21	0.00
Am. Ind. or Alaska Nat., not spec.	5,643	0.46
Albanian	243	0.02
Alsatian	61	0.00
American Indian tribes, specified:	9,990	0.82
Apache (256)	626	0.05
Blackfeet (147)	474	0.04
Cherokee (605)	2,643	0.22
Cheyenne (21)	58	0.00
Chickasaw (62)	136	0.01
Chippewa (116)	253	0.02
Choctaw (167)	495	0.04
Colville (2)	3	0.00
Comanche (31)	98	0.01
Cree (7)	29	0.00
Creek (46)	173	0.01
Crow (5)	29	0.00
Delaware (20)	38	0.00
Houma (7)	7	0.00
Iroquois (88)	241	0.02
Kiowa (12)	27	0.00
Latin American Indians (911)	1,509	0.12
Lumbee (17)	26	0.00
Menominee (12)	15	0.00
Navajo (298)	462	0.04
Osage (17)	56	0.00
Ottawa (14)	27	0.00
Paiute (25)	53	0.00
Pima (24)	41	0.00
Potawatomi (41)	76	0.01
Pueblo (114)	219	0.02
Puget Sound Salish (13)	23	0.00
Seminole (27)	78	0.01
Shoshone (27)	46	0.00
Sioux (174)	372	0.03
Tohono O'Odham (15)	32	0.00
Ute (13)	23	0.00
Yakama (1)	5	0.00
Yaqui (142)	232	0.02
Yuman (25)	53	0.00
All other tribes (761)	1,312	0.11
American Indian tribes, not spec.	827	0.07
Arab:	7,448	0.61
Arab/Arabic	1,375	0.11
Egyptian	561	0.05
Iraqi	579	0.05
Jordanian	89	0.01
Lebanese	2,367	0.19
Moroccan	330	0.03
Palestinian	704	0.06
Syrian	563	0.05
Other Arab	880	0.07
Armenian	1,839	0.15
Asian:	194,228	15.88
Bangladeshi (62)	72	0.01
Cambodian (3,778)	4,545	0.37
Chinese, ex. Taiwanese (21,283)	26,016	2.13
Filipino (75,197)	86,920	7.10
Hmong (1,357)	1,518	0.12
Indian (6,909)	7,936	0.65
Indonesian (332)	634	0.05
Japanese (9,485)	13,953	1.14
Korean (7,139)	8,339	0.68
Laotian (6,054)	7,003	0.57
Malaysian (67)	294	0.02
Pakistani (320)	489	0.04
Sri Lankan (107)	144	0.01
Taiwanese (1,479)	1,793	0.15
Thai (873)	1,300	0.11
Vietnamese (27,473)	29,665	2.42
Other Asian, specified (149)	293	0.02
Other Asian, not specified (1,315)	3,314	0.27
Assyrian/Chaldean/Syriac	633	0.05
Australian	766	0.06
Austrian	3,865	0.32
Basque	479	0.04
Belgian	951	0.08
Brazilian	1,449	0.12
British	6,848	0.56
Bulgarian	432	0.04
Canadian	4,036	0.33
Carpatho Rusyn	6	0.00
Celtic	427	0.03
Croatian	1,379	0.11
Czech	3,804	0.31
Czechoslovakian	2,012	0.16
Danish	6,923	0.57
Dutch	12,943	1.06
Eastern European	1,616	0.13
English	97,807	8.00
Estonian	109	0.01
European	13,053	1.07
Finnish	2,531	0.21
French, except Basque	28,937	2.37
French Canadian	6,337	0.52
German	131,592	10.76
German Russian	83	0.01
Greek	5,588	0.46
Guyanese	80	0.01
Hawaii Native/Pacific Islander:	10,911	0.89
Melanesian: (25)	43	0.00
Fijian (22)	37	0.00
Other Melanesian (3)	6	0.00
Micronesian: (2,405)	3,657	0.30
Guamanian/Chamorro (2,237)	3,450	0.28
Other Micronesian (168)	207	0.02
Polynesian: (2,868)	5,311	0.43
Native Hawaiian (1,016)	2,671	0.22
Samoan (1,701)	2,380	0.19
Tongan (91)	125	0.01
Other Polynesian (60)	135	0.01
Other Pac. Isl., specified	54	0.00
Other Pac. Isl., not spec. (456)	1,846	0.15
Hispanic or Latino:	310,752	25.40
Central American:	5,077	0.41
Costa Rican	462	0.04
Guatemalan	1,320	0.11
Honduran	685	0.06
Nicaraguan	473	0.04
Panamanian	682	0.06
Salvadoran	1,034	0.08
Other Central American	421	0.03
Cuban	1,922	0.16
Dominican Republic	392	0.03
Mexican	259,219	21.19
Puerto Rican	5,938	0.49
South American:	4,410	0.36
Argentinean	642	0.05
Bolivian	154	0.01
Chilean	449	0.04
Colombian	1,152	0.09
Ecuadorian	383	0.03
Paraguayan	26	0.00
Peruvian	987	0.08
Uruguayan	65	0.01
Venezuelan	268	0.02
Other South American	284	0.02
Other Hispanic or Latino	33,794	2.76
Hungarian	5,737	0.47
Icelander	244	0.02
Iranian	7,241	0.59
Irish	105,547	8.63
Israeli	942	0.08
Italian	55,764	4.56
Latvian	367	0.03
Lithuanian	2,707	0.22
Luxemburger	177	0.01
Macedonian	113	0.01
Maltese	150	0.01
New Zealander	210	0.02
Northern European	1,571	0.13
Norwegian	18,681	1.53
Pennsylvania German	267	0.02
Polish	25,207	2.06
Portuguese	8,040	0.66
Romanian	2,063	0.17
Russian	16,955	1.39
Scandinavian	2,586	0.21
Scotch-Irish	16,552	1.35
Scottish	21,965	1.80
Serbian	631	0.05
Slavic	581	0.05
Slovak	1,360	0.11
Slovene	478	0.04
Swedish	17,644	1.44
Swiss	4,349	0.36
Turkish	930	0.08
Ukrainian	3,104	0.25
United States or American	38,557	3.15
Welsh	7,838	0.64
West Indian, excl. Hispanic:	2,390	0.20
Bahamian	11	0.00
Barbadian	141	0.01
Belizean	146	0.01
Bermudan	12	0.00
British West Indian	85	0.01
Dutch West Indian	34	0.00
Haitian	273	0.02
Jamaican	981	0.08
Trinidadian and Tobagonian	239	0.02
U.S. Virgin Islander	45	0.00
West Indian	414	0.03
Other West Indian	9	0.00
White:	781,652	63.89
Not Hispanic (603,892)	632,533	51.70
Hispanic (132,315)	149,119	12.19
Yugoslavian	1,684	0.14

Notes: 1. Figures in the "Number" column do not add up to the total population due to: a) Ancestry/Race overlap — e.g. persons can report being both White and Irish, b) persons of Hispanic origin can report being any race, c) persons reporting two ancestries are counted in both categories. 2. Numbers in parentheses indicate the number of persons reporting this ancestry/race alone, not in combination with any other ancestry/race. 3. Refer to the Explanation of Data in the front of the book for more detailed information.

San Dimas

Place Type: City
County: Los Angeles
Population: 34,980

Ancestry/Race	Number	%
Afghan	40	0.11
African American/Black:	1,341	3.83
Not Hispanic (1,114)	1,256	3.59
Hispanic (42)	85	0.24
African, sub-Saharan:	167	0.48
African	167	0.48
Am. Ind. or Alaska Nat., not spec.	169	0.48
American Indian tribes, specified:	324	0.93
Apache (15)	31	0.09
Blackfeet (3)	16	0.05
Cherokee (23)	78	0.22
Chickasaw	3	0.01
Chippewa (1)	4	0.01
Choctaw (9)	9	0.03
Colville (1)	1	0.00
Comanche (2)	6	0.02
Cree	1	0.00
Creek (2)	4	0.01
Crow	1	0.00
Delaware (1)	1	0.00
Iroquois (3)	11	0.03
Kiowa (1)	1	0.00
Latin American Indians (14)	34	0.10
Lumbee (4)	4	0.01
Navajo (5)	12	0.03
Osage (1)	2	0.01
Ottawa (1)	3	0.01
Potawatomi (6)	10	0.03
Pueblo (12)	18	0.05
Puget Sound Salish	5	0.01
Seminole	6	0.02
Shoshone (2)	2	0.01
Sioux (1)	2	0.01
Tohono O'Odham (5)	8	0.02
Yakama (1)	1	0.00
Yaqui (6)	7	0.02
Yuman (5)	5	0.01
All other tribes (20)	38	0.11
American Indian tribes, not spec.	38	0.11
Arab:	505	1.44
Arab/Arabic	113	0.32
Egyptian	82	0.23
Jordanian	78	0.22
Lebanese	95	0.27
Palestinian	88	0.25
Syrian	49	0.14
Armenian	230	0.66
Asian:	3,910	11.18
Bangladeshi (9)	9	0.03
Cambodian (31)	36	0.10
Chinese, ex. Taiwanese (798)	974	2.78
Filipino (810)	963	2.75
Indian (464)	511	1.46
Indonesian (37)	87	0.25
Japanese (317)	420	1.20
Korean (230)	263	0.75
Laotian (2)	2	0.01
Malaysian (4)	5	0.01
Pakistani (36)	48	0.14
Sri Lankan (13)	15	0.04
Taiwanese (215)	233	0.67
Thai (53)	67	0.19
Vietnamese (116)	130	0.37
Other Asian, specified (12)	14	0.04
Other Asian, not specified (26)	133	0.38
Austrian	179	0.51
Basque	31	0.09
Belgian	60	0.17
Brazilian	18	0.05
British	185	0.53
Canadian	128	0.37
Croatian	122	0.35
Czech	90	0.26
Czechoslovakian	100	0.29
Danish	341	0.97
Dutch	665	1.90
English	3,490	9.95
European	252	0.72
Finnish	31	0.09
French, except Basque	947	2.70
French Canadian	244	0.70
German	4,827	13.77
Greek	261	0.74
Hawaii Native/Pacific Islander:	166	0.47
Micronesian: (11)	15	0.04
Guamanian/Chamorro (11)	15	0.04
Polynesian: (58)	119	0.34
Native Hawaiian (37)	81	0.23
Samoan (20)	35	0.10
Tongan (1)	2	0.01
Other Polynesian	1	0.00
Other Pac. Isl., not spec. (3)	32	0.09
Hispanic or Latino:	8,163	23.34
Central American:	246	0.70
Costa Rican	34	0.10
Guatemalan	28	0.08
Honduran	7	0.02
Nicaraguan	34	0.10
Panamanian	1	0.00
Salvadoran	103	0.29
Other Central American	39	0.11
Cuban	208	0.59
Dominican Republic	8	0.02
Mexican	6,029	17.24
Puerto Rican	190	0.54
South American:	336	0.96
Argentinean	67	0.19
Bolivian	11	0.03
Chilean	19	0.05
Colombian	111	0.32
Ecuadorian	42	0.12
Peruvian	51	0.15
Uruguayan	4	0.01
Venezuelan	10	0.03
Other South American	21	0.06
Other Hispanic or Latino	1,146	3.28
Hungarian	258	0.74
Icelander	22	0.06
Iranian	158	0.45
Irish	4,031	11.50
Italian	2,770	7.90
Latvian	23	0.07
Lithuanian	80	0.23
Luxemburger	12	0.03
Macedonian	16	0.05
Northern European	24	0.07
Norwegian	586	1.67
Pennsylvania German	11	0.03
Polish	886	2.53
Portuguese	196	0.56
Romanian	14	0.04
Russian	309	0.88
Scandinavian	89	0.25
Scotch-Irish	545	1.55
Scottish	627	1.79
Slavic	52	0.15
Slovak	34	0.10
Slovene	7	0.02
Soviet Union	8	0.02
Swedish	626	1.79
Swiss	145	0.41
Turkish	33	0.09
Ukrainian	78	0.22
United States or American	1,700	4.85
Welsh	216	0.62
West Indian, excl. Hispanic:	129	0.37
Jamaican	129	0.37
White:	27,444	78.46
Not Hispanic (21,381)	22,128	63.26
Hispanic (4,735)	5,316	15.20
Yugoslavian	50	0.14

San Fernando

Place Type: City
County: Los Angeles
Population: 23,564

Ancestry/Race	Number	%
African American/Black:	305	1.29
Not Hispanic (176)	202	0.86
Hispanic (55)	103	0.44
African, sub-Saharan:	79	0.34
African	79	0.34
Alaska Native tribes, specified:	1	0.00
Aleut (1)	1	0.00
Am. Ind. or Alaska Nat., not spec.	220	0.93
American Indian tribes, specified:	326	1.38
Apache (25)	37	0.16
Blackfeet (1)	7	0.03
Cherokee (9)	21	0.09
Cheyenne (3)	3	0.01
Chippewa	1	0.00
Choctaw	6	0.03
Comanche	1	0.00
Creek	4	0.02
Latin American Indians (76)	114	0.48
Navajo (8)	12	0.05
Paiute (4)	6	0.03
Pima (1)	1	0.00
Pueblo (9)	15	0.06
Shoshone (2)	3	0.01
Sioux (4)	16	0.07
Tohono O'Odham	3	0.01
Ute	1	0.00
Yaqui (16)	21	0.09
Yuman (4)	5	0.02
All other tribes (41)	49	0.21
American Indian tribes, not spec.	37	0.16
Arab:	18	0.08
Arab/Arabic	6	0.03
Lebanese	12	0.05
Armenian	69	0.29
Asian:	343	1.46
Cambodian (21)	21	0.09
Chinese, ex. Taiwanese (13)	22	0.09
Filipino (101)	131	0.56
Indian (23)	28	0.12
Indonesian (6)	7	0.03
Japanese (56)	69	0.29
Korean (32)	35	0.15
Thai (8)	16	0.07
Vietnamese (1)	1	0.00
Other Asian, not specified (2)	13	0.06
Assyrian/Chaldean/Syriac	10	0.04
Basque	11	0.05
Canadian	18	0.08
Dutch	89	0.38
English	374	1.59
European	18	0.08
French, except Basque	128	0.54
French Canadian	40	0.17
German	463	1.97
Greek	10	0.04
Hawaii Native/Pacific Islander:	43	0.18
Melanesian: (4)	4	0.02
Fijian (4)	4	0.02
Micronesian: (13)	13	0.06
Guamanian/Chamorro (13)	13	0.06
Polynesian: (7)	22	0.09
Native Hawaiian (3)	14	0.06
Samoan (4)	8	0.03
Other Pac. Isl., not spec. (2)	4	0.02
Hispanic or Latino:	21,038	89.28
Central American:	550	2.33
Costa Rican	10	0.04
Guatemalan	122	0.52
Honduran	29	0.12
Nicaraguan	44	0.19
Panamanian	10	0.04
Salvadoran	301	1.28
Other Central American	34	0.14

Notes: 1. Figures in the "Number" column do not add up to the total population due to: a) Ancestry/Race overlap — e.g. persons can report being both White and Irish, b) persons of Hispanic origin can report being any race, c) persons reporting two ancestries are counted in both categories. 2. Numbers in parentheses indicate the number of persons reporting this ancestry/race alone, not in combination with any other ancestry/race. 3. Refer to the Explanation of Data in the front of the book for more detailed information.

Cuban	25	0.11
Dominican Republic	6	0.03
Mexican	18,504	78.53
Puerto Rican	57	0.24
South American:	80	0.34
Argentinean	9	0.04
Bolivian	3	0.01
Chilean	6	0.03
Colombian	17	0.07
Ecuadorian	18	0.08
Paraguayan	3	0.01
Peruvian	12	0.05
Uruguayan	5	0.02
Other South American	7	0.03
Other Hispanic or Latino	1,816	7.71
Hungarian	22	0.09
Irish	323	1.37
Italian	278	1.18
Norwegian	44	0.19
Polish	46	0.20
Portuguese	6	0.03
Russian	36	0.15
Scandinavian	5	0.02
Scotch-Irish	61	0.26
Scottish	84	0.36
Swedish	82	0.35
Swiss	13	0.06
United States or American	459	1.95
Welsh	15	0.06
West Indian, excl. Hispanic:	26	0.11
Belizean	26	0.11
White:	10,893	46.23
Not Hispanic (1,855)	1,979	8.40
Hispanic (8,221)	8,914	37.83

San Francisco

Place Type: City
County: San Francisco
Population: 776,733

Ancestry/Race	Number	%
Acadian/Cajun	176	0.02
Afghan	87	0.01
African American/Black:	67,076	8.64
Not Hispanic (58,791)	64,070	8.25
Hispanic (1,724)	3,006	0.39
African, sub-Saharan:	5,454	0.70
African	3,768	0.49
Cape Verdean	72	0.01
Ethiopian	495	0.06
Liberian	92	0.01
Nigerian	492	0.06
Sierra Leonean	25	0.00
Somalian	113	0.01
South African	202	0.03
Zairian	23	0.00
Zimbabwean	35	0.00
Other sub-Saharan African	137	0.02
Alaska Native tribes, specified:	96	0.01
Alaska Athabascan (6)	10	0.00
Aleut (15)	22	0.00
Eskimo (11)	20	0.00
Tlingit-Haida (23)	35	0.00
All other tribes (2)	9	0.00
Alaska Native tribes, not specified	19	0.00
Am. Ind. or Alaska Nat., not spec.	3,403	0.44
Albanian	173	0.02
Alsatian	156	0.02
American Indian tribes, specified:	5,251	0.68
Apache (97)	236	0.03
Blackfeet (44)	230	0.03
Cherokee (243)	1,352	0.17
Cheyenne (13)	30	0.00
Chickasaw (15)	57	0.01
Chippewa (60)	129	0.02
Choctaw (45)	225	0.03
Colville (1)	3	0.00
Comanche (9)	32	0.00
Cree (3)	31	0.00
Creek (22)	97	0.01
Crow (1)	13	0.00
Delaware (3)	22	0.00
Houma	4	0.00
Iroquois (51)	128	0.02
Kiowa (9)	12	0.00
Latin American Indians (570)	1,080	0.14
Lumbee (10)	12	0.00
Menominee	1	0.00
Navajo (129)	223	0.03
Osage (5)	27	0.00
Ottawa (1)	3	0.00
Paiute (11)	28	0.00
Pima (15)	26	0.00
Potawatomi (11)	25	0.00
Pueblo (61)	108	0.01
Puget Sound Salish (1)	4	0.00
Seminole (4)	54	0.01
Shoshone (4)	16	0.00
Sioux (98)	214	0.03
Tohono O'Odham (20)	29	0.00
Ute (5)	17	0.00
Yakama (2)	6	0.00
Yaqui (33)	74	0.01
Yuman (12)	16	0.00
All other tribes (284)	687	0.09
American Indian tribes, not spec.	478	0.06
Arab:	5,430	0.70
Arab/Arabic	1,311	0.17
Egyptian	423	0.05
Iraqi	110	0.01
Jordanian	266	0.03
Lebanese	1,120	0.14
Moroccan	350	0.05
Palestinian	877	0.11
Syrian	314	0.04
Other Arab	659	0.08
Armenian	2,528	0.33
Asian:	259,403	33.40
Bangladeshi (45)	57	0.01
Cambodian (1,023)	1,358	0.17
Chinese, ex. Taiwanese (151,965)	160,113	20.61
Filipino (40,083)	45,793	5.90
Hmong (30)	33	0.00
Indian (5,524)	6,616	0.85
Indonesian (778)	1,142	0.15
Japanese (11,410)	14,618	1.88
Korean (7,679)	8,706	1.12
Laotian (564)	707	0.09
Malaysian (111)	244	0.03
Pakistani (436)	636	0.08
Sri Lankan (73)	96	0.01
Taiwanese (655)	834	0.11
Thai (1,329)	1,638	0.21
Vietnamese (10,722)	12,874	1.66
Other Asian, specified (845)	1,134	0.15
Other Asian, not specified (1,397)	2,804	0.36
Assyrian/Chaldean/Syriac	308	0.04
Australian	820	0.11
Austrian	2,772	0.36
Basque	549	0.07
Belgian	823	0.11
Brazilian	1,112	0.14
British	5,144	0.66
Bulgarian	146	0.02
Canadian	1,980	0.25
Carpatho Rusyn	8	0.00
Celtic	569	0.07
Croatian	1,272	0.16
Czech	2,062	0.27
Czechoslovakian	869	0.11
Danish	3,970	0.51
Dutch	6,319	0.81
Eastern European	2,626	0.34
English	47,221	6.08
Estonian	155	0.02
European	8,448	1.09
Finnish	1,617	0.21
French, except Basque	17,957	2.31
French Canadian	3,099	0.40
German	60,176	7.75
German Russian	24	0.00
Greek	3,831	0.49
Guyanese	40	0.01
Hawaii Native/Pacific Islander:	6,369	0.82
Melanesian: (161)	218	0.03
Fijian (160)	215	0.03
Other Melanesian (1)	3	0.00
Micronesian: (335)	496	0.06
Guamanian/Chamorro (305)	460	0.06
Other Micronesian (30)	36	0.00
Polynesian: (2,954)	4,363	0.56
Native Hawaiian (473)	1,420	0.18
Samoan (2,311)	2,689	0.35
Tongan (143)	182	0.02
Other Polynesian (27)	72	0.01
Other Pac. Isl., specified	55	0.01
Other Pac. Isl., not spec. (346)	1,237	0.16
Hispanic or Latino:	109,504	14.10
Central American:	23,367	3.01
Costa Rican	326	0.04
Guatemalan	3,196	0.41
Honduran	934	0.12
Nicaraguan	5,459	0.70
Panamanian	261	0.03
Salvadoran	10,655	1.37
Other Central American	2,536	0.33
Cuban	1,632	0.21
Dominican Republic	148	0.02
Mexican	48,935	6.30
Puerto Rican	3,758	0.48
South American:	5,007	0.64
Argentinean	540	0.07
Bolivian	258	0.03
Chilean	405	0.05
Colombian	817	0.11
Ecuadorian	329	0.04
Paraguayan	16	0.00
Peruvian	1,769	0.23
Uruguayan	38	0.00
Venezuelan	234	0.03
Other South American	601	0.08
Other Hispanic or Latino	26,657	3.43
Hungarian	3,711	0.48
Icelander	134	0.02
Iranian	1,662	0.21
Irish	68,307	8.79
Israeli	615	0.08
Italian	39,144	5.04
Latvian	629	0.08
Lithuanian	2,038	0.26
Luxemburger	105	0.01
Macedonian	113	0.01
Maltese	610	0.08
New Zealander	219	0.03
Northern European	1,033	0.13
Norwegian	7,830	1.01
Pennsylvania German	151	0.02
Polish	14,332	1.85
Portuguese	3,679	0.47
Romanian	1,455	0.19
Russian	21,727	2.80
Scandinavian	1,029	0.13
Scotch-Irish	8,129	1.05
Scottish	13,596	1.75
Serbian	396	0.05
Slavic	482	0.06
Slovak	734	0.09
Slovene	559	0.07
Soviet Union	54	0.01
Swedish	9,748	1.26
Swiss	3,381	0.44
Turkish	565	0.07
Ukrainian	5,516	0.71
United States or American	12,520	1.61
Welsh	4,487	0.58
West Indian, excl. Hispanic:	1,639	0.21
Bahamian	22	0.00
Barbadian	30	0.00

Notes: 1. Figures in the "Number" column do not add up to the total population due to: a) Ancestry/Race overlap — e.g. persons can report being both White and Irish, b) persons of Hispanic origin can report being any race, c) persons reporting two ancestries are counted in both categories. 2. Numbers in parentheses indicate the number of persons reporting this ancestry/race alone, not in combination with any other ancestry/race. 3. Refer to the Explanation of Data in the front of the book for more detailed information.

Belizean	97	0.01
Bermudan	9	0.00
British West Indian	128	0.02
Dutch West Indian	18	0.00
Haitian	183	0.02
Jamaican	738	0.10
Trinidadian and Tobagonian	154	0.02
U.S. Virgin Islander	31	0.00
West Indian	212	0.03
Other West Indian	17	0.00
White:	411,427	52.97
Not Hispanic (338,909)	356,374	45.88
Hispanic (46,819)	55,053	7.09
Yugoslavian	1,367	0.18

San Gabriel

Place Type: City
County: Los Angeles
Population: 39,804

Ancestry/Race	Number	%
African American/Black:	516	1.30
Not Hispanic (360)	422	1.06
Hispanic (60)	94	0.24
African, sub-Saharan:	55	0.14
African	17	0.04
Nigerian	38	0.10
Alaska Native tribes, specified:	2	0.01
Alaska Athabascan	1	0.00
Tlingit-Haida	1	0.00
Am. Ind. or Alaska Nat., not spec.	217	0.55
American Indian tribes, specified:	295	0.74
Apache (11)	19	0.05
Blackfeet	2	0.01
Cherokee (12)	27	0.07
Choctaw (2)	7	0.02
Comanche (4)	7	0.02
Creek	1	0.00
Delaware	1	0.00
Iroquois	1	0.00
Latin American Indians (28)	61	0.15
Navajo (11)	13	0.03
Osage (1)	1	0.00
Paiute	2	0.01
Pima (1)	1	0.00
Pueblo (11)	15	0.04
Seminole (2)	2	0.01
Shoshone (2)	3	0.01
Sioux (3)	3	0.01
Tohono O'Odham (1)	2	0.01
Yaqui (6)	8	0.02
Yuman (2)	2	0.01
All other tribes (86)	117	0.29
American Indian tribes, not spec.	25	0.06
Arab:	358	0.91
Arab/Arabic	180	0.46
Egyptian	11	0.03
Jordanian	28	0.07
Lebanese	133	0.34
Syrian	6	0.02
Armenian	70	0.18
Asian:	20,988	52.73
Bangladeshi (3)	3	0.01
Cambodian (167)	234	0.59
Chinese, ex. Taiwanese (12,398)	13,417	33.71
Filipino (886)	1,025	2.58
Indian (156)	195	0.49
Indonesian (106)	154	0.39
Japanese (620)	745	1.87
Korean (235)	264	0.66
Laotian (26)	30	0.08
Malaysian (7)	24	0.06
Pakistani (4)	4	0.01
Sri Lankan (7)	8	0.02
Taiwanese (978)	1,164	2.92
Thai (141)	160	0.40
Vietnamese (2,647)	3,179	7.99
Other Asian, specified (138)	164	0.41
Other Asian, not specified (104)	218	0.55
Austrian	26	0.07
Belgian	6	0.02
Brazilian	15	0.04
British	29	0.07
Canadian	26	0.07
Croatian	4	0.01
Czech	6	0.02
Czechoslovakian	14	0.04
Danish	65	0.17
Dutch	188	0.48
Eastern European	16	0.04
English	1,004	2.55
European	114	0.29
Finnish	24	0.06
French, except Basque	406	1.03
French Canadian	15	0.04
German	1,478	3.76
Greek	36	0.09
Hawaii Native/Pacific Islander:	115	0.29
Micronesian: (8)	15	0.04
Guamanian/Chamorro (8)	15	0.04
Polynesian: (18)	42	0.11
Native Hawaiian (5)	24	0.06
Samoan (11)	14	0.04
Tongan	1	0.00
Other Polynesian (2)	3	0.01
Other Pac. Isl., specified	1	0.00
Other Pac. Isl., not spec. (13)	57	0.14
Hispanic or Latino:	12,223	30.71
Central American:	567	1.42
Costa Rican	16	0.04
Guatemalan	81	0.20
Honduran	11	0.03
Nicaraguan	129	0.32
Panamanian	5	0.01
Salvadoran	251	0.63
Other Central American	74	0.19
Cuban	139	0.35
Dominican Republic	6	0.02
Mexican	9,559	24.02
Puerto Rican	123	0.31
South American:	196	0.49
Argentinean	26	0.07
Bolivian	5	0.01
Chilean	7	0.02
Colombian	35	0.09
Ecuadorian	50	0.13
Peruvian	46	0.12
Uruguayan	3	0.01
Venezuelan	2	0.01
Other South American	22	0.06
Other Hispanic or Latino	1,633	4.10
Hungarian	79	0.20
Icelander	21	0.05
Iranian	57	0.15
Irish	1,128	2.87
Israeli	10	0.03
Italian	914	2.33
Latvian	8	0.02
Lithuanian	21	0.05
Norwegian	185	0.47
Polish	222	0.56
Portuguese	36	0.09
Romanian	12	0.03
Russian	109	0.28
Scandinavian	25	0.06
Scotch-Irish	156	0.40
Scottish	162	0.41
Serbian	15	0.04
Slovak	4	0.01
Swedish	230	0.59
Swiss	19	0.05
Ukrainian	143	0.36
United States or American	678	1.72
Welsh	45	0.11
West Indian, excl. Hispanic:	70	0.18
Belizean	37	0.09
Jamaican	33	0.08
White:	14,290	35.90
Not Hispanic (6,930)	7,378	18.54
Hispanic (6,364)	6,912	17.37
Yugoslavian	29	0.07

San Jacinto

Place Type: City
County: Riverside
Population: 23,779

Ancestry/Race	Number	%
African American/Black:	819	3.44
Not Hispanic (571)	695	2.92
Hispanic (59)	124	0.52
African, sub-Saharan:	18	0.08
African	18	0.08
Alaska Native tribes, specified:	3	0.01
Aleut (1)	1	0.00
Tlingit-Haida (2)	2	0.01
Am. Ind. or Alaska Nat., not spec.	239	1.01
American Indian tribes, specified:	606	2.55
Apache (23)	30	0.13
Blackfeet (1)	27	0.11
Cherokee (54)	133	0.56
Cheyenne (2)	2	0.01
Chickasaw (3)	5	0.02
Chippewa (8)	11	0.05
Choctaw (14)	24	0.10
Comanche (1)	6	0.03
Creek (2)	2	0.01
Iroquois (5)	10	0.04
Latin American Indians (41)	62	0.26
Navajo (13)	17	0.07
Osage (5)	12	0.05
Ottawa	1	0.00
Potawatomi	1	0.00
Pueblo (8)	9	0.04
Seminole	4	0.02
Shoshone (1)	1	0.00
Sioux (7)	9	0.04
Tohono O'Odham (1)	3	0.01
Yakama	1	0.00
Yaqui (6)	12	0.05
Yuman (2)	2	0.01
All other tribes (166)	222	0.93
American Indian tribes, not spec.	28	0.12
Arab:	38	0.16
Arab/Arabic	7	0.03
Lebanese	16	0.07
Moroccan	9	0.04
Syrian	6	0.03
Armenian	31	0.13
Asian:	438	1.84
Cambodian (14)	27	0.11
Chinese, ex. Taiwanese (25)	43	0.18
Filipino (98)	165	0.69
Hmong	2	0.01
Indian (56)	65	0.27
Indonesian (2)	10	0.04
Japanese (21)	59	0.25
Korean (7)	9	0.04
Laotian (8)	8	0.03
Sri Lankan (1)	1	0.00
Taiwanese (5)	5	0.02
Thai (10)	11	0.05
Vietnamese (13)	17	0.07
Other Asian, not specified (3)	16	0.07
Austrian	8	0.03
Basque	26	0.11
Belgian	8	0.03
British	27	0.11
Canadian	117	0.49
Czech	163	0.68
Czechoslovakian	29	0.12
Danish	116	0.48
Dutch	683	2.85
English	2,210	9.24
European	31	0.13
Finnish	86	0.36
French, except Basque	754	3.15
French Canadian	168	0.70

Notes: 1. Figures in the "Number" column do not add up to the total population due to: a) Ancestry/Race overlap — e.g. persons can report being both White and Irish, b) persons of Hispanic origin can report being any race, c) persons reporting two ancestries are counted in both categories. 2. Numbers in parentheses indicate the number of persons reporting this ancestry/race alone, not in combination with any other ancestry/race. 3. Refer to the Explanation of Data in the front of the book for more detailed information.

German	2,579	10.78
Greek	125	0.52
Hawaii Native/Pacific Islander:	94	0.40
Micronesian: (10)	17	0.07
Guamanian/Chamorro (9)	16	0.07
Other Micronesian (1)	1	0.00
Polynesian: (27)	61	0.26
Native Hawaiian (14)	35	0.15
Samoan (3)	14	0.06
Tongan (10)	12	0.05
Other Pac. Isl., not spec. (1)	16	0.07
Hispanic or Latino:	9,583	40.30
Central American:	179	0.75
Costa Rican	5	0.02
Guatemalan	31	0.13
Honduran	12	0.05
Nicaraguan	65	0.27
Panamanian	3	0.01
Salvadoran	54	0.23
Other Central American	9	0.04
Cuban	33	0.14
Dominican Republic	2	0.01
Mexican	7,945	33.41
Puerto Rican	135	0.57
South American:	26	0.11
Argentinean	7	0.03
Bolivian	2	0.01
Chilean	3	0.01
Colombian	2	0.01
Ecuadorian	1	0.00
Peruvian	4	0.02
Venezuelan	3	0.01
Other South American	4	0.02
Other Hispanic or Latino	1,263	5.31
Hungarian	67	0.28
Icelander	13	0.05
Iranian	7	0.03
Irish	2,158	9.02
Italian	714	2.98
Lithuanian	162	0.68
Northern European	17	0.07
Norwegian	209	0.87
Pennsylvania German	8	0.03
Polish	218	0.91
Portuguese	117	0.49
Romanian	34	0.14
Russian	236	0.99
Scandinavian	38	0.16
Scotch-Irish	189	0.79
Scottish	460	1.92
Serbian	9	0.04
Slavic	10	0.04
Slovak	16	0.07
Swedish	390	1.63
Swiss	66	0.28
Turkish	8	0.03
Ukrainian	7	0.03
United States or American	1,370	5.73
Welsh	98	0.41
West Indian, excl. Hispanic:	12	0.05
Jamaican	12	0.05
White:	17,505	73.62
Not Hispanic (12,507)	12,943	54.43
Hispanic (3,981)	4,562	19.18

San Jose

Place Type: City
County: Santa Clara
Population: 894,943

Ancestry/Race	Number	%
Acadian/Cajun	34	0.00
Afghan	566	0.06
African American/Black:	36,928	4.13
Not Hispanic (29,495)	33,571	3.75
Hispanic (1,854)	3,357	0.38
African, sub-Saharan:	5,722	0.64
African	2,605	0.29
Cape Verdean	12	0.00
Ethiopian	1,669	0.19
Ghanian	28	0.00
Kenyan	51	0.01
Liberian	101	0.01
Nigerian	594	0.07
Senegalese	15	0.00
Sierra Leonean	70	0.01
Somalian	186	0.02
South African	166	0.02
Sudanese	25	0.00
Ugandan	4	0.00
Other sub-Saharan African	196	0.02
Alaska Native tribes, specified:	116	0.01
Alaska Athabascan (6)	7	0.00
Aleut (9)	29	0.00
Eskimo (17)	27	0.00
Tlingit-Haida (20)	39	0.00
All other tribes (1)	14	0.00
Alaska Native tribes, not specified	8	0.00
Am. Ind. or Alaska Nat., not spec.	4,974	0.56
Albanian	126	0.01
Alsatian	30	0.00
American Indian tribes, specified:	7,806	0.87
Apache (358)	678	0.08
Blackfeet (53)	260	0.03
Cherokee (435)	1,781	0.20
Cheyenne (13)	30	0.00
Chickasaw (21)	93	0.01
Chippewa (80)	160	0.02
Choctaw (117)	370	0.04
Colville (12)	13	0.00
Comanche (16)	48	0.01
Cree (9)	36	0.00
Creek (27)	97	0.01
Crow (3)	12	0.00
Delaware (19)	37	0.00
Houma (3)	4	0.00
Iroquois (54)	136	0.02
Kiowa (6)	8	0.00
Latin American Indians (883)	1,487	0.17
Lumbee (6)	12	0.00
Menominee (6)	10	0.00
Navajo (192)	353	0.04
Osage (17)	50	0.01
Ottawa (3)	11	0.00
Paiute (69)	100	0.01
Pima (22)	24	0.00
Potawatomi (39)	67	0.01
Pueblo (81)	156	0.02
Puget Sound Salish (2)	6	0.00
Seminole (10)	65	0.01
Shoshone (19)	44	0.00
Sioux (136)	277	0.03
Tohono O'Odham (30)	58	0.01
Ute (7)	21	0.00
Yakama (2)	12	0.00
Yaqui (140)	232	0.03
Yuman (10)	15	0.00
All other tribes (560)	1,043	0.12
American Indian tribes, not spec.	756	0.08
Arab:	4,302	0.48
Arab/Arabic	768	0.09
Egyptian	638	0.07
Iraqi	320	0.04
Jordanian	136	0.02
Lebanese	1,086	0.12
Moroccan	29	0.00
Palestinian	621	0.07
Syrian	384	0.04
Other Arab	320	0.04
Armenian	1,197	0.13
Asian:	263,819	29.48
Bangladeshi (205)	224	0.03
Cambodian (3,955)	4,886	0.55
Chinese, ex. Taiwanese (49,149)	55,543	6.21
Filipino (48,149)	55,120	6.16
Hmong (144)	156	0.02
Indian (26,606)	28,301	3.16
Indonesian (420)	767	0.09
Japanese (11,484)	15,353	1.72
Korean (9,425)	10,393	1.16
Laotian (1,542)	1,813	0.20
Malaysian (107)	198	0.02
Pakistani (961)	1,252	0.14
Sri Lankan (113)	150	0.02
Taiwanese (1,960)	2,431	0.27
Thai (576)	776	0.09
Vietnamese (78,842)	82,834	9.26
Other Asian, specified (275)	397	0.04
Other Asian, not specified (1,268)	3,225	0.36
Assyrian/Chaldean/Syriac	2,200	0.25
Australian	474	0.05
Austrian	1,514	0.17
Basque	311	0.03
Belgian	528	0.06
Brazilian	356	0.04
British	3,299	0.37
Bulgarian	233	0.03
Canadian	2,112	0.24
Celtic	283	0.03
Croatian	1,336	0.15
Cypriot	44	0.00
Czech	1,578	0.18
Czechoslovakian	706	0.08
Danish	4,326	0.48
Dutch	7,920	0.89
Eastern European	492	0.06
English	50,448	5.64
Estonian	35	0.00
European	8,366	0.94
Finnish	1,192	0.13
French, except Basque	15,953	1.78
French Canadian	3,115	0.35
German	67,712	7.57
German Russian	12	0.00
Greek	3,734	0.42
Guyanese	128	0.01
Hawaii Native/Pacific Islander:	7,252	0.81
Melanesian: (215)	302	0.03
Fijian (215)	302	0.03
Micronesian: (727)	1,257	0.14
Guamanian/Chamorro (675)	1,174	0.13
Other Micronesian (52)	83	0.01
Polynesian: (2,199)	3,851	0.43
Native Hawaiian (624)	1,848	0.21
Samoan (1,417)	1,721	0.19
Tongan (134)	199	0.02
Other Polynesian (24)	83	0.01
Other Pac. Isl., specified	25	0.00
Other Pac. Isl., not spec. (370)	1,817	0.20
Hispanic or Latino:	269,989	30.17
Central American:	7,390	0.83
Costa Rican	188	0.02
Guatemalan	917	0.10
Honduran	733	0.08
Nicaraguan	1,705	0.19
Panamanian	187	0.02
Salvadoran	2,963	0.33
Other Central American	697	0.08
Cuban	1,001	0.11
Dominican Republic	77	0.01
Mexican	221,148	24.71
Puerto Rican	4,072	0.46
South American:	3,377	0.38
Argentinean	327	0.04
Bolivian	249	0.03
Chilean	412	0.05
Colombian	597	0.07
Ecuadorian	191	0.02
Paraguayan	15	0.00
Peruvian	1,068	0.12
Uruguayan	14	0.00
Venezuelan	191	0.02
Other South American	313	0.03
Other Hispanic or Latino	32,924	3.68
Hungarian	2,436	0.27
Icelander	116	0.01
Iranian	6,728	0.75
Irish	54,056	6.05
Israeli	399	0.04

Notes: 1. Figures in the "Number" column do not add up to the total population due to: a) Ancestry/Race overlap — e.g. persons can report being both White and Irish, b) persons of Hispanic origin can report being any race, c) persons reporting two ancestries are counted in both categories. 2. Numbers in parentheses indicate the number of persons reporting this ancestry/race alone, not in combination with any other ancestry/race. 3. Refer to the Explanation of Data in the front of the book for more detailed information.

Ancestry/Race	Number	%
Italian	43,165	4.83
Latvian	207	0.02
Lithuanian	919	0.10
Luxemburger	40	0.00
Macedonian	46	0.01
Maltese	261	0.03
New Zealander	125	0.01
Northern European	859	0.10
Norwegian	9,506	1.06
Pennsylvania German	165	0.02
Polish	10,766	1.20
Portuguese	15,285	1.71
Romanian	936	0.10
Russian	6,930	0.78
Scandinavian	1,133	0.13
Scotch-Irish	7,565	0.85
Scottish	11,103	1.24
Serbian	218	0.02
Slavic	223	0.02
Slovak	647	0.07
Slovene	209	0.02
Soviet Union	5	0.00
Swedish	9,350	1.05
Swiss	2,661	0.30
Turkish	391	0.04
Ukrainian	1,423	0.16
United States or American	16,961	1.90
Welsh	3,669	0.41
West Indian, excl. Hispanic:	962	0.11
Barbadian	21	0.00
Belizean	67	0.01
British West Indian	24	0.00
Dutch West Indian	37	0.00
Haitian	190	0.02
Jamaican	487	0.05
Trinidadian and Tobagonian	75	0.01
U.S. Virgin Islander	7	0.00
West Indian	46	0.01
Other West Indian	8	0.00
White:	460,772	51.49
Not Hispanic (322,534)	343,088	38.34
Hispanic (102,483)	117,684	13.15
Yugoslavian	2,222	0.25

San Juan Capistrano

Place Type: City
County: Orange
Population: 33,826

Ancestry/Race	Number	%
African American/Black:	371	1.10
Not Hispanic (151)	217	0.64
Hispanic (114)	154	0.46
African, sub-Saharan:	25	0.07
African	25	0.07
Alaska Native tribes, specified:	3	0.01
Alaska Athabascan (3)	3	0.01
Am. Ind. or Alaska Nat., not spec.	190	0.56
American Indian tribes, specified:	391	1.16
Apache (9)	9	0.03
Blackfeet (2)	16	0.05
Cherokee (24)	80	0.24
Cheyenne	1	0.00
Chickasaw (1)	8	0.02
Chippewa (1)	9	0.03
Choctaw (5)	11	0.03
Comanche	4	0.01
Cree	4	0.01
Creek (5)	5	0.01
Delaware	2	0.01
Iroquois (5)	12	0.04
Latin American Indians (26)	35	0.10
Navajo (2)	14	0.04
Osage (3)	3	0.01
Paiute	2	0.01
Pima	3	0.01
Potawatomi (1)	1	0.00
Pueblo (1)	4	0.01
Sioux (4)	6	0.02
Yaqui (1)	2	0.01
All other tribes (121)	160	0.47
American Indian tribes, not spec.	11	0.03
Arab:	169	0.50
Egyptian	53	0.16
Lebanese	70	0.21
Palestinian	26	0.08
Syrian	14	0.04
Other Arab	6	0.02
Armenian	15	0.04
Asian:	953	2.82
Cambodian (2)	2	0.01
Chinese, ex. Taiwanese (124)	187	0.55
Filipino (134)	218	0.64
Indian (64)	90	0.27
Indonesian (4)	11	0.03
Japanese (147)	233	0.69
Korean (47)	69	0.20
Laotian	2	0.01
Malaysian (1)	1	0.00
Pakistani	5	0.01
Sri Lankan (7)	7	0.02
Taiwanese (11)	12	0.04
Thai (11)	14	0.04
Vietnamese (69)	77	0.23
Other Asian, specified	3	0.01
Other Asian, not specified (11)	22	0.07
Australian	6	0.02
Austrian	183	0.54
Basque	44	0.13
Belgian	25	0.07
British	267	0.79
Bulgarian	8	0.02
Canadian	176	0.52
Celtic	25	0.07
Croatian	27	0.08
Czech	82	0.24
Czechoslovakian	43	0.13
Danish	380	1.12
Dutch	366	1.08
Eastern European	25	0.07
English	4,284	12.62
European	420	1.24
Finnish	41	0.12
French, except Basque	1,188	3.50
French Canadian	235	0.69
German	4,997	14.72
Greek	133	0.39
Hawaii Native/Pacific Islander:	106	0.31
Micronesian: (5)	10	0.03
Guamanian/Chamorro (5)	10	0.03
Polynesian: (27)	74	0.22
Native Hawaiian (9)	40	0.12
Samoan (12)	23	0.07
Other Polynesian (6)	11	0.03
Other Pac. Isl., specified	3	0.01
Other Pac. Isl., not spec. (5)	19	0.06
Hispanic or Latino:	11,206	33.13
Central American:	139	0.41
Costa Rican	9	0.03
Guatemalan	47	0.14
Honduran	9	0.03
Nicaraguan	5	0.01
Panamanian	2	0.01
Salvadoran	61	0.18
Other Central American	6	0.02
Cuban	43	0.13
Dominican Republic	5	0.01
Mexican	9,668	28.58
Puerto Rican	73	0.22
South American:	182	0.54
Argentinean	46	0.14
Bolivian	3	0.01
Chilean	12	0.04
Colombian	30	0.09
Ecuadorian	21	0.06
Peruvian	53	0.16
Uruguayan	5	0.01
Venezuelan	3	0.01
Other South American	9	0.03
Other Hispanic or Latino	1,096	3.24
Hungarian	254	0.75
Iranian	158	0.47
Irish	4,372	12.88
Italian	2,018	5.94
Lithuanian	84	0.25
New Zealander	30	0.09
Northern European	14	0.04
Norwegian	699	2.06
Pennsylvania German	13	0.04
Polish	637	1.88
Portuguese	91	0.27
Romanian	31	0.09
Russian	373	1.10
Scandinavian	125	0.37
Scotch-Irish	597	1.76
Scottish	718	2.12
Serbian	9	0.03
Slavic	7	0.02
Slovak	112	0.33
Slovene	27	0.08
Swedish	552	1.63
Swiss	52	0.15
Ukrainian	73	0.22
United States or American	1,282	3.78
Welsh	201	0.59
West Indian, excl. Hispanic:	45	0.13
Haitian	4	0.01
Jamaican	19	0.06
U.S. Virgin Islander	22	0.06
White:	27,619	81.65
Not Hispanic (21,084)	21,561	63.74
Hispanic (5,459)	6,058	17.91
Yugoslavian	42	0.12

San Leandro

Place Type: City
County: Alameda
Population: 79,452

Ancestry/Race	Number	%
Acadian/Cajun	10	0.01
Afghan	43	0.05
African American/Black:	8,700	10.95
Not Hispanic (7,622)	8,291	10.44
Hispanic (227)	409	0.51
African, sub-Saharan:	875	1.10
African	492	0.62
Cape Verdean	7	0.01
Ethiopian	115	0.15
Kenyan	14	0.02
Liberian	64	0.08
Nigerian	147	0.19
South African	10	0.01
Sudanese	26	0.03
Alaska Native tribes, specified:	24	0.03
Aleut (1)	2	0.00
Eskimo (4)	11	0.01
Tlingit-Haida	3	0.00
All other tribes (7)	8	0.01
Am. Ind. or Alaska Nat., not spec.	441	0.56
Albanian	33	0.04
Alsatian	9	0.01
American Indian tribes, specified:	902	1.14
Apache (10)	24	0.03
Blackfeet (3)	38	0.05
Cherokee (61)	241	0.30
Cheyenne	5	0.01
Chickasaw (2)	12	0.02
Chippewa (4)	14	0.02
Choctaw (14)	42	0.05
Comanche (9)	17	0.02
Cree	2	0.00
Creek (4)	7	0.01
Crow	4	0.01
Delaware	2	0.00
Iroquois (10)	28	0.04
Kiowa (8)	13	0.02
Latin American Indians (56)	91	0.11

Notes: 1. Figures in the "Number" column do not add up to the total population due to: a) Ancestry/Race overlap — e.g. persons can report being both White and Irish, b) persons of Hispanic origin can report being any race, c) persons reporting two ancestries are counted in both categories. 2. Numbers in parentheses indicate the number of persons reporting this ancestry/race alone, not in combination with any other ancestry/race. 3. Refer to the Explanation of Data in the front of the book for more detailed information.

Ancestry/Race	Number	%
Navajo (38)	57	0.07
Osage (2)	5	0.01
Ottawa (2)	2	0.00
Paiute (6)	11	0.01
Potawatomi	1	0.00
Pueblo (10)	19	0.02
Puget Sound Salish (3)	3	0.00
Seminole (3)	8	0.01
Sioux (31)	59	0.07
Tohono O'Odham	3	0.00
Ute	7	0.01
Yakama	1	0.00
Yaqui (3)	8	0.01
Yuman (3)	4	0.01
All other tribes (92)	174	0.22
American Indian tribes, not spec.	60	0.08
Arab:	502	0.63
Arab/Arabic	161	0.20
Egyptian	18	0.02
Jordanian	11	0.01
Lebanese	95	0.12
Moroccan	18	0.02
Palestinian	75	0.09
Syrian	60	0.08
Other Arab	64	0.08
Armenian	124	0.16
Asian:	20,206	25.43
Bangladeshi (2)	2	0.00
Cambodian (112)	165	0.21
Chinese, ex. Taiwanese (7,915)	8,418	10.60
Filipino (6,367)	7,153	9.00
Hmong (4)	4	0.01
Indian (815)	944	1.19
Indonesian (20)	52	0.07
Japanese (607)	871	1.10
Korean (590)	664	0.84
Laotian (30)	35	0.04
Malaysian (4)	12	0.02
Pakistani (20)	41	0.05
Sri Lankan (9)	10	0.01
Taiwanese (72)	105	0.13
Thai (47)	62	0.08
Vietnamese (1,231)	1,371	1.73
Other Asian, specified (16)	30	0.04
Other Asian, not specified (80)	267	0.34
Australian	57	0.07
Austrian	200	0.25
Basque	46	0.06
Belgian	77	0.10
Brazilian	42	0.05
British	189	0.24
Bulgarian	10	0.01
Canadian	131	0.17
Celtic	7	0.01
Croatian	121	0.15
Czech	152	0.19
Czechoslovakian	49	0.06
Danish	514	0.65
Dutch	791	1.00
Eastern European	15	0.02
English	5,161	6.51
Estonian	21	0.03
European	625	0.79
Finnish	162	0.20
French, except Basque	1,589	2.00
French Canadian	254	0.32
German	7,040	8.88
Greek	333	0.42
Hawaii Native/Pacific Islander:	1,262	1.59
Melanesian: (59)	66	0.08
Fijian (59)	66	0.08
Micronesian: (223)	308	0.39
Guamanian/Chamorro (201)	274	0.34
Other Micronesian (22)	34	0.04
Polynesian: (347)	637	0.80
Native Hawaiian (122)	341	0.43
Samoan (167)	223	0.28
Tongan (49)	57	0.07
Other Polynesian (9)	16	0.02
Other Pac. Isl., specified	3	0.00
Other Pac. Isl., not spec. (42)	248	0.31
Hispanic or Latino:	15,939	20.06
Central American:	831	1.05
Costa Rican	36	0.05
Guatemalan	123	0.15
Honduran	35	0.04
Nicaraguan	193	0.24
Panamanian	16	0.02
Salvadoran	342	0.43
Other Central American	86	0.11
Cuban	97	0.12
Dominican Republic	21	0.03
Mexican	10,719	13.49
Puerto Rican	696	0.88
South American:	391	0.49
Argentinean	31	0.04
Bolivian	16	0.02
Chilean	20	0.03
Colombian	76	0.10
Ecuadorian	11	0.01
Paraguayan	1	0.00
Peruvian	152	0.19
Uruguayan	1	0.00
Venezuelan	30	0.04
Other South American	53	0.07
Other Hispanic or Latino	3,184	4.01
Hungarian	254	0.32
Iranian	118	0.15
Irish	5,837	7.36
Italian	4,069	5.13
Latvian	57	0.07
Lithuanian	61	0.08
Luxemburger	21	0.03
Maltese	7	0.01
Northern European	63	0.08
Norwegian	1,068	1.35
Pennsylvania German	19	0.02
Polish	1,035	1.31
Portuguese	5,168	6.52
Romanian	274	0.35
Russian	632	0.80
Scandinavian	16	0.02
Scotch-Irish	965	1.22
Scottish	1,212	1.53
Serbian	60	0.08
Slavic	89	0.11
Slovak	65	0.08
Slovene	31	0.04
Swedish	925	1.17
Swiss	240	0.30
Ukrainian	153	0.19
United States or American	1,646	2.08
Welsh	327	0.41
West Indian, excl. Hispanic:	179	0.23
Belizean	46	0.06
Bermudan	8	0.01
Jamaican	99	0.12
Trinidadian and Tobagonian	16	0.02
West Indian	10	0.01
White:	44,397	55.88
Not Hispanic (33,646)	35,982	45.29
Hispanic (7,108)	8,415	10.59
Yugoslavian	218	0.27

San Lorenzo

Place Type: Census Designated Place
County: Alameda
Population: 21,898

Ancestry/Race	Number	%
Afghan	21	0.10
African American/Black:	778	3.55
Not Hispanic (584)	714	3.26
Hispanic (32)	64	0.29
African, sub-Saharan:	39	0.18
African	21	0.10
Cape Verdean	18	0.08
Alaska Native tribes, specified:	5	0.02
Aleut	3	0.01
Eskimo	1	0.00
Tlingit-Haida	1	0.00
Alaska Native tribes, not specified	2	0.01
Am. Ind. or Alaska Nat., not spec.	107	0.49
Albanian	5	0.02
American Indian tribes, specified:	346	1.58
Apache (18)	26	0.12
Blackfeet (3)	15	0.07
Cherokee (26)	105	0.48
Chickasaw	2	0.01
Chippewa	6	0.03
Choctaw (7)	29	0.13
Colville	1	0.00
Comanche (1)	3	0.01
Creek (1)	2	0.01
Crow	1	0.00
Iroquois	6	0.03
Latin American Indians (18)	26	0.12
Navajo (25)	30	0.14
Osage	3	0.01
Paiute (5)	6	0.03
Pima (1)	1	0.00
Pueblo (7)	7	0.03
Seminole (1)	5	0.02
Shoshone	1	0.00
Sioux (4)	19	0.09
Ute	1	0.00
Yakama (1)	2	0.01
Yuman (1)	1	0.00
All other tribes (21)	48	0.22
American Indian tribes, not spec.	24	0.11
Arab:	50	0.23
Arab/Arabic	14	0.06
Jordanian	7	0.03
Lebanese	17	0.08
Palestinian	12	0.05
Asian:	3,979	18.17
Bangladeshi (4)	4	0.02
Cambodian (50)	51	0.23
Chinese, ex. Taiwanese (982)	1,143	5.22
Filipino (1,534)	1,793	8.19
Hmong (4)	4	0.02
Indian (114)	140	0.64
Indonesian (4)	14	0.06
Japanese (189)	285	1.30
Korean (97)	123	0.56
Laotian (16)	23	0.11
Malaysian (1)	3	0.01
Pakistani (4)	5	0.02
Taiwanese (19)	26	0.12
Thai (3)	3	0.01
Vietnamese (271)	314	1.43
Other Asian, specified (6)	7	0.03
Other Asian, not specified (11)	41	0.19
Austrian	40	0.18
Belgian	25	0.11
British	100	0.46
Canadian	24	0.11
Croatian	12	0.05
Czech	71	0.32
Czechoslovakian	11	0.05
Danish	186	0.85
Dutch	273	1.24
English	1,728	7.87
European	177	0.81
Finnish	55	0.25
French, except Basque	495	2.26
French Canadian	88	0.40
German	2,689	12.25
Greek	67	0.31
Hawaii Native/Pacific Islander:	292	1.33
Melanesian: (6)	9	0.04
Fijian (6)	9	0.04
Micronesian: (24)	52	0.24
Guamanian/Chamorro (24)	52	0.24
Polynesian: (53)	173	0.79
Native Hawaiian (15)	121	0.55
Samoan (29)	40	0.18
Tongan (9)	10	0.05
Other Polynesian	2	0.01

Notes: 1. Figures in the "Number" column do not add up to the total population due to: a) Ancestry/Race overlap — e.g. persons can report being both White and Irish, b) persons of Hispanic origin can report being any race, c) persons reporting two ancestries are counted in both categories. 2. Numbers in parentheses indicate the number of persons reporting this ancestry/race alone, not in combination with any other ancestry/race. 3. Refer to the Explanation of Data in the front of the book for more detailed information.

Ancestry/Race	Number	%
Other Pac. Isl., not spec. (20)	58	0.26
Hispanic or Latino:	5,398	24.65
Central American:	285	1.30
Costa Rican	8	0.04
Guatemalan	60	0.27
Honduran	8	0.04
Nicaraguan	82	0.37
Panamanian	2	0.01
Salvadoran	101	0.46
Other Central American	24	0.11
Cuban	41	0.19
Dominican Republic	6	0.03
Mexican	3,595	16.42
Puerto Rican	255	1.16
South American:	93	0.42
Argentinean	6	0.03
Bolivian	7	0.03
Chilean	9	0.04
Colombian	8	0.04
Ecuadorian	5	0.02
Peruvian	45	0.21
Uruguayan	3	0.01
Venezuelan	1	0.00
Other South American	9	0.04
Other Hispanic or Latino	1,123	5.13
Hungarian	91	0.41
Icelander	36	0.16
Iranian	18	0.08
Irish	2,140	9.75
Italian	1,575	7.18
Lithuanian	32	0.15
Maltese	18	0.08
Northern European	12	0.05
Norwegian	312	1.42
Polish	262	1.19
Portuguese	1,415	6.45
Romanian	5	0.02
Russian	194	0.88
Scandinavian	47	0.21
Scotch-Irish	345	1.57
Scottish	367	1.67
Serbian	4	0.02
Slavic	12	0.05
Slovak	13	0.06
Swedish	316	1.44
Swiss	47	0.21
Turkish	13	0.06
Ukrainian	41	0.19
United States or American	654	2.98
Welsh	92	0.42
White:	15,020	68.59
Not Hispanic (11,475)	12,207	55.74
Hispanic (2,390)	2,813	12.85
Yugoslavian	61	0.28

San Luis Obispo

Place Type: City
County: San Luis Obispo
Population: 44,174

Ancestry/Race	Number	%
African American/Black:	853	1.93
Not Hispanic (594)	757	1.71
Hispanic (50)	96	0.22
African, sub-Saharan:	200	0.45
African	163	0.37
Ethiopian	7	0.02
Nigerian	12	0.03
South African	7	0.02
Other sub-Saharan African	11	0.02
Alaska Native tribes, specified:	7	0.02
Aleut (4)	5	0.01
Tlingit-Haida	2	0.00
Am. Ind. or Alaska Nat., not spec.	206	0.47
Alsatian	7	0.02
American Indian tribes, specified:	470	1.06
Apache (13)	33	0.07
Blackfeet (2)	22	0.05
Cherokee (33)	111	0.25
Cheyenne	5	0.01
Chickasaw (1)	3	0.01
Chippewa (6)	13	0.03
Choctaw (13)	24	0.05
Comanche	6	0.01
Cree (1)	2	0.00
Creek (3)	9	0.02
Crow (1)	1	0.00
Delaware	1	0.00
Iroquois (2)	7	0.02
Latin American Indians (25)	44	0.10
Lumbee (2)	2	0.00
Navajo (5)	12	0.03
Osage (4)	9	0.02
Paiute (4)	8	0.02
Pima (1)	5	0.01
Potawatomi (4)	9	0.02
Pueblo (2)	11	0.02
Seminole (1)	2	0.00
Shoshone (2)	2	0.00
Sioux (3)	12	0.03
Ute	1	0.00
Yaqui (5)	13	0.03
Yuman (2)	5	0.01
All other tribes (43)	98	0.22
American Indian tribes, not spec.	26	0.06
Arab:	261	0.59
Arab/Arabic	13	0.03
Egyptian	31	0.07
Lebanese	167	0.38
Palestinian	6	0.01
Syrian	34	0.08
Other Arab	10	0.02
Armenian	141	0.32
Asian:	2,947	6.67
Cambodian (8)	9	0.02
Chinese, ex. Taiwanese (704)	873	1.98
Filipino (489)	654	1.48
Hmong (2)	3	0.01
Indian (240)	276	0.62
Indonesian (9)	26	0.06
Japanese (292)	428	0.97
Korean (191)	240	0.54
Laotian (41)	45	0.10
Malaysian	3	0.01
Pakistani (28)	40	0.09
Sri Lankan (5)	7	0.02
Taiwanese (22)	27	0.06
Thai (21)	32	0.07
Vietnamese (181)	207	0.47
Other Asian, specified (11)	11	0.02
Other Asian, not specified (27)	66	0.15
Assyrian/Chaldean/Syriac	10	0.02
Australian	40	0.09
Austrian	229	0.52
Basque	114	0.26
Belgian	48	0.11
British	468	1.06
Canadian	91	0.21
Celtic	17	0.04
Croatian	38	0.09
Czech	186	0.42
Czechoslovakian	136	0.31
Danish	518	1.17
Dutch	932	2.11
Eastern European	28	0.06
English	5,696	12.90
Estonian	16	0.04
European	866	1.96
Finnish	150	0.34
French, except Basque	1,924	4.36
French Canadian	229	0.52
German	7,708	17.46
Greek	158	0.36
Guyanese	12	0.03
Hawaii Native/Pacific Islander:	160	0.36
Melanesian: (1)	2	0.00
Fijian (1)	2	0.00
Micronesian: (21)	30	0.07
Guamanian/Chamorro (21)	30	0.07
Polynesian: (33)	94	0.21
Native Hawaiian (24)	73	0.17
Samoan (7)	18	0.04
Tongan (2)	3	0.01
Other Pac. Isl., not spec. (3)	34	0.08
Hispanic or Latino:	5,147	11.65
Central American:	148	0.34
Costa Rican	8	0.02
Guatemalan	45	0.10
Honduran	9	0.02
Nicaraguan	16	0.04
Panamanian	10	0.02
Salvadoran	50	0.11
Other Central American	10	0.02
Cuban	64	0.14
Dominican Republic	1	0.00
Mexican	3,877	8.78
Puerto Rican	118	0.27
South American:	174	0.39
Argentinean	27	0.06
Bolivian	4	0.01
Chilean	23	0.05
Colombian	34	0.08
Ecuadorian	10	0.02
Peruvian	57	0.13
Uruguayan	4	0.01
Venezuelan	2	0.00
Other South American	13	0.03
Other Hispanic or Latino	765	1.73
Hungarian	249	0.56
Icelander	13	0.03
Iranian	96	0.22
Irish	5,943	13.46
Israeli	25	0.06
Italian	3,285	7.44
Lithuanian	80	0.18
Luxemburger	8	0.02
Maltese	10	0.02
Northern European	126	0.29
Norwegian	1,152	2.61
Pennsylvania German	9	0.02
Polish	704	1.59
Portuguese	992	2.25
Romanian	33	0.07
Russian	608	1.38
Scandinavian	184	0.42
Scotch-Irish	922	2.09
Scottish	1,497	3.39
Serbian	11	0.02
Slavic	7	0.02
Slovak	45	0.10
Slovene	10	0.02
Swedish	1,081	2.45
Swiss	723	1.64
Turkish	35	0.08
Ukrainian	96	0.22
United States or American	2,049	4.64
Welsh	508	1.15
West Indian, excl. Hispanic:	28	0.06
Jamaican	20	0.05
Trinidadian and Tobagonian	8	0.02
White:	38,531	87.23
Not Hispanic (34,756)	35,710	80.84
Hispanic (2,399)	2,821	6.39
Yugoslavian	81	0.18

San Marcos

Place Type: City
County: San Diego
Population: 54,977

Ancestry/Race	Number	%
Afghan	64	0.12
African American/Black:	1,514	2.75
Not Hispanic (1,001)	1,279	2.33
Hispanic (98)	235	0.43
African, sub-Saharan:	204	0.37
African	182	0.33
Ethiopian	17	0.03

Notes: 1. Figures in the "Number" column do not add up to the total population due to: a) Ancestry/Race overlap — e.g. persons can report being both White and Irish, b) persons of Hispanic origin can report being any race, c) persons reporting two ancestries are counted in both categories. 2. Numbers in parentheses indicate the number of persons reporting this ancestry/race alone, not in combination with any other ancestry/race. 3. Refer to the Explanation of Data in the front of the book for more detailed information.

Ancestry/Race	Number	%
South African	5	0.01
Alaska Native tribes, specified:	3	0.01
Alaska Athabascan (2)	2	0.00
Aleut	1	0.00
Am. Ind. or Alaska Nat., not spec.	293	0.53
American Indian tribes, specified:	498	0.91
Apache (8)	18	0.03
Blackfeet (1)	14	0.03
Cherokee (34)	113	0.21
Cheyenne	1	0.00
Chickasaw (1)	4	0.01
Chippewa (8)	13	0.02
Choctaw (8)	17	0.03
Comanche (2)	8	0.01
Cree	1	0.00
Creek	3	0.01
Crow	1	0.00
Delaware (1)	2	0.00
Iroquois (11)	14	0.03
Kiowa	2	0.00
Latin American Indians (61)	85	0.15
Navajo (5)	13	0.02
Osage (1)	4	0.01
Paiute (1)	2	0.00
Pima	5	0.01
Potawatomi (3)	3	0.01
Pueblo (14)	21	0.04
Puget Sound Salish (1)	1	0.00
Seminole	5	0.01
Shoshone (1)	5	0.01
Sioux (7)	17	0.03
Tohono O'Odham (1)	4	0.01
Yaqui (7)	9	0.02
Yuman (1)	1	0.00
All other tribes (72)	112	0.20
American Indian tribes, not spec.	39	0.07
Arab:	320	0.58
Arab/Arabic	35	0.06
Egyptian	20	0.04
Lebanese	189	0.34
Moroccan	8	0.01
Syrian	68	0.12
Armenian	19	0.03
Asian:	3,396	6.18
Bangladeshi (3)	3	0.01
Cambodian (24)	27	0.05
Chinese, ex. Taiwanese (390)	523	0.95
Filipino (1,091)	1,391	2.53
Hmong	6	0.01
Indian (147)	182	0.33
Indonesian (10)	26	0.05
Japanese (227)	414	0.75
Korean (129)	186	0.34
Laotian (23)	47	0.09
Malaysian	1	0.00
Pakistani (5)	6	0.01
Sri Lankan (5)	7	0.01
Taiwanese (22)	28	0.05
Thai (25)	44	0.08
Vietnamese (354)	397	0.72
Other Asian, specified (2)	6	0.01
Other Asian, not specified (33)	102	0.19
Australian	31	0.06
Austrian	163	0.30
Basque	23	0.04
Belgian	61	0.11
Brazilian	19	0.03
British	267	0.48
Bulgarian	23	0.04
Canadian	236	0.43
Croatian	94	0.17
Czech	232	0.42
Czechoslovakian	89	0.16
Danish	258	0.47
Dutch	1,067	1.93
Eastern European	9	0.02
English	4,864	8.82
European	545	0.99
Finnish	80	0.15
French, except Basque	1,592	2.89
French Canadian	283	0.51
German	7,366	13.35
Greek	221	0.40
Hawaii Native/Pacific Islander:	258	0.47
Micronesian: (58)	72	0.13
Guamanian/Chamorro (53)	67	0.12
Other Micronesian (5)	5	0.01
Polynesian: (66)	148	0.27
Native Hawaiian (26)	77	0.14
Samoan (37)	58	0.11
Tongan (2)	5	0.01
Other Polynesian (1)	8	0.01
Other Pac. Isl., not spec. (6)	38	0.07
Hispanic or Latino:	20,271	36.87
Central American:	262	0.48
Costa Rican	20	0.04
Guatemalan	98	0.18
Honduran	13	0.02
Nicaraguan	7	0.01
Panamanian	27	0.05
Salvadoran	77	0.14
Other Central American	20	0.04
Cuban	50	0.09
Dominican Republic	5	0.01
Mexican	17,609	32.03
Puerto Rican	258	0.47
South American:	203	0.37
Argentinean	11	0.02
Bolivian	27	0.05
Chilean	26	0.05
Colombian	43	0.08
Ecuadorian	14	0.03
Paraguayan	1	0.00
Peruvian	51	0.09
Uruguayan	2	0.00
Venezuelan	13	0.02
Other South American	15	0.03
Other Hispanic or Latino	1,884	3.43
Hungarian	372	0.67
Iranian	151	0.27
Irish	4,810	8.72
Israeli	31	0.06
Italian	2,474	4.49
Latvian	13	0.02
Lithuanian	121	0.22
Macedonian	33	0.06
New Zealander	42	0.08
Northern European	37	0.07
Norwegian	894	1.62
Pennsylvania German	23	0.04
Polish	848	1.54
Portuguese	140	0.25
Romanian	63	0.11
Russian	467	0.85
Scandinavian	177	0.32
Scotch-Irish	940	1.70
Scottish	1,103	2.00
Serbian	54	0.10
Slavic	23	0.04
Slovak	51	0.09
Slovene	15	0.03
Swedish	890	1.61
Swiss	191	0.35
Turkish	60	0.11
Ukrainian	57	0.10
United States or American	2,232	4.05
Welsh	372	0.67
West Indian, excl. Hispanic:	198	0.36
Dutch West Indian	10	0.02
Jamaican	107	0.19
Trinidadian and Tobagonian	81	0.15
White:	39,198	71.30
Not Hispanic (29,617)	30,653	55.76
Hispanic (7,434)	8,545	15.54
Yugoslavian	96	0.17

San Marino

Place Type: City
County: Los Angeles
Population: 12,945

Ancestry/Race	Number	%
African American/Black:	41	0.32
Not Hispanic (29)	37	0.29
Hispanic (4)	4	0.03
Alaska Native tribes, specified:	1	0.01
All other tribes	1	0.01
Am. Ind. or Alaska Nat., not spec.	18	0.14
American Indian tribes, specified:	12	0.09
Apache (1)	2	0.02
Cherokee	1	0.01
Latin American Indians (1)	1	0.01
Puget Sound Salish	1	0.01
Yaqui	2	0.02
All other tribes (1)	5	0.04
Arab:	19	0.15
Lebanese	6	0.05
Syrian	13	0.10
Armenian	160	1.23
Asian:	6,754	52.17
Cambodian (5)	9	0.07
Chinese, ex. Taiwanese (3,892)	4,186	32.34
Filipino (63)	89	0.69
Indian (114)	119	0.92
Indonesian (35)	62	0.48
Japanese (282)	359	2.77
Korean (196)	222	1.71
Malaysian (9)	10	0.08
Pakistani (4)	6	0.05
Sri Lankan (14)	14	0.11
Taiwanese (1,368)	1,542	11.91
Thai (27)	28	0.22
Vietnamese (35)	56	0.43
Other Asian, specified (13)	20	0.15
Other Asian, not specified (19)	32	0.25
Australian	49	0.38
Austrian	32	0.25
Basque	14	0.11
Belgian	14	0.11
British	107	0.82
Canadian	28	0.22
Croatian	18	0.14
Czech	32	0.25
Czechoslovakian	5	0.04
Danish	45	0.35
Dutch	170	1.31
Eastern European	8	0.06
English	1,609	12.40
European	101	0.78
Finnish	29	0.22
French, except Basque	234	1.80
French Canadian	6	0.05
German	1,451	11.18
Greek	115	0.89
Hawaii Native/Pacific Islander:	57	0.44
Micronesian: (3)	4	0.03
Guamanian/Chamorro (3)	4	0.03
Polynesian: (6)	14	0.11
Native Hawaiian (4)	12	0.09
Samoan (2)	2	0.02
Other Pac. Isl., not spec. (1)	39	0.30
Hispanic or Latino:	571	4.41
Central American:	29	0.22
Costa Rican	3	0.02
Guatemalan	7	0.05
Honduran	2	0.02
Panamanian	4	0.03
Salvadoran	11	0.08
Other Central American	2	0.02
Cuban	16	0.12
Mexican	393	3.04
Puerto Rican	11	0.08
South American:	51	0.39
Argentinean	10	0.08
Chilean	2	0.02

Notes: 1. Figures in the "Number" column do not add up to the total population due to: a) Ancestry/Race overlap — e.g. persons can report being both White and Irish, b) persons of Hispanic origin can report being any race, c) persons reporting two ancestries are counted in both categories. 2. Numbers in parentheses indicate the number of persons reporting this ancestry/race alone, not in combination with any other ancestry/race. 3. Refer to the Explanation of Data in the front of the book for more detailed information.

Ancestry/Race	Number	%
Colombian	11	0.08
Ecuadorian	12	0.09
Peruvian	7	0.05
Venezuelan	4	0.03
Other South American	5	0.04
Other Hispanic or Latino	71	0.55
Hungarian	157	1.21
Iranian	109	0.84
Irish	849	6.54
Italian	295	2.27
Northern European	7	0.05
Norwegian	144	1.11
Polish	105	0.81
Portuguese	13	0.10
Romanian	29	0.22
Russian	41	0.32
Scandinavian	47	0.36
Scotch-Irish	262	2.02
Scottish	286	2.20
Serbian	11	0.08
Slavic	34	0.26
Slovene	4	0.03
Swedish	308	2.37
Swiss	69	0.53
Ukrainian	21	0.16
United States or American	220	1.70
Welsh	177	1.36
White:	6,382	49.30
Not Hispanic (5,771)	5,957	46.02
Hispanic (406)	425	3.28

San Mateo

Place Type: City
County: San Mateo
Population: 92,482

Ancestry/Race	Number	%
Acadian/Cajun	7	0.01
African American/Black:	2,852	3.08
Not Hispanic (2,273)	2,611	2.82
Hispanic (124)	241	0.26
African, sub-Saharan:	211	0.23
African	121	0.13
Ethiopian	28	0.03
Nigerian	15	0.02
South African	39	0.04
Other sub-Saharan African	8	0.01
Alaska Native tribes, specified:	15	0.02
Alaska Athabascan	2	0.00
Aleut (3)	4	0.00
Eskimo (3)	5	0.01
Tlingit-Haida (2)	4	0.00
Am. Ind. or Alaska Nat., not spec.	348	0.38
Alsatian	8	0.01
American Indian tribes, specified:	581	0.63
Apache (9)	30	0.03
Blackfeet (1)	20	0.02
Cherokee (36)	143	0.15
Cheyenne	6	0.01
Chickasaw (2)	9	0.01
Chippewa (5)	18	0.02
Choctaw (6)	25	0.03
Comanche	1	0.00
Cree	4	0.00
Creek (5)	14	0.02
Delaware	1	0.00
Iroquois (6)	14	0.02
Latin American Indians (72)	120	0.13
Lumbee (1)	2	0.00
Navajo (13)	28	0.03
Paiute (1)	3	0.00
Potawatomi (2)	4	0.00
Pueblo (6)	12	0.01
Puget Sound Salish (1)	7	0.01
Seminole (1)	7	0.01
Sioux (8)	19	0.02
Ute (2)	4	0.00
Yakama (1)	2	0.00
Yaqui (5)	10	0.01
Yuman	2	0.00
All other tribes (35)	76	0.08
American Indian tribes, not spec.	60	0.06
Arab:	1,065	1.15
Arab/Arabic	239	0.26
Egyptian	106	0.11
Iraqi	31	0.03
Jordanian	34	0.04
Lebanese	324	0.35
Moroccan	40	0.04
Palestinian	117	0.13
Syrian	67	0.07
Other Arab	107	0.12
Armenian	218	0.24
Asian:	16,363	17.69
Bangladeshi	2	0.00
Cambodian (15)	28	0.03
Chinese, ex. Taiwanese (5,812)	6,451	6.98
Filipino (2,736)	3,478	3.76
Indian (1,652)	2,039	2.20
Indonesian (48)	91	0.10
Japanese (2,214)	2,668	2.88
Korean (583)	678	0.73
Laotian (17)	21	0.02
Malaysian (11)	21	0.02
Pakistani (26)	53	0.06
Sri Lankan (1)	2	0.00
Taiwanese (83)	108	0.12
Thai (122)	147	0.16
Vietnamese (274)	318	0.34
Other Asian, specified (27)	50	0.05
Other Asian, not specified (67)	208	0.22
Assyrian/Chaldean/Syriac	33	0.04
Australian	89	0.10
Austrian	334	0.36
Basque	130	0.14
Belgian	191	0.21
Brazilian	33	0.04
British	531	0.57
Bulgarian	52	0.06
Canadian	351	0.38
Celtic	6	0.01
Croatian	336	0.36
Czech	230	0.25
Czechoslovakian	110	0.12
Danish	581	0.63
Dutch	1,001	1.08
Eastern European	137	0.15
English	7,398	8.01
Estonian	19	0.02
European	1,086	1.18
Finnish	250	0.27
French, except Basque	2,632	2.85
French Canadian	528	0.57
German	10,124	10.96
Greek	839	0.91
Guyanese	12	0.01
Hawaii Native/Pacific Islander:	2,295	2.48
Melanesian: (232)	281	0.30
Fijian (232)	281	0.30
Micronesian: (75)	110	0.12
Guamanian/Chamorro (52)	86	0.09
Other Micronesian (23)	24	0.03
Polynesian: (1,059)	1,493	1.61
Native Hawaiian (97)	271	0.29
Samoan (137)	180	0.19
Tongan (779)	946	1.02
Other Polynesian (46)	96	0.10
Other Pac. Isl., specified	2	0.00
Other Pac. Isl., not spec. (107)	409	0.44
Hispanic or Latino:	18,973	20.52
Central American:	2,826	3.06
Costa Rican	43	0.05
Guatemalan	913	0.99
Honduran	75	0.08
Nicaraguan	363	0.39
Panamanian	17	0.02
Salvadoran	1,156	1.25
Other Central American	259	0.28
Cuban	150	0.16
Dominican Republic	15	0.02
Mexican	10,345	11.19
Puerto Rican	369	0.40
South American:	1,313	1.42
Argentinean	85	0.09
Bolivian	77	0.08
Chilean	148	0.16
Colombian	152	0.16
Ecuadorian	30	0.03
Paraguayan	2	0.00
Peruvian	623	0.67
Uruguayan	17	0.02
Venezuelan	15	0.02
Other South American	164	0.18
Other Hispanic or Latino	3,955	4.28
Hungarian	483	0.52
Icelander	69	0.07
Iranian	723	0.78
Irish	10,242	11.09
Israeli	31	0.03
Italian	8,734	9.46
Latvian	7	0.01
Lithuanian	199	0.22
Luxemburger	26	0.03
Maltese	279	0.30
New Zealander	18	0.02
Northern European	97	0.11
Norwegian	1,206	1.31
Polish	1,671	1.81
Portuguese	916	0.99
Romanian	196	0.21
Russian	1,762	1.91
Scandinavian	124	0.13
Scotch-Irish	1,254	1.36
Scottish	1,828	1.98
Serbian	37	0.04
Slavic	92	0.10
Slovak	146	0.16
Slovene	59	0.06
Swedish	1,584	1.71
Swiss	524	0.57
Turkish	92	0.10
Ukrainian	534	0.58
United States or American	3,213	3.48
Welsh	514	0.56
West Indian, excl. Hispanic:	45	0.05
Haitian	7	0.01
Jamaican	7	0.01
Trinidadian and Tobagonian	5	0.01
West Indian	26	0.03
White:	64,950	70.23
Not Hispanic (52,260)	54,641	59.08
Hispanic (8,991)	10,309	11.15
Yugoslavian	206	0.22

San Pablo

Place Type: City
County: Contra Costa
Population: 30,215

Ancestry/Race	Number	%
African American/Black:	6,019	19.92
Not Hispanic (5,403)	5,748	19.02
Hispanic (136)	271	0.90
African, sub-Saharan:	488	1.62
African	401	1.33
Ethiopian	52	0.17
Nigerian	25	0.08
South African	10	0.03
Alaska Native tribes, specified:	1	0.00
Aleut (1)	1	0.00
Am. Ind. or Alaska Nat., not spec.	236	0.78
American Indian tribes, specified:	367	1.21
Apache (6)	22	0.07
Blackfeet	22	0.07
Cherokee (10)	94	0.31
Cheyenne	3	0.01
Chickasaw (4)	6	0.02
Chippewa (2)	4	0.01

Notes: 1. Figures in the "Number" column do not add up to the total population due to: a) Ancestry/Race overlap — e.g. persons can report being both White and Irish, b) persons of Hispanic origin can report being any race, c) persons reporting two ancestries are counted in both categories. 2. Numbers in parentheses indicate the number of persons reporting this ancestry/race alone, not in combination with any other ancestry/race. 3. Refer to the Explanation of Data in the front of the book for more detailed information.

Ancestry/Race	Number	%
Choctaw (20)	35	0.12
Comanche	1	0.00
Cree	3	0.01
Creek	4	0.01
Delaware	2	0.01
Iroquois (2)	5	0.02
Latin American Indians (50)	66	0.22
Lumbee	1	0.00
Navajo (1)	9	0.03
Paiute (1)	2	0.01
Potawatomi	1	0.00
Pueblo (5)	6	0.02
Seminole	5	0.02
Sioux (4)	26	0.09
Yaqui	1	0.00
All other tribes (33)	49	0.16
American Indian tribes, not spec.	35	0.12
Arab:	63	0.21
Arab/Arabic	49	0.16
Palestinian	6	0.02
Other Arab	8	0.03
Asian:	5,686	18.82
Cambodian (25)	38	0.13
Chinese, ex. Taiwanese (473)	575	1.90
Filipino (1,841)	2,086	6.90
Hmong (15)	16	0.05
Indian (428)	550	1.82
Indonesian (6)	15	0.05
Japanese (84)	122	0.40
Korean (56)	87	0.29
Laotian (1,136)	1,290	4.27
Malaysian	8	0.03
Pakistani (25)	36	0.12
Taiwanese (6)	10	0.03
Thai (34)	39	0.13
Vietnamese (608)	647	2.14
Other Asian, specified (11)	15	0.05
Other Asian, not specified (89)	152	0.50
Austrian	10	0.03
Brazilian	52	0.17
British	39	0.13
Canadian	24	0.08
Croatian	11	0.04
Czech	7	0.02
Danish	9	0.03
Dutch	110	0.37
English	572	1.90
European	62	0.21
Finnish	15	0.05
French, except Basque	257	0.85
French Canadian	13	0.04
German	747	2.48
Greek	73	0.24
Guyanese	6	0.02
Hawaii Native/Pacific Islander:	345	1.14
Melanesian: (41)	54	0.18
Fijian (41)	54	0.18
Micronesian: (19)	35	0.12
Guamanian/Chamorro (19)	35	0.12
Polynesian: (58)	122	0.40
Native Hawaiian (12)	58	0.19
Samoan (34)	45	0.15
Tongan (7)	14	0.05
Other Polynesian (5)	5	0.02
Other Pac. Isl., specified	3	0.01
Other Pac. Isl., not spec. (35)	131	0.43
Hispanic or Latino:	13,490	44.65
Central American:	1,467	4.86
Costa Rican	8	0.03
Guatemalan	218	0.72
Honduran	31	0.10
Nicaraguan	257	0.85
Panamanian	12	0.04
Salvadoran	820	2.71
Other Central American	121	0.40
Cuban	17	0.06
Dominican Republic	7	0.02
Mexican	9,567	31.66
Puerto Rican	166	0.55
South American:	160	0.53
Argentinean	12	0.04
Bolivian	17	0.06
Chilean	8	0.03
Colombian	16	0.05
Ecuadorian	1	0.00
Peruvian	88	0.29
Uruguayan	2	0.01
Other South American	16	0.05
Other Hispanic or Latino	2,106	6.97
Hungarian	9	0.03
Iranian	31	0.10
Irish	965	3.20
Italian	462	1.53
Northern European	39	0.13
Norwegian	58	0.19
Polish	108	0.36
Portuguese	454	1.51
Romanian	4	0.01
Russian	125	0.41
Scotch-Irish	147	0.49
Scottish	191	0.63
Slavic	13	0.04
Slovak	9	0.03
Swedish	61	0.20
Swiss	63	0.21
United States or American	526	1.75
Welsh	36	0.12
West Indian, excl. Hispanic:	22	0.07
Barbadian	8	0.03
Jamaican	14	0.05
White:	10,953	36.25
Not Hispanic (4,886)	5,507	18.23
Hispanic (4,669)	5,446	18.02

San Rafael

Place Type: City
County: Marin
Population: 56,063

Ancestry/Race	Number	%
Acadian/Cajun	15	0.03
Afghan	20	0.04
African American/Black:	1,667	2.97
Not Hispanic (1,175)	1,502	2.68
Hispanic (82)	165	0.29
African, sub-Saharan:	186	0.33
African	120	0.21
Ethiopian	26	0.05
Nigerian	14	0.02
South African	15	0.03
Other sub-Saharan African	11	0.02
Alaska Native tribes, specified:	5	0.01
Eskimo (2)	4	0.01
All other tribes	1	0.00
Alaska Native tribes, not specified	2	0.00
Am. Ind. or Alaska Nat., not spec.	230	0.41
Albanian	7	0.01
American Indian tribes, specified:	456	0.81
Apache (7)	22	0.04
Blackfeet	13	0.02
Cherokee (17)	93	0.17
Cheyenne (2)	4	0.01
Chickasaw (1)	1	0.00
Chippewa (5)	8	0.01
Choctaw (2)	12	0.02
Comanche (1)	2	0.00
Cree (2)	3	0.01
Creek (2)	3	0.01
Crow	2	0.00
Delaware	3	0.01
Iroquois (3)	7	0.01
Kiowa	2	0.00
Latin American Indians (97)	177	0.32
Navajo (6)	17	0.03
Osage (1)	2	0.00
Ottawa (1)	1	0.00
Pima (1)	1	0.00
Potawatomi	5	0.01
Pueblo (3)	7	0.01
Sioux (3)	8	0.01
Ute (1)	1	0.00
Yaqui (4)	9	0.02
All other tribes (14)	53	0.09
American Indian tribes, not spec.	32	0.06
Arab:	444	0.79
Arab/Arabic	45	0.08
Egyptian	64	0.11
Jordanian	182	0.32
Lebanese	63	0.11
Moroccan	19	0.03
Palestinian	13	0.02
Syrian	24	0.04
Other Arab	34	0.06
Armenian	161	0.29
Asian:	3,994	7.12
Cambodian (28)	35	0.06
Chinese, ex. Taiwanese (851)	1,120	2.00
Filipino (252)	402	0.72
Indian (412)	468	0.83
Indonesian (7)	18	0.03
Japanese (348)	539	0.96
Korean (193)	247	0.44
Laotian (18)	21	0.04
Malaysian	1	0.00
Pakistani (14)	23	0.04
Sri Lankan (5)	6	0.01
Taiwanese (7)	11	0.02
Thai (55)	75	0.13
Vietnamese (766)	837	1.49
Other Asian, specified (3)	10	0.02
Other Asian, not specified (48)	181	0.32
Assyrian/Chaldean/Syriac	7	0.01
Australian	117	0.21
Austrian	375	0.67
Basque	77	0.14
Belgian	71	0.13
Brazilian	285	0.51
British	442	0.79
Bulgarian	33	0.06
Canadian	236	0.42
Celtic	16	0.03
Croatian	57	0.10
Czech	228	0.41
Czechoslovakian	92	0.16
Danish	585	1.04
Dutch	898	1.60
Eastern European	191	0.34
English	6,234	11.11
European	783	1.39
Finnish	136	0.24
French, except Basque	2,137	3.81
French Canadian	240	0.43
German	6,884	12.26
Greek	363	0.65
Hawaii Native/Pacific Islander:	256	0.46
Melanesian: (22)	32	0.06
Fijian (22)	32	0.06
Micronesian: (21)	34	0.06
Guamanian/Chamorro (16)	29	0.05
Other Micronesian (5)	5	0.01
Polynesian: (31)	103	0.18
Native Hawaiian (12)	70	0.12
Samoan (13)	26	0.05
Tongan (4)	4	0.01
Other Polynesian (2)	3	0.01
Other Pac. Isl., specified	5	0.01
Other Pac. Isl., not spec. (20)	82	0.15
Hispanic or Latino:	13,070	23.31
Central American:	3,471	6.19
Costa Rican	13	0.02
Guatemalan	2,090	3.73
Honduran	32	0.06
Nicaraguan	117	0.21
Panamanian	5	0.01
Salvadoran	1,072	1.91
Other Central American	142	0.25
Cuban	67	0.12
Dominican Republic	15	0.03
Mexican	6,007	10.71

Notes: 1. Figures in the "Number" column do not add up to the total population due to: a) Ancestry/Race overlap — e.g. persons can report being both White and Irish, b) persons of Hispanic origin can report being any race, c) persons reporting two ancestries are counted in both categories. 2. Numbers in parentheses indicate the number of persons reporting this ancestry/race alone, not in combination with any other ancestry/race. 3. Refer to the Explanation of Data in the front of the book for more detailed information.

Puerto Rican	139	0.25
South American:	473	0.84
Argentinean	44	0.08
Bolivian	20	0.04
Chilean	46	0.08
Colombian	83	0.15
Ecuadorian	17	0.03
Paraguayan	7	0.01
Peruvian	204	0.36
Uruguayan	4	0.01
Venezuelan	9	0.02
Other South American	39	0.07
Other Hispanic or Latino	2,898	5.17
Hungarian	354	0.63
Icelander	22	0.04
Iranian	510	0.91
Irish	7,546	13.44
Israeli	44	0.08
Italian	4,454	7.93
Latvian	20	0.04
Lithuanian	205	0.37
Luxemburger	7	0.01
Macedonian	8	0.01
Maltese	30	0.05
New Zealander	38	0.07
Northern European	141	0.25
Norwegian	1,109	1.98
Pennsylvania German	19	0.03
Polish	1,228	2.19
Portuguese	445	0.79
Romanian	155	0.28
Russian	1,698	3.03
Scandinavian	130	0.23
Scotch-Irish	1,191	2.12
Scottish	1,572	2.80
Serbian	23	0.04
Slavic	34	0.06
Slovak	101	0.18
Slovene	36	0.06
Swedish	1,209	2.15
Swiss	313	0.56
Turkish	36	0.06
Ukrainian	232	0.41
United States or American	1,302	2.32
Welsh	416	0.74
West Indian, excl. Hispanic:	259	0.46
Belizean	7	0.01
British West Indian	8	0.01
Dutch West Indian	7	0.01
Haitian	212	0.38
Jamaican	20	0.04
West Indian	5	0.01
White:	44,631	79.61
Not Hispanic (36,960)	38,114	67.98
Hispanic (5,512)	6,517	11.62
Yugoslavian	99	0.18

San Ramon

Place Type: City
County: Contra Costa
Population: 44,722

Ancestry/Race	Number	%
Afghan	50	0.11
African American/Black:	1,041	2.33
Not Hispanic (842)	985	2.20
Hispanic (20)	56	0.13
African, sub-Saharan:	289	0.65
African	219	0.49
Ethiopian	36	0.08
Nigerian	15	0.03
Other sub-Saharan African	19	0.04
Alaska Native tribes, specified:	9	0.02
Alaska Athabascan (1)	1	0.00
Aleut	3	0.01
Tlingit-Haida (2)	5	0.01
Am. Ind. or Alaska Nat., not spec.	121	0.27
Albanian	13	0.03
Alsatian	7	0.02
American Indian tribes, specified:	260	0.58
Apache (3)	8	0.02
Blackfeet	8	0.02
Cherokee (32)	93	0.21
Chickasaw (1)	3	0.01
Chippewa (7)	9	0.02
Choctaw (13)	35	0.08
Creek (1)	3	0.01
Delaware (1)	2	0.00
Iroquois (3)	8	0.02
Kiowa (9)	12	0.03
Latin American Indians (2)	7	0.02
Lumbee	1	0.00
Menominee (1)	1	0.00
Navajo (3)	8	0.02
Osage	2	0.00
Paiute (1)	2	0.00
Potawatomi	1	0.00
Pueblo (4)	7	0.02
Puget Sound Salish (3)	4	0.01
Seminole	1	0.00
Sioux (3)	13	0.03
Yaqui	4	0.01
All other tribes (15)	28	0.06
American Indian tribes, not spec.	17	0.04
Arab:	392	0.88
Arab/Arabic	76	0.17
Egyptian	66	0.15
Iraqi	21	0.05
Lebanese	112	0.25
Palestinian	31	0.07
Syrian	63	0.14
Other Arab	23	0.05
Armenian	161	0.36
Asian:	7,860	17.58
Bangladeshi	9	0.02
Cambodian (13)	16	0.04
Chinese, ex. Taiwanese (2,546)	2,931	6.55
Filipino (1,134)	1,488	3.33
Indian (1,387)	1,463	3.27
Indonesian (39)	68	0.15
Japanese (497)	760	1.70
Korean (406)	472	1.06
Laotian (2)	4	0.01
Malaysian (10)	14	0.03
Pakistani (57)	79	0.18
Sri Lankan (28)	35	0.08
Taiwanese (56)	66	0.15
Thai (29)	32	0.07
Vietnamese (243)	263	0.59
Other Asian, specified (7)	20	0.04
Other Asian, not specified (49)	140	0.31
Australian	38	0.09
Austrian	159	0.36
Basque	41	0.09
Belgian	96	0.22
Brazilian	19	0.04
British	195	0.44
Bulgarian	24	0.05
Canadian	217	0.49
Celtic	24	0.05
Croatian	87	0.20
Czech	98	0.22
Czechoslovakian	100	0.22
Danish	626	1.41
Dutch	792	1.78
Eastern European	58	0.13
English	5,364	12.06
European	603	1.36
Finnish	195	0.44
French, except Basque	1,509	3.39
French Canadian	228	0.51
German	7,455	16.76
Greek	570	1.28
Hawaii Native/Pacific Islander:	270	0.60
Melanesian: (11)	16	0.04
Fijian (11)	16	0.04
Micronesian: (41)	63	0.14
Guamanian/Chamorro (41)	61	0.14
Other Micronesian	2	0.00
Polynesian: (29)	149	0.33
Native Hawaiian (18)	123	0.28
Samoan (8)	19	0.04
Tongan (2)	3	0.01
Other Polynesian (1)	4	0.01
Other Pac. Isl., specified	1	0.00
Other Pac. Isl., not spec. (11)	41	0.09
Hispanic or Latino:	3,238	7.24
Central American:	179	0.40
Costa Rican	12	0.03
Guatemalan	28	0.06
Honduran	7	0.02
Nicaraguan	31	0.07
Panamanian	20	0.04
Salvadoran	64	0.14
Other Central American	17	0.04
Cuban	69	0.15
Dominican Republic	3	0.01
Mexican	1,844	4.12
Puerto Rican	155	0.35
South American:	232	0.52
Argentinean	34	0.08
Bolivian	10	0.02
Chilean	23	0.05
Colombian	44	0.10
Ecuadorian	11	0.02
Peruvian	76	0.17
Venezuelan	5	0.01
Other South American	29	0.06
Other Hispanic or Latino	756	1.69
Hungarian	253	0.57
Icelander	17	0.04
Iranian	570	1.28
Irish	5,995	13.48
Israeli	27	0.06
Italian	4,048	9.10
Latvian	20	0.04
Lithuanian	119	0.27
Luxemburger	7	0.02
Maltese	34	0.08
New Zealander	6	0.01
Northern European	62	0.14
Norwegian	1,228	2.76
Pennsylvania German	12	0.03
Polish	1,114	2.50
Portuguese	1,555	3.50
Romanian	63	0.14
Russian	842	1.89
Scandinavian	166	0.37
Scotch-Irish	684	1.54
Scottish	985	2.21
Serbian	68	0.15
Slavic	50	0.11
Slovene	6	0.01
Swedish	1,168	2.63
Swiss	229	0.51
Turkish	45	0.10
Ukrainian	156	0.35
United States or American	1,271	2.86
Welsh	462	1.04
West Indian, excl. Hispanic:	34	0.08
Jamaican	34	0.08
White:	35,740	79.92
Not Hispanic (32,356)	33,478	74.86
Hispanic (1,998)	2,262	5.06
Yugoslavian	85	0.19

Sanger

Place Type: City
County: Fresno
Population: 18,931

Ancestry/Race	Number	%
African American/Black:	110	0.58
Not Hispanic (28)	33	0.17
Hispanic (52)	77	0.41
African, sub-Saharan:	3	0.02
African	3	0.02
Am. Ind. or Alaska Nat., not spec.	135	0.71

Notes: 1. Figures in the "Number" column do not add up to the total population due to: a) Ancestry/Race overlap — e.g. persons can report being both White and Irish, b) persons of Hispanic origin can report being any race, c) persons reporting two ancestries are counted in both categories. 2. Numbers in parentheses indicate the number of persons reporting this ancestry/race alone, not in combination with any other ancestry/race. 3. Refer to the Explanation of Data in the front of the book for more detailed information.

American Indian tribes, specified:	156	0.82
Apache (2)	11	0.06
Blackfeet (1)	1	0.01
Cherokee (12)	30	0.16
Cheyenne (1)	1	0.01
Chickasaw (2)	2	0.01
Choctaw (6)	6	0.03
Iroquois	2	0.01
Latin American Indians (59)	66	0.35
Lumbee	1	0.01
Pima	2	0.01
Potawatomi (1)	1	0.01
Pueblo (2)	3	0.02
Yaqui (1)	2	0.01
All other tribes (17)	28	0.15
American Indian tribes, not spec.	50	0.26
Arab:	107	0.56
Arab/Arabic	81	0.43
Lebanese	15	0.08
Other Arab	11	0.06
Armenian	85	0.45
Asian:	486	2.57
Cambodian (23)	24	0.13
Chinese, ex. Taiwanese (59)	67	0.35
Filipino (45)	67	0.35
Hmong (6)	7	0.04
Indian (80)	102	0.54
Japanese (106)	148	0.78
Korean (17)	19	0.10
Laotian (11)	11	0.06
Pakistani (4)	4	0.02
Sri Lankan	4	0.02
Taiwanese (4)	4	0.02
Vietnamese (6)	7	0.04
Other Asian, not specified (2)	22	0.12
Austrian	9	0.05
Basque	8	0.04
British	36	0.19
Canadian	15	0.08
Celtic	5	0.03
Czech	6	0.03
Czechoslovakian	3	0.02
Danish	32	0.17
Dutch	102	0.54
English	514	2.71
European	7	0.04
Finnish	18	0.10
French, except Basque	64	0.34
German	640	3.38
Hawaii Native/Pacific Islander:	36	0.19
Micronesian: (1)	2	0.01
Guamanian/Chamorro (1)	2	0.01
Polynesian: (9)	26	0.14
Native Hawaiian (4)	17	0.09
Tongan	2	0.01
Other Polynesian (5)	7	0.04
Other Pac. Isl., not spec. (4)	8	0.04
Hispanic or Latino:	15,319	80.92
Central American:	43	0.23
Costa Rican	1	0.01
Guatemalan	13	0.07
Honduran	9	0.05
Salvadoran	16	0.08
Other Central American	4	0.02
Cuban	3	0.02
Mexican	13,418	70.88
Puerto Rican	35	0.18
South American:	3	0.02
Chilean	1	0.01
Other South American	2	0.01
Other Hispanic or Latino	1,817	9.60
Hungarian	9	0.05
Irish	375	1.98
Italian	254	1.34
Norwegian	50	0.26
Polish	19	0.10
Portuguese	75	0.40
Romanian	12	0.06
Russian	41	0.22
Scandinavian	9	0.05
Scotch-Irish	34	0.18
Scottish	68	0.36
Serbian	7	0.04
Swedish	118	0.62
Swiss	71	0.37
United States or American	408	2.15
Welsh	15	0.08
White:	9,949	52.55
Not Hispanic (3,015)	3,148	16.63
Hispanic (6,361)	6,801	35.93
Yugoslavian	15	0.08

Santa Ana

Place Type: City
County: Orange
Population: 337,977

Ancestry/Race	Number	%
Acadian/Cajun	14	0.00
Afghan	110	0.03
African American/Black:	7,057	2.09
Not Hispanic (4,309)	4,873	1.44
Hispanic (1,440)	2,184	0.65
African, sub-Saharan:	467	0.14
African	332	0.10
Cape Verdean	11	0.00
Ethiopian	14	0.00
Kenyan	21	0.01
Nigerian	22	0.01
Somalian	7	0.00
South African	41	0.01
Other sub-Saharan African	19	0.01
Alaska Native tribes, specified:	15	0.00
Alaska Athabascan (1)	1	0.00
Aleut (3)	4	0.00
Eskimo (7)	8	0.00
Tlingit-Haida (1)	1	0.00
All other tribes (1)	1	0.00
Alaska Native tribes, not specified	1	0.00
Am. Ind. or Alaska Nat., not spec.	2,903	0.86
American Indian tribes, specified:	2,635	0.78
Apache (66)	157	0.05
Blackfeet (13)	55	0.02
Cherokee (76)	256	0.08
Cheyenne (1)	2	0.00
Chickasaw (2)	8	0.00
Chippewa (12)	27	0.01
Choctaw (18)	60	0.02
Colville (1)	2	0.00
Comanche (2)	3	0.00
Cree (1)	1	0.00
Creek (4)	9	0.00
Crow (1)	2	0.00
Delaware (1)	5	0.00
Iroquois (11)	14	0.00
Kiowa (2)	3	0.00
Latin American Indians (939)	1,300	0.38
Lumbee (2)	2	0.00
Menominee (1)	1	0.00
Navajo (85)	116	0.03
Osage (1)	1	0.00
Paiute (2)	2	0.00
Pima (1)	7	0.00
Potawatomi (1)	1	0.00
Pueblo (38)	69	0.02
Puget Sound Salish (3)	3	0.00
Seminole (1)	3	0.00
Shoshone (17)	19	0.01
Sioux (9)	24	0.01
Tohono O'Odham (8)	14	0.00
Ute (2)	5	0.00
Yaqui (19)	35	0.01
Yuman (5)	6	0.00
All other tribes (301)	423	0.13
American Indian tribes, not spec.	353	0.10
Arab:	465	0.14
Arab/Arabic	136	0.04
Egyptian	75	0.02
Iraqi	6	0.00
Jordanian	5	0.00
Lebanese	94	0.03
Palestinian	60	0.02
Syrian	29	0.01
Other Arab	60	0.02
Armenian	189	0.06
Asian:	32,629	9.65
Bangladeshi (19)	24	0.01
Cambodian (1,767)	2,013	0.60
Chinese, ex. Taiwanese (1,906)	2,533	0.75
Filipino (2,249)	2,693	0.80
Hmong (409)	467	0.14
Indian (553)	818	0.24
Indonesian (55)	109	0.03
Japanese (886)	1,209	0.36
Korean (667)	760	0.22
Laotian (709)	813	0.24
Malaysian (5)	14	0.00
Pakistani (67)	75	0.02
Sri Lankan (7)	11	0.00
Taiwanese (59)	75	0.02
Thai (143)	176	0.05
Vietnamese (19,226)	19,919	5.89
Other Asian, specified (18)	29	0.01
Other Asian, not specified (389)	891	0.26
Assyrian/Chaldean/Syriac	11	0.00
Australian	21	0.01
Austrian	318	0.09
Basque	60	0.02
Belgian	100	0.03
Brazilian	28	0.01
British	326	0.10
Bulgarian	39	0.01
Canadian	446	0.13
Celtic	23	0.01
Croatian	88	0.03
Czech	213	0.06
Czechoslovakian	156	0.05
Danish	440	0.13
Dutch	1,062	0.31
Eastern European	36	0.01
English	5,860	1.74
Estonian	19	0.01
European	763	0.23
Finnish	56	0.02
French, except Basque	2,138	0.63
French Canadian	396	0.12
German	7,893	2.34
Greek	274	0.08
Guyanese	70	0.02
Hawaii Native/Pacific Islander:	1,841	0.54
Melanesian: (9)	12	0.00
Fijian (9)	12	0.00
Micronesian: (164)	323	0.10
Guamanian/Chamorro (134)	289	0.09
Other Micronesian (30)	34	0.01
Polynesian: (876)	1,198	0.35
Native Hawaiian (154)	325	0.10
Samoan (627)	746	0.22
Tongan (76)	91	0.03
Other Polynesian (19)	36	0.01
Other Pac. Isl., specified	5	0.00
Other Pac. Isl., not spec. (100)	303	0.09
Hispanic or Latino:	257,097	76.07
Central American:	7,559	2.24
Costa Rican	87	0.03
Guatemalan	1,931	0.57
Honduran	280	0.08
Nicaraguan	190	0.06
Panamanian	49	0.01
Salvadoran	4,131	1.22
Other Central American	891	0.26
Cuban	551	0.16
Dominican Republic	19	0.01
Mexican	222,719	65.90
Puerto Rican	730	0.22
South American:	1,742	0.52
Argentinean	196	0.06
Bolivian	269	0.08
Chilean	68	0.02

Notes: 1. Figures in the "Number" column do not add up to the total population due to: a) Ancestry/Race overlap — e.g. persons can report being both White and Irish, b) persons of Hispanic origin can report being any race, c) persons reporting two ancestries are counted in both categories. 2. Numbers in parentheses indicate the number of persons reporting this ancestry/race alone, not in combination with any other ancestry/race. 3. Refer to the Explanation of Data in the front of the book for more detailed information.

Ancestry/Race	Number	%
Colombian	397	0.12
Ecuadorian	140	0.04
Paraguayan	1	0.00
Peruvian	420	0.12
Uruguayan	31	0.01
Venezuelan	37	0.01
Other South American	183	0.05
Other Hispanic or Latino	23,777	7.04
Hungarian	362	0.11
Icelander	61	0.02
Iranian	341	0.10
Irish	5,825	1.73
Israeli	14	0.00
Italian	3,239	0.96
Latvian	24	0.01
Lithuanian	192	0.06
Macedonian	11	0.00
New Zealander	32	0.01
Northern European	20	0.01
Norwegian	1,253	0.37
Pennsylvania German	20	0.01
Polish	1,404	0.42
Portuguese	281	0.08
Romanian	129	0.04
Russian	636	0.19
Scandinavian	61	0.02
Scotch-Irish	1,282	0.38
Scottish	1,357	0.40
Serbian	6	0.00
Slavic	100	0.03
Slovak	71	0.02
Slovene	32	0.01
Swedish	993	0.29
Swiss	230	0.07
Turkish	43	0.01
Ukrainian	75	0.02
United States or American	5,832	1.73
Welsh	377	0.11
West Indian, excl. Hispanic:	246	0.07
Belizean	52	0.02
Haitian	87	0.03
Jamaican	64	0.02
Trinidadian and Tobagonian	23	0.01
West Indian	13	0.00
Other West Indian	7	0.00
White:	157,483	46.60
Not Hispanic (41,984)	44,113	13.05
Hispanic (102,441)	113,370	33.54
Yugoslavian	75	0.02

Santa Barbara

Place Type: City
County: Santa Barbara
Population: 92,325

Ancestry/Race	Number	%
Afghan	21	0.02
African American/Black:	2,047	2.22
Not Hispanic (1,418)	1,706	1.85
Hispanic (218)	341	0.37
African, sub-Saharan:	186	0.20
African	153	0.17
South African	33	0.04
Alaska Native tribes, specified:	15	0.02
Alaska Athabascan	3	0.00
Eskimo (5)	6	0.01
Tlingit-Haida (6)	6	0.01
Alaska Native tribes, not specified	1	0.00
Am. Ind. or Alaska Nat., not spec.	620	0.67
Albanian	31	0.03
Alsatian	11	0.01
American Indian tribes, specified:	1,128	1.22
Apache (28)	65	0.07
Blackfeet (4)	22	0.02
Cherokee (51)	178	0.19
Cheyenne	1	0.00
Chickasaw (3)	9	0.01
Chippewa (9)	20	0.02
Choctaw (6)	19	0.02
Colville (1)	1	0.00
Comanche (2)	4	0.00
Cree (1)	2	0.00
Creek (4)	7	0.01
Delaware	2	0.00
Iroquois (4)	14	0.02
Latin American Indians (138)	207	0.22
Navajo (19)	36	0.04
Osage (4)	8	0.01
Ottawa	1	0.00
Pima (2)	4	0.00
Potawatomi	3	0.00
Pueblo (5)	12	0.01
Puget Sound Salish (4)	4	0.00
Seminole	4	0.00
Shoshone (3)	5	0.01
Sioux (7)	23	0.02
Tohono O'Odham (3)	4	0.00
Ute (2)	2	0.00
Yaqui (38)	56	0.06
Yuman (2)	2	0.00
All other tribes (246)	413	0.45
American Indian tribes, not spec.	67	0.07
Arab:	354	0.38
Arab/Arabic	61	0.07
Egyptian	41	0.04
Jordanian	6	0.01
Lebanese	143	0.16
Moroccan	9	0.01
Palestinian	7	0.01
Syrian	45	0.05
Other Arab	42	0.05
Armenian	216	0.23
Asian:	3,378	3.66
Bangladeshi (1)	1	0.00
Cambodian (13)	13	0.01
Chinese, ex. Taiwanese (528)	699	0.76
Filipino (453)	675	0.73
Indian (226)	296	0.32
Indonesian (28)	44	0.05
Japanese (603)	817	0.88
Korean (302)	358	0.39
Laotian (12)	17	0.02
Malaysian (1)	1	0.00
Pakistani (10)	12	0.01
Sri Lankan (44)	47	0.05
Taiwanese (34)	47	0.05
Thai (35)	43	0.05
Vietnamese (124)	141	0.15
Other Asian, specified (8)	17	0.02
Other Asian, not specified (77)	150	0.16
Australian	124	0.13
Austrian	390	0.42
Basque	90	0.10
Belgian	166	0.18
Brazilian	121	0.13
British	1,089	1.18
Bulgarian	73	0.08
Canadian	359	0.39
Celtic	35	0.04
Croatian	42	0.05
Cypriot	8	0.01
Czech	258	0.28
Czechoslovakian	195	0.21
Danish	942	1.02
Dutch	1,258	1.36
Eastern European	162	0.18
English	9,953	10.80
European	1,246	1.35
Finnish	219	0.24
French, except Basque	3,042	3.30
French Canadian	485	0.53
German	10,503	11.39
Greek	382	0.41
Hawaii Native/Pacific Islander:	268	0.29
Micronesian: (10)	16	0.02
Guamanian/Chamorro (10)	15	0.02
Other Micronesian	1	0.00
Polynesian: (90)	177	0.19
Native Hawaiian (49)	118	0.13
Samoan (10)	16	0.02
Tongan (28)	33	0.04
Other Polynesian (3)	10	0.01
Other Pac. Isl., specified	2	0.00
Other Pac. Isl., not spec. (22)	73	0.08
Hispanic or Latino:	32,330	35.02
Central American:	639	0.69
Costa Rican	18	0.02
Guatemalan	329	0.36
Honduran	51	0.06
Nicaraguan	21	0.02
Panamanian	14	0.02
Salvadoran	126	0.14
Other Central American	80	0.09
Cuban	108	0.12
Dominican Republic	3	0.00
Mexican	27,529	29.82
Puerto Rican	198	0.21
South American:	395	0.43
Argentinean	79	0.09
Bolivian	6	0.01
Chilean	65	0.07
Colombian	72	0.08
Ecuadorian	25	0.03
Paraguayan	6	0.01
Peruvian	96	0.10
Uruguayan	5	0.01
Venezuelan	12	0.01
Other South American	29	0.03
Other Hispanic or Latino	3,458	3.75
Hungarian	529	0.57
Icelander	31	0.03
Iranian	232	0.25
Irish	8,203	8.90
Israeli	47	0.05
Italian	4,350	4.72
Latvian	64	0.07
Lithuanian	189	0.20
Luxemburger	18	0.02
Macedonian	5	0.01
Maltese	8	0.01
New Zealander	4	0.00
Northern European	90	0.10
Norwegian	1,562	1.69
Pennsylvania German	21	0.02
Polish	1,798	1.95
Portuguese	395	0.43
Romanian	129	0.14
Russian	1,315	1.43
Scandinavian	193	0.21
Scotch-Irish	1,377	1.49
Scottish	2,475	2.68
Serbian	43	0.05
Slavic	69	0.07
Slovak	135	0.15
Slovene	8	0.01
Swedish	1,733	1.88
Swiss	435	0.47
Turkish	50	0.05
Ukrainian	293	0.32
United States or American	2,522	2.74
Welsh	562	0.61
West Indian, excl. Hispanic:	80	0.09
Bermudan	5	0.01
Haitian	24	0.03
Jamaican	39	0.04
Trinidadian and Tobagonian	12	0.01
White:	71,519	77.46
Not Hispanic (53,849)	55,266	59.86
Hispanic (14,506)	16,253	17.60
Yugoslavian	177	0.19

Santa Clara

Place Type: City
County: Santa Clara
Population: 102,361

Ancestry/Race	Number	%
Afghan	32	0.03

Notes: 1. Figures in the "Number" column do not add up to the total population due to: a) Ancestry/Race overlap — e.g. persons can report being both White and Irish, b) persons of Hispanic origin can report being any race, c) persons reporting two ancestries are counted in both categories. 2. Numbers in parentheses indicate the number of persons reporting this ancestry/race alone, not in combination with any other ancestry/race. 3. Refer to the Explanation of Data in the front of the book for more detailed information.

Ancestry/Race	Number	%
African American/Black:	2,860	2.79
Not Hispanic (2,237)	2,645	2.58
Hispanic (104)	215	0.21
African, sub-Saharan:	618	0.61
African	157	0.15
Ethiopian	363	0.36
Ghanian	11	0.01
Nigerian	40	0.04
Sierra Leonean	7	0.01
South African	33	0.03
Other sub-Saharan African	7	0.01
Alaska Native tribes, specified:	18	0.02
Alaska Athabascan	2	0.00
Aleut (2)	4	0.00
Eskimo (3)	7	0.01
Tlingit-Haida (3)	5	0.00
Alaska Native tribes, not specified	1	0.00
Am. Ind. or Alaska Nat., not spec.	380	0.37
Albanian	8	0.01
Alsatian	7	0.01
American Indian tribes, specified:	695	0.68
Apache (24)	49	0.05
Blackfeet (3)	26	0.03
Cherokee (42)	159	0.16
Cheyenne	1	0.00
Chickasaw	6	0.01
Chippewa (11)	14	0.01
Choctaw (20)	57	0.06
Comanche (4)	11	0.01
Cree (1)	2	0.00
Creek (1)	4	0.00
Crow	1	0.00
Iroquois (9)	13	0.01
Kiowa (1)	2	0.00
Latin American Indians (59)	91	0.09
Menominee	1	0.00
Navajo (24)	37	0.04
Osage (6)	10	0.01
Ottawa	4	0.00
Paiute (1)	1	0.00
Potawatomi (1)	6	0.01
Pueblo (1)	8	0.01
Puget Sound Salish (3)	4	0.00
Seminole (1)	10	0.01
Shoshone (4)	8	0.01
Sioux (19)	33	0.03
Ute	1	0.00
Yakama (2)	2	0.00
Yaqui (12)	20	0.02
Yuman (1)	1	0.00
All other tribes (43)	113	0.11
American Indian tribes, not spec.	74	0.07
Arab:	1,104	1.08
Arab/Arabic	281	0.28
Egyptian	231	0.23
Iraqi	108	0.11
Jordanian	105	0.10
Lebanese	101	0.10
Palestinian	69	0.07
Syrian	118	0.12
Other Arab	91	0.09
Armenian	354	0.35
Asian:	32,707	31.95
Bangladeshi (39)	42	0.04
Cambodian (32)	45	0.04
Chinese, ex. Taiwanese (5,033)	5,644	5.51
Filipino (5,819)	6,592	6.44
Hmong (34)	39	0.04
Indian (8,853)	9,163	8.95
Indonesian (73)	127	0.12
Japanese (1,625)	2,103	2.05
Korean (2,298)	2,471	2.41
Laotian (38)	48	0.05
Malaysian (16)	24	0.02
Pakistani (399)	491	0.48
Sri Lankan (43)	53	0.05
Taiwanese (164)	215	0.21
Thai (84)	125	0.12
Vietnamese (4,803)	5,046	4.93
Other Asian, specified (58)	71	0.07
Other Asian, not specified (152)	408	0.40
Assyrian/Chaldean/Syriac	82	0.08
Australian	102	0.10
Austrian	202	0.20
Basque	57	0.06
Belgian	43	0.04
Brazilian	85	0.08
British	533	0.52
Bulgarian	50	0.05
Canadian	274	0.27
Celtic	45	0.04
Croatian	287	0.28
Czech	244	0.24
Czechoslovakian	161	0.16
Danish	764	0.75
Dutch	1,106	1.08
Eastern European	47	0.05
English	7,272	7.12
European	1,328	1.30
Finnish	130	0.13
French, except Basque	2,574	2.52
French Canadian	554	0.54
German	10,178	9.97
German Russian	5	0.00
Greek	418	0.41
Hawaii Native/Pacific Islander:	929	0.91
Melanesian: (33)	45	0.04
Fijian (32)	44	0.04
Other Melanesian (1)	1	0.00
Micronesian: (64)	115	0.11
Guamanian/Chamorro (58)	105	0.10
Other Micronesian (6)	10	0.01
Polynesian: (274)	532	0.52
Native Hawaiian (64)	248	0.24
Samoan (171)	229	0.22
Tongan (25)	34	0.03
Other Polynesian (14)	21	0.02
Other Pac. Isl., specified	1	0.00
Other Pac. Isl., not spec. (56)	236	0.23
Hispanic or Latino:	16,364	15.99
Central American:	648	0.63
Costa Rican	13	0.01
Guatemalan	152	0.15
Honduran	28	0.03
Nicaraguan	152	0.15
Panamanian	17	0.02
Salvadoran	240	0.23
Other Central American	46	0.04
Cuban	183	0.18
Dominican Republic	12	0.01
Mexican	11,862	11.59
Puerto Rican	343	0.34
South American:	494	0.48
Argentinean	34	0.03
Bolivian	28	0.03
Chilean	56	0.05
Colombian	70	0.07
Ecuadorian	15	0.01
Paraguayan	2	0.00
Peruvian	205	0.20
Uruguayan	1	0.00
Venezuelan	25	0.02
Other South American	58	0.06
Other Hispanic or Latino	2,822	2.76
Hungarian	366	0.36
Icelander	7	0.01
Iranian	758	0.74
Irish	7,687	7.53
Israeli	37	0.04
Italian	5,874	5.75
Latvian	38	0.04
Lithuanian	189	0.19
Macedonian	41	0.04
Maltese	51	0.05
Northern European	93	0.09
Norwegian	1,218	1.19
Pennsylvania German	45	0.04
Polish	1,506	1.47
Portuguese	3,959	3.88
Romanian	176	0.17
Russian	1,010	0.99
Scandinavian	185	0.18
Scotch-Irish	1,016	1.00
Scottish	1,620	1.59
Serbian	117	0.11
Slavic	59	0.06
Slovak	91	0.09
Slovene	86	0.08
Soviet Union	12	0.01
Swedish	1,299	1.27
Swiss	354	0.35
Turkish	61	0.06
Ukrainian	247	0.24
United States or American	3,112	3.05
Welsh	499	0.49
West Indian, excl. Hispanic:	116	0.11
Belizean	22	0.02
Dutch West Indian	5	0.00
Haitian	45	0.04
Jamaican	29	0.03
West Indian	15	0.01
White:	61,000	59.59
Not Hispanic (49,392)	52,239	51.03
Hispanic (7,511)	8,761	8.56
Yugoslavian	723	0.71

Santa Clarita

Place Type: City
County: Los Angeles
Population: 151,088

Ancestry/Race	Number	%
Acadian/Cajun	5	0.00
Afghan	19	0.01
African American/Black:	3,931	2.60
Not Hispanic (2,957)	3,610	2.39
Hispanic (165)	321	0.21
African, sub-Saharan:	413	0.27
African	191	0.13
Ethiopian	31	0.02
Ghanian	59	0.04
Nigerian	50	0.03
South African	54	0.04
Ugandan	17	0.01
Other sub-Saharan African	11	0.01
Alaska Native tribes, specified:	18	0.01
Alaska Athabascan (3)	10	0.01
Aleut	2	0.00
Eskimo (2)	4	0.00
Tlingit-Haida (1)	2	0.00
Am. Ind. or Alaska Nat., not spec.	593	0.39
Albanian	15	0.01
Alsatian	15	0.01
American Indian tribes, specified:	1,372	0.91
Apache (52)	138	0.09
Blackfeet (14)	70	0.05
Cherokee (114)	399	0.26
Cheyenne (1)	5	0.00
Chickasaw (10)	24	0.02
Chippewa (20)	26	0.02
Choctaw (20)	46	0.03
Colville (2)	3	0.00
Comanche (3)	10	0.01
Cree (1)	1	0.00
Creek (7)	26	0.02
Crow (2)	3	0.00
Delaware (6)	10	0.01
Iroquois (26)	51	0.03
Kiowa (3)	6	0.00
Latin American Indians (83)	120	0.08
Lumbee (6)	7	0.00
Menominee (1)	1	0.00
Navajo (28)	59	0.04
Osage (1)	2	0.00
Ottawa (1)	1	0.00
Paiute (4)	8	0.01
Pima (1)	16	0.01
Potawatomi (5)	7	0.00
Pueblo (13)	29	0.02

Notes: 1. Figures in the "Number" column do not add up to the total population due to: a) Ancestry/Race overlap — e.g. persons can report being both White and Irish, b) persons of Hispanic origin can report being any race, c) persons reporting two ancestries are counted in both categories. 2. Numbers in parentheses indicate the number of persons reporting this ancestry/race alone, not in combination with any other ancestry/race. 3. Refer to the Explanation of Data in the front of the book for more detailed information.

Ancestry/Race	Number	%
Seminole (1)	4	0.00
Shoshone (2)	7	0.00
Sioux (32)	67	0.04
Tohono O'Odham	2	0.00
Ute (1)	5	0.00
Yakama	1	0.00
Yaqui (12)	30	0.02
Yuman (1)	1	0.00
All other tribes (72)	187	0.12
American Indian tribes, not spec.	104	0.07
Arab:	1,162	0.77
Arab/Arabic	156	0.10
Egyptian	217	0.14
Iraqi	14	0.01
Jordanian	84	0.06
Lebanese	364	0.24
Moroccan	5	0.00
Palestinian	16	0.01
Syrian	219	0.14
Other Arab	87	0.06
Armenian	664	0.44
Asian:	10,337	6.84
Bangladeshi (28)	32	0.02
Cambodian (28)	45	0.03
Chinese, ex. Taiwanese (939)	1,378	0.91
Filipino (2,848)	3,652	2.42
Hmong (3)	3	0.00
Indian (928)	1,087	0.72
Indonesian (62)	130	0.09
Japanese (1,024)	1,657	1.10
Korean (964)	1,140	0.75
Laotian (7)	11	0.01
Malaysian (3)	14	0.01
Pakistani (44)	70	0.05
Sri Lankan (45)	53	0.04
Taiwanese (68)	82	0.05
Thai (209)	254	0.17
Vietnamese (329)	409	0.27
Other Asian, specified (38)	62	0.04
Other Asian, not specified (101)	258	0.17
Assyrian/Chaldean/Syriac	200	0.13
Australian	156	0.10
Austrian	471	0.31
Basque	98	0.06
Belgian	221	0.15
Brazilian	67	0.04
British	1,021	0.67
Bulgarian	31	0.02
Canadian	871	0.58
Celtic	42	0.03
Croatian	176	0.12
Czech	907	0.60
Czechoslovakian	440	0.29
Danish	1,621	1.07
Dutch	2,713	1.79
Eastern European	185	0.12
English	18,423	12.17
Estonian	17	0.01
European	2,110	1.39
Finnish	386	0.25
French, except Basque	4,837	3.20
French Canadian	1,103	0.73
German	23,526	15.54
German Russian	7	0.00
Greek	775	0.51
Guyanese	32	0.02
Hawaii Native/Pacific Islander:	629	0.42
Melanesian: (12)	20	0.01
Fijian (12)	20	0.01
Micronesian: (39)	75	0.05
Guamanian/Chamorro (34)	67	0.04
Other Micronesian (5)	8	0.01
Polynesian: (149)	385	0.25
Native Hawaiian (87)	281	0.19
Samoan (49)	81	0.05
Tongan (9)	14	0.01
Other Polynesian (4)	9	0.01
Other Pac. Isl., specified	12	0.01
Other Pac. Isl., not spec. (18)	137	0.09
Hispanic or Latino:	30,968	20.50
Central American:	1,922	1.27
Costa Rican	82	0.05
Guatemalan	879	0.58
Honduran	73	0.05
Nicaraguan	93	0.06
Panamanian	76	0.05
Salvadoran	569	0.38
Other Central American	150	0.10
Cuban	704	0.47
Dominican Republic	25	0.02
Mexican	21,603	14.30
Puerto Rican	634	0.42
South American:	1,451	0.96
Argentinean	253	0.17
Bolivian	61	0.04
Chilean	110	0.07
Colombian	299	0.20
Ecuadorian	150	0.10
Peruvian	359	0.24
Uruguayan	16	0.01
Venezuelan	21	0.01
Other South American	182	0.12
Other Hispanic or Latino	4,629	3.06
Hungarian	1,435	0.95
Icelander	36	0.02
Iranian	849	0.56
Irish	18,642	12.31
Israeli	150	0.10
Italian	11,757	7.77
Latvian	79	0.05
Lithuanian	389	0.26
Luxemburger	23	0.02
Macedonian	5	0.00
Maltese	32	0.02
New Zealander	25	0.02
Northern European	162	0.11
Norwegian	3,033	2.00
Pennsylvania German	60	0.04
Polish	4,404	2.91
Portuguese	805	0.53
Romanian	254	0.17
Russian	3,246	2.14
Scandinavian	435	0.29
Scotch-Irish	2,843	1.88
Scottish	4,318	2.85
Serbian	87	0.06
Slavic	78	0.05
Slovak	310	0.20
Slovene	54	0.04
Soviet Union	9	0.01
Swedish	3,400	2.25
Swiss	565	0.37
Turkish	115	0.08
Ukrainian	356	0.24
United States or American	7,414	4.90
Welsh	1,245	0.82
West Indian, excl. Hispanic:	225	0.15
Belizean	72	0.05
Bermudan	9	0.01
Haitian	22	0.01
Jamaican	71	0.05
West Indian	51	0.03
White:	125,345	82.96
Not Hispanic (104,646)	107,908	71.42
Hispanic (15,511)	17,437	11.54
Yugoslavian	334	0.22

Santa Cruz

Place Type: City
County: Santa Cruz
Population: 54,593

Ancestry/Race	Number	%
Acadian/Cajun	21	0.04
Afghan	12	0.02
African American/Black:	1,383	2.53
Not Hispanic (871)	1,247	2.28
Hispanic (74)	136	0.25
African, sub-Saharan:	199	0.37
African	148	0.27
Ethiopian	9	0.02
Nigerian	5	0.01
South African	29	0.05
Other sub-Saharan African	8	0.01
Alaska Native tribes, specified:	17	0.03
Aleut (4)	6	0.01
Eskimo (6)	6	0.01
Tlingit-Haida (2)	3	0.01
All other tribes	2	0.00
Alaska Native tribes, not specified	2	0.00
Am. Ind. or Alaska Nat., not spec.	380	0.70
American Indian tribes, specified:	720	1.32
Apache (21)	50	0.09
Blackfeet (8)	29	0.05
Cherokee (41)	200	0.37
Cheyenne (1)	1	0.00
Chickasaw (2)	8	0.01
Chippewa (6)	17	0.03
Choctaw (7)	25	0.05
Comanche (13)	18	0.03
Cree (1)	5	0.01
Creek (1)	11	0.02
Crow	1	0.00
Iroquois (1)	5	0.01
Kiowa (1)	1	0.00
Latin American Indians (83)	148	0.27
Menominee	1	0.00
Navajo (8)	13	0.02
Osage (1)	2	0.00
Ottawa	1	0.00
Paiute (1)	1	0.00
Pima (1)	1	0.00
Potawatomi (4)	9	0.02
Pueblo (5)	15	0.03
Seminole	2	0.00
Shoshone (1)	8	0.01
Sioux (10)	27	0.05
Ute (1)	1	0.00
Yaqui (5)	14	0.03
All other tribes (53)	106	0.19
American Indian tribes, not spec.	44	0.08
Arab:	304	0.56
Arab/Arabic	38	0.07
Egyptian	14	0.03
Iraqi	16	0.03
Jordanian	3	0.01
Lebanese	147	0.27
Moroccan	29	0.05
Palestinian	19	0.03
Syrian	6	0.01
Other Arab	32	0.06
Armenian	105	0.19
Asian:	3,732	6.84
Bangladeshi (3)	8	0.01
Cambodian (8)	12	0.02
Chinese, ex. Taiwanese (845)	1,100	2.01
Filipino (507)	801	1.47
Hmong (3)	4	0.01
Indian (344)	438	0.80
Indonesian (17)	33	0.06
Japanese (402)	670	1.23
Korean (205)	263	0.48
Laotian (14)	15	0.03
Malaysian	3	0.01
Pakistani (10)	11	0.02
Sri Lankan (7)	8	0.01
Taiwanese (13)	17	0.03
Thai (62)	92	0.17
Vietnamese (119)	143	0.26
Other Asian, specified (14)	22	0.04
Other Asian, not specified (27)	92	0.17
Assyrian/Chaldean/Syriac	7	0.01
Australian	59	0.11
Austrian	219	0.40
Basque	56	0.10
Belgian	104	0.19
Brazilian	38	0.07
British	548	1.01
Canadian	172	0.32

Notes: 1. Figures in the "Number" column do not add up to the total population due to: a) Ancestry/Race overlap — e.g. persons can report being both White and Irish, b) persons of Hispanic origin can report being any race, c) persons reporting two ancestries are counted in both categories. 2. Numbers in parentheses indicate the number of persons reporting this ancestry/race alone, not in combination with any other ancestry/race. 3. Refer to the Explanation of Data in the front of the book for more detailed information.

Ancestry/Race	Number	%
Celtic	129	0.24
Croatian	125	0.23
Czech	204	0.38
Czechoslovakian	46	0.08
Danish	726	1.34
Dutch	1,017	1.87
Eastern European	251	0.46
English	6,461	11.88
Estonian	7	0.01
European	1,322	2.43
Finnish	144	0.26
French, except Basque	1,953	3.59
French Canadian	371	0.68
German	7,708	14.18
Greek	348	0.64
Hawaii Native/Pacific Islander:	233	0.43
Melanesian: (2)	5	0.01
Fijian (1)	4	0.01
Other Melanesian (1)	1	0.00
Micronesian: (8)	17	0.03
Guamanian/Chamorro (8)	17	0.03
Polynesian: (47)	148	0.27
Native Hawaiian (34)	110	0.20
Samoan (10)	32	0.06
Other Polynesian (3)	6	0.01
Other Pac. Isl., specified	4	0.01
Other Pac. Isl., not spec. (13)	59	0.11
Hispanic or Latino:	9,491	17.39
Central American:	538	0.99
Costa Rican	19	0.03
Guatemalan	47	0.09
Honduran	18	0.03
Nicaraguan	41	0.08
Panamanian	7	0.01
Salvadoran	371	0.68
Other Central American	35	0.06
Cuban	77	0.14
Dominican Republic	7	0.01
Mexican	7,184	13.16
Puerto Rican	170	0.31
South American:	251	0.46
Argentinean	43	0.08
Bolivian	8	0.01
Chilean	29	0.05
Colombian	52	0.10
Ecuadorian	12	0.02
Paraguayan	1	0.00
Peruvian	65	0.12
Uruguayan	9	0.02
Venezuelan	21	0.04
Other South American	11	0.02
Other Hispanic or Latino	1,264	2.32
Hungarian	354	0.65
Icelander	25	0.05
Iranian	101	0.19
Irish	6,909	12.71
Israeli	42	0.08
Italian	4,764	8.76
Latvian	36	0.07
Lithuanian	155	0.29
Maltese	11	0.02
New Zealander	4	0.01
Northern European	244	0.45
Norwegian	1,145	2.11
Pennsylvania German	36	0.07
Polish	1,570	2.89
Portuguese	1,126	2.07
Romanian	235	0.43
Russian	1,471	2.71
Scandinavian	225	0.41
Scotch-Irish	1,084	1.99
Scottish	1,956	3.60
Serbian	35	0.06
Slavic	40	0.07
Slovak	46	0.08
Slovene	19	0.03
Swedish	1,132	2.08
Swiss	394	0.72
Turkish	58	0.11
Ukrainian	176	0.32
United States or American	1,414	2.60
Welsh	661	1.22
West Indian, excl. Hispanic:	125	0.23
Barbadian	9	0.02
Belizean	10	0.02
Haitian	13	0.02
Jamaican	59	0.11
U.S. Virgin Islander	16	0.03
West Indian	18	0.03
White:	45,123	82.65
Not Hispanic (39,304)	40,880	74.88
Hispanic (3,680)	4,243	7.77
Yugoslavian	184	0.34

Santa Fe Springs

Place Type: City
County: Los Angeles
Population: 17,438

Ancestry/Race	Number	%
African American/Black:	769	4.41
Not Hispanic (645)	691	3.96
Hispanic (34)	78	0.45
African, sub-Saharan:	127	0.71
African	127	0.71
Alaska Native tribes, not specified	1	0.01
Am. Ind. or Alaska Nat., not spec.	169	0.97
American Indian tribes, specified:	195	1.12
Apache (16)	23	0.13
Blackfeet	4	0.02
Cherokee (11)	32	0.18
Cheyenne (4)	5	0.03
Chippewa (2)	2	0.01
Choctaw (5)	6	0.03
Comanche (7)	9	0.05
Cree (1)	1	0.01
Creek	1	0.01
Iroquois (2)	2	0.01
Latin American Indians (40)	50	0.29
Navajo (1)	7	0.04
Osage	1	0.01
Pima (1)	1	0.01
Pueblo (5)	6	0.03
Shoshone	1	0.01
Sioux (4)	12	0.07
Tohono O'Odham (4)	4	0.02
Ute (1)	1	0.01
Yaqui (5)	5	0.03
All other tribes (16)	22	0.13
American Indian tribes, not spec.	22	0.13
Arab:	11	0.06
Arab/Arabic	5	0.03
Syrian	6	0.03
Armenian	21	0.12
Asian:	843	4.83
Cambodian (6)	14	0.08
Chinese, ex. Taiwanese (65)	102	0.58
Filipino (250)	298	1.71
Hmong (1)	1	0.01
Indian (48)	58	0.33
Indonesian (10)	16	0.09
Japanese (45)	73	0.42
Korean (118)	125	0.72
Laotian (3)	3	0.02
Sri Lankan (1)	1	0.01
Taiwanese (5)	5	0.03
Thai (24)	32	0.18
Vietnamese (94)	99	0.57
Other Asian, not specified (2)	16	0.09
Australian	19	0.11
Basque	8	0.04
Belgian	6	0.03
Brazilian	2	0.01
British	23	0.13
Croatian	6	0.03
Czech	8	0.04
Danish	7	0.04
Dutch	144	0.81
English	416	2.33
European	69	0.39
Finnish	12	0.07
French, except Basque	329	1.84
French Canadian	25	0.14
German	778	4.36
Greek	34	0.19
Hawaii Native/Pacific Islander:	69	0.40
Melanesian:	2	0.01
Fijian	2	0.01
Micronesian: (5)	6	0.03
Guamanian/Chamorro (5)	6	0.03
Polynesian: (25)	47	0.27
Native Hawaiian (10)	21	0.12
Samoan (10)	21	0.12
Other Polynesian (5)	5	0.03
Other Pac. Isl., not spec. (5)	14	0.08
Hispanic or Latino:	12,447	71.38
Central American:	490	2.81
Costa Rican	26	0.15
Guatemalan	88	0.50
Honduran	22	0.13
Nicaraguan	91	0.52
Panamanian	1	0.01
Salvadoran	215	1.23
Other Central American	47	0.27
Cuban	122	0.70
Dominican Republic	3	0.02
Mexican	10,059	57.68
Puerto Rican	112	0.64
South American:	183	1.05
Argentinean	21	0.12
Bolivian	6	0.03
Chilean	4	0.02
Colombian	58	0.33
Ecuadorian	34	0.19
Peruvian	34	0.19
Venezuelan	5	0.03
Other South American	21	0.12
Other Hispanic or Latino	1,478	8.48
Hungarian	31	0.17
Iranian	5	0.03
Irish	565	3.17
Italian	439	2.46
Norwegian	34	0.19
Polish	95	0.53
Portuguese	20	0.11
Romanian	18	0.10
Russian	22	0.12
Scandinavian	18	0.10
Scotch-Irish	166	0.93
Scottish	86	0.48
Slavic	7	0.04
Swedish	169	0.95
Turkish	7	0.04
United States or American	491	2.75
Welsh	10	0.06
West Indian, excl. Hispanic:	17	0.10
Belizean	14	0.08
Jamaican	3	0.02
White:	9,560	54.82
Not Hispanic (3,354)	3,523	20.20
Hispanic (5,578)	6,037	34.62
Yugoslavian	15	0.08

Santa Maria

Place Type: City
County: Santa Barbara
Population: 77,423

Ancestry/Race	Number	%
African American/Black:	1,803	2.33
Not Hispanic (1,246)	1,493	1.93
Hispanic (203)	310	0.40
African, sub-Saharan:	162	0.21
African	144	0.19
Ghanian	18	0.02
Alaska Native tribes, specified:	10	0.01
Aleut	2	0.00
Eskimo (3)	3	0.00

Notes: 1. Figures in the "Number" column do not add up to the total population due to: a) Ancestry/Race overlap — e.g. persons can report being both White and Irish, b) persons of Hispanic origin can report being any race, c) persons reporting two ancestries are counted in both categories. 2. Numbers in parentheses indicate the number of persons reporting this ancestry/race alone, not in combination with any other ancestry/race. 3. Refer to the Explanation of Data in the front of the book for more detailed information.

Tlingit-Haida	5	0.01
Alaska Native tribes, not specified	3	0.00
Am. Ind. or Alaska Nat., not spec.	856	1.11
Albanian	4	0.01
American Indian tribes, specified:	1,493	1.93
Apache (38)	71	0.09
Blackfeet (8)	45	0.06
Cherokee (77)	212	0.27
Cheyenne	1	0.00
Chickasaw (10)	12	0.02
Chippewa (8)	10	0.01
Choctaw (28)	56	0.07
Comanche	5	0.01
Cree (1)	4	0.01
Creek (6)	8	0.01
Delaware (1)	2	0.00
Iroquois (4)	13	0.02
Kiowa (1)	4	0.01
Latin American Indians (436)	642	0.83
Lumbee (5)	5	0.01
Navajo (19)	35	0.05
Osage	3	0.00
Paiute (1)	7	0.01
Pima (2)	4	0.01
Potawatomi (1)	1	0.00
Pueblo (2)	4	0.01
Puget Sound Salish	1	0.00
Seminole (1)	3	0.00
Shoshone (4)	6	0.01
Sioux (13)	35	0.05
Ute (1)	7	0.01
Yaqui (13)	30	0.04
Yuman (4)	6	0.01
All other tribes (159)	261	0.34
American Indian tribes, not spec.	84	0.11
Arab:	86	0.11
Arab/Arabic	7	0.01
Egyptian	22	0.03
Jordanian	41	0.05
Lebanese	6	0.01
Syrian	10	0.01
Armenian	74	0.10
Asian:	4,652	6.01
Cambodian (16)	20	0.03
Chinese, ex. Taiwanese (127)	187	0.24
Filipino (2,656)	3,306	4.27
Hmong (17)	17	0.02
Indian (114)	176	0.23
Indonesian (5)	11	0.01
Japanese (372)	499	0.64
Korean (156)	179	0.23
Laotian (5)	7	0.01
Malaysian (1)	10	0.01
Pakistani (1)	1	0.00
Sri Lankan (6)	10	0.01
Taiwanese (7)	8	0.01
Thai (21)	29	0.04
Vietnamese (81)	100	0.13
Other Asian, specified	3	0.00
Other Asian, not specified (42)	89	0.11
Australian	12	0.02
Austrian	99	0.13
Basque	23	0.03
Belgian	33	0.04
Brazilian	5	0.01
British	143	0.19
Bulgarian	29	0.04
Canadian	131	0.17
Celtic	12	0.02
Croatian	29	0.04
Czech	158	0.20
Czechoslovakian	55	0.07
Danish	572	0.74
Dutch	560	0.73
Eastern European	22	0.03
English	3,757	4.87
European	480	0.62
Finnish	116	0.15
French, except Basque	1,220	1.58
French Canadian	242	0.31
German	4,986	6.47
German Russian	5	0.01
Greek	83	0.11
Guyanese	7	0.01
Hawaii Native/Pacific Islander:	271	0.35
Melanesian: (6)	6	0.01
Fijian (6)	6	0.01
Micronesian: (18)	24	0.03
Guamanian/Chamorro (18)	24	0.03
Polynesian: (92)	167	0.22
Native Hawaiian (42)	109	0.14
Samoan (34)	38	0.05
Tongan (16)	17	0.02
Other Polynesian	3	0.00
Other Pac. Isl., specified	2	0.00
Other Pac. Isl., not spec. (21)	72	0.09
Hispanic or Latino:	46,196	59.67
Central American:	329	0.42
Costa Rican	19	0.02
Guatemalan	75	0.10
Honduran	11	0.01
Nicaraguan	5	0.01
Panamanian	9	0.01
Salvadoran	194	0.25
Other Central American	16	0.02
Cuban	27	0.03
Dominican Republic	4	0.01
Mexican	40,719	52.59
Puerto Rican	235	0.30
South American:	110	0.14
Argentinean	17	0.02
Bolivian	4	0.01
Chilean	14	0.02
Colombian	27	0.03
Ecuadorian	7	0.01
Peruvian	20	0.03
Uruguayan	2	0.00
Venezuelan	11	0.01
Other South American	9	0.01
Other Hispanic or Latino	4,772	6.16
Hungarian	174	0.23
Icelander	9	0.01
Iranian	34	0.04
Irish	4,131	5.36
Israeli	10	0.01
Italian	2,060	2.67
Lithuanian	78	0.10
Luxemburger	8	0.01
Norwegian	680	0.88
Pennsylvania German	12	0.02
Polish	545	0.71
Portuguese	1,202	1.56
Romanian	23	0.03
Russian	215	0.28
Scandinavian	113	0.15
Scotch-Irish	512	0.66
Scottish	616	0.80
Slavic	16	0.02
Slovak	13	0.02
Swedish	629	0.82
Swiss	371	0.48
Turkish	5	0.01
Ukrainian	56	0.07
United States or American	1,972	2.56
Welsh	375	0.49
West Indian, excl. Hispanic:	48	0.06
Dutch West Indian	9	0.01
Jamaican	20	0.03
Trinidadian and Tobagonian	7	0.01
U.S. Virgin Islander	7	0.01
West Indian	5	0.01
White:	48,368	62.47
Not Hispanic (24,742)	25,785	33.30
Hispanic (20,220)	22,583	29.17
Yugoslavian	58	0.08

Santa Monica

Place Type: City
County: Los Angeles
Population: 84,084

Ancestry/Race	Number	%
Afghan	11	0.01
African American/Black:	3,791	4.51
Not Hispanic (3,081)	3,577	4.25
Hispanic (95)	214	0.25
African, sub-Saharan:	746	0.89
African	366	0.44
Ethiopian	60	0.07
Ghanian	27	0.03
Kenyan	17	0.02
Liberian	26	0.03
Nigerian	25	0.03
South African	170	0.20
Ugandan	6	0.01
Zimbabwean	8	0.01
Other sub-Saharan African	41	0.05
Alaska Native tribes, specified:	12	0.01
Alaska Athabascan (2)	2	0.00
Aleut (1)	1	0.00
Tlingit-Haida (2)	8	0.01
All other tribes (1)	1	0.00
Alaska Native tribes, not specified	1	0.00
Am. Ind. or Alaska Nat., not spec.	322	0.38
Albanian	10	0.01
Alsatian	12	0.01
American Indian tribes, specified:	612	0.73
Apache (8)	23	0.03
Blackfeet (2)	22	0.03
Cherokee (27)	160	0.19
Cheyenne (1)	1	0.00
Chickasaw	4	0.00
Chippewa (7)	14	0.02
Choctaw (4)	37	0.04
Comanche (1)	5	0.01
Cree	4	0.00
Creek (1)	15	0.02
Crow	1	0.00
Delaware (1)	4	0.00
Iroquois (2)	14	0.02
Kiowa (2)	2	0.00
Latin American Indians (78)	116	0.14
Lumbee (1)	1	0.00
Navajo (9)	19	0.02
Osage (3)	11	0.01
Ottawa (1)	1	0.00
Paiute (1)	1	0.00
Pima (2)	6	0.01
Potawatomi (1)	3	0.00
Pueblo (5)	15	0.02
Puget Sound Salish	1	0.00
Seminole (4)	13	0.02
Shoshone (2)	4	0.00
Sioux (16)	33	0.04
Yaqui (6)	13	0.02
Yuman (3)	5	0.01
All other tribes (27)	64	0.08
American Indian tribes, not spec.	53	0.06
Arab:	941	1.12
Arab/Arabic	41	0.05
Egyptian	261	0.31
Iraqi	36	0.04
Lebanese	292	0.35
Moroccan	39	0.05
Palestinian	31	0.04
Syrian	87	0.10
Other Arab	154	0.18
Armenian	377	0.45
Asian:	7,501	8.92
Bangladeshi (3)	7	0.01
Cambodian (8)	10	0.01
Chinese, ex. Taiwanese (1,705)	2,009	2.39
Filipino (520)	763	0.91
Indian (719)	848	1.01
Indonesian (28)	48	0.06

Notes: 1. Figures in the "Number" column do not add up to the total population due to: a) Ancestry/Race overlap — e.g. persons can report being both White and Irish, b) persons of Hispanic origin can report being any race, c) persons reporting two ancestries are counted in both categories. 2. Numbers in parentheses indicate the number of persons reporting this ancestry/race alone, not in combination with any other ancestry/race. 3. Refer to the Explanation of Data in the front of the book for more detailed information.

Ancestry/Race	Number	%
Japanese (1,522)	1,928	2.29
Korean (771)	887	1.05
Laotian (6)	7	0.01
Malaysian (6)	10	0.01
Pakistani (62)	101	0.12
Sri Lankan (7)	11	0.01
Taiwanese (217)	260	0.31
Thai (94)	110	0.13
Vietnamese (159)	183	0.22
Other Asian, specified (16)	33	0.04
Other Asian, not specified (99)	286	0.34
Assyrian/Chaldean/Syriac	30	0.04
Australian	213	0.25
Austrian	908	1.08
Basque	84	0.10
Belgian	70	0.08
Brazilian	143	0.17
British	1,171	1.39
Bulgarian	104	0.12
Canadian	395	0.47
Celtic	33	0.04
Croatian	165	0.20
Czech	465	0.55
Czechoslovakian	146	0.17
Danish	696	0.83
Dutch	1,283	1.53
Eastern European	518	0.62
English	8,252	9.81
Estonian	40	0.05
European	1,216	1.45
Finnish	232	0.28
French, except Basque	2,712	3.23
French Canadian	493	0.59
German	9,571	11.38
Greek	622	0.74
Guyanese	10	0.01
Hawaii Native/Pacific Islander:	241	0.29
Melanesian: (17)	21	0.02
Fijian (17)	21	0.02
Micronesian: (11)	18	0.02
Guamanian/Chamorro (9)	16	0.02
Other Micronesian (2)	2	0.00
Polynesian: (47)	113	0.13
Native Hawaiian (30)	85	0.10
Samoan (8)	15	0.02
Tongan (3)	4	0.00
Other Polynesian (6)	9	0.01
Other Pac. Isl., specified	7	0.01
Other Pac. Isl., not spec. (11)	82	0.10
Hispanic or Latino:	11,304	13.44
Central American:	747	0.89
Costa Rican	37	0.04
Guatemalan	196	0.23
Honduran	33	0.04
Nicaraguan	36	0.04
Panamanian	15	0.02
Salvadoran	350	0.42
Other Central American	80	0.10
Cuban	238	0.28
Dominican Republic	14	0.02
Mexican	7,571	9.00
Puerto Rican	257	0.31
South American:	738	0.88
Argentinean	186	0.22
Bolivian	18	0.02
Chilean	71	0.08
Colombian	140	0.17
Ecuadorian	59	0.07
Peruvian	122	0.15
Uruguayan	28	0.03
Venezuelan	49	0.06
Other South American	65	0.08
Other Hispanic or Latino	1,739	2.07
Hungarian	972	1.16
Icelander	18	0.02
Iranian	2,590	3.08
Irish	8,519	10.13
Israeli	221	0.26
Italian	5,523	6.57
Latvian	75	0.09
Lithuanian	780	0.93
Luxemburger	15	0.02
Macedonian	56	0.07
Maltese	39	0.05
New Zealander	5	0.01
Northern European	79	0.09
Norwegian	1,104	1.31
Polish	3,359	3.99
Portuguese	239	0.28
Romanian	459	0.55
Russian	5,774	6.87
Scandinavian	170	0.20
Scotch-Irish	1,340	1.59
Scottish	2,370	2.82
Serbian	167	0.20
Slavic	47	0.06
Slovak	80	0.10
Slovene	5	0.01
Swedish	1,770	2.11
Swiss	509	0.61
Turkish	183	0.22
Ukrainian	854	1.02
United States or American	2,802	3.33
Welsh	658	0.78
West Indian, excl. Hispanic:	258	0.31
Barbadian	9	0.01
Belizean	13	0.02
British West Indian	7	0.01
Dutch West Indian	11	0.01
Haitian	28	0.03
Jamaican	76	0.09
Trinidadian and Tobagonian	46	0.05
West Indian	68	0.08
White:	68,866	81.90
Not Hispanic (60,482)	62,744	74.62
Hispanic (5,350)	6,122	7.28
Yugoslavian	219	0.26

Santa Paula

Place Type: City
County: Ventura
Population: 28,598

Ancestry/Race	Number	%
African American/Black:	212	0.74
Not Hispanic (69)	108	0.38
Hispanic (49)	104	0.36
African, sub-Saharan:	31	0.11
African	31	0.11
Am. Ind. or Alaska Nat., not spec.	209	0.73
Albanian	10	0.03
American Indian tribes, specified:	383	1.34
Apache (11)	31	0.11
Blackfeet	3	0.01
Cherokee (20)	84	0.29
Cheyenne (1)	1	0.00
Chickasaw (3)	7	0.02
Chippewa (2)	5	0.02
Choctaw (10)	18	0.06
Comanche (4)	4	0.01
Creek	4	0.01
Crow	1	0.00
Delaware (1)	1	0.00
Iroquois (1)	2	0.01
Latin American Indians (99)	114	0.40
Lumbee (1)	1	0.00
Navajo (3)	8	0.03
Osage (1)	1	0.00
Pima	2	0.01
Potawatomi (3)	3	0.01
Pueblo	2	0.01
Shoshone	2	0.01
Sioux (3)	10	0.03
Tohono O'Odham	1	0.00
Yaqui (3)	6	0.02
Yuman (3)	3	0.01
All other tribes (41)	69	0.24
American Indian tribes, not spec.	42	0.15
Arab:	7	0.02
Lebanese	7	0.02
Armenian	39	0.14
Asian:	341	1.19
Cambodian (3)	3	0.01
Chinese, ex. Taiwanese (57)	70	0.24
Filipino (37)	75	0.26
Indian (20)	48	0.17
Indonesian	4	0.01
Japanese (32)	54	0.19
Korean (23)	28	0.10
Laotian (2)	3	0.01
Sri Lankan (7)	7	0.02
Thai (1)	1	0.00
Vietnamese (13)	14	0.05
Other Asian, specified	4	0.01
Other Asian, not specified (3)	30	0.10
Austrian	31	0.11
Basque	13	0.05
Belgian	2	0.01
British	50	0.17
Canadian	42	0.15
Croatian	7	0.02
Czech	22	0.08
Czechoslovakian	26	0.09
Danish	46	0.16
Dutch	158	0.55
English	1,229	4.29
European	262	0.92
Finnish	7	0.02
French, except Basque	499	1.74
French Canadian	65	0.23
German	1,520	5.31
Greek	52	0.18
Hawaii Native/Pacific Islander:	107	0.37
Melanesian: (1)	1	0.00
Fijian (1)	1	0.00
Micronesian: (10)	11	0.04
Guamanian/Chamorro (10)	11	0.04
Polynesian: (30)	61	0.21
Native Hawaiian (12)	28	0.10
Samoan (7)	10	0.03
Tongan (11)	18	0.06
Other Polynesian	5	0.02
Other Pac. Isl., specified	4	0.01
Other Pac. Isl., not spec. (12)	30	0.10
Hispanic or Latino:	20,360	71.19
Central American:	173	0.60
Costa Rican	8	0.03
Guatemalan	55	0.19
Honduran	18	0.06
Panamanian	3	0.01
Salvadoran	64	0.22
Other Central American	25	0.09
Cuban	15	0.05
Mexican	18,069	63.18
Puerto Rican	30	0.10
South American:	13	0.05
Chilean	1	0.00
Colombian	5	0.02
Ecuadorian	2	0.01
Peruvian	4	0.01
Other South American	1	0.00
Other Hispanic or Latino	2,060	7.20
Hungarian	42	0.15
Irish	1,062	3.71
Israeli	9	0.03
Italian	282	0.98
Luxemburger	5	0.02
Norwegian	251	0.88
Pennsylvania German	17	0.06
Polish	202	0.71
Portuguese	15	0.05
Romanian	2	0.01
Russian	50	0.17
Scandinavian	28	0.10
Scotch-Irish	297	1.04
Scottish	253	0.88
Slovene	5	0.02
Swedish	175	0.61
Swiss	53	0.19

Notes: 1. Figures in the "Number" column do not add up to the total population due to: a) Ancestry/Race overlap — e.g. persons can report being both White and Irish, b) persons of Hispanic origin can report being any race, c) persons reporting two ancestries are counted in both categories. 2. Numbers in parentheses indicate the number of persons reporting this ancestry/race alone, not in combination with any other ancestry/race. 3. Refer to the Explanation of Data in the front of the book for more detailed information.

Ancestry/Race	Number	%
Turkish	8	0.03
Ukrainian	10	0.03
United States or American	965	3.37
Welsh	71	0.25
West Indian, excl. Hispanic:	4	0.01
Jamaican	4	0.01
White:	16,993	59.42
Not Hispanic (7,551)	7,776	27.19
Hispanic (8,244)	9,217	32.23

Santa Rosa

Place Type: City
County: Sonoma
Population: 147,595

Ancestry/Race	Number	%
Acadian/Cajun	48	0.03
Afghan	94	0.06
African American/Black:	4,345	2.94
Not Hispanic (3,023)	3,982	2.70
Hispanic (154)	363	0.25
African, sub-Saharan:	1,169	0.79
African	331	0.22
Cape Verdean	17	0.01
Ethiopian	650	0.44
Ghanian	15	0.01
Kenyan	97	0.07
Liberian	10	0.01
Sierra Leonean	45	0.03
South African	4	0.00
Alaska Native tribes, specified:	50	0.03
Alaska Athabascan (5)	6	0.00
Aleut (4)	13	0.01
Eskimo (13)	17	0.01
Tlingit-Haida (7)	10	0.01
All other tribes (3)	4	0.00
Alaska Native tribes, not specified	9	0.01
Am. Ind. or Alaska Nat., not spec.	957	0.65
Albanian	5	0.00
Alsatian	23	0.02
American Indian tribes, specified:	2,845	1.93
Apache (38)	96	0.07
Blackfeet (10)	71	0.05
Cherokee (109)	491	0.33
Cheyenne (1)	9	0.01
Chickasaw (5)	22	0.01
Chippewa (19)	40	0.03
Choctaw (34)	101	0.07
Colville	1	0.00
Comanche (8)	18	0.01
Cree (3)	12	0.01
Creek (3)	24	0.02
Crow (1)	4	0.00
Delaware (7)	9	0.01
Iroquois (15)	41	0.03
Kiowa (2)	3	0.00
Latin American Indians (148)	253	0.17
Lumbee (2)	2	0.00
Menominee (1)	2	0.00
Navajo (23)	48	0.03
Osage (5)	17	0.01
Paiute (6)	14	0.01
Pima (8)	16	0.01
Potawatomi (7)	18	0.01
Pueblo (14)	29	0.02
Puget Sound Salish (1)	1	0.00
Seminole (3)	8	0.01
Shoshone (5)	7	0.00
Sioux (39)	94	0.06
Tohono O'Odham (3)	10	0.01
Ute (4)	13	0.01
Yakama (3)	5	0.00
Yaqui (7)	23	0.02
Yuman (2)	2	0.00
All other tribes (867)	1,341	0.91
American Indian tribes, not spec.	155	0.11
Arab:	344	0.23
Arab/Arabic	37	0.03
Egyptian	17	0.01
Iraqi	9	0.01
Lebanese	174	0.12
Moroccan	16	0.01
Palestinian	10	0.01
Syrian	66	0.04
Other Arab	15	0.01
Armenian	187	0.13
Asian:	7,768	5.26
Bangladeshi (2)	2	0.00
Cambodian (554)	654	0.44
Chinese, ex. Taiwanese (1,101)	1,514	1.03
Filipino (922)	1,505	1.02
Hmong (71)	74	0.05
Indian (466)	592	0.40
Indonesian (20)	55	0.04
Japanese (445)	850	0.58
Korean (338)	437	0.30
Laotian (574)	753	0.51
Malaysian (8)	16	0.01
Pakistani (27)	36	0.02
Sri Lankan (1)	2	0.00
Taiwanese (17)	29	0.02
Thai (69)	117	0.08
Vietnamese (757)	852	0.58
Other Asian, specified (12)	35	0.02
Other Asian, not specified (121)	245	0.17
Assyrian/Chaldean/Syriac	23	0.02
Australian	63	0.04
Austrian	701	0.48
Basque	135	0.09
Belgian	183	0.12
Brazilian	87	0.06
British	784	0.53
Bulgarian	16	0.01
Canadian	576	0.39
Celtic	90	0.06
Croatian	182	0.12
Czech	601	0.41
Czechoslovakian	261	0.18
Danish	2,108	1.43
Dutch	2,767	1.88
Eastern European	167	0.11
English	18,380	12.46
Estonian	8	0.01
European	2,189	1.48
Finnish	553	0.37
French, except Basque	5,739	3.89
French Canadian	912	0.62
German	22,672	15.37
German Russian	28	0.02
Greek	648	0.44
Hawaii Native/Pacific Islander:	808	0.55
Melanesian: (15)	19	0.01
Fijian (14)	18	0.01
Other Melanesian (1)	1	0.00
Micronesian: (58)	97	0.07
Guamanian/Chamorro (50)	84	0.06
Other Micronesian (8)	13	0.01
Polynesian: (274)	571	0.39
Native Hawaiian (132)	370	0.25
Samoan (136)	186	0.13
Tongan (5)	7	0.00
Other Polynesian (1)	8	0.01
Other Pac. Isl., specified	3	0.00
Other Pac. Isl., not spec. (30)	118	0.08
Hispanic or Latino:	28,318	19.19
Central American:	919	0.62
Costa Rican	39	0.03
Guatemalan	121	0.08
Honduran	47	0.03
Nicaraguan	135	0.09
Panamanian	19	0.01
Salvadoran	472	0.32
Other Central American	86	0.06
Cuban	111	0.08
Dominican Republic	6	0.00
Mexican	22,779	15.43
Puerto Rican	502	0.34
South American:	359	0.24
Argentinean	33	0.02
Bolivian	20	0.01
Chilean	28	0.02
Colombian	101	0.07
Ecuadorian	30	0.02
Paraguayan	2	0.00
Peruvian	86	0.06
Uruguayan	1	0.00
Venezuelan	20	0.01
Other South American	38	0.03
Other Hispanic or Latino	3,642	2.47
Hungarian	649	0.44
Icelander	86	0.06
Iranian	364	0.25
Irish	19,008	12.88
Israeli	63	0.04
Italian	12,445	8.44
Latvian	48	0.03
Lithuanian	383	0.26
Luxemburger	54	0.04
Maltese	59	0.04
New Zealander	19	0.01
Northern European	378	0.26
Norwegian	3,943	2.67
Pennsylvania German	69	0.05
Polish	2,726	1.85
Portuguese	2,387	1.62
Romanian	201	0.14
Russian	1,944	1.32
Scandinavian	646	0.44
Scotch-Irish	3,049	2.07
Scottish	4,007	2.72
Serbian	32	0.02
Slavic	113	0.08
Slovak	102	0.07
Slovene	64	0.04
Swedish	3,302	2.24
Swiss	974	0.66
Turkish	21	0.01
Ukrainian	300	0.20
United States or American	5,179	3.51
Welsh	1,552	1.05
West Indian, excl. Hispanic:	200	0.14
Barbadian	22	0.01
Belizean	7	0.00
Haitian	121	0.08
Jamaican	50	0.03
White:	120,069	81.35
Not Hispanic (104,581)	108,025	73.19
Hispanic (9,946)	12,044	8.16
Yugoslavian	345	0.23

Santee

Place Type: City
County: San Diego
Population: 52,975

Ancestry/Race	Number	%
Acadian/Cajun	28	0.05
Afghan	10	0.02
African American/Black:	1,051	1.98
Not Hispanic (751)	990	1.87
Hispanic (32)	61	0.12
African, sub-Saharan:	80	0.15
African	28	0.05
Cape Verdean	20	0.04
Ethiopian	13	0.02
South African	19	0.04
Alaska Native tribes, specified:	7	0.01
Alaska Athabascan (1)	1	0.00
Tlingit-Haida (3)	6	0.01
Am. Ind. or Alaska Nat., not spec.	226	0.43
Albanian	7	0.01
American Indian tribes, specified:	657	1.24
Apache (18)	38	0.07
Blackfeet (9)	25	0.05
Cherokee (51)	191	0.36
Cheyenne (1)	3	0.01
Chickasaw (6)	9	0.02
Chippewa (22)	35	0.07

Notes: 1. Figures in the "Number" column do not add up to the total population due to: a) Ancestry/Race overlap — e.g. persons can report being both White and Irish, b) persons of Hispanic origin can report being any race, c) persons reporting two ancestries are counted in both categories. 2. Numbers in parentheses indicate the number of persons reporting this ancestry/race alone, not in combination with any other ancestry/race. 3. Refer to the Explanation of Data in the front of the book for more detailed information.

Choctaw (19)	36	0.07
Cree (2)	2	0.00
Creek (3)	8	0.02
Delaware (2)	2	0.00
Iroquois (1)	14	0.03
Latin American Indians (23)	37	0.07
Lumbee (2)	2	0.00
Menominee (1)	1	0.00
Navajo (17)	29	0.05
Osage (2)	3	0.01
Paiute (1)	2	0.00
Pima	1	0.00
Potawatomi (2)	10	0.02
Pueblo (6)	12	0.02
Puget Sound Salish (2)	3	0.01
Seminole (1)	1	0.00
Shoshone (1)	4	0.01
Sioux (7)	20	0.04
Tohono O'Odham (8)	8	0.02
Ute (1)	1	0.00
Yakama (6)	7	0.01
Yaqui (11)	19	0.04
Yuman (3)	5	0.01
All other tribes (84)	129	0.24
American Indian tribes, not spec.	26	0.05
Arab:	373	0.70
Arab/Arabic	88	0.17
Egyptian	49	0.09
Iraqi	31	0.06
Lebanese	85	0.16
Palestinian	18	0.03
Syrian	23	0.04
Other Arab	79	0.15
Armenian	67	0.13
Asian:	2,204	4.16
Bangladeshi (1)	1	0.00
Cambodian (15)	16	0.03
Chinese, ex. Taiwanese (151)	250	0.47
Filipino (581)	1,005	1.90
Indian (38)	54	0.10
Indonesian (23)	40	0.08
Japanese (176)	344	0.65
Korean (78)	129	0.24
Laotian (6)	9	0.02
Malaysian (2)	6	0.01
Pakistani (2)	12	0.02
Taiwanese (6)	7	0.01
Thai (18)	28	0.05
Vietnamese (196)	225	0.42
Other Asian, specified	4	0.01
Other Asian, not specified (26)	74	0.14
Assyrian/Chaldean/Syriac	56	0.11
Australian	81	0.15
Austrian	153	0.29
Basque	65	0.12
Belgian	45	0.08
Brazilian	28	0.05
British	227	0.43
Canadian	208	0.39
Celtic	13	0.02
Croatian	41	0.08
Czech	254	0.48
Czechoslovakian	99	0.19
Danish	418	0.79
Dutch	1,266	2.38
Eastern European	7	0.01
English	6,451	12.15
European	768	1.45
Finnish	111	0.21
French, except Basque	2,558	4.82
French Canadian	451	0.85
German	10,519	19.81
Greek	204	0.38
Hawaii Native/Pacific Islander:	500	0.94
Melanesian: (3)	11	0.02
Fijian (3)	11	0.02
Micronesian: (92)	160	0.30
Guamanian/Chamorro (91)	157	0.30
Other Micronesian (1)	3	0.01
Polynesian: (62)	219	0.41
Native Hawaiian (37)	157	0.30
Samoan (21)	54	0.10
Tongan (4)	6	0.01
Other Polynesian	2	0.00
Other Pac. Isl., specified	2	0.00
Other Pac. Isl., not spec. (48)	108	0.20
Hispanic or Latino:	6,016	11.36
Central American:	86	0.16
Costa Rican	18	0.03
Guatemalan	12	0.02
Honduran	5	0.01
Nicaraguan	13	0.02
Panamanian	13	0.02
Salvadoran	23	0.04
Other Central American	2	0.00
Cuban	51	0.10
Dominican Republic	7	0.01
Mexican	4,337	8.19
Puerto Rican	210	0.40
South American:	112	0.21
Argentinean	5	0.01
Bolivian	10	0.02
Chilean	16	0.03
Colombian	43	0.08
Ecuadorian	5	0.01
Paraguayan	4	0.01
Peruvian	21	0.04
Venezuelan	6	0.01
Other South American	2	0.00
Other Hispanic or Latino	1,213	2.29
Hungarian	269	0.51
Icelander	29	0.05
Iranian	30	0.06
Irish	7,892	14.87
Israeli	55	0.10
Italian	3,453	6.50
Lithuanian	99	0.19
Northern European	17	0.03
Norwegian	1,391	2.62
Pennsylvania German	16	0.03
Polish	1,351	2.54
Portuguese	514	0.97
Romanian	53	0.10
Russian	380	0.72
Scandinavian	219	0.41
Scotch-Irish	1,126	2.12
Scottish	1,431	2.70
Serbian	36	0.07
Slavic	20	0.04
Slovak	155	0.29
Slovene	19	0.04
Swedish	965	1.82
Swiss	188	0.35
Ukrainian	95	0.18
United States or American	3,695	6.96
Welsh	450	0.85
West Indian, excl. Hispanic:	58	0.11
Jamaican	58	0.11
White:	47,854	90.33
Not Hispanic (42,803)	44,169	83.38
Hispanic (3,126)	3,685	6.96
Yugoslavian	86	0.16

Saratoga

Place Type: City
County: Santa Clara
Population: 29,843

Ancestry/Race	Number	%
African American/Black:	145	0.49
Not Hispanic (110)	133	0.45
Hispanic (5)	12	0.04
African, sub-Saharan:	84	0.28
African	48	0.16
Ethiopian	5	0.02
South African	5	0.02
Other sub-Saharan African	26	0.09
Alaska Native tribes, specified:	1	0.00
Eskimo	1	0.00
Am. Ind. or Alaska Nat., not spec.	39	0.13
Albanian	29	0.10
American Indian tribes, specified:	82	0.27
Apache	2	0.01
Blackfeet (2)	4	0.01
Cherokee (6)	32	0.11
Chickasaw	2	0.01
Chippewa (1)	1	0.00
Choctaw (1)	4	0.01
Colville	1	0.00
Comanche (1)	1	0.00
Creek	1	0.00
Delaware (1)	1	0.00
Iroquois	3	0.01
Latin American Indians (4)	10	0.03
Lumbee (1)	1	0.00
Navajo (4)	5	0.02
Pueblo (1)	2	0.01
All other tribes (2)	12	0.04
American Indian tribes, not spec.	11	0.04
Arab:	67	0.22
Lebanese	33	0.11
Moroccan	6	0.02
Palestinian	6	0.02
Syrian	22	0.07
Armenian	127	0.43
Asian:	9,341	31.30
Cambodian (1)	1	0.00
Chinese, ex. Taiwanese (4,958)	5,237	17.55
Filipino (170)	230	0.77
Indian (1,197)	1,269	4.25
Indonesian (4)	20	0.07
Japanese (734)	896	3.00
Korean (556)	609	2.04
Malaysian (2)	2	0.01
Pakistani (93)	102	0.34
Sri Lankan (4)	10	0.03
Taiwanese (461)	543	1.82
Thai (25)	28	0.09
Vietnamese (278)	296	0.99
Other Asian, specified (1)	4	0.01
Other Asian, not specified (43)	94	0.31
Assyrian/Chaldean/Syriac	7	0.02
Australian	87	0.29
Austrian	251	0.84
Basque	27	0.09
Belgian	35	0.12
Brazilian	4	0.01
British	466	1.56
Canadian	84	0.28
Carpatho Rusyn	22	0.07
Croatian	165	0.55
Czech	122	0.41
Czechoslovakian	97	0.32
Danish	380	1.27
Dutch	415	1.39
Eastern European	54	0.18
English	3,995	13.38
European	342	1.15
Finnish	83	0.28
French, except Basque	842	2.82
French Canadian	155	0.52
German	3,941	13.20
Greek	379	1.27
Hawaii Native/Pacific Islander:	90	0.30
Melanesian: (3)	3	0.01
Fijian (3)	3	0.01
Micronesian: (4)	7	0.02
Guamanian/Chamorro (4)	7	0.02
Polynesian: (13)	58	0.19
Native Hawaiian (8)	45	0.15
Samoan (2)	5	0.02
Tongan (3)	8	0.03
Other Pac. Isl., specified	2	0.01
Other Pac. Isl., not spec. (5)	20	0.07
Hispanic or Latino:	936	3.14
Central American:	36	0.12
Costa Rican	2	0.01
Guatemalan	1	0.00
Nicaraguan	10	0.03

Notes: 1. Figures in the "Number" column do not add up to the total population due to: a) Ancestry/Race overlap — e.g. persons can report being both White and Irish, b) persons of Hispanic origin can report being any race, c) persons reporting two ancestries are counted in both categories. 2. Numbers in parentheses indicate the number of persons reporting this ancestry/race alone, not in combination with any other ancestry/race. 3. Refer to the Explanation of Data in the front of the book for more detailed information.

Panamanian	2	0.01
Salvadoran	14	0.05
Other Central American	7	0.02
Cuban	15	0.05
Mexican	543	1.82
Puerto Rican	14	0.05
South American:	69	0.23
Argentinean	12	0.04
Bolivian	2	0.01
Chilean	7	0.02
Colombian	8	0.03
Ecuadorian	7	0.02
Paraguayan	5	0.02
Peruvian	13	0.04
Uruguayan	3	0.01
Venezuelan	7	0.02
Other South American	5	0.02
Other Hispanic or Latino	259	0.87
Hungarian	190	0.64
Iranian	622	2.08
Irish	2,993	10.03
Israeli	37	0.12
Italian	1,897	6.35
Latvian	13	0.04
Lithuanian	37	0.12
Luxemburger	42	0.14
Maltese	24	0.08
New Zealander	40	0.13
Northern European	99	0.33
Norwegian	500	1.67
Polish	642	2.15
Portuguese	288	0.96
Romanian	90	0.30
Russian	632	2.12
Scandinavian	37	0.12
Scotch-Irish	737	2.47
Scottish	1,086	3.64
Serbian	20	0.07
Slavic	12	0.04
Slovak	42	0.14
Slovene	5	0.02
Swedish	621	2.08
Swiss	162	0.54
Turkish	22	0.07
Ukrainian	121	0.41
United States or American	829	2.78
Welsh	325	1.09
White:	20,724	69.44
Not Hispanic (19,434)	19,965	66.90
Hispanic (677)	759	2.54
Yugoslavian	152	0.51

Scotts Valley

Place Type: City
County: Santa Cruz
Population: 11,385

Ancestry/Race	Number	%
African American/Black:	95	0.83
Not Hispanic (48)	79	0.69
Hispanic (7)	16	0.14
African, sub-Saharan:	9	0.08
African	9	0.08
Alaska Native tribes, specified:	2	0.02
Aleut (1)	1	0.01
Tlingit-Haida (1)	1	0.01
Am. Ind. or Alaska Nat., not spec.	34	0.30
American Indian tribes, specified:	97	0.85
Apache (4)	8	0.07
Blackfeet (1)	3	0.03
Cherokee (6)	44	0.39
Chickasaw (1)	2	0.02
Chippewa (3)	3	0.03
Choctaw	9	0.08
Comanche (2)	2	0.02
Creek (1)	2	0.02
Delaware	1	0.01
Houma (3)	4	0.04
Iroquois (1)	1	0.01
Latin American Indians (2)	2	0.02
Osage	1	0.01
Sioux	2	0.02
Yaqui	3	0.03
All other tribes (6)	10	0.09
American Indian tribes, not spec.	11	0.10
Arab:	34	0.30
Lebanese	8	0.07
Palestinian	8	0.07
Syrian	18	0.16
Armenian	54	0.47
Asian:	704	6.18
Cambodian (1)	3	0.03
Chinese, ex. Taiwanese (138)	194	1.70
Filipino (63)	107	0.94
Hmong (2)	2	0.02
Indian (126)	144	1.26
Indonesian (2)	5	0.04
Japanese (79)	110	0.97
Korean (56)	72	0.63
Pakistani (7)	7	0.06
Taiwanese (1)	1	0.01
Thai (1)	5	0.04
Vietnamese (29)	33	0.29
Other Asian, specified (4)	4	0.04
Other Asian, not specified (7)	17	0.15
Australian	14	0.12
Austrian	15	0.13
Belgian	24	0.21
British	128	1.11
Canadian	39	0.34
Croatian	7	0.06
Czech	25	0.22
Danish	169	1.47
Dutch	291	2.53
English	1,786	15.51
Estonian	8	0.07
European	392	3.40
Finnish	33	0.29
French, except Basque	465	4.04
French Canadian	112	0.97
German	2,433	21.12
Greek	61	0.53
Hawaii Native/Pacific Islander:	57	0.50
Melanesian: (11)	13	0.11
Fijian (11)	13	0.11
Micronesian: (1)	4	0.04
Guamanian/Chamorro (1)	4	0.04
Polynesian: (8)	35	0.31
Native Hawaiian (3)	27	0.24
Samoan (4)	7	0.06
Tongan (1)	1	0.01
Other Pac. Isl., not spec.	5	0.04
Hispanic or Latino:	729	6.40
Central American:	48	0.42
Costa Rican	11	0.10
Guatemalan	1	0.01
Honduran	1	0.01
Nicaraguan	7	0.06
Salvadoran	21	0.18
Other Central American	7	0.06
Cuban	4	0.04
Dominican Republic	1	0.01
Mexican	476	4.18
Puerto Rican	27	0.24
South American:	35	0.31
Argentinean	6	0.05
Bolivian	1	0.01
Chilean	6	0.05
Colombian	2	0.02
Peruvian	20	0.18
Other Hispanic or Latino	138	1.21
Hungarian	27	0.23
Iranian	29	0.25
Irish	1,568	13.61
Italian	1,200	10.42
Latvian	16	0.14
Maltese	42	0.36
New Zealander	9	0.08
Northern European	34	0.30
Norwegian	348	3.02
Pennsylvania German	9	0.08
Polish	186	1.61
Portuguese	340	2.95
Romanian	14	0.12
Russian	141	1.22
Scandinavian	43	0.37
Scotch-Irish	259	2.25
Scottish	531	4.61
Slavic	23	0.20
Slovak	6	0.05
Slovene	14	0.12
Swedish	480	4.17
Swiss	119	1.03
Turkish	9	0.08
Ukrainian	60	0.52
United States or American	403	3.50
Welsh	114	0.99
White:	10,447	91.76
Not Hispanic (9,694)	9,982	87.68
Hispanic (396)	465	4.08
Yugoslavian	15	0.13

Seal Beach

Place Type: City
County: Orange
Population: 24,157

Ancestry/Race	Number	%
African American/Black:	400	1.66
Not Hispanic (329)	369	1.53
Hispanic (18)	31	0.13
African, sub-Saharan:	5	0.02
African	5	0.02
Am. Ind. or Alaska Nat., not spec.	45	0.19
Albanian	16	0.07
American Indian tribes, specified:	135	0.56
Apache (7)	12	0.05
Blackfeet	4	0.02
Cherokee (10)	34	0.14
Chickasaw (2)	5	0.02
Chippewa (2)	4	0.02
Choctaw (2)	14	0.06
Comanche (1)	1	0.00
Cree (1)	2	0.01
Creek	1	0.00
Delaware	4	0.02
Iroquois	1	0.00
Latin American Indians (7)	10	0.04
Navajo (2)	3	0.01
Osage (3)	3	0.01
Ottawa (1)	1	0.00
Potawatomi (2)	2	0.01
Pueblo	1	0.00
Shoshone	2	0.01
Sioux (1)	5	0.02
Yakama	1	0.00
All other tribes (12)	25	0.10
American Indian tribes, not spec.	11	0.05
Arab:	108	0.44
Lebanese	86	0.35
Moroccan	4	0.02
Palestinian	8	0.03
Other Arab	10	0.04
Armenian	26	0.11
Asian:	1,699	7.03
Bangladeshi (2)	3	0.01
Cambodian (7)	9	0.04
Chinese, ex. Taiwanese (334)	392	1.62
Filipino (239)	324	1.34
Indian (71)	89	0.37
Indonesian (2)	10	0.04
Japanese (384)	497	2.06
Korean (164)	186	0.77
Malaysian	2	0.01
Pakistani (1)	1	0.00
Sri Lankan (2)	3	0.01
Taiwanese (37)	43	0.18
Thai (11)	13	0.05

Notes: 1. Figures in the "Number" column do not add up to the total population due to: a) Ancestry/Race overlap — e.g. persons can report being both White and Irish, b) persons of Hispanic origin can report being any race, c) persons reporting two ancestries are counted in both categories. 2. Numbers in parentheses indicate the number of persons reporting this ancestry/race alone, not in combination with any other ancestry/race. 3. Refer to the Explanation of Data in the front of the book for more detailed information.

Vietnamese (90)	95	0.39
Other Asian, specified (1)	3	0.01
Other Asian, not specified (9)	29	0.12
Australian	17	0.07
Austrian	191	0.79
Basque	12	0.05
Belgian	63	0.26
Brazilian	20	0.08
British	195	0.80
Canadian	115	0.47
Celtic	23	0.09
Croatian	57	0.23
Czech	130	0.54
Czechoslovakian	72	0.30
Danish	585	2.41
Dutch	763	3.14
Eastern European	62	0.26
English	3,734	15.38
European	430	1.77
Finnish	65	0.27
French, except Basque	748	3.08
French Canadian	192	0.79
German	4,185	17.23
Greek	139	0.57
Hawaii Native/Pacific Islander:	96	0.40
Melanesian: (1)	1	0.00
Fijian (1)	1	0.00
Micronesian: (15)	20	0.08
Guamanian/Chamorro (14)	18	0.07
Other Micronesian (1)	2	0.01
Polynesian: (17)	49	0.20
Native Hawaiian (10)	38	0.16
Samoan (6)	7	0.03
Tongan	3	0.01
Other Polynesian (1)	1	0.00
Other Pac. Isl., not spec. (10)	26	0.11
Hispanic or Latino:	1,554	6.43
Central American:	45	0.19
Costa Rican	5	0.02
Guatemalan	8	0.03
Honduran	3	0.01
Nicaraguan	8	0.03
Panamanian	6	0.02
Salvadoran	10	0.04
Other Central American	5	0.02
Cuban	85	0.35
Mexican	1,032	4.27
Puerto Rican	58	0.24
South American:	83	0.34
Argentinean	15	0.06
Bolivian	2	0.01
Chilean	3	0.01
Colombian	22	0.09
Ecuadorian	10	0.04
Paraguayan	2	0.01
Peruvian	15	0.06
Venezuelan	8	0.03
Other South American	6	0.02
Other Hispanic or Latino	251	1.04
Hungarian	339	1.40
Iranian	103	0.42
Irish	3,447	14.20
Israeli	33	0.14
Italian	1,377	5.67
Latvian	54	0.22
Lithuanian	89	0.37
Luxemburger	18	0.07
Macedonian	17	0.07
New Zealander	5	0.02
Northern European	16	0.07
Norwegian	601	2.47
Pennsylvania German	4	0.02
Polish	736	3.03
Portuguese	192	0.79
Romanian	61	0.25
Russian	711	2.93
Scandinavian	122	0.50
Scotch-Irish	684	2.82
Scottish	808	3.33
Serbian	14	0.06
Slavic	20	0.08
Slovak	15	0.06
Slovene	18	0.07
Swedish	634	2.61
Swiss	192	0.79
Turkish	6	0.02
Ukrainian	122	0.50
United States or American	1,177	4.85
Welsh	269	1.11
West Indian, excl. Hispanic:	6	0.02
U.S. Virgin Islander	6	0.02
White:	21,944	90.84
Not Hispanic (20,372)	20,757	85.93
Hispanic (1,105)	1,187	4.91
Yugoslavian	33	0.14

Seaside

Place Type: City
County: Monterey
Population: 31,696

Ancestry/Race	Number	%
African American/Black:	4,680	14.77
Not Hispanic (3,836)	4,395	13.87
Hispanic (161)	285	0.90
African, sub-Saharan:	162	0.51
African	134	0.42
Nigerian	22	0.07
South African	6	0.02
Alaska Native tribes, specified:	6	0.02
Alaska Athabascan (2)	4	0.01
Eskimo (1)	1	0.00
Tlingit-Haida (1)	1	0.00
Am. Ind. or Alaska Nat., not spec.	259	0.82
American Indian tribes, specified:	422	1.33
Apache (11)	21	0.07
Blackfeet (4)	21	0.07
Cherokee (29)	130	0.41
Cheyenne	3	0.01
Chickasaw (3)	4	0.01
Chippewa	8	0.03
Choctaw (6)	15	0.05
Cree (1)	4	0.01
Creek (3)	10	0.03
Delaware	1	0.00
Iroquois (5)	7	0.02
Kiowa	1	0.00
Latin American Indians (37)	49	0.15
Lumbee	2	0.01
Navajo (4)	14	0.04
Osage	1	0.00
Paiute (3)	6	0.02
Pima (1)	2	0.01
Potawatomi (3)	5	0.02
Pueblo (4)	4	0.01
Puget Sound Salish (1)	1	0.00
Seminole	2	0.01
Sioux (2)	11	0.03
Yaqui (1)	4	0.01
All other tribes (50)	96	0.30
American Indian tribes, not spec.	14	0.04
Arab:	51	0.16
Arab/Arabic	28	0.09
Iraqi	7	0.02
Moroccan	4	0.01
Other Arab	12	0.04
Asian:	4,355	13.74
Cambodian (3)	4	0.01
Chinese, ex. Taiwanese (106)	176	0.56
Filipino (1,641)	2,074	6.54
Hmong (1)	1	0.00
Indian (163)	318	1.00
Indonesian (2)	6	0.02
Japanese (398)	729	2.30
Korean (224)	345	1.09
Laotian (9)	9	0.03
Malaysian (4)	9	0.03
Pakistani	1	0.00
Taiwanese (1)	2	0.01
Thai (33)	53	0.17
Vietnamese (501)	543	1.71
Other Asian, specified (4)	10	0.03
Other Asian, not specified (44)	75	0.24
Assyrian/Chaldean/Syriac	17	0.05
Australian	14	0.04
Austrian	86	0.27
Belgian	19	0.06
Brazilian	16	0.05
British	172	0.54
Canadian	42	0.13
Croatian	25	0.08
Czech	66	0.21
Czechoslovakian	15	0.05
Danish	116	0.36
Dutch	240	0.76
English	1,570	4.94
European	241	0.76
Finnish	57	0.18
French, except Basque	598	1.88
French Canadian	115	0.36
German	2,471	7.77
German Russian	11	0.03
Greek	112	0.35
Hawaii Native/Pacific Islander:	751	2.37
Melanesian: (100)	133	0.42
Fijian (100)	133	0.42
Micronesian: (88)	140	0.44
Guamanian/Chamorro (85)	137	0.43
Other Micronesian (3)	3	0.01
Polynesian: (166)	272	0.86
Native Hawaiian (32)	112	0.35
Samoan (69)	84	0.27
Tongan (60)	71	0.22
Other Polynesian (5)	5	0.02
Other Pac. Isl., specified	1	0.00
Other Pac. Isl., not spec. (53)	205	0.65
Hispanic or Latino:	10,929	34.48
Central American:	763	2.41
Costa Rican	10	0.03
Guatemalan	38	0.12
Honduran	21	0.07
Nicaraguan	7	0.02
Panamanian	69	0.22
Salvadoran	566	1.79
Other Central American	52	0.16
Cuban	17	0.05
Dominican Republic	2	0.01
Mexican	8,353	26.35
Puerto Rican	281	0.89
South American:	89	0.28
Argentinean	4	0.01
Bolivian	8	0.03
Chilean	8	0.03
Colombian	23	0.07
Ecuadorian	2	0.01
Paraguayan	1	0.00
Peruvian	30	0.09
Venezuelan	4	0.01
Other South American	9	0.03
Other Hispanic or Latino	1,424	4.49
Hungarian	175	0.55
Iranian	33	0.10
Irish	1,953	6.14
Italian	1,000	3.15
Lithuanian	15	0.05
Maltese	18	0.06
Northern European	8	0.03
Norwegian	295	0.93
Pennsylvania German	13	0.04
Polish	190	0.60
Portuguese	303	0.95
Romanian	31	0.10
Russian	136	0.43
Scandinavian	44	0.14
Scotch-Irish	316	0.99
Scottish	253	0.80
Serbian	32	0.10
Slavic	8	0.03
Slovak	55	0.17

Notes: 1. Figures in the "Number" column do not add up to the total population due to: a) Ancestry/Race overlap — e.g. persons can report being both White and Irish, b) persons of Hispanic origin can report being any race, c) persons reporting two ancestries are counted in both categories. 2. Numbers in parentheses indicate the number of persons reporting this ancestry/race alone, not in combination with any other ancestry/race. 3. Refer to the Explanation of Data in the front of the book for more detailed information.

Slovene	7	0.02
Swedish	258	0.81
Swiss	105	0.33
Turkish	14	0.04
Ukrainian	16	0.05
United States or American	960	3.02
Welsh	118	0.37
West Indian, excl. Hispanic:	29	0.09
Jamaican	21	0.07
Trinidadian and Tobagonian	8	0.03
White:	17,285	54.53
Not Hispanic (11,526)	12,606	39.77
Hispanic (4,073)	4,679	14.76
Yugoslavian	18	0.06

Selma

Place Type: City
County: Fresno
Population: 19,444

Ancestry/Race	Number	%
African American/Black:	218	1.12
Not Hispanic (116)	157	0.81
Hispanic (30)	61	0.31
African, sub-Saharan:	10	0.05
African	10	0.05
Alaska Native tribes, specified:	1	0.01
Alaska Athabascan (1)	1	0.01
Am. Ind. or Alaska Nat., not spec.	178	0.92
American Indian tribes, specified:	285	1.47
Apache (5)	9	0.05
Blackfeet (1)	1	0.01
Cherokee (11)	38	0.20
Chickasaw (7)	9	0.05
Chippewa (1)	1	0.01
Choctaw (12)	22	0.11
Creek (13)	21	0.11
Iroquois (1)	1	0.01
Latin American Indians (62)	87	0.45
Navajo (5)	8	0.04
Paiute (1)	1	0.01
Potawatomi (2)	10	0.05
Pueblo (4)	5	0.03
Puget Sound Salish (2)	2	0.01
Seminole (5)	9	0.05
Shoshone (3)	6	0.03
Sioux (1)	1	0.01
Ute	1	0.01
Yaqui (8)	10	0.05
All other tribes (28)	43	0.22
American Indian tribes, not spec.	22	0.11
Arab:	107	0.55
Arab/Arabic	41	0.21
Palestinian	61	0.32
Syrian	5	0.03
Armenian	69	0.36
Asian:	733	3.77
Chinese, ex. Taiwanese (49)	61	0.31
Filipino (41)	67	0.34
Indian (359)	402	2.07
Indonesian (1)	1	0.01
Japanese (135)	155	0.80
Korean (4)	8	0.04
Pakistani (5)	5	0.03
Taiwanese (7)	7	0.04
Vietnamese (6)	10	0.05
Other Asian, not specified (8)	17	0.09
Basque	47	0.24
Belgian	7	0.04
British	3	0.02
Bulgarian	5	0.03
Canadian	10	0.05
Danish	212	1.10
Dutch	294	1.52
English	740	3.82
European	91	0.47
French, except Basque	180	0.93
French Canadian	28	0.14
German	801	4.14
Greek	10	0.05
Hawaii Native/Pacific Islander:	18	0.09
Micronesian:	2	0.01
Guamanian/Chamorro	2	0.01
Polynesian: (4)	10	0.05
Native Hawaiian (1)	4	0.02
Samoan (3)	6	0.03
Other Pac. Isl., not spec. (2)	6	0.03
Hispanic or Latino:	13,952	71.75
Central American:	44	0.23
Costa Rican	2	0.01
Guatemalan	15	0.08
Honduran	3	0.02
Nicaraguan	6	0.03
Salvadoran	14	0.07
Other Central American	4	0.02
Cuban	16	0.08
Mexican	11,953	61.47
Puerto Rican	41	0.21
South American:	8	0.04
Colombian	2	0.01
Ecuadorian	2	0.01
Peruvian	4	0.02
Other Hispanic or Latino	1,890	9.72
Irish	487	2.52
Italian	189	0.98
Norwegian	77	0.40
Pennsylvania German	4	0.02
Polish	35	0.18
Portuguese	179	0.93
Russian	25	0.13
Scandinavian	16	0.08
Scotch-Irish	114	0.59
Scottish	98	0.51
Slovene	8	0.04
Swedish	162	0.84
Swiss	16	0.08
United States or American	426	2.20
Welsh	36	0.19
West Indian, excl. Hispanic:	8	0.04
Jamaican	8	0.04
White:	9,266	47.65
Not Hispanic (4,332)	4,551	23.41
Hispanic (4,204)	4,715	24.25

Shafter

Place Type: City
County: Kern
Population: 12,736

Ancestry/Race	Number	%
African American/Black:	239	1.88
Not Hispanic (181)	187	1.47
Hispanic (23)	52	0.41
African, sub-Saharan:	15	0.12
African	8	0.06
Nigerian	7	0.05
Am. Ind. or Alaska Nat., not spec.	112	0.88
American Indian tribes, specified:	117	0.92
Apache (4)	5	0.04
Cherokee (5)	18	0.14
Chickasaw (2)	3	0.02
Choctaw (6)	7	0.05
Comanche	2	0.02
Latin American Indians (19)	24	0.19
Navajo (1)	2	0.02
Paiute	1	0.01
Pima (1)	2	0.02
Pueblo (2)	2	0.02
Puget Sound Salish (4)	4	0.03
Sioux (3)	5	0.04
Tohono O'Odham (1)	1	0.01
Yaqui (5)	5	0.04
All other tribes (19)	36	0.28
American Indian tribes, not spec.	10	0.08
Arab:	35	0.27
Arab/Arabic	18	0.14
Other Arab	17	0.13
Asian:	71	0.56
Chinese, ex. Taiwanese (2)	4	0.03
Filipino (13)	27	0.21
Indian (11)	11	0.09
Japanese (1)	1	0.01
Korean (8)	16	0.13
Laotian (1)	3	0.02
Vietnamese (1)	1	0.01
Other Asian, specified	1	0.01
Other Asian, not specified (1)	7	0.05
British	15	0.12
Canadian	5	0.04
Dutch	120	0.94
English	407	3.19
European	77	0.60
French, except Basque	58	0.45
German	601	4.71
Greek	6	0.05
Hawaii Native/Pacific Islander:	29	0.23
Micronesian: (8)	12	0.09
Guamanian/Chamorro (8)	12	0.09
Polynesian: (8)	10	0.08
Native Hawaiian (8)	8	0.06
Samoan	2	0.02
Other Pac. Isl., not spec.	7	0.05
Hispanic or Latino:	8,667	68.05
Central American:	52	0.41
Costa Rican	2	0.02
Guatemalan	15	0.12
Honduran	7	0.05
Salvadoran	27	0.21
Other Central American	1	0.01
Cuban	2	0.02
Mexican	7,169	56.29
Puerto Rican	26	0.20
South American:	3	0.02
Ecuadorian	1	0.01
Peruvian	2	0.02
Other Hispanic or Latino	1,415	11.11
Irish	224	1.76
Italian	22	0.17
Norwegian	14	0.11
Polish	15	0.12
Russian	39	0.31
Scandinavian	8	0.06
Scotch-Irish	64	0.50
Scottish	29	0.23
Swedish	50	0.39
Turkish	6	0.05
United States or American	486	3.81
Welsh	7	0.05
West Indian, excl. Hispanic:	9	0.07
Belizean	9	0.07
White:	6,107	47.95
Not Hispanic (3,693)	3,767	29.58
Hispanic (1,977)	2,340	18.37

Sierra Madre

Place Type: City
County: Los Angeles
Population: 10,578

Ancestry/Race	Number	%
Acadian/Cajun	15	0.14
African American/Black:	177	1.67
Not Hispanic (113)	165	1.56
Hispanic (8)	12	0.11
African, sub-Saharan:	44	0.42
African	15	0.14
Cape Verdean	15	0.14
South African	6	0.06
Other sub-Saharan African	8	0.08
Am. Ind. or Alaska Nat., not spec.	23	0.22
Alsatian	15	0.14
American Indian tribes, specified:	94	0.89
Apache (1)	8	0.08
Blackfeet	5	0.05
Cherokee (3)	25	0.24
Chippewa	1	0.01
Choctaw (1)	3	0.03

Notes: 1. Figures in the "Number" column do not add up to the total population due to: a) Ancestry/Race overlap — e.g. persons can report being both White and Irish, b) persons of Hispanic origin can report being any race, c) persons reporting two ancestries are counted in both categories. 2. Numbers in parentheses indicate the number of persons reporting this ancestry/race alone, not in combination with any other ancestry/race. 3. Refer to the Explanation of Data in the front of the book for more detailed information.

Ancestry/Race	Number	%
Comanche	6	0.06
Crow	2	0.02
Iroquois (1)	1	0.01
Latin American Indians (4)	7	0.07
Navajo (3)	14	0.13
Paiute	1	0.01
Pueblo (1)	2	0.02
Sioux (6)	6	0.06
Yaqui	3	0.03
All other tribes (7)	10	0.09
American Indian tribes, not spec.	3	0.03
Arab:	82	0.78
Arab/Arabic	7	0.07
Lebanese	52	0.49
Palestinian	10	0.09
Syrian	9	0.09
Other Arab	4	0.04
Armenian	226	2.14
Asian:	777	7.35
Bangladeshi (2)	2	0.02
Chinese, ex. Taiwanese (194)	241	2.28
Filipino (80)	132	1.25
Indian (37)	53	0.50
Indonesian (18)	19	0.18
Japanese (123)	181	1.71
Korean (45)	56	0.53
Pakistani	1	0.01
Sri Lankan	5	0.05
Taiwanese (33)	37	0.35
Thai (14)	17	0.16
Vietnamese (15)	21	0.20
Other Asian, specified (2)	2	0.02
Other Asian, not specified (4)	10	0.09
Australian	6	0.06
Austrian	31	0.29
Basque	24	0.23
Belgian	12	0.11
Brazilian	26	0.25
British	170	1.61
Canadian	80	0.76
Celtic	27	0.26
Croatian	9	0.09
Czech	66	0.62
Czechoslovakian	25	0.24
Danish	85	0.80
Dutch	152	1.44
Eastern European	22	0.21
English	1,915	18.10
European	157	1.48
Finnish	31	0.29
French, except Basque	456	4.31
French Canadian	60	0.57
German	2,130	20.14
Greek	45	0.43
Hawaii Native/Pacific Islander:	23	0.22
Polynesian: (2)	9	0.09
Native Hawaiian (1)	6	0.06
Samoan (1)	1	0.01
Tongan	1	0.01
Other Polynesian	1	0.01
Other Pac. Isl., not spec. (9)	14	0.13
Hispanic or Latino:	1,054	9.96
Central American:	51	0.48
Costa Rican	8	0.08
Guatemalan	11	0.10
Honduran	4	0.04
Nicaraguan	7	0.07
Panamanian	3	0.03
Salvadoran	17	0.16
Other Central American	1	0.01
Cuban	39	0.37
Mexican	710	6.71
Puerto Rican	13	0.12
South American:	75	0.71
Argentinean	18	0.17
Colombian	10	0.09
Ecuadorian	15	0.14
Peruvian	8	0.08
Uruguayan	1	0.01
Venezuelan	11	0.10
Other South American	12	0.11
Other Hispanic or Latino	166	1.57
Hungarian	53	0.50
Iranian	58	0.55
Irish	1,561	14.76
Italian	810	7.66
Latvian	9	0.09
Lithuanian	38	0.36
Northern European	39	0.37
Norwegian	257	2.43
Pennsylvania German	7	0.07
Polish	346	3.27
Portuguese	34	0.32
Romanian	21	0.20
Russian	261	2.47
Scandinavian	28	0.26
Scotch-Irish	200	1.89
Scottish	375	3.55
Serbian	38	0.36
Slavic	7	0.07
Slovak	20	0.19
Swedish	319	3.02
Swiss	58	0.55
Ukrainian	28	0.26
United States or American	359	3.39
Welsh	144	1.36
West Indian, excl. Hispanic:	13	0.12
Jamaican	10	0.09
West Indian	3	0.03
White:	9,453	89.36
Not Hispanic (8,435)	8,712	82.36
Hispanic (642)	741	7.01
Yugoslavian	30	0.28

Simi Valley

Place Type: City
County: Ventura
Population: 111,351

Ancestry/Race	Number	%
Acadian/Cajun	6	0.01
Afghan	432	0.39
African American/Black:	1,855	1.67
Not Hispanic (1,348)	1,712	1.54
Hispanic (53)	143	0.13
African, sub-Saharan:	187	0.17
African	76	0.07
Cape Verdean	4	0.00
Kenyan	9	0.01
Nigerian	36	0.03
South African	4	0.00
Sudanese	33	0.03
Ugandan	25	0.02
Alaska Native tribes, specified:	7	0.01
Aleut	1	0.00
Eskimo	4	0.00
Tlingit-Haida (2)	2	0.00
Alaska Native tribes, not specified	1	0.00
Am. Ind. or Alaska Nat., not spec.	499	0.45
Albanian	20	0.02
American Indian tribes, specified:	1,244	1.12
Apache (35)	80	0.07
Blackfeet (8)	48	0.04
Cherokee (112)	396	0.36
Cheyenne (3)	6	0.01
Chickasaw	12	0.01
Chippewa (19)	53	0.05
Choctaw (25)	65	0.06
Comanche (3)	18	0.02
Cree	3	0.00
Creek (5)	12	0.01
Delaware (8)	11	0.01
Houma	1	0.00
Iroquois (10)	29	0.03
Kiowa (4)	6	0.01
Latin American Indians (102)	164	0.15
Navajo (15)	39	0.04
Osage (4)	12	0.01
Paiute (6)	11	0.01
Pima (1)	1	0.00
Potawatomi (4)	15	0.01
Pueblo (19)	28	0.03
Puget Sound Salish (1)	1	0.00
Seminole (1)	7	0.01
Shoshone (1)	2	0.00
Sioux (17)	48	0.04
Tohono O'Odham (3)	6	0.01
Ute (4)	11	0.01
Yaqui (12)	37	0.03
Yuman	1	0.00
All other tribes (56)	121	0.11
American Indian tribes, not spec.	52	0.05
Arab:	586	0.53
Arab/Arabic	135	0.12
Egyptian	30	0.03
Lebanese	259	0.23
Palestinian	61	0.05
Syrian	101	0.09
Armenian	323	0.29
Asian:	8,667	7.78
Bangladeshi (6)	7	0.01
Cambodian (45)	63	0.06
Chinese, ex. Taiwanese (975)	1,262	1.13
Filipino (1,754)	2,239	2.01
Hmong (2)	2	0.00
Indian (1,353)	1,463	1.31
Indonesian (93)	152	0.14
Japanese (670)	1,008	0.91
Korean (657)	752	0.68
Laotian (30)	32	0.03
Malaysian (1)	4	0.00
Pakistani (68)	86	0.08
Sri Lankan (27)	38	0.03
Taiwanese (48)	60	0.05
Thai (171)	213	0.19
Vietnamese (940)	1,020	0.92
Other Asian, specified (19)	42	0.04
Other Asian, not specified (56)	224	0.20
Assyrian/Chaldean/Syriac	37	0.03
Australian	38	0.03
Austrian	543	0.49
Basque	87	0.08
Belgian	109	0.10
Brazilian	41	0.04
British	664	0.60
Bulgarian	42	0.04
Canadian	703	0.63
Celtic	6	0.01
Croatian	123	0.11
Czech	347	0.31
Czechoslovakian	262	0.23
Danish	651	0.58
Dutch	2,241	2.01
Eastern European	139	0.12
English	12,657	11.35
Estonian	6	0.01
European	1,111	1.00
Finnish	251	0.23
French, except Basque	3,774	3.38
French Canadian	902	0.81
German	18,626	16.70
German Russian	5	0.00
Greek	629	0.56
Guyanese	8	0.01
Hawaii Native/Pacific Islander:	439	0.39
Melanesian:	3	0.00
Fijian	3	0.00
Micronesian: (30)	47	0.04
Guamanian/Chamorro (26)	41	0.04
Other Micronesian (4)	6	0.01
Polynesian: (83)	251	0.23
Native Hawaiian (47)	171	0.15
Samoan (18)	55	0.05
Tongan (17)	19	0.02
Other Polynesian (1)	6	0.01
Other Pac. Isl., specified	11	0.01
Other Pac. Isl., not spec. (41)	127	0.11
Hispanic or Latino:	18,729	16.82
Central American:	1,113	1.00

Notes: 1. Figures in the "Number" column do not add up to the total population due to: a) Ancestry/Race overlap — e.g. persons can report being both White and Irish, b) persons of Hispanic origin can report being any race, c) persons reporting two ancestries are counted in both categories. 2. Numbers in parentheses indicate the number of persons reporting this ancestry/race alone, not in combination with any other ancestry/race. 3. Refer to the Explanation of Data in the front of the book for more detailed information.

Ancestry/Race	Number	%
Costa Rican	96	0.09
Guatemalan	345	0.31
Honduran	74	0.07
Nicaraguan	96	0.09
Panamanian	20	0.02
Salvadoran	417	0.37
Other Central American	65	0.06
Cuban	302	0.27
Dominican Republic	16	0.01
Mexican	12,501	11.23
Puerto Rican	449	0.40
South American:	980	0.88
Argentinean	174	0.16
Bolivian	24	0.02
Chilean	59	0.05
Colombian	246	0.22
Ecuadorian	112	0.10
Paraguayan	11	0.01
Peruvian	255	0.23
Uruguayan	8	0.01
Venezuelan	16	0.01
Other South American	75	0.07
Other Hispanic or Latino	3,368	3.02
Hungarian	1,224	1.10
Icelander	40	0.04
Iranian	343	0.31
Irish	14,328	12.84
Israeli	22	0.02
Italian	9,481	8.50
Latvian	17	0.02
Lithuanian	195	0.17
Luxemburger	23	0.02
Maltese	4	0.00
Northern European	90	0.08
Norwegian	2,560	2.29
Pennsylvania German	40	0.04
Polish	3,499	3.14
Portuguese	389	0.35
Romanian	204	0.18
Russian	2,158	1.93
Scandinavian	373	0.33
Scotch-Irish	1,840	1.65
Scottish	2,325	2.08
Serbian	117	0.10
Slavic	22	0.02
Slovak	141	0.13
Slovene	18	0.02
Swedish	2,531	2.27
Swiss	353	0.32
Turkish	73	0.07
Ukrainian	270	0.24
United States or American	5,589	5.01
Welsh	982	0.88
West Indian, excl. Hispanic:	174	0.16
Belizean	37	0.03
Dutch West Indian	15	0.01
Jamaican	95	0.09
Trinidadian and Tobagonian	21	0.02
U.S. Virgin Islander	6	0.01
White:	94,259	84.65
Not Hispanic (80,908)	83,267	74.78
Hispanic (9,653)	10,992	9.87
Yugoslavian	184	0.16

Solana Beach

Place Type: City
County: San Diego
Population: 12,979

Ancestry/Race	Number	%
African American/Black:	95	0.73
Not Hispanic (62)	88	0.68
Hispanic (3)	7	0.05
African, sub-Saharan:	27	0.21
African	15	0.12
South African	12	0.09
Alaska Native tribes, specified:	8	0.06
Alaska Athabascan (1)	1	0.01
Aleut (1)	4	0.03
Eskimo	1	0.01
Tlingit-Haida	2	0.02
Am. Ind. or Alaska Nat., not spec.	37	0.29
American Indian tribes, specified:	92	0.71
Apache	3	0.02
Blackfeet	1	0.01
Cherokee (3)	13	0.10
Cheyenne	1	0.01
Chippewa (1)	2	0.02
Choctaw	4	0.03
Iroquois	3	0.02
Latin American Indians (9)	32	0.25
Navajo (1)	4	0.03
Pueblo (1)	1	0.01
Seminole (1)	2	0.02
Sioux	4	0.03
Yaqui (1)	1	0.01
Yuman (3)	3	0.02
All other tribes (8)	18	0.14
American Indian tribes, not spec.	3	0.02
Arab:	12	0.09
Lebanese	9	0.07
Other Arab	3	0.02
Armenian	13	0.10
Asian:	585	4.51
Chinese, ex. Taiwanese (121)	149	1.15
Filipino (49)	84	0.65
Indian (52)	65	0.50
Indonesian	3	0.02
Japanese (105)	133	1.02
Korean (37)	51	0.39
Laotian	3	0.02
Pakistani	2	0.02
Taiwanese (23)	23	0.18
Thai (4)	11	0.08
Vietnamese (36)	38	0.29
Other Asian, specified (4)	4	0.03
Other Asian, not specified (8)	19	0.15
Australian	26	0.20
Austrian	115	0.89
Basque	21	0.16
Belgian	13	0.10
Brazilian	18	0.14
British	127	0.99
Canadian	91	0.71
Croatian	8	0.06
Czech	50	0.39
Czechoslovakian	22	0.17
Danish	111	0.86
Dutch	245	1.90
Eastern European	23	0.18
English	2,313	17.95
Estonian	9	0.07
European	200	1.55
Finnish	17	0.13
French, except Basque	415	3.22
French Canadian	98	0.76
German	2,076	16.11
Greek	99	0.77
Hawaii Native/Pacific Islander:	37	0.29
Micronesian: (2)	4	0.03
Guamanian/Chamorro (2)	4	0.03
Polynesian: (14)	25	0.19
Native Hawaiian (8)	16	0.12
Samoan (4)	6	0.05
Other Polynesian (2)	3	0.02
Other Pac. Isl., not spec. (2)	8	0.06
Hispanic or Latino:	1,922	14.81
Central American:	30	0.23
Costa Rican	3	0.02
Guatemalan	7	0.05
Honduran	3	0.02
Nicaraguan	5	0.04
Panamanian	3	0.02
Salvadoran	9	0.07
Cuban	17	0.13
Dominican Republic	3	0.02
Mexican	1,600	12.33
Puerto Rican	22	0.17
South American:	45	0.35
Argentinean	9	0.07
Chilean	4	0.03
Colombian	7	0.05
Ecuadorian	1	0.01
Peruvian	12	0.09
Venezuelan	5	0.04
Other South American	7	0.05
Other Hispanic or Latino	205	1.58
Hungarian	99	0.77
Icelander	31	0.24
Iranian	12	0.09
Irish	1,861	14.44
Italian	801	6.22
Lithuanian	81	0.63
Northern European	32	0.25
Norwegian	279	2.16
Polish	464	3.60
Portuguese	41	0.32
Romanian	26	0.20
Russian	471	3.65
Scandinavian	32	0.25
Scotch-Irish	445	3.45
Scottish	569	4.42
Serbian	12	0.09
Slavic	23	0.18
Slovak	18	0.14
Slovene	8	0.06
Swedish	487	3.78
Swiss	59	0.46
Turkish	17	0.13
Ukrainian	22	0.17
United States or American	500	3.88
Welsh	127	0.99
White:	11,619	89.52
Not Hispanic (10,250)	10,477	80.72
Hispanic (1,043)	1,142	8.80
Yugoslavian	26	0.20

Soledad

Place Type: City
County: Monterey
Population: 11,263

Ancestry/Race	Number	%
African American/Black:	160	1.42
Not Hispanic (97)	107	0.95
Hispanic (32)	53	0.47
African, sub-Saharan:	13	0.12
African	6	0.05
Cape Verdean	7	0.06
Am. Ind. or Alaska Nat., not spec.	127	1.13
American Indian tribes, specified:	98	0.87
Apache (8)	9	0.08
Blackfeet	1	0.01
Cherokee (1)	4	0.04
Chippewa (5)	5	0.04
Choctaw	4	0.04
Comanche	1	0.01
Creek	1	0.01
Latin American Indians (51)	56	0.50
Pueblo (1)	2	0.02
Yaqui	1	0.01
All other tribes (8)	14	0.12
American Indian tribes, not spec.	5	0.04
Asian:	366	3.25
Chinese, ex. Taiwanese (21)	23	0.20
Filipino (217)	295	2.62
Indian (15)	18	0.16
Indonesian (1)	1	0.01
Japanese (1)	9	0.08
Korean	4	0.04
Taiwanese	3	0.03
Vietnamese (8)	9	0.08
Other Asian, not specified	4	0.04
Canadian	6	0.05
Dutch	5	0.04
English	87	0.77
European	6	0.05
French, except Basque	29	0.26

Notes: 1. Figures in the "Number" column do not add up to the total population due to: a) Ancestry/Race overlap — e.g. persons can report being both White and Irish, b) persons of Hispanic origin can report being any race, c) persons reporting two ancestries are counted in both categories. 2. Numbers in parentheses indicate the number of persons reporting this ancestry/race alone, not in combination with any other ancestry/race. 3. Refer to the Explanation of Data in the front of the book for more detailed information.

Ancestry/Race	Number	%
German	178	1.58
Hawaii Native/Pacific Islander:	31	0.28
Micronesian: (4)	7	0.06
Guamanian/Chamorro (3)	4	0.04
Other Micronesian (1)	3	0.03
Polynesian: (5)	19	0.17
Native Hawaiian (5)	19	0.17
Other Pac. Isl., not spec.	5	0.04
Hispanic or Latino:	9,779	86.82
Central American:	37	0.33
Guatemalan	4	0.04
Honduran	5	0.04
Panamanian	3	0.03
Salvadoran	23	0.20
Other Central American	2	0.02
Cuban	3	0.03
Mexican	8,798	78.11
Puerto Rican	24	0.21
South American:	7	0.06
Argentinean	1	0.01
Peruvian	2	0.02
Uruguayan	1	0.01
Other South American	3	0.03
Other Hispanic or Latino	910	8.08
Irish	125	1.11
Italian	86	0.76
Norwegian	64	0.57
Polish	11	0.10
Portuguese	4	0.04
Romanian	8	0.07
Scottish	7	0.06
Slavic	28	0.25
Swedish	48	0.43
Swiss	92	0.82
United States or American	214	1.90
Welsh	6	0.05
White:	3,997	35.49
Not Hispanic (1,032)	1,112	9.87
Hispanic (2,561)	2,885	25.61

South El Monte

Place Type: City
County: Los Angeles
Population: 21,144

Ancestry/Race	Number	%
African American/Black:	135	0.64
Not Hispanic (29)	38	0.18
Hispanic (51)	97	0.46
African, sub-Saharan:	17	0.08
African	17	0.08
Am. Ind. or Alaska Nat., not spec.	225	1.06
American Indian tribes, specified:	201	0.95
Apache (3)	5	0.02
Blackfeet (3)	5	0.02
Cherokee (8)	12	0.06
Chickasaw	3	0.01
Choctaw (1)	1	0.00
Creek	1	0.00
Latin American Indians (84)	110	0.52
Navajo (16)	18	0.09
Pima (3)	3	0.01
Pueblo (5)	14	0.07
Shoshone	1	0.00
Sioux (2)	4	0.02
Tohono O'Odham	2	0.01
Yaqui	3	0.01
All other tribes (17)	19	0.09
American Indian tribes, not spec.	30	0.14
Arab:	22	0.11
Lebanese	22	0.11
Asian:	1,962	9.28
Bangladeshi (4)	4	0.02
Cambodian (30)	36	0.17
Chinese, ex. Taiwanese (901)	975	4.61
Filipino (90)	112	0.53
Indian (9)	48	0.23
Indonesian (1)	6	0.03
Japanese (30)	41	0.19
Korean (4)	4	0.02
Pakistani (1)	12	0.06
Taiwanese (23)	25	0.12
Thai (10)	15	0.07
Vietnamese (590)	659	3.12
Other Asian, specified (7)	7	0.03
Other Asian, not specified (9)	18	0.09
Canadian	41	0.20
Dutch	85	0.41
English	115	0.55
European	21	0.10
French, except Basque	83	0.40
German	193	0.92
Greek	7	0.03
Hawaii Native/Pacific Islander:	73	0.35
Micronesian: (2)	2	0.01
Guamanian/Chamorro (2)	2	0.01
Polynesian: (34)	60	0.28
Native Hawaiian (15)	34	0.16
Samoan (19)	25	0.12
Tongan	1	0.00
Other Pac. Isl., not spec. (3)	11	0.05
Hispanic or Latino:	18,190	86.03
Central American:	459	2.17
Costa Rican	4	0.02
Guatemalan	120	0.57
Honduran	36	0.17
Nicaraguan	26	0.12
Salvadoran	237	1.12
Other Central American	36	0.17
Cuban	32	0.15
Mexican	15,687	74.19
Puerto Rican	45	0.21
South American:	106	0.50
Argentinean	10	0.05
Chilean	1	0.00
Colombian	23	0.11
Ecuadorian	6	0.03
Peruvian	35	0.17
Uruguayan	1	0.00
Other South American	30	0.14
Other Hispanic or Latino	1,861	8.80
Iranian	7	0.03
Irish	146	0.70
Italian	129	0.62
Norwegian	4	0.02
Pennsylvania German	6	0.03
Portuguese	17	0.08
Russian	9	0.04
Scotch-Irish	16	0.08
Scottish	21	0.10
Swiss	6	0.03
Ukrainian	7	0.03
United States or American	263	1.26
Welsh	16	0.08
White:	9,465	44.76
Not Hispanic (1,005)	1,063	5.03
Hispanic (7,581)	8,402	39.74

South Gate

Place Type: City
County: Los Angeles
Population: 96,375

Ancestry/Race	Number	%
Acadian/Cajun	13	0.01
African American/Black:	1,129	1.17
Not Hispanic (632)	677	0.70
Hispanic (291)	452	0.47
African, sub-Saharan:	59	0.06
African	39	0.04
Nigerian	20	0.02
Am. Ind. or Alaska Nat., not spec.	614	0.64
American Indian tribes, specified:	521	0.54
Apache (15)	26	0.03
Blackfeet (2)	9	0.01
Cherokee (21)	54	0.06
Chickasaw (2)	5	0.01
Chippewa	1	0.00
Choctaw (3)	8	0.01
Colville (1)	1	0.00
Comanche	1	0.00
Creek (6)	10	0.01
Delaware	1	0.00
Iroquois (2)	3	0.00
Latin American Indians (217)	289	0.30
Navajo (20)	28	0.03
Paiute (1)	1	0.00
Pima (3)	6	0.01
Pueblo (26)	33	0.03
Shoshone (1)	2	0.00
Sioux (3)	7	0.01
Tohono O'Odham (2)	5	0.01
Yaqui (1)	2	0.00
All other tribes (21)	29	0.03
American Indian tribes, not spec.	90	0.09
Arab:	153	0.16
Arab/Arabic	134	0.14
Egyptian	6	0.01
Lebanese	4	0.00
Syrian	9	0.01
Asian:	1,048	1.09
Cambodian (7)	7	0.01
Chinese, ex. Taiwanese (76)	110	0.11
Filipino (228)	288	0.30
Hmong	1	0.00
Indian (164)	213	0.22
Indonesian (1)	1	0.00
Japanese (43)	71	0.07
Korean (129)	150	0.16
Laotian (3)	4	0.00
Pakistani (2)	3	0.00
Sri Lankan	2	0.00
Taiwanese (11)	12	0.01
Thai (70)	71	0.07
Vietnamese (36)	41	0.04
Other Asian, specified (2)	4	0.00
Other Asian, not specified (19)	70	0.07
Austrian	18	0.02
British	39	0.04
Canadian	74	0.08
Celtic	6	0.01
Croatian	10	0.01
Czech	16	0.02
Czechoslovakian	6	0.01
Danish	78	0.08
Dutch	189	0.20
English	832	0.86
European	134	0.14
Finnish	9	0.01
French, except Basque	326	0.34
French Canadian	42	0.04
German	1,133	1.18
Greek	24	0.02
Hawaii Native/Pacific Islander:	200	0.21
Melanesian: (1)	1	0.00
Fijian (1)	1	0.00
Micronesian: (18)	22	0.02
Guamanian/Chamorro (18)	22	0.02
Polynesian: (82)	118	0.12
Native Hawaiian (31)	56	0.06
Samoan (51)	62	0.06
Other Pac. Isl., not spec. (13)	59	0.06
Hispanic or Latino:	88,669	92.00
Central American:	6,164	6.40
Costa Rican	123	0.13
Guatemalan	1,488	1.54
Honduran	264	0.27
Nicaraguan	581	0.60
Panamanian	18	0.02
Salvadoran	3,040	3.15
Other Central American	650	0.67
Cuban	761	0.79
Dominican Republic	23	0.02
Mexican	68,181	70.75
Puerto Rican	576	0.60
South American:	1,083	1.12
Argentinean	105	0.11
Bolivian	19	0.02

Notes: 1. Figures in the "Number" column do not add up to the total population due to: a) Ancestry/Race overlap — e.g. persons can report being both White and Irish, b) persons of Hispanic origin can report being any race, c) persons reporting two ancestries are counted in both categories. 2. Numbers in parentheses indicate the number of persons reporting this ancestry/race alone, not in combination with any other ancestry/race. 3. Refer to the Explanation of Data in the front of the book for more detailed information.

Ancestry/Race	Number	%
Chilean	24	0.02
Colombian	198	0.21
Ecuadorian	217	0.23
Paraguayan	1	0.00
Peruvian	380	0.39
Uruguayan	3	0.00
Venezuelan	8	0.01
Other South American	128	0.13
Other Hispanic or Latino	11,881	12.33
Hungarian	113	0.12
Iranian	18	0.02
Irish	853	0.88
Italian	526	0.55
Lithuanian	11	0.01
Norwegian	120	0.12
Pennsylvania German	15	0.02
Polish	105	0.11
Portuguese	41	0.04
Romanian	61	0.06
Russian	23	0.02
Scotch-Irish	225	0.23
Scottish	175	0.18
Serbian	8	0.01
Slavic	23	0.02
Slovak	23	0.02
Swedish	101	0.10
Swiss	32	0.03
Turkish	5	0.01
Ukrainian	22	0.02
United States or American	1,588	1.65
Welsh	24	0.02
West Indian, excl. Hispanic:	89	0.09
Belizean	29	0.03
Haitian	55	0.06
Jamaican	5	0.01
White:	44,110	45.77
Not Hispanic (5,755)	6,015	6.24
Hispanic (34,381)	38,095	39.53
Yugoslavian	19	0.02

South Lake Tahoe

Place Type: City
County: El Dorado
Population: 23,609

Ancestry/Race	Number	%
Afghan	23	0.10
African American/Black:	289	1.22
Not Hispanic (145)	234	0.99
Hispanic (33)	55	0.23
African, sub-Saharan:	4	0.02
African	4	0.02
Alaska Native tribes, specified:	1	0.00
Eskimo (1)	1	0.00
Am. Ind. or Alaska Nat., not spec.	164	0.69
American Indian tribes, specified:	283	1.20
Apache (11)	16	0.07
Blackfeet (2)	18	0.08
Cherokee (26)	79	0.33
Cheyenne	1	0.00
Chickasaw (1)	4	0.02
Chippewa (4)	8	0.03
Choctaw (9)	15	0.06
Colville (1)	3	0.01
Comanche (2)	2	0.01
Crow	7	0.03
Delaware (1)	2	0.01
Iroquois (4)	5	0.02
Latin American Indians (21)	41	0.17
Navajo (3)	7	0.03
Ottawa (1)	2	0.01
Paiute (1)	8	0.03
Potawatomi (3)	5	0.02
Pueblo (2)	3	0.01
Shoshone (1)	2	0.01
Sioux (2)	9	0.04
Yaqui (1)	2	0.01
Yuman (1)	1	0.00
All other tribes (17)	43	0.18
American Indian tribes, not spec.	37	0.16
Arab:	45	0.19
Arab/Arabic	16	0.07
Lebanese	16	0.07
Syrian	5	0.02
Other Arab	8	0.03
Armenian	12	0.05
Asian:	1,666	7.06
Chinese, ex. Taiwanese (112)	142	0.60
Filipino (1,045)	1,168	4.95
Indian (131)	147	0.62
Indonesian (1)	1	0.00
Japanese (80)	130	0.55
Korean (12)	23	0.10
Laotian (1)	1	0.00
Pakistani (4)	4	0.02
Taiwanese (6)	6	0.03
Thai (10)	11	0.05
Vietnamese (9)	18	0.08
Other Asian, specified	1	0.00
Other Asian, not specified (2)	14	0.06
Australian	16	0.07
Austrian	77	0.32
Basque	9	0.04
Belgian	18	0.08
British	125	0.53
Canadian	89	0.38
Croatian	26	0.11
Czech	93	0.39
Czechoslovakian	15	0.06
Danish	120	0.51
Dutch	305	1.29
English	2,558	10.78
European	241	1.02
Finnish	59	0.25
French, except Basque	778	3.28
French Canadian	105	0.44
German	2,892	12.19
Greek	29	0.12
Hawaii Native/Pacific Islander:	74	0.31
Melanesian: (1)	1	0.00
Other Melanesian (1)	1	0.00
Micronesian: (9)	14	0.06
Guamanian/Chamorro (9)	14	0.06
Polynesian: (22)	47	0.20
Native Hawaiian (20)	39	0.17
Samoan (2)	5	0.02
Other Polynesian	3	0.01
Other Pac. Isl., specified	1	0.00
Other Pac. Isl., not spec. (8)	11	0.05
Hispanic or Latino:	6,294	26.66
Central American:	199	0.84
Costa Rican	5	0.02
Guatemalan	14	0.06
Honduran	8	0.03
Nicaraguan	29	0.12
Panamanian	1	0.00
Salvadoran	120	0.51
Other Central American	22	0.09
Cuban	26	0.11
Mexican	5,216	22.09
Puerto Rican	70	0.30
South American:	42	0.18
Argentinean	8	0.03
Bolivian	10	0.04
Chilean	3	0.01
Colombian	6	0.03
Ecuadorian	1	0.00
Peruvian	1	0.00
Other South American	13	0.06
Other Hispanic or Latino	741	3.14
Hungarian	156	0.66
Icelander	7	0.03
Iranian	38	0.16
Irish	2,762	11.64
Italian	1,394	5.88
Lithuanian	53	0.22
Northern European	47	0.20
Norwegian	420	1.77
Pennsylvania German	7	0.03
Polish	406	1.71
Portuguese	248	1.05
Romanian	36	0.15
Russian	263	1.11
Scandinavian	56	0.24
Scotch-Irish	339	1.43
Scottish	629	2.65
Serbian	11	0.05
Slavic	23	0.10
Slovak	34	0.14
Swedish	589	2.48
Swiss	134	0.56
Ukrainian	51	0.22
United States or American	1,235	5.21
Welsh	229	0.97
White:	18,684	79.14
Not Hispanic (15,016)	15,473	65.54
Hispanic (2,862)	3,211	13.60
Yugoslavian	77	0.32

South Pasadena

Place Type: City
County: Los Angeles
Population: 24,292

Ancestry/Race	Number	%
African American/Black:	918	3.78
Not Hispanic (708)	861	3.54
Hispanic (30)	57	0.23
African, sub-Saharan:	140	0.58
African	66	0.27
Cape Verdean	7	0.03
Ghanian	16	0.07
Nigerian	39	0.16
South African	12	0.05
Alaska Native tribes, specified:	6	0.02
Alaska Athabascan	1	0.00
Aleut	1	0.00
Eskimo	1	0.00
Tlingit-Haida (2)	3	0.01
Alaska Native tribes, not specified	1	0.00
Am. Ind. or Alaska Nat., not spec.	100	0.41
American Indian tribes, specified:	140	0.58
Apache (3)	10	0.04
Blackfeet (1)	9	0.04
Cherokee (4)	43	0.18
Chippewa (1)	3	0.01
Choctaw (7)	10	0.04
Comanche (1)	1	0.00
Cree	1	0.00
Creek (1)	6	0.02
Iroquois (1)	10	0.04
Latin American Indians (7)	10	0.04
Navajo (1)	2	0.01
Osage	6	0.02
Paiute (1)	1	0.00
Potawatomi (1)	2	0.01
Pueblo (1)	5	0.02
Shoshone	1	0.00
Sioux (1)	2	0.01
Ute	1	0.00
Yaqui	4	0.02
All other tribes (4)	14	0.06
American Indian tribes, not spec.	5	0.02
Arab:	276	1.14
Arab/Arabic	65	0.27
Egyptian	54	0.22
Lebanese	90	0.37
Syrian	15	0.06
Other Arab	52	0.21
Armenian	117	0.48
Asian:	7,250	29.85
Bangladeshi (1)	1	0.00
Cambodian (2)	2	0.01
Chinese, ex. Taiwanese (3,528)	3,874	15.95
Filipino (351)	442	1.82
Indian (211)	254	1.05
Indonesian (38)	63	0.26
Japanese (777)	998	4.11

Notes: 1. Figures in the "Number" column do not add up to the total population due to: a) Ancestry/Race overlap — e.g. persons can report being both White and Irish, b) persons of Hispanic origin can report being any race, c) persons reporting two ancestries are counted in both categories. 2. Numbers in parentheses indicate the number of persons reporting this ancestry/race alone, not in combination with any other ancestry/race. 3. Refer to the Explanation of Data in the front of the book for more detailed information.

Korean (826)	913	3.76
Malaysian (2)	8	0.03
Pakistani (11)	19	0.08
Sri Lankan (16)	22	0.09
Taiwanese (267)	322	1.33
Thai (63)	75	0.31
Vietnamese (133)	156	0.64
Other Asian, specified (7)	13	0.05
Other Asian, not specified (25)	88	0.36
Assyrian/Chaldean/Syriac	6	0.02
Australian	27	0.11
Austrian	98	0.40
Basque	22	0.09
Belgian	13	0.05
Brazilian	34	0.14
British	123	0.51
Canadian	42	0.17
Croatian	51	0.21
Czech	69	0.28
Czechoslovakian	58	0.24
Danish	191	0.79
Dutch	238	0.98
Eastern European	20	0.08
English	2,697	11.10
European	329	1.35
Finnish	59	0.24
French, except Basque	664	2.73
French Canadian	154	0.63
German	2,751	11.32
German Russian	8	0.03
Greek	172	0.71
Hawaii Native/Pacific Islander:	82	0.34
Micronesian: (4)	7	0.03
Guamanian/Chamorro (4)	6	0.02
Other Micronesian	1	0.00
Polynesian: (13)	40	0.16
Native Hawaiian (10)	37	0.15
Samoan (2)	2	0.01
Tongan (1)	1	0.00
Other Pac. Isl., specified	1	0.00
Other Pac. Isl., not spec. (3)	34	0.14
Hispanic or Latino:	3,903	16.07
Central American:	210	0.86
Costa Rican	22	0.09
Guatemalan	39	0.16
Honduran	11	0.05
Nicaraguan	27	0.11
Panamanian	15	0.06
Salvadoran	74	0.30
Other Central American	22	0.09
Cuban	87	0.36
Dominican Republic	4	0.02
Mexican	2,697	11.10
Puerto Rican	57	0.23
South American:	232	0.96
Argentinean	30	0.12
Bolivian	6	0.02
Chilean	28	0.12
Colombian	44	0.18
Ecuadorian	35	0.14
Peruvian	60	0.25
Uruguayan	1	0.00
Venezuelan	8	0.03
Other South American	20	0.08
Other Hispanic or Latino	616	2.54
Hungarian	195	0.80
Iranian	163	0.67
Irish	2,486	10.23
Israeli	15	0.06
Italian	1,195	4.92
Latvian	28	0.12
Lithuanian	101	0.42
Northern European	30	0.12
Norwegian	336	1.38
Polish	484	1.99
Portuguese	107	0.44
Romanian	71	0.29
Russian	613	2.52
Scandinavian	42	0.17
Scotch-Irish	394	1.62
Scottish	599	2.46
Serbian	36	0.15
Slovak	8	0.03
Slovene	20	0.08
Swedish	458	1.88
Swiss	179	0.74
Ukrainian	66	0.27
United States or American	652	2.68
Welsh	180	0.74
West Indian, excl. Hispanic:	83	0.34
Barbadian	12	0.05
Haitian	8	0.03
Jamaican	34	0.14
Trinidadian and Tobagonian	20	0.08
West Indian	9	0.04
White:	15,558	64.05
Not Hispanic (12,344)	12,996	53.50
Hispanic (2,309)	2,562	10.55
Yugoslavian	71	0.29

South San Francisco

Place Type: City
County: San Mateo
Population: 60,552

Ancestry/Race	Number	%
African American/Black:	2,149	3.55
Not Hispanic (1,621)	1,922	3.17
Hispanic (86)	227	0.37
African, sub-Saharan:	162	0.27
African	63	0.10
Ethiopian	40	0.07
Nigerian	59	0.10
Alaska Native tribes, specified:	10	0.02
Alaska Athabascan (1)	1	0.00
Aleut	3	0.00
Tlingit-Haida (3)	6	0.01
Alaska Native tribes, not specified	9	0.01
Am. Ind. or Alaska Nat., not spec.	267	0.44
Albanian	18	0.03
American Indian tribes, specified:	542	0.90
Apache (30)	66	0.11
Blackfeet (2)	24	0.04
Cherokee (25)	117	0.19
Cheyenne (3)	5	0.01
Chickasaw	1	0.00
Chippewa (6)	15	0.02
Choctaw (12)	34	0.06
Comanche	1	0.00
Creek (8)	14	0.02
Delaware (1)	1	0.00
Iroquois (7)	10	0.02
Kiowa (1)	1	0.00
Latin American Indians (32)	68	0.11
Menominee	1	0.00
Navajo (28)	55	0.09
Osage	4	0.01
Ottawa (2)	2	0.00
Paiute (2)	2	0.00
Pima (2)	4	0.01
Potawatomi (1)	2	0.00
Pueblo (4)	10	0.02
Seminole	3	0.00
Shoshone (2)	2	0.00
Sioux (4)	13	0.02
Ute (1)	2	0.00
Yaqui (1)	8	0.01
All other tribes (22)	77	0.13
American Indian tribes, not spec.	60	0.10
Arab:	1,152	1.90
Arab/Arabic	321	0.53
Egyptian	33	0.05
Iraqi	15	0.02
Jordanian	282	0.46
Lebanese	61	0.10
Palestinian	349	0.57
Syrian	8	0.01
Other Arab	83	0.14
Armenian	190	0.31
Asian:	19,696	32.53
Cambodian (21)	38	0.06
Chinese, ex. Taiwanese (4,711)	5,229	8.64
Filipino (9,987)	11,127	18.38
Indian (1,050)	1,349	2.23
Indonesian (109)	143	0.24
Japanese (498)	724	1.20
Korean (333)	409	0.68
Laotian (3)	6	0.01
Malaysian (10)	18	0.03
Pakistani (30)	74	0.12
Sri Lankan (6)	6	0.01
Taiwanese (28)	40	0.07
Thai (62)	74	0.12
Vietnamese (217)	242	0.40
Other Asian, specified (55)	85	0.14
Other Asian, not specified (45)	132	0.22
Assyrian/Chaldean/Syriac	16	0.03
Australian	6	0.01
Austrian	76	0.13
Basque	43	0.07
Belgian	20	0.03
Brazilian	34	0.06
British	97	0.16
Canadian	70	0.12
Celtic	14	0.02
Croatian	133	0.22
Czech	66	0.11
Czechoslovakian	35	0.06
Danish	252	0.41
Dutch	384	0.63
English	1,913	3.15
European	219	0.36
Finnish	87	0.14
French, except Basque	1,037	1.71
French Canadian	128	0.21
German	3,398	5.60
Greek	521	0.86
Hawaii Native/Pacific Islander:	1,514	2.50
Melanesian: (157)	210	0.35
Fijian (157)	210	0.35
Micronesian: (54)	64	0.11
Guamanian/Chamorro (51)	60	0.10
Other Micronesian (3)	4	0.01
Polynesian: (632)	921	1.52
Native Hawaiian (75)	228	0.38
Samoan (375)	469	0.77
Tongan (179)	210	0.35
Other Polynesian (3)	14	0.02
Other Pac. Isl., specified	1	0.00
Other Pac. Isl., not spec. (76)	318	0.53
Hispanic or Latino:	19,282	31.84
Central American:	3,145	5.19
Costa Rican	30	0.05
Guatemalan	270	0.45
Honduran	52	0.09
Nicaraguan	945	1.56
Panamanian	19	0.03
Salvadoran	1,514	2.50
Other Central American	315	0.52
Cuban	75	0.12
Dominican Republic	14	0.02
Mexican	11,086	18.31
Puerto Rican	504	0.83
South American:	481	0.79
Argentinean	24	0.04
Bolivian	10	0.02
Chilean	46	0.08
Colombian	95	0.16
Ecuadorian	45	0.07
Peruvian	215	0.36
Venezuelan	18	0.03
Other South American	28	0.05
Other Hispanic or Latino	3,977	6.57
Hungarian	72	0.12
Icelander	15	0.02
Iranian	61	0.10
Irish	4,526	7.45
Israeli	16	0.03
Italian	5,107	8.41

Notes: 1. Figures in the "Number" column do not add up to the total population due to: a) Ancestry/Race overlap — e.g. persons can report being both White and Irish, b) persons of Hispanic origin can report being any race, c) persons reporting two ancestries are counted in both categories. 2. Numbers in parentheses indicate the number of persons reporting this ancestry/race alone, not in combination with any other ancestry/race. 3. Refer to the Explanation of Data in the front of the book for more detailed information.

Latvian	39	0.06
Lithuanian	11	0.02
Maltese	279	0.46
Northern European	19	0.03
Norwegian	544	0.90
Pennsylvania German	9	0.01
Polish	497	0.82
Portuguese	446	0.73
Romanian	18	0.03
Russian	431	0.71
Scandinavian	44	0.07
Scotch-Irish	476	0.78
Scottish	449	0.74
Serbian	13	0.02
Slavic	45	0.07
Slovak	47	0.08
Slovene	20	0.03
Swedish	509	0.84
Swiss	106	0.17
Turkish	6	0.01
Ukrainian	213	0.35
United States or American	670	1.10
Welsh	65	0.11
West Indian, excl. Hispanic:	60	0.10
Dutch West Indian	4	0.01
Haitian	14	0.02
Jamaican	42	0.07
White:	30,016	49.57
Not Hispanic (18,487)	20,328	33.57
Hispanic (8,184)	9,688	16.00
Yugoslavian	123	0.20

South San Jose Hills

Place Type: Census Designated Place
County: Los Angeles
Population: 20,218

Ancestry/Race	Number	%
African American/Black:	476	2.35
Not Hispanic (302)	342	1.69
Hispanic (74)	134	0.66
African, sub-Saharan:	4	0.02
African	4	0.02
Alaska Native tribes, specified:	2	0.01
Aleut (1)	1	0.00
Tlingit-Haida (1)	1	0.00
Am. Ind. or Alaska Nat., not spec.	215	1.06
Albanian	7	0.03
American Indian tribes, specified:	191	0.94
Apache (3)	18	0.09
Blackfeet	1	0.00
Cherokee (4)	23	0.11
Choctaw	1	0.00
Creek (3)	3	0.01
Latin American Indians (57)	84	0.42
Navajo (10)	11	0.05
Paiute	2	0.01
Pueblo (7)	9	0.04
Seminole	1	0.00
Sioux (2)	7	0.03
Tohono O'Odham (1)	1	0.00
Ute	1	0.00
Yaqui (6)	8	0.04
Yuman (1)	1	0.00
All other tribes (19)	20	0.10
American Indian tribes, not spec.	30	0.15
Arab:	17	0.08
Egyptian	10	0.05
Lebanese	7	0.03
Asian:	1,450	7.17
Cambodian (2)	3	0.01
Chinese, ex. Taiwanese (218)	236	1.17
Filipino (772)	829	4.10
Indian (44)	50	0.25
Indonesian (7)	10	0.05
Japanese (41)	67	0.33
Korean (27)	30	0.15
Laotian (20)	21	0.10
Malaysian	5	0.02
Pakistani (19)	21	0.10
Sri Lankan (11)	11	0.05
Taiwanese (30)	32	0.16
Thai (18)	22	0.11
Vietnamese (87)	89	0.44
Other Asian, not specified (12)	24	0.12
Belgian	25	0.12
Canadian	6	0.03
Danish	48	0.24
Dutch	26	0.13
English	155	0.77
European	21	0.10
French, except Basque	136	0.67
French Canadian	23	0.11
German	347	1.72
Hawaii Native/Pacific Islander:	94	0.46
Micronesian: (8)	10	0.05
Guamanian/Chamorro (8)	10	0.05
Polynesian: (63)	76	0.38
Native Hawaiian (9)	13	0.06
Samoan (54)	63	0.31
Other Pac. Isl., not spec.	8	0.04
Hispanic or Latino:	16,868	83.43
Central American:	732	3.62
Costa Rican	13	0.06
Guatemalan	169	0.84
Honduran	41	0.20
Nicaraguan	42	0.21
Panamanian	3	0.01
Salvadoran	424	2.10
Other Central American	40	0.20
Cuban	31	0.15
Mexican	13,994	69.22
Puerto Rican	71	0.35
South American:	115	0.57
Argentinean	6	0.03
Bolivian	4	0.02
Colombian	30	0.15
Ecuadorian	35	0.17
Peruvian	23	0.11
Uruguayan	1	0.00
Venezuelan	2	0.01
Other South American	14	0.07
Other Hispanic or Latino	1,925	9.52
Hungarian	11	0.05
Icelander	11	0.05
Irish	289	1.43
Italian	189	0.94
Norwegian	55	0.27
Polish	72	0.36
Scotch-Irish	14	0.07
Scottish	29	0.14
Slovene	21	0.10
Swedish	52	0.26
Ukrainian	17	0.08
United States or American	248	1.23
Welsh	18	0.09
West Indian, excl. Hispanic:	27	0.13
Jamaican	27	0.13
White:	8,598	42.53
Not Hispanic (1,450)	1,581	7.82
Hispanic (6,387)	7,017	34.71

South Whittier

Place Type: Census Designated Place
County: Los Angeles
Population: 55,193

Ancestry/Race	Number	%
Acadian/Cajun	8	0.01
African American/Black:	1,040	1.88
Not Hispanic (616)	715	1.30
Hispanic (196)	325	0.59
African, sub-Saharan:	130	0.24
African	97	0.18
Ethiopian	22	0.04
Ghanian	11	0.02
Alaska Native tribes, specified:	4	0.01
Eskimo	4	0.01
Alaska Native tribes, not specified	1	0.00
Am. Ind. or Alaska Nat., not spec.	415	0.75
Albanian	6	0.01
American Indian tribes, specified:	628	1.14
Apache (51)	88	0.16
Blackfeet (3)	17	0.03
Cherokee (28)	97	0.18
Cheyenne	4	0.01
Chickasaw	6	0.01
Chippewa (3)	3	0.01
Choctaw (12)	22	0.04
Comanche (7)	9	0.02
Delaware (1)	1	0.00
Iroquois (9)	10	0.02
Kiowa (1)	1	0.00
Latin American Indians (101)	142	0.26
Navajo (34)	55	0.10
Osage (1)	1	0.00
Pima	4	0.01
Potawatomi (3)	3	0.01
Pueblo (8)	15	0.03
Seminole (5)	7	0.01
Sioux (10)	19	0.03
Tohono O'Odham (3)	8	0.01
Yakama (1)	1	0.00
Yaqui (14)	34	0.06
All other tribes (48)	81	0.15
American Indian tribes, not spec.	72	0.13
Arab:	213	0.39
Arab/Arabic	58	0.11
Egyptian	77	0.14
Jordanian	14	0.03
Lebanese	54	0.10
Palestinian	10	0.02
Armenian	149	0.27
Asian:	2,193	3.97
Cambodian (43)	57	0.10
Chinese, ex. Taiwanese (160)	267	0.48
Filipino (649)	818	1.48
Hmong (6)	7	0.01
Indian (106)	122	0.22
Indonesian (7)	22	0.04
Japanese (204)	315	0.57
Korean (127)	156	0.28
Laotian (82)	88	0.16
Pakistani (6)	11	0.02
Sri Lankan (1)	2	0.00
Taiwanese (10)	13	0.02
Thai (51)	78	0.14
Vietnamese (147)	160	0.29
Other Asian, specified	17	0.03
Other Asian, not specified (18)	60	0.11
Australian	6	0.01
Austrian	89	0.16
Basque	20	0.04
Brazilian	21	0.04
British	120	0.22
Bulgarian	6	0.01
Canadian	93	0.17
Croatian	80	0.15
Czech	59	0.11
Czechoslovakian	4	0.01
Danish	126	0.23
Dutch	356	0.65
English	2,126	3.86
European	200	0.36
Finnish	45	0.08
French, except Basque	801	1.46
French Canadian	139	0.25
German	3,429	6.23
Greek	89	0.16
Guyanese	4	0.01
Hawaii Native/Pacific Islander:	287	0.52
Micronesian: (34)	48	0.09
Guamanian/Chamorro (34)	48	0.09
Polynesian: (88)	184	0.33
Native Hawaiian (44)	113	0.20
Samoan (16)	25	0.05
Tongan (25)	40	0.07
Other Polynesian (3)	6	0.01

Notes: 1. Figures in the "Number" column do not add up to the total population due to: a) Ancestry/Race overlap — e.g. persons can report being both White and Irish, b) persons of Hispanic origin can report being any race, c) persons reporting two ancestries are counted in both categories. 2. Numbers in parentheses indicate the number of persons reporting this ancestry/race alone, not in combination with any other ancestry/race. 3. Refer to the Explanation of Data in the front of the book for more detailed information.

Ancestry/Race	Number	%
Other Pac. Isl., specified	5	0.01
Other Pac. Isl., not spec. (20)	50	0.09
Hispanic or Latino:	38,256	69.31
Central American:	1,061	1.92
Costa Rican	64	0.12
Guatemalan	218	0.39
Honduran	39	0.07
Nicaraguan	115	0.21
Panamanian	12	0.02
Salvadoran	499	0.90
Other Central American	114	0.21
Cuban	198	0.36
Dominican Republic	5	0.01
Mexican	31,690	57.42
Puerto Rican	251	0.45
South American:	350	0.63
Argentinean	36	0.07
Bolivian	7	0.01
Chilean	14	0.03
Colombian	85	0.15
Ecuadorian	81	0.15
Peruvian	104	0.19
Venezuelan	3	0.01
Other South American	20	0.04
Other Hispanic or Latino	4,701	8.52
Hungarian	57	0.10
Iranian	14	0.03
Irish	3,159	5.74
Israeli	23	0.04
Italian	1,204	2.19
Lithuanian	61	0.11
New Zealander	6	0.01
Northern European	14	0.03
Norwegian	213	0.39
Pennsylvania German	18	0.03
Polish	274	0.50
Portuguese	150	0.27
Romanian	65	0.12
Russian	236	0.43
Scandinavian	37	0.07
Scotch-Irish	523	0.95
Scottish	538	0.98
Serbian	29	0.05
Slavic	6	0.01
Slovak	42	0.08
Slovene	12	0.02
Swedish	532	0.97
Swiss	43	0.08
Turkish	7	0.01
Ukrainian	40	0.07
United States or American	995	1.81
Welsh	112	0.20
West Indian, excl. Hispanic:	104	0.19
Belizean	55	0.10
British West Indian	7	0.01
Jamaican	19	0.03
West Indian	23	0.04
White:	31,425	56.94
Not Hispanic (13,654)	14,258	25.83
Hispanic (15,304)	17,167	31.10
Yugoslavian	37	0.07

South Yuba City

Place Type: Census Designated Place
County: Sutter
Population: 12,651

Ancestry/Race	Number	%
African American/Black:	254	2.01
Not Hispanic (200)	239	1.89
Hispanic (12)	15	0.12
African, sub-Saharan:	15	0.12
African	15	0.12
Alaska Native tribes, specified:	1	0.01
All other tribes	1	0.01
Am. Ind. or Alaska Nat., not spec.	90	0.71
American Indian tribes, specified:	170	1.34
Apache (2)	4	0.03
Blackfeet (3)	9	0.07
Cherokee (29)	93	0.74
Chippewa (1)	1	0.01
Choctaw (8)	14	0.11
Comanche	1	0.01
Cree (1)	1	0.01
Creek (2)	2	0.02
Latin American Indians (1)	1	0.01
Lumbee (2)	4	0.03
Navajo (1)	3	0.02
Pueblo (2)	2	0.02
Seminole	1	0.01
Sioux (4)	5	0.04
Yuman (3)	3	0.02
All other tribes (17)	26	0.21
American Indian tribes, not spec.	5	0.04
Armenian	24	0.19
Asian:	3,210	25.37
Cambodian (4)	4	0.03
Chinese, ex. Taiwanese (52)	74	0.58
Filipino (89)	135	1.07
Hmong (17)	24	0.19
Indian (2,556)	2,713	21.44
Indonesian (1)	1	0.01
Japanese (98)	140	1.11
Korean (31)	39	0.31
Laotian (19)	20	0.16
Pakistani (7)	16	0.13
Thai (4)	7	0.06
Vietnamese (12)	21	0.17
Other Asian, not specified (9)	16	0.13
Austrian	14	0.11
Basque	21	0.16
Brazilian	6	0.05
British	36	0.28
Canadian	16	0.12
Czech	25	0.19
Czechoslovakian	32	0.25
Danish	47	0.36
Dutch	157	1.22
English	1,602	12.43
European	99	0.77
French, except Basque	384	2.98
French Canadian	60	0.47
German	1,794	13.92
Greek	33	0.26
Hawaii Native/Pacific Islander:	55	0.43
Melanesian: (2)	3	0.02
Fijian (2)	3	0.02
Micronesian: (19)	26	0.21
Guamanian/Chamorro (18)	22	0.17
Other Micronesian (1)	4	0.03
Polynesian: (3)	15	0.12
Native Hawaiian (3)	15	0.12
Other Pac. Isl., not spec. (4)	11	0.09
Hispanic or Latino:	1,501	11.86
Central American:	16	0.13
Nicaraguan	7	0.06
Panamanian	7	0.06
Salvadoran	1	0.01
Other Central American	1	0.01
Cuban	8	0.06
Dominican Republic	1	0.01
Mexican	1,240	9.80
Puerto Rican	15	0.12
South American:	5	0.04
Chilean	1	0.01
Colombian	3	0.02
Peruvian	1	0.01
Other Hispanic or Latino	216	1.71
Hungarian	39	0.30
Icelander	7	0.05
Iranian	11	0.09
Irish	1,151	8.93
Italian	548	4.25
Luxemburger	5	0.04
Norwegian	178	1.38
Polish	121	0.94
Portuguese	100	0.78
Romanian	27	0.21
Russian	65	0.50
Scandinavian	7	0.05
Scotch-Irish	105	0.81
Scottish	336	2.61
Slovak	19	0.15
Swedish	145	1.13
Swiss	32	0.25
Ukrainian	13	0.10
United States or American	928	7.20
Welsh	106	0.82
White:	8,450	66.79
Not Hispanic (7,515)	7,784	61.53
Hispanic (575)	666	5.26
Yugoslavian	16	0.12

Spring Valley

Place Type: Census Designated Place
County: San Diego
Population: 26,663

Ancestry/Race	Number	%
Afghan	34	0.13
African American/Black:	3,089	11.59
Not Hispanic (2,632)	2,915	10.93
Hispanic (98)	174	0.65
African, sub-Saharan:	283	1.06
African	241	0.90
Somalian	20	0.08
South African	22	0.08
Alaska Native tribes, specified:	8	0.03
Alaska Athabascan (1)	2	0.01
Aleut (3)	3	0.01
Eskimo (1)	1	0.00
Tlingit-Haida	2	0.01
Am. Ind. or Alaska Nat., not spec.	171	0.64
American Indian tribes, specified:	300	1.13
Apache (5)	11	0.04
Blackfeet (3)	4	0.02
Cherokee (12)	99	0.37
Cheyenne	1	0.00
Chickasaw (3)	7	0.03
Chippewa	6	0.02
Choctaw (13)	25	0.09
Comanche (3)	3	0.01
Cree	6	0.02
Creek (2)	3	0.01
Crow (2)	2	0.01
Iroquois (1)	2	0.01
Latin American Indians (21)	39	0.15
Navajo (3)	6	0.02
Osage (2)	2	0.01
Pueblo (3)	9	0.03
Seminole	7	0.03
Shoshone (1)	1	0.00
Sioux (7)	22	0.08
Yaqui (3)	4	0.02
All other tribes (23)	41	0.15
American Indian tribes, not spec.	23	0.09
Arab:	537	2.02
Arab/Arabic	114	0.43
Egyptian	5	0.02
Iraqi	271	1.02
Lebanese	98	0.37
Palestinian	32	0.12
Syrian	11	0.04
Other Arab	6	0.02
Armenian	61	0.23
Asian:	1,910	7.16
Bangladeshi	2	0.01
Cambodian (22)	28	0.11
Chinese, ex. Taiwanese (83)	169	0.63
Filipino (721)	1,068	4.01
Indian (56)	79	0.30
Indonesian (2)	12	0.05
Japanese (131)	243	0.91
Korean (46)	64	0.24
Laotian (17)	20	0.08
Malaysian	7	0.03
Pakistani (3)	4	0.02
Sri Lankan (1)	1	0.00

Notes: 1. Figures in the "Number" column do not add up to the total population due to: a) Ancestry/Race overlap — e.g. persons can report being both White and Irish, b) persons of Hispanic origin can report being any race, c) persons reporting two ancestries are counted in both categories. 2. Numbers in parentheses indicate the number of persons reporting this ancestry/race alone, not in combination with any other ancestry/race. 3. Refer to the Explanation of Data in the front of the book for more detailed information.

Taiwanese (8)	9	0.03
Thai (11)	21	0.08
Vietnamese (127)	138	0.52
Other Asian, not specified (8)	45	0.17
Assyrian/Chaldean/Syriac	277	1.04
Australian	32	0.12
Austrian	79	0.30
Belgian	33	0.12
Brazilian	7	0.03
British	126	0.47
Canadian	172	0.65
Celtic	19	0.07
Czech	77	0.29
Czechoslovakian	32	0.12
Danish	207	0.78
Dutch	365	1.37
Eastern European	12	0.05
English	2,661	9.99
European	281	1.05
Finnish	143	0.54
French, except Basque	722	2.71
French Canadian	276	1.04
German	3,614	13.56
Greek	58	0.22
Guyanese	15	0.06
Hawaii Native/Pacific Islander:	361	1.35
Micronesian: (89)	162	0.61
Guamanian/Chamorro (88)	161	0.60
Other Micronesian (1)	1	0.00
Polynesian: (42)	160	0.60
Native Hawaiian (28)	114	0.43
Samoan (9)	41	0.15
Tongan (5)	5	0.02
Other Pac. Isl., not spec. (7)	39	0.15
Hispanic or Latino:	5,726	21.48
Central American:	66	0.25
Costa Rican	5	0.02
Guatemalan	26	0.10
Honduran	8	0.03
Nicaraguan	3	0.01
Panamanian	10	0.04
Salvadoran	8	0.03
Other Central American	6	0.02
Cuban	27	0.10
Dominican Republic	12	0.05
Mexican	4,707	17.65
Puerto Rican	214	0.80
South American:	44	0.17
Argentinean	4	0.02
Chilean	9	0.03
Colombian	24	0.09
Ecuadorian	1	0.00
Peruvian	1	0.00
Venezuelan	1	0.00
Other South American	4	0.02
Other Hispanic or Latino	656	2.46
Hungarian	102	0.38
Icelander	57	0.21
Iranian	37	0.14
Irish	2,745	10.30
Italian	1,282	4.81
Lithuanian	116	0.44
New Zealander	24	0.09
Norwegian	398	1.49
Pennsylvania German	3	0.01
Polish	499	1.87
Portuguese	279	1.05
Romanian	6	0.02
Russian	148	0.56
Scandinavian	56	0.21
Scotch-Irish	464	1.74
Scottish	453	1.70
Slavic	5	0.02
Slovak	4	0.02
Slovene	6	0.02
Swedish	382	1.43
Swiss	104	0.39
Ukrainian	30	0.11
United States or American	851	3.19
Welsh	182	0.68
West Indian, excl. Hispanic:	44	0.17
Jamaican	28	0.11
Trinidadian and Tobagonian	8	0.03
West Indian	8	0.03
White:	19,529	73.24
Not Hispanic (15,592)	16,565	62.13
Hispanic (2,561)	2,964	11.12
Yugoslavian	6	0.02

Stanford

Place Type: Census Designated Place
County: Santa Clara
Population: 13,315

Ancestry/Race	Number	%
African American/Black:	764	5.74
Not Hispanic (632)	735	5.52
Hispanic (21)	29	0.22
African, sub-Saharan:	171	1.29
African	6	0.05
Cape Verdean	7	0.05
Ethiopian	22	0.17
Ghanian	17	0.13
Nigerian	82	0.62
South African	29	0.22
Other sub-Saharan African	8	0.06
Alaska Native tribes, specified:	5	0.04
Alaska Athabascan (2)	2	0.02
Eskimo (3)	3	0.02
Am. Ind. or Alaska Nat., not spec.	74	0.56
Albanian	7	0.05
American Indian tribes, specified:	106	0.80
Apache (4)	5	0.04
Blackfeet (1)	3	0.02
Cherokee (1)	18	0.14
Chickasaw	1	0.01
Chippewa (3)	7	0.05
Choctaw (1)	3	0.02
Creek (1)	4	0.03
Delaware	1	0.01
Iroquois (1)	2	0.02
Kiowa (1)	1	0.01
Latin American Indians (2)	7	0.05
Lumbee (1)	1	0.01
Navajo (14)	17	0.13
Pima (1)	1	0.01
Potawatomi	1	0.01
Pueblo (2)	3	0.02
Puget Sound Salish (1)	1	0.01
Sioux (6)	7	0.05
Tohono O'Odham (2)	2	0.02
Yaqui (1)	2	0.02
All other tribes (8)	19	0.14
American Indian tribes, not spec.	11	0.08
Arab:	135	1.01
Egyptian	54	0.41
Jordanian	7	0.05
Lebanese	58	0.44
Syrian	8	0.06
Other Arab	8	0.06
Armenian	67	0.50
Asian:	3,841	28.85
Bangladeshi (4)	4	0.03
Cambodian (6)	7	0.05
Chinese, ex. Taiwanese (1,563)	1,740	13.07
Filipino (54)	105	0.79
Hmong (1)	1	0.01
Indian (602)	642	4.82
Indonesian (4)	10	0.08
Japanese (204)	293	2.20
Korean (480)	522	3.92
Malaysian (7)	8	0.06
Pakistani (27)	31	0.23
Sri Lankan (10)	12	0.09
Taiwanese (175)	200	1.50
Thai (30)	41	0.31
Vietnamese (63)	76	0.57
Other Asian, specified (17)	20	0.15
Other Asian, not specified (84)	129	0.97
Assyrian/Chaldean/Syriac	8	0.06
Australian	43	0.32
Austrian	67	0.50
Basque	21	0.16
Belgian	31	0.23
Brazilian	21	0.16
British	210	1.58
Bulgarian	15	0.11
Canadian	93	0.70
Croatian	56	0.42
Czech	38	0.29
Czechoslovakian	17	0.13
Danish	83	0.62
Dutch	182	1.37
Eastern European	98	0.74
English	1,165	8.75
European	248	1.86
Finnish	63	0.47
French, except Basque	313	2.35
French Canadian	15	0.11
German	1,352	10.16
Greek	93	0.70
Guyanese	4	0.03
Hawaii Native/Pacific Islander:	48	0.36
Micronesian: (3)	4	0.03
Guamanian/Chamorro (3)	4	0.03
Polynesian: (11)	28	0.21
Native Hawaiian (8)	20	0.15
Samoan (3)	8	0.06
Other Pac. Isl., not spec. (6)	16	0.12
Hispanic or Latino:	1,193	8.96
Central American:	38	0.29
Costa Rican	2	0.02
Guatemalan	9	0.07
Honduran	2	0.02
Nicaraguan	5	0.04
Panamanian	10	0.08
Salvadoran	6	0.05
Other Central American	4	0.03
Cuban	18	0.14
Dominican Republic	5	0.04
Mexican	798	5.99
Puerto Rican	38	0.29
South American:	152	1.14
Argentinean	31	0.23
Bolivian	2	0.02
Chilean	19	0.14
Colombian	57	0.43
Ecuadorian	9	0.07
Peruvian	11	0.08
Uruguayan	5	0.04
Venezuelan	15	0.11
Other South American	3	0.02
Other Hispanic or Latino	144	1.08
Hungarian	63	0.47
Icelander	19	0.14
Iranian	43	0.32
Irish	968	7.27
Israeli	60	0.45
Italian	560	4.21
Latvian	31	0.23
Lithuanian	56	0.42
New Zealander	8	0.06
Northern European	13	0.10
Norwegian	309	2.32
Polish	386	2.90
Portuguese	32	0.24
Romanian	48	0.36
Russian	433	3.25
Scandinavian	55	0.41
Scotch-Irish	194	1.46
Scottish	332	2.49
Serbian	7	0.05
Slovak	37	0.28
Slovene	45	0.34
Swedish	213	1.60
Swiss	80	0.60
Turkish	72	0.54
Ukrainian	78	0.59
United States or American	236	1.77

Notes: 1. Figures in the "Number" column do not add up to the total population due to: a) Ancestry/Race overlap — e.g. persons can report being both White and Irish, b) persons of Hispanic origin can report being any race, c) persons reporting two ancestries are counted in both categories. 2. Numbers in parentheses indicate the number of persons reporting this ancestry/race alone, not in combination with any other ancestry/race. 3. Refer to the Explanation of Data in the front of the book for more detailed information.

Welsh	109	0.82
West Indian, excl. Hispanic:	51	0.38
Bermudan	6	0.05
British West Indian	10	0.08
Jamaican	20	0.15
West Indian	15	0.11
White:	8,543	64.16
Not Hispanic (7,453)	7,863	59.05
Hispanic (589)	680	5.11

Stanton

Place Type: City
County: Orange
Population: 37,403

Ancestry/Race	Number	%
Afghan	11	0.03
African American/Black:	1,015	2.71
Not Hispanic (721)	823	2.20
Hispanic (127)	192	0.51
African, sub-Saharan:	122	0.33
African	64	0.17
Ethiopian	19	0.05
Somalian	39	0.11
Alaska Native tribes, specified:	4	0.01
Aleut (1)	1	0.00
Tlingit-Haida (3)	3	0.01
Am. Ind. or Alaska Nat., not spec.	241	0.64
American Indian tribes, specified:	349	0.93
Apache (15)	22	0.06
Blackfeet (1)	6	0.02
Cherokee (19)	60	0.16
Cheyenne (2)	4	0.01
Chickasaw (2)	4	0.01
Chippewa (3)	4	0.01
Choctaw (9)	13	0.03
Comanche (1)	4	0.01
Cree (1)	1	0.00
Creek (3)	5	0.01
Crow (1)	1	0.00
Delaware (3)	7	0.02
Iroquois (3)	6	0.02
Latin American Indians (87)	111	0.30
Lumbee (1)	2	0.01
Menominee	1	0.00
Navajo (7)	9	0.02
Osage	1	0.00
Pima	4	0.01
Pueblo (24)	25	0.07
Seminole	1	0.00
Shoshone	5	0.01
Sioux (5)	5	0.01
Ute (1)	2	0.01
Yuman (3)	5	0.01
All other tribes (27)	41	0.11
American Indian tribes, not spec.	39	0.10
Arab:	157	0.43
Arab/Arabic	39	0.11
Egyptian	9	0.02
Lebanese	77	0.21
Moroccan	4	0.01
Palestinian	21	0.06
Syrian	7	0.02
Armenian	60	0.16
Asian:	6,422	17.17
Bangladeshi (4)	4	0.01
Cambodian (67)	76	0.20
Chinese, ex. Taiwanese (219)	323	0.86
Filipino (972)	1,182	3.16
Hmong (31)	44	0.12
Indian (217)	255	0.68
Indonesian (16)	40	0.11
Japanese (211)	304	0.81
Korean (728)	750	2.01
Laotian (75)	104	0.28
Malaysian (3)	7	0.02
Pakistani (29)	42	0.11
Sri Lankan (23)	27	0.07
Taiwanese (12)	18	0.05
Thai (29)	42	0.11
Vietnamese (3,010)	3,117	8.33
Other Asian, specified (1)	8	0.02
Other Asian, not specified (22)	79	0.21
Assyrian/Chaldean/Syriac	28	0.08
Austrian	21	0.06
Belgian	10	0.03
Brazilian	43	0.12
British	49	0.13
Bulgarian	14	0.04
Canadian	79	0.21
Celtic	26	0.07
Croatian	5	0.01
Czech	49	0.13
Czechoslovakian	8	0.02
Danish	110	0.30
Dutch	339	0.92
English	1,510	4.09
European	182	0.49
Finnish	5	0.01
French, except Basque	427	1.16
French Canadian	153	0.41
German	2,277	6.17
Greek	113	0.31
Hawaii Native/Pacific Islander:	522	1.40
Melanesian:	1	0.00
Fijian	1	0.00
Micronesian: (33)	55	0.15
Guamanian/Chamorro (30)	52	0.14
Other Micronesian (3)	3	0.01
Polynesian: (299)	417	1.11
Native Hawaiian (50)	119	0.32
Samoan (221)	258	0.69
Tongan (22)	30	0.08
Other Polynesian (6)	10	0.03
Other Pac. Isl., specified	5	0.01
Other Pac. Isl., not spec. (2)	44	0.12
Hispanic or Latino:	18,285	48.89
Central American:	422	1.13
Costa Rican	19	0.05
Guatemalan	121	0.32
Honduran	40	0.11
Nicaraguan	33	0.09
Panamanian	7	0.02
Salvadoran	155	0.41
Other Central American	47	0.13
Cuban	56	0.15
Dominican Republic	1	0.00
Mexican	15,496	41.43
Puerto Rican	180	0.48
South American:	218	0.58
Argentinean	19	0.05
Bolivian	17	0.05
Chilean	13	0.03
Colombian	33	0.09
Ecuadorian	22	0.06
Peruvian	93	0.25
Uruguayan	1	0.00
Venezuelan	3	0.01
Other South American	17	0.05
Other Hispanic or Latino	1,912	5.11
Hungarian	87	0.24
Iranian	63	0.17
Irish	1,703	4.61
Italian	863	2.34
Latvian	10	0.03
Lithuanian	17	0.05
Maltese	8	0.02
New Zealander	21	0.06
Northern European	24	0.06
Norwegian	309	0.84
Polish	372	1.01
Portuguese	86	0.23
Romanian	147	0.40
Russian	99	0.27
Scandinavian	4	0.01
Scotch-Irish	241	0.65
Scottish	323	0.87
Serbian	13	0.04
Slovak	18	0.05
Slovene	5	0.01
Swedish	278	0.75
Swiss	96	0.26
Ukrainian	9	0.02
United States or American	968	2.62
Welsh	129	0.35
West Indian, excl. Hispanic:	37	0.10
Barbadian	5	0.01
Jamaican	24	0.06
West Indian	8	0.02
White:	20,065	53.65
Not Hispanic (11,295)	11,948	31.94
Hispanic (7,246)	8,117	21.70
Yugoslavian	6	0.02

Stockton

Place Type: City
County: San Joaquin
Population: 243,771

Ancestry/Race	Number	%
Acadian/Cajun	8	0.00
Afghan	34	0.01
African American/Black:	30,486	12.51
Not Hispanic (26,359)	28,681	11.77
Hispanic (1,058)	1,805	0.74
African, sub-Saharan:	1,833	0.76
African	1,586	0.65
Cape Verdean	9	0.00
Ethiopian	3	0.00
Ghanian	7	0.00
Kenyan	4	0.00
Liberian	89	0.04
Nigerian	122	0.05
South African	8	0.00
Zimbabwean	5	0.00
Alaska Native tribes, specified:	64	0.03
Alaska Athabascan (2)	2	0.00
Aleut (15)	26	0.01
Eskimo (1)	4	0.00
Tlingit-Haida (8)	30	0.01
All other tribes	2	0.00
Alaska Native tribes, not specified	12	0.00
Am. Ind. or Alaska Nat., not spec.	2,027	0.83
Albanian	18	0.01
Alsatian	7	0.00
American Indian tribes, specified:	3,430	1.41
Apache (160)	300	0.12
Blackfeet (23)	135	0.06
Cherokee (267)	1,035	0.42
Cheyenne (3)	20	0.01
Chickasaw (14)	30	0.01
Chippewa (25)	59	0.02
Choctaw (66)	177	0.07
Colville (3)	3	0.00
Comanche (3)	19	0.01
Cree	8	0.00
Creek (17)	38	0.02
Crow (2)	6	0.00
Delaware (20)	23	0.01
Houma	1	0.00
Iroquois (5)	15	0.01
Kiowa (3)	5	0.00
Latin American Indians (229)	374	0.15
Lumbee (3)	10	0.00
Menominee	7	0.00
Navajo (98)	199	0.08
Osage (5)	12	0.00
Ottawa (1)	5	0.00
Paiute (13)	18	0.01
Pima (7)	9	0.00
Potawatomi (28)	47	0.02
Pueblo (21)	41	0.02
Puget Sound Salish (5)	5	0.00
Seminole (4)	16	0.01
Shoshone (19)	25	0.01
Sioux (86)	149	0.06
Tohono O'Odham (4)	10	0.00
Ute (6)	7	0.00

Notes: 1. Figures in the "Number" column do not add up to the total population due to: a) Ancestry/Race overlap — e.g. persons can report being both White and Irish, b) persons of Hispanic origin can report being any race, c) persons reporting two ancestries are counted in both categories. 2. Numbers in parentheses indicate the number of persons reporting this ancestry/race alone, not in combination with any other ancestry/race. 3. Refer to the Explanation of Data in the front of the book for more detailed information.

Ancestry/Race	Number	%
Yakama (2)	3	0.00
Yaqui (28)	65	0.03
Yuman (12)	18	0.01
All other tribes (298)	536	0.22
American Indian tribes, not spec.	353	0.14
Arab:	1,214	0.50
Arab/Arabic	341	0.14
Egyptian	27	0.01
Iraqi	10	0.00
Jordanian	47	0.02
Lebanese	471	0.19
Palestinian	51	0.02
Syrian	168	0.07
Other Arab	99	0.04
Armenian	177	0.07
Asian:	57,387	23.54
Cambodian (9,096)	10,202	4.19
Chinese, ex. Taiwanese (4,216)	5,114	2.10
Filipino (15,219)	19,232	7.89
Hmong (4,896)	5,401	2.22
Indian (2,270)	2,892	1.19
Indonesian (20)	51	0.02
Japanese (1,531)	2,253	0.92
Korean (375)	548	0.22
Laotian (2,790)	3,367	1.38
Malaysian (12)	19	0.01
Pakistani (547)	822	0.34
Sri Lankan (5)	8	0.00
Taiwanese (69)	85	0.03
Thai (119)	205	0.08
Vietnamese (5,477)	5,755	2.36
Other Asian, specified (10)	26	0.01
Other Asian, not specified (720)	1,407	0.58
Assyrian/Chaldean/Syriac	42	0.02
Australian	108	0.04
Austrian	178	0.07
Basque	333	0.14
Belgian	57	0.02
Brazilian	37	0.02
British	488	0.20
Canadian	370	0.15
Celtic	56	0.02
Croatian	131	0.05
Czech	333	0.14
Czechoslovakian	134	0.06
Danish	926	0.38
Dutch	2,334	0.96
Eastern European	30	0.01
English	11,557	4.76
European	1,312	0.54
Finnish	215	0.09
French, except Basque	3,971	1.64
French Canadian	527	0.22
German	18,587	7.66
German Russian	25	0.01
Greek	635	0.26
Hawaii Native/Pacific Islander:	2,477	1.02
Melanesian: (106)	152	0.06
Fijian (106)	151	0.06
Other Melanesian	1	0.00
Micronesian: (232)	317	0.13
Guamanian/Chamorro (197)	272	0.11
Other Micronesian (35)	45	0.02
Polynesian: (461)	1,003	0.41
Native Hawaiian (175)	529	0.22
Samoan (243)	378	0.16
Tongan (37)	71	0.03
Other Polynesian (6)	25	0.01
Other Pac. Isl., specified	9	0.00
Other Pac. Isl., not spec. (168)	996	0.41
Hispanic or Latino:	79,217	32.50
Central American:	1,073	0.44
Costa Rican	29	0.01
Guatemalan	289	0.12
Honduran	40	0.02
Nicaraguan	232	0.10
Panamanian	51	0.02
Salvadoran	340	0.14
Other Central American	92	0.04
Cuban	175	0.07
Dominican Republic	21	0.01
Mexican	66,900	27.44
Puerto Rican	1,056	0.43
South American:	439	0.18
Argentinean	27	0.01
Bolivian	6	0.00
Chilean	128	0.05
Colombian	79	0.03
Ecuadorian	46	0.02
Peruvian	76	0.03
Uruguayan	9	0.00
Venezuelan	26	0.01
Other South American	42	0.02
Other Hispanic or Latino	9,553	3.92
Hungarian	370	0.15
Icelander	38	0.02
Iranian	165	0.07
Irish	13,056	5.38
Israeli	6	0.00
Italian	9,534	3.93
Latvian	6	0.00
Lithuanian	145	0.06
Luxemburger	18	0.01
Maltese	24	0.01
New Zealander	42	0.02
Northern European	142	0.06
Norwegian	2,183	0.90
Pennsylvania German	67	0.03
Polish	1,148	0.47
Portuguese	3,129	1.29
Romanian	92	0.04
Russian	731	0.30
Scandinavian	240	0.10
Scotch-Irish	1,914	0.79
Scottish	2,251	0.93
Serbian	79	0.03
Slavic	59	0.02
Slovak	93	0.04
Slovene	6	0.00
Swedish	2,186	0.90
Swiss	442	0.18
Turkish	15	0.01
Ukrainian	163	0.07
United States or American	4,950	2.04
Welsh	1,183	0.49
West Indian, excl. Hispanic:	213	0.09
British West Indian	12	0.00
Dutch West Indian	21	0.01
Haitian	39	0.02
Jamaican	71	0.03
West Indian	70	0.03
White:	116,389	47.75
Not Hispanic (78,539)	84,503	34.66
Hispanic (26,907)	31,886	13.08
Yugoslavian	135	0.06

Suisun City

Place Type: City
County: Solano
Population: 26,118

Ancestry/Race	Number	%
Acadian/Cajun	3	0.01
Afghan	76	0.29
African American/Black:	5,655	21.65
Not Hispanic (4,904)	5,364	20.54
Hispanic (140)	291	1.11
African, sub-Saharan:	136	0.52
African	136	0.52
Alaska Native tribes, specified:	9	0.03
Alaska Athabascan	1	0.00
Aleut (2)	3	0.01
Eskimo	3	0.01
Tlingit-Haida (1)	2	0.01
Alaska Native tribes, not specified	1	0.00
Am. Ind. or Alaska Nat., not spec.	174	0.67
American Indian tribes, specified:	380	1.45
Apache (6)	22	0.08
Blackfeet (4)	19	0.07
Cherokee (18)	125	0.48
Cheyenne (1)	4	0.02
Chickasaw (7)	8	0.03
Chippewa (1)	2	0.01
Choctaw (8)	24	0.09
Comanche	1	0.00
Cree	1	0.00
Creek (5)	16	0.06
Crow	5	0.02
Delaware	1	0.00
Iroquois (1)	4	0.02
Kiowa (3)	3	0.01
Latin American Indians (11)	12	0.05
Navajo (4)	17	0.07
Osage (1)	4	0.02
Paiute	3	0.01
Pima (1)	2	0.01
Potawatomi (1)	1	0.00
Pueblo (7)	11	0.04
Puget Sound Salish	1	0.00
Seminole (1)	2	0.01
Shoshone (1)	1	0.00
Sioux (1)	13	0.05
Ute	4	0.02
Yuman	1	0.00
All other tribes (30)	73	0.28
American Indian tribes, not spec.	16	0.06
Arab:	125	0.48
Arab/Arabic	15	0.06
Jordanian	14	0.05
Lebanese	19	0.07
Moroccan	5	0.02
Palestinian	72	0.28
Asian:	5,774	22.11
Cambodian (10)	10	0.04
Chinese, ex. Taiwanese (248)	399	1.53
Filipino (2,967)	3,597	13.77
Hmong (135)	136	0.52
Indian (264)	311	1.19
Indonesian (10)	21	0.08
Japanese (172)	362	1.39
Korean (74)	137	0.52
Laotian (249)	268	1.03
Malaysian (2)	12	0.05
Pakistani (11)	11	0.04
Sri Lankan (3)	4	0.02
Taiwanese (4)	4	0.02
Thai (75)	111	0.42
Vietnamese (268)	290	1.11
Other Asian, specified	7	0.03
Other Asian, not specified (41)	94	0.36
Australian	16	0.06
Austrian	10	0.04
Basque	7	0.03
Brazilian	15	0.06
British	60	0.23
Canadian	57	0.22
Celtic	28	0.11
Croatian	15	0.06
Czech	67	0.26
Czechoslovakian	48	0.18
Danish	127	0.49
Dutch	189	0.73
English	1,547	5.94
Estonian	22	0.08
European	226	0.87
Finnish	20	0.08
French, except Basque	731	2.81
French Canadian	120	0.46
German	2,389	9.17
Greek	78	0.30
Hawaii Native/Pacific Islander:	618	2.37
Melanesian: (8)	13	0.05
Fijian (8)	13	0.05
Micronesian: (150)	259	0.99
Guamanian/Chamorro (149)	257	0.98
Other Micronesian (1)	2	0.01
Polynesian: (71)	236	0.90
Native Hawaiian (38)	168	0.64
Samoan (27)	50	0.19

Notes: 1. Figures in the "Number" column do not add up to the total population due to: a) Ancestry/Race overlap — e.g. persons can report being both White and Irish, b) persons of Hispanic origin can report being any race, c) persons reporting two ancestries are counted in both categories. 2. Numbers in parentheses indicate the number of persons reporting this ancestry/race alone, not in combination with any other ancestry/race. 3. Refer to the Explanation of Data in the front of the book for more detailed information.

Tongan (4)	12	0.05
Other Polynesian (2)	6	0.02
Other Pac. Isl., specified	3	0.01
Other Pac. Isl., not spec. (30)	107	0.41
Hispanic or Latino:	4,652	17.81
Central American:	309	1.18
Costa Rican	8	0.03
Guatemalan	25	0.10
Honduran	9	0.03
Nicaraguan	94	0.36
Panamanian	25	0.10
Salvadoran	98	0.38
Other Central American	50	0.19
Cuban	28	0.11
Dominican Republic	5	0.02
Mexican	3,042	11.65
Puerto Rican	246	0.94
South American:	65	0.25
Argentinean	1	0.00
Bolivian	8	0.03
Chilean	9	0.03
Colombian	8	0.03
Ecuadorian	5	0.02
Peruvian	25	0.10
Uruguayan	1	0.00
Venezuelan	4	0.02
Other South American	4	0.02
Other Hispanic or Latino	957	3.66
Hungarian	53	0.20
Iranian	36	0.14
Irish	1,916	7.36
Italian	911	3.50
Lithuanian	22	0.08
Norwegian	442	1.70
Polish	352	1.35
Portuguese	332	1.27
Romanian	5	0.02
Russian	70	0.27
Scandinavian	43	0.17
Scotch-Irish	178	0.68
Scottish	246	0.94
Serbian	18	0.07
Slavic	13	0.05
Slovene	5	0.02
Swedish	303	1.16
Swiss	21	0.08
Turkish	25	0.10
Ukrainian	9	0.03
United States or American	763	2.93
Welsh	144	0.55
West Indian, excl. Hispanic:	124	0.48
Dutch West Indian	7	0.03
Haitian	6	0.02
Jamaican	74	0.28
Trinidadian and Tobagonian	9	0.03
West Indian	17	0.07
Other West Indian	11	0.04
White:	13,209	50.57
Not Hispanic (10,091)	11,178	42.80
Hispanic (1,515)	2,031	7.78
Yugoslavian	11	0.04

Sun City

Place Type: Census Designated Place
County: Riverside
Population: 17,773

Ancestry/Race	Number	%
African American/Black:	435	2.45
Not Hispanic (367)	411	2.31
Hispanic (11)	24	0.14
African, sub-Saharan:	34	0.19
African	34	0.19
Am. Ind. or Alaska Nat., not spec.	86	0.48
Alsatian	9	0.05
American Indian tribes, specified:	167	0.94
Apache (2)	7	0.04
Blackfeet (1)	9	0.05
Cherokee (12)	39	0.22
Chippewa (2)	2	0.01
Choctaw (1)	6	0.03
Comanche	3	0.02
Creek (2)	3	0.02
Crow (1)	1	0.01
Iroquois (2)	8	0.05
Latin American Indians (8)	37	0.21
Lumbee	1	0.01
Navajo (6)	7	0.04
Potawatomi	1	0.01
Pueblo (4)	7	0.04
Seminole	2	0.01
Sioux (3)	7	0.04
Tohono O'Odham (1)	2	0.01
Yaqui (1)	6	0.03
All other tribes (13)	19	0.11
American Indian tribes, not spec.	2	0.01
Arab:	84	0.47
Lebanese	73	0.41
Syrian	11	0.06
Armenian	7	0.04
Asian:	345	1.94
Chinese, ex. Taiwanese (14)	37	0.21
Filipino (84)	119	0.67
Hmong	1	0.01
Indian (10)	23	0.13
Indonesian (5)	13	0.07
Japanese (57)	97	0.55
Korean (17)	24	0.14
Laotian (3)	3	0.02
Malaysian	3	0.02
Taiwanese	1	0.01
Thai (2)	3	0.02
Vietnamese (14)	17	0.10
Other Asian, not specified	4	0.02
Australian	7	0.04
Austrian	88	0.49
Basque	19	0.11
Belgian	47	0.26
British	43	0.24
Canadian	103	0.58
Croatian	15	0.08
Czech	76	0.43
Czechoslovakian	113	0.63
Danish	155	0.87
Dutch	447	2.50
English	2,909	16.30
European	201	1.13
Finnish	44	0.25
French, except Basque	898	5.03
French Canadian	131	0.73
German	3,081	17.26
Greek	47	0.26
Hawaii Native/Pacific Islander:	45	0.25
Melanesian:	1	0.01
Other Melanesian	1	0.01
Micronesian: (8)	9	0.05
Guamanian/Chamorro (8)	9	0.05
Polynesian: (14)	25	0.14
Native Hawaiian (1)	12	0.07
Samoan (13)	13	0.07
Other Pac. Isl., not spec. (4)	10	0.06
Hispanic or Latino:	2,187	12.31
Central American:	44	0.25
Costa Rican	3	0.02
Guatemalan	11	0.06
Honduran	2	0.01
Nicaraguan	7	0.04
Panamanian	8	0.05
Salvadoran	9	0.05
Other Central American	4	0.02
Cuban	30	0.17
Dominican Republic	1	0.01
Mexican	1,628	9.16
Puerto Rican	77	0.43
South American:	43	0.24
Argentinean	4	0.02
Chilean	7	0.04
Colombian	9	0.05
Ecuadorian	6	0.03
Peruvian	12	0.07
Venezuelan	4	0.02
Other South American	1	0.01
Other Hispanic or Latino	364	2.05
Hungarian	214	1.20
Icelander	10	0.06
Iranian	13	0.07
Irish	2,529	14.17
Italian	1,063	5.96
Latvian	8	0.04
Lithuanian	99	0.55
Luxemburger	16	0.09
New Zealander	8	0.04
Norwegian	479	2.68
Pennsylvania German	41	0.23
Polish	568	3.18
Portuguese	20	0.11
Romanian	43	0.24
Russian	133	0.75
Scandinavian	102	0.57
Scotch-Irish	678	3.80
Scottish	470	2.63
Serbian	34	0.19
Slavic	7	0.04
Slovak	7	0.04
Slovene	22	0.12
Swedish	565	3.17
Swiss	54	0.30
Turkish	8	0.04
Ukrainian	25	0.14
United States or American	1,090	6.11
Welsh	105	0.59
White:	16,293	91.67
Not Hispanic (14,684)	14,910	83.89
Hispanic (1,246)	1,383	7.78
Yugoslavian	8	0.04

Sunnyvale

Place Type: City
County: Santa Clara
Population: 131,760

Ancestry/Race	Number	%
Afghan	65	0.05
African American/Black:	3,599	2.73
Not Hispanic (2,790)	3,337	2.53
Hispanic (137)	262	0.20
African, sub-Saharan:	261	0.20
African	155	0.12
Cape Verdean	18	0.01
Ethiopian	19	0.01
Kenyan	33	0.03
Somalian	11	0.01
South African	14	0.01
Other sub-Saharan African	11	0.01
Alaska Native tribes, specified:	11	0.01
Alaska Athabascan	2	0.00
Aleut (3)	4	0.00
Eskimo (1)	1	0.00
Tlingit-Haida (1)	4	0.00
Alaska Native tribes, not specified	1	0.00
Am. Ind. or Alaska Nat., not spec.	459	0.35
Albanian	34	0.03
Alsatian	7	0.01
American Indian tribes, specified:	908	0.69
Apache (19)	44	0.03
Blackfeet (10)	26	0.02
Cherokee (65)	241	0.18
Cheyenne	10	0.01
Chickasaw (4)	13	0.01
Chippewa (15)	26	0.02
Choctaw (18)	55	0.04
Colville (2)	3	0.00
Comanche (2)	4	0.00
Cree (2)	5	0.00
Creek (4)	15	0.01
Crow (2)	3	0.00
Delaware (2)	4	0.00
Iroquois (6)	19	0.01

Notes: 1. Figures in the "Number" column do not add up to the total population due to: a) Ancestry/Race overlap — e.g. persons can report being both White and Irish, b) persons of Hispanic origin can report being any race, c) persons reporting two ancestries are counted in both categories. 2. Numbers in parentheses indicate the number of persons reporting this ancestry/race alone, not in combination with any other ancestry/race. 3. Refer to the Explanation of Data in the front of the book for more detailed information.

Kiowa	4	0.00
Latin American Indians (90)	145	0.11
Lumbee	1	0.00
Menominee	1	0.00
Navajo (25)	45	0.03
Osage (4)	5	0.00
Ottawa (4)	4	0.00
Paiute (1)	4	0.00
Pima (1)	3	0.00
Potawatomi (1)	4	0.00
Pueblo (9)	15	0.01
Puget Sound Salish (2)	6	0.00
Seminole (4)	14	0.01
Shoshone	1	0.00
Sioux (21)	44	0.03
Tohono O'Odham (2)	6	0.00
Ute (2)	4	0.00
Yakama	5	0.00
Yaqui (18)	25	0.02
Yuman	1	0.00
All other tribes (44)	103	0.08
American Indian tribes, not spec.	78	0.06
Arab:	858	0.65
Arab/Arabic	23	0.02
Egyptian	119	0.09
Iraqi	59	0.04
Jordanian	24	0.02
Lebanese	218	0.17
Moroccan	63	0.05
Palestinian	114	0.09
Syrian	128	0.10
Other Arab	110	0.08
Armenian	329	0.25
Asian:	45,822	34.78
Bangladeshi (54)	77	0.06
Cambodian (40)	63	0.05
Chinese, ex. Taiwanese (12,085)	13,063	9.91
Filipino (6,050)	6,880	5.22
Hmong (5)	7	0.01
Indian (13,124)	13,443	10.20
Indonesian (71)	138	0.10
Japanese (3,606)	4,261	3.23
Korean (2,430)	2,618	1.99
Laotian (27)	34	0.03
Malaysian (27)	48	0.04
Pakistani (173)	234	0.18
Sri Lankan (58)	63	0.05
Taiwanese (512)	628	0.48
Thai (118)	139	0.11
Vietnamese (3,249)	3,478	2.64
Other Asian, specified (71)	103	0.08
Other Asian, not specified (243)	545	0.41
Assyrian/Chaldean/Syriac	62	0.05
Australian	115	0.09
Austrian	330	0.25
Basque	21	0.02
Belgian	168	0.13
Brazilian	79	0.06
British	815	0.62
Bulgarian	108	0.08
Canadian	515	0.39
Celtic	74	0.06
Croatian	528	0.40
Cypriot	6	0.00
Czech	453	0.34
Czechoslovakian	219	0.17
Danish	891	0.68
Dutch	1,230	0.93
Eastern European	198	0.15
English	10,023	7.60
Estonian	5	0.00
European	1,631	1.24
Finnish	342	0.26
French, except Basque	3,108	2.36
French Canadian	559	0.42
German	12,640	9.58
German Russian	6	0.00
Greek	633	0.48
Guyanese	6	0.00
Hawaii Native/Pacific Islander:	900	0.68
Melanesian: (30)	33	0.03
Fijian (30)	32	0.02
Other Melanesian	1	0.00
Micronesian: (103)	155	0.12
Guamanian/Chamorro (100)	152	0.12
Other Micronesian (3)	3	0.00
Polynesian: (264)	526	0.40
Native Hawaiian (88)	306	0.23
Samoan (131)	149	0.11
Tongan (36)	55	0.04
Other Polynesian (9)	16	0.01
Other Pac. Isl., specified	5	0.00
Other Pac. Isl., not spec. (30)	181	0.14
Hispanic or Latino:	20,390	15.48
Central American:	1,093	0.83
Costa Rican	17	0.01
Guatemalan	255	0.19
Honduran	46	0.03
Nicaraguan	108	0.08
Panamanian	31	0.02
Salvadoran	527	0.40
Other Central American	109	0.08
Cuban	129	0.10
Dominican Republic	22	0.02
Mexican	14,405	10.93
Puerto Rican	452	0.34
South American:	718	0.54
Argentinean	42	0.03
Bolivian	72	0.05
Chilean	44	0.03
Colombian	114	0.09
Ecuadorian	25	0.02
Paraguayan	2	0.00
Peruvian	295	0.22
Uruguayan	7	0.01
Venezuelan	39	0.03
Other South American	78	0.06
Other Hispanic or Latino	3,571	2.71
Hungarian	531	0.40
Icelander	22	0.02
Iranian	981	0.74
Irish	8,932	6.77
Israeli	1,003	0.76
Italian	5,720	4.34
Latvian	72	0.05
Lithuanian	161	0.12
Luxemburger	11	0.01
Macedonian	24	0.02
Maltese	16	0.01
New Zealander	4	0.00
Northern European	245	0.19
Norwegian	1,746	1.32
Pennsylvania German	42	0.03
Polish	2,239	1.70
Portuguese	1,519	1.15
Romanian	213	0.16
Russian	1,911	1.45
Scandinavian	196	0.15
Scotch-Irish	1,457	1.10
Scottish	2,136	1.62
Serbian	73	0.06
Slavic	79	0.06
Slovak	346	0.26
Slovene	111	0.08
Swedish	2,073	1.57
Swiss	703	0.53
Turkish	184	0.14
Ukrainian	328	0.25
United States or American	3,103	2.35
Welsh	745	0.56
West Indian, excl. Hispanic:	110	0.08
Belizean	4	0.00
British West Indian	16	0.01
Haitian	11	0.01
Jamaican	16	0.01
Trinidadian and Tobagonian	47	0.04
West Indian	16	0.01
White:	74,769	56.75
Not Hispanic (61,221)	64,440	48.91
Hispanic (8,972)	10,329	7.84
Yugoslavian	223	0.17

Susanville

Place Type: City
County: Lassen
Population: 13,541

Ancestry/Race	Number	%
African American/Black:	1,754	12.95
Not Hispanic (1,682)	1,737	12.83
Hispanic (10)	17	0.13
African, sub-Saharan:	35	0.26
African	35	0.26
Alaska Native tribes, specified:	8	0.06
Alaska Athabascan	1	0.01
Aleut (3)	3	0.02
Eskimo (4)	4	0.03
Am. Ind. or Alaska Nat., not spec.	186	1.37
American Indian tribes, specified:	422	3.12
Apache (1)	3	0.02
Blackfeet (3)	8	0.06
Cherokee (21)	65	0.48
Cheyenne (4)	4	0.03
Chippewa (6)	7	0.05
Choctaw (13)	19	0.14
Colville (1)	1	0.01
Comanche (1)	1	0.01
Cree (2)	5	0.04
Creek	1	0.01
Iroquois (3)	6	0.04
Kiowa (3)	3	0.02
Latin American Indians (3)	10	0.07
Navajo (3)	4	0.03
Osage	1	0.01
Ottawa (4)	4	0.03
Paiute (70)	101	0.75
Pueblo (1)	2	0.01
Seminole (1)	2	0.01
Shoshone (4)	11	0.08
Sioux (3)	3	0.02
Yaqui (8)	11	0.08
All other tribes (85)	150	1.11
American Indian tribes, not spec.	17	0.13
Arab:	41	0.30
Lebanese	7	0.05
Syrian	34	0.25
Asian:	219	1.62
Cambodian (2)	2	0.01
Chinese, ex. Taiwanese (34)	43	0.32
Filipino (48)	70	0.52
Hmong (1)	1	0.01
Indian (14)	17	0.13
Japanese (7)	23	0.17
Korean (7)	16	0.12
Malaysian	1	0.01
Taiwanese (2)	2	0.01
Thai (2)	3	0.02
Vietnamese (11)	12	0.09
Other Asian, specified	5	0.04
Other Asian, not specified (23)	24	0.18
Australian	2	0.01
Austrian	17	0.13
Basque	189	1.39
Belgian	10	0.07
British	9	0.07
Canadian	9	0.07
Croatian	8	0.06
Czech	6	0.04
Czechoslovakian	5	0.04
Danish	90	0.66
Dutch	325	2.39
English	932	6.87
European	53	0.39
Finnish	40	0.29
French, except Basque	307	2.26
French Canadian	40	0.29
German	1,375	10.13
Greek	12	0.09
Hawaii Native/Pacific Islander:	158	1.17

Notes: 1. Figures in the "Number" column do not add up to the total population due to: a) Ancestry/Race overlap — e.g. persons can report being both White and Irish, b) persons of Hispanic origin can report being any race, c) persons reporting two ancestries are counted in both categories. 2. Numbers in parentheses indicate the number of persons reporting this ancestry/race alone, not in combination with any other ancestry/race. 3. Refer to the Explanation of Data in the front of the book for more detailed information.

Micronesian: (71)	73	0.54
Guamanian/Chamorro (1)	1	0.01
Other Micronesian (70)	72	0.53
Polynesian: (22)	58	0.43
Native Hawaiian (16)	29	0.21
Samoan (1)	10	0.07
Tongan (5)	13	0.10
Other Polynesian	6	0.04
Other Pac. Isl., specified	5	0.04
Other Pac. Isl., not spec. (21)	22	0.16
Hispanic or Latino:	2,109	15.57
Central American:	12	0.09
Costa Rican	2	0.01
Guatemalan	4	0.03
Nicaraguan	3	0.02
Panamanian	1	0.01
Salvadoran	2	0.01
Cuban	2	0.01
Mexican	1,869	13.80
Puerto Rican	26	0.19
South American:	1	0.01
Colombian	1	0.01
Other Hispanic or Latino	199	1.47
Hungarian	15	0.11
Irish	1,372	10.11
Italian	542	3.99
Lithuanian	35	0.26
Norwegian	98	0.72
Polish	67	0.49
Portuguese	195	1.44
Scandinavian	12	0.09
Scotch-Irish	156	1.15
Scottish	137	1.01
Slavic	10	0.07
Slovak	8	0.06
Slovene	18	0.13
Swedish	171	1.26
Swiss	28	0.21
Ukrainian	21	0.15
United States or American	408	3.01
Welsh	77	0.57
West Indian, excl. Hispanic:	6	0.04
Dutch West Indian	6	0.04
White:	10,623	78.45
Not Hispanic (8,724)	8,951	66.10
Hispanic (1,571)	1,672	12.35
Yugoslavian	12	0.09

Tamalpais-Homestead Valley

Place Type: Census Designated Place
County: Marin
Population: 10,691

Ancestry/Race	Number	%
Acadian/Cajun	8	0.08
African American/Black:	164	1.53
Not Hispanic (97)	157	1.47
Hispanic (4)	7	0.07
African, sub-Saharan:	52	0.49
African	25	0.24
South African	27	0.25
Alaska Native tribes, not specified	1	0.01
Am. Ind. or Alaska Nat., not spec.	33	0.31
American Indian tribes, specified:	58	0.54
Blackfeet	2	0.02
Cherokee (1)	24	0.22
Choctaw (3)	7	0.07
Creek (1)	1	0.01
Iroquois (1)	3	0.03
Latin American Indians (2)	3	0.03
Shoshone	1	0.01
Sioux	1	0.01
Yaqui	1	0.01
All other tribes (5)	15	0.14
American Indian tribes, not spec.	1	0.01
Arab:	78	0.74
Egyptian	15	0.14
Lebanese	46	0.43
Syrian	17	0.16
Armenian	26	0.25
Asian:	699	6.54
Chinese, ex. Taiwanese (216)	272	2.54
Filipino (44)	83	0.78
Indian (57)	67	0.63
Indonesian (3)	4	0.04
Japanese (123)	170	1.59
Korean (41)	53	0.50
Laotian	1	0.01
Taiwanese (3)	3	0.03
Thai (10)	15	0.14
Vietnamese (7)	7	0.07
Other Asian, specified	1	0.01
Other Asian, not specified (12)	23	0.22
Assyrian/Chaldean/Syriac	10	0.09
Australian	7	0.07
Austrian	143	1.35
Belgian	12	0.11
British	226	2.13
Canadian	48	0.45
Celtic	27	0.25
Croatian	31	0.29
Czech	104	0.98
Czechoslovakian	7	0.07
Danish	249	2.35
Dutch	214	2.02
Eastern European	43	0.41
English	1,759	16.60
Estonian	18	0.17
European	245	2.31
Finnish	13	0.12
French, except Basque	423	3.99
French Canadian	81	0.76
German	1,812	17.10
Greek	64	0.60
Hawaii Native/Pacific Islander:	30	0.28
Micronesian: (6)	6	0.06
Guamanian/Chamorro (5)	5	0.05
Other Micronesian (1)	1	0.01
Polynesian: (5)	18	0.17
Native Hawaiian (3)	14	0.13
Samoan (1)	2	0.02
Tongan	1	0.01
Other Polynesian (1)	1	0.01
Other Pac. Isl., not spec.	6	0.06
Hispanic or Latino:	409	3.83
Central American:	38	0.36
Costa Rican	1	0.01
Guatemalan	8	0.07
Nicaraguan	15	0.14
Panamanian	1	0.01
Salvadoran	8	0.07
Other Central American	5	0.05
Cuban	17	0.16
Dominican Republic	1	0.01
Mexican	165	1.54
Puerto Rican	24	0.22
South American:	37	0.35
Argentinean	12	0.11
Bolivian	3	0.03
Colombian	7	0.07
Ecuadorian	3	0.03
Peruvian	4	0.04
Uruguayan	1	0.01
Venezuelan	4	0.04
Other South American	3	0.03
Other Hispanic or Latino	127	1.19
Hungarian	191	1.80
Iranian	13	0.12
Irish	1,931	18.22
Italian	876	8.27
Latvian	22	0.21
Lithuanian	93	0.88
Macedonian	8	0.08
Maltese	7	0.07
Northern European	31	0.29
Norwegian	203	1.92
Polish	583	5.50
Portuguese	50	0.47
Romanian	102	0.96
Russian	608	5.74
Scandinavian	62	0.59
Scotch-Irish	209	1.97
Scottish	405	3.82
Serbian	16	0.15
Swedish	336	3.17
Swiss	88	0.83
Turkish	10	0.09
Ukrainian	26	0.25
United States or American	233	2.20
Welsh	174	1.64
West Indian, excl. Hispanic:	17	0.16
Bahamian	5	0.05
Barbadian	5	0.05
Jamaican	7	0.07
White:	9,914	92.73
Not Hispanic (9,341)	9,582	89.63
Hispanic (285)	332	3.11
Yugoslavian	40	0.38

Tehachapi

Place Type: City
County: Kern
Population: 10,957

Ancestry/Race	Number	%
African American/Black:	1,564	14.27
Not Hispanic (1,497)	1,529	13.95
Hispanic (15)	35	0.32
Alaska Native tribes, specified:	1	0.01
Aleut	1	0.01
Am. Ind. or Alaska Nat., not spec.	110	1.00
American Indian tribes, specified:	198	1.81
Apache	6	0.05
Blackfeet (2)	16	0.15
Cherokee (21)	66	0.60
Cheyenne (2)	2	0.02
Chickasaw (3)	3	0.03
Choctaw (1)	5	0.05
Comanche	4	0.04
Creek	1	0.01
Delaware (1)	1	0.01
Iroquois (2)	6	0.05
Kiowa (1)	1	0.01
Latin American Indians (11)	22	0.20
Navajo (2)	7	0.06
Paiute (12)	17	0.16
Pueblo	2	0.02
Shoshone	1	0.01
Sioux	5	0.05
All other tribes (10)	33	0.30
American Indian tribes, not spec.	15	0.14
Armenian	8	0.07
Asian:	104	0.95
Cambodian (7)	7	0.06
Chinese, ex. Taiwanese (16)	18	0.16
Filipino (31)	40	0.37
Indian (10)	12	0.11
Indonesian	1	0.01
Japanese (9)	10	0.09
Korean (6)	7	0.06
Vietnamese (1)	2	0.02
Other Asian, not specified (1)	7	0.06
British	4	0.04
Canadian	10	0.09
Danish	145	1.33
Dutch	136	1.25
Eastern European	21	0.19
English	683	6.28
European	25	0.23
Finnish	31	0.29
French, except Basque	179	1.65
French Canadian	95	0.87
German	1,031	9.48
Greek	26	0.24
Hawaii Native/Pacific Islander:	28	0.26
Micronesian: (2)	2	0.02
Guamanian/Chamorro (2)	2	0.02

Notes: 1. Figures in the "Number" column do not add up to the total population due to: a) Ancestry/Race overlap — e.g. persons can report being both White and Irish, b) persons of Hispanic origin can report being any race, c) persons reporting two ancestries are counted in both categories. 2. Numbers in parentheses indicate the number of persons reporting this ancestry/race alone, not in combination with any other ancestry/race. 3. Refer to the Explanation of Data in the front of the book for more detailed information.

Polynesian: (14)	23	0.21
Native Hawaiian (4)	9	0.08
Samoan (6)	10	0.09
Tongan (4)	4	0.04
Other Pac. Isl., not spec. (1)	3	0.03
Hispanic or Latino:	3,583	32.70
Central American:	7	0.06
Guatemalan	4	0.04
Honduran	1	0.01
Panamanian	1	0.01
Salvadoran	1	0.01
Mexican	3,347	30.55
Puerto Rican	17	0.16
South American:	4	0.04
Argentinean	1	0.01
Colombian	2	0.02
Peruvian	1	0.01
Other Hispanic or Latino	208	1.90
Irish	794	7.30
Italian	180	1.65
Norwegian	58	0.53
Polish	50	0.46
Portuguese	15	0.14
Russian	38	0.35
Scandinavian	23	0.21
Scotch-Irish	82	0.75
Scottish	106	0.97
Slovak	10	0.09
Swedish	63	0.58
Swiss	19	0.17
United States or American	444	4.08
Welsh	43	0.40
West Indian, excl. Hispanic:	14	0.13
Dutch West Indian	14	0.13
White:	6,552	59.80
Not Hispanic (5,497)	5,657	51.63
Hispanic (767)	895	8.17

Temecula

Place Type: City
County: Riverside
Population: 57,716

Ancestry/Race	Number	%
Afghan	101	0.18
African American/Black:	2,494	4.32
Not Hispanic (1,874)	2,292	3.97
Hispanic (100)	202	0.35
African, sub-Saharan:	140	0.24
African	126	0.22
South African	14	0.02
Alaska Native tribes, specified:	5	0.01
Aleut (1)	2	0.00
Tlingit-Haida	3	0.01
Am. Ind. or Alaska Nat., not spec.	303	0.52
Albanian	8	0.01
American Indian tribes, specified:	667	1.16
Apache (19)	43	0.07
Blackfeet (4)	13	0.02
Cherokee (31)	139	0.24
Chickasaw (5)	6	0.01
Chippewa (8)	13	0.02
Choctaw (10)	26	0.05
Comanche (5)	5	0.01
Cree (1)	2	0.00
Creek (3)	10	0.02
Crow	3	0.01
Delaware (4)	7	0.01
Iroquois (2)	15	0.03
Kiowa (1)	1	0.00
Latin American Indians (33)	59	0.10
Lumbee	1	0.00
Navajo (13)	20	0.03
Osage (2)	3	0.01
Paiute (2)	4	0.01
Pima (1)	3	0.01
Potawatomi (1)	1	0.00
Pueblo (4)	10	0.02
Puget Sound Salish	1	0.00
Seminole (2)	3	0.01
Shoshone (1)	3	0.01
Sioux (2)	8	0.01
Tohono O'Odham (4)	4	0.01
Ute	1	0.00
Yaqui (5)	10	0.02
Yuman (3)	3	0.01
All other tribes (154)	250	0.43
American Indian tribes, not spec.	53	0.09
Arab:	380	0.66
Arab/Arabic	192	0.33
Egyptian	29	0.05
Iraqi	33	0.06
Lebanese	92	0.16
Palestinian	6	0.01
Other Arab	28	0.05
Armenian	136	0.24
Asian:	3,773	6.54
Bangladeshi	5	0.01
Cambodian (10)	16	0.03
Chinese, ex. Taiwanese (219)	333	0.58
Filipino (1,573)	2,034	3.52
Hmong (1)	6	0.01
Indian (134)	172	0.30
Indonesian (30)	56	0.10
Japanese (195)	433	0.75
Korean (231)	300	0.52
Laotian (74)	83	0.14
Malaysian	6	0.01
Pakistani (23)	23	0.04
Taiwanese (13)	17	0.03
Thai (47)	66	0.11
Vietnamese (85)	114	0.20
Other Asian, specified (3)	13	0.02
Other Asian, not specified (39)	96	0.17
Australian	123	0.21
Austrian	212	0.37
Basque	27	0.05
Belgian	62	0.11
Brazilian	9	0.02
British	429	0.75
Bulgarian	10	0.02
Canadian	270	0.47
Celtic	12	0.02
Croatian	45	0.08
Cypriot	7	0.01
Czech	381	0.66
Czechoslovakian	113	0.20
Danish	287	0.50
Dutch	1,179	2.05
English	7,150	12.45
European	726	1.26
Finnish	68	0.12
French, except Basque	2,141	3.73
French Canadian	742	1.29
German	9,744	16.97
Greek	279	0.49
Hawaii Native/Pacific Islander:	393	0.68
Micronesian: (78)	123	0.21
Guamanian/Chamorro (78)	122	0.21
Other Micronesian	1	0.00
Polynesian: (88)	221	0.38
Native Hawaiian (37)	135	0.23
Samoan (49)	83	0.14
Tongan (1)	1	0.00
Other Polynesian (1)	2	0.00
Other Pac. Isl., specified	5	0.01
Other Pac. Isl., not spec. (7)	44	0.08
Hispanic or Latino:	10,974	19.01
Central American:	284	0.49
Costa Rican	16	0.03
Guatemalan	77	0.13
Honduran	13	0.02
Nicaraguan	31	0.05
Panamanian	44	0.08
Salvadoran	76	0.13
Other Central American	27	0.05
Cuban	124	0.21
Dominican Republic	11	0.02
Mexican	8,440	14.62
Puerto Rican	447	0.77
South American:	183	0.32
Argentinean	29	0.05
Bolivian	1	0.00
Chilean	24	0.04
Colombian	55	0.10
Ecuadorian	7	0.01
Peruvian	38	0.07
Venezuelan	5	0.01
Other South American	24	0.04
Other Hispanic or Latino	1,485	2.57
Hungarian	274	0.48
Icelander	20	0.03
Iranian	29	0.05
Irish	7,670	13.36
Israeli	20	0.03
Italian	4,122	7.18
Latvian	32	0.06
Lithuanian	139	0.24
Luxemburger	7	0.01
Macedonian	16	0.03
Northern European	18	0.03
Norwegian	1,384	2.41
Polish	1,725	3.00
Portuguese	314	0.55
Romanian	70	0.12
Russian	424	0.74
Scandinavian	156	0.27
Scotch-Irish	945	1.65
Scottish	1,343	2.34
Serbian	41	0.07
Slavic	15	0.03
Slovak	116	0.20
Swedish	934	1.63
Swiss	243	0.42
Turkish	41	0.07
Ukrainian	184	0.32
United States or American	2,492	4.34
Welsh	309	0.54
West Indian, excl. Hispanic:	59	0.10
Belizean	19	0.03
Jamaican	28	0.05
Trinidadian and Tobagonian	12	0.02
White:	47,695	82.64
Not Hispanic (40,007)	41,406	71.74
Hispanic (5,548)	6,289	10.90
Yugoslavian	99	0.17

Temple City

Place Type: City
County: Los Angeles
Population: 33,377

Ancestry/Race	Number	%
African American/Black:	381	1.14
Not Hispanic (289)	344	1.03
Hispanic (18)	37	0.11
African, sub-Saharan:	38	0.11
African	30	0.09
Sudanese	8	0.02
Am. Ind. or Alaska Nat., not spec.	105	0.31
Albanian	17	0.05
Alsatian	7	0.02
American Indian tribes, specified:	178	0.53
Apache (12)	18	0.05
Blackfeet (4)	8	0.02
Cherokee (4)	40	0.12
Cheyenne (1)	1	0.00
Chickasaw (1)	3	0.01
Chippewa (1)	4	0.01
Choctaw (1)	3	0.01
Comanche (3)	3	0.01
Cree (1)	1	0.00
Creek (2)	2	0.01
Iroquois (1)	3	0.01
Latin American Indians (17)	28	0.08
Navajo (4)	9	0.03
Osage	1	0.00
Potawatomi (2)	3	0.01

Notes: 1. Figures in the "Number" column do not add up to the total population due to: a) Ancestry/Race overlap — e.g. persons can report being both White and Irish, b) persons of Hispanic origin can report being any race, c) persons reporting two ancestries are counted in both categories. 2. Numbers in parentheses indicate the number of persons reporting this ancestry/race alone, not in combination with any other ancestry/race. 3. Refer to the Explanation of Data in the front of the book for more detailed information.

Pueblo (4)	5	0.01
Seminole	1	0.00
Sioux (3)	7	0.02
Tohono O'Odham (2)	2	0.01
Yaqui (4)	5	0.01
Yuman	1	0.00
All other tribes (18)	30	0.09
American Indian tribes, not spec.	20	0.06
Arab:	340	1.02
Arab/Arabic	21	0.06
Egyptian	167	0.50
Jordanian	54	0.16
Lebanese	71	0.21
Palestinian	7	0.02
Syrian	13	0.04
Other Arab	7	0.02
Armenian	294	0.88
Asian:	14,064	42.14
Cambodian (38)	68	0.20
Chinese, ex. Taiwanese (7,912)	8,534	25.57
Filipino (582)	694	2.08
Hmong (1)	1	0.00
Indian (147)	185	0.55
Indonesian (123)	164	0.49
Japanese (507)	640	1.92
Korean (605)	632	1.89
Laotian (4)	4	0.01
Malaysian (9)	29	0.09
Pakistani (12)	12	0.04
Sri Lankan (11)	14	0.04
Taiwanese (1,410)	1,735	5.20
Thai (144)	165	0.49
Vietnamese (814)	985	2.95
Other Asian, specified (42)	50	0.15
Other Asian, not specified (69)	152	0.46
Australian	7	0.02
Austrian	44	0.13
Belgian	30	0.09
British	59	0.18
Canadian	95	0.29
Croatian	57	0.17
Czech	49	0.15
Czechoslovakian	53	0.16
Danish	316	0.95
Dutch	610	1.83
English	2,467	7.41
European	158	0.47
Finnish	67	0.20
French, except Basque	638	1.92
French Canadian	133	0.40
German	2,883	8.66
Greek	106	0.32
Hawaii Native/Pacific Islander:	95	0.28
Micronesian: (10)	14	0.04
Guamanian/Chamorro (10)	14	0.04
Polynesian: (8)	32	0.10
Native Hawaiian (4)	25	0.07
Samoan (4)	7	0.02
Other Pac. Isl., not spec. (1)	49	0.15
Hispanic or Latino:	6,836	20.48
Central American:	330	0.99
Costa Rican	22	0.07
Guatemalan	76	0.23
Honduran	17	0.05
Nicaraguan	46	0.14
Panamanian	4	0.01
Salvadoran	108	0.32
Other Central American	57	0.17
Cuban	154	0.46
Dominican Republic	3	0.01
Mexican	5,032	15.08
Puerto Rican	68	0.20
South American:	255	0.76
Argentinean	49	0.15
Bolivian	3	0.01
Chilean	23	0.07
Colombian	55	0.16
Ecuadorian	33	0.10
Peruvian	60	0.18
Uruguayan	4	0.01
Venezuelan	13	0.04
Other South American	15	0.04
Other Hispanic or Latino	994	2.98
Hungarian	204	0.61
Icelander	4	0.01
Iranian	35	0.11
Irish	2,039	6.12
Israeli	14	0.04
Italian	1,564	4.70
Lithuanian	29	0.09
Macedonian	11	0.03
Northern European	23	0.07
Norwegian	266	0.80
Pennsylvania German	7	0.02
Polish	473	1.42
Portuguese	20	0.06
Romanian	102	0.31
Russian	156	0.47
Scandinavian	30	0.09
Scotch-Irish	396	1.19
Scottish	468	1.41
Serbian	19	0.06
Slavic	16	0.05
Slovak	28	0.08
Slovene	6	0.02
Swedish	601	1.81
Swiss	94	0.28
Ukrainian	71	0.21
United States or American	736	2.21
Welsh	161	0.48
West Indian, excl. Hispanic:	33	0.10
Barbadian	6	0.02
Haitian	6	0.02
Jamaican	14	0.04
Other West Indian	7	0.02
White:	17,203	51.54
Not Hispanic (12,589)	13,102	39.25
Hispanic (3,677)	4,101	12.29
Yugoslavian	39	0.12

Thousand Oaks

Place Type: City
County: Ventura
Population: 117,005

Ancestry/Race	Number	%
Acadian/Cajun	28	0.02
Afghan	157	0.13
African American/Black:	1,642	1.40
Not Hispanic (1,162)	1,494	1.28
Hispanic (79)	148	0.13
African, sub-Saharan:	210	0.18
African	111	0.10
South African	99	0.08
Alaska Native tribes, specified:	6	0.01
Aleut (3)	4	0.00
Eskimo (1)	2	0.00
Alaska Native tribes, not specified	2	0.00
Am. Ind. or Alaska Nat., not spec.	360	0.31
Albanian	14	0.01
Alsatian	8	0.01
American Indian tribes, specified:	809	0.69
Apache (20)	45	0.04
Blackfeet (3)	13	0.01
Cherokee (82)	229	0.20
Cheyenne (2)	3	0.00
Chickasaw (11)	17	0.01
Chippewa (14)	26	0.02
Choctaw (26)	61	0.05
Comanche (2)	5	0.00
Cree (3)	4	0.00
Creek (7)	10	0.01
Crow	1	0.00
Iroquois (6)	22	0.02
Kiowa	1	0.00
Latin American Indians (117)	165	0.14
Lumbee	3	0.00
Navajo (16)	26	0.02
Osage (1)	6	0.01
Paiute (5)	11	0.01
Potawatomi (5)	7	0.01
Pueblo (10)	14	0.01
Seminole (2)	3	0.00
Shoshone (2)	2	0.00
Sioux (22)	41	0.04
Ute	2	0.00
Yaqui (4)	9	0.01
Yuman (1)	1	0.00
All other tribes (44)	82	0.07
American Indian tribes, not spec.	49	0.04
Arab:	824	0.71
Arab/Arabic	127	0.11
Egyptian	105	0.09
Iraqi	45	0.04
Jordanian	22	0.02
Lebanese	331	0.28
Moroccan	29	0.02
Palestinian	61	0.05
Syrian	78	0.07
Other Arab	26	0.02
Armenian	474	0.41
Asian:	8,464	7.23
Bangladeshi (7)	9	0.01
Cambodian (21)	28	0.02
Chinese, ex. Taiwanese (2,175)	2,557	2.19
Filipino (806)	1,161	0.99
Indian (975)	1,094	0.94
Indonesian (44)	79	0.07
Japanese (916)	1,404	1.20
Korean (786)	904	0.77
Laotian (2)	3	0.00
Malaysian (6)	14	0.01
Pakistani (69)	82	0.07
Sri Lankan (26)	30	0.03
Taiwanese (291)	312	0.27
Thai (65)	79	0.07
Vietnamese (395)	443	0.38
Other Asian, specified (6)	15	0.01
Other Asian, not specified (105)	250	0.21
Assyrian/Chaldean/Syriac	9	0.01
Australian	79	0.07
Austrian	772	0.66
Basque	71	0.06
Belgian	156	0.13
Brazilian	73	0.06
British	1,077	0.92
Bulgarian	85	0.07
Canadian	773	0.66
Celtic	49	0.04
Croatian	221	0.19
Czech	555	0.48
Czechoslovakian	313	0.27
Danish	1,312	1.12
Dutch	2,141	1.83
Eastern European	390	0.33
English	16,126	13.82
Estonian	26	0.02
European	1,474	1.26
Finnish	288	0.25
French, except Basque	3,969	3.40
French Canadian	1,109	0.95
German	20,230	17.33
German Russian	6	0.01
Greek	501	0.43
Guyanese	7	0.01
Hawaii Native/Pacific Islander:	330	0.28
Melanesian: (1)	5	0.00
Fijian (1)	5	0.00
Micronesian: (26)	34	0.03
Guamanian/Chamorro (26)	33	0.03
Other Micronesian	1	0.00
Polynesian: (76)	210	0.18
Native Hawaiian (44)	145	0.12
Samoan (17)	43	0.04
Tongan (6)	11	0.01
Other Polynesian (9)	11	0.01
Other Pac. Isl., specified	1	0.00
Other Pac. Isl., not spec. (18)	80	0.07
Hispanic or Latino:	15,328	13.10

Notes: 1. Figures in the "Number" column do not add up to the total population due to: a) Ancestry/Race overlap — e.g. persons can report being both White and Irish, b) persons of Hispanic origin can report being any race, c) persons reporting two ancestries are counted in both categories. 2. Numbers in parentheses indicate the number of persons reporting this ancestry/race alone, not in combination with any other ancestry/race. 3. Refer to the Explanation of Data in the front of the book for more detailed information.

Central American:	1,244	1.06
Costa Rican	36	0.03
Guatemalan	504	0.43
Honduran	78	0.07
Nicaraguan	129	0.11
Panamanian	28	0.02
Salvadoran	373	0.32
Other Central American	96	0.08
Cuban	224	0.19
Dominican Republic	16	0.01
Mexican	10,097	8.63
Puerto Rican	324	0.28
South American:	645	0.55
Argentinean	147	0.13
Bolivian	3	0.00
Chilean	60	0.05
Colombian	137	0.12
Ecuadorian	62	0.05
Paraguayan	2	0.00
Peruvian	176	0.15
Uruguayan	4	0.00
Venezuelan	10	0.01
Other South American	44	0.04
Other Hispanic or Latino	2,778	2.37
Hungarian	1,023	0.88
Icelander	11	0.01
Iranian	1,241	1.06
Irish	15,582	13.35
Israeli	140	0.12
Italian	9,203	7.88
Latvian	123	0.11
Lithuanian	385	0.33
Luxemburger	25	0.02
Macedonian	12	0.01
Maltese	54	0.05
New Zealander	13	0.01
Northern European	140	0.12
Norwegian	3,018	2.59
Pennsylvania German	38	0.03
Polish	4,733	4.05
Portuguese	532	0.46
Romanian	402	0.34
Russian	3,695	3.17
Scandinavian	400	0.34
Scotch-Irish	2,208	1.89
Scottish	3,402	2.91
Serbian	58	0.05
Slavic	84	0.07
Slovak	169	0.14
Slovene	104	0.09
Swedish	2,864	2.45
Swiss	716	0.61
Turkish	43	0.04
Ukrainian	423	0.36
United States or American	5,796	4.97
Welsh	1,075	0.92
West Indian, excl. Hispanic:	50	0.04
Bahamian	5	0.00
British West Indian	11	0.01
Dutch West Indian	10	0.01
Jamaican	11	0.01
Trinidadian and Tobagonian	6	0.01
West Indian	7	0.01
White:	102,573	87.67
Not Hispanic (90,862)	92,891	79.39
Hispanic (8,701)	9,682	8.27
Yugoslavian	223	0.19

Torrance

Place Type: City
County: Los Angeles
Population: 137,946

Ancestry/Race	Number	%
Acadian/Cajun	24	0.02
Afghan	81	0.06
African American/Black:	3,726	2.70
Not Hispanic (2,911)	3,501	2.54
Hispanic (111)	225	0.16
African, sub-Saharan:	545	0.40
African	381	0.28
Ethiopian	18	0.01
Ghanian	7	0.01
Nigerian	50	0.04
Somalian	11	0.01
South African	34	0.02
Sudanese	4	0.00
Ugandan	34	0.02
Other sub-Saharan African	6	0.00
Alaska Native tribes, specified:	15	0.01
Aleut (1)	3	0.00
Eskimo	1	0.00
Tlingit-Haida (7)	9	0.01
All other tribes (2)	2	0.00
Am. Ind. or Alaska Nat., not spec.	487	0.35
Albanian	21	0.02
American Indian tribes, specified:	943	0.68
Apache (26)	60	0.04
Blackfeet (19)	58	0.04
Cherokee (66)	277	0.20
Cheyenne	9	0.01
Chickasaw (4)	15	0.01
Chippewa (8)	22	0.02
Choctaw (20)	53	0.04
Colville (1)	1	0.00
Comanche (1)	5	0.00
Creek (10)	18	0.01
Crow (1)	3	0.00
Delaware (2)	8	0.01
Iroquois (2)	17	0.01
Kiowa	2	0.00
Latin American Indians (48)	89	0.06
Menominee (2)	2	0.00
Navajo (27)	57	0.04
Osage (5)	8	0.01
Ottawa (1)	2	0.00
Paiute (6)	6	0.00
Pima (3)	6	0.00
Potawatomi (7)	14	0.01
Pueblo (10)	28	0.02
Seminole (3)	12	0.01
Shoshone (1)	4	0.00
Sioux (8)	23	0.02
Tohono O'Odham (2)	3	0.00
Ute (1)	7	0.01
Yakama (3)	3	0.00
Yaqui (6)	18	0.01
Yuman (2)	4	0.00
All other tribes (54)	109	0.08
American Indian tribes, not spec.	60	0.04
Arab:	1,642	1.19
Arab/Arabic	228	0.17
Egyptian	499	0.36
Iraqi	7	0.01
Jordanian	56	0.04
Lebanese	544	0.39
Palestinian	13	0.01
Syrian	168	0.12
Other Arab	127	0.09
Armenian	672	0.49
Asian:	44,265	32.09
Bangladeshi (15)	15	0.01
Cambodian (19)	35	0.03
Chinese, ex. Taiwanese (5,399)	6,524	4.73
Filipino (3,036)	4,048	2.93
Hmong (7)	7	0.01
Indian (2,298)	2,523	1.83
Indonesian (118)	199	0.14
Japanese (13,991)	16,048	11.63
Korean (9,481)	9,864	7.15
Laotian (7)	13	0.01
Malaysian (21)	42	0.03
Pakistani (594)	717	0.52
Sri Lankan (118)	152	0.11
Taiwanese (1,159)	1,344	0.97
Thai (299)	373	0.27
Vietnamese (1,603)	1,724	1.25
Other Asian, specified (73)	106	0.08
Other Asian, not specified (176)	531	0.38
Assyrian/Chaldean/Syriac	6	0.00
Australian	111	0.08
Austrian	641	0.46
Basque	68	0.05
Belgian	160	0.12
Brazilian	216	0.16
British	829	0.60
Bulgarian	29	0.02
Canadian	511	0.37
Celtic	31	0.02
Croatian	248	0.18
Czech	423	0.31
Czechoslovakian	204	0.15
Danish	949	0.69
Dutch	2,107	1.53
Eastern European	149	0.11
English	12,256	8.89
Estonian	17	0.01
European	1,387	1.01
Finnish	208	0.15
French, except Basque	3,675	2.66
French Canadian	754	0.55
German	15,786	11.44
German Russian	19	0.01
Greek	887	0.64
Guyanese	6	0.00
Hawaii Native/Pacific Islander:	1,153	0.84
Melanesian: (1)	5	0.00
Fijian (1)	4	0.00
Other Melanesian	1	0.00
Micronesian: (43)	93	0.07
Guamanian/Chamorro (42)	91	0.07
Other Micronesian (1)	2	0.00
Polynesian: (384)	834	0.60
Native Hawaiian (161)	512	0.37
Samoan (198)	275	0.20
Tongan (21)	34	0.02
Other Polynesian (4)	13	0.01
Other Pac. Isl., specified	3	0.00
Other Pac. Isl., not spec. (39)	218	0.16
Hispanic or Latino:	17,637	12.79
Central American:	1,059	0.77
Costa Rican	123	0.09
Guatemalan	274	0.20
Honduran	90	0.07
Nicaraguan	182	0.13
Panamanian	15	0.01
Salvadoran	308	0.22
Other Central American	67	0.05
Cuban	740	0.54
Dominican Republic	33	0.02
Mexican	10,398	7.54
Puerto Rican	549	0.40
South American:	1,521	1.10
Argentinean	189	0.14
Bolivian	10	0.01
Chilean	140	0.10
Colombian	289	0.21
Ecuadorian	163	0.12
Paraguayan	1	0.00
Peruvian	514	0.37
Uruguayan	14	0.01
Venezuelan	33	0.02
Other South American	168	0.12
Other Hispanic or Latino	3,337	2.42
Hungarian	805	0.58
Icelander	112	0.08
Iranian	1,271	0.92
Irish	12,463	9.04
Israeli	76	0.06
Italian	6,870	4.98
Latvian	73	0.05
Lithuanian	300	0.22
Luxemburger	5	0.00
Macedonian	4	0.00
Maltese	26	0.02
Northern European	171	0.12
Norwegian	2,027	1.47
Pennsylvania German	39	0.03
Polish	2,616	1.90

Notes: 1. Figures in the "Number" column do not add up to the total population due to: a) Ancestry/Race overlap — e.g. persons can report being both White and Irish, b) persons of Hispanic origin can report being any race, c) persons reporting two ancestries are counted in both categories. 2. Numbers in parentheses indicate the number of persons reporting this ancestry/race alone, not in combination with any other ancestry/race. 3. Refer to the Explanation of Data in the front of the book for more detailed information.

Portuguese	519	0.38
Romanian	258	0.19
Russian	1,563	1.13
Scandinavian	336	0.24
Scotch-Irish	2,092	1.52
Scottish	2,527	1.83
Serbian	88	0.06
Slavic	97	0.07
Slovak	26	0.02
Slovene	39	0.03
Swedish	2,095	1.52
Swiss	487	0.35
Turkish	98	0.07
Ukrainian	444	0.32
United States or American	4,836	3.51
Welsh	985	0.71
West Indian, excl. Hispanic:	207	0.15
Belizean	13	0.01
Dutch West Indian	12	0.01
Haitian	58	0.04
Jamaican	60	0.04
Trinidadian and Tobagonian	37	0.03
West Indian	27	0.02
White:	87,059	63.11
Not Hispanic (72,234)	76,236	55.27
Hispanic (9,371)	10,823	7.85
Yugoslavian	393	0.28

Tracy

Place Type: City
County: San Joaquin
Population: 56,929

Ancestry/Race	Number	%
Acadian/Cajun	5	0.01
Afghan	182	0.32
African American/Black:	3,625	6.37
Not Hispanic (2,976)	3,370	5.92
Hispanic (141)	255	0.45
African, sub-Saharan:	322	0.57
African	182	0.32
Cape Verdean	23	0.04
Ethiopian	27	0.05
Nigerian	62	0.11
South African	14	0.02
Other sub-Saharan African	14	0.02
Alaska Native tribes, specified:	14	0.02
Alaska Athabascan (3)	6	0.01
Aleut (3)	5	0.01
Eskimo (1)	2	0.00
Tlingit-Haida (1)	1	0.00
Am. Ind. or Alaska Nat., not spec.	372	0.65
American Indian tribes, specified:	726	1.28
Apache (14)	48	0.08
Blackfeet (3)	22	0.04
Cherokee (55)	226	0.40
Cheyenne	1	0.00
Chickasaw (3)	10	0.02
Chippewa (6)	12	0.02
Choctaw (34)	55	0.10
Comanche (1)	5	0.01
Cree (1)	2	0.00
Creek (6)	12	0.02
Delaware (3)	3	0.01
Houma	3	0.01
Iroquois (4)	5	0.01
Latin American Indians (29)	51	0.09
Lumbee	1	0.00
Navajo (10)	27	0.05
Osage (1)	4	0.01
Paiute (21)	28	0.05
Pima (6)	9	0.02
Potawatomi (3)	9	0.02
Pueblo (15)	31	0.05
Seminole (5)	7	0.01
Shoshone (2)	4	0.01
Sioux (15)	25	0.04
Tohono O'Odham (6)	8	0.01
Ute (1)	1	0.00
Yaqui (5)	6	0.01
All other tribes (54)	111	0.19
American Indian tribes, not spec.	66	0.12
Arab:	120	0.21
Arab/Arabic	19	0.03
Egyptian	36	0.06
Lebanese	47	0.08
Other Arab	18	0.03
Armenian	21	0.04
Asian:	6,109	10.73
Cambodian (63)	91	0.16
Chinese, ex. Taiwanese (338)	534	0.94
Filipino (2,279)	2,891	5.08
Hmong (7)	9	0.02
Indian (1,036)	1,166	2.05
Indonesian (16)	26	0.05
Japanese (177)	454	0.80
Korean (172)	244	0.43
Laotian (10)	16	0.03
Pakistani (27)	40	0.07
Sri Lankan (1)	1	0.00
Taiwanese (4)	7	0.01
Thai (31)	55	0.10
Vietnamese (289)	352	0.62
Other Asian, specified (11)	18	0.03
Other Asian, not specified (48)	205	0.36
Assyrian/Chaldean/Syriac	16	0.03
Australian	40	0.07
Austrian	88	0.15
Basque	90	0.16
Belgian	32	0.06
Brazilian	12	0.02
British	151	0.27
Canadian	184	0.32
Celtic	20	0.04
Croatian	77	0.14
Czech	132	0.23
Czechoslovakian	112	0.20
Danish	441	0.78
Dutch	1,047	1.84
Eastern European	50	0.09
English	4,537	7.98
Estonian	11	0.02
European	521	0.92
Finnish	213	0.37
French, except Basque	1,805	3.18
French Canadian	294	0.52
German	7,028	12.36
Greek	346	0.61
Hawaii Native/Pacific Islander:	664	1.17
Melanesian: (32)	44	0.08
Fijian (32)	44	0.08
Micronesian: (64)	121	0.21
Guamanian/Chamorro (64)	121	0.21
Polynesian: (184)	381	0.67
Native Hawaiian (86)	244	0.43
Samoan (74)	101	0.18
Tongan (20)	27	0.05
Other Polynesian (4)	9	0.02
Other Pac. Isl., specified	1	0.00
Other Pac. Isl., not spec. (25)	117	0.21
Hispanic or Latino:	15,765	27.69
Central American:	313	0.55
Costa Rican	17	0.03
Guatemalan	37	0.06
Honduran	11	0.02
Nicaraguan	54	0.09
Panamanian	23	0.04
Salvadoran	131	0.23
Other Central American	40	0.07
Cuban	70	0.12
Dominican Republic	5	0.01
Mexican	12,420	21.82
Puerto Rican	511	0.90
South American:	149	0.26
Argentinean	18	0.03
Bolivian	2	0.00
Chilean	18	0.03
Colombian	18	0.03
Ecuadorian	8	0.01
Peruvian	58	0.10
Venezuelan	11	0.02
Other South American	16	0.03
Other Hispanic or Latino	2,297	4.03
Hungarian	126	0.22
Iranian	133	0.23
Irish	5,277	9.28
Israeli	6	0.01
Italian	3,136	5.52
Latvian	18	0.03
Lithuanian	38	0.07
Luxemburger	9	0.02
Maltese	26	0.05
New Zealander	35	0.06
Northern European	19	0.03
Norwegian	1,005	1.77
Pennsylvania German	12	0.02
Polish	990	1.74
Portuguese	3,217	5.66
Romanian	42	0.07
Russian	246	0.43
Scandinavian	198	0.35
Scotch-Irish	830	1.46
Scottish	967	1.70
Serbian	25	0.04
Slovak	40	0.07
Slovene	37	0.07
Swedish	821	1.44
Swiss	159	0.28
Turkish	22	0.04
Ukrainian	85	0.15
United States or American	2,469	4.34
Welsh	199	0.35
West Indian, excl. Hispanic:	69	0.12
Dutch West Indian	13	0.02
Jamaican	44	0.08
Trinidadian and Tobagonian	12	0.02
White:	40,342	70.86
Not Hispanic (30,723)	32,602	57.27
Hispanic (6,404)	7,740	13.60
Yugoslavian	55	0.10

Truckee

Place Type: Town
County: Nevada
Population: 13,864

Ancestry/Race	Number	%
African American/Black:	56	0.40
Not Hispanic (26)	46	0.33
Hispanic (8)	10	0.07
Alaska Native tribes, specified:	4	0.03
Tlingit-Haida (3)	3	0.02
All other tribes	1	0.01
Am. Ind. or Alaska Nat., not spec.	42	0.30
American Indian tribes, specified:	131	0.94
Apache (3)	15	0.11
Blackfeet (2)	7	0.05
Cherokee (10)	38	0.27
Chickasaw (2)	3	0.02
Chippewa (2)	2	0.01
Choctaw (4)	11	0.08
Latin American Indians (1)	2	0.01
Navajo	3	0.02
Paiute (8)	8	0.06
Potawatomi (1)	1	0.01
Pueblo	2	0.01
Shoshone	5	0.04
Sioux (3)	8	0.06
Ute	2	0.01
Yaqui (2)	2	0.01
All other tribes (15)	22	0.16
American Indian tribes, not spec.	11	0.08
Arab:	21	0.15
Arab/Arabic	21	0.15
Armenian	6	0.04
Asian:	197	1.42
Chinese, ex. Taiwanese (32)	52	0.38
Filipino (23)	49	0.35

Notes: 1. Figures in the "Number" column do not add up to the total population due to: a) Ancestry/Race overlap — e.g. persons can report being both White and Irish, b) persons of Hispanic origin can report being any race, c) persons reporting two ancestries are counted in both categories. 2. Numbers in parentheses indicate the number of persons reporting this ancestry/race alone, not in combination with any other ancestry/race. 3. Refer to the Explanation of Data in the front of the book for more detailed information.

Indian (3)	5	0.04
Indonesian (3)	4	0.03
Japanese (33)	50	0.36
Korean (12)	12	0.09
Malaysian (1)	1	0.01
Taiwanese (1)	1	0.01
Thai	3	0.02
Vietnamese (6)	13	0.09
Other Asian, specified	1	0.01
Other Asian, not specified (3)	6	0.04
Australian	14	0.10
Austrian	18	0.13
Basque	12	0.09
Belgian	53	0.38
British	43	0.31
Canadian	71	0.51
Celtic	19	0.14
Czech	70	0.50
Danish	131	0.94
Dutch	294	2.10
Eastern European	22	0.16
English	2,492	17.84
European	287	2.05
Finnish	58	0.42
French, except Basque	778	5.57
French Canadian	90	0.64
German	2,821	20.20
Greek	37	0.26
Hawaii Native/Pacific Islander:	45	0.32
Micronesian:	2	0.01
Guamanian/Chamorro	1	0.01
Other Micronesian	1	0.01
Polynesian: (23)	39	0.28
Native Hawaiian (5)	16	0.12
Samoan (18)	23	0.17
Other Pac. Isl., not spec. (1)	4	0.03
Hispanic or Latino:	1,773	12.79
Central American:	18	0.13
Costa Rican	1	0.01
Guatemalan	5	0.04
Nicaraguan	1	0.01
Panamanian	2	0.01
Salvadoran	9	0.06
Cuban	10	0.07
Mexican	1,506	10.86
Puerto Rican	23	0.17
South American:	13	0.09
Argentinean	1	0.01
Bolivian	2	0.01
Chilean	2	0.01
Colombian	6	0.04
Peruvian	1	0.01
Other South American	1	0.01
Other Hispanic or Latino	203	1.46
Hungarian	39	0.28
Iranian	11	0.08
Irish	2,465	17.65
Italian	1,180	8.45
Latvian	17	0.12
Lithuanian	26	0.19
Luxemburger	14	0.10
Northern European	24	0.17
Norwegian	409	2.93
Polish	277	1.98
Portuguese	249	1.78
Romanian	24	0.17
Russian	159	1.14
Scandinavian	109	0.78
Scotch-Irish	205	1.47
Scottish	499	3.57
Slavic	5	0.04
Slovak	29	0.21
Swedish	459	3.29
Swiss	82	0.59
Ukrainian	18	0.13
United States or American	707	5.06
Welsh	123	0.88
White:	12,532	90.39
Not Hispanic (11,637)	11,829	85.32
Hispanic (617)	703	5.07
Yugoslavian	70	0.50

Tulare

Place Type: City
County: Tulare
Population: 43,994

Ancestry/Race	Number	%
African American/Black:	2,562	5.82
Not Hispanic (2,051)	2,323	5.28
Hispanic (158)	239	0.54
African, sub-Saharan:	122	0.28
African	122	0.28
Alaska Native tribes, specified:	5	0.01
Tlingit-Haida (1)	5	0.01
Alaska Native tribes, not specified	5	0.01
Am. Ind. or Alaska Nat., not spec.	384	0.87
American Indian tribes, specified:	585	1.33
Apache (17)	28	0.06
Blackfeet (3)	16	0.04
Cherokee (50)	171	0.39
Chickasaw (6)	10	0.02
Chippewa (1)	1	0.00
Choctaw (44)	79	0.18
Comanche (2)	7	0.02
Creek (11)	20	0.05
Delaware	3	0.01
Iroquois (2)	4	0.01
Kiowa	3	0.01
Latin American Indians (61)	73	0.17
Lumbee	2	0.00
Navajo (7)	10	0.02
Osage	3	0.01
Ottawa (3)	3	0.01
Paiute (5)	11	0.03
Pima (1)	1	0.00
Potawatomi (6)	7	0.02
Pueblo (3)	4	0.01
Puget Sound Salish (1)	1	0.00
Seminole (1)	3	0.01
Sioux (9)	11	0.03
Tohono O'Odham (1)	1	0.00
Ute	2	0.00
Yaqui (19)	30	0.07
Yuman	1	0.00
All other tribes (54)	80	0.18
American Indian tribes, not spec.	92	0.21
Arab:	14	0.03
Arab/Arabic	5	0.01
Lebanese	9	0.02
Armenian	158	0.36
Asian:	1,193	2.71
Cambodian (11)	15	0.03
Chinese, ex. Taiwanese (97)	117	0.27
Filipino (114)	217	0.49
Hmong (122)	153	0.35
Indian (156)	192	0.44
Indonesian (1)	4	0.01
Japanese (24)	59	0.13
Korean (41)	64	0.15
Laotian (249)	262	0.60
Pakistani (7)	7	0.02
Taiwanese (1)	2	0.00
Thai (6)	6	0.01
Vietnamese (21)	33	0.08
Other Asian, specified	6	0.01
Other Asian, not specified (15)	56	0.13
Austrian	8	0.02
Basque	30	0.07
Belgian	2	0.00
Brazilian	42	0.10
British	52	0.12
Canadian	43	0.10
Celtic	16	0.04
Croatian	5	0.01
Czech	10	0.02
Czechoslovakian	13	0.03
Danish	97	0.22
Dutch	704	1.60
English	1,949	4.44
European	211	0.48
Finnish	10	0.02
French, except Basque	461	1.05
French Canadian	99	0.23
German	2,295	5.23
Greek	25	0.06
Hawaii Native/Pacific Islander:	163	0.37
Melanesian: (8)	8	0.02
Fijian (8)	8	0.02
Micronesian: (4)	8	0.02
Guamanian/Chamorro (4)	8	0.02
Polynesian: (33)	57	0.13
Native Hawaiian (6)	28	0.06
Samoan (12)	14	0.03
Tongan (15)	15	0.03
Other Pac. Isl., specified	5	0.01
Other Pac. Isl., not spec. (4)	85	0.19
Hispanic or Latino:	20,058	45.59
Central American:	99	0.23
Costa Rican	2	0.00
Guatemalan	29	0.07
Honduran	2	0.00
Nicaraguan	4	0.01
Panamanian	7	0.02
Salvadoran	45	0.10
Other Central American	10	0.02
Cuban	14	0.03
Mexican	17,006	38.66
Puerto Rican	122	0.28
South American:	18	0.04
Bolivian	1	0.00
Chilean	3	0.01
Colombian	7	0.02
Peruvian	7	0.02
Other Hispanic or Latino	2,799	6.36
Hungarian	56	0.13
Icelander	11	0.03
Iranian	39	0.09
Irish	2,302	5.24
Italian	560	1.28
Northern European	11	0.03
Norwegian	110	0.25
Pennsylvania German	21	0.05
Polish	144	0.33
Portuguese	3,760	8.56
Romanian	16	0.04
Russian	49	0.11
Scandinavian	32	0.07
Scotch-Irish	340	0.77
Scottish	307	0.70
Swedish	166	0.38
Swiss	49	0.11
Ukrainian	10	0.02
United States or American	2,832	6.45
Welsh	91	0.21
West Indian, excl. Hispanic:	69	0.16
Dutch West Indian	30	0.07
Jamaican	39	0.09
White:	27,108	61.62
Not Hispanic (19,276)	20,493	46.58
Hispanic (5,528)	6,615	15.04
Yugoslavian	23	0.05

Turlock

Place Type: City
County: Stanislaus
Population: 55,810

Ancestry/Race	Number	%
Acadian/Cajun	32	0.06
African American/Black:	1,021	1.83
Not Hispanic (728)	890	1.59
Hispanic (70)	131	0.23
African, sub-Saharan:	73	0.13
African	73	0.13
Alaska Native tribes, specified:	2	0.00
Tlingit-Haida (1)	2	0.00
Am. Ind. or Alaska Nat., not spec.	307	0.55

Notes: 1. Figures in the "Number" column do not add up to the total population due to: a) Ancestry/Race overlap — e.g. persons can report being both White and Irish, b) persons of Hispanic origin can report being any race, c) persons reporting two ancestries are counted in both categories. 2. Numbers in parentheses indicate the number of persons reporting this ancestry/race alone, not in combination with any other ancestry/race. 3. Refer to the Explanation of Data in the front of the book for more detailed information.

Albanian	9	0.02
American Indian tribes, specified:	674	1.21
Apache (17)	24	0.04
Blackfeet (9)	26	0.05
Cherokee (108)	256	0.46
Chickasaw (5)	9	0.02
Chippewa (4)	13	0.02
Choctaw (20)	51	0.09
Comanche (2)	4	0.01
Creek (5)	14	0.03
Crow	1	0.00
Delaware (1)	3	0.01
Iroquois (6)	12	0.02
Latin American Indians (45)	72	0.13
Navajo (4)	14	0.03
Osage (2)	6	0.01
Paiute (1)	1	0.00
Pima	1	0.00
Potawatomi (1)	1	0.00
Pueblo (17)	21	0.04
Puget Sound Salish (2)	5	0.01
Seminole (3)	4	0.01
Sioux (11)	16	0.03
Tohono O'Odham (2)	3	0.01
Yaqui (10)	14	0.03
All other tribes (47)	103	0.18
American Indian tribes, not spec.	54	0.10
Arab:	140	0.25
Arab/Arabic	31	0.06
Iraqi	51	0.09
Lebanese	13	0.02
Moroccan	9	0.02
Syrian	12	0.02
Other Arab	24	0.04
Armenian	202	0.36
Asian:	3,249	5.82
Cambodian (28)	32	0.06
Chinese, ex. Taiwanese (290)	333	0.60
Filipino (290)	482	0.86
Hmong (82)	88	0.16
Indian (1,448)	1,643	2.94
Indonesian (2)	3	0.01
Japanese (144)	247	0.44
Korean (81)	100	0.18
Laotian (10)	16	0.03
Malaysian	2	0.00
Pakistani (22)	31	0.06
Sri Lankan (5)	5	0.01
Taiwanese (6)	8	0.01
Thai	3	0.01
Vietnamese (62)	86	0.15
Other Asian, specified (1)	5	0.01
Other Asian, not specified (26)	165	0.30
Assyrian/Chaldean/Syriac	2,871	5.17
Australian	16	0.03
Austrian	62	0.11
Basque	49	0.09
Belgian	38	0.07
Brazilian	67	0.12
British	239	0.43
Canadian	102	0.18
Croatian	62	0.11
Czech	37	0.07
Czechoslovakian	46	0.08
Danish	544	0.98
Dutch	992	1.79
English	4,443	8.01
European	382	0.69
Finnish	28	0.05
French, except Basque	1,067	1.92
French Canadian	103	0.19
German	5,594	10.08
Greek	205	0.37
Hawaii Native/Pacific Islander:	354	0.63
Melanesian: (30)	43	0.08
Fijian (30)	43	0.08
Micronesian: (23)	32	0.06
Guamanian/Chamorro (19)	28	0.05
Other Micronesian (4)	4	0.01
Polynesian: (53)	110	0.20
Native Hawaiian (25)	76	0.14
Samoan (25)	31	0.06
Tongan (3)	3	0.01
Other Pac. Isl., specified	4	0.01
Other Pac. Isl., not spec. (46)	165	0.30
Hispanic or Latino:	16,422	29.42
Central American:	175	0.31
Costa Rican	2	0.00
Guatemalan	61	0.11
Honduran	13	0.02
Nicaraguan	29	0.05
Panamanian	4	0.01
Salvadoran	50	0.09
Other Central American	16	0.03
Cuban	41	0.07
Dominican Republic	1	0.00
Mexican	13,965	25.02
Puerto Rican	144	0.26
South American:	104	0.19
Argentinean	2	0.00
Bolivian	2	0.00
Chilean	19	0.03
Colombian	54	0.10
Ecuadorian	2	0.00
Peruvian	14	0.03
Other South American	11	0.02
Other Hispanic or Latino	1,992	3.57
Hungarian	60	0.11
Icelander	27	0.05
Iranian	378	0.68
Irish	4,035	7.27
Italian	1,894	3.41
Lithuanian	14	0.03
Maltese	7	0.01
Northern European	147	0.26
Norwegian	1,009	1.82
Polish	373	0.67
Portuguese	3,995	7.20
Russian	133	0.24
Scandinavian	245	0.44
Scotch-Irish	831	1.50
Scottish	872	1.57
Slavic	10	0.02
Slovak	13	0.02
Slovene	14	0.03
Swedish	1,873	3.38
Swiss	361	0.65
Ukrainian	54	0.10
United States or American	1,871	3.37
Welsh	243	0.44
West Indian, excl. Hispanic:	6	0.01
Dutch West Indian	6	0.01
White:	42,957	76.97
Not Hispanic (33,717)	35,336	63.31
Hispanic (6,653)	7,621	13.66
Yugoslavian	22	0.04

Tustin Foothills

Place Type: Census Designated Place
County: Orange
Population: 24,044

Ancestry/Race	Number	%
African American/Black:	162	0.67
Not Hispanic (121)	148	0.62
Hispanic (13)	14	0.06
African, sub-Saharan:	17	0.07
African	8	0.03
South African	9	0.04
Am. Ind. or Alaska Nat., not spec.	53	0.22
Albanian	13	0.05
American Indian tribes, specified:	146	0.61
Apache (1)	5	0.02
Blackfeet (3)	4	0.02
Cherokee (23)	58	0.24
Chickasaw (1)	2	0.01
Chippewa (2)	4	0.02
Choctaw (2)	15	0.06
Comanche	1	0.00
Creek (1)	1	0.00
Kiowa (1)	1	0.00
Latin American Indians (2)	10	0.04
Navajo	1	0.00
Paiute (1)	1	0.00
Potawatomi	3	0.01
Pueblo (2)	2	0.01
Shoshone (1)	1	0.00
Sioux	3	0.01
Tohono O'Odham (2)	2	0.01
Yaqui (1)	5	0.02
All other tribes (19)	27	0.11
American Indian tribes, not spec.	8	0.03
Arab:	353	1.47
Arab/Arabic	55	0.23
Egyptian	107	0.45
Iraqi	47	0.20
Lebanese	82	0.34
Palestinian	23	0.10
Other Arab	39	0.16
Armenian	168	0.70
Asian:	2,035	8.46
Cambodian (15)	16	0.07
Chinese, ex. Taiwanese (441)	519	2.16
Filipino (123)	193	0.80
Hmong (3)	3	0.01
Indian (134)	154	0.64
Indonesian (5)	11	0.05
Japanese (274)	403	1.68
Korean (199)	220	0.91
Malaysian (1)	2	0.01
Pakistani (6)	11	0.05
Sri Lankan (15)	20	0.08
Taiwanese (156)	179	0.74
Thai (25)	26	0.11
Vietnamese (238)	246	1.02
Other Asian, specified (1)	3	0.01
Other Asian, not specified (10)	29	0.12
Australian	34	0.14
Austrian	130	0.54
Basque	14	0.06
Belgian	26	0.11
British	268	1.12
Bulgarian	15	0.06
Canadian	171	0.71
Croatian	44	0.18
Czech	141	0.59
Czechoslovakian	52	0.22
Danish	191	0.80
Dutch	549	2.29
Eastern European	61	0.25
English	3,892	16.20
European	275	1.14
Finnish	86	0.36
French, except Basque	1,062	4.42
French Canadian	176	0.73
German	4,401	18.32
Greek	151	0.63
Hawaii Native/Pacific Islander:	72	0.30
Micronesian: (9)	14	0.06
Guamanian/Chamorro (9)	14	0.06
Polynesian: (16)	41	0.17
Native Hawaiian (4)	23	0.10
Samoan (12)	15	0.06
Tongan	3	0.01
Other Pac. Isl., not spec. (6)	17	0.07
Hispanic or Latino:	2,037	8.47
Central American:	46	0.19
Costa Rican	3	0.01
Guatemalan	23	0.10
Honduran	3	0.01
Nicaraguan	6	0.02
Panamanian	2	0.01
Salvadoran	9	0.04
Cuban	80	0.33
Mexican	1,392	5.79
Puerto Rican	62	0.26
South American:	122	0.51
Argentinean	15	0.06
Bolivian	12	0.05

Notes: 1. Figures in the "Number" column do not add up to the total population due to: a) Ancestry/Race overlap — e.g. persons can report being both White and Irish, b) persons of Hispanic origin can report being any race, c) persons reporting two ancestries are counted in both categories. 2. Numbers in parentheses indicate the number of persons reporting this ancestry/race alone, not in combination with any other ancestry/race. 3. Refer to the Explanation of Data in the front of the book for more detailed information.

Chilean	11	0.05
Colombian	19	0.08
Ecuadorian	16	0.07
Paraguayan	3	0.01
Peruvian	41	0.17
Other South American	5	0.02
Other Hispanic or Latino	335	1.39
Hungarian	178	0.74
Icelander	47	0.20
Iranian	206	0.86
Irish	3,354	13.96
Israeli	45	0.19
Italian	1,578	6.57
Latvian	10	0.04
Lithuanian	66	0.27
Northern European	32	0.13
Norwegian	565	2.35
Pennsylvania German	4	0.02
Polish	684	2.85
Portuguese	169	0.70
Romanian	97	0.40
Russian	458	1.91
Scandinavian	54	0.22
Scotch-Irish	511	2.13
Scottish	1,046	4.36
Slavic	10	0.04
Slovak	32	0.13
Soviet Union	7	0.03
Swedish	812	3.38
Swiss	107	0.45
Ukrainian	42	0.17
United States or American	955	3.98
Welsh	317	1.32
West Indian, excl. Hispanic:	16	0.07
Belizean	16	0.07
White:	21,413	89.06
Not Hispanic (19,608)	20,033	83.32
Hispanic (1,261)	1,380	5.74
Yugoslavian	48	0.20

Tustin

Place Type: City
County: Orange
Population: 67,504

Ancestry/Race	Number	%
Acadian/Cajun	7	0.01
Afghan	41	0.06
African American/Black:	2,365	3.50
Not Hispanic (1,785)	2,089	3.09
Hispanic (185)	276	0.41
African, sub-Saharan:	296	0.44
African	164	0.24
Ethiopian	27	0.04
Ghanian	7	0.01
Sierra Leonean	8	0.01
South African	72	0.11
Zimbabwean	14	0.02
Other sub-Saharan African	4	0.01
Alaska Native tribes, specified:	3	0.00
Tlingit-Haida (3)	3	0.00
Am. Ind. or Alaska Nat., not spec.	337	0.50
American Indian tribes, specified:	496	0.73
Apache (15)	43	0.06
Blackfeet (2)	18	0.03
Cherokee (36)	91	0.13
Cheyenne (1)	1	0.00
Chickasaw	2	0.00
Chippewa	7	0.01
Choctaw (13)	23	0.03
Comanche (1)	4	0.01
Cree (1)	1	0.00
Creek (1)	10	0.01
Crow (3)	3	0.00
Delaware (1)	1	0.00
Iroquois (6)	12	0.02
Kiowa (1)	2	0.00
Latin American Indians (66)	110	0.16
Menominee	1	0.00
Navajo (8)	31	0.05
Osage (1)	1	0.00
Paiute (1)	3	0.00
Pima (1)	1	0.00
Potawatomi	3	0.00
Pueblo (8)	13	0.02
Seminole (3)	3	0.00
Shoshone (1)	1	0.00
Sioux (8)	19	0.03
Tohono O'Odham (2)	2	0.00
Ute (1)	2	0.00
Yaqui	4	0.01
All other tribes (43)	84	0.12
American Indian tribes, not spec.	66	0.10
Arab:	430	0.64
Arab/Arabic	69	0.10
Egyptian	70	0.10
Jordanian	9	0.01
Lebanese	96	0.14
Palestinian	7	0.01
Syrian	135	0.20
Other Arab	44	0.07
Armenian	206	0.30
Asian:	11,362	16.83
Bangladeshi (31)	48	0.07
Cambodian (168)	194	0.29
Chinese, ex. Taiwanese (1,567)	1,851	2.74
Filipino (1,719)	2,039	3.02
Hmong (5)	7	0.01
Indian (1,286)	1,389	2.06
Indonesian (77)	100	0.15
Japanese (794)	1,079	1.60
Korean (1,141)	1,234	1.83
Laotian (56)	61	0.09
Malaysian (15)	22	0.03
Pakistani (136)	182	0.27
Sri Lankan (31)	39	0.06
Taiwanese (465)	536	0.79
Thai (69)	81	0.12
Vietnamese (2,197)	2,300	3.41
Other Asian, specified (5)	10	0.01
Other Asian, not specified (72)	190	0.28
Assyrian/Chaldean/Syriac	7	0.01
Australian	19	0.03
Austrian	111	0.16
Basque	48	0.07
Belgian	63	0.09
Brazilian	24	0.04
British	229	0.34
Bulgarian	17	0.03
Canadian	231	0.34
Celtic	27	0.04
Croatian	23	0.03
Czech	161	0.24
Czechoslovakian	161	0.24
Danish	295	0.44
Dutch	740	1.10
Eastern European	63	0.09
English	5,111	7.57
European	653	0.97
Finnish	108	0.16
French, except Basque	1,490	2.21
French Canadian	403	0.60
German	7,456	11.04
Greek	229	0.34
Guyanese	6	0.01
Hawaii Native/Pacific Islander:	389	0.58
Melanesian:	2	0.00
Fijian	2	0.00
Micronesian: (53)	92	0.14
Guamanian/Chamorro (44)	79	0.12
Other Micronesian (9)	13	0.02
Polynesian: (137)	238	0.35
Native Hawaiian (40)	107	0.16
Samoan (76)	97	0.14
Tongan (18)	26	0.04
Other Polynesian (3)	8	0.01
Other Pac. Isl., specified	3	0.00
Other Pac. Isl., not spec. (10)	54	0.08
Hispanic or Latino:	23,110	34.24
Central American:	966	1.43
Costa Rican	30	0.04
Guatemalan	255	0.38
Honduran	49	0.07
Nicaraguan	61	0.09
Panamanian	23	0.03
Salvadoran	449	0.67
Other Central American	99	0.15
Cuban	170	0.25
Dominican Republic	19	0.03
Mexican	17,955	26.60
Puerto Rican	214	0.32
South American:	800	1.19
Argentinean	59	0.09
Bolivian	166	0.25
Chilean	38	0.06
Colombian	159	0.24
Ecuadorian	59	0.09
Peruvian	216	0.32
Uruguayan	8	0.01
Venezuelan	18	0.03
Other South American	77	0.11
Other Hispanic or Latino	2,986	4.42
Hungarian	340	0.50
Iranian	582	0.86
Irish	5,260	7.79
Israeli	47	0.07
Italian	3,189	4.72
Latvian	14	0.02
Lithuanian	113	0.17
Luxemburger	32	0.05
Macedonian	62	0.09
New Zealander	12	0.02
Northern European	30	0.04
Norwegian	763	1.13
Pennsylvania German	9	0.01
Polish	1,173	1.74
Portuguese	187	0.28
Romanian	84	0.12
Russian	788	1.17
Scandinavian	52	0.08
Scotch-Irish	827	1.22
Scottish	1,242	1.84
Serbian	20	0.03
Slavic	51	0.08
Slovak	22	0.03
Slovene	41	0.06
Swedish	1,083	1.60
Swiss	120	0.18
Turkish	48	0.07
Ukrainian	166	0.25
United States or American	2,117	3.13
Welsh	485	0.72
West Indian, excl. Hispanic:	134	0.20
Belizean	26	0.04
Jamaican	101	0.15
Other West Indian	7	0.01
White:	42,177	62.48
Not Hispanic (30,264)	31,697	46.96
Hispanic (9,375)	10,480	15.53
Yugoslavian	93	0.14

Twentynine Palms

Place Type: City
County: San Bernardino
Population: 14,764

Ancestry/Race	Number	%
African American/Black:	1,652	11.19
Not Hispanic (1,313)	1,544	10.46
Hispanic (68)	108	0.73
African, sub-Saharan:	42	0.29
African	42	0.29
Alaska Native tribes, specified:	4	0.03
Alaska Athabascan (1)	1	0.01
Aleut (1)	1	0.01
Eskimo (1)	1	0.01
Tlingit-Haida (1)	1	0.01
Am. Ind. or Alaska Nat., not spec.	135	0.91

Notes: 1. Figures in the "Number" column do not add up to the total population due to: a) Ancestry/Race overlap — e.g. persons can report being both White and Irish, b) persons of Hispanic origin can report being any race, c) persons reporting two ancestries are counted in both categories. 2. Numbers in parentheses indicate the number of persons reporting this ancestry/race alone, not in combination with any other ancestry/race. 3. Refer to the Explanation of Data in the front of the book for more detailed information.

American Indian tribes, specified:	329	2.23
Apache (5)	23	0.16
Blackfeet (2)	23	0.16
Cherokee (28)	92	0.62
Cheyenne (3)	3	0.02
Chickasaw (1)	8	0.05
Chippewa (2)	5	0.03
Choctaw (4)	15	0.10
Cree	1	0.01
Creek	6	0.04
Delaware (3)	4	0.03
Iroquois (4)	14	0.09
Kiowa (1)	1	0.01
Latin American Indians (3)	18	0.12
Lumbee (3)	5	0.03
Menominee (1)	1	0.01
Navajo (17)	20	0.14
Osage (1)	1	0.01
Paiute	5	0.03
Pima (1)	1	0.01
Pueblo (8)	14	0.09
Seminole (1)	1	0.01
Shoshone (2)	2	0.01
Sioux (6)	11	0.07
Tohono O'Odham (2)	6	0.04
Ute (1)	1	0.01
Yaqui (3)	9	0.06
Yuman (2)	2	0.01
All other tribes (31)	37	0.25
American Indian tribes, not spec.	41	0.28
Arab:	18	0.12
Lebanese	7	0.05
Palestinian	11	0.08
Armenian	14	0.10
Asian:	891	6.03
Cambodian (2)	6	0.04
Chinese, ex. Taiwanese (37)	69	0.47
Filipino (327)	512	3.47
Hmong (1)	1	0.01
Indian (17)	23	0.16
Indonesian	3	0.02
Japanese (80)	133	0.90
Korean (43)	69	0.47
Laotian (2)	5	0.03
Malaysian (1)	1	0.01
Pakistani (4)	10	0.07
Taiwanese (1)	3	0.02
Thai (1)	7	0.05
Vietnamese (24)	28	0.19
Other Asian, not specified (12)	21	0.14
Australian	19	0.13
Austrian	19	0.13
Basque	15	0.10
Belgian	27	0.18
Brazilian	12	0.08
British	23	0.16
Canadian	21	0.14
Czech	28	0.19
Danish	57	0.39
Dutch	355	2.42
English	1,221	8.33
European	129	0.88
Finnish	18	0.12
French, except Basque	553	3.77
French Canadian	140	0.96
German	2,397	16.36
German Russian	10	0.07
Greek	6	0.04
Hawaii Native/Pacific Islander:	376	2.55
Micronesian: (52)	67	0.45
Guamanian/Chamorro (52)	67	0.45
Polynesian: (190)	282	1.91
Native Hawaiian (16)	52	0.35
Samoan (174)	220	1.49
Tongan	5	0.03
Other Polynesian	5	0.03
Other Pac. Isl., not spec. (10)	27	0.18
Hispanic or Latino:	2,202	14.91
Central American:	78	0.53
Costa Rican	5	0.03
Guatemalan	7	0.05
Honduran	17	0.12
Nicaraguan	13	0.09
Panamanian	21	0.14
Salvadoran	14	0.09
Other Central American	1	0.01
Cuban	35	0.24
Dominican Republic	7	0.05
Mexican	1,512	10.24
Puerto Rican	143	0.97
South American:	25	0.17
Argentinean	1	0.01
Bolivian	2	0.01
Colombian	13	0.09
Ecuadorian	2	0.01
Peruvian	2	0.01
Other South American	5	0.03
Other Hispanic or Latino	402	2.72
Hungarian	101	0.69
Icelander	10	0.07
Irish	2,048	13.98
Italian	617	4.21
Lithuanian	22	0.15
Norwegian	146	1.00
Polish	316	2.16
Portuguese	59	0.40
Russian	87	0.59
Scandinavian	6	0.04
Scotch-Irish	302	2.06
Scottish	232	1.58
Slovene	8	0.05
Swedish	274	1.87
Ukrainian	24	0.16
United States or American	925	6.31
Welsh	83	0.57
West Indian, excl. Hispanic:	120	0.82
Barbadian	35	0.24
Jamaican	77	0.53
West Indian	8	0.05
White:	11,249	76.19
Not Hispanic (9,548)	10,118	68.53
Hispanic (937)	1,131	7.66
Yugoslavian	8	0.05

Ukiah

Place Type: City
County: Mendocino
Population: 15,497

Ancestry/Race	Number	%
Acadian/Cajun	13	0.09
African American/Black:	238	1.54
Not Hispanic (138)	221	1.43
Hispanic (10)	17	0.11
African, sub-Saharan:	19	0.13
African	19	0.13
Alaska Native tribes, specified:	8	0.05
Tlingit-Haida (3)	8	0.05
Alaska Native tribes, not specified	1	0.01
Am. Ind. or Alaska Nat., not spec.	186	1.20
American Indian tribes, specified:	670	4.32
Apache (3)	13	0.08
Blackfeet (3)	13	0.08
Cherokee (17)	75	0.48
Cheyenne (1)	1	0.01
Chippewa (3)	4	0.03
Choctaw (9)	12	0.08
Colville (3)	3	0.02
Comanche	1	0.01
Creek (2)	3	0.02
Iroquois	4	0.03
Latin American Indians (15)	20	0.13
Navajo (2)	4	0.03
Osage	2	0.01
Ottawa	5	0.03
Paiute (1)	1	0.01
Potawatomi	1	0.01
Pueblo (3)	8	0.05
Seminole (1)	6	0.04
Shoshone	5	0.03
Sioux (3)	13	0.08
Tohono O'Odham (1)	2	0.01
Yaqui	2	0.01
Yuman (4)	4	0.03
All other tribes (369)	468	3.02
American Indian tribes, not spec.	32	0.21
Arab:	51	0.34
Arab/Arabic	20	0.13
Egyptian	13	0.09
Lebanese	9	0.06
Palestinian	9	0.06
Armenian	21	0.14
Asian:	370	2.39
Cambodian (4)	4	0.03
Chinese, ex. Taiwanese (77)	90	0.58
Filipino (72)	122	0.79
Hmong (2)	2	0.01
Indian (50)	63	0.41
Indonesian (1)	3	0.02
Japanese (8)	18	0.12
Korean (11)	19	0.12
Pakistani (6)	7	0.05
Taiwanese	4	0.03
Thai (6)	11	0.07
Vietnamese (18)	19	0.12
Other Asian, specified	1	0.01
Other Asian, not specified (1)	7	0.05
Australian	13	0.09
Austrian	42	0.28
Basque	7	0.05
Belgian	9	0.06
British	84	0.56
Canadian	48	0.32
Celtic	12	0.08
Czech	61	0.40
Danish	153	1.01
Dutch	204	1.35
English	1,883	12.46
European	131	0.87
Finnish	102	0.67
French, except Basque	489	3.24
French Canadian	166	1.10
German	2,514	16.63
Greek	78	0.52
Hawaii Native/Pacific Islander:	51	0.33
Melanesian: (2)	2	0.01
Fijian (2)	2	0.01
Micronesian: (1)	2	0.01
Guamanian/Chamorro (1)	2	0.01
Polynesian: (8)	32	0.21
Native Hawaiian (7)	26	0.17
Samoan (1)	4	0.03
Tongan	2	0.01
Other Pac. Isl., specified	1	0.01
Other Pac. Isl., not spec. (4)	14	0.09
Hispanic or Latino:	2,993	19.31
Central American:	7	0.05
Guatemalan	1	0.01
Honduran	1	0.01
Panamanian	2	0.01
Salvadoran	1	0.01
Other Central American	2	0.01
Cuban	15	0.10
Mexican	2,556	16.49
Puerto Rican	23	0.15
South American:	17	0.11
Argentinean	3	0.02
Bolivian	8	0.05
Colombian	2	0.01
Ecuadorian	3	0.02
Other South American	1	0.01
Other Hispanic or Latino	375	2.42
Hungarian	46	0.30
Irish	1,838	12.16
Italian	1,005	6.65
Latvian	49	0.32
Maltese	11	0.07
Northern European	12	0.08
Norwegian	216	1.43

Notes: 1. Figures in the "Number" column do not add up to the total population due to: a) Ancestry/Race overlap — e.g. persons can report being both White and Irish, b) persons of Hispanic origin can report being any race, c) persons reporting two ancestries are counted in both categories. 2. Numbers in parentheses indicate the number of persons reporting this ancestry/race alone, not in combination with any other ancestry/race. 3. Refer to the Explanation of Data in the front of the book for more detailed information.

Ancestry/Race	Number	%
Pennsylvania German	20	0.13
Polish	244	1.61
Portuguese	180	1.19
Romanian	13	0.09
Russian	71	0.47
Scandinavian	92	0.61
Scotch-Irish	364	2.41
Scottish	386	2.55
Slavic	7	0.05
Slovak	17	0.11
Swedish	223	1.48
Swiss	138	0.91
Ukrainian	30	0.20
United States or American	852	5.64
Welsh	108	0.71
White:	12,919	83.36
Not Hispanic (11,220)	11,579	74.72
Hispanic (1,105)	1,340	8.65
Yugoslavian	42	0.28

Union City

Place Type: City
County: Alameda
Population: 66,869

Ancestry/Race	Number	%
Afghan	955	1.43
African American/Black:	5,092	7.61
Not Hispanic (4,321)	4,801	7.18
Hispanic (158)	291	0.44
African, sub-Saharan:	387	0.58
African	188	0.28
Cape Verdean	8	0.01
Ethiopian	47	0.07
Liberian	40	0.06
Nigerian	53	0.08
Sudanese	16	0.02
Other sub-Saharan African	35	0.05
Alaska Native tribes, specified:	6	0.01
Alaska Athabascan (1)	1	0.00
Eskimo (2)	3	0.00
Tlingit-Haida	1	0.00
All other tribes (1)	1	0.00
Am. Ind. or Alaska Nat., not spec.	337	0.50
Albanian	18	0.03
American Indian tribes, specified:	495	0.74
Apache (17)	38	0.06
Blackfeet	17	0.03
Cherokee (31)	134	0.20
Chickasaw (4)	13	0.02
Chippewa (6)	20	0.03
Choctaw (8)	23	0.03
Comanche (5)	6	0.01
Creek (1)	3	0.00
Crow	1	0.00
Delaware (1)	1	0.00
Iroquois (1)	5	0.01
Kiowa (3)	3	0.00
Latin American Indians (48)	76	0.11
Navajo (9)	23	0.03
Ottawa	4	0.01
Potawatomi (3)	9	0.01
Pueblo (11)	13	0.02
Puget Sound Salish	2	0.00
Seminole (1)	4	0.01
Shoshone (2)	2	0.00
Sioux (2)	10	0.01
Tohono O'Odham	2	0.00
Ute	1	0.00
Yakama	2	0.00
Yaqui (4)	15	0.02
All other tribes (26)	68	0.10
American Indian tribes, not spec.	36	0.05
Arab:	325	0.49
Arab/Arabic	158	0.24
Egyptian	77	0.12
Jordanian	43	0.06
Lebanese	9	0.01
Palestinian	22	0.03
Other Arab	16	0.02
Armenian	42	0.06
Asian:	32,098	48.00
Bangladeshi (4)	6	0.01
Cambodian (124)	158	0.24
Chinese, ex. Taiwanese (5,764)	6,438	9.63
Filipino (12,587)	13,716	20.51
Hmong (3)	3	0.00
Indian (5,751)	6,195	9.26
Indonesian (81)	134	0.20
Japanese (414)	710	1.06
Korean (903)	981	1.47
Laotian (58)	60	0.09
Malaysian (6)	18	0.03
Pakistani (196)	260	0.39
Sri Lankan (16)	16	0.02
Taiwanese (146)	184	0.28
Thai (98)	116	0.17
Vietnamese (2,096)	2,309	3.45
Other Asian, specified (89)	126	0.19
Other Asian, not specified (149)	668	1.00
Assyrian/Chaldean/Syriac	8	0.01
Australian	19	0.03
Austrian	27	0.04
Basque	39	0.06
Belgian	8	0.01
Brazilian	11	0.02
British	179	0.27
Canadian	18	0.03
Croatian	34	0.05
Czech	32	0.05
Czechoslovakian	8	0.01
Danish	247	0.37
Dutch	344	0.51
Eastern European	9	0.01
English	1,935	2.89
Estonian	8	0.01
European	303	0.45
Finnish	119	0.18
French, except Basque	756	1.13
French Canadian	175	0.26
German	3,121	4.67
Greek	96	0.14
Guyanese	46	0.07
Hawaii Native/Pacific Islander:	1,261	1.89
Melanesian: (159)	196	0.29
Fijian (159)	196	0.29
Micronesian: (83)	150	0.22
Guamanian/Chamorro (83)	150	0.22
Polynesian: (298)	586	0.88
Native Hawaiian (94)	306	0.46
Samoan (78)	116	0.17
Tongan (107)	145	0.22
Other Polynesian (19)	19	0.03
Other Pac. Isl., specified	2	0.00
Other Pac. Isl., not spec. (68)	327	0.49
Hispanic or Latino:	16,020	23.96
Central American:	730	1.09
Costa Rican	24	0.04
Guatemalan	107	0.16
Honduran	9	0.01
Nicaraguan	169	0.25
Panamanian	29	0.04
Salvadoran	298	0.45
Other Central American	94	0.14
Cuban	42	0.06
Dominican Republic	1	0.00
Mexican	11,960	17.89
Puerto Rican	510	0.76
South American:	261	0.39
Argentinean	17	0.03
Bolivian	30	0.04
Chilean	15	0.02
Colombian	39	0.06
Ecuadorian	10	0.01
Paraguayan	2	0.00
Peruvian	112	0.17
Uruguayan	4	0.01
Venezuelan	5	0.01
Other South American	27	0.04
Other Hispanic or Latino	2,516	3.76
Hungarian	86	0.13
Icelander	21	0.03
Iranian	293	0.44
Irish	2,354	3.52
Italian	1,604	2.40
Latvian	6	0.01
Lithuanian	26	0.04
Maltese	5	0.01
Northern European	13	0.02
Norwegian	302	0.45
Polish	285	0.43
Portuguese	1,572	2.35
Romanian	25	0.04
Russian	197	0.29
Scandinavian	50	0.07
Scotch-Irish	330	0.49
Scottish	261	0.39
Serbian	12	0.02
Slavic	13	0.02
Slovak	41	0.06
Slovene	6	0.01
Swedish	414	0.62
Swiss	26	0.04
Turkish	40	0.06
Ukrainian	26	0.04
United States or American	901	1.35
Welsh	168	0.25
West Indian, excl. Hispanic:	85	0.13
Bahamian	22	0.03
British West Indian	5	0.01
Jamaican	22	0.03
Trinidadian and Tobagonian	15	0.02
West Indian	21	0.03
White:	23,370	34.95
Not Hispanic (13,610)	15,822	23.66
Hispanic (6,588)	7,548	11.29
Yugoslavian	28	0.04

Upland

Place Type: City
County: San Bernardino
Population: 68,393

Ancestry/Race	Number	%
Afghan	61	0.09
African American/Black:	5,747	8.40
Not Hispanic (4,990)	5,429	7.94
Hispanic (174)	318	0.46
African, sub-Saharan:	436	0.64
African	348	0.51
Cape Verdean	23	0.03
Ghanian	21	0.03
Nigerian	15	0.02
Sudanese	10	0.01
Other sub-Saharan African	19	0.03
Alaska Native tribes, specified:	10	0.01
Aleut	2	0.00
All other tribes (5)	8	0.01
Am. Ind. or Alaska Nat., not spec.	347	0.51
Albanian	15	0.02
Alsatian	9	0.01
American Indian tribes, specified:	734	1.07
Apache (13)	60	0.09
Blackfeet (3)	23	0.03
Cherokee (38)	183	0.27
Cheyenne	1	0.00
Chickasaw (5)	8	0.01
Chippewa (1)	7	0.01
Choctaw (12)	42	0.06
Colville (1)	1	0.00
Comanche (4)	10	0.01
Cree	1	0.00
Creek (7)	13	0.02
Crow (1)	1	0.00
Delaware (1)	2	0.00
Iroquois (4)	12	0.02
Kiowa (1)	3	0.00
Latin American Indians (67)	115	0.17

Notes: 1. Figures in the "Number" column do not add up to the total population due to: a) Ancestry/Race overlap — e.g. persons can report being both White and Irish, b) persons of Hispanic origin can report being any race, c) persons reporting two ancestries are counted in both categories. 2. Numbers in parentheses indicate the number of persons reporting this ancestry/race alone, not in combination with any other ancestry/race. 3. Refer to the Explanation of Data in the front of the book for more detailed information.

Lumbee (3)	3	0.00
Navajo (25)	47	0.07
Osage (6)	8	0.01
Ottawa (1)	1	0.00
Paiute	3	0.00
Pima (3)	8	0.01
Potawatomi (4)	6	0.01
Pueblo (13)	22	0.03
Puget Sound Salish (2)	2	0.00
Seminole (3)	10	0.01
Shoshone (1)	3	0.00
Sioux (10)	31	0.05
Tohono O'Odham (1)	6	0.01
Ute (1)	5	0.01
Yaqui (14)	22	0.03
Yuman (7)	9	0.01
All other tribes (35)	66	0.10
American Indian tribes, not spec.	68	0.10
Arab:	653	0.95
Arab/Arabic	167	0.24
Egyptian	144	0.21
Lebanese	185	0.27
Palestinian	116	0.17
Syrian	16	0.02
Other Arab	25	0.04
Armenian	120	0.18
Asian:	5,953	8.70
Bangladeshi (9)	11	0.02
Cambodian (17)	29	0.04
Chinese, ex. Taiwanese (1,015)	1,215	1.78
Filipino (743)	998	1.46
Hmong (1)	1	0.00
Indian (576)	637	0.93
Indonesian (248)	326	0.48
Japanese (262)	398	0.58
Korean (735)	798	1.17
Laotian (4)	4	0.01
Malaysian (3)	6	0.01
Pakistani (75)	105	0.15
Sri Lankan (13)	14	0.02
Taiwanese (361)	425	0.62
Thai (90)	106	0.15
Vietnamese (631)	666	0.97
Other Asian, specified (22)	29	0.04
Other Asian, not specified (58)	185	0.27
Australian	20	0.03
Austrian	127	0.19
Basque	64	0.09
Belgian	82	0.12
Brazilian	44	0.06
British	284	0.42
Canadian	223	0.33
Celtic	10	0.01
Croatian	112	0.16
Czech	148	0.22
Czechoslovakian	122	0.18
Danish	434	0.63
Dutch	984	1.44
Eastern European	44	0.06
English	6,522	9.53
Estonian	8	0.01
European	848	1.24
Finnish	79	0.12
French, except Basque	2,290	3.35
French Canadian	220	0.32
German	8,619	12.60
German Russian	4	0.01
Greek	313	0.46
Hawaii Native/Pacific Islander:	253	0.37
Melanesian: (3)	3	0.00
Fijian (3)	3	0.00
Micronesian: (20)	32	0.05
Guamanian/Chamorro (19)	29	0.04
Other Micronesian (1)	3	0.00
Polynesian: (68)	153	0.22
Native Hawaiian (45)	99	0.14
Samoan (18)	34	0.05
Tongan (4)	12	0.02
Other Polynesian (1)	8	0.01
Other Pac. Isl., not spec. (8)	65	0.10
Hispanic or Latino:	18,830	27.53
Central American:	708	1.04
Costa Rican	36	0.05
Guatemalan	147	0.21
Honduran	35	0.05
Nicaraguan	139	0.20
Panamanian	35	0.05
Salvadoran	248	0.36
Other Central American	68	0.10
Cuban	260	0.38
Dominican Republic	11	0.02
Mexican	14,177	20.73
Puerto Rican	323	0.47
South American:	515	0.75
Argentinean	123	0.18
Bolivian	15	0.02
Chilean	19	0.03
Colombian	109	0.16
Ecuadorian	71	0.10
Paraguayan	2	0.00
Peruvian	109	0.16
Uruguayan	7	0.01
Venezuelan	11	0.02
Other South American	49	0.07
Other Hispanic or Latino	2,836	4.15
Hungarian	315	0.46
Iranian	412	0.60
Irish	6,419	9.38
Israeli	29	0.04
Italian	4,135	6.04
Latvian	6	0.01
Lithuanian	106	0.15
Macedonian	19	0.03
Northern European	72	0.11
Norwegian	1,100	1.61
Pennsylvania German	36	0.05
Polish	1,183	1.73
Portuguese	362	0.53
Romanian	71	0.10
Russian	483	0.71
Scandinavian	85	0.12
Scotch-Irish	990	1.45
Scottish	1,504	2.20
Serbian	28	0.04
Slavic	37	0.05
Slovak	102	0.15
Slovene	110	0.16
Swedish	1,003	1.47
Swiss	289	0.42
Turkish	50	0.07
Ukrainian	116	0.17
United States or American	2,333	3.41
Welsh	557	0.81
West Indian, excl. Hispanic:	237	0.35
Belizean	68	0.10
Haitian	80	0.12
Jamaican	68	0.10
West Indian	21	0.03
White:	48,623	71.09
Not Hispanic (37,456)	38,889	56.86
Hispanic (8,510)	9,734	14.23
Yugoslavian	157	0.23

Vacaville

Place Type: City
County: Solano
Population: 88,625

Ancestry/Race	Number	%
Acadian/Cajun	22	0.02
Afghan	35	0.04
African American/Black:	9,920	11.19
Not Hispanic (8,691)	9,553	10.78
Hispanic (189)	367	0.41
African, sub-Saharan:	543	0.61
African	376	0.42
Cape Verdean	54	0.06
Liberian	17	0.02
Nigerian	57	0.06
Ugandan	18	0.02
Other sub-Saharan African	21	0.02
Alaska Native tribes, specified:	27	0.03
Alaska Athabascan (3)	4	0.00
Aleut (6)	7	0.01
Eskimo (3)	8	0.01
Tlingit-Haida (2)	3	0.00
All other tribes (5)	5	0.01
Alaska Native tribes, not specified	1	0.00
Am. Ind. or Alaska Nat., not spec.	609	0.69
American Indian tribes, specified:	1,172	1.32
Apache (38)	63	0.07
Blackfeet (15)	51	0.06
Cherokee (123)	397	0.45
Cheyenne (1)	4	0.00
Chickasaw (4)	25	0.03
Chippewa (17)	34	0.04
Choctaw (14)	64	0.07
Colville (1)	1	0.00
Comanche (2)	8	0.01
Cree (1)	5	0.01
Creek (21)	38	0.04
Crow	4	0.00
Delaware (2)	3	0.00
Iroquois (10)	20	0.02
Kiowa	2	0.00
Latin American Indians (38)	66	0.07
Lumbee	1	0.00
Menominee (1)	1	0.00
Navajo (31)	58	0.07
Osage	4	0.00
Ottawa (3)	3	0.00
Paiute (9)	18	0.02
Pima	2	0.00
Potawatomi (5)	7	0.01
Pueblo (3)	8	0.01
Puget Sound Salish (1)	5	0.01
Seminole (7)	14	0.02
Shoshone (10)	11	0.01
Sioux (30)	57	0.06
Tohono O'Odham	5	0.01
Yaqui (6)	14	0.02
Yuman (3)	4	0.00
All other tribes (96)	174	0.20
American Indian tribes, not spec.	102	0.12
Arab:	157	0.18
Arab/Arabic	13	0.01
Egyptian	32	0.04
Jordanian	8	0.01
Lebanese	62	0.07
Palestinian	27	0.03
Syrian	6	0.01
Other Arab	9	0.01
Armenian	26	0.03
Asian:	5,808	6.55
Cambodian (11)	24	0.03
Chinese, ex. Taiwanese (484)	766	0.86
Filipino (1,828)	2,674	3.02
Hmong	2	0.00
Indian (302)	367	0.41
Indonesian (5)	21	0.02
Japanese (412)	1,004	1.13
Korean (196)	351	0.40
Laotian (40)	48	0.05
Malaysian	4	0.00
Pakistani (15)	27	0.03
Sri Lankan (3)	4	0.00
Taiwanese (9)	23	0.03
Thai (54)	96	0.11
Vietnamese (193)	240	0.27
Other Asian, specified (13)	30	0.03
Other Asian, not specified (47)	127	0.14
Assyrian/Chaldean/Syriac	10	0.01
Australian	109	0.12
Austrian	157	0.18
Basque	82	0.09
Belgian	50	0.06
Brazilian	48	0.05
British	258	0.29
Canadian	301	0.34

Notes: 1. Figures in the "Number" column do not add up to the total population due to: a) Ancestry/Race overlap — e.g. persons can report being both White and Irish, b) persons of Hispanic origin can report being any race, c) persons reporting two ancestries are counted in both categories. 2. Numbers in parentheses indicate the number of persons reporting this ancestry/race alone, not in combination with any other ancestry/race. 3. Refer to the Explanation of Data in the front of the book for more detailed information.

Celtic	13	0.01
Croatian	20	0.02
Czech	159	0.18
Czechoslovakian	131	0.15
Danish	806	0.91
Dutch	1,610	1.82
Eastern European	17	0.02
English	8,148	9.19
Estonian	16	0.02
European	1,264	1.43
Finnish	222	0.25
French, except Basque	2,589	2.92
French Canadian	595	0.67
German	12,792	14.43
German Russian	7	0.01
Greek	432	0.49
Guyanese	7	0.01
Hawaii Native/Pacific Islander:	884	1.00
Melanesian: (11)	11	0.01
Fijian (11)	11	0.01
Micronesian: (166)	268	0.30
Guamanian/Chamorro (162)	259	0.29
Other Micronesian (4)	9	0.01
Polynesian: (186)	474	0.53
Native Hawaiian (125)	371	0.42
Samoan (56)	94	0.11
Tongan (5)	7	0.01
Other Polynesian	2	0.00
Other Pac. Isl., specified	2	0.00
Other Pac. Isl., not spec. (39)	129	0.15
Hispanic or Latino:	15,847	17.88
Central American:	440	0.50
Costa Rican	15	0.02
Guatemalan	51	0.06
Honduran	17	0.02
Nicaraguan	116	0.13
Panamanian	60	0.07
Salvadoran	144	0.16
Other Central American	37	0.04
Cuban	146	0.16
Dominican Republic	18	0.02
Mexican	11,090	12.51
Puerto Rican	608	0.69
South American:	164	0.19
Argentinean	24	0.03
Bolivian	4	0.00
Chilean	14	0.02
Colombian	27	0.03
Ecuadorian	3	0.00
Peruvian	72	0.08
Uruguayan	4	0.00
Venezuelan	7	0.01
Other South American	9	0.01
Other Hispanic or Latino	3,381	3.81
Hungarian	282	0.32
Icelander	13	0.01
Iranian	92	0.10
Irish	10,140	11.44
Israeli	8	0.01
Italian	5,236	5.91
Latvian	19	0.02
Lithuanian	157	0.18
Luxemburger	10	0.01
Maltese	16	0.02
Northern European	73	0.08
Norwegian	1,654	1.87
Pennsylvania German	8	0.01
Polish	1,418	1.60
Portuguese	1,533	1.73
Romanian	79	0.09
Russian	579	0.65
Scandinavian	327	0.37
Scotch-Irish	1,114	1.26
Scottish	1,897	2.14
Serbian	100	0.11
Slavic	41	0.05
Slovak	29	0.03
Slovene	41	0.05
Swedish	1,615	1.82
Swiss	377	0.43
Turkish	36	0.04
Ukrainian	85	0.10
United States or American	4,778	5.39
Welsh	562	0.63
West Indian, excl. Hispanic:	202	0.23
Belizean	27	0.03
British West Indian	9	0.01
Jamaican	134	0.15
West Indian	32	0.04
White:	68,048	76.78
Not Hispanic (56,031)	58,853	66.41
Hispanic (7,878)	9,195	10.38
Yugoslavian	147	0.17

Valinda

Place Type: Census Designated Place
County: Los Angeles
Population: 21,776

Ancestry/Race	Number	%
African American/Black:	644	2.96
Not Hispanic (508)	577	2.65
Hispanic (28)	67	0.31
African, sub-Saharan:	50	0.23
African	50	0.23
Alaska Native tribes, specified:	1	0.00
Tlingit-Haida	1	0.00
Alaska Native tribes, not specified	1	0.00
Am. Ind. or Alaska Nat., not spec.	175	0.80
Albanian	6	0.03
American Indian tribes, specified:	229	1.05
Apache (17)	25	0.11
Blackfeet (3)	5	0.02
Cherokee (19)	42	0.19
Chickasaw	7	0.03
Chippewa (5)	5	0.02
Choctaw (1)	16	0.07
Comanche (4)	4	0.02
Iroquois	2	0.01
Latin American Indians (41)	68	0.31
Menominee	2	0.01
Navajo (1)	7	0.03
Osage	2	0.01
Pima (4)	4	0.02
Potawatomi (1)	1	0.00
Pueblo (4)	5	0.02
Sioux	4	0.02
Tohono O'Odham (3)	3	0.01
Yakama (1)	1	0.00
Yaqui (7)	8	0.04
All other tribes (4)	18	0.08
American Indian tribes, not spec.	18	0.08
Arab:	74	0.34
Arab/Arabic	14	0.06
Egyptian	14	0.06
Jordanian	46	0.21
Armenian	19	0.09
Asian:	2,320	10.65
Cambodian (16)	17	0.08
Chinese, ex. Taiwanese (351)	394	1.81
Filipino (1,056)	1,153	5.29
Indian (53)	85	0.39
Indonesian (8)	9	0.04
Japanese (75)	124	0.57
Korean (23)	29	0.13
Laotian (21)	23	0.11
Malaysian (4)	4	0.02
Pakistani	7	0.03
Taiwanese (11)	12	0.06
Thai (20)	27	0.12
Vietnamese (353)	383	1.76
Other Asian, specified (15)	21	0.10
Other Asian, not specified (13)	32	0.15
Basque	6	0.03
British	11	0.05
Canadian	99	0.45
Croatian	13	0.06
Danish	30	0.14
Dutch	183	0.84
English	356	1.63
French, except Basque	103	0.47
French Canadian	13	0.06
German	680	3.12
Greek	150	0.69
Hawaii Native/Pacific Islander:	93	0.43
Melanesian: (7)	9	0.04
Fijian (7)	9	0.04
Micronesian: (2)	4	0.02
Guamanian/Chamorro (2)	4	0.02
Polynesian: (18)	50	0.23
Native Hawaiian (9)	29	0.13
Samoan (9)	15	0.07
Other Polynesian	6	0.03
Other Pac. Isl., specified	6	0.03
Other Pac. Isl., not spec. (8)	24	0.11
Hispanic or Latino:	16,271	74.72
Central American:	684	3.14
Costa Rican	16	0.07
Guatemalan	168	0.77
Honduran	20	0.09
Nicaraguan	60	0.28
Panamanian	2	0.01
Salvadoran	345	1.58
Other Central American	73	0.34
Cuban	43	0.20
Dominican Republic	1	0.00
Mexican	13,364	61.37
Puerto Rican	91	0.42
South American:	172	0.79
Argentinean	14	0.06
Chilean	8	0.04
Colombian	34	0.16
Ecuadorian	59	0.27
Peruvian	47	0.22
Venezuelan	2	0.01
Other South American	8	0.04
Other Hispanic or Latino	1,916	8.80
Hungarian	34	0.16
Irish	393	1.80
Italian	187	0.86
Lithuanian	8	0.04
Norwegian	102	0.47
Polish	50	0.23
Portuguese	81	0.37
Romanian	21	0.10
Russian	29	0.13
Scotch-Irish	64	0.29
Scottish	17	0.08
Swedish	73	0.34
United States or American	451	2.07
Welsh	47	0.22
West Indian, excl. Hispanic:	7	0.03
Belizean	7	0.03
White:	9,721	44.64
Not Hispanic (2,522)	2,741	12.59
Hispanic (6,291)	6,980	32.05
Yugoslavian	19	0.09

Valle Vista

Place Type: Census Designated Place
County: Riverside
Population: 10,488

Ancestry/Race	Number	%
African American/Black:	166	1.58
Not Hispanic (125)	149	1.42
Hispanic (5)	17	0.16
African, sub-Saharan:	7	0.07
African	7	0.07
Am. Ind. or Alaska Nat., not spec.	30	0.29
American Indian tribes, specified:	196	1.87
Apache (3)	6	0.06
Blackfeet	1	0.01
Cherokee (11)	37	0.35
Chickasaw	1	0.01
Chippewa (2)	2	0.02
Choctaw (4)	8	0.08
Comanche (1)	4	0.04

Notes: 1. Figures in the "Number" column do not add up to the total population due to: a) Ancestry/Race overlap — e.g. persons can report being both White and Irish, b) persons of Hispanic origin can report being any race, c) persons reporting two ancestries are counted in both categories. 2. Numbers in parentheses indicate the number of persons reporting this ancestry/race alone, not in combination with any other ancestry/race. 3. Refer to the Explanation of Data in the front of the book for more detailed information.

Creek	2	0.02
Iroquois (5)	7	0.07
Kiowa (2)	3	0.03
Latin American Indians (15)	22	0.21
Navajo (4)	9	0.09
Osage (4)	4	0.04
Pueblo (9)	9	0.09
Puget Sound Salish	1	0.01
Shoshone	2	0.02
Sioux (1)	5	0.05
Tohono O'Odham (4)	4	0.04
Yuman	3	0.03
All other tribes (50)	66	0.63
American Indian tribes, not spec.	9	0.09
Arab:	21	0.20
Egyptian	13	0.12
Lebanese	8	0.08
Armenian	9	0.08
Asian:	174	1.66
Chinese, ex. Taiwanese (25)	31	0.30
Filipino (24)	39	0.37
Indian (54)	55	0.52
Japanese (10)	20	0.19
Korean (5)	10	0.10
Pakistani (6)	6	0.06
Thai (2)	5	0.05
Vietnamese (4)	4	0.04
Other Asian, not specified (4)	4	0.04
Australian	31	0.29
Austrian	55	0.52
Basque	31	0.29
Brazilian	20	0.19
British	47	0.44
Canadian	59	0.56
Czech	27	0.25
Czechoslovakian	36	0.34
Danish	130	1.23
Dutch	312	2.94
Eastern European	12	0.11
English	1,433	13.50
European	36	0.34
Finnish	24	0.23
French, except Basque	430	4.05
French Canadian	133	1.25
German	2,166	20.41
Greek	6	0.06
Hawaii Native/Pacific Islander:	29	0.28
Micronesian: (6)	7	0.07
Guamanian/Chamorro (6)	7	0.07
Polynesian: (10)	21	0.20
Native Hawaiian (1)	9	0.09
Samoan (2)	5	0.05
Tongan (7)	7	0.07
Other Pac. Isl., not spec.	1	0.01
Hispanic or Latino:	1,539	14.67
Central American:	24	0.23
Costa Rican	2	0.02
Guatemalan	5	0.05
Honduran	2	0.02
Nicaraguan	2	0.02
Panamanian	1	0.01
Salvadoran	7	0.07
Other Central American	5	0.05
Cuban	10	0.10
Mexican	1,254	11.96
Puerto Rican	23	0.22
South American:	16	0.15
Bolivian	1	0.01
Chilean	4	0.04
Colombian	3	0.03
Peruvian	1	0.01
Other South American	7	0.07
Other Hispanic or Latino	212	2.02
Hungarian	16	0.15
Iranian	8	0.08
Irish	1,341	12.64
Italian	514	4.84
Maltese	7	0.07
Norwegian	194	1.83
Pennsylvania German	10	0.09
Polish	342	3.22
Russian	84	0.79
Scandinavian	16	0.15
Scotch-Irish	379	3.57
Scottish	314	2.96
Slovak	8	0.08
Slovene	8	0.08
Swedish	199	1.88
Swiss	57	0.54
Ukrainian	12	0.11
United States or American	529	4.98
Welsh	120	1.13
White:	9,541	90.97
Not Hispanic (8,408)	8,557	81.59
Hispanic (880)	984	9.38
Yugoslavian	41	0.39

Vallejo

Place Type: City
County: Solano
Population: 116,760

Ancestry/Race	Number	%
Acadian/Cajun	5	0.00
Afghan	9	0.01
African American/Black:	30,138	25.81
Not Hispanic (27,201)	29,288	25.08
Hispanic (454)	850	0.73
African, sub-Saharan:	1,220	1.05
African	1,011	0.87
Cape Verdean	14	0.01
Ethiopian	7	0.01
Liberian	22	0.02
Nigerian	145	0.12
Other sub-Saharan African	21	0.02
Alaska Native tribes, specified:	33	0.03
Aleut (9)	13	0.01
Eskimo (6)	10	0.01
Tlingit-Haida (3)	10	0.01
Alaska Native tribes, not specified	4	0.00
Am. Ind. or Alaska Nat., not spec.	703	0.60
Albanian	7	0.01
American Indian tribes, specified:	1,391	1.19
Apache (33)	74	0.06
Blackfeet (16)	99	0.08
Cherokee (106)	522	0.45
Cheyenne (3)	8	0.01
Chickasaw (6)	23	0.02
Chippewa (11)	19	0.02
Choctaw (32)	116	0.10
Colville (5)	5	0.00
Comanche (5)	9	0.01
Cree	5	0.00
Creek (5)	26	0.02
Crow (2)	17	0.01
Iroquois (7)	21	0.02
Kiowa (1)	7	0.01
Latin American Indians (42)	76	0.07
Lumbee (1)	1	0.00
Menominee	1	0.00
Navajo (18)	37	0.03
Osage (4)	5	0.00
Ottawa (3)	7	0.01
Paiute (5)	7	0.01
Pima (1)	2	0.00
Potawatomi (3)	4	0.00
Pueblo (13)	26	0.02
Puget Sound Salish	3	0.00
Seminole (4)	15	0.01
Shoshone (2)	3	0.00
Sioux (32)	81	0.07
Ute (9)	17	0.01
Yakama (3)	3	0.00
Yaqui (3)	5	0.00
Yuman (1)	8	0.01
All other tribes (45)	139	0.12
American Indian tribes, not spec.	101	0.09
Arab:	300	0.26
Arab/Arabic	44	0.04
Egyptian	72	0.06
Lebanese	90	0.08
Palestinian	51	0.04
Syrian	9	0.01
Other Arab	34	0.03
Armenian	128	0.11
Asian:	32,449	27.79
Bangladeshi (1)	3	0.00
Cambodian (16)	25	0.02
Chinese, ex. Taiwanese (1,029)	1,617	1.38
Filipino (24,215)	27,098	23.21
Hmong (23)	26	0.02
Indian (1,064)	1,340	1.15
Indonesian (32)	66	0.06
Japanese (329)	748	0.64
Korean (242)	360	0.31
Laotian (41)	53	0.05
Malaysian (4)	49	0.04
Pakistani (70)	107	0.09
Sri Lankan (10)	10	0.01
Taiwanese (3)	5	0.00
Thai (45)	80	0.07
Vietnamese (483)	571	0.49
Other Asian, specified (8)	31	0.03
Other Asian, not specified (115)	260	0.22
Australian	63	0.05
Austrian	127	0.11
Basque	51	0.04
Belgian	64	0.06
Brazilian	58	0.05
British	210	0.18
Bulgarian	4	0.00
Canadian	198	0.17
Celtic	16	0.01
Croatian	14	0.01
Czech	151	0.13
Czechoslovakian	139	0.12
Danish	657	0.56
Dutch	848	0.73
Eastern European	37	0.03
English	5,781	4.97
Estonian	8	0.01
European	966	0.83
Finnish	134	0.12
French, except Basque	1,983	1.70
French Canadian	265	0.23
German	7,277	6.25
Greek	314	0.27
Hawaii Native/Pacific Islander:	2,413	2.07
Melanesian: (87)	147	0.13
Fijian (87)	147	0.13
Micronesian: (559)	914	0.78
Guamanian/Chamorro (537)	890	0.76
Other Micronesian (22)	24	0.02
Polynesian: (506)	965	0.83
Native Hawaiian (159)	490	0.42
Samoan (268)	375	0.32
Tongan (66)	84	0.07
Other Polynesian (13)	16	0.01
Other Pac. Isl., specified	3	0.00
Other Pac. Isl., not spec. (105)	384	0.33
Hispanic or Latino:	18,591	15.92
Central American:	1,658	1.42
Costa Rican	17	0.01
Guatemalan	220	0.19
Honduran	59	0.05
Nicaraguan	270	0.23
Panamanian	55	0.05
Salvadoran	893	0.76
Other Central American	144	0.12
Cuban	87	0.07
Dominican Republic	10	0.01
Mexican	12,253	10.49
Puerto Rican	814	0.70
South American:	291	0.25
Argentinean	8	0.01
Bolivian	14	0.01
Chilean	35	0.03
Colombian	47	0.04
Ecuadorian	28	0.02

Notes: 1. Figures in the "Number" column do not add up to the total population due to: a) Ancestry/Race overlap — e.g. persons can report being both White and Irish, b) persons of Hispanic origin can report being any race, c) persons reporting two ancestries are counted in both categories. 2. Numbers in parentheses indicate the number of persons reporting this ancestry/race alone, not in combination with any other ancestry/race. 3. Refer to the Explanation of Data in the front of the book for more detailed information.

Paraguayan	3	0.00
Peruvian	100	0.09
Uruguayan	12	0.01
Venezuelan	15	0.01
Other South American	29	0.02
Other Hispanic or Latino	3,478	2.98
Hungarian	145	0.12
Icelander	15	0.01
Iranian	127	0.11
Irish	6,708	5.77
Israeli	5	0.00
Italian	3,716	3.19
Latvian	7	0.01
Lithuanian	108	0.09
Maltese	7	0.01
Northern European	59	0.05
Norwegian	1,196	1.03
Pennsylvania German	39	0.03
Polish	847	0.73
Portuguese	1,384	1.19
Romanian	21	0.02
Russian	369	0.32
Scandinavian	131	0.11
Scotch-Irish	983	0.84
Scottish	1,186	1.02
Serbian	30	0.03
Slavic	76	0.07
Slovak	35	0.03
Slovene	48	0.04
Swedish	725	0.62
Swiss	160	0.14
Turkish	7	0.01
Ukrainian	82	0.07
United States or American	3,158	2.71
Welsh	415	0.36
West Indian, excl. Hispanic:	192	0.17
Barbadian	21	0.02
British West Indian	10	0.01
Haitian	25	0.02
Jamaican	84	0.07
Trinidadian and Tobagonian	30	0.03
West Indian	22	0.02
White:	47,121	40.36
Not Hispanic (35,533)	39,180	33.56
Hispanic (6,463)	7,941	6.80
Yugoslavian	112	0.10

Victorville

Place Type: City
County: San Bernardino
Population: 64,029

Ancestry/Race	Number	%
African American/Black:	8,611	13.45
Not Hispanic (7,431)	8,194	12.80
Hispanic (199)	417	0.65
African, sub-Saharan:	341	0.53
African	341	0.53
Alaska Native tribes, specified:	6	0.01
Alaska Athabascan	1	0.00
Aleut (1)	1	0.00
Eskimo (3)	4	0.01
Am. Ind. or Alaska Nat., not spec.	510	0.80
American Indian tribes, specified:	1,058	1.65
Apache (34)	61	0.10
Blackfeet (11)	66	0.10
Cherokee (104)	341	0.53
Cheyenne (1)	2	0.00
Chickasaw (5)	9	0.01
Chippewa (8)	20	0.03
Choctaw (14)	50	0.08
Comanche (2)	10	0.02
Cree (1)	6	0.01
Creek (3)	17	0.03
Delaware (2)	2	0.00
Houma	1	0.00
Iroquois (2)	16	0.02
Kiowa	2	0.00
Latin American Indians (45)	101	0.16
Lumbee	9	0.01
Navajo (19)	46	0.07
Osage	3	0.00
Ottawa (1)	1	0.00
Paiute (9)	9	0.01
Pima (2)	6	0.01
Potawatomi (1)	3	0.00
Pueblo (22)	35	0.05
Puget Sound Salish (1)	1	0.00
Seminole (5)	11	0.02
Shoshone (5)	15	0.02
Sioux (10)	42	0.07
Tohono O'Odham (3)	6	0.01
Ute	2	0.00
Yaqui (21)	36	0.06
Yuman (2)	2	0.00
All other tribes (80)	127	0.20
American Indian tribes, not spec.	67	0.10
Arab:	325	0.50
Arab/Arabic	76	0.12
Egyptian	166	0.26
Lebanese	58	0.09
Palestinian	18	0.03
Syrian	7	0.01
Armenian	130	0.20
Asian:	3,114	4.86
Cambodian (43)	65	0.10
Chinese, ex. Taiwanese (190)	286	0.45
Filipino (1,161)	1,467	2.29
Hmong	1	0.00
Indian (128)	181	0.28
Indonesian (18)	61	0.10
Japanese (193)	415	0.65
Korean (158)	213	0.33
Malaysian (9)	13	0.02
Pakistani (2)	8	0.01
Sri Lankan	3	0.00
Taiwanese (23)	29	0.05
Thai (80)	116	0.18
Vietnamese (129)	143	0.22
Other Asian, specified (8)	15	0.02
Other Asian, not specified (31)	98	0.15
Austrian	86	0.13
Basque	14	0.02
Belgian	76	0.12
Brazilian	17	0.03
British	239	0.37
Canadian	278	0.43
Celtic	35	0.05
Croatian	35	0.05
Czech	108	0.17
Czechoslovakian	78	0.12
Danish	278	0.43
Dutch	1,239	1.92
English	3,870	6.00
European	285	0.44
Finnish	169	0.26
French, except Basque	1,737	2.69
French Canadian	461	0.71
German	6,851	10.62
Greek	147	0.23
Guyanese	14	0.02
Hawaii Native/Pacific Islander:	345	0.54
Melanesian: (2)	3	0.00
Fijian (2)	3	0.00
Micronesian: (50)	102	0.16
Guamanian/Chamorro (50)	101	0.16
Other Micronesian	1	0.00
Polynesian: (58)	159	0.25
Native Hawaiian (21)	96	0.15
Samoan (29)	45	0.07
Tongan (8)	14	0.02
Other Polynesian	4	0.01
Other Pac. Isl., specified	1	0.00
Other Pac. Isl., not spec. (18)	80	0.12
Hispanic or Latino:	21,426	33.46
Central American:	588	0.92
Costa Rican	45	0.07
Guatemalan	147	0.23
Honduran	38	0.06
Nicaraguan	58	0.09
Panamanian	22	0.03
Salvadoran	228	0.36
Other Central American	50	0.08
Cuban	185	0.29
Dominican Republic	20	0.03
Mexican	16,091	25.13
Puerto Rican	623	0.97
South American:	191	0.30
Argentinean	22	0.03
Chilean	18	0.03
Colombian	74	0.12
Ecuadorian	37	0.06
Peruvian	24	0.04
Uruguayan	1	0.00
Venezuelan	2	0.00
Other South American	13	0.02
Other Hispanic or Latino	3,728	5.82
Hungarian	222	0.34
Iranian	101	0.16
Irish	5,810	9.01
Italian	2,724	4.22
Lithuanian	25	0.04
Northern European	6	0.01
Norwegian	631	0.98
Pennsylvania German	7	0.01
Polish	1,097	1.70
Portuguese	344	0.53
Romanian	70	0.11
Russian	161	0.25
Scandinavian	17	0.03
Scotch-Irish	757	1.17
Scottish	933	1.45
Serbian	10	0.02
Slavic	15	0.02
Slovak	28	0.04
Slovene	28	0.04
Swedish	705	1.09
Swiss	147	0.23
Turkish	14	0.02
Ukrainian	62	0.10
United States or American	2,955	4.58
Welsh	390	0.60
West Indian, excl. Hispanic:	83	0.13
Bahamian	9	0.01
Belizean	14	0.02
Jamaican	60	0.09
White:	42,264	66.01
Not Hispanic (30,382)	32,044	50.05
Hispanic (8,709)	10,220	15.96
Yugoslavian	16	0.02

View Park-Windsor Hills

Place Type: Census Designated Place
County: Los Angeles
Population: 10,958

Ancestry/Race	Number	%
African American/Black:	10,061	91.81
Not Hispanic (9,557)	9,932	90.64
Hispanic (84)	129	1.18
African, sub-Saharan:	510	4.65
African	341	3.11
Cape Verdean	18	0.16
Ethiopian	69	0.63
Nigerian	60	0.55
Senegalese	22	0.20
Am. Ind. or Alaska Nat., not spec.	105	0.96
American Indian tribes, specified:	110	1.00
Blackfeet	14	0.13
Cherokee (1)	25	0.23
Cheyenne (1)	1	0.01
Chickasaw	5	0.05
Choctaw	12	0.11
Comanche	1	0.01
Cree	2	0.02
Creek	8	0.07
Iroquois	1	0.01
Latin American Indians (3)	7	0.06

Notes: 1. Figures in the "Number" column do not add up to the total population due to: a) Ancestry/Race overlap — e.g. persons can report being both White and Irish, b) persons of Hispanic origin can report being any race, c) persons reporting two ancestries are counted in both categories. 2. Numbers in parentheses indicate the number of persons reporting this ancestry/race alone, not in combination with any other ancestry/race. 3. Refer to the Explanation of Data in the front of the book for more detailed information.

Navajo (1)	4	0.04
Seminole	8	0.07
Sioux	3	0.03
Ute	2	0.02
All other tribes (2)	17	0.16
American Indian tribes, not spec.	13	0.12
Arab:	25	0.23
Egyptian	25	0.23
Asian:	212	1.93
Chinese, ex. Taiwanese (27)	46	0.42
Filipino (30)	65	0.59
Indian (12)	19	0.17
Japanese (42)	61	0.56
Korean (3)	8	0.07
Pakistani (1)	1	0.01
Sri Lankan (1)	1	0.01
Thai (1)	2	0.02
Vietnamese (2)	2	0.02
Other Asian, not specified (2)	7	0.06
British	11	0.10
Dutch	11	0.10
English	128	1.17
European	7	0.06
French, except Basque	73	0.67
German	76	0.69
Greek	18	0.16
Hawaii Native/Pacific Islander:	19	0.17
Melanesian: (1)	1	0.01
Fijian (1)	1	0.01
Micronesian:	2	0.02
Guamanian/Chamorro	2	0.02
Polynesian: (3)	11	0.10
Native Hawaiian	8	0.07
Samoan (2)	2	0.02
Other Polynesian (1)	1	0.01
Other Pac. Isl., not spec. (3)	5	0.05
Hispanic or Latino:	297	2.71
Central American:	41	0.37
Costa Rican	2	0.02
Guatemalan	11	0.10
Honduran	3	0.03
Nicaraguan	2	0.02
Panamanian	13	0.12
Salvadoran	8	0.07
Other Central American	2	0.02
Cuban	6	0.05
Dominican Republic	1	0.01
Mexican	137	1.25
Puerto Rican	29	0.26
South American:	11	0.10
Argentinean	1	0.01
Ecuadorian	1	0.01
Uruguayan	1	0.01
Venezuelan	5	0.05
Other South American	3	0.03
Other Hispanic or Latino	72	0.66
Irish	23	0.21
Italian	138	1.26
Norwegian	5	0.05
Portuguese	9	0.08
Russian	9	0.08
Scandinavian	20	0.18
Scotch-Irish	7	0.06
Swedish	11	0.10
United States or American	108	0.99
West Indian, excl. Hispanic:	286	2.61
Bahamian	6	0.05
Barbadian	12	0.11
Belizean	62	0.57
Haitian	41	0.37
Jamaican	146	1.33
West Indian	19	0.17
White:	841	7.67
Not Hispanic (530)	741	6.76
Hispanic (58)	100	0.91

Vincent

Place Type: Census Designated Place
County: Los Angeles
Population: 15,097

Ancestry/Race	Number	%
African American/Black:	472	3.13
Not Hispanic (377)	409	2.71
Hispanic (26)	63	0.42
African, sub-Saharan:	17	0.11
African	17	0.11
Alaska Native tribes, specified:	1	0.01
Alaska Athabascan	1	0.01
Am. Ind. or Alaska Nat., not spec.	111	0.74
American Indian tribes, specified:	171	1.13
Apache (5)	14	0.09
Blackfeet (2)	5	0.03
Cherokee (12)	34	0.23
Chippewa (3)	3	0.02
Choctaw (3)	5	0.03
Latin American Indians (18)	30	0.20
Navajo (9)	15	0.10
Potawatomi	1	0.01
Pueblo (13)	15	0.10
Seminole	1	0.01
Shoshone (5)	5	0.03
Sioux (8)	8	0.05
Tohono O'Odham (4)	4	0.03
Yaqui (5)	8	0.05
All other tribes (14)	23	0.15
American Indian tribes, not spec.	17	0.11
Arab:	81	0.54
Arab/Arabic	54	0.36
Egyptian	4	0.03
Lebanese	19	0.13
Syrian	4	0.03
Asian:	1,247	8.26
Chinese, ex. Taiwanese (247)	306	2.03
Filipino (455)	511	3.38
Indian (44)	54	0.36
Indonesian (47)	61	0.40
Japanese (64)	116	0.77
Korean (24)	33	0.22
Laotian (1)	10	0.07
Pakistani (9)	9	0.06
Taiwanese (5)	7	0.05
Thai (16)	16	0.11
Vietnamese (78)	98	0.65
Other Asian, specified (3)	3	0.02
Other Asian, not specified (8)	23	0.15
Assyrian/Chaldean/Syriac	5	0.03
Austrian	6	0.04
Basque	7	0.05
Belgian	5	0.03
British	27	0.18
Canadian	11	0.07
Celtic	11	0.07
Czechoslovakian	30	0.20
Danish	15	0.10
Dutch	126	0.83
English	544	3.60
European	56	0.37
Finnish	13	0.09
French, except Basque	280	1.86
French Canadian	74	0.49
German	999	6.62
Greek	38	0.25
Guyanese	40	0.27
Hawaii Native/Pacific Islander:	43	0.28
Melanesian: (4)	4	0.03
Fijian (4)	4	0.03
Micronesian: (5)	9	0.06
Guamanian/Chamorro (5)	9	0.06
Polynesian: (2)	24	0.16
Native Hawaiian (1)	15	0.10
Samoan (1)	9	0.06
Other Pac. Isl., not spec.	6	0.04
Hispanic or Latino:	9,724	64.41
Central American:	429	2.84
Costa Rican	11	0.07
Guatemalan	127	0.84
Honduran	13	0.09
Nicaraguan	68	0.45
Panamanian	8	0.05
Salvadoran	144	0.95
Other Central American	58	0.38
Cuban	59	0.39
Dominican Republic	1	0.01
Mexican	7,888	52.25
Puerto Rican	66	0.44
South American:	134	0.89
Argentinean	22	0.15
Bolivian	2	0.01
Chilean	7	0.05
Colombian	19	0.13
Ecuadorian	21	0.14
Peruvian	41	0.27
Uruguayan	5	0.03
Venezuelan	2	0.01
Other South American	15	0.10
Other Hispanic or Latino	1,147	7.60
Hungarian	28	0.19
Irish	700	4.64
Italian	379	2.51
Lithuanian	34	0.23
Norwegian	147	0.97
Polish	97	0.64
Portuguese	66	0.44
Russian	27	0.18
Scandinavian	6	0.04
Scotch-Irish	137	0.91
Scottish	55	0.36
Slovak	11	0.07
Swedish	93	0.62
Ukrainian	4	0.03
United States or American	251	1.66
Welsh	73	0.48
White:	8,527	56.48
Not Hispanic (3,679)	3,880	25.70
Hispanic (4,132)	4,647	30.78

Vineyard

Place Type: Census Designated Place
County: Sacramento
Population: 10,109

Ancestry/Race	Number	%
African American/Black:	784	7.76
Not Hispanic (653)	751	7.43
Hispanic (18)	33	0.33
African, sub-Saharan:	32	0.32
Nigerian	32	0.32
Alaska Native tribes, specified:	1	0.01
Aleut	1	0.01
Am. Ind. or Alaska Nat., not spec.	57	0.56
American Indian tribes, specified:	130	1.29
Apache	4	0.04
Blackfeet (3)	13	0.13
Cherokee (5)	39	0.39
Chickasaw (1)	2	0.02
Chippewa (1)	2	0.02
Choctaw (7)	18	0.18
Creek (5)	5	0.05
Delaware	1	0.01
Iroquois	1	0.01
Kiowa	1	0.01
Latin American Indians (6)	8	0.08
Lumbee (1)	1	0.01
Navajo (1)	2	0.02
Osage	1	0.01
Pueblo (3)	3	0.03
Shoshone (1)	2	0.02
Sioux (3)	4	0.04
Ute (1)	1	0.01
Yaqui	3	0.03
Yuman	1	0.01
All other tribes (4)	18	0.18
American Indian tribes, not spec.	1	0.01

Notes: 1. Figures in the "Number" column do not add up to the total population due to: a) Ancestry/Race overlap — e.g. persons can report being both White and Irish, b) persons of Hispanic origin can report being any race, c) persons reporting two ancestries are counted in both categories. 2. Numbers in parentheses indicate the number of persons reporting this ancestry/race alone, not in combination with any other ancestry/race. 3. Refer to the Explanation of Data in the front of the book for more detailed information.

Ancestry/Race	Number	%
Arab:	75	0.75
Egyptian	29	0.29
Jordanian	14	0.14
Lebanese	5	0.05
Other Arab	27	0.27
Asian:	1,936	19.15
Cambodian (5)	6	0.06
Chinese, ex. Taiwanese (214)	267	2.64
Filipino (540)	654	6.47
Hmong (10)	11	0.11
Indian (203)	228	2.26
Indonesian	4	0.04
Japanese (106)	184	1.82
Korean (115)	131	1.30
Laotian (24)	24	0.24
Pakistani (24)	24	0.24
Taiwanese (2)	7	0.07
Thai (2)	4	0.04
Vietnamese (333)	351	3.47
Other Asian, specified (4)	10	0.10
Other Asian, not specified (12)	31	0.31
Austrian	15	0.15
Basque	11	0.11
British	19	0.19
Canadian	8	0.08
Czech	7	0.07
Czechoslovakian	21	0.21
Danish	115	1.15
Dutch	106	1.06
English	874	8.73
European	107	1.07
Finnish	84	0.84
French, except Basque	503	5.03
French Canadian	29	0.29
German	1,518	15.17
Greek	79	0.79
Hawaii Native/Pacific Islander:	101	1.00
Melanesian: (12)	12	0.12
Fijian (12)	12	0.12
Micronesian: (17)	26	0.26
Guamanian/Chamorro (16)	25	0.25
Other Micronesian (1)	1	0.01
Polynesian: (12)	24	0.24
Native Hawaiian (2)	11	0.11
Samoan (2)	5	0.05
Tongan (8)	8	0.08
Other Pac. Isl., specified	4	0.04
Other Pac. Isl., not spec. (12)	35	0.35
Hispanic or Latino:	1,243	12.30
Central American:	49	0.48
Costa Rican	3	0.03
Guatemalan	3	0.03
Honduran	5	0.05
Nicaraguan	20	0.20
Panamanian	4	0.04
Salvadoran	12	0.12
Other Central American	2	0.02
Cuban	4	0.04
Mexican	867	8.58
Puerto Rican	35	0.35
South American:	18	0.18
Argentinean	1	0.01
Chilean	1	0.01
Colombian	5	0.05
Peruvian	5	0.05
Venezuelan	5	0.05
Other South American	1	0.01
Other Hispanic or Latino	270	2.67
Hungarian	36	0.36
Iranian	32	0.32
Irish	797	7.96
Italian	758	7.57
Latvian	8	0.08
Luxemburger	12	0.12
Northern European	27	0.27
Norwegian	131	1.31
Pennsylvania German	7	0.07
Polish	101	1.01
Portuguese	207	2.07
Romanian	9	0.09
Russian	112	1.12
Scandinavian	62	0.62
Scotch-Irish	165	1.65
Scottish	208	2.08
Slovak	18	0.18
Slovene	17	0.17
Swedish	202	2.02
Swiss	57	0.57
Ukrainian	29	0.29
United States or American	462	4.62
Welsh	112	1.12
West Indian, excl. Hispanic:	10	0.10
Belizean	10	0.10
White:	7,181	71.04
Not Hispanic (6,105)	6,443	63.74
Hispanic (572)	738	7.30
Yugoslavian	8	0.08

Visalia

Place Type: City
County: Tulare
Population: 91,565

Ancestry/Race	Number	%
African American/Black:	2,133	2.33
Not Hispanic (1,558)	1,797	1.96
Hispanic (196)	336	0.37
African, sub-Saharan:	319	0.35
African	288	0.31
Ethiopian	6	0.01
South African	25	0.03
Alaska Native tribes, specified:	3	0.00
Eskimo (1)	1	0.00
Tlingit-Haida (2)	2	0.00
Am. Ind. or Alaska Nat., not spec.	825	0.90
American Indian tribes, specified:	1,380	1.51
Apache (28)	58	0.06
Blackfeet (5)	18	0.02
Cherokee (167)	426	0.47
Cheyenne (14)	17	0.02
Chickasaw (14)	32	0.03
Chippewa (5)	8	0.01
Choctaw (62)	162	0.18
Comanche (5)	15	0.02
Cree	7	0.01
Creek (7)	18	0.02
Delaware	1	0.00
Iroquois (4)	7	0.01
Latin American Indians (80)	133	0.15
Lumbee (1)	1	0.00
Menominee (2)	2	0.00
Navajo (20)	29	0.03
Osage (5)	5	0.01
Ottawa	3	0.00
Paiute (10)	21	0.02
Pima (2)	7	0.01
Potawatomi (25)	28	0.03
Pueblo (11)	17	0.02
Seminole (12)	32	0.03
Shoshone (3)	4	0.00
Sioux (30)	48	0.05
Tohono O'Odham (3)	3	0.00
Ute	4	0.00
Yakama	1	0.00
Yaqui (13)	32	0.03
Yuman	2	0.00
All other tribes (155)	239	0.26
American Indian tribes, not spec.	109	0.12
Arab:	318	0.35
Arab/Arabic	119	0.13
Egyptian	54	0.06
Jordanian	15	0.02
Lebanese	54	0.06
Palestinian	19	0.02
Syrian	34	0.04
Other Arab	23	0.03
Armenian	354	0.39
Asian:	5,585	6.10
Cambodian (37)	38	0.04
Chinese, ex. Taiwanese (391)	512	0.56
Filipino (645)	858	0.94
Hmong (616)	700	0.76
Indian (271)	350	0.38
Indonesian (7)	13	0.01
Japanese (272)	423	0.46
Korean (160)	189	0.21
Laotian (1,816)	1,962	2.14
Malaysian	2	0.00
Pakistani (54)	66	0.07
Sri Lankan (2)	2	0.00
Taiwanese (13)	15	0.02
Thai (29)	35	0.04
Vietnamese (132)	155	0.17
Other Asian, specified (4)	12	0.01
Other Asian, not specified (156)	253	0.28
Assyrian/Chaldean/Syriac	8	0.01
Australian	10	0.01
Austrian	60	0.07
Basque	74	0.08
Belgian	42	0.05
Brazilian	27	0.03
British	204	0.22
Canadian	180	0.20
Celtic	35	0.04
Croatian	117	0.13
Czech	173	0.19
Czechoslovakian	116	0.13
Danish	493	0.54
Dutch	2,021	2.21
Eastern European	5	0.01
English	7,655	8.36
European	742	0.81
Finnish	120	0.13
French, except Basque	2,171	2.37
French Canadian	261	0.29
German	9,568	10.46
German Russian	21	0.02
Greek	58	0.06
Hawaii Native/Pacific Islander:	252	0.28
Melanesian: (1)	2	0.00
Fijian (1)	2	0.00
Micronesian: (32)	46	0.05
Guamanian/Chamorro (30)	44	0.05
Other Micronesian (2)	2	0.00
Polynesian: (65)	118	0.13
Native Hawaiian (48)	86	0.09
Samoan (7)	21	0.02
Tongan (9)	9	0.01
Other Polynesian (1)	2	0.00
Other Pac. Isl., specified	1	0.00
Other Pac. Isl., not spec. (17)	85	0.09
Hispanic or Latino:	32,619	35.62
Central American:	204	0.22
Costa Rican	13	0.01
Guatemalan	46	0.05
Honduran	11	0.01
Nicaraguan	13	0.01
Panamanian	9	0.01
Salvadoran	89	0.10
Other Central American	23	0.03
Cuban	72	0.08
Dominican Republic	2	0.00
Mexican	27,918	30.49
Puerto Rican	270	0.29
South American:	118	0.13
Argentinean	36	0.04
Bolivian	9	0.01
Chilean	7	0.01
Colombian	20	0.02
Ecuadorian	3	0.00
Peruvian	25	0.03
Uruguayan	1	0.00
Venezuelan	6	0.01
Other South American	11	0.01
Other Hispanic or Latino	4,035	4.41
Hungarian	50	0.05
Icelander	27	0.03
Iranian	86	0.09
Irish	7,882	8.61

Notes: 1. Figures in the "Number" column do not add up to the total population due to: a) Ancestry/Race overlap — e.g. persons can report being both White and Irish, b) persons of Hispanic origin can report being any race, c) persons reporting two ancestries are counted in both categories. 2. Numbers in parentheses indicate the number of persons reporting this ancestry/race alone, not in combination with any other ancestry/race. 3. Refer to the Explanation of Data in the front of the book for more detailed information.

Ancestry/Race	Number	%
Israeli	32	0.03
Italian	3,357	3.67
Lithuanian	64	0.07
Macedonian	7	0.01
Northern European	65	0.07
Norwegian	1,131	1.24
Polish	593	0.65
Portuguese	2,253	2.46
Romanian	27	0.03
Russian	299	0.33
Scandinavian	129	0.14
Scotch-Irish	1,220	1.33
Scottish	1,433	1.57
Serbian	9	0.01
Slavic	47	0.05
Slovak	14	0.02
Slovene	11	0.01
Swedish	1,294	1.41
Swiss	260	0.28
Turkish	27	0.03
Ukrainian	86	0.09
United States or American	4,493	4.91
Welsh	463	0.51
West Indian, excl. Hispanic:	54	0.06
Dutch West Indian	38	0.04
Jamaican	16	0.02
White:	66,895	73.06
Not Hispanic (50,269)	51,761	56.53
Hispanic (13,385)	15,134	16.53
Yugoslavian	62	0.07

Vista

Place Type: City
County: San Diego
Population: 89,857

Ancestry/Race	Number	%
Afghan	19	0.02
African American/Black:	4,549	5.06
Not Hispanic (3,535)	4,064	4.52
Hispanic (279)	485	0.54
African, sub-Saharan:	238	0.26
African	223	0.25
Ethiopian	15	0.02
Alaska Native tribes, specified:	11	0.01
Alaska Athabascan (1)	1	0.00
Aleut (4)	4	0.00
Eskimo (4)	4	0.00
All other tribes (2)	2	0.00
Alaska Native tribes, not specified	1	0.00
Am. Ind. or Alaska Nat., not spec.	493	0.55
American Indian tribes, specified:	1,095	1.22
Apache (20)	34	0.04
Blackfeet (4)	26	0.03
Cherokee (58)	213	0.24
Cheyenne	2	0.00
Chickasaw (7)	21	0.02
Chippewa (12)	22	0.02
Choctaw (20)	51	0.06
Comanche	2	0.00
Cree	3	0.00
Creek (5)	10	0.01
Iroquois (4)	6	0.01
Kiowa (1)	1	0.00
Latin American Indians (178)	299	0.33
Navajo (29)	45	0.05
Osage (9)	15	0.02
Paiute (2)	2	0.00
Pima (2)	2	0.00
Potawatomi (1)	6	0.01
Pueblo (20)	30	0.03
Puget Sound Salish (1)	1	0.00
Seminole	4	0.00
Shoshone (4)	7	0.01
Sioux (5)	29	0.03
Tohono O'Odham (3)	3	0.00
Ute	1	0.00
Yaqui (12)	14	0.02
Yuman (1)	4	0.00
All other tribes (156)	242	0.27
American Indian tribes, not spec.	108	0.12
Arab:	480	0.53
Arab/Arabic	184	0.20
Egyptian	28	0.03
Iraqi	7	0.01
Jordanian	10	0.01
Lebanese	197	0.22
Moroccan	15	0.02
Palestinian	11	0.01
Syrian	28	0.03
Armenian	48	0.05
Asian:	4,656	5.18
Bangladeshi (6)	6	0.01
Cambodian (27)	47	0.05
Chinese, ex. Taiwanese (377)	552	0.61
Filipino (1,060)	1,593	1.77
Hmong (2)	4	0.00
Indian (179)	231	0.26
Indonesian (16)	36	0.04
Japanese (552)	957	1.07
Korean (347)	420	0.47
Laotian (31)	35	0.04
Malaysian (8)	12	0.01
Pakistani (4)	5	0.01
Sri Lankan (9)	9	0.01
Taiwanese (19)	20	0.02
Thai (52)	75	0.08
Vietnamese (486)	543	0.60
Other Asian, specified (11)	20	0.02
Other Asian, not specified (43)	91	0.10
Assyrian/Chaldean/Syriac	11	0.01
Australian	10	0.01
Austrian	257	0.29
Basque	60	0.07
Belgian	151	0.17
Brazilian	150	0.17
British	435	0.48
Canadian	300	0.33
Celtic	45	0.05
Croatian	127	0.14
Czech	359	0.40
Czechoslovakian	90	0.10
Danish	441	0.49
Dutch	1,183	1.31
Eastern European	29	0.03
English	7,456	8.27
European	453	0.50
Finnish	238	0.26
French, except Basque	2,419	2.68
French Canadian	511	0.57
German	10,908	12.10
German Russian	7	0.01
Greek	369	0.41
Hawaii Native/Pacific Islander:	1,066	1.19
Melanesian:	1	0.00
Fijian	1	0.00
Micronesian: (110)	173	0.19
Guamanian/Chamorro (106)	162	0.18
Other Micronesian (4)	11	0.01
Polynesian: (416)	766	0.85
Native Hawaiian (108)	323	0.36
Samoan (302)	422	0.47
Tongan (6)	19	0.02
Other Polynesian	2	0.00
Other Pac. Isl., specified	2	0.00
Other Pac. Isl., not spec. (56)	124	0.14
Hispanic or Latino:	34,990	38.94
Central American:	462	0.51
Costa Rican	16	0.02
Guatemalan	129	0.14
Honduran	46	0.05
Nicaraguan	30	0.03
Panamanian	58	0.06
Salvadoran	151	0.17
Other Central American	32	0.04
Cuban	71	0.08
Dominican Republic	36	0.04
Mexican	29,802	33.17
Puerto Rican	556	0.62
South American:	191	0.21
Argentinean	21	0.02
Bolivian	13	0.01
Chilean	20	0.02
Colombian	51	0.06
Ecuadorian	30	0.03
Paraguayan	1	0.00
Peruvian	32	0.04
Uruguayan	2	0.00
Venezuelan	3	0.00
Other South American	18	0.02
Other Hispanic or Latino	3,872	4.31
Hungarian	311	0.35
Icelander	26	0.03
Iranian	169	0.19
Irish	7,721	8.57
Italian	3,867	4.29
Latvian	51	0.06
Lithuanian	168	0.19
Macedonian	22	0.02
Northern European	34	0.04
Norwegian	1,551	1.72
Pennsylvania German	29	0.03
Polish	1,346	1.49
Portuguese	400	0.44
Romanian	61	0.07
Russian	686	0.76
Scandinavian	261	0.29
Scotch-Irish	1,300	1.44
Scottish	1,817	2.02
Serbian	69	0.08
Slavic	36	0.04
Slovak	101	0.11
Slovene	14	0.02
Swedish	1,185	1.31
Swiss	311	0.35
Ukrainian	110	0.12
United States or American	3,185	3.53
Welsh	491	0.54
West Indian, excl. Hispanic:	132	0.15
Haitian	43	0.05
Jamaican	60	0.07
Trinidadian and Tobagonian	8	0.01
West Indian	21	0.02
White:	61,328	68.25
Not Hispanic (44,844)	46,680	51.95
Hispanic (12,906)	14,648	16.30
Yugoslavian	206	0.23

Walnut Creek

Place Type: City
County: Contra Costa
Population: 64,296

Ancestry/Race	Number	%
Acadian/Cajun	6	0.01
Afghan	172	0.27
African American/Black:	939	1.46
Not Hispanic (666)	885	1.38
Hispanic (22)	54	0.08
African, sub-Saharan:	260	0.40
African	189	0.29
Ethiopian	34	0.05
Ghanian	6	0.01
Nigerian	2	0.00
South African	29	0.04
Alaska Native tribes, specified:	8	0.01
Aleut (1)	5	0.01
Eskimo (1)	1	0.00
Tlingit-Haida (2)	2	0.00
Am. Ind. or Alaska Nat., not spec.	146	0.23
American Indian tribes, specified:	398	0.62
Apache (5)	13	0.02
Blackfeet	13	0.02
Cherokee (32)	129	0.20
Cheyenne	2	0.00
Chickasaw (1)	4	0.01
Chippewa (3)	9	0.01
Choctaw (7)	30	0.05

Notes: 1. Figures in the "Number" column do not add up to the total population due to: a) Ancestry/Race overlap — e.g. persons can report being both White and Irish, b) persons of Hispanic origin can report being any race, c) persons reporting two ancestries are counted in both categories. 2. Numbers in parentheses indicate the number of persons reporting this ancestry/race alone, not in combination with any other ancestry/race. 3. Refer to the Explanation of Data in the front of the book for more detailed information.

Ancestry/Race	Number	%
Colville	1	0.00
Comanche	4	0.01
Cree	1	0.00
Creek (2)	5	0.01
Crow	2	0.00
Delaware (1)	1	0.00
Iroquois (4)	8	0.01
Kiowa (2)	2	0.00
Latin American Indians (37)	65	0.10
Menominee (1)	1	0.00
Navajo (5)	5	0.01
Paiute (4)	5	0.01
Pima	1	0.00
Potawatomi (3)	7	0.01
Pueblo (4)	6	0.01
Puget Sound Salish	1	0.00
Seminole	2	0.00
Shoshone	3	0.00
Sioux (5)	21	0.03
Ute	1	0.00
All other tribes (27)	56	0.09
American Indian tribes, not spec.	36	0.06
Arab:	525	0.81
Arab/Arabic	175	0.27
Egyptian	158	0.24
Lebanese	109	0.17
Moroccan	23	0.04
Syrian	35	0.05
Other Arab	25	0.04
Armenian	282	0.44
Asian:	7,108	11.06
Bangladeshi (4)	5	0.01
Cambodian (4)	4	0.01
Chinese, ex. Taiwanese (2,451)	2,800	4.35
Filipino (1,011)	1,267	1.97
Indian (780)	848	1.32
Indonesian (38)	53	0.08
Japanese (682)	975	1.52
Korean (537)	603	0.94
Laotian (9)	9	0.01
Malaysian (6)	8	0.01
Pakistani (41)	67	0.10
Sri Lankan (15)	17	0.03
Taiwanese (121)	134	0.21
Thai (38)	45	0.07
Vietnamese (106)	125	0.19
Other Asian, specified (6)	14	0.02
Other Asian, not specified (24)	134	0.21
Assyrian/Chaldean/Syriac	47	0.07
Australian	98	0.15
Austrian	317	0.49
Basque	25	0.04
Belgian	143	0.22
Brazilian	41	0.06
British	688	1.07
Bulgarian	79	0.12
Canadian	392	0.61
Carpatho Rusyn	6	0.01
Celtic	27	0.04
Croatian	257	0.40
Czech	336	0.52
Czechoslovakian	233	0.36
Danish	1,050	1.63
Dutch	1,125	1.74
Eastern European	260	0.40
English	9,960	15.42
Estonian	9	0.01
European	1,199	1.86
Finnish	428	0.66
French, except Basque	2,444	3.78
French Canadian	394	0.61
German	10,658	16.50
Greek	375	0.58
Guyanese	3	0.00
Hawaii Native/Pacific Islander:	219	0.34
Melanesian: (3)	6	0.01
Fijian (3)	6	0.01
Micronesian: (20)	30	0.05
Guamanian/Chamorro (19)	29	0.05
Other Micronesian (1)	1	0.00
Polynesian: (55)	124	0.19
Native Hawaiian (29)	87	0.14
Samoan (7)	13	0.02
Tongan (18)	22	0.03
Other Polynesian (1)	2	0.00
Other Pac. Isl., not spec. (15)	59	0.09
Hispanic or Latino:	3,851	5.99
Central American:	259	0.40
Costa Rican	21	0.03
Guatemalan	33	0.05
Honduran	9	0.01
Nicaraguan	35	0.05
Panamanian	33	0.05
Salvadoran	102	0.16
Other Central American	26	0.04
Cuban	63	0.10
Dominican Republic	7	0.01
Mexican	2,099	3.26
Puerto Rican	137	0.21
South American:	378	0.59
Argentinean	60	0.09
Bolivian	16	0.02
Chilean	41	0.06
Colombian	65	0.10
Ecuadorian	13	0.02
Paraguayan	2	0.00
Peruvian	134	0.21
Uruguayan	2	0.00
Venezuelan	15	0.02
Other South American	30	0.05
Other Hispanic or Latino	908	1.41
Hungarian	461	0.71
Icelander	16	0.02
Iranian	895	1.39
Irish	9,237	14.30
Israeli	182	0.28
Italian	5,181	8.02
Latvian	91	0.14
Lithuanian	268	0.41
Luxemburger	12	0.02
Macedonian	27	0.04
Maltese	24	0.04
New Zealander	51	0.08
Northern European	263	0.41
Norwegian	1,574	2.44
Pennsylvania German	104	0.16
Polish	1,813	2.81
Portuguese	849	1.31
Romanian	215	0.33
Russian	2,083	3.23
Scandinavian	265	0.41
Scotch-Irish	1,434	2.22
Scottish	2,303	3.57
Serbian	50	0.08
Slavic	72	0.11
Slovak	66	0.10
Slovene	43	0.07
Swedish	2,079	3.22
Swiss	504	0.78
Turkish	148	0.23
Ukrainian	376	0.58
United States or American	2,220	3.44
Welsh	667	1.03
West Indian, excl. Hispanic:	14	0.02
Bermudan	3	0.00
Trinidadian and Tobagonian	11	0.02
White:	55,811	86.80
Not Hispanic (51,834)	53,270	82.85
Hispanic (2,103)	2,541	3.95
Yugoslavian	232	0.36

Walnut Park

Place Type: Census Designated Place
County: Los Angeles
Population: 16,180

Ancestry/Race	Number	%
African American/Black:	86	0.53
Not Hispanic (15)	19	0.12
Hispanic (43)	67	0.41
African, sub-Saharan:	6	0.04
Ethiopian	6	0.04
Am. Ind. or Alaska Nat., not spec.	86	0.53
American Indian tribes, specified:	128	0.79
Apache (4)	5	0.03
Cherokee (3)	4	0.02
Latin American Indians (54)	99	0.61
Navajo (3)	3	0.02
Seminole (6)	6	0.04
Sioux (4)	4	0.02
Yaqui (2)	5	0.03
All other tribes (2)	2	0.01
American Indian tribes, not spec.	17	0.11
Armenian	11	0.07
Asian:	120	0.74
Chinese, ex. Taiwanese (11)	18	0.11
Filipino (42)	52	0.32
Indian (8)	13	0.08
Indonesian (1)	1	0.01
Japanese (1)	2	0.01
Korean (2)	4	0.02
Laotian (3)	4	0.02
Thai (12)	12	0.07
Vietnamese	5	0.03
Other Asian, not specified (1)	9	0.06
English	51	0.32
European	17	0.11
French, except Basque	24	0.15
German	112	0.69
Greek	66	0.41
Hawaii Native/Pacific Islander:	37	0.23
Micronesian: (10)	12	0.07
Guamanian/Chamorro (1)	3	0.02
Other Micronesian (9)	9	0.06
Polynesian:	4	0.02
Native Hawaiian	3	0.02
Samoan	1	0.01
Other Pac. Isl., not spec. (13)	21	0.13
Hispanic or Latino:	15,496	95.77
Central American:	1,016	6.28
Costa Rican	8	0.05
Guatemalan	192	1.19
Honduran	28	0.17
Nicaraguan	71	0.44
Panamanian	2	0.01
Salvadoran	608	3.76
Other Central American	107	0.66
Cuban	159	0.98
Dominican Republic	3	0.02
Mexican	12,309	76.08
Puerto Rican	92	0.57
South American:	136	0.84
Argentinean	8	0.05
Bolivian	1	0.01
Chilean	1	0.01
Colombian	63	0.39
Ecuadorian	33	0.20
Peruvian	17	0.11
Venezuelan	1	0.01
Other South American	12	0.07
Other Hispanic or Latino	1,781	11.01
Irish	100	0.62
Italian	32	0.20
Polish	40	0.25
Romanian	12	0.07
Scotch-Irish	39	0.24
United States or American	277	1.71
Welsh	12	0.07
West Indian, excl. Hispanic:	18	0.11
Trinidadian and Tobagonian	10	0.06
U.S. Virgin Islander	8	0.05
White:	8,086	49.98
Not Hispanic (533)	562	3.47
Hispanic (6,928)	7,524	46.50

Notes: 1. Figures in the "Number" column do not add up to the total population due to: a) Ancestry/Race overlap — e.g. persons can report being both White and Irish, b) persons of Hispanic origin can report being any race, c) persons reporting two ancestries are counted in both categories. 2. Numbers in parentheses indicate the number of persons reporting this ancestry/race alone, not in combination with any other ancestry/race. 3. Refer to the Explanation of Data in the front of the book for more detailed information.

Walnut

Place Type: City
County: Los Angeles
Population: 30,004

Ancestry/Race	Number	%
Afghan	33	0.11
African American/Black:	1,374	4.58
Not Hispanic (1,237)	1,326	4.42
Hispanic (22)	48	0.16
African, sub-Saharan:	27	0.09
African	27	0.09
Alaska Native tribes, specified:	1	0.00
Eskimo	1	0.00
Am. Ind. or Alaska Nat., not spec.	92	0.31
American Indian tribes, specified:	62	0.21
Apache (1)	6	0.02
Blackfeet	1	0.00
Cherokee	6	0.02
Chippewa	1	0.00
Choctaw (1)	2	0.01
Comanche (1)	1	0.00
Iroquois (1)	1	0.00
Latin American Indians (5)	18	0.06
Navajo (3)	7	0.02
Osage	1	0.00
Pima (1)	1	0.00
Pueblo	6	0.02
Seminole	1	0.00
Shoshone	1	0.00
Tohono O'Odham (2)	2	0.01
Yaqui (2)	2	0.01
Yuman	1	0.00
All other tribes (4)	4	0.01
American Indian tribes, not spec.	18	0.06
Arab:	245	0.82
Arab/Arabic	31	0.10
Egyptian	114	0.38
Iraqi	37	0.12
Lebanese	31	0.10
Palestinian	24	0.08
Syrian	8	0.03
Armenian	43	0.14
Asian:	17,975	59.91
Bangladeshi	3	0.01
Cambodian (46)	51	0.17
Chinese, ex. Taiwanese (6,934)	7,571	25.23
Filipino (3,616)	3,912	13.04
Indian (684)	741	2.47
Indonesian (140)	208	0.69
Japanese (616)	767	2.56
Korean (1,255)	1,307	4.36
Laotian (49)	53	0.18
Malaysian (20)	29	0.10
Pakistani (177)	209	0.70
Sri Lankan (24)	24	0.08
Taiwanese (1,656)	2,028	6.76
Thai (276)	298	0.99
Vietnamese (508)	574	1.91
Other Asian, specified (48)	55	0.18
Other Asian, not specified (61)	145	0.48
Austrian	28	0.09
Basque	27	0.09
Brazilian	35	0.12
British	41	0.14
Canadian	47	0.16
Croatian	6	0.02
Czech	76	0.25
Czechoslovakian	49	0.16
Danish	128	0.43
Dutch	163	0.54
English	1,008	3.36
European	117	0.39
French, except Basque	310	1.03
French Canadian	63	0.21
German	1,583	5.28
Greek	28	0.09
Hawaii Native/Pacific Islander:	142	0.47
Melanesian: (1)	1	0.00
Fijian (1)	1	0.00
Micronesian: (3)	12	0.04
Guamanian/Chamorro (3)	12	0.04
Polynesian: (16)	31	0.10
Native Hawaiian (6)	16	0.05
Samoan (9)	10	0.03
Other Polynesian (1)	5	0.02
Other Pac. Isl., not spec. (4)	98	0.33
Hispanic or Latino:	5,803	19.34
Central American:	213	0.71
Costa Rican	19	0.06
Guatemalan	43	0.14
Honduran	11	0.04
Nicaraguan	48	0.16
Panamanian	8	0.03
Salvadoran	72	0.24
Other Central American	12	0.04
Cuban	96	0.32
Mexican	4,413	14.71
Puerto Rican	101	0.34
South American:	225	0.75
Argentinean	28	0.09
Bolivian	10	0.03
Chilean	27	0.09
Colombian	34	0.11
Ecuadorian	37	0.12
Paraguayan	7	0.02
Peruvian	61	0.20
Uruguayan	1	0.00
Venezuelan	7	0.02
Other South American	13	0.04
Other Hispanic or Latino	755	2.52
Hungarian	116	0.39
Iranian	7	0.02
Irish	829	2.76
Italian	776	2.59
Lithuanian	11	0.04
Norwegian	134	0.45
Polish	308	1.03
Portuguese	68	0.23
Romanian	6	0.02
Russian	87	0.29
Scandinavian	34	0.11
Scotch-Irish	198	0.66
Scottish	208	0.69
Slavic	18	0.06
Slovak	5	0.02
Slovene	5	0.02
Swedish	160	0.53
Swiss	40	0.13
Turkish	7	0.02
Ukrainian	32	0.11
United States or American	425	1.42
Welsh	27	0.09
West Indian, excl. Hispanic:	29	0.10
Belizean	29	0.10
White:	9,245	30.81
Not Hispanic (5,463)	5,880	19.60
Hispanic (3,050)	3,365	11.22

Wasco

Place Type: City
County: Kern
Population: 21,263

Ancestry/Race	Number	%
African American/Black:	2,248	10.57
Not Hispanic (2,088)	2,113	9.94
Hispanic (95)	135	0.63
African, sub-Saharan:	16	0.08
African	16	0.08
Am. Ind. or Alaska Nat., not spec.	130	0.61
American Indian tribes, specified:	132	0.62
Apache (4)	4	0.02
Blackfeet (1)	6	0.03
Cherokee (8)	26	0.12
Choctaw (15)	16	0.08
Creek (4)	4	0.02
Latin American Indians (37)	50	0.24
Puget Sound Salish	1	0.00
All other tribes (23)	25	0.12
American Indian tribes, not spec.	35	0.16
Asian:	187	0.88
Cambodian (12)	12	0.06
Chinese, ex. Taiwanese (22)	23	0.11
Filipino (32)	48	0.23
Indian (48)	48	0.23
Japanese (1)	9	0.04
Korean (12)	15	0.07
Thai (1)	4	0.02
Vietnamese (4)	4	0.02
Other Asian, not specified (10)	24	0.11
British	7	0.03
Bulgarian	8	0.04
Canadian	15	0.07
Czech	22	0.10
Dutch	111	0.52
English	352	1.65
French, except Basque	73	0.34
German	561	2.64
Hawaii Native/Pacific Islander:	53	0.25
Micronesian: (7)	9	0.04
Guamanian/Chamorro (7)	9	0.04
Polynesian: (24)	33	0.16
Native Hawaiian (8)	11	0.05
Samoan (10)	12	0.06
Tongan (6)	10	0.05
Other Pac. Isl., not spec. (1)	11	0.05
Hispanic or Latino:	14,187	66.72
Central American:	83	0.39
Costa Rican	1	0.00
Guatemalan	16	0.08
Honduran	5	0.02
Nicaraguan	4	0.02
Panamanian	5	0.02
Salvadoran	43	0.20
Other Central American	9	0.04
Cuban	2	0.01
Mexican	12,538	58.97
Puerto Rican	111	0.52
South American:	4	0.02
Chilean	1	0.00
Colombian	2	0.01
Peruvian	1	0.00
Other Hispanic or Latino	1,449	6.81
Icelander	8	0.04
Irish	262	1.23
Italian	22	0.10
Norwegian	18	0.08
Pennsylvania German	15	0.07
Polish	27	0.13
Portuguese	31	0.15
Russian	4	0.02
Scandinavian	22	0.10
Scottish	87	0.41
Swedish	41	0.19
Swiss	25	0.12
United States or American	676	3.18
White:	7,855	36.94
Not Hispanic (4,588)	4,677	22.00
Hispanic (2,778)	3,178	14.95

Watsonville

Place Type: City
County: Santa Cruz
Population: 44,265

Ancestry/Race	Number	%
African American/Black:	468	1.06
Not Hispanic (206)	263	0.59
Hispanic (128)	205	0.46
African, sub-Saharan:	36	0.08
African	31	0.07
Nigerian	5	0.01
Alaska Native tribes, specified:	8	0.02
Aleut (1)	1	0.00
Eskimo	5	0.01
Tlingit-Haida	2	0.00

Notes: 1. Figures in the "Number" column do not add up to the total population due to: a) Ancestry/Race overlap — e.g. persons can report being both White and Irish, b) persons of Hispanic origin can report being any race, c) persons reporting two ancestries are counted in both categories. 2. Numbers in parentheses indicate the number of persons reporting this ancestry/race alone, not in combination with any other ancestry/race. 3. Refer to the Explanation of Data in the front of the book for more detailed information.

Am. Ind. or Alaska Nat., not spec.	434	0.98
American Indian tribes, specified:	693	1.57
Apache (13)	37	0.08
Blackfeet (3)	5	0.01
Cherokee (17)	75	0.17
Cheyenne	1	0.00
Chickasaw (1)	2	0.00
Chippewa (2)	5	0.01
Choctaw (7)	24	0.05
Comanche (7)	9	0.02
Cree	2	0.00
Creek (4)	7	0.02
Iroquois	1	0.00
Latin American Indians (289)	372	0.84
Menominee	1	0.00
Navajo (6)	12	0.03
Osage	1	0.00
Paiute	4	0.01
Pueblo (5)	5	0.01
Puget Sound Salish	1	0.00
Sioux (4)	10	0.02
Tohono O'Odham	1	0.00
Yaqui (3)	9	0.02
All other tribes (61)	109	0.25
American Indian tribes, not spec.	47	0.11
Arab:	20	0.04
Lebanese	20	0.04
Armenian	9	0.02
Asian:	1,928	4.36
Chinese, ex. Taiwanese (197)	252	0.57
Filipino (575)	853	1.93
Hmong	1	0.00
Indian (128)	141	0.32
Indonesian (1)	1	0.00
Japanese (457)	547	1.24
Korean (18)	18	0.04
Taiwanese (3)	3	0.01
Thai (6)	11	0.02
Vietnamese (17)	22	0.05
Other Asian, specified (1)	3	0.01
Other Asian, not specified (31)	76	0.17
Austrian	44	0.10
Basque	10	0.02
Brazilian	13	0.03
British	90	0.20
Canadian	24	0.05
Croatian	189	0.42
Czech	7	0.02
Czechoslovakian	13	0.03
Danish	165	0.37
Dutch	240	0.54
English	1,142	2.57
Estonian	8	0.02
European	143	0.32
Finnish	25	0.06
French, except Basque	392	0.88
French Canadian	55	0.12
German	1,564	3.52
Greek	89	0.20
Hawaii Native/Pacific Islander:	140	0.32
Melanesian: (1)	1	0.00
Fijian (1)	1	0.00
Micronesian: (7)	12	0.03
Guamanian/Chamorro (6)	11	0.02
Other Micronesian (1)	1	0.00
Polynesian: (40)	85	0.19
Native Hawaiian (33)	76	0.17
Samoan (7)	9	0.02
Other Pac. Isl., not spec. (5)	42	0.09
Hispanic or Latino:	33,254	75.12
Central American:	209	0.47
Costa Rican	3	0.01
Guatemalan	34	0.08
Honduran	19	0.04
Nicaraguan	19	0.04
Panamanian	2	0.00
Salvadoran	109	0.25
Other Central American	23	0.05
Cuban	25	0.06
Dominican Republic	4	0.01
Mexican	29,953	67.67
Puerto Rican	39	0.09
South American:	51	0.12
Argentinean	4	0.01
Chilean	4	0.01
Colombian	8	0.02
Ecuadorian	9	0.02
Peruvian	19	0.04
Venezuelan	5	0.01
Other South American	2	0.00
Other Hispanic or Latino	2,973	6.72
Hungarian	26	0.06
Irish	1,520	3.42
Italian	948	2.13
Lithuanian	21	0.05
Northern European	7	0.02
Norwegian	107	0.24
Pennsylvania German	7	0.02
Polish	155	0.35
Portuguese	824	1.85
Russian	144	0.32
Scandinavian	15	0.03
Scotch-Irish	194	0.44
Scottish	202	0.45
Slavic	8	0.02
Swedish	215	0.48
Swiss	20	0.04
Turkish	5	0.01
United States or American	704	1.58
Welsh	93	0.21
West Indian, excl. Hispanic:	8	0.02
British West Indian	8	0.02
White:	20,957	47.34
Not Hispanic (8,574)	9,087	20.53
Hispanic (10,462)	11,870	26.82
Yugoslavian	85	0.19

West Carson

Place Type: Census Designated Place
County: Los Angeles
Population: 21,138

Ancestry/Race	Number	%
African American/Black:	2,661	12.59
Not Hispanic (2,439)	2,591	12.26
Hispanic (44)	70	0.33
African, sub-Saharan:	565	2.67
African	335	1.58
Ethiopian	27	0.13
Nigerian	178	0.84
Other sub-Saharan African	25	0.12
Alaska Native tribes, specified:	2	0.01
Tlingit-Haida	1	0.00
All other tribes	1	0.00
Am. Ind. or Alaska Nat., not spec.	117	0.55
American Indian tribes, specified:	197	0.93
Apache (5)	14	0.07
Blackfeet (5)	7	0.03
Cherokee (14)	42	0.20
Cheyenne (1)	1	0.00
Chickasaw (1)	1	0.00
Chippewa	3	0.01
Choctaw (2)	12	0.06
Comanche	1	0.00
Iroquois (3)	4	0.02
Kiowa	1	0.00
Latin American Indians (18)	26	0.12
Lumbee	1	0.00
Navajo (22)	38	0.18
Osage (1)	1	0.00
Pima	3	0.01
Potawatomi	1	0.00
Pueblo (3)	8	0.04
Sioux (7)	16	0.08
Yakama	1	0.00
Yaqui	3	0.01
All other tribes (7)	13	0.06
American Indian tribes, not spec.	12	0.06
Arab:	39	0.18
Arab/Arabic	7	0.03
Lebanese	32	0.15
Armenian	43	0.20
Asian:	5,920	28.01
Bangladeshi (2)	2	0.01
Cambodian (5)	5	0.02
Chinese, ex. Taiwanese (455)	579	2.74
Filipino (2,338)	2,584	12.22
Indian (123)	137	0.65
Indonesian (12)	31	0.15
Japanese (915)	1,093	5.17
Korean (934)	973	4.60
Malaysian (6)	14	0.07
Pakistani (30)	37	0.18
Sri Lankan (15)	15	0.07
Taiwanese (43)	52	0.25
Thai (41)	49	0.23
Vietnamese (235)	259	1.23
Other Asian, specified (15)	19	0.09
Other Asian, not specified (32)	71	0.34
Australian	7	0.03
Austrian	43	0.20
Basque	8	0.04
Belgian	11	0.05
British	34	0.16
Canadian	76	0.36
Croatian	15	0.07
Czech	12	0.06
Czechoslovakian	17	0.08
Danish	57	0.27
Dutch	156	0.74
Eastern European	10	0.05
English	1,000	4.73
European	63	0.30
Finnish	28	0.13
French, except Basque	402	1.90
French Canadian	156	0.74
German	1,139	5.39
German Russian	6	0.03
Greek	29	0.14
Hawaii Native/Pacific Islander:	415	1.96
Micronesian: (10)	13	0.06
Guamanian/Chamorro (9)	12	0.06
Other Micronesian (1)	1	0.00
Polynesian: (219)	355	1.68
Native Hawaiian (41)	109	0.52
Samoan (178)	231	1.09
Tongan	9	0.04
Other Polynesian	6	0.03
Other Pac. Isl., not spec. (22)	47	0.22
Hispanic or Latino:	6,223	29.44
Central American:	304	1.44
Costa Rican	11	0.05
Guatemalan	87	0.41
Honduran	19	0.09
Nicaraguan	36	0.17
Panamanian	7	0.03
Salvadoran	125	0.59
Other Central American	19	0.09
Cuban	140	0.66
Dominican Republic	1	0.00
Mexican	4,614	21.83
Puerto Rican	118	0.56
South American:	183	0.87
Argentinean	46	0.22
Bolivian	6	0.03
Chilean	8	0.04
Colombian	40	0.19
Ecuadorian	11	0.05
Peruvian	59	0.28
Uruguayan	4	0.02
Venezuelan	4	0.02
Other South American	5	0.02
Other Hispanic or Latino	863	4.08
Hungarian	121	0.57
Iranian	155	0.73
Irish	898	4.25
Israeli	18	0.09
Italian	531	2.51
Latvian	8	0.04

Notes: 1. Figures in the "Number" column do not add up to the total population due to: a) Ancestry/Race overlap — e.g. persons can report being both White and Irish, b) persons of Hispanic origin can report being any race, c) persons reporting two ancestries are counted in both categories. 2. Numbers in parentheses indicate the number of persons reporting this ancestry/race alone, not in combination with any other ancestry/race. 3. Refer to the Explanation of Data in the front of the book for more detailed information.

Norwegian	108	0.51
Polish	330	1.56
Portuguese	103	0.49
Romanian	46	0.22
Russian	91	0.43
Scandinavian	22	0.10
Scotch-Irish	134	0.63
Scottish	188	0.89
Slovak	23	0.11
Swedish	123	0.58
Swiss	12	0.06
Turkish	6	0.03
Ukrainian	5	0.02
United States or American	434	2.05
Welsh	79	0.37
West Indian, excl. Hispanic:	74	0.35
Belizean	20	0.09
Jamaican	40	0.19
West Indian	14	0.07
White:	9,748	46.12
Not Hispanic (6,193)	6,672	31.56
Hispanic (2,683)	3,076	14.55
Yugoslavian	22	0.10

West Covina

Place Type: City
County: Los Angeles
Population: 105,080

Ancestry/Race	Number	%
African American/Black:	7,469	7.11
Not Hispanic (6,314)	6,851	6.52
Hispanic (382)	618	0.59
African, sub-Saharan:	540	0.51
African	375	0.36
Ghanian	11	0.01
Kenyan	10	0.01
Nigerian	106	0.10
South African	8	0.01
Other sub-Saharan African	30	0.03
Alaska Native tribes, specified:	4	0.00
Aleut	1	0.00
Tlingit-Haida (1)	1	0.00
All other tribes	2	0.00
Alaska Native tribes, not specified	1	0.00
Am. Ind. or Alaska Nat., not spec.	608	0.58
American Indian tribes, specified:	845	0.80
Apache (40)	77	0.07
Blackfeet (1)	15	0.01
Cherokee (22)	104	0.10
Cheyenne (3)	5	0.00
Chickasaw (1)	1	0.00
Chippewa (12)	16	0.02
Choctaw (9)	22	0.02
Colville (3)	5	0.00
Comanche (1)	4	0.00
Creek (3)	4	0.00
Delaware (4)	4	0.00
Iroquois (2)	14	0.01
Kiowa	3	0.00
Latin American Indians (111)	195	0.19
Lumbee (1)	2	0.00
Navajo (41)	66	0.06
Osage	3	0.00
Ottawa	2	0.00
Paiute (9)	9	0.01
Pima (2)	12	0.01
Pueblo (21)	31	0.03
Seminole	9	0.01
Shoshone (7)	11	0.01
Sioux (17)	36	0.03
Tohono O'Odham (20)	28	0.03
Yakama (1)	1	0.00
Yaqui (17)	25	0.02
Yuman (4)	8	0.01
All other tribes (76)	133	0.13
American Indian tribes, not spec.	101	0.10
Arab:	926	0.88
Arab/Arabic	103	0.10
Egyptian	387	0.37
Iraqi	23	0.02
Lebanese	197	0.19
Moroccan	22	0.02
Syrian	127	0.12
Other Arab	67	0.06
Armenian	127	0.12
Asian:	26,276	25.01
Bangladeshi (14)	18	0.02
Cambodian (79)	115	0.11
Chinese, ex. Taiwanese (6,734)	7,579	7.21
Filipino (9,694)	10,469	9.96
Hmong (3)	5	0.00
Indian (723)	827	0.79
Indonesian (209)	306	0.29
Japanese (809)	1,106	1.05
Korean (728)	808	0.77
Laotian (154)	182	0.17
Malaysian (23)	37	0.04
Pakistani (107)	133	0.13
Sri Lankan (66)	76	0.07
Taiwanese (878)	1,105	1.05
Thai (429)	513	0.49
Vietnamese (2,330)	2,619	2.49
Other Asian, specified (68)	83	0.08
Other Asian, not specified (123)	295	0.28
Australian	18	0.02
Austrian	106	0.10
Basque	58	0.06
Belgian	50	0.05
Brazilian	4	0.00
British	206	0.20
Bulgarian	39	0.04
Canadian	174	0.17
Celtic	16	0.02
Croatian	80	0.08
Czech	152	0.14
Czechoslovakian	40	0.04
Danish	333	0.32
Dutch	909	0.87
Eastern European	10	0.01
English	4,281	4.08
European	232	0.22
Finnish	79	0.08
French, except Basque	1,518	1.45
French Canadian	293	0.28
German	5,607	5.35
Greek	211	0.20
Guyanese	14	0.01
Hawaii Native/Pacific Islander:	530	0.50
Melanesian: (21)	23	0.02
Fijian (21)	23	0.02
Micronesian: (44)	59	0.06
Guamanian/Chamorro (39)	54	0.05
Other Micronesian (5)	5	0.00
Polynesian: (121)	274	0.26
Native Hawaiian (56)	161	0.15
Samoan (56)	96	0.09
Tongan (6)	12	0.01
Other Polynesian (3)	5	0.00
Other Pac. Isl., not spec. (33)	174	0.17
Hispanic or Latino:	48,051	45.73
Central American:	2,212	2.11
Costa Rican	105	0.10
Guatemalan	459	0.44
Honduran	87	0.08
Nicaraguan	383	0.36
Panamanian	44	0.04
Salvadoran	936	0.89
Other Central American	198	0.19
Cuban	482	0.46
Dominican Republic	16	0.02
Mexican	37,206	35.41
Puerto Rican	560	0.53
South American:	1,131	1.08
Argentinean	185	0.18
Bolivian	25	0.02
Chilean	66	0.06
Colombian	240	0.23
Ecuadorian	217	0.21
Paraguayan	2	0.00
Peruvian	256	0.24
Uruguayan	7	0.01
Venezuelan	24	0.02
Other South American	109	0.10
Other Hispanic or Latino	6,444	6.13
Hungarian	445	0.42
Icelander	13	0.01
Iranian	104	0.10
Irish	5,356	5.11
Israeli	6	0.01
Italian	3,404	3.25
Latvian	9	0.01
Lithuanian	53	0.05
Luxemburger	9	0.01
New Zealander	13	0.01
Northern European	18	0.02
Norwegian	519	0.49
Pennsylvania German	13	0.01
Polish	939	0.90
Portuguese	191	0.18
Romanian	50	0.05
Russian	363	0.35
Scandinavian	51	0.05
Scotch-Irish	782	0.75
Scottish	853	0.81
Serbian	39	0.04
Slavic	20	0.02
Slovak	137	0.13
Slovene	9	0.01
Swedish	779	0.74
Swiss	164	0.16
Turkish	26	0.02
Ukrainian	71	0.07
United States or American	1,823	1.74
Welsh	295	0.28
West Indian, excl. Hispanic:	206	0.20
Barbadian	23	0.02
Belizean	25	0.02
British West Indian	14	0.01
Haitian	35	0.03
Jamaican	59	0.06
Trinidadian and Tobagonian	26	0.02
West Indian	24	0.02
White:	49,870	47.46
Not Hispanic (24,124)	25,662	24.42
Hispanic (21,962)	24,208	23.04
Yugoslavian	100	0.10

West Hollywood

Place Type: City
County: Los Angeles
Population: 35,716

Ancestry/Race	Number	%
Acadian/Cajun	11	0.03
Afghan	13	0.04
African American/Black:	1,328	3.72
Not Hispanic (1,033)	1,234	3.46
Hispanic (71)	94	0.26
African, sub-Saharan:	197	0.55
African	118	0.33
Cape Verdean	5	0.01
Ethiopian	6	0.02
Nigerian	9	0.03
South African	51	0.14
Zimbabwean	8	0.02
Alaska Native tribes, specified:	5	0.01
Alaska Athabascan (1)	1	0.00
Eskimo	2	0.01
Tlingit-Haida (2)	2	0.01
Am. Ind. or Alaska Nat., not spec.	73	0.20
Albanian	9	0.03
American Indian tribes, specified:	229	0.64
Apache (6)	10	0.03
Blackfeet (2)	5	0.01
Cherokee (16)	77	0.22
Chickasaw	3	0.01
Chippewa (9)	11	0.03

Notes: 1. Figures in the "Number" column do not add up to the total population due to: a) Ancestry/Race overlap — e.g. persons can report being both White and Irish, b) persons of Hispanic origin can report being any race, c) persons reporting two ancestries are counted in both categories. 2. Numbers in parentheses indicate the number of persons reporting this ancestry/race alone, not in combination with any other ancestry/race. 3. Refer to the Explanation of Data in the front of the book for more detailed information.

Choctaw (3)	12	0.03
Comanche (1)	2	0.01
Creek (2)	7	0.02
Crow	1	0.00
Delaware (1)	1	0.00
Iroquois (1)	9	0.03
Kiowa (1)	2	0.01
Latin American Indians (14)	23	0.06
Lumbee	1	0.00
Navajo (7)	8	0.02
Osage (1)	2	0.01
Ottawa	1	0.00
Pima (1)	1	0.00
Potawatomi (2)	2	0.01
Pueblo (1)	6	0.02
Seminole (1)	5	0.01
Sioux (5)	10	0.03
Tohono O'Odham (1)	1	0.00
Yuman (1)	1	0.00
All other tribes (12)	28	0.08
American Indian tribes, not spec.	14	0.04
Arab:	285	0.80
Arab/Arabic	34	0.10
Egyptian	27	0.08
Iraqi	11	0.03
Lebanese	79	0.22
Moroccan	43	0.12
Syrian	15	0.04
Other Arab	76	0.21
Armenian	207	0.58
Asian:	1,733	4.85
Cambodian (5)	7	0.02
Chinese, ex. Taiwanese (256)	310	0.87
Filipino (316)	384	1.08
Indian (113)	144	0.40
Indonesian (10)	23	0.06
Japanese (273)	343	0.96
Korean (173)	211	0.59
Laotian (4)	5	0.01
Malaysian	2	0.01
Pakistani (1)	8	0.02
Sri Lankan (3)	15	0.04
Taiwanese (13)	15	0.04
Thai (52)	57	0.16
Vietnamese (77)	87	0.24
Other Asian, specified	5	0.01
Other Asian, not specified (21)	117	0.33
Australian	85	0.24
Austrian	298	0.83
Basque	26	0.07
Belgian	55	0.15
Brazilian	61	0.17
British	362	1.01
Bulgarian	30	0.08
Canadian	127	0.36
Celtic	17	0.05
Croatian	52	0.15
Cypriot	16	0.04
Czech	81	0.23
Czechoslovakian	86	0.24
Danish	199	0.56
Dutch	373	1.04
Eastern European	170	0.48
English	2,970	8.32
Estonian	8	0.02
European	368	1.03
Finnish	50	0.14
French, except Basque	1,094	3.06
French Canadian	202	0.57
German	3,883	10.87
Greek	256	0.72
Hawaii Native/Pacific Islander:	120	0.34
Melanesian: (1)	2	0.01
Fijian (1)	1	0.00
Other Melanesian	1	0.00
Micronesian: (5)	10	0.03
Guamanian/Chamorro (5)	10	0.03
Polynesian: (30)	59	0.17
Native Hawaiian (18)	39	0.11
Samoan (11)	13	0.04
Tongan	1	0.00
Other Polynesian (1)	6	0.02
Other Pac. Isl., specified	2	0.01
Other Pac. Isl., not spec. (4)	47	0.13
Hispanic or Latino:	3,142	8.80
Central American:	306	0.86
Costa Rican	11	0.03
Guatemalan	88	0.25
Honduran	13	0.04
Nicaraguan	31	0.09
Panamanian	14	0.04
Salvadoran	122	0.34
Other Central American	27	0.08
Cuban	129	0.36
Dominican Republic	12	0.03
Mexican	1,532	4.29
Puerto Rican	190	0.53
South American:	301	0.84
Argentinean	105	0.29
Bolivian	10	0.03
Chilean	21	0.06
Colombian	44	0.12
Ecuadorian	14	0.04
Peruvian	44	0.12
Uruguayan	8	0.02
Venezuelan	27	0.08
Other South American	28	0.08
Other Hispanic or Latino	672	1.88
Hungarian	429	1.20
Iranian	647	1.81
Irish	3,315	9.28
Israeli	250	0.70
Italian	2,546	7.13
Latvian	38	0.11
Lithuanian	161	0.45
Luxemburger	7	0.02
Macedonian	10	0.03
Maltese	19	0.05
New Zealander	9	0.03
Northern European	65	0.18
Norwegian	318	0.89
Pennsylvania German	14	0.04
Polish	1,433	4.01
Portuguese	173	0.48
Romanian	252	0.71
Russian	4,871	13.64
Scandinavian	84	0.24
Scotch-Irish	429	1.20
Scottish	682	1.91
Serbian	92	0.26
Slavic	8	0.02
Slovak	41	0.11
Slovene	8	0.02
Soviet Union	29	0.08
Swedish	551	1.54
Swiss	106	0.30
Turkish	41	0.11
Ukrainian	1,770	4.96
United States or American	1,147	3.21
Welsh	303	0.85
West Indian, excl. Hispanic:	22	0.06
Jamaican	22	0.06
White:	31,919	89.37
Not Hispanic (29,064)	29,877	83.65
Hispanic (1,804)	2,042	5.72
Yugoslavian	136	0.38

West Puente Valley

Place Type: Census Designated Place
County: Los Angeles
Population: 22,589

Ancestry/Race	Number	%
African American/Black:	643	2.85
Not Hispanic (499)	545	2.41
Hispanic (56)	98	0.43
African, sub-Saharan:	44	0.19
African	4	0.02
Cape Verdean	18	0.08
Nigerian	15	0.07
Other sub-Saharan African	7	0.03
Alaska Native tribes, specified:	8	0.04
Eskimo	1	0.00
Tlingit-Haida (7)	7	0.03
Am. Ind. or Alaska Nat., not spec.	187	0.83
American Indian tribes, specified:	183	0.81
Apache (4)	14	0.06
Blackfeet	1	0.00
Cherokee (8)	17	0.08
Cheyenne (1)	1	0.00
Chickasaw	5	0.02
Chippewa (4)	4	0.02
Choctaw	1	0.00
Colville (4)	4	0.02
Iroquois	3	0.01
Latin American Indians (77)	88	0.39
Navajo (9)	9	0.04
Pima (1)	2	0.01
Potawatomi	2	0.01
Pueblo (5)	8	0.04
Tohono O'Odham	2	0.01
Yaqui (3)	13	0.06
All other tribes (8)	9	0.04
American Indian tribes, not spec.	18	0.08
Arab:	44	0.19
Lebanese	44	0.19
Armenian	11	0.05
Asian:	1,985	8.79
Cambodian (35)	35	0.15
Chinese, ex. Taiwanese (418)	505	2.24
Filipino (694)	748	3.31
Indian (4)	8	0.04
Indonesian (5)	10	0.04
Japanese (44)	66	0.29
Korean (15)	18	0.08
Laotian (6)	12	0.05
Sri Lankan (11)	11	0.05
Taiwanese (12)	20	0.09
Thai (34)	35	0.15
Vietnamese (432)	477	2.11
Other Asian, specified (10)	11	0.05
Other Asian, not specified (10)	29	0.13
Austrian	11	0.05
Basque	5	0.02
Canadian	13	0.06
Czech	6	0.03
Dutch	32	0.14
English	198	0.86
French, except Basque	79	0.34
French Canadian	34	0.15
German	367	1.60
Greek	6	0.03
Hawaii Native/Pacific Islander:	70	0.31
Micronesian: (8)	18	0.08
Guamanian/Chamorro (8)	18	0.08
Polynesian: (31)	41	0.18
Native Hawaiian (9)	18	0.08
Samoan (22)	23	0.10
Other Pac. Isl., not spec. (1)	11	0.05
Hispanic or Latino:	18,416	81.53
Central American:	571	2.53
Costa Rican	14	0.06
Guatemalan	104	0.46
Honduran	19	0.08
Nicaraguan	68	0.30
Panamanian	2	0.01
Salvadoran	302	1.34
Other Central American	62	0.27
Cuban	57	0.25
Dominican Republic	8	0.04
Mexican	15,403	68.19
Puerto Rican	73	0.32
South American:	109	0.48
Argentinean	15	0.07
Chilean	9	0.04
Colombian	27	0.12
Ecuadorian	22	0.10
Paraguayan	3	0.01
Peruvian	22	0.10

Notes: 1. Figures in the "Number" column do not add up to the total population due to: a) Ancestry/Race overlap — e.g. persons can report being both White and Irish, b) persons of Hispanic origin can report being any race, c) persons reporting two ancestries are counted in both categories. 2. Numbers in parentheses indicate the number of persons reporting this ancestry/race alone, not in combination with any other ancestry/race. 3. Refer to the Explanation of Data in the front of the book for more detailed information.

Ancestry/Race	Number	%
Uruguayan	1	0.00
Other South American	10	0.04
Other Hispanic or Latino	2,195	9.72
Hungarian	13	0.06
Irish	183	0.80
Italian	213	0.93
Lithuanian	7	0.03
Norwegian	4	0.02
Polish	85	0.37
Portuguese	13	0.06
Romanian	11	0.05
Russian	7	0.03
Scandinavian	11	0.05
Scotch-Irish	16	0.07
Scottish	55	0.24
Serbian	22	0.10
Slovak	7	0.03
Swedish	91	0.40
Ukrainian	34	0.15
United States or American	296	1.29
Welsh	4	0.02
West Indian, excl. Hispanic:	5	0.02
West Indian	5	0.02
White:	10,756	47.62
Not Hispanic (1,659)	1,783	7.89
Hispanic (8,247)	8,973	39.72
Yugoslavian	11	0.05

West Sacramento

Place Type: City
County: Yolo
Population: 31,615

Ancestry/Race	Number	%
Afghan	178	0.56
African American/Black:	1,028	3.25
Not Hispanic (737)	903	2.86
Hispanic (74)	125	0.40
African, sub-Saharan:	85	0.27
African	58	0.18
Cape Verdean	27	0.09
Alaska Native tribes, specified:	12	0.04
Alaska Athabascan (3)	3	0.01
Aleut (2)	4	0.01
Eskimo	3	0.01
Tlingit-Haida (2)	2	0.01
Alaska Native tribes, not specified	4	0.01
Am. Ind. or Alaska Nat., not spec.	275	0.87
American Indian tribes, specified:	704	2.23
Apache (8)	46	0.15
Blackfeet (3)	27	0.09
Cherokee (50)	163	0.52
Cheyenne (2)	2	0.01
Chickasaw (1)	3	0.01
Chippewa (9)	12	0.04
Choctaw (9)	40	0.13
Comanche	1	0.00
Creek	1	0.00
Crow (1)	2	0.01
Iroquois (2)	8	0.03
Latin American Indians (33)	51	0.16
Navajo (15)	30	0.09
Osage (7)	12	0.04
Ottawa	1	0.00
Paiute (2)	2	0.01
Pima (1)	2	0.01
Potawatomi	2	0.01
Pueblo (1)	9	0.03
Puget Sound Salish (2)	4	0.01
Seminole	1	0.00
Shoshone (5)	7	0.02
Sioux (16)	31	0.10
Tohono O'Odham (5)	5	0.02
Ute (8)	8	0.03
Yakama	1	0.00
Yaqui	10	0.03
All other tribes (169)	223	0.71
American Indian tribes, not spec.	83	0.26
Arab:	75	0.24
Arab/Arabic	43	0.14
Moroccan	13	0.04
Palestinian	10	0.03
Syrian	9	0.03
Armenian	55	0.17
Asian:	3,087	9.76
Bangladeshi (1)	7	0.02
Cambodian (139)	171	0.54
Chinese, ex. Taiwanese (179)	214	0.68
Filipino (197)	398	1.26
Hmong (231)	249	0.79
Indian (438)	617	1.95
Indonesian (2)	6	0.02
Japanese (150)	240	0.76
Korean (27)	44	0.14
Laotian (628)	714	2.26
Pakistani (95)	170	0.54
Sri Lankan (5)	5	0.02
Thai (7)	10	0.03
Vietnamese (67)	79	0.25
Other Asian, specified (1)	2	0.01
Other Asian, not specified (64)	161	0.51
Austrian	39	0.12
Basque	10	0.03
British	63	0.20
Bulgarian	60	0.19
Canadian	24	0.08
Croatian	39	0.12
Czech	7	0.02
Czechoslovakian	18	0.06
Danish	229	0.72
Dutch	372	1.18
English	1,697	5.37
European	187	0.59
Finnish	55	0.17
French, except Basque	682	2.16
French Canadian	183	0.58
German	2,978	9.42
Greek	179	0.57
Hawaii Native/Pacific Islander:	415	1.31
Melanesian: (84)	107	0.34
Fijian (84)	107	0.34
Micronesian: (22)	27	0.09
Guamanian/Chamorro (9)	11	0.03
Other Micronesian (13)	16	0.05
Polynesian: (50)	86	0.27
Native Hawaiian (28)	57	0.18
Samoan (16)	22	0.07
Tongan (6)	7	0.02
Other Pac. Isl., specified	1	0.00
Other Pac. Isl., not spec. (28)	194	0.61
Hispanic or Latino:	9,470	29.95
Central American:	140	0.44
Costa Rican	1	0.00
Guatemalan	56	0.18
Honduran	4	0.01
Nicaraguan	23	0.07
Panamanian	1	0.00
Salvadoran	31	0.10
Other Central American	24	0.08
Cuban	20	0.06
Dominican Republic	7	0.02
Mexican	8,071	25.53
Puerto Rican	110	0.35
South American:	23	0.07
Argentinean	1	0.00
Chilean	6	0.02
Colombian	4	0.01
Ecuadorian	1	0.00
Paraguayan	1	0.00
Peruvian	5	0.02
Venezuelan	5	0.02
Other Hispanic or Latino	1,099	3.48
Hungarian	33	0.10
Icelander	7	0.02
Iranian	31	0.10
Irish	2,498	7.90
Italian	1,239	3.92
Latvian	7	0.02
Lithuanian	19	0.06
New Zealander	10	0.03
Norwegian	397	1.26
Pennsylvania German	29	0.09
Polish	329	1.04
Portuguese	613	1.94
Romanian	23	0.07
Russian	2,228	7.05
Scandinavian	28	0.09
Scotch-Irish	435	1.38
Scottish	471	1.49
Serbian	4	0.01
Slavic	18	0.06
Slovak	10	0.03
Swedish	245	0.78
Swiss	67	0.21
Ukrainian	613	1.94
United States or American	1,763	5.58
Welsh	99	0.31
West Indian, excl. Hispanic:	18	0.06
Dutch West Indian	7	0.02
Jamaican	11	0.03
White:	22,178	70.15
Not Hispanic (17,271)	18,159	57.44
Hispanic (3,277)	4,019	12.71
Yugoslavian	10	0.03

West Whittier-Los Nietos

Place Type: Census Designated Place
County: Los Angeles
Population: 25,129

Ancestry/Race	Number	%
African American/Black:	219	0.87
Not Hispanic (87)	112	0.45
Hispanic (57)	107	0.43
African, sub-Saharan:	10	0.04
African	10	0.04
Am. Ind. or Alaska Nat., not spec.	197	0.78
American Indian tribes, specified:	254	1.01
Apache (27)	33	0.13
Blackfeet (2)	3	0.01
Cherokee (11)	31	0.12
Cheyenne	1	0.00
Chippewa	6	0.02
Choctaw (1)	5	0.02
Creek (6)	6	0.02
Crow (1)	2	0.01
Latin American Indians (69)	92	0.37
Lumbee (7)	7	0.03
Menominee (1)	1	0.00
Navajo (5)	10	0.04
Paiute (2)	2	0.01
Pima (2)	2	0.01
Pueblo (13)	18	0.07
Sioux	1	0.00
Tohono O'Odham (1)	2	0.01
Yakama (3)	3	0.01
Yaqui (4)	10	0.04
All other tribes (9)	19	0.08
American Indian tribes, not spec.	40	0.16
Arab:	37	0.15
Egyptian	29	0.12
Syrian	8	0.03
Armenian	245	0.97
Asian:	562	2.24
Chinese, ex. Taiwanese (46)	69	0.27
Filipino (184)	244	0.97
Indian (23)	37	0.15
Indonesian (3)	6	0.02
Japanese (71)	106	0.42
Korean (24)	30	0.12
Laotian (11)	11	0.04
Pakistani	1	0.00
Taiwanese (3)	3	0.01
Thai (3)	5	0.02
Vietnamese (22)	23	0.09
Other Asian, specified	9	0.04
Other Asian, not specified (8)	18	0.07
Australian	4	0.02

Notes: 1. Figures in the "Number" column do not add up to the total population due to: a) Ancestry/Race overlap — e.g. persons can report being both White and Irish, b) persons of Hispanic origin can report being any race, c) persons reporting two ancestries are counted in both categories. 2. Numbers in parentheses indicate the number of persons reporting this ancestry/race alone, not in combination with any other ancestry/race. 3. Refer to the Explanation of Data in the front of the book for more detailed information.

Brazilian	13	0.05
British	3	0.01
Canadian	54	0.21
Czechoslovakian	6	0.02
Danish	39	0.16
Dutch	75	0.30
English	648	2.58
European	38	0.15
Finnish	10	0.04
French, except Basque	211	0.84
French Canadian	21	0.08
German	718	2.85
Greek	40	0.16
Guyanese	15	0.06
Hawaii Native/Pacific Islander:	92	0.37
Micronesian: (29)	33	0.13
Guamanian/Chamorro (29)	33	0.13
Polynesian: (14)	42	0.17
Native Hawaiian (9)	30	0.12
Samoan (5)	12	0.05
Other Pac. Isl., not spec. (4)	17	0.07
Hispanic or Latino:	20,874	83.07
Central American:	573	2.28
Costa Rican	26	0.10
Guatemalan	115	0.46
Honduran	18	0.07
Nicaraguan	88	0.35
Panamanian	7	0.03
Salvadoran	280	1.11
Other Central American	39	0.16
Cuban	88	0.35
Dominican Republic	6	0.02
Mexican	17,773	70.73
Puerto Rican	141	0.56
South American:	109	0.43
Argentinean	9	0.04
Bolivian	3	0.01
Chilean	2	0.01
Colombian	3	0.01
Ecuadorian	40	0.16
Paraguayan	1	0.00
Peruvian	25	0.10
Uruguayan	7	0.03
Venezuelan	4	0.02
Other South American	15	0.06
Other Hispanic or Latino	2,184	8.69
Hungarian	15	0.06
Iranian	9	0.04
Irish	387	1.54
Italian	424	1.69
Lithuanian	21	0.08
Macedonian	20	0.08
Norwegian	75	0.30
Polish	67	0.27
Portuguese	41	0.16
Russian	92	0.37
Scandinavian	8	0.03
Scotch-Irish	85	0.34
Scottish	49	0.19
Slovak	16	0.06
Swedish	95	0.38
Ukrainian	3	0.01
United States or American	414	1.65
Welsh	102	0.41
White:	14,366	57.17
Not Hispanic (3,488)	3,655	14.54
Hispanic (9,846)	10,711	42.62
Yugoslavian	23	0.09

Westminster

Place Type: City
County: Orange
Population: 88,207

Ancestry/Race	Number	%
Acadian/Cajun	6	0.01
Afghan	33	0.04
African American/Black:	1,203	1.36
Not Hispanic (764)	988	1.12
Hispanic (107)	215	0.24
African, sub-Saharan:	94	0.11
African	66	0.08
Ethiopian	17	0.02
Nigerian	11	0.01
Alaska Native tribes, specified:	5	0.01
Alaska Athabascan (1)	1	0.00
Aleut (1)	2	0.00
Eskimo	1	0.00
Tlingit-Haida (1)	1	0.00
Alaska Native tribes, not specified	1	0.00
Am. Ind. or Alaska Nat., not spec.	472	0.54
Alsatian	4	0.00
American Indian tribes, specified:	759	0.86
Apache (11)	38	0.04
Blackfeet (9)	40	0.05
Cherokee (66)	247	0.28
Cheyenne (1)	3	0.00
Chickasaw (5)	7	0.01
Chippewa (12)	24	0.03
Choctaw (18)	40	0.05
Comanche (2)	7	0.01
Cree	1	0.00
Creek	10	0.01
Crow	1	0.00
Delaware	4	0.00
Iroquois (1)	12	0.01
Kiowa	2	0.00
Latin American Indians (41)	74	0.08
Lumbee (4)	6	0.01
Navajo (12)	24	0.03
Osage (4)	6	0.01
Paiute	2	0.00
Potawatomi (3)	4	0.00
Pueblo (11)	36	0.04
Puget Sound Salish (1)	2	0.00
Seminole (1)	12	0.01
Shoshone	2	0.00
Sioux (20)	54	0.06
Tohono O'Odham	3	0.00
Ute	3	0.00
Yaqui	6	0.01
All other tribes (45)	89	0.10
American Indian tribes, not spec.	53	0.06
Arab:	873	0.99
Arab/Arabic	281	0.32
Egyptian	111	0.13
Jordanian	102	0.12
Lebanese	156	0.18
Palestinian	145	0.16
Syrian	52	0.06
Other Arab	26	0.03
Armenian	213	0.24
Asian:	35,517	40.27
Bangladeshi (1)	1	0.00
Cambodian (257)	301	0.34
Chinese, ex. Taiwanese (1,930)	2,423	2.75
Filipino (1,067)	1,356	1.54
Hmong (68)	76	0.09
Indian (377)	502	0.57
Indonesian (56)	120	0.14
Japanese (1,008)	1,284	1.46
Korean (610)	670	0.76
Laotian (132)	164	0.19
Malaysian (8)	20	0.02
Pakistani (122)	148	0.17
Sri Lankan (15)	16	0.02
Taiwanese (65)	93	0.11
Thai (83)	119	0.13
Vietnamese (27,109)	27,887	31.62
Other Asian, specified (11)	20	0.02
Other Asian, not specified (135)	317	0.36
Australian	22	0.03
Austrian	138	0.16
Basque	51	0.06
Belgian	77	0.09
Brazilian	12	0.01
British	256	0.29
Bulgarian	5	0.01
Canadian	182	0.21
Celtic	11	0.01
Croatian	72	0.08
Czech	209	0.24
Czechoslovakian	108	0.12
Danish	520	0.59
Dutch	1,071	1.22
Eastern European	16	0.02
English	5,234	5.96
Estonian	5	0.01
European	524	0.60
Finnish	122	0.14
French, except Basque	1,517	1.73
French Canadian	411	0.47
German	6,945	7.90
Greek	252	0.29
Hawaii Native/Pacific Islander:	628	0.71
Micronesian: (60)	90	0.10
Guamanian/Chamorro (36)	66	0.07
Other Micronesian (24)	24	0.03
Polynesian: (326)	471	0.53
Native Hawaiian (70)	171	0.19
Samoan (252)	286	0.32
Tongan (1)	3	0.00
Other Polynesian (3)	11	0.01
Other Pac. Isl., not spec. (13)	67	0.08
Hispanic or Latino:	19,138	21.70
Central American:	517	0.59
Costa Rican	53	0.06
Guatemalan	134	0.15
Honduran	25	0.03
Nicaraguan	28	0.03
Panamanian	28	0.03
Salvadoran	197	0.22
Other Central American	52	0.06
Cuban	208	0.24
Dominican Republic	7	0.01
Mexican	15,389	17.45
Puerto Rican	269	0.30
South American:	378	0.43
Argentinean	51	0.06
Bolivian	18	0.02
Chilean	23	0.03
Colombian	62	0.07
Ecuadorian	44	0.05
Paraguayan	2	0.00
Peruvian	108	0.12
Venezuelan	7	0.01
Other South American	63	0.07
Other Hispanic or Latino	2,370	2.69
Hungarian	330	0.38
Icelander	8	0.01
Iranian	106	0.12
Irish	5,556	6.32
Italian	2,920	3.32
Latvian	5	0.01
Lithuanian	95	0.11
Luxemburger	6	0.01
Maltese	30	0.03
New Zealander	28	0.03
Northern European	24	0.03
Norwegian	911	1.04
Pennsylvania German	19	0.02
Polish	835	0.95
Portuguese	253	0.29
Romanian	151	0.17
Russian	588	0.67
Scandinavian	76	0.09
Scotch-Irish	946	1.08
Scottish	931	1.06
Serbian	31	0.04
Slavic	50	0.06
Slovak	34	0.04
Swedish	884	1.01
Swiss	190	0.22
Turkish	44	0.05
Ukrainian	27	0.03
United States or American	2,271	2.58
Welsh	359	0.41
West Indian, excl. Hispanic:	45	0.05
Belizean	16	0.02

Notes: 1. Figures in the "Number" column do not add up to the total population due to: a) Ancestry/Race overlap — e.g. persons can report being both White and Irish, b) persons of Hispanic origin can report being any race, c) persons reporting two ancestries are counted in both categories. 2. Numbers in parentheses indicate the number of persons reporting this ancestry/race alone, not in combination with any other ancestry/race. 3. Refer to the Explanation of Data in the front of the book for more detailed information.

Haitian	11	0.01
Jamaican	4	0.00
West Indian	10	0.01
Other West Indian	4	0.00
White:	43,228	49.01
Not Hispanic (31,962)	33,631	38.13
Hispanic (8,430)	9,597	10.88
Yugoslavian	115	0.13

Westmont

Place Type: Census Designated Place
County: Los Angeles
Population: 31,623

Ancestry/Race	Number	%
African American/Black:	18,684	59.08
Not Hispanic (18,095)	18,363	58.07
Hispanic (241)	321	1.02
African, sub-Saharan:	711	2.25
African	664	2.11
Nigerian	28	0.09
Other sub-Saharan African	19	0.06
Am. Ind. or Alaska Nat., not spec.	161	0.51
American Indian tribes, specified:	169	0.53
Apache	4	0.01
Blackfeet (2)	8	0.03
Cherokee (3)	34	0.11
Choctaw	18	0.06
Comanche	1	0.00
Cree	1	0.00
Creek	1	0.00
Latin American Indians (47)	72	0.23
Navajo (6)	8	0.03
Paiute (1)	1	0.00
Pueblo (1)	1	0.00
Seminole	6	0.02
Sioux	2	0.01
Tohono O'Odham (5)	5	0.02
Yuman	3	0.01
All other tribes (2)	4	0.01
American Indian tribes, not spec.	19	0.06
Arab:	37	0.12
Arab/Arabic	8	0.03
Egyptian	10	0.03
Other Arab	19	0.06
Asian:	204	0.65
Cambodian (9)	9	0.03
Chinese, ex. Taiwanese (20)	31	0.10
Filipino (42)	55	0.17
Hmong	1	0.00
Indian (15)	33	0.10
Japanese (13)	26	0.08
Korean (12)	17	0.05
Thai (3)	3	0.01
Vietnamese (3)	7	0.02
Other Asian, specified	4	0.01
Other Asian, not specified (3)	18	0.06
Austrian	33	0.10
Canadian	30	0.10
English	68	0.22
French, except Basque	35	0.11
French Canadian	30	0.10
German	44	0.14
Hawaii Native/Pacific Islander:	92	0.29
Micronesian: (16)	19	0.06
Guamanian/Chamorro (16)	19	0.06
Polynesian: (31)	41	0.13
Native Hawaiian (4)	13	0.04
Samoan (18)	19	0.06
Tongan (9)	9	0.03
Other Pac. Isl., specified	1	0.00
Other Pac. Isl., not spec. (15)	31	0.10
Hispanic or Latino:	12,499	39.53
Central American:	1,826	5.77
Costa Rican	2	0.01
Guatemalan	515	1.63
Honduran	117	0.37
Nicaraguan	77	0.24
Panamanian	14	0.04
Salvadoran	932	2.95
Other Central American	169	0.53
Cuban	28	0.09
Dominican Republic	1	0.00
Mexican	7,464	23.60
Puerto Rican	109	0.34
South American:	43	0.14
Bolivian	1	0.00
Colombian	5	0.02
Ecuadorian	22	0.07
Peruvian	8	0.03
Other South American	7	0.02
Other Hispanic or Latino	3,028	9.58
Irish	126	0.40
Italian	41	0.13
Maltese	22	0.07
Norwegian	5	0.02
Polish	38	0.12
Portuguese	38	0.12
Scotch-Irish	7	0.02
Scottish	12	0.04
Serbian	8	0.03
United States or American	365	1.16
West Indian, excl. Hispanic:	345	1.09
Barbadian	16	0.05
Belizean	123	0.39
Jamaican	179	0.57
Trinidadian and Tobagonian	15	0.05
West Indian	12	0.04
White:	4,455	14.09
Not Hispanic (381)	519	1.64
Hispanic (3,337)	3,936	12.45

Whittier

Place Type: City
County: Los Angeles
Population: 83,680

Ancestry/Race	Number	%
Acadian/Cajun	8	0.01
African American/Black:	1,305	1.56
Not Hispanic (838)	983	1.17
Hispanic (181)	322	0.38
African, sub-Saharan:	139	0.17
African	139	0.17
Alaska Native tribes, specified:	5	0.01
Aleut (1)	1	0.00
Eskimo (2)	2	0.00
Tlingit-Haida (2)	2	0.00
Alaska Native tribes, not specified	1	0.00
Am. Ind. or Alaska Nat., not spec.	656	0.78
Albanian	6	0.01
Alsatian	7	0.01
American Indian tribes, specified:	1,053	1.26
Apache (58)	121	0.14
Blackfeet (3)	21	0.03
Cherokee (59)	153	0.18
Cheyenne	7	0.01
Chickasaw (4)	8	0.01
Chippewa (4)	19	0.02
Choctaw (7)	34	0.04
Comanche (10)	14	0.02
Cree	1	0.00
Creek (4)	17	0.02
Crow (1)	1	0.00
Delaware (1)	1	0.00
Iroquois (5)	8	0.01
Kiowa (4)	7	0.01
Latin American Indians (156)	216	0.26
Lumbee	3	0.00
Navajo (53)	81	0.10
Osage	4	0.00
Paiute (1)	4	0.00
Pima (15)	17	0.02
Potawatomi (2)	4	0.00
Pueblo (60)	73	0.09
Seminole (1)	5	0.01
Shoshone (1)	9	0.01
Sioux (15)	34	0.04
Tohono O'Odham (6)	8	0.01
Yaqui (18)	32	0.04
Yuman (1)	2	0.00
All other tribes (90)	149	0.18
American Indian tribes, not spec.	79	0.09
Arab:	379	0.45
Arab/Arabic	52	0.06
Egyptian	72	0.09
Lebanese	125	0.15
Moroccan	38	0.05
Palestinian	81	0.10
Other Arab	11	0.01
Armenian	795	0.95
Asian:	3,646	4.36
Bangladeshi	2	0.00
Cambodian (48)	55	0.07
Chinese, ex. Taiwanese (536)	717	0.86
Filipino (660)	891	1.06
Hmong (2)	2	0.00
Indian (216)	259	0.31
Indonesian (17)	42	0.05
Japanese (619)	893	1.07
Korean (247)	302	0.36
Laotian (26)	30	0.04
Malaysian (2)	6	0.01
Pakistani (25)	31	0.04
Sri Lankan (30)	35	0.04
Taiwanese (51)	65	0.08
Thai (54)	69	0.08
Vietnamese (124)	140	0.17
Other Asian, specified (3)	20	0.02
Other Asian, not specified (19)	87	0.10
Assyrian/Chaldean/Syriac	38	0.05
Australian	4	0.00
Austrian	267	0.32
Basque	70	0.08
Belgian	63	0.08
Brazilian	8	0.01
British	310	0.37
Bulgarian	21	0.03
Canadian	122	0.15
Croatian	180	0.21
Czech	114	0.14
Czechoslovakian	103	0.12
Danish	591	0.70
Dutch	1,066	1.27
Eastern European	115	0.14
English	6,042	7.21
European	452	0.54
Finnish	30	0.04
French, except Basque	1,693	2.02
French Canadian	242	0.29
German	7,103	8.47
Greek	143	0.17
Guyanese	18	0.02
Hawaii Native/Pacific Islander:	297	0.35
Melanesian: (1)	1	0.00
Fijian (1)	1	0.00
Micronesian: (18)	35	0.04
Guamanian/Chamorro (18)	35	0.04
Polynesian: (88)	209	0.25
Native Hawaiian (43)	147	0.18
Samoan (44)	59	0.07
Tongan (1)	1	0.00
Other Polynesian	2	0.00
Other Pac. Isl., specified	6	0.01
Other Pac. Isl., not spec. (19)	46	0.05
Hispanic or Latino:	46,765	55.89
Central American:	1,401	1.67
Costa Rican	70	0.08
Guatemalan	296	0.35
Honduran	60	0.07
Nicaraguan	136	0.16
Panamanian	17	0.02
Salvadoran	653	0.78
Other Central American	169	0.20
Cuban	343	0.41
Dominican Republic	14	0.02
Mexican	38,565	46.09
Puerto Rican	393	0.47

Notes: 1. Figures in the "Number" column do not add up to the total population due to: a) Ancestry/Race overlap — e.g. persons can report being both White and Irish, b) persons of Hispanic origin can report being any race, c) persons reporting two ancestries are counted in both categories. 2. Numbers in parentheses indicate the number of persons reporting this ancestry/race alone, not in combination with any other ancestry/race. 3. Refer to the Explanation of Data in the front of the book for more detailed information.

South American:	508	0.61
Argentinean	97	0.12
Bolivian	27	0.03
Chilean	26	0.03
Colombian	98	0.12
Ecuadorian	83	0.10
Peruvian	113	0.14
Uruguayan	12	0.01
Venezuelan	12	0.01
Other South American	40	0.05
Other Hispanic or Latino	5,541	6.62
Hungarian	261	0.31
Icelander	25	0.03
Iranian	35	0.04
Irish	5,634	6.72
Israeli	9	0.01
Italian	3,562	4.25
Latvian	18	0.02
Lithuanian	52	0.06
Macedonian	8	0.01
Maltese	31	0.04
Northern European	42	0.05
Norwegian	911	1.09
Pennsylvania German	13	0.02
Polish	1,042	1.24
Portuguese	109	0.13
Romanian	89	0.11
Russian	847	1.01
Scandinavian	69	0.08
Scotch-Irish	864	1.03
Scottish	1,359	1.62
Serbian	43	0.05
Slavic	7	0.01
Slovak	29	0.03
Slovene	17	0.02
Swedish	941	1.12
Swiss	183	0.22
Turkish	29	0.03
Ukrainian	75	0.09
United States or American	2,237	2.67
Welsh	321	0.38
West Indian, excl. Hispanic:	46	0.05
Belizean	20	0.02
Jamaican	26	0.03
White:	56,590	67.63
Not Hispanic (31,475)	32,748	39.13
Hispanic (21,401)	23,842	28.49
Yugoslavian	89	0.11

Wildomar

Place Type: Census Designated Place
County: Riverside
Population: 14,064

Ancestry/Race	Number	%
African American/Black:	333	2.37
Not Hispanic (229)	299	2.13
Hispanic (19)	34	0.24
Am. Ind. or Alaska Nat., not spec.	72	0.51
American Indian tribes, specified:	195	1.39
Apache (5)	9	0.06
Blackfeet (2)	13	0.09
Cherokee (10)	49	0.35
Cheyenne	1	0.01
Chippewa (2)	2	0.01
Choctaw (3)	11	0.08
Comanche	1	0.01
Creek	4	0.03
Iroquois	2	0.01
Latin American Indians (23)	37	0.26
Navajo	4	0.03
Osage (1)	2	0.01
Pueblo (4)	4	0.03
Seminole (1)	1	0.01
Sioux (4)	10	0.07
Ute	1	0.01
Yaqui (4)	4	0.03
All other tribes (32)	40	0.28
American Indian tribes, not spec.	9	0.06
Armenian	9	0.07
Asian:	421	2.99
Cambodian (4)	4	0.03
Chinese, ex. Taiwanese (21)	44	0.31
Filipino (105)	172	1.22
Indian (5)	19	0.14
Indonesian (6)	16	0.11
Japanese (35)	70	0.50
Korean (16)	31	0.22
Pakistani (5)	5	0.04
Taiwanese (3)	3	0.02
Thai (8)	11	0.08
Vietnamese (40)	42	0.30
Other Asian, specified (1)	1	0.01
Other Asian, not specified (1)	3	0.02
Austrian	56	0.41
Belgian	10	0.07
Brazilian	14	0.10
British	49	0.35
Canadian	74	0.54
Czechoslovakian	20	0.14
Danish	88	0.64
Dutch	478	3.46
English	1,796	13.01
European	241	1.75
Finnish	59	0.43
French, except Basque	522	3.78
French Canadian	114	0.83
German	2,394	17.34
Greek	79	0.57
Hawaii Native/Pacific Islander:	77	0.55
Melanesian:	5	0.04
Fijian	5	0.04
Micronesian: (7)	10	0.07
Guamanian/Chamorro (7)	10	0.07
Polynesian: (25)	45	0.32
Native Hawaiian (8)	27	0.19
Samoan (14)	15	0.11
Tongan (1)	1	0.01
Other Polynesian (2)	2	0.01
Other Pac. Isl., not spec. (4)	17	0.12
Hispanic or Latino:	3,035	21.58
Central American:	38	0.27
Costa Rican	6	0.04
Guatemalan	4	0.03
Nicaraguan	2	0.01
Salvadoran	26	0.18
Cuban	18	0.13
Dominican Republic	3	0.02
Mexican	2,525	17.95
Puerto Rican	48	0.34
South American:	32	0.23
Argentinean	10	0.07
Bolivian	1	0.01
Chilean	2	0.01
Colombian	1	0.01
Ecuadorian	2	0.01
Peruvian	7	0.05
Uruguayan	6	0.04
Other South American	3	0.02
Other Hispanic or Latino	371	2.64
Hungarian	68	0.49
Icelander	29	0.21
Irish	1,408	10.20
Italian	892	6.46
Lithuanian	15	0.11
Norwegian	275	1.99
Pennsylvania German	7	0.05
Polish	314	2.27
Portuguese	38	0.28
Russian	116	0.84
Scandinavian	39	0.28
Scotch-Irish	290	2.10
Scottish	309	2.24
Slavic	21	0.15
Slovak	11	0.08
Swedish	216	1.56
Swiss	28	0.20
Ukrainian	39	0.28
United States or American	863	6.25
Welsh	179	1.30
White:	12,046	85.65
Not Hispanic (10,111)	10,383	73.83
Hispanic (1,429)	1,663	11.82

Willowbrook

Place Type: Census Designated Place
County: Los Angeles
Population: 34,138

Ancestry/Race	Number	%
Acadian/Cajun	5	0.01
African American/Black:	15,612	45.73
Not Hispanic (15,089)	15,280	44.76
Hispanic (242)	332	0.97
African, sub-Saharan:	471	1.38
African	440	1.29
Ethiopian	17	0.05
Nigerian	3	0.01
Senegalese	5	0.01
Other sub-Saharan African	6	0.02
Am. Ind. or Alaska Nat., not spec.	172	0.50
American Indian tribes, specified:	210	0.62
Apache (1)	4	0.01
Blackfeet	22	0.06
Cherokee (13)	35	0.10
Chickasaw	2	0.01
Chippewa	3	0.01
Choctaw (6)	15	0.04
Creek (1)	5	0.01
Latin American Indians (62)	81	0.24
Navajo (24)	30	0.09
Sioux (1)	2	0.01
All other tribes (3)	11	0.03
American Indian tribes, not spec.	17	0.05
Arab:	7	0.02
Lebanese	7	0.02
Armenian	21	0.06
Asian:	149	0.44
Chinese, ex. Taiwanese (14)	21	0.06
Filipino (35)	47	0.14
Indian (8)	16	0.05
Indonesian (3)	3	0.01
Japanese (6)	17	0.05
Korean (8)	10	0.03
Pakistani (1)	3	0.01
Thai (5)	5	0.01
Vietnamese (6)	6	0.02
Other Asian, specified	1	0.00
Other Asian, not specified (2)	20	0.06
English	7	0.02
French, except Basque	43	0.13
German	38	0.11
Hawaii Native/Pacific Islander:	59	0.17
Micronesian: (4)	6	0.02
Guamanian/Chamorro (4)	6	0.02
Polynesian: (36)	46	0.13
Native Hawaiian (6)	6	0.02
Samoan (21)	31	0.09
Tongan (9)	9	0.03
Other Pac. Isl., not spec. (4)	7	0.02
Hispanic or Latino:	18,297	53.60
Central American:	824	2.41
Costa Rican	3	0.01
Guatemalan	201	0.59
Honduran	40	0.12
Nicaraguan	46	0.13
Panamanian	4	0.01
Salvadoran	444	1.30
Other Central American	86	0.25
Cuban	35	0.10
Mexican	14,834	43.45
Puerto Rican	73	0.21
South American:	20	0.06
Argentinean	4	0.01
Colombian	7	0.02
Ecuadorian	4	0.01
Peruvian	4	0.01
Other South American	1	0.00

Notes: 1. Figures in the "Number" column do not add up to the total population due to: a) Ancestry/Race overlap — e.g. persons can report being both White and Irish, b) persons of Hispanic origin can report being any race, c) persons reporting two ancestries are counted in both categories. 2. Numbers in parentheses indicate the number of persons reporting this ancestry/race alone, not in combination with any other ancestry/race. 3. Refer to the Explanation of Data in the front of the book for more detailed information.

Ancestry/Race	Number	%
Other Hispanic or Latino	2,511	7.36
Hungarian	7	0.02
Iranian	7	0.02
Irish	70	0.21
Italian	41	0.12
Polish	11	0.03
Portuguese	17	0.05
Scotch-Irish	9	0.03
Scottish	4	0.01
United States or American	415	1.22
West Indian, excl. Hispanic:	43	0.13
Jamaican	34	0.10
West Indian	9	0.03
White:	6,247	18.30
Not Hispanic (292)	393	1.15
Hispanic (5,190)	5,854	17.15

Windsor

Place Type: Town
County: Sonoma
Population: 22,744

Ancestry/Race	Number	%
African American/Black:	276	1.21
Not Hispanic (150)	226	0.99
Hispanic (28)	50	0.22
Alaska Native tribes, specified:	9	0.04
Aleut (4)	6	0.03
Tlingit-Haida (1)	2	0.01
All other tribes	1	0.00
Am. Ind. or Alaska Nat., not spec.	152	0.67
American Indian tribes, specified:	492	2.16
Apache (3)	17	0.07
Blackfeet (2)	12	0.05
Cherokee (9)	80	0.35
Chippewa (9)	17	0.07
Choctaw (4)	12	0.05
Colville	1	0.00
Cree (1)	1	0.00
Creek (1)	5	0.02
Crow	1	0.00
Delaware	1	0.00
Iroquois (2)	5	0.02
Latin American Indians (35)	69	0.30
Menominee	2	0.01
Navajo (8)	16	0.07
Osage	1	0.00
Ottawa (2)	2	0.01
Paiute (4)	4	0.02
Pima (3)	7	0.03
Potawatomi	1	0.00
Pueblo (1)	2	0.01
Puget Sound Salish (3)	3	0.01
Seminole	1	0.00
Shoshone (1)	1	0.00
Sioux (4)	9	0.04
Yaqui (1)	5	0.02
All other tribes (147)	217	0.95
American Indian tribes, not spec.	14	0.06
Arab:	53	0.23
Egyptian	9	0.04
Lebanese	7	0.03
Palestinian	9	0.04
Other Arab	28	0.12
Armenian	29	0.13
Asian:	749	3.29
Cambodian (2)	2	0.01
Chinese, ex. Taiwanese (102)	141	0.62
Filipino (154)	234	1.03
Hmong (3)	6	0.03
Indian (39)	64	0.28
Indonesian (1)	2	0.01
Japanese (57)	101	0.44
Korean (65)	92	0.40
Laotian (11)	12	0.05
Sri Lankan	1	0.00
Taiwanese	3	0.01
Thai (2)	2	0.01
Vietnamese (55)	63	0.28
Other Asian, specified	5	0.02
Other Asian, not specified (13)	21	0.09
Austrian	81	0.35
Belgian	34	0.15
British	69	0.30
Canadian	125	0.54
Croatian	44	0.19
Czech	46	0.20
Czechoslovakian	16	0.07
Danish	444	1.93
Dutch	396	1.73
Eastern European	15	0.07
English	2,674	11.65
European	448	1.95
Finnish	118	0.51
French, except Basque	828	3.61
French Canadian	134	0.58
German	3,757	16.37
Greek	105	0.46
Hawaii Native/Pacific Islander:	90	0.40
Melanesian: (7)	9	0.04
Fijian (7)	9	0.04
Micronesian: (6)	18	0.08
Guamanian/Chamorro (6)	18	0.08
Polynesian: (19)	57	0.25
Native Hawaiian (9)	36	0.16
Samoan (8)	19	0.08
Other Polynesian (2)	2	0.01
Other Pac. Isl., not spec.	6	0.03
Hispanic or Latino:	5,364	23.58
Central American:	73	0.32
Costa Rican	4	0.02
Guatemalan	22	0.10
Nicaraguan	18	0.08
Panamanian	4	0.02
Salvadoran	17	0.07
Other Central American	8	0.04
Cuban	29	0.13
Dominican Republic	7	0.03
Mexican	4,541	19.97
Puerto Rican	62	0.27
South American:	57	0.25
Argentinean	4	0.02
Bolivian	6	0.03
Chilean	3	0.01
Colombian	12	0.05
Ecuadorian	8	0.04
Peruvian	19	0.08
Uruguayan	4	0.02
Venezuelan	1	0.00
Other Hispanic or Latino	595	2.62
Hungarian	142	0.62
Iranian	48	0.21
Irish	3,173	13.82
Italian	2,642	11.51
Latvian	22	0.10
Lithuanian	49	0.21
Luxemburger	8	0.03
Maltese	43	0.19
Northern European	69	0.30
Norwegian	730	3.18
Polish	369	1.61
Portuguese	409	1.78
Romanian	18	0.08
Russian	315	1.37
Scandinavian	147	0.64
Scotch-Irish	437	1.90
Scottish	550	2.40
Slavic	25	0.11
Slovak	8	0.03
Slovene	20	0.09
Swedish	574	2.50
Swiss	192	0.84
Ukrainian	27	0.12
United States or American	929	4.05
Welsh	270	1.18
White:	18,732	82.36
Not Hispanic (15,989)	16,459	72.37
Hispanic (1,979)	2,273	9.99
Yugoslavian	62	0.27

Winter Gardens

Place Type: Census Designated Place
County: San Diego
Population: 19,771

Ancestry/Race	Number	%
African American/Black:	336	1.70
Not Hispanic (245)	311	1.57
Hispanic (13)	25	0.13
African, sub-Saharan:	26	0.13
African	22	0.11
Ethiopian	4	0.02
Am. Ind. or Alaska Nat., not spec.	93	0.47
American Indian tribes, specified:	344	1.74
Apache (9)	22	0.11
Blackfeet (1)	20	0.10
Cherokee (26)	93	0.47
Cheyenne	7	0.04
Chickasaw	1	0.01
Chippewa (3)	8	0.04
Choctaw (5)	15	0.08
Comanche	4	0.02
Creek (3)	9	0.05
Crow (3)	3	0.02
Delaware	1	0.01
Iroquois (3)	9	0.05
Latin American Indians (7)	14	0.07
Lumbee (1)	3	0.02
Navajo (11)	12	0.06
Osage	2	0.01
Paiute (2)	2	0.01
Pueblo (3)	3	0.02
Puget Sound Salish	1	0.01
Seminole (2)	7	0.04
Shoshone (1)	1	0.01
Sioux (6)	16	0.08
Yaqui (9)	11	0.06
Yuman (3)	5	0.03
All other tribes (44)	75	0.38
American Indian tribes, not spec.	15	0.08
Arab:	4	0.02
Other Arab	4	0.02
Armenian	15	0.07
Asian:	473	2.39
Cambodian (16)	16	0.08
Chinese, ex. Taiwanese (16)	47	0.24
Filipino (141)	226	1.14
Indian (12)	21	0.11
Indonesian (3)	6	0.03
Japanese (27)	74	0.37
Korean (15)	25	0.13
Malaysian (4)	4	0.02
Taiwanese (1)	3	0.02
Thai (4)	4	0.02
Vietnamese (15)	24	0.12
Other Asian, specified	2	0.01
Other Asian, not specified (8)	21	0.11
Austrian	61	0.30
Belgian	23	0.11
British	138	0.69
Canadian	148	0.74
Croatian	7	0.03
Czech	32	0.16
Czechoslovakian	46	0.23
Danish	114	0.57
Dutch	411	2.05
English	2,840	14.19
European	290	1.45
Finnish	51	0.25
French, except Basque	1,018	5.09
French Canadian	191	0.95
German	4,133	20.66
Greek	95	0.47
Hawaii Native/Pacific Islander:	118	0.60
Melanesian: (1)	1	0.01
Fijian (1)	1	0.01
Micronesian: (16)	26	0.13
Guamanian/Chamorro (16)	26	0.13
Polynesian: (34)	75	0.38

Notes: 1. Figures in the "Number" column do not add up to the total population due to: a) Ancestry/Race overlap — e.g. persons can report being both White and Irish, b) persons of Hispanic origin can report being any race, c) persons reporting two ancestries are counted in both categories. 2. Numbers in parentheses indicate the number of persons reporting this ancestry/race alone, not in combination with any other ancestry/race. 3. Refer to the Explanation of Data in the front of the book for more detailed information.

Native Hawaiian (25)	62	0.31
Samoan (9)	13	0.07
Other Pac. Isl., not spec. (3)	16	0.08
Hispanic or Latino:	2,424	12.26
Central American:	60	0.30
Costa Rican	8	0.04
Guatemalan	21	0.11
Honduran	1	0.01
Nicaraguan	8	0.04
Panamanian	14	0.07
Salvadoran	8	0.04
Cuban	18	0.09
Dominican Republic	1	0.01
Mexican	1,859	9.40
Puerto Rican	67	0.34
South American:	32	0.16
Argentinean	3	0.02
Chilean	1	0.01
Colombian	4	0.02
Ecuadorian	11	0.06
Peruvian	8	0.04
Other South American	5	0.03
Other Hispanic or Latino	387	1.96
Hungarian	64	0.32
Irish	2,502	12.50
Italian	1,169	5.84
Lithuanian	35	0.17
Northern European	7	0.03
Norwegian	373	1.86
Polish	313	1.56
Portuguese	193	0.96
Romanian	20	0.10
Russian	68	0.34
Scandinavian	41	0.20
Scotch-Irish	576	2.88
Scottish	474	2.37
Slovak	27	0.13
Slovene	22	0.11
Swedish	535	2.67
Swiss	63	0.31
Ukrainian	16	0.08
United States or American	1,450	7.25
Welsh	178	0.89
White:	18,152	91.81
Not Hispanic (16,139)	16,587	83.90
Hispanic (1,336)	1,565	7.92
Yugoslavian	85	0.42

Woodland

Place Type: City
County: Yolo
Population: 49,151

Ancestry/Race	Number	%
African American/Black:	859	1.75
Not Hispanic (527)	682	1.39
Hispanic (104)	177	0.36
African, sub-Saharan:	35	0.07
African	35	0.07
Alaska Native tribes, specified:	15	0.03
Alaska Athabascan (4)	4	0.01
Eskimo	2	0.00
Tlingit-Haida (6)	8	0.02
All other tribes (1)	1	0.00
Alaska Native tribes, not specified	1	0.00
Am. Ind. or Alaska Nat., not spec.	394	0.80
Alsatian	10	0.02
American Indian tribes, specified:	821	1.67
Apache (16)	43	0.09
Blackfeet (4)	17	0.03
Cherokee (71)	227	0.46
Cheyenne	1	0.00
Chickasaw (1)	5	0.01
Chippewa (6)	11	0.02
Choctaw (27)	55	0.11
Comanche (3)	6	0.01
Cree (1)	4	0.01
Creek (2)	7	0.01
Crow (12)	14	0.03
Delaware (1)	1	0.00
Houma	1	0.00
Iroquois (6)	7	0.01
Kiowa (2)	2	0.00
Latin American Indians (69)	91	0.19
Navajo (12)	26	0.05
Osage (1)	3	0.01
Paiute (1)	6	0.01
Pima (8)	19	0.04
Potawatomi (5)	11	0.02
Pueblo (3)	10	0.02
Puget Sound Salish	2	0.00
Seminole	3	0.01
Shoshone (2)	2	0.00
Sioux (11)	25	0.05
Ute (1)	2	0.00
Yaqui (13)	18	0.04
Yuman	1	0.00
All other tribes (125)	201	0.41
American Indian tribes, not spec.	109	0.22
Arab:	166	0.34
Arab/Arabic	131	0.27
Lebanese	29	0.06
Palestinian	6	0.01
Armenian	15	0.03
Asian:	2,510	5.11
Cambodian (18)	18	0.04
Chinese, ex. Taiwanese (196)	269	0.55
Filipino (284)	455	0.93
Hmong (35)	36	0.07
Indian (541)	646	1.31
Indonesian (2)	2	0.00
Japanese (200)	333	0.68
Korean (50)	76	0.15
Laotian (25)	25	0.05
Malaysian	2	0.00
Pakistani (294)	409	0.83
Sri Lankan (1)	5	0.01
Thai (13)	23	0.05
Vietnamese (108)	127	0.26
Other Asian, specified (1)	2	0.00
Other Asian, not specified (49)	82	0.17
Assyrian/Chaldean/Syriac	8	0.02
Australian	18	0.04
Austrian	26	0.05
Basque	79	0.16
Belgian	46	0.09
British	168	0.34
Canadian	49	0.10
Celtic	7	0.01
Croatian	21	0.04
Czech	85	0.17
Czechoslovakian	139	0.28
Danish	288	0.59
Dutch	639	1.30
Eastern European	9	0.02
English	4,154	8.45
European	633	1.29
Finnish	63	0.13
French, except Basque	955	1.94
French Canadian	148	0.30
German	6,620	13.47
Greek	40	0.08
Hawaii Native/Pacific Islander:	231	0.47
Melanesian: (61)	63	0.13
Fijian (61)	63	0.13
Micronesian: (11)	21	0.04
Guamanian/Chamorro (11)	21	0.04
Polynesian: (46)	78	0.16
Native Hawaiian (21)	49	0.10
Samoan (23)	25	0.05
Tongan (1)	3	0.01
Other Polynesian (1)	1	0.00
Other Pac. Isl., not spec. (18)	69	0.14
Hispanic or Latino:	19,084	38.83
Central American:	111	0.23
Costa Rican	2	0.00
Guatemalan	25	0.05
Honduran	22	0.04
Nicaraguan	8	0.02
Panamanian	3	0.01
Salvadoran	48	0.10
Other Central American	3	0.01
Cuban	40	0.08
Dominican Republic	7	0.01
Mexican	16,642	33.86
Puerto Rican	126	0.26
South American:	73	0.15
Argentinean	9	0.02
Bolivian	4	0.01
Chilean	1	0.00
Colombian	21	0.04
Ecuadorian	6	0.01
Paraguayan	2	0.00
Peruvian	24	0.05
Venezuelan	4	0.01
Other South American	2	0.00
Other Hispanic or Latino	2,085	4.24
Hungarian	69	0.14
Icelander	43	0.09
Iranian	57	0.12
Irish	4,161	8.47
Italian	1,919	3.91
Lithuanian	15	0.03
Maltese	16	0.03
New Zealander	8	0.02
Northern European	41	0.08
Norwegian	822	1.67
Pennsylvania German	9	0.02
Polish	308	0.63
Portuguese	707	1.44
Romanian	14	0.03
Russian	265	0.54
Scandinavian	61	0.12
Scotch-Irish	798	1.62
Scottish	701	1.43
Serbian	27	0.05
Slavic	5	0.01
Slovak	42	0.09
Swedish	695	1.41
Swiss	328	0.67
Ukrainian	102	0.21
United States or American	2,218	4.51
Welsh	213	0.43
West Indian, excl. Hispanic:	16	0.03
British West Indian	7	0.01
Dutch West Indian	9	0.02
White:	34,885	70.98
Not Hispanic (26,064)	26,990	54.91
Hispanic (6,787)	7,895	16.06
Yugoslavian	19	0.04

Yorba Linda

Place Type: City
County: Orange
Population: 58,918

Ancestry/Race	Number	%
Acadian/Cajun	7	0.01
Afghan	15	0.03
African American/Black:	863	1.46
Not Hispanic (638)	774	1.31
Hispanic (50)	89	0.15
African, sub-Saharan:	215	0.37
African	95	0.16
Kenyan	34	0.06
Nigerian	23	0.04
South African	39	0.07
Ugandan	24	0.04
Alaska Native tribes, specified:	3	0.01
Aleut (1)	1	0.00
Eskimo (1)	2	0.00
Alaska Native tribes, not specified	3	0.01
Am. Ind. or Alaska Nat., not spec.	160	0.27
Albanian	8	0.01
American Indian tribes, specified:	382	0.65
Apache (6)	30	0.05
Blackfeet (4)	12	0.02
Cherokee (32)	123	0.21

Notes: 1. Figures in the "Number" column do not add up to the total population due to: a) Ancestry/Race overlap — e.g. persons can report being both White and Irish, b) persons of Hispanic origin can report being any race, c) persons reporting two ancestries are counted in both categories. 2. Numbers in parentheses indicate the number of persons reporting this ancestry/race alone, not in combination with any other ancestry/race. 3. Refer to the Explanation of Data in the front of the book for more detailed information.

Chickasaw (6)	6	0.01
Chippewa (13)	21	0.04
Choctaw (9)	28	0.05
Comanche (2)	3	0.01
Creek (1)	3	0.01
Crow	1	0.00
Delaware (1)	3	0.01
Iroquois (2)	8	0.01
Latin American Indians (9)	23	0.04
Lumbee (1)	3	0.01
Navajo (6)	11	0.02
Osage (4)	6	0.01
Paiute (1)	1	0.00
Pima (1)	1	0.00
Potawatomi	2	0.00
Pueblo (7)	24	0.04
Puget Sound Salish	3	0.01
Shoshone	3	0.01
Sioux (3)	7	0.01
Ute	3	0.01
Yakama	1	0.00
Yaqui (2)	4	0.01
All other tribes (34)	52	0.09
American Indian tribes, not spec.	29	0.05
Arab:	628	1.07
Arab/Arabic	133	0.23
Egyptian	143	0.24
Jordanian	51	0.09
Lebanese	163	0.28
Palestinian	52	0.09
Syrian	66	0.11
Other Arab	20	0.03
Armenian	306	0.52
Asian:	7,611	12.92
Bangladeshi (2)	3	0.01
Cambodian (23)	27	0.05
Chinese, ex. Taiwanese (1,454)	1,736	2.95
Filipino (942)	1,180	2.00
Indian (930)	1,021	1.73
Indonesian (63)	118	0.20
Japanese (806)	1,114	1.89
Korean (787)	838	1.42
Laotian (25)	27	0.05
Malaysian (4)	7	0.01
Pakistani (56)	90	0.15
Sri Lankan (10)	10	0.02
Taiwanese (368)	412	0.70
Thai (88)	99	0.17
Vietnamese (734)	771	1.31
Other Asian, specified (17)	23	0.04
Other Asian, not specified (48)	135	0.23
Assyrian/Chaldean/Syriac	25	0.04
Australian	23	0.04
Austrian	247	0.42
Basque	7	0.01
Belgian	58	0.10
Brazilian	15	0.03
British	313	0.53
Canadian	418	0.71
Carpatho Rusyn	16	0.03
Croatian	76	0.13
Czech	336	0.57
Czechoslovakian	197	0.34
Danish	555	0.95
Dutch	1,270	2.17
Eastern European	49	0.08
English	8,074	13.78
Estonian	31	0.05
European	747	1.27
Finnish	140	0.24
French, except Basque	2,423	4.14
French Canadian	436	0.74
German	11,225	19.16
Greek	487	0.83
Hawaii Native/Pacific Islander:	162	0.27
Melanesian: (1)	1	0.00
Fijian (1)	1	0.00
Micronesian: (3)	4	0.01
Guamanian/Chamorro (3)	4	0.01
Polynesian: (45)	114	0.19
Native Hawaiian (27)	90	0.15
Samoan (17)	21	0.04
Tongan (1)	1	0.00
Other Polynesian	2	0.00
Other Pac. Isl., specified	3	0.01
Other Pac. Isl., not spec. (7)	40	0.07
Hispanic or Latino:	6,044	10.26
Central American:	140	0.24
Costa Rican	21	0.04
Guatemalan	14	0.02
Honduran	11	0.02
Nicaraguan	20	0.03
Panamanian	6	0.01
Salvadoran	32	0.05
Other Central American	36	0.06
Cuban	144	0.24
Dominican Republic	7	0.01
Mexican	4,315	7.32
Puerto Rican	135	0.23
South American:	364	0.62
Argentinean	99	0.17
Bolivian	11	0.02
Chilean	24	0.04
Colombian	58	0.10
Ecuadorian	35	0.06
Peruvian	105	0.18
Uruguayan	2	0.00
Venezuelan	3	0.01
Other South American	27	0.05
Other Hispanic or Latino	939	1.59
Hungarian	347	0.59
Iranian	443	0.76
Irish	7,550	12.89
Israeli	111	0.19
Italian	4,491	7.66
Latvian	60	0.10
Lithuanian	105	0.18
Macedonian	7	0.01
Maltese	40	0.07
New Zealander	40	0.07
Northern European	58	0.10
Norwegian	1,103	1.88
Pennsylvania German	39	0.07
Polish	1,629	2.78
Portuguese	199	0.34
Romanian	229	0.39
Russian	872	1.49
Scandinavian	207	0.35
Scotch-Irish	893	1.52
Scottish	1,446	2.47
Slavic	36	0.06
Slovak	93	0.16
Slovene	31	0.05
Swedish	1,452	2.48
Swiss	457	0.78
Turkish	10	0.02
Ukrainian	92	0.16
United States or American	2,535	4.33
Welsh	615	1.05
West Indian, excl. Hispanic:	13	0.02
Dutch West Indian	13	0.02
White:	49,590	84.17
Not Hispanic (44,071)	45,231	76.77
Hispanic (3,944)	4,359	7.40
Yugoslavian	159	0.27

Yuba City

Place Type: City
County: Sutter
Population: 36,758

Ancestry/Race	Number	%
African American/Black:	1,268	3.45
Not Hispanic (976)	1,160	3.16
Hispanic (59)	108	0.29
African, sub-Saharan:	53	0.14
African	53	0.14
Alaska Native tribes, specified:	1	0.00
Tlingit-Haida (1)	1	0.00
Am. Ind. or Alaska Nat., not spec.	409	1.11
American Indian tribes, specified:	768	2.09
Apache (6)	29	0.08
Blackfeet (5)	20	0.05
Cherokee (148)	320	0.87
Cheyenne	4	0.01
Chickasaw (1)	4	0.01
Chippewa (15)	23	0.06
Choctaw (23)	45	0.12
Comanche (2)	14	0.04
Cree (4)	4	0.01
Creek (6)	10	0.03
Crow (1)	2	0.01
Delaware	2	0.01
Iroquois (1)	2	0.01
Latin American Indians (27)	39	0.11
Lumbee (4)	4	0.01
Menominee (1)	1	0.00
Navajo (4)	21	0.06
Osage	2	0.01
Ottawa	1	0.00
Paiute (3)	6	0.02
Pima	1	0.00
Potawatomi (5)	5	0.01
Pueblo (8)	16	0.04
Puget Sound Salish	1	0.00
Seminole (2)	4	0.01
Shoshone (1)	1	0.00
Sioux (5)	14	0.04
Tohono O'Odham (1)	4	0.01
Yakama (3)	3	0.01
Yaqui (6)	10	0.03
All other tribes (112)	156	0.42
American Indian tribes, not spec.	43	0.12
Arab:	97	0.27
Arab/Arabic	11	0.03
Egyptian	29	0.08
Jordanian	57	0.16
Armenian	91	0.25
Asian:	3,967	10.79
Bangladeshi (1)	1	0.00
Cambodian (23)	31	0.08
Chinese, ex. Taiwanese (157)	215	0.58
Filipino (250)	399	1.09
Hmong (60)	65	0.18
Indian (2,360)	2,636	7.17
Indonesian (3)	7	0.02
Japanese (155)	231	0.63
Korean (84)	124	0.34
Laotian (12)	13	0.04
Malaysian (2)	2	0.01
Pakistani (43)	74	0.20
Taiwanese	1	0.00
Thai (19)	37	0.10
Vietnamese (49)	66	0.18
Other Asian, specified (1)	1	0.00
Other Asian, not specified (37)	64	0.17
Australian	49	0.13
Austrian	36	0.10
Basque	30	0.08
Belgian	15	0.04
British	92	0.25
Canadian	50	0.14
Croatian	8	0.02
Czech	6	0.02
Danish	270	0.74
Dutch	729	1.99
English	2,838	7.76
European	92	0.25
Finnish	37	0.10
French, except Basque	1,009	2.76
French Canadian	165	0.45
German	3,952	10.80
Greek	169	0.46
Hawaii Native/Pacific Islander:	217	0.59
Melanesian: (10)	11	0.03
Fijian (10)	11	0.03
Micronesian: (54)	69	0.19
Guamanian/Chamorro (54)	69	0.19
Polynesian: (35)	82	0.22

Notes: 1. Figures in the "Number" column do not add up to the total population due to: a) Ancestry/Race overlap — e.g. persons can report being both White and Irish, b) persons of Hispanic origin can report being any race, c) persons reporting two ancestries are counted in both categories. 2. Numbers in parentheses indicate the number of persons reporting this ancestry/race alone, not in combination with any other ancestry/race. 3. Refer to the Explanation of Data in the front of the book for more detailed information.

Ancestry/Race	Number	%
Native Hawaiian (21)	57	0.16
Samoan (14)	25	0.07
Other Pac. Isl., not spec. (7)	55	0.15
Hispanic or Latino:	9,029	24.56
Central American:	66	0.18
Costa Rican	4	0.01
Guatemalan	15	0.04
Honduran	4	0.01
Nicaraguan	11	0.03
Panamanian	7	0.02
Salvadoran	21	0.06
Other Central American	4	0.01
Cuban	7	0.02
Dominican Republic	1	0.00
Mexican	7,678	20.89
Puerto Rican	131	0.36
South American:	22	0.06
Argentinean	8	0.02
Colombian	4	0.01
Ecuadorian	1	0.00
Peruvian	6	0.02
Uruguayan	1	0.00
Venezuelan	1	0.00
Other South American	1	0.00
Other Hispanic or Latino	1,124	3.06
Hungarian	22	0.06
Irish	3,076	8.41
Italian	1,497	4.09
Lithuanian	38	0.10
Maltese	28	0.08
Northern European	7	0.02
Norwegian	537	1.47
Pennsylvania German	10	0.03
Polish	327	0.89
Portuguese	409	1.12
Romanian	9	0.02
Russian	68	0.19
Scandinavian	82	0.22
Scotch-Irish	553	1.51
Scottish	550	1.50
Slavic	7	0.02
Slovak	8	0.02
Slovene	10	0.03
Swedish	551	1.51
Swiss	176	0.48
Turkish	6	0.02
Ukrainian	13	0.04
United States or American	2,765	7.56
Welsh	259	0.71
West Indian, excl. Hispanic:	38	0.10
Belizean	9	0.02
Trinidadian and Tobagonian	21	0.06
West Indian	8	0.02
White:	26,003	70.74
Not Hispanic (21,693)	22,502	61.22
Hispanic (2,918)	3,501	9.52
Yugoslavian	115	0.31

Yucaipa

Place Type: City
County: San Bernardino
Population: 41,207

Ancestry/Race	Number	%
African American/Black:	506	1.23
Not Hispanic (353)	452	1.10
Hispanic (16)	54	0.13
African, sub-Saharan:	93	0.23
African	93	0.23
Alaska Native tribes, specified:	7	0.02
Alaska Athabascan (1)	1	0.00
Eskimo (2)	5	0.01
Tlingit-Haida (1)	1	0.00
Alaska Native tribes, not specified	3	0.01
Am. Ind. or Alaska Nat., not spec.	215	0.52
American Indian tribes, specified:	647	1.57
Apache (24)	43	0.10
Blackfeet (5)	17	0.04
Cherokee (51)	187	0.45
Cheyenne (2)	2	0.00
Chickasaw (9)	10	0.02
Chippewa (10)	14	0.03
Choctaw (24)	46	0.11
Comanche (5)	11	0.03
Creek (1)	7	0.02
Crow	2	0.00
Delaware (1)	4	0.01
Iroquois (11)	21	0.05
Latin American Indians (34)	65	0.16
Lumbee	3	0.01
Menominee (1)	2	0.00
Navajo (9)	12	0.03
Osage	1	0.00
Ottawa (4)	4	0.01
Paiute (4)	4	0.01
Pima (3)	3	0.01
Potawatomi (4)	12	0.03
Pueblo (8)	17	0.04
Shoshone (1)	1	0.00
Sioux (8)	18	0.04
Tohono O'Odham (10)	10	0.02
Yaqui (18)	28	0.07
All other tribes (75)	103	0.25
American Indian tribes, not spec.	46	0.11
Arab:	28	0.07
Egyptian	7	0.02
Moroccan	21	0.05
Armenian	71	0.17
Asian:	766	1.86
Cambodian (13)	18	0.04
Chinese, ex. Taiwanese (60)	100	0.24
Filipino (117)	197	0.48
Indian (109)	125	0.30
Indonesian (19)	34	0.08
Japanese (58)	124	0.30
Korean (62)	87	0.21
Malaysian	5	0.01
Pakistani (5)	6	0.01
Sri Lankan (5)	5	0.01
Taiwanese (3)	4	0.01
Thai (7)	11	0.03
Vietnamese (19)	29	0.07
Other Asian, specified	2	0.00
Other Asian, not specified (4)	19	0.05
Australian	27	0.07
Austrian	79	0.19
Basque	8	0.02
Belgian	46	0.11
British	71	0.17
Bulgarian	13	0.03
Canadian	242	0.59
Celtic	8	0.02
Croatian	18	0.04
Czech	132	0.32
Czechoslovakian	81	0.20
Danish	324	0.78
Dutch	1,349	3.27
English	5,290	12.81
European	430	1.04
Finnish	139	0.34
French, except Basque	1,663	4.03
French Canadian	290	0.70
German	7,032	17.03
Greek	115	0.28
Hawaii Native/Pacific Islander:	138	0.33
Melanesian:	2	0.00
Fijian	2	0.00
Micronesian: (18)	27	0.07
Guamanian/Chamorro (18)	27	0.07
Polynesian: (31)	88	0.21
Native Hawaiian (15)	59	0.14
Samoan (16)	28	0.07
Other Polynesian	1	0.00
Other Pac. Isl., not spec. (6)	21	0.05
Hispanic or Latino:	7,561	18.35
Central American:	87	0.21
Costa Rican	13	0.03
Guatemalan	15	0.04
Honduran	6	0.01
Nicaraguan	16	0.04
Panamanian	5	0.01
Salvadoran	25	0.06
Other Central American	7	0.02
Cuban	56	0.14
Mexican	6,206	15.06
Puerto Rican	93	0.23
South American:	38	0.09
Argentinean	4	0.01
Bolivian	1	0.00
Chilean	1	0.00
Colombian	12	0.03
Ecuadorian	3	0.01
Paraguayan	1	0.00
Peruvian	8	0.02
Venezuelan	8	0.02
Other Hispanic or Latino	1,081	2.62
Hungarian	270	0.65
Icelander	15	0.04
Iranian	14	0.03
Irish	5,204	12.60
Israeli	6	0.01
Italian	1,951	4.72
Lithuanian	63	0.15
Northern European	39	0.09
Norwegian	939	2.27
Pennsylvania German	56	0.14
Polish	704	1.70
Portuguese	95	0.23
Romanian	43	0.10
Russian	174	0.42
Scandinavian	27	0.07
Scotch-Irish	1,037	2.51
Scottish	1,074	2.60
Slavic	19	0.05
Slovak	31	0.08
Slovene	8	0.02
Swedish	1,189	2.88
Swiss	145	0.35
Ukrainian	135	0.33
United States or American	2,596	6.29
Welsh	511	1.24
West Indian, excl. Hispanic:	32	0.08
Dutch West Indian	15	0.04
Jamaican	17	0.04
White:	36,393	88.32
Not Hispanic (31,626)	32,393	78.61
Hispanic (3,487)	4,000	9.71
Yugoslavian	62	0.15

Yucca Valley

Place Type: Town
County: San Bernardino
Population: 16,865

Ancestry/Race	Number	%
Afghan	7	0.04
African American/Black:	485	2.88
Not Hispanic (350)	442	2.62
Hispanic (29)	43	0.25
African, sub-Saharan:	39	0.23
African	39	0.23
Alaska Native tribes, specified:	1	0.01
Tlingit-Haida (1)	1	0.01
Am. Ind. or Alaska Nat., not spec.	108	0.64
American Indian tribes, specified:	307	1.82
Apache (11)	19	0.11
Blackfeet (4)	11	0.07
Cherokee (33)	102	0.60
Cheyenne (1)	2	0.01
Chickasaw (11)	11	0.07
Chippewa (3)	3	0.02
Choctaw (9)	21	0.12
Comanche (3)	3	0.02
Creek (2)	4	0.02
Crow (2)	2	0.01
Delaware (1)	1	0.01
Iroquois (3)	10	0.06
Latin American Indians (10)	12	0.07

Notes: 1. Figures in the "Number" column do not add up to the total population due to: a) Ancestry/Race overlap — e.g. persons can report being both White and Irish, b) persons of Hispanic origin can report being any race, c) persons reporting two ancestries are counted in both categories. 2. Numbers in parentheses indicate the number of persons reporting this ancestry/race alone, not in combination with any other ancestry/race. 3. Refer to the Explanation of Data in the front of the book for more detailed information.

Lumbee (2)	4	0.02
Menominee	1	0.01
Navajo (11)	12	0.07
Osage	2	0.01
Pima	2	0.01
Potawatomi (1)	5	0.03
Pueblo (6)	9	0.05
Seminole (1)	4	0.02
Sioux (6)	9	0.05
Yaqui (2)	11	0.07
Yuman	1	0.01
All other tribes (34)	46	0.27
American Indian tribes, not spec.	10	0.06
Arab:	73	0.43
Arab/Arabic	8	0.05
Palestinian	33	0.20
Syrian	15	0.09
Other Arab	17	0.10
Armenian	45	0.27
Asian:	297	1.76
Cambodian (4)	4	0.02
Chinese, ex. Taiwanese (25)	29	0.17
Filipino (57)	80	0.47
Indian (54)	71	0.42
Indonesian	1	0.01
Japanese (28)	44	0.26
Korean (21)	32	0.19
Laotian (1)	2	0.01
Pakistani (5)	5	0.03
Taiwanese (1)	3	0.02
Thai (2)	4	0.02
Vietnamese (5)	8	0.05
Other Asian, not specified (12)	14	0.08
Austrian	16	0.10
Belgian	26	0.15
British	55	0.33
Canadian	76	0.45
Celtic	30	0.18
Czech	74	0.44
Czechoslovakian	24	0.14
Danish	262	1.56
Dutch	225	1.34
English	2,595	15.44
Estonian	7	0.04
European	249	1.48
Finnish	30	0.18
French, except Basque	902	5.37
French Canadian	144	0.86
German	2,993	17.80
Greek	55	0.33
Hawaii Native/Pacific Islander:	74	0.44
Micronesian: (15)	19	0.11
Guamanian/Chamorro (15)	19	0.11
Polynesian: (26)	38	0.23
Native Hawaiian (11)	19	0.11
Samoan (15)	17	0.10
Tongan	2	0.01
Other Pac. Isl., not spec. (10)	17	0.10
Hispanic or Latino:	1,922	11.40
Central American:	47	0.28
Costa Rican	2	0.01
Guatemalan	22	0.13
Nicaraguan	6	0.04
Panamanian	8	0.05
Salvadoran	7	0.04
Other Central American	2	0.01
Cuban	13	0.08
Mexican	1,484	8.80
Puerto Rican	74	0.44
South American:	15	0.09
Chilean	1	0.01
Colombian	5	0.03
Ecuadorian	3	0.02
Peruvian	1	0.01
Uruguayan	1	0.01
Venezuelan	3	0.02
Other South American	1	0.01
Other Hispanic or Latino	289	1.71
Hungarian	124	0.74
Iranian	7	0.04
Irish	2,176	12.94
Italian	965	5.74
Lithuanian	18	0.11
Maltese	13	0.08
Northern European	7	0.04
Norwegian	640	3.81
Pennsylvania German	31	0.18
Polish	269	1.60
Portuguese	35	0.21
Romanian	18	0.11
Russian	111	0.66
Scandinavian	39	0.23
Scotch-Irish	444	2.64
Scottish	436	2.59
Serbian	30	0.18
Slovak	14	0.08
Slovene	9	0.05
Swedish	502	2.99
Swiss	59	0.35
Ukrainian	15	0.09
United States or American	1,485	8.83
Welsh	138	0.82
West Indian, excl. Hispanic:	4	0.02
Jamaican	4	0.02
White:	15,168	89.94
Not Hispanic (13,829)	14,138	83.83
Hispanic (887)	1,030	6.11
Yugoslavian	34	0.20

Arvada

Place Type: City
County: Jefferson
Population: 102,153

Ancestry/Race	Number	%
Acadian/Cajun	15	0.01
Afghan	55	0.05
African American/Black:	1,011	0.99
Not Hispanic (628)	901	0.88
Hispanic (44)	110	0.11
African, sub-Saharan:	47	0.05
African	47	0.05
Alaska Native tribes, specified:	19	0.02
Alaska Athabascan (1)	2	0.00
Aleut (1)	4	0.00
Eskimo (1)	4	0.00
Tlingit-Haida (2)	6	0.01
All other tribes	3	0.00
Alaska Native tribes, not specified	1	0.00
Am. Ind. or Alaska Nat., not spec.	374	0.37
American Indian tribes, specified:	1,011	0.99
Apache (36)	93	0.09
Blackfeet (8)	21	0.02
Cherokee (85)	279	0.27
Cheyenne (6)	14	0.01
Chickasaw (3)	10	0.01
Chippewa (12)	33	0.03
Choctaw (25)	59	0.06
Colville (3)	3	0.00
Comanche (5)	10	0.01
Cree (1)	4	0.00
Creek (5)	6	0.01
Crow (3)	7	0.01
Delaware	1	0.00
Houma (1)	1	0.00
Iroquois (2)	22	0.02
Kiowa (2)	7	0.01
Latin American Indians (26)	60	0.06
Lumbee (1)	1	0.00
Menominee (3)	4	0.00
Navajo (94)	145	0.14
Osage (3)	9	0.01
Ottawa (2)	2	0.00
Paiute (1)	6	0.01
Potawatomi (10)	14	0.01
Pueblo (11)	20	0.02
Puget Sound Salish (3)	4	0.00
Seminole	1	0.00
Shoshone (1)	6	0.01
Sioux (52)	99	0.10
Tohono O'Odham (4)	4	0.00
Ute (3)	9	0.01
Yaqui	5	0.00
All other tribes (17)	52	0.05
American Indian tribes, not spec.	57	0.06
Arab:	364	0.36
Arab/Arabic	103	0.10
Egyptian	50	0.05
Lebanese	165	0.16
Moroccan	10	0.01
Palestinian	4	0.00
Syrian	13	0.01
Other Arab	19	0.02
Armenian	16	0.02
Asian:	2,910	2.85
Cambodian (8)	13	0.01
Chinese, ex. Taiwanese (277)	392	0.38
Filipino (123)	235	0.23
Hmong (193)	215	0.21
Indian (143)	175	0.17
Indonesian (4)	11	0.01
Japanese (369)	580	0.57
Korean (253)	300	0.29
Laotian (277)	325	0.32
Malaysian (1)	2	0.00
Pakistani (9)	9	0.01
Taiwanese (8)	9	0.01
Thai (12)	30	0.03
Vietnamese (400)	432	0.42
Other Asian, specified (10)	16	0.02
Other Asian, not specified (70)	166	0.16
Australian	36	0.04
Austrian	471	0.46
Basque	26	0.03
Belgian	188	0.18
Brazilian	12	0.01
British	393	0.38
Bulgarian	59	0.06
Canadian	225	0.22
Celtic	49	0.05
Croatian	189	0.18
Czech	835	0.81
Czechoslovakian	233	0.23
Danish	1,309	1.28
Dutch	2,118	2.07
Eastern European	31	0.03
English	16,157	15.76
Estonian	6	0.01
European	1,060	1.03
Finnish	255	0.25
French, except Basque	4,041	3.94
French Canadian	701	0.68
German	27,865	27.18
German Russian	35	0.03
Greek	340	0.33
Hawaii Native/Pacific Islander:	177	0.17
Micronesian: (16)	21	0.02
Guamanian/Chamorro (15)	20	0.02
Other Micronesian (1)	1	0.00
Polynesian: (45)	101	0.10
Native Hawaiian (35)	79	0.08
Samoan (9)	16	0.02
Tongan	3	0.00
Other Polynesian (1)	3	0.00
Other Pac. Isl., specified	4	0.00
Other Pac. Isl., not spec. (7)	51	0.05
Hispanic or Latino:	10,031	9.82
Central American:	94	0.09
Costa Rican	10	0.01
Guatemalan	29	0.03
Honduran	8	0.01
Nicaraguan	1	0.00
Panamanian	7	0.01
Salvadoran	31	0.03
Other Central American	8	0.01
Cuban	82	0.08
Dominican Republic	10	0.01
Mexican	5,178	5.07
Puerto Rican	175	0.17

Notes: 1. Figures in the "Number" column do not add up to the total population due to: a) Ancestry/Race overlap — e.g. persons can report being both White and Irish, b) persons of Hispanic origin can report being any race, c) persons reporting two ancestries are counted in both categories. 2. Numbers in parentheses indicate the number of persons reporting this ancestry/race alone, not in combination with any other ancestry/race. 3. Refer to the Explanation of Data in the front of the book for more detailed information.

South American:	118	0.12
Argentinean	15	0.01
Bolivian	7	0.01
Chilean	10	0.01
Colombian	26	0.03
Ecuadorian	13	0.01
Peruvian	26	0.03
Uruguayan	1	0.00
Venezuelan	11	0.01
Other South American	9	0.01
Other Hispanic or Latino	4,374	4.28
Hungarian	479	0.47
Icelander	54	0.05
Iranian	119	0.12
Irish	15,154	14.78
Israeli	23	0.02
Italian	7,804	7.61
Latvian	70	0.07
Lithuanian	180	0.18
Luxemburger	29	0.03
New Zealander	20	0.02
Northern European	100	0.10
Norwegian	2,793	2.72
Pennsylvania German	70	0.07
Polish	2,873	2.80
Portuguese	228	0.22
Romanian	98	0.10
Russian	1,265	1.23
Scandinavian	231	0.23
Scotch-Irish	2,151	2.10
Scottish	2,977	2.90
Serbian	17	0.02
Slavic	114	0.11
Slovak	184	0.18
Slovene	135	0.13
Swedish	4,095	3.99
Swiss	424	0.41
Turkish	7	0.01
Ukrainian	514	0.50
United States or American	5,390	5.26
Welsh	1,076	1.05
West Indian, excl. Hispanic:	34	0.03
Dutch West Indian	8	0.01
Jamaican	26	0.03
White:	95,147	93.14
Not Hispanic (87,302)	88,629	86.76
Hispanic (5,697)	6,518	6.38
Yugoslavian	228	0.22

Aurora

Place Type: City
County: Arapahoe
Population: 276,393

Ancestry/Race	Number	%
Acadian/Cajun	36	0.01
Afghan	76	0.03
African American/Black:	41,519	15.02
Not Hispanic (36,008)	39,688	14.36
Hispanic (1,096)	1,831	0.66
African, sub-Saharan:	4,064	1.47
African	2,400	0.87
Cape Verdean	39	0.01
Ethiopian	651	0.24
Ghanian	170	0.06
Liberian	7	0.00
Nigerian	474	0.17
Sierra Leonean	34	0.01
Somalian	25	0.01
South African	24	0.01
Sudanese	45	0.02
Ugandan	69	0.03
Zimbabwean	23	0.01
Other sub-Saharan African	103	0.04
Alaska Native tribes, specified:	37	0.01
Alaska Athabascan (4)	5	0.00
Aleut (5)	10	0.00
Eskimo (11)	12	0.00
Tlingit-Haida (7)	10	0.00
Alaska Native tribes, not specified	19	0.01
Am. Ind. or Alaska Nat., not spec.	1,534	0.56
Albanian	52	0.02
Alsatian	17	0.01
American Indian tribes, specified:	3,201	1.16
Apache (83)	212	0.08
Blackfeet (36)	157	0.06
Cherokee (214)	841	0.30
Cheyenne (8)	15	0.01
Chickasaw (14)	27	0.01
Chippewa (73)	119	0.04
Choctaw (54)	133	0.05
Colville (3)	8	0.00
Comanche (13)	31	0.01
Cree (1)	14	0.01
Creek (27)	61	0.02
Crow (12)	14	0.01
Delaware (11)	31	0.01
Houma (2)	8	0.00
Iroquois (20)	57	0.02
Kiowa (1)	2	0.00
Latin American Indians (165)	291	0.11
Lumbee (3)	3	0.00
Menominee (5)	8	0.00
Navajo (158)	257	0.09
Osage (8)	24	0.01
Ottawa (4)	6	0.00
Paiute (2)	5	0.00
Pima (9)	11	0.00
Potawatomi (22)	28	0.01
Pueblo (39)	74	0.03
Puget Sound Salish (3)	6	0.00
Seminole (7)	43	0.02
Shoshone (6)	23	0.01
Sioux (210)	341	0.12
Tohono O'Odham (5)	5	0.00
Ute (18)	34	0.01
Yaqui (7)	19	0.01
Yuman (1)	1	0.00
All other tribes (149)	292	0.11
American Indian tribes, not spec.	230	0.08
Arab:	1,329	0.48
Arab/Arabic	366	0.13
Egyptian	165	0.06
Iraqi	47	0.02
Jordanian	98	0.04
Lebanese	178	0.06
Moroccan	173	0.06
Palestinian	121	0.04
Syrian	56	0.02
Other Arab	125	0.05
Armenian	103	0.04
Asian:	15,009	5.43
Bangladeshi (16)	26	0.01
Cambodian (307)	365	0.13
Chinese, ex. Taiwanese (1,422)	1,802	0.65
Filipino (1,388)	2,009	0.73
Hmong (17)	20	0.01
Indian (1,094)	1,362	0.49
Indonesian (125)	164	0.06
Japanese (837)	1,412	0.51
Korean (3,203)	3,641	1.32
Laotian (146)	171	0.06
Malaysian (14)	30	0.01
Pakistani (205)	271	0.10
Sri Lankan (9)	13	0.00
Taiwanese (57)	75	0.03
Thai (270)	400	0.14
Vietnamese (2,381)	2,592	0.94
Other Asian, specified (34)	49	0.02
Other Asian, not specified (260)	607	0.22
Assyrian/Chaldean/Syriac	25	0.01
Australian	116	0.04
Austrian	786	0.28
Basque	82	0.03
Belgian	220	0.08
Brazilian	94	0.03
British	1,140	0.41
Bulgarian	66	0.02
Canadian	654	0.24
Celtic	59	0.02
Croatian	254	0.09
Czech	1,021	0.37
Czechoslovakian	501	0.18
Danish	2,027	0.73
Dutch	4,901	1.78
Eastern European	70	0.03
English	24,340	8.82
Estonian	37	0.01
European	2,577	0.93
Finnish	613	0.22
French, except Basque	7,482	2.71
French Canadian	1,748	0.63
German	50,449	18.28
German Russian	46	0.02
Greek	1,302	0.47
Guyanese	95	0.03
Hawaii Native/Pacific Islander:	1,065	0.39
Melanesian: (6)	8	0.00
Fijian (6)	8	0.00
Micronesian: (120)	213	0.08
Guamanian/Chamorro (92)	182	0.07
Other Micronesian (28)	31	0.01
Polynesian: (321)	639	0.23
Native Hawaiian (129)	374	0.14
Samoan (117)	161	0.06
Tongan (63)	82	0.03
Other Polynesian (12)	22	0.01
Other Pac. Isl., specified	7	0.00
Other Pac. Isl., not spec. (51)	198	0.07
Hispanic or Latino:	54,764	19.81
Central American:	1,888	0.68
Costa Rican	48	0.02
Guatemalan	389	0.14
Honduran	312	0.11
Nicaraguan	43	0.02
Panamanian	152	0.05
Salvadoran	853	0.31
Other Central American	91	0.03
Cuban	325	0.12
Dominican Republic	98	0.04
Mexican	38,276	13.85
Puerto Rican	1,596	0.58
South American:	855	0.31
Argentinean	46	0.02
Bolivian	22	0.01
Chilean	45	0.02
Colombian	172	0.06
Ecuadorian	33	0.01
Paraguayan	12	0.00
Peruvian	395	0.14
Uruguayan	3	0.00
Venezuelan	84	0.03
Other South American	43	0.02
Other Hispanic or Latino	11,726	4.24
Hungarian	1,172	0.42
Icelander	60	0.02
Iranian	292	0.11
Irish	28,267	10.24
Israeli	36	0.01
Italian	9,993	3.62
Latvian	55	0.02
Lithuanian	460	0.17
Luxemburger	34	0.01
Macedonian	11	0.00
Maltese	24	0.01
Northern European	193	0.07
Norwegian	5,964	2.16
Pennsylvania German	147	0.05
Polish	5,612	2.03
Portuguese	457	0.17
Romanian	268	0.10
Russian	3,150	1.14
Scandinavian	534	0.19
Scotch-Irish	4,576	1.66
Scottish	5,481	1.99
Serbian	69	0.03
Slavic	112	0.04
Slovak	342	0.12
Slovene	209	0.08

Notes: 1. Figures in the "Number" column do not add up to the total population due to: a) Ancestry/Race overlap — e.g. persons can report being both White and Irish, b) persons of Hispanic origin can report being any race, c) persons reporting two ancestries are counted in both categories. 2. Numbers in parentheses indicate the number of persons reporting this ancestry/race alone, not in combination with any other ancestry/race. 3. Refer to the Explanation of Data in the front of the book for more detailed information.

Swedish	5,918	2.14
Swiss	954	0.35
Turkish	176	0.06
Ukrainian	856	0.31
United States or American	12,393	4.49
Welsh	2,207	0.80
West Indian, excl. Hispanic:	933	0.34
Bahamian	43	0.02
Barbadian	17	0.01
Belizean	68	0.02
British West Indian	60	0.02
Dutch West Indian	12	0.00
Haitian	70	0.03
Jamaican	424	0.15
Trinidadian and Tobagonian	109	0.04
U.S. Virgin Islander	36	0.01
West Indian	94	0.03
White:	199,729	72.26
Not Hispanic (163,599)	169,688	61.39
Hispanic (26,712)	30,041	10.87
Yugoslavian	660	0.24

Berkley

Place Type: Census Designated Place
County: Adams
Population: 10,743

Ancestry/Race	Number	%
African American/Black:	141	1.31
Not Hispanic (72)	84	0.78
Hispanic (45)	57	0.53
Alaska Native tribes, specified:	2	0.02
Tlingit-Haida	2	0.02
Am. Ind. or Alaska Nat., not spec.	93	0.87
American Indian tribes, specified:	171	1.59
Apache (14)	20	0.19
Blackfeet	2	0.02
Cherokee (9)	46	0.43
Chippewa (3)	8	0.07
Choctaw (3)	3	0.03
Iroquois (5)	6	0.06
Kiowa (1)	1	0.01
Latin American Indians (13)	26	0.24
Navajo (9)	19	0.18
Pueblo	4	0.04
Seminole (1)	1	0.01
Sioux (22)	24	0.22
Ute (3)	3	0.03
All other tribes (7)	8	0.07
American Indian tribes, not spec.	29	0.27
Arab:	6	0.06
Arab/Arabic	6	0.06
Asian:	592	5.51
Chinese, ex. Taiwanese (34)	50	0.47
Filipino (19)	39	0.36
Hmong (137)	156	1.45
Indian (12)	18	0.17
Indonesian (1)	1	0.01
Japanese (33)	43	0.40
Korean (5)	8	0.07
Laotian (82)	99	0.92
Pakistani (4)	4	0.04
Taiwanese (2)	3	0.03
Thai (1)	4	0.04
Vietnamese (142)	145	1.35
Other Asian, not specified (20)	22	0.20
Austrian	24	0.23
Basque	10	0.09
Belgian	5	0.05
British	10	0.09
Czech	11	0.10
Czechoslovakian	5	0.05
Danish	70	0.66
Dutch	170	1.60
English	714	6.74
European	12	0.11
French, except Basque	270	2.55
French Canadian	47	0.44
German	1,268	11.96
Hawaii Native/Pacific Islander:	36	0.34
Micronesian: (8)	12	0.11
Guamanian/Chamorro (6)	8	0.07
Other Micronesian (2)	4	0.04
Polynesian: (10)	17	0.16
Native Hawaiian (7)	14	0.13
Samoan (3)	3	0.03
Other Pac. Isl., not spec. (1)	7	0.07
Hispanic or Latino:	4,643	43.22
Central American:	30	0.28
Guatemalan	10	0.09
Salvadoran	14	0.13
Other Central American	6	0.06
Cuban	11	0.10
Dominican Republic	2	0.02
Mexican	3,093	28.79
Puerto Rican	24	0.22
South American:	11	0.10
Colombian	4	0.04
Peruvian	5	0.05
Venezuelan	2	0.02
Other Hispanic or Latino	1,472	13.70
Hungarian	16	0.15
Iranian	6	0.06
Irish	755	7.12
Italian	437	4.12
Lithuanian	16	0.15
Northern European	10	0.09
Norwegian	152	1.43
Polish	85	0.80
Portuguese	11	0.10
Russian	54	0.51
Scandinavian	13	0.12
Scotch-Irish	103	0.97
Scottish	145	1.37
Swedish	128	1.21
Swiss	20	0.19
Ukrainian	5	0.05
United States or American	312	2.94
Welsh	19	0.18
White:	8,196	76.29
Not Hispanic (5,294)	5,413	50.39
Hispanic (2,531)	2,783	25.91
Yugoslavian	7	0.07

Black Forest

Place Type: Census Designated Place
County: El Paso
Population: 13,247

Ancestry/Race	Number	%
African American/Black:	159	1.20
Not Hispanic (109)	153	1.15
Hispanic (4)	6	0.05
Alaska Native tribes, specified:	2	0.02
Eskimo	1	0.01
All other tribes	1	0.01
Am. Ind. or Alaska Nat., not spec.	49	0.37
American Indian tribes, specified:	123	0.93
Apache (3)	5	0.04
Blackfeet	1	0.01
Cherokee (21)	48	0.36
Chickasaw (1)	3	0.02
Chippewa (2)	5	0.04
Choctaw (6)	7	0.05
Cree	1	0.01
Creek	3	0.02
Crow	5	0.04
Delaware (1)	1	0.01
Iroquois (8)	12	0.09
Latin American Indians (5)	7	0.05
Navajo (4)	4	0.03
Osage	4	0.03
Potawatomi	1	0.01
Pueblo (3)	3	0.02
Seminole (1)	1	0.01
Sioux (1)	2	0.02
Ute (1)	1	0.01
Yaqui (1)	1	0.01
All other tribes (3)	8	0.06
American Indian tribes, not spec.	12	0.09
Arab:	6	0.05
Lebanese	6	0.05
Armenian	35	0.27
Asian:	156	1.18
Cambodian (2)	2	0.02
Chinese, ex. Taiwanese (19)	22	0.17
Filipino (17)	33	0.25
Indian (2)	6	0.05
Japanese (17)	37	0.28
Korean (21)	29	0.22
Pakistani (1)	1	0.01
Thai (3)	3	0.02
Vietnamese (9)	16	0.12
Other Asian, not specified (2)	7	0.05
Australian	3	0.02
Austrian	48	0.36
Belgian	29	0.22
British	202	1.53
Canadian	9	0.07
Celtic	21	0.16
Croatian	21	0.16
Czech	97	0.74
Czechoslovakian	11	0.08
Danish	146	1.11
Dutch	345	2.62
Eastern European	10	0.08
English	2,249	17.05
European	211	1.60
Finnish	112	0.85
French, except Basque	489	3.71
French Canadian	46	0.35
German	3,949	29.94
Greek	73	0.55
Hawaii Native/Pacific Islander:	22	0.17
Micronesian: (4)	10	0.08
Guamanian/Chamorro (4)	10	0.08
Polynesian: (1)	12	0.09
Native Hawaiian (1)	8	0.06
Samoan	4	0.03
Hispanic or Latino:	438	3.31
Central American:	8	0.06
Guatemalan	3	0.02
Panamanian	3	0.02
Salvadoran	2	0.02
Cuban	5	0.04
Mexican	231	1.74
Puerto Rican	35	0.26
South American:	8	0.06
Bolivian	1	0.01
Colombian	2	0.02
Peruvian	3	0.02
Uruguayan	1	0.01
Venezuelan	1	0.01
Other Hispanic or Latino	151	1.14
Hungarian	124	0.94
Irish	1,671	12.67
Italian	675	5.12
Lithuanian	11	0.08
Northern European	19	0.14
Norwegian	445	3.37
Pennsylvania German	6	0.05
Polish	481	3.65
Portuguese	61	0.46
Romanian	35	0.27
Russian	137	1.04
Scandinavian	90	0.68
Scotch-Irish	528	4.00
Scottish	392	2.97
Slovak	23	0.17
Slovene	88	0.67
Swedish	399	3.03
Swiss	100	0.76
Ukrainian	20	0.15
United States or American	902	6.84
Welsh	174	1.32
White:	12,813	96.72
Not Hispanic (12,297)	12,478	94.19
Hispanic (298)	335	2.53

Notes: 1. Figures in the "Number" column do not add up to the total population due to: a) Ancestry/Race overlap — e.g. persons can report being both White and Irish, b) persons of Hispanic origin can report being any race, c) persons reporting two ancestries are counted in both categories. 2. Numbers in parentheses indicate the number of persons reporting this ancestry/race alone, not in combination with any other ancestry/race. 3. Refer to the Explanation of Data in the front of the book for more detailed information.

Yugoslavian	10	0.08

Boulder

Place Type: City
County: Boulder
Population: 94,673

Ancestry/Race	Number	%
Acadian/Cajun	29	0.03
African American/Black:	1,514	1.60
Not Hispanic (1,085)	1,383	1.46
Hispanic (69)	131	0.14
African, sub-Saharan:	279	0.30
African	89	0.09
Ethiopian	31	0.03
Ghanian	8	0.01
Kenyan	13	0.01
South African	106	0.11
Sudanese	7	0.01
Zimbabwean	19	0.02
Other sub-Saharan African	6	0.01
Alaska Native tribes, specified:	7	0.01
Alaska Athabascan (1)	1	0.00
Aleut (1)	1	0.00
Eskimo (3)	3	0.00
Tlingit-Haida (1)	2	0.00
Am. Ind. or Alaska Nat., not spec.	263	0.28
Albanian	18	0.02
Alsatian	25	0.03
American Indian tribes, specified:	644	0.68
Apache (10)	28	0.03
Blackfeet (8)	24	0.03
Cherokee (44)	177	0.19
Cheyenne (1)	6	0.01
Chickasaw (3)	5	0.01
Chippewa (8)	18	0.02
Choctaw (10)	26	0.03
Colville (2)	2	0.00
Comanche (4)	5	0.01
Cree (2)	4	0.00
Creek (2)	9	0.01
Crow (4)	7	0.01
Delaware (1)	2	0.00
Houma	1	0.00
Iroquois (19)	30	0.03
Kiowa (1)	3	0.00
Latin American Indians (21)	52	0.05
Menominee	1	0.00
Navajo (28)	50	0.05
Osage (1)	4	0.00
Ottawa (1)	4	0.00
Paiute (2)	2	0.00
Pima (1)	3	0.00
Potawatomi (2)	4	0.00
Pueblo (14)	18	0.02
Puget Sound Salish (1)	2	0.00
Seminole (2)	7	0.01
Sioux (43)	61	0.06
Yaqui (1)	2	0.00
Yuman (2)	2	0.00
All other tribes (43)	85	0.09
American Indian tribes, not spec.	61	0.06
Arab:	588	0.62
Arab/Arabic	64	0.07
Egyptian	61	0.06
Iraqi	40	0.04
Lebanese	147	0.16
Moroccan	39	0.04
Palestinian	20	0.02
Syrian	32	0.03
Other Arab	185	0.20
Armenian	223	0.24
Asian:	4,820	5.09
Bangladeshi (1)	1	0.00
Cambodian (16)	28	0.03
Chinese, ex. Taiwanese (1,025)	1,268	1.34
Filipino (118)	228	0.24
Hmong (53)	63	0.07
Indian (599)	679	0.72
Indonesian (40)	50	0.05
Japanese (561)	818	0.86
Korean (611)	733	0.77
Laotian (23)	35	0.04
Malaysian (14)	19	0.02
Pakistani (19)	27	0.03
Sri Lankan (14)	18	0.02
Taiwanese (67)	100	0.11
Thai (123)	157	0.17
Vietnamese (252)	281	0.30
Other Asian, specified (71)	85	0.09
Other Asian, not specified (108)	230	0.24
Assyrian/Chaldean/Syriac	5	0.01
Australian	65	0.07
Austrian	668	0.71
Basque	51	0.05
Belgian	229	0.24
Brazilian	84	0.09
British	1,162	1.23
Bulgarian	11	0.01
Canadian	382	0.40
Carpatho Rusyn	13	0.01
Celtic	76	0.08
Croatian	171	0.18
Czech	552	0.58
Czechoslovakian	228	0.24
Danish	939	0.99
Dutch	1,576	1.67
Eastern European	578	0.61
English	14,243	15.07
Estonian	16	0.02
European	2,130	2.25
Finnish	333	0.35
French, except Basque	3,113	3.29
French Canadian	702	0.74
German	19,797	20.95
German Russian	6	0.01
Greek	474	0.50
Hawaii Native/Pacific Islander:	150	0.16
Micronesian: (10)	21	0.02
Guamanian/Chamorro (10)	21	0.02
Polynesian: (34)	95	0.10
Native Hawaiian (25)	74	0.08
Samoan (9)	19	0.02
Other Polynesian	2	0.00
Other Pac. Isl., specified	0	0.00
Other Pac. Isl., not spec. (4)	32	0.03
Hispanic or Latino:	7,801	8.24
Central American:	204	0.22
Costa Rican	30	0.03
Guatemalan	52	0.05
Honduran	20	0.02
Nicaraguan	8	0.01
Panamanian	11	0.01
Salvadoran	79	0.08
Other Central American	4	0.00
Cuban	134	0.14
Dominican Republic	20	0.02
Mexican	5,577	5.89
Puerto Rican	205	0.22
South American:	355	0.37
Argentinean	43	0.05
Bolivian	15	0.02
Chilean	59	0.06
Colombian	74	0.08
Ecuadorian	13	0.01
Paraguayan	1	0.00
Peruvian	53	0.06
Uruguayan	4	0.00
Venezuelan	72	0.08
Other South American	21	0.02
Other Hispanic or Latino	1,306	1.38
Hungarian	810	0.86
Icelander	83	0.09
Iranian	182	0.19
Irish	13,088	13.85
Israeli	88	0.09
Italian	5,256	5.56
Latvian	81	0.09
Lithuanian	434	0.46
Luxemburger	8	0.01
Macedonian	13	0.01
Maltese	40	0.04
New Zealander	8	0.01
Northern European	333	0.35
Norwegian	2,806	2.97
Pennsylvania German	60	0.06
Polish	3,455	3.66
Portuguese	191	0.20
Romanian	253	0.27
Russian	2,693	2.85
Scandinavian	325	0.34
Scotch-Irish	2,809	2.97
Scottish	4,003	4.24
Serbian	70	0.07
Slavic	97	0.10
Slovak	224	0.24
Slovene	117	0.12
Swedish	2,907	3.08
Swiss	777	0.82
Turkish	103	0.11
Ukrainian	381	0.40
United States or American	2,760	2.92
Welsh	1,057	1.12
West Indian, excl. Hispanic:	51	0.05
Belizean	23	0.02
Haitian	18	0.02
Jamaican	10	0.01
White:	85,656	90.48
Not Hispanic (79,721)	81,220	85.79
Hispanic (3,906)	4,436	4.69
Yugoslavian	133	0.14

Brighton

Place Type: City
County: Adams
Population: 20,905

Ancestry/Race	Number	%
African American/Black:	280	1.34
Not Hispanic (180)	219	1.05
Hispanic (26)	61	0.29
African, sub-Saharan:	50	0.24
African	50	0.24
Alaska Native tribes, specified:	1	0.00
Alaska Athabascan (1)	1	0.00
Alaska Native tribes, not specified	1	0.00
Am. Ind. or Alaska Nat., not spec.	209	1.00
American Indian tribes, specified:	277	1.33
Apache (10)	15	0.07
Blackfeet (2)	4	0.02
Cherokee (22)	61	0.29
Cheyenne (2)	7	0.03
Chippewa (4)	10	0.05
Choctaw (1)	2	0.01
Creek (2)	7	0.03
Delaware (1)	1	0.00
Iroquois (2)	2	0.01
Kiowa (1)	2	0.01
Latin American Indians (33)	44	0.21
Lumbee (1)	1	0.00
Navajo (12)	26	0.12
Potawatomi (6)	7	0.03
Pueblo (3)	12	0.06
Puget Sound Salish (2)	2	0.01
Seminole (2)	2	0.01
Shoshone (1)	3	0.01
Sioux (29)	39	0.19
Ute (4)	8	0.04
Yaqui	1	0.00
All other tribes (8)	21	0.10
American Indian tribes, not spec.	20	0.10
Arab:	43	0.21
Lebanese	30	0.14
Other Arab	13	0.06
Asian:	309	1.48
Cambodian (2)	4	0.02
Chinese, ex. Taiwanese (15)	19	0.09
Filipino (18)	28	0.13

Notes: 1. Figures in the "Number" column do not add up to the total population due to: a) Ancestry/Race overlap — e.g. persons can report being both White and Irish, b) persons of Hispanic origin can report being any race, c) persons reporting two ancestries are counted in both categories. 2. Numbers in parentheses indicate the number of persons reporting this ancestry/race alone, not in combination with any other ancestry/race. 3. Refer to the Explanation of Data in the front of the book for more detailed information.

Hmong (25)	28	0.13
Indian (12)	16	0.08
Japanese (110)	146	0.70
Korean (25)	29	0.14
Laotian (4)	5	0.02
Pakistani (1)	1	0.00
Taiwanese	2	0.01
Thai (7)	9	0.04
Vietnamese (5)	13	0.06
Other Asian, not specified (2)	9	0.04
Australian	7	0.03
Austrian	29	0.14
Basque	43	0.21
Canadian	14	0.07
Croatian	26	0.12
Czech	76	0.36
Czechoslovakian	29	0.14
Danish	180	0.86
Dutch	215	1.03
English	1,585	7.59
European	153	0.73
Finnish	45	0.22
French, except Basque	439	2.10
French Canadian	126	0.60
German	4,422	21.18
German Russian	6	0.03
Greek	60	0.29
Hawaii Native/Pacific Islander:	27	0.13
Micronesian: (6)	9	0.04
Guamanian/Chamorro (2)	3	0.01
Other Micronesian (4)	6	0.03
Polynesian: (1)	12	0.06
Native Hawaiian (1)	10	0.05
Samoan	1	0.00
Other Polynesian	1	0.00
Other Pac. Isl., not spec. (2)	6	0.03
Hispanic or Latino:	7,990	38.22
Central American:	10	0.05
Guatemalan	4	0.02
Honduran	1	0.00
Salvadoran	5	0.02
Cuban	17	0.08
Dominican Republic	1	0.00
Mexican	5,439	26.02
Puerto Rican	39	0.19
South American:	14	0.07
Chilean	1	0.00
Colombian	1	0.00
Ecuadorian	1	0.00
Peruvian	10	0.05
Venezuelan	1	0.00
Other Hispanic or Latino	2,470	11.82
Hungarian	82	0.39
Irish	1,977	9.47
Italian	719	3.44
Latvian	8	0.04
Lithuanian	12	0.06
Northern European	12	0.06
Norwegian	435	2.08
Pennsylvania German	19	0.09
Polish	303	1.45
Portuguese	8	0.04
Russian	165	0.79
Scandinavian	19	0.09
Scotch-Irish	272	1.30
Scottish	318	1.52
Serbian	6	0.03
Slavic	56	0.27
Slovak	53	0.25
Slovene	9	0.04
Swedish	362	1.73
Swiss	69	0.33
Ukrainian	12	0.06
United States or American	1,102	5.28
Welsh	156	0.75
West Indian, excl. Hispanic:	7	0.03
Dutch West Indian	7	0.03
White:	16,661	79.70
Not Hispanic (12,175)	12,355	59.10
Hispanic (3,902)	4,306	20.60
Yugoslavian	14	0.07

Broomfield

Place Type: City
County: Boulder
Population: 38,272

Ancestry/Race	Number	%
Acadian/Cajun	6	0.02
African American/Black:	467	1.22
Not Hispanic (329)	431	1.13
Hispanic (23)	36	0.09
African, sub-Saharan:	62	0.16
African	27	0.07
Nigerian	7	0.02
Somalian	11	0.03
South African	17	0.04
Alaska Native tribes, specified:	4	0.01
Aleut (1)	1	0.00
Eskimo (3)	3	0.01
Alaska Native tribes, not specified	1	0.00
Am. Ind. or Alaska Nat., not spec.	122	0.32
American Indian tribes, specified:	370	0.97
Apache (13)	27	0.07
Blackfeet	7	0.02
Cherokee (37)	109	0.28
Cheyenne (2)	5	0.01
Chickasaw	2	0.01
Chippewa (6)	11	0.03
Choctaw (5)	12	0.03
Comanche	2	0.01
Cree (3)	4	0.01
Creek	3	0.01
Delaware	3	0.01
Iroquois (6)	15	0.04
Latin American Indians (8)	20	0.05
Navajo (16)	29	0.08
Osage (4)	8	0.02
Potawatomi (4)	8	0.02
Pueblo (11)	15	0.04
Puget Sound Salish (1)	1	0.00
Seminole	3	0.01
Shoshone	2	0.01
Sioux (23)	52	0.14
Ute (1)	3	0.01
All other tribes (18)	29	0.08
American Indian tribes, not spec.	34	0.09
Arab:	118	0.31
Jordanian	22	0.06
Lebanese	96	0.25
Armenian	25	0.07
Asian:	1,933	5.05
Bangladeshi (2)	2	0.01
Cambodian (42)	48	0.13
Chinese, ex. Taiwanese (273)	316	0.83
Filipino (116)	181	0.47
Hmong (235)	268	0.70
Indian (155)	196	0.51
Indonesian (6)	21	0.05
Japanese (172)	247	0.65
Korean (129)	155	0.40
Laotian (117)	137	0.36
Malaysian	1	0.00
Pakistani (11)	13	0.03
Sri Lankan (4)	4	0.01
Taiwanese (15)	17	0.04
Thai (19)	30	0.08
Vietnamese (206)	216	0.56
Other Asian, specified (19)	24	0.06
Other Asian, not specified (33)	57	0.15
Austrian	139	0.36
Basque	11	0.03
Belgian	24	0.06
Brazilian	33	0.09
British	247	0.64
Canadian	62	0.16
Celtic	34	0.09
Croatian	52	0.14
Czech	487	1.27
Czechoslovakian	115	0.30
Danish	413	1.08
Dutch	757	1.98
Eastern European	7	0.02
English	5,155	13.46
European	667	1.74
Finnish	116	0.30
French, except Basque	1,700	4.44
French Canadian	304	0.79
German	11,020	28.78
Greek	147	0.38
Hawaii Native/Pacific Islander:	80	0.21
Melanesian:	1	0.00
Fijian	1	0.00
Micronesian: (2)	7	0.02
Guamanian/Chamorro (2)	7	0.02
Polynesian: (9)	34	0.09
Native Hawaiian (3)	25	0.07
Samoan (6)	9	0.02
Other Pac. Isl., specified	2	0.01
Other Pac. Isl., not spec. (3)	36	0.09
Hispanic or Latino:	3,471	9.07
Central American:	22	0.06
Guatemalan	2	0.01
Honduran	1	0.00
Nicaraguan	3	0.01
Panamanian	10	0.03
Salvadoran	3	0.01
Other Central American	3	0.01
Cuban	44	0.11
Dominican Republic	1	0.00
Mexican	1,962	5.13
Puerto Rican	80	0.21
South American:	58	0.15
Argentinean	4	0.01
Bolivian	7	0.02
Chilean	7	0.02
Colombian	21	0.05
Peruvian	2	0.01
Venezuelan	14	0.04
Other South American	3	0.01
Other Hispanic or Latino	1,304	3.41
Hungarian	169	0.44
Icelander	36	0.09
Iranian	60	0.16
Irish	5,549	14.49
Italian	2,326	6.07
Lithuanian	175	0.46
Luxemburger	7	0.02
Northern European	46	0.12
Norwegian	1,271	3.32
Pennsylvania German	16	0.04
Polish	1,286	3.36
Portuguese	56	0.15
Romanian	74	0.19
Russian	378	0.99
Scandinavian	191	0.50
Scotch-Irish	867	2.26
Scottish	1,250	3.26
Serbian	5	0.01
Slavic	15	0.04
Slovak	103	0.27
Slovene	46	0.12
Swedish	1,406	3.67
Swiss	142	0.37
Turkish	34	0.09
Ukrainian	99	0.26
United States or American	1,274	3.33
Welsh	530	1.38
West Indian, excl. Hispanic:	55	0.14
Haitian	25	0.07
Jamaican	30	0.08
White:	34,737	90.76
Not Hispanic (32,023)	32,564	85.09
Hispanic (1,895)	2,173	5.68
Yugoslavian	61	0.16

Notes: 1. Figures in the "Number" column do not add up to the total population due to: a) Ancestry/Race overlap — e.g. persons can report being both White and Irish, b) persons of Hispanic origin can report being any race, c) persons reporting two ancestries are counted in both categories. 2. Numbers in parentheses indicate the number of persons reporting this ancestry/race alone, not in combination with any other ancestry/race. 3. Refer to the Explanation of Data in the front of the book for more detailed information.

Canon City

Place Type: City
County: Fremont
Population: 15,431

Ancestry/Race	Number	%
African American/Black:	277	1.80
Not Hispanic (242)	271	1.76
Hispanic (4)	6	0.04
Alaska Native tribes, specified:	5	0.03
Alaska Athabascan (1)	2	0.01
Eskimo (3)	3	0.02
Alaska Native tribes, not specified	2	0.01
Am. Ind. or Alaska Nat., not spec.	127	0.82
Albanian	25	0.16
American Indian tribes, specified:	216	1.40
Apache (20)	24	0.16
Blackfeet (1)	2	0.01
Cherokee (28)	90	0.58
Cheyenne (1)	2	0.01
Chickasaw	7	0.05
Choctaw (4)	15	0.10
Colville	1	0.01
Comanche	1	0.01
Creek (1)	4	0.03
Delaware (2)	2	0.01
Iroquois	1	0.01
Kiowa (4)	6	0.04
Latin American Indians (3)	3	0.02
Navajo (10)	14	0.09
Osage	3	0.02
Potawatomi (1)	3	0.02
Pueblo (2)	3	0.02
Seminole	1	0.01
Shoshone	1	0.01
Sioux (6)	10	0.06
Tohono O'Odham (1)	1	0.01
Ute (2)	5	0.03
Yaqui	1	0.01
All other tribes (5)	16	0.10
American Indian tribes, not spec.	19	0.12
Arab:	21	0.14
Palestinian	21	0.14
Asian:	117	0.76
Cambodian (1)	1	0.01
Chinese, ex. Taiwanese (13)	21	0.14
Filipino (14)	26	0.17
Indian (7)	8	0.05
Japanese (17)	19	0.12
Korean (10)	16	0.10
Pakistani (2)	2	0.01
Thai (3)	3	0.02
Vietnamese (5)	5	0.03
Other Asian, not specified (11)	16	0.10
Austrian	69	0.45
Belgian	14	0.09
British	79	0.51
Canadian	28	0.18
Celtic	15	0.10
Czech	75	0.49
Czechoslovakian	17	0.11
Danish	141	0.92
Dutch	385	2.51
English	2,219	14.44
European	124	0.81
Finnish	46	0.30
French, except Basque	501	3.26
French Canadian	106	0.69
German	3,345	21.77
Greek	34	0.22
Hawaii Native/Pacific Islander:	18	0.12
Micronesian: (1)	5	0.03
Guamanian/Chamorro (1)	5	0.03
Polynesian: (5)	8	0.05
Native Hawaiian (1)	1	0.01
Samoan (4)	6	0.04
Other Polynesian	1	0.01
Other Pac. Isl., not spec. (3)	5	0.03
Hispanic or Latino:	1,285	8.33
Central American:	6	0.04
Nicaraguan	1	0.01
Panamanian	5	0.03
Cuban	13	0.08
Mexican	724	4.69
Puerto Rican	25	0.16
South American:	5	0.03
Colombian	4	0.03
Other South American	1	0.01
Other Hispanic or Latino	512	3.32
Hungarian	12	0.08
Irish	2,148	13.98
Italian	799	5.20
Lithuanian	15	0.10
Maltese	7	0.05
Northern European	7	0.05
Norwegian	196	1.28
Pennsylvania German	17	0.11
Polish	306	1.99
Portuguese	12	0.08
Romanian	7	0.05
Russian	47	0.31
Scandinavian	14	0.09
Scotch-Irish	414	2.69
Scottish	343	2.23
Slavic	93	0.61
Slovak	11	0.07
Slovene	63	0.41
Swedish	330	2.15
Swiss	65	0.42
Ukrainian	6	0.04
United States or American	982	6.39
Welsh	216	1.41
West Indian, excl. Hispanic:	16	0.10
Jamaican	10	0.07
West Indian	6	0.04
White:	14,675	95.10
Not Hispanic (13,430)	13,668	88.57
Hispanic (944)	1,007	6.53
Yugoslavian	65	0.42

Castle Rock

Place Type: Town
County: Douglas
Population: 20,224

Ancestry/Race	Number	%
Acadian/Cajun	8	0.04
African American/Black:	147	0.73
Not Hispanic (84)	134	0.66
Hispanic (11)	13	0.06
Alaska Native tribes, specified:	3	0.01
Aleut (2)	2	0.01
Eskimo	1	0.00
Am. Ind. or Alaska Nat., not spec.	51	0.25
American Indian tribes, specified:	206	1.02
Apache (3)	12	0.06
Blackfeet (5)	11	0.05
Cherokee (17)	62	0.31
Cheyenne	2	0.01
Chickasaw (3)	3	0.01
Chippewa (6)	7	0.03
Choctaw (9)	12	0.06
Comanche (2)	3	0.01
Creek (5)	5	0.02
Crow	1	0.00
Iroquois (3)	9	0.04
Latin American Indians (1)	2	0.01
Navajo (13)	22	0.11
Osage (1)	3	0.01
Potawatomi (5)	6	0.03
Pueblo (4)	9	0.04
Puget Sound Salish (1)	1	0.00
Shoshone (1)	5	0.02
Sioux (13)	22	0.11
Ute (1)	1	0.00
Yakama (1)	1	0.00
All other tribes (3)	7	0.03
American Indian tribes, not spec.	1	0.00
Arab:	27	0.13
Lebanese	27	0.13
Armenian	40	0.20
Asian:	352	1.74
Cambodian (1)	3	0.01
Chinese, ex. Taiwanese (31)	42	0.21
Filipino (43)	81	0.40
Indian (12)	19	0.09
Indonesian (1)	5	0.02
Japanese (26)	47	0.23
Korean (66)	96	0.47
Malaysian	1	0.00
Pakistani (6)	8	0.04
Taiwanese (1)	1	0.00
Thai (3)	3	0.01
Vietnamese (12)	15	0.07
Other Asian, specified	3	0.01
Other Asian, not specified (16)	28	0.14
Australian	6	0.03
Austrian	135	0.67
Belgian	57	0.28
British	234	1.16
Canadian	58	0.29
Celtic	33	0.16
Croatian	26	0.13
Czech	158	0.78
Czechoslovakian	40	0.20
Danish	187	0.92
Dutch	423	2.09
Eastern European	9	0.04
English	2,695	13.31
Estonian	9	0.04
European	233	1.15
Finnish	22	0.11
French, except Basque	1,107	5.47
French Canadian	172	0.85
German	5,774	28.51
Greek	152	0.75
Hawaii Native/Pacific Islander:	36	0.18
Micronesian: (2)	4	0.02
Guamanian/Chamorro (2)	4	0.02
Polynesian: (11)	22	0.11
Native Hawaiian (3)	14	0.07
Samoan (8)	8	0.04
Other Pac. Isl., not spec.	10	0.05
Hispanic or Latino:	1,250	6.18
Central American:	25	0.12
Honduran	5	0.02
Nicaraguan	5	0.02
Panamanian	7	0.03
Salvadoran	6	0.03
Other Central American	2	0.01
Cuban	17	0.08
Mexican	685	3.39
Puerto Rican	51	0.25
South American:	38	0.19
Argentinean	8	0.04
Bolivian	6	0.03
Chilean	2	0.01
Colombian	7	0.03
Ecuadorian	3	0.01
Peruvian	1	0.00
Uruguayan	1	0.00
Venezuelan	5	0.02
Other South American	5	0.02
Other Hispanic or Latino	434	2.15
Hungarian	45	0.22
Irish	2,820	13.92
Italian	1,162	5.74
Lithuanian	108	0.53
Macedonian	7	0.03
Northern European	11	0.05
Norwegian	725	3.58
Pennsylvania German	11	0.05
Polish	751	3.71
Portuguese	36	0.18
Romanian	22	0.11
Russian	210	1.04
Scandinavian	97	0.48
Scotch-Irish	388	1.92

Notes: 1. Figures in the "Number" column do not add up to the total population due to: a) Ancestry/Race overlap — e.g. persons can report being both White and Irish, b) persons of Hispanic origin can report being any race, c) persons reporting two ancestries are counted in both categories. 2. Numbers in parentheses indicate the number of persons reporting this ancestry/race alone, not in combination with any other ancestry/race. 3. Refer to the Explanation of Data in the front of the book for more detailed information.

	Number	%
Scottish	728	3.59
Serbian	6	0.03
Slavic	8	0.04
Slovak	26	0.13
Slovene	20	0.10
Swedish	753	3.72
Swiss	168	0.83
Ukrainian	40	0.20
United States or American	959	4.74
Welsh	181	0.89
White:	19,378	95.82
Not Hispanic (18,253)	18,525	91.60
Hispanic (727)	853	4.22
Yugoslavian	70	0.35

Castlewood

Place Type: Census Designated Place
County: Arapahoe
Population: 25,567

Ancestry/Race	Number	%
African American/Black:	341	1.33
Not Hispanic (269)	330	1.29
Hispanic (5)	11	0.04
African, sub-Saharan:	115	0.45
African	13	0.05
Ghanian	6	0.02
South African	90	0.35
Other sub-Saharan African	6	0.02
Alaska Native tribes, specified:	1	0.00
Aleut (1)	1	0.00
Am. Ind. or Alaska Nat., not spec.	30	0.12
Alsatian	5	0.02
American Indian tribes, specified:	99	0.39
Apache (2)	9	0.04
Blackfeet (1)	3	0.01
Cherokee (10)	27	0.11
Cheyenne (1)	2	0.01
Chickasaw (1)	1	0.00
Chippewa (1)	3	0.01
Choctaw (3)	6	0.02
Creek (1)	1	0.00
Crow	2	0.01
Iroquois (1)	2	0.01
Latin American Indians (5)	6	0.02
Navajo (2)	13	0.05
Osage (2)	5	0.02
Ottawa	1	0.00
Potawatomi (1)	3	0.01
Pueblo (2)	3	0.01
Sioux (6)	7	0.03
All other tribes (3)	5	0.02
American Indian tribes, not spec.	8	0.03
Arab:	112	0.44
Arab/Arabic	43	0.17
Lebanese	53	0.21
Moroccan	6	0.02
Palestinian	10	0.04
Armenian	15	0.06
Asian:	887	3.47
Bangladeshi (3)	3	0.01
Cambodian (3)	3	0.01
Chinese, ex. Taiwanese (164)	205	0.80
Filipino (50)	78	0.31
Hmong (1)	1	0.00
Indian (103)	111	0.43
Indonesian (1)	4	0.02
Japanese (118)	188	0.74
Korean (171)	189	0.74
Laotian (3)	3	0.01
Malaysian (2)	2	0.01
Sri Lankan (2)	2	0.01
Taiwanese (30)	33	0.13
Thai (9)	9	0.04
Vietnamese (31)	34	0.13
Other Asian, specified (1)	1	0.00
Other Asian, not specified (12)	21	0.08
Australian	25	0.10
Austrian	183	0.72
Basque	7	0.03
Belgian	66	0.26
British	299	1.17
Bulgarian	5	0.02
Canadian	185	0.72
Celtic	4	0.02
Croatian	11	0.04
Czech	194	0.76
Czechoslovakian	34	0.13
Danish	255	1.00
Dutch	450	1.76
Eastern European	53	0.21
English	4,625	18.11
European	429	1.68
Finnish	89	0.35
French, except Basque	1,006	3.94
French Canadian	250	0.98
German	6,677	26.15
Greek	131	0.51
Hawaii Native/Pacific Islander:	25	0.10
Micronesian: (1)	1	0.00
Other Micronesian (1)	1	0.00
Polynesian: (3)	17	0.07
Native Hawaiian (3)	13	0.05
Samoan	4	0.02
Other Pac. Isl., not spec. (1)	7	0.03
Hispanic or Latino:	1,098	4.29
Central American:	14	0.05
Costa Rican	1	0.00
Guatemalan	5	0.02
Honduran	2	0.01
Nicaraguan	2	0.01
Panamanian	1	0.00
Salvadoran	2	0.01
Other Central American	1	0.00
Cuban	39	0.15
Mexican	576	2.25
Puerto Rican	39	0.15
South American:	73	0.29
Argentinean	11	0.04
Bolivian	5	0.02
Chilean	8	0.03
Colombian	16	0.06
Ecuadorian	5	0.02
Peruvian	24	0.09
Uruguayan	1	0.00
Venezuelan	2	0.01
Other South American	1	0.00
Other Hispanic or Latino	357	1.40
Hungarian	203	0.80
Icelander	6	0.02
Iranian	45	0.18
Irish	4,137	16.20
Israeli	9	0.04
Italian	1,230	4.82
Latvian	45	0.18
Lithuanian	152	0.60
Northern European	62	0.24
Norwegian	894	3.50
Pennsylvania German	23	0.09
Polish	1,039	4.07
Portuguese	55	0.22
Russian	516	2.02
Scandinavian	98	0.38
Scotch-Irish	674	2.64
Scottish	1,030	4.03
Serbian	18	0.07
Slavic	12	0.05
Slovak	74	0.29
Slovene	57	0.22
Swedish	1,015	3.98
Swiss	141	0.55
Turkish	5	0.02
Ukrainian	133	0.52
United States or American	982	3.85
Welsh	438	1.72
West Indian, excl. Hispanic:	43	0.17
Haitian	12	0.05
Jamaican	11	0.04
West Indian	20	0.08
White:	24,263	94.90
Not Hispanic (23,167)	23,390	91.49
Hispanic (805)	873	3.41
Yugoslavian	7	0.03

Cimarron Hills

Place Type: Census Designated Place
County: El Paso
Population: 15,194

Ancestry/Race	Number	%
Afghan	9	0.06
African American/Black:	1,496	9.85
Not Hispanic (1,186)	1,429	9.41
Hispanic (31)	67	0.44
African, sub-Saharan:	109	0.71
African	79	0.52
Nigerian	30	0.20
Alaska Native tribes, specified:	3	0.02
Tlingit-Haida	3	0.02
Am. Ind. or Alaska Nat., not spec.	106	0.70
American Indian tribes, specified:	245	1.61
Apache (9)	28	0.18
Blackfeet (2)	13	0.09
Cherokee (26)	98	0.64
Cheyenne (2)	6	0.04
Chippewa (3)	4	0.03
Choctaw	13	0.09
Comanche	3	0.02
Cree (3)	3	0.02
Creek (1)	2	0.01
Delaware	1	0.01
Iroquois (2)	2	0.01
Kiowa (1)	4	0.03
Latin American Indians (5)	9	0.06
Menominee (1)	1	0.01
Navajo (6)	17	0.11
Osage (1)	1	0.01
Potawatomi	2	0.01
Pueblo (1)	7	0.05
Shoshone	1	0.01
Sioux (2)	15	0.10
Ute (3)	6	0.04
All other tribes (5)	9	0.06
American Indian tribes, not spec.	20	0.13
Arab:	77	0.50
Egyptian	27	0.18
Lebanese	42	0.28
Syrian	8	0.05
Armenian	10	0.07
Asian:	646	4.25
Chinese, ex. Taiwanese (17)	40	0.26
Filipino (103)	172	1.13
Indian (3)	9	0.06
Japanese (41)	98	0.64
Korean (145)	209	1.38
Laotian (3)	6	0.04
Taiwanese	1	0.01
Thai (12)	26	0.17
Vietnamese (29)	36	0.24
Other Asian, specified (5)	7	0.05
Other Asian, not specified (22)	42	0.28
Australian	13	0.09
Austrian	37	0.24
Belgian	63	0.41
British	166	1.09
Canadian	82	0.54
Czech	115	0.75
Czechoslovakian	43	0.28
Danish	82	0.54
Dutch	197	1.29
Eastern European	12	0.08
English	1,382	9.06
European	79	0.52
Finnish	41	0.27
French, except Basque	442	2.90
French Canadian	158	1.04
German	3,553	23.29
Greek	31	0.20

Notes: 1. Figures in the "Number" column do not add up to the total population due to: a) Ancestry/Race overlap — e.g. persons can report being both White and Irish, b) persons of Hispanic origin can report being any race, c) persons reporting two ancestries are counted in both categories. 2. Numbers in parentheses indicate the number of persons reporting this ancestry/race alone, not in combination with any other ancestry/race. 3. Refer to the Explanation of Data in the front of the book for more detailed information.

Ancestry/Race	Number	%
Hawaii Native/Pacific Islander:	108	0.71
Micronesian: (24)	29	0.19
Guamanian/Chamorro (24)	29	0.19
Polynesian: (36)	75	0.49
Native Hawaiian (8)	38	0.25
Samoan (28)	37	0.24
Other Pac. Isl., not spec.	4	0.03
Hispanic or Latino:	1,798	11.83
Central American:	25	0.16
Costa Rican	2	0.01
Guatemalan	7	0.05
Nicaraguan	1	0.01
Panamanian	7	0.05
Salvadoran	7	0.05
Other Central American	1	0.01
Cuban	20	0.13
Dominican Republic	3	0.02
Mexican	923	6.07
Puerto Rican	147	0.97
South American:	20	0.13
Argentinean	2	0.01
Chilean	1	0.01
Colombian	3	0.02
Ecuadorian	7	0.05
Peruvian	6	0.04
Other South American	1	0.01
Other Hispanic or Latino	660	4.34
Hungarian	14	0.09
Iranian	4	0.03
Irish	1,723	11.29
Italian	601	3.94
Lithuanian	6	0.04
Northern European	18	0.12
Norwegian	389	2.55
Polish	336	2.20
Portuguese	19	0.12
Russian	61	0.40
Scandinavian	33	0.22
Scotch-Irish	168	1.10
Scottish	408	2.67
Serbian	9	0.06
Slavic	9	0.06
Slovak	7	0.05
Slovene	7	0.05
Swedish	188	1.23
Swiss	70	0.46
Ukrainian	33	0.22
United States or American	897	5.88
Welsh	52	0.34
West Indian, excl. Hispanic:	48	0.31
Barbadian	19	0.12
Dutch West Indian	3	0.02
Jamaican	26	0.17
White:	12,599	82.92
Not Hispanic (11,104)	11,557	76.06
Hispanic (849)	1,042	6.86

Clifton

Place Type: Census Designated Place
County: Mesa
Population: 17,345

Ancestry/Race	Number	%
African American/Black:	157	0.91
Not Hispanic (84)	137	0.79
Hispanic (12)	20	0.12
Alaska Native tribes, specified:	1	0.01
Aleut	1	0.01
Am. Ind. or Alaska Nat., not spec.	158	0.91
American Indian tribes, specified:	287	1.65
Apache (10)	21	0.12
Blackfeet (8)	15	0.09
Cherokee (20)	70	0.40
Cheyenne (4)	9	0.05
Chickasaw	2	0.01
Chippewa (11)	17	0.10
Choctaw (12)	13	0.07
Colville	3	0.02
Comanche (2)	2	0.01
Creek (1)	2	0.01
Delaware (4)	4	0.02
Iroquois (2)	4	0.02
Latin American Indians (8)	18	0.10
Lumbee (2)	3	0.02
Navajo (33)	43	0.25
Paiute (1)	1	0.01
Potawatomi (1)	1	0.01
Pueblo (3)	7	0.04
Seminole (1)	1	0.01
Shoshone	2	0.01
Sioux (3)	10	0.06
Tohono O'Odham (4)	4	0.02
Ute (8)	14	0.08
Yakama	1	0.01
Yaqui (1)	1	0.01
Yuman (1)	1	0.01
All other tribes (9)	18	0.10
American Indian tribes, not spec.	37	0.21
Arab:	14	0.08
Lebanese	14	0.08
Asian:	138	0.80
Cambodian (9)	9	0.05
Chinese, ex. Taiwanese (10)	18	0.10
Filipino (20)	35	0.20
Indian (7)	10	0.06
Japanese (9)	27	0.16
Korean (6)	11	0.06
Laotian	1	0.01
Sri Lankan	4	0.02
Thai (2)	6	0.03
Vietnamese (4)	4	0.02
Other Asian, specified	4	0.02
Other Asian, not specified (1)	9	0.05
Australian	6	0.03
Austrian	130	0.76
Basque	31	0.18
Belgian	17	0.10
British	74	0.43
Canadian	50	0.29
Croatian	8	0.05
Czech	60	0.35
Czechoslovakian	32	0.19
Danish	207	1.20
Dutch	382	2.22
English	1,763	10.24
European	164	0.95
Finnish	7	0.04
French, except Basque	656	3.81
French Canadian	202	1.17
German	3,071	17.84
Greek	9	0.05
Hawaii Native/Pacific Islander:	32	0.18
Micronesian: (4)	11	0.06
Guamanian/Chamorro (4)	11	0.06
Polynesian: (4)	11	0.06
Native Hawaiian (1)	7	0.04
Samoan (2)	3	0.02
Tongan (1)	1	0.01
Other Pac. Isl., specified	4	0.02
Other Pac. Isl., not spec.	6	0.03
Hispanic or Latino:	2,448	14.11
Central American:	12	0.07
Guatemalan	1	0.01
Honduran	4	0.02
Nicaraguan	1	0.01
Panamanian	1	0.01
Salvadoran	5	0.03
Cuban	2	0.01
Mexican	1,308	7.54
Puerto Rican	23	0.13
South American:	7	0.04
Chilean	1	0.01
Colombian	2	0.01
Ecuadorian	2	0.01
Peruvian	2	0.01
Other Hispanic or Latino	1,096	6.32
Hungarian	28	0.16
Irish	1,723	10.01
Italian	449	2.61
Norwegian	228	1.32
Pennsylvania German	41	0.24
Polish	298	1.73
Portuguese	37	0.21
Russian	18	0.10
Scandinavian	48	0.28
Scotch-Irish	284	1.65
Scottish	317	1.84
Slavic	11	0.06
Slovene	11	0.06
Swedish	324	1.88
Swiss	34	0.20
United States or American	1,830	10.63
Welsh	123	0.71
West Indian, excl. Hispanic:	23	0.13
Dutch West Indian	11	0.06
Jamaican	12	0.07
White:	15,899	91.66
Not Hispanic (14,271)	14,561	83.95
Hispanic (1,182)	1,338	7.71
Yugoslavian	19	0.11

Colorado Springs

Place Type: City
County: El Paso
Population: 360,890

Ancestry/Race	Number	%
Acadian/Cajun	72	0.02
Afghan	8	0.00
African American/Black:	28,097	7.79
Not Hispanic (22,760)	26,370	7.31
Hispanic (917)	1,727	0.48
African, sub-Saharan:	1,848	0.51
African	1,550	0.43
Cape Verdean	22	0.01
Ethiopian	6	0.00
Ghanian	23	0.01
Kenyan	11	0.00
Nigerian	52	0.01
South African	83	0.02
Other sub-Saharan African	101	0.03
Alaska Native tribes, specified:	77	0.02
Alaska Athabascan (5)	7	0.00
Aleut (7)	10	0.00
Eskimo (19)	31	0.01
Tlingit-Haida (23)	28	0.01
All other tribes (1)	1	0.00
Alaska Native tribes, not specified	5	0.00
Am. Ind. or Alaska Nat., not spec.	1,942	0.54
Albanian	27	0.01
Alsatian	20	0.01
American Indian tribes, specified:	4,932	1.37
Apache (207)	430	0.12
Blackfeet (49)	207	0.06
Cherokee (386)	1,474	0.41
Cheyenne (31)	87	0.02
Chickasaw (15)	64	0.02
Chippewa (94)	158	0.04
Choctaw (54)	208	0.06
Colville (4)	4	0.00
Comanche (16)	61	0.02
Cree (5)	30	0.01
Creek (22)	52	0.01
Crow (4)	10	0.00
Delaware (4)	24	0.01
Houma (3)	3	0.00
Iroquois (59)	125	0.03
Kiowa (4)	13	0.00
Latin American Indians (166)	274	0.08
Lumbee (16)	21	0.01
Menominee (1)	5	0.00
Navajo (294)	458	0.13
Osage (24)	59	0.02
Ottawa (5)	13	0.00
Paiute (7)	11	0.00
Pima (2)	7	0.00
Potawatomi (19)	36	0.01
Pueblo (77)	111	0.03

Notes: 1. Figures in the "Number" column do not add up to the total population due to: a) Ancestry/Race overlap — e.g. persons can report being both White and Irish, b) persons of Hispanic origin can report being any race, c) persons reporting two ancestries are counted in both categories. 2. Numbers in parentheses indicate the number of persons reporting this ancestry/race alone, not in combination with any other ancestry/race. 3. Refer to the Explanation of Data in the front of the book for more detailed information.

Ancestry/Race	Number	%
Puget Sound Salish (7)	10	0.00
Seminole (7)	29	0.01
Shoshone (12)	19	0.01
Sioux (180)	392	0.11
Tohono O'Odham (21)	24	0.01
Ute (57)	111	0.03
Yakama	4	0.00
Yaqui (8)	24	0.01
Yuman (9)	9	0.00
All other tribes (169)	365	0.10
American Indian tribes, not spec.	363	0.10
Arab:	1,046	0.29
Arab/Arabic	71	0.02
Egyptian	99	0.03
Iraqi	20	0.01
Lebanese	457	0.13
Moroccan	99	0.03
Palestinian	60	0.02
Syrian	109	0.03
Other Arab	131	0.04
Armenian	100	0.03
Asian:	14,326	3.97
Bangladeshi (3)	3	0.00
Cambodian (95)	129	0.04
Chinese, ex. Taiwanese (1,113)	1,597	0.44
Filipino (1,660)	2,628	0.73
Hmong (11)	13	0.00
Indian (1,694)	1,908	0.53
Indonesian (37)	73	0.02
Japanese (1,021)	1,888	0.52
Korean (2,907)	3,944	1.09
Laotian (73)	85	0.02
Malaysian (22)	50	0.01
Pakistani (43)	50	0.01
Sri Lankan (4)	4	0.00
Taiwanese (51)	74	0.02
Thai (209)	340	0.09
Vietnamese (808)	978	0.27
Other Asian, specified (30)	76	0.02
Other Asian, not specified (212)	486	0.13
Assyrian/Chaldean/Syriac	7	0.00
Australian	181	0.05
Austrian	1,344	0.37
Basque	51	0.01
Belgian	461	0.13
Brazilian	95	0.03
British	2,388	0.66
Bulgarian	147	0.04
Canadian	991	0.27
Carpatho Rusyn	7	0.00
Celtic	164	0.05
Croatian	446	0.12
Czech	2,521	0.70
Czechoslovakian	941	0.26
Danish	3,068	0.85
Dutch	6,959	1.93
Eastern European	286	0.08
English	44,805	12.42
Estonian	17	0.00
European	5,005	1.39
Finnish	894	0.25
French, except Basque	12,418	3.44
French Canadian	3,002	0.83
German	79,290	21.98
German Russian	60	0.02
Greek	960	0.27
Guyanese	6	0.00
Hawaii Native/Pacific Islander:	1,619	0.45
Melanesian: (2)	4	0.00
Fijian (2)	4	0.00
Micronesian: (241)	389	0.11
Guamanian/Chamorro (221)	363	0.10
Other Micronesian (20)	26	0.01
Polynesian: (433)	915	0.25
Native Hawaiian (210)	590	0.16
Samoan (203)	282	0.08
Tongan (5)	9	0.00
Other Polynesian (15)	34	0.01
Other Pac. Isl., specified	25	0.01
Other Pac. Isl., not spec. (68)	286	0.08
Hispanic or Latino:	43,330	12.01
Central American:	951	0.26
Costa Rican	37	0.01
Guatemalan	148	0.04
Honduran	79	0.02
Nicaraguan	49	0.01
Panamanian	429	0.12
Salvadoran	176	0.05
Other Central American	33	0.01
Cuban	346	0.10
Dominican Republic	106	0.03
Mexican	22,991	6.37
Puerto Rican	2,685	0.74
South American:	593	0.16
Argentinean	61	0.02
Bolivian	12	0.00
Chilean	53	0.01
Colombian	183	0.05
Ecuadorian	66	0.02
Paraguayan	1	0.00
Peruvian	127	0.04
Uruguayan	11	0.00
Venezuelan	46	0.01
Other South American	33	0.01
Other Hispanic or Latino	15,658	4.34
Hungarian	1,669	0.46
Icelander	147	0.04
Iranian	532	0.15
Irish	44,871	12.44
Israeli	35	0.01
Italian	16,692	4.63
Latvian	165	0.05
Lithuanian	929	0.26
Luxemburger	114	0.03
Macedonian	29	0.01
Maltese	32	0.01
New Zealander	10	0.00
Northern European	467	0.13
Norwegian	9,960	2.76
Pennsylvania German	274	0.08
Polish	9,154	2.54
Portuguese	746	0.21
Romanian	360	0.10
Russian	2,341	0.65
Scandinavian	858	0.24
Scotch-Irish	8,284	2.30
Scottish	10,314	2.86
Serbian	122	0.03
Slavic	267	0.07
Slovak	779	0.22
Slovene	276	0.08
Soviet Union	8	0.00
Swedish	8,486	2.35
Swiss	1,721	0.48
Turkish	57	0.02
Ukrainian	915	0.25
United States or American	19,877	5.51
Welsh	3,434	0.95
West Indian, excl. Hispanic:	970	0.27
Barbadian	106	0.03
Belizean	8	0.00
Bermudan	6	0.00
British West Indian	21	0.01
Dutch West Indian	52	0.01
Haitian	79	0.02
Jamaican	433	0.12
Trinidadian and Tobagonian	65	0.02
U.S. Virgin Islander	25	0.01
West Indian	175	0.05
White:	302,662	83.87
Not Hispanic (271,734)	279,961	77.58
Hispanic (19,361)	22,701	6.29
Yugoslavian	503	0.14

Columbine

Place Type: Census Designated Place
County: Jefferson
Population: 24,095

Ancestry/Race	Number	%
African American/Black:	172	0.71
Not Hispanic (113)	162	0.67
Hispanic (1)	10	0.04
African, sub-Saharan:	21	0.09
South African	21	0.09
Alaska Native tribes, specified:	1	0.00
Tlingit-Haida (1)	1	0.00
Am. Ind. or Alaska Nat., not spec.	55	0.23
American Indian tribes, specified:	174	0.72
Apache (12)	25	0.10
Blackfeet (2)	11	0.05
Cherokee (16)	54	0.22
Chickasaw	3	0.01
Chippewa (5)	5	0.02
Choctaw (10)	19	0.08
Comanche	2	0.01
Cree	2	0.01
Creek (3)	3	0.01
Latin American Indians (4)	8	0.03
Navajo (8)	12	0.05
Osage (1)	2	0.01
Potawatomi	3	0.01
Pueblo (2)	6	0.02
Seminole (1)	1	0.00
Sioux (5)	11	0.05
Ute (1)	1	0.00
Yaqui (1)	1	0.00
All other tribes (2)	5	0.02
American Indian tribes, not spec.	5	0.02
Arab:	55	0.23
Lebanese	34	0.14
Syrian	21	0.09
Armenian	14	0.06
Asian:	387	1.61
Cambodian (1)	1	0.00
Chinese, ex. Taiwanese (57)	80	0.33
Filipino (32)	51	0.21
Indian (39)	47	0.20
Indonesian (2)	2	0.01
Japanese (60)	93	0.39
Korean (33)	43	0.18
Taiwanese (4)	4	0.02
Thai (10)	10	0.04
Vietnamese (28)	39	0.16
Other Asian, specified	2	0.01
Other Asian, not specified (7)	15	0.06
Australian	5	0.02
Austrian	115	0.48
Basque	30	0.12
Belgian	20	0.08
British	186	0.77
Canadian	39	0.16
Celtic	11	0.05
Croatian	77	0.32
Czech	306	1.27
Czechoslovakian	60	0.25
Danish	398	1.65
Dutch	690	2.87
Eastern European	10	0.04
English	3,898	16.21
European	278	1.16
Finnish	114	0.47
French, except Basque	1,263	5.25
French Canadian	158	0.66
German	7,431	30.90
Greek	82	0.34
Hawaii Native/Pacific Islander:	43	0.18
Micronesian: (2)	3	0.01
Guamanian/Chamorro (2)	3	0.01
Polynesian: (20)	31	0.13
Native Hawaiian (10)	21	0.09
Samoan (5)	5	0.02
Tongan (1)	1	0.00

Notes: 1. Figures in the "Number" column do not add up to the total population due to: a) Ancestry/Race overlap — e.g. persons can report being both White and Irish, b) persons of Hispanic origin can report being any race, c) persons reporting two ancestries are counted in both categories. 2. Numbers in parentheses indicate the number of persons reporting this ancestry/race alone, not in combination with any other ancestry/race. 3. Refer to the Explanation of Data in the front of the book for more detailed information.

Ancestry/Race	Number	%
Other Polynesian (4)	4	0.02
Other Pac. Isl., specified	2	0.01
Other Pac. Isl., not spec. (6)	7	0.03
Hispanic or Latino:	1,345	5.58
Central American:	7	0.03
Honduran	1	0.00
Panamanian	4	0.02
Salvadoran	2	0.01
Cuban	9	0.04
Mexican	650	2.70
Puerto Rican	52	0.22
South American:	37	0.15
Argentinean	5	0.02
Bolivian	6	0.02
Chilean	2	0.01
Colombian	7	0.03
Ecuadorian	3	0.01
Peruvian	10	0.04
Uruguayan	2	0.01
Venezuelan	1	0.00
Other South American	1	0.00
Other Hispanic or Latino	590	2.45
Hungarian	145	0.60
Icelander	8	0.03
Iranian	5	0.02
Irish	4,284	17.81
Italian	1,534	6.38
Latvian	13	0.05
Lithuanian	49	0.20
Macedonian	6	0.02
Northern European	43	0.18
Norwegian	1,061	4.41
Pennsylvania German	8	0.03
Polish	994	4.13
Portuguese	34	0.14
Romanian	20	0.08
Russian	303	1.26
Scandinavian	29	0.12
Scotch-Irish	533	2.22
Scottish	733	3.05
Serbian	44	0.18
Slavic	67	0.28
Slovak	24	0.10
Slovene	40	0.17
Swedish	1,245	5.18
Swiss	161	0.67
Ukrainian	39	0.16
United States or American	1,348	5.60
Welsh	339	1.41
White:	23,178	96.19
Not Hispanic (22,000)	22,242	92.31
Hispanic (848)	936	3.88
Yugoslavian	30	0.12

Commerce City

Place Type: City
County: Adams
Population: 20,991

Ancestry/Race	Number	%
Acadian/Cajun	11	0.05
African American/Black:	557	2.65
Not Hispanic (371)	450	2.14
Hispanic (57)	107	0.51
African, sub-Saharan:	22	0.10
African	22	0.10
Alaska Native tribes, specified:	8	0.04
Aleut (1)	1	0.00
Eskimo (6)	7	0.03
Am. Ind. or Alaska Nat., not spec.	189	0.90
American Indian tribes, specified:	404	1.92
Apache (27)	58	0.28
Blackfeet (4)	10	0.05
Cherokee (31)	82	0.39
Cheyenne (5)	5	0.02
Chickasaw (1)	2	0.01
Chippewa (8)	10	0.05
Choctaw (2)	5	0.02
Cree (1)	1	0.00
Creek (3)	4	0.02
Iroquois	2	0.01
Latin American Indians (58)	78	0.37
Menominee (1)	1	0.00
Navajo (21)	36	0.17
Potawatomi	4	0.02
Pueblo (5)	7	0.03
Shoshone (2)	3	0.01
Sioux (41)	62	0.30
Tohono O'Odham	1	0.00
Ute (6)	8	0.04
All other tribes (14)	25	0.12
American Indian tribes, not spec.	51	0.24
Asian:	229	1.09
Cambodian (1)	1	0.00
Chinese, ex. Taiwanese (1)	3	0.01
Filipino (31)	59	0.28
Hmong (1)	2	0.01
Indian (8)	16	0.08
Japanese (50)	82	0.39
Korean (20)	30	0.14
Thai (1)	1	0.00
Vietnamese (8)	8	0.04
Other Asian, specified (1)	1	0.00
Other Asian, not specified (7)	26	0.12
Australian	13	0.06
Austrian	20	0.09
Basque	10	0.05
Belgian	12	0.06
British	10	0.05
Canadian	20	0.09
Croatian	8	0.04
Czech	31	0.15
Czechoslovakian	21	0.10
Danish	70	0.33
Dutch	160	0.75
English	952	4.48
European	122	0.57
Finnish	6	0.03
French, except Basque	506	2.38
French Canadian	91	0.43
German	2,763	13.01
Greek	17	0.08
Hawaii Native/Pacific Islander:	23	0.11
Micronesian: (5)	8	0.04
Guamanian/Chamorro (5)	8	0.04
Polynesian: (6)	12	0.06
Native Hawaiian (1)	5	0.02
Samoan (5)	7	0.03
Other Pac. Isl., not spec.	3	0.01
Hispanic or Latino:	11,096	52.86
Central American:	26	0.12
Costa Rican	2	0.01
Guatemalan	8	0.04
Honduran	1	0.00
Panamanian	2	0.01
Salvadoran	12	0.06
Other Central American	1	0.00
Cuban	11	0.05
Mexican	7,556	36.00
Puerto Rican	44	0.21
South American:	12	0.06
Bolivian	2	0.01
Chilean	2	0.01
Colombian	6	0.03
Peruvian	1	0.00
Venezuelan	1	0.00
Other Hispanic or Latino	3,447	16.42
Hungarian	11	0.05
Iranian	9	0.04
Irish	1,509	7.10
Italian	488	2.30
Lithuanian	5	0.02
Northern European	10	0.05
Norwegian	187	0.88
Polish	130	0.61
Portuguese	30	0.14
Russian	63	0.30
Scotch-Irish	358	1.69
Scottish	263	1.24
Slavic	8	0.04
Slovak	13	0.06
Swedish	172	0.81
Swiss	23	0.11
United States or American	870	4.10
Welsh	49	0.23
West Indian, excl. Hispanic:	24	0.11
Barbadian	6	0.03
Trinidadian and Tobagonian	12	0.06
West Indian	6	0.03
White:	14,553	69.33
Not Hispanic (8,931)	9,202	43.84
Hispanic (4,830)	5,351	25.49

Denver

Place Type: City
County: Denver
Population: 554,636

Ancestry/Race	Number	%
Acadian/Cajun	81	0.01
Afghan	33	0.01
African American/Black:	67,375	12.15
Not Hispanic (59,921)	64,370	11.61
Hispanic (1,728)	3,005	0.54
African, sub-Saharan:	5,775	1.04
African	3,758	0.68
Cape Verdean	15	0.00
Ethiopian	718	0.13
Ghanian	192	0.03
Kenyan	18	0.00
Nigerian	327	0.06
Senegalese	20	0.00
Sierra Leonean	32	0.01
Somalian	120	0.02
South African	161	0.03
Sudanese	267	0.05
Ugandan	56	0.01
Zairian	13	0.00
Other sub-Saharan African	78	0.01
Alaska Native tribes, specified:	67	0.01
Alaska Athabascan (6)	10	0.00
Aleut (7)	7	0.00
Eskimo (24)	32	0.01
Tlingit-Haida (13)	17	0.00
All other tribes (1)	1	0.00
Alaska Native tribes, not specified	12	0.00
Am. Ind. or Alaska Nat., not spec.	4,229	0.76
Albanian	77	0.01
Alsatian	54	0.01
American Indian tribes, specified:	7,470	1.35
Apache (337)	648	0.12
Blackfeet (43)	212	0.04
Cherokee (343)	1,390	0.25
Cheyenne (73)	121	0.02
Chickasaw (19)	55	0.01
Chippewa (135)	198	0.04
Choctaw (74)	215	0.04
Comanche (35)	73	0.01
Cree (8)	20	0.00
Creek (42)	92	0.02
Crow (12)	23	0.00
Delaware (9)	16	0.00
Houma (3)	4	0.00
Iroquois (35)	96	0.02
Kiowa (28)	40	0.01
Latin American Indians (582)	907	0.16
Lumbee (11)	13	0.00
Menominee (4)	6	0.00
Navajo (563)	884	0.16
Osage (25)	42	0.01
Ottawa (2)	2	0.00
Paiute (15)	19	0.00
Pima (11)	20	0.00
Potawatomi (39)	58	0.01
Pueblo (201)	277	0.05
Puget Sound Salish (9)	10	0.00
Seminole (27)	54	0.01
Shoshone (32)	47	0.01

Notes: 1. Figures in the "Number" column do not add up to the total population due to: a) Ancestry/Race overlap — e.g. persons can report being both White and Irish, b) persons of Hispanic origin can report being any race, c) persons reporting two ancestries are counted in both categories. 2. Numbers in parentheses indicate the number of persons reporting this ancestry/race alone, not in combination with any other ancestry/race. 3. Refer to the Explanation of Data in the front of the book for more detailed information.

	Number	%
Sioux (817)	1,155	0.21
Tohono O'Odham (19)	22	0.00
Ute (77)	139	0.03
Yakama	1	0.00
Yaqui (29)	45	0.01
Yuman (14)	19	0.00
All other tribes (340)	547	0.10
American Indian tribes, not spec.	840	0.15
Arab:	2,193	0.40
Arab/Arabic	364	0.07
Egyptian	155	0.03
Iraqi	60	0.01
Jordanian	30	0.01
Lebanese	571	0.10
Moroccan	290	0.05
Palestinian	108	0.02
Syrian	242	0.04
Other Arab	373	0.07
Armenian	304	0.05
Asian:	19,513	3.52
Bangladeshi (27)	29	0.01
Cambodian (389)	513	0.09
Chinese, ex. Taiwanese (2,157)	2,757	0.50
Filipino (890)	1,529	0.28
Hmong (69)	84	0.02
Indian (2,240)	2,578	0.46
Indonesian (309)	406	0.07
Japanese (1,941)	2,846	0.51
Korean (1,416)	1,702	0.31
Laotian (119)	143	0.03
Malaysian (19)	36	0.01
Pakistani (98)	142	0.03
Sri Lankan (27)	35	0.01
Taiwanese (122)	147	0.03
Thai (354)	457	0.08
Vietnamese (4,559)	4,849	0.87
Other Asian, specified (79)	142	0.03
Other Asian, not specified (484)	1,118	0.20
Assyrian/Chaldean/Syriac	16	0.00
Australian	199	0.04
Austrian	1,838	0.33
Basque	239	0.04
Belgian	552	0.10
Brazilian	172	0.03
British	2,584	0.47
Bulgarian	194	0.03
Canadian	1,057	0.19
Carpatho Rusyn	40	0.01
Celtic	182	0.03
Croatian	671	0.12
Cypriot	15	0.00
Czech	2,316	0.42
Czechoslovakian	858	0.15
Danish	3,379	0.61
Dutch	8,133	1.47
Eastern European	915	0.16
English	45,841	8.27
Estonian	42	0.01
European	4,893	0.88
Finnish	870	0.16
French, except Basque	13,568	2.45
French Canadian	2,544	0.46
German	76,686	13.83
German Russian	62	0.01
Greek	2,321	0.42
Guyanese	22	0.00
Hawaii Native/Pacific Islander:	1,380	0.25
Melanesian: (1)	2	0.00
Fijian (1)	2	0.00
Micronesian: (181)	283	0.05
Guamanian/Chamorro (108)	182	0.03
Other Micronesian (73)	101	0.02
Polynesian: (349)	701	0.13
Native Hawaiian (178)	412	0.07
Samoan (144)	216	0.04
Tongan (20)	43	0.01
Other Polynesian (7)	30	0.01
Other Pac. Isl., specified	34	0.01
Other Pac. Isl., not spec. (104)	360	0.06
Hispanic or Latino:	175,704	31.68
Central American:	1,997	0.36
Costa Rican	54	0.01
Guatemalan	469	0.08
Honduran	289	0.05
Nicaraguan	82	0.01
Panamanian	135	0.02
Salvadoran	811	0.15
Other Central American	157	0.03
Cuban	669	0.12
Dominican Republic	75	0.01
Mexican	120,664	21.76
Puerto Rican	1,632	0.29
South American:	1,265	0.23
Argentinean	127	0.02
Bolivian	68	0.01
Chilean	133	0.02
Colombian	311	0.06
Ecuadorian	75	0.01
Paraguayan	3	0.00
Peruvian	373	0.07
Uruguayan	7	0.00
Venezuelan	108	0.02
Other South American	60	0.01
Other Hispanic or Latino	49,402	8.91
Hungarian	2,039	0.37
Icelander	150	0.03
Iranian	625	0.11
Irish	52,989	9.55
Israeli	346	0.06
Italian	19,333	3.49
Latvian	283	0.05
Lithuanian	1,213	0.22
Luxemburger	155	0.03
Macedonian	45	0.01
New Zealander	83	0.01
Northern European	667	0.12
Norwegian	8,643	1.56
Pennsylvania German	154	0.03
Polish	11,055	1.99
Portuguese	817	0.15
Romanian	692	0.12
Russian	7,785	1.40
Scandinavian	1,367	0.25
Scotch-Irish	8,810	1.59
Scottish	11,046	1.99
Serbian	180	0.03
Slavic	136	0.02
Slovak	617	0.11
Slovene	474	0.09
Swedish	10,158	1.83
Swiss	1,877	0.34
Turkish	155	0.03
Ukrainian	1,570	0.28
United States or American	18,640	3.36
Welsh	4,039	0.73
West Indian, excl. Hispanic:	672	0.12
Bahamian	26	0.00
Barbadian	5	0.00
Belizean	19	0.00
Bermudan	8	0.00
British West Indian	35	0.01
Dutch West Indian	7	0.00
Haitian	132	0.02
Jamaican	359	0.06
Trinidadian and Tobagonian	38	0.01
West Indian	36	0.01
Other West Indian	7	0.00
White:	378,715	68.28
Not Hispanic (287,997)	296,074	53.38
Hispanic (74,183)	82,641	14.90
Yugoslavian	1,065	0.19

Durango

Place Type: City
County: La Plata
Population: 13,922

Ancestry/Race	Number	%
Acadian/Cajun	5	0.04
African American/Black:	110	0.79
Not Hispanic (64)	93	0.67
Hispanic (6)	17	0.12
African, sub-Saharan:	34	0.24
African	7	0.05
Ethiopian	19	0.14
South African	4	0.03
Zimbabwean	4	0.03
Alaska Native tribes, specified:	59	0.42
Alaska Athabascan (6)	9	0.06
Aleut (6)	8	0.06
Eskimo (10)	18	0.13
Tlingit-Haida (14)	21	0.15
All other tribes (2)	3	0.02
Alaska Native tribes, not specified	11	0.08
Am. Ind. or Alaska Nat., not spec.	78	0.56
American Indian tribes, specified:	741	5.32
Apache (26)	32	0.23
Blackfeet	4	0.03
Cherokee (23)	52	0.37
Cheyenne (2)	5	0.04
Chickasaw	1	0.01
Chippewa (1)	2	0.01
Choctaw (11)	20	0.14
Colville (2)	3	0.02
Comanche (2)	2	0.01
Creek (3)	5	0.04
Crow (1)	1	0.01
Delaware (1)	1	0.01
Iroquois (3)	7	0.05
Kiowa (2)	2	0.01
Latin American Indians (3)	4	0.03
Navajo (397)	411	2.95
Osage	4	0.03
Paiute (9)	9	0.06
Pima (1)	1	0.01
Potawatomi (1)	4	0.03
Pueblo (36)	45	0.32
Shoshone (4)	4	0.03
Sioux (19)	29	0.21
Ute (36)	51	0.37
Yakama (3)	3	0.02
Yuman (3)	3	0.02
All other tribes (23)	36	0.26
American Indian tribes, not spec.	37	0.27
Arab:	13	0.09
Egyptian	7	0.05
Other Arab	6	0.04
Armenian	5	0.04
Asian:	174	1.25
Bangladeshi (2)	2	0.01
Chinese, ex. Taiwanese (11)	23	0.17
Filipino (5)	15	0.11
Indian (7)	8	0.06
Indonesian	1	0.01
Japanese (37)	61	0.44
Korean (20)	26	0.19
Pakistani (1)	2	0.01
Taiwanese (3)	3	0.02
Thai (1)	2	0.01
Vietnamese (12)	17	0.12
Other Asian, specified	2	0.01
Other Asian, not specified (3)	12	0.09
Australian	9	0.06
Austrian	86	0.61
Basque	11	0.08
Belgian	29	0.21
Brazilian	7	0.05
British	123	0.88
Bulgarian	7	0.05
Canadian	24	0.17
Celtic	19	0.14
Croatian	16	0.11
Czech	63	0.45
Czechoslovakian	38	0.27
Danish	91	0.65
Dutch	325	2.32
Eastern European	7	0.05
English	1,944	13.86
European	544	3.88

Notes: 1. Figures in the "Number" column do not add up to the total population due to: a) Ancestry/Race overlap — e.g. persons can report being both White and Irish, b) persons of Hispanic origin can report being any race, c) persons reporting two ancestries are counted in both categories. 2. Numbers in parentheses indicate the number of persons reporting this ancestry/race alone, not in combination with any other ancestry/race. 3. Refer to the Explanation of Data in the front of the book for more detailed information.

Ancestry/Race	Number	%
Finnish	34	0.24
French, except Basque	517	3.69
French Canadian	107	0.76
German	3,014	21.50
Greek	39	0.28
Hawaii Native/Pacific Islander:	33	0.24
Micronesian: (3)	5	0.04
Guamanian/Chamorro (3)	5	0.04
Polynesian: (11)	20	0.14
Native Hawaiian (9)	16	0.11
Samoan (2)	3	0.02
Tongan	1	0.01
Other Pac. Isl., specified	1	0.01
Other Pac. Isl., not spec. (1)	7	0.05
Hispanic or Latino:	1,436	10.31
Central American:	7	0.05
Costa Rican	2	0.01
Honduran	1	0.01
Panamanian	1	0.01
Salvadoran	3	0.02
Cuban	9	0.06
Mexican	543	3.90
Puerto Rican	17	0.12
South American:	15	0.11
Chilean	4	0.03
Ecuadorian	5	0.04
Peruvian	4	0.03
Venezuelan	2	0.01
Other Hispanic or Latino	845	6.07
Hungarian	29	0.21
Iranian	4	0.03
Irish	1,942	13.85
Italian	700	4.99
Latvian	5	0.04
Lithuanian	29	0.21
New Zealander	13	0.09
Northern European	28	0.20
Norwegian	357	2.55
Pennsylvania German	17	0.12
Polish	274	1.95
Portuguese	23	0.16
Romanian	5	0.04
Russian	155	1.11
Scandinavian	63	0.45
Scotch-Irish	429	3.06
Scottish	551	3.93
Slavic	35	0.25
Slovak	15	0.11
Slovene	10	0.07
Swedish	436	3.11
Swiss	84	0.60
Ukrainian	30	0.21
United States or American	552	3.94
Welsh	223	1.59
White:	12,353	88.73
Not Hispanic (11,369)	11,550	82.96
Hispanic (721)	803	5.77

Englewood

Place Type: City
County: Arapahoe
Population: 31,727

Ancestry/Race	Number	%
African American/Black:	604	1.90
Not Hispanic (439)	559	1.76
Hispanic (24)	45	0.14
African, sub-Saharan:	122	0.39
African	78	0.25
Ethiopian	16	0.05
Ghanian	28	0.09
Alaska Native tribes, specified:	7	0.02
Aleut (3)	3	0.01
Eskimo (2)	4	0.01
Alaska Native tribes, not specified	1	0.00
Am. Ind. or Alaska Nat., not spec.	179	0.56
American Indian tribes, specified:	536	1.69
Apache (34)	58	0.18
Blackfeet	4	0.01
Cherokee (51)	156	0.49
Cheyenne (4)	6	0.02
Chickasaw	5	0.02
Chippewa (15)	21	0.07
Choctaw (3)	12	0.04
Comanche (6)	10	0.03
Cree (2)	3	0.01
Creek (7)	10	0.03
Crow	4	0.01
Delaware (2)	2	0.01
Iroquois (3)	7	0.02
Kiowa	1	0.00
Latin American Indians (16)	18	0.06
Lumbee (1)	1	0.00
Navajo (40)	68	0.21
Osage (7)	7	0.02
Paiute	1	0.00
Potawatomi (3)	7	0.02
Pueblo (4)	11	0.03
Seminole (8)	12	0.04
Shoshone (3)	3	0.01
Sioux (39)	51	0.16
Tohono O'Odham	1	0.00
Ute (3)	6	0.02
Yakama	1	0.00
Yaqui	2	0.01
All other tribes (28)	48	0.15
American Indian tribes, not spec.	34	0.11
Arab:	101	0.32
Arab/Arabic	49	0.16
Egyptian	10	0.03
Iraqi	9	0.03
Lebanese	16	0.05
Moroccan	3	0.01
Other Arab	14	0.04
Armenian	7	0.02
Asian:	751	2.37
Bangladeshi (4)	4	0.01
Cambodian (2)	4	0.01
Chinese, ex. Taiwanese (79)	92	0.29
Filipino (37)	60	0.19
Indian (67)	84	0.26
Indonesian (15)	23	0.07
Japanese (88)	123	0.39
Korean (111)	129	0.41
Laotian	2	0.01
Malaysian (3)	3	0.01
Pakistani (5)	7	0.02
Sri Lankan	3	0.01
Taiwanese (6)	6	0.02
Thai (17)	21	0.07
Vietnamese (134)	157	0.49
Other Asian, specified	2	0.01
Other Asian, not specified (15)	31	0.10
Australian	14	0.04
Austrian	122	0.39
Basque	8	0.03
Belgian	30	0.09
British	149	0.47
Bulgarian	28	0.09
Canadian	82	0.26
Celtic	18	0.06
Croatian	32	0.10
Czech	280	0.89
Czechoslovakian	108	0.34
Danish	303	0.96
Dutch	1,011	3.20
Eastern European	25	0.08
English	4,166	13.19
Estonian	10	0.03
European	330	1.04
Finnish	93	0.29
French, except Basque	1,168	3.70
French Canadian	233	0.74
German	7,477	23.67
Greek	270	0.85
Hawaii Native/Pacific Islander:	55	0.17
Micronesian: (14)	16	0.05
Guamanian/Chamorro (2)	3	0.01
Other Micronesian (12)	13	0.04
Polynesian: (13)	22	0.07
Native Hawaiian (9)	18	0.06
Samoan (3)	3	0.01
Other Polynesian (1)	1	0.00
Other Pac. Isl., specified	1	0.00
Other Pac. Isl., not spec. (3)	16	0.05
Hispanic or Latino:	4,140	13.05
Central American:	62	0.20
Costa Rican	3	0.01
Guatemalan	20	0.06
Honduran	7	0.02
Nicaraguan	5	0.02
Panamanian	1	0.00
Salvadoran	18	0.06
Other Central American	8	0.03
Cuban	25	0.08
Dominican Republic	3	0.01
Mexican	2,481	7.82
Puerto Rican	73	0.23
South American:	73	0.23
Argentinean	8	0.03
Bolivian	2	0.01
Chilean	11	0.03
Colombian	12	0.04
Ecuadorian	16	0.05
Peruvian	19	0.06
Venezuelan	3	0.01
Other South American	2	0.01
Other Hispanic or Latino	1,423	4.49
Hungarian	94	0.30
Irish	4,321	13.68
Israeli	9	0.03
Italian	1,156	3.66
Latvian	22	0.07
Lithuanian	38	0.12
Luxemburger	35	0.11
Northern European	37	0.12
Norwegian	886	2.80
Pennsylvania German	22	0.07
Polish	643	2.04
Portuguese	46	0.15
Romanian	29	0.09
Russian	357	1.13
Scandinavian	89	0.28
Scotch-Irish	711	2.25
Scottish	856	2.71
Serbian	6	0.02
Slavic	6	0.02
Slovak	39	0.12
Slovene	22	0.07
Swedish	922	2.92
Swiss	127	0.40
Turkish	9	0.03
Ukrainian	55	0.17
United States or American	1,695	5.37
Welsh	292	0.92
West Indian, excl. Hispanic:	75	0.24
Barbadian	8	0.03
Jamaican	29	0.09
Trinidadian and Tobagonian	38	0.12
White:	28,564	90.03
Not Hispanic (25,708)	26,178	82.51
Hispanic (2,138)	2,386	7.52
Yugoslavian	40	0.13

Federal Heights

Place Type: City
County: Adams
Population: 12,065

Ancestry/Race	Number	%
African American/Black:	243	2.01
Not Hispanic (167)	219	1.82
Hispanic (9)	24	0.20
African, sub-Saharan:	13	0.11
African	13	0.11
Alaska Native tribes, specified:	6	0.05
Eskimo (1)	6	0.05
Alaska Native tribes, not specified	1	0.01

Notes: 1. Figures in the "Number" column do not add up to the total population due to: a) Ancestry/Race overlap — e.g. persons can report being both White and Irish, b) persons of Hispanic origin can report being any race, c) persons reporting two ancestries are counted in both categories. 2. Numbers in parentheses indicate the number of persons reporting this ancestry/race alone, not in combination with any other ancestry/race. 3. Refer to the Explanation of Data in the front of the book for more detailed information.

Ancestry/Race	Number	%
Am. Ind. or Alaska Nat., not spec.	69	0.57
American Indian tribes, specified:	185	1.53
Apache (8)	19	0.16
Blackfeet (1)	3	0.02
Cherokee (15)	53	0.44
Chickasaw	2	0.02
Chippewa (2)	2	0.02
Choctaw	2	0.02
Creek	3	0.02
Delaware (1)	3	0.02
Iroquois	1	0.01
Kiowa (1)	4	0.03
Latin American Indians (24)	25	0.21
Navajo (20)	24	0.20
Ottawa (2)	2	0.02
Potawatomi	2	0.02
Pueblo (8)	9	0.07
Seminole	1	0.01
Shoshone (1)	1	0.01
Sioux (9)	16	0.13
Ute (3)	4	0.03
All other tribes (6)	9	0.07
American Indian tribes, not spec.	15	0.12
Arab:	25	0.21
Iraqi	7	0.06
Other Arab	18	0.15
Asian:	834	6.91
Cambodian (8)	9	0.07
Chinese, ex. Taiwanese (62)	85	0.70
Filipino (22)	39	0.32
Hmong (196)	203	1.68
Indian (16)	20	0.17
Indonesian (4)	6	0.05
Japanese (14)	22	0.18
Korean (55)	65	0.54
Laotian (25)	35	0.29
Pakistani (1)	1	0.01
Taiwanese (1)	1	0.01
Thai (9)	17	0.14
Vietnamese (293)	303	2.51
Other Asian, specified (2)	2	0.02
Other Asian, not specified (10)	26	0.22
Austrian	6	0.05
British	63	0.52
Bulgarian	32	0.27
Canadian	22	0.18
Croatian	9	0.07
Czech	28	0.23
Czechoslovakian	12	0.10
Danish	75	0.62
Dutch	303	2.51
English	1,155	9.57
European	138	1.14
Finnish	42	0.35
French, except Basque	357	2.96
French Canadian	67	0.56
German	1,895	15.71
Greek	7	0.06
Hawaii Native/Pacific Islander:	40	0.33
Micronesian: (4)	6	0.05
Guamanian/Chamorro (4)	6	0.05
Polynesian: (13)	26	0.22
Native Hawaiian (13)	23	0.19
Samoan	3	0.02
Other Pac. Isl., not spec. (5)	8	0.07
Hispanic or Latino:	2,729	22.62
Central American:	16	0.13
Honduran	11	0.09
Nicaraguan	1	0.01
Salvadoran	4	0.03
Cuban	7	0.06
Dominican Republic	1	0.01
Mexican	1,674	13.87
Puerto Rican	32	0.27
South American:	19	0.16
Argentinean	4	0.03
Bolivian	2	0.02
Chilean	1	0.01
Colombian	3	0.02
Peruvian	5	0.04
Venezuelan	4	0.03
Other Hispanic or Latino	980	8.12
Hungarian	20	0.17
Irish	1,320	10.94
Italian	396	3.28
Latvian	6	0.05
Lithuanian	10	0.08
Norwegian	217	1.80
Pennsylvania German	8	0.07
Polish	217	1.80
Portuguese	11	0.09
Russian	39	0.32
Scandinavian	35	0.29
Scotch-Irish	189	1.57
Scottish	221	1.83
Slovak	34	0.28
Slovene	8	0.07
Swedish	316	2.62
Swiss	35	0.29
United States or American	892	7.39
Welsh	116	0.96
West Indian, excl. Hispanic:	16	0.13
Dutch West Indian	7	0.06
Trinidadian and Tobagonian	9	0.07
White:	10,000	82.88
Not Hispanic (8,114)	8,308	68.86
Hispanic (1,542)	1,692	14.02
Yugoslavian	44	0.36

Fort Carson

Place Type: Census Designated Place
County: El Paso
Population: 10,566

Ancestry/Race	Number	%
Acadian/Cajun	13	0.12
African American/Black:	2,320	21.96
Not Hispanic (2,045)	2,207	20.89
Hispanic (69)	113	1.07
African, sub-Saharan:	107	1.01
African	93	0.88
Senegalese	7	0.07
Sudanese	7	0.07
Alaska Native tribes, specified:	4	0.04
Eskimo (2)	4	0.04
Alaska Native tribes, not specified	3	0.03
Am. Ind. or Alaska Nat., not spec.	45	0.43
American Indian tribes, specified:	244	2.31
Apache (8)	13	0.12
Blackfeet (1)	3	0.03
Cherokee (22)	53	0.50
Cheyenne (1)	1	0.01
Chickasaw (5)	5	0.05
Chippewa (3)	4	0.04
Choctaw (8)	15	0.14
Comanche (3)	4	0.04
Crow (1)	4	0.04
Iroquois (5)	12	0.11
Kiowa (1)	1	0.01
Latin American Indians (4)	7	0.07
Lumbee (3)	9	0.09
Menominee (3)	3	0.03
Navajo (38)	43	0.41
Osage (1)	1	0.01
Potawatomi (1)	1	0.01
Pueblo (4)	4	0.04
Puget Sound Salish (4)	4	0.04
Seminole (2)	2	0.02
Sioux (11)	22	0.21
Ute (1)	2	0.02
Yaqui	1	0.01
Yuman (1)	1	0.01
All other tribes (16)	29	0.27
American Indian tribes, not spec.	9	0.09
Arab:	13	0.12
Jordanian	6	0.06
Lebanese	7	0.07
Asian:	355	3.36
Cambodian (6)	6	0.06
Chinese, ex. Taiwanese (9)	20	0.19
Filipino (106)	155	1.47
Hmong (7)	7	0.07
Indian (9)	11	0.10
Japanese (11)	24	0.23
Korean (41)	58	0.55
Laotian (2)	3	0.03
Pakistani (2)	2	0.02
Sri Lankan	3	0.03
Taiwanese (2)	2	0.02
Thai (7)	15	0.14
Vietnamese (14)	23	0.22
Other Asian, not specified (6)	26	0.25
Australian	8	0.08
Austrian	49	0.46
Basque	7	0.07
Belgian	19	0.18
British	50	0.47
Canadian	12	0.11
Celtic	7	0.07
Croatian	7	0.07
Czech	59	0.56
Czechoslovakian	6	0.06
Danish	30	0.28
Dutch	188	1.78
English	619	5.85
European	36	0.34
Finnish	21	0.20
French, except Basque	242	2.29
French Canadian	24	0.23
German	1,704	16.10
Greek	28	0.26
Hawaii Native/Pacific Islander:	144	1.36
Melanesian: (1)	1	0.01
Fijian (1)	1	0.01
Micronesian: (30)	41	0.39
Guamanian/Chamorro (17)	28	0.27
Other Micronesian (13)	13	0.12
Polynesian: (37)	75	0.71
Native Hawaiian (9)	32	0.30
Samoan (27)	41	0.39
Other Polynesian (1)	2	0.02
Other Pac. Isl., not spec. (5)	27	0.26
Hispanic or Latino:	1,626	15.39
Central American:	62	0.59
Costa Rican	2	0.02
Guatemalan	8	0.08
Honduran	15	0.14
Nicaraguan	10	0.09
Panamanian	20	0.19
Salvadoran	7	0.07
Cuban	21	0.20
Dominican Republic	26	0.25
Mexican	827	7.83
Puerto Rican	391	3.70
South American:	42	0.40
Argentinean	1	0.01
Chilean	8	0.08
Colombian	16	0.15
Ecuadorian	3	0.03
Peruvian	11	0.10
Venezuelan	3	0.03
Other Hispanic or Latino	257	2.43
Hungarian	18	0.17
Irish	1,402	13.25
Italian	430	4.06
Latvian	14	0.13
Lithuanian	5	0.05
Macedonian	7	0.07
Northern European	30	0.28
Norwegian	185	1.75
Pennsylvania German	7	0.07
Polish	219	2.07
Portuguese	25	0.24
Russian	50	0.47
Scandinavian	20	0.19
Scotch-Irish	157	1.48
Scottish	234	2.21
Serbian	8	0.08
Slavic	15	0.14

Notes: 1. Figures in the "Number" column do not add up to the total population due to: a) Ancestry/Race overlap — e.g. persons can report being both White and Irish, b) persons of Hispanic origin can report being any race, c) persons reporting two ancestries are counted in both categories. 2. Numbers in parentheses indicate the number of persons reporting this ancestry/race alone, not in combination with any other ancestry/race. 3. Refer to the Explanation of Data in the front of the book for more detailed information.

Slovak	15	0.14
Swedish	85	0.80
Swiss	6	0.06
Ukrainian	7	0.07
United States or American	487	4.60
Welsh	105	0.99
West Indian, excl. Hispanic:	156	1.47
Belizean	14	0.13
Haitian	20	0.19
Jamaican	93	0.88
Trinidadian and Tobagonian	8	0.08
U.S. Virgin Islander	7	0.07
West Indian	14	0.13
White:	7,007	66.32
Not Hispanic (6,098)	6,351	60.11
Hispanic (532)	656	6.21

Fort Collins

Place Type: City
County: Larimer
Population: 118,652

Ancestry/Race	Number	%
Acadian/Cajun	24	0.02
Afghan	19	0.02
African American/Black:	1,697	1.43
Not Hispanic (1,103)	1,520	1.28
Hispanic (110)	177	0.15
African, sub-Saharan:	423	0.36
African	220	0.19
Ethiopian	81	0.07
Nigerian	13	0.01
South African	22	0.02
Sudanese	66	0.06
Ugandan	8	0.01
Other sub-Saharan African	13	0.01
Alaska Native tribes, specified:	32	0.03
Alaska Athabascan (3)	7	0.01
Aleut (2)	5	0.00
Eskimo (4)	8	0.01
Tlingit-Haida (9)	12	0.01
Alaska Native tribes, not specified	3	0.00
Am. Ind. or Alaska Nat., not spec.	393	0.33
Albanian	7	0.01
American Indian tribes, specified:	1,106	0.93
Apache (25)	77	0.06
Blackfeet (7)	34	0.03
Cherokee (90)	328	0.28
Cheyenne (5)	14	0.01
Chickasaw (2)	5	0.00
Chippewa (16)	31	0.03
Choctaw (19)	52	0.04
Comanche (7)	18	0.02
Cree (2)	13	0.01
Creek (7)	22	0.02
Crow (4)	8	0.01
Delaware (5)	8	0.01
Houma	1	0.00
Iroquois (10)	20	0.02
Kiowa (2)	8	0.01
Latin American Indians (29)	71	0.06
Lumbee	5	0.00
Menominee	1	0.00
Navajo (55)	85	0.07
Osage (5)	17	0.01
Paiute	1	0.00
Potawatomi (9)	9	0.01
Pueblo (8)	25	0.02
Puget Sound Salish (1)	4	0.00
Seminole	2	0.00
Shoshone (3)	4	0.00
Sioux (48)	100	0.08
Ute (5)	15	0.01
Yakama	1	0.00
Yaqui (5)	7	0.01
Yuman (1)	1	0.00
All other tribes (73)	119	0.10
American Indian tribes, not spec.	99	0.08
Arab:	763	0.64
Arab/Arabic	223	0.19
Egyptian	27	0.02
Jordanian	6	0.01
Lebanese	256	0.22
Moroccan	31	0.03
Palestinian	17	0.01
Syrian	9	0.01
Other Arab	194	0.16
Armenian	53	0.04
Asian:	3,864	3.26
Bangladeshi (8)	8	0.01
Cambodian (21)	28	0.02
Chinese, ex. Taiwanese (674)	845	0.71
Filipino (182)	325	0.27
Hmong (2)	4	0.00
Indian (526)	588	0.50
Indonesian (42)	54	0.05
Japanese (422)	687	0.58
Korean (474)	589	0.50
Laotian (5)	5	0.00
Malaysian (18)	27	0.02
Pakistani (43)	48	0.04
Sri Lankan (26)	28	0.02
Taiwanese (63)	87	0.07
Thai (56)	73	0.06
Vietnamese (230)	266	0.22
Other Asian, specified (20)	29	0.02
Other Asian, not specified (61)	173	0.15
Australian	68	0.06
Austrian	450	0.38
Basque	73	0.06
Belgian	184	0.16
Brazilian	15	0.01
British	1,138	0.96
Bulgarian	6	0.01
Canadian	257	0.22
Celtic	30	0.03
Croatian	116	0.10
Czech	1,222	1.03
Czechoslovakian	454	0.38
Danish	2,053	1.73
Dutch	2,608	2.20
Eastern European	98	0.08
English	16,836	14.21
Estonian	17	0.01
European	2,036	1.72
Finnish	293	0.25
French, except Basque	4,906	4.14
French Canadian	1,056	0.89
German	34,007	28.71
German Russian	90	0.08
Greek	449	0.38
Hawaii Native/Pacific Islander:	326	0.27
Melanesian: (1)	2	0.00
Other Melanesian (1)	2	0.00
Micronesian: (32)	51	0.04
Guamanian/Chamorro (29)	47	0.04
Other Micronesian (3)	4	0.00
Polynesian: (83)	204	0.17
Native Hawaiian (59)	165	0.14
Samoan (23)	34	0.03
Tongan	2	0.00
Other Polynesian (1)	3	0.00
Other Pac. Isl., specified	5	0.00
Other Pac. Isl., not spec. (25)	64	0.05
Hispanic or Latino:	10,402	8.77
Central American:	163	0.14
Costa Rican	25	0.02
Guatemalan	55	0.05
Honduran	30	0.03
Nicaraguan	6	0.01
Panamanian	15	0.01
Salvadoran	21	0.02
Other Central American	11	0.01
Cuban	87	0.07
Dominican Republic	25	0.02
Mexican	6,222	5.24
Puerto Rican	237	0.20
South American:	254	0.21
Argentinean	55	0.05
Bolivian	18	0.02
Chilean	23	0.02
Colombian	56	0.05
Ecuadorian	12	0.01
Paraguayan	7	0.01
Peruvian	37	0.03
Uruguayan	2	0.00
Venezuelan	32	0.03
Other South American	12	0.01
Other Hispanic or Latino	3,414	2.88
Hungarian	454	0.38
Icelander	121	0.10
Iranian	110	0.09
Irish	16,756	14.15
Israeli	30	0.03
Italian	6,361	5.37
Latvian	74	0.06
Lithuanian	233	0.20
Luxemburger	58	0.05
Macedonian	10	0.01
New Zealander	11	0.01
Northern European	265	0.22
Norwegian	4,302	3.63
Pennsylvania German	29	0.02
Polish	3,416	2.88
Portuguese	240	0.20
Romanian	127	0.11
Russian	1,421	1.20
Scandinavian	678	0.57
Scotch-Irish	2,852	2.41
Scottish	4,277	3.61
Serbian	89	0.08
Slavic	92	0.08
Slovak	193	0.16
Slovene	112	0.09
Swedish	4,795	4.05
Swiss	755	0.64
Turkish	21	0.02
Ukrainian	471	0.40
United States or American	4,750	4.01
Welsh	1,490	1.26
West Indian, excl. Hispanic:	118	0.10
Barbadian	14	0.01
Belizean	21	0.02
Dutch West Indian	32	0.03
Haitian	7	0.01
Jamaican	36	0.03
West Indian	8	0.01
White:	109,122	91.97
Not Hispanic (101,384)	103,324	87.08
Hispanic (4,963)	5,798	4.89
Yugoslavian	157	0.13

Fort Morgan

Place Type: City
County: Morgan
Population: 11,034

Ancestry/Race	Number	%
Acadian/Cajun	7	0.06
African American/Black:	63	0.57
Not Hispanic (15)	36	0.33
Hispanic (16)	27	0.24
Am. Ind. or Alaska Nat., not spec.	59	0.53
American Indian tribes, specified:	123	1.11
Apache (13)	18	0.16
Blackfeet	2	0.02
Cherokee (5)	24	0.22
Cheyenne	5	0.05
Chickasaw (1)	1	0.01
Choctaw (1)	2	0.02
Iroquois	1	0.01
Latin American Indians (20)	33	0.30
Navajo (7)	10	0.09
Osage	1	0.01
Potawatomi (1)	1	0.01
Pueblo (6)	7	0.06
Sioux (6)	11	0.10
All other tribes (1)	7	0.06

Notes: 1. Figures in the "Number" column do not add up to the total population due to: a) Ancestry/Race overlap — e.g. persons can report being both White and Irish, b) persons of Hispanic origin can report being any race, c) persons reporting two ancestries are counted in both categories. 2. Numbers in parentheses indicate the number of persons reporting this ancestry/race alone, not in combination with any other ancestry/race. 3. Refer to the Explanation of Data in the front of the book for more detailed information.

Ancestry/Race	Number	%
American Indian tribes, not spec.	22	0.20
Arab:	5	0.05
Other Arab	5	0.05
Asian:	71	0.64
Chinese, ex. Taiwanese (1)	5	0.05
Filipino (4)	6	0.05
Indian	8	0.07
Indonesian	3	0.03
Japanese (4)	8	0.07
Korean (7)	13	0.12
Pakistani	8	0.07
Thai (2)	2	0.02
Vietnamese (1)	7	0.06
Other Asian, not specified (1)	11	0.10
Austrian	47	0.43
British	19	0.17
Bulgarian	6	0.05
Czech	38	0.34
Danish	31	0.28
Dutch	238	2.15
English	1,046	9.47
European	22	0.20
Finnish	15	0.14
French, except Basque	193	1.75
French Canadian	12	0.11
German	2,327	21.06
Greek	6	0.05
Hawaii Native/Pacific Islander:	42	0.38
Micronesian: (25)	26	0.24
Guamanian/Chamorro (25)	26	0.24
Polynesian:	6	0.05
Native Hawaiian	4	0.04
Samoan	2	0.02
Other Pac. Isl., not spec. (2)	10	0.09
Hispanic or Latino:	4,308	39.04
Central American:	240	2.18
Guatemalan	160	1.45
Honduran	6	0.05
Nicaraguan	5	0.05
Panamanian	3	0.03
Salvadoran	46	0.42
Other Central American	20	0.18
Cuban	2	0.02
Mexican	3,203	29.03
Puerto Rican	11	0.10
South American:	8	0.07
Argentinean	1	0.01
Bolivian	1	0.01
Chilean	1	0.01
Colombian	5	0.05
Other Hispanic or Latino	844	7.65
Hungarian	4	0.04
Irish	891	8.06
Italian	130	1.18
Lithuanian	6	0.05
Norwegian	132	1.19
Polish	99	0.90
Portuguese	6	0.05
Russian	72	0.65
Scandinavian	5	0.05
Scotch-Irish	171	1.55
Scottish	161	1.46
Slavic	6	0.05
Swedish	175	1.58
Swiss	11	0.10
United States or American	852	7.71
Welsh	20	0.18
White:	8,525	77.26
Not Hispanic (6,478)	6,594	59.76
Hispanic (1,735)	1,931	17.50
Yugoslavian	25	0.23

Fountain

Place Type: City
County: El Paso
Population: 15,197

Ancestry/Race	Number	%
African American/Black:	1,613	10.61
Not Hispanic (1,250)	1,484	9.77
Hispanic (78)	129	0.85
African, sub-Saharan:	88	0.58
African	66	0.44
Other sub-Saharan African	22	0.15
Alaska Native tribes, specified:	6	0.04
Alaska Athabascan (1)	1	0.01
Aleut	1	0.01
Tlingit-Haida (4)	4	0.03
Am. Ind. or Alaska Nat., not spec.	132	0.87
Albanian	8	0.05
American Indian tribes, specified:	322	2.12
Apache (16)	33	0.22
Blackfeet (4)	22	0.14
Cherokee (25)	88	0.58
Cheyenne (7)	9	0.06
Chickasaw	1	0.01
Chippewa (6)	10	0.07
Choctaw	5	0.03
Comanche (1)	3	0.02
Cree	1	0.01
Creek (4)	4	0.03
Crow	1	0.01
Delaware (4)	4	0.03
Iroquois (4)	11	0.07
Kiowa (1)	1	0.01
Latin American Indians (9)	15	0.10
Lumbee (3)	3	0.02
Navajo (17)	24	0.16
Osage	1	0.01
Pueblo (5)	7	0.05
Seminole (2)	2	0.01
Shoshone	5	0.03
Sioux (8)	23	0.15
Tohono O'Odham	2	0.01
Ute	6	0.04
Yaqui (1)	7	0.05
Yuman	3	0.02
All other tribes (17)	31	0.20
American Indian tribes, not spec.	14	0.09
Arab:	41	0.27
Lebanese	41	0.27
Asian:	514	3.38
Chinese, ex. Taiwanese (11)	25	0.16
Filipino (89)	144	0.95
Indian (11)	18	0.12
Indonesian (1)	1	0.01
Japanese (36)	81	0.53
Korean (115)	179	1.18
Pakistani	4	0.03
Thai (9)	15	0.10
Vietnamese (11)	20	0.13
Other Asian, specified	3	0.02
Other Asian, not specified (13)	24	0.16
Austrian	20	0.13
Belgian	8	0.05
Brazilian	7	0.05
British	29	0.19
Bulgarian	16	0.11
Canadian	18	0.12
Croatian	13	0.09
Czech	67	0.44
Danish	40	0.26
Dutch	306	2.02
English	990	6.54
Estonian	6	0.04
European	255	1.69
Finnish	37	0.24
French, except Basque	610	4.03
French Canadian	139	0.92
German	3,297	21.79
German Russian	25	0.17
Greek	4	0.03
Guyanese	36	0.24
Hawaii Native/Pacific Islander:	161	1.06
Melanesian: (5)	6	0.04
Fijian (5)	6	0.04
Micronesian: (46)	71	0.47
Guamanian/Chamorro (43)	68	0.45
Other Micronesian (3)	3	0.02
Polynesian: (26)	64	0.42
Native Hawaiian (13)	47	0.31
Samoan (13)	17	0.11
Other Pac. Isl., specified	3	0.02
Other Pac. Isl., not spec. (4)	17	0.11
Hispanic or Latino:	2,289	15.06
Central American:	67	0.44
Costa Rican	3	0.02
Guatemalan	6	0.04
Honduran	5	0.03
Nicaraguan	1	0.01
Panamanian	39	0.26
Salvadoran	13	0.09
Cuban	18	0.12
Dominican Republic	3	0.02
Mexican	1,092	7.19
Puerto Rican	238	1.57
South American:	11	0.07
Colombian	5	0.03
Peruvian	5	0.03
Other South American	1	0.01
Other Hispanic or Latino	860	5.66
Hungarian	29	0.19
Irish	1,746	11.54
Italian	413	2.73
Lithuanian	7	0.05
Norwegian	432	2.85
Pennsylvania German	14	0.09
Polish	284	1.88
Portuguese	18	0.12
Romanian	14	0.09
Russian	57	0.38
Scandinavian	27	0.18
Scotch-Irish	187	1.24
Scottish	280	1.85
Slovak	9	0.06
Slovene	7	0.05
Swedish	228	1.51
Swiss	6	0.04
Ukrainian	24	0.16
United States or American	964	6.37
Welsh	104	0.69
West Indian, excl. Hispanic:	17	0.11
Jamaican	11	0.07
West Indian	6	0.04
White:	12,104	79.65
Not Hispanic (10,539)	11,017	72.49
Hispanic (870)	1,087	7.15

Golden

Place Type: City
County: Jefferson
Population: 17,159

Ancestry/Race	Number	%
Acadian/Cajun	6	0.03
Afghan	21	0.12
African American/Black:	233	1.36
Not Hispanic (154)	203	1.18
Hispanic (22)	30	0.17
African, sub-Saharan:	16	0.09
African	6	0.03
Cape Verdean	10	0.06
Alaska Native tribes, specified:	4	0.02
Aleut (2)	2	0.01
Eskimo	2	0.01
Alaska Native tribes, not specified	1	0.01
Am. Ind. or Alaska Nat., not spec.	80	0.47
Albanian	7	0.04
American Indian tribes, specified:	212	1.24
Apache (7)	14	0.08
Blackfeet (3)	10	0.06
Cherokee (25)	50	0.29
Cheyenne (2)	3	0.02
Chickasaw (5)	5	0.03
Chippewa (10)	11	0.06
Choctaw	8	0.05
Comanche	5	0.03
Cree	2	0.01

Notes: 1. Figures in the "Number" column do not add up to the total population due to: a) Ancestry/Race overlap — e.g. persons can report being both White and Irish, b) persons of Hispanic origin can report being any race, c) persons reporting two ancestries are counted in both categories. 2. Numbers in parentheses indicate the number of persons reporting this ancestry/race alone, not in combination with any other ancestry/race. 3. Refer to the Explanation of Data in the front of the book for more detailed information.

Ancestry/Race	Number	%
Creek (1)	3	0.02
Crow (1)	1	0.01
Delaware (10)	11	0.06
Iroquois	3	0.02
Latin American Indians (10)	12	0.07
Navajo (12)	19	0.11
Osage	1	0.01
Pima (1)	1	0.01
Potawatomi	2	0.01
Pueblo (6)	9	0.05
Seminole	1	0.01
Sioux (21)	31	0.18
Ute	1	0.01
Yaqui (1)	1	0.01
All other tribes (5)	8	0.05
American Indian tribes, not spec.	17	0.10
Arab:	62	0.36
Arab/Arabic	7	0.04
Egyptian	13	0.07
Lebanese	27	0.16
Moroccan	6	0.03
Syrian	9	0.05
Armenian	6	0.03
Asian:	655	3.82
Cambodian (7)	7	0.04
Chinese, ex. Taiwanese (121)	150	0.87
Filipino (31)	46	0.27
Indian (52)	67	0.39
Indonesian (25)	32	0.19
Japanese (62)	91	0.53
Korean (82)	92	0.54
Laotian (1)	1	0.01
Malaysian (13)	13	0.08
Pakistani (1)	2	0.01
Taiwanese (2)	4	0.02
Thai (27)	32	0.19
Vietnamese (32)	35	0.20
Other Asian, specified (14)	23	0.13
Other Asian, not specified (35)	60	0.35
Australian	8	0.05
Austrian	74	0.43
Basque	8	0.05
Belgian	13	0.07
British	157	0.90
Bulgarian	5	0.03
Canadian	46	0.26
Celtic	13	0.07
Croatian	9	0.05
Czech	184	1.06
Czechoslovakian	35	0.20
Danish	244	1.40
Dutch	343	1.97
Eastern European	10	0.06
English	2,741	15.74
European	315	1.81
Finnish	39	0.22
French, except Basque	655	3.76
French Canadian	247	1.42
German	4,975	28.57
German Russian	8	0.05
Greek	85	0.49
Hawaii Native/Pacific Islander:	36	0.21
Micronesian:	1	0.01
Guamanian/Chamorro	1	0.01
Polynesian: (9)	23	0.13
Native Hawaiian (8)	20	0.12
Samoan (1)	3	0.02
Other Pac. Isl., specified	8	0.05
Other Pac. Isl., not spec. (1)	4	0.02
Hispanic or Latino:	1,130	6.59
Central American:	8	0.05
Guatemalan	2	0.01
Nicaraguan	2	0.01
Panamanian	1	0.01
Salvadoran	3	0.02
Cuban	18	0.10
Dominican Republic	2	0.01
Mexican	550	3.21
Puerto Rican	30	0.17
South American:	57	0.33
Argentinean	3	0.02
Bolivian	5	0.03
Chilean	7	0.04
Colombian	11	0.06
Ecuadorian	5	0.03
Peruvian	8	0.05
Venezuelan	15	0.09
Other South American	3	0.02
Other Hispanic or Latino	465	2.71
Hungarian	59	0.34
Icelander	9	0.05
Irish	2,401	13.79
Italian	1,008	5.79
Lithuanian	48	0.28
Luxemburger	6	0.03
Northern European	61	0.35
Norwegian	598	3.43
Pennsylvania German	32	0.18
Polish	489	2.81
Portuguese	32	0.18
Russian	157	0.90
Scandinavian	125	0.72
Scotch-Irish	532	3.06
Scottish	763	4.38
Serbian	14	0.08
Slovak	33	0.19
Slovene	22	0.13
Swedish	846	4.86
Swiss	130	0.75
Turkish	11	0.06
Ukrainian	56	0.32
United States or American	933	5.36
Welsh	179	1.03
White:	15,908	92.71
Not Hispanic (14,922)	15,176	88.44
Hispanic (634)	732	4.27
Yugoslavian	9	0.05

Grand Junction

Place Type: City
County: Mesa
Population: 41,986

Ancestry/Race	Number	%
African American/Black:	363	0.86
Not Hispanic (219)	319	0.76
Hispanic (32)	44	0.10
African, sub-Saharan:	74	0.18
African	74	0.18
Alaska Native tribes, specified:	6	0.01
Alaska Athabascan (3)	3	0.01
Aleut (2)	2	0.00
Eskimo (1)	1	0.00
Alaska Native tribes, not specified	2	0.00
Am. Ind. or Alaska Nat., not spec.	264	0.63
Albanian	6	0.01
Alsatian	51	0.12
American Indian tribes, specified:	441	1.05
Apache (31)	65	0.15
Blackfeet (6)	20	0.05
Cherokee (37)	112	0.27
Cheyenne	2	0.00
Chickasaw (6)	7	0.02
Chippewa (11)	15	0.04
Choctaw (8)	20	0.05
Comanche (2)	2	0.00
Cree	2	0.00
Creek (4)	7	0.02
Crow (3)	3	0.01
Delaware (1)	2	0.00
Iroquois (3)	10	0.02
Kiowa	1	0.00
Latin American Indians (19)	27	0.06
Menominee	2	0.00
Navajo (30)	54	0.13
Osage (1)	2	0.00
Ottawa (1)	1	0.00
Paiute (2)	3	0.01
Pima (1)	2	0.00
Potawatomi (2)	3	0.01
Pueblo	1	0.00
Puget Sound Salish (1)	1	0.00
Seminole	2	0.00
Shoshone (1)	2	0.00
Sioux (5)	23	0.05
Ute (13)	22	0.05
Yaqui	1	0.00
All other tribes (11)	27	0.06
American Indian tribes, not spec.	64	0.15
Arab:	67	0.16
Lebanese	50	0.12
Syrian	8	0.02
Other Arab	9	0.02
Armenian	37	0.09
Asian:	483	1.15
Cambodian (5)	7	0.02
Chinese, ex. Taiwanese (92)	121	0.29
Filipino (45)	86	0.20
Indian (19)	34	0.08
Indonesian (4)	5	0.01
Japanese (69)	112	0.27
Korean (58)	77	0.18
Malaysian	1	0.00
Sri Lankan	1	0.00
Taiwanese	1	0.00
Thai (8)	10	0.02
Vietnamese (11)	13	0.03
Other Asian, not specified (5)	15	0.04
Australian	9	0.02
Austrian	151	0.36
Basque	70	0.17
Belgian	70	0.17
British	266	0.63
Bulgarian	26	0.06
Canadian	77	0.18
Celtic	12	0.03
Croatian	61	0.14
Czech	250	0.59
Czechoslovakian	79	0.19
Danish	588	1.39
Dutch	724	1.71
English	6,396	15.15
European	525	1.24
Finnish	46	0.11
French, except Basque	1,378	3.26
French Canadian	186	0.44
German	9,128	21.62
German Russian	9	0.02
Greek	134	0.32
Hawaii Native/Pacific Islander:	101	0.24
Micronesian: (6)	16	0.04
Guamanian/Chamorro (5)	12	0.03
Other Micronesian (1)	4	0.01
Polynesian: (42)	72	0.17
Native Hawaiian (27)	53	0.13
Samoan (7)	10	0.02
Tongan (8)	8	0.02
Other Polynesian	1	0.00
Other Pac. Isl., not spec. (4)	13	0.03
Hispanic or Latino:	4,561	10.86
Central American:	44	0.10
Costa Rican	1	0.00
Guatemalan	18	0.04
Honduran	9	0.02
Nicaraguan	4	0.01
Panamanian	6	0.01
Salvadoran	4	0.01
Other Central American	2	0.00
Cuban	10	0.02
Dominican Republic	2	0.00
Mexican	2,718	6.47
Puerto Rican	44	0.10
South American:	39	0.09
Argentinean	3	0.01
Bolivian	1	0.00
Chilean	7	0.02
Colombian	8	0.02
Ecuadorian	2	0.00
Peruvian	6	0.01

Notes: 1. Figures in the "Number" column do not add up to the total population due to: a) Ancestry/Race overlap — e.g. persons can report being both White and Irish, b) persons of Hispanic origin can report being any race, c) persons reporting two ancestries are counted in both categories. 2. Numbers in parentheses indicate the number of persons reporting this ancestry/race alone, not in combination with any other ancestry/race. 3. Refer to the Explanation of Data in the front of the book for more detailed information.

Ancestry/Race	Number	%
Venezuelan	11	0.03
Other South American	1	0.00
Other Hispanic or Latino	1,704	4.06
Hungarian	123	0.29
Iranian	13	0.03
Irish	4,777	11.31
Italian	1,825	4.32
Lithuanian	62	0.15
Luxemburger	10	0.02
Macedonian	5	0.01
New Zealander	15	0.04
Northern European	27	0.06
Norwegian	1,181	2.80
Pennsylvania German	16	0.04
Polish	709	1.68
Portuguese	101	0.24
Romanian	61	0.14
Russian	231	0.55
Scandinavian	117	0.28
Scotch-Irish	1,030	2.44
Scottish	1,159	2.74
Serbian	34	0.08
Slavic	45	0.11
Slovak	27	0.06
Slovene	31	0.07
Swedish	1,381	3.27
Swiss	113	0.27
Ukrainian	91	0.22
United States or American	3,327	7.88
Welsh	573	1.36
West Indian, excl. Hispanic:	27	0.06
Belizean	7	0.02
Jamaican	20	0.05
White:	39,293	93.59
Not Hispanic (36,051)	36,539	87.03
Hispanic (2,482)	2,754	6.56
Yugoslavian	72	0.17

Greeley

Place Type: City
County: Weld
Population: 76,930

Ancestry/Race	Number	%
African American/Black:	904	1.18
Not Hispanic (564)	720	0.94
Hispanic (108)	184	0.24
African, sub-Saharan:	70	0.09
African	37	0.05
Ghanian	10	0.01
Nigerian	7	0.01
Sierra Leonean	10	0.01
Other sub-Saharan African	6	0.01
Alaska Native tribes, specified:	6	0.01
Alaska Athabascan (2)	2	0.00
Aleut (1)	1	0.00
Tlingit-Haida (2)	3	0.00
Alaska Native tribes, not specified	2	0.00
Am. Ind. or Alaska Nat., not spec.	435	0.57
Alsatian	10	0.01
American Indian tribes, specified:	679	0.88
Apache (29)	55	0.07
Blackfeet (5)	27	0.04
Cherokee (59)	183	0.24
Cheyenne (8)	16	0.02
Chickasaw (4)	7	0.01
Chippewa (7)	10	0.01
Choctaw (10)	30	0.04
Comanche (7)	9	0.01
Cree	7	0.01
Creek	6	0.01
Crow (2)	2	0.00
Delaware (1)	4	0.01
Iroquois (1)	3	0.00
Kiowa	5	0.01
Latin American Indians (55)	110	0.14
Navajo (17)	31	0.04
Osage	4	0.01
Ottawa	1	0.00
Paiute (1)	1	0.00
Pima (1)	1	0.00
Potawatomi (8)	11	0.01
Pueblo (15)	20	0.03
Puget Sound Salish	1	0.00
Seminole (1)	3	0.00
Shoshone	2	0.00
Sioux (30)	64	0.08
Ute (5)	7	0.01
Yaqui	2	0.00
Yuman (1)	1	0.00
All other tribes (23)	56	0.07
American Indian tribes, not spec.	97	0.13
Arab:	46	0.06
Arab/Arabic	6	0.01
Lebanese	21	0.03
Other Arab	19	0.02
Armenian	28	0.04
Asian:	1,344	1.75
Cambodian (2)	5	0.01
Chinese, ex. Taiwanese (148)	229	0.30
Filipino (91)	185	0.24
Indian (66)	84	0.11
Indonesian (1)	3	0.00
Japanese (287)	447	0.58
Korean (163)	209	0.27
Laotian (6)	6	0.01
Malaysian (1)	2	0.00
Pakistani (9)	10	0.01
Taiwanese (14)	27	0.04
Thai (29)	33	0.04
Vietnamese (20)	30	0.04
Other Asian, specified (5)	9	0.01
Other Asian, not specified (14)	65	0.08
Assyrian/Chaldean/Syriac	6	0.01
Australian	17	0.02
Austrian	119	0.15
Basque	17	0.02
Belgian	104	0.14
Brazilian	8	0.01
British	267	0.35
Bulgarian	14	0.02
Canadian	125	0.16
Celtic	15	0.02
Croatian	63	0.08
Czech	340	0.44
Czechoslovakian	157	0.20
Danish	799	1.04
Dutch	1,491	1.94
Eastern European	6	0.01
English	7,061	9.19
European	728	0.95
Finnish	140	0.18
French, except Basque	1,726	2.25
French Canadian	287	0.37
German	18,581	24.19
German Russian	23	0.03
Greek	108	0.14
Hawaii Native/Pacific Islander:	258	0.34
Micronesian: (9)	20	0.03
Guamanian/Chamorro (7)	18	0.02
Other Micronesian (2)	2	0.00
Polynesian: (79)	189	0.25
Native Hawaiian (68)	170	0.22
Samoan (11)	18	0.02
Tongan	1	0.00
Other Pac. Isl., specified	1	0.00
Other Pac. Isl., not spec. (16)	48	0.06
Hispanic or Latino:	22,683	29.49
Central American:	312	0.41
Costa Rican	2	0.00
Guatemalan	156	0.20
Honduran	15	0.02
Nicaraguan	11	0.01
Panamanian	6	0.01
Salvadoran	103	0.13
Other Central American	19	0.02
Cuban	47	0.06
Dominican Republic	5	0.01
Mexican	16,343	21.24
Puerto Rican	95	0.12
South American:	62	0.08
Argentinean	5	0.01
Bolivian	5	0.01
Chilean	7	0.01
Colombian	15	0.02
Ecuadorian	1	0.00
Paraguayan	2	0.00
Peruvian	15	0.02
Uruguayan	1	0.00
Venezuelan	9	0.01
Other South American	2	0.00
Other Hispanic or Latino	5,819	7.56
Hungarian	102	0.13
Icelander	8	0.01
Iranian	71	0.09
Irish	6,670	8.68
Italian	2,353	3.06
Latvian	19	0.02
Lithuanian	42	0.05
Macedonian	12	0.02
Northern European	73	0.10
Norwegian	1,777	2.31
Pennsylvania German	50	0.07
Polish	1,112	1.45
Portuguese	135	0.18
Romanian	32	0.04
Russian	694	0.90
Scandinavian	171	0.22
Scotch-Irish	1,513	1.97
Scottish	1,661	2.16
Serbian	43	0.06
Slavic	22	0.03
Slovak	134	0.17
Slovene	94	0.12
Swedish	2,216	2.88
Swiss	341	0.44
Ukrainian	121	0.16
United States or American	3,375	4.39
Welsh	782	1.02
West Indian, excl. Hispanic:	90	0.12
Trinidadian and Tobagonian	8	0.01
U.S. Virgin Islander	18	0.02
West Indian	64	0.08
White:	63,769	82.89
Not Hispanic (51,404)	52,242	67.91
Hispanic (10,449)	11,527	14.98
Yugoslavian	65	0.08

Greenwood Village

Place Type: City
County: Arapahoe
Population: 11,035

Ancestry/Race	Number	%
African American/Black:	152	1.38
Not Hispanic (121)	146	1.32
Hispanic (5)	6	0.05
African, sub-Saharan:	12	0.11
Cape Verdean	7	0.06
Nigerian	5	0.05
Am. Ind. or Alaska Nat., not spec.	13	0.12
American Indian tribes, specified:	45	0.41
Apache (1)	2	0.02
Blackfeet	1	0.01
Cherokee (7)	16	0.14
Chippewa (1)	1	0.01
Choctaw	1	0.01
Creek (1)	2	0.02
Crow	1	0.01
Iroquois (1)	2	0.02
Latin American Indians (5)	6	0.05
Osage	3	0.03
Seminole	1	0.01
Sioux (1)	1	0.01
All other tribes (3)	8	0.07
American Indian tribes, not spec.	1	0.01
Arab:	76	0.69
Egyptian	23	0.21

Notes: 1. Figures in the "Number" column do not add up to the total population due to: a) Ancestry/Race overlap — e.g. persons can report being both White and Irish, b) persons of Hispanic origin can report being any race, c) persons reporting two ancestries are counted in both categories. 2. Numbers in parentheses indicate the number of persons reporting this ancestry/race alone, not in combination with any other ancestry/race. 3. Refer to the Explanation of Data in the front of the book for more detailed information.

Ancestry/Race	Number	%
Lebanese	47	0.42
Syrian	6	0.05
Asian:	348	3.15
Chinese, ex. Taiwanese (53)	75	0.68
Filipino (17)	25	0.23
Indian (50)	58	0.53
Indonesian	1	0.01
Japanese (57)	77	0.70
Korean (84)	89	0.81
Taiwanese (3)	3	0.03
Thai (1)	2	0.02
Vietnamese (5)	7	0.06
Other Asian, not specified (5)	11	0.10
Australian	7	0.06
Austrian	91	0.82
Belgian	6	0.05
Brazilian	42	0.38
British	69	0.62
Canadian	68	0.61
Croatian	10	0.09
Czech	98	0.89
Czechoslovakian	29	0.26
Danish	151	1.36
Dutch	343	3.10
Eastern European	91	0.82
English	2,060	18.61
Estonian	6	0.05
European	157	1.42
Finnish	50	0.45
French, except Basque	415	3.75
French Canadian	46	0.42
German	2,563	23.16
German Russian	13	0.12
Greek	194	1.75
Hawaii Native/Pacific Islander:	18	0.16
Micronesian: (1)	9	0.08
Guamanian/Chamorro (1)	9	0.08
Polynesian: (4)	7	0.06
Native Hawaiian (3)	6	0.05
Other Polynesian (1)	1	0.01
Other Pac. Isl., not spec.	2	0.02
Hispanic or Latino:	344	3.12
Central American:	15	0.14
Guatemalan	5	0.05
Honduran	2	0.02
Nicaraguan	3	0.03
Panamanian	3	0.03
Other Central American	2	0.02
Cuban	10	0.09
Dominican Republic	2	0.02
Mexican	162	1.47
Puerto Rican	12	0.11
South American:	36	0.33
Argentinean	3	0.03
Chilean	16	0.14
Colombian	2	0.02
Ecuadorian	1	0.01
Peruvian	9	0.08
Uruguayan	1	0.01
Venezuelan	3	0.03
Other South American	1	0.01
Other Hispanic or Latino	107	0.97
Hungarian	83	0.75
Iranian	82	0.74
Irish	1,506	13.61
Israeli	7	0.06
Italian	661	5.97
Latvian	39	0.35
Lithuanian	52	0.47
Luxemburger	5	0.05
Northern European	37	0.33
Norwegian	352	3.18
Polish	439	3.97
Portuguese	5	0.05
Romanian	29	0.26
Russian	396	3.58
Scandinavian	46	0.42
Scotch-Irish	322	2.91
Scottish	477	4.31
Serbian	9	0.08
Slovak	25	0.23
Slovene	11	0.10
Swedish	383	3.46
Swiss	70	0.63
Turkish	9	0.08
Ukrainian	63	0.57
United States or American	451	4.07
Welsh	121	1.09
West Indian, excl. Hispanic:	24	0.22
Haitian	8	0.07
West Indian	16	0.14
White:	10,524	95.37
Not Hispanic (10,110)	10,251	92.90
Hispanic (252)	273	2.47
Yugoslavian	6	0.05

Highlands Ranch

Place Type: Census Designated Place
County: Douglas
Population: 70,931

Ancestry/Race	Number	%
Acadian/Cajun	19	0.03
African American/Black:	1,183	1.67
Not Hispanic (866)	1,105	1.56
Hispanic (49)	78	0.11
African, sub-Saharan:	277	0.39
African	91	0.13
Ethiopian	42	0.06
South African	144	0.20
Alaska Native tribes, specified:	3	0.00
Alaska Athabascan (1)	1	0.00
Eskimo	1	0.00
Tlingit-Haida (1)	1	0.00
Am. Ind. or Alaska Nat., not spec.	104	0.15
Albanian	34	0.05
Alsatian	6	0.01
American Indian tribes, specified:	374	0.53
Apache (7)	22	0.03
Blackfeet (3)	17	0.02
Cherokee (51)	112	0.16
Cheyenne (1)	1	0.00
Chickasaw (2)	4	0.01
Chippewa (6)	17	0.02
Choctaw (10)	22	0.03
Colville (2)	2	0.00
Comanche (1)	1	0.00
Creek (2)	6	0.01
Crow	1	0.00
Delaware (1)	4	0.01
Iroquois (1)	4	0.01
Latin American Indians (1)	23	0.03
Menominee (5)	6	0.01
Navajo (9)	13	0.02
Osage (1)	2	0.00
Ottawa (2)	4	0.01
Pima (1)	1	0.00
Potawatomi (5)	10	0.01
Pueblo (3)	7	0.01
Sioux (6)	22	0.03
Ute (1)	5	0.01
Yaqui (2)	2	0.00
All other tribes (40)	66	0.09
American Indian tribes, not spec.	28	0.04
Arab:	476	0.67
Arab/Arabic	50	0.07
Egyptian	39	0.06
Lebanese	189	0.27
Moroccan	23	0.03
Palestinian	119	0.17
Syrian	56	0.08
Armenian	21	0.03
Asian:	3,560	5.02
Bangladeshi (2)	5	0.01
Cambodian (8)	8	0.01
Chinese, ex. Taiwanese (809)	958	1.35
Filipino (226)	401	0.57
Hmong (12)	12	0.02
Indian (543)	613	0.86
Indonesian (19)	29	0.04
Japanese (237)	404	0.57
Korean (459)	526	0.74
Laotian (4)	5	0.01
Malaysian (5)	7	0.01
Pakistani (17)	36	0.05
Sri Lankan (2)	2	0.00
Taiwanese (25)	30	0.04
Thai (37)	48	0.07
Vietnamese (332)	367	0.52
Other Asian, specified (2)	5	0.01
Other Asian, not specified (52)	104	0.15
Assyrian/Chaldean/Syriac	27	0.04
Australian	52	0.07
Austrian	437	0.62
Basque	24	0.03
Belgian	158	0.22
Brazilian	42	0.06
British	416	0.59
Bulgarian	18	0.03
Canadian	450	0.64
Celtic	33	0.05
Croatian	93	0.13
Czech	583	0.82
Czechoslovakian	184	0.26
Danish	744	1.05
Dutch	1,692	2.39
Eastern European	98	0.14
English	10,290	14.52
European	1,217	1.72
Finnish	143	0.20
French, except Basque	3,109	4.39
French Canadian	749	1.06
German	18,816	26.55
German Russian	15	0.02
Greek	351	0.50
Guyanese	6	0.01
Hawaii Native/Pacific Islander:	156	0.22
Micronesian: (6)	11	0.02
Guamanian/Chamorro (6)	11	0.02
Polynesian: (39)	111	0.16
Native Hawaiian (23)	85	0.12
Samoan (11)	21	0.03
Tongan (5)	5	0.01
Other Pac. Isl., not spec. (7)	34	0.05
Hispanic or Latino:	3,847	5.42
Central American:	75	0.11
Costa Rican	12	0.02
Guatemalan	21	0.03
Honduran	6	0.01
Nicaraguan	5	0.01
Panamanian	9	0.01
Salvadoran	13	0.02
Other Central American	9	0.01
Cuban	87	0.12
Dominican Republic	14	0.02
Mexican	1,802	2.54
Puerto Rican	248	0.35
South American:	173	0.24
Argentinean	24	0.03
Bolivian	3	0.00
Chilean	15	0.02
Colombian	55	0.08
Ecuadorian	7	0.01
Paraguayan	5	0.01
Peruvian	27	0.04
Uruguayan	4	0.01
Venezuelan	10	0.01
Other South American	23	0.03
Other Hispanic or Latino	1,448	2.04
Hungarian	504	0.71
Icelander	20	0.03
Iranian	215	0.30
Irish	10,938	15.44
Israeli	10	0.01
Italian	4,796	6.77
Latvian	102	0.14
Lithuanian	271	0.38
Luxemburger	36	0.05
Maltese	9	0.01

Notes: 1. Figures in the "Number" column do not add up to the total population due to: a) Ancestry/Race overlap — e.g. persons can report being both White and Irish, b) persons of Hispanic origin can report being any race, c) persons reporting two ancestries are counted in both categories. 2. Numbers in parentheses indicate the number of persons reporting this ancestry/race alone, not in combination with any other ancestry/race. 3. Refer to the Explanation of Data in the front of the book for more detailed information.

Ancestry/Race	Number	%
Northern European	202	0.29
Norwegian	3,074	4.34
Pennsylvania German	55	0.08
Polish	2,435	3.44
Portuguese	184	0.26
Romanian	171	0.24
Russian	994	1.40
Scandinavian	359	0.51
Scotch-Irish	1,448	2.04
Scottish	2,313	3.26
Serbian	23	0.03
Slavic	44	0.06
Slovak	140	0.20
Slovene	100	0.14
Swedish	2,674	3.77
Swiss	402	0.57
Turkish	50	0.07
Ukrainian	200	0.28
United States or American	3,040	4.29
Welsh	888	1.25
West Indian, excl. Hispanic:	145	0.20
Bahamian	7	0.01
Jamaican	80	0.11
Trinidadian and Tobagonian	9	0.01
West Indian	49	0.07
White:	65,680	92.60
Not Hispanic (61,984)	62,985	88.80
Hispanic (2,391)	2,695	3.80
Yugoslavian	167	0.24

Ken Caryl

Place Type: Census Designated Place
County: Jefferson
Population: 30,887

Ancestry/Race	Number	%
Acadian/Cajun	17	0.06
African American/Black:	335	1.08
Not Hispanic (209)	297	0.96
Hispanic (11)	38	0.12
African, sub-Saharan:	73	0.24
African	7	0.02
Ethiopian	22	0.07
South African	44	0.14
Alaska Native tribes, specified:	3	0.01
Tlingit-Haida	3	0.01
Am. Ind. or Alaska Nat., not spec.	91	0.29
American Indian tribes, specified:	236	0.76
Apache (11)	33	0.11
Blackfeet (2)	2	0.01
Cherokee (26)	81	0.26
Chickasaw (1)	6	0.02
Chippewa (8)	18	0.06
Choctaw (7)	11	0.04
Colville (1)	1	0.00
Comanche	3	0.01
Creek (1)	3	0.01
Iroquois (4)	8	0.03
Kiowa	2	0.01
Latin American Indians (5)	10	0.03
Lumbee (1)	3	0.01
Navajo (4)	10	0.03
Osage (1)	2	0.01
Potawatomi	1	0.00
Pueblo (1)	4	0.01
Sioux (6)	18	0.06
Tohono O'Odham	1	0.00
Yuman (1)	1	0.00
All other tribes (12)	18	0.06
American Indian tribes, not spec.	3	0.01
Arab:	154	0.50
Arab/Arabic	25	0.08
Egyptian	30	0.10
Lebanese	66	0.21
Palestinian	6	0.02
Syrian	27	0.09
Asian:	783	2.54
Cambodian (3)	3	0.01
Chinese, ex. Taiwanese (112)	149	0.48
Filipino (62)	112	0.36
Indian (78)	93	0.30
Indonesian	2	0.01
Japanese (80)	158	0.51
Korean (87)	108	0.35
Laotian (5)	5	0.02
Malaysian (2)	4	0.01
Pakistani (8)	13	0.04
Sri Lankan (1)	1	0.00
Taiwanese (3)	3	0.01
Thai (19)	24	0.08
Vietnamese (65)	78	0.25
Other Asian, specified	5	0.02
Other Asian, not specified (8)	25	0.08
Australian	20	0.06
Austrian	100	0.32
Basque	6	0.02
Belgian	99	0.32
Brazilian	15	0.05
British	157	0.51
Bulgarian	78	0.25
Canadian	90	0.29
Celtic	50	0.16
Croatian	81	0.26
Czech	237	0.77
Czechoslovakian	71	0.23
Danish	392	1.27
Dutch	841	2.73
Eastern European	7	0.02
English	5,145	16.68
European	256	0.83
Finnish	137	0.44
French, except Basque	1,359	4.41
French Canadian	276	0.89
German	8,986	29.14
Greek	139	0.45
Hawaii Native/Pacific Islander:	74	0.24
Micronesian: (2)	13	0.04
Guamanian/Chamorro (1)	12	0.04
Other Micronesian (1)	1	0.00
Polynesian: (14)	36	0.12
Native Hawaiian (9)	16	0.05
Samoan (1)	12	0.04
Tongan (3)	3	0.01
Other Polynesian (1)	5	0.02
Other Pac. Isl., specified	3	0.01
Other Pac. Isl., not spec. (7)	22	0.07
Hispanic or Latino:	2,056	6.66
Central American:	23	0.07
Guatemalan	6	0.02
Honduran	4	0.01
Panamanian	2	0.01
Salvadoran	10	0.03
Other Central American	1	0.00
Cuban	20	0.06
Dominican Republic	2	0.01
Mexican	934	3.02
Puerto Rican	52	0.17
South American:	44	0.14
Argentinean	3	0.01
Bolivian	1	0.00
Chilean	9	0.03
Colombian	9	0.03
Ecuadorian	1	0.00
Peruvian	10	0.03
Venezuelan	4	0.01
Other South American	7	0.02
Other Hispanic or Latino	981	3.18
Hungarian	265	0.86
Icelander	4	0.01
Irish	5,263	17.07
Israeli	9	0.03
Italian	2,070	6.71
Lithuanian	51	0.17
Luxemburger	14	0.05
Maltese	6	0.02
New Zealander	7	0.02
Northern European	12	0.04
Norwegian	1,217	3.95
Pennsylvania German	17	0.06
Polish	1,191	3.86
Portuguese	94	0.30
Romanian	81	0.26
Russian	310	1.01
Scandinavian	106	0.34
Scotch-Irish	820	2.66
Scottish	1,003	3.25
Serbian	12	0.04
Slavic	73	0.24
Slovak	56	0.18
Slovene	39	0.13
Swedish	1,013	3.28
Swiss	201	0.65
Turkish	36	0.12
Ukrainian	87	0.28
United States or American	1,728	5.60
Welsh	456	1.48
West Indian, excl. Hispanic:	11	0.04
Jamaican	11	0.04
White:	29,393	95.16
Not Hispanic (27,564)	27,923	90.40
Hispanic (1,299)	1,470	4.76
Yugoslavian	43	0.14

Lafayette

Place Type: City
County: Boulder
Population: 23,197

Ancestry/Race	Number	%
Acadian/Cajun	8	0.03
Afghan	14	0.06
African American/Black:	317	1.37
Not Hispanic (190)	275	1.19
Hispanic (19)	42	0.18
African, sub-Saharan:	33	0.14
African	7	0.03
Cape Verdean	12	0.05
Kenyan	7	0.03
South African	7	0.03
Am. Ind. or Alaska Nat., not spec.	103	0.44
American Indian tribes, specified:	221	0.95
Apache (7)	26	0.11
Blackfeet (2)	3	0.01
Cherokee (19)	45	0.19
Cheyenne (4)	6	0.03
Chickasaw (4)	7	0.03
Chippewa (2)	3	0.01
Choctaw (3)	15	0.06
Creek (1)	2	0.01
Crow (2)	2	0.01
Delaware	3	0.01
Iroquois	3	0.01
Kiowa (2)	2	0.01
Latin American Indians (19)	30	0.13
Navajo (12)	21	0.09
Osage (1)	1	0.00
Potawatomi (4)	4	0.02
Pueblo (3)	7	0.03
Shoshone	8	0.03
Sioux (6)	13	0.06
Ute (4)	8	0.03
Yaqui (2)	3	0.01
All other tribes (6)	9	0.04
American Indian tribes, not spec.	14	0.06
Arab:	44	0.19
Arab/Arabic	6	0.03
Lebanese	24	0.10
Palestinian	9	0.04
Other Arab	5	0.02
Asian:	928	4.00
Bangladeshi (4)	4	0.02
Cambodian (16)	17	0.07
Chinese, ex. Taiwanese (177)	203	0.88
Filipino (48)	84	0.36
Hmong (148)	160	0.69
Indian (95)	104	0.45
Indonesian (6)	11	0.05
Japanese (70)	117	0.50

Notes: 1. Figures in the "Number" column do not add up to the total population due to: a) Ancestry/Race overlap — e.g. persons can report being both White and Irish, b) persons of Hispanic origin can report being any race, c) persons reporting two ancestries are counted in both categories. 2. Numbers in parentheses indicate the number of persons reporting this ancestry/race alone, not in combination with any other ancestry/race. 3. Refer to the Explanation of Data in the front of the book for more detailed information.

Korean (57)	67	0.29
Laotian (29)	29	0.13
Malaysian (4)	4	0.02
Pakistani (3)	4	0.02
Sri Lankan (6)	6	0.03
Taiwanese (3)	4	0.02
Thai (16)	22	0.09
Vietnamese (59)	66	0.28
Other Asian, specified (3)	3	0.01
Other Asian, not specified (15)	23	0.10
Austrian	183	0.78
Basque	8	0.03
Belgian	63	0.27
British	111	0.48
Bulgarian	36	0.15
Canadian	66	0.28
Croatian	53	0.23
Czech	90	0.39
Czechoslovakian	75	0.32
Danish	205	0.88
Dutch	394	1.69
Eastern European	26	0.11
English	3,022	12.94
Estonian	22	0.09
European	318	1.36
Finnish	23	0.10
French, except Basque	895	3.83
French Canadian	190	0.81
German	5,286	22.64
Greek	117	0.50
Hawaii Native/Pacific Islander:	49	0.21
Micronesian: (1)	5	0.02
Guamanian/Chamorro	2	0.01
Other Micronesian (1)	3	0.01
Polynesian: (10)	28	0.12
Native Hawaiian (5)	23	0.10
Samoan (4)	4	0.02
Other Polynesian (1)	1	0.00
Other Pac. Isl., not spec. (9)	16	0.07
Hispanic or Latino:	3,808	16.42
Central American:	46	0.20
Costa Rican	14	0.06
Guatemalan	18	0.08
Honduran	4	0.02
Nicaraguan	1	0.00
Panamanian	1	0.00
Salvadoran	5	0.02
Other Central American	3	0.01
Cuban	19	0.08
Dominican Republic	4	0.02
Mexican	2,803	12.08
Puerto Rican	51	0.22
South American:	54	0.23
Argentinean	5	0.02
Bolivian	3	0.01
Chilean	9	0.04
Colombian	21	0.09
Ecuadorian	3	0.01
Paraguayan	3	0.01
Peruvian	4	0.02
Uruguayan	3	0.01
Venezuelan	3	0.01
Other Hispanic or Latino	831	3.58
Hungarian	162	0.69
Iranian	35	0.15
Irish	3,059	13.10
Israeli	13	0.06
Italian	1,178	5.05
Latvian	17	0.07
Lithuanian	135	0.58
Maltese	8	0.03
Northern European	34	0.15
Norwegian	748	3.20
Pennsylvania German	17	0.07
Polish	716	3.07
Portuguese	20	0.09
Romanian	66	0.28
Russian	318	1.36
Scandinavian	93	0.40
Scotch-Irish	512	2.19
Scottish	961	4.12
Serbian	29	0.12
Slavic	69	0.30
Slovak	78	0.33
Slovene	7	0.03
Swedish	704	3.02
Swiss	161	0.69
Ukrainian	82	0.35
United States or American	1,007	4.31
Welsh	279	1.19
White:	20,368	87.80
Not Hispanic (18,002)	18,280	78.80
Hispanic (1,839)	2,088	9.00

Lakewood

Place Type: City
County: Jefferson
Population: 144,126

Ancestry/Race	Number	%
Acadian/Cajun	32	0.02
Afghan	38	0.03
African American/Black:	2,781	1.93
Not Hispanic (1,910)	2,426	1.68
Hispanic (218)	355	0.25
African, sub-Saharan:	444	0.31
African	129	0.09
Cape Verdean	71	0.05
Ethiopian	54	0.04
Nigerian	15	0.01
Sierra Leonean	7	0.00
South African	131	0.09
Sudanese	18	0.01
Zimbabwean	19	0.01
Alaska Native tribes, specified:	21	0.01
Alaska Athabascan (4)	4	0.00
Aleut (6)	7	0.00
Eskimo (2)	10	0.01
Am. Ind. or Alaska Nat., not spec.	822	0.57
Albanian	8	0.01
American Indian tribes, specified:	1,954	1.36
Apache (54)	132	0.09
Blackfeet (13)	62	0.04
Cherokee (135)	465	0.32
Cheyenne (15)	23	0.02
Chickasaw (10)	18	0.01
Chippewa (43)	75	0.05
Choctaw (30)	70	0.05
Colville (1)	4	0.00
Comanche (8)	18	0.01
Cree	2	0.00
Creek (2)	17	0.01
Crow (5)	12	0.01
Delaware (5)	10	0.01
Iroquois (18)	31	0.02
Kiowa (7)	9	0.01
Latin American Indians (65)	115	0.08
Lumbee (3)	6	0.00
Menominee (9)	10	0.01
Navajo (141)	235	0.16
Osage (7)	14	0.01
Ottawa (1)	3	0.00
Paiute (2)	2	0.00
Potawatomi (9)	18	0.01
Pueblo (56)	85	0.06
Puget Sound Salish (3)	5	0.00
Seminole (2)	8	0.01
Shoshone (12)	15	0.01
Sioux (207)	284	0.20
Tohono O'Odham (1)	2	0.00
Ute (17)	36	0.02
Yakama (2)	2	0.00
Yaqui (7)	8	0.01
Yuman	5	0.00
All other tribes (98)	153	0.11
American Indian tribes, not spec.	189	0.13
Arab:	426	0.30
Arab/Arabic	105	0.07
Egyptian	5	0.00
Iraqi	14	0.01
Lebanese	183	0.13
Palestinian	5	0.00
Syrian	16	0.01
Other Arab	98	0.07
Armenian	117	0.08
Asian:	4,847	3.36
Cambodian (23)	36	0.02
Chinese, ex. Taiwanese (541)	714	0.50
Filipino (287)	447	0.31
Hmong (12)	14	0.01
Indian (535)	606	0.42
Indonesian (12)	26	0.02
Japanese (502)	740	0.51
Korean (446)	531	0.37
Laotian (31)	45	0.03
Malaysian (1)	4	0.00
Pakistani (23)	28	0.02
Sri Lankan (5)	5	0.00
Taiwanese (16)	22	0.02
Thai (47)	70	0.05
Vietnamese (1,236)	1,357	0.94
Other Asian, specified (24)	32	0.02
Other Asian, not specified (78)	170	0.12
Assyrian/Chaldean/Syriac	19	0.01
Australian	29	0.02
Austrian	579	0.40
Basque	71	0.05
Belgian	172	0.12
Brazilian	77	0.05
British	755	0.52
Bulgarian	162	0.11
Canadian	297	0.21
Celtic	114	0.08
Croatian	234	0.16
Czech	926	0.64
Czechoslovakian	639	0.44
Danish	1,633	1.13
Dutch	2,817	1.96
Eastern European	39	0.03
English	19,497	13.53
Estonian	8	0.01
European	1,885	1.31
Finnish	429	0.30
French, except Basque	5,570	3.87
French Canadian	1,071	0.74
German	36,219	25.14
German Russian	11	0.01
Greek	574	0.40
Hawaii Native/Pacific Islander:	282	0.20
Micronesian: (49)	74	0.05
Guamanian/Chamorro (31)	54	0.04
Other Micronesian (18)	20	0.01
Polynesian: (54)	144	0.10
Native Hawaiian (35)	112	0.08
Samoan (15)	20	0.01
Tongan (2)	3	0.00
Other Polynesian (2)	9	0.01
Other Pac. Isl., specified	3	0.00
Other Pac. Isl., not spec. (14)	61	0.04
Hispanic or Latino:	20,949	14.54
Central American:	207	0.14
Costa Rican	13	0.01
Guatemalan	50	0.03
Honduran	28	0.02
Nicaraguan	2	0.00
Panamanian	10	0.01
Salvadoran	72	0.05
Other Central American	32	0.02
Cuban	178	0.12
Dominican Republic	15	0.01
Mexican	11,757	8.16
Puerto Rican	355	0.25
South American:	283	0.20
Argentinean	22	0.02
Bolivian	27	0.02
Chilean	18	0.01
Colombian	73	0.05
Ecuadorian	13	0.01
Peruvian	73	0.05

Notes: 1. Figures in the "Number" column do not add up to the total population due to: a) Ancestry/Race overlap — e.g. persons can report being both White and Irish, b) persons of Hispanic origin can report being any race, c) persons reporting two ancestries are counted in both categories. 2. Numbers in parentheses indicate the number of persons reporting this ancestry/race alone, not in combination with any other ancestry/race. 3. Refer to the Explanation of Data in the front of the book for more detailed information.

Uruguayan	2	0.00
Venezuelan	26	0.02
Other South American	29	0.02
Other Hispanic or Latino	8,154	5.66
Hungarian	872	0.61
Icelander	41	0.03
Iranian	35	0.02
Irish	20,170	14.00
Israeli	35	0.02
Italian	8,014	5.56
Latvian	30	0.02
Lithuanian	290	0.20
Luxemburger	37	0.03
Macedonian	15	0.01
Northern European	202	0.14
Norwegian	4,410	3.06
Pennsylvania German	127	0.09
Polish	3,825	2.65
Portuguese	93	0.06
Romanian	139	0.10
Russian	1,316	0.91
Scandinavian	309	0.21
Scotch-Irish	3,399	2.36
Scottish	4,011	2.78
Serbian	91	0.06
Slavic	104	0.07
Slovak	159	0.11
Slovene	206	0.14
Soviet Union	10	0.01
Swedish	4,776	3.31
Swiss	716	0.50
Turkish	77	0.05
Ukrainian	323	0.22
United States or American	6,700	4.65
Welsh	1,461	1.01
West Indian, excl. Hispanic:	156	0.11
British West Indian	5	0.00
Haitian	7	0.00
Jamaican	58	0.04
Trinidadian and Tobagonian	6	0.00
West Indian	56	0.04
Other West Indian	24	0.02
White:	128,953	89.47
Not Hispanic (113,755)	115,820	80.36
Hispanic (11,856)	13,133	9.11
Yugoslavian	554	0.38

Littleton

Place Type: City
County: Arapahoe
Population: 40,340

Ancestry/Race	Number	%
Afghan	46	0.11
African American/Black:	602	1.49
Not Hispanic (429)	537	1.33
Hispanic (37)	65	0.16
African, sub-Saharan:	96	0.24
African	90	0.22
Ethiopian	6	0.01
Alaska Native tribes, specified:	10	0.02
Alaska Athabascan	3	0.01
Eskimo (1)	1	0.00
Tlingit-Haida (5)	6	0.01
Am. Ind. or Alaska Nat., not spec.	148	0.37
Albanian	28	0.07
American Indian tribes, specified:	398	0.99
Apache (10)	26	0.06
Blackfeet (1)	13	0.03
Cherokee (33)	102	0.25
Cheyenne (2)	4	0.01
Chickasaw (5)	6	0.01
Chippewa (9)	19	0.05
Choctaw (4)	9	0.02
Comanche	3	0.01
Cree (1)	1	0.00
Creek (4)	7	0.02
Delaware (1)	3	0.01
Iroquois (3)	6	0.01
Kiowa (2)	5	0.01
Latin American Indians (7)	14	0.03
Navajo (24)	37	0.09
Ottawa (1)	2	0.00
Pima	1	0.00
Potawatomi (3)	11	0.03
Pueblo (11)	18	0.04
Seminole (3)	5	0.01
Shoshone (4)	4	0.01
Sioux (27)	42	0.10
Ute (1)	6	0.01
Yaqui (2)	7	0.02
All other tribes (34)	47	0.12
American Indian tribes, not spec.	21	0.05
Arab:	119	0.29
Arab/Arabic	17	0.04
Lebanese	75	0.19
Moroccan	4	0.01
Palestinian	2	0.00
Syrian	9	0.02
Other Arab	12	0.03
Armenian	33	0.08
Asian:	906	2.25
Bangladeshi (2)	2	0.00
Cambodian (1)	2	0.00
Chinese, ex. Taiwanese (128)	176	0.44
Filipino (53)	94	0.23
Hmong (12)	12	0.03
Indian (81)	104	0.26
Indonesian (14)	18	0.04
Japanese (97)	169	0.42
Korean (97)	114	0.28
Pakistani (8)	16	0.04
Taiwanese (2)	3	0.01
Thai (10)	14	0.03
Vietnamese (124)	143	0.35
Other Asian, specified	2	0.00
Other Asian, not specified (17)	37	0.09
Australian	78	0.19
Austrian	181	0.45
Basque	40	0.10
Belgian	103	0.25
British	258	0.64
Bulgarian	12	0.03
Canadian	207	0.51
Celtic	64	0.16
Croatian	49	0.12
Czech	307	0.76
Czechoslovakian	116	0.29
Danish	471	1.17
Dutch	766	1.90
Eastern European	12	0.03
English	6,249	15.46
European	467	1.16
Finnish	121	0.30
French, except Basque	1,700	4.21
French Canadian	263	0.65
German	10,055	24.88
Greek	178	0.44
Hawaii Native/Pacific Islander:	75	0.19
Melanesian: (2)	3	0.01
Other Melanesian (2)	3	0.01
Micronesian: (3)	5	0.01
Guamanian/Chamorro (2)	2	0.00
Other Micronesian (1)	3	0.01
Polynesian: (17)	57	0.14
Native Hawaiian (13)	51	0.13
Samoan (4)	6	0.01
Other Pac. Isl., specified	1	0.00
Other Pac. Isl., not spec. (2)	9	0.02
Hispanic or Latino:	3,408	8.45
Central American:	57	0.14
Guatemalan	20	0.05
Honduran	12	0.03
Nicaraguan	2	0.00
Panamanian	5	0.01
Salvadoran	15	0.04
Other Central American	3	0.01
Cuban	36	0.09
Dominican Republic	4	0.01
Mexican	2,024	5.02
Puerto Rican	79	0.20
South American:	65	0.16
Argentinean	6	0.01
Bolivian	2	0.00
Chilean	7	0.02
Colombian	8	0.02
Ecuadorian	4	0.01
Peruvian	17	0.04
Venezuelan	10	0.02
Other South American	11	0.03
Other Hispanic or Latino	1,143	2.83
Hungarian	131	0.32
Icelander	6	0.01
Iranian	23	0.06
Irish	6,373	15.77
Italian	1,880	4.65
Latvian	32	0.08
Lithuanian	120	0.30
Northern European	72	0.18
Norwegian	1,230	3.04
Pennsylvania German	8	0.02
Polish	1,312	3.25
Portuguese	56	0.14
Romanian	13	0.03
Russian	420	1.04
Scandinavian	152	0.38
Scotch-Irish	940	2.33
Scottish	1,147	2.84
Serbian	28	0.07
Slavic	42	0.10
Slovak	91	0.23
Slovene	30	0.07
Swedish	1,473	3.64
Swiss	278	0.69
Ukrainian	187	0.46
United States or American	2,458	6.08
Welsh	559	1.38
West Indian, excl. Hispanic:	19	0.05
Belizean	13	0.03
Jamaican	6	0.01
White:	37,748	93.57
Not Hispanic (35,010)	35,538	88.10
Hispanic (2,011)	2,210	5.48
Yugoslavian	231	0.57

Longmont

Place Type: City
County: Boulder
Population: 71,093

Ancestry/Race	Number	%
Acadian/Cajun	14	0.02
African American/Black:	541	0.76
Not Hispanic (363)	484	0.68
Hispanic (22)	57	0.08
African, sub-Saharan:	136	0.19
African	60	0.08
Nigerian	7	0.01
Senegalese	7	0.01
South African	51	0.07
Other sub-Saharan African	11	0.02
Alaska Native tribes, specified:	17	0.02
Alaska Athabascan (2)	2	0.00
Aleut (4)	6	0.01
Eskimo (1)	6	0.01
All other tribes (3)	3	0.00
Am. Ind. or Alaska Nat., not spec.	329	0.46
American Indian tribes, specified:	745	1.05
Apache (29)	50	0.07
Blackfeet (12)	21	0.03
Cherokee (56)	189	0.27
Cheyenne (2)	3	0.00
Chickasaw (2)	6	0.01
Chippewa (17)	26	0.04
Choctaw (25)	34	0.05
Comanche (1)	2	0.00
Cree	2	0.00
Creek (3)	9	0.01

Notes: 1. Figures in the "Number" column do not add up to the total population due to: a) Ancestry/Race overlap — e.g. persons can report being both White and Irish, b) persons of Hispanic origin can report being any race, c) persons reporting two ancestries are counted in both categories. 2. Numbers in parentheses indicate the number of persons reporting this ancestry/race alone, not in combination with any other ancestry/race. 3. Refer to the Explanation of Data in the front of the book for more detailed information.

Delaware (8)	9	0.01
Houma (1)	3	0.00
Iroquois (12)	24	0.03
Kiowa	1	0.00
Latin American Indians (52)	91	0.13
Lumbee	3	0.00
Menominee (4)	4	0.01
Navajo (54)	85	0.12
Osage (1)	6	0.01
Potawatomi (1)	3	0.00
Pueblo (14)	16	0.02
Seminole (1)	5	0.01
Shoshone	6	0.01
Sioux (65)	84	0.12
Tohono O'Odham (1)	1	0.00
Ute (5)	11	0.02
Yaqui (2)	2	0.00
All other tribes (38)	49	0.07
American Indian tribes, not spec.	57	0.08
Arab:	142	0.20
Iraqi	9	0.01
Jordanian	25	0.04
Lebanese	78	0.11
Moroccan	7	0.01
Palestinian	7	0.01
Other Arab	16	0.02
Armenian	34	0.05
Asian:	1,617	2.27
Bangladeshi (3)	3	0.00
Cambodian (142)	166	0.23
Chinese, ex. Taiwanese (251)	308	0.43
Filipino (107)	177	0.25
Indian (189)	219	0.31
Indonesian (5)	10	0.01
Japanese (145)	245	0.34
Korean (153)	183	0.26
Laotian (15)	16	0.02
Malaysian (6)	8	0.01
Pakistani (5)	6	0.01
Sri Lankan (3)	3	0.00
Taiwanese (6)	6	0.01
Thai (20)	36	0.05
Vietnamese (151)	168	0.24
Other Asian, specified (7)	14	0.02
Other Asian, not specified (26)	49	0.07
Assyrian/Chaldean/Syriac	12	0.02
Australian	8	0.01
Austrian	112	0.16
Basque	22	0.03
Belgian	290	0.41
British	243	0.34
Bulgarian	20	0.03
Canadian	161	0.23
Celtic	66	0.09
Croatian	200	0.28
Czech	435	0.61
Czechoslovakian	187	0.26
Danish	1,022	1.43
Dutch	1,554	2.18
Eastern European	11	0.02
English	9,137	12.81
European	884	1.24
Finnish	105	0.15
French, except Basque	2,330	3.27
French Canadian	533	0.75
German	17,529	24.58
German Russian	6	0.01
Greek	142	0.20
Hawaii Native/Pacific Islander:	103	0.14
Micronesian: (5)	10	0.01
Guamanian/Chamorro (5)	10	0.01
Polynesian: (32)	56	0.08
Native Hawaiian (16)	37	0.05
Samoan (9)	10	0.01
Tongan (7)	8	0.01
Other Polynesian	1	0.00
Other Pac. Isl., not spec. (6)	37	0.05
Hispanic or Latino:	13,558	19.07
Central American:	124	0.17
Costa Rican	2	0.00
Guatemalan	66	0.09
Honduran	17	0.02
Nicaraguan	4	0.01
Panamanian	7	0.01
Salvadoran	18	0.03
Other Central American	10	0.01
Cuban	47	0.07
Dominican Republic	6	0.01
Mexican	10,253	14.42
Puerto Rican	157	0.22
South American:	119	0.17
Argentinean	9	0.01
Bolivian	1	0.00
Chilean	7	0.01
Colombian	27	0.04
Ecuadorian	9	0.01
Peruvian	45	0.06
Uruguayan	2	0.00
Venezuelan	4	0.01
Other South American	15	0.02
Other Hispanic or Latino	2,852	4.01
Hungarian	242	0.34
Icelander	7	0.01
Iranian	40	0.06
Irish	8,821	12.37
Italian	3,009	4.22
Latvian	46	0.06
Lithuanian	107	0.15
Luxemburger	19	0.03
Macedonian	12	0.02
New Zealander	5	0.01
Northern European	122	0.17
Norwegian	2,005	2.81
Pennsylvania German	75	0.11
Polish	1,953	2.74
Portuguese	64	0.09
Romanian	71	0.10
Russian	597	0.84
Scandinavian	274	0.38
Scotch-Irish	1,495	2.10
Scottish	2,116	2.97
Serbian	32	0.04
Slavic	54	0.08
Slovak	121	0.17
Slovene	31	0.04
Swedish	2,189	3.07
Swiss	365	0.51
Ukrainian	250	0.35
United States or American	3,689	5.17
Welsh	923	1.29
West Indian, excl. Hispanic:	20	0.03
Belizean	11	0.02
West Indian	9	0.01
White:	61,639	86.70
Not Hispanic (54,599)	55,352	77.86
Hispanic (5,656)	6,287	8.84
Yugoslavian	117	0.16

Louisville

Place Type: City
County: Boulder
Population: 18,937

Ancestry/Race	Number	%
African American/Black:	245	1.29
Not Hispanic (163)	223	1.18
Hispanic (14)	22	0.12
African, sub-Saharan:	34	0.18
African	5	0.03
Ethiopian	29	0.15
Alaska Native tribes, specified:	2	0.01
Alaska Athabascan (1)	1	0.01
Aleut	1	0.01
Am. Ind. or Alaska Nat., not spec.	63	0.33
American Indian tribes, specified:	142	0.75
Apache (6)	12	0.06
Blackfeet (1)	3	0.02
Cherokee (11)	38	0.20
Cheyenne (1)	4	0.02
Chickasaw (2)	4	0.02
Chippewa	1	0.01
Choctaw (6)	12	0.06
Comanche (2)	4	0.02
Cree	1	0.01
Creek (2)	2	0.01
Iroquois	2	0.01
Kiowa (2)	2	0.01
Latin American Indians (6)	8	0.04
Navajo (6)	10	0.05
Potawatomi (2)	3	0.02
Pueblo (6)	8	0.04
Seminole	2	0.01
Sioux (4)	8	0.04
Ute (1)	3	0.02
Yuman (1)	3	0.02
All other tribes (8)	12	0.06
American Indian tribes, not spec.	9	0.05
Arab:	112	0.59
Iraqi	14	0.07
Lebanese	62	0.33
Syrian	36	0.19
Armenian	50	0.26
Asian:	817	4.31
Cambodian (20)	20	0.11
Chinese, ex. Taiwanese (262)	294	1.55
Filipino (30)	48	0.25
Hmong (16)	16	0.08
Indian (104)	122	0.64
Indonesian (1)	1	0.01
Japanese (90)	132	0.70
Korean (46)	72	0.38
Malaysian (1)	1	0.01
Pakistani (1)	1	0.01
Sri Lankan (5)	12	0.06
Taiwanese (4)	5	0.03
Thai (6)	12	0.06
Vietnamese (58)	60	0.32
Other Asian, specified (2)	2	0.01
Other Asian, not specified (6)	19	0.10
Austrian	135	0.72
Belgian	35	0.19
British	185	0.98
Canadian	91	0.48
Croatian	47	0.25
Czech	165	0.87
Czechoslovakian	60	0.32
Danish	448	2.37
Dutch	493	2.61
Eastern European	32	0.17
English	3,041	16.12
European	450	2.38
Finnish	83	0.44
French, except Basque	616	3.26
French Canadian	230	1.22
German	5,303	28.11
Greek	95	0.50
Hawaii Native/Pacific Islander:	36	0.19
Micronesian: (2)	4	0.02
Guamanian/Chamorro (2)	4	0.02
Polynesian: (11)	24	0.13
Native Hawaiian (11)	23	0.12
Samoan	1	0.01
Other Pac. Isl., not spec. (3)	8	0.04
Hispanic or Latino:	950	5.02
Central American:	20	0.11
Guatemalan	4	0.02
Nicaraguan	5	0.03
Panamanian	3	0.02
Salvadoran	4	0.02
Other Central American	4	0.02
Cuban	20	0.11
Dominican Republic	9	0.05
Mexican	491	2.59
Puerto Rican	34	0.18
South American:	39	0.21
Argentinean	7	0.04
Bolivian	2	0.01
Chilean	2	0.01
Colombian	11	0.06

Notes: 1. Figures in the "Number" column do not add up to the total population due to: a) Ancestry/Race overlap — e.g. persons can report being both White and Irish, b) persons of Hispanic origin can report being any race, c) persons reporting two ancestries are counted in both categories. 2. Numbers in parentheses indicate the number of persons reporting this ancestry/race alone, not in combination with any other ancestry/race. 3. Refer to the Explanation of Data in the front of the book for more detailed information.

Ancestry/Race	Number	%
Ecuadorian	1	0.01
Peruvian	9	0.05
Uruguayan	4	0.02
Venezuelan	3	0.02
Other Hispanic or Latino	337	1.78
Hungarian	128	0.68
Icelander	6	0.03
Iranian	43	0.23
Irish	3,265	17.30
Italian	1,189	6.30
Latvian	52	0.28
Lithuanian	19	0.10
Northern European	20	0.11
Norwegian	609	3.23
Pennsylvania German	8	0.04
Polish	919	4.87
Portuguese	87	0.46
Romanian	46	0.24
Russian	341	1.81
Scandinavian	94	0.50
Scotch-Irish	360	1.91
Scottish	782	4.14
Serbian	10	0.05
Slavic	24	0.13
Slovak	99	0.52
Slovene	16	0.08
Swedish	725	3.84
Swiss	117	0.62
Ukrainian	72	0.38
United States or American	697	3.69
Welsh	307	1.63
West Indian, excl. Hispanic:	32	0.17
Jamaican	8	0.04
West Indian	24	0.13
White:	17,601	92.95
Not Hispanic (16,774)	17,034	89.95
Hispanic (490)	567	2.99
Yugoslavian	66	0.35

Loveland

Place Type: City
County: Larimer
Population: 50,608

Ancestry/Race	Number	%
Acadian/Cajun	18	0.04
African American/Black:	312	0.62
Not Hispanic (175)	278	0.55
Hispanic (13)	34	0.07
African, sub-Saharan:	17	0.03
African	17	0.03
Alaska Native tribes, specified:	6	0.01
Alaska Athabascan	2	0.00
Eskimo (1)	2	0.00
Tlingit-Haida	1	0.00
All other tribes (1)	1	0.00
Am. Ind. or Alaska Nat., not spec.	219	0.43
American Indian tribes, specified:	451	0.89
Apache (17)	51	0.10
Blackfeet (3)	15	0.03
Cherokee (45)	119	0.24
Cheyenne (1)	2	0.00
Chickasaw (1)	2	0.00
Chippewa (12)	19	0.04
Choctaw (8)	18	0.04
Comanche	1	0.00
Cree	2	0.00
Creek	1	0.00
Delaware (1)	1	0.00
Iroquois (4)	5	0.01
Kiowa (1)	5	0.01
Latin American Indians (12)	32	0.06
Menominee (1)	1	0.00
Navajo (23)	37	0.07
Osage (1)	1	0.00
Pima	1	0.00
Potawatomi (2)	9	0.02
Pueblo (6)	9	0.02
Puget Sound Salish (1)	1	0.00
Seminole (2)	2	0.00
Shoshone	2	0.00
Sioux (52)	68	0.13
Ute (4)	8	0.02
Yaqui (2)	2	0.00
All other tribes (18)	37	0.07
American Indian tribes, not spec.	52	0.10
Arab:	16	0.03
Arab/Arabic	8	0.02
Syrian	8	0.02
Asian:	619	1.22
Cambodian	3	0.01
Chinese, ex. Taiwanese (73)	102	0.20
Filipino (64)	102	0.20
Indian (36)	48	0.09
Japanese (63)	128	0.25
Korean (61)	77	0.15
Malaysian (2)	5	0.01
Pakistani (4)	4	0.01
Taiwanese (1)	4	0.01
Thai (6)	10	0.02
Vietnamese (81)	102	0.20
Other Asian, specified	3	0.01
Other Asian, not specified (18)	31	0.06
Assyrian/Chaldean/Syriac	9	0.02
Australian	36	0.07
Austrian	131	0.26
Basque	26	0.05
Belgian	70	0.14
Brazilian	12	0.02
British	206	0.41
Bulgarian	21	0.04
Canadian	140	0.28
Croatian	19	0.04
Czech	369	0.73
Czechoslovakian	144	0.28
Danish	825	1.63
Dutch	1,497	2.95
Eastern European	6	0.01
English	7,163	14.13
Estonian	7	0.01
European	584	1.15
Finnish	118	0.23
French, except Basque	1,959	3.87
French Canadian	444	0.88
German	15,943	31.46
German Russian	6	0.01
Greek	145	0.29
Hawaii Native/Pacific Islander:	50	0.10
Micronesian: (9)	13	0.03
Guamanian/Chamorro (5)	7	0.01
Other Micronesian (4)	6	0.01
Polynesian: (4)	28	0.06
Native Hawaiian (4)	25	0.05
Samoan	3	0.01
Other Pac. Isl., specified	1	0.00
Other Pac. Isl., not spec. (2)	8	0.02
Hispanic or Latino:	4,337	8.57
Central American:	18	0.04
Costa Rican	5	0.01
Guatemalan	8	0.02
Panamanian	2	0.00
Salvadoran	3	0.01
Cuban	17	0.03
Mexican	2,777	5.49
Puerto Rican	51	0.10
South American:	46	0.09
Argentinean	2	0.00
Bolivian	5	0.01
Chilean	1	0.00
Colombian	10	0.02
Peruvian	23	0.05
Other South American	5	0.01
Other Hispanic or Latino	1,428	2.82
Hungarian	150	0.30
Icelander	10	0.02
Iranian	33	0.07
Irish	6,520	12.87
Italian	1,977	3.90
Lithuanian	41	0.08
Northern European	110	0.22
Norwegian	2,101	4.15
Pennsylvania German	34	0.07
Polish	1,070	2.11
Portuguese	117	0.23
Romanian	9	0.02
Russian	631	1.25
Scandinavian	162	0.32
Scotch-Irish	1,203	2.37
Scottish	1,194	2.36
Serbian	15	0.03
Slavic	6	0.01
Slovak	65	0.13
Slovene	23	0.05
Swedish	2,242	4.42
Swiss	287	0.57
Ukrainian	58	0.11
United States or American	2,825	5.57
Welsh	553	1.09
West Indian, excl. Hispanic:	16	0.03
Dutch West Indian	9	0.02
Haitian	7	0.01
White:	47,949	94.75
Not Hispanic (44,853)	45,382	89.67
Hispanic (2,137)	2,567	5.07
Yugoslavian	41	0.08

Montrose

Place Type: City
County: Montrose
Population: 12,344

Ancestry/Race	Number	%
African American/Black:	84	0.68
Not Hispanic (41)	56	0.45
Hispanic (13)	28	0.23
Alaska Native tribes, specified:	1	0.01
Eskimo (1)	1	0.01
Alaska Native tribes, not specified	1	0.01
Am. Ind. or Alaska Nat., not spec.	66	0.53
American Indian tribes, specified:	157	1.27
Apache (7)	15	0.12
Cherokee (13)	38	0.31
Chickasaw	1	0.01
Chippewa	1	0.01
Choctaw (1)	1	0.01
Delaware	1	0.01
Iroquois (1)	8	0.06
Latin American Indians (14)	28	0.23
Navajo (12)	16	0.13
Osage (1)	2	0.02
Pueblo (1)	10	0.08
Sioux (4)	11	0.09
Ute (3)	11	0.09
All other tribes (13)	14	0.11
American Indian tribes, not spec.	14	0.11
Asian:	94	0.76
Chinese, ex. Taiwanese (10)	13	0.11
Filipino (31)	41	0.33
Indian (2)	6	0.05
Japanese (5)	10	0.08
Korean (15)	16	0.13
Vietnamese (7)	8	0.06
Austrian	25	0.20
Basque	19	0.15
Belgian	7	0.06
British	51	0.41
Canadian	29	0.23
Croatian	42	0.34
Czech	48	0.39
Danish	158	1.28
Dutch	317	2.56
English	1,853	14.99
European	173	1.40
Finnish	15	0.12
French, except Basque	315	2.55
French Canadian	142	1.15
German	2,720	22.00
Greek	15	0.12

Notes: 1. Figures in the "Number" column do not add up to the total population due to: a) Ancestry/Race overlap — e.g. persons can report being both White and Irish, b) persons of Hispanic origin can report being any race, c) persons reporting two ancestries are counted in both categories. 2. Numbers in parentheses indicate the number of persons reporting this ancestry/race alone, not in combination with any other ancestry/race. 3. Refer to the Explanation of Data in the front of the book for more detailed information.

Hawaii Native/Pacific Islander:	16	0.13
Melanesian: (1)	1	0.01
Other Melanesian (1)	1	0.01
Polynesian: (7)	12	0.10
Native Hawaiian (3)	8	0.06
Samoan (4)	4	0.03
Other Pac. Isl., not spec. (1)	3	0.02
Hispanic or Latino:	2,143	17.36
Central American:	15	0.12
Costa Rican	2	0.02
Honduran	2	0.02
Panamanian	5	0.04
Salvadoran	5	0.04
Other Central American	1	0.01
Cuban	3	0.02
Dominican Republic	4	0.03
Mexican	1,437	11.64
Puerto Rican	4	0.03
South American:	10	0.08
Argentinean	1	0.01
Colombian	9	0.07
Other Hispanic or Latino	670	5.43
Hungarian	16	0.13
Irish	1,670	13.51
Italian	504	4.08
Lithuanian	7	0.06
Norwegian	120	0.97
Polish	239	1.93
Portuguese	50	0.40
Romanian	6	0.05
Russian	29	0.23
Scandinavian	9	0.07
Scotch-Irish	277	2.24
Scottish	378	3.06
Slovak	16	0.13
Slovene	12	0.10
Swedish	430	3.48
Swiss	54	0.44
United States or American	698	5.64
Welsh	92	0.74
White:	11,241	91.06
Not Hispanic (9,877)	9,981	80.86
Hispanic (1,110)	1,260	10.21
Yugoslavian	7	0.06

Northglenn

Place Type: City
County: Adams
Population: 31,575

Ancestry/Race	Number	%
Afghan	57	0.18
African American/Black:	616	1.95
Not Hispanic (432)	549	1.74
Hispanic (49)	67	0.21
African, sub-Saharan:	101	0.32
African	43	0.14
Cape Verdean	19	0.06
Ethiopian	28	0.09
Liberian	11	0.03
Alaska Native tribes, specified:	7	0.02
Alaska Athabascan	1	0.00
Aleut (2)	2	0.01
Eskimo	4	0.01
Alaska Native tribes, not specified	4	0.01
Am. Ind. or Alaska Nat., not spec.	232	0.73
American Indian tribes, specified:	382	1.21
Apache (27)	56	0.18
Blackfeet (2)	6	0.02
Cherokee (35)	86	0.27
Cheyenne (1)	3	0.01
Chickasaw (1)	2	0.01
Chippewa (3)	8	0.03
Choctaw (8)	14	0.04
Comanche	3	0.01
Creek (1)	2	0.01
Delaware	1	0.00
Iroquois (4)	5	0.02
Kiowa (3)	3	0.01
Latin American Indians (11)	25	0.08
Navajo (26)	42	0.13
Osage (3)	5	0.02
Ottawa	1	0.00
Paiute (1)	2	0.01
Pima (1)	3	0.01
Potawatomi	2	0.01
Pueblo (12)	25	0.08
Puget Sound Salish	5	0.02
Seminole	5	0.02
Shoshone (9)	11	0.03
Sioux (31)	44	0.14
Ute (1)	4	0.01
All other tribes (13)	19	0.06
American Indian tribes, not spec.	24	0.08
Arab:	32	0.10
Iraqi	19	0.06
Lebanese	13	0.04
Asian:	1,207	3.82
Cambodian (10)	14	0.04
Chinese, ex. Taiwanese (125)	163	0.52
Filipino (90)	138	0.44
Hmong (139)	145	0.46
Indian (74)	90	0.29
Indonesian (4)	5	0.02
Japanese (112)	169	0.54
Korean (65)	81	0.26
Laotian (46)	66	0.21
Pakistani (17)	22	0.07
Taiwanese (2)	4	0.01
Thai (2)	2	0.01
Vietnamese (204)	239	0.76
Other Asian, specified (3)	7	0.02
Other Asian, not specified (41)	62	0.20
Australian	20	0.06
Austrian	133	0.42
Basque	4	0.01
British	97	0.31
Bulgarian	73	0.23
Canadian	77	0.24
Croatian	64	0.20
Czech	164	0.52
Czechoslovakian	87	0.28
Danish	292	0.92
Dutch	619	1.96
English	3,520	11.13
Estonian	8	0.03
European	409	1.29
Finnish	100	0.32
French, except Basque	1,236	3.91
French Canadian	202	0.64
German	7,940	25.10
German Russian	13	0.04
Greek	77	0.24
Hawaii Native/Pacific Islander:	86	0.27
Micronesian: (20)	23	0.07
Guamanian/Chamorro (13)	16	0.05
Other Micronesian (7)	7	0.02
Polynesian: (15)	43	0.14
Native Hawaiian (6)	26	0.08
Samoan (7)	11	0.03
Other Polynesian (2)	6	0.02
Other Pac. Isl., specified	3	0.01
Other Pac. Isl., not spec. (12)	17	0.05
Hispanic or Latino:	6,399	20.27
Central American:	50	0.16
Costa Rican	8	0.03
Guatemalan	17	0.05
Honduran	2	0.01
Nicaraguan	3	0.01
Panamanian	5	0.02
Salvadoran	15	0.05
Cuban	15	0.05
Dominican Republic	5	0.02
Mexican	3,356	10.63
Puerto Rican	105	0.33
South American:	34	0.11
Argentinean	8	0.03
Bolivian	2	0.01
Chilean	1	0.00
Colombian	10	0.03
Ecuadorian	2	0.01
Peruvian	7	0.02
Venezuelan	3	0.01
Other South American	1	0.00
Other Hispanic or Latino	2,834	8.98
Hungarian	86	0.27
Iranian	80	0.25
Irish	4,247	13.43
Israeli	4	0.01
Italian	1,672	5.29
Latvian	6	0.02
Lithuanian	14	0.04
Luxemburger	9	0.03
Northern European	7	0.02
Norwegian	983	3.11
Pennsylvania German	13	0.04
Polish	704	2.23
Portuguese	53	0.17
Romanian	35	0.11
Russian	305	0.96
Scandinavian	54	0.17
Scotch-Irish	747	2.36
Scottish	602	1.90
Slavic	43	0.14
Slovak	54	0.17
Slovene	66	0.21
Swedish	752	2.38
Swiss	128	0.40
Ukrainian	76	0.24
United States or American	1,499	4.74
Welsh	243	0.77
West Indian, excl. Hispanic:	8	0.03
Dutch West Indian	8	0.03
White:	27,063	85.71
Not Hispanic (23,031)	23,482	74.37
Hispanic (3,190)	3,581	11.34
Yugoslavian	24	0.08

Parker

Place Type: Town
County: Douglas
Population: 23,558

Ancestry/Race	Number	%
African American/Black:	349	1.48
Not Hispanic (227)	328	1.39
Hispanic (10)	21	0.09
African, sub-Saharan:	11	0.05
African	11	0.05
Am. Ind. or Alaska Nat., not spec.	45	0.19
Albanian	38	0.16
American Indian tribes, specified:	158	0.67
Apache	8	0.03
Cherokee (17)	71	0.30
Cheyenne (1)	1	0.00
Chickasaw (1)	1	0.00
Chippewa (2)	3	0.01
Choctaw (8)	12	0.05
Comanche	1	0.00
Creek	2	0.01
Iroquois	5	0.02
Latin American Indians (5)	6	0.03
Navajo (8)	8	0.03
Osage (3)	4	0.02
Potawatomi (1)	1	0.00
Pueblo (1)	1	0.00
Seminole (1)	2	0.01
Shoshone (1)	1	0.00
Sioux (2)	7	0.03
Ute (3)	5	0.02
All other tribes (15)	19	0.08
American Indian tribes, not spec.	15	0.06
Arab:	61	0.26
Arab/Arabic	20	0.09
Jordanian	10	0.04
Lebanese	31	0.13
Armenian	38	0.16
Asian:	612	2.60

Notes: 1. Figures in the "Number" column do not add up to the total population due to: a) Ancestry/Race overlap — e.g. persons can report being both White and Irish, b) persons of Hispanic origin can report being any race, c) persons reporting two ancestries are counted in both categories. 2. Numbers in parentheses indicate the number of persons reporting this ancestry/race alone, not in combination with any other ancestry/race. 3. Refer to the Explanation of Data in the front of the book for more detailed information.

Ancestry/Race	Number	%
Cambodian (1)	3	0.01
Chinese, ex. Taiwanese (58)	92	0.39
Filipino (65)	121	0.51
Indian (57)	74	0.31
Indonesian (1)	3	0.01
Japanese (48)	98	0.42
Korean (84)	109	0.46
Laotian (4)	4	0.02
Malaysian	5	0.02
Pakistani (2)	4	0.02
Sri Lankan (1)	1	0.00
Taiwanese (5)	5	0.02
Thai (7)	7	0.03
Vietnamese (39)	51	0.22
Other Asian, specified (2)	8	0.03
Other Asian, not specified (13)	27	0.11
Australian	40	0.17
Austrian	42	0.18
Belgian	96	0.41
British	273	1.16
Canadian	106	0.45
Celtic	40	0.17
Croatian	90	0.38
Czech	146	0.62
Czechoslovakian	135	0.57
Danish	266	1.13
Dutch	649	2.76
English	2,666	11.34
Estonian	12	0.05
European	199	0.85
Finnish	72	0.31
French, except Basque	865	3.68
French Canadian	270	1.15
German	6,877	29.25
German Russian	7	0.03
Greek	79	0.34
Hawaii Native/Pacific Islander:	38	0.16
Micronesian: (1)	9	0.04
Guamanian/Chamorro (1)	5	0.02
Other Micronesian	4	0.02
Polynesian: (5)	18	0.08
Native Hawaiian (4)	16	0.07
Samoan (1)	2	0.01
Other Pac. Isl., specified	1	0.00
Other Pac. Isl., not spec. (1)	10	0.04
Hispanic or Latino:	1,366	5.80
Central American:	23	0.10
Costa Rican	4	0.02
Guatemalan	6	0.03
Honduran	8	0.03
Panamanian	1	0.00
Salvadoran	3	0.01
Other Central American	1	0.00
Cuban	21	0.09
Dominican Republic	13	0.06
Mexican	683	2.90
Puerto Rican	82	0.35
South American:	48	0.20
Argentinean	3	0.01
Chilean	5	0.02
Colombian	18	0.08
Ecuadorian	4	0.02
Peruvian	14	0.06
Venezuelan	1	0.00
Other South American	3	0.01
Other Hispanic or Latino	496	2.11
Hungarian	158	0.67
Icelander	28	0.12
Irish	3,855	16.39
Israeli	15	0.06
Italian	1,840	7.83
Latvian	18	0.08
Lithuanian	66	0.28
Northern European	62	0.26
Norwegian	786	3.34
Pennsylvania German	22	0.09
Polish	867	3.69
Portuguese	41	0.17
Romanian	32	0.14
Russian	343	1.46
Scandinavian	159	0.68
Scotch-Irish	560	2.38
Scottish	590	2.51
Serbian	9	0.04
Slavic	17	0.07
Slovak	45	0.19
Slovene	13	0.06
Swedish	1,013	4.31
Swiss	91	0.39
Ukrainian	48	0.20
United States or American	1,694	7.20
Welsh	389	1.65
West Indian, excl. Hispanic:	30	0.13
U.S. Virgin Islander	30	0.13
White:	22,321	94.75
Not Hispanic (21,084)	21,426	90.95
Hispanic (730)	895	3.80
Yugoslavian	40	0.17

Pueblo West

Place Type: Census Designated Place
County: Pueblo
Population: 16,899

Ancestry/Race	Number	%
African American/Black:	189	1.12
Not Hispanic (122)	166	0.98
Hispanic (19)	23	0.14
African, sub-Saharan:	12	0.07
Somalian	12	0.07
Alaska Native tribes, specified:	2	0.01
Aleut	1	0.01
Tlingit-Haida (1)	1	0.01
Am. Ind. or Alaska Nat., not spec.	76	0.45
American Indian tribes, specified:	230	1.36
Apache (13)	31	0.18
Blackfeet (1)	8	0.05
Cherokee (36)	81	0.48
Cheyenne (4)	4	0.02
Chickasaw (2)	6	0.04
Chippewa (4)	5	0.03
Choctaw (5)	13	0.08
Colville	1	0.01
Comanche (5)	8	0.05
Creek (1)	1	0.01
Iroquois (1)	1	0.01
Latin American Indians (5)	6	0.04
Navajo (17)	22	0.13
Ottawa (1)	3	0.02
Pueblo (1)	3	0.02
Seminole (1)	4	0.02
Sioux (3)	13	0.08
Ute (1)	1	0.01
All other tribes (12)	19	0.11
American Indian tribes, not spec.	19	0.11
Asian:	260	1.54
Cambodian (1)	3	0.02
Chinese, ex. Taiwanese (19)	28	0.17
Filipino (33)	51	0.30
Indian (21)	21	0.12
Japanese (23)	47	0.28
Korean (32)	45	0.27
Pakistani (3)	3	0.02
Thai (2)	2	0.01
Vietnamese (29)	32	0.19
Other Asian, not specified (12)	28	0.17
Australian	31	0.18
Austrian	106	0.62
Basque	11	0.06
British	47	0.28
Canadian	19	0.11
Czech	31	0.18
Czechoslovakian	41	0.24
Danish	88	0.52
Dutch	394	2.32
English	2,069	12.17
European	119	0.70
Finnish	17	0.10
French, except Basque	637	3.75
French Canadian	146	0.86
German	3,336	19.63
Greek	11	0.06
Hawaii Native/Pacific Islander:	41	0.24
Micronesian: (6)	6	0.04
Guamanian/Chamorro (6)	6	0.04
Polynesian: (4)	22	0.13
Native Hawaiian (2)	15	0.09
Samoan (2)	7	0.04
Other Pac. Isl., not spec. (2)	13	0.08
Hispanic or Latino:	3,092	18.30
Central American:	11	0.07
Guatemalan	5	0.03
Panamanian	2	0.01
Salvadoran	4	0.02
Cuban	7	0.04
Mexican	1,282	7.59
Puerto Rican	39	0.23
South American:	25	0.15
Chilean	9	0.05
Colombian	5	0.03
Peruvian	10	0.06
Venezuelan	1	0.01
Other Hispanic or Latino	1,728	10.23
Hungarian	65	0.38
Iranian	8	0.05
Irish	2,113	12.43
Italian	1,746	10.27
Latvian	11	0.06
Lithuanian	58	0.34
Northern European	23	0.14
Norwegian	377	2.22
Polish	427	2.51
Portuguese	7	0.04
Russian	44	0.26
Scandinavian	47	0.28
Scotch-Irish	334	1.97
Scottish	475	2.79
Serbian	7	0.04
Slovak	49	0.29
Slovene	127	0.75
Swedish	337	1.98
Swiss	36	0.21
Ukrainian	8	0.05
United States or American	915	5.38
Welsh	133	0.78
West Indian, excl. Hispanic:	11	0.06
Barbadian	11	0.06
White:	15,341	90.78
Not Hispanic (13,122)	13,329	78.87
Hispanic (1,825)	2,012	11.91
Yugoslavian	115	0.68

Pueblo

Place Type: City
County: Pueblo
Population: 102,121

Ancestry/Race	Number	%
Acadian/Cajun	17	0.02
African American/Black:	2,979	2.92
Not Hispanic (2,199)	2,443	2.39
Hispanic (266)	536	0.52
African, sub-Saharan:	206	0.20
African	170	0.17
Nigerian	13	0.01
South African	10	0.01
Other sub-Saharan African	13	0.01
Alaska Native tribes, specified:	10	0.01
Aleut (2)	5	0.00
Eskimo (1)	1	0.00
Tlingit-Haida	4	0.00
Alaska Native tribes, not specified	1	0.00
Am. Ind. or Alaska Nat., not spec.	1,109	1.09
American Indian tribes, specified:	1,527	1.50
Apache (187)	332	0.33
Blackfeet (19)	47	0.05
Cherokee (117)	311	0.30
Cheyenne (6)	23	0.02

Notes: 1. Figures in the "Number" column do not add up to the total population due to: a) Ancestry/Race overlap — e.g. persons can report being both White and Irish, b) persons of Hispanic origin can report being any race, c) persons reporting two ancestries are counted in both categories. 2. Numbers in parentheses indicate the number of persons reporting this ancestry/race alone, not in combination with any other ancestry/race. 3. Refer to the Explanation of Data in the front of the book for more detailed information.

Ancestry/Race	Number	%
Chickasaw (6)	13	0.01
Chippewa (22)	47	0.05
Choctaw (20)	45	0.04
Comanche (7)	17	0.02
Cree (2)	2	0.00
Creek (2)	9	0.01
Crow (1)	2	0.00
Delaware (1)	3	0.00
Houma (1)	1	0.00
Iroquois (6)	11	0.01
Kiowa (14)	17	0.02
Latin American Indians (121)	170	0.17
Navajo (127)	200	0.20
Osage	4	0.00
Paiute (3)	3	0.00
Pima (2)	2	0.00
Potawatomi (17)	18	0.02
Pueblo (43)	61	0.06
Seminole (2)	12	0.01
Shoshone (3)	6	0.01
Sioux (39)	67	0.07
Ute (15)	26	0.03
Yaqui (1)	4	0.00
Yuman (1)	1	0.00
All other tribes (44)	73	0.07
American Indian tribes, not spec.	247	0.24
Arab:	187	0.18
Arab/Arabic	61	0.06
Jordanian	12	0.01
Lebanese	95	0.09
Syrian	19	0.02
Asian:	1,013	0.99
Bangladeshi (2)	2	0.00
Cambodian (8)	8	0.01
Chinese, ex. Taiwanese (111)	145	0.14
Filipino (94)	181	0.18
Hmong (2)	2	0.00
Indian (105)	138	0.14
Indonesian (13)	14	0.01
Japanese (125)	198	0.19
Korean (92)	125	0.12
Malaysian (1)	1	0.00
Pakistani (15)	18	0.02
Taiwanese (7)	11	0.01
Thai (17)	21	0.02
Vietnamese (35)	55	0.05
Other Asian, specified	4	0.00
Other Asian, not specified (44)	90	0.09
Australian	12	0.01
Austrian	489	0.48
Basque	10	0.01
Belgian	69	0.07
Brazilian	10	0.01
British	150	0.15
Bulgarian	23	0.02
Canadian	124	0.12
Celtic	50	0.05
Croatian	223	0.22
Czech	199	0.19
Czechoslovakian	190	0.19
Danish	462	0.45
Dutch	1,005	0.98
Eastern European	23	0.02
English	6,785	6.64
European	365	0.36
Finnish	101	0.10
French, except Basque	2,139	2.09
French Canadian	249	0.24
German	11,989	11.73
Greek	168	0.16
Hawaii Native/Pacific Islander:	177	0.17
Micronesian: (24)	32	0.03
Guamanian/Chamorro (23)	31	0.03
Other Micronesian (1)	1	0.00
Polynesian: (33)	102	0.10
Native Hawaiian (23)	81	0.08
Samoan (10)	21	0.02
Other Pac. Isl., specified	4	0.00
Other Pac. Isl., not spec. (5)	39	0.04
Hispanic or Latino:	45,066	44.13
Central American:	74	0.07
Costa Rican	14	0.01
Guatemalan	6	0.01
Honduran	13	0.01
Nicaraguan	4	0.00
Panamanian	9	0.01
Salvadoran	25	0.02
Other Central American	3	0.00
Cuban	42	0.04
Dominican Republic	1	0.00
Mexican	19,523	19.12
Puerto Rican	350	0.34
South American:	59	0.06
Argentinean	2	0.00
Bolivian	4	0.00
Chilean	7	0.01
Colombian	22	0.02
Ecuadorian	2	0.00
Peruvian	5	0.00
Venezuelan	15	0.01
Other South American	2	0.00
Other Hispanic or Latino	25,017	24.50
Hungarian	256	0.25
Icelander	7	0.01
Iranian	40	0.04
Irish	8,097	7.92
Italian	7,704	7.54
Latvian	20	0.02
Lithuanian	23	0.02
Luxemburger	4	0.00
Northern European	40	0.04
Norwegian	973	0.95
Pennsylvania German	43	0.04
Polish	1,314	1.29
Portuguese	137	0.13
Romanian	8	0.01
Russian	307	0.30
Scandinavian	95	0.09
Scotch-Irish	1,542	1.51
Scottish	1,292	1.26
Serbian	63	0.06
Slavic	365	0.36
Slovak	279	0.27
Slovene	1,298	1.27
Swedish	1,196	1.17
Swiss	245	0.24
Turkish	27	0.03
Ukrainian	65	0.06
United States or American	4,966	4.86
Welsh	644	0.63
West Indian, excl. Hispanic:	15	0.01
Dutch West Indian	12	0.01
Jamaican	3	0.00
White:	81,109	79.42
Not Hispanic (52,202)	53,280	52.17
Hispanic (25,628)	27,829	27.25
Yugoslavian	369	0.36

Security-Widefield

Place Type: Census Designated Place
County: El Paso
Population: 29,845

Ancestry/Race	Number	%
Acadian/Cajun	9	0.03
African American/Black:	3,691	12.37
Not Hispanic (3,046)	3,507	11.75
Hispanic (99)	184	0.62
African, sub-Saharan:	103	0.35
African	103	0.35
Alaska Native tribes, specified:	9	0.03
Alaska Athabascan (1)	1	0.00
Aleut	3	0.01
Eskimo (4)	4	0.01
Tlingit-Haida	1	0.00
Am. Ind. or Alaska Nat., not spec.	172	0.58
American Indian tribes, specified:	490	1.64
Apache (5)	28	0.09
Blackfeet (5)	21	0.07
Cherokee (34)	155	0.52
Cheyenne	4	0.01
Chickasaw	2	0.01
Chippewa (7)	16	0.05
Choctaw (4)	15	0.05
Comanche	3	0.01
Cree	4	0.01
Creek (6)	11	0.04
Iroquois (10)	20	0.07
Latin American Indians (10)	18	0.06
Menominee (1)	1	0.00
Navajo (21)	49	0.16
Osage	6	0.02
Ottawa (1)	5	0.02
Pueblo (11)	18	0.06
Seminole (4)	6	0.02
Shoshone (1)	1	0.00
Sioux (9)	26	0.09
Tohono O'Odham (4)	6	0.02
Ute (8)	15	0.05
Yuman	5	0.02
All other tribes (25)	55	0.18
American Indian tribes, not spec.	17	0.06
Arab:	26	0.09
Arab/Arabic	7	0.02
Lebanese	11	0.04
Syrian	8	0.03
Asian:	1,536	5.15
Chinese, ex. Taiwanese (30)	82	0.27
Filipino (315)	464	1.55
Indian (21)	31	0.10
Indonesian	3	0.01
Japanese (157)	283	0.95
Korean (278)	476	1.59
Malaysian	6	0.02
Taiwanese (2)	4	0.01
Thai (34)	66	0.22
Vietnamese (40)	77	0.26
Other Asian, specified (1)	9	0.03
Other Asian, not specified (15)	35	0.12
Australian	4	0.01
Austrian	98	0.33
Basque	6	0.02
Belgian	15	0.05
British	131	0.44
Canadian	70	0.24
Celtic	23	0.08
Croatian	45	0.15
Czech	78	0.26
Czechoslovakian	20	0.07
Danish	124	0.42
Dutch	500	1.68
Eastern European	13	0.04
English	2,833	9.53
European	370	1.24
Finnish	64	0.22
French, except Basque	999	3.36
French Canadian	290	0.98
German	6,791	22.84
German Russian	4	0.01
Greek	51	0.17
Guyanese	19	0.06
Hawaii Native/Pacific Islander:	348	1.17
Melanesian:	2	0.01
Other Melanesian	2	0.01
Micronesian: (82)	131	0.44
Guamanian/Chamorro (81)	128	0.43
Other Micronesian (1)	3	0.01
Polynesian: (75)	159	0.53
Native Hawaiian (34)	103	0.35
Samoan (37)	51	0.17
Tongan (4)	5	0.02
Other Pac. Isl., not spec. (11)	56	0.19
Hispanic or Latino:	3,763	12.61
Central American:	96	0.32
Costa Rican	8	0.03
Guatemalan	5	0.02
Honduran	13	0.04
Nicaraguan	1	0.00
Panamanian	55	0.18

Notes: 1. Figures in the "Number" column do not add up to the total population due to: a) Ancestry/Race overlap — e.g. persons can report being both White and Irish, b) persons of Hispanic origin can report being any race, c) persons reporting two ancestries are counted in both categories. 2. Numbers in parentheses indicate the number of persons reporting this ancestry/race alone, not in combination with any other ancestry/race. 3. Refer to the Explanation of Data in the front of the book for more detailed information.

Ancestry/Race	Number	%
Salvadoran	9	0.03
Other Central American	5	0.02
Cuban	17	0.06
Dominican Republic	10	0.03
Mexican	1,770	5.93
Puerto Rican	483	1.62
South American:	14	0.05
Argentinean	1	0.00
Chilean	1	0.00
Colombian	6	0.02
Ecuadorian	1	0.00
Peruvian	4	0.01
Venezuelan	1	0.00
Other Hispanic or Latino	1,373	4.60
Hungarian	163	0.55
Icelander	8	0.03
Iranian	7	0.02
Irish	3,123	10.50
Italian	1,002	3.37
Lithuanian	126	0.42
Northern European	47	0.16
Norwegian	602	2.02
Pennsylvania German	28	0.09
Polish	562	1.89
Portuguese	81	0.27
Romanian	61	0.21
Russian	104	0.35
Scandinavian	46	0.15
Scotch-Irish	435	1.46
Scottish	549	1.85
Serbian	23	0.08
Slavic	12	0.04
Slovak	38	0.13
Slovene	13	0.04
Swedish	528	1.78
Swiss	44	0.15
Turkish	7	0.02
Ukrainian	6	0.02
United States or American	2,026	6.81
Welsh	119	0.40
West Indian, excl. Hispanic:	76	0.26
Haitian	22	0.07
Jamaican	54	0.18
White:	23,464	78.62
Not Hispanic (20,535)	21,511	72.08
Hispanic (1,540)	1,953	6.54
Yugoslavian	20	0.07

Sherrelwood

Place Type: Census Designated Place
County: Adams
Population: 17,657

Ancestry/Race	Number	%
African American/Black:	270	1.53
Not Hispanic (192)	231	1.31
Hispanic (22)	39	0.22
African, sub-Saharan:	45	0.26
African	45	0.26
Alaska Native tribes, specified:	3	0.02
Eskimo	2	0.01
Tlingit-Haida (1)	1	0.01
Am. Ind. or Alaska Nat., not spec.	113	0.64
American Indian tribes, specified:	258	1.46
Apache (9)	21	0.12
Blackfeet (1)	10	0.06
Cherokee (19)	49	0.28
Cheyenne (1)	5	0.03
Chickasaw (3)	3	0.02
Chippewa	1	0.01
Choctaw (1)	4	0.02
Comanche	2	0.01
Creek (2)	2	0.01
Delaware	1	0.01
Iroquois (1)	2	0.01
Latin American Indians (14)	34	0.19
Navajo (15)	42	0.24
Ottawa (1)	1	0.01
Potawatomi	3	0.02
Pueblo (1)	3	0.02
Seminole (5)	6	0.03
Shoshone	3	0.02
Sioux (28)	30	0.17
Ute (4)	11	0.06
All other tribes (10)	25	0.14
American Indian tribes, not spec.	27	0.15
Arab:	39	0.22
Arab/Arabic	3	0.02
Lebanese	36	0.20
Asian:	716	4.06
Cambodian (4)	4	0.02
Chinese, ex. Taiwanese (52)	61	0.35
Filipino (42)	65	0.37
Hmong (122)	135	0.76
Indian (5)	16	0.09
Indonesian (1)	1	0.01
Japanese (104)	130	0.74
Korean (14)	17	0.10
Laotian (69)	77	0.44
Pakistani (4)	5	0.03
Taiwanese	2	0.01
Thai (5)	14	0.08
Vietnamese (148)	152	0.86
Other Asian, not specified (15)	37	0.21
Assyrian/Chaldean/Syriac	5	0.03
Austrian	12	0.07
Belgian	11	0.06
British	11	0.06
Canadian	11	0.06
Croatian	8	0.05
Czech	90	0.51
Danish	183	1.04
Dutch	380	2.16
English	1,180	6.69
European	246	1.40
Finnish	26	0.15
French, except Basque	443	2.51
French Canadian	170	0.96
German	3,109	17.63
Greek	34	0.19
Hawaii Native/Pacific Islander:	71	0.40
Micronesian: (11)	13	0.07
Guamanian/Chamorro (3)	4	0.02
Other Micronesian (8)	9	0.05
Polynesian: (17)	25	0.14
Native Hawaiian (11)	19	0.11
Samoan (6)	6	0.03
Other Pac. Isl., not spec. (5)	33	0.19
Hispanic or Latino:	7,032	39.83
Central American:	28	0.16
Costa Rican	1	0.01
Guatemalan	4	0.02
Panamanian	3	0.02
Salvadoran	17	0.10
Other Central American	3	0.02
Cuban	5	0.03
Dominican Republic	1	0.01
Mexican	4,249	24.06
Puerto Rican	40	0.23
South American:	15	0.08
Bolivian	2	0.01
Colombian	2	0.01
Ecuadorian	1	0.01
Peruvian	2	0.01
Venezuelan	6	0.03
Other South American	2	0.01
Other Hispanic or Latino	2,694	15.26
Hungarian	57	0.32
Icelander	5	0.03
Irish	1,744	9.89
Italian	792	4.49
Latvian	7	0.04
Lithuanian	5	0.03
Norwegian	288	1.63
Polish	328	1.86
Portuguese	41	0.23
Romanian	6	0.03
Russian	129	0.73
Scandinavian	21	0.12
Scotch-Irish	182	1.03
Scottish	203	1.15
Slovene	11	0.06
Swedish	218	1.24
Swiss	36	0.20
Ukrainian	25	0.14
United States or American	777	4.41
Welsh	90	0.51
White:	13,328	75.48
Not Hispanic (9,479)	9,674	54.79
Hispanic (3,236)	3,654	20.69

Southglenn

Place Type: Census Designated Place
County: Arapahoe
Population: 43,520

Ancestry/Race	Number	%
Acadian/Cajun	9	0.02
African American/Black:	457	1.05
Not Hispanic (331)	424	0.97
Hispanic (14)	33	0.08
African, sub-Saharan:	142	0.33
African	33	0.08
Cape Verdean	11	0.03
South African	29	0.07
Zimbabwean	69	0.16
Alaska Native tribes, specified:	4	0.01
Eskimo (3)	3	0.01
Tlingit-Haida (1)	1	0.00
Am. Ind. or Alaska Nat., not spec.	91	0.21
American Indian tribes, specified:	261	0.60
Apache (8)	15	0.03
Blackfeet (1)	5	0.01
Cherokee (42)	100	0.23
Cheyenne (1)	1	0.00
Chickasaw (6)	7	0.02
Chippewa (4)	7	0.02
Choctaw (5)	7	0.02
Comanche	1	0.00
Cree	1	0.00
Creek (5)	7	0.02
Delaware (1)	2	0.00
Houma	1	0.00
Iroquois (4)	7	0.02
Latin American Indians (7)	11	0.03
Navajo (14)	16	0.04
Osage (1)	2	0.00
Ottawa (1)	1	0.00
Potawatomi (1)	3	0.01
Pueblo (4)	8	0.02
Shoshone (3)	3	0.01
Sioux (14)	19	0.04
Ute (3)	10	0.02
All other tribes (16)	27	0.06
American Indian tribes, not spec.	18	0.04
Arab:	206	0.47
Arab/Arabic	12	0.03
Egyptian	29	0.07
Iraqi	6	0.01
Lebanese	96	0.22
Palestinian	63	0.14
Armenian	12	0.03
Asian:	1,017	2.34
Cambodian (7)	11	0.03
Chinese, ex. Taiwanese (206)	247	0.57
Filipino (62)	105	0.24
Indian (83)	99	0.23
Indonesian (8)	15	0.03
Japanese (97)	159	0.37
Korean (111)	125	0.29
Laotian (1)	4	0.01
Pakistani (8)	8	0.02
Sri Lankan (1)	1	0.00
Taiwanese (16)	20	0.05
Thai (37)	43	0.10
Vietnamese (136)	149	0.34
Other Asian, specified (5)	5	0.01
Other Asian, not specified (6)	26	0.06

Notes: 1. Figures in the "Number" column do not add up to the total population due to: a) Ancestry/Race overlap — e.g. persons can report being both White and Irish, b) persons of Hispanic origin can report being any race, c) persons reporting two ancestries are counted in both categories. 2. Numbers in parentheses indicate the number of persons reporting this ancestry/race alone, not in combination with any other ancestry/race. 3. Refer to the Explanation of Data in the front of the book for more detailed information.

Ancestry/Race	Number	%
Australian	21	0.05
Austrian	257	0.59
Belgian	73	0.17
British	282	0.65
Canadian	170	0.39
Celtic	40	0.09
Croatian	119	0.27
Czech	505	1.16
Czechoslovakian	93	0.21
Danish	591	1.36
Dutch	1,330	3.06
Eastern European	62	0.14
English	8,285	19.04
European	681	1.56
Finnish	151	0.35
French, except Basque	1,805	4.15
French Canadian	307	0.71
German	12,196	28.03
Greek	187	0.43
Hawaii Native/Pacific Islander:	48	0.11
Micronesian: (9)	15	0.03
Guamanian/Chamorro (7)	12	0.03
Other Micronesian (2)	3	0.01
Polynesian: (15)	26	0.06
Native Hawaiian (8)	17	0.04
Samoan (7)	9	0.02
Other Pac. Isl., not spec.	7	0.02
Hispanic or Latino:	1,758	4.04
Central American:	30	0.07
Costa Rican	7	0.02
Guatemalan	4	0.01
Honduran	4	0.01
Nicaraguan	5	0.01
Salvadoran	6	0.01
Other Central American	4	0.01
Cuban	38	0.09
Dominican Republic	4	0.01
Mexican	917	2.11
Puerto Rican	53	0.12
South American:	94	0.22
Argentinean	16	0.04
Bolivian	8	0.02
Chilean	16	0.04
Colombian	16	0.04
Ecuadorian	10	0.02
Paraguayan	3	0.01
Peruvian	14	0.03
Uruguayan	1	0.00
Venezuelan	2	0.00
Other South American	8	0.02
Other Hispanic or Latino	622	1.43
Hungarian	275	0.63
Icelander	6	0.01
Iranian	57	0.13
Irish	7,797	17.92
Italian	2,078	4.78
Lithuanian	148	0.34
Luxemburger	10	0.02
Northern European	80	0.18
Norwegian	1,643	3.78
Pennsylvania German	31	0.07
Polish	1,344	3.09
Portuguese	39	0.09
Romanian	80	0.18
Russian	557	1.28
Scandinavian	197	0.45
Scotch-Irish	1,319	3.03
Scottish	1,716	3.94
Serbian	42	0.10
Slavic	15	0.03
Slovak	73	0.17
Slovene	41	0.09
Swedish	1,773	4.07
Swiss	353	0.81
Turkish	9	0.02
Ukrainian	118	0.27
United States or American	2,230	5.12
Welsh	734	1.69
West Indian, excl. Hispanic:	45	0.10
Belizean	14	0.03
Jamaican	4	0.01
Trinidadian and Tobagonian	14	0.03
West Indian	13	0.03
White:	41,765	95.97
Not Hispanic (39,972)	40,417	92.87
Hispanic (1,200)	1,348	3.10
Yugoslavian	73	0.17

Sterling

Place Type: City
County: Logan
Population: 11,360

Ancestry/Race	Number	%
African American/Black:	116	1.02
Not Hispanic (83)	106	0.93
Hispanic (2)	10	0.09
African, sub-Saharan:	8	0.07
African	8	0.07
Alaska Native tribes, specified:	1	0.01
Alaska Athabascan (1)	1	0.01
Am. Ind. or Alaska Nat., not spec.	37	0.33
American Indian tribes, specified:	96	0.85
Apache (4)	5	0.04
Blackfeet	3	0.03
Cherokee (4)	15	0.13
Cheyenne (3)	4	0.04
Chippewa (2)	5	0.04
Choctaw	1	0.01
Creek (1)	1	0.01
Latin American Indians (10)	10	0.09
Navajo (3)	9	0.08
Osage (1)	1	0.01
Sioux (28)	34	0.30
Ute	2	0.02
All other tribes (4)	6	0.05
American Indian tribes, not spec.	9	0.08
Arab:	10	0.09
Arab/Arabic	10	0.09
Asian:	64	0.56
Chinese, ex. Taiwanese (12)	13	0.11
Filipino (10)	12	0.11
Indian (1)	6	0.05
Japanese (5)	9	0.08
Korean (9)	9	0.08
Thai (4)	8	0.07
Vietnamese (2)	2	0.02
Other Asian, specified (1)	1	0.01
Other Asian, not specified (3)	4	0.04
Austrian	17	0.15
British	54	0.48
Bulgarian	22	0.19
Canadian	18	0.16
Celtic	26	0.23
Croatian	15	0.13
Czech	114	1.01
Czechoslovakian	17	0.15
Danish	300	2.65
Dutch	269	2.37
Eastern European	6	0.05
English	1,083	9.55
Estonian	7	0.06
European	25	0.22
Finnish	8	0.07
French, except Basque	392	3.46
French Canadian	50	0.44
German	4,161	36.70
German Russian	19	0.17
Greek	6	0.05
Hawaii Native/Pacific Islander:	20	0.18
Melanesian: (2)	4	0.04
Fijian (2)	4	0.04
Micronesian: (3)	3	0.03
Guamanian/Chamorro (3)	3	0.03
Polynesian: (2)	10	0.09
Native Hawaiian	8	0.07
Samoan (2)	2	0.02
Other Pac. Isl., not spec. (2)	3	0.03
Hispanic or Latino:	1,613	14.20
Central American:	4	0.04
Guatemalan	2	0.02
Honduran	2	0.02
Cuban	3	0.03
Mexican	1,242	10.93
Puerto Rican	9	0.08
South American:	2	0.02
Peruvian	1	0.01
Venezuelan	1	0.01
Other Hispanic or Latino	353	3.11
Hungarian	8	0.07
Irish	1,103	9.73
Italian	205	1.81
Lithuanian	8	0.07
Norwegian	191	1.68
Pennsylvania German	5	0.04
Polish	149	1.31
Russian	125	1.10
Scandinavian	35	0.31
Scotch-Irish	242	2.13
Scottish	207	1.83
Serbian	8	0.07
Swedish	448	3.95
Swiss	50	0.44
Ukrainian	5	0.04
United States or American	646	5.70
Welsh	53	0.47
White:	10,483	92.28
Not Hispanic (9,463)	9,555	84.11
Hispanic (846)	928	8.17
Yugoslavian	9	0.08

Thornton

Place Type: City
County: Adams
Population: 82,384

Ancestry/Race	Number	%
Acadian/Cajun	29	0.04
Afghan	62	0.08
African American/Black:	1,576	1.91
Not Hispanic (1,106)	1,366	1.66
Hispanic (100)	210	0.25
African, sub-Saharan:	298	0.36
African	88	0.11
Ethiopian	10	0.01
Nigerian	79	0.10
South African	121	0.15
Alaska Native tribes, specified:	7	0.01
Alaska Athabascan (1)	1	0.00
Aleut (1)	1	0.00
Eskimo (1)	3	0.00
Tlingit-Haida (2)	2	0.00
Am. Ind. or Alaska Nat., not spec.	433	0.53
American Indian tribes, specified:	1,209	1.47
Apache (63)	132	0.16
Blackfeet (13)	33	0.04
Cherokee (107)	321	0.39
Cheyenne (4)	7	0.01
Chickasaw (1)	4	0.00
Chippewa (16)	35	0.04
Choctaw (15)	40	0.05
Comanche (2)	2	0.00
Creek (4)	10	0.01
Crow (6)	8	0.01
Delaware	1	0.00
Houma (1)	4	0.00
Iroquois (7)	16	0.02
Kiowa (10)	11	0.01
Latin American Indians (52)	64	0.08
Lumbee (1)	5	0.01
Menominee (2)	2	0.00
Navajo (91)	157	0.19
Osage (3)	7	0.01
Ottawa (1)	2	0.00
Paiute (5)	6	0.01
Potawatomi (8)	11	0.01
Pueblo (25)	39	0.05
Puget Sound Salish	4	0.00

Notes: 1. Figures in the "Number" column do not add up to the total population due to: a) Ancestry/Race overlap — e.g. persons can report being both White and Irish, b) persons of Hispanic origin can report being any race, c) persons reporting two ancestries are counted in both categories. 2. Numbers in parentheses indicate the number of persons reporting this ancestry/race alone, not in combination with any other ancestry/race. 3. Refer to the Explanation of Data in the front of the book for more detailed information.

Seminole (4)	5	0.01
Shoshone (4)	11	0.01
Sioux (120)	175	0.21
Tohono O'Odham	1	0.00
Ute (12)	21	0.03
Yaqui	1	0.00
Yuman (1)	1	0.00
All other tribes (39)	73	0.09
American Indian tribes, not spec.	98	0.12
Arab:	218	0.26
Arab/Arabic	24	0.03
Egyptian	30	0.04
Lebanese	118	0.14
Syrian	34	0.04
Other Arab	12	0.01
Armenian	42	0.05
Asian:	2,632	3.19
Bangladeshi (3)	3	0.00
Cambodian (50)	57	0.07
Chinese, ex. Taiwanese (266)	342	0.42
Filipino (202)	322	0.39
Hmong (279)	288	0.35
Indian (200)	247	0.30
Indonesian (10)	15	0.02
Japanese (201)	349	0.42
Korean (224)	284	0.34
Laotian (77)	96	0.12
Malaysian (12)	13	0.02
Pakistani (8)	12	0.01
Sri Lankan (1)	1	0.00
Taiwanese (10)	15	0.02
Thai (23)	33	0.04
Vietnamese (388)	423	0.51
Other Asian, specified (9)	16	0.02
Other Asian, not specified (49)	116	0.14
Australian	8	0.01
Austrian	368	0.45
Basque	8	0.01
Belgian	31	0.04
Brazilian	11	0.01
British	313	0.38
Bulgarian	34	0.04
Canadian	130	0.16
Celtic	20	0.02
Croatian	95	0.12
Czech	664	0.81
Czechoslovakian	226	0.27
Danish	744	0.90
Dutch	1,457	1.77
Eastern European	24	0.03
English	8,174	9.92
Estonian	15	0.02
European	733	0.89
Finnish	121	0.15
French, except Basque	3,106	3.77
French Canadian	406	0.49
German	18,942	22.98
German Russian	19	0.02
Greek	340	0.41
Hawaii Native/Pacific Islander:	228	0.28
Micronesian: (32)	48	0.06
Guamanian/Chamorro (19)	35	0.04
Other Micronesian (13)	13	0.02
Polynesian: (32)	117	0.14
Native Hawaiian (12)	79	0.10
Samoan (19)	36	0.04
Other Polynesian (1)	2	0.00
Other Pac. Isl., specified	4	0.00
Other Pac. Isl., not spec. (22)	59	0.07
Hispanic or Latino:	17,583	21.34
Central American:	125	0.15
Costa Rican	6	0.01
Guatemalan	37	0.04
Honduran	10	0.01
Nicaraguan	16	0.02
Panamanian	6	0.01
Salvadoran	43	0.05
Other Central American	7	0.01
Cuban	86	0.10
Dominican Republic	10	0.01
Mexican	9,563	11.61
Puerto Rican	226	0.27
South American:	131	0.16
Argentinean	6	0.01
Bolivian	2	0.00
Chilean	3	0.00
Colombian	27	0.03
Ecuadorian	8	0.01
Peruvian	57	0.07
Venezuelan	15	0.02
Other South American	13	0.02
Other Hispanic or Latino	7,442	9.03
Hungarian	439	0.53
Iranian	73	0.09
Irish	10,829	13.14
Israeli	12	0.01
Italian	4,767	5.78
Latvian	7	0.01
Lithuanian	107	0.13
Maltese	7	0.01
Northern European	46	0.06
Norwegian	2,366	2.87
Pennsylvania German	46	0.06
Polish	2,126	2.58
Portuguese	230	0.28
Romanian	35	0.04
Russian	633	0.77
Scandinavian	191	0.23
Scotch-Irish	1,498	1.82
Scottish	1,448	1.76
Serbian	14	0.02
Slavic	78	0.09
Slovak	99	0.12
Slovene	60	0.07
Swedish	2,110	2.56
Swiss	355	0.43
Turkish	41	0.05
Ukrainian	138	0.17
United States or American	3,939	4.78
Welsh	841	1.02
West Indian, excl. Hispanic:	19	0.02
Jamaican	19	0.02
White:	70,464	85.53
Not Hispanic (59,635)	60,868	73.88
Hispanic (8,502)	9,596	11.65
Yugoslavian	101	0.12

Welby

Place Type: Census Designated Place
County: Adams
Population: 12,973

Ancestry/Race	Number	%
African American/Black:	288	2.22
Not Hispanic (193)	251	1.93
Hispanic (12)	37	0.29
Alaska Native tribes, specified:	2	0.02
Eskimo (1)	2	0.02
Am. Ind. or Alaska Nat., not spec.	129	0.99
American Indian tribes, specified:	254	1.96
Apache (8)	21	0.16
Blackfeet (7)	11	0.08
Cherokee (11)	56	0.43
Cheyenne	1	0.01
Chickasaw (6)	7	0.05
Chippewa (12)	13	0.10
Choctaw	2	0.02
Comanche (1)	2	0.02
Iroquois (7)	11	0.08
Latin American Indians (16)	38	0.29
Navajo (10)	22	0.17
Osage	4	0.03
Pima	3	0.02
Pueblo (4)	5	0.04
Shoshone (1)	1	0.01
Sioux (25)	40	0.31
Ute (1)	5	0.04
Yaqui	1	0.01
All other tribes (7)	11	0.08
American Indian tribes, not spec.	28	0.22
Arab:	16	0.12
Lebanese	9	0.07
Syrian	7	0.05
Asian:	224	1.73
Cambodian (1)	2	0.02
Chinese, ex. Taiwanese (30)	32	0.25
Filipino (14)	32	0.25
Indian (15)	19	0.15
Indonesian (1)	1	0.01
Japanese (29)	55	0.42
Korean (14)	24	0.18
Laotian (4)	4	0.03
Pakistani (8)	9	0.07
Taiwanese	2	0.02
Thai (11)	14	0.11
Vietnamese (19)	20	0.15
Other Asian, not specified (4)	10	0.08
Austrian	29	0.22
Belgian	18	0.14
British	65	0.50
Bulgarian	7	0.05
Canadian	15	0.12
Croatian	16	0.12
Czech	55	0.42
Czechoslovakian	27	0.21
Danish	81	0.62
Dutch	334	2.57
English	707	5.43
European	106	0.81
Finnish	16	0.12
French, except Basque	421	3.24
French Canadian	76	0.58
German	2,334	17.94
German Russian	15	0.12
Greek	56	0.43
Hawaii Native/Pacific Islander:	35	0.27
Micronesian: (1)	8	0.06
Guamanian/Chamorro (1)	8	0.06
Polynesian: (13)	26	0.20
Native Hawaiian (11)	21	0.16
Samoan (2)	5	0.04
Other Pac. Isl., not spec. (1)	1	0.01
Hispanic or Latino:	4,792	36.94
Central American:	40	0.31
Costa Rican	1	0.01
Guatemalan	13	0.10
Nicaraguan	4	0.03
Salvadoran	20	0.15
Other Central American	2	0.02
Cuban	3	0.02
Mexican	2,909	22.42
Puerto Rican	26	0.20
South American:	9	0.07
Chilean	1	0.01
Colombian	1	0.01
Peruvian	2	0.02
Venezuelan	5	0.04
Other Hispanic or Latino	1,805	13.91
Hungarian	45	0.35
Irish	997	7.66
Italian	775	5.96
Lithuanian	6	0.05
Luxemburger	11	0.08
Norwegian	195	1.50
Pennsylvania German	5	0.04
Polish	153	1.18
Portuguese	63	0.48
Romanian	3	0.02
Russian	144	1.11
Scandinavian	53	0.41
Scotch-Irish	144	1.11
Scottish	223	1.71
Slavic	20	0.15
Slovak	34	0.26
Swedish	308	2.37
Swiss	17	0.13
Ukrainian	223	1.71
United States or American	655	5.03
Welsh	84	0.65

Notes: 1. Figures in the "Number" column do not add up to the total population due to: a) Ancestry/Race overlap — e.g. persons can report being both White and Irish, b) persons of Hispanic origin can report being any race, c) persons reporting two ancestries are counted in both categories. 2. Numbers in parentheses indicate the number of persons reporting this ancestry/race alone, not in combination with any other ancestry/race. 3. Refer to the Explanation of Data in the front of the book for more detailed information.

White:	9,771	75.32
Not Hispanic (7,464)	7,677	59.18
Hispanic (1,807)	2,094	16.14
Yugoslavian	7	0.05

Westminster

Place Type: City
County: Adams
Population: 100,940

Ancestry/Race	Number	%
Afghan	124	0.12
African American/Black:	1,610	1.60
Not Hispanic (1,149)	1,451	1.44
Hispanic (88)	159	0.16
African, sub-Saharan:	172	0.17
African	128	0.13
South African	44	0.04
Alaska Native tribes, specified:	20	0.02
Aleut (2)	3	0.00
Eskimo (7)	11	0.01
Tlingit-Haida (2)	5	0.00
All other tribes (1)	1	0.00
Am. Ind. or Alaska Nat., not spec.	429	0.43
American Indian tribes, specified:	1,002	0.99
Apache (48)	117	0.12
Blackfeet (7)	28	0.03
Cherokee (85)	270	0.27
Cheyenne (5)	13	0.01
Chickasaw (2)	7	0.01
Chippewa (11)	21	0.02
Choctaw (17)	35	0.03
Colville (1)	2	0.00
Comanche (7)	10	0.01
Cree (6)	11	0.01
Creek (7)	16	0.02
Crow (1)	3	0.00
Delaware	2	0.00
Iroquois (14)	26	0.03
Kiowa (6)	6	0.01
Latin American Indians (21)	52	0.05
Navajo (47)	79	0.08
Ottawa	1	0.00
Paiute (3)	3	0.00
Pima (1)	1	0.00
Potawatomi (11)	23	0.02
Pueblo (26)	33	0.03
Puget Sound Salish	1	0.00
Seminole (1)	6	0.01
Shoshone (5)	5	0.00
Sioux (78)	127	0.13
Ute (10)	14	0.01
Yakama (1)	1	0.00
Yaqui (2)	2	0.00
Yuman (2)	2	0.00
All other tribes (40)	85	0.08
American Indian tribes, not spec.	115	0.11
Arab:	346	0.34
Arab/Arabic	100	0.10
Egyptian	22	0.02
Jordanian	78	0.08
Lebanese	37	0.04
Palestinian	37	0.04
Syrian	44	0.04
Other Arab	28	0.03
Armenian	15	0.01
Asian:	6,548	6.49
Bangladeshi (3)	5	0.00
Cambodian (121)	146	0.14
Chinese, ex. Taiwanese (680)	820	0.81
Filipino (247)	413	0.41
Hmong (973)	1,123	1.11
Indian (352)	429	0.43
Indonesian (14)	27	0.03
Japanese (349)	541	0.54
Korean (459)	538	0.53
Laotian (785)	884	0.88
Pakistani (10)	12	0.01
Sri Lankan (1)	7	0.01
Taiwanese (26)	35	0.03
Thai (41)	61	0.06
Vietnamese (1,160)	1,246	1.23
Other Asian, specified (8)	17	0.02
Other Asian, not specified (137)	244	0.24
Assyrian/Chaldean/Syriac	11	0.01
Australian	80	0.08
Austrian	329	0.33
Basque	71	0.07
Belgian	94	0.09
Brazilian	25	0.02
British	671	0.66
Bulgarian	61	0.06
Canadian	345	0.34
Celtic	41	0.04
Croatian	84	0.08
Czech	832	0.82
Czechoslovakian	180	0.18
Danish	1,084	1.07
Dutch	2,131	2.11
Eastern European	56	0.06
English	11,383	11.25
European	1,175	1.16
Finnish	257	0.25
French, except Basque	4,084	4.04
French Canadian	658	0.65
German	25,117	24.82
German Russian	21	0.02
Greek	455	0.45
Hawaii Native/Pacific Islander:	233	0.23
Melanesian: (2)	5	0.00
Fijian (1)	4	0.00
Other Melanesian (1)	1	0.00
Micronesian: (21)	37	0.04
Guamanian/Chamorro (19)	35	0.03
Other Micronesian (2)	2	0.00
Polynesian: (42)	84	0.08
Native Hawaiian (15)	51	0.05
Samoan (27)	32	0.03
Other Polynesian	1	0.00
Other Pac. Isl., specified	6	0.01
Other Pac. Isl., not spec. (11)	101	0.10
Hispanic or Latino:	15,369	15.23
Central American:	114	0.11
Costa Rican	5	0.00
Guatemalan	29	0.03
Honduran	10	0.01
Nicaraguan	7	0.01
Panamanian	10	0.01
Salvadoran	45	0.04
Other Central American	8	0.01
Cuban	142	0.14
Dominican Republic	19	0.02
Mexican	8,759	8.68
Puerto Rican	231	0.23
South American:	152	0.15
Argentinean	9	0.01
Bolivian	4	0.00
Chilean	12	0.01
Colombian	54	0.05
Ecuadorian	3	0.00
Peruvian	41	0.04
Uruguayan	4	0.00
Venezuelan	7	0.01
Other South American	18	0.02
Other Hispanic or Latino	5,952	5.90
Hungarian	624	0.62
Icelander	12	0.01
Iranian	95	0.09
Irish	13,875	13.71
Israeli	16	0.02
Italian	6,770	6.69
Latvian	71	0.07
Lithuanian	109	0.11
Luxemburger	35	0.03
Maltese	12	0.01
Northern European	70	0.07
Norwegian	3,098	3.06
Pennsylvania German	46	0.05
Polish	2,641	2.61
Portuguese	115	0.11
Romanian	30	0.03
Russian	622	0.61
Scandinavian	385	0.38
Scotch-Irish	1,773	1.75
Scottish	2,460	2.43
Serbian	45	0.04
Slavic	52	0.05
Slovak	203	0.20
Slovene	69	0.07
Swedish	3,159	3.12
Swiss	452	0.45
Turkish	66	0.07
Ukrainian	181	0.18
United States or American	4,395	4.34
Welsh	1,007	1.00
West Indian, excl. Hispanic:	54	0.05
Jamaican	33	0.03
West Indian	21	0.02
White:	87,374	86.56
Not Hispanic (76,637)	78,101	77.37
Hispanic (8,346)	9,273	9.19
Yugoslavian	215	0.21

Wheat Ridge

Place Type: City
County: Jefferson
Population: 32,913

Ancestry/Race	Number	%
Acadian/Cajun	37	0.11
African American/Black:	400	1.22
Not Hispanic (255)	353	1.07
Hispanic (20)	47	0.14
African, sub-Saharan:	38	0.12
African	26	0.08
Ghanian	12	0.04
Alaska Native tribes, specified:	2	0.01
Eskimo (1)	2	0.01
Am. Ind. or Alaska Nat., not spec.	138	0.42
American Indian tribes, specified:	466	1.42
Apache (11)	40	0.12
Blackfeet (4)	10	0.03
Cherokee (40)	143	0.43
Cheyenne (1)	2	0.01
Chickasaw (2)	6	0.02
Chippewa (10)	13	0.04
Choctaw (11)	19	0.06
Colville (3)	3	0.01
Comanche	2	0.01
Creek (3)	5	0.02
Crow (2)	4	0.01
Delaware (1)	2	0.01
Iroquois	4	0.01
Kiowa (1)	1	0.00
Latin American Indians (15)	44	0.13
Menominee	2	0.01
Navajo (26)	41	0.12
Osage (3)	6	0.02
Potawatomi	4	0.01
Pueblo (7)	11	0.03
Seminole (1)	2	0.01
Shoshone (1)	2	0.01
Sioux (50)	61	0.19
Ute	3	0.01
Yaqui (1)	1	0.00
All other tribes (15)	35	0.11
American Indian tribes, not spec.	34	0.10
Arab:	111	0.34
Lebanese	39	0.12
Syrian	25	0.08
Other Arab	47	0.14
Armenian	17	0.05
Asian:	615	1.87
Chinese, ex. Taiwanese (60)	82	0.25
Filipino (26)	65	0.20
Hmong (12)	12	0.04
Indian (34)	44	0.13
Indonesian	3	0.01

Notes: 1. Figures in the "Number" column do not add up to the total population due to: a) Ancestry/Race overlap — e.g. persons can report being both White and Irish, b) persons of Hispanic origin can report being any race, c) persons reporting two ancestries are counted in both categories. 2. Numbers in parentheses indicate the number of persons reporting this ancestry/race alone, not in combination with any other ancestry/race. 3. Refer to the Explanation of Data in the front of the book for more detailed information.

Ancestry/Race	Number	%
Japanese (129)	175	0.53
Korean (55)	64	0.19
Laotian (30)	35	0.11
Thai (2)	10	0.03
Vietnamese (81)	89	0.27
Other Asian, specified (4)	4	0.01
Other Asian, not specified (8)	32	0.10
Australian	16	0.05
Austrian	143	0.43
Belgian	42	0.13
Brazilian	14	0.04
British	174	0.53
Bulgarian	6	0.02
Canadian	86	0.26
Celtic	43	0.13
Croatian	64	0.19
Czech	263	0.80
Czechoslovakian	56	0.17
Danish	285	0.86
Dutch	687	2.08
English	4,579	13.87
European	357	1.08
Finnish	50	0.15
French, except Basque	1,299	3.93
French Canadian	299	0.91
German	7,914	23.97
German Russian	22	0.07
Greek	45	0.14
Hawaii Native/Pacific Islander:	75	0.23
Micronesian: (8)	12	0.04
Guamanian/Chamorro (7)	11	0.03
Other Micronesian (1)	1	0.00
Polynesian: (19)	47	0.14
Native Hawaiian (14)	38	0.12
Samoan (4)	8	0.02
Other Polynesian (1)	1	0.00
Other Pac. Isl., not spec. (11)	16	0.05
Hispanic or Latino:	4,434	13.47
Central American:	30	0.09
Guatemalan	5	0.02
Honduran	5	0.02
Nicaraguan	2	0.01
Panamanian	2	0.01
Salvadoran	14	0.04
Other Central American	2	0.01
Cuban	22	0.07
Dominican Republic	3	0.01
Mexican	2,569	7.81
Puerto Rican	58	0.18
South American:	39	0.12
Argentinean	6	0.02
Bolivian	2	0.01
Chilean	3	0.01
Colombian	10	0.03
Ecuadorian	1	0.00
Peruvian	4	0.01
Uruguayan	1	0.00
Venezuelan	3	0.01
Other South American	9	0.03
Other Hispanic or Latino	1,713	5.20
Hungarian	119	0.36
Icelander	7	0.02
Iranian	19	0.06
Irish	4,338	13.14
Italian	2,587	7.84
Latvian	15	0.05
Lithuanian	67	0.20
Northern European	49	0.15
Norwegian	762	2.31
Pennsylvania German	33	0.10
Polish	663	2.01
Portuguese	7	0.02
Romanian	8	0.02
Russian	329	1.00
Scandinavian	133	0.40
Scotch-Irish	890	2.70
Scottish	851	2.58
Serbian	9	0.03
Slavic	49	0.15
Slovak	31	0.09
Slovene	67	0.20
Swedish	1,324	4.01
Swiss	120	0.36
Ukrainian	82	0.25
United States or American	1,353	4.10
Welsh	255	0.77
White:	30,121	91.52
Not Hispanic (27,016)	27,474	83.47
Hispanic (2,345)	2,647	8.04
Yugoslavian	103	0.31

Ansonia

Place Type: City
County: New Haven
Population: 18,554

Ancestry/Race	Number	%
African American/Black:	1,733	9.34
Not Hispanic (1,511)	1,659	8.94
Hispanic (51)	74	0.40
African, sub-Saharan:	156	0.84
African	76	0.41
Cape Verdean	73	0.39
Liberian	7	0.04
Alaska Native tribes, specified:	1	0.01
Alaska Athabascan	1	0.01
Am. Ind. or Alaska Nat., not spec.	67	0.36
Albanian	208	1.12
American Indian tribes, specified:	71	0.38
Blackfeet (1)	3	0.02
Cherokee (3)	22	0.12
Chippewa (1)	1	0.01
Choctaw (1)	1	0.01
Iroquois	3	0.02
Latin American Indians (5)	6	0.03
Pueblo	1	0.01
Yuman (1)	1	0.01
All other tribes (19)	33	0.18
American Indian tribes, not spec.	12	0.06
Arab:	69	0.37
Arab/Arabic	14	0.08
Egyptian	9	0.05
Lebanese	22	0.12
Palestinian	24	0.13
Armenian	17	0.09
Asian:	266	1.43
Cambodian (1)	3	0.02
Chinese, ex. Taiwanese (26)	27	0.15
Filipino (12)	26	0.14
Indian (114)	128	0.69
Japanese (3)	5	0.03
Korean (14)	22	0.12
Laotian (3)	3	0.02
Pakistani (10)	14	0.08
Sri Lankan (4)	4	0.02
Taiwanese (3)	3	0.02
Thai (1)	1	0.01
Vietnamese (11)	12	0.06
Other Asian, not specified (7)	18	0.10
Austrian	72	0.39
Belgian	8	0.04
British	28	0.15
Canadian	69	0.37
Czech	73	0.39
Czechoslovakian	85	0.46
Danish	59	0.32
Dutch	95	0.51
English	1,289	6.95
European	12	0.06
Finnish	38	0.20
French, except Basque	961	5.18
French Canadian	445	2.40
German	1,724	9.29
Greek	206	1.11
Guyanese	22	0.12
Hawaii Native/Pacific Islander:	15	0.08
Micronesian: (2)	2	0.01
Guamanian/Chamorro (2)	2	0.01
Polynesian:	2	0.01
Native Hawaiian	2	0.01
Other Pac. Isl., not spec. (1)	11	0.06
Hispanic or Latino:	1,376	7.42
Central American:	42	0.23
Costa Rican	9	0.05
Guatemalan	20	0.11
Nicaraguan	8	0.04
Panamanian	2	0.01
Salvadoran	3	0.02
Cuban	29	0.16
Dominican Republic	37	0.20
Mexican	35	0.19
Puerto Rican	728	3.92
South American:	246	1.33
Argentinean	2	0.01
Bolivian	3	0.02
Chilean	3	0.02
Colombian	41	0.22
Ecuadorian	176	0.95
Peruvian	8	0.04
Venezuelan	5	0.03
Other South American	8	0.04
Other Hispanic or Latino	259	1.40
Hungarian	385	2.08
Iranian	8	0.04
Irish	3,247	17.50
Italian	5,386	29.03
Lithuanian	348	1.88
Macedonian	16	0.09
Norwegian	109	0.59
Pennsylvania German	8	0.04
Polish	2,262	12.19
Portuguese	237	1.28
Russian	346	1.86
Scandinavian	6	0.03
Scotch-Irish	96	0.52
Scottish	185	1.00
Slavic	16	0.09
Slovak	411	2.22
Swedish	320	1.72
Swiss	18	0.10
Turkish	8	0.04
Ukrainian	488	2.63
United States or American	545	2.94
Welsh	49	0.26
West Indian, excl. Hispanic:	107	0.58
Haitian	50	0.27
Jamaican	46	0.25
U.S. Virgin Islander	11	0.06
White:	16,234	87.50
Not Hispanic (15,066)	15,336	82.66
Hispanic (801)	898	4.84
Yugoslavian	33	0.18

Avon

Place Type: Town
County: Hartford
Population: 15,832

Ancestry/Race	Number	%
African American/Black:	182	1.15
Not Hispanic (153)	178	1.12
Hispanic (2)	4	0.03
African, sub-Saharan:	26	0.16
African	12	0.08
South African	14	0.09
Alaska Native tribes, specified:	1	0.01
Eskimo (1)	1	0.01
Am. Ind. or Alaska Nat., not spec.	16	0.10
American Indian tribes, specified:	15	0.09
Cherokee (2)	5	0.03
Latin American Indians (1)	1	0.01
Menominee	3	0.02
Potawatomi	1	0.01
All other tribes (1)	5	0.03
Arab:	48	0.30
Egyptian	8	0.05
Lebanese	29	0.18
Other Arab	11	0.07

Notes: 1. Figures in the "Number" column do not add up to the total population due to: a) Ancestry/Race overlap — e.g. persons can report being both White and Irish, b) persons of Hispanic origin can report being any race, c) persons reporting two ancestries are counted in both categories. 2. Numbers in parentheses indicate the number of persons reporting this ancestry/race alone, not in combination with any other ancestry/race. 3. Refer to the Explanation of Data in the front of the book for more detailed information.

Ancestry/Race	Number	%
Armenian	40	0.25
Asian:	550	3.47
Cambodian (2)	2	0.01
Chinese, ex. Taiwanese (128)	155	0.98
Filipino (24)	32	0.20
Indian (158)	168	1.06
Indonesian (2)	2	0.01
Japanese (20)	34	0.21
Korean (88)	102	0.64
Laotian (1)	1	0.01
Malaysian	4	0.03
Pakistani (11)	14	0.09
Sri Lankan (6)	10	0.06
Vietnamese (10)	13	0.08
Other Asian, specified (2)	5	0.03
Other Asian, not specified (3)	8	0.05
Austrian	156	0.99
Belgian	11	0.07
British	94	0.59
Canadian	142	0.90
Celtic	15	0.09
Croatian	13	0.08
Czech	73	0.46
Czechoslovakian	27	0.17
Danish	168	1.06
Dutch	242	1.53
Eastern European	77	0.49
English	2,446	15.45
European	125	0.79
Finnish	4	0.03
French, except Basque	950	6.00
French Canadian	549	3.47
German	2,557	16.15
Greek	136	0.86
Hawaii Native/Pacific Islander:	7	0.04
Micronesian: (1)	1	0.01
Guamanian/Chamorro (1)	1	0.01
Polynesian: (2)	6	0.04
Native Hawaiian	4	0.03
Samoan (2)	2	0.01
Hispanic or Latino:	249	1.57
Central American:	3	0.02
Guatemalan	3	0.02
Cuban	33	0.21
Dominican Republic	2	0.01
Mexican	40	0.25
Puerto Rican	60	0.38
South American:	60	0.38
Argentinean	17	0.11
Colombian	17	0.11
Ecuadorian	1	0.01
Peruvian	10	0.06
Venezuelan	11	0.07
Other South American	4	0.03
Other Hispanic or Latino	51	0.32
Hungarian	167	1.05
Iranian	16	0.10
Irish	3,183	20.10
Israeli	6	0.04
Italian	2,690	16.99
Lithuanian	110	0.69
Luxemburger	5	0.03
Macedonian	8	0.05
New Zealander	29	0.18
Northern European	5	0.03
Norwegian	119	0.75
Pennsylvania German	7	0.04
Polish	1,401	8.85
Portuguese	192	1.21
Romanian	68	0.43
Russian	667	4.21
Scandinavian	15	0.09
Scotch-Irish	173	1.09
Scottish	454	2.87
Serbian	14	0.09
Slavic	64	0.40
Slovak	104	0.66
Swedish	536	3.39
Swiss	106	0.67
Turkish	21	0.13
Ukrainian	92	0.58
United States or American	655	4.14
Welsh	129	0.81
West Indian, excl. Hispanic:	37	0.23
Jamaican	32	0.20
West Indian	5	0.03
White:	15,142	95.64
Not Hispanic (14,825)	14,927	94.28
Hispanic (205)	215	1.36
Yugoslavian	17	0.11

Berlin

Place Type: Town
County: Hartford
Population: 18,215

Ancestry/Race	Number	%
African American/Black:	97	0.53
Not Hispanic (63)	89	0.49
Hispanic (2)	8	0.04
Am. Ind. or Alaska Nat., not spec.	15	0.08
American Indian tribes, specified:	34	0.19
Blackfeet	3	0.02
Cherokee	7	0.04
Choctaw	4	0.02
Iroquois (1)	6	0.03
Latin American Indians (1)	3	0.02
Sioux	4	0.02
All other tribes (2)	7	0.04
American Indian tribes, not spec.	4	0.02
Arab:	85	0.47
Arab/Arabic	15	0.08
Iraqi	30	0.16
Lebanese	30	0.16
Moroccan	10	0.05
Armenian	92	0.51
Asian:	328	1.80
Cambodian (1)	1	0.01
Chinese, ex. Taiwanese (33)	37	0.20
Filipino (13)	19	0.10
Indian (149)	151	0.83
Japanese (5)	7	0.04
Korean (24)	33	0.18
Laotian (4)	4	0.02
Pakistani (12)	12	0.07
Thai (3)	3	0.02
Vietnamese (54)	55	0.30
Other Asian, not specified (2)	6	0.03
Assyrian/Chaldean/Syriac	48	0.26
Australian	8	0.04
Austrian	155	0.85
Belgian	27	0.15
Brazilian	15	0.08
British	67	0.37
Canadian	63	0.35
Croatian	21	0.12
Czech	29	0.16
Czechoslovakian	83	0.46
Danish	113	0.62
Dutch	164	0.90
English	2,016	11.07
European	17	0.09
French, except Basque	1,777	9.76
French Canadian	703	3.86
German	2,009	11.03
Greek	258	1.42
Hawaii Native/Pacific Islander:	2	0.01
Polynesian: (2)	2	0.01
Native Hawaiian (1)	1	0.01
Samoan (1)	1	0.01
Hispanic or Latino:	267	1.47
Cuban	34	0.19
Dominican Republic	3	0.02
Mexican	13	0.07
Puerto Rican	109	0.60
South American:	39	0.21
Argentinean	5	0.03
Bolivian	2	0.01
Colombian	12	0.07
Ecuadorian	14	0.08
Paraguayan	1	0.01
Peruvian	5	0.03
Other Hispanic or Latino	69	0.38
Hungarian	107	0.59
Irish	3,160	17.35
Italian	5,276	28.97
Latvian	8	0.04
Lithuanian	473	2.60
Norwegian	79	0.43
Polish	3,701	20.32
Portuguese	51	0.28
Russian	279	1.53
Scandinavian	9	0.05
Scotch-Irish	239	1.31
Scottish	297	1.63
Slavic	12	0.07
Slovak	60	0.33
Swedish	714	3.92
Swiss	42	0.23
Ukrainian	242	1.33
United States or American	454	2.49
Welsh	40	0.22
White:	17,804	97.74
Not Hispanic (17,447)	17,568	96.45
Hispanic (227)	236	1.30
Yugoslavian	14	0.08

Bethel

Place Type: Town
County: Fairfield
Population: 18,067

Ancestry/Race	Number	%
African American/Black:	285	1.58
Not Hispanic (219)	270	1.49
Hispanic (9)	15	0.08
African, sub-Saharan:	6	0.03
Somalian	6	0.03
Am. Ind. or Alaska Nat., not spec.	15	0.08
Albanian	16	0.09
American Indian tribes, specified:	58	0.32
Apache	1	0.01
Blackfeet	1	0.01
Cherokee	8	0.04
Choctaw (1)	2	0.01
Iroquois (9)	14	0.08
Latin American Indians (8)	12	0.07
Seminole	1	0.01
All other tribes (7)	19	0.11
American Indian tribes, not spec.	3	0.02
Arab:	96	0.53
Arab/Arabic	31	0.17
Lebanese	65	0.36
Armenian	16	0.09
Asian:	749	4.15
Bangladeshi (12)	12	0.07
Cambodian (82)	95	0.53
Chinese, ex. Taiwanese (116)	128	0.71
Filipino (20)	32	0.18
Indian (172)	198	1.10
Indonesian (2)	5	0.03
Japanese (3)	11	0.06
Korean (40)	45	0.25
Laotian (12)	12	0.07
Malaysian	2	0.01
Pakistani (15)	42	0.23
Taiwanese (4)	6	0.03
Thai (16)	16	0.09
Vietnamese (109)	110	0.61
Other Asian, not specified (30)	35	0.19
Australian	13	0.07
Austrian	133	0.74
Belgian	39	0.22
Brazilian	185	1.02
British	140	0.77
Bulgarian	32	0.18
Canadian	132	0.73
Croatian	71	0.39

Notes: 1. Figures in the "Number" column do not add up to the total population due to: a) Ancestry/Race overlap — e.g. persons can report being both White and Irish, b) persons of Hispanic origin can report being any race, c) persons reporting two ancestries are counted in both categories. 2. Numbers in parentheses indicate the number of persons reporting this ancestry/race alone, not in combination with any other ancestry/race. 3. Refer to the Explanation of Data in the front of the book for more detailed information.

Czech	121	0.67
Czechoslovakian	122	0.68
Danish	103	0.57
Dutch	170	0.94
Eastern European	5	0.03
English	1,889	10.46
European	90	0.50
Finnish	18	0.10
French, except Basque	614	3.40
French Canadian	252	1.39
German	2,600	14.39
Greek	163	0.90
Hawaii Native/Pacific Islander:	13	0.07
Micronesian: (1)	4	0.02
Guamanian/Chamorro (1)	3	0.02
Other Micronesian	1	0.01
Polynesian: (6)	6	0.03
Samoan (5)	5	0.03
Other Polynesian (1)	1	0.01
Other Pac. Isl., not spec.	3	0.02
Hispanic or Latino:	669	3.70
Central American:	59	0.33
Costa Rican	16	0.09
Guatemalan	11	0.06
Honduran	18	0.10
Nicaraguan	1	0.01
Salvadoran	7	0.04
Other Central American	6	0.03
Cuban	19	0.11
Dominican Republic	38	0.21
Mexican	88	0.49
Puerto Rican	180	1.00
South American:	148	0.82
Argentinean	15	0.08
Bolivian	2	0.01
Chilean	20	0.11
Colombian	38	0.21
Ecuadorian	41	0.23
Peruvian	26	0.14
Uruguayan	1	0.01
Venezuelan	4	0.02
Other South American	1	0.01
Other Hispanic or Latino	137	0.76
Hungarian	300	1.66
Irish	3,884	21.50
Israeli	7	0.04
Italian	3,753	20.77
Latvian	31	0.17
Lithuanian	190	1.05
Northern European	19	0.11
Norwegian	240	1.33
Pennsylvania German	12	0.07
Polish	1,485	8.22
Portuguese	279	1.54
Russian	440	2.44
Scandinavian	13	0.07
Scotch-Irish	335	1.85
Scottish	425	2.35
Slavic	28	0.15
Slovak	112	0.62
Slovene	7	0.04
Swedish	472	2.61
Swiss	104	0.58
Turkish	5	0.03
Ukrainian	161	0.89
United States or American	1,073	5.94
Welsh	41	0.23
West Indian, excl. Hispanic:	113	0.63
Haitian	71	0.39
Jamaican	30	0.17
Trinidadian and Tobagonian	12	0.07
White:	16,905	93.57
Not Hispanic (16,237)	16,406	90.81
Hispanic (455)	499	2.76
Yugoslavian	30	0.17

Bloomfield

Place Type: Town
County: Hartford
Population: 19,587

Ancestry/Race	Number	%
African American/Black:	11,035	56.34
Not Hispanic (10,445)	10,846	55.37
Hispanic (144)	189	0.96
African, sub-Saharan:	513	2.62
African	406	2.07
Cape Verdean	47	0.24
Nigerian	60	0.31
Alaska Native tribes, specified:	3	0.02
Alaska Athabascan	3	0.02
Am. Ind. or Alaska Nat., not spec.	96	0.49
Albanian	12	0.06
American Indian tribes, specified:	91	0.46
Blackfeet	4	0.02
Cherokee (2)	35	0.18
Choctaw	1	0.01
Creek	5	0.03
Iroquois	5	0.03
Latin American Indians (2)	5	0.03
Seminole (2)	10	0.05
Sioux	1	0.01
Yuman (1)	1	0.01
All other tribes (3)	24	0.12
American Indian tribes, not spec.	7	0.04
Arab:	16	0.08
Lebanese	8	0.04
Palestinian	8	0.04
Armenian	28	0.14
Asian:	359	1.83
Bangladeshi	3	0.02
Cambodian (1)	1	0.01
Chinese, ex. Taiwanese (40)	63	0.32
Filipino (29)	41	0.21
Hmong (16)	18	0.09
Indian (75)	93	0.47
Indonesian	2	0.01
Japanese (16)	29	0.15
Korean (15)	20	0.10
Laotian (7)	9	0.05
Malaysian (1)	1	0.01
Pakistani (1)	9	0.05
Sri Lankan (3)	3	0.02
Taiwanese (1)	3	0.02
Thai (4)	4	0.02
Vietnamese (18)	25	0.13
Other Asian, specified	2	0.01
Other Asian, not specified (19)	33	0.17
Austrian	32	0.16
Belgian	7	0.04
British	105	0.54
Canadian	36	0.18
Czech	43	0.22
Czechoslovakian	5	0.03
Danish	96	0.49
Dutch	84	0.43
Eastern European	7	0.04
English	1,515	7.73
European	107	0.55
French, except Basque	466	2.38
French Canadian	230	1.17
German	1,082	5.52
German Russian	6	0.03
Greek	22	0.11
Guyanese	112	0.57
Hawaii Native/Pacific Islander:	36	0.18
Micronesian: (1)	1	0.01
Other Micronesian (1)	1	0.01
Polynesian:	1	0.01
Samoan	1	0.01
Other Pac. Isl., specified	2	0.01
Other Pac. Isl., not spec. (2)	32	0.16
Hispanic or Latino:	718	3.67
Central American:	29	0.15
Costa Rican	10	0.05
Guatemalan	4	0.02
Honduran	3	0.02
Nicaraguan	2	0.01
Panamanian	7	0.04
Other Central American	3	0.02
Cuban	19	0.10
Dominican Republic	10	0.05
Mexican	33	0.17
Puerto Rican	522	2.67
South American:	41	0.21
Argentinean	6	0.03
Bolivian	1	0.01
Chilean	4	0.02
Colombian	10	0.05
Ecuadorian	1	0.01
Peruvian	12	0.06
Venezuelan	3	0.02
Other South American	4	0.02
Other Hispanic or Latino	64	0.33
Hungarian	58	0.30
Irish	1,252	6.39
Italian	923	4.71
Lithuanian	77	0.39
Norwegian	58	0.30
Pennsylvania German	28	0.14
Polish	649	3.31
Portuguese	137	0.70
Romanian	45	0.23
Russian	549	2.80
Scandinavian	5	0.03
Scotch-Irish	77	0.39
Scottish	315	1.61
Slovak	4	0.02
Swedish	282	1.44
Swiss	38	0.19
Turkish	15	0.08
Ukrainian	60	0.31
United States or American	604	3.08
Welsh	99	0.51
West Indian, excl. Hispanic:	3,143	16.05
Barbadian	65	0.33
British West Indian	57	0.29
Haitian	70	0.36
Jamaican	2,588	13.21
Trinidadian and Tobagonian	208	1.06
U.S. Virgin Islander	9	0.05
West Indian	146	0.75
White:	8,086	41.28
Not Hispanic (7,599)	7,825	39.95
Hispanic (235)	261	1.33
Yugoslavian	20	0.10

Branford

Place Type: Town
County: New Haven
Population: 28,683

Ancestry/Race	Number	%
African American/Black:	496	1.73
Not Hispanic (374)	473	1.65
Hispanic (12)	23	0.08
African, sub-Saharan:	40	0.14
African	12	0.04
Cape Verdean	23	0.08
South African	5	0.02
Alaska Native tribes, specified:	1	0.00
Tlingit-Haida (1)	1	0.00
Am. Ind. or Alaska Nat., not spec.	63	0.22
Albanian	46	0.16
American Indian tribes, specified:	60	0.21
Blackfeet	8	0.03
Cherokee (4)	16	0.06
Iroquois (1)	6	0.02
Latin American Indians (1)	4	0.01
Puget Sound Salish (1)	1	0.00
Sioux	5	0.02
All other tribes (9)	20	0.07
American Indian tribes, not spec.	12	0.04
Arab:	148	0.52

Notes: 1. Figures in the "Number" column do not add up to the total population due to: a) Ancestry/Race overlap — e.g. persons can report being both White and Irish, b) persons of Hispanic origin can report being any race, c) persons reporting two ancestries are counted in both categories. 2. Numbers in parentheses indicate the number of persons reporting this ancestry/race alone, not in combination with any other ancestry/race. 3. Refer to the Explanation of Data in the front of the book for more detailed information.

Ancestry/Race	Number	%
Lebanese	121	0.42
Syrian	27	0.09
Armenian	22	0.08
Asian:	909	3.17
Bangladeshi	5	0.02
Cambodian (7)	10	0.03
Chinese, ex. Taiwanese (218)	247	0.86
Filipino (44)	61	0.21
Indian (207)	222	0.77
Indonesian (1)	1	0.00
Japanese (64)	78	0.27
Korean (68)	86	0.30
Malaysian (1)	1	0.00
Pakistani (13)	24	0.08
Sri Lankan (1)	1	0.00
Taiwanese (10)	12	0.04
Thai (4)	4	0.01
Vietnamese (106)	117	0.41
Other Asian, specified (14)	19	0.07
Other Asian, not specified (11)	21	0.07
Assyrian/Chaldean/Syriac	10	0.03
Australian	34	0.12
Austrian	113	0.39
Belgian	57	0.20
British	130	0.45
Bulgarian	28	0.10
Canadian	171	0.60
Celtic	5	0.02
Croatian	74	0.26
Czech	27	0.09
Czechoslovakian	19	0.07
Danish	144	0.50
Dutch	280	0.98
Eastern European	82	0.29
English	3,551	12.38
Estonian	5	0.02
European	116	0.40
Finnish	152	0.53
French, except Basque	1,205	4.20
French Canadian	603	2.10
German	3,262	11.37
Greek	283	0.99
Hawaii Native/Pacific Islander:	25	0.09
Micronesian: (7)	7	0.02
Guamanian/Chamorro (7)	7	0.02
Polynesian: (11)	14	0.05
Native Hawaiian (4)	7	0.02
Samoan (7)	7	0.02
Other Pac. Isl., specified	1	0.00
Other Pac. Isl., not spec.	3	0.01
Hispanic or Latino:	737	2.57
Central American:	19	0.07
Costa Rican	4	0.01
Guatemalan	5	0.02
Honduran	1	0.00
Nicaraguan	2	0.01
Salvadoran	7	0.02
Cuban	18	0.06
Dominican Republic	18	0.06
Mexican	73	0.25
Puerto Rican	263	0.92
South American:	162	0.56
Argentinean	15	0.05
Chilean	11	0.04
Colombian	49	0.17
Ecuadorian	74	0.26
Peruvian	9	0.03
Venezuelan	3	0.01
Other South American	1	0.00
Other Hispanic or Latino	184	0.64
Hungarian	324	1.13
Icelander	8	0.03
Irish	6,072	21.17
Israeli	7	0.02
Italian	8,659	30.19
Lithuanian	417	1.45
Northern European	38	0.13
Norwegian	157	0.55
Polish	2,143	7.47
Portuguese	171	0.60
Romanian	41	0.14
Russian	579	2.02
Scandinavian	55	0.19
Scotch-Irish	388	1.35
Scottish	689	2.40
Slavic	5	0.02
Slovak	101	0.35
Swedish	922	3.21
Swiss	61	0.21
Turkish	22	0.08
Ukrainian	259	0.90
United States or American	825	2.88
Welsh	147	0.51
West Indian, excl. Hispanic:	39	0.14
Jamaican	21	0.07
Trinidadian and Tobagonian	6	0.02
West Indian	12	0.04
White:	27,275	95.09
Not Hispanic (26,424)	26,689	93.05
Hispanic (552)	586	2.04
Yugoslavian	68	0.24

Bridgeport

Place Type: City
County: Fairfield
Population: 139,529

Ancestry/Race	Number	%
African American/Black:	46,281	33.17
Not Hispanic (40,974)	43,412	31.11
Hispanic (1,951)	2,869	2.06
African, sub-Saharan:	2,118	1.52
African	921	0.66
Cape Verdean	804	0.58
Ethiopian	20	0.01
Ghanian	12	0.01
Liberian	16	0.01
Nigerian	152	0.11
Senegalese	5	0.00
Somalian	84	0.06
South African	67	0.05
Other sub-Saharan African	37	0.03
Alaska Native tribes, specified:	5	0.00
Aleut	1	0.00
Tlingit-Haida (2)	3	0.00
All other tribes	1	0.00
Am. Ind. or Alaska Nat., not spec.	742	0.53
Albanian	386	0.28
American Indian tribes, specified:	538	0.39
Apache (15)	20	0.01
Blackfeet (15)	46	0.03
Cherokee (33)	142	0.10
Cheyenne	1	0.00
Chickasaw	4	0.00
Chippewa (5)	7	0.01
Choctaw (2)	9	0.01
Comanche (1)	1	0.00
Delaware	1	0.00
Iroquois (11)	27	0.02
Latin American Indians (89)	136	0.10
Navajo (1)	2	0.00
Paiute	1	0.00
Pueblo (1)	3	0.00
Seminole (4)	10	0.01
Sioux (2)	5	0.00
Yuman (1)	1	0.00
All other tribes (62)	122	0.09
American Indian tribes, not spec.	127	0.09
Arab:	588	0.42
Arab/Arabic	71	0.05
Egyptian	15	0.01
Iraqi	96	0.07
Jordanian	6	0.00
Lebanese	99	0.07
Moroccan	50	0.04
Syrian	135	0.10
Other Arab	116	0.08
Armenian	58	0.04
Asian:	5,475	3.92
Bangladeshi (26)	67	0.05
Cambodian (458)	546	0.39
Chinese, ex. Taiwanese (494)	602	0.43
Filipino (143)	186	0.13
Hmong (1)	1	0.00
Indian (801)	976	0.70
Indonesian (10)	11	0.01
Japanese (220)	286	0.20
Korean (219)	250	0.18
Laotian (502)	601	0.43
Malaysian (23)	25	0.02
Pakistani (114)	165	0.12
Sri Lankan (3)	8	0.01
Taiwanese (13)	20	0.01
Thai (42)	57	0.04
Vietnamese (1,189)	1,259	0.90
Other Asian, specified (10)	19	0.01
Other Asian, not specified (178)	396	0.28
Australian	37	0.03
Austrian	177	0.13
Basque	16	0.01
Belgian	22	0.02
Brazilian	1,611	1.15
British	162	0.12
Bulgarian	23	0.02
Canadian	139	0.10
Carpatho Rusyn	24	0.02
Celtic	17	0.01
Croatian	119	0.09
Czech	129	0.09
Czechoslovakian	246	0.18
Danish	142	0.10
Dutch	428	0.31
Eastern European	6	0.00
English	2,942	2.11
Estonian	9	0.01
European	189	0.14
Finnish	28	0.02
French, except Basque	1,610	1.15
French Canadian	958	0.69
German	3,362	2.41
Greek	577	0.41
Guyanese	19	0.01
Hawaii Native/Pacific Islander:	453	0.32
Melanesian: (1)	1	0.00
Fijian (1)	1	0.00
Micronesian: (14)	19	0.01
Guamanian/Chamorro (13)	18	0.01
Other Micronesian (1)	1	0.00
Polynesian: (79)	110	0.08
Native Hawaiian (40)	63	0.05
Samoan (39)	46	0.03
Other Polynesian	1	0.00
Other Pac. Isl., specified	2	0.00
Other Pac. Isl., not spec. (54)	321	0.23
Hispanic or Latino:	44,478	31.88
Central American:	1,443	1.03
Costa Rican	246	0.18
Guatemalan	287	0.21
Honduran	332	0.24
Nicaraguan	44	0.03
Panamanian	73	0.05
Salvadoran	382	0.27
Other Central American	79	0.06
Cuban	994	0.71
Dominican Republic	886	0.63
Mexican	2,687	1.93
Puerto Rican	32,177	23.06
South American:	1,996	1.43
Argentinean	96	0.07
Bolivian	15	0.01
Chilean	64	0.05
Colombian	850	0.61
Ecuadorian	450	0.32
Paraguayan	20	0.01
Peruvian	327	0.23
Uruguayan	17	0.01
Venezuelan	69	0.05
Other South American	88	0.06
Other Hispanic or Latino	4,295	3.08

Notes: 1. Figures in the "Number" column do not add up to the total population due to: a) Ancestry/Race overlap — e.g. persons can report being both White and Irish, b) persons of Hispanic origin can report being any race, c) persons reporting two ancestries are counted in both categories. 2. Numbers in parentheses indicate the number of persons reporting this ancestry/race alone, not in combination with any other ancestry/race. 3. Refer to the Explanation of Data in the front of the book for more detailed information.

Hungarian	2,176	1.56
Iranian	17	0.01
Irish	7,140	5.12
Israeli	26	0.02
Italian	12,051	8.64
Latvian	17	0.01
Lithuanian	265	0.19
Luxemburger	7	0.01
Macedonian	60	0.04
Maltese	6	0.00
Northern European	13	0.01
Norwegian	131	0.09
Pennsylvania German	11	0.01
Polish	3,858	2.77
Portuguese	4,107	2.94
Romanian	376	0.27
Russian	1,112	0.80
Scandinavian	29	0.02
Scotch-Irish	372	0.27
Scottish	510	0.37
Slavic	25	0.02
Slovak	1,569	1.12
Slovene	61	0.04
Swedish	533	0.38
Swiss	79	0.06
Turkish	43	0.03
Ukrainian	401	0.29
United States or American	2,995	2.15
Welsh	189	0.14
West Indian, excl. Hispanic:	8,665	6.21
Barbadian	138	0.10
Belizean	19	0.01
British West Indian	116	0.08
Haitian	1,980	1.42
Jamaican	5,924	4.25
Trinidadian and Tobagonian	180	0.13
West Indian	308	0.22
White:	67,706	48.52
Not Hispanic (43,158)	45,776	32.81
Hispanic (19,664)	21,930	15.72
Yugoslavian	136	0.10

Bristol

Place Type: City
County: Hartford
Population: 60,062

Ancestry/Race	Number	%
African American/Black:	2,041	3.40
Not Hispanic (1,453)	1,800	3.00
Hispanic (159)	241	0.40
African, sub-Saharan:	112	0.19
African	99	0.16
Cape Verdean	13	0.02
Alaska Native tribes, specified:	1	0.00
All other tribes (1)	1	0.00
Alaska Native tribes, not specified	0	0.00
Am. Ind. or Alaska Nat., not spec.	134	0.22
Albanian	106	0.18
American Indian tribes, specified:	266	0.44
Apache	1	0.00
Blackfeet (3)	12	0.02
Cherokee (15)	54	0.09
Chickasaw (2)	3	0.00
Chippewa	9	0.01
Choctaw (1)	2	0.00
Cree (1)	2	0.00
Iroquois (1)	24	0.04
Latin American Indians (4)	14	0.02
Osage	2	0.00
Pima	3	0.00
Potawatomi	1	0.00
Pueblo	1	0.00
Seminole (1)	2	0.00
Shoshone (1)	1	0.00
Sioux (4)	12	0.02
All other tribes (55)	123	0.20
American Indian tribes, not spec.	22	0.04
Arab:	112	0.19
Arab/Arabic	11	0.02
Egyptian	54	0.09
Lebanese	37	0.06
Moroccan	10	0.02
Armenian	107	0.18
Asian:	1,079	1.80
Bangladeshi (1)	6	0.01
Cambodian (73)	83	0.14
Chinese, ex. Taiwanese (141)	165	0.27
Filipino (81)	125	0.21
Indian (276)	326	0.54
Indonesian	2	0.00
Japanese (15)	29	0.05
Korean (65)	71	0.12
Laotian (56)	63	0.10
Malaysian (1)	5	0.01
Pakistani (41)	49	0.08
Taiwanese (3)	4	0.01
Thai (9)	13	0.02
Vietnamese (66)	85	0.14
Other Asian, specified (4)	4	0.01
Other Asian, not specified (23)	49	0.08
Assyrian/Chaldean/Syriac	28	0.05
Australian	15	0.02
Austrian	171	0.28
Belgian	42	0.07
Brazilian	47	0.08
British	158	0.26
Canadian	422	0.70
Carpatho Rusyn	18	0.03
Celtic	10	0.02
Croatian	5	0.01
Czech	83	0.14
Czechoslovakian	122	0.20
Danish	149	0.25
Dutch	309	0.51
English	4,819	8.02
European	45	0.07
Finnish	8	0.01
French, except Basque	11,082	18.45
French Canadian	4,766	7.94
German	6,038	10.05
Greek	394	0.66
Hawaii Native/Pacific Islander:	42	0.07
Melanesian: (2)	2	0.00
Fijian (2)	2	0.00
Micronesian:	3	0.00
Guamanian/Chamorro	2	0.00
Other Micronesian	1	0.00
Polynesian: (11)	21	0.03
Native Hawaiian (2)	11	0.02
Samoan (8)	9	0.01
Other Polynesian (1)	1	0.00
Other Pac. Isl., not spec. (5)	16	0.03
Hispanic or Latino:	3,166	5.27
Central American:	23	0.04
Costa Rican	5	0.01
Guatemalan	6	0.01
Honduran	8	0.01
Other Central American	4	0.01
Cuban	39	0.06
Dominican Republic	32	0.05
Mexican	218	0.36
Puerto Rican	2,150	3.58
South American:	291	0.48
Argentinean	11	0.02
Bolivian	1	0.00
Chilean	12	0.02
Colombian	110	0.18
Ecuadorian	87	0.14
Peruvian	46	0.08
Uruguayan	4	0.01
Venezuelan	3	0.00
Other South American	17	0.03
Other Hispanic or Latino	413	0.69
Hungarian	191	0.32
Icelander	14	0.02
Iranian	23	0.04
Irish	9,122	15.19
Italian	12,595	20.97
Latvian	7	0.01
Lithuanian	812	1.35
Macedonian	62	0.10
Northern European	21	0.03
Norwegian	201	0.33
Pennsylvania German	3	0.00
Polish	7,696	12.81
Portuguese	223	0.37
Romanian	62	0.10
Russian	649	1.08
Scandinavian	8	0.01
Scotch-Irish	679	1.13
Scottish	899	1.50
Serbian	9	0.01
Slavic	33	0.05
Slovak	194	0.32
Slovene	6	0.01
Swedish	1,402	2.33
Swiss	82	0.14
Ukrainian	392	0.65
United States or American	1,864	3.10
Welsh	215	0.36
West Indian, excl. Hispanic:	220	0.37
Barbadian	6	0.01
British West Indian	19	0.03
Haitian	7	0.01
Jamaican	177	0.29
Trinidadian and Tobagonian	11	0.02
White:	55,843	92.98
Not Hispanic (53,610)	54,266	90.35
Hispanic (1,404)	1,577	2.63
Yugoslavian	22	0.04

Brookfield

Place Type: Town
County: Fairfield
Population: 15,664

Ancestry/Race	Number	%
African American/Black:	146	0.93
Not Hispanic (114)	136	0.87
Hispanic (5)	10	0.06
African, sub-Saharan:	7	0.04
Ghanian	7	0.04
Am. Ind. or Alaska Nat., not spec.	14	0.09
Albanian	41	0.26
American Indian tribes, specified:	17	0.11
Apache	2	0.01
Cherokee (1)	5	0.03
Delaware	1	0.01
Iroquois	1	0.01
Latin American Indians (1)	1	0.01
Sioux (1)	1	0.01
All other tribes (6)	6	0.04
American Indian tribes, not spec.	4	0.03
Arab:	111	0.71
Lebanese	80	0.51
Syrian	31	0.20
Armenian	24	0.15
Asian:	450	2.87
Cambodian (7)	7	0.04
Chinese, ex. Taiwanese (114)	129	0.82
Filipino (52)	76	0.49
Indian (136)	141	0.90
Indonesian (7)	8	0.05
Japanese (21)	28	0.18
Korean (28)	29	0.19
Laotian (1)	1	0.01
Taiwanese	3	0.02
Thai (5)	6	0.04
Vietnamese (11)	15	0.10
Other Asian, not specified (3)	7	0.04
Austrian	52	0.33
Belgian	27	0.17
Brazilian	46	0.29
British	178	1.14
Canadian	107	0.68
Carpatho Rusyn	7	0.04
Croatian	15	0.10

Notes: 1. Figures in the "Number" column do not add up to the total population due to: a) Ancestry/Race overlap — e.g. persons can report being both White and Irish, b) persons of Hispanic origin can report being any race, c) persons reporting two ancestries are counted in both categories. 2. Numbers in parentheses indicate the number of persons reporting this ancestry/race alone, not in combination with any other ancestry/race. 3. Refer to the Explanation of Data in the front of the book for more detailed information.

Ancestry/Race	Number	%
Czech	103	0.66
Czechoslovakian	103	0.66
Danish	100	0.64
Dutch	234	1.49
Eastern European	87	0.56
English	2,101	13.41
European	156	1.00
Finnish	58	0.37
French, except Basque	589	3.76
French Canadian	141	0.90
German	2,737	17.47
Greek	82	0.52
Guyanese	30	0.19
Hawaii Native/Pacific Islander:	4	0.03
Polynesian:	4	0.03
Native Hawaiian	4	0.03
Hispanic or Latino:	372	2.37
Central American:	18	0.11
Costa Rican	5	0.03
Guatemalan	7	0.04
Nicaraguan	1	0.01
Panamanian	1	0.01
Salvadoran	3	0.02
Other Central American	1	0.01
Cuban	16	0.10
Dominican Republic	10	0.06
Mexican	61	0.39
Puerto Rican	85	0.54
South American:	80	0.51
Argentinean	15	0.10
Bolivian	3	0.02
Chilean	8	0.05
Colombian	25	0.16
Ecuadorian	6	0.04
Paraguayan	1	0.01
Peruvian	7	0.04
Venezuelan	3	0.02
Other South American	12	0.08
Other Hispanic or Latino	102	0.65
Hungarian	229	1.46
Iranian	16	0.10
Irish	3,805	24.29
Italian	4,026	25.70
Latvian	17	0.11
Lithuanian	112	0.72
Northern European	7	0.04
Norwegian	147	0.94
Polish	1,135	7.25
Portuguese	292	1.86
Romanian	60	0.38
Russian	451	2.88
Scandinavian	15	0.10
Scotch-Irish	250	1.60
Scottish	335	2.14
Serbian	20	0.13
Slavic	32	0.20
Slovak	202	1.29
Swedish	250	1.60
Swiss	140	0.89
Ukrainian	161	1.03
United States or American	602	3.84
Welsh	93	0.59
West Indian, excl. Hispanic:	32	0.20
Barbadian	6	0.04
Haitian	16	0.10
Jamaican	5	0.03
West Indian	5	0.03
White:	15,039	96.01
Not Hispanic (14,666)	14,762	94.24
Hispanic (260)	277	1.77

Central Manchester

Place Type: Census Designated Place
County: Hartford
Population: 30,595

Ancestry/Race	Number	%
African American/Black:	2,850	9.32
Not Hispanic (2,445)	2,677	8.75
Hispanic (95)	173	0.57
African, sub-Saharan:	77	0.25
African	49	0.16
Nigerian	11	0.04
South African	10	0.03
Other sub-Saharan African	7	0.02
Alaska Native tribes, not specified	1	0.00
Am. Ind. or Alaska Nat., not spec.	78	0.25
Albanian	32	0.10
American Indian tribes, specified:	141	0.46
Apache	1	0.00
Blackfeet (1)	8	0.03
Cherokee (2)	30	0.10
Cheyenne	2	0.01
Choctaw	2	0.01
Cree (1)	1	0.00
Creek	1	0.00
Iroquois (3)	5	0.02
Latin American Indians (4)	11	0.04
Navajo	1	0.00
Potawatomi	1	0.00
Shoshone	1	0.00
Sioux (4)	9	0.03
All other tribes (22)	68	0.22
American Indian tribes, not spec.	12	0.04
Arab:	94	0.31
Arab/Arabic	6	0.02
Egyptian	7	0.02
Lebanese	62	0.20
Palestinian	19	0.06
Armenian	20	0.07
Asian:	964	3.15
Bangladeshi (38)	63	0.21
Cambodian (13)	17	0.06
Chinese, ex. Taiwanese (118)	144	0.47
Filipino (71)	104	0.34
Hmong	5	0.02
Indian (175)	221	0.72
Indonesian (1)	3	0.01
Japanese (12)	22	0.07
Korean (42)	52	0.17
Laotian (106)	134	0.44
Malaysian (7)	7	0.02
Pakistani (36)	55	0.18
Sri Lankan (5)	5	0.02
Taiwanese	1	0.00
Thai (2)	7	0.02
Vietnamese (68)	80	0.26
Other Asian, specified (1)	2	0.01
Other Asian, not specified (12)	42	0.14
Australian	23	0.08
Austrian	143	0.47
Belgian	9	0.03
Brazilian	5	0.02
British	64	0.21
Canadian	132	0.43
Celtic	10	0.03
Czech	62	0.20
Czechoslovakian	42	0.14
Danish	198	0.65
Dutch	277	0.90
Eastern European	21	0.07
English	3,615	11.80
European	159	0.52
Finnish	79	0.26
French, except Basque	2,900	9.46
French Canadian	1,318	4.30
German	3,266	10.66
Greek	156	0.51
Guyanese	46	0.15
Hawaii Native/Pacific Islander:	54	0.18
Micronesian: (1)	5	0.02
Guamanian/Chamorro (1)	5	0.02
Polynesian: (10)	27	0.09
Native Hawaiian (3)	10	0.03
Samoan (7)	13	0.04
Other Polynesian	4	0.01
Other Pac. Isl., specified	1	0.00
Other Pac. Isl., not spec. (2)	21	0.07
Hispanic or Latino:	2,130	6.96
Central American:	42	0.14
Costa Rican	1	0.00
Guatemalan	2	0.01
Honduran	2	0.01
Nicaraguan	8	0.03
Panamanian	12	0.04
Salvadoran	12	0.04
Other Central American	5	0.02
Cuban	44	0.14
Dominican Republic	31	0.10
Mexican	131	0.43
Puerto Rican	1,400	4.58
South American:	233	0.76
Argentinean	4	0.01
Bolivian	1	0.00
Chilean	11	0.04
Colombian	104	0.34
Ecuadorian	7	0.02
Paraguayan	2	0.01
Peruvian	93	0.30
Venezuelan	5	0.02
Other South American	6	0.02
Other Hispanic or Latino	249	0.81
Hungarian	189	0.62
Irish	5,922	19.32
Israeli	10	0.03
Italian	4,319	14.09
Latvian	51	0.17
Lithuanian	279	0.91
Northern European	22	0.07
Norwegian	166	0.54
Polish	2,429	7.93
Portuguese	251	0.82
Romanian	46	0.15
Russian	299	0.98
Scandinavian	17	0.06
Scotch-Irish	419	1.37
Scottish	633	2.07
Slavic	12	0.04
Slovak	102	0.33
Slovene	9	0.03
Swedish	788	2.57
Swiss	125	0.41
Turkish	10	0.03
Ukrainian	161	0.53
United States or American	1,209	3.94
Welsh	117	0.38
West Indian, excl. Hispanic:	197	0.64
British West Indian	30	0.10
Jamaican	117	0.38
Trinidadian and Tobagonian	19	0.06
West Indian	31	0.10
White:	26,037	85.10
Not Hispanic (24,570)	25,010	81.75
Hispanic (886)	1,027	3.36
Yugoslavian	67	0.22

Cheshire

Place Type: Town
County: New Haven
Population: 28,543

Ancestry/Race	Number	%
African American/Black:	1,452	5.09
Not Hispanic (1,270)	1,372	4.81
Hispanic (62)	80	0.28
African, sub-Saharan:	155	0.54
African	87	0.31
Cape Verdean	44	0.15
Ethiopian	16	0.06
Other sub-Saharan African	8	0.03
Alaska Native tribes, specified:	2	0.01
Alaska Athabascan (1)	1	0.00
Tlingit-Haida (1)	1	0.00
Alaska Native tribes, not specified	1	0.00
Am. Ind. or Alaska Nat., not spec.	77	0.27
Albanian	27	0.09
American Indian tribes, specified:	100	0.35
Apache	2	0.01

Notes: 1. Figures in the "Number" column do not add up to the total population due to: a) Ancestry/Race overlap — e.g. persons can report being both White and Irish, b) persons of Hispanic origin can report being any race, c) persons reporting two ancestries are counted in both categories. 2. Numbers in parentheses indicate the number of persons reporting this ancestry/race alone, not in combination with any other ancestry/race. 3. Refer to the Explanation of Data in the front of the book for more detailed information.

Ancestry/Race	Number	%
Blackfeet	6	0.02
Cherokee (7)	24	0.08
Chippewa (2)	2	0.01
Iroquois (1)	9	0.03
Latin American Indians (4)	14	0.05
Lumbee (2)	2	0.01
Menominee (1)	1	0.00
Navajo (1)	1	0.00
Paiute (1)	3	0.01
Seminole	3	0.01
Sioux (4)	5	0.02
All other tribes (13)	28	0.10
American Indian tribes, not spec.	16	0.06
Arab:	99	0.35
Egyptian	18	0.06
Lebanese	60	0.21
Syrian	21	0.07
Armenian	60	0.21
Asian:	837	2.93
Cambodian (9)	13	0.05
Chinese, ex. Taiwanese (301)	318	1.11
Filipino (67)	77	0.27
Indian (188)	207	0.73
Indonesian (2)	5	0.02
Japanese (20)	30	0.11
Korean (88)	97	0.34
Laotian (1)	2	0.01
Malaysian (1)	1	0.00
Pakistani (21)	28	0.10
Sri Lankan (4)	4	0.01
Taiwanese (4)	6	0.02
Thai	1	0.00
Vietnamese (22)	31	0.11
Other Asian, not specified (13)	17	0.06
Austrian	295	1.04
Belgian	41	0.14
British	85	0.30
Canadian	129	0.45
Croatian	9	0.03
Czech	88	0.31
Czechoslovakian	34	0.12
Danish	154	0.54
Dutch	202	0.71
Eastern European	69	0.24
English	3,346	11.76
European	136	0.48
Finnish	46	0.16
French, except Basque	1,368	4.81
French Canadian	794	2.79
German	3,581	12.58
Greek	138	0.48
Hawaii Native/Pacific Islander:	21	0.07
Micronesian:	4	0.01
Guamanian/Chamorro	3	0.01
Other Micronesian	1	0.00
Polynesian: (5)	6	0.02
Native Hawaiian (1)	1	0.00
Samoan (3)	4	0.01
Other Polynesian (1)	1	0.00
Other Pac. Isl., not spec. (1)	11	0.04
Hispanic or Latino:	1,097	3.84
Central American:	18	0.06
Costa Rican	2	0.01
Guatemalan	1	0.00
Honduran	2	0.01
Panamanian	9	0.03
Other Central American	4	0.01
Cuban	53	0.19
Dominican Republic	20	0.07
Mexican	101	0.35
Puerto Rican	724	2.54
South American:	76	0.27
Argentinean	5	0.02
Bolivian	2	0.01
Chilean	7	0.02
Colombian	34	0.12
Ecuadorian	7	0.02
Peruvian	9	0.03
Venezuelan	5	0.02
Other South American	7	0.02
Other Hispanic or Latino	105	0.37
Hungarian	313	1.10
Iranian	31	0.11
Irish	6,250	21.96
Italian	7,432	26.11
Latvian	25	0.09
Lithuanian	225	0.79
Luxemburger	6	0.02
Norwegian	222	0.78
Polish	2,155	7.57
Portuguese	250	0.88
Romanian	93	0.33
Russian	875	3.07
Scandinavian	66	0.23
Scotch-Irish	293	1.03
Scottish	649	2.28
Slavic	19	0.07
Slovak	125	0.44
Slovene	28	0.10
Swedish	638	2.24
Swiss	99	0.35
Turkish	23	0.08
Ukrainian	224	0.79
United States or American	601	2.11
Welsh	64	0.22
West Indian, excl. Hispanic:	85	0.30
Belizean	8	0.03
Bermudan	8	0.03
Haitian	7	0.02
Jamaican	42	0.15
West Indian	20	0.07
White:	25,739	90.18
Not Hispanic (25,105)	25,271	88.54
Hispanic (413)	468	1.64
Yugoslavian	21	0.07

Clinton

Place Type: Town
County: Middlesex
Population: 13,094

Ancestry/Race	Number	%
Afghan	90	0.69
African American/Black:	118	0.90
Not Hispanic (67)	110	0.84
Hispanic (7)	8	0.06
African, sub-Saharan:	21	0.16
African	21	0.16
Am. Ind. or Alaska Nat., not spec.	30	0.23
American Indian tribes, specified:	53	0.40
Apache	4	0.03
Cherokee (1)	6	0.05
Chickasaw	1	0.01
Chippewa (1)	2	0.02
Cree	2	0.02
Creek	1	0.01
Delaware (4)	5	0.04
Iroquois (3)	5	0.04
Latin American Indians (4)	5	0.04
All other tribes (12)	22	0.17
American Indian tribes, not spec.	3	0.02
Arab:	18	0.14
Syrian	18	0.14
Armenian	7	0.05
Asian:	180	1.37
Chinese, ex. Taiwanese (36)	42	0.32
Filipino (4)	10	0.08
Indian (34)	39	0.30
Japanese (6)	10	0.08
Korean (13)	20	0.15
Laotian (7)	7	0.05
Thai (1)	1	0.01
Vietnamese (41)	43	0.33
Other Asian, specified (3)	3	0.02
Other Asian, not specified (1)	5	0.04
Austrian	69	0.53
Belgian	6	0.05
Brazilian	7	0.05
British	64	0.49
Canadian	35	0.27
Czech	42	0.32
Czechoslovakian	69	0.53
Danish	75	0.57
Dutch	185	1.41
English	2,412	18.42
European	63	0.48
Finnish	50	0.38
French, except Basque	711	5.43
French Canadian	262	2.00
German	1,778	13.58
Greek	131	1.00
Hawaii Native/Pacific Islander:	5	0.04
Micronesian: (1)	1	0.01
Guamanian/Chamorro (1)	1	0.01
Polynesian:	2	0.02
Samoan	1	0.01
Tongan	1	0.01
Other Pac. Isl., not spec. (1)	2	0.02
Hispanic or Latino:	523	3.99
Central American:	18	0.14
Costa Rican	1	0.01
Guatemalan	4	0.03
Honduran	3	0.02
Panamanian	1	0.01
Salvadoran	6	0.05
Other Central American	3	0.02
Cuban	9	0.07
Dominican Republic	4	0.03
Mexican	35	0.27
Puerto Rican	280	2.14
South American:	101	0.77
Argentinean	5	0.04
Chilean	2	0.02
Colombian	44	0.34
Ecuadorian	40	0.31
Peruvian	2	0.02
Venezuelan	2	0.02
Other South American	6	0.05
Other Hispanic or Latino	76	0.58
Hungarian	142	1.08
Irish	3,611	27.58
Italian	2,867	21.90
Latvian	12	0.09
Lithuanian	164	1.25
Northern European	16	0.12
Norwegian	84	0.64
Polish	1,046	7.99
Portuguese	191	1.46
Romanian	14	0.11
Russian	167	1.28
Scandinavian	5	0.04
Scotch-Irish	168	1.28
Scottish	342	2.61
Serbian	7	0.05
Slovak	22	0.17
Swedish	458	3.50
Swiss	61	0.47
Ukrainian	32	0.24
United States or American	607	4.64
Welsh	117	0.89
West Indian, excl. Hispanic:	18	0.14
Haitian	8	0.06
West Indian	10	0.08
White:	12,690	96.91
Not Hispanic (12,204)	12,316	94.06
Hispanic (346)	374	2.86

Colchester

Place Type: Town
County: New London
Population: 14,551

Ancestry/Race	Number	%
African American/Black:	274	1.88
Not Hispanic (197)	265	1.82
Hispanic (3)	9	0.06
African, sub-Saharan:	12	0.08
Ghanian	12	0.08

Notes: 1. Figures in the "Number" column do not add up to the total population due to: a) Ancestry/Race overlap — e.g. persons can report being both White and Irish, b) persons of Hispanic origin can report being any race, c) persons reporting two ancestries are counted in both categories. 2. Numbers in parentheses indicate the number of persons reporting this ancestry/race alone, not in combination with any other ancestry/race. 3. Refer to the Explanation of Data in the front of the book for more detailed information.

Alaska Native tribes, specified:	3	0.02
Eskimo (3)	3	0.02
Am. Ind. or Alaska Nat., not spec.	38	0.26
Albanian	27	0.19
American Indian tribes, specified:	90	0.62
Blackfeet (1)	5	0.03
Cherokee (2)	17	0.12
Cree	2	0.01
Delaware (1)	1	0.01
Latin American Indians (1)	1	0.01
Potawatomi (2)	5	0.03
All other tribes (30)	59	0.41
American Indian tribes, not spec.	9	0.06
Arab:	29	0.20
Lebanese	21	0.14
Syrian	8	0.05
Armenian	32	0.22
Asian:	119	0.82
Chinese, ex. Taiwanese (22)	26	0.18
Filipino (16)	26	0.18
Indian (30)	34	0.23
Japanese (7)	18	0.12
Korean (5)	5	0.03
Pakistani (1)	1	0.01
Thai (2)	2	0.01
Vietnamese (1)	3	0.02
Other Asian, not specified (2)	4	0.03
Austrian	72	0.49
Basque	13	0.09
British	82	0.56
Canadian	136	0.93
Croatian	8	0.05
Czech	53	0.36
Czechoslovakian	67	0.46
Danish	107	0.74
Dutch	185	1.27
Eastern European	13	0.09
English	2,110	14.50
European	125	0.86
Finnish	17	0.12
French, except Basque	1,510	10.38
French Canadian	1,092	7.50
German	1,843	12.67
Greek	125	0.86
Hawaii Native/Pacific Islander:	10	0.07
Polynesian: (2)	6	0.04
Native Hawaiian (1)	1	0.01
Samoan (1)	5	0.03
Other Pac. Isl., not spec.	4	0.03
Hispanic or Latino:	280	1.92
Central American:	2	0.01
Guatemalan	1	0.01
Honduran	1	0.01
Cuban	17	0.12
Dominican Republic	4	0.03
Mexican	36	0.25
Puerto Rican	129	0.89
South American:	41	0.28
Argentinean	1	0.01
Bolivian	1	0.01
Chilean	4	0.03
Colombian	1	0.01
Ecuadorian	6	0.04
Peruvian	21	0.14
Venezuelan	3	0.02
Other South American	4	0.03
Other Hispanic or Latino	51	0.35
Hungarian	74	0.51
Iranian	6	0.04
Irish	3,134	21.54
Italian	2,304	15.83
Lithuanian	186	1.28
Norwegian	58	0.40
Pennsylvania German	8	0.05
Polish	2,042	14.03
Portuguese	156	1.07
Romanian	14	0.10
Russian	291	2.00
Scotch-Irish	277	1.90
Scottish	339	2.33
Slovak	15	0.10
Swedish	493	3.39
Swiss	16	0.11
Turkish	11	0.08
Ukrainian	234	1.61
United States or American	837	5.75
Welsh	68	0.47
White:	14,062	96.64
Not Hispanic (13,755)	13,883	95.41
Hispanic (145)	179	1.23
Yugoslavian	13	0.09

Conning Towers-Nautilus Park

Place Type: Census Designated Place
County: New London
Population: 10,241

Ancestry/Race	Number	%
African American/Black:	1,107	10.81
Not Hispanic (943)	1,036	10.12
Hispanic (42)	71	0.69
African, sub-Saharan:	104	1.01
African	34	0.33
Cape Verdean	35	0.34
Nigerian	7	0.07
South African	28	0.27
Alaska Native tribes, specified:	1	0.01
Aleut (1)	1	0.01
Am. Ind. or Alaska Nat., not spec.	38	0.37
Albanian	12	0.12
American Indian tribes, specified:	136	1.33
Apache (1)	2	0.02
Blackfeet (1)	13	0.13
Cherokee (9)	48	0.47
Chickasaw (1)	1	0.01
Chippewa	4	0.04
Choctaw	13	0.13
Comanche (3)	3	0.03
Creek	3	0.03
Iroquois	6	0.06
Navajo (4)	6	0.06
Osage	1	0.01
Seminole	1	0.01
Sioux (1)	3	0.03
All other tribes (17)	32	0.31
American Indian tribes, not spec.	1	0.01
Arab:	6	0.06
Lebanese	6	0.06
Asian:	383	3.74
Cambodian (1)	1	0.01
Chinese, ex. Taiwanese (10)	15	0.15
Filipino (161)	254	2.48
Indian (12)	21	0.21
Japanese (15)	36	0.35
Korean (10)	20	0.20
Laotian (1)	1	0.01
Pakistani (8)	8	0.08
Thai (2)	4	0.04
Vietnamese (8)	12	0.12
Other Asian, specified (1)	1	0.01
Other Asian, not specified (6)	10	0.10
Belgian	14	0.14
British	30	0.29
Canadian	47	0.46
Celtic	7	0.07
Croatian	24	0.23
Czech	30	0.29
Czechoslovakian	23	0.22
Danish	8	0.08
Dutch	254	2.47
English	966	9.41
European	169	1.65
Finnish	48	0.47
French, except Basque	511	4.98
French Canadian	173	1.69
German	1,950	19.00
Greek	22	0.21
Hawaii Native/Pacific Islander:	62	0.61
Micronesian: (18)	20	0.20
Guamanian/Chamorro (11)	13	0.13
Other Micronesian (7)	7	0.07
Polynesian: (10)	29	0.28
Native Hawaiian (7)	19	0.19
Samoan (2)	9	0.09
Other Polynesian (1)	1	0.01
Other Pac. Isl., not spec. (5)	13	0.13
Hispanic or Latino:	635	6.20
Central American:	19	0.19
Costa Rican	4	0.04
Guatemalan	3	0.03
Panamanian	7	0.07
Salvadoran	3	0.03
Other Central American	2	0.02
Cuban	23	0.22
Dominican Republic	15	0.15
Mexican	236	2.30
Puerto Rican	212	2.07
South American:	22	0.21
Argentinean	2	0.02
Bolivian	1	0.01
Chilean	2	0.02
Colombian	9	0.09
Ecuadorian	4	0.04
Peruvian	4	0.04
Other Hispanic or Latino	108	1.05
Hungarian	68	0.66
Irish	1,536	14.96
Italian	802	7.81
Lithuanian	75	0.73
Maltese	24	0.23
Norwegian	178	1.73
Polish	258	2.51
Portuguese	84	0.82
Russian	70	0.68
Scandinavian	47	0.46
Scotch-Irish	272	2.65
Scottish	315	3.07
Serbian	27	0.26
Swedish	111	1.08
Swiss	45	0.44
Turkish	6	0.06
Ukrainian	30	0.29
United States or American	995	9.69
Welsh	129	1.26
West Indian, excl. Hispanic:	56	0.55
Bahamian	7	0.07
Haitian	23	0.22
Jamaican	26	0.25
White:	8,631	84.28
Not Hispanic (8,039)	8,280	80.85
Hispanic (288)	351	3.43

Coventry

Place Type: Town
County: Tolland
Population: 11,504

Ancestry/Race	Number	%
African American/Black:	107	0.93
Not Hispanic (58)	99	0.86
Hispanic (8)	8	0.07
Am. Ind. or Alaska Nat., not spec.	28	0.24
American Indian tribes, specified:	46	0.40
Apache	1	0.01
Blackfeet	1	0.01
Cherokee (3)	9	0.08
Cheyenne (1)	1	0.01
Chickasaw	2	0.02
Chippewa (1)	2	0.02
Choctaw	2	0.02
Iroquois	7	0.06
Kiowa	1	0.01
Latin American Indians	3	0.03
Lumbee (1)	1	0.01
Pueblo (1)	2	0.02
Sioux (1)	1	0.01
All other tribes (6)	13	0.11

Notes: 1. Figures in the "Number" column do not add up to the total population due to: a) Ancestry/Race overlap — e.g. persons can report being both White and Irish, b) persons of Hispanic origin can report being any race, c) persons reporting two ancestries are counted in both categories. 2. Numbers in parentheses indicate the number of persons reporting this ancestry/race alone, not in combination with any other ancestry/race. 3. Refer to the Explanation of Data in the front of the book for more detailed information.

American Indian tribes, not spec.	5	0.04
Arab:	18	0.16
Lebanese	7	0.06
Moroccan	11	0.10
Asian:	107	0.93
Cambodian (1)	1	0.01
Chinese, ex. Taiwanese (16)	19	0.17
Filipino (9)	25	0.22
Indian (15)	18	0.16
Japanese (4)	9	0.08
Korean (13)	15	0.13
Pakistani (3)	3	0.03
Taiwanese (2)	2	0.02
Thai (1)	1	0.01
Vietnamese (4)	5	0.04
Other Asian, specified (2)	4	0.03
Other Asian, not specified	5	0.04
Austrian	85	0.74
Belgian	9	0.08
British	54	0.47
Canadian	119	1.03
Croatian	6	0.05
Czech	44	0.38
Czechoslovakian	7	0.06
Danish	59	0.51
Dutch	115	1.00
Eastern European	14	0.12
English	1,879	16.33
European	61	0.53
Finnish	17	0.15
French, except Basque	1,591	13.83
French Canadian	694	6.03
German	1,843	16.02
Greek	58	0.50
Hawaii Native/Pacific Islander:	6	0.05
Polynesian: (1)	3	0.03
Native Hawaiian	2	0.02
Other Polynesian (1)	1	0.01
Other Pac. Isl., specified	2	0.02
Other Pac. Isl., not spec.	1	0.01
Hispanic or Latino:	198	1.72
Central American:	6	0.05
Guatemalan	5	0.04
Other Central American	1	0.01
Cuban	6	0.05
Dominican Republic	1	0.01
Mexican	34	0.30
Puerto Rican	94	0.82
South American:	23	0.20
Argentinean	1	0.01
Chilean	2	0.02
Colombian	5	0.04
Paraguayan	2	0.02
Peruvian	6	0.05
Uruguayan	1	0.01
Venezuelan	1	0.01
Other South American	5	0.04
Other Hispanic or Latino	34	0.30
Hungarian	95	0.83
Iranian	9	0.08
Irish	2,505	21.78
Italian	1,525	13.26
Latvian	19	0.17
Lithuanian	176	1.53
Northern European	3	0.03
Norwegian	83	0.72
Pennsylvania German	7	0.06
Polish	1,158	10.07
Portuguese	183	1.59
Romanian	6	0.05
Russian	111	0.96
Scandinavian	11	0.10
Scotch-Irish	242	2.10
Scottish	320	2.78
Slavic	50	0.43
Slovak	22	0.19
Swedish	391	3.40
Swiss	41	0.36
Ukrainian	100	0.87
United States or American	323	2.81
Welsh	105	0.91
West Indian, excl. Hispanic:	16	0.14
Jamaican	7	0.06
West Indian	9	0.08
White:	11,273	97.99
Not Hispanic (11,021)	11,125	96.71
Hispanic (132)	148	1.29

Cromwell

Place Type: Town
County: Middlesex
Population: 12,871

Ancestry/Race	Number	%
African American/Black:	467	3.63
Not Hispanic (386)	445	3.46
Hispanic (17)	22	0.17
African, sub-Saharan:	68	0.53
African	21	0.16
Nigerian	47	0.37
Am. Ind. or Alaska Nat., not spec.	12	0.09
American Indian tribes, specified:	33	0.26
Apache	4	0.03
Blackfeet	1	0.01
Cherokee (1)	6	0.05
Iroquois (2)	4	0.03
Latin American Indians	1	0.01
Seminole	2	0.02
Yaqui	4	0.03
All other tribes (4)	11	0.09
American Indian tribes, not spec.	6	0.05
Arab:	14	0.11
Egyptian	14	0.11
Armenian	11	0.09
Asian:	207	1.61
Chinese, ex. Taiwanese (43)	47	0.37
Filipino (12)	18	0.14
Indian (49)	63	0.49
Japanese (6)	9	0.07
Korean (13)	20	0.16
Laotian (1)	1	0.01
Pakistani (11)	19	0.15
Sri Lankan (5)	5	0.04
Thai (2)	2	0.02
Vietnamese (16)	16	0.12
Other Asian, not specified (1)	7	0.05
Austrian	97	0.75
British	91	0.71
Canadian	68	0.53
Croatian	5	0.04
Czech	59	0.46
Czechoslovakian	29	0.23
Danish	45	0.35
Dutch	112	0.87
English	1,724	13.39
European	84	0.65
Finnish	44	0.34
French, except Basque	754	5.86
French Canadian	506	3.93
German	1,487	11.55
Greek	150	1.17
Hawaii Native/Pacific Islander:	8	0.06
Polynesian: (1)	1	0.01
Native Hawaiian (1)	1	0.01
Other Pac. Isl., not spec.	7	0.05
Hispanic or Latino:	410	3.19
Central American:	17	0.13
Costa Rican	1	0.01
Guatemalan	3	0.02
Honduran	3	0.02
Panamanian	6	0.05
Salvadoran	2	0.02
Other Central American	2	0.02
Cuban	20	0.16
Dominican Republic	22	0.17
Mexican	58	0.45
Puerto Rican	194	1.51
South American:	42	0.33
Argentinean	2	0.02
Chilean	3	0.02
Colombian	8	0.06
Ecuadorian	5	0.04
Peruvian	17	0.13
Venezuelan	7	0.05
Other Hispanic or Latino	57	0.44
Hungarian	123	0.96
Iranian	21	0.16
Irish	2,537	19.71
Italian	2,930	22.76
Latvian	9	0.07
Lithuanian	95	0.74
Macedonian	44	0.34
Northern European	8	0.06
Norwegian	84	0.65
Polish	1,747	13.57
Portuguese	76	0.59
Romanian	13	0.10
Russian	179	1.39
Scandinavian	36	0.28
Scotch-Irish	48	0.37
Scottish	292	2.27
Slavic	8	0.06
Slovak	33	0.26
Swedish	640	4.97
Swiss	50	0.39
Turkish	19	0.15
Ukrainian	77	0.60
United States or American	580	4.51
Welsh	57	0.44
West Indian, excl. Hispanic:	31	0.24
Jamaican	31	0.24
White:	12,138	94.31
Not Hispanic (11,751)	11,876	92.27
Hispanic (229)	262	2.04
Yugoslavian	8	0.06

Danbury

Place Type: City
County: Fairfield
Population: 74,848

Ancestry/Race	Number	%
Afghan	12	0.02
African American/Black:	5,715	7.64
Not Hispanic (4,743)	5,244	7.01
Hispanic (317)	471	0.63
African, sub-Saharan:	396	0.53
African	218	0.29
Cape Verdean	52	0.07
Nigerian	92	0.12
Sierra Leonean	15	0.02
Other sub-Saharan African	19	0.03
Alaska Native tribes, specified:	3	0.00
Alaska Athabascan (1)	1	0.00
Tlingit-Haida	2	0.00
Am. Ind. or Alaska Nat., not spec.	226	0.30
Albanian	59	0.08
American Indian tribes, specified:	233	0.31
Apache (3)	4	0.01
Blackfeet (1)	22	0.03
Cherokee (11)	63	0.08
Cheyenne	2	0.00
Chippewa (2)	2	0.00
Choctaw	3	0.00
Cree	2	0.00
Iroquois (5)	16	0.02
Latin American Indians (32)	65	0.09
Lumbee (1)	1	0.00
Menominee (1)	1	0.00
Navajo (1)	2	0.00
Osage	1	0.00
Paiute	1	0.00
Pueblo	3	0.00
Seminole (2)	2	0.00
Sioux (3)	4	0.01
Ute (2)	2	0.00
All other tribes (17)	37	0.05
American Indian tribes, not spec.	55	0.07

Notes: 1. Figures in the "Number" column do not add up to the total population due to: a) Ancestry/Race overlap — e.g. persons can report being both White and Irish, b) persons of Hispanic origin can report being any race, c) persons reporting two ancestries are counted in both categories. 2. Numbers in parentheses indicate the number of persons reporting this ancestry/race alone, not in combination with any other ancestry/race. 3. Refer to the Explanation of Data in the front of the book for more detailed information.

Arab:	1,248	1.67
Arab/Arabic	115	0.15
Iraqi	6	0.01
Jordanian	19	0.03
Lebanese	958	1.28
Moroccan	7	0.01
Palestinian	12	0.02
Syrian	99	0.13
Other Arab	32	0.04
Armenian	6	0.01
Asian:	4,698	6.28
Bangladeshi (43)	63	0.08
Cambodian (771)	909	1.21
Chinese, ex. Taiwanese (544)	618	0.83
Filipino (273)	315	0.42
Indian (1,354)	1,503	2.01
Indonesian (3)	4	0.01
Japanese (45)	62	0.08
Korean (110)	127	0.17
Laotian (191)	216	0.29
Malaysian (6)	10	0.01
Pakistani (146)	187	0.25
Sri Lankan (8)	11	0.01
Taiwanese (12)	14	0.02
Thai (32)	52	0.07
Vietnamese (344)	389	0.52
Other Asian, specified (2)	8	0.01
Other Asian, not specified (101)	210	0.28
Assyrian/Chaldean/Syriac	40	0.05
Australian	11	0.01
Austrian	247	0.33
Belgian	65	0.09
Brazilian	4,133	5.52
British	255	0.34
Bulgarian	33	0.04
Canadian	225	0.30
Celtic	31	0.04
Croatian	26	0.03
Czech	341	0.46
Czechoslovakian	245	0.33
Danish	233	0.31
Dutch	664	0.89
Eastern European	150	0.20
English	4,922	6.58
Estonian	6	0.01
European	177	0.24
Finnish	147	0.20
French, except Basque	1,774	2.37
French Canadian	998	1.33
German	7,995	10.68
Greek	350	0.47
Guyanese	32	0.04
Hawaii Native/Pacific Islander:	110	0.15
Micronesian: (7)	13	0.02
Guamanian/Chamorro (7)	13	0.02
Polynesian: (9)	13	0.02
Native Hawaiian (9)	12	0.02
Samoan	1	0.00
Other Pac. Isl., specified	2	0.00
Other Pac. Isl., not spec. (10)	82	0.11
Hispanic or Latino:	11,791	15.75
Central American:	795	1.06
Costa Rican	78	0.10
Guatemalan	319	0.43
Honduran	52	0.07
Nicaraguan	177	0.24
Panamanian	9	0.01
Salvadoran	130	0.17
Other Central American	30	0.04
Cuban	138	0.18
Dominican Republic	2,033	2.72
Mexican	1,294	1.73
Puerto Rican	1,818	2.43
South American:	3,049	4.07
Argentinean	43	0.06
Bolivian	10	0.01
Chilean	27	0.04
Colombian	491	0.66
Ecuadorian	2,183	2.92
Paraguayan	2	0.00
Peruvian	237	0.32
Uruguayan	5	0.01
Venezuelan	21	0.03
Other South American	30	0.04
Other Hispanic or Latino	2,664	3.56
Hungarian	909	1.21
Icelander	11	0.01
Iranian	12	0.02
Irish	11,432	15.27
Israeli	54	0.07
Italian	11,869	15.86
Latvian	10	0.01
Lithuanian	269	0.36
Maltese	21	0.03
Northern European	18	0.02
Norwegian	408	0.55
Pennsylvania German	5	0.01
Polish	3,139	4.19
Portuguese	4,056	5.42
Romanian	101	0.13
Russian	910	1.22
Scandinavian	40	0.05
Scotch-Irish	706	0.94
Scottish	910	1.22
Serbian	8	0.01
Slavic	81	0.11
Slovak	631	0.84
Slovene	20	0.03
Swedish	975	1.30
Swiss	140	0.19
Turkish	58	0.08
Ukrainian	338	0.45
United States or American	2,613	3.49
Welsh	287	0.38
West Indian, excl. Hispanic:	927	1.24
Barbadian	38	0.05
Belizean	51	0.07
British West Indian	45	0.06
Haitian	276	0.37
Jamaican	477	0.64
Trinidadian and Tobagonian	33	0.04
U.S. Virgin Islander	7	0.01
White:	59,302	79.23
Not Hispanic (50,945)	52,615	70.30
Hispanic (5,908)	6,687	8.93
Yugoslavian	24	0.03

Darien

Place Type: Census Designated Place
County: Fairfield
Population: 19,607

Ancestry/Race	Number	%
Afghan	19	0.10
African American/Black:	114	0.58
Not Hispanic (83)	106	0.54
Hispanic (6)	8	0.04
African, sub-Saharan:	15	0.08
Sudanese	15	0.08
Am. Ind. or Alaska Nat., not spec.	12	0.06
Albanian	54	0.28
Alsatian	6	0.03
American Indian tribes, specified:	27	0.14
Blackfeet	1	0.01
Cherokee (2)	11	0.06
Cree (1)	1	0.01
Iroquois	1	0.01
Latin American Indians	2	0.01
Navajo	2	0.01
Sioux	1	0.01
All other tribes (1)	8	0.04
American Indian tribes, not spec.	2	0.01
Arab:	118	0.60
Arab/Arabic	21	0.11
Egyptian	26	0.13
Lebanese	49	0.25
Syrian	22	0.11
Armenian	42	0.21
Asian:	568	2.90
Chinese, ex. Taiwanese (129)	160	0.82
Filipino (25)	41	0.21
Indian (78)	90	0.46
Japanese (168)	189	0.96
Korean (39)	46	0.23
Malaysian (1)	1	0.01
Pakistani (13)	19	0.10
Taiwanese (1)	1	0.01
Thai (2)	2	0.01
Vietnamese (4)	4	0.02
Other Asian, specified (9)	9	0.05
Other Asian, not specified (2)	6	0.03
Australian	65	0.33
Austrian	138	0.70
Belgian	48	0.24
British	320	1.63
Canadian	265	1.35
Croatian	12	0.06
Czech	39	0.20
Czechoslovakian	64	0.33
Danish	184	0.94
Dutch	348	1.77
Eastern European	21	0.11
English	4,239	21.62
European	347	1.77
Finnish	9	0.05
French, except Basque	756	3.86
French Canadian	206	1.05
German	3,249	16.57
Greek	370	1.89
Hawaii Native/Pacific Islander:	10	0.05
Melanesian:	2	0.01
Fijian	2	0.01
Micronesian: (1)	1	0.01
Guamanian/Chamorro (1)	1	0.01
Polynesian: (2)	4	0.02
Native Hawaiian (1)	2	0.01
Samoan (1)	2	0.01
Other Pac. Isl., not spec. (2)	3	0.02
Hispanic or Latino:	429	2.19
Central American:	14	0.07
Costa Rican	3	0.02
Guatemalan	8	0.04
Honduran	1	0.01
Other Central American	2	0.01
Cuban	25	0.13
Dominican Republic	11	0.06
Mexican	86	0.44
Puerto Rican	46	0.23
South American:	136	0.69
Argentinean	13	0.07
Bolivian	1	0.01
Chilean	18	0.09
Colombian	41	0.21
Ecuadorian	13	0.07
Peruvian	28	0.14
Uruguayan	2	0.01
Venezuelan	12	0.06
Other South American	8	0.04
Other Hispanic or Latino	111	0.57
Hungarian	309	1.58
Iranian	26	0.13
Irish	4,663	23.78
Italian	2,933	14.96
Latvian	15	0.08
Lithuanian	101	0.52
New Zealander	6	0.03
Northern European	137	0.70
Norwegian	260	1.33
Pennsylvania German	8	0.04
Polish	658	3.36
Portuguese	52	0.27
Russian	233	1.19
Scandinavian	24	0.12
Scotch-Irish	594	3.03
Scottish	1,029	5.25
Slavic	32	0.16
Slovak	71	0.36
Slovene	7	0.04
Swedish	407	2.08

Notes: 1. Figures in the "Number" column do not add up to the total population due to: a) Ancestry/Race overlap — e.g. persons can report being both White and Irish, b) persons of Hispanic origin can report being any race, c) persons reporting two ancestries are counted in both categories. 2. Numbers in parentheses indicate the number of persons reporting this ancestry/race alone, not in combination with any other ancestry/race. 3. Refer to the Explanation of Data in the front of the book for more detailed information.

Swiss	172	0.88
Ukrainian	134	0.68
United States or American	817	4.17
Welsh	172	0.88
West Indian, excl. Hispanic:	14	0.07
Haitian	6	0.03
Jamaican	8	0.04
White:	18,955	96.67
Not Hispanic (18,445)	18,572	94.72
Hispanic (371)	383	1.95
Yugoslavian	34	0.17

Derby

Place Type: City
County: New Haven
Population: 12,391

Ancestry/Race	Number	%
African American/Black:	521	4.20
Not Hispanic (441)	492	3.97
Hispanic (8)	29	0.23
African, sub-Saharan:	67	0.54
African	8	0.06
Ghanian	59	0.48
Am. Ind. or Alaska Nat., not spec.	24	0.19
Albanian	26	0.21
American Indian tribes, specified:	42	0.34
Apache	2	0.02
Blackfeet (3)	3	0.02
Cherokee (1)	7	0.06
Chippewa (1)	1	0.01
Cree (1)	1	0.01
Iroquois	1	0.01
Latin American Indians (5)	9	0.07
Sioux (1)	1	0.01
All other tribes (5)	17	0.14
Arab:	24	0.19
Lebanese	7	0.06
Syrian	17	0.14
Asian:	237	1.91
Chinese, ex. Taiwanese (48)	50	0.40
Filipino (13)	20	0.16
Indian (101)	109	0.88
Korean (14)	14	0.11
Laotian (4)	5	0.04
Malaysian (4)	4	0.03
Pakistani (8)	13	0.10
Sri Lankan	2	0.02
Vietnamese (12)	13	0.10
Other Asian, not specified (6)	7	0.06
Austrian	30	0.24
Belgian	8	0.06
British	32	0.26
Canadian	24	0.19
Czech	93	0.75
Czechoslovakian	28	0.23
Danish	6	0.05
Dutch	74	0.60
English	920	7.42
European	49	0.40
French, except Basque	439	3.54
French Canadian	156	1.26
German	954	7.70
Greek	80	0.65
Hawaii Native/Pacific Islander:	9	0.07
Micronesian: (5)	5	0.04
Guamanian/Chamorro (5)	5	0.04
Polynesian: (1)	1	0.01
Native Hawaiian (1)	1	0.01
Other Pac. Isl., not spec. (2)	3	0.02
Hispanic or Latino:	950	7.67
Central American:	40	0.32
Costa Rican	11	0.09
Guatemalan	19	0.15
Honduran	3	0.02
Nicaraguan	2	0.02
Salvadoran	5	0.04
Cuban	12	0.10
Dominican Republic	26	0.21
Mexican	113	0.91
Puerto Rican	362	2.92
South American:	200	1.61
Argentinean	3	0.02
Colombian	16	0.13
Ecuadorian	171	1.38
Peruvian	5	0.04
Venezuelan	1	0.01
Other South American	4	0.03
Other Hispanic or Latino	197	1.59
Hungarian	315	2.54
Iranian	14	0.11
Irish	2,093	16.89
Israeli	10	0.08
Italian	4,143	33.44
Lithuanian	148	1.19
Macedonian	11	0.09
Norwegian	21	0.17
Polish	2,228	17.98
Portuguese	99	0.80
Russian	199	1.61
Scandinavian	7	0.06
Scotch-Irish	114	0.92
Scottish	215	1.74
Slavic	26	0.21
Slovak	106	0.86
Swedish	91	0.73
Swiss	7	0.06
Ukrainian	237	1.91
United States or American	343	2.77
Welsh	41	0.33
West Indian, excl. Hispanic:	73	0.59
Barbadian	8	0.06
Haitian	9	0.07
Jamaican	31	0.25
Trinidadian and Tobagonian	11	0.09
West Indian	14	0.11
White:	11,350	91.60
Not Hispanic (10,609)	10,739	86.67
Hispanic (553)	611	4.93
Yugoslavian	100	0.81

East Hampton

Place Type: Town
County: Middlesex
Population: 13,352

Ancestry/Race	Number	%
African American/Black:	322	2.41
Not Hispanic (260)	304	2.28
Hispanic (13)	18	0.13
African, sub-Saharan:	21	0.16
Kenyan	10	0.07
South African	11	0.08
Alaska Native tribes, specified:	6	0.04
Alaska Athabascan (2)	3	0.02
Aleut (1)	2	0.01
Tlingit-Haida (1)	1	0.01
Am. Ind. or Alaska Nat., not spec.	13	0.10
American Indian tribes, specified:	49	0.37
Apache (4)	5	0.04
Cherokee (4)	7	0.05
Chickasaw	1	0.01
Chippewa	1	0.01
Delaware	1	0.01
Iroquois (2)	7	0.05
Latin American Indians	1	0.01
Navajo (1)	1	0.01
All other tribes (8)	25	0.19
American Indian tribes, not spec.	3	0.02
Armenian	12	0.09
Asian:	424	3.18
Bangladeshi (2)	2	0.01
Cambodian (1)	1	0.01
Chinese, ex. Taiwanese (95)	123	0.92
Filipino (27)	37	0.28
Indian (53)	71	0.53
Indonesian (1)	4	0.03
Japanese (16)	37	0.28
Korean (32)	38	0.28
Laotian (10)	10	0.07
Malaysian (2)	2	0.01
Pakistani (4)	7	0.05
Sri Lankan (9)	9	0.07
Taiwanese (18)	22	0.16
Thai (15)	16	0.12
Vietnamese (18)	21	0.16
Other Asian, specified (2)	4	0.03
Other Asian, not specified (4)	20	0.15
Austrian	133	1.00
Belgian	21	0.16
British	58	0.43
Canadian	23	0.17
Celtic	12	0.09
Croatian	10	0.07
Czech	91	0.68
Czechoslovakian	25	0.19
Danish	67	0.50
Dutch	127	0.95
Eastern European	74	0.55
English	1,802	13.50
Estonian	14	0.10
European	85	0.64
Finnish	139	1.04
French, except Basque	1,157	8.67
French Canadian	687	5.15
German	1,494	11.19
Greek	79	0.59
Guyanese	13	0.10
Hawaii Native/Pacific Islander:	17	0.13
Micronesian: (1)	1	0.01
Other Micronesian (1)	1	0.01
Polynesian: (5)	13	0.10
Native Hawaiian (3)	11	0.08
Samoan (2)	2	0.01
Other Pac. Isl., not spec. (1)	3	0.02
Hispanic or Latino:	226	1.69
Central American:	13	0.10
Guatemalan	3	0.02
Panamanian	8	0.06
Other Central American	2	0.01
Cuban	24	0.18
Dominican Republic	12	0.09
Mexican	32	0.24
Puerto Rican	85	0.64
South American:	32	0.24
Argentinean	4	0.03
Bolivian	4	0.03
Chilean	1	0.01
Colombian	8	0.06
Paraguayan	1	0.01
Peruvian	4	0.03
Uruguayan	3	0.02
Venezuelan	6	0.04
Other South American	1	0.01
Other Hispanic or Latino	28	0.21
Hungarian	72	0.54
Irish	2,883	21.59
Italian	2,529	18.94
Latvian	13	0.10
Lithuanian	112	0.84
Norwegian	116	0.87
Polish	1,429	10.70
Portuguese	46	0.34
Romanian	45	0.34
Russian	292	2.19
Scandinavian	34	0.25
Scotch-Irish	266	1.99
Scottish	365	2.73
Slavic	7	0.05
Slovak	11	0.08
Swedish	461	3.45
Swiss	33	0.25
Ukrainian	63	0.47
United States or American	626	4.69
Welsh	110	0.82
West Indian, excl. Hispanic:	42	0.31
Jamaican	19	0.14
West Indian	23	0.17

Notes: 1. Figures in the "Number" column do not add up to the total population due to: a) Ancestry/Race overlap — e.g. persons can report being both White and Irish, b) persons of Hispanic origin can report being any race, c) persons reporting two ancestries are counted in both categories. 2. Numbers in parentheses indicate the number of persons reporting this ancestry/race alone, not in combination with any other ancestry/race. 3. Refer to the Explanation of Data in the front of the book for more detailed information.

Ancestry/Race	Number	%
White:	12,644	94.70
Not Hispanic (12,328)	12,488	93.53
Hispanic (138)	156	1.17
Yugoslavian	15	0.11

East Hartford

Place Type: Census Designated Place
County: Hartford
Population: 49,575

Ancestry/Race	Number	%
African American/Black:	10,155	20.48
Not Hispanic (9,051)	9,700	19.57
Hispanic (284)	455	0.92
African, sub-Saharan:	877	1.77
African	503	1.01
Cape Verdean	2	0.00
Ghanian	298	0.60
Nigerian	64	0.13
Sudanese	10	0.02
Alaska Native tribes, specified:	1	0.00
Tlingit-Haida (1)	1	0.00
Am. Ind. or Alaska Nat., not spec.	179	0.36
Albanian	23	0.05
American Indian tribes, specified:	249	0.50
Apache	3	0.01
Blackfeet (3)	36	0.07
Cherokee (7)	51	0.10
Chickasaw	2	0.00
Chippewa (2)	2	0.00
Choctaw (5)	7	0.01
Cree	1	0.00
Creek (1)	2	0.00
Iroquois (3)	13	0.03
Latin American Indians (21)	31	0.06
Navajo	1	0.00
Ottawa	1	0.00
Potawatomi (2)	5	0.01
Pueblo (1)	1	0.00
Seminole	1	0.00
Sioux (1)	2	0.00
All other tribes (24)	90	0.18
American Indian tribes, not spec.	22	0.04
Arab:	125	0.25
Egyptian	6	0.01
Lebanese	110	0.22
Moroccan	9	0.02
Armenian	34	0.07
Asian:	2,298	4.64
Bangladeshi (5)	23	0.05
Cambodian (28)	31	0.06
Chinese, ex. Taiwanese (117)	154	0.31
Filipino (161)	197	0.40
Hmong (8)	8	0.02
Indian (593)	662	1.34
Indonesian (6)	9	0.02
Japanese (30)	43	0.09
Korean (51)	59	0.12
Laotian (238)	297	0.60
Pakistani (32)	45	0.09
Taiwanese (2)	2	0.00
Thai (1)	4	0.01
Vietnamese (636)	676	1.36
Other Asian, not specified (40)	88	0.18
Assyrian/Chaldean/Syriac	22	0.04
Australian	9	0.02
Austrian	69	0.14
Brazilian	21	0.04
British	99	0.20
Bulgarian	51	0.10
Canadian	175	0.35
Celtic	8	0.02
Croatian	19	0.04
Czech	65	0.13
Czechoslovakian	47	0.09
Danish	122	0.25
Dutch	240	0.48
English	3,304	6.66
Estonian	15	0.03
European	93	0.19
Finnish	89	0.18
French, except Basque	3,940	7.95
French Canadian	2,094	4.22
German	2,840	5.73
Greek	150	0.30
Guyanese	170	0.34
Hawaii Native/Pacific Islander:	93	0.19
Micronesian: (2)	9	0.02
Guamanian/Chamorro (2)	9	0.02
Polynesian: (3)	14	0.03
Native Hawaiian (2)	10	0.02
Samoan (1)	4	0.01
Other Pac. Isl., not spec. (13)	70	0.14
Hispanic or Latino:	7,552	15.23
Central American:	221	0.45
Costa Rican	5	0.01
Guatemalan	15	0.03
Honduran	36	0.07
Nicaraguan	9	0.02
Panamanian	16	0.03
Salvadoran	132	0.27
Other Central American	8	0.02
Cuban	110	0.22
Dominican Republic	137	0.28
Mexican	259	0.52
Puerto Rican	5,121	10.33
South American:	757	1.53
Argentinean	12	0.02
Bolivian	33	0.07
Chilean	6	0.01
Colombian	245	0.49
Ecuadorian	41	0.08
Peruvian	378	0.76
Uruguayan	2	0.00
Venezuelan	12	0.02
Other South American	28	0.06
Other Hispanic or Latino	947	1.91
Hungarian	167	0.34
Irish	6,259	12.63
Israeli	16	0.03
Italian	5,910	11.92
Latvian	8	0.02
Lithuanian	368	0.74
Norwegian	134	0.27
Pennsylvania German	25	0.05
Polish	3,369	6.80
Portuguese	890	1.80
Russian	382	0.77
Scandinavian	21	0.04
Scotch-Irish	438	0.88
Scottish	653	1.32
Slavic	30	0.06
Slovak	61	0.12
Swedish	689	1.39
Swiss	29	0.06
Ukrainian	322	0.65
United States or American	1,262	2.55
Welsh	136	0.27
West Indian, excl. Hispanic:	1,846	3.72
Barbadian	80	0.16
British West Indian	74	0.15
Haitian	111	0.22
Jamaican	1,360	2.74
Trinidadian and Tobagonian	73	0.15
U.S. Virgin Islander	13	0.03
West Indian	121	0.24
Other West Indian	14	0.03
White:	33,127	66.82
Not Hispanic (29,557)	30,268	61.05
Hispanic (2,514)	2,859	5.77
Yugoslavian	28	0.06

East Haven

Place Type: Census Designated Place
County: New Haven
Population: 28,189

Ancestry/Race	Number	%
Acadian/Cajun	8	0.03
African American/Black:	454	1.61
Not Hispanic (377)	420	1.49
Hispanic (19)	34	0.12
African, sub-Saharan:	9	0.03
African	9	0.03
Am. Ind. or Alaska Nat., not spec.	53	0.19
American Indian tribes, specified:	72	0.26
Blackfeet (1)	6	0.02
Cherokee (4)	17	0.06
Iroquois (2)	5	0.02
Latin American Indians (1)	5	0.02
Potawatomi (1)	1	0.00
Pueblo	5	0.02
Sioux	2	0.01
Ute	1	0.00
Yaqui	1	0.00
All other tribes (17)	29	0.10
American Indian tribes, not spec.	3	0.01
Arab:	7	0.02
Arab/Arabic	7	0.02
Armenian	27	0.10
Asian:	620	2.20
Bangladeshi	2	0.01
Cambodian (43)	64	0.23
Chinese, ex. Taiwanese (81)	95	0.34
Filipino (46)	58	0.21
Indian (150)	165	0.59
Japanese (8)	9	0.03
Korean (21)	23	0.08
Laotian (22)	22	0.08
Malaysian (3)	3	0.01
Pakistani (20)	29	0.10
Taiwanese (3)	3	0.01
Thai (6)	6	0.02
Vietnamese (109)	116	0.41
Other Asian, not specified (15)	25	0.09
Australian	7	0.02
Austrian	30	0.11
Belgian	38	0.13
British	26	0.09
Canadian	87	0.31
Croatian	10	0.04
Czech	29	0.10
Czechoslovakian	7	0.02
Danish	6	0.02
Dutch	105	0.37
Eastern European	5	0.02
English	1,870	6.63
European	13	0.05
Finnish	7	0.02
French, except Basque	953	3.38
French Canadian	396	1.40
German	2,248	7.97
Greek	148	0.53
Hawaii Native/Pacific Islander:	8	0.03
Polynesian: (2)	2	0.01
Samoan (2)	2	0.01
Other Pac. Isl., not spec. (2)	6	0.02
Hispanic or Latino:	1,228	4.36
Central American:	55	0.20
Costa Rican	1	0.00
Guatemalan	37	0.13
Honduran	4	0.01
Nicaraguan	5	0.02
Salvadoran	4	0.01
Other Central American	4	0.01
Cuban	49	0.17
Dominican Republic	15	0.05
Mexican	97	0.34
Puerto Rican	604	2.14
South American:	203	0.72
Argentinean	10	0.04
Bolivian	3	0.01
Chilean	7	0.02
Colombian	52	0.18
Ecuadorian	70	0.25
Peruvian	32	0.11
Uruguayan	1	0.00
Venezuelan	9	0.03

Notes: 1. Figures in the "Number" column do not add up to the total population due to: a) Ancestry/Race overlap — e.g. persons can report being both White and Irish, b) persons of Hispanic origin can report being any race, c) persons reporting two ancestries are counted in both categories. 2. Numbers in parentheses indicate the number of persons reporting this ancestry/race alone, not in combination with any other ancestry/race. 3. Refer to the Explanation of Data in the front of the book for more detailed information.

Other South American	19	0.07
Other Hispanic or Latino	205	0.73
Hungarian	210	0.74
Iranian	28	0.10
Irish	5,301	18.81
Israeli	7	0.02
Italian	14,248	50.54
Lithuanian	156	0.55
Norwegian	122	0.43
Polish	2,256	8.00
Portuguese	229	0.81
Romanian	40	0.14
Russian	329	1.17
Scandinavian	41	0.15
Scotch-Irish	287	1.02
Scottish	235	0.83
Serbian	7	0.02
Slavic	6	0.02
Slovak	101	0.36
Swedish	273	0.97
Swiss	37	0.13
Ukrainian	198	0.70
United States or American	333	1.18
Welsh	21	0.07
West Indian, excl. Hispanic:	61	0.22
Haitian	18	0.06
Jamaican	43	0.15
White:	26,738	94.85
Not Hispanic (25,754)	25,959	92.09
Hispanic (721)	779	2.76
Yugoslavian	51	0.18

East Lyme

Place Type: Town
County: New London
Population: 18,118

Ancestry/Race	Number	%
African American/Black:	1,276	7.04
Not Hispanic (1,064)	1,150	6.35
Hispanic (90)	126	0.70
African, sub-Saharan:	167	0.92
African	56	0.31
Ethiopian	8	0.04
Kenyan	8	0.04
Nigerian	95	0.52
Am. Ind. or Alaska Nat., not spec.	70	0.39
American Indian tribes, specified:	114	0.63
Apache	1	0.01
Blackfeet (1)	4	0.02
Cherokee (4)	21	0.12
Chippewa (1)	1	0.01
Choctaw (1)	3	0.02
Iroquois (3)	6	0.03
Kiowa (1)	1	0.01
Latin American Indians (16)	22	0.12
Navajo	1	0.01
Seminole	2	0.01
All other tribes (27)	52	0.29
American Indian tribes, not spec.	6	0.03
Arab:	20	0.11
Lebanese	9	0.05
Syrian	11	0.06
Asian:	609	3.36
Bangladeshi (4)	4	0.02
Cambodian (5)	6	0.03
Chinese, ex. Taiwanese (190)	200	1.10
Filipino (29)	52	0.29
Hmong (6)	6	0.03
Indian (150)	166	0.92
Indonesian (5)	5	0.03
Japanese (16)	39	0.22
Korean (30)	35	0.19
Laotian (6)	6	0.03
Pakistani (9)	9	0.05
Sri Lankan (10)	10	0.06
Taiwanese (17)	17	0.09
Thai	1	0.01
Vietnamese (15)	15	0.08
Other Asian, specified (4)	6	0.03
Other Asian, not specified (12)	32	0.18
Austrian	65	0.36
Belgian	19	0.10
British	47	0.26
Bulgarian	9	0.05
Canadian	59	0.33
Croatian	12	0.07
Cypriot	9	0.05
Czech	72	0.40
Czechoslovakian	71	0.39
Danish	105	0.58
Dutch	262	1.45
Eastern European	23	0.13
English	2,983	16.46
Estonian	8	0.04
European	107	0.59
Finnish	63	0.35
French, except Basque	990	5.46
French Canadian	684	3.78
German	2,334	12.88
Greek	209	1.15
Hawaii Native/Pacific Islander:	20	0.11
Micronesian: (4)	4	0.02
Guamanian/Chamorro (3)	3	0.02
Other Micronesian (1)	1	0.01
Polynesian: (2)	9	0.05
Native Hawaiian (1)	8	0.04
Samoan (1)	1	0.01
Other Pac. Isl., not spec. (2)	7	0.04
Hispanic or Latino:	832	4.59
Central American:	5	0.03
Guatemalan	2	0.01
Honduran	1	0.01
Nicaraguan	1	0.01
Panamanian	1	0.01
Cuban	31	0.17
Dominican Republic	14	0.08
Mexican	52	0.29
Puerto Rican	563	3.11
South American:	75	0.41
Argentinean	3	0.02
Bolivian	5	0.03
Chilean	2	0.01
Colombian	27	0.15
Ecuadorian	4	0.02
Peruvian	25	0.14
Venezuelan	4	0.02
Other South American	5	0.03
Other Hispanic or Latino	92	0.51
Hungarian	115	0.63
Iranian	27	0.15
Irish	3,757	20.74
Italian	2,922	16.13
Lithuanian	168	0.93
Macedonian	7	0.04
Northern European	7	0.04
Norwegian	257	1.42
Polish	1,343	7.41
Portuguese	281	1.55
Romanian	75	0.41
Russian	379	2.09
Scotch-Irish	395	2.18
Scottish	514	2.84
Slavic	7	0.04
Swedish	552	3.05
Swiss	72	0.40
Turkish	27	0.15
Ukrainian	261	1.44
United States or American	558	3.08
Welsh	151	0.83
West Indian, excl. Hispanic:	59	0.33
Jamaican	34	0.19
West Indian	25	0.14
White:	16,077	88.73
Not Hispanic (15,390)	15,600	86.10
Hispanic (425)	477	2.63
Yugoslavian	17	0.09

Ellington

Place Type: Town
County: Tolland
Population: 12,921

Ancestry/Race	Number	%
African American/Black:	163	1.26
Not Hispanic (120)	153	1.18
Hispanic (8)	10	0.08
African, sub-Saharan:	24	0.19
African	7	0.05
Senegalese	17	0.13
Am. Ind. or Alaska Nat., not spec.	16	0.12
American Indian tribes, specified:	47	0.36
Blackfeet (3)	3	0.02
Cherokee (3)	13	0.10
Choctaw	1	0.01
Iroquois (1)	3	0.02
Latin American Indians	5	0.04
All other tribes (9)	23	0.18
American Indian tribes, not spec.	1	0.01
Arab:	81	0.63
Egyptian	8	0.06
Lebanese	73	0.56
Asian:	198	1.53
Chinese, ex. Taiwanese (18)	21	0.16
Filipino (29)	38	0.29
Indian (49)	56	0.43
Indonesian (1)	1	0.01
Japanese (10)	11	0.09
Korean (24)	25	0.19
Laotian (3)	3	0.02
Pakistani (8)	13	0.10
Thai (1)	1	0.01
Vietnamese (19)	19	0.15
Other Asian, not specified (4)	10	0.08
Austrian	90	0.70
Brazilian	40	0.31
British	53	0.41
Canadian	111	0.86
Cypriot	6	0.05
Czech	41	0.32
Czechoslovakian	27	0.21
Danish	121	0.94
Dutch	48	0.37
Eastern European	13	0.10
English	1,611	12.47
European	33	0.26
Finnish	53	0.41
French, except Basque	1,812	14.02
French Canadian	585	4.53
German	2,052	15.88
Greek	159	1.23
Hawaii Native/Pacific Islander:	7	0.05
Melanesian:	2	0.02
Fijian	2	0.02
Polynesian: (1)	3	0.02
Samoan (1)	3	0.02
Other Pac. Isl., not spec.	2	0.02
Hispanic or Latino:	181	1.40
Central American:	5	0.04
Costa Rican	2	0.02
Guatemalan	2	0.02
Panamanian	1	0.01
Cuban	11	0.09
Dominican Republic	1	0.01
Mexican	25	0.19
Puerto Rican	65	0.50
South American:	35	0.27
Chilean	1	0.01
Colombian	15	0.12
Ecuadorian	1	0.01
Peruvian	10	0.08
Venezuelan	8	0.06
Other Hispanic or Latino	39	0.30
Hungarian	136	1.05
Iranian	7	0.05
Irish	2,719	21.04
Israeli	8	0.06

Notes: 1. Figures in the "Number" column do not add up to the total population due to: a) Ancestry/Race overlap — e.g. persons can report being both White and Irish, b) persons of Hispanic origin can report being any race, c) persons reporting two ancestries are counted in both categories. 2. Numbers in parentheses indicate the number of persons reporting this ancestry/race alone, not in combination with any other ancestry/race. 3. Refer to the Explanation of Data in the front of the book for more detailed information.

Italian	1,980	15.32
Latvian	35	0.27
Lithuanian	289	2.24
Norwegian	50	0.39
Polish	1,524	11.79
Portuguese	82	0.63
Romanian	6	0.05
Russian	207	1.60
Scandinavian	7	0.05
Scotch-Irish	164	1.27
Scottish	280	2.17
Serbian	15	0.12
Slovak	81	0.63
Swedish	406	3.14
Swiss	517	4.00
Ukrainian	42	0.33
United States or American	533	4.13
Welsh	98	0.76
West Indian, excl. Hispanic:	8	0.06
British West Indian	8	0.06
White:	12,525	96.94
Not Hispanic (12,333)	12,411	96.05
Hispanic (101)	114	0.88

Enfield

Place Type: Town
County: Hartford
Population: 45,212

Ancestry/Race	Number	%
African American/Black:	2,815	6.23
Not Hispanic (2,382)	2,599	5.75
Hispanic (154)	216	0.48
African, sub-Saharan:	312	0.69
African	226	0.50
Cape Verdean	35	0.08
Ethiopian	9	0.02
Ghanian	8	0.02
Nigerian	12	0.03
South African	22	0.05
Am. Ind. or Alaska Nat., not spec.	115	0.25
Albanian	4	0.01
American Indian tribes, specified:	149	0.33
Apache	2	0.00
Blackfeet (1)	9	0.02
Cherokee (5)	27	0.06
Cheyenne	1	0.00
Chickasaw	1	0.00
Chippewa (5)	6	0.01
Cree (1)	4	0.01
Creek	2	0.00
Iroquois (2)	14	0.03
Latin American Indians (1)	7	0.02
Navajo (2)	5	0.01
Pueblo (2)	2	0.00
Seminole (1)	3	0.01
Sioux (2)	7	0.02
All other tribes (25)	59	0.13
American Indian tribes, not spec.	28	0.06
Arab:	152	0.34
Egyptian	27	0.06
Lebanese	112	0.25
Syrian	13	0.03
Armenian	103	0.23
Asian:	751	1.66
Cambodian (25)	27	0.06
Chinese, ex. Taiwanese (96)	118	0.26
Filipino (80)	109	0.24
Hmong (55)	58	0.13
Indian (150)	174	0.38
Indonesian (9)	9	0.02
Japanese (14)	32	0.07
Korean (46)	53	0.12
Laotian (18)	22	0.05
Pakistani (20)	25	0.06
Taiwanese (2)	4	0.01
Thai (5)	7	0.02
Vietnamese (51)	55	0.12
Other Asian, specified (1)	2	0.00
Other Asian, not specified (22)	56	0.12
Assyrian/Chaldean/Syriac	22	0.05
Australian	3	0.01
Austrian	124	0.27
Belgian	24	0.05
Brazilian	20	0.04
British	136	0.30
Bulgarian	7	0.02
Canadian	237	0.52
Croatian	30	0.07
Czech	194	0.43
Czechoslovakian	98	0.22
Danish	224	0.50
Dutch	246	0.54
Eastern European	21	0.05
English	5,198	11.50
European	81	0.18
Finnish	74	0.16
French, except Basque	6,587	14.57
French Canadian	3,499	7.74
German	4,353	9.63
Greek	358	0.79
Guyanese	75	0.17
Hawaii Native/Pacific Islander:	54	0.12
Micronesian:	1	0.00
Guamanian/Chamorro	1	0.00
Polynesian: (7)	24	0.05
Native Hawaiian (2)	13	0.03
Samoan (4)	7	0.02
Other Polynesian (1)	4	0.01
Other Pac. Isl., specified	1	0.00
Other Pac. Isl., not spec.	28	0.06
Hispanic or Latino:	1,691	3.74
Central American:	23	0.05
Costa Rican	1	0.00
Guatemalan	6	0.01
Honduran	5	0.01
Panamanian	1	0.00
Salvadoran	3	0.01
Other Central American	7	0.02
Cuban	65	0.14
Dominican Republic	26	0.06
Mexican	205	0.45
Puerto Rican	1,128	2.49
South American:	63	0.14
Colombian	29	0.06
Ecuadorian	5	0.01
Peruvian	23	0.05
Venezuelan	4	0.01
Other South American	2	0.00
Other Hispanic or Latino	181	0.40
Hungarian	241	0.53
Iranian	7	0.02
Irish	9,530	21.08
Italian	8,247	18.24
Latvian	9	0.02
Lithuanian	653	1.44
Norwegian	266	0.59
Pennsylvania German	8	0.02
Polish	5,896	13.04
Portuguese	326	0.72
Romanian	24	0.05
Russian	349	0.77
Scandinavian	88	0.19
Scotch-Irish	684	1.51
Scottish	963	2.13
Slavic	39	0.09
Slovak	37	0.08
Slovene	4	0.01
Swedish	635	1.40
Swiss	56	0.12
Turkish	7	0.02
Ukrainian	198	0.44
United States or American	1,029	2.28
Welsh	134	0.30
West Indian, excl. Hispanic:	285	0.63
Bahamian	6	0.01
Barbadian	5	0.01
British West Indian	8	0.02
Haitian	6	0.01
Jamaican	197	0.44
Trinidadian and Tobagonian	14	0.03
U.S. Virgin Islander	9	0.02
West Indian	40	0.09
White:	41,110	90.93
Not Hispanic (39,931)	40,319	89.18
Hispanic (642)	791	1.75
Yugoslavian	14	0.03

Fairfield

Place Type: Town
County: Fairfield
Population: 57,340

Ancestry/Race	Number	%
African American/Black:	734	1.28
Not Hispanic (598)	702	1.22
Hispanic (25)	32	0.06
African, sub-Saharan:	81	0.14
African	28	0.05
Nigerian	12	0.02
South African	41	0.07
Am. Ind. or Alaska Nat., not spec.	50	0.09
Albanian	168	0.29
Alsatian	5	0.01
American Indian tribes, specified:	58	0.10
Apache (1)	1	0.00
Cherokee (5)	25	0.04
Choctaw (1)	6	0.01
Comanche (1)	1	0.00
Iroquois	5	0.01
Latin American Indians (2)	4	0.01
Navajo (3)	3	0.01
Sioux (1)	1	0.00
All other tribes (2)	12	0.02
American Indian tribes, not spec.	3	0.01
Arab:	419	0.73
Arab/Arabic	25	0.04
Egyptian	30	0.05
Iraqi	7	0.01
Lebanese	167	0.29
Moroccan	6	0.01
Palestinian	10	0.02
Syrian	169	0.29
Other Arab	5	0.01
Armenian	172	0.30
Asian:	1,434	2.50
Bangladeshi (12)	12	0.02
Cambodian (18)	19	0.03
Chinese, ex. Taiwanese (334)	392	0.68
Filipino (104)	154	0.27
Indian (338)	364	0.63
Indonesian	3	0.01
Japanese (61)	102	0.18
Korean (148)	158	0.28
Laotian (12)	14	0.02
Malaysian (1)	1	0.00
Pakistani (23)	39	0.07
Sri Lankan (1)	4	0.01
Taiwanese (3)	4	0.01
Thai (20)	25	0.04
Vietnamese (44)	57	0.10
Other Asian, specified	2	0.00
Other Asian, not specified (36)	84	0.15
Australian	45	0.08
Austrian	589	1.03
Belgian	44	0.08
Brazilian	163	0.28
British	394	0.69
Canadian	200	0.35
Carpatho Rusyn	7	0.01
Celtic	42	0.07
Croatian	67	0.12
Czech	311	0.54
Czechoslovakian	217	0.38
Danish	369	0.64
Dutch	672	1.17
Eastern European	263	0.46
English	7,038	12.27

Notes: 1. Figures in the "Number" column do not add up to the total population due to: a) Ancestry/Race overlap — e.g. persons can report being both White and Irish, b) persons of Hispanic origin can report being any race, c) persons reporting two ancestries are counted in both categories. 2. Numbers in parentheses indicate the number of persons reporting this ancestry/race alone, not in combination with any other ancestry/race. 3. Refer to the Explanation of Data in the front of the book for more detailed information.

Estonian	6	0.01
European	334	0.58
Finnish	130	0.23
French, except Basque	1,672	2.92
French Canadian	827	1.44
German	6,647	11.59
Greek	753	1.31
Guyanese	14	0.02
Hawaii Native/Pacific Islander:	33	0.06
Micronesian: (2)	3	0.01
Guamanian/Chamorro (2)	3	0.01
Polynesian: (11)	16	0.03
Native Hawaiian (4)	7	0.01
Samoan (7)	8	0.01
Other Polynesian	1	0.00
Other Pac. Isl., specified	2	0.00
Other Pac. Isl., not spec. (3)	12	0.02
Hispanic or Latino:	1,340	2.34
Central American:	69	0.12
Costa Rican	17	0.03
Guatemalan	9	0.02
Honduran	8	0.01
Nicaraguan	3	0.01
Panamanian	4	0.01
Salvadoran	21	0.04
Other Central American	7	0.01
Cuban	111	0.19
Dominican Republic	20	0.03
Mexican	171	0.30
Puerto Rican	438	0.76
South American:	257	0.45
Argentinean	24	0.04
Bolivian	6	0.01
Chilean	20	0.03
Colombian	65	0.11
Ecuadorian	72	0.13
Paraguayan	10	0.02
Peruvian	39	0.07
Uruguayan	3	0.01
Venezuelan	12	0.02
Other South American	6	0.01
Other Hispanic or Latino	274	0.48
Hungarian	3,088	5.39
Iranian	66	0.12
Irish	13,816	24.09
Israeli	91	0.16
Italian	11,290	19.69
Latvian	72	0.13
Lithuanian	394	0.69
Luxemburger	8	0.01
Macedonian	64	0.11
Maltese	9	0.02
Northern European	35	0.06
Norwegian	532	0.93
Polish	3,904	6.81
Portuguese	441	0.77
Romanian	357	0.62
Russian	1,881	3.28
Scandinavian	87	0.15
Scotch-Irish	920	1.60
Scottish	1,332	2.32
Serbian	8	0.01
Slavic	53	0.09
Slovak	650	1.13
Slovene	173	0.30
Swedish	1,289	2.25
Swiss	223	0.39
Turkish	51	0.09
Ukrainian	463	0.81
United States or American	2,016	3.52
Welsh	405	0.71
West Indian, excl. Hispanic:	196	0.34
Bermudan	8	0.01
Dutch West Indian	4	0.01
Haitian	58	0.10
Jamaican	111	0.19
Trinidadian and Tobagonian	15	0.03
White:	55,107	96.11
Not Hispanic (53,669)	54,057	94.27
Hispanic (961)	1,050	1.83
Yugoslavian	171	0.30

Farmington

Place Type: Town
County: Hartford
Population: 23,641

Ancestry/Race	Number	%
African American/Black:	419	1.77
Not Hispanic (354)	396	1.68
Hispanic (12)	23	0.10
African, sub-Saharan:	8	0.03
African	8	0.03
Am. Ind. or Alaska Nat., not spec.	20	0.08
Albanian	5	0.02
American Indian tribes, specified:	45	0.19
Blackfeet	1	0.00
Cherokee	13	0.05
Comanche	1	0.00
Iroquois (2)	4	0.02
Latin American Indians (2)	7	0.03
Lumbee (1)	1	0.00
Seminole (1)	2	0.01
All other tribes (10)	16	0.07
American Indian tribes, not spec.	6	0.03
Arab:	167	0.71
Arab/Arabic	42	0.18
Egyptian	64	0.27
Lebanese	27	0.11
Palestinian	12	0.05
Syrian	22	0.09
Armenian	187	0.79
Asian:	998	4.22
Bangladeshi (3)	3	0.01
Cambodian (2)	4	0.02
Chinese, ex. Taiwanese (257)	289	1.22
Filipino (38)	55	0.23
Indian (273)	292	1.24
Indonesian (8)	11	0.05
Japanese (49)	67	0.28
Korean (106)	109	0.46
Laotian (9)	9	0.04
Pakistani (48)	64	0.27
Sri Lankan (2)	2	0.01
Taiwanese (19)	19	0.08
Thai (2)	4	0.02
Vietnamese (40)	45	0.19
Other Asian, specified	1	0.00
Other Asian, not specified (14)	24	0.10
Assyrian/Chaldean/Syriac	13	0.05
Australian	36	0.15
Austrian	172	0.73
Belgian	62	0.26
Brazilian	15	0.06
British	112	0.47
Canadian	181	0.77
Croatian	4	0.02
Czech	108	0.46
Czechoslovakian	48	0.20
Danish	150	0.63
Dutch	93	0.39
Eastern European	28	0.12
English	3,133	13.25
European	107	0.45
Finnish	59	0.25
French, except Basque	1,419	6.00
French Canadian	1,004	4.25
German	2,750	11.63
Greek	232	0.98
Hawaii Native/Pacific Islander:	13	0.05
Polynesian: (1)	2	0.01
Native Hawaiian (1)	1	0.00
Samoan	1	0.00
Other Pac. Isl., specified	1	0.00
Other Pac. Isl., not spec.	10	0.04
Hispanic or Latino:	517	2.19
Central American:	12	0.05
Costa Rican	1	0.00
Guatemalan	6	0.03
Panamanian	3	0.01
Salvadoran	2	0.01
Cuban	35	0.15
Dominican Republic	5	0.02
Mexican	66	0.28
Puerto Rican	190	0.80
South American:	91	0.38
Argentinean	15	0.06
Chilean	6	0.03
Colombian	23	0.10
Ecuadorian	2	0.01
Peruvian	32	0.14
Venezuelan	8	0.03
Other South American	5	0.02
Other Hispanic or Latino	118	0.50
Hungarian	157	0.66
Icelander	8	0.03
Iranian	13	0.05
Irish	5,030	21.28
Israeli	24	0.10
Italian	4,451	18.83
Latvian	6	0.03
Lithuanian	159	0.67
Norwegian	198	0.84
Pennsylvania German	6	0.03
Polish	3,372	14.26
Portuguese	188	0.80
Romanian	7	0.03
Russian	760	3.21
Scandinavian	19	0.08
Scotch-Irish	285	1.21
Scottish	503	2.13
Serbian	4	0.02
Slovak	71	0.30
Swedish	768	3.25
Swiss	28	0.12
Turkish	16	0.07
Ukrainian	262	1.11
United States or American	601	2.54
Welsh	138	0.58
West Indian, excl. Hispanic:	19	0.08
Barbadian	9	0.04
Haitian	10	0.04
White:	22,175	93.80
Not Hispanic (21,623)	21,781	92.13
Hispanic (341)	394	1.67
Yugoslavian	14	0.06

Glastonbury

Place Type: Town
County: Hartford
Population: 31,876

Ancestry/Race	Number	%
Acadian/Cajun	8	0.03
African American/Black:	575	1.80
Not Hispanic (454)	529	1.66
Hispanic (35)	46	0.14
African, sub-Saharan:	24	0.08
African	17	0.05
South African	7	0.02
Am. Ind. or Alaska Nat., not spec.	22	0.07
Albanian	75	0.24
American Indian tribes, specified:	69	0.22
Blackfeet (1)	1	0.00
Cherokee	7	0.02
Chippewa (1)	1	0.00
Choctaw	3	0.01
Cree (2)	3	0.01
Iroquois (2)	9	0.03
Latin American Indians (10)	10	0.03
Lumbee	3	0.01
Navajo	1	0.00
Potawatomi (1)	1	0.00
Sioux	1	0.00
All other tribes (18)	29	0.09
American Indian tribes, not spec.	1	0.00
Arab:	106	0.33
Arab/Arabic	50	0.16

Notes: 1. Figures in the "Number" column do not add up to the total population due to: a) Ancestry/Race overlap — e.g. persons can report being both White and Irish, b) persons of Hispanic origin can report being any race, c) persons reporting two ancestries are counted in both categories. 2. Numbers in parentheses indicate the number of persons reporting this ancestry/race alone, not in combination with any other ancestry/race. 3. Refer to the Explanation of Data in the front of the book for more detailed information.

Ancestry/Race	Number	%
Egyptian	6	0.02
Jordanian	20	0.06
Lebanese	11	0.03
Syrian	19	0.06
Armenian	31	0.10
Asian:	1,204	3.78
Bangladeshi (3)	6	0.02
Cambodian (2)	2	0.01
Chinese, ex. Taiwanese (239)	266	0.83
Filipino (73)	93	0.29
Indian (424)	435	1.36
Indonesian	1	0.00
Japanese (51)	76	0.24
Korean (155)	168	0.53
Laotian (5)	6	0.02
Pakistani (35)	38	0.12
Sri Lankan (2)	2	0.01
Taiwanese (18)	24	0.08
Thai (6)	7	0.02
Vietnamese (53)	55	0.17
Other Asian, specified (1)	3	0.01
Other Asian, not specified (11)	22	0.07
Australian	6	0.02
Austrian	269	0.84
Belgian	27	0.08
Brazilian	39	0.12
British	221	0.69
Canadian	59	0.19
Croatian	12	0.04
Czech	118	0.37
Czechoslovakian	85	0.27
Danish	156	0.49
Dutch	355	1.11
Eastern European	123	0.39
English	4,878	15.30
Estonian	8	0.03
European	323	1.01
Finnish	119	0.37
French, except Basque	2,142	6.72
French Canadian	1,247	3.91
German	3,784	11.87
Greek	493	1.55
Hawaii Native/Pacific Islander:	12	0.04
Polynesian: (2)	4	0.01
Native Hawaiian (2)	2	0.01
Samoan	2	0.01
Other Pac. Isl., not spec.	8	0.03
Hispanic or Latino:	799	2.51
Central American:	30	0.09
Costa Rican	7	0.02
Guatemalan	8	0.03
Honduran	2	0.01
Nicaraguan	4	0.01
Panamanian	3	0.01
Salvadoran	5	0.02
Other Central American	1	0.00
Cuban	61	0.19
Dominican Republic	13	0.04
Mexican	62	0.19
Puerto Rican	347	1.09
South American:	162	0.51
Argentinean	6	0.02
Chilean	4	0.01
Colombian	49	0.15
Ecuadorian	7	0.02
Paraguayan	1	0.00
Peruvian	85	0.27
Uruguayan	1	0.00
Venezuelan	3	0.01
Other South American	6	0.02
Other Hispanic or Latino	124	0.39
Hungarian	297	0.93
Iranian	9	0.03
Irish	7,325	22.98
Italian	6,274	19.68
Latvian	8	0.03
Lithuanian	440	1.38
Northern European	79	0.25
Norwegian	303	0.95
Pennsylvania German	7	0.02
Polish	3,190	10.01
Portuguese	544	1.71
Romanian	62	0.19
Russian	699	2.19
Scandinavian	35	0.11
Scotch-Irish	402	1.26
Scottish	847	2.66
Serbian	6	0.02
Slavic	57	0.18
Slovak	95	0.30
Slovene	11	0.03
Swedish	1,053	3.30
Swiss	182	0.57
Turkish	67	0.21
Ukrainian	177	0.56
United States or American	1,004	3.15
Welsh	268	0.84
West Indian, excl. Hispanic:	131	0.41
Barbadian	18	0.06
Haitian	16	0.05
Jamaican	80	0.25
West Indian	17	0.05
White:	29,924	93.88
Not Hispanic (29,228)	29,441	92.36
Hispanic (450)	483	1.52
Yugoslavian	17	0.05

Granby

Place Type: Town
County: Hartford
Population: 10,347

Ancestry/Race	Number	%
Acadian/Cajun	10	0.10
African American/Black:	87	0.84
Not Hispanic (61)	85	0.82
Hispanic (2)	2	0.02
Am. Ind. or Alaska Nat., not spec.	14	0.14
Albanian	31	0.30
American Indian tribes, specified:	31	0.30
Blackfeet (1)	1	0.01
Cherokee (3)	5	0.05
Chippewa (2)	2	0.02
Cree	3	0.03
Creek (2)	2	0.02
Iroquois	1	0.01
Seminole	1	0.01
Sioux (1)	5	0.05
All other tribes (3)	11	0.11
American Indian tribes, not spec.	4	0.04
Arab:	9	0.09
Syrian	9	0.09
Armenian	16	0.15
Asian:	93	0.90
Chinese, ex. Taiwanese (22)	25	0.24
Filipino (7)	12	0.12
Indian (23)	24	0.23
Japanese (1)	2	0.02
Korean (8)	8	0.08
Taiwanese (1)	4	0.04
Thai (2)	2	0.02
Vietnamese (10)	10	0.10
Other Asian, not specified (3)	6	0.06
Austrian	91	0.88
Belgian	7	0.07
British	123	1.19
Canadian	75	0.72
Czech	40	0.39
Czechoslovakian	24	0.23
Danish	105	1.01
Dutch	104	1.01
Eastern European	11	0.11
English	2,100	20.30
Estonian	23	0.22
European	143	1.38
Finnish	50	0.48
French, except Basque	830	8.02
French Canadian	524	5.06
German	1,641	15.86
Greek	87	0.84
Hawaii Native/Pacific Islander:	4	0.04
Polynesian: (1)	2	0.02
Native Hawaiian	1	0.01
Samoan (1)	1	0.01
Other Pac. Isl., not spec. (1)	2	0.02
Hispanic or Latino:	134	1.30
Central American:	6	0.06
Costa Rican	1	0.01
Guatemalan	2	0.02
Panamanian	3	0.03
Cuban	9	0.09
Dominican Republic	1	0.01
Mexican	33	0.32
Puerto Rican	37	0.36
South American:	28	0.27
Argentinean	2	0.02
Colombian	10	0.10
Ecuadorian	2	0.02
Peruvian	6	0.06
Uruguayan	4	0.04
Venezuelan	1	0.01
Other South American	3	0.03
Other Hispanic or Latino	20	0.19
Hungarian	49	0.47
Irish	2,140	20.68
Israeli	25	0.24
Italian	1,393	13.46
Latvian	9	0.09
Lithuanian	96	0.93
New Zealander	10	0.10
Northern European	18	0.17
Norwegian	91	0.88
Polish	941	9.09
Portuguese	49	0.47
Russian	305	2.95
Scandinavian	6	0.06
Scotch-Irish	256	2.47
Scottish	379	3.66
Slavic	37	0.36
Slovak	29	0.28
Slovene	25	0.24
Swedish	268	2.59
Swiss	80	0.77
Ukrainian	19	0.18
United States or American	399	3.86
Welsh	93	0.90
West Indian, excl. Hispanic:	29	0.28
Jamaican	17	0.16
Trinidadian and Tobagonian	3	0.03
West Indian	9	0.09
White:	10,149	98.09
Not Hispanic (10,000)	10,042	97.05
Hispanic (92)	107	1.03

Greenwich

Place Type: Town
County: Fairfield
Population: 61,101

Ancestry/Race	Number	%
African American/Black:	1,204	1.97
Not Hispanic (990)	1,147	1.88
Hispanic (27)	57	0.09
African, sub-Saharan:	122	0.20
African	25	0.04
Cape Verdean	39	0.06
Sierra Leonean	6	0.01
South African	52	0.09
Alaska Native tribes, specified:	1	0.00
Alaska Athabascan (1)	1	0.00
Am. Ind. or Alaska Nat., not spec.	67	0.11
Alsatian	19	0.03
American Indian tribes, specified:	82	0.13
Apache	1	0.00
Blackfeet	9	0.01
Cherokee (2)	18	0.03
Chippewa (1)	1	0.00
Choctaw (1)	1	0.00

Notes: 1. Figures in the "Number" column do not add up to the total population due to: a) Ancestry/Race overlap — e.g. persons can report being both White and Irish, b) persons of Hispanic origin can report being any race, c) persons reporting two ancestries are counted in both categories. 2. Numbers in parentheses indicate the number of persons reporting this ancestry/race alone, not in combination with any other ancestry/race. 3. Refer to the Explanation of Data in the front of the book for more detailed information.

Ancestry/Race	Number	%
Cree	2	0.00
Creek (1)	1	0.00
Delaware (1)	7	0.01
Iroquois (2)	11	0.02
Kiowa	1	0.00
Latin American Indians (7)	14	0.02
Puget Sound Salish (1)	1	0.00
Seminole	1	0.00
Sioux (2)	4	0.01
All other tribes (4)	10	0.02
American Indian tribes, not spec.	17	0.03
Arab:	414	0.68
Arab/Arabic	53	0.09
Egyptian	53	0.09
Iraqi	6	0.01
Lebanese	158	0.26
Moroccan	33	0.05
Palestinian	21	0.03
Syrian	80	0.13
Other Arab	10	0.02
Armenian	157	0.26
Asian:	3,565	5.83
Bangladeshi	3	0.00
Cambodian (1)	1	0.00
Chinese, ex. Taiwanese (612)	720	1.18
Filipino (405)	448	0.73
Indian (334)	399	0.65
Indonesian (5)	9	0.01
Japanese (1,402)	1,506	2.46
Korean (232)	287	0.47
Malaysian (2)	6	0.01
Pakistani (15)	24	0.04
Sri Lankan	2	0.00
Taiwanese (12)	13	0.02
Thai (21)	24	0.04
Vietnamese (50)	62	0.10
Other Asian, specified (5)	5	0.01
Other Asian, not specified (18)	56	0.09
Australian	156	0.26
Austrian	773	1.27
Belgian	55	0.09
Brazilian	239	0.39
British	1,114	1.82
Bulgarian	86	0.14
Canadian	338	0.55
Celtic	6	0.01
Croatian	136	0.22
Cypriot	12	0.02
Czech	423	0.69
Czechoslovakian	203	0.33
Danish	646	1.06
Dutch	939	1.54
Eastern European	193	0.32
English	8,290	13.57
Estonian	11	0.02
European	578	0.95
Finnish	303	0.50
French, except Basque	1,566	2.56
French Canadian	275	0.45
German	7,303	11.95
Greek	524	0.86
Hawaii Native/Pacific Islander:	37	0.06
Micronesian: (1)	1	0.00
Guamanian/Chamorro (1)	1	0.00
Polynesian: (8)	15	0.02
Native Hawaiian (5)	11	0.02
Samoan (3)	4	0.01
Other Pac. Isl., not spec. (7)	21	0.03
Hispanic or Latino:	3,846	6.29
Central American:	259	0.42
Costa Rican	10	0.02
Guatemalan	113	0.18
Honduran	35	0.06
Nicaraguan	6	0.01
Panamanian	15	0.02
Salvadoran	71	0.12
Other Central American	9	0.01
Cuban	120	0.20
Dominican Republic	22	0.04
Mexican	481	0.79
Puerto Rican	302	0.49
South American:	1,697	2.78
Argentinean	172	0.28
Bolivian	17	0.03
Chilean	134	0.22
Colombian	659	1.08
Ecuadorian	175	0.29
Paraguayan	63	0.10
Peruvian	285	0.47
Uruguayan	74	0.12
Venezuelan	55	0.09
Other South American	63	0.10
Other Hispanic or Latino	965	1.58
Hungarian	530	0.87
Iranian	125	0.20
Irish	10,130	16.58
Israeli	34	0.06
Italian	11,245	18.40
Latvian	139	0.23
Lithuanian	308	0.50
Luxemburger	9	0.01
Northern European	55	0.09
Norwegian	928	1.52
Pennsylvania German	13	0.02
Polish	3,425	5.61
Portuguese	236	0.39
Romanian	204	0.33
Russian	1,847	3.02
Scandinavian	108	0.18
Scotch-Irish	999	1.63
Scottish	1,997	3.27
Serbian	34	0.06
Slavic	54	0.09
Slovak	404	0.66
Slovene	6	0.01
Swedish	1,090	1.78
Swiss	424	0.69
Turkish	109	0.18
Ukrainian	234	0.38
United States or American	2,729	4.47
Welsh	246	0.40
West Indian, excl. Hispanic:	339	0.55
Bahamian	15	0.02
British West Indian	20	0.03
Haitian	44	0.07
Jamaican	206	0.34
Trinidadian and Tobagonian	25	0.04
West Indian	29	0.05
White:	55,830	91.37
Not Hispanic (52,229)	52,832	86.47
Hispanic (2,772)	2,998	4.91
Yugoslavian	27	0.04

Griswold

Place Type: Town
County: New London
Population: 10,807

Ancestry/Race	Number	%
Acadian/Cajun	6	0.06
African American/Black:	186	1.72
Not Hispanic (146)	177	1.64
Hispanic (5)	9	0.08
African, sub-Saharan:	29	0.27
Cape Verdean	19	0.18
South African	10	0.09
Am. Ind. or Alaska Nat., not spec.	33	0.31
American Indian tribes, specified:	189	1.75
Apache	3	0.03
Blackfeet	1	0.01
Cherokee (4)	14	0.13
Chippewa	1	0.01
Choctaw	2	0.02
Comanche (4)	4	0.04
Cree	1	0.01
Creek (3)	9	0.08
Iroquois (2)	10	0.09
Latin American Indians	1	0.01
Seminole	2	0.02
Sioux (1)	1	0.01
All other tribes (90)	140	1.30
American Indian tribes, not spec.	4	0.04
Arab:	8	0.07
Lebanese	8	0.07
Asian:	130	1.20
Chinese, ex. Taiwanese (28)	32	0.30
Filipino (17)	35	0.32
Indian (13)	13	0.12
Japanese (3)	7	0.06
Korean (8)	13	0.12
Laotian (3)	3	0.03
Sri Lankan	2	0.02
Taiwanese (1)	1	0.01
Thai	1	0.01
Vietnamese (10)	14	0.13
Other Asian, not specified (7)	9	0.08
Austrian	10	0.09
Brazilian	32	0.30
British	22	0.20
Canadian	47	0.43
Czech	8	0.07
Czechoslovakian	30	0.28
Danish	4	0.04
Dutch	92	0.85
English	1,410	13.05
European	15	0.14
Finnish	50	0.46
French, except Basque	2,043	18.90
French Canadian	1,048	9.70
German	1,293	11.96
Greek	78	0.72
Hawaii Native/Pacific Islander:	5	0.05
Polynesian: (3)	3	0.03
Samoan (3)	3	0.03
Other Pac. Isl., not spec. (2)	2	0.02
Hispanic or Latino:	210	1.94
Central American:	6	0.06
Honduran	2	0.02
Salvadoran	3	0.03
Other Central American	1	0.01
Cuban	4	0.04
Dominican Republic	6	0.06
Mexican	50	0.46
Puerto Rican	107	0.99
South American:	8	0.07
Colombian	3	0.03
Ecuadorian	2	0.02
Peruvian	3	0.03
Other Hispanic or Latino	29	0.27
Hungarian	10	0.09
Icelander	7	0.06
Irish	1,952	18.06
Italian	1,290	11.94
Lithuanian	79	0.73
Norwegian	73	0.68
Pennsylvania German	4	0.04
Polish	1,698	15.71
Portuguese	286	2.65
Russian	178	1.65
Scandinavian	27	0.25
Scotch-Irish	144	1.33
Scottish	271	2.51
Slavic	6	0.06
Swedish	254	2.35
Swiss	31	0.29
Ukrainian	157	1.45
United States or American	321	2.97
Welsh	26	0.24
West Indian, excl. Hispanic:	101	0.93
Haitian	101	0.93
White:	10,356	95.83
Not Hispanic (10,074)	10,228	94.64
Hispanic (115)	128	1.18

Notes: 1. Figures in the "Number" column do not add up to the total population due to: a) Ancestry/Race overlap — e.g. persons can report being both White and Irish, b) persons of Hispanic origin can report being any race, c) persons reporting two ancestries are counted in both categories. 2. Numbers in parentheses indicate the number of persons reporting this ancestry/race alone, not in combination with any other ancestry/race. 3. Refer to the Explanation of Data in the front of the book for more detailed information.

Groton

Place Type: City
County: New London
Population: 10,010

Ancestry/Race	Number	%
African American/Black:	1,258	12.57
Not Hispanic (939)	1,137	11.36
Hispanic (80)	121	1.21
African, sub-Saharan:	147	1.46
African	128	1.27
Cape Verdean	19	0.19
Alaska Native tribes, specified:	1	0.01
Eskimo	1	0.01
Alaska Native tribes, not specified	1	0.01
Am. Ind. or Alaska Nat., not spec.	61	0.61
American Indian tribes, specified:	172	1.72
Apache	2	0.02
Blackfeet (1)	3	0.03
Cherokee (13)	38	0.38
Chickasaw	3	0.03
Chippewa (4)	10	0.10
Choctaw	1	0.01
Creek	2	0.02
Iroquois (3)	10	0.10
Latin American Indians	6	0.06
Lumbee (1)	3	0.03
Navajo (5)	6	0.06
Seminole	2	0.02
Yaqui	4	0.04
All other tribes (44)	82	0.82
American Indian tribes, not spec.	6	0.06
Arab:	77	0.76
Arab/Arabic	14	0.14
Egyptian	35	0.35
Lebanese	28	0.28
Armenian	4	0.04
Asian:	446	4.46
Cambodian (2)	3	0.03
Chinese, ex. Taiwanese (107)	116	1.16
Filipino (77)	126	1.26
Indian (106)	112	1.12
Indonesian (1)	1	0.01
Japanese (7)	19	0.19
Korean (14)	16	0.16
Laotian (7)	11	0.11
Pakistani (6)	6	0.06
Sri Lankan (1)	1	0.01
Taiwanese (1)	1	0.01
Thai (2)	5	0.05
Vietnamese (21)	26	0.26
Other Asian, not specified (1)	3	0.03
Austrian	31	0.31
British	54	0.54
Canadian	45	0.45
Czech	39	0.39
Czechoslovakian	8	0.08
Dutch	116	1.15
English	1,167	11.59
European	105	1.04
Finnish	27	0.27
French, except Basque	599	5.95
French Canadian	381	3.78
German	1,433	14.23
Greek	50	0.50
Hawaii Native/Pacific Islander:	14	0.14
Micronesian: (2)	3	0.03
Guamanian/Chamorro (2)	3	0.03
Polynesian: (1)	6	0.06
Native Hawaiian (1)	5	0.05
Samoan	1	0.01
Other Pac. Isl., not spec. (2)	5	0.05
Hispanic or Latino:	773	7.72
Central American:	26	0.26
Costa Rican	1	0.01
Guatemalan	2	0.02
Honduran	8	0.08
Panamanian	6	0.06
Salvadoran	6	0.06
Other Central American	3	0.03
Cuban	25	0.25
Dominican Republic	36	0.36
Mexican	73	0.73
Puerto Rican	451	4.51
South American:	36	0.36
Argentinean	1	0.01
Colombian	9	0.09
Ecuadorian	8	0.08
Peruvian	9	0.09
Venezuelan	6	0.06
Other South American	3	0.03
Other Hispanic or Latino	126	1.26
Hungarian	75	0.75
Iranian	17	0.17
Irish	1,882	18.69
Italian	1,540	15.30
Lithuanian	22	0.22
Norwegian	134	1.33
Pennsylvania German	6	0.06
Polish	437	4.34
Portuguese	239	2.37
Romanian	6	0.06
Russian	104	1.03
Scandinavian	14	0.14
Scotch-Irish	140	1.39
Scottish	302	3.00
Serbian	13	0.13
Swedish	171	1.70
Swiss	8	0.08
Ukrainian	41	0.41
United States or American	295	2.93
Welsh	95	0.94
West Indian, excl. Hispanic:	89	0.88
Dutch West Indian	7	0.07
Haitian	17	0.17
Jamaican	14	0.14
West Indian	51	0.51
White:	8,162	81.54
Not Hispanic (7,485)	7,774	77.66
Hispanic (295)	388	3.88
Yugoslavian	3	0.03

Groton

Place Type: Town
County: New London
Population: 39,907

Ancestry/Race	Number	%
African American/Black:	3,350	8.39
Not Hispanic (2,608)	3,083	7.73
Hispanic (166)	267	0.67
African, sub-Saharan:	317	0.79
African	178	0.45
Cape Verdean	73	0.18
Ethiopian	17	0.04
Nigerian	15	0.04
South African	34	0.09
Alaska Native tribes, specified:	4	0.01
Alaska Athabascan	1	0.00
Aleut (1)	1	0.00
Eskimo	2	0.01
Alaska Native tribes, not specified	1	0.00
Am. Ind. or Alaska Nat., not spec.	185	0.46
Albanian	34	0.09
American Indian tribes, specified:	613	1.54
Apache (2)	15	0.04
Blackfeet (3)	24	0.06
Cherokee (25)	105	0.26
Chickasaw (1)	5	0.01
Chippewa (5)	15	0.04
Choctaw	21	0.05
Comanche (4)	4	0.01
Cree	1	0.00
Creek	5	0.01
Delaware	1	0.00
Iroquois (6)	27	0.07
Latin American Indians (3)	23	0.06
Lumbee (1)	3	0.01
Navajo (9)	15	0.04
Osage	1	0.00
Ottawa (2)	2	0.01
Pueblo (2)	2	0.01
Seminole (1)	6	0.02
Sioux (5)	7	0.02
Yaqui	4	0.01
All other tribes (178)	327	0.82
American Indian tribes, not spec.	22	0.06
Arab:	218	0.55
Arab/Arabic	35	0.09
Egyptian	63	0.16
Lebanese	111	0.28
Moroccan	6	0.02
Other Arab	3	0.01
Armenian	33	0.08
Asian:	1,715	4.30
Bangladeshi (1)	1	0.00
Cambodian (4)	5	0.01
Chinese, ex. Taiwanese (251)	282	0.71
Filipino (577)	800	2.00
Hmong (1)	1	0.00
Indian (282)	309	0.77
Indonesian (2)	2	0.01
Japanese (38)	89	0.22
Korean (49)	68	0.17
Laotian (13)	17	0.04
Malaysian	4	0.01
Pakistani (14)	14	0.04
Sri Lankan (4)	5	0.01
Taiwanese (5)	5	0.01
Thai (16)	24	0.06
Vietnamese (44)	56	0.14
Other Asian, specified (3)	6	0.02
Other Asian, not specified (14)	27	0.07
Australian	14	0.04
Austrian	97	0.24
Belgian	52	0.13
British	230	0.58
Canadian	180	0.45
Celtic	29	0.07
Croatian	61	0.15
Czech	96	0.24
Czechoslovakian	81	0.20
Danish	108	0.27
Dutch	689	1.73
Eastern European	6	0.02
English	5,733	14.36
European	381	0.95
Finnish	150	0.38
French, except Basque	2,336	5.85
French Canadian	1,237	3.10
German	6,128	15.35
Greek	217	0.54
Hawaii Native/Pacific Islander:	142	0.36
Micronesian: (44)	56	0.14
Guamanian/Chamorro (35)	47	0.12
Other Micronesian (9)	9	0.02
Polynesian: (14)	46	0.12
Native Hawaiian (10)	34	0.09
Samoan (3)	11	0.03
Other Polynesian (1)	1	0.00
Other Pac. Isl., specified	3	0.01
Other Pac. Isl., not spec. (8)	37	0.09
Hispanic or Latino:	2,001	5.01
Central American:	78	0.20
Costa Rican	8	0.02
Guatemalan	5	0.01
Honduran	14	0.04
Panamanian	25	0.06
Salvadoran	21	0.05
Other Central American	5	0.01
Cuban	55	0.14
Dominican Republic	63	0.16
Mexican	407	1.02
Puerto Rican	962	2.41
South American:	102	0.26
Argentinean	5	0.01
Bolivian	2	0.01
Chilean	4	0.01

Notes: 1. Figures in the "Number" column do not add up to the total population due to: a) Ancestry/Race overlap — e.g. persons can report being both White and Irish, b) persons of Hispanic origin can report being any race, c) persons reporting two ancestries are counted in both categories. 2. Numbers in parentheses indicate the number of persons reporting this ancestry/race alone, not in combination with any other ancestry/race. 3. Refer to the Explanation of Data in the front of the book for more detailed information.

Ancestry/Race	Number	%
Colombian	30	0.08
Ecuadorian	13	0.03
Paraguayan	2	0.01
Peruvian	20	0.05
Uruguayan	3	0.01
Venezuelan	8	0.02
Other South American	15	0.04
Other Hispanic or Latino	334	0.84
Hungarian	243	0.61
Iranian	17	0.04
Irish	7,302	18.30
Italian	4,682	11.73
Lithuanian	209	0.52
Maltese	24	0.06
Norwegian	583	1.46
Pennsylvania German	6	0.02
Polish	1,840	4.61
Portuguese	712	1.78
Romanian	40	0.10
Russian	387	0.97
Scandinavian	104	0.26
Scotch-Irish	841	2.11
Scottish	1,388	3.48
Serbian	46	0.12
Slavic	9	0.02
Slovak	96	0.24
Slovene	2	0.01
Swedish	654	1.64
Swiss	118	0.30
Turkish	11	0.03
Ukrainian	141	0.35
United States or American	2,150	5.39
Welsh	408	1.02
West Indian, excl. Hispanic:	187	0.47
Bahamian	7	0.02
Dutch West Indian	7	0.02
Haitian	40	0.10
Jamaican	49	0.12
Trinidadian and Tobagonian	13	0.03
West Indian	70	0.18
Other West Indian	1	0.00
White:	34,490	86.43
Not Hispanic (32,448)	33,355	83.58
Hispanic (920)	1,135	2.84
Yugoslavian	3	0.01

Guilford

Place Type: Town
County: New Haven
Population: 21,398

Ancestry/Race	Number	%
Acadian/Cajun	12	0.06
African American/Black:	247	1.15
Not Hispanic (192)	231	1.08
Hispanic (8)	16	0.07
African, sub-Saharan:	39	0.18
African	20	0.09
Ghanian	19	0.09
Am. Ind. or Alaska Nat., not spec.	35	0.16
Alsatian	8	0.04
American Indian tribes, specified:	42	0.20
Blackfeet	8	0.04
Cherokee	4	0.02
Choctaw	2	0.01
Creek	2	0.01
Delaware	1	0.00
Iroquois (1)	4	0.02
Latin American Indians	1	0.00
Navajo (1)	3	0.01
Seminole	2	0.01
Sioux (1)	1	0.00
All other tribes (4)	14	0.07
American Indian tribes, not spec.	1	0.00
Arab:	84	0.39
Lebanese	55	0.26
Syrian	29	0.14
Armenian	29	0.14
Asian:	401	1.87
Chinese, ex. Taiwanese (163)	174	0.81
Filipino (18)	29	0.14
Indian (73)	83	0.39
Japanese (11)	17	0.08
Korean (52)	60	0.28
Pakistani (1)	1	0.00
Taiwanese (11)	11	0.05
Thai (6)	6	0.03
Vietnamese (12)	14	0.07
Other Asian, specified	1	0.00
Other Asian, not specified (2)	5	0.02
Australian	7	0.03
Austrian	177	0.83
Belgian	107	0.50
British	292	1.36
Bulgarian	25	0.12
Canadian	101	0.47
Carpatho Rusyn	5	0.02
Croatian	13	0.06
Czech	45	0.21
Czechoslovakian	24	0.11
Danish	166	0.78
Dutch	316	1.48
Eastern European	40	0.19
English	3,608	16.86
Estonian	16	0.07
European	77	0.36
Finnish	84	0.39
French, except Basque	890	4.16
French Canadian	408	1.91
German	3,495	16.33
Greek	263	1.23
Hawaii Native/Pacific Islander:	9	0.04
Polynesian:	4	0.02
Native Hawaiian	4	0.02
Other Pac. Isl., not spec.	5	0.02
Hispanic or Latino:	455	2.13
Central American:	19	0.09
Costa Rican	3	0.01
Guatemalan	6	0.03
Honduran	2	0.01
Nicaraguan	1	0.00
Panamanian	1	0.00
Salvadoran	4	0.02
Other Central American	2	0.01
Cuban	19	0.09
Dominican Republic	11	0.05
Mexican	40	0.19
Puerto Rican	183	0.86
South American:	132	0.62
Argentinean	12	0.06
Chilean	37	0.17
Colombian	45	0.21
Ecuadorian	24	0.11
Peruvian	9	0.04
Venezuelan	4	0.02
Other South American	1	0.00
Other Hispanic or Latino	51	0.24
Hungarian	223	1.04
Iranian	29	0.14
Irish	4,747	22.18
Israeli	7	0.03
Italian	5,215	24.37
Latvian	7	0.03
Lithuanian	205	0.96
Luxemburger	15	0.07
Norwegian	267	1.25
Pennsylvania German	8	0.04
Polish	1,337	6.25
Portuguese	122	0.57
Russian	559	2.61
Scandinavian	30	0.14
Scotch-Irish	464	2.17
Scottish	662	3.09
Serbian	7	0.03
Slavic	16	0.07
Slovak	85	0.40
Swedish	878	4.10
Swiss	82	0.38
Ukrainian	139	0.65
United States or American	798	3.73
Welsh	126	0.59
West Indian, excl. Hispanic:	43	0.20
Haitian	7	0.03
Jamaican	19	0.09
Trinidadian and Tobagonian	17	0.08
White:	20,738	96.92
Not Hispanic (20,209)	20,370	95.20
Hispanic (341)	368	1.72
Yugoslavian	40	0.19

Hamden

Place Type: Town
County: New Haven
Population: 56,913

Ancestry/Race	Number	%
African American/Black:	9,351	16.43
Not Hispanic (8,642)	9,092	15.98
Hispanic (198)	259	0.46
African, sub-Saharan:	581	1.02
African	326	0.57
Cape Verdean	90	0.16
Ethiopian	8	0.01
Ghanian	32	0.06
Kenyan	9	0.02
Nigerian	49	0.09
South African	31	0.05
Zimbabwean	36	0.06
Am. Ind. or Alaska Nat., not spec.	136	0.24
Albanian	26	0.05
American Indian tribes, specified:	182	0.32
Apache (1)	4	0.01
Blackfeet (3)	13	0.02
Cherokee (16)	55	0.10
Cheyenne	1	0.00
Chickasaw	1	0.00
Chippewa (2)	6	0.01
Choctaw (2)	2	0.00
Creek	2	0.00
Iroquois	15	0.03
Kiowa	1	0.00
Latin American Indians (1)	12	0.02
Lumbee	1	0.00
Paiute (1)	1	0.00
Pueblo (2)	2	0.00
Seminole	4	0.01
Shoshone (1)	2	0.00
Sioux	4	0.01
All other tribes (7)	56	0.10
American Indian tribes, not spec.	20	0.04
Arab:	237	0.42
Arab/Arabic	45	0.08
Egyptian	23	0.04
Jordanian	22	0.04
Lebanese	126	0.22
Other Arab	21	0.04
Armenian	60	0.11
Asian:	2,256	3.96
Bangladeshi (17)	23	0.04
Cambodian (6)	8	0.01
Chinese, ex. Taiwanese (525)	599	1.05
Filipino (229)	259	0.46
Indian (563)	608	1.07
Indonesian (9)	11	0.02
Japanese (104)	122	0.21
Korean (258)	282	0.50
Laotian (11)	14	0.02
Malaysian (4)	4	0.01
Pakistani (40)	60	0.11
Sri Lankan (7)	7	0.01
Taiwanese (24)	27	0.05
Thai (25)	31	0.05
Vietnamese (107)	132	0.23
Other Asian, specified	6	0.01
Other Asian, not specified (19)	63	0.11
Assyrian/Chaldean/Syriac	6	0.01
Australian	26	0.05
Austrian	238	0.42

Notes: 1. Figures in the "Number" column do not add up to the total population due to: a) Ancestry/Race overlap — e.g. persons can report being both White and Irish, b) persons of Hispanic origin can report being any race, c) persons reporting two ancestries are counted in both categories. 2. Numbers in parentheses indicate the number of persons reporting this ancestry/race alone, not in combination with any other ancestry/race. 3. Refer to the Explanation of Data in the front of the book for more detailed information.

Belgian	114	0.20
Brazilian	5	0.01
British	233	0.41
Bulgarian	36	0.06
Canadian	307	0.54
Croatian	25	0.04
Czech	88	0.15
Czechoslovakian	53	0.09
Danish	185	0.33
Dutch	327	0.57
Eastern European	174	0.31
English	4,278	7.52
Estonian	7	0.01
European	265	0.47
Finnish	33	0.06
French, except Basque	1,660	2.92
French Canadian	1,067	1.87
German	4,959	8.71
Greek	439	0.77
Guyanese	28	0.05
Hawaii Native/Pacific Islander:	64	0.11
Micronesian: (4)	8	0.01
Guamanian/Chamorro (3)	7	0.01
Other Micronesian (1)	1	0.00
Polynesian: (9)	15	0.03
Native Hawaiian (5)	9	0.02
Samoan (4)	4	0.01
Other Polynesian	2	0.00
Other Pac. Isl., specified	6	0.01
Other Pac. Isl., not spec. (5)	35	0.06
Hispanic or Latino:	2,425	4.26
Central American:	51	0.09
Costa Rican	3	0.01
Guatemalan	27	0.05
Honduran	3	0.01
Panamanian	5	0.01
Salvadoran	10	0.02
Other Central American	3	0.01
Cuban	90	0.16
Dominican Republic	53	0.09
Mexican	238	0.42
Puerto Rican	1,247	2.19
South American:	340	0.60
Argentinean	18	0.03
Bolivian	3	0.01
Chilean	33	0.06
Colombian	134	0.24
Ecuadorian	50	0.09
Paraguayan	1	0.00
Peruvian	46	0.08
Venezuelan	40	0.07
Other South American	15	0.03
Other Hispanic or Latino	406	0.71
Hungarian	572	1.01
Icelander	9	0.02
Iranian	10	0.02
Irish	9,913	17.42
Israeli	69	0.12
Italian	15,953	28.03
Latvian	41	0.07
Lithuanian	315	0.55
Macedonian	8	0.01
Norwegian	215	0.38
Pennsylvania German	16	0.03
Polish	3,262	5.73
Portuguese	324	0.57
Romanian	154	0.27
Russian	1,347	2.37
Scandinavian	22	0.04
Scotch-Irish	560	0.98
Scottish	801	1.41
Slavic	17	0.03
Slovak	193	0.34
Slovene	24	0.04
Swedish	667	1.17
Swiss	110	0.19
Turkish	72	0.13
Ukrainian	328	0.58
United States or American	1,655	2.91
Welsh	183	0.32
West Indian, excl. Hispanic:	765	1.34
Barbadian	13	0.02
Bermudan	11	0.02
British West Indian	12	0.02
Haitian	112	0.20
Jamaican	544	0.96
Trinidadian and Tobagonian	20	0.04
West Indian	53	0.09
White:	44,781	78.68
Not Hispanic (42,812)	43,436	76.32
Hispanic (1,184)	1,345	2.36
Yugoslavian	25	0.04

Hartford

Place Type: City
County: Hartford
Population: 121,578

Ancestry/Race	Number	%
African American/Black:	49,412	40.64
Not Hispanic (43,775)	46,085	37.91
Hispanic (2,489)	3,327	2.74
African, sub-Saharan:	1,345	1.11
African	1,095	0.90
Cape Verdean	47	0.04
Ethiopian	15	0.01
Ghanian	107	0.09
Nigerian	29	0.02
Senegalese	9	0.01
Sudanese	38	0.03
Other sub-Saharan African	5	0.00
Alaska Native tribes, specified:	3	0.00
Alaska Athabascan	2	0.00
Eskimo	1	0.00
Am. Ind. or Alaska Nat., not spec.	790	0.65
Albanian	433	0.36
American Indian tribes, specified:	543	0.45
Apache (2)	19	0.02
Blackfeet (3)	25	0.02
Cherokee (26)	117	0.10
Cheyenne	2	0.00
Chippewa (5)	17	0.01
Choctaw	5	0.00
Comanche (1)	3	0.00
Cree	3	0.00
Creek (4)	10	0.01
Crow	1	0.00
Delaware (1)	2	0.00
Iroquois (10)	32	0.03
Kiowa	1	0.00
Latin American Indians (53)	115	0.09
Navajo	2	0.00
Ottawa	1	0.00
Pima (1)	1	0.00
Pueblo (7)	18	0.01
Seminole (2)	9	0.01
Shoshone	2	0.00
Sioux (8)	10	0.01
All other tribes (59)	148	0.12
American Indian tribes, not spec.	105	0.09
Arab:	136	0.11
Arab/Arabic	7	0.01
Egyptian	48	0.04
Lebanese	43	0.04
Moroccan	17	0.01
Syrian	4	0.00
Other Arab	17	0.01
Armenian	180	0.15
Asian:	2,718	2.24
Bangladeshi (5)	8	0.01
Cambodian (9)	11	0.01
Chinese, ex. Taiwanese (325)	422	0.35
Filipino (114)	147	0.12
Indian (644)	897	0.74
Indonesian (18)	23	0.02
Japanese (30)	55	0.05
Korean (107)	127	0.10
Laotian (26)	34	0.03
Malaysian (17)	19	0.02
Pakistani (30)	78	0.06
Sri Lankan (4)	5	0.00
Taiwanese (5)	12	0.01
Thai (19)	31	0.03
Vietnamese (537)	579	0.48
Other Asian, specified (7)	24	0.02
Other Asian, not specified (38)	246	0.20
Assyrian/Chaldean/Syriac	11	0.01
Austrian	54	0.04
Belgian	11	0.01
Brazilian	197	0.16
British	92	0.08
Canadian	151	0.12
Celtic	12	0.01
Croatian	37	0.03
Czech	39	0.03
Czechoslovakian	89	0.07
Danish	53	0.04
Dutch	119	0.10
Eastern European	61	0.05
English	1,624	1.34
Estonian	9	0.01
European	229	0.19
Finnish	34	0.03
French, except Basque	1,518	1.25
French Canadian	644	0.53
German	1,271	1.05
Greek	254	0.21
Guyanese	390	0.32
Hawaii Native/Pacific Islander:	526	0.43
Micronesian: (17)	21	0.02
Guamanian/Chamorro (17)	21	0.02
Polynesian: (65)	101	0.08
Native Hawaiian (36)	52	0.04
Samoan (27)	34	0.03
Tongan (1)	10	0.01
Other Polynesian (1)	5	0.00
Other Pac. Isl., specified	16	0.01
Other Pac. Isl., not spec. (53)	388	0.32
Hispanic or Latino:	49,260	40.52
Central American:	422	0.35
Costa Rican	23	0.02
Guatemalan	68	0.06
Honduran	118	0.10
Nicaraguan	39	0.03
Panamanian	50	0.04
Salvadoran	99	0.08
Other Central American	25	0.02
Cuban	610	0.50
Dominican Republic	1,013	0.83
Mexican	993	0.82
Puerto Rican	39,586	32.56
South American:	2,430	2.00
Argentinean	70	0.06
Bolivian	29	0.02
Chilean	29	0.02
Colombian	829	0.68
Ecuadorian	153	0.13
Paraguayan	3	0.00
Peruvian	1,184	0.97
Uruguayan	1	0.00
Venezuelan	36	0.03
Other South American	96	0.08
Other Hispanic or Latino	4,206	3.46
Hungarian	93	0.08
Icelander	8	0.01
Iranian	24	0.02
Irish	3,191	2.62
Israeli	7	0.01
Italian	4,345	3.57
Latvian	8	0.01
Lithuanian	210	0.17
Northern European	17	0.01
Norwegian	165	0.14
Polish	2,569	2.11
Portuguese	1,429	1.18
Romanian	114	0.09
Russian	470	0.39
Scandinavian	7	0.01
Scotch-Irish	191	0.16

Notes: 1. Figures in the "Number" column do not add up to the total population due to: a) Ancestry/Race overlap — e.g. persons can report being both White and Irish, b) persons of Hispanic origin can report being any race, c) persons reporting two ancestries are counted in both categories. 2. Numbers in parentheses indicate the number of persons reporting this ancestry/race alone, not in combination with any other ancestry/race. 3. Refer to the Explanation of Data in the front of the book for more detailed information.

Scottish	377	0.31
Slavic	17	0.01
Slovak	33	0.03
Soviet Union	7	0.01
Swedish	384	0.32
Swiss	30	0.02
Turkish	53	0.04
Ukrainian	223	0.18
United States or American	2,214	1.82
Welsh	83	0.07
West Indian, excl. Hispanic:	10,114	8.32
Bahamian	5	0.00
Barbadian	278	0.23
Belizean	15	0.01
Bermudan	7	0.01
British West Indian	280	0.23
Haitian	364	0.30
Jamaican	8,293	6.82
Trinidadian and Tobagonian	255	0.21
U.S. Virgin Islander	35	0.03
West Indian	573	0.47
Other West Indian	9	0.01
White:	37,422	30.78
Not Hispanic (21,677)	23,561	19.38
Hispanic (12,028)	13,861	11.40
Yugoslavian	739	0.61

Killingly

Place Type: Town
County: Windham
Population: 16,472

Ancestry/Race	Number	%
African American/Black:	331	2.01
Not Hispanic (211)	300	1.82
Hispanic (19)	31	0.19
African, sub-Saharan:	19	0.12
African	19	0.12
Am. Ind. or Alaska Nat., not spec.	94	0.57
American Indian tribes, specified:	146	0.89
Apache	1	0.01
Blackfeet (6)	13	0.08
Cherokee (8)	26	0.16
Cheyenne (2)	2	0.01
Chippewa	5	0.03
Cree	1	0.01
Houma (2)	3	0.02
Iroquois (2)	5	0.03
Latin American Indians	4	0.02
Lumbee	1	0.01
Pueblo	1	0.01
Seminole	1	0.01
Sioux	2	0.01
All other tribes (35)	81	0.49
American Indian tribes, not spec.	3	0.02
Arab:	24	0.15
Lebanese	16	0.10
Syrian	8	0.05
Armenian	44	0.27
Asian:	326	1.98
Chinese, ex. Taiwanese (21)	23	0.14
Filipino (12)	24	0.15
Indian (37)	51	0.31
Japanese (6)	7	0.04
Korean (6)	10	0.06
Laotian (154)	179	1.09
Thai (1)	2	0.01
Vietnamese (5)	5	0.03
Other Asian, not specified (12)	25	0.15
Belgian	8	0.05
Brazilian	27	0.16
British	71	0.43
Canadian	106	0.64
Czech	24	0.15
Czechoslovakian	27	0.16
Danish	64	0.39
Dutch	194	1.18
Eastern European	17	0.10
English	1,909	11.59
Estonian	31	0.19
Finnish	172	1.04
French, except Basque	4,273	25.94
French Canadian	2,428	14.74
German	1,262	7.66
Greek	72	0.44
Hawaii Native/Pacific Islander:	4	0.02
Polynesian:	1	0.01
Native Hawaiian	1	0.01
Other Pac. Isl., not spec.	3	0.02
Hispanic or Latino:	370	2.25
Central American:	4	0.02
Guatemalan	1	0.01
Salvadoran	1	0.01
Other Central American	2	0.01
Cuban	3	0.02
Dominican Republic	5	0.03
Mexican	38	0.23
Puerto Rican	247	1.50
South American:	11	0.07
Colombian	7	0.04
Ecuadorian	4	0.02
Other Hispanic or Latino	62	0.38
Hungarian	28	0.17
Irish	2,430	14.75
Italian	1,294	7.86
Lithuanian	52	0.32
Northern European	13	0.08
Norwegian	62	0.38
Pennsylvania German	7	0.04
Polish	1,372	8.33
Portuguese	298	1.81
Romanian	7	0.04
Russian	127	0.77
Scandinavian	25	0.15
Scotch-Irish	198	1.20
Scottish	316	1.92
Slavic	6	0.04
Slovak	26	0.16
Swedish	261	1.58
Swiss	20	0.12
Ukrainian	97	0.59
United States or American	520	3.16
Welsh	134	0.81
West Indian, excl. Hispanic:	15	0.09
Jamaican	15	0.09
White:	15,728	95.48
Not Hispanic (15,253)	15,507	94.14
Hispanic (186)	221	1.34
Yugoslavian	6	0.04

Ledyard

Place Type: Town
County: New London
Population: 14,687

Ancestry/Race	Number	%
African American/Black:	535	3.64
Not Hispanic (358)	510	3.47
Hispanic (9)	25	0.17
African, sub-Saharan:	17	0.12
Cape Verdean	5	0.03
Ghanian	12	0.08
Alaska Native tribes, specified:	3	0.02
Aleut (2)	2	0.01
Eskimo	1	0.01
Am. Ind. or Alaska Nat., not spec.	69	0.47
American Indian tribes, specified:	624	4.25
Apache (2)	5	0.03
Blackfeet	9	0.06
Cherokee (14)	47	0.32
Chickasaw (6)	7	0.05
Chippewa (2)	2	0.01
Choctaw	6	0.04
Comanche	1	0.01
Cree	1	0.01
Creek	1	0.01
Crow (1)	1	0.01
Delaware (2)	2	0.01
Houma (2)	5	0.03
Iroquois (11)	11	0.07
Latin American Indians (3)	13	0.09
Lumbee (5)	5	0.03
Seminole	1	0.01
Sioux (5)	10	0.07
Yaqui (2)	2	0.01
All other tribes (396)	495	3.37
American Indian tribes, not spec.	45	0.31
Arab:	77	0.52
Iraqi	6	0.04
Lebanese	68	0.46
Syrian	3	0.02
Armenian	10	0.07
Asian:	426	2.90
Cambodian (1)	1	0.01
Chinese, ex. Taiwanese (98)	111	0.76
Filipino (109)	164	1.12
Indian (41)	43	0.29
Indonesian (2)	3	0.02
Japanese (18)	39	0.27
Korean (18)	26	0.18
Laotian (14)	14	0.10
Malaysian (2)	3	0.02
Taiwanese	2	0.01
Thai (2)	3	0.02
Vietnamese (9)	10	0.07
Other Asian, not specified (2)	7	0.05
Austrian	35	0.24
Belgian	18	0.12
British	67	0.46
Bulgarian	7	0.05
Canadian	48	0.33
Croatian	11	0.07
Czech	99	0.67
Czechoslovakian	46	0.31
Danish	54	0.37
Dutch	192	1.31
Eastern European	7	0.05
English	3,076	20.95
European	97	0.66
Finnish	117	0.80
French, except Basque	1,172	7.98
French Canadian	733	4.99
German	2,550	17.37
Greek	75	0.51
Hawaii Native/Pacific Islander:	21	0.14
Micronesian: (7)	12	0.08
Guamanian/Chamorro (4)	8	0.05
Other Micronesian (3)	4	0.03
Polynesian: (3)	5	0.03
Native Hawaiian (3)	4	0.03
Samoan	1	0.01
Other Pac. Isl., not spec.	4	0.03
Hispanic or Latino:	401	2.73
Central American:	14	0.10
Costa Rican	3	0.02
Guatemalan	1	0.01
Nicaraguan	1	0.01
Salvadoran	7	0.05
Other Central American	2	0.01
Cuban	16	0.11
Dominican Republic	7	0.05
Mexican	77	0.52
Puerto Rican	170	1.16
South American:	51	0.35
Argentinean	1	0.01
Bolivian	1	0.01
Colombian	8	0.05
Ecuadorian	2	0.01
Peruvian	30	0.20
Venezuelan	1	0.01
Other South American	8	0.05
Other Hispanic or Latino	66	0.45
Hungarian	94	0.64
Irish	2,842	19.36
Israeli	8	0.05
Italian	1,887	12.85
Lithuanian	115	0.78
Northern European	13	0.09

Notes: 1. Figures in the "Number" column do not add up to the total population due to: a) Ancestry/Race overlap — e.g. persons can report being both White and Irish, b) persons of Hispanic origin can report being any race, c) persons reporting two ancestries are counted in both categories. 2. Numbers in parentheses indicate the number of persons reporting this ancestry/race alone, not in combination with any other ancestry/race. 3. Refer to the Explanation of Data in the front of the book for more detailed information.

Ancestry/Race	Number	%
Norwegian	98	0.67
Polish	788	5.37
Portuguese	360	2.45
Russian	139	0.95
Scandinavian	73	0.50
Scotch-Irish	470	3.20
Scottish	598	4.07
Slavic	23	0.16
Slovak	42	0.29
Slovene	23	0.16
Swedish	192	1.31
Swiss	45	0.31
Turkish	5	0.03
Ukrainian	69	0.47
United States or American	615	4.19
Welsh	69	0.47
West Indian, excl. Hispanic:	13	0.09
Jamaican	13	0.09
White:	13,236	90.12
Not Hispanic (12,744)	12,977	88.36
Hispanic (215)	259	1.76
Yugoslavian	34	0.23

Madison

Place Type: Town
County: New Haven
Population: 17,858

Ancestry/Race	Number	%
African American/Black:	106	0.59
Not Hispanic (70)	102	0.57
Hispanic (2)	4	0.02
African, sub-Saharan:	6	0.03
African	6	0.03
Am. Ind. or Alaska Nat., not spec.	29	0.16
Albanian	41	0.23
Alsatian	8	0.04
American Indian tribes, specified:	34	0.19
Blackfeet	4	0.02
Cherokee	10	0.06
Latin American Indians (5)	5	0.03
Osage	1	0.01
Pueblo	2	0.01
All other tribes (1)	12	0.07
American Indian tribes, not spec.	2	0.01
Arab:	69	0.39
Arab/Arabic	28	0.16
Lebanese	34	0.19
Other Arab	7	0.04
Armenian	49	0.27
Asian:	366	2.05
Chinese, ex. Taiwanese (134)	142	0.80
Filipino (17)	25	0.14
Indian (96)	117	0.66
Indonesian (1)	1	0.01
Japanese (6)	17	0.10
Korean (20)	21	0.12
Laotian (1)	1	0.01
Thai (2)	2	0.01
Vietnamese (21)	25	0.14
Other Asian, not specified (7)	15	0.08
Australian	17	0.10
Austrian	167	0.94
Belgian	6	0.03
Brazilian	16	0.09
British	120	0.67
Canadian	50	0.28
Celtic	6	0.03
Croatian	30	0.17
Czech	127	0.71
Czechoslovakian	95	0.53
Danish	110	0.62
Dutch	186	1.04
Eastern European	85	0.48
English	3,402	19.05
European	52	0.29
Finnish	21	0.12
French, except Basque	772	4.32
French Canadian	354	1.98
German	2,988	16.73
Greek	124	0.69
Hawaii Native/Pacific Islander:	5	0.03
Polynesian: (1)	4	0.02
Native Hawaiian (1)	3	0.02
Samoan	1	0.01
Other Pac. Isl., not spec.	1	0.01
Hispanic or Latino:	240	1.34
Central American:	10	0.06
Guatemalan	7	0.04
Panamanian	1	0.01
Salvadoran	1	0.01
Other Central American	1	0.01
Cuban	17	0.10
Dominican Republic	4	0.02
Mexican	42	0.24
Puerto Rican	77	0.43
South American:	57	0.32
Argentinean	4	0.02
Chilean	9	0.05
Colombian	18	0.10
Ecuadorian	13	0.07
Paraguayan	2	0.01
Peruvian	9	0.05
Other South American	2	0.01
Other Hispanic or Latino	33	0.18
Hungarian	226	1.27
Iranian	59	0.33
Irish	4,455	24.95
Italian	3,673	20.57
Lithuanian	180	1.01
Northern European	33	0.18
Norwegian	220	1.23
Pennsylvania German	16	0.09
Polish	1,264	7.08
Portuguese	106	0.59
Romanian	21	0.12
Russian	547	3.06
Scandinavian	21	0.12
Scotch-Irish	271	1.52
Scottish	724	4.05
Slavic	126	0.71
Slovak	96	0.54
Slovene	15	0.08
Swedish	739	4.14
Swiss	151	0.85
Ukrainian	139	0.78
United States or American	532	2.98
Welsh	169	0.95
West Indian, excl. Hispanic:	44	0.25
Haitian	26	0.15
Jamaican	5	0.03
West Indian	13	0.07
White:	17,409	97.49
Not Hispanic (17,070)	17,214	96.39
Hispanic (185)	195	1.09
Yugoslavian	9	0.05

Manchester

Place Type: Town
County: Hartford
Population: 54,740

Ancestry/Race	Number	%
Afghan	7	0.01
African American/Black:	5,134	9.38
Not Hispanic (4,430)	4,824	8.81
Hispanic (180)	310	0.57
African, sub-Saharan:	207	0.38
African	104	0.19
Cape Verdean	14	0.03
Ghanian	55	0.10
Nigerian	11	0.02
South African	16	0.03
Other sub-Saharan African	7	0.01
Alaska Native tribes, specified:	3	0.01
Tlingit-Haida (1)	3	0.01
Alaska Native tribes, not specified	1	0.00
Am. Ind. or Alaska Nat., not spec.	132	0.24
Albanian	70	0.13
American Indian tribes, specified:	225	0.41
Apache	1	0.00
Blackfeet (1)	10	0.02
Cherokee (3)	42	0.08
Cheyenne	2	0.00
Chickasaw	1	0.00
Chippewa (2)	4	0.01
Choctaw	2	0.00
Cree (1)	5	0.01
Creek	2	0.00
Crow	1	0.00
Delaware	1	0.00
Iroquois (4)	16	0.03
Latin American Indians (5)	17	0.03
Navajo	2	0.00
Osage	2	0.00
Potawatomi	1	0.00
Shoshone	1	0.00
Sioux (4)	15	0.03
All other tribes (34)	100	0.18
American Indian tribes, not spec.	19	0.03
Arab:	180	0.33
Arab/Arabic	6	0.01
Egyptian	39	0.07
Lebanese	112	0.20
Palestinian	19	0.03
Syrian	4	0.01
Armenian	116	0.21
Asian:	2,105	3.85
Bangladeshi (63)	95	0.17
Cambodian (20)	24	0.04
Chinese, ex. Taiwanese (224)	271	0.50
Filipino (162)	205	0.37
Hmong	5	0.01
Indian (534)	625	1.14
Indonesian (7)	9	0.02
Japanese (35)	50	0.09
Korean (254)	297	0.54
Laotian (115)	143	0.26
Malaysian (7)	7	0.01
Pakistani (62)	88	0.16
Sri Lankan (5)	5	0.01
Taiwanese (2)	4	0.01
Thai (8)	13	0.02
Vietnamese (152)	175	0.32
Other Asian, specified (2)	5	0.01
Other Asian, not specified (27)	84	0.15
Australian	23	0.04
Austrian	256	0.47
Belgian	20	0.04
Brazilian	21	0.04
British	103	0.19
Canadian	292	0.53
Celtic	18	0.03
Croatian	6	0.01
Czech	106	0.19
Czechoslovakian	112	0.20
Danish	367	0.67
Dutch	440	0.80
Eastern European	82	0.15
English	6,148	11.23
Estonian	20	0.04
European	280	0.51
Finnish	152	0.28
French, except Basque	4,882	8.92
French Canadian	2,577	4.71
German	5,612	10.25
Greek	285	0.52
Guyanese	66	0.12
Hawaii Native/Pacific Islander:	67	0.12
Micronesian: (2)	10	0.02
Guamanian/Chamorro (1)	7	0.01
Other Micronesian (1)	3	0.01
Polynesian: (14)	32	0.06
Native Hawaiian (7)	15	0.03
Samoan (7)	13	0.02
Other Polynesian	4	0.01
Other Pac. Isl., specified	2	0.00
Other Pac. Isl., not spec. (2)	23	0.04

Notes: 1. Figures in the "Number" column do not add up to the total population due to: a) Ancestry/Race overlap — e.g. persons can report being both White and Irish, b) persons of Hispanic origin can report being any race, c) persons reporting two ancestries are counted in both categories. 2. Numbers in parentheses indicate the number of persons reporting this ancestry/race alone, not in combination with any other ancestry/race. 3. Refer to the Explanation of Data in the front of the book for more detailed information.

Ancestry/Race	Number	%
Hispanic or Latino:	3,579	6.54
Central American:	69	0.13
Costa Rican	3	0.01
Guatemalan	10	0.02
Honduran	3	0.01
Nicaraguan	9	0.02
Panamanian	17	0.03
Salvadoran	20	0.04
Other Central American	7	0.01
Cuban	93	0.17
Dominican Republic	48	0.09
Mexican	190	0.35
Puerto Rican	2,387	4.36
South American:	368	0.67
Argentinean	11	0.02
Bolivian	3	0.01
Chilean	13	0.02
Colombian	154	0.28
Ecuadorian	13	0.02
Paraguayan	2	0.00
Peruvian	147	0.27
Venezuelan	10	0.02
Other South American	15	0.03
Other Hispanic or Latino	424	0.77
Hungarian	323	0.59
Iranian	36	0.07
Irish	10,990	20.08
Israeli	10	0.02
Italian	7,905	14.44
Latvian	76	0.14
Lithuanian	566	1.03
Northern European	22	0.04
Norwegian	334	0.61
Polish	4,593	8.39
Portuguese	431	0.79
Romanian	108	0.20
Russian	602	1.10
Scandinavian	31	0.06
Scotch-Irish	715	1.31
Scottish	1,123	2.05
Slavic	54	0.10
Slovak	145	0.26
Slovene	9	0.02
Swedish	1,275	2.33
Swiss	200	0.37
Turkish	10	0.02
Ukrainian	262	0.48
United States or American	2,002	3.66
Welsh	231	0.42
West Indian, excl. Hispanic:	549	1.00
Barbadian	47	0.09
British West Indian	63	0.12
Haitian	17	0.03
Jamaican	347	0.63
Trinidadian and Tobagonian	28	0.05
West Indian	47	0.09
White:	46,287	84.56
Not Hispanic (43,820)	44,575	81.43
Hispanic (1,487)	1,712	3.13
Yugoslavian	77	0.14

Mansfield

Place Type: Town
County: Tolland
Population: 20,720

Ancestry/Race	Number	%
Acadian/Cajun	6	0.03
African American/Black:	1,141	5.51
Not Hispanic (971)	1,074	5.18
Hispanic (39)	67	0.32
African, sub-Saharan:	159	0.77
African	88	0.42
Cape Verdean	7	0.03
Ethiopian	5	0.02
Kenyan	42	0.20
Liberian	7	0.03
Nigerian	10	0.05
Am. Ind. or Alaska Nat., not spec.	60	0.29
Albanian	16	0.08
American Indian tribes, specified:	68	0.33
Apache (1)	2	0.01
Blackfeet	5	0.02
Cherokee (2)	13	0.06
Chippewa (1)	1	0.00
Choctaw (1)	1	0.00
Cree	1	0.00
Iroquois (2)	10	0.05
Latin American Indians (6)	12	0.06
Navajo (1)	4	0.02
Potawatomi (1)	1	0.00
Seminole	2	0.01
Shoshone (1)	1	0.00
Sioux (1)	2	0.01
All other tribes (8)	13	0.06
American Indian tribes, not spec.	5	0.02
Arab:	119	0.57
Arab/Arabic	19	0.09
Lebanese	57	0.28
Syrian	9	0.04
Other Arab	34	0.16
Armenian	28	0.14
Asian:	1,632	7.88
Bangladeshi (4)	4	0.02
Cambodian (22)	23	0.11
Chinese, ex. Taiwanese (608)	630	3.04
Filipino (70)	88	0.42
Indian (370)	396	1.91
Indonesian (3)	4	0.02
Japanese (41)	57	0.28
Korean (180)	193	0.93
Laotian (13)	18	0.09
Pakistani (27)	27	0.13
Sri Lankan (9)	9	0.04
Taiwanese (14)	20	0.10
Thai (19)	23	0.11
Vietnamese (57)	68	0.33
Other Asian, specified (18)	19	0.09
Other Asian, not specified (17)	53	0.26
Australian	5	0.02
Austrian	194	0.94
Belgian	38	0.18
Brazilian	7	0.03
British	167	0.81
Bulgarian	10	0.05
Canadian	89	0.43
Celtic	6	0.03
Croatian	13	0.06
Czech	122	0.59
Czechoslovakian	121	0.58
Danish	62	0.30
Dutch	169	0.82
Eastern European	58	0.28
English	2,621	12.65
European	206	0.99
Finnish	94	0.45
French, except Basque	1,472	7.10
French Canadian	1,106	5.34
German	2,490	12.02
Greek	174	0.84
Guyanese	7	0.03
Hawaii Native/Pacific Islander:	39	0.19
Micronesian: (1)	2	0.01
Guamanian/Chamorro (1)	1	0.00
Other Micronesian	1	0.00
Polynesian: (6)	14	0.07
Native Hawaiian (5)	12	0.06
Samoan (1)	2	0.01
Other Pac. Isl., not spec. (3)	23	0.11
Hispanic or Latino:	893	4.31
Central American:	28	0.14
Costa Rican	3	0.01
Guatemalan	10	0.05
Honduran	3	0.01
Nicaraguan	4	0.02
Panamanian	4	0.02
Salvadoran	3	0.01
Other Central American	1	0.00
Cuban	43	0.21
Dominican Republic	24	0.12
Mexican	87	0.42
Puerto Rican	454	2.19
South American:	148	0.71
Argentinean	25	0.12
Bolivian	9	0.04
Chilean	30	0.14
Colombian	40	0.19
Ecuadorian	15	0.07
Paraguayan	1	0.00
Peruvian	24	0.12
Uruguayan	1	0.00
Venezuelan	3	0.01
Other Hispanic or Latino	109	0.53
Hungarian	258	1.25
Iranian	63	0.30
Irish	3,574	17.25
Israeli	7	0.03
Italian	3,029	14.62
Latvian	13	0.06
Lithuanian	144	0.69
Maltese	7	0.03
New Zealander	8	0.04
Northern European	13	0.06
Norwegian	213	1.03
Pennsylvania German	6	0.03
Polish	1,618	7.81
Portuguese	256	1.24
Romanian	117	0.56
Russian	553	2.67
Scandinavian	42	0.20
Scotch-Irish	319	1.54
Scottish	515	2.49
Serbian	7	0.03
Slavic	6	0.03
Slovak	79	0.38
Swedish	508	2.45
Swiss	24	0.12
Turkish	30	0.14
Ukrainian	100	0.48
United States or American	571	2.76
Welsh	126	0.61
West Indian, excl. Hispanic:	232	1.12
British West Indian	15	0.07
Haitian	33	0.16
Jamaican	136	0.66
Trinidadian and Tobagonian	20	0.10
U.S. Virgin Islander	5	0.02
West Indian	17	0.08
Other West Indian	6	0.03
White:	17,710	85.47
Not Hispanic (16,977)	17,240	83.20
Hispanic (410)	470	2.27

Meriden

Place Type: City
County: New Haven
Population: 58,244

Ancestry/Race	Number	%
African American/Black:	4,458	7.65
Not Hispanic (3,321)	3,778	6.49
Hispanic (433)	680	1.17
African, sub-Saharan:	236	0.41
African	149	0.26
Cape Verdean	17	0.03
Ethiopian	8	0.01
Ghanian	6	0.01
Nigerian	24	0.04
South African	32	0.05
Am. Ind. or Alaska Nat., not spec.	195	0.33
Albanian	28	0.05
American Indian tribes, specified:	283	0.49
Apache (1)	2	0.00
Blackfeet (4)	19	0.03
Cherokee (14)	65	0.11
Cheyenne	1	0.00
Chickasaw	1	0.00
Chippewa (2)	4	0.01

Notes: 1. Figures in the "Number" column do not add up to the total population due to: a) Ancestry/Race overlap — e.g. persons can report being both White and Irish, b) persons of Hispanic origin can report being any race, c) persons reporting two ancestries are counted in both categories. 2. Numbers in parentheses indicate the number of persons reporting this ancestry/race alone, not in combination with any other ancestry/race. 3. Refer to the Explanation of Data in the front of the book for more detailed information.

Choctaw	1	0.00
Creek	4	0.01
Iroquois (1)	9	0.02
Latin American Indians (38)	74	0.13
Navajo (2)	3	0.01
Pueblo	8	0.01
Seminole	1	0.00
Sioux (1)	5	0.01
Yakama	1	0.00
All other tribes (43)	85	0.15
American Indian tribes, not spec.	35	0.06
Arab:	147	0.25
Arab/Arabic	10	0.02
Egyptian	16	0.03
Lebanese	45	0.08
Moroccan	9	0.02
Palestinian	33	0.06
Syrian	34	0.06
Armenian	16	0.03
Asian:	969	1.66
Bangladeshi (14)	14	0.02
Cambodian (11)	12	0.02
Chinese, ex. Taiwanese (154)	175	0.30
Filipino (124)	172	0.30
Indian (195)	215	0.37
Indonesian (3)	5	0.01
Japanese (4)	31	0.05
Korean (46)	60	0.10
Laotian (52)	54	0.09
Malaysian	3	0.01
Pakistani (48)	60	0.10
Sri Lankan	3	0.01
Taiwanese	2	0.00
Thai (8)	8	0.01
Vietnamese (91)	97	0.17
Other Asian, specified	2	0.00
Other Asian, not specified (31)	56	0.10
Austrian	142	0.24
Basque	11	0.02
Belgian	36	0.06
Brazilian	33	0.06
British	115	0.20
Bulgarian	6	0.01
Canadian	171	0.29
Celtic	12	0.02
Croatian	22	0.04
Czech	101	0.17
Czechoslovakian	88	0.15
Danish	119	0.20
Dutch	349	0.60
Eastern European	13	0.02
English	4,764	8.18
European	56	0.10
Finnish	46	0.08
French, except Basque	4,538	7.79
French Canadian	2,280	3.91
German	5,994	10.29
Greek	249	0.43
Hawaii Native/Pacific Islander:	40	0.07
Micronesian: (3)	3	0.01
Guamanian/Chamorro (3)	3	0.01
Polynesian: (3)	13	0.02
Native Hawaiian (1)	6	0.01
Samoan (2)	7	0.01
Other Pac. Isl., specified	2	0.00
Other Pac. Isl., not spec. (5)	22	0.04
Hispanic or Latino:	12,296	21.11
Central American:	140	0.24
Costa Rican	8	0.01
Guatemalan	40	0.07
Honduran	7	0.01
Nicaraguan	60	0.10
Panamanian	11	0.02
Salvadoran	9	0.02
Other Central American	5	0.01
Cuban	165	0.28
Dominican Republic	149	0.26
Mexican	948	1.63
Puerto Rican	9,637	16.55
South American:	289	0.50
Argentinean	18	0.03
Bolivian	3	0.01
Chilean	3	0.01
Colombian	60	0.10
Ecuadorian	139	0.24
Paraguayan	2	0.00
Peruvian	35	0.06
Uruguayan	4	0.01
Venezuelan	6	0.01
Other South American	20	0.03
Other Hispanic or Latino	968	1.66
Hungarian	624	1.07
Iranian	7	0.01
Irish	8,187	14.06
Italian	10,382	17.83
Latvian	44	0.08
Lithuanian	298	0.51
Maltese	15	0.03
Northern European	46	0.08
Norwegian	117	0.20
Pennsylvania German	6	0.01
Polish	7,970	13.68
Portuguese	390	0.67
Romanian	45	0.08
Russian	697	1.20
Scandinavian	14	0.02
Scotch-Irish	393	0.67
Scottish	659	1.13
Slavic	39	0.07
Slovak	164	0.28
Slovene	8	0.01
Swedish	678	1.16
Swiss	58	0.10
Ukrainian	193	0.33
United States or American	1,895	3.25
Welsh	278	0.48
West Indian, excl. Hispanic:	371	0.64
British West Indian	9	0.02
Jamaican	286	0.49
West Indian	76	0.13
White:	48,152	82.67
Not Hispanic (40,709)	41,507	71.26
Hispanic (6,025)	6,645	11.41
Yugoslavian	33	0.06

Middletown

Place Type: City
County: Middlesex
Population: 43,167

Ancestry/Race	Number	%
African American/Black:	5,911	13.69
Not Hispanic (5,111)	5,674	13.14
Hispanic (180)	237	0.55
African, sub-Saharan:	297	0.69
African	233	0.54
Cape Verdean	31	0.07
Nigerian	12	0.03
Other sub-Saharan African	21	0.05
Alaska Native tribes, specified:	4	0.01
Alaska Athabascan (1)	1	0.00
Eskimo	2	0.00
Tlingit-Haida	1	0.00
Alaska Native tribes, not specified	1	0.00
Am. Ind. or Alaska Nat., not spec.	143	0.33
Albanian	8	0.02
Alsatian	15	0.03
American Indian tribes, specified:	200	0.46
Apache (2)	5	0.01
Blackfeet (1)	26	0.06
Cherokee (10)	62	0.14
Cheyenne	1	0.00
Chippewa (2)	8	0.02
Choctaw	4	0.01
Comanche (2)	3	0.01
Cree	1	0.00
Creek (2)	2	0.00
Iroquois (3)	17	0.04
Latin American Indians (3)	6	0.01
Navajo (1)	2	0.00
Potawatomi	1	0.00
Seminole	6	0.01
Sioux (5)	6	0.01
All other tribes (25)	50	0.12
American Indian tribes, not spec.	20	0.05
Arab:	181	0.42
Lebanese	117	0.27
Moroccan	19	0.04
Palestinian	8	0.02
Syrian	30	0.07
Other Arab	7	0.02
Armenian	104	0.24
Asian:	1,387	3.21
Bangladeshi (5)	5	0.01
Cambodian (88)	98	0.23
Chinese, ex. Taiwanese (287)	331	0.77
Filipino (79)	105	0.24
Hmong (3)	3	0.01
Indian (367)	409	0.95
Indonesian (11)	15	0.03
Japanese (48)	79	0.18
Korean (76)	94	0.22
Laotian (48)	60	0.14
Malaysian (7)	7	0.02
Pakistani (33)	40	0.09
Sri Lankan (2)	2	0.00
Taiwanese (6)	12	0.03
Thai (11)	13	0.03
Vietnamese (49)	53	0.12
Other Asian, specified	4	0.01
Other Asian, not specified (15)	57	0.13
Assyrian/Chaldean/Syriac	11	0.03
Austrian	127	0.29
Basque	6	0.01
Brazilian	17	0.04
British	233	0.54
Canadian	154	0.36
Celtic	5	0.01
Croatian	24	0.06
Czech	143	0.33
Czechoslovakian	87	0.20
Danish	105	0.24
Dutch	306	0.71
Eastern European	75	0.17
English	4,441	10.29
Estonian	51	0.12
European	228	0.53
Finnish	16	0.04
French, except Basque	2,390	5.54
French Canadian	1,447	3.35
German	4,365	10.11
Greek	301	0.70
Hawaii Native/Pacific Islander:	62	0.14
Micronesian:	2	0.00
Guamanian/Chamorro	2	0.00
Polynesian: (18)	33	0.08
Native Hawaiian (8)	19	0.04
Samoan (9)	10	0.02
Tongan	3	0.01
Other Polynesian (1)	1	0.00
Other Pac. Isl., specified	2	0.00
Other Pac. Isl., not spec. (2)	25	0.06
Hispanic or Latino:	2,287	5.30
Central American:	44	0.10
Costa Rican	6	0.01
Guatemalan	7	0.02
Honduran	6	0.01
Nicaraguan	3	0.01
Panamanian	10	0.02
Salvadoran	11	0.03
Other Central American	1	0.00
Cuban	93	0.22
Dominican Republic	53	0.12
Mexican	162	0.38
Puerto Rican	1,501	3.48
South American:	149	0.35
Argentinean	19	0.04
Bolivian	3	0.01
Chilean	6	0.01

Notes: 1. Figures in the "Number" column do not add up to the total population due to: a) Ancestry/Race overlap — e.g. persons can report being both White and Irish, b) persons of Hispanic origin can report being any race, c) persons reporting two ancestries are counted in both categories. 2. Numbers in parentheses indicate the number of persons reporting this ancestry/race alone, not in combination with any other ancestry/race. 3. Refer to the Explanation of Data in the front of the book for more detailed information.

Ancestry/Race	Number	%
Colombian	49	0.11
Ecuadorian	10	0.02
Paraguayan	2	0.00
Peruvian	42	0.10
Venezuelan	13	0.03
Other South American	5	0.01
Other Hispanic or Latino	285	0.66
Hungarian	301	0.70
Iranian	37	0.09
Irish	6,559	15.19
Italian	9,954	23.06
Latvian	28	0.06
Lithuanian	364	0.84
Northern European	9	0.02
Norwegian	190	0.44
Pennsylvania German	10	0.02
Polish	4,882	11.31
Portuguese	313	0.73
Romanian	69	0.16
Russian	614	1.42
Scandinavian	6	0.01
Scotch-Irish	343	0.79
Scottish	643	1.49
Serbian	7	0.02
Slavic	83	0.19
Slovak	96	0.22
Slovene	5	0.01
Swedish	910	2.11
Swiss	52	0.12
Turkish	50	0.12
Ukrainian	161	0.37
United States or American	1,320	3.06
Welsh	144	0.33
West Indian, excl. Hispanic:	535	1.24
Bahamian	12	0.03
Haitian	39	0.09
Jamaican	429	0.99
Trinidadian and Tobagonian	36	0.08
West Indian	19	0.04
White:	35,488	82.21
Not Hispanic (33,435)	34,261	79.37
Hispanic (1,105)	1,227	2.84
Yugoslavian	73	0.17

Milford

Place Type: Special City
County: New Haven
Population: 50,594

Ancestry/Race	Number	%
African American/Black:	1,132	2.24
Not Hispanic (928)	1,072	2.12
Hispanic (37)	60	0.12
African, sub-Saharan:	110	0.22
African	25	0.05
Cape Verdean	62	0.12
Ethiopian	10	0.02
Liberian	6	0.01
South African	7	0.01
Am. Ind. or Alaska Nat., not spec.	75	0.15
Albanian	19	0.04
Alsatian	4	0.01
American Indian tribes, specified:	134	0.26
Blackfeet (5)	13	0.03
Cherokee (7)	25	0.05
Cheyenne (1)	2	0.00
Chippewa (3)	5	0.01
Choctaw	6	0.01
Cree	1	0.00
Delaware (1)	3	0.01
Iroquois (2)	9	0.02
Latin American Indians (5)	12	0.02
Osage	2	0.00
Seminole	1	0.00
Sioux	2	0.00
Yuman (1)	1	0.00
All other tribes (19)	52	0.10
American Indian tribes, not spec.	7	0.01
Arab:	192	0.38
Arab/Arabic	17	0.03
Egyptian	46	0.09
Lebanese	63	0.12
Palestinian	18	0.04
Syrian	16	0.03
Other Arab	32	0.06
Armenian	100	0.20
Asian:	1,341	2.65
Bangladeshi (1)	2	0.00
Cambodian (8)	10	0.02
Chinese, ex. Taiwanese (258)	287	0.57
Filipino (132)	148	0.29
Indian (466)	491	0.97
Indonesian	4	0.01
Japanese (39)	53	0.10
Korean (106)	121	0.24
Laotian (51)	52	0.10
Malaysian (2)	2	0.00
Pakistani (30)	38	0.08
Sri Lankan (5)	5	0.01
Taiwanese (7)	13	0.03
Thai (16)	17	0.03
Vietnamese (42)	50	0.10
Other Asian, specified	6	0.01
Other Asian, not specified (19)	42	0.08
Australian	20	0.04
Austrian	190	0.38
Basque	19	0.04
Belgian	28	0.06
Brazilian	96	0.19
British	259	0.51
Canadian	151	0.30
Celtic	8	0.02
Croatian	40	0.08
Czech	182	0.36
Czechoslovakian	205	0.41
Danish	275	0.54
Dutch	566	1.12
Eastern European	60	0.12
English	6,579	13.00
Estonian	10	0.02
European	86	0.17
Finnish	53	0.10
French, except Basque	2,447	4.84
French Canadian	1,138	2.25
German	6,180	12.21
Greek	455	0.90
Guyanese	26	0.05
Hawaii Native/Pacific Islander:	36	0.07
Micronesian: (4)	4	0.01
Guamanian/Chamorro (4)	4	0.01
Polynesian: (11)	18	0.04
Native Hawaiian (3)	7	0.01
Samoan (7)	10	0.02
Tongan (1)	1	0.00
Other Pac. Isl., specified	2	0.00
Other Pac. Isl., not spec. (2)	12	0.02
Hispanic or Latino:	1,691	3.34
Central American:	44	0.09
Costa Rican	15	0.03
Guatemalan	10	0.02
Honduran	2	0.00
Panamanian	3	0.01
Salvadoran	9	0.02
Other Central American	5	0.01
Cuban	132	0.26
Dominican Republic	31	0.06
Mexican	95	0.19
Puerto Rican	865	1.71
South American:	262	0.52
Argentinean	19	0.04
Bolivian	5	0.01
Chilean	9	0.02
Colombian	92	0.18
Ecuadorian	58	0.11
Paraguayan	12	0.02
Peruvian	39	0.08
Uruguayan	8	0.02
Venezuelan	3	0.01
Other South American	17	0.03
Other Hispanic or Latino	262	0.52
Hungarian	1,659	3.28
Iranian	15	0.03
Irish	11,819	23.36
Israeli	27	0.05
Italian	11,660	23.04
Latvian	18	0.04
Lithuanian	375	0.74
Luxemburger	5	0.01
Macedonian	14	0.03
Northern European	26	0.05
Norwegian	275	0.54
Pennsylvania German	17	0.03
Polish	5,169	10.22
Portuguese	469	0.93
Romanian	98	0.19
Russian	1,518	3.00
Scandinavian	54	0.11
Scotch-Irish	777	1.54
Scottish	1,091	2.16
Slavic	123	0.24
Slovak	1,520	3.00
Slovene	31	0.06
Swedish	915	1.81
Swiss	87	0.17
Turkish	55	0.11
Ukrainian	474	0.94
United States or American	1,451	2.87
Welsh	233	0.46
West Indian, excl. Hispanic:	259	0.51
Bahamian	8	0.02
Barbadian	6	0.01
Belizean	4	0.01
Bermudan	6	0.01
British West Indian	8	0.02
Haitian	57	0.11
Jamaican	95	0.19
Trinidadian and Tobagonian	22	0.04
West Indian	53	0.10
White:	47,824	94.53
Not Hispanic (46,151)	46,555	92.02
Hispanic (1,181)	1,269	2.51
Yugoslavian	57	0.11

Milford

Place Type: Town
County: New Haven
Population: 52,305

Ancestry/Race	Number	%
African American/Black:	1,159	2.22
Not Hispanic (951)	1,098	2.10
Hispanic (38)	61	0.12
African, sub-Saharan:	110	0.21
African	25	0.05
Cape Verdean	62	0.12
Ethiopian	10	0.02
Liberian	6	0.01
South African	7	0.01
Am. Ind. or Alaska Nat., not spec.	77	0.15
Albanian	19	0.04
Alsatian	4	0.01
American Indian tribes, specified:	138	0.26
Apache (2)	2	0.00
Blackfeet (5)	13	0.02
Cherokee (7)	25	0.05
Cheyenne (1)	2	0.00
Chippewa (5)	7	0.01
Choctaw	6	0.01
Cree	1	0.00
Delaware (1)	3	0.01
Iroquois (2)	9	0.02
Latin American Indians (5)	12	0.02
Osage	2	0.00
Seminole	1	0.00
Sioux	2	0.00
Yuman (1)	1	0.00
All other tribes (19)	52	0.10
American Indian tribes, not spec.	7	0.01

Notes: 1. Figures in the "Number" column do not add up to the total population due to: a) Ancestry/Race overlap — e.g. persons can report being both White and Irish, b) persons of Hispanic origin can report being any race, c) persons reporting two ancestries are counted in both categories. 2. Numbers in parentheses indicate the number of persons reporting this ancestry/race alone, not in combination with any other ancestry/race. 3. Refer to the Explanation of Data in the front of the book for more detailed information.

Arab:	199	0.38
Arab/Arabic	24	0.05
Egyptian	46	0.09
Lebanese	63	0.12
Palestinian	18	0.03
Syrian	16	0.03
Other Arab	32	0.06
Armenian	100	0.19
Asian:	1,367	2.61
Bangladeshi (1)	2	0.00
Cambodian (8)	10	0.02
Chinese, ex. Taiwanese (260)	289	0.55
Filipino (133)	150	0.29
Indian (473)	499	0.95
Indonesian	4	0.01
Japanese (41)	55	0.11
Korean (107)	123	0.24
Laotian (53)	54	0.10
Malaysian (2)	2	0.00
Pakistani (36)	44	0.08
Sri Lankan (5)	5	0.01
Taiwanese (7)	13	0.02
Thai (16)	17	0.03
Vietnamese (44)	52	0.10
Other Asian, specified	6	0.01
Other Asian, not specified (19)	42	0.08
Australian	20	0.04
Austrian	194	0.37
Basque	19	0.04
Belgian	28	0.05
Brazilian	96	0.18
British	263	0.50
Canadian	156	0.30
Celtic	8	0.02
Croatian	46	0.09
Czech	182	0.35
Czechoslovakian	205	0.39
Danish	309	0.59
Dutch	580	1.11
Eastern European	64	0.12
English	6,757	12.92
Estonian	10	0.02
European	90	0.17
Finnish	59	0.11
French, except Basque	2,540	4.86
French Canadian	1,200	2.29
German	6,345	12.13
Greek	480	0.92
Guyanese	26	0.05
Hawaii Native/Pacific Islander:	37	0.07
Micronesian: (4)	4	0.01
Guamanian/Chamorro (4)	4	0.01
Polynesian: (11)	19	0.04
Native Hawaiian (3)	8	0.02
Samoan (7)	10	0.02
Tongan (1)	1	0.00
Other Pac. Isl., specified	2	0.00
Other Pac. Isl., not spec. (2)	12	0.02
Hispanic or Latino:	1,750	3.35
Central American:	47	0.09
Costa Rican	15	0.03
Guatemalan	11	0.02
Honduran	3	0.01
Panamanian	4	0.01
Salvadoran	9	0.02
Other Central American	5	0.01
Cuban	134	0.26
Dominican Republic	32	0.06
Mexican	97	0.19
Puerto Rican	890	1.70
South American:	271	0.52
Argentinean	20	0.04
Bolivian	5	0.01
Chilean	9	0.02
Colombian	95	0.18
Ecuadorian	63	0.12
Paraguayan	12	0.02
Peruvian	39	0.07
Uruguayan	8	0.02
Venezuelan	3	0.01
Other South American	17	0.03
Other Hispanic or Latino	279	0.53
Hungarian	1,684	3.22
Iranian	15	0.03
Irish	12,263	23.45
Israeli	27	0.05
Italian	12,071	23.08
Latvian	18	0.03
Lithuanian	418	0.80
Luxemburger	5	0.01
Macedonian	14	0.03
Northern European	26	0.05
Norwegian	275	0.53
Pennsylvania German	17	0.03
Polish	5,272	10.08
Portuguese	482	0.92
Romanian	119	0.23
Russian	1,565	2.99
Scandinavian	54	0.10
Scotch-Irish	811	1.55
Scottish	1,130	2.16
Slavic	123	0.24
Slovak	1,520	2.91
Slovene	31	0.06
Swedish	940	1.80
Swiss	87	0.17
Turkish	55	0.11
Ukrainian	485	0.93
United States or American	1,511	2.89
Welsh	243	0.46
West Indian, excl. Hispanic:	259	0.50
Bahamian	8	0.02
Barbadian	6	0.01
Belizean	4	0.01
Bermudan	6	0.01
British West Indian	8	0.02
Haitian	57	0.11
Jamaican	95	0.18
Trinidadian and Tobagonian	22	0.04
West Indian	53	0.10
White:	49,470	94.58
Not Hispanic (47,740)	48,151	92.06
Hispanic (1,227)	1,319	2.52
Yugoslavian	57	0.11

Monroe

Place Type: Town
County: Fairfield
Population: 19,247

Ancestry/Race	Number	%
Acadian/Cajun	9	0.05
Afghan	58	0.30
African American/Black:	271	1.41
Not Hispanic (225)	257	1.34
Hispanic (6)	14	0.07
Am. Ind. or Alaska Nat., not spec.	23	0.12
Albanian	76	0.39
American Indian tribes, specified:	35	0.18
Cherokee (3)	7	0.04
Choctaw (1)	10	0.05
Creek	1	0.01
Iroquois (1)	2	0.01
Latin American Indians (2)	8	0.04
Navajo (1)	1	0.01
All other tribes (4)	6	0.03
American Indian tribes, not spec.	4	0.02
Arab:	117	0.61
Lebanese	96	0.50
Palestinian	21	0.11
Armenian	61	0.32
Asian:	364	1.89
Cambodian (4)	4	0.02
Chinese, ex. Taiwanese (60)	76	0.39
Filipino (14)	18	0.09
Indian (154)	184	0.96
Japanese (6)	9	0.05
Korean (28)	34	0.18
Pakistani (12)	14	0.07
Thai (1)	2	0.01
Vietnamese (5)	10	0.05
Other Asian, specified	2	0.01
Other Asian, not specified (4)	11	0.06
Austrian	96	0.50
Belgian	41	0.21
Brazilian	8	0.04
British	129	0.67
Bulgarian	6	0.03
Canadian	83	0.43
Celtic	23	0.12
Croatian	5	0.03
Czech	157	0.82
Czechoslovakian	85	0.44
Danish	86	0.45
Dutch	167	0.87
Eastern European	30	0.16
English	1,813	9.42
Estonian	6	0.03
European	104	0.54
French, except Basque	735	3.82
French Canadian	224	1.16
German	2,811	14.60
Greek	358	1.86
Hawaii Native/Pacific Islander:	3	0.02
Polynesian:	2	0.01
Samoan	1	0.01
Other Polynesian	1	0.01
Other Pac. Isl., not spec.	1	0.01
Hispanic or Latino:	482	2.50
Central American:	22	0.11
Costa Rican	11	0.06
Guatemalan	2	0.01
Honduran	5	0.03
Salvadoran	1	0.01
Other Central American	3	0.02
Cuban	45	0.23
Dominican Republic	18	0.09
Mexican	43	0.22
Puerto Rican	208	1.08
South American:	71	0.37
Argentinean	4	0.02
Chilean	7	0.04
Colombian	33	0.17
Ecuadorian	10	0.05
Paraguayan	1	0.01
Peruvian	4	0.02
Uruguayan	4	0.02
Venezuelan	8	0.04
Other Hispanic or Latino	75	0.39
Hungarian	766	3.98
Iranian	28	0.15
Irish	4,212	21.88
Israeli	11	0.06
Italian	5,642	29.31
Latvian	23	0.12
Lithuanian	260	1.35
Macedonian	23	0.12
Northern European	54	0.28
Norwegian	108	0.56
Polish	2,042	10.61
Portuguese	438	2.28
Romanian	123	0.64
Russian	445	2.31
Scandinavian	63	0.33
Scotch-Irish	153	0.79
Scottish	343	1.78
Serbian	5	0.03
Slovak	646	3.36
Slovene	34	0.18
Swedish	538	2.80
Swiss	36	0.19
Ukrainian	85	0.44
United States or American	678	3.52
Welsh	210	1.09
West Indian, excl. Hispanic:	4	0.02
West Indian	4	0.02
White:	18,598	96.63
Not Hispanic (18,081)	18,203	94.58
Hispanic (372)	395	2.05

Notes: 1. Figures in the "Number" column do not add up to the total population due to: a) Ancestry/Race overlap — e.g. persons can report being both White and Irish, b) persons of Hispanic origin can report being any race, c) persons reporting two ancestries are counted in both categories. 2. Numbers in parentheses indicate the number of persons reporting this ancestry/race alone, not in combination with any other ancestry/race. 3. Refer to the Explanation of Data in the front of the book for more detailed information.

Yugoslavian	16	0.08

Montville

Place Type: Town
County: New London
Population: 18,546

Ancestry/Race	Number	%
African American/Black:	1,217	6.56
Not Hispanic (949)	1,101	5.94
Hispanic (70)	116	0.63
African, sub-Saharan:	207	1.12
African	142	0.77
Cape Verdean	41	0.22
Ethiopian	19	0.10
Sudanese	5	0.03
Am. Ind. or Alaska Nat., not spec.	95	0.51
Albanian	15	0.08
American Indian tribes, specified:	399	2.15
Apache (1)	5	0.03
Blackfeet	13	0.07
Cherokee (12)	37	0.20
Chickasaw	1	0.01
Chippewa	1	0.01
Choctaw	1	0.01
Cree	1	0.01
Crow	1	0.01
Iroquois (3)	5	0.03
Latin American Indians (8)	12	0.06
Navajo (4)	4	0.02
Pueblo	1	0.01
Sioux (1)	15	0.08
All other tribes (185)	302	1.63
American Indian tribes, not spec.	14	0.08
Arab:	55	0.30
Arab/Arabic	7	0.04
Egyptian	34	0.18
Lebanese	14	0.08
Armenian	6	0.03
Asian:	463	2.50
Cambodian (6)	7	0.04
Chinese, ex. Taiwanese (110)	120	0.65
Filipino (97)	158	0.85
Indian (37)	39	0.21
Indonesian (1)	3	0.02
Japanese (11)	28	0.15
Korean (38)	46	0.25
Laotian (2)	6	0.03
Pakistani (15)	15	0.08
Taiwanese	1	0.01
Thai (2)	2	0.01
Vietnamese (20)	21	0.11
Other Asian, not specified (10)	17	0.09
Austrian	54	0.29
Belgian	12	0.06
British	57	0.31
Canadian	62	0.33
Celtic	9	0.05
Croatian	8	0.04
Czech	22	0.12
Czechoslovakian	44	0.24
Danish	45	0.24
Dutch	265	1.43
English	2,612	14.08
Estonian	10	0.05
European	38	0.20
Finnish	25	0.13
French, except Basque	1,953	10.53
French Canadian	834	4.50
German	2,073	11.18
Greek	127	0.68
Hawaii Native/Pacific Islander:	28	0.15
Micronesian: (1)	2	0.01
Guamanian/Chamorro (1)	2	0.01
Polynesian: (6)	16	0.09
Native Hawaiian (4)	11	0.06
Samoan (2)	4	0.02
Other Polynesian	1	0.01
Other Pac. Isl., not spec.	10	0.05
Hispanic or Latino:	1,010	5.45
Central American:	34	0.18
Costa Rican	3	0.02
Guatemalan	4	0.02
Honduran	8	0.04
Nicaraguan	1	0.01
Panamanian	13	0.07
Salvadoran	3	0.02
Other Central American	2	0.01
Cuban	23	0.12
Dominican Republic	12	0.06
Mexican	64	0.35
Puerto Rican	664	3.58
South American:	53	0.29
Argentinean	1	0.01
Bolivian	5	0.03
Chilean	5	0.03
Colombian	18	0.10
Ecuadorian	12	0.06
Peruvian	9	0.05
Venezuelan	3	0.02
Other Hispanic or Latino	160	0.86
Hungarian	162	0.87
Icelander	7	0.04
Irish	3,139	16.93
Italian	2,276	12.27
Latvian	19	0.10
Lithuanian	82	0.44
Northern European	17	0.09
Norwegian	145	0.78
Polish	2,117	11.41
Portuguese	467	2.52
Romanian	7	0.04
Russian	380	2.05
Scandinavian	15	0.08
Scotch-Irish	443	2.39
Scottish	592	3.19
Slovak	42	0.23
Slovene	9	0.05
Swedish	367	1.98
Swiss	12	0.06
Ukrainian	159	0.86
United States or American	532	2.87
Welsh	144	0.78
West Indian, excl. Hispanic:	132	0.71
British West Indian	24	0.13
Haitian	9	0.05
Jamaican	44	0.24
U.S. Virgin Islander	8	0.04
West Indian	40	0.22
Other West Indian	7	0.04
White:	16,392	88.39
Not Hispanic (15,544)	15,896	85.71
Hispanic (412)	496	2.67

Naugatuck

Place Type: Borough
County: New Haven
Population: 30,989

Ancestry/Race	Number	%
Afghan	30	0.10
African American/Black:	1,077	3.48
Not Hispanic (842)	1,023	3.30
Hispanic (40)	54	0.17
African, sub-Saharan:	131	0.42
African	75	0.24
Cape Verdean	24	0.08
Ghanian	16	0.05
Other sub-Saharan African	16	0.05
Alaska Native tribes, specified:	1	0.00
Eskimo	1	0.00
Alaska Native tribes, not specified	1	0.00
Am. Ind. or Alaska Nat., not spec.	75	0.24
Albanian	199	0.64
American Indian tribes, specified:	143	0.46
Apache (1)	5	0.02
Blackfeet (3)	16	0.05
Cherokee (11)	34	0.11
Cheyenne	2	0.01
Comanche	1	0.00
Cree	3	0.01
Creek (3)	4	0.01
Iroquois (2)	7	0.02
Latin American Indians (2)	12	0.04
Lumbee	3	0.01
Paiute (1)	1	0.00
Pueblo (5)	5	0.02
Seminole	1	0.00
Shoshone	2	0.01
Sioux	3	0.01
All other tribes (22)	44	0.14
American Indian tribes, not spec.	12	0.04
Arab:	44	0.14
Arab/Arabic	10	0.03
Lebanese	34	0.11
Armenian	16	0.05
Asian:	604	1.95
Bangladeshi (7)	7	0.02
Cambodian (20)	21	0.07
Chinese, ex. Taiwanese (77)	84	0.27
Filipino (22)	27	0.09
Indian (284)	301	0.97
Indonesian	1	0.00
Japanese (9)	16	0.05
Korean (28)	35	0.11
Laotian (23)	25	0.08
Malaysian (1)	1	0.00
Pakistani (4)	5	0.02
Thai (6)	6	0.02
Vietnamese (32)	34	0.11
Other Asian, not specified (8)	41	0.13
Austrian	84	0.27
Belgian	11	0.04
Brazilian	595	1.92
British	29	0.09
Canadian	73	0.24
Croatian	12	0.04
Czech	67	0.22
Czechoslovakian	104	0.34
Danish	107	0.35
Dutch	233	0.75
Eastern European	15	0.05
English	2,532	8.17
European	16	0.05
French, except Basque	2,185	7.05
French Canadian	1,002	3.23
German	3,240	10.46
Greek	117	0.38
Hawaii Native/Pacific Islander:	7	0.02
Micronesian: (1)	1	0.00
Guamanian/Chamorro (1)	1	0.00
Polynesian: (4)	6	0.02
Native Hawaiian (4)	5	0.02
Samoan	1	0.00
Hispanic or Latino:	1,386	4.47
Central American:	43	0.14
Costa Rican	10	0.03
Guatemalan	10	0.03
Honduran	9	0.03
Panamanian	8	0.03
Salvadoran	6	0.02
Cuban	38	0.12
Dominican Republic	43	0.14
Mexican	80	0.26
Puerto Rican	805	2.60
South American:	137	0.44
Argentinean	6	0.02
Bolivian	2	0.01
Chilean	5	0.02
Colombian	34	0.11
Ecuadorian	54	0.17
Peruvian	8	0.03
Uruguayan	4	0.01
Venezuelan	9	0.03
Other South American	15	0.05
Other Hispanic or Latino	240	0.77
Hungarian	512	1.65
Icelander	22	0.07

Notes: 1. Figures in the "Number" column do not add up to the total population due to: a) Ancestry/Race overlap — e.g. persons can report being both White and Irish, b) persons of Hispanic origin can report being any race, c) persons reporting two ancestries are counted in both categories. 2. Numbers in parentheses indicate the number of persons reporting this ancestry/race alone, not in combination with any other ancestry/race. 3. Refer to the Explanation of Data in the front of the book for more detailed information.

Ancestry/Race	Number	%
Irish	6,939	22.39
Italian	7,011	22.62
Latvian	45	0.15
Lithuanian	751	2.42
Macedonian	26	0.08
New Zealander	12	0.04
Norwegian	87	0.28
Polish	3,461	11.17
Portuguese	2,044	6.60
Romanian	71	0.23
Russian	362	1.17
Scotch-Irish	324	1.05
Scottish	513	1.66
Slavic	39	0.13
Slovak	202	0.65
Slovene	5	0.02
Swedish	691	2.23
Swiss	48	0.15
Turkish	6	0.02
Ukrainian	193	0.62
United States or American	656	2.12
Welsh	114	0.37
West Indian, excl. Hispanic:	84	0.27
Barbadian	7	0.02
Haitian	10	0.03
Jamaican	60	0.19
U.S. Virgin Islander	7	0.02
White:	28,937	93.38
Not Hispanic (27,541)	27,978	90.28
Hispanic (894)	959	3.09
Yugoslavian	38	0.12

New Britain

Place Type: City
County: Hartford
Population: 71,538

Ancestry/Race	Number	%
African American/Black:	8,791	12.29
Not Hispanic (6,965)	7,577	10.59
Hispanic (829)	1,214	1.70
African, sub-Saharan:	458	0.64
African	270	0.38
Cape Verdean	90	0.13
Ethiopian	12	0.02
Ghanian	31	0.04
Nigerian	44	0.06
Somalian	11	0.02
Alaska Native tribes, specified:	1	0.00
Alaska Athabascan (1)	1	0.00
Am. Ind. or Alaska Nat., not spec.	299	0.42
Albanian	53	0.07
American Indian tribes, specified:	255	0.36
Apache	6	0.01
Blackfeet (6)	19	0.03
Cherokee (17)	56	0.08
Cheyenne (1)	1	0.00
Chippewa (2)	5	0.01
Choctaw	2	0.00
Cree	1	0.00
Creek	1	0.00
Iroquois (1)	16	0.02
Latin American Indians (30)	66	0.09
Lumbee	2	0.00
Navajo (1)	1	0.00
Puget Sound Salish	1	0.00
Seminole	2	0.00
Sioux (3)	3	0.00
Tohono O'Odham (5)	5	0.01
Yaqui (1)	1	0.00
All other tribes (23)	67	0.09
American Indian tribes, not spec.	24	0.03
Arab:	150	0.21
Arab/Arabic	33	0.05
Jordanian	8	0.01
Lebanese	67	0.09
Moroccan	5	0.01
Syrian	5	0.01
Other Arab	32	0.04
Armenian	277	0.39
Asian:	1,950	2.73
Bangladeshi (7)	13	0.02
Cambodian (102)	118	0.16
Chinese, ex. Taiwanese (225)	256	0.36
Filipino (129)	155	0.22
Indian (311)	359	0.50
Indonesian (1)	1	0.00
Japanese (26)	45	0.06
Korean (94)	105	0.15
Laotian (326)	375	0.52
Malaysian	2	0.00
Pakistani (76)	100	0.14
Sri Lankan (9)	9	0.01
Taiwanese (6)	6	0.01
Thai (9)	21	0.03
Vietnamese (258)	289	0.40
Other Asian, specified (1)	1	0.00
Other Asian, not specified (53)	95	0.13
Assyrian/Chaldean/Syriac	190	0.27
Austrian	316	0.44
Basque	28	0.04
Belgian	6	0.01
Brazilian	48	0.07
British	212	0.30
Canadian	178	0.25
Celtic	15	0.02
Croatian	16	0.02
Czech	98	0.14
Czechoslovakian	112	0.16
Danish	134	0.19
Dutch	157	0.22
Eastern European	11	0.02
English	2,663	3.72
European	140	0.20
Finnish	30	0.04
French, except Basque	3,985	5.57
French Canadian	1,775	2.48
German	3,059	4.28
Greek	263	0.37
Guyanese	7	0.01
Hawaii Native/Pacific Islander:	97	0.14
Micronesian: (9)	10	0.01
Guamanian/Chamorro (9)	10	0.01
Polynesian: (25)	32	0.04
Native Hawaiian (19)	21	0.03
Samoan (5)	10	0.01
Tongan (1)	1	0.00
Other Pac. Isl., not spec. (9)	55	0.08
Hispanic or Latino:	19,138	26.75
Central American:	137	0.19
Costa Rican	10	0.01
Guatemalan	42	0.06
Honduran	21	0.03
Nicaraguan	13	0.02
Panamanian	23	0.03
Salvadoran	23	0.03
Other Central American	5	0.01
Cuban	226	0.32
Dominican Republic	326	0.46
Mexican	625	0.87
Puerto Rican	15,693	21.94
South American:	486	0.68
Argentinean	62	0.09
Bolivian	2	0.00
Chilean	6	0.01
Colombian	133	0.19
Ecuadorian	72	0.10
Peruvian	162	0.23
Uruguayan	1	0.00
Venezuelan	28	0.04
Other South American	20	0.03
Other Hispanic or Latino	1,645	2.30
Hungarian	183	0.26
Iranian	120	0.17
Irish	5,567	7.78
Italian	9,234	12.91
Latvian	40	0.06
Lithuanian	775	1.08
Northern European	5	0.01
Norwegian	138	0.19
Polish	14,257	19.93
Portuguese	522	0.73
Romanian	51	0.07
Russian	486	0.68
Scandinavian	28	0.04
Scotch-Irish	247	0.35
Scottish	517	0.72
Slavic	22	0.03
Slovak	165	0.23
Slovene	18	0.03
Swedish	1,039	1.45
Swiss	24	0.03
Turkish	10	0.01
Ukrainian	878	1.23
United States or American	1,318	1.84
Welsh	98	0.14
West Indian, excl. Hispanic:	751	1.05
Bahamian	12	0.02
Barbadian	14	0.02
Belizean	6	0.01
British West Indian	86	0.12
Haitian	110	0.15
Jamaican	453	0.63
Trinidadian and Tobagonian	21	0.03
U.S. Virgin Islander	6	0.01
West Indian	43	0.06
White:	51,834	72.46
Not Hispanic (42,083)	43,311	60.54
Hispanic (7,551)	8,523	11.91
Yugoslavian	55	0.08

New Canaan

Place Type: Town
County: Fairfield
Population: 19,395

Ancestry/Race	Number	%
African American/Black:	235	1.21
Not Hispanic (196)	226	1.17
Hispanic (5)	9	0.05
African, sub-Saharan:	59	0.30
African	19	0.10
South African	26	0.13
Zimbabwean	14	0.07
Am. Ind. or Alaska Nat., not spec.	6	0.03
Albanian	8	0.04
Alsatian	6	0.03
American Indian tribes, specified:	22	0.11
Cherokee	9	0.05
Latin American Indians (1)	3	0.02
Navajo (1)	1	0.01
Sioux	1	0.01
All other tribes (2)	8	0.04
American Indian tribes, not spec.	2	0.01
Arab:	55	0.28
Lebanese	39	0.20
Syrian	16	0.08
Armenian	21	0.11
Asian:	570	2.94
Chinese, ex. Taiwanese (159)	205	1.06
Filipino (30)	37	0.19
Indian (78)	97	0.50
Indonesian (2)	2	0.01
Japanese (45)	73	0.38
Korean (90)	106	0.55
Pakistani (1)	1	0.01
Thai (6)	6	0.03
Vietnamese (22)	24	0.12
Other Asian, specified (1)	2	0.01
Other Asian, not specified (7)	17	0.09
Australian	23	0.12
Austrian	253	1.30
Belgian	58	0.30
Brazilian	45	0.23
British	283	1.46
Bulgarian	8	0.04
Canadian	105	0.54
Croatian	21	0.11

Notes: 1. Figures in the "Number" column do not add up to the total population due to: a) Ancestry/Race overlap — e.g. persons can report being both White and Irish, b) persons of Hispanic origin can report being any race, c) persons reporting two ancestries are counted in both categories. 2. Numbers in parentheses indicate the number of persons reporting this ancestry/race alone, not in combination with any other ancestry/race. 3. Refer to the Explanation of Data in the front of the book for more detailed information.

Czech	69	0.36
Czechoslovakian	62	0.32
Danish	145	0.75
Dutch	346	1.78
Eastern European	52	0.27
English	3,874	19.97
Estonian	9	0.05
European	219	1.13
Finnish	9	0.05
French, except Basque	810	4.18
French Canadian	84	0.43
German	3,029	15.62
Greek	316	1.63
Hawaii Native/Pacific Islander:	5	0.03
Polynesian:	1	0.01
Native Hawaiian	1	0.01
Other Pac. Isl., not spec. (1)	4	0.02
Hispanic or Latino:	338	1.74
Central American:	11	0.06
Costa Rican	3	0.02
Guatemalan	3	0.02
Honduran	1	0.01
Nicaraguan	3	0.02
Salvadoran	1	0.01
Cuban	20	0.10
Dominican Republic	8	0.04
Mexican	62	0.32
Puerto Rican	45	0.23
South American:	90	0.46
Argentinean	11	0.06
Bolivian	1	0.01
Chilean	6	0.03
Colombian	40	0.21
Ecuadorian	6	0.03
Paraguayan	3	0.02
Peruvian	20	0.10
Other South American	3	0.02
Other Hispanic or Latino	102	0.53
Hungarian	183	0.94
Iranian	144	0.74
Irish	5,081	26.20
Israeli	19	0.10
Italian	2,651	13.67
Latvian	6	0.03
Lithuanian	105	0.54
Northern European	40	0.21
Norwegian	500	2.58
Polish	818	4.22
Portuguese	26	0.13
Romanian	32	0.16
Russian	420	2.17
Scandinavian	22	0.11
Scotch-Irish	456	2.35
Scottish	905	4.67
Slavic	23	0.12
Slovak	77	0.40
Slovene	13	0.07
Swedish	324	1.67
Swiss	326	1.68
Turkish	8	0.04
Ukrainian	90	0.46
United States or American	843	4.35
Welsh	211	1.09
West Indian, excl. Hispanic:	45	0.23
Haitian	19	0.10
Trinidadian and Tobagonian	26	0.13
White:	18,651	96.16
Not Hispanic (18,220)	18,382	94.78
Hispanic (257)	269	1.39

New Fairfield

Place Type: Town
County: Fairfield
Population: 13,953

Ancestry/Race	Number	%
African American/Black:	76	0.54
Not Hispanic (53)	68	0.49
Hispanic (1)	8	0.06
Am. Ind. or Alaska Nat., not spec.	14	0.10
Albanian	22	0.16
American Indian tribes, specified:	28	0.20
Apache	4	0.03
Blackfeet (1)	4	0.03
Cherokee (1)	5	0.04
Chippewa (1)	3	0.02
Delaware	1	0.01
Iroquois	7	0.05
All other tribes (2)	4	0.03
American Indian tribes, not spec.	1	0.01
Arab:	63	0.45
Lebanese	57	0.41
Syrian	6	0.04
Armenian	8	0.06
Asian:	230	1.65
Chinese, ex. Taiwanese (41)	62	0.44
Filipino (13)	15	0.11
Indian (59)	72	0.52
Indonesian	1	0.01
Japanese (7)	14	0.10
Korean (32)	38	0.27
Pakistani (12)	15	0.11
Sri Lankan (6)	10	0.07
Thai (1)	1	0.01
Vietnamese (1)	1	0.01
Other Asian, not specified	1	0.01
Australian	36	0.26
Austrian	79	0.57
Belgian	33	0.24
Brazilian	13	0.09
British	49	0.35
Canadian	48	0.34
Celtic	20	0.14
Croatian	6	0.04
Czech	73	0.52
Czechoslovakian	58	0.42
Danish	122	0.87
Dutch	142	1.02
Eastern European	25	0.18
English	1,439	10.31
Estonian	23	0.16
European	97	0.70
Finnish	29	0.21
French, except Basque	441	3.16
French Canadian	174	1.25
German	2,962	21.23
Greek	223	1.60
Hawaii Native/Pacific Islander:	4	0.03
Micronesian: (1)	1	0.01
Guamanian/Chamorro (1)	1	0.01
Polynesian:	3	0.02
Native Hawaiian	3	0.02
Hispanic or Latino:	393	2.82
Central American:	23	0.16
Costa Rican	1	0.01
Guatemalan	7	0.05
Honduran	5	0.04
Nicaraguan	2	0.01
Salvadoran	8	0.06
Cuban	29	0.21
Dominican Republic	12	0.09
Mexican	31	0.22
Puerto Rican	146	1.05
South American:	51	0.37
Argentinean	8	0.06
Chilean	11	0.08
Colombian	13	0.09
Ecuadorian	13	0.09
Paraguayan	1	0.01
Peruvian	1	0.01
Uruguayan	2	0.01
Venezuelan	1	0.01
Other South American	1	0.01
Other Hispanic or Latino	101	0.72
Hungarian	270	1.94
Icelander	22	0.16
Iranian	6	0.04
Irish	4,437	31.80
Italian	3,618	25.93
Lithuanian	39	0.28
Norwegian	244	1.75
Pennsylvania German	11	0.08
Polish	963	6.90
Portuguese	179	1.28
Romanian	17	0.12
Russian	294	2.11
Scandinavian	18	0.13
Scotch-Irish	145	1.04
Scottish	156	1.12
Serbian	17	0.12
Slavic	18	0.13
Slovak	119	0.85
Swedish	287	2.06
Swiss	49	0.35
Ukrainian	72	0.52
United States or American	480	3.44
Welsh	132	0.95
West Indian, excl. Hispanic:	30	0.22
Belizean	22	0.16
Bermudan	8	0.06
White:	13,635	97.72
Not Hispanic (13,212)	13,313	95.41
Hispanic (299)	322	2.31
Yugoslavian	33	0.24

New Haven

Place Type: City
County: New Haven
Population: 123,626

Ancestry/Race	Number	%
Acadian/Cajun	7	0.01
Afghan	7	0.01
African American/Black:	48,604	39.32
Not Hispanic (44,598)	46,407	37.54
Hispanic (1,583)	2,197	1.78
African, sub-Saharan:	1,730	1.40
African	1,210	0.98
Cape Verdean	275	0.22
Ethiopian	24	0.02
Ghanian	41	0.03
Nigerian	90	0.07
South African	18	0.01
Ugandan	34	0.03
Other sub-Saharan African	38	0.03
Alaska Native tribes, specified:	4	0.00
Eskimo (3)	3	0.00
Tlingit-Haida (1)	1	0.00
Alaska Native tribes, not specified	1	0.00
Am. Ind. or Alaska Nat., not spec.	711	0.58
Albanian	102	0.08
Alsatian	7	0.01
American Indian tribes, specified:	768	0.62
Apache (3)	9	0.01
Blackfeet (6)	93	0.08
Cherokee (28)	232	0.19
Cheyenne	5	0.00
Chickasaw (2)	7	0.01
Chippewa (2)	17	0.01
Choctaw (2)	6	0.00
Comanche (1)	5	0.00
Cree (1)	2	0.00
Creek (3)	7	0.01
Crow	7	0.01
Delaware (2)	6	0.00
Houma (1)	1	0.00
Iroquois (9)	54	0.04
Kiowa (1)	1	0.00
Latin American Indians (22)	79	0.06
Lumbee	1	0.00
Navajo (4)	6	0.00
Osage	1	0.00
Pueblo (1)	5	0.00
Puget Sound Salish	3	0.00
Seminole (3)	18	0.01
Sioux (2)	16	0.01
Yaqui	3	0.00
All other tribes (61)	184	0.15

Notes: 1. Figures in the "Number" column do not add up to the total population due to: a) Ancestry/Race overlap — e.g. persons can report being both White and Irish, b) persons of Hispanic origin can report being any race, c) persons reporting two ancestries are counted in both categories. 2. Numbers in parentheses indicate the number of persons reporting this ancestry/race alone, not in combination with any other ancestry/race. 3. Refer to the Explanation of Data in the front of the book for more detailed information.

American Indian tribes, not spec.	109	0.09
Arab:	220	0.18
Arab/Arabic	11	0.01
Egyptian	8	0.01
Lebanese	138	0.11
Moroccan	12	0.01
Palestinian	30	0.02
Syrian	15	0.01
Other Arab	6	0.00
Armenian	49	0.04
Asian:	5,579	4.51
Bangladeshi (32)	32	0.03
Cambodian (96)	113	0.09
Chinese, ex. Taiwanese (1,627)	1,785	1.44
Filipino (267)	350	0.28
Hmong (2)	2	0.00
Indian (861)	997	0.81
Indonesian (11)	18	0.01
Japanese (271)	353	0.29
Korean (607)	640	0.52
Laotian (147)	174	0.14
Malaysian (13)	16	0.01
Pakistani (61)	83	0.07
Sri Lankan (10)	10	0.01
Taiwanese (88)	106	0.09
Thai (50)	62	0.05
Vietnamese (139)	151	0.12
Other Asian, specified (20)	24	0.02
Other Asian, not specified (446)	663	0.54
Assyrian/Chaldean/Syriac	8	0.01
Australian	51	0.04
Austrian	366	0.30
Basque	15	0.01
Belgian	22	0.02
Brazilian	83	0.07
British	479	0.39
Bulgarian	47	0.04
Canadian	274	0.22
Celtic	14	0.01
Croatian	65	0.05
Cypriot	6	0.00
Czech	138	0.11
Czechoslovakian	85	0.07
Danish	195	0.16
Dutch	560	0.45
Eastern European	327	0.26
English	4,214	3.41
Estonian	16	0.01
European	647	0.52
Finnish	95	0.08
French, except Basque	1,571	1.27
French Canadian	656	0.53
German	5,056	4.09
Greek	458	0.37
Guyanese	40	0.03
Hawaii Native/Pacific Islander:	350	0.28
Melanesian: (1)	1	0.00
Other Melanesian (1)	1	0.00
Micronesian: (17)	21	0.02
Guamanian/Chamorro (17)	21	0.02
Polynesian: (38)	78	0.06
Native Hawaiian (17)	45	0.04
Samoan (21)	28	0.02
Other Polynesian	5	0.00
Other Pac. Isl., specified	2	0.00
Other Pac. Isl., not spec. (22)	248	0.20
Hispanic or Latino:	26,443	21.39
Central American:	586	0.47
Costa Rican	22	0.02
Guatemalan	240	0.19
Honduran	94	0.08
Nicaraguan	43	0.03
Panamanian	60	0.05
Salvadoran	92	0.07
Other Central American	35	0.03
Cuban	371	0.30
Dominican Republic	460	0.37
Mexican	3,483	2.82
Puerto Rican	17,683	14.30
South American:	1,630	1.32
Argentinean	114	0.09
Bolivian	5	0.00
Chilean	112	0.09
Colombian	386	0.31
Ecuadorian	660	0.53
Paraguayan	2	0.00
Peruvian	235	0.19
Uruguayan	6	0.00
Venezuelan	67	0.05
Other South American	43	0.03
Other Hispanic or Latino	2,230	1.80
Hungarian	496	0.40
Icelander	36	0.03
Iranian	101	0.08
Irish	7,625	6.17
Israeli	251	0.20
Italian	13,038	10.55
Latvian	63	0.05
Lithuanian	222	0.18
New Zealander	52	0.04
Northern European	65	0.05
Norwegian	407	0.33
Polish	3,232	2.61
Portuguese	545	0.44
Romanian	296	0.24
Russian	1,822	1.47
Scandinavian	84	0.07
Scotch-Irish	608	0.49
Scottish	959	0.78
Serbian	17	0.01
Slavic	54	0.04
Slovak	75	0.06
Slovene	27	0.02
Soviet Union	16	0.01
Swedish	757	0.61
Swiss	211	0.17
Turkish	78	0.06
Ukrainian	513	0.41
United States or American	2,306	1.87
Welsh	307	0.25
West Indian, excl. Hispanic:	2,602	2.10
Barbadian	64	0.05
Belizean	3	0.00
Bermudan	9	0.01
British West Indian	72	0.06
Dutch West Indian	13	0.01
Haitian	212	0.17
Jamaican	1,591	1.29
Trinidadian and Tobagonian	248	0.20
U.S. Virgin Islander	7	0.01
West Indian	383	0.31
White:	56,794	45.94
Not Hispanic (43,979)	45,785	37.04
Hispanic (9,744)	11,009	8.91
Yugoslavian	50	0.04

New London

Place Type: City
County: New London
Population: 25,671

Ancestry/Race	Number	%
African American/Black:	5,597	21.80
Not Hispanic (4,393)	5,019	19.55
Hispanic (391)	578	2.25
African, sub-Saharan:	315	1.23
African	218	0.85
Cape Verdean	41	0.16
Ethiopian	5	0.02
Ghanian	11	0.04
Nigerian	23	0.09
Sudanese	5	0.02
Ugandan	12	0.05
Am. Ind. or Alaska Nat., not spec.	184	0.72
Albanian	107	0.42
American Indian tribes, specified:	401	1.56
Apache (3)	4	0.02
Blackfeet (3)	11	0.04
Cherokee (12)	74	0.29
Cheyenne (1)	1	0.00
Chickasaw	1	0.00
Chippewa (3)	9	0.04
Choctaw (2)	14	0.05
Cree	2	0.01
Creek (1)	3	0.01
Iroquois (2)	7	0.03
Kiowa	1	0.00
Latin American Indians (10)	20	0.08
Lumbee (1)	2	0.01
Navajo (1)	4	0.02
Pueblo (1)	1	0.00
Seminole	2	0.01
Sioux (3)	5	0.02
Tohono O'Odham	1	0.00
All other tribes (108)	239	0.93
American Indian tribes, not spec.	16	0.06
Arab:	104	0.41
Lebanese	104	0.41
Asian:	783	3.05
Cambodian (4)	9	0.04
Chinese, ex. Taiwanese (119)	160	0.62
Filipino (143)	237	0.92
Indian (70)	102	0.40
Indonesian (3)	4	0.02
Japanese (27)	61	0.24
Korean (30)	44	0.17
Laotian (15)	16	0.06
Pakistani (30)	42	0.16
Sri Lankan (6)	6	0.02
Taiwanese (3)	4	0.02
Thai (4)	4	0.02
Vietnamese (48)	51	0.20
Other Asian, specified (7)	10	0.04
Other Asian, not specified (9)	33	0.13
Austrian	72	0.28
Belgian	10	0.04
British	138	0.54
Canadian	83	0.32
Croatian	6	0.02
Czech	107	0.42
Czechoslovakian	16	0.06
Danish	60	0.23
Dutch	125	0.49
Eastern European	41	0.16
English	2,216	8.63
Estonian	21	0.08
European	108	0.42
Finnish	15	0.06
French, except Basque	1,044	4.07
French Canadian	557	2.17
German	1,867	7.27
Greek	248	0.97
Guyanese	32	0.12
Hawaii Native/Pacific Islander:	85	0.33
Melanesian: (2)	2	0.01
Fijian (2)	2	0.01
Micronesian: (6)	16	0.06
Guamanian/Chamorro (5)	15	0.06
Other Micronesian (1)	1	0.00
Polynesian: (10)	28	0.11
Native Hawaiian (6)	21	0.08
Samoan (1)	2	0.01
Other Polynesian (3)	5	0.02
Other Pac. Isl., specified	3	0.01
Other Pac. Isl., not spec. (3)	36	0.14
Hispanic or Latino:	5,061	19.71
Central American:	227	0.88
Costa Rican	28	0.11
Guatemalan	8	0.03
Honduran	16	0.06
Nicaraguan	2	0.01
Panamanian	55	0.21
Salvadoran	114	0.44
Other Central American	4	0.02
Cuban	54	0.21
Dominican Republic	280	1.09
Mexican	176	0.69
Puerto Rican	3,382	13.17
South American:	302	1.18

Notes: 1. Figures in the "Number" column do not add up to the total population due to: a) Ancestry/Race overlap — e.g. persons can report being both White and Irish, b) persons of Hispanic origin can report being any race, c) persons reporting two ancestries are counted in both categories. 2. Numbers in parentheses indicate the number of persons reporting this ancestry/race alone, not in combination with any other ancestry/race. 3. Refer to the Explanation of Data in the front of the book for more detailed information.

Argentinean	18	0.07
Bolivian	1	0.00
Chilean	7	0.03
Colombian	53	0.21
Ecuadorian	36	0.14
Paraguayan	1	0.00
Peruvian	169	0.66
Uruguayan	2	0.01
Venezuelan	5	0.02
Other South American	10	0.04
Other Hispanic or Latino	640	2.49
Hungarian	110	0.43
Irish	3,574	13.92
Italian	3,002	11.69
Latvian	14	0.05
Lithuanian	100	0.39
Norwegian	136	0.53
Pennsylvania German	7	0.03
Polish	1,092	4.25
Portuguese	263	1.02
Romanian	23	0.09
Russian	385	1.50
Scandinavian	11	0.04
Scotch-Irish	451	1.76
Scottish	482	1.88
Slavic	14	0.05
Slovak	37	0.14
Swedish	302	1.18
Swiss	16	0.06
Turkish	28	0.11
Ukrainian	102	0.40
United States or American	630	2.45
Welsh	137	0.53
West Indian, excl. Hispanic:	622	2.42
Bahamian	10	0.04
Barbadian	38	0.15
British West Indian	14	0.05
Dutch West Indian	9	0.04
Haitian	152	0.59
Jamaican	95	0.37
Trinidadian and Tobagonian	37	0.14
U.S. Virgin Islander	37	0.14
West Indian	200	0.78
Other West Indian	30	0.12
White:	17,342	67.55
Not Hispanic (14,394)	15,102	58.83
Hispanic (1,905)	2,240	8.73

New Milford

Place Type: Town
County: Litchfield
Population: 27,121

Ancestry/Race	Number	%
African American/Black:	478	1.76
Not Hispanic (371)	458	1.69
Hispanic (12)	20	0.07
African, sub-Saharan:	55	0.20
African	11	0.04
South African	30	0.11
Other sub-Saharan African	14	0.05
Am. Ind. or Alaska Nat., not spec.	55	0.20
American Indian tribes, specified:	75	0.28
Apache	2	0.01
Blackfeet (2)	5	0.02
Cherokee (3)	19	0.07
Chickasaw	4	0.01
Delaware	2	0.01
Iroquois (3)	5	0.02
Latin American Indians (2)	3	0.01
Osage (1)	1	0.00
Pueblo (1)	1	0.00
Sioux (2)	2	0.01
Ute (1)	1	0.00
All other tribes (10)	30	0.11
American Indian tribes, not spec.	7	0.03
Arab:	227	0.84
Arab/Arabic	41	0.15
Egyptian	6	0.02
Lebanese	142	0.52
Moroccan	12	0.04
Syrian	15	0.06
Other Arab	11	0.04
Armenian	51	0.19
Asian:	602	2.22
Bangladeshi (10)	10	0.04
Cambodian (8)	14	0.05
Chinese, ex. Taiwanese (141)	153	0.56
Filipino (66)	93	0.34
Indian (148)	159	0.59
Indonesian	1	0.00
Japanese (15)	18	0.07
Korean (49)	55	0.20
Laotian (26)	28	0.10
Pakistani (3)	3	0.01
Sri Lankan (4)	4	0.01
Taiwanese (5)	5	0.02
Thai (16)	20	0.07
Vietnamese (8)	12	0.04
Other Asian, not specified (16)	27	0.10
Australian	20	0.07
Austrian	183	0.67
Belgian	30	0.11
Brazilian	88	0.32
British	130	0.48
Canadian	111	0.41
Croatian	38	0.14
Czech	154	0.57
Czechoslovakian	122	0.45
Danish	90	0.33
Dutch	317	1.17
Eastern European	9	0.03
English	4,100	15.12
European	115	0.42
Finnish	166	0.61
French, except Basque	1,070	3.95
French Canadian	781	2.88
German	4,866	17.94
Greek	204	0.75
Hawaii Native/Pacific Islander:	12	0.04
Polynesian: (6)	6	0.02
Native Hawaiian (5)	5	0.02
Samoan (1)	1	0.00
Other Pac. Isl., not spec. (1)	6	0.02
Hispanic or Latino:	751	2.77
Central American:	29	0.11
Costa Rican	9	0.03
Guatemalan	13	0.05
Honduran	2	0.01
Panamanian	2	0.01
Salvadoran	1	0.00
Other Central American	2	0.01
Cuban	37	0.14
Dominican Republic	32	0.12
Mexican	108	0.40
Puerto Rican	235	0.87
South American:	135	0.50
Argentinean	4	0.01
Bolivian	1	0.00
Chilean	3	0.01
Colombian	41	0.15
Ecuadorian	41	0.15
Peruvian	26	0.10
Uruguayan	3	0.01
Venezuelan	11	0.04
Other South American	5	0.02
Other Hispanic or Latino	175	0.65
Hungarian	515	1.90
Iranian	12	0.04
Irish	6,238	23.00
Italian	5,063	18.67
Latvian	66	0.24
Lithuanian	138	0.51
Macedonian	33	0.12
Norwegian	270	1.00
Pennsylvania German	14	0.05
Polish	1,967	7.25
Portuguese	147	0.54
Romanian	17	0.06
Russian	555	2.05
Scandinavian	17	0.06
Scotch-Irish	458	1.69
Scottish	557	2.05
Slavic	71	0.26
Slovak	176	0.65
Slovene	44	0.16
Swedish	656	2.42
Swiss	78	0.29
Ukrainian	162	0.60
United States or American	1,643	6.06
Welsh	205	0.76
West Indian, excl. Hispanic:	121	0.45
Belizean	8	0.03
Jamaican	113	0.42
White:	25,950	95.68
Not Hispanic (25,038)	25,357	93.50
Hispanic (545)	593	2.19
Yugoslavian	84	0.31

Newington

Place Type: Census Designated Place
County: Hartford
Population: 29,306

Ancestry/Race	Number	%
African American/Black:	716	2.44
Not Hispanic (581)	658	2.25
Hispanic (28)	58	0.20
African, sub-Saharan:	21	0.07
African	21	0.07
Alaska Native tribes, not specified	4	0.01
Am. Ind. or Alaska Nat., not spec.	48	0.16
American Indian tribes, specified:	75	0.26
Blackfeet (2)	3	0.01
Cherokee (4)	16	0.05
Choctaw	2	0.01
Iroquois (9)	12	0.04
Latin American Indians	12	0.04
Seminole	2	0.01
Sioux (2)	3	0.01
All other tribes (9)	25	0.09
American Indian tribes, not spec.	1	0.00
Arab:	122	0.42
Arab/Arabic	16	0.05
Egyptian	4	0.01
Lebanese	86	0.29
Moroccan	6	0.02
Syrian	10	0.03
Armenian	192	0.66
Asian:	942	3.21
Bangladeshi (1)	2	0.01
Cambodian (7)	7	0.02
Chinese, ex. Taiwanese (135)	150	0.51
Filipino (90)	95	0.32
Indian (372)	412	1.41
Indonesian (3)	3	0.01
Japanese (18)	29	0.10
Korean (44)	48	0.16
Laotian (15)	18	0.06
Pakistani (45)	55	0.19
Taiwanese (4)	4	0.01
Vietnamese (61)	73	0.25
Other Asian, specified (2)	2	0.01
Other Asian, not specified (13)	44	0.15
Assyrian/Chaldean/Syriac	23	0.08
Australian	22	0.08
Austrian	174	0.59
Belgian	5	0.02
Brazilian	7	0.02
British	56	0.19
Canadian	105	0.36
Croatian	34	0.12
Czech	92	0.31
Czechoslovakian	25	0.09
Danish	175	0.60
Dutch	165	0.56
Eastern European	63	0.21
English	2,676	9.13

Notes: 1. Figures in the "Number" column do not add up to the total population due to: a) Ancestry/Race overlap — e.g. persons can report being both White and Irish, b) persons of Hispanic origin can report being any race, c) persons reporting two ancestries are counted in both categories. 2. Numbers in parentheses indicate the number of persons reporting this ancestry/race alone, not in combination with any other ancestry/race. 3. Refer to the Explanation of Data in the front of the book for more detailed information.

Ancestry/Race	Number	%
European	33	0.11
Finnish	28	0.10
French, except Basque	2,096	7.15
French Canadian	1,345	4.59
German	2,321	7.92
Greek	336	1.15
Hawaii Native/Pacific Islander:	23	0.08
Micronesian:	1	0.00
Other Micronesian	1	0.00
Polynesian: (12)	15	0.05
Native Hawaiian (6)	9	0.03
Samoan (5)	5	0.02
Other Polynesian (1)	1	0.00
Other Pac. Isl., not spec. (2)	7	0.02
Hispanic or Latino:	1,079	3.68
Central American:	22	0.08
Costa Rican	3	0.01
Nicaraguan	4	0.01
Salvadoran	15	0.05
Cuban	68	0.23
Dominican Republic	13	0.04
Mexican	67	0.23
Puerto Rican	544	1.86
South American:	184	0.63
Argentinean	21	0.07
Chilean	3	0.01
Colombian	72	0.25
Ecuadorian	7	0.02
Peruvian	72	0.25
Venezuelan	1	0.00
Other South American	8	0.03
Other Hispanic or Latino	181	0.62
Hungarian	143	0.49
Iranian	47	0.16
Irish	4,982	17.00
Italian	6,921	23.62
Lithuanian	418	1.43
New Zealander	9	0.03
Norwegian	204	0.70
Polish	4,404	15.03
Portuguese	1,014	3.46
Romanian	95	0.32
Russian	679	2.32
Scandinavian	24	0.08
Scotch-Irish	344	1.17
Scottish	401	1.37
Slavic	21	0.07
Slovak	23	0.08
Slovene	5	0.02
Swedish	1,005	3.43
Swiss	97	0.33
Ukrainian	300	1.02
United States or American	859	2.93
Welsh	62	0.21
West Indian, excl. Hispanic:	118	0.40
Barbadian	7	0.02
Haitian	23	0.08
Jamaican	53	0.18
West Indian	35	0.12
White:	27,393	93.47
Not Hispanic (26,476)	26,692	91.08
Hispanic (627)	701	2.39
Yugoslavian	18	0.06

Newtown

Place Type: Town
County: Fairfield
Population: 25,031

Ancestry/Race	Number	%
African American/Black:	513	2.05
Not Hispanic (415)	486	1.94
Hispanic (22)	27	0.11
African, sub-Saharan:	30	0.12
African	30	0.12
Am. Ind. or Alaska Nat., not spec.	41	0.16
Albanian	111	0.44
American Indian tribes, specified:	43	0.17
Blackfeet (1)	6	0.02
Cherokee (5)	13	0.05
Chippewa (1)	1	0.00
Cree (1)	1	0.00
Iroquois	1	0.00
Kiowa	1	0.00
Latin American Indians (4)	7	0.03
All other tribes (2)	13	0.05
American Indian tribes, not spec.	3	0.01
Arab:	146	0.58
Egyptian	8	0.03
Lebanese	138	0.55
Armenian	39	0.16
Asian:	449	1.79
Bangladeshi (16)	22	0.09
Cambodian (6)	6	0.02
Chinese, ex. Taiwanese (86)	102	0.41
Filipino (34)	48	0.19
Indian (104)	124	0.50
Japanese (12)	26	0.10
Korean (49)	60	0.24
Malaysian (1)	4	0.02
Sri Lankan (1)	2	0.01
Taiwanese	1	0.00
Thai (6)	14	0.06
Vietnamese (15)	19	0.08
Other Asian, specified (1)	7	0.03
Other Asian, not specified (10)	14	0.06
Assyrian/Chaldean/Syriac	6	0.02
Australian	39	0.16
Austrian	191	0.76
Belgian	31	0.12
Brazilian	28	0.11
British	287	1.15
Canadian	121	0.48
Carpatho Rusyn	11	0.04
Croatian	32	0.13
Czech	176	0.70
Czechoslovakian	149	0.60
Danish	203	0.81
Dutch	387	1.55
Eastern European	69	0.28
English	3,641	14.55
Estonian	26	0.10
European	66	0.26
Finnish	149	0.60
French, except Basque	955	3.82
French Canadian	477	1.91
German	4,557	18.21
Greek	151	0.60
Hawaii Native/Pacific Islander:	21	0.08
Melanesian: (3)	3	0.01
Other Melanesian (3)	3	0.01
Polynesian: (5)	6	0.02
Native Hawaiian (4)	4	0.02
Samoan (1)	2	0.01
Other Pac. Isl., specified	6	0.02
Other Pac. Isl., not spec. (1)	6	0.02
Hispanic or Latino:	590	2.36
Central American:	16	0.06
Costa Rican	2	0.01
Guatemalan	7	0.03
Honduran	2	0.01
Nicaraguan	2	0.01
Salvadoran	3	0.01
Cuban	44	0.18
Dominican Republic	27	0.11
Mexican	53	0.21
Puerto Rican	254	1.01
South American:	82	0.33
Argentinean	10	0.04
Bolivian	3	0.01
Chilean	1	0.00
Colombian	24	0.10
Ecuadorian	14	0.06
Paraguayan	1	0.00
Peruvian	13	0.05
Uruguayan	3	0.01
Venezuelan	2	0.01
Other South American	11	0.04
Other Hispanic or Latino	114	0.46
Hungarian	843	3.37
Iranian	72	0.29
Irish	5,869	23.45
Israeli	28	0.11
Italian	5,218	20.85
Latvian	33	0.13
Lithuanian	226	0.90
Macedonian	10	0.04
New Zealander	6	0.02
Northern European	32	0.13
Norwegian	158	0.63
Pennsylvania German	3	0.01
Polish	1,744	6.97
Portuguese	253	1.01
Romanian	53	0.21
Russian	653	2.61
Scandinavian	22	0.09
Scotch-Irish	514	2.05
Scottish	848	3.39
Serbian	8	0.03
Slavic	26	0.10
Slovak	365	1.46
Slovene	28	0.11
Swedish	650	2.60
Swiss	120	0.48
Turkish	44	0.18
Ukrainian	135	0.54
United States or American	1,027	4.10
Welsh	267	1.07
West Indian, excl. Hispanic:	100	0.40
British West Indian	2	0.01
Haitian	8	0.03
Jamaican	82	0.33
West Indian	8	0.03
White:	24,001	95.89
Not Hispanic (23,441)	23,607	94.31
Hispanic (374)	394	1.57
Yugoslavian	39	0.16

North Branford

Place Type: Town
County: New Haven
Population: 13,906

Ancestry/Race	Number	%
African American/Black:	193	1.39
Not Hispanic (163)	186	1.34
Hispanic (2)	7	0.05
African, sub-Saharan:	39	0.28
African	27	0.19
Cape Verdean	12	0.09
Am. Ind. or Alaska Nat., not spec.	16	0.12
American Indian tribes, specified:	27	0.19
Apache	1	0.01
Blackfeet	2	0.01
Cherokee	7	0.05
Chippewa	1	0.01
Choctaw (1)	6	0.04
Cree	1	0.01
Iroquois (1)	1	0.01
Latin American Indians (3)	3	0.02
Ottawa (1)	1	0.01
Sioux	2	0.01
All other tribes (1)	2	0.01
American Indian tribes, not spec.	3	0.02
Arab:	79	0.57
Egyptian	59	0.42
Lebanese	20	0.14
Armenian	17	0.12
Asian:	148	1.06
Chinese, ex. Taiwanese (45)	50	0.36
Filipino (15)	24	0.17
Indian (19)	19	0.14
Japanese (9)	14	0.10
Korean (23)	25	0.18
Sri Lankan (3)	3	0.02
Thai (3)	5	0.04
Vietnamese (5)	5	0.04
Other Asian, not specified (2)	3	0.02

Notes: 1. Figures in the "Number" column do not add up to the total population due to: a) Ancestry/Race overlap — e.g. persons can report being both White and Irish, b) persons of Hispanic origin can report being any race, c) persons reporting two ancestries are counted in both categories. 2. Numbers in parentheses indicate the number of persons reporting this ancestry/race alone, not in combination with any other ancestry/race. 3. Refer to the Explanation of Data in the front of the book for more detailed information.

Ancestry/Race	Number	%
Austrian	45	0.32
British	157	1.13
Canadian	47	0.34
Czech	14	0.10
Czechoslovakian	28	0.20
Danish	148	1.06
Dutch	113	0.81
Eastern European	8	0.06
English	1,322	9.51
European	66	0.47
Finnish	16	0.12
French, except Basque	441	3.17
French Canadian	256	1.84
German	1,697	12.20
Greek	101	0.73
Hawaii Native/Pacific Islander:	9	0.06
Polynesian: (2)	8	0.06
Native Hawaiian (2)	8	0.06
Other Pac. Isl., not spec. (1)	1	0.01
Hispanic or Latino:	250	1.80
Central American:	1	0.01
Costa Rican	1	0.01
Cuban	7	0.05
Dominican Republic	2	0.01
Mexican	32	0.23
Puerto Rican	122	0.88
South American:	31	0.22
Bolivian	7	0.05
Chilean	4	0.03
Colombian	13	0.09
Ecuadorian	1	0.01
Paraguayan	1	0.01
Peruvian	4	0.03
Venezuelan	1	0.01
Other Hispanic or Latino	55	0.40
Hungarian	70	0.50
Irish	3,019	21.71
Israeli	6	0.04
Italian	5,717	41.11
Lithuanian	182	1.31
Norwegian	137	0.99
Polish	1,355	9.74
Portuguese	113	0.81
Russian	280	2.01
Scandinavian	68	0.49
Scotch-Irish	184	1.32
Scottish	344	2.47
Serbian	11	0.08
Slovak	9	0.06
Swedish	199	1.43
Swiss	18	0.13
Ukrainian	93	0.67
United States or American	328	2.36
Welsh	24	0.17
West Indian, excl. Hispanic:	12	0.09
Jamaican	12	0.09
White:	13,533	97.32
Not Hispanic (13,258)	13,354	96.03
Hispanic (161)	179	1.29
Yugoslavian	18	0.13

North Haven

Place Type: Town
County: New Haven
Population: 23,035

Ancestry/Race	Number	%
African American/Black:	586	2.54
Not Hispanic (502)	566	2.46
Hispanic (10)	20	0.09
African, sub-Saharan:	21	0.09
African	15	0.07
Cape Verdean	6	0.03
Am. Ind. or Alaska Nat., not spec.	31	0.13
Albanian	9	0.04
American Indian tribes, specified:	56	0.24
Apache (1)	1	0.00
Cherokee (1)	13	0.06
Chickasaw (1)	1	0.00
Choctaw (1)	3	0.01
Comanche	1	0.00
Creek	5	0.02
Iroquois	2	0.01
Latin American Indians (1)	3	0.01
Seminole	4	0.02
All other tribes (8)	23	0.10
American Indian tribes, not spec.	4	0.02
Arab:	30	0.13
Arab/Arabic	10	0.04
Lebanese	20	0.09
Armenian	14	0.06
Asian:	876	3.80
Cambodian (14)	19	0.08
Chinese, ex. Taiwanese (300)	337	1.46
Filipino (42)	55	0.24
Indian (132)	150	0.65
Indonesian (1)	1	0.00
Japanese (19)	27	0.12
Korean (107)	127	0.55
Laotian (19)	21	0.09
Malaysian	2	0.01
Pakistani (19)	23	0.10
Taiwanese (13)	32	0.14
Thai (8)	12	0.05
Vietnamese (56)	57	0.25
Other Asian, specified	1	0.00
Other Asian, not specified (9)	12	0.05
Australian	16	0.07
Austrian	75	0.33
Belgian	6	0.03
British	48	0.21
Canadian	50	0.22
Croatian	7	0.03
Czech	64	0.28
Czechoslovakian	10	0.04
Danish	179	0.78
Dutch	161	0.70
Eastern European	23	0.10
English	2,256	9.79
European	38	0.16
Finnish	8	0.03
French, except Basque	645	2.80
French Canadian	375	1.63
German	2,285	9.92
Greek	80	0.35
Hawaii Native/Pacific Islander:	5	0.02
Polynesian: (1)	1	0.00
Samoan (1)	1	0.00
Other Pac. Isl., specified	1	0.00
Other Pac. Isl., not spec. (2)	3	0.01
Hispanic or Latino:	433	1.88
Central American:	12	0.05
Costa Rican	2	0.01
Honduran	3	0.01
Panamanian	1	0.00
Salvadoran	6	0.03
Cuban	19	0.08
Dominican Republic	3	0.01
Mexican	41	0.18
Puerto Rican	182	0.79
South American:	87	0.38
Argentinean	15	0.07
Chilean	4	0.02
Colombian	21	0.09
Ecuadorian	35	0.15
Paraguayan	1	0.00
Peruvian	11	0.05
Other Hispanic or Latino	89	0.39
Hungarian	327	1.42
Iranian	15	0.07
Irish	4,495	19.51
Italian	9,271	40.25
Lithuanian	213	0.92
Maltese	8	0.03
Norwegian	186	0.81
Polish	1,800	7.81
Portuguese	224	0.97
Romanian	95	0.41
Russian	368	1.60
Scandinavian	18	0.08
Scotch-Irish	327	1.42
Scottish	432	1.88
Slovak	50	0.22
Swedish	603	2.62
Swiss	40	0.17
Turkish	49	0.21
Ukrainian	243	1.05
United States or American	354	1.54
Welsh	122	0.53
West Indian, excl. Hispanic:	12	0.05
British West Indian	6	0.03
West Indian	6	0.03
White:	21,567	93.63
Not Hispanic (21,127)	21,265	92.32
Hispanic (291)	302	1.31

Norwalk

Place Type: City
County: Fairfield
Population: 82,951

Ancestry/Race	Number	%
African American/Black:	13,546	16.33
Not Hispanic (12,231)	12,964	15.63
Hispanic (432)	582	0.70
African, sub-Saharan:	583	0.70
African	465	0.56
Cape Verdean	14	0.02
Ethiopian	33	0.04
Nigerian	24	0.03
South African	14	0.02
Sudanese	15	0.02
Zimbabwean	11	0.01
Other sub-Saharan African	7	0.01
Am. Ind. or Alaska Nat., not spec.	236	0.28
Albanian	48	0.06
Alsatian	10	0.01
American Indian tribes, specified:	232	0.28
Apache (1)	1	0.00
Blackfeet	21	0.03
Cherokee (11)	63	0.08
Cheyenne (1)	1	0.00
Chippewa (4)	6	0.01
Choctaw	5	0.01
Cree	1	0.00
Creek	5	0.01
Iroquois (9)	14	0.02
Latin American Indians (19)	69	0.08
Navajo (2)	2	0.00
Pueblo	1	0.00
Seminole (1)	8	0.01
Sioux (1)	7	0.01
All other tribes (10)	28	0.03
American Indian tribes, not spec.	29	0.03
Arab:	247	0.30
Arab/Arabic	58	0.07
Egyptian	96	0.12
Lebanese	31	0.04
Moroccan	12	0.01
Palestinian	7	0.01
Syrian	38	0.05
Other Arab	5	0.01
Armenian	78	0.09
Asian:	3,126	3.77
Bangladeshi (17)	38	0.05
Cambodian	1	0.00
Chinese, ex. Taiwanese (689)	764	0.92
Filipino (341)	386	0.47
Indian (1,132)	1,267	1.53
Indonesian (7)	11	0.01
Japanese (69)	93	0.11
Korean (147)	156	0.19
Laotian (10)	12	0.01
Malaysian	1	0.00
Pakistani (104)	145	0.17
Sri Lankan (14)	14	0.02
Taiwanese (7)	13	0.02
Thai (20)	32	0.04

Notes: 1. Figures in the "Number" column do not add up to the total population due to: a) Ancestry/Race overlap — e.g. persons can report being both White and Irish, b) persons of Hispanic origin can report being any race, c) persons reporting two ancestries are counted in both categories. 2. Numbers in parentheses indicate the number of persons reporting this ancestry/race alone, not in combination with any other ancestry/race. 3. Refer to the Explanation of Data in the front of the book for more detailed information.

Vietnamese (64)	72	0.09
Other Asian, specified (3)	13	0.02
Other Asian, not specified (34)	108	0.13
Australian	48	0.06
Austrian	341	0.41
Basque	7	0.01
Belgian	47	0.06
Brazilian	195	0.24
British	361	0.44
Bulgarian	18	0.02
Canadian	304	0.37
Celtic	10	0.01
Croatian	59	0.07
Czech	289	0.35
Czechoslovakian	177	0.21
Danish	230	0.28
Dutch	613	0.74
Eastern European	202	0.24
English	6,374	7.68
Estonian	22	0.03
European	428	0.52
Finnish	170	0.20
French, except Basque	1,604	1.93
French Canadian	954	1.15
German	6,739	8.12
Greek	1,691	2.04
Guyanese	37	0.04
Hawaii Native/Pacific Islander:	110	0.13
Melanesian: (1)	1	0.00
Fijian (1)	1	0.00
Micronesian: (8)	10	0.01
Guamanian/Chamorro (8)	10	0.01
Polynesian: (17)	27	0.03
Native Hawaiian (10)	19	0.02
Samoan (5)	6	0.01
Tongan (1)	1	0.00
Other Polynesian (1)	1	0.00
Other Pac. Isl., specified	2	0.00
Other Pac. Isl., not spec. (14)	70	0.08
Hispanic or Latino:	12,966	15.63
Central American:	2,117	2.55
Costa Rican	694	0.84
Guatemalan	308	0.37
Honduran	417	0.50
Nicaraguan	180	0.22
Panamanian	16	0.02
Salvadoran	308	0.37
Other Central American	194	0.23
Cuban	191	0.23
Dominican Republic	216	0.26
Mexican	1,897	2.29
Puerto Rican	2,978	3.59
South American:	2,959	3.57
Argentinean	53	0.06
Bolivian	26	0.03
Chilean	54	0.07
Colombian	1,969	2.37
Ecuadorian	330	0.40
Paraguayan	27	0.03
Peruvian	199	0.24
Uruguayan	20	0.02
Venezuelan	183	0.22
Other South American	98	0.12
Other Hispanic or Latino	2,608	3.14
Hungarian	2,259	2.72
Icelander	36	0.04
Iranian	15	0.02
Irish	12,247	14.76
Italian	16,397	19.77
Latvian	26	0.03
Lithuanian	359	0.43
Luxemburger	16	0.02
Maltese	32	0.04
New Zealander	9	0.01
Northern European	48	0.06
Norwegian	688	0.83
Pennsylvania German	20	0.02
Polish	4,102	4.95
Portuguese	194	0.23
Romanian	166	0.20
Russian	1,620	1.95
Scandinavian	79	0.10
Scotch-Irish	752	0.91
Scottish	1,261	1.52
Serbian	5	0.01
Slavic	21	0.03
Slovak	331	0.40
Slovene	9	0.01
Soviet Union	9	0.01
Swedish	914	1.10
Swiss	125	0.15
Turkish	13	0.02
Ukrainian	470	0.57
United States or American	2,531	3.05
Welsh	267	0.32
West Indian, excl. Hispanic:	3,070	3.70
Bahamian	7	0.01
Belizean	11	0.01
British West Indian	66	0.08
Haitian	1,499	1.81
Jamaican	1,358	1.64
Trinidadian and Tobagonian	63	0.08
U.S. Virgin Islander	8	0.01
West Indian	58	0.07
White:	63,158	76.14
Not Hispanic (53,324)	54,299	65.46
Hispanic (8,015)	8,859	10.68
Yugoslavian	92	0.11

Norwich

Place Type: City
County: New London
Population: 36,117

Ancestry/Race	Number	%
Acadian/Cajun	7	0.02
African American/Black:	3,253	9.01
Not Hispanic (2,306)	3,010	8.33
Hispanic (163)	243	0.67
African, sub-Saharan:	498	1.38
African	109	0.30
Cape Verdean	303	0.84
Nigerian	69	0.19
Sierra Leonean	17	0.05
Alaska Native tribes, specified:	3	0.01
Eskimo	1	0.00
Tlingit-Haida	2	0.01
Alaska Native tribes, not specified	3	0.01
Am. Ind. or Alaska Nat., not spec.	161	0.45
Albanian	35	0.10
American Indian tribes, specified:	694	1.92
Apache	5	0.01
Blackfeet (3)	30	0.08
Cherokee (27)	118	0.33
Chickasaw	3	0.01
Chippewa (1)	5	0.01
Choctaw	2	0.01
Comanche (1)	2	0.01
Cree	3	0.01
Creek	2	0.01
Delaware	1	0.00
Iroquois (3)	22	0.06
Latin American Indians (12)	20	0.06
Navajo (3)	7	0.02
Osage	1	0.00
Paiute (1)	1	0.00
Potawatomi (5)	7	0.02
Pueblo (1)	1	0.00
Seminole	1	0.00
Sioux (14)	19	0.05
All other tribes (272)	444	1.23
American Indian tribes, not spec.	30	0.08
Arab:	161	0.45
Egyptian	15	0.04
Lebanese	119	0.33
Syrian	27	0.07
Armenian	48	0.13
Asian:	932	2.58
Cambodian (8)	8	0.02
Chinese, ex. Taiwanese (291)	301	0.83
Filipino (124)	194	0.54
Indian (156)	168	0.47
Indonesian (2)	8	0.02
Japanese (14)	45	0.12
Korean (56)	74	0.20
Laotian (3)	3	0.01
Pakistani (31)	32	0.09
Sri Lankan (16)	16	0.04
Taiwanese	1	0.00
Thai (5)	11	0.03
Vietnamese (23)	28	0.08
Other Asian, specified	1	0.00
Other Asian, not specified (27)	42	0.12
Australian	15	0.04
Austrian	67	0.19
Brazilian	6	0.02
British	82	0.23
Canadian	149	0.41
Celtic	23	0.06
Czech	66	0.18
Czechoslovakian	24	0.07
Danish	133	0.37
Dutch	421	1.17
English	3,618	10.02
Estonian	7	0.02
European	156	0.43
Finnish	78	0.22
French, except Basque	4,667	12.92
French Canadian	2,528	7.00
German	3,250	9.00
Greek	298	0.83
Guyanese	25	0.07
Hawaii Native/Pacific Islander:	51	0.14
Micronesian: (1)	6	0.02
Guamanian/Chamorro (1)	6	0.02
Polynesian: (6)	13	0.04
Native Hawaiian (5)	6	0.02
Samoan (1)	7	0.02
Other Pac. Isl., specified	1	0.00
Other Pac. Isl., not spec. (3)	31	0.09
Hispanic or Latino:	2,208	6.11
Central American:	53	0.15
Costa Rican	5	0.01
Guatemalan	3	0.01
Honduran	12	0.03
Nicaraguan	5	0.01
Panamanian	21	0.06
Salvadoran	7	0.02
Cuban	50	0.14
Dominican Republic	77	0.21
Mexican	226	0.63
Puerto Rican	1,365	3.78
South American:	134	0.37
Argentinean	6	0.02
Chilean	2	0.01
Colombian	24	0.07
Ecuadorian	9	0.02
Paraguayan	4	0.01
Peruvian	67	0.19
Uruguayan	11	0.03
Venezuelan	5	0.01
Other South American	6	0.02
Other Hispanic or Latino	303	0.84
Hungarian	191	0.53
Irish	5,728	15.86
Israeli	6	0.02
Italian	4,242	11.75
Latvian	10	0.03
Lithuanian	125	0.35
Luxemburger	5	0.01
New Zealander	15	0.04
Northern European	8	0.02
Norwegian	311	0.86
Pennsylvania German	5	0.01
Polish	4,324	11.97
Portuguese	529	1.46
Romanian	22	0.06
Russian	691	1.91
Scandinavian	51	0.14

Notes: 1. Figures in the "Number" column do not add up to the total population due to: a) Ancestry/Race overlap — e.g. persons can report being both White and Irish, b) persons of Hispanic origin can report being any race, c) persons reporting two ancestries are counted in both categories. 2. Numbers in parentheses indicate the number of persons reporting this ancestry/race alone, not in combination with any other ancestry/race. 3. Refer to the Explanation of Data in the front of the book for more detailed information.

Ancestry/Race	Number	%
Scotch-Irish	388	1.07
Scottish	805	2.23
Slovak	12	0.03
Swedish	498	1.38
Swiss	16	0.04
Ukrainian	191	0.53
United States or American	1,461	4.05
Welsh	138	0.38
West Indian, excl. Hispanic:	466	1.29
Haitian	389	1.08
Jamaican	35	0.10
Trinidadian and Tobagonian	24	0.07
U.S. Virgin Islander	16	0.04
West Indian	2	0.01
White:	30,983	85.79
Not Hispanic (29,054)	29,844	82.63
Hispanic (975)	1,139	3.15
Yugoslavian	27	0.07

Old Saybrook

Place Type: Town
County: Middlesex
Population: 10,367

Ancestry/Race	Number	%
African American/Black:	138	1.33
Not Hispanic (103)	129	1.24
Hispanic (2)	9	0.09
African, sub-Saharan:	5	0.05
African	5	0.05
Am. Ind. or Alaska Nat., not spec.	9	0.09
American Indian tribes, specified:	31	0.30
Blackfeet	3	0.03
Cherokee (2)	7	0.07
Chippewa	1	0.01
Crow	1	0.01
Iroquois	1	0.01
Seminole	1	0.01
All other tribes (6)	17	0.16
American Indian tribes, not spec.	1	0.01
Arab:	10	0.10
Lebanese	10	0.10
Armenian	21	0.20
Asian:	199	1.92
Chinese, ex. Taiwanese (57)	63	0.61
Filipino (6)	6	0.06
Indian (48)	51	0.49
Indonesian	1	0.01
Japanese (2)	7	0.07
Korean (19)	22	0.21
Laotian (27)	29	0.28
Vietnamese (12)	12	0.12
Other Asian, specified	3	0.03
Other Asian, not specified (4)	5	0.05
Assyrian/Chaldean/Syriac	8	0.08
Australian	28	0.27
Austrian	69	0.67
Belgian	7	0.07
Brazilian	12	0.12
British	52	0.50
Canadian	56	0.54
Croatian	5	0.05
Czech	81	0.78
Czechoslovakian	23	0.22
Danish	61	0.59
Dutch	148	1.43
Eastern European	9	0.09
English	1,936	18.67
Estonian	27	0.26
European	38	0.37
Finnish	25	0.24
French, except Basque	599	5.78
French Canadian	484	4.67
German	1,256	12.12
Greek	41	0.40
Hawaii Native/Pacific Islander:	7	0.07
Micronesian: (1)	1	0.01
Other Micronesian (1)	1	0.01
Polynesian: (2)	2	0.02
Native Hawaiian (1)	1	0.01
Samoan (1)	1	0.01
Other Pac. Isl., not spec. (4)	4	0.04
Hispanic or Latino:	194	1.87
Central American:	9	0.09
Costa Rican	3	0.03
Guatemalan	1	0.01
Salvadoran	4	0.04
Other Central American	1	0.01
Cuban	9	0.09
Dominican Republic	1	0.01
Mexican	19	0.18
Puerto Rican	63	0.61
South American:	41	0.40
Colombian	18	0.17
Ecuadorian	16	0.15
Peruvian	7	0.07
Other Hispanic or Latino	52	0.50
Hungarian	149	1.44
Irish	2,518	24.29
Italian	1,796	17.32
Lithuanian	147	1.42
Norwegian	102	0.98
Pennsylvania German	5	0.05
Polish	731	7.05
Portuguese	66	0.64
Russian	97	0.94
Scandinavian	22	0.21
Scotch-Irish	104	1.00
Scottish	385	3.71
Slovak	58	0.56
Swedish	386	3.72
Swiss	35	0.34
Ukrainian	41	0.40
United States or American	356	3.43
Welsh	49	0.47
White:	10,005	96.51
Not Hispanic (9,795)	9,853	95.04
Hispanic (131)	152	1.47
Yugoslavian	9	0.09

Orange

Place Type: Census Designated Place
County: New Haven
Population: 13,233

Ancestry/Race	Number	%
African American/Black:	126	0.95
Not Hispanic (100)	117	0.88
Hispanic (4)	9	0.07
African, sub-Saharan:	37	0.28
Cape Verdean	9	0.07
Nigerian	28	0.21
Am. Ind. or Alaska Nat., not spec.	22	0.17
Albanian	4	0.03
Alsatian	9	0.07
American Indian tribes, specified:	24	0.18
Cherokee	2	0.02
Chippewa (2)	2	0.02
Iroquois	5	0.04
Latin American Indians	2	0.02
Potawatomi	3	0.02
All other tribes (4)	10	0.08
Arab:	106	0.80
Arab/Arabic	5	0.04
Egyptian	62	0.47
Lebanese	34	0.26
Syrian	5	0.04
Armenian	25	0.19
Asian:	546	4.13
Cambodian (1)	3	0.02
Chinese, ex. Taiwanese (192)	201	1.52
Filipino (16)	16	0.12
Indian (119)	127	0.96
Japanese (7)	12	0.09
Korean (102)	110	0.83
Laotian (1)	3	0.02
Pakistani (19)	19	0.14
Sri Lankan (9)	9	0.07
Taiwanese (20)	24	0.18
Vietnamese (2)	2	0.02
Other Asian, not specified (14)	20	0.15
Austrian	47	0.36
Belgian	6	0.05
Brazilian	18	0.14
British	7	0.05
Canadian	22	0.17
Celtic	23	0.17
Czech	90	0.68
Czechoslovakian	33	0.25
Danish	41	0.31
Dutch	148	1.12
Eastern European	131	0.99
English	1,186	8.96
European	24	0.18
French, except Basque	250	1.89
French Canadian	247	1.87
German	1,105	8.35
Greek	126	0.95
Guyanese	7	0.05
Hawaii Native/Pacific Islander:	9	0.07
Polynesian: (1)	5	0.04
Native Hawaiian (1)	5	0.04
Other Pac. Isl., not spec.	4	0.03
Hispanic or Latino:	190	1.44
Central American:	7	0.05
Costa Rican	2	0.02
Guatemalan	4	0.03
Salvadoran	1	0.01
Cuban	24	0.18
Dominican Republic	2	0.02
Mexican	11	0.08
Puerto Rican	71	0.54
South American:	41	0.31
Argentinean	4	0.03
Chilean	6	0.05
Colombian	19	0.14
Ecuadorian	3	0.02
Paraguayan	1	0.01
Peruvian	5	0.04
Venezuelan	1	0.01
Other South American	2	0.02
Other Hispanic or Latino	34	0.26
Hungarian	267	2.02
Iranian	25	0.19
Irish	2,160	16.32
Italian	4,571	34.54
Latvian	10	0.08
Lithuanian	68	0.51
Macedonian	8	0.06
Norwegian	47	0.36
Pennsylvania German	21	0.16
Polish	1,262	9.54
Portuguese	82	0.62
Romanian	71	0.54
Russian	629	4.75
Scandinavian	16	0.12
Scotch-Irish	139	1.05
Scottish	222	1.68
Slovak	123	0.93
Swedish	156	1.18
Swiss	70	0.53
Turkish	5	0.04
Ukrainian	152	1.15
United States or American	563	4.25
Welsh	57	0.43
West Indian, excl. Hispanic:	20	0.15
Bahamian	8	0.06
Jamaican	12	0.09
White:	12,557	94.89
Not Hispanic (12,312)	12,410	93.78
Hispanic (138)	147	1.11
Yugoslavian	4	0.03

Notes: 1. Figures in the "Number" column do not add up to the total population due to: a) Ancestry/Race overlap — e.g. persons can report being both White and Irish, b) persons of Hispanic origin can report being any race, c) persons reporting two ancestries are counted in both categories. 2. Numbers in parentheses indicate the number of persons reporting this ancestry/race alone, not in combination with any other ancestry/race. 3. Refer to the Explanation of Data in the front of the book for more detailed information.

Plainfield

Place Type: Town
County: Windham
Population: 14,619

Ancestry/Race	Number	%
African American/Black:	173	1.18
Not Hispanic (113)	163	1.11
Hispanic (1)	10	0.07
African, sub-Saharan:	7	0.05
African	7	0.05
Am. Ind. or Alaska Nat., not spec.	22	0.15
Albanian	166	1.14
Alsatian	13	0.09
American Indian tribes, specified:	136	0.93
Blackfeet (2)	4	0.03
Cherokee (4)	19	0.13
Chickasaw	2	0.01
Creek (3)	3	0.02
Iroquois (1)	6	0.04
Latin American Indians (9)	10	0.07
Potawatomi (2)	2	0.01
Pueblo (1)	1	0.01
Sioux (2)	4	0.03
All other tribes (38)	85	0.58
American Indian tribes, not spec.	7	0.05
Arab:	103	0.70
Egyptian	41	0.28
Jordanian	10	0.07
Lebanese	41	0.28
Syrian	11	0.08
Asian:	120	0.82
Cambodian	1	0.01
Chinese, ex. Taiwanese (21)	22	0.15
Filipino (17)	30	0.21
Indian (21)	23	0.16
Japanese (2)	6	0.04
Korean (7)	12	0.08
Laotian (3)	5	0.03
Pakistani (11)	11	0.08
Thai (2)	2	0.01
Vietnamese (3)	5	0.03
Other Asian, not specified	3	0.02
Austrian	33	0.23
Belgian	25	0.17
Brazilian	6	0.04
British	30	0.21
Canadian	215	1.47
Czech	50	0.34
Czechoslovakian	37	0.25
Danish	30	0.21
Dutch	192	1.31
English	1,840	12.59
Estonian	27	0.18
European	39	0.27
Finnish	222	1.52
French, except Basque	3,460	23.67
French Canadian	1,747	11.95
German	1,589	10.87
Greek	26	0.18
Hawaii Native/Pacific Islander:	13	0.09
Micronesian: (4)	5	0.03
Guamanian/Chamorro (4)	5	0.03
Other Pac. Isl., not spec.	8	0.05
Hispanic or Latino:	384	2.63
Central American:	3	0.02
Guatemalan	1	0.01
Honduran	1	0.01
Panamanian	1	0.01
Cuban	4	0.03
Dominican Republic	20	0.14
Mexican	58	0.40
Puerto Rican	229	1.57
South American:	15	0.10
Colombian	10	0.07
Ecuadorian	1	0.01
Peruvian	4	0.03
Other Hispanic or Latino	55	0.38
Hungarian	24	0.16
Irish	2,397	16.40
Italian	1,319	9.02
Lithuanian	139	0.95
Northern European	16	0.11
Norwegian	134	0.92
Polish	1,313	8.98
Portuguese	196	1.34
Romanian	35	0.24
Russian	162	1.11
Scandinavian	30	0.21
Scotch-Irish	279	1.91
Scottish	340	2.33
Serbian	12	0.08
Slavic	13	0.09
Slovak	69	0.47
Swedish	242	1.66
Swiss	51	0.35
Ukrainian	26	0.18
United States or American	740	5.06
Welsh	54	0.37
White:	14,224	97.30
Not Hispanic (13,792)	13,945	95.39
Hispanic (264)	279	1.91
Yugoslavian	34	0.23

Plainville

Place Type: Town
County: Hartford
Population: 17,328

Ancestry/Race	Number	%
African American/Black:	464	2.68
Not Hispanic (377)	440	2.54
Hispanic (13)	24	0.14
African, sub-Saharan:	43	0.25
African	39	0.23
Cape Verdean	4	0.02
Am. Ind. or Alaska Nat., not spec.	37	0.21
American Indian tribes, specified:	54	0.31
Apache	1	0.01
Blackfeet	4	0.02
Cherokee (2)	10	0.06
Chippewa (1)	1	0.01
Houma (1)	1	0.01
Iroquois (1)	6	0.03
Latin American Indians (1)	4	0.02
All other tribes (10)	27	0.16
American Indian tribes, not spec.	1	0.01
Arab:	44	0.25
Lebanese	16	0.09
Syrian	28	0.16
Armenian	31	0.18
Asian:	325	1.88
Cambodian (3)	3	0.02
Chinese, ex. Taiwanese (54)	57	0.33
Filipino (35)	40	0.23
Indian (92)	95	0.55
Indonesian	3	0.02
Japanese (9)	15	0.09
Korean (6)	7	0.04
Laotian (27)	31	0.18
Malaysian (1)	1	0.01
Pakistani (15)	15	0.09
Thai (3)	3	0.02
Vietnamese (33)	37	0.21
Other Asian, specified (1)	1	0.01
Other Asian, not specified (6)	17	0.10
Assyrian/Chaldean/Syriac	45	0.26
Austrian	58	0.33
Belgian	17	0.10
Brazilian	6	0.03
British	42	0.24
Canadian	44	0.25
Croatian	22	0.13
Czech	7	0.04
Czechoslovakian	10	0.06
Danish	29	0.17
Dutch	59	0.34
English	1,468	8.47
European	39	0.23
Finnish	6	0.03
French, except Basque	2,529	14.59
French Canadian	1,045	6.03
German	1,865	10.76
Greek	74	0.43
Hawaii Native/Pacific Islander:	6	0.03
Micronesian: (2)	2	0.01
Guamanian/Chamorro (2)	2	0.01
Polynesian:	1	0.01
Native Hawaiian	1	0.01
Other Pac. Isl., not spec.	3	0.02
Hispanic or Latino:	618	3.57
Central American:	10	0.06
Guatemalan	2	0.01
Honduran	2	0.01
Nicaraguan	1	0.01
Panamanian	3	0.02
Salvadoran	2	0.01
Cuban	12	0.07
Dominican Republic	5	0.03
Mexican	115	0.66
Puerto Rican	338	1.95
South American:	38	0.22
Argentinean	2	0.01
Bolivian	3	0.02
Chilean	3	0.02
Colombian	12	0.07
Ecuadorian	5	0.03
Peruvian	7	0.04
Venezuelan	3	0.02
Other South American	3	0.02
Other Hispanic or Latino	100	0.58
Hungarian	73	0.42
Irish	2,564	14.80
Italian	3,843	22.18
Lithuanian	191	1.10
Northern European	8	0.05
Norwegian	95	0.55
Polish	3,382	19.52
Portuguese	104	0.60
Romanian	13	0.08
Russian	248	1.43
Scandinavian	7	0.04
Scotch-Irish	179	1.03
Scottish	283	1.63
Slavic	5	0.03
Slovak	27	0.16
Slovene	6	0.03
Swedish	567	3.27
Swiss	28	0.16
Turkish	8	0.05
Ukrainian	138	0.80
United States or American	485	2.80
Welsh	27	0.16
West Indian, excl. Hispanic:	68	0.39
Jamaican	57	0.33
West Indian	11	0.06
White:	16,395	94.62
Not Hispanic (15,850)	15,988	92.27
Hispanic (355)	407	2.35
Yugoslavian	6	0.03

Plymouth

Place Type: Town
County: Litchfield
Population: 11,634

Ancestry/Race	Number	%
African American/Black:	117	1.01
Not Hispanic (87)	112	0.96
Hispanic (4)	5	0.04
African, sub-Saharan:	15	0.13
Cape Verdean	15	0.13
Am. Ind. or Alaska Nat., not spec.	33	0.28
Albanian	13	0.11
American Indian tribes, specified:	41	0.35
Apache (1)	1	0.01
Blackfeet (2)	9	0.08

Notes: 1. Figures in the "Number" column do not add up to the total population due to: a) Ancestry/Race overlap — e.g. persons can report being both White and Irish, b) persons of Hispanic origin can report being any race, c) persons reporting two ancestries are counted in both categories. 2. Numbers in parentheses indicate the number of persons reporting this ancestry/race alone, not in combination with any other ancestry/race. 3. Refer to the Explanation of Data in the front of the book for more detailed information.

Ancestry/Race	Number	%
Cherokee (2)	5	0.04
Houma	1	0.01
Sioux (1)	3	0.03
All other tribes (8)	22	0.19
American Indian tribes, not spec.	8	0.07
Arab:	45	0.39
Lebanese	45	0.39
Armenian	24	0.21
Asian:	70	0.60
Chinese, ex. Taiwanese (13)	14	0.12
Filipino (3)	8	0.07
Indian (24)	31	0.27
Japanese (2)	5	0.04
Korean (3)	6	0.05
Laotian (2)	2	0.02
Vietnamese (2)	3	0.03
Other Asian, not specified	1	0.01
Assyrian/Chaldean/Syriac	3	0.03
Austrian	59	0.51
Belgian	8	0.07
British	5	0.04
Canadian	96	0.83
Croatian	6	0.05
Czech	33	0.28
Czechoslovakian	22	0.19
Danish	9	0.08
Dutch	34	0.29
English	1,207	10.37
Estonian	7	0.06
European	10	0.09
French, except Basque	2,092	17.98
French Canadian	817	7.02
German	1,477	12.70
Greek	57	0.49
Hawaii Native/Pacific Islander:	2	0.02
Other Pac. Isl., not spec. (1)	2	0.02
Hispanic or Latino:	147	1.26
Central American:	6	0.05
Costa Rican	1	0.01
Guatemalan	1	0.01
Honduran	1	0.01
Panamanian	3	0.03
Cuban	14	0.12
Mexican	13	0.11
Puerto Rican	89	0.76
South American:	5	0.04
Argentinean	2	0.02
Paraguayan	1	0.01
Venezuelan	1	0.01
Other South American	1	0.01
Other Hispanic or Latino	20	0.17
Hungarian	55	0.47
Iranian	35	0.30
Irish	1,906	16.38
Italian	1,921	16.51
Lithuanian	236	2.03
Norwegian	118	1.01
Polish	1,942	16.69
Portuguese	41	0.35
Russian	253	2.17
Scandinavian	19	0.16
Scotch-Irish	125	1.07
Scottish	156	1.34
Slovak	52	0.45
Swedish	363	3.12
Swiss	19	0.16
Ukrainian	189	1.62
United States or American	408	3.51
Welsh	52	0.45
West Indian, excl. Hispanic:	7	0.06
Bermudan	7	0.06
White:	11,424	98.19
Not Hispanic (11,215)	11,307	97.19
Hispanic (110)	117	1.01

Ridgefield

Place Type: Town
County: Fairfield
Population: 23,643

Ancestry/Race	Number	%
Acadian/Cajun	5	0.02
African American/Black:	181	0.77
Not Hispanic (133)	162	0.69
Hispanic (13)	19	0.08
African, sub-Saharan:	43	0.18
South African	43	0.18
Am. Ind. or Alaska Nat., not spec.	19	0.08
Albanian	16	0.07
American Indian tribes, specified:	40	0.17
Cherokee (5)	12	0.05
Cheyenne	4	0.02
Choctaw (5)	9	0.04
Cree	1	0.00
Iroquois	3	0.01
Latin American Indians (1)	4	0.02
Pueblo	1	0.00
Sioux	1	0.00
All other tribes (2)	5	0.02
American Indian tribes, not spec.	5	0.02
Arab:	74	0.31
Arab/Arabic	18	0.08
Lebanese	35	0.15
Palestinian	10	0.04
Syrian	11	0.05
Asian:	579	2.45
Cambodian (12)	12	0.05
Chinese, ex. Taiwanese (144)	177	0.75
Filipino (37)	49	0.21
Indian (154)	170	0.72
Japanese (30)	52	0.22
Korean (66)	70	0.30
Laotian (1)	1	0.00
Malaysian (5)	6	0.03
Pakistani (5)	5	0.02
Sri Lankan (13)	13	0.05
Taiwanese (1)	1	0.00
Vietnamese (7)	8	0.03
Other Asian, not specified (12)	15	0.06
Australian	65	0.27
Austrian	276	1.17
Basque	4	0.02
Belgian	59	0.25
Brazilian	32	0.14
British	215	0.91
Canadian	232	0.98
Croatian	38	0.16
Czech	102	0.43
Czechoslovakian	103	0.44
Danish	199	0.84
Dutch	265	1.12
Eastern European	162	0.69
English	3,203	13.55
Estonian	13	0.05
European	142	0.60
Finnish	58	0.25
French, except Basque	648	2.74
French Canadian	288	1.22
German	4,225	17.87
Greek	242	1.02
Guyanese	6	0.03
Hawaii Native/Pacific Islander:	7	0.03
Micronesian: (1)	1	0.00
Guamanian/Chamorro (1)	1	0.00
Polynesian: (5)	5	0.02
Native Hawaiian (1)	1	0.00
Samoan (3)	3	0.01
Other Polynesian (1)	1	0.00
Other Pac. Isl., not spec.	1	0.00
Hispanic or Latino:	465	1.97
Central American:	15	0.06
Costa Rican	1	0.00
Guatemalan	7	0.03
Honduran	3	0.01
Nicaraguan	2	0.01
Panamanian	1	0.00
Salvadoran	1	0.00
Cuban	47	0.20
Dominican Republic	16	0.07
Mexican	78	0.33
Puerto Rican	76	0.32
South American:	103	0.44
Argentinean	14	0.06
Bolivian	10	0.04
Chilean	8	0.03
Colombian	27	0.11
Ecuadorian	11	0.05
Paraguayan	9	0.04
Peruvian	19	0.08
Other South American	5	0.02
Other Hispanic or Latino	130	0.55
Hungarian	330	1.40
Icelander	18	0.08
Iranian	46	0.19
Irish	5,846	24.73
Israeli	5	0.02
Italian	5,175	21.89
Latvian	18	0.08
Lithuanian	101	0.43
Macedonian	6	0.03
New Zealander	4	0.02
Northern European	51	0.22
Norwegian	309	1.31
Pennsylvania German	21	0.09
Polish	1,227	5.19
Portuguese	54	0.23
Romanian	49	0.21
Russian	914	3.87
Scandinavian	23	0.10
Scotch-Irish	508	2.15
Scottish	714	3.02
Serbian	8	0.03
Slavic	46	0.19
Slovak	77	0.33
Slovene	12	0.05
Swedish	530	2.24
Swiss	172	0.73
Turkish	6	0.03
Ukrainian	96	0.41
United States or American	922	3.90
Welsh	288	1.22
West Indian, excl. Hispanic:	32	0.14
British West Indian	7	0.03
Haitian	12	0.05
Jamaican	13	0.05
White:	22,878	96.76
Not Hispanic (22,361)	22,485	95.10
Hispanic (365)	393	1.66
Yugoslavian	19	0.08

Rocky Hill

Place Type: Town
County: Hartford
Population: 17,966

Ancestry/Race	Number	%
African American/Black:	683	3.80
Not Hispanic (601)	655	3.65
Hispanic (14)	28	0.16
African, sub-Saharan:	54	0.30
Nigerian	54	0.30
Am. Ind. or Alaska Nat., not spec.	39	0.22
Albanian	19	0.11
American Indian tribes, specified:	38	0.21
Apache	1	0.01
Blackfeet	1	0.01
Cherokee (1)	11	0.06
Creek	1	0.01
Iroquois	2	0.01
Latin American Indians (5)	14	0.08
Sioux (2)	2	0.01
All other tribes (5)	6	0.03
American Indian tribes, not spec.	5	0.03

Notes: 1. Figures in the "Number" column do not add up to the total population due to: a) Ancestry/Race overlap — e.g. persons can report being both White and Irish, b) persons of Hispanic origin can report being any race, c) persons reporting two ancestries are counted in both categories. 2. Numbers in parentheses indicate the number of persons reporting this ancestry/race alone, not in combination with any other ancestry/race. 3. Refer to the Explanation of Data in the front of the book for more detailed information.

Arab:	123	0.69
Lebanese	54	0.30
Palestinian	27	0.15
Other Arab	42	0.23
Armenian	58	0.32
Asian:	775	4.31
Chinese, ex. Taiwanese (102)	116	0.65
Filipino (52)	61	0.34
Indian (391)	414	2.30
Indonesian (7)	9	0.05
Japanese (13)	17	0.09
Korean (38)	40	0.22
Malaysian (5)	6	0.03
Pakistani (42)	50	0.28
Sri Lankan (10)	10	0.06
Taiwanese (2)	5	0.03
Thai (1)	1	0.01
Vietnamese (29)	29	0.16
Other Asian, specified	1	0.01
Other Asian, not specified (11)	16	0.09
Assyrian/Chaldean/Syriac	17	0.09
Austrian	64	0.36
Basque	14	0.08
Belgian	8	0.04
British	51	0.28
Bulgarian	9	0.05
Canadian	64	0.36
Croatian	16	0.09
Czech	73	0.41
Czechoslovakian	44	0.25
Danish	106	0.59
Dutch	137	0.76
Eastern European	8	0.04
English	2,153	12.00
European	78	0.43
Finnish	23	0.13
French, except Basque	1,201	6.69
French Canadian	646	3.60
German	1,677	9.35
Greek	245	1.37
Hawaii Native/Pacific Islander:	15	0.08
Polynesian: (5)	7	0.04
Native Hawaiian (4)	6	0.03
Samoan (1)	1	0.01
Other Pac. Isl., not spec.	8	0.04
Hispanic or Latino:	575	3.20
Central American:	9	0.05
Guatemalan	3	0.02
Honduran	2	0.01
Nicaraguan	1	0.01
Panamanian	1	0.01
Salvadoran	2	0.01
Cuban	47	0.26
Dominican Republic	23	0.13
Mexican	14	0.08
Puerto Rican	287	1.60
South American:	106	0.59
Argentinean	5	0.03
Bolivian	1	0.01
Chilean	9	0.05
Colombian	37	0.21
Ecuadorian	5	0.03
Paraguayan	1	0.01
Peruvian	26	0.14
Uruguayan	6	0.03
Venezuelan	16	0.09
Other Hispanic or Latino	89	0.50
Hungarian	54	0.30
Iranian	49	0.27
Irish	3,137	17.48
Italian	5,344	29.78
Latvian	20	0.11
Lithuanian	201	1.12
Norwegian	39	0.22
Polish	2,040	11.37
Portuguese	309	1.72
Romanian	16	0.09
Russian	260	1.45
Scandinavian	6	0.03
Scotch-Irish	226	1.26
Scottish	282	1.57
Slavic	15	0.08
Slovak	21	0.12
Slovene	6	0.03
Swedish	348	1.94
Swiss	49	0.27
Ukrainian	179	1.00
United States or American	660	3.68
Welsh	105	0.59
West Indian, excl. Hispanic:	71	0.40
Belizean	14	0.08
Bermudan	10	0.06
Jamaican	38	0.21
West Indian	9	0.05
White:	16,387	91.21
Not Hispanic (15,865)	16,019	89.16
Hispanic (340)	368	2.05
Yugoslavian	105	0.59

Seymour

Place Type: Town
County: New Haven
Population: 15,454

Ancestry/Race	Number	%
African American/Black:	242	1.57
Not Hispanic (204)	234	1.51
Hispanic (5)	8	0.05
African, sub-Saharan:	27	0.17
African	27	0.17
Am. Ind. or Alaska Nat., not spec.	24	0.16
American Indian tribes, specified:	49	0.32
Apache (1)	1	0.01
Blackfeet (2)	4	0.03
Cherokee (2)	13	0.08
Delaware	1	0.01
Iroquois	2	0.01
Latin American Indians	1	0.01
Pueblo	1	0.01
All other tribes (17)	26	0.17
Arab:	57	0.37
Arab/Arabic	38	0.25
Lebanese	5	0.03
Palestinian	14	0.09
Asian:	314	2.03
Bangladeshi (1)	1	0.01
Cambodian (2)	2	0.01
Chinese, ex. Taiwanese (33)	44	0.28
Filipino (18)	20	0.13
Indian (149)	159	1.03
Indonesian	1	0.01
Japanese (2)	3	0.02
Korean (26)	32	0.21
Laotian (5)	7	0.05
Malaysian	3	0.02
Pakistani (21)	25	0.16
Thai (1)	1	0.01
Vietnamese (2)	2	0.01
Other Asian, not specified (6)	14	0.09
Austrian	104	0.67
Brazilian	11	0.07
British	10	0.06
Canadian	146	0.94
Croatian	16	0.10
Czech	66	0.43
Czechoslovakian	139	0.90
Danish	46	0.30
Dutch	125	0.81
Eastern European	24	0.16
English	1,885	12.20
European	25	0.16
French, except Basque	811	5.25
French Canadian	408	2.64
German	1,606	10.39
Greek	101	0.65
Hawaii Native/Pacific Islander:	5	0.03
Polynesian: (3)	4	0.03
Native Hawaiian (2)	3	0.02
Other Polynesian (1)	1	0.01
Other Pac. Isl., not spec.	1	0.01
Hispanic or Latino:	470	3.04
Central American:	16	0.10
Costa Rican	5	0.03
Guatemalan	6	0.04
Honduran	3	0.02
Panamanian	2	0.01
Cuban	18	0.12
Dominican Republic	9	0.06
Mexican	29	0.19
Puerto Rican	205	1.33
South American:	100	0.65
Argentinean	8	0.05
Chilean	24	0.16
Colombian	14	0.09
Ecuadorian	43	0.28
Peruvian	6	0.04
Other South American	5	0.03
Other Hispanic or Latino	93	0.60
Hungarian	416	2.69
Irish	2,938	19.01
Italian	3,551	22.98
Latvian	8	0.05
Lithuanian	243	1.57
Northern European	7	0.05
Norwegian	25	0.16
Pennsylvania German	10	0.06
Polish	2,629	17.01
Portuguese	69	0.45
Romanian	32	0.21
Russian	644	4.17
Scotch-Irish	178	1.15
Scottish	296	1.92
Slavic	9	0.06
Slovak	346	2.24
Slovene	8	0.05
Swedish	315	2.04
Swiss	43	0.28
Turkish	67	0.43
Ukrainian	586	3.79
United States or American	355	2.30
Welsh	70	0.45
West Indian, excl. Hispanic:	9	0.06
Jamaican	9	0.06
White:	14,761	95.52
Not Hispanic (14,360)	14,448	93.49
Hispanic (282)	313	2.03
Yugoslavian	12	0.08

Shelton

Place Type: City
County: Fairfield
Population: 38,101

Ancestry/Race	Number	%
African American/Black:	510	1.34
Not Hispanic (393)	465	1.22
Hispanic (35)	45	0.12
African, sub-Saharan:	82	0.22
African	28	0.07
South African	33	0.09
Sudanese	16	0.04
Other sub-Saharan African	5	0.01
Alaska Native tribes, specified:	3	0.01
Alaska Athabascan	1	0.00
Eskimo (2)	2	0.01
Alaska Native tribes, not specified	2	0.01
Am. Ind. or Alaska Nat., not spec.	48	0.13
Albanian	111	0.29
American Indian tribes, specified:	120	0.31
Blackfeet (1)	2	0.01
Cherokee (2)	21	0.06
Chippewa	2	0.01
Choctaw (4)	7	0.02
Creek (1)	8	0.02
Iroquois (5)	17	0.04
Kiowa	3	0.01
Latin American Indians (4)	6	0.02
Navajo	2	0.01

Notes: 1. Figures in the "Number" column do not add up to the total population due to: a) Ancestry/Race overlap — e.g. persons can report being both White and Irish, b) persons of Hispanic origin can report being any race, c) persons reporting two ancestries are counted in both categories. 2. Numbers in parentheses indicate the number of persons reporting this ancestry/race alone, not in combination with any other ancestry/race. 3. Refer to the Explanation of Data in the front of the book for more detailed information.

Sioux	5	0.01
All other tribes (25)	47	0.12
American Indian tribes, not spec.	5	0.01
Arab:	151	0.40
Arab/Arabic	16	0.04
Lebanese	77	0.20
Palestinian	35	0.09
Syrian	23	0.06
Armenian	63	0.17
Asian:	864	2.27
Bangladeshi (2)	3	0.01
Cambodian (5)	5	0.01
Chinese, ex. Taiwanese (170)	176	0.46
Filipino (73)	90	0.24
Indian (286)	301	0.79
Indonesian	2	0.01
Japanese (22)	28	0.07
Korean (49)	56	0.15
Laotian (58)	60	0.16
Pakistani (5)	8	0.02
Sri Lankan (10)	10	0.03
Taiwanese (1)	3	0.01
Thai (9)	9	0.02
Vietnamese (84)	87	0.23
Other Asian, not specified (12)	26	0.07
Austrian	224	0.59
Belgian	22	0.06
Brazilian	41	0.11
British	66	0.17
Canadian	145	0.38
Croatian	36	0.09
Czech	293	0.77
Czechoslovakian	365	0.96
Danish	162	0.43
Dutch	283	0.74
Eastern European	30	0.08
English	4,212	11.05
Estonian	6	0.02
European	179	0.47
Finnish	4	0.01
French, except Basque	1,472	3.86
French Canadian	784	2.06
German	4,267	11.20
Greek	438	1.15
Hawaii Native/Pacific Islander:	4	0.01
Polynesian: (1)	3	0.01
Samoan (1)	3	0.01
Other Pac. Isl., not spec.	1	0.00
Hispanic or Latino:	1,326	3.48
Central American:	49	0.13
Costa Rican	14	0.04
Guatemalan	16	0.04
Honduran	5	0.01
Nicaraguan	3	0.01
Panamanian	3	0.01
Salvadoran	2	0.01
Other Central American	6	0.02
Cuban	89	0.23
Dominican Republic	10	0.03
Mexican	74	0.19
Puerto Rican	598	1.57
South American:	262	0.69
Argentinean	10	0.03
Chilean	4	0.01
Colombian	44	0.12
Ecuadorian	173	0.45
Paraguayan	1	0.00
Peruvian	22	0.06
Uruguayan	1	0.00
Venezuelan	2	0.01
Other South American	5	0.01
Other Hispanic or Latino	244	0.64
Hungarian	1,423	3.73
Iranian	63	0.17
Irish	6,741	17.69
Israeli	23	0.06
Italian	10,816	28.39
Latvian	16	0.04
Lithuanian	314	0.82
Norwegian	199	0.52
Polish	5,228	13.72
Portuguese	1,014	2.66
Romanian	134	0.35
Russian	1,000	2.62
Scandinavian	42	0.11
Scotch-Irish	338	0.89
Scottish	840	2.20
Slavic	38	0.10
Slovak	1,588	4.17
Slovene	61	0.16
Swedish	738	1.94
Swiss	85	0.22
Turkish	73	0.19
Ukrainian	552	1.45
United States or American	1,280	3.36
Welsh	177	0.46
West Indian, excl. Hispanic:	97	0.25
Haitian	24	0.06
Jamaican	36	0.09
Trinidadian and Tobagonian	25	0.07
West Indian	12	0.03
White:	36,436	95.63
Not Hispanic (35,103)	35,484	93.13
Hispanic (881)	952	2.50
Yugoslavian	50	0.13

Simsbury

Place Type: Town
County: Hartford
Population: 23,234

Ancestry/Race	Number	%
African American/Black:	332	1.43
Not Hispanic (266)	320	1.38
Hispanic (5)	12	0.05
African, sub-Saharan:	79	0.34
African	36	0.15
Nigerian	10	0.04
South African	28	0.12
Sudanese	5	0.02
Am. Ind. or Alaska Nat., not spec.	28	0.12
Albanian	44	0.19
American Indian tribes, specified:	41	0.18
Apache	3	0.01
Blackfeet	3	0.01
Cherokee (1)	7	0.03
Chippewa	2	0.01
Cree (2)	2	0.01
Creek	1	0.00
Iroquois (1)	1	0.00
Latin American Indians (1)	5	0.02
Navajo	1	0.00
Sioux	2	0.01
All other tribes (7)	14	0.06
American Indian tribes, not spec.	1	0.00
Arab:	73	0.31
Egyptian	19	0.08
Iraqi	6	0.03
Lebanese	33	0.14
Syrian	15	0.06
Armenian	60	0.26
Asian:	585	2.52
Bangladeshi (1)	2	0.01
Chinese, ex. Taiwanese (131)	151	0.65
Filipino (27)	43	0.19
Hmong (6)	6	0.03
Indian (172)	187	0.80
Indonesian (1)	2	0.01
Japanese (35)	51	0.22
Korean (79)	85	0.37
Taiwanese (2)	3	0.01
Thai (7)	8	0.03
Vietnamese (27)	32	0.14
Other Asian, specified (1)	1	0.00
Other Asian, not specified (2)	14	0.06
Australian	5	0.02
Austrian	163	0.70
Belgian	23	0.10
Brazilian	6	0.03
British	113	0.49
Canadian	116	0.50
Celtic	15	0.06
Croatian	7	0.03
Czech	129	0.56
Czechoslovakian	67	0.29
Danish	184	0.79
Dutch	444	1.91
Eastern European	63	0.27
English	4,053	17.44
Estonian	20	0.09
European	356	1.53
Finnish	74	0.32
French, except Basque	1,223	5.26
French Canadian	902	3.88
German	3,636	15.65
Greek	176	0.76
Guyanese	29	0.12
Hawaii Native/Pacific Islander:	16	0.07
Micronesian: (5)	7	0.03
Guamanian/Chamorro (5)	7	0.03
Polynesian: (1)	7	0.03
Native Hawaiian (1)	5	0.02
Samoan	2	0.01
Other Pac. Isl., not spec. (1)	2	0.01
Hispanic or Latino:	358	1.54
Central American:	7	0.03
Costa Rican	2	0.01
Guatemalan	2	0.01
Honduran	1	0.00
Salvadoran	2	0.01
Cuban	29	0.12
Dominican Republic	10	0.04
Mexican	65	0.28
Puerto Rican	130	0.56
South American:	54	0.23
Bolivian	9	0.04
Chilean	11	0.05
Colombian	14	0.06
Ecuadorian	3	0.01
Paraguayan	1	0.00
Peruvian	7	0.03
Venezuelan	4	0.02
Other South American	5	0.02
Other Hispanic or Latino	63	0.27
Hungarian	178	0.77
Iranian	26	0.11
Irish	5,326	22.92
Israeli	5	0.02
Italian	3,172	13.65
Latvian	40	0.17
Lithuanian	269	1.16
New Zealander	6	0.03
Northern European	85	0.37
Norwegian	229	0.99
Polish	1,775	7.64
Portuguese	91	0.39
Romanian	54	0.23
Russian	797	3.43
Scandinavian	18	0.08
Scotch-Irish	308	1.33
Scottish	853	3.67
Serbian	7	0.03
Slavic	8	0.03
Slovak	126	0.54
Slovene	10	0.04
Swedish	534	2.30
Swiss	220	0.95
Turkish	8	0.03
Ukrainian	208	0.90
United States or American	1,282	5.52
Welsh	120	0.52
West Indian, excl. Hispanic:	67	0.29
Haitian	20	0.09
Jamaican	42	0.18
West Indian	5	0.02
White:	22,350	96.20
Not Hispanic (21,889)	22,068	94.98
Hispanic (253)	282	1.21
Yugoslavian	38	0.16

Notes: 1. Figures in the "Number" column do not add up to the total population due to: a) Ancestry/Race overlap — e.g. persons can report being both White and Irish, b) persons of Hispanic origin can report being any race, c) persons reporting two ancestries are counted in both categories. 2. Numbers in parentheses indicate the number of persons reporting this ancestry/race alone, not in combination with any other ancestry/race. 3. Refer to the Explanation of Data in the front of the book for more detailed information.

Somers

Place Type: Town
County: Tolland
Population: 10,417

Ancestry/Race	Number	%
African American/Black:	1,105	10.61
Not Hispanic (922)	972	9.33
Hispanic (101)	133	1.28
African, sub-Saharan:	159	1.53
African	145	1.39
Cape Verdean	14	0.13
Alaska Native tribes, specified:	1	0.01
Eskimo	1	0.01
Am. Ind. or Alaska Nat., not spec.	45	0.43
American Indian tribes, specified:	77	0.74
Apache (1)	2	0.02
Blackfeet (2)	7	0.07
Cherokee (7)	18	0.17
Cheyenne (2)	2	0.02
Chippewa	1	0.01
Comanche	1	0.01
Delaware (1)	1	0.01
Iroquois	7	0.07
Latin American Indians (9)	18	0.17
Potawatomi (2)	2	0.02
Sioux (3)	3	0.03
Yaqui	1	0.01
All other tribes (4)	14	0.13
American Indian tribes, not spec.	4	0.04
Arab:	9	0.09
Lebanese	4	0.04
Moroccan	5	0.05
Armenian	32	0.31
Asian:	107	1.03
Cambodian (2)	2	0.02
Chinese, ex. Taiwanese (20)	27	0.26
Filipino (9)	20	0.19
Indian (22)	27	0.26
Japanese (1)	3	0.03
Korean (6)	12	0.12
Laotian (2)	3	0.03
Taiwanese (1)	1	0.01
Thai	3	0.03
Vietnamese	2	0.02
Other Asian, specified	3	0.03
Other Asian, not specified (1)	4	0.04
Austrian	14	0.13
British	45	0.43
Canadian	38	0.36
Croatian	19	0.18
Czech	19	0.18
Czechoslovakian	16	0.15
Danish	30	0.29
Dutch	71	0.68
English	1,456	13.98
Estonian	3	0.03
European	72	0.69
Finnish	18	0.17
French, except Basque	1,195	11.47
French Canadian	561	5.39
German	1,022	9.81
Greek	106	1.02
Hawaii Native/Pacific Islander:	33	0.32
Micronesian: (1)	3	0.03
Guamanian/Chamorro (1)	3	0.03
Polynesian: (1)	5	0.05
Native Hawaiian (1)	5	0.05
Other Pac. Isl., specified	3	0.03
Other Pac. Isl., not spec. (4)	22	0.21
Hispanic or Latino:	844	8.10
Central American:	9	0.09
Costa Rican	1	0.01
Guatemalan	4	0.04
Honduran	1	0.01
Nicaraguan	1	0.01
Panamanian	2	0.02
Cuban	21	0.20
Dominican Republic	19	0.18
Mexican	24	0.23
Puerto Rican	656	6.30
South American:	28	0.27
Colombian	13	0.12
Ecuadorian	1	0.01
Peruvian	13	0.12
Other South American	1	0.01
Other Hispanic or Latino	87	0.84
Hungarian	49	0.47
Irish	1,921	18.44
Italian	1,465	14.06
Latvian	11	0.11
Lithuanian	109	1.05
Norwegian	42	0.40
Polish	991	9.51
Portuguese	111	1.07
Russian	106	1.02
Scotch-Irish	160	1.54
Scottish	372	3.57
Slovak	15	0.14
Swedish	240	2.30
Swiss	16	0.15
Ukrainian	29	0.28
United States or American	294	2.82
Welsh	7	0.07
West Indian, excl. Hispanic:	103	0.99
Barbadian	5	0.05
Jamaican	48	0.46
Trinidadian and Tobagonian	7	0.07
West Indian	43	0.41
White:	8,784	84.32
Not Hispanic (8,413)	8,513	81.72
Hispanic (230)	271	2.60

South Windsor

Place Type: Town
County: Hartford
Population: 24,412

Ancestry/Race	Number	%
African American/Black:	788	3.23
Not Hispanic (705)	762	3.12
Hispanic (16)	26	0.11
African, sub-Saharan:	167	0.68
African	87	0.36
Nigerian	7	0.03
South African	46	0.19
Sudanese	13	0.05
Other sub-Saharan African	14	0.06
Am. Ind. or Alaska Nat., not spec.	31	0.13
Albanian	16	0.07
American Indian tribes, specified:	54	0.22
Blackfeet	5	0.02
Cherokee (2)	11	0.05
Chickasaw (1)	1	0.00
Chippewa (2)	2	0.01
Creek	1	0.00
Iroquois (1)	3	0.01
Latin American Indians (10)	10	0.04
Sioux (3)	3	0.01
All other tribes (10)	18	0.07
American Indian tribes, not spec.	5	0.02
Arab:	54	0.22
Egyptian	8	0.03
Lebanese	41	0.17
Syrian	5	0.02
Armenian	29	0.12
Asian:	1,029	4.22
Bangladeshi (2)	2	0.01
Cambodian (1)	2	0.01
Chinese, ex. Taiwanese (170)	185	0.76
Filipino (61)	92	0.38
Indian (287)	314	1.29
Indonesian (1)	6	0.02
Japanese (6)	23	0.09
Korean (144)	150	0.61
Laotian (8)	8	0.03
Malaysian (1)	2	0.01
Pakistani (58)	74	0.30
Sri Lankan (4)	6	0.02
Taiwanese (4)	4	0.02
Thai (1)	1	0.00
Vietnamese (133)	139	0.57
Other Asian, specified (1)	1	0.00
Other Asian, not specified (13)	20	0.08
Austrian	95	0.39
Brazilian	8	0.03
British	123	0.50
Bulgarian	20	0.08
Canadian	230	0.94
Celtic	32	0.13
Croatian	11	0.04
Czech	35	0.14
Czechoslovakian	24	0.10
Danish	138	0.56
Dutch	375	1.53
Eastern European	120	0.49
English	2,992	12.23
Estonian	7	0.03
European	113	0.46
Finnish	41	0.17
French, except Basque	2,464	10.07
French Canadian	1,768	7.22
German	2,620	10.71
Greek	248	1.01
Hawaii Native/Pacific Islander:	14	0.06
Micronesian: (3)	3	0.01
Guamanian/Chamorro (3)	3	0.01
Polynesian: (5)	6	0.02
Native Hawaiian (4)	5	0.02
Samoan (1)	1	0.00
Other Pac. Isl., not spec.	5	0.02
Hispanic or Latino:	554	2.27
Central American:	14	0.06
Costa Rican	3	0.01
Panamanian	7	0.03
Salvadoran	4	0.02
Cuban	22	0.09
Dominican Republic	7	0.03
Mexican	55	0.23
Puerto Rican	250	1.02
South American:	126	0.52
Argentinean	5	0.02
Chilean	4	0.02
Colombian	57	0.23
Ecuadorian	3	0.01
Peruvian	42	0.17
Uruguayan	4	0.02
Venezuelan	2	0.01
Other South American	9	0.04
Other Hispanic or Latino	80	0.33
Hungarian	189	0.77
Iranian	20	0.08
Irish	5,106	20.87
Italian	4,536	18.54
Latvian	8	0.03
Lithuanian	413	1.69
Norwegian	77	0.31
Pennsylvania German	23	0.09
Polish	2,445	9.99
Portuguese	301	1.23
Romanian	17	0.07
Russian	481	1.97
Scandinavian	18	0.07
Scotch-Irish	286	1.17
Scottish	561	2.29
Serbian	25	0.10
Slavic	16	0.07
Slovak	52	0.21
Swedish	705	2.88
Swiss	99	0.40
Turkish	10	0.04
Ukrainian	295	1.21
United States or American	992	4.05
Welsh	130	0.53
West Indian, excl. Hispanic:	234	0.96
Barbadian	11	0.04
Jamaican	209	0.85
West Indian	14	0.06

Notes: 1. Figures in the "Number" column do not add up to the total population due to: a) Ancestry/Race overlap — e.g. persons can report being both White and Irish, b) persons of Hispanic origin can report being any race, c) persons reporting two ancestries are counted in both categories. 2. Numbers in parentheses indicate the number of persons reporting this ancestry/race alone, not in combination with any other ancestry/race. 3. Refer to the Explanation of Data in the front of the book for more detailed information.

White:	22,530	92.29
Not Hispanic (21,987)	22,157	90.76
Hispanic (349)	373	1.53
Yugoslavian	8	0.03

Southbury

Place Type: Town
County: New Haven
Population: 18,567

Ancestry/Race	Number	%
African American/Black:	96	0.52
Not Hispanic (80)	92	0.50
Hispanic (4)	4	0.02
African, sub-Saharan:	7	0.04
African	7	0.04
Am. Ind. or Alaska Nat., not spec.	21	0.11
Albanian	67	0.36
Alsatian	10	0.05
American Indian tribes, specified:	41	0.22
Blackfeet	4	0.02
Cherokee (2)	5	0.03
Creek	1	0.01
Iroquois (1)	2	0.01
Latin American Indians (1)	1	0.01
Pueblo (1)	1	0.01
Seminole	1	0.01
Sioux	5	0.03
All other tribes (5)	21	0.11
American Indian tribes, not spec.	2	0.01
Arab:	109	0.59
Egyptian	27	0.15
Lebanese	66	0.36
Moroccan	16	0.09
Asian:	246	1.32
Cambodian (4)	4	0.02
Chinese, ex. Taiwanese (72)	80	0.43
Filipino (38)	45	0.24
Indian (55)	57	0.31
Indonesian	2	0.01
Japanese (10)	22	0.12
Korean (21)	21	0.11
Vietnamese (5)	5	0.03
Other Asian, not specified (8)	10	0.05
Austrian	178	0.96
Belgian	17	0.09
Brazilian	13	0.07
British	102	0.55
Canadian	72	0.39
Celtic	8	0.04
Croatian	17	0.09
Czech	112	0.60
Czechoslovakian	100	0.54
Danish	82	0.44
Dutch	345	1.86
Eastern European	17	0.09
English	2,747	14.80
Estonian	8	0.04
European	32	0.17
Finnish	32	0.17
French, except Basque	785	4.23
French Canadian	382	2.06
German	3,093	16.66
Greek	155	0.83
Hawaii Native/Pacific Islander:	5	0.03
Micronesian: (1)	1	0.01
Other Micronesian (1)	1	0.01
Polynesian:	1	0.01
Native Hawaiian	1	0.01
Other Pac. Isl., not spec.	3	0.02
Hispanic or Latino:	296	1.59
Central American:	8	0.04
Costa Rican	2	0.01
Guatemalan	1	0.01
Honduran	3	0.02
Panamanian	1	0.01
Salvadoran	1	0.01
Cuban	18	0.10
Dominican Republic	9	0.05
Mexican	65	0.35
Puerto Rican	89	0.48
South American:	40	0.22
Argentinean	5	0.03
Chilean	3	0.02
Colombian	19	0.10
Ecuadorian	9	0.05
Peruvian	2	0.01
Uruguayan	1	0.01
Other South American	1	0.01
Other Hispanic or Latino	67	0.36
Hungarian	294	1.58
Iranian	10	0.05
Irish	4,117	22.17
Israeli	10	0.05
Italian	3,510	18.90
Latvian	17	0.09
Lithuanian	190	1.02
Macedonian	8	0.04
Maltese	22	0.12
Northern European	39	0.21
Norwegian	89	0.48
Polish	1,422	7.66
Portuguese	250	1.35
Romanian	19	0.10
Russian	620	3.34
Scandinavian	30	0.16
Scotch-Irish	366	1.97
Scottish	570	3.07
Slavic	31	0.17
Slovak	104	0.56
Slovene	26	0.14
Swedish	426	2.29
Swiss	145	0.78
Ukrainian	122	0.66
United States or American	667	3.59
Welsh	159	0.86
West Indian, excl. Hispanic:	16	0.09
Belizean	8	0.04
Jamaican	8	0.04
White:	18,185	97.94
Not Hispanic (17,844)	17,946	96.66
Hispanic (229)	239	1.29

Southington

Place Type: Town
County: Hartford
Population: 39,728

Ancestry/Race	Number	%
African American/Black:	460	1.16
Not Hispanic (318)	429	1.08
Hispanic (23)	31	0.08
African, sub-Saharan:	27	0.07
African	16	0.04
Cape Verdean	6	0.02
South African	5	0.01
Alaska Native tribes, specified:	1	0.00
Alaska Athabascan	1	0.00
Am. Ind. or Alaska Nat., not spec.	61	0.15
Albanian	49	0.12
American Indian tribes, specified:	102	0.26
Apache	5	0.01
Blackfeet (4)	10	0.03
Cherokee (4)	31	0.08
Iroquois (1)	8	0.02
Latin American Indians (4)	4	0.01
Navajo (1)	1	0.00
Sioux	5	0.01
All other tribes (12)	38	0.10
American Indian tribes, not spec.	7	0.02
Arab:	132	0.33
Arab/Arabic	5	0.01
Iraqi	9	0.02
Lebanese	71	0.18
Palestinian	9	0.02
Syrian	30	0.08
Other Arab	8	0.02
Armenian	65	0.16
Asian:	493	1.24
Cambodian (3)	3	0.01
Chinese, ex. Taiwanese (95)	103	0.26
Filipino (41)	62	0.16
Indian (155)	167	0.42
Japanese (11)	20	0.05
Korean (54)	74	0.19
Laotian (2)	2	0.01
Pakistani (6)	10	0.03
Taiwanese (4)	4	0.01
Thai (3)	3	0.01
Vietnamese (29)	30	0.08
Other Asian, not specified (7)	15	0.04
Assyrian/Chaldean/Syriac	33	0.08
Austrian	155	0.39
Belgian	51	0.13
Brazilian	11	0.03
British	123	0.31
Canadian	332	0.84
Celtic	19	0.05
Croatian	12	0.03
Czech	177	0.45
Czechoslovakian	116	0.29
Danish	181	0.46
Dutch	348	0.88
Eastern European	25	0.06
English	4,067	10.24
Estonian	15	0.04
European	67	0.17
Finnish	29	0.07
French, except Basque	5,061	12.74
French Canadian	2,215	5.58
German	4,099	10.32
Greek	242	0.61
Hawaii Native/Pacific Islander:	7	0.02
Micronesian: (1)	1	0.00
Guamanian/Chamorro (1)	1	0.00
Other Pac. Isl., not spec. (2)	6	0.02
Hispanic or Latino:	801	2.02
Central American:	10	0.03
Honduran	4	0.01
Panamanian	1	0.00
Salvadoran	5	0.01
Cuban	34	0.09
Dominican Republic	7	0.02
Mexican	66	0.17
Puerto Rican	473	1.19
South American:	79	0.20
Argentinean	9	0.02
Chilean	3	0.01
Colombian	20	0.05
Ecuadorian	26	0.07
Peruvian	17	0.04
Venezuelan	1	0.00
Other South American	3	0.01
Other Hispanic or Latino	132	0.33
Hungarian	390	0.98
Iranian	13	0.03
Irish	7,696	19.37
Italian	11,474	28.88
Latvian	7	0.02
Lithuanian	548	1.38
Northern European	19	0.05
Norwegian	217	0.55
Pennsylvania German	14	0.04
Polish	6,378	16.05
Portuguese	189	0.48
Romanian	43	0.11
Russian	459	1.16
Scandinavian	24	0.06
Scotch-Irish	453	1.14
Scottish	806	2.03
Serbian	22	0.06
Slavic	73	0.18
Slovak	182	0.46
Slovene	34	0.09
Swedish	1,121	2.82
Swiss	44	0.11
Ukrainian	378	0.95
United States or American	1,106	2.78

Notes: 1. Figures in the "Number" column do not add up to the total population due to: a) Ancestry/Race overlap — e.g. persons can report being both White and Irish, b) persons of Hispanic origin can report being any race, c) persons reporting two ancestries are counted in both categories. 2. Numbers in parentheses indicate the number of persons reporting this ancestry/race alone, not in combination with any other ancestry/race. 3. Refer to the Explanation of Data in the front of the book for more detailed information.

Ancestry/Race	Number	%
Welsh	111	0.28
West Indian, excl. Hispanic:	80	0.20
British West Indian	21	0.05
Jamaican	22	0.06
Trinidadian and Tobagonian	32	0.08
West Indian	5	0.01
White:	38,682	97.37
Not Hispanic (37,818)	38,130	95.98
Hispanic (499)	552	1.39
Yugoslavian	12	0.03

Stafford

Place Type: Town
County: Tolland
Population: 11,307

Ancestry/Race	Number	%
African American/Black:	85	0.75
Not Hispanic (60)	73	0.65
Hispanic (12)	12	0.11
Am. Ind. or Alaska Nat., not spec.	25	0.22
American Indian tribes, specified:	49	0.43
Blackfeet (3)	5	0.04
Cherokee	2	0.02
Cree (1)	1	0.01
Iroquois (3)	10	0.09
Latin American Indians	1	0.01
Navajo (3)	4	0.04
Seminole	2	0.02
Shoshone	3	0.03
Sioux	1	0.01
All other tribes (10)	20	0.18
American Indian tribes, not spec.	2	0.02
Arab:	63	0.56
Arab/Arabic	8	0.07
Lebanese	47	0.42
Syrian	8	0.07
Armenian	18	0.16
Asian:	123	1.09
Chinese, ex. Taiwanese (8)	10	0.09
Filipino (8)	10	0.09
Hmong (22)	25	0.22
Indian (15)	15	0.13
Japanese (3)	5	0.04
Korean (4)	6	0.05
Laotian (18)	22	0.19
Pakistani (3)	3	0.03
Thai (3)	5	0.04
Vietnamese (5)	5	0.04
Other Asian, specified	1	0.01
Other Asian, not specified (12)	16	0.14
Australian	8	0.07
Austrian	10	0.09
British	21	0.19
Canadian	49	0.43
Czech	100	0.88
Czechoslovakian	101	0.89
Danish	58	0.51
Dutch	123	1.09
Eastern European	18	0.16
English	1,436	12.70
European	45	0.40
Finnish	37	0.33
French, except Basque	2,111	18.67
French Canadian	672	5.94
German	1,187	10.50
Hawaii Native/Pacific Islander:	2	0.02
Polynesian:	2	0.02
Native Hawaiian	1	0.01
Samoan	1	0.01
Hispanic or Latino:	187	1.65
Central American:	6	0.05
Honduran	1	0.01
Panamanian	4	0.04
Other Central American	1	0.01
Cuban	9	0.08
Mexican	26	0.23
Puerto Rican	96	0.85
South American:	17	0.15
Argentinean	4	0.04
Chilean	3	0.03
Colombian	6	0.05
Peruvian	2	0.02
Uruguayan	2	0.02
Other Hispanic or Latino	33	0.29
Hungarian	102	0.90
Irish	2,208	19.53
Italian	2,177	19.25
Lithuanian	135	1.19
Norwegian	64	0.57
Polish	1,053	9.31
Portuguese	95	0.84
Russian	104	0.92
Scandinavian	11	0.10
Scotch-Irish	182	1.61
Scottish	213	1.88
Slovak	53	0.47
Swedish	231	2.04
Swiss	27	0.24
Ukrainian	24	0.21
United States or American	232	2.05
Welsh	56	0.50
White:	11,040	97.64
Not Hispanic (10,848)	10,922	96.60
Hispanic (108)	118	1.04
Yugoslavian	6	0.05

Stamford

Place Type: City
County: Fairfield
Population: 117,083

Ancestry/Race	Number	%
African American/Black:	19,290	16.48
Not Hispanic (17,421)	18,486	15.79
Hispanic (598)	804	0.69
African, sub-Saharan:	599	0.51
African	415	0.35
Cape Verdean	32	0.03
Ethiopian	11	0.01
Kenyan	10	0.01
Nigerian	22	0.02
South African	13	0.01
Zairian	9	0.01
Other sub-Saharan African	87	0.07
Alaska Native tribes, specified:	8	0.01
Alaska Athabascan	1	0.00
Aleut	3	0.00
Tlingit-Haida (3)	3	0.00
All other tribes	1	0.00
Am. Ind. or Alaska Nat., not spec.	288	0.25
Albanian	508	0.43
Alsatian	8	0.01
American Indian tribes, specified:	247	0.21
Apache	1	0.00
Blackfeet	7	0.01
Cherokee (9)	65	0.06
Cheyenne	1	0.00
Chickasaw	1	0.00
Chippewa (3)	4	0.00
Choctaw	10	0.01
Cree	5	0.00
Creek	3	0.00
Delaware	1	0.00
Houma (2)	2	0.00
Iroquois (1)	4	0.00
Latin American Indians (41)	73	0.06
Lumbee	1	0.00
Navajo	1	0.00
Osage (1)	1	0.00
Ottawa	2	0.00
Pima	1	0.00
Potawatomi	1	0.00
Seminole	2	0.00
Sioux (3)	12	0.01
All other tribes (10)	49	0.04
American Indian tribes, not spec.	49	0.04
Arab:	439	0.37
Arab/Arabic	129	0.11
Egyptian	29	0.02
Iraqi	27	0.02
Jordanian	12	0.01
Lebanese	187	0.16
Moroccan	35	0.03
Syrian	6	0.01
Other Arab	14	0.01
Armenian	196	0.17
Asian:	6,557	5.60
Bangladeshi (81)	100	0.09
Cambodian (2)	2	0.00
Chinese, ex. Taiwanese (1,495)	1,663	1.42
Filipino (702)	807	0.69
Indian (2,577)	2,779	2.37
Indonesian (22)	30	0.03
Japanese (144)	202	0.17
Korean (281)	305	0.26
Laotian (8)	9	0.01
Malaysian (4)	7	0.01
Pakistani (127)	196	0.17
Sri Lankan (22)	30	0.03
Taiwanese (23)	33	0.03
Thai (20)	28	0.02
Vietnamese (187)	203	0.17
Other Asian, specified (8)	19	0.02
Other Asian, not specified (59)	144	0.12
Australian	54	0.05
Austrian	692	0.59
Basque	23	0.02
Belgian	123	0.11
Brazilian	395	0.34
British	697	0.60
Bulgarian	88	0.08
Canadian	312	0.27
Carpatho Rusyn	47	0.04
Celtic	17	0.01
Croatian	166	0.14
Czech	339	0.29
Czechoslovakian	165	0.14
Danish	289	0.25
Dutch	790	0.67
Eastern European	591	0.50
English	6,037	5.16
European	839	0.72
Finnish	81	0.07
French, except Basque	1,997	1.71
French Canadian	586	0.50
German	7,750	6.62
Greek	2,100	1.79
Guyanese	104	0.09
Hawaii Native/Pacific Islander:	146	0.12
Melanesian: (2)	2	0.00
Fijian (2)	2	0.00
Micronesian: (12)	23	0.02
Guamanian/Chamorro (12)	22	0.02
Other Micronesian	1	0.00
Polynesian: (18)	32	0.03
Native Hawaiian (8)	20	0.02
Samoan (10)	11	0.01
Other Polynesian	1	0.00
Other Pac. Isl., specified	6	0.01
Other Pac. Isl., not spec. (14)	83	0.07
Hispanic or Latino:	19,635	16.77
Central American:	4,097	3.50
Costa Rican	79	0.07
Guatemalan	3,067	2.62
Honduran	527	0.45
Nicaraguan	37	0.03
Panamanian	62	0.05
Salvadoran	212	0.18
Other Central American	113	0.10
Cuban	358	0.31
Dominican Republic	656	0.56
Mexican	1,414	1.21
Puerto Rican	3,167	2.70
South American:	5,160	4.41
Argentinean	115	0.10
Bolivian	59	0.05
Chilean	194	0.17

Notes: 1. Figures in the "Number" column do not add up to the total population due to: a) Ancestry/Race overlap — e.g. persons can report being both White and Irish, b) persons of Hispanic origin can report being any race, c) persons reporting two ancestries are counted in both categories. 2. Numbers in parentheses indicate the number of persons reporting this ancestry/race alone, not in combination with any other ancestry/race. 3. Refer to the Explanation of Data in the front of the book for more detailed information.

Ancestry/Race	Number	%
Colombian	1,937	1.65
Ecuadorian	1,170	1.00
Paraguayan	28	0.02
Peruvian	1,268	1.08
Uruguayan	138	0.12
Venezuelan	99	0.08
Other South American	152	0.13
Other Hispanic or Latino	4,783	4.09
Hungarian	1,082	0.92
Icelander	58	0.05
Iranian	147	0.13
Irish	12,330	10.53
Israeli	237	0.20
Italian	19,873	16.97
Latvian	112	0.10
Lithuanian	206	0.18
Luxemburger	15	0.01
Macedonian	9	0.01
Maltese	55	0.05
New Zealander	14	0.01
Northern European	73	0.06
Norwegian	780	0.67
Polish	6,578	5.62
Portuguese	436	0.37
Romanian	464	0.40
Russian	3,590	3.07
Scandinavian	47	0.04
Scotch-Irish	735	0.63
Scottish	1,302	1.11
Serbian	16	0.01
Slavic	36	0.03
Slovak	465	0.40
Slovene	24	0.02
Swedish	1,018	0.87
Swiss	146	0.12
Turkish	54	0.05
Ukrainian	768	0.66
United States or American	3,476	2.97
Welsh	300	0.26
West Indian, excl. Hispanic:	6,319	5.40
Bahamian	19	0.02
Barbadian	95	0.08
Bermudan	36	0.03
British West Indian	69	0.06
Dutch West Indian	18	0.02
Haitian	3,524	3.01
Jamaican	2,289	1.96
Trinidadian and Tobagonian	171	0.15
West Indian	82	0.07
Other West Indian	16	0.01
White:	84,170	71.89
Not Hispanic (71,610)	72,828	62.20
Hispanic (10,108)	11,342	9.69
Yugoslavian	74	0.06

Stonington

Place Type: Town
County: New London
Population: 17,906

Ancestry/Race	Number	%
African American/Black:	186	1.04
Not Hispanic (107)	179	1.00
Hispanic (5)	7	0.04
African, sub-Saharan:	6	0.03
African	6	0.03
Alaska Native tribes, specified:	2	0.01
Alaska Athabascan	2	0.01
Am. Ind. or Alaska Nat., not spec.	43	0.24
Alsatian	5	0.03
American Indian tribes, specified:	115	0.64
Apache (1)	1	0.01
Blackfeet (2)	7	0.04
Cherokee (2)	17	0.09
Choctaw	1	0.01
Cree	3	0.02
Iroquois (1)	6	0.03
Latin American Indians	2	0.01
Lumbee (1)	1	0.01
Navajo (1)	2	0.01
Seminole	2	0.01
All other tribes (43)	73	0.41
American Indian tribes, not spec.	16	0.09
Arab:	45	0.25
Egyptian	27	0.15
Lebanese	18	0.10
Armenian	23	0.13
Asian:	296	1.65
Chinese, ex. Taiwanese (127)	137	0.77
Filipino (31)	54	0.30
Indian (26)	30	0.17
Japanese (10)	23	0.13
Korean (13)	16	0.09
Laotian (4)	6	0.03
Malaysian (1)	1	0.01
Pakistani (5)	5	0.03
Thai (2)	6	0.03
Vietnamese (4)	5	0.03
Other Asian, not specified (1)	13	0.07
Assyrian/Chaldean/Syriac	16	0.09
Austrian	90	0.50
Belgian	2	0.01
Brazilian	45	0.25
British	168	0.94
Canadian	110	0.61
Croatian	25	0.14
Czech	79	0.44
Czechoslovakian	12	0.07
Danish	24	0.13
Dutch	242	1.35
Eastern European	12	0.07
English	3,360	18.76
Estonian	7	0.04
European	95	0.53
Finnish	112	0.63
French, except Basque	1,373	7.67
French Canadian	731	4.08
German	2,170	12.12
Greek	182	1.02
Hawaii Native/Pacific Islander:	17	0.09
Micronesian: (5)	6	0.03
Guamanian/Chamorro (3)	4	0.02
Other Micronesian (2)	2	0.01
Polynesian: (2)	5	0.03
Native Hawaiian (2)	5	0.03
Other Pac. Isl., not spec. (2)	6	0.03
Hispanic or Latino:	233	1.30
Central American:	14	0.08
Costa Rican	8	0.04
Guatemalan	1	0.01
Honduran	1	0.01
Panamanian	4	0.02
Cuban	6	0.03
Dominican Republic	1	0.01
Mexican	39	0.22
Puerto Rican	92	0.51
South American:	21	0.12
Argentinean	4	0.02
Chilean	2	0.01
Colombian	4	0.02
Ecuadorian	2	0.01
Paraguayan	2	0.01
Peruvian	5	0.03
Uruguayan	1	0.01
Other South American	1	0.01
Other Hispanic or Latino	60	0.34
Hungarian	154	0.86
Iranian	3	0.02
Irish	4,037	22.55
Italian	2,937	16.40
Latvian	3	0.02
Lithuanian	132	0.74
Northern European	8	0.04
Norwegian	176	0.98
Pennsylvania German	2	0.01
Polish	1,301	7.27
Portuguese	1,262	7.05
Romanian	6	0.03
Russian	143	0.80
Scandinavian	37	0.21
Scotch-Irish	421	2.35
Scottish	760	4.24
Slavic	7	0.04
Slovak	35	0.20
Slovene	14	0.08
Swedish	346	1.93
Swiss	39	0.22
Ukrainian	107	0.60
United States or American	676	3.78
Welsh	104	0.58
West Indian, excl. Hispanic:	31	0.17
Jamaican	13	0.07
West Indian	5	0.03
Other West Indian	13	0.07
White:	17,369	97.00
Not Hispanic (17,015)	17,207	96.10
Hispanic (141)	162	0.90
Yugoslavian	7	0.04

Storrs

Place Type: Census Designated Place
County: Tolland
Population: 10,996

Ancestry/Race	Number	%
Acadian/Cajun	6	0.05
African American/Black:	691	6.28
Not Hispanic (605)	655	5.96
Hispanic (19)	36	0.33
African, sub-Saharan:	126	1.13
African	60	0.54
Cape Verdean	7	0.06
Ethiopian	5	0.04
Kenyan	42	0.38
Liberian	7	0.06
Nigerian	5	0.04
Am. Ind. or Alaska Nat., not spec.	24	0.22
American Indian tribes, specified:	26	0.24
Apache	1	0.01
Blackfeet	4	0.04
Cherokee (2)	7	0.06
Iroquois	3	0.03
Latin American Indians (3)	5	0.05
Navajo (1)	1	0.01
Sioux	1	0.01
All other tribes (2)	4	0.04
American Indian tribes, not spec.	2	0.02
Arab:	60	0.54
Arab/Arabic	19	0.17
Lebanese	41	0.37
Armenian	17	0.15
Asian:	1,120	10.19
Bangladeshi (4)	4	0.04
Cambodian (21)	22	0.20
Chinese, ex. Taiwanese (426)	447	4.07
Filipino (53)	69	0.63
Indian (236)	252	2.29
Indonesian (3)	4	0.04
Japanese (26)	38	0.35
Korean (107)	119	1.08
Laotian (13)	15	0.14
Pakistani (17)	17	0.15
Sri Lankan (5)	5	0.05
Taiwanese (10)	16	0.15
Thai (9)	13	0.12
Vietnamese (46)	55	0.50
Other Asian, specified (9)	9	0.08
Other Asian, not specified (10)	35	0.32
Austrian	74	0.66
Brazilian	7	0.06
British	76	0.68
Bulgarian	10	0.09
Canadian	39	0.35
Celtic	6	0.05
Croatian	13	0.12
Czech	83	0.74
Czechoslovakian	42	0.38
Danish	39	0.35

Notes: 1. Figures in the "Number" column do not add up to the total population due to: a) Ancestry/Race overlap — e.g. persons can report being both White and Irish, b) persons of Hispanic origin can report being any race, c) persons reporting two ancestries are counted in both categories. 2. Numbers in parentheses indicate the number of persons reporting this ancestry/race alone, not in combination with any other ancestry/race. 3. Refer to the Explanation of Data in the front of the book for more detailed information.

Ancestry/Race	Number	%
Dutch	71	0.64
Eastern European	6	0.05
English	1,083	9.69
European	144	1.29
Finnish	35	0.31
French, except Basque	537	4.81
French Canadian	486	4.35
German	1,198	10.72
Greek	121	1.08
Guyanese	7	0.06
Hawaii Native/Pacific Islander:	31	0.28
Micronesian: (1)	2	0.02
Guamanian/Chamorro (1)	1	0.01
Other Micronesian	1	0.01
Polynesian: (1)	8	0.07
Native Hawaiian (1)	7	0.06
Samoan	1	0.01
Other Pac. Isl., not spec. (3)	21	0.19
Hispanic or Latino:	484	4.40
Central American:	24	0.22
Costa Rican	3	0.03
Guatemalan	9	0.08
Honduran	1	0.01
Nicaraguan	3	0.03
Panamanian	4	0.04
Salvadoran	3	0.03
Other Central American	1	0.01
Cuban	29	0.26
Dominican Republic	16	0.15
Mexican	46	0.42
Puerto Rican	190	1.73
South American:	106	0.96
Argentinean	20	0.18
Bolivian	4	0.04
Chilean	17	0.15
Colombian	30	0.27
Ecuadorian	15	0.14
Peruvian	16	0.15
Uruguayan	1	0.01
Venezuelan	3	0.03
Other Hispanic or Latino	73	0.66
Hungarian	89	0.80
Iranian	12	0.11
Irish	1,841	16.47
Italian	2,134	19.10
Lithuanian	96	0.86
Maltese	7	0.06
New Zealander	8	0.07
Northern European	7	0.06
Norwegian	113	1.01
Pennsylvania German	6	0.05
Polish	1,048	9.38
Portuguese	204	1.83
Romanian	99	0.89
Russian	267	2.39
Scandinavian	17	0.15
Scotch-Irish	137	1.23
Scottish	259	2.32
Serbian	7	0.06
Slavic	6	0.05
Slovak	62	0.55
Swedish	174	1.56
Swiss	19	0.17
Turkish	20	0.18
Ukrainian	76	0.68
United States or American	188	1.68
Welsh	66	0.59
West Indian, excl. Hispanic:	200	1.79
British West Indian	15	0.13
Haitian	28	0.25
Jamaican	121	1.08
Trinidadian and Tobagonian	20	0.18
U.S. Virgin Islander	5	0.04
West Indian	5	0.04
Other West Indian	6	0.05
White:	9,118	82.92
Not Hispanic (8,675)	8,837	80.37
Hispanic (243)	281	2.56

Stratford

Place Type: Census Designated Place
County: Fairfield
Population: 49,976

Ancestry/Race	Number	%
African American/Black:	5,295	10.60
Not Hispanic (4,765)	5,114	10.23
Hispanic (127)	181	0.36
African, sub-Saharan:	334	0.67
African	83	0.17
Cape Verdean	129	0.26
Ghanian	41	0.08
Liberian	39	0.08
Nigerian	42	0.08
Alaska Native tribes, specified:	1	0.00
Tlingit-Haida	1	0.00
Am. Ind. or Alaska Nat., not spec.	92	0.18
Albanian	133	0.27
American Indian tribes, specified:	155	0.31
Apache	1	0.00
Blackfeet (2)	9	0.02
Cherokee (6)	41	0.08
Cheyenne	1	0.00
Chickasaw (1)	1	0.00
Chippewa	1	0.00
Choctaw (1)	7	0.01
Colville (1)	1	0.00
Creek (1)	1	0.00
Iroquois (8)	20	0.04
Latin American Indians (4)	7	0.01
Lumbee	3	0.01
Pima (1)	1	0.00
Pueblo (1)	1	0.00
Seminole	5	0.01
Sioux	1	0.00
All other tribes (28)	54	0.11
American Indian tribes, not spec.	11	0.02
Arab:	336	0.67
Arab/Arabic	32	0.06
Egyptian	10	0.02
Lebanese	82	0.16
Moroccan	16	0.03
Palestinian	11	0.02
Syrian	185	0.37
Armenian	83	0.17
Asian:	896	1.79
Bangladeshi (2)	2	0.00
Cambodian (19)	22	0.04
Chinese, ex. Taiwanese (124)	162	0.32
Filipino (66)	86	0.17
Hmong (5)	5	0.01
Indian (202)	233	0.47
Japanese (32)	47	0.09
Korean (77)	92	0.18
Laotian (36)	50	0.10
Malaysian (2)	2	0.00
Pakistani (15)	29	0.06
Sri Lankan (2)	2	0.00
Taiwanese (5)	9	0.02
Thai (7)	15	0.03
Vietnamese (63)	80	0.16
Other Asian, specified	1	0.00
Other Asian, not specified (18)	59	0.12
Australian	14	0.03
Austrian	214	0.43
Basque	11	0.02
Belgian	32	0.06
Brazilian	58	0.12
British	87	0.17
Canadian	132	0.26
Carpatho Rusyn	33	0.07
Celtic	11	0.02
Croatian	19	0.04
Czech	238	0.48
Czechoslovakian	357	0.71
Danish	134	0.27
Dutch	361	0.72
Eastern European	13	0.03
English	4,020	8.04
European	141	0.28
Finnish	29	0.06
French, except Basque	1,557	3.12
French Canadian	1,021	2.04
German	4,870	9.74
Greek	489	0.98
Guyanese	12	0.02
Hawaii Native/Pacific Islander:	36	0.07
Micronesian: (5)	5	0.01
Guamanian/Chamorro (5)	5	0.01
Polynesian: (8)	16	0.03
Native Hawaiian (5)	8	0.02
Samoan (3)	8	0.02
Other Pac. Isl., not spec. (4)	15	0.03
Hispanic or Latino:	3,399	6.80
Central American:	125	0.25
Costa Rican	19	0.04
Guatemalan	51	0.10
Honduran	11	0.02
Nicaraguan	4	0.01
Panamanian	8	0.02
Salvadoran	31	0.06
Other Central American	1	0.00
Cuban	173	0.35
Dominican Republic	90	0.18
Mexican	173	0.35
Puerto Rican	2,143	4.29
South American:	212	0.42
Argentinean	12	0.02
Bolivian	6	0.01
Chilean	1	0.00
Colombian	90	0.18
Ecuadorian	66	0.13
Paraguayan	5	0.01
Peruvian	20	0.04
Uruguayan	3	0.01
Venezuelan	3	0.01
Other South American	6	0.01
Other Hispanic or Latino	483	0.97
Hungarian	1,559	3.12
Iranian	53	0.11
Irish	9,040	18.09
Israeli	21	0.04
Italian	11,232	22.47
Latvian	5	0.01
Lithuanian	440	0.88
Macedonian	35	0.07
Maltese	8	0.02
Northern European	13	0.03
Norwegian	213	0.43
Pennsylvania German	25	0.05
Polish	5,174	10.35
Portuguese	610	1.22
Romanian	72	0.14
Russian	1,377	2.76
Scandinavian	28	0.06
Scotch-Irish	489	0.98
Scottish	771	1.54
Serbian	31	0.06
Slavic	68	0.14
Slovak	3,173	6.35
Slovene	19	0.04
Swedish	944	1.89
Swiss	73	0.15
Turkish	81	0.16
Ukrainian	478	0.96
United States or American	1,121	2.24
Welsh	179	0.36
West Indian, excl. Hispanic:	763	1.53
Haitian	335	0.67
Jamaican	361	0.72
Trinidadian and Tobagonian	11	0.02
West Indian	56	0.11
White:	42,979	86.00
Not Hispanic (40,327)	40,760	81.56
Hispanic (2,034)	2,219	4.44
Yugoslavian	91	0.18

Notes: 1. Figures in the "Number" column do not add up to the total population due to: a) Ancestry/Race overlap — e.g. persons can report being both White and Irish, b) persons of Hispanic origin can report being any race, c) persons reporting two ancestries are counted in both categories. 2. Numbers in parentheses indicate the number of persons reporting this ancestry/race alone, not in combination with any other ancestry/race. 3. Refer to the Explanation of Data in the front of the book for more detailed information.

Suffield

Place Type: Town
County: Hartford
Population: 13,552

Ancestry/Race	Number	%
African American/Black:	1,000	7.38
Not Hispanic (881)	916	6.76
Hispanic (61)	84	0.62
African, sub-Saharan:	123	0.91
African	103	0.76
Cape Verdean	13	0.10
Kenyan	7	0.05
Alaska Native tribes, specified:	1	0.01
Tlingit-Haida	1	0.01
Am. Ind. or Alaska Nat., not spec.	30	0.22
Albanian	19	0.14
American Indian tribes, specified:	42	0.31
Apache	1	0.01
Blackfeet (3)	3	0.02
Cherokee (4)	9	0.07
Creek	2	0.01
Iroquois (1)	4	0.03
Latin American Indians (4)	6	0.04
All other tribes (9)	17	0.13
American Indian tribes, not spec.	3	0.02
Arab:	41	0.30
Lebanese	34	0.25
Other Arab	7	0.05
Armenian	27	0.20
Asian:	163	1.20
Chinese, ex. Taiwanese (27)	34	0.25
Filipino (23)	32	0.24
Indian (29)	37	0.27
Japanese (5)	6	0.04
Korean (26)	30	0.22
Laotian (4)	4	0.03
Sri Lankan (1)	1	0.01
Thai (2)	2	0.01
Vietnamese (4)	6	0.04
Other Asian, not specified (4)	11	0.08
Austrian	36	0.27
Belgian	4	0.03
British	107	0.79
Bulgarian	5	0.04
Canadian	37	0.27
Celtic	5	0.04
Czech	41	0.30
Czechoslovakian	20	0.15
Danish	75	0.55
Dutch	169	1.25
Eastern European	21	0.15
English	2,074	15.30
European	36	0.27
Finnish	17	0.13
French, except Basque	1,085	8.01
French Canadian	740	5.46
German	1,082	7.98
Greek	72	0.53
Hawaii Native/Pacific Islander:	23	0.17
Polynesian: (4)	14	0.10
Native Hawaiian (1)	10	0.07
Samoan (3)	4	0.03
Other Pac. Isl., not spec. (2)	9	0.07
Hispanic or Latino:	576	4.25
Central American:	3	0.02
Guatemalan	3	0.02
Cuban	15	0.11
Dominican Republic	11	0.08
Mexican	31	0.23
Puerto Rican	383	2.83
South American:	20	0.15
Argentinean	3	0.02
Bolivian	3	0.02
Chilean	3	0.02
Colombian	4	0.03
Ecuadorian	1	0.01
Paraguayan	2	0.01
Peruvian	2	0.01
Venezuelan	2	0.01
Other Hispanic or Latino	113	0.83
Hungarian	55	0.41
Irish	2,488	18.36
Italian	2,476	18.27
Latvian	12	0.09
Lithuanian	172	1.27
Northern European	5	0.04
Norwegian	121	0.89
Polish	2,043	15.08
Portuguese	159	1.17
Romanian	9	0.07
Russian	180	1.33
Scotch-Irish	132	0.97
Scottish	342	2.52
Serbian	7	0.05
Slovak	35	0.26
Slovene	5	0.04
Swedish	290	2.14
Swiss	28	0.21
Ukrainian	37	0.27
United States or American	495	3.65
Welsh	121	0.89
West Indian, excl. Hispanic:	86	0.63
Jamaican	77	0.57
West Indian	9	0.07
White:	12,119	89.43
Not Hispanic (11,841)	11,909	87.88
Hispanic (175)	210	1.55

Tolland

Place Type: Town
County: Tolland
Population: 13,146

Ancestry/Race	Number	%
African American/Black:	122	0.93
Not Hispanic (99)	120	0.91
Hispanic (2)	2	0.02
African, sub-Saharan:	22	0.17
African	5	0.04
Cape Verdean	4	0.03
Ghanian	13	0.10
Alaska Native tribes, specified:	2	0.02
Eskimo	2	0.02
Am. Ind. or Alaska Nat., not spec.	8	0.06
Albanian	11	0.08
American Indian tribes, specified:	40	0.30
Blackfeet	3	0.02
Cherokee (1)	9	0.07
Chippewa (1)	1	0.01
Cree	6	0.05
Iroquois	4	0.03
Menominee	1	0.01
Seminole	1	0.01
All other tribes (4)	16	0.12
American Indian tribes, not spec.	1	0.01
Arab:	7	0.05
Lebanese	7	0.05
Armenian	18	0.14
Asian:	196	1.49
Chinese, ex. Taiwanese (28)	36	0.27
Filipino (7)	10	0.08
Indian (53)	58	0.44
Indonesian (3)	3	0.02
Japanese (1)	3	0.02
Korean (27)	34	0.26
Laotian (8)	8	0.06
Pakistani (8)	17	0.13
Taiwanese (2)	2	0.02
Thai (1)	4	0.03
Vietnamese (7)	10	0.08
Other Asian, specified	2	0.02
Other Asian, not specified (8)	9	0.07
Australian	36	0.27
Austrian	53	0.40
Brazilian	19	0.14
British	65	0.49
Canadian	99	0.75
Croatian	18	0.14
Czech	72	0.55
Czechoslovakian	102	0.78
Danish	77	0.59
Dutch	141	1.07
Eastern European	27	0.21
English	2,078	15.81
Estonian	8	0.06
European	199	1.51
Finnish	58	0.44
French, except Basque	1,631	12.41
French Canadian	987	7.51
German	1,807	13.75
Greek	82	0.62
Hawaii Native/Pacific Islander:	9	0.07
Micronesian: (2)	2	0.02
Guamanian/Chamorro (2)	2	0.02
Polynesian:	4	0.03
Native Hawaiian	4	0.03
Other Pac. Isl., specified	2	0.02
Other Pac. Isl., not spec.	1	0.01
Hispanic or Latino:	151	1.15
Central American:	3	0.02
Guatemalan	1	0.01
Other Central American	2	0.02
Cuban	11	0.08
Dominican Republic	2	0.02
Mexican	17	0.13
Puerto Rican	65	0.49
South American:	43	0.33
Argentinean	1	0.01
Chilean	8	0.06
Colombian	10	0.08
Ecuadorian	5	0.04
Paraguayan	1	0.01
Peruvian	11	0.08
Venezuelan	6	0.05
Other South American	1	0.01
Other Hispanic or Latino	10	0.08
Hungarian	91	0.69
Irish	3,022	22.99
Italian	1,885	14.34
Lithuanian	300	2.28
Northern European	14	0.11
Norwegian	49	0.37
Pennsylvania German	20	0.15
Polish	1,492	11.35
Portuguese	150	1.14
Romanian	15	0.11
Russian	180	1.37
Scandinavian	31	0.24
Scotch-Irish	220	1.67
Scottish	397	3.02
Slavic	4	0.03
Slovak	93	0.71
Swedish	348	2.65
Swiss	136	1.03
Turkish	8	0.06
Ukrainian	75	0.57
United States or American	617	4.69
Welsh	59	0.45
West Indian, excl. Hispanic:	17	0.13
Jamaican	8	0.06
West Indian	9	0.07
White:	12,813	97.47
Not Hispanic (12,620)	12,706	96.65
Hispanic (100)	107	0.81
Yugoslavian	6	0.05

Torrington

Place Type: City
County: Litchfield
Population: 35,202

Ancestry/Race	Number	%
African American/Black:	960	2.73
Not Hispanic (694)	876	2.49
Hispanic (63)	84	0.24
African, sub-Saharan:	77	0.22

Notes: 1. Figures in the "Number" column do not add up to the total population due to: a) Ancestry/Race overlap — e.g. persons can report being both White and Irish, b) persons of Hispanic origin can report being any race, c) persons reporting two ancestries are counted in both categories. 2. Numbers in parentheses indicate the number of persons reporting this ancestry/race alone, not in combination with any other ancestry/race. 3. Refer to the Explanation of Data in the front of the book for more detailed information.

Ancestry/Race	Number	%
African	47	0.13
Cape Verdean	30	0.09
Alaska Native tribes, specified:	1	0.00
Alaska Athabascan (1)	1	0.00
Am. Ind. or Alaska Nat., not spec.	89	0.25
Albanian	47	0.13
Alsatian	15	0.04
American Indian tribes, specified:	107	0.30
Apache (1)	3	0.01
Blackfeet (2)	10	0.03
Cherokee (9)	22	0.06
Cheyenne	1	0.00
Chippewa (1)	1	0.00
Cree	1	0.00
Delaware	1	0.00
Iroquois (6)	13	0.04
Kiowa (2)	2	0.01
Latin American Indians (2)	5	0.01
Osage	2	0.01
Pueblo (1)	2	0.01
Seminole (1)	3	0.01
Sioux	6	0.02
All other tribes (8)	35	0.10
American Indian tribes, not spec.	14	0.04
Arab:	334	0.95
Lebanese	329	0.93
Other Arab	5	0.01
Armenian	20	0.06
Asian:	745	2.12
Cambodian (24)	26	0.07
Chinese, ex. Taiwanese (61)	74	0.21
Filipino (54)	70	0.20
Indian (99)	109	0.31
Indonesian (3)	6	0.02
Japanese (3)	7	0.02
Korean (126)	143	0.41
Laotian (70)	80	0.23
Malaysian (1)	1	0.00
Pakistani (11)	12	0.03
Taiwanese	1	0.00
Thai (3)	7	0.02
Vietnamese (148)	159	0.45
Other Asian, specified	3	0.01
Other Asian, not specified (27)	47	0.13
Australian	14	0.04
Austrian	75	0.21
Belgian	13	0.04
British	82	0.23
Canadian	116	0.33
Czech	113	0.32
Czechoslovakian	87	0.25
Danish	97	0.28
Dutch	170	0.48
Eastern European	5	0.01
English	3,447	9.79
European	29	0.08
Finnish	116	0.33
French, except Basque	3,770	10.71
French Canadian	1,023	2.91
German	4,030	11.45
Greek	155	0.44
Hawaii Native/Pacific Islander:	28	0.08
Micronesian: (1)	1	0.00
Guamanian/Chamorro (1)	1	0.00
Polynesian: (3)	12	0.03
Native Hawaiian (1)	8	0.02
Samoan (2)	3	0.01
Other Polynesian	1	0.00
Other Pac. Isl., specified	3	0.01
Other Pac. Isl., not spec. (3)	12	0.03
Hispanic or Latino:	1,162	3.30
Central American:	12	0.03
Costa Rican	2	0.01
Guatemalan	1	0.00
Panamanian	1	0.00
Salvadoran	8	0.02
Cuban	59	0.17
Dominican Republic	162	0.46
Mexican	73	0.21
Puerto Rican	496	1.41
South American:	121	0.34
Argentinean	2	0.01
Bolivian	4	0.01
Chilean	7	0.02
Colombian	16	0.05
Ecuadorian	75	0.21
Paraguayan	1	0.00
Peruvian	6	0.02
Uruguayan	2	0.01
Venezuelan	3	0.01
Other South American	5	0.01
Other Hispanic or Latino	239	0.68
Hungarian	625	1.78
Iranian	8	0.02
Irish	5,644	16.03
Italian	10,094	28.67
Latvian	41	0.12
Lithuanian	452	1.28
Macedonian	6	0.02
Northern European	10	0.03
Norwegian	165	0.47
Polish	3,027	8.60
Portuguese	161	0.46
Romanian	68	0.19
Russian	369	1.05
Scandinavian	11	0.03
Scotch-Irish	482	1.37
Scottish	665	1.89
Serbian	6	0.02
Slavic	25	0.07
Slovak	1,041	2.96
Swedish	599	1.70
Swiss	177	0.50
Turkish	5	0.01
Ukrainian	147	0.42
United States or American	1,158	3.29
Welsh	130	0.37
West Indian, excl. Hispanic:	198	0.56
British West Indian	17	0.05
Haitian	25	0.07
Jamaican	126	0.36
West Indian	30	0.09
White:	33,201	94.32
Not Hispanic (32,200)	32,573	92.53
Hispanic (549)	628	1.78
Yugoslavian	27	0.08

Trumbull

Place Type: Census Designated Place
County: Fairfield
Population: 34,243

Ancestry/Race	Number	%
African American/Black:	726	2.12
Not Hispanic (613)	688	2.01
Hispanic (32)	38	0.11
African, sub-Saharan:	7	0.02
Nigerian	7	0.02
Alaska Native tribes, not specified	1	0.00
Am. Ind. or Alaska Nat., not spec.	33	0.10
Albanian	91	0.27
Alsatian	6	0.02
American Indian tribes, specified:	50	0.15
Apache	1	0.00
Cherokee (1)	21	0.06
Chickasaw	1	0.00
Iroquois (2)	3	0.01
Latin American Indians (10)	10	0.03
Pima	1	0.00
All other tribes (10)	13	0.04
American Indian tribes, not spec.	13	0.04
Arab:	284	0.83
Arab/Arabic	25	0.07
Lebanese	79	0.23
Syrian	103	0.30
Other Arab	77	0.22
Armenian	78	0.23
Asian:	921	2.69
Cambodian (32)	40	0.12
Chinese, ex. Taiwanese (131)	147	0.43
Filipino (45)	58	0.17
Indian (306)	344	1.00
Indonesian	1	0.00
Japanese (23)	33	0.10
Korean (163)	170	0.50
Laotian (7)	7	0.02
Pakistani (7)	9	0.03
Sri Lankan (10)	12	0.04
Taiwanese (10)	10	0.03
Thai (1)	3	0.01
Vietnamese (57)	61	0.18
Other Asian, specified (5)	8	0.02
Other Asian, not specified (4)	18	0.05
Austrian	424	1.24
Basque	6	0.02
Belgian	25	0.07
Brazilian	18	0.05
British	95	0.28
Canadian	108	0.32
Carpatho Rusyn	29	0.08
Celtic	8	0.02
Croatian	23	0.07
Czech	187	0.55
Czechoslovakian	262	0.77
Danish	188	0.55
Dutch	217	0.63
Eastern European	191	0.56
English	2,808	8.20
Estonian	15	0.04
European	128	0.37
Finnish	27	0.08
French, except Basque	942	2.75
French Canadian	574	1.68
German	3,503	10.23
Greek	448	1.31
Hawaii Native/Pacific Islander:	11	0.03
Micronesian: (3)	3	0.01
Guamanian/Chamorro (3)	3	0.01
Polynesian: (3)	5	0.01
Native Hawaiian (1)	3	0.01
Samoan (2)	2	0.01
Other Pac. Isl., not spec.	3	0.01
Hispanic or Latino:	923	2.70
Central American:	61	0.18
Costa Rican	21	0.06
Guatemalan	19	0.06
Honduran	2	0.01
Nicaraguan	1	0.00
Salvadoran	17	0.05
Other Central American	1	0.00
Cuban	100	0.29
Dominican Republic	18	0.05
Mexican	73	0.21
Puerto Rican	398	1.16
South American:	107	0.31
Argentinean	10	0.03
Bolivian	5	0.01
Chilean	3	0.01
Colombian	39	0.11
Ecuadorian	22	0.06
Paraguayan	1	0.00
Peruvian	13	0.04
Uruguayan	4	0.01
Venezuelan	5	0.01
Other South American	5	0.01
Other Hispanic or Latino	166	0.48
Hungarian	1,322	3.86
Iranian	162	0.47
Irish	7,150	20.88
Israeli	42	0.12
Italian	10,107	29.52
Latvian	6	0.02
Lithuanian	246	0.72
Norwegian	266	0.78
Pennsylvania German	25	0.07
Polish	3,215	9.39
Portuguese	565	1.65
Romanian	57	0.17
Russian	1,538	4.49

Notes: 1. Figures in the "Number" column do not add up to the total population due to: a) Ancestry/Race overlap — e.g. persons can report being both White and Irish, b) persons of Hispanic origin can report being any race, c) persons reporting two ancestries are counted in both categories. 2. Numbers in parentheses indicate the number of persons reporting this ancestry/race alone, not in combination with any other ancestry/race. 3. Refer to the Explanation of Data in the front of the book for more detailed information.

Ancestry/Race	Number	%
Scandinavian	48	0.14
Scotch-Irish	392	1.14
Scottish	659	1.92
Slavic	87	0.25
Slovak	1,121	3.27
Slovene	52	0.15
Swedish	616	1.80
Swiss	127	0.37
Turkish	30	0.09
Ukrainian	302	0.88
United States or American	1,069	3.12
Welsh	87	0.25
West Indian, excl. Hispanic:	105	0.31
Haitian	21	0.06
Jamaican	29	0.08
Trinidadian and Tobagonian	39	0.11
U.S. Virgin Islander	16	0.05
White:	32,448	94.76
Not Hispanic (31,549)	31,769	92.78
Hispanic (645)	679	1.98
Yugoslavian	51	0.15

Vernon

Place Type: Town
County: Tolland
Population: 28,063

Ancestry/Race	Number	%
African American/Black:	1,349	4.81
Not Hispanic (1,070)	1,279	4.56
Hispanic (50)	70	0.25
African, sub-Saharan:	103	0.37
African	85	0.30
Ghanian	12	0.04
Nigerian	6	0.02
Am. Ind. or Alaska Nat., not spec.	82	0.29
American Indian tribes, specified:	109	0.39
Apache	1	0.00
Blackfeet	13	0.05
Cherokee (10)	19	0.07
Chickasaw (1)	1	0.00
Comanche (1)	1	0.00
Delaware (1)	1	0.00
Iroquois (5)	6	0.02
Latin American Indians (4)	9	0.03
Navajo (1)	1	0.00
Ottawa (1)	1	0.00
Pueblo (1)	1	0.00
Seminole	2	0.01
Sioux (1)	3	0.01
All other tribes (19)	50	0.18
American Indian tribes, not spec.	8	0.03
Arab:	73	0.26
Arab/Arabic	8	0.03
Jordanian	6	0.02
Syrian	59	0.21
Armenian	31	0.11
Asian:	904	3.22
Bangladeshi	1	0.00
Cambodian (6)	6	0.02
Chinese, ex. Taiwanese (106)	117	0.42
Filipino (26)	38	0.14
Hmong (20)	25	0.09
Indian (178)	205	0.73
Indonesian (1)	3	0.01
Japanese (11)	26	0.09
Korean (74)	91	0.32
Laotian (33)	40	0.14
Malaysian (1)	2	0.01
Pakistani (114)	158	0.56
Sri Lankan (1)	1	0.00
Taiwanese (4)	4	0.01
Thai (3)	6	0.02
Vietnamese (117)	128	0.46
Other Asian, specified (3)	7	0.02
Other Asian, not specified (25)	46	0.16
Assyrian/Chaldean/Syriac	6	0.02
Australian	6	0.02
Austrian	55	0.20
Belgian	8	0.03
Brazilian	10	0.04
British	156	0.56
Bulgarian	6	0.02
Canadian	203	0.72
Celtic	15	0.05
Croatian	21	0.07
Cypriot	5	0.02
Czech	81	0.29
Czechoslovakian	72	0.26
Danish	135	0.48
Dutch	243	0.87
Eastern European	28	0.10
English	3,555	12.67
Estonian	18	0.06
European	176	0.63
Finnish	63	0.22
French, except Basque	3,254	11.60
French Canadian	1,788	6.37
German	3,381	12.05
German Russian	8	0.03
Greek	177	0.63
Hawaii Native/Pacific Islander:	20	0.07
Micronesian: (5)	7	0.02
Guamanian/Chamorro (5)	7	0.02
Polynesian: (4)	5	0.02
Native Hawaiian (3)	4	0.01
Samoan (1)	1	0.00
Other Pac. Isl., specified	4	0.01
Other Pac. Isl., not spec. (1)	4	0.01
Hispanic or Latino:	1,005	3.58
Central American:	17	0.06
Costa Rican	2	0.01
Guatemalan	1	0.00
Honduran	2	0.01
Nicaraguan	4	0.01
Panamanian	5	0.02
Salvadoran	3	0.01
Cuban	25	0.09
Dominican Republic	18	0.06
Mexican	78	0.28
Puerto Rican	668	2.38
South American:	50	0.18
Argentinean	2	0.01
Bolivian	1	0.00
Chilean	1	0.00
Colombian	17	0.06
Ecuadorian	1	0.00
Peruvian	19	0.07
Uruguayan	4	0.01
Venezuelan	5	0.02
Other Hispanic or Latino	149	0.53
Hungarian	91	0.32
Icelander	35	0.12
Iranian	13	0.05
Irish	5,264	18.76
Italian	3,917	13.96
Latvian	29	0.10
Lithuanian	333	1.19
Norwegian	134	0.48
Polish	2,874	10.24
Portuguese	386	1.38
Romanian	36	0.13
Russian	370	1.32
Scandinavian	35	0.12
Scotch-Irish	446	1.59
Scottish	741	2.64
Slavic	54	0.19
Slovak	156	0.56
Swedish	453	1.61
Swiss	155	0.55
Turkish	33	0.12
Ukrainian	146	0.52
United States or American	1,140	4.06
Welsh	165	0.59
West Indian, excl. Hispanic:	286	1.02
Dutch West Indian	17	0.06
Jamaican	225	0.80
West Indian	44	0.16
White:	25,679	91.50
Not Hispanic (24,711)	25,056	89.28
Hispanic (532)	623	2.22

Wallingford Center

Place Type: Census Designated Place
County: New Haven
Population: 17,509

Ancestry/Race	Number	%
African American/Black:	293	1.67
Not Hispanic (195)	271	1.55
Hispanic (14)	22	0.13
Alaska Native tribes, specified:	2	0.01
Alaska Athabascan (1)	1	0.01
Tlingit-Haida (1)	1	0.01
Am. Ind. or Alaska Nat., not spec.	74	0.42
American Indian tribes, specified:	58	0.33
Blackfeet (3)	4	0.02
Cherokee (2)	18	0.10
Chickasaw	1	0.01
Choctaw (1)	1	0.01
Comanche	1	0.01
Cree	1	0.01
Creek (1)	1	0.01
Crow	1	0.01
Iroquois (2)	7	0.04
Latin American Indians	6	0.03
Ottawa	3	0.02
Sioux	1	0.01
All other tribes (3)	13	0.07
American Indian tribes, not spec.	3	0.02
Arab:	60	0.34
Arab/Arabic	5	0.03
Lebanese	14	0.08
Moroccan	41	0.23
Armenian	48	0.27
Asian:	430	2.46
Bangladeshi (8)	8	0.05
Chinese, ex. Taiwanese (87)	91	0.52
Filipino (34)	39	0.22
Indian (141)	151	0.86
Indonesian (4)	4	0.02
Japanese (8)	16	0.09
Korean (29)	32	0.18
Pakistani (24)	27	0.15
Taiwanese	1	0.01
Thai (3)	7	0.04
Vietnamese (38)	42	0.24
Other Asian, not specified (1)	12	0.07
Australian	17	0.10
Austrian	53	0.30
Brazilian	9	0.05
British	65	0.37
Canadian	90	0.51
Czech	27	0.15
Czechoslovakian	67	0.38
Danish	59	0.34
Dutch	80	0.46
Eastern European	12	0.07
English	1,827	10.43
European	38	0.22
Finnish	27	0.15
French, except Basque	841	4.80
French Canadian	382	2.18
German	1,806	10.31
Greek	123	0.70
Hawaii Native/Pacific Islander:	5	0.03
Other Pac. Isl., not spec.	5	0.03
Hispanic or Latino:	1,403	8.01
Central American:	18	0.10
Costa Rican	5	0.03
Guatemalan	5	0.03
Honduran	5	0.03
Nicaraguan	2	0.01
Salvadoran	1	0.01
Cuban	41	0.23
Dominican Republic	5	0.03
Mexican	649	3.71
Puerto Rican	514	2.94

Notes: 1. Figures in the "Number" column do not add up to the total population due to: a) Ancestry/Race overlap — e.g. persons can report being both White and Irish, b) persons of Hispanic origin can report being any race, c) persons reporting two ancestries are counted in both categories. 2. Numbers in parentheses indicate the number of persons reporting this ancestry/race alone, not in combination with any other ancestry/race. 3. Refer to the Explanation of Data in the front of the book for more detailed information.

Ancestry/Race	Number	%
South American:	65	0.37
Chilean	12	0.07
Colombian	17	0.10
Ecuadorian	24	0.14
Peruvian	12	0.07
Other Hispanic or Latino	111	0.63
Hungarian	426	2.43
Irish	3,420	19.52
Italian	4,097	23.38
Latvian	14	0.08
Lithuanian	129	0.74
Macedonian	9	0.05
Norwegian	51	0.29
Pennsylvania German	9	0.05
Polish	2,136	12.19
Portuguese	446	2.55
Romanian	10	0.06
Russian	267	1.52
Scotch-Irish	204	1.16
Scottish	406	2.32
Serbian	6	0.03
Slovak	60	0.34
Swedish	347	1.98
Swiss	9	0.05
Ukrainian	124	0.71
United States or American	757	4.32
Welsh	63	0.36
White:	16,458	94.00
Not Hispanic (15,292)	15,457	88.28
Hispanic (929)	1,001	5.72
Yugoslavian	17	0.10

Wallingford

Place Type: Town
County: New Haven
Population: 43,026

Ancestry/Race	Number	%
African American/Black:	575	1.34
Not Hispanic (417)	536	1.25
Hispanic (24)	39	0.09
African, sub-Saharan:	53	0.12
African	41	0.10
Cape Verdean	12	0.03
Alaska Native tribes, specified:	5	0.01
Alaska Athabascan (1)	1	0.00
Aleut (1)	1	0.00
Tlingit-Haida (3)	3	0.01
Am. Ind. or Alaska Nat., not spec.	126	0.29
Albanian	8	0.02
American Indian tribes, specified:	111	0.26
Apache	2	0.00
Blackfeet (3)	12	0.03
Cherokee (6)	26	0.06
Chickasaw	1	0.00
Chippewa	3	0.01
Choctaw (1)	1	0.00
Comanche	2	0.00
Cree	1	0.00
Creek (1)	2	0.00
Crow	1	0.00
Iroquois (2)	7	0.02
Kiowa	3	0.01
Latin American Indians	7	0.02
Ottawa	4	0.01
Seminole	1	0.00
Sioux	5	0.01
All other tribes (13)	33	0.08
American Indian tribes, not spec.	5	0.01
Arab:	114	0.26
Arab/Arabic	5	0.01
Lebanese	14	0.03
Moroccan	79	0.18
Syrian	6	0.01
Other Arab	10	0.02
Armenian	64	0.15
Asian:	879	2.04
Bangladeshi (15)	15	0.03
Chinese, ex. Taiwanese (177)	207	0.48
Filipino (57)	75	0.17
Indian (273)	290	0.67
Indonesian (5)	5	0.01
Japanese (18)	33	0.08
Korean (79)	88	0.20
Laotian (1)	1	0.00
Pakistani (37)	41	0.10
Sri Lankan (3)	3	0.01
Taiwanese (3)	7	0.02
Thai (5)	10	0.02
Vietnamese (66)	72	0.17
Other Asian, not specified (7)	32	0.07
Australian	17	0.04
Austrian	142	0.33
Belgian	5	0.01
Brazilian	9	0.02
British	166	0.39
Canadian	204	0.47
Croatian	11	0.03
Czech	95	0.22
Czechoslovakian	99	0.23
Danish	225	0.52
Dutch	239	0.56
Eastern European	23	0.05
English	4,904	11.40
Estonian	5	0.01
European	94	0.22
Finnish	40	0.09
French, except Basque	2,464	5.73
French Canadian	1,251	2.91
German	4,815	11.19
Greek	295	0.69
Hawaii Native/Pacific Islander:	10	0.02
Polynesian:	4	0.01
Native Hawaiian	3	0.01
Samoan	1	0.00
Other Pac. Isl., not spec.	6	0.01
Hispanic or Latino:	1,946	4.52
Central American:	24	0.06
Costa Rican	7	0.02
Guatemalan	6	0.01
Honduran	5	0.01
Nicaraguan	2	0.00
Panamanian	3	0.01
Salvadoran	1	0.00
Cuban	92	0.21
Dominican Republic	16	0.04
Mexican	697	1.62
Puerto Rican	825	1.92
South American:	102	0.24
Argentinean	6	0.01
Bolivian	2	0.00
Chilean	13	0.03
Colombian	33	0.08
Ecuadorian	28	0.07
Peruvian	16	0.04
Uruguayan	2	0.00
Venezuelan	1	0.00
Other South American	1	0.00
Other Hispanic or Latino	190	0.44
Hungarian	1,009	2.35
Irish	9,181	21.34
Israeli	15	0.03
Italian	11,704	27.20
Latvian	77	0.18
Lithuanian	468	1.09
Macedonian	9	0.02
New Zealander	7	0.02
Northern European	5	0.01
Norwegian	221	0.51
Pennsylvania German	17	0.04
Polish	5,200	12.09
Portuguese	815	1.89
Romanian	34	0.08
Russian	656	1.52
Scandinavian	37	0.09
Scotch-Irish	645	1.50
Scottish	913	2.12
Serbian	6	0.01
Slavic	11	0.03
Slovak	116	0.27
Slovene	6	0.01
Swedish	868	2.02
Swiss	87	0.20
Ukrainian	320	0.74
United States or American	1,676	3.90
Welsh	265	0.62
West Indian, excl. Hispanic:	65	0.15
Haitian	5	0.01
Jamaican	60	0.14
White:	41,193	95.74
Not Hispanic (39,458)	39,764	92.42
Hispanic (1,316)	1,429	3.32
Yugoslavian	30	0.07

Waterbury

Place Type: City
County: New Haven
Population: 107,271

Ancestry/Race	Number	%
Afghan	55	0.05
African American/Black:	19,310	18.00
Not Hispanic (16,335)	17,691	16.49
Hispanic (1,165)	1,619	1.51
African, sub-Saharan:	1,658	1.55
African	806	0.75
Cape Verdean	696	0.65
Ethiopian	16	0.01
Nigerian	106	0.10
Sudanese	6	0.01
Ugandan	6	0.01
Other sub-Saharan African	22	0.02
Alaska Native tribes, specified:	1	0.00
Eskimo (1)	1	0.00
Alaska Native tribes, not specified	1	0.00
Am. Ind. or Alaska Nat., not spec.	474	0.44
Albanian	2,174	2.03
American Indian tribes, specified:	562	0.52
Apache (6)	11	0.01
Blackfeet (10)	39	0.04
Cherokee (27)	149	0.14
Cheyenne	4	0.00
Chippewa (8)	12	0.01
Choctaw	12	0.01
Cree	3	0.00
Iroquois (5)	16	0.01
Latin American Indians (37)	84	0.08
Lumbee (1)	2	0.00
Navajo	2	0.00
Osage	1	0.00
Pueblo (1)	10	0.01
Seminole	2	0.00
Sioux (6)	19	0.02
Yaqui (1)	1	0.00
All other tribes (105)	195	0.18
American Indian tribes, not spec.	66	0.06
Arab:	927	0.86
Arab/Arabic	52	0.05
Egyptian	62	0.06
Jordanian	8	0.01
Lebanese	663	0.62
Moroccan	44	0.04
Palestinian	18	0.02
Syrian	28	0.03
Other Arab	52	0.05
Armenian	38	0.04
Asian:	2,022	1.88
Bangladeshi (9)	10	0.01
Cambodian (16)	23	0.02
Chinese, ex. Taiwanese (203)	252	0.23
Filipino (175)	223	0.21
Indian (608)	742	0.69
Indonesian (2)	4	0.00
Japanese (121)	151	0.14
Korean (42)	61	0.06
Laotian (12)	16	0.01
Malaysian	1	0.00
Pakistani (92)	118	0.11

Notes: 1. Figures in the "Number" column do not add up to the total population due to: a) Ancestry/Race overlap — e.g. persons can report being both White and Irish, b) persons of Hispanic origin can report being any race, c) persons reporting two ancestries are counted in both categories. 2. Numbers in parentheses indicate the number of persons reporting this ancestry/race alone, not in combination with any other ancestry/race. 3. Refer to the Explanation of Data in the front of the book for more detailed information.

Ancestry/Race	Number	%
Sri Lankan (10)	11	0.01
Taiwanese	2	0.00
Thai (4)	8	0.01
Vietnamese (231)	243	0.23
Other Asian, specified (4)	9	0.01
Other Asian, not specified (55)	148	0.14
Assyrian/Chaldean/Syriac	7	0.01
Austrian	134	0.12
Belgian	9	0.01
Brazilian	420	0.39
British	155	0.14
Canadian	417	0.39
Celtic	23	0.02
Croatian	9	0.01
Cypriot	10	0.01
Czech	95	0.09
Czechoslovakian	72	0.07
Danish	91	0.08
Dutch	440	0.41
Eastern European	12	0.01
English	4,053	3.78
European	42	0.04
Finnish	7	0.01
French, except Basque	6,087	5.67
French Canadian	2,757	2.57
German	4,360	4.06
Greek	594	0.55
Guyanese	281	0.26
Hawaii Native/Pacific Islander:	183	0.17
Micronesian: (27)	36	0.03
Guamanian/Chamorro (26)	35	0.03
Other Micronesian (1)	1	0.00
Polynesian: (12)	33	0.03
Native Hawaiian (9)	25	0.02
Samoan (3)	8	0.01
Other Pac. Isl., specified	4	0.00
Other Pac. Isl., not spec. (22)	110	0.10
Hispanic or Latino:	23,354	21.77
Central American:	186	0.17
Costa Rican	17	0.02
Guatemalan	55	0.05
Honduran	44	0.04
Nicaraguan	6	0.01
Panamanian	22	0.02
Salvadoran	27	0.03
Other Central American	15	0.01
Cuban	206	0.19
Dominican Republic	1,336	1.25
Mexican	588	0.55
Puerto Rican	18,149	16.92
South American:	568	0.53
Argentinean	31	0.03
Bolivian	1	0.00
Chilean	13	0.01
Colombian	181	0.17
Ecuadorian	238	0.22
Peruvian	47	0.04
Uruguayan	2	0.00
Venezuelan	40	0.04
Other South American	15	0.01
Other Hispanic or Latino	2,321	2.16
Hungarian	475	0.44
Iranian	28	0.03
Irish	12,514	11.67
Israeli	13	0.01
Italian	24,476	22.82
Latvian	12	0.01
Lithuanian	2,475	2.31
Macedonian	100	0.09
Norwegian	192	0.18
Pennsylvania German	30	0.03
Polish	3,329	3.10
Portuguese	2,023	1.89
Romanian	72	0.07
Russian	713	0.66
Scandinavian	12	0.01
Scotch-Irish	533	0.50
Scottish	955	0.89
Serbian	7	0.01
Slavic	7	0.01
Slovak	156	0.15
Swedish	657	0.61
Swiss	84	0.08
Turkish	84	0.08
Ukrainian	227	0.21
United States or American	2,138	1.99
Welsh	198	0.18
West Indian, excl. Hispanic:	1,830	1.71
Barbadian	75	0.07
British West Indian	79	0.07
Haitian	119	0.11
Jamaican	1,122	1.05
Trinidadian and Tobagonian	99	0.09
U.S. Virgin Islander	8	0.01
West Indian	322	0.30
Other West Indian	6	0.01
White:	74,757	69.69
Not Hispanic (62,406)	64,195	59.84
Hispanic (9,612)	10,562	9.85
Yugoslavian	150	0.14

Waterford

Place Type: Town
County: New London
Population: 19,152

Ancestry/Race	Number	%
African American/Black:	534	2.79
Not Hispanic (403)	501	2.62
Hispanic (23)	33	0.17
African, sub-Saharan:	37	0.19
African	23	0.12
Other sub-Saharan African	14	0.07
Alaska Native tribes, specified:	1	0.01
Tlingit-Haida	1	0.01
Am. Ind. or Alaska Nat., not spec.	53	0.28
Albanian	6	0.03
American Indian tribes, specified:	147	0.77
Apache (2)	2	0.01
Blackfeet	3	0.02
Cherokee (9)	25	0.13
Chippewa (1)	4	0.02
Choctaw	1	0.01
Cree	1	0.01
Crow	1	0.01
Iroquois (3)	11	0.06
Latin American Indians	2	0.01
Lumbee (1)	1	0.01
Potawatomi (1)	3	0.02
Pueblo	2	0.01
Sioux (1)	1	0.01
All other tribes (59)	90	0.47
American Indian tribes, not spec.	2	0.01
Arab:	100	0.52
Lebanese	93	0.49
Other Arab	7	0.04
Armenian	17	0.09
Asian:	567	2.96
Cambodian (49)	49	0.26
Chinese, ex. Taiwanese (187)	198	1.03
Filipino (89)	131	0.68
Indian (62)	68	0.36
Japanese (14)	26	0.14
Korean (27)	31	0.16
Laotian (8)	10	0.05
Taiwanese (11)	14	0.07
Thai (2)	2	0.01
Vietnamese (21)	21	0.11
Other Asian, specified (2)	2	0.01
Other Asian, not specified (4)	15	0.08
Austrian	75	0.39
Belgian	6	0.03
British	74	0.39
Canadian	87	0.45
Celtic	6	0.03
Croatian	49	0.26
Czech	27	0.14
Czechoslovakian	12	0.06
Danish	86	0.45
Dutch	261	1.36
Eastern European	23	0.12
English	3,177	16.59
Estonian	16	0.08
European	110	0.57
Finnish	78	0.41
French, except Basque	1,415	7.39
French Canadian	734	3.83
German	1,957	10.22
Greek	481	2.51
Hawaii Native/Pacific Islander:	12	0.06
Micronesian: (2)	8	0.04
Guamanian/Chamorro (2)	8	0.04
Other Pac. Isl., not spec. (1)	4	0.02
Hispanic or Latino:	459	2.40
Central American:	20	0.10
Costa Rican	1	0.01
Guatemalan	3	0.02
Honduran	2	0.01
Panamanian	4	0.02
Salvadoran	9	0.05
Other Central American	1	0.01
Cuban	20	0.10
Dominican Republic	21	0.11
Mexican	35	0.18
Puerto Rican	226	1.18
South American:	54	0.28
Argentinean	6	0.03
Chilean	3	0.02
Colombian	9	0.05
Ecuadorian	2	0.01
Paraguayan	2	0.01
Peruvian	27	0.14
Venezuelan	3	0.02
Other South American	2	0.01
Other Hispanic or Latino	83	0.43
Hungarian	85	0.44
Irish	4,480	23.39
Italian	4,012	20.95
Latvian	6	0.03
Lithuanian	138	0.72
Norwegian	258	1.35
Polish	1,494	7.80
Portuguese	545	2.85
Romanian	16	0.08
Russian	237	1.24
Scandinavian	19	0.10
Scotch-Irish	439	2.29
Scottish	542	2.83
Slavic	24	0.13
Slovak	27	0.14
Swedish	529	2.76
Swiss	63	0.33
Ukrainian	153	0.80
United States or American	583	3.04
Welsh	96	0.50
West Indian, excl. Hispanic:	122	0.64
Dutch West Indian	5	0.03
Haitian	29	0.15
Jamaican	51	0.27
Trinidadian and Tobagonian	14	0.07
West Indian	17	0.09
Other West Indian	6	0.03
White:	17,968	93.82
Not Hispanic (17,437)	17,676	92.29
Hispanic (262)	292	1.52

Watertown

Place Type: Town
County: Litchfield
Population: 21,661

Ancestry/Race	Number	%
African American/Black:	222	1.02
Not Hispanic (149)	204	0.94
Hispanic (13)	18	0.08
African, sub-Saharan:	8	0.04
Other sub-Saharan African	8	0.04
Am. Ind. or Alaska Nat., not spec.	33	0.15

Notes: 1. Figures in the "Number" column do not add up to the total population due to: a) Ancestry/Race overlap — e.g. persons can report being both White and Irish, b) persons of Hispanic origin can report being any race, c) persons reporting two ancestries are counted in both categories. 2. Numbers in parentheses indicate the number of persons reporting this ancestry/race alone, not in combination with any other ancestry/race. 3. Refer to the Explanation of Data in the front of the book for more detailed information.

Albanian	159	0.73
American Indian tribes, specified:	45	0.21
Blackfeet	1	0.00
Cherokee (1)	10	0.05
Chickasaw	2	0.01
Choctaw	1	0.00
Cree	4	0.02
Latin American Indians (1)	1	0.00
Pueblo (6)	6	0.03
Sioux (1)	2	0.01
All other tribes (6)	18	0.08
American Indian tribes, not spec.	3	0.01
Arab:	102	0.47
Lebanese	102	0.47
Armenian	25	0.12
Asian:	325	1.50
Bangladeshi (1)	1	0.00
Cambodian (4)	4	0.02
Chinese, ex. Taiwanese (34)	44	0.20
Filipino (68)	83	0.38
Indian (88)	94	0.43
Indonesian	1	0.00
Japanese (11)	12	0.06
Korean (25)	33	0.15
Laotian	2	0.01
Taiwanese (8)	8	0.04
Thai	2	0.01
Vietnamese (28)	34	0.16
Other Asian, not specified (1)	7	0.03
Australian	6	0.03
Austrian	63	0.29
British	107	0.49
Bulgarian	9	0.04
Canadian	42	0.19
Czech	134	0.62
Czechoslovakian	18	0.08
Danish	28	0.13
Dutch	132	0.61
English	2,194	10.13
European	38	0.18
Finnish	40	0.18
French, except Basque	2,244	10.36
French Canadian	1,200	5.54
German	1,994	9.21
Greek	97	0.45
Hawaii Native/Pacific Islander:	13	0.06
Micronesian: (1)	1	0.00
Guamanian/Chamorro (1)	1	0.00
Polynesian: (5)	8	0.04
Native Hawaiian (3)	6	0.03
Samoan (2)	2	0.01
Other Pac. Isl., not spec. (4)	4	0.02
Hispanic or Latino:	406	1.87
Central American:	6	0.03
Costa Rican	1	0.00
Guatemalan	1	0.00
Honduran	1	0.00
Nicaraguan	1	0.00
Salvadoran	2	0.01
Cuban	15	0.07
Dominican Republic	11	0.05
Mexican	34	0.16
Puerto Rican	240	1.11
South American:	34	0.16
Argentinean	5	0.02
Chilean	1	0.00
Colombian	4	0.02
Ecuadorian	8	0.04
Peruvian	4	0.02
Uruguayan	2	0.01
Venezuelan	8	0.04
Other South American	2	0.01
Other Hispanic or Latino	66	0.30
Hungarian	160	0.74
Irish	4,416	20.39
Italian	7,378	34.06
Latvian	9	0.04
Lithuanian	1,002	4.63
Macedonian	38	0.18
Norwegian	40	0.18
Polish	1,388	6.41
Portuguese	406	1.87
Russian	414	1.91
Scandinavian	53	0.24
Scotch-Irish	166	0.77
Scottish	500	2.31
Slovak	60	0.28
Swedish	327	1.51
Swiss	117	0.54
Ukrainian	133	0.61
United States or American	605	2.79
Welsh	51	0.24
West Indian, excl. Hispanic:	13	0.06
Haitian	13	0.06
White:	21,067	97.26
Not Hispanic (20,628)	20,777	95.92
Hispanic (266)	290	1.34

West Hartford

Place Type: Census Designated Place
County: Hartford
Population: 63,589

Ancestry/Race	Number	%
Afghan	4	0.01
African American/Black:	3,396	5.34
Not Hispanic (2,895)	3,165	4.98
Hispanic (146)	231	0.36
African, sub-Saharan:	407	0.64
African	73	0.11
Cape Verdean	6	0.01
Ethiopian	32	0.05
Ghanian	14	0.02
Liberian	5	0.01
Nigerian	87	0.14
Senegalese	32	0.05
Somalian	22	0.03
South African	104	0.16
Sudanese	6	0.01
Other sub-Saharan African	26	0.04
Alaska Native tribes, specified:	2	0.00
Eskimo	2	0.00
Am. Ind. or Alaska Nat., not spec.	113	0.18
American Indian tribes, specified:	123	0.19
Apache	2	0.00
Blackfeet (1)	5	0.01
Cherokee (2)	29	0.05
Chickasaw	3	0.00
Chippewa (1)	1	0.00
Choctaw (1)	3	0.00
Iroquois (1)	4	0.01
Kiowa (1)	1	0.00
Latin American Indians (11)	31	0.05
Menominee (2)	2	0.00
Potawatomi	1	0.00
Seminole (2)	2	0.00
Shoshone	1	0.00
Sioux (1)	1	0.00
Yaqui	1	0.00
Yuman (1)	1	0.00
All other tribes (13)	35	0.06
American Indian tribes, not spec.	20	0.03
Arab:	243	0.38
Arab/Arabic	8	0.01
Egyptian	15	0.02
Lebanese	174	0.27
Syrian	8	0.01
Other Arab	38	0.06
Armenian	161	0.25
Asian:	3,478	5.47
Bangladeshi (6)	17	0.03
Cambodian (75)	83	0.13
Chinese, ex. Taiwanese (703)	809	1.27
Filipino (120)	156	0.25
Indian (831)	959	1.51
Indonesian (12)	16	0.03
Japanese (60)	87	0.14
Korean (147)	166	0.26
Laotian (64)	67	0.11
Malaysian	2	0.00
Pakistani (54)	75	0.12
Sri Lankan (4)	5	0.01
Taiwanese (63)	69	0.11
Thai (34)	46	0.07
Vietnamese (725)	785	1.23
Other Asian, specified (12)	20	0.03
Other Asian, not specified (53)	116	0.18
Assyrian/Chaldean/Syriac	24	0.04
Australian	17	0.03
Austrian	613	0.96
Belgian	17	0.03
Brazilian	121	0.19
British	274	0.43
Canadian	445	0.70
Celtic	25	0.04
Croatian	26	0.04
Cypriot	8	0.01
Czech	152	0.24
Czechoslovakian	42	0.07
Danish	256	0.40
Dutch	370	0.58
Eastern European	370	0.58
English	6,513	10.24
European	665	1.05
Finnish	105	0.17
French, except Basque	2,640	4.15
French Canadian	1,574	2.48
German	5,645	8.88
Greek	517	0.81
Guyanese	26	0.04
Hawaii Native/Pacific Islander:	99	0.16
Melanesian: (4)	4	0.01
Fijian (4)	4	0.01
Micronesian: (3)	3	0.00
Guamanian/Chamorro (3)	3	0.00
Polynesian: (21)	32	0.05
Native Hawaiian (12)	21	0.03
Samoan (9)	11	0.02
Other Pac. Isl., specified	1	0.00
Other Pac. Isl., not spec. (18)	59	0.09
Hispanic or Latino:	3,990	6.27
Central American:	85	0.13
Costa Rican	10	0.02
Guatemalan	16	0.03
Honduran	8	0.01
Nicaraguan	5	0.01
Panamanian	11	0.02
Salvadoran	29	0.05
Other Central American	6	0.01
Cuban	166	0.26
Dominican Republic	119	0.19
Mexican	190	0.30
Puerto Rican	2,019	3.18
South American:	758	1.19
Argentinean	50	0.08
Bolivian	5	0.01
Chilean	28	0.04
Colombian	213	0.33
Ecuadorian	27	0.04
Paraguayan	3	0.00
Peruvian	363	0.57
Uruguayan	6	0.01
Venezuelan	21	0.03
Other South American	42	0.07
Other Hispanic or Latino	653	1.03
Hungarian	590	0.93
Icelander	18	0.03
Iranian	60	0.09
Irish	10,617	16.70
Israeli	78	0.12
Italian	6,875	10.81
Latvian	54	0.08
Lithuanian	682	1.07
Luxemburger	6	0.01
Northern European	121	0.19
Norwegian	353	0.56
Pennsylvania German	6	0.01
Polish	3,942	6.20
Portuguese	1,489	2.34

Notes: 1. Figures in the "Number" column do not add up to the total population due to: a) Ancestry/Race overlap — e.g. persons can report being both White and Irish, b) persons of Hispanic origin can report being any race, c) persons reporting two ancestries are counted in both categories. 2. Numbers in parentheses indicate the number of persons reporting this ancestry/race alone, not in combination with any other ancestry/race. 3. Refer to the Explanation of Data in the front of the book for more detailed information.

Romanian	269	0.42
Russian	3,662	5.76
Scandinavian	74	0.12
Scotch-Irish	956	1.50
Scottish	1,339	2.11
Serbian	5	0.01
Slavic	65	0.10
Slovak	142	0.22
Swedish	1,371	2.16
Swiss	124	0.20
Turkish	30	0.05
Ukrainian	658	1.03
United States or American	1,976	3.11
Welsh	377	0.59
West Indian, excl. Hispanic:	654	1.03
Barbadian	9	0.01
Haitian	8	0.01
Jamaican	546	0.86
Trinidadian and Tobagonian	10	0.02
U.S. Virgin Islander	23	0.04
West Indian	58	0.09
White:	55,414	87.14
Not Hispanic (52,684)	53,242	83.73
Hispanic (1,974)	2,172	3.42
Yugoslavian	88	0.14

West Haven

Place Type: City
County: New Haven
Population: 52,360

Ancestry/Race	Number	%
Afghan	19	0.04
African American/Black:	9,136	17.45
Not Hispanic (8,257)	8,731	16.67
Hispanic (273)	405	0.77
African, sub-Saharan:	678	1.29
African	209	0.40
Cape Verdean	161	0.31
Ethiopian	13	0.02
Ghanian	73	0.14
Liberian	47	0.09
Nigerian	128	0.24
Senegalese	27	0.05
Ugandan	6	0.01
Zimbabwean	7	0.01
Other sub-Saharan African	7	0.01
Alaska Native tribes, specified:	3	0.01
Aleut	1	0.00
Eskimo	2	0.00
Alaska Native tribes, not specified	1	0.00
Am. Ind. or Alaska Nat., not spec.	143	0.27
American Indian tribes, specified:	186	0.36
Apache (1)	3	0.01
Blackfeet (1)	8	0.02
Cherokee (9)	63	0.12
Chickasaw	1	0.00
Chippewa (2)	3	0.01
Choctaw (2)	2	0.00
Creek (1)	1	0.00
Delaware	1	0.00
Houma	1	0.00
Iroquois (4)	19	0.04
Latin American Indians (4)	13	0.02
Lumbee	1	0.00
Navajo	1	0.00
Pueblo	1	0.00
Seminole (1)	2	0.00
Shoshone (1)	1	0.00
Sioux	2	0.00
All other tribes (32)	63	0.12
American Indian tribes, not spec.	13	0.02
Arab:	561	1.07
Arab/Arabic	102	0.19
Egyptian	92	0.18
Jordanian	138	0.26
Lebanese	88	0.17
Palestinian	36	0.07
Syrian	75	0.14
Other Arab	30	0.06
Armenian	30	0.06
Asian:	1,736	3.32
Bangladeshi (15)	21	0.04
Cambodian (75)	75	0.14
Chinese, ex. Taiwanese (261)	282	0.54
Filipino (169)	189	0.36
Indian (479)	530	1.01
Indonesian (37)	38	0.07
Japanese (29)	42	0.08
Korean (127)	136	0.26
Laotian (24)	25	0.05
Malaysian (79)	87	0.17
Pakistani (73)	90	0.17
Sri Lankan	1	0.00
Taiwanese (3)	3	0.01
Thai (18)	24	0.05
Vietnamese (88)	97	0.19
Other Asian, specified (7)	7	0.01
Other Asian, not specified (33)	89	0.17
Austrian	135	0.26
Basque	11	0.02
Belgian	17	0.03
Brazilian	24	0.05
British	130	0.25
Bulgarian	12	0.02
Canadian	140	0.27
Celtic	28	0.05
Croatian	16	0.03
Cypriot	9	0.02
Czech	60	0.11
Czechoslovakian	143	0.27
Danish	78	0.15
Dutch	312	0.60
Eastern European	54	0.10
English	3,664	7.00
Estonian	24	0.05
European	98	0.19
French, except Basque	2,091	3.99
French Canadian	880	1.68
German	4,022	7.68
Greek	529	1.01
Guyanese	78	0.15
Hawaii Native/Pacific Islander:	69	0.13
Micronesian: (9)	14	0.03
Guamanian/Chamorro (9)	12	0.02
Other Micronesian	2	0.00
Polynesian: (16)	21	0.04
Native Hawaiian (9)	11	0.02
Samoan (6)	8	0.02
Other Polynesian (1)	2	0.00
Other Pac. Isl., not spec. (2)	34	0.06
Hispanic or Latino:	4,757	9.09
Central American:	219	0.42
Costa Rican	15	0.03
Guatemalan	128	0.24
Honduran	11	0.02
Nicaraguan	1	0.00
Panamanian	32	0.06
Salvadoran	26	0.05
Other Central American	6	0.01
Cuban	86	0.16
Dominican Republic	110	0.21
Mexican	451	0.86
Puerto Rican	2,510	4.79
South American:	614	1.17
Argentinean	41	0.08
Bolivian	1	0.00
Chilean	35	0.07
Colombian	332	0.63
Ecuadorian	72	0.14
Paraguayan	3	0.01
Peruvian	62	0.12
Uruguayan	3	0.01
Venezuelan	36	0.07
Other South American	29	0.06
Other Hispanic or Latino	767	1.46
Hungarian	449	0.86
Iranian	40	0.08
Irish	9,331	17.82
Italian	14,395	27.49
Latvian	26	0.05
Lithuanian	242	0.46
Norwegian	139	0.27
Pennsylvania German	30	0.06
Polish	2,824	5.39
Portuguese	797	1.52
Romanian	101	0.19
Russian	628	1.20
Scandinavian	19	0.04
Scotch-Irish	506	0.97
Scottish	486	0.93
Serbian	9	0.02
Slavic	15	0.03
Slovak	221	0.42
Swedish	515	0.98
Swiss	48	0.09
Turkish	256	0.49
Ukrainian	230	0.44
United States or American	1,320	2.52
Welsh	148	0.28
West Indian, excl. Hispanic:	856	1.63
Barbadian	18	0.03
Belizean	10	0.02
British West Indian	63	0.12
Haitian	79	0.15
Jamaican	502	0.96
Trinidadian and Tobagonian	35	0.07
U.S. Virgin Islander	17	0.03
West Indian	132	0.25
White:	39,901	76.21
Not Hispanic (36,521)	37,333	71.30
Hispanic (2,303)	2,568	4.90
Yugoslavian	20	0.04

Weston

Place Type: Town
County: Fairfield
Population: 10,037

Ancestry/Race	Number	%
African American/Black:	106	1.06
Not Hispanic (87)	105	1.05
Hispanic (1)	1	0.01
African, sub-Saharan:	15	0.15
South African	15	0.15
Am. Ind. or Alaska Nat., not spec.	7	0.07
American Indian tribes, specified:	11	0.11
Cherokee	3	0.03
Choctaw	1	0.01
Iroquois	1	0.01
Latin American Indians (3)	5	0.05
All other tribes	1	0.01
American Indian tribes, not spec.	5	0.05
Arab:	82	0.82
Egyptian	25	0.25
Lebanese	37	0.37
Syrian	20	0.20
Armenian	69	0.69
Asian:	255	2.54
Chinese, ex. Taiwanese (73)	96	0.96
Filipino (19)	26	0.26
Indian (51)	56	0.56
Japanese (12)	23	0.23
Korean (23)	37	0.37
Malaysian (1)	1	0.01
Thai (1)	1	0.01
Vietnamese (4)	4	0.04
Other Asian, specified (2)	2	0.02
Other Asian, not specified (7)	9	0.09
Australian	21	0.21
Austrian	133	1.33
Belgian	7	0.07
Brazilian	29	0.29
British	59	0.59
Bulgarian	14	0.14
Canadian	37	0.37
Czech	46	0.46
Czechoslovakian	22	0.22

Notes: 1. Figures in the "Number" column do not add up to the total population due to: a) Ancestry/Race overlap — e.g. persons can report being both White and Irish, b) persons of Hispanic origin can report being any race, c) persons reporting two ancestries are counted in both categories. 2. Numbers in parentheses indicate the number of persons reporting this ancestry/race alone, not in combination with any other ancestry/race. 3. Refer to the Explanation of Data in the front of the book for more detailed information.

Danish	104	1.04
Dutch	263	2.62
Eastern European	287	2.86
English	1,376	13.71
European	97	0.97
Finnish	14	0.14
French, except Basque	450	4.48
French Canadian	70	0.70
German	1,344	13.39
Greek	65	0.65
Guyanese	15	0.15
Hawaii Native/Pacific Islander:	14	0.14
Micronesian: (1)	2	0.02
Guamanian/Chamorro	1	0.01
Other Micronesian (1)	1	0.01
Polynesian: (7)	8	0.08
Native Hawaiian (3)	4	0.04
Samoan (4)	4	0.04
Other Pac. Isl., not spec. (2)	4	0.04
Hispanic or Latino:	206	2.05
Central American:	25	0.25
Costa Rican	8	0.08
Nicaraguan	4	0.04
Panamanian	4	0.04
Salvadoran	7	0.07
Other Central American	2	0.02
Cuban	31	0.31
Dominican Republic	1	0.01
Mexican	30	0.30
Puerto Rican	38	0.38
South American:	38	0.38
Argentinean	5	0.05
Bolivian	2	0.02
Chilean	5	0.05
Colombian	11	0.11
Ecuadorian	7	0.07
Paraguayan	1	0.01
Peruvian	2	0.02
Uruguayan	1	0.01
Venezuelan	4	0.04
Other Hispanic or Latino	43	0.43
Hungarian	197	1.96
Iranian	26	0.26
Irish	1,772	17.65
Italian	1,400	13.95
Latvian	20	0.20
Lithuanian	105	1.05
New Zealander	8	0.08
Northern European	28	0.28
Norwegian	159	1.58
Polish	614	6.12
Portuguese	29	0.29
Romanian	27	0.27
Russian	691	6.88
Scandinavian	12	0.12
Scotch-Irish	127	1.27
Scottish	148	1.47
Serbian	28	0.28
Slavic	6	0.06
Slovak	33	0.33
Slovene	6	0.06
Swedish	270	2.69
Swiss	86	0.86
Ukrainian	76	0.76
United States or American	698	6.95
Welsh	79	0.79
West Indian, excl. Hispanic:	57	0.57
British West Indian	8	0.08
Jamaican	24	0.24
West Indian	25	0.25
White:	9,704	96.68
Not Hispanic (9,443)	9,522	94.87
Hispanic (167)	182	1.81
Yugoslavian	12	0.12

Westport

Place Type: Census Designated Place
County: Fairfield
Population: 25,749

Ancestry/Race	Number	%
African American/Black:	336	1.30
Not Hispanic (279)	316	1.23
Hispanic (13)	20	0.08
African, sub-Saharan:	80	0.31
African	10	0.04
Nigerian	5	0.02
South African	65	0.25
Am. Ind. or Alaska Nat., not spec.	9	0.03
American Indian tribes, specified:	32	0.12
Blackfeet	1	0.00
Cherokee (1)	6	0.02
Chippewa (3)	5	0.02
Iroquois	2	0.01
Latin American Indians (4)	6	0.02
Lumbee (1)	1	0.00
Navajo (1)	1	0.00
Sioux	1	0.00
All other tribes (2)	9	0.03
Arab:	89	0.35
Arab/Arabic	4	0.02
Lebanese	60	0.23
Syrian	13	0.05
Other Arab	12	0.05
Armenian	48	0.19
Asian:	750	2.91
Chinese, ex. Taiwanese (273)	324	1.26
Filipino (30)	40	0.16
Indian (114)	132	0.51
Indonesian (3)	3	0.01
Japanese (64)	91	0.35
Korean (74)	91	0.35
Laotian (1)	1	0.00
Malaysian (1)	1	0.00
Pakistani (9)	11	0.04
Sri Lankan (5)	5	0.02
Taiwanese (3)	4	0.02
Thai (7)	8	0.03
Vietnamese (15)	16	0.06
Other Asian, not specified (13)	23	0.09
Assyrian/Chaldean/Syriac	6	0.02
Australian	27	0.10
Austrian	384	1.49
Basque	5	0.02
Belgian	63	0.24
Brazilian	70	0.27
British	313	1.22
Canadian	113	0.44
Croatian	17	0.07
Czech	133	0.52
Czechoslovakian	69	0.27
Danish	201	0.78
Dutch	287	1.11
Eastern European	508	1.97
English	3,531	13.71
European	415	1.61
Finnish	147	0.57
French, except Basque	858	3.33
French Canadian	148	0.57
German	3,341	12.98
Greek	521	2.02
Hawaii Native/Pacific Islander:	7	0.03
Melanesian: (1)	1	0.00
Fijian (1)	1	0.00
Micronesian: (1)	1	0.00
Guamanian/Chamorro (1)	1	0.00
Polynesian: (2)	4	0.02
Native Hawaiian (1)	2	0.01
Samoan (1)	1	0.00
Other Polynesian	1	0.00
Other Pac. Isl., not spec. (1)	1	0.00
Hispanic or Latino:	602	2.34
Central American:	29	0.11
Costa Rican	7	0.03
Guatemalan	9	0.03
Honduran	5	0.02
Nicaraguan	2	0.01
Salvadoran	6	0.02
Cuban	84	0.33
Dominican Republic	16	0.06
Mexican	81	0.31
Puerto Rican	82	0.32
South American:	132	0.51
Argentinean	18	0.07
Bolivian	9	0.03
Chilean	4	0.02
Colombian	42	0.16
Ecuadorian	19	0.07
Paraguayan	2	0.01
Peruvian	26	0.10
Venezuelan	9	0.03
Other South American	3	0.01
Other Hispanic or Latino	178	0.69
Hungarian	473	1.84
Irish	4,054	15.74
Israeli	41	0.16
Italian	3,789	14.72
Latvian	3	0.01
Lithuanian	181	0.70
Maltese	16	0.06
Northern European	36	0.14
Norwegian	440	1.71
Pennsylvania German	4	0.02
Polish	1,435	5.57
Portuguese	64	0.25
Romanian	179	0.70
Russian	2,012	7.81
Scandinavian	48	0.19
Scotch-Irish	365	1.42
Scottish	727	2.82
Serbian	22	0.09
Slavic	10	0.04
Slovak	191	0.74
Swedish	518	2.01
Swiss	251	0.97
Turkish	21	0.08
Ukrainian	222	0.86
United States or American	1,768	6.87
Welsh	125	0.49
West Indian, excl. Hispanic:	42	0.16
Haitian	5	0.02
Jamaican	33	0.13
Trinidadian and Tobagonian	4	0.02
White:	24,693	95.90
Not Hispanic (24,015)	24,178	93.90
Hispanic (488)	515	2.00
Yugoslavian	65	0.25

Wethersfield

Place Type: Census Designated Place
County: Hartford
Population: 26,271

Ancestry/Race	Number	%
African American/Black:	654	2.49
Not Hispanic (514)	594	2.26
Hispanic (35)	60	0.23
African, sub-Saharan:	46	0.18
African	15	0.06
Cape Verdean	31	0.12
Alaska Native tribes, specified:	1	0.00
Tlingit-Haida (1)	1	0.00
Am. Ind. or Alaska Nat., not spec.	23	0.09
Albanian	35	0.13
Alsatian	6	0.02
American Indian tribes, specified:	32	0.12
Blackfeet	2	0.01
Cherokee (2)	5	0.02
Iroquois	1	0.00
Latin American Indians (9)	13	0.05
Navajo	1	0.00
Sioux (1)	1	0.00
All other tribes (5)	9	0.03

Notes: 1. Figures in the "Number" column do not add up to the total population due to: a) Ancestry/Race overlap — e.g. persons can report being both White and Irish, b) persons of Hispanic origin can report being any race, c) persons reporting two ancestries are counted in both categories. 2. Numbers in parentheses indicate the number of persons reporting this ancestry/race alone, not in combination with any other ancestry/race. 3. Refer to the Explanation of Data in the front of the book for more detailed information.

Ancestry/Race	Number	%
American Indian tribes, not spec.	3	0.01
Arab:	38	0.14
Lebanese	38	0.14
Armenian	110	0.42
Asian:	517	1.97
Bangladeshi	11	0.04
Chinese, ex. Taiwanese (111)	133	0.51
Filipino (50)	60	0.23
Indian (125)	164	0.62
Japanese (7)	10	0.04
Korean (26)	32	0.12
Laotian (8)	10	0.04
Pakistani (16)	20	0.08
Sri Lankan (4)	4	0.02
Taiwanese (3)	5	0.02
Thai (1)	1	0.00
Vietnamese (31)	33	0.13
Other Asian, specified (1)	2	0.01
Other Asian, not specified (10)	32	0.12
Austrian	69	0.26
Belgian	16	0.06
Brazilian	126	0.48
British	75	0.29
Bulgarian	88	0.34
Canadian	124	0.47
Croatian	63	0.24
Czech	47	0.18
Czechoslovakian	71	0.27
Danish	41	0.16
Dutch	196	0.75
Eastern European	17	0.06
English	2,339	8.92
Estonian	6	0.02
European	93	0.35
Finnish	15	0.06
French, except Basque	1,580	6.02
French Canadian	882	3.36
German	1,925	7.34
Greek	405	1.54
Hawaii Native/Pacific Islander:	23	0.09
Micronesian: (2)	4	0.02
Guamanian/Chamorro (2)	4	0.02
Polynesian: (1)	9	0.03
Native Hawaiian (1)	3	0.01
Samoan	6	0.02
Other Pac. Isl., specified	1	0.00
Other Pac. Isl., not spec. (3)	9	0.03
Hispanic or Latino:	1,101	4.19
Central American:	18	0.07
Costa Rican	4	0.02
Guatemalan	3	0.01
Honduran	3	0.01
Nicaraguan	1	0.00
Panamanian	1	0.00
Salvadoran	6	0.02
Cuban	32	0.12
Dominican Republic	34	0.13
Mexican	39	0.15
Puerto Rican	646	2.46
South American:	178	0.68
Argentinean	30	0.11
Bolivian	1	0.00
Chilean	4	0.02
Colombian	53	0.20
Ecuadorian	6	0.02
Paraguayan	3	0.01
Peruvian	57	0.22
Uruguayan	1	0.00
Venezuelan	14	0.05
Other South American	9	0.03
Other Hispanic or Latino	154	0.59
Hungarian	139	0.53
Irish	5,323	20.29
Israeli	7	0.03
Italian	8,333	31.76
Lithuanian	378	1.44
Norwegian	121	0.46
Pennsylvania German	15	0.06
Polish	3,072	11.71
Portuguese	635	2.42
Romanian	118	0.45
Russian	343	1.31
Scotch-Irish	339	1.29
Scottish	461	1.76
Slavic	41	0.16
Slovak	57	0.22
Swedish	481	1.83
Swiss	9	0.03
Ukrainian	472	1.80
United States or American	626	2.39
Welsh	65	0.25
West Indian, excl. Hispanic:	170	0.65
Jamaican	137	0.52
Trinidadian and Tobagonian	15	0.06
West Indian	18	0.07
White:	24,731	94.14
Not Hispanic (23,957)	24,143	91.90
Hispanic (524)	588	2.24
Yugoslavian	55	0.21

Willimantic

Place Type: Census Designated Place
County: Windham
Population: 15,823

Ancestry/Race	Number	%
African American/Black:	1,222	7.72
Not Hispanic (816)	956	6.04
Hispanic (173)	266	1.68
African, sub-Saharan:	64	0.40
African	55	0.35
Kenyan	3	0.02
Nigerian	6	0.04
Alaska Native tribes, specified:	2	0.01
Eskimo (1)	2	0.01
Am. Ind. or Alaska Nat., not spec.	91	0.58
American Indian tribes, specified:	106	0.67
Blackfeet (3)	16	0.10
Cherokee (3)	17	0.11
Chippewa	3	0.02
Choctaw	1	0.01
Iroquois (3)	6	0.04
Latin American Indians (14)	25	0.16
Lumbee (1)	1	0.01
Navajo (1)	1	0.01
Seminole	3	0.02
Sioux (1)	7	0.04
All other tribes (11)	26	0.16
American Indian tribes, not spec.	13	0.08
Arab:	110	0.70
Arab/Arabic	22	0.14
Lebanese	88	0.56
Asian:	331	2.09
Bangladeshi (8)	8	0.05
Chinese, ex. Taiwanese (77)	81	0.51
Filipino (10)	15	0.09
Indian (49)	64	0.40
Indonesian (2)	2	0.01
Japanese (9)	15	0.09
Korean (53)	59	0.37
Laotian (8)	8	0.05
Pakistani (4)	9	0.06
Sri Lankan (4)	4	0.03
Taiwanese (2)	2	0.01
Thai (7)	10	0.06
Vietnamese (29)	31	0.20
Other Asian, not specified (1)	23	0.15
Austrian	22	0.14
Belgian	4	0.03
Brazilian	7	0.04
British	65	0.41
Bulgarian	14	0.09
Canadian	108	0.68
Czech	25	0.16
Czechoslovakian	13	0.08
Danish	41	0.26
Dutch	80	0.51
English	1,006	6.36
European	62	0.39
Finnish	49	0.31
French, except Basque	1,694	10.71
French Canadian	1,032	6.52
German	1,083	6.84
Greek	73	0.46
Hawaii Native/Pacific Islander:	41	0.26
Melanesian:	1	0.01
Fijian	1	0.01
Micronesian: (1)	4	0.03
Guamanian/Chamorro (1)	2	0.01
Other Micronesian	2	0.01
Polynesian: (11)	11	0.07
Native Hawaiian (2)	2	0.01
Samoan (9)	9	0.06
Other Pac. Isl., not spec. (9)	25	0.16
Hispanic or Latino:	4,777	30.19
Central American:	86	0.54
Costa Rican	2	0.01
Guatemalan	48	0.30
Honduran	1	0.01
Panamanian	23	0.15
Salvadoran	12	0.08
Cuban	42	0.27
Dominican Republic	71	0.45
Mexican	902	5.70
Puerto Rican	3,310	20.92
South American:	93	0.59
Argentinean	6	0.04
Bolivian	3	0.02
Chilean	5	0.03
Colombian	32	0.20
Ecuadorian	17	0.11
Peruvian	16	0.10
Venezuelan	13	0.08
Other South American	1	0.01
Other Hispanic or Latino	273	1.73
Hungarian	70	0.44
Iranian	4	0.03
Irish	2,003	12.66
Italian	1,298	8.20
Latvian	58	0.37
Lithuanian	42	0.27
Maltese	21	0.13
Norwegian	59	0.37
Polish	839	5.30
Portuguese	62	0.39
Russian	156	0.99
Scandinavian	18	0.11
Scotch-Irish	197	1.25
Scottish	172	1.09
Serbian	6	0.04
Slovak	15	0.09
Swedish	228	1.44
Swiss	16	0.10
Turkish	9	0.06
Ukrainian	157	0.99
United States or American	397	2.51
Welsh	19	0.12
West Indian, excl. Hispanic:	147	0.93
Bermudan	14	0.09
Haitian	23	0.15
Jamaican	65	0.41
West Indian	45	0.28
White:	11,683	73.84
Not Hispanic (9,589)	9,827	62.11
Hispanic (1,543)	1,856	11.73
Yugoslavian	7	0.04

Wilton

Place Type: Town
County: Fairfield
Population: 17,633

Ancestry/Race	Number	%
African American/Black:	140	0.79
Not Hispanic (97)	127	0.72
Hispanic (9)	13	0.07
African, sub-Saharan:	40	0.23
African	12	0.07

Notes: 1. Figures in the "Number" column do not add up to the total population due to: a) Ancestry/Race overlap — e.g. persons can report being both White and Irish, b) persons of Hispanic origin can report being any race, c) persons reporting two ancestries are counted in both categories. 2. Numbers in parentheses indicate the number of persons reporting this ancestry/race alone, not in combination with any other ancestry/race. 3. Refer to the Explanation of Data in the front of the book for more detailed information.

Ancestry/Race	Number	%
South African	28	0.16
Am. Ind. or Alaska Nat., not spec.	18	0.10
Albanian	34	0.19
American Indian tribes, specified:	26	0.15
Blackfeet	4	0.02
Cherokee	11	0.06
Chickasaw	1	0.01
Choctaw	1	0.01
Iroquois (2)	3	0.02
Latin American Indians	2	0.01
Pueblo (2)	2	0.01
All other tribes	2	0.01
American Indian tribes, not spec.	4	0.02
Arab:	62	0.35
Jordanian	17	0.10
Lebanese	35	0.20
Other Arab	10	0.06
Armenian	86	0.49
Asian:	558	3.16
Bangladeshi (4)	4	0.02
Chinese, ex. Taiwanese (157)	185	1.05
Filipino (48)	57	0.32
Indian (127)	144	0.82
Japanese (36)	56	0.32
Korean (70)	77	0.44
Laotian (1)	2	0.01
Pakistani (1)	1	0.01
Sri Lankan (2)	2	0.01
Thai (7)	10	0.06
Vietnamese (15)	16	0.09
Other Asian, specified	1	0.01
Other Asian, not specified (2)	3	0.02
Austrian	225	1.28
Basque	27	0.15
Belgian	51	0.29
Brazilian	5	0.03
British	127	0.72
Canadian	172	0.98
Croatian	15	0.09
Czech	253	1.43
Czechoslovakian	45	0.26
Danish	135	0.77
Dutch	273	1.55
Eastern European	163	0.92
English	3,104	17.60
Estonian	17	0.10
European	186	1.05
French, except Basque	588	3.33
French Canadian	131	0.74
German	2,973	16.86
Greek	193	1.09
Hawaii Native/Pacific Islander:	9	0.05
Polynesian: (1)	5	0.03
Native Hawaiian	4	0.02
Samoan (1)	1	0.01
Other Pac. Isl., specified	1	0.01
Other Pac. Isl., not spec. (1)	3	0.02
Hispanic or Latino:	269	1.53
Central American:	11	0.06
Costa Rican	4	0.02
Guatemalan	2	0.01
Honduran	2	0.01
Nicaraguan	1	0.01
Panamanian	1	0.01
Salvadoran	1	0.01
Cuban	22	0.12
Dominican Republic	6	0.03
Mexican	40	0.23
Puerto Rican	45	0.26
South American:	65	0.37
Argentinean	5	0.03
Bolivian	2	0.01
Chilean	11	0.06
Colombian	13	0.07
Ecuadorian	3	0.02
Paraguayan	3	0.02
Peruvian	12	0.07
Venezuelan	8	0.05
Other South American	8	0.05
Other Hispanic or Latino	80	0.45
Hungarian	201	1.14
Icelander	20	0.11
Iranian	62	0.35
Irish	3,966	22.49
Israeli	46	0.26
Italian	2,762	15.66
Lithuanian	77	0.44
Macedonian	7	0.04
New Zealander	8	0.05
Norwegian	340	1.93
Pennsylvania German	8	0.05
Polish	1,005	5.70
Portuguese	111	0.63
Romanian	7	0.04
Russian	721	4.09
Scandinavian	57	0.32
Scotch-Irish	321	1.82
Scottish	631	3.58
Slavic	28	0.16
Slovak	86	0.49
Slovene	19	0.11
Swedish	412	2.34
Swiss	83	0.47
Ukrainian	47	0.27
United States or American	970	5.50
Welsh	296	1.68
West Indian, excl. Hispanic:	15	0.09
Belizean	5	0.03
Bermudan	6	0.03
West Indian	4	0.02
White:	16,974	96.26
Not Hispanic (16,640)	16,746	94.97
Hispanic (208)	228	1.29
Yugoslavian	9	0.05

Winchester

Place Type: Town
County: Litchfield
Population: 10,664

Ancestry/Race	Number	%
African American/Black:	184	1.73
Not Hispanic (89)	137	1.28
Hispanic (43)	47	0.44
African, sub-Saharan:	2	0.02
African	2	0.02
Am. Ind. or Alaska Nat., not spec.	29	0.27
American Indian tribes, specified:	39	0.37
Blackfeet	3	0.03
Cherokee (2)	4	0.04
Cheyenne (1)	1	0.01
Creek	3	0.03
Iroquois (1)	3	0.03
Latin American Indians (3)	3	0.03
Seminole	1	0.01
Sioux	1	0.01
All other tribes (9)	20	0.19
American Indian tribes, not spec.	6	0.06
Arab:	54	0.51
Lebanese	48	0.45
Other Arab	6	0.06
Asian:	129	1.21
Cambodian (2)	2	0.02
Chinese, ex. Taiwanese (19)	29	0.27
Filipino (8)	10	0.09
Indian (7)	9	0.08
Indonesian (2)	6	0.06
Japanese (1)	4	0.04
Korean (11)	15	0.14
Laotian	1	0.01
Vietnamese (44)	51	0.48
Other Asian, not specified (1)	2	0.02
Assyrian/Chaldean/Syriac	7	0.07
Austrian	16	0.15
Belgian	17	0.16
Brazilian	44	0.41
British	70	0.66
Canadian	78	0.73
Czech	140	1.31
Czechoslovakian	27	0.25
Danish	71	0.67
Dutch	130	1.22
Eastern European	7	0.07
English	1,521	14.26
European	27	0.25
Finnish	35	0.33
French, except Basque	1,434	13.45
French Canadian	431	4.04
German	1,427	13.38
Greek	161	1.51
Hawaii Native/Pacific Islander:	10	0.09
Micronesian: (1)	1	0.01
Guamanian/Chamorro (1)	1	0.01
Polynesian:	7	0.07
Native Hawaiian	7	0.07
Other Pac. Isl., not spec.	2	0.02
Hispanic or Latino:	338	3.17
Central American:	4	0.04
Guatemalan	2	0.02
Panamanian	1	0.01
Other Central American	1	0.01
Cuban	7	0.07
Dominican Republic	130	1.22
Mexican	20	0.19
Puerto Rican	74	0.69
South American:	27	0.25
Argentinean	5	0.05
Chilean	3	0.03
Colombian	4	0.04
Ecuadorian	11	0.10
Uruguayan	4	0.04
Other Hispanic or Latino	76	0.71
Hungarian	103	0.97
Irish	2,014	18.89
Italian	2,220	20.82
Latvian	21	0.20
Lithuanian	89	0.83
Macedonian	28	0.26
Northern European	12	0.11
Norwegian	114	1.07
Polish	784	7.35
Portuguese	67	0.63
Romanian	22	0.21
Russian	54	0.51
Scotch-Irish	136	1.28
Scottish	211	1.98
Serbian	5	0.05
Slavic	6	0.06
Slovak	113	1.06
Swedish	361	3.39
Swiss	42	0.39
Ukrainian	85	0.80
United States or American	471	4.42
Welsh	86	0.81
West Indian, excl. Hispanic:	26	0.24
Jamaican	24	0.23
West Indian	2	0.02
White:	10,210	95.74
Not Hispanic (9,961)	10,085	94.57
Hispanic (110)	125	1.17

Windham

Place Type: Town
County: Windham
Population: 22,857

Ancestry/Race	Number	%
African American/Black:	1,431	6.26
Not Hispanic (906)	1,078	4.72
Hispanic (250)	353	1.54
African, sub-Saharan:	72	0.32
African	63	0.28
Kenyan	3	0.01
Nigerian	6	0.03
Alaska Native tribes, specified:	2	0.01
Eskimo (1)	2	0.01
Am. Ind. or Alaska Nat., not spec.	113	0.49
American Indian tribes, specified:	150	0.66

Notes: 1. Figures in the "Number" column do not add up to the total population due to: a) Ancestry/Race overlap — e.g. persons can report being both White and Irish, b) persons of Hispanic origin can report being any race, c) persons reporting two ancestries are counted in both categories. 2. Numbers in parentheses indicate the number of persons reporting this ancestry/race alone, not in combination with any other ancestry/race. 3. Refer to the Explanation of Data in the front of the book for more detailed information.

Apache (1)	1	0.00
Blackfeet (5)	20	0.09
Cherokee (10)	32	0.14
Chippewa	3	0.01
Choctaw	1	0.00
Iroquois (6)	10	0.04
Latin American Indians (14)	29	0.13
Lumbee (1)	1	0.00
Navajo (1)	1	0.00
Pueblo	1	0.00
Seminole	3	0.01
Sioux (1)	7	0.03
All other tribes (22)	41	0.18
American Indian tribes, not spec.	18	0.08
Arab:	130	0.57
Arab/Arabic	22	0.10
Lebanese	99	0.43
Other Arab	9	0.04
Asian:	383	1.68
Bangladeshi (8)	8	0.04
Chinese, ex. Taiwanese (87)	91	0.40
Filipino (11)	17	0.07
Indian (52)	67	0.29
Indonesian (2)	2	0.01
Japanese (11)	31	0.14
Korean (67)	73	0.32
Laotian (8)	9	0.04
Pakistani (4)	10	0.04
Sri Lankan (4)	4	0.02
Taiwanese (2)	2	0.01
Thai (7)	10	0.04
Vietnamese (31)	33	0.14
Other Asian, specified	2	0.01
Other Asian, not specified (2)	24	0.11
Australian	8	0.04
Austrian	43	0.19
Belgian	4	0.02
Brazilian	7	0.03
British	81	0.35
Bulgarian	14	0.06
Canadian	174	0.76
Croatian	9	0.04
Czech	77	0.34
Czechoslovakian	39	0.17
Danish	41	0.18
Dutch	180	0.79
English	1,840	8.05
European	114	0.50
Finnish	59	0.26
French, except Basque	2,538	11.10
French Canadian	1,518	6.64
German	1,581	6.92
Greek	80	0.35
Hawaii Native/Pacific Islander:	56	0.25
Melanesian:	1	0.00
Fijian	1	0.00
Micronesian: (6)	9	0.04
Guamanian/Chamorro (6)	7	0.03
Other Micronesian	2	0.01
Polynesian: (13)	18	0.08
Native Hawaiian (3)	7	0.03
Samoan (10)	11	0.05
Other Pac. Isl., not spec. (9)	28	0.12
Hispanic or Latino:	6,136	26.85
Central American:	88	0.39
Costa Rican	2	0.01
Guatemalan	49	0.21
Honduran	1	0.00
Panamanian	23	0.10
Salvadoran	13	0.06
Cuban	44	0.19
Dominican Republic	96	0.42
Mexican	977	4.27
Puerto Rican	4,462	19.52
South American:	106	0.46
Argentinean	7	0.03
Bolivian	3	0.01
Chilean	6	0.03
Colombian	36	0.16
Ecuadorian	18	0.08
Peruvian	19	0.08
Venezuelan	13	0.06
Other South American	4	0.02
Other Hispanic or Latino	363	1.59
Hungarian	121	0.53
Iranian	4	0.02
Irish	3,067	13.42
Italian	1,841	8.05
Latvian	97	0.42
Lithuanian	135	0.59
Maltese	21	0.09
Norwegian	75	0.33
Polish	1,552	6.79
Portuguese	114	0.50
Russian	300	1.31
Scandinavian	27	0.12
Scotch-Irish	302	1.32
Scottish	272	1.19
Serbian	6	0.03
Slovak	24	0.11
Swedish	293	1.28
Swiss	16	0.07
Turkish	9	0.04
Ukrainian	376	1.65
United States or American	666	2.91
Welsh	74	0.32
West Indian, excl. Hispanic:	212	0.93
Bermudan	14	0.06
British West Indian	15	0.07
Haitian	23	0.10
Jamaican	65	0.28
West Indian	95	0.42
White:	17,659	77.26
Not Hispanic (14,999)	15,329	67.06
Hispanic (1,920)	2,330	10.19
Yugoslavian	7	0.03

Windsor Locks

Place Type: Census Designated Place
County: Hartford
Population: 12,043

Ancestry/Race	Number	%
African American/Black:	376	3.12
Not Hispanic (311)	360	2.99
Hispanic (11)	16	0.13
African, sub-Saharan:	52	0.43
African	12	0.10
Ghanian	40	0.33
Am. Ind. or Alaska Nat., not spec.	21	0.17
Alsatian	7	0.06
American Indian tribes, specified:	37	0.31
Blackfeet	1	0.01
Cherokee (1)	11	0.09
Choctaw	1	0.01
Iroquois (1)	4	0.03
Latin American Indians (1)	2	0.02
Seminole (1)	1	0.01
Sioux (1)	1	0.01
All other tribes (5)	16	0.13
American Indian tribes, not spec.	2	0.02
Arab:	105	0.87
Arab/Arabic	98	0.81
Egyptian	7	0.06
Armenian	19	0.16
Asian:	361	3.00
Cambodian (13)	13	0.11
Chinese, ex. Taiwanese (41)	44	0.37
Filipino (16)	28	0.23
Indian (119)	129	1.07
Japanese (3)	6	0.05
Korean (35)	37	0.31
Laotian (21)	23	0.19
Pakistani (15)	30	0.25
Thai (2)	9	0.07
Vietnamese (21)	21	0.17
Other Asian, specified	1	0.01
Other Asian, not specified (15)	20	0.17
Austrian	23	0.19
Basque	11	0.09
Belgian	7	0.06
British	60	0.50
Canadian	11	0.09
Croatian	13	0.11
Czech	69	0.57
Czechoslovakian	32	0.27
Danish	59	0.49
Dutch	78	0.65
English	1,363	11.32
European	38	0.32
French, except Basque	1,232	10.23
French Canadian	712	5.91
German	1,270	10.55
Greek	83	0.69
Guyanese	11	0.09
Hawaii Native/Pacific Islander:	6	0.05
Polynesian:	3	0.02
Native Hawaiian	2	0.02
Samoan	1	0.01
Other Pac. Isl., specified	1	0.01
Other Pac. Isl., not spec.	2	0.02
Hispanic or Latino:	267	2.22
Central American:	7	0.06
Guatemalan	1	0.01
Honduran	2	0.02
Panamanian	3	0.02
Salvadoran	1	0.01
Cuban	5	0.04
Dominican Republic	1	0.01
Mexican	30	0.25
Puerto Rican	171	1.42
South American:	25	0.21
Colombian	6	0.05
Ecuadorian	9	0.07
Peruvian	9	0.07
Venezuelan	1	0.01
Other Hispanic or Latino	28	0.23
Hungarian	69	0.57
Irish	2,414	20.04
Italian	2,318	19.25
Lithuanian	202	1.68
Norwegian	38	0.32
Polish	1,748	14.51
Portuguese	281	2.33
Romanian	10	0.08
Russian	54	0.45
Scotch-Irish	162	1.35
Scottish	206	1.71
Slovak	82	0.68
Swedish	343	2.85
Swiss	38	0.32
Ukrainian	39	0.32
United States or American	482	4.00
Welsh	72	0.60
West Indian, excl. Hispanic:	50	0.42
British West Indian	8	0.07
Jamaican	42	0.35
White:	11,279	93.66
Not Hispanic (11,000)	11,115	92.29
Hispanic (136)	164	1.36

Windsor

Place Type: Town
County: Hartford
Population: 28,237

Ancestry/Race	Number	%
Acadian/Cajun	7	0.02
African American/Black:	8,079	28.61
Not Hispanic (7,529)	7,908	28.01
Hispanic (119)	171	0.61
African, sub-Saharan:	159	0.56
African	102	0.36
Cape Verdean	16	0.06
Nigerian	41	0.15
Am. Ind. or Alaska Nat., not spec.	88	0.31
Albanian	7	0.02
American Indian tribes, specified:	106	0.38

Notes: 1. Figures in the "Number" column do not add up to the total population due to: a) Ancestry/Race overlap — e.g. persons can report being both White and Irish, b) persons of Hispanic origin can report being any race, c) persons reporting two ancestries are counted in both categories. 2. Numbers in parentheses indicate the number of persons reporting this ancestry/race alone, not in combination with any other ancestry/race. 3. Refer to the Explanation of Data in the front of the book for more detailed information.

Apache	1	0.00
Blackfeet	4	0.01
Cherokee (2)	34	0.12
Chickasaw (3)	5	0.02
Choctaw	1	0.00
Crow	1	0.00
Iroquois	8	0.03
Latin American Indians (3)	9	0.03
Pueblo (4)	4	0.01
Seminole	2	0.01
Sioux (1)	5	0.02
All other tribes (7)	32	0.11
American Indian tribes, not spec.	11	0.04
Arab:	95	0.34
Arab/Arabic	14	0.05
Egyptian	37	0.13
Lebanese	38	0.13
Syrian	6	0.02
Armenian	13	0.05
Asian:	1,025	3.63
Bangladeshi (5)	5	0.02
Cambodian (6)	11	0.04
Chinese, ex. Taiwanese (174)	201	0.71
Filipino (69)	81	0.29
Indian (323)	355	1.26
Indonesian (3)	4	0.01
Japanese (14)	20	0.07
Korean (42)	53	0.19
Laotian (15)	17	0.06
Pakistani (21)	36	0.13
Sri Lankan (5)	5	0.02
Taiwanese (13)	14	0.05
Thai (1)	1	0.00
Vietnamese (172)	183	0.65
Other Asian, specified (3)	6	0.02
Other Asian, not specified (9)	33	0.12
Austrian	87	0.31
Basque	29	0.10
Belgian	21	0.07
Brazilian	9	0.03
British	145	0.51
Canadian	107	0.38
Croatian	34	0.12
Czech	15	0.05
Czechoslovakian	36	0.13
Danish	186	0.66
Dutch	151	0.53
Eastern European	24	0.08
English	2,794	9.89
European	68	0.24
Finnish	49	0.17
French, except Basque	1,491	5.28
French Canadian	1,052	3.73
German	2,114	7.49
Greek	127	0.45
Guyanese	139	0.49
Hawaii Native/Pacific Islander:	32	0.11
Micronesian:	1	0.00
Guamanian/Chamorro	1	0.00
Polynesian: (2)	2	0.01
Samoan (2)	2	0.01
Other Pac. Isl., specified	3	0.01
Other Pac. Isl., not spec. (6)	26	0.09
Hispanic or Latino:	1,405	4.98
Central American:	35	0.12
Costa Rican	4	0.01
Guatemalan	11	0.04
Honduran	3	0.01
Panamanian	5	0.02
Salvadoran	10	0.04
Other Central American	2	0.01
Cuban	48	0.17
Dominican Republic	14	0.05
Mexican	78	0.28
Puerto Rican	928	3.29
South American:	127	0.45
Argentinean	8	0.03
Chilean	2	0.01
Colombian	42	0.15
Ecuadorian	13	0.05
Paraguayan	3	0.01
Peruvian	50	0.18
Venezuelan	6	0.02
Other South American	3	0.01
Other Hispanic or Latino	175	0.62
Hungarian	102	0.36
Irish	3,952	14.00
Italian	3,318	11.75
Latvian	7	0.02
Lithuanian	419	1.48
Luxemburger	7	0.02
Macedonian	7	0.02
Maltese	8	0.03
Northern European	39	0.14
Norwegian	148	0.52
Polish	2,256	7.99
Portuguese	525	1.86
Romanian	22	0.08
Russian	388	1.37
Scandinavian	43	0.15
Scotch-Irish	313	1.11
Scottish	525	1.86
Serbian	6	0.02
Slavic	22	0.08
Slovak	92	0.33
Swedish	413	1.46
Swiss	31	0.11
Ukrainian	232	0.82
United States or American	831	2.94
Welsh	188	0.67
West Indian, excl. Hispanic:	1,794	6.35
Barbadian	35	0.12
British West Indian	91	0.32
Haitian	56	0.20
Jamaican	1,442	5.11
Trinidadian and Tobagonian	4	0.01
U.S. Virgin Islander	11	0.04
West Indian	155	0.55
White:	18,769	66.47
Not Hispanic (17,758)	18,087	64.05
Hispanic (629)	682	2.42
Yugoslavian	37	0.13

Wolcott

Place Type: Town
County: New Haven
Population: 15,215

Ancestry/Race	Number	%
African American/Black:	232	1.52
Not Hispanic (185)	225	1.48
Hispanic (4)	7	0.05
African, sub-Saharan:	30	0.20
Cape Verdean	23	0.15
Other sub-Saharan African	7	0.05
Alaska Native tribes, specified:	2	0.01
Alaska Athabascan (2)	2	0.01
Am. Ind. or Alaska Nat., not spec.	26	0.17
Albanian	60	0.39
American Indian tribes, specified:	37	0.24
Blackfeet (2)	2	0.01
Cherokee	6	0.04
Chippewa (1)	1	0.01
Iroquois (2)	2	0.01
Latin American Indians	2	0.01
Shoshone (1)	1	0.01
All other tribes (7)	23	0.15
American Indian tribes, not spec.	4	0.03
Arab:	169	1.11
Jordanian	20	0.13
Lebanese	124	0.81
Palestinian	25	0.16
Armenian	9	0.06
Asian:	144	0.95
Chinese, ex. Taiwanese (19)	23	0.15
Filipino (17)	25	0.16
Indian (41)	43	0.28
Indonesian	1	0.01
Japanese (2)	2	0.01
Korean (16)	22	0.14
Pakistani (3)	10	0.07
Vietnamese (10)	10	0.07
Other Asian, not specified (3)	8	0.05
Austrian	68	0.45
Belgian	10	0.07
Bulgarian	14	0.09
Canadian	48	0.32
Czech	18	0.12
Czechoslovakian	8	0.05
Danish	81	0.53
Dutch	118	0.78
Eastern European	6	0.04
English	1,291	8.49
European	10	0.07
Finnish	7	0.05
French, except Basque	2,172	14.28
French Canadian	912	5.99
German	1,628	10.70
Greek	11	0.07
Hawaii Native/Pacific Islander:	9	0.06
Polynesian: (6)	9	0.06
Native Hawaiian (3)	5	0.03
Samoan (3)	4	0.03
Hispanic or Latino:	273	1.79
Central American:	3	0.02
Salvadoran	3	0.02
Cuban	6	0.04
Dominican Republic	9	0.06
Mexican	23	0.15
Puerto Rican	174	1.14
South American:	19	0.12
Argentinean	1	0.01
Chilean	3	0.02
Colombian	11	0.07
Peruvian	2	0.01
Uruguayan	1	0.01
Other South American	1	0.01
Other Hispanic or Latino	39	0.26
Hungarian	217	1.43
Irish	3,171	20.84
Italian	5,804	38.15
Lithuanian	328	2.16
Norwegian	20	0.13
Polish	1,447	9.51
Portuguese	237	1.56
Romanian	6	0.04
Russian	301	1.98
Scotch-Irish	136	0.89
Scottish	256	1.68
Slavic	8	0.05
Slovak	6	0.04
Slovene	18	0.12
Swedish	249	1.64
Swiss	9	0.06
Turkish	13	0.09
Ukrainian	32	0.21
United States or American	297	1.95
Welsh	58	0.38
West Indian, excl. Hispanic:	7	0.05
U.S. Virgin Islander	7	0.05
White:	14,780	97.14
Not Hispanic (14,486)	14,593	95.91
Hispanic (155)	187	1.23

Bear

Place Type: Census Designated Place
County: New Castle
Population: 17,593

Ancestry/Race	Number	%
Acadian/Cajun	11	0.06
African American/Black:	4,983	28.32
Not Hispanic (4,575)	4,794	27.25
Hispanic (139)	189	1.07
African, sub-Saharan:	108	0.62
African	59	0.34
Nigerian	49	0.28
Am. Ind. or Alaska Nat., not spec.	44	0.25

Notes: 1. Figures in the "Number" column do not add up to the total population due to: a) Ancestry/Race overlap — e.g. persons can report being both White and Irish, b) persons of Hispanic origin can report being any race, c) persons reporting two ancestries are counted in both categories. 2. Numbers in parentheses indicate the number of persons reporting this ancestry/race alone, not in combination with any other ancestry/race. 3. Refer to the Explanation of Data in the front of the book for more detailed information.

American Indian tribes, specified:	65	0.37
Apache (1)	1	0.01
Blackfeet (2)	6	0.03
Cherokee (6)	32	0.18
Choctaw	2	0.01
Iroquois	2	0.01
Latin American Indians (7)	10	0.06
Lumbee (2)	2	0.01
Navajo (2)	2	0.01
Potawatomi (1)	2	0.01
Seminole	2	0.01
Sioux (1)	2	0.01
All other tribes	2	0.01
American Indian tribes, not spec.	3	0.02
Arab:	45	0.26
Arab/Arabic	7	0.04
Egyptian	30	0.17
Syrian	8	0.05
Armenian	9	0.05
Asian:	430	2.44
Cambodian	4	0.02
Chinese, ex. Taiwanese (49)	52	0.30
Filipino (90)	105	0.60
Indian (86)	94	0.53
Indonesian (13)	13	0.07
Japanese (5)	18	0.10
Korean (28)	49	0.28
Laotian	4	0.02
Pakistani (22)	23	0.13
Thai (1)	2	0.01
Vietnamese (49)	52	0.30
Other Asian, specified	1	0.01
Other Asian, not specified (9)	13	0.07
Austrian	17	0.10
British	16	0.09
Canadian	15	0.09
Celtic	5	0.03
Czech	8	0.05
Czechoslovakian	29	0.17
Danish	78	0.45
Dutch	220	1.26
English	1,256	7.20
European	39	0.22
Finnish	8	0.05
French, except Basque	309	1.77
French Canadian	71	0.41
German	2,487	14.26
Greek	161	0.92
Guyanese	26	0.15
Hawaii Native/Pacific Islander:	13	0.07
Polynesian:	1	0.01
Native Hawaiian	1	0.01
Other Pac. Isl., specified	1	0.01
Other Pac. Isl., not spec. (4)	11	0.06
Hispanic or Latino:	968	5.50
Central American:	32	0.18
Honduran	4	0.02
Panamanian	14	0.08
Salvadoran	13	0.07
Other Central American	1	0.01
Cuban	24	0.14
Dominican Republic	50	0.28
Mexican	207	1.18
Puerto Rican	469	2.67
South American:	42	0.24
Argentinean	3	0.02
Bolivian	1	0.01
Chilean	1	0.01
Colombian	25	0.14
Ecuadorian	5	0.03
Peruvian	4	0.02
Venezuelan	2	0.01
Other South American	1	0.01
Other Hispanic or Latino	144	0.82
Hungarian	20	0.11
Irish	3,141	18.01
Italian	1,802	10.33
Latvian	7	0.04
Lithuanian	69	0.40
Norwegian	28	0.16
Pennsylvania German	79	0.45
Polish	807	4.63
Portuguese	8	0.05
Russian	85	0.49
Scandinavian	16	0.09
Scotch-Irish	157	0.90
Scottish	172	0.99
Slavic	5	0.03
Slovak	31	0.18
Swedish	70	0.40
Swiss	48	0.28
Ukrainian	81	0.46
United States or American	732	4.20
Welsh	163	0.93
West Indian, excl. Hispanic:	129	0.74
Jamaican	77	0.44
Trinidadian and Tobagonian	29	0.17
West Indian	23	0.13
White:	12,063	68.57
Not Hispanic (11,338)	11,582	65.83
Hispanic (434)	481	2.73
Yugoslavian	14	0.08

Brookside

Place Type: Census Designated Place
County: New Castle
Population: 14,806

Ancestry/Race	Number	%
Afghan	47	0.32
African American/Black:	2,392	16.16
Not Hispanic (2,174)	2,328	15.72
Hispanic (51)	64	0.43
African, sub-Saharan:	167	1.13
African	149	1.01
Kenyan	18	0.12
Alaska Native tribes, specified:	1	0.01
Eskimo (1)	1	0.01
Am. Ind. or Alaska Nat., not spec.	48	0.32
American Indian tribes, specified:	55	0.37
Blackfeet	1	0.01
Cherokee (6)	24	0.16
Delaware (1)	3	0.02
Iroquois	6	0.04
Latin American Indians (10)	14	0.09
Navajo	2	0.01
Potawatomi (2)	2	0.01
All other tribes	3	0.02
American Indian tribes, not spec.	8	0.05
Arab:	111	0.75
Arab/Arabic	18	0.12
Egyptian	32	0.22
Lebanese	14	0.09
Palestinian	7	0.05
Syrian	20	0.13
Other Arab	20	0.13
Armenian	5	0.03
Asian:	494	3.34
Chinese, ex. Taiwanese (100)	107	0.72
Filipino (59)	76	0.51
Indian (99)	108	0.73
Indonesian (1)	1	0.01
Japanese (8)	17	0.11
Korean (24)	36	0.24
Laotian (18)	19	0.13
Pakistani (16)	21	0.14
Thai (5)	7	0.05
Vietnamese (26)	28	0.19
Other Asian, specified (4)	8	0.05
Other Asian, not specified (20)	66	0.45
Australian	9	0.06
Austrian	24	0.16
Belgian	8	0.05
British	69	0.47
Canadian	13	0.09
Croatian	13	0.09
Czech	10	0.07
Czechoslovakian	14	0.09
Danish	29	0.20
Dutch	260	1.75
English	1,596	10.77
European	22	0.15
French, except Basque	375	2.53
French Canadian	54	0.36
German	2,082	14.05
Greek	83	0.56
Guyanese	24	0.16
Hawaii Native/Pacific Islander:	22	0.15
Micronesian: (4)	8	0.05
Guamanian/Chamorro (4)	8	0.05
Polynesian:	1	0.01
Native Hawaiian	1	0.01
Other Pac. Isl., specified	4	0.03
Other Pac. Isl., not spec. (7)	9	0.06
Hispanic or Latino:	827	5.59
Central American:	15	0.10
Costa Rican	1	0.01
Guatemalan	3	0.02
Nicaraguan	3	0.02
Panamanian	3	0.02
Salvadoran	5	0.03
Cuban	29	0.20
Dominican Republic	22	0.15
Mexican	305	2.06
Puerto Rican	288	1.95
South American:	57	0.38
Chilean	4	0.03
Colombian	32	0.22
Ecuadorian	2	0.01
Peruvian	12	0.08
Venezuelan	2	0.01
Other South American	5	0.03
Other Hispanic or Latino	111	0.75
Hungarian	45	0.30
Iranian	22	0.15
Irish	2,685	18.12
Italian	1,431	9.66
Latvian	12	0.08
Lithuanian	89	0.60
Norwegian	70	0.47
Pennsylvania German	66	0.45
Polish	871	5.88
Romanian	4	0.03
Russian	58	0.39
Scandinavian	13	0.09
Scotch-Irish	387	2.61
Scottish	356	2.40
Slavic	14	0.09
Slovak	18	0.12
Swedish	156	1.05
Swiss	26	0.18
Ukrainian	90	0.61
United States or American	804	5.43
Welsh	119	0.80
West Indian, excl. Hispanic:	48	0.32
Barbadian	8	0.05
Trinidadian and Tobagonian	7	0.05
West Indian	33	0.22
White:	11,755	79.39
Not Hispanic (11,070)	11,332	76.54
Hispanic (382)	423	2.86

Dover

Place Type: City
County: Kent
Population: 32,135

Ancestry/Race	Number	%
African American/Black:	12,467	38.80
Not Hispanic (11,776)	12,207	37.99
Hispanic (185)	260	0.81
African, sub-Saharan:	793	2.44
African	516	1.59
Cape Verdean	18	0.06
Ghanian	74	0.23
Liberian	19	0.06
Nigerian	137	0.42
Sierra Leonean	13	0.04

Notes: 1. Figures in the "Number" column do not add up to the total population due to: a) Ancestry/Race overlap — e.g. persons can report being both White and Irish, b) persons of Hispanic origin can report being any race, c) persons reporting two ancestries are counted in both categories. 2. Numbers in parentheses indicate the number of persons reporting this ancestry/race alone, not in combination with any other ancestry/race. 3. Refer to the Explanation of Data in the front of the book for more detailed information.

South African	9	0.03
Other sub-Saharan African	7	0.02
Am. Ind. or Alaska Nat., not spec.	137	0.43
Albanian	8	0.02
American Indian tribes, specified:	206	0.64
Apache (1)	1	0.00
Blackfeet (5)	28	0.09
Cherokee (17)	48	0.15
Chickasaw	1	0.00
Chippewa (3)	6	0.02
Choctaw (3)	3	0.01
Creek (2)	3	0.01
Crow	1	0.00
Delaware (18)	30	0.09
Iroquois (7)	11	0.03
Kiowa (2)	2	0.01
Latin American Indians (1)	15	0.05
Navajo (4)	10	0.03
Osage (1)	1	0.00
Seminole	3	0.01
Sioux	1	0.00
All other tribes (23)	42	0.13
American Indian tribes, not spec.	44	0.14
Arab:	111	0.34
Arab/Arabic	5	0.02
Egyptian	51	0.16
Lebanese	17	0.05
Moroccan	8	0.02
Other Arab	30	0.09
Asian:	1,236	3.85
Cambodian (2)	2	0.01
Chinese, ex. Taiwanese (101)	118	0.37
Filipino (188)	258	0.80
Indian (267)	281	0.87
Indonesian (1)	1	0.00
Japanese (56)	83	0.26
Korean (233)	255	0.79
Malaysian	3	0.01
Pakistani (29)	30	0.09
Sri Lankan (7)	7	0.02
Taiwanese (2)	4	0.01
Thai (51)	73	0.23
Vietnamese (43)	55	0.17
Other Asian, specified	11	0.03
Other Asian, not specified (27)	55	0.17
Austrian	43	0.13
Belgian	14	0.04
Brazilian	8	0.02
British	255	0.79
Canadian	100	0.31
Croatian	6	0.02
Czech	79	0.24
Czechoslovakian	36	0.11
Danish	42	0.13
Dutch	253	0.78
English	2,987	9.20
European	65	0.20
Finnish	22	0.07
French, except Basque	777	2.39
French Canadian	366	1.13
German	4,232	13.03
Greek	40	0.12
Hawaii Native/Pacific Islander:	63	0.20
Micronesian: (1)	2	0.01
Other Micronesian (1)	2	0.01
Polynesian: (5)	26	0.08
Native Hawaiian (4)	24	0.07
Samoan (1)	2	0.01
Other Pac. Isl., specified	11	0.03
Other Pac. Isl., not spec. (6)	24	0.07
Hispanic or Latino:	1,327	4.13
Central American:	61	0.19
Guatemalan	17	0.05
Honduran	2	0.01
Nicaraguan	1	0.00
Panamanian	31	0.10
Salvadoran	9	0.03
Other Central American	1	0.00
Cuban	49	0.15
Dominican Republic	25	0.08
Mexican	284	0.88
Puerto Rican	616	1.92
South American:	66	0.21
Bolivian	10	0.03
Colombian	13	0.04
Ecuadorian	25	0.08
Peruvian	8	0.02
Venezuelan	9	0.03
Other South American	1	0.00
Other Hispanic or Latino	226	0.70
Hungarian	104	0.32
Iranian	9	0.03
Irish	3,395	10.46
Israeli	23	0.07
Italian	1,831	5.64
Latvian	11	0.03
Lithuanian	58	0.18
Norwegian	239	0.74
Pennsylvania German	44	0.14
Polish	764	2.35
Portuguese	46	0.14
Russian	75	0.23
Scandinavian	9	0.03
Scotch-Irish	496	1.53
Scottish	474	1.46
Slavic	4	0.01
Slovak	125	0.38
Slovene	9	0.03
Soviet Union	7	0.02
Swedish	193	0.59
Swiss	38	0.12
Turkish	15	0.05
Ukrainian	93	0.29
United States or American	1,265	3.90
Welsh	257	0.79
West Indian, excl. Hispanic:	338	1.04
Bahamian	25	0.08
Bermudan	3	0.01
British West Indian	45	0.14
Haitian	105	0.32
Jamaican	96	0.30
Trinidadian and Tobagonian	23	0.07
U.S. Virgin Islander	6	0.02
West Indian	35	0.11
White:	18,214	56.68
Not Hispanic (17,123)	17,580	54.71
Hispanic (532)	634	1.97
Yugoslavian	26	0.08

Glasgow

Place Type: Census Designated Place
County: New Castle
Population: 12,840

Ancestry/Race	Number	%
African American/Black:	2,269	17.67
Not Hispanic (2,160)	2,230	17.37
Hispanic (25)	39	0.30
African, sub-Saharan:	126	0.99
African	99	0.78
Ghanian	21	0.16
Nigerian	6	0.05
Am. Ind. or Alaska Nat., not spec.	25	0.19
American Indian tribes, specified:	31	0.24
Blackfeet (2)	3	0.02
Cherokee (8)	15	0.12
Choctaw (2)	2	0.02
Iroquois	2	0.02
Latin American Indians (2)	5	0.04
Lumbee	1	0.01
Navajo (1)	1	0.01
All other tribes	2	0.02
American Indian tribes, not spec.	2	0.02
Arab:	65	0.51
Egyptian	13	0.10
Jordanian	29	0.23
Lebanese	14	0.11
Syrian	9	0.07
Armenian	20	0.16
Asian:	350	2.73
Bangladeshi (4)	4	0.03
Chinese, ex. Taiwanese (31)	35	0.27
Filipino (47)	67	0.52
Indian (100)	105	0.82
Indonesian (2)	2	0.02
Japanese (2)	7	0.05
Korean (38)	41	0.32
Laotian (12)	12	0.09
Pakistani (21)	25	0.19
Sri Lankan (4)	4	0.03
Taiwanese (7)	8	0.06
Thai (2)	2	0.02
Vietnamese (23)	25	0.19
Other Asian, not specified (5)	13	0.10
Austrian	46	0.36
Brazilian	23	0.18
British	89	0.70
Canadian	18	0.14
Croatian	15	0.12
Czech	35	0.27
Czechoslovakian	19	0.15
Danish	43	0.34
Dutch	202	1.59
English	1,631	12.81
European	61	0.48
French, except Basque	211	1.66
French Canadian	97	0.76
German	2,316	18.19
Greek	36	0.28
Guyanese	11	0.09
Hawaii Native/Pacific Islander:	7	0.05
Micronesian: (3)	6	0.05
Guamanian/Chamorro (3)	6	0.05
Other Pac. Isl., not spec.	1	0.01
Hispanic or Latino:	386	3.01
Central American:	16	0.12
Guatemalan	3	0.02
Honduran	1	0.01
Nicaraguan	2	0.02
Panamanian	9	0.07
Other Central American	1	0.01
Cuban	11	0.09
Dominican Republic	3	0.02
Mexican	80	0.62
Puerto Rican	182	1.42
South American:	26	0.20
Bolivian	1	0.01
Chilean	2	0.02
Colombian	10	0.08
Ecuadorian	8	0.06
Peruvian	2	0.02
Venezuelan	2	0.02
Other South American	1	0.01
Other Hispanic or Latino	68	0.53
Hungarian	49	0.38
Iranian	26	0.20
Irish	2,174	17.07
Italian	1,407	11.05
Lithuanian	43	0.34
Luxemburger	5	0.04
Norwegian	32	0.25
Polish	1,095	8.60
Portuguese	29	0.23
Romanian	12	0.09
Russian	125	0.98
Scotch-Irish	273	2.14
Scottish	274	2.15
Slavic	25	0.20
Slovak	18	0.14
Slovene	33	0.26
Swedish	109	0.86
Swiss	69	0.54
Turkish	30	0.24
Ukrainian	110	0.86
United States or American	588	4.62
Welsh	68	0.53
West Indian, excl. Hispanic:	129	1.01
Barbadian	26	0.20
Bermudan	10	0.08

Notes: 1. Figures in the "Number" column do not add up to the total population due to: a) Ancestry/Race overlap — e.g. persons can report being both White and Irish, b) persons of Hispanic origin can report being any race, c) persons reporting two ancestries are counted in both categories. 2. Numbers in parentheses indicate the number of persons reporting this ancestry/race alone, not in combination with any other ancestry/race. 3. Refer to the Explanation of Data in the front of the book for more detailed information.

Jamaican	87	0.68
West Indian	6	0.05
White:	10,150	79.05
Not Hispanic (9,808)	9,919	77.25
Hispanic (205)	231	1.80

Hockessin

Place Type: Census Designated Place
County: New Castle
Population: 12,902

Ancestry/Race	Number	%
African American/Black:	367	2.84
Not Hispanic (341)	363	2.81
Hispanic (1)	4	0.03
African, sub-Saharan:	43	0.33
Nigerian	43	0.33
Am. Ind. or Alaska Nat., not spec.	11	0.09
Alsatian	10	0.08
American Indian tribes, specified:	16	0.12
Cherokee (4)	11	0.09
Sioux (1)	1	0.01
All other tribes	4	0.03
American Indian tribes, not spec.	1	0.01
Arab:	22	0.17
Lebanese	13	0.10
Syrian	9	0.07
Armenian	13	0.10
Asian:	987	7.65
Chinese, ex. Taiwanese (379)	413	3.20
Filipino (66)	71	0.55
Indian (282)	296	2.29
Indonesian (1)	3	0.02
Japanese (14)	22	0.17
Korean (110)	116	0.90
Pakistani (14)	14	0.11
Taiwanese (39)	40	0.31
Thai (1)	1	0.01
Vietnamese (5)	7	0.05
Other Asian, not specified (2)	4	0.03
Austrian	100	0.78
Belgian	16	0.12
British	115	0.89
Canadian	104	0.81
Celtic	33	0.26
Czech	31	0.24
Czechoslovakian	13	0.10
Danish	85	0.66
Dutch	340	2.64
English	2,148	16.66
Estonian	20	0.16
European	72	0.56
Finnish	8	0.06
French, except Basque	321	2.49
French Canadian	41	0.32
German	1,959	15.19
Greek	144	1.12
Hawaii Native/Pacific Islander:	1	0.01
Micronesian: (1)	1	0.01
Guamanian/Chamorro (1)	1	0.01
Hispanic or Latino:	257	1.99
Central American:	16	0.12
Costa Rican	1	0.01
Guatemalan	3	0.02
Honduran	10	0.08
Nicaraguan	1	0.01
Panamanian	1	0.01
Cuban	40	0.31
Dominican Republic	4	0.03
Mexican	74	0.57
Puerto Rican	43	0.33
South American:	31	0.24
Argentinean	2	0.02
Bolivian	1	0.01
Colombian	15	0.12
Ecuadorian	4	0.03
Paraguayan	2	0.02
Peruvian	4	0.03
Venezuelan	1	0.01
Other South American	2	0.02
Other Hispanic or Latino	49	0.38
Hungarian	134	1.04
Iranian	102	0.79
Irish	2,711	21.02
Israeli	4	0.03
Italian	2,266	17.57
Latvian	7	0.05
Lithuanian	93	0.72
Northern European	16	0.12
Norwegian	78	0.60
Pennsylvania German	31	0.24
Polish	1,049	8.13
Portuguese	90	0.70
Romanian	7	0.05
Russian	188	1.46
Scandinavian	19	0.15
Scotch-Irish	281	2.18
Scottish	393	3.05
Slavic	16	0.12
Slovak	21	0.16
Slovene	9	0.07
Swedish	193	1.50
Swiss	16	0.12
Ukrainian	127	0.98
United States or American	447	3.47
Welsh	166	1.29
White:	11,551	89.53
Not Hispanic (11,280)	11,346	87.94
Hispanic (180)	205	1.59
Yugoslavian	10	0.08

Newark

Place Type: City
County: New Castle
Population: 28,547

Ancestry/Race	Number	%
Afghan	8	0.03
African American/Black:	1,854	6.49
Not Hispanic (1,690)	1,815	6.36
Hispanic (24)	39	0.14
African, sub-Saharan:	234	0.82
African	174	0.61
Ethiopian	14	0.05
Ghanian	21	0.07
South African	25	0.09
Alaska Native tribes, specified:	1	0.00
Eskimo	1	0.00
Am. Ind. or Alaska Nat., not spec.	53	0.19
Albanian	8	0.03
American Indian tribes, specified:	56	0.20
Blackfeet (3)	6	0.02
Cherokee (10)	29	0.10
Choctaw (1)	1	0.00
Cree (1)	1	0.00
Crow	1	0.00
Delaware	2	0.01
Iroquois (3)	6	0.02
Latin American Indians (1)	2	0.01
Lumbee	1	0.00
Potawatomi (1)	1	0.00
Pueblo	1	0.00
Puget Sound Salish	2	0.01
Sioux (1)	1	0.00
All other tribes (1)	2	0.01
American Indian tribes, not spec.	24	0.08
Arab:	178	0.62
Arab/Arabic	66	0.23
Egyptian	23	0.08
Lebanese	43	0.15
Palestinian	13	0.05
Other Arab	33	0.12
Armenian	25	0.09
Asian:	1,347	4.72
Bangladeshi (2)	3	0.01
Cambodian (2)	2	0.01
Chinese, ex. Taiwanese (457)	497	1.74
Filipino (51)	85	0.30
Indian (311)	337	1.18
Indonesian (2)	2	0.01
Japanese (61)	87	0.30
Korean (118)	131	0.46
Laotian (7)	8	0.03
Malaysian (2)	2	0.01
Pakistani (22)	25	0.09
Sri Lankan (5)	5	0.02
Taiwanese (25)	30	0.11
Thai (25)	29	0.10
Vietnamese (28)	32	0.11
Other Asian, specified (4)	5	0.02
Other Asian, not specified (24)	67	0.23
Austrian	173	0.61
Belgian	25	0.09
Brazilian	53	0.19
British	168	0.59
Bulgarian	80	0.28
Canadian	63	0.22
Celtic	6	0.02
Croatian	43	0.15
Czech	87	0.30
Czechoslovakian	67	0.23
Danish	82	0.29
Dutch	362	1.27
Eastern European	77	0.27
English	3,752	13.13
European	415	1.45
Finnish	34	0.12
French, except Basque	744	2.60
French Canadian	165	0.58
German	4,909	17.18
Greek	245	0.86
Guyanese	9	0.03
Hawaii Native/Pacific Islander:	26	0.09
Micronesian: (1)	1	0.00
Guamanian/Chamorro (1)	1	0.00
Polynesian: (6)	10	0.04
Native Hawaiian (3)	7	0.02
Samoan (2)	2	0.01
Other Polynesian (1)	1	0.00
Other Pac. Isl., specified	1	0.00
Other Pac. Isl., not spec. (7)	14	0.05
Hispanic or Latino:	721	2.53
Central American:	29	0.10
Costa Rican	7	0.02
Guatemalan	1	0.00
Honduran	2	0.01
Nicaraguan	4	0.01
Panamanian	11	0.04
Salvadoran	4	0.01
Cuban	45	0.16
Dominican Republic	14	0.05
Mexican	132	0.46
Puerto Rican	195	0.68
South American:	153	0.54
Argentinean	27	0.09
Bolivian	6	0.02
Chilean	9	0.03
Colombian	62	0.22
Ecuadorian	21	0.07
Paraguayan	1	0.00
Peruvian	9	0.03
Uruguayan	1	0.00
Venezuelan	12	0.04
Other South American	5	0.02
Other Hispanic or Latino	153	0.54
Hungarian	334	1.17
Iranian	13	0.05
Irish	5,762	20.17
Israeli	52	0.18
Italian	3,787	13.26
Latvian	18	0.06
Lithuanian	224	0.78
Luxemburger	5	0.02
Northern European	72	0.25
Norwegian	291	1.02
Pennsylvania German	38	0.13
Polish	1,714	6.00
Portuguese	96	0.34

Notes: 1. Figures in the "Number" column do not add up to the total population due to: a) Ancestry/Race overlap — e.g. persons can report being both White and Irish, b) persons of Hispanic origin can report being any race, c) persons reporting two ancestries are counted in both categories. 2. Numbers in parentheses indicate the number of persons reporting this ancestry/race alone, not in combination with any other ancestry/race. 3. Refer to the Explanation of Data in the front of the book for more detailed information.

Ancestry/Race	Number	%
Romanian	63	0.22
Russian	679	2.38
Scandinavian	31	0.11
Scotch-Irish	464	1.62
Scottish	749	2.62
Serbian	27	0.09
Slavic	13	0.05
Slovak	170	0.60
Slovene	4	0.01
Swedish	400	1.40
Swiss	96	0.34
Turkish	50	0.18
Ukrainian	210	0.74
United States or American	1,119	3.92
Welsh	296	1.04
West Indian, excl. Hispanic:	146	0.51
Bermudan	31	0.11
Dutch West Indian	8	0.03
Haitian	21	0.07
Jamaican	77	0.27
West Indian	9	0.03
White:	25,317	88.69
Not Hispanic (24,464)	24,826	86.97
Hispanic (455)	491	1.72
Yugoslavian	11	0.04

Pike Creek

Place Type: Census Designated Place
County: New Castle
Population: 19,751

Ancestry/Race	Number	%
African American/Black:	872	4.41
Not Hispanic (792)	849	4.30
Hispanic (16)	23	0.12
African, sub-Saharan:	50	0.25
African	12	0.06
Nigerian	29	0.15
South African	9	0.05
Am. Ind. or Alaska Nat., not spec.	31	0.16
American Indian tribes, specified:	41	0.21
Apache	1	0.01
Blackfeet (2)	2	0.01
Cherokee (7)	13	0.07
Comanche	2	0.01
Creek (1)	1	0.01
Crow	2	0.01
Delaware (1)	1	0.01
Iroquois	1	0.01
Latin American Indians (2)	2	0.01
Lumbee	1	0.01
Osage	1	0.01
Pueblo	1	0.01
Seminole	1	0.01
Sioux	2	0.01
All other tribes (7)	10	0.05
Arab:	121	0.61
Arab/Arabic	43	0.22
Lebanese	6	0.03
Palestinian	24	0.12
Syrian	48	0.24
Armenian	31	0.16
Asian:	1,201	6.08
Chinese, ex. Taiwanese (300)	328	1.66
Filipino (37)	49	0.25
Hmong (1)	1	0.01
Indian (354)	361	1.83
Indonesian (7)	10	0.05
Japanese (42)	60	0.30
Korean (257)	269	1.36
Laotian (1)	1	0.01
Malaysian (2)	4	0.02
Pakistani (31)	49	0.25
Taiwanese (12)	18	0.09
Thai (2)	2	0.01
Vietnamese (25)	25	0.13
Other Asian, specified (9)	9	0.05
Other Asian, not specified (6)	15	0.08
Austrian	70	0.35
Brazilian	19	0.10
British	84	0.43
Canadian	49	0.25
Croatian	45	0.23
Czech	39	0.20
Czechoslovakian	91	0.46
Danish	55	0.28
Dutch	265	1.34
Eastern European	40	0.20
English	2,591	13.12
Estonian	18	0.09
European	225	1.14
Finnish	27	0.14
French, except Basque	469	2.37
French Canadian	204	1.03
German	3,605	18.26
Greek	236	1.20
Guyanese	12	0.06
Hawaii Native/Pacific Islander:	25	0.13
Micronesian: (2)	2	0.01
Guamanian/Chamorro (2)	2	0.01
Polynesian: (5)	5	0.03
Samoan (5)	5	0.03
Other Pac. Isl., not spec. (12)	18	0.09
Hispanic or Latino:	511	2.59
Central American:	22	0.11
Costa Rican	9	0.05
Guatemalan	2	0.01
Honduran	3	0.02
Panamanian	3	0.02
Salvadoran	3	0.02
Other Central American	2	0.01
Cuban	47	0.24
Dominican Republic	20	0.10
Mexican	109	0.55
Puerto Rican	130	0.66
South American:	99	0.50
Argentinean	8	0.04
Chilean	9	0.05
Colombian	25	0.13
Ecuadorian	9	0.05
Paraguayan	2	0.01
Peruvian	20	0.10
Venezuelan	25	0.13
Other South American	2	0.01
Other Hispanic or Latino	84	0.43
Hungarian	175	0.89
Icelander	6	0.03
Iranian	10	0.05
Irish	4,406	22.31
Italian	3,619	18.33
Lithuanian	154	0.78
Northern European	80	0.41
Norwegian	126	0.64
Pennsylvania German	27	0.14
Polish	1,624	8.22
Portuguese	38	0.19
Romanian	40	0.20
Russian	261	1.32
Scandinavian	20	0.10
Scotch-Irish	321	1.63
Scottish	513	2.60
Serbian	21	0.11
Slavic	14	0.07
Slovak	129	0.65
Swedish	265	1.34
Swiss	65	0.33
Ukrainian	257	1.30
United States or American	752	3.81
Welsh	247	1.25
West Indian, excl. Hispanic:	63	0.32
British West Indian	6	0.03
Haitian	40	0.20
Jamaican	9	0.05
West Indian	8	0.04
White:	17,634	89.28
Not Hispanic (17,099)	17,258	87.38
Hispanic (341)	376	1.90
Yugoslavian	15	0.08

Wilmington

Place Type: City
County: New Castle
Population: 72,664

Ancestry/Race	Number	%
African American/Black:	41,976	57.77
Not Hispanic (40,545)	41,266	56.79
Hispanic (456)	710	0.98
African, sub-Saharan:	1,924	2.65
African	1,833	2.52
Ethiopian	3	0.00
Kenyan	11	0.02
Nigerian	21	0.03
South African	21	0.03
Ugandan	8	0.01
Zimbabwean	10	0.01
Other sub-Saharan African	17	0.02
Am. Ind. or Alaska Nat., not spec.	264	0.36
Albanian	9	0.01
American Indian tribes, specified:	281	0.39
Apache	1	0.00
Blackfeet (3)	30	0.04
Cherokee (25)	110	0.15
Cheyenne (1)	5	0.01
Chippewa	1	0.00
Choctaw (1)	2	0.00
Cree	1	0.00
Creek (1)	4	0.01
Crow	1	0.00
Delaware (1)	7	0.01
Iroquois (3)	5	0.01
Latin American Indians (21)	41	0.06
Lumbee (2)	2	0.00
Navajo (2)	4	0.01
Potawatomi (1)	1	0.00
Pueblo	3	0.00
Seminole (1)	6	0.01
Shoshone	1	0.00
Sioux (1)	4	0.01
Ute	1	0.00
All other tribes (13)	51	0.07
American Indian tribes, not spec.	41	0.06
Arab:	86	0.12
Egyptian	36	0.05
Lebanese	34	0.05
Moroccan	16	0.02
Armenian	19	0.03
Asian:	603	0.83
Bangladeshi (4)	6	0.01
Chinese, ex. Taiwanese (96)	114	0.16
Filipino (73)	98	0.13
Indian (169)	200	0.28
Indonesian (1)	1	0.00
Japanese (19)	35	0.05
Korean (69)	77	0.11
Pakistani (2)	4	0.01
Taiwanese (2)	2	0.00
Thai (5)	7	0.01
Vietnamese (20)	24	0.03
Other Asian, specified	4	0.01
Other Asian, not specified (10)	31	0.04
Australian	7	0.01
Austrian	93	0.13
Brazilian	18	0.02
British	278	0.38
Bulgarian	9	0.01
Canadian	7	0.01
Celtic	7	0.01
Croatian	11	0.02
Czech	60	0.08
Czechoslovakian	86	0.12
Danish	59	0.08
Dutch	253	0.35
Eastern European	58	0.08
English	3,169	4.36
Estonian	23	0.03
European	174	0.24
Finnish	7	0.01

Notes: 1. Figures in the "Number" column do not add up to the total population due to: a) Ancestry/Race overlap — e.g. persons can report being both White and Irish, b) persons of Hispanic origin can report being any race, c) persons reporting two ancestries are counted in both categories. 2. Numbers in parentheses indicate the number of persons reporting this ancestry/race alone, not in combination with any other ancestry/race. 3. Refer to the Explanation of Data in the front of the book for more detailed information.

Ancestry/Race	Number	%
French, except Basque	661	0.91
French Canadian	139	0.19
German	3,760	5.17
Greek	215	0.30
Hawaii Native/Pacific Islander:	74	0.10
Micronesian: (3)	5	0.01
Guamanian/Chamorro (3)	5	0.01
Polynesian: (2)	21	0.03
Native Hawaiian (1)	17	0.02
Samoan (1)	4	0.01
Other Pac. Isl., specified	4	0.01
Other Pac. Isl., not spec. (15)	44	0.06
Hispanic or Latino:	7,148	9.84
Central American:	84	0.12
Costa Rican	5	0.01
Guatemalan	29	0.04
Honduran	6	0.01
Nicaraguan	5	0.01
Panamanian	22	0.03
Salvadoran	10	0.01
Other Central American	7	0.01
Cuban	87	0.12
Dominican Republic	164	0.23
Mexican	1,746	2.40
Puerto Rican	4,328	5.96
South American:	114	0.16
Argentinean	14	0.02
Bolivian	2	0.00
Chilean	6	0.01
Colombian	23	0.03
Ecuadorian	20	0.03
Paraguayan	2	0.00
Peruvian	5	0.01
Venezuelan	40	0.06
Other South American	2	0.00
Other Hispanic or Latino	625	0.86
Hungarian	151	0.21
Iranian	7	0.01
Irish	6,296	8.66
Israeli	18	0.02
Italian	4,164	5.73
Latvian	13	0.02
Lithuanian	190	0.26
New Zealander	3	0.00
Northern European	5	0.01
Norwegian	130	0.18
Pennsylvania German	34	0.05
Polish	2,618	3.60
Portuguese	57	0.08
Romanian	88	0.12
Russian	537	0.74
Scandinavian	6	0.01
Scotch-Irish	504	0.69
Scottish	538	0.74
Serbian	6	0.01
Slavic	12	0.02
Slovak	58	0.08
Slovene	12	0.02
Swedish	372	0.51
Swiss	64	0.09
Turkish	13	0.02
Ukrainian	139	0.19
United States or American	1,299	1.79
Welsh	341	0.47
West Indian, excl. Hispanic:	619	0.85
Barbadian	21	0.03
British West Indian	34	0.05
Haitian	43	0.06
Jamaican	389	0.54
Trinidadian and Tobagonian	11	0.02
U.S. Virgin Islander	13	0.02
West Indian	99	0.14
Other West Indian	9	0.01
White:	26,622	36.64
Not Hispanic (23,352)	23,856	32.83
Hispanic (2,459)	2,766	3.81
Yugoslavian	27	0.04

Washington

Place Type: City
County: District of Columbia
Population: 572,059

Ancestry/Race	Number	%
Acadian/Cajun	78	0.01
Afghan	54	0.01
African American/Black:	350,455	61.26
Not Hispanic (340,088)	346,083	60.50
Hispanic (3,224)	4,372	0.76
African, sub-Saharan:	16,000	2.80
African	9,638	1.68
Cape Verdean	134	0.02
Ethiopian	2,158	0.38
Ghanian	277	0.05
Kenyan	46	0.01
Liberian	82	0.01
Nigerian	1,933	0.34
Senegalese	201	0.04
Sierra Leonean	405	0.07
Somalian	90	0.02
South African	191	0.03
Sudanese	102	0.02
Ugandan	30	0.01
Zairian	17	0.00
Zimbabwean	14	0.00
Other sub-Saharan African	682	0.12
Alaska Native tribes, specified:	24	0.00
Alaska Athabascan	2	0.00
Aleut (3)	6	0.00
Eskimo (2)	7	0.00
Tlingit-Haida (4)	8	0.00
All other tribes (1)	1	0.00
Alaska Native tribes, not specified	3	0.00
Am. Ind. or Alaska Nat., not spec.	2,191	0.38
Albanian	218	0.04
Alsatian	33	0.01
American Indian tribes, specified:	2,355	0.41
Apache (10)	32	0.01
Blackfeet (41)	218	0.04
Cherokee (172)	929	0.16
Cheyenne (3)	9	0.00
Chickasaw (9)	15	0.00
Chippewa (17)	29	0.01
Choctaw (15)	64	0.01
Colville (1)	2	0.00
Comanche (3)	8	0.00
Cree	6	0.00
Creek (7)	35	0.01
Crow (1)	10	0.00
Delaware (2)	6	0.00
Houma	2	0.00
Iroquois (25)	66	0.01
Kiowa (5)	7	0.00
Latin American Indians (172)	365	0.06
Lumbee (13)	19	0.00
Menominee	2	0.00
Navajo (20)	35	0.01
Osage (3)	5	0.00
Ottawa (1)	2	0.00
Pima (2)	3	0.00
Potawatomi (9)	12	0.00
Pueblo (14)	27	0.00
Puget Sound Salish (1)	1	0.00
Seminole (4)	39	0.01
Shoshone (1)	5	0.00
Sioux (20)	62	0.01
Tohono O'Odham (2)	5	0.00
Ute (2)	3	0.00
Yakama (1)	3	0.00
Yaqui (2)	5	0.00
Yuman (1)	2	0.00
All other tribes (120)	322	0.06
American Indian tribes, not spec.	320	0.06
Arab:	3,120	0.55
Arab/Arabic	491	0.09
Egyptian	526	0.09
Iraqi	97	0.02
Jordanian	94	0.02
Lebanese	747	0.13
Moroccan	473	0.08
Palestinian	125	0.02
Syrian	109	0.02
Other Arab	458	0.08
Armenian	372	0.07
Asian:	18,345	3.21
Bangladeshi (116)	151	0.03
Cambodian (34)	47	0.01
Chinese, ex. Taiwanese (3,636)	4,173	0.73
Filipino (2,228)	2,714	0.47
Hmong (6)	6	0.00
Indian (2,845)	3,507	0.61
Indonesian (164)	225	0.04
Japanese (1,117)	1,471	0.26
Korean (1,095)	1,273	0.22
Laotian (56)	62	0.01
Malaysian (42)	66	0.01
Pakistani (188)	276	0.05
Sri Lankan (139)	157	0.03
Taiwanese (98)	129	0.02
Thai (211)	261	0.05
Vietnamese (1,903)	2,035	0.36
Other Asian, specified (151)	225	0.04
Other Asian, not specified (914)	1,567	0.27
Assyrian/Chaldean/Syriac	9	0.00
Australian	257	0.04
Austrian	1,703	0.30
Basque	180	0.03
Belgian	623	0.11
Brazilian	734	0.13
British	3,402	0.59
Bulgarian	207	0.04
Canadian	948	0.17
Carpatho Rusyn	6	0.00
Celtic	126	0.02
Croatian	508	0.09
Cypriot	18	0.00
Czech	1,274	0.22
Czechoslovakian	304	0.05
Danish	1,047	0.18
Dutch	2,879	0.50
Eastern European	2,160	0.38
English	25,214	4.41
Estonian	100	0.02
European	3,445	0.60
Finnish	568	0.10
French, except Basque	6,909	1.21
French Canadian	1,353	0.24
German	27,415	4.79
German Russian	26	0.00
Greek	1,893	0.33
Guyanese	709	0.12
Hawaii Native/Pacific Islander:	808	0.14
Melanesian: (9)	12	0.00
Fijian (2)	4	0.00
Other Melanesian (7)	8	0.00
Micronesian: (70)	115	0.02
Guamanian/Chamorro (62)	104	0.02
Other Micronesian (8)	11	0.00
Polynesian: (194)	327	0.06
Native Hawaiian (138)	231	0.04
Samoan (51)	82	0.01
Tongan (1)	2	0.00
Other Polynesian (4)	12	0.00
Other Pac. Isl., specified	26	0.00
Other Pac. Isl., not spec. (72)	328	0.06
Hispanic or Latino:	44,953	7.86
Central American:	15,803	2.76
Costa Rican	167	0.03
Guatemalan	1,350	0.24
Honduran	853	0.15
Nicaraguan	594	0.10
Panamanian	437	0.08
Salvadoran	11,741	2.05
Other Central American	661	0.12
Cuban	1,101	0.19
Dominican Republic	1,496	0.26
Mexican	5,098	0.89

Notes: 1. Figures in the "Number" column do not add up to the total population due to: a) Ancestry/Race overlap — e.g. persons can report being both White and Irish, b) persons of Hispanic origin can report being any race, c) persons reporting two ancestries are counted in both categories. 2. Numbers in parentheses indicate the number of persons reporting this ancestry/race alone, not in combination with any other ancestry/race. 3. Refer to the Explanation of Data in the front of the book for more detailed information.

Ancestry/Race	Number	%
Puerto Rican	2,328	0.41
South American:	3,721	0.65
Argentinean	510	0.09
Bolivian	310	0.05
Chilean	359	0.06
Colombian	859	0.15
Ecuadorian	348	0.06
Paraguayan	86	0.02
Peruvian	708	0.12
Uruguayan	100	0.02
Venezuelan	247	0.04
Other South American	194	0.03
Other Hispanic or Latino	15,406	2.69
Hungarian	2,048	0.36
Icelander	44	0.01
Iranian	746	0.13
Irish	28,081	4.91
Israeli	229	0.04
Italian	12,587	2.20
Latvian	336	0.06
Lithuanian	1,156	0.20
Luxemburger	44	0.01
Macedonian	7	0.00
Maltese	18	0.00
New Zealander	63	0.01
Northern European	420	0.07
Norwegian	2,336	0.41
Pennsylvania German	79	0.01
Polish	7,910	1.38
Portuguese	682	0.12
Romanian	930	0.16
Russian	8,338	1.46
Scandinavian	515	0.09
Scotch-Irish	4,185	0.73
Scottish	6,536	1.14
Serbian	237	0.04
Slavic	88	0.02
Slovak	640	0.11
Slovene	186	0.03
Soviet Union	11	0.00
Swedish	3,013	0.53
Swiss	1,153	0.20
Turkish	435	0.08
Ukrainian	1,247	0.22
United States or American	9,919	1.73
Welsh	2,067	0.36
West Indian, excl. Hispanic:	7,861	1.37
Bahamian	114	0.02
Barbadian	196	0.03
Belizean	10	0.00
Bermudan	11	0.00
British West Indian	322	0.06
Haitian	896	0.16
Jamaican	4,184	0.73
Trinidadian and Tobagonian	1,249	0.22
U.S. Virgin Islander	71	0.01
West Indian	794	0.14
Other West Indian	14	0.00
White:	184,309	32.22
Not Hispanic (159,178)	164,520	28.76
Hispanic (16,923)	19,789	3.46
Yugoslavian	279	0.05

Altamonte Springs

Place Type: City
County: Seminole
Population: 41,200

Ancestry/Race	Number	%
African American/Black:	4,400	10.68
Not Hispanic (3,795)	4,081	9.91
Hispanic (209)	319	0.77
African, sub-Saharan:	132	0.32
African	107	0.26
Ghanian	10	0.02
Nigerian	8	0.02
Other sub-Saharan African	7	0.02
Am. Ind. or Alaska Nat., not spec.	115	0.28
Albanian	38	0.09
Alsatian	23	0.06
American Indian tribes, specified:	223	0.54
Apache (3)	5	0.01
Blackfeet (5)	15	0.04
Cherokee (39)	97	0.24
Chickasaw (2)	5	0.01
Chippewa (7)	7	0.02
Choctaw (1)	5	0.01
Comanche	2	0.00
Creek (2)	4	0.01
Crow	1	0.00
Delaware	1	0.00
Iroquois (4)	15	0.04
Latin American Indians (9)	27	0.07
Lumbee (3)	3	0.01
Menominee (1)	1	0.00
Navajo (1)	3	0.01
Potawatomi (2)	2	0.00
Pueblo (2)	2	0.00
Puget Sound Salish	2	0.00
Seminole (1)	5	0.01
Shoshone	1	0.00
Sioux (1)	7	0.02
All other tribes (8)	13	0.03
American Indian tribes, not spec.	16	0.04
Arab:	472	1.14
Arab/Arabic	55	0.13
Egyptian	204	0.49
Jordanian	7	0.02
Lebanese	121	0.29
Syrian	38	0.09
Other Arab	47	0.11
Armenian	33	0.08
Asian:	1,534	3.72
Bangladeshi (7)	14	0.03
Cambodian (5)	5	0.01
Chinese, ex. Taiwanese (150)	185	0.45
Filipino (149)	227	0.55
Indian (524)	577	1.40
Indonesian	3	0.01
Japanese (32)	65	0.16
Korean (193)	209	0.51
Laotian (9)	9	0.02
Malaysian (1)	2	0.00
Pakistani (24)	30	0.07
Sri Lankan	2	0.00
Taiwanese (7)	13	0.03
Thai (13)	15	0.04
Vietnamese (56)	77	0.19
Other Asian, specified (1)	2	0.00
Other Asian, not specified (21)	99	0.24
Australian	51	0.12
Austrian	187	0.45
Basque	22	0.05
Belgian	63	0.15
Brazilian	40	0.10
British	318	0.77
Bulgarian	22	0.05
Canadian	143	0.35
Croatian	76	0.18
Czech	63	0.15
Czechoslovakian	62	0.15
Danish	137	0.33
Dutch	576	1.39
Eastern European	71	0.17
English	4,071	9.83
European	255	0.62
Finnish	46	0.11
French, except Basque	1,269	3.07
French Canadian	454	1.10
German	5,951	14.37
Greek	212	0.51
Guyanese	33	0.08
Hawaii Native/Pacific Islander:	77	0.19
Micronesian: (6)	7	0.02
Guamanian/Chamorro (1)	2	0.00
Other Micronesian (5)	5	0.01
Polynesian: (7)	31	0.08
Native Hawaiian (7)	25	0.06
Tongan	3	0.01
Other Polynesian	3	0.01
Other Pac. Isl., not spec. (2)	39	0.09
Hispanic or Latino:	6,563	15.93
Central American:	262	0.64
Costa Rican	32	0.08
Guatemalan	23	0.06
Honduran	36	0.09
Nicaraguan	50	0.12
Panamanian	70	0.17
Salvadoran	36	0.09
Other Central American	15	0.04
Cuban	467	1.13
Dominican Republic	299	0.73
Mexican	485	1.18
Puerto Rican	3,007	7.30
South American:	958	2.33
Argentinean	65	0.16
Bolivian	17	0.04
Chilean	15	0.04
Colombian	459	1.11
Ecuadorian	84	0.20
Paraguayan	1	0.00
Peruvian	115	0.28
Uruguayan	7	0.02
Venezuelan	147	0.36
Other South American	48	0.12
Other Hispanic or Latino	1,085	2.63
Hungarian	300	0.72
Iranian	38	0.09
Irish	5,163	12.47
Israeli	15	0.04
Italian	3,422	8.27
Lithuanian	139	0.34
Luxemburger	8	0.02
Macedonian	8	0.02
Maltese	11	0.03
Norwegian	406	0.98
Pennsylvania German	14	0.03
Polish	1,218	2.94
Portuguese	134	0.32
Romanian	34	0.08
Russian	585	1.41
Scandinavian	66	0.16
Scotch-Irish	794	1.92
Scottish	1,075	2.60
Serbian	10	0.02
Slavic	10	0.02
Slovak	106	0.26
Slovene	43	0.10
Swedish	536	1.29
Swiss	152	0.37
Turkish	22	0.05
Ukrainian	112	0.27
United States or American	2,052	4.96
Welsh	343	0.83
West Indian, excl. Hispanic:	872	2.11
Bahamian	56	0.14
Barbadian	12	0.03
British West Indian	25	0.06
Haitian	80	0.19
Jamaican	437	1.06
Trinidadian and Tobagonian	107	0.26
U.S. Virgin Islander	34	0.08
West Indian	121	0.29
White:	33,601	81.56
Not Hispanic (28,623)	29,243	70.98
Hispanic (4,019)	4,358	10.58
Yugoslavian	11	0.03

Apopka

Place Type: City
County: Orange
Population: 26,642

Ancestry/Race	Number	%
African American/Black:	4,403	16.53
Not Hispanic (4,033)	4,243	15.93
Hispanic (112)	160	0.60
African, sub-Saharan:	116	0.44

Notes: 1. Figures in the "Number" column do not add up to the total population due to: a) Ancestry/Race overlap — e.g. persons can report being both White and Irish, b) persons of Hispanic origin can report being any race, c) persons reporting two ancestries are counted in both categories. 2. Numbers in parentheses indicate the number of persons reporting this ancestry/race alone, not in combination with any other ancestry/race. 3. Refer to the Explanation of Data in the front of the book for more detailed information.

African	83	0.32
Ethiopian	14	0.05
South African	19	0.07
Alaska Native tribes, specified:	3	0.01
Aleut (1)	1	0.00
Eskimo (1)	1	0.00
Tlingit-Haida	1	0.00
Am. Ind. or Alaska Nat., not spec.	64	0.24
American Indian tribes, specified:	127	0.48
Apache (1)	3	0.01
Blackfeet	3	0.01
Cherokee (20)	50	0.19
Chippewa (3)	4	0.02
Choctaw	4	0.02
Creek (2)	5	0.02
Iroquois	1	0.00
Kiowa (1)	1	0.00
Latin American Indians (22)	27	0.10
Ottawa (3)	3	0.01
Pueblo (1)	1	0.00
Seminole (3)	5	0.02
Sioux	2	0.01
Ute	1	0.00
All other tribes (11)	17	0.06
American Indian tribes, not spec.	4	0.02
Arab:	51	0.20
Egyptian	19	0.07
Lebanese	32	0.12
Armenian	34	0.13
Asian:	623	2.34
Bangladeshi (6)	6	0.02
Chinese, ex. Taiwanese (60)	76	0.29
Filipino (81)	105	0.39
Indian (94)	129	0.48
Indonesian (3)	3	0.01
Japanese (11)	22	0.08
Korean (71)	75	0.28
Laotian (23)	23	0.09
Pakistani (2)	2	0.01
Sri Lankan (8)	8	0.03
Thai (11)	11	0.04
Vietnamese (123)	137	0.51
Other Asian, not specified (9)	26	0.10
Austrian	95	0.36
Basque	18	0.07
Belgian	48	0.18
Brazilian	10	0.04
British	41	0.16
Bulgarian	55	0.21
Canadian	127	0.49
Czech	30	0.12
Czechoslovakian	21	0.08
Danish	69	0.26
Dutch	508	1.95
Eastern European	16	0.06
English	2,069	7.93
European	64	0.25
Finnish	18	0.07
French, except Basque	789	3.03
French Canadian	188	0.72
German	3,294	12.63
Greek	39	0.15
Guyanese	20	0.08
Hawaii Native/Pacific Islander:	38	0.14
Micronesian: (4)	6	0.02
Guamanian/Chamorro (4)	6	0.02
Polynesian: (4)	9	0.03
Native Hawaiian (3)	8	0.03
Samoan (1)	1	0.00
Other Pac. Isl., not spec. (16)	23	0.09
Hispanic or Latino:	4,817	18.08
Central American:	143	0.54
Costa Rican	17	0.06
Guatemalan	25	0.09
Honduran	36	0.14
Nicaraguan	11	0.04
Panamanian	23	0.09
Salvadoran	22	0.08
Other Central American	9	0.03
Cuban	161	0.60
Dominican Republic	114	0.43
Mexican	1,883	7.07
Puerto Rican	1,704	6.40
South American:	273	1.02
Argentinean	5	0.02
Bolivian	2	0.01
Chilean	8	0.03
Colombian	132	0.50
Ecuadorian	49	0.18
Peruvian	21	0.08
Uruguayan	3	0.01
Venezuelan	44	0.17
Other South American	9	0.03
Other Hispanic or Latino	539	2.02
Hungarian	129	0.49
Icelander	8	0.03
Iranian	46	0.18
Irish	2,844	10.90
Italian	1,451	5.56
Latvian	7	0.03
Lithuanian	55	0.21
Maltese	13	0.05
Northern European	11	0.04
Norwegian	179	0.69
Pennsylvania German	17	0.07
Polish	510	1.96
Portuguese	104	0.40
Romanian	41	0.16
Russian	81	0.31
Scotch-Irish	384	1.47
Scottish	660	2.53
Slovak	52	0.20
Swedish	220	0.84
Ukrainian	70	0.27
United States or American	2,328	8.93
Welsh	163	0.62
West Indian, excl. Hispanic:	974	3.73
Barbadian	6	0.02
British West Indian	54	0.21
Haitian	143	0.55
Jamaican	417	1.60
Trinidadian and Tobagonian	174	0.67
U.S. Virgin Islander	15	0.06
West Indian	165	0.63
White:	20,261	76.05
Not Hispanic (16,780)	17,066	64.06
Hispanic (2,895)	3,195	11.99
Yugoslavian	43	0.16

Atlantic Beach

Place Type: City
County: Duval
Population: 13,368

Ancestry/Race	Number	%
African American/Black:	1,757	13.14
Not Hispanic (1,669)	1,726	12.91
Hispanic (28)	31	0.23
African, sub-Saharan:	49	0.36
African	27	0.20
Cape Verdean	7	0.05
South African	7	0.05
Other sub-Saharan African	8	0.06
Am. Ind. or Alaska Nat., not spec.	19	0.14
Alsatian	9	0.07
American Indian tribes, specified:	63	0.47
Cherokee (6)	23	0.17
Chippewa (2)	3	0.02
Comanche (1)	4	0.03
Creek (2)	3	0.02
Houma (1)	1	0.01
Iroquois (1)	4	0.03
Latin American Indians (7)	7	0.05
Lumbee	1	0.01
Navajo	1	0.01
Pueblo (2)	2	0.01
Seminole (1)	5	0.04
Sioux (1)	3	0.02
All other tribes (4)	6	0.04
American Indian tribes, not spec.	5	0.04
Arab:	110	0.82
Arab/Arabic	32	0.24
Egyptian	44	0.33
Lebanese	12	0.09
Palestinian	18	0.13
Syrian	4	0.03
Asian:	349	2.61
Cambodian	1	0.01
Chinese, ex. Taiwanese (9)	13	0.10
Filipino (175)	221	1.65
Indian (6)	10	0.07
Indonesian (1)	1	0.01
Japanese (9)	17	0.13
Korean (8)	9	0.07
Laotian (2)	2	0.01
Malaysian	8	0.06
Sri Lankan (5)	5	0.04
Taiwanese (1)	1	0.01
Thai (3)	6	0.04
Vietnamese (21)	24	0.18
Other Asian, specified (3)	3	0.02
Other Asian, not specified (25)	28	0.21
Austrian	35	0.26
Belgian	77	0.57
Brazilian	22	0.16
British	102	0.76
Canadian	45	0.33
Croatian	14	0.10
Czech	21	0.16
Czechoslovakian	11	0.08
Danish	67	0.50
Dutch	224	1.66
Eastern European	16	0.12
English	1,910	14.18
Estonian	9	0.07
European	152	1.13
Finnish	25	0.19
French, except Basque	457	3.39
French Canadian	146	1.08
German	2,122	15.75
Greek	124	0.92
Hawaii Native/Pacific Islander:	24	0.18
Micronesian: (2)	3	0.02
Guamanian/Chamorro (2)	3	0.02
Polynesian: (2)	5	0.04
Native Hawaiian	3	0.02
Samoan (2)	2	0.01
Other Pac. Isl., not spec.	16	0.12
Hispanic or Latino:	559	4.18
Central American:	30	0.22
Costa Rican	1	0.01
Honduran	2	0.01
Nicaraguan	2	0.01
Panamanian	21	0.16
Salvadoran	4	0.03
Cuban	50	0.37
Dominican Republic	4	0.03
Mexican	132	0.99
Puerto Rican	208	1.56
South American:	37	0.28
Argentinean	4	0.03
Chilean	3	0.02
Colombian	18	0.13
Ecuadorian	1	0.01
Peruvian	4	0.03
Venezuelan	2	0.01
Other South American	5	0.04
Other Hispanic or Latino	98	0.73
Hungarian	103	0.76
Iranian	8	0.06
Irish	1,796	13.33
Italian	746	5.54
Lithuanian	34	0.25
Norwegian	181	1.34
Polish	317	2.35
Portuguese	60	0.45
Romanian	30	0.22
Russian	91	0.68
Scandinavian	14	0.10

Notes: 1. Figures in the "Number" column do not add up to the total population due to: a) Ancestry/Race overlap — e.g. persons can report being both White and Irish, b) persons of Hispanic origin can report being any race, c) persons reporting two ancestries are counted in both categories. 2. Numbers in parentheses indicate the number of persons reporting this ancestry/race alone, not in combination with any other ancestry/race. 3. Refer to the Explanation of Data in the front of the book for more detailed information.

Ancestry/Race	Number	%
Scotch-Irish	421	3.12
Scottish	613	4.55
Serbian	8	0.06
Slovak	24	0.18
Swedish	81	0.60
Swiss	46	0.34
Turkish	34	0.25
Ukrainian	104	0.77
United States or American	1,063	7.89
Welsh	135	1.00
West Indian, excl. Hispanic:	41	0.30
British West Indian	23	0.17
Trinidadian and Tobagonian	5	0.04
Other West Indian	13	0.10
White:	11,171	83.57
Not Hispanic (10,627)	10,778	80.63
Hispanic (365)	393	2.94
Yugoslavian	9	0.07

Auburndale

Place Type: City
County: Polk
Population: 11,032

Ancestry/Race	Number	%
African American/Black:	1,453	13.17
Not Hispanic (1,339)	1,430	12.96
Hispanic (14)	23	0.21
African, sub-Saharan:	88	0.78
African	88	0.78
Am. Ind. or Alaska Nat., not spec.	24	0.22
American Indian tribes, specified:	47	0.43
Apache	2	0.02
Blackfeet	2	0.02
Cherokee (4)	17	0.15
Chickasaw (1)	1	0.01
Chippewa	1	0.01
Choctaw (2)	2	0.02
Creek	1	0.01
Houma (4)	4	0.04
Iroquois (2)	2	0.02
Latin American Indians (1)	3	0.03
Lumbee (1)	1	0.01
Pima (3)	3	0.03
Seminole	2	0.02
Sioux (2)	2	0.02
All other tribes (1)	4	0.04
American Indian tribes, not spec.	3	0.03
Arab:	24	0.21
Lebanese	16	0.14
Moroccan	8	0.07
Asian:	120	1.09
Chinese, ex. Taiwanese (5)	6	0.05
Filipino (8)	12	0.11
Indian (30)	34	0.31
Japanese (3)	7	0.06
Korean (1)	3	0.03
Pakistani (1)	1	0.01
Taiwanese (1)	3	0.03
Vietnamese (41)	41	0.37
Other Asian, specified	1	0.01
Other Asian, not specified (6)	12	0.11
Austrian	11	0.10
Belgian	10	0.09
British	11	0.10
Canadian	23	0.21
Czech	9	0.08
Danish	20	0.18
Dutch	161	1.44
English	1,144	10.20
European	14	0.12
French, except Basque	246	2.19
French Canadian	64	0.57
German	1,082	9.65
Greek	15	0.13
Hawaii Native/Pacific Islander:	9	0.08
Micronesian: (5)	5	0.05
Guamanian/Chamorro (5)	5	0.05
Polynesian:	2	0.02
Native Hawaiian	2	0.02
Other Pac. Isl., not spec.	2	0.02
Hispanic or Latino:	894	8.10
Central American:	10	0.09
Guatemalan	4	0.04
Panamanian	1	0.01
Salvadoran	5	0.05
Cuban	35	0.32
Dominican Republic	2	0.02
Mexican	582	5.28
Puerto Rican	130	1.18
South American:	9	0.08
Chilean	1	0.01
Ecuadorian	2	0.02
Peruvian	1	0.01
Venezuelan	5	0.05
Other Hispanic or Latino	126	1.14
Hungarian	38	0.34
Icelander	7	0.06
Irish	902	8.04
Italian	252	2.25
Lithuanian	4	0.04
Norwegian	34	0.30
Pennsylvania German	13	0.12
Polish	163	1.45
Portuguese	11	0.10
Russian	33	0.29
Scotch-Irish	172	1.53
Scottish	181	1.61
Slovak	16	0.14
Swedish	48	0.43
Swiss	46	0.41
United States or American	1,984	17.69
Welsh	25	0.22
West Indian, excl. Hispanic:	163	1.45
Haitian	102	0.91
Jamaican	61	0.54
White:	9,101	82.50
Not Hispanic (8,508)	8,611	78.05
Hispanic (442)	490	4.44
Yugoslavian	7	0.06

Aventura

Place Type: City
County: Miami-Dade
Population: 25,267

Ancestry/Race	Number	%
African American/Black:	499	1.97
Not Hispanic (395)	454	1.80
Hispanic (35)	45	0.18
African, sub-Saharan:	132	0.52
African	35	0.14
South African	88	0.35
Other sub-Saharan African	9	0.04
Am. Ind. or Alaska Nat., not spec.	32	0.13
American Indian tribes, specified:	23	0.09
Cherokee (2)	7	0.03
Chickasaw	1	0.00
Choctaw (1)	1	0.00
Iroquois (1)	1	0.00
Latin American Indians (4)	6	0.02
Potawatomi	1	0.00
Pueblo	1	0.00
Seminole	1	0.00
All other tribes (2)	4	0.02
American Indian tribes, not spec.	4	0.02
Arab:	505	2.00
Arab/Arabic	80	0.32
Egyptian	6	0.02
Iraqi	27	0.11
Lebanese	81	0.32
Moroccan	76	0.30
Palestinian	38	0.15
Syrian	182	0.72
Other Arab	15	0.06
Armenian	8	0.03
Asian:	377	1.49
Bangladeshi (4)	4	0.02
Chinese, ex. Taiwanese (110)	128	0.51
Filipino (32)	39	0.15
Indian (69)	80	0.32
Indonesian (1)	2	0.01
Japanese (30)	31	0.12
Korean (31)	33	0.13
Laotian (2)	3	0.01
Pakistani (7)	11	0.04
Taiwanese (5)	5	0.02
Thai (4)	5	0.02
Vietnamese (7)	12	0.05
Other Asian, not specified (2)	24	0.09
Australian	17	0.07
Austrian	422	1.67
Belgian	52	0.21
Brazilian	463	1.83
British	115	0.46
Bulgarian	26	0.10
Canadian	192	0.76
Croatian	26	0.10
Czech	47	0.19
Czechoslovakian	59	0.23
Danish	20	0.08
Dutch	148	0.59
Eastern European	297	1.18
English	470	1.86
European	282	1.12
Finnish	23	0.09
French, except Basque	348	1.38
French Canadian	79	0.31
German	1,189	4.71
Greek	114	0.45
Hawaii Native/Pacific Islander:	11	0.04
Micronesian: (1)	2	0.01
Guamanian/Chamorro (1)	2	0.01
Polynesian: (3)	3	0.01
Native Hawaiian (2)	2	0.01
Samoan (1)	1	0.00
Other Pac. Isl., not spec. (1)	6	0.02
Hispanic or Latino:	5,218	20.65
Central American:	260	1.03
Costa Rican	47	0.19
Guatemalan	38	0.15
Honduran	56	0.22
Nicaraguan	30	0.12
Panamanian	66	0.26
Salvadoran	15	0.06
Other Central American	8	0.03
Cuban	731	2.89
Dominican Republic	102	0.40
Mexican	325	1.29
Puerto Rican	316	1.25
South American:	2,289	9.06
Argentinean	424	1.68
Bolivian	19	0.08
Chilean	50	0.20
Colombian	1,075	4.25
Ecuadorian	87	0.34
Paraguayan	2	0.01
Peruvian	236	0.93
Uruguayan	24	0.09
Venezuelan	331	1.31
Other South American	41	0.16
Other Hispanic or Latino	1,195	4.73
Hungarian	378	1.50
Iranian	69	0.27
Irish	559	2.21
Israeli	580	2.30
Italian	1,097	4.34
Latvian	26	0.10
Lithuanian	150	0.59
Norwegian	51	0.20
Polish	1,893	7.49
Portuguese	72	0.28
Romanian	446	1.77
Russian	2,998	11.87
Scotch-Irish	93	0.37
Scottish	122	0.48
Slovak	21	0.08
Soviet Union	7	0.03

Notes: 1. Figures in the "Number" column do not add up to the total population due to: a) Ancestry/Race overlap — e.g. persons can report being both White and Irish, b) persons of Hispanic origin can report being any race, c) persons reporting two ancestries are counted in both categories. 2. Numbers in parentheses indicate the number of persons reporting this ancestry/race alone, not in combination with any other ancestry/race. 3. Refer to the Explanation of Data in the front of the book for more detailed information.

Swedish	75	0.30
Swiss	7	0.03
Turkish	140	0.55
Ukrainian	136	0.54
United States or American	2,252	8.91
Welsh	17	0.07
West Indian, excl. Hispanic:	227	0.90
Bahamian	13	0.05
Barbadian	6	0.02
British West Indian	6	0.02
Haitian	98	0.39
Jamaican	65	0.26
Trinidadian and Tobagonian	16	0.06
West Indian	23	0.09
White:	24,092	95.35
Not Hispanic (18,954)	19,206	76.01
Hispanic (4,741)	4,886	19.34

Azalea Park

Place Type: Census Designated Place
County: Orange
Population: 11,073

Ancestry/Race	Number	%
African American/Black:	866	7.82
Not Hispanic (635)	699	6.31
Hispanic (112)	167	1.51
African, sub-Saharan:	24	0.22
African	24	0.22
Alaska Native tribes, specified:	2	0.02
All other tribes (2)	2	0.02
Am. Ind. or Alaska Nat., not spec.	31	0.28
American Indian tribes, specified:	67	0.61
Apache	1	0.01
Blackfeet (2)	6	0.05
Cherokee (14)	26	0.23
Chippewa (3)	3	0.03
Choctaw	3	0.03
Iroquois	1	0.01
Latin American Indians (4)	15	0.14
Menominee	1	0.01
Ottawa	1	0.01
Pueblo (2)	2	0.02
Yaqui (1)	1	0.01
All other tribes (6)	7	0.06
American Indian tribes, not spec.	5	0.05
Arab:	189	1.70
Arab/Arabic	44	0.40
Egyptian	20	0.18
Lebanese	79	0.71
Other Arab	46	0.41
Asian:	498	4.50
Bangladeshi (1)	1	0.01
Cambodian	1	0.01
Chinese, ex. Taiwanese (32)	49	0.44
Filipino (56)	75	0.68
Indian (71)	89	0.80
Japanese (18)	25	0.23
Korean (19)	28	0.25
Laotian	1	0.01
Pakistani (23)	23	0.21
Taiwanese (1)	1	0.01
Thai (5)	6	0.05
Vietnamese (159)	174	1.57
Other Asian, not specified (3)	25	0.23
Brazilian	7	0.06
British	29	0.26
Canadian	24	0.22
Danish	14	0.13
Dutch	93	0.84
English	801	7.19
European	40	0.36
Finnish	25	0.22
French, except Basque	140	1.26
French Canadian	120	1.08
German	879	7.89
Greek	45	0.40
Guyanese	31	0.28
Hawaii Native/Pacific Islander:	29	0.26
Micronesian: (2)	5	0.05
Guamanian/Chamorro (2)	5	0.05
Polynesian: (6)	11	0.10
Native Hawaiian (3)	5	0.05
Samoan (1)	3	0.03
Other Polynesian (2)	3	0.03
Other Pac. Isl., not spec.	13	0.12
Hispanic or Latino:	4,315	38.97
Central American:	145	1.31
Costa Rican	15	0.14
Guatemalan	28	0.25
Honduran	39	0.35
Nicaraguan	20	0.18
Panamanian	12	0.11
Salvadoran	26	0.23
Other Central American	5	0.05
Cuban	383	3.46
Dominican Republic	186	1.68
Mexican	138	1.25
Puerto Rican	2,745	24.79
South American:	261	2.36
Argentinean	10	0.09
Chilean	13	0.12
Colombian	136	1.23
Ecuadorian	48	0.43
Peruvian	18	0.16
Uruguayan	2	0.02
Venezuelan	24	0.22
Other South American	10	0.09
Other Hispanic or Latino	457	4.13
Hungarian	31	0.28
Iranian	13	0.12
Irish	772	6.93
Italian	334	3.00
Lithuanian	13	0.12
Norwegian	204	1.83
Polish	266	2.39
Portuguese	42	0.38
Romanian	4	0.04
Russian	36	0.32
Scotch-Irish	155	1.39
Scottish	159	1.43
Slavic	10	0.09
Slovak	68	0.61
Swedish	6	0.05
Swiss	6	0.05
United States or American	1,102	9.90
Welsh	61	0.55
West Indian, excl. Hispanic:	140	1.26
Barbadian	45	0.40
Haitian	79	0.71
Jamaican	16	0.14
White:	8,168	73.77
Not Hispanic (5,472)	5,637	50.91
Hispanic (2,305)	2,531	22.86
Yugoslavian	12	0.11

Bartow

Place Type: City
County: Polk
Population: 15,340

Ancestry/Race	Number	%
Acadian/Cajun	6	0.04
African American/Black:	4,400	28.68
Not Hispanic (4,321)	4,361	28.43
Hispanic (34)	39	0.25
African, sub-Saharan:	56	0.37
African	56	0.37
Alaska Native tribes, specified:	6	0.04
Aleut (1)	1	0.01
Eskimo (5)	5	0.03
Am. Ind. or Alaska Nat., not spec.	39	0.25
American Indian tribes, specified:	81	0.53
Apache	1	0.01
Blackfeet	1	0.01
Cherokee (17)	43	0.28
Chippewa (2)	2	0.01
Choctaw (1)	2	0.01
Creek (7)	9	0.06
Iroquois (2)	2	0.01
Latin American Indians (2)	8	0.05
Lumbee	1	0.01
Navajo	5	0.03
Potawatomi	2	0.01
Pueblo (1)	1	0.01
Seminole (1)	2	0.01
All other tribes	2	0.01
American Indian tribes, not spec.	9	0.06
Arab:	25	0.16
Other Arab	25	0.16
Armenian	9	0.06
Asian:	164	1.07
Chinese, ex. Taiwanese (3)	9	0.06
Filipino (18)	23	0.15
Indian (56)	59	0.38
Japanese (7)	7	0.05
Korean (5)	8	0.05
Laotian (39)	42	0.27
Taiwanese (3)	3	0.02
Thai (2)	4	0.03
Vietnamese (4)	4	0.03
Other Asian, not specified (3)	5	0.03
British	70	0.46
Bulgarian	12	0.08
Celtic	13	0.08
Czech	11	0.07
Czechoslovakian	7	0.05
Danish	9	0.06
Dutch	282	1.84
English	1,390	9.06
European	50	0.33
French, except Basque	257	1.68
French Canadian	123	0.80
German	1,126	7.34
Greek	19	0.12
Hawaii Native/Pacific Islander:	17	0.11
Micronesian: (1)	3	0.02
Guamanian/Chamorro (1)	3	0.02
Polynesian: (10)	13	0.08
Native Hawaiian (2)	4	0.03
Samoan (8)	9	0.06
Other Pac. Isl., not spec. (1)	1	0.01
Hispanic or Latino:	1,244	8.11
Central American:	13	0.08
Costa Rican	1	0.01
Guatemalan	1	0.01
Honduran	3	0.02
Nicaraguan	1	0.01
Panamanian	6	0.04
Other Central American	1	0.01
Cuban	72	0.47
Mexican	914	5.96
Puerto Rican	92	0.60
South American:	10	0.07
Chilean	3	0.02
Colombian	2	0.01
Ecuadorian	1	0.01
Peruvian	1	0.01
Venezuelan	3	0.02
Other Hispanic or Latino	143	0.93
Hungarian	56	0.37
Irish	1,186	7.73
Italian	286	1.86
Norwegian	46	0.30
Polish	90	0.59
Portuguese	15	0.10
Russian	30	0.20
Scandinavian	9	0.06
Scotch-Irish	255	1.66
Scottish	213	1.39
Slovak	29	0.19
Swedish	33	0.22
Swiss	27	0.18
Ukrainian	10	0.07
United States or American	1,719	11.21
Welsh	65	0.42
West Indian, excl. Hispanic:	128	0.83
British West Indian	18	0.12

Notes: 1. Figures in the "Number" column do not add up to the total population due to: a) Ancestry/Race overlap — e.g. persons can report being both White and Irish, b) persons of Hispanic origin can report being any race, c) persons reporting two ancestries are counted in both categories. 2. Numbers in parentheses indicate the number of persons reporting this ancestry/race alone, not in combination with any other ancestry/race. 3. Refer to the Explanation of Data in the front of the book for more detailed information.

Haitian	13	0.08
Jamaican	97	0.63
White:	10,393	67.75
Not Hispanic (9,445)	9,557	62.30
Hispanic (666)	836	5.45

Bayonet Point

Place Type: Census Designated Place
County: Pasco
Population: 23,577

Ancestry/Race	Number	%
Afghan	4	0.02
African American/Black:	207	0.88
Not Hispanic (142)	182	0.77
Hispanic (17)	25	0.11
Am. Ind. or Alaska Nat., not spec.	52	0.22
American Indian tribes, specified:	99	0.42
Apache (1)	11	0.05
Blackfeet (2)	4	0.02
Cherokee (15)	37	0.16
Chippewa (7)	8	0.03
Choctaw	3	0.01
Comanche	1	0.00
Cree	3	0.01
Creek (2)	3	0.01
Houma (2)	2	0.01
Iroquois (3)	4	0.02
Latin American Indians (1)	1	0.00
Lumbee	1	0.00
Osage	1	0.00
Seminole	2	0.01
Shoshone (1)	1	0.00
Sioux (1)	3	0.01
All other tribes (7)	14	0.06
American Indian tribes, not spec.	8	0.03
Arab:	62	0.26
Egyptian	24	0.10
Jordanian	8	0.03
Lebanese	8	0.03
Syrian	22	0.09
Asian:	192	0.81
Chinese, ex. Taiwanese (11)	17	0.07
Filipino (37)	47	0.20
Indian (38)	46	0.20
Japanese (5)	13	0.06
Korean (14)	19	0.08
Pakistani	1	0.00
Thai (4)	4	0.02
Vietnamese (28)	34	0.14
Other Asian, not specified (1)	11	0.05
Austrian	137	0.58
Belgian	42	0.18
Brazilian	10	0.04
British	47	0.20
Canadian	201	0.85
Croatian	31	0.13
Czech	73	0.31
Czechoslovakian	70	0.30
Danish	97	0.41
Dutch	480	2.03
English	3,046	12.87
European	72	0.30
Finnish	117	0.49
French, except Basque	970	4.10
French Canadian	329	1.39
German	5,079	21.46
Greek	246	1.04
Hawaii Native/Pacific Islander:	11	0.05
Micronesian:	1	0.00
Guamanian/Chamorro	1	0.00
Polynesian: (4)	6	0.03
Native Hawaiian (4)	6	0.03
Other Pac. Isl., not spec. (3)	4	0.02
Hispanic or Latino:	826	3.50
Central American:	39	0.17
Costa Rican	4	0.02
Guatemalan	9	0.04
Honduran	13	0.06
Nicaraguan	2	0.01
Panamanian	2	0.01
Salvadoran	8	0.03
Other Central American	1	0.00
Cuban	62	0.26
Dominican Republic	16	0.07
Mexican	88	0.37
Puerto Rican	344	1.46
South American:	54	0.23
Argentinean	1	0.00
Bolivian	4	0.02
Chilean	3	0.01
Colombian	22	0.09
Ecuadorian	11	0.05
Peruvian	5	0.02
Uruguayan	2	0.01
Venezuelan	5	0.02
Other South American	1	0.00
Other Hispanic or Latino	223	0.95
Hungarian	192	0.81
Irish	4,083	17.25
Italian	3,823	16.15
Lithuanian	122	0.52
Maltese	34	0.14
New Zealander	6	0.03
Norwegian	302	1.28
Pennsylvania German	36	0.15
Polish	1,492	6.30
Portuguese	84	0.35
Romanian	8	0.03
Russian	278	1.17
Scandinavian	32	0.14
Scotch-Irish	447	1.89
Scottish	603	2.55
Slavic	32	0.14
Slovak	77	0.33
Slovene	18	0.08
Swedish	330	1.39
Swiss	67	0.28
Ukrainian	88	0.37
United States or American	1,743	7.36
Welsh	236	1.00
West Indian, excl. Hispanic:	14	0.06
Jamaican	14	0.06
White:	23,054	97.78
Not Hispanic (22,203)	22,384	94.94
Hispanic (629)	670	2.84
Yugoslavian	21	0.09

Bayshore Gardens

Place Type: Census Designated Place
County: Manatee
Population: 17,350

Ancestry/Race	Number	%
African American/Black:	791	4.56
Not Hispanic (677)	761	4.39
Hispanic (13)	30	0.17
African, sub-Saharan:	61	0.35
African	48	0.28
Cape Verdean	13	0.07
Am. Ind. or Alaska Nat., not spec.	50	0.29
American Indian tribes, specified:	87	0.50
Apache	2	0.01
Blackfeet (4)	7	0.04
Cherokee (7)	33	0.19
Cheyenne (2)	2	0.01
Chippewa (3)	4	0.02
Choctaw (5)	9	0.05
Iroquois	2	0.01
Latin American Indians (7)	8	0.05
Lumbee (2)	2	0.01
Sioux (1)	5	0.03
All other tribes (8)	13	0.07
American Indian tribes, not spec.	8	0.05
Arab:	8	0.05
Lebanese	8	0.05
Armenian	12	0.07
Asian:	299	1.72
Bangladeshi	5	0.03
Cambodian (21)	21	0.12
Chinese, ex. Taiwanese (29)	33	0.19
Filipino (35)	56	0.32
Indian (29)	38	0.22
Indonesian (2)	2	0.01
Japanese (5)	13	0.07
Korean (6)	17	0.10
Laotian (7)	11	0.06
Malaysian	1	0.01
Pakistani (1)	1	0.01
Thai (11)	17	0.10
Vietnamese (65)	75	0.43
Other Asian, not specified	9	0.05
Austrian	47	0.27
Belgian	14	0.08
British	18	0.10
Canadian	76	0.44
Celtic	8	0.05
Croatian	36	0.21
Czech	76	0.44
Czechoslovakian	19	0.11
Danish	69	0.40
Dutch	435	2.50
English	2,826	16.26
European	64	0.37
Finnish	41	0.24
French, except Basque	727	4.18
French Canadian	175	1.01
German	3,225	18.55
German Russian	6	0.03
Greek	43	0.25
Hawaii Native/Pacific Islander:	28	0.16
Micronesian: (2)	2	0.01
Guamanian/Chamorro (2)	2	0.01
Polynesian: (10)	17	0.10
Native Hawaiian (6)	13	0.07
Other Polynesian (4)	4	0.02
Other Pac. Isl., not spec. (5)	9	0.05
Hispanic or Latino:	1,426	8.22
Central American:	85	0.49
Costa Rican	2	0.01
Guatemalan	37	0.21
Honduran	24	0.14
Nicaraguan	6	0.03
Panamanian	1	0.01
Salvadoran	10	0.06
Other Central American	5	0.03
Cuban	98	0.56
Dominican Republic	11	0.06
Mexican	537	3.10
Puerto Rican	354	2.04
South American:	119	0.69
Argentinean	4	0.02
Chilean	7	0.04
Colombian	60	0.35
Ecuadorian	20	0.12
Peruvian	17	0.10
Uruguayan	4	0.02
Venezuelan	3	0.02
Other South American	4	0.02
Other Hispanic or Latino	222	1.28
Hungarian	147	0.85
Irish	2,220	12.77
Italian	1,104	6.35
Latvian	10	0.06
Lithuanian	35	0.20
Northern European	20	0.12
Norwegian	189	1.09
Pennsylvania German	31	0.18
Polish	474	2.73
Portuguese	71	0.41
Romanian	47	0.27
Russian	139	0.80
Scandinavian	5	0.03
Scotch-Irish	299	1.72
Scottish	474	2.73
Serbian	26	0.15
Slavic	9	0.05
Slovak	52	0.30

Notes: 1. Figures in the "Number" column do not add up to the total population due to: a) Ancestry/Race overlap — e.g. persons can report being both White and Irish, b) persons of Hispanic origin can report being any race, c) persons reporting two ancestries are counted in both categories. 2. Numbers in parentheses indicate the number of persons reporting this ancestry/race alone, not in combination with any other ancestry/race. 3. Refer to the Explanation of Data in the front of the book for more detailed information.

Slovene	9	0.05
Swedish	259	1.49
Swiss	35	0.20
Ukrainian	47	0.27
United States or American	1,960	11.28
Welsh	77	0.44
West Indian, excl. Hispanic:	105	0.60
Haitian	31	0.18
Jamaican	74	0.43
White:	15,903	91.66
Not Hispanic (14,689)	14,913	85.95
Hispanic (903)	990	5.71
Yugoslavian	14	0.08

Bellair-Meadowbrook Terrace

Place Type: Census Designated Place
County: Clay
Population: 16,539

Ancestry/Race	Number	%
Afghan	14	0.08
African American/Black:	2,022	12.23
Not Hispanic (1,782)	1,925	11.64
Hispanic (67)	97	0.59
African, sub-Saharan:	46	0.28
African	46	0.28
Am. Ind. or Alaska Nat., not spec.	55	0.33
American Indian tribes, specified:	148	0.89
Apache (1)	1	0.01
Blackfeet	2	0.01
Cherokee (22)	80	0.48
Cheyenne	1	0.01
Chickasaw	5	0.03
Chippewa (3)	3	0.02
Creek (5)	11	0.07
Crow	2	0.01
Iroquois (5)	5	0.03
Latin American Indians (5)	6	0.04
Lumbee (3)	3	0.02
Navajo (6)	12	0.07
Osage	1	0.01
Potawatomi (4)	4	0.02
Seminole	3	0.02
Sioux	1	0.01
All other tribes (7)	8	0.05
American Indian tribes, not spec.	7	0.04
Arab:	85	0.51
Arab/Arabic	22	0.13
Lebanese	23	0.14
Syrian	27	0.16
Other Arab	13	0.08
Asian:	799	4.83
Cambodian (4)	5	0.03
Chinese, ex. Taiwanese (20)	37	0.22
Filipino (344)	436	2.64
Hmong (2)	2	0.01
Indian (57)	69	0.42
Japanese (36)	61	0.37
Korean (58)	68	0.41
Laotian (1)	1	0.01
Pakistani (4)	5	0.03
Sri Lankan (7)	7	0.04
Taiwanese (1)	2	0.01
Thai (8)	10	0.06
Vietnamese (42)	46	0.28
Other Asian, specified	1	0.01
Other Asian, not specified (15)	49	0.30
Australian	7	0.04
Austrian	55	0.33
Belgian	6	0.04
Brazilian	20	0.12
British	43	0.26
Canadian	72	0.43
Czech	72	0.43
Czechoslovakian	21	0.13
Danish	45	0.27
Dutch	182	1.10
English	1,698	10.25
European	142	0.86
Finnish	16	0.10
French, except Basque	655	3.95
French Canadian	125	0.75
German	1,998	12.06
Greek	26	0.16
Hawaii Native/Pacific Islander:	50	0.30
Micronesian: (10)	16	0.10
Guamanian/Chamorro (10)	16	0.10
Polynesian: (8)	23	0.14
Native Hawaiian (6)	21	0.13
Samoan (1)	1	0.01
Other Polynesian (1)	1	0.01
Other Pac. Isl., not spec.	11	0.07
Hispanic or Latino:	1,112	6.72
Central American:	48	0.29
Costa Rican	5	0.03
Guatemalan	2	0.01
Honduran	4	0.02
Nicaraguan	5	0.03
Panamanian	19	0.11
Salvadoran	10	0.06
Other Central American	3	0.02
Cuban	58	0.35
Dominican Republic	17	0.10
Mexican	256	1.55
Puerto Rican	410	2.48
South American:	90	0.54
Argentinean	8	0.05
Bolivian	4	0.02
Chilean	14	0.08
Colombian	35	0.21
Ecuadorian	6	0.04
Paraguayan	2	0.01
Peruvian	17	0.10
Uruguayan	1	0.01
Venezuelan	1	0.01
Other South American	2	0.01
Other Hispanic or Latino	233	1.41
Hungarian	77	0.46
Irish	1,823	11.01
Italian	797	4.81
Latvian	5	0.03
Lithuanian	17	0.10
Norwegian	182	1.10
Pennsylvania German	6	0.04
Polish	413	2.49
Portuguese	37	0.22
Romanian	10	0.06
Russian	29	0.18
Scotch-Irish	324	1.96
Scottish	442	2.67
Slavic	10	0.06
Slovak	9	0.05
Slovene	26	0.16
Swedish	106	0.64
Swiss	7	0.04
Ukrainian	20	0.12
United States or American	1,785	10.78
Welsh	241	1.45
West Indian, excl. Hispanic:	187	1.13
Bahamian	4	0.02
British West Indian	12	0.07
Haitian	109	0.66
Jamaican	12	0.07
U.S. Virgin Islander	12	0.07
West Indian	38	0.23
White:	13,448	81.31
Not Hispanic (12,502)	12,849	77.69
Hispanic (522)	599	3.62
Yugoslavian	8	0.05

Belle Glade

Place Type: City
County: Palm Beach
Population: 14,906

Ancestry/Race	Number	%
African American/Black:	8,653	58.05
Not Hispanic (7,471)	8,546	57.33
Hispanic (84)	107	0.72
African, sub-Saharan:	156	1.04
African	156	1.04
Alaska Native tribes, specified:	1	0.01
Aleut	1	0.01
Am. Ind. or Alaska Nat., not spec.	26	0.17
American Indian tribes, specified:	11	0.07
Cherokee	4	0.03
Latin American Indians	3	0.02
All other tribes (4)	4	0.03
American Indian tribes, not spec.	3	0.02
Arab:	141	0.94
Arab/Arabic	115	0.77
Other Arab	26	0.17
Asian:	54	0.36
Bangladeshi	3	0.02
Chinese, ex. Taiwanese	3	0.02
Filipino (1)	4	0.03
Indian (18)	19	0.13
Korean (7)	12	0.08
Thai	1	0.01
Other Asian, not specified (2)	12	0.08
British	39	0.26
Canadian	15	0.10
Danish	6	0.04
Dutch	42	0.28
English	451	3.01
French, except Basque	27	0.18
French Canadian	5	0.03
German	202	1.35
Hawaii Native/Pacific Islander:	145	0.97
Polynesian: (2)	7	0.05
Native Hawaiian (2)	6	0.04
Samoan	1	0.01
Other Pac. Isl., not spec. (4)	138	0.93
Hispanic or Latino:	4,110	27.57
Central American:	204	1.37
Costa Rican	8	0.05
Guatemalan	18	0.12
Honduran	55	0.37
Nicaraguan	76	0.51
Panamanian	1	0.01
Salvadoran	42	0.28
Other Central American	4	0.03
Cuban	891	5.98
Dominican Republic	73	0.49
Mexican	2,302	15.44
Puerto Rican	257	1.72
South American:	19	0.13
Chilean	3	0.02
Colombian	10	0.07
Ecuadorian	3	0.02
Peruvian	1	0.01
Venezuelan	2	0.01
Other Hispanic or Latino	364	2.44
Hungarian	7	0.05
Irish	254	1.69
Italian	64	0.43
Polish	13	0.09
Portuguese	15	0.10
Scotch-Irish	30	0.20
Scottish	40	0.27
Swedish	9	0.06
United States or American	1,271	8.47
Welsh	11	0.07
West Indian, excl. Hispanic:	1,988	13.25
Bahamian	110	0.73
Barbadian	21	0.14
Haitian	1,476	9.84
Jamaican	381	2.54
White:	4,744	31.83
Not Hispanic (2,058)	2,168	14.54
Hispanic (2,457)	2,576	17.28

Notes: 1. Figures in the "Number" column do not add up to the total population due to: a) Ancestry/Race overlap — e.g. persons can report being both White and Irish, b) persons of Hispanic origin can report being any race, c) persons reporting two ancestries are counted in both categories. 2. Numbers in parentheses indicate the number of persons reporting this ancestry/race alone, not in combination with any other ancestry/race. 3. Refer to the Explanation of Data in the front of the book for more detailed information.

Bellview

Place Type: Census Designated Place
County: Escambia
Population: 21,201

Ancestry/Race	Number	%
Acadian/Cajun	42	0.20
African American/Black:	2,581	12.17
Not Hispanic (2,474)	2,568	12.11
Hispanic (5)	13	0.06
African, sub-Saharan:	32	0.15
African	32	0.15
Alaska Native tribes, specified:	1	0.00
Aleut (1)	1	0.00
Am. Ind. or Alaska Nat., not spec.	109	0.51
American Indian tribes, specified:	327	1.54
Apache (1)	1	0.00
Blackfeet (1)	4	0.02
Cherokee (36)	90	0.42
Chickasaw	2	0.01
Chippewa (7)	7	0.03
Choctaw (9)	20	0.09
Colville	1	0.00
Creek (80)	135	0.64
Crow	1	0.00
Delaware (1)	2	0.01
Houma (11)	11	0.05
Latin American Indians (1)	2	0.01
Navajo (5)	8	0.04
Ottawa (1)	1	0.00
Paiute (4)	4	0.02
Potawatomi (2)	3	0.01
Pueblo (1)	2	0.01
Puget Sound Salish (6)	6	0.03
Seminole	2	0.01
Sioux (8)	10	0.05
All other tribes (2)	15	0.07
American Indian tribes, not spec.	8	0.04
Arab:	25	0.12
Arab/Arabic	7	0.03
Egyptian	13	0.06
Lebanese	5	0.02
Armenian	8	0.04
Asian:	917	4.33
Chinese, ex. Taiwanese (19)	36	0.17
Filipino (438)	585	2.76
Indian (13)	19	0.09
Indonesian	1	0.00
Japanese (46)	73	0.34
Korean (23)	31	0.15
Malaysian	9	0.04
Pakistani (1)	1	0.00
Sri Lankan	1	0.00
Taiwanese (3)	3	0.01
Thai (7)	11	0.05
Vietnamese (122)	134	0.63
Other Asian, specified (1)	1	0.00
Other Asian, not specified (7)	12	0.06
Austrian	29	0.14
Brazilian	8	0.04
British	98	0.47
Bulgarian	15	0.07
Canadian	61	0.29
Croatian	8	0.04
Czech	17	0.08
Czechoslovakian	7	0.03
Danish	76	0.36
Dutch	215	1.02
English	2,186	10.38
European	238	1.13
Finnish	5	0.02
French, except Basque	688	3.27
French Canadian	107	0.51
German	2,749	13.05
Greek	56	0.27
Hawaii Native/Pacific Islander:	58	0.27
Micronesian: (16)	24	0.11
Guamanian/Chamorro (16)	24	0.11
Polynesian: (10)	24	0.11
Native Hawaiian (9)	23	0.11
Samoan (1)	1	0.00
Other Pac. Isl., not spec. (6)	10	0.05
Hispanic or Latino:	509	2.40
Central American:	21	0.10
Guatemalan	1	0.00
Honduran	1	0.00
Nicaraguan	1	0.00
Panamanian	16	0.08
Salvadoran	2	0.01
Cuban	19	0.09
Mexican	169	0.80
Puerto Rican	134	0.63
South American:	25	0.12
Argentinean	5	0.02
Bolivian	1	0.00
Chilean	3	0.01
Colombian	10	0.05
Ecuadorian	4	0.02
Peruvian	1	0.00
Venezuelan	1	0.00
Other Hispanic or Latino	141	0.67
Hungarian	75	0.36
Irish	2,321	11.02
Italian	1,007	4.78
Norwegian	130	0.62
Polish	360	1.71
Portuguese	49	0.23
Romanian	15	0.07
Russian	63	0.30
Scandinavian	14	0.07
Scotch-Irish	547	2.60
Scottish	366	1.74
Slovak	39	0.19
Swedish	313	1.49
Swiss	21	0.10
Ukrainian	34	0.16
United States or American	2,863	13.59
Welsh	188	0.89
West Indian, excl. Hispanic:	21	0.10
Trinidadian and Tobagonian	10	0.05
West Indian	11	0.05
White:	17,575	82.90
Not Hispanic (16,771)	17,207	81.16
Hispanic (329)	368	1.74
Yugoslavian	22	0.10

Bloomingdale

Place Type: Census Designated Place
County: Hillsborough
Population: 19,839

Ancestry/Race	Number	%
African American/Black:	1,358	6.85
Not Hispanic (1,237)	1,322	6.66
Hispanic (29)	36	0.18
African, sub-Saharan:	158	0.79
African	54	0.27
Cape Verdean	53	0.27
South African	41	0.21
Zimbabwean	10	0.05
Am. Ind. or Alaska Nat., not spec.	35	0.18
Albanian	8	0.04
American Indian tribes, specified:	104	0.52
Apache	4	0.02
Blackfeet (3)	3	0.02
Cherokee (11)	39	0.20
Chippewa (1)	2	0.01
Choctaw (2)	3	0.02
Cree	1	0.01
Creek (3)	6	0.03
Iroquois (2)	3	0.02
Latin American Indians (1)	4	0.02
Lumbee (2)	2	0.01
Navajo	3	0.02
Pueblo (1)	1	0.01
Puget Sound Salish	6	0.03
Sioux	2	0.01
All other tribes (9)	25	0.13
American Indian tribes, not spec.	9	0.05
Arab:	136	0.68
Arab/Arabic	33	0.17
Egyptian	3	0.02
Lebanese	92	0.46
Syrian	8	0.04
Armenian	9	0.05
Asian:	602	3.03
Chinese, ex. Taiwanese (70)	96	0.48
Filipino (70)	111	0.56
Hmong (6)	6	0.03
Indian (144)	163	0.82
Japanese (17)	39	0.20
Korean (53)	80	0.40
Pakistani	4	0.02
Taiwanese (3)	3	0.02
Thai (15)	18	0.09
Vietnamese (38)	45	0.23
Other Asian, not specified (23)	37	0.19
Australian	9	0.05
Austrian	23	0.12
Brazilian	28	0.14
British	73	0.37
Canadian	135	0.68
Croatian	68	0.34
Czech	46	0.23
Czechoslovakian	41	0.21
Danish	89	0.45
Dutch	356	1.79
Eastern European	7	0.04
English	2,928	14.69
European	241	1.21
Finnish	63	0.32
French, except Basque	721	3.62
French Canadian	148	0.74
German	3,849	19.31
Greek	193	0.97
Guyanese	5	0.03
Hawaii Native/Pacific Islander:	33	0.17
Micronesian: (3)	7	0.04
Guamanian/Chamorro (3)	7	0.04
Polynesian: (2)	10	0.05
Native Hawaiian (1)	7	0.04
Samoan (1)	3	0.02
Other Pac. Isl., not spec. (9)	16	0.08
Hispanic or Latino:	1,375	6.93
Central American:	67	0.34
Costa Rican	8	0.04
Guatemalan	5	0.03
Honduran	14	0.07
Nicaraguan	5	0.03
Panamanian	23	0.12
Salvadoran	12	0.06
Cuban	215	1.08
Dominican Republic	19	0.10
Mexican	136	0.69
Puerto Rican	554	2.79
South American:	80	0.40
Argentinean	6	0.03
Bolivian	1	0.01
Chilean	2	0.01
Colombian	39	0.20
Ecuadorian	6	0.03
Peruvian	11	0.06
Venezuelan	8	0.04
Other South American	7	0.04
Other Hispanic or Latino	304	1.53
Hungarian	109	0.55
Irish	3,238	16.25
Israeli	9	0.05
Italian	1,735	8.71
Lithuanian	37	0.19
Norwegian	207	1.04
Pennsylvania German	10	0.05
Polish	935	4.69
Portuguese	133	0.67
Romanian	20	0.10
Russian	166	0.83
Scandinavian	9	0.05
Scotch-Irish	449	2.25

Notes: 1. Figures in the "Number" column do not add up to the total population due to: a) Ancestry/Race overlap — e.g. persons can report being both White and Irish, b) persons of Hispanic origin can report being any race, c) persons reporting two ancestries are counted in both categories. 2. Numbers in parentheses indicate the number of persons reporting this ancestry/race alone, not in combination with any other ancestry/race. 3. Refer to the Explanation of Data in the front of the book for more detailed information.

Ancestry/Race	Number	%
Scottish	616	3.09
Slavic	18	0.09
Slovak	18	0.09
Slovene	7	0.04
Swedish	362	1.82
Swiss	40	0.20
Turkish	18	0.09
Ukrainian	54	0.27
United States or American	1,387	6.96
Welsh	165	0.83
West Indian, excl. Hispanic:	136	0.68
Haitian	2	0.01
Jamaican	120	0.60
West Indian	14	0.07
White:	17,779	89.62
Not Hispanic (16,421)	16,651	83.93
Hispanic (1,062)	1,128	5.69
Yugoslavian	25	0.13

Boca Del Mar

Place Type: Census Designated Place
County: Palm Beach
Population: 21,832

Ancestry/Race	Number	%
African American/Black:	324	1.48
Not Hispanic (256)	305	1.40
Hispanic (13)	19	0.09
African, sub-Saharan:	98	0.46
Nigerian	9	0.04
South African	89	0.42
Am. Ind. or Alaska Nat., not spec.	22	0.10
American Indian tribes, specified:	18	0.08
Blackfeet	3	0.01
Cherokee	6	0.03
Iroquois	2	0.01
Latin American Indians (1)	3	0.01
All other tribes (3)	4	0.02
American Indian tribes, not spec.	6	0.03
Arab:	190	0.89
Arab/Arabic	18	0.08
Lebanese	43	0.20
Moroccan	41	0.19
Syrian	39	0.18
Other Arab	49	0.23
Armenian	43	0.20
Asian:	474	2.17
Bangladeshi (10)	11	0.05
Chinese, ex. Taiwanese (112)	122	0.56
Filipino (23)	33	0.15
Hmong (1)	1	0.00
Indian (167)	177	0.81
Indonesian (1)	2	0.01
Japanese (30)	34	0.16
Korean (31)	37	0.17
Pakistani	4	0.02
Sri Lankan (2)	2	0.01
Taiwanese (6)	6	0.03
Thai (9)	9	0.04
Vietnamese (13)	13	0.06
Other Asian, specified (1)	1	0.00
Other Asian, not specified (2)	22	0.10
Austrian	281	1.31
Belgian	18	0.08
Brazilian	171	0.80
British	87	0.41
Canadian	115	0.54
Cypriot	12	0.06
Czech	129	0.60
Czechoslovakian	112	0.52
Danish	64	0.30
Dutch	262	1.22
Eastern European	250	1.17
English	1,625	7.58
European	188	0.88
Finnish	18	0.08
French, except Basque	537	2.51
French Canadian	102	0.48
German	2,730	12.74
Greek	195	0.91
Guyanese	57	0.27
Hawaii Native/Pacific Islander:	12	0.05
Melanesian:	3	0.01
Fijian	3	0.01
Micronesian:	1	0.00
Guamanian/Chamorro	1	0.00
Polynesian: (3)	4	0.02
Native Hawaiian (3)	4	0.02
Other Pac. Isl., not spec. (3)	4	0.02
Hispanic or Latino:	1,782	8.16
Central American:	68	0.31
Costa Rican	9	0.04
Guatemalan	10	0.05
Honduran	17	0.08
Nicaraguan	13	0.06
Panamanian	13	0.06
Salvadoran	5	0.02
Other Central American	1	0.00
Cuban	213	0.98
Dominican Republic	38	0.17
Mexican	114	0.52
Puerto Rican	225	1.03
South American:	626	2.87
Argentinean	60	0.27
Bolivian	5	0.02
Chilean	29	0.13
Colombian	262	1.20
Ecuadorian	32	0.15
Paraguayan	2	0.01
Peruvian	116	0.53
Uruguayan	9	0.04
Venezuelan	85	0.39
Other South American	26	0.12
Other Hispanic or Latino	498	2.28
Hungarian	382	1.78
Iranian	53	0.25
Irish	2,063	9.63
Israeli	58	0.27
Italian	2,999	14.00
Latvian	19	0.09
Lithuanian	155	0.72
Macedonian	15	0.07
Northern European	17	0.08
Norwegian	157	0.73
Pennsylvania German	26	0.12
Polish	1,604	7.49
Portuguese	43	0.20
Romanian	208	0.97
Russian	2,027	9.46
Scandinavian	19	0.09
Scotch-Irish	224	1.05
Scottish	316	1.47
Slavic	40	0.19
Slovak	52	0.24
Slovene	16	0.07
Soviet Union	15	0.07
Swedish	117	0.55
Swiss	29	0.14
Turkish	54	0.25
Ukrainian	244	1.14
United States or American	1,306	6.09
Welsh	83	0.39
West Indian, excl. Hispanic:	184	0.86
Bahamian	9	0.04
Haitian	98	0.46
Jamaican	60	0.28
U.S. Virgin Islander	17	0.08
White:	20,849	95.50
Not Hispanic (19,136)	19,280	88.31
Hispanic (1,480)	1,569	7.19
Yugoslavian	49	0.23

Boca Raton

Place Type: City
County: Palm Beach
Population: 74,764

Ancestry/Race	Number	%
African American/Black:	3,251	4.35
Not Hispanic (2,725)	3,131	4.19
Hispanic (85)	120	0.16
African, sub-Saharan:	356	0.47
African	104	0.14
Cape Verdean	14	0.02
Ethiopian	55	0.07
Kenyan	5	0.01
Nigerian	6	0.01
South African	163	0.22
Other sub-Saharan African	9	0.01
Alaska Native tribes, specified:	3	0.00
Tlingit-Haida (1)	3	0.00
Am. Ind. or Alaska Nat., not spec.	106	0.14
Albanian	36	0.05
Alsatian	19	0.03
American Indian tribes, specified:	159	0.21
Blackfeet (2)	6	0.01
Cherokee (19)	62	0.08
Chickasaw	1	0.00
Chippewa (1)	3	0.00
Choctaw	2	0.00
Creek	3	0.00
Iroquois (8)	18	0.02
Latin American Indians (20)	32	0.04
Lumbee (2)	3	0.00
Potawatomi (2)	8	0.01
Pueblo (4)	4	0.01
Seminole (1)	1	0.00
Sioux	1	0.00
All other tribes (11)	19	0.03
American Indian tribes, not spec.	22	0.03
Arab:	704	0.93
Arab/Arabic	80	0.11
Egyptian	71	0.09
Iraqi	11	0.01
Jordanian	29	0.04
Lebanese	375	0.50
Moroccan	39	0.05
Palestinian	7	0.01
Syrian	48	0.06
Other Arab	44	0.06
Armenian	132	0.17
Asian:	1,879	2.51
Bangladeshi (18)	24	0.03
Cambodian (5)	10	0.01
Chinese, ex. Taiwanese (387)	450	0.60
Filipino (159)	215	0.29
Indian (537)	623	0.83
Indonesian (4)	10	0.01
Japanese (52)	97	0.13
Korean (84)	97	0.13
Malaysian (3)	6	0.01
Pakistani (33)	41	0.05
Sri Lankan (11)	17	0.02
Taiwanese (5)	6	0.01
Thai (32)	41	0.05
Vietnamese (102)	119	0.16
Other Asian, specified (7)	14	0.02
Other Asian, not specified (33)	109	0.15
Australian	26	0.03
Austrian	786	1.04
Basque	26	0.03
Belgian	70	0.09
Brazilian	788	1.04
British	558	0.74
Bulgarian	75	0.10
Canadian	582	0.77
Celtic	32	0.04
Croatian	80	0.11
Cypriot	52	0.07
Czech	396	0.52
Czechoslovakian	136	0.18
Danish	240	0.32
Dutch	1,241	1.64
Eastern European	518	0.69
English	7,127	9.43
Estonian	21	0.03
European	735	0.97
Finnish	210	0.28

Notes: 1. Figures in the "Number" column do not add up to the total population due to: a) Ancestry/Race overlap — e.g. persons can report being both White and Irish, b) persons of Hispanic origin can report being any race, c) persons reporting two ancestries are counted in both categories. 2. Numbers in parentheses indicate the number of persons reporting this ancestry/race alone, not in combination with any other ancestry/race. 3. Refer to the Explanation of Data in the front of the book for more detailed information.

Ancestry/Race	Number	%
French, except Basque	2,105	2.78
French Canadian	628	0.83
German	10,855	14.36
Greek	1,065	1.41
Guyanese	6	0.01
Hawaii Native/Pacific Islander:	89	0.12
Micronesian: (7)	18	0.02
Guamanian/Chamorro (7)	18	0.02
Polynesian: (13)	24	0.03
Native Hawaiian (9)	19	0.03
Samoan (4)	4	0.01
Other Polynesian	1	0.00
Other Pac. Isl., specified	4	0.01
Other Pac. Isl., not spec. (9)	43	0.06
Hispanic or Latino:	6,359	8.51
Central American:	397	0.53
Costa Rican	32	0.04
Guatemalan	98	0.13
Honduran	108	0.14
Nicaraguan	57	0.08
Panamanian	42	0.06
Salvadoran	44	0.06
Other Central American	16	0.02
Cuban	1,099	1.47
Dominican Republic	167	0.22
Mexican	778	1.04
Puerto Rican	762	1.02
South American:	1,662	2.22
Argentinean	159	0.21
Bolivian	27	0.04
Chilean	95	0.13
Colombian	685	0.92
Ecuadorian	139	0.19
Paraguayan	10	0.01
Peruvian	202	0.27
Uruguayan	15	0.02
Venezuelan	242	0.32
Other South American	88	0.12
Other Hispanic or Latino	1,494	2.00
Hungarian	1,054	1.39
Iranian	202	0.27
Irish	9,075	12.00
Israeli	237	0.31
Italian	9,386	12.42
Latvian	72	0.10
Lithuanian	343	0.45
Macedonian	70	0.09
Maltese	45	0.06
New Zealander	17	0.02
Northern European	69	0.09
Norwegian	796	1.05
Pennsylvania German	6	0.01
Polish	4,521	5.98
Portuguese	450	0.60
Romanian	365	0.48
Russian	4,066	5.38
Scandinavian	110	0.15
Scotch-Irish	915	1.21
Scottish	1,816	2.40
Serbian	39	0.05
Slavic	51	0.07
Slovak	186	0.25
Slovene	23	0.03
Swedish	1,045	1.38
Swiss	215	0.28
Turkish	147	0.19
Ukrainian	417	0.55
United States or American	4,229	5.59
Welsh	452	0.60
West Indian, excl. Hispanic:	1,352	1.79
Bahamian	34	0.04
Barbadian	23	0.03
British West Indian	7	0.01
Dutch West Indian	7	0.01
Haitian	928	1.23
Jamaican	201	0.27
Trinidadian and Tobagonian	119	0.16
West Indian	33	0.04
White:	68,870	92.12
Not Hispanic (62,925)	63,558	85.01
Hispanic (4,926)	5,312	7.11
Yugoslavian	111	0.15

Bonita Springs

Place Type: City
County: Lee
Population: 32,797

Ancestry/Race	Number	%
Afghan	10	0.03
African American/Black:	169	0.52
Not Hispanic (101)	135	0.41
Hispanic (17)	34	0.10
Alaska Native tribes, not specified	1	0.00
Am. Ind. or Alaska Nat., not spec.	63	0.19
American Indian tribes, specified:	114	0.35
Apache (3)	3	0.01
Blackfeet (1)	4	0.01
Cherokee (6)	30	0.09
Chippewa (2)	4	0.01
Creek (1)	2	0.01
Iroquois (1)	2	0.01
Kiowa (1)	1	0.00
Latin American Indians (22)	48	0.15
Lumbee (1)	1	0.00
Ottawa (1)	1	0.00
Seminole (2)	2	0.01
Sioux (5)	5	0.02
Tohono O'Odham	1	0.00
All other tribes (3)	10	0.03
American Indian tribes, not spec.	4	0.01
Arab:	84	0.26
Egyptian	19	0.06
Lebanese	34	0.10
Syrian	31	0.09
Armenian	13	0.04
Asian:	175	0.53
Chinese, ex. Taiwanese (47)	54	0.16
Filipino (22)	40	0.12
Indian (18)	23	0.07
Japanese (5)	12	0.04
Korean (12)	15	0.05
Laotian	1	0.00
Pakistani	1	0.00
Thai (1)	2	0.01
Vietnamese (8)	9	0.03
Other Asian, specified (1)	1	0.00
Other Asian, not specified (3)	17	0.05
Australian	6	0.02
Austrian	125	0.38
Belgian	42	0.13
British	117	0.36
Bulgarian	5	0.02
Canadian	299	0.91
Croatian	91	0.28
Cypriot	12	0.04
Czech	276	0.84
Czechoslovakian	103	0.31
Danish	211	0.64
Dutch	695	2.11
Eastern European	24	0.07
English	4,884	14.84
European	91	0.28
Finnish	50	0.15
French, except Basque	1,126	3.42
French Canadian	538	1.63
German	6,740	20.48
Greek	68	0.21
Hawaii Native/Pacific Islander:	59	0.18
Micronesian: (22)	31	0.09
Guamanian/Chamorro (22)	31	0.09
Polynesian: (6)	21	0.06
Native Hawaiian (3)	16	0.05
Samoan (3)	5	0.02
Other Pac. Isl., not spec.	7	0.02
Hispanic or Latino:	5,615	17.12
Central American:	663	2.02
Costa Rican	34	0.10
Guatemalan	393	1.20
Honduran	98	0.30
Nicaraguan	6	0.02
Panamanian	1	0.00
Salvadoran	128	0.39
Other Central American	3	0.01
Cuban	163	0.50
Dominican Republic	15	0.05
Mexican	3,955	12.06
Puerto Rican	135	0.41
South American:	143	0.44
Argentinean	30	0.09
Bolivian	1	0.00
Chilean	9	0.03
Colombian	76	0.23
Ecuadorian	5	0.02
Peruvian	12	0.04
Uruguayan	6	0.02
Venezuelan	2	0.01
Other South American	2	0.01
Other Hispanic or Latino	541	1.65
Hungarian	383	1.16
Iranian	16	0.05
Irish	4,475	13.60
Israeli	21	0.06
Italian	1,925	5.85
Latvian	7	0.02
Lithuanian	155	0.47
Luxemburger	9	0.03
Northern European	7	0.02
Norwegian	405	1.23
Pennsylvania German	49	0.15
Polish	1,294	3.93
Portuguese	82	0.25
Romanian	53	0.16
Russian	301	0.91
Scandinavian	76	0.23
Scotch-Irish	626	1.90
Scottish	888	2.70
Serbian	31	0.09
Slavic	12	0.04
Slovak	147	0.45
Slovene	35	0.11
Swedish	630	1.91
Swiss	196	0.60
Turkish	24	0.07
Ukrainian	101	0.31
United States or American	2,057	6.25
Welsh	250	0.76
West Indian, excl. Hispanic:	32	0.10
Jamaican	5	0.02
Trinidadian and Tobagonian	27	0.08
White:	29,787	90.82
Not Hispanic (26,669)	26,851	81.87
Hispanic (2,687)	2,936	8.95
Yugoslavian	8	0.02

Boynton Beach

Place Type: City
County: Palm Beach
Population: 60,389

Ancestry/Race	Number	%
Acadian/Cajun	22	0.04
African American/Black:	14,838	24.57
Not Hispanic (13,585)	14,528	24.06
Hispanic (237)	310	0.51
African, sub-Saharan:	339	0.57
African	221	0.37
Cape Verdean	4	0.01
Liberian	85	0.14
Nigerian	23	0.04
South African	6	0.01
Alaska Native tribes, specified:	2	0.00
Tlingit-Haida (1)	2	0.00
Am. Ind. or Alaska Nat., not spec.	107	0.18
Albanian	11	0.02
Alsatian	21	0.04
American Indian tribes, specified:	126	0.21
Apache (2)	3	0.00

Notes: 1. Figures in the "Number" column do not add up to the total population due to: a) Ancestry/Race overlap — e.g. persons can report being both White and Irish, b) persons of Hispanic origin can report being any race, c) persons reporting two ancestries are counted in both categories. 2. Numbers in parentheses indicate the number of persons reporting this ancestry/race alone, not in combination with any other ancestry/race. 3. Refer to the Explanation of Data in the front of the book for more detailed information.

Ancestry/Race	Number	%
Blackfeet (1)	4	0.01
Cherokee (19)	43	0.07
Chippewa (2)	6	0.01
Choctaw (1)	1	0.00
Comanche (1)	1	0.00
Creek (2)	3	0.00
Iroquois (5)	6	0.01
Latin American Indians (20)	30	0.05
Navajo (4)	6	0.01
Osage	1	0.00
Paiute	1	0.00
Potawatomi	1	0.00
Pueblo	1	0.00
Seminole (4)	7	0.01
Shoshone	1	0.00
Sioux (3)	4	0.01
All other tribes (2)	7	0.01
American Indian tribes, not spec.	20	0.03
Arab:	164	0.27
Egyptian	15	0.03
Iraqi	12	0.02
Lebanese	118	0.20
Syrian	19	0.03
Armenian	32	0.05
Asian:	1,156	1.91
Bangladeshi (33)	50	0.08
Chinese, ex. Taiwanese (207)	254	0.42
Filipino (132)	168	0.28
Indian (371)	415	0.69
Indonesian (4)	5	0.01
Japanese (15)	29	0.05
Korean (31)	47	0.08
Malaysian	1	0.00
Pakistani (7)	8	0.01
Sri Lankan (2)	2	0.00
Taiwanese (1)	3	0.00
Thai (27)	32	0.05
Vietnamese (41)	56	0.09
Other Asian, specified	3	0.00
Other Asian, not specified (30)	83	0.14
Australian	24	0.04
Austrian	322	0.54
Belgian	74	0.12
Brazilian	56	0.09
British	213	0.36
Canadian	201	0.34
Croatian	75	0.13
Czech	188	0.31
Czechoslovakian	92	0.15
Danish	131	0.22
Dutch	932	1.55
Eastern European	66	0.11
English	5,415	9.03
Estonian	11	0.02
European	198	0.33
Finnish	222	0.37
French, except Basque	1,598	2.67
French Canadian	449	0.75
German	7,057	11.77
Greek	304	0.51
Guyanese	25	0.04
Hawaii Native/Pacific Islander:	108	0.18
Micronesian: (15)	27	0.04
Guamanian/Chamorro (15)	27	0.04
Polynesian: (8)	12	0.02
Native Hawaiian (6)	10	0.02
Samoan (2)	2	0.00
Other Pac. Isl., not spec. (7)	69	0.11
Hispanic or Latino:	5,564	9.21
Central American:	525	0.87
Costa Rican	44	0.07
Guatemalan	164	0.27
Honduran	56	0.09
Nicaraguan	60	0.10
Panamanian	2	0.00
Salvadoran	182	0.30
Other Central American	17	0.03
Cuban	530	0.88
Dominican Republic	183	0.30
Mexican	1,199	1.99
Puerto Rican	1,652	2.74
South American:	592	0.98
Argentinean	64	0.11
Bolivian	10	0.02
Chilean	13	0.02
Colombian	271	0.45
Ecuadorian	60	0.10
Paraguayan	3	0.00
Peruvian	93	0.15
Uruguayan	14	0.02
Venezuelan	52	0.09
Other South American	12	0.02
Other Hispanic or Latino	883	1.46
Hungarian	627	1.05
Iranian	27	0.05
Irish	6,976	11.64
Israeli	22	0.04
Italian	5,829	9.72
Latvian	21	0.04
Lithuanian	215	0.36
Macedonian	34	0.06
Norwegian	379	0.63
Pennsylvania German	50	0.08
Polish	2,027	3.38
Portuguese	135	0.23
Romanian	208	0.35
Russian	1,420	2.37
Scandinavian	19	0.03
Scotch-Irish	774	1.29
Scottish	1,197	2.00
Serbian	44	0.07
Slavic	50	0.08
Slovak	196	0.33
Swedish	702	1.17
Swiss	84	0.14
Turkish	86	0.14
Ukrainian	226	0.38
United States or American	3,112	5.19
Welsh	309	0.52
West Indian, excl. Hispanic:	5,221	8.71
Bahamian	84	0.14
Barbadian	67	0.11
Bermudan	5	0.01
British West Indian	53	0.09
Haitian	4,040	6.74
Jamaican	856	1.43
Trinidadian and Tobagonian	62	0.10
U.S. Virgin Islander	6	0.01
West Indian	48	0.08
White:	43,133	71.43
Not Hispanic (38,897)	39,275	65.04
Hispanic (3,590)	3,858	6.39
Yugoslavian	39	0.07

Bradenton

Place Type: City
County: Manatee
Population: 49,504

Ancestry/Race	Number	%
Acadian/Cajun	21	0.04
African American/Black:	7,835	15.83
Not Hispanic (7,381)	7,665	15.48
Hispanic (100)	170	0.34
African, sub-Saharan:	330	0.66
African	302	0.61
Nigerian	2	0.00
South African	12	0.02
Zimbabwean	14	0.03
Alaska Native tribes, specified:	7	0.01
Eskimo (2)	3	0.01
Tlingit-Haida (3)	4	0.01
Alaska Native tribes, not specified	1	0.00
Am. Ind. or Alaska Nat., not spec.	101	0.20
American Indian tribes, specified:	178	0.36
Apache (3)	9	0.02
Blackfeet (5)	24	0.05
Cherokee (26)	67	0.14
Cheyenne (1)	1	0.00
Chippewa (4)	7	0.01
Choctaw	3	0.01
Comanche	1	0.00
Creek (1)	1	0.00
Delaware	1	0.00
Iroquois (2)	8	0.02
Latin American Indians (16)	18	0.04
Lumbee (4)	4	0.01
Navajo (7)	7	0.01
Seminole (1)	4	0.01
Shoshone (1)	1	0.00
Sioux (5)	7	0.01
All other tribes (11)	15	0.03
American Indian tribes, not spec.	16	0.03
Arab:	148	0.30
Arab/Arabic	9	0.02
Egyptian	37	0.07
Lebanese	55	0.11
Moroccan	25	0.05
Palestinian	8	0.02
Syrian	14	0.03
Armenian	32	0.06
Asian:	508	1.03
Bangladeshi (6)	6	0.01
Cambodian (24)	26	0.05
Chinese, ex. Taiwanese (116)	127	0.26
Filipino (51)	76	0.15
Indian (103)	129	0.26
Indonesian	2	0.00
Japanese (20)	30	0.06
Korean (24)	26	0.05
Laotian (3)	7	0.01
Taiwanese (1)	1	0.00
Thai (19)	20	0.04
Vietnamese (15)	18	0.04
Other Asian, specified (3)	5	0.01
Other Asian, not specified (4)	35	0.07
Australian	4	0.01
Austrian	181	0.36
Belgian	20	0.04
British	220	0.44
Canadian	138	0.28
Croatian	88	0.18
Czech	149	0.30
Czechoslovakian	76	0.15
Danish	85	0.17
Dutch	1,185	2.37
English	5,996	12.01
Estonian	10	0.02
European	150	0.30
Finnish	69	0.14
French, except Basque	1,868	3.74
French Canadian	394	0.79
German	7,444	14.92
Greek	190	0.38
Guyanese	25	0.05
Hawaii Native/Pacific Islander:	55	0.11
Micronesian: (2)	7	0.01
Guamanian/Chamorro (2)	7	0.01
Polynesian: (19)	28	0.06
Native Hawaiian (6)	13	0.03
Samoan (4)	6	0.01
Tongan (5)	5	0.01
Other Polynesian (4)	4	0.01
Other Pac. Isl., specified	2	0.00
Other Pac. Isl., not spec. (2)	18	0.04
Hispanic or Latino:	5,574	11.26
Central American:	326	0.66
Costa Rican	2	0.00
Guatemalan	78	0.16
Honduran	130	0.26
Nicaraguan	42	0.08
Panamanian	11	0.02
Salvadoran	40	0.08
Other Central American	23	0.05
Cuban	234	0.47
Dominican Republic	46	0.09
Mexican	3,507	7.08
Puerto Rican	663	1.34
South American:	159	0.32

Notes: 1. Figures in the "Number" column do not add up to the total population due to: a) Ancestry/Race overlap — e.g. persons can report being both White and Irish, b) persons of Hispanic origin can report being any race, c) persons reporting two ancestries are counted in both categories. 2. Numbers in parentheses indicate the number of persons reporting this ancestry/race alone, not in combination with any other ancestry/race. 3. Refer to the Explanation of Data in the front of the book for more detailed information.

Argentinean	16	0.03
Chilean	11	0.02
Colombian	55	0.11
Ecuadorian	13	0.03
Paraguayan	3	0.01
Peruvian	19	0.04
Uruguayan	3	0.01
Venezuelan	25	0.05
Other South American	14	0.03
Other Hispanic or Latino	639	1.29
Hungarian	375	0.75
Iranian	16	0.03
Irish	5,420	10.86
Israeli	33	0.07
Italian	2,705	5.42
Latvian	16	0.03
Lithuanian	126	0.25
Luxemburger	9	0.02
Macedonian	7	0.01
Norwegian	474	0.95
Pennsylvania German	109	0.22
Polish	1,299	2.60
Portuguese	60	0.12
Romanian	16	0.03
Russian	313	0.63
Scandinavian	39	0.08
Scotch-Irish	920	1.84
Scottish	1,220	2.44
Serbian	27	0.05
Slavic	12	0.02
Slovak	137	0.27
Slovene	15	0.03
Swedish	613	1.23
Swiss	192	0.38
Turkish	10	0.02
Ukrainian	158	0.32
United States or American	3,338	6.69
Welsh	501	1.00
West Indian, excl. Hispanic:	548	1.10
Bahamian	68	0.14
Barbadian	5	0.01
Haitian	325	0.65
Jamaican	117	0.23
Trinidadian and Tobagonian	28	0.06
West Indian	5	0.01
White:	39,326	79.44
Not Hispanic (35,450)	35,821	72.36
Hispanic (3,232)	3,505	7.08
Yugoslavian	31	0.06

Brandon

Place Type: Census Designated Place
County: Hillsborough
Population: 77,895

Ancestry/Race	Number	%
African American/Black:	7,766	9.97
Not Hispanic (6,924)	7,358	9.45
Hispanic (289)	408	0.52
African, sub-Saharan:	197	0.25
African	162	0.21
Cape Verdean	7	0.01
Ghanian	12	0.02
Other sub-Saharan African	16	0.02
Alaska Native tribes, specified:	4	0.01
Alaska Athabascan (1)	1	0.00
Eskimo (1)	1	0.00
Tlingit-Haida	2	0.00
Am. Ind. or Alaska Nat., not spec.	202	0.26
American Indian tribes, specified:	471	0.60
Apache (1)	6	0.01
Blackfeet (5)	26	0.03
Cherokee (72)	219	0.28
Cheyenne (1)	1	0.00
Chickasaw (1)	3	0.00
Chippewa (3)	9	0.01
Choctaw (11)	22	0.03
Comanche (3)	3	0.00
Cree	3	0.00
Creek (22)	24	0.03
Delaware	1	0.00
Iroquois (10)	14	0.02
Latin American Indians (11)	27	0.03
Lumbee (4)	5	0.01
Menominee (1)	1	0.00
Navajo (1)	1	0.00
Ottawa (2)	3	0.00
Potawatomi (2)	3	0.00
Pueblo (1)	2	0.00
Seminole (19)	26	0.03
Shoshone	1	0.00
Sioux (20)	28	0.04
Tohono O'Odham	1	0.00
All other tribes (13)	42	0.05
American Indian tribes, not spec.	52	0.07
Arab:	345	0.44
Arab/Arabic	7	0.01
Egyptian	42	0.05
Lebanese	84	0.11
Moroccan	9	0.01
Palestinian	149	0.19
Syrian	24	0.03
Other Arab	30	0.04
Armenian	57	0.07
Asian:	2,438	3.13
Cambodian (4)	4	0.01
Chinese, ex. Taiwanese (187)	256	0.33
Filipino (438)	602	0.77
Indian (566)	629	0.81
Indonesian (13)	19	0.02
Japanese (76)	130	0.17
Korean (235)	313	0.40
Laotian	4	0.01
Malaysian	2	0.00
Pakistani (10)	14	0.02
Taiwanese (1)	4	0.01
Thai (101)	140	0.18
Vietnamese (158)	184	0.24
Other Asian, specified	3	0.00
Other Asian, not specified (54)	134	0.17
Australian	8	0.01
Austrian	115	0.15
Belgian	132	0.17
Brazilian	107	0.14
British	556	0.72
Canadian	267	0.34
Croatian	93	0.12
Cypriot	17	0.02
Czech	272	0.35
Czechoslovakian	127	0.16
Danish	139	0.18
Dutch	1,352	1.74
Eastern European	44	0.06
English	8,848	11.38
European	856	1.10
Finnish	78	0.10
French, except Basque	2,988	3.84
French Canadian	688	0.89
German	11,195	14.40
Greek	352	0.45
Guyanese	8	0.01
Hawaii Native/Pacific Islander:	153	0.20
Melanesian: (1)	1	0.00
Fijian (1)	1	0.00
Micronesian: (20)	29	0.04
Guamanian/Chamorro (16)	25	0.03
Other Micronesian (4)	4	0.01
Polynesian: (34)	66	0.08
Native Hawaiian (14)	38	0.05
Samoan (11)	15	0.02
Tongan (3)	3	0.00
Other Polynesian (6)	10	0.01
Other Pac. Isl., specified	3	0.00
Other Pac. Isl., not spec. (16)	54	0.07
Hispanic or Latino:	9,882	12.69
Central American:	378	0.49
Costa Rican	23	0.03
Guatemalan	30	0.04
Honduran	76	0.10
Nicaraguan	55	0.07
Panamanian	122	0.16
Salvadoran	60	0.08
Other Central American	12	0.02
Cuban	1,078	1.38
Dominican Republic	232	0.30
Mexican	923	1.18
Puerto Rican	4,599	5.90
South American:	658	0.84
Argentinean	35	0.04
Bolivian	9	0.01
Chilean	25	0.03
Colombian	310	0.40
Ecuadorian	67	0.09
Paraguayan	1	0.00
Peruvian	85	0.11
Uruguayan	7	0.01
Venezuelan	89	0.11
Other South American	30	0.04
Other Hispanic or Latino	2,014	2.59
Hungarian	463	0.60
Icelander	9	0.01
Iranian	50	0.06
Irish	9,678	12.45
Italian	5,377	6.92
Lithuanian	260	0.33
Luxemburger	7	0.01
Northern European	14	0.02
Norwegian	699	0.90
Polish	2,333	3.00
Portuguese	424	0.55
Romanian	61	0.08
Russian	494	0.64
Scandinavian	128	0.16
Scotch-Irish	1,380	1.78
Scottish	1,884	2.42
Serbian	23	0.03
Slavic	47	0.06
Slovak	188	0.24
Slovene	17	0.02
Swedish	719	0.92
Swiss	131	0.17
Turkish	52	0.07
Ukrainian	191	0.25
United States or American	6,631	8.53
Welsh	458	0.59
West Indian, excl. Hispanic:	1,124	1.45
Bahamian	9	0.01
Barbadian	17	0.02
Belizean	48	0.06
British West Indian	52	0.07
Dutch West Indian	32	0.04
Haitian	76	0.10
Jamaican	630	0.81
Trinidadian and Tobagonian	165	0.21
U.S. Virgin Islander	26	0.03
West Indian	69	0.09
White:	65,406	83.97
Not Hispanic (57,398)	58,481	75.08
Hispanic (6,400)	6,925	8.89
Yugoslavian	130	0.17

Brent

Place Type: Census Designated Place
County: Escambia
Population: 22,257

Ancestry/Race	Number	%
Acadian/Cajun	5	0.02
African American/Black:	7,760	34.87
Not Hispanic (7,591)	7,715	34.66
Hispanic (31)	45	0.20
African, sub-Saharan:	240	1.08
African	240	1.08
Alaska Native tribes, specified:	1	0.00
All other tribes	1	0.00
Am. Ind. or Alaska Nat., not spec.	83	0.37
American Indian tribes, specified:	246	1.11
Apache (3)	4	0.02

Notes: 1. Figures in the "Number" column do not add up to the total population due to: a) Ancestry/Race overlap — e.g. persons can report being both White and Irish, b) persons of Hispanic origin can report being any race, c) persons reporting two ancestries are counted in both categories. 2. Numbers in parentheses indicate the number of persons reporting this ancestry/race alone, not in combination with any other ancestry/race. 3. Refer to the Explanation of Data in the front of the book for more detailed information.

Blackfeet (4)	12	0.05
Cherokee (20)	80	0.36
Cheyenne	1	0.00
Chippewa (3)	3	0.01
Choctaw (4)	16	0.07
Creek (71)	98	0.44
Houma (3)	4	0.02
Iroquois (2)	3	0.01
Latin American Indians (3)	6	0.03
Navajo (1)	6	0.03
Osage	1	0.00
Potawatomi	2	0.01
Pueblo	1	0.00
Puget Sound Salish (2)	2	0.01
Seminole	1	0.00
Sioux (1)	3	0.01
All other tribes	3	0.01
American Indian tribes, not spec.	43	0.19
Armenian	5	0.02
Asian:	652	2.93
Cambodian (39)	41	0.18
Chinese, ex. Taiwanese (45)	72	0.32
Filipino (141)	185	0.83
Indian (31)	49	0.22
Indonesian (12)	16	0.07
Japanese (14)	30	0.13
Korean (57)	68	0.31
Laotian (11)	11	0.05
Malaysian	2	0.01
Pakistani (1)	2	0.01
Taiwanese (2)	7	0.03
Thai (8)	14	0.06
Vietnamese (128)	131	0.59
Other Asian, specified (2)	4	0.02
Other Asian, not specified (2)	20	0.09
Austrian	7	0.03
Belgian	39	0.18
British	47	0.21
Canadian	27	0.12
Czech	14	0.06
Czechoslovakian	7	0.03
Danish	14	0.06
Dutch	238	1.07
English	941	4.25
European	104	0.47
Finnish	21	0.09
French, except Basque	268	1.21
French Canadian	39	0.18
German	1,169	5.28
Greek	37	0.17
Hawaii Native/Pacific Islander:	103	0.46
Melanesian:	3	0.01
Other Melanesian	3	0.01
Micronesian: (42)	64	0.29
Guamanian/Chamorro (29)	44	0.20
Other Micronesian (13)	20	0.09
Polynesian: (16)	26	0.12
Native Hawaiian (3)	10	0.04
Samoan (13)	16	0.07
Other Pac. Isl., specified	2	0.01
Other Pac. Isl., not spec. (2)	8	0.04
Hispanic or Latino:	433	1.95
Central American:	27	0.12
Costa Rican	3	0.01
Guatemalan	4	0.02
Honduran	8	0.04
Nicaraguan	1	0.00
Panamanian	10	0.04
Salvadoran	1	0.00
Cuban	32	0.14
Dominican Republic	3	0.01
Mexican	127	0.57
Puerto Rican	117	0.53
South American:	24	0.11
Argentinean	6	0.03
Bolivian	1	0.00
Chilean	1	0.00
Colombian	6	0.03
Ecuadorian	2	0.01
Peruvian	3	0.01
Venezuelan	2	0.01
Other South American	3	0.01
Other Hispanic or Latino	103	0.46
Hungarian	36	0.16
Irish	1,131	5.11
Italian	363	1.64
Norwegian	118	0.53
Pennsylvania German	5	0.02
Polish	141	0.64
Portuguese	36	0.16
Romanian	10	0.05
Russian	47	0.21
Scotch-Irish	338	1.53
Scottish	163	0.74
Slavic	8	0.04
Slovak	6	0.03
Swedish	111	0.50
Swiss	19	0.09
United States or American	1,926	8.69
Welsh	144	0.65
West Indian, excl. Hispanic:	27	0.12
Bahamian	7	0.03
Barbadian	4	0.02
Jamaican	6	0.03
Trinidadian and Tobagonian	10	0.05
White:	13,704	61.57
Not Hispanic (13,082)	13,405	60.23
Hispanic (244)	299	1.34

Brownsville

Place Type: Census Designated Place
County: Miami-Dade
Population: 14,393

Ancestry/Race	Number	%
African American/Black:	13,249	92.05
Not Hispanic (12,974)	13,069	90.80
Hispanic (157)	180	1.25
African, sub-Saharan:	307	2.12
African	307	2.12
Am. Ind. or Alaska Nat., not spec.	48	0.33
American Indian tribes, specified:	27	0.19
Blackfeet	1	0.01
Cherokee	17	0.12
Latin American Indians (2)	3	0.02
Pueblo	1	0.01
Seminole	5	0.03
American Indian tribes, not spec.	2	0.01
Asian:	18	0.13
Indian (3)	8	0.06
Other Asian, specified	2	0.01
Other Asian, not specified	8	0.06
British	13	0.09
Canadian	16	0.11
English	16	0.11
German	3	0.02
Hawaii Native/Pacific Islander:	29	0.20
Polynesian: (1)	4	0.03
Native Hawaiian	3	0.02
Samoan (1)	1	0.01
Other Pac. Isl., specified	2	0.01
Other Pac. Isl., not spec. (1)	23	0.16
Hispanic or Latino:	1,183	8.22
Central American:	261	1.81
Costa Rican	1	0.01
Guatemalan	6	0.04
Honduran	75	0.52
Nicaraguan	151	1.05
Panamanian	4	0.03
Salvadoran	8	0.06
Other Central American	16	0.11
Cuban	446	3.10
Dominican Republic	64	0.44
Mexican	16	0.11
Puerto Rican	81	0.56
South American:	27	0.19
Argentinean	5	0.03
Chilean	1	0.01
Colombian	15	0.10
Peruvian	2	0.01
Uruguayan	1	0.01
Venezuelan	3	0.02
Other Hispanic or Latino	288	2.00
Irish	5	0.03
Italian	21	0.15
Norwegian	3	0.02
Polish	8	0.06
Romanian	9	0.06
Russian	23	0.16
Scotch-Irish	6	0.04
United States or American	550	3.81
West Indian, excl. Hispanic:	544	3.76
Bahamian	279	1.93
Barbadian	8	0.06
Belizean	33	0.23
British West Indian	21	0.15
Haitian	52	0.36
Jamaican	114	0.79
Trinidadian and Tobagonian	17	0.12
West Indian	20	0.14
White:	921	6.40
Not Hispanic (102)	131	0.91
Hispanic (727)	790	5.49

Callaway

Place Type: City
County: Bay
Population: 14,233

Ancestry/Race	Number	%
Acadian/Cajun	21	0.15
African American/Black:	2,390	16.79
Not Hispanic (2,227)	2,357	16.56
Hispanic (24)	33	0.23
African, sub-Saharan:	154	1.08
African	154	1.08
Alaska Native tribes, specified:	2	0.01
Alaska Athabascan (1)	1	0.01
Eskimo	1	0.01
Am. Ind. or Alaska Nat., not spec.	48	0.34
American Indian tribes, specified:	147	1.03
Apache	3	0.02
Blackfeet	14	0.10
Cherokee (24)	54	0.38
Cheyenne (1)	2	0.01
Choctaw (2)	3	0.02
Comanche	1	0.01
Creek (21)	30	0.21
Delaware	2	0.01
Houma (2)	2	0.01
Latin American Indians (1)	5	0.04
Navajo (5)	5	0.04
Paiute (1)	1	0.01
Potawatomi (2)	2	0.01
Seminole (2)	3	0.02
Sioux (1)	4	0.03
Yaqui	1	0.01
All other tribes (12)	15	0.11
American Indian tribes, not spec.	18	0.13
Arab:	35	0.25
Egyptian	30	0.21
Lebanese	5	0.04
Asian:	701	4.93
Chinese, ex. Taiwanese (17)	37	0.26
Filipino (170)	257	1.81
Indian (8)	14	0.10
Indonesian	1	0.01
Japanese (30)	58	0.41
Korean (88)	125	0.88
Laotian (1)	1	0.01
Pakistani	4	0.03
Taiwanese (2)	5	0.04
Thai (52)	76	0.53
Vietnamese (84)	94	0.66
Other Asian, specified	1	0.01
Other Asian, not specified (15)	28	0.20
Australian	8	0.06
Austrian	8	0.06

Notes: 1. Figures in the "Number" column do not add up to the total population due to: a) Ancestry/Race overlap — e.g. persons can report being both White and Irish, b) persons of Hispanic origin can report being any race, c) persons reporting two ancestries are counted in both categories. 2. Numbers in parentheses indicate the number of persons reporting this ancestry/race alone, not in combination with any other ancestry/race. 3. Refer to the Explanation of Data in the front of the book for more detailed information.

Basque	9	0.06
British	97	0.68
Canadian	38	0.27
Celtic	64	0.45
Croatian	9	0.06
Czechoslovakian	22	0.15
Danish	22	0.15
Dutch	155	1.09
English	1,198	8.41
European	169	1.19
French, except Basque	315	2.21
French Canadian	190	1.33
German	1,420	9.96
Greek	16	0.11
Hawaii Native/Pacific Islander:	39	0.27
Micronesian: (5)	6	0.04
Guamanian/Chamorro (5)	6	0.04
Polynesian: (5)	23	0.16
Native Hawaiian (5)	21	0.15
Samoan	2	0.01
Other Pac. Isl., not spec. (2)	10	0.07
Hispanic or Latino:	509	3.58
Central American:	21	0.15
Honduran	2	0.01
Panamanian	18	0.13
Other Central American	1	0.01
Cuban	25	0.18
Dominican Republic	1	0.01
Mexican	189	1.33
Puerto Rican	163	1.15
South American:	12	0.08
Bolivian	3	0.02
Chilean	5	0.04
Colombian	1	0.01
Peruvian	1	0.01
Other South American	2	0.01
Other Hispanic or Latino	98	0.69
Hungarian	40	0.28
Icelander	12	0.08
Irish	1,485	10.42
Israeli	5	0.04
Italian	659	4.62
Norwegian	80	0.56
Pennsylvania German	31	0.22
Polish	230	1.61
Portuguese	21	0.15
Scandinavian	17	0.12
Scotch-Irish	298	2.09
Scottish	232	1.63
Serbian	18	0.13
Slovak	14	0.10
Swedish	112	0.79
Swiss	19	0.13
Turkish	12	0.08
United States or American	1,977	13.87
Welsh	22	0.15
West Indian, excl. Hispanic:	53	0.37
Dutch West Indian	9	0.06
Trinidadian and Tobagonian	44	0.31
White:	11,120	78.13
Not Hispanic (10,501)	10,802	75.89
Hispanic (268)	318	2.23

Cape Coral

Place Type: City
County: Lee
Population: 102,286

Ancestry/Race	Number	%
African American/Black:	2,424	2.37
Not Hispanic (1,831)	2,142	2.09
Hispanic (215)	282	0.28
African, sub-Saharan:	87	0.09
African	19	0.02
Cape Verdean	22	0.02
Liberian	22	0.02
South African	24	0.02
Am. Ind. or Alaska Nat., not spec.	191	0.19
Albanian	6	0.01
Alsatian	16	0.02
American Indian tribes, specified:	448	0.44
Apache (6)	12	0.01
Blackfeet (4)	25	0.02
Cherokee (56)	162	0.16
Cheyenne	1	0.00
Chickasaw (3)	5	0.00
Chippewa (10)	26	0.03
Choctaw (4)	22	0.02
Comanche	1	0.00
Cree	6	0.01
Creek (1)	7	0.01
Crow (1)	1	0.00
Delaware (2)	5	0.00
Houma (1)	1	0.00
Iroquois (24)	38	0.04
Latin American Indians (24)	31	0.03
Lumbee (1)	1	0.00
Navajo (2)	6	0.01
Osage	1	0.00
Potawatomi (7)	13	0.01
Pueblo	6	0.01
Puget Sound Salish (1)	2	0.00
Seminole (4)	13	0.01
Sioux (10)	32	0.03
Ute (1)	1	0.00
Yaqui	1	0.00
All other tribes (11)	29	0.03
American Indian tribes, not spec.	27	0.03
Arab:	245	0.24
Arab/Arabic	7	0.01
Egyptian	17	0.02
Lebanese	113	0.11
Moroccan	20	0.02
Syrian	80	0.08
Other Arab	8	0.01
Armenian	26	0.03
Asian:	1,288	1.26
Bangladeshi (11)	16	0.02
Cambodian (2)	2	0.00
Chinese, ex. Taiwanese (114)	157	0.15
Filipino (362)	461	0.45
Indian (112)	169	0.17
Indonesian (2)	14	0.01
Japanese (43)	98	0.10
Korean (103)	141	0.14
Laotian (23)	28	0.03
Malaysian (2)	6	0.01
Pakistani (4)	4	0.00
Taiwanese (1)	2	0.00
Thai (23)	40	0.04
Vietnamese (92)	106	0.10
Other Asian, specified (5)	14	0.01
Other Asian, not specified (10)	30	0.03
Australian	45	0.04
Austrian	370	0.36
Basque	4	0.00
Belgian	160	0.16
Brazilian	18	0.02
British	413	0.40
Bulgarian	24	0.02
Canadian	508	0.50
Croatian	298	0.29
Czech	509	0.50
Czechoslovakian	239	0.23
Danish	473	0.46
Dutch	1,991	1.95
Eastern European	25	0.02
English	12,127	11.87
Estonian	8	0.01
European	439	0.43
Finnish	315	0.31
French, except Basque	4,300	4.21
French Canadian	1,058	1.04
German	21,385	20.92
Greek	670	0.66
Guyanese	23	0.02
Hawaii Native/Pacific Islander:	128	0.13
Micronesian: (12)	13	0.01
Guamanian/Chamorro (8)	9	0.01
Other Micronesian (4)	4	0.00
Polynesian: (31)	69	0.07
Native Hawaiian (28)	62	0.06
Samoan (3)	7	0.01
Other Pac. Isl., specified	8	0.01
Other Pac. Isl., not spec. (12)	38	0.04
Hispanic or Latino:	8,521	8.33
Central American:	432	0.42
Costa Rican	54	0.05
Guatemalan	88	0.09
Honduran	78	0.08
Nicaraguan	49	0.05
Panamanian	41	0.04
Salvadoran	88	0.09
Other Central American	34	0.03
Cuban	1,408	1.38
Dominican Republic	380	0.37
Mexican	822	0.80
Puerto Rican	2,715	2.65
South American:	1,109	1.08
Argentinean	60	0.06
Bolivian	9	0.01
Chilean	31	0.03
Colombian	576	0.56
Ecuadorian	159	0.16
Paraguayan	4	0.00
Peruvian	149	0.15
Uruguayan	22	0.02
Venezuelan	54	0.05
Other South American	45	0.04
Other Hispanic or Latino	1,655	1.62
Hungarian	936	0.92
Icelander	6	0.01
Iranian	12	0.01
Irish	16,271	15.92
Israeli	7	0.01
Italian	13,437	13.15
Latvian	9	0.01
Lithuanian	398	0.39
Luxemburger	8	0.01
Macedonian	12	0.01
Maltese	141	0.14
New Zealander	23	0.02
Northern European	15	0.01
Norwegian	1,299	1.27
Pennsylvania German	110	0.11
Polish	5,055	4.95
Portuguese	536	0.52
Romanian	227	0.22
Russian	855	0.84
Scandinavian	144	0.14
Scotch-Irish	1,735	1.70
Scottish	2,012	1.97
Serbian	101	0.10
Slavic	45	0.04
Slovak	529	0.52
Slovene	138	0.14
Swedish	1,598	1.56
Swiss	336	0.33
Turkish	39	0.04
Ukrainian	370	0.36
United States or American	7,841	7.67
Welsh	773	0.76
West Indian, excl. Hispanic:	491	0.48
Bahamian	11	0.01
Bermudan	17	0.02
British West Indian	10	0.01
Haitian	180	0.18
Jamaican	191	0.19
Trinidadian and Tobagonian	29	0.03
West Indian	53	0.05
White:	96,532	94.37
Not Hispanic (89,535)	90,436	88.41
Hispanic (5,598)	6,096	5.96
Yugoslavian	104	0.10

Notes: 1. Figures in the "Number" column do not add up to the total population due to: a) Ancestry/Race overlap — e.g. persons can report being both White and Irish, b) persons of Hispanic origin can report being any race, c) persons reporting two ancestries are counted in both categories. 2. Numbers in parentheses indicate the number of persons reporting this ancestry/race alone, not in combination with any other ancestry/race. 3. Refer to the Explanation of Data in the front of the book for more detailed information.

Carol City

Place Type: Census Designated Place
County: Miami-Dade
Population: 59,443

Ancestry/Race	Number	%
African American/Black:	31,944	53.74
Not Hispanic (29,560)	30,062	50.57
Hispanic (1,410)	1,882	3.17
African, sub-Saharan:	622	1.05
African	505	0.85
Ethiopian	6	0.01
Ghanian	19	0.03
Nigerian	84	0.14
Other sub-Saharan African	8	0.01
Alaska Native tribes, specified:	1	0.00
Aleut	1	0.00
Am. Ind. or Alaska Nat., not spec.	132	0.22
American Indian tribes, specified:	82	0.14
Apache (4)	4	0.01
Blackfeet (2)	4	0.01
Cherokee (10)	26	0.04
Chippewa	1	0.00
Choctaw	3	0.01
Iroquois	1	0.00
Latin American Indians (12)	28	0.05
Paiute	1	0.00
Potawatomi (1)	3	0.01
Pueblo	2	0.00
Sioux (3)	4	0.01
All other tribes (1)	5	0.01
American Indian tribes, not spec.	19	0.03
Arab:	138	0.23
Arab/Arabic	48	0.08
Egyptian	21	0.04
Lebanese	40	0.07
Palestinian	20	0.03
Syrian	9	0.02
Armenian	4	0.01
Asian:	504	0.85
Bangladeshi (4)	4	0.01
Chinese, ex. Taiwanese (60)	111	0.19
Filipino (85)	99	0.17
Indian (132)	188	0.32
Japanese (6)	16	0.03
Korean (2)	5	0.01
Pakistani (20)	33	0.06
Thai	3	0.01
Vietnamese (5)	7	0.01
Other Asian, specified	3	0.01
Other Asian, not specified (7)	35	0.06
Austrian	6	0.01
Brazilian	43	0.07
British	78	0.13
Canadian	22	0.04
Celtic	5	0.01
Czech	6	0.01
Czechoslovakian	10	0.02
Danish	6	0.01
Dutch	20	0.03
English	255	0.43
European	14	0.02
Finnish	7	0.01
French, except Basque	168	0.28
French Canadian	27	0.05
German	353	0.59
German Russian	8	0.01
Greek	5	0.01
Guyanese	155	0.26
Hawaii Native/Pacific Islander:	75	0.13
Micronesian: (8)	10	0.02
Guamanian/Chamorro (8)	10	0.02
Polynesian: (6)	7	0.01
Native Hawaiian (2)	3	0.01
Samoan (1)	1	0.00
Tongan (2)	2	0.00
Other Polynesian (1)	1	0.00
Other Pac. Isl., specified	3	0.01
Other Pac. Isl., not spec. (10)	55	0.09
Hispanic or Latino:	24,965	42.00
Central American:	2,460	4.14
Costa Rican	128	0.22
Guatemalan	217	0.37
Honduran	428	0.72
Nicaraguan	1,305	2.20
Panamanian	206	0.35
Salvadoran	134	0.23
Other Central American	42	0.07
Cuban	11,146	18.75
Dominican Republic	1,785	3.00
Mexican	377	0.63
Puerto Rican	2,745	4.62
South American:	2,210	3.72
Argentinean	84	0.14
Bolivian	19	0.03
Chilean	92	0.15
Colombian	1,279	2.15
Ecuadorian	318	0.53
Paraguayan	1	0.00
Peruvian	253	0.43
Uruguayan	9	0.02
Venezuelan	131	0.22
Other South American	24	0.04
Other Hispanic or Latino	4,242	7.14
Hungarian	24	0.04
Irish	401	0.67
Israeli	2	0.00
Italian	405	0.68
Lithuanian	6	0.01
Norwegian	14	0.02
Polish	101	0.17
Portuguese	23	0.04
Romanian	36	0.06
Russian	38	0.06
Scotch-Irish	15	0.03
Scottish	38	0.06
Slovak	9	0.02
Swedish	35	0.06
Swiss	18	0.03
Turkish	5	0.01
Ukrainian	17	0.03
United States or American	2,830	4.76
West Indian, excl. Hispanic:	5,829	9.81
Bahamian	437	0.74
Barbadian	54	0.09
Belizean	85	0.14
British West Indian	327	0.55
Haitian	1,357	2.28
Jamaican	3,111	5.23
Trinidadian and Tobagonian	282	0.47
U.S. Virgin Islander	20	0.03
West Indian	122	0.21
Other West Indian	34	0.06
White:	23,995	40.37
Not Hispanic (3,798)	4,020	6.76
Hispanic (18,855)	19,975	33.60

Casselberry

Place Type: City
County: Seminole
Population: 22,629

Ancestry/Race	Number	%
Acadian/Cajun	27	0.12
African American/Black:	1,351	5.97
Not Hispanic (1,137)	1,241	5.48
Hispanic (81)	110	0.49
African, sub-Saharan:	12	0.05
African	12	0.05
Am. Ind. or Alaska Nat., not spec.	45	0.20
Albanian	27	0.12
American Indian tribes, specified:	149	0.66
Apache (1)	2	0.01
Blackfeet (2)	6	0.03
Cherokee (14)	64	0.28
Chippewa	4	0.02
Choctaw (2)	3	0.01
Creek (1)	12	0.05
Iroquois (4)	7	0.03
Latin American Indians (4)	18	0.08
Menominee	1	0.00
Seminole	1	0.00
Sioux (7)	8	0.04
Yaqui	11	0.05
All other tribes (5)	12	0.05
American Indian tribes, not spec.	12	0.05
Arab:	143	0.65
Arab/Arabic	17	0.08
Iraqi	7	0.03
Jordanian	13	0.06
Lebanese	60	0.27
Moroccan	6	0.03
Palestinian	26	0.12
Syrian	14	0.06
Armenian	48	0.22
Asian:	546	2.41
Bangladeshi (3)	3	0.01
Cambodian (1)	1	0.00
Chinese, ex. Taiwanese (95)	114	0.50
Filipino (72)	99	0.44
Indian (77)	94	0.42
Indonesian (1)	2	0.01
Japanese (13)	25	0.11
Korean (32)	39	0.17
Laotian (2)	5	0.02
Pakistani (4)	5	0.02
Taiwanese (4)	5	0.02
Thai (7)	9	0.04
Vietnamese (111)	122	0.54
Other Asian, specified	2	0.01
Other Asian, not specified (2)	21	0.09
Australian	6	0.03
Austrian	53	0.24
Basque	18	0.08
Brazilian	11	0.05
British	78	0.35
Canadian	83	0.37
Croatian	20	0.09
Czech	79	0.36
Czechoslovakian	41	0.19
Danish	141	0.64
Dutch	349	1.57
Eastern European	16	0.07
English	2,720	12.27
European	96	0.43
Finnish	18	0.08
French, except Basque	802	3.62
French Canadian	275	1.24
German	3,532	15.94
Greek	153	0.69
Guyanese	77	0.35
Hawaii Native/Pacific Islander:	37	0.16
Micronesian: (3)	4	0.02
Guamanian/Chamorro (3)	4	0.02
Polynesian: (4)	17	0.08
Native Hawaiian (2)	12	0.05
Samoan (2)	5	0.02
Other Pac. Isl., specified	2	0.01
Other Pac. Isl., not spec. (2)	14	0.06
Hispanic or Latino:	3,424	15.13
Central American:	110	0.49
Costa Rican	16	0.07
Guatemalan	23	0.10
Honduran	19	0.08
Nicaraguan	8	0.04
Panamanian	24	0.11
Salvadoran	16	0.07
Other Central American	4	0.02
Cuban	243	1.07
Dominican Republic	106	0.47
Mexican	278	1.23
Puerto Rican	1,869	8.26
South American:	350	1.55
Argentinean	47	0.21
Bolivian	9	0.04
Chilean	11	0.05
Colombian	157	0.69
Ecuadorian	47	0.21

Notes: 1. Figures in the "Number" column do not add up to the total population due to: a) Ancestry/Race overlap — e.g. persons can report being both White and Irish, b) persons of Hispanic origin can report being any race, c) persons reporting two ancestries are counted in both categories. 2. Numbers in parentheses indicate the number of persons reporting this ancestry/race alone, not in combination with any other ancestry/race. 3. Refer to the Explanation of Data in the front of the book for more detailed information.

Ancestry/Race	Number	%
Peruvian	26	0.11
Venezuelan	46	0.20
Other South American	7	0.03
Other Hispanic or Latino	468	2.07
Hungarian	143	0.65
Iranian	9	0.04
Irish	3,187	14.38
Italian	1,881	8.49
Latvian	23	0.10
Lithuanian	31	0.14
Macedonian	11	0.05
Norwegian	171	0.77
Pennsylvania German	14	0.06
Polish	815	3.68
Portuguese	152	0.69
Romanian	25	0.11
Russian	202	0.91
Scandinavian	32	0.14
Scotch-Irish	401	1.81
Scottish	550	2.48
Serbian	49	0.22
Slavic	18	0.08
Slovak	37	0.17
Swedish	234	1.06
Swiss	83	0.37
Turkish	25	0.11
Ukrainian	81	0.37
United States or American	1,664	7.51
Welsh	169	0.76
West Indian, excl. Hispanic:	255	1.15
Belizean	39	0.18
Bermudan	16	0.07
Jamaican	86	0.39
Trinidadian and Tobagonian	50	0.23
U.S. Virgin Islander	8	0.04
West Indian	49	0.22
Other West Indian	7	0.03
White:	19,867	87.79
Not Hispanic (17,145)	17,452	77.12
Hispanic (2,236)	2,415	10.67
Yugoslavian	110	0.50

Citrus Park

Place Type: Census Designated Place
County: Hillsborough
Population: 20,226

Ancestry/Race	Number	%
African American/Black:	1,680	8.31
Not Hispanic (1,478)	1,588	7.85
Hispanic (54)	92	0.45
African, sub-Saharan:	137	0.68
African	102	0.51
Cape Verdean	35	0.17
Am. Ind. or Alaska Nat., not spec.	40	0.20
American Indian tribes, specified:	92	0.45
Cherokee (18)	35	0.17
Chippewa (6)	6	0.03
Choctaw (2)	3	0.01
Creek (1)	4	0.02
Houma (2)	2	0.01
Iroquois (6)	7	0.03
Kiowa (1)	2	0.01
Latin American Indians (3)	6	0.03
Menominee	1	0.00
Navajo	1	0.00
Osage (2)	2	0.01
Puget Sound Salish (1)	1	0.00
Seminole (1)	3	0.01
Sioux (5)	8	0.04
All other tribes (4)	11	0.05
American Indian tribes, not spec.	13	0.06
Arab:	32	0.16
Lebanese	32	0.16
Armenian	31	0.15
Asian:	797	3.94
Bangladeshi (6)	6	0.03
Cambodian (1)	1	0.00
Chinese, ex. Taiwanese (68)	86	0.43
Filipino (86)	121	0.60
Indian (185)	216	1.07
Indonesian (2)	9	0.04
Japanese (11)	31	0.15
Korean (125)	142	0.70
Pakistani (4)	4	0.02
Taiwanese (8)	9	0.04
Thai (25)	32	0.16
Vietnamese (94)	103	0.51
Other Asian, specified (2)	2	0.01
Other Asian, not specified (21)	35	0.17
Austrian	50	0.25
Belgian	26	0.13
Brazilian	32	0.16
British	100	0.50
Canadian	62	0.31
Czech	22	0.11
Czechoslovakian	55	0.27
Danish	57	0.28
Dutch	327	1.63
English	2,176	10.82
European	95	0.47
Finnish	15	0.07
French, except Basque	515	2.56
French Canadian	231	1.15
German	2,842	14.14
Greek	160	0.80
Guyanese	105	0.52
Hawaii Native/Pacific Islander:	42	0.21
Micronesian: (1)	1	0.00
Guamanian/Chamorro (1)	1	0.00
Polynesian: (14)	23	0.11
Native Hawaiian (7)	13	0.06
Samoan (6)	9	0.04
Other Polynesian (1)	1	0.00
Other Pac. Isl., not spec.	18	0.09
Hispanic or Latino:	4,098	20.26
Central American:	109	0.54
Costa Rican	8	0.04
Guatemalan	15	0.07
Honduran	34	0.17
Nicaraguan	20	0.10
Panamanian	22	0.11
Salvadoran	9	0.04
Other Central American	1	0.00
Cuban	944	4.67
Dominican Republic	78	0.39
Mexican	165	0.82
Puerto Rican	1,442	7.13
South American:	453	2.24
Argentinean	11	0.05
Bolivian	5	0.02
Chilean	6	0.03
Colombian	228	1.13
Ecuadorian	23	0.11
Paraguayan	3	0.01
Peruvian	103	0.51
Venezuelan	49	0.24
Other South American	25	0.12
Other Hispanic or Latino	907	4.48
Hungarian	98	0.49
Iranian	25	0.12
Irish	2,202	10.95
Israeli	13	0.06
Italian	1,815	9.03
Latvian	11	0.05
Lithuanian	38	0.19
Norwegian	78	0.39
Pennsylvania German	20	0.10
Polish	665	3.31
Portuguese	56	0.28
Romanian	23	0.11
Russian	259	1.29
Scotch-Irish	235	1.17
Scottish	404	2.01
Serbian	28	0.14
Slovak	17	0.08
Slovene	10	0.05
Swedish	163	0.81
Swiss	32	0.16
Turkish	14	0.07
Ukrainian	19	0.09
United States or American	2,089	10.39
Welsh	121	0.60
West Indian, excl. Hispanic:	182	0.91
Belizean	7	0.03
British West Indian	10	0.05
Dutch West Indian	11	0.05
Haitian	24	0.12
Jamaican	87	0.43
Trinidadian and Tobagonian	19	0.09
U.S. Virgin Islander	9	0.04
Other West Indian	15	0.07
White:	16,924	83.67
Not Hispanic (13,566)	13,807	68.26
Hispanic (2,918)	3,117	15.41
Yugoslavian	24	0.12

Citrus Ridge

Place Type: Census Designated Place
County: Lake
Population: 12,015

Ancestry/Race	Number	%
Acadian/Cajun	2	0.02
African American/Black:	524	4.36
Not Hispanic (394)	464	3.86
Hispanic (35)	60	0.50
African, sub-Saharan:	25	0.22
African	18	0.16
Nigerian	7	0.06
Am. Ind. or Alaska Nat., not spec.	57	0.47
American Indian tribes, specified:	45	0.37
Apache	1	0.01
Blackfeet (1)	7	0.06
Cherokee (2)	16	0.13
Cheyenne (1)	1	0.01
Chippewa	1	0.01
Choctaw	3	0.02
Creek (1)	1	0.01
Iroquois (1)	1	0.01
Latin American Indians (4)	8	0.07
Navajo	1	0.01
Seminole	1	0.01
Shoshone (1)	1	0.01
All other tribes (1)	3	0.02
American Indian tribes, not spec.	2	0.02
Arab:	106	0.93
Arab/Arabic	27	0.24
Lebanese	22	0.19
Moroccan	27	0.24
Palestinian	21	0.18
Syrian	9	0.08
Asian:	358	2.98
Cambodian (1)	1	0.01
Chinese, ex. Taiwanese (88)	110	0.92
Filipino (44)	76	0.63
Indian (65)	70	0.58
Indonesian (2)	2	0.02
Japanese (12)	25	0.21
Korean (14)	19	0.16
Pakistani (7)	7	0.06
Taiwanese (10)	10	0.08
Thai (4)	4	0.03
Vietnamese (16)	21	0.17
Other Asian, not specified (5)	13	0.11
Austrian	64	0.56
Belgian	22	0.19
British	175	1.53
Canadian	96	0.84
Croatian	21	0.18
Czech	60	0.53
Czechoslovakian	8	0.07
Danish	29	0.25
Dutch	171	1.50
Eastern European	6	0.05
English	1,113	9.75
European	91	0.80
Finnish	37	0.32

Notes: 1. Figures in the "Number" column do not add up to the total population due to: a) Ancestry/Race overlap — e.g. persons can report being both White and Irish, b) persons of Hispanic origin can report being any race, c) persons reporting two ancestries are counted in both categories. 2. Numbers in parentheses indicate the number of persons reporting this ancestry/race alone, not in combination with any other ancestry/race. 3. Refer to the Explanation of Data in the front of the book for more detailed information.

French, except Basque	401	3.51
French Canadian	203	1.78
German	1,779	15.58
Greek	39	0.34
Hawaii Native/Pacific Islander:	27	0.22
Micronesian: (2)	2	0.02
Guamanian/Chamorro (2)	2	0.02
Polynesian: (4)	8	0.07
Native Hawaiian (4)	8	0.07
Other Pac. Isl., not spec. (4)	17	0.14
Hispanic or Latino:	1,874	15.60
Central American:	63	0.52
Costa Rican	4	0.03
Guatemalan	15	0.12
Honduran	10	0.08
Nicaraguan	11	0.09
Panamanian	17	0.14
Salvadoran	3	0.02
Other Central American	3	0.02
Cuban	99	0.82
Dominican Republic	53	0.44
Mexican	139	1.16
Puerto Rican	1,027	8.55
South American:	237	1.97
Argentinean	16	0.13
Bolivian	1	0.01
Chilean	1	0.01
Colombian	121	1.01
Ecuadorian	24	0.20
Paraguayan	1	0.01
Peruvian	39	0.32
Uruguayan	2	0.02
Venezuelan	28	0.23
Other South American	4	0.03
Other Hispanic or Latino	256	2.13
Hungarian	60	0.53
Icelander	2	0.02
Irish	1,495	13.09
Italian	1,283	11.23
Lithuanian	36	0.32
Maltese	10	0.09
Northern European	9	0.08
Norwegian	117	1.02
Pennsylvania German	29	0.25
Polish	390	3.42
Portuguese	102	0.89
Russian	127	1.11
Scandinavian	11	0.10
Scotch-Irish	105	0.92
Scottish	363	3.18
Slavic	2	0.02
Slovak	13	0.11
Slovene	12	0.11
Swedish	126	1.10
Turkish	7	0.06
Ukrainian	58	0.51
United States or American	1,033	9.05
Welsh	62	0.54
West Indian, excl. Hispanic:	122	1.07
Haitian	65	0.57
Jamaican	46	0.40
Trinidadian and Tobagonian	11	0.10
White:	10,706	89.11
Not Hispanic (9,213)	9,381	78.08
Hispanic (1,228)	1,325	11.03

Clearwater

Place Type: City
County: Pinellas
Population: 108,787

Ancestry/Race	Number	%
Acadian/Cajun	11	0.01
African American/Black:	11,315	10.40
Not Hispanic (10,361)	10,931	10.05
Hispanic (290)	384	0.35
African, sub-Saharan:	606	0.56
African	431	0.40
Ghanian	13	0.01
Kenyan	10	0.01
Nigerian	33	0.03
South African	66	0.06
Sudanese	19	0.02
Other sub-Saharan African	34	0.03
Alaska Native tribes, specified:	3	0.00
Eskimo (2)	2	0.00
Tlingit-Haida (1)	1	0.00
Am. Ind. or Alaska Nat., not spec.	260	0.24
Albanian	211	0.20
Alsatian	9	0.01
American Indian tribes, specified:	494	0.45
Apache (10)	20	0.02
Blackfeet (3)	28	0.03
Cherokee (50)	175	0.16
Cheyenne	1	0.00
Chickasaw (2)	6	0.01
Chippewa (12)	17	0.02
Choctaw (9)	23	0.02
Comanche (2)	3	0.00
Cree (1)	3	0.00
Creek (5)	20	0.02
Delaware	2	0.00
Iroquois (22)	36	0.03
Latin American Indians (43)	67	0.06
Lumbee (7)	8	0.01
Menominee (1)	1	0.00
Navajo (4)	7	0.01
Ottawa (5)	8	0.01
Potawatomi	3	0.00
Pueblo (5)	5	0.00
Puget Sound Salish (1)	1	0.00
Seminole (1)	10	0.01
Shoshone	1	0.00
Sioux (5)	12	0.01
Yuman	1	0.00
All other tribes (18)	36	0.03
American Indian tribes, not spec.	45	0.04
Arab:	809	0.75
Arab/Arabic	97	0.09
Egyptian	119	0.11
Iraqi	36	0.03
Jordanian	22	0.02
Lebanese	338	0.31
Moroccan	96	0.09
Palestinian	20	0.02
Syrian	73	0.07
Other Arab	8	0.01
Armenian	152	0.14
Asian:	2,152	1.98
Bangladeshi (4)	5	0.00
Cambodian (15)	19	0.02
Chinese, ex. Taiwanese (234)	309	0.28
Filipino (334)	427	0.39
Hmong (27)	27	0.02
Indian (468)	509	0.47
Indonesian (8)	15	0.01
Japanese (97)	131	0.12
Korean (127)	161	0.15
Laotian (46)	52	0.05
Malaysian (4)	4	0.00
Pakistani (10)	13	0.01
Sri Lankan (1)	1	0.00
Taiwanese (24)	27	0.02
Thai (57)	72	0.07
Vietnamese (254)	282	0.26
Other Asian, specified (3)	9	0.01
Other Asian, not specified (36)	89	0.08
Australian	70	0.06
Austrian	451	0.42
Belgian	118	0.11
Brazilian	71	0.07
British	877	0.81
Bulgarian	58	0.05
Canadian	570	0.53
Celtic	39	0.04
Croatian	120	0.11
Czech	489	0.45
Czechoslovakian	289	0.27
Danish	405	0.38
Dutch	1,684	1.56
Eastern European	25	0.02
English	12,820	11.88
Estonian	6	0.01
European	526	0.49
Finnish	317	0.29
French, except Basque	3,814	3.53
French Canadian	1,290	1.20
German	18,191	16.86
Greek	1,934	1.79
Hawaii Native/Pacific Islander:	160	0.15
Melanesian: (2)	2	0.00
Fijian (2)	2	0.00
Micronesian: (15)	24	0.02
Guamanian/Chamorro (13)	19	0.02
Other Micronesian (2)	5	0.00
Polynesian: (39)	65	0.06
Native Hawaiian (19)	41	0.04
Samoan (19)	23	0.02
Tongan (1)	1	0.00
Other Pac. Isl., specified	5	0.00
Other Pac. Isl., not spec. (19)	64	0.06
Hispanic or Latino:	9,754	8.97
Central American:	274	0.25
Costa Rican	43	0.04
Guatemalan	45	0.04
Honduran	58	0.05
Nicaraguan	18	0.02
Panamanian	42	0.04
Salvadoran	50	0.05
Other Central American	18	0.02
Cuban	469	0.43
Dominican Republic	108	0.10
Mexican	4,771	4.39
Puerto Rican	1,924	1.77
South American:	891	0.82
Argentinean	60	0.06
Bolivian	10	0.01
Chilean	20	0.02
Colombian	394	0.36
Ecuadorian	76	0.07
Paraguayan	8	0.01
Peruvian	131	0.12
Uruguayan	9	0.01
Venezuelan	140	0.13
Other South American	43	0.04
Other Hispanic or Latino	1,317	1.21
Hungarian	810	0.75
Iranian	56	0.05
Irish	14,935	13.84
Israeli	173	0.16
Italian	8,685	8.05
Latvian	52	0.05
Lithuanian	446	0.41
Luxemburger	122	0.11
Macedonian	37	0.03
Maltese	53	0.05
New Zealander	11	0.01
Northern European	61	0.06
Norwegian	1,234	1.14
Pennsylvania German	134	0.12
Polish	3,844	3.56
Portuguese	404	0.37
Romanian	174	0.16
Russian	1,353	1.25
Scandinavian	226	0.21
Scotch-Irish	2,091	1.94
Scottish	2,555	2.37
Serbian	72	0.07
Slavic	43	0.04
Slovak	280	0.26
Slovene	16	0.01
Swedish	1,863	1.73
Swiss	414	0.38
Turkish	66	0.06
Ukrainian	507	0.47
United States or American	5,737	5.32
Welsh	616	0.57
West Indian, excl. Hispanic:	612	0.57
British West Indian	8	0.01

Notes: 1. Figures in the "Number" column do not add up to the total population due to: a) Ancestry/Race overlap — e.g. persons can report being both White and Irish, b) persons of Hispanic origin can report being any race, c) persons reporting two ancestries are counted in both categories. 2. Numbers in parentheses indicate the number of persons reporting this ancestry/race alone, not in combination with any other ancestry/race. 3. Refer to the Explanation of Data in the front of the book for more detailed information.

Ancestry/Race	Number	%
Haitian	19	0.02
Jamaican	353	0.33
Trinidadian and Tobagonian	160	0.15
West Indian	72	0.07
White:	92,947	85.44
Not Hispanic (85,015)	86,260	79.29
Hispanic (6,208)	6,687	6.15
Yugoslavian	585	0.54

Cocoa Beach

Place Type: City
County: Brevard
Population: 12,482

Ancestry/Race	Number	%
African American/Black:	101	0.81
Not Hispanic (71)	89	0.71
Hispanic (7)	12	0.10
African, sub-Saharan:	15	0.12
South African	15	0.12
Am. Ind. or Alaska Nat., not spec.	20	0.16
Albanian	17	0.14
American Indian tribes, specified:	41	0.33
Blackfeet (1)	1	0.01
Cherokee (4)	21	0.17
Cheyenne (1)	1	0.01
Creek	1	0.01
Iroquois	1	0.01
Latin American Indians (2)	2	0.02
Osage (1)	2	0.02
Pueblo (3)	3	0.02
Seminole (6)	6	0.05
Sioux	1	0.01
All other tribes (2)	2	0.02
American Indian tribes, not spec.	5	0.04
Arab:	182	1.47
Egyptian	103	0.83
Iraqi	41	0.33
Lebanese	38	0.31
Armenian	6	0.05
Asian:	182	1.46
Cambodian (1)	1	0.01
Chinese, ex. Taiwanese (41)	46	0.37
Filipino (28)	46	0.37
Indian (24)	31	0.25
Japanese (11)	17	0.14
Korean (5)	7	0.06
Malaysian	2	0.02
Pakistani (1)	1	0.01
Taiwanese (1)	1	0.01
Thai (9)	14	0.11
Vietnamese (5)	7	0.06
Other Asian, specified	1	0.01
Other Asian, not specified (5)	8	0.06
Austrian	65	0.52
Belgian	12	0.10
Brazilian	7	0.06
British	64	0.52
Canadian	58	0.47
Croatian	19	0.15
Czech	27	0.22
Czechoslovakian	59	0.48
Danish	85	0.68
Dutch	214	1.72
English	2,002	16.13
Estonian	5	0.04
European	116	0.93
Finnish	17	0.14
French, except Basque	648	5.22
French Canadian	151	1.22
German	2,285	18.41
Greek	155	1.25
Hawaii Native/Pacific Islander:	19	0.15
Micronesian: (1)	1	0.01
Guamanian/Chamorro (1)	1	0.01
Polynesian: (6)	15	0.12
Native Hawaiian (6)	14	0.11
Samoan	1	0.01
Other Pac. Isl., not spec.	3	0.02
Hispanic or Latino:	314	2.52
Central American:	9	0.07
Costa Rican	1	0.01
Guatemalan	2	0.02
Honduran	2	0.02
Panamanian	2	0.02
Other Central American	2	0.02
Cuban	60	0.48
Mexican	68	0.54
Puerto Rican	44	0.35
South American:	49	0.39
Argentinean	9	0.07
Chilean	3	0.02
Colombian	14	0.11
Ecuadorian	10	0.08
Peruvian	2	0.02
Uruguayan	1	0.01
Venezuelan	7	0.06
Other South American	3	0.02
Other Hispanic or Latino	84	0.67
Hungarian	120	0.97
Irish	2,300	18.53
Italian	1,152	9.28
Lithuanian	56	0.45
Northern European	2	0.02
Norwegian	198	1.60
Pennsylvania German	12	0.10
Polish	441	3.55
Portuguese	52	0.42
Romanian	34	0.27
Russian	203	1.64
Scotch-Irish	471	3.79
Scottish	431	3.47
Slavic	7	0.06
Slovak	45	0.36
Soviet Union	10	0.08
Swedish	233	1.88
Swiss	24	0.19
Turkish	12	0.10
Ukrainian	44	0.35
United States or American	876	7.06
Welsh	153	1.23
West Indian, excl. Hispanic:	12	0.10
Jamaican	12	0.10
White:	12,187	97.64
Not Hispanic (11,805)	11,911	95.43
Hispanic (257)	276	2.21
Yugoslavian	9	0.07

Cocoa

Place Type: City
County: Brevard
Population: 16,412

Ancestry/Race	Number	%
African American/Black:	5,446	33.18
Not Hispanic (5,222)	5,357	32.64
Hispanic (76)	89	0.54
African, sub-Saharan:	87	0.53
African	87	0.53
Alaska Native tribes, specified:	1	0.01
Eskimo	1	0.01
Am. Ind. or Alaska Nat., not spec.	79	0.48
American Indian tribes, specified:	114	0.69
Apache	4	0.02
Blackfeet (1)	3	0.02
Cherokee (35)	64	0.39
Chippewa (1)	2	0.01
Choctaw (2)	4	0.02
Cree	1	0.01
Creek	1	0.01
Delaware	1	0.01
Iroquois (2)	2	0.01
Latin American Indians	4	0.02
Lumbee (8)	8	0.05
Navajo (1)	1	0.01
Potawatomi (1)	2	0.01
Seminole	5	0.03
Sioux	1	0.01
All other tribes (5)	11	0.07
American Indian tribes, not spec.	10	0.06
Arab:	92	0.56
Arab/Arabic	8	0.05
Iraqi	16	0.10
Lebanese	32	0.19
Syrian	19	0.12
Other Arab	17	0.10
Asian:	216	1.32
Bangladeshi (1)	1	0.01
Chinese, ex. Taiwanese (9)	15	0.09
Filipino (36)	49	0.30
Indian (29)	39	0.24
Indonesian (1)	1	0.01
Japanese (10)	21	0.13
Korean (13)	20	0.12
Pakistani (1)	1	0.01
Taiwanese (1)	1	0.01
Thai (4)	6	0.04
Vietnamese (41)	43	0.26
Other Asian, specified (2)	7	0.04
Other Asian, not specified (1)	12	0.07
Austrian	14	0.08
Belgian	9	0.05
Brazilian	22	0.13
British	130	0.79
Canadian	34	0.21
Croatian	6	0.04
Czech	46	0.28
Czechoslovakian	64	0.39
Danish	32	0.19
Dutch	160	0.97
English	1,428	8.65
European	73	0.44
Finnish	8	0.05
French, except Basque	547	3.32
French Canadian	138	0.84
German	1,579	9.57
Greek	4	0.02
Hawaii Native/Pacific Islander:	60	0.37
Micronesian: (35)	38	0.23
Guamanian/Chamorro (35)	38	0.23
Polynesian: (3)	14	0.09
Native Hawaiian (3)	12	0.07
Samoan	2	0.01
Other Pac. Isl., specified	4	0.02
Other Pac. Isl., not spec.	4	0.02
Hispanic or Latino:	809	4.93
Central American:	164	1.00
Costa Rican	1	0.01
Guatemalan	123	0.75
Honduran	12	0.07
Nicaraguan	6	0.04
Panamanian	8	0.05
Salvadoran	10	0.06
Other Central American	4	0.02
Cuban	52	0.32
Dominican Republic	14	0.09
Mexican	199	1.21
Puerto Rican	196	1.19
South American:	47	0.29
Argentinean	4	0.02
Chilean	1	0.01
Colombian	27	0.16
Ecuadorian	3	0.02
Peruvian	2	0.01
Venezuelan	8	0.05
Other South American	2	0.01
Other Hispanic or Latino	137	0.83
Hungarian	76	0.46
Icelander	6	0.04
Irish	1,480	8.97
Italian	927	5.62
Lithuanian	24	0.15
Northern European	14	0.08
Norwegian	32	0.19
Pennsylvania German	10	0.06
Polish	203	1.23
Portuguese	68	0.41
Romanian	5	0.03

Notes: 1. Figures in the "Number" column do not add up to the total population due to: a) Ancestry/Race overlap — e.g. persons can report being both White and Irish, b) persons of Hispanic origin can report being any race, c) persons reporting two ancestries are counted in both categories. 2. Numbers in parentheses indicate the number of persons reporting this ancestry/race alone, not in combination with any other ancestry/race. 3. Refer to the Explanation of Data in the front of the book for more detailed information.

Russian	32	0.19
Scotch-Irish	239	1.45
Scottish	199	1.21
Slovak	13	0.08
Swedish	96	0.58
Swiss	70	0.42
Turkish	19	0.12
Ukrainian	52	0.32
United States or American	1,499	9.08
Welsh	135	0.82
West Indian, excl. Hispanic:	94	0.57
Bahamian	31	0.19
British West Indian	7	0.04
Jamaican	37	0.22
Trinidadian and Tobagonian	11	0.07
West Indian	8	0.05
White:	10,501	63.98
Not Hispanic (9,839)	10,055	61.27
Hispanic (413)	446	2.72
Yugoslavian	15	0.09

Coconut Creek

Place Type: City
County: Broward
Population: 43,566

Ancestry/Race	Number	%
African American/Black:	2,963	6.80
Not Hispanic (2,584)	2,823	6.48
Hispanic (101)	140	0.32
African, sub-Saharan:	222	0.51
African	111	0.26
Cape Verdean	52	0.12
Ghanian	9	0.02
Nigerian	18	0.04
Senegalese	32	0.07
Alaska Native tribes, specified:	1	0.00
Tlingit-Haida (1)	1	0.00
Am. Ind. or Alaska Nat., not spec.	61	0.14
American Indian tribes, specified:	75	0.17
Apache (1)	3	0.01
Blackfeet (1)	1	0.00
Cherokee (5)	18	0.04
Chippewa (4)	10	0.02
Creek	2	0.00
Delaware	1	0.00
Iroquois (8)	11	0.03
Latin American Indians (12)	16	0.04
Lumbee	1	0.00
Navajo	1	0.00
Ottawa	1	0.00
Potawatomi (1)	1	0.00
Seminole (1)	1	0.00
Sioux (1)	2	0.00
Ute	1	0.00
Yuman (1)	1	0.00
All other tribes	4	0.01
American Indian tribes, not spec.	3	0.01
Arab:	459	1.06
Arab/Arabic	88	0.20
Egyptian	13	0.03
Iraqi	6	0.01
Lebanese	236	0.54
Moroccan	20	0.05
Palestinian	14	0.03
Syrian	64	0.15
Other Arab	18	0.04
Armenian	48	0.11
Asian:	1,323	3.04
Bangladeshi (5)	9	0.02
Chinese, ex. Taiwanese (296)	348	0.80
Filipino (96)	144	0.33
Indian (307)	378	0.87
Indonesian (3)	7	0.02
Japanese (29)	48	0.11
Korean (44)	60	0.14
Laotian (4)	4	0.01
Malaysian (3)	5	0.01
Pakistani (49)	72	0.17
Sri Lankan (2)	2	0.00
Taiwanese (4)	4	0.01
Thai (29)	37	0.08
Vietnamese (124)	136	0.31
Other Asian, specified	5	0.01
Other Asian, not specified (18)	64	0.15
Australian	8	0.02
Austrian	491	1.13
Belgian	16	0.04
Brazilian	589	1.36
British	264	0.61
Bulgarian	15	0.03
Canadian	338	0.78
Croatian	27	0.06
Czech	155	0.36
Czechoslovakian	33	0.08
Danish	86	0.20
Dutch	559	1.29
Eastern European	151	0.35
English	2,950	6.81
European	189	0.44
Finnish	48	0.11
French, except Basque	1,068	2.46
French Canadian	467	1.08
German	4,650	10.73
Greek	338	0.78
Guyanese	17	0.04
Hawaii Native/Pacific Islander:	60	0.14
Micronesian: (2)	2	0.00
Guamanian/Chamorro (2)	2	0.00
Polynesian: (16)	32	0.07
Native Hawaiian (9)	20	0.05
Samoan (4)	8	0.02
Tongan (3)	4	0.01
Other Pac. Isl., specified	4	0.01
Other Pac. Isl., not spec. (5)	22	0.05
Hispanic or Latino:	5,076	11.65
Central American:	264	0.61
Costa Rican	42	0.10
Guatemalan	46	0.11
Honduran	45	0.10
Nicaraguan	38	0.09
Panamanian	24	0.06
Salvadoran	57	0.13
Other Central American	12	0.03
Cuban	435	1.00
Dominican Republic	182	0.42
Mexican	688	1.58
Puerto Rican	1,120	2.57
South American:	1,402	3.22
Argentinean	95	0.22
Bolivian	22	0.05
Chilean	54	0.12
Colombian	557	1.28
Ecuadorian	106	0.24
Paraguayan	2	0.00
Peruvian	279	0.64
Uruguayan	26	0.06
Venezuelan	216	0.50
Other South American	45	0.10
Other Hispanic or Latino	985	2.26
Hungarian	566	1.31
Iranian	74	0.17
Irish	4,439	10.25
Israeli	130	0.30
Italian	5,841	13.48
Latvian	32	0.07
Lithuanian	162	0.37
Luxemburger	16	0.04
Macedonian	8	0.02
Maltese	49	0.11
Norwegian	259	0.60
Pennsylvania German	13	0.03
Polish	2,954	6.82
Portuguese	291	0.67
Romanian	257	0.59
Russian	2,804	6.47
Scandinavian	37	0.09
Scotch-Irish	379	0.87
Scottish	518	1.20
Serbian	8	0.02
Slavic	8	0.02
Slovak	97	0.22
Slovene	11	0.03
Swedish	358	0.83
Swiss	15	0.03
Turkish	186	0.43
Ukrainian	230	0.53
United States or American	2,390	5.52
Welsh	173	0.40
West Indian, excl. Hispanic:	1,402	3.24
Bahamian	33	0.08
British West Indian	33	0.08
Haitian	224	0.52
Jamaican	834	1.92
Trinidadian and Tobagonian	226	0.52
U.S. Virgin Islander	12	0.03
West Indian	32	0.07
Other West Indian	8	0.02
White:	38,303	87.92
Not Hispanic (33,909)	34,369	78.89
Hispanic (3,679)	3,934	9.03

Conway

Place Type: Census Designated Place
County: Orange
Population: 14,394

Ancestry/Race	Number	%
Acadian/Cajun	7	0.05
African American/Black:	450	3.13
Not Hispanic (340)	399	2.77
Hispanic (28)	51	0.35
African, sub-Saharan:	5	0.03
African	5	0.03
Alaska Native tribes, specified:	1	0.01
Aleut	1	0.01
Am. Ind. or Alaska Nat., not spec.	23	0.16
American Indian tribes, specified:	80	0.56
Apache (1)	1	0.01
Blackfeet	4	0.03
Cherokee (17)	31	0.22
Cheyenne (1)	1	0.01
Chippewa (3)	8	0.06
Choctaw (1)	3	0.02
Comanche (3)	3	0.02
Cree	1	0.01
Creek (1)	3	0.02
Crow	1	0.01
Iroquois	4	0.03
Latin American Indians (2)	11	0.08
Lumbee (1)	1	0.01
Shoshone	1	0.01
Sioux (1)	2	0.01
Yaqui (1)	1	0.01
All other tribes	4	0.03
American Indian tribes, not spec.	8	0.06
Arab:	170	1.19
Arab/Arabic	70	0.49
Iraqi	8	0.06
Lebanese	57	0.40
Moroccan	10	0.07
Palestinian	25	0.17
Armenian	13	0.09
Asian:	378	2.63
Cambodian (5)	5	0.03
Chinese, ex. Taiwanese (33)	54	0.38
Filipino (92)	100	0.69
Indian (53)	77	0.53
Indonesian (1)	3	0.02
Japanese (21)	36	0.25
Korean (23)	27	0.19
Pakistani (11)	15	0.10
Taiwanese (10)	19	0.13
Thai (7)	8	0.06
Vietnamese (18)	21	0.15
Other Asian, not specified (2)	13	0.09
Australian	12	0.08
Austrian	27	0.19

Notes: 1. Figures in the "Number" column do not add up to the total population due to: a) Ancestry/Race overlap — e.g. persons can report being both White and Irish, b) persons of Hispanic origin can report being any race, c) persons reporting two ancestries are counted in both categories. 2. Numbers in parentheses indicate the number of persons reporting this ancestry/race alone, not in combination with any other ancestry/race. 3. Refer to the Explanation of Data in the front of the book for more detailed information.

Ancestry/Race	Number	%
Basque	10	0.07
Belgian	35	0.24
Brazilian	20	0.14
British	43	0.30
Canadian	52	0.36
Croatian	9	0.06
Czech	75	0.52
Czechoslovakian	51	0.36
Danish	17	0.12
Dutch	285	1.99
English	2,370	16.59
European	89	0.62
Finnish	19	0.13
French, except Basque	541	3.79
French Canadian	139	0.97
German	2,185	15.29
Greek	69	0.48
Guyanese	37	0.26
Hawaii Native/Pacific Islander:	20	0.14
Micronesian: (4)	7	0.05
Guamanian/Chamorro (4)	7	0.05
Polynesian: (3)	6	0.04
Native Hawaiian (2)	5	0.03
Samoan (1)	1	0.01
Other Pac. Isl., not spec. (1)	7	0.05
Hispanic or Latino:	1,661	11.54
Central American:	43	0.30
Costa Rican	2	0.01
Guatemalan	3	0.02
Honduran	14	0.10
Nicaraguan	11	0.08
Panamanian	7	0.05
Salvadoran	6	0.04
Cuban	209	1.45
Dominican Republic	57	0.40
Mexican	92	0.64
Puerto Rican	819	5.69
South American:	178	1.24
Argentinean	18	0.13
Bolivian	2	0.01
Chilean	12	0.08
Colombian	102	0.71
Ecuadorian	26	0.18
Peruvian	4	0.03
Venezuelan	14	0.10
Other Hispanic or Latino	263	1.83
Hungarian	135	0.94
Irish	1,829	12.80
Italian	884	6.19
Lithuanian	46	0.32
Northern European	14	0.10
Norwegian	211	1.48
Pennsylvania German	8	0.06
Polish	412	2.88
Portuguese	5	0.03
Russian	69	0.48
Scandinavian	30	0.21
Scotch-Irish	400	2.80
Scottish	382	2.67
Serbian	5	0.03
Slovak	70	0.49
Slovene	7	0.05
Swedish	203	1.42
Swiss	65	0.45
Ukrainian	27	0.19
United States or American	1,268	8.87
Welsh	126	0.88
West Indian, excl. Hispanic:	96	0.67
Dutch West Indian	8	0.06
Haitian	46	0.32
Jamaican	20	0.14
Trinidadian and Tobagonian	6	0.04
West Indian	16	0.11
White:	13,235	91.95
Not Hispanic (11,862)	11,995	83.33
Hispanic (1,121)	1,240	8.61
Yugoslavian	26	0.18

Cooper City

Place Type: City
County: Broward
Population: 27,939

Ancestry/Race	Number	%
African American/Black:	994	3.56
Not Hispanic (846)	959	3.43
Hispanic (18)	35	0.13
African, sub-Saharan:	150	0.54
African	34	0.12
Nigerian	107	0.39
Other sub-Saharan African	9	0.03
Alaska Native tribes, specified:	4	0.01
Aleut	1	0.00
Eskimo	2	0.01
Tlingit-Haida	1	0.00
Am. Ind. or Alaska Nat., not spec.	35	0.13
Albanian	26	0.09
American Indian tribes, specified:	53	0.19
Apache (1)	1	0.00
Cherokee (7)	22	0.08
Chippewa (1)	3	0.01
Choctaw (4)	4	0.01
Cree (3)	3	0.01
Creek	2	0.01
Latin American Indians	6	0.02
Menominee (1)	1	0.00
Osage (2)	2	0.01
Pueblo (3)	3	0.01
Sioux	1	0.00
All other tribes (3)	5	0.02
American Indian tribes, not spec.	10	0.04
Arab:	395	1.43
Arab/Arabic	127	0.46
Iraqi	32	0.12
Lebanese	157	0.57
Palestinian	28	0.10
Syrian	34	0.12
Other Arab	17	0.06
Armenian	9	0.03
Asian:	1,359	4.86
Bangladeshi (13)	21	0.08
Chinese, ex. Taiwanese (240)	306	1.10
Filipino (94)	120	0.43
Indian (475)	545	1.95
Indonesian (7)	8	0.03
Japanese (17)	26	0.09
Korean (121)	128	0.46
Laotian (1)	1	0.00
Malaysian (1)	1	0.00
Pakistani (26)	37	0.13
Sri Lankan (5)	5	0.02
Taiwanese (12)	20	0.07
Thai (34)	37	0.13
Vietnamese (50)	57	0.20
Other Asian, specified (4)	4	0.01
Other Asian, not specified (15)	43	0.15
Australian	9	0.03
Austrian	184	0.66
Basque	10	0.04
Belgian	35	0.13
Brazilian	108	0.39
British	76	0.27
Canadian	209	0.75
Croatian	20	0.07
Czech	57	0.21
Czechoslovakian	83	0.30
Danish	43	0.16
Dutch	532	1.92
Eastern European	202	0.73
English	2,337	8.44
European	239	0.86
Finnish	71	0.26
French, except Basque	655	2.37
French Canadian	220	0.79
German	4,082	14.74
Greek	179	0.65
Guyanese	23	0.08
Hawaii Native/Pacific Islander:	31	0.11
Polynesian: (10)	17	0.06
Native Hawaiian (8)	13	0.05
Samoan (2)	4	0.01
Other Pac. Isl., not spec. (1)	14	0.05
Hispanic or Latino:	4,349	15.57
Central American:	169	0.60
Costa Rican	19	0.07
Guatemalan	32	0.11
Honduran	31	0.11
Nicaraguan	45	0.16
Panamanian	21	0.08
Salvadoran	12	0.04
Other Central American	9	0.03
Cuban	1,477	5.29
Dominican Republic	115	0.41
Mexican	139	0.50
Puerto Rican	714	2.56
South American:	922	3.30
Argentinean	67	0.24
Bolivian	5	0.02
Chilean	50	0.18
Colombian	496	1.78
Ecuadorian	65	0.23
Paraguayan	4	0.01
Peruvian	131	0.47
Uruguayan	11	0.04
Venezuelan	73	0.26
Other South American	20	0.07
Other Hispanic or Latino	813	2.91
Hungarian	411	1.48
Iranian	77	0.28
Irish	3,855	13.92
Israeli	233	0.84
Italian	3,460	12.50
Latvian	24	0.09
Lithuanian	110	0.40
Macedonian	30	0.11
Northern European	12	0.04
Norwegian	102	0.37
Pennsylvania German	17	0.06
Polish	1,510	5.45
Portuguese	65	0.23
Romanian	176	0.64
Russian	1,453	5.25
Scotch-Irish	332	1.20
Scottish	377	1.36
Slavic	7	0.03
Slovak	61	0.22
Slovene	34	0.12
Swedish	142	0.51
Swiss	100	0.36
Turkish	23	0.08
Ukrainian	83	0.30
United States or American	1,820	6.57
Welsh	198	0.72
West Indian, excl. Hispanic:	593	2.14
Bahamian	11	0.04
British West Indian	10	0.04
Haitian	165	0.60
Jamaican	280	1.01
Trinidadian and Tobagonian	64	0.23
U.S. Virgin Islander	21	0.08
West Indian	42	0.15
White:	25,300	90.55
Not Hispanic (21,147)	21,368	76.48
Hispanic (3,746)	3,932	14.07
Yugoslavian	80	0.29

Coral Gables

Place Type: City
County: Miami-Dade
Population: 42,249

Ancestry/Race	Number	%
African American/Black:	1,518	3.59
Not Hispanic (1,290)	1,367	3.24
Hispanic (104)	151	0.36
African, sub-Saharan:	160	0.38

Notes: 1. Figures in the "Number" column do not add up to the total population due to: a) Ancestry/Race overlap — e.g. persons can report being both White and Irish, b) persons of Hispanic origin can report being any race, c) persons reporting two ancestries are counted in both categories. 2. Numbers in parentheses indicate the number of persons reporting this ancestry/race alone, not in combination with any other ancestry/race. 3. Refer to the Explanation of Data in the front of the book for more detailed information.

Ancestry/Race	Number	%
African	128	0.30
Nigerian	32	0.08
Am. Ind. or Alaska Nat., not spec.	39	0.09
American Indian tribes, specified:	82	0.19
Blackfeet (1)	3	0.01
Cherokee (6)	26	0.06
Choctaw (1)	2	0.00
Creek (2)	3	0.01
Iroquois	1	0.00
Latin American Indians (17)	29	0.07
Navajo (1)	4	0.01
Potawatomi (1)	2	0.00
Seminole (1)	2	0.00
All other tribes (2)	10	0.02
American Indian tribes, not spec.	4	0.01
Arab:	571	1.35
Arab/Arabic	75	0.18
Iraqi	4	0.01
Lebanese	402	0.95
Moroccan	15	0.04
Syrian	46	0.11
Other Arab	29	0.07
Armenian	58	0.14
Asian:	878	2.08
Cambodian (1)	1	0.00
Chinese, ex. Taiwanese (179)	226	0.53
Filipino (63)	90	0.21
Indian (270)	294	0.70
Indonesian (3)	5	0.01
Japanese (61)	88	0.21
Korean (42)	51	0.12
Malaysian (2)	2	0.00
Pakistani (17)	20	0.05
Sri Lankan (3)	3	0.01
Taiwanese (15)	19	0.04
Thai (10)	11	0.03
Vietnamese (18)	23	0.05
Other Asian, specified (1)	1	0.00
Other Asian, not specified (14)	44	0.10
Australian	8	0.02
Austrian	134	0.32
Basque	82	0.19
Belgian	28	0.07
Brazilian	198	0.47
British	287	0.68
Bulgarian	36	0.09
Canadian	145	0.34
Celtic	6	0.01
Croatian	42	0.10
Cypriot	9	0.02
Czech	70	0.17
Czechoslovakian	37	0.09
Danish	61	0.14
Dutch	429	1.02
Eastern European	244	0.58
English	3,132	7.42
Estonian	14	0.03
European	406	0.96
Finnish	40	0.09
French, except Basque	943	2.23
French Canadian	124	0.29
German	2,963	7.02
Greek	234	0.55
Guyanese	22	0.05
Hawaii Native/Pacific Islander:	31	0.07
Micronesian: (1)	1	0.00
Guamanian/Chamorro (1)	1	0.00
Polynesian: (10)	14	0.03
Native Hawaiian (9)	13	0.03
Samoan (1)	1	0.00
Other Pac. Isl., not spec. (4)	16	0.04
Hispanic or Latino:	19,703	46.64
Central American:	936	2.22
Costa Rican	98	0.23
Guatemalan	64	0.15
Honduran	138	0.33
Nicaraguan	400	0.95
Panamanian	113	0.27
Salvadoran	99	0.23
Other Central American	24	0.06
Cuban	12,136	28.72
Dominican Republic	227	0.54
Mexican	482	1.14
Puerto Rican	887	2.10
South American:	2,586	6.12
Argentinean	297	0.70
Bolivian	40	0.09
Chilean	155	0.37
Colombian	961	2.27
Ecuadorian	206	0.49
Paraguayan	26	0.06
Peruvian	286	0.68
Uruguayan	44	0.10
Venezuelan	496	1.17
Other South American	75	0.18
Other Hispanic or Latino	2,449	5.80
Hungarian	226	0.54
Iranian	97	0.23
Irish	2,425	5.75
Israeli	66	0.16
Italian	2,225	5.27
Latvian	9	0.02
Lithuanian	116	0.27
Luxemburger	47	0.11
Northern European	19	0.05
Norwegian	289	0.68
Pennsylvania German	22	0.05
Polish	1,156	2.74
Portuguese	163	0.39
Romanian	132	0.31
Russian	1,050	2.49
Scandinavian	51	0.12
Scotch-Irish	337	0.80
Scottish	806	1.91
Serbian	16	0.04
Slavic	34	0.08
Slovak	39	0.09
Swedish	371	0.88
Swiss	114	0.27
Turkish	51	0.12
Ukrainian	85	0.20
United States or American	2,115	5.01
Welsh	138	0.33
West Indian, excl. Hispanic:	473	1.12
Bahamian	30	0.07
Belizean	7	0.02
British West Indian	31	0.07
Haitian	163	0.39
Jamaican	165	0.39
Trinidadian and Tobagonian	32	0.08
U.S. Virgin Islander	20	0.05
West Indian	25	0.06
White:	39,357	93.15
Not Hispanic (20,168)	20,397	48.28
Hispanic (18,630)	18,960	44.88

Coral Springs

Place Type: City
County: Broward
Population: 117,549

Ancestry/Race	Number	%
Acadian/Cajun	5	0.00
African American/Black:	11,955	10.17
Not Hispanic (10,412)	11,434	9.73
Hispanic (354)	521	0.44
African, sub-Saharan:	389	0.33
African	141	0.12
Cape Verdean	66	0.06
Nigerian	40	0.03
South African	114	0.10
Other sub-Saharan African	28	0.02
Alaska Native tribes, specified:	3	0.00
Tlingit-Haida (2)	3	0.00
Am. Ind. or Alaska Nat., not spec.	161	0.14
Albanian	9	0.01
Alsatian	17	0.01
American Indian tribes, specified:	270	0.23
Apache (1)	8	0.01
Blackfeet (1)	10	0.01
Cherokee (32)	98	0.08
Cheyenne	3	0.00
Chickasaw (2)	2	0.00
Chippewa (1)	2	0.00
Choctaw (7)	7	0.01
Comanche (4)	4	0.00
Creek (1)	1	0.00
Iroquois (6)	16	0.01
Latin American Indians (43)	72	0.06
Menominee (1)	2	0.00
Navajo	1	0.00
Ottawa	1	0.00
Potawatomi (1)	1	0.00
Pueblo (1)	2	0.00
Seminole (5)	5	0.00
Sioux (2)	10	0.01
All other tribes (9)	25	0.02
American Indian tribes, not spec.	32	0.03
Arab:	1,247	1.06
Arab/Arabic	194	0.17
Egyptian	189	0.16
Iraqi	26	0.02
Jordanian	53	0.05
Lebanese	511	0.43
Moroccan	35	0.03
Palestinian	51	0.04
Syrian	77	0.07
Other Arab	111	0.09
Armenian	191	0.16
Asian:	4,925	4.19
Bangladeshi (17)	28	0.02
Cambodian (4)	5	0.00
Chinese, ex. Taiwanese (922)	1,092	0.93
Filipino (303)	413	0.35
Indian (1,922)	2,149	1.83
Indonesian (10)	24	0.02
Japanese (68)	125	0.11
Korean (326)	357	0.30
Laotian (5)	5	0.00
Pakistani (176)	239	0.20
Sri Lankan (15)	18	0.02
Taiwanese (43)	47	0.04
Thai (30)	45	0.04
Vietnamese (170)	184	0.16
Other Asian, specified (16)	19	0.02
Other Asian, not specified (69)	175	0.15
Australian	50	0.04
Austrian	821	0.70
Basque	27	0.02
Belgian	99	0.08
Brazilian	901	0.77
British	653	0.56
Bulgarian	27	0.02
Canadian	599	0.51
Carpatho Rusyn	11	0.01
Croatian	111	0.09
Czech	441	0.38
Czechoslovakian	172	0.15
Danish	357	0.30
Dutch	992	0.84
Eastern European	508	0.43
English	7,115	6.06
Estonian	13	0.01
European	944	0.80
Finnish	210	0.18
French, except Basque	2,802	2.39
French Canadian	709	0.60
German	14,034	11.95
German Russian	7	0.01
Greek	976	0.83
Guyanese	147	0.13
Hawaii Native/Pacific Islander:	167	0.14
Micronesian: (16)	21	0.02
Guamanian/Chamorro (12)	17	0.01
Other Micronesian (4)	4	0.00
Polynesian: (33)	53	0.05
Native Hawaiian (19)	36	0.03
Samoan (7)	8	0.01
Other Polynesian (7)	9	0.01

Notes: 1. Figures in the "Number" column do not add up to the total population due to: a) Ancestry/Race overlap — e.g. persons can report being both White and Irish, b) persons of Hispanic origin can report being any race, c) persons reporting two ancestries are counted in both categories. 2. Numbers in parentheses indicate the number of persons reporting this ancestry/race alone, not in combination with any other ancestry/race. 3. Refer to the Explanation of Data in the front of the book for more detailed information.

Ancestry/Race	Number	%
Other Pac. Isl., not spec. (29)	93	0.08
Hispanic or Latino:	18,233	15.51
Central American:	804	0.68
Costa Rican	118	0.10
Guatemalan	121	0.10
Honduran	118	0.10
Nicaraguan	124	0.11
Panamanian	143	0.12
Salvadoran	157	0.13
Other Central American	23	0.02
Cuban	2,017	1.72
Dominican Republic	630	0.54
Mexican	1,603	1.36
Puerto Rican	4,163	3.54
South American:	5,261	4.48
Argentinean	498	0.42
Bolivian	54	0.05
Chilean	162	0.14
Colombian	2,408	2.05
Ecuadorian	441	0.38
Paraguayan	6	0.01
Peruvian	869	0.74
Uruguayan	99	0.08
Venezuelan	568	0.48
Other South American	156	0.13
Other Hispanic or Latino	3,755	3.19
Hungarian	1,134	0.97
Icelander	8	0.01
Iranian	247	0.21
Irish	13,257	11.28
Israeli	320	0.27
Italian	16,709	14.22
Latvian	99	0.08
Lithuanian	450	0.38
Luxemburger	8	0.01
Macedonian	5	0.00
Maltese	37	0.03
New Zealander	19	0.02
Northern European	19	0.02
Norwegian	894	0.76
Pennsylvania German	25	0.02
Polish	6,741	5.74
Portuguese	848	0.72
Romanian	611	0.52
Russian	5,710	4.86
Scandinavian	152	0.13
Scotch-Irish	1,013	0.86
Scottish	1,441	1.23
Serbian	78	0.07
Slavic	65	0.06
Slovak	172	0.15
Slovene	40	0.03
Swedish	1,324	1.13
Swiss	224	0.19
Turkish	192	0.16
Ukrainian	428	0.36
United States or American	7,594	6.46
Welsh	461	0.39
West Indian, excl. Hispanic:	7,065	6.01
Bahamian	237	0.20
Barbadian	49	0.04
Belizean	47	0.04
British West Indian	158	0.13
Haitian	2,856	2.43
Jamaican	3,019	2.57
Trinidadian and Tobagonian	433	0.37
West Indian	240	0.20
Other West Indian	26	0.02
White:	97,897	83.28
Not Hispanic (82,149)	83,258	70.83
Hispanic (13,711)	14,639	12.45
Yugoslavian	183	0.16

Coral Terrace

Place Type: Census Designated Place
County: Miami-Dade
Population: 24,380

Ancestry/Race	Number	%
Acadian/Cajun	5	0.02
African American/Black:	330	1.35
Not Hispanic (109)	118	0.48
Hispanic (172)	212	0.87
African, sub-Saharan:	55	0.23
African	45	0.18
South African	10	0.04
Am. Ind. or Alaska Nat., not spec.	21	0.09
Albanian	9	0.04
American Indian tribes, specified:	19	0.08
Apache	1	0.00
Cherokee (3)	6	0.02
Cheyenne (1)	1	0.00
Latin American Indians (7)	9	0.04
All other tribes (2)	2	0.01
American Indian tribes, not spec.	5	0.02
Arab:	181	0.74
Arab/Arabic	10	0.04
Lebanese	82	0.34
Moroccan	4	0.02
Palestinian	69	0.28
Syrian	9	0.04
Other Arab	7	0.03
Asian:	184	0.75
Chinese, ex. Taiwanese (45)	68	0.28
Filipino (22)	30	0.12
Indian (27)	35	0.14
Japanese (3)	5	0.02
Korean (8)	8	0.03
Pakistani (2)	5	0.02
Sri Lankan (5)	5	0.02
Taiwanese (3)	5	0.02
Thai (4)	8	0.03
Vietnamese (8)	9	0.04
Other Asian, not specified (1)	6	0.02
Assyrian/Chaldean/Syriac	6	0.02
Austrian	25	0.10
Basque	6	0.02
Brazilian	31	0.13
British	63	0.26
Canadian	31	0.13
Croatian	7	0.03
Czech	13	0.05
Danish	27	0.11
Dutch	59	0.24
English	413	1.70
European	7	0.03
French, except Basque	279	1.15
French Canadian	10	0.04
German	423	1.74
Greek	53	0.22
Hawaii Native/Pacific Islander:	10	0.04
Polynesian: (1)	7	0.03
Samoan (1)	7	0.03
Other Pac. Isl., not spec. (1)	3	0.01
Hispanic or Latino:	20,015	82.10
Central American:	1,057	4.34
Costa Rican	62	0.25
Guatemalan	87	0.36
Honduran	219	0.90
Nicaraguan	553	2.27
Panamanian	33	0.14
Salvadoran	82	0.34
Other Central American	21	0.09
Cuban	15,084	61.87
Dominican Republic	131	0.54
Mexican	111	0.46
Puerto Rican	453	1.86
South American:	1,043	4.28
Argentinean	64	0.26
Bolivian	31	0.13
Chilean	72	0.30
Colombian	414	1.70
Ecuadorian	63	0.26
Paraguayan	7	0.03
Peruvian	213	0.87
Uruguayan	30	0.12
Venezuelan	144	0.59
Other South American	5	0.02
Other Hispanic or Latino	2,136	8.76
Hungarian	30	0.12
Icelander	7	0.03
Irish	425	1.74
Italian	345	1.42
Latvian	5	0.02
Lithuanian	27	0.11
Norwegian	33	0.14
Polish	112	0.46
Portuguese	10	0.04
Russian	26	0.11
Scotch-Irish	93	0.38
Scottish	66	0.27
Swedish	65	0.27
Swiss	4	0.02
Turkish	13	0.05
Ukrainian	38	0.16
United States or American	589	2.42
Welsh	35	0.14
West Indian, excl. Hispanic:	107	0.44
Haitian	79	0.32
Jamaican	17	0.07
West Indian	11	0.05
White:	23,219	95.24
Not Hispanic (4,030)	4,098	16.81
Hispanic (18,657)	19,121	78.43

Country Club

Place Type: Census Designated Place
County: Miami-Dade
Population: 36,310

Ancestry/Race	Number	%
African American/Black:	8,534	23.50
Not Hispanic (7,337)	7,633	21.02
Hispanic (655)	901	2.48
African, sub-Saharan:	300	0.82
African	216	0.59
Cape Verdean	16	0.04
Nigerian	60	0.16
South African	8	0.02
Am. Ind. or Alaska Nat., not spec.	99	0.27
American Indian tribes, specified:	76	0.21
Blackfeet	5	0.01
Cherokee (3)	23	0.06
Chippewa (1)	1	0.00
Choctaw	2	0.01
Latin American Indians (13)	34	0.09
Navajo (2)	2	0.01
Pueblo	1	0.00
Sioux	2	0.01
All other tribes (1)	6	0.02
American Indian tribes, not spec.	13	0.04
Arab:	255	0.70
Arab/Arabic	51	0.14
Egyptian	11	0.03
Iraqi	8	0.02
Lebanese	119	0.33
Moroccan	8	0.02
Palestinian	28	0.08
Syrian	30	0.08
Armenian	29	0.08
Asian:	1,049	2.89
Chinese, ex. Taiwanese (153)	205	0.56
Filipino (170)	203	0.56
Indian (258)	303	0.83
Japanese (19)	36	0.10
Korean (73)	82	0.23
Laotian (9)	10	0.03
Pakistani (36)	89	0.25
Sri Lankan (1)	1	0.00
Taiwanese (4)	5	0.01
Thai (9)	16	0.04
Vietnamese (41)	44	0.12
Other Asian, specified	1	0.00
Other Asian, not specified (22)	54	0.15
Austrian	9	0.02
Belgian	7	0.02
Brazilian	91	0.25
British	45	0.12

Notes: 1. Figures in the "Number" column do not add up to the total population due to: a) Ancestry/Race overlap — e.g. persons can report being both White and Irish, b) persons of Hispanic origin can report being any race, c) persons reporting two ancestries are counted in both categories. 2. Numbers in parentheses indicate the number of persons reporting this ancestry/race alone, not in combination with any other ancestry/race. 3. Refer to the Explanation of Data in the front of the book for more detailed information.

Ancestry/Race	Number	%
Canadian	37	0.10
Carpatho Rusyn	9	0.02
Croatian	19	0.05
Czechoslovakian	5	0.01
Danish	86	0.24
Dutch	123	0.34
English	575	1.58
European	62	0.17
Finnish	9	0.02
French, except Basque	297	0.82
French Canadian	22	0.06
German	691	1.90
Greek	43	0.12
Guyanese	61	0.17
Hawaii Native/Pacific Islander:	71	0.20
Melanesian: (1)	1	0.00
Fijian (1)	1	0.00
Micronesian: (6)	10	0.03
Guamanian/Chamorro (6)	10	0.03
Polynesian: (6)	10	0.03
Native Hawaiian (1)	4	0.01
Samoan (4)	4	0.01
Other Polynesian (1)	2	0.01
Other Pac. Isl., specified	1	0.00
Other Pac. Isl., not spec. (8)	49	0.13
Hispanic or Latino:	21,903	60.32
Central American:	1,398	3.85
Costa Rican	99	0.27
Guatemalan	135	0.37
Honduran	219	0.60
Nicaraguan	585	1.61
Panamanian	240	0.66
Salvadoran	82	0.23
Other Central American	38	0.10
Cuban	7,251	19.97
Dominican Republic	1,309	3.61
Mexican	387	1.07
Puerto Rican	2,152	5.93
South American:	4,843	13.34
Argentinean	175	0.48
Bolivian	41	0.11
Chilean	138	0.38
Colombian	3,134	8.63
Ecuadorian	326	0.90
Paraguayan	2	0.01
Peruvian	454	1.25
Uruguayan	56	0.15
Venezuelan	456	1.26
Other South American	61	0.17
Other Hispanic or Latino	4,563	12.57
Hungarian	34	0.09
Iranian	22	0.06
Irish	769	2.11
Israeli	5	0.01
Italian	756	2.08
Lithuanian	8	0.02
Norwegian	94	0.26
Pennsylvania German	18	0.05
Polish	259	0.71
Portuguese	104	0.29
Romanian	18	0.05
Russian	148	0.41
Scandinavian	10	0.03
Scotch-Irish	98	0.27
Scottish	83	0.23
Slovak	8	0.02
Slovene	18	0.05
Swedish	51	0.14
Swiss	27	0.07
Turkish	37	0.10
Ukrainian	12	0.03
United States or American	1,401	3.85
Welsh	23	0.06
West Indian, excl. Hispanic:	2,555	7.02
Bahamian	313	0.86
Barbadian	21	0.06
British West Indian	88	0.24
Haitian	1,111	3.05
Jamaican	745	2.05
Trinidadian and Tobagonian	123	0.34
U.S. Virgin Islander	52	0.14
West Indian	92	0.25
Other West Indian	10	0.03
White:	24,358	67.08
Not Hispanic (5,643)	5,923	16.31
Hispanic (17,429)	18,435	50.77

Country Walk

Place Type: Census Designated Place
County: Miami-Dade
Population: 10,653

Ancestry/Race	Number	%
Acadian/Cajun	11	0.10
African American/Black:	1,314	12.33
Not Hispanic (1,065)	1,209	11.35
Hispanic (71)	105	0.99
African, sub-Saharan:	95	0.89
African	11	0.10
Nigerian	81	0.76
Sierra Leonean	3	0.03
Am. Ind. or Alaska Nat., not spec.	8	0.08
American Indian tribes, specified:	21	0.20
Cherokee (1)	7	0.07
Creek	4	0.04
Delaware	1	0.01
Latin American Indians (5)	5	0.05
Navajo	2	0.02
Pueblo (1)	1	0.01
All other tribes	1	0.01
American Indian tribes, not spec.	2	0.02
Arab:	86	0.81
Lebanese	45	0.42
Moroccan	41	0.38
Asian:	432	4.06
Bangladeshi	10	0.09
Chinese, ex. Taiwanese (122)	198	1.86
Filipino (31)	41	0.38
Indian (67)	114	1.07
Indonesian (2)	2	0.02
Japanese (9)	14	0.13
Korean (4)	4	0.04
Malaysian	1	0.01
Pakistani (5)	5	0.05
Thai (1)	2	0.02
Vietnamese (12)	21	0.20
Other Asian, not specified (4)	20	0.19
Austrian	13	0.12
Belgian	6	0.06
Brazilian	57	0.54
British	51	0.48
Canadian	29	0.27
Danish	24	0.23
Dutch	66	0.62
Eastern European	9	0.08
English	293	2.75
European	57	0.54
French, except Basque	201	1.89
French Canadian	12	0.11
German	681	6.39
Greek	10	0.09
Guyanese	21	0.20
Hawaii Native/Pacific Islander:	11	0.10
Polynesian: (4)	5	0.05
Native Hawaiian	1	0.01
Samoan (4)	4	0.04
Other Pac. Isl., not spec. (1)	6	0.06
Hispanic or Latino:	5,980	56.13
Central American:	364	3.42
Costa Rican	23	0.22
Guatemalan	27	0.25
Honduran	51	0.48
Nicaraguan	185	1.74
Panamanian	43	0.40
Salvadoran	30	0.28
Other Central American	5	0.05
Cuban	2,366	22.21
Dominican Republic	228	2.14
Mexican	78	0.73
Puerto Rican	589	5.53
South American:	1,243	11.67
Argentinean	66	0.62
Bolivian	18	0.17
Chilean	83	0.78
Colombian	594	5.58
Ecuadorian	93	0.87
Paraguayan	1	0.01
Peruvian	183	1.72
Uruguayan	8	0.08
Venezuelan	178	1.67
Other South American	19	0.18
Other Hispanic or Latino	1,112	10.44
Hungarian	22	0.21
Iranian	25	0.23
Irish	456	4.28
Italian	480	4.51
Norwegian	73	0.69
Polish	67	0.63
Romanian	11	0.10
Russian	126	1.18
Scotch-Irish	10	0.09
Scottish	74	0.69
Swedish	75	0.70
Swiss	34	0.32
Turkish	7	0.07
United States or American	436	4.09
Welsh	11	0.10
West Indian, excl. Hispanic:	980	9.20
Barbadian	18	0.17
British West Indian	27	0.25
Haitian	190	1.78
Jamaican	498	4.67
Trinidadian and Tobagonian	190	1.78
West Indian	57	0.54
White:	8,574	80.48
Not Hispanic (3,049)	3,163	29.69
Hispanic (5,218)	5,411	50.79

Crestview

Place Type: City
County: Okaloosa
Population: 14,766

Ancestry/Race	Number	%
African American/Black:	2,844	19.26
Not Hispanic (2,695)	2,801	18.97
Hispanic (24)	43	0.29
African, sub-Saharan:	247	1.67
African	247	1.67
Am. Ind. or Alaska Nat., not spec.	38	0.26
American Indian tribes, specified:	141	0.95
Apache (1)	5	0.03
Blackfeet	7	0.05
Cherokee (30)	57	0.39
Cheyenne (1)	2	0.01
Chickasaw	1	0.01
Chippewa (3)	5	0.03
Choctaw (1)	4	0.03
Comanche	1	0.01
Cree	1	0.01
Creek (12)	25	0.17
Iroquois (6)	7	0.05
Latin American Indians (2)	3	0.02
Navajo (1)	1	0.01
Ottawa (1)	1	0.01
Potawatomi	2	0.01
Pueblo	2	0.01
Seminole (1)	2	0.01
Shoshone	1	0.01
Sioux (1)	3	0.02
Ute	1	0.01
Yaqui (1)	1	0.01
All other tribes (4)	9	0.06
American Indian tribes, not spec.	9	0.06
Arab:	45	0.30
Lebanese	38	0.26
Moroccan	7	0.05
Asian:	508	3.44

Notes: 1. Figures in the "Number" column do not add up to the total population due to: a) Ancestry/Race overlap — e.g. persons can report being both White and Irish, b) persons of Hispanic origin can report being any race, c) persons reporting two ancestries are counted in both categories. 2. Numbers in parentheses indicate the number of persons reporting this ancestry/race alone, not in combination with any other ancestry/race. 3. Refer to the Explanation of Data in the front of the book for more detailed information.

Ancestry/Race	Number	%
Chinese, ex. Taiwanese (18)	27	0.18
Filipino (165)	249	1.69
Indian (17)	28	0.19
Indonesian (2)	3	0.02
Japanese (16)	37	0.25
Korean (58)	87	0.59
Taiwanese (1)	1	0.01
Thai (26)	36	0.24
Vietnamese (20)	26	0.18
Other Asian, specified	1	0.01
Other Asian, not specified (8)	13	0.09
Australian	11	0.07
British	93	0.63
Canadian	6	0.04
Danish	11	0.07
Dutch	153	1.03
English	1,277	8.62
European	114	0.77
French, except Basque	273	1.84
French Canadian	192	1.30
German	1,645	11.10
Greek	26	0.18
Hawaii Native/Pacific Islander:	42	0.28
Micronesian: (7)	12	0.08
Guamanian/Chamorro (7)	12	0.08
Polynesian: (15)	25	0.17
Native Hawaiian (15)	25	0.17
Other Pac. Isl., specified	1	0.01
Other Pac. Isl., not spec.	4	0.03
Hispanic or Latino:	481	3.26
Central American:	37	0.25
Costa Rican	1	0.01
Guatemalan	1	0.01
Honduran	5	0.03
Nicaraguan	2	0.01
Panamanian	22	0.15
Other Central American	6	0.04
Cuban	15	0.10
Dominican Republic	12	0.08
Mexican	156	1.06
Puerto Rican	127	0.86
South American:	15	0.10
Colombian	12	0.08
Peruvian	1	0.01
Other South American	2	0.01
Other Hispanic or Latino	119	0.81
Hungarian	8	0.05
Irish	1,310	8.84
Italian	648	4.37
Lithuanian	41	0.28
Luxemburger	7	0.05
Northern European	42	0.28
Norwegian	133	0.90
Pennsylvania German	8	0.05
Polish	279	1.88
Russian	9	0.06
Scandinavian	26	0.18
Scotch-Irish	193	1.30
Scottish	293	1.98
Swedish	96	0.65
Swiss	8	0.05
Turkish	24	0.16
United States or American	2,121	14.31
Welsh	38	0.26
West Indian, excl. Hispanic:	45	0.30
Bahamian	3	0.02
Barbadian	6	0.04
Haitian	36	0.24
White:	11,364	76.96
Not Hispanic (10,774)	11,073	74.99
Hispanic (258)	291	1.97

Cutler

Place Type: Census Designated Place
County: Miami-Dade
Population: 17,390

Ancestry/Race	Number	%
African American/Black:	777	4.47
Not Hispanic (645)	727	4.18
Hispanic (34)	50	0.29
African, sub-Saharan:	63	0.36
African	63	0.36
Am. Ind. or Alaska Nat., not spec.	8	0.05
American Indian tribes, specified:	40	0.23
Apache	1	0.01
Blackfeet	2	0.01
Cherokee (10)	23	0.13
Chippewa (3)	3	0.02
Creek	5	0.03
Latin American Indians (4)	5	0.03
Paiute	1	0.01
American Indian tribes, not spec.	1	0.01
Arab:	144	0.82
Egyptian	33	0.19
Lebanese	106	0.60
Syrian	5	0.03
Armenian	14	0.08
Asian:	627	3.61
Cambodian (5)	5	0.03
Chinese, ex. Taiwanese (220)	271	1.56
Filipino (41)	49	0.28
Indian (148)	170	0.98
Japanese (33)	39	0.22
Korean (30)	31	0.18
Laotian (1)	1	0.01
Malaysian	2	0.01
Pakistani (11)	16	0.09
Thai (13)	13	0.07
Vietnamese (10)	11	0.06
Other Asian, not specified (8)	19	0.11
Australian	8	0.05
Austrian	101	0.57
Basque	96	0.54
Belgian	7	0.04
Brazilian	110	0.62
British	159	0.90
Bulgarian	10	0.06
Canadian	63	0.36
Croatian	18	0.10
Czech	107	0.61
Czechoslovakian	41	0.23
Danish	60	0.34
Dutch	189	1.07
Eastern European	132	0.75
English	2,187	12.39
European	319	1.81
French, except Basque	360	2.04
French Canadian	87	0.49
German	2,152	12.19
Greek	204	1.16
Guyanese	14	0.08
Hawaii Native/Pacific Islander:	6	0.03
Micronesian: (2)	2	0.01
Guamanian/Chamorro (2)	2	0.01
Polynesian: (2)	2	0.01
Samoan (2)	2	0.01
Other Pac. Isl., not spec. (1)	2	0.01
Hispanic or Latino:	4,555	26.19
Central American:	354	2.04
Costa Rican	22	0.13
Guatemalan	38	0.22
Honduran	45	0.26
Nicaraguan	120	0.69
Panamanian	36	0.21
Salvadoran	68	0.39
Other Central American	25	0.14
Cuban	1,824	10.49
Dominican Republic	70	0.40
Mexican	144	0.83
Puerto Rican	309	1.78
South American:	978	5.62
Argentinean	107	0.62
Bolivian	33	0.19
Chilean	129	0.74
Colombian	343	1.97
Ecuadorian	78	0.45
Paraguayan	3	0.02
Peruvian	131	0.75
Uruguayan	14	0.08
Venezuelan	130	0.75
Other South American	10	0.06
Other Hispanic or Latino	876	5.04
Hungarian	217	1.23
Iranian	132	0.75
Irish	2,091	11.84
Israeli	18	0.10
Italian	1,390	7.87
Latvian	7	0.04
Lithuanian	36	0.20
Luxemburger	4	0.02
Maltese	31	0.18
Norwegian	100	0.57
Polish	524	2.97
Portuguese	119	0.67
Romanian	201	1.14
Russian	745	4.22
Scandinavian	39	0.22
Scotch-Irish	260	1.47
Scottish	472	2.67
Serbian	12	0.07
Slovak	6	0.03
Slovene	8	0.05
Swedish	212	1.20
Swiss	96	0.54
Turkish	65	0.37
Ukrainian	34	0.19
United States or American	978	5.54
Welsh	99	0.56
West Indian, excl. Hispanic:	211	1.20
Jamaican	165	0.93
Trinidadian and Tobagonian	28	0.16
West Indian	18	0.10
White:	15,782	90.75
Not Hispanic (11,405)	11,554	66.44
Hispanic (4,108)	4,228	24.31
Yugoslavian	15	0.08

Cutler Ridge

Place Type: Census Designated Place
County: Miami-Dade
Population: 24,781

Ancestry/Race	Number	%
African American/Black:	4,280	17.27
Not Hispanic (3,639)	3,936	15.88
Hispanic (246)	344	1.39
African, sub-Saharan:	71	0.29
African	62	0.25
Other sub-Saharan African	9	0.04
Am. Ind. or Alaska Nat., not spec.	69	0.28
American Indian tribes, specified:	85	0.34
Apache	1	0.00
Blackfeet	3	0.01
Cherokee (4)	16	0.06
Cheyenne (1)	1	0.00
Chippewa (1)	2	0.01
Choctaw (2)	4	0.02
Cree (1)	1	0.00
Creek	6	0.02
Crow	1	0.00
Latin American Indians (17)	26	0.10
Navajo (2)	4	0.02
Osage (1)	1	0.00
Seminole	1	0.00
Sioux (4)	9	0.04
Ute	2	0.01
All other tribes (5)	7	0.03
American Indian tribes, not spec.	5	0.02
Arab:	130	0.53
Arab/Arabic	28	0.11
Lebanese	55	0.22
Moroccan	24	0.10
Syrian	23	0.09
Armenian	10	0.04
Asian:	624	2.52
Bangladeshi (4)	4	0.02
Cambodian (1)	1	0.00

Notes: 1. Figures in the "Number" column do not add up to the total population due to: a) Ancestry/Race overlap — e.g. persons can report being both White and Irish, b) persons of Hispanic origin can report being any race, c) persons reporting two ancestries are counted in both categories. 2. Numbers in parentheses indicate the number of persons reporting this ancestry/race alone, not in combination with any other ancestry/race. 3. Refer to the Explanation of Data in the front of the book for more detailed information.

	Number	%
Chinese, ex. Taiwanese (74)	131	0.53
Filipino (33)	64	0.26
Indian (209)	297	1.20
Indonesian (3)	3	0.01
Japanese (10)	23	0.09
Korean (14)	14	0.06
Pakistani (6)	6	0.02
Taiwanese (1)	1	0.00
Thai (29)	30	0.12
Vietnamese (32)	32	0.13
Other Asian, specified (1)	1	0.00
Other Asian, not specified (6)	17	0.07
Australian	7	0.03
Austrian	94	0.38
Belgian	7	0.03
Brazilian	54	0.22
British	165	0.67
Canadian	131	0.53
Croatian	19	0.08
Czech	60	0.24
Czechoslovakian	8	0.03
Danish	63	0.26
Dutch	213	0.86
English	1,408	5.71
European	130	0.53
Finnish	43	0.17
French, except Basque	570	2.31
French Canadian	101	0.41
German	2,014	8.16
Greek	122	0.49
Guyanese	24	0.10
Hawaii Native/Pacific Islander:	58	0.23
Micronesian: (1)	1	0.00
Guamanian/Chamorro (1)	1	0.00
Polynesian: (8)	20	0.08
Native Hawaiian (1)	11	0.04
Samoan (4)	5	0.02
Other Polynesian (3)	4	0.02
Other Pac. Isl., not spec. (9)	37	0.15
Hispanic or Latino:	9,107	36.75
Central American:	701	2.83
Costa Rican	47	0.19
Guatemalan	31	0.13
Honduran	129	0.52
Nicaraguan	355	1.43
Panamanian	55	0.22
Salvadoran	64	0.26
Other Central American	20	0.08
Cuban	3,312	13.37
Dominican Republic	411	1.66
Mexican	332	1.34
Puerto Rican	1,625	6.56
South American:	1,051	4.24
Argentinean	80	0.32
Bolivian	15	0.06
Chilean	63	0.25
Colombian	472	1.90
Ecuadorian	94	0.38
Paraguayan	12	0.05
Peruvian	147	0.59
Uruguayan	22	0.09
Venezuelan	117	0.47
Other South American	29	0.12
Other Hispanic or Latino	1,675	6.76
Hungarian	196	0.79
Icelander	6	0.02
Iranian	17	0.07
Irish	2,133	8.65
Israeli	28	0.11
Italian	1,095	4.44
Latvian	6	0.02
Lithuanian	14	0.06
Maltese	6	0.02
Norwegian	206	0.83
Polish	361	1.46
Portuguese	49	0.20
Romanian	13	0.05
Russian	187	0.76
Scotch-Irish	342	1.39
Scottish	240	0.97
Slavic	13	0.05
Slovak	32	0.13
Swedish	138	0.56
Swiss	37	0.15
Turkish	12	0.05
Ukrainian	43	0.17
United States or American	2,104	8.53
Welsh	83	0.34
West Indian, excl. Hispanic:	1,374	5.57
Bahamian	21	0.09
Barbadian	5	0.02
Bermudan	5	0.02
British West Indian	93	0.38
Haitian	384	1.56
Jamaican	634	2.57
Trinidadian and Tobagonian	154	0.62
U.S. Virgin Islander	9	0.04
West Indian	69	0.28
White:	18,894	76.24
Not Hispanic (11,008)	11,234	45.33
Hispanic (7,260)	7,660	30.91
Yugoslavian	13	0.05

Cypress Lake

Place Type: Census Designated Place
County: Lee
Population: 12,072

Ancestry/Race	Number	%
Acadian/Cajun	7	0.06
African American/Black:	145	1.20
Not Hispanic (112)	123	1.02
Hispanic (14)	22	0.18
Alaska Native tribes, specified:	2	0.02
Tlingit-Haida	2	0.02
Am. Ind. or Alaska Nat., not spec.	13	0.11
American Indian tribes, specified:	25	0.21
Apache (1)	1	0.01
Cherokee (3)	10	0.08
Iroquois	1	0.01
Latin American Indians (4)	4	0.03
Lumbee (3)	3	0.02
Seminole (2)	2	0.02
Shoshone	2	0.02
All other tribes (1)	2	0.02
American Indian tribes, not spec.	3	0.02
Arab:	77	0.64
Egyptian	44	0.36
Lebanese	8	0.07
Palestinian	25	0.21
Asian:	95	0.79
Chinese, ex. Taiwanese (18)	21	0.17
Filipino (12)	17	0.14
Indian (12)	15	0.12
Indonesian (1)	1	0.01
Japanese (5)	6	0.05
Korean (6)	6	0.05
Thai (2)	3	0.02
Vietnamese (7)	10	0.08
Other Asian, not specified (10)	16	0.13
Austrian	71	0.59
Belgian	73	0.60
British	87	0.72
Canadian	61	0.50
Celtic	9	0.07
Croatian	44	0.36
Czech	55	0.45
Czechoslovakian	49	0.40
Danish	75	0.62
Dutch	164	1.36
English	2,121	17.53
Estonian	18	0.15
European	44	0.36
Finnish	41	0.34
French, except Basque	493	4.07
French Canadian	129	1.07
German	2,793	23.08
Greek	87	0.72
Guyanese	9	0.07
Hawaii Native/Pacific Islander:	7	0.06
Polynesian:	1	0.01
Other Polynesian	1	0.01
Other Pac. Isl., not spec. (4)	6	0.05
Hispanic or Latino:	437	3.62
Central American:	19	0.16
Costa Rican	9	0.07
Guatemalan	5	0.04
Honduran	1	0.01
Panamanian	3	0.02
Salvadoran	1	0.01
Cuban	43	0.36
Dominican Republic	13	0.11
Mexican	72	0.60
Puerto Rican	160	1.33
South American:	45	0.37
Argentinean	3	0.02
Chilean	2	0.02
Colombian	14	0.12
Ecuadorian	1	0.01
Peruvian	7	0.06
Uruguayan	1	0.01
Venezuelan	8	0.07
Other South American	9	0.07
Other Hispanic or Latino	85	0.70
Hungarian	66	0.55
Irish	2,122	17.54
Italian	1,052	8.69
Latvian	9	0.07
Lithuanian	14	0.12
Luxemburger	9	0.07
Maltese	10	0.08
Northern European	8	0.07
Norwegian	188	1.55
Pennsylvania German	15	0.12
Polish	650	5.37
Portuguese	81	0.67
Romanian	28	0.23
Russian	160	1.32
Scandinavian	29	0.24
Scotch-Irish	184	1.52
Scottish	340	2.81
Serbian	7	0.06
Slavic	11	0.09
Slovak	38	0.31
Slovene	8	0.07
Swedish	193	1.60
Swiss	122	1.01
Turkish	10	0.08
Ukrainian	51	0.42
United States or American	893	7.38
Welsh	95	0.79
West Indian, excl. Hispanic:	14	0.12
British West Indian	5	0.04
Jamaican	3	0.02
West Indian	6	0.05
White:	11,773	97.52
Not Hispanic (11,358)	11,421	94.61
Hispanic (311)	352	2.92
Yugoslavian	18	0.15

Dania Beach

Place Type: City
County: Broward
Population: 20,061

Ancestry/Race	Number	%
African American/Black:	4,927	24.56
Not Hispanic (4,623)	4,748	23.67
Hispanic (140)	179	0.89
African, sub-Saharan:	289	1.44
African	282	1.40
South African	7	0.03
Am. Ind. or Alaska Nat., not spec.	37	0.18
Albanian	9	0.04
American Indian tribes, specified:	97	0.48
Apache	1	0.00
Blackfeet (2)	4	0.02
Cherokee (14)	46	0.23

Notes: 1. Figures in the "Number" column do not add up to the total population due to: a) Ancestry/Race overlap — e.g. persons can report being both White and Irish, b) persons of Hispanic origin can report being any race, c) persons reporting two ancestries are counted in both categories. 2. Numbers in parentheses indicate the number of persons reporting this ancestry/race alone, not in combination with any other ancestry/race. 3. Refer to the Explanation of Data in the front of the book for more detailed information.

Ancestry/Race	Number	%
Choctaw	1	0.00
Comanche (4)	4	0.02
Creek	1	0.00
Delaware (1)	3	0.01
Iroquois (2)	2	0.01
Latin American Indians (8)	14	0.07
Potawatomi (3)	3	0.01
Seminole (3)	4	0.02
Shoshone (1)	1	0.00
Sioux (1)	4	0.02
All other tribes (4)	9	0.04
American Indian tribes, not spec.	5	0.02
Arab:	264	1.31
Arab/Arabic	47	0.23
Iraqi	22	0.11
Lebanese	120	0.60
Moroccan	7	0.03
Palestinian	43	0.21
Syrian	11	0.05
Other Arab	14	0.07
Armenian	17	0.08
Asian:	372	1.85
Chinese, ex. Taiwanese (38)	58	0.29
Filipino (60)	71	0.35
Indian (86)	99	0.49
Indonesian	4	0.02
Japanese (10)	19	0.09
Korean (57)	60	0.30
Laotian (1)	1	0.00
Pakistani (2)	5	0.02
Taiwanese (2)	2	0.01
Thai (3)	5	0.02
Vietnamese (7)	8	0.04
Other Asian, not specified (5)	40	0.20
Austrian	40	0.20
Basque	7	0.03
Belgian	46	0.23
Brazilian	102	0.51
British	128	0.64
Canadian	147	0.73
Celtic	14	0.07
Czech	57	0.28
Czechoslovakian	42	0.21
Danish	80	0.40
Dutch	171	0.85
Eastern European	7	0.03
English	1,055	5.24
Estonian	43	0.21
European	137	0.68
Finnish	33	0.16
French, except Basque	549	2.73
French Canadian	491	2.44
German	1,955	9.72
Greek	137	0.68
Guyanese	41	0.20
Hawaii Native/Pacific Islander:	24	0.12
Micronesian: (2)	5	0.02
Guamanian/Chamorro (1)	1	0.00
Other Micronesian (1)	4	0.02
Polynesian: (3)	10	0.05
Native Hawaiian (3)	8	0.04
Samoan	2	0.01
Other Pac. Isl., not spec. (1)	9	0.04
Hispanic or Latino:	2,410	12.01
Central American:	173	0.86
Costa Rican	33	0.16
Guatemalan	22	0.11
Honduran	27	0.13
Nicaraguan	34	0.17
Panamanian	21	0.10
Salvadoran	35	0.17
Other Central American	1	0.00
Cuban	340	1.69
Dominican Republic	45	0.22
Mexican	171	0.85
Puerto Rican	669	3.33
South American:	446	2.22
Argentinean	43	0.21
Bolivian	3	0.01
Chilean	11	0.05
Colombian	223	1.11
Ecuadorian	31	0.15
Paraguayan	1	0.00
Peruvian	71	0.35
Uruguayan	5	0.02
Venezuelan	49	0.24
Other South American	9	0.04
Other Hispanic or Latino	566	2.82
Hungarian	81	0.40
Irish	2,048	10.18
Israeli	49	0.24
Italian	2,490	12.38
Latvian	11	0.05
Lithuanian	24	0.12
Macedonian	18	0.09
Maltese	21	0.10
Norwegian	123	0.61
Polish	518	2.57
Portuguese	156	0.78
Romanian	46	0.23
Russian	151	0.75
Scandinavian	39	0.19
Scotch-Irish	168	0.84
Scottish	157	0.78
Serbian	11	0.05
Slovak	28	0.14
Swedish	150	0.75
Swiss	23	0.11
Turkish	11	0.05
Ukrainian	50	0.25
United States or American	1,428	7.10
Welsh	92	0.46
West Indian, excl. Hispanic:	839	4.17
Bahamian	122	0.61
Barbadian	34	0.17
British West Indian	11	0.05
Haitian	341	1.69
Jamaican	285	1.42
Trinidadian and Tobagonian	38	0.19
West Indian	8	0.04
White:	14,375	71.66
Not Hispanic (12,352)	12,540	62.51
Hispanic (1,718)	1,835	9.15
Yugoslavian	21	0.10

Davie

Place Type: Town
County: Broward
Population: 75,720

Ancestry/Race	Number	%
Acadian/Cajun	5	0.01
Afghan	13	0.02
African American/Black:	3,967	5.24
Not Hispanic (3,207)	3,613	4.77
Hispanic (247)	354	0.47
African, sub-Saharan:	216	0.29
African	117	0.15
Nigerian	44	0.06
South African	45	0.06
Other sub-Saharan African	10	0.01
Alaska Native tribes, specified:	6	0.01
Alaska Athabascan (1)	1	0.00
Eskimo (2)	5	0.01
Am. Ind. or Alaska Nat., not spec.	138	0.18
Albanian	36	0.05
Alsatian	8	0.01
American Indian tribes, specified:	287	0.38
Apache (2)	5	0.01
Blackfeet (8)	31	0.04
Cherokee (23)	92	0.12
Chickasaw (3)	4	0.01
Chippewa (4)	6	0.01
Choctaw (9)	10	0.01
Cree	1	0.00
Creek (2)	7	0.01
Delaware	1	0.00
Houma (2)	2	0.00
Iroquois (7)	13	0.02
Latin American Indians (10)	34	0.04
Lumbee (1)	1	0.00
Navajo (5)	7	0.01
Paiute (2)	2	0.00
Potawatomi	1	0.00
Pueblo	2	0.00
Seminole (23)	27	0.04
Sioux (4)	10	0.01
Yaqui (1)	3	0.00
All other tribes (8)	28	0.04
American Indian tribes, not spec.	13	0.02
Arab:	541	0.71
Arab/Arabic	54	0.07
Egyptian	85	0.11
Iraqi	6	0.01
Jordanian	11	0.01
Lebanese	350	0.46
Moroccan	10	0.01
Syrian	25	0.03
Armenian	19	0.03
Asian:	2,634	3.48
Bangladeshi (22)	26	0.03
Cambodian (8)	9	0.01
Chinese, ex. Taiwanese (493)	619	0.82
Filipino (225)	299	0.39
Indian (728)	880	1.16
Indonesian (5)	18	0.02
Japanese (65)	103	0.14
Korean (170)	188	0.25
Laotian (4)	6	0.01
Malaysian	5	0.01
Pakistani (122)	155	0.20
Taiwanese (44)	45	0.06
Thai (28)	39	0.05
Vietnamese (131)	149	0.20
Other Asian, specified (8)	10	0.01
Other Asian, not specified (30)	83	0.11
Australian	43	0.06
Austrian	273	0.36
Basque	9	0.01
Belgian	40	0.05
Brazilian	305	0.40
British	404	0.53
Bulgarian	40	0.05
Canadian	396	0.52
Celtic	6	0.01
Croatian	88	0.12
Cypriot	11	0.01
Czech	295	0.39
Czechoslovakian	121	0.16
Danish	218	0.29
Dutch	827	1.09
Eastern European	123	0.16
English	5,660	7.48
Estonian	12	0.02
European	326	0.43
Finnish	41	0.05
French, except Basque	2,368	3.13
French Canadian	833	1.10
German	10,389	13.73
Greek	544	0.72
Guyanese	136	0.18
Hawaii Native/Pacific Islander:	91	0.12
Micronesian: (5)	12	0.02
Guamanian/Chamorro (5)	12	0.02
Polynesian: (12)	21	0.03
Native Hawaiian (5)	13	0.02
Samoan (7)	8	0.01
Other Pac. Isl., specified	1	0.00
Other Pac. Isl., not spec. (13)	57	0.08
Hispanic or Latino:	14,270	18.85
Central American:	871	1.15
Costa Rican	74	0.10
Guatemalan	144	0.19
Honduran	151	0.20
Nicaraguan	190	0.25
Panamanian	94	0.12
Salvadoran	177	0.23
Other Central American	41	0.05
Cuban	3,275	4.33

Notes: 1. Figures in the "Number" column do not add up to the total population due to: a) Ancestry/Race overlap — e.g. persons can report being both White and Irish, b) persons of Hispanic origin can report being any race, c) persons reporting two ancestries are counted in both categories. 2. Numbers in parentheses indicate the number of persons reporting this ancestry/race alone, not in combination with any other ancestry/race. 3. Refer to the Explanation of Data in the front of the book for more detailed information.

Ancestry/Race	Number	%
Dominican Republic	441	0.58
Mexican	782	1.03
Puerto Rican	3,285	4.34
South American:	2,984	3.94
Argentinean	190	0.25
Bolivian	54	0.07
Chilean	117	0.15
Colombian	1,304	1.72
Ecuadorian	307	0.41
Paraguayan	12	0.02
Peruvian	482	0.64
Uruguayan	30	0.04
Venezuelan	389	0.51
Other South American	99	0.13
Other Hispanic or Latino	2,632	3.48
Hungarian	622	0.82
Iranian	80	0.11
Irish	10,617	14.03
Israeli	83	0.11
Italian	9,477	12.52
Latvian	79	0.10
Lithuanian	138	0.18
Luxemburger	11	0.01
Maltese	28	0.04
Norwegian	512	0.68
Pennsylvania German	59	0.08
Polish	3,184	4.21
Portuguese	434	0.57
Romanian	407	0.54
Russian	2,365	3.12
Scandinavian	91	0.12
Scotch-Irish	990	1.31
Scottish	1,252	1.65
Slavic	57	0.08
Slovak	97	0.13
Slovene	34	0.04
Swedish	730	0.96
Swiss	153	0.20
Turkish	81	0.11
Ukrainian	197	0.26
United States or American	5,248	6.93
Welsh	214	0.28
West Indian, excl. Hispanic:	1,553	2.05
Bahamian	97	0.13
Barbadian	83	0.11
Belizean	7	0.01
British West Indian	33	0.04
Haitian	355	0.47
Jamaican	696	0.92
Trinidadian and Tobagonian	114	0.15
U.S. Virgin Islander	7	0.01
West Indian	119	0.16
Other West Indian	42	0.06
White:	67,335	88.93
Not Hispanic (54,676)	55,419	73.19
Hispanic (11,240)	11,916	15.74
Yugoslavian	97	0.13

Daytona Beach

Place Type: City
County: Volusia
Population: 64,112

Ancestry/Race	Number	%
Acadian/Cajun	10	0.02
African American/Black:	21,462	33.48
Not Hispanic (20,813)	21,234	33.12
Hispanic (181)	228	0.36
African, sub-Saharan:	788	1.23
African	604	0.94
Ethiopian	9	0.01
Ghanian	6	0.01
Kenyan	10	0.02
Liberian	41	0.06
Nigerian	82	0.13
Other sub-Saharan African	36	0.06
Alaska Native tribes, specified:	4	0.01
Aleut (2)	2	0.00
Eskimo (1)	2	0.00
Alaska Native tribes, not specified	4	0.01
Am. Ind. or Alaska Nat., not spec.	158	0.25
American Indian tribes, specified:	331	0.52
Apache (3)	9	0.01
Blackfeet (4)	25	0.04
Cherokee (51)	149	0.23
Cheyenne (2)	4	0.01
Chickasaw	1	0.00
Chippewa (2)	4	0.01
Choctaw (4)	7	0.01
Comanche	2	0.00
Cree	4	0.01
Creek (1)	6	0.01
Crow	2	0.00
Delaware	1	0.00
Iroquois (13)	30	0.05
Kiowa (1)	1	0.00
Latin American Indians (4)	9	0.01
Lumbee (1)	1	0.00
Navajo (1)	6	0.01
Osage (1)	1	0.00
Potawatomi	1	0.00
Pueblo (1)	1	0.00
Puget Sound Salish (1)	2	0.00
Seminole (3)	17	0.03
Shoshone (1)	2	0.00
Sioux (3)	5	0.01
Ute (1)	2	0.00
Yakama	1	0.00
Yaqui (3)	4	0.01
All other tribes (15)	34	0.05
American Indian tribes, not spec.	32	0.05
Arab:	486	0.76
Arab/Arabic	93	0.15
Egyptian	41	0.06
Jordanian	15	0.02
Lebanese	84	0.13
Moroccan	65	0.10
Palestinian	59	0.09
Syrian	41	0.06
Other Arab	88	0.14
Armenian	60	0.09
Asian:	1,375	2.14
Cambodian (2)	6	0.01
Chinese, ex. Taiwanese (139)	163	0.25
Filipino (112)	138	0.22
Indian (436)	490	0.76
Indonesian (1)	4	0.01
Japanese (78)	98	0.15
Korean (181)	202	0.32
Laotian (3)	3	0.00
Malaysian (1)	3	0.00
Pakistani (20)	21	0.03
Sri Lankan (19)	19	0.03
Taiwanese (9)	13	0.02
Thai (14)	28	0.04
Vietnamese (61)	80	0.12
Other Asian, specified	10	0.02
Other Asian, not specified (19)	97	0.15
Australian	17	0.03
Austrian	127	0.20
Basque	38	0.06
Belgian	42	0.07
Brazilian	88	0.14
British	338	0.53
Bulgarian	12	0.02
Canadian	238	0.37
Croatian	33	0.05
Czech	393	0.61
Czechoslovakian	116	0.18
Danish	186	0.29
Dutch	746	1.16
Eastern European	28	0.04
English	5,345	8.34
Estonian	8	0.01
European	343	0.54
Finnish	78	0.12
French, except Basque	1,814	2.83
French Canadian	514	0.80
German	7,065	11.03
Greek	476	0.74
Guyanese	45	0.07
Hawaii Native/Pacific Islander:	122	0.19
Micronesian: (6)	15	0.02
Guamanian/Chamorro (4)	13	0.02
Other Micronesian (2)	2	0.00
Polynesian: (16)	34	0.05
Native Hawaiian (13)	27	0.04
Samoan (3)	7	0.01
Other Pac. Isl., specified	10	0.02
Other Pac. Isl., not spec. (17)	63	0.10
Hispanic or Latino:	2,232	3.48
Central American:	98	0.15
Costa Rican	12	0.02
Guatemalan	9	0.01
Honduran	21	0.03
Nicaraguan	20	0.03
Panamanian	15	0.02
Salvadoran	13	0.02
Other Central American	8	0.01
Cuban	160	0.25
Dominican Republic	32	0.05
Mexican	380	0.59
Puerto Rican	818	1.28
South American:	269	0.42
Argentinean	16	0.02
Bolivian	8	0.01
Chilean	36	0.06
Colombian	88	0.14
Ecuadorian	34	0.05
Peruvian	23	0.04
Uruguayan	11	0.02
Venezuelan	42	0.07
Other South American	11	0.02
Other Hispanic or Latino	475	0.74
Hungarian	372	0.58
Icelander	19	0.03
Iranian	42	0.07
Irish	6,659	10.39
Israeli	20	0.03
Italian	3,811	5.95
Latvian	13	0.02
Lithuanian	132	0.21
Maltese	7	0.01
Norwegian	387	0.60
Pennsylvania German	44	0.07
Polish	1,540	2.40
Portuguese	208	0.32
Romanian	86	0.13
Russian	355	0.55
Scandinavian	33	0.05
Scotch-Irish	857	1.34
Scottish	1,092	1.70
Serbian	22	0.03
Slavic	2	0.00
Slovak	80	0.12
Slovene	8	0.01
Swedish	733	1.14
Swiss	150	0.23
Turkish	53	0.08
Ukrainian	201	0.31
United States or American	3,311	5.17
Welsh	272	0.42
West Indian, excl. Hispanic:	867	1.35
Bahamian	113	0.18
British West Indian	53	0.08
Haitian	37	0.06
Jamaican	432	0.67
Trinidadian and Tobagonian	159	0.25
U.S. Virgin Islander	33	0.05
West Indian	40	0.06
White:	40,792	63.63
Not Hispanic (38,630)	39,365	61.40
Hispanic (1,333)	1,427	2.23
Yugoslavian	33	0.05

Notes: 1. Figures in the "Number" column do not add up to the total population due to: a) Ancestry/Race overlap — e.g. persons can report being both White and Irish, b) persons of Hispanic origin can report being any race, c) persons reporting two ancestries are counted in both categories. 2. Numbers in parentheses indicate the number of persons reporting this ancestry/race alone, not in combination with any other ancestry/race. 3. Refer to the Explanation of Data in the front of the book for more detailed information.

De Bary

Place Type: City
County: Volusia
Population: 15,559

Ancestry/Race	Number	%
African American/Black:	322	2.07
Not Hispanic (293)	308	1.98
Hispanic (3)	14	0.09
Alaska Native tribes, not specified	1	0.01
Am. Ind. or Alaska Nat., not spec.	27	0.17
American Indian tribes, specified:	51	0.33
Blackfeet (4)	5	0.03
Cherokee (8)	23	0.15
Chippewa (1)	2	0.01
Choctaw	2	0.01
Comanche	1	0.01
Creek (3)	3	0.02
Delaware	2	0.01
Iroquois (1)	2	0.01
Lumbee (1)	1	0.01
Seminole	2	0.01
Sioux	3	0.02
All other tribes (5)	5	0.03
American Indian tribes, not spec.	1	0.01
Arab:	53	0.34
Jordanian	10	0.06
Lebanese	28	0.18
Syrian	15	0.10
Armenian	8	0.05
Asian:	218	1.40
Chinese, ex. Taiwanese (34)	38	0.24
Filipino (34)	48	0.31
Indian (51)	58	0.37
Indonesian	2	0.01
Japanese (9)	18	0.12
Korean (11)	14	0.09
Laotian (3)	3	0.02
Pakistani (12)	15	0.10
Sri Lankan (2)	2	0.01
Thai (5)	5	0.03
Vietnamese (6)	6	0.04
Other Asian, not specified (8)	9	0.06
Austrian	39	0.25
Belgian	34	0.22
Brazilian	22	0.14
British	105	0.67
Canadian	131	0.83
Croatian	27	0.17
Czech	51	0.32
Czechoslovakian	77	0.49
Danish	64	0.41
Dutch	307	1.95
English	2,412	15.30
European	66	0.42
Finnish	34	0.22
French, except Basque	573	3.63
French Canadian	400	2.54
German	2,991	18.97
Greek	44	0.28
Hawaii Native/Pacific Islander:	8	0.05
Polynesian: (1)	3	0.02
Native Hawaiian (1)	3	0.02
Other Pac. Isl., not spec.	5	0.03
Hispanic or Latino:	645	4.15
Central American:	25	0.16
Costa Rican	4	0.03
Guatemalan	1	0.01
Honduran	3	0.02
Nicaraguan	9	0.06
Panamanian	7	0.04
Salvadoran	1	0.01
Cuban	64	0.41
Dominican Republic	12	0.08
Mexican	49	0.31
Puerto Rican	365	2.35
South American:	35	0.22
Argentinean	3	0.02
Chilean	2	0.01
Colombian	19	0.12
Ecuadorian	2	0.01
Peruvian	6	0.04
Venezuelan	3	0.02
Other Hispanic or Latino	95	0.61
Hungarian	88	0.56
Iranian	9	0.06
Irish	2,391	15.16
Italian	1,627	10.32
Lithuanian	65	0.41
Norwegian	162	1.03
Pennsylvania German	38	0.24
Polish	584	3.70
Portuguese	10	0.06
Romanian	22	0.14
Russian	52	0.33
Scotch-Irish	431	2.73
Scottish	464	2.94
Serbian	9	0.06
Slovak	82	0.52
Swedish	249	1.58
Swiss	39	0.25
Turkish	7	0.04
Ukrainian	42	0.27
United States or American	1,645	10.43
Welsh	173	1.10
West Indian, excl. Hispanic:	70	0.44
Bahamian	4	0.03
Jamaican	15	0.10
West Indian	33	0.21
Other West Indian	18	0.11
White:	14,904	95.79
Not Hispanic (14,295)	14,382	92.44
Hispanic (477)	522	3.35
Yugoslavian	21	0.13

De Land

Place Type: City
County: Volusia
Population: 20,904

Ancestry/Race	Number	%
African American/Black:	4,145	19.83
Not Hispanic (3,954)	4,072	19.48
Hispanic (56)	73	0.35
African, sub-Saharan:	229	1.09
African	229	1.09
Alaska Native tribes, specified:	1	0.00
Eskimo	1	0.00
Alaska Native tribes, not specified	1	0.00
Am. Ind. or Alaska Nat., not spec.	61	0.29
American Indian tribes, specified:	75	0.36
Apache (4)	4	0.02
Blackfeet (1)	2	0.01
Cherokee (9)	27	0.13
Chippewa (2)	4	0.02
Choctaw (3)	10	0.05
Creek (3)	5	0.02
Delaware (1)	1	0.00
Iroquois (1)	4	0.02
Latin American Indians (3)	6	0.03
Lumbee (1)	1	0.00
Osage	3	0.01
Ottawa (1)	1	0.00
Potawatomi	1	0.00
Seminole (1)	3	0.01
All other tribes (2)	3	0.01
American Indian tribes, not spec.	9	0.04
Arab:	39	0.19
Arab/Arabic	29	0.14
Lebanese	10	0.05
Asian:	256	1.22
Bangladeshi (6)	13	0.06
Chinese, ex. Taiwanese (30)	50	0.24
Filipino (36)	44	0.21
Indian (44)	75	0.36
Japanese (6)	16	0.08
Korean (6)	13	0.06
Laotian (5)	5	0.02
Pakistani (2)	2	0.01
Taiwanese (1)	2	0.01
Thai	2	0.01
Vietnamese (19)	22	0.11
Other Asian, not specified (7)	12	0.06
Austrian	71	0.34
Belgian	35	0.17
Brazilian	19	0.09
British	74	0.35
Bulgarian	31	0.15
Canadian	43	0.20
Czech	26	0.12
Czechoslovakian	55	0.26
Danish	71	0.34
Dutch	387	1.84
Eastern European	7	0.03
English	2,136	10.18
European	114	0.54
Finnish	9	0.04
French, except Basque	641	3.06
French Canadian	163	0.78
German	2,534	12.08
Greek	74	0.35
Hawaii Native/Pacific Islander:	15	0.07
Micronesian: (1)	2	0.01
Guamanian/Chamorro (1)	2	0.01
Polynesian: (2)	10	0.05
Native Hawaiian (1)	9	0.04
Samoan (1)	1	0.00
Other Pac. Isl., not spec.	3	0.01
Hispanic or Latino:	1,824	8.73
Central American:	21	0.10
Honduran	8	0.04
Nicaraguan	3	0.01
Panamanian	4	0.02
Salvadoran	6	0.03
Cuban	71	0.34
Dominican Republic	12	0.06
Mexican	1,060	5.07
Puerto Rican	441	2.11
South American:	34	0.16
Argentinean	10	0.05
Chilean	1	0.00
Colombian	13	0.06
Ecuadorian	1	0.00
Peruvian	2	0.01
Venezuelan	6	0.03
Other South American	1	0.00
Other Hispanic or Latino	185	0.88
Hungarian	118	0.56
Irish	2,191	10.44
Italian	1,085	5.17
Latvian	29	0.14
Lithuanian	23	0.11
Norwegian	193	0.92
Pennsylvania German	14	0.07
Polish	530	2.53
Portuguese	58	0.28
Romanian	15	0.07
Russian	69	0.33
Scandinavian	8	0.04
Scotch-Irish	458	2.18
Scottish	577	2.75
Serbian	26	0.12
Slovak	10	0.05
Swedish	139	0.66
Swiss	71	0.34
Turkish	33	0.16
Ukrainian	89	0.42
United States or American	1,468	7.00
Welsh	168	0.80
West Indian, excl. Hispanic:	194	0.92
Bahamian	13	0.06
Haitian	23	0.11
Jamaican	134	0.64
West Indian	8	0.04
Other West Indian	16	0.08
White:	15,973	76.41
Not Hispanic (14,633)	14,846	71.02
Hispanic (1,037)	1,127	5.39

Notes: 1. Figures in the "Number" column do not add up to the total population due to: a) Ancestry/Race overlap — e.g. persons can report being both White and Irish, b) persons of Hispanic origin can report being any race, c) persons reporting two ancestries are counted in both categories. 2. Numbers in parentheses indicate the number of persons reporting this ancestry/race alone, not in combination with any other ancestry/race. 3. Refer to the Explanation of Data in the front of the book for more detailed information.

Ancestry/Race	Number	%
Yugoslavian	5	0.02

Deerfield Beach

Place Type: City
County: Broward
Population: 64,583

Ancestry/Race	Number	%
African American/Black:	11,094	17.18
Not Hispanic (10,122)	10,807	16.73
Hispanic (217)	287	0.44
African, sub-Saharan:	407	0.63
African	173	0.27
Cape Verdean	7	0.01
Ghanian	105	0.16
Somalian	18	0.03
South African	104	0.16
Alaska Native tribes, specified:	4	0.01
Alaska Athabascan	1	0.00
Tlingit-Haida	3	0.00
Am. Ind. or Alaska Nat., not spec.	122	0.19
American Indian tribes, specified:	129	0.20
Apache (3)	3	0.00
Cherokee (21)	49	0.08
Chickasaw	1	0.00
Chippewa	3	0.00
Choctaw (1)	3	0.00
Cree (1)	1	0.00
Creek (2)	3	0.00
Iroquois (4)	6	0.01
Latin American Indians (17)	28	0.04
Menominee (2)	2	0.00
Navajo (1)	1	0.00
Potawatomi (1)	2	0.00
Pueblo	1	0.00
Shoshone	1	0.00
Sioux	3	0.00
Yakama	1	0.00
All other tribes (7)	21	0.03
American Indian tribes, not spec.	9	0.01
Arab:	430	0.66
Egyptian	44	0.07
Lebanese	214	0.33
Moroccan	53	0.08
Palestinian	9	0.01
Syrian	50	0.08
Other Arab	60	0.09
Armenian	58	0.09
Asian:	1,113	1.72
Bangladeshi (26)	34	0.05
Cambodian (15)	19	0.03
Chinese, ex. Taiwanese (194)	234	0.36
Filipino (109)	141	0.22
Indian (227)	262	0.41
Indonesian (1)	3	0.00
Japanese (38)	60	0.09
Korean (44)	57	0.09
Laotian (3)	3	0.00
Malaysian (5)	7	0.01
Pakistani (22)	38	0.06
Sri Lankan	2	0.00
Taiwanese (3)	4	0.01
Thai (28)	33	0.05
Vietnamese (132)	137	0.21
Other Asian, specified (8)	17	0.03
Other Asian, not specified (28)	62	0.10
Austrian	563	0.87
Basque	11	0.02
Belgian	55	0.08
Brazilian	2,307	3.56
British	266	0.41
Bulgarian	35	0.05
Canadian	708	1.09
Celtic	16	0.02
Croatian	35	0.05
Czech	230	0.36
Czechoslovakian	140	0.22
Danish	152	0.23
Dutch	683	1.06
Eastern European	132	0.20
English	4,659	7.20
European	249	0.38
Finnish	77	0.12
French, except Basque	1,569	2.42
French Canadian	783	1.21
German	6,223	9.62
Greek	440	0.68
Guyanese	33	0.05
Hawaii Native/Pacific Islander:	84	0.13
Micronesian: (5)	10	0.02
Guamanian/Chamorro (5)	10	0.02
Polynesian: (6)	20	0.03
Native Hawaiian (4)	16	0.02
Samoan (2)	4	0.01
Other Pac. Isl., specified	8	0.01
Other Pac. Isl., not spec. (8)	46	0.07
Hispanic or Latino:	5,643	8.74
Central American:	327	0.51
Costa Rican	84	0.13
Guatemalan	43	0.07
Honduran	79	0.12
Nicaraguan	35	0.05
Panamanian	44	0.07
Salvadoran	26	0.04
Other Central American	16	0.02
Cuban	661	1.02
Dominican Republic	298	0.46
Mexican	518	0.80
Puerto Rican	1,177	1.82
South American:	1,309	2.03
Argentinean	102	0.16
Bolivian	30	0.05
Chilean	50	0.08
Colombian	575	0.89
Ecuadorian	113	0.17
Paraguayan	1	0.00
Peruvian	197	0.31
Uruguayan	29	0.04
Venezuelan	158	0.24
Other South American	54	0.08
Other Hispanic or Latino	1,353	2.09
Hungarian	703	1.09
Iranian	26	0.04
Irish	6,957	10.75
Israeli	126	0.19
Italian	6,881	10.63
Latvian	55	0.08
Lithuanian	371	0.57
Luxemburger	11	0.02
Macedonian	14	0.02
Norwegian	439	0.68
Pennsylvania German	33	0.05
Polish	2,667	4.12
Portuguese	655	1.01
Romanian	307	0.47
Russian	2,147	3.32
Scandinavian	31	0.05
Scotch-Irish	535	0.83
Scottish	805	1.24
Slavic	10	0.02
Slovak	173	0.27
Slovene	16	0.02
Swedish	546	0.84
Swiss	116	0.18
Turkish	91	0.14
Ukrainian	277	0.43
United States or American	3,475	5.37
Welsh	196	0.30
West Indian, excl. Hispanic:	3,467	5.36
Bahamian	98	0.15
Barbadian	70	0.11
Belizean	9	0.01
British West Indian	177	0.27
Haitian	2,350	3.63
Jamaican	652	1.01
Trinidadian and Tobagonian	48	0.07
West Indian	63	0.10
White:	50,976	78.93
Not Hispanic (46,014)	46,730	72.36
Hispanic (3,880)	4,246	6.57
Yugoslavian	59	0.09

Delray Beach

Place Type: City
County: Palm Beach
Population: 60,020

Ancestry/Race	Number	%
Acadian/Cajun	8	0.01
African American/Black:	17,847	29.74
Not Hispanic (15,796)	17,609	29.34
Hispanic (185)	238	0.40
African, sub-Saharan:	431	0.72
African	320	0.53
Cape Verdean	19	0.03
Liberian	37	0.06
South African	38	0.06
Other sub-Saharan African	17	0.03
Alaska Native tribes, specified:	3	0.00
Tlingit-Haida	3	0.00
Am. Ind. or Alaska Nat., not spec.	115	0.19
Albanian	44	0.07
American Indian tribes, specified:	105	0.17
Apache (2)	2	0.00
Blackfeet (3)	6	0.01
Cherokee (13)	42	0.07
Chickasaw (2)	2	0.00
Chippewa (1)	7	0.01
Choctaw	1	0.00
Creek (3)	4	0.01
Delaware	1	0.00
Iroquois (9)	14	0.02
Latin American Indians (7)	12	0.02
Navajo (1)	2	0.00
Osage	1	0.00
Pueblo	1	0.00
Puget Sound Salish (1)	1	0.00
Sioux (1)	1	0.00
All other tribes (5)	8	0.01
American Indian tribes, not spec.	22	0.04
Arab:	336	0.56
Arab/Arabic	45	0.08
Egyptian	38	0.06
Jordanian	16	0.03
Lebanese	99	0.17
Moroccan	7	0.01
Palestinian	48	0.08
Syrian	56	0.09
Other Arab	27	0.05
Armenian	120	0.20
Asian:	906	1.51
Bangladeshi (16)	49	0.08
Cambodian	3	0.00
Chinese, ex. Taiwanese (125)	160	0.27
Filipino (95)	123	0.20
Indian (264)	339	0.56
Indonesian (4)	4	0.01
Japanese (31)	43	0.07
Korean (20)	26	0.04
Laotian	2	0.00
Malaysian (1)	2	0.00
Pakistani (2)	2	0.00
Sri Lankan (5)	6	0.01
Taiwanese (3)	3	0.00
Thai (11)	14	0.02
Vietnamese (45)	48	0.08
Other Asian, specified (1)	15	0.02
Other Asian, not specified (24)	67	0.11
Australian	16	0.03
Austrian	428	0.71
Basque	14	0.02
Belgian	77	0.13
Brazilian	156	0.26
British	330	0.55
Bulgarian	45	0.08
Canadian	278	0.46
Celtic	9	0.02
Croatian	54	0.09

Notes: 1. Figures in the "Number" column do not add up to the total population due to: a) Ancestry/Race overlap — e.g. persons can report being both White and Irish, b) persons of Hispanic origin can report being any race, c) persons reporting two ancestries are counted in both categories. 2. Numbers in parentheses indicate the number of persons reporting this ancestry/race alone, not in combination with any other ancestry/race. 3. Refer to the Explanation of Data in the front of the book for more detailed information.

Czech	151	0.25
Czechoslovakian	90	0.15
Danish	175	0.29
Dutch	747	1.25
Eastern European	123	0.21
English	4,856	8.10
Estonian	9	0.02
European	210	0.35
Finnish	98	0.16
French, except Basque	1,495	2.49
French Canadian	412	0.69
German	6,308	10.52
Greek	408	0.68
Hawaii Native/Pacific Islander:	255	0.42
Micronesian: (9)	11	0.02
Guamanian/Chamorro (9)	11	0.02
Polynesian: (34)	47	0.08
Native Hawaiian (12)	19	0.03
Samoan (21)	27	0.04
Other Polynesian (1)	1	0.00
Other Pac. Isl., specified	14	0.02
Other Pac. Isl., not spec. (6)	183	0.30
Hispanic or Latino:	4,184	6.97
Central American:	289	0.48
Costa Rican	24	0.04
Guatemalan	83	0.14
Honduran	48	0.08
Nicaraguan	42	0.07
Panamanian	21	0.03
Salvadoran	58	0.10
Other Central American	13	0.02
Cuban	465	0.77
Dominican Republic	63	0.10
Mexican	1,441	2.40
Puerto Rican	722	1.20
South American:	554	0.92
Argentinean	68	0.11
Bolivian	12	0.02
Chilean	39	0.06
Colombian	187	0.31
Ecuadorian	50	0.08
Paraguayan	13	0.02
Peruvian	75	0.12
Uruguayan	9	0.01
Venezuelan	72	0.12
Other South American	29	0.05
Other Hispanic or Latino	650	1.08
Hungarian	607	1.01
Iranian	9	0.02
Irish	6,173	10.30
Israeli	35	0.06
Italian	4,757	7.94
Latvian	64	0.11
Lithuanian	197	0.33
Northern European	29	0.05
Norwegian	381	0.64
Pennsylvania German	6	0.01
Polish	1,915	3.19
Portuguese	174	0.29
Romanian	281	0.47
Russian	2,001	3.34
Scandinavian	26	0.04
Scotch-Irish	608	1.01
Scottish	1,114	1.86
Serbian	15	0.03
Slavic	21	0.04
Slovak	92	0.15
Slovene	35	0.06
Swedish	745	1.24
Swiss	135	0.23
Turkish	80	0.13
Ukrainian	178	0.30
United States or American	3,128	5.22
Welsh	265	0.44
West Indian, excl. Hispanic:	7,220	12.05
Bahamian	286	0.48
Barbadian	66	0.11
Bermudan	7	0.01
British West Indian	50	0.08
Haitian	6,351	10.60
Jamaican	341	0.57
Trinidadian and Tobagonian	48	0.08
U.S. Virgin Islander	7	0.01
West Indian	51	0.09
Other West Indian	13	0.02
White:	40,506	67.49
Not Hispanic (37,074)	37,436	62.37
Hispanic (2,834)	3,070	5.11
Yugoslavian	67	0.11

Deltona

Place Type: City
County: Volusia
Population: 69,543

Ancestry/Race	Number	%
Acadian/Cajun	21	0.03
African American/Black:	5,345	7.69
Not Hispanic (4,478)	4,797	6.90
Hispanic (370)	548	0.79
African, sub-Saharan:	148	0.21
African	130	0.19
South African	18	0.03
Alaska Native tribes, specified:	3	0.00
Eskimo (1)	1	0.00
Tlingit-Haida (2)	2	0.00
Am. Ind. or Alaska Nat., not spec.	212	0.30
American Indian tribes, specified:	406	0.58
Apache	1	0.00
Blackfeet (2)	31	0.04
Cherokee (62)	188	0.27
Chickasaw (1)	1	0.00
Chippewa (6)	17	0.02
Choctaw (11)	15	0.02
Comanche (1)	1	0.00
Cree (1)	1	0.00
Creek (7)	10	0.01
Crow (1)	1	0.00
Delaware (2)	7	0.01
Iroquois (11)	27	0.04
Latin American Indians (14)	40	0.06
Navajo (1)	5	0.01
Osage (5)	5	0.01
Potawatomi (1)	1	0.00
Pueblo (4)	4	0.01
Seminole	7	0.01
Shoshone	1	0.00
Sioux (3)	9	0.01
Tohono O'Odham (3)	3	0.00
Yuman (1)	1	0.00
All other tribes (16)	30	0.04
American Indian tribes, not spec.	25	0.04
Arab:	141	0.20
Egyptian	23	0.03
Iraqi	6	0.01
Jordanian	25	0.04
Lebanese	52	0.07
Palestinian	23	0.03
Syrian	12	0.02
Asian:	888	1.28
Bangladeshi (1)	5	0.01
Cambodian (9)	9	0.01
Chinese, ex. Taiwanese (86)	123	0.18
Filipino (149)	226	0.32
Hmong	2	0.00
Indian (149)	190	0.27
Indonesian (6)	6	0.01
Japanese (26)	54	0.08
Korean (40)	56	0.08
Laotian (68)	73	0.10
Malaysian (5)	10	0.01
Pakistani (9)	11	0.02
Taiwanese	1	0.00
Thai (18)	23	0.03
Vietnamese (38)	50	0.07
Other Asian, specified	1	0.00
Other Asian, not specified (32)	48	0.07
Australian	16	0.02
Austrian	142	0.20
Belgian	98	0.14
Brazilian	57	0.08
British	305	0.44
Bulgarian	7	0.01
Canadian	261	0.37
Croatian	31	0.04
Czech	197	0.28
Czechoslovakian	117	0.17
Danish	307	0.44
Dutch	1,228	1.76
Eastern European	45	0.06
English	6,760	9.68
European	413	0.59
Finnish	110	0.16
French, except Basque	2,815	4.03
French Canadian	951	1.36
German	11,022	15.79
Greek	257	0.37
Guyanese	120	0.17
Hawaii Native/Pacific Islander:	82	0.12
Melanesian: (4)	4	0.01
Fijian (4)	4	0.01
Micronesian: (5)	8	0.01
Guamanian/Chamorro (5)	8	0.01
Polynesian: (18)	44	0.06
Native Hawaiian (5)	27	0.04
Samoan (5)	9	0.01
Tongan (6)	6	0.01
Other Polynesian (2)	2	0.00
Other Pac. Isl., specified	1	0.00
Other Pac. Isl., not spec. (9)	25	0.04
Hispanic or Latino:	12,747	18.33
Central American:	376	0.54
Costa Rican	32	0.05
Guatemalan	37	0.05
Honduran	75	0.11
Nicaraguan	35	0.05
Panamanian	101	0.15
Salvadoran	75	0.11
Other Central American	21	0.03
Cuban	543	0.78
Dominican Republic	281	0.40
Mexican	546	0.79
Puerto Rican	9,136	13.14
South American:	531	0.76
Argentinean	31	0.04
Bolivian	1	0.00
Chilean	16	0.02
Colombian	244	0.35
Ecuadorian	93	0.13
Paraguayan	5	0.01
Peruvian	62	0.09
Uruguayan	2	0.00
Venezuelan	49	0.07
Other South American	28	0.04
Other Hispanic or Latino	1,334	1.92
Hungarian	358	0.51
Iranian	44	0.06
Irish	10,116	14.49
Italian	6,827	9.78
Latvian	13	0.02
Lithuanian	93	0.13
Norwegian	634	0.91
Pennsylvania German	70	0.10
Polish	2,756	3.95
Portuguese	235	0.34
Romanian	50	0.07
Russian	532	0.76
Scandinavian	72	0.10
Scotch-Irish	1,189	1.70
Scottish	1,472	2.11
Serbian	46	0.07
Slavic	20	0.03
Slovak	127	0.18
Slovene	17	0.02
Swedish	894	1.28
Swiss	103	0.15
Turkish	31	0.04
Ukrainian	275	0.39
United States or American	4,543	6.51

Notes: 1. Figures in the "Number" column do not add up to the total population due to: a) Ancestry/Race overlap — e.g. persons can report being both White and Irish, b) persons of Hispanic origin can report being any race, c) persons reporting two ancestries are counted in both categories. 2. Numbers in parentheses indicate the number of persons reporting this ancestry/race alone, not in combination with any other ancestry/race. 3. Refer to the Explanation of Data in the front of the book for more detailed information.

Welsh	428	0.61
West Indian, excl. Hispanic:	915	1.31
Bahamian	18	0.03
Barbadian	18	0.03
Belizean	10	0.01
British West Indian	76	0.11
Haitian	163	0.23
Jamaican	407	0.58
Trinidadian and Tobagonian	30	0.04
U.S. Virgin Islander	123	0.18
West Indian	70	0.10
White:	60,029	86.32
Not Hispanic (50,540)	51,254	73.70
Hispanic (8,119)	8,775	12.62
Yugoslavian	41	0.06

Destin

Place Type: City
County: Okaloosa
Population: 11,119

Ancestry/Race	Number	%
Acadian/Cajun	16	0.14
African American/Black:	59	0.53
Not Hispanic (40)	53	0.48
Hispanic (1)	6	0.05
Alaska Native tribes, specified:	1	0.01
Eskimo (1)	1	0.01
Am. Ind. or Alaska Nat., not spec.	22	0.20
American Indian tribes, specified:	97	0.87
Apache (3)	7	0.06
Blackfeet (1)	3	0.03
Cherokee (8)	41	0.37
Chickasaw (1)	2	0.02
Choctaw (2)	10	0.09
Cree	3	0.03
Creek (4)	11	0.10
Iroquois	2	0.02
Kiowa (7)	8	0.07
Latin American Indians (1)	1	0.01
Lumbee (1)	3	0.03
Potawatomi	1	0.01
Pueblo	1	0.01
Seminole	1	0.01
Sioux	1	0.01
All other tribes (2)	2	0.02
American Indian tribes, not spec.	10	0.09
Arab:	65	0.58
Egyptian	9	0.08
Jordanian	8	0.07
Lebanese	48	0.43
Armenian	9	0.08
Asian:	170	1.53
Chinese, ex. Taiwanese (7)	10	0.09
Filipino (26)	42	0.38
Indian (9)	10	0.09
Japanese (6)	12	0.11
Korean (18)	26	0.23
Laotian (3)	3	0.03
Taiwanese (1)	2	0.02
Thai (14)	27	0.24
Vietnamese (21)	24	0.22
Other Asian, specified (2)	3	0.03
Other Asian, not specified (7)	11	0.10
Australian	21	0.19
Austrian	14	0.12
Belgian	45	0.40
Brazilian	16	0.14
British	53	0.47
Czech	43	0.38
Czechoslovakian	54	0.48
Danish	37	0.33
Dutch	218	1.94
English	1,663	14.79
European	67	0.60
Finnish	25	0.22
French, except Basque	519	4.61
French Canadian	52	0.46
German	1,864	16.57
Greek	121	1.08
Hawaii Native/Pacific Islander:	17	0.15
Micronesian: (2)	3	0.03
Guamanian/Chamorro (2)	3	0.03
Polynesian: (6)	10	0.09
Native Hawaiian (5)	9	0.08
Other Polynesian (1)	1	0.01
Other Pac. Isl., specified	1	0.01
Other Pac. Isl., not spec. (1)	3	0.03
Hispanic or Latino:	296	2.66
Central American:	11	0.10
Costa Rican	2	0.02
Nicaraguan	4	0.04
Panamanian	5	0.04
Cuban	27	0.24
Dominican Republic	2	0.02
Mexican	167	1.50
Puerto Rican	33	0.30
South American:	10	0.09
Chilean	2	0.02
Colombian	1	0.01
Ecuadorian	1	0.01
Peruvian	1	0.01
Venezuelan	5	0.04
Other Hispanic or Latino	46	0.41
Hungarian	48	0.43
Irish	1,411	12.55
Italian	625	5.56
Lithuanian	31	0.28
Norwegian	129	1.15
Pennsylvania German	9	0.08
Polish	370	3.29
Portuguese	18	0.16
Romanian	8	0.07
Russian	79	0.70
Scandinavian	9	0.08
Scotch-Irish	348	3.09
Scottish	477	4.24
Serbian	9	0.08
Slavic	11	0.10
Slovak	30	0.27
Swedish	121	1.08
Swiss	39	0.35
Ukrainian	25	0.22
United States or American	1,252	11.13
Welsh	108	0.96
White:	10,860	97.67
Not Hispanic (10,461)	10,606	95.39
Hispanic (237)	254	2.28
Yugoslavian	28	0.25

Doral

Place Type: Census Designated Place
County: Miami-Dade
Population: 20,438

Ancestry/Race	Number	%
African American/Black:	650	3.18
Not Hispanic (433)	470	2.30
Hispanic (110)	180	0.88
African, sub-Saharan:	62	0.30
African	35	0.17
South African	13	0.06
Other sub-Saharan African	14	0.07
Alaska Native tribes, specified:	1	0.00
Alaska Athabascan	1	0.00
Am. Ind. or Alaska Nat., not spec.	13	0.06
American Indian tribes, specified:	18	0.09
Blackfeet	2	0.01
Cherokee (2)	4	0.02
Chickasaw	1	0.00
Creek (1)	1	0.00
Latin American Indians (6)	7	0.03
Potawatomi (1)	1	0.00
Sioux (1)	2	0.01
American Indian tribes, not spec.	7	0.03
Arab:	283	1.38
Arab/Arabic	58	0.28
Lebanese	225	1.10
Asian:	1,168	5.71
Cambodian (1)	1	0.00
Chinese, ex. Taiwanese (361)	398	1.95
Filipino (46)	59	0.29
Indian (275)	289	1.41
Indonesian	3	0.01
Japanese (178)	193	0.94
Korean (109)	110	0.54
Laotian (2)	2	0.01
Pakistani (18)	36	0.18
Taiwanese (15)	19	0.09
Thai (16)	16	0.08
Vietnamese (6)	6	0.03
Other Asian, not specified (7)	36	0.18
Austrian	67	0.33
Basque	69	0.34
Brazilian	535	2.61
British	134	0.65
Canadian	27	0.13
Carpatho Rusyn	7	0.03
Czech	8	0.04
Czechoslovakian	41	0.20
Danish	20	0.10
Dutch	15	0.07
English	342	1.67
European	231	1.13
French, except Basque	271	1.32
French Canadian	25	0.12
German	502	2.45
Greek	57	0.28
Hawaii Native/Pacific Islander:	11	0.05
Micronesian: (3)	3	0.01
Guamanian/Chamorro (3)	3	0.01
Polynesian:	1	0.00
Samoan	1	0.00
Other Pac. Isl., not spec.	7	0.03
Hispanic or Latino:	13,784	67.44
Central American:	990	4.84
Costa Rican	66	0.32
Guatemalan	130	0.64
Honduran	135	0.66
Nicaraguan	346	1.69
Panamanian	192	0.94
Salvadoran	77	0.38
Other Central American	44	0.22
Cuban	3,106	15.20
Dominican Republic	540	2.64
Mexican	525	2.57
Puerto Rican	907	4.44
South American:	4,989	24.41
Argentinean	262	1.28
Bolivian	45	0.22
Chilean	224	1.10
Colombian	1,780	8.71
Ecuadorian	241	1.18
Paraguayan	21	0.10
Peruvian	602	2.95
Uruguayan	35	0.17
Venezuelan	1,680	8.22
Other South American	99	0.48
Other Hispanic or Latino	2,727	13.34
Hungarian	52	0.25
Iranian	91	0.44
Irish	518	2.53
Israeli	47	0.23
Italian	1,117	5.45
Lithuanian	23	0.11
Norwegian	46	0.22
Polish	116	0.57
Portuguese	259	1.26
Romanian	23	0.11
Russian	121	0.59
Scandinavian	9	0.04
Scotch-Irish	24	0.12
Scottish	122	0.59
Serbian	10	0.05
Slavic	12	0.06
Swedish	91	0.44
Swiss	57	0.28
Ukrainian	26	0.13

Notes: 1. Figures in the "Number" column do not add up to the total population due to: a) Ancestry/Race overlap — e.g. persons can report being both White and Irish, b) persons of Hispanic origin can report being any race, c) persons reporting two ancestries are counted in both categories. 2. Numbers in parentheses indicate the number of persons reporting this ancestry/race alone, not in combination with any other ancestry/race. 3. Refer to the Explanation of Data in the front of the book for more detailed information.

United States or American	685	3.34
Welsh	25	0.12
West Indian, excl. Hispanic:	170	0.83
Bahamian	13	0.06
Barbadian	17	0.08
British West Indian	39	0.19
Jamaican	87	0.42
Other West Indian	14	0.07
White:	17,849	87.33
Not Hispanic (4,912)	5,119	25.05
Hispanic (12,261)	12,730	62.29

Dunedin

Place Type: City
County: Pinellas
Population: 35,691

Ancestry/Race	Number	%
Acadian/Cajun	15	0.04
Afghan	31	0.09
African American/Black:	798	2.24
Not Hispanic (692)	755	2.12
Hispanic (22)	43	0.12
African, sub-Saharan:	41	0.11
African	15	0.04
Nigerian	8	0.02
South African	18	0.05
Alaska Native tribes, specified:	1	0.00
Eskimo (1)	1	0.00
Am. Ind. or Alaska Nat., not spec.	59	0.17
Albanian	199	0.55
American Indian tribes, specified:	128	0.36
Apache (1)	1	0.00
Blackfeet (3)	6	0.02
Cherokee (13)	58	0.16
Cheyenne (1)	3	0.01
Chippewa (3)	10	0.03
Choctaw (4)	4	0.01
Cree (1)	2	0.01
Creek (2)	3	0.01
Delaware	2	0.01
Iroquois (3)	8	0.02
Latin American Indians (2)	4	0.01
Lumbee (2)	3	0.01
Ottawa	1	0.00
Paiute (1)	1	0.00
Potawatomi	2	0.01
Seminole	2	0.01
Sioux (5)	7	0.02
All other tribes (3)	11	0.03
American Indian tribes, not spec.	11	0.03
Arab:	205	0.57
Arab/Arabic	7	0.02
Egyptian	5	0.01
Lebanese	134	0.37
Syrian	18	0.05
Other Arab	41	0.11
Armenian	40	0.11
Asian:	480	1.34
Cambodian (1)	1	0.00
Chinese, ex. Taiwanese (73)	80	0.22
Filipino (88)	109	0.31
Hmong	1	0.00
Indian (138)	150	0.42
Indonesian (1)	2	0.01
Japanese (19)	30	0.08
Korean (16)	26	0.07
Laotian (10)	10	0.03
Pakistani (2)	4	0.01
Taiwanese (8)	12	0.03
Thai (15)	23	0.06
Vietnamese (15)	16	0.04
Other Asian, specified (2)	2	0.01
Other Asian, not specified (3)	14	0.04
Australian	23	0.06
Austrian	145	0.40
Belgian	59	0.16
Brazilian	15	0.04
British	276	0.77
Bulgarian	45	0.13
Canadian	374	1.04
Celtic	16	0.04
Croatian	65	0.18
Czech	123	0.34
Czechoslovakian	97	0.27
Danish	162	0.45
Dutch	793	2.21
English	5,247	14.61
European	160	0.45
Finnish	58	0.16
French, except Basque	1,411	3.93
French Canadian	513	1.43
German	7,645	21.28
Greek	591	1.65
Guyanese	10	0.03
Hawaii Native/Pacific Islander:	27	0.08
Micronesian: (3)	3	0.01
Guamanian/Chamorro (3)	3	0.01
Polynesian: (6)	14	0.04
Native Hawaiian (2)	7	0.02
Samoan (2)	2	0.01
Tongan (2)	5	0.01
Other Pac. Isl., not spec. (3)	10	0.03
Hispanic or Latino:	1,192	3.34
Central American:	37	0.10
Costa Rican	11	0.03
Guatemalan	2	0.01
Honduran	4	0.01
Nicaraguan	9	0.03
Panamanian	7	0.02
Salvadoran	3	0.01
Other Central American	1	0.00
Cuban	148	0.41
Dominican Republic	26	0.07
Mexican	261	0.73
Puerto Rican	301	0.84
South American:	174	0.49
Argentinean	12	0.03
Bolivian	1	0.00
Chilean	6	0.02
Colombian	87	0.24
Ecuadorian	7	0.02
Paraguayan	1	0.00
Peruvian	24	0.07
Venezuelan	28	0.08
Other South American	8	0.02
Other Hispanic or Latino	245	0.69
Hungarian	344	0.96
Icelander	8	0.02
Irish	6,163	17.15
Israeli	10	0.03
Italian	3,677	10.23
Latvian	18	0.05
Lithuanian	103	0.29
Luxemburger	26	0.07
Northern European	69	0.19
Norwegian	427	1.19
Pennsylvania German	40	0.11
Polish	1,466	4.08
Portuguese	107	0.30
Romanian	81	0.23
Russian	438	1.22
Scandinavian	50	0.14
Scotch-Irish	946	2.63
Scottish	1,413	3.93
Serbian	27	0.08
Slavic	7	0.02
Slovak	170	0.47
Slovene	89	0.25
Swedish	677	1.88
Swiss	74	0.21
Turkish	64	0.18
Ukrainian	247	0.69
United States or American	1,627	4.53
Welsh	423	1.18
West Indian, excl. Hispanic:	254	0.71
Barbadian	16	0.04
British West Indian	46	0.13
Jamaican	156	0.43
Trinidadian and Tobagonian	14	0.04
West Indian	22	0.06
White:	34,223	95.89
Not Hispanic (32,996)	33,271	93.22
Hispanic (868)	952	2.67
Yugoslavian	38	0.11

East Lake

Place Type: Census Designated Place
County: Pinellas
Population: 29,394

Ancestry/Race	Number	%
Acadian/Cajun	7	0.02
African American/Black:	385	1.31
Not Hispanic (313)	363	1.23
Hispanic (14)	22	0.07
African, sub-Saharan:	36	0.12
African	8	0.03
South African	22	0.07
Other sub-Saharan African	6	0.02
Am. Ind. or Alaska Nat., not spec.	35	0.12
Alsatian	9	0.03
American Indian tribes, specified:	49	0.17
Apache (2)	2	0.01
Cherokee (5)	16	0.05
Chickasaw (1)	1	0.00
Chippewa (2)	4	0.01
Choctaw (4)	5	0.02
Comanche	1	0.00
Iroquois	2	0.01
Latin American Indians (1)	3	0.01
Lumbee (1)	1	0.00
Navajo (1)	1	0.00
Sioux (1)	1	0.00
All other tribes (3)	12	0.04
American Indian tribes, not spec.	8	0.03
Arab:	297	1.01
Arab/Arabic	36	0.12
Egyptian	43	0.15
Lebanese	92	0.31
Syrian	117	0.40
Other Arab	9	0.03
Armenian	89	0.30
Asian:	799	2.72
Bangladeshi (2)	2	0.01
Cambodian (6)	7	0.02
Chinese, ex. Taiwanese (83)	108	0.37
Filipino (96)	134	0.46
Indian (277)	294	1.00
Indonesian	1	0.00
Japanese (34)	49	0.17
Korean (56)	63	0.21
Laotian (1)	1	0.00
Pakistani (3)	3	0.01
Sri Lankan (1)	3	0.01
Taiwanese (13)	13	0.04
Thai (13)	14	0.05
Vietnamese (70)	75	0.26
Other Asian, specified (1)	1	0.00
Other Asian, not specified (15)	31	0.11
Assyrian/Chaldean/Syriac	5	0.02
Australian	37	0.13
Austrian	294	1.00
Belgian	31	0.11
Brazilian	45	0.15
British	144	0.49
Canadian	369	1.25
Celtic	11	0.04
Croatian	56	0.19
Czech	198	0.67
Czechoslovakian	77	0.26
Danish	90	0.31
Dutch	510	1.73
Eastern European	35	0.12
English	4,151	14.10
European	175	0.59
Finnish	85	0.29
French, except Basque	1,085	3.68

Notes: 1. Figures in the "Number" column do not add up to the total population due to: a) Ancestry/Race overlap — e.g. persons can report being both White and Irish, b) persons of Hispanic origin can report being any race, c) persons reporting two ancestries are counted in both categories. 2. Numbers in parentheses indicate the number of persons reporting this ancestry/race alone, not in combination with any other ancestry/race. 3. Refer to the Explanation of Data in the front of the book for more detailed information.

Ancestry/Race	Number	%
French Canadian	399	1.35
German	6,235	21.17
Greek	868	2.95
Hawaii Native/Pacific Islander:	15	0.05
Micronesian: (2)	2	0.01
Guamanian/Chamorro (2)	2	0.01
Polynesian:	8	0.03
Native Hawaiian	7	0.02
Samoan	1	0.00
Other Pac. Isl., not spec.	5	0.02
Hispanic or Latino:	1,094	3.72
Central American:	45	0.15
Costa Rican	9	0.03
Guatemalan	11	0.04
Honduran	1	0.00
Nicaraguan	7	0.02
Panamanian	11	0.04
Salvadoran	5	0.02
Other Central American	1	0.00
Cuban	133	0.45
Dominican Republic	18	0.06
Mexican	86	0.29
Puerto Rican	353	1.20
South American:	193	0.66
Argentinean	9	0.03
Bolivian	4	0.01
Chilean	9	0.03
Colombian	96	0.33
Ecuadorian	14	0.05
Paraguayan	1	0.00
Peruvian	23	0.08
Venezuelan	27	0.09
Other South American	10	0.03
Other Hispanic or Latino	266	0.90
Hungarian	420	1.43
Icelander	9	0.03
Iranian	30	0.10
Irish	4,913	16.68
Israeli	34	0.12
Italian	4,083	13.87
Lithuanian	144	0.49
Luxemburger	8	0.03
Macedonian	27	0.09
Northern European	124	0.42
Norwegian	428	1.45
Pennsylvania German	10	0.03
Polish	1,609	5.46
Portuguese	188	0.64
Romanian	56	0.19
Russian	584	1.98
Scandinavian	106	0.36
Scotch-Irish	634	2.15
Scottish	879	2.99
Slovak	181	0.61
Slovene	21	0.07
Swedish	733	2.49
Swiss	168	0.57
Ukrainian	193	0.66
United States or American	1,573	5.34
Welsh	200	0.68
West Indian, excl. Hispanic:	33	0.11
Bermudan	7	0.02
British West Indian	13	0.04
Jamaican	8	0.03
West Indian	5	0.02
White:	28,145	95.75
Not Hispanic (27,007)	27,214	92.58
Hispanic (879)	931	3.17
Yugoslavian	66	0.22

Edgewater

Place Type: City
County: Volusia
Population: 18,668

Ancestry/Race	Number	%
African American/Black:	321	1.72
Not Hispanic (261)	308	1.65
Hispanic (2)	13	0.07
Alaska Native tribes, specified:	2	0.01
Aleut	1	0.01
Eskimo	1	0.01
Am. Ind. or Alaska Nat., not spec.	38	0.20
Alsatian	10	0.05
American Indian tribes, specified:	89	0.48
Blackfeet	3	0.02
Cherokee (11)	33	0.18
Chippewa (3)	4	0.02
Choctaw (5)	13	0.07
Creek (2)	3	0.02
Delaware	2	0.01
Iroquois (8)	9	0.05
Latin American Indians	4	0.02
Navajo (1)	1	0.01
Ottawa (1)	1	0.01
Pueblo	3	0.02
Sioux	2	0.01
All other tribes (5)	11	0.06
Arab:	23	0.12
Lebanese	23	0.12
Asian:	149	0.80
Bangladeshi (1)	3	0.02
Cambodian (3)	3	0.02
Chinese, ex. Taiwanese (23)	31	0.17
Filipino (20)	33	0.18
Indian (30)	31	0.17
Indonesian	1	0.01
Japanese (5)	12	0.06
Korean (5)	12	0.06
Pakistani	1	0.01
Taiwanese (1)	2	0.01
Thai (1)	3	0.02
Vietnamese (3)	6	0.03
Other Asian, specified	1	0.01
Other Asian, not specified (6)	10	0.05
Australian	15	0.08
Austrian	96	0.51
Belgian	37	0.20
Brazilian	6	0.03
British	145	0.77
Canadian	107	0.57
Croatian	10	0.05
Czech	103	0.55
Czechoslovakian	64	0.34
Danish	54	0.29
Dutch	469	2.49
Eastern European	10	0.05
English	2,667	14.14
European	95	0.50
Finnish	14	0.07
French, except Basque	960	5.09
French Canadian	363	1.92
German	3,189	16.91
Greek	59	0.31
Hawaii Native/Pacific Islander:	9	0.05
Micronesian: (1)	2	0.01
Guamanian/Chamorro (1)	2	0.01
Polynesian: (1)	4	0.02
Native Hawaiian (1)	4	0.02
Other Pac. Isl., not spec.	3	0.02
Hispanic or Latino:	365	1.96
Central American:	7	0.04
Honduran	4	0.02
Panamanian	2	0.01
Other Central American	1	0.01
Cuban	31	0.17
Dominican Republic	3	0.02
Mexican	75	0.40
Puerto Rican	134	0.72
South American:	42	0.22
Argentinean	2	0.01
Colombian	17	0.09
Paraguayan	1	0.01
Peruvian	8	0.04
Uruguayan	2	0.01
Venezuelan	11	0.06
Other South American	1	0.01
Other Hispanic or Latino	73	0.39
Hungarian	169	0.90
Irish	3,115	16.52
Italian	1,872	9.93
Latvian	23	0.12
Lithuanian	147	0.78
New Zealander	7	0.04
Norwegian	245	1.30
Pennsylvania German	20	0.11
Polish	846	4.49
Portuguese	60	0.32
Russian	71	0.38
Scotch-Irish	465	2.47
Scottish	412	2.18
Serbian	8	0.04
Slovak	29	0.15
Slovene	15	0.08
Swedish	234	1.24
Swiss	67	0.36
Ukrainian	56	0.30
United States or American	1,541	8.17
Welsh	241	1.28
West Indian, excl. Hispanic:	23	0.12
Jamaican	6	0.03
Trinidadian and Tobagonian	17	0.09
White:	18,176	97.36
Not Hispanic (17,724)	17,874	95.75
Hispanic (263)	302	1.62
Yugoslavian	19	0.10

Egypt Lake-Leto

Place Type: Census Designated Place
County: Hillsborough
Population: 32,782

Ancestry/Race	Number	%
African American/Black:	2,952	9.00
Not Hispanic (2,251)	2,450	7.47
Hispanic (367)	502	1.53
African, sub-Saharan:	226	0.69
African	190	0.58
Ethiopian	26	0.08
Sierra Leonean	10	0.03
Alaska Native tribes, specified:	1	0.00
Aleut (1)	1	0.00
Am. Ind. or Alaska Nat., not spec.	122	0.37
Albanian	8	0.02
American Indian tribes, specified:	135	0.41
Apache (1)	1	0.00
Blackfeet (5)	12	0.04
Cherokee (19)	55	0.17
Cheyenne	1	0.00
Chippewa	3	0.01
Choctaw	2	0.01
Comanche	1	0.00
Cree (7)	8	0.02
Creek (3)	5	0.02
Delaware	2	0.01
Iroquois (2)	8	0.02
Latin American Indians (9)	22	0.07
Lumbee (1)	1	0.00
Seminole (4)	4	0.01
Sioux (1)	1	0.00
All other tribes (4)	9	0.03
American Indian tribes, not spec.	23	0.07
Arab:	259	0.79
Arab/Arabic	107	0.33
Egyptian	24	0.07
Lebanese	43	0.13
Palestinian	75	0.23
Syrian	10	0.03
Armenian	7	0.02
Asian:	1,325	4.04
Cambodian (1)	3	0.01
Chinese, ex. Taiwanese (98)	119	0.36
Filipino (120)	149	0.45
Hmong (1)	4	0.01
Indian (251)	291	0.89
Indonesian (3)	5	0.02
Japanese (24)	37	0.11
Korean (122)	140	0.43

Notes: 1. Figures in the "Number" column do not add up to the total population due to: a) Ancestry/Race overlap — e.g. persons can report being both White and Irish, b) persons of Hispanic origin can report being any race, c) persons reporting two ancestries are counted in both categories. 2. Numbers in parentheses indicate the number of persons reporting this ancestry/race alone, not in combination with any other ancestry/race. 3. Refer to the Explanation of Data in the front of the book for more detailed information.

Ancestry/Race	Number	%
Laotian (4)	6	0.02
Malaysian (1)	1	0.00
Pakistani (15)	21	0.06
Sri Lankan (4)	4	0.01
Taiwanese (1)	1	0.00
Thai (17)	20	0.06
Vietnamese (416)	458	1.40
Other Asian, specified (4)	4	0.01
Other Asian, not specified (12)	62	0.19
Austrian	46	0.14
Belgian	29	0.09
Brazilian	95	0.29
British	83	0.25
Bulgarian	8	0.02
Canadian	85	0.26
Croatian	8	0.02
Czech	50	0.15
Czechoslovakian	13	0.04
Danish	33	0.10
Dutch	216	0.66
Eastern European	12	0.04
English	1,726	5.26
European	50	0.15
Finnish	9	0.03
French, except Basque	692	2.11
French Canadian	130	0.40
German	2,492	7.60
Greek	63	0.19
Guyanese	29	0.09
Hawaii Native/Pacific Islander:	39	0.12
Micronesian: (3)	6	0.02
Guamanian/Chamorro (3)	6	0.02
Polynesian: (14)	16	0.05
Native Hawaiian (6)	8	0.02
Samoan (8)	8	0.02
Other Pac. Isl., not spec.	17	0.05
Hispanic or Latino:	15,015	45.80
Central American:	437	1.33
Costa Rican	71	0.22
Guatemalan	86	0.26
Honduran	74	0.23
Nicaraguan	59	0.18
Panamanian	73	0.22
Salvadoran	44	0.13
Other Central American	30	0.09
Cuban	5,977	18.23
Dominican Republic	471	1.44
Mexican	639	1.95
Puerto Rican	3,559	10.86
South American:	1,087	3.32
Argentinean	31	0.09
Bolivian	13	0.04
Chilean	28	0.09
Colombian	608	1.85
Ecuadorian	82	0.25
Peruvian	128	0.39
Uruguayan	9	0.03
Venezuelan	159	0.49
Other South American	29	0.09
Other Hispanic or Latino	2,845	8.68
Hungarian	150	0.46
Icelander	10	0.03
Iranian	4	0.01
Irish	2,224	6.78
Israeli	10	0.03
Italian	2,066	6.30
Latvian	6	0.02
Lithuanian	60	0.18
Northern European	13	0.04
Norwegian	176	0.54
Pennsylvania German	22	0.07
Polish	465	1.42
Portuguese	74	0.23
Romanian	21	0.06
Russian	210	0.64
Scotch-Irish	373	1.14
Scottish	354	1.08
Slovak	12	0.04
Swedish	163	0.50
Swiss	18	0.05
Turkish	89	0.27
Ukrainian	63	0.19
United States or American	1,802	5.50
Welsh	111	0.34
West Indian, excl. Hispanic:	442	1.35
Bahamian	12	0.04
British West Indian	44	0.13
Haitian	37	0.11
Jamaican	223	0.68
Trinidadian and Tobagonian	34	0.10
West Indian	92	0.28
White:	26,030	79.40
Not Hispanic (13,754)	14,187	43.28
Hispanic (11,192)	11,843	36.13
Yugoslavian	14	0.04

Elfers

Place Type: Census Designated Place
County: Pasco
Population: 13,161

Ancestry/Race	Number	%
African American/Black:	155	1.18
Not Hispanic (116)	140	1.06
Hispanic (10)	15	0.11
Alaska Native tribes, specified:	1	0.01
Eskimo	1	0.01
Am. Ind. or Alaska Nat., not spec.	33	0.25
American Indian tribes, specified:	92	0.70
Apache	7	0.05
Blackfeet	3	0.02
Cherokee (12)	43	0.33
Cheyenne (1)	1	0.01
Chippewa (2)	3	0.02
Choctaw	1	0.01
Cree	1	0.01
Creek (1)	2	0.02
Delaware (5)	5	0.04
Iroquois (1)	3	0.02
Latin American Indians (1)	1	0.01
Lumbee (3)	3	0.02
Osage	1	0.01
Seminole (1)	2	0.02
Sioux	3	0.02
All other tribes (7)	13	0.10
American Indian tribes, not spec.	4	0.03
Arab:	24	0.18
Arab/Arabic	8	0.06
Lebanese	7	0.05
Syrian	9	0.07
Asian:	163	1.24
Chinese, ex. Taiwanese (12)	13	0.10
Filipino (19)	32	0.24
Indian (30)	39	0.30
Japanese (3)	7	0.05
Korean (2)	7	0.05
Laotian (2)	4	0.03
Pakistani (1)	1	0.01
Thai (3)	6	0.05
Vietnamese (43)	45	0.34
Other Asian, not specified (4)	9	0.07
Austrian	37	0.28
Belgian	21	0.16
British	73	0.55
Bulgarian	5	0.04
Canadian	93	0.70
Czech	37	0.28
Czechoslovakian	21	0.16
Danish	59	0.45
Dutch	401	3.04
English	1,732	13.12
Estonian	8	0.06
European	50	0.38
Finnish	7	0.05
French, except Basque	686	5.20
French Canadian	173	1.31
German	2,320	17.57
Greek	196	1.48
Hawaii Native/Pacific Islander:	7	0.05
Polynesian: (3)	3	0.02
Samoan (3)	3	0.02
Other Pac. Isl., not spec. (1)	4	0.03
Hispanic or Latino:	595	4.52
Central American:	23	0.17
Costa Rican	1	0.01
Honduran	12	0.09
Nicaraguan	2	0.02
Panamanian	2	0.02
Salvadoran	6	0.05
Cuban	45	0.34
Dominican Republic	21	0.16
Mexican	85	0.65
Puerto Rican	258	1.96
South American:	42	0.32
Argentinean	4	0.03
Bolivian	3	0.02
Colombian	24	0.18
Ecuadorian	3	0.02
Peruvian	6	0.05
Other South American	2	0.02
Other Hispanic or Latino	121	0.92
Hungarian	123	0.93
Irish	2,160	16.36
Italian	1,772	13.42
Lithuanian	36	0.27
Macedonian	9	0.07
Maltese	7	0.05
Norwegian	168	1.27
Pennsylvania German	22	0.17
Polish	639	4.84
Portuguese	54	0.41
Romanian	10	0.08
Russian	105	0.80
Scandinavian	10	0.08
Scotch-Irish	212	1.61
Scottish	187	1.42
Serbian	33	0.25
Slavic	9	0.07
Slovak	71	0.54
Slovene	17	0.13
Swedish	164	1.24
Swiss	13	0.10
Turkish	10	0.08
Ukrainian	67	0.51
United States or American	1,067	8.08
Welsh	111	0.84
West Indian, excl. Hispanic:	14	0.11
Dutch West Indian	14	0.11
White:	12,725	96.69
Not Hispanic (12,124)	12,271	93.24
Hispanic (404)	454	3.45
Yugoslavian	36	0.27

Englewood

Place Type: Census Designated Place
County: Sarasota
Population: 16,196

Ancestry/Race	Number	%
African American/Black:	50	0.31
Not Hispanic (28)	47	0.29
Hispanic (2)	3	0.02
Am. Ind. or Alaska Nat., not spec.	28	0.17
Alsatian	9	0.06
American Indian tribes, specified:	47	0.29
Apache (1)	1	0.01
Blackfeet	2	0.01
Cherokee (9)	18	0.11
Chippewa (2)	2	0.01
Choctaw (1)	2	0.01
Iroquois (6)	7	0.04
Latin American Indians	1	0.01
Navajo	4	0.02
Osage (1)	1	0.01
Pueblo (1)	1	0.01
Sioux (1)	2	0.01
All other tribes (4)	6	0.04
American Indian tribes, not spec.	4	0.02

Notes: 1. Figures in the "Number" column do not add up to the total population due to: a) Ancestry/Race overlap — e.g. persons can report being both White and Irish, b) persons of Hispanic origin can report being any race, c) persons reporting two ancestries are counted in both categories. 2. Numbers in parentheses indicate the number of persons reporting this ancestry/race alone, not in combination with any other ancestry/race. 3. Refer to the Explanation of Data in the front of the book for more detailed information.

Armenian	18	0.11
Asian:	74	0.46
Cambodian (8)	8	0.05
Chinese, ex. Taiwanese (12)	15	0.09
Filipino (8)	11	0.07
Indian (12)	15	0.09
Japanese (6)	8	0.05
Korean (2)	5	0.03
Sri Lankan (3)	3	0.02
Taiwanese (1)	1	0.01
Thai (6)	6	0.04
Vietnamese (1)	1	0.01
Other Asian, specified	1	0.01
Assyrian/Chaldean/Syriac	9	0.06
Australian	7	0.04
Austrian	38	0.23
Belgian	76	0.47
Brazilian	15	0.09
British	66	0.41
Canadian	244	1.50
Croatian	8	0.05
Czech	43	0.26
Czechoslovakian	78	0.48
Danish	74	0.46
Dutch	564	3.47
English	3,140	19.32
European	53	0.33
Finnish	26	0.16
French, except Basque	813	5.00
French Canadian	280	1.72
German	3,952	24.32
Greek	32	0.20
Hawaii Native/Pacific Islander:	8	0.05
Polynesian: (2)	6	0.04
Native Hawaiian (2)	5	0.03
Samoan	1	0.01
Other Pac. Isl., specified	1	0.01
Other Pac. Isl., not spec.	1	0.01
Hispanic or Latino:	241	1.49
Central American:	3	0.02
Panamanian	2	0.01
Salvadoran	1	0.01
Cuban	9	0.06
Dominican Republic	1	0.01
Mexican	114	0.70
Puerto Rican	55	0.34
South American:	17	0.10
Colombian	4	0.02
Ecuadorian	3	0.02
Peruvian	7	0.04
Other South American	3	0.02
Other Hispanic or Latino	42	0.26
Hungarian	133	0.82
Iranian	8	0.05
Irish	2,362	14.54
Italian	1,025	6.31
Lithuanian	113	0.70
Luxemburger	9	0.06
Macedonian	4	0.02
Northern European	15	0.09
Norwegian	186	1.14
Pennsylvania German	16	0.10
Polish	892	5.49
Portuguese	59	0.36
Romanian	8	0.05
Russian	89	0.55
Scandinavian	19	0.12
Scotch-Irish	448	2.76
Scottish	569	3.50
Slovak	38	0.23
Swedish	462	2.84
Swiss	78	0.48
Turkish	11	0.07
Ukrainian	78	0.48
United States or American	1,060	6.52
Welsh	206	1.27
White:	15,995	98.76
Not Hispanic (15,752)	15,819	97.67
Hispanic (161)	176	1.09
Yugoslavian	9	0.06

Ensley

Place Type: Census Designated Place
County: Escambia
Population: 18,752

Ancestry/Race	Number	%
Acadian/Cajun	18	0.10
African American/Black:	5,432	28.97
Not Hispanic (5,304)	5,388	28.73
Hispanic (29)	44	0.23
African, sub-Saharan:	49	0.26
African	49	0.26
Am. Ind. or Alaska Nat., not spec.	97	0.52
American Indian tribes, specified:	248	1.32
Apache (1)	3	0.02
Blackfeet (1)	11	0.06
Cherokee (15)	62	0.33
Cheyenne	1	0.01
Chickasaw (1)	2	0.01
Chippewa (1)	4	0.02
Choctaw (4)	10	0.05
Comanche	1	0.01
Cree	1	0.01
Creek (73)	125	0.67
Crow	1	0.01
Houma	2	0.01
Iroquois (4)	5	0.03
Latin American Indians	1	0.01
Lumbee (8)	8	0.04
Navajo (1)	1	0.01
Osage	1	0.01
Ottawa (1)	1	0.01
Seminole (3)	3	0.02
Sioux (1)	2	0.01
All other tribes	3	0.02
American Indian tribes, not spec.	8	0.04
Arab:	10	0.05
Lebanese	10	0.05
Asian:	335	1.79
Cambodian (6)	6	0.03
Chinese, ex. Taiwanese (14)	26	0.14
Filipino (86)	133	0.71
Indian (10)	16	0.09
Indonesian (2)	2	0.01
Japanese (22)	42	0.22
Korean (14)	24	0.13
Thai (3)	12	0.06
Vietnamese (50)	56	0.30
Other Asian, specified	2	0.01
Other Asian, not specified (5)	16	0.09
British	71	0.38
Canadian	20	0.11
Croatian	16	0.09
Czech	39	0.21
Danish	32	0.17
Dutch	154	0.83
Eastern European	16	0.09
English	1,481	7.97
European	43	0.23
Finnish	23	0.12
French, except Basque	336	1.81
French Canadian	94	0.51
German	1,657	8.92
Greek	51	0.27
Hawaii Native/Pacific Islander:	18	0.10
Micronesian: (6)	9	0.05
Guamanian/Chamorro (6)	8	0.04
Other Micronesian	1	0.01
Polynesian: (1)	3	0.02
Native Hawaiian	1	0.01
Tongan (1)	2	0.01
Other Pac. Isl., specified	1	0.01
Other Pac. Isl., not spec. (2)	5	0.03
Hispanic or Latino:	390	2.08
Central American:	17	0.09
Guatemalan	2	0.01
Honduran	8	0.04
Nicaraguan	3	0.02
Panamanian	4	0.02
Cuban	19	0.10
Dominican Republic	6	0.03
Mexican	148	0.79
Puerto Rican	78	0.42
South American:	22	0.12
Argentinean	2	0.01
Colombian	13	0.07
Peruvian	3	0.02
Venezuelan	2	0.01
Other South American	2	0.01
Other Hispanic or Latino	100	0.53
Hungarian	74	0.40
Iranian	14	0.08
Irish	1,787	9.61
Italian	496	2.67
Lithuanian	7	0.04
Norwegian	68	0.37
Pennsylvania German	23	0.12
Polish	251	1.35
Portuguese	30	0.16
Russian	27	0.15
Scandinavian	19	0.10
Scotch-Irish	469	2.52
Scottish	293	1.58
Slavic	15	0.08
Slovak	15	0.08
Swedish	71	0.38
Swiss	11	0.06
Ukrainian	4	0.02
United States or American	2,112	11.36
Welsh	36	0.19
White:	12,846	68.50
Not Hispanic (12,336)	12,606	67.22
Hispanic (210)	240	1.28

Eustis

Place Type: City
County: Lake
Population: 15,106

Ancestry/Race	Number	%
African American/Black:	2,932	19.41
Not Hispanic (2,829)	2,886	19.10
Hispanic (38)	46	0.30
African, sub-Saharan:	43	0.28
African	43	0.28
Am. Ind. or Alaska Nat., not spec.	32	0.21
American Indian tribes, specified:	84	0.56
Blackfeet (1)	2	0.01
Cherokee (21)	37	0.24
Chippewa (4)	6	0.04
Choctaw (8)	9	0.06
Creek	1	0.01
Delaware	1	0.01
Iroquois (2)	4	0.03
Latin American Indians (1)	9	0.06
Lumbee	2	0.01
Seminole	2	0.01
Sioux (3)	4	0.03
Yakama (1)	1	0.01
All other tribes (3)	6	0.04
American Indian tribes, not spec.	4	0.03
Arab:	88	0.57
Egyptian	62	0.40
Lebanese	26	0.17
Armenian	17	0.11
Asian:	111	0.73
Chinese, ex. Taiwanese (15)	17	0.11
Filipino (23)	25	0.17
Indian (22)	25	0.17
Indonesian	2	0.01
Japanese (3)	3	0.02
Korean (7)	8	0.05
Malaysian	1	0.01
Sri Lankan (2)	2	0.01
Vietnamese (22)	22	0.15
Other Asian, specified (1)	1	0.01
Other Asian, not specified	5	0.03
Australian	10	0.07

Notes: 1. Figures in the "Number" column do not add up to the total population due to: a) Ancestry/Race overlap — e.g. persons can report being both White and Irish, b) persons of Hispanic origin can report being any race, c) persons reporting two ancestries are counted in both categories. 2. Numbers in parentheses indicate the number of persons reporting this ancestry/race alone, not in combination with any other ancestry/race. 3. Refer to the Explanation of Data in the front of the book for more detailed information.

Ancestry/Race	Number	%
Austrian	11	0.07
Belgian	10	0.07
British	84	0.55
Canadian	22	0.14
Croatian	18	0.12
Czech	72	0.47
Czechoslovakian	18	0.12
Danish	41	0.27
Dutch	216	1.41
Eastern European	9	0.06
English	2,232	14.54
European	34	0.22
Finnish	15	0.10
French, except Basque	394	2.57
French Canadian	123	0.80
German	2,079	13.54
Greek	15	0.10
Hawaii Native/Pacific Islander:	22	0.15
Polynesian: (6)	7	0.05
Native Hawaiian (2)	3	0.02
Samoan (4)	4	0.03
Other Pac. Isl., not spec. (8)	15	0.10
Hispanic or Latino:	962	6.37
Central American:	29	0.19
Costa Rican	1	0.01
Guatemalan	9	0.06
Nicaraguan	3	0.02
Panamanian	4	0.03
Salvadoran	11	0.07
Other Central American	1	0.01
Cuban	35	0.23
Dominican Republic	2	0.01
Mexican	576	3.81
Puerto Rican	192	1.27
South American:	28	0.19
Argentinean	4	0.03
Chilean	1	0.01
Colombian	9	0.06
Peruvian	11	0.07
Uruguayan	1	0.01
Venezuelan	2	0.01
Other Hispanic or Latino	100	0.66
Hungarian	31	0.20
Irish	1,852	12.06
Italian	723	4.71
Latvian	8	0.05
Lithuanian	11	0.07
Northern European	21	0.14
Norwegian	76	0.50
Polish	454	2.96
Romanian	21	0.14
Russian	17	0.11
Scandinavian	41	0.27
Scotch-Irish	291	1.90
Scottish	341	2.22
Serbian	8	0.05
Slovak	9	0.06
Slovene	11	0.07
Swedish	137	0.89
Swiss	38	0.25
Ukrainian	70	0.46
United States or American	1,487	9.69
Welsh	115	0.75
West Indian, excl. Hispanic:	123	0.80
Bahamian	67	0.44
Barbadian	6	0.04
Haitian	7	0.05
Jamaican	43	0.28
White:	11,758	77.84
Not Hispanic (11,040)	11,142	73.76
Hispanic (576)	616	4.08
Yugoslavian	15	0.10

Fairview Shores

Place Type: Census Designated Place
County: Orange
Population: 13,898

Ancestry/Race	Number	%
African American/Black:	1,960	14.10
Not Hispanic (1,809)	1,909	13.74
Hispanic (37)	51	0.37
African, sub-Saharan:	79	0.59
African	29	0.22
Ethiopian	50	0.37
Alaska Native tribes, specified:	1	0.01
Eskimo	1	0.01
Am. Ind. or Alaska Nat., not spec.	44	0.32
American Indian tribes, specified:	74	0.53
Apache (1)	2	0.01
Blackfeet	2	0.01
Cherokee (8)	33	0.24
Chippewa (5)	5	0.04
Choctaw	1	0.01
Creek (1)	3	0.02
Delaware (1)	2	0.01
Iroquois (3)	5	0.04
Latin American Indians (1)	3	0.02
Lumbee	1	0.01
Pueblo	1	0.01
Seminole (3)	4	0.03
Sioux (2)	4	0.03
All other tribes (2)	8	0.06
American Indian tribes, not spec.	11	0.08
Arab:	45	0.34
Arab/Arabic	8	0.06
Lebanese	15	0.11
Moroccan	10	0.07
Syrian	6	0.04
Other Arab	6	0.04
Asian:	459	3.30
Chinese, ex. Taiwanese (30)	41	0.30
Filipino (60)	68	0.49
Indian (9)	17	0.12
Japanese (4)	13	0.09
Korean (39)	51	0.37
Laotian (7)	8	0.06
Pakistani (10)	13	0.09
Thai (9)	13	0.09
Vietnamese (190)	213	1.53
Other Asian, not specified (5)	22	0.16
Australian	30	0.22
Austrian	21	0.16
Belgian	17	0.13
Brazilian	27	0.20
British	60	0.45
Bulgarian	9	0.07
Canadian	49	0.37
Croatian	11	0.08
Czech	28	0.21
Czechoslovakian	14	0.10
Danish	62	0.46
Dutch	229	1.71
English	1,567	11.69
European	55	0.41
Finnish	13	0.10
French, except Basque	428	3.19
French Canadian	203	1.52
German	2,008	14.99
Greek	19	0.14
Hawaii Native/Pacific Islander:	34	0.24
Melanesian: (3)	3	0.02
Other Melanesian (3)	3	0.02
Micronesian:	5	0.04
Guamanian/Chamorro	4	0.03
Other Micronesian	1	0.01
Polynesian: (11)	16	0.12
Native Hawaiian (9)	12	0.09
Samoan (2)	4	0.03
Other Pac. Isl., not spec. (1)	10	0.07
Hispanic or Latino:	1,310	9.43
Central American:	36	0.26
Costa Rican	2	0.01
Guatemalan	5	0.04
Honduran	7	0.05
Nicaraguan	8	0.06
Panamanian	11	0.08
Salvadoran	3	0.02
Cuban	128	0.92
Dominican Republic	62	0.45
Mexican	160	1.15
Puerto Rican	607	4.37
South American:	90	0.65
Argentinean	4	0.03
Bolivian	1	0.01
Chilean	3	0.02
Colombian	51	0.37
Ecuadorian	12	0.09
Peruvian	9	0.06
Uruguayan	3	0.02
Other South American	7	0.05
Other Hispanic or Latino	227	1.63
Hungarian	43	0.32
Irish	1,515	11.31
Italian	679	5.07
Latvian	10	0.07
Lithuanian	26	0.19
Norwegian	128	0.96
Polish	272	2.03
Portuguese	55	0.41
Romanian	31	0.23
Russian	89	0.66
Scandinavian	11	0.08
Scotch-Irish	341	2.54
Scottish	329	2.46
Serbian	5	0.04
Slavic	8	0.06
Slovak	26	0.19
Slovene	7	0.05
Swedish	105	0.78
Swiss	24	0.18
Turkish	4	0.03
Ukrainian	33	0.25
United States or American	1,026	7.66
Welsh	88	0.66
West Indian, excl. Hispanic:	156	1.16
Bahamian	12	0.09
Barbadian	27	0.20
Haitian	12	0.09
Jamaican	65	0.49
Trinidadian and Tobagonian	24	0.18
West Indian	16	0.12
White:	11,091	79.80
Not Hispanic (10,082)	10,263	73.85
Hispanic (771)	828	5.96

Fernandina Beach

Place Type: City
County: Nassau
Population: 10,549

Ancestry/Race	Number	%
African American/Black:	1,726	16.36
Not Hispanic (1,698)	1,714	16.25
Hispanic (10)	12	0.11
African, sub-Saharan:	4	0.04
African	4	0.04
Alaska Native tribes, specified:	5	0.05
Eskimo (1)	4	0.04
Tlingit-Haida (1)	1	0.01
Am. Ind. or Alaska Nat., not spec.	18	0.17
American Indian tribes, specified:	39	0.37
Cherokee (9)	18	0.17
Choctaw (1)	1	0.01
Creek (1)	5	0.05
Iroquois (1)	3	0.03
Latin American Indians (5)	5	0.05
Ottawa	1	0.01
Potawatomi	1	0.01
Seminole	1	0.01
Shoshone	2	0.02
Sioux	1	0.01
All other tribes	1	0.01
American Indian tribes, not spec.	2	0.02
Arab:	14	0.14
Lebanese	14	0.14
Asian:	84	0.80
Chinese, ex. Taiwanese (13)	15	0.14

Notes: 1. Figures in the "Number" column do not add up to the total population due to: a) Ancestry/Race overlap — e.g. persons can report being both White and Irish, b) persons of Hispanic origin can report being any race, c) persons reporting two ancestries are counted in both categories. 2. Numbers in parentheses indicate the number of persons reporting this ancestry/race alone, not in combination with any other ancestry/race. 3. Refer to the Explanation of Data in the front of the book for more detailed information.

Ancestry/Race	Number	%
Filipino (22)	32	0.30
Indian (5)	7	0.07
Japanese (7)	12	0.11
Korean (8)	9	0.09
Laotian (1)	1	0.01
Thai (2)	3	0.03
Vietnamese (2)	2	0.02
Other Asian, specified	1	0.01
Other Asian, not specified (1)	2	0.02
Austrian	48	0.47
Basque	14	0.14
Belgian	18	0.18
British	32	0.31
Canadian	10	0.10
Celtic	6	0.06
Czech	17	0.17
Czechoslovakian	32	0.31
Danish	8	0.08
Dutch	157	1.53
English	1,675	16.35
European	97	0.95
Finnish	43	0.42
French, except Basque	463	4.52
French Canadian	72	0.70
German	1,164	11.36
Greek	64	0.62
Hawaii Native/Pacific Islander:	13	0.12
Micronesian: (2)	2	0.02
Guamanian/Chamorro (2)	2	0.02
Polynesian: (3)	10	0.09
Native Hawaiian (3)	7	0.07
Samoan	3	0.03
Other Pac. Isl., specified	1	0.01
Hispanic or Latino:	246	2.33
Central American:	26	0.25
Costa Rican	9	0.09
Guatemalan	8	0.08
Honduran	8	0.08
Nicaraguan	1	0.01
Cuban	20	0.19
Dominican Republic	1	0.01
Mexican	91	0.86
Puerto Rican	29	0.27
South American:	20	0.19
Argentinean	1	0.01
Colombian	10	0.09
Ecuadorian	1	0.01
Peruvian	1	0.01
Venezuelan	7	0.07
Other Hispanic or Latino	59	0.56
Hungarian	17	0.17
Icelander	8	0.08
Irish	1,273	12.43
Italian	390	3.81
Lithuanian	40	0.39
Northern European	23	0.22
Norwegian	119	1.16
Polish	257	2.51
Portuguese	29	0.28
Romanian	23	0.22
Russian	59	0.58
Scandinavian	9	0.09
Scotch-Irish	279	2.72
Scottish	272	2.66
Slavic	10	0.10
Slovak	9	0.09
Swedish	128	1.25
Swiss	7	0.07
Ukrainian	18	0.18
United States or American	1,372	13.40
Welsh	64	0.62
West Indian, excl. Hispanic:	81	0.79
Bahamian	15	0.15
British West Indian	15	0.15
Haitian	44	0.43
Jamaican	7	0.07
White:	8,685	82.33
Not Hispanic (8,434)	8,499	80.57
Hispanic (168)	186	1.76
Yugoslavian	13	0.13

Ferry Pass

Place Type: Census Designated Place
County: Escambia
Population: 27,176

Ancestry/Race	Number	%
Acadian/Cajun	25	0.09
African American/Black:	3,010	11.08
Not Hispanic (2,852)	2,968	10.92
Hispanic (30)	42	0.15
African, sub-Saharan:	15	0.06
African	11	0.04
Nigerian	4	0.01
Alaska Native tribes, specified:	1	0.00
Tlingit-Haida (1)	1	0.00
Am. Ind. or Alaska Nat., not spec.	75	0.28
Albanian	8	0.03
American Indian tribes, specified:	270	0.99
Apache (3)	5	0.02
Blackfeet	7	0.03
Cherokee (35)	76	0.28
Chickasaw	1	0.00
Chippewa	2	0.01
Choctaw (5)	15	0.06
Comanche	1	0.00
Cree	4	0.01
Creek (60)	108	0.40
Delaware (1)	1	0.00
Houma (2)	2	0.01
Iroquois (1)	1	0.00
Latin American Indians (6)	11	0.04
Lumbee (2)	5	0.02
Navajo (1)	2	0.01
Osage (2)	2	0.01
Paiute	1	0.00
Potawatomi (1)	1	0.00
Puget Sound Salish	1	0.00
Seminole (2)	8	0.03
Sioux (1)	3	0.01
Ute	1	0.00
All other tribes (4)	12	0.04
American Indian tribes, not spec.	15	0.06
Arab:	146	0.54
Arab/Arabic	43	0.16
Egyptian	7	0.03
Jordanian	55	0.20
Lebanese	21	0.08
Syrian	13	0.05
Other Arab	7	0.03
Asian:	757	2.79
Cambodian (2)	3	0.01
Chinese, ex. Taiwanese (67)	97	0.36
Filipino (135)	221	0.81
Indian (63)	73	0.27
Indonesian (6)	9	0.03
Japanese (45)	88	0.32
Korean (43)	53	0.20
Malaysian (1)	1	0.00
Pakistani (11)	12	0.04
Sri Lankan	1	0.00
Taiwanese (7)	10	0.04
Thai (6)	9	0.03
Vietnamese (107)	119	0.44
Other Asian, specified	5	0.02
Other Asian, not specified (19)	56	0.21
Assyrian/Chaldean/Syriac	14	0.05
Australian	47	0.17
Austrian	29	0.11
Belgian	34	0.13
Brazilian	37	0.14
British	253	0.93
Bulgarian	22	0.08
Canadian	76	0.28
Croatian	8	0.03
Czech	86	0.32
Czechoslovakian	62	0.23
Danish	114	0.42
Dutch	395	1.45
English	2,970	10.93
European	203	0.75
Finnish	36	0.13
French, except Basque	1,012	3.72
French Canadian	194	0.71
German	3,630	13.36
Greek	81	0.30
Hawaii Native/Pacific Islander:	40	0.15
Melanesian:	1	0.00
Other Melanesian	1	0.00
Micronesian: (6)	14	0.05
Guamanian/Chamorro (4)	12	0.04
Other Micronesian (2)	2	0.01
Polynesian: (6)	13	0.05
Native Hawaiian (3)	7	0.03
Samoan (3)	6	0.02
Other Pac. Isl., specified	1	0.00
Other Pac. Isl., not spec.	11	0.04
Hispanic or Latino:	740	2.72
Central American:	37	0.14
Costa Rican	5	0.02
Guatemalan	3	0.01
Honduran	4	0.01
Panamanian	17	0.06
Salvadoran	5	0.02
Other Central American	3	0.01
Cuban	65	0.24
Dominican Republic	2	0.01
Mexican	219	0.81
Puerto Rican	177	0.65
South American:	62	0.23
Argentinean	3	0.01
Colombian	30	0.11
Ecuadorian	9	0.03
Peruvian	11	0.04
Venezuelan	5	0.02
Other South American	4	0.01
Other Hispanic or Latino	178	0.65
Hungarian	75	0.28
Iranian	30	0.11
Irish	3,001	11.04
Italian	1,149	4.23
Latvian	8	0.03
Lithuanian	64	0.24
Maltese	12	0.04
Northern European	8	0.03
Norwegian	208	0.77
Pennsylvania German	15	0.06
Polish	363	1.34
Portuguese	23	0.08
Romanian	11	0.04
Russian	180	0.66
Scandinavian	28	0.10
Scotch-Irish	951	3.50
Scottish	624	2.30
Slavic	8	0.03
Slovak	31	0.11
Slovene	7	0.03
Swedish	262	0.96
Swiss	79	0.29
Ukrainian	25	0.09
United States or American	3,297	12.13
Welsh	138	0.51
West Indian, excl. Hispanic:	69	0.25
Bahamian	8	0.03
Haitian	44	0.16
Jamaican	17	0.06
White:	23,310	85.77
Not Hispanic (22,322)	22,791	83.86
Hispanic (449)	519	1.91
Yugoslavian	12	0.04

Florida Ridge

Place Type: Census Designated Place
County: Indian River
Population: 15,217

Ancestry/Race	Number	%
Acadian/Cajun	7	0.05
African American/Black:	1,794	11.79

Notes: 1. Figures in the "Number" column do not add up to the total population due to: a) Ancestry/Race overlap — e.g. persons can report being both White and Irish, b) persons of Hispanic origin can report being any race, c) persons reporting two ancestries are counted in both categories. 2. Numbers in parentheses indicate the number of persons reporting this ancestry/race alone, not in combination with any other ancestry/race. 3. Refer to the Explanation of Data in the front of the book for more detailed information.

Not Hispanic (1,676)	1,780	11.70
Hispanic (13)	14	0.09
African, sub-Saharan:	58	0.38
African	44	0.29
Nigerian	14	0.09
Am. Ind. or Alaska Nat., not spec.	22	0.14
American Indian tribes, specified:	50	0.33
Apache	1	0.01
Blackfeet (1)	3	0.02
Cherokee (10)	28	0.18
Chippewa	2	0.01
Choctaw (1)	2	0.01
Cree	1	0.01
Creek	1	0.01
Houma (1)	1	0.01
Latin American Indians (1)	1	0.01
Lumbee (3)	3	0.02
Navajo (1)	1	0.01
Osage	3	0.02
Potawatomi (1)	1	0.01
All other tribes (1)	2	0.01
American Indian tribes, not spec.	2	0.01
Arab:	12	0.08
Lebanese	6	0.04
Syrian	6	0.04
Armenian	7	0.05
Asian:	138	0.91
Cambodian (1)	3	0.02
Chinese, ex. Taiwanese (25)	29	0.19
Filipino (14)	25	0.16
Indian (17)	22	0.14
Japanese (3)	7	0.05
Korean (9)	9	0.06
Pakistani	4	0.03
Taiwanese	2	0.01
Thai (5)	5	0.03
Vietnamese (20)	23	0.15
Other Asian, specified	2	0.01
Other Asian, not specified (6)	7	0.05
Australian	8	0.05
Austrian	41	0.27
Belgian	6	0.04
British	83	0.54
Canadian	79	0.52
Croatian	11	0.07
Czech	53	0.35
Czechoslovakian	40	0.26
Danish	30	0.20
Dutch	296	1.93
Eastern European	7	0.05
English	2,361	15.41
European	31	0.20
Finnish	6	0.04
French, except Basque	613	4.00
French Canadian	186	1.21
German	2,206	14.40
Greek	53	0.35
Hawaii Native/Pacific Islander:	12	0.08
Micronesian: (1)	1	0.01
Guamanian/Chamorro (1)	1	0.01
Polynesian: (1)	2	0.01
Native Hawaiian (1)	2	0.01
Other Pac. Isl., specified	1	0.01
Other Pac. Isl., not spec.	8	0.05
Hispanic or Latino:	620	4.07
Central American:	21	0.14
Costa Rican	2	0.01
Guatemalan	5	0.03
Honduran	3	0.02
Panamanian	7	0.05
Salvadoran	4	0.03
Cuban	68	0.45
Dominican Republic	4	0.03
Mexican	217	1.43
Puerto Rican	116	0.76
South American:	79	0.52
Argentinean	1	0.01
Bolivian	1	0.01
Chilean	4	0.03
Colombian	42	0.28
Ecuadorian	9	0.06
Peruvian	10	0.07
Uruguayan	2	0.01
Venezuelan	7	0.05
Other South American	3	0.02
Other Hispanic or Latino	115	0.76
Hungarian	136	0.89
Iranian	6	0.04
Irish	2,456	16.03
Italian	1,134	7.40
Latvian	13	0.08
Lithuanian	44	0.29
Macedonian	7	0.05
Norwegian	76	0.50
Pennsylvania German	8	0.05
Polish	617	4.03
Portuguese	50	0.33
Russian	82	0.54
Scandinavian	29	0.19
Scotch-Irish	285	1.86
Scottish	267	1.74
Slovak	47	0.31
Swedish	192	1.25
Swiss	45	0.29
Ukrainian	49	0.32
United States or American	1,275	8.32
Welsh	135	0.88
West Indian, excl. Hispanic:	177	1.16
Bahamian	86	0.56
British West Indian	6	0.04
Haitian	62	0.40
Jamaican	23	0.15
White:	13,167	86.53
Not Hispanic (12,592)	12,707	83.51
Hispanic (425)	460	3.02

Forest City

Place Type: Census Designated Place
County: Seminole
Population: 12,612

Ancestry/Race	Number	%
African American/Black:	717	5.69
Not Hispanic (578)	655	5.19
Hispanic (35)	62	0.49
African, sub-Saharan:	49	0.39
African	26	0.20
Kenyan	23	0.18
Am. Ind. or Alaska Nat., not spec.	17	0.13
American Indian tribes, specified:	56	0.44
Apache	2	0.02
Cherokee (9)	19	0.15
Cheyenne	1	0.01
Chippewa	1	0.01
Choctaw	2	0.02
Creek (1)	1	0.01
Delaware	1	0.01
Iroquois (3)	3	0.02
Latin American Indians (9)	14	0.11
Menominee	1	0.01
Potawatomi (1)	1	0.01
Seminole (1)	3	0.02
Sioux	4	0.03
All other tribes (2)	3	0.02
American Indian tribes, not spec.	10	0.08
Arab:	82	0.65
Arab/Arabic	53	0.42
Lebanese	18	0.14
Palestinian	11	0.09
Asian:	480	3.81
Chinese, ex. Taiwanese (48)	51	0.40
Filipino (39)	49	0.39
Indian (105)	128	1.01
Indonesian (4)	4	0.03
Japanese (13)	21	0.17
Korean (161)	163	1.29
Pakistani (13)	13	0.10
Taiwanese (2)	2	0.02
Thai (2)	3	0.02
Vietnamese (30)	31	0.25
Other Asian, not specified (11)	15	0.12
Austrian	7	0.06
Brazilian	12	0.09
British	64	0.50
Bulgarian	20	0.16
Canadian	74	0.58
Czech	7	0.06
Czechoslovakian	6	0.05
Danish	27	0.21
Dutch	229	1.80
Eastern European	8	0.06
English	1,461	11.49
European	77	0.61
Finnish	32	0.25
French, except Basque	418	3.29
French Canadian	155	1.22
German	1,931	15.19
Greek	74	0.58
Guyanese	18	0.14
Hawaii Native/Pacific Islander:	7	0.06
Melanesian: (1)	1	0.01
Fijian (1)	1	0.01
Polynesian: (4)	6	0.05
Native Hawaiian (4)	6	0.05
Hispanic or Latino:	1,964	15.57
Central American:	85	0.67
Costa Rican	10	0.08
Guatemalan	7	0.06
Honduran	14	0.11
Nicaraguan	24	0.19
Panamanian	14	0.11
Salvadoran	8	0.06
Other Central American	8	0.06
Cuban	416	3.30
Dominican Republic	88	0.70
Mexican	84	0.67
Puerto Rican	735	5.83
South American:	230	1.82
Argentinean	2	0.02
Bolivian	3	0.02
Chilean	9	0.07
Colombian	82	0.65
Ecuadorian	24	0.19
Peruvian	62	0.49
Venezuelan	35	0.28
Other South American	13	0.10
Other Hispanic or Latino	326	2.58
Hungarian	95	0.75
Icelander	7	0.06
Iranian	11	0.09
Irish	1,761	13.85
Italian	927	7.29
Lithuanian	46	0.36
Norwegian	135	1.06
Pennsylvania German	13	0.10
Polish	335	2.64
Portuguese	71	0.56
Romanian	17	0.13
Russian	131	1.03
Scandinavian	14	0.11
Scotch-Irish	193	1.52
Scottish	294	2.31
Slovak	80	0.63
Slovene	12	0.09
Swedish	228	1.79
Swiss	54	0.42
Turkish	39	0.31
Ukrainian	47	0.37
United States or American	859	6.76
Welsh	76	0.60
West Indian, excl. Hispanic:	270	2.12
Dutch West Indian	37	0.29
Haitian	67	0.53
Jamaican	126	0.99
West Indian	40	0.31
White:	11,010	87.30
Not Hispanic (9,386)	9,534	75.59
Hispanic (1,375)	1,476	11.70
Yugoslavian	23	0.18

Notes: 1. Figures in the "Number" column do not add up to the total population due to: a) Ancestry/Race overlap — e.g. persons can report being both White and Irish, b) persons of Hispanic origin can report being any race, c) persons reporting two ancestries are counted in both categories. 2. Numbers in parentheses indicate the number of persons reporting this ancestry/race alone, not in combination with any other ancestry/race. 3. Refer to the Explanation of Data in the front of the book for more detailed information.

Fort Lauderdale

Place Type: City
County: Broward
Population: 152,397

Ancestry/Race	Number	%
Afghan	7	0.00
African American/Black:	48,033	31.52
Not Hispanic (43,441)	47,272	31.02
Hispanic (569)	761	0.50
African, sub-Saharan:	1,802	1.18
African	1,594	1.05
Cape Verdean	11	0.01
Ethiopian	6	0.00
Nigerian	7	0.00
South African	120	0.08
Sudanese	8	0.01
Ugandan	13	0.01
Zimbabwean	36	0.02
Other sub-Saharan African	7	0.00
Alaska Native tribes, specified:	25	0.02
Alaska Athabascan	1	0.00
Aleut (2)	3	0.00
Eskimo (1)	5	0.00
Tlingit-Haida (1)	16	0.01
Am. Ind. or Alaska Nat., not spec.	325	0.21
Albanian	158	0.10
Alsatian	10	0.01
American Indian tribes, specified:	412	0.27
Apache (6)	9	0.01
Blackfeet (8)	19	0.01
Cherokee (50)	157	0.10
Chickasaw (3)	5	0.00
Chippewa (10)	15	0.01
Choctaw (9)	22	0.01
Comanche (1)	1	0.00
Cree (1)	1	0.00
Creek (3)	5	0.00
Delaware	3	0.00
Iroquois (13)	23	0.02
Kiowa (1)	1	0.00
Latin American Indians (39)	67	0.04
Lumbee (4)	4	0.00
Navajo (2)	4	0.00
Ottawa	1	0.00
Paiute	1	0.00
Pueblo	3	0.00
Seminole (13)	16	0.01
Shoshone (1)	1	0.00
Sioux (4)	12	0.01
Yaqui	1	0.00
Yuman	1	0.00
All other tribes (14)	40	0.03
American Indian tribes, not spec.	54	0.04
Arab:	723	0.48
Arab/Arabic	38	0.02
Egyptian	97	0.06
Iraqi	16	0.01
Jordanian	44	0.03
Lebanese	365	0.24
Moroccan	30	0.02
Palestinian	54	0.04
Syrian	26	0.02
Other Arab	53	0.03
Armenian	171	0.11
Asian:	2,194	1.44
Bangladeshi (9)	34	0.02
Cambodian (1)	1	0.00
Chinese, ex. Taiwanese (264)	337	0.22
Filipino (224)	298	0.20
Indian (536)	770	0.51
Indonesian (10)	12	0.01
Japanese (109)	156	0.10
Korean (73)	91	0.06
Laotian (1)	3	0.00
Malaysian (2)	6	0.00
Pakistani (33)	56	0.04
Sri Lankan (9)	10	0.01
Taiwanese (10)	11	0.01
Thai (88)	104	0.07
Vietnamese (100)	115	0.08
Other Asian, specified (4)	14	0.01
Other Asian, not specified (53)	176	0.12
Australian	94	0.06
Austrian	816	0.54
Basque	59	0.04
Belgian	153	0.10
Brazilian	917	0.60
British	882	0.58
Bulgarian	85	0.06
Canadian	655	0.43
Carpatho Rusyn	10	0.01
Celtic	19	0.01
Croatian	110	0.07
Cypriot	14	0.01
Czech	508	0.33
Czechoslovakian	167	0.11
Danish	570	0.37
Dutch	1,580	1.04
Eastern European	211	0.14
English	12,456	8.19
Estonian	9	0.01
European	615	0.40
Finnish	200	0.13
French, except Basque	4,153	2.73
French Canadian	1,163	0.76
German	15,857	10.42
Greek	1,038	0.68
Guyanese	46	0.03
Hawaii Native/Pacific Islander:	274	0.18
Melanesian: (1)	1	0.00
Fijian (1)	1	0.00
Micronesian: (19)	35	0.02
Guamanian/Chamorro (19)	34	0.02
Other Micronesian	1	0.00
Polynesian: (41)	81	0.05
Native Hawaiian (20)	50	0.03
Samoan (16)	20	0.01
Other Polynesian (5)	11	0.01
Other Pac. Isl., specified	8	0.01
Other Pac. Isl., not spec. (13)	149	0.10
Hispanic or Latino:	14,406	9.45
Central American:	1,927	1.26
Costa Rican	93	0.06
Guatemalan	477	0.31
Honduran	381	0.25
Nicaraguan	139	0.09
Panamanian	92	0.06
Salvadoran	674	0.44
Other Central American	71	0.05
Cuban	2,576	1.69
Dominican Republic	272	0.18
Mexican	1,404	0.92
Puerto Rican	2,801	1.84
South American:	2,449	1.61
Argentinean	289	0.19
Bolivian	25	0.02
Chilean	97	0.06
Colombian	988	0.65
Ecuadorian	125	0.08
Paraguayan	13	0.01
Peruvian	476	0.31
Uruguayan	54	0.04
Venezuelan	315	0.21
Other South American	67	0.04
Other Hispanic or Latino	2,977	1.95
Hungarian	1,161	0.76
Icelander	23	0.02
Iranian	101	0.07
Irish	15,639	10.28
Israeli	94	0.06
Italian	11,512	7.57
Latvian	64	0.04
Lithuanian	386	0.25
Luxemburger	26	0.02
Macedonian	66	0.04
Maltese	29	0.02
New Zealander	59	0.04
Northern European	81	0.05
Norwegian	1,204	0.79
Pennsylvania German	93	0.06
Polish	4,344	2.86
Portuguese	468	0.31
Romanian	375	0.25
Russian	2,408	1.58
Scandinavian	106	0.07
Scotch-Irish	1,616	1.06
Scottish	2,689	1.77
Serbian	71	0.05
Slavic	53	0.03
Slovak	265	0.17
Slovene	113	0.07
Swedish	1,518	1.00
Swiss	339	0.22
Turkish	87	0.06
Ukrainian	467	0.31
United States or American	8,904	5.85
Welsh	1,050	0.69
West Indian, excl. Hispanic:	14,964	9.84
Bahamian	607	0.40
Barbadian	84	0.06
Belizean	8	0.01
British West Indian	209	0.14
Dutch West Indian	12	0.01
Haitian	10,869	7.14
Jamaican	2,726	1.79
Trinidadian and Tobagonian	233	0.15
U.S. Virgin Islander	55	0.04
West Indian	124	0.08
Other West Indian	37	0.02
White:	99,898	65.55
Not Hispanic (87,577)	88,757	58.24
Hispanic (10,364)	11,141	7.31
Yugoslavian	109	0.07

Fort Myers

Place Type: City
County: Lee
Population: 48,208

Ancestry/Race	Number	%
African American/Black:	16,989	35.24
Not Hispanic (15,751)	16,533	34.30
Hispanic (344)	456	0.95
African, sub-Saharan:	462	0.96
African	427	0.89
Cape Verdean	11	0.02
Kenyan	8	0.02
Other sub-Saharan African	16	0.03
Alaska Native tribes, specified:	3	0.01
Eskimo (2)	2	0.00
Tlingit-Haida	1	0.00
Am. Ind. or Alaska Nat., not spec.	120	0.25
Albanian	16	0.03
American Indian tribes, specified:	220	0.46
Apache (7)	10	0.02
Blackfeet (4)	9	0.02
Cherokee (20)	55	0.11
Cheyenne (1)	1	0.00
Chippewa (2)	3	0.01
Choctaw (5)	6	0.01
Cree (1)	1	0.00
Creek (3)	7	0.01
Iroquois (4)	11	0.02
Latin American Indians (39)	76	0.16
Navajo (1)	1	0.00
Osage	3	0.01
Potawatomi (2)	2	0.00
Seminole (3)	5	0.01
Sioux (3)	4	0.01
Tohono O'Odham	1	0.00
Yakama	6	0.01
All other tribes (7)	19	0.04
American Indian tribes, not spec.	18	0.04
Arab:	233	0.48
Arab/Arabic	49	0.10
Egyptian	9	0.02
Lebanese	83	0.17

Notes: 1. Figures in the "Number" column do not add up to the total population due to: a) Ancestry/Race overlap — e.g. persons can report being both White and Irish, b) persons of Hispanic origin can report being any race, c) persons reporting two ancestries are counted in both categories. 2. Numbers in parentheses indicate the number of persons reporting this ancestry/race alone, not in combination with any other ancestry/race. 3. Refer to the Explanation of Data in the front of the book for more detailed information.

Moroccan	16	0.03
Syrian	47	0.10
Other Arab	29	0.06
Armenian	10	0.02
Asian:	642	1.33
Bangladeshi (10)	11	0.02
Chinese, ex. Taiwanese (72)	92	0.19
Filipino (60)	91	0.19
Indian (197)	234	0.49
Indonesian (6)	8	0.02
Japanese (11)	22	0.05
Korean (31)	44	0.09
Laotian (9)	22	0.05
Pakistani (7)	11	0.02
Sri Lankan (10)	10	0.02
Taiwanese	1	0.00
Thai (7)	23	0.05
Vietnamese (27)	32	0.07
Other Asian, specified	9	0.02
Other Asian, not specified (18)	32	0.07
Austrian	82	0.17
Belgian	46	0.10
Brazilian	142	0.30
British	217	0.45
Canadian	105	0.22
Croatian	6	0.01
Czech	130	0.27
Czechoslovakian	31	0.06
Danish	62	0.13
Dutch	521	1.08
Eastern European	15	0.03
English	3,823	7.96
Estonian	11	0.02
European	244	0.51
Finnish	85	0.18
French, except Basque	1,064	2.21
French Canadian	235	0.49
German	5,138	10.69
Greek	222	0.46
Guyanese	72	0.15
Hawaii Native/Pacific Islander:	109	0.23
Micronesian: (35)	47	0.10
Guamanian/Chamorro (33)	43	0.09
Other Micronesian (2)	4	0.01
Polynesian: (6)	27	0.06
Native Hawaiian (3)	18	0.04
Samoan (3)	7	0.01
Tongan	1	0.00
Other Polynesian	1	0.00
Other Pac. Isl., specified	9	0.02
Other Pac. Isl., not spec. (7)	26	0.05
Hispanic or Latino:	6,984	14.49
Central American:	670	1.39
Costa Rican	28	0.06
Guatemalan	475	0.99
Honduran	92	0.19
Nicaraguan	20	0.04
Panamanian	21	0.04
Salvadoran	23	0.05
Other Central American	11	0.02
Cuban	261	0.54
Dominican Republic	79	0.16
Mexican	2,588	5.37
Puerto Rican	2,258	4.68
South American:	272	0.56
Argentinean	23	0.05
Bolivian	4	0.01
Chilean	9	0.02
Colombian	117	0.24
Ecuadorian	34	0.07
Paraguayan	2	0.00
Peruvian	28	0.06
Uruguayan	1	0.00
Venezuelan	39	0.08
Other South American	15	0.03
Other Hispanic or Latino	856	1.78
Hungarian	288	0.60
Icelander	10	0.02
Irish	3,718	7.74
Israeli	15	0.03
Italian	1,779	3.70
Latvian	15	0.03
Lithuanian	71	0.15
Macedonian	6	0.01
Northern European	15	0.03
Norwegian	416	0.87
Pennsylvania German	12	0.02
Polish	793	1.65
Portuguese	164	0.34
Romanian	19	0.04
Russian	205	0.43
Scandinavian	34	0.07
Scotch-Irish	533	1.11
Scottish	567	1.18
Serbian	9	0.02
Slavic	11	0.02
Slovak	73	0.15
Swedish	284	0.59
Swiss	68	0.14
Ukrainian	65	0.14
United States or American	3,068	6.39
Welsh	290	0.60
West Indian, excl. Hispanic:	2,509	5.22
Bahamian	14	0.03
Belizean	50	0.10
British West Indian	32	0.07
Haitian	2,202	4.58
Jamaican	150	0.31
Trinidadian and Tobagonian	39	0.08
West Indian	22	0.05
White:	27,877	57.83
Not Hispanic (23,700)	24,111	50.01
Hispanic (3,466)	3,766	7.81
Yugoslavian	32	0.07

Fort Pierce

Place Type: City
County: Saint Lucie
Population: 37,516

Ancestry/Race	Number	%
African American/Black:	16,042	42.76
Not Hispanic (15,109)	15,781	42.06
Hispanic (217)	261	0.70
African, sub-Saharan:	583	1.56
African	542	1.45
Nigerian	30	0.08
South African	11	0.03
Alaska Native tribes, specified:	3	0.01
Alaska Athabascan	1	0.00
Tlingit-Haida	2	0.01
Alaska Native tribes, not specified	1	0.00
Am. Ind. or Alaska Nat., not spec.	130	0.35
American Indian tribes, specified:	108	0.29
Blackfeet (1)	6	0.02
Cherokee (18)	40	0.11
Chippewa (1)	2	0.01
Choctaw (1)	2	0.01
Cree	2	0.01
Creek (3)	3	0.01
Crow (4)	5	0.01
Iroquois (1)	2	0.01
Latin American Indians (23)	23	0.06
Lumbee (1)	1	0.00
Navajo (2)	2	0.01
Pueblo	1	0.00
Seminole (3)	5	0.01
Shoshone	1	0.00
Sioux	1	0.00
Tohono O'Odham	2	0.01
All other tribes (3)	10	0.03
American Indian tribes, not spec.	7	0.02
Arab:	53	0.14
Lebanese	22	0.06
Palestinian	8	0.02
Syrian	8	0.02
Other Arab	15	0.04
Armenian	9	0.02
Asian:	394	1.05
Bangladeshi (7)	11	0.03
Cambodian (1)	2	0.01
Chinese, ex. Taiwanese (25)	31	0.08
Filipino (27)	40	0.11
Indian (121)	140	0.37
Indonesian (3)	3	0.01
Japanese (10)	13	0.03
Korean (31)	40	0.11
Pakistani (10)	11	0.03
Taiwanese (4)	4	0.01
Thai (1)	1	0.00
Vietnamese (37)	45	0.12
Other Asian, specified	2	0.01
Other Asian, not specified (18)	51	0.14
Austrian	6	0.02
Belgian	146	0.39
British	90	0.24
Canadian	86	0.23
Croatian	8	0.02
Czech	105	0.28
Czechoslovakian	29	0.08
Danish	38	0.10
Dutch	344	0.92
Eastern European	11	0.03
English	2,597	6.93
Estonian	11	0.03
European	70	0.19
Finnish	52	0.14
French, except Basque	510	1.36
French Canadian	208	0.55
German	2,971	7.92
Greek	112	0.30
Hawaii Native/Pacific Islander:	61	0.16
Melanesian:	1	0.00
Fijian	1	0.00
Micronesian: (6)	9	0.02
Guamanian/Chamorro (6)	9	0.02
Polynesian: (17)	23	0.06
Native Hawaiian (13)	15	0.04
Samoan (4)	8	0.02
Other Pac. Isl., specified	2	0.01
Other Pac. Isl., not spec. (7)	26	0.07
Hispanic or Latino:	5,629	15.00
Central American:	209	0.56
Costa Rican	3	0.01
Guatemalan	95	0.25
Honduran	70	0.19
Nicaraguan	8	0.02
Panamanian	4	0.01
Salvadoran	28	0.07
Other Central American	1	0.00
Cuban	130	0.35
Dominican Republic	21	0.06
Mexican	4,311	11.49
Puerto Rican	366	0.98
South American:	75	0.20
Argentinean	6	0.02
Bolivian	1	0.00
Chilean	2	0.01
Colombian	33	0.09
Ecuadorian	14	0.04
Paraguayan	1	0.00
Peruvian	8	0.02
Venezuelan	8	0.02
Other South American	2	0.01
Other Hispanic or Latino	517	1.38
Hungarian	130	0.35
Irish	3,084	8.23
Italian	1,171	3.12
Lithuanian	40	0.11
Macedonian	6	0.02
New Zealander	6	0.02
Norwegian	168	0.45
Polish	501	1.34
Portuguese	78	0.21
Romanian	5	0.01
Russian	147	0.39
Scandinavian	21	0.06
Scotch-Irish	381	1.02
Scottish	389	1.04

Notes: 1. Figures in the "Number" column do not add up to the total population due to: a) Ancestry/Race overlap — e.g. persons can report being both White and Irish, b) persons of Hispanic origin can report being any race, c) persons reporting two ancestries are counted in both categories. 2. Numbers in parentheses indicate the number of persons reporting this ancestry/race alone, not in combination with any other ancestry/race. 3. Refer to the Explanation of Data in the front of the book for more detailed information.

Slovak	29	0.08
Slovene	8	0.02
Swedish	184	0.49
Swiss	7	0.02
Ukrainian	24	0.06
United States or American	2,478	6.61
Welsh	213	0.57
West Indian, excl. Hispanic:	2,816	7.51
Bahamian	94	0.25
Barbadian	61	0.16
Belizean	9	0.02
Haitian	2,303	6.14
Jamaican	281	0.75
West Indian	68	0.18
White:	19,113	50.95
Not Hispanic (15,516)	15,732	41.93
Hispanic (3,069)	3,381	9.01
Yugoslavian	7	0.02

Fort Walton Beach

Place Type: City
County: Okaloosa
Population: 19,973

Ancestry/Race	Number	%
African American/Black:	2,861	14.32
Not Hispanic (2,641)	2,821	14.12
Hispanic (23)	40	0.20
African, sub-Saharan:	10	0.05
African	6	0.03
Nigerian	4	0.02
Alaska Native tribes, specified:	3	0.02
Eskimo (3)	3	0.02
Am. Ind. or Alaska Nat., not spec.	78	0.39
American Indian tribes, specified:	165	0.83
Apache	2	0.01
Blackfeet (2)	13	0.07
Cherokee (19)	73	0.37
Chickasaw (1)	1	0.01
Chippewa	3	0.02
Choctaw (4)	10	0.05
Creek (15)	31	0.16
Iroquois (2)	6	0.03
Latin American Indians (2)	2	0.01
Lumbee (4)	5	0.03
Navajo (2)	3	0.02
Osage	1	0.01
Potawatomi (1)	1	0.01
Seminole	1	0.01
Sioux (2)	2	0.01
Tohono O'Odham (1)	1	0.01
All other tribes (5)	10	0.05
American Indian tribes, not spec.	30	0.15
Arab:	20	0.10
Arab/Arabic	5	0.02
Lebanese	10	0.05
Other Arab	5	0.02
Armenian	13	0.06
Asian:	843	4.22
Cambodian (2)	6	0.03
Chinese, ex. Taiwanese (35)	54	0.27
Filipino (182)	302	1.51
Indian (29)	39	0.20
Japanese (43)	92	0.46
Korean (70)	99	0.50
Laotian (7)	7	0.04
Malaysian	1	0.01
Pakistani (1)	1	0.01
Taiwanese (3)	6	0.03
Thai (89)	133	0.67
Vietnamese (59)	65	0.33
Other Asian, specified	9	0.05
Other Asian, not specified (12)	29	0.15
Australian	9	0.04
Austrian	17	0.08
British	153	0.75
Canadian	65	0.32
Croatian	33	0.16
Czech	43	0.21
Czechoslovakian	6	0.03
Danish	102	0.50
Dutch	232	1.14
English	2,495	12.30
European	167	0.82
Finnish	36	0.18
French, except Basque	606	2.99
French Canadian	225	1.11
German	2,829	13.94
Greek	51	0.25
Hawaii Native/Pacific Islander:	68	0.34
Micronesian: (3)	6	0.03
Guamanian/Chamorro (2)	5	0.03
Other Micronesian (1)	1	0.01
Polynesian: (8)	21	0.11
Native Hawaiian (5)	17	0.09
Samoan (3)	3	0.02
Other Polynesian	1	0.01
Other Pac. Isl., specified	6	0.03
Other Pac. Isl., not spec. (5)	35	0.18
Hispanic or Latino:	807	4.04
Central American:	41	0.21
Costa Rican	2	0.01
Guatemalan	4	0.02
Honduran	7	0.04
Nicaraguan	1	0.01
Panamanian	25	0.13
Salvadoran	2	0.01
Cuban	51	0.26
Dominican Republic	5	0.03
Mexican	269	1.35
Puerto Rican	232	1.16
South American:	44	0.22
Argentinean	1	0.01
Chilean	7	0.04
Colombian	15	0.08
Ecuadorian	2	0.01
Paraguayan	1	0.01
Peruvian	12	0.06
Venezuelan	6	0.03
Other Hispanic or Latino	165	0.83
Hungarian	84	0.41
Icelander	11	0.05
Irish	1,970	9.71
Israeli	9	0.04
Italian	542	2.67
Lithuanian	6	0.03
Northern European	8	0.04
Norwegian	246	1.21
Pennsylvania German	8	0.04
Polish	399	1.97
Portuguese	55	0.27
Russian	77	0.38
Scandinavian	17	0.08
Scotch-Irish	490	2.42
Scottish	490	2.42
Serbian	17	0.08
Slovak	45	0.22
Slovene	17	0.08
Swedish	236	1.16
Swiss	34	0.17
Ukrainian	15	0.07
United States or American	1,881	9.27
Welsh	174	0.86
West Indian, excl. Hispanic:	43	0.21
Haitian	4	0.02
Jamaican	39	0.19
White:	16,300	81.61
Not Hispanic (15,274)	15,757	78.89
Hispanic (472)	543	2.72

Fountainbleau

Place Type: Census Designated Place
County: Miami-Dade
Population: 59,549

Ancestry/Race	Number	%
African American/Black:	1,444	2.42
Not Hispanic (611)	662	1.11
Hispanic (603)	782	1.31
African, sub-Saharan:	107	0.18
African	5	0.01
Ethiopian	7	0.01
Nigerian	95	0.16
Am. Ind. or Alaska Nat., not spec.	98	0.16
American Indian tribes, specified:	112	0.19
Cherokee (3)	10	0.02
Chippewa	1	0.00
Choctaw	1	0.00
Iroquois	4	0.01
Latin American Indians (38)	86	0.14
Pueblo	3	0.01
All other tribes (1)	7	0.01
American Indian tribes, not spec.	7	0.01
Arab:	412	0.69
Arab/Arabic	62	0.10
Egyptian	9	0.02
Lebanese	170	0.29
Palestinian	98	0.16
Syrian	73	0.12
Asian:	1,238	2.08
Bangladeshi (7)	7	0.01
Chinese, ex. Taiwanese (314)	382	0.64
Filipino (68)	87	0.15
Indian (448)	481	0.81
Indonesian	1	0.00
Japanese (36)	50	0.08
Korean (51)	54	0.09
Pakistani (48)	54	0.09
Taiwanese (9)	12	0.02
Thai (7)	7	0.01
Vietnamese (37)	38	0.06
Other Asian, specified (8)	9	0.02
Other Asian, not specified (20)	56	0.09
Austrian	14	0.02
Basque	12	0.02
Belgian	12	0.02
Brazilian	286	0.48
British	11	0.02
Canadian	42	0.07
Czech	7	0.01
Czechoslovakian	25	0.04
Danish	22	0.04
Dutch	100	0.17
Eastern European	10	0.02
English	222	0.37
European	126	0.21
Finnish	19	0.03
French, except Basque	293	0.49
French Canadian	9	0.02
German	487	0.82
Greek	93	0.16
Guyanese	11	0.02
Hawaii Native/Pacific Islander:	44	0.07
Melanesian:	1	0.00
Other Melanesian	1	0.00
Micronesian: (11)	13	0.02
Guamanian/Chamorro (11)	13	0.02
Polynesian: (5)	10	0.02
Native Hawaiian (1)	3	0.01
Samoan (4)	4	0.01
Other Polynesian	3	0.01
Other Pac. Isl., not spec. (1)	20	0.03
Hispanic or Latino:	51,948	87.24
Central American:	7,342	12.33
Costa Rican	153	0.26
Guatemalan	235	0.39
Honduran	650	1.09
Nicaraguan	5,624	9.44
Panamanian	293	0.49
Salvadoran	244	0.41
Other Central American	143	0.24
Cuban	22,206	37.29
Dominican Republic	1,779	2.99
Mexican	544	0.91
Puerto Rican	2,015	3.38
South American:	8,100	13.60
Argentinean	518	0.87
Bolivian	153	0.26

Notes: 1. Figures in the "Number" column do not add up to the total population due to: a) Ancestry/Race overlap — e.g. persons can report being both White and Irish, b) persons of Hispanic origin can report being any race, c) persons reporting two ancestries are counted in both categories. 2. Numbers in parentheses indicate the number of persons reporting this ancestry/race alone, not in combination with any other ancestry/race. 3. Refer to the Explanation of Data in the front of the book for more detailed information.

Chilean	550	0.92
Colombian	3,153	5.29
Ecuadorian	564	0.95
Paraguayan	23	0.04
Peruvian	1,044	1.75
Uruguayan	71	0.12
Venezuelan	1,868	3.14
Other South American	156	0.26
Other Hispanic or Latino	9,962	16.73
Hungarian	22	0.04
Iranian	11	0.02
Irish	327	0.55
Italian	992	1.67
Lithuanian	7	0.01
Norwegian	25	0.04
Polish	88	0.15
Portuguese	94	0.16
Russian	85	0.14
Scandinavian	11	0.02
Scotch-Irish	25	0.04
Scottish	54	0.09
Swedish	55	0.09
Swiss	10	0.02
Turkish	7	0.01
Ukrainian	10	0.02
United States or American	1,499	2.52
Welsh	28	0.05
West Indian, excl. Hispanic:	495	0.83
Bahamian	7	0.01
Barbadian	15	0.03
Belizean	33	0.06
British West Indian	32	0.05
Haitian	176	0.30
Jamaican	134	0.23
Trinidadian and Tobagonian	42	0.07
U.S. Virgin Islander	31	0.05
West Indian	25	0.04
White:	52,913	88.86
Not Hispanic (5,618)	5,802	9.74
Hispanic (45,114)	47,111	79.11

Fruit Cove

Place Type: Census Designated Place
County: Saint Johns
Population: 16,077

Ancestry/Race	Number	%
African American/Black:	359	2.23
Not Hispanic (326)	348	2.16
Hispanic (5)	11	0.07
Am. Ind. or Alaska Nat., not spec.	30	0.19
American Indian tribes, specified:	43	0.27
Apache	1	0.01
Blackfeet (2)	3	0.02
Cherokee (6)	16	0.10
Chippewa	1	0.01
Choctaw (1)	1	0.01
Comanche	2	0.01
Creek (2)	3	0.02
Crow	2	0.01
Iroquois (2)	6	0.04
Kiowa	2	0.01
Lumbee (1)	1	0.01
Navajo	1	0.01
Osage (1)	1	0.01
All other tribes (3)	3	0.02
American Indian tribes, not spec.	2	0.01
Armenian	24	0.15
Asian:	310	1.93
Cambodian (4)	4	0.02
Chinese, ex. Taiwanese (57)	65	0.40
Filipino (98)	114	0.71
Indian (42)	48	0.30
Japanese (14)	25	0.16
Korean (24)	32	0.20
Pakistani (4)	4	0.02
Thai (3)	3	0.02
Vietnamese (5)	5	0.03
Other Asian, specified (4)	4	0.02
Other Asian, not specified (3)	6	0.04
Austrian	34	0.21
Belgian	12	0.07
Brazilian	7	0.04
British	156	0.97
Canadian	20	0.12
Celtic	16	0.10
Croatian	16	0.10
Czech	72	0.45
Czechoslovakian	96	0.60
Danish	90	0.56
Dutch	402	2.50
Eastern European	17	0.11
English	2,367	14.75
European	202	1.26
Finnish	39	0.24
French, except Basque	653	4.07
French Canadian	130	0.81
German	3,040	18.94
Greek	92	0.57
Hawaii Native/Pacific Islander:	22	0.14
Micronesian: (15)	15	0.09
Guamanian/Chamorro (15)	15	0.09
Polynesian: (5)	5	0.03
Samoan (5)	5	0.03
Other Pac. Isl., not spec. (2)	2	0.01
Hispanic or Latino:	382	2.38
Central American:	11	0.07
Guatemalan	1	0.01
Honduran	2	0.01
Nicaraguan	3	0.02
Panamanian	4	0.02
Salvadoran	1	0.01
Cuban	36	0.22
Dominican Republic	14	0.09
Mexican	66	0.41
Puerto Rican	121	0.75
South American:	42	0.26
Argentinean	4	0.02
Bolivian	2	0.01
Chilean	7	0.04
Colombian	14	0.09
Ecuadorian	5	0.03
Peruvian	8	0.05
Uruguayan	1	0.01
Venezuelan	1	0.01
Other Hispanic or Latino	92	0.57
Hungarian	140	0.87
Irish	2,671	16.64
Israeli	7	0.04
Italian	1,269	7.91
Latvian	20	0.12
Lithuanian	53	0.33
Maltese	7	0.04
Northern European	10	0.06
Norwegian	186	1.16
Pennsylvania German	4	0.02
Polish	534	3.33
Portuguese	71	0.44
Romanian	9	0.06
Russian	126	0.78
Scotch-Irish	374	2.33
Scottish	399	2.49
Slavic	38	0.24
Slovak	54	0.34
Swedish	189	1.18
Swiss	20	0.12
Ukrainian	98	0.61
United States or American	1,672	10.42
Welsh	166	1.03
West Indian, excl. Hispanic:	52	0.32
Haitian	8	0.05
Jamaican	35	0.22
West Indian	9	0.06
White:	15,350	95.48
Not Hispanic (14,943)	15,047	93.59
Hispanic (292)	303	1.88

Fruitville

Place Type: Census Designated Place
County: Sarasota
Population: 12,741

Ancestry/Race	Number	%
African American/Black:	193	1.51
Not Hispanic (162)	182	1.43
Hispanic (5)	11	0.09
African, sub-Saharan:	38	0.29
African	18	0.14
Nigerian	20	0.16
Am. Ind. or Alaska Nat., not spec.	18	0.14
Albanian	40	0.31
American Indian tribes, specified:	34	0.27
Apache (1)	1	0.01
Blackfeet	2	0.02
Cherokee (1)	6	0.05
Chippewa (1)	1	0.01
Comanche	1	0.01
Creek	5	0.04
Delaware (1)	2	0.02
Iroquois (2)	2	0.02
Latin American Indians (1)	2	0.02
Navajo	1	0.01
Potawatomi (1)	2	0.02
Sioux	2	0.02
All other tribes (3)	7	0.05
American Indian tribes, not spec.	2	0.02
Arab:	123	0.95
Arab/Arabic	36	0.28
Lebanese	26	0.20
Palestinian	52	0.40
Other Arab	9	0.07
Asian:	179	1.40
Chinese, ex. Taiwanese (39)	41	0.32
Filipino (30)	41	0.32
Indian (28)	33	0.26
Japanese (10)	13	0.10
Korean (14)	15	0.12
Taiwanese (4)	4	0.03
Thai (2)	2	0.02
Vietnamese (18)	24	0.19
Other Asian, not specified (4)	6	0.05
Australian	9	0.07
Austrian	73	0.57
Belgian	14	0.11
Brazilian	15	0.12
British	72	0.56
Bulgarian	8	0.06
Canadian	61	0.47
Croatian	27	0.21
Czech	84	0.65
Czechoslovakian	40	0.31
Danish	39	0.30
Dutch	275	2.13
Eastern European	18	0.14
English	1,709	13.26
European	51	0.40
Finnish	37	0.29
French, except Basque	422	3.27
French Canadian	134	1.04
German	3,000	23.27
Greek	38	0.29
Guyanese	25	0.19
Hawaii Native/Pacific Islander:	2	0.02
Polynesian: (1)	1	0.01
Samoan (1)	1	0.01
Other Pac. Isl., not spec.	1	0.01
Hispanic or Latino:	519	4.07
Central American:	24	0.19
Honduran	6	0.05
Nicaraguan	3	0.02
Panamanian	5	0.04
Salvadoran	8	0.06
Other Central American	2	0.02
Cuban	89	0.70
Dominican Republic	5	0.04
Mexican	145	1.14

Notes: 1. Figures in the "Number" column do not add up to the total population due to: a) Ancestry/Race overlap — e.g. persons can report being both White and Irish, b) persons of Hispanic origin can report being any race, c) persons reporting two ancestries are counted in both categories. 2. Numbers in parentheses indicate the number of persons reporting this ancestry/race alone, not in combination with any other ancestry/race. 3. Refer to the Explanation of Data in the front of the book for more detailed information.

Ancestry/Race	Number	%
Puerto Rican	117	0.92
South American:	66	0.52
Argentinean	7	0.05
Chilean	2	0.02
Colombian	25	0.20
Peruvian	8	0.06
Venezuelan	17	0.13
Other South American	7	0.05
Other Hispanic or Latino	73	0.57
Hungarian	140	1.09
Irish	1,937	15.02
Italian	1,242	9.63
Lithuanian	34	0.26
Northern European	9	0.07
Norwegian	126	0.98
Polish	510	3.96
Portuguese	28	0.22
Romanian	20	0.16
Russian	196	1.52
Scotch-Irish	334	2.59
Scottish	394	3.06
Slovak	48	0.37
Slovene	8	0.06
Swedish	263	2.04
Swiss	108	0.84
Ukrainian	42	0.33
United States or American	1,149	8.91
Welsh	81	0.63
West Indian, excl. Hispanic:	40	0.31
Haitian	18	0.14
West Indian	22	0.17
White:	12,289	96.45
Not Hispanic (11,804)	11,882	93.26
Hispanic (381)	407	3.19
Yugoslavian	20	0.16

Gainesville

Place Type: City
County: Alachua
Population: 95,447

Ancestry/Race	Number	%
Acadian/Cajun	37	0.04
African American/Black:	22,929	24.02
Not Hispanic (21,931)	22,594	23.67
Hispanic (250)	335	0.35
African, sub-Saharan:	1,630	1.70
African	1,249	1.31
Ethiopian	135	0.14
Ghanian	7	0.01
Kenyan	30	0.03
Nigerian	74	0.08
South African	81	0.08
Zimbabwean	33	0.03
Other sub-Saharan African	21	0.02
Alaska Native tribes, specified:	3	0.00
Aleut (1)	1	0.00
Eskimo (1)	2	0.00
Alaska Native tribes, not specified	1	0.00
Am. Ind. or Alaska Nat., not spec.	197	0.21
Albanian	36	0.04
Alsatian	38	0.04
American Indian tribes, specified:	424	0.44
Apache (1)	9	0.01
Blackfeet (5)	24	0.03
Cherokee (43)	184	0.19
Chickasaw (3)	3	0.00
Chippewa (4)	5	0.01
Choctaw (5)	23	0.02
Comanche	1	0.00
Cree	2	0.00
Creek (10)	21	0.02
Delaware	4	0.00
Houma (5)	5	0.01
Iroquois (7)	20	0.02
Latin American Indians (14)	35	0.04
Lumbee (2)	3	0.00
Menominee	1	0.00
Navajo (5)	10	0.01
Osage	3	0.00
Ottawa (1)	1	0.00
Potawatomi	1	0.00
Pueblo (3)	9	0.01
Seminole (11)	21	0.02
Shoshone (1)	1	0.00
Sioux (4)	9	0.01
Yaqui (3)	3	0.00
All other tribes (10)	26	0.03
American Indian tribes, not spec.	65	0.07
Arab:	551	0.58
Arab/Arabic	95	0.10
Egyptian	53	0.06
Lebanese	188	0.20
Moroccan	13	0.01
Palestinian	48	0.05
Syrian	79	0.08
Other Arab	75	0.08
Armenian	58	0.06
Asian:	4,976	5.21
Bangladeshi (16)	16	0.02
Cambodian (22)	32	0.03
Chinese, ex. Taiwanese (1,303)	1,411	1.48
Filipino (377)	499	0.52
Indian (1,074)	1,185	1.24
Indonesian (16)	24	0.03
Japanese (203)	293	0.31
Korean (511)	564	0.59
Laotian (8)	10	0.01
Malaysian (14)	21	0.02
Pakistani (47)	58	0.06
Sri Lankan (10)	16	0.02
Taiwanese (69)	87	0.09
Thai (95)	121	0.13
Vietnamese (413)	449	0.47
Other Asian, specified (7)	23	0.02
Other Asian, not specified (60)	167	0.17
Australian	55	0.06
Austrian	271	0.28
Basque	11	0.01
Belgian	107	0.11
Brazilian	172	0.18
British	759	0.79
Bulgarian	80	0.08
Canadian	201	0.21
Celtic	86	0.09
Croatian	43	0.04
Czech	336	0.35
Czechoslovakian	139	0.15
Danish	257	0.27
Dutch	1,228	1.28
Eastern European	161	0.17
English	9,421	9.85
Estonian	13	0.01
European	1,024	1.07
Finnish	191	0.20
French, except Basque	2,862	2.99
French Canadian	821	0.86
German	12,020	12.57
German Russian	5	0.01
Greek	475	0.50
Guyanese	13	0.01
Hawaii Native/Pacific Islander:	128	0.13
Micronesian: (6)	7	0.01
Guamanian/Chamorro (6)	7	0.01
Polynesian: (21)	60	0.06
Native Hawaiian (10)	30	0.03
Samoan (11)	28	0.03
Tongan	2	0.00
Other Pac. Isl., specified	16	0.02
Other Pac. Isl., not spec. (3)	45	0.05
Hispanic or Latino:	6,112	6.40
Central American:	434	0.45
Costa Rican	56	0.06
Guatemalan	41	0.04
Honduran	57	0.06
Nicaraguan	143	0.15
Panamanian	81	0.08
Salvadoran	35	0.04
Other Central American	21	0.02
Cuban	1,278	1.34
Dominican Republic	138	0.14
Mexican	511	0.54
Puerto Rican	1,596	1.67
South American:	1,081	1.13
Argentinean	96	0.10
Bolivian	40	0.04
Chilean	94	0.10
Colombian	342	0.36
Ecuadorian	53	0.06
Paraguayan	4	0.00
Peruvian	153	0.16
Uruguayan	16	0.02
Venezuelan	244	0.26
Other South American	39	0.04
Other Hispanic or Latino	1,074	1.13
Hungarian	380	0.40
Icelander	13	0.01
Iranian	216	0.23
Irish	10,195	10.66
Israeli	75	0.08
Italian	4,654	4.87
Latvian	16	0.02
Lithuanian	211	0.22
Luxemburger	14	0.01
Macedonian	7	0.01
Maltese	14	0.01
New Zealander	7	0.01
Northern European	137	0.14
Norwegian	755	0.79
Polish	2,499	2.61
Portuguese	211	0.22
Romanian	184	0.19
Russian	1,458	1.53
Scandinavian	47	0.05
Scotch-Irish	2,223	2.33
Scottish	2,298	2.40
Serbian	41	0.04
Slavic	59	0.06
Slovak	97	0.10
Slovene	46	0.05
Swedish	1,241	1.30
Swiss	267	0.28
Turkish	163	0.17
Ukrainian	284	0.30
United States or American	5,380	5.63
Welsh	636	0.67
West Indian, excl. Hispanic:	1,025	1.07
Bahamian	61	0.06
Barbadian	8	0.01
Belizean	20	0.02
Bermudan	19	0.02
British West Indian	39	0.04
Dutch West Indian	10	0.01
Haitian	231	0.24
Jamaican	418	0.44
Trinidadian and Tobagonian	110	0.12
West Indian	100	0.10
Other West Indian	9	0.01
White:	66,916	70.11
Not Hispanic (61,156)	62,425	65.40
Hispanic (4,087)	4,491	4.71
Yugoslavian	63	0.07

Gladeview

Place Type: Census Designated Place
County: Miami-Dade
Population: 14,468

Ancestry/Race	Number	%
African American/Black:	11,323	78.26
Not Hispanic (10,967)	11,085	76.62
Hispanic (171)	238	1.65
African, sub-Saharan:	181	1.25
African	151	1.04
Nigerian	30	0.21
Am. Ind. or Alaska Nat., not spec.	38	0.26
American Indian tribes, specified:	14	0.10
Cherokee	2	0.01

Notes: 1. Figures in the "Number" column do not add up to the total population due to: a) Ancestry/Race overlap — e.g. persons can report being both White and Irish, b) persons of Hispanic origin can report being any race, c) persons reporting two ancestries are counted in both categories. 2. Numbers in parentheses indicate the number of persons reporting this ancestry/race alone, not in combination with any other ancestry/race. 3. Refer to the Explanation of Data in the front of the book for more detailed information.

Ancestry/Race	Number	%
Latin American Indians (6)	9	0.06
Pueblo	1	0.01
Seminole	1	0.01
All other tribes (1)	1	0.01
American Indian tribes, not spec.	3	0.02
Arab:	14	0.10
Lebanese	14	0.10
Asian:	51	0.35
Chinese, ex. Taiwanese (1)	4	0.03
Filipino (1)	2	0.01
Indian (17)	23	0.16
Other Asian, specified	2	0.01
Other Asian, not specified (5)	20	0.14
British	49	0.34
Dutch	7	0.05
English	63	0.44
French, except Basque	24	0.17
German	35	0.24
Hawaii Native/Pacific Islander:	35	0.24
Polynesian: (2)	5	0.03
Native Hawaiian (2)	2	0.01
Samoan	3	0.02
Other Pac. Isl., specified	2	0.01
Other Pac. Isl., not spec. (2)	28	0.19
Hispanic or Latino:	3,084	21.32
Central American:	876	6.05
Costa Rican	5	0.03
Guatemalan	48	0.33
Honduran	223	1.54
Nicaraguan	536	3.70
Panamanian	2	0.01
Salvadoran	15	0.10
Other Central American	47	0.32
Cuban	1,003	6.93
Dominican Republic	129	0.89
Mexican	113	0.78
Puerto Rican	197	1.36
South American:	52	0.36
Colombian	25	0.17
Ecuadorian	7	0.05
Peruvian	12	0.08
Venezuelan	6	0.04
Other South American	2	0.01
Other Hispanic or Latino	714	4.94
Hungarian	19	0.13
Irish	35	0.24
Italian	13	0.09
Polish	47	0.32
Russian	17	0.12
Scandinavian	22	0.15
Scottish	14	0.10
United States or American	318	2.20
West Indian, excl. Hispanic:	504	3.48
Bahamian	138	0.95
Haitian	221	1.53
Jamaican	74	0.51
Trinidadian and Tobagonian	60	0.41
West Indian	11	0.08
White:	2,759	19.07
Not Hispanic (256)	281	1.94
Hispanic (2,289)	2,478	17.13

Glenvar Heights

Place Type: Census Designated Place
County: Miami-Dade
Population: 16,243

Ancestry/Race	Number	%
African American/Black:	575	3.54
Not Hispanic (405)	472	2.91
Hispanic (83)	103	0.63
African, sub-Saharan:	28	0.17
African	20	0.12
South African	8	0.05
Am. Ind. or Alaska Nat., not spec.	23	0.14
American Indian tribes, specified:	34	0.21
Apache	6	0.04
Cherokee	9	0.06
Chickasaw	1	0.01
Chippewa	1	0.01
Creek (1)	1	0.01
Latin American Indians (9)	11	0.07
Sioux	2	0.01
All other tribes (1)	3	0.02
American Indian tribes, not spec.	10	0.06
Arab:	221	1.37
Arab/Arabic	51	0.32
Jordanian	10	0.06
Lebanese	100	0.62
Syrian	9	0.06
Other Arab	51	0.32
Asian:	575	3.54
Bangladeshi (3)	3	0.02
Chinese, ex. Taiwanese (184)	210	1.29
Filipino (43)	52	0.32
Indian (133)	160	0.99
Indonesian	1	0.01
Japanese (14)	19	0.12
Korean (11)	13	0.08
Laotian (2)	2	0.01
Malaysian (2)	2	0.01
Pakistani (25)	37	0.23
Sri Lankan (7)	7	0.04
Taiwanese	3	0.02
Thai (20)	22	0.14
Vietnamese (18)	19	0.12
Other Asian, not specified (1)	25	0.15
Assyrian/Chaldean/Syriac	2	0.01
Australian	11	0.07
Austrian	14	0.09
Basque	31	0.19
Belgian	33	0.20
Brazilian	100	0.62
British	79	0.49
Canadian	43	0.27
Croatian	34	0.21
Czech	17	0.11
Danish	23	0.14
Dutch	80	0.50
Eastern European	41	0.25
English	885	5.49
European	125	0.78
Finnish	26	0.16
French, except Basque	309	1.92
French Canadian	41	0.25
German	1,008	6.26
Greek	112	0.70
Guyanese	9	0.06
Hawaii Native/Pacific Islander:	19	0.12
Melanesian: (1)	1	0.01
Fijian (1)	1	0.01
Micronesian: (4)	5	0.03
Guamanian/Chamorro (4)	5	0.03
Polynesian: (2)	2	0.01
Native Hawaiian (2)	2	0.01
Other Pac. Isl., not spec. (2)	11	0.07
Hispanic or Latino:	9,008	55.46
Central American:	569	3.50
Costa Rican	52	0.32
Guatemalan	25	0.15
Honduran	102	0.63
Nicaraguan	274	1.69
Panamanian	46	0.28
Salvadoran	57	0.35
Other Central American	13	0.08
Cuban	4,693	28.89
Dominican Republic	160	0.99
Mexican	150	0.92
Puerto Rican	528	3.25
South American:	1,567	9.65
Argentinean	81	0.50
Bolivian	30	0.18
Chilean	116	0.71
Colombian	563	3.47
Ecuadorian	96	0.59
Paraguayan	4	0.02
Peruvian	292	1.80
Uruguayan	24	0.15
Venezuelan	332	2.04
Other South American	29	0.18
Other Hispanic or Latino	1,341	8.26
Hungarian	126	0.78
Iranian	28	0.17
Irish	763	4.73
Italian	673	4.18
Lithuanian	41	0.25
Macedonian	5	0.03
Norwegian	58	0.36
Pennsylvania German	11	0.07
Polish	218	1.35
Portuguese	50	0.31
Romanian	30	0.19
Russian	360	2.23
Scotch-Irish	114	0.71
Scottish	226	1.40
Serbian	8	0.05
Slavic	10	0.06
Slovak	14	0.09
Swedish	89	0.55
Swiss	58	0.36
Ukrainian	21	0.13
United States or American	652	4.05
Welsh	41	0.25
West Indian, excl. Hispanic:	215	1.33
Bahamian	44	0.27
Belizean	8	0.05
British West Indian	34	0.21
Haitian	32	0.20
Jamaican	54	0.34
Trinidadian and Tobagonian	31	0.19
West Indian	12	0.07
White:	14,613	89.96
Not Hispanic (6,162)	6,294	38.75
Hispanic (8,084)	8,319	51.22
Yugoslavian	8	0.05

Golden Gate

Place Type: Census Designated Place
County: Collier
Population: 20,951

Ancestry/Race	Number	%
Acadian/Cajun	13	0.06
African American/Black:	2,592	12.37
Not Hispanic (2,037)	2,445	11.67
Hispanic (89)	147	0.70
African, sub-Saharan:	62	0.30
African	54	0.26
Sierra Leonean	8	0.04
Am. Ind. or Alaska Nat., not spec.	31	0.15
American Indian tribes, specified:	88	0.42
Apache	2	0.01
Blackfeet	4	0.02
Cherokee (4)	10	0.05
Chippewa (3)	4	0.02
Creek (1)	2	0.01
Delaware	1	0.00
Iroquois	5	0.02
Latin American Indians (32)	44	0.21
Lumbee (1)	1	0.00
Menominee (1)	1	0.00
Seminole (4)	5	0.02
All other tribes (3)	9	0.04
American Indian tribes, not spec.	19	0.09
Arab:	41	0.20
Lebanese	41	0.20
Armenian	15	0.07
Asian:	198	0.95
Chinese, ex. Taiwanese (25)	30	0.14
Filipino (22)	38	0.18
Indian (50)	54	0.26
Indonesian	7	0.03
Japanese	2	0.01
Korean (7)	9	0.04
Thai (2)	2	0.01
Vietnamese (32)	36	0.17
Other Asian, specified (2)	3	0.01
Other Asian, not specified (8)	17	0.08

Notes: 1. Figures in the "Number" column do not add up to the total population due to: a) Ancestry/Race overlap — e.g. persons can report being both White and Irish, b) persons of Hispanic origin can report being any race, c) persons reporting two ancestries are counted in both categories. 2. Numbers in parentheses indicate the number of persons reporting this ancestry/race alone, not in combination with any other ancestry/race. 3. Refer to the Explanation of Data in the front of the book for more detailed information.

Brazilian	49	0.23
British	5	0.02
Canadian	57	0.27
Croatian	16	0.08
Czech	66	0.31
Czechoslovakian	13	0.06
Danish	115	0.55
Dutch	114	0.54
English	1,095	5.21
European	79	0.38
Finnish	5	0.02
French, except Basque	294	1.40
French Canadian	159	0.76
German	1,978	9.41
Greek	65	0.31
Guyanese	11	0.05
Hawaii Native/Pacific Islander:	46	0.22
Micronesian: (23)	31	0.15
Guamanian/Chamorro (23)	31	0.15
Polynesian: (1)	7	0.03
Native Hawaiian	6	0.03
Samoan (1)	1	0.00
Other Pac. Isl., not spec. (1)	8	0.04
Hispanic or Latino:	7,781	37.14
Central American:	428	2.04
Costa Rican	28	0.13
Guatemalan	102	0.49
Honduran	143	0.68
Nicaraguan	44	0.21
Panamanian	10	0.05
Salvadoran	83	0.40
Other Central American	18	0.09
Cuban	1,660	7.92
Dominican Republic	76	0.36
Mexican	3,529	16.84
Puerto Rican	765	3.65
South American:	500	2.39
Argentinean	22	0.11
Bolivian	20	0.10
Chilean	21	0.10
Colombian	240	1.15
Ecuadorian	47	0.22
Peruvian	98	0.47
Uruguayan	4	0.02
Venezuelan	32	0.15
Other South American	16	0.08
Other Hispanic or Latino	823	3.93
Hungarian	87	0.41
Irish	1,644	7.82
Italian	825	3.93
Lithuanian	40	0.19
Norwegian	66	0.31
Polish	407	1.94
Portuguese	54	0.26
Romanian	16	0.08
Russian	69	0.33
Scandinavian	7	0.03
Scotch-Irish	154	0.73
Scottish	240	1.14
Serbian	33	0.16
Slovak	10	0.05
Slovene	21	0.10
Swedish	137	0.65
Swiss	50	0.24
Ukrainian	8	0.04
United States or American	1,552	7.39
Welsh	81	0.39
West Indian, excl. Hispanic:	1,402	6.67
Bahamian	60	0.29
Haitian	1,228	5.84
Jamaican	100	0.48
Trinidadian and Tobagonian	8	0.04
West Indian	6	0.03
White:	16,607	79.27
Not Hispanic (10,402)	10,547	50.34
Hispanic (5,730)	6,060	28.92

Golden Glades

Place Type: Census Designated Place
County: Miami-Dade
Population: 32,623

Ancestry/Race	Number	%
African American/Black:	22,922	70.26
Not Hispanic (20,669)	22,079	67.68
Hispanic (630)	843	2.58
African, sub-Saharan:	400	1.24
African	267	0.83
Ghanian	7	0.02
Nigerian	118	0.37
Sierra Leonean	8	0.02
Alaska Native tribes, specified:	5	0.02
Tlingit-Haida (1)	5	0.02
Am. Ind. or Alaska Nat., not spec.	83	0.25
American Indian tribes, specified:	88	0.27
Cherokee (3)	25	0.08
Cree (1)	2	0.01
Creek (1)	1	0.00
Crow (1)	1	0.00
Latin American Indians (24)	39	0.12
Navajo (1)	1	0.00
Paiute	1	0.00
Pueblo (5)	6	0.02
Seminole	2	0.01
Shoshone (1)	1	0.00
Sioux	1	0.00
All other tribes (4)	8	0.02
American Indian tribes, not spec.	21	0.06
Arab:	25	0.08
Arab/Arabic	17	0.05
Lebanese	8	0.02
Asian:	761	2.33
Bangladeshi (12)	13	0.04
Cambodian (6)	6	0.02
Chinese, ex. Taiwanese (107)	126	0.39
Filipino (183)	199	0.61
Hmong	1	0.00
Indian (162)	256	0.78
Indonesian (5)	6	0.02
Japanese (3)	6	0.02
Korean (6)	6	0.02
Laotian (14)	16	0.05
Pakistani (26)	26	0.08
Sri Lankan (1)	4	0.01
Thai (9)	13	0.04
Vietnamese (34)	34	0.10
Other Asian, specified	1	0.00
Other Asian, not specified (12)	48	0.15
Austrian	45	0.14
Brazilian	20	0.06
British	87	0.27
Canadian	22	0.07
Croatian	8	0.02
Czech	7	0.02
Danish	10	0.03
Dutch	53	0.16
Eastern European	6	0.02
English	414	1.29
European	67	0.21
French, except Basque	199	0.62
French Canadian	63	0.20
German	621	1.93
Greek	54	0.17
Guyanese	96	0.30
Hawaii Native/Pacific Islander:	110	0.34
Micronesian: (5)	6	0.02
Guamanian/Chamorro (5)	6	0.02
Polynesian: (8)	11	0.03
Native Hawaiian (6)	7	0.02
Samoan (1)	3	0.01
Other Polynesian (1)	1	0.00
Other Pac. Isl., not spec. (11)	93	0.29
Hispanic or Latino:	5,753	17.63
Central American:	659	2.02
Costa Rican	32	0.10
Guatemalan	75	0.23
Honduran	199	0.61
Nicaraguan	219	0.67
Panamanian	66	0.20
Salvadoran	40	0.12
Other Central American	28	0.09
Cuban	1,317	4.04
Dominican Republic	560	1.72
Mexican	175	0.54
Puerto Rican	1,275	3.91
South American:	622	1.91
Argentinean	36	0.11
Bolivian	12	0.04
Chilean	15	0.05
Colombian	240	0.74
Ecuadorian	63	0.19
Paraguayan	2	0.01
Peruvian	189	0.58
Uruguayan	7	0.02
Venezuelan	48	0.15
Other South American	10	0.03
Other Hispanic or Latino	1,145	3.51
Hungarian	146	0.45
Iranian	7	0.02
Irish	474	1.47
Israeli	6	0.02
Italian	503	1.56
Lithuanian	15	0.05
Norwegian	20	0.06
Polish	208	0.65
Portuguese	45	0.14
Romanian	28	0.09
Russian	186	0.58
Scotch-Irish	42	0.13
Scottish	133	0.41
Swedish	45	0.14
Swiss	14	0.04
Ukrainian	44	0.14
United States or American	1,686	5.24
Welsh	7	0.02
West Indian, excl. Hispanic:	13,197	41.01
Bahamian	541	1.68
Barbadian	67	0.21
Belizean	25	0.08
Bermudan	8	0.02
British West Indian	197	0.61
Dutch West Indian	12	0.04
Haitian	10,284	31.95
Jamaican	1,739	5.40
Trinidadian and Tobagonian	119	0.37
U.S. Virgin Islander	33	0.10
West Indian	172	0.53
White:	8,169	25.04
Not Hispanic (3,948)	4,160	12.75
Hispanic (3,680)	4,009	12.29

Goldenrod

Place Type: Census Designated Place
County: Seminole
Population: 12,871

Ancestry/Race	Number	%
Acadian/Cajun	12	0.09
African American/Black:	859	6.67
Not Hispanic (648)	738	5.73
Hispanic (64)	121	0.94
African, sub-Saharan:	91	0.70
African	91	0.70
Am. Ind. or Alaska Nat., not spec.	28	0.22
American Indian tribes, specified:	98	0.76
Apache (1)	2	0.02
Blackfeet	3	0.02
Cherokee (19)	40	0.31
Chippewa (1)	2	0.02
Creek	2	0.02
Iroquois (2)	3	0.02
Latin American Indians (14)	23	0.18
Navajo	1	0.01
Ottawa	1	0.01
Potawatomi (3)	5	0.04

Notes: 1. Figures in the "Number" column do not add up to the total population due to: a) Ancestry/Race overlap — e.g. persons can report being both White and Irish, b) persons of Hispanic origin can report being any race, c) persons reporting two ancestries are counted in both categories. 2. Numbers in parentheses indicate the number of persons reporting this ancestry/race alone, not in combination with any other ancestry/race. 3. Refer to the Explanation of Data in the front of the book for more detailed information.

Ancestry/Race	Number	%
Pueblo	1	0.01
Seminole	1	0.01
Sioux (2)	3	0.02
All other tribes (5)	11	0.09
American Indian tribes, not spec.	9	0.07
Arab:	38	0.29
Arab/Arabic	11	0.08
Lebanese	16	0.12
Other Arab	11	0.08
Armenian	5	0.04
Asian:	462	3.59
Cambodian (2)	3	0.02
Chinese, ex. Taiwanese (78)	98	0.76
Filipino (45)	58	0.45
Indian (95)	109	0.85
Indonesian (1)	3	0.02
Japanese (22)	30	0.23
Korean (26)	34	0.26
Laotian (1)	2	0.02
Malaysian (1)	3	0.02
Pakistani (4)	4	0.03
Sri Lankan (1)	1	0.01
Taiwanese (1)	1	0.01
Thai (10)	13	0.10
Vietnamese (65)	75	0.58
Other Asian, specified (2)	2	0.02
Other Asian, not specified (9)	26	0.20
Austrian	38	0.29
Belgian	5	0.04
Brazilian	7	0.05
British	121	0.93
Canadian	26	0.20
Celtic	12	0.09
Croatian	9	0.07
Czech	77	0.59
Czechoslovakian	42	0.32
Danish	42	0.32
Dutch	221	1.69
Eastern European	7	0.05
English	1,559	11.92
Estonian	9	0.07
European	165	1.26
Finnish	19	0.15
French, except Basque	319	2.44
French Canadian	166	1.27
German	1,784	13.65
Greek	70	0.54
Hawaii Native/Pacific Islander:	30	0.23
Micronesian: (1)	4	0.03
Guamanian/Chamorro (1)	4	0.03
Polynesian: (8)	13	0.10
Native Hawaiian (6)	11	0.09
Samoan (2)	2	0.02
Other Pac. Isl., not spec. (3)	13	0.10
Hispanic or Latino:	2,295	17.83
Central American:	118	0.92
Costa Rican	11	0.09
Guatemalan	13	0.10
Honduran	16	0.12
Nicaraguan	8	0.06
Panamanian	21	0.16
Salvadoran	44	0.34
Other Central American	5	0.04
Cuban	195	1.52
Dominican Republic	55	0.43
Mexican	291	2.26
Puerto Rican	1,106	8.59
South American:	221	1.72
Argentinean	7	0.05
Bolivian	3	0.02
Chilean	4	0.03
Colombian	98	0.76
Ecuadorian	22	0.17
Peruvian	22	0.17
Venezuelan	57	0.44
Other South American	8	0.06
Other Hispanic or Latino	309	2.40
Hungarian	33	0.25
Icelander	7	0.05
Iranian	22	0.17
Irish	1,739	13.30
Israeli	18	0.14
Italian	895	6.85
Macedonian	8	0.06
Norwegian	57	0.44
Pennsylvania German	8	0.06
Polish	336	2.57
Portuguese	41	0.31
Romanian	30	0.23
Russian	33	0.25
Scotch-Irish	322	2.46
Scottish	362	2.77
Slovak	82	0.63
Swedish	143	1.09
Swiss	36	0.28
Turkish	10	0.08
Ukrainian	127	0.97
United States or American	827	6.33
Welsh	71	0.54
West Indian, excl. Hispanic:	166	1.27
Belizean	12	0.09
British West Indian	10	0.08
Jamaican	111	0.85
Trinidadian and Tobagonian	25	0.19
U.S. Virgin Islander	8	0.06
White:	10,953	85.10
Not Hispanic (9,237)	9,442	73.36
Hispanic (1,372)	1,511	11.74
Yugoslavian	16	0.12

Gonzalez

Place Type: Census Designated Place
County: Escambia
Population: 11,365

Ancestry/Race	Number	%
Acadian/Cajun	30	0.26
African American/Black:	907	7.98
Not Hispanic (862)	896	7.88
Hispanic (7)	11	0.10
Alaska Native tribes, specified:	1	0.01
Eskimo (1)	1	0.01
Am. Ind. or Alaska Nat., not spec.	41	0.36
American Indian tribes, specified:	148	1.30
Blackfeet	1	0.01
Cherokee (18)	40	0.35
Cheyenne (4)	4	0.04
Chickasaw	1	0.01
Chippewa	3	0.03
Choctaw (1)	5	0.04
Creek (41)	71	0.62
Latin American Indians	1	0.01
Lumbee (2)	6	0.05
Seminole (2)	2	0.02
Sioux (1)	10	0.09
All other tribes (3)	4	0.04
American Indian tribes, not spec.	2	0.02
Arab:	10	0.09
Lebanese	10	0.09
Asian:	222	1.95
Chinese, ex. Taiwanese (21)	24	0.21
Filipino (47)	74	0.65
Indian (7)	13	0.11
Indonesian	1	0.01
Japanese (6)	10	0.09
Korean (13)	23	0.20
Taiwanese (1)	1	0.01
Thai (1)	1	0.01
Vietnamese (68)	69	0.61
Other Asian, specified	1	0.01
Other Asian, not specified (3)	5	0.04
Austrian	11	0.09
Belgian	20	0.17
British	49	0.42
Canadian	37	0.32
Czech	62	0.53
Czechoslovakian	40	0.34
Danish	95	0.81
Dutch	170	1.46
English	1,006	8.62
European	67	0.57
French, except Basque	403	3.45
French Canadian	55	0.47
German	1,230	10.54
Greek	7	0.06
Hawaii Native/Pacific Islander:	11	0.10
Micronesian: (1)	7	0.06
Guamanian/Chamorro (1)	7	0.06
Polynesian: (1)	2	0.02
Samoan (1)	2	0.02
Other Pac. Isl., not spec.	2	0.02
Hispanic or Latino:	190	1.67
Central American:	17	0.15
Costa Rican	1	0.01
Guatemalan	7	0.06
Honduran	1	0.01
Panamanian	4	0.04
Salvadoran	3	0.03
Other Central American	1	0.01
Cuban	22	0.19
Mexican	52	0.46
Puerto Rican	40	0.35
South American:	11	0.10
Bolivian	5	0.04
Chilean	1	0.01
Colombian	5	0.04
Other Hispanic or Latino	48	0.42
Hungarian	38	0.33
Icelander	11	0.09
Iranian	63	0.54
Irish	1,184	10.14
Italian	454	3.89
Northern European	10	0.09
Norwegian	19	0.16
Pennsylvania German	9	0.08
Polish	177	1.52
Russian	46	0.39
Scandinavian	7	0.06
Scotch-Irish	266	2.28
Scottish	382	3.27
Serbian	17	0.15
Slovak	16	0.14
Swedish	56	0.48
Swiss	37	0.32
Turkish	8	0.07
Ukrainian	9	0.08
United States or American	1,540	13.19
Welsh	79	0.68
West Indian, excl. Hispanic:	12	0.10
Belizean	12	0.10
White:	10,169	89.48
Not Hispanic (9,874)	10,025	88.21
Hispanic (130)	144	1.27

Greater Carrollwood

Place Type: Census Designated Place
County: Hillsborough
Population: 33,519

Ancestry/Race	Number	%
African American/Black:	2,195	6.55
Not Hispanic (1,834)	1,981	5.91
Hispanic (126)	214	0.64
African, sub-Saharan:	185	0.55
African	106	0.32
Ethiopian	17	0.05
Liberian	12	0.04
South African	50	0.15
Am. Ind. or Alaska Nat., not spec.	59	0.18
American Indian tribes, specified:	131	0.39
Apache (5)	7	0.02
Blackfeet (1)	3	0.01
Cherokee (27)	58	0.17
Choctaw	1	0.00
Cree (1)	1	0.00
Creek	1	0.00
Delaware	2	0.01
Iroquois (2)	6	0.02

Notes: 1. Figures in the "Number" column do not add up to the total population due to: a) Ancestry/Race overlap — e.g. persons can report being both White and Irish, b) persons of Hispanic origin can report being any race, c) persons reporting two ancestries are counted in both categories. 2. Numbers in parentheses indicate the number of persons reporting this ancestry/race alone, not in combination with any other ancestry/race. 3. Refer to the Explanation of Data in the front of the book for more detailed information.

Ancestry/Race	Number	%
Latin American Indians (13)	29	0.09
Lumbee	4	0.01
Navajo (1)	1	0.00
Paiute	1	0.00
Pueblo (1)	2	0.01
Seminole	4	0.01
Sioux (1)	1	0.00
Tohono O'Odham (1)	1	0.00
All other tribes (6)	9	0.03
American Indian tribes, not spec.	11	0.03
Arab:	205	0.61
Arab/Arabic	9	0.03
Egyptian	23	0.07
Lebanese	115	0.34
Moroccan	19	0.06
Syrian	39	0.12
Armenian	23	0.07
Asian:	1,411	4.21
Cambodian (2)	4	0.01
Chinese, ex. Taiwanese (147)	192	0.57
Filipino (164)	212	0.63
Indian (421)	468	1.40
Indonesian (8)	10	0.03
Japanese (28)	48	0.14
Korean (151)	176	0.53
Laotian (1)	1	0.00
Malaysian (1)	1	0.00
Pakistani (12)	22	0.07
Sri Lankan (6)	9	0.03
Taiwanese (10)	10	0.03
Thai (30)	38	0.11
Vietnamese (155)	178	0.53
Other Asian, specified	1	0.00
Other Asian, not specified (13)	41	0.12
Australian	40	0.12
Austrian	79	0.24
Belgian	46	0.14
Brazilian	67	0.20
British	173	0.51
Bulgarian	129	0.38
Canadian	126	0.37
Croatian	44	0.13
Czech	173	0.51
Czechoslovakian	69	0.21
Danish	123	0.37
Dutch	493	1.47
Eastern European	140	0.42
English	3,432	10.21
European	83	0.25
Finnish	29	0.09
French, except Basque	1,252	3.72
French Canadian	231	0.69
German	4,675	13.91
Greek	256	0.76
Hawaii Native/Pacific Islander:	35	0.10
Micronesian: (1)	4	0.01
Guamanian/Chamorro (1)	2	0.01
Other Micronesian	2	0.01
Polynesian: (6)	10	0.03
Native Hawaiian (6)	10	0.03
Other Pac. Isl., specified	1	0.00
Other Pac. Isl., not spec. (10)	20	0.06
Hispanic or Latino:	6,131	18.29
Central American:	228	0.68
Costa Rican	31	0.09
Guatemalan	37	0.11
Honduran	45	0.13
Nicaraguan	19	0.06
Panamanian	73	0.22
Salvadoran	16	0.05
Other Central American	7	0.02
Cuban	1,128	3.37
Dominican Republic	138	0.41
Mexican	230	0.69
Puerto Rican	1,942	5.79
South American:	829	2.47
Argentinean	27	0.08
Bolivian	15	0.04
Chilean	26	0.08
Colombian	444	1.32
Ecuadorian	119	0.36
Paraguayan	2	0.01
Peruvian	67	0.20
Uruguayan	5	0.01
Venezuelan	104	0.31
Other South American	20	0.06
Other Hispanic or Latino	1,636	4.88
Hungarian	299	0.89
Iranian	119	0.35
Irish	4,281	12.73
Italian	2,992	8.90
Latvian	20	0.06
Lithuanian	45	0.13
Luxemburger	14	0.04
Norwegian	167	0.50
Pennsylvania German	10	0.03
Polish	962	2.86
Portuguese	111	0.33
Romanian	62	0.18
Russian	543	1.62
Scandinavian	35	0.10
Scotch-Irish	565	1.68
Scottish	798	2.37
Serbian	35	0.10
Slovak	124	0.37
Slovene	34	0.10
Swedish	340	1.01
Swiss	25	0.07
Turkish	14	0.04
Ukrainian	116	0.35
United States or American	2,306	6.86
Welsh	254	0.76
West Indian, excl. Hispanic:	390	1.16
Belizean	10	0.03
British West Indian	20	0.06
Haitian	45	0.13
Jamaican	244	0.73
Trinidadian and Tobagonian	67	0.20
West Indian	4	0.01
White:	29,006	86.54
Not Hispanic (23,808)	24,182	72.14
Hispanic (4,512)	4,824	14.39
Yugoslavian	16	0.05

Greater Northdale

Place Type: Census Designated Place
County: Hillsborough
Population: 20,461

Ancestry/Race	Number	%
African American/Black:	1,278	6.25
Not Hispanic (1,106)	1,197	5.85
Hispanic (43)	81	0.40
African, sub-Saharan:	61	0.30
African	41	0.20
Ethiopian	16	0.08
Nigerian	4	0.02
Am. Ind. or Alaska Nat., not spec.	37	0.18
American Indian tribes, specified:	59	0.29
Apache (2)	2	0.01
Blackfeet (4)	6	0.03
Cherokee (11)	19	0.09
Chippewa (2)	2	0.01
Choctaw (1)	2	0.01
Creek (1)	1	0.00
Latin American Indians	18	0.09
Osage (1)	1	0.00
Seminole	4	0.02
Sioux (2)	2	0.01
Ute (1)	1	0.00
All other tribes (1)	1	0.00
American Indian tribes, not spec.	11	0.05
Arab:	292	1.44
Arab/Arabic	42	0.21
Egyptian	8	0.04
Jordanian	7	0.03
Lebanese	132	0.65
Palestinian	55	0.27
Syrian	48	0.24
Asian:	917	4.48
Chinese, ex. Taiwanese (105)	139	0.68
Filipino (114)	141	0.69
Hmong (2)	2	0.01
Indian (256)	289	1.41
Indonesian (1)	3	0.01
Japanese (20)	40	0.20
Korean (126)	139	0.68
Laotian (8)	9	0.04
Pakistani (7)	8	0.04
Sri Lankan (7)	7	0.03
Taiwanese (12)	12	0.06
Thai (29)	29	0.14
Vietnamese (40)	42	0.21
Other Asian, specified (1)	5	0.02
Other Asian, not specified (15)	52	0.25
Austrian	68	0.34
Belgian	6	0.03
Brazilian	27	0.13
British	150	0.74
Canadian	99	0.49
Celtic	9	0.04
Croatian	24	0.12
Czech	33	0.16
Czechoslovakian	107	0.53
Danish	81	0.40
Dutch	357	1.76
Eastern European	10	0.05
English	2,328	11.48
Estonian	6	0.03
European	146	0.72
Finnish	30	0.15
French, except Basque	766	3.78
French Canadian	252	1.24
German	3,378	16.66
Greek	57	0.28
Guyanese	10	0.05
Hawaii Native/Pacific Islander:	29	0.14
Micronesian: (12)	12	0.06
Guamanian/Chamorro (12)	12	0.06
Polynesian: (4)	6	0.03
Native Hawaiian (4)	6	0.03
Other Pac. Isl., not spec. (2)	11	0.05
Hispanic or Latino:	3,074	15.02
Central American:	104	0.51
Costa Rican	18	0.09
Guatemalan	11	0.05
Honduran	31	0.15
Nicaraguan	9	0.04
Panamanian	20	0.10
Salvadoran	9	0.04
Other Central American	6	0.03
Cuban	731	3.57
Dominican Republic	62	0.30
Mexican	155	0.76
Puerto Rican	861	4.21
South American:	396	1.94
Argentinean	11	0.05
Bolivian	5	0.02
Chilean	6	0.03
Colombian	166	0.81
Ecuadorian	50	0.24
Peruvian	75	0.37
Uruguayan	5	0.02
Venezuelan	54	0.26
Other South American	24	0.12
Other Hispanic or Latino	765	3.74
Hungarian	137	0.68
Iranian	105	0.52
Irish	3,029	14.93
Israeli	8	0.04
Italian	2,223	10.96
Lithuanian	91	0.45
Macedonian	8	0.04
Maltese	8	0.04
Norwegian	162	0.80
Pennsylvania German	8	0.04
Polish	680	3.35
Portuguese	45	0.22
Romanian	35	0.17

Notes: 1. Figures in the "Number" column do not add up to the total population due to: a) Ancestry/Race overlap — e.g. persons can report being both White and Irish, b) persons of Hispanic origin can report being any race, c) persons reporting two ancestries are counted in both categories. 2. Numbers in parentheses indicate the number of persons reporting this ancestry/race alone, not in combination with any other ancestry/race. 3. Refer to the Explanation of Data in the front of the book for more detailed information.

Ancestry/Race	Number	%
Russian	193	0.95
Scandinavian	28	0.14
Scotch-Irish	252	1.24
Scottish	448	2.21
Slavic	9	0.04
Slovak	43	0.21
Slovene	10	0.05
Swedish	205	1.01
Swiss	60	0.30
Turkish	9	0.04
Ukrainian	62	0.31
United States or American	1,244	6.13
Welsh	203	1.00
West Indian, excl. Hispanic:	278	1.37
Barbadian	8	0.04
British West Indian	6	0.03
Haitian	25	0.12
Jamaican	137	0.68
Trinidadian and Tobagonian	13	0.06
West Indian	30	0.15
Other West Indian	59	0.29
White:	17,941	87.68
Not Hispanic (15,125)	15,372	75.13
Hispanic (2,408)	2,569	12.56

Greater Sun Center

Place Type: Census Designated Place
County: Hillsborough
Population: 16,321

Ancestry/Race	Number	%
African American/Black:	33	0.20
Not Hispanic (22)	32	0.20
Hispanic	1	0.01
African, sub-Saharan:	10	0.06
African	10	0.06
Am. Ind. or Alaska Nat., not spec.	5	0.03
Alsatian	8	0.05
American Indian tribes, specified:	19	0.12
Blackfeet	2	0.01
Cherokee (5)	10	0.06
Chippewa (1)	1	0.01
Choctaw	1	0.01
Iroquois (4)	4	0.02
Sioux (1)	1	0.01
American Indian tribes, not spec.	4	0.02
Arab:	7	0.04
Lebanese	7	0.04
Armenian	25	0.15
Asian:	72	0.44
Chinese, ex. Taiwanese (10)	12	0.07
Filipino (16)	18	0.11
Indian (4)	6	0.04
Indonesian (1)	1	0.01
Japanese (17)	17	0.10
Korean (4)	4	0.02
Vietnamese (13)	13	0.08
Other Asian, not specified	1	0.01
Assyrian/Chaldean/Syriac	8	0.05
Australian	17	0.10
Austrian	148	0.91
Belgian	25	0.15
Brazilian	9	0.06
British	108	0.66
Bulgarian	8	0.05
Canadian	113	0.69
Croatian	8	0.05
Czech	90	0.55
Czechoslovakian	84	0.52
Danish	100	0.61
Dutch	387	2.38
English	3,336	20.48
European	68	0.42
Finnish	24	0.15
French, except Basque	807	4.96
French Canadian	332	2.04
German	3,737	22.95
Greek	29	0.18
Hawaii Native/Pacific Islander:	11	0.07
Micronesian: (4)	4	0.02
Guamanian/Chamorro (2)	2	0.01
Other Micronesian (2)	2	0.01
Polynesian: (6)	6	0.04
Native Hawaiian (4)	4	0.02
Samoan (2)	2	0.01
Other Pac. Isl., not spec. (1)	1	0.01
Hispanic or Latino:	195	1.19
Central American:	5	0.03
Costa Rican	1	0.01
Guatemalan	2	0.01
Nicaraguan	1	0.01
Panamanian	1	0.01
Cuban	12	0.07
Dominican Republic	2	0.01
Mexican	43	0.26
Puerto Rican	65	0.40
South American:	8	0.05
Argentinean	1	0.01
Colombian	6	0.04
Other South American	1	0.01
Other Hispanic or Latino	60	0.37
Hungarian	186	1.14
Irish	2,386	14.65
Italian	817	5.02
Lithuanian	48	0.29
Macedonian	29	0.18
Norwegian	230	1.41
Pennsylvania German	30	0.18
Polish	739	4.54
Portuguese	17	0.10
Romanian	23	0.14
Russian	207	1.27
Scandinavian	15	0.09
Scotch-Irish	557	3.42
Scottish	672	4.13
Slovak	60	0.37
Slovene	23	0.14
Swedish	423	2.60
Swiss	142	0.87
Ukrainian	60	0.37
United States or American	922	5.66
Welsh	253	1.55
West Indian, excl. Hispanic:	8	0.05
Jamaican	8	0.05
White:	16,181	99.14
Not Hispanic (15,986)	16,012	98.11
Hispanic (166)	169	1.04
Yugoslavian	8	0.05

Greenacres

Place Type: City
County: Palm Beach
Population: 27,569

Ancestry/Race	Number	%
African American/Black:	2,007	7.28
Not Hispanic (1,673)	1,848	6.70
Hispanic (117)	159	0.58
African, sub-Saharan:	40	0.15
African	35	0.13
Sierra Leonean	5	0.02
Am. Ind. or Alaska Nat., not spec.	42	0.15
Albanian	9	0.03
Alsatian	30	0.11
American Indian tribes, specified:	111	0.40
Apache	5	0.02
Blackfeet (3)	7	0.03
Cherokee (9)	30	0.11
Cheyenne (1)	4	0.01
Chickasaw (2)	3	0.01
Chippewa	1	0.00
Choctaw (1)	9	0.03
Comanche (2)	2	0.01
Cree (1)	2	0.01
Iroquois (3)	3	0.01
Latin American Indians (12)	27	0.10
Navajo (1)	1	0.00
Paiute (1)	1	0.00
Pueblo (1)	1	0.00
Sioux (3)	4	0.01
Yaqui	2	0.01
All other tribes (6)	9	0.03
American Indian tribes, not spec.	17	0.06
Arab:	92	0.34
Arab/Arabic	67	0.25
Egyptian	6	0.02
Lebanese	19	0.07
Armenian	23	0.08
Asian:	640	2.32
Bangladeshi (19)	23	0.08
Chinese, ex. Taiwanese (95)	115	0.42
Filipino (81)	98	0.36
Indian (185)	222	0.81
Japanese (8)	17	0.06
Korean (25)	26	0.09
Pakistani (28)	42	0.15
Sri Lankan (2)	2	0.01
Thai (12)	15	0.05
Vietnamese (33)	35	0.13
Other Asian, specified (5)	9	0.03
Other Asian, not specified (10)	36	0.13
Austrian	223	0.82
Belgian	12	0.04
Brazilian	19	0.07
British	167	0.61
Canadian	145	0.53
Croatian	34	0.12
Czech	45	0.17
Czechoslovakian	44	0.16
Danish	66	0.24
Dutch	434	1.59
Eastern European	9	0.03
English	2,022	7.42
Estonian	22	0.08
European	84	0.31
Finnish	232	0.85
French, except Basque	737	2.70
French Canadian	151	0.55
German	3,266	11.98
Greek	151	0.55
Guyanese	23	0.08
Hawaii Native/Pacific Islander:	37	0.13
Micronesian: (3)	5	0.02
Guamanian/Chamorro (3)	5	0.02
Polynesian: (3)	8	0.03
Native Hawaiian (3)	8	0.03
Other Pac. Isl., not spec. (5)	24	0.09
Hispanic or Latino:	5,858	21.25
Central American:	517	1.88
Costa Rican	14	0.05
Guatemalan	111	0.40
Honduran	180	0.65
Nicaraguan	112	0.41
Panamanian	21	0.08
Salvadoran	66	0.24
Other Central American	13	0.05
Cuban	665	2.41
Dominican Republic	198	0.72
Mexican	1,439	5.22
Puerto Rican	1,169	4.24
South American:	893	3.24
Argentinean	69	0.25
Bolivian	26	0.09
Chilean	51	0.18
Colombian	461	1.67
Ecuadorian	82	0.30
Paraguayan	1	0.00
Peruvian	85	0.31
Uruguayan	48	0.17
Venezuelan	50	0.18
Other South American	20	0.07
Other Hispanic or Latino	977	3.54
Hungarian	229	0.84
Irish	2,972	10.90
Italian	3,581	13.13
Lithuanian	52	0.19
Norwegian	158	0.58
Pennsylvania German	41	0.15

Notes: 1. Figures in the "Number" column do not add up to the total population due to: a) Ancestry/Race overlap — e.g. persons can report being both White and Irish, b) persons of Hispanic origin can report being any race, c) persons reporting two ancestries are counted in both categories. 2. Numbers in parentheses indicate the number of persons reporting this ancestry/race alone, not in combination with any other ancestry/race. 3. Refer to the Explanation of Data in the front of the book for more detailed information.

Polish	912	3.34
Portuguese	156	0.57
Romanian	87	0.32
Russian	648	2.38
Scandinavian	49	0.18
Scotch-Irish	223	0.82
Scottish	318	1.17
Serbian	27	0.10
Slavic	14	0.05
Slovak	53	0.19
Slovene	10	0.04
Swedish	217	0.80
Swiss	73	0.27
Turkish	9	0.03
Ukrainian	109	0.40
United States or American	1,453	5.33
Welsh	187	0.69
West Indian, excl. Hispanic:	680	2.49
Bahamian	13	0.05
Barbadian	12	0.04
Haitian	299	1.10
Jamaican	285	1.05
Trinidadian and Tobagonian	61	0.22
West Indian	10	0.04
White:	23,425	84.97
Not Hispanic (19,066)	19,244	69.80
Hispanic (3,873)	4,181	15.17
Yugoslavian	13	0.05

Gulf Gate Estates

Place Type: Census Designated Place
County: Sarasota
Population: 11,647

Ancestry/Race	Number	%
African American/Black:	113	0.97
Not Hispanic (84)	105	0.90
Hispanic (7)	8	0.07
African, sub-Saharan:	25	0.22
African	7	0.06
South African	18	0.16
Am. Ind. or Alaska Nat., not spec.	15	0.13
Alsatian	11	0.10
American Indian tribes, specified:	39	0.33
Apache	4	0.03
Blackfeet (2)	4	0.03
Cherokee (2)	17	0.15
Cheyenne (1)	1	0.01
Choctaw	3	0.03
Comanche	1	0.01
Creek (1)	1	0.01
Iroquois	2	0.02
Latin American Indians (2)	2	0.02
Sioux (1)	2	0.02
Ute	1	0.01
All other tribes	1	0.01
American Indian tribes, not spec.	4	0.03
Arab:	63	0.55
Lebanese	47	0.41
Moroccan	6	0.05
Syrian	10	0.09
Asian:	127	1.09
Chinese, ex. Taiwanese (25)	30	0.26
Filipino (15)	19	0.16
Indian (21)	25	0.21
Indonesian (1)	1	0.01
Japanese (4)	10	0.09
Korean (11)	17	0.15
Laotian (7)	7	0.06
Pakistani (1)	1	0.01
Thai (2)	6	0.05
Vietnamese (2)	3	0.03
Other Asian, not specified (4)	8	0.07
Austrian	23	0.20
Belgian	17	0.15
Brazilian	54	0.47
British	129	1.12
Bulgarian	21	0.18
Canadian	64	0.55
Croatian	22	0.19
Czech	58	0.50
Czechoslovakian	31	0.27
Danish	30	0.26
Dutch	175	1.51
English	1,731	14.98
European	7	0.06
Finnish	57	0.49
French, except Basque	544	4.71
French Canadian	195	1.69
German	2,248	19.45
Greek	82	0.71
Hawaii Native/Pacific Islander:	4	0.03
Micronesian: (3)	3	0.03
Guamanian/Chamorro (2)	2	0.02
Other Micronesian (1)	1	0.01
Polynesian:	1	0.01
Native Hawaiian	1	0.01
Hispanic or Latino:	373	3.20
Central American:	11	0.09
Costa Rican	1	0.01
Guatemalan	1	0.01
Honduran	1	0.01
Nicaraguan	1	0.01
Panamanian	3	0.03
Other Central American	4	0.03
Cuban	51	0.44
Dominican Republic	11	0.09
Mexican	96	0.82
Puerto Rican	66	0.57
South American:	72	0.62
Argentinean	3	0.03
Bolivian	3	0.03
Chilean	2	0.02
Colombian	46	0.39
Ecuadorian	3	0.03
Peruvian	12	0.10
Venezuelan	2	0.02
Other South American	1	0.01
Other Hispanic or Latino	66	0.57
Hungarian	222	1.92
Icelander	12	0.10
Irish	1,606	13.90
Israeli	9	0.08
Italian	1,087	9.40
Lithuanian	15	0.13
Norwegian	166	1.44
Pennsylvania German	6	0.05
Polish	470	4.07
Portuguese	26	0.22
Romanian	32	0.28
Russian	259	2.24
Scandinavian	18	0.16
Scotch-Irish	250	2.16
Scottish	270	2.34
Serbian	9	0.08
Slovak	70	0.61
Swedish	155	1.34
Swiss	114	0.99
Ukrainian	13	0.11
United States or American	739	6.39
Welsh	151	1.31
West Indian, excl. Hispanic:	17	0.15
Jamaican	17	0.15
White:	11,333	97.30
Not Hispanic (10,967)	11,053	94.90
Hispanic (268)	280	2.40
Yugoslavian	121	1.05

Gulfport

Place Type: City
County: Pinellas
Population: 12,527

Ancestry/Race	Number	%
African American/Black:	948	7.57
Not Hispanic (861)	913	7.29
Hispanic (23)	35	0.28
African, sub-Saharan:	62	0.49
African	62	0.49
Alaska Native tribes, specified:	1	0.01
Alaska Athabascan (1)	1	0.01
Alaska Native tribes, not specified	1	0.01
Am. Ind. or Alaska Nat., not spec.	26	0.21
Alsatian	6	0.05
American Indian tribes, specified:	111	0.89
Apache	2	0.02
Blackfeet (2)	15	0.12
Cherokee (22)	54	0.43
Cheyenne	1	0.01
Chickasaw (1)	3	0.02
Chippewa (1)	2	0.02
Choctaw	4	0.03
Comanche (2)	3	0.02
Cree	1	0.01
Creek (1)	1	0.01
Delaware (2)	2	0.02
Iroquois (1)	3	0.02
Latin American Indians (1)	4	0.03
Pueblo (1)	1	0.01
Seminole	1	0.01
Sioux	2	0.02
All other tribes (2)	12	0.10
American Indian tribes, not spec.	9	0.07
Arab:	70	0.55
Arab/Arabic	22	0.17
Egyptian	12	0.10
Lebanese	20	0.16
Syrian	10	0.08
Other Arab	6	0.05
Armenian	7	0.06
Asian:	96	0.77
Cambodian	1	0.01
Chinese, ex. Taiwanese (4)	7	0.06
Filipino (18)	29	0.23
Indian (14)	18	0.14
Japanese (8)	10	0.08
Korean (4)	6	0.05
Laotian (1)	1	0.01
Thai (2)	2	0.02
Vietnamese (14)	15	0.12
Other Asian, specified	1	0.01
Other Asian, not specified (2)	6	0.05
Austrian	35	0.28
Belgian	7	0.06
British	103	0.82
Bulgarian	5	0.04
Canadian	56	0.44
Celtic	6	0.05
Croatian	13	0.10
Czech	23	0.18
Czechoslovakian	21	0.17
Danish	64	0.51
Dutch	260	2.06
English	1,621	12.84
European	57	0.45
Finnish	39	0.31
French, except Basque	533	4.22
French Canadian	111	0.88
German	2,189	17.34
German Russian	5	0.04
Greek	108	0.86
Hawaii Native/Pacific Islander:	11	0.09
Micronesian: (3)	3	0.02
Other Micronesian (3)	3	0.02
Polynesian: (5)	5	0.04
Native Hawaiian (1)	1	0.01
Samoan (4)	4	0.03
Other Pac. Isl., specified	1	0.01
Other Pac. Isl., not spec.	2	0.02
Hispanic or Latino:	435	3.47
Central American:	6	0.05
Costa Rican	3	0.02
Guatemalan	1	0.01
Honduran	1	0.01
Panamanian	1	0.01
Cuban	62	0.49
Dominican Republic	5	0.04
Mexican	72	0.57

Notes: 1. Figures in the "Number" column do not add up to the total population due to: a) Ancestry/Race overlap — e.g. persons can report being both White and Irish, b) persons of Hispanic origin can report being any race, c) persons reporting two ancestries are counted in both categories. 2. Numbers in parentheses indicate the number of persons reporting this ancestry/race alone, not in combination with any other ancestry/race. 3. Refer to the Explanation of Data in the front of the book for more detailed information.

Puerto Rican	134	1.07
South American:	39	0.31
Argentinean	6	0.05
Chilean	1	0.01
Colombian	21	0.17
Ecuadorian	5	0.04
Peruvian	2	0.02
Venezuelan	3	0.02
Other South American	1	0.01
Other Hispanic or Latino	117	0.93
Hungarian	194	1.54
Irish	1,683	13.33
Italian	1,042	8.25
Latvian	7	0.06
Lithuanian	115	0.91
Luxemburger	5	0.04
Maltese	8	0.06
Norwegian	194	1.54
Pennsylvania German	29	0.23
Polish	420	3.33
Portuguese	38	0.30
Romanian	48	0.38
Russian	196	1.55
Scotch-Irish	253	2.00
Scottish	417	3.30
Serbian	21	0.17
Slavic	11	0.09
Slovak	34	0.27
Slovene	11	0.09
Swedish	260	2.06
Swiss	74	0.59
Ukrainian	216	1.71
United States or American	980	7.76
Welsh	117	0.93
West Indian, excl. Hispanic:	55	0.44
Bahamian	4	0.03
Jamaican	30	0.24
Trinidadian and Tobagonian	14	0.11
West Indian	7	0.06
White:	11,401	91.01
Not Hispanic (10,917)	11,083	88.47
Hispanic (282)	318	2.54
Yugoslavian	12	0.10

Haines City

Place Type: City
County: Polk
Population: 13,174

Ancestry/Race	Number	%
African American/Black:	4,316	32.76
Not Hispanic (4,143)	4,253	32.28
Hispanic (54)	63	0.48
African, sub-Saharan:	184	1.40
African	184	1.40
Am. Ind. or Alaska Nat., not spec.	38	0.29
American Indian tribes, specified:	59	0.45
Apache	4	0.03
Blackfeet	2	0.02
Cherokee (2)	19	0.14
Choctaw (1)	1	0.01
Cree (1)	1	0.01
Iroquois (2)	2	0.02
Latin American Indians (18)	19	0.14
Lumbee	1	0.01
Potawatomi (1)	1	0.01
Pueblo	1	0.01
All other tribes (6)	8	0.06
American Indian tribes, not spec.	9	0.07
Asian:	69	0.52
Bangladeshi (6)	7	0.05
Cambodian	1	0.01
Chinese, ex. Taiwanese (2)	2	0.02
Filipino (7)	10	0.08
Indian (14)	20	0.15
Japanese (9)	10	0.08
Korean (2)	3	0.02
Thai (1)	1	0.01
Vietnamese (3)	4	0.03
Other Asian, specified	2	0.02
Other Asian, not specified (5)	9	0.07
Austrian	21	0.16
Belgian	7	0.05
British	40	0.30
Canadian	19	0.14
Czech	25	0.19
Czechoslovakian	7	0.05
Dutch	90	0.69
English	755	5.75
European	57	0.43
French, except Basque	186	1.42
French Canadian	88	0.67
German	1,157	8.81
Greek	7	0.05
Hawaii Native/Pacific Islander:	20	0.15
Micronesian: (2)	3	0.02
Guamanian/Chamorro (2)	3	0.02
Polynesian: (2)	3	0.02
Native Hawaiian (1)	2	0.02
Samoan (1)	1	0.01
Other Pac. Isl., specified	2	0.02
Other Pac. Isl., not spec. (1)	12	0.09
Hispanic or Latino:	3,074	23.33
Central American:	48	0.36
Costa Rican	3	0.02
Guatemalan	5	0.04
Honduran	6	0.05
Nicaraguan	22	0.17
Panamanian	6	0.05
Salvadoran	3	0.02
Other Central American	4	0.03
Cuban	21	0.16
Dominican Republic	25	0.19
Mexican	2,309	17.53
Puerto Rican	473	3.59
South American:	27	0.20
Argentinean	3	0.02
Colombian	5	0.04
Ecuadorian	10	0.08
Peruvian	8	0.06
Venezuelan	1	0.01
Other Hispanic or Latino	171	1.30
Hungarian	44	0.34
Irish	646	4.92
Italian	171	1.30
Lithuanian	62	0.47
Luxemburger	11	0.08
Norwegian	31	0.24
Polish	85	0.65
Russian	7	0.05
Scotch-Irish	106	0.81
Scottish	124	0.94
Serbian	26	0.20
Slovak	18	0.14
Swedish	83	0.63
Swiss	35	0.27
Ukrainian	7	0.05
United States or American	1,145	8.72
Welsh	51	0.39
West Indian, excl. Hispanic:	510	3.88
Haitian	359	2.73
Jamaican	151	1.15
White:	7,371	55.95
Not Hispanic (5,688)	5,753	43.67
Hispanic (1,541)	1,618	12.28

Hallandale

Place Type: City
County: Broward
Population: 34,282

Ancestry/Race	Number	%
African American/Black:	5,828	17.00
Not Hispanic (5,353)	5,644	16.46
Hispanic (140)	184	0.54
African, sub-Saharan:	153	0.44
African	119	0.34
South African	19	0.05
Ugandan	7	0.02
Other sub-Saharan African	8	0.02
Alaska Native tribes, specified:	1	0.00
Aleut (1)	1	0.00
Am. Ind. or Alaska Nat., not spec.	77	0.22
Albanian	10	0.03
American Indian tribes, specified:	78	0.23
Blackfeet	5	0.01
Cherokee (8)	20	0.06
Chickasaw	1	0.00
Chippewa	4	0.01
Delaware	2	0.01
Iroquois (4)	5	0.01
Latin American Indians (6)	17	0.05
Navajo (1)	1	0.00
Paiute (1)	1	0.00
Potawatomi (1)	2	0.01
Pueblo (1)	2	0.01
Yaqui (3)	3	0.01
All other tribes (6)	15	0.04
American Indian tribes, not spec.	11	0.03
Arab:	303	0.88
Arab/Arabic	9	0.03
Egyptian	37	0.11
Iraqi	19	0.05
Lebanese	61	0.18
Moroccan	72	0.21
Palestinian	7	0.02
Syrian	9	0.03
Other Arab	89	0.26
Armenian	19	0.05
Asian:	485	1.41
Bangladeshi	2	0.01
Chinese, ex. Taiwanese (87)	114	0.33
Filipino (19)	35	0.10
Indian (152)	188	0.55
Indonesian (8)	16	0.05
Japanese (14)	24	0.07
Korean (7)	14	0.04
Pakistani (9)	13	0.04
Taiwanese (4)	6	0.02
Thai (13)	13	0.04
Vietnamese (6)	7	0.02
Other Asian, specified (4)	10	0.03
Other Asian, not specified (10)	43	0.13
Austrian	490	1.42
Belgian	23	0.07
Brazilian	125	0.36
British	123	0.36
Bulgarian	9	0.03
Canadian	475	1.37
Croatian	18	0.05
Cypriot	11	0.03
Czech	65	0.19
Czechoslovakian	86	0.25
Danish	19	0.05
Dutch	145	0.42
Eastern European	46	0.13
English	948	2.74
European	112	0.32
Finnish	21	0.06
French, except Basque	482	1.40
French Canadian	934	2.70
German	2,037	5.90
German Russian	17	0.05
Greek	243	0.70
Guyanese	6	0.02
Hawaii Native/Pacific Islander:	57	0.17
Micronesian: (2)	3	0.01
Guamanian/Chamorro (2)	3	0.01
Polynesian: (7)	15	0.04
Native Hawaiian (2)	9	0.03
Samoan (5)	6	0.02
Other Pac. Isl., specified	5	0.01
Other Pac. Isl., not spec. (5)	34	0.10
Hispanic or Latino:	6,447	18.81
Central American:	459	1.34
Costa Rican	63	0.18
Guatemalan	27	0.08
Honduran	136	0.40

Notes: 1. Figures in the "Number" column do not add up to the total population due to: a) Ancestry/Race overlap — e.g. persons can report being both White and Irish, b) persons of Hispanic origin can report being any race, c) persons reporting two ancestries are counted in both categories. 2. Numbers in parentheses indicate the number of persons reporting this ancestry/race alone, not in combination with any other ancestry/race. 3. Refer to the Explanation of Data in the front of the book for more detailed information.

Ancestry/Race	Number	%
Nicaraguan	111	0.32
Panamanian	48	0.14
Salvadoran	51	0.15
Other Central American	23	0.07
Cuban	1,308	3.82
Dominican Republic	228	0.67
Mexican	348	1.02
Puerto Rican	1,027	3.00
South American:	1,731	5.05
Argentinean	205	0.60
Bolivian	7	0.02
Chilean	98	0.29
Colombian	669	1.95
Ecuadorian	121	0.35
Paraguayan	1	0.00
Peruvian	391	1.14
Uruguayan	28	0.08
Venezuelan	147	0.43
Other South American	64	0.19
Other Hispanic or Latino	1,346	3.93
Hungarian	644	1.86
Irish	1,589	4.60
Israeli	126	0.36
Italian	3,171	9.18
Latvian	18	0.05
Lithuanian	126	0.36
Luxemburger	9	0.03
Norwegian	46	0.13
Polish	1,573	4.55
Portuguese	47	0.14
Romanian	1,056	3.06
Russian	1,750	5.06
Scotch-Irish	145	0.42
Scottish	270	0.78
Serbian	39	0.11
Slovak	32	0.09
Swedish	209	0.60
Swiss	38	0.11
Turkish	97	0.28
Ukrainian	242	0.70
United States or American	1,874	5.42
Welsh	73	0.21
West Indian, excl. Hispanic:	1,623	4.70
Bahamian	210	0.61
Belizean	8	0.02
Bermudan	6	0.02
British West Indian	33	0.10
Haitian	849	2.46
Jamaican	464	1.34
Trinidadian and Tobagonian	21	0.06
U.S. Virgin Islander	6	0.02
West Indian	26	0.08
White:	27,105	79.06
Not Hispanic (21,456)	21,783	63.54
Hispanic (5,028)	5,322	15.52
Yugoslavian	85	0.25

Hamptons at Boca Raton

Place Type: Census Designated Place
County: Palm Beach
Population: 11,306

Ancestry/Race	Number	%
African American/Black:	230	2.03
Not Hispanic (186)	227	2.01
Hispanic (2)	3	0.03
Alaska Native tribes, specified:	2	0.02
Eskimo (1)	1	0.01
Tlingit-Haida (1)	1	0.01
Am. Ind. or Alaska Nat., not spec.	13	0.11
American Indian tribes, specified:	12	0.11
Apache (1)	1	0.01
Cherokee (1)	3	0.03
Sioux	5	0.04
All other tribes	3	0.03
American Indian tribes, not spec.	3	0.03
Arab:	48	0.42
Moroccan	20	0.18
Syrian	28	0.25
Asian:	210	1.86
Cambodian	1	0.01
Chinese, ex. Taiwanese (22)	28	0.25
Filipino (10)	18	0.16
Indian (76)	82	0.73
Indonesian (1)	1	0.01
Japanese (8)	11	0.10
Korean (4)	7	0.06
Pakistani (7)	7	0.06
Thai (12)	15	0.13
Vietnamese (23)	26	0.23
Other Asian, specified (2)	5	0.04
Other Asian, not specified (1)	9	0.08
Austrian	391	3.42
Belgian	8	0.07
Brazilian	49	0.43
British	22	0.19
Canadian	61	0.53
Croatian	19	0.17
Czech	35	0.31
Czechoslovakian	47	0.41
Danish	47	0.41
Dutch	49	0.43
Eastern European	28	0.25
English	340	2.98
European	106	0.93
Finnish	5	0.04
French, except Basque	104	0.91
French Canadian	82	0.72
German	592	5.18
Greek	69	0.60
Hawaii Native/Pacific Islander:	12	0.11
Polynesian: (1)	5	0.04
Native Hawaiian (1)	3	0.03
Samoan	1	0.01
Other Polynesian	1	0.01
Other Pac. Isl., specified	3	0.03
Other Pac. Isl., not spec.	4	0.04
Hispanic or Latino:	522	4.62
Central American:	26	0.23
Costa Rican	2	0.02
Guatemalan	4	0.04
Honduran	6	0.05
Nicaraguan	2	0.02
Panamanian	3	0.03
Salvadoran	9	0.08
Cuban	74	0.65
Dominican Republic	12	0.11
Mexican	44	0.39
Puerto Rican	104	0.92
South American:	158	1.40
Argentinean	33	0.29
Bolivian	4	0.04
Chilean	12	0.11
Colombian	60	0.53
Ecuadorian	9	0.08
Peruvian	15	0.13
Uruguayan	1	0.01
Venezuelan	13	0.11
Other South American	11	0.10
Other Hispanic or Latino	104	0.92
Hungarian	187	1.64
Iranian	32	0.28
Irish	786	6.88
Israeli	96	0.84
Italian	872	7.63
Latvian	46	0.40
Lithuanian	51	0.45
Norwegian	33	0.29
Polish	1,143	10.01
Portuguese	17	0.15
Romanian	183	1.60
Russian	1,035	9.06
Scotch-Irish	61	0.53
Scottish	124	1.09
Slavic	9	0.08
Slovak	19	0.17
Swedish	19	0.17
Swiss	65	0.57
Turkish	28	0.25
Ukrainian	93	0.81
United States or American	952	8.33
Welsh	25	0.22
West Indian, excl. Hispanic:	31	0.27
Haitian	31	0.27
White:	10,810	95.61
Not Hispanic (10,315)	10,380	91.81
Hispanic (403)	430	3.80

Hialeah Gardens

Place Type: City
County: Miami-Dade
Population: 19,297

Ancestry/Race	Number	%
African American/Black:	416	2.16
Not Hispanic (70)	79	0.41
Hispanic (278)	337	1.75
Am. Ind. or Alaska Nat., not spec.	15	0.08
American Indian tribes, specified:	27	0.14
Cherokee	1	0.01
Latin American Indians (9)	21	0.11
All other tribes	5	0.03
American Indian tribes, not spec.	2	0.01
Arab:	44	0.23
Jordanian	18	0.09
Lebanese	18	0.09
Syrian	8	0.04
Asian:	217	1.12
Chinese, ex. Taiwanese (88)	108	0.56
Filipino (2)	2	0.01
Indian (36)	45	0.23
Japanese (2)	7	0.04
Korean (5)	6	0.03
Pakistani (6)	10	0.05
Taiwanese (5)	5	0.03
Thai (1)	4	0.02
Vietnamese (3)	15	0.08
Other Asian, not specified	15	0.08
Dutch	13	0.07
English	65	0.34
French, except Basque	27	0.14
German	50	0.26
Greek	16	0.08
Hawaii Native/Pacific Islander:	12	0.06
Polynesian:	1	0.01
Native Hawaiian	1	0.01
Other Pac. Isl., not spec.	11	0.06
Hispanic or Latino:	17,324	89.78
Central American:	1,472	7.63
Costa Rican	30	0.16
Guatemalan	92	0.48
Honduran	223	1.16
Nicaraguan	939	4.87
Panamanian	54	0.28
Salvadoran	86	0.45
Other Central American	48	0.25
Cuban	10,480	54.31
Dominican Republic	551	2.86
Mexican	138	0.72
Puerto Rican	641	3.32
South American:	1,471	7.62
Argentinean	47	0.24
Bolivian	25	0.13
Chilean	43	0.22
Colombian	892	4.62
Ecuadorian	161	0.83
Paraguayan	1	0.01
Peruvian	146	0.76
Uruguayan	10	0.05
Venezuelan	138	0.72
Other South American	8	0.04
Other Hispanic or Latino	2,571	13.32
Iranian	19	0.10
Irish	30	0.16
Italian	220	1.14
Portuguese	39	0.20
Russian	20	0.10
Scotch-Irish	17	0.09

Notes: 1. Figures in the "Number" column do not add up to the total population due to: a) Ancestry/Race overlap — e.g. persons can report being both White and Irish, b) persons of Hispanic origin can report being any race, c) persons reporting two ancestries are counted in both categories. 2. Numbers in parentheses indicate the number of persons reporting this ancestry/race alone, not in combination with any other ancestry/race. 3. Refer to the Explanation of Data in the front of the book for more detailed information.

Scottish	10	0.05
Ukrainian	8	0.04
United States or American	364	1.89
West Indian, excl. Hispanic:	18	0.09
British West Indian	7	0.04
Haitian	11	0.06
White:	17,690	91.67
Not Hispanic (1,683)	1,736	9.00
Hispanic (15,377)	15,954	82.68

Hialeah

Place Type: City
County: Miami-Dade
Population: 226,419

Ancestry/Race	Number	%
African American/Black:	6,580	2.91
Not Hispanic (2,127)	2,259	1.00
Hispanic (3,326)	4,321	1.91
African, sub-Saharan:	197	0.09
African	197	0.09
Alaska Native tribes, specified:	3	0.00
Alaska Athabascan (2)	2	0.00
Eskimo	1	0.00
Alaska Native tribes, not specified	1	0.00
Am. Ind. or Alaska Nat., not spec.	327	0.14
American Indian tribes, specified:	235	0.10
Blackfeet	1	0.00
Cherokee (3)	15	0.01
Chippewa (5)	5	0.00
Choctaw (3)	3	0.00
Iroquois (2)	3	0.00
Latin American Indians (86)	178	0.08
Navajo (3)	3	0.00
Paiute	1	0.00
Pueblo (2)	10	0.00
Seminole	1	0.00
Sioux (1)	3	0.00
All other tribes (3)	12	0.01
American Indian tribes, not spec.	59	0.03
Arab:	669	0.30
Arab/Arabic	106	0.05
Egyptian	20	0.01
Jordanian	7	0.00
Lebanese	429	0.19
Palestinian	68	0.03
Syrian	19	0.01
Other Arab	20	0.01
Armenian	15	0.01
Asian:	1,290	0.57
Bangladeshi (4)	6	0.00
Chinese, ex. Taiwanese (345)	497	0.22
Filipino (85)	116	0.05
Indian (234)	315	0.14
Indonesian (1)	1	0.00
Japanese (34)	53	0.02
Korean (11)	17	0.01
Laotian (1)	1	0.00
Malaysian	3	0.00
Pakistani (84)	117	0.05
Sri Lankan	1	0.00
Thai (5)	9	0.00
Vietnamese (73)	78	0.03
Other Asian, not specified (9)	76	0.03
Assyrian/Chaldean/Syriac	10	0.00
Austrian	38	0.02
Basque	40	0.02
Brazilian	131	0.06
British	157	0.07
Canadian	27	0.01
Celtic	14	0.01
Croatian	21	0.01
Czech	7	0.00
Czechoslovakian	43	0.02
Danish	95	0.04
Dutch	151	0.07
Eastern European	8	0.00
English	907	0.40
European	227	0.10
Finnish	11	0.00
French, except Basque	807	0.36
French Canadian	34	0.02
German	1,344	0.59
Greek	42	0.02
Guyanese	25	0.01
Hawaii Native/Pacific Islander:	170	0.08
Melanesian: (2)	2	0.00
Fijian (2)	2	0.00
Micronesian: (10)	14	0.01
Guamanian/Chamorro (10)	14	0.01
Polynesian: (8)	22	0.01
Native Hawaiian (4)	9	0.00
Samoan (4)	12	0.01
Other Polynesian	1	0.00
Other Pac. Isl., not spec. (33)	132	0.06
Hispanic or Latino:	204,543	90.34
Central American:	14,668	6.48
Costa Rican	473	0.21
Guatemalan	823	0.36
Honduran	2,593	1.15
Nicaraguan	9,211	4.07
Panamanian	379	0.17
Salvadoran	763	0.34
Other Central American	426	0.19
Cuban	140,651	62.12
Dominican Republic	4,106	1.81
Mexican	1,719	0.76
Puerto Rican	6,584	2.91
South American:	12,510	5.53
Argentinean	632	0.28
Bolivian	113	0.05
Chilean	611	0.27
Colombian	7,152	3.16
Ecuadorian	1,159	0.51
Paraguayan	16	0.01
Peruvian	1,418	0.63
Uruguayan	118	0.05
Venezuelan	1,117	0.49
Other South American	174	0.08
Other Hispanic or Latino	24,305	10.73
Hungarian	82	0.04
Iranian	18	0.01
Irish	1,027	0.45
Italian	1,583	0.70
Latvian	16	0.01
Lithuanian	58	0.03
Norwegian	97	0.04
Pennsylvania German	7	0.00
Polish	334	0.15
Portuguese	183	0.08
Romanian	19	0.01
Russian	144	0.06
Scandinavian	5	0.00
Scotch-Irish	193	0.09
Scottish	147	0.06
Slovak	8	0.00
Swedish	26	0.01
Swiss	15	0.01
Turkish	22	0.01
Ukrainian	69	0.03
United States or American	5,822	2.57
Welsh	41	0.02
West Indian, excl. Hispanic:	803	0.35
Bahamian	57	0.03
Belizean	8	0.00
British West Indian	30	0.01
Dutch West Indian	8	0.00
Haitian	423	0.19
Jamaican	186	0.08
Trinidadian and Tobagonian	67	0.03
U.S. Virgin Islander	8	0.00
West Indian	16	0.01
White:	206,539	91.22
Not Hispanic (18,267)	18,674	8.25
Hispanic (181,009)	187,865	82.97
Yugoslavian	7	0.00

Hobe Sound

Place Type: Census Designated Place
County: Martin
Population: 11,376

Ancestry/Race	Number	%
African American/Black:	684	6.01
Not Hispanic (656)	679	5.97
Hispanic (3)	5	0.04
African, sub-Saharan:	26	0.23
African	26	0.23
Am. Ind. or Alaska Nat., not spec.	12	0.11
American Indian tribes, specified:	27	0.24
Apache	1	0.01
Blackfeet (1)	1	0.01
Cherokee (3)	10	0.09
Chippewa (2)	2	0.02
Comanche	1	0.01
Crow (1)	1	0.01
Iroquois (1)	2	0.02
Latin American Indians (5)	5	0.04
Seminole	1	0.01
Sioux	1	0.01
All other tribes	2	0.02
American Indian tribes, not spec.	1	0.01
Arab:	49	0.44
Lebanese	7	0.06
Moroccan	42	0.38
Armenian	7	0.06
Asian:	90	0.79
Chinese, ex. Taiwanese (23)	27	0.24
Filipino (11)	15	0.13
Indian (18)	23	0.20
Indonesian (1)	2	0.02
Japanese (2)	2	0.02
Korean (4)	5	0.04
Sri Lankan (2)	2	0.02
Taiwanese (2)	2	0.02
Thai (2)	2	0.02
Vietnamese (3)	4	0.04
Other Asian, not specified	6	0.05
Austrian	16	0.14
Belgian	34	0.30
British	36	0.32
Canadian	44	0.39
Carpatho Rusyn	15	0.13
Croatian	25	0.22
Czech	63	0.56
Czechoslovakian	18	0.16
Danish	82	0.73
Dutch	265	2.37
Eastern European	31	0.28
English	1,583	14.14
European	36	0.32
Finnish	64	0.57
French, except Basque	545	4.87
French Canadian	256	2.29
German	1,975	17.64
Greek	78	0.70
Hawaii Native/Pacific Islander:	14	0.12
Melanesian: (1)	6	0.05
Other Melanesian (1)	6	0.05
Micronesian: (1)	1	0.01
Guamanian/Chamorro (1)	1	0.01
Polynesian: (1)	1	0.01
Native Hawaiian (1)	1	0.01
Other Pac. Isl., not spec.	6	0.05
Hispanic or Latino:	253	2.22
Central American:	11	0.10
Costa Rican	1	0.01
Guatemalan	2	0.02
Salvadoran	3	0.03
Other Central American	5	0.04
Cuban	47	0.41
Dominican Republic	3	0.03
Mexican	64	0.56
Puerto Rican	69	0.61
South American:	22	0.19
Argentinean	4	0.04

Notes: 1. Figures in the "Number" column do not add up to the total population due to: a) Ancestry/Race overlap — e.g. persons can report being both White and Irish, b) persons of Hispanic origin can report being any race, c) persons reporting two ancestries are counted in both categories. 2. Numbers in parentheses indicate the number of persons reporting this ancestry/race alone, not in combination with any other ancestry/race. 3. Refer to the Explanation of Data in the front of the book for more detailed information.

Chilean	1	0.01
Colombian	6	0.05
Paraguayan	1	0.01
Peruvian	2	0.02
Venezuelan	2	0.02
Other South American	6	0.05
Other Hispanic or Latino	37	0.33
Hungarian	65	0.58
Irish	1,691	15.11
Italian	868	7.75
Lithuanian	73	0.65
Norwegian	112	1.00
Pennsylvania German	32	0.29
Polish	431	3.85
Portuguese	26	0.23
Romanian	7	0.06
Russian	26	0.23
Scandinavian	14	0.13
Scotch-Irish	270	2.41
Scottish	301	2.69
Serbian	19	0.17
Slovak	69	0.62
Swedish	166	1.48
Swiss	56	0.50
Ukrainian	66	0.59
United States or American	967	8.64
Welsh	57	0.51
West Indian, excl. Hispanic:	47	0.42
Bermudan	8	0.07
Haitian	31	0.28
Jamaican	8	0.07
White:	10,535	92.61
Not Hispanic (10,286)	10,349	90.97
Hispanic (178)	186	1.64
Yugoslavian	9	0.08

Holiday

Place Type: Census Designated Place
County: Pasco
Population: 21,904

Ancestry/Race	Number	%
African American/Black:	360	1.64
Not Hispanic (291)	326	1.49
Hispanic (18)	34	0.16
African, sub-Saharan:	17	0.08
African	6	0.03
South African	11	0.05
Am. Ind. or Alaska Nat., not spec.	36	0.16
Albanian	41	0.19
American Indian tribes, specified:	123	0.56
Apache (2)	2	0.01
Blackfeet	8	0.04
Cherokee (22)	54	0.25
Chippewa (13)	14	0.06
Choctaw (2)	2	0.01
Cree	1	0.00
Creek (1)	6	0.03
Iroquois (2)	6	0.03
Latin American Indians	6	0.03
Navajo (1)	5	0.02
Pueblo	6	0.03
Sioux (6)	7	0.03
All other tribes	6	0.03
American Indian tribes, not spec.	9	0.04
Arab:	194	0.89
Arab/Arabic	13	0.06
Lebanese	64	0.29
Syrian	117	0.53
Armenian	32	0.15
Asian:	270	1.23
Chinese, ex. Taiwanese (11)	20	0.09
Filipino (34)	56	0.26
Indian (34)	42	0.19
Japanese (10)	15	0.07
Korean (6)	10	0.05
Laotian (7)	7	0.03
Pakistani (2)	7	0.03
Thai (6)	10	0.05
Vietnamese (71)	79	0.36
Other Asian, specified	2	0.01
Other Asian, not specified (7)	22	0.10
Austrian	106	0.48
Belgian	25	0.11
Brazilian	8	0.04
British	115	0.52
Canadian	227	1.04
Croatian	39	0.18
Czech	129	0.59
Czechoslovakian	81	0.37
Danish	100	0.46
Dutch	427	1.95
Eastern European	8	0.04
English	2,402	10.96
European	94	0.43
Finnish	45	0.21
French, except Basque	889	4.06
French Canadian	388	1.77
German	4,074	18.59
Greek	1,247	5.69
Guyanese	22	0.10
Hawaii Native/Pacific Islander:	24	0.11
Micronesian: (5)	10	0.05
Guamanian/Chamorro	2	0.01
Other Micronesian (5)	8	0.04
Polynesian: (3)	3	0.01
Native Hawaiian (3)	3	0.01
Other Pac. Isl., specified	1	0.00
Other Pac. Isl., not spec. (4)	10	0.05
Hispanic or Latino:	883	4.03
Central American:	25	0.11
Costa Rican	5	0.02
Guatemalan	5	0.02
Honduran	10	0.05
Panamanian	3	0.01
Other Central American	2	0.01
Cuban	107	0.49
Dominican Republic	29	0.13
Mexican	121	0.55
Puerto Rican	394	1.80
South American:	45	0.21
Argentinean	4	0.02
Chilean	1	0.00
Colombian	18	0.08
Ecuadorian	6	0.03
Peruvian	9	0.04
Venezuelan	4	0.02
Other South American	3	0.01
Other Hispanic or Latino	162	0.74
Hungarian	258	1.18
Irish	3,711	16.93
Israeli	7	0.03
Italian	2,528	11.53
Lithuanian	122	0.56
Maltese	7	0.03
Northern European	7	0.03
Norwegian	273	1.25
Pennsylvania German	15	0.07
Polish	1,123	5.12
Portuguese	147	0.67
Romanian	9	0.04
Russian	176	0.80
Scandinavian	38	0.17
Scotch-Irish	303	1.38
Scottish	375	1.71
Slovak	101	0.46
Slovene	5	0.02
Swedish	420	1.92
Swiss	78	0.36
Ukrainian	59	0.27
United States or American	1,141	5.21
Welsh	147	0.67
West Indian, excl. Hispanic:	69	0.31
Bahamian	6	0.03
Barbadian	8	0.04
Jamaican	44	0.20
Trinidadian and Tobagonian	11	0.05
White:	21,098	96.32
Not Hispanic (20,227)	20,432	93.28
Hispanic (611)	666	3.04
Yugoslavian	61	0.28

Holly Hill

Place Type: City
County: Volusia
Population: 12,119

Ancestry/Race	Number	%
African American/Black:	1,146	9.46
Not Hispanic (1,063)	1,104	9.11
Hispanic (24)	42	0.35
African, sub-Saharan:	51	0.42
African	43	0.36
Nigerian	8	0.07
Alaska Native tribes, specified:	1	0.01
Alaska Athabascan (1)	1	0.01
Am. Ind. or Alaska Nat., not spec.	48	0.40
American Indian tribes, specified:	94	0.78
Apache	1	0.01
Blackfeet (1)	3	0.02
Cherokee (8)	43	0.35
Chickasaw	1	0.01
Chippewa (3)	8	0.07
Creek (3)	9	0.07
Iroquois	4	0.03
Kiowa (1)	1	0.01
Latin American Indians	3	0.02
Lumbee (1)	1	0.01
Navajo (1)	1	0.01
Seminole (2)	8	0.07
Sioux	2	0.02
All other tribes (2)	9	0.07
American Indian tribes, not spec.	11	0.09
Arab:	51	0.42
Lebanese	38	0.31
Palestinian	13	0.11
Asian:	147	1.21
Chinese, ex. Taiwanese (14)	18	0.15
Filipino (27)	33	0.27
Indian (36)	42	0.35
Japanese (4)	5	0.04
Korean (14)	21	0.17
Thai (2)	2	0.02
Vietnamese (20)	23	0.19
Other Asian, not specified	3	0.02
Austrian	46	0.38
Brazilian	10	0.08
British	77	0.64
Canadian	13	0.11
Celtic	18	0.15
Czech	11	0.09
Czechoslovakian	24	0.20
Danish	36	0.30
Dutch	230	1.90
English	1,418	11.73
European	52	0.43
Finnish	10	0.08
French, except Basque	412	3.41
French Canadian	111	0.92
German	1,659	13.73
Greek	30	0.25
Hawaii Native/Pacific Islander:	3	0.02
Micronesian: (1)	1	0.01
Guamanian/Chamorro (1)	1	0.01
Polynesian: (2)	2	0.02
Samoan (2)	2	0.02
Hispanic or Latino:	447	3.69
Central American:	16	0.13
Costa Rican	7	0.06
Honduran	4	0.03
Nicaraguan	1	0.01
Panamanian	2	0.02
Other Central American	2	0.02
Cuban	65	0.54
Dominican Republic	11	0.09
Mexican	107	0.88
Puerto Rican	129	1.06
South American:	50	0.41

Notes: 1. Figures in the "Number" column do not add up to the total population due to: a) Ancestry/Race overlap — e.g. persons can report being both White and Irish, b) persons of Hispanic origin can report being any race, c) persons reporting two ancestries are counted in both categories. 2. Numbers in parentheses indicate the number of persons reporting this ancestry/race alone, not in combination with any other ancestry/race. 3. Refer to the Explanation of Data in the front of the book for more detailed information.

Argentinean	2	0.02
Bolivian	1	0.01
Chilean	8	0.07
Colombian	20	0.17
Ecuadorian	5	0.04
Peruvian	2	0.02
Uruguayan	2	0.02
Venezuelan	8	0.07
Other South American	2	0.02
Other Hispanic or Latino	69	0.57
Hungarian	54	0.45
Irish	1,466	12.13
Italian	899	7.44
Latvian	14	0.12
Lithuanian	15	0.12
Norwegian	156	1.29
Polish	438	3.62
Portuguese	56	0.46
Russian	13	0.11
Scandinavian	35	0.29
Scotch-Irish	254	2.10
Scottish	230	1.90
Serbian	9	0.07
Slovak	6	0.05
Swedish	111	0.92
Swiss	14	0.12
Ukrainian	17	0.14
United States or American	1,366	11.30
Welsh	45	0.37
West Indian, excl. Hispanic:	44	0.36
Bahamian	7	0.06
Trinidadian and Tobagonian	29	0.24
West Indian	8	0.07
White:	10,734	88.57
Not Hispanic (10,282)	10,424	86.01
Hispanic (274)	310	2.56
Yugoslavian	23	0.19

Hollywood

Place Type: City
County: Broward
Population: 139,357

Ancestry/Race	Number	%
Acadian/Cajun	9	0.01
African American/Black:	18,405	13.21
Not Hispanic (15,972)	17,170	12.32
Hispanic (881)	1,235	0.89
African, sub-Saharan:	961	0.69
African	554	0.40
Cape Verdean	18	0.01
Liberian	37	0.03
Nigerian	285	0.20
South African	56	0.04
Other sub-Saharan African	11	0.01
Alaska Native tribes, specified:	2	0.00
Aleut (2)	2	0.00
Alaska Native tribes, not specified	2	0.00
Am. Ind. or Alaska Nat., not spec.	314	0.23
Albanian	20	0.01
Alsatian	9	0.01
American Indian tribes, specified:	483	0.35
Apache (5)	10	0.01
Blackfeet (3)	23	0.02
Cherokee (57)	159	0.11
Cheyenne	3	0.00
Chickasaw	1	0.00
Chippewa (10)	14	0.01
Choctaw (8)	21	0.02
Comanche (1)	2	0.00
Cree (4)	4	0.00
Creek (5)	8	0.01
Crow (4)	5	0.00
Delaware	2	0.00
Iroquois (10)	27	0.02
Latin American Indians (38)	99	0.07
Lumbee (2)	2	0.00
Navajo	3	0.00
Paiute	3	0.00
Pueblo	6	0.00
Seminole (33)	38	0.03
Sioux (10)	18	0.01
Tohono O'Odham (1)	1	0.00
Ute (1)	1	0.00
All other tribes (12)	33	0.02
American Indian tribes, not spec.	53	0.04
Arab:	1,183	0.85
Arab/Arabic	158	0.11
Egyptian	85	0.06
Iraqi	15	0.01
Jordanian	100	0.07
Lebanese	394	0.28
Moroccan	107	0.08
Palestinian	49	0.04
Syrian	186	0.13
Other Arab	89	0.06
Armenian	95	0.07
Asian:	3,469	2.49
Bangladeshi (15)	17	0.01
Cambodian (3)	4	0.00
Chinese, ex. Taiwanese (640)	778	0.56
Filipino (259)	355	0.25
Indian (1,168)	1,410	1.01
Indonesian (11)	17	0.01
Japanese (83)	129	0.09
Korean (164)	181	0.13
Laotian (9)	10	0.01
Malaysian (3)	7	0.01
Pakistani (117)	166	0.12
Sri Lankan (2)	2	0.00
Taiwanese (15)	18	0.01
Thai (33)	40	0.03
Vietnamese (152)	162	0.12
Other Asian, specified (1)	8	0.01
Other Asian, not specified (55)	165	0.12
Australian	61	0.04
Austrian	790	0.57
Basque	8	0.01
Belgian	57	0.04
Brazilian	731	0.52
British	564	0.40
Bulgarian	58	0.04
Canadian	1,156	0.83
Croatian	121	0.09
Czech	228	0.16
Czechoslovakian	330	0.24
Danish	293	0.21
Dutch	1,419	1.02
Eastern European	494	0.35
English	7,354	5.28
European	872	0.63
Finnish	180	0.13
French, except Basque	3,601	2.59
French Canadian	1,696	1.22
German	11,959	8.59
German Russian	20	0.01
Greek	1,097	0.79
Guyanese	281	0.20
Hawaii Native/Pacific Islander:	260	0.19
Micronesian: (18)	27	0.02
Guamanian/Chamorro (12)	19	0.01
Other Micronesian (6)	8	0.01
Polynesian: (60)	87	0.06
Native Hawaiian (28)	51	0.04
Samoan (11)	14	0.01
Tongan (18)	18	0.01
Other Polynesian (3)	4	0.00
Other Pac. Isl., specified	3	0.00
Other Pac. Isl., not spec. (39)	143	0.10
Hispanic or Latino:	31,392	22.53
Central American:	2,021	1.45
Costa Rican	256	0.18
Guatemalan	272	0.20
Honduran	418	0.30
Nicaraguan	501	0.36
Panamanian	241	0.17
Salvadoran	272	0.20
Other Central American	61	0.04
Cuban	5,891	4.23
Dominican Republic	1,681	1.21
Mexican	1,288	0.92
Puerto Rican	7,463	5.36
South American:	6,952	4.99
Argentinean	456	0.33
Bolivian	100	0.07
Chilean	302	0.22
Colombian	3,152	2.26
Ecuadorian	592	0.42
Paraguayan	15	0.01
Peruvian	1,466	1.05
Uruguayan	113	0.08
Venezuelan	568	0.41
Other South American	188	0.13
Other Hispanic or Latino	6,096	4.37
Hungarian	1,703	1.22
Iranian	76	0.05
Irish	12,650	9.08
Israeli	742	0.53
Italian	13,206	9.48
Latvian	89	0.06
Lithuanian	490	0.35
Luxemburger	18	0.01
Macedonian	73	0.05
Maltese	11	0.01
Northern European	33	0.02
Norwegian	677	0.49
Pennsylvania German	61	0.04
Polish	5,026	3.61
Portuguese	588	0.42
Romanian	1,613	1.16
Russian	4,464	3.21
Scandinavian	31	0.02
Scotch-Irish	1,311	0.94
Scottish	1,402	1.01
Serbian	117	0.08
Slavic	49	0.04
Slovak	181	0.13
Slovene	32	0.02
Swedish	861	0.62
Swiss	421	0.30
Turkish	218	0.16
Ukrainian	753	0.54
United States or American	9,762	7.01
Welsh	440	0.32
West Indian, excl. Hispanic:	7,171	5.15
Bahamian	435	0.31
Barbadian	86	0.06
Belizean	38	0.03
Bermudan	7	0.01
British West Indian	224	0.16
Haitian	2,140	1.54
Jamaican	3,105	2.23
Trinidadian and Tobagonian	727	0.52
U.S. Virgin Islander	67	0.05
West Indian	324	0.23
Other West Indian	18	0.01
White:	112,460	80.70
Not Hispanic (85,808)	87,426	62.74
Hispanic (23,382)	25,034	17.96
Yugoslavian	245	0.18

Homestead

Place Type: City
County: Miami-Dade
Population: 31,909

Ancestry/Race	Number	%
African American/Black:	7,977	25.00
Not Hispanic (6,886)	7,534	23.61
Hispanic (308)	443	1.39
African, sub-Saharan:	103	0.32
African	103	0.32
Alaska Native tribes, specified:	3	0.01
Alaska Athabascan	1	0.00
Eskimo (1)	1	0.00
Tlingit-Haida	1	0.00
Am. Ind. or Alaska Nat., not spec.	68	0.21
American Indian tribes, specified:	180	0.56

Notes: 1. Figures in the "Number" column do not add up to the total population due to: a) Ancestry/Race overlap — e.g. persons can report being both White and Irish, b) persons of Hispanic origin can report being any race, c) persons reporting two ancestries are counted in both categories. 2. Numbers in parentheses indicate the number of persons reporting this ancestry/race alone, not in combination with any other ancestry/race. 3. Refer to the Explanation of Data in the front of the book for more detailed information.

Blackfeet (3)	5	0.02
Cherokee (12)	28	0.09
Cheyenne	1	0.00
Choctaw (1)	7	0.02
Crow (1)	1	0.00
Iroquois	2	0.01
Kiowa (1)	1	0.00
Latin American Indians (82)	104	0.33
Lumbee	1	0.00
Navajo	2	0.01
Potawatomi (1)	1	0.00
Seminole	1	0.00
Sioux (5)	5	0.02
All other tribes (6)	21	0.07
American Indian tribes, not spec.	14	0.04
Arab:	22	0.07
Arab/Arabic	8	0.02
Egyptian	14	0.04
Armenian	21	0.07
Asian:	351	1.10
Bangladeshi (17)	18	0.06
Cambodian (9)	9	0.03
Chinese, ex. Taiwanese (35)	46	0.14
Filipino (27)	49	0.15
Indian (72)	94	0.29
Indonesian	4	0.01
Japanese (11)	21	0.07
Korean (12)	21	0.07
Pakistani	2	0.01
Taiwanese (4)	4	0.01
Thai (9)	11	0.03
Vietnamese (30)	32	0.10
Other Asian, specified (7)	7	0.02
Other Asian, not specified (10)	33	0.10
British	28	0.09
Canadian	24	0.07
Croatian	9	0.03
Czech	26	0.08
Czechoslovakian	26	0.08
Danish	20	0.06
Dutch	247	0.77
Eastern European	9	0.03
English	871	2.72
European	25	0.08
Finnish	16	0.05
French, except Basque	323	1.01
French Canadian	27	0.08
German	1,289	4.02
Greek	55	0.17
Guyanese	6	0.02
Hawaii Native/Pacific Islander:	82	0.26
Melanesian:	1	0.00
Fijian	1	0.00
Micronesian: (10)	12	0.04
Guamanian/Chamorro (10)	12	0.04
Polynesian: (11)	19	0.06
Native Hawaiian (8)	14	0.04
Samoan (3)	5	0.02
Other Pac. Isl., not spec. (6)	50	0.16
Hispanic or Latino:	16,537	51.83
Central American:	2,595	8.13
Costa Rican	47	0.15
Guatemalan	1,059	3.32
Honduran	343	1.07
Nicaraguan	228	0.71
Panamanian	39	0.12
Salvadoran	859	2.69
Other Central American	20	0.06
Cuban	2,171	6.80
Dominican Republic	263	0.82
Mexican	7,279	22.81
Puerto Rican	2,084	6.53
South American:	425	1.33
Argentinean	21	0.07
Bolivian	2	0.01
Chilean	11	0.03
Colombian	195	0.61
Ecuadorian	57	0.18
Peruvian	59	0.18
Uruguayan	2	0.01
Venezuelan	74	0.23
Other South American	4	0.01
Other Hispanic or Latino	1,720	5.39
Hungarian	98	0.31
Irish	1,336	4.17
Italian	579	1.81
Lithuanian	8	0.02
Norwegian	25	0.08
Polish	287	0.90
Portuguese	35	0.11
Romanian	16	0.05
Russian	63	0.20
Scotch-Irish	108	0.34
Scottish	208	0.65
Slavic	9	0.03
Slovak	9	0.03
Swedish	187	0.58
Swiss	36	0.11
Turkish	30	0.09
Ukrainian	37	0.12
United States or American	1,680	5.24
Welsh	60	0.19
West Indian, excl. Hispanic:	1,923	6.00
Bahamian	52	0.16
British West Indian	21	0.07
Haitian	1,531	4.78
Jamaican	229	0.71
Trinidadian and Tobagonian	75	0.23
West Indian	15	0.05
White:	20,447	64.08
Not Hispanic (7,295)	7,542	23.64
Hispanic (12,170)	12,905	40.44

Homosassa Springs

Place Type: Census Designated Place
County: Citrus
Population: 12,458

Ancestry/Race	Number	%
African American/Black:	130	1.04
Not Hispanic (108)	125	1.00
Hispanic (4)	5	0.04
African, sub-Saharan:	43	0.34
African	43	0.34
Am. Ind. or Alaska Nat., not spec.	48	0.39
American Indian tribes, specified:	117	0.94
Apache (1)	1	0.01
Blackfeet (1)	5	0.04
Cherokee (16)	53	0.43
Chippewa (5)	9	0.07
Comanche (1)	1	0.01
Creek (7)	8	0.06
Delaware (1)	1	0.01
Iroquois (3)	7	0.06
Lumbee (1)	1	0.01
Navajo (3)	3	0.02
Osage	1	0.01
Ottawa	1	0.01
Paiute (1)	1	0.01
Potawatomi (1)	1	0.01
Pueblo (1)	1	0.01
Seminole (1)	2	0.02
Sioux (3)	3	0.02
All other tribes (13)	18	0.14
American Indian tribes, not spec.	6	0.05
Arab:	35	0.27
Lebanese	35	0.27
Armenian	10	0.08
Asian:	96	0.77
Chinese, ex. Taiwanese (4)	8	0.06
Filipino (10)	25	0.20
Indian (33)	42	0.34
Japanese (5)	6	0.05
Korean (3)	8	0.06
Pakistani	1	0.01
Vietnamese (3)	3	0.02
Other Asian, not specified (1)	3	0.02
Austrian	10	0.08
Belgian	7	0.05
British	49	0.38
Canadian	35	0.27
Croatian	6	0.05
Czech	34	0.27
Danish	49	0.38
Dutch	413	3.24
English	1,936	15.18
European	41	0.32
Finnish	40	0.31
French, except Basque	546	4.28
French Canadian	141	1.11
German	2,692	21.11
Greek	47	0.37
Hawaii Native/Pacific Islander:	2	0.02
Micronesian: (1)	2	0.02
Guamanian/Chamorro (1)	2	0.02
Hispanic or Latino:	260	2.09
Central American:	6	0.05
Honduran	1	0.01
Nicaraguan	3	0.02
Panamanian	2	0.02
Cuban	36	0.29
Dominican Republic	1	0.01
Mexican	35	0.28
Puerto Rican	119	0.96
South American:	13	0.10
Colombian	2	0.02
Ecuadorian	4	0.03
Peruvian	2	0.02
Venezuelan	3	0.02
Other South American	2	0.02
Other Hispanic or Latino	50	0.40
Hungarian	101	0.79
Irish	2,223	17.44
Italian	877	6.88
Latvian	17	0.13
Northern European	28	0.22
Norwegian	54	0.42
Pennsylvania German	17	0.13
Polish	443	3.47
Portuguese	31	0.24
Russian	33	0.26
Scandinavian	47	0.37
Scotch-Irish	310	2.43
Scottish	409	3.21
Serbian	11	0.09
Slavic	7	0.05
Slovak	8	0.06
Swedish	201	1.58
Swiss	61	0.48
Ukrainian	44	0.35
United States or American	1,449	11.36
Welsh	142	1.11
West Indian, excl. Hispanic:	25	0.20
Bahamian	8	0.06
Jamaican	17	0.13
White:	12,170	97.69
Not Hispanic (11,822)	11,942	95.86
Hispanic (219)	228	1.83
Yugoslavian	22	0.17

Hudson

Place Type: Census Designated Place
County: Pasco
Population: 12,765

Ancestry/Race	Number	%
African American/Black:	65	0.51
Not Hispanic (44)	59	0.46
Hispanic (2)	6	0.05
Am. Ind. or Alaska Nat., not spec.	28	0.22
Alsatian	9	0.07
American Indian tribes, specified:	87	0.68
Apache (1)	1	0.01
Blackfeet (1)	5	0.04
Cherokee (9)	42	0.33
Cheyenne	1	0.01
Chickasaw	1	0.01
Chippewa (2)	4	0.03

Notes: 1. Figures in the "Number" column do not add up to the total population due to: a) Ancestry/Race overlap — e.g. persons can report being both White and Irish, b) persons of Hispanic origin can report being any race, c) persons reporting two ancestries are counted in both categories. 2. Numbers in parentheses indicate the number of persons reporting this ancestry/race alone, not in combination with any other ancestry/race. 3. Refer to the Explanation of Data in the front of the book for more detailed information.

Choctaw (1)	1	0.01
Comanche	1	0.01
Creek	4	0.03
Iroquois (2)	7	0.05
Kiowa (1)	1	0.01
Lumbee	2	0.02
Ottawa	4	0.03
Paiute (1)	1	0.01
Seminole (1)	5	0.04
Shoshone	1	0.01
Sioux	1	0.01
Yaqui	4	0.03
All other tribes	1	0.01
American Indian tribes, not spec.	5	0.04
Arab:	34	0.27
Egyptian	16	0.13
Lebanese	11	0.09
Syrian	7	0.06
Asian:	153	1.20
Chinese, ex. Taiwanese (27)	32	0.25
Filipino (26)	27	0.21
Hmong (1)	1	0.01
Indian (36)	47	0.37
Japanese (6)	11	0.09
Korean (5)	9	0.07
Laotian (1)	1	0.01
Malaysian	2	0.02
Pakistani	4	0.03
Taiwanese (1)	1	0.01
Thai (4)	5	0.04
Vietnamese (5)	9	0.07
Other Asian, not specified (1)	4	0.03
Austrian	51	0.40
Belgian	42	0.33
British	71	0.56
Canadian	149	1.17
Croatian	30	0.24
Czech	191	1.50
Czechoslovakian	66	0.52
Danish	74	0.58
Dutch	284	2.23
English	1,687	13.26
Estonian	8	0.06
European	7	0.06
Finnish	18	0.14
French, except Basque	638	5.01
French Canadian	218	1.71
German	2,536	19.93
Greek	169	1.33
Hawaii Native/Pacific Islander:	9	0.07
Micronesian: (2)	2	0.02
Guamanian/Chamorro (2)	2	0.02
Polynesian: (2)	7	0.05
Native Hawaiian (1)	5	0.04
Tongan (1)	2	0.02
Hispanic or Latino:	332	2.60
Central American:	13	0.10
Costa Rican	5	0.04
Guatemalan	1	0.01
Honduran	5	0.04
Panamanian	1	0.01
Other Central American	1	0.01
Cuban	29	0.23
Mexican	56	0.44
Puerto Rican	175	1.37
South American:	16	0.13
Chilean	3	0.02
Colombian	9	0.07
Ecuadorian	1	0.01
Peruvian	2	0.02
Venezuelan	1	0.01
Other Hispanic or Latino	43	0.34
Hungarian	112	0.88
Icelander	6	0.05
Irish	2,259	17.75
Italian	1,529	12.02
Latvian	14	0.11
Lithuanian	137	1.08
Macedonian	8	0.06
Norwegian	174	1.37
Pennsylvania German	16	0.13
Polish	744	5.85
Portuguese	81	0.64
Romanian	44	0.35
Russian	52	0.41
Scandinavian	20	0.16
Scotch-Irish	152	1.19
Scottish	284	2.23
Slavic	109	0.86
Slovak	47	0.37
Slovene	9	0.07
Swedish	333	2.62
Swiss	75	0.59
Ukrainian	106	0.83
United States or American	627	4.93
Welsh	137	1.08
White:	12,512	98.02
Not Hispanic (12,109)	12,232	95.82
Hispanic (256)	280	2.19

Immokalee

Place Type: Census Designated Place
County: Collier
Population: 19,763

Ancestry/Race	Number	%
African American/Black:	4,331	21.91
Not Hispanic (3,491)	4,218	21.34
Hispanic (73)	113	0.57
African, sub-Saharan:	67	0.35
African	60	0.31
Cape Verdean	7	0.04
Alaska Native tribes, specified:	2	0.01
Alaska Athabascan	1	0.01
Tlingit-Haida	1	0.01
Am. Ind. or Alaska Nat., not spec.	63	0.32
American Indian tribes, specified:	174	0.88
Cherokee (4)	8	0.04
Choctaw (3)	3	0.02
Latin American Indians (19)	31	0.16
Osage (1)	1	0.01
Seminole (117)	123	0.62
All other tribes (1)	8	0.04
American Indian tribes, not spec.	12	0.06
Arab:	7	0.04
Syrian	7	0.04
Asian:	79	0.40
Chinese, ex. Taiwanese	2	0.01
Indian (23)	35	0.18
Japanese (1)	3	0.02
Korean (2)	2	0.01
Thai	2	0.01
Vietnamese (2)	2	0.01
Other Asian, not specified (11)	33	0.17
Dutch	6	0.03
English	92	0.47
European	20	0.10
Finnish	21	0.11
French, except Basque	63	0.32
German	48	0.25
Hawaii Native/Pacific Islander:	49	0.25
Micronesian: (34)	41	0.21
Guamanian/Chamorro (34)	41	0.21
Polynesian: (2)	6	0.03
Native Hawaiian (2)	5	0.03
Samoan	1	0.01
Other Pac. Isl., not spec. (1)	2	0.01
Hispanic or Latino:	14,027	70.98
Central American:	930	4.71
Guatemalan	861	4.36
Honduran	38	0.19
Nicaraguan	6	0.03
Panamanian	1	0.01
Salvadoran	19	0.10
Other Central American	5	0.03
Cuban	40	0.20
Dominican Republic	8	0.04
Mexican	11,354	57.45
Puerto Rican	377	1.91
South American:	23	0.12
Colombian	2	0.01
Paraguayan	1	0.01
Peruvian	19	0.10
Venezuelan	1	0.01
Other Hispanic or Latino	1,295	6.55
Irish	165	0.85
Italian	32	0.16
Norwegian	10	0.05
Polish	8	0.04
Portuguese	17	0.09
Russian	7	0.04
Scotch-Irish	4	0.02
Scottish	8	0.04
United States or American	646	3.33
West Indian, excl. Hispanic:	2,135	11.00
Bahamian	15	0.08
Haitian	2,095	10.79
Trinidadian and Tobagonian	25	0.13
White:	8,084	40.90
Not Hispanic (1,254)	1,291	6.53
Hispanic (6,356)	6,793	34.37

Iona

Place Type: Census Designated Place
County: Lee
Population: 11,756

Ancestry/Race	Number	%
African American/Black:	62	0.53
Not Hispanic (43)	54	0.46
Hispanic (5)	8	0.07
Alaska Native tribes, specified:	2	0.02
Eskimo (2)	2	0.02
Am. Ind. or Alaska Nat., not spec.	11	0.09
American Indian tribes, specified:	28	0.24
Blackfeet (4)	4	0.03
Cherokee (2)	11	0.09
Chippewa	2	0.02
Choctaw (1)	1	0.01
Lumbee (3)	3	0.03
Ottawa (2)	2	0.02
Shoshone	3	0.03
All other tribes (1)	2	0.02
American Indian tribes, not spec.	4	0.03
Arab:	20	0.17
Lebanese	13	0.11
Syrian	7	0.06
Asian:	73	0.62
Chinese, ex. Taiwanese (9)	12	0.10
Filipino (8)	11	0.09
Indian (18)	19	0.16
Indonesian	2	0.02
Japanese (6)	8	0.07
Korean (5)	5	0.04
Malaysian	1	0.01
Thai	2	0.02
Vietnamese (2)	2	0.02
Other Asian, specified (8)	9	0.08
Other Asian, not specified	3	0.03
Austrian	63	0.53
Belgian	10	0.08
British	72	0.61
Canadian	71	0.60
Croatian	45	0.38
Czech	71	0.60
Czechoslovakian	28	0.24
Danish	77	0.65
Dutch	252	2.13
English	1,995	16.83
European	15	0.13
Finnish	26	0.22
French, except Basque	392	3.31
French Canadian	251	2.12
German	2,970	25.06
Greek	18	0.15
Hawaii Native/Pacific Islander:	4	0.03
Polynesian: (1)	1	0.01
Native Hawaiian (1)	1	0.01

Notes: 1. Figures in the "Number" column do not add up to the total population due to: a) Ancestry/Race overlap — e.g. persons can report being both White and Irish, b) persons of Hispanic origin can report being any race, c) persons reporting two ancestries are counted in both categories. 2. Numbers in parentheses indicate the number of persons reporting this ancestry/race alone, not in combination with any other ancestry/race. 3. Refer to the Explanation of Data in the front of the book for more detailed information.

Ancestry/Race	Number	%
Other Pac. Isl., specified	1	0.01
Other Pac. Isl., not spec.	2	0.02
Hispanic or Latino:	463	3.94
Central American:	5	0.04
Honduran	2	0.02
Nicaraguan	1	0.01
Salvadoran	1	0.01
Other Central American	1	0.01
Cuban	13	0.11
Dominican Republic	3	0.03
Mexican	314	2.67
Puerto Rican	54	0.46
South American:	24	0.20
Argentinean	7	0.06
Chilean	1	0.01
Colombian	4	0.03
Ecuadorian	4	0.03
Peruvian	1	0.01
Venezuelan	7	0.06
Other Hispanic or Latino	50	0.43
Hungarian	142	1.20
Irish	1,871	15.79
Italian	800	6.75
Lithuanian	47	0.40
Norwegian	167	1.41
Pennsylvania German	10	0.08
Polish	360	3.04
Portuguese	15	0.13
Russian	167	1.41
Scotch-Irish	323	2.73
Scottish	274	2.31
Serbian	11	0.09
Slavic	16	0.13
Slovak	76	0.64
Slovene	8	0.07
Swedish	289	2.44
Swiss	56	0.47
Ukrainian	77	0.65
United States or American	1,044	8.81
Welsh	110	0.93
White:	11,524	98.03
Not Hispanic (11,128)	11,166	94.98
Hispanic (331)	358	3.05
Yugoslavian	28	0.24

Ives Estates

Place Type: Census Designated Place
County: Miami-Dade
Population: 17,586

Ancestry/Race	Number	%
African American/Black:	6,714	38.18
Not Hispanic (5,957)	6,385	36.31
Hispanic (217)	329	1.87
African, sub-Saharan:	242	1.39
African	188	1.08
Kenyan	26	0.15
Nigerian	17	0.10
South African	11	0.06
Alaska Native tribes, specified:	2	0.01
Aleut	1	0.01
Tlingit-Haida	1	0.01
Am. Ind. or Alaska Nat., not spec.	41	0.23
American Indian tribes, specified:	36	0.20
Blackfeet	6	0.03
Cherokee (3)	16	0.09
Choctaw (1)	1	0.01
Latin American Indians (2)	6	0.03
Seminole	1	0.01
All other tribes (3)	6	0.03
American Indian tribes, not spec.	5	0.03
Arab:	297	1.71
Arab/Arabic	127	0.73
Iraqi	7	0.04
Lebanese	44	0.25
Moroccan	5	0.03
Palestinian	40	0.23
Syrian	74	0.42
Asian:	1,024	5.82
Bangladeshi (3)	3	0.02
Cambodian (4)	4	0.02
Chinese, ex. Taiwanese (220)	273	1.55
Filipino (97)	120	0.68
Indian (276)	337	1.92
Indonesian (12)	13	0.07
Japanese (13)	24	0.14
Korean (32)	33	0.19
Laotian (4)	4	0.02
Malaysian	1	0.01
Pakistani (80)	93	0.53
Taiwanese (4)	4	0.02
Thai (15)	15	0.09
Vietnamese (25)	30	0.17
Other Asian, specified	1	0.01
Other Asian, not specified (20)	69	0.39
Austrian	115	0.66
Brazilian	161	0.92
British	66	0.38
Canadian	47	0.27
Croatian	18	0.10
Czech	34	0.20
Danish	14	0.08
Dutch	121	0.69
Eastern European	39	0.22
English	309	1.77
European	79	0.45
Finnish	33	0.19
French, except Basque	163	0.94
French Canadian	13	0.07
German	592	3.40
Greek	84	0.48
Guyanese	76	0.44
Hawaii Native/Pacific Islander:	49	0.28
Polynesian: (7)	8	0.05
Samoan (7)	8	0.05
Other Pac. Isl., specified	1	0.01
Other Pac. Isl., not spec. (2)	40	0.23
Hispanic or Latino:	4,234	24.08
Central American:	420	2.39
Costa Rican	45	0.26
Guatemalan	46	0.26
Honduran	94	0.53
Nicaraguan	120	0.68
Panamanian	70	0.40
Salvadoran	35	0.20
Other Central American	10	0.06
Cuban	617	3.51
Dominican Republic	269	1.53
Mexican	71	0.40
Puerto Rican	695	3.95
South American:	1,175	6.68
Argentinean	183	1.04
Bolivian	5	0.03
Chilean	36	0.20
Colombian	486	2.76
Ecuadorian	63	0.36
Paraguayan	1	0.01
Peruvian	230	1.31
Uruguayan	25	0.14
Venezuelan	120	0.68
Other South American	26	0.15
Other Hispanic or Latino	987	5.61
Hungarian	95	0.55
Iranian	18	0.10
Irish	588	3.38
Israeli	116	0.67
Italian	639	3.67
Latvian	10	0.06
Lithuanian	14	0.08
Norwegian	14	0.08
Pennsylvania German	17	0.10
Polish	346	1.99
Portuguese	62	0.36
Romanian	99	0.57
Russian	707	4.06
Scandinavian	24	0.14
Scotch-Irish	83	0.48
Scottish	166	0.95
Slavic	18	0.10
Swedish	9	0.05
Swiss	11	0.06
Turkish	34	0.20
Ukrainian	52	0.30
United States or American	917	5.26
Welsh	32	0.18
West Indian, excl. Hispanic:	3,901	22.40
Bahamian	146	0.84
Barbadian	15	0.09
Belizean	7	0.04
British West Indian	43	0.25
Haitian	2,449	14.06
Jamaican	1,000	5.74
Trinidadian and Tobagonian	108	0.62
U.S. Virgin Islander	32	0.18
West Indian	101	0.58
White:	9,443	53.70
Not Hispanic (5,863)	6,117	34.78
Hispanic (3,123)	3,326	18.91
Yugoslavian	6	0.03

Jacksonville Beach

Place Type: City
County: Duval
Population: 20,990

Ancestry/Race	Number	%
African American/Black:	1,074	5.12
Not Hispanic (996)	1,045	4.98
Hispanic (15)	29	0.14
African, sub-Saharan:	120	0.57
African	103	0.49
Ghanian	7	0.03
South African	10	0.05
Alaska Native tribes, specified:	1	0.00
Aleut (1)	1	0.00
Am. Ind. or Alaska Nat., not spec.	50	0.24
American Indian tribes, specified:	89	0.42
Apache	1	0.00
Blackfeet	1	0.00
Cherokee (17)	47	0.22
Chickasaw (1)	1	0.00
Chippewa (4)	4	0.02
Choctaw (2)	3	0.01
Comanche (1)	2	0.01
Creek (4)	11	0.05
Delaware	2	0.01
Iroquois	2	0.01
Latin American Indians (1)	2	0.01
Lumbee (3)	3	0.01
Ottawa (1)	1	0.00
Seminole (1)	1	0.00
Sioux	3	0.01
All other tribes (2)	5	0.02
American Indian tribes, not spec.	4	0.02
Arab:	172	0.82
Arab/Arabic	62	0.30
Lebanese	88	0.42
Moroccan	10	0.05
Palestinian	12	0.06
Armenian	38	0.18
Asian:	482	2.30
Cambodian (8)	8	0.04
Chinese, ex. Taiwanese (18)	34	0.16
Filipino (204)	267	1.27
Indian (38)	44	0.21
Indonesian (2)	2	0.01
Japanese (21)	44	0.21
Korean (9)	16	0.08
Laotian (2)	3	0.01
Taiwanese (1)	1	0.00
Thai (8)	12	0.06
Vietnamese (12)	23	0.11
Other Asian, not specified (12)	28	0.13
Austrian	32	0.15
Belgian	12	0.06
British	180	0.86
Bulgarian	12	0.06
Canadian	45	0.21

Notes: 1. Figures in the "Number" column do not add up to the total population due to: a) Ancestry/Race overlap — e.g. persons can report being both White and Irish, b) persons of Hispanic origin can report being any race, c) persons reporting two ancestries are counted in both categories. 2. Numbers in parentheses indicate the number of persons reporting this ancestry/race alone, not in combination with any other ancestry/race. 3. Refer to the Explanation of Data in the front of the book for more detailed information.

Croatian	23	0.11
Czech	133	0.63
Czechoslovakian	39	0.19
Danish	35	0.17
Dutch	500	2.38
Eastern European	15	0.07
English	3,246	15.46
European	260	1.24
Finnish	59	0.28
French, except Basque	932	4.44
French Canadian	262	1.25
German	2,732	13.02
Greek	186	0.89
Hawaii Native/Pacific Islander:	20	0.10
Micronesian: (1)	2	0.01
Guamanian/Chamorro	1	0.00
Other Micronesian (1)	1	0.00
Polynesian: (6)	10	0.05
Native Hawaiian (4)	7	0.03
Samoan (1)	2	0.01
Other Polynesian (1)	1	0.00
Other Pac. Isl., not spec. (2)	8	0.04
Hispanic or Latino:	628	2.99
Central American:	25	0.12
Costa Rican	2	0.01
Guatemalan	4	0.02
Honduran	6	0.03
Nicaraguan	5	0.02
Panamanian	5	0.02
Salvadoran	1	0.00
Other Central American	2	0.01
Cuban	57	0.27
Dominican Republic	4	0.02
Mexican	161	0.77
Puerto Rican	160	0.76
South American:	66	0.31
Bolivian	2	0.01
Chilean	16	0.08
Colombian	13	0.06
Ecuadorian	3	0.01
Peruvian	20	0.10
Uruguayan	1	0.00
Venezuelan	9	0.04
Other South American	2	0.01
Other Hispanic or Latino	155	0.74
Hungarian	116	0.55
Irish	3,347	15.95
Italian	1,676	7.98
Lithuanian	106	0.51
Maltese	8	0.04
Norwegian	218	1.04
Pennsylvania German	22	0.10
Polish	733	3.49
Portuguese	62	0.30
Romanian	35	0.17
Russian	244	1.16
Scandinavian	11	0.05
Scotch-Irish	567	2.70
Scottish	783	3.73
Slavic	9	0.04
Slovak	54	0.26
Slovene	13	0.06
Swedish	158	0.75
Swiss	52	0.25
Turkish	28	0.13
Ukrainian	33	0.16
United States or American	1,356	6.46
Welsh	187	0.89
West Indian, excl. Hispanic:	9	0.04
Jamaican	9	0.04
White:	19,376	92.31
Not Hispanic (18,675)	18,924	90.16
Hispanic (414)	452	2.15
Yugoslavian	16	0.08

Jacksonville

Place Type: Special City
County: Duval
Population: 735,617

Ancestry/Race	Number	%
Acadian/Cajun	179	0.02
Afghan	205	0.03
African American/Black:	218,451	29.70
Not Hispanic (211,252)	215,484	29.29
Hispanic (2,262)	2,967	0.40
African, sub-Saharan:	8,010	1.09
African	6,995	0.95
Cape Verdean	72	0.01
Ethiopian	99	0.01
Ghanian	112	0.02
Kenyan	7	0.00
Liberian	10	0.00
Nigerian	281	0.04
Sierra Leonean	49	0.01
South African	154	0.02
Sudanese	64	0.01
Other sub-Saharan African	167	0.02
Alaska Native tribes, specified:	46	0.01
Alaska Athabascan (4)	5	0.00
Aleut (11)	11	0.00
Eskimo (7)	12	0.00
Tlingit-Haida (10)	17	0.00
All other tribes (1)	1	0.00
Alaska Native tribes, not specified	9	0.00
Am. Ind. or Alaska Nat., not spec.	1,954	0.27
Albanian	855	0.12
Alsatian	43	0.01
American Indian tribes, specified:	3,545	0.48
Apache (36)	97	0.01
Blackfeet (42)	186	0.03
Cherokee (615)	1,717	0.23
Cheyenne (7)	15	0.00
Chickasaw (15)	23	0.00
Chippewa (54)	97	0.01
Choctaw (60)	131	0.02
Colville (3)	3	0.00
Comanche (2)	12	0.00
Cree (5)	10	0.00
Creek (100)	188	0.03
Crow (2)	7	0.00
Delaware (8)	10	0.00
Houma (13)	14	0.00
Iroquois (65)	131	0.02
Kiowa (3)	6	0.00
Latin American Indians (60)	141	0.02
Lumbee (81)	108	0.01
Menominee (1)	1	0.00
Navajo (35)	64	0.01
Osage (3)	14	0.00
Ottawa (11)	12	0.00
Paiute (6)	6	0.00
Pima	2	0.00
Potawatomi (7)	11	0.00
Pueblo (1)	9	0.00
Seminole (46)	124	0.02
Shoshone (3)	7	0.00
Sioux (58)	108	0.01
Ute (1)	3	0.00
Yaqui (4)	12	0.00
Yuman	1	0.00
All other tribes (151)	275	0.04
American Indian tribes, not spec.	288	0.04
Arab:	5,861	0.80
Arab/Arabic	1,602	0.22
Egyptian	167	0.02
Iraqi	169	0.02
Jordanian	81	0.01
Lebanese	1,623	0.22
Moroccan	94	0.01
Palestinian	789	0.11
Syrian	1,182	0.16
Other Arab	154	0.02
Armenian	397	0.05
Asian:	25,465	3.46
Bangladeshi (11)	16	0.00
Cambodian (891)	1,064	0.14
Chinese, ex. Taiwanese (1,376)	1,879	0.26
Filipino (9,958)	12,295	1.67
Hmong (5)	10	0.00
Indian (2,758)	3,163	0.43
Indonesian (32)	44	0.01
Japanese (486)	930	0.13
Korean (1,085)	1,366	0.19
Laotian (227)	273	0.04
Malaysian (15)	56	0.01
Pakistani (108)	147	0.02
Sri Lankan (27)	27	0.00
Taiwanese (66)	96	0.01
Thai (177)	271	0.04
Vietnamese (2,324)	2,566	0.35
Other Asian, specified (61)	152	0.02
Other Asian, not specified (470)	1,110	0.15
Assyrian/Chaldean/Syriac	29	0.00
Australian	137	0.02
Austrian	1,086	0.15
Basque	49	0.01
Belgian	645	0.09
Brazilian	116	0.02
British	3,160	0.43
Bulgarian	26	0.00
Canadian	1,400	0.19
Carpatho Rusyn	8	0.00
Celtic	195	0.03
Croatian	659	0.09
Cypriot	35	0.00
Czech	1,244	0.17
Czechoslovakian	741	0.10
Danish	1,337	0.18
Dutch	7,635	1.04
Eastern European	323	0.04
English	62,798	8.54
Estonian	28	0.00
European	5,173	0.70
Finnish	665	0.09
French, except Basque	16,196	2.20
French Canadian	4,238	0.58
German	70,440	9.58
Greek	2,314	0.31
Guyanese	358	0.05
Hawaii Native/Pacific Islander:	1,290	0.18
Melanesian: (1)	1	0.00
Other Melanesian (1)	1	0.00
Micronesian: (169)	300	0.04
Guamanian/Chamorro (145)	263	0.04
Other Micronesian (24)	37	0.01
Polynesian: (176)	493	0.07
Native Hawaiian (111)	369	0.05
Samoan (57)	105	0.01
Tongan (2)	2	0.00
Other Polynesian (6)	17	0.00
Other Pac. Isl., specified	59	0.01
Other Pac. Isl., not spec. (100)	437	0.06
Hispanic or Latino:	30,594	4.16
Central American:	1,651	0.22
Costa Rican	259	0.04
Guatemalan	172	0.02
Honduran	267	0.04
Nicaraguan	263	0.04
Panamanian	461	0.06
Salvadoran	169	0.02
Other Central American	60	0.01
Cuban	3,229	0.44
Dominican Republic	601	0.08
Mexican	6,076	0.83
Puerto Rican	11,066	1.50
South American:	2,037	0.28
Argentinean	117	0.02
Bolivian	55	0.01
Chilean	117	0.02
Colombian	924	0.13
Ecuadorian	201	0.03
Paraguayan	6	0.00
Peruvian	303	0.04

Notes: 1. Figures in the "Number" column do not add up to the total population due to: a) Ancestry/Race overlap — e.g. persons can report being both White and Irish, b) persons of Hispanic origin can report being any race, c) persons reporting two ancestries are counted in both categories. 2. Numbers in parentheses indicate the number of persons reporting this ancestry/race alone, not in combination with any other ancestry/race. 3. Refer to the Explanation of Data in the front of the book for more detailed information.

Uruguayan	24	0.00
Venezuelan	209	0.03
Other South American	81	0.01
Other Hispanic or Latino	5,934	0.81
Hungarian	2,485	0.34
Icelander	64	0.01
Iranian	407	0.06
Irish	66,148	8.99
Israeli	97	0.01
Italian	25,385	3.45
Latvian	103	0.01
Lithuanian	1,014	0.14
Luxemburger	42	0.01
Macedonian	6	0.00
Maltese	8	0.00
New Zealander	31	0.00
Northern European	188	0.03
Norwegian	4,816	0.65
Pennsylvania German	217	0.03
Polish	10,500	1.43
Portuguese	1,184	0.16
Romanian	707	0.10
Russian	3,705	0.50
Scandinavian	560	0.08
Scotch-Irish	13,064	1.78
Scottish	13,558	1.84
Serbian	155	0.02
Slavic	227	0.03
Slovak	564	0.08
Slovene	163	0.02
Swedish	4,774	0.65
Swiss	1,064	0.14
Turkish	324	0.04
Ukrainian	1,294	0.18
United States or American	68,488	9.31
Welsh	3,699	0.50
West Indian, excl. Hispanic:	4,952	0.67
Bahamian	264	0.04
Barbadian	76	0.01
Belizean	122	0.02
Bermudan	90	0.01
British West Indian	161	0.02
Dutch West Indian	37	0.01
Haitian	996	0.14
Jamaican	2,010	0.27
Trinidadian and Tobagonian	297	0.04
U.S. Virgin Islander	107	0.01
West Indian	750	0.10
Other West Indian	42	0.01
White:	485,785	66.04
Not Hispanic (457,478)	467,111	63.50
Hispanic (16,829)	18,674	2.54
Yugoslavian	2,655	0.36

Jasmine Estates

Place Type: Census Designated Place
County: Pasco
Population: 18,213

Ancestry/Race	Number	%
Acadian/Cajun	11	0.06
African American/Black:	370	2.03
Not Hispanic (286)	344	1.89
Hispanic (10)	26	0.14
African, sub-Saharan:	16	0.09
Sudanese	16	0.09
Alaska Native tribes, specified:	3	0.02
Eskimo	3	0.02
Am. Ind. or Alaska Nat., not spec.	37	0.20
American Indian tribes, specified:	91	0.50
Blackfeet (2)	9	0.05
Cherokee (18)	43	0.24
Cheyenne	1	0.01
Chippewa (5)	5	0.03
Choctaw	4	0.02
Creek (1)	1	0.01
Crow (1)	1	0.01
Iroquois (1)	4	0.02
Latin American Indians (1)	9	0.05
Navajo (1)	2	0.01
Ottawa (3)	3	0.02
Seminole	2	0.01
Sioux	3	0.02
All other tribes (4)	4	0.02
American Indian tribes, not spec.	12	0.07
Arab:	8	0.04
Lebanese	8	0.04
Armenian	29	0.16
Asian:	226	1.24
Chinese, ex. Taiwanese (40)	46	0.25
Filipino (45)	58	0.32
Indian (24)	38	0.21
Indonesian	4	0.02
Japanese (3)	8	0.04
Korean (5)	9	0.05
Pakistani (3)	9	0.05
Thai (4)	7	0.04
Vietnamese (21)	23	0.13
Other Asian, specified (1)	4	0.02
Other Asian, not specified (7)	20	0.11
Austrian	142	0.79
British	34	0.19
Canadian	85	0.47
Croatian	16	0.09
Czech	143	0.79
Czechoslovakian	30	0.17
Danish	47	0.26
Dutch	226	1.25
English	1,434	7.94
European	49	0.27
Finnish	64	0.35
French, except Basque	812	4.50
French Canadian	168	0.93
German	2,968	16.44
Greek	222	1.23
Guyanese	31	0.17
Hawaii Native/Pacific Islander:	14	0.08
Micronesian: (2)	3	0.02
Guamanian/Chamorro (2)	3	0.02
Polynesian: (1)	6	0.03
Native Hawaiian (1)	6	0.03
Other Pac. Isl., specified	1	0.01
Other Pac. Isl., not spec.	4	0.02
Hispanic or Latino:	1,105	6.07
Central American:	22	0.12
Costa Rican	3	0.02
Guatemalan	1	0.01
Honduran	7	0.04
Nicaraguan	2	0.01
Panamanian	4	0.02
Salvadoran	4	0.02
Other Central American	1	0.01
Cuban	83	0.46
Dominican Republic	15	0.08
Mexican	114	0.63
Puerto Rican	608	3.34
South American:	66	0.36
Argentinean	4	0.02
Bolivian	2	0.01
Chilean	1	0.01
Colombian	24	0.13
Ecuadorian	8	0.04
Peruvian	9	0.05
Uruguayan	5	0.03
Venezuelan	5	0.03
Other South American	8	0.04
Other Hispanic or Latino	197	1.08
Hungarian	260	1.44
Irish	2,861	15.85
Italian	3,432	19.01
Lithuanian	66	0.37
Maltese	19	0.11
Norwegian	112	0.62
Pennsylvania German	21	0.12
Polish	1,287	7.13
Portuguese	76	0.42
Romanian	8	0.04
Russian	176	0.97
Scandinavian	43	0.24
Scotch-Irish	320	1.77
Scottish	412	2.28
Slovak	51	0.28
Swedish	234	1.30
Swiss	48	0.27
Ukrainian	144	0.80
United States or American	1,489	8.25
Welsh	68	0.38
West Indian, excl. Hispanic:	99	0.55
Dutch West Indian	11	0.06
Haitian	13	0.07
Jamaican	30	0.17
West Indian	45	0.25
White:	17,436	95.73
Not Hispanic (16,401)	16,583	91.05
Hispanic (803)	853	4.68
Yugoslavian	54	0.30

Jensen Beach

Place Type: Census Designated Place
County: Martin
Population: 11,100

Ancestry/Race	Number	%
Acadian/Cajun	5	0.05
African American/Black:	271	2.44
Not Hispanic (230)	248	2.23
Hispanic (20)	23	0.21
Am. Ind. or Alaska Nat., not spec.	18	0.16
Alsatian	9	0.08
American Indian tribes, specified:	36	0.32
Blackfeet	1	0.01
Cherokee (5)	15	0.14
Chippewa (1)	2	0.02
Iroquois	2	0.02
Latin American Indians (2)	2	0.02
Lumbee (1)	1	0.01
Navajo	1	0.01
Pueblo	4	0.04
Seminole	1	0.01
Sioux (1)	1	0.01
All other tribes (4)	6	0.05
American Indian tribes, not spec.	5	0.05
Arab:	15	0.14
Lebanese	15	0.14
Armenian	6	0.05
Asian:	73	0.66
Chinese, ex. Taiwanese (13)	17	0.15
Filipino (8)	14	0.13
Indian (10)	12	0.11
Japanese (2)	9	0.08
Korean (1)	1	0.01
Pakistani (3)	3	0.03
Thai (1)	1	0.01
Vietnamese (7)	10	0.09
Other Asian, specified (5)	5	0.05
Other Asian, not specified (1)	1	0.01
Austrian	87	0.78
Belgian	56	0.50
British	45	0.41
Canadian	33	0.30
Czech	52	0.47
Czechoslovakian	10	0.09
Danish	51	0.46
Dutch	283	2.55
English	1,914	17.24
Estonian	7	0.06
European	71	0.64
Finnish	29	0.26
French, except Basque	485	4.37
French Canadian	114	1.03
German	2,316	20.86
Greek	8	0.07
Hawaii Native/Pacific Islander:	11	0.10
Micronesian:	1	0.01
Guamanian/Chamorro	1	0.01
Polynesian: (4)	8	0.07
Native Hawaiian (2)	6	0.05
Samoan (2)	2	0.02

Notes: 1. Figures in the "Number" column do not add up to the total population due to: a) Ancestry/Race overlap — e.g. persons can report being both White and Irish, b) persons of Hispanic origin can report being any race, c) persons reporting two ancestries are counted in both categories. 2. Numbers in parentheses indicate the number of persons reporting this ancestry/race alone, not in combination with any other ancestry/race. 3. Refer to the Explanation of Data in the front of the book for more detailed information.

Other Pac. Isl., not spec.	2	0.02
Hispanic or Latino:	307	2.77
Central American:	13	0.12
Costa Rican	1	0.01
Guatemalan	4	0.04
Honduran	3	0.03
Panamanian	4	0.04
Salvadoran	1	0.01
Cuban	76	0.68
Dominican Republic	3	0.03
Mexican	69	0.62
Puerto Rican	59	0.53
South American:	31	0.28
Argentinean	1	0.01
Chilean	1	0.01
Colombian	14	0.13
Ecuadorian	3	0.03
Peruvian	5	0.05
Venezuelan	5	0.05
Other South American	2	0.02
Other Hispanic or Latino	56	0.50
Hungarian	71	0.64
Irish	2,214	19.94
Italian	1,422	12.81
Latvian	2	0.02
Lithuanian	61	0.55
Maltese	18	0.16
Norwegian	83	0.75
Pennsylvania German	8	0.07
Polish	553	4.98
Portuguese	40	0.36
Russian	109	0.98
Scotch-Irish	217	1.95
Scottish	360	3.24
Serbian	4	0.04
Slavic	8	0.07
Slovak	33	0.30
Slovene	37	0.33
Swedish	246	2.22
Swiss	46	0.41
Ukrainian	25	0.23
United States or American	734	6.61
Welsh	121	1.09
West Indian, excl. Hispanic:	97	0.87
British West Indian	10	0.09
Haitian	34	0.31
Jamaican	53	0.48
White:	10,726	96.63
Not Hispanic (10,414)	10,483	94.44
Hispanic (220)	243	2.19

Jupiter

Place Type: Town
County: Palm Beach
Population: 39,328

Ancestry/Race	Number	%
African American/Black:	555	1.41
Not Hispanic (461)	513	1.30
Hispanic (19)	42	0.11
African, sub-Saharan:	54	0.14
Nigerian	24	0.06
South African	25	0.06
Other sub-Saharan African	5	0.01
Am. Ind. or Alaska Nat., not spec.	39	0.10
Albanian	22	0.06
American Indian tribes, specified:	131	0.33
Apache (1)	3	0.01
Blackfeet (1)	4	0.01
Cherokee (11)	38	0.10
Chippewa (6)	6	0.02
Choctaw (7)	10	0.03
Delaware (1)	2	0.01
Iroquois (4)	15	0.04
Latin American Indians (11)	25	0.06
Lumbee (3)	3	0.01
Navajo (1)	2	0.01
Pueblo	1	0.00
Shoshone	3	0.01
Sioux (3)	6	0.02
Ute	1	0.00
All other tribes (3)	12	0.03
American Indian tribes, not spec.	8	0.02
Arab:	130	0.33
Arab/Arabic	7	0.02
Lebanese	87	0.22
Palestinian	13	0.03
Syrian	23	0.06
Armenian	77	0.20
Asian:	594	1.51
Bangladeshi (10)	10	0.03
Chinese, ex. Taiwanese (104)	148	0.38
Filipino (58)	91	0.23
Indian (155)	176	0.45
Japanese (16)	29	0.07
Korean (24)	37	0.09
Laotian (9)	9	0.02
Malaysian (1)	2	0.01
Pakistani (5)	7	0.02
Taiwanese (1)	3	0.01
Thai (15)	18	0.05
Vietnamese (29)	32	0.08
Other Asian, specified	3	0.01
Other Asian, not specified (6)	29	0.07
Assyrian/Chaldean/Syriac	16	0.04
Australian	6	0.02
Austrian	295	0.75
Belgian	49	0.12
Brazilian	36	0.09
British	254	0.65
Canadian	210	0.53
Celtic	7	0.02
Croatian	74	0.19
Cypriot	8	0.02
Czech	169	0.43
Czechoslovakian	85	0.22
Danish	137	0.35
Dutch	727	1.85
Eastern European	33	0.08
English	5,363	13.64
Estonian	8	0.02
European	283	0.72
Finnish	164	0.42
French, except Basque	1,651	4.20
French Canadian	382	0.97
German	7,055	17.95
Greek	293	0.75
Hawaii Native/Pacific Islander:	75	0.19
Micronesian: (34)	34	0.09
Guamanian/Chamorro (34)	34	0.09
Polynesian: (5)	24	0.06
Native Hawaiian (3)	19	0.05
Samoan (1)	2	0.01
Other Polynesian (1)	3	0.01
Other Pac. Isl., specified	3	0.01
Other Pac. Isl., not spec. (6)	14	0.04
Hispanic or Latino:	2,881	7.33
Central American:	501	1.27
Costa Rican	15	0.04
Guatemalan	427	1.09
Honduran	18	0.05
Nicaraguan	12	0.03
Panamanian	8	0.02
Salvadoran	21	0.05
Cuban	262	0.67
Dominican Republic	17	0.04
Mexican	912	2.32
Puerto Rican	362	0.92
South American:	285	0.72
Argentinean	33	0.08
Bolivian	6	0.02
Chilean	10	0.03
Colombian	106	0.27
Ecuadorian	14	0.04
Paraguayan	8	0.02
Peruvian	51	0.13
Uruguayan	7	0.02
Venezuelan	39	0.10
Other South American	11	0.03
Other Hispanic or Latino	542	1.38
Hungarian	547	1.39
Icelander	8	0.02
Iranian	6	0.02
Irish	7,303	18.58
Israeli	7	0.02
Italian	6,586	16.75
Latvian	65	0.17
Lithuanian	310	0.79
Luxemburger	8	0.02
Macedonian	10	0.03
Maltese	12	0.03
New Zealander	15	0.04
Northern European	13	0.03
Norwegian	473	1.20
Pennsylvania German	14	0.04
Polish	1,922	4.89
Portuguese	230	0.59
Romanian	127	0.32
Russian	1,088	2.77
Scandinavian	31	0.08
Scotch-Irish	700	1.78
Scottish	1,105	2.81
Serbian	15	0.04
Slovak	120	0.31
Slovene	20	0.05
Swedish	424	1.08
Swiss	181	0.46
Turkish	32	0.08
Ukrainian	223	0.57
United States or American	1,942	4.94
Welsh	323	0.82
West Indian, excl. Hispanic:	198	0.50
Bahamian	16	0.04
Jamaican	157	0.40
Trinidadian and Tobagonian	10	0.03
West Indian	6	0.02
Other West Indian	9	0.02
White:	37,690	95.84
Not Hispanic (35,152)	35,402	90.02
Hispanic (2,155)	2,288	5.82
Yugoslavian	141	0.36

Kendale Lakes

Place Type: Census Designated Place
County: Miami-Dade
Population: 56,901

Ancestry/Race	Number	%
African American/Black:	1,569	2.76
Not Hispanic (997)	1,112	1.95
Hispanic (315)	457	0.80
African, sub-Saharan:	56	0.10
African	16	0.03
Ethiopian	11	0.02
Sierra Leonean	29	0.05
Am. Ind. or Alaska Nat., not spec.	72	0.13
Albanian	8	0.01
American Indian tribes, specified:	63	0.11
Apache	1	0.00
Cherokee	3	0.01
Chippewa (5)	6	0.01
Comanche	1	0.00
Creek	1	0.00
Iroquois	1	0.00
Latin American Indians (15)	38	0.07
Lumbee (1)	2	0.00
Navajo (1)	2	0.00
Pueblo	3	0.01
All other tribes (4)	5	0.01
American Indian tribes, not spec.	15	0.03
Arab:	207	0.36
Arab/Arabic	12	0.02
Egyptian	22	0.04
Lebanese	137	0.24
Syrian	27	0.05
Other Arab	9	0.02
Armenian	57	0.10
Asian:	1,428	2.51

Notes: 1. Figures in the "Number" column do not add up to the total population due to: a) Ancestry/Race overlap — e.g. persons can report being both White and Irish, b) persons of Hispanic origin can report being any race, c) persons reporting two ancestries are counted in both categories. 2. Numbers in parentheses indicate the number of persons reporting this ancestry/race alone, not in combination with any other ancestry/race. 3. Refer to the Explanation of Data in the front of the book for more detailed information.

Bangladeshi (5)	5	0.01
Cambodian (2)	2	0.00
Chinese, ex. Taiwanese (455)	561	0.99
Filipino (94)	121	0.21
Indian (266)	351	0.62
Indonesian	2	0.00
Japanese (36)	62	0.11
Korean (13)	21	0.04
Laotian (1)	2	0.00
Pakistani (94)	158	0.28
Sri Lankan (5)	5	0.01
Taiwanese (11)	13	0.02
Thai (7)	7	0.01
Vietnamese (36)	52	0.09
Other Asian, not specified (25)	66	0.12
Austrian	169	0.30
Belgian	35	0.06
Brazilian	215	0.38
British	182	0.32
Canadian	43	0.08
Czech	20	0.04
Czechoslovakian	9	0.02
Danish	44	0.08
Dutch	88	0.15
Eastern European	6	0.01
English	978	1.72
European	191	0.34
Finnish	16	0.03
French, except Basque	590	1.04
French Canadian	95	0.17
German	1,017	1.79
Greek	62	0.11
Guyanese	27	0.05
Hawaii Native/Pacific Islander:	30	0.05
Polynesian: (2)	6	0.01
Native Hawaiian	3	0.01
Samoan (2)	3	0.01
Other Pac. Isl., not spec. (12)	24	0.04
Hispanic or Latino:	43,574	76.58
Central American:	3,640	6.40
Costa Rican	108	0.19
Guatemalan	143	0.25
Honduran	284	0.50
Nicaraguan	2,612	4.59
Panamanian	221	0.39
Salvadoran	182	0.32
Other Central American	90	0.16
Cuban	21,953	38.58
Dominican Republic	858	1.51
Mexican	573	1.01
Puerto Rican	1,995	3.51
South American:	7,076	12.44
Argentinean	346	0.61
Bolivian	96	0.17
Chilean	381	0.67
Colombian	3,619	6.36
Ecuadorian	372	0.65
Paraguayan	7	0.01
Peruvian	1,157	2.03
Uruguayan	100	0.18
Venezuelan	875	1.54
Other South American	123	0.22
Other Hispanic or Latino	7,479	13.14
Hungarian	76	0.13
Iranian	25	0.04
Irish	954	1.68
Israeli	9	0.02
Italian	1,298	2.28
Latvian	28	0.05
Lithuanian	50	0.09
Norwegian	56	0.10
Pennsylvania German	11	0.02
Polish	340	0.60
Portuguese	39	0.07
Romanian	39	0.07
Russian	559	0.98
Scotch-Irish	187	0.33
Scottish	118	0.21
Slavic	22	0.04
Slovak	16	0.03
Swedish	130	0.23
Ukrainian	27	0.05
United States or American	1,614	2.84
Welsh	180	0.32
West Indian, excl. Hispanic:	1,216	2.14
Bahamian	22	0.04
British West Indian	18	0.03
Dutch West Indian	40	0.07
Haitian	644	1.13
Jamaican	440	0.77
Trinidadian and Tobagonian	17	0.03
West Indian	35	0.06
White:	51,341	90.23
Not Hispanic (10,765)	11,092	19.49
Hispanic (38,727)	40,249	70.74
Yugoslavian	10	0.02

Kendall

Place Type: Census Designated Place
County: Miami-Dade
Population: 75,226

Ancestry/Race	Number	%
Acadian/Cajun	14	0.02
African American/Black:	3,906	5.19
Not Hispanic (3,030)	3,404	4.53
Hispanic (318)	502	0.67
African, sub-Saharan:	113	0.15
African	52	0.07
Ghanian	15	0.02
Nigerian	28	0.04
Other sub-Saharan African	18	0.02
Alaska Native tribes, specified:	2	0.00
Aleut (1)	1	0.00
Eskimo (1)	1	0.00
Am. Ind. or Alaska Nat., not spec.	110	0.15
Albanian	18	0.02
Alsatian	10	0.01
American Indian tribes, specified:	131	0.17
Apache (3)	4	0.01
Blackfeet	6	0.01
Cherokee (9)	32	0.04
Choctaw (1)	1	0.00
Creek	2	0.00
Iroquois (1)	1	0.00
Latin American Indians (19)	66	0.09
Navajo (1)	1	0.00
Pueblo	2	0.00
Seminole (3)	4	0.01
Sioux (1)	2	0.00
All other tribes (7)	10	0.01
American Indian tribes, not spec.	10	0.01
Arab:	1,315	1.75
Arab/Arabic	41	0.05
Egyptian	60	0.08
Lebanese	755	1.00
Moroccan	24	0.03
Palestinian	52	0.07
Syrian	335	0.45
Other Arab	48	0.06
Armenian	46	0.06
Asian:	2,810	3.74
Chinese, ex. Taiwanese (796)	990	1.32
Filipino (196)	253	0.34
Indian (597)	714	0.95
Indonesian (5)	10	0.01
Japanese (162)	196	0.26
Korean (162)	176	0.23
Laotian (7)	8	0.01
Malaysian (2)	7	0.01
Pakistani (112)	153	0.20
Sri Lankan (4)	4	0.01
Taiwanese (8)	11	0.01
Thai (43)	51	0.07
Vietnamese (87)	105	0.14
Other Asian, specified (9)	10	0.01
Other Asian, not specified (25)	122	0.16
Australian	21	0.03
Austrian	451	0.60
Basque	69	0.09
Belgian	55	0.07
Brazilian	680	0.90
British	312	0.41
Bulgarian	25	0.03
Canadian	229	0.30
Celtic	17	0.02
Croatian	52	0.07
Czech	204	0.27
Czechoslovakian	65	0.09
Danish	110	0.15
Dutch	503	0.67
Eastern European	316	0.42
English	3,469	4.61
European	450	0.60
Finnish	73	0.10
French, except Basque	1,363	1.81
French Canadian	240	0.32
German	4,256	5.65
Greek	256	0.34
Guyanese	42	0.06
Hawaii Native/Pacific Islander:	81	0.11
Melanesian: (3)	3	0.00
Fijian (3)	3	0.00
Micronesian: (3)	4	0.01
Guamanian/Chamorro (3)	4	0.01
Polynesian: (9)	22	0.03
Native Hawaiian (6)	16	0.02
Samoan (2)	3	0.00
Other Polynesian (1)	3	0.00
Other Pac. Isl., specified	1	0.00
Other Pac. Isl., not spec. (6)	51	0.07
Hispanic or Latino:	37,549	49.91
Central American:	3,310	4.40
Costa Rican	171	0.23
Guatemalan	199	0.26
Honduran	387	0.51
Nicaraguan	1,869	2.48
Panamanian	268	0.36
Salvadoran	337	0.45
Other Central American	79	0.11
Cuban	16,029	21.31
Dominican Republic	821	1.09
Mexican	582	0.77
Puerto Rican	2,298	3.05
South American:	7,961	10.58
Argentinean	605	0.80
Bolivian	170	0.23
Chilean	479	0.64
Colombian	3,429	4.56
Ecuadorian	415	0.55
Paraguayan	31	0.04
Peruvian	1,512	2.01
Uruguayan	65	0.09
Venezuelan	1,108	1.47
Other South American	147	0.20
Other Hispanic or Latino	6,548	8.70
Hungarian	575	0.76
Icelander	22	0.03
Iranian	167	0.22
Irish	3,776	5.02
Israeli	65	0.09
Italian	3,842	5.10
Latvian	39	0.05
Lithuanian	175	0.23
Macedonian	4	0.01
Northern European	50	0.07
Norwegian	383	0.51
Pennsylvania German	19	0.03
Polish	1,583	2.10
Portuguese	489	0.65
Romanian	230	0.31
Russian	2,409	3.20
Scandinavian	64	0.09
Scotch-Irish	566	0.75
Scottish	593	0.79
Serbian	14	0.02
Slavic	65	0.09
Slovak	83	0.11
Swedish	624	0.83

Notes: 1. Figures in the "Number" column do not add up to the total population due to: a) Ancestry/Race overlap — e.g. persons can report being both White and Irish, b) persons of Hispanic origin can report being any race, c) persons reporting two ancestries are counted in both categories. 2. Numbers in parentheses indicate the number of persons reporting this ancestry/race alone, not in combination with any other ancestry/race. 3. Refer to the Explanation of Data in the front of the book for more detailed information.

Ancestry/Race	Number	%
Swiss	199	0.26
Turkish	56	0.07
Ukrainian	205	0.27
United States or American	4,036	5.36
Welsh	221	0.29
West Indian, excl. Hispanic:	2,298	3.05
Bahamian	51	0.07
Barbadian	27	0.04
Belizean	16	0.02
British West Indian	32	0.04
Haitian	974	1.29
Jamaican	894	1.19
Trinidadian and Tobagonian	205	0.27
U.S. Virgin Islander	10	0.01
West Indian	81	0.11
Other West Indian	8	0.01
White:	66,968	89.02
Not Hispanic (31,270)	31,885	42.39
Hispanic (33,785)	35,083	46.64
Yugoslavian	64	0.09

Kendall West

Place Type: Census Designated Place
County: Miami-Dade
Population: 38,034

Ancestry/Race	Number	%
African American/Black:	1,877	4.94
Not Hispanic (1,232)	1,372	3.61
Hispanic (377)	505	1.33
African, sub-Saharan:	82	0.22
African	30	0.08
Nigerian	47	0.12
South African	5	0.01
Am. Ind. or Alaska Nat., not spec.	87	0.23
American Indian tribes, specified:	56	0.15
Blackfeet (1)	1	0.00
Cherokee (3)	12	0.03
Choctaw (3)	3	0.01
Cree	1	0.00
Latin American Indians (15)	33	0.09
Lumbee (2)	2	0.01
Pueblo (1)	2	0.01
Seminole	1	0.00
All other tribes	1	0.00
American Indian tribes, not spec.	13	0.03
Arab:	131	0.35
Arab/Arabic	27	0.07
Egyptian	22	0.06
Lebanese	82	0.22
Armenian	18	0.05
Asian:	757	1.99
Chinese, ex. Taiwanese (190)	251	0.66
Filipino (111)	138	0.36
Hmong	1	0.00
Indian (144)	198	0.52
Indonesian (1)	1	0.00
Japanese (19)	28	0.07
Korean (13)	13	0.03
Pakistani (14)	44	0.12
Sri Lankan (1)	5	0.01
Taiwanese (11)	11	0.03
Thai (18)	19	0.05
Vietnamese (11)	18	0.05
Other Asian, specified	1	0.00
Other Asian, not specified (4)	29	0.08
Austrian	16	0.04
Basque	31	0.08
Brazilian	137	0.36
British	52	0.14
Canadian	16	0.04
Croatian	6	0.02
Czech	10	0.03
Czechoslovakian	13	0.03
Danish	34	0.09
Dutch	33	0.09
English	448	1.18
European	124	0.33
Finnish	12	0.03
French, except Basque	171	0.45
French Canadian	42	0.11
German	604	1.59
German Russian	8	0.02
Greek	38	0.10
Guyanese	38	0.10
Hawaii Native/Pacific Islander:	35	0.09
Polynesian: (1)	3	0.01
Native Hawaiian (1)	1	0.00
Samoan	2	0.01
Other Pac. Isl., not spec. (12)	32	0.08
Hispanic or Latino:	30,060	79.03
Central American:	2,511	6.60
Costa Rican	105	0.28
Guatemalan	84	0.22
Honduran	259	0.68
Nicaraguan	1,670	4.39
Panamanian	143	0.38
Salvadoran	200	0.53
Other Central American	50	0.13
Cuban	11,092	29.16
Dominican Republic	982	2.58
Mexican	445	1.17
Puerto Rican	2,142	5.63
South American:	7,073	18.60
Argentinean	294	0.77
Bolivian	79	0.21
Chilean	249	0.65
Colombian	3,778	9.93
Ecuadorian	417	1.10
Paraguayan	6	0.02
Peruvian	1,084	2.85
Uruguayan	48	0.13
Venezuelan	1,015	2.67
Other South American	103	0.27
Other Hispanic or Latino	5,815	15.29
Hungarian	8	0.02
Irish	396	1.04
Israeli	26	0.07
Italian	802	2.11
Latvian	22	0.06
Lithuanian	5	0.01
Norwegian	15	0.04
Pennsylvania German	22	0.06
Polish	198	0.52
Portuguese	44	0.12
Romanian	4	0.01
Russian	156	0.41
Scandinavian	6	0.02
Scotch-Irish	64	0.17
Scottish	111	0.29
Swedish	39	0.10
Ukrainian	26	0.07
United States or American	944	2.49
Welsh	33	0.09
West Indian, excl. Hispanic:	948	2.50
Bahamian	9	0.02
Belizean	18	0.05
British West Indian	44	0.12
Haitian	336	0.89
Jamaican	389	1.02
Trinidadian and Tobagonian	59	0.16
West Indian	79	0.21
Other West Indian	14	0.04
White:	33,110	87.05
Not Hispanic (5,812)	5,969	15.69
Hispanic (25,896)	27,141	71.36
Yugoslavian	10	0.03

Key Biscayne

Place Type: Village
County: Miami-Dade
Population: 10,507

Ancestry/Race	Number	%
African American/Black:	65	0.62
Not Hispanic (28)	42	0.40
Hispanic (20)	23	0.22
African, sub-Saharan:	17	0.16
African	8	0.08
South African	9	0.09
Am. Ind. or Alaska Nat., not spec.	8	0.08
American Indian tribes, specified:	13	0.12
Cherokee (2)	4	0.04
Latin American Indians (4)	7	0.07
Pueblo	1	0.01
Sioux (1)	1	0.01
American Indian tribes, not spec.	5	0.05
Arab:	127	1.21
Arab/Arabic	16	0.15
Egyptian	25	0.24
Iraqi	3	0.03
Lebanese	63	0.60
Syrian	20	0.19
Asian:	135	1.28
Chinese, ex. Taiwanese (28)	38	0.36
Filipino (10)	14	0.13
Indian (27)	37	0.35
Indonesian (1)	1	0.01
Japanese (22)	34	0.32
Pakistani (1)	1	0.01
Sri Lankan (1)	1	0.01
Vietnamese (4)	5	0.05
Other Asian, not specified (2)	4	0.04
Australian	35	0.33
Austrian	74	0.71
Basque	35	0.33
Belgian	33	0.31
Brazilian	180	1.72
British	96	0.92
Canadian	69	0.66
Celtic	8	0.08
Croatian	20	0.19
Czech	41	0.39
Czechoslovakian	18	0.17
Danish	23	0.22
Dutch	163	1.56
English	722	6.89
European	124	1.18
Finnish	7	0.07
French, except Basque	483	4.61
French Canadian	62	0.59
German	985	9.40
Greek	88	0.84
Hawaii Native/Pacific Islander:	3	0.03
Polynesian:	3	0.03
Native Hawaiian	2	0.02
Other Polynesian	1	0.01
Hispanic or Latino:	5,231	49.79
Central American:	303	2.88
Costa Rican	30	0.29
Guatemalan	35	0.33
Honduran	32	0.30
Nicaraguan	107	1.02
Panamanian	15	0.14
Salvadoran	67	0.64
Other Central American	17	0.16
Cuban	1,632	15.53
Dominican Republic	12	0.11
Mexican	193	1.84
Puerto Rican	116	1.10
South American:	1,793	17.06
Argentinean	282	2.68
Bolivian	27	0.26
Chilean	76	0.72
Colombian	743	7.07
Ecuadorian	102	0.97
Paraguayan	13	0.12
Peruvian	261	2.48
Uruguayan	6	0.06
Venezuelan	248	2.36
Other South American	35	0.33
Other Hispanic or Latino	1,182	11.25
Hungarian	70	0.67
Icelander	9	0.09
Iranian	20	0.19
Irish	504	4.81
Israeli	7	0.07
Italian	626	5.97

Notes: 1. Figures in the "Number" column do not add up to the total population due to: a) Ancestry/Race overlap — e.g. persons can report being both White and Irish, b) persons of Hispanic origin can report being any race, c) persons reporting two ancestries are counted in both categories. 2. Numbers in parentheses indicate the number of persons reporting this ancestry/race alone, not in combination with any other ancestry/race. 3. Refer to the Explanation of Data in the front of the book for more detailed information.

Ancestry/Race	Number	%
Lithuanian	12	0.11
Norwegian	32	0.31
Polish	120	1.15
Portuguese	67	0.64
Romanian	11	0.10
Russian	285	2.72
Scotch-Irish	82	0.78
Scottish	183	1.75
Slovak	12	0.11
Slovene	10	0.10
Swedish	160	1.53
Swiss	104	0.99
Turkish	26	0.25
United States or American	421	4.02
Welsh	26	0.25
West Indian, excl. Hispanic:	67	0.64
Jamaican	67	0.64
White:	10,182	96.91
Not Hispanic (5,058)	5,122	48.75
Hispanic (4,972)	5,060	48.16
Yugoslavian	7	0.07

Key Largo

Place Type: Census Designated Place
County: Monroe
Population: 11,886

Ancestry/Race	Number	%
African American/Black:	278	2.34
Not Hispanic (227)	238	2.00
Hispanic (16)	40	0.34
African, sub-Saharan:	24	0.20
African	24	0.20
Am. Ind. or Alaska Nat., not spec.	34	0.29
American Indian tribes, specified:	54	0.45
Apache	1	0.01
Blackfeet (1)	8	0.07
Cherokee (7)	23	0.19
Chippewa	1	0.01
Choctaw (3)	3	0.03
Comanche (1)	1	0.01
Creek	1	0.01
Iroquois (2)	5	0.04
Latin American Indians (2)	4	0.03
Lumbee (1)	1	0.01
Sioux	2	0.02
All other tribes (3)	4	0.03
American Indian tribes, not spec.	11	0.09
Arab:	16	0.13
Lebanese	16	0.13
Armenian	39	0.33
Asian:	86	0.72
Chinese, ex. Taiwanese (15)	21	0.18
Filipino (3)	9	0.08
Indian (13)	13	0.11
Indonesian (2)	2	0.02
Japanese (3)	6	0.05
Korean (6)	7	0.06
Thai (4)	5	0.04
Vietnamese (2)	3	0.03
Other Asian, specified (6)	8	0.07
Other Asian, not specified (2)	12	0.10
Austrian	30	0.25
Belgian	9	0.08
British	77	0.64
Canadian	118	0.98
Czech	72	0.60
Czechoslovakian	46	0.38
Danish	44	0.37
Dutch	266	2.22
Eastern European	9	0.08
English	1,723	14.38
European	147	1.23
Finnish	37	0.31
French, except Basque	606	5.06
French Canadian	79	0.66
German	2,273	18.97
Greek	60	0.50
Hawaii Native/Pacific Islander:	4	0.03
Micronesian:	1	0.01
Guamanian/Chamorro	1	0.01
Other Pac. Isl., not spec.	3	0.03
Hispanic or Latino:	1,979	16.65
Central American:	99	0.83
Costa Rican	23	0.19
Guatemalan	9	0.08
Honduran	27	0.23
Nicaraguan	18	0.15
Panamanian	2	0.02
Salvadoran	20	0.17
Cuban	1,160	9.76
Dominican Republic	10	0.08
Mexican	444	3.74
Puerto Rican	91	0.77
South American:	93	0.78
Argentinean	1	0.01
Bolivian	4	0.03
Chilean	5	0.04
Colombian	59	0.50
Ecuadorian	2	0.02
Paraguayan	1	0.01
Peruvian	14	0.12
Uruguayan	1	0.01
Venezuelan	6	0.05
Other Hispanic or Latino	82	0.69
Hungarian	49	0.41
Irish	1,588	13.26
Italian	1,013	8.46
Lithuanian	51	0.43
Maltese	5	0.04
Norwegian	96	0.80
Polish	428	3.57
Portuguese	14	0.12
Romanian	39	0.33
Russian	30	0.25
Scandinavian	17	0.14
Scotch-Irish	257	2.15
Scottish	337	2.81
Serbian	20	0.17
Slavic	8	0.07
Slovak	17	0.14
Slovene	10	0.08
Swedish	197	1.64
Swiss	59	0.49
Ukrainian	12	0.10
United States or American	967	8.07
Welsh	77	0.64
West Indian, excl. Hispanic:	53	0.44
Bahamian	17	0.14
Jamaican	19	0.16
West Indian	17	0.14
White:	11,407	95.97
Not Hispanic (9,446)	9,564	80.46
Hispanic (1,772)	1,843	15.51

Key West

Place Type: City
County: Monroe
Population: 25,478

Ancestry/Race	Number	%
Acadian/Cajun	12	0.05
African American/Black:	2,552	10.02
Not Hispanic (2,237)	2,381	9.35
Hispanic (128)	171	0.67
African, sub-Saharan:	104	0.41
African	71	0.28
Nigerian	18	0.07
South African	8	0.03
Other sub-Saharan African	7	0.03
Alaska Native tribes, specified:	1	0.00
Eskimo (1)	1	0.00
Alaska Native tribes, not specified	1	0.00
Am. Ind. or Alaska Nat., not spec.	68	0.27
American Indian tribes, specified:	132	0.52
Apache (1)	1	0.00
Blackfeet (1)	6	0.02
Cherokee (22)	43	0.17
Cheyenne	1	0.00
Chippewa (5)	6	0.02
Choctaw (5)	6	0.02
Comanche	3	0.01
Cree	1	0.00
Creek (2)	3	0.01
Delaware (1)	2	0.01
Iroquois (2)	6	0.02
Latin American Indians (8)	17	0.07
Navajo	1	0.00
Ottawa (1)	1	0.00
Seminole (1)	4	0.02
Sioux (1)	7	0.03
All other tribes (12)	24	0.09
American Indian tribes, not spec.	12	0.05
Arab:	124	0.49
Egyptian	16	0.06
Lebanese	83	0.33
Moroccan	12	0.05
Syrian	13	0.05
Armenian	93	0.36
Asian:	458	1.80
Bangladeshi	11	0.04
Cambodian (2)	2	0.01
Chinese, ex. Taiwanese (54)	68	0.27
Filipino (92)	135	0.53
Indian (66)	87	0.34
Japanese (35)	49	0.19
Korean (26)	35	0.14
Laotian (1)	1	0.00
Malaysian (1)	5	0.02
Pakistani	1	0.00
Sri Lankan (2)	3	0.01
Taiwanese (7)	7	0.03
Thai (6)	12	0.05
Vietnamese (7)	12	0.05
Other Asian, specified (13)	14	0.05
Other Asian, not specified (8)	16	0.06
Austrian	127	0.50
Belgian	15	0.06
British	107	0.42
Bulgarian	10	0.04
Canadian	55	0.22
Celtic	16	0.06
Czech	170	0.67
Czechoslovakian	92	0.36
Danish	66	0.26
Dutch	276	1.08
Eastern European	10	0.04
English	3,158	12.39
European	196	0.77
Finnish	23	0.09
French, except Basque	927	3.64
French Canadian	361	1.42
German	3,106	12.19
Greek	198	0.78
Guyanese	9	0.04
Hawaii Native/Pacific Islander:	31	0.12
Melanesian: (1)	1	0.00
Fijian (1)	1	0.00
Micronesian: (6)	7	0.03
Guamanian/Chamorro (2)	3	0.01
Other Micronesian (4)	4	0.02
Polynesian: (5)	15	0.06
Native Hawaiian (4)	13	0.05
Samoan (1)	2	0.01
Other Pac. Isl., specified	1	0.00
Other Pac. Isl., not spec. (2)	7	0.03
Hispanic or Latino:	4,215	16.54
Central American:	459	1.80
Costa Rican	33	0.13
Guatemalan	34	0.13
Honduran	21	0.08
Nicaraguan	311	1.22
Panamanian	28	0.11
Salvadoran	29	0.11
Other Central American	3	0.01
Cuban	1,977	7.76
Dominican Republic	23	0.09
Mexican	371	1.46

Notes: 1. Figures in the "Number" column do not add up to the total population due to: a) Ancestry/Race overlap — e.g. persons can report being both White and Irish, b) persons of Hispanic origin can report being any race, c) persons reporting two ancestries are counted in both categories. 2. Numbers in parentheses indicate the number of persons reporting this ancestry/race alone, not in combination with any other ancestry/race. 3. Refer to the Explanation of Data in the front of the book for more detailed information.

Ancestry/Race	Number	%
Puerto Rican	284	1.11
South American:	168	0.66
Argentinean	26	0.10
Bolivian	12	0.05
Chilean	5	0.02
Colombian	59	0.23
Ecuadorian	6	0.02
Peruvian	35	0.14
Uruguayan	2	0.01
Venezuelan	20	0.08
Other South American	3	0.01
Other Hispanic or Latino	933	3.66
Hungarian	110	0.43
Iranian	13	0.05
Irish	2,869	11.26
Israeli	52	0.20
Italian	1,730	6.79
Latvian	6	0.02
Lithuanian	92	0.36
Luxemburger	16	0.06
New Zealander	12	0.05
Northern European	49	0.19
Norwegian	229	0.90
Pennsylvania German	49	0.19
Polish	890	3.49
Portuguese	80	0.31
Romanian	19	0.07
Russian	283	1.11
Scandinavian	26	0.10
Scotch-Irish	465	1.82
Scottish	700	2.75
Slavic	16	0.06
Slovak	136	0.53
Swedish	404	1.59
Swiss	109	0.43
Turkish	10	0.04
Ukrainian	126	0.49
United States or American	1,522	5.97
Welsh	159	0.62
West Indian, excl. Hispanic:	580	2.28
Bahamian	269	1.06
Barbadian	8	0.03
British West Indian	30	0.12
Haitian	130	0.51
Jamaican	100	0.39
Trinidadian and Tobagonian	9	0.04
West Indian	34	0.13
White:	22,084	86.68
Not Hispanic (18,195)	18,482	72.54
Hispanic (3,447)	3,602	14.14
Yugoslavian	28	0.11

Keystone

Place Type: Census Designated Place
County: Hillsborough
Population: 14,627

Ancestry/Race	Number	%
African American/Black:	562	3.84
Not Hispanic (489)	528	3.61
Hispanic (23)	34	0.23
African, sub-Saharan:	6	0.04
African	6	0.04
Am. Ind. or Alaska Nat., not spec.	33	0.23
American Indian tribes, specified:	62	0.42
Cherokee (11)	37	0.25
Chickasaw (3)	3	0.02
Chippewa (3)	4	0.03
Creek (2)	2	0.01
Iroquois (1)	1	0.01
Latin American Indians (5)	5	0.03
Sioux (1)	3	0.02
All other tribes (7)	7	0.05
American Indian tribes, not spec.	9	0.06
Arab:	26	0.18
Egyptian	7	0.05
Palestinian	6	0.04
Syrian	13	0.09
Asian:	439	3.00
Chinese, ex. Taiwanese (43)	62	0.42
Filipino (52)	72	0.49
Indian (141)	143	0.98
Indonesian	3	0.02
Japanese (6)	18	0.12
Korean (58)	68	0.46
Malaysian	1	0.01
Sri Lankan (1)	1	0.01
Taiwanese (12)	12	0.08
Thai (6)	8	0.05
Vietnamese (29)	31	0.21
Other Asian, specified (1)	3	0.02
Other Asian, not specified (4)	17	0.12
Australian	7	0.05
Austrian	69	0.47
Belgian	30	0.20
Brazilian	36	0.24
British	54	0.37
Canadian	54	0.37
Croatian	9	0.06
Czech	46	0.31
Czechoslovakian	6	0.04
Danish	82	0.56
Dutch	241	1.64
Eastern European	74	0.50
English	2,191	14.88
European	79	0.54
French, except Basque	397	2.70
French Canadian	139	0.94
German	3,009	20.43
Greek	213	1.45
Hawaii Native/Pacific Islander:	17	0.12
Micronesian: (7)	9	0.06
Guamanian/Chamorro (7)	9	0.06
Polynesian:	6	0.04
Native Hawaiian	6	0.04
Other Pac. Isl., not spec.	2	0.01
Hispanic or Latino:	1,240	8.48
Central American:	31	0.21
Costa Rican	5	0.03
Honduran	8	0.05
Nicaraguan	3	0.02
Panamanian	4	0.03
Salvadoran	8	0.05
Other Central American	3	0.02
Cuban	288	1.97
Dominican Republic	16	0.11
Mexican	78	0.53
Puerto Rican	342	2.34
South American:	137	0.94
Argentinean	13	0.09
Bolivian	1	0.01
Chilean	4	0.03
Colombian	69	0.47
Ecuadorian	16	0.11
Paraguayan	4	0.03
Peruvian	7	0.05
Venezuelan	8	0.05
Other South American	15	0.10
Other Hispanic or Latino	348	2.38
Hungarian	117	0.79
Iranian	73	0.50
Irish	2,050	13.92
Italian	1,786	12.13
Lithuanian	51	0.35
Luxemburger	22	0.15
Norwegian	259	1.76
Polish	551	3.74
Portuguese	44	0.30
Romanian	26	0.18
Russian	158	1.07
Scandinavian	39	0.26
Scotch-Irish	224	1.52
Scottish	571	3.88
Serbian	20	0.14
Slovak	16	0.11
Swedish	223	1.51
Swiss	22	0.15
Ukrainian	53	0.36
United States or American	1,232	8.37
Welsh	142	0.96
West Indian, excl. Hispanic:	63	0.43
Belizean	14	0.10
Haitian	7	0.05
Jamaican	28	0.19
West Indian	7	0.05
Other West Indian	7	0.05
White:	13,528	92.49
Not Hispanic (12,328)	12,457	85.16
Hispanic (1,027)	1,071	7.32

Kings Point

Place Type: Census Designated Place
County: Palm Beach
Population: 12,207

Ancestry/Race	Number	%
African American/Black:	41	0.34
Not Hispanic (32)	40	0.33
Hispanic (1)	1	0.01
Alaska Native tribes, specified:	1	0.01
Eskimo (1)	1	0.01
Am. Ind. or Alaska Nat., not spec.	18	0.15
Albanian	22	0.18
Alsatian	6	0.05
American Indian tribes, specified:	1	0.01
Chippewa	1	0.01
American Indian tribes, not spec.	4	0.03
Arab:	6	0.05
Lebanese	6	0.05
Armenian	32	0.26
Asian:	35	0.29
Chinese, ex. Taiwanese (14)	16	0.13
Filipino	2	0.02
Indian (1)	3	0.02
Japanese (1)	1	0.01
Korean (2)	2	0.02
Thai (1)	1	0.01
Vietnamese (3)	3	0.02
Other Asian, specified	5	0.04
Other Asian, not specified	2	0.02
Austrian	420	3.39
Belgian	15	0.12
British	16	0.13
Canadian	16	0.13
Czech	34	0.27
Czechoslovakian	44	0.36
Danish	24	0.19
Dutch	16	0.13
Eastern European	23	0.19
English	202	1.63
Estonian	16	0.13
European	37	0.30
French, except Basque	13	0.10
French Canadian	15	0.12
German	424	3.42
Greek	74	0.60
Hawaii Native/Pacific Islander:	8	0.07
Micronesian: (1)	2	0.02
Guamanian/Chamorro (1)	2	0.02
Other Pac. Isl., specified	5	0.04
Other Pac. Isl., not spec.	1	0.01
Hispanic or Latino:	138	1.13
Central American:	1	0.01
Salvadoran	1	0.01
Cuban	16	0.13
Dominican Republic	2	0.02
Mexican	6	0.05
Puerto Rican	41	0.34
South American:	28	0.23
Argentinean	4	0.03
Chilean	5	0.04
Colombian	16	0.13
Ecuadorian	2	0.02
Other South American	1	0.01
Other Hispanic or Latino	44	0.36
Hungarian	341	2.75
Iranian	8	0.06
Irish	146	1.18

Notes: 1. Figures in the "Number" column do not add up to the total population due to: a) Ancestry/Race overlap — e.g. persons can report being both White and Irish, b) persons of Hispanic origin can report being any race, c) persons reporting two ancestries are counted in both categories. 2. Numbers in parentheses indicate the number of persons reporting this ancestry/race alone, not in combination with any other ancestry/race. 3. Refer to the Explanation of Data in the front of the book for more detailed information.

Ancestry/Race	Number	%
Israeli	12	0.10
Italian	886	7.15
Latvian	16	0.13
Lithuanian	93	0.75
Norwegian	17	0.14
Polish	1,345	10.86
Romanian	239	1.93
Russian	2,005	16.19
Scotch-Irish	9	0.07
Scottish	14	0.11
Slovak	8	0.06
Turkish	85	0.69
Ukrainian	138	1.11
United States or American	1,208	9.75
Welsh	18	0.15
White:	12,134	99.40
Not Hispanic (11,976)	12,007	98.36
Hispanic (121)	127	1.04

Kissimmee

Place Type: City
County: Osceola
Population: 47,814

Ancestry/Race	Number	%
Acadian/Cajun	16	0.03
African American/Black:	5,423	11.34
Not Hispanic (4,074)	4,411	9.23
Hispanic (701)	1,012	2.12
African, sub-Saharan:	293	0.62
African	191	0.40
Cape Verdean	56	0.12
Other sub-Saharan African	46	0.10
Am. Ind. or Alaska Nat., not spec.	227	0.47
Albanian	10	0.02
American Indian tribes, specified:	249	0.52
Apache (7)	11	0.02
Blackfeet (3)	7	0.01
Cherokee (17)	60	0.13
Cheyenne	1	0.00
Chippewa (2)	8	0.02
Choctaw (4)	11	0.02
Comanche (2)	2	0.00
Creek	3	0.01
Delaware	2	0.00
Houma (1)	1	0.00
Iroquois (3)	16	0.03
Latin American Indians (31)	70	0.15
Lumbee (3)	3	0.01
Menominee (3)	3	0.01
Navajo (4)	7	0.01
Osage (3)	3	0.01
Potawatomi (1)	1	0.00
Pueblo (1)	2	0.00
Puget Sound Salish (1)	1	0.00
Seminole (5)	9	0.02
Shoshone (1)	2	0.00
Sioux (1)	6	0.01
Yaqui (1)	1	0.00
All other tribes (13)	19	0.04
American Indian tribes, not spec.	11	0.02
Arab:	684	1.44
Arab/Arabic	201	0.42
Egyptian	12	0.03
Jordanian	6	0.01
Lebanese	111	0.23
Moroccan	249	0.52
Palestinian	7	0.01
Syrian	48	0.10
Other Arab	50	0.11
Armenian	11	0.02
Asian:	1,998	4.18
Bangladeshi (24)	44	0.09
Cambodian (3)	3	0.01
Chinese, ex. Taiwanese (226)	258	0.54
Filipino (374)	452	0.95
Indian (560)	640	1.34
Indonesian (2)	3	0.01
Japanese (26)	42	0.09
Korean (45)	65	0.14
Laotian (4)	7	0.01
Malaysian	1	0.00
Pakistani (112)	178	0.37
Sri Lankan (13)	13	0.03
Taiwanese (11)	17	0.04
Thai (24)	33	0.07
Vietnamese (103)	120	0.25
Other Asian, specified (2)	6	0.01
Other Asian, not specified (46)	116	0.24
Austrian	168	0.35
Brazilian	291	0.61
British	196	0.41
Canadian	156	0.33
Celtic	18	0.04
Croatian	15	0.03
Czech	241	0.51
Czechoslovakian	80	0.17
Danish	45	0.09
Dutch	393	0.83
English	2,984	6.27
Estonian	10	0.02
European	152	0.32
Finnish	59	0.12
French, except Basque	888	1.87
French Canadian	390	0.82
German	4,202	8.84
Greek	159	0.33
Guyanese	120	0.25
Hawaii Native/Pacific Islander:	132	0.28
Melanesian: (2)	4	0.01
Fijian (2)	4	0.01
Micronesian: (8)	19	0.04
Guamanian/Chamorro (5)	14	0.03
Other Micronesian (3)	5	0.01
Polynesian: (17)	38	0.08
Native Hawaiian (12)	25	0.05
Samoan (5)	13	0.03
Other Pac. Isl., specified	4	0.01
Other Pac. Isl., not spec. (19)	67	0.14
Hispanic or Latino:	19,954	41.73
Central American:	853	1.78
Costa Rican	69	0.14
Guatemalan	89	0.19
Honduran	141	0.29
Nicaraguan	148	0.31
Panamanian	91	0.19
Salvadoran	276	0.58
Other Central American	39	0.08
Cuban	817	1.71
Dominican Republic	964	2.02
Mexican	1,573	3.29
Puerto Rican	11,312	23.66
South American:	2,047	4.28
Argentinean	63	0.13
Bolivian	15	0.03
Chilean	54	0.11
Colombian	960	2.01
Ecuadorian	179	0.37
Paraguayan	3	0.01
Peruvian	250	0.52
Uruguayan	22	0.05
Venezuelan	454	0.95
Other South American	47	0.10
Other Hispanic or Latino	2,388	4.99
Hungarian	233	0.49
Iranian	25	0.05
Irish	3,393	7.13
Israeli	8	0.02
Italian	2,483	5.22
Lithuanian	28	0.06
Luxemburger	8	0.02
Northern European	16	0.03
Norwegian	145	0.30
Pennsylvania German	48	0.10
Polish	1,057	2.22
Portuguese	120	0.25
Romanian	6	0.01
Russian	321	0.67
Scandinavian	26	0.05
Scotch-Irish	376	0.79
Scottish	520	1.09
Serbian	12	0.03
Slavic	6	0.01
Slovak	63	0.13
Swedish	282	0.59
Swiss	19	0.04
Turkish	6	0.01
Ukrainian	134	0.28
United States or American	3,005	6.32
Welsh	176	0.37
West Indian, excl. Hispanic:	929	1.95
Bahamian	16	0.03
Barbadian	43	0.09
Belizean	6	0.01
British West Indian	87	0.18
Haitian	272	0.57
Jamaican	302	0.64
Trinidadian and Tobagonian	95	0.20
West Indian	108	0.23
White:	33,855	70.81
Not Hispanic (20,887)	21,564	45.10
Hispanic (11,252)	12,291	25.71
Yugoslavian	5	0.01

Lady Lake

Place Type: Town
County: Lake
Population: 11,828

Ancestry/Race	Number	%
African American/Black:	389	3.29
Not Hispanic (375)	380	3.21
Hispanic (8)	9	0.08
Alaska Native tribes, specified:	1	0.01
Aleut (1)	1	0.01
Am. Ind. or Alaska Nat., not spec.	19	0.16
American Indian tribes, specified:	44	0.37
Apache (1)	1	0.01
Blackfeet (2)	3	0.03
Cherokee (4)	20	0.17
Chickasaw	2	0.02
Chippewa (1)	3	0.03
Choctaw	4	0.03
Iroquois	3	0.03
Sioux	6	0.05
All other tribes (1)	2	0.02
American Indian tribes, not spec.	2	0.02
Arab:	17	0.15
Lebanese	8	0.07
Syrian	9	0.08
Asian:	44	0.37
Chinese, ex. Taiwanese (13)	18	0.15
Filipino (4)	6	0.05
Indian (4)	4	0.03
Japanese (9)	9	0.08
Korean (1)	1	0.01
Thai (4)	4	0.03
Vietnamese (1)	1	0.01
Other Asian, not specified	1	0.01
Austrian	18	0.15
Belgian	17	0.15
Brazilian	4	0.03
British	49	0.42
Bulgarian	8	0.07
Canadian	40	0.34
Croatian	34	0.29
Czech	49	0.42
Czechoslovakian	35	0.30
Danish	80	0.69
Dutch	302	2.59
English	2,130	18.24
European	8	0.07
Finnish	8	0.07
French, except Basque	640	5.48
French Canadian	182	1.56
German	2,232	19.11
Greek	27	0.23
Hawaii Native/Pacific Islander:	9	0.08

Notes: 1. Figures in the "Number" column do not add up to the total population due to: a) Ancestry/Race overlap — e.g. persons can report being both White and Irish, b) persons of Hispanic origin can report being any race, c) persons reporting two ancestries are counted in both categories. 2. Numbers in parentheses indicate the number of persons reporting this ancestry/race alone, not in combination with any other ancestry/race. 3. Refer to the Explanation of Data in the front of the book for more detailed information.

Polynesian: (5)	7	0.06
Native Hawaiian (4)	6	0.05
Samoan (1)	1	0.01
Other Pac. Isl., not spec. (2)	2	0.02
Hispanic or Latino:	217	1.83
Central American:	4	0.03
Panamanian	3	0.03
Other Central American	1	0.01
Cuban	9	0.08
Dominican Republic	5	0.04
Mexican	74	0.63
Puerto Rican	59	0.50
South American:	8	0.07
Chilean	1	0.01
Colombian	7	0.06
Other Hispanic or Latino	58	0.49
Hungarian	37	0.32
Irish	1,778	15.23
Italian	873	7.48
Latvian	8	0.07
Lithuanian	39	0.33
Maltese	8	0.07
Northern European	8	0.07
Norwegian	153	1.31
Polish	504	4.32
Portuguese	8	0.07
Romanian	16	0.14
Russian	74	0.63
Scandinavian	9	0.08
Scotch-Irish	298	2.55
Scottish	411	3.52
Serbian	9	0.08
Slavic	8	0.07
Slovak	49	0.42
Slovene	17	0.15
Swedish	168	1.44
Swiss	47	0.40
Ukrainian	40	0.34
United States or American	1,186	10.16
Welsh	187	1.60
West Indian, excl. Hispanic:	23	0.20
Jamaican	23	0.20
White:	11,328	95.77
Not Hispanic (11,116)	11,161	94.36
Hispanic (158)	167	1.41
Yugoslavian	7	0.06

Lake Magdalene

Place Type: Census Designated Place
County: Hillsborough
Population: 28,755

Ancestry/Race	Number	%
African American/Black:	1,873	6.51
Not Hispanic (1,598)	1,723	5.99
Hispanic (100)	150	0.52
African, sub-Saharan:	131	0.45
African	69	0.24
Nigerian	7	0.02
Sierra Leonean	8	0.03
South African	47	0.16
Alaska Native tribes, specified:	1	0.00
Tlingit-Haida	1	0.00
Am. Ind. or Alaska Nat., not spec.	70	0.24
American Indian tribes, specified:	127	0.44
Apache (1)	4	0.01
Blackfeet (1)	8	0.03
Cherokee (32)	72	0.25
Chickasaw (1)	3	0.01
Choctaw (3)	4	0.01
Creek (1)	3	0.01
Delaware	1	0.00
Iroquois (1)	4	0.01
Latin American Indians (5)	12	0.04
Lumbee	1	0.00
Navajo (1)	1	0.00
Pueblo (2)	2	0.01
Seminole (1)	1	0.00
Sioux	1	0.00
All other tribes (9)	10	0.03
American Indian tribes, not spec.	16	0.06
Arab:	436	1.51
Arab/Arabic	100	0.35
Egyptian	25	0.09
Jordanian	29	0.10
Lebanese	235	0.82
Moroccan	26	0.09
Syrian	21	0.07
Asian:	842	2.93
Chinese, ex. Taiwanese (91)	125	0.43
Filipino (131)	171	0.59
Indian (242)	262	0.91
Indonesian	2	0.01
Japanese (24)	56	0.19
Korean (48)	60	0.21
Laotian (7)	7	0.02
Malaysian (2)	3	0.01
Pakistani (5)	5	0.02
Taiwanese (1)	1	0.00
Thai (25)	32	0.11
Vietnamese (73)	78	0.27
Other Asian, specified (5)	6	0.02
Other Asian, not specified (13)	34	0.12
Austrian	124	0.43
Basque	8	0.03
Belgian	27	0.09
Brazilian	42	0.15
British	316	1.10
Bulgarian	7	0.02
Canadian	112	0.39
Croatian	14	0.05
Czech	199	0.69
Czechoslovakian	52	0.18
Danish	94	0.33
Dutch	504	1.75
Eastern European	30	0.10
English	3,437	11.92
European	294	1.02
Finnish	48	0.17
French, except Basque	917	3.18
French Canadian	227	0.79
German	4,343	15.06
Greek	269	0.93
Guyanese	8	0.03
Hawaii Native/Pacific Islander:	35	0.12
Melanesian: (1)	1	0.00
Other Melanesian (1)	1	0.00
Polynesian: (6)	11	0.04
Native Hawaiian (4)	9	0.03
Samoan (2)	2	0.01
Other Pac. Isl., specified	1	0.00
Other Pac. Isl., not spec. (2)	22	0.08
Hispanic or Latino:	3,886	13.51
Central American:	179	0.62
Costa Rican	24	0.08
Guatemalan	17	0.06
Honduran	61	0.21
Nicaraguan	24	0.08
Panamanian	35	0.12
Salvadoran	12	0.04
Other Central American	6	0.02
Cuban	665	2.31
Dominican Republic	63	0.22
Mexican	217	0.75
Puerto Rican	1,313	4.57
South American:	309	1.07
Argentinean	10	0.03
Bolivian	2	0.01
Chilean	2	0.01
Colombian	146	0.51
Ecuadorian	31	0.11
Peruvian	62	0.22
Uruguayan	4	0.01
Venezuelan	35	0.12
Other South American	17	0.06
Other Hispanic or Latino	1,140	3.96
Hungarian	200	0.69
Iranian	69	0.24
Irish	3,895	13.51
Italian	2,400	8.32
Latvian	6	0.02
Lithuanian	119	0.41
Northern European	30	0.10
Norwegian	268	0.93
Polish	736	2.55
Portuguese	55	0.19
Romanian	31	0.11
Russian	277	0.96
Scandinavian	18	0.06
Scotch-Irish	638	2.21
Scottish	656	2.28
Slavic	18	0.06
Slovak	98	0.34
Slovene	14	0.05
Soviet Union	7	0.02
Swedish	542	1.88
Swiss	55	0.19
Ukrainian	88	0.31
United States or American	2,370	8.22
Welsh	224	0.78
West Indian, excl. Hispanic:	432	1.50
Bahamian	58	0.20
Barbadian	6	0.02
British West Indian	11	0.04
Haitian	74	0.26
Jamaican	190	0.66
Trinidadian and Tobagonian	72	0.25
U.S. Virgin Islander	11	0.04
Other West Indian	10	0.03
White:	25,403	88.34
Not Hispanic (22,079)	22,407	77.92
Hispanic (2,836)	2,996	10.42
Yugoslavian	38	0.13

Lake Mary

Place Type: City
County: Seminole
Population: 11,458

Ancestry/Race	Number	%
Afghan	8	0.07
African American/Black:	469	4.09
Not Hispanic (396)	450	3.93
Hispanic (17)	19	0.17
African, sub-Saharan:	50	0.44
African	29	0.26
South African	9	0.08
Other sub-Saharan African	12	0.11
Am. Ind. or Alaska Nat., not spec.	22	0.19
American Indian tribes, specified:	50	0.44
Blackfeet (1)	1	0.01
Cherokee (4)	23	0.20
Choctaw (4)	5	0.04
Creek (1)	6	0.05
Latin American Indians (5)	8	0.07
Osage (1)	1	0.01
Seminole (3)	4	0.03
All other tribes (2)	2	0.02
Arab:	104	0.92
Egyptian	15	0.13
Lebanese	76	0.67
Palestinian	13	0.12
Armenian	132	1.17
Asian:	491	4.29
Cambodian (5)	10	0.09
Chinese, ex. Taiwanese (62)	73	0.64
Filipino (83)	95	0.83
Indian (124)	130	1.13
Indonesian (10)	10	0.09
Japanese (13)	19	0.17
Korean (55)	56	0.49
Laotian (1)	1	0.01
Pakistani (15)	15	0.13
Taiwanese (8)	8	0.07
Thai (7)	8	0.07
Vietnamese (48)	53	0.46
Other Asian, not specified (2)	13	0.11
Australian	38	0.34

Notes: 1. Figures in the "Number" column do not add up to the total population due to: a) Ancestry/Race overlap — e.g. persons can report being both White and Irish, b) persons of Hispanic origin can report being any race, c) persons reporting two ancestries are counted in both categories. 2. Numbers in parentheses indicate the number of persons reporting this ancestry/race alone, not in combination with any other ancestry/race. 3. Refer to the Explanation of Data in the front of the book for more detailed information.

Ancestry/Race	Number	%
Belgian	54	0.48
British	41	0.36
Canadian	32	0.28
Celtic	7	0.06
Czech	69	0.61
Czechoslovakian	29	0.26
Danish	30	0.27
Dutch	142	1.26
English	1,627	14.41
European	48	0.43
Finnish	5	0.04
French, except Basque	368	3.26
French Canadian	155	1.37
German	2,528	22.39
Greek	57	0.50
Guyanese	12	0.11
Hawaii Native/Pacific Islander:	15	0.13
Micronesian: (1)	1	0.01
Guamanian/Chamorro (1)	1	0.01
Polynesian: (5)	8	0.07
Native Hawaiian (4)	7	0.06
Samoan (1)	1	0.01
Other Pac. Isl., not spec. (4)	6	0.05
Hispanic or Latino:	713	6.22
Central American:	25	0.22
Costa Rican	3	0.03
Guatemalan	2	0.02
Honduran	1	0.01
Nicaraguan	1	0.01
Panamanian	11	0.10
Salvadoran	7	0.06
Cuban	58	0.51
Dominican Republic	11	0.10
Mexican	72	0.63
Puerto Rican	331	2.89
South American:	113	0.99
Argentinean	14	0.12
Bolivian	3	0.03
Chilean	1	0.01
Colombian	65	0.57
Ecuadorian	3	0.03
Peruvian	14	0.12
Venezuelan	6	0.05
Other South American	7	0.06
Other Hispanic or Latino	103	0.90
Hungarian	86	0.76
Iranian	33	0.29
Irish	1,575	13.95
Italian	1,143	10.12
Lithuanian	17	0.15
Luxemburger	9	0.08
Norwegian	184	1.63
Pennsylvania German	8	0.07
Polish	388	3.44
Portuguese	60	0.53
Romanian	22	0.19
Russian	186	1.65
Scotch-Irish	249	2.21
Scottish	323	2.86
Slovak	85	0.75
Swedish	83	0.74
Swiss	22	0.19
Ukrainian	63	0.56
United States or American	1,024	9.07
Welsh	64	0.57
West Indian, excl. Hispanic:	143	1.27
Bahamian	25	0.22
Bermudan	46	0.41
Haitian	38	0.34
Jamaican	34	0.30
White:	10,359	90.41
Not Hispanic (9,734)	9,827	85.77
Hispanic (502)	532	4.64
Yugoslavian	36	0.32

Lake Wales

Place Type: City
County: Polk
Population: 10,194

Ancestry/Race	Number	%
African American/Black:	3,610	35.41
Not Hispanic (3,492)	3,569	35.01
Hispanic (34)	41	0.40
African, sub-Saharan:	45	0.44
African	37	0.36
Cape Verdean	8	0.08
Am. Ind. or Alaska Nat., not spec.	14	0.14
American Indian tribes, specified:	42	0.41
Blackfeet	1	0.01
Cherokee (3)	19	0.19
Chippewa (1)	1	0.01
Choctaw	2	0.02
Creek (2)	3	0.03
Latin American Indians (2)	5	0.05
Navajo (1)	1	0.01
Potawatomi (1)	1	0.01
Seminole (6)	6	0.06
Sioux (1)	1	0.01
All other tribes (1)	2	0.02
American Indian tribes, not spec.	1	0.01
Arab:	38	0.37
Egyptian	38	0.37
Asian:	60	0.59
Chinese, ex. Taiwanese (4)	5	0.05
Filipino (7)	8	0.08
Indian (19)	19	0.19
Indonesian (1)	1	0.01
Japanese (5)	7	0.07
Korean (1)	1	0.01
Taiwanese (5)	5	0.05
Thai (3)	3	0.03
Vietnamese (6)	6	0.06
Other Asian, not specified (1)	5	0.05
Austrian	25	0.24
Belgian	20	0.19
British	45	0.44
Canadian	15	0.15
Celtic	10	0.10
Czech	26	0.25
Czechoslovakian	10	0.10
Danish	59	0.57
Dutch	175	1.70
English	888	8.62
Finnish	8	0.08
French, except Basque	246	2.39
French Canadian	24	0.23
German	806	7.82
Hawaii Native/Pacific Islander:	15	0.15
Micronesian: (7)	7	0.07
Guamanian/Chamorro (7)	7	0.07
Polynesian: (2)	3	0.03
Native Hawaiian	1	0.01
Samoan (2)	2	0.02
Other Pac. Isl., not spec. (1)	5	0.05
Hispanic or Latino:	1,014	9.95
Central American:	24	0.24
Guatemalan	5	0.05
Honduran	1	0.01
Nicaraguan	8	0.08
Panamanian	5	0.05
Salvadoran	4	0.04
Other Central American	1	0.01
Cuban	36	0.35
Dominican Republic	9	0.09
Mexican	575	5.64
Puerto Rican	237	2.32
South American:	31	0.30
Argentinean	2	0.02
Colombian	1	0.01
Ecuadorian	14	0.14
Peruvian	9	0.09
Uruguayan	2	0.02
Venezuelan	3	0.03
Other Hispanic or Latino	102	1.00
Hungarian	6	0.06
Irish	793	7.70
Italian	255	2.48
Lithuanian	8	0.08
Norwegian	100	0.97
Polish	199	1.93
Russian	43	0.42
Scotch-Irish	127	1.23
Scottish	95	0.92
Swedish	79	0.77
United States or American	1,149	11.15
Welsh	45	0.44
West Indian, excl. Hispanic:	92	0.89
Bahamian	11	0.11
Haitian	16	0.16
Jamaican	65	0.63
White:	6,157	60.40
Not Hispanic (5,484)	5,550	54.44
Hispanic (580)	607	5.95

Lake Worth Corridor

Place Type: Census Designated Place
County: Palm Beach
Population: 18,663

Ancestry/Race	Number	%
African American/Black:	2,936	15.73
Not Hispanic (2,378)	2,714	14.54
Hispanic (164)	222	1.19
African, sub-Saharan:	133	0.72
African	133	0.72
Am. Ind. or Alaska Nat., not spec.	66	0.35
Albanian	49	0.27
American Indian tribes, specified:	126	0.68
Blackfeet (1)	4	0.02
Cherokee (11)	28	0.15
Cheyenne (1)	1	0.01
Chippewa (4)	4	0.02
Choctaw	4	0.02
Crow (4)	4	0.02
Iroquois	3	0.02
Latin American Indians (35)	64	0.34
Lumbee (1)	1	0.01
Navajo (1)	1	0.01
Pima (1)	1	0.01
Pueblo	2	0.01
Seminole	1	0.01
Sioux (1)	2	0.01
All other tribes (2)	6	0.03
American Indian tribes, not spec.	18	0.10
Arab:	17	0.09
Egyptian	9	0.05
Lebanese	8	0.04
Asian:	304	1.63
Bangladeshi (25)	44	0.24
Chinese, ex. Taiwanese (19)	25	0.13
Filipino (16)	22	0.12
Indian (88)	112	0.60
Indonesian (3)	5	0.03
Japanese (5)	7	0.04
Korean (9)	9	0.05
Pakistani (11)	20	0.11
Sri Lankan (1)	1	0.01
Thai (5)	5	0.03
Vietnamese (14)	21	0.11
Other Asian, specified	1	0.01
Other Asian, not specified (17)	32	0.17
Austrian	72	0.39
Belgian	23	0.13
Brazilian	25	0.14
British	13	0.07
Canadian	38	0.21
Croatian	6	0.03
Czech	30	0.16
Czechoslovakian	23	0.13
Danish	42	0.23
Dutch	80	0.44
English	827	4.50

Notes: 1. Figures in the "Number" column do not add up to the total population due to: a) Ancestry/Race overlap — e.g. persons can report being both White and Irish, b) persons of Hispanic origin can report being any race, c) persons reporting two ancestries are counted in both categories. 2. Numbers in parentheses indicate the number of persons reporting this ancestry/race alone, not in combination with any other ancestry/race. 3. Refer to the Explanation of Data in the front of the book for more detailed information.

Estonian	8	0.04
European	15	0.08
Finnish	109	0.59
French, except Basque	524	2.85
French Canadian	110	0.60
German	1,495	8.13
Greek	38	0.21
Guyanese	26	0.14
Hawaii Native/Pacific Islander:	71	0.38
Micronesian: (7)	22	0.12
Guamanian/Chamorro (7)	21	0.11
Other Micronesian	1	0.01
Polynesian: (1)	7	0.04
Native Hawaiian	3	0.02
Samoan (1)	3	0.02
Other Polynesian	1	0.01
Other Pac. Isl., not spec. (6)	42	0.23
Hispanic or Latino:	7,613	40.79
Central American:	1,051	5.63
Costa Rican	21	0.11
Guatemalan	459	2.46
Honduran	216	1.16
Nicaraguan	97	0.52
Panamanian	10	0.05
Salvadoran	235	1.26
Other Central American	13	0.07
Cuban	608	3.26
Dominican Republic	180	0.96
Mexican	3,032	16.25
Puerto Rican	1,356	7.27
South American:	368	1.97
Argentinean	32	0.17
Bolivian	33	0.18
Chilean	14	0.08
Colombian	142	0.76
Ecuadorian	42	0.23
Paraguayan	3	0.02
Peruvian	52	0.28
Uruguayan	13	0.07
Venezuelan	31	0.17
Other South American	6	0.03
Other Hispanic or Latino	1,018	5.45
Hungarian	58	0.32
Irish	1,727	9.39
Israeli	11	0.06
Italian	966	5.25
Lithuanian	7	0.04
Norwegian	57	0.31
Pennsylvania German	25	0.14
Polish	338	1.84
Portuguese	32	0.17
Romanian	101	0.55
Russian	121	0.66
Scandinavian	10	0.05
Scotch-Irish	332	1.81
Scottish	115	0.63
Slavic	10	0.05
Slovak	18	0.10
Swedish	134	0.73
Swiss	4	0.02
Ukrainian	49	0.27
United States or American	918	4.99
Welsh	151	0.82
West Indian, excl. Hispanic:	989	5.38
Bahamian	87	0.47
Barbadian	23	0.13
Haitian	627	3.41
Jamaican	166	0.90
Trinidadian and Tobagonian	63	0.34
West Indian	23	0.13
White:	12,403	66.46
Not Hispanic (7,837)	8,028	43.02
Hispanic (3,976)	4,375	23.44

Lake Worth

Place Type: City
County: Palm Beach
Population: 35,133

Ancestry/Race	Number	%
African American/Black:	7,476	21.28
Not Hispanic (6,320)	7,106	20.23
Hispanic (307)	370	1.05
African, sub-Saharan:	59	0.17
African	48	0.14
Ethiopian	11	0.03
Alaska Native tribes, specified:	1	0.00
Tlingit-Haida	1	0.00
Am. Ind. or Alaska Nat., not spec.	84	0.24
American Indian tribes, specified:	412	1.17
Apache	1	0.00
Blackfeet	6	0.02
Cherokee (12)	33	0.09
Chickasaw (1)	1	0.00
Chippewa	1	0.00
Choctaw (1)	2	0.01
Cree	1	0.00
Creek (1)	3	0.01
Crow	3	0.01
Delaware	1	0.00
Iroquois (1)	4	0.01
Latin American Indians (181)	318	0.91
Lumbee (2)	3	0.01
Navajo (2)	2	0.01
Ottawa (1)	2	0.01
Paiute	1	0.00
Pueblo (6)	7	0.02
Sioux (3)	5	0.01
All other tribes (2)	18	0.05
American Indian tribes, not spec.	18	0.05
Arab:	149	0.42
Arab/Arabic	28	0.08
Egyptian	13	0.04
Lebanese	87	0.25
Palestinian	15	0.04
Other Arab	6	0.02
Armenian	40	0.11
Asian:	399	1.14
Bangladeshi (6)	6	0.02
Cambodian (2)	2	0.01
Chinese, ex. Taiwanese (29)	43	0.12
Filipino (43)	66	0.19
Indian (97)	144	0.41
Indonesian (10)	10	0.03
Japanese (4)	9	0.03
Korean (8)	11	0.03
Laotian (1)	3	0.01
Malaysian (2)	2	0.01
Pakistani	1	0.00
Taiwanese	1	0.00
Thai (13)	17	0.05
Vietnamese (26)	35	0.10
Other Asian, not specified (14)	49	0.14
Australian	11	0.03
Austrian	115	0.33
Belgian	14	0.04
Brazilian	52	0.15
British	218	0.62
Canadian	199	0.56
Croatian	28	0.08
Czech	80	0.23
Czechoslovakian	45	0.13
Danish	62	0.18
Dutch	389	1.10
Eastern European	9	0.03
English	2,159	6.13
Estonian	5	0.01
European	80	0.23
Finnish	1,026	2.91
French, except Basque	895	2.54
French Canadian	342	0.97
German	3,083	8.75
Greek	142	0.40
Hawaii Native/Pacific Islander:	106	0.30
Micronesian: (20)	33	0.09
Guamanian/Chamorro (20)	33	0.09
Polynesian: (8)	11	0.03
Native Hawaiian (1)	3	0.01
Samoan (6)	7	0.02
Other Polynesian (1)	1	0.00
Other Pac. Isl., not spec. (9)	62	0.18
Hispanic or Latino:	10,437	29.71
Central American:	2,965	8.44
Costa Rican	51	0.15
Guatemalan	1,711	4.87
Honduran	559	1.59
Nicaraguan	122	0.35
Panamanian	14	0.04
Salvadoran	433	1.23
Other Central American	75	0.21
Cuban	1,218	3.47
Dominican Republic	172	0.49
Mexican	2,400	6.83
Puerto Rican	1,652	4.70
South American:	522	1.49
Argentinean	62	0.18
Bolivian	63	0.18
Chilean	19	0.05
Colombian	154	0.44
Ecuadorian	78	0.22
Peruvian	80	0.23
Uruguayan	28	0.08
Venezuelan	31	0.09
Other South American	7	0.02
Other Hispanic or Latino	1,508	4.29
Hungarian	243	0.69
Irish	2,985	8.47
Italian	1,594	4.52
Lithuanian	127	0.36
Luxemburger	10	0.03
Maltese	11	0.03
Norwegian	185	0.53
Pennsylvania German	41	0.12
Polish	691	1.96
Portuguese	84	0.24
Romanian	48	0.14
Russian	240	0.68
Scandinavian	17	0.05
Scotch-Irish	303	0.86
Scottish	478	1.36
Serbian	7	0.02
Slavic	25	0.07
Slovak	52	0.15
Swedish	157	0.45
Swiss	29	0.08
Ukrainian	43	0.12
United States or American	1,610	4.57
Welsh	226	0.64
West Indian, excl. Hispanic:	3,512	9.97
Bahamian	39	0.11
Belizean	46	0.13
British West Indian	110	0.31
Haitian	2,763	7.84
Jamaican	442	1.25
Trinidadian and Tobagonian	91	0.26
West Indian	21	0.06
White:	23,684	67.41
Not Hispanic (16,884)	17,188	48.92
Hispanic (5,993)	6,496	18.49
Yugoslavian	34	0.10

Lakeland Highlands

Place Type: Census Designated Place
County: Polk
Population: 12,557

Ancestry/Race	Number	%
African American/Black:	342	2.72
Not Hispanic (302)	330	2.63
Hispanic (8)	12	0.10
African, sub-Saharan:	63	0.49
African	7	0.05

Notes: 1. Figures in the "Number" column do not add up to the total population due to: a) Ancestry/Race overlap — e.g. persons can report being both White and Irish, b) persons of Hispanic origin can report being any race, c) persons reporting two ancestries are counted in both categories. 2. Numbers in parentheses indicate the number of persons reporting this ancestry/race alone, not in combination with any other ancestry/race. 3. Refer to the Explanation of Data in the front of the book for more detailed information.

Ghanian	12	0.09
South African	44	0.35
Alaska Native tribes, not specified	1	0.01
Am. Ind. or Alaska Nat., not spec.	9	0.07
American Indian tribes, specified:	42	0.33
Blackfeet (2)	2	0.02
Cherokee (4)	14	0.11
Choctaw (7)	7	0.06
Creek	3	0.02
Latin American Indians (1)	3	0.02
Lumbee (1)	3	0.02
Osage	1	0.01
Potawatomi (1)	1	0.01
Seminole	1	0.01
Sioux (3)	7	0.06
American Indian tribes, not spec.	2	0.02
Arab:	69	0.54
Arab/Arabic	50	0.39
Palestinian	9	0.07
Syrian	10	0.08
Asian:	255	2.03
Cambodian	2	0.02
Chinese, ex. Taiwanese (26)	39	0.31
Filipino (52)	57	0.45
Indian (57)	64	0.51
Indonesian (3)	3	0.02
Japanese (4)	8	0.06
Korean (23)	32	0.25
Laotian	1	0.01
Pakistani (5)	5	0.04
Taiwanese	4	0.03
Thai (8)	11	0.09
Vietnamese (20)	25	0.20
Other Asian, not specified (4)	4	0.03
Austrian	75	0.59
British	111	0.87
Canadian	85	0.67
Celtic	32	0.25
Croatian	10	0.08
Czech	28	0.22
Czechoslovakian	41	0.32
Danish	8	0.06
Dutch	300	2.35
English	1,690	13.26
European	119	0.93
Finnish	8	0.06
French, except Basque	366	2.87
French Canadian	200	1.57
German	2,211	17.35
Greek	17	0.13
Hawaii Native/Pacific Islander:	7	0.06
Polynesian: (1)	1	0.01
Samoan (1)	1	0.01
Other Pac. Isl., not spec. (1)	6	0.05
Hispanic or Latino:	484	3.85
Central American:	17	0.14
Costa Rican	2	0.02
Guatemalan	2	0.02
Honduran	1	0.01
Nicaraguan	3	0.02
Panamanian	9	0.07
Cuban	162	1.29
Dominican Republic	10	0.08
Mexican	40	0.32
Puerto Rican	108	0.86
South American:	33	0.26
Argentinean	3	0.02
Bolivian	1	0.01
Colombian	16	0.13
Peruvian	6	0.05
Other South American	7	0.06
Other Hispanic or Latino	114	0.91
Hungarian	45	0.35
Iranian	44	0.35
Irish	1,701	13.34
Italian	770	6.04
Latvian	9	0.07
Northern European	9	0.07
Norwegian	138	1.08
Pennsylvania German	18	0.14
Polish	376	2.95
Portuguese	54	0.42
Romanian	32	0.25
Russian	78	0.61
Scandinavian	15	0.12
Scotch-Irish	342	2.68
Scottish	392	3.08
Slavic	36	0.28
Slovak	11	0.09
Slovene	10	0.08
Swedish	164	1.29
Swiss	24	0.19
Ukrainian	19	0.15
United States or American	1,943	15.24
Welsh	127	1.00
West Indian, excl. Hispanic:	65	0.51
Belizean	17	0.13
Haitian	20	0.16
Jamaican	17	0.13
Trinidadian and Tobagonian	11	0.09
White:	11,927	94.98
Not Hispanic (11,444)	11,518	91.73
Hispanic (386)	409	3.26

Lakeland

Place Type: City
County: Polk
Population: 78,452

Ancestry/Race	Number	%
Acadian/Cajun	23	0.03
African American/Black:	17,316	22.07
Not Hispanic (16,500)	17,022	21.70
Hispanic (182)	294	0.37
African, sub-Saharan:	401	0.51
African	312	0.40
Cape Verdean	10	0.01
Nigerian	74	0.09
South African	5	0.01
Alaska Native tribes, specified:	5	0.01
Alaska Athabascan (1)	1	0.00
Aleut (1)	1	0.00
Eskimo (1)	3	0.00
Am. Ind. or Alaska Nat., not spec.	196	0.25
Albanian	47	0.06
Alsatian	15	0.02
American Indian tribes, specified:	268	0.34
Apache (4)	9	0.01
Blackfeet (7)	23	0.03
Cherokee (49)	124	0.16
Chickasaw	1	0.00
Chippewa (4)	10	0.01
Choctaw (4)	14	0.02
Comanche	1	0.00
Cree (1)	2	0.00
Creek (1)	7	0.01
Delaware	1	0.00
Houma (1)	1	0.00
Iroquois (1)	10	0.01
Latin American Indians (5)	12	0.02
Lumbee (2)	3	0.00
Menominee (1)	1	0.00
Navajo (1)	5	0.01
Potawatomi	1	0.00
Seminole (1)	8	0.01
Sioux (8)	12	0.02
Ute (1)	3	0.00
All other tribes (8)	20	0.03
American Indian tribes, not spec.	56	0.07
Arab:	131	0.17
Arab/Arabic	35	0.04
Egyptian	5	0.01
Jordanian	7	0.01
Lebanese	39	0.05
Moroccan	25	0.03
Syrian	20	0.03
Armenian	21	0.03
Asian:	1,349	1.72
Cambodian (10)	24	0.03
Chinese, ex. Taiwanese (157)	197	0.25
Filipino (125)	156	0.20
Indian (412)	476	0.61
Indonesian (12)	18	0.02
Japanese (66)	98	0.12
Korean (79)	110	0.14
Laotian (25)	33	0.04
Pakistani (3)	16	0.02
Sri Lankan (16)	16	0.02
Taiwanese (11)	13	0.02
Thai (24)	32	0.04
Vietnamese (49)	63	0.08
Other Asian, specified (2)	9	0.01
Other Asian, not specified (34)	88	0.11
Austrian	109	0.14
Belgian	42	0.05
Brazilian	33	0.04
British	394	0.50
Bulgarian	15	0.02
Canadian	206	0.26
Celtic	19	0.02
Croatian	52	0.07
Czech	141	0.18
Czechoslovakian	93	0.12
Danish	122	0.16
Dutch	1,389	1.78
English	8,672	11.09
European	442	0.57
Finnish	68	0.09
French, except Basque	2,478	3.17
French Canadian	579	0.74
German	9,773	12.50
Greek	285	0.36
Guyanese	12	0.02
Hawaii Native/Pacific Islander:	100	0.13
Micronesian: (4)	7	0.01
Guamanian/Chamorro (4)	7	0.01
Polynesian: (33)	40	0.05
Native Hawaiian (18)	23	0.03
Samoan (15)	17	0.02
Other Pac. Isl., not spec. (8)	53	0.07
Hispanic or Latino:	5,032	6.41
Central American:	164	0.21
Costa Rican	17	0.02
Guatemalan	18	0.02
Honduran	27	0.03
Nicaraguan	36	0.05
Panamanian	28	0.04
Salvadoran	24	0.03
Other Central American	14	0.02
Cuban	688	0.88
Dominican Republic	71	0.09
Mexican	1,279	1.63
Puerto Rican	1,852	2.36
South American:	247	0.31
Argentinean	16	0.02
Bolivian	7	0.01
Chilean	8	0.01
Colombian	95	0.12
Ecuadorian	13	0.02
Peruvian	48	0.06
Uruguayan	1	0.00
Venezuelan	40	0.05
Other South American	19	0.02
Other Hispanic or Latino	731	0.93
Hungarian	472	0.60
Iranian	7	0.01
Irish	8,027	10.27
Israeli	6	0.01
Italian	2,494	3.19
Latvian	24	0.03
Lithuanian	75	0.10
Northern European	92	0.12
Norwegian	594	0.76
Pennsylvania German	61	0.08
Polish	1,494	1.91
Portuguese	161	0.21
Romanian	79	0.10
Russian	327	0.42
Scandinavian	54	0.07

Notes: 1. Figures in the "Number" column do not add up to the total population due to: a) Ancestry/Race overlap — e.g. persons can report being both White and Irish, b) persons of Hispanic origin can report being any race, c) persons reporting two ancestries are counted in both categories. 2. Numbers in parentheses indicate the number of persons reporting this ancestry/race alone, not in combination with any other ancestry/race. 3. Refer to the Explanation of Data in the front of the book for more detailed information.

Scotch-Irish	1,645	2.10
Scottish	1,591	2.04
Serbian	4	0.01
Slavic	27	0.03
Slovak	125	0.16
Slovene	15	0.02
Swedish	779	1.00
Swiss	164	0.21
Turkish	35	0.04
Ukrainian	75	0.10
United States or American	7,715	9.87
Welsh	494	0.63
West Indian, excl. Hispanic:	838	1.07
Bahamian	19	0.02
British West Indian	10	0.01
Dutch West Indian	5	0.01
Haitian	214	0.27
Jamaican	438	0.56
Trinidadian and Tobagonian	17	0.02
U.S. Virgin Islander	8	0.01
West Indian	127	0.16
White:	58,683	74.80
Not Hispanic (54,555)	55,286	70.47
Hispanic (3,122)	3,397	4.33
Yugoslavian	57	0.07

Lakeside

Place Type: Census Designated Place
County: Clay
Population: 30,927

Ancestry/Race	Number	%
Acadian/Cajun	16	0.05
African American/Black:	2,389	7.72
Not Hispanic (2,149)	2,301	7.44
Hispanic (50)	88	0.28
African, sub-Saharan:	97	0.31
African	38	0.12
Ghanian	28	0.09
Liberian	6	0.02
South African	25	0.08
Am. Ind. or Alaska Nat., not spec.	91	0.29
American Indian tribes, specified:	219	0.71
Apache (2)	7	0.02
Blackfeet	5	0.02
Cherokee (34)	109	0.35
Cheyenne	1	0.00
Chickasaw (1)	2	0.01
Chippewa (4)	8	0.03
Choctaw (7)	12	0.04
Comanche	4	0.01
Cree	1	0.00
Creek (6)	8	0.03
Crow	1	0.00
Delaware	1	0.00
Houma (1)	1	0.00
Iroquois (3)	7	0.02
Kiowa (2)	2	0.01
Latin American Indians (2)	4	0.01
Lumbee (8)	10	0.03
Navajo (2)	8	0.03
Potawatomi	1	0.00
Seminole (4)	9	0.03
Shoshone (1)	1	0.00
Sioux (3)	3	0.01
All other tribes (3)	14	0.05
American Indian tribes, not spec.	11	0.04
Arab:	27	0.09
Palestinian	14	0.05
Syrian	13	0.04
Armenian	15	0.05
Asian:	1,144	3.70
Cambodian (16)	16	0.05
Chinese, ex. Taiwanese (68)	97	0.31
Filipino (501)	659	2.13
Indian (73)	92	0.30
Indonesian (1)	7	0.02
Japanese (36)	78	0.25
Korean (52)	57	0.18
Malaysian	2	0.01
Pakistani (9)	21	0.07
Sri Lankan (1)	1	0.00
Taiwanese (1)	2	0.01
Thai (16)	19	0.06
Vietnamese (53)	65	0.21
Other Asian, specified (1)	1	0.00
Other Asian, not specified (6)	27	0.09
Austrian	75	0.24
Belgian	58	0.19
Brazilian	9	0.03
British	184	0.60
Canadian	144	0.47
Celtic	10	0.03
Croatian	8	0.03
Czech	39	0.13
Danish	81	0.26
Dutch	560	1.82
English	3,362	10.90
European	238	0.77
Finnish	106	0.34
French, except Basque	1,122	3.64
French Canadian	269	0.87
German	4,529	14.68
Greek	133	0.43
Guyanese	8	0.03
Hawaii Native/Pacific Islander:	64	0.21
Micronesian: (10)	23	0.07
Guamanian/Chamorro (10)	23	0.07
Polynesian: (11)	26	0.08
Native Hawaiian (5)	18	0.06
Samoan (6)	8	0.03
Other Pac. Isl., not spec. (5)	15	0.05
Hispanic or Latino:	1,638	5.30
Central American:	103	0.33
Costa Rican	11	0.04
Guatemalan	15	0.05
Honduran	9	0.03
Nicaraguan	7	0.02
Panamanian	36	0.12
Salvadoran	19	0.06
Other Central American	6	0.02
Cuban	52	0.17
Dominican Republic	43	0.14
Mexican	321	1.04
Puerto Rican	627	2.03
South American:	141	0.46
Argentinean	7	0.02
Chilean	12	0.04
Colombian	61	0.20
Ecuadorian	28	0.09
Peruvian	14	0.05
Uruguayan	3	0.01
Venezuelan	15	0.05
Other South American	1	0.00
Other Hispanic or Latino	351	1.13
Hungarian	196	0.64
Iranian	11	0.04
Irish	3,828	12.41
Italian	1,810	5.87
Lithuanian	42	0.14
Macedonian	6	0.02
Northern European	7	0.02
Norwegian	304	0.99
Pennsylvania German	16	0.05
Polish	878	2.85
Portuguese	129	0.42
Romanian	9	0.03
Russian	109	0.35
Scandinavian	16	0.05
Scotch-Irish	783	2.54
Scottish	749	2.43
Slovak	17	0.06
Swedish	208	0.67
Swiss	44	0.14
Ukrainian	135	0.44
United States or American	3,658	11.86
Welsh	247	0.80
West Indian, excl. Hispanic:	227	0.74
Bahamian	6	0.02
Barbadian	5	0.02
Belizean	24	0.08
British West Indian	8	0.03
Haitian	124	0.40
Jamaican	35	0.11
Trinidadian and Tobagonian	18	0.06
West Indian	7	0.02
White:	27,132	87.73
Not Hispanic (25,536)	26,015	84.12
Hispanic (984)	1,117	3.61
Yugoslavian	25	0.08

Lakewood Park

Place Type: Census Designated Place
County: Saint Lucie
Population: 10,458

Ancestry/Race	Number	%
African American/Black:	595	5.69
Not Hispanic (542)	584	5.58
Hispanic (10)	11	0.11
Alaska Native tribes, specified:	3	0.03
Aleut (1)	1	0.01
All other tribes	2	0.02
Am. Ind. or Alaska Nat., not spec.	28	0.27
American Indian tribes, specified:	55	0.53
Apache	3	0.03
Blackfeet	1	0.01
Cherokee (13)	25	0.24
Chippewa (2)	3	0.03
Iroquois (1)	4	0.04
Latin American Indians (2)	4	0.04
Navajo (3)	7	0.07
All other tribes (5)	8	0.08
American Indian tribes, not spec.	1	0.01
Arab:	15	0.14
Lebanese	15	0.14
Armenian	9	0.09
Asian:	86	0.82
Chinese, ex. Taiwanese (7)	10	0.10
Filipino (8)	17	0.16
Indian (10)	17	0.16
Japanese (6)	6	0.06
Korean (11)	11	0.11
Pakistani (11)	11	0.11
Thai (1)	1	0.01
Vietnamese (9)	9	0.09
Other Asian, not specified (1)	4	0.04
Assyrian/Chaldean/Syriac	6	0.06
Australian	8	0.08
Austrian	57	0.55
Belgian	16	0.15
British	40	0.38
Canadian	48	0.46
Croatian	6	0.06
Czechoslovakian	13	0.12
Danish	62	0.60
Dutch	259	2.49
English	1,373	13.19
European	16	0.15
Finnish	34	0.33
French, except Basque	562	5.40
French Canadian	181	1.74
German	1,708	16.41
Greek	204	1.96
Hawaii Native/Pacific Islander:	14	0.13
Polynesian: (4)	6	0.06
Native Hawaiian (4)	6	0.06
Other Pac. Isl., not spec. (2)	8	0.08
Hispanic or Latino:	266	2.54
Central American:	7	0.07
Costa Rican	1	0.01
Guatemalan	1	0.01
Honduran	2	0.02
Panamanian	2	0.02
Other Central American	1	0.01
Cuban	24	0.23
Dominican Republic	2	0.02
Mexican	116	1.11

Notes: 1. Figures in the "Number" column do not add up to the total population due to: a) Ancestry/Race overlap — e.g. persons can report being both White and Irish, b) persons of Hispanic origin can report being any race, c) persons reporting two ancestries are counted in both categories. 2. Numbers in parentheses indicate the number of persons reporting this ancestry/race alone, not in combination with any other ancestry/race. 3. Refer to the Explanation of Data in the front of the book for more detailed information.

Puerto Rican	53	0.51
South American:	22	0.21
Bolivian	1	0.01
Chilean	2	0.02
Colombian	9	0.09
Peruvian	6	0.06
Venezuelan	4	0.04
Other Hispanic or Latino	42	0.40
Hungarian	130	1.25
Icelander	13	0.12
Iranian	10	0.10
Irish	1,760	16.91
Israeli	52	0.50
Italian	1,021	9.81
Lithuanian	47	0.45
Norwegian	34	0.33
Polish	248	2.38
Portuguese	106	1.02
Russian	61	0.59
Scandinavian	5	0.05
Scotch-Irish	296	2.84
Scottish	347	3.33
Slavic	8	0.08
Slovak	16	0.15
Slovene	6	0.06
Swedish	202	1.94
Swiss	32	0.31
Ukrainian	31	0.30
United States or American	1,132	10.88
Welsh	92	0.88
West Indian, excl. Hispanic:	76	0.73
Bahamian	8	0.08
Haitian	47	0.45
Jamaican	21	0.20
White:	9,709	92.84
Not Hispanic (9,428)	9,524	91.07
Hispanic (174)	185	1.77
Yugoslavian	39	0.37

Land O' Lakes

Place Type: Census Designated Place
County: Pasco
Population: 20,971

Ancestry/Race	Number	%
African American/Black:	524	2.50
Not Hispanic (408)	467	2.23
Hispanic (34)	57	0.27
Alaska Native tribes, specified:	1	0.00
Tlingit-Haida	1	0.00
Am. Ind. or Alaska Nat., not spec.	31	0.15
American Indian tribes, specified:	121	0.58
Apache (9)	9	0.04
Blackfeet (1)	7	0.03
Cherokee (15)	65	0.31
Chippewa (3)	5	0.02
Cree	2	0.01
Creek (4)	5	0.02
Iroquois (1)	6	0.03
Latin American Indians (1)	4	0.02
Menominee	2	0.01
Pueblo (2)	2	0.01
Seminole (1)	1	0.00
Sioux (1)	2	0.01
Ute (1)	1	0.00
All other tribes (5)	10	0.05
American Indian tribes, not spec.	6	0.03
Arab:	75	0.36
Lebanese	26	0.13
Moroccan	49	0.24
Armenian	19	0.09
Asian:	354	1.69
Chinese, ex. Taiwanese (46)	57	0.27
Filipino (82)	99	0.47
Indian (79)	86	0.41
Indonesian (6)	9	0.04
Japanese (8)	22	0.10
Korean (16)	25	0.12
Pakistani (5)	11	0.05
Taiwanese (2)	2	0.01
Thai (5)	5	0.02
Vietnamese (19)	19	0.09
Other Asian, not specified (10)	19	0.09
Australian	13	0.06
Austrian	91	0.44
Belgian	93	0.45
British	117	0.56
Bulgarian	10	0.05
Canadian	34	0.16
Croatian	54	0.26
Czech	139	0.67
Czechoslovakian	46	0.22
Danish	22	0.11
Dutch	453	2.18
Eastern European	8	0.04
English	2,862	13.76
Estonian	8	0.04
European	155	0.75
Finnish	32	0.15
French, except Basque	965	4.64
French Canadian	263	1.26
German	4,231	20.35
Greek	100	0.48
Hawaii Native/Pacific Islander:	13	0.06
Micronesian: (1)	2	0.01
Guamanian/Chamorro (1)	2	0.01
Polynesian:	6	0.03
Native Hawaiian	6	0.03
Other Pac. Isl., not spec.	5	0.02
Hispanic or Latino:	1,836	8.75
Central American:	65	0.31
Costa Rican	11	0.05
Guatemalan	5	0.02
Honduran	17	0.08
Nicaraguan	7	0.03
Panamanian	14	0.07
Salvadoran	10	0.05
Other Central American	1	0.00
Cuban	248	1.18
Dominican Republic	12	0.06
Mexican	134	0.64
Puerto Rican	863	4.12
South American:	84	0.40
Argentinean	1	0.00
Bolivian	2	0.01
Chilean	1	0.00
Colombian	42	0.20
Ecuadorian	15	0.07
Paraguayan	1	0.00
Peruvian	4	0.02
Uruguayan	1	0.00
Venezuelan	5	0.02
Other South American	12	0.06
Other Hispanic or Latino	430	2.05
Hungarian	164	0.79
Irish	3,064	14.74
Israeli	32	0.15
Italian	1,611	7.75
Lithuanian	40	0.19
Luxemburger	11	0.05
Maltese	6	0.03
Northern European	9	0.04
Norwegian	313	1.51
Pennsylvania German	24	0.12
Polish	741	3.56
Portuguese	69	0.33
Romanian	23	0.11
Russian	150	0.72
Scandinavian	9	0.04
Scotch-Irish	539	2.59
Scottish	544	2.62
Slovak	6	0.03
Slovene	9	0.04
Swedish	382	1.84
Swiss	69	0.33
Turkish	24	0.12
Ukrainian	67	0.32
United States or American	1,806	8.69
Welsh	281	1.35
West Indian, excl. Hispanic:	99	0.48
Jamaican	41	0.20
Trinidadian and Tobagonian	41	0.20
West Indian	17	0.08
White:	19,881	94.80
Not Hispanic (18,147)	18,334	87.43
Hispanic (1,483)	1,547	7.38
Yugoslavian	25	0.12

Largo

Place Type: City
County: Pinellas
Population: 69,371

Ancestry/Race	Number	%
Acadian/Cajun	17	0.02
African American/Black:	2,144	3.09
Not Hispanic (1,806)	2,042	2.94
Hispanic (63)	102	0.15
African, sub-Saharan:	182	0.26
African	137	0.20
Cape Verdean	41	0.06
Other sub-Saharan African	4	0.01
Alaska Native tribes, specified:	11	0.02
Alaska Athabascan (1)	2	0.00
Eskimo (6)	6	0.01
Tlingit-Haida (1)	2	0.00
All other tribes (1)	1	0.00
Alaska Native tribes, not specified	2	0.00
Am. Ind. or Alaska Nat., not spec.	182	0.26
Albanian	312	0.45
Alsatian	9	0.01
American Indian tribes, specified:	297	0.43
Apache (2)	5	0.01
Blackfeet (8)	19	0.03
Cherokee (49)	126	0.18
Cheyenne	1	0.00
Chippewa (16)	24	0.03
Choctaw (5)	8	0.01
Cree (1)	1	0.00
Creek (3)	8	0.01
Delaware (2)	2	0.00
Iroquois (18)	31	0.04
Latin American Indians (11)	15	0.02
Lumbee (5)	5	0.01
Navajo (2)	2	0.00
Potawatomi (1)	1	0.00
Pueblo (2)	2	0.00
Seminole (2)	8	0.01
Sioux (3)	7	0.01
Ute	1	0.00
All other tribes (18)	31	0.04
American Indian tribes, not spec.	35	0.05
Arab:	262	0.38
Arab/Arabic	49	0.07
Egyptian	29	0.04
Jordanian	10	0.01
Lebanese	88	0.13
Moroccan	37	0.05
Palestinian	24	0.03
Syrian	18	0.03
Other Arab	7	0.01
Armenian	84	0.12
Asian:	1,427	2.06
Bangladeshi (10)	29	0.04
Cambodian (10)	11	0.02
Chinese, ex. Taiwanese (98)	126	0.18
Filipino (286)	346	0.50
Hmong	1	0.00
Indian (341)	403	0.58
Indonesian (2)	4	0.01
Japanese (40)	69	0.10
Korean (53)	67	0.10
Laotian (28)	33	0.05
Malaysian	1	0.00
Pakistani (10)	11	0.02
Sri Lankan (3)	3	0.00
Taiwanese (11)	15	0.02
Thai (32)	49	0.07

Notes: 1. Figures in the "Number" column do not add up to the total population due to: a) Ancestry/Race overlap — e.g. persons can report being both White and Irish, b) persons of Hispanic origin can report being any race, c) persons reporting two ancestries are counted in both categories. 2. Numbers in parentheses indicate the number of persons reporting this ancestry/race alone, not in combination with any other ancestry/race. 3. Refer to the Explanation of Data in the front of the book for more detailed information.

Ancestry/Race	Number	%
Vietnamese (197)	213	0.31
Other Asian, specified (2)	2	0.00
Other Asian, not specified (26)	44	0.06
Australian	16	0.02
Austrian	191	0.27
Belgian	65	0.09
Brazilian	66	0.10
British	466	0.67
Canadian	699	1.01
Croatian	178	0.26
Czech	268	0.39
Czechoslovakian	195	0.28
Danish	379	0.55
Dutch	1,412	2.03
Eastern European	15	0.02
English	9,669	13.92
European	278	0.40
Finnish	195	0.28
French, except Basque	3,167	4.56
French Canadian	1,079	1.55
German	12,735	18.33
Greek	731	1.05
Guyanese	37	0.05
Hawaii Native/Pacific Islander:	113	0.16
Micronesian: (20)	28	0.04
Guamanian/Chamorro (6)	10	0.01
Other Micronesian (14)	18	0.03
Polynesian: (23)	64	0.09
Native Hawaiian (5)	15	0.02
Samoan (2)	13	0.02
Tongan (14)	24	0.03
Other Polynesian (2)	12	0.02
Other Pac. Isl., not spec. (10)	21	0.03
Hispanic or Latino:	2,902	4.18
Central American:	104	0.15
Costa Rican	21	0.03
Guatemalan	12	0.02
Honduran	19	0.03
Nicaraguan	6	0.01
Panamanian	20	0.03
Salvadoran	22	0.03
Other Central American	4	0.01
Cuban	190	0.27
Dominican Republic	50	0.07
Mexican	910	1.31
Puerto Rican	800	1.15
South American:	326	0.47
Argentinean	17	0.02
Bolivian	7	0.01
Chilean	7	0.01
Colombian	139	0.20
Ecuadorian	68	0.10
Peruvian	37	0.05
Uruguayan	4	0.01
Venezuelan	34	0.05
Other South American	13	0.02
Other Hispanic or Latino	522	0.75
Hungarian	597	0.86
Iranian	79	0.11
Irish	10,696	15.40
Israeli	25	0.04
Italian	6,661	9.59
Latvian	28	0.04
Lithuanian	269	0.39
Luxemburger	16	0.02
Macedonian	9	0.01
Maltese	17	0.02
Northern European	30	0.04
Norwegian	1,128	1.62
Pennsylvania German	45	0.06
Polish	2,980	4.29
Portuguese	393	0.57
Romanian	103	0.15
Russian	578	0.83
Scandinavian	105	0.15
Scotch-Irish	1,632	2.35
Scottish	2,040	2.94
Serbian	26	0.04
Slavic	34	0.05
Slovak	200	0.29
Slovene	52	0.07
Swedish	905	1.30
Swiss	180	0.26
Turkish	68	0.10
Ukrainian	340	0.49
United States or American	5,100	7.34
Welsh	596	0.86
West Indian, excl. Hispanic:	158	0.23
Bermudan	13	0.02
Haitian	31	0.04
Jamaican	69	0.10
Trinidadian and Tobagonian	16	0.02
U.S. Virgin Islander	4	0.01
West Indian	25	0.04
White:	65,198	93.98
Not Hispanic (62,359)	63,050	90.89
Hispanic (1,955)	2,148	3.10
Yugoslavian	106	0.15

Lauderdale Lakes

Place Type: City
County: Broward
Population: 31,705

Ancestry/Race	Number	%
African American/Black:	22,834	72.02
Not Hispanic (21,243)	22,531	71.06
Hispanic (233)	303	0.96
African, sub-Saharan:	390	1.24
African	382	1.21
Ghanian	8	0.03
Alaska Native tribes, specified:	6	0.02
Alaska Athabascan	3	0.01
Tlingit-Haida (1)	3	0.01
Am. Ind. or Alaska Nat., not spec.	69	0.22
Alsatian	14	0.04
American Indian tribes, specified:	55	0.17
Blackfeet (1)	2	0.01
Cherokee	9	0.03
Iroquois (3)	7	0.02
Latin American Indians (2)	21	0.07
Lumbee (2)	2	0.01
Osage (4)	4	0.01
Pueblo	1	0.00
Sioux (1)	1	0.00
Yakama	4	0.01
All other tribes	4	0.01
American Indian tribes, not spec.	5	0.02
Arab:	49	0.16
Egyptian	40	0.13
Jordanian	9	0.03
Asian:	473	1.49
Bangladeshi (3)	5	0.02
Cambodian (1)	2	0.01
Chinese, ex. Taiwanese (75)	102	0.32
Filipino (15)	19	0.06
Hmong	1	0.00
Indian (154)	216	0.68
Indonesian (2)	3	0.01
Japanese (8)	8	0.03
Korean (11)	15	0.05
Laotian	1	0.00
Pakistani (9)	11	0.03
Taiwanese	1	0.00
Thai (5)	7	0.02
Vietnamese (33)	33	0.10
Other Asian, specified	5	0.02
Other Asian, not specified (8)	44	0.14
Austrian	71	0.23
Brazilian	109	0.35
British	85	0.27
Bulgarian	7	0.02
Canadian	132	0.42
Croatian	32	0.10
Czechoslovakian	14	0.04
Danish	24	0.08
Dutch	56	0.18
English	372	1.18
European	143	0.45
Finnish	9	0.03
French, except Basque	172	0.55
French Canadian	473	1.50
German	701	2.22
Greek	61	0.19
Guyanese	163	0.52
Hawaii Native/Pacific Islander:	100	0.32
Micronesian: (1)	1	0.00
Guamanian/Chamorro (1)	1	0.00
Polynesian: (4)	10	0.03
Native Hawaiian (3)	6	0.02
Samoan (1)	4	0.01
Other Pac. Isl., specified	5	0.02
Other Pac. Isl., not spec. (14)	84	0.26
Hispanic or Latino:	1,755	5.54
Central American:	154	0.49
Costa Rican	8	0.03
Guatemalan	12	0.04
Honduran	49	0.15
Nicaraguan	12	0.04
Panamanian	32	0.10
Salvadoran	36	0.11
Other Central American	5	0.02
Cuban	155	0.49
Dominican Republic	84	0.26
Mexican	212	0.67
Puerto Rican	484	1.53
South American:	255	0.80
Argentinean	4	0.01
Bolivian	3	0.01
Chilean	14	0.04
Colombian	134	0.42
Ecuadorian	18	0.06
Peruvian	41	0.13
Uruguayan	3	0.01
Venezuelan	30	0.09
Other South American	8	0.03
Other Hispanic or Latino	411	1.30
Hungarian	77	0.24
Iranian	8	0.03
Irish	536	1.70
Italian	781	2.48
Latvian	10	0.03
Lithuanian	22	0.07
Norwegian	32	0.10
Polish	358	1.14
Portuguese	25	0.08
Romanian	38	0.12
Russian	323	1.02
Scotch-Irish	53	0.17
Scottish	142	0.45
Serbian	25	0.08
Slovak	8	0.03
Slovene	9	0.03
Swedish	41	0.13
Swiss	10	0.03
Turkish	41	0.13
Ukrainian	78	0.25
United States or American	1,801	5.71
Welsh	7	0.02
West Indian, excl. Hispanic:	11,455	36.35
Bahamian	291	0.92
Barbadian	22	0.07
British West Indian	238	0.76
Haitian	4,732	15.01
Jamaican	5,646	17.91
Trinidadian and Tobagonian	217	0.69
U.S. Virgin Islander	159	0.50
West Indian	141	0.45
Other West Indian	9	0.03
White:	7,956	25.09
Not Hispanic (6,726)	6,994	22.06
Hispanic (870)	962	3.03

Notes: 1. Figures in the "Number" column do not add up to the total population due to: a) Ancestry/Race overlap — e.g. persons can report being both White and Irish, b) persons of Hispanic origin can report being any race, c) persons reporting two ancestries are counted in both categories. 2. Numbers in parentheses indicate the number of persons reporting this ancestry/race alone, not in combination with any other ancestry/race. 3. Refer to the Explanation of Data in the front of the book for more detailed information.

Lauderhill

Place Type: City
County: Broward
Population: 57,585

Ancestry/Race	Number	%
African American/Black:	35,657	61.92
Not Hispanic (33,355)	35,041	60.85
Hispanic (485)	616	1.07
African, sub-Saharan:	668	1.17
African	638	1.11
Ethiopian	10	0.02
Ghanian	7	0.01
Nigerian	5	0.01
South African	8	0.01
Alaska Native tribes, specified:	6	0.01
Tlingit-Haida	6	0.01
Am. Ind. or Alaska Nat., not spec.	121	0.21
American Indian tribes, specified:	83	0.14
Apache (1)	1	0.00
Blackfeet (1)	2	0.00
Cherokee (2)	27	0.05
Chippewa (1)	5	0.01
Comanche (1)	1	0.00
Cree (1)	1	0.00
Creek (1)	1	0.00
Delaware (1)	1	0.00
Iroquois (2)	6	0.01
Latin American Indians (5)	16	0.03
Navajo	1	0.00
Seminole (1)	2	0.00
Shoshone	1	0.00
Sioux (5)	8	0.01
All other tribes (3)	10	0.02
American Indian tribes, not spec.	8	0.01
Arab:	280	0.49
Arab/Arabic	44	0.08
Lebanese	62	0.11
Moroccan	84	0.15
Palestinian	58	0.10
Syrian	21	0.04
Other Arab	11	0.02
Armenian	12	0.02
Asian:	1,254	2.18
Bangladeshi (4)	4	0.01
Chinese, ex. Taiwanese (224)	313	0.54
Filipino (106)	126	0.22
Indian (365)	493	0.86
Indonesian (1)	1	0.00
Japanese (21)	29	0.05
Korean (66)	72	0.13
Malaysian (1)	1	0.00
Pakistani (21)	27	0.05
Taiwanese (1)	3	0.01
Thai (8)	10	0.02
Vietnamese (60)	70	0.12
Other Asian, specified (1)	15	0.03
Other Asian, not specified (18)	90	0.16
Austrian	241	0.42
Belgian	4	0.01
Brazilian	143	0.25
British	195	0.34
Bulgarian	12	0.02
Canadian	251	0.44
Czech	45	0.08
Czechoslovakian	52	0.09
Danish	42	0.07
Dutch	160	0.28
Eastern European	116	0.20
English	1,104	1.93
European	116	0.20
Finnish	16	0.03
French, except Basque	372	0.65
French Canadian	444	0.78
German	1,947	3.40
German Russian	7	0.01
Greek	123	0.21
Guyanese	217	0.38
Hawaii Native/Pacific Islander:	189	0.33
Micronesian: (2)	4	0.01
Guamanian/Chamorro (2)	4	0.01
Polynesian: (11)	19	0.03
Native Hawaiian (5)	12	0.02
Samoan (6)	7	0.01
Other Pac. Isl., specified	14	0.02
Other Pac. Isl., not spec. (22)	152	0.26
Hispanic or Latino:	3,995	6.94
Central American:	284	0.49
Costa Rican	35	0.06
Guatemalan	29	0.05
Honduran	86	0.15
Nicaraguan	13	0.02
Panamanian	76	0.13
Salvadoran	33	0.06
Other Central American	12	0.02
Cuban	436	0.76
Dominican Republic	144	0.25
Mexican	199	0.35
Puerto Rican	1,028	1.79
South American:	1,006	1.75
Argentinean	73	0.13
Bolivian	13	0.02
Chilean	26	0.05
Colombian	497	0.86
Ecuadorian	85	0.15
Peruvian	140	0.24
Uruguayan	26	0.05
Venezuelan	111	0.19
Other South American	35	0.06
Other Hispanic or Latino	898	1.56
Hungarian	277	0.48
Iranian	64	0.11
Irish	1,544	2.70
Israeli	141	0.25
Italian	2,157	3.77
Latvian	16	0.03
Lithuanian	145	0.25
Norwegian	78	0.14
Pennsylvania German	11	0.02
Polish	1,257	2.20
Portuguese	85	0.15
Romanian	205	0.36
Russian	1,379	2.41
Scotch-Irish	222	0.39
Scottish	415	0.72
Slovak	43	0.08
Swedish	101	0.18
Swiss	44	0.08
Turkish	8	0.01
Ukrainian	77	0.13
United States or American	4,316	7.54
Welsh	195	0.34
West Indian, excl. Hispanic:	16,626	29.04
Bahamian	473	0.83
Barbadian	168	0.29
Belizean	33	0.06
British West Indian	254	0.44
Haitian	5,034	8.79
Jamaican	9,723	16.98
Trinidadian and Tobagonian	480	0.84
U.S. Virgin Islander	82	0.14
West Indian	365	0.64
Other West Indian	14	0.02
White:	20,153	35.00
Not Hispanic (17,014)	17,476	30.35
Hispanic (2,468)	2,677	4.65
Yugoslavian	25	0.04

Leesburg

Place Type: City
County: Lake
Population: 15,956

Ancestry/Race	Number	%
African American/Black:	4,728	29.63
Not Hispanic (4,609)	4,689	29.39
Hispanic (37)	39	0.24
African, sub-Saharan:	417	2.63
African	417	2.63
Am. Ind. or Alaska Nat., not spec.	48	0.30
American Indian tribes, specified:	77	0.48
Apache	3	0.02
Blackfeet (1)	5	0.03
Cherokee (12)	39	0.24
Chippewa (1)	2	0.01
Choctaw	2	0.01
Creek	5	0.03
Iroquois (1)	5	0.03
Latin American Indians	6	0.04
Potawatomi (1)	1	0.01
Seminole (1)	5	0.03
Sioux (3)	3	0.02
All other tribes	1	0.01
American Indian tribes, not spec.	2	0.01
Arab:	17	0.11
Egyptian	6	0.04
Lebanese	11	0.07
Asian:	245	1.54
Chinese, ex. Taiwanese (26)	32	0.20
Filipino (46)	50	0.31
Indian (76)	80	0.50
Indonesian	1	0.01
Japanese (3)	4	0.03
Korean (16)	17	0.11
Laotian (5)	5	0.03
Malaysian	1	0.01
Pakistani (2)	7	0.04
Taiwanese (2)	2	0.01
Thai (6)	6	0.04
Vietnamese (27)	27	0.17
Other Asian, specified	3	0.02
Other Asian, not specified (3)	10	0.06
Austrian	28	0.18
Basque	4	0.03
British	47	0.30
Canadian	66	0.42
Celtic	31	0.20
Croatian	17	0.11
Czech	31	0.20
Czechoslovakian	27	0.17
Danish	77	0.48
Dutch	194	1.22
English	1,878	11.82
European	81	0.51
Finnish	31	0.20
French, except Basque	561	3.53
French Canadian	133	0.84
German	1,872	11.79
German Russian	9	0.06
Greek	70	0.44
Guyanese	9	0.06
Hawaii Native/Pacific Islander:	10	0.06
Micronesian:	1	0.01
Guamanian/Chamorro	1	0.01
Polynesian: (1)	1	0.01
Native Hawaiian (1)	1	0.01
Other Pac. Isl., specified	3	0.02
Other Pac. Isl., not spec.	5	0.03
Hispanic or Latino:	657	4.12
Central American:	52	0.33
Costa Rican	1	0.01
Guatemalan	20	0.13
Honduran	7	0.04
Panamanian	13	0.08
Salvadoran	10	0.06
Other Central American	1	0.01
Cuban	47	0.29
Dominican Republic	3	0.02
Mexican	280	1.75
Puerto Rican	151	0.95
South American:	25	0.16
Argentinean	1	0.01
Colombian	15	0.09
Ecuadorian	1	0.01
Peruvian	4	0.03
Venezuelan	4	0.03
Other Hispanic or Latino	99	0.62
Hungarian	49	0.31

Notes: 1. Figures in the "Number" column do not add up to the total population due to: a) Ancestry/Race overlap — e.g. persons can report being both White and Irish, b) persons of Hispanic origin can report being any race, c) persons reporting two ancestries are counted in both categories. 2. Numbers in parentheses indicate the number of persons reporting this ancestry/race alone, not in combination with any other ancestry/race. 3. Refer to the Explanation of Data in the front of the book for more detailed information.

Ancestry/Race	Number	%
Irish	1,189	7.49
Italian	358	2.25
Latvian	10	0.06
Lithuanian	20	0.13
Norwegian	130	0.82
Pennsylvania German	10	0.06
Polish	216	1.36
Portuguese	46	0.29
Romanian	8	0.05
Russian	37	0.23
Scandinavian	35	0.22
Scotch-Irish	196	1.23
Scottish	309	1.95
Slovak	48	0.30
Swedish	108	0.68
Swiss	5	0.03
Ukrainian	8	0.05
United States or American	1,313	8.27
Welsh	73	0.46
West Indian, excl. Hispanic:	152	0.96
Bahamian	11	0.07
Haitian	24	0.15
Jamaican	117	0.74
White:	10,809	67.74
Not Hispanic (10,265)	10,408	65.23
Hispanic (362)	401	2.51
Yugoslavian	34	0.21

Lehigh Acres

Place Type: Census Designated Place
County: Lee
Population: 33,430

Ancestry/Race	Number	%
African American/Black:	3,192	9.55
Not Hispanic (2,835)	3,044	9.11
Hispanic (103)	148	0.44
African, sub-Saharan:	110	0.33
African	110	0.33
Alaska Native tribes, specified:	2	0.01
Eskimo	2	0.01
Am. Ind. or Alaska Nat., not spec.	84	0.25
American Indian tribes, specified:	114	0.34
Apache	5	0.01
Blackfeet (1)	3	0.01
Cherokee (13)	39	0.12
Chippewa (1)	5	0.01
Choctaw (1)	1	0.00
Comanche	2	0.01
Cree (1)	2	0.01
Creek (1)	2	0.01
Delaware (1)	1	0.00
Iroquois (18)	20	0.06
Latin American Indians (7)	14	0.04
Lumbee (1)	1	0.00
Navajo (2)	2	0.01
Ottawa (1)	2	0.01
Potawatomi	3	0.01
Seminole	1	0.00
Shoshone (1)	1	0.00
Sioux (1)	4	0.01
All other tribes (5)	6	0.02
American Indian tribes, not spec.	20	0.06
Arab:	64	0.19
Arab/Arabic	13	0.04
Egyptian	15	0.05
Lebanese	31	0.09
Syrian	5	0.02
Armenian	17	0.05
Asian:	402	1.20
Cambodian (2)	3	0.01
Chinese, ex. Taiwanese (64)	80	0.24
Filipino (59)	91	0.27
Indian (58)	84	0.25
Indonesian (2)	9	0.03
Japanese (12)	22	0.07
Korean (25)	38	0.11
Laotian (21)	21	0.06
Thai (3)	6	0.02
Vietnamese (21)	27	0.08
Other Asian, not specified (10)	21	0.06
Austrian	74	0.22
Belgian	61	0.18
British	120	0.36
Canadian	169	0.51
Croatian	21	0.06
Czech	85	0.26
Czechoslovakian	81	0.24
Danish	120	0.36
Dutch	410	1.24
English	3,514	10.60
European	50	0.15
Finnish	40	0.12
French, except Basque	932	2.81
French Canadian	393	1.19
German	4,991	15.06
Greek	112	0.34
Guyanese	50	0.15
Hawaii Native/Pacific Islander:	54	0.16
Melanesian: (1)	1	0.00
Fijian (1)	1	0.00
Micronesian: (1)	6	0.02
Guamanian/Chamorro (1)	6	0.02
Polynesian: (1)	16	0.05
Native Hawaiian	11	0.03
Samoan (1)	5	0.01
Other Pac. Isl., not spec. (3)	31	0.09
Hispanic or Latino:	4,466	13.36
Central American:	135	0.40
Costa Rican	22	0.07
Guatemalan	35	0.10
Honduran	22	0.07
Nicaraguan	12	0.04
Panamanian	26	0.08
Salvadoran	15	0.04
Other Central American	3	0.01
Cuban	239	0.71
Dominican Republic	38	0.11
Mexican	1,169	3.50
Puerto Rican	2,098	6.28
South American:	164	0.49
Argentinean	4	0.01
Chilean	8	0.02
Colombian	82	0.25
Ecuadorian	14	0.04
Paraguayan	10	0.03
Peruvian	23	0.07
Venezuelan	16	0.05
Other South American	7	0.02
Other Hispanic or Latino	623	1.86
Hungarian	207	0.62
Irish	4,115	12.42
Israeli	9	0.03
Italian	2,627	7.93
Lithuanian	24	0.07
Macedonian	4	0.01
Northern European	13	0.04
Norwegian	368	1.11
Pennsylvania German	44	0.13
Polish	976	2.94
Portuguese	159	0.48
Romanian	24	0.07
Russian	149	0.45
Scandinavian	18	0.05
Scotch-Irish	524	1.58
Scottish	747	2.25
Serbian	6	0.02
Slovak	116	0.35
Slovene	20	0.06
Swedish	304	0.92
Swiss	99	0.30
Turkish	33	0.10
Ukrainian	42	0.13
United States or American	3,935	11.87
Welsh	185	0.56
West Indian, excl. Hispanic:	962	2.90
Bahamian	20	0.06
Barbadian	6	0.02
British West Indian	61	0.18
Dutch West Indian	7	0.02
Haitian	285	0.86
Jamaican	545	1.64
Trinidadian and Tobagonian	10	0.03
West Indian	28	0.08
White:	28,699	85.85
Not Hispanic (25,287)	25,600	76.58
Hispanic (2,896)	3,099	9.27
Yugoslavian	18	0.05

Leisure City

Place Type: Census Designated Place
County: Miami-Dade
Population: 22,152

Ancestry/Race	Number	%
African American/Black:	4,278	19.31
Not Hispanic (3,769)	3,975	17.94
Hispanic (218)	303	1.37
African, sub-Saharan:	171	0.79
African	159	0.73
Cape Verdean	12	0.06
Am. Ind. or Alaska Nat., not spec.	45	0.20
American Indian tribes, specified:	59	0.27
Blackfeet	1	0.00
Cherokee (4)	21	0.09
Choctaw	1	0.00
Cree (1)	1	0.00
Iroquois	5	0.02
Latin American Indians (8)	21	0.09
Lumbee (1)	1	0.00
Seminole (2)	2	0.01
All other tribes (2)	6	0.03
American Indian tribes, not spec.	7	0.03
Arab:	13	0.06
Arab/Arabic	13	0.06
Asian:	276	1.25
Bangladeshi	3	0.01
Chinese, ex. Taiwanese (13)	21	0.09
Filipino (18)	37	0.17
Indian (32)	42	0.19
Japanese (11)	15	0.07
Korean (17)	30	0.14
Laotian (25)	25	0.11
Malaysian (1)	1	0.00
Pakistani (8)	8	0.04
Sri Lankan (1)	1	0.00
Taiwanese	7	0.03
Thai (29)	39	0.18
Vietnamese (16)	22	0.10
Other Asian, not specified (10)	25	0.11
Brazilian	10	0.05
British	26	0.12
Czechoslovakian	17	0.08
Dutch	96	0.44
English	261	1.20
European	22	0.10
Finnish	6	0.03
French, except Basque	166	0.76
French Canadian	40	0.18
German	629	2.89
Greek	12	0.06
Hawaii Native/Pacific Islander:	26	0.12
Micronesian: (1)	1	0.00
Guamanian/Chamorro (1)	1	0.00
Polynesian: (3)	6	0.03
Native Hawaiian (1)	3	0.01
Samoan (2)	3	0.01
Other Pac. Isl., not spec. (3)	19	0.09
Hispanic or Latino:	14,465	65.30
Central American:	1,154	5.21
Costa Rican	52	0.23
Guatemalan	236	1.07
Honduran	213	0.96
Nicaraguan	304	1.37
Panamanian	34	0.15
Salvadoran	286	1.29
Other Central American	29	0.13
Cuban	3,799	17.15

Notes: 1. Figures in the "Number" column do not add up to the total population due to: a) Ancestry/Race overlap — e.g. persons can report being both White and Irish, b) persons of Hispanic origin can report being any race, c) persons reporting two ancestries are counted in both categories. 2. Numbers in parentheses indicate the number of persons reporting this ancestry/race alone, not in combination with any other ancestry/race. 3. Refer to the Explanation of Data in the front of the book for more detailed information.

Ancestry/Race	Number	%
Dominican Republic	221	1.00
Mexican	5,259	23.74
Puerto Rican	1,960	8.85
South American:	464	2.09
Argentinean	11	0.05
Bolivian	23	0.10
Chilean	28	0.13
Colombian	224	1.01
Ecuadorian	55	0.25
Peruvian	65	0.29
Uruguayan	8	0.04
Venezuelan	40	0.18
Other South American	10	0.05
Other Hispanic or Latino	1,608	7.26
Hungarian	22	0.10
Irish	648	2.98
Italian	234	1.07
Norwegian	32	0.15
Polish	60	0.28
Portuguese	83	0.38
Russian	26	0.12
Scandinavian	7	0.03
Scotch-Irish	58	0.27
Scottish	89	0.41
Serbian	7	0.03
Slovak	6	0.03
Swedish	49	0.23
Swiss	5	0.02
United States or American	1,119	5.14
Welsh	13	0.06
West Indian, excl. Hispanic:	1,067	4.90
Bahamian	32	0.15
British West Indian	18	0.08
Dutch West Indian	9	0.04
Haitian	765	3.51
Jamaican	170	0.78
Trinidadian and Tobagonian	73	0.34
White:	15,146	68.37
Not Hispanic (3,356)	3,498	15.79
Hispanic (11,050)	11,648	52.58
Yugoslavian	23	0.11

Lighthouse Point

Place Type: City
County: Broward
Population: 10,767

Ancestry/Race	Number	%
African American/Black:	61	0.57
Not Hispanic (46)	61	0.57
Am. Ind. or Alaska Nat., not spec.	10	0.09
Alsatian	9	0.08
American Indian tribes, specified:	30	0.28
Blackfeet (1)	2	0.02
Cherokee (3)	11	0.10
Comanche	1	0.01
Cree (1)	1	0.01
Iroquois (2)	2	0.02
Potawatomi	1	0.01
Seminole	1	0.01
Sioux	5	0.05
Ute	1	0.01
All other tribes (2)	5	0.05
American Indian tribes, not spec.	6	0.06
Arab:	78	0.73
Egyptian	15	0.14
Iraqi	9	0.08
Jordanian	9	0.08
Lebanese	31	0.29
Syrian	14	0.13
Armenian	26	0.24
Asian:	116	1.08
Chinese, ex. Taiwanese (29)	33	0.31
Filipino (5)	17	0.16
Indian (9)	11	0.10
Japanese (2)	2	0.02
Korean (18)	21	0.20
Taiwanese (3)	3	0.03
Thai (8)	8	0.07
Vietnamese (9)	11	0.10
Other Asian, specified	1	0.01
Other Asian, not specified (2)	9	0.08
Austrian	87	0.82
Belgian	9	0.08
Brazilian	38	0.36
British	173	1.62
Bulgarian	9	0.08
Canadian	75	0.70
Croatian	14	0.13
Czech	23	0.22
Czechoslovakian	71	0.67
Danish	36	0.34
Dutch	154	1.44
Eastern European	18	0.17
English	1,600	15.00
European	88	0.82
Finnish	61	0.57
French, except Basque	429	4.02
French Canadian	152	1.42
German	1,771	16.60
Greek	115	1.08
Hawaii Native/Pacific Islander:	6	0.06
Micronesian:	3	0.03
Guamanian/Chamorro	3	0.03
Polynesian: (1)	3	0.03
Native Hawaiian (1)	2	0.02
Other Polynesian	1	0.01
Hispanic or Latino:	450	4.18
Central American:	24	0.22
Costa Rican	6	0.06
Guatemalan	2	0.02
Honduran	6	0.06
Nicaraguan	5	0.05
Panamanian	1	0.01
Salvadoran	1	0.01
Other Central American	3	0.03
Cuban	100	0.93
Dominican Republic	2	0.02
Mexican	34	0.32
Puerto Rican	87	0.81
South American:	103	0.96
Argentinean	18	0.17
Chilean	2	0.02
Colombian	45	0.42
Ecuadorian	7	0.07
Paraguayan	1	0.01
Peruvian	16	0.15
Uruguayan	1	0.01
Venezuelan	3	0.03
Other South American	10	0.09
Other Hispanic or Latino	100	0.93
Hungarian	148	1.39
Icelander	13	0.12
Irish	2,023	18.96
Israeli	45	0.42
Italian	1,891	17.73
Latvian	6	0.06
Lithuanian	73	0.68
Macedonian	9	0.08
Maltese	17	0.16
Norwegian	158	1.48
Polish	573	5.37
Portuguese	49	0.46
Romanian	31	0.29
Russian	228	2.14
Scandinavian	9	0.08
Scotch-Irish	258	2.42
Scottish	396	3.71
Slavic	13	0.12
Slovak	29	0.27
Slovene	23	0.22
Swedish	242	2.27
Swiss	45	0.42
Turkish	29	0.27
Ukrainian	39	0.37
United States or American	697	6.53
Welsh	104	0.97
West Indian, excl. Hispanic:	38	0.36
Bahamian	11	0.10
Jamaican	27	0.25
White:	10,562	98.10
Not Hispanic (10,071)	10,149	94.26
Hispanic (378)	413	3.84
Yugoslavian	17	0.16

Lockhart

Place Type: Census Designated Place
County: Orange
Population: 12,944

Ancestry/Race	Number	%
African American/Black:	2,230	17.23
Not Hispanic (2,010)	2,102	16.24
Hispanic (71)	128	0.99
African, sub-Saharan:	119	0.95
African	73	0.58
Nigerian	16	0.13
Other sub-Saharan African	30	0.24
Am. Ind. or Alaska Nat., not spec.	51	0.39
American Indian tribes, specified:	88	0.68
Blackfeet	1	0.01
Cherokee (13)	41	0.32
Chippewa (2)	4	0.03
Choctaw (2)	6	0.05
Cree (1)	1	0.01
Creek (5)	6	0.05
Iroquois (8)	9	0.07
Latin American Indians (6)	10	0.08
Navajo (6)	6	0.05
Yuman	1	0.01
All other tribes (2)	3	0.02
American Indian tribes, not spec.	16	0.12
Arab:	33	0.26
Lebanese	25	0.20
Syrian	8	0.06
Asian:	354	2.73
Chinese, ex. Taiwanese (23)	30	0.23
Filipino (91)	119	0.92
Indian (38)	43	0.33
Indonesian (6)	6	0.05
Japanese (11)	19	0.15
Korean (2)	8	0.06
Laotian	4	0.03
Sri Lankan (1)	1	0.01
Thai (3)	7	0.05
Vietnamese (107)	112	0.87
Other Asian, not specified (2)	5	0.04
Austrian	27	0.22
British	62	0.49
Celtic	21	0.17
Croatian	9	0.07
Czechoslovakian	51	0.41
Danish	24	0.19
Dutch	179	1.43
English	922	7.36
European	68	0.54
French, except Basque	389	3.10
French Canadian	132	1.05
German	1,600	12.77
Greek	17	0.14
Guyanese	51	0.41
Hawaii Native/Pacific Islander:	25	0.19
Micronesian: (1)	3	0.02
Other Micronesian (1)	3	0.02
Polynesian: (2)	6	0.05
Native Hawaiian (1)	5	0.04
Samoan (1)	1	0.01
Other Pac. Isl., not spec. (2)	16	0.12
Hispanic or Latino:	2,083	16.09
Central American:	60	0.46
Costa Rican	9	0.07
Guatemalan	3	0.02
Honduran	24	0.19
Nicaraguan	4	0.03
Panamanian	8	0.06
Salvadoran	4	0.03
Other Central American	8	0.06
Cuban	163	1.26

Notes: 1. Figures in the "Number" column do not add up to the total population due to: a) Ancestry/Race overlap — e.g. persons can report being both White and Irish, b) persons of Hispanic origin can report being any race, c) persons reporting two ancestries are counted in both categories. 2. Numbers in parentheses indicate the number of persons reporting this ancestry/race alone, not in combination with any other ancestry/race. 3. Refer to the Explanation of Data in the front of the book for more detailed information.

Dominican Republic	76	0.59
Mexican	256	1.98
Puerto Rican	1,123	8.68
South American:	135	1.04
Argentinean	3	0.02
Chilean	10	0.08
Colombian	53	0.41
Ecuadorian	19	0.15
Paraguayan	1	0.01
Peruvian	16	0.12
Uruguayan	1	0.01
Venezuelan	18	0.14
Other South American	14	0.11
Other Hispanic or Latino	270	2.09
Hungarian	68	0.54
Irish	1,320	10.53
Italian	540	4.31
Latvian	9	0.07
Lithuanian	12	0.10
Norwegian	84	0.67
Polish	247	1.97
Portuguese	42	0.34
Romanian	9	0.07
Russian	63	0.50
Scandinavian	9	0.07
Scotch-Irish	149	1.19
Scottish	289	2.31
Slovak	43	0.34
Swedish	83	0.66
Swiss	18	0.14
United States or American	1,317	10.51
Welsh	50	0.40
West Indian, excl. Hispanic:	394	3.14
British West Indian	9	0.07
Haitian	108	0.86
Jamaican	209	1.67
Trinidadian and Tobagonian	57	0.45
West Indian	11	0.09
White:	9,871	76.26
Not Hispanic (8,244)	8,432	65.14
Hispanic (1,308)	1,439	11.12
Yugoslavian	50	0.40

Longwood

Place Type: City
County: Seminole
Population: 13,745

Ancestry/Race	Number	%
African American/Black:	584	4.25
Not Hispanic (450)	514	3.74
Hispanic (45)	70	0.51
African, sub-Saharan:	37	0.27
African	31	0.23
South African	6	0.04
Am. Ind. or Alaska Nat., not spec.	40	0.29
American Indian tribes, specified:	90	0.65
Apache	2	0.01
Blackfeet (2)	3	0.02
Cherokee (8)	50	0.36
Chippewa (1)	1	0.01
Choctaw	2	0.01
Comanche	1	0.01
Cree	1	0.01
Creek (4)	6	0.04
Iroquois (1)	6	0.04
Latin American Indians (3)	6	0.04
Ottawa	2	0.01
Pueblo (1)	1	0.01
Shoshone	5	0.04
Sioux	2	0.01
All other tribes	2	0.01
American Indian tribes, not spec.	3	0.02
Arab:	132	0.96
Lebanese	56	0.41
Moroccan	7	0.05
Palestinian	21	0.15
Syrian	48	0.35
Asian:	426	3.10
Bangladeshi (13)	13	0.09
Chinese, ex. Taiwanese (44)	51	0.37
Filipino (38)	57	0.41
Hmong (6)	6	0.04
Indian (83)	114	0.83
Indonesian (1)	1	0.01
Japanese (2)	3	0.02
Korean (48)	52	0.38
Laotian (26)	28	0.20
Malaysian (5)	5	0.04
Taiwanese	4	0.03
Thai (4)	7	0.05
Vietnamese (61)	70	0.51
Other Asian, specified (1)	1	0.01
Other Asian, not specified (2)	14	0.10
Austrian	57	0.42
Basque	6	0.04
Belgian	49	0.36
Brazilian	43	0.31
British	44	0.32
Bulgarian	8	0.06
Canadian	127	0.93
Celtic	7	0.05
Croatian	17	0.12
Czech	60	0.44
Czechoslovakian	35	0.26
Danish	17	0.12
Dutch	349	2.55
English	1,808	13.19
European	77	0.56
Finnish	16	0.12
French, except Basque	438	3.19
French Canadian	91	0.66
German	2,474	18.04
Greek	61	0.44
Guyanese	7	0.05
Hawaii Native/Pacific Islander:	22	0.16
Polynesian: (1)	3	0.02
Native Hawaiian (1)	2	0.01
Samoan	1	0.01
Other Pac. Isl., not spec. (5)	19	0.14
Hispanic or Latino:	1,519	11.05
Central American:	86	0.63
Costa Rican	19	0.14
Guatemalan	6	0.04
Honduran	15	0.11
Nicaraguan	6	0.04
Panamanian	13	0.09
Salvadoran	24	0.17
Other Central American	3	0.02
Cuban	162	1.18
Dominican Republic	48	0.35
Mexican	145	1.05
Puerto Rican	653	4.75
South American:	152	1.11
Argentinean	10	0.07
Bolivian	1	0.01
Chilean	4	0.03
Colombian	72	0.52
Ecuadorian	23	0.17
Peruvian	23	0.17
Uruguayan	1	0.01
Venezuelan	6	0.04
Other South American	12	0.09
Other Hispanic or Latino	273	1.99
Hungarian	183	1.33
Icelander	35	0.26
Irish	2,192	15.99
Italian	1,255	9.15
Latvian	4	0.03
Lithuanian	42	0.31
Northern European	13	0.09
Norwegian	127	0.93
Pennsylvania German	7	0.05
Polish	456	3.33
Portuguese	92	0.67
Romanian	12	0.09
Russian	259	1.89
Scotch-Irish	190	1.39
Scottish	285	2.08
Serbian	22	0.16
Slovak	101	0.74
Slovene	9	0.07
Swedish	262	1.91
Swiss	64	0.47
Turkish	16	0.12
Ukrainian	6	0.04
United States or American	949	6.92
Welsh	72	0.53
West Indian, excl. Hispanic:	98	0.71
Belizean	20	0.15
Jamaican	33	0.24
Trinidadian and Tobagonian	45	0.33
White:	12,249	89.12
Not Hispanic (11,145)	11,294	82.17
Hispanic (854)	955	6.95

Lutz

Place Type: Census Designated Place
County: Hillsborough
Population: 17,081

Ancestry/Race	Number	%
African American/Black:	565	3.31
Not Hispanic (491)	527	3.09
Hispanic (21)	38	0.22
Alaska Native tribes, specified:	2	0.01
Alaska Athabascan (1)	1	0.01
Aleut (1)	1	0.01
Am. Ind. or Alaska Nat., not spec.	38	0.22
American Indian tribes, specified:	99	0.58
Apache	1	0.01
Blackfeet	4	0.02
Cherokee (13)	45	0.26
Cheyenne (1)	1	0.01
Chippewa (1)	1	0.01
Choctaw (2)	7	0.04
Creek (3)	5	0.03
Crow	2	0.01
Iroquois (2)	7	0.04
Latin American Indians	7	0.04
Lumbee (2)	2	0.01
Menominee (1)	1	0.01
Navajo (1)	1	0.01
Seminole (2)	2	0.01
Sioux (3)	5	0.03
All other tribes (2)	8	0.05
American Indian tribes, not spec.	5	0.03
Arab:	37	0.22
Arab/Arabic	12	0.07
Lebanese	16	0.09
Syrian	9	0.05
Armenian	13	0.08
Asian:	320	1.87
Chinese, ex. Taiwanese (32)	40	0.23
Filipino (58)	74	0.43
Indian (43)	63	0.37
Indonesian (2)	9	0.05
Japanese (13)	27	0.16
Korean (30)	36	0.21
Malaysian (1)	2	0.01
Taiwanese (5)	5	0.03
Thai (8)	14	0.08
Vietnamese (35)	37	0.22
Other Asian, specified (2)	2	0.01
Other Asian, not specified (9)	11	0.06
Austrian	22	0.13
Basque	9	0.05
Belgian	77	0.45
Brazilian	24	0.14
British	123	0.72
Canadian	32	0.19
Croatian	39	0.23
Czech	108	0.63
Czechoslovakian	48	0.28
Danish	83	0.49
Dutch	456	2.67
Eastern European	13	0.08
English	2,517	14.76

Notes: 1. Figures in the "Number" column do not add up to the total population due to: a) Ancestry/Race overlap — e.g. persons can report being both White and Irish, b) persons of Hispanic origin can report being any race, c) persons reporting two ancestries are counted in both categories. 2. Numbers in parentheses indicate the number of persons reporting this ancestry/race alone, not in combination with any other ancestry/race. 3. Refer to the Explanation of Data in the front of the book for more detailed information.

Ancestry/Race	Number	%
European	63	0.37
Finnish	53	0.31
French, except Basque	596	3.49
French Canadian	116	0.68
German	3,091	18.12
Greek	100	0.59
Hawaii Native/Pacific Islander:	14	0.08
Polynesian:	3	0.02
Native Hawaiian	3	0.02
Other Pac. Isl., not spec. (1)	11	0.06
Hispanic or Latino:	1,343	7.86
Central American:	40	0.23
Costa Rican	7	0.04
Honduran	9	0.05
Nicaraguan	8	0.05
Panamanian	12	0.07
Salvadoran	3	0.02
Other Central American	1	0.01
Cuban	255	1.49
Dominican Republic	18	0.11
Mexican	84	0.49
Puerto Rican	362	2.12
South American:	114	0.67
Argentinean	6	0.04
Bolivian	2	0.01
Colombian	55	0.32
Ecuadorian	14	0.08
Peruvian	15	0.09
Uruguayan	1	0.01
Venezuelan	18	0.11
Other South American	3	0.02
Other Hispanic or Latino	470	2.75
Hungarian	186	1.09
Irish	2,793	16.38
Italian	1,385	8.12
Lithuanian	131	0.77
Maltese	8	0.05
Norwegian	152	0.89
Pennsylvania German	29	0.17
Polish	524	3.07
Portuguese	135	0.79
Romanian	11	0.06
Russian	90	0.53
Scandinavian	24	0.14
Scotch-Irish	311	1.82
Scottish	488	2.86
Serbian	28	0.16
Slavic	7	0.04
Slovak	9	0.05
Slovene	20	0.12
Swedish	220	1.29
Swiss	34	0.20
Ukrainian	26	0.15
United States or American	1,714	10.05
Welsh	197	1.16
West Indian, excl. Hispanic:	88	0.52
Belizean	21	0.12
British West Indian	27	0.16
Jamaican	20	0.12
Trinidadian and Tobagonian	12	0.07
West Indian	8	0.05
White:	16,021	93.79
Not Hispanic (14,752)	14,917	87.33
Hispanic (1,042)	1,104	6.46
Yugoslavian	36	0.21

Lynn Haven

Place Type: City
County: Bay
Population: 12,451

Ancestry/Race	Number	%
Acadian/Cajun	11	0.09
African American/Black:	1,218	9.78
Not Hispanic (1,157)	1,208	9.70
Hispanic (7)	10	0.08
African, sub-Saharan:	22	0.18
African	22	0.18
Alaska Native tribes, specified:	3	0.02
Alaska Athabascan (1)	1	0.01
Aleut	1	0.01
Tlingit-Haida (1)	1	0.01
Am. Ind. or Alaska Nat., not spec.	30	0.24
American Indian tribes, specified:	119	0.96
Apache	2	0.02
Blackfeet (1)	1	0.01
Cherokee (22)	45	0.36
Chippewa (3)	3	0.02
Choctaw (2)	3	0.02
Cree (1)	1	0.01
Creek (26)	44	0.35
Crow (1)	1	0.01
Houma (2)	2	0.02
Latin American Indians (1)	1	0.01
Lumbee (5)	5	0.04
Sioux (8)	8	0.06
All other tribes (2)	3	0.02
American Indian tribes, not spec.	8	0.06
Arab:	75	0.61
Egyptian	11	0.09
Palestinian	9	0.07
Syrian	55	0.45
Asian:	258	2.07
Cambodian (8)	8	0.06
Chinese, ex. Taiwanese (17)	23	0.18
Filipino (48)	70	0.56
Indian (36)	40	0.32
Indonesian (1)	1	0.01
Japanese (9)	17	0.14
Korean (36)	41	0.33
Malaysian	1	0.01
Pakistani (7)	8	0.06
Taiwanese	1	0.01
Thai (3)	5	0.04
Vietnamese (17)	25	0.20
Other Asian, not specified (13)	18	0.14
Austrian	31	0.25
Belgian	8	0.06
British	69	0.56
Canadian	7	0.06
Czech	27	0.22
Danish	36	0.29
Dutch	272	2.20
English	1,433	11.60
European	141	1.14
Finnish	9	0.07
French, except Basque	426	3.45
French Canadian	47	0.38
German	1,598	12.94
Hawaii Native/Pacific Islander:	32	0.26
Micronesian: (3)	4	0.03
Guamanian/Chamorro (3)	4	0.03
Polynesian: (11)	26	0.21
Native Hawaiian (9)	23	0.18
Samoan	1	0.01
Other Polynesian (2)	2	0.02
Other Pac. Isl., not spec.	2	0.02
Hispanic or Latino:	202	1.62
Central American:	15	0.12
Costa Rican	9	0.07
Guatemalan	1	0.01
Honduran	1	0.01
Panamanian	4	0.03
Cuban	22	0.18
Dominican Republic	5	0.04
Mexican	51	0.41
Puerto Rican	63	0.51
South American:	5	0.04
Argentinean	1	0.01
Colombian	2	0.02
Peruvian	1	0.01
Venezuelan	1	0.01
Other Hispanic or Latino	41	0.33
Icelander	15	0.12
Irish	1,776	14.38
Italian	306	2.48
Lithuanian	9	0.07
Northern European	13	0.11
Norwegian	73	0.59
Polish	230	1.86
Portuguese	49	0.40
Russian	31	0.25
Scandinavian	44	0.36
Scotch-Irish	300	2.43
Scottish	294	2.38
Serbian	8	0.06
Slavic	23	0.19
Slovene	7	0.06
Swedish	97	0.79
United States or American	1,838	14.88
Welsh	33	0.27
West Indian, excl. Hispanic:	45	0.36
Bahamian	6	0.05
Trinidadian and Tobagonian	39	0.32
White:	10,913	87.65
Not Hispanic (10,604)	10,762	86.43
Hispanic (134)	151	1.21
Yugoslavian	5	0.04

Maitland

Place Type: City
County: Orange
Population: 12,019

Ancestry/Race	Number	%
African American/Black:	1,249	10.39
Not Hispanic (1,135)	1,202	10.00
Hispanic (34)	47	0.39
African, sub-Saharan:	100	0.84
African	78	0.65
Nigerian	22	0.18
Alaska Native tribes, specified:	1	0.01
Aleut (1)	1	0.01
Am. Ind. or Alaska Nat., not spec.	15	0.12
American Indian tribes, specified:	32	0.27
Apache	1	0.01
Cherokee (3)	13	0.11
Chippewa	1	0.01
Choctaw	1	0.01
Creek	6	0.05
Iroquois	1	0.01
Latin American Indians (1)	2	0.02
Lumbee (1)	1	0.01
Menominee	1	0.01
Seminole (1)	4	0.03
Sioux (1)	1	0.01
American Indian tribes, not spec.	2	0.02
Arab:	77	0.65
Arab/Arabic	8	0.07
Egyptian	24	0.20
Iraqi	9	0.08
Lebanese	14	0.12
Palestinian	8	0.07
Syrian	8	0.07
Other Arab	6	0.05
Armenian	20	0.17
Asian:	312	2.60
Bangladeshi (2)	2	0.02
Cambodian (1)	1	0.01
Chinese, ex. Taiwanese (39)	49	0.41
Filipino (16)	29	0.24
Indian (95)	104	0.87
Indonesian (1)	1	0.01
Japanese (8)	20	0.17
Korean (20)	21	0.17
Laotian (6)	6	0.05
Malaysian	1	0.01
Pakistani (1)	2	0.02
Thai (4)	8	0.07
Vietnamese (48)	50	0.42
Other Asian, specified (1)	1	0.01
Other Asian, not specified (14)	17	0.14
Australian	8	0.07
Austrian	50	0.42
Belgian	12	0.10
Brazilian	16	0.13
British	84	0.70
Bulgarian	30	0.25

Notes: 1. Figures in the "Number" column do not add up to the total population due to: a) Ancestry/Race overlap — e.g. persons can report being both White and Irish, b) persons of Hispanic origin can report being any race, c) persons reporting two ancestries are counted in both categories. 2. Numbers in parentheses indicate the number of persons reporting this ancestry/race alone, not in combination with any other ancestry/race. 3. Refer to the Explanation of Data in the front of the book for more detailed information.

Canadian	60	0.50
Croatian	19	0.16
Czech	45	0.38
Czechoslovakian	6	0.05
Danish	35	0.29
Dutch	75	0.63
Eastern European	88	0.74
English	1,988	16.66
Estonian	7	0.06
European	247	2.07
Finnish	29	0.24
French, except Basque	485	4.06
French Canadian	121	1.01
German	1,694	14.19
Greek	47	0.39
Guyanese	10	0.08
Hawaii Native/Pacific Islander:	8	0.07
Polynesian:	1	0.01
Native Hawaiian	1	0.01
Other Pac. Isl., not spec. (1)	7	0.06
Hispanic or Latino:	717	5.97
Central American:	17	0.14
Guatemalan	1	0.01
Honduran	1	0.01
Nicaraguan	3	0.02
Panamanian	11	0.09
Other Central American	1	0.01
Cuban	71	0.59
Dominican Republic	18	0.15
Mexican	45	0.37
Puerto Rican	328	2.73
South American:	105	0.87
Argentinean	19	0.16
Chilean	4	0.03
Colombian	44	0.37
Ecuadorian	14	0.12
Peruvian	7	0.06
Venezuelan	17	0.14
Other Hispanic or Latino	133	1.11
Hungarian	117	0.98
Icelander	10	0.08
Iranian	24	0.20
Irish	1,318	11.04
Italian	626	5.25
Latvian	7	0.06
Lithuanian	46	0.39
Northern European	14	0.12
Norwegian	131	1.10
Pennsylvania German	13	0.11
Polish	300	2.51
Portuguese	45	0.38
Romanian	68	0.57
Russian	300	2.51
Scandinavian	17	0.14
Scotch-Irish	377	3.16
Scottish	393	3.29
Serbian	7	0.06
Slovak	26	0.22
Slovene	29	0.24
Swedish	156	1.31
Swiss	11	0.09
Ukrainian	32	0.27
United States or American	900	7.54
Welsh	79	0.66
West Indian, excl. Hispanic:	115	0.96
Haitian	8	0.07
Jamaican	87	0.73
Trinidadian and Tobagonian	5	0.04
U.S. Virgin Islander	15	0.13
White:	10,395	86.49
Not Hispanic (9,732)	9,855	82.00
Hispanic (511)	540	4.49
Yugoslavian	39	0.33

Marathon

Place Type: City
County: Monroe
Population: 10,255

Ancestry/Race	Number	%
African American/Black:	529	5.16
Not Hispanic (449)	499	4.87
Hispanic (28)	30	0.29
African, sub-Saharan:	30	0.29
African	30	0.29
Am. Ind. or Alaska Nat., not spec.	24	0.23
American Indian tribes, specified:	43	0.42
Apache (2)	2	0.02
Blackfeet (3)	4	0.04
Cherokee (8)	18	0.18
Chickasaw	1	0.01
Chippewa (2)	2	0.02
Cree (1)	2	0.02
Creek (1)	1	0.01
Iroquois	3	0.03
Latin American Indians	2	0.02
Ottawa	1	0.01
Sioux (1)	4	0.04
All other tribes (2)	3	0.03
American Indian tribes, not spec.	5	0.05
Arab:	25	0.25
Lebanese	25	0.25
Armenian	7	0.07
Asian:	68	0.66
Cambodian (2)	4	0.04
Chinese, ex. Taiwanese (13)	17	0.17
Filipino (10)	14	0.14
Indian (8)	8	0.08
Japanese (2)	2	0.02
Korean (6)	6	0.06
Laotian	2	0.02
Thai (1)	3	0.03
Vietnamese (5)	5	0.05
Other Asian, not specified (1)	7	0.07
Austrian	27	0.26
Belgian	17	0.17
British	55	0.54
Bulgarian	37	0.36
Canadian	46	0.45
Croatian	14	0.14
Czech	42	0.41
Czechoslovakian	21	0.21
Danish	55	0.54
Dutch	106	1.04
English	1,293	12.68
European	101	0.99
Finnish	30	0.29
French, except Basque	454	4.45
French Canadian	111	1.09
German	1,752	17.19
Greek	16	0.16
Hawaii Native/Pacific Islander:	12	0.12
Micronesian:	2	0.02
Guamanian/Chamorro	2	0.02
Polynesian: (4)	4	0.04
Native Hawaiian (4)	4	0.04
Other Pac. Isl., not spec.	6	0.06
Hispanic or Latino:	2,095	20.43
Central American:	300	2.93
Costa Rican	9	0.09
Guatemalan	120	1.17
Honduran	31	0.30
Nicaraguan	133	1.30
Salvadoran	7	0.07
Cuban	1,212	11.82
Dominican Republic	24	0.23
Mexican	270	2.63
Puerto Rican	92	0.90
South American:	80	0.78
Argentinean	18	0.18
Bolivian	2	0.02
Chilean	1	0.01
Colombian	27	0.26
Ecuadorian	7	0.07
Peruvian	3	0.03
Uruguayan	1	0.01
Venezuelan	16	0.16
Other South American	5	0.05
Other Hispanic or Latino	117	1.14
Hungarian	35	0.34
Irish	1,600	15.70
Israeli	7	0.07
Italian	557	5.46
Latvian	10	0.10
Lithuanian	35	0.34
Macedonian	5	0.05
Northern European	10	0.10
Norwegian	54	0.53
Polish	396	3.88
Portuguese	11	0.11
Romanian	17	0.17
Russian	81	0.79
Scandinavian	9	0.09
Scotch-Irish	246	2.41
Scottish	363	3.56
Serbian	6	0.06
Slavic	8	0.08
Slovak	16	0.16
Slovene	19	0.19
Swedish	205	2.01
Swiss	54	0.53
Turkish	7	0.07
Ukrainian	45	0.44
United States or American	596	5.85
Welsh	76	0.75
West Indian, excl. Hispanic:	82	0.80
Bahamian	39	0.38
Belizean	13	0.13
Haitian	9	0.09
Jamaican	21	0.21
White:	9,432	91.97
Not Hispanic (7,513)	7,573	73.85
Hispanic (1,828)	1,859	18.13
Yugoslavian	7	0.07

Marco Island

Place Type: City
County: Collier
Population: 14,879

Ancestry/Race	Number	%
African American/Black:	42	0.28
Not Hispanic (35)	39	0.26
Hispanic	3	0.02
Alaska Native tribes, specified:	2	0.01
Tlingit-Haida (1)	2	0.01
Am. Ind. or Alaska Nat., not spec.	15	0.10
Alsatian	7	0.05
American Indian tribes, specified:	26	0.17
Apache (1)	2	0.01
Blackfeet (1)	1	0.01
Cherokee (3)	5	0.03
Latin American Indians (10)	10	0.07
Pueblo (1)	1	0.01
Sioux (2)	5	0.03
All other tribes (1)	2	0.01
American Indian tribes, not spec.	1	0.01
Arab:	106	0.71
Lebanese	52	0.35
Palestinian	49	0.33
Syrian	5	0.03
Armenian	51	0.34
Asian:	111	0.75
Chinese, ex. Taiwanese (18)	23	0.15
Filipino (22)	33	0.22
Indian (16)	18	0.12
Indonesian	2	0.01
Japanese (4)	4	0.03
Korean (11)	12	0.08
Pakistani (1)	1	0.01
Sri Lankan (1)	1	0.01
Taiwanese (1)	1	0.01

Notes: 1. Figures in the "Number" column do not add up to the total population due to: a) Ancestry/Race overlap — e.g. persons can report being both White and Irish, b) persons of Hispanic origin can report being any race, c) persons reporting two ancestries are counted in both categories. 2. Numbers in parentheses indicate the number of persons reporting this ancestry/race alone, not in combination with any other ancestry/race. 3. Refer to the Explanation of Data in the front of the book for more detailed information.

Vietnamese (10)	11	0.07
Other Asian, not specified (2)	5	0.03
Assyrian/Chaldean/Syriac	8	0.05
Australian	9	0.06
Austrian	107	0.71
Basque	19	0.13
Belgian	7	0.05
Brazilian	22	0.15
British	79	0.53
Canadian	117	0.78
Croatian	67	0.45
Czech	79	0.53
Czechoslovakian	67	0.45
Danish	137	0.91
Dutch	271	1.81
English	2,235	14.92
European	121	0.81
Finnish	127	0.85
French, except Basque	467	3.12
French Canadian	150	1.00
German	3,498	23.35
Greek	107	0.71
Hawaii Native/Pacific Islander:	3	0.02
Polynesian: (1)	1	0.01
Native Hawaiian (1)	1	0.01
Other Pac. Isl., not spec.	2	0.01
Hispanic or Latino:	608	4.09
Central American:	61	0.41
Costa Rican	9	0.06
Guatemalan	33	0.22
Honduran	4	0.03
Nicaraguan	1	0.01
Panamanian	2	0.01
Salvadoran	12	0.08
Cuban	157	1.06
Dominican Republic	6	0.04
Mexican	233	1.57
Puerto Rican	44	0.30
South American:	32	0.22
Argentinean	2	0.01
Colombian	17	0.11
Ecuadorian	4	0.03
Uruguayan	2	0.01
Venezuelan	6	0.04
Other South American	1	0.01
Other Hispanic or Latino	75	0.50
Hungarian	167	1.11
Iranian	8	0.05
Irish	2,892	19.31
Italian	2,014	13.44
Lithuanian	107	0.71
Luxemburger	6	0.04
Northern European	23	0.15
Norwegian	294	1.96
Polish	751	5.01
Portuguese	12	0.08
Romanian	37	0.25
Russian	216	1.44
Scandinavian	27	0.18
Scotch-Irish	350	2.34
Scottish	438	2.92
Slavic	25	0.17
Slovak	49	0.33
Slovene	9	0.06
Swedish	437	2.92
Swiss	109	0.73
Ukrainian	38	0.25
United States or American	758	5.06
Welsh	183	1.22
West Indian, excl. Hispanic:	10	0.07
British West Indian	10	0.07
White:	14,650	98.46
Not Hispanic (14,077)	14,125	94.93
Hispanic (517)	525	3.53
Yugoslavian	9	0.06

Margate

Place Type: City
County: Broward
Population: 53,909

Ancestry/Race	Number	%
African American/Black:	7,054	13.09
Not Hispanic (6,069)	6,760	12.54
Hispanic (199)	294	0.55
African, sub-Saharan:	286	0.53
African	232	0.43
Ethiopian	36	0.07
Nigerian	18	0.03
Alaska Native tribes, specified:	1	0.00
Tlingit-Haida (1)	1	0.00
Am. Ind. or Alaska Nat., not spec.	132	0.24
American Indian tribes, specified:	172	0.32
Apache (8)	10	0.02
Blackfeet	4	0.01
Cherokee (16)	62	0.12
Chippewa (2)	3	0.01
Choctaw (1)	5	0.01
Creek	4	0.01
Iroquois (4)	7	0.01
Latin American Indians (20)	42	0.08
Lumbee (4)	5	0.01
Navajo	4	0.01
Ottawa (1)	1	0.00
Seminole (1)	1	0.00
Sioux (1)	4	0.01
Tohono O'Odham	3	0.01
All other tribes (12)	17	0.03
American Indian tribes, not spec.	17	0.03
Arab:	250	0.46
Arab/Arabic	35	0.06
Egyptian	19	0.04
Jordanian	31	0.06
Lebanese	109	0.20
Moroccan	8	0.01
Palestinian	40	0.07
Syrian	8	0.01
Armenian	34	0.06
Asian:	1,916	3.55
Bangladeshi (17)	26	0.05
Cambodian (1)	2	0.00
Chinese, ex. Taiwanese (296)	386	0.72
Filipino (127)	186	0.35
Indian (550)	691	1.28
Indonesian (1)	1	0.00
Japanese (21)	40	0.07
Korean (43)	55	0.10
Laotian (2)	2	0.00
Malaysian (4)	4	0.01
Pakistani (23)	37	0.07
Taiwanese (2)	3	0.01
Thai (45)	49	0.09
Vietnamese (321)	345	0.64
Other Asian, specified	3	0.01
Other Asian, not specified (24)	86	0.16
Austrian	232	0.43
Belgian	13	0.02
Brazilian	258	0.48
British	205	0.38
Bulgarian	10	0.02
Canadian	272	0.51
Croatian	53	0.10
Czech	96	0.18
Czechoslovakian	104	0.19
Danish	122	0.23
Dutch	546	1.01
Eastern European	67	0.12
English	3,508	6.51
European	181	0.34
Finnish	73	0.14
French, except Basque	1,220	2.27
French Canadian	713	1.32
German	6,057	11.25
Greek	341	0.63
Guyanese	16	0.03

Ancestry/Race	Number	%
Hawaii Native/Pacific Islander:	118	0.22
Micronesian: (3)	6	0.01
Guamanian/Chamorro (3)	6	0.01
Polynesian: (9)	28	0.05
Native Hawaiian (4)	20	0.04
Samoan (2)	5	0.01
Tongan (1)	1	0.00
Other Polynesian (2)	2	0.00
Other Pac. Isl., specified	2	0.00
Other Pac. Isl., not spec. (19)	82	0.15
Hispanic or Latino:	8,238	15.28
Central American:	530	0.98
Costa Rican	36	0.07
Guatemalan	48	0.09
Honduran	104	0.19
Nicaraguan	62	0.12
Panamanian	37	0.07
Salvadoran	214	0.40
Other Central American	29	0.05
Cuban	796	1.48
Dominican Republic	247	0.46
Mexican	820	1.52
Puerto Rican	2,154	4.00
South American:	2,029	3.76
Argentinean	89	0.17
Bolivian	15	0.03
Chilean	51	0.09
Colombian	1,199	2.22
Ecuadorian	135	0.25
Paraguayan	5	0.01
Peruvian	315	0.58
Uruguayan	24	0.04
Venezuelan	136	0.25
Other South American	60	0.11
Other Hispanic or Latino	1,662	3.08
Hungarian	545	1.01
Iranian	26	0.05
Irish	6,034	11.20
Israeli	39	0.07
Italian	6,867	12.75
Latvian	27	0.05
Lithuanian	186	0.35
Luxemburger	8	0.01
Maltese	7	0.01
Norwegian	300	0.56
Pennsylvania German	23	0.04
Polish	2,393	4.44
Portuguese	189	0.35
Romanian	185	0.34
Russian	1,650	3.06
Scotch-Irish	440	0.82
Scottish	666	1.24
Slavic	35	0.06
Slovak	252	0.47
Swedish	400	0.74
Swiss	64	0.12
Turkish	27	0.05
Ukrainian	249	0.46
United States or American	3,332	6.19
Welsh	261	0.48
West Indian, excl. Hispanic:	4,094	7.60
Bahamian	33	0.06
Barbadian	35	0.06
Bermudan	10	0.02
British West Indian	25	0.05
Haitian	1,853	3.44
Jamaican	1,734	3.22
Trinidadian and Tobagonian	333	0.62
U.S. Virgin Islander	10	0.02
West Indian	61	0.11
White:	43,693	81.05
Not Hispanic (36,534)	37,165	68.94
Hispanic (5,944)	6,528	12.11
Yugoslavian	67	0.12

Notes: 1. Figures in the "Number" column do not add up to the total population due to: a) Ancestry/Race overlap — e.g. persons can report being both White and Irish, b) persons of Hispanic origin can report being any race, c) persons reporting two ancestries are counted in both categories. 2. Numbers in parentheses indicate the number of persons reporting this ancestry/race alone, not in combination with any other ancestry/race. 3. Refer to the Explanation of Data in the front of the book for more detailed information.

Meadow Woods

Place Type: Census Designated Place
County: Orange
Population: 11,286

Ancestry/Race	Number	%
African American/Black:	1,498	13.27
Not Hispanic (1,150)	1,241	11.00
Hispanic (199)	257	2.28
African, sub-Saharan:	49	0.43
African	24	0.21
Cape Verdean	16	0.14
Nigerian	9	0.08
Am. Ind. or Alaska Nat., not spec.	57	0.51
American Indian tribes, specified:	58	0.51
Blackfeet	3	0.03
Cherokee (12)	19	0.17
Choctaw (2)	4	0.04
Creek	1	0.01
Iroquois (1)	1	0.01
Latin American Indians (8)	22	0.19
Sioux (1)	1	0.01
All other tribes (2)	7	0.06
American Indian tribes, not spec.	5	0.04
Arab:	131	1.14
Arab/Arabic	30	0.26
Iraqi	30	0.26
Lebanese	9	0.08
Palestinian	44	0.38
Other Arab	18	0.16
Asian:	358	3.17
Bangladeshi (3)	3	0.03
Cambodian (2)	10	0.09
Chinese, ex. Taiwanese (58)	68	0.60
Filipino (79)	88	0.78
Indian (64)	77	0.68
Japanese (7)	15	0.13
Korean (12)	14	0.12
Laotian	2	0.02
Pakistani (9)	13	0.12
Taiwanese (11)	13	0.12
Thai (5)	8	0.07
Vietnamese (17)	19	0.17
Other Asian, specified	1	0.01
Other Asian, not specified (1)	27	0.24
British	54	0.47
Bulgarian	20	0.17
Canadian	34	0.30
Czech	20	0.17
Czechoslovakian	8	0.07
Danish	24	0.21
Dutch	58	0.51
English	492	4.28
European	31	0.27
Finnish	13	0.11
French, except Basque	164	1.43
French Canadian	47	0.41
German	796	6.93
Greek	44	0.38
Guyanese	28	0.24
Hawaii Native/Pacific Islander:	36	0.32
Polynesian: (12)	29	0.26
Native Hawaiian (8)	19	0.17
Samoan (1)	5	0.04
Tongan	1	0.01
Other Polynesian (3)	4	0.04
Other Pac. Isl., specified	1	0.01
Other Pac. Isl., not spec.	6	0.05
Hispanic or Latino:	5,964	52.84
Central American:	149	1.32
Costa Rican	19	0.17
Guatemalan	15	0.13
Honduran	7	0.06
Nicaraguan	24	0.21
Panamanian	44	0.39
Salvadoran	29	0.26
Other Central American	11	0.10
Cuban	225	1.99
Dominican Republic	228	2.02
Mexican	161	1.43
Puerto Rican	3,772	33.42
South American:	714	6.33
Argentinean	20	0.18
Bolivian	1	0.01
Chilean	7	0.06
Colombian	408	3.62
Ecuadorian	95	0.84
Peruvian	72	0.64
Uruguayan	8	0.07
Venezuelan	79	0.70
Other South American	24	0.21
Other Hispanic or Latino	715	6.34
Hungarian	29	0.25
Irish	747	6.50
Italian	623	5.42
Lithuanian	16	0.14
Northern European	10	0.09
Norwegian	7	0.06
Pennsylvania German	19	0.17
Polish	200	1.74
Russian	7	0.06
Scotch-Irish	94	0.82
Scottish	110	0.96
Slovak	57	0.50
Swedish	19	0.17
Swiss	30	0.26
Ukrainian	23	0.20
United States or American	412	3.59
Welsh	18	0.16
West Indian, excl. Hispanic:	482	4.20
Barbadian	41	0.36
Belizean	45	0.39
Haitian	130	1.13
Jamaican	145	1.26
Trinidadian and Tobagonian	28	0.24
West Indian	93	0.81
White:	7,947	70.41
Not Hispanic (3,592)	3,735	33.09
Hispanic (3,969)	4,212	37.32

Melbourne

Place Type: City
County: Brevard
Population: 71,382

Ancestry/Race	Number	%
African American/Black:	7,176	10.05
Not Hispanic (6,493)	6,920	9.69
Hispanic (165)	256	0.36
African, sub-Saharan:	438	0.61
African	299	0.42
Nigerian	124	0.17
Other sub-Saharan African	15	0.02
Alaska Native tribes, specified:	5	0.01
Aleut (1)	1	0.00
Eskimo (3)	4	0.01
Alaska Native tribes, not specified	4	0.01
Am. Ind. or Alaska Nat., not spec.	201	0.28
American Indian tribes, specified:	447	0.63
Apache (6)	8	0.01
Blackfeet (4)	22	0.03
Cherokee (69)	243	0.34
Cheyenne (7)	7	0.01
Chickasaw	1	0.00
Chippewa (12)	17	0.02
Choctaw (3)	16	0.02
Comanche (1)	1	0.00
Cree (2)	5	0.01
Creek (4)	9	0.01
Houma (1)	1	0.00
Iroquois (10)	14	0.02
Latin American Indians (3)	11	0.02
Lumbee (3)	3	0.00
Menominee	1	0.00
Navajo	3	0.00
Osage (1)	3	0.00
Ottawa	2	0.00
Potawatomi (1)	1	0.00
Pueblo (3)	6	0.01
Seminole (2)	10	0.01
Sioux (11)	25	0.04
Yaqui (2)	4	0.01
All other tribes (23)	34	0.05
American Indian tribes, not spec.	16	0.02
Arab:	486	0.68
Arab/Arabic	175	0.25
Egyptian	7	0.01
Lebanese	107	0.15
Moroccan	19	0.03
Palestinian	40	0.06
Syrian	44	0.06
Other Arab	94	0.13
Armenian	32	0.04
Asian:	2,188	3.07
Bangladeshi (2)	2	0.00
Cambodian (21)	25	0.04
Chinese, ex. Taiwanese (218)	274	0.38
Filipino (341)	471	0.66
Indian (393)	452	0.63
Indonesian (11)	18	0.03
Japanese (116)	177	0.25
Korean (130)	191	0.27
Laotian (5)	5	0.01
Malaysian	6	0.01
Pakistani (17)	24	0.03
Sri Lankan (1)	1	0.00
Taiwanese (12)	17	0.02
Thai (114)	158	0.22
Vietnamese (175)	214	0.30
Other Asian, specified (11)	14	0.02
Other Asian, not specified (55)	139	0.19
Australian	19	0.03
Austrian	259	0.36
Basque	9	0.01
Belgian	34	0.05
Brazilian	36	0.05
British	656	0.92
Bulgarian	9	0.01
Canadian	367	0.51
Celtic	44	0.06
Croatian	69	0.10
Czech	250	0.35
Czechoslovakian	199	0.28
Danish	294	0.41
Dutch	1,624	2.28
Eastern European	33	0.05
English	9,106	12.76
European	568	0.80
Finnish	221	0.31
French, except Basque	3,126	4.38
French Canadian	863	1.21
German	11,896	16.67
Greek	303	0.42
Guyanese	37	0.05
Hawaii Native/Pacific Islander:	113	0.16
Melanesian: (3)	4	0.01
Fijian (3)	4	0.01
Micronesian: (13)	17	0.02
Guamanian/Chamorro (13)	17	0.02
Polynesian: (18)	51	0.07
Native Hawaiian (14)	39	0.05
Samoan (2)	7	0.01
Other Polynesian (2)	5	0.01
Other Pac. Isl., specified	2	0.00
Other Pac. Isl., not spec. (10)	39	0.05
Hispanic or Latino:	3,958	5.54
Central American:	171	0.24
Costa Rican	25	0.04
Guatemalan	27	0.04
Honduran	40	0.06
Nicaraguan	8	0.01
Panamanian	58	0.08
Salvadoran	12	0.02
Other Central American	1	0.00
Cuban	332	0.47
Dominican Republic	95	0.13
Mexican	694	0.97
Puerto Rican	1,529	2.14

Notes: 1. Figures in the "Number" column do not add up to the total population due to: a) Ancestry/Race overlap — e.g. persons can report being both White and Irish, b) persons of Hispanic origin can report being any race, c) persons reporting two ancestries are counted in both categories. 2. Numbers in parentheses indicate the number of persons reporting this ancestry/race alone, not in combination with any other ancestry/race. 3. Refer to the Explanation of Data in the front of the book for more detailed information.

Ancestry/Race	Number	%
South American:	399	0.56
Argentinean	27	0.04
Bolivian	6	0.01
Chilean	28	0.04
Colombian	125	0.18
Ecuadorian	54	0.08
Paraguayan	2	0.00
Peruvian	52	0.07
Uruguayan	9	0.01
Venezuelan	68	0.10
Other South American	30	0.04
Other Hispanic or Latino	738	1.03
Hungarian	324	0.45
Icelander	10	0.01
Iranian	102	0.14
Irish	10,484	14.69
Israeli	17	0.02
Italian	5,842	8.19
Lithuanian	305	0.43
Luxemburger	19	0.03
Maltese	36	0.05
New Zealander	8	0.01
Northern European	46	0.06
Norwegian	786	1.10
Pennsylvania German	78	0.11
Polish	2,407	3.37
Portuguese	209	0.29
Romanian	46	0.06
Russian	597	0.84
Scandinavian	130	0.18
Scotch-Irish	1,357	1.90
Scottish	1,906	2.67
Serbian	15	0.02
Slavic	50	0.07
Slovak	171	0.24
Slovene	74	0.10
Swedish	834	1.17
Swiss	164	0.23
Turkish	30	0.04
Ukrainian	252	0.35
United States or American	5,124	7.18
Welsh	537	0.75
West Indian, excl. Hispanic:	504	0.71
Bahamian	23	0.03
Barbadian	14	0.02
Bermudan	6	0.01
British West Indian	59	0.08
Dutch West Indian	9	0.01
Haitian	18	0.03
Jamaican	284	0.40
Trinidadian and Tobagonian	40	0.06
U.S. Virgin Islander	15	0.02
West Indian	36	0.05
White:	61,652	86.37
Not Hispanic (57,600)	58,702	82.24
Hispanic (2,739)	2,950	4.13
Yugoslavian	40	0.06

Merritt Island

Place Type: Census Designated Place
County: Brevard
Population: 36,090

Ancestry/Race	Number	%
Acadian/Cajun	12	0.03
African American/Black:	2,068	5.73
Not Hispanic (1,871)	2,002	5.55
Hispanic (47)	66	0.18
African, sub-Saharan:	106	0.29
African	94	0.26
South African	12	0.03
Alaska Native tribes, specified:	7	0.02
Eskimo (2)	4	0.01
Tlingit-Haida (3)	3	0.01
Am. Ind. or Alaska Nat., not spec.	78	0.22
American Indian tribes, specified:	244	0.68
Apache (2)	3	0.01
Blackfeet (1)	12	0.03
Cherokee (26)	91	0.25
Chickasaw (3)	3	0.01
Chippewa (6)	11	0.03
Choctaw (2)	4	0.01
Cree	1	0.00
Creek (6)	10	0.03
Iroquois (10)	18	0.05
Kiowa (2)	2	0.01
Latin American Indians (6)	19	0.05
Lumbee (9)	9	0.02
Navajo	3	0.01
Osage (1)	1	0.00
Paiute (1)	1	0.00
Pueblo (7)	10	0.03
Seminole (1)	8	0.02
Sioux (4)	8	0.02
Tohono O'Odham (1)	4	0.01
Ute	1	0.00
All other tribes (9)	25	0.07
American Indian tribes, not spec.	10	0.03
Arab:	107	0.30
Egyptian	13	0.04
Jordanian	7	0.02
Lebanese	28	0.08
Moroccan	4	0.01
Palestinian	33	0.09
Syrian	22	0.06
Armenian	49	0.14
Asian:	784	2.17
Cambodian (4)	7	0.02
Chinese, ex. Taiwanese (73)	108	0.30
Filipino (101)	145	0.40
Indian (158)	180	0.50
Indonesian	1	0.00
Japanese (52)	81	0.22
Korean (48)	66	0.18
Laotian (2)	2	0.01
Malaysian	1	0.00
Pakistani (1)	1	0.00
Sri Lankan (1)	3	0.01
Taiwanese (11)	11	0.03
Thai (24)	28	0.08
Vietnamese (105)	125	0.35
Other Asian, specified (1)	3	0.01
Other Asian, not specified (10)	22	0.06
Australian	41	0.11
Austrian	117	0.32
Basque	5	0.01
Belgian	71	0.20
Brazilian	59	0.16
British	264	0.73
Canadian	198	0.55
Celtic	21	0.06
Croatian	16	0.04
Czech	266	0.74
Czechoslovakian	55	0.15
Danish	206	0.57
Dutch	752	2.08
Eastern European	12	0.03
English	5,788	16.04
Estonian	22	0.06
European	381	1.06
Finnish	106	0.29
French, except Basque	1,674	4.64
French Canadian	508	1.41
German	7,083	19.63
Greek	235	0.65
Hawaii Native/Pacific Islander:	60	0.17
Micronesian: (9)	10	0.03
Guamanian/Chamorro (9)	10	0.03
Polynesian: (11)	33	0.09
Native Hawaiian (9)	28	0.08
Samoan (2)	5	0.01
Other Pac. Isl., not spec. (1)	17	0.05
Hispanic or Latino:	1,381	3.83
Central American:	75	0.21
Costa Rican	10	0.03
Guatemalan	9	0.02
Honduran	16	0.04
Nicaraguan	7	0.02
Panamanian	23	0.06
Salvadoran	6	0.02
Other Central American	4	0.01
Cuban	221	0.61
Dominican Republic	24	0.07
Mexican	215	0.60
Puerto Rican	470	1.30
South American:	102	0.28
Argentinean	10	0.03
Bolivian	1	0.00
Chilean	10	0.03
Colombian	28	0.08
Ecuadorian	10	0.03
Peruvian	19	0.05
Venezuelan	8	0.02
Other South American	16	0.04
Other Hispanic or Latino	274	0.76
Hungarian	325	0.90
Irish	5,584	15.47
Israeli	19	0.05
Italian	3,137	8.69
Latvian	39	0.11
Lithuanian	86	0.24
Luxemburger	6	0.02
Maltese	7	0.02
New Zealander	11	0.03
Northern European	22	0.06
Norwegian	504	1.40
Pennsylvania German	44	0.12
Polish	1,108	3.07
Portuguese	178	0.49
Romanian	78	0.22
Russian	379	1.05
Scandinavian	55	0.15
Scotch-Irish	1,199	3.32
Scottish	964	2.67
Serbian	39	0.11
Slavic	33	0.09
Slovak	67	0.19
Slovene	15	0.04
Swedish	600	1.66
Swiss	231	0.64
Ukrainian	197	0.55
United States or American	2,391	6.62
Welsh	311	0.86
West Indian, excl. Hispanic:	110	0.30
Bahamian	18	0.05
Barbadian	7	0.02
British West Indian	4	0.01
Jamaican	12	0.03
Trinidadian and Tobagonian	26	0.07
West Indian	43	0.12
White:	33,076	91.65
Not Hispanic (31,565)	31,983	88.62
Hispanic (995)	1,093	3.03
Yugoslavian	35	0.10

Miami Beach

Place Type: City
County: Miami-Dade
Population: 87,933

Ancestry/Race	Number	%
African American/Black:	4,218	4.80
Not Hispanic (2,491)	2,762	3.14
Hispanic (1,057)	1,456	1.66
African, sub-Saharan:	351	0.40
African	256	0.29
Cape Verdean	21	0.02
Ghanian	9	0.01
Nigerian	19	0.02
Somalian	9	0.01
South African	19	0.02
Zairian	12	0.01
Other sub-Saharan African	6	0.01
Alaska Native tribes, specified:	4	0.00
Alaska Athabascan (3)	3	0.00
Tlingit-Haida	1	0.00
Alaska Native tribes, not specified	1	0.00
Am. Ind. or Alaska Nat., not spec.	206	0.23

Notes: 1. Figures in the "Number" column do not add up to the total population due to: a) Ancestry/Race overlap — e.g. persons can report being both White and Irish, b) persons of Hispanic origin can report being any race, c) persons reporting two ancestries are counted in both categories. 2. Numbers in parentheses indicate the number of persons reporting this ancestry/race alone, not in combination with any other ancestry/race. 3. Refer to the Explanation of Data in the front of the book for more detailed information.

Albanian	47	0.05
Alsatian	12	0.01
American Indian tribes, specified:	232	0.26
Apache (3)	9	0.01
Blackfeet	2	0.00
Cherokee (19)	47	0.05
Chippewa (1)	4	0.00
Choctaw (2)	2	0.00
Comanche (1)	1	0.00
Creek	1	0.00
Iroquois (1)	5	0.01
Latin American Indians (57)	124	0.14
Lumbee (1)	2	0.00
Navajo (1)	2	0.00
Pueblo (1)	6	0.01
Seminole	2	0.00
Sioux (2)	8	0.01
All other tribes (5)	17	0.02
American Indian tribes, not spec.	24	0.03
Arab:	934	1.06
Arab/Arabic	139	0.16
Egyptian	100	0.11
Iraqi	41	0.05
Lebanese	271	0.31
Moroccan	120	0.14
Palestinian	56	0.06
Syrian	69	0.08
Other Arab	138	0.16
Armenian	104	0.12
Asian:	1,639	1.86
Bangladeshi (20)	49	0.06
Cambodian (3)	3	0.00
Chinese, ex. Taiwanese (188)	277	0.32
Filipino (272)	315	0.36
Indian (386)	499	0.57
Indonesian (23)	28	0.03
Japanese (102)	134	0.15
Korean (49)	63	0.07
Laotian (1)	1	0.00
Malaysian (4)	4	0.00
Pakistani (19)	32	0.04
Sri Lankan (8)	9	0.01
Taiwanese	2	0.00
Thai (35)	50	0.06
Vietnamese (33)	46	0.05
Other Asian, specified (8)	12	0.01
Other Asian, not specified (24)	115	0.13
Australian	59	0.07
Austrian	816	0.93
Basque	77	0.09
Belgian	201	0.23
Brazilian	1,949	2.21
British	333	0.38
Bulgarian	91	0.10
Canadian	387	0.44
Celtic	12	0.01
Croatian	110	0.12
Czech	113	0.13
Czechoslovakian	106	0.12
Danish	85	0.10
Dutch	532	0.60
Eastern European	414	0.47
English	2,185	2.48
Estonian	8	0.01
European	988	1.12
Finnish	23	0.03
French, except Basque	1,704	1.94
French Canadian	184	0.21
German	3,811	4.33
Greek	379	0.43
Guyanese	30	0.03
Hawaii Native/Pacific Islander:	133	0.15
Melanesian:	1	0.00
Fijian	1	0.00
Micronesian: (4)	9	0.01
Guamanian/Chamorro (4)	9	0.01
Polynesian: (18)	40	0.05
Native Hawaiian (8)	21	0.02
Samoan (9)	17	0.02
Other Polynesian (1)	2	0.00
Other Pac. Isl., specified	3	0.00
Other Pac. Isl., not spec. (17)	80	0.09
Hispanic or Latino:	47,000	53.45
Central American:	3,096	3.52
Costa Rican	293	0.33
Guatemalan	328	0.37
Honduran	1,062	1.21
Nicaraguan	905	1.03
Panamanian	224	0.25
Salvadoran	201	0.23
Other Central American	83	0.09
Cuban	18,038	20.51
Dominican Republic	1,084	1.23
Mexican	1,183	1.35
Puerto Rican	3,596	4.09
South American:	11,589	13.18
Argentinean	2,680	3.05
Bolivian	176	0.20
Chilean	623	0.71
Colombian	3,872	4.40
Ecuadorian	493	0.56
Paraguayan	64	0.07
Peruvian	1,630	1.85
Uruguayan	222	0.25
Venezuelan	1,572	1.79
Other South American	257	0.29
Other Hispanic or Latino	8,414	9.57
Hungarian	897	1.02
Iranian	106	0.12
Irish	2,881	3.27
Israeli	237	0.27
Italian	4,441	5.04
Latvian	96	0.11
Lithuanian	263	0.30
New Zealander	11	0.01
Northern European	18	0.02
Norwegian	283	0.32
Pennsylvania German	7	0.01
Polish	2,533	2.88
Portuguese	655	0.74
Romanian	400	0.45
Russian	3,286	3.73
Scandinavian	40	0.05
Scotch-Irish	301	0.34
Scottish	611	0.69
Serbian	24	0.03
Slavic	20	0.02
Slovak	86	0.10
Slovene	6	0.01
Swedish	244	0.28
Swiss	116	0.13
Turkish	342	0.39
Ukrainian	460	0.52
United States or American	4,437	5.04
Welsh	227	0.26
West Indian, excl. Hispanic:	1,240	1.41
Bahamian	39	0.04
Belizean	21	0.02
British West Indian	36	0.04
Haitian	422	0.48
Jamaican	527	0.60
Trinidadian and Tobagonian	114	0.13
West Indian	52	0.06
Other West Indian	29	0.03
White:	78,945	89.78
Not Hispanic (35,959)	36,764	41.81
Hispanic (40,317)	42,181	47.97
Yugoslavian	135	0.15

Miami Lakes

Place Type: Census Designated Place
County: Miami-Dade
Population: 22,676

Ancestry/Race	Number	%
Acadian/Cajun	8	0.04
African American/Black:	729	3.21
Not Hispanic (530)	575	2.54
Hispanic (105)	154	0.68
African, sub-Saharan:	47	0.21
Nigerian	28	0.12
South African	19	0.08
Alaska Native tribes, specified:	2	0.01
Alaska Athabascan	1	0.00
Eskimo	1	0.00
Am. Ind. or Alaska Nat., not spec.	27	0.12
American Indian tribes, specified:	28	0.12
Cherokee (2)	7	0.03
Chickasaw	1	0.00
Creek (3)	3	0.01
Delaware	1	0.00
Latin American Indians (8)	11	0.05
Sioux (1)	1	0.00
All other tribes (1)	4	0.02
American Indian tribes, not spec.	4	0.02
Arab:	396	1.74
Arab/Arabic	261	1.15
Egyptian	8	0.04
Lebanese	86	0.38
Moroccan	7	0.03
Palestinian	23	0.10
Syrian	11	0.05
Armenian	6	0.03
Asian:	624	2.75
Chinese, ex. Taiwanese (164)	200	0.88
Filipino (62)	68	0.30
Indian (94)	121	0.53
Japanese (19)	27	0.12
Korean (72)	81	0.36
Pakistani (35)	60	0.26
Sri Lankan (3)	3	0.01
Taiwanese (11)	11	0.05
Thai (8)	9	0.04
Vietnamese (14)	15	0.07
Other Asian, not specified (6)	29	0.13
Austrian	19	0.08
Brazilian	133	0.59
British	34	0.15
Canadian	45	0.20
Croatian	16	0.07
Czech	67	0.29
Danish	16	0.07
Dutch	97	0.43
Eastern European	9	0.04
English	490	2.16
European	39	0.17
French, except Basque	282	1.24
French Canadian	11	0.05
German	862	3.79
Greek	41	0.18
Hawaii Native/Pacific Islander:	12	0.05
Polynesian: (5)	10	0.04
Native Hawaiian (3)	3	0.01
Samoan (2)	7	0.03
Other Pac. Isl., not spec. (1)	2	0.01
Hispanic or Latino:	15,083	66.52
Central American:	485	2.14
Costa Rican	37	0.16
Guatemalan	31	0.14
Honduran	70	0.31
Nicaraguan	243	1.07
Panamanian	68	0.30
Salvadoran	28	0.12
Other Central American	8	0.04
Cuban	9,588	42.28
Dominican Republic	375	1.65
Mexican	161	0.71
Puerto Rican	701	3.09
South American:	1,879	8.29
Argentinean	100	0.44
Bolivian	24	0.11
Chilean	95	0.42
Colombian	1,005	4.43
Ecuadorian	170	0.75
Paraguayan	1	0.00
Peruvian	215	0.95
Uruguayan	12	0.05
Venezuelan	240	1.06
Other South American	17	0.07

Notes: 1. Figures in the "Number" column do not add up to the total population due to: a) Ancestry/Race overlap — e.g. persons can report being both White and Irish, b) persons of Hispanic origin can report being any race, c) persons reporting two ancestries are counted in both categories. 2. Numbers in parentheses indicate the number of persons reporting this ancestry/race alone, not in combination with any other ancestry/race. 3. Refer to the Explanation of Data in the front of the book for more detailed information.

Ancestry/Race	Number	%
Other Hispanic or Latino	1,894	8.35
Hungarian	66	0.29
Iranian	18	0.08
Irish	987	4.34
Israeli	14	0.06
Italian	784	3.45
Lithuanian	53	0.23
Maltese	6	0.03
Norwegian	53	0.23
Polish	133	0.59
Portuguese	102	0.45
Romanian	15	0.07
Russian	87	0.38
Scotch-Irish	113	0.50
Scottish	143	0.63
Slavic	15	0.07
Slovak	33	0.15
Swedish	76	0.33
Swiss	35	0.15
Turkish	40	0.18
Ukrainian	23	0.10
United States or American	870	3.83
Welsh	28	0.12
West Indian, excl. Hispanic:	125	0.55
Bahamian	22	0.10
Dutch West Indian	14	0.06
Haitian	9	0.04
Jamaican	64	0.28
Trinidadian and Tobagonian	9	0.04
U.S. Virgin Islander	7	0.03
White:	20,791	91.69
Not Hispanic (6,362)	6,493	28.63
Hispanic (13,877)	14,298	63.05
Yugoslavian	13	0.06

Miami Shores

Place Type: Village
County: Miami-Dade
Population: 10,380

Ancestry/Race	Number	%
African American/Black:	2,816	27.13
Not Hispanic (2,440)	2,688	25.90
Hispanic (101)	128	1.23
African, sub-Saharan:	88	0.84
African	66	0.63
Kenyan	22	0.21
Am. Ind. or Alaska Nat., not spec.	8	0.08
Albanian	6	0.06
American Indian tribes, specified:	22	0.21
Apache	2	0.02
Cherokee	6	0.06
Choctaw	1	0.01
Creek (1)	1	0.01
Kiowa (1)	1	0.01
Latin American Indians (3)	6	0.06
Seminole (1)	3	0.03
Sioux	1	0.01
All other tribes	1	0.01
American Indian tribes, not spec.	1	0.01
Arab:	51	0.49
Arab/Arabic	5	0.05
Lebanese	28	0.27
Palestinian	7	0.07
Syrian	11	0.11
Armenian	32	0.31
Asian:	355	3.42
Chinese, ex. Taiwanese (48)	80	0.77
Filipino (86)	116	1.12
Indian (59)	70	0.67
Indonesian	2	0.02
Japanese (9)	23	0.22
Korean (8)	8	0.08
Pakistani (4)	4	0.04
Taiwanese (4)	9	0.09
Thai (16)	16	0.15
Vietnamese (5)	8	0.08
Other Asian, not specified (4)	19	0.18
Australian	13	0.12
Austrian	39	0.37
Basque	8	0.08
Belgian	10	0.10
Brazilian	47	0.45
British	36	0.34
Canadian	36	0.34
Cypriot	7	0.07
Czech	31	0.30
Czechoslovakian	16	0.15
Danish	44	0.42
Dutch	91	0.87
Eastern European	9	0.09
English	769	7.36
European	95	0.91
French, except Basque	274	2.62
French Canadian	112	1.07
German	963	9.22
Greek	41	0.39
Guyanese	11	0.11
Hawaii Native/Pacific Islander:	27	0.26
Polynesian: (2)	5	0.05
Native Hawaiian	1	0.01
Samoan (1)	2	0.02
Other Polynesian (1)	2	0.02
Other Pac. Isl., not spec. (6)	22	0.21
Hispanic or Latino:	2,257	21.74
Central American:	241	2.32
Costa Rican	19	0.18
Guatemalan	45	0.43
Honduran	64	0.62
Nicaraguan	76	0.73
Panamanian	24	0.23
Salvadoran	12	0.12
Other Central American	1	0.01
Cuban	651	6.27
Dominican Republic	133	1.28
Mexican	61	0.59
Puerto Rican	345	3.32
South American:	405	3.90
Argentinean	48	0.46
Bolivian	5	0.05
Chilean	27	0.26
Colombian	170	1.64
Ecuadorian	17	0.16
Paraguayan	1	0.01
Peruvian	67	0.65
Uruguayan	5	0.05
Venezuelan	51	0.49
Other South American	14	0.13
Other Hispanic or Latino	421	4.06
Hungarian	104	1.00
Irish	1,234	11.82
Italian	831	7.96
Latvian	7	0.07
Lithuanian	30	0.29
Northern European	11	0.11
Norwegian	17	0.16
Polish	308	2.95
Portuguese	66	0.63
Russian	81	0.78
Scotch-Irish	149	1.43
Scottish	212	2.03
Slavic	13	0.12
Slovak	13	0.12
Slovene	17	0.16
Swedish	186	1.78
Swiss	58	0.56
Ukrainian	20	0.19
United States or American	319	3.05
Welsh	51	0.49
West Indian, excl. Hispanic:	1,377	13.19
Bahamian	29	0.28
Barbadian	6	0.06
British West Indian	5	0.05
Dutch West Indian	14	0.13
Haitian	969	9.28
Jamaican	242	2.32
Trinidadian and Tobagonian	47	0.45
U.S. Virgin Islander	7	0.07
West Indian	58	0.56
White:	7,054	67.96
Not Hispanic (5,043)	5,185	49.95
Hispanic (1,710)	1,869	18.01

Miami Springs

Place Type: City
County: Miami-Dade
Population: 13,712

Ancestry/Race	Number	%
African American/Black:	335	2.44
Not Hispanic (163)	194	1.41
Hispanic (117)	141	1.03
African, sub-Saharan:	3	0.02
African	3	0.02
Am. Ind. or Alaska Nat., not spec.	24	0.18
American Indian tribes, specified:	44	0.32
Blackfeet (1)	1	0.01
Cherokee (11)	26	0.19
Chickasaw (1)	1	0.01
Chippewa (1)	2	0.01
Cree (1)	1	0.01
Creek	1	0.01
Latin American Indians (4)	10	0.07
All other tribes (1)	2	0.01
American Indian tribes, not spec.	9	0.07
Arab:	89	0.65
Iraqi	29	0.21
Lebanese	33	0.24
Palestinian	10	0.07
Syrian	17	0.12
Armenian	6	0.04
Asian:	228	1.66
Chinese, ex. Taiwanese (31)	43	0.31
Filipino (18)	26	0.19
Indian (61)	82	0.60
Indonesian	3	0.02
Japanese (10)	13	0.09
Korean (2)	3	0.02
Pakistani (20)	28	0.20
Sri Lankan	3	0.02
Taiwanese (1)	1	0.01
Thai (4)	5	0.04
Vietnamese (5)	9	0.07
Other Asian, not specified (5)	12	0.09
Australian	7	0.05
Austrian	45	0.33
Brazilian	62	0.45
British	97	0.71
Canadian	59	0.43
Croatian	12	0.09
Czech	84	0.61
Czechoslovakian	21	0.15
Danish	51	0.37
Dutch	74	0.54
Eastern European	8	0.06
English	800	5.85
European	14	0.10
Finnish	11	0.08
French, except Basque	221	1.62
French Canadian	57	0.42
German	955	6.98
Greek	39	0.29
Hawaii Native/Pacific Islander:	8	0.06
Micronesian: (4)	4	0.03
Guamanian/Chamorro (2)	2	0.01
Other Micronesian (2)	2	0.01
Polynesian: (1)	1	0.01
Native Hawaiian (1)	1	0.01
Other Pac. Isl., not spec.	3	0.02
Hispanic or Latino:	8,173	59.60
Central American:	643	4.69
Costa Rican	109	0.79
Guatemalan	39	0.28
Honduran	129	0.94
Nicaraguan	283	2.06
Panamanian	25	0.18
Salvadoran	46	0.34
Other Central American	12	0.09

Notes: 1. Figures in the "Number" column do not add up to the total population due to: a) Ancestry/Race overlap — e.g. persons can report being both White and Irish, b) persons of Hispanic origin can report being any race, c) persons reporting two ancestries are counted in both categories. 2. Numbers in parentheses indicate the number of persons reporting this ancestry/race alone, not in combination with any other ancestry/race. 3. Refer to the Explanation of Data in the front of the book for more detailed information.

Ancestry/Race	Number	%
Cuban	4,364	31.83
Dominican Republic	158	1.15
Mexican	110	0.80
Puerto Rican	500	3.65
South American:	1,228	8.96
Argentinean	73	0.53
Bolivian	31	0.23
Chilean	46	0.34
Colombian	533	3.89
Ecuadorian	101	0.74
Paraguayan	7	0.05
Peruvian	260	1.90
Uruguayan	9	0.07
Venezuelan	139	1.01
Other South American	29	0.21
Other Hispanic or Latino	1,170	8.53
Hungarian	74	0.54
Icelander	24	0.18
Irish	858	6.27
Israeli	7	0.05
Italian	447	3.27
Lithuanian	59	0.43
Maltese	12	0.09
Norwegian	33	0.24
Pennsylvania German	15	0.11
Polish	172	1.26
Portuguese	26	0.19
Romanian	7	0.05
Russian	70	0.51
Scandinavian	18	0.13
Scotch-Irish	108	0.79
Scottish	169	1.24
Slovak	7	0.05
Swedish	100	0.73
Swiss	51	0.37
Ukrainian	19	0.14
United States or American	592	4.33
Welsh	16	0.12
West Indian, excl. Hispanic:	126	0.92
Bahamian	16	0.12
Belizean	25	0.18
Haitian	19	0.14
Jamaican	31	0.23
Trinidadian and Tobagonian	21	0.15
West Indian	6	0.04
Other West Indian	8	0.06
White:	12,765	93.09
Not Hispanic (5,073)	5,151	37.57
Hispanic (7,379)	7,614	55.53

Miami

Place Type: City
County: Miami-Dade
Population: 362,470

Ancestry/Race	Number	%
African American/Black:	87,857	24.24
Not Hispanic (72,190)	77,247	21.31
Hispanic (8,668)	10,610	2.93
African, sub-Saharan:	2,816	0.78
African	2,661	0.73
Ethiopian	8	0.00
Ghanian	7	0.00
Liberian	9	0.00
Nigerian	99	0.03
Sudanese	6	0.00
Zairian	7	0.00
Zimbabwean	12	0.00
Other sub-Saharan African	7	0.00
Alaska Native tribes, specified:	11	0.00
Eskimo	5	0.00
Tlingit-Haida	6	0.00
Alaska Native tribes, not specified	1	0.00
Am. Ind. or Alaska Nat., not spec.	897	0.25
Albanian	38	0.01
Alsatian	11	0.00
American Indian tribes, specified:	825	0.23
Apache (1)	4	0.00
Blackfeet (1)	11	0.00
Cherokee (34)	93	0.03
Chickasaw (1)	1	0.00
Chippewa	2	0.00
Choctaw (1)	6	0.00
Comanche	1	0.00
Creek (1)	12	0.00
Delaware	1	0.00
Iroquois (3)	14	0.00
Kiowa	1	0.00
Latin American Indians (191)	535	0.15
Lumbee (4)	7	0.00
Menominee	1	0.00
Navajo (2)	3	0.00
Osage (1)	1	0.00
Pima	1	0.00
Pueblo (5)	42	0.01
Seminole (1)	4	0.00
Shoshone	6	0.00
Sioux (6)	8	0.00
Yakama	1	0.00
All other tribes (17)	70	0.02
American Indian tribes, not spec.	157	0.04
Arab:	1,864	0.51
Arab/Arabic	333	0.09
Egyptian	10	0.00
Iraqi	89	0.02
Jordanian	55	0.02
Lebanese	855	0.24
Moroccan	80	0.02
Palestinian	119	0.03
Syrian	236	0.07
Other Arab	87	0.02
Armenian	138	0.04
Asian:	3,238	0.89
Bangladeshi (11)	12	0.00
Cambodian (4)	4	0.00
Chinese, ex. Taiwanese (813)	1,021	0.28
Filipino (382)	454	0.13
Indian (629)	859	0.24
Indonesian (17)	39	0.01
Japanese (124)	156	0.04
Korean (83)	115	0.03
Laotian (2)	2	0.00
Malaysian (3)	7	0.00
Pakistani (36)	56	0.02
Sri Lankan (4)	7	0.00
Taiwanese (31)	33	0.01
Thai (20)	32	0.01
Vietnamese (90)	117	0.03
Other Asian, specified (2)	26	0.01
Other Asian, not specified (83)	298	0.08
Assyrian/Chaldean/Syriac	5	0.00
Australian	94	0.03
Austrian	421	0.12
Basque	118	0.03
Belgian	79	0.02
Brazilian	802	0.22
British	414	0.11
Bulgarian	74	0.02
Canadian	377	0.10
Celtic	7	0.00
Croatian	73	0.02
Czech	158	0.04
Czechoslovakian	109	0.03
Danish	242	0.07
Dutch	573	0.16
Eastern European	160	0.04
English	3,893	1.07
European	637	0.18
Finnish	37	0.01
French, except Basque	2,799	0.77
French Canadian	247	0.07
German	4,411	1.22
Greek	628	0.17
Guyanese	53	0.01
Hawaii Native/Pacific Islander:	681	0.19
Micronesian: (34)	48	0.01
Guamanian/Chamorro (34)	45	0.01
Other Micronesian	3	0.00
Polynesian: (40)	103	0.03
Native Hawaiian (19)	71	0.02
Samoan (15)	25	0.01
Tongan (5)	5	0.00
Other Polynesian (1)	2	0.00
Other Pac. Isl., specified	21	0.01
Other Pac. Isl., not spec. (55)	509	0.14
Hispanic or Latino:	238,351	65.76
Central American:	40,158	11.08
Costa Rican	775	0.21
Guatemalan	2,475	0.68
Honduran	12,118	3.34
Nicaraguan	20,543	5.67
Panamanian	657	0.18
Salvadoran	2,482	0.68
Other Central American	1,108	0.31
Cuban	123,763	34.14
Dominican Republic	6,370	1.76
Mexican	3,669	1.01
Puerto Rican	10,257	2.83
South American:	15,076	4.16
Argentinean	1,669	0.46
Bolivian	355	0.10
Chilean	939	0.26
Colombian	5,784	1.60
Ecuadorian	1,408	0.39
Paraguayan	45	0.01
Peruvian	2,447	0.68
Uruguayan	221	0.06
Venezuelan	1,959	0.54
Other South American	249	0.07
Other Hispanic or Latino	39,058	10.78
Hungarian	457	0.13
Icelander	36	0.01
Iranian	111	0.03
Irish	3,626	1.00
Israeli	142	0.04
Italian	5,169	1.43
Latvian	81	0.02
Lithuanian	233	0.06
Macedonian	20	0.01
Northern European	7	0.00
Norwegian	380	0.10
Pennsylvania German	11	0.00
Polish	1,492	0.41
Portuguese	488	0.13
Romanian	208	0.06
Russian	1,888	0.52
Scandinavian	63	0.02
Scotch-Irish	663	0.18
Scottish	1,019	0.28
Serbian	42	0.01
Slavic	35	0.01
Slovak	53	0.01
Swedish	389	0.11
Swiss	170	0.05
Turkish	160	0.04
Ukrainian	202	0.06
United States or American	11,317	3.12
Welsh	333	0.09
West Indian, excl. Hispanic:	22,904	6.32
Bahamian	1,470	0.41
Barbadian	13	0.00
Belizean	105	0.03
British West Indian	189	0.05
Dutch West Indian	27	0.01
Haitian	18,309	5.05
Jamaican	2,080	0.57
Trinidadian and Tobagonian	229	0.06
U.S. Virgin Islander	107	0.03
West Indian	350	0.10
Other West Indian	25	0.01
White:	251,993	69.52
Not Hispanic (42,897)	44,105	12.17
Hispanic (198,573)	207,888	57.35
Yugoslavian	91	0.03

Notes: 1. Figures in the "Number" column do not add up to the total population due to: a) Ancestry/Race overlap — e.g. persons can report being both White and Irish, b) persons of Hispanic origin can report being any race, c) persons reporting two ancestries are counted in both categories. 2. Numbers in parentheses indicate the number of persons reporting this ancestry/race alone, not in combination with any other ancestry/race. 3. Refer to the Explanation of Data in the front of the book for more detailed information.

Middleburg

Place Type: Census Designated Place
County: Clay
Population: 10,338

Ancestry/Race	Number	%
African American/Black:	371	3.59
Not Hispanic (329)	361	3.49
Hispanic (5)	10	0.10
African, sub-Saharan:	41	0.39
African	41	0.39
Am. Ind. or Alaska Nat., not spec.	25	0.24
American Indian tribes, specified:	145	1.40
Apache (3)	10	0.10
Blackfeet (4)	5	0.05
Cherokee (24)	77	0.74
Chickasaw (1)	1	0.01
Choctaw (1)	5	0.05
Creek	2	0.02
Crow	2	0.02
Delaware	1	0.01
Iroquois (2)	8	0.08
Latin American Indians (1)	1	0.01
Lumbee	1	0.01
Menominee (4)	4	0.04
Pueblo	1	0.01
Seminole	6	0.06
Sioux	5	0.05
All other tribes (10)	16	0.15
American Indian tribes, not spec.	7	0.07
Asian:	109	1.05
Bangladeshi (5)	5	0.05
Chinese, ex. Taiwanese (3)	3	0.03
Filipino (33)	60	0.58
Indian (2)	3	0.03
Japanese (6)	12	0.12
Korean (3)	6	0.06
Pakistani (8)	8	0.08
Vietnamese (2)	5	0.05
Other Asian, specified	4	0.04
Other Asian, not specified	3	0.03
Austrian	14	0.13
British	29	0.28
Canadian	29	0.28
Celtic	5	0.05
Czechoslovakian	10	0.10
Danish	79	0.76
Dutch	116	1.11
English	1,390	13.36
European	72	0.69
Finnish	42	0.40
French, except Basque	610	5.86
French Canadian	134	1.29
German	1,473	14.16
Greek	19	0.18
Hawaii Native/Pacific Islander:	20	0.19
Micronesian: (3)	3	0.03
Guamanian/Chamorro (1)	1	0.01
Other Micronesian (2)	2	0.02
Polynesian: (2)	10	0.10
Native Hawaiian (2)	10	0.10
Other Pac. Isl., specified	4	0.04
Other Pac. Isl., not spec.	3	0.03
Hispanic or Latino:	266	2.57
Central American:	10	0.10
Guatemalan	2	0.02
Honduran	3	0.03
Panamanian	4	0.04
Salvadoran	1	0.01
Cuban	19	0.18
Dominican Republic	4	0.04
Mexican	69	0.67
Puerto Rican	97	0.94
South American:	7	0.07
Chilean	5	0.05
Peruvian	2	0.02
Other Hispanic or Latino	60	0.58
Hungarian	27	0.26
Irish	1,367	13.14
Italian	439	4.22
Lithuanian	6	0.06
Norwegian	108	1.04
Polish	273	2.62
Portuguese	47	0.45
Romanian	25	0.24
Russian	38	0.37
Scotch-Irish	182	1.75
Scottish	174	1.67
Slavic	6	0.06
Slovak	35	0.34
Swedish	125	1.20
Ukrainian	8	0.08
United States or American	1,502	14.43
Welsh	43	0.41
White:	9,765	94.46
Not Hispanic (9,460)	9,579	92.66
Hispanic (172)	186	1.80
Yugoslavian	29	0.28

Miramar

Place Type: City
County: Broward
Population: 72,739

Ancestry/Race	Number	%
African American/Black:	33,627	46.23
Not Hispanic (30,561)	32,317	44.43
Hispanic (937)	1,310	1.80
African, sub-Saharan:	818	1.13
African	514	0.71
Nigerian	267	0.37
South African	16	0.02
Sudanese	16	0.02
Other sub-Saharan African	5	0.01
Alaska Native tribes, specified:	3	0.00
Aleut	1	0.00
Eskimo	1	0.00
Tlingit-Haida	1	0.00
Am. Ind. or Alaska Nat., not spec.	134	0.18
Albanian	9	0.01
American Indian tribes, specified:	163	0.22
Apache	3	0.00
Blackfeet	12	0.02
Cherokee (12)	49	0.07
Chippewa (3)	5	0.01
Choctaw (1)	2	0.00
Creek (2)	10	0.01
Iroquois	7	0.01
Latin American Indians (16)	46	0.06
Lumbee (1)	1	0.00
Pueblo	1	0.00
Seminole (1)	3	0.00
Shoshone (2)	2	0.00
Sioux (1)	3	0.00
All other tribes (5)	19	0.03
American Indian tribes, not spec.	23	0.03
Arab:	167	0.23
Arab/Arabic	76	0.10
Jordanian	12	0.02
Lebanese	36	0.05
Syrian	36	0.05
Other Arab	7	0.01
Armenian	14	0.02
Asian:	2,893	3.98
Bangladeshi (12)	12	0.02
Cambodian (10)	13	0.02
Chinese, ex. Taiwanese (413)	618	0.85
Filipino (526)	586	0.81
Indian (828)	1,055	1.45
Indonesian (3)	10	0.01
Japanese (28)	48	0.07
Korean (54)	69	0.09
Laotian	3	0.00
Pakistani (63)	125	0.17
Sri Lankan (2)	2	0.00
Taiwanese (4)	4	0.01
Thai (18)	26	0.04
Vietnamese (179)	198	0.27
Other Asian, specified (1)	4	0.01
Other Asian, not specified (36)	120	0.16
Australian	5	0.01
Austrian	129	0.18
Belgian	18	0.02
Brazilian	242	0.33
British	334	0.46
Bulgarian	7	0.01
Canadian	168	0.23
Croatian	7	0.01
Czech	69	0.09
Czechoslovakian	82	0.11
Danish	104	0.14
Dutch	258	0.36
Eastern European	39	0.05
English	1,704	2.34
European	90	0.12
Finnish	7	0.01
French, except Basque	688	0.95
French Canadian	276	0.38
German	2,838	3.91
Greek	128	0.18
Guyanese	469	0.65
Hawaii Native/Pacific Islander:	251	0.35
Micronesian: (4)	8	0.01
Guamanian/Chamorro (4)	5	0.01
Other Micronesian	3	0.00
Polynesian: (23)	34	0.05
Native Hawaiian (17)	23	0.03
Samoan (6)	9	0.01
Other Polynesian	2	0.00
Other Pac. Isl., not spec. (45)	209	0.29
Hispanic or Latino:	21,374	29.38
Central American:	1,622	2.23
Costa Rican	122	0.17
Guatemalan	130	0.18
Honduran	287	0.39
Nicaraguan	589	0.81
Panamanian	336	0.46
Salvadoran	86	0.12
Other Central American	72	0.10
Cuban	6,377	8.77
Dominican Republic	1,439	1.98
Mexican	469	0.64
Puerto Rican	3,800	5.22
South American:	3,696	5.08
Argentinean	149	0.20
Bolivian	16	0.02
Chilean	143	0.20
Colombian	1,827	2.51
Ecuadorian	297	0.41
Paraguayan	1	0.00
Peruvian	614	0.84
Uruguayan	45	0.06
Venezuelan	499	0.69
Other South American	105	0.14
Other Hispanic or Latino	3,971	5.46
Hungarian	271	0.37
Iranian	11	0.02
Irish	2,206	3.04
Israeli	28	0.04
Italian	2,795	3.85
Lithuanian	83	0.11
New Zealander	10	0.01
Norwegian	128	0.18
Polish	668	0.92
Portuguese	122	0.17
Romanian	222	0.31
Russian	340	0.47
Scandinavian	13	0.02
Scotch-Irish	324	0.45
Scottish	204	0.28
Slavic	8	0.01
Swedish	189	0.26
Swiss	43	0.06
Ukrainian	48	0.07
United States or American	3,565	4.91
Welsh	34	0.05
West Indian, excl. Hispanic:	18,445	25.38
Bahamian	578	0.80

Notes: 1. Figures in the "Number" column do not add up to the total population due to: a) Ancestry/Race overlap — e.g. persons can report being both White and Irish, b) persons of Hispanic origin can report being any race, c) persons reporting two ancestries are counted in both categories. 2. Numbers in parentheses indicate the number of persons reporting this ancestry/race alone, not in combination with any other ancestry/race. 3. Refer to the Explanation of Data in the front of the book for more detailed information.

Barbadian	139	0.19
Belizean	42	0.06
Bermudan	11	0.02
British West Indian	428	0.59
Dutch West Indian	10	0.01
Haitian	4,359	6.00
Jamaican	11,263	15.50
Trinidadian and Tobagonian	897	1.23
U.S. Virgin Islander	207	0.28
West Indian	493	0.68
Other West Indian	18	0.02
White:	33,571	46.15
Not Hispanic (15,716)	16,444	22.61
Hispanic (15,988)	17,127	23.55
Yugoslavian	48	0.07

Myrtle Grove

Place Type: Census Designated Place
County: Escambia
Population: 17,211

Ancestry/Race	Number	%
Acadian/Cajun	15	0.09
African American/Black:	2,489	14.46
Not Hispanic (2,282)	2,426	14.10
Hispanic (40)	63	0.37
African, sub-Saharan:	20	0.12
African	20	0.12
Alaska Native tribes, specified:	3	0.02
Alaska Athabascan (2)	2	0.01
Aleut (1)	1	0.01
Am. Ind. or Alaska Nat., not spec.	90	0.52
American Indian tribes, specified:	245	1.42
Apache (1)	4	0.02
Blackfeet (4)	9	0.05
Cherokee (24)	74	0.43
Chippewa (3)	6	0.03
Choctaw (1)	5	0.03
Comanche (3)	3	0.02
Creek (41)	76	0.44
Crow (1)	1	0.01
Houma (3)	3	0.02
Iroquois (2)	13	0.08
Kiowa	1	0.01
Latin American Indians (1)	6	0.03
Lumbee (1)	1	0.01
Menominee (1)	1	0.01
Navajo (6)	10	0.06
Osage	1	0.01
Potawatomi (1)	4	0.02
Pueblo	4	0.02
Seminole	4	0.02
Shoshone (1)	1	0.01
Sioux (2)	3	0.02
Tohono O'Odham	1	0.01
Yaqui	1	0.01
All other tribes (4)	13	0.08
American Indian tribes, not spec.	14	0.08
Arab:	76	0.44
Arab/Arabic	29	0.17
Lebanese	7	0.04
Other Arab	40	0.23
Asian:	1,107	6.43
Cambodian (1)	1	0.01
Chinese, ex. Taiwanese (35)	51	0.30
Filipino (527)	683	3.97
Indian (36)	45	0.26
Indonesian (2)	2	0.01
Japanese (42)	68	0.40
Korean (31)	43	0.25
Laotian (1)	1	0.01
Thai (6)	8	0.05
Vietnamese (162)	178	1.03
Other Asian, specified	3	0.02
Other Asian, not specified (7)	24	0.14
Austrian	20	0.12
Belgian	14	0.08
Brazilian	29	0.17
British	66	0.38
Canadian	34	0.20
Celtic	11	0.06
Croatian	6	0.03
Czech	21	0.12
Danish	19	0.11
Dutch	215	1.24
Eastern European	9	0.05
English	1,588	9.18
European	178	1.03
Finnish	35	0.20
French, except Basque	574	3.32
French Canadian	95	0.55
German	2,144	12.39
Greek	63	0.36
Hawaii Native/Pacific Islander:	102	0.59
Micronesian: (13)	31	0.18
Guamanian/Chamorro (12)	27	0.16
Other Micronesian (1)	4	0.02
Polynesian: (29)	48	0.28
Native Hawaiian (12)	23	0.13
Samoan (16)	23	0.13
Tongan (1)	1	0.01
Other Polynesian	1	0.01
Other Pac. Isl., not spec. (9)	23	0.13
Hispanic or Latino:	740	4.30
Central American:	41	0.24
Costa Rican	8	0.05
Guatemalan	1	0.01
Honduran	1	0.01
Nicaraguan	2	0.01
Panamanian	26	0.15
Salvadoran	3	0.02
Cuban	29	0.17
Dominican Republic	10	0.06
Mexican	316	1.84
Puerto Rican	169	0.98
South American:	26	0.15
Argentinean	2	0.01
Bolivian	2	0.01
Colombian	9	0.05
Ecuadorian	3	0.02
Uruguayan	1	0.01
Venezuelan	9	0.05
Other Hispanic or Latino	149	0.87
Hungarian	7	0.04
Irish	2,153	12.44
Israeli	5	0.03
Italian	691	3.99
Lithuanian	18	0.10
Northern European	24	0.14
Norwegian	216	1.25
Polish	286	1.65
Portuguese	109	0.63
Romanian	7	0.04
Russian	103	0.60
Scandinavian	13	0.08
Scotch-Irish	446	2.58
Scottish	376	2.17
Soviet Union	5	0.03
Swedish	184	1.06
Swiss	9	0.05
Ukrainian	39	0.23
United States or American	1,641	9.48
Welsh	87	0.50
West Indian, excl. Hispanic:	61	0.35
Bahamian	5	0.03
Barbadian	7	0.04
Haitian	8	0.05
Jamaican	32	0.18
West Indian	9	0.05
White:	13,428	78.02
Not Hispanic (12,631)	13,039	75.76
Hispanic (319)	389	2.26
Yugoslavian	12	0.07

Naples

Place Type: City
County: Collier
Population: 20,976

Ancestry/Race	Number	%
African American/Black:	1,310	6.25
Not Hispanic (953)	1,285	6.13
Hispanic (22)	25	0.12
African, sub-Saharan:	47	0.22
African	15	0.07
South African	32	0.15
Alaska Native tribes, specified:	2	0.01
Tlingit-Haida	1	0.00
All other tribes (1)	1	0.00
Am. Ind. or Alaska Nat., not spec.	37	0.18
Alsatian	14	0.07
American Indian tribes, specified:	29	0.14
Apache (1)	1	0.00
Blackfeet	1	0.00
Cherokee (7)	14	0.07
Chippewa (1)	3	0.01
Choctaw	1	0.00
Creek (1)	1	0.00
Iroquois	1	0.00
Latin American Indians (1)	1	0.00
Navajo	1	0.00
Yaqui	2	0.01
All other tribes (2)	3	0.01
American Indian tribes, not spec.	9	0.04
Arab:	58	0.28
Arab/Arabic	23	0.11
Lebanese	20	0.10
Syrian	15	0.07
Armenian	46	0.22
Asian:	95	0.45
Bangladeshi (1)	1	0.00
Cambodian (1)	1	0.00
Chinese, ex. Taiwanese (22)	25	0.12
Filipino (7)	13	0.06
Indian (14)	23	0.11
Indonesian (1)	1	0.00
Japanese (3)	6	0.03
Korean (15)	16	0.08
Thai (2)	3	0.01
Vietnamese (3)	4	0.02
Other Asian, not specified (1)	2	0.01
Australian	7	0.03
Austrian	128	0.61
Belgian	72	0.34
Brazilian	19	0.09
British	238	1.13
Canadian	143	0.68
Croatian	19	0.09
Czech	88	0.42
Czechoslovakian	38	0.18
Danish	168	0.80
Dutch	454	2.16
Eastern European	14	0.07
English	3,920	18.68
Estonian	10	0.05
European	154	0.73
Finnish	47	0.22
French, except Basque	888	4.23
French Canadian	188	0.90
German	4,191	19.97
Greek	141	0.67
Hawaii Native/Pacific Islander:	15	0.07
Micronesian: (1)	2	0.01
Guamanian/Chamorro (1)	2	0.01
Polynesian: (3)	5	0.02
Native Hawaiian (1)	2	0.01
Samoan (2)	2	0.01
Tongan	1	0.00
Other Pac. Isl., not spec. (1)	8	0.04
Hispanic or Latino:	467	2.23
Central American:	17	0.08
Costa Rican	4	0.02
Guatemalan	7	0.03

Notes: 1. Figures in the "Number" column do not add up to the total population due to: a) Ancestry/Race overlap — e.g. persons can report being both White and Irish, b) persons of Hispanic origin can report being any race, c) persons reporting two ancestries are counted in both categories. 2. Numbers in parentheses indicate the number of persons reporting this ancestry/race alone, not in combination with any other ancestry/race. 3. Refer to the Explanation of Data in the front of the book for more detailed information.

Honduran	1	0.00
Nicaraguan	2	0.01
Panamanian	2	0.01
Other Central American	1	0.00
Cuban	155	0.74
Dominican Republic	7	0.03
Mexican	87	0.41
Puerto Rican	49	0.23
South American:	44	0.21
Argentinean	10	0.05
Bolivian	2	0.01
Chilean	2	0.01
Colombian	15	0.07
Ecuadorian	1	0.00
Paraguayan	5	0.02
Peruvian	2	0.01
Uruguayan	3	0.01
Venezuelan	4	0.02
Other Hispanic or Latino	108	0.51
Hungarian	280	1.33
Irish	3,246	15.47
Italian	1,522	7.25
Lithuanian	102	0.49
Luxemburger	7	0.03
Maltese	12	0.06
Northern European	7	0.03
Norwegian	428	2.04
Pennsylvania German	14	0.07
Polish	625	2.98
Portuguese	46	0.22
Romanian	65	0.31
Russian	234	1.11
Scandinavian	31	0.15
Scotch-Irish	670	3.19
Scottish	921	4.39
Slovak	77	0.37
Swedish	654	3.12
Swiss	213	1.01
Ukrainian	93	0.44
United States or American	1,180	5.62
Welsh	303	1.44
West Indian, excl. Hispanic:	278	1.32
Bahamian	37	0.18
Haitian	234	1.11
Trinidadian and Tobagonian	7	0.03
White:	19,510	93.01
Not Hispanic (19,048)	19,131	91.20
Hispanic (354)	379	1.81
Yugoslavian	20	0.10

New Port Richey

Place Type: City
County: Pasco
Population: 16,117

Ancestry/Race	Number	%
African American/Black:	193	1.20
Not Hispanic (145)	173	1.07
Hispanic (16)	20	0.12
African, sub-Saharan:	15	0.10
African	15	0.10
Am. Ind. or Alaska Nat., not spec.	69	0.43
American Indian tribes, specified:	125	0.78
Apache (2)	2	0.01
Blackfeet (2)	15	0.09
Cherokee (18)	56	0.35
Chippewa (4)	6	0.04
Choctaw (2)	3	0.02
Creek	4	0.02
Delaware	3	0.02
Iroquois (2)	4	0.02
Latin American Indians (5)	5	0.03
Lumbee (1)	1	0.01
Menominee (3)	3	0.02
Navajo (2)	2	0.01
Ottawa (1)	1	0.01
Sioux (5)	8	0.05
All other tribes	12	0.07
American Indian tribes, not spec.	12	0.07
Arab:	23	0.15
Lebanese	23	0.15
Armenian	5	0.03
Asian:	231	1.43
Cambodian (1)	1	0.01
Chinese, ex. Taiwanese (20)	28	0.17
Filipino (42)	65	0.40
Indian (17)	25	0.16
Indonesian (1)	1	0.01
Japanese (5)	8	0.05
Korean (5)	5	0.03
Laotian (1)	5	0.03
Pakistani (1)	1	0.01
Thai	3	0.02
Vietnamese (56)	72	0.45
Other Asian, specified	1	0.01
Other Asian, not specified (2)	16	0.10
Austrian	50	0.32
British	32	0.20
Bulgarian	29	0.18
Canadian	37	0.24
Croatian	68	0.43
Czech	94	0.60
Czechoslovakian	17	0.11
Danish	69	0.44
Dutch	188	1.20
Eastern European	26	0.17
English	2,084	13.29
European	65	0.41
Finnish	35	0.22
French, except Basque	621	3.96
French Canadian	193	1.23
German	2,817	17.96
Greek	100	0.64
Hawaii Native/Pacific Islander:	20	0.12
Polynesian: (14)	17	0.11
Native Hawaiian (3)	6	0.04
Samoan (11)	11	0.07
Other Pac. Isl., specified	1	0.01
Other Pac. Isl., not spec.	2	0.01
Hispanic or Latino:	846	5.25
Central American:	34	0.21
Costa Rican	2	0.01
Guatemalan	7	0.04
Honduran	14	0.09
Nicaraguan	4	0.02
Panamanian	3	0.02
Salvadoran	2	0.01
Other Central American	2	0.01
Cuban	32	0.20
Dominican Republic	13	0.08
Mexican	279	1.73
Puerto Rican	332	2.06
South American:	63	0.39
Argentinean	2	0.01
Chilean	4	0.02
Colombian	24	0.15
Ecuadorian	13	0.08
Peruvian	13	0.08
Uruguayan	1	0.01
Other South American	6	0.04
Other Hispanic or Latino	93	0.58
Hungarian	113	0.72
Icelander	7	0.04
Irish	2,637	16.81
Italian	1,764	11.25
Lithuanian	31	0.20
Macedonian	10	0.06
Norwegian	167	1.06
Pennsylvania German	16	0.10
Polish	853	5.44
Portuguese	81	0.52
Romanian	18	0.11
Russian	134	0.85
Scandinavian	24	0.15
Scotch-Irish	204	1.30
Scottish	244	1.56
Serbian	35	0.22
Slavic	11	0.07
Slovak	61	0.39
Slovene	6	0.04
Swedish	274	1.75
Ukrainian	70	0.45
United States or American	1,433	9.14
Welsh	151	0.96
West Indian, excl. Hispanic:	86	0.55
Dutch West Indian	6	0.04
Haitian	36	0.23
Jamaican	44	0.28
White:	15,455	95.89
Not Hispanic (14,606)	14,865	92.23
Hispanic (559)	590	3.66
Yugoslavian	164	1.05

New Smyrna Beach

Place Type: City
County: Volusia
Population: 20,048

Ancestry/Race	Number	%
African American/Black:	1,331	6.64
Not Hispanic (1,250)	1,319	6.58
Hispanic (7)	12	0.06
African, sub-Saharan:	23	0.11
African	23	0.11
Alaska Native tribes, specified:	3	0.01
Eskimo	3	0.01
Am. Ind. or Alaska Nat., not spec.	33	0.16
American Indian tribes, specified:	115	0.57
Apache (1)	3	0.01
Blackfeet	5	0.02
Cherokee (11)	37	0.18
Cheyenne	1	0.00
Chippewa	7	0.03
Choctaw (2)	2	0.01
Comanche	4	0.02
Creek (2)	3	0.01
Delaware	1	0.00
Iroquois (10)	16	0.08
Kiowa (2)	2	0.01
Latin American Indians (2)	2	0.01
Lumbee (2)	3	0.01
Menominee (1)	1	0.00
Ottawa	1	0.00
Potawatomi (4)	4	0.02
Pueblo	1	0.00
Seminole (2)	2	0.01
Shoshone	4	0.02
Sioux (2)	2	0.01
Ute (3)	3	0.01
All other tribes (6)	11	0.05
American Indian tribes, not spec.	6	0.03
Arab:	117	0.58
Egyptian	42	0.21
Iraqi	8	0.04
Lebanese	56	0.28
Syrian	11	0.05
Asian:	122	0.61
Bangladeshi (3)	3	0.01
Chinese, ex. Taiwanese (27)	29	0.14
Filipino (15)	20	0.10
Indian (18)	22	0.11
Japanese (11)	18	0.09
Korean (16)	16	0.08
Laotian (1)	1	0.00
Thai (2)	2	0.01
Vietnamese (4)	5	0.02
Other Asian, not specified (2)	6	0.03
Australian	23	0.11
Austrian	83	0.41
Belgian	36	0.18
Brazilian	19	0.09
British	184	0.91
Canadian	62	0.31
Croatian	18	0.09
Czech	61	0.30
Czechoslovakian	50	0.25
Danish	156	0.77
Dutch	483	2.38

Notes: 1. Figures in the "Number" column do not add up to the total population due to: a) Ancestry/Race overlap — e.g. persons can report being both White and Irish, b) persons of Hispanic origin can report being any race, c) persons reporting two ancestries are counted in both categories. 2. Numbers in parentheses indicate the number of persons reporting this ancestry/race alone, not in combination with any other ancestry/race. 3. Refer to the Explanation of Data in the front of the book for more detailed information.

English	3,429	16.90
European	103	0.51
Finnish	53	0.26
French, except Basque	776	3.82
French Canadian	260	1.28
German	3,730	18.38
Greek	85	0.42
Hawaii Native/Pacific Islander:	10	0.05
Micronesian: (1)	1	0.00
Guamanian/Chamorro (1)	1	0.00
Polynesian: (4)	5	0.02
Native Hawaiian (3)	4	0.02
Samoan (1)	1	0.00
Other Pac. Isl., not spec. (2)	4	0.02
Hispanic or Latino:	301	1.50
Central American:	13	0.06
Costa Rican	4	0.02
Guatemalan	1	0.00
Honduran	3	0.01
Nicaraguan	2	0.01
Panamanian	3	0.01
Cuban	35	0.17
Dominican Republic	12	0.06
Mexican	79	0.39
Puerto Rican	73	0.36
South American:	44	0.22
Argentinean	5	0.02
Bolivian	4	0.02
Chilean	4	0.02
Colombian	20	0.10
Ecuadorian	1	0.00
Uruguayan	5	0.02
Venezuelan	5	0.02
Other Hispanic or Latino	45	0.22
Hungarian	127	0.63
Irish	3,317	16.34
Israeli	7	0.03
Italian	1,784	8.79
Latvian	27	0.13
Lithuanian	40	0.20
Norwegian	184	0.91
Pennsylvania German	38	0.19
Polish	671	3.31
Portuguese	58	0.29
Romanian	53	0.26
Russian	128	0.63
Scotch-Irish	561	2.76
Scottish	572	2.82
Slavic	9	0.04
Slovak	112	0.55
Slovene	39	0.19
Swedish	263	1.30
Swiss	99	0.49
Ukrainian	68	0.34
United States or American	1,721	8.48
Welsh	279	1.37
West Indian, excl. Hispanic:	68	0.34
Bahamian	13	0.06
Haitian	33	0.16
Jamaican	13	0.06
West Indian	9	0.04
White:	18,538	92.47
Not Hispanic (18,141)	18,303	91.30
Hispanic (217)	235	1.17

Niceville

Place Type: City
County: Okaloosa
Population: 11,684

Ancestry/Race	Number	%
Acadian/Cajun	21	0.18
African American/Black:	626	5.36
Not Hispanic (529)	608	5.20
Hispanic (6)	18	0.15
African, sub-Saharan:	12	0.10
Ghanian	12	0.10
Alaska Native tribes, specified:	5	0.04
Tlingit-Haida	5	0.04
Am. Ind. or Alaska Nat., not spec.	58	0.50
American Indian tribes, specified:	107	0.92
Apache	1	0.01
Blackfeet	2	0.02
Cherokee (34)	52	0.45
Chickasaw	1	0.01
Chippewa (5)	5	0.04
Choctaw (6)	10	0.09
Comanche	1	0.01
Creek (12)	18	0.15
Iroquois	1	0.01
Latin American Indians (1)	2	0.02
Lumbee (2)	2	0.02
Menominee	1	0.01
Navajo (1)	1	0.01
Potawatomi	3	0.03
Seminole (2)	2	0.02
Sioux	2	0.02
Ute (1)	1	0.01
All other tribes (2)	2	0.02
American Indian tribes, not spec.	1	0.01
Arab:	42	0.36
Arab/Arabic	6	0.05
Egyptian	10	0.08
Lebanese	26	0.22
Asian:	579	4.96
Cambodian (5)	5	0.04
Chinese, ex. Taiwanese (25)	40	0.34
Filipino (147)	224	1.92
Indian (10)	12	0.10
Indonesian (1)	1	0.01
Japanese (36)	69	0.59
Korean (67)	101	0.86
Laotian (1)	1	0.01
Pakistani (1)	1	0.01
Taiwanese (1)	8	0.07
Thai (39)	60	0.51
Vietnamese (24)	27	0.23
Other Asian, specified (1)	2	0.02
Other Asian, not specified (8)	28	0.24
Austrian	5	0.04
Belgian	29	0.25
Brazilian	16	0.14
British	81	0.69
Canadian	56	0.47
Croatian	61	0.52
Czech	40	0.34
Czechoslovakian	9	0.08
Danish	21	0.18
Dutch	259	2.20
English	1,347	11.42
European	251	2.13
Finnish	12	0.10
French, except Basque	424	3.59
French Canadian	96	0.81
German	1,697	14.39
Greek	56	0.47
Hawaii Native/Pacific Islander:	39	0.33
Micronesian: (2)	5	0.04
Guamanian/Chamorro (2)	5	0.04
Polynesian: (9)	18	0.15
Native Hawaiian (9)	17	0.15
Samoan	1	0.01
Other Pac. Isl., specified	1	0.01
Other Pac. Isl., not spec. (2)	15	0.13
Hispanic or Latino:	434	3.71
Central American:	18	0.15
Costa Rican	5	0.04
Guatemalan	1	0.01
Honduran	1	0.01
Panamanian	11	0.09
Cuban	20	0.17
Dominican Republic	10	0.09
Mexican	128	1.10
Puerto Rican	144	1.23
South American:	12	0.10
Argentinean	1	0.01
Bolivian	1	0.01
Colombian	2	0.02
Peruvian	8	0.07
Other Hispanic or Latino	102	0.87
Hungarian	19	0.16
Irish	1,523	12.91
Italian	392	3.32
Northern European	26	0.22
Norwegian	275	2.33
Pennsylvania German	12	0.10
Polish	238	2.02
Romanian	9	0.08
Russian	42	0.36
Scandinavian	7	0.06
Scotch-Irish	371	3.15
Scottish	244	2.07
Slovak	21	0.18
Swedish	269	2.28
Swiss	26	0.22
Ukrainian	47	0.40
United States or American	1,522	12.90
Welsh	80	0.68
West Indian, excl. Hispanic:	52	0.44
Jamaican	44	0.37
West Indian	8	0.07
White:	10,475	89.65
Not Hispanic (9,941)	10,181	87.14
Hispanic (253)	294	2.52

Norland

Place Type: Census Designated Place
County: Miami-Dade
Population: 22,995

Ancestry/Race	Number	%
African American/Black:	18,992	82.59
Not Hispanic (17,916)	18,523	80.55
Hispanic (369)	469	2.04
African, sub-Saharan:	531	2.31
African	487	2.12
Nigerian	44	0.19
Am. Ind. or Alaska Nat., not spec.	67	0.29
American Indian tribes, specified:	47	0.20
Blackfeet (1)	2	0.01
Cherokee (3)	17	0.07
Cree	3	0.01
Latin American Indians (4)	16	0.07
Pueblo	1	0.00
Seminole	2	0.01
All other tribes	6	0.03
American Indian tribes, not spec.	10	0.04
Arab:	16	0.07
Lebanese	11	0.05
Syrian	5	0.02
Asian:	358	1.56
Bangladeshi (7)	7	0.03
Chinese, ex. Taiwanese (55)	85	0.37
Filipino (36)	38	0.17
Indian (107)	150	0.65
Japanese (10)	17	0.07
Korean (1)	7	0.03
Laotian	1	0.00
Pakistani	1	0.00
Thai	1	0.00
Vietnamese (26)	32	0.14
Other Asian, specified	5	0.02
Other Asian, not specified (4)	14	0.06
Austrian	16	0.07
Belgian	10	0.04
Brazilian	10	0.04
British	51	0.22
Canadian	7	0.03
Croatian	9	0.04
Dutch	32	0.14
English	229	0.99
European	20	0.09
French, except Basque	129	0.56
French Canadian	9	0.04
German	170	0.74
Greek	41	0.18
Guyanese	33	0.14
Hawaii Native/Pacific Islander:	81	0.35

Notes: 1. Figures in the "Number" column do not add up to the total population due to: a) Ancestry/Race overlap — e.g. persons can report being both White and Irish, b) persons of Hispanic origin can report being any race, c) persons reporting two ancestries are counted in both categories. 2. Numbers in parentheses indicate the number of persons reporting this ancestry/race alone, not in combination with any other ancestry/race. 3. Refer to the Explanation of Data in the front of the book for more detailed information.

Ancestry/Race	Number	%
Micronesian:	4	0.02
Guamanian/Chamorro	4	0.02
Polynesian:	2	0.01
Native Hawaiian	1	0.00
Samoan	1	0.00
Other Pac. Isl., specified	5	0.02
Other Pac. Isl., not spec. (1)	70	0.30
Hispanic or Latino:	2,285	9.94
Central American:	352	1.53
Costa Rican	11	0.05
Guatemalan	27	0.12
Honduran	72	0.31
Nicaraguan	163	0.71
Panamanian	45	0.20
Salvadoran	5	0.02
Other Central American	29	0.13
Cuban	456	1.98
Dominican Republic	249	1.08
Mexican	54	0.23
Puerto Rican	473	2.06
South American:	186	0.81
Argentinean	10	0.04
Bolivian	5	0.02
Chilean	14	0.06
Colombian	96	0.42
Ecuadorian	9	0.04
Peruvian	27	0.12
Venezuelan	11	0.05
Other South American	14	0.06
Other Hispanic or Latino	515	2.24
Hungarian	20	0.09
Irish	203	0.88
Italian	223	0.97
Norwegian	16	0.07
Polish	68	0.30
Russian	44	0.19
Scotch-Irish	16	0.07
Scottish	88	0.38
United States or American	872	3.79
West Indian, excl. Hispanic:	8,976	38.98
Bahamian	513	2.23
Barbadian	57	0.25
Belizean	18	0.08
British West Indian	305	1.32
Dutch West Indian	19	0.08
Haitian	2,789	12.11
Jamaican	4,849	21.06
Trinidadian and Tobagonian	328	1.42
U.S. Virgin Islander	24	0.10
West Indian	66	0.29
Other West Indian	8	0.03
White:	3,310	14.39
Not Hispanic (1,764)	1,931	8.40
Hispanic (1,225)	1,379	6.00

North Fort Myers

Place Type: Census Designated Place
County: Lee
Population: 40,214

Ancestry/Race	Number	%
Acadian/Cajun	18	0.04
African American/Black:	438	1.09
Not Hispanic (341)	397	0.99
Hispanic (34)	41	0.10
African, sub-Saharan:	27	0.07
African	15	0.04
Cape Verdean	7	0.02
South African	5	0.01
Alaska Native tribes, specified:	3	0.01
Eskimo	3	0.01
Am. Ind. or Alaska Nat., not spec.	97	0.24
Alsatian	4	0.01
American Indian tribes, specified:	187	0.47
Apache (1)	6	0.01
Blackfeet (1)	8	0.02
Cherokee (26)	84	0.21
Cheyenne	1	0.00
Chickasaw	1	0.00
Chippewa (12)	16	0.04
Choctaw (2)	3	0.01
Creek (3)	4	0.01
Delaware (1)	1	0.00
Iroquois (5)	8	0.02
Latin American Indians (7)	10	0.02
Lumbee	2	0.00
Menominee	1	0.00
Navajo (1)	2	0.00
Osage (1)	2	0.00
Ottawa (2)	3	0.01
Paiute (1)	1	0.00
Potawatomi	3	0.01
Seminole	1	0.00
Sioux (4)	12	0.03
Yuman (2)	2	0.00
All other tribes (13)	16	0.04
American Indian tribes, not spec.	13	0.03
Arab:	50	0.12
Lebanese	31	0.08
Syrian	19	0.05
Armenian	58	0.14
Asian:	269	0.67
Chinese, ex. Taiwanese (29)	36	0.09
Filipino (32)	50	0.12
Indian (37)	46	0.11
Japanese (11)	23	0.06
Korean (17)	22	0.05
Laotian (36)	42	0.10
Malaysian	1	0.00
Pakistani (5)	5	0.01
Taiwanese (1)	1	0.00
Thai (13)	16	0.04
Vietnamese (8)	10	0.02
Other Asian, specified	2	0.00
Other Asian, not specified (5)	15	0.04
Australian	6	0.01
Austrian	110	0.27
Belgian	22	0.05
British	148	0.37
Bulgarian	4	0.01
Canadian	259	0.64
Croatian	90	0.22
Czech	239	0.59
Czechoslovakian	86	0.21
Danish	208	0.52
Dutch	1,098	2.72
Eastern European	13	0.03
English	6,343	15.73
Estonian	6	0.01
European	166	0.41
Finnish	117	0.29
French, except Basque	1,754	4.35
French Canadian	630	1.56
German	8,078	20.03
Greek	127	0.31
Hawaii Native/Pacific Islander:	43	0.11
Micronesian: (14)	15	0.04
Guamanian/Chamorro (3)	3	0.01
Other Micronesian (11)	12	0.03
Polynesian: (6)	7	0.02
Native Hawaiian (5)	6	0.01
Samoan (1)	1	0.00
Other Pac. Isl., not spec. (2)	21	0.05
Hispanic or Latino:	1,166	2.90
Central American:	42	0.10
Costa Rican	8	0.02
Guatemalan	10	0.02
Honduran	3	0.01
Nicaraguan	9	0.02
Panamanian	4	0.01
Salvadoran	7	0.02
Other Central American	1	0.00
Cuban	93	0.23
Dominican Republic	26	0.06
Mexican	348	0.87
Puerto Rican	446	1.11
South American:	28	0.07
Argentinean	6	0.01
Chilean	4	0.01
Colombian	13	0.03
Ecuadorian	1	0.00
Paraguayan	1	0.00
Venezuelan	2	0.00
Other South American	1	0.00
Other Hispanic or Latino	183	0.46
Hungarian	355	0.88
Icelander	8	0.02
Irish	5,653	14.02
Israeli	10	0.02
Italian	2,327	5.77
Lithuanian	92	0.23
Luxemburger	15	0.04
Norwegian	423	1.05
Pennsylvania German	66	0.16
Polish	1,375	3.41
Portuguese	199	0.49
Romanian	33	0.08
Russian	173	0.43
Scandinavian	42	0.10
Scotch-Irish	874	2.17
Scottish	1,071	2.66
Serbian	6	0.01
Slavic	20	0.05
Slovak	148	0.37
Slovene	47	0.12
Swedish	632	1.57
Swiss	144	0.36
Turkish	5	0.01
Ukrainian	103	0.26
United States or American	4,012	9.95
Welsh	414	1.03
West Indian, excl. Hispanic:	135	0.33
Bahamian	9	0.02
Barbadian	7	0.02
Bermudan	12	0.03
Haitian	70	0.17
Jamaican	16	0.04
Trinidadian and Tobagonian	9	0.02
West Indian	12	0.03
White:	39,104	97.24
Not Hispanic (38,078)	38,317	95.28
Hispanic (726)	787	1.96
Yugoslavian	24	0.06

North Lauderdale

Place Type: City
County: Broward
Population: 32,264

Ancestry/Race	Number	%
African American/Black:	12,345	38.26
Not Hispanic (11,050)	11,971	37.10
Hispanic (293)	374	1.16
African, sub-Saharan:	441	1.36
African	380	1.18
Cape Verdean	23	0.07
Liberian	8	0.02
Nigerian	24	0.07
South African	6	0.02
Am. Ind. or Alaska Nat., not spec.	84	0.26
American Indian tribes, specified:	91	0.28
Blackfeet (4)	7	0.02
Cherokee (14)	37	0.11
Chippewa (2)	4	0.01
Choctaw (1)	2	0.01
Comanche (1)	1	0.00
Creek (2)	2	0.01
Iroquois (2)	4	0.01
Latin American Indians (17)	29	0.09
Navajo (1)	1	0.00
Ottawa	2	0.01
Sioux (1)	1	0.00
All other tribes	1	0.00
American Indian tribes, not spec.	14	0.04
Arab:	115	0.36
Arab/Arabic	8	0.02
Egyptian	48	0.15
Lebanese	50	0.15

Notes: 1. Figures in the "Number" column do not add up to the total population due to: a) Ancestry/Race overlap — e.g. persons can report being both White and Irish, b) persons of Hispanic origin can report being any race, c) persons reporting two ancestries are counted in both categories. 2. Numbers in parentheses indicate the number of persons reporting this ancestry/race alone, not in combination with any other ancestry/race. 3. Refer to the Explanation of Data in the front of the book for more detailed information.

Palestinian	9	0.03
Asian:	1,273	3.95
Bangladeshi (7)	7	0.02
Chinese, ex. Taiwanese (116)	180	0.56
Filipino (54)	77	0.24
Indian (382)	472	1.46
Indonesian (1)	3	0.01
Japanese (11)	23	0.07
Korean (16)	23	0.07
Laotian (9)	16	0.05
Pakistani (26)	30	0.09
Taiwanese (3)	3	0.01
Thai (27)	31	0.10
Vietnamese (339)	360	1.12
Other Asian, specified	2	0.01
Other Asian, not specified (6)	46	0.14
Australian	10	0.03
Austrian	51	0.16
Brazilian	283	0.88
British	64	0.20
Bulgarian	7	0.02
Canadian	82	0.25
Celtic	8	0.02
Czech	44	0.14
Czechoslovakian	44	0.14
Danish	14	0.04
Dutch	167	0.52
Eastern European	11	0.03
English	1,115	3.45
European	61	0.19
Finnish	25	0.08
French, except Basque	609	1.88
French Canadian	177	0.55
German	1,824	5.64
Greek	28	0.09
Guyanese	84	0.26
Hawaii Native/Pacific Islander:	100	0.31
Micronesian:	6	0.02
Guamanian/Chamorro	5	0.02
Other Micronesian	1	0.00
Polynesian: (4)	6	0.02
Native Hawaiian	1	0.00
Samoan (4)	4	0.01
Other Polynesian	1	0.00
Other Pac. Isl., specified	1	0.00
Other Pac. Isl., not spec. (17)	87	0.27
Hispanic or Latino:	6,816	21.13
Central American:	721	2.23
Costa Rican	25	0.08
Guatemalan	74	0.23
Honduran	145	0.45
Nicaraguan	68	0.21
Panamanian	60	0.19
Salvadoran	336	1.04
Other Central American	13	0.04
Cuban	334	1.04
Dominican Republic	246	0.76
Mexican	811	2.51
Puerto Rican	1,552	4.81
South American:	1,713	5.31
Argentinean	72	0.22
Bolivian	13	0.04
Chilean	39	0.12
Colombian	1,071	3.32
Ecuadorian	115	0.36
Paraguayan	2	0.01
Peruvian	240	0.74
Uruguayan	13	0.04
Venezuelan	102	0.32
Other South American	46	0.14
Other Hispanic or Latino	1,439	4.46
Hungarian	74	0.23
Iranian	43	0.13
Irish	2,030	6.28
Israeli	14	0.04
Italian	2,234	6.91
Latvian	10	0.03
Lithuanian	37	0.11
Norwegian	94	0.29
Pennsylvania German	11	0.03
Polish	799	2.47
Portuguese	162	0.50
Romanian	27	0.08
Russian	351	1.09
Scandinavian	33	0.10
Scotch-Irish	144	0.45
Scottish	246	0.76
Slovak	20	0.06
Swedish	153	0.47
Turkish	13	0.04
Ukrainian	49	0.15
United States or American	2,601	8.05
Welsh	106	0.33
West Indian, excl. Hispanic:	6,828	21.12
Bahamian	70	0.22
Barbadian	7	0.02
Belizean	19	0.06
British West Indian	82	0.25
Dutch West Indian	10	0.03
Haitian	2,223	6.88
Jamaican	3,688	11.41
Trinidadian and Tobagonian	357	1.10
U.S. Virgin Islander	65	0.20
West Indian	307	0.95
White:	16,994	52.67
Not Hispanic (11,831)	12,228	37.90
Hispanic (4,306)	4,766	14.77
Yugoslavian	8	0.02

North Miami Beach

Place Type: City
County: Miami-Dade
Population: 40,786

Ancestry/Race	Number	%
African American/Black:	17,066	41.84
Not Hispanic (15,273)	16,218	39.76
Hispanic (622)	848	2.08
African, sub-Saharan:	344	0.85
African	249	0.61
Ghanian	26	0.06
Nigerian	43	0.11
Senegalese	6	0.01
Ugandan	20	0.05
Alaska Native tribes, specified:	3	0.01
Eskimo (1)	1	0.00
Tlingit-Haida	2	0.00
Am. Ind. or Alaska Nat., not spec.	116	0.28
American Indian tribes, specified:	101	0.25
Apache (1)	1	0.00
Blackfeet	3	0.01
Cherokee (11)	20	0.05
Chippewa	2	0.00
Choctaw	1	0.00
Latin American Indians (22)	46	0.11
Pueblo (1)	1	0.00
Seminole	2	0.00
All other tribes (5)	25	0.06
American Indian tribes, not spec.	17	0.04
Arab:	188	0.46
Arab/Arabic	37	0.09
Lebanese	55	0.14
Moroccan	76	0.19
Syrian	9	0.02
Other Arab	11	0.03
Armenian	20	0.05
Asian:	2,031	4.98
Bangladeshi (21)	36	0.09
Cambodian (1)	3	0.01
Chinese, ex. Taiwanese (606)	677	1.66
Filipino (261)	303	0.74
Indian (408)	528	1.29
Indonesian (5)	9	0.02
Japanese (31)	42	0.10
Korean (17)	18	0.04
Laotian (2)	2	0.00
Pakistani (73)	90	0.22
Taiwanese (4)	4	0.01
Thai (41)	67	0.16
Vietnamese (108)	112	0.27
Other Asian, specified (3)	12	0.03
Other Asian, not specified (33)	128	0.31
Assyrian/Chaldean/Syriac	75	0.18
Australian	4	0.01
Austrian	77	0.19
Belgian	9	0.02
Brazilian	335	0.82
British	76	0.19
Bulgarian	19	0.05
Canadian	71	0.17
Croatian	15	0.04
Czech	32	0.08
Czechoslovakian	45	0.11
Danish	16	0.04
Dutch	96	0.24
Eastern European	45	0.11
English	628	1.54
Estonian	26	0.06
European	122	0.30
French, except Basque	253	0.62
French Canadian	45	0.11
German	996	2.45
Greek	89	0.22
Guyanese	72	0.18
Hawaii Native/Pacific Islander:	142	0.35
Micronesian: (5)	5	0.01
Guamanian/Chamorro (5)	5	0.01
Polynesian: (16)	23	0.06
Native Hawaiian (6)	9	0.02
Samoan (9)	11	0.03
Tongan (1)	2	0.00
Other Polynesian	1	0.00
Other Pac. Isl., specified	4	0.01
Other Pac. Isl., not spec. (6)	110	0.27
Hispanic or Latino:	12,245	30.02
Central American:	1,253	3.07
Costa Rican	74	0.18
Guatemalan	202	0.50
Honduran	394	0.97
Nicaraguan	374	0.92
Panamanian	84	0.21
Salvadoran	74	0.18
Other Central American	51	0.13
Cuban	2,008	4.92
Dominican Republic	976	2.39
Mexican	207	0.51
Puerto Rican	1,789	4.39
South American:	2,936	7.20
Argentinean	304	0.75
Bolivian	34	0.08
Chilean	186	0.46
Colombian	1,154	2.83
Ecuadorian	171	0.42
Paraguayan	13	0.03
Peruvian	733	1.80
Uruguayan	40	0.10
Venezuelan	222	0.54
Other South American	79	0.19
Other Hispanic or Latino	3,076	7.54
Hungarian	180	0.44
Iranian	20	0.05
Irish	1,001	2.46
Israeli	128	0.31
Italian	1,203	2.96
Lithuanian	14	0.03
Norwegian	35	0.09
Polish	614	1.51
Portuguese	126	0.31
Romanian	54	0.13
Russian	726	1.78
Scotch-Irish	132	0.32
Scottish	123	0.30
Serbian	8	0.02
Swedish	78	0.19
Swiss	20	0.05
Turkish	130	0.32
Ukrainian	125	0.31
United States or American	2,446	6.01
Welsh	34	0.08

Notes: 1. Figures in the "Number" column do not add up to the total population due to: a) Ancestry/Race overlap — e.g. persons can report being both White and Irish, b) persons of Hispanic origin can report being any race, c) persons reporting two ancestries are counted in both categories. 2. Numbers in parentheses indicate the number of persons reporting this ancestry/race alone, not in combination with any other ancestry/race. 3. Refer to the Explanation of Data in the front of the book for more detailed information.

Ancestry/Race	Number	%
West Indian, excl. Hispanic:	11,041	27.15
Bahamian	441	1.08
Barbadian	17	0.04
Belizean	85	0.21
British West Indian	64	0.16
Haitian	7,864	19.33
Jamaican	2,178	5.35
Trinidadian and Tobagonian	215	0.53
U.S. Virgin Islander	35	0.09
West Indian	117	0.29
Other West Indian	25	0.06
White:	20,106	49.30
Not Hispanic (10,104)	10,494	25.73
Hispanic (8,936)	9,612	23.57
Yugoslavian	27	0.07

North Miami

Place Type: City
County: Miami-Dade
Population: 59,880

Ancestry/Race	Number	%
African American/Black:	34,778	58.08
Not Hispanic (31,758)	33,411	55.80
Hispanic (1,109)	1,367	2.28
African, sub-Saharan:	662	1.10
African	499	0.83
Cape Verdean	7	0.01
Ethiopian	36	0.06
Ghanian	8	0.01
Kenyan	8	0.01
Nigerian	82	0.14
South African	12	0.02
Sudanese	10	0.02
Alaska Native tribes, specified:	13	0.02
Tlingit-Haida (1)	13	0.02
Alaska Native tribes, not specified	1	0.00
Am. Ind. or Alaska Nat., not spec.	231	0.39
American Indian tribes, specified:	150	0.25
Apache (6)	7	0.01
Blackfeet	3	0.01
Cherokee (10)	29	0.05
Chickasaw	1	0.00
Choctaw (1)	6	0.01
Cree	3	0.01
Creek (1)	2	0.00
Houma	1	0.00
Iroquois	1	0.00
Latin American Indians (35)	55	0.09
Lumbee	1	0.00
Menominee (3)	3	0.01
Navajo (1)	1	0.00
Paiute (1)	1	0.00
Pima (1)	1	0.00
Pueblo	3	0.01
Seminole	8	0.01
Shoshone (2)	2	0.00
All other tribes (2)	22	0.04
American Indian tribes, not spec.	24	0.04
Arab:	231	0.38
Arab/Arabic	20	0.03
Egyptian	14	0.02
Iraqi	9	0.01
Lebanese	97	0.16
Moroccan	13	0.02
Syrian	15	0.02
Other Arab	63	0.10
Armenian	11	0.02
Asian:	1,597	2.67
Bangladeshi (8)	19	0.03
Chinese, ex. Taiwanese (199)	270	0.45
Filipino (317)	371	0.62
Hmong	3	0.01
Indian (333)	511	0.85
Indonesian (8)	10	0.02
Japanese (45)	52	0.09
Korean (55)	63	0.11
Laotian (7)	7	0.01
Malaysian (1)	2	0.00
Pakistani (44)	80	0.13
Sri Lankan (1)	1	0.00
Taiwanese (9)	12	0.02
Thai (17)	23	0.04
Vietnamese (28)	30	0.05
Other Asian, specified	4	0.01
Other Asian, not specified (53)	139	0.23
Australian	8	0.01
Austrian	139	0.23
Basque	12	0.02
Brazilian	276	0.46
British	84	0.14
Bulgarian	13	0.02
Canadian	144	0.24
Croatian	41	0.07
Czech	80	0.13
Czechoslovakian	23	0.04
Danish	16	0.03
Dutch	224	0.37
Eastern European	74	0.12
English	938	1.56
European	116	0.19
Finnish	21	0.03
French, except Basque	454	0.76
French Canadian	44	0.07
German	1,451	2.42
German Russian	6	0.01
Greek	160	0.27
Guyanese	116	0.19
Hawaii Native/Pacific Islander:	247	0.41
Melanesian: (1)	1	0.00
Fijian (1)	1	0.00
Micronesian: (1)	3	0.01
Guamanian/Chamorro (1)	2	0.00
Other Micronesian	1	0.00
Polynesian: (10)	30	0.05
Native Hawaiian (9)	21	0.04
Samoan (1)	4	0.01
Other Polynesian	5	0.01
Other Pac. Isl., specified	4	0.01
Other Pac. Isl., not spec. (16)	209	0.35
Hispanic or Latino:	13,869	23.16
Central American:	1,709	2.85
Costa Rican	115	0.19
Guatemalan	217	0.36
Honduran	565	0.94
Nicaraguan	553	0.92
Panamanian	97	0.16
Salvadoran	108	0.18
Other Central American	54	0.09
Cuban	2,655	4.43
Dominican Republic	1,032	1.72
Mexican	367	0.61
Puerto Rican	2,660	4.44
South American:	2,009	3.36
Argentinean	223	0.37
Bolivian	33	0.06
Chilean	74	0.12
Colombian	858	1.43
Ecuadorian	118	0.20
Paraguayan	9	0.02
Peruvian	384	0.64
Uruguayan	26	0.04
Venezuelan	215	0.36
Other South American	69	0.12
Other Hispanic or Latino	3,437	5.74
Hungarian	148	0.25
Iranian	35	0.06
Irish	1,263	2.10
Israeli	82	0.14
Italian	1,171	1.95
Latvian	89	0.15
Lithuanian	76	0.13
Northern European	44	0.07
Norwegian	72	0.12
Pennsylvania German	6	0.01
Polish	638	1.06
Portuguese	107	0.18
Romanian	108	0.18
Russian	576	0.96
Scandinavian	10	0.02
Scotch-Irish	99	0.16
Scottish	240	0.40
Serbian	9	0.01
Slovak	33	0.05
Slovene	19	0.03
Swedish	223	0.37
Swiss	42	0.07
Turkish	48	0.08
Ukrainian	69	0.11
United States or American	3,319	5.53
Welsh	70	0.12
West Indian, excl. Hispanic:	22,034	36.70
Bahamian	675	1.12
Barbadian	149	0.25
Belizean	56	0.09
British West Indian	246	0.41
Dutch West Indian	18	0.03
Haitian	18,656	31.07
Jamaican	1,837	3.06
Trinidadian and Tobagonian	267	0.44
U.S. Virgin Islander	32	0.05
West Indian	98	0.16
White:	21,977	36.70
Not Hispanic (10,860)	11,283	18.84
Hispanic (9,982)	10,694	17.86
Yugoslavian	40	0.07

North Palm Beach

Place Type: Village
County: Palm Beach
Population: 12,064

Ancestry/Race	Number	%
African American/Black:	126	1.04
Not Hispanic (108)	122	1.01
Hispanic (4)	4	0.03
African, sub-Saharan:	8	0.07
Other sub-Saharan African	8	0.07
Am. Ind. or Alaska Nat., not spec.	17	0.14
Albanian	10	0.08
Alsatian	7	0.06
American Indian tribes, specified:	21	0.17
Blackfeet (1)	2	0.02
Cherokee (3)	5	0.04
Cheyenne	1	0.01
Chippewa (1)	2	0.02
Creek (2)	2	0.02
Delaware	1	0.01
Iroquois	2	0.02
Latin American Indians (1)	1	0.01
Osage	1	0.01
Sioux	1	0.01
All other tribes	3	0.02
Armenian	32	0.26
Asian:	191	1.58
Chinese, ex. Taiwanese (30)	34	0.28
Filipino (5)	16	0.13
Indian (31)	36	0.30
Japanese (6)	9	0.07
Korean (6)	7	0.06
Laotian (1)	1	0.01
Thai (4)	5	0.04
Vietnamese (56)	63	0.52
Other Asian, not specified (8)	20	0.17
Australian	9	0.07
Austrian	80	0.66
Belgian	30	0.25
British	74	0.61
Canadian	153	1.26
Croatian	9	0.07
Czech	43	0.35
Czechoslovakian	14	0.12
Danish	85	0.70
Dutch	363	2.99
Eastern European	43	0.35
English	1,836	15.14
European	72	0.59
Finnish	84	0.69

Notes: 1. Figures in the "Number" column do not add up to the total population due to: a) Ancestry/Race overlap — e.g. persons can report being both White and Irish, b) persons of Hispanic origin can report being any race, c) persons reporting two ancestries are counted in both categories. 2. Numbers in parentheses indicate the number of persons reporting this ancestry/race alone, not in combination with any other ancestry/race. 3. Refer to the Explanation of Data in the front of the book for more detailed information.

Ancestry/Race	Number	%
French, except Basque	576	4.75
French Canadian	106	0.87
German	2,469	20.36
Greek	183	1.51
Hawaii Native/Pacific Islander:	9	0.07
Micronesian: (1)	1	0.01
Guamanian/Chamorro (1)	1	0.01
Polynesian: (1)	7	0.06
Native Hawaiian (1)	6	0.05
Other Polynesian	1	0.01
Other Pac. Isl., not spec. (1)	1	0.01
Hispanic or Latino:	426	3.53
Central American:	16	0.13
Guatemalan	3	0.02
Honduran	3	0.02
Nicaraguan	6	0.05
Panamanian	1	0.01
Salvadoran	3	0.02
Cuban	93	0.77
Dominican Republic	2	0.02
Mexican	46	0.38
Puerto Rican	93	0.77
South American:	82	0.68
Argentinean	6	0.05
Chilean	5	0.04
Colombian	33	0.27
Ecuadorian	14	0.12
Paraguayan	1	0.01
Peruvian	10	0.08
Uruguayan	2	0.02
Venezuelan	11	0.09
Other Hispanic or Latino	94	0.78
Hungarian	83	0.68
Iranian	9	0.07
Irish	2,686	22.15
Israeli	10	0.08
Italian	1,393	11.48
Lithuanian	61	0.50
Norwegian	117	0.96
Pennsylvania German	18	0.15
Polish	451	3.72
Portuguese	41	0.34
Romanian	41	0.34
Russian	327	2.70
Scandinavian	9	0.07
Scotch-Irish	345	2.84
Scottish	416	3.43
Serbian	11	0.09
Slavic	37	0.31
Slovak	15	0.12
Slovene	8	0.07
Swedish	154	1.27
Swiss	52	0.43
Turkish	46	0.38
Ukrainian	85	0.70
United States or American	810	6.68
Welsh	132	1.09
West Indian, excl. Hispanic:	109	0.90
Haitian	72	0.59
Jamaican	28	0.23
West Indian	9	0.07
White:	11,715	97.11
Not Hispanic (11,265)	11,344	94.03
Hispanic (343)	371	3.08
Yugoslavian	26	0.21

North Port

Place Type: City
County: Sarasota
Population: 22,797

Ancestry/Race	Number	%
African American/Black:	1,069	4.69
Not Hispanic (912)	1,005	4.41
Hispanic (42)	64	0.28
African, sub-Saharan:	58	0.26
African	58	0.26
Alaska Native tribes, specified:	2	0.01
Eskimo (1)	2	0.01
Am. Ind. or Alaska Nat., not spec.	54	0.24
American Indian tribes, specified:	108	0.47
Blackfeet	6	0.03
Cherokee (15)	56	0.25
Chickasaw (1)	1	0.00
Chippewa (3)	7	0.03
Choctaw	1	0.00
Creek	6	0.03
Iroquois	6	0.03
Latin American Indians (1)	3	0.01
Lumbee (1)	7	0.03
Pueblo	1	0.00
Seminole	1	0.00
Sioux	2	0.01
All other tribes (2)	11	0.05
American Indian tribes, not spec.	6	0.03
Arab:	138	0.61
Arab/Arabic	36	0.16
Jordanian	23	0.10
Lebanese	74	0.33
Syrian	5	0.02
Armenian	18	0.08
Asian:	207	0.91
Cambodian (1)	1	0.00
Chinese, ex. Taiwanese (6)	15	0.07
Filipino (37)	73	0.32
Indian (21)	32	0.14
Indonesian (1)	2	0.01
Japanese (12)	21	0.09
Korean (14)	16	0.07
Laotian (2)	2	0.01
Pakistani	3	0.01
Sri Lankan (1)	1	0.00
Thai (2)	2	0.01
Vietnamese (12)	13	0.06
Other Asian, not specified (1)	26	0.11
Austrian	23	0.10
Belgian	48	0.21
Brazilian	19	0.08
British	129	0.57
Canadian	144	0.63
Croatian	52	0.23
Czech	118	0.52
Czechoslovakian	40	0.18
Danish	112	0.49
Dutch	544	2.39
Eastern European	32	0.14
English	2,700	11.89
Estonian	8	0.04
European	111	0.49
Finnish	50	0.22
French, except Basque	1,112	4.90
French Canadian	326	1.44
German	4,955	21.81
Greek	121	0.53
Hawaii Native/Pacific Islander:	19	0.08
Polynesian: (2)	12	0.05
Native Hawaiian (1)	11	0.05
Samoan (1)	1	0.00
Other Pac. Isl., not spec. (1)	7	0.03
Hispanic or Latino:	739	3.24
Central American:	51	0.22
Costa Rican	2	0.01
Guatemalan	12	0.05
Honduran	8	0.04
Nicaraguan	8	0.04
Panamanian	13	0.06
Salvadoran	8	0.04
Cuban	91	0.40
Dominican Republic	8	0.04
Mexican	139	0.61
Puerto Rican	259	1.14
South American:	39	0.17
Argentinean	2	0.01
Chilean	8	0.04
Colombian	10	0.04
Ecuadorian	2	0.01
Peruvian	13	0.06
Uruguayan	1	0.00
Venezuelan	1	0.00
Other South American	2	0.01
Other Hispanic or Latino	152	0.67
Hungarian	238	1.05
Irish	3,596	15.83
Israeli	24	0.11
Italian	1,934	8.51
Latvian	8	0.04
Lithuanian	119	0.52
Northern European	9	0.04
Norwegian	165	0.73
Pennsylvania German	8	0.04
Polish	1,075	4.73
Portuguese	207	0.91
Romanian	15	0.07
Russian	346	1.52
Scandinavian	9	0.04
Scotch-Irish	319	1.40
Scottish	470	2.07
Serbian	47	0.21
Slavic	8	0.04
Slovak	65	0.29
Slovene	9	0.04
Swedish	270	1.19
Swiss	43	0.19
Turkish	13	0.06
Ukrainian	612	2.69
United States or American	1,870	8.23
Welsh	182	0.80
West Indian, excl. Hispanic:	434	1.91
British West Indian	59	0.26
Haitian	10	0.04
Jamaican	329	1.45
Trinidadian and Tobagonian	28	0.12
West Indian	8	0.04
White:	21,461	94.14
Not Hispanic (20,625)	20,908	91.71
Hispanic (502)	553	2.43
Yugoslavian	52	0.23

Oak Ridge

Place Type: Census Designated Place
County: Orange
Population: 22,349

Ancestry/Race	Number	%
Acadian/Cajun	9	0.04
African American/Black:	7,397	33.10
Not Hispanic (5,946)	6,791	30.39
Hispanic (411)	606	2.71
African, sub-Saharan:	275	1.23
African	252	1.12
Cape Verdean	9	0.04
Ethiopian	14	0.06
Alaska Native tribes, specified:	1	0.00
Tlingit-Haida	1	0.00
Am. Ind. or Alaska Nat., not spec.	117	0.52
American Indian tribes, specified:	74	0.33
Blackfeet (1)	3	0.01
Cherokee (6)	27	0.12
Cheyenne	1	0.00
Chickasaw	2	0.01
Chippewa (1)	2	0.01
Creek (1)	1	0.00
Crow	1	0.00
Delaware	1	0.00
Iroquois	1	0.00
Latin American Indians (17)	28	0.13
Potawatomi (1)	1	0.00
Pueblo (1)	2	0.01
Seminole	1	0.00
All other tribes	3	0.01
American Indian tribes, not spec.	12	0.05
Arab:	46	0.21
Arab/Arabic	17	0.08
Egyptian	29	0.13
Asian:	1,525	6.82
Bangladeshi (14)	25	0.11
Cambodian (34)	50	0.22
Chinese, ex. Taiwanese (111)	146	0.65

Notes: 1. Figures in the "Number" column do not add up to the total population due to: a) Ancestry/Race overlap — e.g. persons can report being both White and Irish, b) persons of Hispanic origin can report being any race, c) persons reporting two ancestries are counted in both categories. 2. Numbers in parentheses indicate the number of persons reporting this ancestry/race alone, not in combination with any other ancestry/race. 3. Refer to the Explanation of Data in the front of the book for more detailed information.

Ancestry/Race	Number	%
Filipino (74)	97	0.43
Indian (212)	285	1.28
Indonesian (3)	4	0.02
Japanese (12)	15	0.07
Korean (26)	32	0.14
Laotian (48)	52	0.23
Malaysian (4)	4	0.02
Pakistani (12)	32	0.14
Taiwanese	2	0.01
Thai (5)	7	0.03
Vietnamese (644)	706	3.16
Other Asian, not specified (24)	68	0.30
Austrian	19	0.08
Brazilian	161	0.72
British	9	0.04
Canadian	18	0.08
Czech	17	0.08
Czechoslovakian	23	0.10
Dutch	80	0.36
English	683	3.05
Estonian	8	0.04
European	7	0.03
French, except Basque	168	0.75
French Canadian	80	0.36
German	866	3.86
Greek	82	0.37
Guyanese	18	0.08
Hawaii Native/Pacific Islander:	141	0.63
Melanesian: (3)	3	0.01
Fijian (3)	3	0.01
Micronesian: (20)	20	0.09
Guamanian/Chamorro (9)	9	0.04
Other Micronesian (11)	11	0.05
Polynesian: (36)	65	0.29
Native Hawaiian (6)	21	0.09
Samoan (5)	7	0.03
Tongan (23)	31	0.14
Other Polynesian (2)	6	0.03
Other Pac. Isl., not spec. (5)	53	0.24
Hispanic or Latino:	9,257	41.42
Central American:	403	1.80
Costa Rican	28	0.13
Guatemalan	62	0.28
Honduran	107	0.48
Nicaraguan	59	0.26
Panamanian	38	0.17
Salvadoran	98	0.44
Other Central American	11	0.05
Cuban	707	3.16
Dominican Republic	677	3.03
Mexican	967	4.33
Puerto Rican	4,249	19.01
South American:	865	3.87
Argentinean	35	0.16
Bolivian	3	0.01
Chilean	42	0.19
Colombian	431	1.93
Ecuadorian	91	0.41
Peruvian	108	0.48
Uruguayan	8	0.04
Venezuelan	115	0.51
Other South American	32	0.14
Other Hispanic or Latino	1,389	6.22
Hungarian	65	0.29
Irish	778	3.47
Italian	389	1.74
Latvian	14	0.06
Lithuanian	9	0.04
Polish	151	0.67
Portuguese	56	0.25
Russian	90	0.40
Scotch-Irish	47	0.21
Scottish	100	0.45
Slavic	37	0.17
Slovak	24	0.11
Swedish	43	0.19
Swiss	4	0.02
United States or American	989	4.41
Welsh	46	0.21
West Indian, excl. Hispanic:	2,824	12.60
Bahamian	14	0.06
Barbadian	13	0.06
British West Indian	13	0.06
Dutch West Indian	5	0.02
Haitian	2,240	10.00
Jamaican	296	1.32
Trinidadian and Tobagonian	119	0.53
U.S. Virgin Islander	23	0.10
West Indian	101	0.45
White:	10,547	47.19
Not Hispanic (4,542)	4,901	21.93
Hispanic (5,086)	5,646	25.26
Yugoslavian	23	0.10

Oakland Park

Place Type: City
County: Broward
Population: 30,966

Ancestry/Race	Number	%
African American/Black:	7,783	25.13
Not Hispanic (6,858)	7,551	24.38
Hispanic (155)	232	0.75
African, sub-Saharan:	379	1.21
African	360	1.15
South African	19	0.06
Alaska Native tribes, specified:	3	0.01
Tlingit-Haida (1)	3	0.01
Am. Ind. or Alaska Nat., not spec.	69	0.22
Albanian	24	0.08
American Indian tribes, specified:	119	0.38
Apache (1)	1	0.00
Blackfeet	6	0.02
Cherokee (7)	42	0.14
Chippewa	4	0.01
Choctaw	7	0.02
Comanche	1	0.00
Creek (1)	1	0.00
Delaware	2	0.01
Iroquois (2)	6	0.02
Latin American Indians (10)	25	0.08
Ottawa (1)	1	0.00
Potawatomi	1	0.00
Pueblo (1)	2	0.01
Seminole (1)	1	0.00
Sioux (1)	5	0.02
Yaqui (1)	1	0.00
All other tribes (1)	13	0.04
American Indian tribes, not spec.	12	0.04
Arab:	108	0.35
Arab/Arabic	9	0.03
Egyptian	30	0.10
Lebanese	61	0.20
Palestinian	8	0.03
Armenian	31	0.10
Asian:	783	2.53
Bangladeshi (14)	26	0.08
Cambodian (1)	3	0.01
Chinese, ex. Taiwanese (133)	164	0.53
Filipino (32)	43	0.14
Indian (228)	286	0.92
Indonesian (2)	3	0.01
Japanese (38)	54	0.17
Korean (19)	23	0.07
Laotian (3)	6	0.02
Malaysian (1)	1	0.00
Pakistani (10)	22	0.07
Sri Lankan (1)	1	0.00
Taiwanese (1)	1	0.00
Thai (38)	46	0.15
Vietnamese (56)	61	0.20
Other Asian, specified (5)	7	0.02
Other Asian, not specified (5)	36	0.12
Australian	18	0.06
Austrian	123	0.39
Basque	16	0.05
Brazilian	704	2.26
British	131	0.42
Bulgarian	16	0.05
Canadian	138	0.44
Croatian	105	0.34
Cypriot	9	0.03
Czech	79	0.25
Czechoslovakian	38	0.12
Danish	52	0.17
Dutch	285	0.91
Eastern European	43	0.14
English	2,101	6.73
European	115	0.37
Finnish	18	0.06
French, except Basque	823	2.64
French Canadian	146	0.47
German	3,217	10.31
Greek	134	0.43
Guyanese	48	0.15
Hawaii Native/Pacific Islander:	110	0.36
Micronesian: (14)	18	0.06
Guamanian/Chamorro (14)	17	0.05
Other Micronesian	1	0.00
Polynesian: (16)	33	0.11
Native Hawaiian (10)	21	0.07
Samoan (3)	8	0.03
Other Polynesian (3)	4	0.01
Other Pac. Isl., not spec. (11)	59	0.19
Hispanic or Latino:	5,556	17.94
Central American:	846	2.73
Costa Rican	26	0.08
Guatemalan	122	0.39
Honduran	163	0.53
Nicaraguan	43	0.14
Panamanian	35	0.11
Salvadoran	425	1.37
Other Central American	32	0.10
Cuban	629	2.03
Dominican Republic	140	0.45
Mexican	861	2.78
Puerto Rican	1,038	3.35
South American:	930	3.00
Argentinean	34	0.11
Bolivian	15	0.05
Chilean	90	0.29
Colombian	347	1.12
Ecuadorian	51	0.16
Paraguayan	4	0.01
Peruvian	196	0.63
Uruguayan	43	0.14
Venezuelan	104	0.34
Other South American	46	0.15
Other Hispanic or Latino	1,112	3.59
Hungarian	244	0.78
Iranian	31	0.10
Irish	2,995	9.60
Israeli	24	0.08
Italian	2,508	8.04
Lithuanian	57	0.18
Maltese	10	0.03
Northern European	31	0.10
Norwegian	172	0.55
Pennsylvania German	7	0.02
Polish	859	2.75
Portuguese	243	0.78
Romanian	23	0.07
Russian	271	0.87
Scandinavian	15	0.05
Scotch-Irish	230	0.74
Scottish	388	1.24
Serbian	30	0.10
Slavic	6	0.02
Slovak	94	0.30
Slovene	14	0.04
Swedish	329	1.05
Swiss	85	0.27
Turkish	131	0.42
Ukrainian	93	0.30
United States or American	1,393	4.46
Welsh	219	0.70
West Indian, excl. Hispanic:	3,501	11.22
Bahamian	138	0.44
Barbadian	7	0.02

Notes: 1. Figures in the "Number" column do not add up to the total population due to: a) Ancestry/Race overlap — e.g. persons can report being both White and Irish, b) persons of Hispanic origin can report being any race, c) persons reporting two ancestries are counted in both categories. 2. Numbers in parentheses indicate the number of persons reporting this ancestry/race alone, not in combination with any other ancestry/race. 3. Refer to the Explanation of Data in the front of the book for more detailed information.

Ancestry/Race	Number	%
Belizean	46	0.15
British West Indian	70	0.22
Haitian	2,299	7.37
Jamaican	743	2.38
Trinidadian and Tobagonian	141	0.45
U.S. Virgin Islander	9	0.03
West Indian	48	0.15
White:	21,173	68.37
Not Hispanic (16,703)	17,108	55.25
Hispanic (3,729)	4,065	13.13
Yugoslavian	14	0.04

Ocala

Place Type: City
County: Marion
Population: 45,943

Ancestry/Race	Number	%
Acadian/Cajun	24	0.05
African American/Black:	10,408	22.65
Not Hispanic (10,055)	10,253	22.32
Hispanic (119)	155	0.34
African, sub-Saharan:	256	0.56
African	186	0.41
Ethiopian	17	0.04
Kenyan	53	0.12
Am. Ind. or Alaska Nat., not spec.	129	0.28
Alsatian	7	0.02
American Indian tribes, specified:	262	0.57
Apache	3	0.01
Blackfeet (6)	17	0.04
Cherokee (50)	143	0.31
Chickasaw (1)	1	0.00
Chippewa (2)	4	0.01
Choctaw (1)	5	0.01
Comanche (2)	2	0.00
Creek (6)	11	0.02
Crow	2	0.00
Iroquois (6)	9	0.02
Latin American Indians (13)	21	0.05
Lumbee (5)	10	0.02
Navajo (3)	4	0.01
Potawatomi (1)	1	0.00
Pueblo	1	0.00
Seminole	5	0.01
Sioux (3)	5	0.01
All other tribes (7)	18	0.04
American Indian tribes, not spec.	19	0.04
Arab:	412	0.90
Arab/Arabic	149	0.33
Egyptian	8	0.02
Jordanian	29	0.06
Lebanese	142	0.31
Palestinian	7	0.02
Syrian	57	0.12
Other Arab	20	0.04
Asian:	665	1.45
Chinese, ex. Taiwanese (56)	68	0.15
Filipino (84)	113	0.25
Indian (229)	249	0.54
Indonesian (1)	3	0.01
Japanese (35)	43	0.09
Korean (59)	71	0.15
Laotian (1)	2	0.00
Malaysian (1)	1	0.00
Pakistani (9)	13	0.03
Sri Lankan (1)	1	0.00
Taiwanese (10)	11	0.02
Thai (3)	6	0.01
Vietnamese (46)	51	0.11
Other Asian, not specified (21)	33	0.07
Australian	7	0.02
Austrian	117	0.26
Belgian	52	0.11
Brazilian	19	0.04
British	246	0.54
Bulgarian	9	0.02
Canadian	171	0.37
Celtic	15	0.03
Croatian	55	0.12
Czech	55	0.12
Czechoslovakian	64	0.14
Danish	55	0.12
Dutch	797	1.75
English	5,056	11.08
European	253	0.55
Finnish	69	0.15
French, except Basque	1,450	3.18
French Canadian	307	0.67
German	6,040	13.24
German Russian	6	0.01
Greek	164	0.36
Hawaii Native/Pacific Islander:	30	0.07
Micronesian: (1)	3	0.01
Guamanian/Chamorro (1)	3	0.01
Polynesian: (8)	21	0.05
Native Hawaiian (3)	10	0.02
Samoan (5)	11	0.02
Other Pac. Isl., not spec.	6	0.01
Hispanic or Latino:	2,636	5.74
Central American:	105	0.23
Costa Rican	9	0.02
Guatemalan	30	0.07
Honduran	12	0.03
Nicaraguan	5	0.01
Panamanian	43	0.09
Salvadoran	3	0.01
Other Central American	3	0.01
Cuban	193	0.42
Dominican Republic	36	0.08
Mexican	606	1.32
Puerto Rican	1,040	2.26
South American:	189	0.41
Argentinean	9	0.02
Bolivian	1	0.00
Chilean	10	0.02
Colombian	87	0.19
Ecuadorian	35	0.08
Peruvian	18	0.04
Uruguayan	7	0.02
Venezuelan	17	0.04
Other South American	5	0.01
Other Hispanic or Latino	467	1.02
Hungarian	77	0.17
Iranian	35	0.08
Irish	5,378	11.79
Italian	2,486	5.45
Latvian	11	0.02
Lithuanian	55	0.12
Macedonian	6	0.01
Norwegian	340	0.75
Pennsylvania German	26	0.06
Polish	1,009	2.21
Portuguese	135	0.30
Romanian	26	0.06
Russian	236	0.52
Scandinavian	65	0.14
Scotch-Irish	796	1.74
Scottish	1,122	2.46
Serbian	8	0.02
Slovak	49	0.11
Slovene	42	0.09
Swedish	441	0.97
Swiss	99	0.22
Turkish	15	0.03
Ukrainian	81	0.18
United States or American	3,084	6.76
Welsh	310	0.68
West Indian, excl. Hispanic:	285	0.62
Bahamian	24	0.05
British West Indian	18	0.04
Haitian	38	0.08
Jamaican	168	0.37
Trinidadian and Tobagonian	19	0.04
West Indian	18	0.04
White:	34,097	74.22
Not Hispanic (31,982)	32,415	70.55
Hispanic (1,492)	1,682	3.66
Yugoslavian	37	0.08

Ocoee

Place Type: City
County: Orange
Population: 24,391

Ancestry/Race	Number	%
African American/Black:	1,775	7.28
Not Hispanic (1,538)	1,686	6.91
Hispanic (69)	89	0.36
African, sub-Saharan:	26	0.11
African	10	0.04
Nigerian	16	0.07
Alaska Native tribes, specified:	1	0.00
Eskimo (1)	1	0.00
Am. Ind. or Alaska Nat., not spec.	53	0.22
American Indian tribes, specified:	139	0.57
Apache	4	0.02
Blackfeet	3	0.01
Cherokee (25)	58	0.24
Chippewa (1)	4	0.02
Choctaw (1)	5	0.02
Comanche (3)	3	0.01
Creek (5)	7	0.03
Crow	1	0.00
Iroquois	7	0.03
Latin American Indians (8)	10	0.04
Navajo (6)	6	0.02
Pueblo (3)	3	0.01
Seminole (7)	14	0.06
Shoshone	1	0.00
Sioux (6)	7	0.03
All other tribes	6	0.02
American Indian tribes, not spec.	6	0.02
Arab:	75	0.32
Arab/Arabic	17	0.07
Jordanian	32	0.14
Moroccan	20	0.08
Syrian	6	0.03
Asian:	883	3.62
Cambodian (2)	2	0.01
Chinese, ex. Taiwanese (61)	73	0.30
Filipino (111)	144	0.59
Indian (288)	368	1.51
Japanese (31)	40	0.16
Korean (67)	72	0.30
Laotian (4)	4	0.02
Pakistani (11)	14	0.06
Sri Lankan (2)	2	0.01
Taiwanese (1)	1	0.00
Thai (1)	1	0.00
Vietnamese (116)	123	0.50
Other Asian, specified	4	0.02
Other Asian, not specified (16)	35	0.14
Brazilian	7	0.03
British	113	0.48
Canadian	124	0.52
Celtic	6	0.03
Croatian	24	0.10
Czech	107	0.45
Czechoslovakian	24	0.10
Danish	124	0.52
Dutch	394	1.67
Eastern European	6	0.03
English	2,373	10.04
European	174	0.74
Finnish	31	0.13
French, except Basque	833	3.53
French Canadian	271	1.15
German	3,325	14.07
Greek	88	0.37
Guyanese	41	0.17
Hawaii Native/Pacific Islander:	41	0.17
Micronesian: (2)	2	0.01
Guamanian/Chamorro (2)	2	0.01
Polynesian: (9)	22	0.09
Native Hawaiian (5)	13	0.05
Samoan (4)	4	0.02
Other Polynesian	5	0.02
Other Pac. Isl., specified	4	0.02

Notes: 1. Figures in the "Number" column do not add up to the total population due to: a) Ancestry/Race overlap — e.g. persons can report being both White and Irish, b) persons of Hispanic origin can report being any race, c) persons reporting two ancestries are counted in both categories. 2. Numbers in parentheses indicate the number of persons reporting this ancestry/race alone, not in combination with any other ancestry/race. 3. Refer to the Explanation of Data in the front of the book for more detailed information.

Other Pac. Isl., not spec. (3)	13	0.05
Hispanic or Latino:	3,707	15.20
Central American:	130	0.53
Costa Rican	6	0.02
Guatemalan	79	0.32
Honduran	8	0.03
Nicaraguan	11	0.05
Panamanian	17	0.07
Salvadoran	4	0.02
Other Central American	5	0.02
Cuban	162	0.66
Dominican Republic	46	0.19
Mexican	1,753	7.19
Puerto Rican	1,013	4.15
South American:	234	0.96
Argentinean	10	0.04
Bolivian	3	0.01
Chilean	6	0.02
Colombian	127	0.52
Ecuadorian	17	0.07
Peruvian	21	0.09
Uruguayan	9	0.04
Venezuelan	32	0.13
Other South American	9	0.04
Other Hispanic or Latino	369	1.51
Hungarian	105	0.44
Icelander	6	0.03
Irish	2,666	11.28
Italian	1,595	6.75
Lithuanian	36	0.15
Norwegian	272	1.15
Pennsylvania German	8	0.03
Polish	654	2.77
Portuguese	232	0.98
Romanian	52	0.22
Russian	121	0.51
Scandinavian	31	0.13
Scotch-Irish	350	1.48
Scottish	540	2.29
Slovak	41	0.17
Swedish	284	1.20
Swiss	57	0.24
Ukrainian	56	0.24
United States or American	2,344	9.92
Welsh	105	0.44
West Indian, excl. Hispanic:	376	1.59
Bahamian	15	0.06
Barbadian	10	0.04
Dutch West Indian	8	0.03
Haitian	30	0.13
Jamaican	271	1.15
Trinidadian and Tobagonian	11	0.05
West Indian	31	0.13
White:	20,271	83.11
Not Hispanic (17,909)	18,132	74.34
Hispanic (1,962)	2,139	8.77

Ojus

Place Type: Census Designated Place
County: Miami-Dade
Population: 16,642

Ancestry/Race	Number	%
African American/Black:	1,274	7.66
Not Hispanic (1,066)	1,132	6.80
Hispanic (108)	142	0.85
African, sub-Saharan:	82	0.49
African	34	0.20
South African	36	0.22
Other sub-Saharan African	12	0.07
Am. Ind. or Alaska Nat., not spec.	25	0.15
American Indian tribes, specified:	29	0.17
Cherokee (1)	6	0.04
Latin American Indians (8)	19	0.11
Pueblo	1	0.01
Sioux (1)	1	0.01
All other tribes (1)	2	0.01
American Indian tribes, not spec.	3	0.02
Arab:	365	2.19
Arab/Arabic	9	0.05
Egyptian	164	0.98
Jordanian	91	0.55
Lebanese	44	0.26
Moroccan	28	0.17
Syrian	14	0.08
Other Arab	15	0.09
Armenian	9	0.05
Asian:	378	2.27
Chinese, ex. Taiwanese (105)	125	0.75
Filipino (38)	51	0.31
Indian (76)	103	0.62
Japanese (4)	8	0.05
Korean (14)	22	0.13
Laotian (2)	4	0.02
Pakistani (16)	22	0.13
Sri Lankan (2)	2	0.01
Thai (13)	15	0.09
Vietnamese (4)	7	0.04
Other Asian, not specified (11)	19	0.11
Austrian	169	1.01
Basque	5	0.03
Brazilian	268	1.61
British	63	0.38
Canadian	59	0.35
Czech	46	0.28
Czechoslovakian	43	0.26
Dutch	65	0.39
Eastern European	157	0.94
English	404	2.42
Estonian	6	0.04
European	320	1.92
French, except Basque	369	2.21
French Canadian	130	0.78
German	780	4.68
Greek	166	1.00
Guyanese	27	0.16
Hawaii Native/Pacific Islander:	13	0.08
Micronesian: (2)	2	0.01
Guamanian/Chamorro (2)	2	0.01
Polynesian: (1)	2	0.01
Native Hawaiian (1)	1	0.01
Other Polynesian	1	0.01
Other Pac. Isl., not spec. (4)	9	0.05
Hispanic or Latino:	5,093	30.60
Central American:	336	2.02
Costa Rican	34	0.20
Guatemalan	51	0.31
Honduran	91	0.55
Nicaraguan	93	0.56
Panamanian	28	0.17
Salvadoran	24	0.14
Other Central American	15	0.09
Cuban	1,126	6.77
Dominican Republic	237	1.42
Mexican	89	0.53
Puerto Rican	487	2.93
South American:	1,609	9.67
Argentinean	249	1.50
Bolivian	33	0.20
Chilean	51	0.31
Colombian	618	3.71
Ecuadorian	71	0.43
Paraguayan	1	0.01
Peruvian	381	2.29
Uruguayan	31	0.19
Venezuelan	131	0.79
Other South American	43	0.26
Other Hispanic or Latino	1,209	7.26
Hungarian	202	1.21
Iranian	27	0.16
Irish	421	2.52
Israeli	295	1.77
Italian	795	4.77
Latvian	13	0.08
Lithuanian	118	0.71
Northern European	8	0.05
Norwegian	38	0.23
Polish	830	4.98
Portuguese	58	0.35
Romanian	177	1.06
Russian	1,256	7.53
Scandinavian	9	0.05
Scotch-Irish	32	0.19
Scottish	60	0.36
Swedish	29	0.17
Turkish	132	0.79
Ukrainian	206	1.23
United States or American	1,171	7.02
Welsh	29	0.17
West Indian, excl. Hispanic:	836	5.01
Bahamian	18	0.11
Barbadian	9	0.05
British West Indian	8	0.05
Haitian	505	3.03
Jamaican	181	1.09
Trinidadian and Tobagonian	108	0.65
West Indian	7	0.04
White:	14,542	87.38
Not Hispanic (9,894)	10,059	60.44
Hispanic (4,267)	4,483	26.94

Oldsmar

Place Type: City
County: Pinellas
Population: 11,910

Ancestry/Race	Number	%
African American/Black:	417	3.50
Not Hispanic (338)	396	3.32
Hispanic (14)	21	0.18
African, sub-Saharan:	11	0.09
African	11	0.09
Alaska Native tribes, specified:	1	0.01
Tlingit-Haida	1	0.01
Am. Ind. or Alaska Nat., not spec.	19	0.16
Albanian	75	0.64
American Indian tribes, specified:	61	0.51
Apache (1)	1	0.01
Blackfeet (1)	1	0.01
Cherokee (2)	16	0.13
Cheyenne (2)	2	0.02
Chickasaw (1)	1	0.01
Chippewa (3)	4	0.03
Choctaw (1)	1	0.01
Creek	1	0.01
Delaware (1)	2	0.02
Iroquois (4)	7	0.06
Latin American Indians (7)	8	0.07
Lumbee (3)	3	0.03
Ottawa (1)	1	0.01
Seminole	2	0.02
Shoshone (2)	3	0.03
Sioux	1	0.01
All other tribes (1)	7	0.06
American Indian tribes, not spec.	2	0.02
Arab:	172	1.47
Arab/Arabic	44	0.37
Egyptian	25	0.21
Lebanese	15	0.13
Moroccan	14	0.12
Syrian	65	0.55
Other Arab	9	0.08
Armenian	9	0.08
Asian:	409	3.43
Chinese, ex. Taiwanese (47)	56	0.47
Filipino (65)	85	0.71
Indian (110)	120	1.01
Japanese (8)	12	0.10
Korean (18)	26	0.22
Laotian (7)	13	0.11
Malaysian (1)	1	0.01
Pakistani (2)	2	0.02
Taiwanese	4	0.03
Thai (6)	6	0.05
Vietnamese (58)	60	0.50
Other Asian, not specified (4)	24	0.20
Austrian	51	0.43
Belgian	12	0.10

Notes: 1. Figures in the "Number" column do not add up to the total population due to: a) Ancestry/Race overlap — e.g. persons can report being both White and Irish, b) persons of Hispanic origin can report being any race, c) persons reporting two ancestries are counted in both categories. 2. Numbers in parentheses indicate the number of persons reporting this ancestry/race alone, not in combination with any other ancestry/race. 3. Refer to the Explanation of Data in the front of the book for more detailed information.

Brazilian	7	0.06
British	43	0.37
Canadian	98	0.84
Croatian	65	0.55
Cypriot	25	0.21
Czech	85	0.72
Czechoslovakian	9	0.08
Danish	75	0.64
Dutch	253	2.16
English	1,420	12.10
European	51	0.43
Finnish	20	0.17
French, except Basque	584	4.98
French Canadian	220	1.87
German	2,641	22.50
Greek	79	0.67
Hawaii Native/Pacific Islander:	23	0.19
Micronesian: (5)	5	0.04
Guamanian/Chamorro (5)	5	0.04
Polynesian: (8)	10	0.08
Native Hawaiian (4)	5	0.04
Samoan (4)	5	0.04
Other Pac. Isl., not spec. (6)	8	0.07
Hispanic or Latino:	794	6.67
Central American:	21	0.18
Costa Rican	5	0.04
Guatemalan	3	0.03
Honduran	4	0.03
Nicaraguan	2	0.02
Panamanian	4	0.03
Salvadoran	2	0.02
Other Central American	1	0.01
Cuban	75	0.63
Dominican Republic	15	0.13
Mexican	117	0.98
Puerto Rican	287	2.41
South American:	118	0.99
Argentinean	8	0.07
Bolivian	3	0.03
Chilean	2	0.02
Colombian	43	0.36
Ecuadorian	23	0.19
Peruvian	23	0.19
Uruguayan	2	0.02
Venezuelan	13	0.11
Other South American	1	0.01
Other Hispanic or Latino	161	1.35
Hungarian	65	0.55
Irish	2,223	18.94
Italian	1,544	13.16
Latvian	41	0.35
Norwegian	75	0.64
Polish	556	4.74
Portuguese	131	1.12
Romanian	38	0.32
Russian	99	0.84
Scotch-Irish	153	1.30
Scottish	303	2.58
Slavic	10	0.09
Slovak	43	0.37
Swedish	100	0.85
Swiss	49	0.42
Turkish	16	0.14
Ukrainian	34	0.29
United States or American	812	6.92
Welsh	121	1.03
West Indian, excl. Hispanic:	52	0.44
Barbadian	17	0.14
British West Indian	8	0.07
Haitian	8	0.07
West Indian	19	0.16
White:	10,990	92.28
Not Hispanic (10,210)	10,367	87.04
Hispanic (561)	623	5.23
Yugoslavian	12	0.10

Olympia Heights

Place Type: Census Designated Place
County: Miami-Dade
Population: 13,452

Ancestry/Race	Number	%
African American/Black:	141	1.05
Not Hispanic (20)	25	0.19
Hispanic (92)	116	0.86
African, sub-Saharan:	10	0.07
African	10	0.07
Am. Ind. or Alaska Nat., not spec.	12	0.09
American Indian tribes, specified:	17	0.13
Cherokee (5)	9	0.07
Latin American Indians (4)	8	0.06
American Indian tribes, not spec.	3	0.02
Arab:	75	0.56
Arab/Arabic	20	0.15
Lebanese	29	0.21
Moroccan	7	0.05
Palestinian	19	0.14
Asian:	139	1.03
Chinese, ex. Taiwanese (70)	76	0.56
Filipino (2)	2	0.01
Indian (30)	30	0.22
Japanese (3)	3	0.02
Korean (3)	3	0.02
Pakistani (5)	14	0.10
Taiwanese (4)	5	0.04
Vietnamese (2)	2	0.01
Other Asian, not specified (3)	4	0.03
Austrian	52	0.39
Belgian	21	0.16
Brazilian	19	0.14
British	9	0.07
Croatian	6	0.04
Czech	8	0.06
Czechoslovakian	7	0.05
Dutch	16	0.12
English	351	2.60
European	19	0.14
French, except Basque	121	0.90
French Canadian	35	0.26
German	362	2.68
Greek	14	0.10
Hawaii Native/Pacific Islander:	2	0.01
Micronesian:	2	0.01
Guamanian/Chamorro	2	0.01
Hispanic or Latino:	10,268	76.33
Central American:	432	3.21
Costa Rican	22	0.16
Guatemalan	41	0.30
Honduran	63	0.47
Nicaraguan	242	1.80
Panamanian	16	0.12
Salvadoran	34	0.25
Other Central American	14	0.10
Cuban	7,755	57.65
Dominican Republic	118	0.88
Mexican	101	0.75
Puerto Rican	272	2.02
South American:	570	4.24
Argentinean	31	0.23
Bolivian	7	0.05
Chilean	41	0.30
Colombian	268	1.99
Ecuadorian	40	0.30
Paraguayan	1	0.01
Peruvian	101	0.75
Uruguayan	3	0.02
Venezuelan	67	0.50
Other South American	11	0.08
Other Hispanic or Latino	1,020	7.58
Hungarian	29	0.21
Irish	480	3.56
Italian	218	1.62
Lithuanian	49	0.36
Norwegian	10	0.07
Polish	65	0.48
Romanian	23	0.17
Russian	105	0.78
Scotch-Irish	118	0.87
Scottish	89	0.66
Swiss	6	0.04
Ukrainian	9	0.07
United States or American	397	2.94
Welsh	15	0.11
White:	12,860	95.60
Not Hispanic (2,997)	3,024	22.48
Hispanic (9,581)	9,836	73.12
Yugoslavian	7	0.05

Opa-locka

Place Type: City
County: Miami-Dade
Population: 14,951

Ancestry/Race	Number	%
African American/Black:	10,705	71.60
Not Hispanic (9,933)	10,127	67.73
Hispanic (479)	578	3.87
African, sub-Saharan:	202	1.33
African	193	1.27
Cape Verdean	9	0.06
Alaska Native tribes, specified:	2	0.01
Eskimo	2	0.01
Am. Ind. or Alaska Nat., not spec.	52	0.35
American Indian tribes, specified:	40	0.27
Cherokee (5)	7	0.05
Crow	1	0.01
Iroquois	1	0.01
Latin American Indians (12)	18	0.12
Navajo (3)	3	0.02
Pueblo	1	0.01
Sioux (1)	1	0.01
All other tribes (1)	8	0.05
American Indian tribes, not spec.	6	0.04
Arab:	15	0.10
Lebanese	15	0.10
Asian:	78	0.52
Chinese, ex. Taiwanese (7)	18	0.12
Filipino (1)	1	0.01
Indian (10)	30	0.20
Japanese (1)	3	0.02
Korean (2)	3	0.02
Pakistani	1	0.01
Thai (4)	4	0.03
Vietnamese (2)	2	0.01
Other Asian, not specified (4)	16	0.11
Brazilian	11	0.07
British	13	0.09
Canadian	6	0.04
Czech	6	0.04
Dutch	8	0.05
English	154	1.01
European	7	0.05
French, except Basque	23	0.15
German	93	0.61
Hawaii Native/Pacific Islander:	42	0.28
Micronesian: (1)	7	0.05
Guamanian/Chamorro (1)	7	0.05
Polynesian: (2)	5	0.03
Native Hawaiian (2)	3	0.02
Samoan	2	0.01
Other Pac. Isl., not spec.	30	0.20
Hispanic or Latino:	4,268	28.55
Central American:	594	3.97
Costa Rican	12	0.08
Guatemalan	56	0.37
Honduran	133	0.89
Nicaraguan	332	2.22
Panamanian	13	0.09
Salvadoran	29	0.19
Other Central American	19	0.13
Cuban	1,432	9.58
Dominican Republic	387	2.59
Mexican	152	1.02
Puerto Rican	707	4.73

Notes: 1. Figures in the "Number" column do not add up to the total population due to: a) Ancestry/Race overlap — e.g. persons can report being both White and Irish, b) persons of Hispanic origin can report being any race, c) persons reporting two ancestries are counted in both categories. 2. Numbers in parentheses indicate the number of persons reporting this ancestry/race alone, not in combination with any other ancestry/race. 3. Refer to the Explanation of Data in the front of the book for more detailed information.

Ancestry/Race	Number	%
South American:	219	1.46
Argentinean	1	0.01
Bolivian	7	0.05
Chilean	3	0.02
Colombian	124	0.83
Ecuadorian	48	0.32
Paraguayan	1	0.01
Peruvian	20	0.13
Uruguayan	1	0.01
Venezuelan	8	0.05
Other South American	6	0.04
Other Hispanic or Latino	777	5.20
Icelander	13	0.09
Irish	125	0.82
Italian	64	0.42
Norwegian	20	0.13
Polish	5	0.03
Scotch-Irish	8	0.05
United States or American	457	3.00
West Indian, excl. Hispanic:	1,079	7.08
Bahamian	79	0.52
Barbadian	7	0.05
Belizean	8	0.05
British West Indian	36	0.24
Dutch West Indian	28	0.18
Haitian	364	2.39
Jamaican	389	2.55
Trinidadian and Tobagonian	49	0.32
U.S. Virgin Islander	7	0.05
West Indian	105	0.69
Other West Indian	7	0.05
White:	3,664	24.51
Not Hispanic (469)	507	3.39
Hispanic (2,945)	3,157	21.12

Orlando

Place Type: City
County: Orange
Population: 185,951

Ancestry/Race	Number	%
Acadian/Cajun	20	0.01
African American/Black:	52,652	28.31
Not Hispanic (48,547)	50,745	27.29
Hispanic (1,386)	1,907	1.03
African, sub-Saharan:	1,786	0.96
African	1,598	0.86
Cape Verdean	84	0.05
Nigerian	25	0.01
Sierra Leonean	12	0.01
South African	16	0.01
Zairian	10	0.01
Zimbabwean	10	0.01
Other sub-Saharan African	31	0.02
Alaska Native tribes, specified:	8	0.00
Alaska Athabascan (2)	4	0.00
Eskimo (1)	1	0.00
Tlingit-Haida (1)	1	0.00
All other tribes	2	0.00
Alaska Native tribes, not specified	1	0.00
Am. Ind. or Alaska Nat., not spec.	499	0.27
Albanian	114	0.06
Alsatian	13	0.01
American Indian tribes, specified:	807	0.43
Apache (12)	24	0.01
Blackfeet (7)	41	0.02
Cherokee (122)	349	0.19
Cheyenne	2	0.00
Chickasaw (2)	5	0.00
Chippewa (14)	27	0.01
Choctaw (19)	32	0.02
Colville	2	0.00
Comanche (1)	3	0.00
Creek (3)	22	0.01
Crow	1	0.00
Delaware (2)	3	0.00
Iroquois (26)	41	0.02
Kiowa (1)	1	0.00
Latin American Indians (38)	91	0.05
Lumbee (1)	3	0.00
Menominee	2	0.00
Navajo (5)	6	0.00
Osage	1	0.00
Ottawa	2	0.00
Paiute (2)	3	0.00
Potawatomi (3)	4	0.00
Pueblo (3)	8	0.00
Seminole (7)	36	0.02
Shoshone	1	0.00
Sioux (10)	23	0.01
Yakama (1)	1	0.00
Yaqui (4)	6	0.00
All other tribes (25)	67	0.04
American Indian tribes, not spec.	102	0.05
Arab:	1,693	0.91
Arab/Arabic	254	0.14
Egyptian	85	0.05
Jordanian	25	0.01
Lebanese	587	0.32
Moroccan	272	0.15
Palestinian	169	0.09
Syrian	204	0.11
Other Arab	97	0.05
Armenian	126	0.07
Asian:	6,259	3.37
Bangladeshi (17)	17	0.01
Cambodian (27)	29	0.02
Chinese, ex. Taiwanese (683)	873	0.47
Filipino (876)	1,138	0.61
Hmong (2)	5	0.00
Indian (1,247)	1,464	0.79
Indonesian (11)	19	0.01
Japanese (328)	447	0.24
Korean (437)	524	0.28
Laotian (34)	42	0.02
Malaysian (4)	7	0.00
Pakistani (133)	190	0.10
Sri Lankan (20)	21	0.01
Taiwanese (26)	30	0.02
Thai (73)	112	0.06
Vietnamese (849)	939	0.50
Other Asian, specified (15)	34	0.02
Other Asian, not specified (92)	368	0.20
Assyrian/Chaldean/Syriac	5	0.00
Australian	63	0.03
Austrian	362	0.19
Basque	27	0.01
Belgian	144	0.08
Brazilian	1,355	0.73
British	1,080	0.58
Bulgarian	13	0.01
Canadian	457	0.25
Carpatho Rusyn	17	0.01
Celtic	6	0.00
Croatian	145	0.08
Czech	255	0.14
Czechoslovakian	197	0.11
Danish	514	0.28
Dutch	2,223	1.20
Eastern European	101	0.05
English	14,663	7.88
Estonian	38	0.02
European	1,110	0.60
Finnish	330	0.18
French, except Basque	4,327	2.33
French Canadian	1,240	0.67
German	18,259	9.82
German Russian	9	0.00
Greek	682	0.37
Guyanese	131	0.07
Hawaii Native/Pacific Islander:	487	0.26
Melanesian: (2)	3	0.00
Fijian (2)	3	0.00
Micronesian: (49)	71	0.04
Guamanian/Chamorro (22)	33	0.02
Other Micronesian (27)	38	0.02
Polynesian: (66)	149	0.08
Native Hawaiian (32)	103	0.06
Samoan (22)	28	0.02
Tongan (6)	6	0.00
Other Polynesian (6)	12	0.01
Other Pac. Isl., specified	13	0.01
Other Pac. Isl., not spec. (33)	251	0.13
Hispanic or Latino:	32,510	17.48
Central American:	1,183	0.64
Costa Rican	119	0.06
Guatemalan	179	0.10
Honduran	329	0.18
Nicaraguan	123	0.07
Panamanian	230	0.12
Salvadoran	132	0.07
Other Central American	71	0.04
Cuban	2,696	1.45
Dominican Republic	1,191	0.64
Mexican	2,279	1.23
Puerto Rican	17,029	9.16
South American:	3,494	1.88
Argentinean	179	0.10
Bolivian	38	0.02
Chilean	84	0.05
Colombian	1,663	0.89
Ecuadorian	376	0.20
Paraguayan	7	0.00
Peruvian	336	0.18
Uruguayan	18	0.01
Venezuelan	674	0.36
Other South American	119	0.06
Other Hispanic or Latino	4,638	2.49
Hungarian	912	0.49
Icelander	91	0.05
Iranian	104	0.06
Irish	16,241	8.73
Israeli	13	0.01
Italian	8,557	4.60
Latvian	47	0.03
Lithuanian	319	0.17
Luxemburger	10	0.01
Maltese	18	0.01
New Zealander	6	0.00
Northern European	89	0.05
Norwegian	1,225	0.66
Pennsylvania German	35	0.02
Polish	3,297	1.77
Portuguese	514	0.28
Romanian	121	0.07
Russian	1,178	0.63
Scandinavian	192	0.10
Scotch-Irish	2,634	1.42
Scottish	3,164	1.70
Serbian	105	0.06
Slavic	54	0.03
Slovak	246	0.13
Slovene	43	0.02
Swedish	1,552	0.83
Swiss	377	0.20
Turkish	47	0.03
Ukrainian	388	0.21
United States or American	12,426	6.68
Welsh	1,046	0.56
West Indian, excl. Hispanic:	6,955	3.74
Bahamian	207	0.11
Barbadian	156	0.08
Belizean	36	0.02
British West Indian	279	0.15
Haitian	3,514	1.89
Jamaican	1,955	1.05
Trinidadian and Tobagonian	236	0.13
U.S. Virgin Islander	166	0.09
West Indian	369	0.20
Other West Indian	37	0.02
White:	117,957	63.43
Not Hispanic (94,452)	96,921	52.12
Hispanic (19,159)	21,036	11.31
Yugoslavian	118	0.06

Notes: 1. Figures in the "Number" column do not add up to the total population due to: a) Ancestry/Race overlap — e.g. persons can report being both White and Irish, b) persons of Hispanic origin can report being any race, c) persons reporting two ancestries are counted in both categories. 2. Numbers in parentheses indicate the number of persons reporting this ancestry/race alone, not in combination with any other ancestry/race. 3. Refer to the Explanation of Data in the front of the book for more detailed information.

Ormond Beach

Place Type: City
County: Volusia
Population: 36,301

Ancestry/Race	Number	%
Acadian/Cajun	26	0.07
African American/Black:	1,067	2.94
Not Hispanic (990)	1,053	2.90
Hispanic (10)	14	0.04
African, sub-Saharan:	113	0.31
African	101	0.28
Cape Verdean	6	0.02
Nigerian	6	0.02
Am. Ind. or Alaska Nat., not spec.	60	0.17
Alsatian	7	0.02
American Indian tribes, specified:	116	0.32
Blackfeet (1)	5	0.01
Cherokee (13)	58	0.16
Cheyenne (1)	1	0.00
Chickasaw (1)	1	0.00
Chippewa (2)	3	0.01
Choctaw (1)	2	0.01
Comanche (1)	1	0.00
Cree (1)	1	0.00
Creek (2)	6	0.02
Delaware	4	0.01
Iroquois (6)	12	0.03
Latin American Indians (1)	1	0.00
Pima (1)	2	0.01
Potawatomi	3	0.01
Pueblo	1	0.00
Seminole	1	0.00
Shoshone	1	0.00
Sioux (2)	5	0.01
All other tribes (5)	8	0.02
American Indian tribes, not spec.	5	0.01
Arab:	269	0.74
Arab/Arabic	18	0.05
Egyptian	119	0.33
Jordanian	29	0.08
Lebanese	92	0.25
Other Arab	11	0.03
Armenian	50	0.14
Asian:	619	1.71
Bangladeshi (1)	1	0.00
Chinese, ex. Taiwanese (73)	84	0.23
Filipino (75)	107	0.29
Indian (231)	261	0.72
Indonesian (2)	2	0.01
Japanese (22)	39	0.11
Korean (42)	45	0.12
Malaysian (1)	1	0.00
Pakistani (12)	12	0.03
Sri Lankan (4)	4	0.01
Taiwanese (5)	5	0.01
Thai (4)	5	0.01
Vietnamese (28)	28	0.08
Other Asian, specified	1	0.00
Other Asian, not specified (15)	24	0.07
Austrian	171	0.47
Belgian	33	0.09
Brazilian	43	0.12
British	259	0.71
Bulgarian	13	0.04
Canadian	231	0.64
Celtic	5	0.01
Croatian	38	0.10
Czech	90	0.25
Czechoslovakian	98	0.27
Danish	106	0.29
Dutch	732	2.01
Eastern European	20	0.06
English	6,146	16.91
Estonian	25	0.07
European	108	0.30
Finnish	90	0.25
French, except Basque	1,329	3.66
French Canadian	361	0.99
German	6,400	17.61
Greek	343	0.94
Hawaii Native/Pacific Islander:	15	0.04
Polynesian: (7)	15	0.04
Native Hawaiian (3)	11	0.03
Samoan (4)	4	0.01
Hispanic or Latino:	797	2.20
Central American:	45	0.12
Costa Rican	20	0.06
Guatemalan	10	0.03
Honduran	7	0.02
Nicaraguan	1	0.00
Panamanian	3	0.01
Salvadoran	4	0.01
Cuban	101	0.28
Dominican Republic	11	0.03
Mexican	87	0.24
Puerto Rican	275	0.76
South American:	123	0.34
Argentinean	14	0.04
Bolivian	1	0.00
Chilean	7	0.02
Colombian	28	0.08
Ecuadorian	22	0.06
Peruvian	14	0.04
Uruguayan	9	0.02
Venezuelan	13	0.04
Other South American	15	0.04
Other Hispanic or Latino	155	0.43
Hungarian	365	1.00
Icelander	6	0.02
Iranian	137	0.38
Irish	5,394	14.84
Italian	3,451	9.49
Latvian	6	0.02
Lithuanian	196	0.54
Luxemburger	6	0.02
Maltese	87	0.24
Northern European	57	0.16
Norwegian	459	1.26
Pennsylvania German	7	0.02
Polish	1,515	4.17
Portuguese	132	0.36
Romanian	23	0.06
Russian	543	1.49
Scandinavian	89	0.24
Scotch-Irish	1,127	3.10
Scottish	1,142	3.14
Serbian	60	0.17
Slavic	41	0.11
Slovak	109	0.30
Slovene	55	0.15
Swedish	572	1.57
Swiss	111	0.31
Ukrainian	227	0.62
United States or American	3,522	9.69
Welsh	331	0.91
West Indian, excl. Hispanic:	51	0.14
Bahamian	29	0.08
Jamaican	14	0.04
Trinidadian and Tobagonian	8	0.02
White:	34,566	95.22
Not Hispanic (33,564)	33,863	93.28
Hispanic (659)	703	1.94
Yugoslavian	28	0.08

Oviedo

Place Type: City
County: Seminole
Population: 26,316

Ancestry/Race	Number	%
African American/Black:	2,491	9.47
Not Hispanic (2,242)	2,363	8.98
Hispanic (83)	128	0.49
African, sub-Saharan:	104	0.38
African	87	0.32
Other sub-Saharan African	17	0.06
Alaska Native tribes, specified:	2	0.01
Eskimo (1)	1	0.00
Tlingit-Haida (1)	1	0.00
Am. Ind. or Alaska Nat., not spec.	61	0.23
Albanian	7	0.03
American Indian tribes, specified:	102	0.39
Apache (1)	2	0.01
Cherokee (11)	47	0.18
Chickasaw (1)	1	0.00
Chippewa	5	0.02
Choctaw (4)	7	0.03
Creek (2)	6	0.02
Iroquois (1)	3	0.01
Latin American Indians (7)	20	0.08
Navajo	2	0.01
Osage (1)	1	0.00
Ottawa	1	0.00
Seminole	3	0.01
Sioux	2	0.01
All other tribes (2)	2	0.01
American Indian tribes, not spec.	20	0.08
Arab:	215	0.80
Egyptian	44	0.16
Jordanian	55	0.20
Lebanese	36	0.13
Palestinian	36	0.13
Syrian	35	0.13
Other Arab	9	0.03
Armenian	32	0.12
Asian:	839	3.19
Cambodian (7)	7	0.03
Chinese, ex. Taiwanese (97)	150	0.57
Filipino (111)	161	0.61
Indian (174)	205	0.78
Indonesian (2)	4	0.02
Japanese (39)	64	0.24
Korean (76)	90	0.34
Laotian (2)	2	0.01
Pakistani (2)	13	0.05
Taiwanese (3)	4	0.02
Thai (7)	8	0.03
Vietnamese (97)	102	0.39
Other Asian, not specified (14)	29	0.11
Australian	8	0.03
Austrian	91	0.34
Basque	8	0.03
Belgian	74	0.27
British	307	1.14
Canadian	73	0.27
Celtic	21	0.08
Croatian	9	0.03
Czech	81	0.30
Czechoslovakian	52	0.19
Danish	103	0.38
Dutch	468	1.73
English	3,175	11.75
European	191	0.71
Finnish	85	0.31
French, except Basque	796	2.95
French Canadian	260	0.96
German	4,890	18.10
Greek	104	0.38
Guyanese	51	0.19
Hawaii Native/Pacific Islander:	40	0.15
Micronesian: (7)	12	0.05
Guamanian/Chamorro (7)	12	0.05
Polynesian: (3)	13	0.05
Native Hawaiian (3)	13	0.05
Other Pac. Isl., not spec.	15	0.06
Hispanic or Latino:	3,209	12.19
Central American:	130	0.49
Costa Rican	22	0.08
Guatemalan	7	0.03
Honduran	19	0.07
Nicaraguan	11	0.04
Panamanian	43	0.16
Salvadoran	16	0.06
Other Central American	12	0.05
Cuban	220	0.84
Dominican Republic	50	0.19
Mexican	308	1.17

Notes: 1. Figures in the "Number" column do not add up to the total population due to: a) Ancestry/Race overlap — e.g. persons can report being both White and Irish, b) persons of Hispanic origin can report being any race, c) persons reporting two ancestries are counted in both categories. 2. Numbers in parentheses indicate the number of persons reporting this ancestry/race alone, not in combination with any other ancestry/race. 3. Refer to the Explanation of Data in the front of the book for more detailed information.

Ancestry/Race	Number	%
Puerto Rican	1,807	6.87
South American:	318	1.21
Argentinean	10	0.04
Bolivian	9	0.03
Chilean	7	0.03
Colombian	148	0.56
Ecuadorian	49	0.19
Paraguayan	1	0.00
Peruvian	45	0.17
Uruguayan	3	0.01
Venezuelan	42	0.16
Other South American	4	0.02
Other Hispanic or Latino	376	1.43
Hungarian	156	0.58
Irish	3,621	13.40
Italian	3,136	11.60
Lithuanian	33	0.12
Maltese	8	0.03
Northern European	77	0.28
Norwegian	291	1.08
Pennsylvania German	10	0.04
Polish	1,243	4.60
Portuguese	81	0.30
Romanian	42	0.16
Russian	170	0.63
Scandinavian	7	0.03
Scotch-Irish	599	2.22
Scottish	659	2.44
Serbian	10	0.04
Slavic	29	0.11
Slovak	123	0.46
Slovene	28	0.10
Swedish	244	0.90
Swiss	77	0.28
Turkish	26	0.10
Ukrainian	27	0.10
United States or American	1,575	5.83
Welsh	248	0.92
West Indian, excl. Hispanic:	528	1.95
Belizean	3	0.01
British West Indian	47	0.17
Haitian	192	0.71
Jamaican	219	0.81
Trinidadian and Tobagonian	24	0.09
U.S. Virgin Islander	14	0.05
West Indian	29	0.11
White:	22,450	85.31
Not Hispanic (19,734)	20,053	76.20
Hispanic (2,252)	2,397	9.11
Yugoslavian	22	0.08

Palatka

Place Type: City
County: Putnam
Population: 10,033

Ancestry/Race	Number	%
African American/Black:	4,907	48.91
Not Hispanic (4,840)	4,880	48.64
Hispanic (19)	27	0.27
African, sub-Saharan:	62	0.61
African	62	0.61
Am. Ind. or Alaska Nat., not spec.	27	0.27
American Indian tribes, specified:	37	0.37
Apache (1)	3	0.03
Blackfeet	4	0.04
Cherokee (3)	23	0.23
Cree	1	0.01
Iroquois	1	0.01
Latin American Indians	1	0.01
Seminole	4	0.04
American Indian tribes, not spec.	1	0.01
Armenian	12	0.12
Asian:	60	0.60
Chinese, ex. Taiwanese (3)	3	0.03
Filipino (5)	9	0.09
Indian (12)	12	0.12
Japanese (3)	5	0.05
Korean (1)	1	0.01
Pakistani (12)	15	0.15
Thai	2	0.02
Vietnamese (3)	3	0.03
Other Asian, not specified (5)	10	0.10
British	22	0.22
Canadian	16	0.16
Celtic	9	0.09
Croatian	21	0.21
Danish	12	0.12
Dutch	84	0.82
English	565	5.54
European	12	0.12
French, except Basque	85	0.83
French Canadian	14	0.14
German	453	4.44
Greek	7	0.07
Guyanese	10	0.10
Hawaii Native/Pacific Islander:	2	0.02
Polynesian: (1)	2	0.02
Native Hawaiian (1)	2	0.02
Hispanic or Latino:	284	2.83
Central American:	2	0.02
Nicaraguan	2	0.02
Cuban	21	0.21
Dominican Republic	2	0.02
Mexican	65	0.65
Puerto Rican	131	1.31
South American:	10	0.10
Argentinean	1	0.01
Colombian	4	0.04
Ecuadorian	1	0.01
Peruvian	3	0.03
Venezuelan	1	0.01
Other Hispanic or Latino	53	0.53
Hungarian	8	0.08
Irish	555	5.44
Italian	114	1.12
Lithuanian	11	0.11
Norwegian	29	0.28
Polish	97	0.95
Portuguese	57	0.56
Russian	5	0.05
Scandinavian	22	0.22
Scotch-Irish	193	1.89
Scottish	192	1.88
Serbian	11	0.11
Slovak	11	0.11
Swedish	46	0.45
United States or American	1,045	10.24
Welsh	27	0.26
West Indian, excl. Hispanic:	64	0.63
Haitian	37	0.36
Jamaican	27	0.26
White:	4,982	49.66
Not Hispanic (4,762)	4,822	48.06
Hispanic (147)	160	1.59
Yugoslavian	8	0.08

Palm Bay

Place Type: City
County: Brevard
Population: 79,413

Ancestry/Race	Number	%
Acadian/Cajun	22	0.03
African American/Black:	9,697	12.21
Not Hispanic (8,634)	9,186	11.57
Hispanic (349)	511	0.64
African, sub-Saharan:	450	0.57
African	399	0.50
Cape Verdean	39	0.05
South African	12	0.02
Alaska Native tribes, specified:	9	0.01
Aleut (1)	1	0.00
Eskimo (3)	6	0.01
Tlingit-Haida (1)	1	0.00
All other tribes	1	0.00
Am. Ind. or Alaska Nat., not spec.	197	0.25
Albanian	8	0.01
American Indian tribes, specified:	449	0.57
Apache (6)	12	0.02
Blackfeet (7)	35	0.04
Cherokee (67)	183	0.23
Cheyenne (1)	3	0.00
Chickasaw (3)	7	0.01
Chippewa (10)	18	0.02
Choctaw (5)	6	0.01
Comanche (2)	3	0.00
Cree	1	0.00
Creek (2)	9	0.01
Iroquois (19)	32	0.04
Kiowa (3)	3	0.00
Latin American Indians (21)	39	0.05
Lumbee (1)	1	0.00
Menominee	2	0.00
Navajo (5)	12	0.02
Potawatomi (3)	5	0.01
Pueblo	4	0.01
Puget Sound Salish	1	0.00
Seminole (2)	20	0.03
Sioux (5)	15	0.02
Yuman (1)	1	0.00
All other tribes (14)	37	0.05
American Indian tribes, not spec.	36	0.05
Arab:	598	0.75
Arab/Arabic	226	0.28
Egyptian	91	0.11
Lebanese	166	0.21
Moroccan	27	0.03
Syrian	24	0.03
Other Arab	64	0.08
Armenian	43	0.05
Asian:	1,888	2.38
Bangladeshi (10)	11	0.01
Cambodian (12)	13	0.02
Chinese, ex. Taiwanese (156)	230	0.29
Filipino (316)	458	0.58
Indian (362)	419	0.53
Indonesian (9)	19	0.02
Japanese (92)	171	0.22
Korean (126)	162	0.20
Laotian (1)	1	0.00
Malaysian (3)	3	0.00
Pakistani (12)	17	0.02
Sri Lankan	1	0.00
Taiwanese (16)	24	0.03
Thai (58)	87	0.11
Vietnamese (135)	165	0.21
Other Asian, specified (3)	6	0.01
Other Asian, not specified (29)	101	0.13
Australian	37	0.05
Austrian	236	0.30
Basque	19	0.02
Belgian	31	0.04
Brazilian	62	0.08
British	378	0.48
Canadian	261	0.33
Celtic	6	0.01
Croatian	62	0.08
Cypriot	16	0.02
Czech	304	0.38
Czechoslovakian	144	0.18
Danish	262	0.33
Dutch	1,671	2.10
Eastern European	7	0.01
English	8,038	10.12
European	454	0.57
Finnish	136	0.17
French, except Basque	3,337	4.20
French Canadian	1,257	1.58
German	14,240	17.92
German Russian	11	0.01
Greek	438	0.55
Guyanese	211	0.27
Hawaii Native/Pacific Islander:	133	0.17
Melanesian: (1)	3	0.00
Fijian (1)	3	0.00
Micronesian: (11)	18	0.02
Guamanian/Chamorro (11)	18	0.02

Notes: 1. Figures in the "Number" column do not add up to the total population due to: a) Ancestry/Race overlap — e.g. persons can report being both White and Irish, b) persons of Hispanic origin can report being any race, c) persons reporting two ancestries are counted in both categories. 2. Numbers in parentheses indicate the number of persons reporting this ancestry/race alone, not in combination with any other ancestry/race. 3. Refer to the Explanation of Data in the front of the book for more detailed information.

Polynesian: (16)	40	0.05
Native Hawaiian (12)	28	0.04
Samoan (1)	5	0.01
Tongan (2)	6	0.01
Other Polynesian (1)	1	0.00
Other Pac. Isl., not spec. (8)	72	0.09
Hispanic or Latino:	6,850	8.63
Central American:	312	0.39
Costa Rican	36	0.05
Guatemalan	35	0.04
Honduran	40	0.05
Nicaraguan	22	0.03
Panamanian	127	0.16
Salvadoran	40	0.05
Other Central American	12	0.02
Cuban	404	0.51
Dominican Republic	182	0.23
Mexican	549	0.69
Puerto Rican	3,767	4.74
South American:	489	0.62
Argentinean	32	0.04
Bolivian	8	0.01
Chilean	15	0.02
Colombian	211	0.27
Ecuadorian	39	0.05
Paraguayan	10	0.01
Peruvian	70	0.09
Uruguayan	3	0.00
Venezuelan	79	0.10
Other South American	22	0.03
Other Hispanic or Latino	1,147	1.44
Hungarian	499	0.63
Iranian	34	0.04
Irish	11,603	14.60
Israeli	9	0.01
Italian	7,318	9.21
Lithuanian	281	0.35
Luxemburger	4	0.01
Maltese	27	0.03
Northern European	5	0.01
Norwegian	731	0.92
Pennsylvania German	47	0.06
Polish	3,059	3.85
Portuguese	445	0.56
Romanian	25	0.03
Russian	440	0.55
Scandinavian	52	0.07
Scotch-Irish	1,317	1.66
Scottish	1,636	2.06
Serbian	21	0.03
Slavic	23	0.03
Slovak	187	0.24
Slovene	9	0.01
Swedish	1,042	1.31
Swiss	222	0.28
Turkish	50	0.06
Ukrainian	282	0.35
United States or American	6,286	7.91
Welsh	719	0.90
West Indian, excl. Hispanic:	2,785	3.51
Bahamian	11	0.01
Barbadian	92	0.12
Belizean	13	0.02
British West Indian	75	0.09
Dutch West Indian	59	0.07
Haitian	175	0.22
Jamaican	1,756	2.21
Trinidadian and Tobagonian	356	0.45
U.S. Virgin Islander	32	0.04
West Indian	197	0.25
Other West Indian	19	0.02
White:	66,399	83.61
Not Hispanic (60,549)	61,781	77.80
Hispanic (4,206)	4,618	5.82
Yugoslavian	10	0.01

Palm Beach Gardens

Place Type: City
County: Palm Beach
Population: 35,058

Ancestry/Race	Number	%
Acadian/Cajun	14	0.04
Afghan	14	0.04
African American/Black:	904	2.58
Not Hispanic (736)	816	2.33
Hispanic (70)	88	0.25
African, sub-Saharan:	51	0.15
African	32	0.09
South African	19	0.06
Alaska Native tribes, specified:	1	0.00
Aleut	1	0.00
Am. Ind. or Alaska Nat., not spec.	40	0.11
Albanian	24	0.07
American Indian tribes, specified:	47	0.13
Blackfeet (1)	2	0.01
Cherokee (6)	14	0.04
Chippewa	1	0.00
Choctaw	3	0.01
Creek	5	0.01
Iroquois (1)	3	0.01
Latin American Indians (3)	6	0.02
Lumbee (1)	1	0.00
Pueblo	1	0.00
Seminole	2	0.01
All other tribes (4)	9	0.03
American Indian tribes, not spec.	10	0.03
Arab:	301	0.87
Arab/Arabic	89	0.26
Iraqi	17	0.05
Lebanese	54	0.16
Palestinian	39	0.11
Syrian	102	0.30
Armenian	92	0.27
Asian:	868	2.48
Bangladeshi (13)	17	0.05
Chinese, ex. Taiwanese (135)	154	0.44
Filipino (45)	62	0.18
Indian (256)	286	0.82
Indonesian (2)	2	0.01
Japanese (38)	57	0.16
Korean (91)	98	0.28
Laotian (2)	2	0.01
Malaysian (1)	2	0.01
Pakistani (8)	13	0.04
Sri Lankan (1)	1	0.00
Thai (8)	11	0.03
Vietnamese (130)	135	0.39
Other Asian, specified	1	0.00
Other Asian, not specified (8)	27	0.08
Austrian	195	0.57
Belgian	56	0.16
Brazilian	8	0.02
British	199	0.58
Bulgarian	7	0.02
Canadian	199	0.58
Celtic	23	0.07
Croatian	10	0.03
Czech	170	0.49
Czechoslovakian	116	0.34
Danish	213	0.62
Dutch	503	1.46
Eastern European	169	0.49
English	4,579	13.28
European	458	1.33
Finnish	109	0.32
French, except Basque	1,441	4.18
French Canadian	413	1.20
German	5,937	17.22
Greek	481	1.40
Hawaii Native/Pacific Islander:	28	0.08
Micronesian: (8)	12	0.03
Guamanian/Chamorro (8)	12	0.03
Polynesian: (2)	9	0.03
Native Hawaiian (1)	6	0.02
Samoan (1)	3	0.01
Other Pac. Isl., not spec. (1)	7	0.02
Hispanic or Latino:	1,973	5.63
Central American:	129	0.37
Costa Rican	11	0.03
Guatemalan	41	0.12
Honduran	19	0.05
Nicaraguan	9	0.03
Panamanian	9	0.03
Salvadoran	32	0.09
Other Central American	8	0.02
Cuban	429	1.22
Dominican Republic	23	0.07
Mexican	137	0.39
Puerto Rican	345	0.98
South American:	448	1.28
Argentinean	39	0.11
Bolivian	3	0.01
Chilean	48	0.14
Colombian	150	0.43
Ecuadorian	49	0.14
Peruvian	93	0.27
Uruguayan	3	0.01
Venezuelan	45	0.13
Other South American	18	0.05
Other Hispanic or Latino	462	1.32
Hungarian	643	1.87
Iranian	65	0.19
Irish	5,248	15.22
Israeli	48	0.14
Italian	4,451	12.91
Latvian	46	0.13
Lithuanian	156	0.45
Maltese	9	0.03
Northern European	6	0.02
Norwegian	295	0.86
Pennsylvania German	20	0.06
Polish	1,952	5.66
Portuguese	164	0.48
Romanian	165	0.48
Russian	1,548	4.49
Scandinavian	36	0.10
Scotch-Irish	635	1.84
Scottish	796	2.31
Serbian	11	0.03
Slovak	168	0.49
Swedish	471	1.37
Swiss	122	0.35
Turkish	32	0.09
Ukrainian	185	0.54
United States or American	2,125	6.16
Welsh	308	0.89
West Indian, excl. Hispanic:	325	0.94
Bahamian	52	0.15
Barbadian	14	0.04
Bermudan	15	0.04
British West Indian	26	0.08
Haitian	95	0.28
Jamaican	80	0.23
Trinidadian and Tobagonian	43	0.12
White:	33,157	94.58
Not Hispanic (31,252)	31,461	89.74
Hispanic (1,626)	1,696	4.84
Yugoslavian	10	0.03

Palm Beach

Place Type: Town
County: Palm Beach
Population: 10,468

Ancestry/Race	Number	%
African American/Black:	285	2.72
Not Hispanic (262)	278	2.66
Hispanic (7)	7	0.07
Alaska Native tribes, specified:	1	0.01
Aleut (1)	1	0.01
Am. Ind. or Alaska Nat., not spec.	4	0.04
Albanian	13	0.13
American Indian tribes, specified:	6	0.06

Notes: 1. Figures in the "Number" column do not add up to the total population due to: a) Ancestry/Race overlap — e.g. persons can report being both White and Irish, b) persons of Hispanic origin can report being any race, c) persons reporting two ancestries are counted in both categories. 2. Numbers in parentheses indicate the number of persons reporting this ancestry/race alone, not in combination with any other ancestry/race. 3. Refer to the Explanation of Data in the front of the book for more detailed information.

Ancestry/Race	Number	%
Cherokee	1	0.01
Chickasaw	1	0.01
Chippewa (1)	1	0.01
Comanche	1	0.01
Latin American Indians (1)	1	0.01
All other tribes (1)	1	0.01
American Indian tribes, not spec.	9	0.09
Arab:	151	1.46
Arab/Arabic	11	0.11
Egyptian	5	0.05
Iraqi	21	0.20
Lebanese	62	0.60
Moroccan	12	0.12
Palestinian	14	0.13
Syrian	26	0.25
Armenian	19	0.18
Asian:	78	0.75
Chinese, ex. Taiwanese (9)	11	0.11
Filipino (22)	26	0.25
Indian (9)	9	0.09
Japanese (7)	23	0.22
Korean (5)	5	0.05
Thai (2)	2	0.02
Other Asian, specified (1)	1	0.01
Other Asian, not specified (1)	1	0.01
Australian	5	0.05
Austrian	224	2.16
Basque	4	0.04
Belgian	10	0.10
Brazilian	11	0.11
British	99	0.95
Bulgarian	6	0.06
Canadian	48	0.46
Czech	5	0.05
Czechoslovakian	12	0.12
Danish	34	0.33
Dutch	102	0.98
Eastern European	68	0.66
English	1,323	12.75
Estonian	9	0.09
European	110	1.06
Finnish	34	0.33
French, except Basque	472	4.55
French Canadian	73	0.70
German	1,198	11.55
Greek	147	1.42
Hawaii Native/Pacific Islander:	6	0.06
Micronesian:	2	0.02
Guamanian/Chamorro	2	0.02
Polynesian: (1)	1	0.01
Tongan (1)	1	0.01
Other Pac. Isl., not spec. (1)	3	0.03
Hispanic or Latino:	268	2.56
Central American:	20	0.19
Guatemalan	6	0.06
Honduran	6	0.06
Nicaraguan	5	0.05
Panamanian	2	0.02
Salvadoran	1	0.01
Cuban	82	0.78
Dominican Republic	9	0.09
Mexican	19	0.18
Puerto Rican	13	0.12
South American:	53	0.51
Argentinean	14	0.13
Bolivian	3	0.03
Chilean	3	0.03
Colombian	15	0.14
Ecuadorian	2	0.02
Paraguayan	3	0.03
Peruvian	5	0.05
Uruguayan	1	0.01
Venezuelan	5	0.05
Other South American	2	0.02
Other Hispanic or Latino	72	0.69
Hungarian	136	1.31
Iranian	16	0.15
Irish	904	8.71
Israeli	12	0.12
Italian	646	6.23
Latvian	19	0.18
Lithuanian	155	1.49
Luxemburger	9	0.09
Maltese	12	0.12
Northern European	7	0.07
Norwegian	48	0.46
Polish	531	5.12
Portuguese	33	0.32
Romanian	102	0.98
Russian	1,089	10.50
Scandinavian	13	0.13
Scotch-Irish	89	0.86
Scottish	190	1.83
Serbian	36	0.35
Slovak	8	0.08
Slovene	14	0.13
Swedish	51	0.49
Swiss	27	0.26
Ukrainian	82	0.79
United States or American	777	7.49
Welsh	54	0.52
West Indian, excl. Hispanic:	37	0.36
British West Indian	32	0.31
Haitian	5	0.05
White:	10,104	96.52
Not Hispanic (9,817)	9,859	94.18
Hispanic (232)	245	2.34

Palm City

Place Type: Census Designated Place
County: Martin
Population: 20,097

Ancestry/Race	Number	%
Acadian/Cajun	12	0.06
African American/Black:	249	1.24
Not Hispanic (207)	235	1.17
Hispanic (10)	14	0.07
African, sub-Saharan:	16	0.08
African	16	0.08
Am. Ind. or Alaska Nat., not spec.	27	0.13
American Indian tribes, specified:	46	0.23
Apache (1)	3	0.01
Cherokee (5)	16	0.08
Chippewa (1)	1	0.00
Choctaw	1	0.00
Iroquois (4)	8	0.04
Latin American Indians	8	0.04
Osage	1	0.00
Pueblo (3)	3	0.01
Sioux	2	0.01
All other tribes (2)	3	0.01
American Indian tribes, not spec.	3	0.01
Arab:	70	0.35
Lebanese	45	0.22
Moroccan	9	0.04
Syrian	16	0.08
Armenian	41	0.20
Asian:	276	1.37
Chinese, ex. Taiwanese (66)	85	0.42
Filipino (23)	40	0.20
Indian (65)	73	0.36
Japanese (10)	19	0.09
Korean (14)	18	0.09
Malaysian (1)	2	0.01
Sri Lankan (2)	2	0.01
Thai (5)	7	0.03
Vietnamese (9)	13	0.06
Other Asian, not specified (6)	17	0.08
Australian	7	0.03
Austrian	203	1.01
Belgian	14	0.07
British	153	0.76
Canadian	58	0.29
Croatian	44	0.22
Czech	38	0.19
Czechoslovakian	57	0.28
Danish	183	0.91
Dutch	365	1.82
Eastern European	63	0.31
English	3,372	16.77
European	97	0.48
Finnish	63	0.31
French, except Basque	749	3.72
French Canadian	382	1.90
German	3,836	19.08
Greek	165	0.82
Guyanese	18	0.09
Hawaii Native/Pacific Islander:	4	0.02
Polynesian: (1)	3	0.01
Native Hawaiian (1)	3	0.01
Other Pac. Isl., not spec.	1	0.00
Hispanic or Latino:	556	2.77
Central American:	19	0.09
Costa Rican	2	0.01
Guatemalan	10	0.05
Nicaraguan	1	0.00
Panamanian	1	0.00
Salvadoran	3	0.01
Other Central American	2	0.01
Cuban	88	0.44
Dominican Republic	6	0.03
Mexican	82	0.41
Puerto Rican	150	0.75
South American:	91	0.45
Argentinean	6	0.03
Bolivian	10	0.05
Chilean	2	0.01
Colombian	25	0.12
Ecuadorian	14	0.07
Peruvian	7	0.03
Venezuelan	15	0.07
Other South American	12	0.06
Other Hispanic or Latino	120	0.60
Hungarian	290	1.44
Irish	3,470	17.26
Italian	2,992	14.88
Latvian	18	0.09
Lithuanian	40	0.20
Norwegian	277	1.38
Pennsylvania German	10	0.05
Polish	1,037	5.16
Portuguese	70	0.35
Romanian	37	0.18
Russian	432	2.15
Scandinavian	70	0.35
Scotch-Irish	476	2.37
Scottish	497	2.47
Slavic	60	0.30
Slovak	60	0.30
Slovene	26	0.13
Swedish	542	2.70
Swiss	131	0.65
Turkish	9	0.04
Ukrainian	104	0.52
United States or American	1,566	7.79
Welsh	157	0.78
West Indian, excl. Hispanic:	103	0.51
Bahamian	19	0.09
Haitian	36	0.18
Jamaican	39	0.19
West Indian	9	0.04
White:	19,535	97.20
Not Hispanic (18,971)	19,073	94.90
Hispanic (435)	462	2.30
Yugoslavian	24	0.12

Palm Coast

Place Type: City
County: Flagler
Population: 32,732

Ancestry/Race	Number	%
Acadian/Cajun	6	0.02
African American/Black:	3,592	10.97
Not Hispanic (3,261)	3,451	10.54
Hispanic (99)	141	0.43
African, sub-Saharan:	82	0.24

Notes: 1. Figures in the "Number" column do not add up to the total population due to: a) Ancestry/Race overlap — e.g. persons can report being both White and Irish, b) persons of Hispanic origin can report being any race, c) persons reporting two ancestries are counted in both categories. 2. Numbers in parentheses indicate the number of persons reporting this ancestry/race alone, not in combination with any other ancestry/race. 3. Refer to the Explanation of Data in the front of the book for more detailed information.

African	79	0.24
Cape Verdean	3	0.01
Alaska Native tribes, specified:	4	0.01
Eskimo	1	0.00
Tlingit-Haida (3)	3	0.01
Am. Ind. or Alaska Nat., not spec.	74	0.23
American Indian tribes, specified:	135	0.41
Apache (2)	2	0.01
Blackfeet (4)	7	0.02
Cherokee (22)	63	0.19
Cheyenne (1)	2	0.01
Chippewa (1)	2	0.01
Choctaw (1)	8	0.02
Comanche (1)	3	0.01
Creek	10	0.03
Delaware (1)	2	0.01
Iroquois (1)	5	0.02
Latin American Indians (4)	8	0.02
Potawatomi	1	0.00
Sioux (3)	4	0.01
All other tribes (7)	18	0.05
American Indian tribes, not spec.	16	0.05
Arab:	68	0.20
Egyptian	23	0.07
Lebanese	45	0.13
Armenian	32	0.10
Asian:	618	1.89
Cambodian (13)	17	0.05
Chinese, ex. Taiwanese (60)	85	0.26
Filipino (259)	304	0.93
Indian (68)	84	0.26
Indonesian (2)	5	0.02
Japanese (14)	24	0.07
Korean (31)	36	0.11
Laotian	1	0.00
Malaysian	2	0.01
Pakistani (1)	6	0.02
Taiwanese (11)	12	0.04
Thai (9)	12	0.04
Vietnamese (16)	20	0.06
Other Asian, not specified (6)	10	0.03
Australian	7	0.02
Austrian	177	0.53
Belgian	37	0.11
Brazilian	9	0.03
British	205	0.61
Canadian	91	0.27
Celtic	11	0.03
Croatian	60	0.18
Czech	168	0.50
Czechoslovakian	98	0.29
Danish	96	0.29
Dutch	612	1.83
English	3,975	11.86
European	75	0.22
Finnish	109	0.33
French, except Basque	1,067	3.18
French Canadian	318	0.95
German	5,341	15.94
Greek	160	0.48
Guyanese	115	0.34
Hawaii Native/Pacific Islander:	35	0.11
Melanesian: (2)	2	0.01
Other Melanesian (2)	2	0.01
Micronesian: (1)	1	0.00
Guamanian/Chamorro (1)	1	0.00
Polynesian: (5)	12	0.04
Native Hawaiian	2	0.01
Samoan (5)	10	0.03
Other Pac. Isl., not spec. (1)	20	0.06
Hispanic or Latino:	2,196	6.71
Central American:	85	0.26
Costa Rican	4	0.01
Guatemalan	17	0.05
Honduran	15	0.05
Nicaraguan	5	0.02
Panamanian	28	0.09
Salvadoran	11	0.03
Other Central American	5	0.02
Cuban	249	0.76
Dominican Republic	36	0.11
Mexican	172	0.53
Puerto Rican	912	2.79
South American:	305	0.93
Argentinean	24	0.07
Bolivian	6	0.02
Chilean	6	0.02
Colombian	139	0.42
Ecuadorian	25	0.08
Peruvian	49	0.15
Uruguayan	22	0.07
Venezuelan	19	0.06
Other South American	15	0.05
Other Hispanic or Latino	437	1.34
Hungarian	254	0.76
Icelander	24	0.07
Iranian	24	0.07
Irish	5,666	16.91
Israeli	27	0.08
Italian	5,128	15.31
Lithuanian	105	0.31
Macedonian	13	0.04
Maltese	30	0.09
New Zealander	48	0.14
Norwegian	262	0.78
Pennsylvania German	33	0.10
Polish	1,633	4.87
Portuguese	486	1.45
Romanian	7	0.02
Russian	446	1.33
Scandinavian	30	0.09
Scotch-Irish	519	1.55
Scottish	804	2.40
Serbian	83	0.25
Slavic	38	0.11
Slovak	130	0.39
Slovene	13	0.04
Swedish	466	1.39
Swiss	92	0.27
Turkish	58	0.17
Ukrainian	307	0.92
United States or American	1,473	4.40
Welsh	352	1.05
West Indian, excl. Hispanic:	839	2.50
Bahamian	15	0.04
Barbadian	43	0.13
Belizean	24	0.07
Bermudan	8	0.02
British West Indian	19	0.06
Haitian	37	0.11
Jamaican	492	1.47
Trinidadian and Tobagonian	72	0.21
West Indian	129	0.39
White:	28,261	86.34
Not Hispanic (26,217)	26,532	81.06
Hispanic (1,617)	1,729	5.28
Yugoslavian	33	0.10

Palm Harbor

Place Type: Census Designated Place
County: Pinellas
Population: 59,248

Ancestry/Race	Number	%
Acadian/Cajun	53	0.09
African American/Black:	695	1.17
Not Hispanic (545)	648	1.09
Hispanic (29)	47	0.08
African, sub-Saharan:	125	0.21
African	72	0.12
Kenyan	5	0.01
South African	48	0.08
Alaska Native tribes, specified:	3	0.01
Eskimo (2)	2	0.00
Tlingit-Haida	1	0.00
Am. Ind. or Alaska Nat., not spec.	65	0.11
Albanian	105	0.18
American Indian tribes, specified:	189	0.32
Apache	3	0.01
Blackfeet (7)	13	0.02
Cherokee (25)	82	0.14
Chickasaw	1	0.00
Chippewa (5)	7	0.01
Choctaw (4)	4	0.01
Creek (3)	11	0.02
Crow	1	0.00
Delaware	1	0.00
Houma (1)	1	0.00
Iroquois (4)	16	0.03
Latin American Indians (7)	8	0.01
Navajo	1	0.00
Osage (1)	1	0.00
Ottawa	1	0.00
Potawatomi (1)	1	0.00
Seminole (2)	5	0.01
Sioux (5)	12	0.02
Yaqui	3	0.01
All other tribes (9)	17	0.03
American Indian tribes, not spec.	40	0.07
Arab:	572	0.97
Arab/Arabic	54	0.09
Egyptian	129	0.22
Iraqi	8	0.01
Lebanese	215	0.36
Palestinian	105	0.18
Syrian	50	0.08
Other Arab	11	0.02
Armenian	44	0.07
Asian:	930	1.57
Cambodian (6)	6	0.01
Chinese, ex. Taiwanese (126)	145	0.24
Filipino (120)	159	0.27
Indian (268)	285	0.48
Indonesian (7)	8	0.01
Japanese (59)	98	0.17
Korean (47)	69	0.12
Laotian (9)	9	0.02
Malaysian (1)	2	0.00
Pakistani (18)	21	0.04
Taiwanese (3)	4	0.01
Thai (13)	14	0.02
Vietnamese (59)	71	0.12
Other Asian, specified (5)	7	0.01
Other Asian, not specified (16)	32	0.05
Australian	48	0.08
Austrian	238	0.40
Belgian	66	0.11
Brazilian	51	0.09
British	432	0.73
Bulgarian	14	0.02
Canadian	438	0.74
Celtic	12	0.02
Croatian	216	0.37
Cypriot	30	0.05
Czech	366	0.62
Czechoslovakian	222	0.38
Danish	531	0.90
Dutch	1,377	2.33
Eastern European	20	0.03
English	8,244	13.94
European	365	0.62
Finnish	195	0.33
French, except Basque	2,569	4.35
French Canadian	639	1.08
German	11,510	19.47
Greek	1,707	2.89
Hawaii Native/Pacific Islander:	41	0.07
Micronesian: (2)	5	0.01
Guamanian/Chamorro (2)	5	0.01
Polynesian: (12)	24	0.04
Native Hawaiian (12)	21	0.04
Samoan	2	0.00
Tongan	1	0.00
Other Pac. Isl., not spec.	12	0.02
Hispanic or Latino:	2,047	3.45
Central American:	71	0.12
Costa Rican	20	0.03
Guatemalan	15	0.03
Honduran	3	0.01

Notes: 1. Figures in the "Number" column do not add up to the total population due to: a) Ancestry/Race overlap — e.g. persons can report being both White and Irish, b) persons of Hispanic origin can report being any race, c) persons reporting two ancestries are counted in both categories. 2. Numbers in parentheses indicate the number of persons reporting this ancestry/race alone, not in combination with any other ancestry/race. 3. Refer to the Explanation of Data in the front of the book for more detailed information.

Nicaraguan	7	0.01
Panamanian	10	0.02
Salvadoran	13	0.02
Other Central American	3	0.01
Cuban	240	0.41
Dominican Republic	46	0.08
Mexican	268	0.45
Puerto Rican	611	1.03
South American:	352	0.59
Argentinean	20	0.03
Bolivian	9	0.02
Chilean	8	0.01
Colombian	145	0.24
Ecuadorian	55	0.09
Paraguayan	1	0.00
Peruvian	49	0.08
Uruguayan	2	0.00
Venezuelan	47	0.08
Other South American	16	0.03
Other Hispanic or Latino	459	0.77
Hungarian	792	1.34
Icelander	26	0.04
Iranian	44	0.07
Irish	9,754	16.50
Israeli	37	0.06
Italian	7,548	12.77
Latvian	8	0.01
Lithuanian	313	0.53
Macedonian	9	0.02
Maltese	44	0.07
Northern European	51	0.09
Norwegian	604	1.02
Pennsylvania German	29	0.05
Polish	3,230	5.46
Portuguese	299	0.51
Romanian	173	0.29
Russian	849	1.44
Scandinavian	61	0.10
Scotch-Irish	1,226	2.07
Scottish	1,780	3.01
Serbian	19	0.03
Slavic	51	0.09
Slovak	137	0.23
Slovene	26	0.04
Swedish	1,264	2.14
Swiss	233	0.39
Turkish	15	0.03
Ukrainian	253	0.43
United States or American	3,674	6.21
Welsh	604	1.02
West Indian, excl. Hispanic:	97	0.16
Jamaican	97	0.16
White:	57,366	96.82
Not Hispanic (55,198)	55,679	93.98
Hispanic (1,582)	1,687	2.85
Yugoslavian	89	0.15

Palm River-Clair Mel

Place Type: Census Designated Place
County: Hillsborough
Population: 17,589

Ancestry/Race	Number	%
African American/Black:	6,282	35.72
Not Hispanic (5,933)	6,061	34.46
Hispanic (154)	221	1.26
African, sub-Saharan:	105	0.60
African	83	0.47
South African	22	0.13
Am. Ind. or Alaska Nat., not spec.	73	0.42
Albanian	6	0.03
American Indian tribes, specified:	127	0.72
Apache (4)	5	0.03
Blackfeet (2)	4	0.02
Cherokee (16)	55	0.31
Cheyenne (1)	2	0.01
Chippewa (5)	5	0.03
Choctaw (1)	5	0.03
Comanche (4)	4	0.02
Cree	1	0.01
Crow	1	0.01
Iroquois (5)	7	0.04
Latin American Indians (5)	16	0.09
Lumbee (1)	1	0.01
Navajo	1	0.01
Pueblo (3)	3	0.02
Seminole	4	0.02
Sioux (1)	4	0.02
Yakama	2	0.01
All other tribes (2)	7	0.04
American Indian tribes, not spec.	9	0.05
Arab:	58	0.33
Lebanese	7	0.04
Moroccan	7	0.04
Palestinian	27	0.15
Other Arab	17	0.10
Asian:	295	1.68
Chinese, ex. Taiwanese (4)	7	0.04
Filipino (59)	71	0.40
Indian (57)	71	0.40
Japanese (13)	18	0.10
Korean (7)	14	0.08
Pakistani (2)	2	0.01
Thai (21)	28	0.16
Vietnamese (43)	51	0.29
Other Asian, specified	1	0.01
Other Asian, not specified (5)	32	0.18
British	20	0.11
Canadian	72	0.41
Croatian	6	0.03
Czech	10	0.06
Dutch	107	0.61
English	885	5.03
European	57	0.32
French, except Basque	154	0.88
French Canadian	59	0.34
German	1,059	6.02
Greek	47	0.27
Hawaii Native/Pacific Islander:	22	0.13
Micronesian: (1)	4	0.02
Guamanian/Chamorro (1)	4	0.02
Polynesian: (1)	7	0.04
Native Hawaiian (1)	5	0.03
Samoan	2	0.01
Other Pac. Isl., specified	1	0.01
Other Pac. Isl., not spec. (2)	10	0.06
Hispanic or Latino:	3,958	22.50
Central American:	155	0.88
Costa Rican	43	0.24
Guatemalan	23	0.13
Honduran	30	0.17
Nicaraguan	15	0.09
Panamanian	15	0.09
Salvadoran	14	0.08
Other Central American	15	0.09
Cuban	914	5.20
Dominican Republic	113	0.64
Mexican	525	2.98
Puerto Rican	1,462	8.31
South American:	110	0.63
Argentinean	1	0.01
Chilean	3	0.02
Colombian	40	0.23
Ecuadorian	22	0.13
Peruvian	12	0.07
Uruguayan	1	0.01
Venezuelan	29	0.16
Other South American	2	0.01
Other Hispanic or Latino	679	3.86
Hungarian	43	0.24
Irish	920	5.23
Italian	508	2.89
Lithuanian	12	0.07
Norwegian	47	0.27
Polish	187	1.06
Portuguese	32	0.18
Scandinavian	28	0.16
Scotch-Irish	224	1.27
Scottish	112	0.64
Slavic	10	0.06
Swedish	69	0.39
Ukrainian	19	0.11
United States or American	1,684	9.57
Welsh	51	0.29
West Indian, excl. Hispanic:	500	2.84
Barbadian	12	0.07
British West Indian	10	0.06
Dutch West Indian	9	0.05
Haitian	208	1.18
Jamaican	158	0.90
Trinidadian and Tobagonian	41	0.23
West Indian	62	0.35
White:	9,938	56.50
Not Hispanic (7,095)	7,275	41.36
Hispanic (2,461)	2,663	15.14

Palm Springs

Place Type: Village
County: Palm Beach
Population: 11,699

Ancestry/Race	Number	%
African American/Black:	857	7.33
Not Hispanic (736)	798	6.82
Hispanic (45)	59	0.50
African, sub-Saharan:	56	0.47
African	56	0.47
Am. Ind. or Alaska Nat., not spec.	30	0.26
Albanian	8	0.07
American Indian tribes, specified:	28	0.24
Cherokee (7)	13	0.11
Chickasaw (1)	1	0.01
Choctaw (1)	1	0.01
Iroquois (1)	1	0.01
Latin American Indians (4)	6	0.05
Lumbee	1	0.01
Sioux	1	0.01
Yuman (1)	1	0.01
All other tribes (2)	3	0.03
American Indian tribes, not spec.	8	0.07
Arab:	71	0.60
Lebanese	71	0.60
Asian:	216	1.85
Bangladeshi (6)	6	0.05
Chinese, ex. Taiwanese (15)	18	0.15
Filipino (26)	30	0.26
Indian (43)	62	0.53
Japanese (3)	4	0.03
Korean (19)	23	0.20
Pakistani (1)	9	0.08
Sri Lankan (4)	4	0.03
Taiwanese (2)	2	0.02
Thai (17)	27	0.23
Vietnamese (13)	15	0.13
Other Asian, specified (9)	9	0.08
Other Asian, not specified (3)	7	0.06
Austrian	45	0.38
Brazilian	93	0.79
British	18	0.15
Bulgarian	35	0.30
Canadian	49	0.41
Croatian	5	0.04
Czech	71	0.60
Czechoslovakian	26	0.22
Danish	6	0.05
Dutch	141	1.19
English	1,109	9.38
European	34	0.29
Finnish	48	0.41
French, except Basque	363	3.07
French Canadian	111	0.94
German	1,328	11.23
Greek	74	0.63
Hawaii Native/Pacific Islander:	8	0.07
Micronesian: (1)	2	0.02
Guamanian/Chamorro (1)	2	0.02
Polynesian: (2)	2	0.02
Samoan (2)	2	0.02

Notes: 1. Figures in the "Number" column do not add up to the total population due to: a) Ancestry/Race overlap — e.g. persons can report being both White and Irish, b) persons of Hispanic origin can report being any race, c) persons reporting two ancestries are counted in both categories. 2. Numbers in parentheses indicate the number of persons reporting this ancestry/race alone, not in combination with any other ancestry/race. 3. Refer to the Explanation of Data in the front of the book for more detailed information.

Other Pac. Isl., not spec.	4	0.03
Hispanic or Latino:	2,929	25.04
Central American:	194	1.66
Costa Rican	8	0.07
Guatemalan	29	0.25
Honduran	87	0.74
Nicaraguan	29	0.25
Panamanian	6	0.05
Salvadoran	25	0.21
Other Central American	10	0.09
Cuban	891	7.62
Dominican Republic	140	1.20
Mexican	233	1.99
Puerto Rican	532	4.55
South American:	425	3.63
Argentinean	14	0.12
Bolivian	6	0.05
Chilean	22	0.19
Colombian	223	1.91
Ecuadorian	61	0.52
Peruvian	44	0.38
Uruguayan	14	0.12
Venezuelan	26	0.22
Other South American	15	0.13
Other Hispanic or Latino	514	4.39
Hungarian	26	0.22
Icelander	6	0.05
Irish	1,368	11.57
Israeli	8	0.07
Italian	1,015	8.59
Lithuanian	46	0.39
Norwegian	41	0.35
Polish	358	3.03
Portuguese	36	0.30
Romanian	46	0.39
Russian	90	0.76
Scotch-Irish	263	2.22
Scottish	210	1.78
Serbian	9	0.08
Slavic	9	0.08
Swedish	94	0.80
Swiss	11	0.09
Ukrainian	17	0.14
United States or American	802	6.78
Welsh	43	0.36
West Indian, excl. Hispanic:	575	4.86
Bahamian	7	0.06
Haitian	365	3.09
Jamaican	152	1.29
Trinidadian and Tobagonian	40	0.34
U.S. Virgin Islander	11	0.09
White:	10,088	86.23
Not Hispanic (7,679)	7,785	66.54
Hispanic (2,176)	2,303	19.69
Yugoslavian	8	0.07

Palm Valley

Place Type: Census Designated Place
County: Saint Johns
Population: 19,860

Ancestry/Race	Number	%
Acadian/Cajun	39	0.20
African American/Black:	291	1.47
Not Hispanic (245)	280	1.41
Hispanic (4)	11	0.06
African, sub-Saharan:	55	0.28
African	29	0.15
Cape Verdean	11	0.06
South African	15	0.08
Am. Ind. or Alaska Nat., not spec.	15	0.08
Albanian	8	0.04
American Indian tribes, specified:	57	0.29
Apache (1)	2	0.01
Blackfeet	1	0.01
Cherokee (9)	24	0.12
Chickasaw (1)	2	0.01
Chippewa (1)	1	0.01
Choctaw (1)	2	0.01
Creek (2)	5	0.03
Delaware	3	0.02
Iroquois (6)	6	0.03
Latin American Indians (4)	4	0.02
Navajo	1	0.01
Osage	1	0.01
Sioux (1)	1	0.01
All other tribes (3)	4	0.02
American Indian tribes, not spec.	1	0.01
Arab:	103	0.52
Arab/Arabic	14	0.07
Egyptian	10	0.05
Lebanese	35	0.18
Syrian	44	0.22
Armenian	33	0.17
Asian:	337	1.70
Chinese, ex. Taiwanese (73)	86	0.43
Filipino (52)	75	0.38
Indian (65)	72	0.36
Indonesian (1)	3	0.02
Japanese (19)	37	0.19
Korean (15)	22	0.11
Laotian (1)	1	0.01
Pakistani (3)	3	0.02
Sri Lankan (4)	4	0.02
Taiwanese (2)	3	0.02
Thai (2)	2	0.01
Vietnamese (3)	8	0.04
Other Asian, specified (10)	10	0.05
Other Asian, not specified (1)	11	0.06
Australian	41	0.21
Austrian	155	0.78
Belgian	8	0.04
Brazilian	8	0.04
British	192	0.97
Bulgarian	9	0.05
Canadian	37	0.19
Croatian	18	0.09
Czech	68	0.34
Czechoslovakian	40	0.20
Danish	74	0.37
Dutch	262	1.32
Eastern European	16	0.08
English	3,584	18.05
European	160	0.81
Finnish	74	0.37
French, except Basque	760	3.83
French Canadian	185	0.93
German	3,558	17.92
Greek	140	0.71
Hawaii Native/Pacific Islander:	15	0.08
Micronesian: (1)	2	0.01
Guamanian/Chamorro (1)	2	0.01
Polynesian: (3)	5	0.03
Native Hawaiian (2)	4	0.02
Samoan (1)	1	0.01
Other Pac. Isl., not spec. (1)	8	0.04
Hispanic or Latino:	557	2.80
Central American:	29	0.15
Costa Rican	4	0.02
Guatemalan	6	0.03
Honduran	1	0.01
Nicaraguan	3	0.02
Panamanian	8	0.04
Salvadoran	1	0.01
Other Central American	6	0.03
Cuban	92	0.46
Dominican Republic	3	0.02
Mexican	101	0.51
Puerto Rican	152	0.77
South American:	65	0.33
Argentinean	3	0.02
Bolivian	6	0.03
Chilean	8	0.04
Colombian	18	0.09
Ecuadorian	9	0.05
Peruvian	9	0.05
Uruguayan	3	0.02
Venezuelan	6	0.03
Other South American	3	0.02
Other Hispanic or Latino	115	0.58
Hungarian	286	1.44
Icelander	16	0.08
Iranian	37	0.19
Irish	3,379	17.02
Israeli	59	0.30
Italian	1,719	8.66
Latvian	8	0.04
Lithuanian	107	0.54
Northern European	19	0.10
Norwegian	275	1.39
Pennsylvania German	19	0.10
Polish	711	3.58
Portuguese	19	0.10
Romanian	50	0.25
Russian	251	1.26
Scandinavian	11	0.06
Scotch-Irish	521	2.62
Scottish	858	4.32
Serbian	43	0.22
Slovak	84	0.42
Slovene	26	0.13
Swedish	391	1.97
Swiss	92	0.46
Ukrainian	102	0.51
United States or American	1,572	7.92
Welsh	154	0.78
West Indian, excl. Hispanic:	17	0.09
Jamaican	17	0.09
White:	19,195	96.65
Not Hispanic (18,591)	18,741	94.37
Hispanic (443)	454	2.29

Palmetto Estates

Place Type: Census Designated Place
County: Miami-Dade
Population: 13,675

Ancestry/Race	Number	%
African American/Black:	7,082	51.79
Not Hispanic (6,405)	6,742	49.30
Hispanic (264)	340	2.49
African, sub-Saharan:	190	1.39
African	190	1.39
Am. Ind. or Alaska Nat., not spec.	21	0.15
American Indian tribes, specified:	35	0.26
Blackfeet	2	0.01
Cherokee (4)	10	0.07
Cheyenne	2	0.01
Iroquois (1)	1	0.01
Latin American Indians (13)	17	0.12
Navajo	1	0.01
Seminole	1	0.01
All other tribes	1	0.01
American Indian tribes, not spec.	6	0.04
Arab:	28	0.20
Arab/Arabic	28	0.20
Asian:	611	4.47
Chinese, ex. Taiwanese (75)	140	1.02
Filipino (54)	60	0.44
Indian (213)	301	2.20
Indonesian	2	0.01
Japanese (5)	6	0.04
Korean (7)	15	0.11
Laotian (4)	4	0.03
Pakistani (4)	16	0.12
Sri Lankan (2)	2	0.01
Thai (5)	7	0.05
Vietnamese (43)	43	0.31
Other Asian, not specified	15	0.11
Austrian	44	0.32
Brazilian	67	0.49
British	96	0.70
Canadian	9	0.07
Czech	24	0.18
Danish	19	0.14
Dutch	45	0.33
Eastern European	6	0.04
English	256	1.87

Notes: 1. Figures in the "Number" column do not add up to the total population due to: a) Ancestry/Race overlap — e.g. persons can report being both White and Irish, b) persons of Hispanic origin can report being any race, c) persons reporting two ancestries are counted in both categories. 2. Numbers in parentheses indicate the number of persons reporting this ancestry/race alone, not in combination with any other ancestry/race. 3. Refer to the Explanation of Data in the front of the book for more detailed information.

Ancestry/Race	Number	%
European	13	0.10
French, except Basque	101	0.74
French Canadian	23	0.17
German	433	3.17
Guyanese	113	0.83
Hawaii Native/Pacific Islander:	48	0.35
Polynesian: (2)	3	0.02
Native Hawaiian (2)	3	0.02
Other Pac. Isl., not spec.	45	0.33
Hispanic or Latino:	3,953	28.91
Central American:	673	4.92
Costa Rican	28	0.20
Guatemalan	30	0.22
Honduran	141	1.03
Nicaraguan	326	2.38
Panamanian	80	0.59
Salvadoran	49	0.36
Other Central American	19	0.14
Cuban	1,180	8.63
Dominican Republic	150	1.10
Mexican	68	0.50
Puerto Rican	592	4.33
South American:	501	3.66
Argentinean	44	0.32
Bolivian	4	0.03
Chilean	23	0.17
Colombian	258	1.89
Ecuadorian	34	0.25
Paraguayan	1	0.01
Peruvian	90	0.66
Uruguayan	5	0.04
Venezuelan	33	0.24
Other South American	9	0.07
Other Hispanic or Latino	789	5.77
Hungarian	13	0.10
Irish	391	2.86
Italian	264	1.93
Norwegian	34	0.25
Polish	153	1.12
Portuguese	65	0.48
Romanian	25	0.18
Russian	44	0.32
Scotch-Irish	92	0.67
Scottish	36	0.26
Swedish	31	0.23
Ukrainian	28	0.20
United States or American	566	4.14
Welsh	10	0.07
West Indian, excl. Hispanic:	3,497	25.57
Bahamian	97	0.71
Barbadian	50	0.37
Belizean	40	0.29
British West Indian	35	0.26
Haitian	469	3.43
Jamaican	2,359	17.25
Trinidadian and Tobagonian	413	3.02
West Indian	34	0.25
White:	5,507	40.27
Not Hispanic (2,311)	2,465	18.03
Hispanic (2,842)	3,042	22.24

Palmetto

Place Type: City
County: Manatee
Population: 12,571

Ancestry/Race	Number	%
African American/Black:	1,702	13.54
Not Hispanic (1,547)	1,611	12.82
Hispanic (60)	91	0.72
African, sub-Saharan:	30	0.24
African	21	0.17
Ethiopian	9	0.07
Alaska Native tribes, specified:	2	0.02
Alaska Athabascan	1	0.01
Eskimo	1	0.01
Am. Ind. or Alaska Nat., not spec.	59	0.47
American Indian tribes, specified:	55	0.44
Apache (1)	1	0.01
Blackfeet (9)	9	0.07
Cherokee (5)	15	0.12
Chippewa	1	0.01
Creek	4	0.03
Iroquois	3	0.02
Latin American Indians (5)	5	0.04
Lumbee (4)	4	0.03
Pueblo (5)	5	0.04
Seminole (4)	4	0.03
Sioux	2	0.02
All other tribes	2	0.02
American Indian tribes, not spec.	9	0.07
Arab:	24	0.19
Arab/Arabic	24	0.19
Armenian	6	0.05
Asian:	60	0.48
Chinese, ex. Taiwanese (8)	13	0.10
Filipino (17)	18	0.14
Indian (7)	8	0.06
Japanese (2)	3	0.02
Korean (1)	1	0.01
Thai (5)	6	0.05
Vietnamese (2)	3	0.02
Other Asian, specified	3	0.02
Other Asian, not specified (2)	5	0.04
Austrian	31	0.25
Belgian	8	0.06
British	7	0.06
Canadian	14	0.11
Celtic	12	0.10
Croatian	10	0.08
Czech	26	0.21
Czechoslovakian	16	0.13
Danish	82	0.66
Dutch	169	1.37
English	1,391	11.28
European	32	0.26
Finnish	10	0.08
French, except Basque	310	2.51
French Canadian	84	0.68
German	1,419	11.50
Greek	78	0.63
Hawaii Native/Pacific Islander:	26	0.21
Micronesian: (2)	2	0.02
Guamanian/Chamorro (2)	2	0.02
Polynesian: (11)	13	0.10
Native Hawaiian (10)	11	0.09
Samoan (1)	2	0.02
Other Pac. Isl., specified	2	0.02
Other Pac. Isl., not spec.	9	0.07
Hispanic or Latino:	3,358	26.71
Central American:	88	0.70
Guatemalan	37	0.29
Honduran	39	0.31
Nicaraguan	7	0.06
Salvadoran	5	0.04
Cuban	42	0.33
Dominican Republic	1	0.01
Mexican	2,821	22.44
Puerto Rican	100	0.80
South American:	22	0.18
Bolivian	1	0.01
Colombian	12	0.10
Peruvian	9	0.07
Other Hispanic or Latino	284	2.26
Hungarian	30	0.24
Irish	971	7.87
Israeli	2	0.02
Italian	311	2.52
Northern European	9	0.07
Norwegian	98	0.79
Polish	153	1.24
Portuguese	12	0.10
Russian	23	0.19
Scotch-Irish	167	1.35
Scottish	234	1.90
Slovak	16	0.13
Swedish	90	0.73
Swiss	32	0.26
Ukrainian	43	0.35
United States or American	1,244	10.09
Welsh	106	0.86
West Indian, excl. Hispanic:	93	0.75
Bahamian	3	0.02
Haitian	90	0.73
White:	9,688	77.07
Not Hispanic (7,449)	7,541	59.99
Hispanic (2,005)	2,147	17.08

Panama City

Place Type: City
County: Bay
Population: 36,417

Ancestry/Race	Number	%
African American/Black:	8,028	22.04
Not Hispanic (7,648)	7,819	21.47
Hispanic (165)	209	0.57
African, sub-Saharan:	136	0.37
African	120	0.33
Ethiopian	7	0.02
Nigerian	9	0.02
Alaska Native tribes, specified:	7	0.02
Alaska Athabascan (4)	6	0.02
Eskimo	1	0.00
Am. Ind. or Alaska Nat., not spec.	133	0.37
American Indian tribes, specified:	351	0.96
Apache (2)	4	0.01
Blackfeet (5)	16	0.04
Cherokee (69)	139	0.38
Cheyenne (1)	2	0.01
Chickasaw (1)	1	0.00
Chippewa (11)	12	0.03
Choctaw (5)	14	0.04
Comanche	1	0.00
Cree (3)	4	0.01
Creek (39)	87	0.24
Delaware (1)	1	0.00
Houma (2)	2	0.01
Iroquois (4)	7	0.02
Kiowa	1	0.00
Latin American Indians (4)	11	0.03
Lumbee (6)	6	0.02
Navajo (1)	1	0.00
Potawatomi	1	0.00
Pueblo	1	0.00
Puget Sound Salish (1)	3	0.01
Seminole (4)	8	0.02
Shoshone (1)	1	0.00
Sioux (5)	14	0.04
Ute	1	0.00
Yakama (1)	1	0.00
Yaqui (1)	1	0.00
All other tribes (7)	11	0.03
American Indian tribes, not spec.	26	0.07
Arab:	148	0.41
Arab/Arabic	40	0.11
Egyptian	53	0.15
Lebanese	35	0.10
Palestinian	20	0.05
Asian:	786	2.16
Chinese, ex. Taiwanese (53)	67	0.18
Filipino (90)	136	0.37
Indian (51)	83	0.23
Indonesian	1	0.00
Japanese (31)	58	0.16
Korean (29)	38	0.10
Laotian (3)	3	0.01
Pakistani (20)	27	0.07
Taiwanese (1)	1	0.00
Thai (27)	37	0.10
Vietnamese (231)	259	0.71
Other Asian, specified	6	0.02
Other Asian, not specified (18)	70	0.19
Australian	9	0.02
Austrian	35	0.10
British	198	0.54
Bulgarian	6	0.02
Canadian	100	0.27

Notes: 1. Figures in the "Number" column do not add up to the total population due to: a) Ancestry/Race overlap — e.g. persons can report being both White and Irish, b) persons of Hispanic origin can report being any race, c) persons reporting two ancestries are counted in both categories. 2. Numbers in parentheses indicate the number of persons reporting this ancestry/race alone, not in combination with any other ancestry/race. 3. Refer to the Explanation of Data in the front of the book for more detailed information.

Ancestry/Race	Number	%
Czech	115	0.32
Czechoslovakian	28	0.08
Danish	79	0.22
Dutch	476	1.31
English	3,294	9.06
Estonian	4	0.01
European	270	0.74
Finnish	46	0.13
French, except Basque	929	2.55
French Canadian	247	0.68
German	3,551	9.76
German Russian	7	0.02
Greek	134	0.37
Guyanese	12	0.03
Hawaii Native/Pacific Islander:	70	0.19
Micronesian: (9)	18	0.05
Guamanian/Chamorro (9)	18	0.05
Polynesian: (14)	30	0.08
Native Hawaiian (14)	27	0.07
Samoan	3	0.01
Other Pac. Isl., specified	6	0.02
Other Pac. Isl., not spec. (5)	16	0.04
Hispanic or Latino:	1,060	2.91
Central American:	50	0.14
Costa Rican	10	0.03
Guatemalan	2	0.01
Honduran	5	0.01
Nicaraguan	1	0.00
Panamanian	24	0.07
Salvadoran	7	0.02
Other Central American	1	0.00
Cuban	182	0.50
Dominican Republic	5	0.01
Mexican	300	0.82
Puerto Rican	287	0.79
South American:	34	0.09
Bolivian	2	0.01
Chilean	3	0.01
Colombian	4	0.01
Paraguayan	2	0.01
Peruvian	22	0.06
Venezuelan	1	0.00
Other Hispanic or Latino	202	0.55
Hungarian	107	0.29
Iranian	5	0.01
Irish	3,731	10.26
Italian	1,074	2.95
Lithuanian	45	0.12
Luxemburger	8	0.02
Northern European	70	0.19
Norwegian	293	0.81
Pennsylvania German	6	0.02
Polish	437	1.20
Portuguese	132	0.36
Russian	65	0.18
Scandinavian	9	0.02
Scotch-Irish	800	2.20
Scottish	875	2.41
Slavic	28	0.08
Slovak	39	0.11
Slovene	5	0.01
Swedish	279	0.77
Swiss	53	0.15
Turkish	4	0.01
Ukrainian	24	0.07
United States or American	4,695	12.91
Welsh	327	0.90
West Indian, excl. Hispanic:	67	0.18
Bahamian	7	0.02
Haitian	16	0.04
Jamaican	37	0.10
West Indian	7	0.02
White:	27,379	75.18
Not Hispanic (26,317)	26,803	73.60
Hispanic (502)	576	1.58
Yugoslavian	4	0.01

Parkland

Place Type: City
County: Broward
Population: 13,835

Ancestry/Race	Number	%
African American/Black:	478	3.46
Not Hispanic (420)	468	3.38
Hispanic (5)	10	0.07
African, sub-Saharan:	82	0.59
African	8	0.06
Liberian	24	0.17
Nigerian	19	0.14
South African	31	0.22
Alaska Native tribes, specified:	1	0.01
Tlingit-Haida (1)	1	0.01
Am. Ind. or Alaska Nat., not spec.	15	0.11
American Indian tribes, specified:	23	0.17
Apache	1	0.01
Cherokee (4)	13	0.09
Chickasaw (1)	1	0.01
Chippewa	2	0.01
Lumbee (1)	1	0.01
Pueblo	4	0.03
All other tribes (1)	1	0.01
Arab:	111	0.79
Egyptian	14	0.10
Iraqi	7	0.05
Lebanese	14	0.10
Moroccan	15	0.11
Palestinian	37	0.26
Syrian	24	0.17
Armenian	105	0.75
Asian:	521	3.77
Chinese, ex. Taiwanese (168)	189	1.37
Filipino (35)	51	0.37
Indian (158)	170	1.23
Indonesian (1)	1	0.01
Japanese (11)	18	0.13
Korean (25)	31	0.22
Pakistani (9)	10	0.07
Taiwanese (6)	10	0.07
Thai (6)	7	0.05
Vietnamese (13)	22	0.16
Other Asian, not specified (7)	12	0.09
Australian	9	0.06
Austrian	90	0.64
Brazilian	73	0.52
British	94	0.67
Canadian	41	0.29
Croatian	47	0.34
Czech	88	0.63
Czechoslovakian	7	0.05
Danish	32	0.23
Dutch	201	1.44
Eastern European	100	0.71
English	919	6.57
European	67	0.48
French, except Basque	418	2.99
French Canadian	70	0.50
German	1,809	12.93
Greek	116	0.83
Guyanese	57	0.41
Hawaii Native/Pacific Islander:	9	0.07
Polynesian: (1)	9	0.07
Native Hawaiian (1)	6	0.04
Samoan	3	0.02
Hispanic or Latino:	1,152	8.33
Central American:	46	0.33
Costa Rican	9	0.07
Guatemalan	3	0.02
Honduran	2	0.01
Nicaraguan	19	0.14
Panamanian	10	0.07
Salvadoran	3	0.02
Cuban	234	1.69
Dominican Republic	24	0.17
Mexican	98	0.71
Puerto Rican	207	1.50
South American:	348	2.52
Argentinean	14	0.10
Bolivian	10	0.07
Chilean	13	0.09
Colombian	148	1.07
Ecuadorian	35	0.25
Peruvian	68	0.49
Uruguayan	2	0.01
Venezuelan	46	0.33
Other South American	12	0.09
Other Hispanic or Latino	195	1.41
Hungarian	178	1.27
Iranian	167	1.19
Irish	1,751	12.52
Israeli	26	0.19
Italian	2,293	16.39
Lithuanian	109	0.78
Norwegian	84	0.60
Polish	877	6.27
Portuguese	54	0.39
Romanian	112	0.80
Russian	976	6.98
Scandinavian	43	0.31
Scotch-Irish	45	0.32
Scottish	176	1.26
Slovak	21	0.15
Swedish	130	0.93
Swiss	20	0.14
Turkish	45	0.32
Ukrainian	49	0.35
United States or American	1,306	9.34
Welsh	9	0.06
West Indian, excl. Hispanic:	204	1.46
Bahamian	23	0.16
Jamaican	162	1.16
Trinidadian and Tobagonian	10	0.07
Other West Indian	9	0.06
White:	12,780	92.37
Not Hispanic (11,638)	11,731	84.79
Hispanic (1,010)	1,049	7.58
Yugoslavian	34	0.24

Pembroke Pines

Place Type: City
County: Broward
Population: 137,427

Ancestry/Race	Number	%
African American/Black:	20,115	14.64
Not Hispanic (17,471)	19,021	13.84
Hispanic (739)	1,094	0.80
African, sub-Saharan:	642	0.47
African	278	0.20
Ghanian	69	0.05
Nigerian	188	0.14
Somalian	22	0.02
South African	24	0.02
Sudanese	44	0.03
Other sub-Saharan African	17	0.01
Alaska Native tribes, specified:	1	0.00
Alaska Athabascan (1)	1	0.00
Alaska Native tribes, not specified	1	0.00
Am. Ind. or Alaska Nat., not spec.	236	0.17
Albanian	53	0.04
Alsatian	9	0.01
American Indian tribes, specified:	306	0.22
Apache (2)	6	0.00
Blackfeet (3)	13	0.01
Cherokee (35)	93	0.07
Cheyenne	1	0.00
Chickasaw	1	0.00
Chippewa (3)	4	0.00
Choctaw (1)	7	0.01
Comanche	1	0.00
Creek (2)	3	0.00
Crow (1)	1	0.00
Delaware (2)	3	0.00
Iroquois (6)	11	0.01
Latin American Indians (46)	104	0.08

Notes: 1. Figures in the "Number" column do not add up to the total population due to: a) Ancestry/Race overlap — e.g. persons can report being both White and Irish, b) persons of Hispanic origin can report being any race, c) persons reporting two ancestries are counted in both categories. 2. Numbers in parentheses indicate the number of persons reporting this ancestry/race alone, not in combination with any other ancestry/race. 3. Refer to the Explanation of Data in the front of the book for more detailed information.

Ancestry/Race	Number	%
Lumbee (3)	5	0.00
Navajo (1)	8	0.01
Potawatomi (1)	1	0.00
Pueblo (1)	5	0.00
Seminole (13)	13	0.01
Sioux (6)	8	0.01
All other tribes (8)	18	0.01
American Indian tribes, not spec.	28	0.02
Arab:	1,230	0.90
Arab/Arabic	220	0.16
Egyptian	72	0.05
Iraqi	9	0.01
Jordanian	44	0.03
Lebanese	421	0.31
Moroccan	99	0.07
Palestinian	68	0.05
Syrian	155	0.11
Other Arab	142	0.10
Armenian	54	0.04
Asian:	6,553	4.77
Bangladeshi (13)	18	0.01
Cambodian (6)	6	0.00
Chinese, ex. Taiwanese (1,199)	1,622	1.18
Filipino (891)	1,062	0.77
Indian (1,851)	2,237	1.63
Indonesian (11)	17	0.01
Japanese (121)	188	0.14
Korean (369)	428	0.31
Laotian (8)	9	0.01
Malaysian (2)	3	0.00
Pakistani (197)	307	0.22
Taiwanese (35)	45	0.03
Thai (52)	76	0.06
Vietnamese (220)	253	0.18
Other Asian, specified (7)	14	0.01
Other Asian, not specified (93)	268	0.20
Australian	31	0.02
Austrian	837	0.61
Basque	30	0.02
Belgian	91	0.07
Brazilian	751	0.55
British	552	0.40
Bulgarian	33	0.02
Canadian	544	0.40
Croatian	111	0.08
Czech	241	0.18
Czechoslovakian	140	0.10
Danish	225	0.16
Dutch	836	0.61
Eastern European	224	0.16
English	6,310	4.60
Estonian	7	0.01
European	614	0.45
Finnish	148	0.11
French, except Basque	2,256	1.65
French Canadian	851	0.62
German	11,085	8.08
Greek	582	0.42
Guyanese	508	0.37
Hawaii Native/Pacific Islander:	228	0.17
Micronesian: (15)	21	0.02
Guamanian/Chamorro (11)	17	0.01
Other Micronesian (4)	4	0.00
Polynesian: (27)	59	0.04
Native Hawaiian (18)	41	0.03
Samoan (9)	15	0.01
Tongan	2	0.00
Other Polynesian	1	0.00
Other Pac. Isl., specified	3	0.00
Other Pac. Isl., not spec. (25)	145	0.11
Hispanic or Latino:	38,700	28.16
Central American:	1,896	1.38
Costa Rican	227	0.17
Guatemalan	214	0.16
Honduran	273	0.20
Nicaraguan	533	0.39
Panamanian	367	0.27
Salvadoran	234	0.17
Other Central American	48	0.03
Cuban	11,901	8.66
Dominican Republic	1,637	1.19
Mexican	960	0.70
Puerto Rican	6,887	5.01
South American:	8,292	6.03
Argentinean	463	0.34
Bolivian	66	0.05
Chilean	298	0.22
Colombian	4,124	3.00
Ecuadorian	734	0.53
Paraguayan	20	0.01
Peruvian	1,082	0.79
Uruguayan	78	0.06
Venezuelan	1,242	0.90
Other South American	185	0.13
Other Hispanic or Latino	7,127	5.19
Hungarian	1,052	0.77
Iranian	98	0.07
Irish	11,272	8.22
Israeli	94	0.07
Italian	12,850	9.37
Latvian	19	0.01
Lithuanian	390	0.28
Maltese	22	0.02
Northern European	9	0.01
Norwegian	523	0.38
Pennsylvania German	20	0.01
Polish	4,881	3.56
Portuguese	592	0.43
Romanian	684	0.50
Russian	4,179	3.05
Scandinavian	139	0.10
Scotch-Irish	944	0.69
Scottish	1,289	0.94
Serbian	37	0.03
Slavic	63	0.05
Slovak	162	0.12
Slovene	54	0.04
Swedish	821	0.60
Swiss	126	0.09
Turkish	136	0.10
Ukrainian	374	0.27
United States or American	8,380	6.11
Welsh	505	0.37
West Indian, excl. Hispanic:	12,327	8.99
Bahamian	518	0.38
Barbadian	49	0.04
Belizean	54	0.04
British West Indian	270	0.20
Dutch West Indian	22	0.02
Haitian	2,583	1.88
Jamaican	7,648	5.58
Trinidadian and Tobagonian	592	0.43
U.S. Virgin Islander	46	0.03
West Indian	522	0.38
Other West Indian	23	0.02
White:	107,142	77.96
Not Hispanic (72,464)	74,076	53.90
Hispanic (31,406)	33,066	24.06
Yugoslavian	93	0.07

Pensacola

Place Type: City
County: Escambia
Population: 56,255

Ancestry/Race	Number	%
Acadian/Cajun	59	0.10
African American/Black:	17,551	31.20
Not Hispanic (17,086)	17,393	30.92
Hispanic (117)	158	0.28
African, sub-Saharan:	411	0.73
African	368	0.65
Nigerian	43	0.08
Alaska Native tribes, specified:	2	0.00
Tlingit-Haida (2)	2	0.00
Am. Ind. or Alaska Nat., not spec.	186	0.33
Alsatian	12	0.02
American Indian tribes, specified:	454	0.81
Apache (1)	1	0.00
Blackfeet (3)	10	0.02
Cherokee (64)	184	0.33
Chickasaw (1)	2	0.00
Chippewa (1)	3	0.01
Choctaw (4)	15	0.03
Comanche	1	0.00
Cree (2)	2	0.00
Creek (87)	160	0.28
Delaware	3	0.01
Iroquois (6)	10	0.02
Latin American Indians (1)	5	0.01
Navajo (1)	3	0.01
Ottawa (2)	2	0.00
Potawatomi (2)	2	0.00
Pueblo (2)	2	0.00
Seminole (2)	10	0.02
Sioux (1)	5	0.01
Ute	1	0.00
All other tribes (16)	33	0.06
American Indian tribes, not spec.	29	0.05
Arab:	208	0.37
Arab/Arabic	49	0.09
Lebanese	85	0.15
Other Arab	74	0.13
Armenian	5	0.01
Asian:	1,289	2.29
Bangladeshi (5)	5	0.01
Cambodian (15)	22	0.04
Chinese, ex. Taiwanese (148)	169	0.30
Filipino (184)	288	0.51
Indian (106)	127	0.23
Indonesian (4)	4	0.01
Japanese (52)	95	0.17
Korean (67)	98	0.17
Laotian (4)	4	0.01
Malaysian	4	0.01
Pakistani	1	0.00
Sri Lankan	4	0.01
Taiwanese (14)	17	0.03
Thai (11)	16	0.03
Vietnamese (340)	377	0.67
Other Asian, specified	8	0.01
Other Asian, not specified (19)	50	0.09
Australian	29	0.05
Austrian	103	0.18
Basque	14	0.02
Belgian	35	0.06
Brazilian	16	0.03
British	498	0.88
Canadian	110	0.20
Celtic	10	0.02
Croatian	20	0.04
Czech	204	0.36
Czechoslovakian	71	0.13
Danish	166	0.29
Dutch	587	1.04
Eastern European	20	0.04
English	6,180	10.98
European	512	0.91
Finnish	93	0.17
French, except Basque	1,786	3.17
French Canadian	495	0.88
German	5,902	10.49
Greek	245	0.44
Hawaii Native/Pacific Islander:	90	0.16
Melanesian: (2)	2	0.00
Fijian (2)	2	0.00
Micronesian: (10)	18	0.03
Guamanian/Chamorro (10)	15	0.03
Other Micronesian	3	0.01
Polynesian: (11)	33	0.06
Native Hawaiian (8)	21	0.04
Samoan (3)	12	0.02
Other Pac. Isl., specified	7	0.01
Other Pac. Isl., not spec. (6)	30	0.05
Hispanic or Latino:	1,167	2.07
Central American:	54	0.10
Costa Rican	8	0.01
Guatemalan	12	0.02
Honduran	9	0.02

Notes: 1. Figures in the "Number" column do not add up to the total population due to: a) Ancestry/Race overlap — e.g. persons can report being both White and Irish, b) persons of Hispanic origin can report being any race, c) persons reporting two ancestries are counted in both categories. 2. Numbers in parentheses indicate the number of persons reporting this ancestry/race alone, not in combination with any other ancestry/race. 3. Refer to the Explanation of Data in the front of the book for more detailed information.

Ancestry/Race	Number	%
Nicaraguan	1	0.00
Panamanian	19	0.03
Salvadoran	5	0.01
Cuban	138	0.25
Dominican Republic	16	0.03
Mexican	358	0.64
Puerto Rican	254	0.45
South American:	68	0.12
Argentinean	16	0.03
Bolivian	7	0.01
Chilean	2	0.00
Colombian	21	0.04
Ecuadorian	2	0.00
Peruvian	10	0.02
Uruguayan	4	0.01
Venezuelan	4	0.01
Other South American	2	0.00
Other Hispanic or Latino	279	0.50
Hungarian	174	0.31
Icelander	8	0.01
Iranian	37	0.07
Irish	5,604	9.96
Israeli	8	0.01
Italian	1,728	3.07
Latvian	22	0.04
Lithuanian	38	0.07
Maltese	6	0.01
Northern European	68	0.12
Norwegian	428	0.76
Pennsylvania German	9	0.02
Polish	1,084	1.93
Portuguese	111	0.20
Romanian	46	0.08
Russian	262	0.47
Scandinavian	59	0.10
Scotch-Irish	1,609	2.86
Scottish	1,395	2.48
Serbian	4	0.01
Slavic	50	0.09
Slovak	34	0.06
Slovene	19	0.03
Swedish	497	0.88
Swiss	65	0.12
Ukrainian	80	0.14
United States or American	4,332	7.70
Welsh	358	0.64
West Indian, excl. Hispanic:	331	0.59
Bahamian	36	0.06
Belizean	50	0.09
Dutch West Indian	8	0.01
Haitian	15	0.03
Jamaican	101	0.18
Trinidadian and Tobagonian	49	0.09
West Indian	72	0.13
White:	37,212	66.15
Not Hispanic (35,824)	36,438	64.77
Hispanic (690)	774	1.38

Pine Hills

Place Type: Census Designated Place
County: Orange
Population: 41,764

Ancestry/Race	Number	%
African American/Black:	23,135	55.39
Not Hispanic (21,004)	22,486	53.84
Hispanic (469)	649	1.55
African, sub-Saharan:	964	2.30
African	903	2.15
Nigerian	45	0.11
South African	16	0.04
Alaska Native tribes, specified:	2	0.00
Tlingit-Haida (1)	2	0.00
Am. Ind. or Alaska Nat., not spec.	133	0.32
American Indian tribes, specified:	160	0.38
Apache	4	0.01
Blackfeet	8	0.02
Cherokee (17)	82	0.20
Chippewa (1)	3	0.01
Choctaw (1)	4	0.01
Cree (2)	4	0.01
Creek (4)	8	0.02
Iroquois (2)	7	0.02
Kiowa (1)	1	0.00
Latin American Indians (9)	16	0.04
Lumbee (2)	2	0.00
Pueblo	4	0.01
Seminole (1)	7	0.02
Sioux (2)	3	0.01
All other tribes (3)	7	0.02
American Indian tribes, not spec.	22	0.05
Arab:	26	0.06
Egyptian	18	0.04
Lebanese	8	0.02
Asian:	1,509	3.61
Chinese, ex. Taiwanese (57)	90	0.22
Filipino (57)	82	0.20
Indian (383)	497	1.19
Indonesian (1)	1	0.00
Japanese (4)	18	0.04
Korean (28)	37	0.09
Laotian (6)	9	0.02
Malaysian (2)	2	0.00
Pakistani (8)	10	0.02
Thai (9)	11	0.03
Vietnamese (606)	646	1.55
Other Asian, specified (1)	6	0.01
Other Asian, not specified (19)	100	0.24
Austrian	22	0.05
Belgian	8	0.02
Brazilian	18	0.04
British	120	0.29
Canadian	173	0.41
Croatian	14	0.03
Czech	51	0.12
Czechoslovakian	18	0.04
Danish	19	0.05
Dutch	363	0.86
English	1,641	3.91
European	60	0.14
Finnish	51	0.12
French, except Basque	477	1.14
French Canadian	181	0.43
German	2,024	4.82
Greek	36	0.09
Guyanese	385	0.92
Hawaii Native/Pacific Islander:	165	0.40
Micronesian: (10)	10	0.02
Guamanian/Chamorro (10)	10	0.02
Polynesian: (4)	13	0.03
Native Hawaiian (3)	12	0.03
Samoan (1)	1	0.00
Other Pac. Isl., specified	4	0.01
Other Pac. Isl., not spec. (9)	138	0.33
Hispanic or Latino:	5,875	14.07
Central American:	267	0.64
Costa Rican	7	0.02
Guatemalan	45	0.11
Honduran	86	0.21
Nicaraguan	34	0.08
Panamanian	34	0.08
Salvadoran	36	0.09
Other Central American	25	0.06
Cuban	221	0.53
Dominican Republic	412	0.99
Mexican	861	2.06
Puerto Rican	2,958	7.08
South American:	226	0.54
Argentinean	5	0.01
Bolivian	1	0.00
Chilean	11	0.03
Colombian	104	0.25
Ecuadorian	29	0.07
Peruvian	23	0.06
Uruguayan	1	0.00
Venezuelan	44	0.11
Other South American	8	0.02
Other Hispanic or Latino	930	2.23
Hungarian	77	0.18
Irish	1,754	4.18
Italian	694	1.65
Lithuanian	19	0.05
Northern European	18	0.04
Norwegian	56	0.13
Pennsylvania German	34	0.08
Polish	289	0.69
Portuguese	67	0.16
Romanian	42	0.10
Russian	54	0.13
Scandinavian	9	0.02
Scotch-Irish	370	0.88
Scottish	190	0.45
Slavic	7	0.02
Slovak	25	0.06
Swedish	214	0.51
Turkish	12	0.03
Ukrainian	27	0.06
United States or American	2,778	6.62
Welsh	74	0.18
West Indian, excl. Hispanic:	7,145	17.02
Bahamian	59	0.14
Barbadian	112	0.27
British West Indian	176	0.42
Haitian	4,817	11.47
Jamaican	1,472	3.51
Trinidadian and Tobagonian	134	0.32
U.S. Virgin Islander	100	0.24
West Indian	275	0.65
White:	15,008	35.94
Not Hispanic (11,591)	12,042	28.83
Hispanic (2,581)	2,966	7.10
Yugoslavian	9	0.02

Pinecrest

Place Type: Village
County: Miami-Dade
Population: 19,055

Ancestry/Race	Number	%
African American/Black:	409	2.15
Not Hispanic (295)	357	1.87
Hispanic (32)	52	0.27
African, sub-Saharan:	42	0.22
African	36	0.19
South African	6	0.03
Am. Ind. or Alaska Nat., not spec.	26	0.14
American Indian tribes, specified:	46	0.24
Blackfeet	1	0.01
Cherokee (1)	17	0.09
Choctaw	2	0.01
Creek (3)	3	0.02
Delaware	1	0.01
Latin American Indians (6)	10	0.05
Navajo (1)	1	0.01
Paiute (1)	1	0.01
Pueblo (1)	2	0.01
Sioux (1)	5	0.03
All other tribes	3	0.02
American Indian tribes, not spec.	4	0.02
Arab:	477	2.49
Arab/Arabic	72	0.38
Egyptian	74	0.39
Jordanian	17	0.09
Lebanese	209	1.09
Palestinian	7	0.04
Syrian	55	0.29
Other Arab	43	0.22
Armenian	19	0.10
Asian:	1,019	5.35
Chinese, ex. Taiwanese (339)	405	2.13
Filipino (55)	75	0.39
Indian (242)	278	1.46
Indonesian (1)	2	0.01
Japanese (31)	46	0.24
Korean (75)	79	0.41
Pakistani (16)	16	0.08
Taiwanese (23)	24	0.13
Thai (36)	42	0.22

Notes: 1. Figures in the "Number" column do not add up to the total population due to: a) Ancestry/Race overlap — e.g. persons can report being both White and Irish, b) persons of Hispanic origin can report being any race, c) persons reporting two ancestries are counted in both categories. 2. Numbers in parentheses indicate the number of persons reporting this ancestry/race alone, not in combination with any other ancestry/race. 3. Refer to the Explanation of Data in the front of the book for more detailed information.

Ancestry/Race	Number	%
Vietnamese (12)	14	0.07
Other Asian, not specified (20)	38	0.20
Austrian	351	1.83
Basque	16	0.08
Belgian	38	0.20
Brazilian	175	0.91
British	249	1.30
Canadian	58	0.30
Croatian	10	0.05
Czech	71	0.37
Czechoslovakian	46	0.24
Danish	150	0.78
Dutch	127	0.66
Eastern European	64	0.33
English	1,895	9.88
European	315	1.64
French, except Basque	444	2.31
French Canadian	75	0.39
German	1,651	8.61
Greek	217	1.13
Guyanese	16	0.08
Hawaii Native/Pacific Islander:	9	0.05
Polynesian: (1)	6	0.03
Native Hawaiian (1)	6	0.03
Other Pac. Isl., not spec. (1)	3	0.02
Hispanic or Latino:	5,652	29.66
Central American:	518	2.72
Costa Rican	45	0.24
Guatemalan	25	0.13
Honduran	83	0.44
Nicaraguan	228	1.20
Panamanian	39	0.20
Salvadoran	84	0.44
Other Central American	14	0.07
Cuban	2,613	13.71
Dominican Republic	73	0.38
Mexican	201	1.05
Puerto Rican	281	1.47
South American:	1,006	5.28
Argentinean	113	0.59
Bolivian	22	0.12
Chilean	119	0.62
Colombian	340	1.78
Ecuadorian	42	0.22
Paraguayan	8	0.04
Peruvian	173	0.91
Uruguayan	12	0.06
Venezuelan	156	0.82
Other South American	21	0.11
Other Hispanic or Latino	960	5.04
Hungarian	165	0.86
Irish	1,285	6.70
Italian	827	4.31
Lithuanian	115	0.60
New Zealander	9	0.05
Northern European	15	0.08
Norwegian	61	0.32
Polish	688	3.59
Portuguese	50	0.26
Romanian	127	0.66
Russian	1,331	6.94
Scandinavian	22	0.11
Scotch-Irish	228	1.19
Scottish	284	1.48
Slavic	9	0.05
Slovak	47	0.25
Swedish	221	1.15
Swiss	63	0.33
Turkish	5	0.03
Ukrainian	65	0.34
United States or American	1,199	6.25
Welsh	58	0.30
West Indian, excl. Hispanic:	248	1.29
Bahamian	9	0.05
Belizean	11	0.06
British West Indian	6	0.03
Haitian	116	0.60
Jamaican	52	0.27
Trinidadian and Tobagonian	54	0.28
White:	17,533	92.01
Not Hispanic (11,961)	12,158	63.80
Hispanic (5,245)	5,375	28.21
Yugoslavian	23	0.12

Pinellas Park

Place Type: City
County: Pinellas
Population: 45,658

Ancestry/Race	Number	%
African American/Black:	1,123	2.46
Not Hispanic (892)	1,036	2.27
Hispanic (60)	87	0.19
African, sub-Saharan:	99	0.22
African	99	0.22
Alaska Native tribes, specified:	2	0.00
Eskimo	1	0.00
Tlingit-Haida (1)	1	0.00
Am. Ind. or Alaska Nat., not spec.	124	0.27
Alsatian	6	0.01
American Indian tribes, specified:	362	0.79
Apache (3)	8	0.02
Blackfeet (3)	21	0.05
Cherokee (64)	172	0.38
Cheyenne	4	0.01
Chickasaw (1)	2	0.00
Chippewa (9)	12	0.03
Choctaw (7)	14	0.03
Cree	7	0.02
Creek (2)	4	0.01
Crow (1)	2	0.00
Delaware (1)	3	0.01
Iroquois (15)	31	0.07
Latin American Indians (6)	10	0.02
Lumbee (1)	1	0.00
Navajo (5)	5	0.01
Osage	4	0.01
Paiute (1)	2	0.00
Potawatomi	2	0.00
Seminole (3)	10	0.02
Shoshone	5	0.01
Sioux (1)	11	0.02
All other tribes (8)	32	0.07
American Indian tribes, not spec.	17	0.04
Arab:	111	0.24
Egyptian	6	0.01
Iraqi	20	0.04
Lebanese	61	0.13
Palestinian	6	0.01
Syrian	18	0.04
Armenian	28	0.06
Asian:	2,217	4.86
Bangladeshi (5)	7	0.02
Cambodian (47)	58	0.13
Chinese, ex. Taiwanese (150)	184	0.40
Filipino (309)	383	0.84
Indian (139)	162	0.35
Indonesian (2)	3	0.01
Japanese (27)	58	0.13
Korean (87)	100	0.22
Laotian (277)	296	0.65
Malaysian (1)	11	0.02
Pakistani (14)	19	0.04
Thai (28)	48	0.11
Vietnamese (788)	839	1.84
Other Asian, specified	2	0.00
Other Asian, not specified (29)	47	0.10
Australian	8	0.02
Austrian	101	0.22
Belgian	59	0.13
Brazilian	25	0.06
British	191	0.42
Bulgarian	15	0.03
Canadian	180	0.40
Celtic	14	0.03
Croatian	138	0.30
Czech	102	0.22
Czechoslovakian	105	0.23
Danish	242	0.53
Dutch	1,004	2.21
English	5,254	11.57
European	319	0.70
Finnish	57	0.13
French, except Basque	1,984	4.37
French Canadian	823	1.81
German	8,383	18.46
Greek	263	0.58
Guyanese	12	0.03
Hawaii Native/Pacific Islander:	28	0.06
Micronesian: (1)	1	0.00
Guamanian/Chamorro (1)	1	0.00
Polynesian: (6)	16	0.04
Native Hawaiian (5)	8	0.02
Samoan	3	0.01
Tongan (1)	5	0.01
Other Pac. Isl., specified	1	0.00
Other Pac. Isl., not spec. (1)	10	0.02
Hispanic or Latino:	2,856	6.26
Central American:	102	0.22
Costa Rican	14	0.03
Guatemalan	27	0.06
Honduran	16	0.04
Nicaraguan	4	0.01
Panamanian	16	0.04
Salvadoran	24	0.05
Other Central American	1	0.00
Cuban	262	0.57
Dominican Republic	78	0.17
Mexican	612	1.34
Puerto Rican	1,219	2.67
South American:	146	0.32
Argentinean	2	0.00
Bolivian	2	0.00
Chilean	2	0.00
Colombian	76	0.17
Ecuadorian	22	0.05
Peruvian	18	0.04
Uruguayan	1	0.00
Venezuelan	22	0.05
Other South American	1	0.00
Other Hispanic or Latino	437	0.96
Hungarian	311	0.68
Iranian	22	0.05
Irish	7,197	15.85
Italian	3,836	8.45
Latvian	15	0.03
Lithuanian	193	0.42
Northern European	39	0.09
Norwegian	385	0.85
Pennsylvania German	30	0.07
Polish	1,588	3.50
Portuguese	277	0.61
Romanian	84	0.18
Russian	211	0.46
Scandinavian	14	0.03
Scotch-Irish	795	1.75
Scottish	1,168	2.57
Serbian	94	0.21
Slavic	48	0.11
Slovak	101	0.22
Slovene	19	0.04
Swedish	691	1.52
Swiss	146	0.32
Turkish	7	0.02
Ukrainian	76	0.17
United States or American	3,765	8.29
Welsh	285	0.63
West Indian, excl. Hispanic:	85	0.19
Bermudan	13	0.03
British West Indian	12	0.03
Jamaican	40	0.09
Trinidadian and Tobagonian	20	0.04
White:	41,598	91.11
Not Hispanic (38,962)	39,734	87.03
Hispanic (1,690)	1,864	4.08
Yugoslavian	338	0.74

Notes: 1. Figures in the "Number" column do not add up to the total population due to: a) Ancestry/Race overlap — e.g. persons can report being both White and Irish, b) persons of Hispanic origin can report being any race, c) persons reporting two ancestries are counted in both categories. 2. Numbers in parentheses indicate the number of persons reporting this ancestry/race alone, not in combination with any other ancestry/race. 3. Refer to the Explanation of Data in the front of the book for more detailed information.

Pinewood

Place Type: Census Designated Place
County: Miami-Dade
Population: 16,523

Ancestry/Race	Number	%
African American/Black:	12,422	75.18
Not Hispanic (11,434)	12,043	72.89
Hispanic (305)	379	2.29
African, sub-Saharan:	152	0.90
African	133	0.79
Ethiopian	11	0.07
Nigerian	8	0.05
Alaska Native tribes, specified:	4	0.02
Eskimo	2	0.01
Tlingit-Haida (1)	2	0.01
Am. Ind. or Alaska Nat., not spec.	56	0.34
American Indian tribes, specified:	39	0.24
Apache (4)	4	0.02
Blackfeet	2	0.01
Cherokee (3)	6	0.04
Chippewa (2)	2	0.01
Iroquois (1)	1	0.01
Latin American Indians (1)	7	0.04
Lumbee (1)	1	0.01
Pueblo (5)	12	0.07
All other tribes	4	0.02
American Indian tribes, not spec.	3	0.02
Arab:	23	0.14
Arab/Arabic	23	0.14
Armenian	7	0.04
Asian:	111	0.67
Chinese, ex. Taiwanese (7)	10	0.06
Filipino (16)	24	0.15
Indian (17)	35	0.21
Japanese	1	0.01
Korean (2)	7	0.04
Thai (1)	1	0.01
Vietnamese (1)	5	0.03
Other Asian, specified	6	0.04
Other Asian, not specified (9)	22	0.13
Brazilian	9	0.05
Czech	75	0.45
Danish	8	0.05
English	52	0.31
French, except Basque	50	0.30
French Canadian	13	0.08
German	69	0.41
Greek	35	0.21
Guyanese	10	0.06
Hawaii Native/Pacific Islander:	56	0.34
Polynesian: (5)	8	0.05
Native Hawaiian	3	0.02
Samoan (5)	5	0.03
Other Pac. Isl., specified	2	0.01
Other Pac. Isl., not spec.	46	0.28
Hispanic or Latino:	3,775	22.85
Central American:	715	4.33
Costa Rican	17	0.10
Guatemalan	46	0.28
Honduran	276	1.67
Nicaraguan	331	2.00
Panamanian	7	0.04
Salvadoran	20	0.12
Other Central American	18	0.11
Cuban	881	5.33
Dominican Republic	254	1.54
Mexican	95	0.57
Puerto Rican	894	5.41
South American:	111	0.67
Argentinean	5	0.03
Chilean	2	0.01
Colombian	40	0.24
Ecuadorian	31	0.19
Peruvian	13	0.08
Venezuelan	15	0.09
Other South American	5	0.03
Other Hispanic or Latino	825	4.99
Irish	22	0.13
Italian	59	0.35
Polish	20	0.12
Scottish	12	0.07
Swedish	12	0.07
Ukrainian	7	0.04
United States or American	920	5.47
West Indian, excl. Hispanic:	5,402	32.12
Bahamian	304	1.81
British West Indian	65	0.39
Haitian	4,315	25.66
Jamaican	576	3.42
Trinidadian and Tobagonian	59	0.35
U.S. Virgin Islander	14	0.08
West Indian	50	0.30
Other West Indian	19	0.11
White:	3,442	20.83
Not Hispanic (588)	628	3.80
Hispanic (2,594)	2,814	17.03

Plant City

Place Type: City
County: Hillsborough
Population: 29,915

Ancestry/Race	Number	%
Acadian/Cajun	25	0.08
African American/Black:	4,959	16.58
Not Hispanic (4,751)	4,858	16.24
Hispanic (82)	101	0.34
African, sub-Saharan:	99	0.33
African	89	0.30
Sudanese	10	0.03
Am. Ind. or Alaska Nat., not spec.	89	0.30
American Indian tribes, specified:	110	0.37
Blackfeet (1)	4	0.01
Cherokee (23)	54	0.18
Chippewa (1)	1	0.00
Choctaw	1	0.00
Comanche	2	0.01
Cree	2	0.01
Creek (1)	1	0.00
Crow	1	0.00
Houma (1)	1	0.00
Iroquois (2)	2	0.01
Latin American Indians (13)	15	0.05
Lumbee (4)	4	0.01
Navajo	1	0.00
Potawatomi	2	0.01
Pueblo (1)	1	0.00
Seminole (2)	5	0.02
Sioux (2)	2	0.01
All other tribes (5)	11	0.04
American Indian tribes, not spec.	20	0.07
Arab:	72	0.24
Arab/Arabic	27	0.09
Lebanese	27	0.09
Syrian	18	0.06
Armenian	16	0.05
Asian:	374	1.25
Chinese, ex. Taiwanese (22)	23	0.08
Filipino (31)	40	0.13
Indian (111)	139	0.46
Indonesian (1)	1	0.00
Japanese (8)	23	0.08
Korean (13)	21	0.07
Laotian (1)	1	0.00
Pakistani (10)	22	0.07
Taiwanese (4)	4	0.01
Thai (19)	20	0.07
Vietnamese (35)	42	0.14
Other Asian, specified	5	0.02
Other Asian, not specified (9)	33	0.11
Austrian	42	0.14
Belgian	7	0.02
Brazilian	7	0.02
British	145	0.48
Canadian	36	0.12
Czech	55	0.18
Danish	67	0.22
Dutch	379	1.26
Eastern European	9	0.03
English	3,215	10.68
Estonian	7	0.02
European	74	0.25
Finnish	36	0.12
French, except Basque	750	2.49
French Canadian	223	0.74
German	3,310	10.99
Greek	36	0.12
Hawaii Native/Pacific Islander:	44	0.15
Micronesian: (1)	12	0.04
Guamanian/Chamorro (1)	12	0.04
Polynesian: (11)	15	0.05
Native Hawaiian (8)	11	0.04
Samoan (3)	3	0.01
Other Polynesian	1	0.00
Other Pac. Isl., specified	5	0.02
Other Pac. Isl., not spec. (1)	12	0.04
Hispanic or Latino:	5,211	17.42
Central American:	148	0.49
Costa Rican	7	0.02
Guatemalan	76	0.25
Honduran	47	0.16
Nicaraguan	4	0.01
Panamanian	9	0.03
Salvadoran	5	0.02
Cuban	133	0.44
Dominican Republic	28	0.09
Mexican	3,681	12.30
Puerto Rican	635	2.12
South American:	74	0.25
Argentinean	8	0.03
Bolivian	1	0.00
Chilean	2	0.01
Colombian	25	0.08
Ecuadorian	12	0.04
Peruvian	19	0.06
Venezuelan	4	0.01
Other South American	3	0.01
Other Hispanic or Latino	512	1.71
Hungarian	154	0.51
Irish	3,393	11.27
Italian	911	3.03
Lithuanian	28	0.09
Macedonian	8	0.03
Norwegian	121	0.40
Pennsylvania German	10	0.03
Polish	499	1.66
Portuguese	175	0.58
Romanian	20	0.07
Russian	84	0.28
Scandinavian	43	0.14
Scotch-Irish	427	1.42
Scottish	653	2.17
Serbian	7	0.02
Slovak	81	0.27
Slovene	7	0.02
Swedish	143	0.47
Swiss	14	0.05
Ukrainian	78	0.26
United States or American	2,763	9.18
Welsh	143	0.47
West Indian, excl. Hispanic:	216	0.72
Dutch West Indian	16	0.05
Haitian	51	0.17
Jamaican	115	0.38
Trinidadian and Tobagonian	28	0.09
West Indian	6	0.02
White:	21,838	73.00
Not Hispanic (19,250)	19,471	65.09
Hispanic (2,190)	2,367	7.91
Yugoslavian	33	0.11

Notes: 1. Figures in the "Number" column do not add up to the total population due to: a) Ancestry/Race overlap — e.g. persons can report being both White and Irish, b) persons of Hispanic origin can report being any race, c) persons reporting two ancestries are counted in both categories. 2. Numbers in parentheses indicate the number of persons reporting this ancestry/race alone, not in combination with any other ancestry/race. 3. Refer to the Explanation of Data in the front of the book for more detailed information.

Plantation

Place Type: City
County: Broward
Population: 82,934

Ancestry/Race	Number	%
Acadian/Cajun	16	0.02
African American/Black:	12,497	15.07
Not Hispanic (11,101)	12,053	14.53
Hispanic (325)	444	0.54
African, sub-Saharan:	684	0.82
African	465	0.56
Kenyan	28	0.03
Nigerian	50	0.06
South African	119	0.14
Sudanese	10	0.01
Other sub-Saharan African	12	0.01
Alaska Native tribes, specified:	4	0.00
Alaska Athabascan	1	0.00
Tlingit-Haida (3)	3	0.00
Am. Ind. or Alaska Nat., not spec.	129	0.16
Albanian	26	0.03
American Indian tribes, specified:	188	0.23
Apache	8	0.01
Blackfeet	8	0.01
Cherokee (29)	74	0.09
Cheyenne (3)	3	0.00
Chickasaw (1)	1	0.00
Chippewa (6)	7	0.01
Choctaw (6)	9	0.01
Comanche (3)	3	0.00
Creek	2	0.00
Crow	1	0.00
Delaware (1)	1	0.00
Iroquois (2)	8	0.01
Latin American Indians (7)	32	0.04
Lumbee (2)	2	0.00
Navajo (2)	6	0.01
Potawatomi (1)	1	0.00
Seminole (2)	5	0.01
Sioux (1)	3	0.00
All other tribes (3)	14	0.02
American Indian tribes, not spec.	15	0.02
Arab:	703	0.84
Arab/Arabic	132	0.16
Egyptian	51	0.06
Iraqi	9	0.01
Jordanian	25	0.03
Lebanese	159	0.19
Moroccan	56	0.07
Palestinian	156	0.19
Syrian	29	0.03
Other Arab	86	0.10
Armenian	107	0.13
Asian:	3,021	3.64
Bangladeshi (19)	30	0.04
Cambodian (1)	1	0.00
Chinese, ex. Taiwanese (488)	646	0.78
Filipino (268)	351	0.42
Indian (1,090)	1,230	1.48
Indonesian (6)	14	0.02
Japanese (65)	106	0.13
Korean (123)	153	0.18
Laotian (3)	10	0.01
Malaysian (4)	4	0.00
Pakistani (86)	111	0.13
Sri Lankan	1	0.00
Taiwanese (28)	30	0.04
Thai (25)	33	0.04
Vietnamese (116)	139	0.17
Other Asian, specified (12)	16	0.02
Other Asian, not specified (28)	146	0.18
Australian	12	0.01
Austrian	735	0.88
Belgian	21	0.03
Brazilian	349	0.42
British	449	0.54
Bulgarian	8	0.01
Canadian	528	0.63
Croatian	111	0.13
Czech	311	0.37
Czechoslovakian	216	0.26
Danish	231	0.28
Dutch	687	0.82
Eastern European	525	0.63
English	5,894	7.08
Estonian	11	0.01
European	834	1.00
Finnish	25	0.03
French, except Basque	1,928	2.32
French Canadian	562	0.67
German	8,959	10.76
German Russian	14	0.02
Greek	776	0.93
Guyanese	158	0.19
Hawaii Native/Pacific Islander:	132	0.16
Micronesian: (5)	11	0.01
Guamanian/Chamorro (4)	10	0.01
Other Micronesian (1)	1	0.00
Polynesian: (14)	30	0.04
Native Hawaiian (8)	20	0.02
Samoan (1)	2	0.00
Other Polynesian (5)	8	0.01
Other Pac. Isl., specified	4	0.00
Other Pac. Isl., not spec. (18)	87	0.10
Hispanic or Latino:	10,860	13.09
Central American:	621	0.75
Costa Rican	55	0.07
Guatemalan	80	0.10
Honduran	135	0.16
Nicaraguan	90	0.11
Panamanian	100	0.12
Salvadoran	142	0.17
Other Central American	19	0.02
Cuban	2,043	2.46
Dominican Republic	387	0.47
Mexican	559	0.67
Puerto Rican	1,915	2.31
South American:	3,137	3.78
Argentinean	177	0.21
Bolivian	25	0.03
Chilean	72	0.09
Colombian	1,502	1.81
Ecuadorian	256	0.31
Paraguayan	8	0.01
Peruvian	484	0.58
Uruguayan	50	0.06
Venezuelan	468	0.56
Other South American	95	0.11
Other Hispanic or Latino	2,198	2.65
Hungarian	1,070	1.28
Iranian	149	0.18
Irish	8,473	10.17
Israeli	439	0.53
Italian	7,382	8.86
Latvian	39	0.05
Lithuanian	188	0.23
Macedonian	45	0.05
Northern European	48	0.06
Norwegian	553	0.66
Pennsylvania German	12	0.01
Polish	3,518	4.22
Portuguese	454	0.55
Romanian	469	0.56
Russian	3,428	4.12
Scandinavian	97	0.12
Scotch-Irish	1,054	1.27
Scottish	1,234	1.48
Serbian	30	0.04
Slavic	7	0.01
Slovak	79	0.09
Slovene	45	0.05
Swedish	707	0.85
Swiss	160	0.19
Turkish	62	0.07
Ukrainian	258	0.31
United States or American	6,631	7.96
Welsh	426	0.51
West Indian, excl. Hispanic:	7,276	8.74
Bahamian	223	0.27
Barbadian	55	0.07
Belizean	91	0.11
Bermudan	11	0.01
British West Indian	58	0.07
Dutch West Indian	50	0.06
Haitian	2,307	2.77
Jamaican	3,657	4.39
Trinidadian and Tobagonian	461	0.55
U.S. Virgin Islander	56	0.07
West Indian	288	0.35
Other West Indian	19	0.02
White:	66,357	80.01
Not Hispanic (56,411)	57,301	69.09
Hispanic (8,556)	9,056	10.92
Yugoslavian	65	0.08

Poinciana

Place Type: Census Designated Place
County: Osceola
Population: 13,647

Ancestry/Race	Number	%
African American/Black:	2,759	20.22
Not Hispanic (2,178)	2,405	17.62
Hispanic (242)	354	2.59
African, sub-Saharan:	155	1.14
African	65	0.48
Cape Verdean	90	0.66
Alaska Native tribes, specified:	6	0.04
Eskimo (2)	6	0.04
Am. Ind. or Alaska Nat., not spec.	49	0.36
Albanian	11	0.08
American Indian tribes, specified:	61	0.45
Apache (1)	2	0.01
Blackfeet (1)	4	0.03
Cherokee (6)	18	0.13
Cheyenne	1	0.01
Choctaw (1)	2	0.01
Delaware	2	0.01
Iroquois (2)	2	0.01
Latin American Indians (4)	15	0.11
Navajo (2)	2	0.01
Pueblo	3	0.02
Sioux (2)	3	0.02
Tohono O'Odham	3	0.02
Ute	3	0.02
All other tribes	1	0.01
American Indian tribes, not spec.	17	0.12
Arab:	81	0.60
Egyptian	29	0.21
Lebanese	13	0.10
Moroccan	39	0.29
Asian:	270	1.98
Chinese, ex. Taiwanese (20)	53	0.39
Filipino (52)	69	0.51
Indian (46)	82	0.60
Japanese	7	0.05
Korean (6)	13	0.10
Laotian (3)	3	0.02
Pakistani (3)	3	0.02
Thai (1)	1	0.01
Vietnamese (4)	18	0.13
Other Asian, not specified (2)	21	0.15
Australian	22	0.16
Austrian	35	0.26
Belgian	20	0.15
Brazilian	19	0.14
British	111	0.82
Canadian	8	0.06
Czech	13	0.10
Czechoslovakian	22	0.16
Dutch	206	1.52
English	598	4.40
European	93	0.68
Finnish	13	0.10
French, except Basque	538	3.96
French Canadian	165	1.21
German	1,335	9.83

Notes: 1. Figures in the "Number" column do not add up to the total population due to: a) Ancestry/Race overlap — e.g. persons can report being both White and Irish, b) persons of Hispanic origin can report being any race, c) persons reporting two ancestries are counted in both categories. 2. Numbers in parentheses indicate the number of persons reporting this ancestry/race alone, not in combination with any other ancestry/race. 3. Refer to the Explanation of Data in the front of the book for more detailed information.

Greek	18	0.13
Guyanese	70	0.52
Hawaii Native/Pacific Islander:	55	0.40
Micronesian: (1)	2	0.01
Guamanian/Chamorro (1)	2	0.01
Polynesian: (12)	23	0.17
Native Hawaiian (2)	8	0.06
Samoan (5)	9	0.07
Tongan (5)	5	0.04
Other Polynesian	1	0.01
Other Pac. Isl., not spec.	30	0.22
Hispanic or Latino:	5,393	39.52
Central American:	196	1.44
Costa Rican	18	0.13
Guatemalan	25	0.18
Honduran	27	0.20
Nicaraguan	23	0.17
Panamanian	58	0.43
Salvadoran	35	0.26
Other Central American	10	0.07
Cuban	135	0.99
Dominican Republic	217	1.59
Mexican	136	1.00
Puerto Rican	3,789	27.76
South American:	301	2.21
Argentinean	22	0.16
Bolivian	4	0.03
Chilean	13	0.10
Colombian	147	1.08
Ecuadorian	43	0.32
Peruvian	16	0.12
Uruguayan	3	0.02
Venezuelan	26	0.19
Other South American	27	0.20
Other Hispanic or Latino	619	4.54
Hungarian	118	0.87
Irish	1,164	8.57
Italian	979	7.21
Luxemburger	8	0.06
Norwegian	71	0.52
Pennsylvania German	10	0.07
Polish	355	2.61
Portuguese	87	0.64
Romanian	46	0.34
Russian	100	0.74
Scotch-Irish	62	0.46
Scottish	83	0.61
Slovak	25	0.18
Swedish	71	0.52
Swiss	9	0.07
Ukrainian	12	0.09
United States or American	424	3.12
Welsh	6	0.04
West Indian, excl. Hispanic:	1,088	8.01
Barbadian	44	0.32
British West Indian	20	0.15
Haitian	195	1.44
Jamaican	545	4.01
Trinidadian and Tobagonian	102	0.75
U.S. Virgin Islander	8	0.06
West Indian	162	1.19
Other West Indian	12	0.09
White:	9,382	68.75
Not Hispanic (5,450)	5,609	41.10
Hispanic (3,434)	3,773	27.65
Yugoslavian	9	0.07

Pompano Beach

Place Type: City
County: Broward
Population: 78,191

Ancestry/Race	Number	%
African American/Black:	21,687	27.74
Not Hispanic (19,520)	21,238	27.16
Hispanic (377)	449	0.57
African, sub-Saharan:	401	0.51
African	303	0.39
Kenyan	29	0.04
Nigerian	22	0.03
Senegalese	24	0.03
South African	23	0.03
Alaska Native tribes, specified:	7	0.01
Alaska Athabascan	2	0.00
Aleut (1)	3	0.00
Eskimo (1)	2	0.00
Am. Ind. or Alaska Nat., not spec.	173	0.22
American Indian tribes, specified:	194	0.25
Apache	2	0.00
Blackfeet (1)	6	0.01
Cherokee (24)	71	0.09
Chippewa (7)	7	0.01
Choctaw (5)	10	0.01
Cree (1)	1	0.00
Creek	3	0.00
Delaware (3)	3	0.00
Iroquois (7)	11	0.01
Kiowa (1)	1	0.00
Latin American Indians (32)	43	0.05
Navajo (1)	1	0.00
Pueblo (1)	1	0.00
Seminole (3)	7	0.01
Sioux (2)	4	0.01
Ute	1	0.00
All other tribes (6)	22	0.03
American Indian tribes, not spec.	29	0.04
Arab:	398	0.51
Arab/Arabic	24	0.03
Egyptian	37	0.05
Jordanian	10	0.01
Lebanese	149	0.19
Moroccan	29	0.04
Palestinian	30	0.04
Syrian	71	0.09
Other Arab	48	0.06
Armenian	75	0.10
Asian:	1,016	1.30
Bangladeshi (23)	32	0.04
Cambodian (3)	3	0.00
Chinese, ex. Taiwanese (103)	144	0.18
Filipino (77)	136	0.17
Indian (270)	377	0.48
Indonesian (1)	2	0.00
Japanese (28)	66	0.08
Korean (37)	61	0.08
Laotian (1)	1	0.00
Malaysian (1)	1	0.00
Pakistani (8)	10	0.01
Sri Lankan (1)	2	0.00
Thai (16)	17	0.02
Vietnamese (29)	46	0.06
Other Asian, specified (2)	14	0.02
Other Asian, not specified (13)	104	0.13
Assyrian/Chaldean/Syriac	12	0.02
Australian	44	0.06
Austrian	413	0.53
Belgian	67	0.09
Brazilian	919	1.17
British	506	0.65
Bulgarian	28	0.04
Canadian	516	0.66
Croatian	61	0.08
Czech	171	0.22
Czechoslovakian	82	0.10
Danish	197	0.25
Dutch	940	1.20
Eastern European	70	0.09
English	5,122	6.54
Estonian	20	0.03
European	339	0.43
Finnish	73	0.09
French, except Basque	2,105	2.69
French Canadian	964	1.23
German	7,615	9.73
Greek	523	0.67
Guyanese	25	0.03
Hawaii Native/Pacific Islander:	133	0.17
Micronesian: (3)	14	0.02
Guamanian/Chamorro (3)	14	0.02
Polynesian: (13)	41	0.05
Native Hawaiian (8)	32	0.04
Samoan (4)	8	0.01
Other Polynesian (1)	1	0.00
Other Pac. Isl., specified	9	0.01
Other Pac. Isl., not spec. (6)	69	0.09
Hispanic or Latino:	7,770	9.94
Central American:	342	0.44
Costa Rican	43	0.05
Guatemalan	72	0.09
Honduran	105	0.13
Nicaraguan	34	0.04
Panamanian	18	0.02
Salvadoran	63	0.08
Other Central American	7	0.01
Cuban	562	0.72
Dominican Republic	84	0.11
Mexican	2,795	3.57
Puerto Rican	1,275	1.63
South American:	1,461	1.87
Argentinean	81	0.10
Bolivian	27	0.03
Chilean	56	0.07
Colombian	479	0.61
Ecuadorian	82	0.10
Paraguayan	4	0.01
Peruvian	156	0.20
Uruguayan	25	0.03
Venezuelan	496	0.63
Other South American	55	0.07
Other Hispanic or Latino	1,251	1.60
Hungarian	781	1.00
Iranian	35	0.04
Irish	7,578	9.68
Israeli	36	0.05
Italian	6,975	8.91
Latvian	70	0.09
Lithuanian	295	0.38
Macedonian	8	0.01
New Zealander	22	0.03
Northern European	8	0.01
Norwegian	475	0.61
Pennsylvania German	61	0.08
Polish	2,624	3.35
Portuguese	333	0.43
Romanian	293	0.37
Russian	2,066	2.64
Scandinavian	37	0.05
Scotch-Irish	774	0.99
Scottish	1,246	1.59
Serbian	30	0.04
Slavic	40	0.05
Slovak	92	0.12
Slovene	32	0.04
Swedish	888	1.13
Swiss	188	0.24
Turkish	165	0.21
Ukrainian	335	0.43
United States or American	4,633	5.92
Welsh	325	0.42
West Indian, excl. Hispanic:	5,453	6.96
Bahamian	110	0.14
Barbadian	10	0.01
Belizean	21	0.03
British West Indian	91	0.12
Haitian	4,718	6.03
Jamaican	402	0.51
Trinidadian and Tobagonian	49	0.06
West Indian	52	0.07
White:	54,200	69.32
Not Hispanic (47,549)	48,331	61.81
Hispanic (5,440)	5,869	7.51
Yugoslavian	76	0.10

Notes: 1. Figures in the "Number" column do not add up to the total population due to: a) Ancestry/Race overlap — e.g. persons can report being both White and Irish, b) persons of Hispanic origin can report being any race, c) persons reporting two ancestries are counted in both categories. 2. Numbers in parentheses indicate the number of persons reporting this ancestry/race alone, not in combination with any other ancestry/race. 3. Refer to the Explanation of Data in the front of the book for more detailed information.

Port Charlotte

Place Type: Census Designated Place
County: Charlotte
Population: 46,451

Ancestry/Race	Number	%
African American/Black:	3,320	7.15
Not Hispanic (2,895)	3,128	6.73
Hispanic (138)	192	0.41
African, sub-Saharan:	160	0.34
African	150	0.32
Cape Verdean	10	0.02
Alaska Native tribes, specified:	1	0.00
Tlingit-Haida (1)	1	0.00
Alaska Native tribes, not specified	1	0.00
Am. Ind. or Alaska Nat., not spec.	95	0.20
American Indian tribes, specified:	223	0.48
Apache (2)	3	0.01
Blackfeet (5)	7	0.02
Cherokee (33)	92	0.20
Cheyenne	2	0.00
Chickasaw (2)	2	0.00
Chippewa (16)	26	0.06
Choctaw	4	0.01
Creek (1)	3	0.01
Crow (1)	2	0.00
Delaware (1)	1	0.00
Iroquois (9)	20	0.04
Latin American Indians (4)	20	0.04
Navajo (2)	3	0.01
Osage	1	0.00
Potawatomi	1	0.00
Pueblo	2	0.00
Seminole (4)	6	0.01
Sioux (2)	12	0.03
All other tribes (7)	16	0.03
American Indian tribes, not spec.	18	0.04
Arab:	239	0.51
Arab/Arabic	70	0.15
Egyptian	55	0.12
Lebanese	30	0.06
Palestinian	69	0.15
Syrian	15	0.03
Armenian	13	0.03
Asian:	701	1.51
Cambodian (1)	1	0.00
Chinese, ex. Taiwanese (90)	117	0.25
Filipino (136)	198	0.43
Indian (135)	174	0.37
Indonesian (1)	4	0.01
Japanese (26)	35	0.08
Korean (27)	32	0.07
Laotian (5)	5	0.01
Malaysian	3	0.01
Pakistani (10)	10	0.02
Sri Lankan (2)	2	0.00
Thai (21)	30	0.06
Vietnamese (48)	54	0.12
Other Asian, specified (1)	9	0.02
Other Asian, not specified (13)	27	0.06
Assyrian/Chaldean/Syriac	8	0.02
Austrian	147	0.32
Belgian	62	0.13
Brazilian	28	0.06
British	270	0.58
Bulgarian	6	0.01
Canadian	257	0.55
Celtic	20	0.04
Croatian	87	0.19
Czech	305	0.66
Czechoslovakian	117	0.25
Danish	178	0.38
Dutch	869	1.87
Eastern European	7	0.02
English	5,833	12.55
Estonian	8	0.02
European	229	0.49
Finnish	227	0.49
French, except Basque	2,390	5.14
French Canadian	580	1.25
German	8,981	19.33
Greek	193	0.42
Guyanese	125	0.27
Hawaii Native/Pacific Islander:	80	0.17
Micronesian: (4)	6	0.01
Guamanian/Chamorro (4)	6	0.01
Polynesian: (16)	34	0.07
Native Hawaiian (5)	19	0.04
Samoan (11)	13	0.03
Other Polynesian	2	0.00
Other Pac. Isl., specified	7	0.02
Other Pac. Isl., not spec. (2)	33	0.07
Hispanic or Latino:	2,395	5.16
Central American:	93	0.20
Costa Rican	15	0.03
Guatemalan	11	0.02
Honduran	14	0.03
Nicaraguan	10	0.02
Panamanian	29	0.06
Salvadoran	6	0.01
Other Central American	8	0.02
Cuban	322	0.69
Dominican Republic	62	0.13
Mexican	367	0.79
Puerto Rican	870	1.87
South American:	215	0.46
Argentinean	14	0.03
Chilean	2	0.00
Colombian	108	0.23
Ecuadorian	27	0.06
Peruvian	36	0.08
Uruguayan	4	0.01
Venezuelan	16	0.03
Other South American	8	0.02
Other Hispanic or Latino	466	1.00
Hungarian	450	0.97
Icelander	11	0.02
Irish	7,395	15.91
Israeli	9	0.02
Italian	4,833	10.40
Latvian	11	0.02
Lithuanian	177	0.38
Maltese	30	0.06
Northern European	9	0.02
Norwegian	409	0.88
Pennsylvania German	48	0.10
Polish	2,063	4.44
Portuguese	298	0.64
Romanian	63	0.14
Russian	325	0.70
Scandinavian	68	0.15
Scotch-Irish	757	1.63
Scottish	1,239	2.67
Serbian	40	0.09
Slavic	22	0.05
Slovak	161	0.35
Slovene	8	0.02
Swedish	648	1.39
Swiss	109	0.23
Ukrainian	310	0.67
United States or American	3,368	7.25
Welsh	441	0.95
West Indian, excl. Hispanic:	1,537	3.31
Barbadian	39	0.08
Belizean	12	0.03
British West Indian	18	0.04
Haitian	391	0.84
Jamaican	820	1.76
Trinidadian and Tobagonian	71	0.15
U.S. Virgin Islander	9	0.02
West Indian	177	0.38
White:	41,988	90.39
Not Hispanic (39,890)	40,298	86.75
Hispanic (1,558)	1,690	3.64
Yugoslavian	36	0.08

Port Orange

Place Type: City
County: Volusia
Population: 45,823

Ancestry/Race	Number	%
Acadian/Cajun	16	0.04
African American/Black:	800	1.75
Not Hispanic (695)	769	1.68
Hispanic (27)	31	0.07
African, sub-Saharan:	132	0.29
African	54	0.12
Cape Verdean	33	0.07
Ghanian	9	0.02
South African	9	0.02
Other sub-Saharan African	27	0.06
Alaska Native tribes, specified:	1	0.00
Eskimo	1	0.00
Am. Ind. or Alaska Nat., not spec.	59	0.13
Albanian	6	0.01
American Indian tribes, specified:	193	0.42
Apache	2	0.00
Blackfeet (5)	12	0.03
Cherokee (28)	73	0.16
Cheyenne	2	0.00
Chickasaw (2)	3	0.01
Chippewa (3)	4	0.01
Choctaw	2	0.00
Cree	1	0.00
Creek (2)	7	0.02
Delaware (4)	7	0.02
Iroquois (12)	29	0.06
Latin American Indians (5)	5	0.01
Lumbee (8)	9	0.02
Navajo	1	0.00
Pueblo (1)	1	0.00
Seminole (5)	7	0.02
Shoshone	1	0.00
Sioux (3)	3	0.01
Tohono O'Odham	1	0.00
All other tribes (11)	23	0.05
American Indian tribes, not spec.	13	0.03
Arab:	352	0.78
Arab/Arabic	55	0.12
Egyptian	73	0.16
Lebanese	95	0.21
Syrian	98	0.22
Other Arab	31	0.07
Armenian	25	0.06
Asian:	650	1.42
Cambodian	1	0.00
Chinese, ex. Taiwanese (91)	111	0.24
Filipino (103)	131	0.29
Indian (139)	151	0.33
Indonesian (4)	5	0.01
Japanese (24)	31	0.07
Korean (67)	84	0.18
Pakistani (12)	19	0.04
Taiwanese (2)	2	0.00
Thai (10)	13	0.03
Vietnamese (46)	56	0.12
Other Asian, specified	1	0.00
Other Asian, not specified (18)	45	0.10
Australian	7	0.02
Austrian	124	0.27
Belgian	73	0.16
Brazilian	9	0.02
British	191	0.42
Bulgarian	9	0.02
Canadian	225	0.50
Celtic	8	0.02
Croatian	131	0.29
Czech	174	0.38
Czechoslovakian	75	0.17
Danish	117	0.26
Dutch	906	2.00
Eastern European	17	0.04
English	6,354	14.00
European	218	0.48

Notes: 1. Figures in the "Number" column do not add up to the total population due to: a) Ancestry/Race overlap — e.g. persons can report being both White and Irish, b) persons of Hispanic origin can report being any race, c) persons reporting two ancestries are counted in both categories. 2. Numbers in parentheses indicate the number of persons reporting this ancestry/race alone, not in combination with any other ancestry/race. 3. Refer to the Explanation of Data in the front of the book for more detailed information.

Ancestry/Race	Number	%
Finnish	71	0.16
French, except Basque	1,850	4.08
French Canadian	792	1.75
German	8,246	18.18
Greek	353	0.78
Hawaii Native/Pacific Islander:	27	0.06
Micronesian: (3)	5	0.01
Guamanian/Chamorro (3)	3	0.01
Other Micronesian	2	0.00
Polynesian: (4)	17	0.04
Native Hawaiian (1)	8	0.02
Samoan (3)	8	0.02
Other Polynesian	1	0.00
Other Pac. Isl., not spec. (3)	5	0.01
Hispanic or Latino:	1,151	2.51
Central American:	36	0.08
Costa Rican	7	0.02
Guatemalan	6	0.01
Nicaraguan	5	0.01
Panamanian	11	0.02
Salvadoran	5	0.01
Other Central American	2	0.00
Cuban	94	0.21
Dominican Republic	16	0.03
Mexican	157	0.34
Puerto Rican	441	0.96
South American:	152	0.33
Argentinean	19	0.04
Bolivian	5	0.01
Chilean	8	0.02
Colombian	55	0.12
Ecuadorian	22	0.05
Peruvian	2	0.00
Uruguayan	7	0.02
Venezuelan	23	0.05
Other South American	11	0.02
Other Hispanic or Latino	255	0.56
Hungarian	254	0.56
Iranian	41	0.09
Irish	7,137	15.73
Italian	5,028	11.08
Latvian	8	0.02
Lithuanian	160	0.35
Luxemburger	17	0.04
Macedonian	13	0.03
New Zealander	8	0.02
Norwegian	319	0.70
Pennsylvania German	43	0.09
Polish	1,986	4.38
Portuguese	159	0.35
Romanian	45	0.10
Russian	360	0.79
Scandinavian	15	0.03
Scotch-Irish	997	2.20
Scottish	1,094	2.41
Serbian	28	0.06
Slavic	36	0.08
Slovak	224	0.49
Slovene	21	0.05
Swedish	648	1.43
Swiss	162	0.36
Turkish	10	0.02
Ukrainian	186	0.41
United States or American	3,612	7.96
Welsh	461	1.02
West Indian, excl. Hispanic:	144	0.32
Barbadian	9	0.02
British West Indian	8	0.02
Dutch West Indian	11	0.02
Haitian	71	0.16
Jamaican	34	0.07
Trinidadian and Tobagonian	6	0.01
West Indian	5	0.01
White:	44,167	96.39
Not Hispanic (42,941)	43,260	94.41
Hispanic (862)	907	1.98
Yugoslavian	45	0.10

Port Saint John

Place Type: Census Designated Place
County: Brevard
Population: 12,112

Ancestry/Race	Number	%
African American/Black:	659	5.44
Not Hispanic (593)	640	5.28
Hispanic (14)	19	0.16
Am. Ind. or Alaska Nat., not spec.	42	0.35
American Indian tribes, specified:	110	0.91
Apache	3	0.02
Blackfeet (1)	4	0.03
Cherokee (23)	61	0.50
Chickasaw (1)	1	0.01
Chippewa (1)	6	0.05
Choctaw	5	0.04
Creek (2)	4	0.03
Latin American Indians (1)	1	0.01
Lumbee (1)	1	0.01
Navajo (2)	2	0.02
Potawatomi (1)	1	0.01
Pueblo	1	0.01
Puget Sound Salish	1	0.01
Seminole (1)	2	0.02
Sioux (4)	7	0.06
All other tribes (5)	10	0.08
American Indian tribes, not spec.	1	0.01
Armenian	31	0.26
Asian:	174	1.44
Chinese, ex. Taiwanese (5)	5	0.04
Filipino (39)	57	0.47
Indian (20)	26	0.21
Indonesian (1)	1	0.01
Japanese (12)	37	0.31
Korean (7)	16	0.13
Malaysian (1)	1	0.01
Thai (6)	7	0.06
Vietnamese (11)	13	0.11
Other Asian, not specified (7)	11	0.09
Austrian	45	0.38
Belgian	62	0.52
Brazilian	18	0.15
British	11	0.09
Canadian	4	0.03
Cypriot	8	0.07
Czech	27	0.23
Czechoslovakian	30	0.25
Danish	35	0.29
Dutch	286	2.39
English	1,623	13.56
European	87	0.73
Finnish	11	0.09
French, except Basque	575	4.80
French Canadian	192	1.60
German	2,103	17.57
Greek	86	0.72
Hawaii Native/Pacific Islander:	33	0.27
Micronesian: (15)	21	0.17
Guamanian/Chamorro (14)	18	0.15
Other Micronesian (1)	3	0.02
Polynesian: (6)	10	0.08
Native Hawaiian (1)	5	0.04
Samoan (5)	5	0.04
Other Pac. Isl., not spec.	2	0.02
Hispanic or Latino:	397	3.28
Central American:	21	0.17
Costa Rican	3	0.02
Guatemalan	3	0.02
Honduran	3	0.02
Nicaraguan	2	0.02
Panamanian	8	0.07
Salvadoran	2	0.02
Cuban	31	0.26
Dominican Republic	4	0.03
Mexican	88	0.73
Puerto Rican	166	1.37
South American:	28	0.23
Argentinean	4	0.03
Colombian	13	0.11
Peruvian	4	0.03
Venezuelan	7	0.06
Other Hispanic or Latino	59	0.49
Hungarian	22	0.18
Irish	1,954	16.33
Italian	857	7.16
Latvian	8	0.07
Lithuanian	19	0.16
Norwegian	96	0.80
Pennsylvania German	16	0.13
Polish	318	2.66
Portuguese	8	0.07
Russian	58	0.48
Scandinavian	23	0.19
Scotch-Irish	297	2.48
Scottish	403	3.37
Slavic	12	0.10
Swedish	180	1.50
Swiss	29	0.24
Turkish	32	0.27
Ukrainian	37	0.31
United States or American	1,216	10.16
Welsh	65	0.54
West Indian, excl. Hispanic:	103	0.86
Bahamian	16	0.13
Jamaican	46	0.38
Trinidadian and Tobagonian	20	0.17
West Indian	21	0.18
White:	11,182	92.32
Not Hispanic (10,712)	10,893	89.94
Hispanic (273)	289	2.39

Port Saint Lucie

Place Type: City
County: Saint Lucie
Population: 88,769

Ancestry/Race	Number	%
Acadian/Cajun	7	0.01
African American/Black:	6,848	7.71
Not Hispanic (6,035)	6,509	7.33
Hispanic (260)	339	0.38
African, sub-Saharan:	282	0.32
African	220	0.25
Ghanian	16	0.02
Nigerian	12	0.01
South African	26	0.03
Zimbabwean	8	0.01
Alaska Native tribes, specified:	8	0.01
Eskimo (1)	1	0.00
Tlingit-Haida (1)	7	0.01
Am. Ind. or Alaska Nat., not spec.	171	0.19
American Indian tribes, specified:	378	0.43
Apache (6)	12	0.01
Blackfeet (2)	32	0.04
Cherokee (38)	149	0.17
Cheyenne (2)	4	0.00
Chickasaw (8)	12	0.01
Chippewa (6)	22	0.02
Choctaw	3	0.00
Comanche (1)	1	0.00
Cree (1)	1	0.00
Creek (1)	2	0.00
Delaware	3	0.00
Iroquois (11)	31	0.03
Latin American Indians (9)	26	0.03
Lumbee (1)	1	0.00
Menominee (1)	1	0.00
Navajo (1)	3	0.00
Osage (2)	4	0.00
Pueblo	2	0.00
Seminole (13)	17	0.02
Sioux (5)	12	0.01
All other tribes (9)	40	0.05
American Indian tribes, not spec.	24	0.03
Arab:	380	0.43
Arab/Arabic	136	0.15
Jordanian	21	0.02

Notes: 1. Figures in the "Number" column do not add up to the total population due to: a) Ancestry/Race overlap — e.g. persons can report being both White and Irish, b) persons of Hispanic origin can report being any race, c) persons reporting two ancestries are counted in both categories. 2. Numbers in parentheses indicate the number of persons reporting this ancestry/race alone, not in combination with any other ancestry/race. 3. Refer to the Explanation of Data in the front of the book for more detailed information.

Lebanese	121	0.14
Moroccan	7	0.01
Palestinian	11	0.01
Syrian	50	0.06
Other Arab	34	0.04
Armenian	17	0.02
Asian:	1,437	1.62
Bangladeshi (2)	9	0.01
Cambodian (40)	44	0.05
Chinese, ex. Taiwanese (230)	275	0.31
Filipino (285)	372	0.42
Indian (247)	323	0.36
Indonesian (7)	8	0.01
Japanese (40)	82	0.09
Korean (72)	96	0.11
Laotian (2)	2	0.00
Malaysian (5)	5	0.01
Pakistani (37)	38	0.04
Sri Lankan (4)	4	0.00
Taiwanese (1)	9	0.01
Thai (25)	33	0.04
Vietnamese (57)	62	0.07
Other Asian, specified (1)	2	0.00
Other Asian, not specified (25)	73	0.08
Australian	7	0.01
Austrian	392	0.44
Basque	45	0.05
Belgian	71	0.08
Brazilian	81	0.09
British	307	0.35
Bulgarian	19	0.02
Canadian	268	0.30
Carpatho Rusyn	16	0.02
Celtic	7	0.01
Croatian	71	0.08
Czech	260	0.29
Czechoslovakian	167	0.19
Danish	256	0.29
Dutch	1,624	1.83
Eastern European	33	0.04
English	10,173	11.46
Estonian	14	0.02
European	286	0.32
Finnish	201	0.23
French, except Basque	3,402	3.83
French Canadian	1,357	1.53
German	14,983	16.87
German Russian	11	0.01
Greek	524	0.59
Guyanese	57	0.06
Hawaii Native/Pacific Islander:	104	0.12
Micronesian: (10)	16	0.02
Guamanian/Chamorro (9)	15	0.02
Other Micronesian (1)	1	0.00
Polynesian: (16)	44	0.05
Native Hawaiian (10)	36	0.04
Samoan (5)	7	0.01
Other Polynesian (1)	1	0.00
Other Pac. Isl., specified	1	0.00
Other Pac. Isl., not spec. (5)	43	0.05
Hispanic or Latino:	6,677	7.52
Central American:	378	0.43
Costa Rican	24	0.03
Guatemalan	110	0.12
Honduran	91	0.10
Nicaraguan	32	0.04
Panamanian	80	0.09
Salvadoran	27	0.03
Other Central American	14	0.02
Cuban	786	0.89
Dominican Republic	193	0.22
Mexican	648	0.73
Puerto Rican	2,811	3.17
South American:	634	0.71
Argentinean	36	0.04
Bolivian	4	0.00
Chilean	30	0.03
Colombian	280	0.32
Ecuadorian	112	0.13
Paraguayan	1	0.00
Peruvian	83	0.09
Uruguayan	13	0.01
Venezuelan	51	0.06
Other South American	24	0.03
Other Hispanic or Latino	1,227	1.38
Hungarian	973	1.10
Icelander	7	0.01
Iranian	16	0.02
Irish	15,466	17.42
Israeli	6	0.01
Italian	13,966	15.73
Latvian	37	0.04
Lithuanian	342	0.39
Maltese	14	0.02
Norwegian	977	1.10
Pennsylvania German	57	0.06
Polish	4,487	5.05
Portuguese	537	0.60
Romanian	69	0.08
Russian	1,082	1.22
Scandinavian	168	0.19
Scotch-Irish	1,167	1.31
Scottish	1,916	2.16
Slavic	50	0.06
Slovak	429	0.48
Slovene	63	0.07
Swedish	1,129	1.27
Swiss	199	0.22
Turkish	38	0.04
Ukrainian	382	0.43
United States or American	5,962	6.71
Welsh	360	0.41
West Indian, excl. Hispanic:	2,798	3.15
Bahamian	130	0.15
Barbadian	38	0.04
British West Indian	48	0.05
Haitian	702	0.79
Jamaican	1,584	1.78
Trinidadian and Tobagonian	165	0.19
West Indian	131	0.15
White:	79,199	89.22
Not Hispanic (73,489)	74,290	83.69
Hispanic (4,522)	4,909	5.53
Yugoslavian	83	0.09

Port Salerno

Place Type: Census Designated Place
County: Martin
Population: 10,141

Ancestry/Race	Number	%
African American/Black:	755	7.45
Not Hispanic (694)	742	7.32
Hispanic (11)	13	0.13
Am. Ind. or Alaska Nat., not spec.	10	0.10
American Indian tribes, specified:	32	0.32
Blackfeet (1)	2	0.02
Cherokee (1)	11	0.11
Chippewa (1)	3	0.03
Cree (1)	1	0.01
Creek	1	0.01
Iroquois (3)	5	0.05
Latin American Indians (2)	4	0.04
Navajo (1)	1	0.01
Seminole	1	0.01
Shoshone	1	0.01
All other tribes	2	0.02
American Indian tribes, not spec.	3	0.03
Asian:	87	0.86
Chinese, ex. Taiwanese (15)	16	0.16
Filipino (13)	21	0.21
Indian (16)	17	0.17
Indonesian	2	0.02
Japanese	4	0.04
Korean (5)	5	0.05
Laotian (8)	8	0.08
Pakistani (2)	3	0.03
Sri Lankan (5)	5	0.05
Thai (1)	2	0.02
Vietnamese (3)	3	0.03
Other Asian, not specified (1)	1	0.01
Australian	10	0.10
Austrian	41	0.41
Belgian	11	0.11
British	61	0.60
Canadian	21	0.21
Croatian	7	0.07
Czech	39	0.39
Danish	24	0.24
Dutch	274	2.71
English	1,541	15.25
European	40	0.40
Finnish	18	0.18
French, except Basque	389	3.85
French Canadian	179	1.77
German	1,881	18.62
Greek	18	0.18
Hawaii Native/Pacific Islander:	17	0.17
Melanesian: (3)	3	0.03
Fijian (3)	3	0.03
Micronesian: (5)	6	0.06
Guamanian/Chamorro (5)	6	0.06
Polynesian: (4)	6	0.06
Native Hawaiian (3)	5	0.05
Samoan (1)	1	0.01
Other Pac. Isl., not spec.	2	0.02
Hispanic or Latino:	827	8.16
Central American:	96	0.95
Costa Rican	2	0.02
Guatemalan	63	0.62
Honduran	12	0.12
Panamanian	4	0.04
Salvadoran	13	0.13
Other Central American	2	0.02
Cuban	36	0.35
Dominican Republic	8	0.08
Mexican	359	3.54
Puerto Rican	195	1.92
South American:	29	0.29
Bolivian	1	0.01
Colombian	11	0.11
Ecuadorian	4	0.04
Paraguayan	4	0.04
Peruvian	6	0.06
Venezuelan	3	0.03
Other Hispanic or Latino	104	1.03
Hungarian	25	0.25
Irish	1,723	17.05
Italian	956	9.46
Lithuanian	31	0.31
Northern European	20	0.20
Norwegian	120	1.19
Polish	309	3.06
Portuguese	49	0.48
Russian	38	0.38
Scotch-Irish	254	2.51
Scottish	317	3.14
Serbian	11	0.11
Slovak	7	0.07
Swedish	137	1.36
Swiss	58	0.57
Ukrainian	31	0.31
United States or American	865	8.56
Welsh	35	0.35
West Indian, excl. Hispanic:	79	0.78
Bahamian	7	0.07
Haitian	65	0.64
Jamaican	7	0.07
White:	9,093	89.67
Not Hispanic (8,440)	8,519	84.01
Hispanic (535)	574	5.66

Princeton

Place Type: Census Designated Place
County: Miami-Dade
Population: 10,090

Ancestry/Race	Number	%

Notes: 1. Figures in the "Number" column do not add up to the total population due to: a) Ancestry/Race overlap — e.g. persons can report being both White and Irish, b) persons of Hispanic origin can report being any race, c) persons reporting two ancestries are counted in both categories. 2. Numbers in parentheses indicate the number of persons reporting this ancestry/race alone, not in combination with any other ancestry/race. 3. Refer to the Explanation of Data in the front of the book for more detailed information.

African American/Black:	3,433	34.02
Not Hispanic (3,143)	3,242	32.13
Hispanic (140)	191	1.89
African, sub-Saharan:	194	1.91
African	194	1.91
Alaska Native tribes, specified:	1	0.01
Tlingit-Haida (1)	1	0.01
Am. Ind. or Alaska Nat., not spec.	17	0.17
American Indian tribes, specified:	54	0.54
Blackfeet	13	0.13
Cherokee (2)	14	0.14
Chippewa (1)	1	0.01
Latin American Indians (21)	24	0.24
Puget Sound Salish	1	0.01
All other tribes (1)	1	0.01
American Indian tribes, not spec.	3	0.03
Asian:	227	2.25
Cambodian (1)	2	0.02
Chinese, ex. Taiwanese (27)	55	0.55
Filipino (13)	25	0.25
Indian (27)	40	0.40
Japanese (7)	15	0.15
Korean (14)	27	0.27
Laotian (11)	14	0.14
Pakistani (5)	7	0.07
Taiwanese (1)	4	0.04
Thai (11)	12	0.12
Vietnamese (14)	17	0.17
Other Asian, not specified (3)	9	0.09
Brazilian	27	0.27
British	32	0.32
Canadian	31	0.31
Czech	43	0.42
Dutch	8	0.08
English	120	1.18
French, except Basque	102	1.01
French Canadian	62	0.61
German	377	3.72
Greek	15	0.15
Hawaii Native/Pacific Islander:	19	0.19
Micronesian: (3)	6	0.06
Guamanian/Chamorro (3)	6	0.06
Polynesian: (3)	6	0.06
Native Hawaiian (2)	5	0.05
Samoan (1)	1	0.01
Other Pac. Isl., not spec.	7	0.07
Hispanic or Latino:	4,792	47.49
Central American:	533	5.28
Costa Rican	30	0.30
Guatemalan	79	0.78
Honduran	96	0.95
Nicaraguan	217	2.15
Panamanian	35	0.35
Salvadoran	54	0.54
Other Central American	22	0.22
Cuban	1,306	12.94
Dominican Republic	134	1.33
Mexican	844	8.36
Puerto Rican	1,009	10.00
South American:	345	3.42
Argentinean	16	0.16
Bolivian	3	0.03
Chilean	14	0.14
Colombian	179	1.77
Ecuadorian	30	0.30
Peruvian	48	0.48
Uruguayan	12	0.12
Venezuelan	36	0.36
Other South American	7	0.07
Other Hispanic or Latino	621	6.15
Hungarian	25	0.25
Irish	277	2.73
Italian	274	2.70
Lithuanian	7	0.07
Norwegian	16	0.16
Polish	69	0.68
Portuguese	11	0.11
Scotch-Irish	19	0.19
Scottish	31	0.31
Swedish	16	0.16
Turkish	5	0.05
Ukrainian	7	0.07
United States or American	282	2.78
Welsh	17	0.17
West Indian, excl. Hispanic:	414	4.08
Bahamian	61	0.60
Dutch West Indian	20	0.20
Haitian	75	0.74
Jamaican	171	1.69
Trinidadian and Tobagonian	80	0.79
West Indian	7	0.07
White:	5,736	56.85
Not Hispanic (1,811)	1,887	18.70
Hispanic (3,615)	3,849	38.15

Punta Gorda

Place Type: City
County: Charlotte
Population: 14,344

Ancestry/Race	Number	%
African American/Black:	489	3.41
Not Hispanic (447)	471	3.28
Hispanic (7)	18	0.13
African, sub-Saharan:	19	0.13
African	10	0.07
Liberian	9	0.06
Am. Ind. or Alaska Nat., not spec.	12	0.08
Albanian	9	0.06
American Indian tribes, specified:	40	0.28
Blackfeet	4	0.03
Cherokee (9)	12	0.08
Chippewa (5)	8	0.06
Creek	1	0.01
Iroquois (1)	1	0.01
Osage (1)	1	0.01
Ottawa (1)	5	0.03
Sioux (1)	2	0.01
All other tribes (2)	6	0.04
American Indian tribes, not spec.	1	0.01
Arab:	69	0.48
Arab/Arabic	20	0.14
Palestinian	39	0.27
Syrian	10	0.07
Asian:	134	0.93
Chinese, ex. Taiwanese (12)	16	0.11
Filipino (33)	42	0.29
Indian (35)	39	0.27
Japanese (4)	4	0.03
Korean (7)	7	0.05
Laotian	1	0.01
Malaysian	1	0.01
Taiwanese (2)	2	0.01
Thai (3)	3	0.02
Vietnamese (11)	11	0.08
Other Asian, not specified (4)	8	0.06
Austrian	132	0.91
Belgian	27	0.19
British	176	1.22
Canadian	129	0.89
Croatian	9	0.06
Czech	61	0.42
Czechoslovakian	50	0.35
Danish	150	1.04
Dutch	321	2.22
English	2,556	17.71
European	104	0.72
Finnish	48	0.33
French, except Basque	442	3.06
French Canadian	184	1.27
German	3,419	23.69
Greek	95	0.66
Guyanese	22	0.15
Hawaii Native/Pacific Islander:	10	0.07
Micronesian: (2)	3	0.02
Guamanian/Chamorro (2)	3	0.02
Polynesian: (2)	3	0.02
Native Hawaiian (2)	2	0.01
Samoan	1	0.01
Other Pac. Isl., not spec.	4	0.03
Hispanic or Latino:	285	1.99
Central American:	5	0.03
Costa Rican	5	0.03
Cuban	52	0.36
Mexican	47	0.33
Puerto Rican	120	0.84
South American:	12	0.08
Argentinean	2	0.01
Chilean	3	0.02
Colombian	2	0.01
Ecuadorian	2	0.01
Peruvian	1	0.01
Venezuelan	1	0.01
Other South American	1	0.01
Other Hispanic or Latino	49	0.34
Hungarian	183	1.27
Irish	2,430	16.84
Italian	1,244	8.62
Latvian	23	0.16
Lithuanian	86	0.60
Maltese	11	0.08
Northern European	16	0.11
Norwegian	316	2.19
Pennsylvania German	9	0.06
Polish	674	4.67
Portuguese	43	0.30
Romanian	48	0.33
Russian	158	1.09
Scandinavian	15	0.10
Scotch-Irish	320	2.22
Scottish	469	3.25
Slovak	64	0.44
Swedish	301	2.09
Swiss	164	1.14
Ukrainian	8	0.06
United States or American	809	5.61
Welsh	139	0.96
West Indian, excl. Hispanic:	83	0.58
Bermudan	24	0.17
Haitian	19	0.13
Jamaican	14	0.10
West Indian	26	0.18
White:	13,649	95.15
Not Hispanic (13,373)	13,449	93.76
Hispanic (196)	200	1.39
Yugoslavian	40	0.28

Richmond West

Place Type: Census Designated Place
County: Miami-Dade
Population: 28,082

Ancestry/Race	Number	%
African American/Black:	2,735	9.74
Not Hispanic (2,042)	2,237	7.97
Hispanic (349)	498	1.77
African, sub-Saharan:	223	0.80
African	123	0.44
Nigerian	91	0.32
Other sub-Saharan African	9	0.03
Am. Ind. or Alaska Nat., not spec.	32	0.11
American Indian tribes, specified:	66	0.24
Blackfeet (1)	4	0.01
Cherokee (1)	4	0.01
Comanche	1	0.00
Creek	1	0.00
Iroquois (2)	2	0.01
Latin American Indians (25)	40	0.14
All other tribes (3)	14	0.05
American Indian tribes, not spec.	1	0.00
Arab:	141	0.50
Arab/Arabic	11	0.04
Lebanese	76	0.27
Palestinian	54	0.19
Armenian	10	0.04
Asian:	893	3.18
Chinese, ex. Taiwanese (216)	322	1.15
Filipino (143)	161	0.57

Notes: 1. Figures in the "Number" column do not add up to the total population due to: a) Ancestry/Race overlap — e.g. persons can report being both White and Irish, b) persons of Hispanic origin can report being any race, c) persons reporting two ancestries are counted in both categories. 2. Numbers in parentheses indicate the number of persons reporting this ancestry/race alone, not in combination with any other ancestry/race. 3. Refer to the Explanation of Data in the front of the book for more detailed information.

Indian (148)	206	0.73
Indonesian (4)	6	0.02
Japanese (8)	19	0.07
Korean (9)	25	0.09
Laotian (1)	3	0.01
Malaysian (1)	1	0.00
Pakistani (30)	49	0.17
Thai (18)	24	0.09
Vietnamese (33)	41	0.15
Other Asian, specified (1)	1	0.00
Other Asian, not specified (8)	35	0.12
Austrian	19	0.07
Basque	17	0.06
Brazilian	43	0.15
British	142	0.51
Czechoslovakian	7	0.02
Dutch	112	0.40
English	362	1.29
European	78	0.28
Finnish	9	0.03
French, except Basque	162	0.58
French Canadian	38	0.14
German	469	1.67
Greek	48	0.17
Guyanese	139	0.50
Hawaii Native/Pacific Islander:	43	0.15
Micronesian: (6)	6	0.02
Guamanian/Chamorro (6)	6	0.02
Polynesian: (1)	5	0.02
Native Hawaiian	4	0.01
Other Polynesian (1)	1	0.00
Other Pac. Isl., not spec. (11)	32	0.11
Hispanic or Latino:	19,663	70.02
Central American:	1,963	6.99
Costa Rican	82	0.29
Guatemalan	80	0.28
Honduran	229	0.82
Nicaraguan	1,178	4.19
Panamanian	210	0.75
Salvadoran	121	0.43
Other Central American	63	0.22
Cuban	8,227	29.30
Dominican Republic	696	2.48
Mexican	269	0.96
Puerto Rican	2,045	7.28
South American:	2,906	10.35
Argentinean	111	0.40
Bolivian	38	0.14
Chilean	129	0.46
Colombian	1,441	5.13
Ecuadorian	197	0.70
Paraguayan	5	0.02
Peruvian	506	1.80
Uruguayan	14	0.05
Venezuelan	381	1.36
Other South American	84	0.30
Other Hispanic or Latino	3,557	12.67
Hungarian	67	0.24
Irish	615	2.20
Italian	750	2.68
Lithuanian	10	0.04
Norwegian	76	0.27
Polish	247	0.88
Portuguese	59	0.21
Romanian	9	0.03
Russian	118	0.42
Scotch-Irish	70	0.25
Scottish	153	0.55
Swedish	12	0.04
Turkish	6	0.02
United States or American	1,521	5.43
Welsh	14	0.05
West Indian, excl. Hispanic:	1,635	5.84
Bahamian	21	0.07
Barbadian	9	0.03
British West Indian	57	0.20
Haitian	415	1.48
Jamaican	947	3.38
Trinidadian and Tobagonian	177	0.63
West Indian	9	0.03
White:	22,930	81.65
Not Hispanic (5,269)	5,476	19.50
Hispanic (16,727)	17,454	62.15
Yugoslavian	8	0.03

Riverview

Place Type: Census Designated Place
County: Hillsborough
Population: 12,035

Ancestry/Race	Number	%
African American/Black:	1,081	8.98
Not Hispanic (958)	1,014	8.43
Hispanic (44)	67	0.56
African, sub-Saharan:	77	0.64
African	62	0.52
Sierra Leonean	15	0.12
Am. Ind. or Alaska Nat., not spec.	51	0.42
Albanian	10	0.08
American Indian tribes, specified:	86	0.71
Apache	3	0.02
Blackfeet	1	0.01
Cherokee (9)	35	0.29
Chickasaw	1	0.01
Chippewa (1)	3	0.02
Comanche	3	0.02
Creek (3)	4	0.03
Crow	2	0.02
Iroquois (2)	3	0.02
Latin American Indians (1)	1	0.01
Pueblo	3	0.02
Seminole (3)	7	0.06
Sioux (6)	7	0.06
Yakama	1	0.01
All other tribes (4)	12	0.10
American Indian tribes, not spec.	7	0.06
Arab:	47	0.39
Lebanese	47	0.39
Armenian	9	0.07
Asian:	228	1.89
Chinese, ex. Taiwanese (30)	34	0.28
Filipino (42)	53	0.44
Hmong (4)	6	0.05
Indian (22)	32	0.27
Japanese (5)	14	0.12
Korean (23)	34	0.28
Taiwanese (1)	1	0.01
Thai (3)	9	0.07
Vietnamese (17)	22	0.18
Other Asian, specified (2)	2	0.02
Other Asian, not specified (9)	21	0.17
Austrian	16	0.13
Belgian	8	0.07
British	55	0.46
Canadian	17	0.14
Croatian	15	0.12
Czechoslovakian	17	0.14
Danish	62	0.52
Dutch	243	2.02
Eastern European	8	0.07
English	1,327	11.06
Estonian	11	0.09
European	86	0.72
Finnish	42	0.35
French, except Basque	480	4.00
French Canadian	123	1.02
German	2,149	17.90
Greek	20	0.17
Guyanese	33	0.27
Hawaii Native/Pacific Islander:	19	0.16
Micronesian:	1	0.01
Guamanian/Chamorro	1	0.01
Polynesian: (5)	7	0.06
Native Hawaiian (5)	7	0.06
Other Pac. Isl., not spec. (3)	11	0.09
Hispanic or Latino:	1,085	9.02
Central American:	58	0.48
Costa Rican	2	0.02
Guatemalan	13	0.11
Honduran	5	0.04
Nicaraguan	1	0.01
Panamanian	32	0.27
Salvadoran	5	0.04
Cuban	130	1.08
Dominican Republic	10	0.08
Mexican	165	1.37
Puerto Rican	427	3.55
South American:	36	0.30
Argentinean	4	0.03
Chilean	1	0.01
Colombian	11	0.09
Ecuadorian	2	0.02
Venezuelan	15	0.12
Other South American	3	0.02
Other Hispanic or Latino	259	2.15
Hungarian	19	0.16
Irish	1,317	10.97
Italian	685	5.71
New Zealander	10	0.08
Northern European	21	0.17
Norwegian	79	0.66
Pennsylvania German	23	0.19
Polish	245	2.04
Portuguese	26	0.22
Russian	46	0.38
Scandinavian	51	0.42
Scotch-Irish	231	1.92
Scottish	288	2.40
Slovak	15	0.12
Swedish	105	0.87
Swiss	7	0.06
Ukrainian	7	0.06
United States or American	1,239	10.32
Welsh	73	0.61
West Indian, excl. Hispanic:	180	1.50
Barbadian	7	0.06
Bermudan	8	0.07
British West Indian	8	0.07
Haitian	8	0.07
Jamaican	143	1.19
West Indian	6	0.05
White:	10,521	87.42
Not Hispanic (9,562)	9,709	80.67
Hispanic (765)	812	6.75
Yugoslavian	8	0.07

Riviera Beach

Place Type: City
County: Palm Beach
Population: 29,884

Ancestry/Race	Number	%
African American/Black:	20,735	69.38
Not Hispanic (20,066)	20,476	68.52
Hispanic (198)	259	0.87
African, sub-Saharan:	344	1.13
African	313	1.03
Kenyan	7	0.02
Nigerian	2	0.01
South African	8	0.03
Other sub-Saharan African	14	0.05
Alaska Native tribes, not specified	1	0.00
Am. Ind. or Alaska Nat., not spec.	64	0.21
Albanian	13	0.04
Alsatian	4	0.01
American Indian tribes, specified:	68	0.23
Blackfeet (1)	1	0.00
Cherokee (5)	23	0.08
Chickasaw	3	0.01
Choctaw	1	0.00
Creek (1)	1	0.00
Iroquois (2)	2	0.01
Latin American Indians (3)	22	0.07
Paiute (1)	1	0.00
Pima (1)	2	0.01
Seminole	2	0.01
Sioux (1)	3	0.01
All other tribes (3)	7	0.02

Notes: 1. Figures in the "Number" column do not add up to the total population due to: a) Ancestry/Race overlap — e.g. persons can report being both White and Irish, b) persons of Hispanic origin can report being any race, c) persons reporting two ancestries are counted in both categories. 2. Numbers in parentheses indicate the number of persons reporting this ancestry/race alone, not in combination with any other ancestry/race. 3. Refer to the Explanation of Data in the front of the book for more detailed information.

American Indian tribes, not spec.	11	0.04
Arab:	68	0.22
Egyptian	8	0.03
Lebanese	39	0.13
Syrian	13	0.04
Other Arab	8	0.03
Armenian	8	0.03
Asian:	365	1.22
Bangladeshi (3)	3	0.01
Chinese, ex. Taiwanese (41)	53	0.18
Filipino (47)	53	0.18
Indian (78)	103	0.34
Japanese (8)	9	0.03
Korean (38)	41	0.14
Pakistani (2)	2	0.01
Taiwanese (1)	1	0.00
Thai (12)	14	0.05
Vietnamese (58)	63	0.21
Other Asian, specified	8	0.03
Other Asian, not specified (6)	15	0.05
Austrian	73	0.24
Basque	13	0.04
British	44	0.14
Bulgarian	9	0.03
Canadian	109	0.36
Croatian	3	0.01
Czech	53	0.17
Czechoslovakian	11	0.04
Danish	26	0.09
Dutch	108	0.36
Eastern European	8	0.03
English	1,244	4.09
European	48	0.16
Finnish	7	0.02
French, except Basque	374	1.23
French Canadian	142	0.47
German	1,331	4.38
Greek	80	0.26
Hawaii Native/Pacific Islander:	49	0.16
Micronesian: (8)	10	0.03
Guamanian/Chamorro (7)	9	0.03
Other Micronesian (1)	1	0.00
Polynesian: (3)	7	0.02
Native Hawaiian (3)	5	0.02
Other Polynesian	2	0.01
Other Pac. Isl., specified	8	0.03
Other Pac. Isl., not spec. (4)	24	0.08
Hispanic or Latino:	1,348	4.51
Central American:	176	0.59
Costa Rican	7	0.02
Guatemalan	98	0.33
Honduran	12	0.04
Nicaraguan	37	0.12
Panamanian	12	0.04
Salvadoran	8	0.03
Other Central American	2	0.01
Cuban	171	0.57
Dominican Republic	26	0.09
Mexican	182	0.61
Puerto Rican	341	1.14
South American:	125	0.42
Argentinean	12	0.04
Bolivian	3	0.01
Chilean	3	0.01
Colombian	61	0.20
Ecuadorian	8	0.03
Peruvian	17	0.06
Uruguayan	1	0.00
Venezuelan	9	0.03
Other South American	11	0.04
Other Hispanic or Latino	327	1.09
Hungarian	65	0.21
Iranian	21	0.07
Irish	1,150	3.78
Israeli	21	0.07
Italian	752	2.47
Lithuanian	43	0.14
Norwegian	136	0.45
Pennsylvania German	6	0.02
Polish	389	1.28
Portuguese	71	0.23
Romanian	6	0.02
Russian	200	0.66
Scotch-Irish	154	0.51
Scottish	239	0.79
Serbian	21	0.07
Slavic	18	0.06
Slovak	34	0.11
Slovene	4	0.01
Swedish	189	0.62
Swiss	30	0.10
Turkish	7	0.02
Ukrainian	48	0.16
United States or American	1,032	3.39
Welsh	94	0.31
West Indian, excl. Hispanic:	1,533	5.04
Bahamian	151	0.50
Barbadian	17	0.06
Belizean	27	0.09
British West Indian	40	0.13
Haitian	582	1.91
Jamaican	646	2.12
Trinidadian and Tobagonian	34	0.11
U.S. Virgin Islander	22	0.07
West Indian	14	0.05
White:	8,520	28.51
Not Hispanic (7,586)	7,729	25.86
Hispanic (711)	791	2.65
Yugoslavian	16	0.05

Rockledge

Place Type: City
County: Brevard
Population: 20,170

Ancestry/Race	Number	%
Acadian/Cajun	47	0.23
African American/Black:	3,073	15.24
Not Hispanic (2,928)	3,041	15.08
Hispanic (24)	32	0.16
African, sub-Saharan:	178	0.88
African	63	0.31
Nigerian	115	0.57
Am. Ind. or Alaska Nat., not spec.	45	0.22
Albanian	6	0.03
American Indian tribes, specified:	80	0.40
Apache (2)	4	0.02
Blackfeet (3)	4	0.02
Cherokee (17)	39	0.19
Chickasaw (1)	1	0.00
Chippewa (1)	2	0.01
Choctaw	1	0.00
Creek	2	0.01
Iroquois (3)	9	0.04
Latin American Indians (1)	3	0.01
Lumbee (1)	1	0.00
Menominee	2	0.01
Navajo (3)	4	0.02
Seminole	1	0.00
Sioux (1)	3	0.01
All other tribes (3)	4	0.02
American Indian tribes, not spec.	5	0.02
Arab:	71	0.35
Lebanese	60	0.30
Syrian	11	0.05
Asian:	450	2.23
Chinese, ex. Taiwanese (51)	70	0.35
Filipino (63)	93	0.46
Indian (94)	105	0.52
Indonesian (4)	4	0.02
Japanese (18)	39	0.19
Korean (35)	57	0.28
Pakistani (7)	7	0.03
Taiwanese (1)	1	0.00
Thai (19)	22	0.11
Vietnamese (41)	42	0.21
Other Asian, not specified (2)	10	0.05
Assyrian/Chaldean/Syriac	8	0.04
Austrian	50	0.25
Belgian	14	0.07
Brazilian	34	0.17
British	46	0.23
Canadian	20	0.10
Celtic	8	0.04
Croatian	31	0.15
Czech	136	0.68
Czechoslovakian	76	0.38
Danish	91	0.45
Dutch	376	1.87
English	2,888	14.35
European	91	0.45
Finnish	22	0.11
French, except Basque	692	3.44
French Canadian	208	1.03
German	3,358	16.69
Greek	98	0.49
Guyanese	44	0.22
Hawaii Native/Pacific Islander:	34	0.17
Polynesian: (13)	21	0.10
Native Hawaiian (6)	14	0.07
Samoan (7)	7	0.03
Other Pac. Isl., not spec. (4)	13	0.06
Hispanic or Latino:	662	3.28
Central American:	47	0.23
Costa Rican	3	0.01
Guatemalan	15	0.07
Honduran	4	0.02
Nicaraguan	2	0.01
Panamanian	22	0.11
Salvadoran	1	0.00
Cuban	79	0.39
Dominican Republic	11	0.05
Mexican	176	0.87
Puerto Rican	203	1.01
South American:	39	0.19
Argentinean	8	0.04
Chilean	3	0.01
Colombian	11	0.05
Peruvian	7	0.03
Uruguayan	2	0.01
Venezuelan	4	0.02
Other South American	4	0.02
Other Hispanic or Latino	107	0.53
Hungarian	124	0.62
Iranian	25	0.12
Irish	2,764	13.74
Italian	1,389	6.90
Lithuanian	48	0.24
Luxemburger	5	0.02
Northern European	15	0.07
Norwegian	289	1.44
Pennsylvania German	16	0.08
Polish	599	2.98
Portuguese	139	0.69
Romanian	7	0.03
Russian	141	0.70
Scandinavian	9	0.04
Scotch-Irish	522	2.59
Scottish	439	2.18
Slavic	20	0.10
Slovak	29	0.14
Swedish	371	1.84
Swiss	104	0.52
Turkish	18	0.09
Ukrainian	43	0.21
United States or American	1,590	7.90
Welsh	198	0.98
West Indian, excl. Hispanic:	72	0.36
Barbadian	10	0.05
Haitian	36	0.18
Trinidadian and Tobagonian	10	0.05
West Indian	16	0.08
White:	16,610	82.35
Not Hispanic (15,885)	16,101	79.83
Hispanic (464)	509	2.52
Yugoslavian	16	0.08

Notes: 1. Figures in the "Number" column do not add up to the total population due to: a) Ancestry/Race overlap — e.g. persons can report being both White and Irish, b) persons of Hispanic origin can report being any race, c) persons reporting two ancestries are counted in both categories. 2. Numbers in parentheses indicate the number of persons reporting this ancestry/race alone, not in combination with any other ancestry/race. 3. Refer to the Explanation of Data in the front of the book for more detailed information.

Royal Palm Beach

Place Type: Village
County: Palm Beach
Population: 21,523

Ancestry/Race	Number	%
African American/Black:	3,256	15.13
Not Hispanic (2,990)	3,162	14.69
Hispanic (69)	94	0.44
African, sub-Saharan:	150	0.70
African	49	0.23
Cape Verdean	18	0.08
Liberian	61	0.28
Nigerian	22	0.10
Alaska Native tribes, specified:	2	0.01
Eskimo (2)	2	0.01
Am. Ind. or Alaska Nat., not spec.	42	0.20
American Indian tribes, specified:	52	0.24
Apache (1)	1	0.00
Blackfeet (3)	5	0.02
Cherokee (10)	20	0.09
Chippewa (5)	5	0.02
Delaware (1)	1	0.00
Iroquois (7)	7	0.03
Latin American Indians (2)	2	0.01
Navajo	2	0.01
Pueblo	5	0.02
Sioux (1)	1	0.00
All other tribes (2)	3	0.01
American Indian tribes, not spec.	2	0.01
Arab:	93	0.43
Arab/Arabic	23	0.11
Lebanese	37	0.17
Moroccan	7	0.03
Palestinian	10	0.05
Syrian	16	0.07
Armenian	14	0.06
Asian:	702	3.26
Cambodian (2)	2	0.01
Chinese, ex. Taiwanese (79)	100	0.46
Filipino (197)	215	1.00
Indian (165)	210	0.98
Japanese (8)	19	0.09
Korean (37)	46	0.21
Laotian (1)	2	0.01
Pakistani	5	0.02
Sri Lankan (3)	3	0.01
Thai (20)	26	0.12
Vietnamese (40)	46	0.21
Other Asian, not specified (10)	28	0.13
Austrian	65	0.30
Belgian	36	0.17
Brazilian	37	0.17
British	88	0.41
Canadian	90	0.42
Celtic	8	0.04
Croatian	8	0.04
Czech	146	0.68
Czechoslovakian	14	0.06
Danish	71	0.33
Dutch	225	1.04
Eastern European	18	0.08
English	1,699	7.88
European	125	0.58
Finnish	24	0.11
French, except Basque	604	2.80
French Canadian	252	1.17
German	3,011	13.96
Greek	72	0.33
Guyanese	13	0.06
Hawaii Native/Pacific Islander:	33	0.15
Micronesian: (2)	3	0.01
Guamanian/Chamorro (1)	2	0.01
Other Micronesian (1)	1	0.00
Polynesian: (6)	14	0.07
Native Hawaiian (5)	10	0.05
Samoan (1)	4	0.02
Other Pac. Isl., not spec. (1)	16	0.07
Hispanic or Latino:	2,546	11.83
Central American:	148	0.69
Costa Rican	20	0.09
Guatemalan	26	0.12
Honduran	21	0.10
Nicaraguan	33	0.15
Panamanian	15	0.07
Salvadoran	17	0.08
Other Central American	16	0.07
Cuban	635	2.95
Dominican Republic	63	0.29
Mexican	267	1.24
Puerto Rican	684	3.18
South American:	312	1.45
Argentinean	12	0.06
Bolivian	1	0.00
Chilean	4	0.02
Colombian	168	0.78
Ecuadorian	37	0.17
Paraguayan	1	0.00
Peruvian	40	0.19
Uruguayan	5	0.02
Venezuelan	34	0.16
Other South American	10	0.05
Other Hispanic or Latino	437	2.03
Hungarian	183	0.85
Irish	2,555	11.85
Israeli	8	0.04
Italian	2,858	13.25
Latvian	25	0.12
Lithuanian	64	0.30
Maltese	5	0.02
Norwegian	127	0.59
Pennsylvania German	21	0.10
Polish	841	3.90
Portuguese	92	0.43
Romanian	56	0.26
Russian	573	2.66
Scandinavian	22	0.10
Scotch-Irish	141	0.65
Scottish	300	1.39
Slovak	81	0.38
Slovene	9	0.04
Swedish	205	0.95
Swiss	52	0.24
Turkish	21	0.10
Ukrainian	94	0.44
United States or American	1,840	8.53
Welsh	120	0.56
West Indian, excl. Hispanic:	1,385	6.42
Bahamian	21	0.10
Barbadian	34	0.16
British West Indian	15	0.07
Dutch West Indian	42	0.19
Haitian	180	0.83
Jamaican	970	4.50
Trinidadian and Tobagonian	81	0.38
West Indian	42	0.19
White:	17,184	79.84
Not Hispanic (14,934)	15,170	70.48
Hispanic (1,887)	2,014	9.36
Yugoslavian	25	0.12

Safety Harbor

Place Type: City
County: Pinellas
Population: 17,203

Ancestry/Race	Number	%
Acadian/Cajun	8	0.05
African American/Black:	774	4.50
Not Hispanic (698)	739	4.30
Hispanic (14)	35	0.20
Am. Ind. or Alaska Nat., not spec.	29	0.17
Albanian	27	0.16
American Indian tribes, specified:	74	0.43
Blackfeet	4	0.02
Cherokee (11)	39	0.23
Choctaw (1)	1	0.01
Comanche	1	0.01
Creek (1)	1	0.01
Delaware	1	0.01
Iroquois (3)	4	0.02
Latin American Indians (4)	4	0.02
Lumbee	1	0.01
Navajo (1)	1	0.01
Sioux (5)	12	0.07
All other tribes (4)	5	0.03
American Indian tribes, not spec.	6	0.03
Arab:	193	1.13
Arab/Arabic	40	0.23
Egyptian	19	0.11
Lebanese	85	0.50
Palestinian	8	0.05
Syrian	41	0.24
Armenian	40	0.23
Asian:	339	1.97
Bangladeshi (4)	4	0.02
Cambodian (6)	10	0.06
Chinese, ex. Taiwanese (81)	93	0.54
Filipino (54)	66	0.38
Hmong (8)	8	0.05
Indian (64)	73	0.42
Indonesian (5)	7	0.04
Japanese (8)	14	0.08
Korean (24)	25	0.15
Laotian	2	0.01
Sri Lankan (1)	1	0.01
Taiwanese (2)	3	0.02
Thai (5)	5	0.03
Vietnamese (22)	22	0.13
Other Asian, specified	1	0.01
Other Asian, not specified	5	0.03
Australian	12	0.07
Austrian	128	0.75
Belgian	16	0.09
British	159	0.93
Bulgarian	15	0.09
Canadian	89	0.52
Croatian	48	0.28
Czech	53	0.31
Czechoslovakian	12	0.07
Danish	73	0.43
Dutch	338	1.98
Eastern European	22	0.13
English	2,127	12.45
Estonian	8	0.05
European	185	1.08
Finnish	37	0.22
French, except Basque	556	3.25
French Canadian	284	1.66
German	3,302	19.32
Greek	241	1.41
Hawaii Native/Pacific Islander:	22	0.13
Micronesian: (1)	4	0.02
Guamanian/Chamorro (1)	4	0.02
Polynesian: (7)	13	0.08
Native Hawaiian (4)	10	0.06
Samoan (3)	3	0.02
Other Pac. Isl., specified	1	0.01
Other Pac. Isl., not spec.	4	0.02
Hispanic or Latino:	628	3.65
Central American:	43	0.25
Costa Rican	3	0.02
Guatemalan	5	0.03
Honduran	4	0.02
Nicaraguan	6	0.03
Panamanian	17	0.10
Salvadoran	8	0.05
Cuban	75	0.44
Dominican Republic	8	0.05
Mexican	115	0.67
Puerto Rican	169	0.98
South American:	68	0.40
Argentinean	1	0.01
Colombian	35	0.20
Ecuadorian	10	0.06
Peruvian	9	0.05
Venezuelan	8	0.05
Other South American	5	0.03

Notes: 1. Figures in the "Number" column do not add up to the total population due to: a) Ancestry/Race overlap — e.g. persons can report being both White and Irish, b) persons of Hispanic origin can report being any race, c) persons reporting two ancestries are counted in both categories. 2. Numbers in parentheses indicate the number of persons reporting this ancestry/race alone, not in combination with any other ancestry/race. 3. Refer to the Explanation of Data in the front of the book for more detailed information.

Other Hispanic or Latino	150	0.87
Hungarian	141	0.83
Iranian	7	0.04
Irish	2,774	16.23
Israeli	14	0.08
Italian	1,660	9.71
Latvian	4	0.02
Lithuanian	16	0.09
Macedonian	4	0.02
Norwegian	212	1.24
Polish	896	5.24
Portuguese	67	0.39
Romanian	19	0.11
Russian	271	1.59
Scandinavian	62	0.36
Scotch-Irish	406	2.38
Scottish	506	2.96
Slavic	23	0.13
Slovak	70	0.41
Slovene	10	0.06
Swedish	235	1.38
Swiss	104	0.61
Turkish	32	0.19
Ukrainian	104	0.61
United States or American	1,312	7.68
Welsh	127	0.74
West Indian, excl. Hispanic:	123	0.72
Barbadian	8	0.05
Haitian	26	0.15
Jamaican	49	0.29
West Indian	39	0.23
White:	16,052	93.31
Not Hispanic (15,390)	15,531	90.28
Hispanic (477)	521	3.03
Yugoslavian	48	0.28

Saint Augustine

Place Type: City
County: Saint Johns
Population: 11,592

Ancestry/Race	Number	%
Acadian/Cajun	5	0.04
African American/Black:	1,797	15.50
Not Hispanic (1,741)	1,788	15.42
Hispanic (6)	9	0.08
African, sub-Saharan:	45	0.39
African	22	0.19
Ghanian	23	0.20
Alaska Native tribes, not specified	1	0.01
Am. Ind. or Alaska Nat., not spec.	24	0.21
American Indian tribes, specified:	99	0.85
Apache (9)	9	0.08
Blackfeet	2	0.02
Cherokee (10)	57	0.49
Chippewa (2)	2	0.02
Choctaw (2)	3	0.03
Cree (2)	2	0.02
Creek (1)	3	0.03
Delaware	1	0.01
Iroquois (2)	3	0.03
Latin American Indians	1	0.01
Navajo	1	0.01
Seminole (2)	2	0.02
Shoshone (1)	1	0.01
Sioux (2)	5	0.04
All other tribes (3)	7	0.06
American Indian tribes, not spec.	5	0.04
Arab:	44	0.38
Jordanian	7	0.06
Lebanese	21	0.18
Syrian	8	0.07
Other Arab	8	0.07
Armenian	26	0.23
Asian:	121	1.04
Chinese, ex. Taiwanese (10)	10	0.09
Filipino (25)	27	0.23
Indian (30)	43	0.37
Japanese (3)	9	0.08
Korean (4)	6	0.05
Taiwanese (1)	1	0.01
Thai	1	0.01
Vietnamese (6)	9	0.08
Other Asian, specified	2	0.02
Other Asian, not specified (4)	13	0.11
Australian	17	0.15
Austrian	62	0.54
Belgian	23	0.20
British	94	0.82
Celtic	31	0.27
Croatian	6	0.05
Czech	65	0.56
Czechoslovakian	23	0.20
Danish	44	0.38
Dutch	188	1.63
English	1,571	13.65
European	101	0.88
Finnish	24	0.21
French, except Basque	503	4.37
French Canadian	152	1.32
German	1,679	14.58
Greek	81	0.70
Hawaii Native/Pacific Islander:	17	0.15
Micronesian: (4)	4	0.03
Guamanian/Chamorro (4)	4	0.03
Polynesian: (5)	5	0.04
Native Hawaiian (1)	1	0.01
Samoan (4)	4	0.03
Other Pac. Isl., specified	2	0.02
Other Pac. Isl., not spec. (2)	6	0.05
Hispanic or Latino:	361	3.11
Central American:	28	0.24
Costa Rican	2	0.02
Guatemalan	12	0.10
Honduran	7	0.06
Panamanian	6	0.05
Salvadoran	1	0.01
Cuban	37	0.32
Dominican Republic	3	0.03
Mexican	75	0.65
Puerto Rican	103	0.89
South American:	24	0.21
Argentinean	5	0.04
Bolivian	1	0.01
Chilean	3	0.03
Colombian	7	0.06
Ecuadorian	1	0.01
Peruvian	1	0.01
Venezuelan	4	0.03
Other South American	2	0.02
Other Hispanic or Latino	91	0.79
Hungarian	66	0.57
Irish	1,586	13.78
Italian	682	5.92
Lithuanian	35	0.30
Luxemburger	17	0.15
New Zealander	7	0.06
Norwegian	142	1.23
Pennsylvania German	19	0.17
Polish	274	2.38
Portuguese	63	0.55
Romanian	6	0.05
Russian	140	1.22
Scandinavian	47	0.41
Scotch-Irish	407	3.54
Scottish	316	2.74
Slavic	35	0.30
Slovene	8	0.07
Swedish	182	1.58
Swiss	40	0.35
Ukrainian	26	0.23
United States or American	755	6.56
Welsh	100	0.87
West Indian, excl. Hispanic:	29	0.25
Jamaican	29	0.25
White:	9,563	82.50
Not Hispanic (9,193)	9,307	80.29
Hispanic (221)	256	2.21

Saint Cloud

Place Type: City
County: Osceola
Population: 20,074

Ancestry/Race	Number	%
African American/Black:	476	2.37
Not Hispanic (319)	366	1.82
Hispanic (96)	110	0.55
African, sub-Saharan:	30	0.15
African	21	0.10
South African	9	0.04
Alaska Native tribes, specified:	1	0.00
Alaska Athabascan (1)	1	0.00
Am. Ind. or Alaska Nat., not spec.	47	0.23
American Indian tribes, specified:	150	0.75
Apache (1)	9	0.04
Blackfeet (3)	8	0.04
Cherokee (19)	68	0.34
Chickasaw	1	0.00
Chippewa (2)	4	0.02
Choctaw	1	0.00
Creek	1	0.00
Delaware (2)	2	0.01
Iroquois (4)	6	0.03
Latin American Indians (10)	12	0.06
Lumbee (3)	6	0.03
Osage	1	0.00
Pueblo (1)	1	0.00
Seminole (7)	9	0.04
Sioux (1)	3	0.01
All other tribes (11)	18	0.09
American Indian tribes, not spec.	7	0.03
Armenian	9	0.04
Asian:	278	1.38
Cambodian	1	0.00
Chinese, ex. Taiwanese (14)	24	0.12
Filipino (45)	69	0.34
Indian (51)	67	0.33
Indonesian	1	0.00
Japanese (10)	20	0.10
Korean (9)	18	0.09
Malaysian (1)	2	0.01
Pakistani (16)	23	0.11
Taiwanese (2)	2	0.01
Thai (11)	14	0.07
Vietnamese (18)	19	0.09
Other Asian, specified (1)	4	0.02
Other Asian, not specified (9)	14	0.07
Austrian	65	0.32
Belgian	40	0.20
British	146	0.73
Canadian	49	0.24
Croatian	15	0.07
Czech	126	0.63
Czechoslovakian	25	0.12
Danish	48	0.24
Dutch	489	2.43
English	2,127	10.58
European	115	0.57
Finnish	44	0.22
French, except Basque	778	3.87
French Canadian	273	1.36
German	3,466	17.24
Greek	90	0.45
Guyanese	8	0.04
Hawaii Native/Pacific Islander:	35	0.17
Micronesian: (2)	10	0.05
Guamanian/Chamorro (2)	10	0.05
Polynesian: (4)	14	0.07
Native Hawaiian (2)	11	0.05
Samoan (1)	2	0.01
Tongan (1)	1	0.00
Other Pac. Isl., specified	1	0.00
Other Pac. Isl., not spec. (8)	10	0.05
Hispanic or Latino:	2,681	13.36
Central American:	91	0.45
Costa Rican	14	0.07
Guatemalan	13	0.06

Notes: 1. Figures in the "Number" column do not add up to the total population due to: a) Ancestry/Race overlap — e.g. persons can report being both White and Irish, b) persons of Hispanic origin can report being any race, c) persons reporting two ancestries are counted in both categories. 2. Numbers in parentheses indicate the number of persons reporting this ancestry/race alone, not in combination with any other ancestry/race. 3. Refer to the Explanation of Data in the front of the book for more detailed information.

Honduran	18	0.09
Nicaraguan	5	0.02
Panamanian	16	0.08
Salvadoran	18	0.09
Other Central American	7	0.03
Cuban	152	0.76
Dominican Republic	58	0.29
Mexican	247	1.23
Puerto Rican	1,653	8.23
South American:	172	0.86
Bolivian	9	0.04
Chilean	15	0.07
Colombian	89	0.44
Ecuadorian	22	0.11
Peruvian	12	0.06
Venezuelan	21	0.10
Other South American	4	0.02
Other Hispanic or Latino	308	1.53
Hungarian	178	0.89
Irish	3,294	16.39
Italian	1,455	7.24
Lithuanian	13	0.06
Norwegian	182	0.91
Pennsylvania German	53	0.26
Polish	703	3.50
Portuguese	23	0.11
Russian	87	0.43
Scandinavian	8	0.04
Scotch-Irish	502	2.50
Scottish	395	1.97
Serbian	15	0.07
Slovak	66	0.33
Swedish	156	0.78
Swiss	27	0.13
Turkish	8	0.04
Ukrainian	44	0.22
United States or American	1,773	8.82
Welsh	236	1.17
West Indian, excl. Hispanic:	132	0.66
Haitian	24	0.12
Jamaican	69	0.34
Trinidadian and Tobagonian	9	0.04
West Indian	30	0.15
White:	18,505	92.18
Not Hispanic (16,513)	16,755	83.47
Hispanic (1,608)	1,750	8.72
Yugoslavian	39	0.19

Saint Petersburg

Place Type: City
County: Pinellas
Population: 248,232

Ancestry/Race	Number	%
Acadian/Cajun	30	0.01
African American/Black:	57,483	23.16
Not Hispanic (54,884)	56,642	22.82
Hispanic (618)	841	0.34
African, sub-Saharan:	2,394	0.97
African	2,107	0.85
Cape Verdean	5	0.00
Ethiopian	15	0.01
Ghanian	22	0.01
Kenyan	9	0.00
Liberian	5	0.00
Nigerian	136	0.05
Sierra Leonean	7	0.00
South African	55	0.02
Sudanese	5	0.00
Zimbabwean	19	0.01
Other sub-Saharan African	9	0.00
Alaska Native tribes, specified:	7	0.00
Aleut (2)	2	0.00
Eskimo (4)	5	0.00
Alaska Native tribes, not specified	6	0.00
Am. Ind. or Alaska Nat., not spec.	709	0.29
Albanian	311	0.13
Alsatian	11	0.00
American Indian tribes, specified:	1,364	0.55
Apache (17)	28	0.01
Blackfeet (16)	76	0.03
Cherokee (162)	619	0.25
Cheyenne	4	0.00
Chickasaw (3)	6	0.00
Chippewa (33)	52	0.02
Choctaw (26)	52	0.02
Colville (1)	1	0.00
Comanche (8)	12	0.00
Cree (6)	10	0.00
Creek (13)	33	0.01
Crow (1)	5	0.00
Delaware (6)	12	0.00
Houma (2)	2	0.00
Iroquois (39)	67	0.03
Kiowa	3	0.00
Latin American Indians (35)	82	0.03
Lumbee (14)	22	0.01
Navajo (7)	9	0.00
Osage (4)	11	0.00
Ottawa (1)	1	0.00
Paiute (1)	2	0.00
Potawatomi (7)	8	0.00
Pueblo (2)	8	0.00
Seminole (11)	41	0.02
Shoshone (1)	1	0.00
Sioux (21)	53	0.02
Tohono O'Odham (1)	1	0.00
Yakama (1)	1	0.00
Yuman (1)	1	0.00
All other tribes (68)	141	0.06
American Indian tribes, not spec.	103	0.04
Arab:	1,229	0.50
Arab/Arabic	172	0.07
Egyptian	55	0.02
Iraqi	34	0.01
Lebanese	565	0.23
Moroccan	87	0.04
Palestinian	127	0.05
Syrian	153	0.06
Other Arab	36	0.01
Armenian	146	0.06
Asian:	8,101	3.26
Bangladeshi (9)	25	0.01
Cambodian (437)	538	0.22
Chinese, ex. Taiwanese (531)	723	0.29
Filipino (798)	1,030	0.41
Hmong (1)	1	0.00
Indian (867)	1,067	0.43
Indonesian (28)	40	0.02
Japanese (151)	296	0.12
Korean (317)	393	0.16
Laotian (1,052)	1,178	0.47
Malaysian (10)	12	0.00
Pakistani (27)	36	0.01
Sri Lankan (3)	4	0.00
Taiwanese (13)	18	0.01
Thai (132)	191	0.08
Vietnamese (1,910)	2,108	0.85
Other Asian, specified (5)	34	0.01
Other Asian, not specified (181)	407	0.16
Assyrian/Chaldean/Syriac	7	0.00
Australian	84	0.03
Austrian	931	0.38
Basque	42	0.02
Belgian	269	0.11
Brazilian	134	0.05
British	1,607	0.65
Bulgarian	268	0.11
Canadian	963	0.39
Celtic	41	0.02
Croatian	284	0.11
Czech	990	0.40
Czechoslovakian	493	0.20
Danish	906	0.37
Dutch	4,000	1.61
Eastern European	129	0.05
English	27,556	11.12
Estonian	16	0.01
European	1,372	0.55
Finnish	407	0.16
French, except Basque	9,438	3.81
French Canadian	2,528	1.02
German	36,327	14.66
Greek	1,436	0.58
Guyanese	161	0.06
Hawaii Native/Pacific Islander:	369	0.15
Melanesian: (6)	10	0.00
Fijian (6)	10	0.00
Micronesian: (14)	32	0.01
Guamanian/Chamorro (13)	30	0.01
Other Micronesian (1)	2	0.00
Polynesian: (78)	155	0.06
Native Hawaiian (27)	71	0.03
Samoan (13)	28	0.01
Tongan (23)	33	0.01
Other Polynesian (15)	23	0.01
Other Pac. Isl., specified	26	0.01
Other Pac. Isl., not spec. (27)	146	0.06
Hispanic or Latino:	10,502	4.23
Central American:	462	0.19
Costa Rican	88	0.04
Guatemalan	76	0.03
Honduran	72	0.03
Nicaraguan	54	0.02
Panamanian	115	0.05
Salvadoran	47	0.02
Other Central American	10	0.00
Cuban	1,560	0.63
Dominican Republic	229	0.09
Mexican	1,474	0.59
Puerto Rican	3,574	1.44
South American:	1,127	0.45
Argentinean	84	0.03
Bolivian	44	0.02
Chilean	52	0.02
Colombian	377	0.15
Ecuadorian	89	0.04
Paraguayan	3	0.00
Peruvian	137	0.06
Uruguayan	8	0.00
Venezuelan	284	0.11
Other South American	49	0.02
Other Hispanic or Latino	2,076	0.84
Hungarian	1,673	0.68
Icelander	29	0.01
Iranian	74	0.03
Irish	30,759	12.41
Israeli	63	0.03
Italian	16,736	6.75
Latvian	350	0.14
Lithuanian	873	0.35
Macedonian	23	0.01
Maltese	11	0.00
New Zealander	43	0.02
Northern European	111	0.04
Norwegian	2,489	1.00
Pennsylvania German	35	0.01
Polish	7,542	3.04
Portuguese	882	0.36
Romanian	273	0.11
Russian	2,236	0.90
Scandinavian	210	0.08
Scotch-Irish	4,625	1.87
Scottish	6,317	2.55
Serbian	206	0.08
Slavic	116	0.05
Slovak	530	0.21
Slovene	92	0.04
Swedish	3,150	1.27
Swiss	615	0.25
Turkish	129	0.05
Ukrainian	943	0.38
United States or American	14,062	5.67
Welsh	1,985	0.80
West Indian, excl. Hispanic:	3,261	1.32
Bahamian	49	0.02
Barbadian	240	0.10
Belizean	44	0.02
Bermudan	15	0.01

Notes: 1. Figures in the "Number" column do not add up to the total population due to: a) Ancestry/Race overlap — e.g. persons can report being both White and Irish, b) persons of Hispanic origin can report being any race, c) persons reporting two ancestries are counted in both categories. 2. Numbers in parentheses indicate the number of persons reporting this ancestry/race alone, not in combination with any other ancestry/race. 3. Refer to the Explanation of Data in the front of the book for more detailed information.

British West Indian	113	0.05
Haitian	339	0.14
Jamaican	1,649	0.67
Trinidadian and Tobagonian	273	0.11
U.S. Virgin Islander	197	0.08
West Indian	268	0.11
Other West Indian	74	0.03
White:	181,278	73.03
Not Hispanic (170,396)	173,878	70.05
Hispanic (6,737)	7,400	2.98
Yugoslavian	1,459	0.59

San Carlos Park

Place Type: Census Designated Place
County: Lee
Population: 16,317

Ancestry/Race	Number	%
Acadian/Cajun	15	0.09
African American/Black:	257	1.58
Not Hispanic (173)	221	1.35
Hispanic (32)	36	0.22
African, sub-Saharan:	4	0.02
African	4	0.02
Am. Ind. or Alaska Nat., not spec.	42	0.26
Albanian	17	0.11
American Indian tribes, specified:	90	0.55
Apache	3	0.02
Blackfeet	3	0.02
Cherokee (15)	38	0.23
Chickasaw (4)	4	0.02
Chippewa (1)	3	0.02
Choctaw (4)	5	0.03
Comanche	1	0.01
Cree	1	0.01
Iroquois (2)	2	0.01
Latin American Indians (2)	2	0.01
Menominee	1	0.01
Navajo	2	0.01
Potawatomi (1)	2	0.01
Pueblo	1	0.01
Seminole	2	0.01
Sioux	3	0.02
All other tribes (10)	17	0.10
American Indian tribes, not spec.	3	0.02
Arab:	7	0.04
Lebanese	7	0.04
Armenian	6	0.04
Asian:	168	1.03
Chinese, ex. Taiwanese (43)	52	0.32
Filipino (35)	59	0.36
Indian (6)	7	0.04
Indonesian (1)	1	0.01
Japanese (4)	8	0.05
Korean (10)	16	0.10
Laotian (1)	1	0.01
Thai (1)	2	0.01
Vietnamese (5)	9	0.06
Other Asian, not specified (9)	13	0.08
Austrian	45	0.28
Belgian	17	0.11
Brazilian	34	0.21
British	76	0.47
Canadian	67	0.42
Croatian	22	0.14
Czech	61	0.38
Danish	40	0.25
Dutch	363	2.25
Eastern European	11	0.07
English	1,652	10.25
European	68	0.42
Finnish	44	0.27
French, except Basque	721	4.47
French Canadian	228	1.41
German	4,108	25.48
Greek	118	0.73
Hawaii Native/Pacific Islander:	14	0.09
Micronesian:	4	0.02
Guamanian/Chamorro	4	0.02
Polynesian: (1)	7	0.04
Native Hawaiian	6	0.04
Samoan (1)	1	0.01
Other Pac. Isl., not spec.	3	0.02
Hispanic or Latino:	1,329	8.14
Central American:	50	0.31
Costa Rican	6	0.04
Guatemalan	3	0.02
Honduran	16	0.10
Nicaraguan	11	0.07
Panamanian	3	0.02
Salvadoran	9	0.06
Other Central American	2	0.01
Cuban	85	0.52
Dominican Republic	14	0.09
Mexican	547	3.35
Puerto Rican	417	2.56
South American:	61	0.37
Argentinean	5	0.03
Bolivian	10	0.06
Chilean	10	0.06
Colombian	14	0.09
Ecuadorian	7	0.04
Paraguayan	1	0.01
Peruvian	4	0.02
Uruguayan	2	0.01
Venezuelan	5	0.03
Other South American	3	0.02
Other Hispanic or Latino	155	0.95
Hungarian	193	1.20
Irish	2,823	17.51
Italian	1,788	11.09
Lithuanian	54	0.33
Luxemburger	10	0.06
Norwegian	217	1.35
Pennsylvania German	38	0.24
Polish	830	5.15
Portuguese	134	0.83
Romanian	22	0.14
Russian	128	0.79
Scotch-Irish	200	1.24
Scottish	420	2.61
Serbian	6	0.04
Slavic	28	0.17
Slovak	25	0.16
Swedish	185	1.15
Swiss	27	0.17
Turkish	37	0.23
Ukrainian	67	0.42
United States or American	1,189	7.38
Welsh	176	1.09
West Indian, excl. Hispanic:	23	0.14
Haitian	11	0.07
Jamaican	12	0.07
White:	15,530	95.18
Not Hispanic (14,457)	14,612	89.55
Hispanic (855)	918	5.63

Sandalfoot Cove

Place Type: Census Designated Place
County: Palm Beach
Population: 16,582

Ancestry/Race	Number	%
African American/Black:	761	4.59
Not Hispanic (628)	708	4.27
Hispanic (29)	53	0.32
African, sub-Saharan:	85	0.51
South African	85	0.51
Am. Ind. or Alaska Nat., not spec.	43	0.26
Albanian	8	0.05
American Indian tribes, specified:	43	0.26
Apache	1	0.01
Blackfeet	5	0.03
Cherokee (1)	10	0.06
Chippewa	1	0.01
Choctaw	5	0.03
Delaware (1)	1	0.01
Iroquois	1	0.01
Latin American Indians (1)	5	0.03
Lumbee (1)	1	0.01
Sioux (3)	4	0.02
All other tribes (3)	9	0.05
American Indian tribes, not spec.	3	0.02
Arab:	154	0.93
Egyptian	8	0.05
Lebanese	98	0.59
Moroccan	10	0.06
Syrian	38	0.23
Armenian	17	0.10
Asian:	577	3.48
Bangladeshi (14)	22	0.13
Chinese, ex. Taiwanese (149)	168	1.01
Filipino (28)	39	0.24
Indian (119)	133	0.80
Japanese (15)	23	0.14
Korean (39)	43	0.26
Pakistani (12)	14	0.08
Sri Lankan (6)	6	0.04
Taiwanese (3)	3	0.02
Thai (16)	19	0.11
Vietnamese (74)	76	0.46
Other Asian, specified (6)	6	0.04
Other Asian, not specified (7)	25	0.15
Austrian	210	1.27
Belgian	13	0.08
Brazilian	340	2.05
British	58	0.35
Canadian	56	0.34
Celtic	11	0.07
Croatian	10	0.06
Czech	54	0.33
Czechoslovakian	58	0.35
Danish	21	0.13
Dutch	74	0.45
Eastern European	129	0.78
English	999	6.02
European	134	0.81
Finnish	18	0.11
French, except Basque	497	3.00
French Canadian	61	0.37
German	1,769	10.66
Greek	171	1.03
Hawaii Native/Pacific Islander:	22	0.13
Melanesian: (1)	1	0.01
Fijian (1)	1	0.01
Micronesian: (2)	3	0.02
Guamanian/Chamorro (2)	2	0.01
Other Micronesian	1	0.01
Other Pac. Isl., not spec. (6)	18	0.11
Hispanic or Latino:	2,397	14.46
Central American:	117	0.71
Costa Rican	11	0.07
Guatemalan	22	0.13
Honduran	15	0.09
Nicaraguan	20	0.12
Panamanian	9	0.05
Salvadoran	26	0.16
Other Central American	14	0.08
Cuban	235	1.42
Dominican Republic	86	0.52
Mexican	195	1.18
Puerto Rican	414	2.50
South American:	729	4.40
Argentinean	49	0.30
Bolivian	1	0.01
Chilean	29	0.17
Colombian	324	1.95
Ecuadorian	98	0.59
Paraguayan	9	0.05
Peruvian	152	0.92
Uruguayan	16	0.10
Venezuelan	49	0.30
Other South American	2	0.01
Other Hispanic or Latino	621	3.75
Hungarian	154	0.93
Iranian	27	0.16
Irish	1,777	10.71
Israeli	48	0.29

Notes: 1. Figures in the "Number" column do not add up to the total population due to: a) Ancestry/Race overlap — e.g. persons can report being both White and Irish, b) persons of Hispanic origin can report being any race, c) persons reporting two ancestries are counted in both categories. 2. Numbers in parentheses indicate the number of persons reporting this ancestry/race alone, not in combination with any other ancestry/race. 3. Refer to the Explanation of Data in the front of the book for more detailed information.

Italian	2,489	15.00
Lithuanian	56	0.34
Norwegian	135	0.81
Polish	757	4.56
Portuguese	94	0.57
Romanian	75	0.45
Russian	558	3.36
Scotch-Irish	205	1.24
Scottish	254	1.53
Slovak	38	0.23
Slovene	8	0.05
Swedish	201	1.21
Swiss	11	0.07
Turkish	43	0.26
Ukrainian	77	0.46
United States or American	1,142	6.88
Welsh	95	0.57
West Indian, excl. Hispanic:	316	1.90
Bahamian	12	0.07
Barbadian	31	0.19
British West Indian	93	0.56
Haitian	18	0.11
Jamaican	91	0.55
Trinidadian and Tobagonian	11	0.07
West Indian	60	0.36
White:	14,782	89.14
Not Hispanic (12,671)	12,887	77.72
Hispanic (1,790)	1,895	11.43
Yugoslavian	12	0.07

Sanford

Place Type: City
County: Seminole
Population: 38,291

Ancestry/Race	Number	%
African American/Black:	12,686	33.13
Not Hispanic (12,167)	12,474	32.58
Hispanic (141)	212	0.55
African, sub-Saharan:	607	1.61
African	607	1.61
Am. Ind. or Alaska Nat., not spec.	139	0.36
American Indian tribes, specified:	250	0.65
Apache	2	0.01
Blackfeet (6)	17	0.04
Cherokee (30)	97	0.25
Cheyenne (1)	1	0.00
Chippewa (2)	5	0.01
Choctaw (3)	8	0.02
Cree	4	0.01
Creek (8)	12	0.03
Crow	3	0.01
Delaware	2	0.01
Iroquois (7)	18	0.05
Latin American Indians (15)	23	0.06
Lumbee	1	0.00
Menominee (1)	2	0.01
Navajo (1)	6	0.02
Ottawa (1)	2	0.01
Pueblo	1	0.00
Puget Sound Salish (1)	1	0.00
Seminole (4)	15	0.04
Sioux (5)	8	0.02
Yakama (3)	3	0.01
Yaqui	2	0.01
All other tribes (11)	17	0.04
American Indian tribes, not spec.	21	0.05
Arab:	105	0.28
Arab/Arabic	17	0.05
Lebanese	64	0.17
Moroccan	17	0.05
Syrian	7	0.02
Armenian	64	0.17
Asian:	558	1.46
Bangladeshi (1)	1	0.00
Cambodian (2)	2	0.01
Chinese, ex. Taiwanese (50)	74	0.19
Filipino (70)	98	0.26
Indian (108)	137	0.36
Indonesian (4)	7	0.02
Japanese (20)	46	0.12
Korean (10)	25	0.07
Laotian (33)	34	0.09
Malaysian (1)	1	0.00
Pakistani (9)	11	0.03
Sri Lankan (1)	2	0.01
Taiwanese (2)	2	0.01
Thai (13)	21	0.05
Vietnamese (51)	55	0.14
Other Asian, specified (4)	6	0.02
Other Asian, not specified (20)	36	0.09
Austrian	52	0.14
Belgian	8	0.02
Brazilian	11	0.03
British	123	0.33
Canadian	115	0.31
Croatian	17	0.05
Czech	40	0.11
Czechoslovakian	39	0.10
Danish	52	0.14
Dutch	391	1.04
Eastern European	10	0.03
English	3,439	9.15
European	139	0.37
Finnish	5	0.01
French, except Basque	949	2.52
French Canadian	282	0.75
German	4,032	10.72
Greek	46	0.12
Guyanese	49	0.13
Hawaii Native/Pacific Islander:	56	0.15
Micronesian: (8)	8	0.02
Guamanian/Chamorro (8)	8	0.02
Polynesian: (8)	22	0.06
Native Hawaiian (6)	15	0.04
Samoan (1)	4	0.01
Other Polynesian (1)	3	0.01
Other Pac. Isl., specified	2	0.01
Other Pac. Isl., not spec. (4)	24	0.06
Hispanic or Latino:	3,974	10.38
Central American:	192	0.50
Costa Rican	18	0.05
Guatemalan	12	0.03
Honduran	26	0.07
Nicaraguan	12	0.03
Panamanian	57	0.15
Salvadoran	49	0.13
Other Central American	18	0.05
Cuban	126	0.33
Dominican Republic	73	0.19
Mexican	868	2.27
Puerto Rican	1,974	5.16
South American:	266	0.69
Argentinean	18	0.05
Bolivian	6	0.02
Chilean	10	0.03
Colombian	118	0.31
Ecuadorian	39	0.10
Peruvian	28	0.07
Uruguayan	7	0.02
Venezuelan	28	0.07
Other South American	12	0.03
Other Hispanic or Latino	475	1.24
Hungarian	92	0.24
Icelander	8	0.02
Irish	3,441	9.15
Italian	1,733	4.61
Lithuanian	57	0.15
New Zealander	5	0.01
Northern European	14	0.04
Norwegian	220	0.59
Pennsylvania German	13	0.03
Polish	770	2.05
Portuguese	106	0.28
Romanian	35	0.09
Russian	206	0.55
Scandinavian	32	0.09
Scotch-Irish	487	1.30
Scottish	563	1.50
Serbian	13	0.03
Slavic	28	0.07
Slovak	26	0.07
Slovene	13	0.03
Swedish	243	0.65
Swiss	53	0.14
Ukrainian	36	0.10
United States or American	2,326	6.19
Welsh	172	0.46
West Indian, excl. Hispanic:	501	1.33
Bahamian	75	0.20
Barbadian	24	0.06
Bermudan	6	0.02
Haitian	103	0.27
Jamaican	248	0.66
Trinidadian and Tobagonian	25	0.07
U.S. Virgin Islander	8	0.02
West Indian	12	0.03
White:	23,563	61.54
Not Hispanic (20,911)	21,381	55.84
Hispanic (1,961)	2,182	5.70
Yugoslavian	9	0.02

Sarasota Springs

Place Type: Census Designated Place
County: Sarasota
Population: 15,875

Ancestry/Race	Number	%
African American/Black:	159	1.00
Not Hispanic (110)	153	0.96
Hispanic (6)	6	0.04
Am. Ind. or Alaska Nat., not spec.	32	0.20
American Indian tribes, specified:	54	0.34
Apache	2	0.01
Blackfeet (1)	1	0.01
Cherokee (5)	19	0.12
Chippewa (1)	3	0.02
Choctaw (1)	1	0.01
Iroquois (1)	4	0.03
Latin American Indians (4)	4	0.03
Lumbee (2)	3	0.02
Pueblo (2)	2	0.01
Seminole	4	0.03
Shoshone	1	0.01
Sioux (5)	6	0.04
All other tribes (2)	4	0.03
American Indian tribes, not spec.	7	0.04
Arab:	27	0.17
Iraqi	8	0.05
Lebanese	13	0.08
Palestinian	6	0.04
Armenian	44	0.28
Asian:	173	1.09
Chinese, ex. Taiwanese (20)	24	0.15
Filipino (20)	30	0.19
Indian (15)	18	0.11
Japanese (8)	18	0.11
Korean (9)	12	0.08
Laotian (1)	1	0.01
Thai (5)	11	0.07
Vietnamese (38)	43	0.27
Other Asian, specified (1)	1	0.01
Other Asian, not specified (1)	15	0.09
Austrian	81	0.51
Belgian	39	0.25
Brazilian	38	0.24
British	67	0.42
Canadian	89	0.56
Czech	100	0.63
Czechoslovakian	36	0.23
Danish	96	0.61
Dutch	262	1.65
English	2,056	12.97
European	132	0.83
Finnish	61	0.38
French, except Basque	754	4.76
French Canadian	183	1.15
German	3,520	22.21

Notes: 1. Figures in the "Number" column do not add up to the total population due to: a) Ancestry/Race overlap — e.g. persons can report being both White and Irish, b) persons of Hispanic origin can report being any race, c) persons reporting two ancestries are counted in both categories. 2. Numbers in parentheses indicate the number of persons reporting this ancestry/race alone, not in combination with any other ancestry/race. 3. Refer to the Explanation of Data in the front of the book for more detailed information.

Ancestry/Race	Number	%
Greek	71	0.45
Guyanese	18	0.11
Hawaii Native/Pacific Islander:	7	0.04
Micronesian:	2	0.01
Guamanian/Chamorro	2	0.01
Polynesian: (4)	4	0.03
Native Hawaiian (3)	3	0.02
Samoan (1)	1	0.01
Other Pac. Isl., not spec.	1	0.01
Hispanic or Latino:	759	4.78
Central American:	22	0.14
Guatemalan	6	0.04
Honduran	2	0.01
Nicaraguan	6	0.04
Panamanian	3	0.02
Salvadoran	4	0.03
Other Central American	1	0.01
Cuban	130	0.82
Dominican Republic	5	0.03
Mexican	263	1.66
Puerto Rican	106	0.67
South American:	107	0.67
Argentinean	7	0.04
Bolivian	4	0.03
Chilean	14	0.09
Colombian	55	0.35
Ecuadorian	1	0.01
Peruvian	17	0.11
Uruguayan	1	0.01
Venezuelan	8	0.05
Other Hispanic or Latino	126	0.79
Hungarian	194	1.22
Iranian	6	0.04
Irish	2,232	14.08
Italian	1,284	8.10
Lithuanian	27	0.17
Maltese	6	0.04
Norwegian	216	1.36
Pennsylvania German	18	0.11
Polish	624	3.94
Portuguese	105	0.66
Romanian	17	0.11
Russian	198	1.25
Scotch-Irish	353	2.23
Scottish	376	2.37
Serbian	17	0.11
Slavic	10	0.06
Slovak	97	0.61
Slovene	16	0.10
Swedish	469	2.96
Swiss	83	0.52
Ukrainian	39	0.25
United States or American	1,469	9.27
Welsh	187	1.18
White:	15,386	96.92
Not Hispanic (14,672)	14,827	93.40
Hispanic (513)	559	3.52
Yugoslavian	41	0.26

Sarasota

Place Type: City
County: Sarasota
Population: 52,715

Ancestry/Race	Number	%
African American/Black:	8,852	16.79
Not Hispanic (8,250)	8,566	16.25
Hispanic (197)	286	0.54
African, sub-Saharan:	407	0.77
African	345	0.66
Cape Verdean	10	0.02
Ethiopian	28	0.05
South African	24	0.05
Alaska Native tribes, specified:	4	0.01
Aleut	1	0.00
Eskimo	2	0.00
Tlingit-Haida (1)	1	0.00
Am. Ind. or Alaska Nat., not spec.	146	0.28
Albanian	33	0.06
Alsatian	11	0.02
American Indian tribes, specified:	322	0.61
Apache (4)	7	0.01
Blackfeet (3)	15	0.03
Cherokee (33)	121	0.23
Chippewa (7)	17	0.03
Choctaw (6)	9	0.02
Cree	3	0.01
Creek (3)	16	0.03
Crow	1	0.00
Delaware (1)	1	0.00
Iroquois (8)	14	0.03
Latin American Indians (28)	44	0.08
Lumbee (5)	5	0.01
Navajo (4)	9	0.02
Paiute	2	0.00
Potawatomi	2	0.00
Seminole (7)	11	0.02
Sioux (7)	17	0.03
Ute	1	0.00
All other tribes (13)	27	0.05
American Indian tribes, not spec.	27	0.05
Arab:	317	0.60
Arab/Arabic	12	0.02
Egyptian	16	0.03
Lebanese	96	0.18
Moroccan	128	0.24
Palestinian	39	0.07
Syrian	8	0.02
Other Arab	18	0.03
Armenian	84	0.16
Asian:	713	1.35
Bangladeshi (4)	4	0.01
Chinese, ex. Taiwanese (86)	115	0.22
Filipino (49)	76	0.14
Indian (113)	130	0.25
Indonesian (1)	4	0.01
Japanese (25)	43	0.08
Korean (30)	38	0.07
Laotian (19)	19	0.04
Malaysian (1)	2	0.00
Pakistani (3)	3	0.01
Taiwanese (1)	1	0.00
Thai (25)	30	0.06
Vietnamese (163)	184	0.35
Other Asian, specified	2	0.00
Other Asian, not specified (7)	62	0.12
Australian	55	0.10
Austrian	221	0.42
Basque	26	0.05
Belgian	59	0.11
Brazilian	69	0.13
British	328	0.62
Bulgarian	10	0.02
Canadian	204	0.39
Croatian	14	0.03
Czech	130	0.25
Czechoslovakian	81	0.15
Danish	198	0.38
Dutch	905	1.72
Eastern European	32	0.06
English	5,501	10.47
Estonian	8	0.02
European	304	0.58
Finnish	102	0.19
French, except Basque	1,707	3.25
French Canadian	415	0.79
German	7,341	13.97
Greek	165	0.31
Hawaii Native/Pacific Islander:	72	0.14
Melanesian: (1)	1	0.00
Fijian (1)	1	0.00
Micronesian: (11)	15	0.03
Guamanian/Chamorro (7)	10	0.02
Other Micronesian (4)	5	0.01
Polynesian: (14)	42	0.08
Native Hawaiian (12)	29	0.06
Samoan (2)	9	0.02
Tongan	3	0.01
Other Polynesian	1	0.00
Other Pac. Isl., not spec.	14	0.03
Hispanic or Latino:	6,283	11.92
Central American:	223	0.42
Costa Rican	18	0.03
Guatemalan	27	0.05
Honduran	73	0.14
Nicaraguan	45	0.09
Panamanian	29	0.06
Salvadoran	26	0.05
Other Central American	5	0.01
Cuban	656	1.24
Dominican Republic	69	0.13
Mexican	3,587	6.80
Puerto Rican	572	1.09
South American:	417	0.79
Argentinean	42	0.08
Bolivian	4	0.01
Chilean	10	0.02
Colombian	181	0.34
Ecuadorian	18	0.03
Paraguayan	3	0.01
Peruvian	102	0.19
Uruguayan	2	0.00
Venezuelan	50	0.09
Other South American	5	0.01
Other Hispanic or Latino	759	1.44
Hungarian	506	0.96
Icelander	10	0.02
Iranian	8	0.02
Irish	5,496	10.46
Israeli	6	0.01
Italian	2,923	5.56
Latvian	28	0.05
Lithuanian	158	0.30
Luxemburger	9	0.02
New Zealander	7	0.01
Norwegian	490	0.93
Pennsylvania German	72	0.14
Polish	1,550	2.95
Portuguese	55	0.10
Romanian	103	0.20
Russian	679	1.29
Scandinavian	126	0.24
Scotch-Irish	857	1.63
Scottish	1,208	2.30
Serbian	58	0.11
Slavic	27	0.05
Slovak	149	0.28
Slovene	15	0.03
Swedish	861	1.64
Swiss	280	0.53
Ukrainian	192	0.37
United States or American	3,256	6.20
Welsh	362	0.69
West Indian, excl. Hispanic:	347	0.66
Barbadian	7	0.01
Belizean	11	0.02
British West Indian	6	0.01
Haitian	89	0.17
Jamaican	181	0.34
Trinidadian and Tobagonian	6	0.01
U.S. Virgin Islander	14	0.03
West Indian	33	0.06
White:	41,325	78.39
Not Hispanic (36,786)	37,256	70.67
Hispanic (3,756)	4,069	7.72
Yugoslavian	49	0.09

Scott Lake

Place Type: Census Designated Place
County: Miami-Dade
Population: 14,401

Ancestry/Race	Number	%
African American/Black:	13,445	93.36
Not Hispanic (12,916)	13,177	91.50
Hispanic (217)	268	1.86
African, sub-Saharan:	189	1.31
African	158	1.10

Notes: 1. Figures in the "Number" column do not add up to the total population due to: a) Ancestry/Race overlap — e.g. persons can report being both White and Irish, b) persons of Hispanic origin can report being any race, c) persons reporting two ancestries are counted in both categories. 2. Numbers in parentheses indicate the number of persons reporting this ancestry/race alone, not in combination with any other ancestry/race. 3. Refer to the Explanation of Data in the front of the book for more detailed information.

Nigerian	31	0.22
Am. Ind. or Alaska Nat., not spec.	33	0.23
American Indian tribes, specified:	27	0.19
Apache (1)	1	0.01
Blackfeet (2)	5	0.03
Cherokee (1)	9	0.06
Chippewa	1	0.01
Latin American Indians (2)	2	0.01
Seminole	3	0.02
Sioux	2	0.01
All other tribes (1)	4	0.03
Arab:	18	0.13
Egyptian	7	0.05
Lebanese	11	0.08
Asian:	94	0.65
Chinese, ex. Taiwanese (21)	36	0.25
Filipino (9)	13	0.09
Indian (18)	27	0.19
Japanese (1)	1	0.01
Pakistani	1	0.01
Thai (1)	1	0.01
Vietnamese	1	0.01
Other Asian, not specified (8)	14	0.10
Brazilian	10	0.07
Canadian	16	0.11
Croatian	7	0.05
English	64	0.44
European	11	0.08
Finnish	5	0.03
German	27	0.19
Greek	27	0.19
Guyanese	5	0.03
Hawaii Native/Pacific Islander:	43	0.30
Micronesian: (1)	1	0.01
Other Micronesian (1)	1	0.01
Polynesian: (1)	6	0.04
Native Hawaiian	5	0.03
Samoan (1)	1	0.01
Other Pac. Isl., not spec. (4)	36	0.25
Hispanic or Latino:	789	5.48
Central American:	129	0.90
Costa Rican	5	0.03
Guatemalan	3	0.02
Honduran	15	0.10
Nicaraguan	74	0.51
Panamanian	21	0.15
Salvadoran	3	0.02
Other Central American	8	0.06
Cuban	221	1.53
Dominican Republic	52	0.36
Mexican	21	0.15
Puerto Rican	131	0.91
South American:	57	0.40
Argentinean	1	0.01
Bolivian	6	0.04
Chilean	3	0.02
Colombian	26	0.18
Ecuadorian	8	0.06
Peruvian	10	0.07
Venezuelan	2	0.01
Other South American	1	0.01
Other Hispanic or Latino	178	1.24
Iranian	6	0.04
Irish	40	0.28
Lithuanian	13	0.09
Norwegian	18	0.13
Polish	5	0.03
Russian	6	0.04
Scotch-Irish	5	0.03
Slavic	9	0.06
United States or American	317	2.20
West Indian, excl. Hispanic:	3,269	22.72
Bahamian	223	1.55
Barbadian	8	0.06
Belizean	15	0.10
British West Indian	134	0.93
Haitian	788	5.48
Jamaican	1,870	13.00
Trinidadian and Tobagonian	104	0.72
U.S. Virgin Islander	85	0.59
West Indian	42	0.29
White:	740	5.14
Not Hispanic (287)	323	2.24
Hispanic (383)	417	2.90

Sebastian

Place Type: City
County: Indian River
Population: 16,181

Ancestry/Race	Number	%
African American/Black:	574	3.55
Not Hispanic (503)	552	3.41
Hispanic (12)	22	0.14
African, sub-Saharan:	123	0.75
African	114	0.69
South African	9	0.05
Am. Ind. or Alaska Nat., not spec.	17	0.11
American Indian tribes, specified:	59	0.36
Apache	3	0.02
Blackfeet (1)	2	0.01
Cherokee (15)	34	0.21
Chickasaw	1	0.01
Chippewa (1)	2	0.01
Choctaw	1	0.01
Delaware (2)	3	0.02
Iroquois	2	0.01
Kiowa (1)	2	0.01
Latin American Indians (1)	1	0.01
Lumbee (1)	1	0.01
Navajo	2	0.01
Osage	1	0.01
Yakama (1)	1	0.01
All other tribes (2)	3	0.02
American Indian tribes, not spec.	11	0.07
Arab:	82	0.50
Lebanese	32	0.19
Syrian	50	0.30
Armenian	11	0.07
Asian:	164	1.01
Cambodian (3)	3	0.02
Chinese, ex. Taiwanese (5)	10	0.06
Filipino (25)	36	0.22
Indian (31)	42	0.26
Indonesian (1)	2	0.01
Japanese (8)	18	0.11
Korean (9)	10	0.06
Pakistani (1)	4	0.02
Taiwanese (4)	4	0.02
Thai (1)	3	0.02
Vietnamese (26)	26	0.16
Other Asian, not specified (5)	6	0.04
Australian	10	0.06
Austrian	71	0.43
Belgian	18	0.11
Brazilian	45	0.27
British	40	0.24
Canadian	132	0.80
Croatian	11	0.07
Czech	47	0.29
Czechoslovakian	16	0.10
Danish	109	0.66
Dutch	355	2.16
English	2,254	13.70
European	125	0.76
Finnish	156	0.95
French, except Basque	783	4.76
French Canadian	194	1.18
German	3,252	19.77
Greek	77	0.47
Hawaii Native/Pacific Islander:	13	0.08
Micronesian:	1	0.01
Other Micronesian	1	0.01
Polynesian:	5	0.03
Native Hawaiian	5	0.03
Other Pac. Isl., not spec.	7	0.04
Hispanic or Latino:	625	3.86
Central American:	14	0.09
Costa Rican	1	0.01
Guatemalan	3	0.02
Nicaraguan	5	0.03
Panamanian	5	0.03
Cuban	64	0.40
Dominican Republic	8	0.05
Mexican	199	1.23
Puerto Rican	174	1.08
South American:	59	0.36
Argentinean	1	0.01
Colombian	45	0.28
Ecuadorian	8	0.05
Peruvian	1	0.01
Venezuelan	3	0.02
Other South American	1	0.01
Other Hispanic or Latino	107	0.66
Hungarian	77	0.47
Irish	2,457	14.94
Italian	2,249	13.67
Lithuanian	85	0.52
Norwegian	158	0.96
Pennsylvania German	17	0.10
Polish	705	4.29
Portuguese	210	1.28
Romanian	23	0.14
Russian	209	1.27
Scandinavian	21	0.13
Scotch-Irish	420	2.55
Scottish	475	2.89
Serbian	16	0.10
Slavic	17	0.10
Slovak	41	0.25
Swedish	223	1.36
Swiss	28	0.17
Ukrainian	38	0.23
United States or American	1,143	6.95
Welsh	167	1.02
West Indian, excl. Hispanic:	161	0.98
Bahamian	25	0.15
Bermudan	12	0.07
British West Indian	9	0.05
Jamaican	115	0.70
White:	15,322	94.69
Not Hispanic (14,748)	14,866	91.87
Hispanic (407)	456	2.82
Yugoslavian	8	0.05

Seminole

Place Type: City
County: Pinellas
Population: 10,890

Ancestry/Race	Number	%
African American/Black:	69	0.63
Not Hispanic (47)	61	0.56
Hispanic (5)	8	0.07
Am. Ind. or Alaska Nat., not spec.	23	0.21
Albanian	19	0.18
American Indian tribes, specified:	58	0.53
Apache	1	0.01
Blackfeet (1)	2	0.02
Cherokee (10)	26	0.24
Chippewa	2	0.02
Choctaw	1	0.01
Cree	1	0.01
Delaware	1	0.01
Iroquois (3)	7	0.06
Latin American Indians	1	0.01
Osage	1	0.01
Seminole (1)	1	0.01
Sioux (1)	3	0.03
All other tribes (9)	11	0.10
American Indian tribes, not spec.	11	0.10
Armenian	18	0.17
Asian:	109	1.00
Bangladeshi	2	0.02
Chinese, ex. Taiwanese (7)	8	0.07
Filipino (39)	45	0.41
Indian (28)	30	0.28
Japanese (2)	2	0.02

Notes: 1. Figures in the "Number" column do not add up to the total population due to: a) Ancestry/Race overlap — e.g. persons can report being both White and Irish, b) persons of Hispanic origin can report being any race, c) persons reporting two ancestries are counted in both categories. 2. Numbers in parentheses indicate the number of persons reporting this ancestry/race alone, not in combination with any other ancestry/race. 3. Refer to the Explanation of Data in the front of the book for more detailed information.

Korean (6)	8	0.07
Laotian (4)	4	0.04
Taiwanese (1)	3	0.03
Vietnamese (3)	3	0.03
Other Asian, not specified (3)	4	0.04
Austrian	37	0.34
Belgian	8	0.07
Brazilian	8	0.07
British	51	0.47
Canadian	70	0.65
Croatian	42	0.39
Czech	35	0.32
Czechoslovakian	100	0.93
Danish	85	0.79
Dutch	331	3.07
Eastern European	8	0.07
English	1,570	14.57
European	12	0.11
Finnish	13	0.12
French, except Basque	439	4.07
French Canadian	64	0.59
German	2,397	22.24
Greek	95	0.88
Guyanese	6	0.06
Hawaii Native/Pacific Islander:	4	0.04
Micronesian: (1)	1	0.01
Guamanian/Chamorro (1)	1	0.01
Polynesian: (2)	2	0.02
Native Hawaiian (1)	1	0.01
Samoan (1)	1	0.01
Other Pac. Isl., not spec.	1	0.01
Hispanic or Latino:	245	2.25
Central American:	22	0.20
Costa Rican	1	0.01
Honduran	3	0.03
Nicaraguan	5	0.05
Panamanian	5	0.05
Salvadoran	8	0.07
Cuban	19	0.17
Dominican Republic	7	0.06
Mexican	47	0.43
Puerto Rican	88	0.81
South American:	9	0.08
Argentinean	1	0.01
Bolivian	1	0.01
Colombian	6	0.06
Ecuadorian	1	0.01
Other Hispanic or Latino	53	0.49
Hungarian	166	1.54
Iranian	5	0.05
Irish	1,712	15.89
Italian	1,031	9.57
Latvian	9	0.08
Lithuanian	30	0.28
Norwegian	153	1.42
Pennsylvania German	20	0.19
Polish	394	3.66
Portuguese	38	0.35
Romanian	24	0.22
Russian	107	0.99
Scotch-Irish	288	2.67
Scottish	248	2.30
Slavic	6	0.06
Slovak	83	0.77
Slovene	7	0.06
Swedish	240	2.23
Swiss	30	0.28
Ukrainian	74	0.69
United States or American	797	7.40
Welsh	81	0.75
West Indian, excl. Hispanic:	29	0.27
Barbadian	8	0.07
British West Indian	8	0.07
Jamaican	9	0.08
Trinidadian and Tobagonian	4	0.04
White:	10,652	97.81
Not Hispanic (10,340)	10,458	96.03
Hispanic (181)	194	1.78
Yugoslavian	25	0.23

South Bradenton

Place Type: Census Designated Place
County: Manatee
Population: 21,587

Ancestry/Race	Number	%
African American/Black:	1,110	5.14
Not Hispanic (904)	1,007	4.66
Hispanic (93)	103	0.48
African, sub-Saharan:	10	0.05
African	10	0.05
Am. Ind. or Alaska Nat., not spec.	35	0.16
Albanian	12	0.06
Alsatian	10	0.05
American Indian tribes, specified:	109	0.50
Blackfeet (4)	11	0.05
Cherokee (16)	44	0.20
Chickasaw (1)	1	0.00
Chippewa (3)	4	0.02
Comanche	2	0.01
Creek (1)	2	0.01
Iroquois (2)	3	0.01
Latin American Indians (5)	5	0.02
Lumbee (1)	1	0.00
Menominee (1)	1	0.00
Navajo	3	0.01
Paiute	1	0.00
Potawatomi (1)	1	0.00
Pueblo (3)	3	0.01
Seminole	1	0.00
Sioux (3)	3	0.01
All other tribes (5)	23	0.11
American Indian tribes, not spec.	10	0.05
Arab:	64	0.30
Egyptian	7	0.03
Lebanese	24	0.11
Moroccan	11	0.05
Syrian	8	0.04
Other Arab	14	0.07
Asian:	336	1.56
Cambodian (29)	30	0.14
Chinese, ex. Taiwanese (72)	79	0.37
Filipino (38)	57	0.26
Indian (61)	74	0.34
Japanese (11)	15	0.07
Korean (18)	20	0.09
Laotian (1)	1	0.00
Pakistani	2	0.01
Taiwanese (1)	1	0.00
Thai (8)	10	0.05
Vietnamese (31)	36	0.17
Other Asian, not specified (8)	11	0.05
Australian	12	0.06
Austrian	60	0.28
Belgian	15	0.07
Brazilian	7	0.03
British	68	0.32
Canadian	71	0.33
Croatian	22	0.10
Czech	94	0.44
Czechoslovakian	50	0.23
Danish	17	0.08
Dutch	591	2.76
English	3,007	14.04
European	32	0.15
Finnish	19	0.09
French, except Basque	811	3.79
French Canadian	245	1.14
German	3,510	16.38
Greek	84	0.39
Hawaii Native/Pacific Islander:	31	0.14
Micronesian: (6)	6	0.03
Guamanian/Chamorro (6)	6	0.03
Polynesian: (12)	13	0.06
Native Hawaiian (6)	6	0.03
Samoan (6)	7	0.03
Other Pac. Isl., not spec. (3)	12	0.06
Hispanic or Latino:	1,870	8.66
Central American:	159	0.74
Costa Rican	6	0.03
Guatemalan	24	0.11
Honduran	84	0.39
Nicaraguan	17	0.08
Panamanian	5	0.02
Salvadoran	12	0.06
Other Central American	11	0.05
Cuban	92	0.43
Dominican Republic	21	0.10
Mexican	976	4.52
Puerto Rican	302	1.40
South American:	67	0.31
Argentinean	4	0.02
Chilean	6	0.03
Colombian	33	0.15
Ecuadorian	6	0.03
Peruvian	10	0.05
Uruguayan	5	0.02
Venezuelan	3	0.01
Other Hispanic or Latino	253	1.17
Hungarian	204	0.95
Iranian	8	0.04
Irish	2,747	12.82
Italian	1,435	6.70
Lithuanian	73	0.34
Northern European	18	0.08
Norwegian	107	0.50
Pennsylvania German	20	0.09
Polish	571	2.67
Portuguese	47	0.22
Russian	200	0.93
Scandinavian	39	0.18
Scotch-Irish	336	1.57
Scottish	519	2.42
Serbian	11	0.05
Slovak	93	0.43
Slovene	12	0.06
Swedish	330	1.54
Swiss	84	0.39
Turkish	22	0.10
Ukrainian	59	0.28
United States or American	1,718	8.02
Welsh	164	0.77
West Indian, excl. Hispanic:	96	0.45
Haitian	82	0.38
West Indian	14	0.07
White:	19,695	91.24
Not Hispanic (18,208)	18,400	85.24
Hispanic (1,202)	1,295	6.00
Yugoslavian	18	0.08

South Daytona

Place Type: City
County: Volusia
Population: 13,177

Ancestry/Race	Number	%
African American/Black:	1,104	8.38
Not Hispanic (1,021)	1,088	8.26
Hispanic (13)	16	0.12
African, sub-Saharan:	95	0.72
African	95	0.72
Am. Ind. or Alaska Nat., not spec.	15	0.11
Albanian	9	0.07
American Indian tribes, specified:	52	0.39
Blackfeet	1	0.01
Cherokee (2)	16	0.12
Chickasaw	3	0.02
Chippewa	1	0.01
Creek	3	0.02
Delaware	1	0.01
Iroquois	8	0.06
Kiowa	1	0.01
Latin American Indians (4)	4	0.03
Seminole	1	0.01
Sioux (6)	9	0.07
All other tribes (3)	4	0.03
American Indian tribes, not spec.	4	0.03
Arab:	109	0.83

Notes: 1. Figures in the "Number" column do not add up to the total population due to: a) Ancestry/Race overlap — e.g. persons can report being both White and Irish, b) persons of Hispanic origin can report being any race, c) persons reporting two ancestries are counted in both categories. 2. Numbers in parentheses indicate the number of persons reporting this ancestry/race alone, not in combination with any other ancestry/race. 3. Refer to the Explanation of Data in the front of the book for more detailed information.

Ancestry/Race	Number	%
Arab/Arabic	24	0.18
Lebanese	13	0.10
Palestinian	53	0.40
Syrian	19	0.14
Armenian	12	0.09
Asian:	209	1.59
Chinese, ex. Taiwanese (18)	21	0.16
Filipino (21)	42	0.32
Indian (46)	51	0.39
Indonesian (1)	3	0.02
Japanese (11)	11	0.08
Korean (19)	23	0.17
Laotian (1)	1	0.01
Sri Lankan (3)	3	0.02
Taiwanese	1	0.01
Thai (2)	4	0.03
Vietnamese (31)	36	0.27
Other Asian, not specified (6)	13	0.10
Austrian	47	0.36
Belgian	24	0.18
Brazilian	7	0.05
British	82	0.62
Canadian	102	0.78
Celtic	6	0.05
Croatian	5	0.04
Czech	53	0.40
Czechoslovakian	28	0.21
Danish	60	0.46
Dutch	214	1.63
English	1,933	14.69
European	49	0.37
Finnish	31	0.24
French, except Basque	533	4.05
French Canadian	242	1.84
German	1,906	14.49
Greek	48	0.36
Hawaii Native/Pacific Islander:	26	0.20
Melanesian:	1	0.01
Other Melanesian	1	0.01
Micronesian: (5)	13	0.10
Guamanian/Chamorro (5)	13	0.10
Polynesian: (2)	8	0.06
Native Hawaiian (2)	8	0.06
Other Pac. Isl., not spec.	4	0.03
Hispanic or Latino:	381	2.89
Central American:	7	0.05
Honduran	2	0.02
Panamanian	2	0.02
Other Central American	3	0.02
Cuban	27	0.20
Dominican Republic	5	0.04
Mexican	51	0.39
Puerto Rican	166	1.26
South American:	36	0.27
Argentinean	8	0.06
Bolivian	2	0.02
Colombian	13	0.10
Ecuadorian	2	0.02
Paraguayan	1	0.01
Uruguayan	4	0.03
Venezuelan	4	0.03
Other South American	2	0.02
Other Hispanic or Latino	89	0.68
Hungarian	106	0.81
Irish	2,173	16.52
Italian	970	7.37
Lithuanian	63	0.48
Northern European	5	0.04
Norwegian	88	0.67
Pennsylvania German	32	0.24
Polish	440	3.34
Portuguese	29	0.22
Romanian	7	0.05
Russian	55	0.42
Scandinavian	31	0.24
Scotch-Irish	246	1.87
Scottish	301	2.29
Slavic	6	0.05
Slovak	33	0.25
Slovene	14	0.11
Swedish	139	1.06
Swiss	51	0.39
Turkish	7	0.05
Ukrainian	76	0.58
United States or American	1,418	10.78
Welsh	79	0.60
West Indian, excl. Hispanic:	158	1.20
Bahamian	10	0.08
Belizean	13	0.10
British West Indian	12	0.09
Dutch West Indian	6	0.05
Haitian	57	0.43
Jamaican	60	0.46
White:	11,876	90.13
Not Hispanic (11,407)	11,573	87.83
Hispanic (277)	303	2.30
Yugoslavian	42	0.32

South Miami Heights

Place Type: Census Designated Place
County: Miami-Dade
Population: 33,522

Ancestry/Race	Number	%
African American/Black:	10,786	32.18
Not Hispanic (9,507)	9,910	29.56
Hispanic (656)	876	2.61
African, sub-Saharan:	76	0.23
African	50	0.15
Nigerian	26	0.08
Alaska Native tribes, specified:	1	0.00
All other tribes (1)	1	0.00
Am. Ind. or Alaska Nat., not spec.	100	0.30
American Indian tribes, specified:	79	0.24
Blackfeet	1	0.00
Cherokee (2)	28	0.08
Chippewa (1)	1	0.00
Choctaw	2	0.01
Creek (2)	2	0.01
Crow (1)	1	0.00
Latin American Indians (15)	28	0.08
Lumbee (1)	1	0.00
Osage (1)	1	0.00
Pueblo	2	0.01
Sioux	2	0.01
All other tribes (2)	10	0.03
American Indian tribes, not spec.	32	0.10
Arab:	61	0.18
Arab/Arabic	33	0.10
Lebanese	9	0.03
Palestinian	10	0.03
Syrian	9	0.03
Asian:	828	2.47
Bangladeshi	1	0.00
Chinese, ex. Taiwanese (54)	116	0.35
Filipino (65)	94	0.28
Hmong	3	0.01
Indian (406)	511	1.52
Japanese (7)	12	0.04
Korean (4)	9	0.03
Laotian (4)	4	0.01
Malaysian (2)	2	0.01
Pakistani (13)	19	0.06
Thai (13)	14	0.04
Vietnamese (16)	17	0.05
Other Asian, not specified (15)	26	0.08
Austrian	19	0.06
Brazilian	26	0.08
British	69	0.21
Canadian	7	0.02
Croatian	9	0.03
Danish	19	0.06
Dutch	155	0.46
English	587	1.75
European	43	0.13
Finnish	10	0.03
French, except Basque	237	0.71
French Canadian	17	0.05
German	543	1.62
Greek	29	0.09
Guyanese	337	1.00
Hawaii Native/Pacific Islander:	75	0.22
Micronesian: (1)	5	0.01
Guamanian/Chamorro	3	0.01
Other Micronesian (1)	2	0.01
Polynesian: (2)	9	0.03
Native Hawaiian (2)	6	0.02
Samoan	2	0.01
Other Polynesian	1	0.00
Other Pac. Isl., not spec. (4)	61	0.18
Hispanic or Latino:	18,829	56.17
Central American:	1,868	5.57
Costa Rican	80	0.24
Guatemalan	147	0.44
Honduran	366	1.09
Nicaraguan	936	2.79
Panamanian	98	0.29
Salvadoran	218	0.65
Other Central American	23	0.07
Cuban	8,616	25.70
Dominican Republic	851	2.54
Mexican	867	2.59
Puerto Rican	2,285	6.82
South American:	1,441	4.30
Argentinean	60	0.18
Bolivian	1	0.00
Chilean	56	0.17
Colombian	798	2.38
Ecuadorian	127	0.38
Paraguayan	4	0.01
Peruvian	243	0.72
Uruguayan	22	0.07
Venezuelan	106	0.32
Other South American	24	0.07
Other Hispanic or Latino	2,901	8.65
Hungarian	30	0.09
Iranian	44	0.13
Irish	413	1.23
Italian	355	1.06
Maltese	11	0.03
Norwegian	39	0.12
Polish	155	0.46
Portuguese	13	0.04
Russian	23	0.07
Scotch-Irish	24	0.07
Scottish	56	0.17
Swedish	23	0.07
Ukrainian	16	0.05
United States or American	1,482	4.41
Welsh	11	0.03
West Indian, excl. Hispanic:	2,956	8.80
Bahamian	124	0.37
British West Indian	133	0.40
Haitian	403	1.20
Jamaican	1,909	5.69
Trinidadian and Tobagonian	229	0.68
U.S. Virgin Islander	33	0.10
West Indian	101	0.30
Other West Indian	24	0.07
White:	19,771	58.98
Not Hispanic (3,746)	3,964	11.83
Hispanic (14,848)	15,807	47.15

South Miami

Place Type: City
County: Miami-Dade
Population: 10,741

Ancestry/Race	Number	%
Acadian/Cajun	14	0.13
African American/Black:	2,716	25.29
Not Hispanic (2,589)	2,643	24.61
Hispanic (64)	73	0.68
African, sub-Saharan:	48	0.44
African	38	0.35
South African	10	0.09
Am. Ind. or Alaska Nat., not spec.	10	0.09
Albanian	7	0.06

Notes: 1. Figures in the "Number" column do not add up to the total population due to: a) Ancestry/Race overlap — e.g. persons can report being both White and Irish, b) persons of Hispanic origin can report being any race, c) persons reporting two ancestries are counted in both categories. 2. Numbers in parentheses indicate the number of persons reporting this ancestry/race alone, not in combination with any other ancestry/race. 3. Refer to the Explanation of Data in the front of the book for more detailed information.

American Indian tribes, specified:	22	0.20
Apache	1	0.01
Cherokee	5	0.05
Comanche	1	0.01
Iroquois	1	0.01
Latin American Indians (6)	10	0.09
Pueblo (1)	1	0.01
Sioux	1	0.01
All other tribes	2	0.02
American Indian tribes, not spec.	6	0.06
Arab:	115	1.05
Arab/Arabic	9	0.08
Jordanian	9	0.08
Lebanese	38	0.35
Moroccan	24	0.22
Syrian	24	0.22
Other Arab	11	0.10
Asian:	205	1.91
Chinese, ex. Taiwanese (49)	62	0.58
Filipino (12)	14	0.13
Indian (51)	64	0.60
Indonesian (4)	4	0.04
Japanese (8)	12	0.11
Korean (3)	10	0.09
Malaysian (4)	5	0.05
Pakistani (1)	7	0.07
Sri Lankan (2)	2	0.02
Thai (7)	8	0.07
Vietnamese (4)	6	0.06
Other Asian, specified (1)	1	0.01
Other Asian, not specified (2)	10	0.09
Australian	10	0.09
Austrian	25	0.23
Basque	10	0.09
Belgian	67	0.61
Brazilian	12	0.11
British	69	0.63
Bulgarian	18	0.16
Czechoslovakian	22	0.20
Danish	28	0.26
Dutch	120	1.10
Eastern European	54	0.49
English	650	5.94
European	30	0.27
Finnish	19	0.17
French, except Basque	143	1.31
French Canadian	33	0.30
German	665	6.08
Greek	40	0.37
Hawaii Native/Pacific Islander:	15	0.14
Micronesian:	1	0.01
Guamanian/Chamorro	1	0.01
Polynesian: (3)	4	0.04
Native Hawaiian (2)	2	0.02
Samoan (1)	2	0.02
Other Pac. Isl., not spec. (1)	10	0.09
Hispanic or Latino:	3,692	34.37
Central American:	245	2.28
Costa Rican	23	0.21
Guatemalan	18	0.17
Honduran	33	0.31
Nicaraguan	112	1.04
Panamanian	29	0.27
Salvadoran	28	0.26
Other Central American	2	0.02
Cuban	2,103	19.58
Dominican Republic	64	0.60
Mexican	116	1.08
Puerto Rican	190	1.77
South American:	448	4.17
Argentinean	33	0.31
Bolivian	6	0.06
Chilean	25	0.23
Colombian	190	1.77
Ecuadorian	19	0.18
Paraguayan	5	0.05
Peruvian	75	0.70
Uruguayan	10	0.09
Venezuelan	81	0.75
Other South American	4	0.04
Other Hispanic or Latino	526	4.90
Hungarian	58	0.53
Iranian	10	0.09
Irish	712	6.51
Israeli	13	0.12
Italian	453	4.14
Latvian	15	0.14
Lithuanian	18	0.16
Norwegian	45	0.41
Polish	217	1.98
Portuguese	8	0.07
Romanian	9	0.08
Russian	244	2.23
Scotch-Irish	90	0.82
Scottish	205	1.87
Serbian	13	0.12
Swedish	80	0.73
Swiss	26	0.24
Turkish	20	0.18
United States or American	495	4.53
Welsh	44	0.40
West Indian, excl. Hispanic:	462	4.22
Bahamian	50	0.46
Haitian	67	0.61
Jamaican	312	2.85
Trinidadian and Tobagonian	3	0.03
West Indian	30	0.27
White:	7,675	71.46
Not Hispanic (4,174)	4,243	39.50
Hispanic (3,328)	3,432	31.95
Yugoslavian	21	0.19

South Venice

Place Type: Census Designated Place
County: Sarasota
Population: 13,539

Ancestry/Race	Number	%
African American/Black:	70	0.52
Not Hispanic (44)	57	0.42
Hispanic (10)	13	0.10
Alaska Native tribes, specified:	2	0.01
Eskimo	2	0.01
Am. Ind. or Alaska Nat., not spec.	30	0.22
American Indian tribes, specified:	59	0.44
Blackfeet	4	0.03
Cherokee (6)	18	0.13
Cheyenne	1	0.01
Chippewa (2)	3	0.02
Choctaw (2)	3	0.02
Comanche	1	0.01
Iroquois (5)	6	0.04
Latin American Indians	5	0.04
Lumbee (2)	2	0.01
Osage	1	0.01
Puget Sound Salish	1	0.01
Seminole	1	0.01
Sioux (3)	6	0.04
All other tribes	7	0.05
American Indian tribes, not spec.	2	0.01
Arab:	21	0.16
Lebanese	21	0.16
Asian:	91	0.67
Cambodian (7)	11	0.08
Chinese, ex. Taiwanese (13)	17	0.13
Filipino (24)	30	0.22
Indian (3)	3	0.02
Indonesian (1)	1	0.01
Japanese (2)	3	0.02
Korean (8)	13	0.10
Laotian (1)	1	0.01
Malaysian (1)	1	0.01
Vietnamese (6)	6	0.04
Other Asian, not specified (2)	5	0.04
Austrian	50	0.37
Belgian	89	0.66
British	25	0.19
Canadian	41	0.30
Croatian	17	0.13
Czech	40	0.30
Czechoslovakian	48	0.36
Danish	81	0.60
Dutch	306	2.26
English	2,345	17.36
European	65	0.48
Finnish	29	0.21
French, except Basque	838	6.20
French Canadian	221	1.64
German	2,807	20.78
Greek	54	0.40
Hawaii Native/Pacific Islander:	7	0.05
Polynesian: (2)	4	0.03
Native Hawaiian	2	0.01
Samoan (2)	2	0.01
Other Pac. Isl., not spec.	3	0.02
Hispanic or Latino:	236	1.74
Central American:	10	0.07
Costa Rican	3	0.02
Guatemalan	4	0.03
Honduran	1	0.01
Nicaraguan	2	0.01
Cuban	22	0.16
Dominican Republic	1	0.01
Mexican	47	0.35
Puerto Rican	63	0.47
South American:	44	0.32
Argentinean	12	0.09
Bolivian	1	0.01
Chilean	2	0.01
Colombian	11	0.08
Peruvian	12	0.09
Venezuelan	4	0.03
Other South American	2	0.01
Other Hispanic or Latino	49	0.36
Hungarian	184	1.36
Irish	2,372	17.56
Italian	1,300	9.62
Lithuanian	26	0.19
Norwegian	174	1.29
Pennsylvania German	27	0.20
Polish	697	5.16
Portuguese	26	0.19
Romanian	45	0.33
Russian	83	0.61
Scotch-Irish	278	2.06
Scottish	357	2.64
Serbian	11	0.08
Slavic	24	0.18
Slovak	22	0.16
Slovene	16	0.12
Swedish	306	2.26
Swiss	100	0.74
Turkish	8	0.06
Ukrainian	91	0.67
United States or American	1,077	7.97
Welsh	159	1.18
West Indian, excl. Hispanic:	36	0.27
Haitian	24	0.18
Trinidadian and Tobagonian	12	0.09
White:	13,319	98.38
Not Hispanic (13,066)	13,140	97.05
Hispanic (157)	179	1.32
Yugoslavian	17	0.13

Spring Hill

Place Type: Census Designated Place
County: Hernando
Population: 69,078

Ancestry/Race	Number	%
African American/Black:	2,345	3.39
Not Hispanic (1,940)	2,146	3.11
Hispanic (133)	199	0.29
African, sub-Saharan:	86	0.12
African	53	0.08
Cape Verdean	33	0.05
Alaska Native tribes, specified:	4	0.01
Alaska Athabascan (4)	4	0.01

Notes: 1. Figures in the "Number" column do not add up to the total population due to: a) Ancestry/Race overlap — e.g. persons can report being both White and Irish, b) persons of Hispanic origin can report being any race, c) persons reporting two ancestries are counted in both categories. 2. Numbers in parentheses indicate the number of persons reporting this ancestry/race alone, not in combination with any other ancestry/race. 3. Refer to the Explanation of Data in the front of the book for more detailed information.

Ancestry/Race	Number	%
Am. Ind. or Alaska Nat., not spec.	113	0.16
Albanian	12	0.02
Alsatian	9	0.01
American Indian tribes, specified:	285	0.41
Apache (5)	10	0.01
Blackfeet (4)	20	0.03
Cherokee (25)	119	0.17
Chickasaw	1	0.00
Chippewa (12)	16	0.02
Choctaw (6)	6	0.01
Cree (2)	2	0.00
Creek (2)	7	0.01
Delaware	2	0.00
Iroquois (9)	25	0.04
Kiowa (1)	1	0.00
Latin American Indians (9)	18	0.03
Lumbee (2)	4	0.01
Navajo (1)	2	0.00
Potawatomi (1)	2	0.00
Pueblo (4)	5	0.01
Seminole (1)	6	0.01
Sioux (11)	12	0.02
All other tribes (13)	27	0.04
American Indian tribes, not spec.	28	0.04
Arab:	418	0.60
Arab/Arabic	111	0.16
Egyptian	28	0.04
Iraqi	8	0.01
Lebanese	17	0.02
Syrian	239	0.35
Other Arab	15	0.02
Armenian	84	0.12
Asian:	722	1.05
Cambodian	2	0.00
Chinese, ex. Taiwanese (100)	145	0.21
Filipino (151)	199	0.29
Indian (164)	188	0.27
Indonesian (2)	3	0.00
Japanese (25)	40	0.06
Korean (27)	39	0.06
Laotian	3	0.00
Pakistani (1)	1	0.00
Taiwanese (1)	1	0.00
Thai (10)	19	0.03
Vietnamese (34)	44	0.06
Other Asian, specified	1	0.00
Other Asian, not specified (14)	37	0.05
Assyrian/Chaldean/Syriac	9	0.01
Austrian	319	0.46
Belgian	128	0.18
Brazilian	50	0.07
British	276	0.40
Canadian	294	0.42
Carpatho Rusyn	7	0.01
Croatian	75	0.11
Czech	294	0.42
Czechoslovakian	327	0.47
Danish	223	0.32
Dutch	1,524	2.20
Eastern European	39	0.06
English	7,629	11.03
European	96	0.14
Finnish	118	0.17
French, except Basque	2,582	3.73
French Canadian	983	1.42
German	13,617	19.68
Greek	391	0.57
Guyanese	31	0.04
Hawaii Native/Pacific Islander:	49	0.07
Micronesian: (3)	7	0.01
Guamanian/Chamorro (3)	7	0.01
Polynesian: (11)	23	0.03
Native Hawaiian (5)	16	0.02
Samoan (5)	6	0.01
Tongan (1)	1	0.00
Other Pac. Isl., specified	1	0.00
Other Pac. Isl., not spec. (1)	18	0.03
Hispanic or Latino:	4,720	6.83
Central American:	139	0.20
Costa Rican	11	0.02
Guatemalan	15	0.02
Honduran	23	0.03
Nicaraguan	9	0.01
Panamanian	43	0.06
Salvadoran	30	0.04
Other Central American	8	0.01
Cuban	276	0.40
Dominican Republic	76	0.11
Mexican	310	0.45
Puerto Rican	3,067	4.44
South American:	224	0.32
Argentinean	13	0.02
Chilean	8	0.01
Colombian	118	0.17
Ecuadorian	21	0.03
Peruvian	21	0.03
Uruguayan	3	0.00
Venezuelan	20	0.03
Other South American	20	0.03
Other Hispanic or Latino	628	0.91
Hungarian	744	1.08
Irish	11,765	17.00
Italian	12,431	17.96
Latvian	47	0.07
Lithuanian	388	0.56
Luxemburger	7	0.01
Macedonian	25	0.04
Maltese	20	0.03
Northern European	19	0.03
Norwegian	694	1.00
Pennsylvania German	132	0.19
Polish	4,108	5.94
Portuguese	410	0.59
Romanian	85	0.12
Russian	635	0.92
Scandinavian	119	0.17
Scotch-Irish	1,214	1.75
Scottish	1,232	1.78
Serbian	25	0.04
Slavic	44	0.06
Slovak	320	0.46
Slovene	72	0.10
Swedish	1,131	1.63
Swiss	182	0.26
Turkish	10	0.01
Ukrainian	444	0.64
United States or American	3,631	5.25
Welsh	520	0.75
West Indian, excl. Hispanic:	431	0.62
Belizean	7	0.01
Bermudan	9	0.01
British West Indian	2	0.00
Haitian	25	0.04
Jamaican	253	0.37
Trinidadian and Tobagonian	53	0.08
West Indian	82	0.12
White:	65,304	94.54
Not Hispanic (61,097)	61,575	89.14
Hispanic (3,494)	3,729	5.40
Yugoslavian	9	0.01

Stuart

Place Type: City
County: Martin
Population: 14,633

Ancestry/Race	Number	%
African American/Black:	1,892	12.93
Not Hispanic (1,793)	1,848	12.63
Hispanic (11)	44	0.30
African, sub-Saharan:	36	0.24
African	25	0.17
Nigerian	11	0.07
Alaska Native tribes, specified:	2	0.01
Tlingit-Haida (2)	2	0.01
Am. Ind. or Alaska Nat., not spec.	33	0.23
American Indian tribes, specified:	59	0.40
Apache	1	0.01
Blackfeet	1	0.01
Cherokee (5)	21	0.14
Chippewa	1	0.01
Choctaw (2)	2	0.01
Comanche	1	0.01
Creek	3	0.02
Latin American Indians (15)	25	0.17
Seminole	1	0.01
All other tribes (3)	3	0.02
American Indian tribes, not spec.	1	0.01
Asian:	129	0.88
Chinese, ex. Taiwanese (20)	25	0.17
Filipino (16)	25	0.17
Indian (20)	27	0.18
Japanese (8)	16	0.11
Korean (13)	14	0.10
Pakistani	3	0.02
Taiwanese (1)	1	0.01
Thai (1)	1	0.01
Vietnamese (11)	11	0.08
Other Asian, not specified (1)	6	0.04
Austrian	68	0.46
Basque	8	0.05
Belgian	15	0.10
British	38	0.26
Canadian	40	0.27
Czech	48	0.33
Czechoslovakian	22	0.15
Danish	70	0.48
Dutch	194	1.32
English	2,095	14.23
European	26	0.18
Finnish	12	0.08
French, except Basque	615	4.18
French Canadian	297	2.02
German	2,164	14.70
Greek	30	0.20
Hawaii Native/Pacific Islander:	24	0.16
Micronesian: (3)	12	0.08
Guamanian/Chamorro (3)	12	0.08
Polynesian: (1)	6	0.04
Native Hawaiian	3	0.02
Samoan (1)	3	0.02
Other Pac. Isl., not spec. (1)	6	0.04
Hispanic or Latino:	920	6.29
Central American:	242	1.65
Costa Rican	2	0.01
Guatemalan	186	1.27
Honduran	41	0.28
Salvadoran	9	0.06
Other Central American	4	0.03
Cuban	98	0.67
Dominican Republic	13	0.09
Mexican	181	1.24
Puerto Rican	202	1.38
South American:	52	0.36
Argentinean	5	0.03
Chilean	4	0.03
Colombian	25	0.17
Ecuadorian	2	0.01
Peruvian	7	0.05
Uruguayan	2	0.01
Venezuelan	4	0.03
Other South American	3	0.02
Other Hispanic or Latino	132	0.90
Hungarian	149	1.01
Iranian	9	0.06
Irish	2,318	15.74
Israeli	9	0.06
Italian	1,464	9.94
Latvian	14	0.10
Lithuanian	63	0.43
Norwegian	135	0.92
Pennsylvania German	9	0.06
Polish	378	2.57
Portuguese	89	0.60
Romanian	6	0.04
Russian	116	0.79
Scandinavian	77	0.52
Scotch-Irish	363	2.47
Scottish	268	1.82

Notes: 1. Figures in the "Number" column do not add up to the total population due to: a) Ancestry/Race overlap — e.g. persons can report being both White and Irish, b) persons of Hispanic origin can report being any race, c) persons reporting two ancestries are counted in both categories. 2. Numbers in parentheses indicate the number of persons reporting this ancestry/race alone, not in combination with any other ancestry/race. 3. Refer to the Explanation of Data in the front of the book for more detailed information.

Ancestry/Race	Number	%
Serbian	9	0.06
Slovak	27	0.18
Slovene	25	0.17
Swedish	167	1.13
Swiss	91	0.62
Turkish	6	0.04
Ukrainian	72	0.49
United States or American	815	5.53
Welsh	218	1.48
West Indian, excl. Hispanic:	120	0.81
Bahamian	35	0.24
Haitian	36	0.24
Jamaican	29	0.20
Trinidadian and Tobagonian	12	0.08
West Indian	8	0.05
White:	12,331	84.27
Not Hispanic (11,659)	11,759	80.36
Hispanic (530)	572	3.91

Sunny Isles Beach

Place Type: City
County: Miami-Dade
Population: 15,315

Ancestry/Race	Number	%
African American/Black:	344	2.25
Not Hispanic (271)	293	1.91
Hispanic (40)	51	0.33
African, sub-Saharan:	169	1.11
African	107	0.70
Ethiopian	24	0.16
South African	38	0.25
Alaska Native tribes, specified:	1	0.01
Tlingit-Haida	1	0.01
Am. Ind. or Alaska Nat., not spec.	29	0.19
Albanian	24	0.16
American Indian tribes, specified:	14	0.09
Cherokee	1	0.01
Chippewa	2	0.01
Crow (1)	1	0.01
Iroquois (1)	1	0.01
Latin American Indians (3)	6	0.04
Seminole (1)	1	0.01
All other tribes	2	0.01
American Indian tribes, not spec.	7	0.05
Arab:	380	2.49
Arab/Arabic	88	0.58
Egyptian	87	0.57
Lebanese	28	0.18
Moroccan	108	0.71
Syrian	57	0.37
Other Arab	12	0.08
Asian:	272	1.78
Chinese, ex. Taiwanese (56)	73	0.48
Filipino (30)	33	0.22
Indian (37)	42	0.27
Indonesian (8)	9	0.06
Japanese (27)	31	0.20
Korean (13)	17	0.11
Malaysian	1	0.01
Pakistani (14)	14	0.09
Taiwanese (5)	5	0.03
Thai (3)	4	0.03
Vietnamese (6)	10	0.07
Other Asian, specified (1)	5	0.03
Other Asian, not specified (3)	28	0.18
Austrian	99	0.65
Belgian	11	0.07
Brazilian	222	1.45
British	189	1.24
Bulgarian	34	0.22
Canadian	123	0.81
Czech	31	0.20
Czechoslovakian	55	0.36
Dutch	52	0.34
Eastern European	55	0.36
English	322	2.11
Estonian	25	0.16
European	143	0.94
French, except Basque	238	1.56
French Canadian	177	1.16
German	419	2.74
Greek	82	0.54
Hawaii Native/Pacific Islander:	13	0.08
Micronesian:	1	0.01
Guamanian/Chamorro	1	0.01
Polynesian:	1	0.01
Samoan	1	0.01
Other Pac. Isl., specified	3	0.02
Other Pac. Isl., not spec. (1)	8	0.05
Hispanic or Latino:	5,607	36.61
Central American:	163	1.06
Costa Rican	31	0.20
Guatemalan	23	0.15
Honduran	19	0.12
Nicaraguan	39	0.25
Panamanian	18	0.12
Salvadoran	30	0.20
Other Central American	3	0.02
Cuban	1,493	9.75
Dominican Republic	83	0.54
Mexican	135	0.88
Puerto Rican	322	2.10
South American:	2,150	14.04
Argentinean	371	2.42
Bolivian	26	0.17
Chilean	93	0.61
Colombian	930	6.07
Ecuadorian	81	0.53
Paraguayan	12	0.08
Peruvian	271	1.77
Uruguayan	29	0.19
Venezuelan	300	1.96
Other South American	37	0.24
Other Hispanic or Latino	1,261	8.23
Hungarian	124	0.81
Iranian	30	0.20
Irish	450	2.95
Israeli	260	1.70
Italian	895	5.86
Latvian	39	0.26
Lithuanian	79	0.52
Norwegian	30	0.20
Polish	770	5.04
Portuguese	68	0.45
Romanian	219	1.43
Russian	1,447	9.47
Scotch-Irish	93	0.61
Scottish	52	0.34
Swedish	39	0.26
Swiss	67	0.44
Turkish	59	0.39
Ukrainian	203	1.33
United States or American	753	4.93
Welsh	12	0.08
West Indian, excl. Hispanic:	159	1.04
British West Indian	16	0.10
Haitian	92	0.60
Jamaican	51	0.33
White:	14,383	93.91
Not Hispanic (9,010)	9,167	59.86
Hispanic (5,057)	5,216	34.06
Yugoslavian	9	0.06

Sunrise

Place Type: City
County: Broward
Population: 85,779

Ancestry/Race	Number	%
African American/Black:	18,825	21.95
Not Hispanic (17,176)	18,258	21.28
Hispanic (381)	567	0.66
African, sub-Saharan:	331	0.39
African	231	0.27
Cape Verdean	23	0.03
Nigerian	31	0.04
South African	46	0.05
Alaska Native tribes, specified:	5	0.01
Alaska Athabascan (1)	1	0.00
Aleut (1)	1	0.00
Tlingit-Haida	3	0.00
Alaska Native tribes, not specified	2	0.00
Am. Ind. or Alaska Nat., not spec.	133	0.16
Albanian	40	0.05
American Indian tribes, specified:	177	0.21
Apache (5)	7	0.01
Blackfeet (1)	6	0.01
Cherokee (22)	57	0.07
Chickasaw (1)	1	0.00
Chippewa (7)	8	0.01
Cree	1	0.00
Creek	5	0.01
Delaware (2)	3	0.00
Iroquois (8)	13	0.02
Latin American Indians (16)	35	0.04
Lumbee	2	0.00
Navajo	1	0.00
Pueblo (1)	4	0.00
Seminole (5)	6	0.01
Sioux (1)	4	0.00
Ute	4	0.00
All other tribes (5)	20	0.02
American Indian tribes, not spec.	18	0.02
Arab:	602	0.70
Arab/Arabic	17	0.02
Egyptian	25	0.03
Jordanian	43	0.05
Lebanese	282	0.33
Moroccan	26	0.03
Palestinian	61	0.07
Syrian	123	0.14
Other Arab	25	0.03
Armenian	77	0.09
Asian:	3,294	3.84
Bangladeshi (15)	22	0.03
Cambodian (1)	3	0.00
Chinese, ex. Taiwanese (682)	832	0.97
Filipino (323)	396	0.46
Indian (1,037)	1,217	1.42
Indonesian (9)	19	0.02
Japanese (42)	81	0.09
Korean (109)	136	0.16
Laotian (5)	5	0.01
Pakistani (147)	187	0.22
Sri Lankan (5)	5	0.01
Taiwanese (6)	8	0.01
Thai (45)	67	0.08
Vietnamese (150)	158	0.18
Other Asian, specified (1)	10	0.01
Other Asian, not specified (36)	148	0.17
Australian	12	0.01
Austrian	573	0.67
Belgian	99	0.12
Brazilian	617	0.72
British	422	0.49
Bulgarian	7	0.01
Canadian	327	0.38
Croatian	99	0.12
Czech	210	0.25
Czechoslovakian	130	0.15
Danish	119	0.14
Dutch	602	0.70
Eastern European	91	0.11
English	3,779	4.41
Estonian	19	0.02
European	344	0.40
Finnish	13	0.02
French, except Basque	1,562	1.82
French Canadian	382	0.45
German	6,357	7.42
Greek	253	0.30
Guyanese	218	0.25
Hawaii Native/Pacific Islander:	228	0.27
Micronesian: (4)	11	0.01
Guamanian/Chamorro (3)	8	0.01
Other Micronesian (1)	3	0.00
Polynesian: (17)	39	0.05

Notes: 1. Figures in the "Number" column do not add up to the total population due to: a) Ancestry/Race overlap — e.g. persons can report being both White and Irish, b) persons of Hispanic origin can report being any race, c) persons reporting two ancestries are counted in both categories. 2. Numbers in parentheses indicate the number of persons reporting this ancestry/race alone, not in combination with any other ancestry/race. 3. Refer to the Explanation of Data in the front of the book for more detailed information.

Native Hawaiian (7)	21	0.02
Samoan (10)	18	0.02
Other Pac. Isl., specified	4	0.00
Other Pac. Isl., not spec. (40)	174	0.20
Hispanic or Latino:	14,655	17.08
Central American:	784	0.91
Costa Rican	97	0.11
Guatemalan	76	0.09
Honduran	142	0.17
Nicaraguan	132	0.15
Panamanian	135	0.16
Salvadoran	158	0.18
Other Central American	44	0.05
Cuban	1,965	2.29
Dominican Republic	573	0.67
Mexican	570	0.66
Puerto Rican	3,223	3.76
South American:	4,320	5.04
Argentinean	233	0.27
Bolivian	40	0.05
Chilean	134	0.16
Colombian	2,090	2.44
Ecuadorian	392	0.46
Paraguayan	3	0.00
Peruvian	688	0.80
Uruguayan	92	0.11
Venezuelan	543	0.63
Other South American	105	0.12
Other Hispanic or Latino	3,220	3.75
Hungarian	679	0.79
Iranian	252	0.29
Irish	6,368	7.44
Israeli	434	0.51
Italian	8,815	10.29
Latvian	39	0.05
Lithuanian	252	0.29
Luxemburger	37	0.04
Macedonian	13	0.02
Maltese	25	0.03
Norwegian	287	0.34
Pennsylvania German	13	0.02
Polish	3,758	4.39
Portuguese	397	0.46
Romanian	559	0.65
Russian	3,533	4.13
Scandinavian	106	0.12
Scotch-Irish	590	0.69
Scottish	865	1.01
Slovak	169	0.20
Slovene	31	0.04
Swedish	466	0.54
Swiss	70	0.08
Turkish	140	0.16
Ukrainian	372	0.43
United States or American	5,325	6.22
Welsh	217	0.25
West Indian, excl. Hispanic:	11,027	12.88
Bahamian	227	0.27
Barbadian	74	0.09
Belizean	21	0.02
Bermudan	30	0.04
British West Indian	172	0.20
Haitian	2,524	2.95
Jamaican	6,888	8.04
Trinidadian and Tobagonian	694	0.81
U.S. Virgin Islander	47	0.05
West Indian	337	0.39
Other West Indian	13	0.02
White:	61,323	71.49
Not Hispanic (48,863)	49,791	58.05
Hispanic (10,734)	11,532	13.44
Yugoslavian	74	0.09

Sunset

Place Type: Census Designated Place
County: Miami-Dade
Population: 17,150

Ancestry/Race	Number	%
African American/Black:	317	1.85
Not Hispanic (193)	215	1.25
Hispanic (66)	102	0.59
Am. Ind. or Alaska Nat., not spec.	25	0.15
American Indian tribes, specified:	22	0.13
Blackfeet	1	0.01
Cherokee (1)	4	0.02
Chippewa	1	0.01
Creek (5)	5	0.03
Crow	1	0.01
Iroquois	2	0.01
Latin American Indians (4)	8	0.05
American Indian tribes, not spec.	6	0.03
Arab:	230	1.34
Arab/Arabic	92	0.54
Lebanese	128	0.75
Palestinian	10	0.06
Asian:	513	2.99
Chinese, ex. Taiwanese (188)	230	1.34
Filipino (31)	55	0.32
Hmong (1)	1	0.01
Indian (105)	112	0.65
Japanese (8)	24	0.14
Korean (6)	7	0.04
Laotian (7)	8	0.05
Pakistani (9)	13	0.08
Sri Lankan (4)	4	0.02
Thai (10)	11	0.06
Vietnamese (30)	36	0.21
Other Asian, not specified (8)	12	0.07
Austrian	28	0.16
Basque	6	0.04
Belgian	18	0.11
Brazilian	55	0.32
British	88	0.51
Canadian	30	0.18
Croatian	7	0.04
Czech	16	0.09
Czechoslovakian	10	0.06
Danish	13	0.08
Dutch	117	0.68
English	552	3.23
European	20	0.12
French, except Basque	199	1.16
French Canadian	6	0.04
German	795	4.65
Greek	41	0.24
Hawaii Native/Pacific Islander:	8	0.05
Polynesian:	2	0.01
Native Hawaiian	1	0.01
Samoan	1	0.01
Other Pac. Isl., not spec.	6	0.03
Hispanic or Latino:	11,952	69.69
Central American:	644	3.76
Costa Rican	25	0.15
Guatemalan	32	0.19
Honduran	96	0.56
Nicaraguan	370	2.16
Panamanian	45	0.26
Salvadoran	56	0.33
Other Central American	20	0.12
Cuban	7,989	46.58
Dominican Republic	119	0.69
Mexican	220	1.28
Puerto Rican	432	2.52
South American:	1,162	6.78
Argentinean	88	0.51
Bolivian	37	0.22
Chilean	54	0.31
Colombian	459	2.68
Ecuadorian	88	0.51
Paraguayan	1	0.01
Peruvian	248	1.45
Uruguayan	9	0.05
Venezuelan	146	0.85
Other South American	32	0.19
Other Hispanic or Latino	1,386	8.08
Hungarian	145	0.85
Iranian	53	0.31
Irish	599	3.50
Italian	644	3.76
Latvian	4	0.02
Lithuanian	28	0.16
Norwegian	6	0.04
Polish	136	0.79
Romanian	22	0.13
Russian	171	1.00
Scotch-Irish	80	0.47
Scottish	182	1.06
Slovak	7	0.04
Swedish	47	0.27
Swiss	5	0.03
Turkish	6	0.04
Ukrainian	5	0.03
United States or American	588	3.44
Welsh	7	0.04
West Indian, excl. Hispanic:	102	0.60
Bahamian	4	0.02
Haitian	75	0.44
Jamaican	23	0.13
White:	15,991	93.24
Not Hispanic (4,468)	4,564	26.61
Hispanic (11,179)	11,427	66.63

Sweetwater

Place Type: City
County: Miami-Dade
Population: 14,226

Ancestry/Race	Number	%
African American/Black:	156	1.10
Not Hispanic (14)	15	0.11
Hispanic (112)	141	0.99
African, sub-Saharan:	56	0.39
African	4	0.03
Nigerian	52	0.36
Am. Ind. or Alaska Nat., not spec.	38	0.27
American Indian tribes, specified:	11	0.08
Choctaw	1	0.01
Latin American Indians (9)	9	0.06
Osage (1)	1	0.01
American Indian tribes, not spec.	1	0.01
Arab:	29	0.20
Jordanian	24	0.17
Lebanese	5	0.04
Asian:	41	0.29
Chinese, ex. Taiwanese (13)	18	0.13
Filipino (2)	8	0.06
Indian (5)	6	0.04
Korean (1)	2	0.01
Pakistani (7)	7	0.05
Canadian	29	0.20
English	51	0.36
French, except Basque	29	0.20
French Canadian	12	0.08
German	40	0.28
Greek	16	0.11
Hawaii Native/Pacific Islander:	6	0.04
Polynesian: (2)	2	0.01
Native Hawaiian (2)	2	0.01
Other Pac. Isl., not spec.	4	0.03
Hispanic or Latino:	13,253	93.16
Central American:	2,818	19.81
Costa Rican	33	0.23
Guatemalan	49	0.34
Honduran	187	1.31
Nicaraguan	2,366	16.63
Panamanian	41	0.29
Salvadoran	74	0.52
Other Central American	68	0.48
Cuban	7,101	49.92
Dominican Republic	133	0.93
Mexican	69	0.49
Puerto Rican	286	2.01
South American:	582	4.09
Argentinean	32	0.22
Bolivian	4	0.03
Chilean	50	0.35
Colombian	244	1.72

Notes: 1. Figures in the "Number" column do not add up to the total population due to: a) Ancestry/Race overlap — e.g. persons can report being both White and Irish, b) persons of Hispanic origin can report being any race, c) persons reporting two ancestries are counted in both categories. 2. Numbers in parentheses indicate the number of persons reporting this ancestry/race alone, not in combination with any other ancestry/race. 3. Refer to the Explanation of Data in the front of the book for more detailed information.

Ancestry/Race	Number	%
Ecuadorian	56	0.39
Paraguayan	2	0.01
Peruvian	92	0.65
Uruguayan	5	0.04
Venezuelan	89	0.63
Other South American	8	0.06
Other Hispanic or Latino	2,264	15.91
Irish	59	0.41
Italian	71	0.50
Polish	10	0.07
Swiss	13	0.09
United States or American	330	2.31
Welsh	9	0.06
West Indian, excl. Hispanic:	14	0.10
Haitian	14	0.10
White:	12,984	91.27
Not Hispanic (884)	928	6.52
Hispanic (11,514)	12,056	84.75

Tallahassee

Place Type: City
County: Leon
Population: 150,624

Ancestry/Race	Number	%
Acadian/Cajun	70	0.05
African American/Black:	52,611	34.93
Not Hispanic (51,025)	51,926	34.47
Hispanic (544)	685	0.45
African, sub-Saharan:	2,240	1.49
African	1,726	1.15
Cape Verdean	8	0.01
Ethiopian	28	0.02
Ghanian	82	0.05
Kenyan	8	0.01
Nigerian	250	0.17
South African	18	0.01
Other sub-Saharan African	120	0.08
Alaska Native tribes, specified:	14	0.01
Aleut (4)	4	0.00
Eskimo (2)	9	0.01
All other tribes (1)	1	0.00
Am. Ind. or Alaska Nat., not spec.	333	0.22
Albanian	6	0.00
Alsatian	8	0.01
American Indian tribes, specified:	595	0.40
Apache (10)	23	0.02
Blackfeet (3)	15	0.01
Cherokee (65)	237	0.16
Cheyenne (1)	2	0.00
Chickasaw (1)	4	0.00
Chippewa (3)	7	0.00
Choctaw (6)	17	0.01
Comanche (2)	5	0.00
Cree (1)	1	0.00
Creek (58)	107	0.07
Delaware (7)	9	0.01
Houma (2)	2	0.00
Iroquois (10)	23	0.02
Kiowa (2)	2	0.00
Latin American Indians (9)	34	0.02
Lumbee (7)	8	0.01
Menominee (2)	3	0.00
Navajo (4)	7	0.00
Osage (1)	1	0.00
Ottawa (1)	1	0.00
Potawatomi (2)	2	0.00
Pueblo (2)	6	0.00
Seminole (7)	22	0.01
Sioux (5)	21	0.01
All other tribes (11)	36	0.02
American Indian tribes, not spec.	58	0.04
Arab:	651	0.43
Arab/Arabic	135	0.09
Egyptian	51	0.03
Jordanian	16	0.01
Lebanese	303	0.20
Moroccan	18	0.01
Syrian	79	0.05
Other Arab	49	0.03
Armenian	29	0.02
Asian:	4,417	2.93
Bangladeshi (9)	14	0.01
Cambodian (17)	18	0.01
Chinese, ex. Taiwanese (983)	1,118	0.74
Filipino (345)	489	0.32
Hmong (4)	4	0.00
Indian (1,010)	1,098	0.73
Indonesian (12)	14	0.01
Japanese (183)	306	0.20
Korean (446)	508	0.34
Laotian (5)	5	0.00
Malaysian (4)	8	0.01
Pakistani (46)	61	0.04
Sri Lankan (5)	7	0.00
Taiwanese (75)	106	0.07
Thai (56)	81	0.05
Vietnamese (255)	305	0.20
Other Asian, specified (3)	38	0.03
Other Asian, not specified (127)	237	0.16
Australian	86	0.06
Austrian	292	0.19
Belgian	134	0.09
Brazilian	62	0.04
British	1,136	0.75
Bulgarian	52	0.03
Canadian	347	0.23
Carpatho Rusyn	8	0.01
Celtic	125	0.08
Croatian	94	0.06
Czech	228	0.15
Czechoslovakian	140	0.09
Danish	421	0.28
Dutch	1,586	1.05
Eastern European	149	0.10
English	13,888	9.22
Estonian	7	0.00
European	1,416	0.94
Finnish	130	0.09
French, except Basque	3,382	2.25
French Canadian	660	0.44
German	14,091	9.36
Greek	772	0.51
Guyanese	116	0.08
Hawaii Native/Pacific Islander:	224	0.15
Melanesian:	1	0.00
Other Melanesian	1	0.00
Micronesian: (24)	32	0.02
Guamanian/Chamorro (21)	29	0.02
Other Micronesian (3)	3	0.00
Polynesian: (40)	91	0.06
Native Hawaiian (16)	52	0.03
Samoan (20)	32	0.02
Tongan (2)	2	0.00
Other Polynesian (2)	5	0.00
Other Pac. Isl., specified	21	0.01
Other Pac. Isl., not spec. (18)	79	0.05
Hispanic or Latino:	6,309	4.19
Central American:	437	0.29
Costa Rican	51	0.03
Guatemalan	36	0.02
Honduran	60	0.04
Nicaraguan	97	0.06
Panamanian	130	0.09
Salvadoran	45	0.03
Other Central American	18	0.01
Cuban	1,338	0.89
Dominican Republic	131	0.09
Mexican	1,102	0.73
Puerto Rican	1,302	0.86
South American:	741	0.49
Argentinean	60	0.04
Bolivian	29	0.02
Chilean	28	0.02
Colombian	365	0.24
Ecuadorian	52	0.03
Paraguayan	12	0.01
Peruvian	83	0.06
Uruguayan	8	0.01
Venezuelan	92	0.06
Other South American	12	0.01
Other Hispanic or Latino	1,258	0.84
Hungarian	503	0.33
Icelander	90	0.06
Iranian	64	0.04
Irish	13,276	8.82
Israeli	79	0.05
Italian	5,035	3.34
Latvian	39	0.03
Lithuanian	201	0.13
Luxemburger	7	0.00
Maltese	19	0.01
New Zealander	4	0.00
Northern European	84	0.06
Norwegian	961	0.64
Pennsylvania German	16	0.01
Polish	2,264	1.50
Portuguese	221	0.15
Romanian	181	0.12
Russian	1,128	0.75
Scandinavian	189	0.13
Scotch-Irish	3,309	2.20
Scottish	3,513	2.33
Serbian	41	0.03
Slavic	11	0.01
Slovak	217	0.14
Slovene	19	0.01
Swedish	1,110	0.74
Swiss	339	0.23
Turkish	108	0.07
Ukrainian	294	0.20
United States or American	7,976	5.30
Welsh	1,061	0.70
West Indian, excl. Hispanic:	2,340	1.55
Bahamian	187	0.12
Barbadian	32	0.02
Belizean	26	0.02
Bermudan	13	0.01
British West Indian	111	0.07
Dutch West Indian	6	0.00
Haitian	512	0.34
Jamaican	1,045	0.69
Trinidadian and Tobagonian	105	0.07
U.S. Virgin Islander	153	0.10
West Indian	132	0.09
Other West Indian	18	0.01
White:	92,887	61.67
Not Hispanic (87,047)	88,527	58.77
Hispanic (3,960)	4,360	2.89
Yugoslavian	38	0.03

Tamarac

Place Type: City
County: Broward
Population: 55,588

Ancestry/Race	Number	%
African American/Black:	6,460	11.62
Not Hispanic (5,623)	6,150	11.06
Hispanic (222)	310	0.56
African, sub-Saharan:	333	0.59
African	333	0.59
Alaska Native tribes, specified:	3	0.01
Aleut (1)	1	0.00
Eskimo	2	0.00
Am. Ind. or Alaska Nat., not spec.	88	0.16
Albanian	7	0.01
American Indian tribes, specified:	113	0.20
Apache (4)	6	0.01
Blackfeet (2)	3	0.01
Cherokee (7)	41	0.07
Chippewa (2)	4	0.01
Choctaw	1	0.00
Crow (1)	1	0.00
Iroquois (1)	7	0.01
Latin American Indians (10)	22	0.04
Lumbee	1	0.00
Ottawa (3)	3	0.01

Notes: 1. Figures in the "Number" column do not add up to the total population due to: a) Ancestry/Race overlap — e.g. persons can report being both White and Irish, b) persons of Hispanic origin can report being any race, c) persons reporting two ancestries are counted in both categories. 2. Numbers in parentheses indicate the number of persons reporting this ancestry/race alone, not in combination with any other ancestry/race. 3. Refer to the Explanation of Data in the front of the book for more detailed information.

Pueblo (2)	5	0.01
Seminole (2)	3	0.01
Sioux (3)	4	0.01
All other tribes (7)	12	0.02
American Indian tribes, not spec.	11	0.02
Arab:	222	0.40
Egyptian	43	0.08
Lebanese	108	0.19
Moroccan	19	0.03
Palestinian	19	0.03
Syrian	9	0.02
Other Arab	24	0.04
Armenian	7	0.01
Asian:	1,076	1.94
Bangladeshi (5)	5	0.01
Chinese, ex. Taiwanese (241)	303	0.55
Filipino (87)	116	0.21
Indian (293)	370	0.67
Indonesian (4)	5	0.01
Japanese (19)	30	0.05
Korean (53)	55	0.10
Pakistani (12)	31	0.06
Sri Lankan (3)	3	0.01
Taiwanese (4)	4	0.01
Thai (9)	14	0.03
Vietnamese (65)	85	0.15
Other Asian, specified	4	0.01
Other Asian, not specified (10)	51	0.09
Australian	51	0.09
Austrian	862	1.54
Basque	25	0.04
Belgian	54	0.10
Brazilian	164	0.29
British	145	0.26
Canadian	282	0.50
Croatian	17	0.03
Czech	78	0.14
Czechoslovakian	78	0.14
Danish	91	0.16
Dutch	511	0.91
Eastern European	177	0.32
English	2,706	4.83
European	305	0.54
Finnish	22	0.04
French, except Basque	1,233	2.20
French Canadian	273	0.49
German	4,326	7.71
Greek	217	0.39
Guyanese	31	0.06
Hawaii Native/Pacific Islander:	103	0.19
Micronesian: (4)	5	0.01
Guamanian/Chamorro (4)	5	0.01
Polynesian: (13)	17	0.03
Native Hawaiian (7)	10	0.02
Samoan (6)	6	0.01
Other Polynesian	1	0.00
Other Pac. Isl., specified	3	0.01
Other Pac. Isl., not spec. (3)	78	0.14
Hispanic or Latino:	8,274	14.88
Central American:	408	0.73
Costa Rican	55	0.10
Guatemalan	36	0.06
Honduran	130	0.23
Nicaraguan	53	0.10
Panamanian	55	0.10
Salvadoran	61	0.11
Other Central American	18	0.03
Cuban	790	1.42
Dominican Republic	263	0.47
Mexican	507	0.91
Puerto Rican	1,955	3.52
South American:	2,496	4.49
Argentinean	112	0.20
Bolivian	9	0.02
Chilean	51	0.09
Colombian	1,523	2.74
Ecuadorian	155	0.28
Peruvian	342	0.62
Uruguayan	32	0.06
Venezuelan	195	0.35
Other South American	77	0.14
Other Hispanic or Latino	1,855	3.34
Hungarian	725	1.29
Iranian	76	0.14
Irish	4,432	7.90
Israeli	122	0.22
Italian	6,122	10.92
Latvian	49	0.09
Lithuanian	159	0.28
Macedonian	11	0.02
Norwegian	232	0.41
Pennsylvania German	22	0.04
Polish	2,795	4.98
Portuguese	159	0.28
Romanian	452	0.81
Russian	3,431	6.12
Scotch-Irish	345	0.62
Scottish	427	0.76
Serbian	22	0.04
Slavic	10	0.02
Slovak	157	0.28
Slovene	24	0.04
Swedish	324	0.58
Swiss	123	0.22
Turkish	65	0.12
Ukrainian	293	0.52
United States or American	5,079	9.06
Welsh	110	0.20
West Indian, excl. Hispanic:	3,834	6.84
Bahamian	58	0.10
Barbadian	16	0.03
Belizean	59	0.11
British West Indian	72	0.13
Haitian	809	1.44
Jamaican	2,398	4.28
Trinidadian and Tobagonian	271	0.48
West Indian	151	0.27
White:	46,694	84.00
Not Hispanic (39,688)	40,225	72.36
Hispanic (5,937)	6,469	11.64
Yugoslavian	96	0.17

Tamiami

Place Type: Census Designated Place
County: Miami-Dade
Population: 54,788

Ancestry/Race	Number	%
African American/Black:	599	1.09
Not Hispanic (189)	209	0.38
Hispanic (297)	390	0.71
African, sub-Saharan:	62	0.11
African	24	0.04
Nigerian	31	0.06
Other sub-Saharan African	7	0.01
Am. Ind. or Alaska Nat., not spec.	47	0.09
American Indian tribes, specified:	44	0.08
Cherokee (4)	6	0.01
Choctaw	1	0.00
Iroquois	2	0.00
Latin American Indians (14)	27	0.05
Paiute	1	0.00
Sioux (1)	1	0.00
All other tribes (1)	6	0.01
American Indian tribes, not spec.	15	0.03
Arab:	425	0.78
Arab/Arabic	74	0.14
Lebanese	229	0.42
Palestinian	27	0.05
Syrian	95	0.17
Armenian	11	0.02
Asian:	415	0.76
Bangladeshi	1	0.00
Chinese, ex. Taiwanese (122)	159	0.29
Filipino (45)	46	0.08
Indian (75)	97	0.18
Indonesian (1)	1	0.00
Japanese (11)	17	0.03
Korean (8)	8	0.01
Malaysian (3)	3	0.01
Pakistani (11)	17	0.03
Taiwanese (15)	24	0.04
Vietnamese (15)	17	0.03
Other Asian, specified (1)	1	0.00
Other Asian, not specified (10)	24	0.04
Austrian	30	0.05
Basque	14	0.03
Brazilian	91	0.17
British	47	0.09
Bulgarian	15	0.03
Canadian	43	0.08
Czech	12	0.02
Czechoslovakian	7	0.01
Danish	9	0.02
Dutch	44	0.08
English	466	0.85
European	120	0.22
French, except Basque	397	0.73
German	475	0.87
Greek	76	0.14
Guyanese	12	0.02
Hawaii Native/Pacific Islander:	18	0.03
Micronesian: (2)	2	0.00
Guamanian/Chamorro (2)	2	0.00
Other Pac. Isl., not spec. (8)	16	0.03
Hispanic or Latino:	47,654	86.98
Central American:	3,451	6.30
Costa Rican	97	0.18
Guatemalan	122	0.22
Honduran	358	0.65
Nicaraguan	2,551	4.66
Panamanian	142	0.26
Salvadoran	86	0.16
Other Central American	95	0.17
Cuban	31,029	56.63
Dominican Republic	836	1.53
Mexican	377	0.69
Puerto Rican	1,382	2.52
South American:	4,322	7.89
Argentinean	251	0.46
Bolivian	82	0.15
Chilean	262	0.48
Colombian	2,161	3.94
Ecuadorian	322	0.59
Paraguayan	7	0.01
Peruvian	526	0.96
Uruguayan	56	0.10
Venezuelan	583	1.06
Other South American	72	0.13
Other Hispanic or Latino	6,257	11.42
Hungarian	24	0.04
Iranian	27	0.05
Irish	483	0.88
Italian	733	1.34
Polish	89	0.16
Portuguese	89	0.16
Romanian	37	0.07
Russian	99	0.18
Scotch-Irish	56	0.10
Scottish	33	0.06
Slavic	10	0.02
Swedish	49	0.09
Swiss	41	0.07
Turkish	68	0.12
Ukrainian	9	0.02
United States or American	1,052	1.92
Welsh	14	0.03
West Indian, excl. Hispanic:	93	0.17
Belizean	5	0.01
Haitian	8	0.01
Jamaican	80	0.15
White:	51,161	93.38
Not Hispanic (6,445)	6,589	12.03
Hispanic (43,174)	44,572	81.35
Yugoslavian	7	0.01

Notes: 1. Figures in the "Number" column do not add up to the total population due to: a) Ancestry/Race overlap — e.g. persons can report being both White and Irish, b) persons of Hispanic origin can report being any race, c) persons reporting two ancestries are counted in both categories. 2. Numbers in parentheses indicate the number of persons reporting this ancestry/race alone, not in combination with any other ancestry/race. 3. Refer to the Explanation of Data in the front of the book for more detailed information.

Tampa

Place Type: City
County: Hillsborough
Population: 303,447

Ancestry/Race	Number	%
Acadian/Cajun	47	0.02
African American/Black:	82,470	27.18
Not Hispanic (76,711)	79,161	26.09
Hispanic (2,407)	3,309	1.09
African, sub-Saharan:	2,718	0.90
African	2,282	0.75
Ethiopian	106	0.03
Ghanian	126	0.04
Nigerian	20	0.01
Somalian	11	0.00
South African	139	0.05
Sudanese	7	0.00
Ugandan	22	0.01
Other sub-Saharan African	5	0.00
Alaska Native tribes, specified:	22	0.01
Alaska Athabascan (5)	7	0.00
Aleut	1	0.00
Eskimo (1)	12	0.00
Tlingit-Haida	1	0.00
All other tribes (1)	1	0.00
Alaska Native tribes, not specified	8	0.00
Am. Ind. or Alaska Nat., not spec.	1,030	0.34
Albanian	65	0.02
American Indian tribes, specified:	1,559	0.51
Apache (22)	66	0.02
Blackfeet (19)	86	0.03
Cherokee (189)	651	0.21
Cheyenne (2)	4	0.00
Chickasaw (4)	9	0.00
Chippewa (18)	36	0.01
Choctaw (15)	34	0.01
Colville	1	0.00
Comanche (2)	5	0.00
Cree (6)	9	0.00
Creek (33)	56	0.02
Delaware	3	0.00
Houma	5	0.00
Iroquois (39)	77	0.03
Latin American Indians (101)	226	0.07
Lumbee (15)	18	0.01
Menominee (1)	1	0.00
Navajo (9)	18	0.01
Osage (6)	14	0.00
Ottawa (1)	1	0.00
Pima	1	0.00
Potawatomi (1)	2	0.00
Pueblo (3)	11	0.00
Puget Sound Salish (5)	6	0.00
Seminole (33)	74	0.02
Shoshone	7	0.00
Sioux (19)	44	0.01
Tohono O'Odham (1)	1	0.00
Ute (1)	1	0.00
Yaqui	2	0.00
Yuman (3)	3	0.00
All other tribes (45)	87	0.03
American Indian tribes, not spec.	172	0.06
Arab:	1,118	0.37
Arab/Arabic	333	0.11
Egyptian	81	0.03
Iraqi	10	0.00
Jordanian	10	0.00
Lebanese	315	0.10
Moroccan	84	0.03
Palestinian	43	0.01
Syrian	111	0.04
Other Arab	131	0.04
Armenian	222	0.07
Asian:	8,363	2.76
Bangladeshi (20)	29	0.01
Cambodian (13)	16	0.01
Chinese, ex. Taiwanese (678)	895	0.29
Filipino (1,025)	1,450	0.48
Hmong (1)	1	0.00
Indian (1,707)	1,955	0.64
Indonesian (19)	41	0.01
Japanese (231)	410	0.14
Korean (612)	772	0.25
Laotian (17)	22	0.01
Malaysian (2)	4	0.00
Pakistani (103)	150	0.05
Sri Lankan (12)	13	0.00
Taiwanese (46)	66	0.02
Thai (248)	376	0.12
Vietnamese (1,512)	1,677	0.55
Other Asian, specified (12)	45	0.01
Other Asian, not specified (156)	441	0.15
Australian	64	0.02
Austrian	585	0.19
Basque	76	0.03
Belgian	127	0.04
Brazilian	366	0.12
British	1,535	0.51
Bulgarian	61	0.02
Canadian	531	0.17
Celtic	111	0.04
Croatian	247	0.08
Czech	592	0.20
Czechoslovakian	308	0.10
Danish	591	0.19
Dutch	3,035	1.00
Eastern European	206	0.07
English	23,319	7.68
Estonian	7	0.00
European	1,958	0.65
Finnish	227	0.07
French, except Basque	7,198	2.37
French Canadian	1,892	0.62
German	27,990	9.22
German Russian	6	0.00
Greek	1,022	0.34
Guyanese	220	0.07
Hawaii Native/Pacific Islander:	643	0.21
Melanesian:	1	0.00
Fijian	1	0.00
Micronesian: (126)	168	0.06
Guamanian/Chamorro (45)	72	0.02
Other Micronesian (81)	96	0.03
Polynesian: (112)	189	0.06
Native Hawaiian (65)	117	0.04
Samoan (44)	64	0.02
Tongan (1)	1	0.00
Other Polynesian (2)	7	0.00
Other Pac. Isl., specified	25	0.01
Other Pac. Isl., not spec. (42)	260	0.09
Hispanic or Latino:	58,522	19.29
Central American:	2,362	0.78
Costa Rican	233	0.08
Guatemalan	225	0.07
Honduran	778	0.26
Nicaraguan	267	0.09
Panamanian	407	0.13
Salvadoran	362	0.12
Other Central American	90	0.03
Cuban	14,674	4.84
Dominican Republic	1,397	0.46
Mexican	6,272	2.07
Puerto Rican	17,527	5.78
South American:	2,791	0.92
Argentinean	117	0.04
Bolivian	64	0.02
Chilean	68	0.02
Colombian	1,401	0.46
Ecuadorian	311	0.10
Paraguayan	7	0.00
Peruvian	365	0.12
Uruguayan	10	0.00
Venezuelan	353	0.12
Other South American	95	0.03
Other Hispanic or Latino	13,499	4.45
Hungarian	1,218	0.40
Icelander	17	0.01
Iranian	122	0.04
Irish	25,499	8.40
Israeli	42	0.01
Italian	17,096	5.63
Latvian	49	0.02
Lithuanian	365	0.12
Macedonian	8	0.00
Northern European	81	0.03
Norwegian	1,786	0.59
Pennsylvania German	92	0.03
Polish	5,130	1.69
Portuguese	618	0.20
Romanian	217	0.07
Russian	2,419	0.80
Scandinavian	294	0.10
Scotch-Irish	4,497	1.48
Scottish	5,312	1.75
Serbian	85	0.03
Slavic	114	0.04
Slovak	228	0.08
Slovene	54	0.02
Swedish	2,521	0.83
Swiss	549	0.18
Turkish	208	0.07
Ukrainian	551	0.18
United States or American	18,834	6.21
Welsh	1,346	0.44
West Indian, excl. Hispanic:	4,748	1.56
Bahamian	252	0.08
Barbadian	99	0.03
Belizean	38	0.01
British West Indian	106	0.03
Dutch West Indian	34	0.01
Haitian	1,619	0.53
Jamaican	1,680	0.55
Trinidadian and Tobagonian	359	0.12
U.S. Virgin Islander	108	0.04
West Indian	415	0.14
Other West Indian	38	0.01
White:	201,268	66.33
Not Hispanic (154,872)	158,426	52.21
Hispanic (39,999)	42,842	14.12
Yugoslavian	345	0.11

Tarpon Springs

Place Type: City
County: Pinellas
Population: 21,003

Ancestry/Race	Number	%
African American/Black:	1,378	6.56
Not Hispanic (1,265)	1,341	6.38
Hispanic (27)	37	0.18
African, sub-Saharan:	147	0.70
African	114	0.54
South African	33	0.16
Alaska Native tribes, specified:	2	0.01
Aleut	1	0.00
Tlingit-Haida (1)	1	0.00
Am. Ind. or Alaska Nat., not spec.	28	0.13
Albanian	36	0.17
Alsatian	8	0.04
American Indian tribes, specified:	81	0.39
Apache (1)	4	0.02
Blackfeet (5)	6	0.03
Cherokee (17)	39	0.19
Chippewa (5)	6	0.03
Choctaw	2	0.01
Comanche	1	0.00
Creek (2)	2	0.01
Houma (1)	1	0.00
Iroquois (2)	3	0.01
Kiowa	1	0.00
Latin American Indians (3)	7	0.03
Lumbee	1	0.00
Navajo (1)	1	0.00
Ottawa	1	0.00
Pueblo	1	0.00
Shoshone	1	0.00
All other tribes (2)	4	0.02

Notes: 1. Figures in the "Number" column do not add up to the total population due to: a) Ancestry/Race overlap — e.g. persons can report being both White and Irish, b) persons of Hispanic origin can report being any race, c) persons reporting two ancestries are counted in both categories. 2. Numbers in parentheses indicate the number of persons reporting this ancestry/race alone, not in combination with any other ancestry/race. 3. Refer to the Explanation of Data in the front of the book for more detailed information.

American Indian tribes, not spec.	5	0.02
Arab:	126	0.60
Egyptian	54	0.26
Lebanese	61	0.29
Syrian	11	0.05
Armenian	22	0.10
Asian:	293	1.40
Chinese, ex. Taiwanese (25)	28	0.13
Filipino (28)	45	0.21
Indian (37)	48	0.23
Indonesian (3)	6	0.03
Japanese (15)	25	0.12
Korean (14)	21	0.10
Laotian (5)	14	0.07
Pakistani (2)	2	0.01
Thai (11)	20	0.10
Vietnamese (64)	70	0.33
Other Asian, specified (3)	5	0.02
Other Asian, not specified	9	0.04
Australian	7	0.03
Austrian	102	0.48
Belgian	16	0.08
British	154	0.73
Bulgarian	4	0.02
Canadian	112	0.53
Croatian	19	0.09
Czech	160	0.76
Czechoslovakian	80	0.38
Danish	60	0.28
Dutch	458	2.17
Eastern European	16	0.08
English	2,588	12.29
Estonian	10	0.05
European	84	0.40
Finnish	15	0.07
French, except Basque	841	3.99
French Canadian	225	1.07
German	3,726	17.69
Greek	2,479	11.77
Hawaii Native/Pacific Islander:	28	0.13
Micronesian: (5)	8	0.04
Guamanian/Chamorro (5)	8	0.04
Polynesian: (6)	10	0.05
Native Hawaiian (5)	8	0.04
Samoan (1)	2	0.01
Other Pac. Isl., specified	2	0.01
Other Pac. Isl., not spec. (2)	8	0.04
Hispanic or Latino:	909	4.33
Central American:	24	0.11
Costa Rican	8	0.04
Guatemalan	1	0.00
Honduran	1	0.00
Nicaraguan	2	0.01
Panamanian	5	0.02
Salvadoran	3	0.01
Other Central American	4	0.02
Cuban	74	0.35
Dominican Republic	2	0.01
Mexican	181	0.86
Puerto Rican	366	1.74
South American:	97	0.46
Argentinean	1	0.00
Chilean	2	0.01
Colombian	45	0.21
Ecuadorian	16	0.08
Peruvian	19	0.09
Uruguayan	2	0.01
Venezuelan	7	0.03
Other South American	5	0.02
Other Hispanic or Latino	165	0.79
Hungarian	117	0.56
Irish	3,132	14.87
Italian	1,991	9.45
Latvian	5	0.02
Lithuanian	47	0.22
Macedonian	11	0.05
New Zealander	11	0.05
Norwegian	228	1.08
Pennsylvania German	34	0.16
Polish	837	3.97
Portuguese	121	0.57
Romanian	28	0.13
Russian	236	1.12
Scandinavian	15	0.07
Scotch-Irish	436	2.07
Scottish	629	2.99
Serbian	8	0.04
Slovak	61	0.29
Slovene	8	0.04
Swedish	333	1.58
Swiss	98	0.47
Turkish	6	0.03
Ukrainian	24	0.11
United States or American	895	4.25
Welsh	230	1.09
West Indian, excl. Hispanic:	103	0.49
Bahamian	8	0.04
British West Indian	13	0.06
Haitian	23	0.11
Jamaican	55	0.26
West Indian	4	0.02
White:	19,208	91.45
Not Hispanic (18,263)	18,505	88.11
Hispanic (655)	703	3.35
Yugoslavian	8	0.04

Temple Terrace

Place Type: City
County: Hillsborough
Population: 20,918

Ancestry/Race	Number	%
African American/Black:	2,497	11.94
Not Hispanic (2,267)	2,385	11.40
Hispanic (67)	112	0.54
African, sub-Saharan:	83	0.40
African	83	0.40
Am. Ind. or Alaska Nat., not spec.	43	0.21
American Indian tribes, specified:	131	0.63
Apache (4)	6	0.03
Blackfeet (5)	14	0.07
Cherokee (21)	52	0.25
Chickasaw	1	0.00
Chippewa	2	0.01
Choctaw (4)	4	0.02
Creek (2)	3	0.01
Iroquois (1)	4	0.02
Latin American Indians (8)	20	0.10
Navajo	1	0.00
Osage (1)	1	0.00
Potawatomi (1)	1	0.00
Seminole (4)	5	0.02
Sioux	2	0.01
All other tribes (8)	15	0.07
American Indian tribes, not spec.	3	0.01
Arab:	428	2.05
Arab/Arabic	231	1.11
Jordanian	8	0.04
Lebanese	16	0.08
Moroccan	8	0.04
Palestinian	35	0.17
Syrian	32	0.15
Other Arab	98	0.47
Armenian	5	0.02
Asian:	668	3.19
Bangladeshi (5)	10	0.05
Chinese, ex. Taiwanese (70)	89	0.43
Filipino (65)	89	0.43
Indian (243)	253	1.21
Indonesian (10)	14	0.07
Japanese (28)	49	0.23
Korean (36)	36	0.17
Malaysian (1)	1	0.00
Pakistani (16)	23	0.11
Taiwanese (25)	32	0.15
Thai (7)	9	0.04
Vietnamese (18)	25	0.12
Other Asian, specified (6)	7	0.03
Other Asian, not specified (8)	31	0.15
Australian	10	0.05
Austrian	90	0.43
Belgian	12	0.06
Brazilian	9	0.04
British	139	0.67
Canadian	106	0.51
Croatian	7	0.03
Czech	49	0.23
Czechoslovakian	25	0.12
Danish	102	0.49
Dutch	417	2.00
English	2,563	12.28
European	202	0.97
Finnish	52	0.25
French, except Basque	671	3.21
French Canadian	136	0.65
German	3,228	15.47
Greek	87	0.42
Guyanese	102	0.49
Hawaii Native/Pacific Islander:	52	0.25
Micronesian: (11)	14	0.07
Guamanian/Chamorro (11)	14	0.07
Polynesian: (6)	12	0.06
Native Hawaiian (4)	7	0.03
Samoan (2)	2	0.01
Other Polynesian	3	0.01
Other Pac. Isl., not spec. (11)	26	0.12
Hispanic or Latino:	2,373	11.34
Central American:	108	0.52
Costa Rican	25	0.12
Guatemalan	6	0.03
Honduran	26	0.12
Nicaraguan	12	0.06
Panamanian	23	0.11
Salvadoran	12	0.06
Other Central American	4	0.02
Cuban	302	1.44
Dominican Republic	43	0.21
Mexican	274	1.31
Puerto Rican	690	3.30
South American:	323	1.54
Argentinean	12	0.06
Bolivian	4	0.02
Chilean	4	0.02
Colombian	191	0.91
Ecuadorian	14	0.07
Peruvian	39	0.19
Uruguayan	2	0.01
Venezuelan	51	0.24
Other South American	6	0.03
Other Hispanic or Latino	633	3.03
Hungarian	224	1.07
Irish	2,469	11.83
Italian	1,739	8.33
Lithuanian	46	0.22
Northern European	7	0.03
Norwegian	214	1.03
Pennsylvania German	18	0.09
Polish	504	2.41
Portuguese	47	0.23
Romanian	29	0.14
Russian	234	1.12
Scandinavian	14	0.07
Scotch-Irish	549	2.63
Scottish	651	3.12
Serbian	22	0.11
Slovak	42	0.20
Swedish	199	0.95
Swiss	80	0.38
Ukrainian	14	0.07
United States or American	1,201	5.75
Welsh	229	1.10
West Indian, excl. Hispanic:	361	1.73
Bahamian	30	0.14
British West Indian	30	0.14
Dutch West Indian	9	0.04
Haitian	25	0.12
Jamaican	217	1.04
Trinidadian and Tobagonian	31	0.15
U.S. Virgin Islander	9	0.04

Notes: 1. Figures in the "Number" column do not add up to the total population due to: a) Ancestry/Race overlap — e.g. persons can report being both White and Irish, b) persons of Hispanic origin can report being any race, c) persons reporting two ancestries are counted in both categories. 2. Numbers in parentheses indicate the number of persons reporting this ancestry/race alone, not in combination with any other ancestry/race. 3. Refer to the Explanation of Data in the front of the book for more detailed information.

West Indian	10	0.05
White:	17,323	82.81
Not Hispanic (15,163)	15,505	74.12
Hispanic (1,668)	1,818	8.69
Yugoslavian	41	0.20

The Crossings

Place Type: Census Designated Place
County: Miami-Dade
Population: 23,557

Ancestry/Race	Number	%
African American/Black:	1,314	5.58
Not Hispanic (1,016)	1,198	5.09
Hispanic (78)	116	0.49
Am. Ind. or Alaska Nat., not spec.	33	0.14
American Indian tribes, specified:	31	0.13
Cherokee (4)	14	0.06
Chippewa	1	0.00
Crow	3	0.01
Latin American Indians (4)	9	0.04
Pueblo	2	0.01
All other tribes (1)	2	0.01
American Indian tribes, not spec.	4	0.02
Arab:	302	1.28
Arab/Arabic	73	0.31
Egyptian	50	0.21
Lebanese	155	0.66
Palestinian	7	0.03
Other Arab	17	0.07
Armenian	18	0.08
Asian:	1,060	4.50
Chinese, ex. Taiwanese (299)	382	1.62
Filipino (38)	51	0.22
Indian (224)	297	1.26
Indonesian (1)	1	0.00
Japanese (78)	91	0.39
Korean (29)	37	0.16
Laotian (1)	1	0.00
Malaysian	2	0.01
Pakistani (28)	64	0.27
Sri Lankan (2)	2	0.01
Taiwanese (9)	13	0.06
Thai (15)	18	0.08
Vietnamese (37)	39	0.17
Other Asian, not specified (12)	62	0.26
Australian	11	0.05
Austrian	162	0.69
Brazilian	362	1.54
British	104	0.44
Canadian	42	0.18
Czech	37	0.16
Czechoslovakian	50	0.21
Danish	45	0.19
Dutch	80	0.34
Eastern European	29	0.12
English	603	2.56
European	143	0.61
Finnish	8	0.03
French, except Basque	490	2.08
French Canadian	34	0.14
German	1,132	4.81
Greek	149	0.63
Hawaii Native/Pacific Islander:	30	0.13
Micronesian: (4)	4	0.02
Guamanian/Chamorro (4)	4	0.02
Polynesian: (4)	10	0.04
Native Hawaiian	5	0.02
Samoan (3)	3	0.01
Other Polynesian (1)	2	0.01
Other Pac. Isl., not spec. (3)	16	0.07
Hispanic or Latino:	13,219	56.11
Central American:	1,004	4.26
Costa Rican	46	0.20
Guatemalan	56	0.24
Honduran	98	0.42
Nicaraguan	592	2.51
Panamanian	88	0.37
Salvadoran	105	0.45
Other Central American	19	0.08
Cuban	4,821	20.47
Dominican Republic	371	1.57
Mexican	203	0.86
Puerto Rican	910	3.86
South American:	3,326	14.12
Argentinean	233	0.99
Bolivian	69	0.29
Chilean	212	0.90
Colombian	1,454	6.17
Ecuadorian	122	0.52
Paraguayan	18	0.08
Peruvian	634	2.69
Uruguayan	48	0.20
Venezuelan	453	1.92
Other South American	83	0.35
Other Hispanic or Latino	2,584	10.97
Hungarian	198	0.84
Iranian	202	0.86
Irish	1,092	4.64
Israeli	38	0.16
Italian	1,074	4.56
Latvian	10	0.04
Lithuanian	37	0.16
Norwegian	52	0.22
Polish	437	1.86
Portuguese	52	0.22
Romanian	39	0.17
Russian	496	2.11
Scotch-Irish	101	0.43
Scottish	230	0.98
Serbian	5	0.02
Slavic	15	0.06
Slovak	34	0.14
Swedish	111	0.47
Swiss	39	0.17
Turkish	8	0.03
Ukrainian	26	0.11
United States or American	823	3.50
Welsh	36	0.15
West Indian, excl. Hispanic:	907	3.85
Bahamian	8	0.03
Belizean	11	0.05
British West Indian	37	0.16
Dutch West Indian	10	0.04
Haitian	348	1.48
Jamaican	369	1.57
Trinidadian and Tobagonian	124	0.53
White:	20,705	87.89
Not Hispanic (8,001)	8,280	35.15
Hispanic (12,070)	12,425	52.74
Yugoslavian	47	0.20

The Hammocks

Place Type: Census Designated Place
County: Miami-Dade
Population: 47,379

Ancestry/Race	Number	%
African American/Black:	3,842	8.11
Not Hispanic (2,899)	3,364	7.10
Hispanic (360)	478	1.01
African, sub-Saharan:	178	0.38
African	92	0.19
Cape Verdean	6	0.01
Kenyan	5	0.01
Nigerian	10	0.02
South African	8	0.02
Other sub-Saharan African	57	0.12
Am. Ind. or Alaska Nat., not spec.	88	0.19
American Indian tribes, specified:	100	0.21
Apache	1	0.00
Blackfeet	6	0.01
Cherokee (12)	22	0.05
Chippewa (3)	3	0.01
Choctaw (1)	2	0.00
Comanche	2	0.00
Creek	1	0.00
Delaware (1)	1	0.00
Iroquois	1	0.00
Latin American Indians (18)	38	0.08
Navajo (1)	1	0.00
Seminole (5)	5	0.01
All other tribes (12)	17	0.04
American Indian tribes, not spec.	19	0.04
Arab:	671	1.41
Arab/Arabic	199	0.42
Iraqi	11	0.02
Lebanese	174	0.37
Palestinian	112	0.24
Syrian	84	0.18
Other Arab	91	0.19
Asian:	1,960	4.14
Bangladeshi (6)	6	0.01
Chinese, ex. Taiwanese (577)	764	1.61
Filipino (220)	250	0.53
Indian (400)	525	1.11
Indonesian (4)	4	0.01
Japanese (54)	70	0.15
Korean (48)	58	0.12
Laotian (4)	6	0.01
Malaysian	1	0.00
Pakistani (103)	120	0.25
Taiwanese (16)	21	0.04
Thai (22)	23	0.05
Vietnamese (39)	44	0.09
Other Asian, specified (2)	2	0.00
Other Asian, not specified (17)	66	0.14
Austrian	56	0.12
Basque	38	0.08
Belgian	12	0.03
Brazilian	206	0.43
British	127	0.27
Canadian	79	0.17
Croatian	66	0.14
Cypriot	10	0.02
Czech	41	0.09
Danish	22	0.05
Dutch	180	0.38
Eastern European	30	0.06
English	739	1.56
European	262	0.55
Finnish	15	0.03
French, except Basque	537	1.13
French Canadian	43	0.09
German	1,443	3.04
Greek	86	0.18
Guyanese	55	0.12
Hawaii Native/Pacific Islander:	81	0.17
Micronesian: (1)	10	0.02
Guamanian/Chamorro (1)	7	0.01
Other Micronesian	3	0.01
Polynesian: (15)	29	0.06
Native Hawaiian (12)	23	0.05
Samoan (3)	6	0.01
Other Pac. Isl., not spec. (11)	42	0.09
Hispanic or Latino:	30,953	65.33
Central American:	2,324	4.91
Costa Rican	126	0.27
Guatemalan	120	0.25
Honduran	233	0.49
Nicaraguan	1,364	2.88
Panamanian	226	0.48
Salvadoran	201	0.42
Other Central American	54	0.11
Cuban	8,334	17.59
Dominican Republic	1,167	2.46
Mexican	504	1.06
Puerto Rican	2,763	5.83
South American:	9,494	20.04
Argentinean	401	0.85
Bolivian	93	0.20
Chilean	409	0.86
Colombian	4,749	10.02
Ecuadorian	522	1.10
Paraguayan	5	0.01
Peruvian	1,591	3.36
Uruguayan	79	0.17
Venezuelan	1,488	3.14

Notes: 1. Figures in the "Number" column do not add up to the total population due to: a) Ancestry/Race overlap — e.g. persons can report being both White and Irish, b) persons of Hispanic origin can report being any race, c) persons reporting two ancestries are counted in both categories. 2. Numbers in parentheses indicate the number of persons reporting this ancestry/race alone, not in combination with any other ancestry/race. 3. Refer to the Explanation of Data in the front of the book for more detailed information.

Other South American	157	0.33
Other Hispanic or Latino	6,367	13.44
Hungarian	140	0.30
Iranian	94	0.20
Irish	1,316	2.77
Israeli	31	0.07
Italian	1,914	4.04
Lithuanian	53	0.11
Northern European	11	0.02
Norwegian	116	0.24
Polish	428	0.90
Portuguese	193	0.41
Romanian	32	0.07
Russian	263	0.55
Scandinavian	19	0.04
Scotch-Irish	156	0.33
Scottish	168	0.35
Slovak	3	0.01
Swedish	37	0.08
Swiss	85	0.18
Turkish	53	0.11
Ukrainian	16	0.03
United States or American	1,491	3.14
Welsh	46	0.10
West Indian, excl. Hispanic:	2,670	5.63
Bahamian	113	0.24
Barbadian	28	0.06
Belizean	34	0.07
British West Indian	77	0.16
Dutch West Indian	9	0.02
Haitian	861	1.82
Jamaican	1,410	2.97
Trinidadian and Tobagonian	99	0.21
West Indian	39	0.08
White:	38,875	82.05
Not Hispanic (10,913)	11,396	24.05
Hispanic (26,347)	27,479	58.00
Yugoslavian	9	0.02

Titusville

Place Type: City
County: Brevard
Population: 40,670

Ancestry/Race	Number	%
Afghan	8	0.02
African American/Black:	5,382	13.23
Not Hispanic (5,073)	5,289	13.00
Hispanic (69)	93	0.23
African, sub-Saharan:	515	1.27
African	504	1.24
Nigerian	6	0.01
Other sub-Saharan African	5	0.01
Alaska Native tribes, specified:	5	0.01
Aleut (3)	3	0.01
Eskimo (2)	2	0.00
Am. Ind. or Alaska Nat., not spec.	111	0.27
American Indian tribes, specified:	262	0.64
Apache (2)	6	0.01
Blackfeet (2)	12	0.03
Cherokee (34)	130	0.32
Cheyenne (1)	1	0.00
Chickasaw (4)	7	0.02
Chippewa (4)	5	0.01
Choctaw (1)	10	0.02
Comanche	1	0.00
Cree	1	0.00
Creek (6)	9	0.02
Crow	1	0.00
Delaware (2)	3	0.01
Iroquois (14)	24	0.06
Latin American Indians (1)	4	0.01
Lumbee (2)	2	0.00
Navajo (2)	2	0.00
Pueblo (7)	8	0.02
Seminole (1)	8	0.02
Sioux (4)	5	0.01
Yaqui	1	0.00
All other tribes (12)	22	0.05
American Indian tribes, not spec.	17	0.04
Arab:	91	0.22
Arab/Arabic	9	0.02
Jordanian	5	0.01
Lebanese	69	0.17
Syrian	8	0.02
Armenian	15	0.04
Asian:	526	1.29
Chinese, ex. Taiwanese (56)	78	0.19
Filipino (61)	105	0.26
Indian (143)	166	0.41
Indonesian (1)	2	0.00
Japanese (26)	41	0.10
Korean (30)	37	0.09
Malaysian (1)	1	0.00
Thai (22)	28	0.07
Vietnamese (28)	37	0.09
Other Asian, specified (1)	5	0.01
Other Asian, not specified (11)	26	0.06
Assyrian/Chaldean/Syriac	9	0.02
Australian	7	0.02
Austrian	50	0.12
Belgian	89	0.22
Brazilian	17	0.04
British	272	0.67
Bulgarian	8	0.02
Canadian	140	0.34
Celtic	16	0.04
Croatian	24	0.06
Czech	67	0.16
Czechoslovakian	69	0.17
Danish	181	0.45
Dutch	692	1.70
English	5,048	12.41
Estonian	9	0.02
European	356	0.88
Finnish	70	0.17
French, except Basque	1,409	3.47
French Canadian	466	1.15
German	6,797	16.72
German Russian	8	0.02
Greek	108	0.27
Hawaii Native/Pacific Islander:	41	0.10
Melanesian:	1	0.00
Fijian	1	0.00
Micronesian: (6)	12	0.03
Guamanian/Chamorro (5)	10	0.02
Other Micronesian (1)	2	0.00
Polynesian: (8)	15	0.04
Native Hawaiian (4)	9	0.02
Samoan (4)	6	0.01
Other Pac. Isl., specified	4	0.01
Other Pac. Isl., not spec. (2)	9	0.02
Hispanic or Latino:	1,430	3.52
Central American:	59	0.15
Costa Rican	4	0.01
Guatemalan	8	0.02
Honduran	7	0.02
Nicaraguan	13	0.03
Panamanian	21	0.05
Salvadoran	3	0.01
Other Central American	3	0.01
Cuban	179	0.44
Dominican Republic	16	0.04
Mexican	200	0.49
Puerto Rican	654	1.61
South American:	62	0.15
Argentinean	7	0.02
Chilean	3	0.01
Colombian	32	0.08
Ecuadorian	4	0.01
Peruvian	4	0.01
Venezuelan	11	0.03
Other South American	1	0.00
Other Hispanic or Latino	260	0.64
Hungarian	280	0.69
Iranian	22	0.05
Irish	5,448	13.40
Italian	2,242	5.51
Latvian	14	0.03
Lithuanian	107	0.26
Maltese	9	0.02
Northern European	77	0.19
Norwegian	416	1.02
Pennsylvania German	32	0.08
Polish	938	2.31
Portuguese	121	0.30
Romanian	14	0.03
Russian	184	0.45
Scandinavian	46	0.11
Scotch-Irish	1,012	2.49
Scottish	966	2.38
Slavic	20	0.05
Slovak	95	0.23
Slovene	26	0.06
Swedish	465	1.14
Swiss	184	0.45
Ukrainian	77	0.19
United States or American	3,621	8.91
Welsh	268	0.66
West Indian, excl. Hispanic:	483	1.19
Bahamian	7	0.02
Belizean	8	0.02
British West Indian	98	0.24
Haitian	54	0.13
Jamaican	224	0.55
Trinidadian and Tobagonian	8	0.02
West Indian	84	0.21
White:	34,587	85.04
Not Hispanic (33,058)	33,509	82.39
Hispanic (1,022)	1,078	2.65
Yugoslavian	23	0.06

Town 'n' Country

Place Type: Census Designated Place
County: Hillsborough
Population: 72,523

Ancestry/Race	Number	%
African American/Black:	6,321	8.72
Not Hispanic (5,225)	5,638	7.77
Hispanic (499)	683	0.94
African, sub-Saharan:	337	0.47
African	276	0.38
Ethiopian	28	0.04
Nigerian	33	0.05
Alaska Native tribes, specified:	2	0.00
Alaska Athabascan (1)	2	0.00
Am. Ind. or Alaska Nat., not spec.	173	0.24
Albanian	6	0.01
American Indian tribes, specified:	356	0.49
Apache (5)	8	0.01
Blackfeet (4)	21	0.03
Cherokee (51)	139	0.19
Chickasaw (1)	2	0.00
Chippewa (5)	8	0.01
Choctaw (4)	12	0.02
Comanche (1)	1	0.00
Cree	1	0.00
Creek (8)	11	0.02
Crow	1	0.00
Delaware (1)	4	0.01
Iroquois (8)	18	0.02
Kiowa (1)	1	0.00
Latin American Indians (28)	60	0.08
Lumbee (5)	5	0.01
Menominee (1)	1	0.00
Navajo (3)	5	0.01
Osage (1)	2	0.00
Potawatomi	6	0.01
Pueblo (2)	3	0.00
Seminole (3)	7	0.01
Shoshone (2)	3	0.00
Sioux (6)	13	0.02
Tohono O'Odham (1)	1	0.00
Ute	1	0.00
All other tribes (9)	22	0.03
American Indian tribes, not spec.	27	0.04
Arab:	332	0.46

Notes: 1. Figures in the "Number" column do not add up to the total population due to: a) Ancestry/Race overlap — e.g. persons can report being both White and Irish, b) persons of Hispanic origin can report being any race, c) persons reporting two ancestries are counted in both categories. 2. Numbers in parentheses indicate the number of persons reporting this ancestry/race alone, not in combination with any other ancestry/race. 3. Refer to the Explanation of Data in the front of the book for more detailed information.

Arab/Arabic	100	0.14
Egyptian	24	0.03
Lebanese	140	0.19
Moroccan	22	0.03
Palestinian	6	0.01
Syrian	40	0.06
Armenian	18	0.02
Asian:	2,878	3.97
Bangladeshi (2)	5	0.01
Cambodian (11)	12	0.02
Chinese, ex. Taiwanese (243)	326	0.45
Filipino (350)	435	0.60
Indian (415)	487	0.67
Indonesian (6)	9	0.01
Japanese (58)	104	0.14
Korean (381)	444	0.61
Laotian (1)	3	0.00
Malaysian (4)	5	0.01
Pakistani (3)	7	0.01
Sri Lankan (5)	5	0.01
Taiwanese (7)	16	0.02
Thai (60)	82	0.11
Vietnamese (720)	807	1.11
Other Asian, specified (8)	14	0.02
Other Asian, not specified (38)	117	0.16
Australian	15	0.02
Austrian	129	0.18
Basque	5	0.01
Belgian	86	0.12
Brazilian	106	0.15
British	315	0.44
Canadian	187	0.26
Croatian	42	0.06
Czech	255	0.35
Czechoslovakian	82	0.11
Danish	162	0.22
Dutch	749	1.03
Eastern European	10	0.01
English	5,928	8.19
Estonian	11	0.02
European	379	0.52
Finnish	132	0.18
French, except Basque	1,935	2.67
French Canadian	622	0.86
German	9,554	13.20
Greek	521	0.72
Guyanese	354	0.49
Hawaii Native/Pacific Islander:	112	0.15
Micronesian: (8)	11	0.02
Guamanian/Chamorro (8)	11	0.02
Polynesian: (34)	48	0.07
Native Hawaiian (23)	35	0.05
Samoan (8)	10	0.01
Tongan (1)	1	0.00
Other Polynesian (2)	2	0.00
Other Pac. Isl., specified	1	0.00
Other Pac. Isl., not spec. (18)	52	0.07
Hispanic or Latino:	21,010	28.97
Central American:	691	0.95
Costa Rican	91	0.13
Guatemalan	59	0.08
Honduran	135	0.19
Nicaraguan	123	0.17
Panamanian	132	0.18
Salvadoran	105	0.14
Other Central American	46	0.06
Cuban	5,146	7.10
Dominican Republic	876	1.21
Mexican	829	1.14
Puerto Rican	7,505	10.35
South American:	2,008	2.77
Argentinean	65	0.09
Bolivian	28	0.04
Chilean	32	0.04
Colombian	1,057	1.46
Ecuadorian	226	0.31
Paraguayan	3	0.00
Peruvian	356	0.49
Uruguayan	19	0.03
Venezuelan	160	0.22
Other South American	62	0.09
Other Hispanic or Latino	3,955	5.45
Hungarian	322	0.44
Irish	7,491	10.35
Israeli	10	0.01
Italian	5,259	7.26
Latvian	9	0.01
Lithuanian	279	0.39
Maltese	19	0.03
Northern European	9	0.01
Norwegian	334	0.46
Pennsylvania German	8	0.01
Polish	2,256	3.12
Portuguese	195	0.27
Romanian	84	0.12
Russian	380	0.52
Scandinavian	56	0.08
Scotch-Irish	949	1.31
Scottish	1,083	1.50
Serbian	16	0.02
Slavic	39	0.05
Slovak	118	0.16
Swedish	637	0.88
Swiss	146	0.20
Turkish	25	0.03
Ukrainian	152	0.21
United States or American	4,570	6.31
Welsh	469	0.65
West Indian, excl. Hispanic:	997	1.38
Bahamian	27	0.04
Belizean	2	0.00
British West Indian	163	0.23
Haitian	161	0.22
Jamaican	457	0.63
Trinidadian and Tobagonian	34	0.05
U.S. Virgin Islander	48	0.07
West Indian	98	0.14
Other West Indian	7	0.01
White:	58,591	80.79
Not Hispanic (42,405)	43,240	59.62
Hispanic (14,508)	15,351	21.17
Yugoslavian	73	0.10

Union Park

Place Type: Census Designated Place
County: Orange
Population: 10,191

Ancestry/Race	Number	%
African American/Black:	614	6.02
Not Hispanic (434)	498	4.89
Hispanic (69)	116	1.14
African, sub-Saharan:	82	0.80
African	82	0.80
Am. Ind. or Alaska Nat., not spec.	33	0.32
Albanian	10	0.10
American Indian tribes, specified:	54	0.53
Apache (1)	6	0.06
Blackfeet	3	0.03
Cherokee (6)	21	0.21
Creek (2)	5	0.05
Crow (1)	1	0.01
Delaware	5	0.05
Houma (1)	1	0.01
Iroquois (1)	1	0.01
Latin American Indians (2)	7	0.07
Seminole (1)	1	0.01
All other tribes (2)	3	0.03
American Indian tribes, not spec.	3	0.03
Arab:	25	0.25
Egyptian	7	0.07
Lebanese	12	0.12
Moroccan	6	0.06
Armenian	6	0.06
Asian:	436	4.28
Cambodian	1	0.01
Chinese, ex. Taiwanese (22)	29	0.28
Filipino (108)	151	1.48
Indian (71)	82	0.80
Indonesian (3)	6	0.06
Japanese (27)	36	0.35
Korean (16)	17	0.17
Pakistani (2)	3	0.03
Thai (12)	15	0.15
Vietnamese (79)	83	0.81
Other Asian, not specified (7)	13	0.13
Austrian	9	0.09
Belgian	25	0.25
Brazilian	24	0.24
British	74	0.73
Croatian	7	0.07
Czech	34	0.33
Czechoslovakian	23	0.23
Danish	5	0.05
Dutch	160	1.57
English	827	8.11
European	42	0.41
Finnish	16	0.16
French, except Basque	233	2.28
French Canadian	64	0.63
German	1,258	12.34
Greek	24	0.24
Guyanese	15	0.15
Hawaii Native/Pacific Islander:	32	0.31
Micronesian: (1)	3	0.03
Guamanian/Chamorro (1)	3	0.03
Polynesian: (2)	4	0.04
Native Hawaiian (2)	4	0.04
Other Pac. Isl., not spec. (3)	25	0.25
Hispanic or Latino:	2,657	26.07
Central American:	64	0.63
Costa Rican	5	0.05
Guatemalan	5	0.05
Honduran	9	0.09
Nicaraguan	11	0.11
Panamanian	15	0.15
Salvadoran	15	0.15
Other Central American	4	0.04
Cuban	160	1.57
Dominican Republic	110	1.08
Mexican	125	1.23
Puerto Rican	1,730	16.98
South American:	202	1.98
Argentinean	3	0.03
Bolivian	9	0.09
Chilean	2	0.02
Colombian	122	1.20
Ecuadorian	13	0.13
Peruvian	16	0.16
Uruguayan	1	0.01
Venezuelan	27	0.26
Other South American	9	0.09
Other Hispanic or Latino	266	2.61
Hungarian	16	0.16
Irish	1,066	10.45
Israeli	13	0.13
Italian	676	6.63
Lithuanian	78	0.76
Norwegian	107	1.05
Polish	324	3.18
Portuguese	9	0.09
Russian	36	0.35
Scandinavian	43	0.42
Scotch-Irish	131	1.28
Scottish	141	1.38
Slovak	12	0.12
Swedish	54	0.53
Swiss	10	0.10
Ukrainian	21	0.21
United States or American	693	6.80
Welsh	42	0.41
West Indian, excl. Hispanic:	120	1.18
Haitian	12	0.12
Jamaican	85	0.83
Trinidadian and Tobagonian	23	0.23
White:	8,281	81.26
Not Hispanic (6,508)	6,669	65.44
Hispanic (1,457)	1,612	15.82
Yugoslavian	11	0.11

Notes: 1. Figures in the "Number" column do not add up to the total population due to: a) Ancestry/Race overlap — e.g. persons can report being both White and Irish, b) persons of Hispanic origin can report being any race, c) persons reporting two ancestries are counted in both categories. 2. Numbers in parentheses indicate the number of persons reporting this ancestry/race alone, not in combination with any other ancestry/race. 3. Refer to the Explanation of Data in the front of the book for more detailed information.

University

Place Type: Census Designated Place
County: Hillsborough
Population: 30,736

Ancestry/Race	Number	%
African American/Black:	11,027	35.88
Not Hispanic (10,141)	10,575	34.41
Hispanic (328)	452	1.47
African, sub-Saharan:	574	1.87
African	439	1.43
Cape Verdean	18	0.06
Nigerian	108	0.35
Other sub-Saharan African	9	0.03
Alaska Native tribes, specified:	2	0.01
Alaska Athabascan	1	0.00
Tlingit-Haida (1)	1	0.00
Am. Ind. or Alaska Nat., not spec.	136	0.44
American Indian tribes, specified:	162	0.53
Apache (2)	6	0.02
Blackfeet (3)	14	0.05
Cherokee (22)	80	0.26
Chickasaw (1)	2	0.01
Chippewa	1	0.00
Choctaw (1)	2	0.01
Creek	2	0.01
Delaware (4)	4	0.01
Iroquois (3)	7	0.02
Latin American Indians (14)	22	0.07
Seminole (2)	4	0.01
Sioux	3	0.01
All other tribes (7)	15	0.05
American Indian tribes, not spec.	22	0.07
Arab:	322	1.05
Arab/Arabic	71	0.23
Egyptian	33	0.11
Jordanian	44	0.14
Lebanese	35	0.11
Moroccan	17	0.06
Palestinian	31	0.10
Syrian	41	0.13
Other Arab	50	0.16
Armenian	24	0.08
Asian:	1,335	4.34
Bangladeshi (4)	5	0.02
Cambodian (3)	5	0.02
Chinese, ex. Taiwanese (310)	342	1.11
Filipino (94)	122	0.40
Indian (419)	470	1.53
Indonesian (6)	11	0.04
Japanese (26)	43	0.14
Korean (51)	67	0.22
Laotian (5)	7	0.02
Malaysian (1)	1	0.00
Pakistani (14)	18	0.06
Sri Lankan (19)	19	0.06
Taiwanese (14)	15	0.05
Thai (15)	23	0.07
Vietnamese (103)	115	0.37
Other Asian, specified	3	0.01
Other Asian, not specified (16)	69	0.22
Austrian	14	0.05
Belgian	8	0.03
Brazilian	10	0.03
British	98	0.32
Bulgarian	8	0.03
Canadian	51	0.17
Celtic	23	0.07
Croatian	41	0.13
Czech	69	0.22
Czechoslovakian	27	0.09
Danish	44	0.14
Dutch	236	0.77
English	1,256	4.09
European	201	0.66
Finnish	38	0.12
French, except Basque	443	1.44
French Canadian	215	0.70
German	2,065	6.73
Greek	42	0.14
Guyanese	14	0.05
Hawaii Native/Pacific Islander:	80	0.26
Micronesian: (7)	14	0.05
Guamanian/Chamorro (7)	14	0.05
Polynesian: (9)	15	0.05
Native Hawaiian (3)	6	0.02
Samoan (6)	9	0.03
Other Pac. Isl., specified	2	0.01
Other Pac. Isl., not spec. (6)	49	0.16
Hispanic or Latino:	5,935	19.31
Central American:	386	1.26
Costa Rican	16	0.05
Guatemalan	22	0.07
Honduran	222	0.72
Nicaraguan	32	0.10
Panamanian	45	0.15
Salvadoran	37	0.12
Other Central American	12	0.04
Cuban	403	1.31
Dominican Republic	92	0.30
Mexican	1,224	3.98
Puerto Rican	2,699	8.78
South American:	277	0.90
Argentinean	21	0.07
Bolivian	6	0.02
Chilean	9	0.03
Colombian	129	0.42
Ecuadorian	26	0.08
Peruvian	42	0.14
Venezuelan	29	0.09
Other South American	15	0.05
Other Hispanic or Latino	854	2.78
Hungarian	73	0.24
Iranian	42	0.14
Irish	1,882	6.13
Italian	1,200	3.91
Lithuanian	16	0.05
Northern European	32	0.10
Norwegian	170	0.55
Polish	514	1.68
Portuguese	23	0.07
Romanian	23	0.07
Russian	140	0.46
Scandinavian	25	0.08
Scotch-Irish	368	1.20
Scottish	347	1.13
Slavic	9	0.03
Slovak	64	0.21
Slovene	16	0.05
Swedish	59	0.19
Swiss	62	0.20
Turkish	62	0.20
United States or American	1,381	4.50
Welsh	81	0.26
West Indian, excl. Hispanic:	1,344	4.38
Bahamian	71	0.23
Barbadian	25	0.08
Belizean	27	0.09
British West Indian	67	0.22
Dutch West Indian	12	0.04
Haitian	545	1.78
Jamaican	372	1.21
Trinidadian and Tobagonian	49	0.16
U.S. Virgin Islander	11	0.04
West Indian	133	0.43
Other West Indian	32	0.10
White:	16,667	54.23
Not Hispanic (12,488)	13,035	42.41
Hispanic (3,280)	3,632	11.82
Yugoslavian	44	0.14

University Park

Place Type: Census Designated Place
County: Miami-Dade
Population: 26,538

Ancestry/Race	Number	%
African American/Black:	978	3.69
Not Hispanic (717)	754	2.84
Hispanic (186)	224	0.84
African, sub-Saharan:	28	0.11
African	28	0.11
Am. Ind. or Alaska Nat., not spec.	17	0.06
Albanian	23	0.09
American Indian tribes, specified:	16	0.06
Apache (1)	1	0.00
Blackfeet	2	0.01
Cherokee (3)	6	0.02
Creek	1	0.00
Latin American Indians	3	0.01
Navajo	1	0.00
Sioux	1	0.00
All other tribes	1	0.00
American Indian tribes, not spec.	8	0.03
Arab:	214	0.81
Arab/Arabic	61	0.23
Lebanese	107	0.40
Syrian	46	0.17
Asian:	519	1.96
Bangladeshi (3)	3	0.01
Chinese, ex. Taiwanese (162)	201	0.76
Filipino (41)	46	0.17
Indian (93)	129	0.49
Indonesian (1)	1	0.00
Japanese (40)	43	0.16
Korean (12)	14	0.05
Pakistani (11)	20	0.08
Sri Lankan (6)	6	0.02
Taiwanese (7)	12	0.05
Thai (6)	6	0.02
Vietnamese (15)	15	0.06
Other Asian, specified (1)	1	0.00
Other Asian, not specified (4)	22	0.08
Belgian	8	0.03
Brazilian	83	0.31
British	19	0.07
Canadian	44	0.17
Croatian	8	0.03
Czech	11	0.04
Dutch	15	0.06
English	245	0.93
European	51	0.19
Finnish	9	0.03
French, except Basque	161	0.61
French Canadian	13	0.05
German	259	0.98
Greek	30	0.11
Guyanese	16	0.06
Hawaii Native/Pacific Islander:	18	0.07
Micronesian: (3)	4	0.02
Guamanian/Chamorro (3)	4	0.02
Polynesian: (2)	7	0.03
Native Hawaiian (1)	3	0.01
Samoan (1)	3	0.01
Other Polynesian	1	0.00
Other Pac. Isl., not spec.	7	0.03
Hispanic or Latino:	21,945	82.69
Central American:	1,240	4.67
Costa Rican	43	0.16
Guatemalan	70	0.26
Honduran	147	0.55
Nicaraguan	767	2.89
Panamanian	76	0.29
Salvadoran	114	0.43
Other Central American	23	0.09
Cuban	15,871	59.80
Dominican Republic	280	1.06
Mexican	168	0.63
Puerto Rican	573	2.16
South American:	1,560	5.88
Argentinean	126	0.47
Bolivian	38	0.14
Chilean	64	0.24
Colombian	701	2.64
Ecuadorian	91	0.34
Paraguayan	4	0.02
Peruvian	227	0.86
Uruguayan	27	0.10

Notes: 1. Figures in the "Number" column do not add up to the total population due to: a) Ancestry/Race overlap — e.g. persons can report being both White and Irish, b) persons of Hispanic origin can report being any race, c) persons reporting two ancestries are counted in both categories. 2. Numbers in parentheses indicate the number of persons reporting this ancestry/race alone, not in combination with any other ancestry/race. 3. Refer to the Explanation of Data in the front of the book for more detailed information.

Ancestry/Race	Number	%
Venezuelan	264	0.99
Other South American	18	0.07
Other Hispanic or Latino	2,253	8.49
Iranian	13	0.05
Irish	185	0.70
Italian	615	2.32
Polish	61	0.23
Portuguese	110	0.42
Russian	106	0.40
Scotch-Irish	29	0.11
Scottish	19	0.07
Swedish	20	0.08
Swiss	29	0.11
Turkish	14	0.05
Ukrainian	8	0.03
United States or American	378	1.43
West Indian, excl. Hispanic:	332	1.25
Bahamian	61	0.23
Belizean	6	0.02
British West Indian	13	0.05
Dutch West Indian	6	0.02
Haitian	37	0.14
Jamaican	145	0.55
Trinidadian and Tobagonian	43	0.16
West Indian	7	0.03
Other West Indian	14	0.05
White:	24,230	91.30
Not Hispanic (3,329)	3,405	12.83
Hispanic (20,301)	20,825	78.47

Upper Grand Lagoon

Place Type: Census Designated Place
County: Bay
Population: 10,889

Ancestry/Race	Number	%
African American/Black:	186	1.71
Not Hispanic (151)	180	1.65
Hispanic (3)	6	0.06
African, sub-Saharan:	28	0.25
Cape Verdean	28	0.25
Alaska Native tribes, specified:	2	0.02
Eskimo (1)	1	0.01
Tlingit-Haida (1)	1	0.01
Alaska Native tribes, not specified	1	0.01
Am. Ind. or Alaska Nat., not spec.	25	0.23
American Indian tribes, specified:	124	1.14
Apache (3)	5	0.05
Blackfeet	2	0.02
Cherokee (24)	51	0.47
Chippewa (8)	14	0.13
Choctaw (2)	6	0.06
Creek (22)	31	0.28
Iroquois (1)	2	0.02
Navajo	2	0.02
Seminole	5	0.05
Sioux	2	0.02
Ute (3)	3	0.03
All other tribes	1	0.01
American Indian tribes, not spec.	7	0.06
Arab:	49	0.45
Lebanese	7	0.06
Moroccan	9	0.08
Palestinian	7	0.06
Other Arab	26	0.24
Asian:	234	2.15
Cambodian	1	0.01
Chinese, ex. Taiwanese (15)	19	0.17
Filipino (36)	58	0.53
Indian (38)	42	0.39
Japanese (20)	26	0.24
Korean (22)	31	0.28
Sri Lankan (1)	1	0.01
Thai (3)	8	0.07
Vietnamese (34)	35	0.32
Other Asian, not specified (7)	13	0.12
Austrian	35	0.32
British	78	0.71
Canadian	24	0.22
Czech	31	0.28
Czechoslovakian	26	0.24
Danish	62	0.56
Dutch	218	1.98
Eastern European	10	0.09
English	1,732	15.77
European	88	0.80
French, except Basque	460	4.19
French Canadian	208	1.89
German	1,482	13.49
Greek	73	0.66
Hawaii Native/Pacific Islander:	21	0.19
Micronesian: (7)	14	0.13
Guamanian/Chamorro (7)	14	0.13
Polynesian: (3)	5	0.05
Native Hawaiian (1)	3	0.03
Samoan (2)	2	0.02
Other Pac. Isl., not spec.	2	0.02
Hispanic or Latino:	267	2.45
Central American:	11	0.10
Costa Rican	2	0.02
Nicaraguan	2	0.02
Panamanian	5	0.05
Salvadoran	2	0.02
Cuban	42	0.39
Dominican Republic	4	0.04
Mexican	69	0.63
Puerto Rican	93	0.85
South American:	7	0.06
Colombian	1	0.01
Peruvian	3	0.03
Venezuelan	3	0.03
Other Hispanic or Latino	41	0.38
Hungarian	64	0.58
Irish	1,649	15.01
Israeli	9	0.08
Italian	416	3.79
Lithuanian	10	0.09
Norwegian	45	0.41
Polish	306	2.79
Portuguese	8	0.07
Russian	95	0.86
Scandinavian	7	0.06
Scotch-Irish	373	3.40
Scottish	364	3.31
Slovak	47	0.43
Slovene	18	0.16
Swedish	164	1.49
Swiss	17	0.15
Turkish	35	0.32
Ukrainian	19	0.17
United States or American	1,822	16.59
Welsh	63	0.57
West Indian, excl. Hispanic:	46	0.42
Belizean	28	0.25
Jamaican	9	0.08
Other West Indian	9	0.08
White:	10,373	95.26
Not Hispanic (10,026)	10,177	93.46
Hispanic (173)	196	1.80

Venice

Place Type: City
County: Sarasota
Population: 17,764

Ancestry/Race	Number	%
African American/Black:	113	0.64
Not Hispanic (90)	102	0.57
Hispanic (7)	11	0.06
Am. Ind. or Alaska Nat., not spec.	8	0.05
American Indian tribes, specified:	40	0.23
Apache	1	0.01
Blackfeet (1)	1	0.01
Cherokee (12)	23	0.13
Chickasaw	2	0.01
Chippewa	1	0.01
Iroquois (2)	3	0.02
Navajo	1	0.01
Ottawa	1	0.01
Seminole	1	0.01
Sioux (1)	2	0.01
All other tribes	4	0.02
American Indian tribes, not spec.	3	0.02
Arab:	59	0.33
Lebanese	59	0.33
Armenian	20	0.11
Asian:	99	0.56
Chinese, ex. Taiwanese (12)	18	0.10
Filipino (15)	23	0.13
Indian (7)	15	0.08
Indonesian (2)	2	0.01
Japanese (6)	7	0.04
Korean (6)	8	0.05
Thai (1)	1	0.01
Vietnamese (23)	23	0.13
Other Asian, not specified	2	0.01
Austrian	122	0.68
British	153	0.86
Bulgarian	8	0.04
Canadian	179	1.00
Croatian	33	0.18
Czech	138	0.77
Czechoslovakian	46	0.26
Danish	92	0.52
Dutch	394	2.21
English	3,402	19.06
Estonian	16	0.09
European	124	0.69
Finnish	21	0.12
French, except Basque	867	4.86
French Canadian	182	1.02
German	3,705	20.76
Greek	103	0.58
Hawaii Native/Pacific Islander:	6	0.03
Micronesian: (1)	1	0.01
Guamanian/Chamorro (1)	1	0.01
Polynesian: (1)	3	0.02
Native Hawaiian	1	0.01
Samoan (1)	1	0.01
Other Polynesian	1	0.01
Other Pac. Isl., not spec. (2)	2	0.01
Hispanic or Latino:	195	1.10
Central American:	10	0.06
Costa Rican	1	0.01
Honduran	3	0.02
Nicaraguan	1	0.01
Panamanian	3	0.02
Salvadoran	2	0.01
Cuban	21	0.12
Dominican Republic	5	0.03
Mexican	60	0.34
Puerto Rican	34	0.19
South American:	17	0.10
Argentinean	1	0.01
Bolivian	1	0.01
Chilean	1	0.01
Colombian	1	0.01
Ecuadorian	2	0.01
Paraguayan	1	0.01
Peruvian	6	0.03
Venezuelan	2	0.01
Other South American	2	0.01
Other Hispanic or Latino	48	0.27
Hungarian	113	0.63
Irish	3,104	17.39
Italian	1,402	7.85
Latvian	13	0.07
Lithuanian	81	0.45
Luxemburger	19	0.11
Macedonian	9	0.05
Maltese	8	0.04
Norwegian	244	1.37
Pennsylvania German	8	0.04
Polish	883	4.95
Portuguese	74	0.41
Russian	103	0.58
Scandinavian	28	0.16
Scotch-Irish	517	2.90

Notes: 1. Figures in the "Number" column do not add up to the total population due to: a) Ancestry/Race overlap — e.g. persons can report being both White and Irish, b) persons of Hispanic origin can report being any race, c) persons reporting two ancestries are counted in both categories. 2. Numbers in parentheses indicate the number of persons reporting this ancestry/race alone, not in combination with any other ancestry/race. 3. Refer to the Explanation of Data in the front of the book for more detailed information.

Ancestry/Race	Number	%
Scottish	744	4.17
Slovak	37	0.21
Slovene	8	0.04
Swedish	307	1.72
Swiss	99	0.55
Ukrainian	92	0.52
United States or American	1,174	6.58
Welsh	140	0.78
White:	17,519	98.62
Not Hispanic (17,299)	17,360	97.73
Hispanic (134)	159	0.90
Yugoslavian	7	0.04

Vero Beach South

Place Type: Census Designated Place
County: Indian River
Population: 20,362

Ancestry/Race	Number	%
African American/Black:	533	2.62
Not Hispanic (460)	523	2.57
Hispanic (7)	10	0.05
African, sub-Saharan:	16	0.08
African	9	0.04
Kenyan	7	0.03
Am. Ind. or Alaska Nat., not spec.	53	0.26
American Indian tribes, specified:	98	0.48
Apache	3	0.01
Blackfeet	2	0.01
Cherokee (27)	52	0.26
Chippewa (2)	4	0.02
Choctaw (4)	8	0.04
Creek	2	0.01
Crow	3	0.01
Iroquois (1)	9	0.04
Latin American Indians	2	0.01
Lumbee	3	0.01
Potawatomi (2)	2	0.01
Pueblo	1	0.00
Seminole	1	0.00
All other tribes	6	0.03
American Indian tribes, not spec.	3	0.01
Arab:	73	0.36
Arab/Arabic	31	0.15
Lebanese	21	0.10
Syrian	6	0.03
Other Arab	15	0.07
Armenian	45	0.22
Asian:	269	1.32
Bangladeshi (2)	2	0.01
Chinese, ex. Taiwanese (19)	31	0.15
Filipino (26)	42	0.21
Indian (76)	89	0.44
Indonesian (1)	1	0.00
Japanese (11)	22	0.11
Korean (18)	19	0.09
Laotian (2)	3	0.01
Pakistani (6)	6	0.03
Sri Lankan (2)	2	0.01
Vietnamese (21)	22	0.11
Other Asian, specified (1)	1	0.00
Other Asian, not specified (5)	29	0.14
Austrian	84	0.41
Belgian	24	0.12
Brazilian	6	0.03
British	111	0.54
Canadian	58	0.28
Celtic	10	0.05
Croatian	10	0.05
Czech	101	0.50
Czechoslovakian	57	0.28
Danish	116	0.57
Dutch	469	2.30
English	3,209	15.75
European	67	0.33
Finnish	70	0.34
French, except Basque	812	3.99
French Canadian	296	1.45
German	3,521	17.28
Greek	130	0.64
Hawaii Native/Pacific Islander:	30	0.15
Micronesian: (8)	9	0.04
Guamanian/Chamorro (8)	9	0.04
Polynesian: (6)	14	0.07
Native Hawaiian (3)	9	0.04
Samoan (1)	1	0.00
Tongan (1)	1	0.00
Other Polynesian (1)	3	0.01
Other Pac. Isl., not spec. (1)	7	0.03
Hispanic or Latino:	686	3.37
Central American:	22	0.11
Costa Rican	7	0.03
Guatemalan	1	0.00
Honduran	4	0.02
Nicaraguan	1	0.00
Panamanian	4	0.02
Salvadoran	5	0.02
Cuban	97	0.48
Dominican Republic	3	0.01
Mexican	203	1.00
Puerto Rican	136	0.67
South American:	104	0.51
Argentinean	6	0.03
Chilean	9	0.04
Colombian	61	0.30
Ecuadorian	4	0.02
Peruvian	12	0.06
Venezuelan	3	0.01
Other South American	9	0.04
Other Hispanic or Latino	121	0.59
Hungarian	147	0.72
Irish	3,954	19.41
Italian	1,970	9.67
Latvian	5	0.02
Lithuanian	46	0.23
Maltese	5	0.02
New Zealander	8	0.04
Northern European	7	0.03
Norwegian	147	0.72
Pennsylvania German	24	0.12
Polish	590	2.90
Portuguese	81	0.40
Romanian	15	0.07
Russian	148	0.73
Scandinavian	78	0.38
Scotch-Irish	390	1.91
Scottish	592	2.91
Serbian	13	0.06
Slavic	36	0.18
Slovak	67	0.33
Slovene	15	0.07
Swedish	466	2.29
Swiss	58	0.28
Turkish	8	0.04
Ukrainian	63	0.31
United States or American	2,047	10.05
Welsh	247	1.21
West Indian, excl. Hispanic:	45	0.22
Haitian	8	0.04
Jamaican	37	0.18
White:	19,423	95.39
Not Hispanic (18,692)	18,901	92.82
Hispanic (485)	522	2.56

Vero Beach

Place Type: City
County: Indian River
Population: 17,705

Ancestry/Race	Number	%
African American/Black:	654	3.69
Not Hispanic (581)	627	3.54
Hispanic (25)	27	0.15
African, sub-Saharan:	80	0.45
African	60	0.34
South African	20	0.11
Alaska Native tribes, specified:	3	0.02
Aleut	1	0.01
Eskimo (1)	1	0.01
All other tribes (1)	1	0.01
Am. Ind. or Alaska Nat., not spec.	14	0.08
Alsatian	8	0.04
American Indian tribes, specified:	41	0.23
Apache (1)	1	0.01
Blackfeet	1	0.01
Cherokee (14)	23	0.13
Choctaw	1	0.01
Delaware	1	0.01
Houma	1	0.01
Iroquois	2	0.01
Latin American Indians (2)	2	0.01
Lumbee (1)	1	0.01
Seminole	1	0.01
All other tribes (5)	7	0.04
American Indian tribes, not spec.	2	0.01
Arab:	40	0.22
Arab/Arabic	14	0.08
Lebanese	12	0.07
Syrian	14	0.08
Armenian	6	0.03
Asian:	265	1.50
Bangladeshi (9)	9	0.05
Cambodian (1)	1	0.01
Chinese, ex. Taiwanese (48)	52	0.29
Filipino (22)	32	0.18
Indian (58)	64	0.36
Indonesian (1)	2	0.01
Japanese (9)	18	0.10
Korean (20)	21	0.12
Malaysian	1	0.01
Pakistani (8)	8	0.05
Taiwanese (1)	3	0.02
Thai (2)	4	0.02
Vietnamese (23)	27	0.15
Other Asian, specified (1)	1	0.01
Other Asian, not specified (11)	22	0.12
Australian	11	0.06
Austrian	102	0.57
Belgian	22	0.12
British	239	1.34
Canadian	105	0.59
Celtic	6	0.03
Czech	71	0.40
Czechoslovakian	4	0.02
Danish	52	0.29
Dutch	394	2.21
English	2,880	16.14
European	211	1.18
Finnish	81	0.45
French, except Basque	605	3.39
French Canadian	91	0.51
German	2,925	16.39
Greek	109	0.61
Hawaii Native/Pacific Islander:	12	0.07
Micronesian: (4)	4	0.02
Guamanian/Chamorro (3)	3	0.02
Other Micronesian (1)	1	0.01
Polynesian: (1)	5	0.03
Native Hawaiian (1)	4	0.02
Samoan	1	0.01
Other Pac. Isl., not spec.	3	0.02
Hispanic or Latino:	1,025	5.79
Central American:	89	0.50
Costa Rican	5	0.03
Guatemalan	11	0.06
Honduran	37	0.21
Nicaraguan	6	0.03
Panamanian	3	0.02
Salvadoran	24	0.14
Other Central American	3	0.02
Cuban	77	0.43
Dominican Republic	7	0.04
Mexican	410	2.32
Puerto Rican	146	0.82
South American:	144	0.81
Argentinean	13	0.07
Bolivian	4	0.02
Chilean	7	0.04

Notes: 1. Figures in the "Number" column do not add up to the total population due to: a) Ancestry/Race overlap — e.g. persons can report being both White and Irish, b) persons of Hispanic origin can report being any race, c) persons reporting two ancestries are counted in both categories. 2. Numbers in parentheses indicate the number of persons reporting this ancestry/race alone, not in combination with any other ancestry/race. 3. Refer to the Explanation of Data in the front of the book for more detailed information.

Ancestry/Race	Number	%
Colombian	72	0.41
Ecuadorian	10	0.06
Peruvian	22	0.12
Uruguayan	1	0.01
Venezuelan	12	0.07
Other South American	3	0.02
Other Hispanic or Latino	152	0.86
Hungarian	118	0.66
Irish	3,191	17.88
Israeli	18	0.10
Italian	1,555	8.71
Lithuanian	11	0.06
Macedonian	8	0.04
Maltese	9	0.05
New Zealander	3	0.02
Norwegian	221	1.24
Polish	691	3.87
Portuguese	32	0.18
Russian	135	0.76
Scandinavian	43	0.24
Scotch-Irish	513	2.87
Scottish	607	3.40
Slovak	18	0.10
Swedish	320	1.79
Swiss	60	0.34
Turkish	20	0.11
Ukrainian	74	0.41
United States or American	1,173	6.57
Welsh	216	1.21
West Indian, excl. Hispanic:	87	0.49
Bahamian	8	0.04
Haitian	46	0.26
Jamaican	33	0.18
White:	16,570	93.59
Not Hispanic (15,695)	15,807	89.28
Hispanic (723)	763	4.31
Yugoslavian	17	0.10

Villas

Place Type: Census Designated Place
County: Lee
Population: 11,346

Ancestry/Race	Number	%
Afghan	6	0.05
African American/Black:	239	2.11
Not Hispanic (161)	208	1.83
Hispanic (26)	31	0.27
African, sub-Saharan:	7	0.06
African	7	0.06
Alaska Native tribes, specified:	6	0.05
Aleut (2)	2	0.02
Eskimo	4	0.04
Alaska Native tribes, not specified	1	0.01
Am. Ind. or Alaska Nat., not spec.	12	0.11
American Indian tribes, specified:	19	0.17
Apache	1	0.01
Blackfeet	1	0.01
Cherokee (2)	7	0.06
Creek (2)	2	0.02
Iroquois (1)	2	0.02
Latin American Indians	2	0.02
Sioux (1)	1	0.01
All other tribes	3	0.03
American Indian tribes, not spec.	2	0.02
Arab:	31	0.28
Egyptian	18	0.16
Lebanese	13	0.12
Asian:	183	1.61
Cambodian	1	0.01
Chinese, ex. Taiwanese (20)	26	0.23
Filipino (26)	43	0.38
Indian (38)	48	0.42
Japanese (2)	7	0.06
Korean (11)	17	0.15
Pakistani (3)	4	0.04
Sri Lankan (2)	2	0.02
Thai (2)	2	0.02
Vietnamese (20)	25	0.22
Other Asian, not specified (4)	8	0.07
Austrian	26	0.23
Belgian	24	0.21
Brazilian	54	0.48
British	82	0.73
Bulgarian	6	0.05
Canadian	49	0.44
Croatian	23	0.21
Czech	53	0.47
Czechoslovakian	14	0.13
Danish	57	0.51
Dutch	286	2.56
English	1,927	17.25
European	61	0.55
Finnish	44	0.39
French, except Basque	571	5.11
French Canadian	128	1.15
German	2,283	20.44
Greek	139	1.24
Hawaii Native/Pacific Islander:	9	0.08
Polynesian: (5)	8	0.07
Native Hawaiian (5)	8	0.07
Other Pac. Isl., not spec.	1	0.01
Hispanic or Latino:	634	5.59
Central American:	36	0.32
Costa Rican	6	0.05
Guatemalan	5	0.04
Honduran	6	0.05
Nicaraguan	6	0.05
Panamanian	6	0.05
Salvadoran	4	0.04
Other Central American	3	0.03
Cuban	81	0.71
Dominican Republic	5	0.04
Mexican	206	1.82
Puerto Rican	151	1.33
South American:	70	0.62
Argentinean	10	0.09
Chilean	4	0.04
Colombian	28	0.25
Ecuadorian	4	0.04
Peruvian	10	0.09
Venezuelan	3	0.03
Other South American	11	0.10
Other Hispanic or Latino	85	0.75
Hungarian	106	0.95
Irish	1,711	15.32
Israeli	9	0.08
Italian	1,125	10.07
Latvian	18	0.16
Lithuanian	66	0.59
Norwegian	174	1.56
Pennsylvania German	26	0.23
Polish	526	4.71
Portuguese	35	0.31
Romanian	21	0.19
Russian	116	1.04
Scandinavian	9	0.08
Scotch-Irish	205	1.84
Scottish	357	3.20
Serbian	10	0.09
Slovak	51	0.46
Slovene	23	0.21
Swedish	169	1.51
Swiss	37	0.33
Turkish	7	0.06
Ukrainian	29	0.26
United States or American	638	5.71
Welsh	129	1.16
West Indian, excl. Hispanic:	72	0.64
Dutch West Indian	12	0.11
Haitian	30	0.27
Jamaican	30	0.27
White:	10,827	95.43
Not Hispanic (10,266)	10,367	91.37
Hispanic (425)	460	4.05

Warrington

Place Type: Census Designated Place
County: Escambia
Population: 15,207

Ancestry/Race	Number	%
Acadian/Cajun	18	0.12
African American/Black:	3,410	22.42
Not Hispanic (3,278)	3,383	22.25
Hispanic (21)	27	0.18
African, sub-Saharan:	54	0.36
African	54	0.36
Am. Ind. or Alaska Nat., not spec.	65	0.43
American Indian tribes, specified:	293	1.93
Apache (4)	12	0.08
Blackfeet (1)	8	0.05
Cherokee (36)	116	0.76
Chippewa (3)	4	0.03
Choctaw (5)	14	0.09
Colville (1)	1	0.01
Creek (58)	89	0.59
Houma (4)	5	0.03
Iroquois	1	0.01
Latin American Indians (1)	4	0.03
Lumbee (5)	7	0.05
Navajo (2)	2	0.01
Paiute (3)	3	0.02
Puget Sound Salish (1)	1	0.01
Seminole (3)	4	0.03
Sioux (2)	11	0.07
All other tribes (2)	11	0.07
American Indian tribes, not spec.	14	0.09
Arab:	16	0.11
Arab/Arabic	4	0.03
Lebanese	4	0.03
Syrian	8	0.05
Asian:	417	2.74
Cambodian (2)	4	0.03
Chinese, ex. Taiwanese (10)	18	0.12
Filipino (150)	204	1.34
Indian (9)	17	0.11
Japanese (14)	23	0.15
Korean (8)	11	0.07
Malaysian	1	0.01
Thai (4)	5	0.03
Vietnamese (111)	119	0.78
Other Asian, specified	3	0.02
Other Asian, not specified (1)	12	0.08
Australian	11	0.07
Austrian	16	0.11
Belgian	35	0.23
Brazilian	28	0.18
British	27	0.18
Canadian	34	0.22
Croatian	10	0.07
Danish	44	0.29
Dutch	283	1.86
English	1,372	9.04
European	53	0.35
Finnish	26	0.17
French, except Basque	619	4.08
French Canadian	152	1.00
German	1,561	10.28
Greek	46	0.30
Hawaii Native/Pacific Islander:	50	0.33
Micronesian: (13)	18	0.12
Guamanian/Chamorro (9)	13	0.09
Other Micronesian (4)	5	0.03
Polynesian: (8)	17	0.11
Native Hawaiian (4)	12	0.08
Samoan (4)	5	0.03
Other Pac. Isl., specified	3	0.02
Other Pac. Isl., not spec. (2)	12	0.08
Hispanic or Latino:	438	2.88
Central American:	17	0.11
Guatemalan	1	0.01
Honduran	7	0.05
Nicaraguan	1	0.01
Panamanian	7	0.05

Notes: 1. Figures in the "Number" column do not add up to the total population due to: a) Ancestry/Race overlap — e.g. persons can report being both White and Irish, b) persons of Hispanic origin can report being any race, c) persons reporting two ancestries are counted in both categories. 2. Numbers in parentheses indicate the number of persons reporting this ancestry/race alone, not in combination with any other ancestry/race. 3. Refer to the Explanation of Data in the front of the book for more detailed information.

Salvadoran	1	0.01
Cuban	32	0.21
Dominican Republic	2	0.01
Mexican	145	0.95
Puerto Rican	117	0.77
South American:	11	0.07
Bolivian	1	0.01
Chilean	3	0.02
Colombian	6	0.04
Venezuelan	1	0.01
Other Hispanic or Latino	114	0.75
Hungarian	76	0.50
Irish	1,451	9.56
Italian	457	3.01
Lithuanian	25	0.16
Luxemburger	10	0.07
Norwegian	75	0.49
Pennsylvania German	9	0.06
Polish	171	1.13
Portuguese	29	0.19
Russian	30	0.20
Scandinavian	16	0.11
Scotch-Irish	511	3.37
Scottish	245	1.61
Serbian	7	0.05
Slavic	10	0.07
Slovak	5	0.03
Slovene	7	0.05
Swedish	146	0.96
Swiss	26	0.17
Ukrainian	17	0.11
United States or American	2,204	14.51
Welsh	35	0.23
West Indian, excl. Hispanic:	42	0.28
Bahamian	8	0.05
Dutch West Indian	7	0.05
Jamaican	16	0.11
West Indian	11	0.07
White:	11,211	73.72
Not Hispanic (10,658)	10,957	72.05
Hispanic (225)	254	1.67

Wekiwa Springs

Place Type: Census Designated Place
County: Seminole
Population: 23,169

Ancestry/Race	Number	%
Acadian/Cajun	11	0.05
African American/Black:	386	1.67
Not Hispanic (330)	364	1.57
Hispanic (13)	22	0.09
African, sub-Saharan:	107	0.46
African	56	0.24
South African	43	0.18
Other sub-Saharan African	8	0.03
Am. Ind. or Alaska Nat., not spec.	19	0.08
American Indian tribes, specified:	74	0.32
Blackfeet	4	0.02
Cherokee (8)	31	0.13
Chickasaw (4)	4	0.02
Chippewa (1)	1	0.00
Comanche (1)	1	0.00
Creek (1)	2	0.01
Delaware	1	0.00
Iroquois	2	0.01
Latin American Indians (5)	11	0.05
Lumbee (1)	1	0.00
Potawatomi (4)	5	0.02
Pueblo (1)	1	0.00
Seminole	2	0.01
Sioux (1)	1	0.00
All other tribes (4)	7	0.03
American Indian tribes, not spec.	1	0.00
Arab:	220	0.95
Egyptian	5	0.02
Iraqi	9	0.04
Jordanian	6	0.03
Lebanese	107	0.46
Syrian	93	0.40
Armenian	12	0.05
Asian:	607	2.62
Chinese, ex. Taiwanese (65)	79	0.34
Filipino (40)	48	0.21
Indian (248)	269	1.16
Indonesian (1)	1	0.00
Japanese (17)	30	0.13
Korean (86)	96	0.41
Pakistani (11)	18	0.08
Taiwanese (3)	4	0.02
Thai (9)	9	0.04
Vietnamese (25)	29	0.13
Other Asian, not specified (9)	24	0.10
Australian	7	0.03
Austrian	212	0.91
Belgian	24	0.10
Brazilian	7	0.03
British	275	1.18
Canadian	128	0.55
Croatian	19	0.08
Czech	99	0.43
Czechoslovakian	69	0.30
Danish	208	0.89
Dutch	396	1.70
Eastern European	158	0.68
English	3,654	15.70
Estonian	9	0.04
European	378	1.62
Finnish	63	0.27
French, except Basque	930	4.00
French Canadian	219	0.94
German	4,525	19.44
Greek	178	0.76
Hawaii Native/Pacific Islander:	17	0.07
Micronesian: (3)	3	0.01
Guamanian/Chamorro (3)	3	0.01
Polynesian: (3)	7	0.03
Native Hawaiian (2)	6	0.03
Samoan (1)	1	0.00
Other Pac. Isl., not spec.	7	0.03
Hispanic or Latino:	1,139	4.92
Central American:	32	0.14
Costa Rican	3	0.01
Guatemalan	5	0.02
Honduran	1	0.00
Nicaraguan	1	0.00
Panamanian	9	0.04
Salvadoran	8	0.03
Other Central American	5	0.02
Cuban	205	0.88
Dominican Republic	24	0.10
Mexican	83	0.36
Puerto Rican	371	1.60
South American:	219	0.95
Argentinean	45	0.19
Bolivian	3	0.01
Chilean	5	0.02
Colombian	94	0.41
Ecuadorian	9	0.04
Peruvian	38	0.16
Uruguayan	1	0.00
Venezuelan	16	0.07
Other South American	8	0.03
Other Hispanic or Latino	205	0.88
Hungarian	264	1.13
Icelander	10	0.04
Iranian	69	0.30
Irish	3,458	14.86
Israeli	32	0.14
Italian	2,069	8.89
Latvian	15	0.06
Lithuanian	143	0.61
New Zealander	10	0.04
Northern European	55	0.24
Norwegian	346	1.49
Pennsylvania German	13	0.06
Polish	1,208	5.19
Portuguese	59	0.25
Romanian	123	0.53
Russian	730	3.14
Scandinavian	45	0.19
Scotch-Irish	482	2.07
Scottish	535	2.30
Slovak	65	0.28
Slovene	17	0.07
Swedish	466	2.00
Swiss	108	0.46
Ukrainian	61	0.26
United States or American	1,274	5.47
Welsh	215	0.92
West Indian, excl. Hispanic:	80	0.34
Jamaican	80	0.34
White:	22,085	95.32
Not Hispanic (20,924)	21,082	90.99
Hispanic (954)	1,003	4.33

Wellington

Place Type: Village
County: Palm Beach
Population: 38,216

Ancestry/Race	Number	%
African American/Black:	2,286	5.98
Not Hispanic (1,957)	2,158	5.65
Hispanic (100)	128	0.33
African, sub-Saharan:	234	0.62
African	206	0.54
Ghanian	28	0.07
Am. Ind. or Alaska Nat., not spec.	31	0.08
American Indian tribes, specified:	113	0.30
Apache (2)	2	0.01
Blackfeet (2)	11	0.03
Cherokee (10)	48	0.13
Chickasaw (1)	1	0.00
Chippewa (2)	11	0.03
Choctaw	1	0.00
Cree	1	0.00
Houma	3	0.01
Iroquois (4)	5	0.01
Latin American Indians (3)	11	0.03
Menominee	2	0.01
Navajo	1	0.00
Ottawa	1	0.00
Potawatomi (1)	1	0.00
Pueblo (3)	3	0.01
Seminole	1	0.00
Sioux (1)	5	0.01
All other tribes (3)	5	0.01
American Indian tribes, not spec.	7	0.02
Arab:	232	0.61
Arab/Arabic	45	0.12
Egyptian	18	0.05
Lebanese	93	0.24
Moroccan	6	0.02
Palestinian	53	0.14
Syrian	17	0.04
Armenian	51	0.13
Asian:	979	2.56
Bangladeshi (12)	17	0.04
Chinese, ex. Taiwanese (169)	208	0.54
Filipino (101)	143	0.37
Indian (285)	349	0.91
Indonesian (3)	5	0.01
Japanese (24)	36	0.09
Korean (44)	64	0.17
Pakistani (18)	22	0.06
Sri Lankan (10)	10	0.03
Taiwanese (1)	5	0.01
Thai (19)	27	0.07
Vietnamese (42)	50	0.13
Other Asian, specified (7)	8	0.02
Other Asian, not specified (13)	35	0.09
Australian	11	0.03
Austrian	202	0.53
Basque	32	0.08
Belgian	27	0.07
Brazilian	14	0.04
British	273	0.72

Notes: 1. Figures in the "Number" column do not add up to the total population due to: a) Ancestry/Race overlap — e.g. persons can report being both White and Irish, b) persons of Hispanic origin can report being any race, c) persons reporting two ancestries are counted in both categories. 2. Numbers in parentheses indicate the number of persons reporting this ancestry/race alone, not in combination with any other ancestry/race. 3. Refer to the Explanation of Data in the front of the book for more detailed information.

Bulgarian	16	0.04
Canadian	230	0.60
Celtic	16	0.04
Croatian	32	0.08
Cypriot	20	0.05
Czech	176	0.46
Czechoslovakian	67	0.18
Danish	98	0.26
Dutch	332	0.87
Eastern European	225	0.59
English	4,245	11.16
Estonian	49	0.13
European	336	0.88
Finnish	146	0.38
French, except Basque	1,384	3.64
French Canadian	434	1.14
German	5,175	13.61
Greek	235	0.62
Guyanese	58	0.15
Hawaii Native/Pacific Islander:	37	0.10
Melanesian: (2)	2	0.01
Fijian (2)	2	0.01
Micronesian: (1)	3	0.01
Guamanian/Chamorro (1)	3	0.01
Polynesian: (3)	10	0.03
Native Hawaiian (1)	3	0.01
Samoan (1)	3	0.01
Other Polynesian (1)	4	0.01
Other Pac. Isl., not spec. (4)	22	0.06
Hispanic or Latino:	4,395	11.50
Central American:	171	0.45
Costa Rican	29	0.08
Guatemalan	17	0.04
Honduran	30	0.08
Nicaraguan	36	0.09
Panamanian	28	0.07
Salvadoran	21	0.05
Other Central American	10	0.03
Cuban	1,248	3.27
Dominican Republic	146	0.38
Mexican	451	1.18
Puerto Rican	769	2.01
South American:	840	2.20
Argentinean	103	0.27
Bolivian	15	0.04
Chilean	31	0.08
Colombian	362	0.95
Ecuadorian	76	0.20
Paraguayan	8	0.02
Peruvian	73	0.19
Uruguayan	31	0.08
Venezuelan	117	0.31
Other South American	24	0.06
Other Hispanic or Latino	770	2.01
Hungarian	453	1.19
Iranian	6	0.02
Irish	5,728	15.06
Israeli	77	0.20
Italian	5,550	14.59
Latvian	56	0.15
Lithuanian	140	0.37
Luxemburger	7	0.02
Maltese	12	0.03
Norwegian	348	0.91
Pennsylvania German	41	0.11
Polish	1,769	4.65
Portuguese	204	0.54
Romanian	98	0.26
Russian	1,463	3.85
Scandinavian	27	0.07
Scotch-Irish	550	1.45
Scottish	723	1.90
Serbian	9	0.02
Slovak	98	0.26
Slovene	17	0.04
Swedish	389	1.02
Swiss	95	0.25
Turkish	15	0.04
Ukrainian	205	0.54
United States or American	2,588	6.80
Welsh	217	0.57
West Indian, excl. Hispanic:	879	2.31
Bahamian	9	0.02
British West Indian	12	0.03
Haitian	422	1.11
Jamaican	373	0.98
Trinidadian and Tobagonian	24	0.06
West Indian	39	0.10
White:	34,456	90.16
Not Hispanic (30,473)	30,836	80.69
Hispanic (3,445)	3,620	9.47
Yugoslavian	51	0.13

West Little River

Place Type: Census Designated Place
County: Miami-Dade
Population: 32,498

Ancestry/Race	Number	%
African American/Black:	19,129	58.86
Not Hispanic (17,819)	18,206	56.02
Hispanic (775)	923	2.84
African, sub-Saharan:	539	1.67
African	539	1.67
Am. Ind. or Alaska Nat., not spec.	125	0.38
American Indian tribes, specified:	58	0.18
Apache	2	0.01
Cherokee (1)	10	0.03
Creek	1	0.00
Iroquois	1	0.00
Latin American Indians (16)	34	0.10
Pueblo	2	0.01
Sioux	1	0.00
All other tribes (3)	7	0.02
American Indian tribes, not spec.	11	0.03
Arab:	27	0.08
Arab/Arabic	14	0.04
Lebanese	5	0.02
Other Arab	8	0.02
Asian:	141	0.43
Cambodian (6)	6	0.02
Chinese, ex. Taiwanese (9)	25	0.08
Filipino (12)	14	0.04
Indian (17)	55	0.17
Indonesian	1	0.00
Japanese	1	0.00
Korean (7)	8	0.02
Vietnamese (2)	3	0.01
Other Asian, specified	7	0.02
Other Asian, not specified (6)	21	0.06
Brazilian	5	0.02
British	11	0.03
Canadian	13	0.04
English	42	0.13
European	30	0.09
French, except Basque	26	0.08
French Canadian	11	0.03
German	42	0.13
Guyanese	9	0.03
Hawaii Native/Pacific Islander:	86	0.26
Micronesian: (3)	5	0.02
Guamanian/Chamorro (3)	5	0.02
Polynesian: (1)	5	0.02
Native Hawaiian (1)	2	0.01
Samoan	3	0.01
Other Pac. Isl., specified	7	0.02
Other Pac. Isl., not spec. (18)	69	0.21
Hispanic or Latino:	13,016	40.05
Central American:	2,528	7.78
Costa Rican	14	0.04
Guatemalan	391	1.20
Honduran	709	2.18
Nicaraguan	1,163	3.58
Panamanian	34	0.10
Salvadoran	127	0.39
Other Central American	90	0.28
Cuban	5,452	16.78
Dominican Republic	786	2.42
Mexican	187	0.58
Puerto Rican	1,117	3.44
South American:	429	1.32
Argentinean	32	0.10
Bolivian	2	0.01
Chilean	11	0.03
Colombian	186	0.57
Ecuadorian	71	0.22
Peruvian	77	0.24
Uruguayan	4	0.01
Venezuelan	42	0.13
Other South American	4	0.01
Other Hispanic or Latino	2,517	7.75
Iranian	40	0.12
Irish	87	0.27
Italian	51	0.16
Lithuanian	16	0.05
Polish	6	0.02
Russian	6	0.02
Scottish	10	0.03
Swedish	25	0.08
United States or American	1,527	4.73
Welsh	12	0.04
West Indian, excl. Hispanic:	2,654	8.22
Bahamian	339	1.05
Belizean	6	0.02
British West Indian	18	0.06
Haitian	1,687	5.23
Jamaican	565	1.75
Trinidadian and Tobagonian	21	0.07
U.S. Virgin Islander	8	0.02
West Indian	10	0.03
White:	11,461	35.27
Not Hispanic (1,089)	1,173	3.61
Hispanic (9,483)	10,288	31.66
Yugoslavian	15	0.05

West Palm Beach

Place Type: City
County: Palm Beach
Population: 82,103

Ancestry/Race	Number	%
Acadian/Cajun	4	0.00
African American/Black:	27,925	34.01
Not Hispanic (25,958)	27,307	33.26
Hispanic (488)	618	0.75
African, sub-Saharan:	779	0.96
African	705	0.86
South African	52	0.06
Zimbabwean	7	0.01
Other sub-Saharan African	15	0.02
Alaska Native tribes, specified:	5	0.01
Alaska Athabascan	1	0.00
Eskimo	2	0.00
Tlingit-Haida	2	0.00
Am. Ind. or Alaska Nat., not spec.	198	0.24
Albanian	33	0.04
American Indian tribes, specified:	446	0.54
Apache (3)	4	0.00
Blackfeet (1)	6	0.01
Cherokee (29)	74	0.09
Cheyenne (2)	2	0.00
Chippewa (4)	7	0.01
Choctaw (2)	6	0.01
Comanche	4	0.00
Delaware	2	0.00
Iroquois (16)	19	0.02
Kiowa	1	0.00
Latin American Indians (76)	265	0.32
Lumbee (1)	1	0.00
Navajo (6)	9	0.01
Ottawa (1)	1	0.00
Paiute (1)	1	0.00
Potawatomi (2)	2	0.00
Pueblo (4)	5	0.01
Seminole (2)	7	0.01
Shoshone (1)	1	0.00
Sioux	5	0.01
Tohono O'Odham	1	0.00

Notes: 1. Figures in the "Number" column do not add up to the total population due to: a) Ancestry/Race overlap — e.g. persons can report being both White and Irish, b) persons of Hispanic origin can report being any race, c) persons reporting two ancestries are counted in both categories. 2. Numbers in parentheses indicate the number of persons reporting this ancestry/race alone, not in combination with any other ancestry/race. 3. Refer to the Explanation of Data in the front of the book for more detailed information.

Yuman (1)	2	0.00
All other tribes (11)	21	0.03
American Indian tribes, not spec.	39	0.05
Arab:	839	1.03
Arab/Arabic	123	0.15
Egyptian	58	0.07
Iraqi	41	0.05
Jordanian	15	0.02
Lebanese	307	0.38
Moroccan	23	0.03
Palestinian	149	0.18
Syrian	70	0.09
Other Arab	53	0.06
Armenian	33	0.04
Asian:	1,516	1.85
Bangladeshi (12)	21	0.03
Cambodian (7)	9	0.01
Chinese, ex. Taiwanese (162)	203	0.25
Filipino (200)	239	0.29
Indian (382)	446	0.54
Indonesian (3)	4	0.00
Japanese (52)	75	0.09
Korean (107)	129	0.16
Laotian (1)	1	0.00
Malaysian (3)	4	0.00
Pakistani (10)	25	0.03
Sri Lankan (9)	9	0.01
Taiwanese (2)	4	0.00
Thai (56)	71	0.09
Vietnamese (130)	139	0.17
Other Asian, specified (8)	14	0.02
Other Asian, not specified (38)	123	0.15
Australian	64	0.08
Austrian	445	0.55
Basque	9	0.01
Belgian	127	0.16
Brazilian	174	0.21
British	384	0.47
Bulgarian	11	0.01
Canadian	338	0.41
Croatian	41	0.05
Czech	164	0.20
Czechoslovakian	104	0.13
Danish	176	0.22
Dutch	764	0.94
Eastern European	141	0.17
English	5,016	6.15
European	365	0.45
Finnish	104	0.13
French, except Basque	1,740	2.13
French Canadian	406	0.50
German	6,078	7.45
Greek	379	0.46
Guyanese	62	0.08
Hawaii Native/Pacific Islander:	262	0.32
Melanesian:	3	0.00
Other Melanesian	3	0.00
Micronesian: (84)	98	0.12
Guamanian/Chamorro (84)	98	0.12
Polynesian: (24)	54	0.07
Native Hawaiian (15)	26	0.03
Samoan (8)	25	0.03
Other Polynesian (1)	3	0.00
Other Pac. Isl., specified	6	0.01
Other Pac. Isl., not spec. (23)	101	0.12
Hispanic or Latino:	14,955	18.21
Central American:	2,745	3.34
Costa Rican	116	0.14
Guatemalan	1,841	2.24
Honduran	308	0.38
Nicaraguan	265	0.32
Panamanian	37	0.05
Salvadoran	111	0.14
Other Central American	67	0.08
Cuban	4,343	5.29
Dominican Republic	418	0.51
Mexican	1,975	2.41
Puerto Rican	2,130	2.59
South American:	1,171	1.43
Argentinean	72	0.09
Bolivian	18	0.02
Chilean	31	0.04
Colombian	587	0.71
Ecuadorian	130	0.16
Paraguayan	8	0.01
Peruvian	131	0.16
Uruguayan	56	0.07
Venezuelan	98	0.12
Other South American	40	0.05
Other Hispanic or Latino	2,173	2.65
Hungarian	576	0.71
Iranian	61	0.07
Irish	5,742	7.04
Israeli	24	0.03
Italian	4,034	4.95
Latvian	32	0.04
Lithuanian	168	0.21
Maltese	5	0.01
Norwegian	346	0.42
Pennsylvania German	21	0.03
Polish	1,834	2.25
Portuguese	334	0.41
Romanian	109	0.13
Russian	1,425	1.75
Scandinavian	31	0.04
Scotch-Irish	835	1.02
Scottish	1,041	1.28
Serbian	28	0.03
Slavic	7	0.01
Slovak	89	0.11
Slovene	8	0.01
Swedish	538	0.66
Swiss	94	0.12
Turkish	63	0.08
Ukrainian	218	0.27
United States or American	4,276	5.24
Welsh	324	0.40
West Indian, excl. Hispanic:	6,338	7.77
Bahamian	327	0.40
Barbadian	50	0.06
Belizean	17	0.02
Bermudan	11	0.01
British West Indian	106	0.13
Haitian	3,389	4.16
Jamaican	2,134	2.62
Trinidadian and Tobagonian	132	0.16
U.S. Virgin Islander	34	0.04
West Indian	119	0.15
Other West Indian	19	0.02
White:	49,003	59.68
Not Hispanic (37,771)	38,444	46.82
Hispanic (9,925)	10,559	12.86
Yugoslavian	26	0.03

West Pensacola

Place Type: Census Designated Place
County: Escambia
Population: 21,939

Ancestry/Race	Number	%
African American/Black:	7,584	34.57
Not Hispanic (7,339)	7,508	34.22
Hispanic (52)	76	0.35
African, sub-Saharan:	177	0.81
African	129	0.59
Cape Verdean	32	0.15
Ghanian	7	0.03
Nigerian	9	0.04
Alaska Native tribes, specified:	3	0.01
Aleut (2)	2	0.01
Eskimo	1	0.00
Alaska Native tribes, not specified	1	0.00
Am. Ind. or Alaska Nat., not spec.	130	0.59
American Indian tribes, specified:	370	1.69
Apache (5)	7	0.03
Blackfeet (3)	13	0.06
Cherokee (40)	112	0.51
Cheyenne (2)	2	0.01
Chippewa (3)	3	0.01
Choctaw (2)	9	0.04
Creek (94)	150	0.68
Delaware (1)	1	0.00
Houma (4)	4	0.02
Iroquois (1)	6	0.03
Kiowa (1)	1	0.00
Latin American Indians (5)	7	0.03
Lumbee	2	0.01
Navajo (1)	2	0.01
Ottawa	1	0.00
Paiute	3	0.01
Potawatomi	1	0.00
Seminole (6)	8	0.04
Sioux (8)	14	0.06
All other tribes (11)	24	0.11
American Indian tribes, not spec.	18	0.08
Arab:	14	0.06
Syrian	14	0.06
Armenian	27	0.12
Asian:	933	4.25
Cambodian (7)	7	0.03
Chinese, ex. Taiwanese (14)	24	0.11
Filipino (257)	344	1.57
Indian (19)	33	0.15
Indonesian	1	0.00
Japanese (26)	49	0.22
Korean (16)	21	0.10
Laotian (2)	4	0.02
Taiwanese (1)	1	0.00
Thai (3)	4	0.02
Vietnamese (389)	412	1.88
Other Asian, specified	1	0.00
Other Asian, not specified (7)	32	0.15
Australian	8	0.04
Austrian	40	0.18
Brazilian	34	0.15
British	104	0.47
Czech	7	0.03
Czechoslovakian	14	0.06
Danish	21	0.10
Dutch	170	0.77
English	1,217	5.54
European	165	0.75
French, except Basque	537	2.45
French Canadian	90	0.41
German	1,274	5.80
German Russian	6	0.03
Greek	103	0.47
Hawaii Native/Pacific Islander:	88	0.40
Micronesian: (21)	24	0.11
Guamanian/Chamorro (21)	24	0.11
Polynesian: (21)	50	0.23
Native Hawaiian (9)	33	0.15
Samoan (12)	17	0.08
Other Pac. Isl., specified	1	0.00
Other Pac. Isl., not spec.	13	0.06
Hispanic or Latino:	571	2.60
Central American:	17	0.08
Costa Rican	1	0.00
Guatemalan	4	0.02
Honduran	3	0.01
Panamanian	9	0.04
Cuban	35	0.16
Dominican Republic	11	0.05
Mexican	173	0.79
Puerto Rican	135	0.62
South American:	17	0.08
Bolivian	2	0.01
Colombian	7	0.03
Ecuadorian	3	0.01
Peruvian	3	0.01
Venezuelan	1	0.00
Other South American	1	0.00
Other Hispanic or Latino	183	0.83
Hungarian	45	0.20
Icelander	9	0.04
Irish	1,564	7.12
Israeli	13	0.06
Italian	471	2.15
Lithuanian	19	0.09

Notes: 1. Figures in the "Number" column do not add up to the total population due to: a) Ancestry/Race overlap — e.g. persons can report being both White and Irish, b) persons of Hispanic origin can report being any race, c) persons reporting two ancestries are counted in both categories. 2. Numbers in parentheses indicate the number of persons reporting this ancestry/race alone, not in combination with any other ancestry/race. 3. Refer to the Explanation of Data in the front of the book for more detailed information.

Ancestry/Race	Number	%
Norwegian	114	0.52
Polish	211	0.96
Portuguese	48	0.22
Scotch-Irish	427	1.94
Scottish	279	1.27
Swedish	139	0.63
Swiss	11	0.05
United States or American	2,240	10.20
Welsh	58	0.26
West Indian, excl. Hispanic:	175	0.80
Haitian	146	0.66
Jamaican	17	0.08
West Indian	12	0.05
White:	13,222	60.27
Not Hispanic (12,432)	12,864	58.64
Hispanic (305)	358	1.63

West and East Lealman

Place Type: Census Designated Place
County: Pinellas
Population: 21,753

Ancestry/Race	Number	%
African American/Black:	802	3.69
Not Hispanic (673)	750	3.45
Hispanic (28)	52	0.24
African, sub-Saharan:	13	0.06
African	13	0.06
Am. Ind. or Alaska Nat., not spec.	73	0.34
Albanian	9	0.04
Alsatian	8	0.04
American Indian tribes, specified:	222	1.02
Apache	7	0.03
Blackfeet (7)	16	0.07
Cherokee (29)	103	0.47
Chippewa (5)	9	0.04
Choctaw (3)	6	0.03
Comanche (2)	4	0.02
Creek (2)	3	0.01
Crow (1)	1	0.00
Iroquois (20)	37	0.17
Latin American Indians (7)	8	0.04
Lumbee (2)	2	0.01
Seminole (2)	3	0.01
Sioux	8	0.04
Ute	1	0.00
All other tribes (8)	14	0.06
American Indian tribes, not spec.	21	0.10
Arab:	38	0.17
Lebanese	31	0.14
Syrian	7	0.03
Asian:	1,025	4.71
Bangladeshi (2)	2	0.01
Cambodian (40)	65	0.30
Chinese, ex. Taiwanese (22)	30	0.14
Filipino (44)	64	0.29
Indian (33)	44	0.20
Indonesian (1)	1	0.00
Japanese (7)	17	0.08
Korean (29)	36	0.17
Laotian (110)	120	0.55
Taiwanese (2)	2	0.01
Thai (20)	23	0.11
Vietnamese (539)	584	2.68
Other Asian, not specified (7)	37	0.17
Austrian	37	0.17
Belgian	13	0.06
British	139	0.64
Bulgarian	6	0.03
Canadian	133	0.61
Croatian	5	0.02
Czech	76	0.35
Czechoslovakian	17	0.08
Danish	38	0.17
Dutch	542	2.48
English	2,726	12.47
European	127	0.58
Finnish	35	0.16
French, except Basque	1,045	4.78
French Canadian	353	1.62
German	3,706	16.96
Greek	92	0.42
Hawaii Native/Pacific Islander:	28	0.13
Polynesian: (4)	7	0.03
Native Hawaiian (3)	5	0.02
Tongan (1)	2	0.01
Other Pac. Isl., not spec. (12)	21	0.10
Hispanic or Latino:	1,067	4.91
Central American:	38	0.17
Costa Rican	8	0.04
Guatemalan	1	0.00
Honduran	10	0.05
Nicaraguan	3	0.01
Panamanian	9	0.04
Salvadoran	7	0.03
Cuban	122	0.56
Dominican Republic	14	0.06
Mexican	261	1.20
Puerto Rican	432	1.99
South American:	62	0.29
Argentinean	5	0.02
Bolivian	4	0.02
Chilean	5	0.02
Colombian	22	0.10
Ecuadorian	8	0.04
Peruvian	4	0.02
Venezuelan	3	0.01
Other South American	11	0.05
Other Hispanic or Latino	138	0.63
Hungarian	147	0.67
Irish	3,318	15.18
Italian	1,672	7.65
Lithuanian	54	0.25
Norwegian	100	0.46
Pennsylvania German	8	0.04
Polish	925	4.23
Portuguese	75	0.34
Romanian	7	0.03
Russian	125	0.57
Scandinavian	17	0.08
Scotch-Irish	509	2.33
Scottish	468	2.14
Serbian	28	0.13
Slovak	46	0.21
Swedish	289	1.32
Swiss	41	0.19
Ukrainian	37	0.17
United States or American	2,025	9.27
Welsh	156	0.71
West Indian, excl. Hispanic:	145	0.66
Haitian	70	0.32
Jamaican	9	0.04
Trinidadian and Tobagonian	55	0.25
West Indian	11	0.05
White:	19,605	90.13
Not Hispanic (18,581)	18,903	86.90
Hispanic (629)	702	3.23
Yugoslavian	94	0.43

Westchase

Place Type: Census Designated Place
County: Hillsborough
Population: 11,116

Ancestry/Race	Number	%
Acadian/Cajun	7	0.06
African American/Black:	607	5.46
Not Hispanic (551)	586	5.27
Hispanic (12)	21	0.19
African, sub-Saharan:	94	0.85
African	62	0.56
Other sub-Saharan African	32	0.29
Am. Ind. or Alaska Nat., not spec.	6	0.05
American Indian tribes, specified:	21	0.19
Blackfeet	2	0.02
Cherokee (1)	5	0.04
Cheyenne	1	0.01
Chippewa (1)	1	0.01
Choctaw	2	0.02
Delaware (1)	1	0.01
Latin American Indians (3)	3	0.03
Lumbee (1)	1	0.01
Ottawa (2)	2	0.02
Sioux	1	0.01
All other tribes (2)	2	0.02
Arab:	20	0.18
Lebanese	20	0.18
Asian:	526	4.73
Cambodian	1	0.01
Chinese, ex. Taiwanese (72)	96	0.86
Filipino (97)	115	1.03
Hmong (4)	4	0.04
Indian (110)	122	1.10
Japanese (17)	25	0.22
Korean (64)	69	0.62
Laotian (3)	3	0.03
Sri Lankan (1)	1	0.01
Thai (8)	9	0.08
Vietnamese (62)	64	0.58
Other Asian, specified (6)	9	0.08
Other Asian, not specified (6)	8	0.07
Austrian	44	0.40
Basque	7	0.06
Belgian	23	0.21
Brazilian	4	0.04
British	62	0.56
Canadian	46	0.41
Croatian	10	0.09
Czech	78	0.70
Czechoslovakian	14	0.13
Danish	39	0.35
Dutch	137	1.23
Eastern European	26	0.23
English	1,413	12.71
European	49	0.44
Finnish	45	0.40
French, except Basque	421	3.79
French Canadian	94	0.85
German	2,018	18.15
Greek	128	1.15
Hawaii Native/Pacific Islander:	11	0.10
Polynesian: (1)	5	0.04
Native Hawaiian	4	0.04
Samoan (1)	1	0.01
Other Pac. Isl., specified	1	0.01
Other Pac. Isl., not spec.	5	0.04
Hispanic or Latino:	1,322	11.89
Central American:	33	0.30
Costa Rican	3	0.03
Guatemalan	6	0.05
Honduran	1	0.01
Nicaraguan	3	0.03
Panamanian	7	0.06
Salvadoran	8	0.07
Other Central American	5	0.04
Cuban	290	2.61
Dominican Republic	29	0.26
Mexican	75	0.67
Puerto Rican	422	3.80
South American:	189	1.70
Argentinean	8	0.07
Bolivian	6	0.05
Chilean	5	0.04
Colombian	76	0.68
Ecuadorian	14	0.13
Peruvian	48	0.43
Uruguayan	1	0.01
Venezuelan	12	0.11
Other South American	19	0.17
Other Hispanic or Latino	284	2.55
Hungarian	97	0.87
Iranian	9	0.08
Irish	1,883	16.94
Italian	1,290	11.60
Latvian	8	0.07
Lithuanian	34	0.31
Luxemburger	7	0.06
Norwegian	81	0.73

Notes: 1. Figures in the "Number" column do not add up to the total population due to: a) Ancestry/Race overlap — e.g. persons can report being both White and Irish, b) persons of Hispanic origin can report being any race, c) persons reporting two ancestries are counted in both categories. 2. Numbers in parentheses indicate the number of persons reporting this ancestry/race alone, not in combination with any other ancestry/race. 3. Refer to the Explanation of Data in the front of the book for more detailed information.

Ancestry/Race	Number	%
Pennsylvania German	26	0.23
Polish	540	4.86
Portuguese	19	0.17
Romanian	16	0.14
Russian	168	1.51
Scotch-Irish	232	2.09
Scottish	386	3.47
Serbian	23	0.21
Swedish	222	2.00
Swiss	58	0.52
Turkish	6	0.05
Ukrainian	44	0.40
United States or American	592	5.33
Welsh	98	0.88
West Indian, excl. Hispanic:	49	0.44
Dutch West Indian	23	0.21
Jamaican	26	0.23
White:	9,827	88.40
Not Hispanic (8,650)	8,759	78.80
Hispanic (1,011)	1,068	9.61

Westchester

Place Type: Census Designated Place
County: Miami-Dade
Population: 30,271

Ancestry/Race	Number	%
Afghan	5	0.02
African American/Black:	292	0.96
Not Hispanic (53)	72	0.24
Hispanic (133)	220	0.73
African, sub-Saharan:	9	0.03
African	9	0.03
Am. Ind. or Alaska Nat., not spec.	26	0.09
American Indian tribes, specified:	20	0.07
Apache (1)	2	0.01
Cherokee	1	0.00
Iroquois	2	0.01
Latin American Indians (9)	11	0.04
All other tribes	4	0.01
American Indian tribes, not spec.	1	0.00
Arab:	158	0.52
Arab/Arabic	47	0.16
Lebanese	111	0.37
Armenian	7	0.02
Asian:	195	0.64
Chinese, ex. Taiwanese (72)	85	0.28
Filipino (3)	7	0.02
Indian (37)	52	0.17
Japanese (12)	13	0.04
Korean (6)	9	0.03
Pakistani (4)	6	0.02
Vietnamese (15)	15	0.05
Other Asian, not specified (2)	8	0.03
Austrian	6	0.02
Basque	32	0.11
Belgian	7	0.02
Brazilian	16	0.05
Canadian	10	0.03
Czech	19	0.06
Danish	9	0.03
Dutch	10	0.03
English	338	1.12
European	19	0.06
French, except Basque	275	0.91
French Canadian	81	0.27
German	290	0.96
Greek	47	0.16
Hawaii Native/Pacific Islander:	17	0.06
Micronesian:	4	0.01
Guamanian/Chamorro	4	0.01
Polynesian: (1)	5	0.02
Native Hawaiian (1)	5	0.02
Other Pac. Isl., not spec.	8	0.03
Hispanic or Latino:	25,824	85.31
Central American:	1,230	4.06
Costa Rican	68	0.22
Guatemalan	130	0.43
Honduran	159	0.53
Nicaraguan	682	2.25
Panamanian	58	0.19
Salvadoran	106	0.35
Other Central American	27	0.09
Cuban	19,886	65.69
Dominican Republic	317	1.05
Mexican	199	0.66
Puerto Rican	509	1.68
South American:	1,329	4.39
Argentinean	91	0.30
Bolivian	18	0.06
Chilean	74	0.24
Colombian	536	1.77
Ecuadorian	119	0.39
Paraguayan	7	0.02
Peruvian	236	0.78
Uruguayan	29	0.10
Venezuelan	182	0.60
Other South American	37	0.12
Other Hispanic or Latino	2,354	7.78
Hungarian	8	0.03
Irish	280	0.93
Italian	473	1.56
Lithuanian	12	0.04
Norwegian	46	0.15
Polish	162	0.54
Romanian	19	0.06
Russian	187	0.62
Scotch-Irish	50	0.17
Scottish	46	0.15
Swedish	10	0.03
Turkish	10	0.03
Ukrainian	23	0.08
United States or American	737	2.44
Welsh	16	0.05
West Indian, excl. Hispanic:	44	0.15
Bahamian	15	0.05
Haitian	22	0.07
Jamaican	7	0.02
White:	29,004	95.81
Not Hispanic (4,142)	4,231	13.98
Hispanic (24,247)	24,773	81.84
Yugoslavian	17	0.06

Weston

Place Type: City
County: Broward
Population: 49,286

Ancestry/Race	Number	%
Acadian/Cajun	49	0.10
Afghan	11	0.02
African American/Black:	2,085	4.23
Not Hispanic (1,699)	1,892	3.84
Hispanic (133)	193	0.39
African, sub-Saharan:	262	0.53
African	31	0.06
Ethiopian	21	0.04
South African	210	0.43
Alaska Native tribes, specified:	2	0.00
Alaska Athabascan (1)	1	0.00
Eskimo (1)	1	0.00
Am. Ind. or Alaska Nat., not spec.	40	0.08
Albanian	7	0.01
American Indian tribes, specified:	59	0.12
Apache	3	0.01
Blackfeet	2	0.00
Cherokee (4)	13	0.03
Chippewa (1)	1	0.00
Choctaw	1	0.00
Comanche (1)	1	0.00
Latin American Indians (20)	24	0.05
Osage (3)	3	0.01
Seminole (2)	2	0.00
Sioux	2	0.00
Tohono O'Odham (1)	1	0.00
All other tribes (3)	6	0.01
American Indian tribes, not spec.	7	0.01
Arab:	428	0.87
Arab/Arabic	8	0.02
Egyptian	20	0.04
Iraqi	7	0.01
Jordanian	6	0.01
Lebanese	309	0.63
Moroccan	24	0.05
Palestinian	17	0.03
Syrian	22	0.04
Other Arab	15	0.03
Armenian	78	0.16
Asian:	1,850	3.75
Cambodian (3)	3	0.01
Chinese, ex. Taiwanese (369)	458	0.93
Filipino (144)	184	0.37
Indian (540)	598	1.21
Indonesian (3)	8	0.02
Japanese (95)	130	0.26
Korean (248)	262	0.53
Laotian (1)	1	0.00
Pakistani (32)	44	0.09
Sri Lankan (2)	2	0.00
Taiwanese (16)	22	0.04
Thai (10)	13	0.03
Vietnamese (43)	52	0.11
Other Asian, not specified (33)	73	0.15
Australian	10	0.02
Austrian	305	0.62
Basque	10	0.02
Belgian	117	0.24
Brazilian	471	0.96
British	374	0.76
Bulgarian	40	0.08
Canadian	272	0.55
Celtic	10	0.02
Croatian	26	0.05
Czech	60	0.12
Czechoslovakian	58	0.12
Danish	212	0.43
Dutch	383	0.78
Eastern European	328	0.67
English	2,994	6.09
Estonian	7	0.01
European	392	0.80
Finnish	61	0.12
French, except Basque	1,177	2.40
French Canadian	159	0.32
German	4,526	9.21
Greek	242	0.49
Guyanese	27	0.05
Hawaii Native/Pacific Islander:	28	0.06
Melanesian:	1	0.00
Other Melanesian	1	0.00
Micronesian: (3)	3	0.01
Guamanian/Chamorro (2)	2	0.00
Other Micronesian (1)	1	0.00
Polynesian: (3)	10	0.02
Native Hawaiian (2)	9	0.02
Samoan (1)	1	0.00
Other Pac. Isl., not spec. (2)	14	0.03
Hispanic or Latino:	14,880	30.19
Central American:	427	0.87
Costa Rican	53	0.11
Guatemalan	62	0.13
Honduran	52	0.11
Nicaraguan	105	0.21
Panamanian	84	0.17
Salvadoran	50	0.10
Other Central American	21	0.04
Cuban	1,995	4.05
Dominican Republic	364	0.74
Mexican	594	1.21
Puerto Rican	1,632	3.31
South American:	6,620	13.43
Argentinean	306	0.62
Bolivian	34	0.07
Chilean	116	0.24
Colombian	3,052	6.19
Ecuadorian	319	0.65
Paraguayan	11	0.02
Peruvian	588	1.19

Notes: 1. Figures in the "Number" column do not add up to the total population due to: a) Ancestry/Race overlap — e.g. persons can report being both White and Irish, b) persons of Hispanic origin can report being any race, c) persons reporting two ancestries are counted in both categories. 2. Numbers in parentheses indicate the number of persons reporting this ancestry/race alone, not in combination with any other ancestry/race. 3. Refer to the Explanation of Data in the front of the book for more detailed information.

Ancestry/Race	Number	%
Uruguayan	44	0.09
Venezuelan	2,020	4.10
Other South American	130	0.26
Other Hispanic or Latino	3,248	6.59
Hungarian	401	0.82
Iranian	157	0.32
Irish	3,894	7.93
Israeli	63	0.13
Italian	4,837	9.84
Latvian	44	0.09
Lithuanian	134	0.27
Macedonian	7	0.01
Maltese	18	0.04
Northern European	8	0.02
Norwegian	261	0.53
Polish	2,345	4.77
Portuguese	151	0.31
Romanian	289	0.59
Russian	2,784	5.67
Scandinavian	76	0.15
Scotch-Irish	363	0.74
Scottish	679	1.38
Serbian	19	0.04
Slavic	25	0.05
Slovak	140	0.28
Slovene	9	0.02
Swedish	469	0.95
Swiss	136	0.28
Turkish	183	0.37
Ukrainian	207	0.42
United States or American	3,355	6.83
Welsh	112	0.23
West Indian, excl. Hispanic:	1,262	2.57
Bahamian	59	0.12
Barbadian	26	0.05
British West Indian	10	0.02
Haitian	136	0.28
Jamaican	944	1.92
Trinidadian and Tobagonian	79	0.16
West Indian	8	0.02
White:	44,202	89.68
Not Hispanic (30,465)	30,847	62.59
Hispanic (12,821)	13,355	27.10
Yugoslavian	86	0.18

Westwood Lakes

Place Type: Census Designated Place
County: Miami-Dade
Population: 12,005

Ancestry/Race	Number	%
African American/Black:	119	0.99
Not Hispanic (31)	34	0.28
Hispanic (64)	85	0.71
African, sub-Saharan:	7	0.06
African	7	0.06
Am. Ind. or Alaska Nat., not spec.	12	0.10
American Indian tribes, specified:	9	0.07
Cherokee	2	0.02
Iroquois (1)	1	0.01
Latin American Indians (3)	6	0.05
American Indian tribes, not spec.	1	0.01
Arab:	26	0.22
Arab/Arabic	16	0.13
Jordanian	10	0.08
Asian:	179	1.49
Chinese, ex. Taiwanese (37)	57	0.47
Filipino (3)	7	0.06
Hmong	1	0.01
Indian (16)	21	0.17
Japanese (1)	4	0.03
Korean (2)	3	0.02
Pakistani (21)	32	0.27
Thai	1	0.01
Vietnamese (34)	46	0.38
Other Asian, not specified (2)	7	0.06
Belgian	8	0.07
Canadian	21	0.17
Croatian	8	0.07
Czech	16	0.13
Danish	18	0.15
Dutch	39	0.32
English	308	2.57
French, except Basque	163	1.36
French Canadian	19	0.16
German	421	3.51
Greek	24	0.20
Hispanic or Latino:	9,164	76.33
Central American:	512	4.26
Costa Rican	37	0.31
Guatemalan	52	0.43
Honduran	54	0.45
Nicaraguan	305	2.54
Panamanian	14	0.12
Salvadoran	24	0.20
Other Central American	26	0.22
Cuban	6,730	56.06
Dominican Republic	65	0.54
Mexican	183	1.52
Puerto Rican	233	1.94
South American:	515	4.29
Argentinean	40	0.33
Bolivian	10	0.08
Chilean	28	0.23
Colombian	253	2.11
Ecuadorian	28	0.23
Peruvian	91	0.76
Uruguayan	9	0.07
Venezuelan	53	0.44
Other South American	3	0.02
Other Hispanic or Latino	926	7.71
Hungarian	42	0.35
Irish	440	3.67
Italian	282	2.35
Lithuanian	37	0.31
Norwegian	29	0.24
Polish	59	0.49
Russian	13	0.11
Scotch-Irish	10	0.08
Scottish	30	0.25
Swedish	69	0.57
Ukrainian	7	0.06
United States or American	511	4.26
Welsh	47	0.39
West Indian, excl. Hispanic:	35	0.29
Trinidadian and Tobagonian	35	0.29
White:	11,408	95.03
Not Hispanic (2,637)	2,667	22.22
Hispanic (8,522)	8,741	72.81

Wilton Manors

Place Type: City
County: Broward
Population: 12,697

Ancestry/Race	Number	%
Acadian/Cajun	20	0.16
African American/Black:	1,989	15.67
Not Hispanic (1,624)	1,930	15.20
Hispanic (50)	59	0.46
African, sub-Saharan:	68	0.54
African	68	0.54
Am. Ind. or Alaska Nat., not spec.	14	0.11
American Indian tribes, specified:	48	0.38
Apache	1	0.01
Blackfeet	3	0.02
Cherokee (11)	24	0.19
Chickasaw (1)	1	0.01
Chippewa (2)	2	0.02
Choctaw (1)	1	0.01
Iroquois (2)	3	0.02
Lumbee (1)	1	0.01
Navajo	1	0.01
Osage (1)	1	0.01
Ottawa (2)	2	0.02
Pueblo	1	0.01
Seminole (1)	1	0.01
Sioux (2)	4	0.03
All other tribes	2	0.02
American Indian tribes, not spec.	4	0.03
Arab:	49	0.39
Lebanese	40	0.32
Syrian	9	0.07
Asian:	273	2.15
Bangladeshi (3)	10	0.08
Cambodian	1	0.01
Chinese, ex. Taiwanese (39)	48	0.38
Filipino (18)	19	0.15
Indian (98)	119	0.94
Indonesian	1	0.01
Japanese (9)	14	0.11
Korean (6)	7	0.06
Laotian (1)	1	0.01
Pakistani (5)	5	0.04
Taiwanese (1)	1	0.01
Thai (20)	29	0.23
Vietnamese (1)	2	0.02
Other Asian, specified	7	0.06
Other Asian, not specified (2)	9	0.07
Austrian	39	0.31
Basque	14	0.11
Brazilian	51	0.40
British	93	0.73
Bulgarian	10	0.08
Canadian	29	0.23
Celtic	8	0.06
Czech	109	0.86
Czechoslovakian	8	0.06
Danish	44	0.35
Dutch	286	2.25
English	1,539	12.12
European	96	0.76
Finnish	20	0.16
French, except Basque	442	3.48
French Canadian	158	1.24
German	1,693	13.33
Greek	64	0.50
Guyanese	25	0.20
Hawaii Native/Pacific Islander:	22	0.17
Micronesian: (3)	3	0.02
Guamanian/Chamorro (3)	3	0.02
Polynesian: (4)	7	0.06
Native Hawaiian (2)	3	0.02
Samoan (2)	4	0.03
Other Pac. Isl., specified	5	0.04
Other Pac. Isl., not spec.	7	0.06
Hispanic or Latino:	1,228	9.67
Central American:	145	1.14
Costa Rican	7	0.06
Guatemalan	28	0.22
Honduran	37	0.29
Nicaraguan	11	0.09
Panamanian	7	0.06
Salvadoran	47	0.37
Other Central American	8	0.06
Cuban	201	1.58
Dominican Republic	25	0.20
Mexican	204	1.61
Puerto Rican	226	1.78
South American:	158	1.24
Argentinean	14	0.11
Chilean	11	0.09
Colombian	59	0.46
Ecuadorian	9	0.07
Peruvian	36	0.28
Uruguayan	1	0.01
Venezuelan	25	0.20
Other South American	3	0.02
Other Hispanic or Latino	269	2.12
Hungarian	79	0.62
Irish	1,791	14.11
Israeli	11	0.09
Italian	1,149	9.05
Lithuanian	25	0.20
Norwegian	168	1.32
Pennsylvania German	11	0.09
Polish	385	3.03
Portuguese	15	0.12

Notes: 1. Figures in the "Number" column do not add up to the total population due to: a) Ancestry/Race overlap — e.g. persons can report being both White and Irish, b) persons of Hispanic origin can report being any race, c) persons reporting two ancestries are counted in both categories. 2. Numbers in parentheses indicate the number of persons reporting this ancestry/race alone, not in combination with any other ancestry/race. 3. Refer to the Explanation of Data in the front of the book for more detailed information.

Ancestry/Race	Number	%
Romanian	8	0.06
Russian	118	0.93
Scandinavian	67	0.53
Scotch-Irish	268	2.11
Scottish	227	1.79
Serbian	7	0.06
Slavic	13	0.10
Slovak	53	0.42
Slovene	9	0.07
Swedish	195	1.54
Swiss	7	0.06
Turkish	10	0.08
Ukrainian	70	0.55
United States or American	567	4.47
Welsh	105	0.83
West Indian, excl. Hispanic:	1,082	8.52
Bahamian	53	0.42
Haitian	925	7.29
Jamaican	15	0.12
Trinidadian and Tobagonian	85	0.67
West Indian	4	0.03
White:	10,266	80.85
Not Hispanic (9,159)	9,289	73.16
Hispanic (899)	977	7.69
Yugoslavian	16	0.13

Winter Garden

Place Type: City
County: Orange
Population: 14,351

Ancestry/Race	Number	%
Acadian/Cajun	7	0.05
African American/Black:	2,003	13.96
Not Hispanic (1,846)	1,920	13.38
Hispanic (56)	83	0.58
African, sub-Saharan:	48	0.34
African	48	0.34
Alaska Native tribes, specified:	2	0.01
Alaska Athabascan (1)	1	0.01
Tlingit-Haida	1	0.01
Am. Ind. or Alaska Nat., not spec.	44	0.31
American Indian tribes, specified:	96	0.67
Apache (2)	5	0.03
Blackfeet	6	0.04
Cherokee (14)	46	0.32
Chickasaw	1	0.01
Choctaw (2)	8	0.06
Comanche	2	0.01
Cree	1	0.01
Creek (3)	8	0.06
Iroquois (2)	8	0.06
Latin American Indians (2)	2	0.01
Paiute (1)	1	0.01
Potawatomi (1)	1	0.01
Seminole (1)	4	0.03
Sioux (1)	1	0.01
Yakama	1	0.01
All other tribes	1	0.01
American Indian tribes, not spec.	5	0.03
Arab:	9	0.06
Lebanese	9	0.06
Armenian	26	0.19
Asian:	196	1.37
Chinese, ex. Taiwanese (14)	20	0.14
Filipino (15)	18	0.13
Indian (55)	87	0.61
Japanese (3)	8	0.06
Korean (24)	27	0.19
Laotian (7)	7	0.05
Pakistani	1	0.01
Taiwanese (3)	3	0.02
Thai (4)	5	0.03
Vietnamese (9)	9	0.06
Other Asian, specified (4)	4	0.03
Other Asian, not specified (3)	7	0.05
Brazilian	47	0.34
British	36	0.26
Bulgarian	33	0.24
Canadian	10	0.07
Carpatho Rusyn	7	0.05
Celtic	12	0.09
Czechoslovakian	14	0.10
Danish	29	0.21
Dutch	195	1.39
English	1,619	11.57
European	104	0.74
Finnish	29	0.21
French, except Basque	317	2.26
French Canadian	156	1.11
German	1,597	11.41
Greek	31	0.22
Hawaii Native/Pacific Islander:	33	0.23
Micronesian: (1)	4	0.03
Guamanian/Chamorro (1)	4	0.03
Polynesian: (5)	15	0.10
Native Hawaiian	3	0.02
Samoan (3)	7	0.05
Tongan (1)	1	0.01
Other Polynesian (1)	4	0.03
Other Pac. Isl., not spec. (1)	14	0.10
Hispanic or Latino:	2,511	17.50
Central American:	75	0.52
Costa Rican	8	0.06
Guatemalan	23	0.16
Honduran	12	0.08
Nicaraguan	13	0.09
Panamanian	6	0.04
Salvadoran	13	0.09
Cuban	114	0.79
Dominican Republic	40	0.28
Mexican	1,137	7.92
Puerto Rican	772	5.38
South American:	113	0.79
Argentinean	1	0.01
Bolivian	5	0.03
Colombian	58	0.40
Ecuadorian	12	0.08
Peruvian	17	0.12
Venezuelan	14	0.10
Other South American	6	0.04
Other Hispanic or Latino	260	1.81
Hungarian	35	0.25
Irish	1,395	9.96
Italian	699	4.99
Maltese	8	0.06
Norwegian	99	0.71
Pennsylvania German	4	0.03
Polish	168	1.20
Portuguese	12	0.09
Romanian	43	0.31
Scandinavian	13	0.09
Scotch-Irish	266	1.90
Scottish	367	2.62
Slovak	61	0.44
Slovene	7	0.05
Swedish	112	0.80
Swiss	21	0.15
United States or American	1,539	10.99
Welsh	37	0.26
West Indian, excl. Hispanic:	162	1.16
Haitian	15	0.11
Jamaican	84	0.60
Trinidadian and Tobagonian	34	0.24
West Indian	29	0.21
White:	11,235	78.29
Not Hispanic (9,587)	9,726	67.77
Hispanic (1,406)	1,509	10.51

Winter Haven

Place Type: City
County: Polk
Population: 26,487

Ancestry/Race	Number	%
African American/Black:	6,499	24.54
Not Hispanic (6,050)	6,382	24.09
Hispanic (84)	117	0.44
African, sub-Saharan:	277	1.07
African	270	1.04
Nigerian	7	0.03
Alaska Native tribes, specified:	1	0.00
Tlingit-Haida	1	0.00
Am. Ind. or Alaska Nat., not spec.	44	0.17
American Indian tribes, specified:	82	0.31
Apache (1)	1	0.00
Blackfeet (1)	2	0.01
Cherokee (18)	45	0.17
Chippewa (1)	1	0.00
Choctaw (1)	8	0.03
Creek	2	0.01
Iroquois (2)	4	0.02
Latin American Indians	1	0.00
Lumbee (3)	3	0.01
Ottawa (2)	2	0.01
Seminole (1)	5	0.02
Sioux (2)	3	0.01
All other tribes (3)	5	0.02
American Indian tribes, not spec.	8	0.03
Arab:	34	0.13
Lebanese	23	0.09
Syrian	11	0.04
Armenian	3	0.01
Asian:	364	1.37
Chinese, ex. Taiwanese (36)	47	0.18
Filipino (51)	69	0.26
Indian (71)	84	0.32
Japanese (7)	15	0.06
Korean (7)	8	0.03
Sri Lankan (3)	3	0.01
Taiwanese (5)	5	0.02
Thai (3)	4	0.02
Vietnamese (78)	86	0.32
Other Asian, specified	1	0.00
Other Asian, not specified (7)	42	0.16
Australian	17	0.07
Austrian	24	0.09
Belgian	17	0.07
Brazilian	4	0.02
British	122	0.47
Canadian	109	0.42
Croatian	28	0.11
Czech	8	0.03
Czechoslovakian	33	0.13
Danish	95	0.37
Dutch	361	1.39
English	2,749	10.60
European	99	0.38
Finnish	82	0.32
French, except Basque	553	2.13
French Canadian	191	0.74
German	2,978	11.48
Greek	63	0.24
Hawaii Native/Pacific Islander:	28	0.11
Micronesian: (1)	1	0.00
Guamanian/Chamorro (1)	1	0.00
Polynesian: (7)	10	0.04
Native Hawaiian (4)	5	0.02
Samoan (3)	5	0.02
Other Pac. Isl., specified	1	0.00
Other Pac. Isl., not spec. (2)	16	0.06
Hispanic or Latino:	1,309	4.94
Central American:	25	0.09
Costa Rican	5	0.02
Guatemalan	1	0.00
Honduran	2	0.01
Panamanian	13	0.05
Salvadoran	4	0.02
Cuban	84	0.32
Dominican Republic	11	0.04
Mexican	339	1.28
Puerto Rican	627	2.37
South American:	41	0.15
Argentinean	3	0.01
Colombian	8	0.03
Ecuadorian	14	0.05
Peruvian	5	0.02
Uruguayan	6	0.02

Notes: 1. Figures in the "Number" column do not add up to the total population due to: a) Ancestry/Race overlap — e.g. persons can report being both White and Irish, b) persons of Hispanic origin can report being any race, c) persons reporting two ancestries are counted in both categories. 2. Numbers in parentheses indicate the number of persons reporting this ancestry/race alone, not in combination with any other ancestry/race. 3. Refer to the Explanation of Data in the front of the book for more detailed information.

Ancestry/Race	Number	%
Venezuelan	5	0.02
Other Hispanic or Latino	182	0.69
Hungarian	51	0.20
Irish	2,454	9.46
Italian	650	2.51
Lithuanian	9	0.03
Norwegian	144	0.56
Pennsylvania German	25	0.10
Polish	563	2.17
Portuguese	117	0.45
Russian	64	0.25
Scotch-Irish	380	1.46
Scottish	399	1.54
Slavic	12	0.05
Slovak	71	0.27
Slovene	14	0.05
Swedish	349	1.35
Swiss	93	0.36
Ukrainian	30	0.12
United States or American	3,798	14.64
Welsh	176	0.68
West Indian, excl. Hispanic:	723	2.79
British West Indian	15	0.06
Dutch West Indian	7	0.03
Haitian	550	2.12
Jamaican	151	0.58
White:	19,216	72.55
Not Hispanic (18,299)	18,501	69.85
Hispanic (642)	715	2.70

Winter Park

Place Type: City
County: Orange
Population: 24,090

Ancestry/Race	Number	%
Acadian/Cajun	5	0.02
African American/Black:	2,627	10.90
Not Hispanic (2,513)	2,591	10.76
Hispanic (21)	36	0.15
African, sub-Saharan:	141	0.58
African	111	0.46
South African	30	0.12
Alaska Native tribes, specified:	3	0.01
Tlingit-Haida (3)	3	0.01
Am. Ind. or Alaska Nat., not spec.	40	0.17
Albanian	6	0.02
American Indian tribes, specified:	57	0.24
Apache (1)	2	0.01
Blackfeet	2	0.01
Cherokee (8)	26	0.11
Chippewa (1)	3	0.01
Choctaw	2	0.01
Creek	2	0.01
Crow	1	0.00
Delaware (2)	2	0.01
Iroquois	1	0.00
Latin American Indians (5)	6	0.02
Lumbee (2)	2	0.01
Seminole	1	0.00
Yaqui	1	0.00
All other tribes (2)	6	0.02
American Indian tribes, not spec.	5	0.02
Arab:	62	0.26
Iraqi	7	0.03
Lebanese	55	0.23
Armenian	5	0.02
Asian:	414	1.72
Chinese, ex. Taiwanese (79)	100	0.42
Filipino (35)	59	0.24
Indian (54)	69	0.29
Japanese (28)	43	0.18
Korean (26)	37	0.15
Laotian (1)	1	0.00
Sri Lankan (3)	5	0.02
Taiwanese (4)	4	0.02
Thai (8)	11	0.05
Vietnamese (71)	77	0.32
Other Asian, specified	1	0.00
Other Asian, not specified (3)	7	0.03
Assyrian/Chaldean/Syriac	5	0.02
Australian	24	0.10
Austrian	102	0.42
Basque	31	0.13
Belgian	20	0.08
Brazilian	19	0.08
British	348	1.44
Canadian	130	0.54
Croatian	32	0.13
Czech	82	0.34
Czechoslovakian	34	0.14
Danish	180	0.74
Dutch	311	1.28
Eastern European	22	0.09
English	4,347	17.94
Estonian	6	0.02
European	265	1.09
Finnish	35	0.14
French, except Basque	1,161	4.79
French Canadian	190	0.78
German	3,709	15.31
Greek	153	0.63
Hawaii Native/Pacific Islander:	18	0.07
Polynesian: (6)	17	0.07
Native Hawaiian (6)	16	0.07
Samoan	1	0.00
Other Pac. Isl., specified	1	0.00
Hispanic or Latino:	1,039	4.31
Central American:	42	0.17
Guatemalan	4	0.02
Honduran	6	0.02
Nicaraguan	6	0.02
Panamanian	18	0.07
Salvadoran	6	0.02
Other Central American	2	0.01
Cuban	145	0.60
Dominican Republic	21	0.09
Mexican	142	0.59
Puerto Rican	394	1.64
South American:	120	0.50
Argentinean	13	0.05
Bolivian	2	0.01
Chilean	6	0.02
Colombian	46	0.19
Ecuadorian	13	0.05
Peruvian	14	0.06
Venezuelan	24	0.10
Other South American	2	0.01
Other Hispanic or Latino	175	0.73
Hungarian	94	0.39
Iranian	19	0.08
Irish	2,937	12.12
Israeli	65	0.27
Italian	1,206	4.98
Latvian	15	0.06
Lithuanian	44	0.18
Northern European	82	0.34
Norwegian	319	1.32
Pennsylvania German	26	0.11
Polish	536	2.21
Portuguese	44	0.18
Romanian	52	0.21
Russian	362	1.49
Scandinavian	68	0.28
Scotch-Irish	667	2.75
Scottish	1,229	5.07
Serbian	27	0.11
Slavic	27	0.11
Slovak	57	0.24
Swedish	365	1.51
Swiss	115	0.47
Turkish	7	0.03
Ukrainian	136	0.56
United States or American	1,469	6.06
Welsh	309	1.28
West Indian, excl. Hispanic:	179	0.74
Bahamian	8	0.03
British West Indian	12	0.05
Haitian	56	0.23
Jamaican	91	0.38
West Indian	12	0.05
White:	20,908	86.79
Not Hispanic (19,940)	20,112	83.49
Hispanic (754)	796	3.30
Yugoslavian	71	0.29

Winter Springs

Place Type: City
County: Seminole
Population: 31,666

Ancestry/Race	Number	%
Acadian/Cajun	10	0.03
African American/Black:	1,635	5.16
Not Hispanic (1,363)	1,503	4.75
Hispanic (89)	132	0.42
African, sub-Saharan:	66	0.21
South African	66	0.21
Alaska Native tribes, specified:	4	0.01
Eskimo (1)	3	0.01
Tlingit-Haida	1	0.00
Am. Ind. or Alaska Nat., not spec.	49	0.15
American Indian tribes, specified:	138	0.44
Apache (1)	7	0.02
Blackfeet	5	0.02
Cherokee (16)	54	0.17
Chickasaw	1	0.00
Chippewa (1)	9	0.03
Choctaw (1)	2	0.01
Comanche (1)	3	0.01
Creek (4)	9	0.03
Houma	1	0.00
Iroquois (2)	8	0.03
Latin American Indians (3)	17	0.05
Lumbee (4)	4	0.01
Menominee	1	0.00
Navajo	1	0.00
Pueblo	1	0.00
Seminole (2)	4	0.01
Sioux (1)	1	0.00
All other tribes (2)	10	0.03
American Indian tribes, not spec.	4	0.01
Arab:	361	1.15
Arab/Arabic	40	0.13
Egyptian	65	0.21
Jordanian	42	0.13
Lebanese	157	0.50
Palestinian	14	0.04
Syrian	24	0.08
Other Arab	19	0.06
Armenian	17	0.05
Asian:	748	2.36
Bangladeshi (2)	2	0.01
Cambodian (3)	3	0.01
Chinese, ex. Taiwanese (123)	149	0.47
Filipino (98)	134	0.42
Hmong (4)	4	0.01
Indian (138)	152	0.48
Indonesian (1)	6	0.02
Japanese (28)	49	0.15
Korean (78)	87	0.27
Laotian (12)	14	0.04
Malaysian (1)	1	0.00
Pakistani (10)	12	0.04
Sri Lankan (4)	4	0.01
Taiwanese (2)	3	0.01
Thai (14)	15	0.05
Vietnamese (84)	88	0.28
Other Asian, specified	1	0.00
Other Asian, not specified (9)	24	0.08
Australian	7	0.02
Austrian	125	0.40
Basque	7	0.02
Belgian	37	0.12
British	330	1.05
Bulgarian	14	0.04
Canadian	101	0.32
Celtic	8	0.03

Notes: 1. Figures in the "Number" column do not add up to the total population due to: a) Ancestry/Race overlap — e.g. persons can report being both White and Irish, b) persons of Hispanic origin can report being any race, c) persons reporting two ancestries are counted in both categories. 2. Numbers in parentheses indicate the number of persons reporting this ancestry/race alone, not in combination with any other ancestry/race. 3. Refer to the Explanation of Data in the front of the book for more detailed information.

Croatian	62	0.20
Czech	137	0.44
Czechoslovakian	129	0.41
Danish	164	0.52
Dutch	623	1.98
Eastern European	9	0.03
English	4,028	12.82
European	359	1.14
Finnish	94	0.30
French, except Basque	1,056	3.36
French Canadian	436	1.39
German	5,722	18.21
Greek	191	0.61
Guyanese	45	0.14
Hawaii Native/Pacific Islander:	26	0.08
Micronesian: (8)	11	0.03
Guamanian/Chamorro (5)	8	0.03
Other Micronesian (3)	3	0.01
Polynesian: (5)	9	0.03
Native Hawaiian (3)	6	0.02
Samoan (2)	3	0.01
Other Pac. Isl., specified	1	0.00
Other Pac. Isl., not spec. (1)	5	0.02
Hispanic or Latino:	3,330	10.52
Central American:	100	0.32
Costa Rican	5	0.02
Guatemalan	21	0.07
Honduran	10	0.03
Nicaraguan	13	0.04
Panamanian	28	0.09
Salvadoran	16	0.05
Other Central American	7	0.02
Cuban	284	0.90
Dominican Republic	90	0.28
Mexican	219	0.69
Puerto Rican	1,762	5.56
South American:	338	1.07
Argentinean	30	0.09
Bolivian	2	0.01
Chilean	2	0.01
Colombian	173	0.55
Ecuadorian	34	0.11
Paraguayan	2	0.01
Peruvian	42	0.13
Uruguayan	5	0.02
Venezuelan	36	0.11
Other South American	12	0.04
Other Hispanic or Latino	537	1.70
Hungarian	268	0.85
Iranian	39	0.12
Irish	4,909	15.62
Israeli	5	0.02
Italian	3,399	10.82
Latvian	13	0.04
Lithuanian	163	0.52
Macedonian	20	0.06
Maltese	7	0.02
Northern European	9	0.03
Norwegian	333	1.06
Polish	1,275	4.06
Portuguese	100	0.32
Romanian	22	0.07
Russian	506	1.61
Scandinavian	38	0.12
Scotch-Irish	727	2.31
Scottish	953	3.03
Serbian	19	0.06
Slavic	19	0.06
Slovak	123	0.39
Slovene	33	0.11
Swedish	551	1.75
Swiss	125	0.40
Turkish	20	0.06
Ukrainian	107	0.34
United States or American	2,405	7.65
Welsh	295	0.94
West Indian, excl. Hispanic:	358	1.14
Bahamian	18	0.06
Belizean	17	0.05
Haitian	58	0.18
Jamaican	180	0.57
Trinidadian and Tobagonian	32	0.10
U.S. Virgin Islander	28	0.09
West Indian	25	0.08
White:	28,644	90.46
Not Hispanic (25,851)	26,189	82.70
Hispanic (2,247)	2,455	7.75
Yugoslavian	98	0.31

Wright

Place Type: Census Designated Place
County: Okaloosa
Population: 21,697

Ancestry/Race	Number	%
Acadian/Cajun	21	0.10
African American/Black:	3,355	15.46
Not Hispanic (2,993)	3,269	15.07
Hispanic (52)	86	0.40
African, sub-Saharan:	79	0.37
African	79	0.37
Alaska Native tribes, specified:	1	0.00
Alaska Athabascan (1)	1	0.00
Am. Ind. or Alaska Nat., not spec.	110	0.51
American Indian tribes, specified:	235	1.08
Apache (3)	6	0.03
Blackfeet (3)	19	0.09
Cherokee (46)	111	0.51
Cheyenne (2)	4	0.02
Chickasaw (1)	4	0.02
Chippewa (2)	6	0.03
Choctaw	4	0.02
Creek (6)	18	0.08
Delaware (1)	1	0.00
Iroquois (8)	15	0.07
Kiowa (1)	1	0.00
Latin American Indians (6)	8	0.04
Lumbee (1)	1	0.00
Navajo (1)	1	0.00
Osage	4	0.02
Ottawa (3)	3	0.01
Pueblo	1	0.00
Puget Sound Salish (1)	1	0.00
Seminole	4	0.02
Shoshone	1	0.00
Sioux (2)	6	0.03
All other tribes (4)	16	0.07
American Indian tribes, not spec.	8	0.04
Arab:	56	0.26
Lebanese	44	0.20
Syrian	6	0.03
Other Arab	6	0.03
Armenian	23	0.11
Asian:	1,162	5.36
Chinese, ex. Taiwanese (34)	62	0.29
Filipino (266)	418	1.93
Hmong (1)	1	0.00
Indian (11)	18	0.08
Indonesian (1)	6	0.03
Japanese (58)	118	0.54
Korean (127)	182	0.84
Laotian (6)	8	0.04
Malaysian	1	0.00
Pakistani	2	0.01
Sri Lankan (1)	1	0.00
Taiwanese (4)	6	0.03
Thai (115)	193	0.89
Vietnamese (68)	83	0.38
Other Asian, specified	2	0.01
Other Asian, not specified (32)	61	0.28
Australian	59	0.27
British	122	0.57
Canadian	8	0.04
Croatian	16	0.07
Czech	6	0.03
Czechoslovakian	45	0.21
Danish	55	0.26
Dutch	285	1.32
English	2,018	9.36
European	182	0.84
Finnish	12	0.06
French, except Basque	617	2.86
French Canadian	150	0.70
German	2,801	13.00
Greek	142	0.66
Hawaii Native/Pacific Islander:	102	0.47
Micronesian: (20)	33	0.15
Guamanian/Chamorro (18)	30	0.14
Other Micronesian (2)	3	0.01
Polynesian: (16)	42	0.19
Native Hawaiian (15)	39	0.18
Samoan (1)	3	0.01
Other Pac. Isl., not spec. (4)	27	0.12
Hispanic or Latino:	1,136	5.24
Central American:	147	0.68
Costa Rican	2	0.01
Guatemalan	20	0.09
Honduran	43	0.20
Nicaraguan	20	0.09
Panamanian	54	0.25
Salvadoran	6	0.03
Other Central American	2	0.01
Cuban	43	0.20
Dominican Republic	5	0.02
Mexican	404	1.86
Puerto Rican	265	1.22
South American:	35	0.16
Bolivian	3	0.01
Chilean	2	0.01
Colombian	15	0.07
Paraguayan	3	0.01
Peruvian	8	0.04
Other South American	4	0.02
Other Hispanic or Latino	237	1.09
Hungarian	47	0.22
Irish	2,653	12.31
Italian	922	4.28
Lithuanian	36	0.17
Norwegian	139	0.64
Pennsylvania German	42	0.19
Polish	361	1.67
Portuguese	70	0.32
Romanian	32	0.15
Russian	88	0.41
Scandinavian	13	0.06
Scotch-Irish	503	2.33
Scottish	677	3.14
Serbian	10	0.05
Slovak	47	0.22
Swedish	244	1.13
Swiss	33	0.15
Ukrainian	44	0.20
United States or American	2,020	9.37
Welsh	86	0.40
West Indian, excl. Hispanic:	120	0.56
Barbadian	9	0.04
Jamaican	90	0.42
Trinidadian and Tobagonian	9	0.04
West Indian	12	0.06
White:	17,229	79.41
Not Hispanic (15,861)	16,500	76.05
Hispanic (630)	729	3.36
Yugoslavian	10	0.05

Yeehaw Junction

Place Type: Census Designated Place
County: Osceola
Population: 21,778

Ancestry/Race	Number	%
African American/Black:	2,943	13.51
Not Hispanic (2,203)	2,393	10.99
Hispanic (362)	550	2.53
African, sub-Saharan:	50	0.23
African	50	0.23
Am. Ind. or Alaska Nat., not spec.	78	0.36
American Indian tribes, specified:	95	0.44
Apache	1	0.00

Notes: 1. Figures in the "Number" column do not add up to the total population due to: a) Ancestry/Race overlap — e.g. persons can report being both White and Irish, b) persons of Hispanic origin can report being any race, c) persons reporting two ancestries are counted in both categories. 2. Numbers in parentheses indicate the number of persons reporting this ancestry/race alone, not in combination with any other ancestry/race. 3. Refer to the Explanation of Data in the front of the book for more detailed information.

Ancestry/Race	Number	%
Cherokee (7)	20	0.09
Choctaw (1)	1	0.00
Cree (1)	1	0.00
Delaware (1)	1	0.00
Iroquois (4)	7	0.03
Latin American Indians (27)	50	0.23
Sioux (1)	3	0.01
All other tribes (5)	11	0.05
American Indian tribes, not spec.	11	0.05
Arab:	26	0.12
Moroccan	6	0.03
Syrian	20	0.09
Armenian	23	0.10
Asian:	767	3.52
Cambodian (3)	3	0.01
Chinese, ex. Taiwanese (62)	88	0.40
Filipino (234)	291	1.34
Indian (186)	231	1.06
Indonesian (5)	7	0.03
Japanese (22)	35	0.16
Korean (11)	14	0.06
Laotian (6)	7	0.03
Malaysian	3	0.01
Pakistani (6)	11	0.05
Taiwanese (7)	8	0.04
Thai (20)	20	0.09
Vietnamese (15)	20	0.09
Other Asian, not specified (3)	29	0.13
Austrian	25	0.11
Belgian	6	0.03
Brazilian	25	0.11
British	102	0.46
Canadian	72	0.32
Celtic	11	0.05
Czechoslovakian	10	0.05
Danish	24	0.11
Dutch	47	0.21
English	757	3.42
European	114	0.51
Finnish	10	0.05
French, except Basque	330	1.49
French Canadian	155	0.70
German	1,131	5.10
Guyanese	42	0.19
Hawaii Native/Pacific Islander:	55	0.25
Micronesian:	2	0.01
Guamanian/Chamorro	2	0.01
Polynesian: (17)	26	0.12
Native Hawaiian (7)	16	0.07
Samoan (10)	10	0.05
Other Pac. Isl., not spec. (3)	27	0.12
Hispanic or Latino:	11,898	54.63
Central American:	348	1.60
Costa Rican	36	0.17
Guatemalan	41	0.19
Honduran	47	0.22
Nicaraguan	68	0.31
Panamanian	33	0.15
Salvadoran	102	0.47
Other Central American	21	0.10
Cuban	420	1.93
Dominican Republic	609	2.80
Mexican	288	1.32
Puerto Rican	7,980	36.64
South American:	812	3.73
Argentinean	51	0.23
Bolivian	4	0.02
Chilean	7	0.03
Colombian	476	2.19
Ecuadorian	107	0.49
Peruvian	84	0.39
Uruguayan	5	0.02
Venezuelan	58	0.27
Other South American	20	0.09
Other Hispanic or Latino	1,441	6.62
Hungarian	49	0.22
Irish	1,247	5.63
Israeli	22	0.10
Italian	961	4.34
Lithuanian	43	0.19
Norwegian	56	0.25
Pennsylvania German	11	0.05
Polish	215	0.97
Portuguese	149	0.67
Romanian	9	0.04
Russian	37	0.17
Scandinavian	17	0.08
Scotch-Irish	156	0.70
Scottish	235	1.06
Slavic	11	0.05
Slovak	14	0.06
Swedish	87	0.39
Swiss	6	0.03
Ukrainian	53	0.24
United States or American	1,067	4.81
Welsh	101	0.46
West Indian, excl. Hispanic:	1,150	5.19
Barbadian	29	0.13
Belizean	25	0.11
British West Indian	18	0.08
Haitian	441	1.99
Jamaican	378	1.71
Trinidadian and Tobagonian	53	0.24
U.S. Virgin Islander	50	0.23
West Indian	156	0.70
White:	14,442	66.31
Not Hispanic (6,530)	6,796	31.21
Hispanic (7,117)	7,646	35.11

Zephyrhills

Place Type: City
County: Pasco
Population: 10,833

Ancestry/Race	Number	%
African American/Black:	340	3.14
Not Hispanic (288)	324	2.99
Hispanic (14)	16	0.15
African, sub-Saharan:	7	0.07
Nigerian	7	0.07
Alaska Native tribes, not specified	1	0.01
Am. Ind. or Alaska Nat., not spec.	23	0.21
American Indian tribes, specified:	78	0.72
Apache	5	0.05
Blackfeet (1)	9	0.08
Cherokee (6)	34	0.31
Chippewa (3)	5	0.05
Choctaw	1	0.01
Comanche	2	0.02
Creek (1)	6	0.06
Iroquois	3	0.03
Latin American Indians	3	0.03
Osage	4	0.04
Seminole (1)	1	0.01
Sioux (1)	1	0.01
All other tribes (2)	4	0.04
American Indian tribes, not spec.	6	0.06
Arab:	35	0.33
Lebanese	35	0.33
Armenian	8	0.07
Asian:	142	1.31
Chinese, ex. Taiwanese (12)	13	0.12
Filipino (43)	49	0.45
Indian (33)	34	0.31
Indonesian (4)	4	0.04
Japanese (1)	10	0.09
Korean (3)	4	0.04
Thai (1)	2	0.02
Vietnamese (15)	16	0.15
Other Asian, specified (1)	3	0.03
Other Asian, not specified (6)	7	0.06
Austrian	26	0.24
Belgian	55	0.51
British	28	0.26
Canadian	58	0.54
Croatian	11	0.10
Czech	32	0.30
Czechoslovakian	16	0.15
Danish	29	0.27
Dutch	330	3.09
English	1,775	16.60
European	18	0.17
Finnish	61	0.57
French, except Basque	449	4.20
French Canadian	177	1.66
German	2,056	19.23
Greek	24	0.22
Hawaii Native/Pacific Islander:	9	0.08
Micronesian:	2	0.02
Other Micronesian	2	0.02
Polynesian: (3)	6	0.06
Native Hawaiian (1)	3	0.03
Samoan (2)	3	0.03
Other Pac. Isl., specified	1	0.01
Hispanic or Latino:	545	5.03
Central American:	14	0.13
Costa Rican	2	0.02
Guatemalan	3	0.03
Nicaraguan	4	0.04
Other Central American	5	0.05
Cuban	32	0.30
Dominican Republic	5	0.05
Mexican	121	1.12
Puerto Rican	267	2.46
South American:	14	0.13
Argentinean	2	0.02
Chilean	2	0.02
Colombian	4	0.04
Ecuadorian	2	0.02
Peruvian	3	0.03
Venezuelan	1	0.01
Other Hispanic or Latino	92	0.85
Hungarian	100	0.94
Irish	1,346	12.59
Italian	610	5.71
Lithuanian	36	0.34
Norwegian	89	0.83
Pennsylvania German	18	0.17
Polish	233	2.18
Portuguese	34	0.32
Russian	22	0.21
Scandinavian	23	0.22
Scotch-Irish	214	2.00
Scottish	332	3.11
Slovak	34	0.32
Slovene	7	0.07
Swedish	116	1.09
Swiss	7	0.07
Ukrainian	9	0.08
United States or American	1,388	12.98
Welsh	148	1.38
West Indian, excl. Hispanic:	74	0.69
Haitian	62	0.58
U.S. Virgin Islander	12	0.11
White:	10,204	94.19
Not Hispanic (9,720)	9,838	90.82
Hispanic (315)	366	3.38

Acworth

Place Type: City
County: Cobb
Population: 13,422

Ancestry/Race	Number	%
African American/Black:	1,776	13.23
Not Hispanic (1,662)	1,724	12.84
Hispanic (34)	52	0.39
African, sub-Saharan:	167	1.24
African	56	0.41
Ethiopian	12	0.09
Nigerian	88	0.65
Zairian	11	0.08
Am. Ind. or Alaska Nat., not spec.	25	0.19
American Indian tribes, specified:	63	0.47
Apache	3	0.02
Blackfeet (3)	5	0.04
Cherokee (6)	39	0.29
Chippewa (1)	1	0.01

Notes: 1. Figures in the "Number" column do not add up to the total population due to: a) Ancestry/Race overlap — e.g. persons can report being both White and Irish, b) persons of Hispanic origin can report being any race, c) persons reporting two ancestries are counted in both categories. 2. Numbers in parentheses indicate the number of persons reporting this ancestry/race alone, not in combination with any other ancestry/race. 3. Refer to the Explanation of Data in the front of the book for more detailed information.

Choctaw (1)	2	0.01
Iroquois (1)	2	0.01
Latin American Indians (3)	3	0.02
Lumbee (1)	2	0.01
Navajo	2	0.01
Sioux	2	0.01
All other tribes (1)	2	0.01
American Indian tribes, not spec.	3	0.02
Arab:	68	0.50
Arab/Arabic	8	0.06
Egyptian	44	0.33
Lebanese	7	0.05
Syrian	9	0.07
Armenian	8	0.06
Asian:	380	2.83
Cambodian (7)	7	0.05
Chinese, ex. Taiwanese (64)	75	0.56
Filipino (45)	67	0.50
Indian (71)	79	0.59
Japanese (13)	20	0.15
Korean (53)	72	0.54
Laotian (13)	14	0.10
Pakistani (3)	5	0.04
Taiwanese (6)	6	0.04
Thai (2)	3	0.02
Vietnamese (26)	26	0.19
Other Asian, specified	1	0.01
Other Asian, not specified (1)	5	0.04
Austrian	9	0.07
Belgian	17	0.13
Brazilian	22	0.16
British	70	0.52
Bulgarian	17	0.13
Canadian	74	0.55
Croatian	10	0.07
Czech	44	0.33
Czechoslovakian	19	0.14
Danish	35	0.26
Dutch	172	1.27
English	1,420	10.52
European	76	0.56
Finnish	33	0.24
French, except Basque	329	2.44
French Canadian	99	0.73
German	1,906	14.12
Greek	29	0.21
Guyanese	11	0.08
Hawaii Native/Pacific Islander:	13	0.10
Micronesian: (1)	1	0.01
Guamanian/Chamorro (1)	1	0.01
Polynesian: (2)	5	0.04
Native Hawaiian (1)	4	0.03
Samoan (1)	1	0.01
Other Pac. Isl., specified	1	0.01
Other Pac. Isl., not spec.	6	0.04
Hispanic or Latino:	812	6.05
Central American:	40	0.30
Costa Rican	1	0.01
Guatemalan	15	0.11
Honduran	3	0.02
Panamanian	11	0.08
Salvadoran	10	0.07
Cuban	44	0.33
Dominican Republic	9	0.07
Mexican	475	3.54
Puerto Rican	100	0.75
South American:	42	0.31
Argentinean	3	0.02
Chilean	3	0.02
Colombian	26	0.19
Peruvian	4	0.03
Uruguayan	1	0.01
Venezuelan	1	0.01
Other South American	4	0.03
Other Hispanic or Latino	102	0.76
Hungarian	19	0.14
Iranian	64	0.47
Irish	1,694	12.55
Israeli	9	0.07
Italian	418	3.10
Lithuanian	8	0.06
Norwegian	98	0.73
Polish	240	1.78
Russian	15	0.11
Scandinavian	11	0.08
Scotch-Irish	203	1.50
Scottish	489	3.62
Serbian	7	0.05
Slovak	20	0.15
Swedish	137	1.02
Swiss	14	0.10
Turkish	13	0.10
Ukrainian	24	0.18
United States or American	1,732	12.84
Welsh	85	0.63
West Indian, excl. Hispanic:	98	0.73
Barbadian	21	0.16
Jamaican	39	0.29
Trinidadian and Tobagonian	15	0.11
West Indian	23	0.17
White:	10,912	81.30
Not Hispanic (10,377)	10,535	78.49
Hispanic (315)	377	2.81
Yugoslavian	15	0.11

Albany

Place Type: City
County: Dougherty
Population: 76,939

Ancestry/Race	Number	%
Acadian/Cajun	20	0.03
African American/Black:	50,177	65.22
Not Hispanic (49,643)	49,941	64.91
Hispanic (212)	236	0.31
African, sub-Saharan:	1,294	1.68
African	920	1.19
Kenyan	7	0.01
Liberian	10	0.01
Nigerian	347	0.45
Sudanese	10	0.01
Alaska Native tribes, specified:	1	0.00
Eskimo	1	0.00
Am. Ind. or Alaska Nat., not spec.	164	0.21
American Indian tribes, specified:	162	0.21
Apache (1)	4	0.01
Blackfeet	4	0.01
Cherokee (34)	80	0.10
Chickasaw (1)	3	0.00
Chippewa (1)	2	0.00
Choctaw	3	0.00
Comanche (1)	1	0.00
Creek (15)	27	0.04
Iroquois	1	0.00
Latin American Indians (5)	7	0.01
Lumbee (3)	6	0.01
Navajo	2	0.00
Pima (1)	1	0.00
Potawatomi (3)	3	0.00
Seminole (1)	5	0.01
Sioux	1	0.00
All other tribes (6)	12	0.02
American Indian tribes, not spec.	37	0.05
Arab:	41	0.05
Egyptian	9	0.01
Lebanese	24	0.03
Syrian	8	0.01
Asian:	625	0.81
Chinese, ex. Taiwanese (74)	91	0.12
Filipino (43)	77	0.10
Indian (210)	247	0.32
Japanese (21)	40	0.05
Korean (35)	47	0.06
Laotian (1)	1	0.00
Pakistani (4)	4	0.01
Taiwanese (2)	4	0.01
Thai (5)	9	0.01
Vietnamese (25)	38	0.05
Other Asian, specified (2)	22	0.03
Other Asian, not specified (23)	45	0.06
Austrian	56	0.07
Belgian	32	0.04
British	172	0.22
Canadian	96	0.12
Croatian	15	0.02
Czech	26	0.03
Czechoslovakian	36	0.05
Danish	41	0.05
Dutch	206	0.27
Eastern European	6	0.01
English	3,516	4.56
Estonian	20	0.03
European	467	0.61
Finnish	31	0.04
French, except Basque	581	0.75
French Canadian	119	0.15
German	2,462	3.20
Greek	19	0.02
Guyanese	7	0.01
Hawaii Native/Pacific Islander:	72	0.09
Micronesian: (8)	11	0.01
Guamanian/Chamorro (8)	11	0.01
Polynesian: (14)	33	0.04
Native Hawaiian (12)	30	0.04
Samoan (2)	3	0.00
Other Pac. Isl., specified	19	0.02
Other Pac. Isl., not spec.	9	0.01
Hispanic or Latino:	950	1.23
Central American:	39	0.05
Costa Rican	4	0.01
Guatemalan	25	0.03
Honduran	3	0.00
Nicaraguan	3	0.00
Panamanian	4	0.01
Cuban	36	0.05
Dominican Republic	7	0.01
Mexican	458	0.60
Puerto Rican	117	0.15
South American:	33	0.04
Argentinean	1	0.00
Chilean	3	0.00
Colombian	15	0.02
Peruvian	3	0.00
Uruguayan	1	0.00
Venezuelan	7	0.01
Other South American	3	0.00
Other Hispanic or Latino	260	0.34
Hungarian	103	0.13
Irish	2,735	3.55
Italian	524	0.68
Lithuanian	18	0.02
Norwegian	211	0.27
Polish	354	0.46
Portuguese	6	0.01
Romanian	21	0.03
Russian	19	0.02
Scandinavian	18	0.02
Scotch-Irish	965	1.25
Scottish	658	0.85
Slovak	16	0.02
Slovene	12	0.02
Swedish	142	0.18
Swiss	63	0.08
Ukrainian	14	0.02
United States or American	5,613	7.28
Welsh	192	0.25
West Indian, excl. Hispanic:	155	0.20
Bahamian	19	0.02
British West Indian	11	0.01
Dutch West Indian	8	0.01
Haitian	9	0.01
Jamaican	91	0.12
U.S. Virgin Islander	17	0.02
White:	25,895	33.66
Not Hispanic (25,193)	25,499	33.14
Hispanic (360)	396	0.51
Yugoslavian	9	0.01

Notes: 1. Figures in the "Number" column do not add up to the total population due to: a) Ancestry/Race overlap — e.g. persons can report being both White and Irish, b) persons of Hispanic origin can report being any race, c) persons reporting two ancestries are counted in both categories. 2. Numbers in parentheses indicate the number of persons reporting this ancestry/race alone, not in combination with any other ancestry/race. 3. Refer to the Explanation of Data in the front of the book for more detailed information.

Alpharetta

Place Type: City
County: Fulton
Population: 34,854

Ancestry/Race	Number	%
African American/Black:	2,369	6.80
Not Hispanic (2,224)	2,310	6.63
Hispanic (32)	59	0.17
African, sub-Saharan:	250	0.72
African	109	0.31
Ethiopian	6	0.02
Ghanian	13	0.04
Nigerian	24	0.07
South African	98	0.28
Am. Ind. or Alaska Nat., not spec.	49	0.14
American Indian tribes, specified:	135	0.39
Apache (5)	5	0.01
Blackfeet	1	0.00
Cherokee (16)	57	0.16
Chippewa (1)	2	0.01
Choctaw	1	0.00
Comanche	1	0.00
Creek	1	0.00
Delaware	4	0.01
Iroquois (1)	2	0.01
Latin American Indians (5)	39	0.11
Lumbee (3)	3	0.01
Navajo (1)	1	0.00
Ottawa (1)	1	0.00
Potawatomi (1)	1	0.00
Seminole (1)	5	0.01
Sioux (1)	3	0.01
Ute (1)	3	0.01
All other tribes (3)	5	0.01
American Indian tribes, not spec.	4	0.01
Arab:	153	0.44
Arab/Arabic	28	0.08
Jordanian	10	0.03
Lebanese	64	0.18
Other Arab	51	0.15
Armenian	41	0.12
Asian:	2,182	6.26
Bangladeshi (5)	7	0.02
Cambodian (5)	5	0.01
Chinese, ex. Taiwanese (454)	490	1.41
Filipino (79)	112	0.32
Hmong (2)	2	0.01
Indian (857)	890	2.55
Indonesian (11)	12	0.03
Japanese (67)	95	0.27
Korean (285)	300	0.86
Laotian (4)	4	0.01
Malaysian (9)	12	0.03
Pakistani (50)	60	0.17
Sri Lankan (1)	1	0.00
Taiwanese (29)	30	0.09
Thai (24)	30	0.09
Vietnamese (70)	73	0.21
Other Asian, specified (5)	5	0.01
Other Asian, not specified (21)	54	0.15
Australian	67	0.19
Austrian	148	0.43
Belgian	37	0.11
Brazilian	298	0.86
British	326	0.94
Canadian	258	0.75
Carpatho Rusyn	16	0.05
Celtic	11	0.03
Croatian	41	0.12
Czech	91	0.26
Czechoslovakian	18	0.05
Danish	150	0.43
Dutch	503	1.45
Eastern European	45	0.13
English	4,132	11.94
Estonian	6	0.02
European	436	1.26
Finnish	48	0.14
French, except Basque	1,135	3.28
French Canadian	378	1.09
German	5,388	15.57
Greek	257	0.74
Hawaii Native/Pacific Islander:	18	0.05
Melanesian: (3)	3	0.01
Fijian (3)	3	0.01
Micronesian:	2	0.01
Other Micronesian	2	0.01
Polynesian: (3)	10	0.03
Native Hawaiian (1)	7	0.02
Samoan (2)	3	0.01
Other Pac. Isl., not spec. (1)	3	0.01
Hispanic or Latino:	1,927	5.53
Central American:	101	0.29
Costa Rican	6	0.02
Guatemalan	13	0.04
Honduran	23	0.07
Nicaraguan	9	0.03
Panamanian	15	0.04
Salvadoran	35	0.10
Cuban	139	0.40
Dominican Republic	10	0.03
Mexican	997	2.86
Puerto Rican	200	0.57
South American:	230	0.66
Argentinean	7	0.02
Bolivian	3	0.01
Chilean	4	0.01
Colombian	131	0.38
Ecuadorian	6	0.02
Paraguayan	1	0.00
Peruvian	27	0.08
Uruguayan	1	0.00
Venezuelan	37	0.11
Other South American	13	0.04
Other Hispanic or Latino	250	0.72
Hungarian	182	0.53
Iranian	28	0.08
Irish	4,596	13.28
Italian	2,502	7.23
Latvian	39	0.11
Lithuanian	119	0.34
Luxemburger	33	0.10
Northern European	101	0.29
Norwegian	416	1.20
Pennsylvania German	19	0.05
Polish	921	2.66
Portuguese	34	0.10
Romanian	19	0.05
Russian	369	1.07
Scandinavian	74	0.21
Scotch-Irish	868	2.51
Scottish	1,148	3.32
Serbian	13	0.04
Slavic	15	0.04
Slovak	67	0.19
Slovene	13	0.04
Swedish	531	1.53
Swiss	107	0.31
Turkish	24	0.07
Ukrainian	76	0.22
United States or American	3,071	8.87
Welsh	208	0.60
West Indian, excl. Hispanic:	169	0.49
Bahamian	22	0.06
Haitian	44	0.13
Jamaican	97	0.28
Trinidadian and Tobagonian	6	0.02
White:	29,593	84.91
Not Hispanic (28,143)	28,469	81.68
Hispanic (1,007)	1,124	3.22
Yugoslavian	18	0.05

Americus

Place Type: City
County: Sumter
Population: 17,013

Ancestry/Race	Number	%
African American/Black:	9,972	58.61
Not Hispanic (9,851)	9,905	58.22
Hispanic (61)	67	0.39
African, sub-Saharan:	34	0.20
African	34	0.20
Am. Ind. or Alaska Nat., not spec.	35	0.21
American Indian tribes, specified:	44	0.26
Apache	2	0.01
Cherokee (4)	17	0.10
Comanche (1)	1	0.01
Creek (7)	10	0.06
Crow	1	0.01
Latin American Indians (5)	6	0.04
Seminole (1)	3	0.02
All other tribes (3)	4	0.02
American Indian tribes, not spec.	9	0.05
Arab:	20	0.12
Syrian	20	0.12
Asian:	166	0.98
Bangladeshi (2)	2	0.01
Chinese, ex. Taiwanese (24)	28	0.16
Filipino (16)	21	0.12
Indian (51)	54	0.32
Japanese (8)	9	0.05
Korean (30)	31	0.18
Laotian (1)	1	0.01
Vietnamese (7)	9	0.05
Other Asian, specified	1	0.01
Other Asian, not specified (3)	10	0.06
Austrian	17	0.10
Brazilian	18	0.11
British	63	0.37
Czech	6	0.04
Czechoslovakian	8	0.05
Danish	32	0.19
Dutch	75	0.45
English	788	4.69
European	78	0.46
French, except Basque	210	1.25
French Canadian	16	0.10
German	739	4.40
Greek	51	0.30
Hawaii Native/Pacific Islander:	7	0.04
Micronesian: (1)	1	0.01
Guamanian/Chamorro (1)	1	0.01
Polynesian: (1)	1	0.01
Native Hawaiian (1)	1	0.01
Other Pac. Isl., specified	1	0.01
Other Pac. Isl., not spec.	4	0.02
Hispanic or Latino:	423	2.49
Central American:	15	0.09
Guatemalan	5	0.03
Honduran	4	0.02
Panamanian	5	0.03
Other Central American	1	0.01
Cuban	11	0.06
Mexican	278	1.63
Puerto Rican	17	0.10
South American:	18	0.11
Argentinean	2	0.01
Chilean	1	0.01
Colombian	4	0.02
Ecuadorian	3	0.02
Venezuelan	7	0.04
Other South American	1	0.01
Other Hispanic or Latino	84	0.49
Irish	630	3.75
Italian	169	1.01
Lithuanian	27	0.16
New Zealander	16	0.10
Northern European	13	0.08
Norwegian	32	0.19
Polish	144	0.86

Notes: 1. Figures in the "Number" column do not add up to the total population due to: a) Ancestry/Race overlap — e.g. persons can report being both White and Irish, b) persons of Hispanic origin can report being any race, c) persons reporting two ancestries are counted in both categories. 2. Numbers in parentheses indicate the number of persons reporting this ancestry/race alone, not in combination with any other ancestry/race. 3. Refer to the Explanation of Data in the front of the book for more detailed information.

Scandinavian	3	0.02
Scotch-Irish	258	1.53
Scottish	181	1.08
Slovak	6	0.04
Swedish	32	0.19
Swiss	72	0.43
United States or American	1,539	9.15
Welsh	46	0.27
White:	6,725	39.53
Not Hispanic (6,472)	6,541	38.45
Hispanic (172)	184	1.08

Athens-Clarke County

Place Type: Special City
County: Clarke
Population: 100,266

Ancestry/Race	Number	%
Acadian/Cajun	29	0.03
African American/Black:	27,945	27.87
Not Hispanic (27,284)	27,739	27.67
Hispanic (158)	206	0.21
African, sub-Saharan:	1,393	1.39
African	861	0.86
Cape Verdean	11	0.01
Ethiopian	47	0.05
Ghanian	50	0.05
Kenyan	73	0.07
Nigerian	145	0.14
Sierra Leonean	13	0.01
South African	47	0.05
Sudanese	45	0.04
Other sub-Saharan African	101	0.10
Alaska Native tribes, specified:	3	0.00
Alaska Athabascan	1	0.00
Eskimo (1)	2	0.00
Alaska Native tribes, not specified	1	0.00
Am. Ind. or Alaska Nat., not spec.	209	0.21
Albanian	40	0.04
American Indian tribes, specified:	281	0.28
Apache	2	0.00
Blackfeet (8)	15	0.01
Cherokee (42)	158	0.16
Chickasaw	1	0.00
Chippewa (4)	7	0.01
Choctaw (5)	8	0.01
Creek (8)	16	0.02
Delaware (1)	7	0.01
Iroquois (1)	3	0.00
Latin American Indians (17)	28	0.03
Lumbee (3)	4	0.00
Menominee (1)	1	0.00
Navajo (3)	4	0.00
Ottawa (5)	5	0.00
Paiute (1)	1	0.00
Potawatomi	2	0.00
Pueblo (1)	2	0.00
Seminole	1	0.00
Sioux (1)	2	0.00
Ute	2	0.00
Yaqui	1	0.00
All other tribes (6)	11	0.01
American Indian tribes, not spec.	34	0.03
Arab:	422	0.42
Arab/Arabic	66	0.07
Egyptian	92	0.09
Iraqi	7	0.01
Lebanese	216	0.22
Moroccan	10	0.01
Palestinian	8	0.01
Syrian	15	0.01
Other Arab	8	0.01
Armenian	33	0.03
Asian:	3,663	3.65
Bangladeshi (6)	6	0.01
Cambodian (10)	14	0.01
Chinese, ex. Taiwanese (851)	917	0.91
Filipino (226)	323	0.32
Hmong (5)	5	0.00
Indian (889)	967	0.96
Indonesian (4)	10	0.01
Japanese (161)	215	0.21
Korean (630)	712	0.71
Laotian (20)	29	0.03
Malaysian (22)	23	0.02
Pakistani (55)	65	0.06
Sri Lankan (13)	13	0.01
Taiwanese (68)	79	0.08
Thai (53)	63	0.06
Vietnamese (87)	119	0.12
Other Asian, specified (3)	13	0.01
Other Asian, not specified (25)	90	0.09
Assyrian/Chaldean/Syriac	8	0.01
Australian	94	0.09
Austrian	313	0.31
Basque	15	0.01
Belgian	87	0.09
Brazilian	109	0.11
British	842	0.84
Bulgarian	25	0.02
Canadian	188	0.19
Celtic	33	0.03
Croatian	137	0.14
Czech	196	0.20
Czechoslovakian	146	0.15
Danish	202	0.20
Dutch	849	0.85
Eastern European	80	0.08
English	10,478	10.45
Estonian	17	0.02
European	1,639	1.63
Finnish	78	0.08
French, except Basque	2,266	2.26
French Canadian	416	0.41
German	9,414	9.39
Greek	298	0.30
Guyanese	45	0.04
Hawaii Native/Pacific Islander:	101	0.10
Micronesian: (20)	29	0.03
Guamanian/Chamorro (16)	24	0.02
Other Micronesian (4)	5	0.00
Polynesian: (22)	41	0.04
Native Hawaiian (11)	25	0.02
Samoan (8)	12	0.01
Tongan (1)	1	0.00
Other Polynesian (2)	3	0.00
Other Pac. Isl., specified	9	0.01
Other Pac. Isl., not spec. (3)	22	0.02
Hispanic or Latino:	6,402	6.39
Central American:	483	0.48
Costa Rican	12	0.01
Guatemalan	104	0.10
Honduran	40	0.04
Nicaraguan	14	0.01
Panamanian	23	0.02
Salvadoran	257	0.26
Other Central American	33	0.03
Cuban	174	0.17
Dominican Republic	24	0.02
Mexican	4,091	4.08
Puerto Rican	370	0.37
South American:	530	0.53
Argentinean	33	0.03
Bolivian	6	0.01
Chilean	12	0.01
Colombian	119	0.12
Ecuadorian	19	0.02
Paraguayan	6	0.01
Peruvian	266	0.27
Uruguayan	10	0.01
Venezuelan	34	0.03
Other South American	25	0.02
Other Hispanic or Latino	730	0.73
Hungarian	258	0.26
Icelander	10	0.01
Iranian	118	0.12
Irish	8,916	8.89
Israeli	26	0.03
Italian	2,426	2.42
Latvian	15	0.01
Lithuanian	162	0.16
New Zealander	19	0.02
Northern European	107	0.11
Norwegian	745	0.74
Pennsylvania German	39	0.04
Polish	1,596	1.59
Portuguese	154	0.15
Romanian	40	0.04
Russian	591	0.59
Scandinavian	92	0.09
Scotch-Irish	2,787	2.78
Scottish	2,695	2.69
Serbian	12	0.01
Slavic	6	0.01
Slovak	52	0.05
Swedish	690	0.69
Swiss	189	0.19
Turkish	20	0.02
Ukrainian	145	0.14
United States or American	6,401	6.38
Welsh	689	0.69
West Indian, excl. Hispanic:	322	0.32
Bahamian	30	0.03
Barbadian	7	0.01
Belizean	9	0.01
British West Indian	7	0.01
Haitian	23	0.02
Jamaican	212	0.21
U.S. Virgin Islander	11	0.01
West Indian	23	0.02
White:	66,057	65.88
Not Hispanic (61,950)	62,858	62.69
Hispanic (2,928)	3,199	3.19
Yugoslavian	69	0.07

Atlanta

Place Type: City
County: Fulton
Population: 416,474

Ancestry/Race	Number	%
Acadian/Cajun	90	0.02
Afghan	28	0.01
African American/Black:	258,610	62.10
Not Hispanic (254,062)	256,605	61.61
Hispanic (1,627)	2,005	0.48
African, sub-Saharan:	7,699	1.85
African	5,549	1.33
Cape Verdean	33	0.01
Ethiopian	580	0.14
Ghanian	166	0.04
Kenyan	4	0.00
Liberian	75	0.02
Nigerian	630	0.15
Senegalese	25	0.01
Sierra Leonean	50	0.01
Somalian	58	0.01
South African	92	0.02
Sudanese	230	0.06
Zairian	21	0.01
Other sub-Saharan African	186	0.04
Alaska Native tribes, specified:	10	0.00
Alaska Athabascan (2)	2	0.00
Aleut (2)	3	0.00
Eskimo (1)	2	0.00
Tlingit-Haida (2)	3	0.00
Alaska Native tribes, not specified	1	0.00
Am. Ind. or Alaska Nat., not spec.	1,003	0.24
Albanian	45	0.01
American Indian tribes, specified:	1,111	0.27
Apache (13)	28	0.01
Blackfeet (8)	61	0.01
Cherokee (123)	579	0.14
Cheyenne	2	0.00
Chickasaw (6)	11	0.00
Chippewa (4)	13	0.00
Choctaw (9)	39	0.01
Comanche (3)	4	0.00

Notes: 1. Figures in the "Number" column do not add up to the total population due to: a) Ancestry/Race overlap — e.g. persons can report being both White and Irish, b) persons of Hispanic origin can report being any race, c) persons reporting two ancestries are counted in both categories. 2. Numbers in parentheses indicate the number of persons reporting this ancestry/race alone, not in combination with any other ancestry/race. 3. Refer to the Explanation of Data in the front of the book for more detailed information.

Cree (4)	7	0.00
Creek (10)	65	0.02
Crow (1)	1	0.00
Delaware	1	0.00
Iroquois (8)	22	0.01
Kiowa (1)	1	0.00
Latin American Indians (60)	116	0.03
Lumbee (15)	20	0.00
Navajo (5)	7	0.00
Osage	2	0.00
Ottawa	3	0.00
Paiute (1)	2	0.00
Pima (1)	1	0.00
Potawatomi (4)	6	0.00
Pueblo (1)	9	0.00
Seminole (4)	16	0.00
Shoshone (1)	2	0.00
Sioux (10)	27	0.01
Ute (1)	1	0.00
Yuman	1	0.00
All other tribes (25)	64	0.02
American Indian tribes, not spec.	150	0.04
Arab:	963	0.23
Arab/Arabic	55	0.01
Egyptian	91	0.02
Iraqi	80	0.02
Lebanese	444	0.11
Moroccan	109	0.03
Palestinian	29	0.01
Syrian	65	0.02
Other Arab	90	0.02
Armenian	222	0.05
Asian:	9,310	2.24
Bangladeshi (102)	144	0.03
Cambodian (29)	35	0.01
Chinese, ex. Taiwanese (1,567)	1,758	0.42
Filipino (354)	496	0.12
Indian (2,361)	2,617	0.63
Indonesian (26)	41	0.01
Japanese (408)	539	0.13
Korean (748)	872	0.21
Laotian (41)	46	0.01
Malaysian (9)	18	0.00
Pakistani (76)	100	0.02
Sri Lankan (18)	24	0.01
Taiwanese (71)	79	0.02
Thai (144)	171	0.04
Vietnamese (1,783)	1,881	0.45
Other Asian, specified (17)	110	0.03
Other Asian, not specified (198)	379	0.09
Australian	99	0.02
Austrian	509	0.12
Basque	18	0.00
Belgian	242	0.06
Brazilian	141	0.03
British	2,174	0.52
Bulgarian	16	0.00
Canadian	556	0.13
Celtic	93	0.02
Croatian	141	0.03
Czech	537	0.13
Czechoslovakian	244	0.06
Danish	613	0.15
Dutch	2,090	0.50
Eastern European	465	0.11
English	24,686	5.93
Estonian	13	0.00
European	3,012	0.72
Finnish	205	0.05
French, except Basque	4,984	1.20
French Canadian	760	0.18
German	18,709	4.49
German Russian	13	0.00
Greek	913	0.22
Guyanese	78	0.02
Hawaii Native/Pacific Islander:	472	0.11
Melanesian:	1	0.00
Other Melanesian	1	0.00
Micronesian: (36)	57	0.01
Guamanian/Chamorro (34)	53	0.01
Other Micronesian (2)	4	0.00
Polynesian: (91)	172	0.04
Native Hawaiian (62)	118	0.03
Samoan (27)	51	0.01
Tongan	1	0.00
Other Polynesian (2)	2	0.00
Other Pac. Isl., specified	79	0.02
Other Pac. Isl., not spec. (45)	163	0.04
Hispanic or Latino:	18,720	4.49
Central American:	796	0.19
Costa Rican	47	0.01
Guatemalan	120	0.03
Honduran	267	0.06
Nicaraguan	44	0.01
Panamanian	119	0.03
Salvadoran	163	0.04
Other Central American	36	0.01
Cuban	887	0.21
Dominican Republic	144	0.03
Mexican	12,715	3.05
Puerto Rican	1,147	0.28
South American:	853	0.20
Argentinean	100	0.02
Bolivian	16	0.00
Chilean	62	0.01
Colombian	293	0.07
Ecuadorian	51	0.01
Paraguayan	10	0.00
Peruvian	127	0.03
Uruguayan	28	0.01
Venezuelan	129	0.03
Other South American	37	0.01
Other Hispanic or Latino	2,178	0.52
Hungarian	809	0.19
Icelander	37	0.01
Iranian	223	0.05
Irish	18,503	4.44
Israeli	96	0.02
Italian	6,609	1.59
Latvian	98	0.02
Lithuanian	509	0.12
Luxemburger	11	0.00
Macedonian	9	0.00
Maltese	5	0.00
New Zealander	16	0.00
Northern European	265	0.06
Norwegian	1,310	0.31
Pennsylvania German	19	0.00
Polish	3,441	0.83
Portuguese	222	0.05
Romanian	177	0.04
Russian	3,233	0.78
Scandinavian	156	0.04
Scotch-Irish	6,088	1.46
Scottish	6,711	1.61
Serbian	90	0.02
Slavic	54	0.01
Slovak	239	0.06
Slovene	47	0.01
Swedish	1,738	0.42
Swiss	621	0.15
Turkish	161	0.04
Ukrainian	419	0.10
United States or American	12,412	2.98
Welsh	1,472	0.35
West Indian, excl. Hispanic:	2,406	0.58
Bahamian	65	0.02
Barbadian	83	0.02
Belizean	4	0.00
Bermudan	50	0.01
British West Indian	89	0.02
Dutch West Indian	12	0.00
Haitian	468	0.11
Jamaican	1,189	0.29
Trinidadian and Tobagonian	199	0.05
U.S. Virgin Islander	76	0.02
West Indian	166	0.04
Other West Indian	5	0.00
White:	141,429	33.96
Not Hispanic (130,222)	132,645	31.85
Hispanic (8,130)	8,784	2.11
Yugoslavian	181	0.04

Augusta-Richmond County

Place Type: Special City
County: Richmond
Population: 195,182

Ancestry/Race	Number	%
Acadian/Cajun	29	0.01
African American/Black:	100,233	51.35
Not Hispanic (97,517)	99,150	50.80
Hispanic (803)	1,083	0.55
African, sub-Saharan:	2,417	1.24
African	2,105	1.08
Cape Verdean	66	0.03
Ethiopian	39	0.02
Ghanian	7	0.00
Kenyan	8	0.00
Nigerian	146	0.07
South African	13	0.01
Sudanese	13	0.01
Other sub-Saharan African	20	0.01
Alaska Native tribes, specified:	7	0.00
Alaska Athabascan (1)	1	0.00
Aleut	1	0.00
Eskimo (1)	1	0.00
Tlingit-Haida (4)	4	0.00
Am. Ind. or Alaska Nat., not spec.	594	0.30
American Indian tribes, specified:	774	0.40
Apache (12)	33	0.02
Blackfeet (17)	41	0.02
Cherokee (114)	429	0.22
Cheyenne (3)	6	0.00
Chickasaw (5)	10	0.01
Chippewa (6)	16	0.01
Choctaw (10)	22	0.01
Comanche (4)	9	0.00
Creek (10)	28	0.01
Delaware (1)	2	0.00
Houma (1)	1	0.00
Iroquois (5)	17	0.01
Kiowa (1)	1	0.00
Latin American Indians (9)	27	0.01
Lumbee (9)	10	0.01
Navajo (3)	7	0.00
Osage (2)	4	0.00
Ottawa	1	0.00
Paiute (1)	1	0.00
Pima (1)	1	0.00
Potawatomi	2	0.00
Pueblo (6)	8	0.00
Puget Sound Salish (2)	2	0.00
Seminole (1)	16	0.01
Sioux (11)	24	0.01
Ute	1	0.00
Yaqui (3)	3	0.00
All other tribes (23)	52	0.03
American Indian tribes, not spec.	103	0.05
Arab:	260	0.13
Arab/Arabic	13	0.01
Egyptian	48	0.02
Lebanese	105	0.05
Palestinian	8	0.00
Syrian	86	0.04
Armenian	16	0.01
Asian:	4,089	2.09
Bangladeshi (5)	5	0.00
Cambodian (7)	9	0.00
Chinese, ex. Taiwanese (505)	603	0.31
Filipino (372)	581	0.30
Indian (390)	498	0.26
Indonesian (6)	9	0.00
Japanese (215)	345	0.18
Korean (927)	1,258	0.64
Laotian (28)	32	0.02
Malaysian (5)	5	0.00
Pakistani (22)	33	0.02

Notes: 1. Figures in the "Number" column do not add up to the total population due to: a) Ancestry/Race overlap — e.g. persons can report being both White and Irish, b) persons of Hispanic origin can report being any race, c) persons reporting two ancestries are counted in both categories. 2. Numbers in parentheses indicate the number of persons reporting this ancestry/race alone, not in combination with any other ancestry/race. 3. Refer to the Explanation of Data in the front of the book for more detailed information.

Ancestry/Race	Number	%
Taiwanese (18)	25	0.01
Thai (101)	141	0.07
Vietnamese (237)	279	0.14
Other Asian, specified (9)	62	0.03
Other Asian, not specified (86)	204	0.10
Assyrian/Chaldean/Syriac	2	0.00
Australian	37	0.02
Austrian	122	0.06
Belgian	33	0.02
Brazilian	27	0.01
British	541	0.28
Canadian	198	0.10
Celtic	12	0.01
Croatian	47	0.02
Czech	102	0.05
Czechoslovakian	129	0.07
Danish	218	0.11
Dutch	896	0.46
Eastern European	27	0.01
English	11,364	5.82
Estonian	8	0.00
European	959	0.49
Finnish	94	0.05
French, except Basque	2,407	1.23
French Canadian	646	0.33
German	11,163	5.71
German Russian	15	0.01
Greek	286	0.15
Guyanese	64	0.03
Hawaii Native/Pacific Islander:	470	0.24
Melanesian:	1	0.00
Fijian	1	0.00
Micronesian: (118)	152	0.08
Guamanian/Chamorro (103)	134	0.07
Other Micronesian (15)	18	0.01
Polynesian: (90)	185	0.09
Native Hawaiian (41)	109	0.06
Samoan (41)	64	0.03
Tongan (2)	3	0.00
Other Polynesian (6)	9	0.00
Other Pac. Isl., specified	51	0.03
Other Pac. Isl., not spec. (25)	81	0.04
Hispanic or Latino:	5,447	2.79
Central American:	435	0.22
Costa Rican	22	0.01
Guatemalan	18	0.01
Honduran	38	0.02
Nicaraguan	10	0.01
Panamanian	306	0.16
Salvadoran	19	0.01
Other Central American	22	0.01
Cuban	137	0.07
Dominican Republic	85	0.04
Mexican	1,511	0.77
Puerto Rican	2,068	1.06
South American:	167	0.09
Argentinean	2	0.00
Bolivian	8	0.00
Chilean	11	0.01
Colombian	58	0.03
Ecuadorian	21	0.01
Paraguayan	4	0.00
Peruvian	19	0.01
Uruguayan	2	0.00
Venezuelan	35	0.02
Other South American	7	0.00
Other Hispanic or Latino	1,044	0.53
Hungarian	292	0.15
Icelander	4	0.00
Iranian	121	0.06
Irish	11,184	5.72
Israeli	6	0.00
Italian	2,698	1.38
Lithuanian	73	0.04
Macedonian	8	0.00
Northern European	68	0.03
Norwegian	720	0.37
Pennsylvania German	66	0.03
Polish	1,252	0.64
Portuguese	263	0.13
Romanian	12	0.01
Russian	265	0.14
Scandinavian	77	0.04
Scotch-Irish	2,373	1.21
Scottish	2,749	1.41
Serbian	39	0.02
Slavic	5	0.00
Slovak	35	0.02
Slovene	23	0.01
Swedish	634	0.32
Swiss	75	0.04
Turkish	31	0.02
Ukrainian	177	0.09
United States or American	17,803	9.11
Welsh	651	0.33
West Indian, excl. Hispanic:	768	0.39
Bahamian	11	0.01
Barbadian	75	0.04
Belizean	6	0.00
Bermudan	17	0.01
British West Indian	6	0.00
Dutch West Indian	9	0.00
Haitian	124	0.06
Jamaican	302	0.15
Trinidadian and Tobagonian	42	0.02
U.S. Virgin Islander	45	0.02
West Indian	131	0.07
White:	90,069	46.15
Not Hispanic (85,340)	87,437	44.80
Hispanic (2,311)	2,632	1.35
Yugoslavian	58	0.03

Bainbridge

Place Type: City
County: Decatur
Population: 11,722

Ancestry/Race	Number	%
African American/Black:	5,929	50.58
Not Hispanic (5,887)	5,911	50.43
Hispanic (14)	18	0.15
African, sub-Saharan:	96	0.82
African	85	0.73
Liberian	11	0.09
Am. Ind. or Alaska Nat., not spec.	17	0.15
American Indian tribes, specified:	27	0.23
Blackfeet	1	0.01
Cherokee (1)	13	0.11
Comanche (1)	1	0.01
Creek (5)	5	0.04
Navajo (2)	7	0.06
American Indian tribes, not spec.	2	0.02
Arab:	7	0.06
Syrian	7	0.06
Asian:	96	0.82
Chinese, ex. Taiwanese (10)	15	0.13
Filipino (6)	10	0.09
Indian (37)	42	0.36
Japanese (2)	5	0.04
Korean (10)	11	0.09
Thai (1)	1	0.01
Vietnamese (2)	6	0.05
Other Asian, specified	2	0.02
Other Asian, not specified (3)	4	0.03
British	6	0.05
Canadian	8	0.07
Croatian	19	0.16
Danish	6	0.05
Dutch	84	0.72
English	909	7.77
European	72	0.62
French, except Basque	130	1.11
French Canadian	27	0.23
German	410	3.51
Hawaii Native/Pacific Islander:	13	0.11
Micronesian:	1	0.01
Guamanian/Chamorro	1	0.01
Polynesian: (2)	5	0.04
Native Hawaiian (2)	5	0.04
Other Pac. Isl., specified	2	0.02
Other Pac. Isl., not spec.	5	0.04
Hispanic or Latino:	234	2.00
Central American:	6	0.05
Costa Rican	2	0.02
Guatemalan	4	0.03
Cuban	10	0.09
Dominican Republic	1	0.01
Mexican	162	1.38
Puerto Rican	24	0.20
South American:	3	0.03
Colombian	1	0.01
Peruvian	1	0.01
Venezuelan	1	0.01
Other Hispanic or Latino	28	0.24
Hungarian	11	0.09
Irish	593	5.07
Italian	51	0.44
Northern European	21	0.18
Norwegian	16	0.14
Polish	49	0.42
Russian	22	0.19
Scotch-Irish	133	1.14
Scottish	95	0.81
Swedish	17	0.15
United States or American	1,473	12.60
Welsh	39	0.33
West Indian, excl. Hispanic:	9	0.08
Haitian	4	0.03
Jamaican	5	0.04
White:	5,618	47.93
Not Hispanic (5,452)	5,500	46.92
Hispanic (114)	118	1.01
Yugoslavian	15	0.13

Belvedere Park

Place Type: Census Designated Place
County: De Kalb
Population: 18,945

Ancestry/Race	Number	%
African American/Black:	15,797	83.38
Not Hispanic (15,542)	15,687	82.80
Hispanic (65)	110	0.58
African, sub-Saharan:	436	2.30
African	306	1.61
Ethiopian	26	0.14
Ghanian	71	0.37
Liberian	9	0.05
Nigerian	11	0.06
South African	6	0.03
Other sub-Saharan African	7	0.04
Am. Ind. or Alaska Nat., not spec.	45	0.24
Albanian	23	0.12
American Indian tribes, specified:	72	0.38
Apache	2	0.01
Blackfeet (2)	6	0.03
Cherokee (9)	40	0.21
Chippewa	2	0.01
Choctaw	1	0.01
Creek	1	0.01
Latin American Indians (9)	10	0.05
Lumbee	2	0.01
Navajo	2	0.01
Sioux	1	0.01
All other tribes (3)	5	0.03
Arab:	8	0.04
Other Arab	8	0.04
Asian:	245	1.29
Cambodian (15)	15	0.08
Chinese, ex. Taiwanese (14)	20	0.11
Filipino (8)	17	0.09
Hmong (35)	35	0.18
Indian (33)	44	0.23
Japanese (5)	15	0.08
Korean (15)	20	0.11
Laotian (19)	19	0.10
Pakistani (1)	1	0.01
Thai (1)	1	0.01

Notes: 1. Figures in the "Number" column do not add up to the total population due to: a) Ancestry/Race overlap — e.g. persons can report being both White and Irish, b) persons of Hispanic origin can report being any race, c) persons reporting two ancestries are counted in both categories. 2. Numbers in parentheses indicate the number of persons reporting this ancestry/race alone, not in combination with any other ancestry/race. 3. Refer to the Explanation of Data in the front of the book for more detailed information.

Vietnamese (23)	34	0.18
Other Asian, specified (1)	2	0.01
Other Asian, not specified (8)	22	0.12
British	24	0.13
Canadian	14	0.07
Croatian	25	0.13
Czechoslovakian	5	0.03
Danish	20	0.11
Dutch	30	0.16
English	334	1.76
European	126	0.66
French, except Basque	140	0.74
French Canadian	19	0.10
German	189	1.00
Greek	18	0.09
Hawaii Native/Pacific Islander:	14	0.07
Micronesian: (1)	1	0.01
Guamanian/Chamorro (1)	1	0.01
Polynesian: (2)	4	0.02
Native Hawaiian (2)	4	0.02
Other Pac. Isl., specified	1	0.01
Other Pac. Isl., not spec. (1)	8	0.04
Hispanic or Latino:	660	3.48
Central American:	24	0.13
Costa Rican	2	0.01
Guatemalan	5	0.03
Honduran	6	0.03
Panamanian	8	0.04
Other Central American	3	0.02
Cuban	20	0.11
Dominican Republic	4	0.02
Mexican	447	2.36
Puerto Rican	56	0.30
South American:	14	0.07
Argentinean	1	0.01
Chilean	2	0.01
Colombian	1	0.01
Ecuadorian	2	0.01
Peruvian	8	0.04
Other Hispanic or Latino	95	0.50
Hungarian	10	0.05
Irish	345	1.82
Italian	168	0.89
Latvian	5	0.03
Lithuanian	5	0.03
Northern European	7	0.04
Polish	87	0.46
Russian	10	0.05
Scotch-Irish	92	0.49
Scottish	89	0.47
Serbian	33	0.17
Slovak	7	0.04
Swedish	54	0.28
Turkish	6	0.03
United States or American	406	2.14
Welsh	23	0.12
West Indian, excl. Hispanic:	336	1.77
Barbadian	8	0.04
Haitian	52	0.27
Jamaican	191	1.01
Trinidadian and Tobagonian	22	0.12
U.S. Virgin Islander	17	0.09
West Indian	46	0.24
White:	2,656	14.02
Not Hispanic (2,286)	2,412	12.73
Hispanic (208)	244	1.29
Yugoslavian	30	0.16

Brunswick

Place Type: City
County: Glynn
Population: 15,600

Ancestry/Race	Number	%
African American/Black:	9,452	60.59
Not Hispanic (9,247)	9,361	60.01
Hispanic (83)	91	0.58
African, sub-Saharan:	660	4.28
African	660	4.28
Am. Ind. or Alaska Nat., not spec.	43	0.28
American Indian tribes, specified:	49	0.31
Blackfeet	2	0.01
Cherokee (7)	20	0.13
Cree	1	0.01
Iroquois	7	0.04
Latin American Indians (3)	12	0.08
Lumbee (3)	3	0.02
Seminole	2	0.01
Sioux (1)	1	0.01
All other tribes	1	0.01
American Indian tribes, not spec.	7	0.04
Arab:	13	0.08
Lebanese	5	0.03
Palestinian	8	0.05
Asian:	99	0.63
Chinese, ex. Taiwanese (14)	20	0.13
Filipino (5)	12	0.08
Indian (22)	28	0.18
Japanese (10)	23	0.15
Korean (1)	4	0.03
Thai (1)	2	0.01
Vietnamese	2	0.01
Other Asian, specified	5	0.03
Other Asian, not specified (2)	3	0.02
Austrian	9	0.06
British	49	0.32
Canadian	18	0.12
Dutch	119	0.77
English	780	5.06
European	42	0.27
Finnish	11	0.07
French, except Basque	169	1.10
French Canadian	46	0.30
German	549	3.56
Greek	49	0.32
Guyanese	25	0.16
Hawaii Native/Pacific Islander:	26	0.17
Micronesian: (1)	7	0.04
Guamanian/Chamorro (1)	6	0.04
Other Micronesian	1	0.01
Polynesian: (2)	7	0.04
Native Hawaiian (1)	3	0.02
Samoan (1)	4	0.03
Other Pac. Isl., specified	4	0.03
Other Pac. Isl., not spec. (2)	8	0.05
Hispanic or Latino:	908	5.82
Central American:	45	0.29
Guatemalan	32	0.21
Honduran	9	0.06
Panamanian	4	0.03
Cuban	15	0.10
Dominican Republic	4	0.03
Mexican	704	4.51
Puerto Rican	43	0.28
South American:	6	0.04
Argentinean	1	0.01
Colombian	1	0.01
Ecuadorian	2	0.01
Peruvian	2	0.01
Other Hispanic or Latino	91	0.58
Irish	635	4.12
Italian	119	0.77
Norwegian	36	0.23
Polish	133	0.86
Portuguese	67	0.43
Russian	26	0.17
Scotch-Irish	187	1.21
Scottish	72	0.47
Slovak	12	0.08
Swedish	44	0.29
United States or American	810	5.25
Welsh	43	0.28
West Indian, excl. Hispanic:	16	0.10
West Indian	16	0.10
White:	5,834	37.40
Not Hispanic (5,162)	5,289	33.90
Hispanic (518)	545	3.49

Buford

Place Type: City
County: Gwinnett
Population: 10,668

Ancestry/Race	Number	%
African American/Black:	1,472	13.80
Not Hispanic (1,404)	1,451	13.60
Hispanic (18)	21	0.20
African, sub-Saharan:	133	1.24
African	120	1.12
Ghanian	7	0.07
Nigerian	6	0.06
Am. Ind. or Alaska Nat., not spec.	35	0.33
American Indian tribes, specified:	38	0.36
Blackfeet (1)	1	0.01
Cherokee (6)	19	0.18
Choctaw (4)	4	0.04
Creek (1)	1	0.01
Houma (3)	3	0.03
Iroquois (2)	2	0.02
Lumbee (1)	1	0.01
Navajo (1)	1	0.01
Sioux	1	0.01
All other tribes	5	0.05
Arab:	18	0.17
Jordanian	10	0.09
Palestinian	8	0.07
Asian:	126	1.18
Bangladeshi (6)	6	0.06
Cambodian (5)	5	0.05
Chinese, ex. Taiwanese (16)	27	0.25
Filipino (13)	23	0.22
Hmong (1)	1	0.01
Indian (19)	27	0.25
Indonesian (1)	1	0.01
Japanese (2)	5	0.05
Korean (7)	8	0.07
Thai (2)	4	0.04
Vietnamese (12)	14	0.13
Other Asian, not specified (1)	5	0.05
Austrian	23	0.21
Belgian	12	0.11
British	86	0.80
Croatian	9	0.08
Czech	12	0.11
Dutch	70	0.65
English	1,147	10.71
European	130	1.21
French, except Basque	205	1.91
French Canadian	16	0.15
German	706	6.59
Greek	4	0.04
Hawaii Native/Pacific Islander:	6	0.06
Polynesian: (4)	6	0.06
Native Hawaiian (4)	5	0.05
Samoan	1	0.01
Hispanic or Latino:	1,842	17.27
Central American:	119	1.12
Honduran	37	0.35
Nicaraguan	5	0.05
Salvadoran	75	0.70
Other Central American	2	0.02
Cuban	30	0.28
Dominican Republic	9	0.08
Mexican	1,479	13.86
Puerto Rican	43	0.40
South American:	33	0.31
Chilean	1	0.01
Colombian	26	0.24
Uruguayan	3	0.03
Venezuelan	2	0.02
Other South American	1	0.01
Other Hispanic or Latino	129	1.21
Hungarian	36	0.34
Irish	897	8.38
Italian	193	1.80
Polish	59	0.55
Portuguese	8	0.07

Notes: 1. Figures in the "Number" column do not add up to the total population due to: a) Ancestry/Race overlap — e.g. persons can report being both White and Irish, b) persons of Hispanic origin can report being any race, c) persons reporting two ancestries are counted in both categories. 2. Numbers in parentheses indicate the number of persons reporting this ancestry/race alone, not in combination with any other ancestry/race. 3. Refer to the Explanation of Data in the front of the book for more detailed information.

Romanian	31	0.29
Russian	10	0.09
Scotch-Irish	107	1.00
Scottish	169	1.58
Serbian	8	0.07
Slovak	10	0.09
Slovene	7	0.07
Swedish	46	0.43
Ukrainian	9	0.08
United States or American	1,969	18.39
Welsh	24	0.22
West Indian, excl. Hispanic:	1	0.01
Jamaican	1	0.01
White:	8,307	77.87
Not Hispanic (7,147)	7,290	68.34
Hispanic (978)	1,017	9.53
Yugoslavian	57	0.53

Calhoun

Place Type: City
County: Gordon
Population: 10,667

Ancestry/Race	Number	%
African American/Black:	851	7.98
Not Hispanic (794)	835	7.83
Hispanic (12)	16	0.15
Am. Ind. or Alaska Nat., not spec.	30	0.28
Albanian	31	0.30
American Indian tribes, specified:	36	0.34
Apache (2)	3	0.03
Cherokee (2)	6	0.06
Latin American Indians (18)	19	0.18
All other tribes (1)	8	0.07
American Indian tribes, not spec.	13	0.12
Arab:	42	0.40
Arab/Arabic	32	0.31
Egyptian	10	0.10
Asian:	128	1.20
Chinese, ex. Taiwanese (7)	8	0.07
Filipino (5)	12	0.11
Indian (38)	42	0.39
Indonesian	1	0.01
Japanese (32)	32	0.30
Korean (8)	9	0.08
Pakistani (5)	9	0.08
Thai (2)	2	0.02
Vietnamese (7)	7	0.07
Other Asian, not specified (3)	6	0.06
Austrian	2	0.02
British	76	0.73
Canadian	3	0.03
Czech	49	0.47
Dutch	77	0.74
English	965	9.28
French, except Basque	228	2.19
French Canadian	31	0.30
German	659	6.34
Hawaii Native/Pacific Islander:	19	0.18
Micronesian: (6)	7	0.07
Guamanian/Chamorro (4)	5	0.05
Other Micronesian (2)	2	0.02
Polynesian: (1)	2	0.02
Native Hawaiian (1)	2	0.02
Other Pac. Isl., not spec. (8)	10	0.09
Hispanic or Latino:	1,821	17.07
Central American:	284	2.66
Costa Rican	8	0.07
Guatemalan	227	2.13
Honduran	26	0.24
Salvadoran	14	0.13
Other Central American	9	0.08
Cuban	4	0.04
Dominican Republic	2	0.02
Mexican	1,265	11.86
Puerto Rican	13	0.12
South American:	11	0.10
Chilean	1	0.01
Colombian	3	0.03
Ecuadorian	1	0.01
Peruvian	6	0.06
Other Hispanic or Latino	242	2.27
Irish	610	5.87
Italian	132	1.27
Lithuanian	6	0.06
Norwegian	58	0.56
Polish	57	0.55
Portuguese	2	0.02
Russian	9	0.09
Scotch-Irish	234	2.25
Scottish	189	1.82
Swedish	46	0.44
Ukrainian	20	0.19
United States or American	1,670	16.07
Welsh	30	0.29
West Indian, excl. Hispanic:	46	0.44
Dutch West Indian	6	0.06
Jamaican	26	0.25
West Indian	14	0.13
White:	8,440	79.12
Not Hispanic (7,807)	7,894	74.00
Hispanic (504)	546	5.12

Candler-McAfee

Place Type: Census Designated Place
County: De Kalb
Population: 28,294

Ancestry/Race	Number	%
African American/Black:	27,113	95.83
Not Hispanic (26,802)	26,972	95.33
Hispanic (124)	141	0.50
African, sub-Saharan:	1,057	3.75
African	843	2.99
Nigerian	85	0.30
Sierra Leonean	17	0.06
Somalian	49	0.17
Zimbabwean	8	0.03
Other sub-Saharan African	55	0.20
Alaska Native tribes, specified:	2	0.01
Aleut	1	0.00
Tlingit-Haida	1	0.00
Alaska Native tribes, not specified	1	0.00
Am. Ind. or Alaska Nat., not spec.	90	0.32
American Indian tribes, specified:	62	0.22
Blackfeet	2	0.01
Cherokee (4)	33	0.12
Choctaw	1	0.00
Creek	7	0.02
Latin American Indians	4	0.01
Pueblo	1	0.00
Seminole	3	0.01
Shoshone	3	0.01
Sioux	1	0.00
All other tribes	7	0.02
American Indian tribes, not spec.	4	0.01
Arab:	24	0.09
Moroccan	24	0.09
Asian:	72	0.25
Cambodian (8)	8	0.03
Chinese, ex. Taiwanese (2)	9	0.03
Filipino (5)	11	0.04
Indian (13)	17	0.06
Japanese (1)	6	0.02
Korean (3)	5	0.02
Laotian (5)	5	0.02
Pakistani (1)	1	0.00
Vietnamese (2)	4	0.01
Other Asian, specified	1	0.00
Other Asian, not specified (2)	5	0.02
Brazilian	9	0.03
British	15	0.05
Canadian	11	0.04
English	44	0.16
European	17	0.06
French, except Basque	32	0.11
French Canadian	24	0.09
German	144	0.51
Greek	9	0.03
Hawaii Native/Pacific Islander:	8	0.03
Micronesian: (1)	1	0.00
Guamanian/Chamorro (1)	1	0.00
Polynesian: (2)	2	0.01
Native Hawaiian (2)	2	0.01
Other Pac. Isl., specified	1	0.00
Other Pac. Isl., not spec.	4	0.01
Hispanic or Latino:	264	0.93
Central American:	18	0.06
Panamanian	16	0.06
Other Central American	2	0.01
Cuban	20	0.07
Dominican Republic	6	0.02
Mexican	116	0.41
Puerto Rican	43	0.15
South American:	4	0.01
Colombian	4	0.01
Other Hispanic or Latino	57	0.20
Hungarian	5	0.02
Irish	138	0.49
Italian	32	0.11
Lithuanian	8	0.03
Norwegian	7	0.02
Polish	7	0.02
Portuguese	11	0.04
Scotch-Irish	55	0.20
Scottish	19	0.07
Swedish	8	0.03
United States or American	573	2.03
Welsh	9	0.03
West Indian, excl. Hispanic:	384	1.36
Bahamian	21	0.07
Barbadian	11	0.04
Haitian	58	0.21
Jamaican	241	0.85
Trinidadian and Tobagonian	21	0.07
U.S. Virgin Islander	7	0.02
West Indian	25	0.09
White:	1,012	3.58
Not Hispanic (888)	964	3.41
Hispanic (48)	48	0.17

Carrollton

Place Type: City
County: Carroll
Population: 19,843

Ancestry/Race	Number	%
African American/Black:	6,317	31.83
Not Hispanic (6,146)	6,255	31.52
Hispanic (38)	62	0.31
African, sub-Saharan:	212	1.06
African	168	0.84
Cape Verdean	15	0.08
Nigerian	20	0.10
South African	9	0.05
Alaska Native tribes, specified:	2	0.01
Tlingit-Haida (1)	2	0.01
Am. Ind. or Alaska Nat., not spec.	50	0.25
American Indian tribes, specified:	79	0.40
Apache	3	0.02
Blackfeet	1	0.01
Cherokee (4)	44	0.22
Choctaw (1)	5	0.03
Creek (1)	1	0.01
Latin American Indians	9	0.05
Lumbee	10	0.05
Sioux (1)	2	0.01
All other tribes (3)	4	0.02
American Indian tribes, not spec.	13	0.07
Arab:	14	0.07
Arab/Arabic	14	0.07
Armenian	7	0.04
Asian:	315	1.59
Chinese, ex. Taiwanese (45)	51	0.26
Filipino (23)	30	0.15
Indian (95)	111	0.56
Indonesian (1)	3	0.02

Notes: 1. Figures in the "Number" column do not add up to the total population due to: a) Ancestry/Race overlap — e.g. persons can report being both White and Irish, b) persons of Hispanic origin can report being any race, c) persons reporting two ancestries are counted in both categories. 2. Numbers in parentheses indicate the number of persons reporting this ancestry/race alone, not in combination with any other ancestry/race. 3. Refer to the Explanation of Data in the front of the book for more detailed information.

Japanese (22)	36	0.18
Korean (14)	23	0.12
Laotian (1)	1	0.01
Malaysian (1)	2	0.01
Pakistani (12)	12	0.06
Sri Lankan (1)	1	0.01
Taiwanese (2)	2	0.01
Thai (4)	4	0.02
Vietnamese (19)	20	0.10
Other Asian, specified	2	0.01
Other Asian, not specified (9)	17	0.09
Austrian	7	0.04
Basque	9	0.05
British	86	0.43
Canadian	41	0.21
Celtic	22	0.11
Czech	25	0.13
Czechoslovakian	11	0.06
Danish	8	0.04
Dutch	139	0.70
Eastern European	11	0.06
English	1,436	7.19
European	206	1.03
French, except Basque	186	0.93
French Canadian	63	0.32
German	1,174	5.88
Hawaii Native/Pacific Islander:	14	0.07
Micronesian:	1	0.01
Guamanian/Chamorro	1	0.01
Polynesian: (1)	4	0.02
Native Hawaiian (1)	4	0.02
Other Pac. Isl., specified	2	0.01
Other Pac. Isl., not spec.	7	0.04
Hispanic or Latino:	1,120	5.64
Central American:	287	1.45
Costa Rican	1	0.01
Guatemalan	51	0.26
Honduran	143	0.72
Nicaraguan	64	0.32
Panamanian	4	0.02
Salvadoran	16	0.08
Other Central American	8	0.04
Cuban	26	0.13
Dominican Republic	6	0.03
Mexican	544	2.74
Puerto Rican	44	0.22
South American:	27	0.14
Chilean	3	0.02
Colombian	10	0.05
Ecuadorian	1	0.01
Peruvian	3	0.02
Venezuelan	3	0.02
Other South American	7	0.04
Other Hispanic or Latino	186	0.94
Hungarian	10	0.05
Icelander	9	0.05
Irish	1,494	7.48
Italian	324	1.62
Lithuanian	17	0.09
Norwegian	107	0.54
Polish	72	0.36
Portuguese	7	0.04
Russian	7	0.04
Scandinavian	44	0.22
Scotch-Irish	463	2.32
Scottish	408	2.04
Slavic	10	0.05
Slovak	15	0.08
Swedish	45	0.23
Swiss	14	0.07
Turkish	20	0.10
United States or American	2,492	12.48
Welsh	49	0.25
West Indian, excl. Hispanic:	163	0.82
Belizean	8	0.04
Haitian	9	0.05
Jamaican	34	0.17
Trinidadian and Tobagonian	13	0.07
U.S. Virgin Islander	89	0.45
West Indian	10	0.05
White:	12,725	64.13
Not Hispanic (12,018)	12,208	61.52
Hispanic (381)	517	2.61

Cartersville

Place Type: City
County: Bartow
Population: 15,925

Ancestry/Race	Number	%
African American/Black:	2,788	17.51
Not Hispanic (2,682)	2,745	17.24
Hispanic (32)	43	0.27
African, sub-Saharan:	115	0.72
African	115	0.72
Am. Ind. or Alaska Nat., not spec.	33	0.21
American Indian tribes, specified:	54	0.34
Blackfeet (3)	3	0.02
Cherokee (16)	36	0.23
Choctaw (1)	2	0.01
Creek (1)	1	0.01
Iroquois	1	0.01
Latin American Indians (5)	5	0.03
Sioux (2)	2	0.01
Tohono O'Odham (3)	3	0.02
All other tribes (1)	1	0.01
American Indian tribes, not spec.	4	0.03
Arab:	60	0.37
Egyptian	12	0.07
Lebanese	48	0.30
Asian:	188	1.18
Chinese, ex. Taiwanese (24)	32	0.20
Filipino (7)	26	0.16
Indian (41)	45	0.28
Japanese (8)	12	0.08
Korean (24)	33	0.21
Laotian (2)	5	0.03
Thai (2)	2	0.01
Vietnamese (15)	16	0.10
Other Asian, specified	10	0.06
Other Asian, not specified (7)	7	0.04
British	29	0.18
Canadian	11	0.07
Croatian	11	0.07
Czech	15	0.09
Czechoslovakian	7	0.04
Danish	11	0.07
Dutch	133	0.83
English	1,799	11.19
European	223	1.39
French, except Basque	200	1.24
French Canadian	13	0.08
German	901	5.60
Hawaii Native/Pacific Islander:	34	0.21
Micronesian: (1)	7	0.04
Guamanian/Chamorro (1)	7	0.04
Polynesian: (1)	9	0.06
Native Hawaiian (1)	2	0.01
Samoan	7	0.04
Other Pac. Isl., specified	10	0.06
Other Pac. Isl., not spec. (5)	8	0.05
Hispanic or Latino:	1,160	7.28
Central American:	81	0.51
Costa Rican	4	0.03
Guatemalan	44	0.28
Honduran	4	0.03
Panamanian	7	0.04
Salvadoran	11	0.07
Other Central American	11	0.07
Cuban	14	0.09
Mexican	849	5.33
Puerto Rican	27	0.17
South American:	15	0.09
Ecuadorian	11	0.07
Venezuelan	1	0.01
Other South American	3	0.02
Other Hispanic or Latino	174	1.09
Hungarian	11	0.07
Irish	1,364	8.48
Italian	289	1.80
Lithuanian	21	0.13
Norwegian	114	0.71
Polish	127	0.79
Russian	34	0.21
Scotch-Irish	294	1.83
Scottish	370	2.30
Slovak	19	0.12
Swedish	115	0.72
Swiss	47	0.29
United States or American	2,939	18.28
Welsh	55	0.34
West Indian, excl. Hispanic:	65	0.40
British West Indian	16	0.10
Haitian	35	0.22
Jamaican	14	0.09
White:	12,394	77.83
Not Hispanic (11,758)	11,871	74.54
Hispanic (429)	523	3.28

College Park

Place Type: City
County: Fulton
Population: 20,382

Ancestry/Race	Number	%
African American/Black:	16,923	83.03
Not Hispanic (16,545)	16,740	82.13
Hispanic (129)	183	0.90
African, sub-Saharan:	1,036	4.99
African	539	2.60
Ethiopian	61	0.29
Ghanian	38	0.18
Liberian	25	0.12
Nigerian	241	1.16
Senegalese	19	0.09
Sierra Leonean	36	0.17
Other sub-Saharan African	77	0.37
Am. Ind. or Alaska Nat., not spec.	47	0.23
American Indian tribes, specified:	43	0.21
Blackfeet	2	0.01
Cherokee (6)	21	0.10
Creek	1	0.00
Iroquois (3)	3	0.01
Latin American Indians	4	0.02
Pueblo	1	0.00
Sioux (2)	2	0.01
All other tribes (4)	9	0.04
American Indian tribes, not spec.	9	0.04
Asian:	164	0.80
Cambodian (20)	26	0.13
Chinese, ex. Taiwanese (19)	26	0.13
Filipino (13)	21	0.10
Indian (45)	50	0.25
Japanese (2)	3	0.01
Korean (1)	4	0.02
Laotian (2)	4	0.02
Thai (1)	1	0.00
Vietnamese (17)	17	0.08
Other Asian, specified	2	0.01
Other Asian, not specified (3)	10	0.05
Austrian	10	0.05
Belgian	19	0.09
British	17	0.08
Dutch	6	0.03
English	277	1.34
European	51	0.25
Finnish	9	0.04
French, except Basque	138	0.67
French Canadian	60	0.29
German	176	0.85
Greek	7	0.03
Guyanese	23	0.11
Hawaii Native/Pacific Islander:	27	0.13
Micronesian:	3	0.01
Guamanian/Chamorro	2	0.01
Other Micronesian	1	0.00
Polynesian:	5	0.02
Native Hawaiian	2	0.01

Notes: 1. Figures in the "Number" column do not add up to the total population due to: a) Ancestry/Race overlap — e.g. persons can report being both White and Irish, b) persons of Hispanic origin can report being any race, c) persons reporting two ancestries are counted in both categories. 2. Numbers in parentheses indicate the number of persons reporting this ancestry/race alone, not in combination with any other ancestry/race. 3. Refer to the Explanation of Data in the front of the book for more detailed information.

Samoan	3	0.01
Other Pac. Isl., specified	2	0.01
Other Pac. Isl., not spec. (1)	17	0.08
Hispanic or Latino:	1,398	6.86
Central American:	96	0.47
Costa Rican	5	0.02
Guatemalan	5	0.02
Honduran	46	0.23
Panamanian	14	0.07
Salvadoran	19	0.09
Other Central American	7	0.03
Cuban	31	0.15
Dominican Republic	17	0.08
Mexican	1,017	4.99
Puerto Rican	71	0.35
South American:	14	0.07
Colombian	9	0.04
Venezuelan	5	0.02
Other Hispanic or Latino	152	0.75
Hungarian	8	0.04
Irish	204	0.98
Israeli	13	0.06
Italian	54	0.26
Norwegian	29	0.14
Polish	17	0.08
Portuguese	5	0.02
Scotch-Irish	105	0.51
Scottish	76	0.37
Slovak	6	0.03
Swiss	20	0.10
United States or American	493	2.38
Welsh	21	0.10
West Indian, excl. Hispanic:	331	1.60
Bahamian	14	0.07
Haitian	55	0.27
Jamaican	154	0.74
Trinidadian and Tobagonian	16	0.08
U.S. Virgin Islander	23	0.11
West Indian	69	0.33
White:	2,701	13.25
Not Hispanic (2,026)	2,118	10.39
Hispanic (499)	583	2.86

Columbus

Place Type: Special City
County: Muscogee
Population: 185,781

Ancestry/Race	Number	%
Acadian/Cajun	21	0.01
African American/Black:	83,134	44.75
Not Hispanic (80,698)	82,038	44.16
Hispanic (768)	1,096	0.59
African, sub-Saharan:	2,526	1.36
African	2,328	1.25
Cape Verdean	5	0.00
Ghanian	28	0.02
Liberian	5	0.00
Nigerian	121	0.07
Somalian	23	0.01
Sudanese	6	0.00
Other sub-Saharan African	10	0.01
Alaska Native tribes, specified:	17	0.01
Alaska Athabascan	3	0.00
Aleut	2	0.00
Eskimo (11)	11	0.01
Tlingit-Haida	1	0.00
Alaska Native tribes, not specified	12	0.01
Am. Ind. or Alaska Nat., not spec.	464	0.25
Albanian	5	0.00
American Indian tribes, specified:	943	0.51
Apache (21)	38	0.02
Blackfeet (13)	54	0.03
Cherokee (180)	419	0.23
Cheyenne (1)	1	0.00
Chickasaw (7)	8	0.00
Chippewa (13)	22	0.01
Choctaw (27)	53	0.03
Comanche	1	0.00
Cree (2)	3	0.00
Creek (27)	56	0.03
Crow (2)	4	0.00
Delaware	2	0.00
Houma (5)	7	0.00
Iroquois (7)	14	0.01
Latin American Indians (20)	42	0.02
Lumbee (16)	18	0.01
Menominee (1)	1	0.00
Navajo (22)	31	0.02
Osage (4)	9	0.00
Ottawa (1)	1	0.00
Paiute (1)	1	0.00
Potawatomi (2)	6	0.00
Pueblo (11)	14	0.01
Puget Sound Salish (5)	5	0.00
Seminole (4)	24	0.01
Shoshone (1)	2	0.00
Sioux (24)	40	0.02
Ute	1	0.00
Yaqui	4	0.00
All other tribes (28)	62	0.03
American Indian tribes, not spec.	68	0.04
Arab:	79	0.04
Arab/Arabic	29	0.02
Lebanese	27	0.01
Moroccan	23	0.01
Armenian	8	0.00
Asian:	3,863	2.08
Bangladeshi	1	0.00
Cambodian (35)	42	0.02
Chinese, ex. Taiwanese (217)	320	0.17
Filipino (558)	756	0.41
Hmong (2)	3	0.00
Indian (470)	543	0.29
Indonesian (5)	7	0.00
Japanese (266)	420	0.23
Korean (932)	1,252	0.67
Laotian (7)	8	0.00
Malaysian (3)	9	0.00
Pakistani (33)	37	0.02
Sri Lankan (12)	12	0.01
Taiwanese (9)	9	0.00
Thai (39)	64	0.03
Vietnamese (165)	217	0.12
Other Asian, specified (2)	8	0.00
Other Asian, not specified (75)	155	0.08
Australian	78	0.04
Austrian	159	0.09
Basque	16	0.01
Belgian	102	0.05
Brazilian	17	0.01
British	640	0.34
Canadian	205	0.11
Celtic	50	0.03
Croatian	60	0.03
Czech	172	0.09
Czechoslovakian	172	0.09
Danish	189	0.10
Dutch	1,258	0.68
Eastern European	13	0.01
English	11,560	6.22
Estonian	6	0.00
European	1,440	0.78
Finnish	77	0.04
French, except Basque	2,527	1.36
French Canadian	546	0.29
German	12,529	6.74
German Russian	12	0.01
Greek	210	0.11
Hawaii Native/Pacific Islander:	507	0.27
Melanesian: (1)	2	0.00
Fijian (1)	2	0.00
Micronesian: (93)	152	0.08
Guamanian/Chamorro (80)	131	0.07
Other Micronesian (13)	21	0.01
Polynesian: (139)	243	0.13
Native Hawaiian (53)	123	0.07
Samoan (79)	100	0.05
Tongan (1)	5	0.00
Other Polynesian (6)	15	0.01
Other Pac. Isl., specified	3	0.00
Other Pac. Isl., not spec. (31)	107	0.06
Hispanic or Latino:	8,368	4.50
Central American:	831	0.45
Costa Rican	23	0.01
Guatemalan	176	0.09
Honduran	63	0.03
Nicaraguan	29	0.02
Panamanian	480	0.26
Salvadoran	44	0.02
Other Central American	16	0.01
Cuban	186	0.10
Dominican Republic	109	0.06
Mexican	2,749	1.48
Puerto Rican	2,682	1.44
South American:	386	0.21
Argentinean	14	0.01
Bolivian	40	0.02
Chilean	6	0.00
Colombian	152	0.08
Ecuadorian	25	0.01
Paraguayan	6	0.00
Peruvian	47	0.03
Uruguayan	8	0.00
Venezuelan	76	0.04
Other South American	12	0.01
Other Hispanic or Latino	1,425	0.77
Hungarian	386	0.21
Icelander	65	0.03
Iranian	54	0.03
Irish	12,173	6.55
Israeli	7	0.00
Italian	3,008	1.62
Latvian	6	0.00
Lithuanian	99	0.05
Luxemburger	8	0.00
Macedonian	8	0.00
Maltese	32	0.02
Northern European	31	0.02
Norwegian	762	0.41
Pennsylvania German	55	0.03
Polish	1,567	0.84
Portuguese	289	0.16
Romanian	105	0.06
Russian	284	0.15
Scandinavian	147	0.08
Scotch-Irish	2,742	1.48
Scottish	2,328	1.25
Serbian	7	0.00
Slavic	33	0.02
Slovak	93	0.05
Slovene	14	0.01
Swedish	508	0.27
Swiss	106	0.06
Turkish	26	0.01
Ukrainian	79	0.04
United States or American	18,200	9.80
Welsh	547	0.29
West Indian, excl. Hispanic:	979	0.53
Bahamian	31	0.02
Barbadian	30	0.02
Belizean	46	0.02
British West Indian	98	0.05
Dutch West Indian	6	0.00
Haitian	169	0.09
Jamaican	416	0.22
Trinidadian and Tobagonian	45	0.02
U.S. Virgin Islander	28	0.02
West Indian	110	0.06
White:	95,946	51.64
Not Hispanic (90,200)	92,112	49.58
Hispanic (3,266)	3,834	2.06
Yugoslavian	27	0.01

Notes: 1. Figures in the "Number" column do not add up to the total population due to: a) Ancestry/Race overlap — e.g. persons can report being both White and Irish, b) persons of Hispanic origin can report being any race, c) persons reporting two ancestries are counted in both categories. 2. Numbers in parentheses indicate the number of persons reporting this ancestry/race alone, not in combination with any other ancestry/race. 3. Refer to the Explanation of Data in the front of the book for more detailed information.

Conyers

Place Type: City
County: Rockdale
Population: 10,689

Ancestry/Race	Number	%
African American/Black:	3,653	34.18
Not Hispanic (3,552)	3,617	33.84
Hispanic (20)	36	0.34
African, sub-Saharan:	100	0.88
African	100	0.88
Am. Ind. or Alaska Nat., not spec.	26	0.24
American Indian tribes, specified:	51	0.48
Apache	1	0.01
Blackfeet (1)	2	0.02
Cherokee (13)	28	0.26
Chippewa (2)	2	0.02
Choctaw (1)	1	0.01
Creek (1)	1	0.01
Latin American Indians (2)	8	0.07
Navajo	1	0.01
Sioux (2)	2	0.02
All other tribes (4)	5	0.05
American Indian tribes, not spec.	5	0.05
Asian:	310	2.90
Cambodian (10)	13	0.12
Chinese, ex. Taiwanese (36)	37	0.35
Filipino (12)	14	0.13
Indian (83)	89	0.83
Indonesian (2)	2	0.02
Japanese (2)	7	0.07
Korean (34)	42	0.39
Laotian (7)	8	0.07
Malaysian (1)	1	0.01
Pakistani (7)	7	0.07
Thai (3)	3	0.03
Vietnamese (62)	64	0.60
Other Asian, specified	4	0.04
Other Asian, not specified (13)	19	0.18
Austrian	15	0.13
Belgian	6	0.05
Brazilian	5	0.04
British	33	0.29
Dutch	79	0.69
English	725	6.37
European	37	0.33
Finnish	10	0.09
French, except Basque	251	2.21
French Canadian	30	0.26
German	697	6.13
Greek	10	0.09
Guyanese	61	0.54
Hawaii Native/Pacific Islander:	14	0.13
Micronesian:	1	0.01
Guamanian/Chamorro	1	0.01
Polynesian: (3)	3	0.03
Native Hawaiian (1)	1	0.01
Samoan (2)	2	0.02
Other Pac. Isl., specified	1	0.01
Other Pac. Isl., not spec. (2)	9	0.08
Hispanic or Latino:	1,153	10.79
Central American:	24	0.22
Costa Rican	5	0.05
Guatemalan	1	0.01
Honduran	2	0.02
Nicaraguan	9	0.08
Panamanian	2	0.02
Salvadoran	5	0.05
Cuban	17	0.16
Mexican	998	9.34
Puerto Rican	46	0.43
South American:	14	0.13
Bolivian	1	0.01
Chilean	2	0.02
Colombian	6	0.06
Ecuadorian	3	0.03
Venezuelan	1	0.01
Other South American	1	0.01
Other Hispanic or Latino	54	0.51
Hungarian	3	0.03
Irish	948	8.34
Italian	142	1.25
Norwegian	29	0.25
Polish	67	0.59
Portuguese	56	0.49
Russian	18	0.16
Scandinavian	16	0.14
Scotch-Irish	100	0.88
Scottish	131	1.15
Swedish	31	0.27
United States or American	1,172	10.31
Welsh	38	0.33
West Indian, excl. Hispanic:	85	0.75
Haitian	33	0.29
Jamaican	52	0.46
White:	6,350	59.41
Not Hispanic (5,536)	5,623	52.61
Hispanic (695)	727	6.80

Cordele

Place Type: City
County: Crisp
Population: 11,608

Ancestry/Race	Number	%
African American/Black:	7,611	65.57
Not Hispanic (7,515)	7,564	65.16
Hispanic (34)	47	0.40
African, sub-Saharan:	229	1.99
African	223	1.94
Nigerian	6	0.05
Am. Ind. or Alaska Nat., not spec.	17	0.15
American Indian tribes, specified:	16	0.14
Cherokee (1)	14	0.12
Pueblo (2)	2	0.02
Asian:	138	1.19
Chinese, ex. Taiwanese (10)	16	0.14
Filipino (5)	9	0.08
Indian (71)	81	0.70
Japanese (2)	6	0.05
Korean	4	0.03
Pakistani	1	0.01
Thai	4	0.03
Vietnamese (7)	8	0.07
Other Asian, not specified	9	0.08
Austrian	6	0.05
British	7	0.06
Canadian	25	0.22
Dutch	48	0.42
English	386	3.36
European	23	0.20
French, except Basque	16	0.14
French Canadian	10	0.09
German	244	2.13
Hawaii Native/Pacific Islander:	18	0.16
Micronesian: (7)	7	0.06
Guamanian/Chamorro (7)	7	0.06
Polynesian:	5	0.04
Native Hawaiian	5	0.04
Other Pac. Isl., not spec.	6	0.05
Hispanic or Latino:	226	1.95
Central American:	3	0.03
Guatemalan	1	0.01
Honduran	1	0.01
Panamanian	1	0.01
Cuban	4	0.03
Dominican Republic	1	0.01
Mexican	170	1.46
Puerto Rican	11	0.09
Other Hispanic or Latino	37	0.32
Irish	401	3.49
Italian	40	0.35
Polish	18	0.16
Russian	18	0.16
Scotch-Irish	189	1.65
Scottish	44	0.38
Swedish	6	0.05
United States or American	1,371	11.94
Welsh	37	0.32
West Indian, excl. Hispanic:	7	0.06
West Indian	7	0.06
White:	3,772	32.49
Not Hispanic (3,664)	3,719	32.04
Hispanic (39)	53	0.46

Covington

Place Type: City
County: Newton
Population: 11,547

Ancestry/Race	Number	%
African American/Black:	5,323	46.10
Not Hispanic (5,229)	5,292	45.83
Hispanic (30)	31	0.27
African, sub-Saharan:	120	1.04
African	98	0.85
Kenyan	15	0.13
Other sub-Saharan African	7	0.06
Am. Ind. or Alaska Nat., not spec.	20	0.17
American Indian tribes, specified:	21	0.18
Apache (1)	1	0.01
Cherokee (8)	18	0.16
Houma (1)	1	0.01
Latin American Indians (1)	1	0.01
American Indian tribes, not spec.	16	0.14
Asian:	79	0.68
Chinese, ex. Taiwanese (5)	5	0.04
Filipino (3)	8	0.07
Hmong (1)	3	0.03
Indian (10)	16	0.14
Japanese (4)	4	0.03
Korean (5)	7	0.06
Pakistani	1	0.01
Vietnamese (33)	34	0.29
Other Asian, not specified (1)	1	0.01
Australian	8	0.07
Austrian	5	0.04
British	32	0.28
Czech	16	0.14
Czechoslovakian	14	0.12
Dutch	83	0.72
English	699	6.06
European	73	0.63
French, except Basque	92	0.80
French Canadian	8	0.07
German	564	4.89
Greek	23	0.20
Hawaii Native/Pacific Islander:	12	0.10
Micronesian: (2)	7	0.06
Guamanian/Chamorro (2)	7	0.06
Polynesian: (2)	2	0.02
Native Hawaiian (2)	2	0.02
Other Pac. Isl., not spec. (1)	3	0.03
Hispanic or Latino:	331	2.87
Central American:	9	0.08
Guatemalan	3	0.03
Panamanian	3	0.03
Salvadoran	2	0.02
Other Central American	1	0.01
Cuban	7	0.06
Mexican	220	1.91
Puerto Rican	30	0.26
South American:	7	0.06
Colombian	6	0.05
Peruvian	1	0.01
Other Hispanic or Latino	58	0.50
Irish	713	6.18
Italian	36	0.31
Lithuanian	7	0.06
Norwegian	53	0.46
Polish	28	0.24
Romanian	9	0.08
Scotch-Irish	319	2.77
Scottish	148	1.28
Swedish	20	0.17
Ukrainian	42	0.36
United States or American	1,378	11.95

Notes: 1. Figures in the "Number" column do not add up to the total population due to: a) Ancestry/Race overlap — e.g. persons can report being both White and Irish, b) persons of Hispanic origin can report being any race, c) persons reporting two ancestries are counted in both categories. 2. Numbers in parentheses indicate the number of persons reporting this ancestry/race alone, not in combination with any other ancestry/race. 3. Refer to the Explanation of Data in the front of the book for more detailed information.

Welsh	74	0.64
White:	6,065	52.52
Not Hispanic (5,775)	5,863	50.78
Hispanic (178)	202	1.75

Dalton

Place Type: City
County: Whitfield
Population: 27,912

Ancestry/Race	Number	%
Acadian/Cajun	5	0.02
African American/Black:	2,301	8.24
Not Hispanic (2,042)	2,143	7.68
Hispanic (111)	158	0.57
African, sub-Saharan:	62	0.22
African	45	0.16
South African	17	0.06
Alaska Native tribes, specified:	1	0.00
Eskimo	1	0.00
Am. Ind. or Alaska Nat., not spec.	71	0.25
American Indian tribes, specified:	118	0.42
Cherokee (9)	34	0.12
Cheyenne	2	0.01
Chickasaw (1)	1	0.00
Choctaw	1	0.00
Creek (1)	1	0.00
Iroquois	1	0.00
Latin American Indians (50)	67	0.24
Ottawa	1	0.00
Potawatomi	1	0.00
Seminole (3)	3	0.01
Sioux	1	0.00
Tohono O'Odham (1)	1	0.00
All other tribes (3)	4	0.01
American Indian tribes, not spec.	17	0.06
Arab:	54	0.19
Arab/Arabic	28	0.10
Egyptian	17	0.06
Jordanian	9	0.03
Asian:	556	1.99
Cambodian (9)	10	0.04
Chinese, ex. Taiwanese (70)	75	0.27
Filipino (11)	23	0.08
Indian (168)	181	0.65
Japanese (10)	20	0.07
Korean (41)	43	0.15
Malaysian (1)	1	0.00
Pakistani (40)	43	0.15
Thai (2)	2	0.01
Vietnamese (114)	119	0.43
Other Asian, not specified (11)	39	0.14
Australian	20	0.07
Austrian	7	0.02
Belgian	12	0.04
British	55	0.19
Czech	49	0.17
Danish	9	0.03
Dutch	257	0.91
English	2,085	7.38
European	103	0.36
French, except Basque	269	0.95
French Canadian	93	0.33
German	1,226	4.34
Greek	24	0.09
Hawaii Native/Pacific Islander:	50	0.18
Micronesian: (6)	19	0.07
Guamanian/Chamorro (2)	11	0.04
Other Micronesian (4)	8	0.03
Polynesian: (5)	23	0.08
Native Hawaiian (5)	15	0.05
Samoan	8	0.03
Other Pac. Isl., not spec. (4)	8	0.03
Hispanic or Latino:	11,219	40.19
Central American:	567	2.03
Costa Rican	13	0.05
Guatemalan	279	1.00
Honduran	44	0.16
Nicaraguan	31	0.11
Panamanian	1	0.00
Salvadoran	190	0.68
Other Central American	9	0.03
Cuban	76	0.27
Dominican Republic	45	0.16
Mexican	9,431	33.79
Puerto Rican	170	0.61
South American:	54	0.19
Chilean	5	0.02
Colombian	12	0.04
Ecuadorian	11	0.04
Peruvian	16	0.06
Venezuelan	7	0.03
Other South American	3	0.01
Other Hispanic or Latino	876	3.14
Hungarian	29	0.10
Irish	1,472	5.21
Italian	209	0.74
Norwegian	75	0.27
Polish	43	0.15
Russian	9	0.03
Scandinavian	9	0.03
Scotch-Irish	504	1.79
Scottish	359	1.27
Slovak	18	0.06
Swedish	67	0.24
Swiss	19	0.07
Turkish	10	0.04
United States or American	3,265	11.56
Welsh	68	0.24
West Indian, excl. Hispanic:	80	0.28
Barbadian	24	0.09
Belizean	24	0.09
Dutch West Indian	8	0.03
West Indian	24	0.09
White:	19,146	68.59
Not Hispanic (13,867)	14,080	50.44
Hispanic (4,601)	5,066	18.15

Decatur

Place Type: City
County: De Kalb
Population: 18,147

Ancestry/Race	Number	%
Acadian/Cajun	19	0.10
Afghan	15	0.08
African American/Black:	5,655	31.16
Not Hispanic (5,505)	5,612	30.93
Hispanic (27)	43	0.24
African, sub-Saharan:	192	1.05
African	89	0.49
Ethiopian	12	0.07
Nigerian	28	0.15
Somalian	56	0.31
South African	7	0.04
Alaska Native tribes, specified:	2	0.01
Eskimo (1)	2	0.01
Am. Ind. or Alaska Nat., not spec.	38	0.21
Albanian	8	0.04
Alsatian	23	0.13
American Indian tribes, specified:	83	0.46
Blackfeet (2)	6	0.03
Cherokee (5)	41	0.23
Cheyenne (1)	1	0.01
Chickasaw	1	0.01
Chippewa (2)	2	0.01
Choctaw (2)	6	0.03
Creek (4)	7	0.04
Latin American Indians	7	0.04
Lumbee	1	0.01
Navajo (1)	1	0.01
Seminole	2	0.01
Sioux (2)	3	0.02
Yakama (1)	1	0.01
All other tribes	4	0.02
American Indian tribes, not spec.	4	0.02
Arab:	24	0.13
Lebanese	14	0.08
Syrian	10	0.05
Asian:	366	2.02
Bangladeshi (4)	4	0.02
Cambodian (2)	2	0.01
Chinese, ex. Taiwanese (64)	82	0.45
Filipino (14)	19	0.10
Indian (89)	98	0.54
Indonesian (3)	5	0.03
Japanese (20)	36	0.20
Korean (58)	66	0.36
Laotian (2)	2	0.01
Malaysian	2	0.01
Pakistani (5)	7	0.04
Sri Lankan (1)	1	0.01
Taiwanese (4)	4	0.02
Thai (8)	8	0.04
Vietnamese (4)	6	0.03
Other Asian, specified (2)	3	0.02
Other Asian, not specified (16)	21	0.12
Austrian	30	0.16
Belgian	65	0.36
British	201	1.10
Bulgarian	7	0.04
Canadian	42	0.23
Celtic	21	0.12
Croatian	20	0.11
Czech	47	0.26
Czechoslovakian	23	0.13
Danish	39	0.21
Dutch	137	0.75
Eastern European	104	0.57
English	2,504	13.75
European	396	2.18
Finnish	19	0.10
French, except Basque	767	4.21
French Canadian	69	0.38
German	2,045	11.23
Greek	34	0.19
Guyanese	25	0.14
Hawaii Native/Pacific Islander:	22	0.12
Micronesian: (2)	2	0.01
Guamanian/Chamorro (2)	2	0.01
Polynesian: (4)	10	0.06
Native Hawaiian (1)	5	0.03
Samoan (3)	5	0.03
Other Pac. Isl., specified	1	0.01
Other Pac. Isl., not spec.	9	0.05
Hispanic or Latino:	304	1.68
Central American:	30	0.17
Costa Rican	7	0.04
Guatemalan	2	0.01
Honduran	6	0.03
Nicaraguan	7	0.04
Panamanian	5	0.03
Salvadoran	1	0.01
Other Central American	2	0.01
Cuban	39	0.21
Mexican	59	0.33
Puerto Rican	57	0.31
South American:	50	0.28
Argentinean	5	0.03
Bolivian	3	0.02
Chilean	6	0.03
Colombian	16	0.09
Ecuadorian	3	0.02
Paraguayan	3	0.02
Peruvian	9	0.05
Venezuelan	5	0.03
Other Hispanic or Latino	69	0.38
Hungarian	52	0.29
Iranian	33	0.18
Irish	1,902	10.45
Israeli	7	0.04
Italian	494	2.71
Lithuanian	60	0.33
Northern European	18	0.10
Norwegian	142	0.78
Polish	442	2.43
Portuguese	7	0.04
Romanian	31	0.17

Notes: 1. Figures in the "Number" column do not add up to the total population due to: a) Ancestry/Race overlap — e.g. persons can report being both White and Irish, b) persons of Hispanic origin can report being any race, c) persons reporting two ancestries are counted in both categories. 2. Numbers in parentheses indicate the number of persons reporting this ancestry/race alone, not in combination with any other ancestry/race. 3. Refer to the Explanation of Data in the front of the book for more detailed information.

Ancestry/Race	Number	%
Russian	162	0.89
Scandinavian	23	0.13
Scotch-Irish	925	5.08
Scottish	765	4.20
Serbian	15	0.08
Slovak	9	0.05
Slovene	5	0.03
Swedish	114	0.63
Swiss	86	0.47
Turkish	25	0.14
Ukrainian	15	0.08
United States or American	877	4.82
Welsh	276	1.52
West Indian, excl. Hispanic:	138	0.76
Belizean	23	0.13
British West Indian	27	0.15
Jamaican	4	0.02
Trinidadian and Tobagonian	9	0.05
U.S. Virgin Islander	66	0.36
West Indian	9	0.05
White:	12,105	66.71
Not Hispanic (11,733)	11,894	65.54
Hispanic (173)	211	1.16
Yugoslavian	56	0.31

Douglas

Place Type: City
County: Coffee
Population: 10,639

Ancestry/Race	Number	%
African American/Black:	4,872	45.79
Not Hispanic (4,809)	4,846	45.55
Hispanic (14)	26	0.24
African, sub-Saharan:	144	1.42
African	144	1.42
Am. Ind. or Alaska Nat., not spec.	37	0.35
American Indian tribes, specified:	22	0.21
Apache	1	0.01
Blackfeet (1)	1	0.01
Cherokee (1)	13	0.12
Choctaw	1	0.01
Creek (2)	2	0.02
Iroquois	1	0.01
Pueblo	1	0.01
All other tribes (2)	2	0.02
American Indian tribes, not spec.	6	0.06
Arab:	41	0.40
Jordanian	24	0.24
Lebanese	17	0.17
Asian:	138	1.30
Chinese, ex. Taiwanese (10)	17	0.16
Filipino (11)	12	0.11
Indian (71)	77	0.72
Japanese (2)	8	0.08
Korean (5)	7	0.07
Pakistani (2)	2	0.02
Sri Lankan (3)	3	0.03
Vietnamese (4)	4	0.04
Other Asian, specified	3	0.03
Other Asian, not specified (4)	5	0.05
Dutch	40	0.39
English	499	4.91
European	142	1.40
French, except Basque	49	0.48
German	234	2.30
Hawaii Native/Pacific Islander:	21	0.20
Micronesian: (3)	7	0.07
Guamanian/Chamorro (3)	7	0.07
Polynesian:	3	0.03
Native Hawaiian	2	0.02
Samoan	1	0.01
Other Pac. Isl., specified	3	0.03
Other Pac. Isl., not spec. (2)	8	0.08
Hispanic or Latino:	736	6.92
Central American:	57	0.54
Costa Rican	1	0.01
Guatemalan	35	0.33
Honduran	8	0.08
Panamanian	2	0.02
Salvadoran	11	0.10
Cuban	5	0.05
Dominican Republic	4	0.04
Mexican	574	5.40
Puerto Rican	22	0.21
South American:	6	0.06
Argentinean	4	0.04
Peruvian	1	0.01
Venezuelan	1	0.01
Other Hispanic or Latino	68	0.64
Irish	433	4.26
Italian	89	0.88
Norwegian	20	0.20
Polish	28	0.28
Scotch-Irish	93	0.92
Scottish	135	1.33
Swedish	6	0.06
Swiss	8	0.08
Ukrainian	20	0.20
United States or American	1,017	10.01
Welsh	9	0.09
West Indian, excl. Hispanic:	58	0.57
Jamaican	17	0.17
Trinidadian and Tobagonian	36	0.35
West Indian	5	0.05
White:	5,229	49.15
Not Hispanic (4,868)	4,925	46.29
Hispanic (282)	304	2.86

Douglasville

Place Type: City
County: Douglas
Population: 20,065

Ancestry/Race	Number	%
Acadian/Cajun	5	0.02
African American/Black:	6,302	31.41
Not Hispanic (6,054)	6,249	31.14
Hispanic (23)	53	0.26
African, sub-Saharan:	490	2.43
African	427	2.12
Ethiopian	21	0.10
Nigerian	42	0.21
Am. Ind. or Alaska Nat., not spec.	65	0.32
Alsatian	10	0.05
American Indian tribes, specified:	107	0.53
Apache (1)	3	0.01
Blackfeet	7	0.03
Cherokee (19)	45	0.22
Cheyenne	2	0.01
Chickasaw (2)	3	0.01
Chippewa	5	0.02
Choctaw	3	0.01
Creek	2	0.01
Iroquois (1)	1	0.00
Latin American Indians	13	0.06
Lumbee (1)	9	0.04
Navajo	2	0.01
Osage	1	0.00
Ottawa (1)	1	0.00
Potawatomi (1)	1	0.00
Seminole	1	0.00
Sioux	2	0.01
All other tribes (4)	6	0.03
American Indian tribes, not spec.	5	0.02
Arab:	8	0.04
Palestinian	8	0.04
Armenian	7	0.03
Asian:	449	2.24
Chinese, ex. Taiwanese (74)	86	0.43
Filipino (33)	54	0.27
Indian (166)	182	0.91
Indonesian (6)	7	0.03
Japanese (21)	31	0.15
Korean (21)	25	0.12
Pakistani (4)	11	0.05
Taiwanese (6)	6	0.03
Thai (2)	4	0.02
Vietnamese (3)	8	0.04
Other Asian, specified	1	0.00
Other Asian, not specified (8)	34	0.17
Belgian	6	0.03
British	117	0.58
Canadian	20	0.10
Czech	29	0.14
Czechoslovakian	17	0.08
Danish	75	0.37
Dutch	166	0.82
English	1,648	8.18
European	91	0.45
Finnish	9	0.04
French, except Basque	291	1.44
French Canadian	66	0.33
German	1,509	7.49
Greek	14	0.07
Guyanese	22	0.11
Hawaii Native/Pacific Islander:	33	0.16
Micronesian:	2	0.01
Guamanian/Chamorro	2	0.01
Polynesian: (3)	16	0.08
Native Hawaiian	9	0.04
Samoan (3)	7	0.03
Other Pac. Isl., specified	1	0.00
Other Pac. Isl., not spec.	14	0.07
Hispanic or Latino:	800	3.99
Central American:	41	0.20
Costa Rican	1	0.00
Guatemalan	3	0.01
Honduran	2	0.01
Nicaraguan	5	0.02
Panamanian	5	0.02
Salvadoran	22	0.11
Other Central American	3	0.01
Cuban	8	0.04
Dominican Republic	7	0.03
Mexican	463	2.31
Puerto Rican	114	0.57
South American:	34	0.17
Argentinean	1	0.00
Chilean	1	0.00
Colombian	11	0.05
Ecuadorian	6	0.03
Peruvian	9	0.04
Venezuelan	6	0.03
Other Hispanic or Latino	133	0.66
Hungarian	67	0.33
Iranian	23	0.11
Irish	2,020	10.02
Italian	475	2.36
Lithuanian	21	0.10
Northern European	12	0.06
Norwegian	65	0.32
Pennsylvania German	23	0.11
Polish	127	0.63
Portuguese	17	0.08
Romanian	11	0.05
Russian	37	0.18
Scandinavian	14	0.07
Scotch-Irish	277	1.37
Scottish	284	1.41
Slavic	23	0.11
Swedish	70	0.35
Swiss	32	0.16
Turkish	9	0.04
Ukrainian	15	0.07
United States or American	2,812	13.95
Welsh	135	0.67
West Indian, excl. Hispanic:	161	0.80
Bahamian	9	0.04
Barbadian	12	0.06
Bermudan	20	0.10
Haitian	48	0.24
Jamaican	35	0.17
Trinidadian and Tobagonian	29	0.14
U.S. Virgin Islander	8	0.04
White:	13,150	65.54
Not Hispanic (12,425)	12,723	63.41
Hispanic (384)	427	2.13

Notes: 1. Figures in the "Number" column do not add up to the total population due to: a) Ancestry/Race overlap — e.g. persons can report being both White and Irish, b) persons of Hispanic origin can report being any race, c) persons reporting two ancestries are counted in both categories. 2. Numbers in parentheses indicate the number of persons reporting this ancestry/race alone, not in combination with any other ancestry/race. 3. Refer to the Explanation of Data in the front of the book for more detailed information.

Druid Hills

Place Type: Census Designated Place
County: De Kalb
Population: 12,741

Ancestry/Race	Number	%
African American/Black:	815	6.40
Not Hispanic (748)	799	6.27
Hispanic (16)	16	0.13
African, sub-Saharan:	104	0.82
African	25	0.20
Ethiopian	9	0.07
Nigerian	50	0.39
South African	14	0.11
Ugandan	6	0.05
Alaska Native tribes, specified:	1	0.01
Eskimo (1)	1	0.01
Am. Ind. or Alaska Nat., not spec.	18	0.14
American Indian tribes, specified:	42	0.33
Cherokee (9)	24	0.19
Choctaw	2	0.02
Creek	6	0.05
Delaware	1	0.01
Iroquois	1	0.01
Latin American Indians (4)	4	0.03
Sioux (2)	3	0.02
All other tribes	1	0.01
American Indian tribes, not spec.	3	0.02
Arab:	105	0.83
Arab/Arabic	12	0.09
Egyptian	48	0.38
Lebanese	25	0.20
Palestinian	7	0.06
Syrian	13	0.10
Armenian	15	0.12
Asian:	1,069	8.39
Bangladeshi (1)	1	0.01
Cambodian (4)	4	0.03
Chinese, ex. Taiwanese (270)	307	2.41
Filipino (29)	42	0.33
Indian (325)	350	2.75
Indonesian (2)	3	0.02
Japanese (39)	50	0.39
Korean (145)	164	1.29
Laotian	1	0.01
Malaysian (6)	7	0.05
Pakistani (10)	17	0.13
Sri Lankan (3)	3	0.02
Taiwanese (20)	24	0.19
Thai (5)	13	0.10
Vietnamese (35)	39	0.31
Other Asian, specified (6)	10	0.08
Other Asian, not specified (11)	34	0.27
Austrian	83	0.65
Belgian	11	0.09
Brazilian	28	0.22
British	222	1.75
Bulgarian	13	0.10
Canadian	41	0.32
Celtic	32	0.25
Croatian	48	0.38
Czech	45	0.35
Czechoslovakian	3	0.02
Danish	72	0.57
Dutch	171	1.35
Eastern European	107	0.84
English	2,082	16.41
Estonian	10	0.08
European	267	2.10
Finnish	20	0.16
French, except Basque	461	3.63
French Canadian	12	0.09
German	1,748	13.78
Greek	65	0.51
Guyanese	18	0.14
Hawaii Native/Pacific Islander:	19	0.15
Micronesian: (1)	2	0.02
Guamanian/Chamorro	1	0.01
Other Micronesian (1)	1	0.01
Polynesian: (3)	3	0.02
Native Hawaiian (3)	3	0.02
Other Pac. Isl., not spec. (5)	14	0.11
Hispanic or Latino:	309	2.43
Central American:	21	0.16
Costa Rican	5	0.04
Guatemalan	6	0.05
Honduran	3	0.02
Nicaraguan	2	0.02
Panamanian	2	0.02
Salvadoran	3	0.02
Cuban	47	0.37
Dominican Republic	7	0.05
Mexican	49	0.38
Puerto Rican	36	0.28
South American:	86	0.67
Argentinean	8	0.06
Chilean	19	0.15
Colombian	21	0.16
Ecuadorian	11	0.09
Paraguayan	5	0.04
Peruvian	11	0.09
Venezuelan	9	0.07
Other South American	2	0.02
Other Hispanic or Latino	63	0.49
Hungarian	75	0.59
Iranian	35	0.28
Irish	1,576	12.42
Israeli	23	0.18
Italian	489	3.85
Latvian	6	0.05
Lithuanian	54	0.43
Northern European	15	0.12
Norwegian	117	0.92
Polish	487	3.84
Portuguese	41	0.32
Romanian	38	0.30
Russian	604	4.76
Scandinavian	34	0.27
Scotch-Irish	447	3.52
Scottish	710	5.60
Slavic	8	0.06
Slovak	41	0.32
Swedish	172	1.36
Swiss	65	0.51
Turkish	42	0.33
Ukrainian	38	0.30
United States or American	650	5.12
Welsh	84	0.66
West Indian, excl. Hispanic:	133	1.05
British West Indian	9	0.07
Haitian	9	0.07
Jamaican	79	0.62
Trinidadian and Tobagonian	21	0.17
U.S. Virgin Islander	5	0.04
West Indian	10	0.08
White:	10,898	85.53
Not Hispanic (10,511)	10,676	83.79
Hispanic (210)	222	1.74

Dublin

Place Type: City
County: Laurens
Population: 15,857

Ancestry/Race	Number	%
African American/Black:	8,218	51.83
Not Hispanic (8,110)	8,167	51.50
Hispanic (44)	51	0.32
African, sub-Saharan:	223	1.40
African	223	1.40
Am. Ind. or Alaska Nat., not spec.	32	0.20
American Indian tribes, specified:	27	0.17
Cherokee (8)	20	0.13
Chickasaw	2	0.01
Choctaw (1)	1	0.01
Creek (1)	1	0.01
Lumbee (2)	2	0.01
Yakama (1)	1	0.01
Asian:	313	1.97
Bangladeshi (2)	2	0.01
Chinese, ex. Taiwanese (36)	40	0.25
Filipino (21)	26	0.16
Indian (143)	150	0.95
Japanese (35)	41	0.26
Korean (10)	17	0.11
Pakistani (6)	6	0.04
Thai (2)	2	0.01
Vietnamese (13)	16	0.10
Other Asian, specified (4)	8	0.05
Other Asian, not specified (5)	5	0.03
Austrian	23	0.14
Belgian	40	0.25
British	70	0.44
Canadian	7	0.04
Czech	6	0.04
Czechoslovakian	13	0.08
Danish	7	0.04
Dutch	125	0.78
English	1,363	8.55
European	65	0.41
Finnish	14	0.09
French, except Basque	157	0.98
German	344	2.16
Hawaii Native/Pacific Islander:	25	0.16
Micronesian:	13	0.08
Guamanian/Chamorro	8	0.05
Other Micronesian	5	0.03
Polynesian: (2)	2	0.01
Native Hawaiian (2)	2	0.01
Other Pac. Isl., specified	4	0.03
Other Pac. Isl., not spec.	6	0.04
Hispanic or Latino:	181	1.14
Central American:	2	0.01
Panamanian	2	0.01
Cuban	12	0.08
Dominican Republic	4	0.03
Mexican	90	0.57
Puerto Rican	30	0.19
South American:	1	0.01
Venezuelan	1	0.01
Other Hispanic or Latino	42	0.26
Hungarian	23	0.14
Irish	693	4.35
Italian	87	0.55
Lithuanian	15	0.09
New Zealander	9	0.06
Northern European	41	0.26
Pennsylvania German	7	0.04
Polish	10	0.06
Russian	15	0.09
Scotch-Irish	210	1.32
Scottish	249	1.56
Slovene	11	0.07
Swedish	14	0.09
Swiss	33	0.21
United States or American	1,672	10.48
Welsh	35	0.22
West Indian, excl. Hispanic:	16	0.10
Bahamian	7	0.04
Haitian	9	0.06
White:	7,300	46.04
Not Hispanic (7,143)	7,202	45.42
Hispanic (79)	98	0.62
Yugoslavian	8	0.05

Duluth

Place Type: City
County: Gwinnett
Population: 22,122

Ancestry/Race	Number	%
Acadian/Cajun	10	0.04
African American/Black:	2,770	12.52
Not Hispanic (2,578)	2,690	12.16
Hispanic (45)	80	0.36
African, sub-Saharan:	125	0.56
African	62	0.28

Notes: 1. Figures in the "Number" column do not add up to the total population due to: a) Ancestry/Race overlap — e.g. persons can report being both White and Irish, b) persons of Hispanic origin can report being any race, c) persons reporting two ancestries are counted in both categories. 2. Numbers in parentheses indicate the number of persons reporting this ancestry/race alone, not in combination with any other ancestry/race. 3. Refer to the Explanation of Data in the front of the book for more detailed information.

Ancestry/Race	Number	%
Ethiopian	9	0.04
Ghanian	17	0.08
Kenyan	14	0.06
Liberian	8	0.04
Nigerian	15	0.07
Am. Ind. or Alaska Nat., not spec.	44	0.20
Albanian	19	0.08
American Indian tribes, specified:	127	0.57
Apache (1)	1	0.00
Blackfeet	3	0.01
Cherokee (8)	32	0.14
Chippewa (1)	1	0.00
Choctaw (2)	3	0.01
Creek (1)	1	0.00
Houma	1	0.00
Iroquois	1	0.00
Latin American Indians (20)	73	0.33
Lumbee (3)	3	0.01
Sioux (3)	4	0.02
All other tribes (2)	4	0.02
American Indian tribes, not spec.	9	0.04
Arab:	249	1.11
Arab/Arabic	14	0.06
Egyptian	99	0.44
Lebanese	123	0.55
Syrian	13	0.06
Armenian	6	0.03
Asian:	3,029	13.69
Bangladeshi (3)	9	0.04
Cambodian	3	0.01
Chinese, ex. Taiwanese (655)	677	3.06
Filipino (52)	73	0.33
Hmong (2)	2	0.01
Indian (858)	887	4.01
Indonesian (21)	25	0.11
Japanese (139)	165	0.75
Korean (763)	785	3.55
Laotian (35)	37	0.17
Malaysian (5)	8	0.04
Pakistani (58)	64	0.29
Sri Lankan (1)	1	0.00
Taiwanese (29)	38	0.17
Thai (16)	18	0.08
Vietnamese (158)	165	0.75
Other Asian, specified (3)	3	0.01
Other Asian, not specified (29)	69	0.31
Australian	8	0.04
Austrian	84	0.38
Belgian	61	0.27
Brazilian	50	0.22
British	155	0.69
Bulgarian	45	0.20
Canadian	41	0.18
Croatian	49	0.22
Czech	29	0.13
Czechoslovakian	5	0.02
Danish	68	0.30
Dutch	279	1.25
Eastern European	12	0.05
English	2,398	10.71
European	201	0.90
Finnish	65	0.29
French, except Basque	571	2.55
French Canadian	153	0.68
German	2,710	12.10
German Russian	5	0.02
Greek	90	0.40
Guyanese	17	0.08
Hawaii Native/Pacific Islander:	30	0.14
Micronesian: (5)	5	0.02
Other Micronesian (5)	5	0.02
Polynesian: (2)	9	0.04
Native Hawaiian	7	0.03
Samoan (1)	1	0.00
Other Polynesian (1)	1	0.00
Other Pac. Isl., not spec. (2)	16	0.07
Hispanic or Latino:	2,002	9.05
Central American:	76	0.34
Costa Rican	6	0.03
Guatemalan	11	0.05
Honduran	10	0.05
Nicaraguan	1	0.00
Panamanian	7	0.03
Salvadoran	39	0.18
Other Central American	2	0.01
Cuban	60	0.27
Dominican Republic	9	0.04
Mexican	1,183	5.35
Puerto Rican	148	0.67
South American:	236	1.07
Argentinean	4	0.02
Bolivian	2	0.01
Chilean	3	0.01
Colombian	106	0.48
Ecuadorian	15	0.07
Paraguayan	5	0.02
Peruvian	64	0.29
Uruguayan	12	0.05
Venezuelan	20	0.09
Other South American	5	0.02
Other Hispanic or Latino	290	1.31
Hungarian	95	0.42
Iranian	103	0.46
Irish	2,308	10.31
Italian	799	3.57
Lithuanian	24	0.11
Northern European	9	0.04
Norwegian	168	0.75
Pennsylvania German	9	0.04
Polish	368	1.64
Portuguese	41	0.18
Romanian	35	0.16
Russian	220	0.98
Scandinavian	23	0.10
Scotch-Irish	459	2.05
Scottish	649	2.90
Slovak	11	0.05
Swedish	131	0.59
Swiss	51	0.23
Turkish	6	0.03
Ukrainian	53	0.24
United States or American	1,953	8.72
Welsh	133	0.59
West Indian, excl. Hispanic:	164	0.73
Barbadian	25	0.11
Haitian	14	0.06
Jamaican	75	0.34
West Indian	50	0.22
White:	15,551	70.30
Not Hispanic (14,203)	14,510	65.59
Hispanic (983)	1,041	4.71

Dunwoody

Place Type: Census Designated Place
County: De Kalb
Population: 32,808

Ancestry/Race	Number	%
African American/Black:	1,567	4.78
Not Hispanic (1,423)	1,526	4.65
Hispanic (29)	41	0.12
African, sub-Saharan:	339	1.03
African	111	0.34
Ethiopian	73	0.22
Ghanian	19	0.06
Liberian	10	0.03
Nigerian	33	0.10
Somalian	50	0.15
South African	28	0.09
Other sub-Saharan African	15	0.05
Am. Ind. or Alaska Nat., not spec.	70	0.21
Alsatian	8	0.02
American Indian tribes, specified:	81	0.25
Apache	1	0.00
Blackfeet	3	0.01
Cherokee (8)	31	0.09
Cheyenne	1	0.00
Chickasaw	2	0.01
Chippewa	2	0.01
Choctaw (4)	10	0.03
Comanche (1)	1	0.00
Creek	1	0.00
Kiowa	1	0.00
Latin American Indians (6)	8	0.02
Seminole	1	0.00
Sioux	8	0.02
All other tribes (3)	11	0.03
American Indian tribes, not spec.	13	0.04
Arab:	206	0.63
Iraqi	21	0.06
Lebanese	142	0.43
Palestinian	15	0.05
Other Arab	28	0.09
Armenian	45	0.14
Asian:	2,771	8.45
Bangladeshi (3)	3	0.01
Cambodian (1)	3	0.01
Chinese, ex. Taiwanese (447)	502	1.53
Filipino (47)	82	0.25
Indian (1,030)	1,052	3.21
Indonesian (13)	13	0.04
Japanese (172)	199	0.61
Korean (537)	561	1.71
Laotian (4)	4	0.01
Malaysian	1	0.00
Pakistani (49)	49	0.15
Sri Lankan (9)	9	0.03
Taiwanese (58)	69	0.21
Thai (14)	17	0.05
Vietnamese (110)	128	0.39
Other Asian, specified	6	0.02
Other Asian, not specified (22)	73	0.22
Australian	32	0.10
Austrian	182	0.55
Belgian	127	0.39
Brazilian	42	0.13
British	360	1.10
Bulgarian	10	0.03
Canadian	156	0.48
Celtic	10	0.03
Croatian	37	0.11
Czech	115	0.35
Czechoslovakian	75	0.23
Danish	103	0.31
Dutch	385	1.17
Eastern European	304	0.93
English	5,101	15.55
European	536	1.63
Finnish	37	0.11
French, except Basque	781	2.38
French Canadian	160	0.49
German	5,099	15.54
Greek	216	0.66
Hawaii Native/Pacific Islander:	13	0.04
Melanesian: (1)	1	0.00
Fijian (1)	1	0.00
Micronesian: (1)	1	0.00
Guamanian/Chamorro (1)	1	0.00
Polynesian:	4	0.01
Native Hawaiian	2	0.01
Samoan	2	0.01
Other Pac. Isl., specified	5	0.02
Other Pac. Isl., not spec. (2)	2	0.01
Hispanic or Latino:	1,514	4.61
Central American:	108	0.33
Costa Rican	9	0.03
Guatemalan	23	0.07
Honduran	26	0.08
Nicaraguan	12	0.04
Panamanian	13	0.04
Salvadoran	25	0.08
Cuban	92	0.28
Dominican Republic	9	0.03
Mexican	705	2.15
Puerto Rican	85	0.26
South American:	259	0.79
Argentinean	29	0.09
Chilean	13	0.04
Colombian	102	0.31

Notes: 1. Figures in the "Number" column do not add up to the total population due to: a) Ancestry/Race overlap — e.g. persons can report being both White and Irish, b) persons of Hispanic origin can report being any race, c) persons reporting two ancestries are counted in both categories. 2. Numbers in parentheses indicate the number of persons reporting this ancestry/race alone, not in combination with any other ancestry/race. 3. Refer to the Explanation of Data in the front of the book for more detailed information.

Ecuadorian	19	0.06
Peruvian	41	0.12
Uruguayan	5	0.02
Venezuelan	33	0.10
Other South American	17	0.05
Other Hispanic or Latino	256	0.78
Hungarian	196	0.60
Iranian	28	0.09
Irish	3,996	12.18
Israeli	39	0.12
Italian	1,388	4.23
Latvian	45	0.14
Lithuanian	82	0.25
Maltese	9	0.03
Northern European	10	0.03
Norwegian	298	0.91
Pennsylvania German	5	0.02
Polish	1,121	3.42
Portuguese	93	0.28
Romanian	92	0.28
Russian	785	2.39
Scandinavian	37	0.11
Scotch-Irish	1,200	3.66
Scottish	1,115	3.40
Slavic	29	0.09
Slovak	103	0.31
Slovene	18	0.05
Swedish	392	1.19
Swiss	158	0.48
Turkish	66	0.20
Ukrainian	137	0.42
United States or American	2,124	6.47
Welsh	475	1.45
West Indian, excl. Hispanic:	74	0.23
Dutch West Indian	10	0.03
Jamaican	52	0.16
West Indian	12	0.04
White:	28,209	85.98
Not Hispanic (26,833)	27,098	82.60
Hispanic (1,060)	1,111	3.39
Yugoslavian	29	0.09

East Point

Place Type: City
County: Fulton
Population: 39,595

Ancestry/Race	Number	%
African American/Black:	31,294	79.04
Not Hispanic (30,728)	31,044	78.40
Hispanic (221)	250	0.63
African, sub-Saharan:	628	1.59
African	469	1.19
Ethiopian	54	0.14
Liberian	2	0.01
Nigerian	56	0.14
Zairian	7	0.02
Zimbabwean	21	0.05
Other sub-Saharan African	19	0.05
Alaska Native tribes, specified:	1	0.00
All other tribes (1)	1	0.00
Am. Ind. or Alaska Nat., not spec.	108	0.27
American Indian tribes, specified:	117	0.30
Blackfeet	4	0.01
Cherokee (10)	47	0.12
Chickasaw	4	0.01
Choctaw	3	0.01
Cree	4	0.01
Creek	6	0.02
Crow	1	0.00
Iroquois	2	0.01
Latin American Indians (7)	24	0.06
Navajo	1	0.00
Pueblo (1)	3	0.01
Seminole (1)	2	0.01
Shoshone (3)	3	0.01
Sioux	1	0.00
All other tribes (2)	12	0.03
American Indian tribes, not spec.	7	0.02
Arab:	24	0.06
Lebanese	15	0.04
Moroccan	9	0.02
Asian:	344	0.87
Bangladeshi	1	0.00
Cambodian (6)	10	0.03
Chinese, ex. Taiwanese (32)	45	0.11
Filipino (25)	41	0.10
Indian (70)	88	0.22
Indonesian (4)	8	0.02
Japanese (9)	18	0.05
Korean (17)	21	0.05
Laotian	1	0.00
Pakistani (9)	10	0.03
Thai (2)	3	0.01
Vietnamese (53)	57	0.14
Other Asian, specified	2	0.01
Other Asian, not specified (13)	39	0.10
Belgian	26	0.07
Brazilian	12	0.03
British	73	0.19
Canadian	8	0.02
Croatian	9	0.02
Czech	9	0.02
Danish	11	0.03
Dutch	84	0.21
English	797	2.02
European	59	0.15
French, except Basque	136	0.34
German	351	0.89
Greek	13	0.03
Guyanese	69	0.17
Hawaii Native/Pacific Islander:	80	0.20
Melanesian: (3)	3	0.01
Other Melanesian (3)	3	0.01
Micronesian: (11)	14	0.04
Guamanian/Chamorro (11)	14	0.04
Polynesian: (12)	21	0.05
Native Hawaiian (3)	10	0.03
Samoan (9)	11	0.03
Other Pac. Isl., specified	2	0.01
Other Pac. Isl., not spec. (10)	40	0.10
Hispanic or Latino:	2,998	7.57
Central American:	49	0.12
Costa Rican	1	0.00
Guatemalan	9	0.02
Honduran	3	0.01
Nicaraguan	1	0.00
Panamanian	20	0.05
Salvadoran	12	0.03
Other Central American	3	0.01
Cuban	67	0.17
Dominican Republic	8	0.02
Mexican	2,504	6.32
Puerto Rican	90	0.23
South American:	27	0.07
Chilean	3	0.01
Colombian	8	0.02
Peruvian	6	0.02
Venezuelan	8	0.02
Other South American	2	0.01
Other Hispanic or Latino	253	0.64
Hungarian	5	0.01
Irish	565	1.43
Italian	76	0.19
Lithuanian	18	0.05
Norwegian	5	0.01
Polish	12	0.03
Scotch-Irish	199	0.50
Scottish	145	0.37
Swedish	38	0.10
United States or American	1,078	2.73
Welsh	35	0.09
West Indian, excl. Hispanic:	583	1.48
Bahamian	7	0.02
Belizean	12	0.03
British West Indian	41	0.10
Haitian	121	0.31
Jamaican	277	0.70
Trinidadian and Tobagonian	80	0.20
U.S. Virgin Islander	19	0.05
West Indian	26	0.07
White:	6,692	16.90
Not Hispanic (5,135)	5,320	13.44
Hispanic (1,241)	1,372	3.47

Evans

Place Type: Census Designated Place
County: Columbia
Population: 17,727

Ancestry/Race	Number	%
African American/Black:	1,895	10.69
Not Hispanic (1,785)	1,861	10.50
Hispanic (26)	34	0.19
African, sub-Saharan:	99	0.56
African	99	0.56
Am. Ind. or Alaska Nat., not spec.	26	0.15
American Indian tribes, specified:	78	0.44
Apache (2)	3	0.02
Blackfeet	1	0.01
Cherokee (8)	40	0.23
Chippewa	2	0.01
Choctaw	5	0.03
Comanche	1	0.01
Creek (1)	2	0.01
Iroquois (1)	1	0.01
Latin American Indians (2)	2	0.01
Lumbee	1	0.01
Navajo	1	0.01
Ottawa (1)	2	0.01
Pueblo (2)	2	0.01
Sioux (3)	3	0.02
All other tribes (9)	12	0.07
American Indian tribes, not spec.	5	0.03
Arab:	105	0.59
Iraqi	7	0.04
Lebanese	65	0.37
Moroccan	7	0.04
Syrian	19	0.11
Other Arab	7	0.04
Asian:	598	3.37
Bangladeshi	1	0.01
Chinese, ex. Taiwanese (39)	53	0.30
Filipino (58)	82	0.46
Indian (122)	130	0.73
Japanese (28)	58	0.33
Korean (111)	147	0.83
Laotian (2)	2	0.01
Pakistani (5)	5	0.03
Taiwanese (6)	7	0.04
Thai (16)	20	0.11
Vietnamese (68)	72	0.41
Other Asian, not specified (14)	21	0.12
Austrian	46	0.26
Belgian	23	0.13
British	88	0.50
Bulgarian	7	0.04
Croatian	9	0.05
Czech	23	0.13
Czechoslovakian	18	0.10
Danish	18	0.10
Dutch	265	1.50
English	2,100	11.87
European	226	1.28
French, except Basque	401	2.27
French Canadian	107	0.60
German	2,180	12.32
Greek	19	0.11
Hawaii Native/Pacific Islander:	21	0.12
Melanesian:	3	0.02
Fijian	3	0.02
Micronesian: (5)	5	0.03
Guamanian/Chamorro (5)	5	0.03
Polynesian: (2)	10	0.06
Native Hawaiian (1)	8	0.05
Other Polynesian (1)	2	0.01
Other Pac. Isl., not spec. (1)	3	0.02
Hispanic or Latino:	396	2.23

Notes: 1. Figures in the "Number" column do not add up to the total population due to: a) Ancestry/Race overlap — e.g. persons can report being both White and Irish, b) persons of Hispanic origin can report being any race, c) persons reporting two ancestries are counted in both categories. 2. Numbers in parentheses indicate the number of persons reporting this ancestry/race alone, not in combination with any other ancestry/race. 3. Refer to the Explanation of Data in the front of the book for more detailed information.

Ancestry/Race	Number	%
Central American:	44	0.25
Costa Rican	5	0.03
Honduran	2	0.01
Nicaraguan	1	0.01
Panamanian	28	0.16
Salvadoran	8	0.05
Cuban	7	0.04
Dominican Republic	1	0.01
Mexican	109	0.61
Puerto Rican	132	0.74
South American:	16	0.09
Colombian	10	0.06
Ecuadorian	1	0.01
Paraguayan	1	0.01
Peruvian	1	0.01
Other South American	3	0.02
Other Hispanic or Latino	87	0.49
Hungarian	168	0.95
Iranian	28	0.16
Irish	2,271	12.83
Israeli	7	0.04
Italian	638	3.61
Lithuanian	34	0.19
Norwegian	169	0.96
Polish	341	1.93
Portuguese	37	0.21
Russian	86	0.49
Scotch-Irish	475	2.68
Scottish	379	2.14
Slavic	27	0.15
Slovak	11	0.06
Swedish	97	0.55
Swiss	55	0.31
Turkish	46	0.26
Ukrainian	27	0.15
United States or American	2,817	15.92
Welsh	50	0.28
West Indian, excl. Hispanic:	47	0.27
Barbadian	8	0.05
Jamaican	32	0.18
West Indian	7	0.04
White:	15,248	86.02
Not Hispanic (14,748)	14,972	84.46
Hispanic (251)	276	1.56
Yugoslavian	9	0.05

Fayetteville

Place Type: City
County: Fayette
Population: 11,148

Ancestry/Race	Number	%
African American/Black:	1,598	14.33
Not Hispanic (1,544)	1,579	14.16
Hispanic (13)	19	0.17
African, sub-Saharan:	131	1.16
African	52	0.46
Nigerian	79	0.70
Am. Ind. or Alaska Nat., not spec.	20	0.18
American Indian tribes, specified:	41	0.37
Apache (1)	1	0.01
Blackfeet	3	0.03
Cherokee (5)	17	0.15
Choctaw	1	0.01
Comanche (1)	1	0.01
Creek (2)	5	0.04
Latin American Indians (4)	4	0.04
Lumbee	1	0.01
Ottawa (2)	2	0.02
Potawatomi (1)	1	0.01
Seminole (3)	3	0.03
Sioux (1)	2	0.02
American Indian tribes, not spec.	2	0.02
Arab:	67	0.59
Lebanese	7	0.06
Other Arab	60	0.53
Armenian	33	0.29
Asian:	423	3.79
Cambodian (1)	1	0.01
Chinese, ex. Taiwanese (59)	69	0.62
Filipino (40)	51	0.46
Indian (148)	154	1.38
Indonesian (1)	1	0.01
Japanese (19)	27	0.24
Korean (47)	55	0.49
Laotian (10)	16	0.14
Pakistani (19)	19	0.17
Thai (3)	3	0.03
Vietnamese (13)	17	0.15
Other Asian, specified	5	0.04
Other Asian, not specified (5)	5	0.04
Austrian	17	0.15
British	65	0.58
Canadian	39	0.35
Croatian	8	0.07
Czech	27	0.24
Czechoslovakian	10	0.09
Danish	110	0.98
Dutch	193	1.71
English	1,308	11.59
European	52	0.46
French, except Basque	316	2.80
French Canadian	105	0.93
German	1,131	10.03
Greek	34	0.30
Hawaii Native/Pacific Islander:	10	0.09
Micronesian: (1)	1	0.01
Guamanian/Chamorro (1)	1	0.01
Other Pac. Isl., specified	5	0.04
Other Pac. Isl., not spec.	4	0.04
Hispanic or Latino:	310	2.78
Central American:	18	0.16
Costa Rican	1	0.01
Guatemalan	1	0.01
Honduran	1	0.01
Panamanian	6	0.05
Salvadoran	2	0.02
Other Central American	7	0.06
Cuban	32	0.29
Dominican Republic	12	0.11
Mexican	90	0.81
Puerto Rican	68	0.61
South American:	32	0.29
Argentinean	3	0.03
Chilean	1	0.01
Colombian	8	0.07
Ecuadorian	7	0.06
Peruvian	12	0.11
Venezuelan	1	0.01
Other Hispanic or Latino	58	0.52
Hungarian	41	0.36
Irish	1,513	13.41
Italian	373	3.31
Lithuanian	32	0.28
Norwegian	38	0.34
Polish	208	1.84
Portuguese	16	0.14
Russian	10	0.09
Scandinavian	14	0.12
Scotch-Irish	300	2.66
Scottish	207	1.83
Slovak	18	0.16
Swedish	47	0.42
Swiss	12	0.11
United States or American	1,506	13.35
Welsh	57	0.51
West Indian, excl. Hispanic:	84	0.74
British West Indian	7	0.06
Jamaican	77	0.68
White:	9,073	81.39
Not Hispanic (8,772)	8,861	79.49
Hispanic (195)	212	1.90

Forest Park

Place Type: City
County: Clayton
Population: 21,447

Ancestry/Race	Number	%
African American/Black:	8,215	38.30
Not Hispanic (7,883)	8,055	37.56
Hispanic (135)	160	0.75
African, sub-Saharan:	192	0.90
African	192	0.90
Alaska Native tribes, specified:	2	0.01
Tlingit-Haida (2)	2	0.01
Alaska Native tribes, not specified	1	0.00
Am. Ind. or Alaska Nat., not spec.	125	0.58
American Indian tribes, specified:	75	0.35
Apache	4	0.02
Blackfeet	2	0.01
Cherokee (10)	39	0.18
Chickasaw	4	0.02
Chippewa (1)	1	0.00
Houma (4)	4	0.02
Latin American Indians (13)	16	0.07
Lumbee (1)	1	0.00
Sioux (1)	2	0.01
All other tribes (1)	2	0.01
American Indian tribes, not spec.	10	0.05
Arab:	26	0.12
Lebanese	26	0.12
Asian:	1,413	6.59
Bangladeshi (1)	1	0.00
Cambodian (26)	35	0.16
Chinese, ex. Taiwanese (19)	23	0.11
Filipino (36)	39	0.18
Indian (58)	79	0.37
Korean (27)	34	0.16
Laotian (137)	160	0.75
Pakistani (2)	9	0.04
Taiwanese	1	0.00
Thai (4)	6	0.03
Vietnamese (919)	965	4.50
Other Asian, specified (1)	1	0.00
Other Asian, not specified (33)	60	0.28
British	4	0.02
Czechoslovakian	6	0.03
Danish	12	0.06
Dutch	104	0.49
English	706	3.32
European	49	0.23
French, except Basque	106	0.50
French Canadian	62	0.29
German	580	2.72
Hawaii Native/Pacific Islander:	14	0.07
Micronesian: (1)	1	0.00
Guamanian/Chamorro (1)	1	0.00
Polynesian: (3)	6	0.03
Native Hawaiian (3)	6	0.03
Other Pac. Isl., not spec.	7	0.03
Hispanic or Latino:	4,322	20.15
Central American:	180	0.84
Costa Rican	2	0.01
Guatemalan	32	0.15
Honduran	49	0.23
Nicaraguan	4	0.02
Panamanian	12	0.06
Salvadoran	78	0.36
Other Central American	3	0.01
Cuban	38	0.18
Dominican Republic	30	0.14
Mexican	3,539	16.50
Puerto Rican	153	0.71
South American:	22	0.10
Chilean	2	0.01
Colombian	5	0.02
Ecuadorian	1	0.00
Peruvian	1	0.00
Venezuelan	4	0.02
Other South American	9	0.04
Other Hispanic or Latino	360	1.68

Notes: 1. Figures in the "Number" column do not add up to the total population due to: a) Ancestry/Race overlap — e.g. persons can report being both White and Irish, b) persons of Hispanic origin can report being any race, c) persons reporting two ancestries are counted in both categories. 2. Numbers in parentheses indicate the number of persons reporting this ancestry/race alone, not in combination with any other ancestry/race. 3. Refer to the Explanation of Data in the front of the book for more detailed information.

Hungarian	8	0.04
Irish	878	4.12
Italian	212	1.00
Northern European	9	0.04
Norwegian	41	0.19
Polish	22	0.10
Romanian	9	0.04
Russian	7	0.03
Scotch-Irish	226	1.06
Scottish	199	0.93
Swedish	20	0.09
Swiss	8	0.04
United States or American	2,050	9.63
Welsh	25	0.12
West Indian, excl. Hispanic:	206	0.97
Bahamian	16	0.08
Dutch West Indian	8	0.04
Haitian	58	0.27
Jamaican	79	0.37
Trinidadian and Tobagonian	33	0.15
U.S. Virgin Islander	12	0.06
White:	10,065	46.93
Not Hispanic (7,557)	7,774	36.25
Hispanic (2,118)	2,291	10.68

Fort Benning South

Place Type: Census Designated Place
County: Chattahoochee
Population: 11,737

Ancestry/Race	Number	%
African American/Black:	3,659	31.17
Not Hispanic (3,335)	3,510	29.91
Hispanic (89)	149	1.27
African, sub-Saharan:	210	1.79
African	192	1.64
Kenyan	6	0.05
Nigerian	7	0.06
South African	5	0.04
Alaska Native tribes, specified:	5	0.04
Aleut (1)	1	0.01
Eskimo (4)	4	0.03
Am. Ind. or Alaska Nat., not spec.	53	0.45
American Indian tribes, specified:	127	1.08
Apache (2)	2	0.02
Blackfeet (2)	3	0.03
Cherokee (5)	38	0.32
Chippewa (1)	2	0.02
Choctaw (6)	10	0.09
Colville (1)	1	0.01
Creek (4)	5	0.04
Delaware	1	0.01
Iroquois (1)	2	0.02
Latin American Indians (5)	13	0.11
Lumbee (7)	7	0.06
Navajo (13)	14	0.12
Pima (1)	1	0.01
Potawatomi (1)	1	0.01
Pueblo (3)	4	0.03
Seminole (2)	2	0.02
Sioux (1)	5	0.04
Ute (2)	2	0.02
Yaqui (1)	1	0.01
All other tribes (9)	13	0.11
American Indian tribes, not spec.	8	0.07
Asian:	385	3.28
Bangladeshi (1)	1	0.01
Cambodian (1)	2	0.02
Chinese, ex. Taiwanese (19)	25	0.21
Filipino (62)	119	1.01
Indian (12)	18	0.15
Japanese (22)	53	0.45
Korean (72)	95	0.81
Laotian (3)	3	0.03
Malaysian (1)	1	0.01
Sri Lankan (1)	1	0.01
Taiwanese (2)	2	0.02
Thai (8)	18	0.15
Vietnamese (16)	18	0.15
Other Asian, specified (2)	3	0.03
Other Asian, not specified (10)	26	0.22
Australian	35	0.30
Austrian	37	0.32
British	28	0.24
Celtic	6	0.05
Croatian	16	0.14
Czech	10	0.09
Czechoslovakian	12	0.10
Danish	30	0.26
Dutch	97	0.83
English	530	4.53
European	165	1.41
French, except Basque	250	2.14
French Canadian	97	0.83
German	1,488	12.71
Greek	64	0.55
Hawaii Native/Pacific Islander:	114	0.97
Micronesian: (24)	40	0.34
Guamanian/Chamorro (15)	27	0.23
Other Micronesian (9)	13	0.11
Polynesian: (29)	52	0.44
Native Hawaiian (8)	23	0.20
Samoan (21)	28	0.24
Tongan	1	0.01
Other Pac. Isl., not spec. (1)	22	0.19
Hispanic or Latino:	1,461	12.45
Central American:	112	0.95
Costa Rican	8	0.07
Guatemalan	6	0.05
Honduran	6	0.05
Nicaraguan	7	0.06
Panamanian	63	0.54
Salvadoran	17	0.14
Other Central American	5	0.04
Cuban	35	0.30
Dominican Republic	38	0.32
Mexican	503	4.29
Puerto Rican	457	3.89
South American:	77	0.66
Chilean	5	0.04
Colombian	33	0.28
Ecuadorian	17	0.14
Peruvian	10	0.09
Venezuelan	10	0.09
Other South American	2	0.02
Other Hispanic or Latino	239	2.04
Hungarian	46	0.39
Irish	1,283	10.96
Israeli	10	0.09
Italian	460	3.93
Lithuanian	18	0.15
Maltese	25	0.21
Northern European	5	0.04
Norwegian	158	1.35
Polish	180	1.54
Portuguese	20	0.17
Russian	23	0.20
Scandinavian	17	0.15
Scotch-Irish	199	1.70
Scottish	192	1.64
Slovak	73	0.62
Swedish	91	0.78
Swiss	14	0.12
United States or American	750	6.41
Welsh	56	0.48
West Indian, excl. Hispanic:	244	2.08
Barbadian	6	0.05
British West Indian	13	0.11
Haitian	13	0.11
Jamaican	140	1.20
Trinidadian and Tobagonian	22	0.19
West Indian	50	0.43
White:	7,030	59.90
Not Hispanic (6,229)	6,462	55.06
Hispanic (440)	568	4.84

Fort Stewart

Place Type: Census Designated Place
County: Liberty
Population: 11,205

Ancestry/Race	Number	%
African American/Black:	4,321	38.56
Not Hispanic (4,024)	4,164	37.16
Hispanic (94)	157	1.40
African, sub-Saharan:	286	2.51
African	215	1.89
Cape Verdean	37	0.33
Ghanian	7	0.06
Nigerian	19	0.17
Sudanese	8	0.07
Alaska Native tribes, specified:	3	0.03
Alaska Athabascan (2)	2	0.02
Eskimo (1)	1	0.01
Am. Ind. or Alaska Nat., not spec.	30	0.27
American Indian tribes, specified:	108	0.96
Apache (1)	1	0.01
Blackfeet (2)	13	0.12
Cherokee (7)	17	0.15
Cheyenne (2)	2	0.02
Chickasaw	3	0.03
Chippewa (2)	2	0.02
Choctaw (5)	14	0.12
Cree (1)	1	0.01
Creek (1)	1	0.01
Iroquois	1	0.01
Latin American Indians (7)	8	0.07
Lumbee (10)	10	0.09
Navajo (8)	9	0.08
Paiute	1	0.01
Seminole (5)	5	0.04
Sioux (1)	1	0.01
Tohono O'Odham (1)	1	0.01
Yaqui (1)	1	0.01
All other tribes (12)	17	0.15
American Indian tribes, not spec.	7	0.06
Asian:	344	3.07
Bangladeshi (1)	1	0.01
Cambodian (5)	7	0.06
Chinese, ex. Taiwanese (11)	27	0.24
Filipino (72)	117	1.04
Hmong (8)	9	0.08
Indian (16)	17	0.15
Japanese (12)	30	0.27
Korean (55)	81	0.72
Laotian (3)	3	0.03
Taiwanese	2	0.02
Thai (5)	12	0.11
Vietnamese (6)	7	0.06
Other Asian, specified	6	0.05
Other Asian, not specified (12)	25	0.22
Austrian	18	0.16
Belgian	10	0.09
British	27	0.24
Croatian	10	0.09
Czech	9	0.08
Czechoslovakian	17	0.15
Danish	18	0.16
Dutch	154	1.35
English	387	3.40
European	21	0.18
Finnish	47	0.41
French, except Basque	167	1.47
French Canadian	36	0.32
German	1,105	9.72
Greek	21	0.18
Hawaii Native/Pacific Islander:	91	0.81
Micronesian: (20)	22	0.20
Guamanian/Chamorro (17)	18	0.16
Other Micronesian (3)	4	0.04
Polynesian: (25)	45	0.40
Native Hawaiian (7)	22	0.20
Samoan (18)	22	0.20
Tongan	1	0.01
Other Pac. Isl., specified	5	0.04

Notes: 1. Figures in the "Number" column do not add up to the total population due to: a) Ancestry/Race overlap — e.g. persons can report being both White and Irish, b) persons of Hispanic origin can report being any race, c) persons reporting two ancestries are counted in both categories. 2. Numbers in parentheses indicate the number of persons reporting this ancestry/race alone, not in combination with any other ancestry/race. 3. Refer to the Explanation of Data in the front of the book for more detailed information.

Ancestry/Race	Number	%
Other Pac. Isl., not spec. (1)	19	0.17
Hispanic or Latino:	1,358	12.12
Central American:	117	1.04
Costa Rican	4	0.04
Guatemalan	15	0.13
Honduran	8	0.07
Nicaraguan	3	0.03
Panamanian	78	0.70
Salvadoran	7	0.06
Other Central American	2	0.02
Cuban	24	0.21
Dominican Republic	58	0.52
Mexican	514	4.59
Puerto Rican	484	4.32
South American:	35	0.31
Argentinean	1	0.01
Chilean	1	0.01
Colombian	12	0.11
Ecuadorian	10	0.09
Peruvian	9	0.08
Venezuelan	2	0.02
Other Hispanic or Latino	126	1.12
Hungarian	7	0.06
Iranian	15	0.13
Irish	905	7.96
Italian	432	3.80
Lithuanian	29	0.25
Northern European	38	0.33
Norwegian	70	0.62
Pennsylvania German	20	0.18
Polish	177	1.56
Portuguese	10	0.09
Romanian	9	0.08
Russian	17	0.15
Scandinavian	10	0.09
Scotch-Irish	211	1.86
Scottish	133	1.17
Slovak	10	0.09
Swedish	60	0.53
Ukrainian	55	0.48
United States or American	1,039	9.14
Welsh	27	0.24
West Indian, excl. Hispanic:	294	2.59
Bahamian	8	0.07
Belizean	19	0.17
British West Indian	77	0.68
Haitian	15	0.13
Jamaican	132	1.16
Trinidadian and Tobagonian	4	0.04
U.S. Virgin Islander	19	0.17
West Indian	20	0.18
White:	5,851	52.22
Not Hispanic (5,216)	5,397	48.17
Hispanic (387)	454	4.05

Gainesville

Place Type: City
County: Hall
Population: 25,578

Ancestry/Race	Number	%
African American/Black:	4,111	16.07
Not Hispanic (3,952)	4,024	15.73
Hispanic (71)	87	0.34
African, sub-Saharan:	167	0.66
African	102	0.40
Ghanian	5	0.02
Nigerian	10	0.04
Other sub-Saharan African	50	0.20
Am. Ind. or Alaska Nat., not spec.	64	0.25
American Indian tribes, specified:	86	0.34
Apache	3	0.01
Cherokee (16)	52	0.20
Chippewa (3)	4	0.02
Cree	1	0.00
Creek (4)	5	0.02
Crow	1	0.00
Delaware (1)	1	0.00
Latin American Indians (7)	12	0.05
Pueblo (1)	1	0.00
Sioux	2	0.01
Yuman (1)	1	0.00
All other tribes (1)	3	0.01
American Indian tribes, not spec.	8	0.03
Arab:	38	0.15
Arab/Arabic	11	0.04
Lebanese	7	0.03
Other Arab	20	0.08
Asian:	767	3.00
Chinese, ex. Taiwanese (20)	29	0.11
Filipino (26)	38	0.15
Hmong (1)	1	0.00
Indian (55)	68	0.27
Japanese (32)	45	0.18
Korean (22)	28	0.11
Laotian (1)	3	0.01
Malaysian (1)	1	0.00
Pakistani (1)	3	0.01
Taiwanese	6	0.02
Thai (5)	5	0.02
Vietnamese (501)	519	2.03
Other Asian, specified	3	0.01
Other Asian, not specified (13)	18	0.07
Austrian	26	0.10
Belgian	12	0.05
British	62	0.24
Canadian	24	0.09
Czech	46	0.18
Czechoslovakian	13	0.05
Danish	25	0.10
Dutch	110	0.43
English	2,208	8.67
European	195	0.77
Finnish	5	0.02
French, except Basque	272	1.07
French Canadian	147	0.58
German	1,255	4.93
Greek	110	0.43
Guyanese	6	0.02
Hawaii Native/Pacific Islander:	49	0.19
Micronesian: (28)	29	0.11
Guamanian/Chamorro (28)	28	0.11
Other Micronesian	1	0.00
Polynesian: (4)	7	0.03
Native Hawaiian (4)	5	0.02
Samoan	2	0.01
Other Pac. Isl., specified	3	0.01
Other Pac. Isl., not spec. (2)	10	0.04
Hispanic or Latino:	8,484	33.17
Central American:	449	1.76
Costa Rican	1	0.00
Guatemalan	27	0.11
Honduran	66	0.26
Nicaraguan	13	0.05
Panamanian	7	0.03
Salvadoran	323	1.26
Other Central American	12	0.05
Cuban	20	0.08
Dominican Republic	11	0.04
Mexican	7,083	27.69
Puerto Rican	83	0.32
South American:	91	0.36
Argentinean	3	0.01
Bolivian	2	0.01
Chilean	1	0.00
Colombian	56	0.22
Ecuadorian	2	0.01
Paraguayan	2	0.01
Peruvian	14	0.05
Uruguayan	4	0.02
Venezuelan	7	0.03
Other Hispanic or Latino	747	2.92
Iranian	16	0.06
Irish	1,513	5.94
Italian	441	1.73
Lithuanian	17	0.07
Norwegian	89	0.35
Polish	112	0.44
Portuguese	8	0.03
Russian	34	0.13
Scandinavian	26	0.10
Scotch-Irish	542	2.13
Scottish	470	1.85
Swedish	87	0.34
Swiss	45	0.18
Ukrainian	5	0.02
United States or American	2,307	9.06
Welsh	51	0.20
West Indian, excl. Hispanic:	18	0.07
Bermudan	5	0.02
Jamaican	8	0.03
Trinidadian and Tobagonian	5	0.02
White:	17,022	66.55
Not Hispanic (12,218)	12,352	48.29
Hispanic (4,462)	4,670	18.26
Yugoslavian	8	0.03

Garden City

Place Type: City
County: Chatham
Population: 11,289

Ancestry/Race	Number	%
Acadian/Cajun	38	0.34
African American/Black:	4,602	40.77
Not Hispanic (4,484)	4,556	40.36
Hispanic (30)	46	0.41
African, sub-Saharan:	169	1.51
African	115	1.02
Ghanian	26	0.23
Kenyan	18	0.16
Nigerian	10	0.09
Am. Ind. or Alaska Nat., not spec.	58	0.51
American Indian tribes, specified:	61	0.54
Apache (1)	4	0.04
Blackfeet (1)	2	0.02
Cherokee (7)	23	0.20
Chickasaw	1	0.01
Chippewa (3)	3	0.03
Choctaw (1)	1	0.01
Comanche (1)	1	0.01
Creek	1	0.01
Iroquois	1	0.01
Latin American Indians (17)	20	0.18
Navajo	1	0.01
Seminole	2	0.02
All other tribes (1)	1	0.01
American Indian tribes, not spec.	8	0.07
Asian:	153	1.36
Chinese, ex. Taiwanese (12)	16	0.14
Filipino (21)	29	0.26
Indian (43)	45	0.40
Japanese	2	0.02
Korean (6)	7	0.06
Laotian	4	0.04
Thai (2)	2	0.02
Vietnamese (16)	16	0.14
Other Asian, specified	17	0.15
Other Asian, not specified (3)	15	0.13
Austrian	48	0.43
British	11	0.10
Canadian	7	0.06
Croatian	4	0.04
Czech	12	0.11
Czechoslovakian	6	0.05
Danish	21	0.19
Dutch	71	0.63
Eastern European	9	0.08
English	439	3.91
European	42	0.37
French, except Basque	247	2.20
French Canadian	45	0.40
German	702	6.25
Greek	18	0.16
Guyanese	23	0.20
Hawaii Native/Pacific Islander:	26	0.23
Polynesian:	1	0.01
Native Hawaiian	1	0.01

Notes: 1. Figures in the "Number" column do not add up to the total population due to: a) Ancestry/Race overlap — e.g. persons can report being both White and Irish, b) persons of Hispanic origin can report being any race, c) persons reporting two ancestries are counted in both categories. 2. Numbers in parentheses indicate the number of persons reporting this ancestry/race alone, not in combination with any other ancestry/race. 3. Refer to the Explanation of Data in the front of the book for more detailed information.

Ancestry/Race	Number	%
Other Pac. Isl., specified	17	0.15
Other Pac. Isl., not spec. (5)	8	0.07
Hispanic or Latino:	675	5.98
Central American:	46	0.41
Guatemalan	1	0.01
Honduran	31	0.27
Nicaraguan	3	0.03
Panamanian	4	0.04
Salvadoran	7	0.06
Cuban	8	0.07
Dominican Republic	1	0.01
Mexican	484	4.29
Puerto Rican	28	0.25
South American:	4	0.04
Colombian	1	0.01
Peruvian	3	0.03
Other Hispanic or Latino	104	0.92
Hungarian	9	0.08
Irish	784	6.99
Italian	166	1.48
Lithuanian	10	0.09
Norwegian	32	0.29
Polish	127	1.13
Romanian	38	0.34
Russian	15	0.13
Scotch-Irish	94	0.84
Scottish	78	0.69
Swedish	22	0.20
Ukrainian	14	0.12
United States or American	1,389	12.38
Welsh	19	0.17
West Indian, excl. Hispanic:	44	0.39
Haitian	6	0.05
Jamaican	38	0.34
White:	6,292	55.74
Not Hispanic (5,841)	5,934	52.56
Hispanic (274)	358	3.17

Georgetown

Place Type: Census Designated Place
County: Chatham
Population: 10,599

Ancestry/Race	Number	%
Acadian/Cajun	10	0.09
African American/Black:	2,165	20.43
Not Hispanic (2,093)	2,142	20.21
Hispanic (15)	23	0.22
African, sub-Saharan:	7	0.07
African	7	0.07
Am. Ind. or Alaska Nat., not spec.	21	0.20
American Indian tribes, specified:	70	0.66
Apache (2)	2	0.02
Blackfeet (2)	4	0.04
Cherokee (12)	42	0.40
Choctaw (1)	1	0.01
Iroquois (2)	2	0.02
Latin American Indians (7)	7	0.07
Lumbee (3)	3	0.03
Sioux (2)	3	0.03
All other tribes (3)	6	0.06
American Indian tribes, not spec.	3	0.03
Arab:	52	0.49
Egyptian	11	0.10
Lebanese	41	0.39
Asian:	419	3.95
Chinese, ex. Taiwanese (49)	54	0.51
Filipino (70)	85	0.80
Indian (84)	97	0.92
Japanese (15)	31	0.29
Korean (48)	69	0.65
Laotian (1)	1	0.01
Thai (10)	13	0.12
Vietnamese (35)	45	0.42
Other Asian, specified	1	0.01
Other Asian, not specified (10)	23	0.22
Australian	11	0.10
Austrian	45	0.43
British	29	0.27
Canadian	10	0.09
Czech	43	0.41
Czechoslovakian	41	0.39
Dutch	202	1.92
English	968	9.18
European	94	0.89
French, except Basque	238	2.26
French Canadian	51	0.48
German	1,531	14.52
Greek	43	0.41
Hawaii Native/Pacific Islander:	14	0.13
Melanesian: (1)	1	0.01
Fijian (1)	1	0.01
Micronesian: (1)	3	0.03
Guamanian/Chamorro (1)	3	0.03
Polynesian: (4)	5	0.05
Native Hawaiian (3)	4	0.04
Samoan (1)	1	0.01
Other Pac. Isl., not spec.	5	0.05
Hispanic or Latino:	490	4.62
Central American:	27	0.25
Costa Rican	2	0.02
Guatemalan	1	0.01
Honduran	4	0.04
Nicaraguan	2	0.02
Panamanian	18	0.17
Cuban	49	0.46
Dominican Republic	2	0.02
Mexican	134	1.26
Puerto Rican	159	1.50
South American:	28	0.26
Argentinean	4	0.04
Chilean	4	0.04
Colombian	6	0.06
Ecuadorian	1	0.01
Peruvian	4	0.04
Venezuelan	9	0.08
Other Hispanic or Latino	91	0.86
Hungarian	42	0.40
Iranian	42	0.40
Irish	1,332	12.63
Italian	398	3.77
Latvian	10	0.09
Norwegian	79	0.75
Pennsylvania German	15	0.14
Polish	138	1.31
Portuguese	29	0.27
Russian	34	0.32
Scandinavian	8	0.08
Scotch-Irish	275	2.61
Scottish	146	1.38
Slavic	11	0.10
Slovak	45	0.43
Slovene	8	0.08
Swedish	50	0.47
Ukrainian	18	0.17
United States or American	1,089	10.33
Welsh	40	0.38
West Indian, excl. Hispanic:	49	0.46
Dutch West Indian	9	0.09
Jamaican	10	0.09
Trinidadian and Tobagonian	30	0.28
White:	7,900	74.54
Not Hispanic (7,458)	7,605	71.75
Hispanic (256)	295	2.78
Yugoslavian	7	0.07

Griffin

Place Type: City
County: Spalding
Population: 23,451

Ancestry/Race	Number	%
African American/Black:	11,817	50.39
Not Hispanic (11,647)	11,749	50.10
Hispanic (50)	68	0.29
African, sub-Saharan:	385	1.64
African	297	1.27
Ghanian	16	0.07
Nigerian	72	0.31
Am. Ind. or Alaska Nat., not spec.	45	0.19
American Indian tribes, specified:	44	0.19
Apache (4)	4	0.02
Cherokee (14)	29	0.12
Creek (4)	5	0.02
Navajo (1)	1	0.00
Sioux (4)	4	0.02
All other tribes	1	0.00
American Indian tribes, not spec.	3	0.01
Arab:	153	0.65
Arab/Arabic	144	0.61
Lebanese	9	0.04
Asian:	299	1.27
Bangladeshi (5)	5	0.02
Cambodian (1)	1	0.00
Chinese, ex. Taiwanese (19)	24	0.10
Filipino (11)	21	0.09
Indian (124)	124	0.53
Indonesian	3	0.01
Japanese (1)	4	0.02
Korean (34)	42	0.18
Laotian (1)	1	0.00
Pakistani (8)	12	0.05
Taiwanese (5)	5	0.02
Thai (4)	6	0.03
Vietnamese (16)	17	0.07
Other Asian, specified (3)	28	0.12
Other Asian, not specified (1)	6	0.03
Austrian	14	0.06
Belgian	24	0.10
British	101	0.43
Canadian	7	0.03
Danish	16	0.07
Dutch	71	0.30
Eastern European	10	0.04
English	1,451	6.19
European	271	1.16
Finnish	8	0.03
French, except Basque	183	0.78
French Canadian	55	0.23
German	861	3.67
Guyanese	19	0.08
Hawaii Native/Pacific Islander:	45	0.19
Micronesian:	1	0.00
Guamanian/Chamorro	1	0.00
Polynesian: (6)	8	0.03
Native Hawaiian (4)	5	0.02
Samoan (2)	3	0.01
Other Pac. Isl., specified	25	0.11
Other Pac. Isl., not spec.	11	0.05
Hispanic or Latino:	520	2.22
Central American:	2	0.01
Costa Rican	1	0.00
Honduran	1	0.00
Cuban	14	0.06
Dominican Republic	4	0.02
Mexican	372	1.59
Puerto Rican	47	0.20
South American:	11	0.05
Argentinean	3	0.01
Colombian	2	0.01
Peruvian	1	0.00
Other South American	5	0.02
Other Hispanic or Latino	70	0.30
Hungarian	12	0.05
Iranian	10	0.04
Irish	1,009	4.31
Italian	81	0.35
Lithuanian	7	0.03
Norwegian	74	0.32
Polish	62	0.26
Romanian	5	0.02
Russian	19	0.08
Scandinavian	37	0.16
Scotch-Irish	415	1.77
Scottish	412	1.76
Swedish	8	0.03
Swiss	9	0.04
United States or American	2,992	12.77

Notes: 1. Figures in the "Number" column do not add up to the total population due to: a) Ancestry/Race overlap — e.g. persons can report being both White and Irish, b) persons of Hispanic origin can report being any race, c) persons reporting two ancestries are counted in both categories. 2. Numbers in parentheses indicate the number of persons reporting this ancestry/race alone, not in combination with any other ancestry/race. 3. Refer to the Explanation of Data in the front of the book for more detailed information.

Welsh	90	0.38
West Indian, excl. Hispanic:	14	0.06
British West Indian	14	0.06
White:	11,171	47.64
Not Hispanic (10,830)	10,941	46.65
Hispanic (188)	230	0.98

Hinesville

Place Type: City
County: Liberty
Population: 30,392

Ancestry/Race	Number	%
African American/Black:	14,654	48.22
Not Hispanic (13,792)	14,317	47.11
Hispanic (200)	337	1.11
African, sub-Saharan:	257	0.84
African	180	0.59
Cape Verdean	8	0.03
Nigerian	60	0.20
Other sub-Saharan African	9	0.03
Alaska Native tribes, specified:	3	0.01
Alaska Athabascan (1)	1	0.00
Eskimo (2)	2	0.01
Am. Ind. or Alaska Nat., not spec.	86	0.28
American Indian tribes, specified:	235	0.77
Apache (3)	5	0.02
Blackfeet (4)	17	0.06
Cherokee (37)	112	0.37
Chippewa (2)	5	0.02
Choctaw (3)	9	0.03
Colville	2	0.01
Cree	1	0.00
Creek (5)	8	0.03
Iroquois (5)	7	0.02
Latin American Indians (9)	28	0.09
Lumbee (10)	11	0.04
Navajo	2	0.01
Osage (1)	1	0.00
Ottawa	2	0.01
Paiute (1)	1	0.00
Potawatomi (3)	5	0.02
Sioux (7)	9	0.03
All other tribes (7)	10	0.03
American Indian tribes, not spec.	28	0.09
Arab:	72	0.24
Arab/Arabic	38	0.12
Egyptian	14	0.05
Lebanese	10	0.03
Syrian	10	0.03
Armenian	16	0.05
Asian:	1,037	3.41
Cambodian (2)	3	0.01
Chinese, ex. Taiwanese (28)	69	0.23
Filipino (116)	170	0.56
Hmong (3)	4	0.01
Indian (71)	85	0.28
Indonesian (1)	2	0.01
Japanese (34)	88	0.29
Korean (334)	456	1.50
Laotian (3)	4	0.01
Malaysian (1)	1	0.00
Sri Lankan (3)	3	0.01
Taiwanese (1)	1	0.00
Thai (31)	41	0.13
Vietnamese (25)	39	0.13
Other Asian, not specified (23)	71	0.23
Austrian	96	0.31
Belgian	6	0.02
British	122	0.40
Canadian	40	0.13
Celtic	9	0.03
Czech	20	0.07
Czechoslovakian	24	0.08
Danish	107	0.35
Dutch	172	0.56
English	1,336	4.38
European	342	1.12
Finnish	9	0.03
French, except Basque	552	1.81
French Canadian	114	0.37
German	2,677	8.77
Greek	58	0.19
Guyanese	32	0.10
Hawaii Native/Pacific Islander:	279	0.92
Melanesian: (1)	1	0.00
Fijian (1)	1	0.00
Micronesian: (52)	61	0.20
Guamanian/Chamorro (37)	46	0.15
Other Micronesian (15)	15	0.05
Polynesian: (94)	157	0.52
Native Hawaiian (19)	62	0.20
Samoan (75)	95	0.31
Other Pac. Isl., not spec. (23)	60	0.20
Hispanic or Latino:	2,769	9.11
Central American:	299	0.98
Costa Rican	7	0.02
Guatemalan	9	0.03
Honduran	25	0.08
Nicaraguan	3	0.01
Panamanian	239	0.79
Salvadoran	12	0.04
Other Central American	4	0.01
Cuban	47	0.15
Dominican Republic	57	0.19
Mexican	619	2.04
Puerto Rican	1,317	4.33
South American:	64	0.21
Chilean	1	0.00
Colombian	25	0.08
Ecuadorian	12	0.04
Paraguayan	1	0.00
Peruvian	20	0.07
Venezuelan	3	0.01
Other South American	2	0.01
Other Hispanic or Latino	366	1.20
Hungarian	23	0.08
Irish	1,828	5.99
Italian	570	1.87
Latvian	13	0.04
Lithuanian	16	0.05
Maltese	6	0.02
Northern European	22	0.07
Norwegian	159	0.52
Pennsylvania German	10	0.03
Polish	371	1.22
Portuguese	29	0.09
Romanian	13	0.04
Russian	4	0.01
Scandinavian	17	0.06
Scotch-Irish	317	1.04
Scottish	377	1.23
Serbian	2	0.01
Slavic	4	0.01
Slovak	10	0.03
Swedish	116	0.38
Swiss	7	0.02
Turkish	24	0.08
Ukrainian	24	0.08
United States or American	2,255	7.39
Welsh	112	0.37
West Indian, excl. Hispanic:	296	0.97
Bahamian	16	0.05
British West Indian	23	0.08
Haitian	45	0.15
Jamaican	142	0.47
Trinidadian and Tobagonian	38	0.12
West Indian	16	0.05
Other West Indian	16	0.05
White:	13,443	44.23
Not Hispanic (11,796)	12,425	40.88
Hispanic (817)	1,018	3.35

Kennesaw

Place Type: City
County: Cobb
Population: 21,675

Ancestry/Race	Number	%
Acadian/Cajun	7	0.03
African American/Black:	2,298	10.60
Not Hispanic (2,122)	2,246	10.36
Hispanic (24)	52	0.24
African, sub-Saharan:	158	0.72
African	51	0.23
Ghanian	27	0.12
Kenyan	23	0.10
Nigerian	49	0.22
South African	8	0.04
Alaska Native tribes, not specified	2	0.01
Am. Ind. or Alaska Nat., not spec.	52	0.24
American Indian tribes, specified:	91	0.42
Apache (1)	2	0.01
Blackfeet (1)	2	0.01
Cherokee (12)	53	0.24
Chippewa (1)	1	0.00
Choctaw (1)	2	0.01
Comanche	1	0.00
Creek (2)	3	0.01
Iroquois (1)	3	0.01
Latin American Indians (4)	16	0.07
Navajo (1)	1	0.00
Ottawa	1	0.00
Sioux (2)	4	0.02
All other tribes (2)	2	0.01
American Indian tribes, not spec.	5	0.02
Arab:	116	0.53
Arab/Arabic	7	0.03
Lebanese	109	0.50
Asian:	799	3.69
Bangladeshi	1	0.00
Cambodian	2	0.01
Chinese, ex. Taiwanese (103)	141	0.65
Filipino (57)	88	0.41
Indian (152)	181	0.84
Indonesian	2	0.01
Japanese (30)	49	0.23
Korean (134)	148	0.68
Laotian (18)	18	0.08
Malaysian	1	0.00
Pakistani (24)	25	0.12
Sri Lankan (1)	1	0.00
Taiwanese (2)	2	0.01
Thai (8)	13	0.06
Vietnamese (71)	85	0.39
Other Asian, not specified (15)	42	0.19
Austrian	35	0.16
Belgian	8	0.04
Brazilian	19	0.09
British	96	0.44
Canadian	21	0.10
Celtic	7	0.03
Czech	78	0.36
Czechoslovakian	42	0.19
Danish	55	0.25
Dutch	300	1.37
Eastern European	14	0.06
English	2,270	10.36
European	307	1.40
Finnish	44	0.20
French, except Basque	722	3.30
French Canadian	144	0.66
German	2,765	12.62
Greek	145	0.66
Guyanese	23	0.10
Hawaii Native/Pacific Islander:	24	0.11
Micronesian: (1)	6	0.03
Guamanian/Chamorro (1)	6	0.03
Polynesian:	8	0.04
Native Hawaiian	8	0.04
Other Pac. Isl., not spec. (3)	10	0.05
Hispanic or Latino:	1,344	6.20

Notes: 1. Figures in the "Number" column do not add up to the total population due to: a) Ancestry/Race overlap — e.g. persons can report being both White and Irish, b) persons of Hispanic origin can report being any race, c) persons reporting two ancestries are counted in both categories. 2. Numbers in parentheses indicate the number of persons reporting this ancestry/race alone, not in combination with any other ancestry/race. 3. Refer to the Explanation of Data in the front of the book for more detailed information.

Ancestry/Race	Number	%
Central American:	83	0.38
Costa Rican	10	0.05
Guatemalan	17	0.08
Honduran	35	0.16
Nicaraguan	4	0.02
Panamanian	7	0.03
Salvadoran	9	0.04
Other Central American	1	0.00
Cuban	46	0.21
Dominican Republic	6	0.03
Mexican	768	3.54
Puerto Rican	149	0.69
South American:	122	0.56
Argentinean	2	0.01
Bolivian	4	0.02
Chilean	4	0.02
Colombian	37	0.17
Ecuadorian	22	0.10
Peruvian	20	0.09
Venezuelan	31	0.14
Other South American	2	0.01
Other Hispanic or Latino	170	0.78
Hungarian	80	0.37
Icelander	11	0.05
Iranian	8	0.04
Irish	3,074	14.03
Italian	1,186	5.41
Lithuanian	14	0.06
Northern European	17	0.08
Norwegian	156	0.71
Polish	699	3.19
Portuguese	47	0.21
Romanian	9	0.04
Russian	205	0.94
Scandinavian	49	0.22
Scotch-Irish	431	1.97
Scottish	537	2.45
Serbian	23	0.10
Slavic	17	0.08
Slovak	45	0.21
Swedish	288	1.31
Swiss	27	0.12
Turkish	11	0.05
United States or American	2,189	9.99
Welsh	157	0.72
West Indian, excl. Hispanic:	185	0.84
Bahamian	7	0.03
Haitian	10	0.05
Jamaican	161	0.73
West Indian	7	0.03
White:	18,189	83.92
Not Hispanic (17,128)	17,426	80.40
Hispanic (639)	763	3.52
Yugoslavian	16	0.07

Kingsland

Place Type: City
County: Camden
Population: 10,506

Ancestry/Race	Number	%
African American/Black:	2,301	21.90
Not Hispanic (2,210)	2,276	21.66
Hispanic (11)	25	0.24
African, sub-Saharan:	97	0.92
African	97	0.92
Alaska Native tribes, specified:	3	0.03
Eskimo	3	0.03
Am. Ind. or Alaska Nat., not spec.	28	0.27
American Indian tribes, specified:	92	0.88
Blackfeet (1)	3	0.03
Cherokee (14)	39	0.37
Choctaw (4)	8	0.08
Comanche	1	0.01
Creek (1)	2	0.02
Houma	1	0.01
Iroquois (5)	9	0.09
Lumbee (4)	4	0.04
Navajo	2	0.02
Pueblo (6)	6	0.06
Seminole (1)	2	0.02
Sioux (2)	2	0.02
All other tribes (10)	13	0.12
American Indian tribes, not spec.	1	0.01
Arab:	6	0.06
Syrian	6	0.06
Asian:	249	2.37
Chinese, ex. Taiwanese (27)	28	0.27
Filipino (71)	119	1.13
Indian (28)	36	0.34
Indonesian (1)	1	0.01
Japanese (5)	26	0.25
Korean (4)	9	0.09
Pakistani (11)	11	0.10
Thai (1)	2	0.02
Vietnamese (11)	12	0.11
Other Asian, specified	2	0.02
Other Asian, not specified (2)	3	0.03
Australian	7	0.07
Austrian	16	0.15
Belgian	7	0.07
British	10	0.10
Canadian	25	0.24
Celtic	41	0.39
Cypriot	8	0.08
Czech	15	0.14
Czechoslovakian	13	0.12
Danish	54	0.51
Dutch	118	1.12
English	830	7.89
European	89	0.85
Finnish	43	0.41
French, except Basque	289	2.75
French Canadian	93	0.88
German	1,302	12.38
Greek	29	0.28
Hawaii Native/Pacific Islander:	14	0.13
Micronesian: (4)	4	0.04
Guamanian/Chamorro (4)	4	0.04
Polynesian: (2)	5	0.05
Native Hawaiian (2)	5	0.05
Other Pac. Isl., specified	2	0.02
Other Pac. Isl., not spec.	3	0.03
Hispanic or Latino:	379	3.61
Central American:	19	0.18
Costa Rican	3	0.03
Guatemalan	4	0.04
Honduran	3	0.03
Panamanian	5	0.05
Salvadoran	2	0.02
Other Central American	2	0.02
Cuban	13	0.12
Dominican Republic	6	0.06
Mexican	173	1.65
Puerto Rican	105	1.00
South American:	13	0.12
Bolivian	2	0.02
Colombian	3	0.03
Ecuadorian	1	0.01
Venezuelan	6	0.06
Other South American	1	0.01
Other Hispanic or Latino	50	0.48
Hungarian	45	0.43
Irish	1,073	10.20
Italian	668	6.35
Lithuanian	19	0.18
Norwegian	167	1.59
Polish	226	2.15
Portuguese	16	0.15
Russian	23	0.22
Scandinavian	8	0.08
Scotch-Irish	138	1.31
Scottish	296	2.81
Slavic	26	0.25
Slovak	8	0.08
Swedish	115	1.09
Ukrainian	28	0.27
United States or American	1,024	9.74
Welsh	136	1.29
West Indian, excl. Hispanic:	58	0.55
Jamaican	19	0.18
West Indian	39	0.37
White:	7,894	75.14
Not Hispanic (7,475)	7,648	72.80
Hispanic (221)	246	2.34

La Grange

Place Type: City
County: Troup
Population: 25,998

Ancestry/Race	Number	%
African American/Black:	12,466	47.95
Not Hispanic (12,289)	12,395	47.68
Hispanic (64)	71	0.27
African, sub-Saharan:	192	0.73
African	192	0.73
Am. Ind. or Alaska Nat., not spec.	66	0.25
American Indian tribes, specified:	54	0.21
Apache	1	0.00
Cherokee (15)	34	0.13
Chickasaw (1)	1	0.00
Chippewa	1	0.00
Choctaw (3)	3	0.01
Creek (1)	5	0.02
Latin American Indians (2)	2	0.01
Pueblo (1)	1	0.00
Seminole (3)	5	0.02
All other tribes (1)	1	0.00
American Indian tribes, not spec.	12	0.05
Arab:	43	0.16
Lebanese	28	0.11
Syrian	7	0.03
Other Arab	8	0.03
Asian:	264	1.02
Bangladeshi (5)	5	0.02
Chinese, ex. Taiwanese (22)	28	0.11
Filipino (10)	10	0.04
Indian (79)	86	0.33
Japanese (33)	43	0.17
Korean (35)	41	0.16
Laotian (1)	1	0.00
Malaysian (2)	2	0.01
Pakistani (5)	5	0.02
Thai	2	0.01
Vietnamese (14)	14	0.05
Other Asian, specified	14	0.05
Other Asian, not specified (6)	13	0.05
Austrian	27	0.10
British	66	0.25
Canadian	9	0.03
Czech	5	0.02
Danish	40	0.15
Dutch	125	0.47
English	1,617	6.13
European	72	0.27
Finnish	7	0.03
French, except Basque	273	1.03
French Canadian	65	0.25
German	863	3.27
Greek	42	0.16
Hawaii Native/Pacific Islander:	59	0.23
Micronesian: (20)	24	0.09
Guamanian/Chamorro (20)	24	0.09
Polynesian: (5)	12	0.05
Native Hawaiian (4)	9	0.03
Samoan (1)	3	0.01
Other Pac. Isl., specified	14	0.05
Other Pac. Isl., not spec. (1)	9	0.03
Hispanic or Latino:	635	2.44
Central American:	118	0.45
Guatemalan	86	0.33
Honduran	8	0.03
Nicaraguan	2	0.01
Panamanian	7	0.03
Salvadoran	15	0.06
Cuban	27	0.10
Dominican Republic	3	0.01

Notes: 1. Figures in the "Number" column do not add up to the total population due to: a) Ancestry/Race overlap — e.g. persons can report being both White and Irish, b) persons of Hispanic origin can report being any race, c) persons reporting two ancestries are counted in both categories. 2. Numbers in parentheses indicate the number of persons reporting this ancestry/race alone, not in combination with any other ancestry/race. 3. Refer to the Explanation of Data in the front of the book for more detailed information.

Mexican	342	1.32
Puerto Rican	26	0.10
South American:	5	0.02
Argentinean	1	0.00
Colombian	2	0.01
Peruvian	1	0.00
Venezuelan	1	0.00
Other Hispanic or Latino	114	0.44
Hungarian	15	0.06
Irish	1,388	5.26
Italian	252	0.95
Norwegian	86	0.33
Polish	117	0.44
Portuguese	19	0.07
Russian	8	0.03
Scotch-Irish	516	1.96
Scottish	461	1.75
Swedish	98	0.37
United States or American	3,573	13.54
Welsh	31	0.12
White:	12,993	49.98
Not Hispanic (12,588)	12,740	49.00
Hispanic (208)	253	0.97

Lawrenceville

Place Type: City
County: Gwinnett
Population: 22,397

Ancestry/Race	Number	%
African American/Black:	3,166	14.14
Not Hispanic (2,987)	3,091	13.80
Hispanic (61)	75	0.33
African, sub-Saharan:	574	2.55
African	472	2.10
Ethiopian	10	0.04
Liberian	6	0.03
Nigerian	51	0.23
Somalian	20	0.09
Other sub-Saharan African	15	0.07
Alaska Native tribes, specified:	1	0.00
Aleut (1)	1	0.00
Am. Ind. or Alaska Nat., not spec.	53	0.24
American Indian tribes, specified:	96	0.43
Blackfeet (2)	4	0.02
Cherokee (9)	43	0.19
Choctaw	3	0.01
Comanche (1)	1	0.00
Creek	1	0.00
Iroquois	5	0.02
Latin American Indians (8)	20	0.09
Lumbee (5)	7	0.03
Pueblo	1	0.00
Sioux	4	0.02
Tohono O'Odham (1)	1	0.00
All other tribes (3)	6	0.03
American Indian tribes, not spec.	3	0.01
Arab:	46	0.20
Arab/Arabic	24	0.11
Lebanese	22	0.10
Asian:	822	3.67
Bangladeshi (4)	4	0.02
Cambodian (10)	11	0.05
Chinese, ex. Taiwanese (46)	58	0.26
Filipino (45)	62	0.28
Hmong (6)	9	0.04
Indian (106)	117	0.52
Indonesian (1)	1	0.00
Japanese (8)	15	0.07
Korean (101)	122	0.54
Laotian (124)	139	0.62
Pakistani (45)	45	0.20
Taiwanese (1)	1	0.00
Thai (14)	17	0.08
Vietnamese (173)	179	0.80
Other Asian, not specified (21)	42	0.19
Austrian	7	0.03
British	75	0.33
Canadian	41	0.18
Celtic	43	0.19
Croatian	38	0.17
Czech	78	0.35
Czechoslovakian	20	0.09
Danish	36	0.16
Dutch	223	0.99
Eastern European	9	0.04
English	2,278	10.12
European	200	0.89
Finnish	17	0.08
French, except Basque	305	1.35
French Canadian	123	0.55
German	1,856	8.24
Greek	50	0.22
Hawaii Native/Pacific Islander:	37	0.17
Micronesian: (11)	15	0.07
Guamanian/Chamorro (6)	10	0.04
Other Micronesian (5)	5	0.02
Polynesian: (1)	7	0.03
Native Hawaiian (1)	5	0.02
Samoan	2	0.01
Other Pac. Isl., not spec. (10)	15	0.07
Hispanic or Latino:	2,720	12.14
Central American:	131	0.58
Costa Rican	7	0.03
Guatemalan	59	0.26
Honduran	24	0.11
Panamanian	15	0.07
Salvadoran	20	0.09
Other Central American	6	0.03
Cuban	87	0.39
Dominican Republic	40	0.18
Mexican	1,817	8.11
Puerto Rican	158	0.71
South American:	108	0.48
Argentinean	5	0.02
Bolivian	6	0.03
Chilean	5	0.02
Colombian	46	0.21
Ecuadorian	8	0.04
Paraguayan	3	0.01
Peruvian	20	0.09
Venezuelan	13	0.06
Other South American	2	0.01
Other Hispanic or Latino	379	1.69
Hungarian	50	0.22
Irish	2,310	10.26
Italian	413	1.83
Lithuanian	8	0.04
Norwegian	145	0.64
Polish	269	1.19
Portuguese	9	0.04
Romanian	236	1.05
Russian	39	0.17
Scandinavian	18	0.08
Scotch-Irish	422	1.87
Scottish	460	2.04
Serbian	25	0.11
Slovak	29	0.13
Swedish	157	0.70
Swiss	18	0.08
Ukrainian	27	0.12
United States or American	2,849	12.66
Welsh	136	0.60
West Indian, excl. Hispanic:	126	0.56
Haitian	8	0.04
Jamaican	118	0.52
White:	17,485	78.07
Not Hispanic (15,513)	15,807	70.58
Hispanic (1,517)	1,678	7.49
Yugoslavian	530	2.35

Lilburn

Place Type: City
County: Gwinnett
Population: 11,307

Ancestry/Race	Number	%
African American/Black:	1,425	12.60
Not Hispanic (1,322)	1,376	12.17
Hispanic (27)	49	0.43
African, sub-Saharan:	246	2.17
African	80	0.70
Ethiopian	65	0.57
Nigerian	101	0.89
Am. Ind. or Alaska Nat., not spec.	49	0.43
American Indian tribes, specified:	27	0.24
Apache (1)	1	0.01
Cherokee (6)	20	0.18
Creek	2	0.02
Sioux (1)	2	0.02
All other tribes (2)	2	0.02
American Indian tribes, not spec.	5	0.04
Arab:	30	0.26
Other Arab	30	0.26
Asian:	1,437	12.71
Bangladeshi (23)	27	0.24
Cambodian (36)	39	0.34
Chinese, ex. Taiwanese (191)	215	1.90
Filipino (31)	41	0.36
Hmong (29)	37	0.33
Indian (411)	449	3.97
Indonesian (4)	4	0.04
Japanese (7)	12	0.11
Korean (133)	139	1.23
Laotian (7)	15	0.13
Pakistani (27)	40	0.35
Taiwanese (26)	36	0.32
Thai (13)	16	0.14
Vietnamese (311)	331	2.93
Other Asian, specified (2)	2	0.02
Other Asian, not specified (27)	34	0.30
Australian	8	0.07
Austrian	19	0.17
Brazilian	16	0.14
British	29	0.26
Canadian	20	0.18
Croatian	18	0.16
Czech	14	0.12
Czechoslovakian	18	0.16
Danish	19	0.17
Dutch	93	0.82
English	1,223	10.78
Estonian	11	0.10
European	257	2.26
French, except Basque	274	2.41
French Canadian	10	0.09
German	1,142	10.06
Greek	43	0.38
Guyanese	48	0.42
Hawaii Native/Pacific Islander:	20	0.18
Micronesian:	1	0.01
Guamanian/Chamorro	1	0.01
Polynesian: (3)	5	0.04
Native Hawaiian (2)	4	0.04
Samoan (1)	1	0.01
Other Pac. Isl., not spec.	14	0.12
Hispanic or Latino:	1,495	13.22
Central American:	116	1.03
Costa Rican	10	0.09
Guatemalan	17	0.15
Honduran	10	0.09
Nicaraguan	1	0.01
Panamanian	1	0.01
Salvadoran	68	0.60
Other Central American	9	0.08
Cuban	59	0.52
Dominican Republic	3	0.03
Mexican	814	7.20
Puerto Rican	93	0.82
South American:	176	1.56
Argentinean	8	0.07
Bolivian	1	0.01
Chilean	8	0.07
Colombian	112	0.99
Ecuadorian	3	0.03
Peruvian	11	0.10
Uruguayan	15	0.13
Venezuelan	18	0.16

Notes: 1. Figures in the "Number" column do not add up to the total population due to: a) Ancestry/Race overlap — e.g. persons can report being both White and Irish, b) persons of Hispanic origin can report being any race, c) persons reporting two ancestries are counted in both categories. 2. Numbers in parentheses indicate the number of persons reporting this ancestry/race alone, not in combination with any other ancestry/race. 3. Refer to the Explanation of Data in the front of the book for more detailed information.

Other Hispanic or Latino	234	2.07
Hungarian	9	0.08
Irish	906	7.98
Italian	314	2.77
Lithuanian	25	0.22
Maltese	14	0.12
Northern European	6	0.05
Norwegian	31	0.27
Pennsylvania German	6	0.05
Polish	156	1.37
Portuguese	39	0.34
Romanian	34	0.30
Russian	86	0.76
Scotch-Irish	152	1.34
Scottish	192	1.69
Slavic	8	0.07
Slovak	11	0.10
Swedish	104	0.92
Swiss	115	1.01
Turkish	5	0.04
Ukrainian	42	0.37
United States or American	1,170	10.31
Welsh	52	0.46
West Indian, excl. Hispanic:	34	0.30
Bahamian	10	0.09
West Indian	24	0.21
White:	7,977	70.55
Not Hispanic (6,974)	7,067	62.50
Hispanic (838)	910	8.05
Yugoslavian	6	0.05

Mableton

Place Type: Census Designated Place
County: Cobb
Population: 29,733

Ancestry/Race	Number	%
Acadian/Cajun	6	0.02
African American/Black:	8,935	30.05
Not Hispanic (8,633)	8,851	29.77
Hispanic (66)	84	0.28
African, sub-Saharan:	670	2.27
African	220	0.74
Cape Verdean	6	0.02
Ghanian	217	0.73
Kenyan	9	0.03
Nigerian	145	0.49
Zairian	36	0.12
Zimbabwean	10	0.03
Other sub-Saharan African	27	0.09
Alaska Native tribes, specified:	4	0.01
Eskimo (4)	4	0.01
Am. Ind. or Alaska Nat., not spec.	80	0.27
American Indian tribes, specified:	141	0.47
Blackfeet	2	0.01
Cherokee (35)	92	0.31
Chickasaw	1	0.00
Chippewa (1)	2	0.01
Choctaw (1)	5	0.02
Comanche	1	0.00
Cree	1	0.00
Creek (1)	4	0.01
Houma (1)	1	0.00
Iroquois	2	0.01
Latin American Indians (2)	5	0.02
Lumbee (4)	5	0.02
Shoshone	5	0.02
Sioux (3)	6	0.02
All other tribes (2)	9	0.03
American Indian tribes, not spec.	16	0.05
Arab:	93	0.31
Arab/Arabic	30	0.10
Egyptian	10	0.03
Lebanese	33	0.11
Moroccan	12	0.04
Syrian	8	0.03
Armenian	25	0.08
Asian:	522	1.76
Cambodian (6)	6	0.02
Chinese, ex. Taiwanese (49)	65	0.22
Filipino (52)	71	0.24
Indian (175)	203	0.68
Indonesian (1)	8	0.03
Japanese (14)	28	0.09
Korean (34)	51	0.17
Laotian (9)	9	0.03
Pakistani (6)	8	0.03
Sri Lankan (4)	4	0.01
Taiwanese (2)	3	0.01
Vietnamese (53)	56	0.19
Other Asian, not specified (2)	10	0.03
Austrian	64	0.22
Belgian	22	0.07
Brazilian	12	0.04
British	145	0.49
Canadian	50	0.17
Croatian	30	0.10
Czech	35	0.12
Czechoslovakian	24	0.08
Danish	84	0.28
Dutch	213	0.72
English	2,023	6.85
European	219	0.74
French, except Basque	367	1.24
French Canadian	71	0.24
German	1,827	6.18
Greek	28	0.09
Guyanese	10	0.03
Hawaii Native/Pacific Islander:	23	0.08
Micronesian: (3)	8	0.03
Guamanian/Chamorro (3)	8	0.03
Polynesian:	6	0.02
Native Hawaiian	6	0.02
Other Pac. Isl., not spec. (4)	9	0.03
Hispanic or Latino:	2,915	9.80
Central American:	237	0.80
Costa Rican	2	0.01
Guatemalan	61	0.21
Honduran	14	0.05
Nicaraguan	13	0.04
Panamanian	13	0.04
Salvadoran	132	0.44
Other Central American	2	0.01
Cuban	42	0.14
Dominican Republic	7	0.02
Mexican	2,071	6.97
Puerto Rican	148	0.50
South American:	98	0.33
Argentinean	7	0.02
Colombian	20	0.07
Ecuadorian	13	0.04
Peruvian	45	0.15
Uruguayan	1	0.00
Venezuelan	1	0.00
Other South American	11	0.04
Other Hispanic or Latino	312	1.05
Hungarian	33	0.11
Iranian	11	0.04
Irish	2,371	8.02
Israeli	9	0.03
Italian	581	1.97
Lithuanian	22	0.07
Northern European	15	0.05
Norwegian	194	0.66
Polish	258	0.87
Portuguese	21	0.07
Romanian	21	0.07
Russian	39	0.13
Scotch-Irish	488	1.65
Scottish	429	1.45
Slovak	9	0.03
Swedish	114	0.39
Swiss	32	0.11
Ukrainian	28	0.09
United States or American	3,303	11.18
Welsh	34	0.12
West Indian, excl. Hispanic:	421	1.42
Barbadian	13	0.04
Bermudan	7	0.02
Haitian	203	0.69
Jamaican	53	0.18
Trinidadian and Tobagonian	71	0.24
U.S. Virgin Islander	17	0.06
West Indian	31	0.10
Other West Indian	26	0.09
White:	19,017	63.96
Not Hispanic (17,165)	17,479	58.79
Hispanic (1,385)	1,538	5.17
Yugoslavian	55	0.19

Macon

Place Type: City
County: Bibb
Population: 97,255

Ancestry/Race	Number	%
African American/Black:	61,185	62.91
Not Hispanic (60,503)	60,916	62.64
Hispanic (237)	269	0.28
African, sub-Saharan:	954	0.98
African	908	0.93
Cape Verdean	4	0.00
Kenyan	20	0.02
Nigerian	22	0.02
Alaska Native tribes, specified:	3	0.00
Tlingit-Haida (1)	3	0.00
Am. Ind. or Alaska Nat., not spec.	196	0.20
Albanian	7	0.01
American Indian tribes, specified:	216	0.22
Apache (1)	7	0.01
Blackfeet (3)	6	0.01
Cherokee (58)	134	0.14
Chickasaw	1	0.00
Choctaw (5)	10	0.01
Creek (8)	12	0.01
Delaware	1	0.00
Latin American Indians (4)	9	0.01
Lumbee (2)	3	0.00
Menominee (1)	1	0.00
Navajo (2)	2	0.00
Osage	1	0.00
Pueblo (1)	2	0.00
Seminole (1)	6	0.01
Sioux (1)	4	0.00
Tohono O'Odham (2)	2	0.00
Ute	3	0.00
Yaqui	1	0.00
All other tribes (4)	11	0.01
American Indian tribes, not spec.	28	0.03
Arab:	143	0.15
Egyptian	7	0.01
Jordanian	9	0.01
Lebanese	68	0.07
Moroccan	6	0.01
Syrian	53	0.05
Armenian	7	0.01
Asian:	802	0.82
Bangladeshi (1)	1	0.00
Chinese, ex. Taiwanese (85)	98	0.10
Filipino (73)	106	0.11
Indian (178)	214	0.22
Indonesian (4)	4	0.00
Japanese (43)	51	0.05
Korean (60)	80	0.08
Laotian (9)	11	0.01
Pakistani (11)	13	0.01
Taiwanese (3)	6	0.01
Thai (11)	11	0.01
Vietnamese (36)	50	0.05
Other Asian, specified	18	0.02
Other Asian, not specified (112)	139	0.14
Australian	18	0.02
Austrian	32	0.03
Belgian	8	0.01
British	174	0.18
Canadian	55	0.06
Celtic	7	0.01
Croatian	34	0.03

Notes: 1. Figures in the "Number" column do not add up to the total population due to: a) Ancestry/Race overlap — e.g. persons can report being both White and Irish, b) persons of Hispanic origin can report being any race, c) persons reporting two ancestries are counted in both categories. 2. Numbers in parentheses indicate the number of persons reporting this ancestry/race alone, not in combination with any other ancestry/race. 3. Refer to the Explanation of Data in the front of the book for more detailed information.

Czech	74	0.08
Czechoslovakian	25	0.03
Danish	35	0.04
Dutch	477	0.49
Eastern European	43	0.04
English	5,530	5.66
European	569	0.58
Finnish	30	0.03
French, except Basque	721	0.74
French Canadian	102	0.10
German	2,497	2.56
Greek	79	0.08
Hawaii Native/Pacific Islander:	77	0.08
Micronesian: (12)	21	0.02
Guamanian/Chamorro (1)	10	0.01
Other Micronesian (11)	11	0.01
Polynesian: (10)	23	0.02
Native Hawaiian (8)	16	0.02
Samoan (1)	6	0.01
Other Polynesian (1)	1	0.00
Other Pac. Isl., specified	16	0.02
Other Pac. Isl., not spec. (6)	17	0.02
Hispanic or Latino:	1,166	1.20
Central American:	39	0.04
Costa Rican	3	0.00
Guatemalan	5	0.01
Honduran	9	0.01
Nicaraguan	6	0.01
Salvadoran	9	0.01
Other Central American	7	0.01
Cuban	65	0.07
Dominican Republic	13	0.01
Mexican	591	0.61
Puerto Rican	135	0.14
South American:	36	0.04
Argentinean	4	0.00
Bolivian	2	0.00
Chilean	1	0.00
Colombian	18	0.02
Ecuadorian	7	0.01
Peruvian	3	0.00
Venezuelan	1	0.00
Other Hispanic or Latino	287	0.30
Hungarian	50	0.05
Iranian	13	0.01
Irish	3,866	3.96
Italian	738	0.76
Latvian	8	0.01
Lithuanian	12	0.01
Northern European	33	0.03
Norwegian	147	0.15
Polish	331	0.34
Portuguese	61	0.06
Russian	82	0.08
Scandinavian	18	0.02
Scotch-Irish	1,139	1.17
Scottish	1,114	1.14
Slavic	19	0.02
Slovak	20	0.02
Swedish	77	0.08
Swiss	14	0.01
Ukrainian	27	0.03
United States or American	7,121	7.29
Welsh	182	0.19
West Indian, excl. Hispanic:	127	0.13
Bermudan	5	0.01
Jamaican	73	0.07
Trinidadian and Tobagonian	32	0.03
West Indian	17	0.02
White:	34,934	35.92
Not Hispanic (34,050)	34,457	35.43
Hispanic (432)	477	0.49
Yugoslavian	21	0.02

Marietta

Place Type: City
County: Cobb
Population: 58,748

Ancestry/Race	Number	%
Acadian/Cajun	11	0.02
Afghan	12	0.02
African American/Black:	17,913	30.49
Not Hispanic (17,090)	17,581	29.93
Hispanic (240)	332	0.57
African, sub-Saharan:	1,423	2.44
African	848	1.45
Cape Verdean	42	0.07
Ethiopian	35	0.06
Ghanian	36	0.06
Kenyan	175	0.30
Nigerian	123	0.21
Senegalese	10	0.02
South African	43	0.07
Zimbabwean	13	0.02
Other sub-Saharan African	98	0.17
Alaska Native tribes, specified:	4	0.01
Alaska Athabascan (1)	1	0.00
Eskimo (1)	3	0.01
Am. Ind. or Alaska Nat., not spec.	205	0.35
Albanian	26	0.04
American Indian tribes, specified:	259	0.44
Apache (1)	3	0.01
Blackfeet (1)	9	0.02
Cherokee (30)	140	0.24
Cheyenne	1	0.00
Chippewa (1)	7	0.01
Choctaw (3)	13	0.02
Colville (2)	2	0.00
Creek (2)	15	0.03
Delaware	1	0.00
Iroquois (5)	9	0.02
Kiowa (1)	1	0.00
Latin American Indians (20)	29	0.05
Lumbee	1	0.00
Navajo (1)	2	0.00
Potawatomi (2)	3	0.01
Pueblo (2)	2	0.00
Seminole (1)	1	0.00
Sioux	4	0.01
All other tribes (3)	16	0.03
American Indian tribes, not spec.	27	0.05
Arab:	258	0.44
Arab/Arabic	85	0.15
Iraqi	12	0.02
Jordanian	9	0.02
Lebanese	60	0.10
Moroccan	8	0.01
Palestinian	25	0.04
Syrian	18	0.03
Other Arab	41	0.07
Armenian	12	0.02
Asian:	2,051	3.49
Bangladeshi (4)	5	0.01
Cambodian (5)	11	0.02
Chinese, ex. Taiwanese (301)	358	0.61
Filipino (92)	131	0.22
Hmong (2)	2	0.00
Indian (622)	669	1.14
Indonesian (12)	15	0.03
Japanese (68)	96	0.16
Korean (318)	350	0.60
Laotian (29)	42	0.07
Malaysian (2)	6	0.01
Pakistani (67)	87	0.15
Sri Lankan (3)	3	0.01
Taiwanese (15)	16	0.03
Thai (27)	38	0.06
Vietnamese (111)	119	0.20
Other Asian, specified (1)	11	0.02
Other Asian, not specified (38)	92	0.16
Austrian	103	0.18
Belgian	88	0.15
Brazilian	157	0.27
British	296	0.51
Bulgarian	17	0.03
Canadian	84	0.14
Celtic	18	0.03
Croatian	48	0.08
Czech	83	0.14
Danish	54	0.09
Dutch	477	0.82
English	5,041	8.64
European	592	1.01
Finnish	25	0.04
French, except Basque	1,047	1.79
French Canadian	227	0.39
German	4,367	7.48
Greek	201	0.34
Guyanese	60	0.10
Hawaii Native/Pacific Islander:	121	0.21
Micronesian: (21)	30	0.05
Guamanian/Chamorro (21)	30	0.05
Polynesian: (12)	25	0.04
Native Hawaiian (5)	11	0.02
Samoan (7)	14	0.02
Other Pac. Isl., specified	7	0.01
Other Pac. Isl., not spec. (18)	59	0.10
Hispanic or Latino:	9,947	16.93
Central American:	893	1.52
Costa Rican	31	0.05
Guatemalan	473	0.81
Honduran	146	0.25
Nicaraguan	31	0.05
Panamanian	24	0.04
Salvadoran	152	0.26
Other Central American	36	0.06
Cuban	117	0.20
Dominican Republic	42	0.07
Mexican	7,170	12.20
Puerto Rican	531	0.90
South American:	306	0.52
Argentinean	15	0.03
Bolivian	6	0.01
Chilean	14	0.02
Colombian	134	0.23
Ecuadorian	34	0.06
Paraguayan	5	0.01
Peruvian	43	0.07
Uruguayan	4	0.01
Venezuelan	30	0.05
Other South American	21	0.04
Other Hispanic or Latino	888	1.51
Hungarian	117	0.20
Iranian	152	0.26
Irish	4,079	6.99
Italian	1,699	2.91
Latvian	43	0.07
Lithuanian	53	0.09
Northern European	27	0.05
Norwegian	206	0.35
Pennsylvania German	8	0.01
Polish	583	1.00
Portuguese	76	0.13
Romanian	18	0.03
Russian	291	0.50
Scandinavian	40	0.07
Scotch-Irish	928	1.59
Scottish	970	1.66
Serbian	26	0.04
Slavic	4	0.01
Slovak	57	0.10
Soviet Union	10	0.02
Swedish	208	0.36
Swiss	125	0.21
Ukrainian	68	0.12
United States or American	3,627	6.21
Welsh	255	0.44
West Indian, excl. Hispanic:	764	1.31
Bahamian	9	0.02
Barbadian	22	0.04
Belizean	14	0.02
British West Indian	16	0.03

Notes: 1. Figures in the "Number" column do not add up to the total population due to: a) Ancestry/Race overlap — e.g. persons can report being both White and Irish, b) persons of Hispanic origin can report being any race, c) persons reporting two ancestries are counted in both categories. 2. Numbers in parentheses indicate the number of persons reporting this ancestry/race alone, not in combination with any other ancestry/race. 3. Refer to the Explanation of Data in the front of the book for more detailed information.

Haitian	262	0.45
Jamaican	334	0.57
Trinidadian and Tobagonian	62	0.11
West Indian	45	0.08
White:	34,307	58.40
Not Hispanic (28,544)	29,227	49.75
Hispanic (4,641)	5,080	8.65
Yugoslavian	90	0.15

Martinez

Place Type: Census Designated Place
County: Columbia
Population: 27,749

Ancestry/Race	Number	%
Acadian/Cajun	21	0.08
African American/Black:	2,324	8.38
Not Hispanic (2,196)	2,289	8.25
Hispanic (29)	35	0.13
African, sub-Saharan:	77	0.28
African	45	0.16
Nigerian	18	0.07
South African	14	0.05
Am. Ind. or Alaska Nat., not spec.	27	0.10
Albanian	30	0.11
American Indian tribes, specified:	104	0.37
Apache (1)	2	0.01
Blackfeet	3	0.01
Cherokee (30)	61	0.22
Chippewa (3)	7	0.03
Choctaw (1)	4	0.01
Cree	1	0.00
Creek (1)	2	0.01
Delaware (1)	2	0.01
Latin American Indians (1)	2	0.01
Lumbee (2)	5	0.02
Menominee (3)	3	0.01
Sioux (3)	5	0.02
All other tribes (2)	7	0.03
American Indian tribes, not spec.	1	0.00
Arab:	48	0.17
Egyptian	41	0.15
Syrian	7	0.03
Armenian	8	0.03
Asian:	1,766	6.36
Bangladeshi (14)	18	0.06
Cambodian (4)	4	0.01
Chinese, ex. Taiwanese (201)	237	0.85
Filipino (118)	157	0.57
Hmong	1	0.00
Indian (726)	750	2.70
Indonesian (1)	5	0.02
Japanese (34)	66	0.24
Korean (258)	306	1.10
Laotian (2)	2	0.01
Malaysian (1)	2	0.01
Pakistani (55)	58	0.21
Sri Lankan (8)	8	0.03
Taiwanese (10)	10	0.04
Thai (15)	18	0.06
Vietnamese (75)	84	0.30
Other Asian, not specified (17)	40	0.14
Austrian	29	0.11
Belgian	6	0.02
Brazilian	16	0.06
British	114	0.41
Canadian	36	0.13
Croatian	8	0.03
Czech	118	0.43
Czechoslovakian	6	0.02
Danish	67	0.24
Dutch	336	1.22
Eastern European	14	0.05
English	3,277	11.89
European	317	1.15
Finnish	71	0.26
French, except Basque	965	3.50
French Canadian	114	0.41
German	3,785	13.74
Greek	75	0.27
Hawaii Native/Pacific Islander:	39	0.14
Micronesian: (9)	10	0.04
Guamanian/Chamorro (9)	10	0.04
Polynesian: (11)	14	0.05
Native Hawaiian (6)	9	0.03
Samoan (5)	5	0.02
Other Pac. Isl., not spec.	15	0.05
Hispanic or Latino:	640	2.31
Central American:	28	0.10
Honduran	1	0.00
Nicaraguan	5	0.02
Panamanian	19	0.07
Salvadoran	1	0.00
Other Central American	2	0.01
Cuban	21	0.08
Dominican Republic	2	0.01
Mexican	224	0.81
Puerto Rican	208	0.75
South American:	42	0.15
Argentinean	2	0.01
Chilean	1	0.00
Colombian	10	0.04
Ecuadorian	4	0.01
Paraguayan	1	0.00
Peruvian	15	0.05
Uruguayan	1	0.00
Venezuelan	7	0.03
Other South American	1	0.00
Other Hispanic or Latino	115	0.41
Hungarian	64	0.23
Iranian	14	0.05
Irish	3,525	12.79
Italian	1,101	4.00
Lithuanian	76	0.28
Norwegian	259	0.94
Polish	617	2.24
Portuguese	53	0.19
Romanian	19	0.07
Russian	116	0.42
Scandinavian	35	0.13
Scotch-Irish	639	2.32
Scottish	597	2.17
Slavic	9	0.03
Slovak	10	0.04
Swedish	136	0.49
Swiss	30	0.11
Ukrainian	75	0.27
United States or American	3,921	14.23
Welsh	194	0.70
West Indian, excl. Hispanic:	18	0.07
Jamaican	18	0.07
White:	23,640	85.19
Not Hispanic (22,883)	23,183	83.55
Hispanic (421)	457	1.65
Yugoslavian	22	0.08

Milledgeville

Place Type: City
County: Baldwin
Population: 18,757

Ancestry/Race	Number	%
African American/Black:	8,996	47.96
Not Hispanic (8,921)	8,964	47.79
Hispanic (22)	32	0.17
African, sub-Saharan:	215	1.13
African	205	1.08
Other sub-Saharan African	10	0.05
Am. Ind. or Alaska Nat., not spec.	28	0.15
American Indian tribes, specified:	25	0.13
Cherokee (13)	17	0.09
Choctaw	1	0.01
Creek (2)	3	0.02
Iroquois (1)	1	0.01
Sioux (3)	3	0.02
American Indian tribes, not spec.	4	0.02
Arab:	49	0.26
Egyptian	34	0.18
Lebanese	9	0.05
Moroccan	6	0.03
Asian:	317	1.69
Cambodian	1	0.01
Chinese, ex. Taiwanese (38)	40	0.21
Filipino (96)	101	0.54
Hmong (1)	1	0.01
Indian (104)	111	0.59
Japanese (3)	3	0.02
Korean (24)	25	0.13
Taiwanese (1)	1	0.01
Thai (1)	2	0.01
Vietnamese (14)	15	0.08
Other Asian, specified	10	0.05
Other Asian, not specified (5)	7	0.04
Belgian	6	0.03
Brazilian	5	0.03
British	96	0.50
Bulgarian	14	0.07
Canadian	6	0.03
Czech	6	0.03
Czechoslovakian	4	0.02
Dutch	47	0.25
English	891	4.69
European	204	1.07
French, except Basque	234	1.23
French Canadian	35	0.18
German	752	3.95
Greek	19	0.10
Hawaii Native/Pacific Islander:	16	0.09
Polynesian: (1)	3	0.02
Native Hawaiian (1)	3	0.02
Other Pac. Isl., specified	10	0.05
Other Pac. Isl., not spec.	3	0.02
Hispanic or Latino:	231	1.23
Central American:	5	0.03
Panamanian	2	0.01
Salvadoran	3	0.02
Cuban	47	0.25
Mexican	109	0.58
Puerto Rican	26	0.14
South American:	10	0.05
Argentinean	1	0.01
Chilean	1	0.01
Colombian	6	0.03
Peruvian	1	0.01
Other South American	1	0.01
Other Hispanic or Latino	34	0.18
Hungarian	32	0.17
Iranian	7	0.04
Irish	1,023	5.38
Italian	210	1.10
Luxemburger	5	0.03
Norwegian	35	0.18
Polish	41	0.22
Russian	18	0.09
Scandinavian	24	0.13
Scotch-Irish	218	1.15
Scottish	319	1.68
Swedish	82	0.43
Ukrainian	5	0.03
United States or American	1,796	9.44
Welsh	77	0.40
West Indian, excl. Hispanic:	12	0.06
Bahamian	7	0.04
Haitian	5	0.03
White:	9,425	50.25
Not Hispanic (9,217)	9,262	49.38
Hispanic (151)	163	0.87

Monroe

Place Type: City
County: Walton
Population: 11,407

Ancestry/Race	Number	%
African American/Black:	4,878	42.76
Not Hispanic (4,786)	4,846	42.48
Hispanic (32)	32	0.28

Notes: 1. Figures in the "Number" column do not add up to the total population due to: a) Ancestry/Race overlap — e.g. persons can report being both White and Irish, b) persons of Hispanic origin can report being any race, c) persons reporting two ancestries are counted in both categories. 2. Numbers in parentheses indicate the number of persons reporting this ancestry/race alone, not in combination with any other ancestry/race. 3. Refer to the Explanation of Data in the front of the book for more detailed information.

Ancestry/Race	Number	%
African, sub-Saharan:	76	0.66
African	76	0.66
Am. Ind. or Alaska Nat., not spec.	36	0.32
American Indian tribes, specified:	39	0.34
Blackfeet (3)	3	0.03
Cherokee (9)	29	0.25
Choctaw	1	0.01
Comanche	3	0.03
Latin American Indians (1)	1	0.01
Seminole	1	0.01
All other tribes (1)	1	0.01
American Indian tribes, not spec.	1	0.01
Asian:	64	0.56
Chinese, ex. Taiwanese (8)	12	0.11
Filipino (16)	22	0.19
Indian (16)	21	0.18
Japanese	2	0.02
Korean	2	0.02
Thai (1)	1	0.01
Other Asian, specified	2	0.02
Other Asian, not specified	2	0.02
Austrian	8	0.07
Belgian	6	0.05
British	33	0.29
Canadian	16	0.14
Czech	7	0.06
Dutch	43	0.37
English	745	6.44
European	36	0.31
French, except Basque	73	0.63
German	341	2.95
Hawaii Native/Pacific Islander:	7	0.06
Micronesian: (4)	4	0.04
Guamanian/Chamorro (4)	4	0.04
Polynesian:	1	0.01
Samoan	1	0.01
Other Pac. Isl., specified	2	0.02
Hispanic or Latino:	287	2.52
Central American:	16	0.14
Guatemalan	4	0.04
Honduran	5	0.04
Nicaraguan	7	0.06
Cuban	11	0.10
Mexican	183	1.60
Puerto Rican	18	0.16
South American:	4	0.04
Chilean	1	0.01
Colombian	1	0.01
Peruvian	2	0.02
Other Hispanic or Latino	55	0.48
Irish	516	4.46
Italian	76	0.66
Norwegian	13	0.11
Polish	22	0.19
Scotch-Irish	102	0.88
Scottish	131	1.13
United States or American	2,184	18.88
Welsh	13	0.11
West Indian, excl. Hispanic:	12	0.10
West Indian	12	0.10
White:	6,343	55.61
Not Hispanic (6,143)	6,226	54.58
Hispanic (96)	117	1.03

Moultrie

Place Type: City
County: Colquitt
Population: 14,387

Ancestry/Race	Number	%
African American/Black:	7,148	49.68
Not Hispanic (7,052)	7,104	49.38
Hispanic (37)	44	0.31
African, sub-Saharan:	78	0.56
African	78	0.56
Am. Ind. or Alaska Nat., not spec.	52	0.36
American Indian tribes, specified:	49	0.34
Blackfeet	1	0.01
Cherokee (2)	16	0.11
Cree (1)	1	0.01
Creek (3)	5	0.03
Iroquois (3)	3	0.02
Latin American Indians (10)	12	0.08
Lumbee (2)	2	0.01
Seminole	1	0.01
Sioux (1)	2	0.01
All other tribes (1)	6	0.04
American Indian tribes, not spec.	2	0.01
Asian:	98	0.68
Chinese, ex. Taiwanese (12)	19	0.13
Filipino (5)	6	0.04
Indian (13)	24	0.17
Japanese	2	0.01
Korean (11)	11	0.08
Vietnamese (10)	11	0.08
Other Asian, specified	14	0.10
Other Asian, not specified (2)	11	0.08
Austrian	7	0.05
Belgian	12	0.09
British	8	0.06
Danish	7	0.05
Dutch	83	0.59
English	663	4.75
European	92	0.66
French, except Basque	39	0.28
French Canadian	7	0.05
German	267	1.91
Hawaii Native/Pacific Islander:	26	0.18
Micronesian: (3)	3	0.02
Other Micronesian (3)	3	0.02
Polynesian: (4)	8	0.06
Samoan (4)	8	0.06
Other Pac. Isl., specified	14	0.10
Other Pac. Isl., not spec.	1	0.01
Hispanic or Latino:	866	6.02
Central American:	9	0.06
Honduran	7	0.05
Nicaraguan	1	0.01
Panamanian	1	0.01
Cuban	76	0.53
Mexican	675	4.69
Puerto Rican	10	0.07
South American:	7	0.05
Colombian	3	0.02
Ecuadorian	4	0.03
Other Hispanic or Latino	89	0.62
Hungarian	11	0.08
Irish	529	3.79
Italian	93	0.67
Lithuanian	7	0.05
Norwegian	32	0.23
Polish	13	0.09
Russian	6	0.04
Scotch-Irish	121	0.87
Scottish	154	1.10
Swedish	14	0.10
Ukrainian	7	0.05
United States or American	1,978	14.16
Welsh	11	0.08
West Indian, excl. Hispanic:	13	0.09
Haitian	6	0.04
Jamaican	7	0.05
White:	6,717	46.69
Not Hispanic (6,287)	6,343	44.09
Hispanic (332)	374	2.60

Mountain Park

Place Type: Census Designated Place
County: Gwinnett
Population: 11,753

Ancestry/Race	Number	%
Acadian/Cajun	11	0.10
African American/Black:	744	6.33
Not Hispanic (694)	730	6.21
Hispanic (6)	14	0.12
African, sub-Saharan:	94	0.82
African	51	0.44
South African	17	0.15
Other sub-Saharan African	26	0.23
Am. Ind. or Alaska Nat., not spec.	13	0.11
American Indian tribes, specified:	39	0.33
Cherokee (11)	24	0.20
Choctaw	1	0.01
Creek (2)	4	0.03
Latin American Indians (2)	3	0.03
Navajo (2)	2	0.02
Ottawa (1)	1	0.01
Seminole	1	0.01
All other tribes	3	0.03
American Indian tribes, not spec.	3	0.03
Arab:	9	0.08
Lebanese	9	0.08
Asian:	1,155	9.83
Bangladeshi (4)	5	0.04
Cambodian (17)	18	0.15
Chinese, ex. Taiwanese (189)	192	1.63
Filipino (19)	26	0.22
Indian (519)	540	4.59
Japanese (20)	30	0.26
Korean (147)	148	1.26
Laotian (16)	16	0.14
Pakistani (36)	47	0.40
Sri Lankan (1)	1	0.01
Taiwanese (12)	12	0.10
Thai (1)	1	0.01
Vietnamese (74)	74	0.63
Other Asian, specified (1)	1	0.01
Other Asian, not specified (9)	44	0.37
Austrian	55	0.48
British	68	0.59
Canadian	10	0.09
Croatian	51	0.44
Czech	16	0.14
Czechoslovakian	15	0.13
Danish	26	0.23
Dutch	157	1.37
English	1,425	12.41
European	260	2.26
French, except Basque	230	2.00
French Canadian	51	0.44
German	1,404	12.22
Greek	15	0.13
Hawaii Native/Pacific Islander:	11	0.09
Polynesian: (2)	3	0.03
Samoan (2)	3	0.03
Other Pac. Isl., not spec. (1)	8	0.07
Hispanic or Latino:	313	2.66
Central American:	43	0.37
Costa Rican	1	0.01
Guatemalan	10	0.09
Honduran	6	0.05
Nicaraguan	2	0.02
Salvadoran	8	0.07
Other Central American	16	0.14
Cuban	30	0.26
Dominican Republic	6	0.05
Mexican	95	0.81
Puerto Rican	54	0.46
South American:	30	0.26
Argentinean	2	0.02
Chilean	3	0.03
Colombian	9	0.08
Ecuadorian	2	0.02
Paraguayan	1	0.01
Peruvian	5	0.04
Venezuelan	3	0.03
Other South American	5	0.04
Other Hispanic or Latino	55	0.47
Hungarian	63	0.55
Iranian	18	0.16
Irish	1,519	13.23
Italian	207	1.80
Lithuanian	4	0.03
Northern European	28	0.24
Norwegian	176	1.53
Polish	216	1.88
Portuguese	57	0.50

Notes: 1. Figures in the "Number" column do not add up to the total population due to: a) Ancestry/Race overlap — e.g. persons can report being both White and Irish, b) persons of Hispanic origin can report being any race, c) persons reporting two ancestries are counted in both categories. 2. Numbers in parentheses indicate the number of persons reporting this ancestry/race alone, not in combination with any other ancestry/race. 3. Refer to the Explanation of Data in the front of the book for more detailed information.

Romanian	66	0.57
Russian	106	0.92
Scotch-Irish	484	4.21
Scottish	361	3.14
Slovak	9	0.08
Swedish	63	0.55
Swiss	130	1.13
Ukrainian	19	0.17
United States or American	1,091	9.50
Welsh	203	1.77
West Indian, excl. Hispanic:	42	0.37
Bermudan	11	0.10
Haitian	21	0.18
Jamaican	10	0.09
White:	9,780	83.21
Not Hispanic (9,475)	9,576	81.48
Hispanic (180)	204	1.74

Newnan

Place Type: City
County: Coweta
Population: 16,242

Ancestry/Race	Number	%
African American/Black:	6,910	42.54
Not Hispanic (6,790)	6,848	42.16
Hispanic (56)	62	0.38
African, sub-Saharan:	240	1.49
African	234	1.45
Zimbabwean	6	0.04
Am. Ind. or Alaska Nat., not spec.	14	0.09
Albanian	9	0.06
American Indian tribes, specified:	64	0.39
Apache	1	0.01
Blackfeet	1	0.01
Cherokee (7)	39	0.24
Chickasaw	1	0.01
Choctaw	3	0.02
Creek (3)	3	0.02
Latin American Indians (4)	4	0.02
Lumbee	2	0.01
Navajo	1	0.01
Sioux	5	0.03
All other tribes (3)	4	0.02
American Indian tribes, not spec.	6	0.04
Arab:	91	0.57
Arab/Arabic	10	0.06
Egyptian	38	0.24
Lebanese	43	0.27
Asian:	156	0.96
Chinese, ex. Taiwanese (15)	15	0.09
Filipino (10)	17	0.10
Indian (49)	52	0.32
Indonesian (1)	1	0.01
Japanese (5)	17	0.10
Korean (13)	18	0.11
Laotian (6)	7	0.04
Malaysian (1)	1	0.01
Pakistani (7)	12	0.07
Sri Lankan (1)	1	0.01
Vietnamese (9)	11	0.07
Other Asian, not specified (1)	4	0.02
Australian	20	0.12
British	93	0.58
Canadian	66	0.41
Czechoslovakian	22	0.14
Danish	23	0.14
Dutch	86	0.53
English	1,153	7.16
European	52	0.32
French, except Basque	280	1.74
French Canadian	27	0.17
German	808	5.02
Greek	62	0.39
Hawaii Native/Pacific Islander:	9	0.06
Micronesian: (2)	2	0.01
Guamanian/Chamorro (2)	2	0.01
Polynesian: (1)	4	0.02
Native Hawaiian (1)	4	0.02
Other Pac. Isl., not spec.	3	0.02
Hispanic or Latino:	806	4.96
Central American:	14	0.09
Costa Rican	2	0.01
Guatemalan	3	0.02
Honduran	8	0.05
Nicaraguan	1	0.01
Cuban	12	0.07
Dominican Republic	1	0.01
Mexican	580	3.57
Puerto Rican	48	0.30
South American:	29	0.18
Chilean	1	0.01
Colombian	14	0.09
Ecuadorian	1	0.01
Peruvian	9	0.06
Venezuelan	2	0.01
Other South American	1	0.01
Other Hispanic or Latino	122	0.75
Iranian	10	0.06
Irish	1,041	6.47
Italian	242	1.50
Latvian	9	0.06
Lithuanian	8	0.05
Norwegian	28	0.17
Pennsylvania German	5	0.03
Polish	75	0.47
Russian	21	0.13
Scotch-Irish	316	1.96
Scottish	247	1.53
Slovene	8	0.05
Swedish	25	0.16
Ukrainian	9	0.06
United States or American	1,604	9.96
Welsh	75	0.47
West Indian, excl. Hispanic:	88	0.55
Jamaican	79	0.49
Trinidadian and Tobagonian	9	0.06
White:	8,952	55.12
Not Hispanic (8,347)	8,462	52.10
Hispanic (436)	490	3.02
Yugoslavian	8	0.05

North Atlanta

Place Type: Census Designated Place
County: De Kalb
Population: 38,579

Ancestry/Race	Number	%
Acadian/Cajun	21	0.05
African American/Black:	7,124	18.47
Not Hispanic (6,615)	6,891	17.86
Hispanic (158)	233	0.60
African, sub-Saharan:	1,892	4.93
African	480	1.25
Cape Verdean	4	0.01
Ethiopian	844	2.20
Ghanian	10	0.03
Kenyan	31	0.08
Liberian	10	0.03
Nigerian	128	0.33
Senegalese	101	0.26
Somalian	89	0.23
South African	17	0.04
Other sub-Saharan African	178	0.46
Am. Ind. or Alaska Nat., not spec.	123	0.32
Albanian	9	0.02
Alsatian	6	0.02
American Indian tribes, specified:	200	0.52
Apache (1)	2	0.01
Blackfeet	3	0.01
Cherokee (17)	66	0.17
Cheyenne (2)	2	0.01
Chippewa	1	0.00
Choctaw (3)	6	0.02
Creek (4)	11	0.03
Iroquois	2	0.01
Latin American Indians (43)	86	0.22
Lumbee (2)	3	0.01
Menominee (1)	2	0.01
Pueblo (1)	1	0.00
Seminole	2	0.01
Sioux	5	0.01
Yaqui (1)	1	0.00
All other tribes (2)	7	0.02
American Indian tribes, not spec.	21	0.05
Arab:	123	0.32
Iraqi	9	0.02
Jordanian	16	0.04
Lebanese	62	0.16
Moroccan	36	0.09
Armenian	11	0.03
Asian:	2,160	5.60
Bangladeshi (206)	276	0.72
Cambodian (1)	1	0.00
Chinese, ex. Taiwanese (413)	450	1.17
Filipino (40)	57	0.15
Indian (599)	674	1.75
Indonesian (24)	25	0.06
Japanese (110)	133	0.34
Korean (109)	124	0.32
Laotian (14)	14	0.04
Malaysian (4)	5	0.01
Pakistani (29)	46	0.12
Sri Lankan (2)	4	0.01
Taiwanese (13)	18	0.05
Thai (23)	29	0.08
Vietnamese (199)	204	0.53
Other Asian, specified (1)	1	0.00
Other Asian, not specified (51)	99	0.26
Assyrian/Chaldean/Syriac	4	0.01
Australian	7	0.02
Austrian	115	0.30
Belgian	17	0.04
Brazilian	17	0.04
British	377	0.98
Bulgarian	19	0.05
Canadian	40	0.10
Celtic	8	0.02
Croatian	93	0.24
Czech	56	0.15
Czechoslovakian	33	0.09
Danish	112	0.29
Dutch	289	0.75
Eastern European	46	0.12
English	3,316	8.63
European	285	0.74
Finnish	7	0.02
French, except Basque	998	2.60
French Canadian	106	0.28
German	3,449	8.98
German Russian	6	0.02
Greek	68	0.18
Hawaii Native/Pacific Islander:	49	0.13
Micronesian: (8)	8	0.02
Guamanian/Chamorro (5)	5	0.01
Other Micronesian (3)	3	0.01
Polynesian: (7)	13	0.03
Native Hawaiian (2)	5	0.01
Samoan (5)	8	0.02
Other Pac. Isl., not spec. (5)	28	0.07
Hispanic or Latino:	10,574	27.41
Central American:	1,182	3.06
Costa Rican	10	0.03
Guatemalan	148	0.38
Honduran	447	1.16
Nicaraguan	140	0.36
Panamanian	26	0.07
Salvadoran	358	0.93
Other Central American	53	0.14
Cuban	181	0.47
Dominican Republic	70	0.18
Mexican	7,372	19.11
Puerto Rican	242	0.63
South American:	397	1.03
Argentinean	23	0.06
Bolivian	13	0.03
Chilean	11	0.03
Colombian	149	0.39

Notes: 1. Figures in the "Number" column do not add up to the total population due to: a) Ancestry/Race overlap — e.g. persons can report being both White and Irish, b) persons of Hispanic origin can report being any race, c) persons reporting two ancestries are counted in both categories. 2. Numbers in parentheses indicate the number of persons reporting this ancestry/race alone, not in combination with any other ancestry/race. 3. Refer to the Explanation of Data in the front of the book for more detailed information.

Ancestry/Race	Number	%
Ecuadorian	38	0.10
Paraguayan	1	0.00
Peruvian	97	0.25
Uruguayan	19	0.05
Venezuelan	32	0.08
Other South American	14	0.04
Other Hispanic or Latino	1,130	2.93
Hungarian	140	0.36
Icelander	5	0.01
Iranian	31	0.08
Irish	2,860	7.45
Israeli	23	0.06
Italian	953	2.48
Latvian	17	0.04
Lithuanian	130	0.34
Northern European	71	0.18
Norwegian	190	0.49
Pennsylvania German	6	0.02
Polish	608	1.58
Portuguese	22	0.06
Romanian	22	0.06
Russian	390	1.02
Scandinavian	28	0.07
Scotch-Irish	775	2.02
Scottish	681	1.77
Slavic	43	0.11
Slovak	27	0.07
Slovene	9	0.02
Swedish	344	0.90
Swiss	59	0.15
Turkish	44	0.11
Ukrainian	36	0.09
United States or American	1,905	4.96
Welsh	267	0.70
West Indian, excl. Hispanic:	271	0.71
British West Indian	15	0.04
Haitian	34	0.09
Jamaican	126	0.33
Trinidadian and Tobagonian	31	0.08
West Indian	65	0.17
White:	24,463	63.41
Not Hispanic (18,770)	19,084	49.47
Hispanic (4,963)	5,379	13.94
Yugoslavian	136	0.35

North Decatur

Place Type: Census Designated Place
County: De Kalb
Population: 15,270

Ancestry/Race	Number	%
Afghan	13	0.09
African American/Black:	1,281	8.39
Not Hispanic (1,212)	1,258	8.24
Hispanic (15)	23	0.15
African, sub-Saharan:	208	1.37
African	72	0.48
Ethiopian	110	0.73
Liberian	14	0.09
Nigerian	12	0.08
Alaska Native tribes, specified:	4	0.03
Aleut (2)	2	0.01
Eskimo (2)	2	0.01
Alaska Native tribes, not specified	2	0.01
Am. Ind. or Alaska Nat., not spec.	34	0.22
American Indian tribes, specified:	40	0.26
Blackfeet	2	0.01
Cherokee (5)	17	0.11
Chickasaw (1)	4	0.03
Chippewa (1)	1	0.01
Choctaw (2)	7	0.05
Cree	1	0.01
Creek (1)	1	0.01
Iroquois	2	0.01
Latin American Indians (1)	1	0.01
Navajo	1	0.01
Pueblo (1)	1	0.01
All other tribes	2	0.01
American Indian tribes, not spec.	6	0.04
Arab:	131	0.86
Lebanese	110	0.73
Syrian	11	0.07
Other Arab	10	0.07
Armenian	7	0.05
Asian:	988	6.47
Bangladeshi (30)	44	0.29
Chinese, ex. Taiwanese (193)	220	1.44
Filipino (22)	30	0.20
Hmong (2)	2	0.01
Indian (353)	382	2.50
Indonesian (6)	6	0.04
Japanese (44)	61	0.40
Korean (94)	98	0.64
Laotian (1)	1	0.01
Malaysian	2	0.01
Pakistani (27)	41	0.27
Sri Lankan	1	0.01
Taiwanese (5)	5	0.03
Thai (7)	9	0.06
Vietnamese (47)	57	0.37
Other Asian, specified (10)	12	0.08
Other Asian, not specified (11)	17	0.11
Austrian	111	0.73
Basque	5	0.03
Belgian	16	0.11
British	204	1.35
Canadian	29	0.19
Celtic	22	0.15
Croatian	12	0.08
Czech	54	0.36
Czechoslovakian	33	0.22
Danish	38	0.25
Dutch	269	1.77
Eastern European	94	0.62
English	2,344	15.47
European	256	1.69
Finnish	44	0.29
French, except Basque	505	3.33
French Canadian	15	0.10
German	1,865	12.31
Greek	142	0.94
Guyanese	39	0.26
Hawaii Native/Pacific Islander:	24	0.16
Melanesian: (2)	2	0.01
Fijian (2)	2	0.01
Micronesian: (1)	1	0.01
Guamanian/Chamorro (1)	1	0.01
Polynesian: (2)	16	0.10
Native Hawaiian (1)	9	0.06
Samoan (1)	3	0.02
Tongan	2	0.01
Other Polynesian	2	0.01
Other Pac. Isl., specified	2	0.01
Other Pac. Isl., not spec. (3)	3	0.02
Hispanic or Latino:	429	2.81
Central American:	20	0.13
Costa Rican	3	0.02
Guatemalan	6	0.04
Nicaraguan	1	0.01
Panamanian	6	0.04
Salvadoran	4	0.03
Cuban	67	0.44
Dominican Republic	9	0.06
Mexican	107	0.70
Puerto Rican	67	0.44
South American:	65	0.43
Argentinean	6	0.04
Bolivian	1	0.01
Chilean	11	0.07
Colombian	26	0.17
Ecuadorian	6	0.04
Peruvian	6	0.04
Venezuelan	4	0.03
Other South American	5	0.03
Other Hispanic or Latino	94	0.62
Hungarian	135	0.89
Iranian	20	0.13
Irish	1,577	10.41
Italian	507	3.35
Lithuanian	62	0.41
Northern European	55	0.36
Norwegian	167	1.10
Polish	486	3.21
Portuguese	8	0.05
Romanian	19	0.13
Russian	282	1.86
Scandinavian	69	0.46
Scotch-Irish	700	4.62
Scottish	642	4.24
Slavic	9	0.06
Slovak	34	0.22
Slovene	14	0.09
Swedish	258	1.70
Swiss	82	0.54
Turkish	16	0.11
Ukrainian	69	0.46
United States or American	1,156	7.63
Welsh	138	0.91
West Indian, excl. Hispanic:	73	0.48
Barbadian	14	0.09
Jamaican	52	0.34
Trinidadian and Tobagonian	7	0.05
White:	12,983	85.02
Not Hispanic (12,499)	12,655	82.87
Hispanic (296)	328	2.15
Yugoslavian	17	0.11

North Druid Hills

Place Type: Census Designated Place
County: De Kalb
Population: 18,852

Ancestry/Race	Number	%
Acadian/Cajun	16	0.08
African American/Black:	1,456	7.72
Not Hispanic (1,363)	1,437	7.62
Hispanic (13)	19	0.10
African, sub-Saharan:	189	1.00
African	57	0.30
Ethiopian	9	0.05
Kenyan	11	0.06
Liberian	12	0.06
Nigerian	28	0.15
Senegalese	10	0.05
South African	33	0.18
Sudanese	21	0.11
Zimbabwean	8	0.04
Alaska Native tribes, specified:	1	0.01
Eskimo	1	0.01
Am. Ind. or Alaska Nat., not spec.	37	0.20
American Indian tribes, specified:	68	0.36
Apache	2	0.01
Cherokee (11)	33	0.18
Cheyenne	1	0.01
Chickasaw	1	0.01
Choctaw (2)	4	0.02
Comanche	1	0.01
Creek	4	0.02
Delaware (1)	1	0.01
Latin American Indians (2)	9	0.05
Lumbee	1	0.01
Navajo	3	0.02
Sioux	1	0.01
Ute	2	0.01
All other tribes (2)	5	0.03
American Indian tribes, not spec.	10	0.05
Arab:	214	1.14
Arab/Arabic	17	0.09
Egyptian	57	0.30
Jordanian	9	0.05
Lebanese	44	0.23
Moroccan	32	0.17
Palestinian	15	0.08
Syrian	40	0.21
Armenian	12	0.06
Asian:	1,430	7.59
Bangladeshi (10)	18	0.10
Cambodian (5)	11	0.06

Notes: 1. Figures in the "Number" column do not add up to the total population due to: a) Ancestry/Race overlap — e.g. persons can report being both White and Irish, b) persons of Hispanic origin can report being any race, c) persons reporting two ancestries are counted in both categories. 2. Numbers in parentheses indicate the number of persons reporting this ancestry/race alone, not in combination with any other ancestry/race. 3. Refer to the Explanation of Data in the front of the book for more detailed information.

Ancestry/Race	Number	%
Chinese, ex. Taiwanese (324)	347	1.84
Filipino (44)	62	0.33
Hmong (1)	1	0.01
Indian (537)	569	3.02
Indonesian (2)	2	0.01
Japanese (75)	95	0.50
Korean (107)	111	0.59
Laotian (3)	3	0.02
Malaysian (7)	8	0.04
Pakistani (28)	37	0.20
Sri Lankan (4)	4	0.02
Taiwanese (16)	26	0.14
Thai (37)	44	0.23
Vietnamese (23)	30	0.16
Other Asian, specified (8)	9	0.05
Other Asian, not specified (18)	53	0.28
Australian	44	0.23
Austrian	93	0.49
Basque	11	0.06
Belgian	31	0.16
British	354	1.88
Bulgarian	10	0.05
Canadian	43	0.23
Celtic	10	0.05
Croatian	11	0.06
Czech	74	0.39
Czechoslovakian	8	0.04
Danish	79	0.42
Dutch	234	1.24
Eastern European	47	0.25
English	2,391	12.68
Estonian	8	0.04
European	143	0.76
Finnish	10	0.05
French, except Basque	612	3.25
French Canadian	125	0.66
German	2,262	12.00
Greek	80	0.42
Hawaii Native/Pacific Islander:	25	0.13
Melanesian: (2)	2	0.01
Fijian (2)	2	0.01
Micronesian: (1)	3	0.02
Guamanian/Chamorro (1)	3	0.02
Polynesian: (2)	10	0.05
Native Hawaiian (2)	4	0.02
Samoan	5	0.03
Other Polynesian	1	0.01
Other Pac. Isl., specified	1	0.01
Other Pac. Isl., not spec. (1)	9	0.05
Hispanic or Latino:	815	4.32
Central American:	52	0.28
Costa Rican	1	0.01
Guatemalan	7	0.04
Honduran	15	0.08
Nicaraguan	4	0.02
Panamanian	17	0.09
Salvadoran	3	0.02
Other Central American	5	0.03
Cuban	145	0.77
Dominican Republic	10	0.05
Mexican	268	1.42
Puerto Rican	49	0.26
South American:	166	0.88
Argentinean	10	0.05
Bolivian	7	0.04
Chilean	12	0.06
Colombian	57	0.30
Ecuadorian	9	0.05
Peruvian	31	0.16
Uruguayan	1	0.01
Venezuelan	31	0.16
Other South American	8	0.04
Other Hispanic or Latino	125	0.66
Hungarian	125	0.66
Icelander	7	0.04
Iranian	71	0.38
Irish	1,916	10.16
Israeli	79	0.42
Italian	656	3.48
Lithuanian	72	0.38
Luxemburger	7	0.04
New Zealander	7	0.04
Northern European	20	0.11
Norwegian	239	1.27
Polish	709	3.76
Portuguese	10	0.05
Romanian	62	0.33
Russian	716	3.80
Scandinavian	7	0.04
Scotch-Irish	396	2.10
Scottish	707	3.75
Slavic	22	0.12
Slovak	28	0.15
Slovene	7	0.04
Swedish	192	1.02
Swiss	162	0.86
Turkish	29	0.15
Ukrainian	83	0.44
United States or American	1,356	7.19
Welsh	231	1.23
West Indian, excl. Hispanic:	39	0.21
Jamaican	26	0.14
Trinidadian and Tobagonian	13	0.07
White:	15,798	83.80
Not Hispanic (15,008)	15,196	80.61
Hispanic (545)	602	3.19
Yugoslavian	8	0.04

Panthersville

Place Type: Census Designated Place
County: De Kalb
Population: 11,791

Ancestry/Race	Number	%
Acadian/Cajun	11	0.09
African American/Black:	11,474	97.31
Not Hispanic (11,275)	11,377	96.49
Hispanic (85)	97	0.82
African, sub-Saharan:	361	3.09
African	314	2.69
Cape Verdean	8	0.07
Kenyan	6	0.05
Nigerian	9	0.08
Sierra Leonean	24	0.21
Am. Ind. or Alaska Nat., not spec.	33	0.28
American Indian tribes, specified:	17	0.14
Apache (1)	1	0.01
Cherokee (1)	8	0.07
Creek	1	0.01
Iroquois (1)	1	0.01
Latin American Indians	1	0.01
Lumbee (2)	2	0.02
Navajo	1	0.01
Sioux	1	0.01
All other tribes (1)	1	0.01
American Indian tribes, not spec.	3	0.03
Arab:	14	0.12
Moroccan	14	0.12
Asian:	40	0.34
Bangladeshi	1	0.01
Cambodian (1)	1	0.01
Chinese, ex. Taiwanese (3)	7	0.06
Filipino (2)	2	0.02
Indian (6)	8	0.07
Japanese (2)	3	0.03
Korean (3)	5	0.04
Sri Lankan (1)	1	0.01
Thai (5)	5	0.04
Vietnamese	1	0.01
Other Asian, specified	3	0.03
Other Asian, not specified (1)	3	0.03
Dutch	7	0.06
English	59	0.51
French Canadian	9	0.08
German	37	0.32
Guyanese	25	0.21
Hawaii Native/Pacific Islander:	15	0.13
Polynesian: (2)	2	0.02
Native Hawaiian (2)	2	0.02
Other Pac. Isl., specified	3	0.03
Other Pac. Isl., not spec. (4)	10	0.08
Hispanic or Latino:	140	1.19
Central American:	9	0.08
Costa Rican	2	0.02
Panamanian	7	0.06
Cuban	15	0.13
Dominican Republic	1	0.01
Mexican	46	0.39
Puerto Rican	47	0.40
South American:	1	0.01
Bolivian	1	0.01
Other Hispanic or Latino	21	0.18
Irish	51	0.44
Italian	18	0.15
Polish	20	0.17
Scotch-Irish	18	0.15
United States or American	195	1.67
West Indian, excl. Hispanic:	333	2.85
Dutch West Indian	10	0.09
Haitian	154	1.32
Jamaican	100	0.86
Trinidadian and Tobagonian	10	0.09
U.S. Virgin Islander	50	0.43
West Indian	9	0.08
White:	268	2.27
Not Hispanic (215)	254	2.15
Hispanic (10)	14	0.12

Peachtree City

Place Type: City
County: Fayette
Population: 31,580

Ancestry/Race	Number	%
Acadian/Cajun	45	0.14
African American/Black:	2,050	6.49
Not Hispanic (1,894)	2,009	6.36
Hispanic (35)	41	0.13
African, sub-Saharan:	137	0.43
African	66	0.21
Nigerian	40	0.13
South African	31	0.10
Am. Ind. or Alaska Nat., not spec.	69	0.22
Albanian	8	0.03
American Indian tribes, specified:	107	0.34
Apache	1	0.00
Blackfeet (1)	3	0.01
Cherokee (12)	62	0.20
Cheyenne (1)	1	0.00
Chippewa (1)	3	0.01
Choctaw (3)	7	0.02
Cree (2)	2	0.01
Creek	7	0.02
Iroquois (1)	2	0.01
Latin American Indians (1)	1	0.00
Lumbee (2)	2	0.01
Seminole	1	0.00
Sioux	2	0.01
All other tribes (6)	13	0.04
American Indian tribes, not spec.	2	0.01
Arab:	47	0.15
Arab/Arabic	8	0.03
Lebanese	39	0.12
Armenian	62	0.19
Asian:	1,348	4.27
Chinese, ex. Taiwanese (162)	181	0.57
Filipino (101)	142	0.45
Indian (224)	236	0.75
Indonesian	5	0.02
Japanese (459)	492	1.56
Korean (77)	108	0.34
Laotian (2)	2	0.01
Pakistani (26)	26	0.08
Taiwanese (18)	29	0.09
Thai (14)	21	0.07
Vietnamese (54)	62	0.20
Other Asian, specified (6)	15	0.05
Other Asian, not specified (12)	29	0.09

Notes: 1. Figures in the "Number" column do not add up to the total population due to: a) Ancestry/Race overlap — e.g. persons can report being both White and Irish, b) persons of Hispanic origin can report being any race, c) persons reporting two ancestries are counted in both categories. 2. Numbers in parentheses indicate the number of persons reporting this ancestry/race alone, not in combination with any other ancestry/race. 3. Refer to the Explanation of Data in the front of the book for more detailed information.

Australian	19	0.06
Austrian	76	0.24
Belgian	49	0.15
Brazilian	54	0.17
British	401	1.26
Canadian	188	0.59
Celtic	50	0.16
Croatian	58	0.18
Czech	109	0.34
Czechoslovakian	65	0.20
Danish	264	0.83
Dutch	587	1.84
Eastern European	6	0.02
English	4,613	14.46
Estonian	8	0.03
European	575	1.80
Finnish	84	0.26
French, except Basque	1,507	4.72
French Canadian	481	1.51
German	5,365	16.82
Greek	214	0.67
Hawaii Native/Pacific Islander:	44	0.14
Micronesian: (3)	7	0.02
Guamanian/Chamorro (2)	6	0.02
Other Micronesian (1)	1	0.00
Polynesian: (4)	21	0.07
Native Hawaiian (4)	17	0.05
Samoan	3	0.01
Other Polynesian	1	0.00
Other Pac. Isl., specified	4	0.01
Other Pac. Isl., not spec. (2)	12	0.04
Hispanic or Latino:	1,184	3.75
Central American:	101	0.32
Costa Rican	42	0.13
Guatemalan	9	0.03
Honduran	11	0.03
Nicaraguan	9	0.03
Panamanian	17	0.05
Salvadoran	7	0.02
Other Central American	6	0.02
Cuban	84	0.27
Dominican Republic	8	0.03
Mexican	405	1.28
Puerto Rican	259	0.82
South American:	133	0.42
Argentinean	7	0.02
Bolivian	1	0.00
Chilean	17	0.05
Colombian	71	0.22
Ecuadorian	2	0.01
Peruvian	18	0.06
Uruguayan	2	0.01
Venezuelan	12	0.04
Other South American	3	0.01
Other Hispanic or Latino	194	0.61
Hungarian	133	0.42
Icelander	45	0.14
Irish	4,593	14.40
Italian	1,876	5.88
Latvian	43	0.13
Lithuanian	58	0.18
Northern European	100	0.31
Norwegian	259	0.81
Pennsylvania German	7	0.02
Polish	972	3.05
Portuguese	62	0.19
Romanian	84	0.26
Russian	127	0.40
Scandinavian	127	0.40
Scotch-Irish	822	2.58
Scottish	1,229	3.85
Serbian	11	0.03
Slavic	14	0.04
Slovak	129	0.40
Swedish	510	1.60
Swiss	126	0.40
Turkish	7	0.02
Ukrainian	78	0.24
United States or American	2,874	9.01
Welsh	265	0.83
West Indian, excl. Hispanic:	84	0.26
Barbadian	9	0.03
Dutch West Indian	11	0.03
Jamaican	50	0.16
Trinidadian and Tobagonian	5	0.02
West Indian	9	0.03
White:	28,072	88.89
Not Hispanic (26,873)	27,185	86.08
Hispanic (810)	887	2.81
Yugoslavian	15	0.05

Powder Springs

Place Type: City
County: Cobb
Population: 12,481

Ancestry/Race	Number	%
Acadian/Cajun	11	0.08
African American/Black:	4,762	38.15
Not Hispanic (4,615)	4,703	37.68
Hispanic (51)	59	0.47
African, sub-Saharan:	410	3.16
African	222	1.71
Ethiopian	38	0.29
Ghanian	12	0.09
Kenyan	8	0.06
Nigerian	130	1.00
Am. Ind. or Alaska Nat., not spec.	11	0.09
American Indian tribes, specified:	63	0.50
Blackfeet	3	0.02
Cherokee (6)	32	0.26
Choctaw	1	0.01
Creek (2)	4	0.03
Houma (1)	1	0.01
Iroquois	1	0.01
Latin American Indians (9)	9	0.07
Lumbee (1)	1	0.01
Navajo	3	0.02
Potawatomi (1)	1	0.01
All other tribes (1)	7	0.06
American Indian tribes, not spec.	2	0.02
Arab:	22	0.17
Lebanese	15	0.12
Syrian	7	0.05
Armenian	6	0.05
Asian:	181	1.45
Bangladeshi (7)	7	0.06
Chinese, ex. Taiwanese (8)	10	0.08
Filipino (33)	46	0.37
Indian (26)	34	0.27
Indonesian (4)	8	0.06
Japanese (6)	16	0.13
Korean (11)	13	0.10
Laotian (6)	6	0.05
Pakistani (13)	15	0.12
Vietnamese (3)	9	0.07
Other Asian, specified (12)	14	0.11
Other Asian, not specified (2)	3	0.02
Austrian	32	0.25
British	90	0.69
Canadian	19	0.15
Czech	37	0.29
Danish	49	0.38
Dutch	80	0.62
English	833	6.42
Estonian	35	0.27
European	37	0.29
French, except Basque	208	1.60
French Canadian	31	0.24
German	960	7.40
Greek	26	0.20
Guyanese	55	0.42
Hawaii Native/Pacific Islander:	11	0.09
Micronesian: (4)	4	0.03
Guamanian/Chamorro (2)	2	0.02
Other Micronesian (2)	2	0.02
Polynesian: (3)	4	0.03
Native Hawaiian (2)	3	0.02
Samoan (1)	1	0.01
Other Pac. Isl., not spec.	3	0.02
Hispanic or Latino:	539	4.32
Central American:	44	0.35
Costa Rican	6	0.05
Guatemalan	21	0.17
Honduran	3	0.02
Panamanian	8	0.06
Salvadoran	3	0.02
Other Central American	3	0.02
Cuban	26	0.21
Dominican Republic	7	0.06
Mexican	211	1.69
Puerto Rican	108	0.87
South American:	38	0.30
Argentinean	2	0.02
Bolivian	1	0.01
Chilean	1	0.01
Colombian	13	0.10
Ecuadorian	8	0.06
Peruvian	11	0.09
Uruguayan	1	0.01
Other South American	1	0.01
Other Hispanic or Latino	105	0.84
Hungarian	89	0.69
Iranian	20	0.15
Irish	956	7.37
Italian	251	1.93
Lithuanian	10	0.08
Norwegian	33	0.25
Polish	219	1.69
Portuguese	17	0.13
Russian	48	0.37
Scandinavian	9	0.07
Scotch-Irish	242	1.86
Scottish	319	2.46
Slovak	15	0.12
Swedish	29	0.22
Swiss	11	0.08
United States or American	1,746	13.45
Welsh	57	0.44
West Indian, excl. Hispanic:	321	2.47
Bahamian	9	0.07
Barbadian	6	0.05
British West Indian	17	0.13
Haitian	121	0.93
Jamaican	150	1.16
West Indian	18	0.14
White:	7,387	59.19
Not Hispanic (6,997)	7,103	56.91
Hispanic (228)	284	2.28

Redan

Place Type: Census Designated Place
County: De Kalb
Population: 33,841

Ancestry/Race	Number	%
African American/Black:	31,322	92.56
Not Hispanic (30,668)	31,040	91.72
Hispanic (218)	282	0.83
African, sub-Saharan:	1,696	5.01
African	812	2.40
Cape Verdean	19	0.06
Ethiopian	116	0.34
Ghanian	38	0.11
Liberian	48	0.14
Nigerian	564	1.67
Senegalese	14	0.04
Sierra Leonean	62	0.18
Sudanese	6	0.02
Other sub-Saharan African	17	0.05
Alaska Native tribes, specified:	1	0.00
Tlingit-Haida	1	0.00
Am. Ind. or Alaska Nat., not spec.	91	0.27
American Indian tribes, specified:	81	0.24
Blackfeet	8	0.02
Cherokee (11)	48	0.14
Choctaw	4	0.01
Creek	3	0.01

Notes: 1. Figures in the "Number" column do not add up to the total population due to: a) Ancestry/Race overlap — e.g. persons can report being both White and Irish, b) persons of Hispanic origin can report being any race, c) persons reporting two ancestries are counted in both categories. 2. Numbers in parentheses indicate the number of persons reporting this ancestry/race alone, not in combination with any other ancestry/race. 3. Refer to the Explanation of Data in the front of the book for more detailed information.

Iroquois	6	0.02
Osage	1	0.00
Seminole	1	0.00
All other tribes (3)	10	0.03
American Indian tribes, not spec.	9	0.03
Asian:	326	0.96
Cambodian (11)	13	0.04
Chinese, ex. Taiwanese (20)	32	0.09
Filipino (40)	53	0.16
Hmong (25)	26	0.08
Indian (32)	60	0.18
Japanese (9)	13	0.04
Korean (18)	23	0.07
Laotian (37)	46	0.14
Malaysian (1)	3	0.01
Sri Lankan (2)	2	0.01
Thai (1)	5	0.01
Vietnamese (26)	31	0.09
Other Asian, not specified (8)	19	0.06
Australian	12	0.04
Austrian	6	0.02
British	34	0.10
Croatian	8	0.02
Dutch	121	0.36
English	222	0.66
European	105	0.31
Finnish	8	0.02
French, except Basque	46	0.14
French Canadian	17	0.05
German	425	1.26
Greek	15	0.04
Guyanese	122	0.36
Hawaii Native/Pacific Islander:	38	0.11
Melanesian: (1)	1	0.00
Fijian (1)	1	0.00
Micronesian: (1)	2	0.01
Guamanian/Chamorro (1)	2	0.01
Polynesian: (2)	8	0.02
Native Hawaiian (2)	5	0.01
Samoan	3	0.01
Other Pac. Isl., not spec. (7)	27	0.08
Hispanic or Latino:	603	1.78
Central American:	47	0.14
Costa Rican	5	0.01
Guatemalan	2	0.01
Honduran	3	0.01
Nicaraguan	2	0.01
Panamanian	34	0.10
Salvadoran	1	0.00
Cuban	24	0.07
Dominican Republic	28	0.08
Mexican	210	0.62
Puerto Rican	153	0.45
South American:	17	0.05
Argentinean	1	0.00
Chilean	1	0.00
Colombian	9	0.03
Peruvian	2	0.01
Venezuelan	3	0.01
Other South American	1	0.00
Other Hispanic or Latino	124	0.37
Irish	475	1.40
Israeli	17	0.05
Italian	66	0.20
Norwegian	8	0.02
Polish	45	0.13
Scotch-Irish	103	0.30
Scottish	81	0.24
Slovak	11	0.03
Swedish	19	0.06
Swiss	9	0.03
United States or American	758	2.24
Welsh	9	0.03
West Indian, excl. Hispanic:	1,805	5.33
Bahamian	19	0.06
Barbadian	102	0.30
Belizean	26	0.08
British West Indian	51	0.15
Haitian	75	0.22
Jamaican	1,231	3.64
Trinidadian and Tobagonian	142	0.42
West Indian	159	0.47
White:	2,112	6.24
Not Hispanic (1,791)	1,967	5.81
Hispanic (131)	145	0.43

Riverdale

Place Type: City
County: Clayton
Population: 12,478

Ancestry/Race	Number	%
African American/Black:	8,551	68.53
Not Hispanic (8,339)	8,460	67.80
Hispanic (74)	91	0.73
African, sub-Saharan:	403	3.24
African	155	1.24
Nigerian	201	1.61
Sierra Leonean	9	0.07
Sudanese	38	0.31
Alaska Native tribes, specified:	3	0.02
Alaska Athabascan	2	0.02
Tlingit-Haida	1	0.01
Am. Ind. or Alaska Nat., not spec.	55	0.44
American Indian tribes, specified:	45	0.36
Blackfeet	5	0.04
Cherokee (3)	25	0.20
Chippewa	1	0.01
Choctaw	1	0.01
Iroquois	1	0.01
Latin American Indians	6	0.05
Seminole	3	0.02
Sioux (3)	3	0.02
American Indian tribes, not spec.	6	0.05
Arab:	25	0.20
Moroccan	15	0.12
Palestinian	10	0.08
Asian:	1,076	8.62
Cambodian (159)	180	1.44
Chinese, ex. Taiwanese (32)	41	0.33
Filipino (33)	40	0.32
Indian (161)	165	1.32
Japanese (1)	2	0.02
Korean (14)	19	0.15
Laotian (138)	157	1.26
Pakistani (55)	65	0.52
Thai (5)	9	0.07
Vietnamese (337)	361	2.89
Other Asian, specified	2	0.02
Other Asian, not specified (17)	35	0.28
British	15	0.12
Dutch	22	0.18
English	249	2.00
European	14	0.11
French, except Basque	13	0.10
German	239	1.92
Greek	8	0.06
Hawaii Native/Pacific Islander:	26	0.21
Micronesian: (4)	4	0.03
Guamanian/Chamorro (4)	4	0.03
Polynesian: (5)	9	0.07
Native Hawaiian (1)	5	0.04
Samoan (4)	4	0.03
Other Pac. Isl., specified	2	0.02
Other Pac. Isl., not spec. (1)	11	0.09
Hispanic or Latino:	600	4.81
Central American:	47	0.38
Costa Rican	3	0.02
Guatemalan	3	0.02
Honduran	15	0.12
Panamanian	20	0.16
Salvadoran	6	0.05
Cuban	25	0.20
Dominican Republic	8	0.06
Mexican	318	2.55
Puerto Rican	64	0.51
South American:	33	0.26
Chilean	1	0.01
Colombian	19	0.15
Ecuadorian	10	0.08
Peruvian	2	0.02
Venezuelan	1	0.01
Other Hispanic or Latino	105	0.84
Hungarian	6	0.05
Irish	274	2.20
Italian	26	0.21
Polish	7	0.06
Portuguese	10	0.08
Russian	10	0.08
Scotch-Irish	75	0.60
Scottish	50	0.40
Swedish	17	0.14
United States or American	595	4.78
Welsh	18	0.14
West Indian, excl. Hispanic:	154	1.24
Barbadian	9	0.07
British West Indian	19	0.15
Dutch West Indian	10	0.08
Haitian	40	0.32
Jamaican	60	0.48
Trinidadian and Tobagonian	16	0.13
White:	2,622	21.01
Not Hispanic (2,298)	2,392	19.17
Hispanic (209)	230	1.84

Rome

Place Type: City
County: Floyd
Population: 34,980

Ancestry/Race	Number	%
African American/Black:	9,870	28.22
Not Hispanic (9,638)	9,814	28.06
Hispanic (39)	56	0.16
African, sub-Saharan:	442	1.26
African	435	1.24
Nigerian	7	0.02
Alaska Native tribes, specified:	3	0.01
Alaska Athabascan (3)	3	0.01
Am. Ind. or Alaska Nat., not spec.	89	0.25
American Indian tribes, specified:	150	0.43
Apache (1)	1	0.00
Blackfeet (1)	4	0.01
Cherokee (22)	65	0.19
Chippewa	1	0.00
Choctaw	1	0.00
Creek	5	0.01
Delaware (1)	1	0.00
Iroquois	3	0.01
Latin American Indians (56)	62	0.18
Navajo	1	0.00
Pueblo	1	0.00
Sioux (1)	1	0.00
Yaqui (2)	2	0.01
All other tribes (1)	2	0.01
American Indian tribes, not spec.	11	0.03
Arab:	196	0.56
Arab/Arabic	45	0.13
Lebanese	6	0.02
Palestinian	67	0.19
Other Arab	78	0.22
Asian:	604	1.73
Bangladeshi (9)	9	0.03
Cambodian (1)	1	0.00
Chinese, ex. Taiwanese (35)	43	0.12
Filipino (25)	45	0.13
Indian (188)	210	0.60
Indonesian	1	0.00
Japanese (11)	14	0.04
Korean (39)	45	0.13
Pakistani (6)	11	0.03
Sri Lankan (13)	13	0.04
Thai	3	0.01
Vietnamese (149)	166	0.47
Other Asian, specified (1)	2	0.01
Other Asian, not specified (11)	41	0.12
Assyrian/Chaldean/Syriac	8	0.02
Austrian	5	0.01

Notes: 1. Figures in the "Number" column do not add up to the total population due to: a) Ancestry/Race overlap — e.g. persons can report being both White and Irish, b) persons of Hispanic origin can report being any race, c) persons reporting two ancestries are counted in both categories. 2. Numbers in parentheses indicate the number of persons reporting this ancestry/race alone, not in combination with any other ancestry/race. 3. Refer to the Explanation of Data in the front of the book for more detailed information.

Ancestry/Race	Number	%
Belgian	9	0.03
British	220	0.63
Canadian	51	0.15
Celtic	8	0.02
Croatian	30	0.09
Czech	34	0.10
Czechoslovakian	6	0.02
Danish	22	0.06
Dutch	288	0.82
English	2,423	6.91
European	289	0.82
Finnish	11	0.03
French, except Basque	267	0.76
French Canadian	74	0.21
German	1,474	4.20
Greek	67	0.19
Guyanese	6	0.02
Hawaii Native/Pacific Islander:	78	0.22
Micronesian: (50)	60	0.17
Guamanian/Chamorro (50)	60	0.17
Polynesian: (4)	9	0.03
Native Hawaiian (3)	6	0.02
Samoan (1)	3	0.01
Other Pac. Isl., specified	1	0.00
Other Pac. Isl., not spec. (2)	8	0.02
Hispanic or Latino:	3,620	10.35
Central American:	1,055	3.02
Costa Rican	1	0.00
Guatemalan	992	2.84
Honduran	9	0.03
Nicaraguan	1	0.00
Panamanian	4	0.01
Salvadoran	30	0.09
Other Central American	18	0.05
Cuban	31	0.09
Dominican Republic	10	0.03
Mexican	1,747	4.99
Puerto Rican	86	0.25
South American:	49	0.14
Argentinean	1	0.00
Chilean	3	0.01
Colombian	27	0.08
Ecuadorian	4	0.01
Paraguayan	2	0.01
Peruvian	4	0.01
Venezuelan	6	0.02
Other South American	2	0.01
Other Hispanic or Latino	642	1.84
Hungarian	12	0.03
Irish	2,328	6.64
Israeli	10	0.03
Italian	248	0.71
Lithuanian	5	0.01
Norwegian	88	0.25
Pennsylvania German	10	0.03
Polish	162	0.46
Russian	29	0.08
Scandinavian	60	0.17
Scotch-Irish	578	1.65
Scottish	623	1.78
Swedish	100	0.29
Ukrainian	8	0.02
United States or American	4,615	13.17
Welsh	100	0.29
West Indian, excl. Hispanic:	8	0.02
Jamaican	8	0.02
White:	22,559	64.49
Not Hispanic (20,704)	21,018	60.09
Hispanic (1,377)	1,541	4.41

Roswell

Place Type: City
County: Fulton
Population: 79,334

Ancestry/Race	Number	%
Acadian/Cajun	10	0.01
African American/Black:	7,240	9.13
Not Hispanic (6,620)	7,029	8.86
Hispanic (153)	211	0.27
African, sub-Saharan:	373	0.47
African	201	0.25
Cape Verdean	9	0.01
Ethiopian	13	0.02
Ghanian	24	0.03
Kenyan	1	0.00
Nigerian	75	0.09
South African	41	0.05
Other sub-Saharan African	9	0.01
Alaska Native tribes, specified:	7	0.01
Alaska Athabascan (1)	4	0.01
Eskimo	2	0.00
Tlingit-Haida	1	0.00
Am. Ind. or Alaska Nat., not spec.	156	0.20
American Indian tribes, specified:	285	0.36
Apache	4	0.01
Blackfeet (2)	10	0.01
Cherokee (20)	130	0.16
Cheyenne (2)	2	0.00
Chickasaw	2	0.00
Chippewa (3)	5	0.01
Choctaw (4)	20	0.03
Colville	1	0.00
Comanche (1)	2	0.00
Cree	3	0.00
Creek (4)	4	0.01
Delaware (4)	4	0.01
Iroquois (6)	11	0.01
Kiowa (2)	2	0.00
Latin American Indians (17)	28	0.04
Lumbee (1)	1	0.00
Navajo (6)	7	0.01
Osage (3)	4	0.01
Paiute	1	0.00
Pueblo	1	0.00
Seminole (3)	7	0.01
Sioux (3)	5	0.01
All other tribes (9)	31	0.04
American Indian tribes, not spec.	34	0.04
Arab:	530	0.66
Arab/Arabic	9	0.01
Egyptian	22	0.03
Iraqi	11	0.01
Jordanian	7	0.01
Lebanese	308	0.39
Palestinian	24	0.03
Syrian	69	0.09
Other Arab	80	0.10
Armenian	70	0.09
Asian:	3,445	4.34
Bangladeshi (27)	33	0.04
Cambodian (9)	12	0.02
Chinese, ex. Taiwanese (586)	691	0.87
Filipino (147)	208	0.26
Indian (961)	1,046	1.32
Indonesian (67)	108	0.14
Japanese (127)	171	0.22
Korean (661)	696	0.88
Laotian (3)	3	0.00
Malaysian (1)	8	0.01
Pakistani (58)	80	0.10
Sri Lankan (4)	7	0.01
Taiwanese (47)	57	0.07
Thai (37)	44	0.06
Vietnamese (122)	138	0.17
Other Asian, specified (13)	19	0.02
Other Asian, not specified (46)	124	0.16
Assyrian/Chaldean/Syriac	6	0.01
Australian	31	0.04
Austrian	208	0.26
Belgian	150	0.19
Brazilian	142	0.18
British	772	0.97
Bulgarian	43	0.05
Canadian	359	0.45
Croatian	98	0.12
Cypriot	11	0.01
Czech	256	0.32
Czechoslovakian	115	0.14
Danish	315	0.39
Dutch	968	1.21
Eastern European	179	0.22
English	11,508	14.41
Estonian	23	0.03
European	1,109	1.39
Finnish	185	0.23
French, except Basque	2,032	2.54
French Canadian	456	0.57
German	10,290	12.89
German Russian	8	0.01
Greek	471	0.59
Guyanese	32	0.04
Hawaii Native/Pacific Islander:	67	0.08
Micronesian: (9)	11	0.01
Guamanian/Chamorro (8)	10	0.01
Other Micronesian (1)	1	0.00
Polynesian: (12)	29	0.04
Native Hawaiian (5)	15	0.02
Samoan (7)	12	0.02
Tongan	1	0.00
Other Polynesian	1	0.00
Other Pac. Isl., not spec. (2)	27	0.03
Hispanic or Latino:	8,421	10.61
Central American:	311	0.39
Costa Rican	21	0.03
Guatemalan	45	0.06
Honduran	86	0.11
Nicaraguan	19	0.02
Panamanian	17	0.02
Salvadoran	122	0.15
Other Central American	1	0.00
Cuban	250	0.32
Dominican Republic	45	0.06
Mexican	5,833	7.35
Puerto Rican	401	0.51
South American:	634	0.80
Argentinean	48	0.06
Bolivian	11	0.01
Chilean	18	0.02
Colombian	333	0.42
Ecuadorian	30	0.04
Paraguayan	2	0.00
Peruvian	88	0.11
Uruguayan	8	0.01
Venezuelan	78	0.10
Other South American	18	0.02
Other Hispanic or Latino	947	1.19
Hungarian	409	0.51
Iranian	290	0.36
Irish	9,731	12.19
Israeli	61	0.08
Italian	4,427	5.54
Latvian	30	0.04
Lithuanian	130	0.16
Luxemburger	10	0.01
Macedonian	13	0.02
New Zealander	9	0.01
Northern European	64	0.08
Norwegian	841	1.05
Pennsylvania German	6	0.01
Polish	2,162	2.71
Portuguese	123	0.15
Romanian	317	0.40
Russian	1,298	1.63
Scandinavian	69	0.09
Scotch-Irish	2,655	3.33
Scottish	2,517	3.15
Serbian	71	0.09
Slavic	50	0.06
Slovak	200	0.25
Slovene	29	0.04
Swedish	858	1.07
Swiss	283	0.35
Turkish	105	0.13
Ukrainian	326	0.41
United States or American	6,151	7.70
Welsh	740	0.93
West Indian, excl. Hispanic:	523	0.66
Barbadian	10	0.01

Notes: 1. Figures in the "Number" column do not add up to the total population due to: a) Ancestry/Race overlap — e.g. persons can report being both White and Irish, b) persons of Hispanic origin can report being any race, c) persons reporting two ancestries are counted in both categories. 2. Numbers in parentheses indicate the number of persons reporting this ancestry/race alone, not in combination with any other ancestry/race. 3. Refer to the Explanation of Data in the front of the book for more detailed information.

British West Indian	6	0.01
Dutch West Indian	11	0.01
Haitian	263	0.33
Jamaican	177	0.22
Trinidadian and Tobagonian	22	0.03
U.S. Virgin Islander	31	0.04
Other West Indian	3	0.00
White:	65,783	82.92
Not Hispanic (59,870)	60,701	76.51
Hispanic (4,796)	5,082	6.41
Yugoslavian	261	0.33

Saint Marys

Place Type: City
County: Camden
Population: 13,761

Ancestry/Race	Number	%
African American/Black:	2,868	20.84
Not Hispanic (2,710)	2,803	20.37
Hispanic (41)	65	0.47
African, sub-Saharan:	48	0.36
African	48	0.36
Alaska Native tribes, specified:	1	0.01
Aleut (1)	1	0.01
Am. Ind. or Alaska Nat., not spec.	29	0.21
American Indian tribes, specified:	101	0.73
Apache	3	0.02
Blackfeet (1)	2	0.01
Cherokee (22)	59	0.43
Chippewa (3)	4	0.03
Choctaw (1)	1	0.01
Creek (4)	6	0.04
Iroquois (1)	2	0.01
Latin American Indians (3)	3	0.02
Navajo (2)	2	0.01
Osage (1)	1	0.01
Sioux (5)	9	0.07
Ute (1)	1	0.01
All other tribes (4)	8	0.06
American Indian tribes, not spec.	2	0.01
Arab:	49	0.36
Lebanese	36	0.27
Moroccan	13	0.10
Asian:	256	1.86
Chinese, ex. Taiwanese (3)	16	0.12
Filipino (105)	155	1.13
Indian (8)	13	0.09
Indonesian (2)	3	0.02
Japanese (3)	13	0.09
Korean (16)	19	0.14
Laotian (1)	1	0.01
Pakistani (4)	4	0.03
Thai (1)	1	0.01
Vietnamese (12)	19	0.14
Other Asian, not specified (6)	12	0.09
Austrian	18	0.13
Belgian	39	0.29
British	112	0.83
Canadian	49	0.36
Croatian	8	0.06
Czech	46	0.34
Danish	41	0.30
Dutch	116	0.86
English	1,327	9.87
European	97	0.72
Finnish	10	0.07
French, except Basque	483	3.59
French Canadian	189	1.41
German	1,793	13.34
Greek	47	0.35
Guyanese	7	0.05
Hawaii Native/Pacific Islander:	22	0.16
Micronesian: (5)	7	0.05
Guamanian/Chamorro (5)	7	0.05
Polynesian: (4)	10	0.07
Native Hawaiian (4)	9	0.07
Samoan	1	0.01
Other Pac. Isl., not spec.	5	0.04
Hispanic or Latino:	614	4.46
Central American:	16	0.12
Costa Rican	2	0.01
Guatemalan	1	0.01
Nicaraguan	1	0.01
Panamanian	6	0.04
Salvadoran	4	0.03
Other Central American	2	0.01
Cuban	9	0.07
Dominican Republic	6	0.04
Mexican	203	1.48
Puerto Rican	281	2.04
South American:	20	0.15
Argentinean	1	0.01
Chilean	2	0.01
Colombian	5	0.04
Ecuadorian	8	0.06
Peruvian	2	0.01
Other South American	2	0.01
Other Hispanic or Latino	79	0.57
Hungarian	38	0.28
Iranian	22	0.16
Irish	1,731	12.87
Italian	600	4.46
Lithuanian	35	0.26
Maltese	8	0.06
Norwegian	124	0.92
Pennsylvania German	10	0.07
Polish	228	1.70
Portuguese	27	0.20
Russian	131	0.97
Scandinavian	25	0.19
Scotch-Irish	321	2.39
Scottish	561	4.17
Swedish	174	1.29
Swiss	20	0.15
Turkish	12	0.09
Ukrainian	61	0.45
United States or American	1,353	10.06
Welsh	98	0.73
West Indian, excl. Hispanic:	94	0.70
Barbadian	21	0.16
Haitian	5	0.04
Jamaican	58	0.43
West Indian	10	0.07
White:	10,504	76.33
Not Hispanic (9,969)	10,152	73.77
Hispanic (298)	352	2.56
Yugoslavian	14	0.10

Saint Simons

Place Type: Census Designated Place
County: Glynn
Population: 13,381

Ancestry/Race	Number	%
African American/Black:	507	3.79
Not Hispanic (486)	496	3.71
Hispanic (8)	11	0.08
African, sub-Saharan:	31	0.23
African	14	0.10
Ethiopian	17	0.13
Alaska Native tribes, specified:	1	0.01
Eskimo (1)	1	0.01
Alaska Native tribes, not specified	1	0.01
Am. Ind. or Alaska Nat., not spec.	20	0.15
American Indian tribes, specified:	30	0.22
Cherokee (2)	16	0.12
Chippewa	1	0.01
Choctaw (1)	1	0.01
Comanche	1	0.01
Delaware	1	0.01
Iroquois	2	0.01
Lumbee (1)	1	0.01
Sioux	2	0.01
Yaqui	1	0.01
All other tribes (2)	4	0.03
American Indian tribes, not spec.	1	0.01
Arab:	44	0.33
Egyptian	8	0.06
Lebanese	36	0.27
Asian:	160	1.20
Chinese, ex. Taiwanese (30)	35	0.26
Filipino (21)	26	0.19
Indian (19)	21	0.16
Indonesian (1)	1	0.01
Japanese (24)	33	0.25
Korean (6)	11	0.08
Thai (4)	5	0.04
Vietnamese (13)	21	0.16
Other Asian, not specified (4)	7	0.05
Austrian	50	0.37
British	331	2.46
Canadian	209	1.55
Croatian	8	0.06
Czech	6	0.04
Czechoslovakian	114	0.85
Danish	17	0.13
Dutch	219	1.63
Eastern European	7	0.05
English	3,196	23.77
European	189	1.41
Finnish	17	0.13
French, except Basque	546	4.06
French Canadian	78	0.58
German	1,585	11.79
Greek	11	0.08
Guyanese	33	0.25
Hawaii Native/Pacific Islander:	6	0.04
Micronesian: (1)	1	0.01
Guamanian/Chamorro (1)	1	0.01
Polynesian: (1)	2	0.01
Native Hawaiian (1)	2	0.01
Other Pac. Isl., not spec.	3	0.02
Hispanic or Latino:	253	1.89
Central American:	11	0.08
Guatemalan	1	0.01
Honduran	1	0.01
Salvadoran	8	0.06
Other Central American	1	0.01
Cuban	14	0.10
Dominican Republic	3	0.02
Mexican	138	1.03
Puerto Rican	27	0.20
South American:	19	0.14
Bolivian	1	0.01
Chilean	2	0.01
Colombian	6	0.04
Ecuadorian	3	0.02
Peruvian	6	0.04
Venezuelan	1	0.01
Other Hispanic or Latino	41	0.31
Hungarian	58	0.43
Irish	1,681	12.50
Italian	353	2.62
Lithuanian	36	0.27
Northern European	7	0.05
Norwegian	65	0.48
Pennsylvania German	8	0.06
Polish	176	1.31
Portuguese	21	0.16
Russian	50	0.37
Scandinavian	7	0.05
Scotch-Irish	728	5.41
Scottish	634	4.71
Slovak	81	0.60
Slovene	17	0.13
Swedish	220	1.64
Swiss	8	0.06
Ukrainian	72	0.54
United States or American	1,604	11.93
Welsh	236	1.75
West Indian, excl. Hispanic:	17	0.13
Jamaican	17	0.13
White:	12,689	94.83
Not Hispanic (12,426)	12,489	93.33
Hispanic (191)	200	1.49
Yugoslavian	29	0.22

Notes: 1. Figures in the "Number" column do not add up to the total population due to: a) Ancestry/Race overlap — e.g. persons can report being both White and Irish, b) persons of Hispanic origin can report being any race, c) persons reporting two ancestries are counted in both categories. 2. Numbers in parentheses indicate the number of persons reporting this ancestry/race alone, not in combination with any other ancestry/race. 3. Refer to the Explanation of Data in the front of the book for more detailed information.

Sandy Springs

Place Type: Census Designated Place
County: Fulton
Population: 85,781

Ancestry/Race	Number	%
Acadian/Cajun	12	0.01
Afghan	17	0.02
African American/Black:	10,875	12.68
Not Hispanic (10,139)	10,579	12.33
Hispanic (193)	296	0.35
African, sub-Saharan:	1,661	1.94
African	976	1.14
Ethiopian	21	0.02
Ghanian	26	0.03
Kenyan	40	0.05
Liberian	8	0.01
Nigerian	94	0.11
Sierra Leonean	17	0.02
Somalian	19	0.02
South African	315	0.37
Sudanese	23	0.03
Zimbabwean	28	0.03
Other sub-Saharan African	94	0.11
Alaska Native tribes, specified:	1	0.00
Alaska Athabascan	1	0.00
Am. Ind. or Alaska Nat., not spec.	158	0.18
Albanian	15	0.02
Alsatian	12	0.01
American Indian tribes, specified:	228	0.27
Apache	3	0.00
Blackfeet	1	0.00
Cherokee (26)	108	0.13
Chickasaw	1	0.00
Chippewa (3)	3	0.00
Choctaw (5)	15	0.02
Cree (1)	2	0.00
Creek (5)	17	0.02
Crow	1	0.00
Houma (1)	1	0.00
Iroquois (7)	12	0.01
Kiowa	1	0.00
Latin American Indians (15)	28	0.03
Lumbee	1	0.00
Osage	2	0.00
Pueblo	2	0.00
Seminole	1	0.00
Sioux (1)	4	0.00
Ute (1)	1	0.00
Yakama (1)	1	0.00
All other tribes (13)	25	0.03
American Indian tribes, not spec.	20	0.02
Arab:	358	0.42
Arab/Arabic	51	0.06
Egyptian	34	0.04
Jordanian	7	0.01
Lebanese	170	0.20
Moroccan	29	0.03
Palestinian	27	0.03
Syrian	28	0.03
Other Arab	12	0.01
Armenian	32	0.04
Asian:	3,264	3.81
Bangladeshi (9)	10	0.01
Cambodian (8)	9	0.01
Chinese, ex. Taiwanese (543)	624	0.73
Filipino (161)	200	0.23
Indian (1,154)	1,216	1.42
Indonesian (49)	56	0.07
Japanese (183)	244	0.28
Korean (342)	380	0.44
Laotian (6)	6	0.01
Malaysian (9)	28	0.03
Pakistani (36)	51	0.06
Sri Lankan (3)	3	0.00
Taiwanese (28)	32	0.04
Thai (52)	65	0.08
Vietnamese (105)	123	0.14
Other Asian, specified (15)	20	0.02
Other Asian, not specified (82)	197	0.23
Australian	60	0.07
Austrian	541	0.63
Basque	21	0.02
Belgian	67	0.08
Brazilian	720	0.84
British	675	0.79
Bulgarian	44	0.05
Canadian	302	0.35
Celtic	32	0.04
Croatian	133	0.16
Cypriot	12	0.01
Czech	133	0.16
Czechoslovakian	133	0.16
Danish	327	0.38
Dutch	1,099	1.29
Eastern European	401	0.47
English	10,833	12.67
Estonian	22	0.03
European	1,242	1.45
Finnish	113	0.13
French, except Basque	2,327	2.72
French Canadian	387	0.45
German	9,942	11.62
Greek	508	0.59
Guyanese	29	0.03
Hawaii Native/Pacific Islander:	113	0.13
Melanesian: (1)	1	0.00
Fijian (1)	1	0.00
Micronesian: (9)	13	0.02
Guamanian/Chamorro (9)	13	0.02
Polynesian: (22)	49	0.06
Native Hawaiian (5)	19	0.02
Samoan (15)	26	0.03
Other Polynesian (2)	4	0.00
Other Pac. Isl., specified	2	0.00
Other Pac. Isl., not spec. (12)	48	0.06
Hispanic or Latino:	8,514	9.93
Central American:	447	0.52
Costa Rican	25	0.03
Guatemalan	62	0.07
Honduran	48	0.06
Nicaraguan	15	0.02
Panamanian	45	0.05
Salvadoran	227	0.26
Other Central American	25	0.03
Cuban	216	0.25
Dominican Republic	56	0.07
Mexican	5,761	6.72
Puerto Rican	422	0.49
South American:	635	0.74
Argentinean	52	0.06
Bolivian	20	0.02
Chilean	26	0.03
Colombian	253	0.29
Ecuadorian	33	0.04
Paraguayan	7	0.01
Peruvian	90	0.10
Uruguayan	11	0.01
Venezuelan	116	0.14
Other South American	27	0.03
Other Hispanic or Latino	977	1.14
Hungarian	464	0.54
Iranian	109	0.13
Irish	9,377	10.96
Israeli	57	0.07
Italian	3,431	4.01
Latvian	21	0.02
Lithuanian	277	0.32
Macedonian	27	0.03
New Zealander	11	0.01
Northern European	154	0.18
Norwegian	568	0.66
Pennsylvania German	15	0.02
Polish	2,291	2.68
Portuguese	283	0.33
Romanian	280	0.33
Russian	2,350	2.75
Scandinavian	103	0.12
Scotch-Irish	2,430	2.84
Scottish	2,775	3.24
Serbian	67	0.08
Slavic	32	0.04
Slovak	148	0.17
Slovene	73	0.09
Swedish	921	1.08
Swiss	221	0.26
Turkish	305	0.36
Ukrainian	354	0.41
United States or American	5,908	6.91
Welsh	555	0.65
West Indian, excl. Hispanic:	538	0.63
Bahamian	13	0.02
Belizean	13	0.02
Bermudan	10	0.01
British West Indian	28	0.03
Haitian	106	0.12
Jamaican	244	0.29
Trinidadian and Tobagonian	37	0.04
U.S. Virgin Islander	43	0.05
West Indian	44	0.05
White:	67,806	79.05
Not Hispanic (62,657)	63,574	74.11
Hispanic (3,865)	4,232	4.93
Yugoslavian	230	0.27

Savannah

Place Type: City
County: Chatham
Population: 131,510

Ancestry/Race	Number	%
Acadian/Cajun	10	0.01
African American/Black:	75,953	57.75
Not Hispanic (74,691)	75,441	57.37
Hispanic (381)	512	0.39
African, sub-Saharan:	2,405	1.83
African	2,244	1.71
Ethiopian	50	0.04
Kenyan	9	0.01
Nigerian	61	0.05
South African	13	0.01
Sudanese	5	0.00
Ugandan	8	0.01
Other sub-Saharan African	15	0.01
Alaska Native tribes, specified:	7	0.01
Alaska Athabascan (3)	3	0.00
Eskimo (3)	4	0.00
Alaska Native tribes, not specified	1	0.00
Am. Ind. or Alaska Nat., not spec.	338	0.26
Albanian	15	0.01
Alsatian	4	0.00
American Indian tribes, specified:	399	0.30
Apache (6)	15	0.01
Blackfeet (3)	17	0.01
Cherokee (51)	206	0.16
Chickasaw (2)	2	0.00
Chippewa (5)	5	0.00
Choctaw (3)	12	0.01
Comanche (6)	6	0.00
Creek (2)	16	0.01
Crow (1)	4	0.00
Delaware (2)	5	0.00
Iroquois (4)	7	0.01
Latin American Indians (5)	15	0.01
Lumbee (1)	7	0.01
Menominee (3)	3	0.00
Navajo (15)	17	0.01
Paiute (1)	1	0.00
Pueblo (1)	4	0.00
Seminole	4	0.00
Shoshone	1	0.00
Sioux (7)	15	0.01
All other tribes (23)	37	0.03
American Indian tribes, not spec.	60	0.05
Arab:	264	0.20
Arab/Arabic	7	0.01
Egyptian	25	0.02
Lebanese	149	0.11

Notes: 1. Figures in the "Number" column do not add up to the total population due to: a) Ancestry/Race overlap — e.g. persons can report being both White and Irish, b) persons of Hispanic origin can report being any race, c) persons reporting two ancestries are counted in both categories. 2. Numbers in parentheses indicate the number of persons reporting this ancestry/race alone, not in combination with any other ancestry/race. 3. Refer to the Explanation of Data in the front of the book for more detailed information.

Ancestry/Race	Number	%
Moroccan	36	0.03
Syrian	30	0.02
Other Arab	17	0.01
Armenian	50	0.04
Asian:	2,525	1.92
Cambodian (1)	1	0.00
Chinese, ex. Taiwanese (321)	400	0.30
Filipino (227)	308	0.23
Indian (340)	419	0.32
Indonesian (11)	19	0.01
Japanese (96)	163	0.12
Korean (298)	383	0.29
Laotian (20)	23	0.02
Malaysian (2)	2	0.00
Pakistani (18)	22	0.02
Sri Lankan (5)	5	0.00
Taiwanese (13)	19	0.01
Thai (51)	70	0.05
Vietnamese (518)	540	0.41
Other Asian, specified (1)	28	0.02
Other Asian, not specified (44)	123	0.09
Australian	22	0.02
Austrian	251	0.19
Belgian	54	0.04
Brazilian	17	0.01
British	400	0.30
Canadian	230	0.17
Celtic	5	0.00
Croatian	43	0.03
Czech	87	0.07
Czechoslovakian	109	0.08
Danish	156	0.12
Dutch	701	0.53
Eastern European	26	0.02
English	7,701	5.85
Estonian	8	0.01
European	775	0.59
Finnish	29	0.02
French, except Basque	1,742	1.32
French Canadian	376	0.29
German	6,823	5.18
Greek	461	0.35
Guyanese	13	0.01
Hawaii Native/Pacific Islander:	240	0.18
Micronesian: (28)	53	0.04
Guamanian/Chamorro (19)	37	0.03
Other Micronesian (9)	16	0.01
Polynesian: (43)	104	0.08
Native Hawaiian (15)	59	0.04
Samoan (26)	38	0.03
Tongan (1)	1	0.00
Other Polynesian (1)	6	0.00
Other Pac. Isl., specified	27	0.02
Other Pac. Isl., not spec. (18)	56	0.04
Hispanic or Latino:	2,938	2.23
Central American:	181	0.14
Costa Rican	15	0.01
Guatemalan	9	0.01
Honduran	21	0.02
Nicaraguan	2	0.00
Panamanian	124	0.09
Salvadoran	8	0.01
Other Central American	2	0.00
Cuban	150	0.11
Dominican Republic	38	0.03
Mexican	1,104	0.84
Puerto Rican	803	0.61
South American:	154	0.12
Argentinean	7	0.01
Bolivian	7	0.01
Chilean	8	0.01
Colombian	61	0.05
Ecuadorian	5	0.00
Paraguayan	4	0.00
Peruvian	28	0.02
Venezuelan	29	0.02
Other South American	5	0.00
Other Hispanic or Latino	508	0.39
Hungarian	300	0.23
Iranian	145	0.11
Irish	7,770	5.90
Italian	2,171	1.65
Latvian	11	0.01
Lithuanian	164	0.12
Maltese	6	0.00
New Zealander	31	0.02
Northern European	16	0.01
Norwegian	442	0.34
Pennsylvania German	5	0.00
Polish	1,019	0.77
Portuguese	90	0.07
Romanian	64	0.05
Russian	492	0.37
Scandinavian	14	0.01
Scotch-Irish	1,663	1.26
Scottish	2,454	1.86
Slavic	18	0.01
Slovak	33	0.03
Swedish	526	0.40
Swiss	168	0.13
Turkish	43	0.03
Ukrainian	101	0.08
United States or American	6,758	5.14
Welsh	378	0.29
West Indian, excl. Hispanic:	660	0.50
Bahamian	31	0.02
Barbadian	4	0.00
Belizean	30	0.02
British West Indian	20	0.02
Haitian	134	0.10
Jamaican	225	0.17
Trinidadian and Tobagonian	116	0.09
U.S. Virgin Islander	74	0.06
West Indian	26	0.02
White:	52,295	39.77
Not Hispanic (49,903)	50,939	38.73
Hispanic (1,205)	1,356	1.03
Yugoslavian	6	0.00

Smyrna

Place Type: City
County: Cobb
Population: 40,999

Ancestry/Race	Number	%
African American/Black:	11,526	28.11
Not Hispanic (10,963)	11,278	27.51
Hispanic (184)	248	0.60
African, sub-Saharan:	904	2.22
African	615	1.51
Ethiopian	18	0.04
Kenyan	107	0.26
Nigerian	99	0.24
South African	18	0.04
Sudanese	11	0.03
Other sub-Saharan African	36	0.09
Am. Ind. or Alaska Nat., not spec.	121	0.30
Alsatian	5	0.01
American Indian tribes, specified:	223	0.54
Apache (2)	5	0.01
Blackfeet (2)	2	0.00
Cherokee (18)	91	0.22
Chickasaw	1	0.00
Chippewa (8)	8	0.02
Choctaw (1)	6	0.01
Comanche	1	0.00
Creek (12)	13	0.03
Crow	4	0.01
Delaware (1)	1	0.00
Iroquois (2)	6	0.01
Latin American Indians (45)	55	0.13
Lumbee (1)	1	0.00
Navajo (1)	1	0.00
Osage	1	0.00
Pueblo (3)	5	0.01
Puget Sound Salish	1	0.00
Seminole	3	0.01
Sioux (2)	5	0.01
Tohono O'Odham (3)	4	0.01
Yakama (1)	1	0.00
All other tribes (2)	8	0.02
American Indian tribes, not spec.	22	0.05
Arab:	153	0.38
Arab/Arabic	33	0.08
Egyptian	27	0.07
Iraqi	9	0.02
Lebanese	63	0.15
Syrian	21	0.05
Asian:	1,839	4.49
Bangladeshi (2)	6	0.01
Cambodian (30)	43	0.10
Chinese, ex. Taiwanese (213)	248	0.60
Filipino (105)	141	0.34
Hmong (1)	1	0.00
Indian (642)	690	1.68
Indonesian (5)	9	0.02
Japanese (56)	80	0.20
Korean (203)	223	0.54
Laotian (9)	10	0.02
Malaysian (1)	2	0.00
Pakistani (31)	33	0.08
Sri Lankan (1)	2	0.00
Taiwanese (13)	14	0.03
Thai (13)	18	0.04
Vietnamese (189)	213	0.52
Other Asian, specified (25)	32	0.08
Other Asian, not specified (38)	74	0.18
Australian	8	0.02
Austrian	73	0.18
Belgian	32	0.08
Brazilian	72	0.18
British	269	0.66
Bulgarian	39	0.10
Canadian	68	0.17
Croatian	24	0.06
Czech	62	0.15
Czechoslovakian	66	0.16
Danish	60	0.15
Dutch	366	0.90
Eastern European	20	0.05
English	3,502	8.59
European	381	0.93
Finnish	18	0.04
French, except Basque	703	1.72
French Canadian	204	0.50
German	3,446	8.45
Greek	116	0.28
Guyanese	9	0.02
Hawaii Native/Pacific Islander:	74	0.18
Micronesian: (4)	6	0.01
Guamanian/Chamorro (4)	6	0.01
Polynesian: (8)	15	0.04
Native Hawaiian (5)	12	0.03
Samoan (2)	2	0.00
Other Polynesian (1)	1	0.00
Other Pac. Isl., specified	7	0.02
Other Pac. Isl., not spec. (2)	46	0.11
Hispanic or Latino:	5,659	13.80
Central American:	328	0.80
Costa Rican	9	0.02
Guatemalan	25	0.06
Honduran	46	0.11
Nicaraguan	14	0.03
Panamanian	40	0.10
Salvadoran	183	0.45
Other Central American	11	0.03
Cuban	125	0.30
Dominican Republic	46	0.11
Mexican	4,143	10.11
Puerto Rican	301	0.73
South American:	153	0.37
Argentinean	10	0.02
Bolivian	4	0.01
Chilean	3	0.01
Colombian	75	0.18
Ecuadorian	5	0.01
Peruvian	28	0.07
Uruguayan	1	0.00
Venezuelan	23	0.06

Notes: 1. Figures in the "Number" column do not add up to the total population due to: a) Ancestry/Race overlap — e.g. persons can report being both White and Irish, b) persons of Hispanic origin can report being any race, c) persons reporting two ancestries are counted in both categories. 2. Numbers in parentheses indicate the number of persons reporting this ancestry/race alone, not in combination with any other ancestry/race. 3. Refer to the Explanation of Data in the front of the book for more detailed information.

Ancestry/Race	Number	%
Other South American	4	0.01
Other Hispanic or Latino	563	1.37
Hungarian	77	0.19
Iranian	61	0.15
Irish	3,188	7.82
Israeli	20	0.05
Italian	973	2.39
Latvian	9	0.02
Lithuanian	30	0.07
Northern European	20	0.05
Norwegian	142	0.35
Polish	622	1.53
Portuguese	43	0.11
Romanian	38	0.09
Russian	250	0.61
Scandinavian	38	0.09
Scotch-Irish	692	1.70
Scottish	707	1.73
Serbian	11	0.03
Slavic	56	0.14
Slovak	38	0.09
Slovene	8	0.02
Soviet Union	8	0.02
Swedish	191	0.47
Swiss	74	0.18
Turkish	47	0.12
Ukrainian	50	0.12
United States or American	3,223	7.90
Welsh	280	0.69
West Indian, excl. Hispanic:	474	1.16
Bahamian	15	0.04
Barbadian	8	0.02
British West Indian	17	0.04
Haitian	164	0.40
Jamaican	174	0.43
Trinidadian and Tobagonian	18	0.04
U.S. Virgin Islander	20	0.05
West Indian	58	0.14
White:	25,114	61.26
Not Hispanic (21,936)	22,413	54.67
Hispanic (2,432)	2,701	6.59
Yugoslavian	71	0.17

Snellville

Place Type: City
County: Gwinnett
Population: 15,351

Ancestry/Race	Number	%
African American/Black:	882	5.75
Not Hispanic (823)	874	5.69
Hispanic (5)	8	0.05
African, sub-Saharan:	81	0.54
African	81	0.54
Am. Ind. or Alaska Nat., not spec.	25	0.16
American Indian tribes, specified:	50	0.33
Blackfeet	1	0.01
Cherokee (6)	29	0.19
Chippewa (3)	4	0.03
Choctaw (1)	3	0.02
Creek	1	0.01
Iroquois (1)	2	0.01
Latin American Indians (2)	2	0.01
Lumbee (5)	5	0.03
Sioux (1)	1	0.01
All other tribes (1)	2	0.01
American Indian tribes, not spec.	3	0.02
Arab:	19	0.13
Egyptian	9	0.06
Lebanese	10	0.07
Armenian	13	0.09
Asian:	366	2.38
Bangladeshi	2	0.01
Cambodian (6)	6	0.04
Chinese, ex. Taiwanese (33)	41	0.27
Filipino (14)	28	0.18
Indian (182)	190	1.24
Japanese (5)	8	0.05
Korean (38)	46	0.30
Laotian (1)	1	0.01
Malaysian (1)	1	0.01
Pakistani (7)	13	0.08
Taiwanese (3)	3	0.02
Thai (4)	5	0.03
Vietnamese (10)	14	0.09
Other Asian, specified	1	0.01
Other Asian, not specified (4)	7	0.05
British	187	1.25
Canadian	26	0.17
Croatian	14	0.09
Czech	55	0.37
Czechoslovakian	7	0.05
Danish	39	0.26
Dutch	306	2.05
Eastern European	11	0.07
English	2,245	15.01
European	150	1.00
French, except Basque	288	1.93
French Canadian	124	0.83
German	1,781	11.91
Greek	44	0.29
Guyanese	13	0.09
Hawaii Native/Pacific Islander:	9	0.06
Micronesian: (1)	1	0.01
Guamanian/Chamorro (1)	1	0.01
Polynesian: (2)	7	0.05
Native Hawaiian (1)	5	0.03
Other Polynesian (1)	2	0.01
Other Pac. Isl., not spec.	1	0.01
Hispanic or Latino:	628	4.09
Central American:	21	0.14
Guatemalan	1	0.01
Honduran	2	0.01
Nicaraguan	8	0.05
Panamanian	7	0.05
Salvadoran	3	0.02
Cuban	42	0.27
Dominican Republic	12	0.08
Mexican	334	2.18
Puerto Rican	69	0.45
South American:	66	0.43
Argentinean	1	0.01
Colombian	28	0.18
Ecuadorian	6	0.04
Peruvian	10	0.07
Uruguayan	3	0.02
Venezuelan	11	0.07
Other South American	7	0.05
Other Hispanic or Latino	84	0.55
Hungarian	76	0.51
Iranian	9	0.06
Irish	1,512	10.11
Israeli	19	0.13
Italian	655	4.38
Latvian	9	0.06
Lithuanian	23	0.15
Norwegian	65	0.43
Pennsylvania German	17	0.11
Polish	390	2.61
Portuguese	27	0.18
Romanian	20	0.13
Russian	89	0.60
Scandinavian	24	0.16
Scotch-Irish	467	3.12
Scottish	434	2.90
Slovak	31	0.21
Swedish	92	0.62
Swiss	52	0.35
Ukrainian	33	0.22
United States or American	2,309	15.44
Welsh	136	0.91
West Indian, excl. Hispanic:	116	0.78
Barbadian	10	0.07
Haitian	6	0.04
Jamaican	74	0.49
Trinidadian and Tobagonian	11	0.07
West Indian	15	0.10
White:	13,896	90.52
Not Hispanic (13,400)	13,506	87.98
Hispanic (361)	390	2.54

Statesboro

Place Type: City
County: Bulloch
Population: 22,698

Ancestry/Race	Number	%
African American/Black:	9,253	40.77
Not Hispanic (9,071)	9,176	40.43
Hispanic (65)	77	0.34
African, sub-Saharan:	636	2.81
African	493	2.18
Ethiopian	18	0.08
Nigerian	125	0.55
Alaska Native tribes, specified:	1	0.00
Aleut	1	0.00
Am. Ind. or Alaska Nat., not spec.	32	0.14
Albanian	12	0.05
American Indian tribes, specified:	23	0.10
Cherokee (2)	17	0.07
Choctaw	1	0.00
Latin American Indians (1)	1	0.00
Lumbee	1	0.00
Sioux	1	0.00
All other tribes (1)	2	0.01
American Indian tribes, not spec.	4	0.02
Arab:	63	0.28
Egyptian	29	0.13
Lebanese	23	0.10
Syrian	11	0.05
Asian:	402	1.77
Cambodian (2)	3	0.01
Chinese, ex. Taiwanese (67)	80	0.35
Filipino (20)	41	0.18
Indian (76)	94	0.41
Indonesian (1)	1	0.00
Japanese (45)	57	0.25
Korean (36)	54	0.24
Laotian (3)	3	0.01
Pakistani	1	0.00
Taiwanese (3)	3	0.01
Thai (7)	7	0.03
Vietnamese (16)	21	0.09
Other Asian, specified (1)	1	0.00
Other Asian, not specified (18)	36	0.16
Brazilian	15	0.07
British	113	0.50
Canadian	33	0.15
Croatian	10	0.04
Czechoslovakian	8	0.04
Danish	26	0.11
Dutch	130	0.57
English	1,702	7.52
European	400	1.77
Finnish	8	0.04
French, except Basque	309	1.37
French Canadian	15	0.07
German	1,324	5.85
Greek	61	0.27
Hawaii Native/Pacific Islander:	38	0.17
Micronesian: (2)	8	0.04
Guamanian/Chamorro (2)	8	0.04
Polynesian: (4)	11	0.05
Native Hawaiian (3)	9	0.04
Samoan	1	0.00
Other Polynesian (1)	1	0.00
Other Pac. Isl., not spec. (6)	19	0.08
Hispanic or Latino:	487	2.15
Central American:	31	0.14
Costa Rican	5	0.02
Guatemalan	1	0.00
Honduran	12	0.05
Nicaraguan	2	0.01
Panamanian	6	0.03
Salvadoran	2	0.01
Other Central American	3	0.01
Cuban	37	0.16
Dominican Republic	5	0.02

Notes: 1. Figures in the "Number" column do not add up to the total population due to: a) Ancestry/Race overlap — e.g. persons can report being both White and Irish, b) persons of Hispanic origin can report being any race, c) persons reporting two ancestries are counted in both categories. 2. Numbers in parentheses indicate the number of persons reporting this ancestry/race alone, not in combination with any other ancestry/race. 3. Refer to the Explanation of Data in the front of the book for more detailed information.

Mexican	235	1.04
Puerto Rican	77	0.34
South American:	24	0.11
Argentinean	1	0.00
Chilean	2	0.01
Colombian	10	0.04
Ecuadorian	2	0.01
Venezuelan	8	0.04
Other South American	1	0.00
Other Hispanic or Latino	78	0.34
Hungarian	14	0.06
Irish	1,714	7.57
Italian	442	1.95
Latvian	9	0.04
Lithuanian	10	0.04
Norwegian	122	0.54
Polish	108	0.48
Russian	81	0.36
Scandinavian	30	0.13
Scotch-Irish	432	1.91
Scottish	302	1.33
Slavic	11	0.05
Slovak	9	0.04
Swedish	102	0.45
Swiss	18	0.08
Turkish	12	0.05
United States or American	1,090	4.82
Welsh	97	0.43
West Indian, excl. Hispanic:	113	0.50
Bahamian	18	0.08
Belizean	6	0.03
British West Indian	9	0.04
Haitian	11	0.05
Jamaican	69	0.30
White:	12,953	57.07
Not Hispanic (12,571)	12,735	56.11
Hispanic (187)	218	0.96

Sugar Hill

Place Type: City
County: Gwinnett
Population: 11,399

Ancestry/Race	Number	%
African American/Black:	570	5.00
Not Hispanic (524)	558	4.90
Hispanic (9)	12	0.11
African, sub-Saharan:	105	0.93
African	77	0.69
Cape Verdean	11	0.10
Nigerian	17	0.15
Am. Ind. or Alaska Nat., not spec.	26	0.23
American Indian tribes, specified:	33	0.29
Blackfeet	2	0.02
Cherokee (2)	19	0.17
Creek (1)	1	0.01
Iroquois (1)	3	0.03
Latin American Indians	3	0.03
Seminole	1	0.01
Sioux (1)	1	0.01
All other tribes (3)	3	0.03
American Indian tribes, not spec.	1	0.01
Arab:	33	0.29
Arab/Arabic	8	0.07
Egyptian	8	0.07
Other Arab	17	0.15
Asian:	240	2.11
Bangladeshi (3)	3	0.03
Cambodian	2	0.02
Chinese, ex. Taiwanese (22)	25	0.22
Filipino (7)	18	0.16
Indian (36)	37	0.32
Japanese (16)	27	0.24
Korean (63)	70	0.61
Laotian	3	0.03
Thai (1)	4	0.04
Vietnamese (33)	35	0.31
Other Asian, not specified (4)	16	0.14
Austrian	29	0.26
Belgian	22	0.20
British	46	0.41
Canadian	23	0.20
Celtic	6	0.05
Croatian	12	0.11
Czech	19	0.17
Czechoslovakian	9	0.08
Danish	36	0.32
Dutch	210	1.87
English	1,278	11.38
European	192	1.71
Finnish	19	0.17
French, except Basque	307	2.73
French Canadian	77	0.69
German	1,396	12.43
Greek	8	0.07
Guyanese	24	0.21
Hawaii Native/Pacific Islander:	8	0.07
Melanesian:	1	0.01
Other Melanesian	1	0.01
Polynesian: (1)	6	0.05
Native Hawaiian (1)	6	0.05
Other Pac. Isl., not spec. (1)	1	0.01
Hispanic or Latino:	1,039	9.11
Central American:	28	0.25
Honduran	4	0.04
Nicaraguan	6	0.05
Panamanian	2	0.02
Salvadoran	16	0.14
Cuban	15	0.13
Mexican	619	5.43
Puerto Rican	77	0.68
South American:	122	1.07
Argentinean	18	0.16
Bolivian	1	0.01
Chilean	3	0.03
Colombian	63	0.55
Ecuadorian	3	0.03
Peruvian	12	0.11
Uruguayan	3	0.03
Venezuelan	19	0.17
Other Hispanic or Latino	178	1.56
Hungarian	81	0.72
Iranian	80	0.71
Irish	1,488	13.25
Italian	509	4.53
Lithuanian	9	0.08
Norwegian	189	1.68
Polish	222	1.98
Portuguese	24	0.21
Russian	25	0.22
Scandinavian	25	0.22
Scotch-Irish	190	1.69
Scottish	200	1.78
Slavic	7	0.06
Slovak	10	0.09
Swedish	81	0.72
Swiss	11	0.10
Turkish	9	0.08
Ukrainian	20	0.18
United States or American	1,590	14.16
Welsh	52	0.46
West Indian, excl. Hispanic:	78	0.69
Haitian	33	0.29
Trinidadian and Tobagonian	35	0.31
West Indian	10	0.09
White:	10,172	89.24
Not Hispanic (9,496)	9,598	84.20
Hispanic (502)	574	5.04

Thomasville

Place Type: City
County: Thomas
Population: 18,162

Ancestry/Race	Number	%
African American/Black:	10,123	55.74
Not Hispanic (9,990)	10,043	55.30
Hispanic (70)	80	0.44
African, sub-Saharan:	167	0.92
African	162	0.89
Other sub-Saharan African	5	0.03
Am. Ind. or Alaska Nat., not spec.	41	0.23
American Indian tribes, specified:	56	0.31
Blackfeet	3	0.02
Cherokee (10)	29	0.16
Chickasaw	2	0.01
Choctaw (1)	1	0.01
Cree	1	0.01
Creek (9)	12	0.07
Iroquois	1	0.01
Navajo	2	0.01
Seminole	2	0.01
Sioux	1	0.01
All other tribes	2	0.01
American Indian tribes, not spec.	6	0.03
Asian:	138	0.76
Chinese, ex. Taiwanese (18)	20	0.11
Filipino (8)	12	0.07
Indian (48)	71	0.39
Japanese (6)	9	0.05
Korean (7)	12	0.07
Thai (1)	1	0.01
Vietnamese (8)	8	0.04
Other Asian, specified	5	0.03
Austrian	12	0.07
British	38	0.21
Danish	25	0.14
Dutch	147	0.81
English	1,163	6.40
European	76	0.42
French, except Basque	220	1.21
French Canadian	7	0.04
German	765	4.21
Greek	55	0.30
Hawaii Native/Pacific Islander:	8	0.04
Micronesian: (1)	1	0.01
Guamanian/Chamorro (1)	1	0.01
Polynesian: (1)	2	0.01
Native Hawaiian (1)	2	0.01
Other Pac. Isl., specified	5	0.03
Hispanic or Latino:	232	1.28
Central American:	4	0.02
Salvadoran	4	0.02
Cuban	27	0.15
Dominican Republic	1	0.01
Mexican	80	0.44
Puerto Rican	32	0.18
South American:	3	0.02
Colombian	1	0.01
Venezuelan	2	0.01
Other Hispanic or Latino	85	0.47
Irish	932	5.13
Israeli	17	0.09
Italian	140	0.77
Norwegian	24	0.13
Polish	91	0.50
Russian	20	0.11
Scotch-Irish	283	1.56
Scottish	357	1.97
Slovak	8	0.04
Swedish	23	0.13
Swiss	47	0.26
United States or American	1,670	9.20
Welsh	50	0.28
White:	7,873	43.35
Not Hispanic (7,677)	7,756	42.70
Hispanic (102)	117	0.64

Tifton

Place Type: City
County: Tift
Population: 15,060

Ancestry/Race	Number	%
African American/Black:	4,804	31.90
Not Hispanic (4,716)	4,759	31.60
Hispanic (39)	45	0.30

Notes: 1. Figures in the "Number" column do not add up to the total population due to: a) Ancestry/Race overlap — e.g. persons can report being both White and Irish, b) persons of Hispanic origin can report being any race, c) persons reporting two ancestries are counted in both categories. 2. Numbers in parentheses indicate the number of persons reporting this ancestry/race alone, not in combination with any other ancestry/race. 3. Refer to the Explanation of Data in the front of the book for more detailed information.

Ancestry/Race	Number	%
African, sub-Saharan:	268	1.80
African	268	1.80
Alaska Native tribes, specified:	1	0.01
Alaska Athabascan (1)	1	0.01
Am. Ind. or Alaska Nat., not spec.	24	0.16
American Indian tribes, specified:	18	0.12
Cherokee (3)	9	0.06
Chippewa (1)	1	0.01
Creek	1	0.01
Latin American Indians (5)	5	0.03
Ottawa (1)	1	0.01
All other tribes (1)	1	0.01
American Indian tribes, not spec.	7	0.05
Arab:	12	0.08
Lebanese	12	0.08
Asian:	263	1.75
Cambodian (4)	4	0.03
Chinese, ex. Taiwanese (38)	39	0.26
Filipino (8)	8	0.05
Indian (92)	95	0.63
Japanese (15)	19	0.13
Korean (12)	14	0.09
Pakistani (13)	15	0.10
Thai (1)	1	0.01
Vietnamese (58)	59	0.39
Other Asian, not specified (4)	9	0.06
British	17	0.11
Bulgarian	9	0.06
Canadian	33	0.22
Croatian	17	0.11
Czech	18	0.12
Danish	14	0.09
Dutch	99	0.67
English	1,146	7.71
European	253	1.70
French, except Basque	151	1.02
French Canadian	21	0.14
German	535	3.60
Hawaii Native/Pacific Islander:	9	0.06
Micronesian: (3)	3	0.02
Guamanian/Chamorro (2)	2	0.01
Other Micronesian (1)	1	0.01
Polynesian: (2)	6	0.04
Samoan (2)	6	0.04
Hispanic or Latino:	1,139	7.56
Central American:	18	0.12
Guatemalan	3	0.02
Honduran	7	0.05
Nicaraguan	1	0.01
Salvadoran	7	0.05
Cuban	1	0.01
Dominican Republic	1	0.01
Mexican	913	6.06
Puerto Rican	29	0.19
South American:	18	0.12
Bolivian	3	0.02
Colombian	14	0.09
Peruvian	1	0.01
Other Hispanic or Latino	159	1.06
Hungarian	42	0.28
Iranian	9	0.06
Irish	888	5.97
Italian	232	1.56
Norwegian	9	0.06
Polish	117	0.79
Russian	8	0.05
Scotch-Irish	260	1.75
Scottish	121	0.81
Swedish	27	0.18
Turkish	11	0.07
United States or American	2,225	14.97
Welsh	56	0.38
White:	9,298	61.74
Not Hispanic (8,852)	8,906	59.14
Hispanic (374)	392	2.60
Yugoslavian	12	0.08

Tucker

Place Type: Census Designated Place
County: De Kalb
Population: 26,532

Ancestry/Race	Number	%
Acadian/Cajun	28	0.11
Afghan	7	0.03
African American/Black:	3,861	14.55
Not Hispanic (3,670)	3,784	14.26
Hispanic (59)	77	0.29
African, sub-Saharan:	327	1.23
African	99	0.37
Ethiopian	206	0.77
Somalian	11	0.04
South African	7	0.03
Other sub-Saharan African	4	0.02
Alaska Native tribes, specified:	1	0.00
Aleut	1	0.00
Am. Ind. or Alaska Nat., not spec.	53	0.20
American Indian tribes, specified:	77	0.29
Blackfeet	3	0.01
Cherokee (6)	32	0.12
Chippewa	1	0.00
Choctaw (1)	4	0.02
Creek (2)	6	0.02
Iroquois	2	0.01
Latin American Indians (8)	12	0.05
Lumbee (2)	2	0.01
Navajo (2)	4	0.02
Sioux (4)	5	0.02
Ute	1	0.00
All other tribes (2)	5	0.02
American Indian tribes, not spec.	13	0.05
Arab:	211	0.79
Arab/Arabic	86	0.32
Egyptian	6	0.02
Lebanese	62	0.23
Moroccan	57	0.21
Armenian	26	0.10
Asian:	2,291	8.63
Bangladeshi (18)	23	0.09
Cambodian (79)	83	0.31
Chinese, ex. Taiwanese (320)	357	1.35
Filipino (48)	61	0.23
Indian (551)	585	2.20
Indonesian (14)	16	0.06
Japanese (27)	40	0.15
Korean (429)	445	1.68
Laotian (42)	44	0.17
Malaysian	6	0.02
Pakistani (38)	46	0.17
Sri Lankan (9)	9	0.03
Taiwanese (62)	73	0.28
Thai (25)	29	0.11
Vietnamese (368)	391	1.47
Other Asian, specified (1)	5	0.02
Other Asian, not specified (24)	78	0.29
Australian	7	0.03
Austrian	62	0.23
Belgian	16	0.06
British	265	1.00
Canadian	62	0.23
Croatian	12	0.05
Czech	79	0.30
Czechoslovakian	40	0.15
Danish	144	0.54
Dutch	276	1.04
Eastern European	10	0.04
English	3,316	12.46
European	427	1.60
Finnish	37	0.14
French, except Basque	706	2.65
French Canadian	88	0.33
German	2,659	9.99
Greek	149	0.56
Hawaii Native/Pacific Islander:	35	0.13
Micronesian: (4)	5	0.02
Guamanian/Chamorro (4)	5	0.02
Polynesian: (6)	16	0.06
Native Hawaiian (5)	7	0.03
Samoan (1)	8	0.03
Other Polynesian	1	0.00
Other Pac. Isl., not spec. (3)	14	0.05
Hispanic or Latino:	2,047	7.72
Central American:	480	1.81
Costa Rican	4	0.02
Guatemalan	137	0.52
Honduran	45	0.17
Nicaraguan	9	0.03
Panamanian	10	0.04
Salvadoran	252	0.95
Other Central American	23	0.09
Cuban	133	0.50
Dominican Republic	57	0.21
Mexican	704	2.65
Puerto Rican	137	0.52
South American:	191	0.72
Argentinean	4	0.02
Chilean	13	0.05
Colombian	94	0.35
Ecuadorian	13	0.05
Paraguayan	2	0.01
Peruvian	30	0.11
Uruguayan	6	0.02
Venezuelan	20	0.08
Other South American	9	0.03
Other Hispanic or Latino	345	1.30
Hungarian	108	0.41
Iranian	59	0.22
Irish	2,706	10.17
Italian	764	2.87
Lithuanian	51	0.19
Macedonian	9	0.03
New Zealander	10	0.04
Northern European	9	0.03
Norwegian	139	0.52
Pennsylvania German	8	0.03
Polish	315	1.18
Portuguese	50	0.19
Romanian	97	0.36
Russian	314	1.18
Scandinavian	6	0.02
Scotch-Irish	1,004	3.77
Scottish	826	3.10
Serbian	45	0.17
Slavic	5	0.02
Slovak	7	0.03
Swedish	299	1.12
Swiss	98	0.37
Ukrainian	134	0.50
United States or American	2,241	8.42
Welsh	116	0.44
West Indian, excl. Hispanic:	173	0.65
Bahamian	11	0.04
Barbadian	42	0.16
British West Indian	30	0.11
Haitian	35	0.13
Jamaican	26	0.10
Trinidadian and Tobagonian	29	0.11
White:	19,820	74.70
Not Hispanic (18,239)	18,541	69.88
Hispanic (1,199)	1,279	4.82
Yugoslavian	63	0.24

Union City

Place Type: City
County: Fulton
Population: 11,621

Ancestry/Race	Number	%
African American/Black:	8,176	70.36
Not Hispanic (7,998)	8,100	69.70
Hispanic (59)	76	0.65
African, sub-Saharan:	315	2.76
African	242	2.12
Liberian	7	0.06
Nigerian	66	0.58

Notes: 1. Figures in the "Number" column do not add up to the total population due to: a) Ancestry/Race overlap — e.g. persons can report being both White and Irish, b) persons of Hispanic origin can report being any race, c) persons reporting two ancestries are counted in both categories. 2. Numbers in parentheses indicate the number of persons reporting this ancestry/race alone, not in combination with any other ancestry/race. 3. Refer to the Explanation of Data in the front of the book for more detailed information.

Ancestry/Race	Number	%
Am. Ind. or Alaska Nat., not spec.	36	0.31
American Indian tribes, specified:	40	0.34
Apache	5	0.04
Blackfeet	5	0.04
Cherokee (4)	26	0.22
All other tribes (1)	4	0.03
American Indian tribes, not spec.	11	0.09
Arab:	6	0.05
Other Arab	6	0.05
Asian:	171	1.47
Cambodian (8)	8	0.07
Chinese, ex. Taiwanese (18)	21	0.18
Filipino (9)	9	0.08
Indian (32)	41	0.35
Indonesian (1)	1	0.01
Japanese (5)	6	0.05
Korean (8)	12	0.10
Laotian (42)	42	0.36
Pakistani (1)	1	0.01
Thai (9)	10	0.09
Vietnamese (8)	9	0.08
Other Asian, not specified (6)	11	0.09
Belgian	16	0.14
British	9	0.08
Canadian	8	0.07
Dutch	8	0.07
English	430	3.76
European	38	0.33
French, except Basque	48	0.42
French Canadian	17	0.15
German	118	1.03
Guyanese	8	0.07
Hawaii Native/Pacific Islander:	8	0.07
Polynesian: (3)	3	0.03
Native Hawaiian (2)	2	0.02
Samoan (1)	1	0.01
Other Pac. Isl., not spec.	5	0.04
Hispanic or Latino:	607	5.22
Central American:	22	0.19
Costa Rican	3	0.03
Guatemalan	3	0.03
Panamanian	12	0.10
Salvadoran	2	0.02
Other Central American	2	0.02
Cuban	12	0.10
Dominican Republic	2	0.02
Mexican	467	4.02
Puerto Rican	41	0.35
South American:	6	0.05
Argentinean	1	0.01
Peruvian	2	0.02
Uruguayan	2	0.02
Venezuelan	1	0.01
Other Hispanic or Latino	57	0.49
Irish	274	2.40
Italian	23	0.20
Norwegian	9	0.08
Polish	35	0.31
Portuguese	9	0.08
Scotch-Irish	27	0.24
Scottish	96	0.84
United States or American	530	4.64
Welsh	4	0.04
West Indian, excl. Hispanic:	120	1.05
Jamaican	63	0.55
Trinidadian and Tobagonian	34	0.30
West Indian	23	0.20
White:	3,050	26.25
Not Hispanic (2,690)	2,740	23.58
Hispanic (257)	310	2.67

Valdosta

Place Type: City
County: Lowndes
Population: 43,724

Ancestry/Race	Number	%
Acadian/Cajun	5	0.01
African American/Black:	21,439	49.03
Not Hispanic (21,091)	21,297	48.71
Hispanic (110)	142	0.32
African, sub-Saharan:	818	1.87
African	793	1.81
Ethiopian	10	0.02
Nigerian	6	0.01
Somalian	9	0.02
Alaska Native tribes, specified:	1	0.00
Eskimo	1	0.00
Am. Ind. or Alaska Nat., not spec.	100	0.23
American Indian tribes, specified:	149	0.34
Apache	3	0.01
Blackfeet	4	0.01
Cherokee (18)	80	0.18
Chippewa (6)	6	0.01
Choctaw (7)	11	0.03
Creek (4)	6	0.01
Delaware	1	0.00
Iroquois	1	0.00
Latin American Indians (1)	8	0.02
Menominee (1)	1	0.00
Ottawa	1	0.00
Pueblo (2)	2	0.00
Seminole (1)	3	0.01
Sioux (1)	2	0.00
Yaqui (2)	2	0.00
All other tribes (14)	18	0.04
American Indian tribes, not spec.	18	0.04
Arab:	114	0.26
Arab/Arabic	5	0.01
Egyptian	4	0.01
Lebanese	89	0.20
Palestinian	7	0.02
Syrian	9	0.02
Asian:	776	1.77
Bangladeshi (2)	2	0.00
Cambodian (2)	3	0.01
Chinese, ex. Taiwanese (70)	89	0.20
Filipino (121)	175	0.40
Indian (224)	239	0.55
Indonesian	1	0.00
Japanese (23)	40	0.09
Korean (71)	96	0.22
Laotian (4)	4	0.01
Malaysian (1)	2	0.00
Pakistani (7)	7	0.02
Taiwanese (5)	5	0.01
Thai (23)	31	0.07
Vietnamese (28)	30	0.07
Other Asian, specified	9	0.02
Other Asian, not specified (22)	43	0.10
Austrian	66	0.15
Belgian	6	0.01
Brazilian	5	0.01
British	172	0.39
Canadian	29	0.07
Celtic	13	0.03
Croatian	32	0.07
Czech	22	0.05
Czechoslovakian	15	0.03
Danish	12	0.03
Dutch	300	0.68
Eastern European	12	0.03
English	3,523	8.04
European	490	1.12
Finnish	33	0.08
French, except Basque	718	1.64
French Canadian	57	0.13
German	2,443	5.57
Greek	144	0.33
Hawaii Native/Pacific Islander:	51	0.12
Micronesian: (4)	4	0.01
Guamanian/Chamorro (2)	2	0.00
Other Micronesian (2)	2	0.00
Polynesian: (8)	29	0.07
Native Hawaiian (6)	25	0.06
Samoan (2)	4	0.01
Other Pac. Isl., specified	7	0.02
Other Pac. Isl., not spec. (1)	11	0.03
Hispanic or Latino:	954	2.18
Central American:	82	0.19
Costa Rican	1	0.00
Guatemalan	39	0.09
Honduran	7	0.02
Nicaraguan	4	0.01
Panamanian	22	0.05
Salvadoran	5	0.01
Other Central American	4	0.01
Cuban	52	0.12
Dominican Republic	13	0.03
Mexican	354	0.81
Puerto Rican	156	0.36
South American:	62	0.14
Argentinean	1	0.00
Bolivian	8	0.02
Chilean	3	0.01
Colombian	43	0.10
Paraguayan	1	0.00
Peruvian	1	0.00
Venezuelan	1	0.00
Other South American	4	0.01
Other Hispanic or Latino	235	0.54
Hungarian	80	0.18
Irish	2,623	5.99
Italian	853	1.95
Lithuanian	15	0.03
Luxemburger	6	0.01
Maltese	4	0.01
Northern European	55	0.13
Norwegian	179	0.41
Polish	281	0.64
Portuguese	33	0.08
Russian	77	0.18
Scandinavian	25	0.06
Scotch-Irish	925	2.11
Scottish	821	1.87
Serbian	6	0.01
Slovak	32	0.07
Swedish	132	0.30
Swiss	43	0.10
Ukrainian	41	0.09
United States or American	3,338	7.62
Welsh	123	0.28
West Indian, excl. Hispanic:	72	0.16
Belizean	23	0.05
British West Indian	17	0.04
Jamaican	32	0.07
White:	21,237	48.57
Not Hispanic (20,440)	20,755	47.47
Hispanic (420)	482	1.10
Yugoslavian	5	0.01

Vidalia

Place Type: City
County: Toombs
Population: 10,491

Ancestry/Race	Number	%
African American/Black:	3,895	37.13
Not Hispanic (3,859)	3,883	37.01
Hispanic (10)	12	0.11
African, sub-Saharan:	192	1.81
African	192	1.81
Am. Ind. or Alaska Nat., not spec.	18	0.17
American Indian tribes, specified:	25	0.24
Blackfeet	2	0.02
Cherokee (7)	15	0.14
Chippewa (4)	4	0.04
Latin American Indians	4	0.04
Asian:	101	0.96
Chinese, ex. Taiwanese (22)	22	0.21
Filipino (26)	32	0.31
Indian (28)	28	0.27
Indonesian (3)	3	0.03
Korean (8)	8	0.08
Vietnamese (4)	4	0.04
Other Asian, specified	2	0.02
Other Asian, not specified (2)	2	0.02
British	6	0.06

Notes: 1. Figures in the "Number" column do not add up to the total population due to: a) Ancestry/Race overlap — e.g. persons can report being both White and Irish, b) persons of Hispanic origin can report being any race, c) persons reporting two ancestries are counted in both categories. 2. Numbers in parentheses indicate the number of persons reporting this ancestry/race alone, not in combination with any other ancestry/race. 3. Refer to the Explanation of Data in the front of the book for more detailed information.

Canadian	36	0.34
Czechoslovakian	13	0.12
Danish	18	0.17
Dutch	34	0.32
English	852	8.03
European	104	0.98
French, except Basque	178	1.68
French Canadian	38	0.36
German	340	3.21
Greek	11	0.10
Hawaii Native/Pacific Islander:	2	0.02
Other Pac. Isl., specified	2	0.02
Hispanic or Latino:	340	3.24
Central American:	10	0.10
Guatemalan	1	0.01
Honduran	3	0.03
Nicaraguan	6	0.06
Cuban	15	0.14
Dominican Republic	2	0.02
Mexican	255	2.43
Puerto Rican	19	0.18
South American:	3	0.03
Colombian	2	0.02
Venezuelan	1	0.01
Other Hispanic or Latino	36	0.34
Irish	600	5.66
Italian	45	0.42
Northern European	18	0.17
Norwegian	9	0.08
Portuguese	17	0.16
Romanian	7	0.07
Russian	6	0.06
Scandinavian	6	0.06
Scotch-Irish	130	1.23
Scottish	143	1.35
Slavic	5	0.05
Swedish	27	0.25
United States or American	2,152	20.29
Welsh	20	0.19
White:	6,314	60.18
Not Hispanic (6,129)	6,177	58.88
Hispanic (125)	137	1.31
Yugoslavian	6	0.06

Warner Robins

Place Type: City
County: Houston
Population: 48,804

Ancestry/Race	Number	%
Acadian/Cajun	16	0.03
African American/Black:	16,032	32.85
Not Hispanic (15,504)	15,834	32.44
Hispanic (159)	198	0.41
African, sub-Saharan:	692	1.42
African	677	1.38
Nigerian	5	0.01
Somalian	10	0.02
Alaska Native tribes, specified:	2	0.00
Eskimo (1)	1	0.00
Tlingit-Haida	1	0.00
Am. Ind. or Alaska Nat., not spec.	130	0.27
Albanian	12	0.02
American Indian tribes, specified:	258	0.53
Apache (4)	11	0.02
Blackfeet (2)	11	0.02
Cherokee (41)	125	0.26
Chickasaw (1)	1	0.00
Chippewa (6)	6	0.01
Choctaw (4)	11	0.02
Comanche	1	0.00
Creek (14)	23	0.05
Crow	2	0.00
Iroquois	5	0.01
Latin American Indians (5)	10	0.02
Lumbee (5)	5	0.01
Navajo (3)	11	0.02
Pueblo (1)	2	0.00
Seminole (2)	3	0.01
Sioux (6)	14	0.03
Yakama	1	0.00
All other tribes (3)	16	0.03
American Indian tribes, not spec.	36	0.07
Arab:	71	0.15
Arab/Arabic	20	0.04
Lebanese	51	0.10
Armenian	7	0.01
Asian:	1,232	2.52
Bangladeshi (1)	1	0.00
Cambodian (4)	4	0.01
Chinese, ex. Taiwanese (73)	100	0.20
Filipino (254)	380	0.78
Indian (113)	133	0.27
Indonesian (2)	5	0.01
Japanese (54)	85	0.17
Korean (128)	184	0.38
Laotian (1)	1	0.00
Malaysian (2)	4	0.01
Pakistani (10)	10	0.02
Taiwanese	4	0.01
Thai (65)	102	0.21
Vietnamese (132)	137	0.28
Other Asian, specified (5)	13	0.03
Other Asian, not specified (20)	69	0.14
Australian	9	0.02
Austrian	39	0.08
Brazilian	18	0.04
British	290	0.59
Canadian	46	0.09
Czech	37	0.08
Czechoslovakian	44	0.09
Danish	67	0.14
Dutch	539	1.10
English	3,874	7.92
European	446	0.91
Finnish	52	0.11
French, except Basque	925	1.89
French Canadian	203	0.42
German	3,740	7.65
Greek	41	0.08
Hawaii Native/Pacific Islander:	79	0.16
Melanesian: (3)	3	0.01
Fijian (3)	3	0.01
Micronesian: (12)	13	0.03
Guamanian/Chamorro (12)	13	0.03
Polynesian: (16)	33	0.07
Native Hawaiian (11)	23	0.05
Samoan (5)	10	0.02
Other Pac. Isl., specified	3	0.01
Other Pac. Isl., not spec. (3)	27	0.06
Hispanic or Latino:	1,856	3.80
Central American:	94	0.19
Costa Rican	3	0.01
Guatemalan	4	0.01
Honduran	15	0.03
Nicaraguan	8	0.02
Panamanian	57	0.12
Salvadoran	6	0.01
Other Central American	1	0.00
Cuban	57	0.12
Dominican Republic	13	0.03
Mexican	969	1.99
Puerto Rican	282	0.58
South American:	41	0.08
Argentinean	2	0.00
Bolivian	5	0.01
Colombian	17	0.03
Ecuadorian	4	0.01
Peruvian	10	0.02
Venezuelan	1	0.00
Other South American	2	0.00
Other Hispanic or Latino	400	0.82
Hungarian	95	0.19
Iranian	8	0.02
Irish	3,747	7.66
Italian	852	1.74
Lithuanian	16	0.03
Northern European	7	0.01
Norwegian	232	0.47
Pennsylvania German	22	0.05
Polish	421	0.86
Portuguese	45	0.09
Romanian	8	0.02
Russian	79	0.16
Scandinavian	49	0.10
Scotch-Irish	892	1.82
Scottish	596	1.22
Slovak	25	0.05
Swedish	174	0.36
Swiss	61	0.12
Turkish	43	0.09
United States or American	6,408	13.11
Welsh	191	0.39
West Indian, excl. Hispanic:	132	0.27
Belizean	8	0.02
Dutch West Indian	4	0.01
Haitian	9	0.02
Jamaican	77	0.16
Trinidadian and Tobagonian	9	0.02
West Indian	25	0.05
White:	31,267	64.07
Not Hispanic (29,538)	30,155	61.79
Hispanic (966)	1,112	2.28
Yugoslavian	41	0.08

Waycross

Place Type: City
County: Ware
Population: 15,333

Ancestry/Race	Number	%
African American/Black:	8,264	53.90
Not Hispanic (8,184)	8,240	53.74
Hispanic (21)	24	0.16
African, sub-Saharan:	314	2.00
African	298	1.90
Nigerian	9	0.06
South African	7	0.04
Am. Ind. or Alaska Nat., not spec.	17	0.11
American Indian tribes, specified:	33	0.22
Blackfeet	1	0.01
Cherokee (9)	22	0.14
Choctaw	1	0.01
Creek	1	0.01
Iroquois (1)	1	0.01
Potawatomi	1	0.01
Pueblo (1)	1	0.01
Seminole	1	0.01
Sioux (1)	3	0.02
All other tribes	1	0.01
American Indian tribes, not spec.	5	0.03
Arab:	39	0.25
Iraqi	8	0.05
Other Arab	31	0.20
Asian:	120	0.78
Chinese, ex. Taiwanese (4)	7	0.05
Filipino (14)	22	0.14
Indian (31)	31	0.20
Japanese (3)	7	0.05
Korean (13)	13	0.08
Laotian (4)	4	0.03
Pakistani (4)	4	0.03
Thai (1)	2	0.01
Vietnamese (16)	24	0.16
Other Asian, not specified (3)	6	0.04
Brazilian	18	0.11
British	10	0.06
Canadian	7	0.04
Czechoslovakian	8	0.05
Dutch	130	0.83
English	872	5.55
European	29	0.18
French, except Basque	195	1.24
French Canadian	15	0.10
German	491	3.13
Hawaii Native/Pacific Islander:	10	0.07
Micronesian: (1)	1	0.01
Guamanian/Chamorro (1)	1	0.01

Notes: 1. Figures in the "Number" column do not add up to the total population due to: a) Ancestry/Race overlap — e.g. persons can report being both White and Irish, b) persons of Hispanic origin can report being any race, c) persons reporting two ancestries are counted in both categories. 2. Numbers in parentheses indicate the number of persons reporting this ancestry/race alone, not in combination with any other ancestry/race. 3. Refer to the Explanation of Data in the front of the book for more detailed information.

Polynesian: (2)	5	0.03
Native Hawaiian (1)	3	0.02
Samoan (1)	2	0.01
Other Pac. Isl., not spec.	4	0.03
Hispanic or Latino:	210	1.37
Central American:	4	0.03
Panamanian	4	0.03
Cuban	5	0.03
Mexican	101	0.66
Puerto Rican	35	0.23
South American:	6	0.04
Colombian	4	0.03
Ecuadorian	2	0.01
Other Hispanic or Latino	59	0.38
Irish	586	3.73
Italian	76	0.48
Norwegian	17	0.11
Polish	54	0.34
Portuguese	49	0.31
Russian	19	0.12
Scotch-Irish	253	1.61
Scottish	174	1.11
Swedish	36	0.23
United States or American	1,887	12.01
Welsh	55	0.35
West Indian, excl. Hispanic:	11	0.07
Bermudan	11	0.07
White:	6,885	44.90
Not Hispanic (6,716)	6,795	44.32
Hispanic (78)	90	0.59

Wilmington Island

Place Type: Census Designated Place
County: Chatham
Population: 14,213

Ancestry/Race	Number	%
African American/Black:	583	4.10
Not Hispanic (559)	583	4.10
African, sub-Saharan:	34	0.24
Cape Verdean	8	0.06
Ghanian	26	0.18
Am. Ind. or Alaska Nat., not spec.	16	0.11
American Indian tribes, specified:	39	0.27
Cherokee (6)	31	0.22
Choctaw (1)	1	0.01
Creek	1	0.01
Iroquois	1	0.01
Navajo (1)	1	0.01
Seminole	1	0.01
All other tribes (2)	3	0.02
American Indian tribes, not spec.	4	0.03
Arab:	89	0.63
Lebanese	81	0.57
Syrian	8	0.06
Asian:	405	2.85
Chinese, ex. Taiwanese (85)	100	0.70
Filipino (15)	24	0.17
Indian (44)	48	0.34
Indonesian	4	0.03
Japanese (13)	16	0.11
Korean (11)	14	0.10
Malaysian (3)	3	0.02
Pakistani (1)	2	0.01
Taiwanese (4)	4	0.03
Thai (12)	13	0.09
Vietnamese (160)	160	1.13
Other Asian, specified	1	0.01
Other Asian, not specified (5)	16	0.11
Austrian	52	0.37
Belgian	10	0.07
British	146	1.03
Canadian	58	0.41
Celtic	11	0.08
Croatian	20	0.14
Czech	29	0.20
Czechoslovakian	5	0.04
Danish	57	0.40
Dutch	190	1.34
English	2,193	15.43
European	45	0.32
Finnish	88	0.62
French, except Basque	669	4.71
French Canadian	26	0.18
German	2,131	14.99
Greek	69	0.49
Hawaii Native/Pacific Islander:	7	0.05
Micronesian: (1)	1	0.01
Guamanian/Chamorro (1)	1	0.01
Polynesian: (4)	6	0.04
Native Hawaiian (1)	3	0.02
Samoan (3)	3	0.02
Hispanic or Latino:	188	1.32
Central American:	9	0.06
Costa Rican	4	0.03
Honduran	3	0.02
Salvadoran	1	0.01
Other Central American	1	0.01
Cuban	13	0.09
Dominican Republic	3	0.02
Mexican	46	0.32
Puerto Rican	41	0.29
South American:	36	0.25
Argentinean	1	0.01
Bolivian	2	0.01
Chilean	1	0.01
Colombian	16	0.11
Ecuadorian	4	0.03
Peruvian	3	0.02
Venezuelan	9	0.06
Other Hispanic or Latino	40	0.28
Hungarian	33	0.23
Irish	2,136	15.03
Italian	586	4.12
Lithuanian	17	0.12
Norwegian	32	0.23
Polish	310	2.18
Portuguese	46	0.32
Russian	146	1.03
Scandinavian	8	0.06
Scotch-Irish	615	4.33
Scottish	779	5.48
Serbian	8	0.06
Slovak	69	0.49
Swedish	122	0.86
Swiss	41	0.29
Turkish	8	0.06
United States or American	1,789	12.59
Welsh	94	0.66
West Indian, excl. Hispanic:	48	0.34
Jamaican	31	0.22
West Indian	17	0.12
White:	13,213	92.96
Not Hispanic (12,969)	13,059	91.88
Hispanic (144)	154	1.08

Winder

Place Type: City
County: Barrow
Population: 10,201

Ancestry/Race	Number	%
African American/Black:	1,917	18.79
Not Hispanic (1,826)	1,901	18.64
Hispanic (12)	16	0.16
African, sub-Saharan:	25	0.25
African	25	0.25
Am. Ind. or Alaska Nat., not spec.	42	0.41
American Indian tribes, specified:	28	0.27
Apache (1)	2	0.02
Cherokee (10)	18	0.18
Choctaw	5	0.05
Seminole	1	0.01
Sioux (1)	1	0.01
All other tribes	1	0.01
American Indian tribes, not spec.	3	0.03
Arab:	9	0.09
Lebanese	9	0.09
Asian:	168	1.65
Cambodian (9)	10	0.10
Chinese, ex. Taiwanese (13)	21	0.21
Filipino (5)	10	0.10
Hmong (37)	41	0.40
Indian (23)	25	0.25
Indonesian (3)	5	0.05
Japanese (1)	2	0.02
Korean (1)	1	0.01
Laotian (17)	17	0.17
Thai	1	0.01
Vietnamese (8)	12	0.12
Other Asian, not specified (7)	23	0.23
British	98	0.98
Canadian	10	0.10
Czechoslovakian	16	0.16
Danish	21	0.21
Dutch	64	0.64
English	855	8.51
European	81	0.81
French, except Basque	88	0.88
French Canadian	5	0.05
German	763	7.60
Hawaii Native/Pacific Islander:	3	0.03
Micronesian: (1)	1	0.01
Other Micronesian (1)	1	0.01
Polynesian: (2)	2	0.02
Native Hawaiian (2)	2	0.02
Hispanic or Latino:	385	3.77
Central American:	8	0.08
Guatemalan	3	0.03
Nicaraguan	1	0.01
Panamanian	3	0.03
Salvadoran	1	0.01
Cuban	14	0.14
Mexican	256	2.51
Puerto Rican	57	0.56
South American:	4	0.04
Chilean	1	0.01
Colombian	3	0.03
Other Hispanic or Latino	46	0.45
Hungarian	22	0.22
Irish	700	6.97
Italian	135	1.34
Norwegian	23	0.23
Polish	62	0.62
Scotch-Irish	179	1.78
Scottish	191	1.90
Slovak	9	0.09
Swedish	32	0.32
Swiss	19	0.19
Ukrainian	23	0.23
United States or American	1,708	17.01
Welsh	111	1.11
White:	7,984	78.27
Not Hispanic (7,701)	7,787	76.34
Hispanic (145)	197	1.93

Woodstock

Place Type: City
County: Cherokee
Population: 10,050

Ancestry/Race	Number	%
Acadian/Cajun	11	0.11
African American/Black:	550	5.47
Not Hispanic (506)	544	5.41
Hispanic (2)	6	0.06
Am. Ind. or Alaska Nat., not spec.	21	0.21
American Indian tribes, specified:	57	0.57
Blackfeet	2	0.02
Cherokee (14)	41	0.41
Chippewa (1)	2	0.02
Choctaw	1	0.01
Creek (3)	3	0.03
Latin American Indians	2	0.02
Menominee (1)	1	0.01
Osage (1)	1	0.01
Potawatomi (3)	4	0.04

Notes: 1. Figures in the "Number" column do not add up to the total population due to: a) Ancestry/Race overlap — e.g. persons can report being both White and Irish, b) persons of Hispanic origin can report being any race, c) persons reporting two ancestries are counted in both categories. 2. Numbers in parentheses indicate the number of persons reporting this ancestry/race alone, not in combination with any other ancestry/race. 3. Refer to the Explanation of Data in the front of the book for more detailed information.

American Indian tribes, not spec.	4	0.04
Arab:	4	0.04
Lebanese	4	0.04
Asian:	215	2.14
Chinese, ex. Taiwanese (20)	30	0.30
Filipino (15)	23	0.23
Indian (54)	64	0.64
Indonesian (1)	1	0.01
Japanese (10)	15	0.15
Korean (36)	38	0.38
Laotian (6)	12	0.12
Pakistani (1)	1	0.01
Thai (2)	3	0.03
Vietnamese (15)	15	0.15
Other Asian, specified (4)	9	0.09
Other Asian, not specified (2)	4	0.04
Austrian	78	0.80
Brazilian	26	0.27
British	58	0.59
Canadian	4	0.04
Czech	22	0.23
Czechoslovakian	9	0.09
Danish	24	0.25
Dutch	145	1.49
English	1,171	12.01
European	97	0.99
Finnish	7	0.07
French, except Basque	393	4.03
French Canadian	65	0.67
German	1,589	16.30
Greek	52	0.53
Hawaii Native/Pacific Islander:	7	0.07
Micronesian: (2)	2	0.02
Guamanian/Chamorro (2)	2	0.02
Polynesian:	3	0.03
Native Hawaiian	3	0.03
Other Pac. Isl., specified	1	0.01
Other Pac. Isl., not spec.	1	0.01
Hispanic or Latino:	496	4.94
Central American:	25	0.25
Costa Rican	8	0.08
Guatemalan	9	0.09
Honduran	1	0.01
Panamanian	5	0.05
Salvadoran	2	0.02
Cuban	23	0.23
Dominican Republic	2	0.02
Mexican	306	3.04
Puerto Rican	44	0.44
South American:	37	0.37
Argentinean	1	0.01
Bolivian	2	0.02
Chilean	2	0.02
Colombian	17	0.17
Ecuadorian	4	0.04
Paraguayan	1	0.01
Peruvian	7	0.07
Venezuelan	3	0.03
Other Hispanic or Latino	59	0.59
Hungarian	62	0.64
Irish	1,352	13.87
Italian	433	4.44
Latvian	10	0.10
Lithuanian	16	0.16
Northern European	13	0.13
Norwegian	125	1.28
Polish	221	2.27
Portuguese	30	0.31
Romanian	26	0.27
Russian	38	0.39
Scotch-Irish	279	2.86
Scottish	360	3.69
Swedish	82	0.84
Swiss	15	0.15
Ukrainian	10	0.10
United States or American	1,000	10.26
Welsh	121	1.24
West Indian, excl. Hispanic:	29	0.30
Haitian	2	0.02
Jamaican	14	0.14
West Indian	13	0.13
White:	9,131	90.86
Not Hispanic (8,710)	8,822	87.78
Hispanic (277)	309	3.07

Ewa Beach

Place Type: Census Designated Place
County: Honolulu
Population: 14,650

Ancestry/Race	Number	%
African American/Black:	308	2.10
Not Hispanic (94)	262	1.79
Hispanic (2)	46	0.31
Alaska Native tribes, specified:	1	0.01
All other tribes (1)	1	0.01
Am. Ind. or Alaska Nat., not spec.	157	1.07
American Indian tribes, specified:	127	0.87
Apache	8	0.05
Blackfeet (1)	6	0.04
Cherokee (1)	66	0.45
Cheyenne	5	0.03
Choctaw (1)	8	0.05
Cree	1	0.01
Delaware	1	0.01
Iroquois	4	0.03
Latin American Indians	2	0.01
Navajo (1)	2	0.01
Ottawa	3	0.02
Pueblo	1	0.01
Yakama	2	0.01
All other tribes (1)	18	0.12
American Indian tribes, not spec.	13	0.09
Asian:	11,864	80.98
Chinese, ex. Taiwanese (225)	1,888	12.89
Filipino (5,723)	7,835	53.48
Indian (9)	38	0.26
Indonesian	1	0.01
Japanese (759)	1,731	11.82
Korean (31)	209	1.43
Malaysian (5)	11	0.08
Taiwanese (2)	2	0.01
Thai (7)	11	0.08
Vietnamese (64)	82	0.56
Other Asian, specified (8)	40	0.27
Other Asian, not specified (4)	16	0.11
Austrian	19	0.13
British	4	0.03
Canadian	9	0.06
Dutch	25	0.17
English	259	1.77
European	45	0.31
Finnish	14	0.10
French, except Basque	110	0.75
French Canadian	17	0.12
German	289	1.97
Greek	8	0.05
Hawaii Native/Pacific Islander:	4,529	30.91
Melanesian: (4)	4	0.03
Fijian (4)	4	0.03
Micronesian: (68)	145	0.99
Guamanian/Chamorro (29)	85	0.58
Other Micronesian (39)	60	0.41
Polynesian: (1,407)	4,310	29.42
Native Hawaiian (889)	3,473	23.71
Samoan (473)	751	5.13
Tongan (34)	56	0.38
Other Polynesian (11)	30	0.20
Other Pac. Isl., not spec. (20)	70	0.48
Hispanic or Latino:	1,421	9.70
Central American:	4	0.03
Nicaraguan	2	0.01
Salvadoran	2	0.01
Cuban	5	0.03
Dominican Republic	2	0.01
Mexican	159	1.09
Puerto Rican	648	4.42
South American:	2	0.01
Peruvian	2	0.01
Other Hispanic or Latino	602	4.11
Hungarian	15	0.10
Irish	284	1.94
Italian	88	0.60
Norwegian	46	0.31
Polish	51	0.35
Portuguese	809	5.52
Russian	16	0.11
Scotch-Irish	54	0.37
Scottish	89	0.61
Swedish	46	0.31
United States or American	162	1.11
Welsh	26	0.18
White:	4,370	29.83
Not Hispanic (1,416)	3,614	24.67
Hispanic (217)	756	5.16

Halawa

Place Type: Census Designated Place
County: Honolulu
Population: 13,891

Ancestry/Race	Number	%
African American/Black:	414	2.98
Not Hispanic (245)	362	2.61
Hispanic (9)	52	0.37
African, sub-Saharan:	28	0.20
African	18	0.13
Liberian	10	0.07
Alaska Native tribes, specified:	6	0.04
Alaska Athabascan (1)	1	0.01
Eskimo	5	0.04
Am. Ind. or Alaska Nat., not spec.	124	0.89
American Indian tribes, specified:	136	0.98
Apache	7	0.05
Blackfeet (1)	7	0.05
Cherokee (1)	78	0.56
Chippewa (1)	4	0.03
Choctaw	3	0.02
Comanche (3)	3	0.02
Cree	1	0.01
Creek	3	0.02
Iroquois (1)	2	0.01
Latin American Indians	9	0.06
Lumbee	2	0.01
Navajo	1	0.01
Pueblo (1)	2	0.01
Seminole	1	0.01
Shoshone	3	0.02
Sioux (1)	8	0.06
All other tribes	2	0.01
American Indian tribes, not spec.	16	0.12
Asian:	10,705	77.06
Cambodian (2)	20	0.14
Chinese, ex. Taiwanese (681)	2,102	15.13
Filipino (2,555)	3,735	26.89
Indian (6)	28	0.20
Indonesian	2	0.01
Japanese (2,802)	3,911	28.15
Korean (229)	468	3.37
Laotian (12)	17	0.12
Malaysian (5)	8	0.06
Pakistani (2)	3	0.02
Taiwanese (2)	7	0.05
Thai (29)	42	0.30
Vietnamese (202)	250	1.80
Other Asian, specified (31)	82	0.59
Other Asian, not specified (7)	30	0.22
Austrian	6	0.04
Belgian	6	0.04
British	60	0.43
Canadian	39	0.28
Czech	12	0.09
Czechoslovakian	16	0.11
Danish	34	0.24
Dutch	73	0.52
English	302	2.16
European	55	0.39
Finnish	12	0.09

Notes: 1. Figures in the "Number" column do not add up to the total population due to: a) Ancestry/Race overlap — e.g. persons can report being both White and Irish, b) persons of Hispanic origin can report being any race, c) persons reporting two ancestries are counted in both categories. 2. Numbers in parentheses indicate the number of persons reporting this ancestry/race alone, not in combination with any other ancestry/race. 3. Refer to the Explanation of Data in the front of the book for more detailed information.

French, except Basque	129	0.92
French Canadian	20	0.14
German	657	4.71
Hawaii Native/Pacific Islander:	3,488	25.11
Melanesian:	4	0.03
Fijian	4	0.03
Micronesian: (132)	208	1.50
Guamanian/Chamorro (22)	66	0.48
Other Micronesian (110)	142	1.02
Polynesian: (1,259)	3,221	23.19
Native Hawaiian (630)	2,245	16.16
Samoan (605)	894	6.44
Tongan (7)	32	0.23
Other Polynesian (17)	50	0.36
Other Pac. Isl., not spec. (9)	55	0.40
Hispanic or Latino:	905	6.52
Central American:	8	0.06
Honduran	1	0.01
Nicaraguan	2	0.01
Panamanian	4	0.03
Salvadoran	1	0.01
Cuban	7	0.05
Dominican Republic	2	0.01
Mexican	173	1.25
Puerto Rican	307	2.21
South American:	8	0.06
Argentinean	1	0.01
Colombian	3	0.02
Ecuadorian	1	0.01
Peruvian	1	0.01
Venezuelan	2	0.01
Other Hispanic or Latino	400	2.88
Hungarian	31	0.22
Irish	410	2.94
Italian	218	1.56
Norwegian	37	0.27
Polish	96	0.69
Portuguese	401	2.87
Russian	23	0.16
Scandinavian	4	0.03
Scotch-Irish	74	0.53
Scottish	111	0.80
Swedish	32	0.23
Ukrainian	19	0.14
United States or American	151	1.08
Welsh	18	0.13
West Indian, excl. Hispanic:	7	0.05
Jamaican	7	0.05
White:	3,981	28.66
Not Hispanic (2,021)	3,573	25.72
Hispanic (132)	408	2.94

Hilo

Place Type: Census Designated Place
County: Hawaii
Population: 40,759

Ancestry/Race	Number	%
Acadian/Cajun	16	0.04
Afghan	5	0.01
African American/Black:	471	1.16
Not Hispanic (162)	366	0.90
Hispanic (21)	105	0.26
African, sub-Saharan:	51	0.13
African	45	0.11
Other sub-Saharan African	6	0.01
Alaska Native tribes, specified:	28	0.07
Alaska Athabascan (1)	7	0.02
Aleut (1)	1	0.00
Eskimo	11	0.03
Tlingit-Haida (5)	9	0.02
Alaska Native tribes, not specified	5	0.01
Am. Ind. or Alaska Nat., not spec.	417	1.02
American Indian tribes, specified:	601	1.47
Apache (3)	28	0.07
Blackfeet (2)	41	0.10
Cherokee (22)	284	0.70
Cheyenne	6	0.01
Chippewa (5)	15	0.04
Choctaw (1)	35	0.09
Comanche	5	0.01
Cree	2	0.00
Creek (1)	1	0.00
Crow (1)	3	0.01
Delaware	1	0.00
Iroquois	15	0.04
Kiowa	2	0.00
Latin American Indians (1)	20	0.05
Navajo	17	0.04
Osage (2)	5	0.01
Paiute	4	0.01
Potawatomi (1)	7	0.02
Pueblo (5)	14	0.03
Seminole (1)	15	0.04
Shoshone (1)	2	0.00
Sioux (8)	25	0.06
Tohono O'Odham	1	0.00
Ute	4	0.01
Yaqui (1)	1	0.00
All other tribes (11)	48	0.12
American Indian tribes, not spec.	61	0.15
Arab:	17	0.04
Lebanese	8	0.02
Syrian	9	0.02
Armenian	11	0.03
Asian:	30,372	74.52
Cambodian (1)	1	0.00
Chinese, ex. Taiwanese (624)	5,709	14.01
Filipino (2,364)	7,329	17.98
Indian (19)	106	0.26
Indonesian (11)	18	0.04
Japanese (10,863)	15,639	38.37
Korean (410)	1,068	2.62
Laotian (1)	6	0.01
Malaysian (4)	7	0.02
Pakistani	1	0.00
Sri Lankan (1)	1	0.00
Taiwanese (17)	27	0.07
Thai (28)	39	0.10
Vietnamese (52)	94	0.23
Other Asian, specified (59)	222	0.54
Other Asian, not specified (15)	105	0.26
Austrian	26	0.06
Brazilian	24	0.06
British	91	0.22
Canadian	25	0.06
Celtic	13	0.03
Croatian	15	0.04
Czech	38	0.09
Czechoslovakian	5	0.01
Danish	93	0.23
Dutch	200	0.49
Eastern European	16	0.04
English	1,211	2.97
European	116	0.28
Finnish	14	0.03
French, except Basque	393	0.96
French Canadian	90	0.22
German	1,278	3.13
Greek	55	0.13
Hawaii Native/Pacific Islander:	14,401	35.33
Melanesian: (9)	44	0.11
Fijian (7)	41	0.10
Other Melanesian (2)	3	0.01
Micronesian: (403)	564	1.38
Guamanian/Chamorro (23)	95	0.23
Other Micronesian (380)	469	1.15
Polynesian: (4,790)	13,514	33.16
Native Hawaiian (4,606)	12,951	31.77
Samoan (84)	307	0.75
Tongan (90)	172	0.42
Other Polynesian (10)	84	0.21
Other Pac. Isl., not spec. (36)	279	0.68
Hispanic or Latino:	3,579	8.78
Central American:	19	0.05
Costa Rican	2	0.00
Guatemalan	3	0.01
Honduran	1	0.00
Nicaraguan	1	0.00
Panamanian	7	0.02
Salvadoran	3	0.01
Other Central American	2	0.00
Cuban	14	0.03
Dominican Republic	2	0.00
Mexican	500	1.23
Puerto Rican	1,660	4.07
South American:	27	0.07
Argentinean	3	0.01
Chilean	2	0.00
Colombian	8	0.02
Ecuadorian	5	0.01
Peruvian	7	0.02
Other South American	2	0.00
Other Hispanic or Latino	1,357	3.33
Hungarian	36	0.09
Iranian	16	0.04
Irish	973	2.38
Italian	505	1.24
Luxemburger	11	0.03
Northern European	40	0.10
Norwegian	221	0.54
Pennsylvania German	21	0.05
Polish	185	0.45
Portuguese	3,664	8.98
Romanian	16	0.04
Russian	188	0.46
Scandinavian	7	0.02
Scotch-Irish	187	0.46
Scottish	245	0.60
Serbian	17	0.04
Slavic	5	0.01
Slovak	14	0.03
Swedish	169	0.41
Swiss	26	0.06
Turkish	21	0.05
Ukrainian	33	0.08
United States or American	430	1.05
Welsh	97	0.24
West Indian, excl. Hispanic:	17	0.04
West Indian	17	0.04
White:	15,764	38.68
Not Hispanic (6,491)	13,788	33.83
Hispanic (485)	1,976	4.85
Yugoslavian	8	0.02

Honolulu

Place Type: Census Designated Place
County: Honolulu
Population: 371,657

Ancestry/Race	Number	%
Acadian/Cajun	12	0.00
Afghan	58	0.02
African American/Black:	8,980	2.42
Not Hispanic (5,706)	8,236	2.22
Hispanic (332)	744	0.20
African, sub-Saharan:	469	0.13
African	337	0.09
Cape Verdean	6	0.00
Ethiopian	19	0.01
Nigerian	18	0.00
South African	27	0.01
Ugandan	12	0.00
Other sub-Saharan African	50	0.01
Alaska Native tribes, specified:	91	0.02
Alaska Athabascan (9)	13	0.00
Aleut (3)	7	0.00
Eskimo (8)	48	0.01
Tlingit-Haida (14)	21	0.01
All other tribes	2	0.00
Alaska Native tribes, not specified	13	0.00
Am. Ind. or Alaska Nat., not spec.	2,149	0.58
Albanian	7	0.00
Alsatian	15	0.00
American Indian tribes, specified:	2,831	0.76
Apache (25)	132	0.04
Blackfeet (16)	197	0.05
Cherokee (73)	1,286	0.35

Notes: 1. Figures in the "Number" column do not add up to the total population due to: a) Ancestry/Race overlap — e.g. persons can report being both White and Irish, b) persons of Hispanic origin can report being any race, c) persons reporting two ancestries are counted in both categories. 2. Numbers in parentheses indicate the number of persons reporting this ancestry/race alone, not in combination with any other ancestry/race. 3. Refer to the Explanation of Data in the front of the book for more detailed information.

Ancestry/Race	Number	%
Cheyenne (4)	26	0.01
Chickasaw (3)	29	0.01
Chippewa (9)	47	0.01
Choctaw (13)	112	0.03
Colville (2)	4	0.00
Comanche (5)	19	0.01
Cree (4)	27	0.01
Creek (12)	39	0.01
Crow (1)	12	0.00
Delaware (2)	12	0.00
Iroquois (5)	74	0.02
Kiowa (2)	7	0.00
Latin American Indians (26)	95	0.03
Lumbee (2)	4	0.00
Menominee	3	0.00
Navajo (29)	78	0.02
Osage	9	0.00
Ottawa	1	0.00
Paiute (1)	6	0.00
Pima (4)	13	0.00
Potawatomi	5	0.00
Pueblo (14)	71	0.02
Puget Sound Salish (3)	10	0.00
Seminole (4)	56	0.02
Shoshone (2)	11	0.00
Sioux (25)	157	0.04
Tohono O'Odham (2)	6	0.00
Ute	8	0.00
Yakama (1)	1	0.00
Yaqui (3)	11	0.00
Yuman	1	0.00
All other tribes (83)	262	0.07
American Indian tribes, not spec.	190	0.05
Arab:	769	0.21
Arab/Arabic	156	0.04
Egyptian	150	0.04
Iraqi	10	0.00
Jordanian	48	0.01
Lebanese	251	0.07
Moroccan	10	0.00
Palestinian	14	0.00
Syrian	55	0.01
Other Arab	75	0.02
Armenian	118	0.03
Asian:	279,450	75.19
Bangladeshi (5)	6	0.00
Cambodian (121)	163	0.04
Chinese, ex. Taiwanese (38,989)	68,070	18.32
Filipino (43,187)	60,922	16.39
Hmong (9)	10	0.00
Indian (816)	1,313	0.35
Indonesian (154)	267	0.07
Japanese (86,612)	112,778	30.34
Korean (15,586)	21,576	5.81
Laotian (1,062)	1,399	0.38
Malaysian (47)	138	0.04
Pakistani (26)	54	0.01
Sri Lankan (77)	118	0.03
Taiwanese (611)	779	0.21
Thai (505)	852	0.23
Vietnamese (5,978)	7,227	1.94
Other Asian, specified (1,108)	2,560	0.69
Other Asian, not specified (360)	1,218	0.33
Australian	204	0.05
Austrian	551	0.15
Basque	52	0.01
Belgian	190	0.05
Brazilian	181	0.05
British	875	0.24
Bulgarian	79	0.02
Canadian	479	0.13
Celtic	61	0.02
Croatian	226	0.06
Cypriot	7	0.00
Czech	429	0.12
Czechoslovakian	208	0.06
Danish	742	0.20
Dutch	1,770	0.48
Eastern European	59	0.02
English	14,124	3.80
Estonian	5	0.00
European	1,323	0.36
Finnish	304	0.08
French, except Basque	4,931	1.33
French Canadian	848	0.23
German	17,238	4.64
Greek	524	0.14
Guyanese	9	0.00
Hawaii Native/Pacific Islander:	60,586	16.30
Melanesian: (82)	130	0.03
Fijian (73)	121	0.03
Other Melanesian (9)	9	0.00
Micronesian: (3,990)	5,327	1.43
Guamanian/Chamorro (611)	1,221	0.33
Other Micronesian (3,379)	4,106	1.10
Polynesian: (20,353)	53,905	14.50
Native Hawaiian (13,558)	43,363	11.67
Samoan (5,619)	8,474	2.28
Tongan (1,021)	1,381	0.37
Other Polynesian (155)	687	0.18
Other Pac. Isl., specified	25	0.01
Other Pac. Isl., not spec. (303)	1,199	0.32
Hispanic or Latino:	16,229	4.37
Central American:	284	0.08
Costa Rican	32	0.01
Guatemalan	41	0.01
Honduran	15	0.00
Nicaraguan	36	0.01
Panamanian	98	0.03
Salvadoran	46	0.01
Other Central American	16	0.00
Cuban	200	0.05
Dominican Republic	71	0.02
Mexican	4,033	1.09
Puerto Rican	4,607	1.24
South American:	462	0.12
Argentinean	56	0.02
Bolivian	8	0.00
Chilean	42	0.01
Colombian	130	0.03
Ecuadorian	31	0.01
Paraguayan	2	0.00
Peruvian	134	0.04
Uruguayan	2	0.00
Venezuelan	36	0.01
Other South American	21	0.01
Other Hispanic or Latino	6,572	1.77
Hungarian	579	0.16
Icelander	13	0.00
Iranian	106	0.03
Irish	12,576	3.38
Israeli	58	0.02
Italian	5,697	1.53
Latvian	50	0.01
Lithuanian	268	0.07
Luxemburger	6	0.00
Macedonian	6	0.00
New Zealander	50	0.01
Northern European	88	0.02
Norwegian	2,561	0.69
Pennsylvania German	30	0.01
Polish	2,616	0.70
Portuguese	8,033	2.16
Romanian	126	0.03
Russian	1,368	0.37
Scandinavian	137	0.04
Scotch-Irish	2,612	0.70
Scottish	3,222	0.87
Serbian	75	0.02
Slavic	13	0.00
Slovak	153	0.04
Slovene	84	0.02
Swedish	2,651	0.71
Swiss	475	0.13
Turkish	62	0.02
Ukrainian	391	0.11
United States or American	4,416	1.19
Welsh	1,280	0.34
West Indian, excl. Hispanic:	523	0.14
Bahamian	7	0.00
Barbadian	26	0.01
Belizean	14	0.00
Bermudan	11	0.00
British West Indian	13	0.00
Dutch West Indian	5	0.00
Haitian	83	0.02
Jamaican	191	0.05
Trinidadian and Tobagonian	85	0.02
U.S. Virgin Islander	9	0.00
West Indian	79	0.02
White:	111,687	30.05
Not Hispanic (69,503)	103,539	27.86
Hispanic (3,590)	8,148	2.19
Yugoslavian	193	0.05

Kahului

Place Type: Census Designated Place
County: Maui
Population: 20,146

Ancestry/Race	Number	%
African American/Black:	172	0.85
Not Hispanic (42)	136	0.68
Hispanic (7)	36	0.18
African, sub-Saharan:	18	0.09
African	18	0.09
Alaska Native tribes, specified:	16	0.08
Alaska Athabascan	3	0.01
Eskimo	12	0.06
Tlingit-Haida	1	0.00
Am. Ind. or Alaska Nat., not spec.	217	1.08
American Indian tribes, specified:	145	0.72
Apache (2)	6	0.03
Blackfeet	12	0.06
Cherokee (3)	61	0.30
Cheyenne	1	0.00
Chippewa (1)	3	0.01
Choctaw	1	0.00
Colville (1)	2	0.01
Comanche (2)	2	0.01
Creek	6	0.03
Crow (2)	5	0.02
Iroquois	4	0.02
Latin American Indians (4)	5	0.02
Navajo	1	0.00
Pueblo	1	0.00
Seminole	1	0.00
Sioux (2)	4	0.02
All other tribes (11)	30	0.15
American Indian tribes, not spec.	25	0.12
Arab:	13	0.06
Lebanese	13	0.06
Asian:	16,742	83.10
Chinese, ex. Taiwanese (173)	2,103	10.44
Filipino (6,388)	8,940	44.38
Indian (11)	40	0.20
Indonesian	12	0.06
Japanese (3,514)	5,087	25.25
Korean (129)	378	1.88
Malaysian	7	0.03
Taiwanese (2)	7	0.03
Thai (4)	5	0.02
Vietnamese (52)	62	0.31
Other Asian, specified (26)	53	0.26
Other Asian, not specified (26)	48	0.24
Austrian	5	0.02
Basque	4	0.02
Belgian	8	0.04
Brazilian	6	0.03
British	14	0.07
Canadian	18	0.09
Danish	37	0.18
Dutch	35	0.17
English	267	1.33
European	13	0.06
Finnish	11	0.05
French, except Basque	169	0.84
French Canadian	41	0.20
German	477	2.38

Notes: 1. Figures in the "Number" column do not add up to the total population due to: a) Ancestry/Race overlap — e.g. persons can report being both White and Irish, b) persons of Hispanic origin can report being any race, c) persons reporting two ancestries are counted in both categories. 2. Numbers in parentheses indicate the number of persons reporting this ancestry/race alone, not in combination with any other ancestry/race. 3. Refer to the Explanation of Data in the front of the book for more detailed information.

Hawaii Native/Pacific Islander:	5,547	27.53
Melanesian:	1	0.00
Fijian	1	0.00
Micronesian: (330)	467	2.32
Guamanian/Chamorro (2)	35	0.17
Other Micronesian (328)	432	2.14
Polynesian: (1,596)	4,986	24.75
Native Hawaiian (1,355)	4,566	22.66
Samoan (54)	174	0.86
Tongan (182)	220	1.09
Other Polynesian (5)	26	0.13
Other Pac. Isl., not spec. (18)	93	0.46
Hispanic or Latino:	1,763	8.75
Central American:	59	0.29
Guatemalan	49	0.24
Honduran	5	0.02
Salvadoran	4	0.02
Other Central American	1	0.00
Cuban	3	0.01
Dominican Republic	2	0.01
Mexican	347	1.72
Puerto Rican	731	3.63
South American:	2	0.01
Argentinean	2	0.01
Other Hispanic or Latino	619	3.07
Irish	293	1.46
Italian	115	0.57
Luxemburger	6	0.03
Norwegian	65	0.32
Polish	32	0.16
Portuguese	1,058	5.28
Romanian	16	0.08
Scotch-Irish	53	0.26
Scottish	39	0.19
Swedish	96	0.48
Swiss	6	0.03
United States or American	122	0.61
West Indian, excl. Hispanic:	9	0.04
Other West Indian	9	0.04
White:	5,026	24.95
Not Hispanic (1,733)	4,177	20.73
Hispanic (294)	849	4.21

Kailua

Place Type: Census Designated Place
County: Honolulu
Population: 36,513

Ancestry/Race	Number	%
African American/Black:	602	1.65
Not Hispanic (257)	530	1.45
Hispanic (20)	72	0.20
African, sub-Saharan:	10	0.03
African	7	0.02
Sudanese	3	0.01
Alaska Native tribes, specified:	16	0.04
Alaska Athabascan (2)	2	0.01
Aleut (3)	8	0.02
Eskimo (3)	3	0.01
Tlingit-Haida	3	0.01
Alaska Native tribes, not specified	1	0.00
Am. Ind. or Alaska Nat., not spec.	274	0.75
American Indian tribes, specified:	562	1.54
Apache (2)	10	0.03
Blackfeet	32	0.09
Cherokee (22)	290	0.79
Cheyenne (1)	1	0.00
Chickasaw (1)	3	0.01
Chippewa (2)	2	0.01
Choctaw (1)	22	0.06
Colville (1)	1	0.00
Comanche (1)	2	0.01
Cree	1	0.00
Creek (2)	8	0.02
Crow	1	0.00
Delaware (1)	5	0.01
Iroquois (2)	19	0.05
Kiowa	3	0.01
Latin American Indians (6)	16	0.04
Menominee	2	0.01
Navajo (5)	12	0.03
Osage (1)	6	0.02
Paiute (3)	3	0.01
Potawatomi	3	0.01
Pueblo	5	0.01
Puget Sound Salish	1	0.00
Seminole (1)	13	0.04
Shoshone (1)	2	0.01
Sioux (3)	17	0.05
Yakama (3)	12	0.03
Yaqui (2)	5	0.01
All other tribes (12)	65	0.18
American Indian tribes, not spec.	38	0.10
Arab:	22	0.06
Egyptian	4	0.01
Lebanese	18	0.05
Armenian	38	0.10
Asian:	17,087	46.80
Cambodian (11)	16	0.04
Chinese, ex. Taiwanese (1,040)	5,000	13.69
Filipino (1,002)	2,969	8.13
Hmong (1)	1	0.00
Indian (35)	83	0.23
Indonesian (10)	34	0.09
Japanese (4,385)	7,534	20.63
Korean (318)	933	2.56
Laotian (3)	9	0.02
Malaysian (2)	9	0.02
Pakistani	1	0.00
Sri Lankan (9)	12	0.03
Taiwanese (10)	10	0.03
Thai (16)	35	0.10
Vietnamese (80)	133	0.36
Other Asian, specified (84)	244	0.67
Other Asian, not specified (18)	64	0.18
Australian	48	0.13
Austrian	138	0.38
Belgian	39	0.11
Brazilian	6	0.02
British	187	0.51
Bulgarian	5	0.01
Canadian	79	0.22
Carpatho Rusyn	8	0.02
Croatian	56	0.15
Czech	184	0.50
Czechoslovakian	73	0.20
Danish	112	0.31
Dutch	552	1.51
Eastern European	8	0.02
English	3,759	10.27
European	269	0.74
Finnish	102	0.28
French, except Basque	1,306	3.57
French Canadian	150	0.41
German	3,633	9.93
Greek	104	0.28
Hawaii Native/Pacific Islander:	9,341	25.58
Melanesian: (1)	12	0.03
Fijian (1)	12	0.03
Micronesian: (63)	188	0.51
Guamanian/Chamorro (34)	137	0.38
Other Micronesian (29)	51	0.14
Polynesian: (2,815)	9,008	24.67
Native Hawaiian (2,574)	8,390	22.98
Samoan (133)	349	0.96
Tongan (98)	160	0.44
Other Polynesian (10)	109	0.30
Other Pac. Isl., specified	2	0.01
Other Pac. Isl., not spec. (24)	131	0.36
Hispanic or Latino:	2,228	6.10
Central American:	43	0.12
Costa Rican	9	0.02
Guatemalan	6	0.02
Nicaraguan	5	0.01
Panamanian	10	0.03
Salvadoran	12	0.03
Other Central American	1	0.00
Cuban	32	0.09
Dominican Republic	1	0.00
Mexican	589	1.61
Puerto Rican	537	1.47
South American:	58	0.16
Argentinean	9	0.02
Chilean	8	0.02
Colombian	21	0.06
Ecuadorian	6	0.02
Peruvian	5	0.01
Venezuelan	8	0.02
Other South American	1	0.00
Other Hispanic or Latino	968	2.65
Hungarian	119	0.33
Icelander	5	0.01
Iranian	6	0.02
Irish	3,403	9.30
Israeli	10	0.03
Italian	1,099	3.00
Latvian	27	0.07
Lithuanian	36	0.10
Luxemburger	6	0.02
New Zealander	23	0.06
Northern European	46	0.13
Norwegian	393	1.07
Polish	655	1.79
Portuguese	2,425	6.63
Romanian	12	0.03
Russian	309	0.84
Scandinavian	91	0.25
Scotch-Irish	573	1.57
Scottish	823	2.25
Serbian	13	0.04
Slavic	20	0.05
Slovak	46	0.13
Slovene	28	0.08
Soviet Union	3	0.01
Swedish	528	1.44
Swiss	129	0.35
Ukrainian	75	0.21
United States or American	636	1.74
Welsh	300	0.82
West Indian, excl. Hispanic:	49	0.13
British West Indian	6	0.02
Jamaican	43	0.12
White:	23,491	64.34
Not Hispanic (15,433)	22,014	60.29
Hispanic (575)	1,477	4.05
Yugoslavian	53	0.14

Kaneohe

Place Type: Census Designated Place
County: Honolulu
Population: 34,970

Ancestry/Race	Number	%
African American/Black:	514	1.47
Not Hispanic (263)	444	1.27
Hispanic (22)	70	0.20
African, sub-Saharan:	30	0.09
African	15	0.04
South African	15	0.04
Alaska Native tribes, specified:	1	0.00
Eskimo (1)	1	0.00
Am. Ind. or Alaska Nat., not spec.	339	0.97
American Indian tribes, specified:	390	1.12
Apache (2)	17	0.05
Blackfeet (2)	26	0.07
Cherokee (5)	209	0.60
Chickasaw	2	0.01
Chippewa (1)	7	0.02
Choctaw	9	0.03
Colville	1	0.00
Comanche	3	0.01
Creek (6)	12	0.03
Crow (1)	1	0.00
Iroquois (3)	9	0.03
Latin American Indians (2)	11	0.03
Navajo (2)	13	0.04
Osage	2	0.01
Ottawa	1	0.00

Notes: 1. Figures in the "Number" column do not add up to the total population due to: a) Ancestry/Race overlap — e.g. persons can report being both White and Irish, b) persons of Hispanic origin can report being any race, c) persons reporting two ancestries are counted in both categories. 2. Numbers in parentheses indicate the number of persons reporting this ancestry/race alone, not in combination with any other ancestry/race. 3. Refer to the Explanation of Data in the front of the book for more detailed information.

Ancestry/Race	Number	%
Pueblo (3)	4	0.01
Seminole (1)	12	0.03
Shoshone	3	0.01
Sioux (5)	21	0.06
Ute (1)	2	0.01
Yaqui (9)	10	0.03
All other tribes	15	0.04
American Indian tribes, not spec.	33	0.09
Arab:	9	0.03
Lebanese	9	0.03
Asian:	25,800	73.78
Cambodian (3)	4	0.01
Chinese, ex. Taiwanese (1,597)	6,965	19.92
Filipino (1,600)	4,513	12.91
Hmong (1)	1	0.00
Indian (26)	66	0.19
Indonesian (9)	23	0.07
Japanese (8,259)	12,518	35.80
Korean (367)	1,054	3.01
Laotian (15)	18	0.05
Malaysian (2)	4	0.01
Pakistani	2	0.01
Sri Lankan (1)	5	0.01
Taiwanese (2)	4	0.01
Thai (23)	39	0.11
Vietnamese (70)	111	0.32
Other Asian, specified (133)	389	1.11
Other Asian, not specified (23)	84	0.24
Austrian	38	0.11
Basque	8	0.02
Belgian	4	0.01
Brazilian	12	0.03
British	62	0.18
Canadian	30	0.09
Czech	42	0.12
Czechoslovakian	12	0.03
Danish	99	0.28
Dutch	146	0.42
English	1,479	4.23
European	119	0.34
Finnish	38	0.11
French, except Basque	567	1.62
French Canadian	33	0.09
German	1,925	5.50
German Russian	5	0.01
Greek	35	0.10
Guyanese	10	0.03
Hawaii Native/Pacific Islander:	11,296	32.30
Melanesian: (16)	32	0.09
Fijian (16)	31	0.09
Other Melanesian	1	0.00
Micronesian: (92)	182	0.52
Guamanian/Chamorro (27)	90	0.26
Other Micronesian (65)	92	0.26
Polynesian: (3,787)	10,918	31.22
Native Hawaiian (3,443)	10,067	28.79
Samoan (282)	649	1.86
Tongan (57)	108	0.31
Other Polynesian (5)	94	0.27
Other Pac. Isl., not spec. (7)	164	0.47
Hispanic or Latino:	2,523	7.21
Central American:	25	0.07
Costa Rican	3	0.01
Guatemalan	2	0.01
Honduran	3	0.01
Nicaraguan	4	0.01
Panamanian	7	0.02
Salvadoran	6	0.02
Cuban	10	0.03
Dominican Republic	1	0.00
Mexican	386	1.10
Puerto Rican	846	2.42
South American:	31	0.09
Argentinean	1	0.00
Chilean	2	0.01
Colombian	10	0.03
Ecuadorian	3	0.01
Peruvian	13	0.04
Venezuelan	1	0.00
Other South American	1	0.00
Other Hispanic or Latino	1,224	3.50
Hungarian	17	0.05
Irish	1,533	4.38
Italian	504	1.44
Latvian	8	0.02
Lithuanian	55	0.16
Northern European	81	0.23
Norwegian	226	0.65
Pennsylvania German	12	0.03
Polish	214	0.61
Portuguese	1,805	5.16
Romanian	27	0.08
Russian	68	0.19
Scotch-Irish	217	0.62
Scottish	335	0.96
Swedish	270	0.77
Swiss	75	0.21
Turkish	5	0.01
Ukrainian	49	0.14
United States or American	327	0.93
Welsh	62	0.18
West Indian, excl. Hispanic:	63	0.18
Jamaican	47	0.13
West Indian	7	0.02
Other West Indian	9	0.03
White:	14,446	41.31
Not Hispanic (6,756)	12,924	36.96
Hispanic (410)	1,522	4.35
Yugoslavian	8	0.02

Kaneohe Station

Place Type: Census Designated Place
County: Honolulu
Population: 11,827

Ancestry/Race	Number	%
African American/Black:	1,628	13.77
Not Hispanic (1,384)	1,539	13.01
Hispanic (44)	89	0.75
African, sub-Saharan:	125	1.06
African	125	1.06
Alaska Native tribes, specified:	3	0.03
Alaska Athabascan (1)	1	0.01
Tlingit-Haida (1)	2	0.02
Am. Ind. or Alaska Nat., not spec.	82	0.69
American Indian tribes, specified:	170	1.44
Apache (3)	5	0.04
Blackfeet	3	0.03
Cherokee (26)	56	0.47
Chickasaw (2)	5	0.04
Chippewa (4)	5	0.04
Choctaw (2)	4	0.03
Comanche	1	0.01
Creek (2)	2	0.02
Crow (1)	1	0.01
Delaware (1)	1	0.01
Iroquois (8)	12	0.10
Latin American Indians (7)	13	0.11
Lumbee (4)	5	0.04
Navajo (14)	14	0.12
Osage (1)	1	0.01
Potawatomi (3)	3	0.03
Pueblo (2)	6	0.05
Seminole	1	0.01
Shoshone	2	0.02
Sioux (5)	11	0.09
Tohono O'Odham (1)	1	0.01
Ute	2	0.02
Yakama (1)	3	0.03
Yaqui (1)	3	0.03
All other tribes (5)	10	0.08
American Indian tribes, not spec.	12	0.10
Arab:	19	0.16
Lebanese	8	0.07
Moroccan	11	0.09
Armenian	7	0.06
Asian:	1,057	8.94
Cambodian (2)	3	0.03
Chinese, ex. Taiwanese (28)	99	0.84
Filipino (341)	523	4.42
Hmong (4)	4	0.03
Indian (22)	31	0.26
Japanese (92)	218	1.84
Korean (36)	58	0.49
Laotian (33)	38	0.32
Malaysian	4	0.03
Pakistani	1	0.01
Thai (16)	21	0.18
Vietnamese (28)	35	0.30
Other Asian, specified (3)	6	0.05
Other Asian, not specified (9)	16	0.14
Australian	23	0.19
Austrian	8	0.07
Belgian	9	0.08
Brazilian	13	0.11
British	35	0.30
Canadian	19	0.16
Croatian	10	0.08
Czech	103	0.87
Czechoslovakian	16	0.14
Danish	36	0.30
Dutch	119	1.01
English	774	6.54
European	66	0.56
Finnish	10	0.08
French, except Basque	292	2.47
French Canadian	118	1.00
German	2,039	17.24
Greek	54	0.46
Guyanese	10	0.08
Hawaii Native/Pacific Islander:	324	2.74
Melanesian: (1)	3	0.03
Fijian (1)	3	0.03
Micronesian: (54)	84	0.71
Guamanian/Chamorro (45)	68	0.57
Other Micronesian (9)	16	0.14
Polynesian: (72)	217	1.83
Native Hawaiian (54)	171	1.45
Samoan (15)	42	0.36
Tongan (2)	2	0.02
Other Polynesian (1)	2	0.02
Other Pac. Isl., not spec. (3)	20	0.17
Hispanic or Latino:	1,731	14.64
Central American:	84	0.71
Costa Rican	5	0.04
Guatemalan	15	0.13
Honduran	16	0.14
Nicaraguan	5	0.04
Panamanian	15	0.13
Salvadoran	26	0.22
Other Central American	2	0.02
Cuban	32	0.27
Dominican Republic	27	0.23
Mexican	942	7.96
Puerto Rican	283	2.39
South American:	78	0.66
Argentinean	6	0.05
Chilean	4	0.03
Colombian	33	0.28
Ecuadorian	9	0.08
Peruvian	22	0.19
Venezuelan	2	0.02
Other South American	2	0.02
Other Hispanic or Latino	285	2.41
Hungarian	33	0.28
Icelander	11	0.09
Iranian	10	0.08
Irish	1,546	13.07
Israeli	6	0.05
Italian	622	5.26
Lithuanian	7	0.06
Norwegian	220	1.86
Polish	332	2.81
Portuguese	41	0.35
Russian	69	0.58
Scandinavian	27	0.23
Scotch-Irish	157	1.33
Scottish	220	1.86
Serbian	29	0.25

Notes: 1. Figures in the "Number" column do not add up to the total population due to: a) Ancestry/Race overlap — e.g. persons can report being both White and Irish, b) persons of Hispanic origin can report being any race, c) persons reporting two ancestries are counted in both categories. 2. Numbers in parentheses indicate the number of persons reporting this ancestry/race alone, not in combination with any other ancestry/race. 3. Refer to the Explanation of Data in the front of the book for more detailed information.

Slavic	38	0.32
Slovak	21	0.18
Swedish	145	1.23
Swiss	21	0.18
Ukrainian	10	0.08
United States or American	648	5.48
Welsh	15	0.13
West Indian, excl. Hispanic:	78	0.66
Haitian	29	0.25
Jamaican	34	0.29
West Indian	15	0.13
White:	8,437	71.34
Not Hispanic (7,297)	7,728	65.34
Hispanic (580)	709	5.99
Yugoslavian	6	0.05

Kihei

Place Type: Census Designated Place
County: Maui
Population: 16,749

Ancestry/Race	Number	%
African American/Black:	273	1.63
Not Hispanic (121)	249	1.49
Hispanic (3)	24	0.14
African, sub-Saharan:	19	0.11
African	8	0.05
South African	11	0.07
Alaska Native tribes, specified:	16	0.10
Alaska Athabascan (1)	1	0.01
Aleut (1)	1	0.01
Eskimo (1)	4	0.02
Tlingit-Haida (5)	7	0.04
All other tribes	3	0.02
Alaska Native tribes, not specified	1	0.01
Am. Ind. or Alaska Nat., not spec.	122	0.73
Albanian	12	0.07
American Indian tribes, specified:	194	1.16
Apache (1)	10	0.06
Blackfeet (5)	12	0.07
Cherokee (6)	76	0.45
Chickasaw (2)	2	0.01
Chippewa (2)	3	0.02
Choctaw (3)	11	0.07
Colville	1	0.01
Comanche	4	0.02
Cree (1)	3	0.02
Delaware (1)	1	0.01
Iroquois	4	0.02
Latin American Indians (3)	10	0.06
Navajo (3)	8	0.05
Osage	1	0.01
Paiute (2)	4	0.02
Pueblo (1)	1	0.01
Seminole (2)	3	0.02
Shoshone	1	0.01
Sioux (2)	6	0.04
Yaqui (1)	3	0.02
All other tribes (16)	30	0.18
American Indian tribes, not spec.	9	0.05
Arab:	25	0.15
Lebanese	25	0.15
Armenian	43	0.26
Asian:	7,176	42.84
Cambodian (4)	7	0.04
Chinese, ex. Taiwanese (121)	1,072	6.40
Filipino (2,933)	4,246	25.35
Indian (20)	52	0.31
Indonesian (10)	13	0.08
Japanese (615)	1,362	8.13
Korean (82)	221	1.32
Laotian (11)	11	0.07
Malaysian	2	0.01
Taiwanese (4)	5	0.03
Thai (15)	24	0.14
Vietnamese (47)	58	0.35
Other Asian, specified (9)	42	0.25
Other Asian, not specified (24)	61	0.36
Australian	13	0.08
Austrian	55	0.33
Basque	20	0.12
Belgian	35	0.21
Brazilian	36	0.21
British	80	0.48
Canadian	48	0.29
Celtic	8	0.05
Croatian	2	0.01
Czech	15	0.09
Czechoslovakian	8	0.05
Danish	91	0.54
Dutch	144	0.86
Eastern European	11	0.07
English	1,320	7.84
Estonian	19	0.11
European	128	0.76
Finnish	22	0.13
French, except Basque	517	3.07
French Canadian	70	0.42
German	1,816	10.79
Greek	38	0.23
Guyanese	6	0.04
Hawaii Native/Pacific Islander:	3,116	18.60
Melanesian: (8)	11	0.07
Fijian (8)	11	0.07
Micronesian: (44)	80	0.48
Guamanian/Chamorro (20)	47	0.28
Other Micronesian (24)	33	0.20
Polynesian: (1,190)	2,929	17.49
Native Hawaiian (920)	2,487	14.85
Samoan (55)	140	0.84
Tongan (206)	266	1.59
Other Polynesian (9)	36	0.21
Other Pac. Isl., not spec. (29)	96	0.57
Hispanic or Latino:	1,259	7.52
Central American:	18	0.11
Costa Rican	8	0.05
Guatemalan	2	0.01
Honduran	2	0.01
Nicaraguan	5	0.03
Salvadoran	1	0.01
Cuban	20	0.12
Dominican Republic	1	0.01
Mexican	480	2.87
Puerto Rican	294	1.76
South American:	47	0.28
Argentinean	11	0.07
Chilean	8	0.05
Colombian	4	0.02
Ecuadorian	6	0.04
Peruvian	13	0.08
Uruguayan	1	0.01
Other South American	4	0.02
Other Hispanic or Latino	399	2.38
Hungarian	51	0.30
Iranian	10	0.06
Irish	1,760	10.46
Israeli	19	0.11
Italian	769	4.57
Lithuanian	54	0.32
Luxemburger	9	0.05
Maltese	8	0.05
New Zealander	6	0.04
Northern European	17	0.10
Norwegian	258	1.53
Polish	262	1.56
Portuguese	596	3.54
Romanian	11	0.07
Russian	104	0.62
Scandinavian	22	0.13
Scotch-Irish	181	1.08
Scottish	253	1.50
Slovak	18	0.11
Slovene	19	0.11
Swedish	158	0.94
Swiss	37	0.22
Turkish	35	0.21
Ukrainian	58	0.34
United States or American	236	1.40
Welsh	111	0.66
West Indian, excl. Hispanic:	8	0.05
Jamaican	8	0.05
White:	10,026	59.86
Not Hispanic (7,575)	9,303	55.54
Hispanic (424)	723	4.32
Yugoslavian	38	0.23

Makakilo City

Place Type: Census Designated Place
County: Honolulu
Population: 13,156

Ancestry/Race	Number	%
Acadian/Cajun	9	0.07
African American/Black:	533	4.05
Not Hispanic (318)	484	3.68
Hispanic (15)	49	0.37
African, sub-Saharan:	58	0.44
African	58	0.44
Alaska Native tribes, specified:	8	0.06
Aleut	4	0.03
Eskimo (1)	4	0.03
Am. Ind. or Alaska Nat., not spec.	119	0.90
American Indian tribes, specified:	159	1.21
Apache (3)	13	0.10
Blackfeet (1)	9	0.07
Cherokee (5)	72	0.55
Cheyenne (1)	1	0.01
Chickasaw	3	0.02
Chippewa (4)	4	0.03
Choctaw (1)	9	0.07
Cree	5	0.04
Crow	3	0.02
Iroquois	3	0.02
Latin American Indians	3	0.02
Lumbee (1)	1	0.01
Navajo	1	0.01
Pima (1)	1	0.01
Pueblo (1)	1	0.01
Seminole	1	0.01
Shoshone	1	0.01
Sioux (1)	3	0.02
Ute	3	0.02
All other tribes (4)	22	0.17
American Indian tribes, not spec.	16	0.12
Arab:	21	0.16
Arab/Arabic	21	0.16
Armenian	9	0.07
Asian:	9,001	68.42
Cambodian (1)	5	0.04
Chinese, ex. Taiwanese (250)	1,855	14.10
Filipino (2,224)	4,112	31.26
Indian (7)	39	0.30
Indonesian (9)	17	0.13
Japanese (1,008)	2,318	17.62
Korean (175)	409	3.11
Laotian (12)	16	0.12
Malaysian	1	0.01
Pakistani	4	0.03
Sri Lankan (2)	2	0.02
Taiwanese	1	0.01
Thai (27)	56	0.43
Vietnamese (20)	36	0.27
Other Asian, specified (22)	111	0.84
Other Asian, not specified (8)	19	0.14
Austrian	6	0.05
Belgian	54	0.41
British	29	0.22
Canadian	22	0.17
Croatian	15	0.11
Czech	16	0.12
Dutch	97	0.74
English	501	3.81
Estonian	9	0.07
European	92	0.70
Finnish	7	0.05
French, except Basque	219	1.66
French Canadian	69	0.52
German	729	5.54

Notes: 1. Figures in the "Number" column do not add up to the total population due to: a) Ancestry/Race overlap — e.g. persons can report being both White and Irish, b) persons of Hispanic origin can report being any race, c) persons reporting two ancestries are counted in both categories. 2. Numbers in parentheses indicate the number of persons reporting this ancestry/race alone, not in combination with any other ancestry/race. 3. Refer to the Explanation of Data in the front of the book for more detailed information.

Hawaii Native/Pacific Islander:	3,947	30.00
Melanesian:	4	0.03
Fijian	4	0.03
Micronesian: (52)	137	1.04
Guamanian/Chamorro (37)	102	0.78
Other Micronesian (15)	35	0.27
Polynesian: (1,249)	3,757	28.56
Native Hawaiian (997)	3,188	24.23
Samoan (244)	509	3.87
Tongan (3)	16	0.12
Other Polynesian (5)	44	0.33
Other Pac. Isl., not spec. (5)	49	0.37
Hispanic or Latino:	1,327	10.09
Central American:	9	0.07
Guatemalan	6	0.05
Honduran	1	0.01
Panamanian	1	0.01
Salvadoran	1	0.01
Cuban	12	0.09
Mexican	225	1.71
Puerto Rican	485	3.69
South American:	12	0.09
Chilean	2	0.02
Colombian	3	0.02
Ecuadorian	4	0.03
Peruvian	1	0.01
Other South American	2	0.02
Other Hispanic or Latino	584	4.44
Hungarian	14	0.11
Irish	700	5.32
Italian	199	1.51
Lithuanian	20	0.15
Norwegian	158	1.20
Pennsylvania German	37	0.28
Polish	129	0.98
Portuguese	557	4.23
Russian	36	0.27
Scandinavian	60	0.46
Scotch-Irish	77	0.59
Scottish	99	0.75
Slovene	10	0.08
Swedish	85	0.65
Swiss	20	0.15
Ukrainian	21	0.16
United States or American	341	2.59
Welsh	14	0.11
White:	5,959	45.29
Not Hispanic (2,986)	5,301	40.29
Hispanic (193)	658	5.00
Yugoslavian	10	0.08

Mililani Town

Place Type: Census Designated Place
County: Honolulu
Population: 28,608

Ancestry/Race	Number	%
African American/Black:	1,237	4.32
Not Hispanic (832)	1,140	3.98
Hispanic (47)	97	0.34
African, sub-Saharan:	13	0.05
African	8	0.03
Ghanian	5	0.02
Alaska Native tribes, specified:	20	0.07
Alaska Athabascan	3	0.01
Aleut	4	0.01
Eskimo	6	0.02
Tlingit-Haida (3)	7	0.02
Am. Ind. or Alaska Nat., not spec.	208	0.73
American Indian tribes, specified:	321	1.12
Apache (2)	13	0.05
Blackfeet (1)	33	0.12
Cherokee (7)	155	0.54
Cheyenne	2	0.01
Chippewa (1)	8	0.03
Choctaw (1)	10	0.03
Comanche (1)	5	0.02
Cree	3	0.01
Creek	3	0.01
Delaware	3	0.01
Iroquois	9	0.03
Latin American Indians (4)	21	0.07
Lumbee (2)	2	0.01
Navajo (3)	9	0.03
Pima (1)	3	0.01
Potawatomi	1	0.00
Pueblo (1)	9	0.03
Shoshone (1)	2	0.01
Sioux	12	0.04
Yaqui	2	0.01
All other tribes (7)	16	0.06
American Indian tribes, not spec.	21	0.07
Arab:	7	0.02
Arab/Arabic	7	0.02
Asian:	23,130	80.85
Cambodian (4)	9	0.03
Chinese, ex. Taiwanese (912)	4,194	14.66
Filipino (2,974)	6,134	21.44
Hmong (4)	4	0.01
Indian (35)	70	0.24
Indonesian (4)	10	0.03
Japanese (7,126)	10,739	37.54
Korean (633)	1,413	4.94
Laotian (14)	24	0.08
Malaysian (4)	4	0.01
Taiwanese (20)	28	0.10
Thai (60)	93	0.33
Vietnamese (55)	95	0.33
Other Asian, specified (103)	252	0.88
Other Asian, not specified (26)	61	0.21
Austrian	68	0.24
Basque	4	0.01
British	94	0.33
Canadian	66	0.23
Croatian	13	0.05
Czech	11	0.04
Czechoslovakian	28	0.10
Danish	19	0.07
Dutch	138	0.48
Eastern European	7	0.02
English	1,233	4.32
European	178	0.62
Finnish	65	0.23
French, except Basque	269	0.94
French Canadian	76	0.27
German	1,960	6.86
Greek	49	0.17
Hawaii Native/Pacific Islander:	5,331	18.63
Melanesian: (2)	3	0.01
Fijian (2)	3	0.01
Micronesian: (97)	208	0.73
Guamanian/Chamorro (81)	163	0.57
Other Micronesian (16)	45	0.16
Polynesian: (1,149)	4,993	17.45
Native Hawaiian (943)	4,483	15.67
Samoan (194)	434	1.52
Tongan (6)	23	0.08
Other Polynesian (6)	53	0.19
Other Pac. Isl., specified	11	0.04
Other Pac. Isl., not spec. (11)	116	0.41
Hispanic or Latino:	2,222	7.77
Central American:	54	0.19
Guatemalan	3	0.01
Honduran	5	0.02
Nicaraguan	7	0.02
Panamanian	36	0.13
Salvadoran	3	0.01
Cuban	8	0.03
Dominican Republic	7	0.02
Mexican	488	1.71
Puerto Rican	707	2.47
South American:	18	0.06
Colombian	8	0.03
Ecuadorian	1	0.00
Peruvian	7	0.02
Venezuelan	1	0.00
Other South American	1	0.00
Other Hispanic or Latino	940	3.29
Hungarian	107	0.37
Iranian	60	0.21
Irish	1,403	4.91
Italian	459	1.61
Lithuanian	8	0.03
Northern European	8	0.03
Norwegian	270	0.95
Polish	255	0.89
Portuguese	1,218	4.26
Russian	40	0.14
Scandinavian	38	0.13
Scotch-Irish	140	0.49
Scottish	242	0.85
Slovak	8	0.03
Swedish	230	0.81
Swiss	44	0.15
Ukrainian	21	0.07
United States or American	387	1.35
Welsh	87	0.30
West Indian, excl. Hispanic:	40	0.14
Jamaican	17	0.06
Trinidadian and Tobagonian	15	0.05
West Indian	8	0.03
White:	10,957	38.30
Not Hispanic (5,483)	9,765	34.13
Hispanic (346)	1,192	4.17

Nanakuli

Place Type: Census Designated Place
County: Honolulu
Population: 10,814

Ancestry/Race	Number	%
African American/Black:	255	2.36
Not Hispanic (75)	215	1.99
Hispanic (10)	40	0.37
Alaska Native tribes, not specified	2	0.02
Am. Ind. or Alaska Nat., not spec.	156	1.44
American Indian tribes, specified:	142	1.31
Apache	25	0.23
Blackfeet	4	0.04
Cherokee (4)	81	0.75
Cheyenne	1	0.01
Chippewa	3	0.03
Choctaw	7	0.06
Kiowa	2	0.02
Latin American Indians (1)	1	0.01
Pueblo	1	0.01
Seminole	1	0.01
Sioux	8	0.07
All other tribes (1)	8	0.07
American Indian tribes, not spec.	22	0.20
Asian:	5,293	48.95
Chinese, ex. Taiwanese (125)	1,956	18.09
Filipino (844)	2,289	21.17
Indian (6)	31	0.29
Indonesian	3	0.03
Japanese (160)	861	7.96
Korean (3)	93	0.86
Laotian (9)	12	0.11
Thai (3)	6	0.06
Vietnamese (6)	7	0.06
Other Asian, specified (1)	12	0.11
Other Asian, not specified (6)	23	0.21
Austrian	50	0.47
Danish	9	0.08
Dutch	5	0.05
Eastern European	10	0.09
English	72	0.67
French, except Basque	24	0.22
German	256	2.39
Hawaii Native/Pacific Islander:	8,684	80.30
Melanesian: (1)	5	0.05
Fijian (1)	5	0.05
Micronesian: (24)	69	0.64
Guamanian/Chamorro (5)	38	0.35
Other Micronesian (19)	31	0.29
Polynesian: (4,117)	8,559	79.15
Native Hawaiian (3,367)	7,171	66.31
Samoan (692)	1,224	11.32

Notes: 1. Figures in the "Number" column do not add up to the total population due to: a) Ancestry/Race overlap — e.g. persons can report being both White and Irish, b) persons of Hispanic origin can report being any race, c) persons reporting two ancestries are counted in both categories. 2. Numbers in parentheses indicate the number of persons reporting this ancestry/race alone, not in combination with any other ancestry/race. 3. Refer to the Explanation of Data in the front of the book for more detailed information.

Tongan (55)	102	0.94
Other Polynesian (3)	62	0.57
Other Pac. Isl., not spec. (9)	51	0.47
Hispanic or Latino:	1,202	11.12
Central American:	6	0.06
Honduran	3	0.03
Nicaraguan	2	0.02
Panamanian	1	0.01
Cuban	3	0.03
Dominican Republic	1	0.01
Mexican	149	1.38
Puerto Rican	493	4.56
South American:	2	0.02
Chilean	1	0.01
Other South American	1	0.01
Other Hispanic or Latino	548	5.07
Irish	133	1.24
Italian	113	1.06
Lithuanian	20	0.19
Polish	27	0.25
Portuguese	504	4.71
Russian	13	0.12
Scotch-Irish	24	0.22
Scottish	14	0.13
Swiss	4	0.04
United States or American	68	0.64
Welsh	11	0.10
White:	3,369	31.15
Not Hispanic (533)	2,820	26.08
Hispanic (83)	549	5.08

Pearl City

Place Type: Census Designated Place
County: Honolulu
Population: 30,976

Ancestry/Race	Number	%
Acadian/Cajun	17	0.06
African American/Black:	1,122	3.62
Not Hispanic (796)	1,035	3.34
Hispanic (42)	87	0.28
African, sub-Saharan:	59	0.19
African	53	0.17
Cape Verdean	6	0.02
Alaska Native tribes, specified:	3	0.01
Eskimo (1)	3	0.01
Alaska Native tribes, not specified	1	0.00
Am. Ind. or Alaska Nat., not spec.	172	0.56
American Indian tribes, specified:	302	0.97
Apache (5)	8	0.03
Blackfeet (4)	19	0.06
Cherokee (14)	132	0.43
Cheyenne (1)	7	0.02
Chickasaw	6	0.02
Chippewa (2)	10	0.03
Choctaw (4)	11	0.04
Comanche (1)	5	0.02
Cree	5	0.02
Creek (3)	11	0.04
Crow (1)	2	0.01
Iroquois	6	0.02
Latin American Indians (2)	5	0.02
Lumbee	4	0.01
Navajo (5)	8	0.03
Osage	6	0.02
Pueblo	1	0.00
Seminole	7	0.02
Shoshone	4	0.01
Sioux (3)	24	0.08
All other tribes (8)	21	0.07
American Indian tribes, not spec.	44	0.14
Arab:	29	0.09
Arab/Arabic	17	0.06
Lebanese	12	0.04
Asian:	24,718	79.80
Cambodian	4	0.01
Chinese, ex. Taiwanese (1,204)	4,131	13.34
Filipino (3,764)	6,460	20.85
Hmong (1)	2	0.01
Indian (21)	65	0.21
Indonesian (2)	23	0.07
Japanese (9,621)	12,499	40.35
Korean (403)	953	3.08
Laotian (10)	15	0.05
Malaysian (1)	7	0.02
Pakistani (1)	1	0.00
Sri Lankan	1	0.00
Taiwanese (6)	6	0.02
Thai (33)	63	0.20
Vietnamese (114)	167	0.54
Other Asian, specified (93)	217	0.70
Other Asian, not specified (26)	104	0.34
Brazilian	9	0.03
British	35	0.11
Canadian	28	0.09
Croatian	10	0.03
Czech	17	0.06
Czechoslovakian	9	0.03
Danish	66	0.21
Dutch	150	0.49
English	742	2.41
European	61	0.20
Finnish	16	0.05
French, except Basque	246	0.80
French Canadian	80	0.26
German	1,236	4.01
Greek	64	0.21
Hawaii Native/Pacific Islander:	5,775	18.64
Melanesian: (5)	15	0.05
Fijian (5)	15	0.05
Micronesian: (137)	247	0.80
Guamanian/Chamorro (46)	113	0.36
Other Micronesian (91)	134	0.43
Polynesian: (1,683)	5,386	17.39
Native Hawaiian (1,240)	4,596	14.84
Samoan (399)	669	2.16
Tongan (35)	57	0.18
Other Polynesian (9)	64	0.21
Other Pac. Isl., specified	1	0.00
Other Pac. Isl., not spec. (19)	126	0.41
Hispanic or Latino:	2,260	7.30
Central American:	22	0.07
Costa Rican	1	0.00
Guatemalan	1	0.00
Honduran	3	0.01
Nicaraguan	1	0.00
Panamanian	6	0.02
Salvadoran	9	0.03
Other Central American	1	0.00
Cuban	2	0.01
Dominican Republic	2	0.01
Mexican	512	1.65
Puerto Rican	687	2.22
South American:	29	0.09
Argentinean	1	0.00
Chilean	4	0.01
Colombian	6	0.02
Ecuadorian	7	0.02
Peruvian	9	0.03
Venezuelan	2	0.01
Other Hispanic or Latino	1,006	3.25
Hungarian	46	0.15
Irish	986	3.20
Italian	421	1.37
Lithuanian	16	0.05
Norwegian	233	0.76
Polish	203	0.66
Portuguese	1,012	3.28
Russian	95	0.31
Scandinavian	26	0.08
Scotch-Irish	158	0.51
Scottish	231	0.75
Slovak	5	0.02
Swedish	184	0.60
Ukrainian	5	0.02
United States or American	217	0.70
West Indian, excl. Hispanic:	35	0.11
Haitian	9	0.03
Jamaican	26	0.08
White:	9,337	30.14
Not Hispanic (4,952)	8,246	26.62
Hispanic (388)	1,091	3.52

Schofield Barracks

Place Type: Census Designated Place
County: Honolulu
Population: 14,428

Ancestry/Race	Number	%
Afghan	6	0.04
African American/Black:	3,515	24.36
Not Hispanic (3,017)	3,286	22.78
Hispanic (137)	229	1.59
African, sub-Saharan:	195	1.35
African	173	1.20
Ghanian	12	0.08
Nigerian	5	0.03
Other sub-Saharan African	5	0.03
Alaska Native tribes, specified:	11	0.08
Alaska Athabascan (1)	2	0.01
Aleut	1	0.01
Eskimo (1)	4	0.03
Tlingit-Haida	4	0.03
Am. Ind. or Alaska Nat., not spec.	74	0.51
American Indian tribes, specified:	240	1.66
Apache (8)	14	0.10
Blackfeet	12	0.08
Cherokee (18)	77	0.53
Cheyenne (1)	1	0.01
Chippewa	2	0.01
Choctaw (4)	12	0.08
Colville (1)	1	0.01
Comanche	1	0.01
Cree	1	0.01
Creek (5)	6	0.04
Iroquois (4)	5	0.03
Kiowa (5)	5	0.03
Latin American Indians (13)	16	0.11
Lumbee (2)	2	0.01
Menominee	1	0.01
Navajo (26)	33	0.23
Ottawa (2)	2	0.01
Potawatomi (2)	2	0.01
Pueblo (4)	6	0.04
Seminole (6)	7	0.05
Shoshone (1)	1	0.01
Sioux (3)	5	0.03
Tohono O'Odham (1)	2	0.01
Yaqui	1	0.01
All other tribes (13)	25	0.17
American Indian tribes, not spec.	11	0.08
Arab:	17	0.12
Arab/Arabic	7	0.05
Lebanese	10	0.07
Armenian	5	0.03
Asian:	999	6.92
Bangladeshi (1)	4	0.03
Cambodian (7)	7	0.05
Chinese, ex. Taiwanese (37)	128	0.89
Filipino (236)	403	2.79
Indian (19)	24	0.17
Indonesian	3	0.02
Japanese (33)	99	0.69
Korean (139)	222	1.54
Laotian (14)	16	0.11
Malaysian	1	0.01
Pakistani (1)	1	0.01
Sri Lankan (3)	3	0.02
Taiwanese	1	0.01
Thai (7)	17	0.12
Vietnamese (19)	33	0.23
Other Asian, specified (4)	4	0.03
Other Asian, not specified (18)	33	0.23
Austrian	18	0.12
Belgian	5	0.03
British	6	0.04
Canadian	41	0.28
Czech	17	0.12

Notes: 1. Figures in the "Number" column do not add up to the total population due to: a) Ancestry/Race overlap — e.g. persons can report being both White and Irish, b) persons of Hispanic origin can report being any race, c) persons reporting two ancestries are counted in both categories. 2. Numbers in parentheses indicate the number of persons reporting this ancestry/race alone, not in combination with any other ancestry/race. 3. Refer to the Explanation of Data in the front of the book for more detailed information.

Ancestry/Race	Number	%
Czechoslovakian	7	0.05
Danish	30	0.21
Dutch	55	0.38
Eastern European	9	0.06
English	596	4.13
European	108	0.75
Finnish	18	0.12
French, except Basque	416	2.88
French Canadian	154	1.07
German	2,084	14.44
Greek	35	0.24
Hawaii Native/Pacific Islander:	443	3.07
Micronesian: (79)	105	0.73
Guamanian/Chamorro (57)	82	0.57
Other Micronesian (22)	23	0.16
Polynesian: (137)	293	2.03
Native Hawaiian (67)	171	1.19
Samoan (67)	107	0.74
Tongan (2)	6	0.04
Other Polynesian (1)	9	0.06
Other Pac. Isl., not spec. (13)	45	0.31
Hispanic or Latino:	2,337	16.20
Central American:	109	0.76
Costa Rican	1	0.01
Guatemalan	7	0.05
Honduran	9	0.06
Nicaraguan	4	0.03
Panamanian	69	0.48
Salvadoran	18	0.12
Other Central American	1	0.01
Cuban	37	0.26
Dominican Republic	39	0.27
Mexican	1,143	7.92
Puerto Rican	649	4.50
South American:	70	0.49
Argentinean	3	0.02
Bolivian	1	0.01
Chilean	1	0.01
Colombian	25	0.17
Ecuadorian	19	0.13
Paraguayan	3	0.02
Peruvian	12	0.08
Venezuelan	4	0.03
Other South American	2	0.01
Other Hispanic or Latino	290	2.01
Hungarian	30	0.21
Icelander	6	0.04
Irish	1,587	10.99
Italian	672	4.66
Lithuanian	33	0.23
Maltese	9	0.06
Norwegian	147	1.02
Polish	369	2.56
Portuguese	76	0.53
Romanian	25	0.17
Russian	27	0.19
Scandinavian	34	0.24
Scotch-Irish	140	0.97
Scottish	295	2.04
Slovak	6	0.04
Swedish	77	0.53
Swiss	19	0.13
United States or American	945	6.55
Welsh	60	0.42
West Indian, excl. Hispanic:	152	1.05
British West Indian	12	0.08
Dutch West Indian	9	0.06
Haitian	24	0.17
Jamaican	80	0.55
Trinidadian and Tobagonian	17	0.12
West Indian	10	0.07
White:	8,827	61.18
Not Hispanic (7,506)	8,019	55.58
Hispanic (631)	808	5.60
Yugoslavian	7	0.05

Wahiawa

Place Type: Census Designated Place
County: Honolulu
Population: 16,151

Ancestry/Race	Number	%
African American/Black:	674	4.17
Not Hispanic (306)	567	3.51
Hispanic (20)	107	0.66
African, sub-Saharan:	65	0.40
African	65	0.40
Alaska Native tribes, specified:	7	0.04
Aleut (1)	2	0.01
Eskimo (2)	5	0.03
Am. Ind. or Alaska Nat., not spec.	178	1.10
American Indian tribes, specified:	287	1.78
Apache (7)	25	0.15
Blackfeet	21	0.13
Cherokee (7)	157	0.97
Cheyenne	3	0.02
Chippewa	3	0.02
Choctaw (1)	10	0.06
Comanche	2	0.01
Cree	2	0.01
Iroquois (2)	11	0.07
Latin American Indians (2)	3	0.02
Lumbee	1	0.01
Navajo (1)	3	0.02
Pueblo (1)	3	0.02
Seminole	4	0.02
Sioux	21	0.13
Ute	3	0.02
Yaqui	2	0.01
Yuman	1	0.01
All other tribes (4)	12	0.07
American Indian tribes, not spec.	27	0.17
Asian:	13,282	82.24
Cambodian (5)	5	0.03
Chinese, ex. Taiwanese (245)	2,084	12.90
Filipino (2,855)	5,362	33.20
Indian (2)	42	0.26
Indonesian (1)	2	0.01
Japanese (3,342)	4,888	30.26
Korean (313)	668	4.14
Laotian (14)	26	0.16
Malaysian	10	0.06
Taiwanese	4	0.02
Thai (5)	27	0.17
Vietnamese (18)	27	0.17
Other Asian, specified (27)	98	0.61
Other Asian, not specified (20)	39	0.24
Austrian	14	0.09
Brazilian	7	0.04
British	30	0.19
Celtic	7	0.04
Czechoslovakian	7	0.04
Dutch	25	0.15
English	385	2.38
European	27	0.17
Finnish	7	0.04
French, except Basque	169	1.05
French Canadian	39	0.24
German	554	3.43
Greek	17	0.11
Hawaii Native/Pacific Islander:	4,951	30.65
Melanesian: (1)	5	0.03
Fijian (1)	5	0.03
Micronesian: (163)	250	1.55
Guamanian/Chamorro (32)	99	0.61
Other Micronesian (131)	151	0.93
Polynesian: (1,317)	4,577	28.34
Native Hawaiian (911)	3,776	23.38
Samoan (366)	668	4.14
Tongan (18)	32	0.20
Other Polynesian (22)	101	0.63
Other Pac. Isl., specified	1	0.01
Other Pac. Isl., not spec. (10)	118	0.73
Hispanic or Latino:	1,777	11.00
Central American:	17	0.11
Guatemalan	1	0.01
Nicaraguan	2	0.01
Panamanian	11	0.07
Salvadoran	3	0.02
Cuban	11	0.07
Dominican Republic	1	0.01
Mexican	306	1.89
Puerto Rican	734	4.54
South American:	7	0.04
Colombian	6	0.04
Peruvian	1	0.01
Other Hispanic or Latino	701	4.34
Hungarian	13	0.08
Irish	331	2.05
Italian	191	1.18
Lithuanian	3	0.02
Norwegian	77	0.48
Polish	48	0.30
Portuguese	510	3.16
Scotch-Irish	44	0.27
Scottish	74	0.46
Swedish	106	0.66
Swiss	8	0.05
United States or American	195	1.21
White:	4,845	30.00
Not Hispanic (1,640)	4,056	25.11
Hispanic (186)	789	4.89

Waianae

Place Type: Census Designated Place
County: Honolulu
Population: 10,506

Ancestry/Race	Number	%
African American/Black:	250	2.38
Not Hispanic (69)	199	1.89
Hispanic (16)	51	0.49
African, sub-Saharan:	38	0.36
African	12	0.11
Somalian	26	0.24
Am. Ind. or Alaska Nat., not spec.	142	1.35
American Indian tribes, specified:	237	2.26
Apache (1)	15	0.14
Blackfeet	12	0.11
Cherokee (11)	144	1.37
Cheyenne	10	0.10
Chickasaw	2	0.02
Choctaw	2	0.02
Comanche	2	0.02
Crow	2	0.02
Kiowa	1	0.01
Latin American Indians	2	0.02
Navajo	5	0.05
Seminole	3	0.03
Shoshone	1	0.01
Sioux	19	0.18
Yakama	4	0.04
All other tribes (6)	13	0.12
American Indian tribes, not spec.	20	0.19
Asian:	6,628	63.09
Chinese, ex. Taiwanese (156)	2,024	19.27
Filipino (1,155)	2,970	28.27
Indian (5)	20	0.19
Japanese (474)	1,317	12.54
Korean (18)	199	1.89
Laotian (37)	43	0.41
Malaysian	2	0.02
Thai (7)	13	0.12
Vietnamese (1)	8	0.08
Other Asian, specified (3)	12	0.11
Other Asian, not specified (2)	20	0.19
Belgian	7	0.07
Czech	10	0.09
Czechoslovakian	15	0.14
Danish	8	0.08
Dutch	18	0.17
English	143	1.34
European	14	0.13
French, except Basque	17	0.16

Notes: 1. Figures in the "Number" column do not add up to the total population due to: a) Ancestry/Race overlap — e.g. persons can report being both White and Irish, b) persons of Hispanic origin can report being any race, c) persons reporting two ancestries are counted in both categories. 2. Numbers in parentheses indicate the number of persons reporting this ancestry/race alone, not in combination with any other ancestry/race. 3. Refer to the Explanation of Data in the front of the book for more detailed information.

Ancestry/Race	Number	%
German	369	3.47
Hawaii Native/Pacific Islander:	6,839	65.10
Melanesian:	1	0.01
Fijian	1	0.01
Micronesian: (29)	68	0.65
Guamanian/Chamorro (11)	42	0.40
Other Micronesian (18)	26	0.25
Polynesian: (2,724)	6,701	63.78
Native Hawaiian (2,417)	6,021	57.31
Samoan (273)	555	5.28
Tongan (29)	75	0.71
Other Polynesian (5)	50	0.48
Other Pac. Isl., not spec. (4)	69	0.66
Hispanic or Latino:	1,471	14.00
Cuban	9	0.09
Mexican	146	1.39
Puerto Rican	600	5.71
Other Hispanic or Latino	716	6.82
Irish	302	2.84
Italian	48	0.45
Polish	31	0.29
Portuguese	604	5.67
Russian	26	0.24
Scotch-Irish	25	0.23
Scottish	67	0.63
Swedish	34	0.32
United States or American	29	0.27
Welsh	14	0.13
White:	3,879	36.92
Not Hispanic (844)	3,148	29.96
Hispanic (138)	731	6.96

Wailuku

Place Type: Census Designated Place
County: Maui
Population: 12,296

Ancestry/Race	Number	%
African American/Black:	81	0.66
Not Hispanic (29)	72	0.59
Hispanic	9	0.07
Am. Ind. or Alaska Nat., not spec.	129	1.05
American Indian tribes, specified:	84	0.68
Apache (2)	3	0.02
Blackfeet (1)	7	0.06
Cherokee (11)	34	0.28
Cheyenne (1)	1	0.01
Chickasaw	2	0.02
Chippewa	1	0.01
Choctaw (3)	8	0.07
Cree	1	0.01
Iroquois	2	0.02
Latin American Indians	2	0.02
Navajo	4	0.03
Osage	1	0.01
Sioux (1)	1	0.01
Yaqui	2	0.02
All other tribes (1)	15	0.12
American Indian tribes, not spec.	6	0.05
Arab:	3	0.02
Lebanese	2	0.02
Palestinian	1	0.01
Asian:	9,111	74.10
Cambodian (1)	2	0.02
Chinese, ex. Taiwanese (158)	1,514	12.31
Filipino (1,587)	3,001	24.41
Indian (13)	31	0.25
Indonesian	6	0.05
Japanese (2,799)	3,984	32.40
Korean (225)	410	3.33
Laotian (4)	5	0.04
Malaysian (1)	4	0.03
Sri Lankan (1)	1	0.01
Thai (8)	9	0.07
Vietnamese (56)	72	0.59
Other Asian, specified (15)	50	0.41
Other Asian, not specified (11)	22	0.18
Austrian	11	0.09
British	17	0.14
Croatian	21	0.17
Czech	10	0.08
Danish	27	0.22
Dutch	49	0.39
English	283	2.28
European	52	0.42
Finnish	11	0.09
French, except Basque	72	0.58
French Canadian	20	0.16
German	361	2.91
Hawaii Native/Pacific Islander:	3,813	31.01
Melanesian: (1)	5	0.04
Fijian (1)	5	0.04
Micronesian: (92)	128	1.04
Guamanian/Chamorro (8)	27	0.22
Other Micronesian (84)	101	0.82
Polynesian: (1,317)	3,630	29.52
Native Hawaiian (1,256)	3,453	28.08
Samoan (16)	74	0.60
Tongan (44)	85	0.69
Other Polynesian (1)	18	0.15
Other Pac. Isl., specified	1	0.01
Other Pac. Isl., not spec. (10)	49	0.40
Hispanic or Latino:	953	7.75
Central American:	20	0.16
Guatemalan	12	0.10
Nicaraguan	2	0.02
Salvadoran	3	0.02
Other Central American	3	0.02
Cuban	1	0.01
Mexican	189	1.54
Puerto Rican	402	3.27
South American:	4	0.03
Argentinean	1	0.01
Colombian	1	0.01
Venezuelan	1	0.01
Other South American	1	0.01
Other Hispanic or Latino	337	2.74
Hungarian	23	0.19
Irish	282	2.27
Italian	117	0.94
Norwegian	96	0.77
Polish	128	1.03
Portuguese	773	6.22
Russian	35	0.28
Scandinavian	3	0.02
Scotch-Irish	48	0.39
Scottish	58	0.47
Swedish	51	0.41
Swiss	6	0.05
United States or American	94	0.76
Welsh	40	0.32
White:	4,329	35.21
Not Hispanic (2,055)	3,847	31.29
Hispanic (178)	482	3.92

Waimalu

Place Type: Census Designated Place
County: Honolulu
Population: 29,371

Ancestry/Race	Number	%
Acadian/Cajun	24	0.08
African American/Black:	1,023	3.48
Not Hispanic (668)	950	3.23
Hispanic (16)	73	0.25
African, sub-Saharan:	123	0.42
African	99	0.34
Other sub-Saharan African	24	0.08
Alaska Native tribes, specified:	2	0.01
Tlingit-Haida (2)	2	0.01
Alaska Native tribes, not specified	1	0.00
Am. Ind. or Alaska Nat., not spec.	171	0.58
American Indian tribes, specified:	257	0.88
Apache (2)	19	0.06
Blackfeet (2)	31	0.11
Cherokee (10)	97	0.33
Cheyenne	2	0.01
Chickasaw (1)	2	0.01
Chippewa (2)	6	0.02
Choctaw (1)	6	0.02
Comanche	1	0.00
Creek (3)	7	0.02
Crow	2	0.01
Delaware	1	0.00
Iroquois (1)	14	0.05
Latin American Indians (4)	9	0.03
Navajo (2)	8	0.03
Osage (1)	2	0.01
Potawatomi (2)	3	0.01
Pueblo (8)	10	0.03
Seminole	3	0.01
Shoshone	4	0.01
Sioux (2)	3	0.01
Tohono O'Odham (1)	2	0.01
Yakama	2	0.01
Yaqui (2)	3	0.01
All other tribes (9)	20	0.07
American Indian tribes, not spec.	33	0.11
Arab:	18	0.06
Moroccan	8	0.03
Other Arab	10	0.03
Armenian	11	0.04
Asian:	24,215	82.45
Cambodian (6)	7	0.02
Chinese, ex. Taiwanese (1,379)	4,253	14.48
Filipino (3,511)	5,951	20.26
Indian (19)	58	0.20
Indonesian (5)	10	0.03
Japanese (8,473)	11,537	39.28
Korean (1,025)	1,708	5.82
Laotian (16)	31	0.11
Malaysian (4)	19	0.06
Pakistani (1)	1	0.00
Taiwanese (24)	36	0.12
Thai (43)	79	0.27
Vietnamese (119)	176	0.60
Other Asian, specified (104)	297	1.01
Other Asian, not specified (14)	52	0.18
Austrian	44	0.15
Belgian	8	0.03
British	25	0.08
Canadian	38	0.13
Celtic	6	0.02
Croatian	31	0.11
Czech	51	0.17
Czechoslovakian	25	0.08
Danish	45	0.15
Dutch	113	0.38
Eastern European	6	0.02
English	969	3.28
European	48	0.16
French, except Basque	432	1.46
French Canadian	20	0.07
German	1,559	5.28
Greek	9	0.03
Hawaii Native/Pacific Islander:	4,888	16.64
Melanesian:	3	0.01
Fijian	2	0.01
Other Melanesian	1	0.00
Micronesian: (227)	373	1.27
Guamanian/Chamorro (61)	135	0.46
Other Micronesian (166)	238	0.81
Polynesian: (1,354)	4,430	15.08
Native Hawaiian (995)	3,746	12.75
Samoan (346)	619	2.11
Tongan (8)	24	0.08
Other Polynesian (5)	41	0.14
Other Pac. Isl., specified	1	0.00
Other Pac. Isl., not spec. (17)	81	0.28
Hispanic or Latino:	1,753	5.97
Central American:	12	0.04
Costa Rican	1	0.00
Guatemalan	2	0.01
Honduran	2	0.01
Nicaraguan	2	0.01
Panamanian	4	0.01
Other Central American	1	0.00
Cuban	18	0.06

Notes: 1. Figures in the "Number" column do not add up to the total population due to: a) Ancestry/Race overlap — e.g. persons can report being both White and Irish, b) persons of Hispanic origin can report being any race, c) persons reporting two ancestries are counted in both categories. 2. Numbers in parentheses indicate the number of persons reporting this ancestry/race alone, not in combination with any other ancestry/race. 3. Refer to the Explanation of Data in the front of the book for more detailed information.

Dominican Republic	3	0.01
Mexican	373	1.27
Puerto Rican	526	1.79
South American:	26	0.09
Bolivian	2	0.01
Chilean	2	0.01
Colombian	9	0.03
Ecuadorian	1	0.00
Peruvian	5	0.02
Uruguayan	2	0.01
Venezuelan	3	0.01
Other South American	2	0.01
Other Hispanic or Latino	795	2.71
Hungarian	96	0.33
Irish	978	3.31
Israeli	7	0.02
Italian	275	0.93
Norwegian	126	0.43
Pennsylvania German	6	0.02
Polish	252	0.85
Portuguese	742	2.51
Russian	57	0.19
Scandinavian	5	0.02
Scotch-Irish	134	0.45
Scottish	183	0.62
Slovak	10	0.03
Slovene	6	0.02
Swedish	159	0.54
Swiss	30	0.10
Ukrainian	39	0.13
United States or American	329	1.12
Welsh	16	0.05
West Indian, excl. Hispanic:	54	0.18
Barbadian	7	0.02
Jamaican	24	0.08
Trinidadian and Tobagonian	14	0.05
West Indian	9	0.03
White:	8,727	29.71
Not Hispanic (4,726)	7,858	26.75
Hispanic (291)	869	2.96

Waipahu

Place Type: Census Designated Place
County: Honolulu
Population: 33,108

Ancestry/Race	Number	%
African American/Black:	569	1.72
Not Hispanic (281)	488	1.47
Hispanic (27)	81	0.24
African, sub-Saharan:	4	0.01
African	4	0.01
Alaska Native tribes, specified:	1	0.00
Eskimo	1	0.00
Alaska Native tribes, not specified	6	0.02
Am. Ind. or Alaska Nat., not spec.	253	0.76
American Indian tribes, specified:	189	0.57
Apache (2)	16	0.05
Blackfeet (2)	20	0.06
Cherokee (3)	94	0.28
Cheyenne (1)	2	0.01
Chickasaw	1	0.00
Chippewa	1	0.00
Comanche	2	0.01
Cree	3	0.01
Creek (1)	2	0.01
Crow	1	0.00
Delaware	1	0.00
Latin American Indians (3)	14	0.04
Navajo	1	0.00
Pueblo (2)	2	0.01
Seminole	1	0.00
Shoshone (1)	2	0.01
Sioux (4)	11	0.03
Tohono O'Odham (1)	1	0.00
Yuman (1)	1	0.00
All other tribes (1)	13	0.04
American Indian tribes, not spec.	16	0.05
Asian:	28,120	84.93
Chinese, ex. Taiwanese (444)	2,669	8.06
Filipino (16,668)	19,727	59.58
Indian (11)	38	0.11
Indonesian	2	0.01
Japanese (3,481)	4,874	14.72
Korean (181)	409	1.24
Laotian (42)	58	0.18
Malaysian	15	0.05
Pakistani	2	0.01
Taiwanese (1)	6	0.02
Thai (14)	36	0.11
Vietnamese (93)	114	0.34
Other Asian, specified (53)	89	0.27
Other Asian, not specified (20)	81	0.24
Canadian	11	0.03
Danish	9	0.03
Dutch	6	0.02
English	58	0.18
Finnish	17	0.05
French, except Basque	113	0.34
German	223	0.67
German Russian	6	0.02
Greek	16	0.05
Hawaii Native/Pacific Islander:	7,867	23.76
Melanesian: (1)	9	0.03
Fijian (1)	9	0.03
Micronesian: (396)	521	1.57
Guamanian/Chamorro (18)	78	0.24
Other Micronesian (378)	443	1.34
Polynesian: (3,499)	7,226	21.83
Native Hawaiian (1,072)	4,006	12.10
Samoan (2,198)	2,845	8.59
Tongan (214)	302	0.91
Other Polynesian (15)	73	0.22
Other Pac. Isl., not spec. (23)	111	0.34
Hispanic or Latino:	2,016	6.09
Central American:	14	0.04
Costa Rican	1	0.00
Guatemalan	1	0.00
Honduran	1	0.00
Nicaraguan	1	0.00
Panamanian	10	0.03
Cuban	8	0.02
Dominican Republic	5	0.02
Mexican	250	0.76
Puerto Rican	766	2.31
South American:	3	0.01
Ecuadorian	2	0.01
Paraguayan	1	0.00
Other Hispanic or Latino	970	2.93
Irish	158	0.48
Italian	107	0.32
Norwegian	34	0.10
Polish	20	0.06
Portuguese	742	2.24
Scotch-Irish	26	0.08
Scottish	6	0.02
Slovak	26	0.08
Slovene	7	0.02
United States or American	227	0.69
West Indian, excl. Hispanic:	19	0.06
Haitian	12	0.04
Jamaican	7	0.02
White:	4,524	13.66
Not Hispanic (1,362)	3,785	11.43
Hispanic (204)	739	2.23

Waipio

Place Type: Census Designated Place
County: Honolulu
Population: 11,672

Ancestry/Race	Number	%
African American/Black:	449	3.85
Not Hispanic (316)	410	3.51
Hispanic (13)	39	0.33
African, sub-Saharan:	32	0.27
African	32	0.27
Alaska Native tribes, specified:	2	0.02
Alaska Athabascan	1	0.01
Aleut (1)	1	0.01
Alaska Native tribes, not specified	2	0.02
Am. Ind. or Alaska Nat., not spec.	61	0.52
American Indian tribes, specified:	111	0.95
Apache	4	0.03
Blackfeet	1	0.01
Cherokee	43	0.37
Cheyenne	2	0.02
Chippewa (2)	6	0.05
Choctaw	9	0.08
Comanche	5	0.04
Creek (2)	5	0.04
Latin American Indians (2)	2	0.02
Pueblo (2)	3	0.03
Sioux (4)	13	0.11
Tohono O'Odham (1)	1	0.01
All other tribes (3)	17	0.15
American Indian tribes, not spec.	5	0.04
Arab:	33	0.28
Arab/Arabic	33	0.28
Armenian	7	0.06
Asian:	10,342	88.61
Chinese, ex. Taiwanese (379)	1,770	15.16
Filipino (2,199)	3,535	30.29
Indian (17)	38	0.33
Indonesian	5	0.04
Japanese (2,734)	4,205	36.03
Korean (234)	534	4.58
Laotian (12)	20	0.17
Malaysian (4)	6	0.05
Pakistani	4	0.03
Sri Lankan (5)	5	0.04
Taiwanese (1)	1	0.01
Thai (10)	19	0.16
Vietnamese (30)	57	0.49
Other Asian, specified (45)	125	1.07
Other Asian, not specified (6)	18	0.15
Austrian	17	0.15
Canadian	8	0.07
Czech	23	0.20
Danish	12	0.10
Dutch	13	0.11
English	278	2.39
European	64	0.55
French, except Basque	74	0.64
French Canadian	17	0.15
German	328	2.82
Greek	10	0.09
Hawaii Native/Pacific Islander:	2,211	18.94
Melanesian: (2)	4	0.03
Fijian (2)	4	0.03
Micronesian: (41)	95	0.81
Guamanian/Chamorro (17)	55	0.47
Other Micronesian (24)	40	0.34
Polynesian: (558)	2,073	17.76
Native Hawaiian (431)	1,799	15.41
Samoan (97)	210	1.80
Tongan (20)	33	0.28
Other Polynesian (10)	31	0.27
Other Pac. Isl., specified	1	0.01
Other Pac. Isl., not spec. (9)	38	0.33
Hispanic or Latino:	789	6.76
Central American:	3	0.03
Costa Rican	1	0.01
Salvadoran	2	0.02
Cuban	1	0.01
Dominican Republic	1	0.01
Mexican	166	1.42
Puerto Rican	213	1.82
South American:	11	0.09
Argentinean	1	0.01
Chilean	2	0.02
Ecuadorian	3	0.03
Peruvian	4	0.03
Other South American	1	0.01
Other Hispanic or Latino	394	3.38
Hungarian	7	0.06
Irish	263	2.26
Italian	168	1.44

Notes: 1. Figures in the "Number" column do not add up to the total population due to: a) Ancestry/Race overlap — e.g. persons can report being both White and Irish, b) persons of Hispanic origin can report being any race, c) persons reporting two ancestries are counted in both categories. 2. Numbers in parentheses indicate the number of persons reporting this ancestry/race alone, not in combination with any other ancestry/race. 3. Refer to the Explanation of Data in the front of the book for more detailed information.

Ancestry/Race	Number	%
Lithuanian	17	0.15
Norwegian	42	0.36
Polish	51	0.44
Portuguese	230	1.98
Russian	21	0.18
Scandinavian	17	0.15
Scotch-Irish	41	0.35
Scottish	35	0.30
Slavic	9	0.08
Swedish	45	0.39
Swiss	23	0.20
Ukrainian	9	0.08
United States or American	114	0.98
Welsh	40	0.34
West Indian, excl. Hispanic:	21	0.18
Belizean	13	0.11
Jamaican	8	0.07
White:	3,482	29.83
Not Hispanic (1,565)	3,108	26.63
Hispanic (118)	374	3.20

Blackfoot

Place Type: City
County: Bingham
Population: 10,419

Ancestry/Race	Number	%
African American/Black:	54	0.52
Not Hispanic (16)	41	0.39
Hispanic (6)	13	0.12
Alaska Native tribes, specified:	1	0.01
Alaska Athabascan (1)	1	0.01
Alaska Native tribes, not specified	2	0.02
Am. Ind. or Alaska Nat., not spec.	75	0.72
American Indian tribes, specified:	272	2.61
Apache	1	0.01
Blackfeet	2	0.02
Cherokee (1)	4	0.04
Cheyenne (4)	4	0.04
Chippewa (5)	6	0.06
Choctaw (2)	2	0.02
Comanche	1	0.01
Cree (3)	3	0.03
Crow (1)	1	0.01
Iroquois (1)	7	0.07
Latin American Indians (5)	11	0.11
Navajo (19)	19	0.18
Osage	1	0.01
Pueblo (1)	1	0.01
Shoshone (36)	47	0.45
Sioux (4)	10	0.10
Ute (3)	3	0.03
Yakama	1	0.01
Yaqui (2)	3	0.03
All other tribes (122)	145	1.39
American Indian tribes, not spec.	6	0.06
Arab:	36	0.34
Arab/Arabic	36	0.34
Armenian	8	0.08
Asian:	186	1.79
Chinese, ex. Taiwanese (19)	28	0.27
Filipino (6)	14	0.13
Indian (5)	8	0.08
Japanese (49)	74	0.71
Korean (6)	12	0.12
Laotian (5)	14	0.13
Thai (1)	1	0.01
Vietnamese (19)	24	0.23
Other Asian, specified	1	0.01
Other Asian, not specified (4)	10	0.10
Basque	9	0.09
Belgian	18	0.17
British	34	0.33
Bulgarian	11	0.11
Canadian	36	0.34
Croatian	7	0.07
Czech	38	0.36
Czechoslovakian	11	0.11
Danish	632	6.06
Dutch	142	1.36
English	2,283	21.88
European	134	1.28
Finnish	65	0.62
French, except Basque	86	0.82
French Canadian	21	0.20
German	1,043	9.99
Greek	24	0.23
Hawaii Native/Pacific Islander:	24	0.23
Micronesian: (1)	3	0.03
Other Micronesian (1)	3	0.03
Polynesian: (1)	11	0.11
Native Hawaiian (1)	6	0.06
Samoan	1	0.01
Tongan	3	0.03
Other Polynesian	1	0.01
Other Pac. Isl., not spec.	10	0.10
Hispanic or Latino:	1,372	13.17
Central American:	11	0.11
Guatemalan	9	0.09
Salvadoran	1	0.01
Other Central American	1	0.01
Dominican Republic	4	0.04
Mexican	1,121	10.76
Puerto Rican	17	0.16
South American:	19	0.18
Bolivian	1	0.01
Chilean	3	0.03
Colombian	3	0.03
Peruvian	11	0.11
Other South American	1	0.01
Other Hispanic or Latino	200	1.92
Hungarian	9	0.09
Irish	639	6.12
Italian	225	2.16
Lithuanian	6	0.06
Norwegian	89	0.85
Pennsylvania German	9	0.09
Polish	84	0.80
Russian	39	0.37
Scandinavian	150	1.44
Scotch-Irish	191	1.83
Scottish	242	2.32
Swedish	312	2.99
Swiss	57	0.55
United States or American	939	9.00
Welsh	332	3.18
White:	9,333	89.58
Not Hispanic (8,540)	8,679	83.30
Hispanic (500)	654	6.28

Boise City

Place Type: City
County: Ada
Population: 185,787

Ancestry/Race	Number	%
Acadian/Cajun	8	0.00
Afghan	7	0.00
African American/Black:	2,133	1.15
Not Hispanic (1,363)	1,978	1.06
Hispanic (74)	155	0.08
African, sub-Saharan:	258	0.14
African	103	0.06
Nigerian	25	0.01
Somalian	57	0.03
South African	12	0.01
Sudanese	37	0.02
Zairian	7	0.00
Zimbabwean	10	0.01
Other sub-Saharan African	7	0.00
Alaska Native tribes, specified:	72	0.04
Alaska Athabascan (3)	7	0.00
Aleut (15)	22	0.01
Eskimo (10)	17	0.01
Tlingit-Haida (19)	25	0.01
All other tribes	1	0.00
Alaska Native tribes, not specified	14	0.01
Am. Ind. or Alaska Nat., not spec.	642	0.35
Albanian	269	0.14
American Indian tribes, specified:	1,797	0.97
Apache (18)	51	0.03
Blackfeet (13)	71	0.04
Cherokee (139)	484	0.26
Cheyenne (15)	19	0.01
Chickasaw (5)	13	0.01
Chippewa (53)	79	0.04
Choctaw (45)	78	0.04
Colville (3)	5	0.00
Comanche (6)	12	0.01
Cree (5)	10	0.01
Creek (9)	28	0.02
Crow (6)	13	0.01
Delaware (17)	29	0.02
Iroquois (20)	30	0.02
Kiowa (2)	3	0.00
Latin American Indians (25)	78	0.04
Lumbee (3)	5	0.00
Menominee (2)	2	0.00
Navajo (54)	90	0.05
Osage (5)	5	0.00
Ottawa (3)	5	0.00
Paiute (6)	19	0.01
Pima (3)	6	0.00
Potawatomi (12)	23	0.01
Pueblo (10)	21	0.01
Puget Sound Salish (7)	8	0.00
Seminole (8)	20	0.01
Shoshone (39)	67	0.04
Sioux (42)	98	0.05
Tohono O'Odham	2	0.00
Ute (4)	11	0.01
Yakama (3)	5	0.00
Yaqui (1)	1	0.00
Yuman	2	0.00
All other tribes (278)	404	0.22
American Indian tribes, not spec.	107	0.06
Arab:	519	0.28
Arab/Arabic	104	0.06
Egyptian	45	0.02
Iraqi	50	0.03
Lebanese	241	0.13
Moroccan	35	0.02
Syrian	26	0.01
Other Arab	18	0.01
Armenian	126	0.07
Asian:	5,204	2.80
Bangladeshi (3)	3	0.00
Cambodian (36)	42	0.02
Chinese, ex. Taiwanese (766)	967	0.52
Filipino (359)	655	0.35
Hmong (16)	23	0.01
Indian (593)	664	0.36
Indonesian (10)	20	0.01
Japanese (532)	933	0.50
Korean (335)	476	0.26
Laotian (240)	284	0.15
Malaysian	4	0.00
Pakistani (33)	34	0.02
Sri Lankan (2)	2	0.00
Taiwanese (22)	26	0.01
Thai (61)	95	0.05
Vietnamese (677)	736	0.40
Other Asian, specified (6)	28	0.02
Other Asian, not specified (127)	212	0.11
Australian	69	0.04
Austrian	537	0.29
Basque	1,965	1.06
Belgian	183	0.10
Brazilian	49	0.03
British	1,360	0.73
Bulgarian	7	0.00
Canadian	469	0.25
Celtic	88	0.05
Croatian	255	0.14
Czech	1,080	0.58
Czechoslovakian	434	0.23
Danish	3,900	2.10
Dutch	4,673	2.51

Notes: 1. Figures in the "Number" column do not add up to the total population due to: a) Ancestry/Race overlap — e.g. persons can report being both White and Irish, b) persons of Hispanic origin can report being any race, c) persons reporting two ancestries are counted in both categories. 2. Numbers in parentheses indicate the number of persons reporting this ancestry/race alone, not in combination with any other ancestry/race. 3. Refer to the Explanation of Data in the front of the book for more detailed information.

Ancestry/Race	Number	%
Eastern European	44	0.02
English	32,070	17.25
Estonian	24	0.01
European	3,594	1.93
Finnish	797	0.43
French, except Basque	6,701	3.60
French Canadian	1,410	0.76
German	38,259	20.58
German Russian	7	0.00
Greek	672	0.36
Hawaii Native/Pacific Islander:	642	0.35
Melanesian: (1)	1	0.00
Fijian (1)	1	0.00
Micronesian: (104)	157	0.08
Guamanian/Chamorro (84)	122	0.07
Other Micronesian (20)	35	0.02
Polynesian: (153)	362	0.19
Native Hawaiian (77)	219	0.12
Samoan (57)	106	0.06
Tongan (10)	22	0.01
Other Polynesian (9)	15	0.01
Other Pac. Isl., specified	19	0.01
Other Pac. Isl., not spec. (32)	103	0.06
Hispanic or Latino:	8,410	4.53
Central American:	150	0.08
Costa Rican	19	0.01
Guatemalan	43	0.02
Honduran	19	0.01
Nicaraguan	7	0.00
Panamanian	30	0.02
Salvadoran	27	0.01
Other Central American	5	0.00
Cuban	107	0.06
Dominican Republic	7	0.00
Mexican	5,756	3.10
Puerto Rican	297	0.16
South American:	235	0.13
Argentinean	22	0.01
Bolivian	7	0.00
Chilean	27	0.01
Colombian	59	0.03
Ecuadorian	30	0.02
Paraguayan	2	0.00
Peruvian	45	0.02
Uruguayan	2	0.00
Venezuelan	27	0.01
Other South American	14	0.01
Other Hispanic or Latino	1,858	1.00
Hungarian	523	0.28
Icelander	99	0.05
Iranian	161	0.09
Irish	23,146	12.45
Italian	5,843	3.14
Latvian	41	0.02
Lithuanian	306	0.16
Luxemburger	47	0.03
Macedonian	5	0.00
Maltese	16	0.01
New Zealander	5	0.00
Northern European	330	0.18
Norwegian	6,957	3.74
Pennsylvania German	83	0.04
Polish	2,839	1.53
Portuguese	647	0.35
Romanian	84	0.05
Russian	1,386	0.75
Scandinavian	975	0.52
Scotch-Irish	4,215	2.27
Scottish	7,186	3.86
Serbian	80	0.04
Slavic	62	0.03
Slovak	162	0.09
Slovene	110	0.06
Swedish	6,140	3.30
Swiss	1,560	0.84
Turkish	25	0.01
Ukrainian	428	0.23
United States or American	13,208	7.10
Welsh	3,344	1.80
West Indian, excl. Hispanic:	174	0.09
Dutch West Indian	14	0.01
Haitian	10	0.01
Jamaican	131	0.07
U.S. Virgin Islander	5	0.00
West Indian	14	0.01
White:	175,314	94.36
Not Hispanic (167,022)	170,284	91.66
Hispanic (4,182)	5,030	2.71
Yugoslavian	1,444	0.78

Caldwell

Place Type: City
County: Canyon
Population: 25,967

Ancestry/Race	Number	%
Acadian/Cajun	9	0.03
African American/Black:	210	0.81
Not Hispanic (86)	146	0.56
Hispanic (35)	64	0.25
African, sub-Saharan:	16	0.06
Ethiopian	16	0.06
Alaska Native tribes, specified:	2	0.01
Aleut	1	0.00
Eskimo	1	0.00
Am. Ind. or Alaska Nat., not spec.	147	0.57
American Indian tribes, specified:	314	1.21
Apache (6)	16	0.06
Blackfeet (1)	5	0.02
Cherokee (33)	92	0.35
Cheyenne	1	0.00
Chickasaw (3)	8	0.03
Chippewa (10)	20	0.08
Choctaw (8)	19	0.07
Creek (2)	4	0.02
Crow	1	0.00
Delaware	10	0.04
Iroquois (1)	2	0.01
Latin American Indians (14)	23	0.09
Menominee	3	0.01
Navajo (14)	21	0.08
Osage (1)	1	0.00
Paiute (8)	11	0.04
Seminole (1)	3	0.01
Shoshone (2)	3	0.01
Sioux (2)	11	0.04
Ute (1)	4	0.02
Yaqui	1	0.00
All other tribes (37)	55	0.21
American Indian tribes, not spec.	23	0.09
Arab:	9	0.03
Lebanese	9	0.03
Armenian	22	0.09
Asian:	370	1.42
Chinese, ex. Taiwanese (56)	74	0.28
Filipino (34)	100	0.39
Indian (10)	13	0.05
Indonesian	2	0.01
Japanese (82)	122	0.47
Korean (10)	15	0.06
Laotian	1	0.00
Thai (4)	9	0.03
Vietnamese (15)	15	0.06
Other Asian, specified	1	0.00
Other Asian, not specified (2)	18	0.07
Austrian	15	0.06
Basque	322	1.25
British	68	0.26
Bulgarian	30	0.12
Canadian	49	0.19
Croatian	9	0.03
Czech	68	0.26
Czechoslovakian	40	0.16
Danish	407	1.58
Dutch	617	2.40
English	2,743	10.66
European	217	0.84
Finnish	30	0.12
French, except Basque	492	1.91
French Canadian	214	0.83
German	3,921	15.24
Greek	14	0.05
Hawaii Native/Pacific Islander:	89	0.34
Micronesian: (10)	15	0.06
Guamanian/Chamorro (9)	14	0.05
Other Micronesian (1)	1	0.00
Polynesian: (15)	57	0.22
Native Hawaiian (8)	41	0.16
Samoan (2)	6	0.02
Tongan (3)	4	0.02
Other Polynesian (2)	6	0.02
Other Pac. Isl., not spec.	17	0.07
Hispanic or Latino:	7,307	28.14
Central American:	33	0.13
Costa Rican	1	0.00
Guatemalan	16	0.06
Honduran	1	0.00
Nicaraguan	2	0.01
Salvadoran	11	0.04
Other Central American	2	0.01
Cuban	8	0.03
Dominican Republic	1	0.00
Mexican	5,703	21.96
Puerto Rican	43	0.17
South American:	36	0.14
Argentinean	13	0.05
Bolivian	3	0.01
Chilean	8	0.03
Colombian	2	0.01
Ecuadorian	2	0.01
Peruvian	3	0.01
Venezuelan	3	0.01
Other South American	2	0.01
Other Hispanic or Latino	1,483	5.71
Hungarian	17	0.07
Icelander	11	0.04
Iranian	11	0.04
Irish	2,142	8.33
Italian	484	1.88
Lithuanian	21	0.08
Norwegian	502	1.95
Pennsylvania German	42	0.16
Polish	163	0.63
Portuguese	28	0.11
Russian	73	0.28
Scandinavian	51	0.20
Scotch-Irish	371	1.44
Scottish	628	2.44
Serbian	15	0.06
Slovene	8	0.03
Swedish	548	2.13
Swiss	132	0.51
United States or American	1,679	6.53
Welsh	203	0.79
West Indian, excl. Hispanic:	7	0.03
West Indian	7	0.03
White:	20,149	77.59
Not Hispanic (17,746)	18,127	69.81
Hispanic (1,747)	2,022	7.79
Yugoslavian	12	0.05

Coeur d'Alene

Place Type: City
County: Kootenai
Population: 34,514

Ancestry/Race	Number	%
African American/Black:	141	0.41
Not Hispanic (73)	133	0.39
Hispanic (4)	8	0.02
African, sub-Saharan:	9	0.03
African	9	0.03
Alaska Native tribes, specified:	18	0.05
Alaska Athabascan (2)	4	0.01
Aleut (3)	4	0.01
Eskimo	1	0.00
Tlingit-Haida (4)	6	0.02
All other tribes (1)	3	0.01

Notes: 1. Figures in the "Number" column do not add up to the total population due to: a) Ancestry/Race overlap — e.g. persons can report being both White and Irish, b) persons of Hispanic origin can report being any race, c) persons reporting two ancestries are counted in both categories. 2. Numbers in parentheses indicate the number of persons reporting this ancestry/race alone, not in combination with any other ancestry/race. 3. Refer to the Explanation of Data in the front of the book for more detailed information.

Alaska Native tribes, not specified	1	0.00
Am. Ind. or Alaska Nat., not spec.	158	0.46
American Indian tribes, specified:	454	1.32
Apache (2)	17	0.05
Blackfeet (10)	22	0.06
Cherokee (26)	122	0.35
Cheyenne (1)	6	0.02
Chickasaw	1	0.00
Chippewa (16)	33	0.10
Choctaw (4)	25	0.07
Colville (7)	9	0.03
Comanche (1)	5	0.01
Cree (3)	7	0.02
Creek	1	0.00
Crow (1)	2	0.01
Delaware	1	0.00
Iroquois (1)	3	0.01
Kiowa (1)	1	0.00
Latin American Indians (2)	9	0.03
Menominee	1	0.00
Navajo (6)	9	0.03
Osage (1)	2	0.01
Ottawa (2)	3	0.01
Paiute	3	0.01
Pima	1	0.00
Potawatomi	1	0.00
Pueblo (4)	8	0.02
Puget Sound Salish (3)	4	0.01
Shoshone (9)	11	0.03
Sioux (12)	29	0.08
Yaqui (1)	1	0.00
All other tribes (66)	117	0.34
American Indian tribes, not spec.	20	0.06
Arab:	17	0.05
Lebanese	7	0.02
Syrian	10	0.03
Asian:	370	1.07
Chinese, ex. Taiwanese (38)	54	0.16
Filipino (45)	95	0.28
Hmong (1)	1	0.00
Indian (11)	26	0.08
Indonesian (1)	2	0.01
Japanese (58)	101	0.29
Korean (21)	34	0.10
Malaysian (1)	1	0.00
Thai (4)	7	0.02
Vietnamese (17)	28	0.08
Other Asian, specified (2)	6	0.02
Other Asian, not specified (5)	15	0.04
Australian	16	0.05
Austrian	129	0.37
Basque	18	0.05
Belgian	40	0.11
Brazilian	6	0.02
British	194	0.56
Bulgarian	11	0.03
Canadian	119	0.34
Croatian	8	0.02
Czech	205	0.59
Czechoslovakian	124	0.36
Danish	353	1.01
Dutch	913	2.62
English	4,584	13.18
Estonian	8	0.02
European	414	1.19
Finnish	182	0.52
French, except Basque	1,643	4.72
French Canadian	362	1.04
German	8,158	23.45
German Russian	11	0.03
Greek	60	0.17
Hawaii Native/Pacific Islander:	63	0.18
Micronesian: (8)	9	0.03
Guamanian/Chamorro (8)	9	0.03
Polynesian: (20)	43	0.12
Native Hawaiian (17)	40	0.12
Samoan (3)	3	0.01
Other Pac. Isl., not spec. (3)	11	0.03
Hispanic or Latino:	932	2.70
Central American:	15	0.04
Guatemalan	4	0.01
Honduran	1	0.00
Panamanian	2	0.01
Salvadoran	8	0.02
Cuban	16	0.05
Dominican Republic	1	0.00
Mexican	566	1.64
Puerto Rican	67	0.19
South American:	15	0.04
Argentinean	1	0.00
Colombian	8	0.02
Peruvian	5	0.01
Other South American	1	0.00
Other Hispanic or Latino	252	0.73
Hungarian	128	0.37
Icelander	8	0.02
Irish	4,906	14.10
Italian	1,318	3.79
Lithuanian	74	0.21
Luxemburger	9	0.03
Northern European	11	0.03
Norwegian	1,915	5.51
Pennsylvania German	36	0.10
Polish	561	1.61
Portuguese	140	0.40
Russian	257	0.74
Scandinavian	253	0.73
Scotch-Irish	616	1.77
Scottish	1,022	2.94
Serbian	39	0.11
Slavic	17	0.05
Slovak	5	0.01
Slovene	14	0.04
Swedish	1,414	4.06
Swiss	149	0.43
Turkish	46	0.13
Ukrainian	115	0.33
United States or American	2,848	8.19
Welsh	374	1.08
West Indian, excl. Hispanic:	11	0.03
Dutch West Indian	11	0.03
White:	33,680	97.58
Not Hispanic (32,463)	32,982	95.56
Hispanic (601)	698	2.02
Yugoslavian	56	0.16

Eagle

Place Type: City
County: Ada
Population: 11,085

Ancestry/Race	Number	%
African American/Black:	53	0.48
Not Hispanic (40)	50	0.45
Hispanic (1)	3	0.03
Alaska Native tribes, specified:	3	0.03
Aleut (1)	1	0.01
Tlingit-Haida	2	0.02
Alaska Native tribes, not specified	1	0.01
Am. Ind. or Alaska Nat., not spec.	32	0.29
American Indian tribes, specified:	88	0.79
Apache (1)	5	0.05
Blackfeet (1)	2	0.02
Cherokee (7)	25	0.23
Chickasaw	2	0.02
Chippewa	1	0.01
Choctaw (3)	7	0.06
Colville (3)	4	0.04
Delaware	2	0.02
Iroquois	1	0.01
Latin American Indians (1)	5	0.05
Navajo (2)	5	0.05
Pueblo (1)	1	0.01
Sioux (5)	7	0.06
All other tribes (11)	21	0.19
American Indian tribes, not spec.	5	0.05
Arab:	16	0.14
Other Arab	16	0.14
Asian:	137	1.24
Chinese, ex. Taiwanese (12)	21	0.19
Filipino (7)	16	0.14
Indian (23)	23	0.21
Japanese (13)	34	0.31
Korean (13)	23	0.21
Pakistani (4)	4	0.04
Thai (2)	3	0.03
Vietnamese (7)	13	0.12
Austrian	41	0.37
Basque	140	1.26
Belgian	5	0.04
British	60	0.54
Canadian	38	0.34
Czech	132	1.18
Czechoslovakian	39	0.35
Danish	281	2.52
Dutch	203	1.82
English	2,065	18.53
European	122	1.09
Finnish	25	0.22
French, except Basque	491	4.41
French Canadian	36	0.32
German	2,232	20.03
Greek	43	0.39
Hawaii Native/Pacific Islander:	29	0.26
Micronesian: (10)	12	0.11
Guamanian/Chamorro (10)	12	0.11
Polynesian: (3)	12	0.11
Native Hawaiian (2)	9	0.08
Samoan (1)	3	0.03
Other Pac. Isl., not spec. (1)	5	0.05
Hispanic or Latino:	291	2.63
Central American:	6	0.05
Guatemalan	2	0.02
Salvadoran	3	0.03
Other Central American	1	0.01
Cuban	6	0.05
Mexican	182	1.64
Puerto Rican	17	0.15
South American:	12	0.11
Paraguayan	1	0.01
Peruvian	7	0.06
Uruguayan	2	0.02
Venezuelan	2	0.02
Other Hispanic or Latino	68	0.61
Hungarian	35	0.31
Irish	1,164	10.45
Italian	380	3.41
Lithuanian	9	0.08
Northern European	29	0.26
Norwegian	508	4.56
Pennsylvania German	12	0.11
Polish	156	1.40
Portuguese	29	0.26
Romanian	10	0.09
Russian	39	0.35
Scandinavian	42	0.38
Scotch-Irish	210	1.88
Scottish	436	3.91
Slavic	7	0.06
Slovak	26	0.23
Swedish	454	4.07
Swiss	120	1.08
Ukrainian	35	0.31
United States or American	950	8.53
Welsh	162	1.45
West Indian, excl. Hispanic:	5	0.04
West Indian	5	0.04
White:	10,825	97.65
Not Hispanic (10,452)	10,608	95.70
Hispanic (179)	217	1.96
Yugoslavian	10	0.09

Garden City

Place Type: City
County: Ada
Population: 10,624

Ancestry/Race	Number	%

Notes: 1. Figures in the "Number" column do not add up to the total population due to: a) Ancestry/Race overlap — e.g. persons can report being both White and Irish, b) persons of Hispanic origin can report being any race, c) persons reporting two ancestries are counted in both categories. 2. Numbers in parentheses indicate the number of persons reporting this ancestry/race alone, not in combination with any other ancestry/race. 3. Refer to the Explanation of Data in the front of the book for more detailed information.

African American/Black:	92	0.87
Not Hispanic (47)	74	0.70
Hispanic (3)	18	0.17
African, sub-Saharan:	3	0.03
African	3	0.03
Alaska Native tribes, specified:	5	0.05
Aleut (3)	3	0.03
Tlingit-Haida	2	0.02
Am. Ind. or Alaska Nat., not spec.	57	0.54
American Indian tribes, specified:	146	1.37
Apache	9	0.08
Blackfeet (3)	4	0.04
Cherokee (9)	48	0.45
Cheyenne	1	0.01
Chippewa (1)	3	0.03
Choctaw (1)	7	0.07
Colville (1)	1	0.01
Cree (1)	1	0.01
Creek	2	0.02
Iroquois	2	0.02
Latin American Indians	8	0.08
Navajo	8	0.08
Ottawa (4)	4	0.04
Potawatomi (4)	4	0.04
Pueblo (1)	2	0.02
Seminole (4)	5	0.05
Shoshone (4)	5	0.05
Sioux	2	0.02
Ute (1)	2	0.02
All other tribes (23)	28	0.26
American Indian tribes, not spec.	9	0.08
Asian:	249	2.34
Chinese, ex. Taiwanese (11)	21	0.20
Filipino (17)	44	0.41
Indian (30)	36	0.34
Japanese (28)	51	0.48
Korean (14)	23	0.22
Laotian	7	0.07
Thai (2)	3	0.03
Vietnamese (38)	55	0.52
Other Asian, specified	2	0.02
Other Asian, not specified	7	0.07
Australian	11	0.10
Austrian	7	0.06
Basque	28	0.26
Belgian	22	0.20
British	73	0.67
Canadian	45	0.41
Croatian	7	0.06
Czech	38	0.35
Danish	215	1.97
Dutch	208	1.91
English	1,640	15.03
European	262	2.40
Finnish	101	0.93
French, except Basque	306	2.80
French Canadian	66	0.60
German	2,218	20.33
Greek	21	0.19
Hawaii Native/Pacific Islander:	28	0.26
Micronesian: (5)	5	0.05
Guamanian/Chamorro (5)	5	0.05
Polynesian: (6)	18	0.17
Native Hawaiian (2)	14	0.13
Samoan (4)	4	0.04
Other Pac. Isl., specified	2	0.02
Other Pac. Isl., not spec. (1)	3	0.03
Hispanic or Latino:	1,018	9.58
Central American:	17	0.16
Guatemalan	3	0.03
Nicaraguan	5	0.05
Salvadoran	9	0.08
Dominican Republic	1	0.01
Mexican	840	7.91
Puerto Rican	10	0.09
South American:	5	0.05
Ecuadorian	3	0.03
Peruvian	1	0.01
Other South American	1	0.01
Other Hispanic or Latino	145	1.36
Hungarian	19	0.17
Icelander	30	0.27
Irish	1,309	12.00
Italian	277	2.54
Norwegian	501	4.59
Pennsylvania German	25	0.23
Polish	142	1.30
Portuguese	13	0.12
Russian	24	0.22
Scandinavian	35	0.32
Scotch-Irish	260	2.38
Scottish	433	3.97
Slavic	19	0.17
Swedish	216	1.98
Swiss	60	0.55
United States or American	714	6.54
Welsh	156	1.43
White:	9,772	91.98
Not Hispanic (9,101)	9,298	87.52
Hispanic (390)	474	4.46
Yugoslavian	38	0.35

Idaho Falls

Place Type: City
County: Bonneville
Population: 50,730

Ancestry/Race	Number	%
African American/Black:	445	0.88
Not Hispanic (297)	413	0.81
Hispanic (18)	32	0.06
African, sub-Saharan:	41	0.08
African	34	0.07
South African	7	0.01
Alaska Native tribes, specified:	10	0.02
Alaska Athabascan	1	0.00
Eskimo (1)	2	0.00
Tlingit-Haida	1	0.00
All other tribes (5)	6	0.01
Am. Ind. or Alaska Nat., not spec.	160	0.32
Alsatian	14	0.03
American Indian tribes, specified:	514	1.01
Apache (1)	3	0.01
Blackfeet (15)	24	0.05
Cherokee (27)	96	0.19
Cheyenne	1	0.00
Chickasaw	3	0.01
Chippewa (15)	32	0.06
Choctaw (2)	11	0.02
Comanche (4)	11	0.02
Cree (1)	3	0.01
Creek (1)	1	0.00
Crow	2	0.00
Delaware (1)	2	0.00
Iroquois	1	0.00
Latin American Indians (14)	28	0.06
Lumbee (1)	2	0.00
Navajo (38)	49	0.10
Osage	5	0.01
Paiute (2)	2	0.00
Pima (3)	3	0.01
Potawatomi (3)	3	0.01
Shoshone (16)	21	0.04
Sioux (21)	43	0.08
Tohono O'Odham	3	0.01
Ute (7)	9	0.02
Yaqui (1)	1	0.00
All other tribes (101)	155	0.31
American Indian tribes, not spec.	16	0.03
Arab:	7	0.01
Moroccan	7	0.01
Armenian	62	0.12
Asian:	728	1.44
Chinese, ex. Taiwanese (144)	166	0.33
Filipino (45)	86	0.17
Indian (64)	75	0.15
Indonesian (3)	5	0.01
Japanese (184)	256	0.50
Korean (56)	82	0.16
Laotian	1	0.00
Pakistani (1)	1	0.00
Taiwanese (1)	1	0.00
Thai (4)	6	0.01
Vietnamese (15)	16	0.03
Other Asian, specified (2)	9	0.02
Other Asian, not specified (6)	24	0.05
Australian	21	0.04
Austrian	143	0.28
Basque	47	0.09
Belgian	47	0.09
British	481	0.95
Canadian	51	0.10
Carpatho Rusyn	39	0.08
Celtic	18	0.04
Croatian	30	0.06
Czech	94	0.19
Czechoslovakian	58	0.11
Danish	2,158	4.27
Dutch	922	1.83
Eastern European	6	0.01
English	11,718	23.21
European	1,109	2.20
Finnish	124	0.25
French, except Basque	1,404	2.78
French Canadian	408	0.81
German	8,534	16.90
Greek	169	0.33
Hawaii Native/Pacific Islander:	67	0.13
Melanesian: (3)	3	0.01
Fijian (3)	3	0.01
Micronesian: (11)	20	0.04
Guamanian/Chamorro (11)	20	0.04
Polynesian: (12)	27	0.05
Native Hawaiian (6)	14	0.03
Samoan (2)	4	0.01
Tongan (2)	5	0.01
Other Polynesian (2)	4	0.01
Other Pac. Isl., specified	7	0.01
Other Pac. Isl., not spec. (6)	10	0.02
Hispanic or Latino:	3,641	7.18
Central American:	53	0.10
Costa Rican	7	0.01
Guatemalan	13	0.03
Honduran	3	0.01
Panamanian	4	0.01
Salvadoran	13	0.03
Other Central American	13	0.03
Cuban	16	0.03
Dominican Republic	1	0.00
Mexican	2,776	5.47
Puerto Rican	58	0.11
South American:	57	0.11
Argentinean	7	0.01
Bolivian	1	0.00
Chilean	11	0.02
Colombian	7	0.01
Ecuadorian	10	0.02
Peruvian	14	0.03
Venezuelan	2	0.00
Other South American	5	0.01
Other Hispanic or Latino	680	1.34
Hungarian	143	0.28
Icelander	31	0.06
Iranian	6	0.01
Irish	3,795	7.52
Israeli	13	0.03
Italian	1,182	2.34
Latvian	18	0.04
Lithuanian	30	0.06
Northern European	77	0.15
Norwegian	1,581	3.13
Pennsylvania German	71	0.14
Polish	593	1.17
Portuguese	63	0.12
Romanian	50	0.10
Russian	118	0.23
Scandinavian	318	0.63
Scotch-Irish	583	1.15
Scottish	2,151	4.26

Notes: 1. Figures in the "Number" column do not add up to the total population due to: a) Ancestry/Race overlap — e.g. persons can report being both White and Irish, b) persons of Hispanic origin can report being any race, c) persons reporting two ancestries are counted in both categories. 2. Numbers in parentheses indicate the number of persons reporting this ancestry/race alone, not in combination with any other ancestry/race. 3. Refer to the Explanation of Data in the front of the book for more detailed information.

Ancestry/Race	Number	%
Serbian	29	0.06
Slavic	7	0.01
Slovak	15	0.03
Slovene	5	0.01
Swedish	2,287	4.53
Swiss	468	0.93
Turkish	8	0.02
Ukrainian	43	0.09
United States or American	4,790	9.49
Welsh	1,167	2.31
West Indian, excl. Hispanic:	21	0.04
Bahamian	16	0.03
Jamaican	5	0.01
White:	47,485	93.60
Not Hispanic (45,330)	45,856	90.39
Hispanic (1,387)	1,629	3.21
Yugoslavian	96	0.19

Lewiston

Place Type: City
County: Nez Perce
Population: 30,904

Ancestry/Race	Number	%
Acadian/Cajun	6	0.02
African American/Black:	129	0.42
Not Hispanic (89)	118	0.38
Hispanic (3)	11	0.04
African, sub-Saharan:	10	0.03
Nigerian	10	0.03
Alaska Native tribes, specified:	36	0.12
Alaska Athabascan (8)	13	0.04
Aleut (3)	5	0.02
Tlingit-Haida (11)	16	0.05
All other tribes (1)	2	0.01
Alaska Native tribes, not specified	2	0.01
Am. Ind. or Alaska Nat., not spec.	134	0.43
American Indian tribes, specified:	616	1.99
Apache (1)	6	0.02
Blackfeet (7)	10	0.03
Cherokee (25)	79	0.26
Cheyenne (4)	4	0.01
Chippewa (19)	35	0.11
Choctaw (4)	16	0.05
Colville (9)	11	0.04
Comanche	2	0.01
Cree (1)	3	0.01
Creek (3)	4	0.01
Crow	1	0.00
Delaware	3	0.01
Iroquois (6)	8	0.03
Kiowa	1	0.00
Latin American Indians (1)	2	0.01
Menominee (1)	1	0.00
Navajo (7)	7	0.02
Paiute (3)	4	0.01
Potawatomi	1	0.00
Puget Sound Salish	3	0.01
Shoshone (5)	5	0.02
Sioux (16)	37	0.12
Ute (3)	3	0.01
Yakama (8)	15	0.05
Yaqui (1)	2	0.01
All other tribes (236)	353	1.14
American Indian tribes, not spec.	27	0.09
Arab:	8	0.03
Syrian	8	0.03
Asian:	344	1.11
Cambodian	1	0.00
Chinese, ex. Taiwanese (46)	59	0.19
Filipino (28)	65	0.21
Indian (15)	25	0.08
Indonesian (6)	6	0.02
Japanese (94)	134	0.43
Korean (32)	36	0.12
Pakistani	1	0.00
Taiwanese	1	0.00
Thai (2)	3	0.01
Vietnamese (2)	2	0.01
Other Asian, specified (4)	5	0.02
Other Asian, not specified (4)	6	0.02
Australian	32	0.10
Austrian	64	0.21
Basque	17	0.05
Belgian	29	0.09
Brazilian	8	0.03
British	211	0.68
Bulgarian	31	0.10
Canadian	127	0.41
Celtic	33	0.11
Czech	59	0.19
Czechoslovakian	22	0.07
Danish	286	0.92
Dutch	769	2.48
English	4,119	13.27
European	405	1.30
Finnish	163	0.53
French, except Basque	963	3.10
French Canadian	244	0.79
German	8,068	25.99
Greek	37	0.12
Hawaii Native/Pacific Islander:	60	0.19
Micronesian: (4)	7	0.02
Guamanian/Chamorro (2)	2	0.01
Other Micronesian (2)	5	0.02
Polynesian: (17)	43	0.14
Native Hawaiian (9)	31	0.10
Samoan (8)	12	0.04
Other Pac. Isl., not spec. (3)	10	0.03
Hispanic or Latino:	590	1.91
Central American:	11	0.04
Costa Rican	4	0.01
Guatemalan	1	0.00
Honduran	4	0.01
Salvadoran	2	0.01
Cuban	16	0.05
Dominican Republic	1	0.00
Mexican	355	1.15
Puerto Rican	36	0.12
South American:	20	0.06
Argentinean	1	0.00
Colombian	5	0.02
Ecuadorian	3	0.01
Peruvian	3	0.01
Venezuelan	7	0.02
Other South American	1	0.00
Other Hispanic or Latino	151	0.49
Hungarian	42	0.14
Irish	3,877	12.49
Italian	776	2.50
Lithuanian	22	0.07
Maltese	7	0.02
Northern European	33	0.11
Norwegian	1,803	5.81
Pennsylvania German	15	0.05
Polish	329	1.06
Portuguese	38	0.12
Romanian	23	0.07
Russian	95	0.31
Scandinavian	121	0.39
Scotch-Irish	695	2.24
Scottish	887	2.86
Slavic	13	0.04
Slovak	9	0.03
Slovene	6	0.02
Swedish	1,267	4.08
Swiss	195	0.63
Ukrainian	35	0.11
United States or American	2,669	8.60
Welsh	296	0.95
West Indian, excl. Hispanic:	9	0.03
Jamaican	9	0.03
White:	29,877	96.68
Not Hispanic (29,069)	29,466	95.35
Hispanic (334)	411	1.33
Yugoslavian	26	0.08

Meridian

Place Type: City
County: Ada
Population: 34,919

Ancestry/Race	Number	%
Afghan	5	0.01
African American/Black:	259	0.74
Not Hispanic (155)	242	0.69
Hispanic (9)	17	0.05
Alaska Native tribes, specified:	15	0.04
Alaska Athabascan	1	0.00
Aleut (1)	3	0.01
Eskimo (2)	3	0.01
Tlingit-Haida (5)	8	0.02
Am. Ind. or Alaska Nat., not spec.	92	0.26
Albanian	6	0.02
American Indian tribes, specified:	218	0.62
Apache	4	0.01
Blackfeet (3)	8	0.02
Cherokee (24)	85	0.24
Chickasaw (1)	2	0.01
Chippewa (2)	7	0.02
Choctaw (8)	11	0.03
Colville (1)	1	0.00
Comanche (1)	2	0.01
Creek	3	0.01
Delaware (1)	5	0.01
Iroquois (1)	2	0.01
Latin American Indians (7)	10	0.03
Navajo (1)	2	0.01
Osage	1	0.00
Ottawa	1	0.00
Pima (1)	1	0.00
Potawatomi (3)	5	0.01
Pueblo (5)	5	0.01
Shoshone (2)	7	0.02
Sioux (8)	10	0.03
Ute (1)	1	0.00
Yakama (2)	2	0.01
All other tribes (26)	43	0.12
American Indian tribes, not spec.	23	0.07
Arab:	35	0.10
Lebanese	25	0.07
Other Arab	10	0.03
Asian:	752	2.15
Bangladeshi (1)	1	0.00
Cambodian (1)	3	0.01
Chinese, ex. Taiwanese (78)	117	0.34
Filipino (71)	143	0.41
Hmong (7)	7	0.02
Indian (42)	46	0.13
Indonesian (1)	4	0.01
Japanese (60)	157	0.45
Korean (68)	118	0.34
Laotian (29)	39	0.11
Pakistani (1)	2	0.01
Sri Lankan (1)	1	0.00
Taiwanese	5	0.01
Thai (6)	9	0.03
Vietnamese (33)	41	0.12
Other Asian, specified (1)	4	0.01
Other Asian, not specified (25)	55	0.16
Australian	17	0.05
Austrian	88	0.25
Basque	433	1.24
Belgian	36	0.10
Brazilian	7	0.02
British	241	0.69
Bulgarian	26	0.07
Canadian	68	0.20
Croatian	6	0.02
Czech	164	0.47
Czechoslovakian	37	0.11
Danish	686	1.97
Dutch	921	2.64
English	5,414	15.53
European	380	1.09
Finnish	154	0.44

Notes: 1. Figures in the "Number" column do not add up to the total population due to: a) Ancestry/Race overlap — e.g. persons can report being both White and Irish, b) persons of Hispanic origin can report being any race, c) persons reporting two ancestries are counted in both categories. 2. Numbers in parentheses indicate the number of persons reporting this ancestry/race alone, not in combination with any other ancestry/race. 3. Refer to the Explanation of Data in the front of the book for more detailed information.

French, except Basque	1,162	3.33
French Canadian	256	0.73
German	7,410	21.26
Greek	89	0.26
Hawaii Native/Pacific Islander:	114	0.33
Micronesian: (8)	12	0.03
Guamanian/Chamorro (7)	11	0.03
Other Micronesian (1)	1	0.00
Polynesian: (28)	80	0.23
Native Hawaiian (17)	55	0.16
Samoan (8)	19	0.05
Tongan (2)	4	0.01
Other Polynesian (1)	2	0.01
Other Pac. Isl., not spec. (6)	22	0.06
Hispanic or Latino:	1,291	3.70
Central American:	15	0.04
Costa Rican	3	0.01
Honduran	3	0.01
Panamanian	4	0.01
Salvadoran	4	0.01
Other Central American	1	0.00
Cuban	13	0.04
Dominican Republic	1	0.00
Mexican	833	2.39
Puerto Rican	36	0.10
South American:	41	0.12
Argentinean	3	0.01
Bolivian	1	0.00
Chilean	3	0.01
Colombian	18	0.05
Ecuadorian	2	0.01
Paraguayan	1	0.00
Uruguayan	1	0.00
Venezuelan	4	0.01
Other South American	8	0.02
Other Hispanic or Latino	352	1.01
Hungarian	83	0.24
Icelander	52	0.15
Irish	3,969	11.39
Italian	1,402	4.02
Lithuanian	60	0.17
Luxemburger	27	0.08
Norwegian	1,774	5.09
Pennsylvania German	11	0.03
Polish	318	0.91
Portuguese	119	0.34
Russian	146	0.42
Scandinavian	137	0.39
Scotch-Irish	489	1.40
Scottish	1,182	3.39
Slovak	8	0.02
Swedish	1,201	3.45
Swiss	237	0.68
Ukrainian	200	0.57
United States or American	3,229	9.26
Welsh	578	1.66
West Indian, excl. Hispanic:	8	0.02
Jamaican	8	0.02
White:	33,611	96.25
Not Hispanic (32,270)	32,789	93.90
Hispanic (657)	822	2.35
Yugoslavian	57	0.16

Moscow

Place Type: City
County: Latah
Population: 21,291

Ancestry/Race	Number	%
African American/Black:	264	1.24
Not Hispanic (191)	256	1.20
Hispanic (3)	8	0.04
African, sub-Saharan:	46	0.22
African	11	0.05
Kenyan	7	0.03
Nigerian	28	0.13
Alaska Native tribes, specified:	12	0.06
Alaska Athabascan (1)	2	0.01
Aleut (4)	5	0.02
Eskimo (1)	1	0.00
Tlingit-Haida (1)	3	0.01
All other tribes (1)	1	0.00
Alaska Native tribes, not specified	3	0.01
Am. Ind. or Alaska Nat., not spec.	50	0.23
American Indian tribes, specified:	176	0.83
Apache (1)	2	0.01
Blackfeet	3	0.01
Cherokee (13)	36	0.17
Cheyenne (3)	5	0.02
Chickasaw	1	0.00
Chippewa (3)	5	0.02
Choctaw (1)	2	0.01
Colville (2)	2	0.01
Comanche (1)	1	0.00
Cree (2)	2	0.01
Creek	1	0.00
Crow (1)	1	0.00
Delaware (1)	1	0.00
Iroquois (1)	7	0.03
Latin American Indians (4)	5	0.02
Navajo (1)	2	0.01
Osage (1)	1	0.00
Potawatomi	2	0.01
Puget Sound Salish (4)	5	0.02
Seminole (2)	2	0.01
Sioux (9)	12	0.06
Yaqui (1)	2	0.01
All other tribes (61)	76	0.36
American Indian tribes, not spec.	26	0.12
Arab:	104	0.49
Arab/Arabic	8	0.04
Lebanese	67	0.32
Other Arab	29	0.14
Armenian	11	0.05
Asian:	842	3.95
Cambodian (1)	1	0.00
Chinese, ex. Taiwanese (237)	276	1.30
Filipino (35)	72	0.34
Indian (79)	88	0.41
Indonesian	2	0.01
Japanese (101)	159	0.75
Korean (138)	148	0.70
Laotian (1)	1	0.00
Pakistani (10)	11	0.05
Sri Lankan (1)	1	0.00
Taiwanese (6)	7	0.03
Thai (15)	19	0.09
Vietnamese (18)	21	0.10
Other Asian, specified (2)	3	0.01
Other Asian, not specified (13)	33	0.15
Australian	8	0.04
Austrian	91	0.43
Basque	51	0.24
Belgian	14	0.07
Brazilian	13	0.06
British	193	0.91
Bulgarian	10	0.05
Canadian	142	0.67
Celtic	6	0.03
Croatian	34	0.16
Czech	130	0.61
Czechoslovakian	57	0.27
Danish	468	2.21
Dutch	528	2.49
English	3,604	16.99
European	604	2.85
Finnish	103	0.49
French, except Basque	652	3.07
French Canadian	198	0.93
German	5,009	23.62
Greek	122	0.58
Hawaii Native/Pacific Islander:	53	0.25
Micronesian: (2)	3	0.01
Guamanian/Chamorro (1)	1	0.00
Other Micronesian (1)	2	0.01
Polynesian: (23)	38	0.18
Native Hawaiian (11)	22	0.10
Samoan (11)	15	0.07
Tongan (1)	1	0.00
Other Pac. Isl., not spec. (5)	12	0.06
Hispanic or Latino:	525	2.47
Central American:	19	0.09
Costa Rican	4	0.02
Guatemalan	2	0.01
Honduran	5	0.02
Nicaraguan	7	0.03
Salvadoran	1	0.00
Cuban	16	0.08
Mexican	292	1.37
Puerto Rican	28	0.13
South American:	42	0.20
Argentinean	2	0.01
Bolivian	2	0.01
Chilean	9	0.04
Colombian	5	0.02
Ecuadorian	10	0.05
Peruvian	3	0.01
Uruguayan	2	0.01
Venezuelan	9	0.04
Other Hispanic or Latino	128	0.60
Hungarian	83	0.39
Iranian	8	0.04
Irish	2,460	11.60
Israeli	13	0.06
Italian	910	4.29
Lithuanian	43	0.20
New Zealander	9	0.04
Northern European	36	0.17
Norwegian	1,268	5.98
Pennsylvania German	6	0.03
Polish	500	2.36
Portuguese	33	0.16
Romanian	13	0.06
Russian	101	0.48
Scandinavian	140	0.66
Scotch-Irish	457	2.15
Scottish	913	4.31
Serbian	29	0.14
Slovak	6	0.03
Slovene	14	0.07
Swedish	1,120	5.28
Swiss	252	1.19
Turkish	32	0.15
Ukrainian	35	0.17
United States or American	1,127	5.31
Welsh	316	1.49
White:	20,000	93.94
Not Hispanic (19,376)	19,685	92.46
Hispanic (260)	315	1.48

Mountain Home

Place Type: City
County: Elmore
Population: 11,143

Ancestry/Race	Number	%
African American/Black:	350	3.14
Not Hispanic (278)	335	3.01
Hispanic (13)	15	0.13
African, sub-Saharan:	15	0.13
African	15	0.13
Alaska Native tribes, specified:	2	0.02
Alaska Athabascan	1	0.01
Eskimo (1)	1	0.01
Am. Ind. or Alaska Nat., not spec.	58	0.52
American Indian tribes, specified:	151	1.36
Blackfeet	4	0.04
Cherokee (13)	39	0.35
Cheyenne (1)	5	0.04
Chickasaw	1	0.01
Chippewa (5)	8	0.07
Choctaw	3	0.03
Creek (2)	2	0.02
Delaware	2	0.02
Iroquois (1)	2	0.02
Latin American Indians (2)	5	0.04
Navajo (9)	20	0.18
Osage (2)	2	0.02

Notes: 1. Figures in the "Number" column do not add up to the total population due to: a) Ancestry/Race overlap — e.g. persons can report being both White and Irish, b) persons of Hispanic origin can report being any race, c) persons reporting two ancestries are counted in both categories. 2. Numbers in parentheses indicate the number of persons reporting this ancestry/race alone, not in combination with any other ancestry/race. 3. Refer to the Explanation of Data in the front of the book for more detailed information.

Paiute (4)	4	0.04
Pueblo (2)	2	0.02
Puget Sound Salish	1	0.01
Seminole (1)	1	0.01
Shoshone (4)	9	0.08
Sioux (8)	10	0.09
Tohono O'Odham (2)	6	0.05
Ute (1)	1	0.01
All other tribes (18)	24	0.22
American Indian tribes, not spec.	12	0.11
Arab:	18	0.16
Lebanese	18	0.16
Asian:	303	2.72
Chinese, ex. Taiwanese (14)	24	0.22
Filipino (77)	114	1.02
Indian (10)	15	0.13
Indonesian (1)	1	0.01
Japanese (19)	48	0.43
Korean (36)	49	0.44
Taiwanese (1)	1	0.01
Thai (22)	31	0.28
Vietnamese (6)	9	0.08
Other Asian, specified (1)	1	0.01
Other Asian, not specified (4)	10	0.09
Australian	17	0.15
Austrian	20	0.17
Basque	60	0.52
Belgian	11	0.10
British	114	0.99
Canadian	29	0.25
Celtic	5	0.04
Czech	35	0.31
Czechoslovakian	30	0.26
Danish	137	1.20
Dutch	255	2.23
Eastern European	10	0.09
English	1,700	14.84
European	133	1.16
Finnish	42	0.37
French, except Basque	346	3.02
French Canadian	134	1.17
German	2,130	18.59
Greek	19	0.17
Hawaii Native/Pacific Islander:	71	0.64
Micronesian: (15)	19	0.17
Guamanian/Chamorro (15)	19	0.17
Polynesian: (16)	40	0.36
Native Hawaiian (15)	32	0.29
Samoan	4	0.04
Other Polynesian (1)	4	0.04
Other Pac. Isl., not spec. (3)	12	0.11
Hispanic or Latino:	928	8.33
Central American:	8	0.07
Guatemalan	1	0.01
Honduran	3	0.03
Panamanian	2	0.02
Salvadoran	2	0.02
Cuban	15	0.13
Dominican Republic	2	0.02
Mexican	628	5.64
Puerto Rican	62	0.56
South American:	12	0.11
Argentinean	1	0.01
Chilean	1	0.01
Colombian	2	0.02
Ecuadorian	6	0.05
Peruvian	1	0.01
Uruguayan	1	0.01
Other Hispanic or Latino	201	1.80
Hungarian	47	0.41
Irish	1,025	8.95
Italian	427	3.73
Lithuanian	32	0.28
Norwegian	414	3.61
Polish	158	1.38
Portuguese	30	0.26
Romanian	16	0.14
Russian	31	0.27
Scandinavian	97	0.85
Scotch-Irish	129	1.13
Scottish	301	2.63
Slavic	29	0.25
Slovak	9	0.08
Slovene	8	0.07
Swedish	301	2.63
Swiss	33	0.29
Ukrainian	39	0.34
United States or American	1,057	9.22
Welsh	99	0.86
West Indian, excl. Hispanic:	8	0.07
Jamaican	8	0.07
White:	10,107	90.70
Not Hispanic (9,320)	9,573	85.91
Hispanic (474)	534	4.79

Nampa

Place Type: City
County: Canyon
Population: 51,867

Ancestry/Race	Number	%
African American/Black:	342	0.66
Not Hispanic (173)	283	0.55
Hispanic (33)	59	0.11
African, sub-Saharan:	19	0.04
African	9	0.02
South African	10	0.02
Alaska Native tribes, specified:	20	0.04
Aleut (2)	4	0.01
Eskimo (1)	7	0.01
Tlingit-Haida (8)	9	0.02
Am. Ind. or Alaska Nat., not spec.	262	0.51
Albanian	7	0.01
American Indian tribes, specified:	619	1.19
Apache (7)	20	0.04
Blackfeet (3)	19	0.04
Cherokee (68)	199	0.38
Cheyenne (4)	5	0.01
Chickasaw (1)	7	0.01
Chippewa (10)	15	0.03
Choctaw (14)	27	0.05
Comanche	1	0.00
Cree	2	0.00
Creek (2)	7	0.01
Delaware (7)	17	0.03
Iroquois (8)	16	0.03
Kiowa	1	0.00
Latin American Indians (22)	32	0.06
Navajo (10)	17	0.03
Osage (1)	3	0.01
Ottawa (2)	2	0.00
Paiute (17)	20	0.04
Pima (1)	3	0.01
Potawatomi	3	0.01
Pueblo (5)	6	0.01
Puget Sound Salish (1)	3	0.01
Seminole (2)	4	0.01
Shoshone (9)	22	0.04
Sioux (22)	43	0.08
Tohono O'Odham (5)	7	0.01
Ute (2)	3	0.01
Yakama (1)	2	0.00
Yaqui	1	0.00
All other tribes (57)	112	0.22
American Indian tribes, not spec.	25	0.05
Arab:	89	0.17
Arab/Arabic	47	0.09
Egyptian	5	0.01
Iraqi	8	0.02
Lebanese	9	0.02
Syrian	20	0.04
Asian:	823	1.59
Cambodian (9)	12	0.02
Chinese, ex. Taiwanese (83)	110	0.21
Filipino (73)	189	0.36
Indian (70)	87	0.17
Indonesian (2)	5	0.01
Japanese (62)	148	0.29
Korean (34)	67	0.13
Laotian (21)	32	0.06
Pakistani	1	0.00
Taiwanese (1)	3	0.01
Thai (30)	46	0.09
Vietnamese (71)	79	0.15
Other Asian, specified	2	0.00
Other Asian, not specified (14)	42	0.08
Austrian	147	0.28
Basque	284	0.54
Belgian	7	0.01
Brazilian	4	0.01
British	301	0.57
Bulgarian	24	0.05
Canadian	65	0.12
Celtic	9	0.02
Czech	158	0.30
Czechoslovakian	78	0.15
Danish	774	1.48
Dutch	1,108	2.11
English	6,334	12.08
European	653	1.25
Finnish	102	0.19
French, except Basque	1,413	2.70
French Canadian	200	0.38
German	8,455	16.13
Greek	46	0.09
Hawaii Native/Pacific Islander:	183	0.35
Micronesian: (10)	17	0.03
Guamanian/Chamorro	7	0.01
Other Micronesian (10)	10	0.02
Polynesian: (73)	128	0.25
Native Hawaiian (14)	51	0.10
Samoan (11)	16	0.03
Tongan (46)	55	0.11
Other Polynesian (2)	6	0.01
Other Pac. Isl., specified	1	0.00
Other Pac. Isl., not spec. (7)	37	0.07
Hispanic or Latino:	9,282	17.90
Central American:	103	0.20
Costa Rican	4	0.01
Guatemalan	20	0.04
Honduran	22	0.04
Nicaraguan	3	0.01
Panamanian	1	0.00
Salvadoran	48	0.09
Other Central American	5	0.01
Cuban	9	0.02
Dominican Republic	6	0.01
Mexican	7,388	14.24
Puerto Rican	78	0.15
South American:	59	0.11
Argentinean	6	0.01
Bolivian	5	0.01
Chilean	4	0.01
Colombian	14	0.03
Ecuadorian	8	0.02
Peruvian	18	0.03
Venezuelan	3	0.01
Other South American	1	0.00
Other Hispanic or Latino	1,639	3.16
Hungarian	28	0.05
Icelander	29	0.06
Irish	4,583	8.74
Italian	1,088	2.08
Latvian	12	0.02
Lithuanian	24	0.05
Luxemburger	7	0.01
Northern European	33	0.06
Norwegian	1,286	2.45
Pennsylvania German	13	0.02
Polish	519	0.99
Portuguese	166	0.32
Romanian	134	0.26
Russian	111	0.21
Scandinavian	273	0.52
Scotch-Irish	972	1.85
Scottish	1,329	2.54
Swedish	1,237	2.36
Swiss	403	0.77
Turkish	8	0.02

Notes: 1. Figures in the "Number" column do not add up to the total population due to: a) Ancestry/Race overlap — e.g. persons can report being both White and Irish, b) persons of Hispanic origin can report being any race, c) persons reporting two ancestries are counted in both categories. 2. Numbers in parentheses indicate the number of persons reporting this ancestry/race alone, not in combination with any other ancestry/race. 3. Refer to the Explanation of Data in the front of the book for more detailed information.

Ancestry/Race	Number	%
Ukrainian	6	0.01
United States or American	3,828	7.30
Welsh	475	0.91
West Indian, excl. Hispanic:	27	0.05
British West Indian	8	0.02
Dutch West Indian	11	0.02
Jamaican	8	0.02
White:	44,650	86.09
Not Hispanic (40,555)	41,371	79.76
Hispanic (2,726)	3,279	6.32
Yugoslavian	29	0.06

Pocatello

Place Type: City
County: Bannock
Population: 51,466

Ancestry/Race	Number	%
Acadian/Cajun	8	0.02
African American/Black:	524	1.02
Not Hispanic (345)	479	0.93
Hispanic (24)	45	0.09
African, sub-Saharan:	19	0.04
African	14	0.03
South African	5	0.01
Alaska Native tribes, specified:	14	0.03
Alaska Athabascan (3)	3	0.01
Aleut	1	0.00
Eskimo (8)	8	0.02
Tlingit-Haida	1	0.00
All other tribes	1	0.00
Alaska Native tribes, not specified	2	0.00
Am. Ind. or Alaska Nat., not spec.	195	0.38
American Indian tribes, specified:	817	1.59
Apache (14)	23	0.04
Blackfeet (1)	4	0.01
Cherokee (26)	97	0.19
Cheyenne (5)	9	0.02
Chickasaw	1	0.00
Chippewa (31)	42	0.08
Choctaw (5)	7	0.01
Comanche (1)	2	0.00
Cree (2)	2	0.00
Creek (1)	7	0.01
Delaware (1)	1	0.00
Iroquois (9)	13	0.03
Latin American Indians (13)	28	0.05
Lumbee (1)	2	0.00
Navajo (37)	45	0.09
Osage	2	0.00
Paiute	2	0.00
Pueblo (7)	11	0.02
Puget Sound Salish	4	0.01
Seminole (1)	2	0.00
Shoshone (50)	70	0.14
Sioux (54)	81	0.16
Yakama (1)	2	0.00
All other tribes (270)	360	0.70
American Indian tribes, not spec.	49	0.10
Arab:	57	0.11
Arab/Arabic	8	0.02
Lebanese	39	0.08
Palestinian	10	0.02
Armenian	36	0.07
Asian:	879	1.71
Bangladeshi (6)	6	0.01
Cambodian (1)	3	0.01
Chinese, ex. Taiwanese (122)	160	0.31
Filipino (63)	104	0.20
Indian (84)	93	0.18
Indonesian (2)	7	0.01
Japanese (173)	277	0.54
Korean (39)	84	0.16
Laotian (31)	33	0.06
Malaysian (7)	8	0.02
Pakistani (4)	7	0.01
Sri Lankan (6)	6	0.01
Taiwanese (9)	20	0.04
Thai (6)	8	0.02
Vietnamese (17)	17	0.03
Other Asian, specified	9	0.02
Other Asian, not specified (11)	37	0.07
Assyrian/Chaldean/Syriac	27	0.05
Australian	13	0.03
Austrian	77	0.15
Basque	73	0.14
Belgian	20	0.04
Brazilian	5	0.01
British	583	1.13
Canadian	94	0.18
Celtic	43	0.08
Croatian	52	0.10
Czech	282	0.55
Czechoslovakian	135	0.26
Danish	2,370	4.60
Dutch	1,263	2.45
English	11,533	22.37
Estonian	5	0.01
European	679	1.32
Finnish	68	0.13
French, except Basque	1,434	2.78
French Canadian	269	0.52
German	8,756	16.98
Greek	242	0.47
Hawaii Native/Pacific Islander:	204	0.40
Micronesian: (15)	30	0.06
Guamanian/Chamorro (7)	15	0.03
Other Micronesian (8)	15	0.03
Polynesian: (82)	150	0.29
Native Hawaiian (23)	65	0.13
Samoan (47)	62	0.12
Tongan (3)	11	0.02
Other Polynesian (9)	12	0.02
Other Pac. Isl., specified	4	0.01
Other Pac. Isl., not spec. (2)	20	0.04
Hispanic or Latino:	2,544	4.94
Central American:	23	0.04
Costa Rican	4	0.01
Guatemalan	8	0.02
Honduran	1	0.00
Nicaraguan	2	0.00
Panamanian	5	0.01
Salvadoran	2	0.00
Other Central American	1	0.00
Cuban	20	0.04
Mexican	1,865	3.62
Puerto Rican	57	0.11
South American:	58	0.11
Argentinean	2	0.00
Bolivian	4	0.01
Chilean	7	0.01
Colombian	12	0.02
Peruvian	26	0.05
Uruguayan	2	0.00
Venezuelan	3	0.01
Other South American	2	0.00
Other Hispanic or Latino	521	1.01
Hungarian	78	0.15
Icelander	29	0.06
Iranian	40	0.08
Irish	5,040	9.77
Israeli	11	0.02
Italian	1,746	3.39
Latvian	7	0.01
Lithuanian	49	0.10
New Zealander	9	0.02
Northern European	46	0.09
Norwegian	1,729	3.35
Pennsylvania German	19	0.04
Polish	813	1.58
Portuguese	135	0.26
Romanian	7	0.01
Russian	237	0.46
Scandinavian	476	0.92
Scotch-Irish	875	1.70
Scottish	1,621	3.14
Slavic	8	0.02
Slovak	40	0.08
Slovene	33	0.06
Swedish	2,049	3.97
Swiss	571	1.11
Ukrainian	35	0.07
United States or American	4,517	8.76
Welsh	1,309	2.54
West Indian, excl. Hispanic:	34	0.07
Dutch West Indian	11	0.02
Jamaican	6	0.01
West Indian	17	0.03
White:	48,505	94.25
Not Hispanic (46,502)	47,223	91.76
Hispanic (1,011)	1,282	2.49
Yugoslavian	27	0.05

Post Falls

Place Type: City
County: Kootenai
Population: 17,247

Ancestry/Race	Number	%
African American/Black:	76	0.44
Not Hispanic (30)	72	0.42
Hispanic (1)	4	0.02
Alaska Native tribes, specified:	7	0.04
Aleut	2	0.01
Eskimo	2	0.01
Tlingit-Haida (2)	2	0.01
All other tribes (1)	1	0.01
Am. Ind. or Alaska Nat., not spec.	89	0.52
American Indian tribes, specified:	208	1.21
Apache (3)	4	0.02
Blackfeet (7)	13	0.08
Cherokee (15)	35	0.20
Cheyenne (3)	3	0.02
Chippewa (13)	18	0.10
Choctaw (4)	6	0.03
Colville (6)	6	0.03
Comanche (1)	1	0.01
Crow (3)	4	0.02
Iroquois	1	0.01
Latin American Indians (2)	10	0.06
Menominee (1)	1	0.01
Navajo (2)	2	0.01
Osage	4	0.02
Paiute	1	0.01
Pima	1	0.01
Potawatomi (4)	6	0.03
Puget Sound Salish (4)	5	0.03
Seminole (1)	3	0.02
Shoshone (1)	5	0.03
Sioux (9)	14	0.08
Yakama (3)	3	0.02
All other tribes (32)	62	0.36
American Indian tribes, not spec.	12	0.07
Arab:	65	0.38
Arab/Arabic	10	0.06
Lebanese	25	0.15
Other Arab	30	0.18
Asian:	170	0.99
Chinese, ex. Taiwanese (5)	15	0.09
Filipino (34)	57	0.33
Indian (7)	11	0.06
Indonesian (1)	1	0.01
Japanese (22)	42	0.24
Korean (13)	19	0.11
Laotian (1)	2	0.01
Thai (3)	5	0.03
Vietnamese (8)	9	0.05
Other Asian, specified	2	0.01
Other Asian, not specified (2)	7	0.04
Austrian	112	0.66
Belgian	7	0.04
British	60	0.35
Canadian	65	0.38
Celtic	8	0.05
Croatian	9	0.05
Czech	54	0.32
Czechoslovakian	81	0.48
Danish	258	1.52

Notes: 1. Figures in the "Number" column do not add up to the total population due to: a) Ancestry/Race overlap — e.g. persons can report being both White and Irish, b) persons of Hispanic origin can report being any race, c) persons reporting two ancestries are counted in both categories. 2. Numbers in parentheses indicate the number of persons reporting this ancestry/race alone, not in combination with any other ancestry/race. 3. Refer to the Explanation of Data in the front of the book for more detailed information.

Dutch	327	1.92
English	1,883	11.06
European	131	0.77
Finnish	149	0.88
French, except Basque	835	4.90
French Canadian	229	1.34
German	4,298	25.24
Greek	41	0.24
Hawaii Native/Pacific Islander:	31	0.18
Micronesian:	1	0.01
Guamanian/Chamorro	1	0.01
Polynesian: (7)	21	0.12
Native Hawaiian (7)	19	0.11
Samoan	2	0.01
Other Pac. Isl., specified	1	0.01
Other Pac. Isl., not spec. (4)	8	0.05
Hispanic or Latino:	439	2.55
Central American:	11	0.06
Costa Rican	4	0.02
Guatemalan	1	0.01
Nicaraguan	1	0.01
Panamanian	1	0.01
Salvadoran	4	0.02
Cuban	3	0.02
Mexican	291	1.69
Puerto Rican	39	0.23
South American:	7	0.04
Argentinean	1	0.01
Bolivian	1	0.01
Chilean	1	0.01
Peruvian	3	0.02
Venezuelan	1	0.01
Other Hispanic or Latino	88	0.51
Hungarian	49	0.29
Irish	2,363	13.88
Italian	954	5.60
Latvian	10	0.06
Lithuanian	30	0.18
New Zealander	10	0.06
Norwegian	959	5.63
Pennsylvania German	9	0.05
Polish	193	1.13
Portuguese	63	0.37
Romanian	78	0.46
Russian	70	0.41
Scandinavian	55	0.32
Scotch-Irish	378	2.22
Scottish	497	2.92
Slovak	9	0.05
Slovene	9	0.05
Swedish	733	4.30
Swiss	107	0.63
Ukrainian	73	0.43
United States or American	1,245	7.31
Welsh	194	1.14
White:	16,827	97.56
Not Hispanic (16,293)	16,508	95.72
Hispanic (286)	319	1.85
Yugoslavian	41	0.24

Rexburg

Place Type: City
County: Madison
Population: 17,257

Ancestry/Race	Number	%
African American/Black:	64	0.37
Not Hispanic (43)	54	0.31
Hispanic (8)	10	0.06
African, sub-Saharan:	5	0.03
Nigerian	5	0.03
Alaska Native tribes, specified:	8	0.05
Aleut (4)	4	0.02
Eskimo (2)	2	0.01
Tlingit-Haida (2)	2	0.01
Alaska Native tribes, not specified	1	0.01
Am. Ind. or Alaska Nat., not spec.	34	0.20
American Indian tribes, specified:	60	0.35
Apache (1)	1	0.01
Cherokee (2)	15	0.09
Chippewa (1)	1	0.01
Choctaw (1)	3	0.02
Cree (1)	1	0.01
Crow (1)	1	0.01
Iroquois (1)	1	0.01
Latin American Indians (2)	3	0.02
Navajo (8)	8	0.05
Osage	2	0.01
Ottawa	4	0.02
Pueblo (2)	3	0.02
Shoshone (1)	1	0.01
All other tribes (4)	16	0.09
American Indian tribes, not spec.	4	0.02
Armenian	18	0.10
Asian:	182	1.05
Cambodian (2)	2	0.01
Chinese, ex. Taiwanese (22)	34	0.20
Filipino (14)	29	0.17
Indian (9)	10	0.06
Indonesian (1)	7	0.04
Japanese (36)	59	0.34
Korean (16)	17	0.10
Laotian (2)	5	0.03
Vietnamese (2)	11	0.06
Other Asian, not specified (6)	8	0.05
Australian	5	0.03
Basque	21	0.12
Brazilian	29	0.17
British	398	2.31
Bulgarian	23	0.13
Canadian	104	0.60
Croatian	16	0.09
Czech	39	0.23
Czechoslovakian	20	0.12
Danish	1,183	6.88
Dutch	214	1.24
English	4,890	28.43
European	541	3.14
Finnish	21	0.12
French, except Basque	279	1.62
French Canadian	47	0.27
German	1,977	11.49
Greek	21	0.12
Hawaii Native/Pacific Islander:	94	0.54
Melanesian: (7)	7	0.04
Fijian (7)	7	0.04
Micronesian: (2)	5	0.03
Guamanian/Chamorro (1)	4	0.02
Other Micronesian (1)	1	0.01
Polynesian: (34)	72	0.42
Native Hawaiian (11)	33	0.19
Samoan (16)	27	0.16
Tongan (4)	9	0.05
Other Polynesian (3)	3	0.02
Other Pac. Isl., not spec. (4)	10	0.06
Hispanic or Latino:	697	4.04
Central American:	20	0.12
Costa Rican	3	0.02
Guatemalan	7	0.04
Honduran	4	0.02
Panamanian	4	0.02
Salvadoran	2	0.01
Cuban	4	0.02
Dominican Republic	2	0.01
Mexican	541	3.13
Puerto Rican	9	0.05
South American:	27	0.16
Argentinean	8	0.05
Chilean	7	0.04
Colombian	2	0.01
Paraguayan	1	0.01
Peruvian	4	0.02
Venezuelan	5	0.03
Other Hispanic or Latino	94	0.54
Hungarian	47	0.27
Icelander	13	0.08
Irish	676	3.93
Italian	211	1.23
Luxemburger	5	0.03
New Zealander	15	0.09
Northern European	62	0.36
Norwegian	564	3.28
Polish	106	0.62
Portuguese	27	0.16
Russian	71	0.41
Scandinavian	263	1.53
Scotch-Irish	295	1.71
Scottish	855	4.97
Swedish	790	4.59
Swiss	384	2.23
Ukrainian	33	0.19
United States or American	1,224	7.12
Welsh	405	2.35
West Indian, excl. Hispanic:	7	0.04
Haitian	7	0.04
White:	16,590	96.13
Not Hispanic (16,183)	16,300	94.45
Hispanic (246)	290	1.68

Twin Falls

Place Type: City
County: Twin Falls
Population: 34,469

Ancestry/Race	Number	%
African American/Black:	137	0.40
Not Hispanic (64)	117	0.34
Hispanic (12)	20	0.06
African, sub-Saharan:	20	0.06
African	20	0.06
Alaska Native tribes, specified:	8	0.02
Alaska Athabascan (2)	3	0.01
Aleut (1)	1	0.00
Eskimo	1	0.00
Tlingit-Haida (1)	1	0.00
All other tribes (1)	2	0.01
Am. Ind. or Alaska Nat., not spec.	143	0.41
Albanian	4	0.01
Alsatian	19	0.06
American Indian tribes, specified:	344	1.00
Apache (10)	22	0.06
Blackfeet (3)	12	0.03
Cherokee (29)	100	0.29
Cheyenne (2)	4	0.01
Chickasaw (2)	5	0.01
Chippewa (8)	10	0.03
Choctaw (4)	12	0.03
Colville (1)	4	0.01
Comanche (2)	4	0.01
Cree	1	0.00
Creek (4)	5	0.01
Crow	1	0.00
Delaware (1)	1	0.00
Iroquois (6)	11	0.03
Latin American Indians (8)	12	0.03
Navajo (6)	12	0.03
Osage	1	0.00
Ottawa (1)	2	0.01
Paiute (3)	7	0.02
Potawatomi (2)	4	0.01
Pueblo (2)	2	0.01
Puget Sound Salish (6)	6	0.02
Seminole	3	0.01
Shoshone (15)	17	0.05
Sioux (10)	18	0.05
Tohono O'Odham (1)	1	0.00
Yakama (1)	1	0.00
All other tribes (48)	66	0.19
American Indian tribes, not spec.	12	0.03
Arab:	28	0.08
Egyptian	10	0.03
Lebanese	18	0.05
Armenian	59	0.17
Asian:	484	1.40
Cambodian (10)	11	0.03
Chinese, ex. Taiwanese (60)	70	0.20
Filipino (29)	48	0.14
Indian (19)	29	0.08

Notes: 1. Figures in the "Number" column do not add up to the total population due to: a) Ancestry/Race overlap — e.g. persons can report being both White and Irish, b) persons of Hispanic origin can report being any race, c) persons reporting two ancestries are counted in both categories. 2. Numbers in parentheses indicate the number of persons reporting this ancestry/race alone, not in combination with any other ancestry/race. 3. Refer to the Explanation of Data in the front of the book for more detailed information.

Ancestry/Race	Number	%
Indonesian (1)	1	0.00
Japanese (80)	108	0.31
Korean (17)	24	0.07
Laotian (56)	61	0.18
Malaysian (1)	1	0.00
Taiwanese (1)	1	0.00
Thai (20)	26	0.08
Vietnamese (72)	82	0.24
Other Asian, not specified (8)	22	0.06
Australian	13	0.04
Austrian	48	0.14
Basque	216	0.63
Belgian	22	0.06
British	224	0.66
Bulgarian	27	0.08
Canadian	80	0.23
Croatian	19	0.06
Czech	204	0.60
Czechoslovakian	35	0.10
Danish	847	2.48
Dutch	869	2.54
English	6,529	19.11
European	391	1.14
Finnish	91	0.27
French, except Basque	1,048	3.07
French Canadian	267	0.78
German	6,363	18.62
Greek	96	0.28
Hawaii Native/Pacific Islander:	67	0.19
Micronesian: (8)	8	0.02
Guamanian/Chamorro (1)	1	0.00
Other Micronesian (7)	7	0.02
Polynesian: (26)	38	0.11
Native Hawaiian (12)	21	0.06
Samoan (8)	11	0.03
Tongan (6)	6	0.02
Other Pac. Isl., not spec. (5)	21	0.06
Hispanic or Latino:	3,066	8.89
Central American:	32	0.09
Costa Rican	4	0.01
Guatemalan	6	0.02
Nicaraguan	1	0.00
Panamanian	1	0.00
Salvadoran	18	0.05
Other Central American	2	0.01
Cuban	12	0.03
Dominican Republic	1	0.00
Mexican	2,328	6.75
Puerto Rican	42	0.12
South American:	44	0.13
Argentinean	1	0.00
Chilean	6	0.02
Colombian	10	0.03
Peruvian	16	0.05
Venezuelan	11	0.03
Other Hispanic or Latino	607	1.76
Hungarian	12	0.04
Icelander	19	0.06
Irish	3,429	10.04
Italian	795	2.33
Lithuanian	29	0.08
Northern European	17	0.05
Norwegian	993	2.91
Polish	249	0.73
Portuguese	174	0.51
Romanian	125	0.37
Russian	145	0.42
Scandinavian	95	0.28
Scotch-Irish	778	2.28
Scottish	979	2.87
Serbian	16	0.05
Slavic	25	0.07
Slovak	9	0.03
Swedish	1,067	3.12
Swiss	138	0.40
Ukrainian	75	0.22
United States or American	2,657	7.78
Welsh	453	1.33
White:	32,404	94.01
Not Hispanic (30,199)	30,675	88.99
Hispanic (1,434)	1,729	5.02
Yugoslavian	401	1.17

Addison

Place Type: Village
County: Du Page
Population: 35,914

Ancestry/Race	Number	%
African American/Black:	971	2.70
Not Hispanic (874)	921	2.56
Hispanic (28)	50	0.14
African, sub-Saharan:	103	0.29
African	80	0.22
Other sub-Saharan African	23	0.06
Am. Ind. or Alaska Nat., not spec.	107	0.30
Albanian	267	0.75
American Indian tribes, specified:	102	0.28
Apache (4)	5	0.01
Blackfeet	8	0.02
Cherokee (5)	29	0.08
Chippewa (3)	5	0.01
Choctaw	1	0.00
Creek	2	0.01
Delaware	1	0.00
Iroquois (1)	2	0.01
Latin American Indians (28)	32	0.09
Navajo	1	0.00
Osage	1	0.00
Potawatomi	1	0.00
Sioux	4	0.01
Tohono O'Odham (4)	4	0.01
Yaqui (1)	1	0.00
All other tribes (3)	5	0.01
American Indian tribes, not spec.	18	0.05
Arab:	54	0.15
Arab/Arabic	7	0.02
Egyptian	8	0.02
Jordanian	27	0.08
Palestinian	12	0.03
Armenian	53	0.15
Asian:	3,059	8.52
Bangladeshi	4	0.01
Cambodian (2)	4	0.01
Chinese, ex. Taiwanese (133)	152	0.42
Filipino (535)	577	1.61
Indian (1,645)	1,711	4.76
Indonesian (1)	1	0.00
Japanese (25)	36	0.10
Korean (87)	97	0.27
Laotian (2)	2	0.01
Pakistani (137)	167	0.46
Sri Lankan (2)	2	0.01
Taiwanese (13)	13	0.04
Thai (18)	20	0.06
Vietnamese (187)	193	0.54
Other Asian, specified (1)	4	0.01
Other Asian, not specified (42)	76	0.21
Assyrian/Chaldean/Syriac	35	0.10
Austrian	63	0.18
Belgian	9	0.03
British	40	0.11
Bulgarian	65	0.18
Canadian	43	0.12
Croatian	111	0.31
Czech	400	1.12
Czechoslovakian	84	0.24
Danish	138	0.39
Dutch	310	0.87
English	1,050	2.94
European	24	0.07
Finnish	78	0.22
French, except Basque	421	1.18
French Canadian	142	0.40
German	5,111	14.31
Greek	783	2.19
Hawaii Native/Pacific Islander:	32	0.09
Micronesian:	1	0.00
Guamanian/Chamorro	1	0.00
Polynesian: (1)	14	0.04
Native Hawaiian (1)	14	0.04
Other Pac. Isl., not spec. (4)	17	0.05
Hispanic or Latino:	10,198	28.40
Central American:	256	0.71
Costa Rican	1	0.00
Guatemalan	189	0.53
Honduran	13	0.04
Nicaraguan	3	0.01
Panamanian	5	0.01
Salvadoran	40	0.11
Other Central American	5	0.01
Cuban	96	0.27
Dominican Republic	1	0.00
Mexican	8,741	24.34
Puerto Rican	351	0.98
South American:	135	0.38
Argentinean	6	0.02
Bolivian	2	0.01
Chilean	6	0.02
Colombian	65	0.18
Ecuadorian	11	0.03
Paraguayan	1	0.00
Peruvian	15	0.04
Uruguayan	2	0.01
Venezuelan	17	0.05
Other South American	10	0.03
Other Hispanic or Latino	618	1.72
Hungarian	250	0.70
Irish	3,159	8.85
Italian	5,835	16.34
Lithuanian	207	0.58
Luxemburger	6	0.02
Macedonian	12	0.03
Maltese	5	0.01
Norwegian	373	1.04
Pennsylvania German	28	0.08
Polish	4,645	13.01
Romanian	94	0.26
Russian	58	0.16
Scandinavian	53	0.15
Scotch-Irish	324	0.91
Scottish	222	0.62
Serbian	70	0.20
Slovak	132	0.37
Swedish	648	1.81
Swiss	27	0.08
Ukrainian	229	0.64
United States or American	631	1.77
Welsh	66	0.18
West Indian, excl. Hispanic:	17	0.05
Belizean	7	0.02
Jamaican	10	0.03
White:	27,823	77.47
Not Hispanic (21,540)	21,832	60.79
Hispanic (5,536)	5,991	16.68
Yugoslavian	12	0.03

Algonquin

Place Type: Village
County: McHenry
Population: 23,276

Ancestry/Race	Number	%
Acadian/Cajun	14	0.06
African American/Black:	264	1.13
Not Hispanic (194)	240	1.03
Hispanic (20)	24	0.10
Am. Ind. or Alaska Nat., not spec.	31	0.13
American Indian tribes, specified:	38	0.16
Apache	4	0.02
Blackfeet (1)	1	0.00
Cherokee	13	0.06
Chippewa (3)	4	0.02
Choctaw (1)	2	0.01
Iroquois (2)	3	0.01
Latin American Indians (3)	3	0.01
Menominee	1	0.00
Ottawa (2)	2	0.01

Notes: 1. Figures in the "Number" column do not add up to the total population due to: a) Ancestry/Race overlap — e.g. persons can report being both White and Irish, b) persons of Hispanic origin can report being any race, c) persons reporting two ancestries are counted in both categories. 2. Numbers in parentheses indicate the number of persons reporting this ancestry/race alone, not in combination with any other ancestry/race. 3. Refer to the Explanation of Data in the front of the book for more detailed information.

Ancestry/Race	Number	%
Potawatomi (1)	1	0.00
Pueblo (1)	1	0.00
Shoshone	1	0.00
Sioux (1)	1	0.00
All other tribes	1	0.00
American Indian tribes, not spec.	3	0.01
Arab:	79	0.34
Lebanese	32	0.14
Syrian	47	0.20
Armenian	25	0.11
Asian:	655	2.81
Bangladeshi (1)	1	0.00
Cambodian (5)	5	0.02
Chinese, ex. Taiwanese (106)	126	0.54
Filipino (132)	158	0.68
Hmong (1)	1	0.00
Indian (143)	148	0.64
Japanese (21)	34	0.15
Korean (50)	64	0.27
Laotian (10)	10	0.04
Malaysian (1)	2	0.01
Pakistani (27)	31	0.13
Taiwanese (1)	1	0.00
Thai (8)	10	0.04
Vietnamese (32)	40	0.17
Other Asian, specified (1)	4	0.02
Other Asian, not specified (1)	20	0.09
Assyrian/Chaldean/Syriac	20	0.09
Austrian	145	0.62
Belgian	55	0.23
British	121	0.52
Canadian	68	0.29
Croatian	69	0.29
Czech	528	2.25
Czechoslovakian	130	0.56
Danish	230	0.98
Dutch	473	2.02
Eastern European	10	0.04
English	2,139	9.13
Estonian	9	0.04
European	153	0.65
Finnish	98	0.42
French, except Basque	659	2.81
French Canadian	178	0.76
German	7,746	33.08
Greek	267	1.14
Hawaii Native/Pacific Islander:	7	0.03
Polynesian: (1)	1	0.00
Native Hawaiian (1)	1	0.00
Other Pac. Isl., not spec. (2)	6	0.03
Hispanic or Latino:	948	4.07
Central American:	43	0.18
Guatemalan	20	0.09
Honduran	11	0.05
Nicaraguan	3	0.01
Panamanian	2	0.01
Salvadoran	2	0.01
Other Central American	5	0.02
Cuban	29	0.12
Mexican	554	2.38
Puerto Rican	133	0.57
South American:	75	0.32
Argentinean	4	0.02
Bolivian	2	0.01
Colombian	39	0.17
Ecuadorian	21	0.09
Paraguayan	2	0.01
Peruvian	4	0.02
Venezuelan	1	0.00
Other South American	2	0.01
Other Hispanic or Latino	114	0.49
Hungarian	252	1.08
Irish	3,991	17.04
Italian	2,842	12.14
Latvian	19	0.08
Lithuanian	132	0.56
Luxemburger	19	0.08
Northern European	33	0.14
Norwegian	925	3.95
Polish	4,352	18.58
Portuguese	9	0.04
Romanian	41	0.18
Russian	192	0.82
Scandinavian	68	0.29
Scotch-Irish	256	1.09
Scottish	334	1.43
Serbian	19	0.08
Slavic	11	0.05
Slovak	25	0.11
Swedish	1,179	5.03
Swiss	31	0.13
Ukrainian	185	0.79
United States or American	594	2.54
Welsh	175	0.75
West Indian, excl. Hispanic:	54	0.23
Haitian	24	0.10
Jamaican	11	0.05
West Indian	19	0.08
White:	22,189	95.33
Not Hispanic (21,327)	21,511	92.42
Hispanic (612)	678	2.91
Yugoslavian	36	0.15

Alsip

Place Type: Village
County: Cook
Population: 19,725

Ancestry/Race	Number	%
African American/Black:	2,052	10.40
Not Hispanic (1,982)	2,033	10.31
Hispanic (9)	19	0.10
African, sub-Saharan:	189	0.95
African	156	0.79
Ethiopian	27	0.14
Nigerian	6	0.03
Am. Ind. or Alaska Nat., not spec.	44	0.22
American Indian tribes, specified:	62	0.31
Blackfeet (2)	6	0.03
Cherokee (9)	33	0.17
Chippewa (2)	7	0.04
Choctaw	1	0.01
Iroquois (1)	1	0.01
Kiowa	1	0.01
Latin American Indians (1)	2	0.01
Navajo	1	0.01
Potawatomi (3)	3	0.02
Sioux (1)	4	0.02
All other tribes (1)	3	0.02
American Indian tribes, not spec.	6	0.03
Arab:	388	1.95
Arab/Arabic	338	1.70
Egyptian	5	0.03
Jordanian	6	0.03
Palestinian	39	0.20
Armenian	15	0.08
Asian:	544	2.76
Chinese, ex. Taiwanese (14)	18	0.09
Filipino (220)	248	1.26
Indian (93)	98	0.50
Indonesian (1)	1	0.01
Japanese (6)	14	0.07
Korean (24)	37	0.19
Laotian (6)	6	0.03
Pakistani (8)	14	0.07
Thai (12)	12	0.06
Vietnamese (25)	28	0.14
Other Asian, not specified (6)	68	0.34
Austrian	57	0.29
Belgian	8	0.04
Brazilian	10	0.05
British	13	0.07
Croatian	227	1.14
Czech	309	1.56
Czechoslovakian	92	0.46
Danish	90	0.45
Dutch	570	2.87
English	685	3.45
Estonian	6	0.03
European	19	0.10
Finnish	17	0.09
French, except Basque	329	1.66
French Canadian	134	0.67
German	4,110	20.69
Greek	563	2.83
Hawaii Native/Pacific Islander:	16	0.08
Melanesian: (4)	4	0.02
Fijian (4)	4	0.02
Micronesian: (1)	2	0.01
Guamanian/Chamorro	1	0.01
Other Micronesian (1)	1	0.01
Polynesian: (1)	2	0.01
Native Hawaiian	1	0.01
Samoan (1)	1	0.01
Other Pac. Isl., not spec.	8	0.04
Hispanic or Latino:	1,727	8.76
Central American:	41	0.21
Costa Rican	2	0.01
Guatemalan	24	0.12
Honduran	1	0.01
Nicaraguan	3	0.02
Salvadoran	4	0.02
Other Central American	7	0.04
Cuban	13	0.07
Dominican Republic	2	0.01
Mexican	1,395	7.07
Puerto Rican	107	0.54
South American:	30	0.15
Argentinean	2	0.01
Colombian	15	0.08
Ecuadorian	2	0.01
Peruvian	11	0.06
Other Hispanic or Latino	139	0.70
Hungarian	87	0.44
Irish	4,804	24.19
Italian	2,338	11.77
Lithuanian	476	2.40
Northern European	5	0.03
Norwegian	147	0.74
Pennsylvania German	7	0.04
Polish	3,434	17.29
Portuguese	6	0.03
Romanian	10	0.05
Russian	84	0.42
Scandinavian	13	0.07
Scotch-Irish	165	0.83
Scottish	150	0.76
Serbian	73	0.37
Slovak	187	0.94
Slovene	7	0.04
Swedish	635	3.20
Swiss	38	0.19
Turkish	13	0.07
Ukrainian	41	0.21
United States or American	303	1.53
Welsh	34	0.17
West Indian, excl. Hispanic:	8	0.04
Jamaican	8	0.04
White:	16,600	84.16
Not Hispanic (15,122)	15,504	78.60
Hispanic (982)	1,096	5.56
Yugoslavian	35	0.18

Alton

Place Type: City
County: Madison
Population: 30,496

Ancestry/Race	Number	%
African American/Black:	7,851	25.74
Not Hispanic (7,504)	7,808	25.60
Hispanic (34)	43	0.14
African, sub-Saharan:	398	1.31
African	374	1.23
South African	14	0.05
Other sub-Saharan African	10	0.03
Am. Ind. or Alaska Nat., not spec.	76	0.25
American Indian tribes, specified:	118	0.39

Notes: 1. Figures in the "Number" column do not add up to the total population due to: a) Ancestry/Race overlap — e.g. persons can report being both White and Irish, b) persons of Hispanic origin can report being any race, c) persons reporting two ancestries are counted in both categories. 2. Numbers in parentheses indicate the number of persons reporting this ancestry/race alone, not in combination with any other ancestry/race. 3. Refer to the Explanation of Data in the front of the book for more detailed information.

Ancestry/Race	Number	%
Apache (1)	1	0.00
Blackfeet (1)	8	0.03
Cherokee (21)	72	0.24
Cheyenne	2	0.01
Chippewa (1)	1	0.00
Choctaw (1)	4	0.01
Comanche	1	0.00
Creek (1)	2	0.01
Crow	4	0.01
Kiowa (1)	1	0.00
Menominee (1)	1	0.00
Potawatomi	1	0.00
Pueblo	1	0.00
Sioux (2)	10	0.03
Ute	1	0.00
Yakama	1	0.00
All other tribes (2)	7	0.02
American Indian tribes, not spec.	13	0.04
Arab:	35	0.12
Arab/Arabic	8	0.03
Lebanese	20	0.07
Moroccan	7	0.02
Asian:	197	0.65
Chinese, ex. Taiwanese (24)	39	0.13
Filipino (18)	33	0.11
Indian (12)	18	0.06
Japanese (8)	19	0.06
Korean (17)	25	0.08
Malaysian (1)	1	0.00
Pakistani (1)	1	0.00
Thai (2)	3	0.01
Vietnamese (21)	23	0.08
Other Asian, specified	4	0.01
Other Asian, not specified (9)	31	0.10
Austrian	49	0.16
Belgian	25	0.08
British	58	0.19
Bulgarian	16	0.05
Canadian	12	0.04
Celtic	3	0.01
Croatian	99	0.33
Czech	79	0.26
Czechoslovakian	24	0.08
Dutch	460	1.51
Eastern European	16	0.05
English	2,390	7.86
European	360	1.18
Finnish	13	0.04
French, except Basque	811	2.67
French Canadian	102	0.34
German	6,716	22.07
Greek	147	0.48
Hawaii Native/Pacific Islander:	18	0.06
Polynesian: (3)	13	0.04
Native Hawaiian (1)	8	0.03
Samoan (2)	5	0.02
Other Pac. Isl., specified	3	0.01
Other Pac. Isl., not spec.	2	0.01
Hispanic or Latino:	454	1.49
Central American:	12	0.04
Guatemalan	3	0.01
Honduran	1	0.00
Panamanian	7	0.02
Salvadoran	1	0.00
Cuban	12	0.04
Dominican Republic	2	0.01
Mexican	283	0.93
Puerto Rican	39	0.13
South American:	13	0.04
Chilean	8	0.03
Colombian	2	0.01
Ecuadorian	1	0.00
Venezuelan	2	0.01
Other Hispanic or Latino	93	0.30
Hungarian	30	0.10
Icelander	21	0.07
Iranian	12	0.04
Irish	3,704	12.17
Italian	1,055	3.47
Lithuanian	33	0.11
Luxemburger	6	0.02
Macedonian	23	0.08
Northern European	12	0.04
Norwegian	49	0.16
Pennsylvania German	7	0.02
Polish	230	0.76
Portuguese	13	0.04
Romanian	4	0.01
Russian	26	0.09
Scandinavian	10	0.03
Scotch-Irish	385	1.27
Scottish	330	1.08
Slavic	7	0.02
Slovak	32	0.11
Slovene	12	0.04
Swedish	118	0.39
Swiss	157	0.52
Ukrainian	22	0.07
United States or American	2,504	8.23
Welsh	126	0.41
West Indian, excl. Hispanic:	77	0.25
Jamaican	69	0.23
West Indian	8	0.03
White:	22,505	73.80
Not Hispanic (21,825)	22,229	72.89
Hispanic (231)	276	0.91
Yugoslavian	11	0.04

Arlington Heights

Place Type: Village
County: Cook
Population: 76,031

Ancestry/Race	Number	%
African American/Black:	868	1.14
Not Hispanic (706)	813	1.07
Hispanic (22)	55	0.07
African, sub-Saharan:	44	0.06
African	19	0.02
Kenyan	7	0.01
Nigerian	11	0.01
South African	7	0.01
Am. Ind. or Alaska Nat., not spec.	75	0.10
Albanian	72	0.09
Alsatian	7	0.01
American Indian tribes, specified:	103	0.14
Apache (1)	1	0.00
Cherokee (11)	35	0.05
Chickasaw (2)	2	0.00
Chippewa	8	0.01
Choctaw	5	0.01
Cree (1)	1	0.00
Iroquois (2)	6	0.01
Latin American Indians (1)	19	0.02
Menominee (1)	1	0.00
Navajo (2)	2	0.00
Osage (1)	1	0.00
Ottawa (1)	2	0.00
Seminole	2	0.00
Sioux (3)	4	0.01
All other tribes (2)	13	0.02
American Indian tribes, not spec.	10	0.01
Arab:	316	0.42
Arab/Arabic	16	0.02
Egyptian	73	0.10
Iraqi	44	0.06
Jordanian	64	0.08
Lebanese	55	0.07
Moroccan	21	0.03
Syrian	31	0.04
Other Arab	12	0.02
Armenian	60	0.08
Asian:	5,006	6.58
Bangladeshi (3)	3	0.00
Cambodian (9)	10	0.01
Chinese, ex. Taiwanese (701)	818	1.08
Filipino (568)	667	0.88
Indian (933)	969	1.27
Indonesian (12)	19	0.02
Japanese (999)	1,108	1.46
Korean (926)	958	1.26
Laotian (6)	6	0.01
Malaysian (1)	1	0.00
Pakistani (68)	76	0.10
Sri Lankan (1)	1	0.00
Taiwanese (56)	64	0.08
Thai (30)	40	0.05
Vietnamese (145)	178	0.23
Other Asian, specified (4)	7	0.01
Other Asian, not specified (25)	81	0.11
Assyrian/Chaldean/Syriac	79	0.10
Austrian	712	0.94
Basque	15	0.02
Belgian	158	0.21
Brazilian	22	0.03
British	286	0.38
Bulgarian	25	0.03
Canadian	248	0.33
Celtic	33	0.04
Croatian	240	0.32
Cypriot	7	0.01
Czech	995	1.31
Czechoslovakian	292	0.38
Danish	667	0.88
Dutch	788	1.04
Eastern European	56	0.07
English	6,298	8.28
Estonian	46	0.06
European	486	0.64
Finnish	218	0.29
French, except Basque	1,617	2.12
French Canadian	340	0.45
German	20,899	27.46
Greek	1,442	1.89
Guyanese	9	0.01
Hawaii Native/Pacific Islander:	65	0.09
Micronesian: (4)	7	0.01
Guamanian/Chamorro (4)	7	0.01
Polynesian: (13)	24	0.03
Native Hawaiian (6)	11	0.01
Samoan (6)	10	0.01
Tongan	1	0.00
Other Polynesian (1)	2	0.00
Other Pac. Isl., not spec. (13)	34	0.04
Hispanic or Latino:	3,393	4.46
Central American:	106	0.14
Costa Rican	7	0.01
Guatemalan	52	0.07
Honduran	3	0.00
Nicaraguan	5	0.01
Panamanian	10	0.01
Salvadoran	19	0.02
Other Central American	10	0.01
Cuban	109	0.14
Dominican Republic	10	0.01
Mexican	2,311	3.04
Puerto Rican	277	0.36
South American:	207	0.27
Argentinean	18	0.02
Bolivian	6	0.01
Chilean	5	0.01
Colombian	67	0.09
Ecuadorian	62	0.08
Paraguayan	2	0.00
Peruvian	31	0.04
Uruguayan	1	0.00
Venezuelan	10	0.01
Other South American	5	0.01
Other Hispanic or Latino	373	0.49
Hungarian	670	0.88
Iranian	121	0.16
Irish	14,592	19.18
Italian	8,456	11.11
Latvian	76	0.10
Lithuanian	432	0.57
Luxemburger	141	0.19
Macedonian	15	0.02
Northern European	5	0.01
Norwegian	2,053	2.70

Notes: 1. Figures in the "Number" column do not add up to the total population due to: a) Ancestry/Race overlap — e.g. persons can report being both White and Irish, b) persons of Hispanic origin can report being any race, c) persons reporting two ancestries are counted in both categories. 2. Numbers in parentheses indicate the number of persons reporting this ancestry/race alone, not in combination with any other ancestry/race. 3. Refer to the Explanation of Data in the front of the book for more detailed information.

Ancestry/Race	Number	%
Pennsylvania German	8	0.01
Polish	11,001	14.46
Portuguese	31	0.04
Romanian	290	0.38
Russian	2,046	2.69
Scandinavian	168	0.22
Scotch-Irish	869	1.14
Scottish	1,296	1.70
Serbian	147	0.19
Slavic	45	0.06
Slovak	377	0.50
Slovene	149	0.20
Swedish	3,307	4.35
Swiss	274	0.36
Turkish	26	0.03
Ukrainian	617	0.81
United States or American	2,232	2.93
Welsh	367	0.48
West Indian, excl. Hispanic:	29	0.04
Barbadian	29	0.04
White:	69,645	91.60
Not Hispanic (66,612)	67,192	88.37
Hispanic (2,242)	2,453	3.23
Yugoslavian	162	0.21

Aurora

Place Type: City
County: Kane
Population: 142,990

Ancestry/Race	Number	%
African American/Black:	17,058	11.93
Not Hispanic (15,389)	16,343	11.43
Hispanic (428)	715	0.50
African, sub-Saharan:	748	0.52
African	466	0.32
Ethiopian	17	0.01
Ghanian	26	0.02
Liberian	74	0.05
Nigerian	56	0.04
South African	61	0.04
Zimbabwean	9	0.01
Other sub-Saharan African	39	0.03
Alaska Native tribes, specified:	11	0.01
Alaska Athabascan	3	0.00
Aleut	2	0.00
Eskimo (2)	4	0.00
Tlingit-Haida (1)	2	0.00
Alaska Native tribes, not specified	1	0.00
Am. Ind. or Alaska Nat., not spec.	461	0.32
Albanian	20	0.01
Alsatian	4	0.00
American Indian tribes, specified:	493	0.34
Apache (2)	15	0.01
Blackfeet (3)	28	0.02
Cherokee (29)	164	0.11
Cheyenne (1)	1	0.00
Chickasaw (1)	2	0.00
Chippewa (11)	22	0.02
Choctaw (1)	16	0.01
Comanche (2)	3	0.00
Cree	1	0.00
Creek (1)	3	0.00
Crow (2)	6	0.00
Delaware	2	0.00
Houma (1)	1	0.00
Iroquois (3)	8	0.01
Latin American Indians (100)	125	0.09
Navajo (15)	20	0.01
Osage	3	0.00
Ottawa	4	0.00
Pima (1)	1	0.00
Potawatomi	1	0.00
Pueblo	1	0.00
Seminole	4	0.00
Sioux (13)	37	0.03
Ute (1)	3	0.00
Yakama	1	0.00
All other tribes (6)	21	0.01
American Indian tribes, not spec.	81	0.06
Arab:	390	0.27
Arab/Arabic	9	0.01
Egyptian	106	0.07
Iraqi	25	0.02
Jordanian	6	0.00
Lebanese	169	0.12
Moroccan	27	0.02
Palestinian	23	0.02
Syrian	9	0.01
Other Arab	16	0.01
Armenian	56	0.04
Asian:	5,106	3.57
Bangladeshi (6)	6	0.00
Cambodian (2)	13	0.01
Chinese, ex. Taiwanese (677)	793	0.55
Filipino (865)	1,045	0.73
Hmong (77)	95	0.07
Indian (1,742)	1,841	1.29
Indonesian (4)	14	0.01
Japanese (87)	180	0.13
Korean (276)	325	0.23
Laotian (97)	125	0.09
Malaysian (2)	4	0.00
Pakistani (114)	140	0.10
Sri Lankan (7)	8	0.01
Taiwanese (11)	16	0.01
Thai (35)	47	0.03
Vietnamese (222)	243	0.17
Other Asian, specified (3)	6	0.00
Other Asian, not specified (72)	205	0.14
Assyrian/Chaldean/Syriac	7	0.00
Australian	59	0.04
Austrian	263	0.18
Basque	17	0.01
Belgian	270	0.19
Brazilian	24	0.02
British	434	0.30
Bulgarian	42	0.03
Canadian	163	0.11
Celtic	24	0.02
Croatian	275	0.19
Czech	1,112	0.77
Czechoslovakian	282	0.20
Danish	757	0.53
Dutch	1,831	1.27
Eastern European	55	0.04
English	8,014	5.58
Estonian	6	0.00
European	635	0.44
Finnish	253	0.18
French, except Basque	2,482	1.73
French Canadian	669	0.47
German	25,070	17.46
Greek	935	0.65
Guyanese	7	0.00
Hawaii Native/Pacific Islander:	126	0.09
Melanesian:	1	0.00
Fijian	1	0.00
Micronesian: (19)	35	0.02
Guamanian/Chamorro (11)	23	0.02
Other Micronesian (8)	12	0.01
Polynesian: (7)	23	0.02
Native Hawaiian (4)	11	0.01
Samoan (3)	11	0.01
Other Polynesian	1	0.00
Other Pac. Isl., not spec. (21)	67	0.05
Hispanic or Latino:	46,557	32.56
Central American:	329	0.23
Costa Rican	12	0.01
Guatemalan	108	0.08
Honduran	58	0.04
Nicaraguan	37	0.03
Panamanian	21	0.01
Salvadoran	82	0.06
Other Central American	11	0.01
Cuban	207	0.14
Dominican Republic	47	0.03
Mexican	39,351	27.52
Puerto Rican	2,611	1.83
South American:	358	0.25
Argentinean	43	0.03
Bolivian	24	0.02
Chilean	24	0.02
Colombian	119	0.08
Ecuadorian	35	0.02
Peruvian	47	0.03
Venezuelan	52	0.04
Other South American	14	0.01
Other Hispanic or Latino	3,654	2.56
Hungarian	819	0.57
Icelander	10	0.01
Iranian	88	0.06
Irish	13,998	9.75
Italian	6,704	4.67
Latvian	23	0.02
Lithuanian	753	0.52
Luxemburger	597	0.42
New Zealander	30	0.02
Northern European	15	0.01
Norwegian	2,733	1.90
Pennsylvania German	55	0.04
Polish	6,644	4.63
Portuguese	98	0.07
Romanian	711	0.50
Russian	562	0.39
Scandinavian	295	0.21
Scotch-Irish	1,278	0.89
Scottish	1,947	1.36
Serbian	79	0.06
Slavic	29	0.02
Slovak	389	0.27
Slovene	171	0.12
Swedish	3,129	2.18
Swiss	291	0.20
Turkish	7	0.00
Ukrainian	410	0.29
United States or American	4,260	2.97
Welsh	568	0.40
West Indian, excl. Hispanic:	197	0.14
Bahamian	7	0.00
Haitian	50	0.03
Jamaican	54	0.04
Trinidadian and Tobagonian	55	0.04
West Indian	31	0.02
White:	100,854	70.53
Not Hispanic (74,457)	76,031	53.17
Hispanic (22,883)	24,823	17.36
Yugoslavian	114	0.08

Barrington

Place Type: Village
County: Cook
Population: 10,168

Ancestry/Race	Number	%
African American/Black:	68	0.67
Not Hispanic (63)	67	0.66
Hispanic	1	0.01
Am. Ind. or Alaska Nat., not spec.	14	0.14
American Indian tribes, specified:	25	0.25
Cherokee	5	0.05
Choctaw (2)	7	0.07
Kiowa (1)	1	0.01
Latin American Indians (1)	1	0.01
Menominee	5	0.05
Sioux (1)	2	0.02
All other tribes (4)	4	0.04
Arab:	18	0.18
Arab/Arabic	18	0.18
Asian:	240	2.36
Chinese, ex. Taiwanese (47)	54	0.53
Filipino (12)	24	0.24
Indian (82)	89	0.88
Japanese (20)	29	0.29
Korean (22)	23	0.23
Laotian (1)	1	0.01
Pakistani (1)	1	0.01
Taiwanese (2)	3	0.03

Notes: 1. Figures in the "Number" column do not add up to the total population due to: a) Ancestry/Race overlap — e.g. persons can report being both White and Irish, b) persons of Hispanic origin can report being any race, c) persons reporting two ancestries are counted in both categories. 2. Numbers in parentheses indicate the number of persons reporting this ancestry/race alone, not in combination with any other ancestry/race. 3. Refer to the Explanation of Data in the front of the book for more detailed information.

Vietnamese (9)	9	0.09
Other Asian, specified (2)	2	0.02
Other Asian, not specified (3)	5	0.05
Austrian	88	0.88
Belgian	27	0.27
British	91	0.91
Canadian	48	0.48
Croatian	26	0.26
Czech	132	1.32
Czechoslovakian	30	0.30
Danish	55	0.55
Dutch	239	2.39
Eastern European	7	0.07
English	1,226	12.24
European	131	1.31
Finnish	42	0.42
French, except Basque	335	3.34
French Canadian	131	1.31
German	2,860	28.55
Greek	210	2.10
Hawaii Native/Pacific Islander:	3	0.03
Micronesian:	1	0.01
Guamanian/Chamorro	1	0.01
Polynesian: (1)	2	0.02
Native Hawaiian (1)	2	0.02
Hispanic or Latino:	237	2.33
Central American:	4	0.04
Costa Rican	2	0.02
Guatemalan	2	0.02
Cuban	6	0.06
Mexican	178	1.75
Puerto Rican	6	0.06
South American:	12	0.12
Chilean	6	0.06
Colombian	3	0.03
Peruvian	2	0.02
Other South American	1	0.01
Other Hispanic or Latino	31	0.30
Hungarian	66	0.66
Iranian	10	0.10
Irish	2,338	23.34
Italian	872	8.70
Latvian	6	0.06
Lithuanian	49	0.49
Northern European	30	0.30
Norwegian	285	2.84
Polish	798	7.97
Portuguese	31	0.31
Romanian	9	0.09
Russian	168	1.68
Scandinavian	83	0.83
Scotch-Irish	120	1.20
Scottish	343	3.42
Serbian	14	0.14
Slovak	37	0.37
Slovene	23	0.23
Swedish	479	4.78
Swiss	67	0.67
Ukrainian	53	0.53
United States or American	496	4.95
Welsh	107	1.07
White:	9,854	96.91
Not Hispanic (9,570)	9,643	94.84
Hispanic (208)	211	2.08
Yugoslavian	15	0.15

Bartlett

Place Type: Village
County: Du Page
Population: 36,706

Ancestry/Race	Number	%
African American/Black:	843	2.30
Not Hispanic (706)	812	2.21
Hispanic (19)	31	0.08
African, sub-Saharan:	29	0.08
African	29	0.08
Am. Ind. or Alaska Nat., not spec.	64	0.17
Albanian	7	0.02
American Indian tribes, specified:	84	0.23
Apache (2)	6	0.02
Blackfeet	5	0.01
Cherokee (8)	28	0.08
Chippewa (3)	8	0.02
Creek	1	0.00
Iroquois (5)	6	0.02
Latin American Indians (5)	12	0.03
Navajo	2	0.01
Pima	1	0.00
Pueblo	1	0.00
Sioux (2)	5	0.01
All other tribes (2)	9	0.02
American Indian tribes, not spec.	3	0.01
Arab:	121	0.33
Arab/Arabic	8	0.02
Jordanian	10	0.03
Lebanese	23	0.06
Palestinian	13	0.04
Other Arab	67	0.18
Armenian	68	0.18
Asian:	3,115	8.49
Bangladeshi (3)	3	0.01
Cambodian (7)	8	0.02
Chinese, ex. Taiwanese (233)	255	0.69
Filipino (1,061)	1,149	3.13
Indian (938)	984	2.68
Indonesian (3)	3	0.01
Japanese (71)	103	0.28
Korean (231)	241	0.66
Laotian (20)	30	0.08
Malaysian (7)	9	0.02
Pakistani (152)	179	0.49
Sri Lankan	1	0.00
Taiwanese (3)	4	0.01
Thai (4)	4	0.01
Vietnamese (60)	67	0.18
Other Asian, specified (1)	5	0.01
Other Asian, not specified (45)	70	0.19
Assyrian/Chaldean/Syriac	88	0.24
Austrian	301	0.82
Belgian	84	0.23
British	51	0.14
Bulgarian	8	0.02
Canadian	80	0.22
Croatian	134	0.36
Czech	694	1.88
Czechoslovakian	175	0.48
Danish	376	1.02
Dutch	498	1.35
English	2,237	6.07
European	222	0.60
Finnish	72	0.20
French, except Basque	928	2.52
French Canadian	256	0.69
German	10,493	28.48
Greek	436	1.18
Hawaii Native/Pacific Islander:	27	0.07
Micronesian:	2	0.01
Other Micronesian	2	0.01
Polynesian: (3)	6	0.02
Native Hawaiian (2)	4	0.01
Samoan (1)	1	0.00
Other Polynesian	1	0.00
Other Pac. Isl., specified	2	0.01
Other Pac. Isl., not spec. (5)	17	0.05
Hispanic or Latino:	2,024	5.51
Central American:	70	0.19
Costa Rican	7	0.02
Guatemalan	29	0.08
Honduran	10	0.03
Panamanian	4	0.01
Salvadoran	16	0.04
Other Central American	4	0.01
Cuban	86	0.23
Dominican Republic	3	0.01
Mexican	1,332	3.63
Puerto Rican	243	0.66
South American:	97	0.26
Argentinean	6	0.02
Bolivian	4	0.01
Chilean	8	0.02
Colombian	31	0.08
Ecuadorian	25	0.07
Peruvian	14	0.04
Uruguayan	5	0.01
Venezuelan	1	0.00
Other South American	3	0.01
Other Hispanic or Latino	193	0.53
Hungarian	160	0.43
Iranian	18	0.05
Irish	6,014	16.32
Italian	6,333	17.19
Lithuanian	314	0.85
Luxemburger	11	0.03
Northern European	36	0.10
Norwegian	1,119	3.04
Polish	5,619	15.25
Portuguese	10	0.03
Romanian	140	0.38
Russian	242	0.66
Scandinavian	91	0.25
Scotch-Irish	282	0.77
Scottish	492	1.34
Serbian	41	0.11
Slavic	10	0.03
Slovak	186	0.50
Slovene	62	0.17
Swedish	1,356	3.68
Swiss	117	0.32
Turkish	5	0.01
Ukrainian	241	0.65
United States or American	978	2.65
Welsh	179	0.49
West Indian, excl. Hispanic:	29	0.08
Belizean	7	0.02
Haitian	22	0.06
White:	32,443	88.39
Not Hispanic (30,673)	30,961	84.35
Hispanic (1,347)	1,482	4.04
Yugoslavian	67	0.18

Batavia

Place Type: City
County: Kane
Population: 23,866

Ancestry/Race	Number	%
African American/Black:	704	2.95
Not Hispanic (540)	648	2.72
Hispanic (37)	56	0.23
African, sub-Saharan:	56	0.23
African	56	0.23
Alaska Native tribes, specified:	4	0.02
Eskimo	4	0.02
Am. Ind. or Alaska Nat., not spec.	35	0.15
Albanian	28	0.12
Alsatian	8	0.03
American Indian tribes, specified:	42	0.18
Apache	2	0.01
Blackfeet	2	0.01
Cherokee (3)	16	0.07
Chippewa (1)	3	0.01
Choctaw	2	0.01
Iroquois (2)	5	0.02
Latin American Indians (3)	5	0.02
Menominee (1)	1	0.00
Navajo	1	0.00
Shoshone	1	0.00
Sioux	2	0.01
All other tribes	2	0.01
American Indian tribes, not spec.	3	0.01
Arab:	49	0.20
Arab/Arabic	14	0.06
Egyptian	26	0.11
Syrian	9	0.04
Asian:	395	1.66
Chinese, ex. Taiwanese (94)	115	0.48
Filipino (18)	28	0.12

Notes: 1. Figures in the "Number" column do not add up to the total population due to: a) Ancestry/Race overlap — e.g. persons can report being both White and Irish, b) persons of Hispanic origin can report being any race, c) persons reporting two ancestries are counted in both categories. 2. Numbers in parentheses indicate the number of persons reporting this ancestry/race alone, not in combination with any other ancestry/race. 3. Refer to the Explanation of Data in the front of the book for more detailed information.

Hmong	1	0.00
Indian (66)	75	0.31
Indonesian (2)	2	0.01
Japanese (15)	30	0.13
Korean (54)	60	0.25
Laotian (11)	13	0.05
Malaysian (1)	1	0.00
Pakistani (19)	20	0.08
Taiwanese (1)	1	0.00
Thai (2)	4	0.02
Vietnamese (25)	28	0.12
Other Asian, specified	8	0.03
Other Asian, not specified (7)	9	0.04
Assyrian/Chaldean/Syriac	6	0.03
Austrian	194	0.81
Belgian	71	0.30
British	167	0.70
Canadian	53	0.22
Croatian	92	0.38
Czech	404	1.69
Czechoslovakian	30	0.13
Danish	270	1.13
Dutch	444	1.86
Eastern European	8	0.03
English	2,751	11.50
European	256	1.07
Finnish	43	0.18
French, except Basque	756	3.16
French Canadian	183	0.77
German	7,549	31.56
Greek	227	0.95
Hawaii Native/Pacific Islander:	13	0.05
Polynesian: (1)	5	0.02
Native Hawaiian (1)	5	0.02
Other Pac. Isl., specified	8	0.03
Hispanic or Latino:	1,257	5.27
Central American:	14	0.06
Guatemalan	2	0.01
Honduran	1	0.00
Salvadoran	10	0.04
Other Central American	1	0.00
Cuban	50	0.21
Mexican	976	4.09
Puerto Rican	62	0.26
South American:	42	0.18
Argentinean	4	0.02
Chilean	1	0.00
Colombian	19	0.08
Ecuadorian	10	0.04
Paraguayan	1	0.00
Peruvian	4	0.02
Venezuelan	1	0.00
Other South American	2	0.01
Other Hispanic or Latino	113	0.47
Hungarian	164	0.69
Icelander	31	0.13
Iranian	10	0.04
Irish	4,320	18.06
Italian	2,101	8.78
Latvian	11	0.05
Lithuanian	133	0.56
Luxemburger	69	0.29
Northern European	5	0.02
Norwegian	843	3.52
Pennsylvania German	8	0.03
Polish	2,064	8.63
Portuguese	6	0.03
Romanian	103	0.43
Russian	295	1.23
Scandinavian	84	0.35
Scotch-Irish	424	1.77
Scottish	685	2.86
Serbian	8	0.03
Slovak	127	0.53
Slovene	77	0.32
Swedish	1,930	8.07
Swiss	133	0.56
Ukrainian	45	0.19
United States or American	712	2.98
Welsh	253	1.06
West Indian, excl. Hispanic:	18	0.08
Barbadian	5	0.02
Jamaican	13	0.05
White:	22,555	94.51
Not Hispanic (21,504)	21,706	90.95
Hispanic (741)	849	3.56
Yugoslavian	38	0.16

Beach Park

Place Type: Village
County: Lake
Population: 10,072

Ancestry/Race	Number	%
African American/Black:	522	5.18
Not Hispanic (450)	503	4.99
Hispanic (7)	19	0.19
African, sub-Saharan:	31	0.32
Cape Verdean	13	0.13
Nigerian	11	0.11
South African	7	0.07
Alaska Native tribes, specified:	4	0.04
Aleut	4	0.04
Am. Ind. or Alaska Nat., not spec.	37	0.37
American Indian tribes, specified:	70	0.69
Blackfeet (1)	6	0.06
Cherokee (1)	31	0.31
Chickasaw	1	0.01
Chippewa (5)	10	0.10
Cree	2	0.02
Latin American Indians	7	0.07
Navajo	1	0.01
Sioux (1)	6	0.06
All other tribes (5)	6	0.06
American Indian tribes, not spec.	1	0.01
Arab:	12	0.12
Arab/Arabic	6	0.06
Palestinian	6	0.06
Asian:	200	1.99
Cambodian (6)	8	0.08
Chinese, ex. Taiwanese (1)	2	0.02
Filipino (104)	130	1.29
Indian (11)	12	0.12
Japanese (10)	21	0.21
Korean (12)	12	0.12
Sri Lankan	1	0.01
Taiwanese (2)	2	0.02
Thai (2)	2	0.02
Other Asian, specified	4	0.04
Other Asian, not specified (2)	6	0.06
Austrian	50	0.51
Belgian	43	0.44
British	56	0.58
Canadian	7	0.07
Croatian	27	0.28
Czech	111	1.14
Czechoslovakian	25	0.26
Danish	146	1.50
Dutch	232	2.38
English	915	9.40
European	35	0.36
Finnish	187	1.92
French, except Basque	415	4.26
French Canadian	110	1.13
German	2,669	27.41
Greek	12	0.12
Hawaii Native/Pacific Islander:	9	0.09
Micronesian: (1)	1	0.01
Guamanian/Chamorro (1)	1	0.01
Polynesian: (2)	2	0.02
Native Hawaiian (2)	2	0.02
Other Pac. Isl., specified	4	0.04
Other Pac. Isl., not spec.	2	0.02
Hispanic or Latino:	1,368	13.58
Central American:	24	0.24
Guatemalan	4	0.04
Honduran	12	0.12
Salvadoran	7	0.07
Other Central American	1	0.01
Cuban	4	0.04
Dominican Republic	3	0.03
Mexican	976	9.69
Puerto Rican	220	2.18
South American:	26	0.26
Colombian	22	0.22
Peruvian	3	0.03
Other South American	1	0.01
Other Hispanic or Latino	115	1.14
Hungarian	73	0.75
Irish	1,567	16.09
Italian	505	5.19
Latvian	7	0.07
Lithuanian	187	1.92
Norwegian	306	3.14
Polish	849	8.72
Portuguese	12	0.12
Romanian	42	0.43
Russian	71	0.73
Scandinavian	21	0.22
Scotch-Irish	113	1.16
Scottish	178	1.83
Slavic	6	0.06
Slovak	14	0.14
Slovene	105	1.08
Swedish	367	3.77
Swiss	24	0.25
Ukrainian	29	0.30
United States or American	393	4.04
Welsh	66	0.68
West Indian, excl. Hispanic:	11	0.11
Belizean	11	0.11
White:	8,795	87.32
Not Hispanic (7,922)	8,056	79.98
Hispanic (670)	739	7.34
Yugoslavian	62	0.64

Belleville

Place Type: City
County: Saint Clair
Population: 41,410

Ancestry/Race	Number	%
Acadian/Cajun	13	0.03
African American/Black:	6,681	16.13
Not Hispanic (6,377)	6,630	16.01
Hispanic (44)	51	0.12
African, sub-Saharan:	350	0.83
African	286	0.68
Ethiopian	6	0.01
Kenyan	13	0.03
Nigerian	5	0.01
South African	17	0.04
Other sub-Saharan African	23	0.05
Alaska Native tribes, specified:	10	0.02
Alaska Athabascan (2)	7	0.02
Eskimo (2)	3	0.01
Alaska Native tribes, not specified	1	0.00
Am. Ind. or Alaska Nat., not spec.	82	0.20
American Indian tribes, specified:	151	0.36
Apache	3	0.01
Blackfeet (2)	8	0.02
Cherokee (20)	70	0.17
Cheyenne (1)	1	0.00
Chickasaw (5)	5	0.01
Chippewa (3)	6	0.01
Choctaw (6)	9	0.02
Comanche (5)	5	0.01
Cree	1	0.00
Creek	1	0.00
Iroquois (4)	5	0.01
Latin American Indians (2)	3	0.01
Navajo (6)	7	0.02
Osage (1)	2	0.00
Potawatomi (6)	6	0.01
Pueblo (2)	2	0.00
Seminole (1)	1	0.00
Sioux (3)	7	0.02
Yaqui (2)	2	0.00

Notes: 1. Figures in the "Number" column do not add up to the total population due to: a) Ancestry/Race overlap — e.g. persons can report being both White and Irish, b) persons of Hispanic origin can report being any race, c) persons reporting two ancestries are counted in both categories. 2. Numbers in parentheses indicate the number of persons reporting this ancestry/race alone, not in combination with any other ancestry/race. 3. Refer to the Explanation of Data in the front of the book for more detailed information.

All other tribes (5)	7	0.02
American Indian tribes, not spec.	9	0.02
Arab:	156	0.37
Arab/Arabic	18	0.04
Egyptian	34	0.08
Lebanese	65	0.15
Moroccan	7	0.02
Palestinian	18	0.04
Syrian	14	0.03
Armenian	100	0.24
Asian:	462	1.12
Bangladeshi (5)	6	0.01
Cambodian (4)	5	0.01
Chinese, ex. Taiwanese (38)	49	0.12
Filipino (102)	144	0.35
Indian (32)	39	0.09
Japanese (21)	47	0.11
Korean (37)	55	0.13
Laotian (2)	2	0.00
Pakistani (11)	11	0.03
Taiwanese (3)	5	0.01
Thai (26)	39	0.09
Vietnamese (33)	41	0.10
Other Asian, not specified (14)	19	0.05
Assyrian/Chaldean/Syriac	11	0.03
Australian	7	0.02
Austrian	71	0.17
Belgian	46	0.11
British	113	0.27
Canadian	38	0.09
Celtic	6	0.01
Croatian	127	0.30
Czech	237	0.56
Czechoslovakian	43	0.10
Danish	120	0.28
Dutch	380	0.90
English	3,540	8.40
European	164	0.39
Finnish	41	0.10
French, except Basque	2,141	5.08
French Canadian	110	0.26
German	14,000	33.20
Greek	57	0.14
Hawaii Native/Pacific Islander:	62	0.15
Micronesian: (12)	19	0.05
Guamanian/Chamorro (11)	18	0.04
Other Micronesian (1)	1	0.00
Polynesian: (12)	26	0.06
Native Hawaiian (9)	20	0.05
Samoan (3)	6	0.01
Other Pac. Isl., not spec. (3)	17	0.04
Hispanic or Latino:	677	1.63
Central American:	10	0.02
Guatemalan	2	0.00
Honduran	1	0.00
Panamanian	6	0.01
Salvadoran	1	0.00
Cuban	15	0.04
Mexican	372	0.90
Puerto Rican	94	0.23
South American:	13	0.03
Argentinean	1	0.00
Bolivian	3	0.01
Chilean	1	0.00
Colombian	6	0.01
Peruvian	1	0.00
Venezuelan	1	0.00
Other Hispanic or Latino	173	0.42
Hungarian	109	0.26
Icelander	8	0.02
Iranian	33	0.08
Irish	4,854	11.51
Italian	1,177	2.79
Lithuanian	197	0.47
Macedonian	20	0.05
Northern European	24	0.06
Norwegian	219	0.52
Pennsylvania German	11	0.03
Polish	1,266	3.00
Portuguese	25	0.06
Romanian	8	0.02
Russian	65	0.15
Scandinavian	13	0.03
Scotch-Irish	710	1.68
Scottish	566	1.34
Serbian	5	0.01
Slavic	57	0.14
Slovak	122	0.29
Swedish	188	0.45
Swiss	62	0.15
Turkish	8	0.02
Ukrainian	71	0.17
United States or American	2,531	6.00
Welsh	179	0.42
West Indian, excl. Hispanic:	11	0.03
Trinidadian and Tobagonian	11	0.03
White:	34,292	82.81
Not Hispanic (33,341)	33,810	81.65
Hispanic (413)	482	1.16
Yugoslavian	26	0.06

Bellwood

Place Type: Village
County: Cook
Population: 20,535

Ancestry/Race	Number	%
African American/Black:	16,995	82.76
Not Hispanic (16,673)	16,848	82.05
Hispanic (110)	147	0.72
African, sub-Saharan:	412	2.01
African	359	1.75
Ethiopian	14	0.07
Ghanian	39	0.19
Am. Ind. or Alaska Nat., not spec.	67	0.33
American Indian tribes, specified:	61	0.30
Apache	2	0.01
Blackfeet	9	0.04
Cherokee (1)	11	0.05
Choctaw	2	0.01
Iroquois	3	0.01
Latin American Indians (21)	28	0.14
Seminole	2	0.01
Sioux	2	0.01
All other tribes	2	0.01
American Indian tribes, not spec.	10	0.05
Armenian	22	0.11
Asian:	225	1.10
Chinese, ex. Taiwanese (5)	13	0.06
Filipino (49)	54	0.26
Indian (92)	101	0.49
Japanese (4)	5	0.02
Korean (2)	5	0.02
Pakistani (25)	27	0.13
Sri Lankan (1)	1	0.00
Vietnamese (13)	13	0.06
Other Asian, not specified (4)	6	0.03
Austrian	12	0.06
Canadian	6	0.03
Celtic	15	0.07
Croatian	22	0.11
Czech	52	0.25
Czechoslovakian	4	0.02
Danish	10	0.05
Dutch	21	0.10
English	117	0.57
European	4	0.02
French, except Basque	34	0.17
French Canadian	19	0.09
German	664	3.23
German Russian	11	0.05
Greek	19	0.09
Guyanese	12	0.06
Hawaii Native/Pacific Islander:	15	0.07
Micronesian: (1)	2	0.01
Guamanian/Chamorro (1)	2	0.01
Polynesian: (2)	7	0.03
Native Hawaiian	1	0.00
Samoan (2)	6	0.03
Other Pac. Isl., not spec. (1)	6	0.03
Hispanic or Latino:	1,631	7.94
Central American:	42	0.20
Guatemalan	22	0.11
Honduran	3	0.01
Panamanian	8	0.04
Salvadoran	6	0.03
Other Central American	3	0.01
Cuban	20	0.10
Dominican Republic	9	0.04
Mexican	1,297	6.32
Puerto Rican	151	0.74
South American:	6	0.03
Colombian	2	0.01
Peruvian	4	0.02
Other Hispanic or Latino	106	0.52
Hungarian	5	0.02
Irish	360	1.75
Italian	387	1.88
Latvian	12	0.06
Lithuanian	28	0.14
Norwegian	9	0.04
Polish	270	1.31
Romanian	7	0.03
Russian	85	0.41
Scotch-Irish	31	0.15
Scottish	39	0.19
Serbian	35	0.17
Slovak	6	0.03
Slovene	41	0.20
Swedish	24	0.12
Ukrainian	16	0.08
United States or American	164	0.80
West Indian, excl. Hispanic:	187	0.91
Belizean	15	0.07
Haitian	14	0.07
Jamaican	158	0.77
White:	2,633	12.82
Not Hispanic (1,803)	1,938	9.44
Hispanic (609)	695	3.38
Yugoslavian	12	0.06

Belvidere

Place Type: City
County: Boone
Population: 20,820

Ancestry/Race	Number	%
African American/Black:	320	1.54
Not Hispanic (217)	279	1.34
Hispanic (22)	41	0.20
African, sub-Saharan:	7	0.03
African	7	0.03
Alaska Native tribes, specified:	2	0.01
Alaska Athabascan (1)	1	0.00
Tlingit-Haida (1)	1	0.00
Alaska Native tribes, not specified	1	0.00
Am. Ind. or Alaska Nat., not spec.	76	0.37
Albanian	21	0.10
American Indian tribes, specified:	87	0.42
Apache (4)	4	0.02
Blackfeet (2)	5	0.02
Cherokee (5)	32	0.15
Cheyenne	1	0.00
Chippewa (4)	7	0.03
Choctaw	1	0.00
Delaware (2)	2	0.01
Iroquois (3)	4	0.02
Latin American Indians (6)	12	0.06
Sioux (3)	11	0.05
All other tribes (2)	8	0.04
American Indian tribes, not spec.	6	0.03
Asian:	164	0.79
Chinese, ex. Taiwanese (16)	17	0.08
Filipino (21)	40	0.19
Indian (14)	22	0.11
Indonesian	4	0.02
Japanese (5)	20	0.10
Korean (9)	16	0.08

Notes: 1. Figures in the "Number" column do not add up to the total population due to: a) Ancestry/Race overlap — e.g. persons can report being both White and Irish, b) persons of Hispanic origin can report being any race, c) persons reporting two ancestries are counted in both categories. 2. Numbers in parentheses indicate the number of persons reporting this ancestry/race alone, not in combination with any other ancestry/race. 3. Refer to the Explanation of Data in the front of the book for more detailed information.

Laotian (12)	13	0.06
Malaysian (2)	2	0.01
Pakistani (4)	4	0.02
Thai (4)	12	0.06
Vietnamese (1)	3	0.01
Other Asian, not specified (1)	11	0.05
Austrian	34	0.16
Belgian	38	0.18
British	25	0.12
Croatian	32	0.15
Czech	212	1.02
Czechoslovakian	17	0.08
Danish	122	0.59
Dutch	365	1.76
English	1,868	9.03
European	71	0.34
Finnish	22	0.11
French, except Basque	476	2.30
French Canadian	50	0.24
German	6,325	30.56
Greek	88	0.43
Hawaii Native/Pacific Islander:	11	0.05
Micronesian: (1)	1	0.00
Guamanian/Chamorro (1)	1	0.00
Polynesian: (3)	3	0.01
Native Hawaiian (1)	1	0.00
Samoan (2)	2	0.01
Other Pac. Isl., not spec.	7	0.03
Hispanic or Latino:	4,179	20.07
Central American:	16	0.08
Guatemalan	11	0.05
Honduran	2	0.01
Salvadoran	1	0.00
Other Central American	2	0.01
Cuban	15	0.07
Dominican Republic	16	0.08
Mexican	3,656	17.56
Puerto Rican	126	0.61
South American:	33	0.16
Chilean	1	0.00
Colombian	14	0.07
Ecuadorian	3	0.01
Peruvian	12	0.06
Uruguayan	2	0.01
Other South American	1	0.00
Other Hispanic or Latino	317	1.52
Hungarian	117	0.57
Irish	2,725	13.17
Italian	830	4.01
Lithuanian	73	0.35
Luxemburger	8	0.04
Northern European	41	0.20
Norwegian	869	4.20
Pennsylvania German	12	0.06
Polish	978	4.73
Romanian	12	0.06
Russian	103	0.50
Scandinavian	33	0.16
Scotch-Irish	190	0.92
Scottish	312	1.51
Serbian	13	0.06
Slavic	9	0.04
Slovak	6	0.03
Swedish	1,427	6.89
Swiss	102	0.49
Ukrainian	103	0.50
United States or American	1,087	5.25
Welsh	146	0.71
White:	17,964	86.28
Not Hispanic (16,063)	16,263	78.11
Hispanic (1,537)	1,701	8.17
Yugoslavian	15	0.07

Bensenville

Place Type: Village
County: Du Page
Population: 20,703

Ancestry/Race	Number	%
African American/Black:	655	3.16
Not Hispanic (537)	583	2.82
Hispanic (42)	72	0.35
African, sub-Saharan:	71	0.35
African	71	0.35
Am. Ind. or Alaska Nat., not spec.	97	0.47
Albanian	32	0.16
American Indian tribes, specified:	73	0.35
Apache (1)	2	0.01
Cherokee (1)	16	0.08
Chippewa	1	0.00
Choctaw (1)	1	0.00
Comanche (2)	2	0.01
Creek	2	0.01
Houma (1)	1	0.00
Iroquois	2	0.01
Latin American Indians (12)	33	0.16
Pueblo	3	0.01
Sioux (1)	4	0.02
Yaqui	1	0.00
All other tribes	5	0.02
American Indian tribes, not spec.	6	0.03
Arab:	127	0.62
Arab/Arabic	99	0.48
Jordanian	22	0.11
Palestinian	6	0.03
Asian:	1,466	7.08
Chinese, ex. Taiwanese (35)	53	0.26
Filipino (236)	270	1.30
Indian (757)	794	3.84
Japanese (23)	35	0.17
Korean (52)	62	0.30
Laotian (5)	5	0.02
Malaysian	3	0.01
Pakistani (144)	187	0.90
Taiwanese (12)	12	0.06
Thai (2)	2	0.01
Vietnamese (21)	26	0.13
Other Asian, not specified (10)	17	0.08
Austrian	123	0.60
Belgian	19	0.09
British	6	0.03
Canadian	52	0.25
Croatian	65	0.32
Czech	245	1.19
Czechoslovakian	51	0.25
Danish	180	0.88
Dutch	219	1.07
English	603	2.94
European	42	0.20
Finnish	13	0.06
French, except Basque	235	1.15
French Canadian	86	0.42
German	3,614	17.62
Greek	204	0.99
Hawaii Native/Pacific Islander:	16	0.08
Micronesian: (5)	6	0.03
Guamanian/Chamorro (5)	6	0.03
Polynesian:	3	0.01
Native Hawaiian	3	0.01
Other Pac. Isl., not spec.	7	0.03
Hispanic or Latino:	7,690	37.14
Central American:	226	1.09
Guatemalan	187	0.90
Honduran	17	0.08
Nicaraguan	7	0.03
Panamanian	1	0.00
Salvadoran	12	0.06
Other Central American	2	0.01
Cuban	54	0.26
Dominican Republic	5	0.02
Mexican	6,524	31.51
Puerto Rican	221	1.07
South American:	121	0.58
Argentinean	8	0.04
Bolivian	1	0.00
Chilean	3	0.01
Colombian	58	0.28
Ecuadorian	33	0.16
Peruvian	15	0.07
Venezuelan	1	0.00
Other South American	2	0.01
Other Hispanic or Latino	539	2.60
Hungarian	92	0.45
Icelander	29	0.14
Iranian	11	0.05
Irish	2,008	9.79
Italian	1,908	9.30
Lithuanian	131	0.64
Luxemburger	17	0.08
Norwegian	351	1.71
Polish	2,195	10.70
Portuguese	33	0.16
Romanian	47	0.23
Russian	69	0.34
Scandinavian	9	0.04
Scotch-Irish	107	0.52
Scottish	133	0.65
Serbian	27	0.13
Slavic	6	0.03
Slovak	48	0.23
Slovene	27	0.13
Swedish	426	2.08
Swiss	36	0.18
Ukrainian	54	0.26
United States or American	517	2.52
West Indian, excl. Hispanic:	60	0.29
British West Indian	41	0.20
Jamaican	10	0.05
Trinidadian and Tobagonian	9	0.04
White:	15,158	73.22
Not Hispanic (10,779)	11,041	53.33
Hispanic (3,836)	4,117	19.89
Yugoslavian	52	0.25

Berwyn

Place Type: City
County: Cook
Population: 54,016

Ancestry/Race	Number	%
Afghan	10	0.02
African American/Black:	872	1.61
Not Hispanic (588)	675	1.25
Hispanic (114)	197	0.36
African, sub-Saharan:	46	0.09
African	46	0.09
Alaska Native tribes, specified:	2	0.00
Eskimo (1)	2	0.00
Am. Ind. or Alaska Nat., not spec.	205	0.38
American Indian tribes, specified:	250	0.46
Apache	1	0.00
Blackfeet (1)	3	0.01
Cherokee (20)	78	0.14
Chippewa (18)	28	0.05
Choctaw (4)	14	0.03
Cree	2	0.00
Creek	1	0.00
Delaware	2	0.00
Iroquois (9)	11	0.02
Latin American Indians (58)	75	0.14
Lumbee	1	0.00
Menominee (3)	5	0.01
Ottawa	1	0.00
Pima	2	0.00
Potawatomi	1	0.00
Seminole (1)	1	0.00
Shoshone	2	0.00
Sioux (3)	8	0.01
Yaqui	1	0.00
All other tribes (3)	13	0.02
American Indian tribes, not spec.	21	0.04
Arab:	509	0.94
Arab/Arabic	222	0.41
Egyptian	16	0.03
Jordanian	74	0.14
Lebanese	10	0.02
Moroccan	45	0.08
Palestinian	78	0.14

Notes: 1. Figures in the "Number" column do not add up to the total population due to: a) Ancestry/Race overlap — e.g. persons can report being both White and Irish, b) persons of Hispanic origin can report being any race, c) persons reporting two ancestries are counted in both categories. 2. Numbers in parentheses indicate the number of persons reporting this ancestry/race alone, not in combination with any other ancestry/race. 3. Refer to the Explanation of Data in the front of the book for more detailed information.

Ancestry/Race	Number	%
Syrian	64	0.12
Asian:	1,665	3.08
Cambodian (18)	22	0.04
Chinese, ex. Taiwanese (176)	208	0.39
Filipino (787)	871	1.61
Hmong	1	0.00
Indian (122)	153	0.28
Indonesian (2)	2	0.00
Japanese (36)	50	0.09
Korean (48)	63	0.12
Laotian (8)	8	0.01
Malaysian (1)	3	0.01
Pakistani (33)	55	0.10
Taiwanese	1	0.00
Thai (23)	30	0.06
Vietnamese (122)	126	0.23
Other Asian, specified	7	0.01
Other Asian, not specified (12)	65	0.12
Assyrian/Chaldean/Syriac	13	0.02
Austrian	265	0.49
Belgian	44	0.08
Brazilian	41	0.08
British	16	0.03
Bulgarian	23	0.04
Canadian	15	0.03
Croatian	415	0.77
Czech	2,982	5.52
Czechoslovakian	717	1.33
Danish	169	0.31
Dutch	404	0.75
Eastern European	12	0.02
English	1,324	2.45
European	136	0.25
Finnish	37	0.07
French, except Basque	878	1.63
French Canadian	129	0.24
German	6,389	11.83
Greek	744	1.38
Hawaii Native/Pacific Islander:	43	0.08
Melanesian:	1	0.00
Other Melanesian	1	0.00
Micronesian: (4)	7	0.01
Guamanian/Chamorro (4)	7	0.01
Polynesian: (8)	14	0.03
Native Hawaiian (6)	8	0.01
Samoan (2)	6	0.01
Other Pac. Isl., specified	6	0.01
Other Pac. Isl., not spec. (2)	15	0.03
Hispanic or Latino:	20,543	38.03
Central American:	350	0.65
Costa Rican	2	0.00
Guatemalan	169	0.31
Honduran	51	0.09
Nicaraguan	11	0.02
Panamanian	16	0.03
Salvadoran	76	0.14
Other Central American	25	0.05
Cuban	127	0.24
Dominican Republic	16	0.03
Mexican	16,745	31.00
Puerto Rican	1,392	2.58
South American:	445	0.82
Argentinean	33	0.06
Bolivian	13	0.02
Chilean	37	0.07
Colombian	120	0.22
Ecuadorian	141	0.26
Paraguayan	8	0.01
Peruvian	58	0.11
Uruguayan	13	0.02
Venezuelan	11	0.02
Other South American	11	0.02
Other Hispanic or Latino	1,468	2.72
Hungarian	182	0.34
Iranian	15	0.03
Irish	6,005	11.12
Israeli	4	0.01
Italian	5,591	10.35
Lithuanian	556	1.03
Luxemburger	7	0.01
Macedonian	47	0.09
Northern European	41	0.08
Norwegian	374	0.69
Polish	6,480	12.00
Portuguese	79	0.15
Romanian	41	0.08
Russian	315	0.58
Scandinavian	7	0.01
Scotch-Irish	218	0.40
Scottish	343	0.63
Serbian	357	0.66
Slavic	36	0.07
Slovak	515	0.95
Slovene	67	0.12
Swedish	510	0.94
Swiss	16	0.03
Turkish	8	0.01
Ukrainian	457	0.85
United States or American	898	1.66
Welsh	104	0.19
West Indian, excl. Hispanic:	115	0.21
Belizean	60	0.11
Haitian	33	0.06
Jamaican	12	0.02
West Indian	10	0.02
White:	41,499	76.83
Not Hispanic (30,476)	31,318	57.98
Hispanic (9,191)	10,181	18.85
Yugoslavian	301	0.56

Bloomingdale

Place Type: Village
County: Du Page
Population: 21,675

Ancestry/Race	Number	%
African American/Black:	595	2.75
Not Hispanic (551)	584	2.69
Hispanic (6)	11	0.05
African, sub-Saharan:	84	0.39
African	84	0.39
Am. Ind. or Alaska Nat., not spec.	39	0.18
Albanian	30	0.14
American Indian tribes, specified:	42	0.19
Apache (1)	2	0.01
Blackfeet	1	0.00
Cherokee (2)	9	0.04
Chippewa (1)	1	0.00
Choctaw	1	0.00
Creek	2	0.01
Iroquois (1)	8	0.04
Latin American Indians (1)	3	0.01
Menominee (2)	2	0.01
Ottawa	5	0.02
Pueblo (1)	2	0.01
Sioux	3	0.01
Yaqui	1	0.00
All other tribes (1)	2	0.01
American Indian tribes, not spec.	1	0.00
Arab:	168	0.78
Arab/Arabic	142	0.66
Iraqi	7	0.03
Lebanese	7	0.03
Palestinian	6	0.03
Syrian	6	0.03
Armenian	98	0.45
Asian:	2,090	9.64
Bangladeshi (2)	4	0.02
Cambodian (1)	1	0.00
Chinese, ex. Taiwanese (221)	236	1.09
Filipino (434)	490	2.26
Indian (806)	835	3.85
Indonesian (1)	3	0.01
Japanese (125)	146	0.67
Korean (153)	166	0.77
Pakistani (83)	102	0.47
Sri Lankan (1)	1	0.00
Taiwanese (13)	17	0.08
Thai (7)	7	0.03
Vietnamese (39)	43	0.20
Other Asian, not specified (12)	39	0.18
Austrian	115	0.53
Belgian	69	0.32
Brazilian	8	0.04
British	9	0.04
Bulgarian	7	0.03
Canadian	38	0.18
Croatian	119	0.55
Czech	365	1.69
Czechoslovakian	74	0.34
Danish	219	1.01
Dutch	250	1.16
Eastern European	66	0.31
English	1,085	5.03
European	52	0.24
Finnish	122	0.57
French, except Basque	389	1.80
French Canadian	112	0.52
German	4,525	20.97
Greek	484	2.24
Hawaii Native/Pacific Islander:	23	0.11
Micronesian: (2)	2	0.01
Guamanian/Chamorro (2)	2	0.01
Polynesian:	8	0.04
Native Hawaiian	7	0.03
Samoan	1	0.00
Other Pac. Isl., not spec. (1)	13	0.06
Hispanic or Latino:	1,074	4.96
Central American:	54	0.25
Costa Rican	5	0.02
Guatemalan	36	0.17
Honduran	3	0.01
Nicaraguan	5	0.02
Panamanian	2	0.01
Salvadoran	2	0.01
Other Central American	1	0.00
Cuban	56	0.26
Mexican	629	2.90
Puerto Rican	134	0.62
South American:	67	0.31
Argentinean	12	0.06
Bolivian	1	0.00
Chilean	2	0.01
Colombian	23	0.11
Ecuadorian	23	0.11
Peruvian	3	0.01
Uruguayan	1	0.00
Venezuelan	1	0.00
Other South American	1	0.00
Other Hispanic or Latino	134	0.62
Hungarian	95	0.44
Icelander	8	0.04
Iranian	70	0.32
Irish	3,422	15.86
Israeli	13	0.06
Italian	4,471	20.72
Lithuanian	196	0.91
Luxemburger	17	0.08
Norwegian	425	1.97
Polish	2,691	12.47
Romanian	15	0.07
Russian	250	1.16
Scandinavian	16	0.07
Scotch-Irish	172	0.80
Scottish	227	1.05
Serbian	36	0.17
Slavic	9	0.04
Slovak	107	0.50
Slovene	46	0.21
Swedish	639	2.96
Swiss	65	0.30
Ukrainian	173	0.80
United States or American	549	2.54
Welsh	76	0.35
West Indian, excl. Hispanic:	32	0.15
Haitian	25	0.12
Jamaican	7	0.03
White:	18,771	86.60
Not Hispanic (17,854)	18,041	83.23

Notes: 1. Figures in the "Number" column do not add up to the total population due to: a) Ancestry/Race overlap — e.g. persons can report being both White and Irish, b) persons of Hispanic origin can report being any race, c) persons reporting two ancestries are counted in both categories. 2. Numbers in parentheses indicate the number of persons reporting this ancestry/race alone, not in combination with any other ancestry/race. 3. Refer to the Explanation of Data in the front of the book for more detailed information.

Hispanic (651)	730	3.37
Yugoslavian	39	0.18

Bloomington

Place Type: City
County: McLean
Population: 64,808

Ancestry/Race	Number	%
African American/Black:	6,153	9.49
Not Hispanic (5,527)	6,049	9.33
Hispanic (75)	104	0.16
African, sub-Saharan:	198	0.30
African	128	0.20
Ghanian	15	0.02
Kenyan	10	0.02
Nigerian	17	0.03
Somalian	20	0.03
South African	8	0.01
Alaska Native tribes, specified:	4	0.01
Alaska Athabascan (1)	3	0.00
Eskimo (1)	1	0.00
Am. Ind. or Alaska Nat., not spec.	133	0.21
Alsatian	7	0.01
American Indian tribes, specified:	216	0.33
Apache (1)	5	0.01
Blackfeet (8)	16	0.02
Cherokee (20)	92	0.14
Chickasaw	1	0.00
Chippewa (6)	17	0.03
Choctaw (4)	12	0.02
Colville (3)	3	0.00
Comanche	2	0.00
Creek (2)	2	0.00
Iroquois (3)	5	0.01
Kiowa (3)	4	0.01
Latin American Indians (5)	5	0.01
Navajo	1	0.00
Osage (1)	2	0.00
Potawatomi (6)	20	0.03
Seminole	4	0.01
Shoshone (1)	1	0.00
Sioux (6)	12	0.02
All other tribes (1)	12	0.02
American Indian tribes, not spec.	11	0.02
Arab:	105	0.16
Arab/Arabic	9	0.01
Lebanese	87	0.13
Syrian	9	0.01
Armenian	15	0.02
Asian:	2,219	3.42
Cambodian (1)	1	0.00
Chinese, ex. Taiwanese (281)	315	0.49
Filipino (103)	170	0.26
Indian (1,030)	1,070	1.65
Indonesian	1	0.00
Japanese (187)	232	0.36
Korean (134)	159	0.25
Laotian (3)	4	0.01
Malaysian (4)	4	0.01
Pakistani (19)	21	0.03
Sri Lankan (5)	5	0.01
Taiwanese (14)	18	0.03
Thai (25)	37	0.06
Vietnamese (114)	131	0.20
Other Asian, specified (4)	4	0.01
Other Asian, not specified (16)	47	0.07
Australian	11	0.02
Austrian	171	0.26
Belgian	136	0.21
British	179	0.28
Bulgarian	8	0.01
Canadian	94	0.14
Croatian	121	0.19
Czech	504	0.77
Czechoslovakian	97	0.15
Danish	345	0.53
Dutch	1,118	1.72
Eastern European	22	0.03
English	7,025	10.80
Estonian	24	0.04
European	377	0.58
Finnish	21	0.03
French, except Basque	2,019	3.10
French Canadian	288	0.44
German	18,245	28.05
Greek	214	0.33
Hawaii Native/Pacific Islander:	53	0.08
Melanesian: (4)	4	0.01
Fijian (4)	4	0.01
Micronesian: (6)	9	0.01
Guamanian/Chamorro (6)	7	0.01
Other Micronesian	2	0.00
Polynesian: (12)	26	0.04
Native Hawaiian (6)	17	0.03
Samoan (6)	9	0.01
Other Pac. Isl., not spec. (6)	14	0.02
Hispanic or Latino:	2,150	3.32
Central American:	105	0.16
Guatemalan	78	0.12
Honduran	4	0.01
Nicaraguan	1	0.00
Panamanian	6	0.01
Salvadoran	16	0.02
Cuban	36	0.06
Dominican Republic	7	0.01
Mexican	1,453	2.24
Puerto Rican	136	0.21
South American:	47	0.07
Argentinean	2	0.00
Bolivian	9	0.01
Chilean	2	0.00
Colombian	15	0.02
Ecuadorian	3	0.00
Paraguayan	7	0.01
Peruvian	5	0.01
Venezuelan	2	0.00
Other South American	2	0.00
Other Hispanic or Latino	366	0.56
Hungarian	467	0.72
Icelander	10	0.02
Iranian	27	0.04
Irish	9,189	14.13
Israeli	13	0.02
Italian	2,839	4.36
Lithuanian	271	0.42
Macedonian	28	0.04
Northern European	58	0.09
Norwegian	1,397	2.15
Pennsylvania German	12	0.02
Polish	2,318	3.56
Portuguese	93	0.14
Romanian	33	0.05
Russian	260	0.40
Scandinavian	150	0.23
Scotch-Irish	1,117	1.72
Scottish	1,283	1.97
Serbian	41	0.06
Slavic	24	0.04
Slovak	245	0.38
Slovene	10	0.02
Swedish	1,681	2.58
Swiss	307	0.47
Turkish	20	0.03
Ukrainian	165	0.25
United States or American	4,589	7.06
Welsh	437	0.67
West Indian, excl. Hispanic:	44	0.07
Belizean	25	0.04
Dutch West Indian	7	0.01
Haitian	8	0.01
West Indian	4	0.01
White:	56,091	86.55
Not Hispanic (54,011)	54,896	84.71
Hispanic (1,021)	1,195	1.84
Yugoslavian	131	0.20

Blue Island

Place Type: City
County: Cook
Population: 23,463

Ancestry/Race	Number	%
African American/Black:	5,808	24.75
Not Hispanic (5,599)	5,718	24.37
Hispanic (56)	90	0.38
African, sub-Saharan:	104	0.45
African	104	0.45
Alaska Native tribes, specified:	1	0.00
Eskimo	1	0.00
Am. Ind. or Alaska Nat., not spec.	120	0.51
American Indian tribes, specified:	119	0.51
Blackfeet	8	0.03
Cherokee (4)	33	0.14
Cheyenne (1)	1	0.00
Chickasaw	1	0.00
Chippewa (4)	8	0.03
Choctaw	2	0.01
Iroquois (1)	1	0.00
Latin American Indians (38)	51	0.22
Menominee	1	0.00
Navajo	1	0.00
Pueblo	1	0.00
Sioux (1)	7	0.03
Yaqui (2)	2	0.01
All other tribes (1)	2	0.01
American Indian tribes, not spec.	25	0.11
Arab:	99	0.42
Arab/Arabic	18	0.08
Jordanian	4	0.02
Palestinian	64	0.27
Other Arab	13	0.06
Asian:	161	0.69
Chinese, ex. Taiwanese (6)	11	0.05
Filipino (27)	49	0.21
Indian (18)	38	0.16
Indonesian	1	0.00
Japanese (3)	7	0.03
Korean (9)	12	0.05
Pakistani (12)	17	0.07
Sri Lankan	1	0.00
Vietnamese (7)	9	0.04
Other Asian, not specified (4)	16	0.07
Austrian	44	0.19
Belgian	5	0.02
Canadian	12	0.05
Croatian	26	0.11
Czech	154	0.66
Czechoslovakian	38	0.16
Danish	47	0.20
Dutch	254	1.09
English	550	2.36
European	15	0.06
Finnish	8	0.03
French, except Basque	307	1.32
French Canadian	133	0.57
German	2,735	11.72
Greek	137	0.59
Hawaii Native/Pacific Islander:	26	0.11
Micronesian: (1)	1	0.00
Guamanian/Chamorro (1)	1	0.00
Polynesian: (2)	9	0.04
Native Hawaiian (2)	3	0.01
Samoan	3	0.01
Other Polynesian	3	0.01
Other Pac. Isl., not spec. (4)	16	0.07
Hispanic or Latino:	8,899	37.93
Central American:	110	0.47
Costa Rican	5	0.02
Guatemalan	73	0.31
Nicaraguan	8	0.03
Salvadoran	17	0.07
Other Central American	7	0.03
Cuban	20	0.09
Dominican Republic	4	0.02
Mexican	7,975	33.99

Notes: 1. Figures in the "Number" column do not add up to the total population due to: a) Ancestry/Race overlap — e.g. persons can report being both White and Irish, b) persons of Hispanic origin can report being any race, c) persons reporting two ancestries are counted in both categories. 2. Numbers in parentheses indicate the number of persons reporting this ancestry/race alone, not in combination with any other ancestry/race. 3. Refer to the Explanation of Data in the front of the book for more detailed information.

Ancestry/Race	Number	%
Puerto Rican	129	0.55
South American:	49	0.21
Argentinean	21	0.09
Colombian	6	0.03
Ecuadorian	1	0.00
Paraguayan	3	0.01
Peruvian	15	0.06
Uruguayan	3	0.01
Other Hispanic or Latino	612	2.61
Hungarian	84	0.36
Irish	2,438	10.45
Italian	1,550	6.64
Lithuanian	149	0.64
Northern European	6	0.03
Norwegian	71	0.30
Polish	1,562	6.69
Portuguese	30	0.13
Russian	43	0.18
Scandinavian	4	0.02
Scotch-Irish	63	0.27
Scottish	118	0.51
Serbian	20	0.09
Slavic	28	0.12
Slovak	176	0.75
Swedish	346	1.48
Swiss	10	0.04
Ukrainian	22	0.09
United States or American	269	1.15
Welsh	11	0.05
West Indian, excl. Hispanic:	39	0.17
Belizean	22	0.09
British West Indian	9	0.04
Jamaican	8	0.03
White:	13,321	56.77
Not Hispanic (8,498)	8,762	37.34
Hispanic (4,098)	4,559	19.43
Yugoslavian	9	0.04

Bolingbrook

Place Type: Village
County: Will
Population: 56,321

Ancestry/Race	Number	%
African American/Black:	12,159	21.59
Not Hispanic (11,324)	11,928	21.18
Hispanic (170)	231	0.41
African, sub-Saharan:	1,084	1.92
African	614	1.09
Cape Verdean	23	0.04
Ghanian	301	0.53
Kenyan	12	0.02
Nigerian	114	0.20
Zimbabwean	10	0.02
Other sub-Saharan African	10	0.02
Alaska Native tribes, specified:	2	0.00
Tlingit-Haida (2)	2	0.00
Am. Ind. or Alaska Nat., not spec.	188	0.33
Albanian	3	0.01
American Indian tribes, specified:	186	0.33
Apache	5	0.01
Blackfeet (6)	15	0.03
Cherokee (19)	78	0.14
Cheyenne (2)	2	0.00
Chickasaw	4	0.01
Chippewa (2)	8	0.01
Choctaw	6	0.01
Cree	3	0.01
Creek (1)	4	0.01
Crow	1	0.00
Delaware	4	0.01
Iroquois (1)	4	0.01
Kiowa (1)	1	0.00
Latin American Indians (10)	22	0.04
Lumbee (1)	1	0.00
Menominee	1	0.00
Navajo	2	0.00
Ottawa (1)	2	0.00
Potawatomi (6)	11	0.02
Sioux (1)	2	0.00
All other tribes (2)	11	0.02
American Indian tribes, not spec.	21	0.04
Arab:	252	0.45
Arab/Arabic	51	0.09
Egyptian	20	0.04
Lebanese	72	0.13
Moroccan	23	0.04
Palestinian	22	0.04
Syrian	49	0.09
Other Arab	15	0.03
Asian:	4,114	7.30
Bangladeshi (19)	24	0.04
Cambodian (52)	75	0.13
Chinese, ex. Taiwanese (306)	376	0.67
Filipino (1,315)	1,529	2.71
Hmong (5)	5	0.01
Indian (1,146)	1,213	2.15
Indonesian (5)	5	0.01
Japanese (50)	91	0.16
Korean (137)	165	0.29
Laotian (48)	59	0.10
Malaysian (9)	10	0.02
Pakistani (209)	256	0.45
Sri Lankan (9)	9	0.02
Taiwanese (1)	9	0.02
Thai (29)	51	0.09
Vietnamese (118)	127	0.23
Other Asian, specified (4)	8	0.01
Other Asian, not specified (63)	102	0.18
Assyrian/Chaldean/Syriac	36	0.06
Austrian	193	0.34
Belgian	77	0.14
Brazilian	11	0.02
British	56	0.10
Bulgarian	13	0.02
Canadian	162	0.29
Celtic	20	0.04
Croatian	175	0.31
Czech	1,532	2.71
Czechoslovakian	225	0.40
Danish	326	0.58
Dutch	857	1.52
Eastern European	16	0.03
English	2,752	4.87
European	468	0.83
Finnish	48	0.09
French, except Basque	1,029	1.82
French Canadian	264	0.47
German	11,087	19.64
Greek	246	0.44
Guyanese	13	0.02
Hawaii Native/Pacific Islander:	75	0.13
Melanesian: (2)	2	0.00
Fijian (2)	2	0.00
Micronesian: (1)	1	0.00
Guamanian/Chamorro (1)	1	0.00
Polynesian: (10)	24	0.04
Native Hawaiian (3)	16	0.03
Samoan (6)	7	0.01
Other Polynesian (1)	1	0.00
Other Pac. Isl., specified	4	0.01
Other Pac. Isl., not spec. (23)	44	0.08
Hispanic or Latino:	7,371	13.09
Central American:	136	0.24
Costa Rican	10	0.02
Guatemalan	56	0.10
Honduran	19	0.03
Nicaraguan	6	0.01
Panamanian	13	0.02
Salvadoran	22	0.04
Other Central American	10	0.02
Cuban	101	0.18
Dominican Republic	15	0.03
Mexican	5,717	10.15
Puerto Rican	626	1.11
South American:	161	0.29
Argentinean	16	0.03
Bolivian	3	0.01
Chilean	8	0.01
Colombian	65	0.12
Ecuadorian	15	0.03
Paraguayan	1	0.00
Peruvian	27	0.05
Venezuelan	18	0.03
Other South American	8	0.01
Other Hispanic or Latino	615	1.09
Hungarian	370	0.66
Iranian	21	0.04
Irish	7,240	12.82
Italian	4,328	7.67
Latvian	20	0.04
Lithuanian	533	0.94
Luxemburger	10	0.02
Macedonian	30	0.05
New Zealander	10	0.02
Northern European	27	0.05
Norwegian	990	1.75
Pennsylvania German	15	0.03
Polish	5,515	9.77
Portuguese	53	0.09
Romanian	51	0.09
Russian	299	0.53
Scandinavian	86	0.15
Scotch-Irish	469	0.83
Scottish	525	0.93
Serbian	51	0.09
Slovak	163	0.29
Slovene	36	0.06
Swedish	1,280	2.27
Swiss	59	0.10
Turkish	8	0.01
Ukrainian	113	0.20
United States or American	1,631	2.89
Welsh	196	0.35
West Indian, excl. Hispanic:	355	0.63
Barbadian	9	0.02
Belizean	25	0.04
British West Indian	20	0.04
Dutch West Indian	12	0.02
Haitian	65	0.12
Jamaican	220	0.39
West Indian	4	0.01
White:	37,589	66.74
Not Hispanic (32,618)	33,553	59.57
Hispanic (3,712)	4,036	7.17
Yugoslavian	28	0.05

Bourbonnais

Place Type: Village
County: Kankakee
Population: 15,256

Ancestry/Race	Number	%
African American/Black:	787	5.16
Not Hispanic (685)	765	5.01
Hispanic (16)	22	0.14
African, sub-Saharan:	34	0.22
African	30	0.20
Ghanian	4	0.03
Alaska Native tribes, specified:	2	0.01
Aleut	2	0.01
Am. Ind. or Alaska Nat., not spec.	20	0.13
American Indian tribes, specified:	46	0.30
Blackfeet	1	0.01
Cherokee (7)	29	0.19
Chickasaw	3	0.02
Choctaw	1	0.01
Comanche	5	0.03
Crow	1	0.01
Potawatomi	3	0.02
Seminole	1	0.01
Sioux (1)	2	0.01
American Indian tribes, not spec.	1	0.01
Arab:	55	0.36
Arab/Arabic	34	0.22
Syrian	21	0.14
Armenian	13	0.08
Asian:	456	2.99

Notes: 1. Figures in the "Number" column do not add up to the total population due to: a) Ancestry/Race overlap — e.g. persons can report being both White and Irish, b) persons of Hispanic origin can report being any race, c) persons reporting two ancestries are counted in both categories. 2. Numbers in parentheses indicate the number of persons reporting this ancestry/race alone, not in combination with any other ancestry/race. 3. Refer to the Explanation of Data in the front of the book for more detailed information.

Ancestry/Race	Number	%
Chinese, ex. Taiwanese (34)	42	0.28
Filipino (86)	106	0.69
Hmong (3)	3	0.02
Indian (150)	162	1.06
Japanese (14)	22	0.14
Korean (16)	34	0.22
Laotian (1)	1	0.01
Pakistani (9)	9	0.06
Taiwanese (8)	9	0.06
Thai (3)	9	0.06
Vietnamese (20)	25	0.16
Other Asian, specified (8)	9	0.06
Other Asian, not specified (11)	25	0.16
Austrian	8	0.05
Belgian	4	0.03
British	87	0.57
Canadian	64	0.42
Croatian	54	0.35
Czech	141	0.92
Czechoslovakian	7	0.05
Danish	94	0.61
Dutch	499	3.25
English	1,258	8.19
European	91	0.59
French, except Basque	1,854	12.08
French Canadian	337	2.20
German	3,902	25.42
Greek	130	0.85
Hawaii Native/Pacific Islander:	11	0.07
Micronesian:	1	0.01
Guamanian/Chamorro	1	0.01
Polynesian: (1)	1	0.01
Samoan (1)	1	0.01
Other Pac. Isl., specified	1	0.01
Other Pac. Isl., not spec. (3)	8	0.05
Hispanic or Latino:	345	2.26
Central American:	8	0.05
Guatemalan	2	0.01
Honduran	1	0.01
Nicaraguan	1	0.01
Panamanian	1	0.01
Other Central American	3	0.02
Cuban	16	0.10
Dominican Republic	1	0.01
Mexican	213	1.40
Puerto Rican	43	0.28
South American:	12	0.08
Chilean	2	0.01
Colombian	9	0.06
Uruguayan	1	0.01
Other Hispanic or Latino	52	0.34
Hungarian	47	0.31
Irish	2,260	14.72
Italian	709	4.62
Latvian	34	0.22
Lithuanian	110	0.72
Norwegian	253	1.65
Pennsylvania German	17	0.11
Polish	650	4.23
Russian	40	0.26
Scotch-Irish	201	1.31
Scottish	310	2.02
Slavic	7	0.05
Slovak	14	0.09
Slovene	7	0.05
Swedish	382	2.49
Swiss	13	0.08
Ukrainian	41	0.27
United States or American	716	4.66
Welsh	64	0.42
West Indian, excl. Hispanic:	22	0.14
British West Indian	22	0.14
White:	14,031	91.97
Not Hispanic (13,640)	13,808	90.51
Hispanic (199)	223	1.46
Yugoslavian	5	0.03

Bradley

Place Type: Village
County: Kankakee
Population: 12,784

Ancestry/Race	Number	%
African American/Black:	198	1.55
Not Hispanic (154)	192	1.50
Hispanic (3)	6	0.05
African, sub-Saharan:	2	0.02
African	2	0.02
Am. Ind. or Alaska Nat., not spec.	18	0.14
American Indian tribes, specified:	27	0.21
Apache	1	0.01
Cherokee (9)	15	0.12
Chippewa (1)	1	0.01
Iroquois (1)	3	0.02
Latin American Indians	1	0.01
Menominee	3	0.02
Ottawa (2)	2	0.02
Shoshone	1	0.01
American Indian tribes, not spec.	1	0.01
Asian:	112	0.88
Chinese, ex. Taiwanese (19)	24	0.19
Filipino (23)	31	0.24
Indian (24)	29	0.23
Japanese (6)	6	0.05
Korean (14)	16	0.13
Thai	3	0.02
Other Asian, not specified (1)	3	0.02
Austrian	31	0.24
Belgian	39	0.31
British	8	0.06
Canadian	45	0.35
Celtic	4	0.03
Croatian	26	0.20
Czech	99	0.78
Czechoslovakian	17	0.13
Danish	156	1.23
Dutch	463	3.64
English	1,172	9.21
European	42	0.33
French, except Basque	1,713	13.46
French Canadian	639	5.02
German	3,429	26.95
Greek	67	0.53
Hawaii Native/Pacific Islander:	6	0.05
Micronesian: (1)	1	0.01
Guamanian/Chamorro (1)	1	0.01
Polynesian:	1	0.01
Native Hawaiian	1	0.01
Other Pac. Isl., not spec. (2)	4	0.03
Hispanic or Latino:	461	3.61
Central American:	10	0.08
Honduran	5	0.04
Panamanian	3	0.02
Other Central American	2	0.02
Cuban	2	0.02
Mexican	377	2.95
Puerto Rican	10	0.08
South American:	1	0.01
Chilean	1	0.01
Other Hispanic or Latino	61	0.48
Hungarian	2	0.02
Irish	2,089	16.42
Italian	720	5.66
Lithuanian	116	0.91
Northern European	13	0.10
Norwegian	75	0.59
Pennsylvania German	8	0.06
Polish	755	5.93
Romanian	2	0.02
Russian	12	0.09
Scandinavian	4	0.03
Scotch-Irish	117	0.92
Scottish	111	0.87
Serbian	8	0.06
Slovak	67	0.53
Swedish	185	1.45
Swiss	36	0.28
Ukrainian	11	0.09
United States or American	793	6.23
Welsh	46	0.36
White:	12,344	96.56
Not Hispanic (11,956)	12,046	94.23
Hispanic (268)	298	2.33

Bridgeview

Place Type: Village
County: Cook
Population: 15,335

Ancestry/Race	Number	%
African American/Black:	132	0.86
Not Hispanic (126)	132	0.86
African, sub-Saharan:	16	0.10
African	16	0.10
Alaska Native tribes, specified:	2	0.01
Alaska Athabascan (2)	2	0.01
Am. Ind. or Alaska Nat., not spec.	48	0.31
Albanian	70	0.46
American Indian tribes, specified:	29	0.19
Cherokee (3)	11	0.07
Chippewa (1)	1	0.01
Choctaw	1	0.01
Latin American Indians (1)	1	0.01
Navajo (8)	9	0.06
Pueblo (1)	1	0.01
Shoshone	1	0.01
Sioux (2)	2	0.01
All other tribes	2	0.01
American Indian tribes, not spec.	5	0.03
Arab:	1,104	7.18
Arab/Arabic	743	4.83
Egyptian	45	0.29
Jordanian	65	0.42
Palestinian	141	0.92
Syrian	91	0.59
Other Arab	19	0.12
Asian:	453	2.95
Bangladeshi (4)	9	0.06
Chinese, ex. Taiwanese (11)	17	0.11
Filipino (127)	136	0.89
Indian (116)	132	0.86
Indonesian	1	0.01
Japanese (4)	7	0.05
Korean (16)	16	0.10
Laotian (5)	5	0.03
Pakistani (39)	66	0.43
Thai (2)	5	0.03
Vietnamese (1)	2	0.01
Other Asian, not specified (7)	57	0.37
Austrian	48	0.31
Belgian	5	0.03
Brazilian	28	0.18
Canadian	19	0.12
Croatian	126	0.82
Czech	557	3.62
Czechoslovakian	54	0.35
Danish	26	0.17
Dutch	77	0.50
Eastern European	7	0.05
English	464	3.02
European	19	0.12
Finnish	7	0.05
French, except Basque	247	1.61
French Canadian	92	0.60
German	2,322	15.11
Greek	309	2.01
Hawaii Native/Pacific Islander:	13	0.08
Polynesian:	6	0.04
Native Hawaiian	6	0.04
Other Pac. Isl., not spec.	7	0.05
Hispanic or Latino:	1,445	9.42
Central American:	8	0.05
Costa Rican	2	0.01
Honduran	3	0.02
Nicaraguan	2	0.01

Notes: 1. Figures in the "Number" column do not add up to the total population due to: a) Ancestry/Race overlap — e.g. persons can report being both White and Irish, b) persons of Hispanic origin can report being any race, c) persons reporting two ancestries are counted in both categories. 2. Numbers in parentheses indicate the number of persons reporting this ancestry/race alone, not in combination with any other ancestry/race. 3. Refer to the Explanation of Data in the front of the book for more detailed information.

Ancestry/Race	Number	%
Other Central American	1	0.01
Cuban	7	0.05
Dominican Republic	3	0.02
Mexican	1,178	7.68
Puerto Rican	79	0.52
South American:	34	0.22
Bolivian	3	0.02
Colombian	14	0.09
Ecuadorian	10	0.07
Peruvian	7	0.05
Other Hispanic or Latino	136	0.89
Hungarian	96	0.62
Icelander	10	0.07
Irish	2,642	17.19
Italian	1,378	8.97
Lithuanian	386	2.51
Luxemburger	5	0.03
Macedonian	40	0.26
Northern European	16	0.10
Norwegian	44	0.29
Polish	3,942	25.65
Portuguese	17	0.11
Romanian	13	0.08
Russian	73	0.48
Scandinavian	18	0.12
Scotch-Irish	114	0.74
Scottish	96	0.62
Serbian	7	0.05
Slovak	88	0.57
Slovene	5	0.03
Swedish	308	2.00
Swiss	2	0.01
Ukrainian	68	0.44
United States or American	589	3.83
Welsh	17	0.11
White:	14,184	92.49
Not Hispanic (12,589)	13,291	86.67
Hispanic (817)	893	5.82
Yugoslavian	30	0.20

Brookfield

Place Type: Village
County: Cook
Population: 19,085

Ancestry/Race	Number	%
African American/Black:	202	1.06
Not Hispanic (165)	196	1.03
Hispanic (4)	6	0.03
African, sub-Saharan:	3	0.02
African	3	0.02
Alaska Native tribes, specified:	1	0.01
Tlingit-Haida (1)	1	0.01
Am. Ind. or Alaska Nat., not spec.	30	0.16
Albanian	50	0.26
American Indian tribes, specified:	47	0.25
Apache (2)	2	0.01
Blackfeet (1)	1	0.01
Cherokee (3)	13	0.07
Cheyenne (1)	1	0.01
Chippewa (2)	4	0.02
Cree	3	0.02
Iroquois	5	0.03
Latin American Indians (1)	2	0.01
Ottawa (2)	2	0.01
Paiute	1	0.01
Pueblo (1)	1	0.01
Sioux	1	0.01
All other tribes (5)	11	0.06
American Indian tribes, not spec.	5	0.03
Arab:	123	0.65
Arab/Arabic	37	0.19
Lebanese	39	0.21
Palestinian	14	0.07
Syrian	33	0.17
Asian:	314	1.65
Cambodian (3)	3	0.02
Chinese, ex. Taiwanese (28)	34	0.18
Filipino (68)	95	0.50
Indian (80)	89	0.47
Japanese (13)	25	0.13
Korean (12)	20	0.10
Laotian (1)	1	0.01
Malaysian	4	0.02
Pakistani (7)	7	0.04
Thai (6)	9	0.05
Vietnamese (9)	10	0.05
Other Asian, specified (1)	1	0.01
Other Asian, not specified (3)	16	0.08
Australian	17	0.09
Austrian	172	0.90
British	25	0.13
Canadian	26	0.14
Celtic	26	0.14
Croatian	197	1.04
Cypriot	18	0.09
Czech	1,802	9.48
Czechoslovakian	318	1.67
Danish	51	0.27
Dutch	349	1.84
English	1,007	5.30
Estonian	12	0.06
European	59	0.31
Finnish	8	0.04
French, except Basque	398	2.09
French Canadian	75	0.39
German	4,418	23.24
Greek	153	0.80
Hawaii Native/Pacific Islander:	12	0.06
Micronesian:	6	0.03
Guamanian/Chamorro	6	0.03
Polynesian: (2)	2	0.01
Native Hawaiian (2)	2	0.01
Other Pac. Isl., not spec.	4	0.02
Hispanic or Latino:	1,537	8.05
Central American:	46	0.24
Costa Rican	2	0.01
Guatemalan	18	0.09
Honduran	8	0.04
Panamanian	4	0.02
Salvadoran	11	0.06
Other Central American	3	0.02
Cuban	17	0.09
Dominican Republic	1	0.01
Mexican	1,169	6.13
Puerto Rican	87	0.46
South American:	66	0.35
Argentinean	8	0.04
Bolivian	8	0.04
Colombian	21	0.11
Ecuadorian	11	0.06
Paraguayan	6	0.03
Peruvian	2	0.01
Venezuelan	4	0.02
Other South American	6	0.03
Other Hispanic or Latino	151	0.79
Hungarian	101	0.53
Irish	3,823	20.11
Israeli	14	0.07
Italian	2,462	12.95
Latvian	19	0.10
Lithuanian	503	2.65
Luxemburger	7	0.04
Macedonian	48	0.25
Northern European	23	0.12
Norwegian	281	1.48
Polish	3,430	18.05
Portuguese	33	0.17
Romanian	26	0.14
Russian	267	1.40
Scandinavian	11	0.06
Scotch-Irish	398	2.09
Scottish	350	1.84
Serbian	7	0.04
Slavic	28	0.15
Slovak	186	0.98
Slovene	58	0.31
Swedish	408	2.15
Swiss	58	0.31
Ukrainian	100	0.53
United States or American	431	2.27
Welsh	35	0.18
White:	18,077	94.72
Not Hispanic (16,961)	17,111	89.66
Hispanic (889)	966	5.06
Yugoslavian	151	0.79

Buffalo Grove

Place Type: Village
County: Lake
Population: 42,909

Ancestry/Race	Number	%
African American/Black:	385	0.90
Not Hispanic (317)	370	0.86
Hispanic (8)	15	0.03
African, sub-Saharan:	84	0.20
African	10	0.02
South African	68	0.16
Other sub-Saharan African	6	0.01
Am. Ind. or Alaska Nat., not spec.	17	0.04
American Indian tribes, specified:	34	0.08
Blackfeet (1)	3	0.01
Cherokee	5	0.01
Chippewa (1)	2	0.00
Choctaw	1	0.00
Iroquois (8)	8	0.02
Latin American Indians (1)	3	0.01
Osage	1	0.00
Potawatomi	3	0.01
Sioux (1)	1	0.00
All other tribes (3)	7	0.02
American Indian tribes, not spec.	4	0.01
Arab:	168	0.39
Arab/Arabic	19	0.04
Egyptian	39	0.09
Jordanian	8	0.02
Lebanese	16	0.04
Moroccan	25	0.06
Syrian	54	0.13
Other Arab	7	0.02
Armenian	26	0.06
Asian:	3,927	9.15
Bangladeshi	1	0.00
Chinese, ex. Taiwanese (725)	791	1.84
Filipino (341)	379	0.88
Indian (749)	793	1.85
Indonesian (10)	10	0.02
Japanese (526)	600	1.40
Korean (1,072)	1,135	2.65
Malaysian	1	0.00
Pakistani (33)	45	0.10
Sri Lankan (2)	2	0.00
Taiwanese (33)	41	0.10
Thai (27)	32	0.07
Vietnamese (40)	50	0.12
Other Asian, specified (4)	5	0.01
Other Asian, not specified (16)	42	0.10
Assyrian/Chaldean/Syriac	73	0.17
Austrian	335	0.79
Belgian	95	0.22
Brazilian	13	0.03
British	111	0.26
Bulgarian	32	0.08
Canadian	137	0.32
Croatian	34	0.08
Czech	371	0.87
Czechoslovakian	117	0.27
Danish	209	0.49
Dutch	463	1.09
Eastern European	521	1.22
English	2,250	5.28
European	541	1.27
Finnish	69	0.16
French, except Basque	592	1.39
French Canadian	307	0.72
German	6,876	16.14
German Russian	19	0.04

Notes: 1. Figures in the "Number" column do not add up to the total population due to: a) Ancestry/Race overlap — e.g. persons can report being both White and Irish, b) persons of Hispanic origin can report being any race, c) persons reporting two ancestries are counted in both categories. 2. Numbers in parentheses indicate the number of persons reporting this ancestry/race alone, not in combination with any other ancestry/race. 3. Refer to the Explanation of Data in the front of the book for more detailed information.

Greek	316	0.74
Hawaii Native/Pacific Islander:	22	0.05
Polynesian: (3)	9	0.02
Native Hawaiian (3)	9	0.02
Other Pac. Isl., not spec. (3)	13	0.03
Hispanic or Latino:	1,425	3.32
Central American:	42	0.10
Costa Rican	2	0.00
Guatemalan	17	0.04
Honduran	5	0.01
Nicaraguan	2	0.00
Panamanian	3	0.01
Salvadoran	6	0.01
Other Central American	7	0.02
Cuban	45	0.10
Dominican Republic	5	0.01
Mexican	889	2.07
Puerto Rican	89	0.21
South American:	184	0.43
Argentinean	23	0.05
Bolivian	4	0.01
Chilean	8	0.02
Colombian	87	0.20
Ecuadorian	29	0.07
Paraguayan	2	0.00
Peruvian	20	0.05
Venezuelan	6	0.01
Other South American	5	0.01
Other Hispanic or Latino	171	0.40
Hungarian	547	1.28
Iranian	116	0.27
Irish	4,127	9.69
Israeli	234	0.55
Italian	2,396	5.63
Latvian	97	0.23
Lithuanian	367	0.86
Luxemburger	45	0.11
Northern European	17	0.04
Norwegian	753	1.77
Polish	5,428	12.74
Portuguese	19	0.04
Romanian	302	0.71
Russian	6,542	15.36
Scandinavian	7	0.02
Scotch-Irish	289	0.68
Scottish	525	1.23
Serbian	69	0.16
Slavic	29	0.07
Slovak	109	0.26
Slovene	12	0.03
Swedish	859	2.02
Swiss	50	0.12
Turkish	62	0.15
Ukrainian	1,017	2.39
United States or American	2,459	5.77
Welsh	119	0.28
West Indian, excl. Hispanic:	73	0.17
Belizean	9	0.02
Haitian	30	0.07
Jamaican	15	0.04
West Indian	19	0.04
White:	38,478	89.67
Not Hispanic (37,121)	37,429	87.23
Hispanic (938)	1,049	2.44
Yugoslavian	8	0.02

Burbank

Place Type: City
County: Cook
Population: 27,902

Ancestry/Race	Number	%
African American/Black:	106	0.38
Not Hispanic (67)	92	0.33
Hispanic (6)	14	0.05
African, sub-Saharan:	14	0.05
African	14	0.05
Am. Ind. or Alaska Nat., not spec.	50	0.18
Albanian	33	0.12
American Indian tribes, specified:	98	0.35
Apache (2)	13	0.05
Blackfeet (6)	12	0.04
Cherokee (3)	33	0.12
Chippewa (3)	7	0.03
Choctaw	12	0.04
Iroquois	1	0.00
Latin American Indians (1)	5	0.02
Lumbee (1)	1	0.00
Menominee (1)	3	0.01
Navajo	4	0.01
Paiute	2	0.01
Sioux (2)	2	0.01
Yaqui (1)	1	0.00
All other tribes	2	0.01
American Indian tribes, not spec.	8	0.03
Arab:	1,273	4.58
Arab/Arabic	788	2.83
Egyptian	30	0.11
Jordanian	96	0.35
Lebanese	41	0.15
Palestinian	311	1.12
Syrian	7	0.03
Armenian	7	0.03
Asian:	595	2.13
Cambodian	1	0.00
Chinese, ex. Taiwanese (18)	23	0.08
Filipino (212)	243	0.87
Indian (94)	99	0.35
Japanese (9)	13	0.05
Korean (26)	27	0.10
Laotian	2	0.01
Pakistani (27)	29	0.10
Sri Lankan (2)	2	0.01
Thai (27)	30	0.11
Vietnamese (65)	66	0.24
Other Asian, not specified (6)	60	0.22
Austrian	136	0.49
Basque	8	0.03
Belgian	9	0.03
Bulgarian	19	0.07
Canadian	8	0.03
Croatian	228	0.82
Czech	712	2.56
Czechoslovakian	93	0.33
Danish	51	0.18
Dutch	276	0.99
English	1,050	3.77
European	21	0.08
Finnish	49	0.18
French, except Basque	510	1.83
French Canadian	64	0.23
German	4,484	16.12
Greek	336	1.21
Hawaii Native/Pacific Islander:	14	0.05
Micronesian: (2)	7	0.03
Guamanian/Chamorro (2)	7	0.03
Polynesian: (4)	4	0.01
Native Hawaiian (3)	3	0.01
Samoan (1)	1	0.00
Other Pac. Isl., not spec.	3	0.01
Hispanic or Latino:	3,095	11.09
Central American:	44	0.16
Guatemalan	17	0.06
Honduran	2	0.01
Panamanian	8	0.03
Salvadoran	11	0.04
Other Central American	6	0.02
Cuban	10	0.04
Dominican Republic	1	0.00
Mexican	2,465	8.83
Puerto Rican	254	0.91
South American:	76	0.27
Argentinean	3	0.01
Bolivian	4	0.01
Chilean	1	0.00
Colombian	33	0.12
Ecuadorian	22	0.08
Paraguayan	3	0.01
Peruvian	9	0.03
Venezuelan	1	0.00
Other Hispanic or Latino	245	0.88
Hungarian	109	0.39
Iranian	18	0.06
Irish	5,207	18.71
Israeli	32	0.12
Italian	2,582	9.28
Latvian	6	0.02
Lithuanian	960	3.45
Luxemburger	15	0.05
Norwegian	136	0.49
Polish	8,427	30.29
Portuguese	6	0.02
Russian	117	0.42
Scandinavian	13	0.05
Scotch-Irish	213	0.77
Scottish	151	0.54
Slovak	418	1.50
Slovene	73	0.26
Swedish	314	1.13
Swiss	24	0.09
Ukrainian	67	0.24
United States or American	618	2.22
Welsh	78	0.28
West Indian, excl. Hispanic:	6	0.02
Trinidadian and Tobagonian	6	0.02
White:	26,162	93.76
Not Hispanic (23,515)	24,185	86.68
Hispanic (1,784)	1,977	7.09
Yugoslavian	6	0.02

Burr Ridge

Place Type: Village
County: Du Page
Population: 10,408

Ancestry/Race	Number	%
African American/Black:	120	1.15
Not Hispanic (102)	119	1.14
Hispanic	1	0.01
Am. Ind. or Alaska Nat., not spec.	1	0.01
American Indian tribes, specified:	9	0.09
Apache	1	0.01
Cherokee	4	0.04
Comanche	1	0.01
Latin American Indians (1)	1	0.01
Sioux	1	0.01
All other tribes	1	0.01
American Indian tribes, not spec.	4	0.04
Arab:	167	1.62
Arab/Arabic	35	0.34
Egyptian	64	0.62
Lebanese	11	0.11
Syrian	57	0.55
Armenian	27	0.26
Asian:	1,251	12.02
Chinese, ex. Taiwanese (159)	185	1.78
Filipino (174)	187	1.80
Indian (637)	664	6.38
Japanese (6)	12	0.12
Korean (36)	36	0.35
Malaysian (1)	1	0.01
Pakistani (77)	97	0.93
Taiwanese (17)	17	0.16
Thai (12)	13	0.12
Vietnamese (6)	8	0.08
Other Asian, specified (3)	3	0.03
Other Asian, not specified (3)	28	0.27
Austrian	28	0.27
Belgian	6	0.06
British	13	0.13
Bulgarian	28	0.27
Canadian	7	0.07
Croatian	108	1.05
Czech	493	4.77
Czechoslovakian	170	1.65
Danish	58	0.56
Dutch	328	3.18
Eastern European	11	0.11

Notes: 1. Figures in the "Number" column do not add up to the total population due to: a) Ancestry/Race overlap — e.g. persons can report being both White and Irish, b) persons of Hispanic origin can report being any race, c) persons reporting two ancestries are counted in both categories. 2. Numbers in parentheses indicate the number of persons reporting this ancestry/race alone, not in combination with any other ancestry/race. 3. Refer to the Explanation of Data in the front of the book for more detailed information.

Ancestry/Race	Number	%
English	965	9.34
Estonian	23	0.22
European	29	0.28
Finnish	30	0.29
French, except Basque	212	2.05
French Canadian	19	0.18
German	2,188	21.19
German Russian	7	0.07
Greek	214	2.07
Hawaii Native/Pacific Islander:	3	0.03
Other Pac. Isl., not spec. (3)	3	0.03
Hispanic or Latino:	304	2.92
Central American:	5	0.05
Honduran	3	0.03
Panamanian	1	0.01
Other Central American	1	0.01
Cuban	42	0.40
Mexican	181	1.74
Puerto Rican	21	0.20
South American:	19	0.18
Argentinean	1	0.01
Bolivian	4	0.04
Chilean	3	0.03
Colombian	2	0.02
Ecuadorian	2	0.02
Peruvian	4	0.04
Venezuelan	1	0.01
Other South American	2	0.02
Other Hispanic or Latino	36	0.35
Hungarian	141	1.37
Iranian	42	0.41
Irish	1,794	17.37
Italian	1,257	12.17
Latvian	12	0.12
Lithuanian	143	1.38
Northern European	31	0.30
Norwegian	172	1.67
Pennsylvania German	20	0.19
Polish	1,008	9.76
Romanian	38	0.37
Russian	61	0.59
Scandinavian	59	0.57
Scotch-Irish	58	0.56
Scottish	117	1.13
Serbian	96	0.93
Slovak	100	0.97
Slovene	36	0.35
Swedish	192	1.86
Swiss	27	0.26
Ukrainian	18	0.17
United States or American	333	3.22
Welsh	31	0.30
West Indian, excl. Hispanic:	19	0.18
Haitian	19	0.18
White:	9,067	87.12
Not Hispanic (8,698)	8,839	84.93
Hispanic (221)	228	2.19
Yugoslavian	52	0.50

Cahokia

Place Type: Village
County: Saint Clair
Population: 16,391

Ancestry/Race	Number	%
African American/Black:	6,491	39.60
Not Hispanic (6,299)	6,445	39.32
Hispanic (43)	46	0.28
African, sub-Saharan:	511	3.10
African	511	3.10
Am. Ind. or Alaska Nat., not spec.	58	0.35
Albanian	9	0.05
American Indian tribes, specified:	69	0.42
Apache	6	0.04
Blackfeet (2)	3	0.02
Cherokee (18)	48	0.29
Choctaw	1	0.01
Latin American Indians (1)	2	0.01
Menominee (3)	3	0.02
Navajo (1)	1	0.01
Sioux	3	0.02
All other tribes	2	0.01
American Indian tribes, not spec.	8	0.05
Asian:	103	0.63
Chinese, ex. Taiwanese (25)	28	0.17
Filipino (12)	20	0.12
Indian (3)	8	0.05
Indonesian	3	0.02
Japanese (4)	8	0.05
Korean (11)	17	0.10
Pakistani	3	0.02
Thai (5)	7	0.04
Vietnamese (1)	2	0.01
Other Asian, not specified (2)	7	0.04
Austrian	51	0.31
Belgian	10	0.06
Celtic	59	0.36
Croatian	3	0.02
Czech	50	0.30
Czechoslovakian	2	0.01
Dutch	219	1.33
English	851	5.17
European	37	0.22
French, except Basque	525	3.19
French Canadian	23	0.14
German	2,309	14.01
Greek	72	0.44
Hawaii Native/Pacific Islander:	7	0.04
Micronesian: (2)	2	0.01
Guamanian/Chamorro (2)	2	0.01
Polynesian: (3)	4	0.02
Native Hawaiian (1)	2	0.01
Samoan (2)	2	0.01
Other Pac. Isl., not spec.	1	0.01
Hispanic or Latino:	369	2.25
Central American:	8	0.05
Guatemalan	2	0.01
Panamanian	1	0.01
Salvadoran	4	0.02
Other Central American	1	0.01
Mexican	261	1.59
Puerto Rican	21	0.13
South American:	2	0.01
Colombian	1	0.01
Venezuelan	1	0.01
Other Hispanic or Latino	77	0.47
Hungarian	59	0.36
Irish	1,483	9.00
Italian	329	2.00
Lithuanian	32	0.19
Norwegian	63	0.38
Polish	286	1.74
Romanian	7	0.04
Russian	18	0.11
Scotch-Irish	84	0.51
Scottish	211	1.28
Serbian	5	0.03
Swedish	83	0.50
Swiss	20	0.12
Ukrainian	6	0.04
United States or American	1,280	7.77
Welsh	33	0.20
West Indian, excl. Hispanic:	32	0.19
Jamaican	32	0.19
White:	9,765	59.58
Not Hispanic (9,363)	9,557	58.31
Hispanic (189)	208	1.27
Yugoslavian	2	0.01

Calumet City

Place Type: City
County: Cook
Population: 39,071

Ancestry/Race	Number	%
African American/Black:	21,043	53.86
Not Hispanic (20,530)	20,855	53.38
Hispanic (143)	188	0.48
African, sub-Saharan:	659	1.69
African	470	1.21
Liberian	6	0.02
Nigerian	179	0.46
South African	4	0.01
Alaska Native tribes, specified:	1	0.00
Tlingit-Haida	1	0.00
Am. Ind. or Alaska Nat., not spec.	132	0.34
American Indian tribes, specified:	105	0.27
Blackfeet (3)	24	0.06
Cherokee (2)	29	0.07
Chippewa (6)	13	0.03
Choctaw	10	0.03
Comanche (1)	2	0.01
Latin American Indians (7)	7	0.02
Menominee (1)	1	0.00
Navajo	5	0.01
Potawatomi (1)	1	0.00
Seminole	1	0.00
Sioux	8	0.02
All other tribes (2)	4	0.01
American Indian tribes, not spec.	29	0.07
Arab:	165	0.42
Arab/Arabic	47	0.12
Jordanian	73	0.19
Lebanese	40	0.10
Palestinian	5	0.01
Asian:	298	0.76
Chinese, ex. Taiwanese (34)	43	0.11
Filipino (57)	73	0.19
Hmong (2)	3	0.01
Indian (27)	54	0.14
Japanese (4)	17	0.04
Korean (21)	25	0.06
Laotian (8)	8	0.02
Pakistani (5)	9	0.02
Sri Lankan	5	0.01
Thai (5)	5	0.01
Vietnamese (33)	34	0.09
Other Asian, not specified (2)	22	0.06
Assyrian/Chaldean/Syriac	44	0.11
Austrian	69	0.18
Belgian	63	0.16
Brazilian	9	0.02
British	9	0.02
Canadian	10	0.03
Croatian	280	0.72
Czech	89	0.23
Czechoslovakian	6	0.02
Danish	64	0.16
Dutch	189	0.48
English	607	1.56
European	7	0.02
French, except Basque	239	0.61
French Canadian	54	0.14
German	2,543	6.52
Greek	317	0.81
Guyanese	11	0.03
Hawaii Native/Pacific Islander:	32	0.08
Micronesian: (5)	5	0.01
Guamanian/Chamorro (5)	5	0.01
Polynesian: (4)	9	0.02
Native Hawaiian (4)	7	0.02
Samoan	2	0.01
Other Pac. Isl., not spec. (12)	18	0.05
Hispanic or Latino:	4,242	10.86
Central American:	54	0.14
Costa Rican	5	0.01
Guatemalan	30	0.08
Honduran	1	0.00
Nicaraguan	1	0.00
Panamanian	5	0.01
Salvadoran	6	0.02
Other Central American	6	0.02
Cuban	10	0.03
Dominican Republic	2	0.01
Mexican	3,667	9.39
Puerto Rican	253	0.65
South American:	13	0.03
Colombian	5	0.01

Notes: 1. Figures in the "Number" column do not add up to the total population due to: a) Ancestry/Race overlap — e.g. persons can report being both White and Irish, b) persons of Hispanic origin can report being any race, c) persons reporting two ancestries are counted in both categories. 2. Numbers in parentheses indicate the number of persons reporting this ancestry/race alone, not in combination with any other ancestry/race. 3. Refer to the Explanation of Data in the front of the book for more detailed information.

Ecuadorian	1	0.00
Peruvian	7	0.02
Other Hispanic or Latino	243	0.62
Hungarian	227	0.58
Irish	1,992	5.11
Israeli	61	0.16
Italian	1,494	3.83
Lithuanian	207	0.53
Luxemburger	19	0.05
Norwegian	149	0.38
Pennsylvania German	6	0.02
Polish	4,964	12.73
Portuguese	8	0.02
Romanian	60	0.15
Russian	80	0.21
Scotch-Irish	108	0.28
Scottish	128	0.33
Serbian	118	0.30
Slovak	214	0.55
Slovene	13	0.03
Swedish	349	0.90
Swiss	45	0.12
Ukrainian	108	0.28
United States or American	529	1.36
Welsh	28	0.07
West Indian, excl. Hispanic:	313	0.80
Bahamian	11	0.03
Belizean	24	0.06
Dutch West Indian	11	0.03
Haitian	133	0.34
Jamaican	117	0.30
West Indian	17	0.04
White:	15,753	40.32
Not Hispanic (13,421)	13,829	35.39
Hispanic (1,716)	1,924	4.92
Yugoslavian	47	0.12

Canton

Place Type: City
County: Fulton
Population: 15,288

Ancestry/Race	Number	%
African American/Black:	1,386	9.07
Not Hispanic (1,344)	1,377	9.01
Hispanic (9)	9	0.06
African, sub-Saharan:	8	0.05
Nigerian	8	0.05
Am. Ind. or Alaska Nat., not spec.	23	0.15
American Indian tribes, specified:	29	0.19
Apache	1	0.01
Blackfeet (3)	4	0.03
Cherokee (3)	15	0.10
Chippewa (2)	3	0.02
Choctaw (2)	2	0.01
Navajo	1	0.01
Pueblo	1	0.01
Sioux (2)	2	0.01
American Indian tribes, not spec.	1	0.01
Asian:	80	0.52
Chinese, ex. Taiwanese (17)	20	0.13
Filipino (3)	5	0.03
Indian (8)	13	0.09
Japanese (4)	6	0.04
Korean (7)	7	0.05
Pakistani (4)	6	0.04
Vietnamese (11)	14	0.09
Other Asian, specified (3)	3	0.02
Other Asian, not specified (3)	6	0.04
Austrian	14	0.09
Belgian	23	0.15
British	63	0.41
Canadian	7	0.05
Croatian	264	1.73
Czech	29	0.19
Czechoslovakian	19	0.12
Danish	36	0.24
Dutch	454	2.98
English	1,603	10.52
Estonian	16	0.10
European	64	0.42
Finnish	28	0.18
French, except Basque	288	1.89
French Canadian	24	0.16
German	2,647	17.37
Greek	32	0.21
Hawaii Native/Pacific Islander:	6	0.04
Micronesian: (1)	1	0.01
Guamanian/Chamorro (1)	1	0.01
Other Pac. Isl., not spec. (2)	5	0.03
Hispanic or Latino:	320	2.09
Central American:	3	0.02
Panamanian	3	0.02
Cuban	4	0.03
Mexican	43	0.28
Puerto Rican	11	0.07
South American:	1	0.01
Colombian	1	0.01
Other Hispanic or Latino	258	1.69
Hungarian	11	0.07
Irish	1,178	7.73
Italian	312	2.05
Lithuanian	40	0.26
Northern European	13	0.09
Norwegian	55	0.36
Pennsylvania German	12	0.08
Polish	170	1.12
Russian	21	0.14
Scandinavian	7	0.05
Scotch-Irish	169	1.11
Scottish	280	1.84
Slovak	7	0.05
Swedish	250	1.64
Swiss	19	0.12
Ukrainian	7	0.05
United States or American	1,732	11.36
Welsh	106	0.70
White:	13,776	90.11
Not Hispanic (13,456)	13,531	88.51
Hispanic (240)	245	1.60
Yugoslavian	31	0.20

Carbondale

Place Type: City
County: Jackson
Population: 20,681

Ancestry/Race	Number	%
Acadian/Cajun	31	0.15
African American/Black:	5,006	24.21
Not Hispanic (4,750)	4,949	23.93
Hispanic (35)	57	0.28
African, sub-Saharan:	389	1.88
African	211	1.02
Ethiopian	11	0.05
Kenyan	5	0.02
Nigerian	132	0.64
Other sub-Saharan African	30	0.14
Alaska Native tribes, specified:	1	0.00
Eskimo (1)	1	0.00
Am. Ind. or Alaska Nat., not spec.	47	0.23
American Indian tribes, specified:	112	0.54
Apache	1	0.00
Blackfeet	8	0.04
Cherokee (12)	70	0.34
Chickasaw (1)	1	0.00
Chippewa (2)	5	0.02
Choctaw (5)	6	0.03
Comanche (1)	1	0.00
Latin American Indians (2)	9	0.04
Sioux (3)	4	0.02
All other tribes	7	0.03
American Indian tribes, not spec.	13	0.06
Arab:	267	1.29
Arab/Arabic	75	0.36
Egyptian	18	0.09
Jordanian	56	0.27
Lebanese	28	0.14
Palestinian	25	0.12
Other Arab	65	0.31
Armenian	8	0.04
Asian:	1,525	7.37
Bangladeshi (15)	18	0.09
Cambodian	1	0.00
Chinese, ex. Taiwanese (355)	376	1.82
Filipino (23)	41	0.20
Hmong (2)	2	0.01
Indian (312)	333	1.61
Indonesian (19)	21	0.10
Japanese (217)	229	1.11
Korean (233)	248	1.20
Laotian (2)	3	0.01
Malaysian (52)	55	0.27
Pakistani (20)	24	0.12
Sri Lankan (2)	2	0.01
Taiwanese (39)	43	0.21
Thai (36)	41	0.20
Vietnamese (27)	29	0.14
Other Asian, specified (3)	5	0.02
Other Asian, not specified (18)	54	0.26
Austrian	66	0.32
Belgian	17	0.08
Brazilian	10	0.05
British	110	0.53
Bulgarian	51	0.25
Canadian	48	0.23
Croatian	44	0.21
Cypriot	25	0.12
Czech	68	0.33
Czechoslovakian	61	0.29
Danish	122	0.59
Dutch	240	1.16
English	1,875	9.06
European	296	1.43
Finnish	61	0.29
French, except Basque	384	1.86
French Canadian	88	0.43
German	3,818	18.44
Greek	63	0.30
Hawaii Native/Pacific Islander:	22	0.11
Micronesian: (2)	2	0.01
Guamanian/Chamorro (2)	2	0.01
Polynesian: (10)	10	0.05
Native Hawaiian (3)	3	0.01
Samoan (7)	7	0.03
Other Pac. Isl., specified	1	0.00
Other Pac. Isl., not spec. (4)	9	0.04
Hispanic or Latino:	630	3.05
Central American:	48	0.23
Costa Rican	2	0.01
Guatemalan	16	0.08
Honduran	11	0.05
Nicaraguan	5	0.02
Panamanian	2	0.01
Salvadoran	5	0.02
Other Central American	7	0.03
Cuban	20	0.10
Dominican Republic	5	0.02
Mexican	267	1.29
Puerto Rican	90	0.44
South American:	68	0.33
Argentinean	4	0.02
Bolivian	4	0.02
Chilean	4	0.02
Colombian	24	0.12
Ecuadorian	5	0.02
Peruvian	14	0.07
Uruguayan	2	0.01
Venezuelan	8	0.04
Other South American	3	0.01
Other Hispanic or Latino	132	0.64
Hungarian	68	0.33
Iranian	27	0.13
Irish	2,358	11.39
Italian	840	4.06
Lithuanian	18	0.09
Luxemburger	9	0.04
Northern European	60	0.29

Notes: 1. Figures in the "Number" column do not add up to the total population due to: a) Ancestry/Race overlap — e.g. persons can report being both White and Irish, b) persons of Hispanic origin can report being any race, c) persons reporting two ancestries are counted in both categories. 2. Numbers in parentheses indicate the number of persons reporting this ancestry/race alone, not in combination with any other ancestry/race. 3. Refer to the Explanation of Data in the front of the book for more detailed information.

Norwegian	219	1.06
Pennsylvania German	8	0.04
Polish	737	3.56
Portuguese	62	0.30
Romanian	11	0.05
Russian	130	0.63
Scandinavian	27	0.13
Scotch-Irish	331	1.60
Scottish	428	2.07
Serbian	10	0.05
Slavic	8	0.04
Slovak	74	0.36
Slovene	10	0.05
Swedish	341	1.65
Swiss	62	0.30
Turkish	20	0.10
Ukrainian	15	0.07
United States or American	958	4.63
Welsh	158	0.76
West Indian, excl. Hispanic:	41	0.20
Bahamian	8	0.04
Haitian	6	0.03
Jamaican	27	0.13
White:	14,077	68.07
Not Hispanic (13,384)	13,748	66.48
Hispanic (281)	329	1.59
Yugoslavian	9	0.04

Carol Stream

Place Type: Village
County: Du Page
Population: 40,438

Ancestry/Race	Number	%
African American/Black:	1,901	4.70
Not Hispanic (1,689)	1,844	4.56
Hispanic (27)	57	0.14
African, sub-Saharan:	159	0.40
African	124	0.31
Ethiopian	11	0.03
Nigerian	8	0.02
South African	16	0.04
Am. Ind. or Alaska Nat., not spec.	71	0.18
Albanian	148	0.37
American Indian tribes, specified:	118	0.29
Apache	2	0.00
Blackfeet	6	0.01
Cherokee (6)	48	0.12
Chippewa (4)	5	0.01
Choctaw (1)	3	0.01
Cree	1	0.00
Iroquois (3)	3	0.01
Latin American Indians (20)	31	0.08
Lumbee	1	0.00
Navajo (1)	1	0.00
Osage	1	0.00
Potawatomi (2)	2	0.00
Pueblo	1	0.00
Seminole	1	0.00
Sioux (1)	8	0.02
Yakama (1)	2	0.00
All other tribes	2	0.00
American Indian tribes, not spec.	9	0.02
Arab:	128	0.32
Arab/Arabic	38	0.10
Iraqi	13	0.03
Lebanese	18	0.05
Moroccan	26	0.07
Syrian	25	0.06
Other Arab	8	0.02
Armenian	5	0.01
Asian:	4,863	12.03
Cambodian (76)	93	0.23
Chinese, ex. Taiwanese (227)	251	0.62
Filipino (1,035)	1,127	2.79
Hmong (3)	4	0.01
Indian (1,995)	2,063	5.10
Indonesian	4	0.01
Japanese (44)	78	0.19
Korean (198)	214	0.53
Laotian (24)	25	0.06
Pakistani (214)	245	0.61
Taiwanese (15)	15	0.04
Thai (24)	32	0.08
Vietnamese (586)	605	1.50
Other Asian, specified (6)	6	0.01
Other Asian, not specified (44)	101	0.25
Austrian	175	0.44
Belgian	109	0.27
British	75	0.19
Canadian	79	0.20
Croatian	142	0.36
Czech	935	2.35
Czechoslovakian	146	0.37
Danish	260	0.65
Dutch	551	1.38
English	2,255	5.67
European	165	0.41
Finnish	139	0.35
French, except Basque	995	2.50
French Canadian	184	0.46
German	9,677	24.32
Greek	502	1.26
Hawaii Native/Pacific Islander:	35	0.09
Polynesian: (1)	9	0.02
Native Hawaiian (1)	9	0.02
Other Pac. Isl., not spec. (3)	26	0.06
Hispanic or Latino:	4,055	10.03
Central American:	138	0.34
Costa Rican	8	0.02
Guatemalan	62	0.15
Honduran	11	0.03
Nicaraguan	6	0.01
Panamanian	6	0.01
Salvadoran	37	0.09
Other Central American	8	0.02
Cuban	99	0.24
Dominican Republic	2	0.00
Mexican	2,892	7.15
Puerto Rican	330	0.82
South American:	183	0.45
Argentinean	3	0.01
Bolivian	1	0.00
Chilean	10	0.02
Colombian	93	0.23
Ecuadorian	25	0.06
Paraguayan	1	0.00
Peruvian	37	0.09
Venezuelan	12	0.03
Other South American	1	0.00
Other Hispanic or Latino	411	1.02
Hungarian	213	0.54
Iranian	14	0.04
Irish	5,705	14.34
Italian	5,633	14.16
Latvian	26	0.07
Lithuanian	542	1.36
Luxemburger	9	0.02
Northern European	19	0.05
Norwegian	1,059	2.66
Pennsylvania German	22	0.06
Polish	5,034	12.65
Portuguese	38	0.10
Romanian	63	0.16
Russian	507	1.27
Scandinavian	82	0.21
Scotch-Irish	275	0.69
Scottish	646	1.62
Serbian	180	0.45
Slavic	13	0.03
Slovak	77	0.19
Slovene	31	0.08
Swedish	1,228	3.09
Swiss	174	0.44
Ukrainian	285	0.72
United States or American	939	2.36
Welsh	271	0.68
West Indian, excl. Hispanic:	60	0.15
Jamaican	60	0.15
White:	32,412	80.15
Not Hispanic (29,524)	29,967	74.11
Hispanic (2,225)	2,445	6.05
Yugoslavian	233	0.59

Carpentersville

Place Type: Village
County: Kane
Population: 30,586

Ancestry/Race	Number	%
African American/Black:	1,437	4.70
Not Hispanic (1,234)	1,343	4.39
Hispanic (45)	94	0.31
African, sub-Saharan:	86	0.28
African	86	0.28
Alaska Native tribes, specified:	1	0.00
Eskimo	1	0.00
Am. Ind. or Alaska Nat., not spec.	115	0.38
Albanian	30	0.10
American Indian tribes, specified:	186	0.61
Apache (6)	11	0.04
Blackfeet	12	0.04
Cherokee (9)	48	0.16
Chippewa (10)	17	0.06
Choctaw (9)	11	0.04
Creek	3	0.01
Crow	1	0.00
Iroquois	2	0.01
Latin American Indians (37)	43	0.14
Navajo (7)	10	0.03
Ottawa	1	0.00
Pima (6)	6	0.02
Potawatomi (2)	2	0.01
Seminole (2)	2	0.01
Sioux (6)	9	0.03
Tohono O'Odham (1)	1	0.00
All other tribes (3)	7	0.02
American Indian tribes, not spec.	19	0.06
Arab:	38	0.13
Arab/Arabic	9	0.03
Jordanian	13	0.04
Lebanese	16	0.05
Asian:	732	2.39
Cambodian (2)	2	0.01
Chinese, ex. Taiwanese (74)	94	0.31
Filipino (166)	210	0.69
Hmong (15)	15	0.05
Indian (128)	140	0.46
Indonesian	5	0.02
Japanese (27)	42	0.14
Korean (48)	55	0.18
Laotian (59)	65	0.21
Pakistani (37)	38	0.12
Taiwanese (1)	1	0.00
Thai (7)	12	0.04
Vietnamese (30)	32	0.10
Other Asian, specified (1)	5	0.02
Other Asian, not specified (5)	16	0.05
Assyrian/Chaldean/Syriac	70	0.23
Austrian	148	0.49
Belgian	15	0.05
British	65	0.21
Canadian	55	0.18
Croatian	25	0.08
Czech	261	0.86
Czechoslovakian	31	0.10
Danish	149	0.49
Dutch	222	0.73
English	1,363	4.50
European	43	0.14
Finnish	41	0.14
French, except Basque	634	2.09
French Canadian	189	0.62
German	5,416	17.88
Greek	133	0.44
Hawaii Native/Pacific Islander:	48	0.16
Micronesian: (6)	6	0.02
Guamanian/Chamorro (6)	6	0.02

Notes: 1. Figures in the "Number" column do not add up to the total population due to: a) Ancestry/Race overlap — e.g. persons can report being both White and Irish, b) persons of Hispanic origin can report being any race, c) persons reporting two ancestries are counted in both categories. 2. Numbers in parentheses indicate the number of persons reporting this ancestry/race alone, not in combination with any other ancestry/race. 3. Refer to the Explanation of Data in the front of the book for more detailed information.

Polynesian: (6)	11	0.04
Native Hawaiian (5)	9	0.03
Samoan (1)	2	0.01
Other Pac. Isl., specified	1	0.00
Other Pac. Isl., not spec. (18)	30	0.10
Hispanic or Latino:	12,410	40.57
Central American:	282	0.92
Costa Rican	9	0.03
Guatemalan	79	0.26
Honduran	17	0.06
Nicaraguan	10	0.03
Panamanian	7	0.02
Salvadoran	157	0.51
Other Central American	3	0.01
Cuban	24	0.08
Dominican Republic	6	0.02
Mexican	10,755	35.16
Puerto Rican	349	1.14
South American:	67	0.22
Argentinean	2	0.01
Bolivian	6	0.02
Chilean	8	0.03
Colombian	24	0.08
Ecuadorian	7	0.02
Peruvian	13	0.04
Venezuelan	4	0.01
Other South American	3	0.01
Other Hispanic or Latino	927	3.03
Hungarian	97	0.32
Irish	2,900	9.58
Italian	1,575	5.20
Latvian	23	0.08
Lithuanian	69	0.23
Norwegian	565	1.87
Pennsylvania German	6	0.02
Polish	2,329	7.69
Portuguese	10	0.03
Romanian	11	0.04
Russian	159	0.52
Scandinavian	9	0.03
Scotch-Irish	192	0.63
Scottish	290	0.96
Serbian	25	0.08
Slavic	10	0.03
Slovak	96	0.32
Slovene	5	0.02
Swedish	573	1.89
Swiss	40	0.13
Turkish	15	0.05
Ukrainian	94	0.31
United States or American	827	2.73
Welsh	79	0.26
West Indian, excl. Hispanic:	15	0.05
Haitian	5	0.02
Jamaican	10	0.03
White:	22,009	71.96
Not Hispanic (15,862)	16,224	53.04
Hispanic (5,169)	5,785	18.91
Yugoslavian	9	0.03

Cary

Place Type: Village
County: McHenry
Population: 15,531

Ancestry/Race	Number	%
African American/Black:	78	0.50
Not Hispanic (60)	77	0.50
Hispanic (1)	1	0.01
Am. Ind. or Alaska Nat., not spec.	17	0.11
American Indian tribes, specified:	30	0.19
Apache	2	0.01
Cherokee (1)	14	0.09
Chippewa (4)	4	0.03
Choctaw	1	0.01
Menominee (4)	4	0.03
Paiute (1)	1	0.01
Potawatomi (1)	1	0.01
Yaqui (1)	1	0.01
All other tribes (2)	2	0.01
American Indian tribes, not spec.	1	0.01
Arab:	67	0.44
Arab/Arabic	29	0.19
Lebanese	38	0.25
Armenian	30	0.20
Asian:	250	1.61
Chinese, ex. Taiwanese (35)	47	0.30
Filipino (46)	53	0.34
Indian (39)	40	0.26
Japanese (10)	25	0.16
Korean (49)	51	0.33
Pakistani (14)	14	0.09
Thai (2)	5	0.03
Vietnamese (10)	10	0.06
Other Asian, not specified (3)	5	0.03
Assyrian/Chaldean/Syriac	28	0.18
Austrian	73	0.47
Brazilian	7	0.05
British	25	0.16
Bulgarian	1	0.01
Canadian	75	0.49
Croatian	57	0.37
Czech	362	2.35
Czechoslovakian	63	0.41
Danish	208	1.35
Dutch	231	1.50
English	1,578	10.26
European	33	0.21
Finnish	24	0.16
French, except Basque	619	4.02
French Canadian	194	1.26
German	5,207	33.85
Greek	194	1.26
Hawaii Native/Pacific Islander:	5	0.03
Polynesian: (2)	2	0.01
Native Hawaiian (2)	2	0.01
Other Pac. Isl., not spec. (2)	3	0.02
Hispanic or Latino:	843	5.43
Central American:	8	0.05
Costa Rican	4	0.03
Guatemalan	1	0.01
Honduran	2	0.01
Panamanian	1	0.01
Cuban	10	0.06
Mexican	729	4.69
Puerto Rican	24	0.15
South American:	16	0.10
Colombian	7	0.05
Ecuadorian	5	0.03
Peruvian	2	0.01
Venezuelan	2	0.01
Other Hispanic or Latino	56	0.36
Hungarian	96	0.62
Iranian	6	0.04
Irish	3,687	23.97
Israeli	21	0.14
Italian	1,884	12.25
Latvian	12	0.08
Lithuanian	75	0.49
Luxemburger	42	0.27
Northern European	17	0.11
Norwegian	407	2.65
Polish	2,110	13.72
Portuguese	10	0.07
Romanian	45	0.29
Russian	238	1.55
Scandinavian	100	0.65
Scotch-Irish	200	1.30
Scottish	395	2.57
Serbian	7	0.05
Slavic	13	0.08
Slovak	75	0.49
Swedish	701	4.56
Swiss	99	0.64
Ukrainian	107	0.70
United States or American	587	3.82
Welsh	107	0.70
White:	14,946	96.23
Not Hispanic (14,311)	14,393	92.67
Hispanic (526)	553	3.56
Yugoslavian	42	0.27

Centralia

Place Type: City
County: Marion
Population: 14,136

Ancestry/Race	Number	%
African American/Black:	1,593	11.27
Not Hispanic (1,456)	1,582	11.19
Hispanic (6)	11	0.08
African, sub-Saharan:	17	0.12
African	17	0.12
Am. Ind. or Alaska Nat., not spec.	61	0.43
American Indian tribes, specified:	62	0.44
Apache (2)	7	0.05
Blackfeet (1)	6	0.04
Cherokee (9)	33	0.23
Chippewa (1)	1	0.01
Choctaw (4)	5	0.04
Crow	1	0.01
Iroquois	1	0.01
Sioux	5	0.04
All other tribes (1)	3	0.02
American Indian tribes, not spec.	17	0.12
Arab:	5	0.04
Egyptian	5	0.04
Asian:	134	0.95
Chinese, ex. Taiwanese (7)	7	0.05
Filipino (24)	32	0.23
Indian (31)	36	0.25
Indonesian	4	0.03
Japanese (2)	2	0.01
Korean (6)	9	0.06
Pakistani (11)	17	0.12
Thai (4)	4	0.03
Vietnamese (3)	6	0.04
Other Asian, not specified (14)	17	0.12
Australian	19	0.13
Austrian	5	0.04
British	42	0.30
Croatian	11	0.08
Czech	38	0.27
Czechoslovakian	19	0.13
Danish	34	0.24
Dutch	430	3.04
English	1,405	9.93
European	23	0.16
Finnish	2	0.01
French, except Basque	350	2.47
French Canadian	50	0.35
German	3,312	23.40
Hawaii Native/Pacific Islander:	17	0.12
Micronesian: (1)	2	0.01
Guamanian/Chamorro (1)	2	0.01
Polynesian: (7)	7	0.05
Native Hawaiian (2)	2	0.01
Samoan (5)	5	0.04
Other Pac. Isl., not spec. (1)	8	0.06
Hispanic or Latino:	170	1.20
Central American:	3	0.02
Honduran	1	0.01
Nicaraguan	1	0.01
Salvadoran	1	0.01
Cuban	4	0.03
Mexican	114	0.81
Puerto Rican	6	0.04
South American:	5	0.04
Chilean	2	0.01
Peruvian	2	0.01
Other South American	1	0.01
Other Hispanic or Latino	38	0.27
Hungarian	7	0.05
Irish	1,413	9.98
Italian	342	2.42
Lithuanian	35	0.25
Northern European	12	0.08
Norwegian	17	0.12

Notes: 1. Figures in the "Number" column do not add up to the total population due to: a) Ancestry/Race overlap — e.g. persons can report being both White and Irish, b) persons of Hispanic origin can report being any race, c) persons reporting two ancestries are counted in both categories. 2. Numbers in parentheses indicate the number of persons reporting this ancestry/race alone, not in combination with any other ancestry/race. 3. Refer to the Explanation of Data in the front of the book for more detailed information.

Ancestry/Race	Number	%
Polish	241	1.70
Russian	28	0.20
Scotch-Irish	246	1.74
Scottish	168	1.19
Slovak	10	0.07
Swedish	15	0.11
Swiss	15	0.11
Turkish	10	0.07
United States or American	1,575	11.13
Welsh	65	0.46
White:	12,420	87.86
Not Hispanic (12,128)	12,300	87.01
Hispanic (99)	120	0.85
Yugoslavian	12	0.08

Champaign

Place Type: City
County: Champaign
Population: 67,518

Ancestry/Race	Number	%
Afghan	41	0.06
African American/Black:	11,158	16.53
Not Hispanic (10,471)	11,048	16.36
Hispanic (72)	110	0.16
African, sub-Saharan:	798	1.18
African	545	0.80
Ethiopian	20	0.03
Ghanian	21	0.03
Kenyan	8	0.01
Liberian	95	0.14
Nigerian	54	0.08
South African	20	0.03
Sudanese	6	0.01
Zairian	7	0.01
Zimbabwean	12	0.02
Other sub-Saharan African	10	0.01
Alaska Native tribes, specified:	3	0.00
Alaska Athabascan (1)	1	0.00
Aleut (2)	2	0.00
Am. Ind. or Alaska Nat., not spec.	164	0.24
Albanian	21	0.03
American Indian tribes, specified:	229	0.34
Apache (4)	7	0.01
Blackfeet (1)	13	0.02
Cherokee (29)	102	0.15
Chickasaw	3	0.00
Chippewa (6)	10	0.01
Choctaw (3)	11	0.02
Comanche (1)	1	0.00
Creek (4)	5	0.01
Iroquois	5	0.01
Latin American Indians (12)	28	0.04
Lumbee (1)	2	0.00
Navajo (1)	4	0.01
Osage (1)	2	0.00
Ottawa (1)	1	0.00
Paiute (1)	1	0.00
Potawatomi	1	0.00
Pueblo (1)	2	0.00
Sioux (2)	12	0.02
All other tribes (12)	19	0.03
American Indian tribes, not spec.	35	0.05
Arab:	331	0.49
Arab/Arabic	96	0.14
Egyptian	17	0.03
Iraqi	22	0.03
Jordanian	13	0.02
Lebanese	71	0.10
Palestinian	82	0.12
Other Arab	30	0.04
Armenian	22	0.03
Asian:	5,184	7.68
Bangladeshi (6)	6	0.01
Cambodian (16)	20	0.03
Chinese, ex. Taiwanese (1,131)	1,251	1.85
Filipino (373)	454	0.67
Hmong (11)	19	0.03
Indian (1,118)	1,201	1.78
Indonesian (17)	18	0.03
Japanese (231)	322	0.48
Korean (885)	959	1.42
Laotian (49)	66	0.10
Malaysian (26)	27	0.04
Pakistani (47)	64	0.09
Sri Lankan (3)	4	0.01
Taiwanese (67)	96	0.14
Thai (107)	124	0.18
Vietnamese (392)	416	0.62
Other Asian, specified (12)	18	0.03
Other Asian, not specified (43)	119	0.18
Assyrian/Chaldean/Syriac	15	0.02
Austrian	309	0.46
Belgian	128	0.19
Brazilian	23	0.03
British	474	0.70
Bulgarian	34	0.05
Canadian	168	0.25
Celtic	42	0.06
Croatian	145	0.21
Czech	458	0.67
Czechoslovakian	172	0.25
Danish	289	0.43
Dutch	1,077	1.59
Eastern European	59	0.09
English	7,102	10.46
European	936	1.38
Finnish	91	0.13
French, except Basque	1,648	2.43
French Canadian	297	0.44
German	16,445	24.23
German Russian	4	0.01
Greek	399	0.59
Guyanese	6	0.01
Hawaii Native/Pacific Islander:	86	0.13
Micronesian: (2)	10	0.01
Guamanian/Chamorro (2)	10	0.01
Polynesian: (14)	28	0.04
Native Hawaiian (5)	12	0.02
Samoan (8)	12	0.02
Other Polynesian (1)	4	0.01
Other Pac. Isl., not spec. (7)	48	0.07
Hispanic or Latino:	2,724	4.03
Central American:	172	0.25
Costa Rican	29	0.04
Guatemalan	85	0.13
Honduran	9	0.01
Nicaraguan	16	0.02
Panamanian	10	0.01
Salvadoran	1	0.01
Other Central American	17	0.03
Cuban	73	0.11
Dominican Republic	14	0.02
Mexican	1,645	2.44
Puerto Rican	255	0.38
South American:	269	0.40
Argentinean	29	0.04
Bolivian	11	0.02
Chilean	26	0.04
Colombian	69	0.10
Ecuadorian	54	0.08
Paraguayan	1	0.00
Peruvian	37	0.05
Uruguayan	2	0.00
Venezuelan	23	0.03
Other South American	17	0.03
Other Hispanic or Latino	296	0.44
Hungarian	254	0.37
Icelander	7	0.01
Iranian	54	0.08
Irish	9,070	13.36
Israeli	28	0.04
Italian	2,975	4.38
Latvian	17	0.03
Lithuanian	320	0.47
Luxemburger	6	0.01
New Zealander	21	0.03
Northern European	106	0.16
Norwegian	1,289	1.90
Pennsylvania German	24	0.04
Polish	3,109	4.58
Portuguese	113	0.17
Romanian	126	0.19
Russian	854	1.26
Scandinavian	156	0.23
Scotch-Irish	1,033	1.52
Scottish	1,368	2.02
Serbian	95	0.14
Slavic	53	0.08
Slovak	156	0.23
Slovene	43	0.06
Swedish	1,714	2.53
Swiss	370	0.55
Turkish	70	0.10
Ukrainian	150	0.22
United States or American	2,350	3.46
Welsh	370	0.55
West Indian, excl. Hispanic:	137	0.20
Bahamian	5	0.01
Belizean	14	0.02
Bermudan	5	0.01
British West Indian	7	0.01
Haitian	43	0.06
Jamaican	34	0.05
Trinidadian and Tobagonian	21	0.03
West Indian	8	0.01
White:	50,587	74.92
Not Hispanic (48,168)	49,197	72.87
Hispanic (1,230)	1,390	2.06
Yugoslavian	87	0.13

Charleston

Place Type: City
County: Coles
Population: 21,039

Ancestry/Race	Number	%
African American/Black:	951	4.52
Not Hispanic (889)	936	4.45
Hispanic (5)	15	0.07
African, sub-Saharan:	66	0.31
African	66	0.31
Am. Ind. or Alaska Nat., not spec.	49	0.23
Albanian	6	0.03
American Indian tribes, specified:	55	0.26
Apache (1)	1	0.00
Blackfeet (2)	4	0.02
Cherokee (7)	26	0.12
Chickasaw	1	0.00
Chippewa	4	0.02
Choctaw (2)	5	0.02
Creek	2	0.01
Iroquois	1	0.00
Latin American Indians (3)	3	0.01
Osage	2	0.01
Potawatomi (4)	4	0.02
Sioux (1)	1	0.00
All other tribes	1	0.00
American Indian tribes, not spec.	8	0.04
Arab:	63	0.30
Palestinian	52	0.25
Syrian	11	0.05
Asian:	352	1.67
Chinese, ex. Taiwanese (67)	74	0.35
Filipino (26)	35	0.17
Indian (55)	65	0.31
Indonesian (7)	7	0.03
Japanese (38)	52	0.25
Korean (32)	45	0.21
Laotian	2	0.01
Pakistani (7)	11	0.05
Sri Lankan (7)	7	0.03
Taiwanese (9)	13	0.06
Thai (5)	5	0.02
Vietnamese (10)	12	0.06
Other Asian, specified (6)	6	0.03
Other Asian, not specified (10)	18	0.09
Australian	6	0.03

Notes: 1. Figures in the "Number" column do not add up to the total population due to: a) Ancestry/Race overlap — e.g. persons can report being both White and Irish, b) persons of Hispanic origin can report being any race, c) persons reporting two ancestries are counted in both categories. 2. Numbers in parentheses indicate the number of persons reporting this ancestry/race alone, not in combination with any other ancestry/race. 3. Refer to the Explanation of Data in the front of the book for more detailed information.

Ancestry/Race	Number	%
Austrian	38	0.18
Belgian	60	0.29
British	86	0.41
Canadian	15	0.07
Celtic	20	0.10
Croatian	39	0.19
Czech	154	0.73
Czechoslovakian	39	0.19
Danish	117	0.56
Dutch	300	1.43
English	2,331	11.08
European	239	1.14
Finnish	32	0.15
French, except Basque	531	2.52
French Canadian	48	0.23
German	5,879	27.95
Greek	170	0.81
Hawaii Native/Pacific Islander:	25	0.12
Micronesian: (4)	5	0.02
Guamanian/Chamorro (2)	3	0.01
Other Micronesian (2)	2	0.01
Polynesian: (3)	7	0.03
Native Hawaiian (2)	6	0.03
Samoan (1)	1	0.00
Other Pac. Isl., not spec. (11)	13	0.06
Hispanic or Latino:	370	1.76
Central American:	11	0.05
Costa Rican	1	0.00
Guatemalan	7	0.03
Nicaraguan	2	0.01
Panamanian	1	0.00
Cuban	22	0.10
Mexican	229	1.09
Puerto Rican	38	0.18
South American:	22	0.10
Argentinean	3	0.01
Chilean	1	0.00
Colombian	9	0.04
Ecuadorian	5	0.02
Peruvian	3	0.01
Venezuelan	1	0.00
Other Hispanic or Latino	48	0.23
Hungarian	73	0.35
Irish	3,596	17.10
Italian	1,025	4.87
Latvian	6	0.03
Lithuanian	127	0.60
Luxemburger	11	0.05
Maltese	15	0.07
Norwegian	238	1.13
Pennsylvania German	5	0.02
Polish	873	4.15
Portuguese	18	0.09
Romanian	14	0.07
Russian	137	0.65
Scandinavian	17	0.08
Scotch-Irish	384	1.83
Scottish	414	1.97
Slovak	49	0.23
Slovene	30	0.14
Swedish	476	2.26
Swiss	79	0.38
Turkish	16	0.08
Ukrainian	18	0.09
United States or American	1,468	6.98
Welsh	113	0.54
West Indian, excl. Hispanic:	10	0.05
Haitian	4	0.02
Jamaican	6	0.03
White:	19,662	93.46
Not Hispanic (19,252)	19,403	92.22
Hispanic (210)	259	1.23
Yugoslavian	76	0.36

Chicago Heights

Place Type: City
County: Cook
Population: 32,776

Ancestry/Race	Number	%
African American/Black:	12,747	38.89
Not Hispanic (12,305)	12,542	38.27
Hispanic (116)	205	0.63
African, sub-Saharan:	298	0.90
African	272	0.82
Nigerian	17	0.05
Sudanese	9	0.03
Am. Ind. or Alaska Nat., not spec.	114	0.35
American Indian tribes, specified:	136	0.41
Apache (5)	13	0.04
Blackfeet (3)	10	0.03
Cherokee (9)	42	0.13
Cheyenne (1)	1	0.00
Chippewa (1)	1	0.00
Choctaw	3	0.01
Creek	1	0.00
Kiowa	2	0.01
Latin American Indians (28)	53	0.16
Navajo	1	0.00
Pueblo	1	0.00
Sioux	2	0.01
All other tribes	6	0.02
American Indian tribes, not spec.	24	0.07
Arab:	7	0.02
Palestinian	7	0.02
Asian:	208	0.63
Chinese, ex. Taiwanese (16)	32	0.10
Filipino (28)	40	0.12
Indian (39)	49	0.15
Japanese (4)	16	0.05
Korean (14)	19	0.06
Laotian (4)	4	0.01
Pakistani (4)	6	0.02
Taiwanese (1)	1	0.00
Vietnamese (20)	24	0.07
Other Asian, not specified (11)	17	0.05
Austrian	128	0.39
Belgian	43	0.13
British	30	0.09
Canadian	11	0.03
Croatian	60	0.18
Czech	105	0.32
Czechoslovakian	69	0.21
Danish	58	0.18
Dutch	240	0.73
English	823	2.49
Estonian	17	0.05
European	30	0.09
Finnish	27	0.08
French, except Basque	345	1.04
French Canadian	78	0.24
German	3,355	10.15
Greek	148	0.45
Hawaii Native/Pacific Islander:	25	0.08
Micronesian: (1)	2	0.01
Guamanian/Chamorro (1)	2	0.01
Polynesian: (8)	13	0.04
Native Hawaiian (1)	3	0.01
Samoan (7)	9	0.03
Tongan	1	0.00
Other Pac. Isl., not spec. (3)	10	0.03
Hispanic or Latino:	7,790	23.77
Central American:	23	0.07
Guatemalan	7	0.02
Honduran	10	0.03
Nicaraguan	3	0.01
Salvadoran	3	0.01
Cuban	19	0.06
Mexican	6,847	20.89
Puerto Rican	192	0.59
South American:	60	0.18
Argentinean	1	0.00
Colombian	24	0.07
Ecuadorian	1	0.00
Peruvian	20	0.06
Uruguayan	14	0.04
Other Hispanic or Latino	649	1.98
Hungarian	181	0.55
Iranian	7	0.02
Irish	2,179	6.59
Italian	3,757	11.37
Latvian	6	0.02
Lithuanian	196	0.59
Macedonian	6	0.02
Norwegian	56	0.17
Polish	2,043	6.18
Portuguese	6	0.02
Romanian	6	0.02
Russian	21	0.06
Scandinavian	53	0.16
Scotch-Irish	208	0.63
Scottish	212	0.64
Serbian	4	0.01
Slavic	7	0.02
Slovak	201	0.61
Swedish	325	0.98
Swiss	5	0.02
Turkish	9	0.03
Ukrainian	28	0.08
United States or American	514	1.56
Welsh	53	0.16
West Indian, excl. Hispanic:	20	0.06
Haitian	16	0.05
Jamaican	4	0.01
White:	15,486	47.25
Not Hispanic (12,062)	12,377	37.76
Hispanic (2,694)	3,109	9.49
Yugoslavian	16	0.05

Chicago Ridge

Place Type: Village
County: Cook
Population: 14,127

Ancestry/Race	Number	%
African American/Black:	365	2.58
Not Hispanic (337)	356	2.52
Hispanic (8)	9	0.06
Am. Ind. or Alaska Nat., not spec.	27	0.19
Albanian	19	0.14
American Indian tribes, specified:	47	0.33
Apache	8	0.06
Blackfeet	2	0.01
Cherokee (1)	18	0.13
Chippewa (1)	1	0.01
Latin American Indians (1)	2	0.01
Menominee (1)	3	0.02
Navajo (1)	1	0.01
Ottawa (2)	2	0.01
Sioux	3	0.02
Yuman (1)	1	0.01
All other tribes (1)	6	0.04
American Indian tribes, not spec.	6	0.04
Arab:	963	6.94
Arab/Arabic	539	3.88
Jordanian	192	1.38
Lebanese	26	0.19
Palestinian	183	1.32
Syrian	5	0.04
Other Arab	18	0.13
Armenian	12	0.09
Asian:	303	2.14
Cambodian (1)	1	0.01
Chinese, ex. Taiwanese (14)	22	0.16
Filipino (103)	123	0.87
Indian (44)	50	0.35
Japanese (7)	13	0.09
Korean (7)	12	0.08
Pakistani (1)	4	0.03
Thai (2)	3	0.02
Vietnamese (4)	4	0.03
Other Asian, not specified (19)	71	0.50

Notes: 1. Figures in the "Number" column do not add up to the total population due to: a) Ancestry/Race overlap — e.g. persons can report being both White and Irish, b) persons of Hispanic origin can report being any race, c) persons reporting two ancestries are counted in both categories. 2. Numbers in parentheses indicate the number of persons reporting this ancestry/race alone, not in combination with any other ancestry/race. 3. Refer to the Explanation of Data in the front of the book for more detailed information.

Ancestry/Race	Number	%
Austrian	127	0.92
Basque	6	0.04
Belgian	25	0.18
Brazilian	10	0.07
Canadian	31	0.22
Croatian	36	0.26
Czech	322	2.32
Czechoslovakian	79	0.57
Danish	144	1.04
Dutch	227	1.64
English	481	3.47
European	16	0.12
French, except Basque	259	1.87
French Canadian	73	0.53
German	2,649	19.09
Greek	108	0.78
Hawaii Native/Pacific Islander:	4	0.03
Polynesian:	1	0.01
Samoan	1	0.01
Other Pac. Isl., not spec.	3	0.02
Hispanic or Latino:	883	6.25
Central American:	11	0.08
Costa Rican	1	0.01
Guatemalan	8	0.06
Panamanian	1	0.01
Other Central American	1	0.01
Cuban	5	0.04
Mexican	666	4.71
Puerto Rican	56	0.40
South American:	32	0.23
Argentinean	4	0.03
Bolivian	2	0.01
Colombian	9	0.06
Ecuadorian	3	0.02
Peruvian	5	0.04
Other South American	9	0.06
Other Hispanic or Latino	113	0.80
Hungarian	33	0.24
Iranian	11	0.08
Irish	3,538	25.49
Italian	1,559	11.23
Lithuanian	534	3.85
Macedonian	36	0.26
Norwegian	119	0.86
Polish	2,823	20.34
Portuguese	26	0.19
Russian	32	0.23
Scotch-Irish	95	0.68
Scottish	86	0.62
Serbian	9	0.06
Slovak	97	0.70
Swedish	445	3.21
Ukrainian	51	0.37
United States or American	421	3.03
Welsh	79	0.57
White:	13,251	93.80
Not Hispanic (12,052)	12,659	89.61
Hispanic (540)	592	4.19

Chicago

Place Type: City
County: Cook
Population: 2,896,016

Ancestry/Race	Number	%
Acadian/Cajun	68	0.00
Afghan	381	0.01
African American/Black:	1,084,221	37.44
Not Hispanic (1,053,739)	1,068,054	36.88
Hispanic (11,270)	16,167	0.56
African, sub-Saharan:	36,985	1.28
African	26,959	0.93
Cape Verdean	66	0.00
Ethiopian	1,186	0.04
Ghanian	1,522	0.05
Kenyan	130	0.00
Liberian	171	0.01
Nigerian	5,464	0.19
Senegalese	26	0.00
Sierra Leonean	55	0.00
Somalian	222	0.01
South African	223	0.01
Sudanese	117	0.00
Ugandan	24	0.00
Zimbabwean	64	0.00
Other sub-Saharan African	756	0.03
Alaska Native tribes, specified:	68	0.00
Alaska Athabascan (3)	9	0.00
Aleut (5)	11	0.00
Eskimo (20)	32	0.00
Tlingit-Haida (6)	15	0.00
All other tribes	1	0.00
Alaska Native tribes, not specified	8	0.00
Am. Ind. or Alaska Nat., not spec.	9,741	0.34
Albanian	1,368	0.05
Alsatian	137	0.00
American Indian tribes, specified:	10,059	0.35
Apache (146)	278	0.01
Blackfeet (44)	425	0.01
Cherokee (423)	2,337	0.08
Cheyenne (10)	44	0.00
Chickasaw (8)	46	0.00
Chippewa (417)	636	0.02
Choctaw (112)	401	0.01
Colville (3)	3	0.00
Comanche (17)	53	0.00
Cree (25)	62	0.00
Creek (28)	102	0.00
Crow (4)	22	0.00
Delaware (8)	26	0.00
Houma (1)	5	0.00
Iroquois (230)	401	0.01
Kiowa (12)	18	0.00
Latin American Indians (1,926)	3,250	0.11
Lumbee (20)	26	0.00
Menominee (126)	183	0.01
Navajo (144)	245	0.01
Osage (4)	20	0.00
Ottawa (20)	40	0.00
Paiute (5)	10	0.00
Pima (13)	21	0.00
Potawatomi (48)	105	0.00
Pueblo (46)	103	0.00
Puget Sound Salish (2)	3	0.00
Seminole (12)	81	0.00
Shoshone (3)	15	0.00
Sioux (206)	439	0.02
Tohono O'Odham (8)	11	0.00
Ute (2)	12	0.00
Yakama (1)	3	0.00
Yaqui (4)	14	0.00
Yuman (4)	7	0.00
All other tribes (260)	612	0.02
American Indian tribes, not spec.	1,394	0.05
Arab:	14,971	0.52
Arab/Arabic	5,458	0.19
Egyptian	556	0.02
Iraqi	931	0.03
Jordanian	1,078	0.04
Lebanese	2,027	0.07
Moroccan	733	0.03
Palestinian	2,052	0.07
Syrian	1,124	0.04
Other Arab	1,012	0.03
Armenian	1,674	0.06
Asian:	143,175	4.94
Bangladeshi (284)	376	0.01
Cambodian (1,427)	1,751	0.06
Chinese, ex. Taiwanese (31,280)	33,701	1.16
Filipino (28,423)	32,266	1.11
Hmong (132)	173	0.01
Indian (25,004)	27,889	0.96
Indonesian (250)	359	0.01
Japanese (5,467)	7,114	0.25
Korean (11,895)	12,867	0.44
Laotian (433)	517	0.02
Malaysian (100)	186	0.01
Pakistani (5,920)	7,606	0.26
Sri Lankan (120)	144	0.00
Taiwanese (533)	669	0.02
Thai (1,967)	2,385	0.08
Vietnamese (8,221)	8,925	0.31
Other Asian, specified (188)	404	0.01
Other Asian, not specified (2,212)	5,843	0.20
Assyrian/Chaldean/Syriac	7,121	0.25
Australian	486	0.02
Austrian	8,080	0.28
Basque	141	0.00
Belgian	2,366	0.08
Brazilian	833	0.03
British	4,653	0.16
Bulgarian	2,045	0.07
Canadian	2,050	0.07
Carpatho Rusyn	37	0.00
Celtic	269	0.01
Croatian	7,819	0.27
Cypriot	52	0.00
Czech	13,790	0.48
Czechoslovakian	3,296	0.11
Danish	5,922	0.20
Dutch	11,906	0.41
Eastern European	3,388	0.12
English	57,579	1.99
Estonian	233	0.01
European	7,652	0.26
Finnish	2,163	0.07
French, except Basque	24,043	0.83
French Canadian	4,945	0.17
German	189,618	6.55
German Russian	73	0.00
Greek	18,249	0.63
Guyanese	370	0.01
Hawaii Native/Pacific Islander:	4,661	0.16
Melanesian: (5)	23	0.00
Fijian (5)	19	0.00
Other Melanesian	4	0.00
Micronesian: (490)	663	0.02
Guamanian/Chamorro (480)	637	0.02
Other Micronesian (10)	26	0.00
Polynesian: (781)	1,303	0.04
Native Hawaiian (336)	643	0.02
Samoan (436)	618	0.02
Tongan (1)	7	0.00
Other Polynesian (8)	35	0.00
Other Pac. Isl., specified	132	0.00
Other Pac. Isl., not spec. (501)	2,540	0.09
Hispanic or Latino:	753,644	26.02
Central American:	23,339	0.81
Costa Rican	609	0.02
Guatemalan	13,610	0.47
Honduran	3,049	0.11
Nicaraguan	778	0.03
Panamanian	637	0.02
Salvadoran	3,468	0.12
Other Central American	1,188	0.04
Cuban	8,084	0.28
Dominican Republic	1,651	0.06
Mexican	530,462	18.32
Puerto Rican	113,055	3.90
South American:	20,828	0.72
Argentinean	908	0.03
Bolivian	414	0.01
Chilean	640	0.02
Colombian	5,625	0.19
Ecuadorian	8,941	0.31
Paraguayan	68	0.00
Peruvian	2,737	0.09
Uruguayan	134	0.00
Venezuelan	600	0.02
Other South American	761	0.03
Other Hispanic or Latino	56,225	1.94
Hungarian	9,418	0.33
Icelander	176	0.01
Iranian	1,944	0.07
Irish	191,729	6.62
Israeli	1,033	0.04
Italian	101,903	3.52
Latvian	1,383	0.05
Lithuanian	15,383	0.53

Notes: 1. Figures in the "Number" column do not add up to the total population due to: a) Ancestry/Race overlap — e.g. persons can report being both White and Irish, b) persons of Hispanic origin can report being any race, c) persons reporting two ancestries are counted in both categories. 2. Numbers in parentheses indicate the number of persons reporting this ancestry/race alone, not in combination with any other ancestry/race. 3. Refer to the Explanation of Data in the front of the book for more detailed information.

Ancestry/Race	Number	%
Luxemburger	756	0.03
Macedonian	450	0.02
Maltese	96	0.00
New Zealander	62	0.00
Northern European	783	0.03
Norwegian	14,890	0.51
Pennsylvania German	94	0.00
Polish	210,421	7.27
Portuguese	915	0.03
Romanian	8,227	0.28
Russian	28,845	1.00
Scandinavian	1,649	0.06
Scotch-Irish	11,142	0.38
Scottish	14,285	0.49
Serbian	5,044	0.17
Slavic	846	0.03
Slovak	6,238	0.22
Slovene	1,555	0.05
Soviet Union	60	0.00
Swedish	24,882	0.86
Swiss	3,008	0.10
Turkish	1,178	0.04
Ukrainian	13,579	0.47
United States or American	38,779	1.34
Welsh	5,226	0.18
West Indian, excl. Hispanic:	11,698	0.40
Bahamian	114	0.00
Barbadian	144	0.00
Belizean	2,244	0.08
Bermudan	17	0.00
British West Indian	143	0.00
Dutch West Indian	32	0.00
Haitian	3,104	0.11
Jamaican	4,778	0.16
Trinidadian and Tobagonian	407	0.01
U.S. Virgin Islander	154	0.01
West Indian	552	0.02
Other West Indian	9	0.00
White:	1,282,320	44.28
Not Hispanic (907,166)	943,299	32.57
Hispanic (308,149)	339,021	11.71
Yugoslavian	10,130	0.35

Cicero

Place Type: Town
County: Cook
Population: 85,616

Ancestry/Race	Number	%
African American/Black:	1,113	1.30
Not Hispanic (674)	739	0.86
Hispanic (282)	374	0.44
African, sub-Saharan:	75	0.09
African	53	0.06
Nigerian	22	0.03
Alaska Native tribes, specified:	1	0.00
Eskimo	1	0.00
Alaska Native tribes, not specified	3	0.00
Am. Ind. or Alaska Nat., not spec.	592	0.69
American Indian tribes, specified:	464	0.54
Apache (4)	11	0.01
Blackfeet (5)	15	0.02
Cherokee (19)	70	0.08
Cheyenne (2)	2	0.00
Chickasaw	1	0.00
Chippewa (12)	20	0.02
Choctaw (1)	1	0.00
Colville (1)	1	0.00
Comanche (3)	4	0.00
Creek	8	0.01
Iroquois (9)	12	0.01
Latin American Indians (175)	249	0.29
Menominee	4	0.00
Navajo (3)	3	0.00
Osage	1	0.00
Ottawa (1)	4	0.00
Pueblo (5)	7	0.01
Sioux (7)	20	0.02
All other tribes (18)	31	0.04
American Indian tribes, not spec.	65	0.08
Arab:	253	0.30
Arab/Arabic	83	0.10
Jordanian	62	0.07
Palestinian	86	0.10
Syrian	8	0.01
Other Arab	14	0.02
Asian:	1,071	1.25
Cambodian (27)	36	0.04
Chinese, ex. Taiwanese (56)	67	0.08
Filipino (394)	445	0.52
Indian (67)	118	0.14
Japanese (21)	36	0.04
Korean (23)	34	0.04
Laotian	1	0.00
Pakistani (23)	35	0.04
Taiwanese (2)	2	0.00
Thai (60)	73	0.09
Vietnamese (123)	125	0.15
Other Asian, not specified (16)	99	0.12
Assyrian/Chaldean/Syriac	12	0.01
Austrian	216	0.25
Belgian	11	0.01
British	84	0.10
Bulgarian	7	0.01
Canadian	12	0.01
Croatian	223	0.26
Czech	1,714	2.00
Czechoslovakian	249	0.29
Danish	94	0.11
Dutch	197	0.23
English	704	0.82
European	58	0.07
Finnish	18	0.02
French, except Basque	439	0.51
French Canadian	106	0.12
German	3,178	3.71
Greek	287	0.34
Hawaii Native/Pacific Islander:	87	0.10
Micronesian: (22)	29	0.03
Guamanian/Chamorro (22)	29	0.03
Polynesian:	11	0.01
Native Hawaiian	10	0.01
Samoan	1	0.00
Other Pac. Isl., not spec. (16)	47	0.05
Hispanic or Latino:	66,299	77.44
Central American:	879	1.03
Costa Rican	12	0.01
Guatemalan	478	0.56
Honduran	134	0.16
Nicaraguan	44	0.05
Panamanian	25	0.03
Salvadoran	151	0.18
Other Central American	35	0.04
Cuban	123	0.14
Dominican Republic	96	0.11
Mexican	58,542	68.38
Puerto Rican	2,331	2.72
South American:	544	0.64
Argentinean	18	0.02
Bolivian	1	0.00
Chilean	22	0.03
Colombian	171	0.20
Ecuadorian	208	0.24
Paraguayan	5	0.01
Peruvian	72	0.08
Venezuelan	24	0.03
Other South American	23	0.03
Other Hispanic or Latino	3,784	4.42
Hungarian	100	0.12
Iranian	5	0.01
Irish	3,206	3.74
Israeli	12	0.01
Italian	2,597	3.03
Latvian	9	0.01
Lithuanian	443	0.52
Norwegian	249	0.29
Polish	3,984	4.65
Portuguese	27	0.03
Romanian	84	0.10
Russian	143	0.17
Scotch-Irish	107	0.12
Scottish	115	0.13
Serbian	79	0.09
Slavic	6	0.01
Slovak	252	0.29
Slovene	80	0.09
Swedish	236	0.28
Swiss	9	0.01
Ukrainian	89	0.10
United States or American	1,254	1.46
West Indian, excl. Hispanic:	68	0.08
Belizean	29	0.03
Haitian	34	0.04
West Indian	5	0.01
White:	44,429	51.89
Not Hispanic (16,787)	17,592	20.55
Hispanic (24,540)	26,837	31.35
Yugoslavian	50	0.06

Collinsville

Place Type: City
County: Madison
Population: 24,707

Ancestry/Race	Number	%
African American/Black:	1,552	6.28
Not Hispanic (1,429)	1,531	6.20
Hispanic (17)	21	0.08
African, sub-Saharan:	95	0.39
African	95	0.39
Alaska Native tribes, specified:	1	0.00
Aleut	1	0.00
Am. Ind. or Alaska Nat., not spec.	37	0.15
American Indian tribes, specified:	113	0.46
Apache (1)	1	0.00
Blackfeet (1)	9	0.04
Cherokee (27)	69	0.28
Chippewa (1)	1	0.00
Choctaw (7)	7	0.03
Comanche	1	0.00
Creek (1)	1	0.00
Iroquois (1)	2	0.01
Latin American Indians	4	0.02
Lumbee	2	0.01
Menominee (2)	2	0.01
Osage	2	0.01
Seminole (1)	1	0.00
Sioux (2)	5	0.02
All other tribes (5)	6	0.02
American Indian tribes, not spec.	4	0.02
Arab:	44	0.18
Arab/Arabic	11	0.05
Lebanese	22	0.09
Syrian	11	0.05
Armenian	9	0.04
Asian:	217	0.88
Cambodian (1)	1	0.00
Chinese, ex. Taiwanese (15)	22	0.09
Filipino (25)	40	0.16
Indian (15)	23	0.09
Japanese (7)	13	0.05
Korean (54)	65	0.26
Laotian (1)	1	0.00
Malaysian (1)	1	0.00
Pakistani (1)	1	0.00
Sri Lankan	1	0.00
Taiwanese (4)	8	0.03
Thai (5)	11	0.04
Vietnamese (5)	6	0.02
Other Asian, not specified (8)	24	0.10
Austrian	106	0.43
Basque	10	0.04
Belgian	6	0.02
British	115	0.47
Bulgarian	26	0.11
Canadian	16	0.07
Croatian	118	0.48
Czech	209	0.86

Notes: 1. Figures in the "Number" column do not add up to the total population due to: a) Ancestry/Race overlap — e.g. persons can report being both White and Irish, b) persons of Hispanic origin can report being any race, c) persons reporting two ancestries are counted in both categories. 2. Numbers in parentheses indicate the number of persons reporting this ancestry/race alone, not in combination with any other ancestry/race. 3. Refer to the Explanation of Data in the front of the book for more detailed information.

Ancestry/Race	Number	%
Czechoslovakian	60	0.25
Danish	29	0.12
Dutch	542	2.22
English	2,945	12.06
European	81	0.33
Finnish	47	0.19
French, except Basque	1,336	5.47
French Canadian	31	0.13
German	7,932	32.49
Greek	43	0.18
Hawaii Native/Pacific Islander:	9	0.04
Polynesian: (5)	6	0.02
Native Hawaiian (5)	6	0.02
Other Pac. Isl., not spec.	3	0.01
Hispanic or Latino:	534	2.16
Central American:	17	0.07
Guatemalan	4	0.02
Honduran	1	0.00
Panamanian	6	0.02
Other Central American	6	0.02
Cuban	7	0.03
Mexican	337	1.36
Puerto Rican	51	0.21
South American:	7	0.03
Bolivian	1	0.00
Colombian	4	0.02
Peruvian	2	0.01
Other Hispanic or Latino	115	0.47
Hungarian	194	0.79
Iranian	21	0.09
Irish	3,991	16.35
Israeli	10	0.04
Italian	2,261	9.26
Lithuanian	333	1.36
Macedonian	17	0.07
Maltese	5	0.02
Northern European	14	0.06
Norwegian	164	0.67
Pennsylvania German	9	0.04
Polish	909	3.72
Portuguese	10	0.04
Romanian	9	0.04
Russian	67	0.27
Scotch-Irish	305	1.25
Scottish	232	0.95
Serbian	32	0.13
Slavic	34	0.14
Slovak	78	0.32
Slovene	7	0.03
Swedish	177	0.72
Swiss	137	0.56
Ukrainian	31	0.13
United States or American	1,605	6.57
Welsh	142	0.58
White:	22,854	92.50
Not Hispanic (22,274)	22,488	91.02
Hispanic (329)	366	1.48
Yugoslavian	44	0.18

Country Club Hills

Place Type: City
County: Cook
Population: 16,169

Ancestry/Race	Number	%
African American/Black:	13,468	83.30
Not Hispanic (13,167)	13,379	82.74
Hispanic (76)	89	0.55
African, sub-Saharan:	542	3.35
African	501	3.09
Nigerian	41	0.25
Alaska Native tribes, specified:	4	0.02
Eskimo	4	0.02
Am. Ind. or Alaska Nat., not spec.	57	0.35
American Indian tribes, specified:	69	0.43
Blackfeet (3)	11	0.07
Cherokee (4)	32	0.20
Choctaw	11	0.07
Cree	2	0.01
Creek (1)	1	0.01
Iroquois	1	0.01
Latin American Indians	1	0.01
Ottawa	2	0.01
Sioux (1)	2	0.01
All other tribes	6	0.04
American Indian tribes, not spec.	8	0.05
Arab:	5	0.03
Arab/Arabic	5	0.03
Armenian	7	0.04
Asian:	216	1.34
Chinese, ex. Taiwanese (10)	17	0.11
Filipino (67)	83	0.51
Indian (42)	46	0.28
Indonesian	2	0.01
Japanese (3)	11	0.07
Korean (7)	12	0.07
Laotian (18)	19	0.12
Malaysian	3	0.02
Thai (1)	1	0.01
Vietnamese (2)	3	0.02
Other Asian, not specified (10)	19	0.12
Belgian	19	0.12
British	14	0.09
Bulgarian	4	0.02
Croatian	19	0.12
Czech	66	0.41
Czechoslovakian	17	0.10
Danish	9	0.06
Dutch	26	0.16
English	164	1.01
Finnish	20	0.12
French, except Basque	92	0.57
French Canadian	14	0.09
German	654	4.04
Greek	55	0.34
Hawaii Native/Pacific Islander:	4	0.02
Other Pac. Isl., not spec.	4	0.02
Hispanic or Latino:	280	1.73
Central American:	2	0.01
Honduran	1	0.01
Panamanian	1	0.01
Cuban	3	0.02
Mexican	151	0.93
Puerto Rican	58	0.36
South American:	5	0.03
Argentinean	2	0.01
Chilean	1	0.01
Ecuadorian	1	0.01
Uruguayan	1	0.01
Other Hispanic or Latino	61	0.38
Hungarian	41	0.25
Irish	630	3.89
Italian	264	1.63
Lithuanian	25	0.15
Norwegian	48	0.30
Polish	405	2.50
Russian	68	0.42
Scandinavian	8	0.05
Scotch-Irish	37	0.23
Scottish	32	0.20
Slovak	21	0.13
Slovene	8	0.05
Swedish	129	0.80
United States or American	190	1.17
Welsh	33	0.20
West Indian, excl. Hispanic:	262	1.62
Belizean	36	0.22
Haitian	70	0.43
Jamaican	145	0.89
U.S. Virgin Islander	7	0.04
West Indian	4	0.02
White:	2,525	15.62
Not Hispanic (2,248)	2,406	14.88
Hispanic (98)	119	0.74

Crest Hill

Place Type: City
County: Will
Population: 13,329

Ancestry/Race	Number	%
African American/Black:	2,671	20.04
Not Hispanic (2,591)	2,652	19.90
Hispanic (15)	19	0.14
African, sub-Saharan:	6	0.05
Other sub-Saharan African	6	0.05
Am. Ind. or Alaska Nat., not spec.	22	0.17
American Indian tribes, specified:	46	0.35
Apache (1)	5	0.04
Blackfeet	3	0.02
Cherokee (2)	13	0.10
Cheyenne	3	0.02
Chippewa (4)	6	0.05
Choctaw (1)	3	0.02
Crow (1)	1	0.01
Iroquois (1)	1	0.01
Latin American Indians (1)	4	0.03
Lumbee	1	0.01
Navajo (2)	4	0.03
Sioux (1)	1	0.01
All other tribes	1	0.01
American Indian tribes, not spec.	4	0.03
Asian:	186	1.40
Cambodian (1)	2	0.02
Chinese, ex. Taiwanese (25)	26	0.20
Filipino (24)	34	0.26
Indian (36)	40	0.30
Indonesian	3	0.02
Japanese (14)	18	0.14
Korean (31)	36	0.27
Laotian (5)	5	0.04
Pakistani (6)	6	0.05
Thai (1)	2	0.02
Vietnamese (3)	3	0.02
Other Asian, specified	2	0.02
Other Asian, not specified (3)	9	0.07
Austrian	30	0.23
Belgian	7	0.05
British	30	0.23
Canadian	26	0.20
Croatian	437	3.35
Czech	149	1.14
Czechoslovakian	53	0.41
Danish	113	0.87
Dutch	77	0.59
English	775	5.95
European	107	0.82
French, except Basque	261	2.00
French Canadian	124	0.95
German	2,744	21.06
Greek	101	0.78
Hawaii Native/Pacific Islander:	26	0.20
Micronesian: (2)	2	0.02
Guamanian/Chamorro (2)	2	0.02
Polynesian: (14)	19	0.14
Native Hawaiian (8)	13	0.10
Samoan (6)	6	0.05
Other Pac. Isl., not spec. (1)	5	0.04
Hispanic or Latino:	1,174	8.81
Central American:	9	0.07
Costa Rican	3	0.02
Guatemalan	2	0.02
Honduran	1	0.01
Panamanian	1	0.01
Other Central American	2	0.02
Cuban	6	0.05
Dominican Republic	1	0.01
Mexican	668	5.01
Puerto Rican	48	0.36
South American:	25	0.19
Argentinean	1	0.01
Chilean	6	0.05
Colombian	3	0.02
Ecuadorian	1	0.01

Notes: 1. Figures in the "Number" column do not add up to the total population due to: a) Ancestry/Race overlap — e.g. persons can report being both White and Irish, b) persons of Hispanic origin can report being any race, c) persons reporting two ancestries are counted in both categories. 2. Numbers in parentheses indicate the number of persons reporting this ancestry/race alone, not in combination with any other ancestry/race. 3. Refer to the Explanation of Data in the front of the book for more detailed information.

Peruvian	14	0.11
Other Hispanic or Latino	417	3.13
Hungarian	3	0.02
Irish	1,609	12.35
Italian	1,189	9.12
Lithuanian	55	0.42
Maltese	13	0.10
Norwegian	130	1.00
Polish	1,213	9.31
Romanian	28	0.21
Russian	34	0.26
Scandinavian	9	0.07
Scotch-Irish	179	1.37
Scottish	116	0.89
Slavic	43	0.33
Slovak	162	1.24
Slovene	349	2.68
Swedish	247	1.90
Swiss	8	0.06
Ukrainian	8	0.06
United States or American	544	4.17
Welsh	65	0.50
White:	10,080	75.62
Not Hispanic (9,246)	9,352	70.16
Hispanic (666)	728	5.46

Crestwood

Place Type: Village
County: Cook
Population: 11,251

Ancestry/Race	Number	%
African American/Black:	522	4.64
Not Hispanic (498)	510	4.53
Hispanic (10)	12	0.11
Am. Ind. or Alaska Nat., not spec.	14	0.12
American Indian tribes, specified:	18	0.16
Apache (2)	2	0.02
Cherokee (3)	6	0.05
Chickasaw	1	0.01
Chippewa (4)	4	0.04
Menominee (2)	2	0.02
Navajo (1)	2	0.02
All other tribes	1	0.01
American Indian tribes, not spec.	1	0.01
Arab:	32	0.29
Arab/Arabic	25	0.22
Jordanian	7	0.06
Asian:	107	0.95
Cambodian (2)	2	0.02
Chinese, ex. Taiwanese (6)	9	0.08
Filipino (29)	32	0.28
Indian (17)	20	0.18
Indonesian	2	0.02
Japanese (7)	13	0.12
Korean (11)	12	0.11
Pakistani (2)	2	0.02
Taiwanese	2	0.02
Vietnamese (7)	9	0.08
Other Asian, not specified (1)	4	0.04
Assyrian/Chaldean/Syriac	7	0.06
Austrian	155	1.38
Belgian	10	0.09
Croatian	193	1.72
Czech	225	2.01
Czechoslovakian	26	0.23
Danish	119	1.06
Dutch	466	4.15
English	544	4.85
Estonian	55	0.49
French, except Basque	202	1.80
French Canadian	93	0.83
German	2,675	23.84
Greek	77	0.69
Hawaii Native/Pacific Islander:	5	0.04
Polynesian:	1	0.01
Native Hawaiian	1	0.01
Other Pac. Isl., not spec.	4	0.04
Hispanic or Latino:	414	3.68
Central American:	5	0.04
Guatemalan	1	0.01
Salvadoran	4	0.04
Cuban	1	0.01
Mexican	312	2.77
Puerto Rican	35	0.31
South American:	20	0.18
Argentinean	2	0.02
Colombian	1	0.01
Ecuadorian	12	0.11
Peruvian	2	0.02
Other South American	3	0.03
Other Hispanic or Latino	41	0.36
Hungarian	37	0.33
Irish	3,301	29.42
Israeli	5	0.04
Italian	1,343	11.97
Lithuanian	236	2.10
Norwegian	123	1.10
Pennsylvania German	17	0.15
Polish	2,224	19.82
Romanian	7	0.06
Russian	49	0.44
Scotch-Irish	68	0.61
Scottish	81	0.72
Serbian	17	0.15
Slavic	10	0.09
Slovak	106	0.94
Swedish	506	4.51
Ukrainian	56	0.50
United States or American	120	1.07
Welsh	7	0.06
White:	10,524	93.54
Not Hispanic (10,139)	10,236	90.98
Hispanic (264)	288	2.56
Yugoslavian	16	0.14

Crystal Lake

Place Type: City
County: McHenry
Population: 38,000

Ancestry/Race	Number	%
African American/Black:	283	0.74
Not Hispanic (193)	257	0.68
Hispanic (19)	26	0.07
African, sub-Saharan:	129	0.34
African	129	0.34
Am. Ind. or Alaska Nat., not spec.	46	0.12
American Indian tribes, specified:	98	0.26
Blackfeet	2	0.01
Cherokee (11)	32	0.08
Cheyenne	2	0.01
Chickasaw	2	0.01
Chippewa (11)	14	0.04
Choctaw (1)	2	0.01
Creek	1	0.00
Iroquois (1)	11	0.03
Latin American Indians	1	0.00
Lumbee (3)	3	0.01
Menominee	5	0.01
Seminole (1)	2	0.01
Sioux (2)	4	0.01
Yaqui	1	0.00
All other tribes (4)	16	0.04
American Indian tribes, not spec.	9	0.02
Arab:	28	0.07
Lebanese	28	0.07
Armenian	46	0.12
Asian:	911	2.40
Cambodian (1)	1	0.00
Chinese, ex. Taiwanese (126)	155	0.41
Filipino (125)	171	0.45
Indian (281)	296	0.78
Indonesian (2)	5	0.01
Japanese (28)	47	0.12
Korean (84)	101	0.27
Laotian (20)	23	0.06
Pakistani (22)	34	0.09
Taiwanese (5)	6	0.02
Thai (4)	8	0.02
Vietnamese (27)	33	0.09
Other Asian, specified (1)	4	0.01
Other Asian, not specified (14)	27	0.07
Assyrian/Chaldean/Syriac	53	0.14
Australian	5	0.01
Austrian	148	0.39
Belgian	73	0.19
British	144	0.38
Canadian	125	0.33
Carpatho Rusyn	10	0.03
Croatian	114	0.30
Czech	644	1.70
Czechoslovakian	95	0.25
Danish	568	1.50
Dutch	629	1.66
Eastern European	13	0.03
English	3,787	10.01
Estonian	20	0.05
European	250	0.66
Finnish	117	0.31
French, except Basque	875	2.31
French Canadian	224	0.59
German	13,035	34.45
Greek	431	1.14
Hawaii Native/Pacific Islander:	27	0.07
Micronesian: (1)	2	0.01
Guamanian/Chamorro (1)	2	0.01
Polynesian: (5)	11	0.03
Native Hawaiian (1)	5	0.01
Samoan (4)	4	0.01
Other Polynesian	2	0.01
Other Pac. Isl., specified	1	0.00
Other Pac. Isl., not spec. (2)	13	0.03
Hispanic or Latino:	2,662	7.01
Central American:	46	0.12
Costa Rican	4	0.01
Guatemalan	16	0.04
Honduran	2	0.01
Nicaraguan	1	0.00
Panamanian	1	0.00
Salvadoran	11	0.03
Other Central American	11	0.03
Cuban	47	0.12
Dominican Republic	8	0.02
Mexican	2,056	5.41
Puerto Rican	175	0.46
South American:	66	0.17
Argentinean	5	0.01
Bolivian	4	0.01
Chilean	4	0.01
Colombian	37	0.10
Ecuadorian	5	0.01
Peruvian	5	0.01
Venezuelan	5	0.01
Other South American	1	0.00
Other Hispanic or Latino	264	0.69
Hungarian	234	0.62
Icelander	7	0.02
Iranian	19	0.05
Irish	7,965	21.05
Israeli	34	0.09
Italian	3,420	9.04
Latvian	29	0.08
Lithuanian	436	1.15
Maltese	8	0.02
Northern European	58	0.15
Norwegian	1,475	3.90
Pennsylvania German	9	0.02
Polish	4,491	11.87
Portuguese	42	0.11
Romanian	41	0.11
Russian	503	1.33
Scandinavian	122	0.32
Scotch-Irish	666	1.76
Scottish	643	1.70
Serbian	40	0.11
Slavic	21	0.06
Slovak	81	0.21

Notes: 1. Figures in the "Number" column do not add up to the total population due to: a) Ancestry/Race overlap — e.g. persons can report being both White and Irish, b) persons of Hispanic origin can report being any race, c) persons reporting two ancestries are counted in both categories. 2. Numbers in parentheses indicate the number of persons reporting this ancestry/race alone, not in combination with any other ancestry/race. 3. Refer to the Explanation of Data in the front of the book for more detailed information.

Slovene	35	0.09
Swedish	1,627	4.30
Swiss	117	0.31
Ukrainian	308	0.81
United States or American	1,111	2.94
Welsh	358	0.95
West Indian, excl. Hispanic:	22	0.06
Trinidadian and Tobagonian	22	0.06
White:	36,093	94.98
Not Hispanic (34,067)	34,294	90.25
Hispanic (1,679)	1,799	4.73
Yugoslavian	65	0.17

Danville

Place Type: City
County: Vermilion
Population: 33,904

Ancestry/Race	Number	%
African American/Black:	8,629	25.45
Not Hispanic (8,193)	8,509	25.10
Hispanic (68)	120	0.35
African, sub-Saharan:	200	0.59
African	191	0.56
Nigerian	9	0.03
Am. Ind. or Alaska Nat., not spec.	113	0.33
American Indian tribes, specified:	96	0.28
Apache (1)	5	0.01
Blackfeet (2)	13	0.04
Cherokee (15)	53	0.16
Chippewa (1)	2	0.01
Choctaw (1)	2	0.01
Comanche	1	0.00
Iroquois	1	0.00
Latin American Indians (4)	4	0.01
Sioux (4)	5	0.01
All other tribes (4)	10	0.03
American Indian tribes, not spec.	13	0.04
Arab:	138	0.41
Arab/Arabic	40	0.12
Egyptian	62	0.18
Lebanese	7	0.02
Palestinian	16	0.05
Syrian	7	0.02
Other Arab	6	0.02
Asian:	469	1.38
Chinese, ex. Taiwanese (54)	59	0.17
Filipino (65)	79	0.23
Hmong (35)	35	0.10
Indian (167)	186	0.55
Japanese (19)	27	0.08
Korean (21)	26	0.08
Pakistani (4)	5	0.01
Taiwanese (1)	1	0.00
Thai (5)	7	0.02
Vietnamese (23)	26	0.08
Other Asian, specified (2)	2	0.01
Other Asian, not specified (6)	16	0.05
Austrian	14	0.04
Belgian	110	0.32
British	68	0.20
Canadian	25	0.07
Croatian	15	0.04
Czech	41	0.12
Czechoslovakian	28	0.08
Danish	41	0.12
Dutch	691	2.04
English	2,651	7.83
European	134	0.40
Finnish	22	0.06
French, except Basque	646	1.91
French Canadian	69	0.20
German	5,323	15.72
Greek	78	0.23
Hawaii Native/Pacific Islander:	21	0.06
Micronesian: (2)	8	0.02
Guamanian/Chamorro	3	0.01
Other Micronesian (2)	5	0.01
Polynesian: (7)	9	0.03
Native Hawaiian	2	0.01
Samoan (7)	7	0.02
Other Pac. Isl., not spec. (1)	4	0.01
Hispanic or Latino:	1,549	4.57
Central American:	13	0.04
Costa Rican	1	0.00
Guatemalan	2	0.01
Honduran	3	0.01
Nicaraguan	1	0.00
Panamanian	2	0.01
Salvadoran	3	0.01
Other Central American	1	0.00
Cuban	19	0.06
Dominican Republic	1	0.00
Mexican	1,055	3.11
Puerto Rican	64	0.19
South American:	9	0.03
Argentinean	1	0.00
Chilean	3	0.01
Colombian	1	0.00
Peruvian	3	0.01
Other South American	1	0.00
Other Hispanic or Latino	388	1.14
Hungarian	92	0.27
Irish	3,261	9.63
Italian	775	2.29
Lithuanian	189	0.56
Northern European	43	0.13
Norwegian	143	0.42
Pennsylvania German	25	0.07
Polish	580	1.71
Portuguese	37	0.11
Russian	36	0.11
Scandinavian	5	0.01
Scotch-Irish	388	1.15
Scottish	482	1.42
Serbian	6	0.02
Slavic	8	0.02
Slovak	31	0.09
Swedish	372	1.10
Swiss	80	0.24
Turkish	9	0.03
Ukrainian	6	0.02
United States or American	3,023	8.93
Welsh	121	0.36
West Indian, excl. Hispanic:	70	0.21
Barbadian	4	0.01
Haitian	44	0.13
Jamaican	22	0.06
White:	24,349	71.82
Not Hispanic (23,140)	23,574	69.53
Hispanic (656)	775	2.29

Darien

Place Type: City
County: Du Page
Population: 22,860

Ancestry/Race	Number	%
African American/Black:	480	2.10
Not Hispanic (437)	465	2.03
Hispanic (14)	15	0.07
African, sub-Saharan:	6	0.03
African	6	0.03
Am. Ind. or Alaska Nat., not spec.	24	0.10
Albanian	74	0.32
American Indian tribes, specified:	41	0.18
Blackfeet (1)	1	0.00
Cherokee	6	0.03
Chippewa (10)	16	0.07
Choctaw	2	0.01
Iroquois	5	0.02
Latin American Indians	1	0.00
Menominee (1)	1	0.00
Navajo (1)	1	0.00
Ottawa	1	0.00
Seminole	1	0.00
Shoshone	1	0.00
Sioux	3	0.01
All other tribes (2)	2	0.01
American Indian tribes, not spec.	5	0.02
Arab:	52	0.23
Arab/Arabic	10	0.04
Lebanese	42	0.18
Armenian	7	0.03
Asian:	2,873	12.57
Bangladeshi (4)	4	0.02
Chinese, ex. Taiwanese (471)	530	2.32
Filipino (818)	930	4.07
Indian (936)	972	4.25
Indonesian (1)	2	0.01
Japanese (32)	48	0.21
Korean (111)	119	0.52
Malaysian (1)	4	0.02
Pakistani (60)	67	0.29
Sri Lankan (10)	10	0.04
Taiwanese (43)	56	0.24
Thai (68)	79	0.35
Vietnamese (17)	19	0.08
Other Asian, specified (2)	3	0.01
Other Asian, not specified (13)	30	0.13
Austrian	99	0.43
Belgian	77	0.34
British	109	0.47
Bulgarian	11	0.05
Canadian	67	0.29
Croatian	228	0.99
Czech	1,176	5.12
Czechoslovakian	225	0.98
Danish	91	0.40
Dutch	341	1.48
Eastern European	39	0.17
English	1,429	6.22
European	67	0.29
Finnish	48	0.21
French, except Basque	419	1.82
French Canadian	99	0.43
German	4,570	19.90
Greek	375	1.63
Hawaii Native/Pacific Islander:	34	0.15
Micronesian: (1)	3	0.01
Guamanian/Chamorro	1	0.00
Other Micronesian (1)	2	0.01
Polynesian: (4)	5	0.02
Native Hawaiian (1)	2	0.01
Samoan (3)	3	0.01
Other Pac. Isl., not spec.	26	0.11
Hispanic or Latino:	831	3.64
Central American:	18	0.08
Guatemalan	6	0.03
Honduran	8	0.03
Panamanian	2	0.01
Salvadoran	2	0.01
Cuban	32	0.14
Dominican Republic	7	0.03
Mexican	586	2.56
Puerto Rican	54	0.24
South American:	44	0.19
Argentinean	3	0.01
Bolivian	4	0.02
Chilean	5	0.02
Colombian	18	0.08
Ecuadorian	7	0.03
Peruvian	3	0.01
Venezuelan	2	0.01
Other South American	2	0.01
Other Hispanic or Latino	90	0.39
Hungarian	148	0.64
Iranian	20	0.09
Irish	3,697	16.10
Italian	3,402	14.81
Latvian	5	0.02
Lithuanian	770	3.35
Luxemburger	15	0.07
Macedonian	22	0.10
Norwegian	335	1.46
Pennsylvania German	11	0.05
Polish	4,415	19.22
Portuguese	34	0.15

Notes: 1. Figures in the "Number" column do not add up to the total population due to: a) Ancestry/Race overlap — e.g. persons can report being both White and Irish, b) persons of Hispanic origin can report being any race, c) persons reporting two ancestries are counted in both categories. 2. Numbers in parentheses indicate the number of persons reporting this ancestry/race alone, not in combination with any other ancestry/race. 3. Refer to the Explanation of Data in the front of the book for more detailed information.

Ancestry/Race	Number	%
Russian	255	1.11
Scandinavian	52	0.23
Scotch-Irish	182	0.79
Scottish	227	0.99
Serbian	52	0.23
Slavic	29	0.13
Slovak	215	0.94
Slovene	95	0.41
Swedish	675	2.94
Swiss	67	0.29
Turkish	6	0.03
Ukrainian	97	0.42
United States or American	218	0.95
Welsh	203	0.88
West Indian, excl. Hispanic:	31	0.13
Belizean	15	0.07
Haitian	4	0.02
Jamaican	7	0.03
Trinidadian and Tobagonian	5	0.02
White:	19,454	85.10
Not Hispanic (18,673)	18,847	82.45
Hispanic (552)	607	2.66
Yugoslavian	63	0.27

De Kalb

Place Type: City
County: De Kalb
Population: 39,018

Ancestry/Race	Number	%
African American/Black:	3,788	9.71
Not Hispanic (3,508)	3,725	9.55
Hispanic (35)	63	0.16
African, sub-Saharan:	417	1.07
African	240	0.62
Ghanian	27	0.07
Nigerian	29	0.07
Somalian	63	0.16
Other sub-Saharan African	58	0.15
Am. Ind. or Alaska Nat., not spec.	85	0.22
American Indian tribes, specified:	134	0.34
Apache (1)	2	0.01
Blackfeet	7	0.02
Cherokee (11)	51	0.13
Cheyenne (1)	2	0.01
Chippewa (3)	7	0.02
Choctaw (1)	4	0.01
Comanche (1)	5	0.01
Creek (1)	1	0.00
Delaware (1)	1	0.00
Iroquois (7)	12	0.03
Latin American Indians (7)	8	0.02
Osage	1	0.00
Ottawa	3	0.01
Potawatomi	1	0.00
Pueblo (1)	4	0.01
Puget Sound Salish	1	0.00
Sioux (2)	10	0.03
All other tribes (8)	14	0.04
American Indian tribes, not spec.	30	0.08
Arab:	174	0.45
Arab/Arabic	21	0.05
Egyptian	40	0.10
Iraqi	9	0.02
Jordanian	9	0.02
Lebanese	59	0.15
Moroccan	24	0.06
Palestinian	12	0.03
Armenian	51	0.13
Asian:	2,035	5.22
Cambodian (32)	36	0.09
Chinese, ex. Taiwanese (424)	463	1.19
Filipino (248)	281	0.72
Hmong (2)	2	0.01
Indian (532)	577	1.48
Indonesian (13)	14	0.04
Japanese (48)	75	0.19
Korean (197)	229	0.59
Laotian (19)	22	0.06
Malaysian (8)	18	0.05
Pakistani (45)	52	0.13
Sri Lankan (1)	4	0.01
Taiwanese (27)	35	0.09
Thai (46)	56	0.14
Vietnamese (95)	106	0.27
Other Asian, specified (14)	20	0.05
Other Asian, not specified (24)	45	0.12
Assyrian/Chaldean/Syriac	47	0.12
Australian	7	0.02
Austrian	144	0.37
Belgian	117	0.30
Brazilian	33	0.08
British	120	0.31
Bulgarian	27	0.07
Canadian	63	0.16
Croatian	255	0.66
Czech	406	1.05
Czechoslovakian	95	0.24
Danish	227	0.58
Dutch	622	1.60
Eastern European	18	0.05
English	2,932	7.55
European	198	0.51
Finnish	217	0.56
French, except Basque	946	2.44
French Canadian	189	0.49
German	9,520	24.51
Greek	420	1.08
Hawaii Native/Pacific Islander:	84	0.22
Melanesian: (3)	3	0.01
Other Melanesian (3)	3	0.01
Micronesian: (4)	5	0.01
Guamanian/Chamorro (4)	5	0.01
Polynesian: (23)	29	0.07
Native Hawaiian (4)	6	0.02
Samoan (19)	23	0.06
Other Pac. Isl., specified	4	0.01
Other Pac. Isl., not spec. (19)	43	0.11
Hispanic or Latino:	3,527	9.04
Central American:	67	0.17
Costa Rican	2	0.01
Guatemalan	25	0.06
Honduran	9	0.02
Nicaraguan	11	0.03
Panamanian	6	0.02
Salvadoran	6	0.02
Other Central American	8	0.02
Cuban	51	0.13
Dominican Republic	1	0.00
Mexican	2,928	7.50
Puerto Rican	195	0.50
South American:	84	0.22
Argentinean	4	0.01
Bolivian	2	0.01
Chilean	3	0.01
Colombian	27	0.07
Ecuadorian	11	0.03
Peruvian	19	0.05
Uruguayan	1	0.00
Venezuelan	11	0.03
Other South American	6	0.02
Other Hispanic or Latino	201	0.52
Hungarian	203	0.52
Icelander	9	0.02
Iranian	20	0.05
Irish	5,626	14.49
Israeli	10	0.03
Italian	2,176	5.60
Latvian	9	0.02
Lithuanian	247	0.64
Luxemburger	58	0.15
Macedonian	6	0.02
Northern European	97	0.25
Norwegian	1,329	3.42
Pennsylvania German	10	0.03
Polish	2,383	6.14
Portuguese	46	0.12
Romanian	63	0.16
Russian	322	0.83
Scandinavian	140	0.36
Scotch-Irish	332	0.85
Scottish	513	1.32
Serbian	81	0.21
Slavic	47	0.12
Slovak	90	0.23
Slovene	30	0.08
Swedish	1,767	4.55
Swiss	128	0.33
Turkish	25	0.06
Ukrainian	130	0.33
United States or American	1,293	3.33
Welsh	190	0.49
West Indian, excl. Hispanic:	117	0.30
Haitian	12	0.03
Jamaican	78	0.20
Trinidadian and Tobagonian	27	0.07
White:	31,684	81.20
Not Hispanic (29,479)	29,922	76.69
Hispanic (1,536)	1,762	4.52
Yugoslavian	51	0.13

Decatur

Place Type: City
County: Macon
Population: 81,860

Ancestry/Race	Number	%
Acadian/Cajun	42	0.05
African American/Black:	16,845	20.58
Not Hispanic (15,846)	16,718	20.42
Hispanic (94)	127	0.16
African, sub-Saharan:	626	0.76
African	529	0.64
Liberian	28	0.03
Nigerian	7	0.01
South African	43	0.05
Other sub-Saharan African	19	0.02
Alaska Native tribes, specified:	1	0.00
Eskimo (1)	1	0.00
Alaska Native tribes, not specified	1	0.00
Am. Ind. or Alaska Nat., not spec.	198	0.24
Alsatian	6	0.01
American Indian tribes, specified:	244	0.30
Apache (2)	5	0.01
Blackfeet (4)	19	0.02
Cherokee (36)	140	0.17
Cheyenne	2	0.00
Chickasaw	1	0.00
Chippewa (1)	3	0.00
Choctaw (5)	9	0.01
Comanche (1)	2	0.00
Creek	3	0.00
Crow	2	0.00
Delaware (1)	5	0.01
Iroquois (2)	5	0.01
Latin American Indians	4	0.00
Lumbee	1	0.00
Navajo (1)	2	0.00
Paiute (2)	3	0.00
Potawatomi	3	0.00
Seminole	2	0.00
Shoshone (1)	1	0.00
Sioux (9)	14	0.02
All other tribes (3)	18	0.02
American Indian tribes, not spec.	19	0.02
Arab:	77	0.09
Arab/Arabic	13	0.02
Egyptian	21	0.03
Lebanese	14	0.02
Moroccan	6	0.01
Syrian	23	0.03
Asian:	706	0.86
Chinese, ex. Taiwanese (96)	121	0.15
Filipino (106)	153	0.19
Indian (133)	158	0.19
Indonesian (2)	6	0.01
Japanese (48)	62	0.08
Korean (54)	63	0.08

Notes: 1. Figures in the "Number" column do not add up to the total population due to: a) Ancestry/Race overlap — e.g. persons can report being both White and Irish, b) persons of Hispanic origin can report being any race, c) persons reporting two ancestries are counted in both categories. 2. Numbers in parentheses indicate the number of persons reporting this ancestry/race alone, not in combination with any other ancestry/race. 3. Refer to the Explanation of Data in the front of the book for more detailed information.

Laotian (1)	2	0.00
Malaysian (2)	2	0.00
Pakistani (12)	12	0.01
Taiwanese (2)	2	0.00
Thai (10)	12	0.01
Vietnamese (46)	57	0.07
Other Asian, specified (3)	7	0.01
Other Asian, not specified (14)	49	0.06
Australian	12	0.01
Austrian	89	0.11
Belgian	51	0.06
British	290	0.35
Bulgarian	5	0.01
Canadian	55	0.07
Celtic	5	0.01
Croatian	55	0.07
Czech	131	0.16
Czechoslovakian	49	0.06
Danish	151	0.18
Dutch	1,342	1.63
Eastern European	6	0.01
English	7,668	9.34
Estonian	12	0.01
European	729	0.89
Finnish	11	0.01
French, except Basque	1,898	2.31
French Canadian	262	0.32
German	15,879	19.34
German Russian	7	0.01
Greek	151	0.18
Hawaii Native/Pacific Islander:	48	0.06
Micronesian: (4)	6	0.01
Guamanian/Chamorro (1)	3	0.00
Other Micronesian (3)	3	0.00
Polynesian: (8)	13	0.02
Native Hawaiian (4)	6	0.01
Samoan (4)	7	0.01
Other Pac. Isl., specified	4	0.00
Other Pac. Isl., not spec. (3)	25	0.03
Hispanic or Latino:	978	1.19
Central American:	45	0.05
Costa Rican	7	0.01
Guatemalan	7	0.01
Honduran	4	0.00
Nicaraguan	6	0.01
Panamanian	10	0.01
Salvadoran	4	0.00
Other Central American	7	0.01
Cuban	35	0.04
Dominican Republic	6	0.01
Mexican	525	0.64
Puerto Rican	81	0.10
South American:	28	0.03
Bolivian	1	0.00
Chilean	3	0.00
Colombian	14	0.02
Peruvian	5	0.01
Venezuelan	4	0.00
Other South American	1	0.00
Other Hispanic or Latino	258	0.32
Hungarian	125	0.15
Iranian	68	0.08
Irish	9,183	11.18
Italian	1,292	1.57
Latvian	7	0.01
Lithuanian	75	0.09
Luxemburger	29	0.04
Northern European	18	0.02
Norwegian	633	0.77
Pennsylvania German	88	0.11
Polish	1,340	1.63
Portuguese	25	0.03
Romanian	15	0.02
Russian	147	0.18
Scandinavian	76	0.09
Scotch-Irish	1,227	1.49
Scottish	1,034	1.26
Serbian	24	0.03
Slavic	7	0.01
Slovak	70	0.09
Slovene	19	0.02
Swedish	774	0.94
Swiss	226	0.28
Ukrainian	30	0.04
United States or American	8,418	10.25
Welsh	485	0.59
West Indian, excl. Hispanic:	63	0.08
Dutch West Indian	9	0.01
Haitian	7	0.01
Jamaican	35	0.04
U.S. Virgin Islander	4	0.00
West Indian	8	0.01
White:	64,742	79.09
Not Hispanic (62,993)	64,156	78.37
Hispanic (526)	586	0.72
Yugoslavian	51	0.06

Deerfield

Place Type: Village
County: Lake
Population: 18,420

Ancestry/Race	Number	%
Acadian/Cajun	12	0.06
African American/Black:	81	0.44
Not Hispanic (58)	75	0.41
Hispanic (3)	6	0.03
African, sub-Saharan:	22	0.12
African	5	0.03
South African	17	0.09
Am. Ind. or Alaska Nat., not spec.	8	0.04
American Indian tribes, specified:	17	0.09
Cherokee (5)	12	0.07
Latin American Indians (1)	1	0.01
Osage	3	0.02
Sioux	1	0.01
American Indian tribes, not spec.	4	0.02
Arab:	22	0.12
Lebanese	15	0.08
Moroccan	2	0.01
Other Arab	5	0.03
Armenian	18	0.10
Asian:	546	2.96
Bangladeshi (1)	2	0.01
Chinese, ex. Taiwanese (86)	103	0.56
Filipino (69)	79	0.43
Indian (58)	71	0.39
Japanese (82)	105	0.57
Korean (151)	163	0.88
Pakistani (1)	3	0.02
Sri Lankan	1	0.01
Taiwanese (5)	8	0.04
Thai (3)	3	0.02
Vietnamese (2)	2	0.01
Other Asian, not specified (5)	6	0.03
Assyrian/Chaldean/Syriac	30	0.16
Australian	12	0.06
Austrian	312	1.69
Belgian	10	0.05
British	84	0.45
Bulgarian	23	0.12
Canadian	77	0.42
Croatian	28	0.15
Czech	132	0.71
Czechoslovakian	22	0.12
Danish	98	0.53
Dutch	267	1.44
Eastern European	444	2.40
English	1,336	7.22
European	478	2.58
Finnish	51	0.28
French, except Basque	334	1.81
French Canadian	18	0.10
German	3,264	17.65
Greek	274	1.48
Hawaii Native/Pacific Islander:	8	0.04
Micronesian: (1)	1	0.01
Guamanian/Chamorro (1)	1	0.01
Polynesian: (1)	4	0.02
Native Hawaiian (1)	4	0.02
Other Pac. Isl., not spec. (2)	3	0.02
Hispanic or Latino:	312	1.69
Central American:	22	0.12
Costa Rican	5	0.03
Guatemalan	12	0.07
Honduran	1	0.01
Salvadoran	1	0.01
Other Central American	3	0.02
Cuban	18	0.10
Dominican Republic	4	0.02
Mexican	152	0.83
Puerto Rican	24	0.13
South American:	45	0.24
Argentinean	9	0.05
Bolivian	1	0.01
Colombian	19	0.10
Ecuadorian	7	0.04
Paraguayan	1	0.01
Peruvian	1	0.01
Uruguayan	4	0.02
Venezuelan	1	0.01
Other South American	2	0.01
Other Hispanic or Latino	47	0.26
Hungarian	268	1.45
Icelander	26	0.14
Iranian	32	0.17
Irish	2,078	11.23
Israeli	119	0.64
Italian	1,217	6.58
Latvian	69	0.37
Lithuanian	317	1.71
Luxemburger	24	0.13
Northern European	33	0.18
Norwegian	343	1.85
Pennsylvania German	9	0.05
Polish	1,667	9.01
Romanian	135	0.73
Russian	2,473	13.37
Scandinavian	35	0.19
Scotch-Irish	186	1.01
Scottish	310	1.68
Slavic	19	0.10
Slovak	50	0.27
Slovene	7	0.04
Swedish	416	2.25
Swiss	54	0.29
Turkish	10	0.05
Ukrainian	179	0.97
United States or American	1,612	8.71
Welsh	108	0.58
West Indian, excl. Hispanic:	7	0.04
Belizean	7	0.04
White:	17,790	96.58
Not Hispanic (17,434)	17,544	95.24
Hispanic (228)	246	1.34
Yugoslavian	58	0.31

Des Plaines

Place Type: City
County: Cook
Population: 58,720

Ancestry/Race	Number	%
Acadian/Cajun	10	0.02
Afghan	8	0.01
African American/Black:	686	1.17
Not Hispanic (558)	630	1.07
Hispanic (36)	56	0.10
African, sub-Saharan:	23	0.04
African	23	0.04
Alaska Native tribes, specified:	3	0.01
Aleut (2)	2	0.00
Eskimo	1	0.00
Am. Ind. or Alaska Nat., not spec.	163	0.28
Albanian	80	0.14
American Indian tribes, specified:	182	0.31
Apache (3)	5	0.01
Blackfeet (1)	13	0.02

Notes: 1. Figures in the "Number" column do not add up to the total population due to: a) Ancestry/Race overlap — e.g. persons can report being both White and Irish, b) persons of Hispanic origin can report being any race, c) persons reporting two ancestries are counted in both categories. 2. Numbers in parentheses indicate the number of persons reporting this ancestry/race alone, not in combination with any other ancestry/race. 3. Refer to the Explanation of Data in the front of the book for more detailed information.

Cherokee (9)	54	0.09
Chippewa (5)	11	0.02
Choctaw (2)	4	0.01
Creek (1)	2	0.00
Crow	3	0.01
Iroquois (8)	12	0.02
Latin American Indians (16)	36	0.06
Menominee (1)	4	0.01
Navajo (1)	2	0.00
Paiute (1)	1	0.00
Pima (1)	2	0.00
Potawatomi	3	0.01
Pueblo (3)	3	0.01
Sioux (2)	4	0.01
Tohono O'Odham (2)	2	0.00
Yaqui (2)	2	0.00
Yuman	1	0.00
All other tribes (4)	18	0.03
American Indian tribes, not spec.	13	0.02
Arab:	266	0.45
Arab/Arabic	30	0.05
Egyptian	19	0.03
Iraqi	58	0.10
Jordanian	104	0.18
Lebanese	25	0.04
Palestinian	25	0.04
Syrian	5	0.01
Armenian	63	0.11
Asian:	4,885	8.32
Bangladeshi (1)	1	0.00
Cambodian (47)	50	0.09
Chinese, ex. Taiwanese (318)	356	0.61
Filipino (1,029)	1,118	1.90
Indian (2,216)	2,339	3.98
Indonesian (1)	8	0.01
Japanese (152)	204	0.35
Korean (426)	441	0.75
Laotian (1)	1	0.00
Malaysian (1)	1	0.00
Pakistani (66)	101	0.17
Sri Lankan (1)	4	0.01
Taiwanese (15)	15	0.03
Thai (29)	33	0.06
Vietnamese (122)	126	0.21
Other Asian, specified (1)	1	0.00
Other Asian, not specified (34)	86	0.15
Assyrian/Chaldean/Syriac	152	0.26
Australian	4	0.01
Austrian	462	0.79
Belgian	172	0.29
Brazilian	32	0.05
British	193	0.33
Bulgarian	149	0.25
Canadian	48	0.08
Croatian	164	0.28
Cypriot	17	0.03
Czech	509	0.87
Czechoslovakian	219	0.37
Danish	558	0.95
Dutch	583	0.99
Eastern European	14	0.02
English	3,038	5.18
European	269	0.46
Finnish	178	0.30
French, except Basque	1,065	1.81
French Canadian	212	0.36
German	12,622	21.50
Greek	1,423	2.42
Hawaii Native/Pacific Islander:	42	0.07
Micronesian:	1	0.00
Guamanian/Chamorro	1	0.00
Polynesian: (7)	25	0.04
Native Hawaiian (6)	23	0.04
Samoan (1)	2	0.00
Other Pac. Isl., not spec. (6)	16	0.03
Hispanic or Latino:	8,229	14.01
Central American:	255	0.43
Costa Rican	15	0.03
Guatemalan	103	0.18
Honduran	25	0.04
Nicaraguan	5	0.01
Panamanian	12	0.02
Salvadoran	73	0.12
Other Central American	22	0.04
Cuban	124	0.21
Dominican Republic	6	0.01
Mexican	6,538	11.13
Puerto Rican	419	0.71
South American:	304	0.52
Argentinean	12	0.02
Bolivian	25	0.04
Chilean	13	0.02
Colombian	78	0.13
Ecuadorian	87	0.15
Paraguayan	2	0.00
Peruvian	38	0.06
Uruguayan	6	0.01
Venezuelan	10	0.02
Other South American	34	0.06
Other Hispanic or Latino	583	0.99
Hungarian	340	0.58
Iranian	58	0.10
Irish	8,100	13.80
Israeli	5	0.01
Italian	6,207	10.58
Latvian	105	0.18
Lithuanian	353	0.60
Luxemburger	129	0.22
Macedonian	22	0.04
Northern European	18	0.03
Norwegian	1,140	1.94
Polish	10,703	18.23
Portuguese	43	0.07
Romanian	408	0.70
Russian	513	0.87
Scandinavian	175	0.30
Scotch-Irish	454	0.77
Scottish	707	1.20
Serbian	122	0.21
Slavic	20	0.03
Slovak	258	0.44
Slovene	26	0.04
Swedish	1,938	3.30
Swiss	149	0.25
Turkish	34	0.06
Ukrainian	532	0.91
United States or American	1,381	2.35
Welsh	220	0.37
West Indian, excl. Hispanic:	20	0.03
Bahamian	5	0.01
Haitian	15	0.03
White:	50,563	86.11
Not Hispanic (44,635)	45,194	76.97
Hispanic (4,951)	5,369	9.14
Yugoslavian	181	0.31

Dixon

Place Type: City
County: Lee
Population: 15,941

Ancestry/Race	Number	%
African American/Black:	1,757	11.02
Not Hispanic (1,660)	1,733	10.87
Hispanic (11)	24	0.15
African, sub-Saharan:	12	0.08
African	12	0.08
Am. Ind. or Alaska Nat., not spec.	32	0.20
Albanian	34	0.21
American Indian tribes, specified:	54	0.34
Blackfeet	2	0.01
Cherokee (1)	29	0.18
Cheyenne	1	0.01
Chickasaw	1	0.01
Chippewa (1)	5	0.03
Choctaw (1)	2	0.01
Crow	1	0.01
Latin American Indians (2)	3	0.02
Seminole (1)	1	0.01
Shoshone	1	0.01
Sioux (2)	8	0.05
American Indian tribes, not spec.	6	0.04
Arab:	9	0.06
Arab/Arabic	6	0.04
Jordanian	3	0.02
Asian:	176	1.10
Chinese, ex. Taiwanese (29)	29	0.18
Filipino (23)	30	0.19
Hmong (4)	17	0.11
Indian (17)	23	0.14
Japanese (4)	11	0.07
Korean (7)	10	0.06
Laotian (10)	16	0.10
Pakistani (5)	5	0.03
Vietnamese (8)	8	0.05
Other Asian, specified (1)	7	0.04
Other Asian, not specified (16)	20	0.13
Assyrian/Chaldean/Syriac	6	0.04
Austrian	68	0.43
Belgian	18	0.11
British	77	0.48
Canadian	16	0.10
Czech	62	0.39
Danish	106	0.66
Dutch	520	3.26
English	1,385	8.67
European	54	0.34
Finnish	30	0.19
French, except Basque	432	2.71
French Canadian	75	0.47
German	4,355	27.27
Greek	32	0.20
Hawaii Native/Pacific Islander:	14	0.09
Polynesian: (8)	8	0.05
Native Hawaiian (1)	1	0.01
Samoan (7)	7	0.04
Other Pac. Isl., specified	6	0.04
Hispanic or Latino:	685	4.30
Central American:	7	0.04
Guatemalan	3	0.02
Salvadoran	4	0.03
Cuban	9	0.06
Mexican	309	1.94
Puerto Rican	19	0.12
South American:	2	0.01
Peruvian	2	0.01
Other Hispanic or Latino	339	2.13
Hungarian	143	0.90
Irish	2,501	15.66
Italian	453	2.84
Lithuanian	17	0.11
Norwegian	349	2.19
Pennsylvania German	20	0.13
Polish	249	1.56
Romanian	20	0.13
Russian	12	0.08
Scandinavian	26	0.16
Scotch-Irish	200	1.25
Scottish	292	1.83
Slovak	15	0.09
Slovene	6	0.04
Swedish	511	3.20
Swiss	120	0.75
Ukrainian	8	0.05
United States or American	931	5.83
Welsh	61	0.38
White:	13,920	87.32
Not Hispanic (13,290)	13,420	84.19
Hispanic (472)	500	3.14

Dolton

Place Type: Village
County: Cook
Population: 25,614

Ancestry/Race	Number	%
African American/Black:	21,293	83.13
Not Hispanic (20,973)	21,159	82.61

Notes: 1. Figures in the "Number" column do not add up to the total population due to: a) Ancestry/Race overlap — e.g. persons can report being both White and Irish, b) persons of Hispanic origin can report being any race, c) persons reporting two ancestries are counted in both categories. 2. Numbers in parentheses indicate the number of persons reporting this ancestry/race alone, not in combination with any other ancestry/race. 3. Refer to the Explanation of Data in the front of the book for more detailed information.

Ancestry/Race	Number	%
Hispanic (125)	134	0.52
African, sub-Saharan:	655	2.54
African	414	1.61
Kenyan	17	0.07
Nigerian	224	0.87
Am. Ind. or Alaska Nat., not spec.	74	0.29
American Indian tribes, specified:	51	0.20
Apache	1	0.00
Blackfeet	5	0.02
Cherokee	27	0.11
Choctaw	2	0.01
Crow	1	0.00
Latin American Indians	4	0.02
Menominee	1	0.00
Potawatomi	4	0.02
Sioux	2	0.01
All other tribes (1)	4	0.02
American Indian tribes, not spec.	4	0.02
Asian:	204	0.80
Chinese, ex. Taiwanese (5)	13	0.05
Filipino (85)	117	0.46
Indian (3)	14	0.05
Japanese (3)	3	0.01
Korean (11)	15	0.06
Laotian (1)	1	0.00
Pakistani (5)	8	0.03
Thai (2)	3	0.01
Vietnamese (25)	26	0.10
Other Asian, not specified (1)	4	0.02
Belgian	7	0.03
British	23	0.09
Bulgarian	6	0.02
Czech	65	0.25
Czechoslovakian	27	0.10
Danish	60	0.23
Dutch	155	0.60
English	315	1.22
European	22	0.09
French, except Basque	77	0.30
French Canadian	35	0.14
German	937	3.64
Greek	27	0.10
Hawaii Native/Pacific Islander:	11	0.04
Micronesian:	2	0.01
Guamanian/Chamorro	2	0.01
Polynesian: (3)	4	0.02
Native Hawaiian (1)	1	0.00
Samoan (2)	3	0.01
Other Pac. Isl., not spec. (1)	5	0.02
Hispanic or Latino:	791	3.09
Central American:	15	0.06
Guatemalan	7	0.03
Honduran	4	0.02
Panamanian	3	0.01
Salvadoran	1	0.00
Cuban	19	0.07
Dominican Republic	2	0.01
Mexican	581	2.27
Puerto Rican	78	0.30
South American:	18	0.07
Bolivian	5	0.02
Chilean	1	0.00
Colombian	2	0.01
Ecuadorian	9	0.04
Peruvian	1	0.00
Other Hispanic or Latino	78	0.30
Hungarian	35	0.14
Irish	616	2.39
Italian	370	1.44
Lithuanian	40	0.16
Norwegian	39	0.15
Polish	657	2.55
Russian	16	0.06
Scandinavian	8	0.03
Scotch-Irish	55	0.21
Scottish	94	0.37
Serbian	7	0.03
Slovak	49	0.19
Swedish	322	1.25
Swiss	13	0.05
Ukrainian	30	0.12
United States or American	170	0.66
Welsh	17	0.07
West Indian, excl. Hispanic:	259	1.01
Belizean	10	0.04
Haitian	108	0.42
Jamaican	141	0.55
White:	3,837	14.98
Not Hispanic (3,390)	3,529	13.78
Hispanic (281)	308	1.20
Yugoslavian	55	0.21

Downers Grove

Place Type: Village
County: Du Page
Population: 48,724

Ancestry/Race	Number	%
Acadian/Cajun	8	0.02
African American/Black:	1,043	2.14
Not Hispanic (911)	998	2.05
Hispanic (25)	45	0.09
African, sub-Saharan:	83	0.17
African	71	0.15
Nigerian	4	0.01
Other sub-Saharan African	8	0.02
Alaska Native tribes, specified:	4	0.01
Aleut (4)	4	0.01
Am. Ind. or Alaska Nat., not spec.	60	0.12
Albanian	40	0.08
American Indian tribes, specified:	85	0.17
Blackfeet (1)	2	0.00
Cherokee (7)	29	0.06
Cheyenne	1	0.00
Chippewa (6)	15	0.03
Choctaw (2)	2	0.00
Iroquois (7)	11	0.02
Latin American Indians (5)	8	0.02
Ottawa	1	0.00
Potawatomi	2	0.00
Pueblo (2)	2	0.00
Sioux	3	0.01
All other tribes (3)	9	0.02
American Indian tribes, not spec.	9	0.02
Arab:	269	0.55
Arab/Arabic	27	0.06
Egyptian	143	0.29
Lebanese	50	0.10
Syrian	26	0.05
Other Arab	23	0.05
Armenian	8	0.02
Asian:	3,069	6.30
Bangladeshi (4)	4	0.01
Cambodian (15)	19	0.04
Chinese, ex. Taiwanese (506)	573	1.18
Filipino (545)	620	1.27
Indian (1,211)	1,274	2.61
Indonesian (1)	2	0.00
Japanese (46)	73	0.15
Korean (150)	173	0.36
Malaysian (1)	2	0.00
Pakistani (97)	108	0.22
Sri Lankan (3)	5	0.01
Taiwanese (44)	49	0.10
Thai (38)	50	0.10
Vietnamese (54)	58	0.12
Other Asian, specified (8)	8	0.02
Other Asian, not specified (12)	51	0.10
Australian	8	0.02
Austrian	291	0.60
Belgian	163	0.34
British	171	0.35
Bulgarian	39	0.08
Canadian	112	0.23
Celtic	11	0.02
Croatian	488	1.00
Czech	2,563	5.27
Czechoslovakian	374	0.77
Danish	602	1.24
Dutch	969	1.99
Eastern European	55	0.11
English	4,200	8.64
European	573	1.18
Finnish	104	0.21
French, except Basque	1,268	2.61
French Canadian	346	0.71
German	12,388	25.47
Greek	395	0.81
Hawaii Native/Pacific Islander:	17	0.03
Micronesian: (2)	2	0.00
Guamanian/Chamorro (2)	2	0.00
Polynesian: (2)	7	0.01
Native Hawaiian (2)	7	0.01
Other Pac. Isl., not spec. (2)	8	0.02
Hispanic or Latino:	1,747	3.59
Central American:	26	0.05
Costa Rican	1	0.00
Guatemalan	11	0.02
Honduran	6	0.01
Nicaraguan	1	0.00
Salvadoran	1	0.00
Other Central American	6	0.01
Cuban	42	0.09
Dominican Republic	3	0.01
Mexican	1,225	2.51
Puerto Rican	151	0.31
South American:	97	0.20
Argentinean	13	0.03
Bolivian	7	0.01
Chilean	14	0.03
Colombian	14	0.03
Ecuadorian	6	0.01
Peruvian	24	0.05
Uruguayan	1	0.00
Venezuelan	12	0.02
Other South American	6	0.01
Other Hispanic or Latino	203	0.42
Hungarian	446	0.92
Iranian	154	0.32
Irish	9,867	20.29
Italian	5,271	10.84
Latvian	15	0.03
Lithuanian	911	1.87
Luxemburger	36	0.07
Macedonian	26	0.05
Northern European	57	0.12
Norwegian	933	1.92
Polish	7,247	14.90
Portuguese	16	0.03
Romanian	94	0.19
Russian	364	0.75
Scandinavian	158	0.32
Scotch-Irish	846	1.74
Scottish	874	1.80
Serbian	45	0.09
Slavic	5	0.01
Slovak	448	0.92
Slovene	206	0.42
Swedish	2,072	4.26
Swiss	191	0.39
Turkish	28	0.06
Ukrainian	401	0.82
United States or American	1,294	2.66
Welsh	356	0.73
White:	44,397	91.12
Not Hispanic (42,777)	43,142	88.54
Hispanic (1,147)	1,255	2.58
Yugoslavian	116	0.24

East Moline

Place Type: City
County: Rock Island
Population: 20,333

Ancestry/Race	Number	%
African American/Black:	1,719	8.45
Not Hispanic (1,446)	1,627	8.00
Hispanic (47)	92	0.45

Notes: 1. Figures in the "Number" column do not add up to the total population due to: a) Ancestry/Race overlap — e.g. persons can report being both White and Irish, b) persons of Hispanic origin can report being any race, c) persons reporting two ancestries are counted in both categories. 2. Numbers in parentheses indicate the number of persons reporting this ancestry/race alone, not in combination with any other ancestry/race. 3. Refer to the Explanation of Data in the front of the book for more detailed information.

African, sub-Saharan:	85	0.42
African	85	0.42
Alaska Native tribes, not specified	1	0.00
Am. Ind. or Alaska Nat., not spec.	62	0.30
Albanian	41	0.20
American Indian tribes, specified:	92	0.45
Apache (1)	1	0.00
Blackfeet (2)	6	0.03
Cherokee (9)	35	0.17
Chippewa (1)	1	0.00
Choctaw (1)	5	0.02
Colville	1	0.00
Cree	1	0.00
Creek	1	0.00
Crow	2	0.01
Latin American Indians (2)	11	0.05
Sioux (12)	15	0.07
Yaqui	3	0.01
All other tribes (6)	10	0.05
American Indian tribes, not spec.	8	0.04
Arab:	20	0.10
Lebanese	8	0.04
Syrian	12	0.06
Armenian	8	0.04
Asian:	533	2.62
Cambodian (3)	3	0.01
Chinese, ex. Taiwanese (40)	57	0.28
Filipino (21)	35	0.17
Indian (214)	226	1.11
Japanese (12)	20	0.10
Korean (12)	21	0.10
Laotian (34)	35	0.17
Pakistani (3)	4	0.02
Thai (5)	8	0.04
Vietnamese (92)	98	0.48
Other Asian, specified	1	0.00
Other Asian, not specified (14)	25	0.12
Austrian	6	0.03
Belgian	1,490	7.32
British	35	0.17
Bulgarian	19	0.09
Canadian	19	0.09
Celtic	7	0.03
Croatian	64	0.31
Czech	129	0.63
Czechoslovakian	46	0.23
Danish	85	0.42
Dutch	395	1.94
English	1,834	9.01
European	121	0.59
French, except Basque	323	1.59
French Canadian	54	0.27
German	4,545	22.32
Greek	133	0.65
Hawaii Native/Pacific Islander:	7	0.03
Polynesian: (1)	1	0.00
Samoan (1)	1	0.00
Other Pac. Isl., not spec.	6	0.03
Hispanic or Latino:	3,081	15.15
Central American:	31	0.15
Guatemalan	5	0.02
Honduran	8	0.04
Nicaraguan	1	0.00
Salvadoran	3	0.01
Other Central American	14	0.07
Cuban	15	0.07
Mexican	2,718	13.37
Puerto Rican	32	0.16
South American:	10	0.05
Argentinean	5	0.02
Bolivian	3	0.01
Colombian	1	0.00
Venezuelan	1	0.00
Other Hispanic or Latino	275	1.35
Hungarian	53	0.26
Irish	2,231	10.96
Italian	385	1.89
Lithuanian	68	0.33
Luxemburger	7	0.03
Northern European	31	0.15
Norwegian	309	1.52
Pennsylvania German	107	0.53
Polish	361	1.77
Romanian	9	0.04
Russian	40	0.20
Scandinavian	30	0.15
Scotch-Irish	296	1.45
Scottish	287	1.41
Slovak	8	0.04
Slovene	34	0.17
Swedish	1,293	6.35
Swiss	60	0.29
Ukrainian	51	0.25
United States or American	1,162	5.71
Welsh	139	0.68
White:	16,732	82.29
Not Hispanic (14,979)	15,269	75.09
Hispanic (1,295)	1,463	7.20
Yugoslavian	17	0.08

East Peoria

Place Type: City
County: Tazewell
Population: 22,638

Ancestry/Race	Number	%
African American/Black:	153	0.68
Not Hispanic (101)	145	0.64
Hispanic (5)	8	0.04
African, sub-Saharan:	16	0.07
African	16	0.07
Alaska Native tribes, specified:	3	0.01
Eskimo (3)	3	0.01
Am. Ind. or Alaska Nat., not spec.	43	0.19
Alsatian	6	0.03
American Indian tribes, specified:	96	0.42
Apache	8	0.04
Blackfeet	10	0.04
Cherokee (12)	50	0.22
Cheyenne	1	0.00
Chippewa (1)	1	0.00
Choctaw	2	0.01
Comanche (5)	5	0.02
Iroquois (1)	2	0.01
Navajo (2)	2	0.01
Osage	1	0.00
Potawatomi (5)	5	0.02
Sioux (3)	3	0.01
All other tribes (3)	6	0.03
American Indian tribes, not spec.	8	0.04
Arab:	187	0.82
Lebanese	187	0.82
Asian:	184	0.81
Chinese, ex. Taiwanese (22)	27	0.12
Filipino (25)	31	0.14
Hmong (2)	2	0.01
Indian (23)	26	0.11
Japanese (8)	20	0.09
Korean (24)	25	0.11
Laotian (2)	3	0.01
Taiwanese	1	0.00
Thai (2)	3	0.01
Vietnamese (30)	34	0.15
Other Asian, not specified (8)	12	0.05
Australian	9	0.04
Austrian	15	0.07
Belgian	17	0.07
British	79	0.35
Croatian	28	0.12
Czech	66	0.29
Czechoslovakian	50	0.22
Danish	70	0.31
Dutch	484	2.11
English	3,013	13.16
European	169	0.74
Finnish	16	0.07
French, except Basque	805	3.52
French Canadian	56	0.24
German	6,814	29.77
Greek	60	0.26
Hawaii Native/Pacific Islander:	4	0.02
Micronesian: (1)	2	0.01
Guamanian/Chamorro (1)	2	0.01
Polynesian: (1)	1	0.00
Samoan (1)	1	0.00
Other Pac. Isl., not spec.	1	0.00
Hispanic or Latino:	293	1.29
Central American:	10	0.04
Costa Rican	4	0.02
Nicaraguan	3	0.01
Panamanian	1	0.00
Salvadoran	2	0.01
Cuban	2	0.01
Mexican	194	0.86
Puerto Rican	21	0.09
South American:	3	0.01
Argentinean	1	0.00
Bolivian	1	0.00
Paraguayan	1	0.00
Other Hispanic or Latino	63	0.28
Hungarian	84	0.37
Iranian	11	0.05
Irish	3,246	14.18
Italian	597	2.61
Lithuanian	22	0.10
Macedonian	10	0.04
Northern European	30	0.13
Norwegian	274	1.20
Pennsylvania German	40	0.17
Polish	377	1.65
Portuguese	11	0.05
Romanian	13	0.06
Russian	54	0.24
Scandinavian	41	0.18
Scotch-Irish	446	1.95
Scottish	459	2.01
Serbian	15	0.07
Slovene	8	0.03
Swedish	415	1.81
Swiss	118	0.52
United States or American	2,795	12.21
Welsh	127	0.55
White:	22,216	98.14
Not Hispanic (21,867)	22,025	97.29
Hispanic (164)	191	0.84
Yugoslavian	36	0.16

East Saint Louis

Place Type: City
County: Saint Clair
Population: 31,542

Ancestry/Race	Number	%
African American/Black:	30,983	98.23
Not Hispanic (30,702)	30,845	97.79
Hispanic (127)	138	0.44
African, sub-Saharan:	350	1.11
African	350	1.11
Am. Ind. or Alaska Nat., not spec.	89	0.28
American Indian tribes, specified:	50	0.16
Blackfeet	10	0.03
Cherokee (7)	30	0.10
Chickasaw	1	0.00
Choctaw	1	0.00
Comanche	2	0.01
Latin American Indians	3	0.01
Pueblo	1	0.00
Sioux (1)	1	0.00
All other tribes	1	0.00
American Indian tribes, not spec.	13	0.04
Arab:	4	0.01
Palestinian	4	0.01
Asian:	53	0.17
Chinese, ex. Taiwanese (2)	3	0.01
Filipino (3)	7	0.02
Indian (12)	22	0.07
Japanese (2)	6	0.02
Korean (4)	4	0.01

Notes: 1. Figures in the "Number" column do not add up to the total population due to: a) Ancestry/Race overlap — e.g. persons can report being both White and Irish, b) persons of Hispanic origin can report being any race, c) persons reporting two ancestries are counted in both categories. 2. Numbers in parentheses indicate the number of persons reporting this ancestry/race alone, not in combination with any other ancestry/race. 3. Refer to the Explanation of Data in the front of the book for more detailed information.

Ancestry/Race	Number	%
Thai	1	0.00
Vietnamese (1)	2	0.01
Other Asian, specified	2	0.01
Other Asian, not specified	6	0.02
English	86	0.27
French, except Basque	20	0.06
French Canadian	24	0.08
German	117	0.37
Hawaii Native/Pacific Islander:	12	0.04
Polynesian: (4)	5	0.02
Native Hawaiian (4)	4	0.01
Samoan	1	0.00
Other Pac. Isl., specified	2	0.01
Other Pac. Isl., not spec. (5)	5	0.02
Hispanic or Latino:	230	0.73
Central American:	1	0.00
Other Central American	1	0.00
Cuban	7	0.02
Mexican	131	0.42
Puerto Rican	8	0.03
Other Hispanic or Latino	83	0.26
Irish	117	0.37
Italian	6	0.02
Lithuanian	16	0.05
Polish	21	0.07
Scotch-Irish	3	0.01
Ukrainian	8	0.03
United States or American	182	0.58
West Indian, excl. Hispanic:	20	0.06
Haitian	11	0.03
Jamaican	9	0.03
White:	472	1.50
Not Hispanic (363)	442	1.40
Hispanic (24)	30	0.10

Edwardsville

Place Type: City
County: Madison
Population: 21,491

Ancestry/Race	Number	%
African American/Black:	1,988	9.25
Not Hispanic (1,845)	1,970	9.17
Hispanic (16)	18	0.08
African, sub-Saharan:	38	0.18
African	17	0.08
Zimbabwean	10	0.05
Other sub-Saharan African	11	0.05
Alaska Native tribes, specified:	1	0.00
Alaska Athabascan (1)	1	0.00
Am. Ind. or Alaska Nat., not spec.	21	0.10
Albanian	23	0.11
American Indian tribes, specified:	95	0.44
Apache (2)	2	0.01
Blackfeet (1)	4	0.02
Cherokee (15)	59	0.27
Cheyenne	1	0.00
Chickasaw (1)	1	0.00
Chippewa (1)	1	0.00
Choctaw (2)	5	0.02
Creek (1)	1	0.00
Iroquois (1)	2	0.01
Latin American Indians (3)	4	0.02
Navajo	1	0.00
Potawatomi (1)	2	0.01
Seminole (3)	3	0.01
Sioux	5	0.02
All other tribes (2)	4	0.02
American Indian tribes, not spec.	20	0.09
Arab:	104	0.50
Arab/Arabic	35	0.17
Jordanian	10	0.05
Lebanese	22	0.11
Syrian	37	0.18
Armenian	7	0.03
Asian:	445	2.07
Bangladeshi (3)	3	0.01
Cambodian (1)	1	0.00
Chinese, ex. Taiwanese (112)	128	0.60
Filipino (18)	24	0.11
Indian (111)	125	0.58
Indonesian (2)	2	0.01
Japanese (14)	31	0.14
Korean (33)	40	0.19
Laotian (3)	3	0.01
Malaysian (1)	5	0.02
Pakistani (18)	24	0.11
Sri Lankan (1)	1	0.00
Taiwanese (8)	15	0.07
Thai (10)	11	0.05
Vietnamese (8)	9	0.04
Other Asian, specified (4)	4	0.02
Other Asian, not specified (10)	19	0.09
Australian	8	0.04
Austrian	133	0.64
Belgian	7	0.03
British	59	0.28
Bulgarian	9	0.04
Canadian	34	0.16
Croatian	123	0.59
Czech	301	1.44
Czechoslovakian	70	0.34
Danish	107	0.51
Dutch	330	1.58
Eastern European	8	0.04
English	2,421	11.60
European	164	0.79
Finnish	8	0.04
French, except Basque	749	3.59
French Canadian	34	0.16
German	7,068	33.86
Greek	19	0.09
Hawaii Native/Pacific Islander:	20	0.09
Micronesian: (2)	2	0.01
Guamanian/Chamorro (2)	2	0.01
Polynesian: (3)	14	0.07
Native Hawaiian (1)	9	0.04
Samoan (2)	5	0.02
Other Pac. Isl., not spec. (1)	4	0.02
Hispanic or Latino:	215	1.00
Central American:	17	0.08
Costa Rican	1	0.00
Guatemalan	6	0.03
Nicaraguan	4	0.02
Panamanian	3	0.01
Other Central American	3	0.01
Cuban	6	0.03
Dominican Republic	2	0.01
Mexican	105	0.49
Puerto Rican	14	0.07
South American:	17	0.08
Argentinean	1	0.00
Colombian	6	0.03
Ecuadorian	7	0.03
Peruvian	2	0.01
Venezuelan	1	0.00
Other Hispanic or Latino	54	0.25
Hungarian	81	0.39
Iranian	14	0.07
Irish	2,699	12.93
Italian	1,115	5.34
Lithuanian	134	0.64
Macedonian	15	0.07
Maltese	39	0.19
Northern European	24	0.11
Norwegian	201	0.96
Polish	851	4.08
Portuguese	20	0.10
Romanian	25	0.12
Russian	86	0.41
Scandinavian	19	0.09
Scotch-Irish	428	2.05
Scottish	321	1.54
Slavic	32	0.15
Slovak	104	0.50
Slovene	13	0.06
Swedish	170	0.81
Swiss	67	0.32
Turkish	24	0.11
Ukrainian	9	0.04
United States or American	1,057	5.06
Welsh	133	0.64
West Indian, excl. Hispanic:	52	0.25
Belizean	6	0.03
Bermudan	10	0.05
Jamaican	29	0.14
West Indian	7	0.03
White:	19,101	88.88
Not Hispanic (18,720)	18,954	88.20
Hispanic (127)	147	0.68

Effingham

Place Type: City
County: Effingham
Population: 12,384

Ancestry/Race	Number	%
Acadian/Cajun	25	0.20
African American/Black:	62	0.50
Not Hispanic (44)	58	0.47
Hispanic	4	0.03
African, sub-Saharan:	26	0.21
Ghanian	26	0.21
Am. Ind. or Alaska Nat., not spec.	24	0.19
American Indian tribes, specified:	31	0.25
Cherokee (2)	19	0.15
Comanche (1)	1	0.01
Kiowa (6)	7	0.06
Latin American Indians	2	0.02
Potawatomi (1)	1	0.01
All other tribes (1)	1	0.01
American Indian tribes, not spec.	5	0.04
Arab:	6	0.05
Syrian	6	0.05
Armenian	7	0.06
Asian:	91	0.73
Chinese, ex. Taiwanese (15)	22	0.18
Filipino (8)	11	0.09
Indian (27)	29	0.23
Japanese	1	0.01
Korean (9)	9	0.07
Pakistani (3)	3	0.02
Sri Lankan (2)	2	0.02
Vietnamese (6)	9	0.07
Other Asian, not specified (1)	5	0.04
Australian	13	0.10
Austrian	20	0.16
Belgian	23	0.18
British	61	0.49
Croatian	7	0.06
Czech	33	0.27
Czechoslovakian	11	0.09
Danish	17	0.14
Dutch	236	1.90
Eastern European	21	0.17
English	1,267	10.19
European	68	0.55
Finnish	6	0.05
French, except Basque	322	2.59
French Canadian	59	0.47
German	4,633	37.25
Greek	5	0.04
Hawaii Native/Pacific Islander:	8	0.06
Micronesian:	1	0.01
Guamanian/Chamorro	1	0.01
Polynesian:	7	0.06
Native Hawaiian	7	0.06
Hispanic or Latino:	129	1.04
Central American:	2	0.02
Honduran	1	0.01
Panamanian	1	0.01
Cuban	1	0.01
Mexican	84	0.68
Puerto Rican	5	0.04
South American:	2	0.02
Bolivian	1	0.01
Peruvian	1	0.01
Other Hispanic or Latino	35	0.28

Notes: 1. Figures in the "Number" column do not add up to the total population due to: a) Ancestry/Race overlap — e.g. persons can report being both White and Irish, b) persons of Hispanic origin can report being any race, c) persons reporting two ancestries are counted in both categories. 2. Numbers in parentheses indicate the number of persons reporting this ancestry/race alone, not in combination with any other ancestry/race. 3. Refer to the Explanation of Data in the front of the book for more detailed information.

Hungarian	5	0.04
Irish	1,275	10.25
Italian	296	2.38
Norwegian	96	0.77
Pennsylvania German	6	0.05
Polish	155	1.25
Russian	19	0.15
Scandinavian	16	0.13
Scotch-Irish	257	2.07
Scottish	115	0.92
Slavic	5	0.04
Swedish	96	0.77
Swiss	41	0.33
Ukrainian	30	0.24
United States or American	1,120	9.01
Welsh	87	0.70
White:	12,185	98.39
Not Hispanic (12,049)	12,110	97.79
Hispanic (61)	75	0.61
Yugoslavian	13	0.10

Elgin

Place Type: City
County: Kane
Population: 94,487

Ancestry/Race	Number	%
African American/Black:	7,108	7.52
Not Hispanic (6,100)	6,621	7.01
Hispanic (327)	487	0.52
African, sub-Saharan:	283	0.30
African	245	0.26
Ethiopian	38	0.04
Alaska Native tribes, specified:	4	0.00
Aleut (1)	1	0.00
Eskimo (1)	3	0.00
Am. Ind. or Alaska Nat., not spec.	347	0.37
Albanian	116	0.12
American Indian tribes, specified:	344	0.36
Apache (2)	9	0.01
Blackfeet (1)	12	0.01
Cherokee (15)	84	0.09
Cheyenne	2	0.00
Chippewa (12)	24	0.03
Choctaw (4)	18	0.02
Comanche	1	0.00
Creek	1	0.00
Delaware (2)	2	0.00
Iroquois (4)	11	0.01
Latin American Indians (99)	113	0.12
Menominee (3)	4	0.00
Navajo (1)	1	0.00
Osage	1	0.00
Ottawa (1)	2	0.00
Potawatomi (6)	12	0.01
Pueblo (4)	4	0.00
Seminole	1	0.00
Shoshone	1	0.00
Sioux (2)	9	0.01
Tohono O'Odham	1	0.00
All other tribes (6)	31	0.03
American Indian tribes, not spec.	30	0.03
Arab:	188	0.20
Arab/Arabic	12	0.01
Egyptian	22	0.02
Iraqi	21	0.02
Jordanian	10	0.01
Lebanese	25	0.03
Syrian	89	0.09
Other Arab	9	0.01
Armenian	87	0.09
Asian:	4,265	4.51
Cambodian (69)	69	0.07
Chinese, ex. Taiwanese (237)	301	0.32
Filipino (540)	648	0.69
Hmong (7)	9	0.01
Indian (604)	682	0.72
Indonesian (2)	2	0.00
Japanese (62)	104	0.11
Korean (124)	162	0.17
Laotian (1,355)	1,507	1.59
Malaysian (6)	9	0.01
Pakistani (152)	198	0.21
Taiwanese (7)	8	0.01
Thai (62)	84	0.09
Vietnamese (188)	221	0.23
Other Asian, specified (10)	14	0.01
Other Asian, not specified (153)	247	0.26
Assyrian/Chaldean/Syriac	334	0.36
Australian	52	0.06
Austrian	301	0.32
Belgian	163	0.17
Brazilian	35	0.04
British	240	0.26
Bulgarian	62	0.07
Canadian	173	0.18
Croatian	65	0.07
Czech	833	0.89
Czechoslovakian	265	0.28
Danish	516	0.55
Dutch	1,115	1.19
English	5,289	5.63
Estonian	13	0.01
European	474	0.50
Finnish	80	0.09
French, except Basque	1,667	1.78
French Canadian	454	0.48
German	20,620	21.96
Greek	520	0.55
Hawaii Native/Pacific Islander:	133	0.14
Micronesian: (19)	23	0.02
Guamanian/Chamorro (19)	23	0.02
Polynesian: (25)	41	0.04
Native Hawaiian (10)	23	0.02
Samoan (14)	17	0.02
Other Polynesian (1)	1	0.00
Other Pac. Isl., not spec. (14)	69	0.07
Hispanic or Latino:	32,430	34.32
Central American:	295	0.31
Costa Rican	1	0.00
Guatemalan	116	0.12
Honduran	32	0.03
Nicaraguan	5	0.01
Panamanian	10	0.01
Salvadoran	107	0.11
Other Central American	24	0.03
Cuban	112	0.12
Dominican Republic	33	0.03
Mexican	27,444	29.05
Puerto Rican	2,355	2.49
South American:	182	0.19
Argentinean	6	0.01
Bolivian	2	0.00
Chilean	9	0.01
Colombian	95	0.10
Ecuadorian	32	0.03
Paraguayan	1	0.00
Peruvian	28	0.03
Venezuelan	4	0.00
Other South American	5	0.01
Other Hispanic or Latino	2,009	2.13
Hungarian	553	0.59
Icelander	16	0.02
Iranian	61	0.06
Irish	9,239	9.84
Italian	4,584	4.88
Latvian	14	0.01
Lithuanian	296	0.32
Luxemburger	60	0.06
Macedonian	30	0.03
Northern European	20	0.02
Norwegian	1,822	1.94
Pennsylvania German	28	0.03
Polish	5,910	6.29
Portuguese	23	0.02
Romanian	46	0.05
Russian	427	0.45
Scandinavian	133	0.14
Scotch-Irish	997	1.06
Scottish	1,098	1.17
Serbian	123	0.13
Slavic	33	0.04
Slovak	184	0.20
Slovene	48	0.05
Swedish	2,978	3.17
Swiss	530	0.56
Turkish	22	0.02
Ukrainian	255	0.27
United States or American	2,753	2.93
Welsh	355	0.38
West Indian, excl. Hispanic:	86	0.09
Jamaican	86	0.09
White:	68,992	73.02
Not Hispanic (50,831)	51,894	54.92
Hispanic (15,769)	17,098	18.10
Yugoslavian	138	0.15

Elk Grove Village

Place Type: Village
County: Cook
Population: 34,727

Ancestry/Race	Number	%
African American/Black:	559	1.61
Not Hispanic (481)	541	1.56
Hispanic (9)	18	0.05
African, sub-Saharan:	20	0.06
African	7	0.02
Nigerian	13	0.04
Am. Ind. or Alaska Nat., not spec.	49	0.14
American Indian tribes, specified:	55	0.16
Apache (1)	3	0.01
Blackfeet (1)	3	0.01
Cherokee (5)	17	0.05
Chippewa (3)	6	0.02
Choctaw (5)	5	0.01
Creek	4	0.01
Iroquois (1)	1	0.00
Latin American Indians (2)	5	0.01
Menominee (2)	4	0.01
Sioux (1)	3	0.01
Tohono O'Odham	1	0.00
All other tribes	3	0.01
American Indian tribes, not spec.	9	0.03
Arab:	160	0.46
Arab/Arabic	39	0.11
Egyptian	21	0.06
Lebanese	47	0.14
Palestinian	10	0.03
Syrian	43	0.12
Armenian	39	0.11
Asian:	3,301	9.51
Cambodian	2	0.01
Chinese, ex. Taiwanese (331)	389	1.12
Filipino (462)	514	1.48
Indian (1,135)	1,161	3.34
Indonesian (6)	6	0.02
Japanese (605)	676	1.95
Korean (364)	381	1.10
Laotian (1)	1	0.00
Malaysian (1)	1	0.00
Pakistani (42)	63	0.18
Taiwanese (10)	10	0.03
Thai (12)	17	0.05
Vietnamese (22)	32	0.09
Other Asian, specified (3)	3	0.01
Other Asian, not specified (23)	45	0.13
Assyrian/Chaldean/Syriac	169	0.49
Australian	9	0.03
Austrian	260	0.75
Belgian	93	0.27
Brazilian	34	0.10
British	110	0.32
Bulgarian	68	0.20
Canadian	20	0.06
Celtic	13	0.04
Croatian	51	0.15
Czech	467	1.34

Notes: 1. Figures in the "Number" column do not add up to the total population due to: a) Ancestry/Race overlap — e.g. persons can report being both White and Irish, b) persons of Hispanic origin can report being any race, c) persons reporting two ancestries are counted in both categories. 2. Numbers in parentheses indicate the number of persons reporting this ancestry/race alone, not in combination with any other ancestry/race. 3. Refer to the Explanation of Data in the front of the book for more detailed information.

Czechoslovakian	160	0.46
Danish	336	0.97
Dutch	342	0.98
English	2,350	6.76
Estonian	10	0.03
European	188	0.54
Finnish	110	0.32
French, except Basque	832	2.39
French Canadian	139	0.40
German	8,876	25.54
Greek	543	1.56
Hawaii Native/Pacific Islander:	26	0.07
Micronesian: (4)	4	0.01
Guamanian/Chamorro (4)	4	0.01
Polynesian: (8)	10	0.03
Native Hawaiian (7)	9	0.03
Samoan (1)	1	0.00
Other Pac. Isl., not spec. (3)	12	0.03
Hispanic or Latino:	2,165	6.23
Central American:	53	0.15
Guatemalan	27	0.08
Honduran	5	0.01
Nicaraguan	1	0.00
Panamanian	11	0.03
Salvadoran	7	0.02
Other Central American	2	0.01
Cuban	42	0.12
Dominican Republic	9	0.03
Mexican	1,458	4.20
Puerto Rican	223	0.64
South American:	145	0.42
Argentinean	26	0.07
Bolivian	3	0.01
Chilean	10	0.03
Colombian	47	0.14
Ecuadorian	43	0.12
Paraguayan	1	0.00
Peruvian	8	0.02
Venezuelan	6	0.02
Other South American	1	0.00
Other Hispanic or Latino	235	0.68
Hungarian	225	0.65
Iranian	9	0.03
Irish	5,934	17.07
Israeli	10	0.03
Italian	5,122	14.74
Latvian	7	0.02
Lithuanian	187	0.54
Luxemburger	60	0.17
Northern European	26	0.07
Norwegian	789	2.27
Polish	6,725	19.35
Portuguese	9	0.03
Romanian	80	0.23
Russian	241	0.69
Scandinavian	26	0.07
Scotch-Irish	296	0.85
Scottish	391	1.12
Serbian	101	0.29
Slavic	12	0.03
Slovak	122	0.35
Slovene	56	0.16
Swedish	1,581	4.55
Swiss	134	0.39
Ukrainian	113	0.33
United States or American	870	2.50
Welsh	170	0.49
White:	30,264	87.15
Not Hispanic (28,599)	28,901	83.22
Hispanic (1,275)	1,363	3.92
Yugoslavian	66	0.19

Elmhurst

Place Type: City
County: Du Page
Population: 42,762

Ancestry/Race	Number	%
African American/Black:	444	1.04
Not Hispanic (388)	429	1.00
Hispanic (12)	15	0.04
African, sub-Saharan:	87	0.20
African	31	0.07
Ghanian	25	0.06
Kenyan	10	0.02
South African	6	0.01
Ugandan	15	0.03
Am. Ind. or Alaska Nat., not spec.	33	0.08
Albanian	29	0.07
Alsatian	16	0.04
American Indian tribes, specified:	67	0.16
Apache (1)	4	0.01
Blackfeet	6	0.01
Cherokee (2)	29	0.07
Chippewa (3)	3	0.01
Creek	2	0.00
Iroquois (5)	6	0.01
Latin American Indians (2)	2	0.00
Navajo	1	0.00
Seminole	1	0.00
Shoshone	1	0.00
Sioux	3	0.01
All other tribes (3)	9	0.02
American Indian tribes, not spec.	10	0.02
Arab:	73	0.17
Arab/Arabic	6	0.01
Lebanese	61	0.14
Palestinian	6	0.01
Armenian	21	0.05
Asian:	1,786	4.18
Chinese, ex. Taiwanese (187)	227	0.53
Filipino (273)	316	0.74
Indian (772)	815	1.91
Indonesian	2	0.00
Japanese (53)	79	0.18
Korean (121)	128	0.30
Laotian (2)	2	0.00
Malaysian (5)	7	0.02
Pakistani (54)	73	0.17
Sri Lankan (1)	1	0.00
Taiwanese (41)	44	0.10
Thai (12)	13	0.03
Vietnamese (21)	29	0.07
Other Asian, not specified (15)	50	0.12
Assyrian/Chaldean/Syriac	20	0.05
Australian	23	0.05
Austrian	233	0.54
Belgian	76	0.18
Brazilian	13	0.03
British	114	0.27
Bulgarian	37	0.09
Canadian	60	0.14
Croatian	253	0.59
Cypriot	6	0.01
Czech	1,128	2.63
Czechoslovakian	233	0.54
Danish	333	0.78
Dutch	1,216	2.83
Eastern European	33	0.08
English	3,804	8.85
Estonian	8	0.02
European	250	0.58
Finnish	146	0.34
French, except Basque	1,254	2.92
French Canadian	181	0.42
German	11,381	26.49
Greek	725	1.69
Hawaii Native/Pacific Islander:	25	0.06
Polynesian: (4)	13	0.03
Native Hawaiian (2)	9	0.02
Samoan (2)	4	0.01
Other Pac. Isl., not spec. (4)	12	0.03
Hispanic or Latino:	1,717	4.02
Central American:	44	0.10
Costa Rican	8	0.02
Guatemalan	24	0.06
Honduran	5	0.01
Panamanian	5	0.01
Salvadoran	1	0.00
Other Central American	1	0.00
Cuban	151	0.35
Dominican Republic	6	0.01
Mexican	1,028	2.40
Puerto Rican	183	0.43
South American:	96	0.22
Argentinean	6	0.01
Bolivian	8	0.02
Colombian	28	0.07
Ecuadorian	17	0.04
Paraguayan	8	0.02
Peruvian	7	0.02
Venezuelan	15	0.04
Other South American	7	0.02
Other Hispanic or Latino	209	0.49
Hungarian	208	0.48
Icelander	17	0.04
Iranian	3	0.01
Irish	9,236	21.50
Italian	6,110	14.22
Latvian	44	0.10
Lithuanian	411	0.96
Luxemburger	44	0.10
Northern European	15	0.03
Norwegian	1,111	2.59
Pennsylvania German	6	0.01
Polish	5,677	13.21
Portuguese	16	0.04
Romanian	149	0.35
Russian	524	1.22
Scandinavian	37	0.09
Scotch-Irish	576	1.34
Scottish	819	1.91
Serbian	262	0.61
Slavic	26	0.06
Slovak	204	0.47
Slovene	131	0.30
Swedish	1,729	4.02
Swiss	286	0.67
Ukrainian	354	0.82
United States or American	1,123	2.61
Welsh	333	0.78
West Indian, excl. Hispanic:	5	0.01
Trinidadian and Tobagonian	5	0.01
White:	40,274	94.18
Not Hispanic (38,706)	38,988	91.17
Hispanic (1,234)	1,286	3.01
Yugoslavian	143	0.33

Elmwood Park

Place Type: Village
County: Cook
Population: 25,405

Ancestry/Race	Number	%
African American/Black:	166	0.65
Not Hispanic (129)	154	0.61
Hispanic (3)	12	0.05
Alaska Native tribes, not specified	1	0.00
Am. Ind. or Alaska Nat., not spec.	52	0.20
Albanian	202	0.80
American Indian tribes, specified:	54	0.21
Apache	1	0.00
Blackfeet	2	0.01
Cherokee (7)	23	0.09
Chippewa (3)	4	0.02
Iroquois	3	0.01
Latin American Indians (3)	5	0.02
Lumbee (1)	1	0.00
Ottawa	1	0.00
Pima (1)	1	0.00
Potawatomi	1	0.00
Sioux	3	0.01
All other tribes (1)	9	0.04
American Indian tribes, not spec.	1	0.00
Arab:	210	0.83
Arab/Arabic	144	0.57
Egyptian	29	0.11
Jordanian	9	0.04

Notes: 1. Figures in the "Number" column do not add up to the total population due to: a) Ancestry/Race overlap — e.g. persons can report being both White and Irish, b) persons of Hispanic origin can report being any race, c) persons reporting two ancestries are counted in both categories. 2. Numbers in parentheses indicate the number of persons reporting this ancestry/race alone, not in combination with any other ancestry/race. 3. Refer to the Explanation of Data in the front of the book for more detailed information.

Lebanese	7	0.03
Palestinian	9	0.04
Syrian	12	0.05
Armenian	17	0.07
Asian:	608	2.39
Chinese, ex. Taiwanese (33)	36	0.14
Filipino (354)	382	1.50
Indian (78)	86	0.34
Japanese (12)	32	0.13
Korean (13)	16	0.06
Pakistani (1)	5	0.02
Taiwanese (6)	6	0.02
Thai (20)	23	0.09
Vietnamese (6)	6	0.02
Other Asian, specified	3	0.01
Other Asian, not specified (3)	13	0.05
Austrian	98	0.39
Belgian	52	0.20
Brazilian	13	0.05
British	10	0.04
Bulgarian	106	0.42
Canadian	16	0.06
Croatian	89	0.35
Czech	370	1.46
Czechoslovakian	66	0.26
Danish	91	0.36
Dutch	164	0.65
English	545	2.15
Estonian	7	0.03
European	26	0.10
Finnish	14	0.06
French, except Basque	270	1.06
French Canadian	44	0.17
German	3,039	11.96
Greek	598	2.35
Hawaii Native/Pacific Islander:	13	0.05
Micronesian: (2)	2	0.01
Guamanian/Chamorro (2)	2	0.01
Polynesian: (3)	3	0.01
Native Hawaiian (1)	1	0.00
Samoan (2)	2	0.01
Other Pac. Isl., not spec. (2)	8	0.03
Hispanic or Latino:	2,798	11.01
Central American:	93	0.37
Costa Rican	7	0.03
Guatemalan	53	0.21
Honduran	15	0.06
Panamanian	1	0.00
Salvadoran	11	0.04
Other Central American	6	0.02
Cuban	76	0.30
Dominican Republic	14	0.06
Mexican	1,434	5.64
Puerto Rican	656	2.58
South American:	216	0.85
Argentinean	52	0.20
Bolivian	3	0.01
Chilean	2	0.01
Colombian	64	0.25
Ecuadorian	62	0.24
Peruvian	27	0.11
Uruguayan	1	0.00
Other South American	5	0.02
Other Hispanic or Latino	309	1.22
Hungarian	78	0.31
Iranian	23	0.09
Irish	3,134	12.34
Italian	7,293	28.71
Latvian	15	0.06
Lithuanian	166	0.65
Luxemburger	19	0.07
Macedonian	4	0.02
Norwegian	425	1.67
Pennsylvania German	8	0.03
Polish	6,270	24.68
Portuguese	7	0.03
Romanian	124	0.49
Russian	194	0.76
Scandinavian	10	0.04
Scotch-Irish	93	0.37
Scottish	112	0.44
Serbian	34	0.13
Slovak	36	0.14
Swedish	362	1.42
Swiss	19	0.07
Turkish	29	0.11
Ukrainian	390	1.54
United States or American	605	2.38
Welsh	13	0.05
White:	23,821	93.77
Not Hispanic (21,490)	21,900	86.20
Hispanic (1,765)	1,921	7.56
Yugoslavian	23	0.09

Evanston

Place Type: City
County: Cook
Population: 74,239

Ancestry/Race	Number	%
African American/Black:	17,883	24.09
Not Hispanic (16,449)	17,506	23.58
Hispanic (255)	377	0.51
African, sub-Saharan:	899	1.21
African	659	0.89
Cape Verdean	6	0.01
Ethiopian	67	0.09
Ghanian	53	0.07
Kenyan	25	0.03
Nigerian	42	0.06
South African	7	0.01
Ugandan	27	0.04
Other sub-Saharan African	13	0.02
Alaska Native tribes, specified:	5	0.01
Eskimo (1)	1	0.00
Tlingit-Haida	4	0.01
Am. Ind. or Alaska Nat., not spec.	206	0.28
Albanian	66	0.09
Alsatian	6	0.01
American Indian tribes, specified:	264	0.36
Apache (2)	3	0.00
Blackfeet (4)	22	0.03
Cherokee (13)	104	0.14
Cheyenne	2	0.00
Chickasaw	5	0.01
Chippewa (12)	22	0.03
Choctaw (3)	11	0.01
Cree	6	0.01
Creek	1	0.00
Iroquois (3)	6	0.01
Latin American Indians (7)	32	0.04
Menominee	1	0.00
Navajo (5)	7	0.01
Ottawa	1	0.00
Pueblo (1)	3	0.00
Puget Sound Salish	2	0.00
Seminole	12	0.02
Sioux (6)	9	0.01
Yakama	1	0.00
All other tribes (2)	14	0.02
American Indian tribes, not spec.	19	0.03
Arab:	435	0.59
Arab/Arabic	111	0.15
Egyptian	90	0.12
Iraqi	15	0.02
Lebanese	107	0.14
Moroccan	13	0.02
Palestinian	55	0.07
Syrian	41	0.06
Other Arab	3	0.00
Armenian	136	0.18
Asian:	5,260	7.09
Bangladeshi (2)	2	0.00
Cambodian (3)	14	0.02
Chinese, ex. Taiwanese (1,296)	1,464	1.97
Filipino (433)	551	0.74
Indian (1,149)	1,278	1.72
Indonesian (3)	9	0.01
Japanese (454)	597	0.80
Korean (659)	726	0.98
Laotian (9)	11	0.01
Malaysian (15)	17	0.02
Pakistani (79)	104	0.14
Sri Lankan (10)	10	0.01
Taiwanese (130)	161	0.22
Thai (80)	88	0.12
Vietnamese (49)	71	0.10
Other Asian, specified (19)	24	0.03
Other Asian, not specified (58)	133	0.18
Assyrian/Chaldean/Syriac	67	0.09
Australian	49	0.07
Austrian	482	0.65
Basque	15	0.02
Belgian	163	0.22
Brazilian	76	0.10
British	596	0.80
Bulgarian	71	0.10
Canadian	118	0.16
Croatian	150	0.20
Cypriot	9	0.01
Czech	451	0.61
Czechoslovakian	157	0.21
Danish	556	0.75
Dutch	960	1.29
Eastern European	585	0.79
English	6,690	9.01
Estonian	30	0.04
European	1,153	1.55
Finnish	174	0.23
French, except Basque	1,684	2.27
French Canadian	376	0.51
German	12,027	16.20
Greek	553	0.74
Hawaii Native/Pacific Islander:	150	0.20
Melanesian: (1)	1	0.00
Fijian (1)	1	0.00
Micronesian: (20)	27	0.04
Guamanian/Chamorro (19)	26	0.04
Other Micronesian (1)	1	0.00
Polynesian: (20)	40	0.05
Native Hawaiian (14)	27	0.04
Samoan (5)	9	0.01
Other Polynesian (1)	4	0.01
Other Pac. Isl., specified	2	0.00
Other Pac. Isl., not spec. (23)	80	0.11
Hispanic or Latino:	4,539	6.11
Central American:	230	0.31
Costa Rican	13	0.02
Guatemalan	73	0.10
Honduran	20	0.03
Nicaraguan	10	0.01
Panamanian	57	0.08
Salvadoran	37	0.05
Other Central American	20	0.03
Cuban	209	0.28
Dominican Republic	37	0.05
Mexican	2,794	3.76
Puerto Rican	329	0.44
South American:	372	0.50
Argentinean	66	0.09
Bolivian	10	0.01
Chilean	41	0.06
Colombian	93	0.13
Ecuadorian	26	0.04
Paraguayan	3	0.00
Peruvian	82	0.11
Uruguayan	4	0.01
Venezuelan	31	0.04
Other South American	16	0.02
Other Hispanic or Latino	568	0.77
Hungarian	713	0.96
Icelander	24	0.03
Iranian	145	0.20
Irish	9,283	12.50
Israeli	92	0.12
Italian	3,106	4.18
Latvian	124	0.17
Lithuanian	590	0.79
Luxemburger	66	0.09

Notes: 1. Figures in the "Number" column do not add up to the total population due to: a) Ancestry/Race overlap — e.g. persons can report being both White and Irish, b) persons of Hispanic origin can report being any race, c) persons reporting two ancestries are counted in both categories. 2. Numbers in parentheses indicate the number of persons reporting this ancestry/race alone, not in combination with any other ancestry/race. 3. Refer to the Explanation of Data in the front of the book for more detailed information.

Ancestry/Race	Number	%
Macedonian	9	0.01
Maltese	34	0.05
New Zealander	23	0.03
Northern European	106	0.14
Norwegian	1,259	1.70
Pennsylvania German	18	0.02
Polish	4,125	5.56
Portuguese	165	0.22
Romanian	372	0.50
Russian	2,892	3.90
Scandinavian	121	0.16
Scotch-Irish	1,201	1.62
Scottish	1,568	2.11
Serbian	126	0.17
Slavic	46	0.06
Slovak	136	0.18
Slovene	63	0.08
Swedish	2,323	3.13
Swiss	463	0.62
Turkish	185	0.25
Ukrainian	465	0.63
United States or American	1,926	2.59
Welsh	523	0.70
West Indian, excl. Hispanic:	3,448	4.64
Bahamian	24	0.03
Belizean	488	0.66
British West Indian	46	0.06
Dutch West Indian	11	0.01
Haitian	856	1.15
Jamaican	1,937	2.61
Trinidadian and Tobagonian	32	0.04
West Indian	43	0.06
Other West Indian	11	0.01
White:	50,045	67.41
Not Hispanic (46,444)	47,748	64.32
Hispanic (1,985)	2,297	3.09
Yugoslavian	108	0.15

Evergreen Park

Place Type: Village
County: Cook
Population: 20,821

Ancestry/Race	Number	%
Afghan	11	0.05
African American/Black:	1,702	8.17
Not Hispanic (1,627)	1,676	8.05
Hispanic (17)	26	0.12
African, sub-Saharan:	124	0.60
African	98	0.47
Nigerian	26	0.12
Am. Ind. or Alaska Nat., not spec.	16	0.08
Albanian	23	0.11
American Indian tribes, specified:	53	0.25
Apache	1	0.00
Cherokee (11)	28	0.13
Chickasaw	1	0.00
Chippewa (4)	5	0.02
Cree (1)	2	0.01
Iroquois (8)	8	0.04
Latin American Indians	2	0.01
Navajo	2	0.01
Pueblo	1	0.00
Ute	1	0.00
All other tribes	2	0.01
American Indian tribes, not spec.	2	0.01
Arab:	213	1.02
Arab/Arabic	67	0.32
Egyptian	16	0.08
Jordanian	42	0.20
Lebanese	13	0.06
Palestinian	75	0.36
Asian:	321	1.54
Chinese, ex. Taiwanese (17)	29	0.14
Filipino (156)	189	0.91
Indian (44)	52	0.25
Japanese (9)	14	0.07
Korean (8)	9	0.04
Pakistani (4)	5	0.02
Thai (2)	2	0.01
Vietnamese (16)	16	0.08
Other Asian, not specified (1)	5	0.02
Austrian	280	1.34
Belgian	9	0.04
British	12	0.06
Croatian	209	1.00
Czech	452	2.17
Czechoslovakian	53	0.25
Danish	41	0.20
Dutch	677	3.25
Eastern European	28	0.13
English	1,096	5.26
European	20	0.10
Finnish	24	0.12
French, except Basque	468	2.25
French Canadian	111	0.53
German	4,464	21.44
Greek	258	1.24
Hawaii Native/Pacific Islander:	7	0.03
Micronesian: (1)	1	0.00
Guamanian/Chamorro (1)	1	0.00
Polynesian: (2)	4	0.02
Native Hawaiian (2)	4	0.02
Other Pac. Isl., not spec.	2	0.01
Hispanic or Latino:	831	3.99
Central American:	7	0.03
Nicaraguan	4	0.02
Salvadoran	2	0.01
Other Central American	1	0.00
Cuban	9	0.04
Mexican	606	2.91
Puerto Rican	116	0.56
South American:	27	0.13
Argentinean	1	0.00
Colombian	5	0.02
Ecuadorian	5	0.02
Paraguayan	1	0.00
Peruvian	7	0.03
Uruguayan	7	0.03
Other South American	1	0.00
Other Hispanic or Latino	66	0.32
Hungarian	59	0.28
Iranian	16	0.08
Irish	8,250	39.62
Israeli	4	0.02
Italian	2,122	10.19
Lithuanian	570	2.74
Norwegian	121	0.58
Pennsylvania German	10	0.05
Polish	2,746	13.19
Portuguese	5	0.02
Romanian	23	0.11
Russian	79	0.38
Scandinavian	23	0.11
Scotch-Irish	300	1.44
Scottish	201	0.97
Serbian	37	0.18
Slavic	8	0.04
Slovak	90	0.43
Slovene	8	0.04
Swedish	749	3.60
Swiss	21	0.10
Ukrainian	72	0.35
United States or American	296	1.42
Welsh	35	0.17
West Indian, excl. Hispanic:	53	0.25
Belizean	32	0.15
Jamaican	21	0.10
White:	18,609	89.38
Not Hispanic (17,895)	18,060	86.74
Hispanic (493)	549	2.64
Yugoslavian	5	0.02

Fairview Heights

Place Type: City
County: Saint Clair
Population: 15,034

Ancestry/Race	Number	%
African American/Black:	2,637	17.54
Not Hispanic (2,559)	2,626	17.47
Hispanic (8)	11	0.07
African, sub-Saharan:	72	0.47
African	72	0.47
Alaska Native tribes, specified:	1	0.01
Tlingit-Haida (1)	1	0.01
Am. Ind. or Alaska Nat., not spec.	37	0.25
American Indian tribes, specified:	51	0.34
Blackfeet	1	0.01
Cherokee (8)	27	0.18
Chippewa (1)	2	0.01
Choctaw	2	0.01
Iroquois	3	0.02
Navajo	2	0.01
Pueblo (1)	2	0.01
Seminole (1)	2	0.01
Sioux (1)	3	0.02
Yaqui	4	0.03
All other tribes (2)	3	0.02
American Indian tribes, not spec.	8	0.05
Armenian	46	0.30
Asian:	411	2.73
Chinese, ex. Taiwanese (44)	58	0.39
Filipino (67)	97	0.65
Indian (66)	72	0.48
Japanese (30)	45	0.30
Korean (31)	44	0.29
Malaysian (1)	1	0.01
Pakistani	6	0.04
Taiwanese (1)	7	0.05
Thai (16)	16	0.11
Vietnamese (52)	55	0.37
Other Asian, not specified (3)	10	0.07
Austrian	82	0.54
Belgian	22	0.14
British	40	0.26
Bulgarian	8	0.05
Croatian	105	0.69
Czech	190	1.24
Czechoslovakian	11	0.07
Danish	30	0.20
Dutch	388	2.54
English	1,483	9.70
European	119	0.78
Finnish	8	0.05
French, except Basque	817	5.34
French Canadian	106	0.69
German	4,387	28.68
Greek	42	0.27
Hawaii Native/Pacific Islander:	22	0.15
Micronesian:	5	0.03
Guamanian/Chamorro	5	0.03
Polynesian: (1)	10	0.07
Native Hawaiian (1)	9	0.06
Samoan	1	0.01
Other Pac. Isl., not spec.	7	0.05
Hispanic or Latino:	289	1.92
Central American:	16	0.11
Costa Rican	2	0.01
Guatemalan	2	0.01
Nicaraguan	2	0.01
Panamanian	10	0.07
Cuban	1	0.01
Mexican	139	0.92
Puerto Rican	54	0.36
South American:	8	0.05
Argentinean	2	0.01
Peruvian	4	0.03
Other South American	2	0.01
Other Hispanic or Latino	71	0.47
Hungarian	78	0.51
Iranian	35	0.23

Notes: 1. Figures in the "Number" column do not add up to the total population due to: a) Ancestry/Race overlap — e.g. persons can report being both White and Irish, b) persons of Hispanic origin can report being any race, c) persons reporting two ancestries are counted in both categories. 2. Numbers in parentheses indicate the number of persons reporting this ancestry/race alone, not in combination with any other ancestry/race. 3. Refer to the Explanation of Data in the front of the book for more detailed information.

Irish	2,193	14.34
Italian	419	2.74
Lithuanian	85	0.56
Macedonian	7	0.05
Norwegian	124	0.81
Polish	643	4.20
Russian	58	0.38
Scandinavian	26	0.17
Scotch-Irish	271	1.77
Scottish	239	1.56
Serbian	16	0.10
Slavic	7	0.05
Slovak	31	0.20
Slovene	17	0.11
Swedish	108	0.71
Swiss	82	0.54
Ukrainian	8	0.05
United States or American	603	3.94
Welsh	179	1.17
West Indian, excl. Hispanic:	16	0.10
Jamaican	8	0.05
Trinidadian and Tobagonian	8	0.05
White:	11,975	79.65
Not Hispanic (11,628)	11,786	78.40
Hispanic (159)	189	1.26
Yugoslavian	34	0.22

Forest Park

Place Type: Village
County: Cook
Population: 15,688

Ancestry/Race	Number	%
Acadian/Cajun	3	0.02
African American/Black:	5,128	32.69
Not Hispanic (4,824)	5,020	32.00
Hispanic (68)	108	0.69
African, sub-Saharan:	245	1.56
African	126	0.80
Ethiopian	38	0.24
Ghanian	17	0.11
Kenyan	38	0.24
Zimbabwean	15	0.10
Other sub-Saharan African	11	0.07
Am. Ind. or Alaska Nat., not spec.	56	0.36
American Indian tribes, specified:	81	0.52
Blackfeet	13	0.08
Cherokee (3)	28	0.18
Chickasaw	5	0.03
Chippewa	6	0.04
Choctaw	6	0.04
Comanche	3	0.02
Creek (1)	2	0.01
Iroquois	2	0.01
Latin American Indians	4	0.03
Navajo	2	0.01
Ottawa (1)	1	0.01
Potawatomi	1	0.01
Seminole	4	0.03
Sioux (1)	3	0.02
Ute	2	0.01
All other tribes (1)	1	0.01
American Indian tribes, not spec.	5	0.03
Arab:	43	0.27
Arab/Arabic	14	0.09
Egyptian	23	0.15
Lebanese	6	0.04
Asian:	1,202	7.66
Bangladeshi (2)	6	0.04
Cambodian (2)	2	0.01
Chinese, ex. Taiwanese (124)	142	0.91
Filipino (312)	358	2.28
Indian (402)	424	2.70
Japanese (26)	35	0.22
Korean (59)	65	0.41
Laotian (2)	3	0.02
Malaysian	6	0.04
Pakistani (55)	64	0.41
Sri Lankan (4)	4	0.03
Taiwanese (3)	4	0.03
Thai (36)	43	0.27
Vietnamese (13)	27	0.17
Other Asian, specified (4)	4	0.03
Other Asian, not specified (6)	15	0.10
Australian	5	0.03
Austrian	90	0.57
Basque	3	0.02
Belgian	26	0.17
British	45	0.29
Bulgarian	41	0.26
Canadian	5	0.03
Croatian	37	0.24
Czech	178	1.13
Czechoslovakian	57	0.36
Danish	42	0.27
Dutch	136	0.87
Eastern European	14	0.09
English	926	5.90
European	78	0.50
Finnish	8	0.05
French, except Basque	239	1.52
French Canadian	136	0.87
German	2,487	15.85
Greek	122	0.78
Hawaii Native/Pacific Islander:	24	0.15
Micronesian: (5)	5	0.03
Guamanian/Chamorro (5)	5	0.03
Polynesian: (6)	9	0.06
Native Hawaiian (4)	7	0.04
Samoan (1)	1	0.01
Other Polynesian (1)	1	0.01
Other Pac. Isl., not spec.	10	0.06
Hispanic or Latino:	1,230	7.84
Central American:	40	0.25
Costa Rican	3	0.02
Guatemalan	14	0.09
Honduran	2	0.01
Nicaraguan	15	0.10
Panamanian	1	0.01
Salvadoran	2	0.01
Other Central American	3	0.02
Cuban	34	0.22
Dominican Republic	2	0.01
Mexican	876	5.58
Puerto Rican	159	1.01
South American:	47	0.30
Argentinean	4	0.03
Chilean	5	0.03
Colombian	9	0.06
Ecuadorian	3	0.02
Paraguayan	3	0.02
Peruvian	21	0.13
Other South American	2	0.01
Other Hispanic or Latino	72	0.46
Hungarian	41	0.26
Iranian	21	0.13
Irish	2,292	14.61
Italian	1,264	8.06
Latvian	18	0.11
Lithuanian	69	0.44
Luxemburger	32	0.20
Northern European	4	0.03
Norwegian	190	1.21
Polish	839	5.35
Portuguese	12	0.08
Romanian	19	0.12
Russian	63	0.40
Scandinavian	21	0.13
Scotch-Irish	117	0.75
Scottish	181	1.15
Slavic	9	0.06
Slovak	12	0.08
Slovene	9	0.06
Swedish	243	1.55
Swiss	84	0.54
Ukrainian	56	0.36
United States or American	314	2.00
Welsh	44	0.28
West Indian, excl. Hispanic:	60	0.38
Haitian	16	0.10
Jamaican	29	0.18
West Indian	15	0.10
White:	9,103	58.03
Not Hispanic (8,169)	8,390	53.48
Hispanic (639)	713	4.54
Yugoslavian	35	0.22

Frankfort

Place Type: Village
County: Will
Population: 10,391

Ancestry/Race	Number	%
African American/Black:	284	2.73
Not Hispanic (257)	283	2.72
Hispanic (1)	1	0.01
Am. Ind. or Alaska Nat., not spec.	9	0.09
American Indian tribes, specified:	33	0.32
Apache	2	0.02
Blackfeet	2	0.02
Cherokee (7)	12	0.12
Chickasaw (1)	1	0.01
Chippewa (2)	2	0.02
Choctaw	4	0.04
Latin American Indians (4)	4	0.04
Navajo (1)	3	0.03
Potawatomi (1)	1	0.01
All other tribes (1)	2	0.02
Arab:	7	0.07
Jordanian	7	0.07
Armenian	9	0.09
Asian:	246	2.37
Chinese, ex. Taiwanese (37)	43	0.41
Filipino (38)	49	0.47
Indian (82)	84	0.81
Japanese (14)	19	0.18
Korean (26)	28	0.27
Pakistani (1)	1	0.01
Thai (9)	9	0.09
Vietnamese (1)	1	0.01
Other Asian, not specified (9)	12	0.12
Australian	16	0.16
Austrian	109	1.06
Belgian	13	0.13
Canadian	8	0.08
Croatian	148	1.44
Czech	117	1.14
Czechoslovakian	35	0.34
Danish	29	0.28
Dutch	474	4.63
English	800	7.81
European	73	0.71
French, except Basque	230	2.24
French Canadian	46	0.45
German	2,713	26.48
Greek	219	2.14
Hispanic or Latino:	240	2.31
Central American:	6	0.06
Guatemalan	5	0.05
Nicaraguan	1	0.01
Cuban	3	0.03
Dominican Republic	1	0.01
Mexican	171	1.65
Puerto Rican	23	0.22
South American:	9	0.09
Ecuadorian	1	0.01
Peruvian	4	0.04
Venezuelan	3	0.03
Other South American	1	0.01
Other Hispanic or Latino	27	0.26
Hungarian	31	0.30
Iranian	13	0.13
Irish	2,235	21.81
Italian	1,305	12.74
Lithuanian	255	2.49
Macedonian	6	0.06
Norwegian	158	1.54
Pennsylvania German	5	0.05

Notes: 1. Figures in the "Number" column do not add up to the total population due to: a) Ancestry/Race overlap — e.g. persons can report being both White and Irish, b) persons of Hispanic origin can report being any race, c) persons reporting two ancestries are counted in both categories. 2. Numbers in parentheses indicate the number of persons reporting this ancestry/race alone, not in combination with any other ancestry/race. 3. Refer to the Explanation of Data in the front of the book for more detailed information.

Ancestry/Race	Number	%
Polish	1,460	14.25
Portuguese	26	0.25
Romanian	35	0.34
Russian	61	0.60
Scotch-Irish	88	0.86
Scottish	198	1.93
Serbian	18	0.18
Slovak	58	0.57
Slovene	20	0.20
Swedish	599	5.85
Swiss	47	0.46
Ukrainian	36	0.35
United States or American	292	2.85
Welsh	98	0.96
West Indian, excl. Hispanic:	8	0.08
Haitian	8	0.08
White:	9,824	94.54
Not Hispanic (9,592)	9,640	92.77
Hispanic (161)	184	1.77
Yugoslavian	29	0.28

Franklin Park

Place Type: Village
County: Cook
Population: 19,434

Ancestry/Race	Number	%
African American/Black:	191	0.98
Not Hispanic (112)	128	0.66
Hispanic (35)	63	0.32
Am. Ind. or Alaska Nat., not spec.	37	0.19
Albanian	62	0.32
American Indian tribes, specified:	64	0.33
Apache (1)	1	0.01
Cherokee (1)	13	0.07
Chippewa	1	0.01
Comanche	2	0.01
Iroquois	1	0.01
Latin American Indians (20)	31	0.16
Lumbee	1	0.01
Menominee (1)	5	0.03
Navajo	4	0.02
Sioux	2	0.01
All other tribes (1)	3	0.02
American Indian tribes, not spec.	9	0.05
Arab:	69	0.35
Arab/Arabic	34	0.17
Lebanese	28	0.14
Palestinian	7	0.04
Armenian	9	0.05
Asian:	545	2.80
Cambodian (21)	21	0.11
Chinese, ex. Taiwanese (25)	34	0.17
Filipino (252)	274	1.41
Indian (64)	67	0.34
Japanese (4)	16	0.08
Korean (18)	19	0.10
Laotian (22)	24	0.12
Pakistani (15)	24	0.12
Thai (14)	14	0.07
Vietnamese (41)	41	0.21
Other Asian, not specified	11	0.06
Assyrian/Chaldean/Syriac	15	0.08
Australian	5	0.03
Austrian	82	0.42
Belgian	34	0.17
British	37	0.19
Canadian	5	0.03
Croatian	37	0.19
Czech	253	1.30
Czechoslovakian	28	0.14
Danish	101	0.52
Dutch	155	0.80
English	427	2.20
European	63	0.32
Finnish	12	0.06
French, except Basque	179	0.92
French Canadian	41	0.21
German	2,791	14.36
Greek	126	0.65
Hawaii Native/Pacific Islander:	15	0.08
Micronesian: (1)	1	0.01
Guamanian/Chamorro (1)	1	0.01
Polynesian: (3)	5	0.03
Native Hawaiian (3)	3	0.02
Samoan	2	0.01
Other Pac. Isl., not spec. (5)	9	0.05
Hispanic or Latino:	7,399	38.07
Central American:	175	0.90
Guatemalan	127	0.65
Honduran	20	0.10
Nicaraguan	2	0.01
Panamanian	4	0.02
Salvadoran	16	0.08
Other Central American	6	0.03
Cuban	99	0.51
Dominican Republic	8	0.04
Mexican	6,104	31.41
Puerto Rican	466	2.40
South American:	105	0.54
Argentinean	3	0.02
Bolivian	9	0.05
Chilean	6	0.03
Colombian	46	0.24
Ecuadorian	16	0.08
Peruvian	21	0.11
Other South American	4	0.02
Other Hispanic or Latino	442	2.27
Hungarian	78	0.40
Irish	1,589	8.17
Israeli	16	0.08
Italian	2,536	13.05
Latvian	23	0.12
Lithuanian	69	0.35
Luxemburger	14	0.07
Northern European	6	0.03
Norwegian	287	1.48
Polish	3,812	19.61
Portuguese	11	0.06
Romanian	9	0.05
Russian	42	0.22
Scandinavian	25	0.13
Scotch-Irish	63	0.32
Scottish	67	0.34
Slovak	62	0.32
Slovene	12	0.06
Swedish	194	1.00
Swiss	10	0.05
Ukrainian	184	0.95
United States or American	554	2.85
Welsh	21	0.11
White:	15,867	81.65
Not Hispanic (11,251)	11,415	58.74
Hispanic (4,150)	4,452	22.91
Yugoslavian	33	0.17

Freeport

Place Type: City
County: Stephenson
Population: 26,443

Ancestry/Race	Number	%
African American/Black:	4,012	15.17
Not Hispanic (3,623)	3,968	15.01
Hispanic (28)	44	0.17
African, sub-Saharan:	71	0.27
African	50	0.19
Nigerian	11	0.04
South African	10	0.04
Alaska Native tribes, specified:	3	0.01
Alaska Athabascan	3	0.01
Am. Ind. or Alaska Nat., not spec.	60	0.23
Albanian	46	0.17
American Indian tribes, specified:	78	0.29
Blackfeet	10	0.04
Cherokee (9)	36	0.14
Chippewa (3)	7	0.03
Creek (1)	2	0.01
Latin American Indians (4)	8	0.03
Navajo (1)	1	0.00
Pima (1)	2	0.01
Seminole	1	0.00
Sioux (3)	7	0.03
All other tribes (2)	4	0.02
American Indian tribes, not spec.	4	0.02
Arab:	48	0.18
Arab/Arabic	4	0.02
Egyptian	41	0.16
Iraqi	3	0.01
Armenian	6	0.02
Asian:	354	1.34
Cambodian (1)	1	0.00
Chinese, ex. Taiwanese (27)	40	0.15
Filipino (51)	83	0.31
Hmong	1	0.00
Indian (92)	108	0.41
Japanese (9)	25	0.09
Korean (31)	33	0.12
Laotian (18)	18	0.07
Pakistani	2	0.01
Thai (3)	4	0.02
Vietnamese (12)	14	0.05
Other Asian, specified	2	0.01
Other Asian, not specified (11)	23	0.09
Austrian	7	0.03
Belgian	33	0.12
Brazilian	10	0.04
British	44	0.17
Canadian	25	0.09
Croatian	15	0.06
Czech	41	0.16
Czechoslovakian	31	0.12
Danish	154	0.58
Dutch	772	2.92
English	2,148	8.12
European	101	0.38
Finnish	43	0.16
French, except Basque	519	1.96
French Canadian	70	0.26
German	9,600	36.31
Greek	94	0.36
Guyanese	26	0.10
Hawaii Native/Pacific Islander:	27	0.10
Micronesian:	1	0.00
Guamanian/Chamorro	1	0.00
Polynesian: (7)	13	0.05
Native Hawaiian (2)	5	0.02
Samoan (5)	8	0.03
Other Pac. Isl., specified	2	0.01
Other Pac. Isl., not spec. (2)	11	0.04
Hispanic or Latino:	561	2.12
Central American:	7	0.03
Guatemalan	2	0.01
Honduran	2	0.01
Panamanian	3	0.01
Cuban	23	0.09
Mexican	401	1.52
Puerto Rican	42	0.16
South American:	9	0.03
Bolivian	1	0.00
Colombian	7	0.03
Peruvian	1	0.00
Other Hispanic or Latino	79	0.30
Hungarian	90	0.34
Irish	2,904	10.98
Italian	788	2.98
Lithuanian	69	0.26
Northern European	19	0.07
Norwegian	739	2.80
Pennsylvania German	51	0.19
Polish	653	2.47
Portuguese	15	0.06
Romanian	16	0.06
Russian	67	0.25
Scandinavian	5	0.02
Scotch-Irish	269	1.02
Scottish	205	0.78
Slovak	7	0.03

Notes: 1. Figures in the "Number" column do not add up to the total population due to: a) Ancestry/Race overlap — e.g. persons can report being both White and Irish, b) persons of Hispanic origin can report being any race, c) persons reporting two ancestries are counted in both categories. 2. Numbers in parentheses indicate the number of persons reporting this ancestry/race alone, not in combination with any other ancestry/race. 3. Refer to the Explanation of Data in the front of the book for more detailed information.

Ancestry/Race	Number	%
Swedish	567	2.14
Swiss	478	1.81
Turkish	13	0.05
United States or American	1,365	5.16
Welsh	90	0.34
West Indian, excl. Hispanic:	6	0.02
Jamaican	6	0.02
White:	22,153	83.78
Not Hispanic (21,399)	21,870	82.71
Hispanic (224)	283	1.07
Yugoslavian	66	0.25

Gages Lake

Place Type: Census Designated Place
County: Lake
Population: 10,415

Ancestry/Race	Number	%
African American/Black:	244	2.34
Not Hispanic (206)	237	2.28
Hispanic (4)	7	0.07
African, sub-Saharan:	12	0.11
South African	12	0.11
Am. Ind. or Alaska Nat., not spec.	20	0.19
American Indian tribes, specified:	38	0.36
Apache (1)	2	0.02
Cherokee (4)	11	0.11
Chippewa (2)	5	0.05
Choctaw (1)	2	0.02
Crow	4	0.04
Iroquois (2)	5	0.05
Kiowa (1)	1	0.01
Latin American Indians (2)	2	0.02
Menominee (1)	1	0.01
Sioux (1)	1	0.01
All other tribes (3)	4	0.04
American Indian tribes, not spec.	1	0.01
Arab:	23	0.22
Lebanese	1	0.01
Palestinian	10	0.10
Syrian	12	0.11
Armenian	9	0.09
Asian:	379	3.64
Chinese, ex. Taiwanese (47)	50	0.48
Filipino (112)	135	1.30
Indian (82)	91	0.87
Japanese (21)	30	0.29
Korean (32)	34	0.33
Malaysian (4)	4	0.04
Taiwanese (2)	2	0.02
Thai (12)	18	0.17
Vietnamese (6)	6	0.06
Other Asian, specified	1	0.01
Other Asian, not specified (3)	8	0.08
Assyrian/Chaldean/Syriac	11	0.11
Austrian	31	0.30
Belgian	6	0.06
Brazilian	7	0.07
British	47	0.45
Canadian	36	0.34
Croatian	11	0.11
Czech	88	0.84
Czechoslovakian	9	0.09
Danish	100	0.96
Dutch	193	1.85
English	1,048	10.02
European	106	1.01
Finnish	114	1.09
French, except Basque	245	2.34
French Canadian	28	0.27
German	3,676	35.15
German Russian	3	0.03
Greek	90	0.86
Hawaii Native/Pacific Islander:	18	0.17
Polynesian: (1)	18	0.17
Native Hawaiian (1)	10	0.10
Samoan	7	0.07
Other Polynesian	1	0.01
Hispanic or Latino:	436	4.19
Central American:	13	0.12
Honduran	5	0.05
Salvadoran	6	0.06
Other Central American	2	0.02
Cuban	17	0.16
Dominican Republic	3	0.03
Mexican	291	2.79
Puerto Rican	53	0.51
South American:	21	0.20
Argentinean	6	0.06
Colombian	9	0.09
Ecuadorian	2	0.02
Peruvian	3	0.03
Uruguayan	1	0.01
Other Hispanic or Latino	38	0.36
Hungarian	102	0.98
Irish	1,817	17.37
Italian	1,033	9.88
Lithuanian	89	0.85
Luxemburger	38	0.36
Norwegian	347	3.32
Polish	1,191	11.39
Portuguese	9	0.09
Romanian	2	0.02
Russian	76	0.73
Scandinavian	28	0.27
Scotch-Irish	55	0.53
Scottish	206	1.97
Serbian	61	0.58
Slovak	48	0.46
Slovene	22	0.21
Swedish	730	6.98
Swiss	14	0.13
Ukrainian	51	0.49
United States or American	403	3.85
Welsh	83	0.79
West Indian, excl. Hispanic:	10	0.10
Jamaican	10	0.10
White:	9,689	93.03
Not Hispanic (9,317)	9,411	90.36
Hispanic (257)	278	2.67
Yugoslavian	32	0.31

Galesburg

Place Type: City
County: Knox
Population: 33,706

Ancestry/Race	Number	%
African American/Black:	3,803	11.28
Not Hispanic (3,402)	3,728	11.06
Hispanic (35)	75	0.22
African, sub-Saharan:	212	0.63
African	180	0.53
South African	24	0.07
Zimbabwean	8	0.02
Alaska Native tribes, specified:	1	0.00
Eskimo	1	0.00
Alaska Native tribes, not specified	1	0.00
Am. Ind. or Alaska Nat., not spec.	82	0.24
American Indian tribes, specified:	120	0.36
Apache (2)	6	0.02
Blackfeet (3)	8	0.02
Cherokee (17)	59	0.18
Cheyenne	2	0.01
Chickasaw (1)	1	0.00
Chippewa	2	0.01
Choctaw (7)	8	0.02
Iroquois (1)	2	0.01
Latin American Indians (4)	5	0.01
Menominee	3	0.01
Navajo (4)	8	0.02
Pueblo	2	0.01
Sioux (1)	5	0.01
All other tribes (1)	9	0.03
American Indian tribes, not spec.	5	0.01
Arab:	76	0.22
Arab/Arabic	18	0.05
Egyptian	8	0.02
Lebanese	39	0.12
Moroccan	11	0.03
Asian:	407	1.21
Bangladeshi (3)	3	0.01
Chinese, ex. Taiwanese (56)	73	0.22
Filipino (43)	52	0.15
Indian (120)	123	0.36
Indonesian (1)	1	0.00
Japanese (23)	36	0.11
Korean (29)	37	0.11
Laotian	2	0.01
Malaysian	1	0.00
Pakistani (10)	10	0.03
Sri Lankan (2)	2	0.01
Taiwanese (3)	3	0.01
Thai (5)	7	0.02
Vietnamese (17)	20	0.06
Other Asian, not specified (29)	37	0.11
Australian	7	0.02
Austrian	12	0.04
Belgian	100	0.30
British	87	0.26
Canadian	16	0.05
Croatian	118	0.35
Cypriot	5	0.01
Czech	43	0.13
Czechoslovakian	36	0.11
Danish	180	0.53
Dutch	852	2.52
Eastern European	7	0.02
English	3,399	10.05
European	218	0.64
Finnish	30	0.09
French, except Basque	932	2.76
French Canadian	64	0.19
German	6,093	18.01
Greek	30	0.09
Hawaii Native/Pacific Islander:	21	0.06
Micronesian: (2)	4	0.01
Guamanian/Chamorro (2)	4	0.01
Polynesian: (5)	14	0.04
Native Hawaiian (3)	9	0.03
Samoan (2)	4	0.01
Other Polynesian	1	0.00
Other Pac. Isl., not spec. (1)	3	0.01
Hispanic or Latino:	1,688	5.01
Central American:	16	0.05
Guatemalan	3	0.01
Honduran	3	0.01
Nicaraguan	7	0.02
Panamanian	3	0.01
Cuban	15	0.04
Dominican Republic	1	0.00
Mexican	1,231	3.65
Puerto Rican	39	0.12
South American:	18	0.05
Chilean	1	0.00
Colombian	4	0.01
Peruvian	7	0.02
Venezuelan	4	0.01
Other South American	2	0.01
Other Hispanic or Latino	368	1.09
Hungarian	55	0.16
Irish	4,155	12.28
Italian	940	2.78
Latvian	9	0.03
Lithuanian	38	0.11
Luxemburger	10	0.03
Northern European	9	0.03
Norwegian	481	1.42
Pennsylvania German	25	0.07
Polish	374	1.11
Portuguese	7	0.02
Russian	69	0.20
Scandinavian	55	0.16
Scotch-Irish	704	2.08
Scottish	608	1.80
Serbian	22	0.07
Slavic	5	0.01
Slovak	29	0.09

Notes: 1. Figures in the "Number" column do not add up to the total population due to: a) Ancestry/Race overlap — e.g. persons can report being both White and Irish, b) persons of Hispanic origin can report being any race, c) persons reporting two ancestries are counted in both categories. 2. Numbers in parentheses indicate the number of persons reporting this ancestry/race alone, not in combination with any other ancestry/race. 3. Refer to the Explanation of Data in the front of the book for more detailed information.

Slovene	15	0.04
Swedish	3,374	9.97
Swiss	117	0.35
Turkish	8	0.02
Ukrainian	9	0.03
United States or American	2,962	8.76
Welsh	222	0.66
West Indian, excl. Hispanic:	5	0.01
Dutch West Indian	5	0.01
White:	28,944	85.87
Not Hispanic (27,688)	28,141	83.49
Hispanic (702)	803	2.38
Yugoslavian	62	0.18

Geneva

Place Type: City
County: Kane
Population: 19,515

Ancestry/Race	Number	%
African American/Black:	218	1.12
Not Hispanic (196)	213	1.09
Hispanic (3)	5	0.03
Am. Ind. or Alaska Nat., not spec.	9	0.05
American Indian tribes, specified:	27	0.14
Apache	1	0.01
Cherokee (4)	14	0.07
Chippewa	1	0.01
Choctaw	1	0.01
Crow	1	0.01
Iroquois (1)	1	0.01
Latin American Indians (1)	1	0.01
Osage	1	0.01
Potawatomi	1	0.01
All other tribes (1)	5	0.03
American Indian tribes, not spec.	4	0.02
Arab:	7	0.04
Lebanese	7	0.04
Asian:	284	1.46
Cambodian (10)	10	0.05
Chinese, ex. Taiwanese (73)	82	0.42
Filipino (24)	29	0.15
Indian (61)	64	0.33
Japanese (30)	46	0.24
Korean (23)	28	0.14
Laotian (1)	1	0.01
Taiwanese (4)	4	0.02
Vietnamese (14)	14	0.07
Other Asian, not specified (4)	6	0.03
Austrian	117	0.60
Belgian	222	1.14
British	124	0.63
Canadian	75	0.38
Croatian	124	0.63
Czech	311	1.59
Czechoslovakian	69	0.35
Danish	191	0.98
Dutch	288	1.47
Eastern European	19	0.10
English	2,008	10.27
Estonian	9	0.05
European	136	0.70
Finnish	20	0.10
French, except Basque	642	3.28
French Canadian	171	0.87
German	5,806	29.70
Greek	196	1.00
Hawaii Native/Pacific Islander:	9	0.05
Micronesian: (3)	3	0.02
Guamanian/Chamorro (3)	3	0.02
Polynesian:	3	0.02
Native Hawaiian	3	0.02
Other Pac. Isl., not spec. (2)	3	0.02
Hispanic or Latino:	541	2.77
Central American:	11	0.06
Guatemalan	7	0.04
Nicaraguan	1	0.01
Panamanian	1	0.01
Salvadoran	2	0.01
Cuban	19	0.10
Dominican Republic	1	0.01
Mexican	408	2.09
Puerto Rican	23	0.12
South American:	13	0.07
Argentinean	2	0.01
Bolivian	1	0.01
Ecuadorian	2	0.01
Paraguayan	1	0.01
Peruvian	7	0.04
Other Hispanic or Latino	66	0.34
Hungarian	220	1.13
Irish	4,672	23.90
Israeli	40	0.20
Italian	1,919	9.81
Lithuanian	164	0.84
Luxemburger	11	0.06
Northern European	21	0.11
Norwegian	481	2.46
Polish	2,145	10.97
Portuguese	6	0.03
Romanian	32	0.16
Russian	140	0.72
Scandinavian	39	0.20
Scotch-Irish	320	1.64
Scottish	465	2.38
Serbian	26	0.13
Slovak	121	0.62
Slovene	68	0.35
Swedish	1,479	7.56
Swiss	111	0.57
Ukrainian	23	0.12
United States or American	716	3.66
Welsh	146	0.75
West Indian, excl. Hispanic:	18	0.09
Bahamian	10	0.05
Belizean	8	0.04
White:	18,934	97.02
Not Hispanic (18,436)	18,512	94.86
Hispanic (396)	422	2.16
Yugoslavian	54	0.28

Glen Carbon

Place Type: Village
County: Madison
Population: 10,425

Ancestry/Race	Number	%
African American/Black:	756	7.25
Not Hispanic (722)	750	7.19
Hispanic (4)	6	0.06
African, sub-Saharan:	22	0.21
African	22	0.21
Am. Ind. or Alaska Nat., not spec.	16	0.15
American Indian tribes, specified:	47	0.45
Apache (1)	2	0.02
Blackfeet	2	0.02
Cherokee (7)	20	0.19
Cheyenne	1	0.01
Chickasaw	2	0.02
Choctaw (6)	9	0.09
Creek (1)	1	0.01
Iroquois	3	0.03
Latin American Indians (2)	2	0.02
Osage	1	0.01
Sioux (2)	3	0.03
All other tribes (1)	1	0.01
Arab:	24	0.23
Egyptian	10	0.10
Lebanese	9	0.09
Moroccan	5	0.05
Armenian	21	0.20
Asian:	258	2.47
Chinese, ex. Taiwanese (51)	55	0.53
Filipino (17)	23	0.22
Indian (56)	59	0.57
Japanese (9)	16	0.15
Korean (23)	29	0.28
Pakistani (32)	34	0.33
Taiwanese (16)	16	0.15
Thai (3)	6	0.06
Vietnamese (2)	4	0.04
Other Asian, specified (8)	8	0.08
Other Asian, not specified (2)	8	0.08
Austrian	16	0.15
Belgian	24	0.23
British	32	0.31
Bulgarian	28	0.27
Croatian	49	0.47
Czech	145	1.39
Czechoslovakian	32	0.31
Danish	42	0.40
Dutch	235	2.25
English	1,257	12.04
Estonian	5	0.05
European	74	0.71
Finnish	8	0.08
French, except Basque	371	3.55
French Canadian	54	0.52
German	3,410	32.66
Hawaii Native/Pacific Islander:	5	0.05
Polynesian: (3)	4	0.04
Native Hawaiian (3)	4	0.04
Other Pac. Isl., not spec. (1)	1	0.01
Hispanic or Latino:	156	1.50
Central American:	4	0.04
Costa Rican	1	0.01
Guatemalan	1	0.01
Honduran	2	0.02
Cuban	2	0.02
Dominican Republic	2	0.02
Mexican	88	0.84
Puerto Rican	13	0.12
South American:	14	0.13
Argentinean	1	0.01
Bolivian	2	0.02
Colombian	8	0.08
Ecuadorian	1	0.01
Peruvian	1	0.01
Venezuelan	1	0.01
Other Hispanic or Latino	33	0.32
Hungarian	61	0.58
Irish	1,580	15.13
Italian	449	4.30
Lithuanian	25	0.24
Macedonian	8	0.08
Norwegian	104	1.00
Polish	405	3.88
Russian	42	0.40
Scandinavian	13	0.12
Scotch-Irish	117	1.12
Scottish	178	1.70
Slovak	10	0.10
Swedish	112	1.07
Swiss	45	0.43
Ukrainian	18	0.17
United States or American	515	4.93
Welsh	111	1.06
West Indian, excl. Hispanic:	10	0.10
West Indian	10	0.10
White:	9,399	90.16
Not Hispanic (9,188)	9,287	89.08
Hispanic (100)	112	1.07

Glen Ellyn

Place Type: Village
County: Du Page
Population: 26,999

Ancestry/Race	Number	%
African American/Black:	643	2.38
Not Hispanic (570)	634	2.35
Hispanic (5)	9	0.03
African, sub-Saharan:	57	0.21
African	20	0.07
Ethiopian	37	0.14
Am. Ind. or Alaska Nat., not spec.	27	0.10
Albanian	111	0.41

Notes: 1. Figures in the "Number" column do not add up to the total population due to: a) Ancestry/Race overlap — e.g. persons can report being both White and Irish, b) persons of Hispanic origin can report being any race, c) persons reporting two ancestries are counted in both categories. 2. Numbers in parentheses indicate the number of persons reporting this ancestry/race alone, not in combination with any other ancestry/race. 3. Refer to the Explanation of Data in the front of the book for more detailed information.

Ancestry/Race	Number	%
American Indian tribes, specified:	44	0.16
Apache (1)	2	0.01
Blackfeet (1)	2	0.01
Cherokee (3)	13	0.05
Cheyenne	1	0.00
Chippewa (1)	1	0.00
Creek (1)	1	0.00
Iroquois (1)	1	0.00
Latin American Indians (8)	11	0.04
Menominee	1	0.00
Navajo (2)	2	0.01
Pima	4	0.01
Pueblo	1	0.00
Sioux (2)	2	0.01
All other tribes (1)	2	0.01
American Indian tribes, not spec.	11	0.04
Arab:	116	0.43
Iraqi	8	0.03
Jordanian	8	0.03
Lebanese	74	0.27
Palestinian	8	0.03
Syrian	13	0.05
Other Arab	5	0.02
Armenian	16	0.06
Asian:	1,483	5.49
Cambodian (10)	10	0.04
Chinese, ex. Taiwanese (149)	180	0.67
Filipino (136)	178	0.66
Indian (614)	646	2.39
Indonesian (1)	2	0.01
Japanese (45)	76	0.28
Korean (78)	82	0.30
Malaysian (1)	2	0.01
Pakistani (140)	174	0.64
Sri Lankan (1)	2	0.01
Taiwanese (16)	24	0.09
Thai (4)	12	0.04
Vietnamese (31)	37	0.14
Other Asian, specified (11)	12	0.04
Other Asian, not specified (22)	46	0.17
Assyrian/Chaldean/Syriac	42	0.16
Austrian	141	0.52
Belgian	58	0.21
Brazilian	16	0.06
British	111	0.41
Bulgarian	17	0.06
Canadian	62	0.23
Croatian	154	0.57
Czech	684	2.53
Czechoslovakian	203	0.75
Danish	318	1.18
Dutch	442	1.63
Eastern European	13	0.05
English	3,588	13.27
Estonian	44	0.16
European	238	0.88
Finnish	33	0.12
French, except Basque	698	2.58
French Canadian	244	0.90
German	7,525	27.83
Greek	341	1.26
Hawaii Native/Pacific Islander:	18	0.07
Micronesian: (2)	2	0.01
Guamanian/Chamorro (1)	1	0.00
Other Micronesian (1)	1	0.00
Polynesian:	2	0.01
Native Hawaiian	2	0.01
Other Pac. Isl., not spec.	14	0.05
Hispanic or Latino:	1,275	4.72
Central American:	30	0.11
Costa Rican	4	0.01
Guatemalan	12	0.04
Honduran	5	0.02
Nicaraguan	1	0.00
Panamanian	1	0.00
Salvadoran	5	0.02
Other Central American	2	0.01
Cuban	56	0.21
Dominican Republic	2	0.01
Mexican	919	3.40
Puerto Rican	69	0.26
South American:	88	0.33
Argentinean	2	0.01
Bolivian	20	0.07
Chilean	6	0.02
Colombian	21	0.08
Ecuadorian	14	0.05
Paraguayan	1	0.00
Peruvian	21	0.08
Venezuelan	3	0.01
Other Hispanic or Latino	111	0.41
Hungarian	187	0.69
Iranian	32	0.12
Irish	6,088	22.51
Israeli	17	0.06
Italian	2,789	10.31
Latvian	44	0.16
Lithuanian	415	1.53
Luxemburger	6	0.02
Macedonian	9	0.03
Northern European	14	0.05
Norwegian	786	2.91
Pennsylvania German	19	0.07
Polish	2,409	8.91
Portuguese	14	0.05
Romanian	54	0.20
Russian	191	0.71
Scandinavian	74	0.27
Scotch-Irish	463	1.71
Scottish	975	3.61
Serbian	30	0.11
Slavic	38	0.14
Slovak	110	0.41
Slovene	19	0.07
Swedish	1,235	4.57
Swiss	126	0.47
Turkish	37	0.14
Ukrainian	107	0.40
United States or American	628	2.32
Welsh	273	1.01
White:	24,536	90.88
Not Hispanic (23,476)	23,759	88.00
Hispanic (687)	777	2.88
Yugoslavian	43	0.16

Glendale Heights

Place Type: Village
County: Du Page
Population: 31,765

Ancestry/Race	Number	%
African American/Black:	1,718	5.41
Not Hispanic (1,494)	1,652	5.20
Hispanic (43)	66	0.21
African, sub-Saharan:	194	0.61
African	107	0.34
Cape Verdean	4	0.01
Ethiopian	15	0.05
Liberian	14	0.04
Nigerian	48	0.15
Other sub-Saharan African	6	0.02
Am. Ind. or Alaska Nat., not spec.	88	0.28
Albanian	65	0.21
American Indian tribes, specified:	88	0.28
Apache (1)	1	0.00
Cherokee (9)	23	0.07
Cheyenne	1	0.00
Chippewa (3)	5	0.02
Choctaw (2)	3	0.01
Crow	1	0.00
Latin American Indians (32)	34	0.11
Navajo (1)	1	0.00
Ottawa (1)	1	0.00
Potawatomi (1)	3	0.01
Seminole (1)	1	0.00
Sioux (8)	8	0.03
All other tribes (3)	6	0.02
American Indian tribes, not spec.	13	0.04
Arab:	127	0.40
Iraqi	13	0.04
Jordanian	21	0.07
Lebanese	54	0.17
Moroccan	22	0.07
Palestinian	17	0.05
Armenian	77	0.24
Asian:	6,764	21.29
Bangladeshi (5)	5	0.02
Cambodian (75)	91	0.29
Chinese, ex. Taiwanese (230)	263	0.83
Filipino (1,803)	1,926	6.06
Hmong (5)	5	0.02
Indian (2,728)	2,840	8.94
Indonesian	1	0.00
Japanese (54)	67	0.21
Korean (166)	187	0.59
Laotian (28)	30	0.09
Malaysian (6)	6	0.02
Pakistani (300)	354	1.11
Sri Lankan	2	0.01
Taiwanese (22)	24	0.08
Thai (23)	38	0.12
Vietnamese (762)	805	2.53
Other Asian, specified (6)	7	0.02
Other Asian, not specified (56)	113	0.36
Austrian	106	0.33
Belgian	54	0.17
British	50	0.16
Bulgarian	25	0.08
Canadian	29	0.09
Croatian	44	0.14
Czech	449	1.42
Czechoslovakian	52	0.16
Danish	55	0.17
Dutch	266	0.84
English	1,452	4.58
European	73	0.23
Finnish	35	0.11
French, except Basque	640	2.02
French Canadian	131	0.41
German	5,323	16.80
Greek	317	1.00
Hawaii Native/Pacific Islander:	50	0.16
Melanesian: (3)	3	0.01
Fijian (3)	3	0.01
Micronesian: (1)	2	0.01
Guamanian/Chamorro (1)	2	0.01
Polynesian: (8)	12	0.04
Native Hawaiian (1)	4	0.01
Samoan (7)	8	0.03
Other Pac. Isl., not spec. (13)	33	0.10
Hispanic or Latino:	5,842	18.39
Central American:	290	0.91
Costa Rican	6	0.02
Guatemalan	219	0.69
Honduran	11	0.03
Nicaraguan	5	0.02
Panamanian	2	0.01
Salvadoran	29	0.09
Other Central American	18	0.06
Cuban	53	0.17
Dominican Republic	2	0.01
Mexican	4,622	14.55
Puerto Rican	234	0.74
South American:	132	0.42
Argentinean	3	0.01
Bolivian	5	0.02
Chilean	12	0.04
Colombian	46	0.14
Ecuadorian	14	0.04
Paraguayan	2	0.01
Peruvian	27	0.08
Venezuelan	13	0.04
Other South American	10	0.03
Other Hispanic or Latino	509	1.60
Hungarian	145	0.46
Irish	3,022	9.54
Israeli	4	0.01
Italian	3,212	10.14
Latvian	40	0.13

Notes: 1. Figures in the "Number" column do not add up to the total population due to: a) Ancestry/Race overlap — e.g. persons can report being both White and Irish, b) persons of Hispanic origin can report being any race, c) persons reporting two ancestries are counted in both categories. 2. Numbers in parentheses indicate the number of persons reporting this ancestry/race alone, not in combination with any other ancestry/race. 3. Refer to the Explanation of Data in the front of the book for more detailed information.

Lithuanian	106	0.33
Luxemburger	14	0.04
Macedonian	11	0.03
Northern European	7	0.02
Norwegian	315	0.99
Polish	3,604	11.38
Portuguese	21	0.07
Romanian	40	0.13
Russian	151	0.48
Scandinavian	5	0.02
Scotch-Irish	177	0.56
Scottish	315	0.99
Serbian	51	0.16
Slavic	26	0.08
Slovak	62	0.20
Slovene	12	0.04
Swedish	580	1.83
Swiss	40	0.13
Ukrainian	329	1.04
United States or American	618	1.95
Welsh	81	0.26
West Indian, excl. Hispanic:	15	0.05
Jamaican	15	0.05
White:	20,981	66.05
Not Hispanic (17,409)	17,829	56.13
Hispanic (2,854)	3,152	9.92
Yugoslavian	176	0.56

Glenview

Place Type: Village
County: Cook
Population: 41,847

Ancestry/Race	Number	%
African American/Black:	721	1.72
Not Hispanic (646)	693	1.66
Hispanic (19)	28	0.07
African, sub-Saharan:	72	0.17
African	24	0.06
Ethiopian	21	0.05
Zimbabwean	27	0.06
Am. Ind. or Alaska Nat., not spec.	38	0.09
Albanian	53	0.13
American Indian tribes, specified:	74	0.18
Apache	1	0.00
Cherokee (4)	25	0.06
Chippewa (6)	9	0.02
Creek	2	0.00
Crow	1	0.00
Houma	1	0.00
Iroquois	2	0.00
Latin American Indians (7)	13	0.03
Menominee (1)	2	0.00
Navajo (1)	3	0.01
Osage (2)	2	0.00
Pueblo (1)	1	0.00
Sioux	4	0.01
Yuman	2	0.00
All other tribes (2)	6	0.01
American Indian tribes, not spec.	6	0.01
Arab:	198	0.48
Arab/Arabic	31	0.07
Egyptian	49	0.12
Iraqi	5	0.01
Lebanese	46	0.11
Moroccan	21	0.05
Palestinian	46	0.11
Armenian	136	0.33
Asian:	4,589	10.97
Bangladeshi (3)	3	0.01
Cambodian (3)	3	0.01
Chinese, ex. Taiwanese (541)	643	1.54
Filipino (493)	569	1.36
Indian (667)	707	1.69
Indonesian (2)	2	0.00
Japanese (319)	406	0.97
Korean (1,866)	1,929	4.61
Laotian (1)	2	0.00
Malaysian (4)	4	0.01
Pakistani (47)	54	0.13
Sri Lankan (10)	10	0.02
Taiwanese (53)	61	0.15
Thai (66)	83	0.20
Vietnamese (34)	36	0.09
Other Asian, specified (1)	5	0.01
Other Asian, not specified (28)	72	0.17
Assyrian/Chaldean/Syriac	203	0.49
Australian	36	0.09
Austrian	324	0.78
Basque	13	0.03
Belgian	190	0.46
British	193	0.46
Bulgarian	37	0.09
Canadian	69	0.17
Croatian	94	0.23
Cypriot	4	0.01
Czech	338	0.81
Czechoslovakian	97	0.23
Danish	228	0.55
Dutch	525	1.26
Eastern European	143	0.34
English	3,110	7.46
European	346	0.83
Finnish	140	0.34
French, except Basque	858	2.06
French Canadian	179	0.43
German	8,580	20.59
Greek	1,420	3.41
Hawaii Native/Pacific Islander:	26	0.06
Polynesian: (6)	9	0.02
Native Hawaiian	3	0.01
Samoan (6)	6	0.01
Other Pac. Isl., not spec. (1)	17	0.04
Hispanic or Latino:	1,702	4.07
Central American:	46	0.11
Costa Rican	6	0.01
Guatemalan	20	0.05
Honduran	8	0.02
Nicaraguan	1	0.00
Panamanian	1	0.00
Salvadoran	10	0.02
Cuban	138	0.33
Dominican Republic	6	0.01
Mexican	1,036	2.48
Puerto Rican	110	0.26
South American:	185	0.44
Argentinean	16	0.04
Bolivian	9	0.02
Chilean	12	0.03
Colombian	68	0.16
Ecuadorian	17	0.04
Paraguayan	2	0.00
Peruvian	29	0.07
Uruguayan	1	0.00
Venezuelan	6	0.01
Other South American	25	0.06
Other Hispanic or Latino	181	0.43
Hungarian	462	1.11
Icelander	13	0.03
Iranian	115	0.28
Irish	7,068	16.96
Israeli	68	0.16
Italian	2,853	6.85
Latvian	7	0.02
Lithuanian	367	0.88
Luxemburger	112	0.27
Maltese	5	0.01
Northern European	35	0.08
Norwegian	874	2.10
Polish	3,856	9.25
Portuguese	42	0.10
Romanian	223	0.54
Russian	2,510	6.02
Scandinavian	96	0.23
Scotch-Irish	558	1.34
Scottish	824	1.98
Serbian	124	0.30
Slavic	42	0.10
Slovak	151	0.36
Slovene	56	0.13
Swedish	1,615	3.87
Swiss	192	0.46
Turkish	49	0.12
Ukrainian	546	1.31
United States or American	1,748	4.19
Welsh	106	0.25
West Indian, excl. Hispanic:	40	0.10
Belizean	30	0.07
Jamaican	10	0.02
White:	36,329	86.81
Not Hispanic (34,778)	35,195	84.10
Hispanic (1,039)	1,134	2.71
Yugoslavian	120	0.29

Godfrey

Place Type: Village
County: Madison
Population: 16,286

Ancestry/Race	Number	%
Acadian/Cajun	15	0.09
African American/Black:	699	4.29
Not Hispanic (653)	693	4.26
Hispanic (5)	6	0.04
African, sub-Saharan:	72	0.44
African	72	0.44
Am. Ind. or Alaska Nat., not spec.	29	0.18
American Indian tribes, specified:	83	0.51
Blackfeet (3)	6	0.04
Cherokee (13)	40	0.25
Cheyenne (1)	1	0.01
Chickasaw	3	0.02
Latin American Indians (1)	1	0.01
Navajo (3)	7	0.04
Pueblo (2)	5	0.03
Sioux (11)	14	0.09
All other tribes	6	0.04
American Indian tribes, not spec.	5	0.03
Arab:	25	0.15
Egyptian	17	0.10
Lebanese	8	0.05
Asian:	149	0.91
Chinese, ex. Taiwanese (15)	21	0.13
Filipino (10)	22	0.14
Indian (13)	15	0.09
Japanese (8)	12	0.07
Korean (19)	26	0.16
Laotian (4)	4	0.02
Taiwanese (4)	4	0.02
Thai (10)	10	0.06
Vietnamese (18)	19	0.12
Other Asian, specified	6	0.04
Other Asian, not specified (5)	10	0.06
Austrian	49	0.30
Belgian	17	0.10
British	36	0.22
Canadian	58	0.36
Celtic	7	0.04
Croatian	129	0.79
Czech	25	0.15
Czechoslovakian	45	0.28
Danish	40	0.25
Dutch	220	1.35
English	2,220	13.60
European	415	2.54
Finnish	33	0.20
French, except Basque	723	4.43
French Canadian	35	0.21
German	5,575	34.16
Greek	71	0.44
Hawaii Native/Pacific Islander:	11	0.07
Micronesian:	1	0.01
Guamanian/Chamorro	1	0.01
Polynesian: (1)	4	0.02
Native Hawaiian (1)	4	0.02
Other Pac. Isl., specified	6	0.04
Hispanic or Latino:	159	0.98
Central American:	3	0.02

Notes: 1. Figures in the "Number" column do not add up to the total population due to: a) Ancestry/Race overlap — e.g. persons can report being both White and Irish, b) persons of Hispanic origin can report being any race, c) persons reporting two ancestries are counted in both categories. 2. Numbers in parentheses indicate the number of persons reporting this ancestry/race alone, not in combination with any other ancestry/race. 3. Refer to the Explanation of Data in the front of the book for more detailed information.

Ancestry/Race	Number	%
Honduran	1	0.01
Panamanian	1	0.01
Other Central American	1	0.01
Cuban	2	0.01
Mexican	93	0.57
Puerto Rican	16	0.10
South American:	16	0.10
Argentinean	4	0.02
Chilean	6	0.04
Ecuadorian	1	0.01
Peruvian	5	0.03
Other Hispanic or Latino	29	0.18
Hungarian	7	0.04
Iranian	6	0.04
Irish	2,314	14.18
Italian	534	3.27
Lithuanian	38	0.23
Macedonian	7	0.04
Norwegian	87	0.53
Pennsylvania German	8	0.05
Polish	252	1.54
Portuguese	9	0.06
Scandinavian	7	0.04
Scotch-Irish	343	2.10
Scottish	314	1.92
Serbian	10	0.06
Slovak	35	0.21
Swedish	194	1.19
Swiss	104	0.64
Ukrainian	7	0.04
United States or American	1,376	8.43
Welsh	111	0.68
White:	15,423	94.70
Not Hispanic (15,200)	15,296	93.92
Hispanic (119)	127	0.78
Yugoslavian	17	0.10

Goodings Grove

Place Type: Census Designated Place
County: Will
Population: 17,084

Ancestry/Race	Number	%
African American/Black:	47	0.28
Not Hispanic (35)	47	0.28
Am. Ind. or Alaska Nat., not spec.	9	0.05
American Indian tribes, specified:	16	0.09
Blackfeet	1	0.01
Cherokee	5	0.03
Cheyenne	3	0.02
Latin American Indians (1)	5	0.03
All other tribes	2	0.01
Arab:	254	1.48
Arab/Arabic	73	0.43
Egyptian	33	0.19
Jordanian	30	0.18
Palestinian	111	0.65
Other Arab	7	0.04
Asian:	385	2.25
Chinese, ex. Taiwanese (25)	32	0.19
Filipino (119)	136	0.80
Hmong (5)	10	0.06
Indian (81)	96	0.56
Japanese (4)	15	0.09
Korean (41)	48	0.28
Laotian	5	0.03
Malaysian (1)	2	0.01
Thai (10)	12	0.07
Vietnamese (2)	6	0.04
Other Asian, not specified	23	0.13
Australian	19	0.11
Austrian	103	0.60
Belgian	15	0.09
British	66	0.39
Canadian	8	0.05
Croatian	316	1.85
Czech	592	3.46
Czechoslovakian	27	0.16
Danish	106	0.62
Dutch	421	2.46
Eastern European	10	0.06
English	838	4.90
European	57	0.33
Finnish	28	0.16
French, except Basque	527	3.08
French Canadian	67	0.39
German	4,019	23.50
Greek	438	2.56
Hawaii Native/Pacific Islander:	3	0.02
Micronesian:	1	0.01
Guamanian/Chamorro	1	0.01
Other Pac. Isl., not spec.	2	0.01
Hispanic or Latino:	601	3.52
Central American:	12	0.07
Costa Rican	1	0.01
Guatemalan	2	0.01
Salvadoran	8	0.05
Other Central American	1	0.01
Cuban	3	0.02
Mexican	476	2.79
Puerto Rican	47	0.28
South American:	9	0.05
Argentinean	1	0.01
Colombian	4	0.02
Ecuadorian	1	0.01
Peruvian	1	0.01
Other South American	2	0.01
Other Hispanic or Latino	54	0.32
Hungarian	111	0.65
Iranian	10	0.06
Irish	4,217	24.65
Italian	2,691	15.73
Latvian	6	0.04
Lithuanian	934	5.46
Norwegian	197	1.15
Pennsylvania German	10	0.06
Polish	4,825	28.21
Romanian	9	0.05
Russian	189	1.10
Scotch-Irish	104	0.61
Scottish	213	1.25
Serbian	23	0.13
Slovak	147	0.86
Slovene	45	0.26
Swedish	428	2.50
Ukrainian	70	0.41
United States or American	175	1.02
Welsh	32	0.19
West Indian, excl. Hispanic:	53	0.31
Jamaican	53	0.31
White:	16,636	97.38
Not Hispanic (16,012)	16,135	94.45
Hispanic (472)	501	2.93
Yugoslavian	60	0.35

Granite City

Place Type: City
County: Madison
Population: 31,301

Ancestry/Race	Number	%
African American/Black:	695	2.22
Not Hispanic (616)	687	2.19
Hispanic (6)	8	0.03
African, sub-Saharan:	4	0.01
African	4	0.01
Alaska Native tribes, specified:	1	0.00
Alaska Athabascan (1)	1	0.00
Am. Ind. or Alaska Nat., not spec.	130	0.42
American Indian tribes, specified:	186	0.59
Apache (4)	11	0.04
Blackfeet (10)	11	0.04
Cherokee (41)	115	0.37
Cheyenne	2	0.01
Chickasaw	4	0.01
Chippewa (1)	2	0.01
Choctaw (4)	5	0.02
Iroquois (1)	1	0.00
Latin American Indians (3)	4	0.01
Lumbee (2)	2	0.01
Osage	3	0.01
Puget Sound Salish (3)	3	0.01
Seminole	1	0.00
Shoshone (7)	7	0.02
Sioux (5)	9	0.03
All other tribes (2)	6	0.02
American Indian tribes, not spec.	12	0.04
Arab:	22	0.07
Lebanese	22	0.07
Armenian	82	0.26
Asian:	228	0.73
Chinese, ex. Taiwanese (6)	16	0.05
Filipino (31)	54	0.17
Indian (14)	26	0.08
Japanese (19)	35	0.11
Korean (44)	51	0.16
Laotian (11)	12	0.04
Thai (1)	1	0.00
Vietnamese (5)	9	0.03
Other Asian, specified (7)	7	0.02
Other Asian, not specified (7)	17	0.05
Austrian	95	0.30
Belgian	8	0.03
Brazilian	7	0.02
British	96	0.30
Bulgarian	58	0.18
Canadian	7	0.02
Croatian	378	1.19
Czech	102	0.32
Czechoslovakian	44	0.14
Danish	40	0.13
Dutch	793	2.51
Eastern European	7	0.02
English	3,060	9.67
European	340	1.07
Finnish	33	0.10
French, except Basque	1,310	4.14
French Canadian	86	0.27
German	6,513	20.59
Greek	58	0.18
Hawaii Native/Pacific Islander:	30	0.10
Micronesian: (2)	9	0.03
Guamanian/Chamorro (2)	9	0.03
Polynesian: (5)	19	0.06
Native Hawaiian (4)	15	0.05
Samoan (1)	4	0.01
Other Pac. Isl., not spec.	2	0.01
Hispanic or Latino:	894	2.86
Central American:	22	0.07
Costa Rican	1	0.00
Guatemalan	2	0.01
Honduran	2	0.01
Nicaraguan	6	0.02
Panamanian	10	0.03
Other Central American	1	0.00
Cuban	5	0.02
Mexican	641	2.05
Puerto Rican	58	0.19
South American:	3	0.01
Ecuadorian	1	0.00
Peruvian	2	0.01
Other Hispanic or Latino	165	0.53
Hungarian	387	1.22
Iranian	4	0.01
Irish	5,329	16.85
Italian	1,243	3.93
Lithuanian	69	0.22
Macedonian	173	0.55
Norwegian	146	0.46
Polish	1,161	3.67
Portuguese	6	0.02
Romanian	71	0.22
Russian	128	0.40
Scandinavian	9	0.03
Scotch-Irish	429	1.36
Scottish	325	1.03
Serbian	15	0.05
Slavic	9	0.03

Notes: 1. Figures in the "Number" column do not add up to the total population due to: a) Ancestry/Race overlap — e.g. persons can report being both White and Irish, b) persons of Hispanic origin can report being any race, c) persons reporting two ancestries are counted in both categories. 2. Numbers in parentheses indicate the number of persons reporting this ancestry/race alone, not in combination with any other ancestry/race. 3. Refer to the Explanation of Data in the front of the book for more detailed information.

Ancestry/Race	Number	%
Slovak	185	0.58
Swedish	123	0.39
Swiss	65	0.21
Ukrainian	23	0.07
United States or American	3,263	10.32
Welsh	319	1.01
White:	30,070	96.07
Not Hispanic (29,142)	29,471	94.15
Hispanic (511)	599	1.91
Yugoslavian	89	0.28

Grayslake

Place Type: Village
County: Lake
Population: 18,506

Ancestry/Race	Number	%
African American/Black:	336	1.82
Not Hispanic (288)	325	1.76
Hispanic (5)	11	0.06
African, sub-Saharan:	28	0.15
African	28	0.15
Alaska Native tribes, specified:	3	0.02
Eskimo (3)	3	0.02
Am. Ind. or Alaska Nat., not spec.	26	0.14
Albanian	14	0.08
American Indian tribes, specified:	46	0.25
Blackfeet	4	0.02
Cherokee (3)	14	0.08
Cheyenne	1	0.01
Chippewa	2	0.01
Choctaw (2)	4	0.02
Creek (1)	1	0.01
Iroquois (2)	2	0.01
Latin American Indians (3)	5	0.03
Lumbee (1)	1	0.01
Menominee (1)	1	0.01
Navajo (2)	2	0.01
Sioux (1)	6	0.03
All other tribes (1)	3	0.02
American Indian tribes, not spec.	5	0.03
Arab:	99	0.54
Arab/Arabic	32	0.17
Egyptian	7	0.04
Lebanese	16	0.09
Palestinian	34	0.18
Syrian	10	0.05
Armenian	14	0.08
Asian:	884	4.78
Chinese, ex. Taiwanese (153)	172	0.93
Filipino (166)	194	1.05
Indian (243)	252	1.36
Indonesian (2)	3	0.02
Japanese (32)	62	0.34
Korean (103)	114	0.62
Pakistani (24)	29	0.16
Thai (8)	9	0.05
Vietnamese (24)	25	0.14
Other Asian, specified (2)	6	0.03
Other Asian, not specified (15)	18	0.10
Assyrian/Chaldean/Syriac	47	0.25
Australian	26	0.14
Austrian	194	1.05
Belgian	32	0.17
Brazilian	25	0.14
British	77	0.42
Bulgarian	64	0.35
Canadian	49	0.27
Croatian	85	0.46
Czech	253	1.37
Czechoslovakian	110	0.60
Danish	318	1.72
Dutch	401	2.17
Eastern European	10	0.05
English	1,711	9.26
Estonian	35	0.19
European	61	0.33
Finnish	104	0.56
French, except Basque	621	3.36
French Canadian	140	0.76
German	5,804	31.41
Greek	178	0.96
Hawaii Native/Pacific Islander:	14	0.08
Micronesian: (2)	2	0.01
Guamanian/Chamorro (2)	2	0.01
Polynesian: (2)	4	0.02
Native Hawaiian	1	0.01
Samoan (2)	3	0.02
Other Pac. Isl., not spec. (2)	8	0.04
Hispanic or Latino:	920	4.97
Central American:	34	0.18
Costa Rican	2	0.01
Guatemalan	1	0.01
Nicaraguan	2	0.01
Panamanian	5	0.03
Salvadoran	23	0.12
Other Central American	1	0.01
Cuban	56	0.30
Dominican Republic	9	0.05
Mexican	521	2.82
Puerto Rican	125	0.68
South American:	83	0.45
Argentinean	4	0.02
Bolivian	3	0.02
Chilean	2	0.01
Colombian	29	0.16
Ecuadorian	31	0.17
Paraguayan	3	0.02
Peruvian	7	0.04
Venezuelan	1	0.01
Other South American	3	0.02
Other Hispanic or Latino	92	0.50
Hungarian	177	0.96
Iranian	30	0.16
Irish	3,121	16.89
Israeli	30	0.16
Italian	1,882	10.18
Lithuanian	194	1.05
Luxemburger	35	0.19
Macedonian	11	0.06
New Zealander	14	0.08
Norwegian	526	2.85
Pennsylvania German	5	0.03
Polish	1,991	10.77
Portuguese	49	0.27
Romanian	26	0.14
Russian	292	1.58
Scandinavian	55	0.30
Scotch-Irish	241	1.30
Scottish	282	1.53
Serbian	56	0.30
Slavic	9	0.05
Slovak	30	0.16
Slovene	53	0.29
Swedish	692	3.74
Swiss	64	0.35
Ukrainian	70	0.38
United States or American	753	4.07
Welsh	120	0.65
White:	17,049	92.13
Not Hispanic (16,293)	16,449	88.88
Hispanic (547)	600	3.24
Yugoslavian	21	0.11

Gurnee

Place Type: Village
County: Lake
Population: 28,834

Ancestry/Race	Number	%
African American/Black:	1,625	5.64
Not Hispanic (1,442)	1,577	5.47
Hispanic (17)	48	0.17
African, sub-Saharan:	74	0.26
African	38	0.13
Ghanian	12	0.04
Liberian	21	0.07
Other sub-Saharan African	3	0.01
Alaska Native tribes, not specified	3	0.01
Am. Ind. or Alaska Nat., not spec.	55	0.19
Albanian	6	0.02
American Indian tribes, specified:	106	0.37
Apache (1)	4	0.01
Blackfeet (1)	2	0.01
Cherokee (1)	35	0.12
Cheyenne (1)	1	0.00
Chippewa (18)	19	0.07
Choctaw (2)	9	0.03
Creek (2)	2	0.01
Delaware	1	0.00
Iroquois (1)	8	0.03
Latin American Indians (1)	5	0.02
Menominee	1	0.00
Navajo	3	0.01
Osage (1)	1	0.00
Ottawa (2)	2	0.01
Pima (1)	1	0.00
Sioux	4	0.01
All other tribes (5)	8	0.03
American Indian tribes, not spec.	5	0.02
Arab:	79	0.28
Egyptian	9	0.03
Lebanese	8	0.03
Moroccan	6	0.02
Palestinian	18	0.06
Syrian	17	0.06
Other Arab	21	0.07
Armenian	121	0.42
Asian:	2,624	9.10
Bangladeshi (3)	4	0.01
Cambodian (15)	20	0.07
Chinese, ex. Taiwanese (407)	465	1.61
Filipino (874)	977	3.39
Hmong (2)	2	0.01
Indian (597)	630	2.18
Indonesian	2	0.01
Japanese (66)	92	0.32
Korean (223)	238	0.83
Laotian	1	0.00
Malaysian (5)	7	0.02
Pakistani (41)	47	0.16
Sri Lankan (2)	2	0.01
Taiwanese (24)	28	0.10
Thai (18)	20	0.07
Vietnamese (35)	42	0.15
Other Asian, specified (2)	2	0.01
Other Asian, not specified (27)	45	0.16
Assyrian/Chaldean/Syriac	9	0.03
Austrian	188	0.66
Belgian	68	0.24
British	120	0.42
Bulgarian	46	0.16
Canadian	52	0.18
Croatian	204	0.71
Czech	279	0.98
Czechoslovakian	69	0.24
Danish	328	1.15
Dutch	548	1.92
Eastern European	24	0.08
English	2,349	8.21
European	243	0.85
Finnish	384	1.34
French, except Basque	527	1.84
French Canadian	252	0.88
German	7,821	27.33
Greek	363	1.27
Hawaii Native/Pacific Islander:	41	0.14
Micronesian:	5	0.02
Guamanian/Chamorro	5	0.02
Polynesian: (7)	15	0.05
Native Hawaiian (3)	9	0.03
Samoan (4)	6	0.02
Other Pac. Isl., not spec. (8)	21	0.07
Hispanic or Latino:	1,738	6.03
Central American:	71	0.25
Guatemalan	14	0.05
Honduran	11	0.04
Nicaraguan	1	0.00

Notes: 1. Figures in the "Number" column do not add up to the total population due to: a) Ancestry/Race overlap — e.g. persons can report being both White and Irish, b) persons of Hispanic origin can report being any race, c) persons reporting two ancestries are counted in both categories. 2. Numbers in parentheses indicate the number of persons reporting this ancestry/race alone, not in combination with any other ancestry/race. 3. Refer to the Explanation of Data in the front of the book for more detailed information.

Panamanian	7	0.02
Salvadoran	30	0.10
Other Central American	8	0.03
Cuban	37	0.13
Dominican Republic	9	0.03
Mexican	962	3.34
Puerto Rican	351	1.22
South American:	137	0.48
Argentinean	14	0.05
Bolivian	6	0.02
Chilean	3	0.01
Colombian	62	0.22
Ecuadorian	24	0.08
Peruvian	14	0.05
Uruguayan	1	0.00
Venezuelan	9	0.03
Other South American	4	0.01
Other Hispanic or Latino	171	0.59
Hungarian	199	0.70
Icelander	9	0.03
Iranian	5	0.02
Irish	4,140	14.47
Italian	2,468	8.62
Latvian	11	0.04
Lithuanian	308	1.08
Luxemburger	28	0.10
Macedonian	39	0.14
Norwegian	902	3.15
Polish	2,645	9.24
Portuguese	12	0.04
Romanian	88	0.31
Russian	403	1.41
Scandinavian	82	0.29
Scotch-Irish	387	1.35
Scottish	360	1.26
Serbian	140	0.49
Slavic	103	0.36
Slovak	162	0.57
Slovene	95	0.33
Swedish	907	3.17
Swiss	131	0.46
Ukrainian	112	0.39
United States or American	737	2.58
Welsh	105	0.37
West Indian, excl. Hispanic:	93	0.33
Belizean	9	0.03
Haitian	45	0.16
Jamaican	39	0.14
White:	24,204	83.94
Not Hispanic (22,705)	23,115	80.17
Hispanic (974)	1,089	3.78
Yugoslavian	98	0.34

Hanover Park

Place Type: Village
County: Cook
Population: 38,278

Ancestry/Race	Number	%
Acadian/Cajun	20	0.05
African American/Black:	2,529	6.61
Not Hispanic (2,243)	2,406	6.29
Hispanic (105)	123	0.32
African, sub-Saharan:	157	0.41
African	90	0.23
Nigerian	67	0.17
Am. Ind. or Alaska Nat., not spec.	143	0.37
Albanian	21	0.05
American Indian tribes, specified:	113	0.30
Apache (2)	4	0.01
Blackfeet (1)	2	0.01
Cherokee (15)	47	0.12
Chippewa (2)	8	0.02
Choctaw (4)	7	0.02
Cree	1	0.00
Delaware	1	0.00
Iroquois	4	0.01
Latin American Indians (12)	16	0.04
Osage	1	0.00
Potawatomi	5	0.01
Seminole	1	0.00
Sioux	6	0.02
All other tribes (5)	10	0.03
American Indian tribes, not spec.	27	0.07
Arab:	212	0.55
Arab/Arabic	121	0.32
Lebanese	49	0.13
Palestinian	20	0.05
Other Arab	22	0.06
Armenian	23	0.06
Asian:	4,991	13.04
Cambodian (53)	68	0.18
Chinese, ex. Taiwanese (141)	166	0.43
Filipino (1,180)	1,274	3.33
Hmong (8)	8	0.02
Indian (2,193)	2,313	6.04
Indonesian (1)	3	0.01
Japanese (70)	111	0.29
Korean (228)	248	0.65
Laotian (136)	147	0.38
Malaysian (1)	1	0.00
Pakistani (308)	351	0.92
Taiwanese	2	0.01
Thai (14)	21	0.05
Vietnamese (138)	152	0.40
Other Asian, specified (10)	11	0.03
Other Asian, not specified (52)	115	0.30
Assyrian/Chaldean/Syriac	51	0.13
Austrian	77	0.20
Belgian	76	0.20
Brazilian	40	0.10
British	77	0.20
Canadian	67	0.17
Croatian	165	0.43
Czech	383	1.00
Czechoslovakian	45	0.12
Danish	204	0.53
Dutch	258	0.67
English	1,481	3.86
Estonian	8	0.02
European	108	0.28
Finnish	30	0.08
French, except Basque	688	1.79
French Canadian	200	0.52
German	5,965	15.55
Greek	358	0.93
Guyanese	56	0.15
Hawaii Native/Pacific Islander:	46	0.12
Micronesian: (1)	2	0.01
Guamanian/Chamorro (1)	1	0.00
Other Micronesian	1	0.00
Polynesian: (2)	18	0.05
Native Hawaiian (2)	13	0.03
Samoan	4	0.01
Other Polynesian	1	0.00
Other Pac. Isl., not spec. (2)	26	0.07
Hispanic or Latino:	10,233	26.73
Central American:	270	0.71
Costa Rican	11	0.03
Guatemalan	123	0.32
Honduran	19	0.05
Nicaraguan	6	0.02
Panamanian	4	0.01
Salvadoran	94	0.25
Other Central American	13	0.03
Cuban	99	0.26
Dominican Republic	17	0.04
Mexican	8,548	22.33
Puerto Rican	365	0.95
South American:	197	0.51
Argentinean	13	0.03
Bolivian	4	0.01
Chilean	11	0.03
Colombian	90	0.24
Ecuadorian	39	0.10
Paraguayan	1	0.00
Peruvian	20	0.05
Venezuelan	6	0.02
Other South American	13	0.03
Other Hispanic or Latino	737	1.93
Hungarian	85	0.22
Icelander	7	0.02
Iranian	6	0.02
Irish	4,842	12.62
Italian	3,353	8.74
Latvian	29	0.08
Lithuanian	156	0.41
Luxemburger	34	0.09
Norwegian	578	1.51
Pennsylvania German	8	0.02
Polish	4,221	11.00
Portuguese	51	0.13
Romanian	54	0.14
Russian	415	1.08
Scandinavian	140	0.36
Scotch-Irish	239	0.62
Scottish	473	1.23
Serbian	31	0.08
Slovak	108	0.28
Slovene	11	0.03
Swedish	1,061	2.77
Swiss	14	0.04
Turkish	11	0.03
Ukrainian	168	0.44
United States or American	663	1.73
Welsh	152	0.40
West Indian, excl. Hispanic:	187	0.49
Barbadian	24	0.06
Haitian	15	0.04
Jamaican	118	0.31
Trinidadian and Tobagonian	30	0.08
White:	27,055	70.68
Not Hispanic (20,474)	20,979	54.81
Hispanic (5,603)	6,076	15.87
Yugoslavian	29	0.08

Harvey

Place Type: City
County: Cook
Population: 30,000

Ancestry/Race	Number	%
African American/Black:	24,232	80.77
Not Hispanic (23,732)	24,027	80.09
Hispanic (139)	205	0.68
African, sub-Saharan:	757	2.51
African	757	2.51
Am. Ind. or Alaska Nat., not spec.	116	0.39
American Indian tribes, specified:	76	0.25
Apache (4)	7	0.02
Blackfeet	7	0.02
Cherokee (8)	36	0.12
Choctaw	1	0.00
Iroquois	6	0.02
Latin American Indians (10)	12	0.04
Seminole	3	0.01
Sioux (1)	3	0.01
All other tribes	1	0.00
American Indian tribes, not spec.	22	0.07
Arab:	22	0.07
Arab/Arabic	11	0.04
Iraqi	11	0.04
Asian:	182	0.61
Chinese, ex. Taiwanese	11	0.04
Filipino (5)	17	0.06
Indian (99)	129	0.43
Japanese (2)	3	0.01
Korean (2)	5	0.02
Pakistani	2	0.01
Vietnamese (5)	5	0.02
Other Asian, not specified	10	0.03
Belgian	7	0.02
Czech	38	0.13
Danish	13	0.04
Dutch	38	0.13
English	98	0.33
European	10	0.03
French, except Basque	73	0.24

Notes: 1. Figures in the "Number" column do not add up to the total population due to: a) Ancestry/Race overlap — e.g. persons can report being both White and Irish, b) persons of Hispanic origin can report being any race, c) persons reporting two ancestries are counted in both categories. 2. Numbers in parentheses indicate the number of persons reporting this ancestry/race alone, not in combination with any other ancestry/race. 3. Refer to the Explanation of Data in the front of the book for more detailed information.

French Canadian	5	0.02
German	357	1.19
Greek	31	0.10
Hawaii Native/Pacific Islander:	33	0.11
Micronesian: (10)	10	0.03
Guamanian/Chamorro (10)	10	0.03
Polynesian: (2)	12	0.04
Native Hawaiian (1)	10	0.03
Samoan (1)	1	0.00
Other Polynesian	1	0.00
Other Pac. Isl., not spec. (4)	11	0.04
Hispanic or Latino:	3,834	12.78
Central American:	21	0.07
Guatemalan	16	0.05
Honduran	1	0.00
Panamanian	3	0.01
Salvadoran	1	0.00
Cuban	17	0.06
Mexican	3,420	11.40
Puerto Rican	90	0.30
South American:	3	0.01
Ecuadorian	3	0.01
Other Hispanic or Latino	283	0.94
Hungarian	6	0.02
Irish	279	0.93
Italian	191	0.63
Lithuanian	8	0.03
Norwegian	29	0.10
Polish	486	1.61
Scotch-Irish	27	0.09
Scottish	51	0.17
Slovak	10	0.03
Swedish	75	0.25
Ukrainian	5	0.02
United States or American	318	1.06
West Indian, excl. Hispanic:	176	0.58
Belizean	23	0.08
Haitian	7	0.02
Jamaican	90	0.30
Trinidadian and Tobagonian	29	0.10
West Indian	27	0.09
White:	3,329	11.10
Not Hispanic (1,903)	2,108	7.03
Hispanic (1,102)	1,221	4.07

Hazel Crest

Place Type: Village
County: Cook
Population: 14,816

Ancestry/Race	Number	%
African American/Black:	11,482	77.50
Not Hispanic (11,227)	11,384	76.84
Hispanic (81)	98	0.66
African, sub-Saharan:	330	2.24
African	213	1.45
Ghanian	28	0.19
Nigerian	79	0.54
Other sub-Saharan African	10	0.07
Am. Ind. or Alaska Nat., not spec.	55	0.37
American Indian tribes, specified:	48	0.32
Apache	4	0.03
Blackfeet (2)	3	0.02
Cherokee (2)	20	0.13
Chickasaw	2	0.01
Chippewa (1)	2	0.01
Creek	1	0.01
Iroquois (1)	1	0.01
Menominee	1	0.01
Navajo (1)	2	0.01
Pueblo	7	0.05
Seminole	1	0.01
Sioux	1	0.01
All other tribes (1)	3	0.02
American Indian tribes, not spec.	2	0.01
Asian:	181	1.22
Chinese, ex. Taiwanese (7)	15	0.10
Filipino (41)	59	0.40
Hmong	1	0.01
Indian (40)	50	0.34
Japanese (3)	8	0.05
Korean (4)	9	0.06
Laotian (10)	10	0.07
Pakistani (12)	13	0.09
Thai (4)	5	0.03
Vietnamese (8)	8	0.05
Other Asian, not specified (3)	3	0.02
Australian	8	0.05
Austrian	9	0.06
Brazilian	9	0.06
British	7	0.05
Canadian	6	0.04
Croatian	5	0.03
Czech	71	0.48
Czechoslovakian	9	0.06
Danish	4	0.03
Dutch	73	0.50
English	451	3.06
European	30	0.20
French, except Basque	83	0.56
French Canadian	24	0.16
German	638	4.33
Greek	12	0.08
Hawaii Native/Pacific Islander:	4	0.03
Polynesian: (3)	3	0.02
Samoan (3)	3	0.02
Other Pac. Isl., not spec.	1	0.01
Hispanic or Latino:	494	3.33
Central American:	8	0.05
Costa Rican	1	0.01
Guatemalan	2	0.01
Panamanian	3	0.02
Salvadoran	1	0.01
Other Central American	1	0.01
Cuban	8	0.05
Mexican	338	2.28
Puerto Rican	86	0.58
South American:	4	0.03
Colombian	2	0.01
Uruguayan	2	0.01
Other Hispanic or Latino	50	0.34
Hungarian	69	0.47
Irish	596	4.05
Italian	203	1.38
Lithuanian	45	0.31
Norwegian	124	0.84
Polish	329	2.23
Russian	83	0.56
Scandinavian	11	0.07
Scotch-Irish	73	0.50
Scottish	73	0.50
Slovak	18	0.12
Swedish	159	1.08
Swiss	5	0.03
Ukrainian	45	0.31
United States or American	105	0.71
Welsh	27	0.18
West Indian, excl. Hispanic:	55	0.37
Bahamian	7	0.05
Haitian	26	0.18
Jamaican	22	0.15
White:	3,044	20.55
Not Hispanic (2,708)	2,851	19.24
Hispanic (177)	193	1.30

Herrin

Place Type: City
County: Williamson
Population: 11,298

Ancestry/Race	Number	%
African American/Black:	144	1.27
Not Hispanic (103)	143	1.27
Hispanic (1)	1	0.01
African, sub-Saharan:	7	0.06
African	7	0.06
Alaska Native tribes, specified:	3	0.03
Aleut (3)	3	0.03
Alaska Native tribes, not specified	1	0.01
Am. Ind. or Alaska Nat., not spec.	25	0.22
American Indian tribes, specified:	44	0.39
Apache	2	0.02
Blackfeet	2	0.02
Cherokee (8)	24	0.21
Choctaw	1	0.01
Creek	1	0.01
Crow	2	0.02
Latin American Indians	1	0.01
Pueblo	2	0.02
Sioux	4	0.04
All other tribes (4)	5	0.04
American Indian tribes, not spec.	11	0.10
Asian:	112	0.99
Chinese, ex. Taiwanese (17)	26	0.23
Filipino (18)	30	0.27
Indian	2	0.02
Japanese (4)	8	0.07
Korean (10)	13	0.12
Malaysian (4)	4	0.04
Pakistani (5)	6	0.05
Thai (10)	10	0.09
Vietnamese	6	0.05
Other Asian, not specified (2)	7	0.06
Austrian	7	0.06
Belgian	17	0.15
Canadian	45	0.41
Croatian	11	0.10
Czech	20	0.18
Czechoslovakian	15	0.14
Dutch	363	3.27
English	1,293	11.66
European	52	0.47
French, except Basque	230	2.07
French Canadian	51	0.46
German	1,618	14.59
German Russian	5	0.05
Greek	13	0.12
Hawaii Native/Pacific Islander:	5	0.04
Polynesian: (2)	3	0.03
Native Hawaiian (2)	3	0.03
Other Pac. Isl., not spec. (1)	2	0.02
Hispanic or Latino:	107	0.95
Central American:	9	0.08
Guatemalan	2	0.02
Honduran	6	0.05
Panamanian	1	0.01
Cuban	1	0.01
Mexican	34	0.30
Puerto Rican	2	0.02
South American:	6	0.05
Chilean	2	0.02
Colombian	2	0.02
Peruvian	2	0.02
Other Hispanic or Latino	55	0.49
Hungarian	36	0.32
Iranian	13	0.12
Irish	1,467	13.23
Italian	979	8.83
Lithuanian	58	0.52
Norwegian	15	0.14
Pennsylvania German	6	0.05
Polish	136	1.23
Romanian	3	0.03
Russian	22	0.20
Scandinavian	8	0.07
Scotch-Irish	356	3.21
Scottish	188	1.70
Serbian	3	0.03
Slavic	2	0.02
Slovak	11	0.10
Slovene	7	0.06
Swedish	71	0.64
United States or American	1,449	13.07
Welsh	96	0.87
White:	11,035	97.67
Not Hispanic (10,850)	10,952	96.94
Hispanic (77)	83	0.73
Yugoslavian	6	0.05

Notes: 1. Figures in the "Number" column do not add up to the total population due to: a) Ancestry/Race overlap — e.g. persons can report being both White and Irish, b) persons of Hispanic origin can report being any race, c) persons reporting two ancestries are counted in both categories. 2. Numbers in parentheses indicate the number of persons reporting this ancestry/race alone, not in combination with any other ancestry/race. 3. Refer to the Explanation of Data in the front of the book for more detailed information.

Hickory Hills

Place Type: City
County: Cook
Population: 13,926

Ancestry/Race	Number	%
African American/Black:	188	1.35
Not Hispanic (161)	174	1.25
Hispanic (11)	14	0.10
Am. Ind. or Alaska Nat., not spec.	40	0.29
Albanian	52	0.37
American Indian tribes, specified:	24	0.17
Apache	1	0.01
Cherokee (4)	14	0.10
Chippewa (2)	2	0.01
Choctaw	1	0.01
Iroquois (1)	2	0.01
Kiowa (1)	1	0.01
Latin American Indians	1	0.01
Menominee (1)	1	0.01
Sioux (1)	1	0.01
American Indian tribes, not spec.	6	0.04
Arab:	763	5.48
Arab/Arabic	381	2.73
Egyptian	29	0.21
Jordanian	82	0.59
Lebanese	31	0.22
Palestinian	203	1.46
Syrian	12	0.09
Other Arab	25	0.18
Armenian	11	0.08
Asian:	371	2.66
Chinese, ex. Taiwanese (15)	24	0.17
Filipino (96)	106	0.76
Indian (104)	109	0.78
Indonesian (4)	4	0.03
Japanese (14)	22	0.16
Korean (24)	29	0.21
Malaysian (1)	1	0.01
Pakistani (1)	6	0.04
Thai (11)	11	0.08
Vietnamese (6)	7	0.05
Other Asian, not specified (9)	52	0.37
Assyrian/Chaldean/Syriac	32	0.23
Austrian	159	1.14
Belgian	59	0.42
Canadian	13	0.09
Croatian	122	0.88
Czech	417	2.99
Czechoslovakian	94	0.67
Danish	57	0.41
Dutch	139	1.00
English	654	4.69
European	41	0.29
French, except Basque	356	2.55
French Canadian	75	0.54
German	2,402	17.24
Greek	392	2.81
Hawaii Native/Pacific Islander:	3	0.02
Polynesian: (1)	2	0.01
Native Hawaiian (1)	2	0.01
Other Pac. Isl., not spec.	1	0.01
Hispanic or Latino:	1,129	8.11
Central American:	10	0.07
Costa Rican	2	0.01
Guatemalan	6	0.04
Honduran	1	0.01
Nicaraguan	1	0.01
Cuban	1	0.01
Mexican	925	6.64
Puerto Rican	81	0.58
South American:	10	0.07
Argentinean	2	0.01
Bolivian	4	0.03
Chilean	1	0.01
Colombian	1	0.01
Venezuelan	2	0.01
Other Hispanic or Latino	102	0.73
Hungarian	67	0.48
Irish	2,768	19.86
Italian	1,488	10.68
Lithuanian	685	4.92
Luxemburger	22	0.16
Norwegian	91	0.65
Polish	3,750	26.91
Romanian	8	0.06
Russian	162	1.16
Scotch-Irish	92	0.66
Scottish	92	0.66
Slovak	94	0.67
Slovene	19	0.14
Swedish	340	2.44
Swiss	19	0.14
Turkish	6	0.04
Ukrainian	51	0.37
United States or American	285	2.05
Welsh	5	0.04
White:	13,083	93.95
Not Hispanic (11,949)	12,293	88.27
Hispanic (708)	790	5.67
Yugoslavian	16	0.11

Highland Park

Place Type: City
County: Lake
Population: 31,365

Ancestry/Race	Number	%
African American/Black:	653	2.08
Not Hispanic (488)	552	1.76
Hispanic (71)	101	0.32
African, sub-Saharan:	99	0.32
African	35	0.11
South African	64	0.20
Am. Ind. or Alaska Nat., not spec.	48	0.15
Albanian	6	0.02
Alsatian	6	0.02
American Indian tribes, specified:	35	0.11
Apache (1)	3	0.01
Cherokee	9	0.03
Chickasaw	2	0.01
Chippewa (2)	5	0.02
Choctaw	3	0.01
Creek	1	0.00
Latin American Indians (3)	3	0.01
Menominee (1)	1	0.00
Navajo (1)	5	0.02
Osage	1	0.00
Ottawa (1)	1	0.00
All other tribes (1)	1	0.00
American Indian tribes, not spec.	15	0.05
Arab:	122	0.39
Egyptian	9	0.03
Jordanian	7	0.02
Lebanese	33	0.11
Moroccan	21	0.07
Palestinian	10	0.03
Syrian	42	0.13
Armenian	17	0.05
Asian:	862	2.75
Chinese, ex. Taiwanese (168)	188	0.60
Filipino (141)	186	0.59
Indian (152)	161	0.51
Indonesian (1)	1	0.00
Japanese (71)	92	0.29
Korean (122)	136	0.43
Pakistani (16)	22	0.07
Sri Lankan (2)	2	0.01
Taiwanese (6)	8	0.03
Thai (7)	12	0.04
Vietnamese (8)	12	0.04
Other Asian, specified (1)	2	0.01
Other Asian, not specified (13)	40	0.13
Assyrian/Chaldean/Syriac	24	0.08
Australian	9	0.03
Austrian	456	1.45
Basque	40	0.13
Belgian	38	0.12
British	206	0.66
Canadian	165	0.53
Croatian	55	0.18
Czech	238	0.76
Czechoslovakian	113	0.36
Danish	184	0.59
Dutch	253	0.81
Eastern European	797	2.54
English	1,613	5.14
European	627	2.00
Finnish	71	0.23
French, except Basque	253	0.81
French Canadian	97	0.31
German	3,948	12.58
Greek	152	0.48
Hawaii Native/Pacific Islander:	31	0.10
Melanesian: (1)	1	0.00
Fijian (1)	1	0.00
Micronesian: (2)	5	0.02
Guamanian/Chamorro (2)	5	0.02
Polynesian: (1)	8	0.03
Native Hawaiian (1)	6	0.02
Samoan	2	0.01
Other Pac. Isl., not spec.	17	0.05
Hispanic or Latino:	2,792	8.90
Central American:	91	0.29
Costa Rican	3	0.01
Guatemalan	48	0.15
Honduran	14	0.04
Nicaraguan	1	0.00
Panamanian	3	0.01
Salvadoran	22	0.07
Cuban	51	0.16
Dominican Republic	3	0.01
Mexican	2,221	7.08
Puerto Rican	80	0.26
South American:	141	0.45
Argentinean	15	0.05
Bolivian	3	0.01
Chilean	5	0.02
Colombian	57	0.18
Ecuadorian	15	0.05
Paraguayan	10	0.03
Peruvian	15	0.05
Venezuelan	7	0.02
Other South American	14	0.04
Other Hispanic or Latino	205	0.65
Hungarian	439	1.40
Iranian	60	0.19
Irish	1,848	5.89
Israeli	251	0.80
Italian	2,447	7.80
Latvian	76	0.24
Lithuanian	398	1.27
Luxemburger	29	0.09
Macedonian	6	0.02
Maltese	38	0.12
Northern European	76	0.24
Norwegian	314	1.00
Polish	2,742	8.74
Portuguese	16	0.05
Romanian	314	1.00
Russian	5,157	16.43
Scandinavian	10	0.03
Scotch-Irish	202	0.64
Scottish	358	1.14
Serbian	5	0.02
Slovak	65	0.21
Slovene	58	0.18
Soviet Union	28	0.09
Swedish	434	1.38
Swiss	121	0.39
Turkish	37	0.12
Ukrainian	465	1.48
United States or American	2,751	8.77
Welsh	70	0.22
West Indian, excl. Hispanic:	12	0.04
Haitian	12	0.04
White:	28,912	92.18
Not Hispanic (27,112)	27,314	87.08

Notes: 1. Figures in the "Number" column do not add up to the total population due to: a) Ancestry/Race overlap — e.g. persons can report being both White and Irish, b) persons of Hispanic origin can report being any race, c) persons reporting two ancestries are counted in both categories. 2. Numbers in parentheses indicate the number of persons reporting this ancestry/race alone, not in combination with any other ancestry/race. 3. Refer to the Explanation of Data in the front of the book for more detailed information.

Hispanic (1,494)	1,598	5.09
Yugoslavian	31	0.10

Hinsdale

Place Type: Village
County: Du Page
Population: 17,349

Ancestry/Race	Number	%
African American/Black:	158	0.91
Not Hispanic (136)	158	0.91
African, sub-Saharan:	31	0.18
African	8	0.05
Ghanian	7	0.04
Kenyan	9	0.05
South African	7	0.04
Alaska Native tribes, specified:	2	0.01
Alaska Athabascan	1	0.01
Aleut (1)	1	0.01
Am. Ind. or Alaska Nat., not spec.	19	0.11
Albanian	7	0.04
Alsatian	8	0.05
American Indian tribes, specified:	29	0.17
Cherokee (1)	13	0.07
Chippewa (1)	2	0.01
Choctaw (3)	4	0.02
Comanche	1	0.01
Iroquois	1	0.01
Latin American Indians (1)	1	0.01
Navajo (1)	1	0.01
Potawatomi (1)	1	0.01
Sioux (1)	1	0.01
Ute	4	0.02
Arab:	76	0.43
Arab/Arabic	5	0.03
Jordanian	27	0.15
Lebanese	44	0.25
Armenian	57	0.33
Asian:	873	5.03
Bangladeshi (1)	1	0.01
Cambodian (1)	3	0.02
Chinese, ex. Taiwanese (236)	271	1.56
Filipino (151)	165	0.95
Indian (180)	192	1.11
Indonesian (1)	2	0.01
Japanese (39)	52	0.30
Korean (109)	122	0.70
Pakistani (12)	12	0.07
Sri Lankan (6)	6	0.03
Taiwanese (19)	26	0.15
Thai (2)	3	0.02
Vietnamese (6)	6	0.03
Other Asian, specified	3	0.02
Other Asian, not specified (4)	9	0.05
Austrian	75	0.43
Belgian	95	0.54
Brazilian	33	0.19
British	92	0.53
Bulgarian	32	0.18
Canadian	82	0.47
Croatian	114	0.65
Czech	547	3.13
Czechoslovakian	81	0.46
Danish	156	0.89
Dutch	352	2.01
Eastern European	27	0.15
English	2,430	13.90
Estonian	9	0.05
European	234	1.34
Finnish	48	0.27
French, except Basque	338	1.93
French Canadian	126	0.72
German	4,286	24.52
Greek	210	1.20
Hawaii Native/Pacific Islander:	12	0.07
Polynesian: (4)	5	0.03
Native Hawaiian (4)	4	0.02
Other Polynesian	1	0.01
Other Pac. Isl., not spec.	7	0.04
Hispanic or Latino:	414	2.39
Central American:	20	0.12
Costa Rican	1	0.01
Guatemalan	3	0.02
Honduran	8	0.05
Nicaraguan	2	0.01
Panamanian	1	0.01
Salvadoran	4	0.02
Other Central American	1	0.01
Cuban	39	0.22
Dominican Republic	2	0.01
Mexican	189	1.09
Puerto Rican	48	0.28
South American:	52	0.30
Argentinean	7	0.04
Bolivian	1	0.01
Chilean	4	0.02
Colombian	17	0.10
Ecuadorian	3	0.02
Paraguayan	2	0.01
Peruvian	10	0.06
Venezuelan	3	0.02
Other South American	5	0.03
Other Hispanic or Latino	64	0.37
Hungarian	41	0.23
Iranian	9	0.05
Irish	4,100	23.45
Italian	1,729	9.89
Latvian	17	0.10
Lithuanian	345	1.97
Luxemburger	33	0.19
Northern European	26	0.15
Norwegian	529	3.03
Pennsylvania German	7	0.04
Polish	1,356	7.76
Portuguese	6	0.03
Romanian	92	0.53
Russian	265	1.52
Scandinavian	82	0.47
Scotch-Irish	315	1.80
Scottish	464	2.65
Serbian	31	0.18
Slovak	84	0.48
Slovene	24	0.14
Swedish	845	4.83
Swiss	34	0.19
Ukrainian	71	0.41
United States or American	602	3.44
Welsh	135	0.77
West Indian, excl. Hispanic:	5	0.03
Trinidadian and Tobagonian	5	0.03
White:	16,314	94.03
Not Hispanic (15,884)	15,989	92.16
Hispanic (303)	325	1.87
Yugoslavian	27	0.15

Hoffman Estates

Place Type: Village
County: Cook
Population: 49,495

Ancestry/Race	Number	%
African American/Black:	2,373	4.79
Not Hispanic (2,141)	2,310	4.67
Hispanic (25)	63	0.13
African, sub-Saharan:	183	0.36
African	88	0.17
Nigerian	95	0.19
Am. Ind. or Alaska Nat., not spec.	108	0.22
Albanian	14	0.03
American Indian tribes, specified:	136	0.27
Apache	2	0.00
Blackfeet	8	0.02
Cherokee (8)	47	0.09
Chippewa (8)	13	0.03
Choctaw	4	0.01
Comanche (1)	1	0.00
Cree	3	0.01
Delaware	5	0.01
Iroquois (2)	2	0.00
Latin American Indians (16)	25	0.05
Osage (1)	1	0.00
Potawatomi (1)	1	0.00
Pueblo (5)	5	0.01
Sioux (3)	8	0.02
All other tribes (3)	11	0.02
American Indian tribes, not spec.	22	0.04
Arab:	342	0.68
Arab/Arabic	175	0.35
Egyptian	60	0.12
Jordanian	16	0.03
Lebanese	40	0.08
Moroccan	10	0.02
Palestinian	31	0.06
Other Arab	10	0.02
Armenian	137	0.27
Asian:	8,046	16.26
Bangladeshi (3)	3	0.01
Cambodian (7)	10	0.02
Chinese, ex. Taiwanese (825)	907	1.83
Filipino (964)	1,060	2.14
Hmong (1)	1	0.00
Indian (3,233)	3,371	6.81
Indonesian (7)	17	0.03
Japanese (705)	796	1.61
Korean (1,122)	1,144	2.31
Laotian (3)	5	0.01
Malaysian (1)	4	0.01
Pakistani (277)	351	0.71
Sri Lankan (10)	13	0.03
Taiwanese (71)	79	0.16
Thai (49)	57	0.12
Vietnamese (60)	78	0.16
Other Asian, specified (3)	6	0.01
Other Asian, not specified (33)	144	0.29
Assyrian/Chaldean/Syriac	100	0.20
Austrian	400	0.79
Basque	8	0.02
Belgian	161	0.32
Brazilian	26	0.05
British	58	0.12
Bulgarian	24	0.05
Canadian	107	0.21
Celtic	5	0.01
Croatian	113	0.22
Czech	561	1.11
Czechoslovakian	147	0.29
Danish	419	0.83
Dutch	430	0.85
Eastern European	63	0.13
English	2,740	5.44
Estonian	6	0.01
European	211	0.42
Finnish	174	0.35
French, except Basque	1,076	2.14
French Canadian	281	0.56
German	11,040	21.93
Greek	745	1.48
Guyanese	12	0.02
Hawaii Native/Pacific Islander:	53	0.11
Micronesian: (4)	4	0.01
Other Micronesian (4)	4	0.01
Polynesian: (6)	14	0.03
Native Hawaiian (4)	7	0.01
Samoan (2)	7	0.01
Other Pac. Isl., not spec. (2)	35	0.07
Hispanic or Latino:	5,198	10.50
Central American:	159	0.32
Guatemalan	80	0.16
Honduran	2	0.00
Nicaraguan	5	0.01
Panamanian	13	0.03
Salvadoran	55	0.11
Other Central American	4	0.01
Cuban	98	0.20
Dominican Republic	15	0.03
Mexican	3,830	7.74
Puerto Rican	332	0.67
South American:	259	0.52

Notes: 1. Figures in the "Number" column do not add up to the total population due to: a) Ancestry/Race overlap — e.g. persons can report being both White and Irish, b) persons of Hispanic origin can report being any race, c) persons reporting two ancestries are counted in both categories. 2. Numbers in parentheses indicate the number of persons reporting this ancestry/race alone, not in combination with any other ancestry/race. 3. Refer to the Explanation of Data in the front of the book for more detailed information.

Ancestry/Race	Number	%
Argentinean	15	0.03
Bolivian	5	0.01
Chilean	6	0.01
Colombian	104	0.21
Ecuadorian	72	0.15
Peruvian	33	0.07
Uruguayan	2	0.00
Venezuelan	4	0.01
Other South American	18	0.04
Other Hispanic or Latino	505	1.02
Hungarian	370	0.73
Iranian	243	0.48
Irish	7,400	14.70
Israeli	33	0.07
Italian	5,432	10.79
Latvian	74	0.15
Lithuanian	384	0.76
Luxemburger	35	0.07
Macedonian	41	0.08
Maltese	21	0.04
Northern European	19	0.04
Norwegian	1,175	2.33
Pennsylvania German	7	0.01
Polish	6,721	13.35
Portuguese	9	0.02
Romanian	163	0.32
Russian	782	1.55
Scandinavian	113	0.22
Scotch-Irish	430	0.85
Scottish	586	1.16
Serbian	68	0.14
Slavic	35	0.07
Slovak	131	0.26
Slovene	64	0.13
Swedish	1,461	2.90
Swiss	160	0.32
Turkish	130	0.26
Ukrainian	282	0.56
United States or American	1,199	2.38
Welsh	241	0.48
West Indian, excl. Hispanic:	116	0.23
Haitian	53	0.11
Jamaican	63	0.13
White:	37,672	76.11
Not Hispanic (33,789)	34,395	69.49
Hispanic (3,048)	3,277	6.62
Yugoslavian	200	0.40

Homewood

Place Type: Village
County: Cook
Population: 19,543

Ancestry/Race	Number	%
African American/Black:	3,561	18.22
Not Hispanic (3,403)	3,535	18.09
Hispanic (19)	26	0.13
African, sub-Saharan:	183	0.94
African	85	0.44
Nigerian	98	0.50
Alaska Native tribes, specified:	1	0.01
Aleut (1)	1	0.01
Am. Ind. or Alaska Nat., not spec.	33	0.17
American Indian tribes, specified:	41	0.21
Apache	1	0.01
Blackfeet	1	0.01
Cherokee (4)	16	0.08
Chippewa (2)	2	0.01
Choctaw	4	0.02
Iroquois (1)	4	0.02
Latin American Indians (2)	2	0.01
Navajo (1)	5	0.03
Pueblo	1	0.01
Sioux (1)	5	0.03
Arab:	18	0.09
Lebanese	12	0.06
Other Arab	6	0.03
Asian:	381	1.95
Chinese, ex. Taiwanese (64)	74	0.38
Filipino (49)	81	0.41
Indian (84)	96	0.49
Indonesian	1	0.01
Japanese (11)	14	0.07
Korean (47)	54	0.28
Pakistani (12)	14	0.07
Taiwanese (2)	2	0.01
Thai (15)	18	0.09
Vietnamese (10)	13	0.07
Other Asian, specified (4)	6	0.03
Other Asian, not specified (4)	8	0.04
Australian	16	0.08
Austrian	82	0.42
Belgian	12	0.06
British	59	0.30
Canadian	16	0.08
Croatian	81	0.42
Czech	227	1.16
Czechoslovakian	40	0.21
Danish	197	1.01
Dutch	602	3.09
Eastern European	10	0.05
English	1,412	7.24
European	121	0.62
Finnish	47	0.24
French, except Basque	518	2.66
French Canadian	123	0.63
German	4,428	22.72
Greek	124	0.64
Hawaii Native/Pacific Islander:	26	0.13
Micronesian: (7)	7	0.04
Other Micronesian (7)	7	0.04
Polynesian: (1)	4	0.02
Native Hawaiian	3	0.02
Samoan (1)	1	0.01
Other Pac. Isl., not spec. (5)	15	0.08
Hispanic or Latino:	597	3.05
Central American:	9	0.05
Guatemalan	3	0.02
Honduran	2	0.01
Nicaraguan	3	0.02
Salvadoran	1	0.01
Cuban	15	0.08
Dominican Republic	1	0.01
Mexican	451	2.31
Puerto Rican	49	0.25
South American:	22	0.11
Argentinean	9	0.05
Chilean	1	0.01
Colombian	3	0.02
Paraguayan	1	0.01
Peruvian	7	0.04
Other South American	1	0.01
Other Hispanic or Latino	50	0.26
Hungarian	232	1.19
Iranian	12	0.06
Irish	3,707	19.02
Israeli	13	0.07
Italian	1,883	9.66
Latvian	4	0.02
Lithuanian	120	0.62
Luxemburger	13	0.07
Northern European	24	0.12
Norwegian	187	0.96
Polish	2,010	10.31
Romanian	42	0.22
Russian	299	1.53
Scotch-Irish	306	1.57
Scottish	443	2.27
Serbian	47	0.24
Slavic	11	0.06
Slovak	79	0.41
Slovene	49	0.25
Swedish	864	4.43
Swiss	92	0.47
Turkish	21	0.11
Ukrainian	74	0.38
United States or American	732	3.76
Welsh	167	0.86
West Indian, excl. Hispanic:	55	0.28
Belizean	15	0.08
Jamaican	40	0.21
White:	15,524	79.44
Not Hispanic (14,936)	15,133	77.43
Hispanic (334)	391	2.00
Yugoslavian	27	0.14

Jacksonville

Place Type: City
County: Morgan
Population: 18,940

Ancestry/Race	Number	%
African American/Black:	1,399	7.39
Not Hispanic (1,253)	1,389	7.33
Hispanic (8)	10	0.05
African, sub-Saharan:	42	0.22
African	28	0.15
Nigerian	7	0.04
Other sub-Saharan African	7	0.04
Am. Ind. or Alaska Nat., not spec.	36	0.19
American Indian tribes, specified:	73	0.39
Apache (11)	12	0.06
Blackfeet	4	0.02
Cherokee (6)	27	0.14
Chickasaw (1)	4	0.02
Chippewa (3)	3	0.02
Choctaw	1	0.01
Colville	1	0.01
Creek	1	0.01
Delaware	1	0.01
Latin American Indians	3	0.02
Seminole (8)	9	0.05
Sioux (2)	5	0.03
All other tribes	2	0.01
American Indian tribes, not spec.	6	0.03
Arab:	5	0.03
Lebanese	5	0.03
Asian:	174	0.92
Chinese, ex. Taiwanese (20)	27	0.14
Filipino (38)	45	0.24
Hmong (1)	1	0.01
Indian (41)	59	0.31
Japanese (6)	12	0.06
Korean (6)	10	0.05
Laotian (1)	2	0.01
Pakistani (4)	4	0.02
Vietnamese (5)	5	0.03
Other Asian, not specified (7)	9	0.05
Austrian	9	0.05
Belgian	16	0.08
British	74	0.39
Canadian	24	0.13
Croatian	15	0.08
Czech	11	0.06
Czechoslovakian	33	0.17
Danish	35	0.18
Dutch	477	2.52
Eastern European	14	0.07
English	2,612	13.80
Estonian	7	0.04
European	93	0.49
French, except Basque	378	2.00
French Canadian	58	0.31
German	3,704	19.58
Greek	12	0.06
Hawaii Native/Pacific Islander:	8	0.04
Micronesian:	2	0.01
Guamanian/Chamorro	2	0.01
Polynesian: (1)	2	0.01
Native Hawaiian (1)	2	0.01
Other Pac. Isl., not spec. (1)	4	0.02
Hispanic or Latino:	291	1.54
Central American:	16	0.08
Costa Rican	1	0.01
Guatemalan	2	0.01
Honduran	3	0.02
Panamanian	6	0.03
Salvadoran	4	0.02

Notes: 1. Figures in the "Number" column do not add up to the total population due to: a) Ancestry/Race overlap — e.g. persons can report being both White and Irish, b) persons of Hispanic origin can report being any race, c) persons reporting two ancestries are counted in both categories. 2. Numbers in parentheses indicate the number of persons reporting this ancestry/race alone, not in combination with any other ancestry/race. 3. Refer to the Explanation of Data in the front of the book for more detailed information.

Cuban	5	0.03
Mexican	191	1.01
Puerto Rican	17	0.09
South American:	16	0.08
Argentinean	1	0.01
Bolivian	8	0.04
Colombian	4	0.02
Ecuadorian	1	0.01
Paraguayan	1	0.01
Venezuelan	1	0.01
Other Hispanic or Latino	46	0.24
Hungarian	11	0.06
Irish	1,898	10.03
Italian	421	2.23
Lithuanian	7	0.04
Luxemburger	7	0.04
Norwegian	150	0.79
Polish	251	1.33
Portuguese	154	0.81
Romanian	3	0.02
Russian	39	0.21
Scandinavian	12	0.06
Scotch-Irish	383	2.02
Scottish	407	2.15
Serbian	14	0.07
Slavic	3	0.02
Slovak	30	0.16
Swedish	229	1.21
Swiss	17	0.09
Turkish	6	0.03
United States or American	1,994	10.54
Welsh	156	0.82
West Indian, excl. Hispanic:	10	0.05
Dutch West Indian	10	0.05
White:	17,358	91.65
Not Hispanic (16,969)	17,196	90.79
Hispanic (140)	162	0.86
Yugoslavian	14	0.07

Joliet

Place Type: City
County: Will
Population: 106,221

Ancestry/Race	Number	%
Afghan	7	0.01
African American/Black:	20,012	18.84
Not Hispanic (19,125)	19,763	18.61
Hispanic (169)	249	0.23
African, sub-Saharan:	572	0.54
African	509	0.48
Ethiopian	10	0.01
Nigerian	53	0.05
Alaska Native tribes, specified:	1	0.00
Eskimo	1	0.00
Am. Ind. or Alaska Nat., not spec.	324	0.31
Albanian	98	0.09
American Indian tribes, specified:	329	0.31
Apache (6)	12	0.01
Blackfeet (4)	17	0.02
Cherokee (11)	115	0.11
Cheyenne (4)	4	0.00
Chickasaw	3	0.00
Chippewa (13)	23	0.02
Choctaw (1)	5	0.00
Cree	1	0.00
Creek (10)	12	0.01
Crow	1	0.00
Delaware (2)	2	0.00
Iroquois	3	0.00
Latin American Indians (45)	67	0.06
Menominee (2)	3	0.00
Navajo (4)	8	0.01
Ottawa (1)	1	0.00
Potawatomi (3)	3	0.00
Pueblo	1	0.00
Seminole (1)	2	0.00
Shoshone	1	0.00
Sioux (3)	8	0.01
Yaqui	1	0.00
All other tribes (14)	36	0.03
American Indian tribes, not spec.	50	0.05
Arab:	254	0.24
Arab/Arabic	49	0.05
Jordanian	21	0.02
Lebanese	85	0.08
Palestinian	36	0.03
Syrian	29	0.03
Other Arab	34	0.03
Asian:	1,629	1.53
Cambodian (81)	95	0.09
Chinese, ex. Taiwanese (91)	143	0.13
Filipino (317)	440	0.41
Indian (217)	262	0.25
Indonesian (1)	3	0.00
Japanese (41)	100	0.09
Korean (84)	122	0.11
Laotian (202)	222	0.21
Malaysian (2)	5	0.00
Pakistani (29)	40	0.04
Sri Lankan (1)	1	0.00
Taiwanese (3)	3	0.00
Thai (14)	17	0.02
Vietnamese (78)	97	0.09
Other Asian, specified	9	0.01
Other Asian, not specified (26)	70	0.07
Australian	32	0.03
Austrian	274	0.26
Belgian	130	0.12
Brazilian	21	0.02
British	124	0.12
Canadian	50	0.05
Celtic	7	0.01
Croatian	1,536	1.45
Czech	1,201	1.13
Czechoslovakian	231	0.22
Danish	505	0.48
Dutch	1,254	1.18
Eastern European	30	0.03
English	4,874	4.59
European	261	0.25
Finnish	175	0.16
French, except Basque	2,207	2.08
French Canadian	324	0.31
German	19,079	17.97
Greek	1,005	0.95
Hawaii Native/Pacific Islander:	92	0.09
Micronesian: (3)	6	0.01
Guamanian/Chamorro (3)	6	0.01
Polynesian: (12)	39	0.04
Native Hawaiian (6)	27	0.03
Samoan (6)	12	0.01
Other Pac. Isl., specified	8	0.01
Other Pac. Isl., not spec. (6)	39	0.04
Hispanic or Latino:	19,552	18.41
Central American:	76	0.07
Costa Rican	3	0.00
Guatemalan	35	0.03
Honduran	6	0.01
Nicaraguan	2	0.00
Panamanian	14	0.01
Salvadoran	15	0.01
Other Central American	1	0.00
Cuban	57	0.05
Dominican Republic	20	0.02
Mexican	16,939	15.95
Puerto Rican	586	0.55
South American:	114	0.11
Argentinean	7	0.01
Bolivian	4	0.00
Chilean	5	0.00
Colombian	31	0.03
Ecuadorian	20	0.02
Paraguayan	4	0.00
Peruvian	38	0.04
Venezuelan	4	0.00
Other South American	1	0.00
Other Hispanic or Latino	1,760	1.66
Hungarian	648	0.61
Irish	14,609	13.76
Israeli	13	0.01
Italian	9,271	8.73
Lithuanian	749	0.71
Luxemburger	44	0.04
Norwegian	1,186	1.12
Pennsylvania German	34	0.03
Polish	8,153	7.68
Portuguese	76	0.07
Romanian	73	0.07
Russian	544	0.51
Scandinavian	59	0.06
Scotch-Irish	947	0.89
Scottish	1,019	0.96
Serbian	108	0.10
Slavic	134	0.13
Slovak	1,456	1.37
Slovene	1,770	1.67
Swedish	2,645	2.49
Swiss	199	0.19
Ukrainian	282	0.27
United States or American	2,941	2.77
Welsh	352	0.33
West Indian, excl. Hispanic:	147	0.14
Haitian	8	0.01
Jamaican	90	0.08
Trinidadian and Tobagonian	35	0.03
West Indian	14	0.01
White:	75,537	71.11
Not Hispanic (64,811)	65,854	62.00
Hispanic (8,822)	9,683	9.12
Yugoslavian	191	0.18

Justice

Place Type: Village
County: Cook
Population: 12,193

Ancestry/Race	Number	%
African American/Black:	2,528	20.73
Not Hispanic (2,420)	2,487	20.40
Hispanic (36)	41	0.34
African, sub-Saharan:	470	3.89
African	431	3.56
Sudanese	30	0.25
Other sub-Saharan African	9	0.07
Am. Ind. or Alaska Nat., not spec.	40	0.33
Albanian	57	0.47
American Indian tribes, specified:	37	0.30
Apache (3)	3	0.02
Blackfeet	2	0.02
Cherokee (2)	19	0.16
Chippewa	2	0.02
Creek	3	0.02
Iroquois (2)	3	0.02
Latin American Indians (1)	1	0.01
Sioux (2)	2	0.02
All other tribes	2	0.02
American Indian tribes, not spec.	1	0.01
Arab:	507	4.19
Arab/Arabic	290	2.40
Egyptian	50	0.41
Jordanian	13	0.11
Palestinian	94	0.78
Other Arab	60	0.50
Asian:	320	2.62
Chinese, ex. Taiwanese (9)	12	0.10
Filipino (58)	68	0.56
Indian (82)	91	0.75
Japanese (6)	12	0.10
Korean (10)	19	0.16
Malaysian (5)	5	0.04
Pakistani (17)	18	0.15
Thai (2)	2	0.02
Vietnamese (12)	15	0.12
Other Asian, specified	1	0.01
Other Asian, not specified (9)	77	0.63
Austrian	46	0.38
British	11	0.09

Notes: 1. Figures in the "Number" column do not add up to the total population due to: a) Ancestry/Race overlap — e.g. persons can report being both White and Irish, b) persons of Hispanic origin can report being any race, c) persons reporting two ancestries are counted in both categories. 2. Numbers in parentheses indicate the number of persons reporting this ancestry/race alone, not in combination with any other ancestry/race. 3. Refer to the Explanation of Data in the front of the book for more detailed information.

Ancestry/Race	Number	%
Canadian	9	0.07
Croatian	56	0.46
Czech	229	1.89
Czechoslovakian	51	0.42
Dutch	186	1.54
English	511	4.23
European	52	0.43
Finnish	31	0.26
French, except Basque	194	1.60
French Canadian	39	0.32
German	1,586	13.12
Greek	27	0.22
Hawaii Native/Pacific Islander:	11	0.09
Polynesian: (2)	2	0.02
Native Hawaiian (2)	2	0.02
Other Pac. Isl., specified	1	0.01
Other Pac. Isl., not spec. (1)	8	0.07
Hispanic or Latino:	928	7.61
Central American:	4	0.03
Costa Rican	1	0.01
Guatemalan	1	0.01
Nicaraguan	1	0.01
Panamanian	1	0.01
Cuban	15	0.12
Dominican Republic	1	0.01
Mexican	754	6.18
Puerto Rican	91	0.75
South American:	11	0.09
Argentinean	7	0.06
Colombian	4	0.03
Other Hispanic or Latino	52	0.43
Hungarian	53	0.44
Irish	1,430	11.83
Italian	684	5.66
Latvian	17	0.14
Lithuanian	211	1.75
Norwegian	27	0.22
Pennsylvania German	6	0.05
Polish	2,931	24.24
Romanian	58	0.48
Russian	49	0.41
Scotch-Irish	72	0.60
Scottish	43	0.36
Slavic	19	0.16
Slovak	107	0.89
Slovene	13	0.11
Swedish	237	1.96
Swiss	9	0.07
Ukrainian	34	0.28
United States or American	236	1.95
Welsh	6	0.05
White:	9,133	74.90
Not Hispanic (8,127)	8,577	70.34
Hispanic (512)	556	4.56
Yugoslavian	37	0.31

Kankakee

Place Type: City
County: Kankakee
Population: 27,491

Ancestry/Race	Number	%
African American/Black:	11,586	42.14
Not Hispanic (11,216)	11,487	41.78
Hispanic (75)	99	0.36
African, sub-Saharan:	174	0.63
African	140	0.51
Cape Verdean	11	0.04
Liberian	17	0.06
Zimbabwean	6	0.02
Am. Ind. or Alaska Nat., not spec.	92	0.33
Alsatian	6	0.02
American Indian tribes, specified:	118	0.43
Apache (1)	7	0.03
Blackfeet	9	0.03
Cherokee (11)	48	0.17
Chippewa	4	0.01
Choctaw	3	0.01
Iroquois (1)	1	0.00
Latin American Indians (10)	11	0.04
Menominee (2)	2	0.01
Navajo	4	0.01
Potawatomi	5	0.02
Sioux (4)	5	0.02
Ute (1)	1	0.00
All other tribes (8)	18	0.07
American Indian tribes, not spec.	16	0.06
Arab:	20	0.07
Arab/Arabic	20	0.07
Asian:	149	0.54
Chinese, ex. Taiwanese (18)	25	0.09
Filipino (19)	29	0.11
Hmong (1)	3	0.01
Indian (24)	32	0.12
Indonesian (1)	1	0.00
Japanese (3)	15	0.05
Korean (9)	14	0.05
Sri Lankan (1)	4	0.01
Taiwanese (1)	1	0.00
Vietnamese (8)	8	0.03
Other Asian, not specified (2)	17	0.06
Austrian	6	0.02
Belgian	49	0.18
British	64	0.23
Canadian	74	0.27
Croatian	14	0.05
Czech	77	0.28
Czechoslovakian	25	0.09
Danish	134	0.49
Dutch	493	1.79
Eastern European	8	0.03
English	1,163	4.22
European	44	0.16
Finnish	14	0.05
French, except Basque	1,786	6.48
French Canadian	496	1.80
German	3,850	13.97
Greek	36	0.13
Guyanese	4	0.01
Hawaii Native/Pacific Islander:	15	0.05
Micronesian: (1)	1	0.00
Guamanian/Chamorro (1)	1	0.00
Polynesian: (5)	9	0.03
Native Hawaiian (2)	6	0.02
Samoan (3)	3	0.01
Other Pac. Isl., not spec. (1)	5	0.02
Hispanic or Latino:	2,544	9.25
Central American:	13	0.05
Honduran	2	0.01
Nicaraguan	1	0.00
Panamanian	10	0.04
Cuban	14	0.05
Mexican	2,152	7.83
Puerto Rican	93	0.34
South American:	5	0.02
Bolivian	2	0.01
Colombian	3	0.01
Other Hispanic or Latino	267	0.97
Hungarian	31	0.11
Iranian	14	0.05
Irish	2,127	7.72
Italian	854	3.10
Lithuanian	97	0.35
Norwegian	282	1.02
Polish	701	2.54
Portuguese	42	0.15
Romanian	15	0.05
Russian	21	0.08
Scandinavian	9	0.03
Scotch-Irish	165	0.60
Scottish	213	0.77
Slovak	25	0.09
Slovene	8	0.03
Swedish	251	0.91
Swiss	82	0.30
Ukrainian	26	0.09
United States or American	910	3.30
Welsh	41	0.15
West Indian, excl. Hispanic:	37	0.13
Haitian	5	0.02
Jamaican	32	0.12
White:	14,422	52.46
Not Hispanic (13,130)	13,451	48.93
Hispanic (868)	971	3.53
Yugoslavian	9	0.03

Kewanee

Place Type: City
County: Henry
Population: 12,944

Ancestry/Race	Number	%
African American/Black:	596	4.60
Not Hispanic (463)	569	4.40
Hispanic (13)	27	0.21
African, sub-Saharan:	11	0.08
African	11	0.08
Am. Ind. or Alaska Nat., not spec.	30	0.23
American Indian tribes, specified:	41	0.32
Apache	1	0.01
Blackfeet	9	0.07
Cherokee (2)	23	0.18
Chickasaw	1	0.01
Chippewa (1)	6	0.05
All other tribes (1)	1	0.01
American Indian tribes, not spec.	2	0.02
Arab:	38	0.29
Arab/Arabic	5	0.04
Lebanese	33	0.25
Asian:	72	0.56
Chinese, ex. Taiwanese (9)	12	0.09
Filipino (11)	15	0.12
Indian (9)	12	0.09
Japanese (5)	8	0.06
Korean (6)	10	0.08
Taiwanese (3)	3	0.02
Vietnamese (2)	4	0.03
Other Asian, specified	6	0.05
Other Asian, not specified	2	0.02
Austrian	17	0.13
Belgian	805	6.22
British	7	0.05
Canadian	17	0.13
Croatian	7	0.05
Czech	5	0.04
Danish	63	0.49
Dutch	389	3.01
English	1,408	10.88
European	76	0.59
French, except Basque	436	3.37
French Canadian	30	0.23
German	3,008	23.24
Greek	29	0.22
Hawaii Native/Pacific Islander:	11	0.08
Polynesian: (1)	4	0.03
Native Hawaiian (1)	4	0.03
Other Pac. Isl., specified	6	0.05
Other Pac. Isl., not spec. (1)	1	0.01
Hispanic or Latino:	790	6.10
Central American:	23	0.18
Costa Rican	1	0.01
Guatemalan	1	0.01
Nicaraguan	5	0.04
Salvadoran	16	0.12
Dominican Republic	1	0.01
Mexican	664	5.13
Puerto Rican	20	0.15
South American:	4	0.03
Colombian	1	0.01
Ecuadorian	3	0.02
Other Hispanic or Latino	78	0.60
Hungarian	6	0.05
Irish	1,508	11.65
Italian	139	1.07
Lithuanian	115	0.89
Luxemburger	6	0.05
Northern European	5	0.04
Norwegian	119	0.92

Notes: 1. Figures in the "Number" column do not add up to the total population due to: a) Ancestry/Race overlap — e.g. persons can report being both White and Irish, b) persons of Hispanic origin can report being any race, c) persons reporting two ancestries are counted in both categories. 2. Numbers in parentheses indicate the number of persons reporting this ancestry/race alone, not in combination with any other ancestry/race. 3. Refer to the Explanation of Data in the front of the book for more detailed information.

Pennsylvania German	15	0.12
Polish	555	4.29
Portuguese	11	0.08
Russian	66	0.51
Scandinavian	32	0.25
Scotch-Irish	225	1.74
Scottish	230	1.78
Serbian	16	0.12
Slavic	21	0.16
Swedish	987	7.63
Swiss	24	0.19
Ukrainian	6	0.05
United States or American	1,344	10.38
Welsh	37	0.29
West Indian, excl. Hispanic:	21	0.16
Haitian	7	0.05
Jamaican	14	0.11
White:	11,918	92.07
Not Hispanic (11,445)	11,617	89.75
Hispanic (239)	301	2.33
Yugoslavian	7	0.05

La Grange Park

Place Type: Village
County: Cook
Population: 13,295

Ancestry/Race	Number	%
African American/Black:	440	3.31
Not Hispanic (399)	421	3.17
Hispanic (10)	19	0.14
African, sub-Saharan:	10	0.08
African	10	0.08
Am. Ind. or Alaska Nat., not spec.	3	0.02
American Indian tribes, specified:	25	0.19
Apache (3)	3	0.02
Cherokee (4)	14	0.11
Cheyenne	1	0.01
Chippewa (2)	2	0.02
Latin American Indians (1)	2	0.02
Sioux (1)	1	0.01
All other tribes (1)	2	0.02
American Indian tribes, not spec.	1	0.01
Arab:	70	0.53
Arab/Arabic	35	0.26
Jordanian	19	0.14
Other Arab	16	0.12
Asian:	283	2.13
Cambodian (1)	1	0.01
Chinese, ex. Taiwanese (65)	78	0.59
Filipino (58)	87	0.65
Indian (31)	33	0.25
Indonesian	3	0.02
Japanese (9)	20	0.15
Korean (21)	25	0.19
Pakistani (5)	5	0.04
Taiwanese (1)	1	0.01
Thai (11)	18	0.14
Vietnamese (5)	6	0.05
Other Asian, not specified (5)	6	0.05
Austrian	89	0.67
Belgian	55	0.42
British	87	0.66
Bulgarian	13	0.10
Canadian	31	0.23
Croatian	46	0.35
Cypriot	6	0.05
Czech	1,072	8.10
Czechoslovakian	250	1.89
Danish	93	0.70
Dutch	209	1.58
Eastern European	14	0.11
English	985	7.44
European	87	0.66
Finnish	42	0.32
French, except Basque	296	2.24
French Canadian	36	0.27
German	2,911	21.99
Greek	163	1.23
Hawaii Native/Pacific Islander:	13	0.10
Polynesian: (5)	5	0.04
Native Hawaiian (2)	2	0.02
Samoan (3)	3	0.02
Other Pac. Isl., not spec.	8	0.06
Hispanic or Latino:	472	3.55
Central American:	15	0.11
Costa Rican	3	0.02
Guatemalan	7	0.05
Honduran	1	0.01
Panamanian	2	0.02
Salvadoran	2	0.02
Cuban	27	0.20
Dominican Republic	1	0.01
Mexican	287	2.16
Puerto Rican	52	0.39
South American:	35	0.26
Argentinean	1	0.01
Bolivian	2	0.02
Colombian	17	0.13
Ecuadorian	2	0.02
Paraguayan	1	0.01
Peruvian	4	0.03
Venezuelan	3	0.02
Other South American	5	0.04
Other Hispanic or Latino	55	0.41
Hungarian	102	0.77
Irish	2,994	22.62
Italian	1,544	11.66
Lithuanian	276	2.08
Luxemburger	17	0.13
Macedonian	7	0.05
Northern European	16	0.12
Norwegian	146	1.10
Polish	2,126	16.06
Romanian	66	0.50
Russian	179	1.35
Scandinavian	6	0.05
Scotch-Irish	162	1.22
Scottish	172	1.30
Serbian	32	0.24
Slavic	30	0.23
Slovak	68	0.51
Slovene	49	0.37
Swedish	412	3.11
Swiss	9	0.07
Ukrainian	80	0.60
United States or American	355	2.68
Welsh	50	0.38
West Indian, excl. Hispanic:	7	0.05
Jamaican	7	0.05
White:	12,510	94.10
Not Hispanic (12,061)	12,160	91.46
Hispanic (333)	350	2.63
Yugoslavian	69	0.52

La Grange

Place Type: Village
County: Cook
Population: 15,608

Ancestry/Race	Number	%
African American/Black:	967	6.20
Not Hispanic (935)	957	6.13
Hispanic (4)	10	0.06
African, sub-Saharan:	94	0.60
African	94	0.60
Alaska Native tribes, specified:	3	0.02
Tlingit-Haida (3)	3	0.02
Am. Ind. or Alaska Nat., not spec.	9	0.06
Albanian	8	0.05
American Indian tribes, specified:	33	0.21
Blackfeet	1	0.01
Cherokee (2)	12	0.08
Chippewa (1)	1	0.01
Choctaw	2	0.01
Iroquois	1	0.01
Latin American Indians	3	0.02
Lumbee (1)	1	0.01
Sioux (1)	1	0.01
All other tribes (3)	11	0.07
American Indian tribes, not spec.	2	0.01
Arab:	68	0.43
Arab/Arabic	23	0.15
Lebanese	40	0.25
Syrian	5	0.03
Asian:	215	1.38
Cambodian (1)	1	0.01
Chinese, ex. Taiwanese (43)	57	0.37
Filipino (31)	52	0.33
Indian (27)	30	0.19
Indonesian (2)	6	0.04
Japanese (10)	24	0.15
Korean (29)	37	0.24
Thai (4)	4	0.03
Vietnamese (2)	2	0.01
Other Asian, not specified	2	0.01
Austrian	154	0.98
Belgian	52	0.33
British	69	0.44
Canadian	34	0.22
Croatian	128	0.81
Czech	853	5.42
Czechoslovakian	159	1.01
Danish	89	0.57
Dutch	379	2.41
Eastern European	5	0.03
English	1,523	9.69
Estonian	25	0.16
European	89	0.57
Finnish	31	0.20
French, except Basque	510	3.24
French Canadian	104	0.66
German	3,907	24.85
Greek	223	1.42
Hawaii Native/Pacific Islander:	7	0.04
Micronesian: (1)	1	0.01
Guamanian/Chamorro (1)	1	0.01
Polynesian: (2)	5	0.03
Native Hawaiian (1)	3	0.02
Other Polynesian (1)	2	0.01
Other Pac. Isl., not spec.	1	0.01
Hispanic or Latino:	572	3.66
Central American:	10	0.06
Costa Rican	1	0.01
Guatemalan	3	0.02
Honduran	1	0.01
Nicaraguan	1	0.01
Panamanian	2	0.01
Salvadoran	2	0.01
Cuban	23	0.15
Dominican Republic	3	0.02
Mexican	393	2.52
Puerto Rican	37	0.24
South American:	51	0.33
Argentinean	10	0.06
Colombian	33	0.21
Ecuadorian	5	0.03
Paraguayan	1	0.01
Peruvian	1	0.01
Venezuelan	1	0.01
Other Hispanic or Latino	55	0.35
Hungarian	36	0.23
Irish	3,962	25.20
Italian	1,597	10.16
Latvian	28	0.18
Lithuanian	274	1.74
Luxemburger	6	0.04
Macedonian	23	0.15
Northern European	12	0.08
Norwegian	449	2.86
Polish	1,651	10.50
Portuguese	6	0.04
Romanian	12	0.08
Russian	178	1.13
Scandinavian	14	0.09
Scotch-Irish	178	1.13
Scottish	264	1.68
Serbian	23	0.15

Notes: 1. Figures in the "Number" column do not add up to the total population due to: a) Ancestry/Race overlap—e.g. persons can report being both White and Irish, b) persons of Hispanic origin can report being any race, c) persons reporting two ancestries are counted in both categories. 2. Numbers in parentheses indicate the number of persons reporting this ancestry/race alone, not in combination with any other ancestry/race. 3. Refer to the Explanation of Data in the front of the book for more detailed information.

Slavic	16	0.10
Slovak	119	0.76
Slovene	50	0.32
Swedish	639	4.06
Swiss	57	0.36
Ukrainian	134	0.85
United States or American	477	3.03
Welsh	129	0.82
White:	14,330	91.81
Not Hispanic (13,816)	13,910	89.12
Hispanic (390)	420	2.69
Yugoslavian	28	0.18

Lake Forest

Place Type: City
County: Lake
Population: 20,059

Ancestry/Race	Number	%
African American/Black:	295	1.47
Not Hispanic (263)	287	1.43
Hispanic (8)	8	0.04
African, sub-Saharan:	24	0.12
South African	24	0.12
Alaska Native tribes, specified:	1	0.00
Alaska Athabascan	1	0.00
Am. Ind. or Alaska Nat., not spec.	9	0.04
Alsatian	20	0.10
American Indian tribes, specified:	18	0.09
Cherokee (3)	7	0.03
Chickasaw (1)	1	0.00
Chippewa	2	0.01
Choctaw	1	0.00
Iroquois (1)	2	0.01
Latin American Indians (1)	3	0.01
All other tribes	2	0.01
American Indian tribes, not spec.	1	0.00
Arab:	94	0.47
Arab/Arabic	1	0.00
Egyptian	28	0.14
Lebanese	14	0.07
Syrian	51	0.25
Armenian	234	1.17
Asian:	825	4.11
Cambodian	1	0.00
Chinese, ex. Taiwanese (136)	166	0.83
Filipino (72)	92	0.46
Indian (188)	204	1.02
Indonesian (6)	6	0.03
Japanese (31)	51	0.25
Korean (173)	181	0.90
Laotian (2)	4	0.02
Pakistani (18)	18	0.09
Sri Lankan (5)	5	0.02
Taiwanese (20)	22	0.11
Thai (12)	15	0.07
Vietnamese (4)	5	0.02
Other Asian, specified	1	0.00
Other Asian, not specified (8)	54	0.27
Assyrian/Chaldean/Syriac	7	0.03
Austrian	122	0.61
Belgian	103	0.51
British	83	0.41
Bulgarian	24	0.12
Canadian	37	0.18
Croatian	131	0.65
Czech	233	1.16
Czechoslovakian	57	0.28
Danish	160	0.80
Dutch	465	2.32
Eastern European	51	0.25
English	3,288	16.43
European	155	0.77
Finnish	55	0.27
French, except Basque	734	3.67
French Canadian	45	0.22
German	4,472	22.34
Greek	586	2.93
Hawaii Native/Pacific Islander:	75	0.37
Polynesian: (2)	4	0.02
Native Hawaiian (1)	3	0.01
Samoan (1)	1	0.00
Other Pac. Isl., not spec. (24)	71	0.35
Hispanic or Latino:	376	1.87
Central American:	16	0.08
Costa Rican	1	0.00
Guatemalan	5	0.02
Honduran	1	0.00
Nicaraguan	7	0.03
Other Central American	2	0.01
Cuban	18	0.09
Dominican Republic	4	0.02
Mexican	160	0.80
Puerto Rican	28	0.14
South American:	49	0.24
Argentinean	2	0.01
Chilean	3	0.01
Colombian	20	0.10
Ecuadorian	3	0.01
Paraguayan	3	0.01
Peruvian	8	0.04
Venezuelan	7	0.03
Other South American	3	0.01
Other Hispanic or Latino	101	0.50
Hungarian	114	0.57
Icelander	7	0.03
Iranian	49	0.24
Irish	4,007	20.02
Italian	1,682	8.40
Latvian	8	0.04
Lithuanian	153	0.76
Macedonian	2	0.01
Maltese	8	0.04
Northern European	23	0.11
Norwegian	511	2.55
Pennsylvania German	11	0.05
Polish	1,145	5.72
Romanian	21	0.10
Russian	345	1.72
Scandinavian	44	0.22
Scotch-Irish	468	2.34
Scottish	720	3.60
Serbian	33	0.16
Slovak	159	0.79
Slovene	5	0.02
Swedish	787	3.93
Swiss	178	0.89
Ukrainian	87	0.43
United States or American	925	4.62
Welsh	151	0.75
White:	18,915	94.30
Not Hispanic (18,537)	18,633	92.89
Hispanic (278)	282	1.41
Yugoslavian	77	0.38

Lake Zurich

Place Type: Village
County: Lake
Population: 18,104

Ancestry/Race	Number	%
African American/Black:	179	0.99
Not Hispanic (142)	171	0.94
Hispanic (4)	8	0.04
Am. Ind. or Alaska Nat., not spec.	25	0.14
Albanian	5	0.03
American Indian tribes, specified:	41	0.23
Blackfeet	2	0.01
Cherokee (1)	16	0.09
Chippewa (1)	4	0.02
Iroquois (3)	8	0.04
Latin American Indians (3)	3	0.02
All other tribes (2)	8	0.04
American Indian tribes, not spec.	2	0.01
Arab:	19	0.10
Egyptian	19	0.10
Armenian	31	0.17
Asian:	777	4.29
Chinese, ex. Taiwanese (234)	248	1.37
Filipino (53)	69	0.38
Indian (209)	215	1.19
Japanese (26)	43	0.24
Korean (103)	119	0.66
Malaysian	4	0.02
Pakistani (14)	27	0.15
Taiwanese (12)	14	0.08
Thai (9)	9	0.05
Vietnamese (18)	18	0.10
Other Asian, specified	3	0.02
Other Asian, not specified (2)	8	0.04
Assyrian/Chaldean/Syriac	25	0.14
Australian	15	0.08
Austrian	109	0.60
Basque	8	0.04
Belgian	99	0.55
Brazilian	40	0.22
British	86	0.47
Canadian	37	0.20
Celtic	7	0.04
Croatian	105	0.58
Czech	240	1.32
Czechoslovakian	66	0.36
Danish	180	0.99
Dutch	140	0.77
Eastern European	30	0.17
English	1,321	7.28
European	96	0.53
Finnish	48	0.26
French, except Basque	579	3.19
French Canadian	125	0.69
German	5,623	30.99
Greek	301	1.66
Hawaii Native/Pacific Islander:	11	0.06
Polynesian: (1)	2	0.01
Native Hawaiian (1)	2	0.01
Other Pac. Isl., specified	3	0.02
Other Pac. Isl., not spec. (1)	6	0.03
Hispanic or Latino:	1,005	5.55
Central American:	21	0.12
Costa Rican	5	0.03
Guatemalan	3	0.02
Nicaraguan	1	0.01
Panamanian	5	0.03
Salvadoran	6	0.03
Other Central American	1	0.01
Cuban	22	0.12
Dominican Republic	2	0.01
Mexican	730	4.03
Puerto Rican	69	0.38
South American:	52	0.29
Argentinean	2	0.01
Bolivian	5	0.03
Chilean	3	0.02
Colombian	19	0.10
Ecuadorian	8	0.04
Peruvian	3	0.02
Venezuelan	8	0.04
Other South American	4	0.02
Other Hispanic or Latino	109	0.60
Hungarian	163	0.90
Irish	3,000	16.53
Italian	1,919	10.58
Lithuanian	136	0.75
Luxemburger	31	0.17
Norwegian	417	2.30
Pennsylvania German	7	0.04
Polish	3,000	16.53
Portuguese	9	0.05
Romanian	13	0.07
Russian	267	1.47
Scandinavian	41	0.23
Scotch-Irish	111	0.61
Scottish	329	1.81
Serbian	54	0.30
Slovak	112	0.62
Slovene	11	0.06
Swedish	879	4.84
Swiss	120	0.66

Notes: 1. Figures in the "Number" column do not add up to the total population due to: a) Ancestry/Race overlap — e.g. persons can report being both White and Irish, b) persons of Hispanic origin can report being any race, c) persons reporting two ancestries are counted in both categories. 2. Numbers in parentheses indicate the number of persons reporting this ancestry/race alone, not in combination with any other ancestry/race. 3. Refer to the Explanation of Data in the front of the book for more detailed information.

Ukrainian	40	0.22
United States or American	740	4.08
Welsh	95	0.52
West Indian, excl. Hispanic:	11	0.06
Haitian	11	0.06
White:	16,861	93.13
Not Hispanic (16,115)	16,227	89.63
Hispanic (596)	634	3.50
Yugoslavian	59	0.33

Lake in the Hills

Place Type: Village
County: McHenry
Population: 23,152

Ancestry/Race	Number	%
Afghan	8	0.03
African American/Black:	427	1.84
Not Hispanic (337)	398	1.72
Hispanic (10)	29	0.13
African, sub-Saharan:	45	0.19
African	6	0.03
Ghanian	39	0.17
Alaska Native tribes, specified:	3	0.01
Aleut (1)	1	0.00
Eskimo	2	0.01
Am. Ind. or Alaska Nat., not spec.	40	0.17
American Indian tribes, specified:	59	0.25
Apache (2)	2	0.01
Blackfeet (1)	8	0.03
Cherokee (3)	9	0.04
Cheyenne (1)	1	0.00
Chippewa (1)	2	0.01
Choctaw (2)	4	0.02
Creek	2	0.01
Iroquois (1)	4	0.02
Latin American Indians (1)	9	0.04
Menominee (1)	1	0.00
Ottawa (2)	2	0.01
Pima	5	0.02
Potawatomi (1)	2	0.01
Sioux (4)	5	0.02
All other tribes (2)	3	0.01
American Indian tribes, not spec.	3	0.01
Arab:	93	0.40
Egyptian	28	0.12
Jordanian	47	0.20
Lebanese	18	0.08
Asian:	920	3.97
Cambodian (2)	2	0.01
Chinese, ex. Taiwanese (72)	94	0.41
Filipino (253)	290	1.25
Indian (206)	247	1.07
Indonesian (1)	1	0.00
Japanese (34)	58	0.25
Korean (101)	112	0.48
Laotian (5)	9	0.04
Pakistani (30)	36	0.16
Thai (4)	5	0.02
Vietnamese (21)	25	0.11
Other Asian, specified (1)	1	0.00
Other Asian, not specified (33)	40	0.17
Austrian	115	0.49
Belgian	89	0.38
British	161	0.69
Canadian	41	0.17
Croatian	102	0.43
Czech	434	1.85
Czechoslovakian	64	0.27
Danish	198	0.84
Dutch	267	1.14
English	1,751	7.46
European	179	0.76
Finnish	110	0.47
French, except Basque	429	1.83
French Canadian	122	0.52
German	7,214	30.75
Greek	242	1.03
Hawaii Native/Pacific Islander:	18	0.08
Micronesian: (3)	3	0.01
Guamanian/Chamorro (3)	3	0.01
Polynesian:	12	0.05
Native Hawaiian	11	0.05
Samoan	1	0.00
Other Pac. Isl., not spec. (1)	3	0.01
Hispanic or Latino:	1,462	6.31
Central American:	62	0.27
Guatemalan	37	0.16
Honduran	8	0.03
Nicaraguan	1	0.00
Panamanian	3	0.01
Salvadoran	11	0.05
Other Central American	2	0.01
Cuban	50	0.22
Dominican Republic	8	0.03
Mexican	842	3.64
Puerto Rican	225	0.97
South American:	98	0.42
Argentinean	8	0.03
Bolivian	1	0.00
Chilean	5	0.02
Colombian	33	0.14
Ecuadorian	21	0.09
Peruvian	24	0.10
Venezuelan	5	0.02
Other South American	1	0.00
Other Hispanic or Latino	177	0.76
Hungarian	96	0.41
Iranian	18	0.08
Irish	4,292	18.29
Italian	4,179	17.81
Latvian	10	0.04
Lithuanian	184	0.78
Luxemburger	11	0.05
Northern European	26	0.11
Norwegian	608	2.59
Polish	3,886	16.56
Portuguese	7	0.03
Russian	244	1.04
Scandinavian	133	0.57
Scotch-Irish	312	1.33
Scottish	302	1.29
Serbian	25	0.11
Slavic	11	0.05
Slovak	11	0.05
Swedish	899	3.83
Swiss	106	0.45
Ukrainian	202	0.86
United States or American	637	2.72
Welsh	74	0.32
White:	21,526	92.98
Not Hispanic (20,324)	20,526	88.66
Hispanic (882)	1,000	4.32
Yugoslavian	8	0.03

Lansing

Place Type: Village
County: Cook
Population: 28,332

Ancestry/Race	Number	%
African American/Black:	3,114	10.99
Not Hispanic (2,983)	3,058	10.79
Hispanic (46)	56	0.20
African, sub-Saharan:	184	0.65
African	74	0.26
Nigerian	89	0.32
Other sub-Saharan African	21	0.07
Alaska Native tribes, specified:	5	0.02
Alaska Athabascan	3	0.01
Tlingit-Haida (1)	2	0.01
Am. Ind. or Alaska Nat., not spec.	48	0.17
American Indian tribes, specified:	86	0.30
Apache	1	0.00
Blackfeet	3	0.01
Cherokee (7)	41	0.14
Chippewa (1)	6	0.02
Choctaw (1)	1	0.00
Cree	1	0.00
Iroquois (7)	21	0.07
Latin American Indians	2	0.01
Pueblo	3	0.01
Sioux (2)	2	0.01
Tohono O'Odham	1	0.00
All other tribes (3)	4	0.01
American Indian tribes, not spec.	6	0.02
Arab:	112	0.40
Arab/Arabic	15	0.05
Egyptian	19	0.07
Jordanian	45	0.16
Moroccan	17	0.06
Palestinian	16	0.06
Asian:	246	0.87
Chinese, ex. Taiwanese (13)	14	0.05
Filipino (59)	72	0.25
Indian (77)	77	0.27
Indonesian	1	0.00
Japanese (11)	23	0.08
Korean (15)	18	0.06
Laotian (4)	4	0.01
Pakistani (2)	5	0.02
Thai (2)	2	0.01
Vietnamese (11)	11	0.04
Other Asian, not specified (9)	19	0.07
Austrian	223	0.79
Belgian	34	0.12
British	59	0.21
Canadian	117	0.42
Croatian	564	2.00
Czech	146	0.52
Czechoslovakian	75	0.27
Danish	146	0.52
Dutch	3,857	13.70
English	1,532	5.44
European	92	0.33
Finnish	44	0.16
French, except Basque	549	1.95
French Canadian	142	0.50
German	5,753	20.43
Greek	246	0.87
Hawaii Native/Pacific Islander:	14	0.05
Polynesian: (9)	9	0.03
Native Hawaiian (2)	2	0.01
Samoan (6)	6	0.02
Other Polynesian (1)	1	0.00
Other Pac. Isl., not spec. (4)	5	0.02
Hispanic or Latino:	1,624	5.73
Central American:	16	0.06
Guatemalan	5	0.02
Honduran	2	0.01
Nicaraguan	1	0.00
Salvadoran	5	0.02
Other Central American	3	0.01
Cuban	12	0.04
Dominican Republic	2	0.01
Mexican	1,355	4.78
Puerto Rican	65	0.23
South American:	21	0.07
Argentinean	1	0.00
Colombian	4	0.01
Ecuadorian	7	0.02
Peruvian	4	0.01
Venezuelan	5	0.02
Other Hispanic or Latino	153	0.54
Hungarian	402	1.43
Iranian	7	0.02
Irish	4,354	15.46
Italian	2,410	8.56
Latvian	10	0.04
Lithuanian	255	0.91
Luxemburger	7	0.02
Macedonian	71	0.25
Maltese	50	0.18
Northern European	20	0.07
Norwegian	235	0.83
Pennsylvania German	7	0.02
Polish	4,429	15.73
Romanian	81	0.29

Notes: 1. Figures in the "Number" column do not add up to the total population due to: a) Ancestry/Race overlap — e.g. persons can report being both White and Irish, b) persons of Hispanic origin can report being any race, c) persons reporting two ancestries are counted in both categories. 2. Numbers in parentheses indicate the number of persons reporting this ancestry/race alone, not in combination with any other ancestry/race. 3. Refer to the Explanation of Data in the front of the book for more detailed information.

Russian	115	0.41
Scandinavian	35	0.12
Scotch-Irish	321	1.14
Scottish	392	1.39
Serbian	385	1.37
Slavic	11	0.04
Slovak	261	0.93
Slovene	30	0.11
Swedish	902	3.20
Swiss	35	0.12
Ukrainian	84	0.30
United States or American	737	2.62
Welsh	176	0.62
West Indian, excl. Hispanic:	21	0.07
Belizean	21	0.07
White:	24,569	86.72
Not Hispanic (23,238)	23,435	82.72
Hispanic (1,057)	1,134	4.00
Yugoslavian	81	0.29

Lemont

Place Type: Village
County: Cook
Population: 13,098

Ancestry/Race	Number	%
African American/Black:	58	0.44
Not Hispanic (39)	52	0.40
Hispanic (1)	6	0.05
African, sub-Saharan:	28	0.21
Nigerian	28	0.21
Alaska Native tribes, specified:	2	0.02
Tlingit-Haida (2)	2	0.02
Am. Ind. or Alaska Nat., not spec.	10	0.08
Alsatian	8	0.06
American Indian tribes, specified:	24	0.18
Apache (1)	1	0.01
Cherokee	7	0.05
Chippewa (2)	2	0.02
Colville	1	0.01
Comanche (1)	1	0.01
Latin American Indians (3)	3	0.02
Lumbee (1)	1	0.01
Navajo	3	0.02
Ottawa	4	0.03
All other tribes	1	0.01
American Indian tribes, not spec.	6	0.05
Arab:	16	0.12
Lebanese	16	0.12
Asian:	132	1.01
Chinese, ex. Taiwanese (22)	25	0.19
Filipino (25)	31	0.24
Indian (31)	32	0.24
Japanese (1)	3	0.02
Korean (19)	24	0.18
Pakistani	3	0.02
Thai (5)	5	0.04
Vietnamese (3)	4	0.03
Other Asian, not specified (1)	5	0.04
Austrian	98	0.74
British	32	0.24
Croatian	202	1.53
Czech	349	2.65
Czechoslovakian	50	0.38
Danish	70	0.53
Dutch	98	0.74
English	595	4.52
European	16	0.12
Finnish	30	0.23
French, except Basque	435	3.30
French Canadian	132	1.00
German	3,364	25.53
Greek	304	2.31
Hawaii Native/Pacific Islander:	4	0.03
Micronesian: (2)	2	0.02
Guamanian/Chamorro (1)	1	0.01
Other Micronesian (1)	1	0.01
Polynesian: (1)	1	0.01
Native Hawaiian (1)	1	0.01
Other Pac. Isl., not spec. (1)	1	0.01
Hispanic or Latino:	393	3.00
Central American:	6	0.05
Costa Rican	1	0.01
Guatemalan	4	0.03
Panamanian	1	0.01
Cuban	13	0.10
Dominican Republic	8	0.06
Mexican	276	2.11
Puerto Rican	38	0.29
South American:	13	0.10
Argentinean	1	0.01
Chilean	1	0.01
Colombian	5	0.04
Ecuadorian	1	0.01
Peruvian	5	0.04
Other Hispanic or Latino	39	0.30
Hungarian	28	0.21
Irish	2,718	20.63
Italian	1,588	12.05
Lithuanian	539	4.09
Luxemburger	16	0.12
Macedonian	83	0.63
Norwegian	82	0.62
Polish	4,327	32.84
Romanian	13	0.10
Russian	63	0.48
Scandinavian	19	0.14
Scotch-Irish	96	0.73
Scottish	117	0.89
Serbian	5	0.04
Slovak	110	0.83
Slovene	94	0.71
Swedish	400	3.04
Swiss	30	0.23
Ukrainian	40	0.30
United States or American	171	1.30
Welsh	29	0.22
White:	12,834	97.98
Not Hispanic (12,469)	12,534	95.69
Hispanic (288)	300	2.29
Yugoslavian	45	0.34

Libertyville

Place Type: Village
County: Lake
Population: 20,742

Ancestry/Race	Number	%
African American/Black:	259	1.25
Not Hispanic (209)	252	1.21
Hispanic (2)	7	0.03
Am. Ind. or Alaska Nat., not spec.	6	0.03
Albanian	6	0.03
Alsatian	7	0.03
American Indian tribes, specified:	27	0.13
Apache (1)	1	0.00
Blackfeet	3	0.01
Cherokee (5)	15	0.07
Choctaw (1)	3	0.01
Latin American Indians (1)	2	0.01
All other tribes (3)	3	0.01
American Indian tribes, not spec.	10	0.05
Arab:	100	0.48
Arab/Arabic	19	0.09
Egyptian	27	0.13
Iraqi	18	0.09
Lebanese	36	0.17
Armenian	36	0.17
Asian:	1,046	5.04
Bangladeshi (1)	1	0.00
Chinese, ex. Taiwanese (320)	339	1.63
Filipino (75)	92	0.44
Indian (301)	317	1.53
Japanese (44)	61	0.29
Korean (106)	112	0.54
Pakistani (17)	23	0.11
Sri Lankan (2)	2	0.01
Taiwanese (23)	26	0.13
Thai (11)	11	0.05
Vietnamese (36)	43	0.21
Other Asian, not specified (8)	19	0.09
Assyrian/Chaldean/Syriac	18	0.09
Austrian	100	0.48
Basque	15	0.07
Belgian	30	0.14
Brazilian	79	0.38
British	86	0.42
Bulgarian	9	0.04
Canadian	53	0.26
Croatian	133	0.64
Czech	195	0.94
Czechoslovakian	118	0.57
Danish	171	0.83
Dutch	354	1.71
Eastern European	12	0.06
English	2,597	12.55
Estonian	12	0.06
European	160	0.77
Finnish	77	0.37
French, except Basque	689	3.33
French Canadian	106	0.51
German	5,617	27.14
Greek	275	1.33
Hawaii Native/Pacific Islander:	14	0.07
Melanesian: (1)	4	0.02
Fijian (1)	4	0.02
Polynesian: (1)	5	0.02
Native Hawaiian (1)	4	0.02
Samoan	1	0.00
Other Pac. Isl., not spec. (4)	5	0.02
Hispanic or Latino:	566	2.73
Central American:	21	0.10
Costa Rican	1	0.00
Guatemalan	5	0.02
Honduran	1	0.00
Salvadoran	14	0.07
Cuban	28	0.13
Mexican	389	1.88
Puerto Rican	33	0.16
South American:	41	0.20
Argentinean	8	0.04
Colombian	16	0.08
Ecuadorian	3	0.01
Peruvian	13	0.06
Uruguayan	1	0.00
Other Hispanic or Latino	54	0.26
Hungarian	60	0.29
Iranian	13	0.06
Irish	3,792	18.32
Israeli	17	0.08
Italian	1,971	9.52
Latvian	10	0.05
Lithuanian	94	0.45
Luxemburger	23	0.11
Maltese	17	0.08
Northern European	11	0.05
Norwegian	683	3.30
Polish	1,940	9.37
Romanian	52	0.25
Russian	285	1.38
Scandinavian	7	0.03
Scotch-Irish	514	2.48
Scottish	500	2.42
Serbian	87	0.42
Slovak	139	0.67
Slovene	93	0.45
Swedish	1,516	7.33
Swiss	125	0.60
Turkish	17	0.08
Ukrainian	114	0.55
United States or American	611	2.95
Welsh	121	0.58
White:	19,295	93.02
Not Hispanic (18,812)	18,954	91.38
Hispanic (309)	341	1.64
Yugoslavian	105	0.51

Notes: 1. Figures in the "Number" column do not add up to the total population due to: a) Ancestry/Race overlap — e.g. persons can report being both White and Irish, b) persons of Hispanic origin can report being any race, c) persons reporting two ancestries are counted in both categories. 2. Numbers in parentheses indicate the number of persons reporting this ancestry/race alone, not in combination with any other ancestry/race. 3. Refer to the Explanation of Data in the front of the book for more detailed information.

Lincoln

Place Type: City
County: Logan
Population: 15,369

Ancestry/Race	Number	%
African American/Black:	487	3.17
Not Hispanic (434)	483	3.14
Hispanic	4	0.03
African, sub-Saharan:	29	0.19
African	29	0.19
Alaska Native tribes, specified:	5	0.03
Alaska Athabascan (1)	1	0.01
Eskimo (1)	1	0.01
Tlingit-Haida	3	0.02
Am. Ind. or Alaska Nat., not spec.	29	0.19
American Indian tribes, specified:	34	0.22
Apache (1)	1	0.01
Blackfeet	2	0.01
Cherokee (4)	21	0.14
Creek	1	0.01
Crow	1	0.01
Iroquois (3)	3	0.02
Latin American Indians (2)	2	0.01
Sioux	2	0.01
All other tribes	1	0.01
American Indian tribes, not spec.	6	0.04
Arab:	6	0.04
Lebanese	6	0.04
Asian:	173	1.13
Bangladeshi (2)	2	0.01
Cambodian (1)	1	0.01
Chinese, ex. Taiwanese (20)	25	0.16
Filipino (34)	50	0.33
Indian (18)	23	0.15
Japanese (6)	9	0.06
Korean (12)	13	0.08
Malaysian (1)	1	0.01
Thai (1)	4	0.03
Vietnamese (33)	33	0.21
Other Asian, specified (1)	2	0.01
Other Asian, not specified (7)	10	0.07
Austrian	26	0.17
Belgian	48	0.31
British	47	0.31
Canadian	15	0.10
Celtic	2	0.01
Croatian	15	0.10
Czech	30	0.20
Czechoslovakian	6	0.04
Danish	38	0.25
Dutch	365	2.37
English	1,541	10.03
European	211	1.37
French, except Basque	376	2.45
French Canadian	25	0.16
German	4,390	28.56
Greek	17	0.11
Hawaii Native/Pacific Islander:	11	0.07
Micronesian: (1)	1	0.01
Guamanian/Chamorro (1)	1	0.01
Polynesian: (3)	7	0.05
Native Hawaiian (3)	7	0.05
Other Pac. Isl., specified	1	0.01
Other Pac. Isl., not spec.	2	0.01
Hispanic or Latino:	183	1.19
Central American:	3	0.02
Guatemalan	1	0.01
Panamanian	1	0.01
Other Central American	1	0.01
Cuban	3	0.02
Dominican Republic	2	0.01
Mexican	103	0.67
Puerto Rican	31	0.20
South American:	3	0.02
Chilean	2	0.01
Colombian	1	0.01
Other Hispanic or Latino	38	0.25
Hungarian	34	0.22
Iranian	13	0.08
Irish	1,813	11.80
Italian	318	2.07
Lithuanian	36	0.23
Northern European	5	0.03
Norwegian	98	0.64
Polish	289	1.88
Portuguese	8	0.05
Russian	13	0.08
Scandinavian	26	0.17
Scotch-Irish	289	1.88
Scottish	213	1.39
Slovak	8	0.05
Slovene	4	0.03
Swedish	143	0.93
Swiss	15	0.10
Ukrainian	17	0.11
United States or American	1,905	12.39
Welsh	35	0.23
West Indian, excl. Hispanic:	40	0.26
Haitian	40	0.26
White:	14,683	95.54
Not Hispanic (14,466)	14,577	94.85
Hispanic (103)	106	0.69
Yugoslavian	47	0.31

Lincolnwood

Place Type: Village
County: Cook
Population: 12,359

Ancestry/Race	Number	%
Afghan	9	0.07
African American/Black:	71	0.57
Not Hispanic (46)	70	0.57
Hispanic (1)	1	0.01
Am. Ind. or Alaska Nat., not spec.	8	0.06
Albanian	19	0.15
American Indian tribes, specified:	12	0.10
Cherokee	3	0.02
Chippewa	1	0.01
Pueblo (1)	1	0.01
All other tribes (1)	7	0.06
Arab:	118	0.95
Arab/Arabic	77	0.62
Egyptian	6	0.05
Palestinian	25	0.20
Syrian	10	0.08
Armenian	98	0.79
Asian:	2,822	22.83
Cambodian (2)	2	0.02
Chinese, ex. Taiwanese (235)	268	2.17
Filipino (538)	575	4.65
Indian (762)	795	6.43
Indonesian (4)	8	0.06
Japanese (112)	151	1.22
Korean (568)	586	4.74
Pakistani (183)	203	1.64
Taiwanese (10)	11	0.09
Thai (57)	62	0.50
Vietnamese (67)	74	0.60
Other Asian, specified (2)	2	0.02
Other Asian, not specified (22)	85	0.69
Assyrian/Chaldean/Syriac	438	3.54
Austrian	94	0.76
British	13	0.11
Bulgarian	9	0.07
Canadian	26	0.21
Croatian	144	1.17
Cypriot	18	0.15
Czech	49	0.40
Czechoslovakian	30	0.24
Dutch	31	0.25
Eastern European	133	1.08
English	264	2.14
European	82	0.66
Finnish	11	0.09
French, except Basque	94	0.76
French Canadian	12	0.10
German	827	6.69
Greek	963	7.79
Hawaii Native/Pacific Islander:	14	0.11
Micronesian:	1	0.01
Guamanian/Chamorro	1	0.01
Other Pac. Isl., not spec. (3)	13	0.11
Hispanic or Latino:	517	4.18
Central American:	36	0.29
Costa Rican	8	0.06
Guatemalan	19	0.15
Honduran	2	0.02
Nicaraguan	5	0.04
Salvadoran	2	0.02
Cuban	84	0.68
Mexican	167	1.35
Puerto Rican	41	0.33
South American:	113	0.91
Argentinean	18	0.15
Bolivian	11	0.09
Chilean	4	0.03
Colombian	36	0.29
Ecuadorian	13	0.11
Paraguayan	2	0.02
Peruvian	18	0.15
Venezuelan	5	0.04
Other South American	6	0.05
Other Hispanic or Latino	76	0.61
Hungarian	152	1.23
Icelander	6	0.05
Iranian	66	0.53
Irish	558	4.51
Israeli	7	0.06
Italian	441	3.57
Latvian	13	0.11
Lithuanian	92	0.74
Macedonian	20	0.16
Northern European	5	0.04
Norwegian	36	0.29
Pennsylvania German	6	0.05
Polish	864	6.99
Romanian	382	3.09
Russian	1,078	8.72
Scandinavian	20	0.16
Scotch-Irish	32	0.26
Scottish	23	0.19
Serbian	123	1.00
Slovak	24	0.19
Slovene	7	0.06
Soviet Union	5	0.04
Swedish	122	0.99
Swiss	23	0.19
Turkish	41	0.33
Ukrainian	110	0.89
United States or American	740	5.99
Welsh	16	0.13
West Indian, excl. Hispanic:	11	0.09
Belizean	5	0.04
Jamaican	6	0.05
White:	9,510	76.95
Not Hispanic (8,866)	9,136	73.92
Hispanic (345)	374	3.03
Yugoslavian	84	0.68

Lindenhurst

Place Type: Village
County: Lake
Population: 12,539

Ancestry/Race	Number	%
African American/Black:	221	1.76
Not Hispanic (169)	202	1.61
Hispanic (15)	19	0.15
African, sub-Saharan:	2	0.02
African	2	0.02
Am. Ind. or Alaska Nat., not spec.	15	0.12
American Indian tribes, specified:	33	0.26
Blackfeet	5	0.04
Cherokee	5	0.04
Chippewa	10	0.08

Notes: 1. Figures in the "Number" column do not add up to the total population due to: a) Ancestry/Race overlap — e.g. persons can report being both White and Irish, b) persons of Hispanic origin can report being any race, c) persons reporting two ancestries are counted in both categories. 2. Numbers in parentheses indicate the number of persons reporting this ancestry/race alone, not in combination with any other ancestry/race. 3. Refer to the Explanation of Data in the front of the book for more detailed information.

Iroquois	1	0.01
Latin American Indians (1)	1	0.01
Potawatomi (5)	5	0.04
Pueblo (1)	1	0.01
Sioux	2	0.02
All other tribes (1)	3	0.02
Arab:	8	0.06
Arab/Arabic	3	0.02
Lebanese	5	0.04
Armenian	50	0.40
Asian:	448	3.57
Bangladeshi (5)	5	0.04
Chinese, ex. Taiwanese (37)	43	0.34
Filipino (137)	157	1.25
Hmong (5)	5	0.04
Indian (86)	92	0.73
Japanese (11)	27	0.22
Korean (57)	69	0.55
Pakistani (13)	13	0.10
Sri Lankan (4)	5	0.04
Taiwanese (2)	2	0.02
Thai (1)	2	0.02
Vietnamese (11)	11	0.09
Other Asian, not specified (3)	17	0.14
Assyrian/Chaldean/Syriac	5	0.04
Austrian	95	0.75
Belgian	61	0.48
British	23	0.18
Canadian	13	0.10
Croatian	18	0.14
Czech	213	1.68
Czechoslovakian	56	0.44
Danish	230	1.82
Dutch	365	2.89
English	1,149	9.09
Estonian	9	0.07
European	60	0.47
Finnish	56	0.44
French, except Basque	364	2.88
French Canadian	82	0.65
German	3,843	30.39
Greek	215	1.70
Hawaii Native/Pacific Islander:	8	0.06
Micronesian: (1)	2	0.02
Guamanian/Chamorro (1)	2	0.02
Polynesian:	4	0.03
Native Hawaiian	4	0.03
Other Pac. Isl., not spec.	2	0.02
Hispanic or Latino:	508	4.05
Central American:	10	0.08
Guatemalan	8	0.06
Salvadoran	2	0.02
Cuban	28	0.22
Mexican	280	2.23
Puerto Rican	58	0.46
South American:	35	0.28
Argentinean	5	0.04
Chilean	3	0.02
Colombian	22	0.18
Ecuadorian	4	0.03
Peruvian	1	0.01
Other Hispanic or Latino	97	0.77
Hungarian	136	1.08
Iranian	13	0.10
Irish	2,282	18.05
Italian	902	7.13
Lithuanian	100	0.79
Luxemburger	14	0.11
Northern European	6	0.05
Norwegian	469	3.71
Pennsylvania German	6	0.05
Polish	1,734	13.71
Portuguese	17	0.13
Romanian	86	0.68
Russian	155	1.23
Scandinavian	40	0.32
Scotch-Irish	81	0.64
Scottish	237	1.87
Serbian	34	0.27
Slavic	5	0.04
Slovak	56	0.44
Slovene	131	1.04
Swedish	513	4.06
Swiss	27	0.21
Ukrainian	51	0.40
United States or American	580	4.59
Welsh	60	0.47
West Indian, excl. Hispanic:	23	0.18
Belizean	11	0.09
Haitian	12	0.09
White:	11,776	93.91
Not Hispanic (11,320)	11,442	91.25
Hispanic (320)	334	2.66
Yugoslavian	3	0.02

Lisle

Place Type: Village
County: Du Page
Population: 21,182

Ancestry/Race	Number	%
African American/Black:	795	3.75
Not Hispanic (727)	778	3.67
Hispanic (9)	17	0.08
African, sub-Saharan:	89	0.42
African	89	0.42
Am. Ind. or Alaska Nat., not spec.	33	0.16
Albanian	31	0.15
Alsatian	9	0.04
American Indian tribes, specified:	69	0.33
Apache	4	0.02
Blackfeet	1	0.00
Cherokee (10)	35	0.17
Chippewa (4)	5	0.02
Choctaw (1)	1	0.00
Creek (2)	2	0.01
Iroquois (2)	2	0.01
Latin American Indians	2	0.01
Navajo	4	0.02
Potawatomi (1)	1	0.00
Pueblo (5)	5	0.02
Ute	1	0.00
Yaqui (1)	1	0.00
All other tribes (3)	5	0.02
American Indian tribes, not spec.	2	0.01
Arab:	217	1.03
Arab/Arabic	50	0.24
Egyptian	52	0.25
Lebanese	20	0.09
Moroccan	60	0.28
Palestinian	12	0.06
Syrian	23	0.11
Armenian	11	0.05
Asian:	2,251	10.63
Chinese, ex. Taiwanese (590)	645	3.05
Filipino (185)	213	1.01
Hmong (4)	4	0.02
Indian (806)	831	3.92
Indonesian (7)	7	0.03
Japanese (50)	75	0.35
Korean (209)	228	1.08
Laotian (1)	1	0.00
Malaysian (4)	11	0.05
Pakistani (44)	56	0.26
Sri Lankan (11)	11	0.05
Taiwanese (57)	66	0.31
Thai (7)	11	0.05
Vietnamese (53)	60	0.28
Other Asian, specified (2)	3	0.01
Other Asian, not specified (11)	29	0.14
Australian	11	0.05
Austrian	182	0.86
Belgian	35	0.17
British	38	0.18
Canadian	70	0.33
Croatian	147	0.70
Czech	689	3.26
Czechoslovakian	162	0.77
Danish	218	1.03
Dutch	279	1.32
English	1,601	7.58
European	95	0.45
Finnish	36	0.17
French, except Basque	585	2.77
French Canadian	134	0.63
German	4,709	22.30
Greek	296	1.40
Hawaii Native/Pacific Islander:	19	0.09
Micronesian: (2)	2	0.01
Guamanian/Chamorro (2)	2	0.01
Polynesian: (2)	4	0.02
Native Hawaiian	2	0.01
Samoan (2)	2	0.01
Other Pac. Isl., specified	1	0.00
Other Pac. Isl., not spec. (2)	12	0.06
Hispanic or Latino:	1,163	5.49
Central American:	17	0.08
Costa Rican	1	0.00
Guatemalan	6	0.03
Nicaraguan	2	0.01
Panamanian	1	0.00
Salvadoran	3	0.01
Other Central American	4	0.02
Cuban	47	0.22
Dominican Republic	2	0.01
Mexican	869	4.10
Puerto Rican	78	0.37
South American:	67	0.32
Bolivian	11	0.05
Chilean	7	0.03
Colombian	21	0.10
Ecuadorian	10	0.05
Paraguayan	5	0.02
Peruvian	11	0.05
Venezuelan	2	0.01
Other Hispanic or Latino	83	0.39
Hungarian	90	0.43
Iranian	6	0.03
Irish	3,373	15.97
Italian	2,168	10.27
Lithuanian	355	1.68
Luxemburger	15	0.07
Maltese	5	0.02
Northern European	18	0.09
Norwegian	384	1.82
Polish	2,704	12.80
Portuguese	15	0.07
Romanian	101	0.48
Russian	164	0.78
Scandinavian	26	0.12
Scotch-Irish	305	1.44
Scottish	353	1.67
Serbian	26	0.12
Slavic	16	0.08
Slovak	312	1.48
Slovene	50	0.24
Swedish	713	3.38
Swiss	51	0.24
Turkish	29	0.14
Ukrainian	92	0.44
United States or American	479	2.27
Welsh	167	0.79
West Indian, excl. Hispanic:	23	0.11
Haitian	6	0.03
Jamaican	8	0.04
U.S. Virgin Islander	9	0.04
White:	17,933	84.66
Not Hispanic (16,954)	17,172	81.07
Hispanic (707)	761	3.59
Yugoslavian	37	0.18

Lockport

Place Type: City
County: Will
Population: 15,191

Ancestry/Race	Number	%
African American/Black:	202	1.33

Notes: 1. Figures in the "Number" column do not add up to the total population due to: a) Ancestry/Race overlap — e.g. persons can report being both White and Irish, b) persons of Hispanic origin can report being any race, c) persons reporting two ancestries are counted in both categories. 2. Numbers in parentheses indicate the number of persons reporting this ancestry/race alone, not in combination with any other ancestry/race. 3. Refer to the Explanation of Data in the front of the book for more detailed information.

Ancestry/Race	Number	%
Not Hispanic (164)	191	1.26
Hispanic (4)	11	0.07
Am. Ind. or Alaska Nat., not spec.	30	0.20
Albanian	38	0.26
Alsatian	7	0.05
American Indian tribes, specified:	77	0.51
Apache (2)	9	0.06
Blackfeet (2)	6	0.04
Cherokee (6)	36	0.24
Chippewa (2)	4	0.03
Iroquois (4)	7	0.05
Latin American Indians	2	0.01
Potawatomi (1)	1	0.01
Pueblo (1)	7	0.05
Shoshone	2	0.01
Sioux	3	0.02
American Indian tribes, not spec.	7	0.05
Arab:	19	0.13
Arab/Arabic	7	0.05
Lebanese	12	0.08
Armenian	6	0.04
Asian:	146	0.96
Chinese, ex. Taiwanese (22)	25	0.16
Filipino (30)	44	0.29
Indian (16)	19	0.13
Indonesian (1)	2	0.01
Japanese (4)	10	0.07
Korean (25)	29	0.19
Laotian (2)	2	0.01
Malaysian (2)	2	0.01
Pakistani (7)	7	0.05
Other Asian, specified (1)	1	0.01
Other Asian, not specified (4)	5	0.03
Australian	40	0.27
Austrian	156	1.05
Belgian	12	0.08
British	20	0.14
Canadian	7	0.05
Croatian	169	1.14
Czech	410	2.77
Czechoslovakian	50	0.34
Danish	54	0.36
Dutch	473	3.20
English	1,154	7.80
European	43	0.29
Finnish	30	0.20
French, except Basque	393	2.65
French Canadian	72	0.49
German	4,594	31.03
Greek	139	0.94
Hawaii Native/Pacific Islander:	4	0.03
Polynesian:	3	0.02
Samoan	3	0.02
Other Pac. Isl., not spec. (1)	1	0.01
Hispanic or Latino:	660	4.34
Central American:	1	0.01
Guatemalan	1	0.01
Cuban	9	0.06
Mexican	519	3.42
Puerto Rican	41	0.27
South American:	13	0.09
Chilean	1	0.01
Colombian	6	0.04
Ecuadorian	4	0.03
Peruvian	1	0.01
Other South American	1	0.01
Other Hispanic or Latino	77	0.51
Hungarian	108	0.73
Irish	3,631	24.53
Italian	2,399	16.21
Lithuanian	269	1.82
Luxemburger	3	0.02
Macedonian	28	0.19
New Zealander	7	0.05
Norwegian	122	0.82
Pennsylvania German	7	0.05
Polish	3,031	20.48
Portuguese	22	0.15
Romanian	13	0.09
Russian	194	1.31
Scotch-Irish	117	0.79
Scottish	219	1.48
Serbian	60	0.41
Slavic	15	0.10
Slovak	232	1.57
Slovene	190	1.28
Swedish	678	4.58
Swiss	20	0.14
Turkish	5	0.03
Ukrainian	34	0.23
United States or American	478	3.23
Welsh	34	0.23
West Indian, excl. Hispanic:	7	0.05
Belizean	7	0.05
White:	14,715	96.87
Not Hispanic (14,080)	14,198	93.46
Hispanic (476)	517	3.40
Yugoslavian	21	0.14

Lombard

Place Type: Village
County: Du Page
Population: 42,322

Ancestry/Race	Number	%
African American/Black:	1,255	2.97
Not Hispanic (1,125)	1,222	2.89
Hispanic (16)	33	0.08
African, sub-Saharan:	63	0.15
African	53	0.13
Nigerian	10	0.02
Alaska Native tribes, specified:	2	0.00
All other tribes (2)	2	0.00
Am. Ind. or Alaska Nat., not spec.	77	0.18
Albanian	76	0.18
Alsatian	12	0.03
American Indian tribes, specified:	114	0.27
Apache (1)	1	0.00
Blackfeet (3)	11	0.03
Cherokee (7)	41	0.10
Chippewa (2)	9	0.02
Choctaw	2	0.00
Cree (1)	1	0.00
Iroquois	2	0.00
Latin American Indians (1)	7	0.02
Lumbee	2	0.00
Navajo (1)	3	0.01
Osage	7	0.02
Ottawa (1)	1	0.00
Pueblo	2	0.00
Seminole	1	0.00
Sioux (1)	7	0.02
Yaqui	3	0.01
All other tribes (3)	15	0.04
American Indian tribes, not spec.	26	0.06
Arab:	269	0.64
Arab/Arabic	89	0.21
Egyptian	49	0.12
Lebanese	23	0.05
Palestinian	49	0.12
Syrian	59	0.14
Armenian	63	0.15
Asian:	3,326	7.86
Bangladeshi (7)	7	0.02
Cambodian (1)	2	0.00
Chinese, ex. Taiwanese (211)	243	0.57
Filipino (663)	742	1.75
Indian (1,471)	1,564	3.70
Indonesian (3)	3	0.01
Japanese (69)	108	0.26
Korean (143)	163	0.39
Laotian (8)	8	0.02
Malaysian (1)	6	0.01
Pakistani (223)	285	0.67
Taiwanese (14)	16	0.04
Thai (27)	36	0.09
Vietnamese (43)	47	0.11
Other Asian, specified (3)	3	0.01
Other Asian, not specified (59)	93	0.22
Australian	7	0.02
Austrian	257	0.61
Belgian	133	0.32
British	165	0.39
Canadian	90	0.22
Celtic	10	0.02
Croatian	129	0.31
Czech	1,229	2.94
Czechoslovakian	197	0.47
Danish	367	0.88
Dutch	926	2.21
English	3,409	8.14
Estonian	22	0.05
European	215	0.51
Finnish	180	0.43
French, except Basque	871	2.08
French Canadian	252	0.60
German	11,330	27.07
Greek	556	1.33
Hawaii Native/Pacific Islander:	28	0.07
Micronesian: (2)	6	0.01
Guamanian/Chamorro (2)	6	0.01
Polynesian:	8	0.02
Native Hawaiian	8	0.02
Other Pac. Isl., not spec. (5)	14	0.03
Hispanic or Latino:	2,012	4.75
Central American:	59	0.14
Costa Rican	11	0.03
Guatemalan	23	0.05
Honduran	8	0.02
Nicaraguan	4	0.01
Panamanian	6	0.01
Salvadoran	7	0.02
Cuban	52	0.12
Dominican Republic	10	0.02
Mexican	1,261	2.98
Puerto Rican	217	0.51
South American:	183	0.43
Argentinean	7	0.02
Bolivian	6	0.01
Chilean	15	0.04
Colombian	72	0.17
Ecuadorian	34	0.08
Paraguayan	1	0.00
Peruvian	13	0.03
Venezuelan	24	0.06
Other South American	11	0.03
Other Hispanic or Latino	230	0.54
Hungarian	311	0.74
Iranian	49	0.12
Irish	8,246	19.70
Israeli	37	0.09
Italian	6,030	14.41
Latvian	83	0.20
Lithuanian	406	0.97
Luxemburger	28	0.07
Macedonian	6	0.01
New Zealander	7	0.02
Northern European	48	0.11
Norwegian	822	1.96
Pennsylvania German	38	0.09
Polish	4,591	10.97
Portuguese	13	0.03
Romanian	53	0.13
Russian	342	0.82
Scandinavian	72	0.17
Scotch-Irish	628	1.50
Scottish	589	1.41
Serbian	35	0.08
Slavic	8	0.02
Slovak	240	0.57
Slovene	77	0.18
Swedish	1,422	3.40
Swiss	112	0.27
Turkish	18	0.04
Ukrainian	240	0.57
United States or American	726	1.73
Welsh	235	0.56
West Indian, excl. Hispanic:	58	0.14
Dutch West Indian	8	0.02

Notes: 1. Figures in the "Number" column do not add up to the total population due to: a) Ancestry/Race overlap — e.g. persons can report being both White and Irish, b) persons of Hispanic origin can report being any race, c) persons reporting two ancestries are counted in both categories. 2. Numbers in parentheses indicate the number of persons reporting this ancestry/race alone, not in combination with any other ancestry/race. 3. Refer to the Explanation of Data in the front of the book for more detailed information.

	Number	%
Haitian	9	0.02
Jamaican	41	0.10
White:	37,383	88.33
Not Hispanic (35,591)	36,022	85.11
Hispanic (1,238)	1,361	3.22
Yugoslavian	31	0.07

Loves Park

Place Type: City
County: Winnebago
Population: 20,044

Ancestry/Race	Number	%
African American/Black:	552	2.75
Not Hispanic (463)	543	2.71
Hispanic (4)	9	0.04
Alaska Native tribes, specified:	6	0.03
Eskimo	6	0.03
Am. Ind. or Alaska Nat., not spec.	35	0.17
American Indian tribes, specified:	77	0.38
Apache (1)	3	0.01
Blackfeet (2)	5	0.02
Cherokee (5)	38	0.19
Chippewa (2)	5	0.02
Cree	1	0.00
Crow (1)	1	0.00
Kiowa (1)	1	0.00
Latin American Indians (1)	3	0.01
Navajo	2	0.01
Pueblo	2	0.01
Sioux (3)	6	0.03
All other tribes (7)	10	0.05
American Indian tribes, not spec.	6	0.03
Arab:	23	0.12
Arab/Arabic	6	0.03
Lebanese	6	0.03
Syrian	11	0.06
Asian:	439	2.19
Chinese, ex. Taiwanese (39)	45	0.22
Filipino (66)	84	0.42
Indian (60)	66	0.33
Indonesian	6	0.03
Japanese (11)	25	0.12
Korean (66)	74	0.37
Laotian (48)	51	0.25
Malaysian	1	0.00
Pakistani (9)	11	0.05
Sri Lankan (1)	1	0.00
Thai (12)	13	0.06
Vietnamese (42)	51	0.25
Other Asian, specified (1)	1	0.00
Other Asian, not specified (6)	10	0.05
Austrian	38	0.19
Belgian	23	0.12
Brazilian	17	0.09
British	29	0.15
Bulgarian	11	0.06
Canadian	12	0.06
Croatian	30	0.15
Czech	177	0.89
Czechoslovakian	39	0.20
Danish	148	0.74
Dutch	494	2.48
English	1,983	9.96
European	38	0.19
Finnish	23	0.12
French, except Basque	690	3.47
French Canadian	30	0.15
German	5,789	29.08
German Russian	5	0.03
Greek	30	0.15
Hawaii Native/Pacific Islander:	18	0.09
Polynesian: (4)	4	0.02
Native Hawaiian (2)	2	0.01
Samoan (2)	2	0.01
Other Pac. Isl., not spec. (1)	14	0.07
Hispanic or Latino:	655	3.27
Central American:	12	0.06
Costa Rican	5	0.02
Guatemalan	2	0.01
Honduran	4	0.02
Panamanian	1	0.00
Cuban	23	0.11
Dominican Republic	2	0.01
Mexican	442	2.21
Puerto Rican	52	0.26
South American:	41	0.20
Argentinean	2	0.01
Bolivian	1	0.00
Chilean	12	0.06
Colombian	21	0.10
Ecuadorian	1	0.00
Peruvian	4	0.02
Other Hispanic or Latino	83	0.41
Hungarian	89	0.45
Icelander	7	0.04
Iranian	15	0.08
Irish	2,919	14.67
Italian	1,552	7.80
Lithuanian	94	0.47
Luxemburger	5	0.03
Norwegian	1,146	5.76
Pennsylvania German	13	0.07
Polish	958	4.81
Portuguese	10	0.05
Russian	62	0.31
Scandinavian	47	0.24
Scotch-Irish	439	2.21
Scottish	201	1.01
Serbian	42	0.21
Slavic	13	0.07
Slovak	9	0.05
Slovene	48	0.24
Swedish	2,149	10.80
Swiss	44	0.22
Turkish	34	0.17
Ukrainian	19	0.10
United States or American	817	4.10
Welsh	121	0.61
West Indian, excl. Hispanic:	16	0.08
Bahamian	16	0.08
White:	18,923	94.41
Not Hispanic (18,247)	18,503	92.31
Hispanic (371)	420	2.10
Yugoslavian	158	0.79

Lyons

Place Type: Village
County: Cook
Population: 10,255

Ancestry/Race	Number	%
African American/Black:	132	1.29
Not Hispanic (98)	121	1.18
Hispanic (5)	11	0.11
African, sub-Saharan:	12	0.12
Nigerian	12	0.12
Am. Ind. or Alaska Nat., not spec.	22	0.21
Albanian	74	0.73
American Indian tribes, specified:	47	0.46
Apache	1	0.01
Blackfeet (1)	2	0.02
Cherokee	17	0.17
Chippewa (4)	6	0.06
Iroquois (1)	2	0.02
Latin American Indians (4)	6	0.06
Menominee (6)	6	0.06
All other tribes (2)	7	0.07
American Indian tribes, not spec.	1	0.01
Arab:	143	1.41
Arab/Arabic	53	0.52
Jordanian	25	0.25
Lebanese	9	0.09
Palestinian	12	0.12
Other Arab	44	0.43
Asian:	227	2.21
Cambodian (6)	6	0.06
Chinese, ex. Taiwanese (11)	21	0.20
Filipino (43)	71	0.69
Indian (47)	57	0.56
Japanese (5)	6	0.06
Korean (7)	10	0.10
Pakistani (11)	21	0.20
Thai (5)	6	0.06
Vietnamese (2)	2	0.02
Other Asian, not specified (2)	27	0.26
Austrian	47	0.46
Belgian	12	0.12
Bulgarian	19	0.19
Canadian	5	0.05
Croatian	157	1.55
Czech	991	9.78
Czechoslovakian	164	1.62
Danish	21	0.21
Dutch	96	0.95
English	334	3.30
European	79	0.78
French, except Basque	159	1.57
French Canadian	33	0.33
German	1,516	14.96
Greek	164	1.62
Hawaii Native/Pacific Islander:	9	0.09
Polynesian: (4)	9	0.09
Native Hawaiian (3)	8	0.08
Samoan (1)	1	0.01
Hispanic or Latino:	1,668	16.27
Central American:	41	0.40
Costa Rican	4	0.04
Guatemalan	17	0.17
Honduran	5	0.05
Nicaraguan	5	0.05
Panamanian	2	0.02
Salvadoran	7	0.07
Other Central American	1	0.01
Cuban	7	0.07
Mexican	1,343	13.10
Puerto Rican	128	1.25
South American:	35	0.34
Argentinean	1	0.01
Bolivian	2	0.02
Chilean	3	0.03
Colombian	17	0.17
Ecuadorian	6	0.06
Peruvian	5	0.05
Other South American	1	0.01
Other Hispanic or Latino	114	1.11
Hungarian	59	0.58
Irish	1,419	14.00
Italian	1,147	11.32
Latvian	54	0.53
Lithuanian	140	1.38
Macedonian	16	0.16
Norwegian	139	1.37
Polish	1,580	15.59
Romanian	20	0.20
Russian	67	0.66
Scotch-Irish	169	1.67
Scottish	86	0.85
Serbian	248	2.45
Slavic	6	0.06
Slovak	67	0.66
Slovene	42	0.41
Swedish	125	1.23
Ukrainian	95	0.94
United States or American	231	2.28
Welsh	34	0.34
West Indian, excl. Hispanic:	14	0.14
British West Indian	7	0.07
Dutch West Indian	7	0.07
White:	9,257	90.27
Not Hispanic (8,079)	8,303	80.97
Hispanic (832)	954	9.30
Yugoslavian	160	1.58

Notes: 1. Figures in the "Number" column do not add up to the total population due to: a) Ancestry/Race overlap — e.g. persons can report being both White and Irish, b) persons of Hispanic origin can report being any race, c) persons reporting two ancestries are counted in both categories. 2. Numbers in parentheses indicate the number of persons reporting this ancestry/race alone, not in combination with any other ancestry/race. 3. Refer to the Explanation of Data in the front of the book for more detailed information.

Machesney Park

Place Type: Village
County: Winnebago
Population: 20,759

Ancestry/Race	Number	%
African American/Black:	362	1.74
Not Hispanic (283)	356	1.71
Hispanic (1)	6	0.03
African, sub-Saharan:	12	0.06
African	12	0.06
Alaska Native tribes, specified:	1	0.00
Aleut	1	0.00
Am. Ind. or Alaska Nat., not spec.	42	0.20
American Indian tribes, specified:	79	0.38
Apache (2)	2	0.01
Blackfeet (1)	3	0.01
Cherokee (10)	42	0.20
Chippewa (4)	4	0.02
Iroquois (5)	5	0.02
Latin American Indians (2)	3	0.01
Menominee	2	0.01
Navajo (1)	2	0.01
Osage (2)	3	0.01
Pueblo (5)	5	0.02
Sioux (3)	3	0.01
All other tribes (3)	5	0.02
American Indian tribes, not spec.	7	0.03
Arab:	7	0.03
Syrian	7	0.03
Asian:	264	1.27
Chinese, ex. Taiwanese (35)	43	0.21
Filipino (41)	59	0.28
Indian (26)	33	0.16
Japanese (8)	22	0.11
Korean (14)	22	0.11
Laotian (10)	11	0.05
Pakistani	6	0.03
Taiwanese (1)	1	0.00
Thai (16)	20	0.10
Vietnamese (28)	31	0.15
Other Asian, not specified (13)	16	0.08
Austrian	4	0.02
Basque	7	0.03
Belgian	29	0.14
Brazilian	4	0.02
British	7	0.03
Bulgarian	6	0.03
Canadian	51	0.25
Croatian	9	0.04
Czech	55	0.27
Danish	131	0.63
Dutch	686	3.32
Eastern European	9	0.04
English	1,947	9.41
European	130	0.63
Finnish	58	0.28
French, except Basque	692	3.35
French Canadian	115	0.56
German	5,990	28.96
Greek	38	0.18
Hawaii Native/Pacific Islander:	9	0.04
Other Pac. Isl., not spec. (7)	9	0.04
Hispanic or Latino:	584	2.81
Central American:	4	0.02
Nicaraguan	1	0.00
Panamanian	1	0.00
Salvadoran	2	0.01
Cuban	29	0.14
Dominican Republic	2	0.01
Mexican	406	1.96
Puerto Rican	44	0.21
South American:	17	0.08
Argentinean	2	0.01
Chilean	4	0.02
Colombian	5	0.02
Ecuadorian	4	0.02
Peruvian	2	0.01
Other Hispanic or Latino	82	0.40
Hungarian	12	0.06
Irish	3,055	14.77
Italian	1,476	7.14
Lithuanian	115	0.56
Luxemburger	9	0.04
Norwegian	1,110	5.37
Pennsylvania German	16	0.08
Polish	773	3.74
Romanian	15	0.07
Russian	24	0.12
Scandinavian	109	0.53
Scotch-Irish	241	1.17
Scottish	369	1.78
Serbian	36	0.17
Slavic	8	0.04
Slovak	9	0.04
Slovene	8	0.04
Swedish	1,847	8.93
Swiss	84	0.41
Turkish	23	0.11
Ukrainian	49	0.24
United States or American	1,369	6.62
Welsh	52	0.25
White:	20,026	96.47
Not Hispanic (19,443)	19,625	94.54
Hispanic (362)	401	1.93
Yugoslavian	7	0.03

Macomb

Place Type: City
County: McDonough
Population: 18,558

Ancestry/Race	Number	%
Acadian/Cajun	7	0.04
African American/Black:	1,193	6.43
Not Hispanic (1,090)	1,176	6.34
Hispanic (11)	17	0.09
African, sub-Saharan:	104	0.56
African	81	0.44
Kenyan	19	0.10
Sudanese	4	0.02
Alaska Native tribes, specified:	1	0.01
Aleut (1)	1	0.01
Am. Ind. or Alaska Nat., not spec.	60	0.32
American Indian tribes, specified:	55	0.30
Apache (1)	2	0.01
Blackfeet (1)	5	0.03
Cherokee (5)	21	0.11
Cheyenne	3	0.02
Chippewa (2)	3	0.02
Creek (1)	1	0.01
Crow	1	0.01
Iroquois (2)	3	0.02
Latin American Indians (4)	4	0.02
Menominee	1	0.01
Osage	1	0.01
Sioux	8	0.04
All other tribes	2	0.01
American Indian tribes, not spec.	6	0.03
Arab:	104	0.56
Egyptian	4	0.02
Lebanese	23	0.12
Moroccan	8	0.04
Palestinian	12	0.06
Other Arab	57	0.31
Armenian	7	0.04
Asian:	645	3.48
Bangladeshi (2)	2	0.01
Chinese, ex. Taiwanese (108)	126	0.68
Filipino (32)	43	0.23
Indian (88)	97	0.52
Indonesian (3)	5	0.03
Japanese (111)	126	0.68
Korean (128)	135	0.73
Laotian (3)	3	0.02
Malaysian (10)	10	0.05
Pakistani (12)	13	0.07
Taiwanese (6)	7	0.04
Thai (12)	12	0.06
Vietnamese (7)	9	0.05
Other Asian, specified (35)	35	0.19
Other Asian, not specified (8)	22	0.12
Austrian	24	0.13
Belgian	83	0.45
Brazilian	6	0.03
British	102	0.55
Canadian	40	0.22
Croatian	105	0.57
Czech	77	0.42
Czechoslovakian	49	0.26
Danish	75	0.41
Dutch	496	2.68
English	2,158	11.67
European	192	1.04
Finnish	33	0.18
French, except Basque	453	2.45
French Canadian	50	0.27
German	4,902	26.51
Greek	21	0.11
Hawaii Native/Pacific Islander:	11	0.06
Micronesian: (1)	2	0.01
Guamanian/Chamorro (1)	2	0.01
Polynesian: (3)	4	0.02
Native Hawaiian (1)	2	0.01
Samoan (2)	2	0.01
Other Pac. Isl., not spec. (2)	5	0.03
Hispanic or Latino:	389	2.10
Central American:	21	0.11
Costa Rican	4	0.02
Guatemalan	5	0.03
Honduran	2	0.01
Nicaraguan	1	0.01
Panamanian	7	0.04
Salvadoran	1	0.01
Other Central American	1	0.01
Cuban	6	0.03
Dominican Republic	6	0.03
Mexican	250	1.35
Puerto Rican	38	0.20
South American:	20	0.11
Argentinean	1	0.01
Bolivian	4	0.02
Chilean	1	0.01
Colombian	6	0.03
Ecuadorian	1	0.01
Peruvian	4	0.02
Other South American	3	0.02
Other Hispanic or Latino	48	0.26
Hungarian	55	0.30
Irish	2,898	15.67
Italian	715	3.87
Lithuanian	79	0.43
Macedonian	7	0.04
Norwegian	456	2.47
Pennsylvania German	18	0.10
Polish	776	4.20
Portuguese	16	0.09
Romanian	7	0.04
Russian	51	0.28
Scandinavian	7	0.04
Scotch-Irish	354	1.91
Scottish	358	1.94
Serbian	21	0.11
Slavic	5	0.03
Slovene	7	0.04
Swedish	703	3.80
Swiss	64	0.35
Turkish	5	0.03
Ukrainian	24	0.13
United States or American	1,209	6.54
Welsh	162	0.88
West Indian, excl. Hispanic:	16	0.09
Haitian	7	0.04
Jamaican	5	0.03
West Indian	4	0.02
White:	16,701	89.99
Not Hispanic (16,241)	16,454	88.66
Hispanic (226)	247	1.33

Notes: 1. Figures in the "Number" column do not add up to the total population due to: a) Ancestry/Race overlap — e.g. persons can report being both White and Irish, b) persons of Hispanic origin can report being any race, c) persons reporting two ancestries are counted in both categories. 2. Numbers in parentheses indicate the number of persons reporting this ancestry/race alone, not in combination with any other ancestry/race. 3. Refer to the Explanation of Data in the front of the book for more detailed information.

Yugoslavian	29	0.16

Marion

Place Type: City
County: Williamson
Population: 16,035

Ancestry/Race	Number	%
African American/Black:	792	4.94
Not Hispanic (679)	767	4.78
Hispanic (17)	25	0.16
African, sub-Saharan:	29	0.18
African	29	0.18
Alaska Native tribes, specified:	1	0.01
Tlingit-Haida	1	0.01
Am. Ind. or Alaska Nat., not spec.	36	0.22
American Indian tribes, specified:	64	0.40
Apache (1)	1	0.01
Blackfeet (3)	6	0.04
Cherokee (10)	27	0.17
Cheyenne (1)	1	0.01
Choctaw (3)	3	0.02
Cree	5	0.03
Creek (1)	1	0.01
Iroquois	3	0.02
Kiowa	1	0.01
Latin American Indians (1)	1	0.01
Navajo (1)	2	0.01
Pueblo	1	0.01
Sioux (6)	7	0.04
All other tribes (3)	5	0.03
American Indian tribes, not spec.	1	0.01
Arab:	34	0.21
Arab/Arabic	8	0.05
Lebanese	26	0.16
Asian:	161	1.00
Cambodian (7)	10	0.06
Chinese, ex. Taiwanese (14)	16	0.10
Filipino (35)	43	0.27
Indian (38)	39	0.24
Japanese (1)	7	0.04
Korean (4)	5	0.03
Laotian (1)	1	0.01
Malaysian (1)	1	0.01
Pakistani (2)	3	0.02
Taiwanese	1	0.01
Thai (5)	6	0.04
Vietnamese (21)	22	0.14
Other Asian, not specified (1)	7	0.04
Austrian	10	0.06
Belgian	12	0.08
British	33	0.21
Canadian	16	0.10
Croatian	12	0.08
Czech	27	0.17
Czechoslovakian	47	0.29
Danish	33	0.21
Dutch	235	1.47
English	2,104	13.16
European	181	1.13
French, except Basque	386	2.41
French Canadian	76	0.48
German	2,477	15.49
Greek	6	0.04
Hawaii Native/Pacific Islander:	13	0.08
Polynesian: (8)	10	0.06
Native Hawaiian (8)	8	0.05
Samoan	2	0.01
Other Pac. Isl., not spec.	3	0.02
Hispanic or Latino:	257	1.60
Central American:	8	0.05
Costa Rican	1	0.01
Honduran	1	0.01
Nicaraguan	2	0.01
Panamanian	2	0.01
Salvadoran	2	0.01
Cuban	8	0.05
Mexican	145	0.90
Puerto Rican	30	0.19
South American:	16	0.10
Bolivian	3	0.02
Colombian	4	0.02
Paraguayan	2	0.01
Other South American	7	0.04
Other Hispanic or Latino	50	0.31
Hungarian	41	0.26
Irish	1,775	11.10
Israeli	8	0.05
Italian	549	3.43
Lithuanian	58	0.36
Norwegian	118	0.74
Pennsylvania German	11	0.07
Polish	206	1.29
Russian	8	0.05
Scandinavian	10	0.06
Scotch-Irish	388	2.43
Scottish	234	1.46
Serbian	15	0.09
Slavic	11	0.07
Slovene	6	0.04
Swedish	93	0.58
Swiss	62	0.39
Ukrainian	4	0.03
United States or American	1,786	11.17
Welsh	100	0.63
West Indian, excl. Hispanic:	13	0.08
Jamaican	13	0.08
White:	15,070	93.98
Not Hispanic (14,760)	14,912	93.00
Hispanic (135)	158	0.99
Yugoslavian	9	0.06

Markham

Place Type: City
County: Cook
Population: 12,620

Ancestry/Race	Number	%
African American/Black:	10,089	79.94
Not Hispanic (9,903)	10,030	79.48
Hispanic (49)	59	0.47
African, sub-Saharan:	138	1.09
African	122	0.96
Nigerian	8	0.06
Other sub-Saharan African	8	0.06
Am. Ind. or Alaska Nat., not spec.	32	0.25
American Indian tribes, specified:	34	0.27
Blackfeet	8	0.06
Cherokee (5)	15	0.12
Choctaw	1	0.01
Creek	1	0.01
Iroquois	1	0.01
Latin American Indians (2)	6	0.05
Navajo (1)	1	0.01
Seminole	1	0.01
American Indian tribes, not spec.	9	0.07
Asian:	91	0.72
Cambodian (1)	1	0.01
Chinese, ex. Taiwanese (5)	6	0.05
Filipino (8)	10	0.08
Hmong	1	0.01
Indian (10)	18	0.14
Indonesian (1)	1	0.01
Japanese (1)	1	0.01
Korean (1)	2	0.02
Laotian (26)	26	0.21
Vietnamese (10)	10	0.08
Other Asian, specified (7)	7	0.06
Other Asian, not specified (5)	8	0.06
Austrian	13	0.10
Belgian	7	0.06
Czech	78	0.62
Danish	14	0.11
Dutch	115	0.91
English	140	1.11
Finnish	5	0.04
French, except Basque	77	0.61
French Canadian	47	0.37
German	648	5.12
Greek	18	0.14
Hawaii Native/Pacific Islander:	3	0.02
Micronesian: (1)	1	0.01
Guamanian/Chamorro (1)	1	0.01
Polynesian: (1)	1	0.01
Native Hawaiian (1)	1	0.01
Other Pac. Isl., not spec. (1)	1	0.01
Hispanic or Latino:	396	3.14
Central American:	7	0.06
Guatemalan	4	0.03
Honduran	3	0.02
Cuban	7	0.06
Mexican	305	2.42
Puerto Rican	31	0.25
South American:	3	0.02
Ecuadorian	1	0.01
Peruvian	1	0.01
Other South American	1	0.01
Other Hispanic or Latino	43	0.34
Hungarian	37	0.29
Irish	690	5.45
Italian	232	1.83
Lithuanian	29	0.23
Luxemburger	7	0.06
Norwegian	16	0.13
Polish	395	3.12
Russian	43	0.34
Scandinavian	7	0.06
Scotch-Irish	79	0.62
Scottish	38	0.30
Slavic	6	0.05
Slovak	13	0.10
Slovene	9	0.07
Swedish	65	0.51
Ukrainian	5	0.04
United States or American	117	0.92
Welsh	4	0.03
West Indian, excl. Hispanic:	74	0.58
Belizean	27	0.21
Jamaican	16	0.13
Trinidadian and Tobagonian	5	0.04
West Indian	26	0.21
White:	2,317	18.36
Not Hispanic (2,062)	2,185	17.31
Hispanic (121)	132	1.05

Matteson

Place Type: Village
County: Cook
Population: 12,928

Ancestry/Race	Number	%
African American/Black:	8,284	64.08
Not Hispanic (8,033)	8,194	63.38
Hispanic (65)	90	0.70
African, sub-Saharan:	303	2.35
African	268	2.08
Nigerian	35	0.27
Am. Ind. or Alaska Nat., not spec.	19	0.15
American Indian tribes, specified:	61	0.47
Apache	1	0.01
Blackfeet	10	0.08
Cherokee (2)	23	0.18
Chippewa	3	0.02
Choctaw (3)	3	0.02
Creek	3	0.02
Iroquois	4	0.03
Latin American Indians (1)	4	0.03
Navajo	1	0.01
Potawatomi (1)	1	0.01
Seminole	3	0.02
Sioux (2)	3	0.02
All other tribes	2	0.02
American Indian tribes, not spec.	10	0.08
Armenian	4	0.03
Asian:	234	1.81
Chinese, ex. Taiwanese (20)	28	0.22
Filipino (58)	69	0.53

Notes: 1. Figures in the "Number" column do not add up to the total population due to: a) Ancestry/Race overlap — e.g. persons can report being both White and Irish, b) persons of Hispanic origin can report being any race, c) persons reporting two ancestries are counted in both categories. 2. Numbers in parentheses indicate the number of persons reporting this ancestry/race alone, not in combination with any other ancestry/race. 3. Refer to the Explanation of Data in the front of the book for more detailed information.

Indian (80)	86	0.67
Japanese (9)	11	0.09
Korean (10)	11	0.09
Laotian (3)	3	0.02
Pakistani (6)	7	0.05
Thai (2)	3	0.02
Vietnamese (6)	7	0.05
Other Asian, not specified (4)	9	0.07
Australian	6	0.05
Belgian	18	0.14
British	97	0.75
Celtic	7	0.05
Croatian	21	0.16
Czech	50	0.39
Czechoslovakian	20	0.16
Danish	103	0.80
Dutch	219	1.70
English	378	2.93
Finnish	6	0.05
French, except Basque	202	1.57
French Canadian	31	0.24
German	1,449	11.25
Greek	6	0.05
Guyanese	6	0.05
Hawaii Native/Pacific Islander:	4	0.03
Other Pac. Isl., not spec.	4	0.03
Hispanic or Latino:	436	3.37
Central American:	3	0.02
Costa Rican	1	0.01
Panamanian	2	0.02
Cuban	5	0.04
Mexican	305	2.36
Puerto Rican	48	0.37
South American:	2	0.02
Colombian	1	0.01
Peruvian	1	0.01
Other Hispanic or Latino	73	0.56
Hungarian	47	0.36
Irish	1,058	8.21
Italian	334	2.59
Lithuanian	88	0.68
Norwegian	56	0.43
Polish	563	4.37
Portuguese	11	0.09
Romanian	11	0.09
Russian	18	0.14
Scotch-Irish	99	0.77
Scottish	127	0.99
Slovak	21	0.16
Swedish	239	1.86
Ukrainian	43	0.33
United States or American	291	2.26
Welsh	23	0.18
West Indian, excl. Hispanic:	97	0.75
Belizean	11	0.09
Haitian	19	0.15
Jamaican	62	0.48
West Indian	5	0.04
White:	4,380	33.88
Not Hispanic (4,031)	4,164	32.21
Hispanic (199)	216	1.67

Mattoon

Place Type: City
County: Coles
Population: 18,291

Ancestry/Race	Number	%
African American/Black:	339	1.85
Not Hispanic (259)	337	1.84
Hispanic (1)	2	0.01
African, sub-Saharan:	18	0.10
African	18	0.10
Alaska Native tribes, specified:	1	0.01
Tlingit-Haida (1)	1	0.01
Am. Ind. or Alaska Nat., not spec.	32	0.17
American Indian tribes, specified:	41	0.22
Apache (5)	6	0.03
Cherokee (6)	20	0.11
Chippewa (4)	4	0.02
Comanche (2)	2	0.01
Latin American Indians (3)	4	0.02
Osage	2	0.01
Paiute (1)	1	0.01
Sioux	1	0.01
Yuman	1	0.01
American Indian tribes, not spec.	5	0.03
Arab:	7	0.04
Syrian	7	0.04
Armenian	6	0.03
Asian:	99	0.54
Bangladeshi (4)	4	0.02
Cambodian (1)	1	0.01
Chinese, ex. Taiwanese (12)	14	0.08
Filipino (5)	10	0.05
Indian (19)	20	0.11
Indonesian (1)	5	0.03
Japanese (7)	8	0.04
Korean (14)	20	0.11
Taiwanese (2)	2	0.01
Thai (4)	6	0.03
Vietnamese (6)	6	0.03
Other Asian, not specified	3	0.02
Austrian	26	0.14
Belgian	13	0.07
British	58	0.32
Canadian	6	0.03
Celtic	6	0.03
Czech	5	0.03
Czechoslovakian	50	0.27
Danish	89	0.49
Dutch	410	2.24
Eastern European	13	0.07
English	2,142	11.68
European	131	0.71
French, except Basque	473	2.58
French Canadian	38	0.21
German	3,779	20.61
Greek	31	0.17
Hawaii Native/Pacific Islander:	6	0.03
Micronesian: (1)	4	0.02
Guamanian/Chamorro (1)	4	0.02
Polynesian:	1	0.01
Native Hawaiian	1	0.01
Other Pac. Isl., not spec. (1)	1	0.01
Hispanic or Latino:	232	1.27
Central American:	3	0.02
Guatemalan	1	0.01
Panamanian	1	0.01
Salvadoran	1	0.01
Dominican Republic	2	0.01
Mexican	166	0.91
Puerto Rican	25	0.14
South American:	2	0.01
Argentinean	1	0.01
Ecuadorian	1	0.01
Other Hispanic or Latino	34	0.19
Hungarian	66	0.36
Iranian	13	0.07
Irish	2,273	12.40
Italian	237	1.29
Lithuanian	48	0.26
Northern European	13	0.07
Norwegian	39	0.21
Pennsylvania German	25	0.14
Polish	277	1.51
Russian	40	0.22
Scandinavian	6	0.03
Scotch-Irish	356	1.94
Scottish	290	1.58
Slavic	12	0.07
Swedish	102	0.56
Swiss	37	0.20
Ukrainian	15	0.08
United States or American	2,907	15.85
Welsh	79	0.43
West Indian, excl. Hispanic:	6	0.03
West Indian	6	0.03
White:	17,837	97.52
Not Hispanic (17,528)	17,671	96.61
Hispanic (148)	166	0.91
Yugoslavian	9	0.05

Maywood

Place Type: Village
County: Cook
Population: 26,987

Ancestry/Race	Number	%
African American/Black:	22,612	83.79
Not Hispanic (22,208)	22,485	83.32
Hispanic (100)	127	0.47
African, sub-Saharan:	295	1.09
African	285	1.06
Nigerian	10	0.04
Am. Ind. or Alaska Nat., not spec.	83	0.31
American Indian tribes, specified:	67	0.25
Blackfeet	6	0.02
Cherokee (1)	30	0.11
Choctaw	12	0.04
Creek	3	0.01
Iroquois	3	0.01
Kiowa (1)	1	0.00
Latin American Indians (1)	2	0.01
Potawatomi	3	0.01
Sioux	4	0.01
All other tribes	3	0.01
American Indian tribes, not spec.	8	0.03
Asian:	108	0.40
Chinese, ex. Taiwanese (3)	9	0.03
Filipino (46)	55	0.20
Indian (14)	23	0.09
Indonesian (4)	5	0.02
Japanese (4)	4	0.01
Korean (2)	2	0.01
Pakistani	2	0.01
Thai (1)	1	0.00
Vietnamese (3)	4	0.01
Other Asian, specified	3	0.01
Austrian	24	0.09
Belgian	3	0.01
British	7	0.03
Croatian	14	0.05
Czech	28	0.10
Czechoslovakian	22	0.08
Danish	21	0.08
Dutch	11	0.04
English	76	0.28
European	6	0.02
Finnish	11	0.04
French, except Basque	31	0.11
French Canadian	6	0.02
German	370	1.37
Greek	15	0.06
Hawaii Native/Pacific Islander:	7	0.03
Polynesian: (1)	2	0.01
Native Hawaiian (1)	2	0.01
Other Pac. Isl., specified	3	0.01
Other Pac. Isl., not spec.	2	0.01
Hispanic or Latino:	2,843	10.53
Central American:	56	0.21
Guatemalan	32	0.12
Honduran	6	0.02
Panamanian	8	0.03
Salvadoran	5	0.02
Other Central American	5	0.02
Cuban	51	0.19
Dominican Republic	5	0.02
Mexican	2,443	9.05
Puerto Rican	96	0.36
South American:	9	0.03
Colombian	1	0.00
Ecuadorian	2	0.01
Peruvian	4	0.01
Venezuelan	1	0.00
Other South American	1	0.00
Other Hispanic or Latino	183	0.68
Hungarian	11	0.04

Notes: 1. Figures in the "Number" column do not add up to the total population due to: a) Ancestry/Race overlap — e.g. persons can report being both White and Irish, b) persons of Hispanic origin can report being any race, c) persons reporting two ancestries are counted in both categories. 2. Numbers in parentheses indicate the number of persons reporting this ancestry/race alone, not in combination with any other ancestry/race. 3. Refer to the Explanation of Data in the front of the book for more detailed information.

Irish	310	1.15
Italian	208	0.77
Lithuanian	7	0.03
Norwegian	58	0.21
Polish	154	0.57
Portuguese	11	0.04
Russian	23	0.09
Scandinavian	26	0.10
Scotch-Irish	26	0.10
Scottish	32	0.12
Slovak	5	0.02
Swedish	70	0.26
Swiss	11	0.04
Ukrainian	13	0.05
United States or American	185	0.69
West Indian, excl. Hispanic:	194	0.72
Barbadian	26	0.10
Belizean	48	0.18
Haitian	11	0.04
Jamaican	89	0.33
Trinidadian and Tobagonian	16	0.06
West Indian	4	0.01
White:	2,905	10.76
Not Hispanic (1,488)	1,655	6.13
Hispanic (1,137)	1,250	4.63

McHenry

Place Type: City
County: McHenry
Population: 21,501

Ancestry/Race	Number	%
African American/Black:	108	0.50
Not Hispanic (62)	87	0.40
Hispanic (13)	21	0.10
Alaska Native tribes, specified:	1	0.00
Alaska Athabascan (1)	1	0.00
Am. Ind. or Alaska Nat., not spec.	32	0.15
American Indian tribes, specified:	63	0.29
Apache	2	0.01
Blackfeet	1	0.00
Cherokee (16)	33	0.15
Chippewa	1	0.00
Iroquois (2)	2	0.01
Latin American Indians (1)	8	0.04
Menominee	1	0.00
Ottawa	1	0.00
Pima	2	0.01
Potawatomi (2)	3	0.01
Seminole	2	0.01
Sioux (1)	1	0.00
Tohono O'Odham	2	0.01
Yaqui	1	0.00
All other tribes (3)	3	0.01
American Indian tribes, not spec.	5	0.02
Arab:	25	0.12
Lebanese	13	0.06
Palestinian	2	0.01
Syrian	10	0.05
Armenian	18	0.08
Asian:	236	1.10
Chinese, ex. Taiwanese (46)	51	0.24
Filipino (87)	101	0.47
Indian (24)	25	0.12
Japanese (8)	14	0.07
Korean (16)	19	0.09
Laotian (1)	1	0.00
Pakistani (1)	3	0.01
Thai (3)	4	0.02
Vietnamese (2)	6	0.03
Other Asian, specified (1)	6	0.03
Other Asian, not specified (1)	6	0.03
Austrian	98	0.45
Belgian	51	0.24
British	28	0.13
Canadian	71	0.33
Celtic	3	0.01
Croatian	85	0.39
Czech	264	1.22
Czechoslovakian	85	0.39
Danish	124	0.57
Dutch	316	1.47
English	1,608	7.46
European	85	0.39
Finnish	174	0.81
French, except Basque	765	3.55
French Canadian	159	0.74
German	7,904	36.65
Greek	146	0.68
Hawaii Native/Pacific Islander:	20	0.09
Polynesian: (8)	11	0.05
Native Hawaiian (3)	3	0.01
Samoan (5)	8	0.04
Other Pac. Isl., specified	5	0.02
Other Pac. Isl., not spec.	4	0.02
Hispanic or Latino:	1,527	7.10
Central American:	22	0.10
Guatemalan	14	0.07
Honduran	1	0.00
Panamanian	1	0.00
Salvadoran	4	0.02
Other Central American	2	0.01
Cuban	24	0.11
Mexican	1,317	6.13
Puerto Rican	50	0.23
South American:	8	0.04
Chilean	1	0.00
Colombian	1	0.00
Ecuadorian	1	0.00
Peruvian	4	0.02
Venezuelan	1	0.00
Other Hispanic or Latino	106	0.49
Hungarian	134	0.62
Icelander	6	0.03
Irish	4,509	20.91
Italian	1,871	8.67
Latvian	54	0.25
Lithuanian	221	1.02
Luxemburger	27	0.13
Northern European	2	0.01
Norwegian	939	4.35
Pennsylvania German	17	0.08
Polish	2,826	13.10
Portuguese	5	0.02
Romanian	46	0.21
Russian	116	0.54
Scandinavian	57	0.26
Scotch-Irish	177	0.82
Scottish	388	1.80
Slovak	25	0.12
Swedish	871	4.04
Swiss	60	0.28
Ukrainian	61	0.28
United States or American	707	3.28
Welsh	181	0.84
West Indian, excl. Hispanic:	6	0.03
Haitian	6	0.03
White:	20,462	95.17
Not Hispanic (19,536)	19,653	91.41
Hispanic (714)	809	3.76
Yugoslavian	54	0.25

Melrose Park

Place Type: Village
County: Cook
Population: 23,171

Ancestry/Race	Number	%
African American/Black:	725	3.13
Not Hispanic (634)	652	2.81
Hispanic (42)	73	0.32
African, sub-Saharan:	35	0.15
African	35	0.15
Alaska Native tribes, specified:	1	0.00
Eskimo	1	0.00
Am. Ind. or Alaska Nat., not spec.	90	0.39
American Indian tribes, specified:	73	0.32
Apache	1	0.00
Blackfeet	1	0.00
Cherokee (5)	17	0.07
Chippewa (1)	2	0.01
Comanche	1	0.00
Iroquois (1)	1	0.00
Latin American Indians (35)	45	0.19
Navajo	1	0.00
Osage	1	0.00
Sioux	1	0.00
All other tribes	2	0.01
American Indian tribes, not spec.	10	0.04
Arab:	72	0.31
Arab/Arabic	11	0.05
Lebanese	21	0.09
Moroccan	11	0.05
Syrian	29	0.12
Asian:	525	2.27
Chinese, ex. Taiwanese (22)	33	0.14
Filipino (158)	170	0.73
Indian (163)	175	0.76
Indonesian (3)	3	0.01
Japanese (14)	20	0.09
Korean (10)	15	0.06
Pakistani (17)	26	0.11
Thai (12)	16	0.07
Vietnamese (53)	54	0.23
Other Asian, not specified (4)	13	0.06
Assyrian/Chaldean/Syriac	8	0.03
Austrian	71	0.31
Belgian	26	0.11
Brazilian	21	0.09
Bulgarian	9	0.04
Canadian	44	0.19
Croatian	10	0.04
Czech	166	0.72
Czechoslovakian	6	0.03
Danish	25	0.11
Dutch	31	0.13
English	319	1.37
Estonian	5	0.02
European	12	0.05
French, except Basque	160	0.69
French Canadian	42	0.18
German	1,799	7.75
Greek	155	0.67
Hawaii Native/Pacific Islander:	10	0.04
Micronesian:	2	0.01
Guamanian/Chamorro	2	0.01
Polynesian: (3)	6	0.03
Native Hawaiian (3)	5	0.02
Samoan	1	0.00
Other Pac. Isl., not spec.	2	0.01
Hispanic or Latino:	12,485	53.88
Central American:	243	1.05
Costa Rican	6	0.03
Guatemalan	177	0.76
Honduran	12	0.05
Nicaraguan	22	0.09
Panamanian	2	0.01
Salvadoran	18	0.08
Other Central American	6	0.03
Cuban	345	1.49
Dominican Republic	15	0.06
Mexican	10,500	45.32
Puerto Rican	448	1.93
South American:	186	0.80
Argentinean	8	0.03
Bolivian	12	0.05
Chilean	5	0.02
Colombian	53	0.23
Ecuadorian	32	0.14
Peruvian	37	0.16
Uruguayan	13	0.06
Venezuelan	14	0.06
Other South American	12	0.05
Other Hispanic or Latino	748	3.23
Hungarian	73	0.31
Icelander	6	0.03
Iranian	17	0.07
Irish	1,252	5.39

Notes: 1. Figures in the "Number" column do not add up to the total population due to: a) Ancestry/Race overlap — e.g. persons can report being both White and Irish, b) persons of Hispanic origin can report being any race, c) persons reporting two ancestries are counted in both categories. 2. Numbers in parentheses indicate the number of persons reporting this ancestry/race alone, not in combination with any other ancestry/race. 3. Refer to the Explanation of Data in the front of the book for more detailed information.

Ancestry/Race	Number	%
Italian	4,368	18.82
Lithuanian	168	0.72
Norwegian	97	0.42
Polish	934	4.02
Portuguese	13	0.06
Romanian	27	0.12
Russian	50	0.22
Scandinavian	22	0.09
Scotch-Irish	49	0.21
Scottish	57	0.25
Serbian	36	0.16
Slovak	87	0.37
Swedish	189	0.81
Swiss	5	0.02
United States or American	488	2.10
Welsh	17	0.07
White:	17,201	74.24
Not Hispanic (9,380)	9,539	41.17
Hispanic (7,195)	7,662	33.07
Yugoslavian	41	0.18

Midlothian

Place Type: Village
County: Cook
Population: 14,315

Ancestry/Race	Number	%
African American/Black:	919	6.42
Not Hispanic (869)	906	6.33
Hispanic (8)	13	0.09
African, sub-Saharan:	49	0.34
African	43	0.30
Nigerian	6	0.04
Alaska Native tribes, specified:	2	0.01
Eskimo	2	0.01
Am. Ind. or Alaska Nat., not spec.	30	0.21
American Indian tribes, specified:	52	0.36
Apache	1	0.01
Blackfeet (3)	7	0.05
Cherokee (2)	22	0.15
Chippewa	1	0.01
Cree	4	0.03
Crow (1)	3	0.02
Iroquois (1)	3	0.02
Latin American Indians (1)	2	0.01
Navajo (1)	1	0.01
Osage	4	0.03
Sioux (1)	2	0.01
All other tribes (2)	2	0.01
American Indian tribes, not spec.	2	0.01
Arab:	5	0.04
Lebanese	5	0.04
Asian:	292	2.04
Chinese, ex. Taiwanese (18)	28	0.20
Filipino (120)	141	0.98
Indian (74)	82	0.57
Japanese (4)	5	0.03
Korean (9)	14	0.10
Laotian (4)	4	0.03
Malaysian	2	0.01
Thai	1	0.01
Vietnamese (4)	5	0.03
Other Asian, not specified (1)	10	0.07
Assyrian/Chaldean/Syriac	11	0.08
Austrian	96	0.68
Belgian	61	0.43
British	12	0.08
Canadian	27	0.19
Croatian	68	0.48
Czech	317	2.23
Czechoslovakian	36	0.25
Danish	72	0.51
Dutch	381	2.68
English	735	5.17
European	66	0.46
Finnish	28	0.20
French, except Basque	337	2.37
French Canadian	120	0.84
German	3,909	27.49
German Russian	9	0.06
Greek	177	1.24
Hawaii Native/Pacific Islander:	4	0.03
Micronesian: (1)	1	0.01
Guamanian/Chamorro (1)	1	0.01
Polynesian: (1)	2	0.01
Native Hawaiian	1	0.01
Samoan (1)	1	0.01
Other Pac. Isl., not spec. (1)	1	0.01
Hispanic or Latino:	976	6.82
Central American:	21	0.15
Costa Rican	7	0.05
Guatemalan	12	0.08
Panamanian	2	0.01
Cuban	7	0.05
Mexican	800	5.59
Puerto Rican	42	0.29
South American:	17	0.12
Argentinean	2	0.01
Ecuadorian	6	0.04
Peruvian	6	0.04
Uruguayan	3	0.02
Other Hispanic or Latino	89	0.62
Hungarian	104	0.73
Irish	3,773	26.53
Italian	1,481	10.41
Lithuanian	371	2.61
Norwegian	123	0.86
Pennsylvania German	12	0.08
Polish	2,190	15.40
Portuguese	25	0.18
Romanian	9	0.06
Russian	36	0.25
Scandinavian	15	0.11
Scotch-Irish	224	1.58
Scottish	138	0.97
Serbian	25	0.18
Slovak	89	0.63
Slovene	7	0.05
Swedish	426	3.00
Ukrainian	23	0.16
United States or American	490	3.45
Welsh	45	0.32
West Indian, excl. Hispanic:	11	0.08
Belizean	11	0.08
White:	12,829	89.62
Not Hispanic (12,037)	12,178	85.07
Hispanic (599)	651	4.55
Yugoslavian	7	0.05

Mokena

Place Type: Village
County: Will
Population: 14,583

Ancestry/Race	Number	%
African American/Black:	86	0.59
Not Hispanic (71)	85	0.58
Hispanic (1)	1	0.01
Am. Ind. or Alaska Nat., not spec.	15	0.10
American Indian tribes, specified:	13	0.09
Blackfeet	1	0.01
Cherokee	4	0.03
Chippewa (1)	1	0.01
Creek	1	0.01
Latin American Indians (1)	1	0.01
Potawatomi (3)	3	0.02
Seminole (1)	1	0.01
All other tribes (1)	1	0.01
American Indian tribes, not spec.	1	0.01
Arab:	95	0.65
Arab/Arabic	66	0.45
Palestinian	21	0.14
Syrian	8	0.05
Armenian	11	0.07
Asian:	200	1.37
Chinese, ex. Taiwanese (27)	31	0.21
Filipino (37)	39	0.27
Indian (55)	59	0.40
Japanese (7)	7	0.05
Korean (44)	50	0.34
Pakistani (6)	6	0.04
Vietnamese (3)	3	0.02
Other Asian, not specified (3)	5	0.03
Australian	20	0.14
Austrian	50	0.34
Belgian	18	0.12
British	33	0.22
Bulgarian	7	0.05
Canadian	7	0.05
Croatian	164	1.12
Czech	466	3.18
Czechoslovakian	67	0.46
Danish	73	0.50
Dutch	563	3.84
English	916	6.24
European	45	0.31
Finnish	43	0.29
French, except Basque	366	2.49
French Canadian	125	0.85
German	4,265	29.06
Greek	121	0.82
Hawaii Native/Pacific Islander:	10	0.07
Micronesian: (1)	3	0.02
Guamanian/Chamorro (1)	3	0.02
Polynesian: (4)	4	0.03
Other Polynesian (4)	4	0.03
Other Pac. Isl., not spec. (3)	3	0.02
Hispanic or Latino:	421	2.89
Central American:	1	0.01
Guatemalan	1	0.01
Cuban	12	0.08
Mexican	324	2.22
Puerto Rican	32	0.22
South American:	8	0.05
Colombian	4	0.03
Ecuadorian	3	0.02
Venezuelan	1	0.01
Other Hispanic or Latino	44	0.30
Hungarian	160	1.09
Irish	4,316	29.41
Italian	2,122	14.46
Lithuanian	276	1.88
Norwegian	249	1.70
Polish	2,710	18.46
Portuguese	4	0.03
Russian	144	0.98
Scandinavian	23	0.16
Scotch-Irish	212	1.44
Scottish	191	1.30
Serbian	75	0.51
Slovak	129	0.88
Slovene	61	0.42
Swedish	476	3.24
Swiss	42	0.29
Ukrainian	179	1.22
United States or American	358	2.44
Welsh	49	0.33
West Indian, excl. Hispanic:	5	0.03
Jamaican	5	0.03
White:	14,216	97.48
Not Hispanic (13,812)	13,888	95.23
Hispanic (314)	328	2.25
Yugoslavian	34	0.23

Moline

Place Type: City
County: Rock Island
Population: 43,768

Ancestry/Race	Number	%
African American/Black:	1,603	3.66
Not Hispanic (1,325)	1,531	3.50
Hispanic (26)	72	0.16
African, sub-Saharan:	104	0.24
African	100	0.23
Other sub-Saharan African	4	0.01
Alaska Native tribes, specified:	3	0.01

Notes: 1. Figures in the "Number" column do not add up to the total population due to: a) Ancestry/Race overlap — e.g. persons can report being both White and Irish, b) persons of Hispanic origin can report being any race, c) persons reporting two ancestries are counted in both categories. 2. Numbers in parentheses indicate the number of persons reporting this ancestry/race alone, not in combination with any other ancestry/race. 3. Refer to the Explanation of Data in the front of the book for more detailed information.

Ancestry/Race	Number	%
Eskimo (2)	3	0.01
Am. Ind. or Alaska Nat., not spec.	90	0.21
Albanian	15	0.03
American Indian tribes, specified:	167	0.38
Apache (2)	9	0.02
Blackfeet	6	0.01
Cherokee (10)	66	0.15
Cheyenne (1)	2	0.00
Chickasaw	3	0.01
Chippewa (1)	4	0.01
Choctaw	2	0.00
Creek	5	0.01
Delaware (1)	1	0.00
Iroquois (3)	4	0.01
Latin American Indians (6)	14	0.03
Menominee (2)	3	0.01
Navajo (4)	4	0.01
Osage	1	0.00
Potawatomi	3	0.01
Sioux (6)	22	0.05
Tohono O'Odham (1)	1	0.00
All other tribes (6)	17	0.04
American Indian tribes, not spec.	11	0.03
Arab:	82	0.19
Arab/Arabic	12	0.03
Egyptian	18	0.04
Lebanese	13	0.03
Moroccan	7	0.02
Syrian	32	0.07
Asian:	717	1.64
Cambodian (7)	10	0.02
Chinese, ex. Taiwanese (40)	59	0.13
Filipino (54)	90	0.21
Indian (335)	346	0.79
Japanese (18)	29	0.07
Korean (55)	66	0.15
Laotian (3)	3	0.01
Pakistani (15)	17	0.04
Taiwanese (1)	1	0.00
Thai (7)	10	0.02
Vietnamese (45)	57	0.13
Other Asian, specified (4)	4	0.01
Other Asian, not specified (19)	25	0.06
Assyrian/Chaldean/Syriac	26	0.06
Australian	10	0.02
Austrian	58	0.13
Belgian	2,686	6.14
British	131	0.30
Bulgarian	19	0.04
Canadian	67	0.15
Croatian	73	0.17
Czech	239	0.55
Czechoslovakian	66	0.15
Danish	279	0.64
Dutch	804	1.84
Eastern European	17	0.04
English	4,361	9.98
Estonian	7	0.02
European	194	0.44
Finnish	34	0.08
French, except Basque	1,077	2.46
French Canadian	191	0.44
German	10,514	24.05
Greek	221	0.51
Hawaii Native/Pacific Islander:	21	0.05
Micronesian: (1)	1	0.00
Guamanian/Chamorro (1)	1	0.00
Polynesian: (5)	12	0.03
Native Hawaiian (1)	6	0.01
Samoan (4)	5	0.01
Other Polynesian	1	0.00
Other Pac. Isl., not spec. (5)	8	0.02
Hispanic or Latino:	5,212	11.91
Central American:	46	0.11
Costa Rican	5	0.01
Guatemalan	8	0.02
Honduran	14	0.03
Nicaraguan	1	0.00
Salvadoran	13	0.03
Other Central American	5	0.01
Cuban	27	0.06
Dominican Republic	6	0.01
Mexican	4,637	10.59
Puerto Rican	73	0.17
South American:	40	0.09
Argentinean	3	0.01
Chilean	3	0.01
Colombian	18	0.04
Ecuadorian	6	0.01
Peruvian	1	0.00
Venezuelan	8	0.02
Other South American	1	0.00
Other Hispanic or Latino	383	0.88
Hungarian	108	0.25
Iranian	7	0.02
Irish	6,083	13.91
Italian	1,038	2.37
Lithuanian	77	0.18
Macedonian	13	0.03
Northern European	24	0.05
Norwegian	945	2.16
Pennsylvania German	36	0.08
Polish	699	1.60
Portuguese	29	0.07
Romanian	38	0.09
Russian	74	0.17
Scandinavian	76	0.17
Scotch-Irish	648	1.48
Scottish	855	1.96
Serbian	40	0.09
Slavic	46	0.11
Slovak	43	0.10
Slovene	21	0.05
Swedish	4,073	9.32
Swiss	176	0.40
Ukrainian	28	0.06
United States or American	2,531	5.79
Welsh	301	0.69
West Indian, excl. Hispanic:	18	0.04
Haitian	6	0.01
Jamaican	6	0.01
West Indian	6	0.01
White:	39,421	90.07
Not Hispanic (36,030)	36,496	83.39
Hispanic (2,652)	2,925	6.68
Yugoslavian	132	0.30

Morris

Place Type: City
County: Grundy
Population: 11,928

Ancestry/Race	Number	%
African American/Black:	57	0.48
Not Hispanic (41)	56	0.47
Hispanic	1	0.01
African, sub-Saharan:	7	0.06
African	7	0.06
Am. Ind. or Alaska Nat., not spec.	21	0.18
American Indian tribes, specified:	35	0.29
Blackfeet	1	0.01
Cherokee (9)	20	0.17
Chippewa (3)	3	0.03
Choctaw (1)	1	0.01
Latin American Indians (3)	3	0.03
Pueblo (1)	1	0.01
Sioux (1)	2	0.02
Yaqui (1)	1	0.01
All other tribes (3)	3	0.03
American Indian tribes, not spec.	4	0.03
Arab:	42	0.35
Lebanese	42	0.35
Asian:	80	0.67
Cambodian (1)	6	0.05
Chinese, ex. Taiwanese (10)	10	0.08
Filipino (14)	15	0.13
Indian (12)	13	0.11
Japanese (1)	7	0.06
Korean (11)	13	0.11
Laotian (1)	1	0.01
Taiwanese (1)	1	0.01
Thai (2)	2	0.02
Vietnamese (6)	7	0.06
Other Asian, not specified (2)	5	0.04
Austrian	27	0.23
British	14	0.12
Canadian	29	0.24
Croatian	35	0.29
Czech	96	0.80
Czechoslovakian	37	0.31
Danish	170	1.42
Dutch	265	2.22
English	1,058	8.86
European	72	0.60
Finnish	5	0.04
French, except Basque	398	3.33
French Canadian	64	0.54
German	2,575	21.57
Greek	30	0.25
Hawaii Native/Pacific Islander:	5	0.04
Polynesian: (3)	5	0.04
Native Hawaiian	1	0.01
Samoan (3)	4	0.03
Hispanic or Latino:	828	6.94
Cuban	5	0.04
Mexican	737	6.18
Puerto Rican	30	0.25
South American:	5	0.04
Argentinean	1	0.01
Chilean	1	0.01
Paraguayan	3	0.03
Other Hispanic or Latino	51	0.43
Hungarian	39	0.33
Irish	2,400	20.11
Italian	816	6.84
Lithuanian	57	0.48
Luxemburger	13	0.11
Northern European	13	0.11
Norwegian	1,595	13.36
Polish	645	5.40
Portuguese	8	0.07
Romanian	40	0.34
Russian	34	0.28
Scotch-Irish	243	2.04
Scottish	239	2.00
Serbian	20	0.17
Slovak	96	0.80
Slovene	25	0.21
Swedish	393	3.29
Swiss	45	0.38
Ukrainian	8	0.07
United States or American	812	6.80
Welsh	75	0.63
White:	11,499	96.40
Not Hispanic (10,903)	10,971	91.98
Hispanic (470)	528	4.43
Yugoslavian	4	0.03

Morton Grove

Place Type: Village
County: Cook
Population: 22,451

Ancestry/Race	Number	%
Afghan	22	0.10
African American/Black:	181	0.81
Not Hispanic (135)	166	0.74
Hispanic (7)	15	0.07
African, sub-Saharan:	30	0.13
African	12	0.05
South African	18	0.08
Am. Ind. or Alaska Nat., not spec.	37	0.16
Albanian	11	0.05
American Indian tribes, specified:	38	0.17
Blackfeet	1	0.00
Cherokee (1)	14	0.06
Chickasaw	4	0.02
Chippewa (2)	2	0.01

Notes: 1. Figures in the "Number" column do not add up to the total population due to: a) Ancestry/Race overlap — e.g. persons can report being both White and Irish, b) persons of Hispanic origin can report being any race, c) persons reporting two ancestries are counted in both categories. 2. Numbers in parentheses indicate the number of persons reporting this ancestry/race alone, not in combination with any other ancestry/race. 3. Refer to the Explanation of Data in the front of the book for more detailed information.

Ancestry/Race	Number	%
Iroquois (1)	1	0.00
Latin American Indians (3)	12	0.05
Sioux (3)	3	0.01
All other tribes (1)	1	0.00
American Indian tribes, not spec.	13	0.06
Arab:	303	1.35
Iraqi	41	0.18
Jordanian	189	0.84
Lebanese	18	0.08
Moroccan	5	0.02
Syrian	35	0.16
Other Arab	15	0.07
Armenian	169	0.75
Asian:	5,345	23.81
Bangladeshi (4)	4	0.02
Cambodian (3)	4	0.02
Chinese, ex. Taiwanese (438)	511	2.28
Filipino (1,445)	1,569	6.99
Indian (1,497)	1,565	6.97
Indonesian (1)	1	0.00
Japanese (153)	192	0.86
Korean (1,042)	1,065	4.74
Laotian (1)	1	0.00
Pakistani (107)	146	0.65
Sri Lankan (4)	6	0.03
Taiwanese (17)	25	0.11
Thai (88)	97	0.43
Vietnamese (79)	88	0.39
Other Asian, specified (4)	8	0.04
Other Asian, not specified (31)	63	0.28
Assyrian/Chaldean/Syriac	496	2.21
Austrian	196	0.87
Belgian	44	0.20
British	17	0.08
Bulgarian	32	0.14
Canadian	34	0.15
Croatian	176	0.78
Czech	114	0.51
Czechoslovakian	66	0.29
Danish	106	0.47
Dutch	127	0.57
Eastern European	32	0.14
English	941	4.19
European	19	0.08
Finnish	70	0.31
French, except Basque	323	1.44
French Canadian	31	0.14
German	3,602	16.04
Greek	859	3.83
Hawaii Native/Pacific Islander:	22	0.10
Micronesian:	2	0.01
Guamanian/Chamorro	2	0.01
Polynesian: (1)	6	0.03
Native Hawaiian	4	0.02
Samoan (1)	2	0.01
Other Pac. Isl., not spec.	14	0.06
Hispanic or Latino:	988	4.40
Central American:	39	0.17
Costa Rican	3	0.01
Guatemalan	24	0.11
Honduran	2	0.01
Nicaraguan	8	0.04
Panamanian	1	0.00
Salvadoran	1	0.00
Cuban	71	0.32
Dominican Republic	6	0.03
Mexican	453	2.02
Puerto Rican	125	0.56
South American:	179	0.80
Argentinean	9	0.04
Bolivian	14	0.06
Chilean	1	0.00
Colombian	57	0.25
Ecuadorian	43	0.19
Paraguayan	1	0.00
Peruvian	32	0.14
Uruguayan	6	0.03
Venezuelan	3	0.01
Other South American	13	0.06
Other Hispanic or Latino	115	0.51
Hungarian	222	0.99
Iranian	50	0.22
Irish	1,945	8.66
Israeli	7	0.03
Italian	1,323	5.89
Latvian	31	0.14
Lithuanian	155	0.69
Luxemburger	87	0.39
Macedonian	25	0.11
Norwegian	273	1.22
Pennsylvania German	8	0.04
Polish	2,666	11.87
Portuguese	7	0.03
Romanian	376	1.67
Russian	1,199	5.34
Scandinavian	21	0.09
Scotch-Irish	168	0.75
Scottish	172	0.77
Serbian	130	0.58
Slavic	22	0.10
Slovak	23	0.10
Slovene	21	0.09
Soviet Union	15	0.07
Swedish	515	2.29
Swiss	40	0.18
Turkish	14	0.06
Ukrainian	294	1.31
United States or American	633	2.82
Welsh	53	0.24
West Indian, excl. Hispanic:	5	0.02
Trinidadian and Tobagonian	5	0.02
White:	16,901	75.28
Not Hispanic (15,938)	16,192	72.12
Hispanic (668)	709	3.16
Yugoslavian	80	0.36

Morton

Place Type: Village
County: Tazewell
Population: 15,198

Ancestry/Race	Number	%
African American/Black:	31	0.20
Not Hispanic (20)	31	0.20
African, sub-Saharan:	12	0.08
Sierra Leonean	12	0.08
Am. Ind. or Alaska Nat., not spec.	15	0.10
American Indian tribes, specified:	26	0.17
Apache (5)	5	0.03
Blackfeet	1	0.01
Cherokee (10)	16	0.11
Sioux (4)	4	0.03
Arab:	40	0.27
Lebanese	33	0.22
Syrian	7	0.05
Asian:	205	1.35
Chinese, ex. Taiwanese (29)	36	0.24
Filipino (20)	25	0.16
Indian (83)	85	0.56
Japanese (5)	11	0.07
Korean (18)	25	0.16
Taiwanese (5)	5	0.03
Vietnamese (12)	12	0.08
Other Asian, not specified (2)	6	0.04
Australian	4	0.03
Austrian	32	0.21
Belgian	72	0.48
Brazilian	30	0.20
British	70	0.47
Canadian	12	0.08
Celtic	18	0.12
Croatian	31	0.21
Czech	167	1.11
Czechoslovakian	20	0.13
Danish	69	0.46
Dutch	219	1.46
English	1,985	13.19
European	135	0.90
Finnish	15	0.10
French, except Basque	352	2.34
French Canadian	43	0.29
German	6,055	40.25
Greek	59	0.39
Hawaii Native/Pacific Islander:	2	0.01
Polynesian: (1)	2	0.01
Native Hawaiian	1	0.01
Samoan (1)	1	0.01
Hispanic or Latino:	122	0.80
Central American:	2	0.01
Panamanian	1	0.01
Salvadoran	1	0.01
Cuban	4	0.03
Mexican	86	0.57
Puerto Rican	10	0.07
South American:	6	0.04
Chilean	2	0.01
Colombian	2	0.01
Peruvian	2	0.01
Other Hispanic or Latino	14	0.09
Hungarian	31	0.21
Iranian	7	0.05
Irish	2,012	13.37
Israeli	7	0.05
Italian	389	2.59
Lithuanian	41	0.27
Luxemburger	6	0.04
Northern European	13	0.09
Norwegian	322	2.14
Polish	275	1.83
Russian	38	0.25
Scotch-Irish	187	1.24
Scottish	330	2.19
Serbian	33	0.22
Slovak	46	0.31
Slovene	11	0.07
Swedish	496	3.30
Swiss	456	3.03
Ukrainian	35	0.23
United States or American	874	5.81
Welsh	151	1.00
White:	14,930	98.24
Not Hispanic (14,806)	14,853	97.73
Hispanic (68)	77	0.51
Yugoslavian	7	0.05

Mount Prospect

Place Type: Village
County: Cook
Population: 56,265

Ancestry/Race	Number	%
African American/Black:	1,184	2.10
Not Hispanic (979)	1,124	2.00
Hispanic (47)	60	0.11
African, sub-Saharan:	182	0.32
African	110	0.19
Nigerian	17	0.03
Senegalese	13	0.02
South African	8	0.01
Ugandan	13	0.02
Zimbabwean	12	0.02
Other sub-Saharan African	9	0.02
Am. Ind. or Alaska Nat., not spec.	144	0.26
Albanian	148	0.26
Alsatian	14	0.02
American Indian tribes, specified:	104	0.18
Blackfeet	4	0.01
Cherokee (5)	31	0.06
Chickasaw	3	0.01
Chippewa (5)	8	0.01
Choctaw (1)	3	0.01
Cree (1)	1	0.00
Creek	2	0.00
Delaware	3	0.01
Iroquois (4)	7	0.01
Kiowa (1)	1	0.00
Latin American Indians (14)	21	0.04
Navajo (2)	4	0.01

Notes: 1. Figures in the "Number" column do not add up to the total population due to: a) Ancestry/Race overlap — e.g. persons can report being both White and Irish, b) persons of Hispanic origin can report being any race, c) persons reporting two ancestries are counted in both categories. 2. Numbers in parentheses indicate the number of persons reporting this ancestry/race alone, not in combination with any other ancestry/race. 3. Refer to the Explanation of Data in the front of the book for more detailed information.

Ancestry/Race	Number	%
Ottawa (1)	1	0.00
Potawatomi (1)	4	0.01
Sioux (1)	7	0.01
All other tribes (1)	4	0.01
American Indian tribes, not spec.	19	0.03
Arab:	177	0.31
Arab/Arabic	35	0.06
Egyptian	16	0.03
Iraqi	9	0.02
Jordanian	80	0.14
Lebanese	13	0.02
Moroccan	7	0.01
Palestinian	11	0.02
Syrian	6	0.01
Armenian	93	0.16
Asian:	6,731	11.96
Bangladeshi (11)	15	0.03
Cambodian (7)	7	0.01
Chinese, ex. Taiwanese (511)	561	1.00
Filipino (594)	682	1.21
Indian (3,166)	3,325	5.91
Indonesian (9)	11	0.02
Japanese (347)	408	0.73
Korean (1,189)	1,232	2.19
Laotian (26)	26	0.05
Malaysian (2)	3	0.01
Pakistani (114)	124	0.22
Taiwanese (11)	14	0.02
Thai (40)	50	0.09
Vietnamese (176)	185	0.33
Other Asian, specified (4)	10	0.02
Other Asian, not specified (28)	78	0.14
Assyrian/Chaldean/Syriac	220	0.39
Australian	26	0.05
Austrian	391	0.69
Belgian	73	0.13
British	132	0.23
Bulgarian	164	0.29
Canadian	63	0.11
Croatian	145	0.26
Czech	533	0.94
Czechoslovakian	164	0.29
Danish	410	0.72
Dutch	547	0.96
Eastern European	10	0.02
English	3,174	5.60
European	96	0.17
Finnish	131	0.23
French, except Basque	1,035	1.83
French Canadian	244	0.43
German	11,965	21.10
Greek	1,654	2.92
Hawaii Native/Pacific Islander:	59	0.10
Micronesian: (4)	7	0.01
Guamanian/Chamorro (4)	5	0.01
Other Micronesian	2	0.00
Polynesian: (15)	21	0.04
Native Hawaiian (6)	12	0.02
Samoan (9)	9	0.02
Other Pac. Isl., specified	1	0.00
Other Pac. Isl., not spec. (9)	30	0.05
Hispanic or Latino:	6,620	11.77
Central American:	185	0.33
Costa Rican	5	0.01
Guatemalan	57	0.10
Honduran	13	0.02
Nicaraguan	3	0.01
Panamanian	12	0.02
Salvadoran	85	0.15
Other Central American	10	0.02
Cuban	106	0.19
Dominican Republic	16	0.03
Mexican	5,323	9.46
Puerto Rican	290	0.52
South American:	203	0.36
Argentinean	18	0.03
Bolivian	4	0.01
Chilean	2	0.00
Colombian	66	0.12
Ecuadorian	66	0.12
Paraguayan	1	0.00
Peruvian	34	0.06
Venezuelan	8	0.01
Other South American	4	0.01
Other Hispanic or Latino	497	0.88
Hungarian	349	0.62
Iranian	36	0.06
Irish	7,605	13.41
Israeli	11	0.02
Italian	6,196	10.93
Latvian	100	0.18
Lithuanian	237	0.42
Luxemburger	86	0.15
Macedonian	105	0.19
Northern European	81	0.14
Norwegian	1,140	2.01
Pennsylvania German	9	0.02
Polish	9,216	16.25
Portuguese	89	0.16
Romanian	243	0.43
Russian	719	1.27
Scandinavian	42	0.07
Scotch-Irish	341	0.60
Scottish	550	0.97
Serbian	108	0.19
Slavic	17	0.03
Slovak	321	0.57
Slovene	29	0.05
Swedish	1,594	2.81
Swiss	195	0.34
Turkish	35	0.06
Ukrainian	421	0.74
United States or American	1,170	2.06
Welsh	203	0.36
West Indian, excl. Hispanic:	246	0.43
Haitian	50	0.09
Jamaican	138	0.24
Trinidadian and Tobagonian	40	0.07
West Indian	18	0.03
White:	46,271	82.24
Not Hispanic (41,548)	42,103	74.83
Hispanic (3,790)	4,168	7.41
Yugoslavian	232	0.41

Mount Vernon

Place Type: City
County: Jefferson
Population: 16,269

Ancestry/Race	Number	%
African American/Black:	2,154	13.24
Not Hispanic (1,976)	2,113	12.99
Hispanic (35)	41	0.25
African, sub-Saharan:	100	0.62
African	100	0.62
Am. Ind. or Alaska Nat., not spec.	70	0.43
American Indian tribes, specified:	85	0.52
Blackfeet (3)	8	0.05
Cherokee (12)	61	0.37
Choctaw	2	0.01
Comanche (2)	3	0.02
Creek (1)	1	0.01
Crow	2	0.01
Iroquois	1	0.01
Osage	1	0.01
Seminole	1	0.01
All other tribes (2)	5	0.03
American Indian tribes, not spec.	6	0.04
Arab:	33	0.20
Jordanian	20	0.12
Lebanese	4	0.02
Syrian	9	0.06
Asian:	181	1.11
Chinese, ex. Taiwanese (22)	33	0.20
Filipino (17)	31	0.19
Indian (29)	34	0.21
Japanese (5)	6	0.04
Korean (12)	14	0.09
Laotian (1)	2	0.01
Pakistani (4)	12	0.07
Sri Lankan	1	0.01
Taiwanese (2)	8	0.05
Thai (4)	5	0.03
Vietnamese (16)	16	0.10
Other Asian, not specified (9)	19	0.12
Austrian	7	0.04
British	52	0.32
Canadian	6	0.04
Celtic	7	0.04
Croatian	11	0.07
Czech	27	0.17
Danish	31	0.19
Dutch	275	1.69
Eastern European	16	0.10
English	1,756	10.81
European	54	0.33
French, except Basque	275	1.69
French Canadian	26	0.16
German	2,693	16.58
Greek	22	0.14
Hawaii Native/Pacific Islander:	13	0.08
Polynesian: (3)	9	0.06
Native Hawaiian (2)	5	0.03
Tongan (1)	4	0.02
Other Pac. Isl., not spec.	4	0.02
Hispanic or Latino:	242	1.49
Central American:	8	0.05
Guatemalan	1	0.01
Panamanian	5	0.03
Salvadoran	2	0.01
Cuban	1	0.01
Mexican	94	0.58
Puerto Rican	95	0.58
South American:	5	0.03
Argentinean	1	0.01
Chilean	1	0.01
Venezuelan	3	0.02
Other Hispanic or Latino	39	0.24
Hungarian	33	0.20
Iranian	7	0.04
Irish	1,476	9.09
Italian	308	1.90
Lithuanian	16	0.10
Luxemburger	8	0.05
New Zealander	5	0.03
Norwegian	67	0.41
Pennsylvania German	7	0.04
Polish	225	1.39
Russian	11	0.07
Scandinavian	9	0.06
Scotch-Irish	265	1.63
Scottish	193	1.19
Serbian	7	0.04
Slovak	5	0.03
Slovene	7	0.04
Swedish	69	0.42
Swiss	2	0.01
Turkish	9	0.06
United States or American	2,594	15.97
Welsh	33	0.20
West Indian, excl. Hispanic:	20	0.12
Dutch West Indian	20	0.12
White:	13,983	85.95
Not Hispanic (13,589)	13,841	85.08
Hispanic (117)	142	0.87

Mundelein

Place Type: Village
County: Lake
Population: 30,935

Ancestry/Race	Number	%
African American/Black:	585	1.89
Not Hispanic (464)	536	1.73
Hispanic (30)	49	0.16
African, sub-Saharan:	28	0.09
African	6	0.02
Nigerian	22	0.07

Notes: 1. Figures in the "Number" column do not add up to the total population due to: a) Ancestry/Race overlap — e.g. persons can report being both White and Irish, b) persons of Hispanic origin can report being any race, c) persons reporting two ancestries are counted in both categories. 2. Numbers in parentheses indicate the number of persons reporting this ancestry/race alone, not in combination with any other ancestry/race. 3. Refer to the Explanation of Data in the front of the book for more detailed information.

Ancestry/Race	Number	%
Am. Ind. or Alaska Nat., not spec.	76	0.25
Albanian	19	0.06
American Indian tribes, specified:	96	0.31
Apache (1)	3	0.01
Blackfeet (1)	2	0.01
Cherokee (2)	21	0.07
Chickasaw (1)	1	0.00
Chippewa (2)	7	0.02
Creek	3	0.01
Iroquois	5	0.02
Latin American Indians (17)	39	0.13
Paiute	1	0.00
Pueblo	2	0.01
Sioux (3)	4	0.01
All other tribes	8	0.03
American Indian tribes, not spec.	10	0.03
Arab:	141	0.46
Arab/Arabic	63	0.21
Lebanese	57	0.19
Palestinian	9	0.03
Syrian	12	0.04
Asian:	2,271	7.34
Bangladeshi (3)	3	0.01
Cambodian (74)	83	0.27
Chinese, ex. Taiwanese (358)	409	1.32
Filipino (649)	740	2.39
Indian (424)	440	1.42
Indonesian (1)	2	0.01
Japanese (77)	114	0.37
Korean (275)	298	0.96
Laotian (1)	1	0.00
Malaysian	4	0.01
Pakistani (24)	25	0.08
Sri Lankan	1	0.00
Taiwanese (2)	2	0.01
Thai (19)	30	0.10
Vietnamese (89)	97	0.31
Other Asian, specified (2)	5	0.02
Other Asian, not specified (9)	17	0.05
Assyrian/Chaldean/Syriac	9	0.03
Austrian	180	0.59
Belgian	52	0.17
Brazilian	37	0.12
British	33	0.11
Canadian	69	0.23
Celtic	9	0.03
Croatian	83	0.27
Czech	222	0.73
Czechoslovakian	151	0.49
Danish	145	0.47
Dutch	406	1.33
Eastern European	64	0.21
English	1,862	6.09
Estonian	26	0.09
European	202	0.66
Finnish	217	0.71
French, except Basque	757	2.47
French Canadian	260	0.85
German	6,963	22.76
Greek	245	0.80
Hawaii Native/Pacific Islander:	39	0.13
Micronesian: (2)	2	0.01
Guamanian/Chamorro (2)	2	0.01
Polynesian: (7)	13	0.04
Native Hawaiian (5)	10	0.03
Samoan (2)	3	0.01
Other Pac. Isl., not spec. (14)	24	0.08
Hispanic or Latino:	7,487	24.20
Central American:	204	0.66
Costa Rican	4	0.01
Guatemalan	49	0.16
Honduran	21	0.07
Nicaraguan	4	0.01
Panamanian	3	0.01
Salvadoran	107	0.35
Other Central American	16	0.05
Cuban	33	0.11
Dominican Republic	1	0.00
Mexican	6,540	21.14
Puerto Rican	195	0.63
South American:	114	0.37
Argentinean	1	0.00
Bolivian	1	0.00
Chilean	6	0.02
Colombian	44	0.14
Ecuadorian	37	0.12
Paraguayan	2	0.01
Peruvian	19	0.06
Venezuelan	2	0.01
Other South American	2	0.01
Other Hispanic or Latino	400	1.29
Hungarian	146	0.48
Irish	4,238	13.86
Israeli	28	0.09
Italian	2,289	7.48
Latvian	23	0.08
Lithuanian	188	0.61
Luxemburger	40	0.13
Norwegian	607	1.98
Polish	3,273	10.70
Portuguese	11	0.04
Romanian	150	0.49
Russian	526	1.72
Scandinavian	89	0.29
Scotch-Irish	366	1.20
Scottish	197	0.64
Serbian	42	0.14
Slavic	10	0.03
Slovak	122	0.40
Slovene	13	0.04
Swedish	716	2.34
Swiss	138	0.45
Ukrainian	226	0.74
United States or American	855	2.80
Welsh	172	0.56
West Indian, excl. Hispanic:	38	0.12
Belizean	9	0.03
Haitian	4	0.01
Jamaican	25	0.08
White:	24,910	80.52
Not Hispanic (20,566)	20,854	67.41
Hispanic (3,774)	4,056	13.11
Yugoslavian	58	0.19

Murphysboro

Place Type: City
County: Jackson
Population: 13,295

Ancestry/Race	Number	%
African American/Black:	2,208	16.61
Not Hispanic (2,073)	2,175	16.36
Hispanic (28)	33	0.25
African, sub-Saharan:	133	1.00
African	75	0.56
Kenyan	9	0.07
Nigerian	26	0.19
Other sub-Saharan African	23	0.17
Am. Ind. or Alaska Nat., not spec.	55	0.41
Albanian	10	0.07
American Indian tribes, specified:	77	0.58
Apache	3	0.02
Blackfeet (1)	11	0.08
Cherokee (26)	52	0.39
Chickasaw (1)	2	0.02
Chippewa (1)	1	0.01
Choctaw (1)	2	0.02
Creek	1	0.01
Sioux	1	0.01
All other tribes (1)	4	0.03
American Indian tribes, not spec.	7	0.05
Arab:	19	0.14
Arab/Arabic	7	0.05
Lebanese	8	0.06
Other Arab	4	0.03
Asian:	193	1.45
Chinese, ex. Taiwanese (21)	26	0.20
Filipino (16)	25	0.19
Hmong (3)	3	0.02
Indian (37)	47	0.35
Indonesian (2)	3	0.02
Japanese (25)	32	0.24
Korean (22)	34	0.26
Laotian (1)	1	0.01
Pakistani (1)	2	0.02
Taiwanese (1)	2	0.02
Thai (3)	5	0.04
Vietnamese (3)	4	0.03
Other Asian, specified	2	0.02
Other Asian, not specified (1)	7	0.05
Austrian	14	0.10
Belgian	8	0.06
British	44	0.33
Bulgarian	8	0.06
Croatian	22	0.16
Cypriot	15	0.11
Czech	24	0.18
Czechoslovakian	20	0.15
Danish	24	0.18
Dutch	302	2.26
English	944	7.08
European	94	0.70
Finnish	5	0.04
French, except Basque	422	3.16
French Canadian	16	0.12
German	2,929	21.95
Greek	57	0.43
Hawaii Native/Pacific Islander:	23	0.17
Micronesian: (7)	9	0.07
Guamanian/Chamorro (5)	5	0.04
Other Micronesian (2)	4	0.03
Polynesian: (4)	9	0.07
Native Hawaiian (1)	5	0.04
Samoan (3)	4	0.03
Other Pac. Isl., specified	2	0.02
Other Pac. Isl., not spec. (1)	3	0.02
Hispanic or Latino:	361	2.72
Central American:	14	0.11
Guatemalan	3	0.02
Honduran	2	0.02
Nicaraguan	6	0.05
Salvadoran	3	0.02
Cuban	7	0.05
Dominican Republic	4	0.03
Mexican	225	1.69
Puerto Rican	44	0.33
South American:	10	0.08
Colombian	5	0.04
Peruvian	5	0.04
Other Hispanic or Latino	57	0.43
Hungarian	50	0.37
Icelander	7	0.05
Irish	1,775	13.30
Israeli	18	0.13
Italian	649	4.86
Lithuanian	61	0.46
Norwegian	170	1.27
Polish	410	3.07
Romanian	10	0.07
Russian	64	0.48
Scandinavian	23	0.17
Scotch-Irish	121	0.91
Scottish	191	1.43
Serbian	18	0.13
Slavic	5	0.04
Slovak	15	0.11
Swedish	166	1.24
Swiss	28	0.21
Ukrainian	4	0.03
United States or American	566	4.24
Welsh	93	0.70
West Indian, excl. Hispanic:	58	0.43
Haitian	28	0.21
Jamaican	16	0.12
West Indian	14	0.10
White:	10,813	81.33
Not Hispanic (10,444)	10,629	79.95
Hispanic (168)	184	1.38
Yugoslavian	15	0.11

Notes: 1. Figures in the "Number" column do not add up to the total population due to: a) Ancestry/Race overlap — e.g. persons can report being both White and Irish, b) persons of Hispanic origin can report being any race, c) persons reporting two ancestries are counted in both categories. 2. Numbers in parentheses indicate the number of persons reporting this ancestry/race alone, not in combination with any other ancestry/race. 3. Refer to the Explanation of Data in the front of the book for more detailed information.

Naperville

Place Type: City
County: Du Page
Population: 128,358

Ancestry/Race	Number	%
Acadian/Cajun	9	0.01
Afghan	31	0.02
African American/Black:	4,209	3.28
Not Hispanic (3,828)	4,113	3.20
Hispanic (59)	96	0.07
African, sub-Saharan:	281	0.22
African	188	0.15
Ghanian	40	0.03
Kenyan	16	0.01
Nigerian	5	0.00
South African	32	0.02
Alaska Native tribes, specified:	7	0.01
Alaska Athabascan	4	0.00
Eskimo (1)	1	0.00
Tlingit-Haida (1)	2	0.00
Am. Ind. or Alaska Nat., not spec.	142	0.11
Albanian	180	0.14
Alsatian	30	0.02
American Indian tribes, specified:	248	0.19
Apache (1)	15	0.01
Blackfeet	14	0.01
Cherokee (30)	107	0.08
Chickasaw (2)	3	0.00
Chippewa (14)	22	0.02
Choctaw (2)	10	0.01
Cree	2	0.00
Creek (2)	6	0.00
Delaware (1)	3	0.00
Iroquois (5)	10	0.01
Latin American Indians (9)	11	0.01
Lumbee	5	0.00
Navajo (2)	2	0.00
Osage (1)	2	0.00
Potawatomi (4)	5	0.00
Pueblo (1)	1	0.00
Sioux (5)	11	0.01
All other tribes (7)	19	0.01
American Indian tribes, not spec.	21	0.02
Arab:	948	0.74
Arab/Arabic	150	0.12
Egyptian	147	0.11
Iraqi	27	0.02
Jordanian	91	0.07
Lebanese	374	0.29
Palestinian	65	0.05
Syrian	78	0.06
Other Arab	16	0.01
Armenian	24	0.02
Asian:	13,377	10.42
Bangladeshi (21)	25	0.02
Cambodian (46)	50	0.04
Chinese, ex. Taiwanese (3,820)	4,072	3.17
Filipino (797)	979	0.76
Indian (5,126)	5,261	4.10
Indonesian (11)	24	0.02
Japanese (223)	356	0.28
Korean (1,141)	1,215	0.95
Laotian (5)	8	0.01
Malaysian (3)	3	0.00
Pakistani (343)	403	0.31
Sri Lankan (19)	22	0.02
Taiwanese (378)	455	0.35
Thai (46)	79	0.06
Vietnamese (181)	203	0.16
Other Asian, specified (10)	21	0.02
Other Asian, not specified (73)	201	0.16
Assyrian/Chaldean/Syriac	58	0.05
Australian	49	0.04
Austrian	806	0.63
Basque	21	0.02
Belgian	251	0.20
Brazilian	37	0.03
British	711	0.55
Bulgarian	83	0.06
Canadian	554	0.43
Celtic	7	0.01
Croatian	680	0.53
Cypriot	8	0.01
Czech	2,803	2.18
Czechoslovakian	827	0.64
Danish	1,328	1.04
Dutch	2,808	2.19
Eastern European	74	0.06
English	12,672	9.88
Estonian	45	0.04
European	962	0.75
Finnish	381	0.30
French, except Basque	3,566	2.78
French Canadian	811	0.63
German	34,638	27.00
German Russian	9	0.01
Greek	1,606	1.25
Hawaii Native/Pacific Islander:	103	0.08
Micronesian: (5)	6	0.00
Guamanian/Chamorro (5)	6	0.00
Polynesian: (13)	19	0.01
Native Hawaiian (8)	14	0.01
Samoan (5)	5	0.00
Other Pac. Isl., not spec. (6)	78	0.06
Hispanic or Latino:	4,160	3.24
Central American:	79	0.06
Costa Rican	9	0.01
Guatemalan	29	0.02
Honduran	6	0.00
Nicaraguan	12	0.01
Panamanian	10	0.01
Salvadoran	12	0.01
Other Central American	1	0.00
Cuban	211	0.16
Dominican Republic	30	0.02
Mexican	2,490	1.94
Puerto Rican	491	0.38
South American:	336	0.26
Argentinean	42	0.03
Bolivian	17	0.01
Chilean	23	0.02
Colombian	100	0.08
Ecuadorian	44	0.03
Paraguayan	4	0.00
Peruvian	40	0.03
Uruguayan	1	0.00
Venezuelan	17	0.01
Other South American	48	0.04
Other Hispanic or Latino	523	0.41
Hungarian	1,042	0.81
Icelander	68	0.05
Iranian	479	0.37
Irish	23,688	18.46
Israeli	12	0.01
Italian	13,611	10.61
Latvian	34	0.03
Lithuanian	1,291	1.01
Luxemburger	108	0.08
Macedonian	38	0.03
New Zealander	44	0.03
Northern European	54	0.04
Norwegian	2,972	2.32
Pennsylvania German	74	0.06
Polish	13,936	10.86
Portuguese	160	0.12
Romanian	111	0.09
Russian	1,467	1.14
Scandinavian	347	0.27
Scotch-Irish	1,913	1.49
Scottish	2,178	1.70
Serbian	286	0.22
Slavic	157	0.12
Slovak	809	0.63
Slovene	351	0.27
Soviet Union	9	0.01
Swedish	4,529	3.53
Swiss	681	0.53
Turkish	211	0.16
Ukrainian	658	0.51
United States or American	3,264	2.54
Welsh	945	0.74
West Indian, excl. Hispanic:	102	0.08
Bahamian	9	0.01
Jamaican	34	0.03
Trinidadian and Tobagonian	51	0.04
West Indian	8	0.01
White:	110,648	86.20
Not Hispanic (106,386)	107,484	83.74
Hispanic (2,960)	3,164	2.46
Yugoslavian	210	0.16

New Lenox

Place Type: Village
County: Will
Population: 17,771

Ancestry/Race	Number	%
African American/Black:	68	0.38
Not Hispanic (53)	67	0.38
Hispanic (1)	1	0.01
Alaska Native tribes, specified:	1	0.01
Alaska Athabascan (1)	1	0.01
Am. Ind. or Alaska Nat., not spec.	12	0.07
American Indian tribes, specified:	29	0.16
Apache	2	0.01
Blackfeet	3	0.02
Cherokee (5)	13	0.07
Chippewa	4	0.02
Creek (1)	1	0.01
Iroquois (1)	1	0.01
Latin American Indians (2)	2	0.01
Sioux	3	0.02
American Indian tribes, not spec.	1	0.01
Arab:	33	0.19
Arab/Arabic	12	0.07
Jordanian	7	0.04
Lebanese	8	0.05
Syrian	6	0.03
Armenian	5	0.03
Asian:	102	0.57
Chinese, ex. Taiwanese (16)	22	0.12
Filipino (18)	22	0.12
Indian (3)	4	0.02
Indonesian	4	0.02
Japanese (5)	16	0.09
Korean (18)	24	0.14
Thai (1)	1	0.01
Vietnamese (1)	2	0.01
Other Asian, specified	6	0.03
Other Asian, not specified (1)	1	0.01
Austrian	117	0.66
Belgian	38	0.22
British	35	0.20
Canadian	32	0.18
Celtic	30	0.17
Croatian	174	0.99
Czech	350	1.99
Czechoslovakian	57	0.32
Danish	113	0.64
Dutch	602	3.42
English	1,398	7.94
European	94	0.53
Finnish	28	0.16
French, except Basque	589	3.34
French Canadian	93	0.53
German	5,557	31.54
Greek	219	1.24
Hawaii Native/Pacific Islander:	14	0.08
Micronesian: (2)	3	0.02
Guamanian/Chamorro (2)	3	0.02
Other Pac. Isl., specified	6	0.03
Other Pac. Isl., not spec.	5	0.03
Hispanic or Latino:	563	3.17
Central American:	4	0.02
Guatemalan	3	0.02
Honduran	1	0.01
Cuban	18	0.10

Notes: 1. Figures in the "Number" column do not add up to the total population due to: a) Ancestry/Race overlap — e.g. persons can report being both White and Irish, b) persons of Hispanic origin can report being any race, c) persons reporting two ancestries are counted in both categories. 2. Numbers in parentheses indicate the number of persons reporting this ancestry/race alone, not in combination with any other ancestry/race. 3. Refer to the Explanation of Data in the front of the book for more detailed information.

Mexican	421	2.37
Puerto Rican	48	0.27
South American:	11	0.06
Chilean	2	0.01
Colombian	4	0.02
Ecuadorian	1	0.01
Peruvian	4	0.02
Other Hispanic or Latino	61	0.34
Hungarian	226	1.28
Irish	4,917	27.91
Italian	2,358	13.38
Latvian	1	0.01
Lithuanian	508	2.88
Norwegian	336	1.91
Pennsylvania German	8	0.05
Polish	2,955	16.77
Portuguese	27	0.15
Romanian	19	0.11
Russian	192	1.09
Scandinavian	9	0.05
Scotch-Irish	195	1.11
Scottish	206	1.17
Serbian	8	0.05
Slavic	6	0.03
Slovak	241	1.37
Slovene	137	0.78
Swedish	695	3.95
Swiss	29	0.16
Ukrainian	88	0.50
United States or American	529	3.00
Welsh	36	0.20
White:	17,478	98.35
Not Hispanic (16,991)	17,074	96.08
Hispanic (363)	404	2.27
Yugoslavian	38	0.22

Niles

Place Type: Village
County: Cook
Population: 30,068

Ancestry/Race	Number	%
African American/Black:	180	0.60
Not Hispanic (123)	164	0.55
Hispanic (16)	16	0.05
African, sub-Saharan:	55	0.18
African	47	0.16
Nigerian	8	0.03
Am. Ind. or Alaska Nat., not spec.	44	0.15
Albanian	6	0.02
Alsatian	24	0.08
American Indian tribes, specified:	57	0.19
Apache (1)	5	0.02
Blackfeet	2	0.01
Cherokee (1)	23	0.08
Chippewa (2)	6	0.02
Iroquois	1	0.00
Latin American Indians (9)	11	0.04
Sioux	2	0.01
Yakama (1)	1	0.00
All other tribes (2)	6	0.02
American Indian tribes, not spec.	11	0.04
Arab:	392	1.30
Arab/Arabic	74	0.25
Iraqi	52	0.17
Jordanian	89	0.30
Lebanese	28	0.09
Palestinian	64	0.21
Syrian	46	0.15
Other Arab	39	0.13
Armenian	55	0.18
Asian:	4,098	13.63
Bangladeshi (6)	6	0.02
Cambodian (2)	2	0.01
Chinese, ex. Taiwanese (236)	282	0.94
Filipino (890)	958	3.19
Indian (1,322)	1,380	4.59
Japanese (89)	107	0.36
Korean (938)	949	3.16
Laotian (4)	4	0.01
Pakistani (133)	167	0.56
Sri Lankan (4)	6	0.02
Taiwanese (7)	13	0.04
Thai (57)	57	0.19
Vietnamese (33)	35	0.12
Other Asian, specified (16)	20	0.07
Other Asian, not specified (41)	112	0.37
Assyrian/Chaldean/Syriac	458	1.52
Austrian	128	0.42
Belgian	11	0.04
British	6	0.02
Canadian	61	0.20
Celtic	12	0.04
Croatian	75	0.25
Czech	179	0.59
Czechoslovakian	22	0.07
Danish	70	0.23
Dutch	69	0.23
Eastern European	8	0.03
English	746	2.47
Estonian	15	0.05
European	30	0.10
Finnish	48	0.16
French, except Basque	228	0.76
French Canadian	52	0.17
German	4,287	14.22
Greek	990	3.28
Hawaii Native/Pacific Islander:	29	0.10
Micronesian: (1)	1	0.00
Guamanian/Chamorro (1)	1	0.00
Polynesian: (3)	5	0.02
Native Hawaiian	2	0.01
Samoan (3)	3	0.01
Other Pac. Isl., not spec.	23	0.08
Hispanic or Latino:	1,512	5.03
Central American:	94	0.31
Costa Rican	1	0.00
Guatemalan	63	0.21
Honduran	2	0.01
Nicaraguan	1	0.00
Panamanian	2	0.01
Salvadoran	22	0.07
Other Central American	3	0.01
Cuban	56	0.19
Dominican Republic	1	0.00
Mexican	806	2.68
Puerto Rican	157	0.52
South American:	185	0.62
Argentinean	3	0.01
Bolivian	7	0.02
Chilean	10	0.03
Colombian	46	0.15
Ecuadorian	94	0.31
Peruvian	18	0.06
Uruguayan	1	0.00
Other South American	6	0.02
Other Hispanic or Latino	213	0.71
Hungarian	140	0.46
Iranian	22	0.07
Irish	2,962	9.83
Israeli	17	0.06
Italian	2,686	8.91
Latvian	26	0.09
Lithuanian	116	0.38
Luxemburger	49	0.16
Norwegian	224	0.74
Polish	6,880	22.82
Portuguese	9	0.03
Romanian	266	0.88
Russian	1,133	3.76
Scandinavian	28	0.09
Scotch-Irish	127	0.42
Scottish	112	0.37
Serbian	439	1.46
Slavic	21	0.07
Slovak	126	0.42
Slovene	8	0.03
Swedish	633	2.10
Swiss	21	0.07
Turkish	14	0.05
Ukrainian	507	1.68
United States or American	581	1.93
Welsh	37	0.12
West Indian, excl. Hispanic:	80	0.27
Haitian	80	0.27
White:	25,467	84.70
Not Hispanic (24,133)	24,509	81.51
Hispanic (889)	958	3.19
Yugoslavian	214	0.71

Normal

Place Type: Town
County: McLean
Population: 45,386

Ancestry/Race	Number	%
African American/Black:	3,829	8.44
Not Hispanic (3,460)	3,769	8.30
Hispanic (39)	60	0.13
African, sub-Saharan:	198	0.44
African	116	0.26
Ghanian	21	0.05
Kenyan	26	0.06
Nigerian	23	0.05
South African	12	0.03
Alaska Native tribes, not specified	1	0.00
Am. Ind. or Alaska Nat., not spec.	82	0.18
Albanian	9	0.02
American Indian tribes, specified:	71	0.16
Apache (1)	1	0.00
Blackfeet (1)	1	0.00
Cherokee (17)	36	0.08
Chickasaw	1	0.00
Chippewa (3)	5	0.01
Choctaw	1	0.00
Iroquois (1)	2	0.00
Latin American Indians (1)	1	0.00
Navajo (2)	2	0.00
Osage	1	0.00
Potawatomi (2)	3	0.01
Shoshone (1)	1	0.00
Sioux (2)	6	0.01
All other tribes (6)	10	0.02
American Indian tribes, not spec.	18	0.04
Arab:	207	0.46
Arab/Arabic	35	0.08
Egyptian	8	0.02
Lebanese	95	0.21
Syrian	69	0.15
Armenian	11	0.02
Asian:	1,177	2.59
Bangladeshi (9)	9	0.02
Cambodian (5)	9	0.02
Chinese, ex. Taiwanese (282)	318	0.70
Filipino (76)	109	0.24
Indian (233)	245	0.54
Indonesian (3)	10	0.02
Japanese (131)	161	0.35
Korean (83)	112	0.25
Laotian (14)	15	0.03
Malaysian (3)	4	0.01
Pakistani (4)	5	0.01
Sri Lankan (9)	12	0.03
Taiwanese (5)	6	0.01
Thai (31)	40	0.09
Vietnamese (73)	78	0.17
Other Asian, specified (12)	12	0.03
Other Asian, not specified (11)	32	0.07
Assyrian/Chaldean/Syriac	39	0.09
Austrian	121	0.27
Basque	16	0.04
Belgian	172	0.38
Brazilian	10	0.02
British	250	0.55
Canadian	124	0.27
Celtic	28	0.06
Croatian	50	0.11
Czech	262	0.58

Notes: 1. Figures in the "Number" column do not add up to the total population due to: a) Ancestry/Race overlap — e.g. persons can report being both White and Irish, b) persons of Hispanic origin can report being any race, c) persons reporting two ancestries are counted in both categories. 2. Numbers in parentheses indicate the number of persons reporting this ancestry/race alone, not in combination with any other ancestry/race. 3. Refer to the Explanation of Data in the front of the book for more detailed information.

Ancestry/Race	Number	%
Czechoslovakian	116	0.26
Danish	155	0.34
Dutch	883	1.95
Eastern European	13	0.03
English	4,487	9.90
European	442	0.97
Finnish	21	0.05
French, except Basque	1,073	2.37
French Canadian	156	0.34
German	14,200	31.32
Greek	245	0.54
Hawaii Native/Pacific Islander:	44	0.10
Micronesian: (5)	8	0.02
Guamanian/Chamorro (5)	7	0.02
Other Micronesian	1	0.00
Polynesian: (8)	12	0.03
Native Hawaiian (4)	7	0.02
Samoan (4)	5	0.01
Other Pac. Isl., not spec. (5)	24	0.05
Hispanic or Latino:	1,162	2.56
Central American:	32	0.07
Guatemalan	10	0.02
Honduran	6	0.01
Nicaraguan	1	0.00
Panamanian	11	0.02
Salvadoran	4	0.01
Cuban	52	0.11
Dominican Republic	10	0.02
Mexican	736	1.62
Puerto Rican	133	0.29
South American:	87	0.19
Argentinean	4	0.01
Bolivian	3	0.01
Chilean	13	0.03
Colombian	36	0.08
Ecuadorian	7	0.02
Paraguayan	1	0.00
Peruvian	20	0.04
Venezuelan	3	0.01
Other Hispanic or Latino	112	0.25
Hungarian	176	0.39
Iranian	42	0.09
Irish	6,844	15.10
Italian	2,313	5.10
Latvian	5	0.01
Lithuanian	115	0.25
Luxemburger	25	0.06
Northern European	68	0.15
Norwegian	867	1.91
Pennsylvania German	13	0.03
Polish	2,006	4.42
Portuguese	21	0.05
Romanian	30	0.07
Russian	181	0.40
Scandinavian	82	0.18
Scotch-Irish	894	1.97
Scottish	907	2.00
Serbian	31	0.07
Slavic	8	0.02
Slovak	92	0.20
Slovene	23	0.05
Swedish	1,328	2.93
Swiss	215	0.47
Turkish	39	0.09
Ukrainian	95	0.21
United States or American	1,791	3.95
Welsh	267	0.59
West Indian, excl. Hispanic:	60	0.13
Dutch West Indian	8	0.02
Haitian	13	0.03
Jamaican	30	0.07
West Indian	9	0.02
White:	40,301	88.80
Not Hispanic (39,121)	39,589	87.23
Hispanic (624)	712	1.57
Yugoslavian	86	0.19

Norridge

Place Type: Village
County: Cook
Population: 14,582

Ancestry/Race	Number	%
African American/Black:	21	0.14
Not Hispanic (13)	18	0.12
Hispanic (2)	3	0.02
Am. Ind. or Alaska Nat., not spec.	12	0.08
Albanian	28	0.19
American Indian tribes, specified:	13	0.09
Cherokee (1)	8	0.05
Choctaw	2	0.01
Comanche (3)	3	0.02
American Indian tribes, not spec.	5	0.03
Arab:	113	0.77
Arab/Arabic	29	0.20
Egyptian	46	0.31
Jordanian	20	0.14
Palestinian	10	0.07
Syrian	8	0.05
Armenian	42	0.29
Asian:	445	3.05
Bangladeshi (2)	2	0.01
Chinese, ex. Taiwanese (34)	38	0.26
Filipino (179)	193	1.32
Hmong (8)	8	0.05
Indian (113)	120	0.82
Indonesian (1)	1	0.01
Japanese (13)	14	0.10
Korean (24)	24	0.16
Pakistani	1	0.01
Thai (6)	14	0.10
Vietnamese (11)	12	0.08
Other Asian, specified (3)	3	0.02
Other Asian, not specified (4)	15	0.10
Assyrian/Chaldean/Syriac	4	0.03
Austrian	127	0.86
Belgian	19	0.13
Croatian	80	0.54
Cypriot	4	0.03
Czech	201	1.37
Czechoslovakian	9	0.06
Danish	54	0.37
Dutch	89	0.61
English	293	1.99
European	15	0.10
Finnish	5	0.03
French, except Basque	113	0.77
French Canadian	3	0.02
German	1,961	13.35
Greek	556	3.78
Hawaii Native/Pacific Islander:	3	0.02
Polynesian: (1)	1	0.01
Native Hawaiian (1)	1	0.01
Other Pac. Isl., not spec.	2	0.01
Hispanic or Latino:	553	3.79
Central American:	18	0.12
Guatemalan	4	0.03
Honduran	5	0.03
Salvadoran	4	0.03
Other Central American	5	0.03
Cuban	40	0.27
Dominican Republic	1	0.01
Mexican	274	1.88
Puerto Rican	115	0.79
South American:	46	0.32
Argentinean	8	0.05
Bolivian	3	0.02
Colombian	13	0.09
Ecuadorian	15	0.10
Peruvian	3	0.02
Venezuelan	3	0.02
Other South American	1	0.01
Other Hispanic or Latino	59	0.40
Hungarian	52	0.35
Irish	1,095	7.45
Italian	3,740	25.46
Lithuanian	68	0.46
Luxemburger	25	0.17
Macedonian	18	0.12
Norwegian	138	0.94
Polish	4,673	31.81
Romanian	42	0.29
Russian	68	0.46
Scandinavian	9	0.06
Scotch-Irish	83	0.57
Scottish	96	0.65
Serbian	109	0.74
Slavic	11	0.07
Slovak	73	0.50
Slovene	37	0.25
Swedish	243	1.65
Swiss	21	0.14
Ukrainian	94	0.64
United States or American	271	1.84
Welsh	9	0.06
West Indian, excl. Hispanic:	26	0.18
Haitian	19	0.13
Jamaican	7	0.05
White:	13,969	95.80
Not Hispanic (13,492)	13,595	93.23
Hispanic (337)	374	2.56
Yugoslavian	106	0.72

North Aurora

Place Type: Village
County: Kane
Population: 10,585

Ancestry/Race	Number	%
African American/Black:	536	5.06
Not Hispanic (464)	513	4.85
Hispanic (10)	23	0.22
African, sub-Saharan:	7	0.07
African	7	0.07
Am. Ind. or Alaska Nat., not spec.	12	0.11
American Indian tribes, specified:	31	0.29
Apache (1)	1	0.01
Blackfeet	1	0.01
Cherokee (2)	7	0.07
Chickasaw (1)	1	0.01
Chippewa (1)	2	0.02
Creek	1	0.01
Crow	1	0.01
Iroquois (3)	3	0.03
Latin American Indians (2)	6	0.06
Lumbee (1)	1	0.01
Potawatomi (1)	1	0.01
All other tribes	6	0.06
American Indian tribes, not spec.	6	0.06
Arab:	29	0.27
Arab/Arabic	29	0.27
Armenian	7	0.07
Asian:	314	2.97
Chinese, ex. Taiwanese (21)	25	0.24
Filipino (29)	40	0.38
Indian (84)	88	0.83
Japanese (10)	16	0.15
Korean (17)	27	0.26
Laotian (51)	56	0.53
Pakistani (19)	19	0.18
Taiwanese (2)	2	0.02
Thai (4)	6	0.06
Vietnamese (17)	20	0.19
Other Asian, specified (3)	3	0.03
Other Asian, not specified (8)	12	0.11
Assyrian/Chaldean/Syriac	8	0.08
Austrian	30	0.28
Belgian	29	0.27
British	26	0.25
Canadian	20	0.19
Celtic	6	0.06
Croatian	50	0.47
Czech	188	1.77
Czechoslovakian	30	0.28
Danish	77	0.73

Notes: 1. Figures in the "Number" column do not add up to the total population due to: a) Ancestry/Race overlap — e.g. persons can report being both White and Irish, b) persons of Hispanic origin can report being any race, c) persons reporting two ancestries are counted in both categories. 2. Numbers in parentheses indicate the number of persons reporting this ancestry/race alone, not in combination with any other ancestry/race. 3. Refer to the Explanation of Data in the front of the book for more detailed information.

Ancestry/Race	Number	%
Dutch	138	1.30
English	840	7.92
European	73	0.69
Finnish	23	0.22
French, except Basque	315	2.97
French Canadian	26	0.25
German	3,482	32.84
Greek	31	0.29
Hawaii Native/Pacific Islander:	4	0.04
Micronesian: (1)	1	0.01
Other Micronesian (1)	1	0.01
Polynesian:	1	0.01
Samoan	1	0.01
Other Pac. Isl., not spec. (2)	2	0.02
Hispanic or Latino:	1,025	9.68
Central American:	5	0.05
Honduran	4	0.04
Salvadoran	1	0.01
Cuban	23	0.22
Mexican	779	7.36
Puerto Rican	83	0.78
South American:	21	0.20
Chilean	8	0.08
Colombian	11	0.10
Ecuadorian	1	0.01
Peruvian	1	0.01
Other Hispanic or Latino	114	1.08
Hungarian	68	0.64
Irish	1,821	17.17
Italian	541	5.10
Lithuanian	127	1.20
Luxemburger	81	0.76
Northern European	22	0.21
Norwegian	335	3.16
Polish	968	9.13
Romanian	84	0.79
Russian	42	0.40
Scandinavian	35	0.33
Scotch-Irish	118	1.11
Scottish	107	1.01
Slavic	4	0.04
Slovak	5	0.05
Slovene	6	0.06
Swedish	495	4.67
Swiss	21	0.20
United States or American	301	2.84
Welsh	70	0.66
West Indian, excl. Hispanic:	8	0.08
Belizean	8	0.08
White:	9,446	89.24
Not Hispanic (8,671)	8,785	82.99
Hispanic (613)	661	6.24
Yugoslavian	13	0.12

North Chicago

Place Type: City
County: Lake
Population: 35,918

Ancestry/Race	Number	%
Acadian/Cajun	37	0.10
African American/Black:	13,528	37.66
Not Hispanic (12,853)	13,239	36.86
Hispanic (171)	289	0.80
African, sub-Saharan:	496	1.38
African	455	1.26
Cape Verdean	6	0.02
Ghanian	5	0.01
Nigerian	23	0.06
Other sub-Saharan African	7	0.02
Alaska Native tribes, specified:	9	0.03
Aleut (1)	1	0.00
Eskimo (4)	4	0.01
Tlingit-Haida (1)	1	0.00
All other tribes (3)	3	0.01
Am. Ind. or Alaska Nat., not spec.	183	0.51
American Indian tribes, specified:	410	1.14
Apache (4)	17	0.05
Blackfeet (5)	29	0.08
Cherokee (64)	175	0.49
Cheyenne (1)	3	0.01
Chickasaw (1)	1	0.00
Chippewa (11)	15	0.04
Choctaw (10)	20	0.06
Comanche (1)	5	0.01
Cree	1	0.00
Creek (3)	4	0.01
Crow (1)	4	0.01
Delaware	1	0.00
Iroquois (4)	7	0.02
Kiowa (1)	1	0.00
Latin American Indians (15)	18	0.05
Lumbee (2)	2	0.01
Navajo (17)	20	0.06
Osage (1)	2	0.01
Paiute	1	0.00
Potawatomi (2)	3	0.01
Pueblo (2)	3	0.01
Puget Sound Salish (1)	2	0.01
Seminole (1)	6	0.02
Shoshone	1	0.00
Sioux (14)	25	0.07
Yaqui	3	0.01
Yuman (2)	2	0.01
All other tribes (16)	39	0.11
American Indian tribes, not spec.	17	0.05
Arab:	54	0.15
Arab/Arabic	6	0.02
Egyptian	14	0.04
Lebanese	14	0.04
Moroccan	20	0.06
Asian:	1,689	4.70
Cambodian (8)	13	0.04
Chinese, ex. Taiwanese (116)	155	0.43
Filipino (761)	964	2.68
Hmong (7)	8	0.02
Indian (119)	141	0.39
Indonesian	5	0.01
Japanese (49)	102	0.28
Korean (85)	119	0.33
Laotian (11)	13	0.04
Pakistani (4)	5	0.01
Taiwanese (5)	7	0.02
Thai (15)	22	0.06
Vietnamese (69)	77	0.21
Other Asian, specified (3)	3	0.01
Other Asian, not specified (16)	55	0.15
Austrian	79	0.22
Belgian	19	0.05
Brazilian	13	0.04
British	113	0.31
Canadian	40	0.11
Celtic	23	0.06
Croatian	98	0.27
Czech	136	0.38
Czechoslovakian	41	0.11
Danish	80	0.22
Dutch	289	0.80
English	1,443	4.01
European	140	0.39
Finnish	28	0.08
French, except Basque	604	1.68
French Canadian	191	0.53
German	3,616	10.04
German Russian	16	0.04
Greek	73	0.20
Guyanese	28	0.08
Hawaii Native/Pacific Islander:	184	0.51
Micronesian: (26)	66	0.18
Guamanian/Chamorro (18)	55	0.15
Other Micronesian (8)	11	0.03
Polynesian: (16)	72	0.20
Native Hawaiian (9)	60	0.17
Samoan (7)	11	0.03
Tongan	1	0.00
Other Pac. Isl., not spec. (10)	46	0.13
Hispanic or Latino:	6,552	18.24
Central American:	233	0.65
Costa Rican	8	0.02
Guatemalan	16	0.04
Honduran	73	0.20
Nicaraguan	27	0.08
Panamanian	24	0.07
Salvadoran	65	0.18
Other Central American	20	0.06
Cuban	62	0.17
Dominican Republic	64	0.18
Mexican	4,615	12.85
Puerto Rican	775	2.16
South American:	127	0.35
Argentinean	1	0.00
Bolivian	4	0.01
Chilean	5	0.01
Colombian	50	0.14
Ecuadorian	25	0.07
Peruvian	30	0.08
Venezuelan	7	0.02
Other South American	5	0.01
Other Hispanic or Latino	676	1.88
Hungarian	105	0.29
Iranian	73	0.20
Irish	2,776	7.71
Israeli	80	0.22
Italian	1,176	3.27
Latvian	7	0.02
Lithuanian	29	0.08
New Zealander	9	0.02
Norwegian	304	0.84
Pennsylvania German	16	0.04
Polish	947	2.63
Portuguese	65	0.18
Romanian	35	0.10
Russian	118	0.33
Scandinavian	51	0.14
Scotch-Irish	247	0.69
Scottish	442	1.23
Serbian	15	0.04
Slavic	14	0.04
Slovak	62	0.17
Slovene	56	0.16
Swedish	357	0.99
Swiss	21	0.06
Turkish	46	0.13
Ukrainian	43	0.12
United States or American	1,244	3.46
Welsh	143	0.40
West Indian, excl. Hispanic:	433	1.20
Bahamian	8	0.02
Barbadian	17	0.05
Belizean	56	0.16
British West Indian	30	0.08
Haitian	47	0.13
Jamaican	225	0.62
Trinidadian and Tobagonian	16	0.04
West Indian	34	0.09
White:	18,212	50.70
Not Hispanic (14,028)	14,681	40.87
Hispanic (3,112)	3,531	9.83
Yugoslavian	36	0.10

Northbrook

Place Type: Village
County: Cook
Population: 33,435

Ancestry/Race	Number	%
Afghan	5	0.01
African American/Black:	225	0.67
Not Hispanic (190)	224	0.67
Hispanic	1	0.00
African, sub-Saharan:	30	0.09
African	6	0.02
South African	24	0.07
Am. Ind. or Alaska Nat., not spec.	22	0.07
American Indian tribes, specified:	19	0.06
Cherokee (3)	10	0.03
Chippewa	2	0.01
Latin American Indians (1)	2	0.01

Notes: 1. Figures in the "Number" column do not add up to the total population due to: a) Ancestry/Race overlap — e.g. persons can report being both White and Irish, b) persons of Hispanic origin can report being any race, c) persons reporting two ancestries are counted in both categories. 2. Numbers in parentheses indicate the number of persons reporting this ancestry/race alone, not in combination with any other ancestry/race. 3. Refer to the Explanation of Data in the front of the book for more detailed information.

Menominee (1)	1	0.00
All other tribes (1)	4	0.01
American Indian tribes, not spec.	6	0.02
Arab:	168	0.50
Lebanese	71	0.21
Moroccan	12	0.04
Palestinian	19	0.06
Syrian	60	0.18
Other Arab	6	0.02
Armenian	159	0.48
Asian:	3,174	9.49
Bangladeshi (5)	5	0.01
Cambodian (1)	1	0.00
Chinese, ex. Taiwanese (541)	596	1.78
Filipino (198)	229	0.68
Indian (378)	407	1.22
Japanese (172)	205	0.61
Korean (1,480)	1,520	4.55
Malaysian (1)	1	0.00
Pakistani (17)	28	0.08
Sri Lankan (6)	6	0.02
Taiwanese (51)	57	0.17
Thai (42)	46	0.14
Vietnamese (27)	29	0.09
Other Asian, specified (1)	1	0.00
Other Asian, not specified (7)	43	0.13
Assyrian/Chaldean/Syriac	29	0.09
Australian	7	0.02
Austrian	510	1.53
Belgian	103	0.31
Brazilian	5	0.01
British	96	0.29
Canadian	110	0.33
Croatian	79	0.24
Czech	342	1.02
Czechoslovakian	69	0.21
Danish	172	0.51
Dutch	575	1.72
Eastern European	331	0.99
English	2,694	8.06
Estonian	25	0.07
European	306	0.92
Finnish	36	0.11
French, except Basque	633	1.89
French Canadian	50	0.15
German	6,119	18.31
Greek	628	1.88
Hawaii Native/Pacific Islander:	25	0.07
Micronesian:	4	0.01
Guamanian/Chamorro	4	0.01
Polynesian: (3)	10	0.03
Native Hawaiian (1)	6	0.02
Samoan (2)	4	0.01
Other Pac. Isl., not spec.	11	0.03
Hispanic or Latino:	616	1.84
Central American:	19	0.06
Costa Rican	2	0.01
Guatemalan	6	0.02
Honduran	4	0.01
Panamanian	1	0.00
Salvadoran	6	0.02
Cuban	64	0.19
Mexican	285	0.85
Puerto Rican	52	0.16
South American:	102	0.31
Argentinean	11	0.03
Bolivian	1	0.00
Chilean	4	0.01
Colombian	31	0.09
Ecuadorian	11	0.03
Paraguayan	5	0.01
Peruvian	18	0.05
Uruguayan	1	0.00
Venezuelan	8	0.02
Other South American	12	0.04
Other Hispanic or Latino	94	0.28
Hungarian	388	1.16
Icelander	11	0.03
Iranian	78	0.23
Irish	4,058	12.14
Israeli	29	0.09
Italian	2,090	6.25
Latvian	88	0.26
Lithuanian	345	1.03
Luxemburger	169	0.51
Norwegian	670	2.00
Pennsylvania German	6	0.02
Polish	3,339	9.99
Portuguese	25	0.07
Romanian	297	0.89
Russian	4,101	12.27
Scandinavian	31	0.09
Scotch-Irish	358	1.07
Scottish	733	2.19
Serbian	85	0.25
Slavic	7	0.02
Slovak	50	0.15
Slovene	22	0.07
Soviet Union	34	0.10
Swedish	982	2.94
Swiss	130	0.39
Turkish	53	0.16
Ukrainian	320	0.96
United States or American	2,201	6.58
Welsh	98	0.29
West Indian, excl. Hispanic:	15	0.04
Belizean	8	0.02
Jamaican	7	0.02
White:	30,121	90.09
Not Hispanic (29,346)	29,606	88.55
Hispanic (484)	515	1.54
Yugoslavian	66	0.20

Northlake

Place Type: City
County: Cook
Population: 11,878

Ancestry/Race	Number	%
African American/Black:	316	2.66
Not Hispanic (277)	303	2.55
Hispanic (8)	13	0.11
African, sub-Saharan:	29	0.25
African	10	0.08
Nigerian	19	0.16
Am. Ind. or Alaska Nat., not spec.	44	0.37
American Indian tribes, specified:	61	0.51
Apache (1)	2	0.02
Blackfeet	2	0.02
Cherokee (1)	11	0.09
Chippewa (3)	4	0.03
Choctaw (1)	2	0.02
Iroquois	2	0.02
Latin American Indians (22)	27	0.23
Lumbee (1)	3	0.03
Potawatomi	3	0.03
Sioux	2	0.02
All other tribes (2)	3	0.03
American Indian tribes, not spec.	3	0.03
Armenian	3	0.03
Asian:	483	4.07
Chinese, ex. Taiwanese (1)	4	0.03
Filipino (196)	212	1.78
Indian (115)	123	1.04
Japanese (11)	20	0.17
Korean (9)	15	0.13
Laotian (7)	7	0.06
Pakistani (11)	12	0.10
Thai (3)	3	0.03
Vietnamese (66)	71	0.60
Other Asian, not specified (10)	16	0.13
Austrian	50	0.42
Belgian	11	0.09
British	32	0.27
Canadian	23	0.19
Croatian	10	0.08
Czech	152	1.29
Czechoslovakian	13	0.11
Danish	111	0.94
Dutch	142	1.20
Eastern European	6	0.05
English	486	4.12
European	25	0.21
Finnish	11	0.09
French, except Basque	169	1.43
French Canadian	61	0.52
German	2,091	17.71
Greek	81	0.69
Hawaii Native/Pacific Islander:	9	0.08
Micronesian: (1)	2	0.02
Guamanian/Chamorro (1)	2	0.02
Polynesian: (1)	1	0.01
Samoan (1)	1	0.01
Other Pac. Isl., not spec. (4)	6	0.05
Hispanic or Latino:	4,133	34.80
Central American:	146	1.23
Costa Rican	1	0.01
Guatemalan	112	0.94
Honduran	13	0.11
Nicaraguan	1	0.01
Panamanian	2	0.02
Salvadoran	6	0.05
Other Central American	11	0.09
Cuban	158	1.33
Mexican	3,205	26.98
Puerto Rican	279	2.35
South American:	68	0.57
Argentinean	5	0.04
Bolivian	7	0.06
Chilean	1	0.01
Colombian	12	0.10
Ecuadorian	23	0.19
Peruvian	20	0.17
Other Hispanic or Latino	277	2.33
Hungarian	77	0.65
Irish	1,675	14.18
Italian	1,407	11.91
Latvian	4	0.03
Lithuanian	58	0.49
Norwegian	178	1.51
Pennsylvania German	14	0.12
Polish	1,395	11.81
Portuguese	5	0.04
Russian	40	0.34
Scandinavian	7	0.06
Scotch-Irish	67	0.57
Scottish	54	0.46
Serbian	19	0.16
Slovak	39	0.33
Slovene	18	0.15
Swedish	316	2.68
Swiss	17	0.14
Ukrainian	33	0.28
United States or American	131	1.11
Welsh	13	0.11
White:	9,247	77.85
Not Hispanic (6,913)	7,009	59.01
Hispanic (2,051)	2,238	18.84

O'Fallon

Place Type: City
County: Saint Clair
Population: 21,910

Ancestry/Race	Number	%
African American/Black:	2,737	12.49
Not Hispanic (2,603)	2,707	12.36
Hispanic (24)	30	0.14
African, sub-Saharan:	59	0.27
African	59	0.27
Alaska Native tribes, specified:	4	0.02
Tlingit-Haida (1)	4	0.02
Am. Ind. or Alaska Nat., not spec.	40	0.18
American Indian tribes, specified:	115	0.52
Apache	1	0.00
Blackfeet (1)	3	0.01
Cherokee (20)	68	0.31
Cheyenne	2	0.01

Notes: 1. Figures in the "Number" column do not add up to the total population due to: a) Ancestry/Race overlap — e.g. persons can report being both White and Irish, b) persons of Hispanic origin can report being any race, c) persons reporting two ancestries are counted in both categories. 2. Numbers in parentheses indicate the number of persons reporting this ancestry/race alone, not in combination with any other ancestry/race. 3. Refer to the Explanation of Data in the front of the book for more detailed information.

Ancestry/Race	Number	%
Chickasaw	2	0.01
Choctaw (4)	8	0.04
Comanche	2	0.01
Cree (2)	2	0.01
Delaware (1)	1	0.00
Iroquois	1	0.00
Kiowa (1)	2	0.01
Latin American Indians (2)	4	0.02
Navajo	5	0.02
Potawatomi (1)	2	0.01
Pueblo (3)	3	0.01
Sioux	3	0.01
Yaqui	1	0.00
All other tribes (2)	5	0.02
American Indian tribes, not spec.	7	0.03
Arab:	42	0.19
Arab/Arabic	42	0.19
Armenian	15	0.07
Asian:	723	3.30
Bangladeshi (11)	11	0.05
Chinese, ex. Taiwanese (43)	61	0.28
Filipino (113)	174	0.79
Indian (77)	83	0.38
Indonesian (1)	1	0.00
Japanese (45)	85	0.39
Korean (155)	192	0.88
Pakistani (15)	16	0.07
Taiwanese (11)	12	0.05
Thai (20)	26	0.12
Vietnamese (24)	28	0.13
Other Asian, specified (1)	1	0.00
Other Asian, not specified (20)	33	0.15
Assyrian/Chaldean/Syriac	17	0.08
Austrian	52	0.24
Belgian	21	0.10
British	117	0.54
Canadian	65	0.30
Celtic	8	0.04
Croatian	33	0.15
Czech	369	1.69
Czechoslovakian	60	0.27
Danish	94	0.43
Dutch	429	1.96
Eastern European	15	0.07
English	2,431	11.12
European	318	1.45
Finnish	9	0.04
French, except Basque	1,146	5.24
French Canadian	69	0.32
German	6,728	30.78
Greek	89	0.41
Hawaii Native/Pacific Islander:	41	0.19
Micronesian: (2)	9	0.04
Guamanian/Chamorro (2)	9	0.04
Polynesian: (10)	23	0.10
Native Hawaiian (7)	18	0.08
Samoan (3)	4	0.02
Tongan	1	0.00
Other Pac. Isl., not spec. (3)	9	0.04
Hispanic or Latino:	488	2.23
Central American:	24	0.11
Guatemalan	4	0.02
Honduran	3	0.01
Nicaraguan	6	0.03
Panamanian	8	0.04
Other Central American	3	0.01
Cuban	15	0.07
Dominican Republic	4	0.02
Mexican	244	1.11
Puerto Rican	88	0.40
South American:	11	0.05
Chilean	5	0.02
Colombian	2	0.01
Paraguayan	1	0.00
Peruvian	3	0.01
Other Hispanic or Latino	102	0.47
Hungarian	82	0.38
Irish	2,763	12.64
Italian	786	3.60
Lithuanian	27	0.12
Macedonian	7	0.03
Northern European	10	0.05
Norwegian	306	1.40
Polish	630	2.88
Portuguese	25	0.11
Romanian	6	0.03
Russian	21	0.10
Scandinavian	53	0.24
Scotch-Irish	374	1.71
Scottish	517	2.37
Slavic	14	0.06
Slovak	38	0.17
Slovene	32	0.15
Swedish	284	1.30
Swiss	98	0.45
Turkish	8	0.04
Ukrainian	8	0.04
United States or American	1,332	6.09
Welsh	101	0.46
West Indian, excl. Hispanic:	31	0.14
Jamaican	15	0.07
West Indian	8	0.04
Other West Indian	8	0.04
White:	18,446	84.19
Not Hispanic (17,831)	18,126	82.73
Hispanic (282)	320	1.46
Yugoslavian	15	0.07

Oak Forest

Place Type: City
County: Cook
Population: 28,051

Ancestry/Race	Number	%
African American/Black:	1,063	3.79
Not Hispanic (1,006)	1,044	3.72
Hispanic (15)	19	0.07
African, sub-Saharan:	48	0.17
African	42	0.15
South African	6	0.02
Alaska Native tribes, specified:	1	0.00
Eskimo (1)	1	0.00
Am. Ind. or Alaska Nat., not spec.	36	0.13
American Indian tribes, specified:	75	0.27
Apache (5)	5	0.02
Blackfeet	1	0.00
Cherokee (11)	44	0.16
Chippewa (1)	2	0.01
Delaware	1	0.00
Latin American Indians (5)	6	0.02
Menominee	1	0.00
Osage	2	0.01
Ottawa	1	0.00
Potawatomi (1)	1	0.00
Pueblo	1	0.00
Sioux (1)	2	0.01
Yaqui	4	0.01
All other tribes (3)	4	0.01
American Indian tribes, not spec.	16	0.06
Arab:	389	1.39
Arab/Arabic	211	0.75
Egyptian	19	0.07
Jordanian	138	0.49
Palestinian	21	0.08
Armenian	28	0.10
Asian:	887	3.16
Chinese, ex. Taiwanese (36)	61	0.22
Filipino (236)	275	0.98
Indian (357)	396	1.41
Indonesian (1)	1	0.00
Japanese (10)	17	0.06
Korean (26)	40	0.14
Laotian (1)	1	0.00
Pakistani (22)	27	0.10
Taiwanese (3)	3	0.01
Thai (16)	23	0.08
Vietnamese (5)	6	0.02
Other Asian, not specified (16)	37	0.13
Austrian	321	1.15
Belgian	54	0.19
British	17	0.06
Canadian	18	0.06
Croatian	222	0.79
Czech	556	1.99
Czechoslovakian	60	0.21
Danish	111	0.40
Dutch	1,439	5.15
English	1,298	4.64
Estonian	8	0.03
European	57	0.20
Finnish	15	0.05
French, except Basque	777	2.78
French Canadian	101	0.36
German	7,020	25.11
Greek	342	1.22
Guyanese	9	0.03
Hawaii Native/Pacific Islander:	13	0.05
Micronesian: (2)	4	0.01
Guamanian/Chamorro (2)	4	0.01
Polynesian: (1)	4	0.01
Native Hawaiian (1)	4	0.01
Other Pac. Isl., not spec. (1)	5	0.02
Hispanic or Latino:	1,645	5.86
Central American:	21	0.07
Guatemalan	8	0.03
Honduran	3	0.01
Nicaraguan	5	0.02
Panamanian	5	0.02
Cuban	12	0.04
Dominican Republic	3	0.01
Mexican	1,350	4.81
Puerto Rican	96	0.34
South American:	31	0.11
Argentinean	4	0.01
Chilean	1	0.00
Colombian	8	0.03
Ecuadorian	7	0.02
Peruvian	5	0.02
Venezuelan	3	0.01
Other South American	3	0.01
Other Hispanic or Latino	132	0.47
Hungarian	238	0.85
Iranian	6	0.02
Irish	7,362	26.34
Italian	3,634	13.00
Lithuanian	869	3.11
Luxemburger	23	0.08
Norwegian	349	1.25
Pennsylvania German	9	0.03
Polish	5,116	18.30
Portuguese	8	0.03
Romanian	26	0.09
Russian	172	0.62
Scandinavian	19	0.07
Scotch-Irish	260	0.93
Scottish	305	1.09
Serbian	18	0.06
Slovak	140	0.50
Slovene	17	0.06
Swedish	1,077	3.85
Swiss	50	0.18
Turkish	26	0.09
Ukrainian	98	0.35
United States or American	598	2.14
Welsh	72	0.26
West Indian, excl. Hispanic:	11	0.04
Jamaican	11	0.04
White:	25,729	91.72
Not Hispanic (24,297)	24,577	87.62
Hispanic (1,056)	1,152	4.11
Yugoslavian	10	0.04

Oak Lawn

Place Type: Village
County: Cook
Population: 55,245

Ancestry/Race	Number	%

Notes: 1. Figures in the "Number" column do not add up to the total population due to: a) Ancestry/Race overlap — e.g. persons can report being both White and Irish, b) persons of Hispanic origin can report being any race, c) persons reporting two ancestries are counted in both categories. 2. Numbers in parentheses indicate the number of persons reporting this ancestry/race alone, not in combination with any other ancestry/race. 3. Refer to the Explanation of Data in the front of the book for more detailed information.

Ancestry/Race	Number	%
Acadian/Cajun	7	0.01
African American/Black:	718	1.30
Not Hispanic (666)	708	1.28
Hispanic (7)	10	0.02
African, sub-Saharan:	33	0.06
African	33	0.06
Alaska Native tribes, specified:	1	0.00
Tlingit-Haida (1)	1	0.00
Alaska Native tribes, not specified	1	0.00
Am. Ind. or Alaska Nat., not spec.	79	0.14
Albanian	32	0.06
American Indian tribes, specified:	132	0.24
Apache (2)	3	0.01
Blackfeet	10	0.02
Cherokee (11)	67	0.12
Chickasaw	1	0.00
Chippewa (5)	9	0.02
Choctaw	3	0.01
Comanche	1	0.00
Iroquois (4)	7	0.01
Latin American Indians (6)	11	0.02
Menominee (1)	2	0.00
Navajo	2	0.00
Potawatomi	1	0.00
Seminole	1	0.00
Sioux (3)	8	0.01
Yaqui (2)	2	0.00
All other tribes (1)	4	0.01
American Indian tribes, not spec.	12	0.02
Arab:	2,142	3.87
Arab/Arabic	1,070	1.93
Egyptian	29	0.05
Jordanian	194	0.35
Lebanese	63	0.11
Moroccan	50	0.09
Palestinian	577	1.04
Syrian	114	0.21
Other Arab	45	0.08
Armenian	25	0.05
Asian:	1,201	2.17
Bangladeshi (1)	1	0.00
Chinese, ex. Taiwanese (76)	94	0.17
Filipino (367)	439	0.79
Indian (204)	227	0.41
Indonesian (1)	1	0.00
Japanese (30)	58	0.10
Korean (40)	53	0.10
Pakistani (19)	31	0.06
Taiwanese (2)	3	0.01
Thai (55)	63	0.11
Vietnamese (105)	109	0.20
Other Asian, specified (11)	15	0.03
Other Asian, not specified (33)	107	0.19
Assyrian/Chaldean/Syriac	34	0.06
Austrian	619	1.12
Belgian	71	0.13
Brazilian	7	0.01
British	65	0.12
Bulgarian	5	0.01
Canadian	119	0.21
Croatian	713	1.29
Czech	1,233	2.23
Czechoslovakian	253	0.46
Danish	367	0.66
Dutch	1,013	1.83
English	2,411	4.35
European	46	0.08
Finnish	44	0.08
French, except Basque	1,211	2.19
French Canadian	289	0.52
German	10,823	19.54
Greek	1,378	2.49
Hawaii Native/Pacific Islander:	24	0.04
Micronesian: (1)	1	0.00
Guamanian/Chamorro (1)	1	0.00
Polynesian: (4)	8	0.01
Native Hawaiian (1)	5	0.01
Samoan (3)	3	0.01
Other Pac. Isl., not spec.	15	0.03
Hispanic or Latino:	2,942	5.33
Central American:	10	0.02
Costa Rican	4	0.01
Guatemalan	3	0.01
Honduran	2	0.00
Panamanian	1	0.00
Cuban	21	0.04
Dominican Republic	2	0.00
Mexican	2,356	4.26
Puerto Rican	212	0.38
South American:	107	0.19
Argentinean	13	0.02
Bolivian	25	0.05
Chilean	8	0.01
Colombian	21	0.04
Ecuadorian	18	0.03
Paraguayan	1	0.00
Peruvian	11	0.02
Uruguayan	1	0.00
Venezuelan	4	0.01
Other South American	5	0.01
Other Hispanic or Latino	234	0.42
Hungarian	279	0.50
Icelander	6	0.01
Iranian	24	0.04
Irish	16,841	30.40
Italian	5,388	9.73
Latvian	13	0.02
Lithuanian	2,101	3.79
Luxemburger	7	0.01
Macedonian	6	0.01
Northern European	19	0.03
Norwegian	381	0.69
Pennsylvania German	9	0.02
Polish	10,667	19.26
Romanian	26	0.05
Russian	388	0.70
Scandinavian	93	0.17
Scotch-Irish	493	0.89
Scottish	517	0.93
Serbian	64	0.12
Slavic	33	0.06
Slovak	533	0.96
Slovene	95	0.17
Swedish	1,646	2.97
Swiss	82	0.15
Ukrainian	355	0.64
United States or American	1,240	2.24
Welsh	112	0.20
West Indian, excl. Hispanic:	22	0.04
Belizean	5	0.01
Jamaican	17	0.03
White:	52,557	95.13
Not Hispanic (49,689)	50,548	91.50
Hispanic (1,881)	2,009	3.64
Yugoslavian	52	0.09

Oak Park

Place Type: Village
County: Cook
Population: 52,524

Ancestry/Race	Number	%
African American/Black:	12,552	23.90
Not Hispanic (11,685)	12,369	23.55
Hispanic (103)	183	0.35
African, sub-Saharan:	899	1.71
African	601	1.14
Ethiopian	10	0.02
Ghanian	17	0.03
Kenyan	27	0.05
Liberian	14	0.03
Nigerian	185	0.35
South African	33	0.06
Other sub-Saharan African	12	0.02
Alaska Native tribes, not specified	1	0.00
Am. Ind. or Alaska Nat., not spec.	135	0.26
Albanian	6	0.01
Alsatian	28	0.05
American Indian tribes, specified:	219	0.42
Apache (1)	1	0.00
Blackfeet	17	0.03
Cherokee (8)	85	0.16
Chippewa (4)	15	0.03
Choctaw	8	0.02
Comanche	1	0.00
Cree	4	0.01
Creek	1	0.00
Iroquois (5)	12	0.02
Latin American Indians (10)	34	0.06
Menominee (1)	1	0.00
Navajo (1)	2	0.00
Ottawa (2)	2	0.00
Potawatomi (3)	4	0.01
Pueblo	1	0.00
Seminole	6	0.01
Sioux (3)	9	0.02
All other tribes (3)	16	0.03
American Indian tribes, not spec.	12	0.02
Arab:	449	0.85
Arab/Arabic	205	0.39
Egyptian	44	0.08
Jordanian	8	0.02
Lebanese	91	0.17
Moroccan	8	0.02
Palestinian	37	0.07
Syrian	37	0.07
Other Arab	19	0.04
Armenian	75	0.14
Asian:	2,676	5.09
Bangladeshi (1)	3	0.01
Cambodian (1)	1	0.00
Chinese, ex. Taiwanese (458)	567	1.08
Filipino (395)	523	1.00
Indian (669)	764	1.45
Indonesian (2)	7	0.01
Japanese (192)	273	0.52
Korean (188)	233	0.44
Laotian (13)	13	0.02
Malaysian (2)	4	0.01
Pakistani (33)	43	0.08
Sri Lankan (7)	8	0.02
Taiwanese (8)	18	0.03
Thai (69)	77	0.15
Vietnamese (51)	64	0.12
Other Asian, specified (5)	10	0.02
Other Asian, not specified (28)	68	0.13
Assyrian/Chaldean/Syriac	16	0.03
Australian	5	0.01
Austrian	351	0.67
Basque	27	0.05
Belgian	169	0.32
Brazilian	42	0.08
British	175	0.33
Bulgarian	8	0.02
Canadian	141	0.27
Celtic	31	0.06
Croatian	212	0.40
Czech	1,044	1.99
Czechoslovakian	194	0.37
Danish	335	0.64
Dutch	748	1.42
Eastern European	200	0.38
English	4,547	8.66
Estonian	17	0.03
European	572	1.09
Finnish	64	0.12
French, except Basque	1,211	2.31
French Canadian	236	0.45
German	9,475	18.04
Greek	662	1.26
Guyanese	15	0.03
Hawaii Native/Pacific Islander:	56	0.11
Melanesian:	1	0.00
Fijian	1	0.00
Micronesian: (3)	3	0.01
Guamanian/Chamorro (3)	3	0.01
Polynesian: (9)	20	0.04
Native Hawaiian (5)	13	0.02
Samoan (4)	4	0.01

Notes: 1. Figures in the "Number" column do not add up to the total population due to: a) Ancestry/Race overlap — e.g. persons can report being both White and Irish, b) persons of Hispanic origin can report being any race, c) persons reporting two ancestries are counted in both categories. 2. Numbers in parentheses indicate the number of persons reporting this ancestry/race alone, not in combination with any other ancestry/race. 3. Refer to the Explanation of Data in the front of the book for more detailed information.

Tongan	3	0.01
Other Pac. Isl., specified	4	0.01
Other Pac. Isl., not spec. (4)	28	0.05
Hispanic or Latino:	2,374	4.52
Central American:	113	0.22
Costa Rican	6	0.01
Guatemalan	34	0.06
Honduran	9	0.02
Nicaraguan	21	0.04
Panamanian	21	0.04
Salvadoran	16	0.03
Other Central American	6	0.01
Cuban	116	0.22
Dominican Republic	17	0.03
Mexican	1,221	2.32
Puerto Rican	329	0.63
South American:	281	0.53
Argentinean	42	0.08
Bolivian	7	0.01
Chilean	31	0.06
Colombian	58	0.11
Ecuadorian	23	0.04
Paraguayan	10	0.02
Peruvian	63	0.12
Uruguayan	11	0.02
Venezuelan	29	0.06
Other South American	7	0.01
Other Hispanic or Latino	297	0.57
Hungarian	310	0.59
Icelander	32	0.06
Iranian	36	0.07
Irish	9,148	17.42
Israeli	15	0.03
Italian	3,954	7.53
Latvian	146	0.28
Lithuanian	340	0.65
Luxemburger	36	0.07
Northern European	38	0.07
Norwegian	1,026	1.95
Pennsylvania German	12	0.02
Polish	3,281	6.25
Portuguese	26	0.05
Romanian	188	0.36
Russian	1,286	2.45
Scandinavian	120	0.23
Scotch-Irish	763	1.45
Scottish	902	1.72
Serbian	74	0.14
Slavic	18	0.03
Slovak	164	0.31
Slovene	94	0.18
Swedish	1,399	2.66
Swiss	306	0.58
Turkish	43	0.08
Ukrainian	307	0.58
United States or American	960	1.83
Welsh	424	0.81
West Indian, excl. Hispanic:	271	0.52
Barbadian	34	0.06
Belizean	9	0.02
British West Indian	30	0.06
Haitian	51	0.10
Jamaican	96	0.18
Trinidadian and Tobagonian	6	0.01
West Indian	36	0.07
Other West Indian	9	0.02
White:	37,334	71.08
Not Hispanic (34,767)	35,807	68.17
Hispanic (1,357)	1,527	2.91
Yugoslavian	166	0.32

Orland Park

Place Type: Village
County: Cook
Population: 51,077

Ancestry/Race	Number	%
African American/Black:	412	0.81
Not Hispanic (367)	404	0.79
Hispanic (7)	8	0.02
African, sub-Saharan:	37	0.07
African	6	0.01
Cape Verdean	8	0.02
Nigerian	23	0.05
Alaska Native tribes, specified:	1	0.00
Eskimo	1	0.00
Am. Ind. or Alaska Nat., not spec.	37	0.07
Albanian	62	0.12
American Indian tribes, specified:	58	0.11
Blackfeet	1	0.00
Cherokee (7)	21	0.04
Cheyenne	3	0.01
Chippewa (3)	7	0.01
Iroquois (1)	3	0.01
Latin American Indians (2)	9	0.02
Menominee (1)	1	0.00
Navajo (1)	1	0.00
Ottawa (3)	3	0.01
Potawatomi	1	0.00
Pueblo (1)	1	0.00
Seminole (1)	1	0.00
All other tribes (2)	6	0.01
American Indian tribes, not spec.	5	0.01
Arab:	960	1.88
Arab/Arabic	401	0.78
Iraqi	23	0.05
Jordanian	89	0.17
Lebanese	20	0.04
Palestinian	394	0.77
Syrian	14	0.03
Other Arab	19	0.04
Armenian	32	0.06
Asian:	1,981	3.88
Bangladeshi (1)	3	0.01
Chinese, ex. Taiwanese (182)	201	0.39
Filipino (495)	535	1.05
Indian (638)	672	1.32
Indonesian	1	0.00
Japanese (16)	30	0.06
Korean (278)	300	0.59
Laotian	1	0.00
Malaysian (3)	5	0.01
Pakistani (35)	44	0.09
Taiwanese (14)	23	0.05
Thai (18)	27	0.05
Vietnamese (27)	31	0.06
Other Asian, specified (7)	8	0.02
Other Asian, not specified (33)	100	0.20
Austrian	628	1.23
Belgian	79	0.15
British	49	0.10
Bulgarian	17	0.03
Canadian	34	0.07
Carpatho Rusyn	10	0.02
Croatian	868	1.70
Czech	1,138	2.23
Czechoslovakian	158	0.31
Danish	206	0.40
Dutch	1,658	3.24
Eastern European	6	0.01
English	2,599	5.09
European	131	0.26
Finnish	72	0.14
French, except Basque	975	1.91
French Canadian	214	0.42
German	9,979	19.53
Greek	1,797	3.52
Hawaii Native/Pacific Islander:	39	0.08
Polynesian: (3)	7	0.01
Native Hawaiian (3)	7	0.01
Other Pac. Isl., specified	1	0.00
Other Pac. Isl., not spec. (15)	31	0.06
Hispanic or Latino:	1,874	3.67
Central American:	36	0.07
Guatemalan	26	0.05
Honduran	7	0.01
Salvadoran	3	0.01
Cuban	36	0.07
Dominican Republic	2	0.00
Mexican	1,460	2.86
Puerto Rican	103	0.20
South American:	56	0.11
Argentinean	3	0.01
Bolivian	1	0.00
Chilean	7	0.01
Colombian	20	0.04
Ecuadorian	9	0.02
Paraguayan	2	0.00
Peruvian	6	0.01
Venezuelan	5	0.01
Other South American	3	0.01
Other Hispanic or Latino	181	0.35
Hungarian	334	0.65
Iranian	24	0.05
Irish	13,550	26.52
Israeli	47	0.09
Italian	7,568	14.81
Latvian	9	0.02
Lithuanian	1,500	2.94
Luxemburger	23	0.05
Macedonian	15	0.03
Norwegian	429	0.84
Pennsylvania German	18	0.04
Polish	9,430	18.45
Portuguese	7	0.01
Romanian	117	0.23
Russian	337	0.66
Scandinavian	49	0.10
Scotch-Irish	503	0.98
Scottish	485	0.95
Serbian	62	0.12
Slavic	9	0.02
Slovak	388	0.76
Slovene	157	0.31
Swedish	1,340	2.62
Swiss	41	0.08
Turkish	11	0.02
Ukrainian	201	0.39
United States or American	645	1.26
Welsh	125	0.24
White:	48,300	94.56
Not Hispanic (46,478)	46,927	91.88
Hispanic (1,294)	1,373	2.69
Yugoslavian	55	0.11

Oswego

Place Type: Village
County: Kendall
Population: 13,326

Ancestry/Race	Number	%
African American/Black:	278	2.09
Not Hispanic (236)	272	2.04
Hispanic (3)	6	0.05
African, sub-Saharan:	26	0.20
Senegalese	26	0.20
Am. Ind. or Alaska Nat., not spec.	15	0.11
American Indian tribes, specified:	47	0.35
Cherokee (10)	23	0.17
Chippewa (1)	4	0.03
Crow (3)	3	0.02
Iroquois (1)	1	0.01
Latin American Indians	3	0.02
Navajo (1)	1	0.01
Osage	1	0.01
Potawatomi	2	0.02
Sioux (5)	5	0.04
All other tribes	4	0.03
Arab:	4	0.03
Lebanese	4	0.03
Armenian	9	0.07
Asian:	239	1.79
Cambodian (2)	4	0.03
Chinese, ex. Taiwanese (32)	41	0.31
Filipino (62)	84	0.63
Indian (32)	34	0.26
Indonesian	1	0.01
Japanese (6)	8	0.06

Notes: 1. Figures in the "Number" column do not add up to the total population due to: a) Ancestry/Race overlap — e.g. persons can report being both White and Irish, b) persons of Hispanic origin can report being any race, c) persons reporting two ancestries are counted in both categories. 2. Numbers in parentheses indicate the number of persons reporting this ancestry/race alone, not in combination with any other ancestry/race. 3. Refer to the Explanation of Data in the front of the book for more detailed information.

Ancestry/Race	Number	%
Korean (13)	21	0.16
Laotian (4)	4	0.03
Pakistani (6)	13	0.10
Taiwanese (1)	2	0.02
Thai (1)	3	0.02
Vietnamese (11)	14	0.11
Other Asian, specified (1)	1	0.01
Other Asian, not specified (5)	9	0.07
Austrian	56	0.42
Belgian	109	0.82
British	45	0.34
Canadian	17	0.13
Croatian	15	0.11
Czech	414	3.11
Czechoslovakian	79	0.59
Danish	198	1.49
Dutch	385	2.89
English	1,497	11.26
European	110	0.83
Finnish	58	0.44
French, except Basque	431	3.24
French Canadian	58	0.44
German	4,504	33.86
Greek	41	0.31
Hawaii Native/Pacific Islander:	6	0.05
Other Pac. Isl., not spec. (4)	6	0.05
Hispanic or Latino:	665	4.99
Central American:	3	0.02
Guatemalan	2	0.02
Panamanian	1	0.01
Cuban	13	0.10
Mexican	496	3.72
Puerto Rican	85	0.64
South American:	5	0.04
Bolivian	1	0.01
Colombian	2	0.02
Ecuadorian	1	0.01
Peruvian	1	0.01
Other Hispanic or Latino	63	0.47
Hungarian	71	0.53
Iranian	16	0.12
Irish	2,665	20.04
Italian	1,194	8.98
Lithuanian	217	1.63
Luxemburger	34	0.26
Norwegian	571	4.29
Pennsylvania German	46	0.35
Polish	1,508	11.34
Portuguese	8	0.06
Romanian	92	0.69
Russian	84	0.63
Scotch-Irish	188	1.41
Scottish	209	1.57
Serbian	5	0.04
Slavic	8	0.06
Slovak	113	0.85
Swedish	563	4.23
Swiss	74	0.56
Ukrainian	21	0.16
United States or American	411	3.09
Welsh	59	0.44
West Indian, excl. Hispanic:	10	0.08
West Indian	10	0.08
White:	12,627	94.75
Not Hispanic (12,079)	12,190	91.48
Hispanic (380)	437	3.28
Yugoslavian	8	0.06

Ottawa

Place Type: City
County: La Salle
Population: 18,307

Ancestry/Race	Number	%
African American/Black:	292	1.60
Not Hispanic (241)	280	1.53
Hispanic (10)	12	0.07
African, sub-Saharan:	13	0.07
African	13	0.07
Alaska Native tribes, specified:	1	0.01
Alaska Athabascan (1)	1	0.01
Alaska Native tribes, not specified	1	0.01
Am. Ind. or Alaska Nat., not spec.	27	0.15
Alsatian	3	0.02
American Indian tribes, specified:	63	0.34
Blackfeet (1)	3	0.02
Cherokee (9)	31	0.17
Chickasaw (1)	5	0.03
Choctaw (2)	7	0.04
Cree (1)	1	0.01
Iroquois (1)	7	0.04
Latin American Indians (1)	1	0.01
Potawatomi (1)	2	0.01
Sioux	1	0.01
All other tribes (2)	5	0.03
American Indian tribes, not spec.	3	0.02
Arab:	12	0.07
Arab/Arabic	8	0.04
Other Arab	4	0.02
Armenian	20	0.11
Asian:	210	1.15
Bangladeshi (1)	1	0.01
Cambodian (3)	3	0.02
Chinese, ex. Taiwanese (5)	8	0.04
Filipino (26)	39	0.21
Hmong	4	0.02
Indian (39)	51	0.28
Japanese (18)	27	0.15
Korean (21)	27	0.15
Laotian (1)	5	0.03
Pakistani (8)	8	0.04
Taiwanese (5)	5	0.03
Thai (3)	4	0.02
Vietnamese (11)	11	0.06
Other Asian, specified	4	0.02
Other Asian, not specified (4)	13	0.07
Australian	4	0.02
Austrian	64	0.35
Belgian	70	0.38
British	25	0.14
Canadian	41	0.22
Croatian	95	0.52
Czech	64	0.35
Czechoslovakian	40	0.22
Danish	194	1.06
Dutch	340	1.85
English	1,654	9.01
European	38	0.21
Finnish	12	0.07
French, except Basque	953	5.19
French Canadian	29	0.16
German	5,032	27.42
Greek	44	0.24
Hawaii Native/Pacific Islander:	18	0.10
Polynesian: (11)	13	0.07
Native Hawaiian (5)	7	0.04
Samoan (6)	6	0.03
Other Pac. Isl., specified	4	0.02
Other Pac. Isl., not spec.	1	0.01
Hispanic or Latino:	954	5.21
Central American:	3	0.02
Guatemalan	2	0.01
Other Central American	1	0.01
Cuban	2	0.01
Mexican	816	4.46
Puerto Rican	37	0.20
South American:	21	0.11
Colombian	19	0.10
Ecuadorian	2	0.01
Other Hispanic or Latino	75	0.41
Hungarian	109	0.59
Iranian	7	0.04
Irish	3,820	20.81
Italian	1,544	8.41
Lithuanian	70	0.38
Norwegian	1,455	7.93
Pennsylvania German	5	0.03
Polish	781	4.26
Portuguese	22	0.12
Romanian	16	0.09
Russian	57	0.31
Scandinavian	30	0.16
Scotch-Irish	255	1.39
Scottish	271	1.48
Slavic	11	0.06
Slovak	106	0.58
Slovene	33	0.18
Swedish	399	2.17
Swiss	22	0.12
Turkish	21	0.11
Ukrainian	56	0.31
United States or American	796	4.34
Welsh	82	0.45
White:	17,684	96.60
Not Hispanic (16,756)	16,901	92.32
Hispanic (684)	783	4.28
Yugoslavian	49	0.27

Palatine

Place Type: Village
County: Cook
Population: 65,479

Ancestry/Race	Number	%
African American/Black:	1,613	2.46
Not Hispanic (1,343)	1,502	2.29
Hispanic (64)	111	0.17
African, sub-Saharan:	155	0.24
African	67	0.10
Ethiopian	3	0.00
Kenyan	3	0.00
Nigerian	17	0.03
South African	55	0.08
Other sub-Saharan African	10	0.02
Alaska Native tribes, specified:	2	0.00
Aleut (1)	1	0.00
Eskimo	1	0.00
Am. Ind. or Alaska Nat., not spec.	131	0.20
Albanian	30	0.05
American Indian tribes, specified:	144	0.22
Apache (1)	3	0.00
Blackfeet	11	0.02
Cherokee (14)	46	0.07
Chickasaw (1)	1	0.00
Chippewa (10)	14	0.02
Comanche (5)	5	0.01
Delaware	1	0.00
Iroquois	6	0.01
Latin American Indians (24)	38	0.06
Lumbee (1)	1	0.00
Menominee (2)	2	0.00
Navajo (2)	2	0.00
Osage	1	0.00
Potawatomi (1)	1	0.00
Sioux (3)	5	0.01
All other tribes (3)	7	0.01
American Indian tribes, not spec.	14	0.02
Arab:	177	0.27
Egyptian	34	0.05
Jordanian	10	0.02
Lebanese	39	0.06
Palestinian	31	0.05
Syrian	46	0.07
Other Arab	17	0.03
Armenian	105	0.16
Asian:	5,439	8.31
Bangladeshi (21)	21	0.03
Cambodian (5)	5	0.01
Chinese, ex. Taiwanese (796)	882	1.35
Filipino (469)	575	0.88
Hmong (2)	2	0.00
Indian (2,132)	2,229	3.40
Indonesian (10)	11	0.02
Japanese (413)	490	0.75
Korean (602)	645	0.99
Laotian (5)	5	0.01
Malaysian (3)	7	0.01
Pakistani (184)	212	0.32

Notes: 1. Figures in the "Number" column do not add up to the total population due to: a) Ancestry/Race overlap — e.g. persons can report being both White and Irish, b) persons of Hispanic origin can report being any race, c) persons reporting two ancestries are counted in both categories. 2. Numbers in parentheses indicate the number of persons reporting this ancestry/race alone, not in combination with any other ancestry/race. 3. Refer to the Explanation of Data in the front of the book for more detailed information.

Ancestry/Race	Number	%
Sri Lankan (4)	7	0.01
Taiwanese (50)	59	0.09
Thai (31)	42	0.06
Vietnamese (137)	148	0.23
Other Asian, specified (3)	8	0.01
Other Asian, not specified (38)	91	0.14
Assyrian/Chaldean/Syriac	64	0.10
Australian	35	0.05
Austrian	397	0.61
Belgian	194	0.30
Brazilian	73	0.11
British	198	0.30
Bulgarian	32	0.05
Canadian	142	0.22
Celtic	11	0.02
Croatian	225	0.35
Cypriot	8	0.01
Czech	688	1.06
Czechoslovakian	159	0.24
Danish	728	1.12
Dutch	846	1.30
Eastern European	56	0.09
English	4,916	7.54
Estonian	25	0.04
European	335	0.51
Finnish	188	0.29
French, except Basque	1,275	1.96
French Canadian	292	0.45
German	16,328	25.06
Greek	660	1.01
Hawaii Native/Pacific Islander:	64	0.10
Micronesian: (11)	11	0.02
Guamanian/Chamorro (11)	11	0.02
Polynesian: (12)	26	0.04
Native Hawaiian (6)	19	0.03
Samoan (5)	6	0.01
Tongan (1)	1	0.00
Other Pac. Isl., specified	2	0.00
Other Pac. Isl., not spec. (4)	25	0.04
Hispanic or Latino:	9,247	14.12
Central American:	237	0.36
Costa Rican	11	0.02
Guatemalan	95	0.15
Honduran	21	0.03
Nicaraguan	24	0.04
Panamanian	9	0.01
Salvadoran	74	0.11
Other Central American	3	0.00
Cuban	96	0.15
Dominican Republic	20	0.03
Mexican	7,587	11.59
Puerto Rican	312	0.48
South American:	279	0.43
Argentinean	13	0.02
Bolivian	12	0.02
Chilean	8	0.01
Colombian	75	0.11
Ecuadorian	45	0.07
Paraguayan	3	0.00
Peruvian	79	0.12
Uruguayan	1	0.00
Venezuelan	22	0.03
Other South American	21	0.03
Other Hispanic or Latino	716	1.09
Hungarian	539	0.83
Icelander	7	0.01
Iranian	74	0.11
Irish	9,654	14.82
Israeli	9	0.01
Italian	5,948	9.13
Latvian	172	0.26
Lithuanian	430	0.66
Luxemburger	131	0.20
Macedonian	9	0.01
New Zealander	6	0.01
Northern European	86	0.13
Norwegian	1,354	2.08
Pennsylvania German	8	0.01
Polish	7,846	12.04
Portuguese	63	0.10
Romanian	120	0.18
Russian	924	1.42
Scandinavian	166	0.25
Scotch-Irish	829	1.27
Scottish	1,012	1.55
Serbian	120	0.18
Slavic	44	0.07
Slovak	217	0.33
Slovene	67	0.10
Swedish	2,243	3.44
Swiss	278	0.43
Turkish	48	0.07
Ukrainian	785	1.20
United States or American	1,964	3.01
Welsh	378	0.58
West Indian, excl. Hispanic:	92	0.14
Belizean	38	0.06
Haitian	28	0.04
Jamaican	16	0.02
West Indian	10	0.02
White:	55,467	84.71
Not Hispanic (49,029)	49,694	75.89
Hispanic (5,352)	5,773	8.82
Yugoslavian	133	0.20

Palos Heights

Place Type: City
County: Cook
Population: 11,260

Ancestry/Race	Number	%
African American/Black:	63	0.56
Not Hispanic (47)	61	0.54
Hispanic (2)	2	0.02
Am. Ind. or Alaska Nat., not spec.	10	0.09
Albanian	8	0.07
American Indian tribes, specified:	15	0.13
Cherokee (2)	9	0.08
Latin American Indians (3)	3	0.03
Navajo (2)	3	0.03
Arab:	30	0.27
Egyptian	4	0.04
Lebanese	22	0.19
Palestinian	4	0.04
Armenian	6	0.05
Asian:	264	2.34
Cambodian (4)	5	0.04
Chinese, ex. Taiwanese (31)	32	0.28
Filipino (55)	76	0.67
Indian (48)	50	0.44
Japanese (8)	9	0.08
Korean (42)	42	0.37
Malaysian (1)	1	0.01
Pakistani (12)	12	0.11
Taiwanese (11)	11	0.10
Thai (12)	12	0.11
Vietnamese (5)	5	0.04
Other Asian, not specified (3)	9	0.08
Austrian	188	1.66
Belgian	6	0.05
British	12	0.11
Canadian	31	0.27
Croatian	105	0.93
Czech	301	2.66
Czechoslovakian	42	0.37
Danish	80	0.71
Dutch	1,032	9.12
English	726	6.41
European	29	0.26
Finnish	18	0.16
French, except Basque	164	1.45
French Canadian	71	0.63
German	2,323	20.52
Greek	315	2.78
Hawaii Native/Pacific Islander:	2	0.02
Other Pac. Isl., not spec.	2	0.02
Hispanic or Latino:	161	1.43
Central American:	3	0.03
Honduran	2	0.02
Salvadoran	1	0.01
Cuban	9	0.08
Mexican	114	1.01
Puerto Rican	4	0.04
South American:	20	0.18
Argentinean	3	0.03
Colombian	8	0.07
Ecuadorian	5	0.04
Peruvian	1	0.01
Uruguayan	1	0.01
Venezuelan	2	0.02
Other Hispanic or Latino	11	0.10
Hungarian	95	0.84
Iranian	10	0.09
Irish	3,078	27.19
Italian	1,184	10.46
Lithuanian	360	3.18
Luxemburger	19	0.17
Norwegian	139	1.23
Polish	1,599	14.13
Romanian	11	0.10
Russian	116	1.02
Scotch-Irish	121	1.07
Scottish	112	0.99
Serbian	19	0.17
Slovak	89	0.79
Slovene	11	0.10
Swedish	394	3.48
Swiss	32	0.28
Ukrainian	82	0.72
United States or American	224	1.98
Welsh	12	0.11
White:	10,939	97.15
Not Hispanic (10,727)	10,803	95.94
Hispanic (126)	136	1.21
Yugoslavian	7	0.06

Palos Hills

Place Type: City
County: Cook
Population: 17,665

Ancestry/Race	Number	%
African American/Black:	1,010	5.72
Not Hispanic (960)	992	5.62
Hispanic (8)	18	0.10
African, sub-Saharan:	20	0.11
African	12	0.07
Ethiopian	8	0.05
Am. Ind. or Alaska Nat., not spec.	19	0.11
Albanian	64	0.36
American Indian tribes, specified:	44	0.25
Blackfeet	7	0.04
Cherokee (6)	19	0.11
Chippewa	1	0.01
Choctaw	3	0.02
Creek (5)	5	0.03
Delaware	1	0.01
Iroquois (1)	2	0.01
Latin American Indians (1)	1	0.01
All other tribes	5	0.03
American Indian tribes, not spec.	3	0.02
Arab:	578	3.26
Arab/Arabic	253	1.42
Egyptian	68	0.38
Jordanian	102	0.57
Palestinian	155	0.87
Armenian	31	0.17
Asian:	539	3.05
Bangladeshi (3)	3	0.02
Chinese, ex. Taiwanese (38)	52	0.29
Filipino (126)	139	0.79
Indian (125)	135	0.76
Indonesian (4)	6	0.03
Japanese (7)	8	0.05
Korean (95)	100	0.57
Pakistani (32)	45	0.25
Taiwanese	2	0.01
Thai (15)	16	0.09

Notes: 1. Figures in the "Number" column do not add up to the total population due to: a) Ancestry/Race overlap — e.g. persons can report being both White and Irish, b) persons of Hispanic origin can report being any race, c) persons reporting two ancestries are counted in both categories. 2. Numbers in parentheses indicate the number of persons reporting this ancestry/race alone, not in combination with any other ancestry/race. 3. Refer to the Explanation of Data in the front of the book for more detailed information.

Ancestry/Race	Number	%
Vietnamese (10)	10	0.06
Other Asian, specified (1)	4	0.02
Other Asian, not specified (4)	19	0.11
Australian	17	0.10
Austrian	178	1.00
Belgian	24	0.14
British	25	0.14
Celtic	11	0.06
Croatian	351	1.98
Czech	633	3.57
Czechoslovakian	96	0.54
Danish	97	0.55
Dutch	298	1.68
English	821	4.62
European	78	0.44
Finnish	7	0.04
French, except Basque	267	1.50
French Canadian	45	0.25
German	2,886	16.25
Greek	1,141	6.43
Hawaii Native/Pacific Islander:	10	0.06
Micronesian: (1)	2	0.01
Guamanian/Chamorro	1	0.01
Other Micronesian (1)	1	0.01
Polynesian:	3	0.02
Native Hawaiian	2	0.01
Other Polynesian	1	0.01
Other Pac. Isl., specified	3	0.02
Other Pac. Isl., not spec. (1)	2	0.01
Hispanic or Latino:	854	4.83
Central American:	8	0.05
Costa Rican	2	0.01
Guatemalan	5	0.03
Salvadoran	1	0.01
Cuban	19	0.11
Dominican Republic	1	0.01
Mexican	702	3.97
Puerto Rican	23	0.13
South American:	18	0.10
Argentinean	4	0.02
Colombian	3	0.02
Ecuadorian	2	0.01
Paraguayan	1	0.01
Peruvian	5	0.03
Venezuelan	3	0.02
Other Hispanic or Latino	83	0.47
Hungarian	30	0.17
Irish	3,389	19.09
Italian	1,867	10.52
Latvian	23	0.13
Lithuanian	759	4.27
Macedonian	6	0.03
Maltese	5	0.03
Northern European	23	0.13
Norwegian	189	1.06
Pennsylvania German	10	0.06
Polish	3,364	18.95
Russian	66	0.37
Scandinavian	24	0.14
Scotch-Irish	146	0.82
Scottish	219	1.23
Serbian	31	0.17
Slavic	11	0.06
Slovak	161	0.91
Slovene	62	0.35
Swedish	364	2.05
Ukrainian	53	0.30
United States or American	394	2.22
Welsh	70	0.39
White:	15,906	90.04
Not Hispanic (14,897)	15,335	86.81
Hispanic (504)	571	3.23
Yugoslavian	8	0.05

Park Forest

Place Type: Village
County: Cook
Population: 23,462

Ancestry/Race	Number	%
African American/Black:	9,643	41.10
Not Hispanic (9,144)	9,487	40.44
Hispanic (103)	156	0.66
African, sub-Saharan:	319	1.37
African	257	1.10
Nigerian	52	0.22
Other sub-Saharan African	10	0.04
Am. Ind. or Alaska Nat., not spec.	81	0.35
Alsatian	13	0.06
American Indian tribes, specified:	107	0.46
Blackfeet	10	0.04
Cherokee (3)	43	0.18
Cheyenne	1	0.00
Chippewa (8)	8	0.03
Choctaw (1)	6	0.03
Cree (1)	1	0.00
Iroquois	1	0.00
Latin American Indians (5)	9	0.04
Navajo (8)	8	0.03
Potawatomi	1	0.00
Sioux	11	0.05
All other tribes (1)	8	0.03
American Indian tribes, not spec.	2	0.01
Arab:	46	0.20
Arab/Arabic	40	0.17
Palestinian	6	0.03
Asian:	278	1.18
Chinese, ex. Taiwanese (34)	45	0.19
Filipino (40)	55	0.23
Indian (56)	70	0.30
Japanese (27)	38	0.16
Korean (11)	22	0.09
Laotian (6)	6	0.03
Malaysian	1	0.00
Pakistani (6)	6	0.03
Sri Lankan (2)	2	0.01
Thai (8)	13	0.06
Vietnamese (2)	8	0.03
Other Asian, not specified (1)	12	0.05
Austrian	70	0.30
Belgian	22	0.09
British	82	0.35
Bulgarian	5	0.02
Canadian	24	0.10
Croatian	49	0.21
Czech	109	0.47
Czechoslovakian	54	0.23
Danish	113	0.49
Dutch	354	1.52
Eastern European	9	0.04
English	1,904	8.18
European	50	0.21
Finnish	8	0.03
French, except Basque	506	2.17
French Canadian	130	0.56
German	4,521	19.42
German Russian	9	0.04
Greek	71	0.31
Hawaii Native/Pacific Islander:	24	0.10
Polynesian: (16)	19	0.08
Native Hawaiian (3)	6	0.03
Samoan (13)	13	0.06
Other Pac. Isl., not spec. (1)	5	0.02
Hispanic or Latino:	1,169	4.98
Central American:	15	0.06
Costa Rican	2	0.01
Guatemalan	9	0.04
Honduran	1	0.00
Panamanian	2	0.01
Salvadoran	1	0.00
Cuban	22	0.09
Dominican Republic	8	0.03
Mexican	777	3.31
Puerto Rican	173	0.74
South American:	24	0.10
Chilean	4	0.02
Colombian	3	0.01
Ecuadorian	3	0.01
Peruvian	11	0.05
Other South American	3	0.01
Other Hispanic or Latino	150	0.64
Hungarian	184	0.79
Icelander	13	0.06
Iranian	7	0.03
Irish	2,776	11.93
Italian	1,553	6.67
Lithuanian	165	0.71
Norwegian	239	1.03
Polish	1,544	6.63
Portuguese	16	0.07
Romanian	21	0.09
Russian	102	0.44
Scandinavian	59	0.25
Scotch-Irish	237	1.02
Scottish	373	1.60
Serbian	36	0.15
Slavic	15	0.06
Slovak	173	0.74
Slovene	22	0.09
Swedish	423	1.82
Swiss	59	0.25
Ukrainian	53	0.23
United States or American	545	2.34
Welsh	74	0.32
West Indian, excl. Hispanic:	46	0.20
Bahamian	4	0.02
Haitian	20	0.09
Jamaican	22	0.09
White:	13,476	57.44
Not Hispanic (12,412)	12,780	54.47
Hispanic (591)	696	2.97
Yugoslavian	5	0.02

Park Ridge

Place Type: City
County: Cook
Population: 37,775

Ancestry/Race	Number	%
African American/Black:	128	0.34
Not Hispanic (85)	115	0.30
Hispanic (5)	13	0.03
Am. Ind. or Alaska Nat., not spec.	31	0.08
Albanian	19	0.05
American Indian tribes, specified:	45	0.12
Apache	3	0.01
Cherokee (3)	14	0.04
Chippewa	2	0.01
Creek	1	0.00
Iroquois (4)	4	0.01
Latin American Indians (7)	10	0.03
Lumbee (1)	1	0.00
Osage	1	0.00
Sioux (3)	8	0.02
All other tribes	1	0.00
American Indian tribes, not spec.	4	0.01
Arab:	275	0.73
Arab/Arabic	111	0.29
Egyptian	56	0.15
Lebanese	39	0.10
Palestinian	30	0.08
Syrian	6	0.02
Other Arab	33	0.09
Armenian	49	0.13
Asian:	1,172	3.10
Cambodian (1)	1	0.00
Chinese, ex. Taiwanese (185)	238	0.63
Filipino (280)	320	0.85
Indian (153)	168	0.44
Japanese (108)	140	0.37
Korean (144)	164	0.43
Malaysian (1)	1	0.00

Notes: 1. Figures in the "Number" column do not add up to the total population due to: a) Ancestry/Race overlap — e.g. persons can report being both White and Irish, b) persons of Hispanic origin can report being any race, c) persons reporting two ancestries are counted in both categories. 2. Numbers in parentheses indicate the number of persons reporting this ancestry/race alone, not in combination with any other ancestry/race. 3. Refer to the Explanation of Data in the front of the book for more detailed information.

Ancestry/Race	Number	%
Pakistani (34)	44	0.12
Taiwanese (17)	17	0.05
Thai (18)	20	0.05
Vietnamese (11)	11	0.03
Other Asian, specified (1)	4	0.01
Other Asian, not specified (22)	44	0.12
Assyrian/Chaldean/Syriac	137	0.36
Austrian	408	1.08
Basque	7	0.02
Belgian	150	0.40
British	103	0.27
Bulgarian	26	0.07
Canadian	53	0.14
Croatian	80	0.21
Czech	539	1.43
Czechoslovakian	208	0.55
Danish	365	0.97
Dutch	324	0.86
Eastern European	7	0.02
English	2,458	6.51
Estonian	23	0.06
European	140	0.37
Finnish	60	0.16
French, except Basque	666	1.76
French Canadian	114	0.30
German	9,111	24.14
Greek	1,288	3.41
Hawaii Native/Pacific Islander:	28	0.07
Micronesian: (1)	1	0.00
Guamanian/Chamorro (1)	1	0.00
Polynesian: (15)	19	0.05
Native Hawaiian (7)	8	0.02
Samoan (8)	9	0.02
Tongan	2	0.01
Other Pac. Isl., specified	2	0.01
Other Pac. Isl., not spec. (2)	6	0.02
Hispanic or Latino:	1,113	2.95
Central American:	23	0.06
Costa Rican	4	0.01
Guatemalan	14	0.04
Honduran	1	0.00
Panamanian	3	0.01
Salvadoran	1	0.00
Cuban	108	0.29
Dominican Republic	6	0.02
Mexican	628	1.66
Puerto Rican	145	0.38
South American:	108	0.29
Argentinean	10	0.03
Chilean	2	0.01
Colombian	34	0.09
Ecuadorian	11	0.03
Paraguayan	1	0.00
Peruvian	24	0.06
Uruguayan	6	0.02
Venezuelan	6	0.02
Other South American	14	0.04
Other Hispanic or Latino	95	0.25
Hungarian	296	0.78
Icelander	28	0.07
Iranian	22	0.06
Irish	8,445	22.38
Italian	6,140	16.27
Latvian	13	0.03
Lithuanian	253	0.67
Luxemburger	83	0.22
Northern European	31	0.08
Norwegian	1,169	3.10
Polish	7,855	20.82
Portuguese	55	0.15
Romanian	156	0.41
Russian	471	1.25
Scandinavian	78	0.21
Scotch-Irish	432	1.14
Scottish	417	1.11
Serbian	97	0.26
Slavic	6	0.02
Slovak	318	0.84
Slovene	87	0.23
Swedish	1,558	4.13
Swiss	201	0.53
Turkish	23	0.06
Ukrainian	420	1.11
United States or American	885	2.35
Welsh	128	0.34
West Indian, excl. Hispanic:	22	0.06
Jamaican	22	0.06
White:	36,294	96.08
Not Hispanic (35,307)	35,508	94.00
Hispanic (724)	786	2.08
Yugoslavian	102	0.27

Pekin

Place Type: City
County: Tazewell
Population: 33,857

Ancestry/Race	Number	%
African American/Black:	910	2.69
Not Hispanic (857)	904	2.67
Hispanic (6)	6	0.02
Alaska Native tribes, specified:	4	0.01
All other tribes (1)	4	0.01
Am. Ind. or Alaska Nat., not spec.	97	0.29
American Indian tribes, specified:	147	0.43
Apache	3	0.01
Blackfeet (3)	19	0.06
Cherokee (28)	70	0.21
Chickasaw	1	0.00
Chippewa (4)	6	0.02
Choctaw (7)	9	0.03
Cree (1)	1	0.00
Creek	2	0.01
Delaware (1)	3	0.01
Iroquois (3)	6	0.02
Latin American Indians (2)	2	0.01
Navajo (1)	1	0.00
Potawatomi	1	0.00
Seminole (1)	2	0.01
Sioux (9)	11	0.03
All other tribes (2)	8	0.02
American Indian tribes, not spec.	10	0.03
Arab:	22	0.07
Lebanese	22	0.07
Asian:	175	0.52
Chinese, ex. Taiwanese (14)	15	0.04
Filipino (16)	21	0.06
Indian (30)	34	0.10
Japanese (12)	22	0.06
Korean (12)	16	0.05
Laotian (1)	1	0.00
Taiwanese (1)	2	0.01
Thai (8)	9	0.03
Vietnamese (25)	32	0.09
Other Asian, specified	1	0.00
Other Asian, not specified (19)	22	0.06
Austrian	17	0.05
Belgian	44	0.13
British	47	0.14
Canadian	23	0.07
Celtic	18	0.05
Croatian	75	0.22
Czech	115	0.34
Czechoslovakian	55	0.16
Danish	103	0.30
Dutch	645	1.91
English	3,809	11.26
European	142	0.42
Finnish	3	0.01
French, except Basque	1,251	3.70
French Canadian	49	0.14
German	9,621	28.43
Greek	187	0.55
Hawaii Native/Pacific Islander:	11	0.03
Polynesian: (4)	7	0.02
Native Hawaiian	3	0.01
Samoan (4)	4	0.01
Other Pac. Isl., specified	1	0.00
Other Pac. Isl., not spec.	3	0.01
Hispanic or Latino:	445	1.31
Central American:	3	0.01
Panamanian	2	0.01
Salvadoran	1	0.00
Dominican Republic	1	0.00
Mexican	210	0.62
Puerto Rican	38	0.11
South American:	11	0.03
Chilean	1	0.00
Colombian	5	0.01
Ecuadorian	2	0.01
Peruvian	3	0.01
Other Hispanic or Latino	182	0.54
Hungarian	86	0.25
Irish	3,888	11.49
Italian	1,478	4.37
Lithuanian	36	0.11
Macedonian	16	0.05
Maltese	12	0.04
Norwegian	344	1.02
Pennsylvania German	30	0.09
Polish	404	1.19
Portuguese	47	0.14
Romanian	29	0.09
Russian	60	0.18
Scandinavian	32	0.09
Scotch-Irish	522	1.54
Scottish	665	1.97
Serbian	27	0.08
Slavic	11	0.03
Slovak	18	0.05
Slovene	14	0.04
Swedish	499	1.47
Swiss	115	0.34
United States or American	3,443	10.17
Welsh	205	0.61
White:	32,659	96.46
Not Hispanic (32,088)	32,291	95.37
Hispanic (346)	368	1.09
Yugoslavian	29	0.09

Peoria

Place Type: City
County: Peoria
Population: 112,936

Ancestry/Race	Number	%
Acadian/Cajun	7	0.01
African American/Black:	29,553	26.17
Not Hispanic (27,783)	29,235	25.89
Hispanic (209)	318	0.28
African, sub-Saharan:	1,264	1.12
African	1,071	0.95
Ethiopian	21	0.02
Ghanian	8	0.01
Nigerian	83	0.07
Sierra Leonean	29	0.03
South African	18	0.02
Sudanese	9	0.01
Other sub-Saharan African	25	0.02
Alaska Native tribes, specified:	4	0.00
Alaska Athabascan	1	0.00
Aleut (1)	1	0.00
Eskimo	1	0.00
Tlingit-Haida (1)	1	0.00
Am. Ind. or Alaska Nat., not spec.	277	0.25
Alsatian	15	0.01
American Indian tribes, specified:	408	0.36
Apache (5)	20	0.02
Blackfeet (4)	33	0.03
Cherokee (67)	221	0.20
Cheyenne (1)	4	0.00
Chippewa (3)	12	0.01
Choctaw (3)	5	0.00
Comanche (1)	1	0.00
Cree (1)	1	0.00
Creek (1)	4	0.00
Crow (1)	2	0.00
Houma (2)	2	0.00

Notes: 1. Figures in the "Number" column do not add up to the total population due to: a) Ancestry/Race overlap — e.g. persons can report being both White and Irish, b) persons of Hispanic origin can report being any race, c) persons reporting two ancestries are counted in both categories. 2. Numbers in parentheses indicate the number of persons reporting this ancestry/race alone, not in combination with any other ancestry/race. 3. Refer to the Explanation of Data in the front of the book for more detailed information.

Ancestry/Race	Number	%
Iroquois (4)	7	0.01
Latin American Indians (11)	25	0.02
Lumbee (1)	6	0.01
Menominee (2)	2	0.00
Navajo (2)	2	0.00
Osage	3	0.00
Paiute (1)	1	0.00
Pima (1)	3	0.00
Potawatomi (2)	2	0.00
Pueblo	1	0.00
Puget Sound Salish (3)	4	0.00
Shoshone (2)	2	0.00
Sioux (10)	27	0.02
Tohono O'Odham	2	0.00
All other tribes (5)	16	0.01
American Indian tribes, not spec.	46	0.04
Arab:	1,576	1.40
Arab/Arabic	61	0.05
Egyptian	46	0.04
Jordanian	13	0.01
Lebanese	1,300	1.15
Moroccan	15	0.01
Palestinian	37	0.03
Syrian	104	0.09
Armenian	28	0.02
Asian:	3,045	2.70
Bangladeshi (9)	11	0.01
Cambodian (7)	9	0.01
Chinese, ex. Taiwanese (524)	584	0.52
Filipino (244)	323	0.29
Hmong (1)	1	0.00
Indian (982)	1,057	0.94
Indonesian (15)	21	0.02
Japanese (90)	145	0.13
Korean (184)	214	0.19
Laotian (56)	65	0.06
Malaysian (8)	9	0.01
Pakistani (60)	72	0.06
Sri Lankan (2)	7	0.01
Taiwanese (20)	22	0.02
Thai (21)	26	0.02
Vietnamese (341)	382	0.34
Other Asian, specified (9)	19	0.02
Other Asian, not specified (15)	78	0.07
Austrian	251	0.22
Belgian	380	0.34
Brazilian	97	0.09
British	347	0.31
Bulgarian	7	0.01
Canadian	152	0.13
Celtic	12	0.01
Croatian	256	0.23
Czech	422	0.37
Czechoslovakian	162	0.14
Danish	477	0.42
Dutch	1,821	1.61
Eastern European	53	0.05
English	9,938	8.80
European	853	0.76
Finnish	84	0.07
French, except Basque	2,428	2.15
French Canadian	368	0.33
German	24,774	21.94
German Russian	6	0.01
Greek	381	0.34
Hawaii Native/Pacific Islander:	107	0.09
Micronesian: (4)	13	0.01
Guamanian/Chamorro (3)	12	0.01
Other Micronesian (1)	1	0.00
Polynesian: (25)	49	0.04
Native Hawaiian (14)	30	0.03
Samoan (11)	19	0.02
Other Pac. Isl., specified	6	0.01
Other Pac. Isl., not spec. (13)	39	0.03
Hispanic or Latino:	2,839	2.51
Central American:	49	0.04
Costa Rican	5	0.00
Guatemalan	14	0.01
Honduran	5	0.00
Nicaraguan	7	0.01
Panamanian	8	0.01
Salvadoran	4	0.00
Other Central American	6	0.01
Cuban	77	0.07
Dominican Republic	14	0.01
Mexican	1,974	1.75
Puerto Rican	221	0.20
South American:	94	0.08
Argentinean	13	0.01
Bolivian	3	0.00
Chilean	9	0.01
Colombian	37	0.03
Ecuadorian	4	0.00
Peruvian	15	0.01
Uruguayan	3	0.00
Venezuelan	5	0.00
Other South American	5	0.00
Other Hispanic or Latino	410	0.36
Hungarian	386	0.34
Iranian	37	0.03
Irish	13,790	12.22
Italian	3,474	3.08
Latvian	56	0.05
Lithuanian	227	0.20
Luxemburger	5	0.00
Northern European	19	0.02
Norwegian	1,290	1.14
Pennsylvania German	63	0.06
Polish	2,169	1.92
Portuguese	135	0.12
Romanian	82	0.07
Russian	456	0.40
Scandinavian	68	0.06
Scotch-Irish	1,547	1.37
Scottish	1,663	1.47
Serbian	28	0.02
Slavic	30	0.03
Slovak	124	0.11
Slovene	100	0.09
Swedish	2,495	2.21
Swiss	649	0.57
Turkish	25	0.02
Ukrainian	124	0.11
United States or American	6,366	5.64
Welsh	502	0.44
West Indian, excl. Hispanic:	88	0.08
Haitian	41	0.04
Jamaican	47	0.04
White:	80,323	71.12
Not Hispanic (77,138)	78,976	69.93
Hispanic (1,116)	1,347	1.19
Yugoslavian	149	0.13

Plainfield

Place Type: Village
County: Will
Population: 13,038

Ancestry/Race	Number	%
African American/Black:	126	0.97
Not Hispanic (109)	125	0.96
Hispanic (1)	1	0.01
Am. Ind. or Alaska Nat., not spec.	16	0.12
Alsatian	18	0.14
American Indian tribes, specified:	35	0.27
Apache	1	0.01
Blackfeet (3)	4	0.03
Cherokee (3)	18	0.14
Cree	2	0.02
Creek (1)	1	0.01
Iroquois	6	0.05
Latin American Indians	1	0.01
Menominee	1	0.01
Sioux	1	0.01
American Indian tribes, not spec.	1	0.01
Arab:	51	0.39
Lebanese	51	0.39
Asian:	205	1.57
Cambodian (7)	7	0.05
Chinese, ex. Taiwanese (36)	38	0.29
Filipino (38)	52	0.40
Hmong (10)	10	0.08
Indian (31)	32	0.25
Japanese (7)	23	0.18
Korean (22)	29	0.22
Pakistani (2)	2	0.02
Taiwanese (1)	1	0.01
Thai (3)	4	0.03
Vietnamese (1)	3	0.02
Other Asian, not specified (1)	4	0.03
Austrian	13	0.10
British	33	0.25
Canadian	41	0.32
Croatian	91	0.70
Czech	464	3.57
Czechoslovakian	104	0.80
Danish	78	0.60
Dutch	355	2.73
English	1,202	9.24
European	8	0.06
Finnish	66	0.51
French, except Basque	318	2.44
French Canadian	32	0.25
German	4,052	31.15
Greek	190	1.46
Hawaii Native/Pacific Islander:	11	0.08
Polynesian:	5	0.04
Native Hawaiian	5	0.04
Other Pac. Isl., not spec. (1)	6	0.05
Hispanic or Latino:	504	3.87
Central American:	3	0.02
Guatemalan	2	0.02
Other Central American	1	0.01
Cuban	16	0.12
Mexican	371	2.85
Puerto Rican	51	0.39
South American:	7	0.05
Chilean	1	0.01
Colombian	3	0.02
Ecuadorian	2	0.02
Peruvian	1	0.01
Other Hispanic or Latino	56	0.43
Hungarian	161	1.24
Irish	2,628	20.20
Italian	2,076	15.96
Lithuanian	167	1.28
Luxemburger	29	0.22
Norwegian	382	2.94
Polish	2,006	15.42
Romanian	79	0.61
Russian	34	0.26
Scandinavian	11	0.08
Scotch-Irish	191	1.47
Scottish	219	1.68
Serbian	14	0.11
Slavic	23	0.18
Slovak	152	1.17
Slovene	71	0.55
Swedish	618	4.75
Swiss	119	0.91
Ukrainian	29	0.22
United States or American	426	3.27
Welsh	100	0.77
White:	12,613	96.74
Not Hispanic (12,144)	12,230	93.80
Hispanic (353)	383	2.94
Yugoslavian	71	0.55

Pontiac

Place Type: City
County: Livingston
Population: 11,864

Ancestry/Race	Number	%
African American/Black:	1,325	11.17
Not Hispanic (1,278)	1,306	11.01
Hispanic (15)	19	0.16
African, sub-Saharan:	10	0.08

Notes: 1. Figures in the "Number" column do not add up to the total population due to: a) Ancestry/Race overlap — e.g. persons can report being both White and Irish, b) persons of Hispanic origin can report being any race, c) persons reporting two ancestries are counted in both categories. 2. Numbers in parentheses indicate the number of persons reporting this ancestry/race alone, not in combination with any other ancestry/race. 3. Refer to the Explanation of Data in the front of the book for more detailed information.

Ancestry/Race	Number	%
African	10	0.08
Am. Ind. or Alaska Nat., not spec.	19	0.16
American Indian tribes, specified:	42	0.35
Blackfeet	1	0.01
Cherokee (12)	29	0.24
Cheyenne	3	0.03
Choctaw	1	0.01
Iroquois (1)	2	0.02
Navajo (1)	1	0.01
Osage	1	0.01
Pima (1)	1	0.01
Sioux	1	0.01
All other tribes (1)	2	0.02
American Indian tribes, not spec.	1	0.01
Arab:	46	0.39
Arab/Arabic	43	0.36
Lebanese	3	0.03
Asian:	73	0.62
Chinese, ex. Taiwanese (11)	15	0.13
Filipino (14)	15	0.13
Indian (11)	13	0.11
Japanese (2)	7	0.06
Korean (6)	9	0.08
Laotian	2	0.02
Pakistani (1)	1	0.01
Vietnamese (1)	1	0.01
Other Asian, not specified (4)	10	0.08
Austrian	9	0.08
British	9	0.08
Canadian	36	0.30
Czech	39	0.33
Czechoslovakian	6	0.05
Danish	140	1.18
Dutch	214	1.80
English	1,155	9.70
European	21	0.18
French, except Basque	282	2.37
French Canadian	28	0.24
German	3,107	26.10
Hawaii Native/Pacific Islander:	6	0.05
Polynesian:	6	0.05
Native Hawaiian	6	0.05
Hispanic or Latino:	519	4.37
Central American:	4	0.03
Costa Rican	4	0.03
Cuban	1	0.01
Mexican	261	2.20
Puerto Rican	10	0.08
South American:	12	0.10
Colombian	1	0.01
Ecuadorian	1	0.01
Venezuelan	9	0.08
Other South American	1	0.01
Other Hispanic or Latino	231	1.95
Hungarian	15	0.13
Irish	1,755	14.75
Italian	295	2.48
Lithuanian	21	0.18
Northern European	8	0.07
Norwegian	316	2.66
Polish	154	1.29
Scandinavian	19	0.16
Scotch-Irish	122	1.03
Scottish	250	2.10
Slavic	9	0.08
Slovak	9	0.08
Slovene	3	0.03
Swedish	198	1.66
Swiss	102	0.86
Ukrainian	2	0.02
United States or American	1,206	10.13
Welsh	70	0.59
West Indian, excl. Hispanic:	5	0.04
Dutch West Indian	5	0.04
White:	10,249	86.39
Not Hispanic (9,905)	9,997	84.26
Hispanic (226)	252	2.12

Prospect Heights

Place Type: City
County: Cook
Population: 17,081

Ancestry/Race	Number	%
African American/Black:	344	2.01
Not Hispanic (272)	293	1.72
Hispanic (28)	51	0.30
African, sub-Saharan:	22	0.13
African	15	0.09
Kenyan	7	0.04
Am. Ind. or Alaska Nat., not spec.	37	0.22
Albanian	6	0.03
American Indian tribes, specified:	34	0.20
Apache	1	0.01
Cherokee (2)	10	0.06
Choctaw	1	0.01
Cree	2	0.01
Delaware	1	0.01
Iroquois (3)	3	0.02
Latin American Indians (11)	12	0.07
Sioux (1)	1	0.01
All other tribes (2)	3	0.02
American Indian tribes, not spec.	8	0.05
Arab:	97	0.55
Arab/Arabic	70	0.40
Syrian	27	0.15
Armenian	37	0.21
Asian:	825	4.83
Chinese, ex. Taiwanese (68)	82	0.48
Filipino (133)	151	0.88
Indian (231)	244	1.43
Indonesian (2)	3	0.02
Japanese (43)	59	0.35
Korean (190)	200	1.17
Pakistani (29)	32	0.19
Sri Lankan (1)	1	0.01
Taiwanese (3)	3	0.02
Thai (1)	4	0.02
Vietnamese (27)	32	0.19
Other Asian, not specified (6)	14	0.08
Assyrian/Chaldean/Syriac	51	0.29
Australian	13	0.07
Austrian	86	0.49
Belgian	48	0.27
Brazilian	8	0.05
British	33	0.19
Canadian	25	0.14
Croatian	21	0.12
Czech	108	0.62
Czechoslovakian	75	0.43
Danish	147	0.84
Dutch	148	0.84
English	787	4.49
Finnish	24	0.14
French, except Basque	306	1.74
French Canadian	38	0.22
German	3,461	19.73
Greek	352	2.01
Guyanese	8	0.05
Hawaii Native/Pacific Islander:	18	0.11
Polynesian:	1	0.01
Native Hawaiian	1	0.01
Other Pac. Isl., not spec. (8)	17	0.10
Hispanic or Latino:	4,711	27.58
Central American:	91	0.53
Costa Rican	4	0.02
Guatemalan	14	0.08
Honduran	7	0.04
Nicaraguan	1	0.01
Salvadoran	63	0.37
Other Central American	2	0.01
Cuban	30	0.18
Mexican	4,181	24.48
Puerto Rican	60	0.35
South American:	49	0.29
Bolivian	3	0.02
Chilean	1	0.01
Colombian	24	0.14
Ecuadorian	17	0.10
Peruvian	3	0.02
Other South American	1	0.01
Other Hispanic or Latino	300	1.76
Hungarian	230	1.31
Iranian	37	0.21
Irish	1,511	8.61
Italian	1,197	6.82
Latvian	21	0.12
Lithuanian	33	0.19
Luxemburger	8	0.05
Norwegian	112	0.64
Polish	3,575	20.38
Romanian	87	0.50
Russian	217	1.24
Scandinavian	7	0.04
Scotch-Irish	191	1.09
Scottish	178	1.01
Serbian	90	0.51
Slavic	7	0.04
Slovak	70	0.40
Slovene	24	0.14
Swedish	450	2.57
Swiss	24	0.14
Ukrainian	124	0.71
United States or American	306	1.74
Welsh	17	0.10
West Indian, excl. Hispanic:	98	0.56
Jamaican	91	0.52
Trinidadian and Tobagonian	7	0.04
White:	13,587	79.54
Not Hispanic (11,139)	11,306	66.19
Hispanic (2,084)	2,281	13.35
Yugoslavian	45	0.26

Quincy

Place Type: City
County: Adams
Population: 40,366

Ancestry/Race	Number	%
African American/Black:	2,167	5.37
Not Hispanic (1,862)	2,144	5.31
Hispanic (17)	23	0.06
African, sub-Saharan:	235	0.58
African	228	0.57
Nigerian	7	0.02
Am. Ind. or Alaska Nat., not spec.	81	0.20
Albanian	7	0.02
American Indian tribes, specified:	117	0.29
Apache	4	0.01
Blackfeet (3)	11	0.03
Cherokee (29)	76	0.19
Chickasaw (1)	2	0.00
Chippewa (4)	5	0.01
Cree (1)	1	0.00
Iroquois (1)	4	0.01
Latin American Indians (1)	1	0.00
Lumbee (1)	1	0.00
Ottawa (1)	1	0.00
Pueblo (1)	1	0.00
Seminole	1	0.00
Sioux (1)	4	0.01
All other tribes (3)	5	0.01
American Indian tribes, not spec.	19	0.05
Arab:	40	0.10
Lebanese	40	0.10
Asian:	290	0.72
Chinese, ex. Taiwanese (50)	58	0.14
Filipino (36)	53	0.13
Indian (42)	56	0.14
Indonesian (3)	3	0.01
Japanese (12)	27	0.07
Korean (6)	12	0.03
Laotian (19)	22	0.05
Pakistani (6)	6	0.01
Taiwanese (14)	17	0.04
Thai (2)	2	0.00

Notes: 1. Figures in the "Number" column do not add up to the total population due to: a) Ancestry/Race overlap — e.g. persons can report being both White and Irish, b) persons of Hispanic origin can report being any race, c) persons reporting two ancestries are counted in both categories. 2. Numbers in parentheses indicate the number of persons reporting this ancestry/race alone, not in combination with any other ancestry/race. 3. Refer to the Explanation of Data in the front of the book for more detailed information.

	Number	%
Vietnamese (12)	16	0.04
Other Asian, specified (4)	5	0.01
Other Asian, not specified (6)	13	0.03
Australian	3	0.01
Austrian	56	0.14
Belgian	15	0.04
British	48	0.12
Canadian	18	0.04
Celtic	6	0.01
Croatian	12	0.03
Czech	50	0.12
Czechoslovakian	37	0.09
Danish	146	0.36
Dutch	645	1.60
Eastern European	5	0.01
English	3,435	8.53
European	134	0.33
Finnish	23	0.06
French, except Basque	912	2.26
French Canadian	155	0.38
German	14,757	36.64
Greek	110	0.27
Hawaii Native/Pacific Islander:	18	0.04
Micronesian:	2	0.00
Guamanian/Chamorro	2	0.00
Polynesian: (4)	9	0.02
Native Hawaiian (3)	7	0.02
Samoan (1)	2	0.00
Other Pac. Isl., specified	1	0.00
Other Pac. Isl., not spec. (1)	6	0.01
Hispanic or Latino:	381	0.94
Central American:	9	0.02
Honduran	2	0.00
Nicaraguan	1	0.00
Panamanian	5	0.01
Salvadoran	1	0.00
Cuban	24	0.06
Dominican Republic	6	0.01
Mexican	196	0.49
Puerto Rican	31	0.08
South American:	25	0.06
Colombian	18	0.04
Paraguayan	1	0.00
Peruvian	1	0.00
Venezuelan	2	0.00
Other South American	3	0.01
Other Hispanic or Latino	90	0.22
Hungarian	88	0.22
Irish	4,861	12.07
Italian	930	2.31
Lithuanian	65	0.16
Northern European	13	0.03
Norwegian	312	0.77
Pennsylvania German	64	0.16
Polish	339	0.84
Portuguese	23	0.06
Romanian	7	0.02
Russian	69	0.17
Scandinavian	40	0.10
Scotch-Irish	546	1.36
Scottish	526	1.31
Serbian	9	0.02
Slovak	34	0.08
Slovene	12	0.03
Swedish	427	1.06
Swiss	104	0.26
Turkish	5	0.01
Ukrainian	26	0.06
United States or American	3,626	9.00
Welsh	163	0.40
West Indian, excl. Hispanic:	11	0.03
West Indian	11	0.03
White:	37,991	94.12
Not Hispanic (37,332)	37,746	93.51
Hispanic (218)	245	0.61
Yugoslavian	7	0.02

Rantoul

Place Type: Village
County: Champaign
Population: 12,857

Ancestry/Race	Number	%
African American/Black:	2,422	18.84
Not Hispanic (2,133)	2,373	18.46
Hispanic (37)	49	0.38
African, sub-Saharan:	92	0.72
African	85	0.66
Kenyan	7	0.05
Alaska Native tribes, specified:	4	0.03
Eskimo (1)	4	0.03
Am. Ind. or Alaska Nat., not spec.	51	0.40
American Indian tribes, specified:	100	0.78
Apache (5)	5	0.04
Blackfeet (2)	11	0.09
Cherokee (17)	42	0.33
Cheyenne (1)	1	0.01
Chippewa (3)	6	0.05
Choctaw	8	0.06
Cree	1	0.01
Iroquois (1)	2	0.02
Latin American Indians (4)	6	0.05
Navajo	2	0.02
Potawatomi (2)	3	0.02
Sioux (3)	6	0.05
All other tribes (1)	7	0.05
American Indian tribes, not spec.	6	0.05
Arab:	25	0.19
Lebanese	25	0.19
Asian:	317	2.47
Cambodian (1)	1	0.01
Chinese, ex. Taiwanese (17)	21	0.16
Filipino (53)	85	0.66
Indian (56)	67	0.52
Indonesian	1	0.01
Japanese (36)	55	0.43
Korean (12)	27	0.21
Laotian (7)	10	0.08
Taiwanese (1)	1	0.01
Thai (7)	11	0.09
Vietnamese (11)	15	0.12
Other Asian, specified	1	0.01
Other Asian, not specified (16)	22	0.17
Austrian	13	0.10
Belgian	7	0.05
British	99	0.77
Canadian	30	0.23
Croatian	19	0.15
Czech	23	0.18
Czechoslovakian	9	0.07
Danish	77	0.60
Dutch	198	1.54
English	945	7.35
European	33	0.26
French, except Basque	344	2.67
French Canadian	112	0.87
German	2,851	22.17
Greek	4	0.03
Hawaii Native/Pacific Islander:	15	0.12
Micronesian: (2)	2	0.02
Guamanian/Chamorro (2)	2	0.02
Polynesian: (3)	10	0.08
Native Hawaiian (2)	9	0.07
Samoan (1)	1	0.01
Other Pac. Isl., not spec. (2)	3	0.02
Hispanic or Latino:	346	2.69
Central American:	8	0.06
Honduran	1	0.01
Nicaraguan	3	0.02
Other Central American	4	0.03
Cuban	5	0.04
Mexican	214	1.66
Puerto Rican	34	0.26
South American:	7	0.05
Colombian	7	0.05
Other Hispanic or Latino	78	0.61
Hungarian	28	0.22
Iranian	17	0.13
Irish	1,467	11.41
Italian	334	2.60
Lithuanian	30	0.23
Norwegian	98	0.76
Pennsylvania German	3	0.02
Polish	175	1.36
Portuguese	16	0.12
Russian	22	0.17
Scandinavian	17	0.13
Scotch-Irish	201	1.56
Scottish	187	1.45
Slovak	10	0.08
Swedish	302	2.35
Swiss	13	0.10
Ukrainian	23	0.18
United States or American	1,225	9.52
Welsh	52	0.40
West Indian, excl. Hispanic:	14	0.11
Haitian	14	0.11
White:	10,212	79.43
Not Hispanic (9,709)	10,031	78.02
Hispanic (151)	181	1.41

Richton Park

Place Type: Village
County: Cook
Population: 12,533

Ancestry/Race	Number	%
African American/Black:	7,578	60.46
Not Hispanic (7,374)	7,514	59.95
Hispanic (33)	64	0.51
African, sub-Saharan:	127	1.02
African	84	0.68
Cape Verdean	10	0.08
Ghanian	23	0.19
Nigerian	10	0.08
Am. Ind. or Alaska Nat., not spec.	40	0.32
American Indian tribes, specified:	50	0.40
Blackfeet	9	0.07
Cherokee (2)	25	0.20
Chippewa (1)	2	0.02
Choctaw	2	0.02
Creek	1	0.01
Crow	1	0.01
Latin American Indians	1	0.01
Navajo	1	0.01
Potawatomi (2)	2	0.02
Sioux (2)	5	0.04
Yaqui	1	0.01
American Indian tribes, not spec.	10	0.08
Asian:	246	1.96
Chinese, ex. Taiwanese (26)	30	0.24
Filipino (75)	95	0.76
Indian (45)	50	0.40
Japanese (12)	27	0.22
Korean (4)	7	0.06
Laotian (8)	8	0.06
Pakistani (10)	10	0.08
Thai (2)	2	0.02
Vietnamese (10)	10	0.08
Other Asian, not specified	7	0.06
Australian	7	0.06
Austrian	54	0.44
Belgian	6	0.05
British	33	0.27
Canadian	23	0.19
Croatian	14	0.11
Czech	63	0.51
Danish	63	0.51
Dutch	151	1.22
English	590	4.76
European	16	0.13
Finnish	13	0.10
French, except Basque	136	1.10
German	1,312	10.57
Greek	38	0.31

Notes: 1. Figures in the "Number" column do not add up to the total population due to: a) Ancestry/Race overlap — e.g. persons can report being both White and Irish, b) persons of Hispanic origin can report being any race, c) persons reporting two ancestries are counted in both categories. 2. Numbers in parentheses indicate the number of persons reporting this ancestry/race alone, not in combination with any other ancestry/race. 3. Refer to the Explanation of Data in the front of the book for more detailed information.

	Number	%
Hawaii Native/Pacific Islander:	14	0.11
Micronesian:	1	0.01
Guamanian/Chamorro	1	0.01
Polynesian: (2)	10	0.08
Native Hawaiian (2)	2	0.02
Samoan	5	0.04
Other Polynesian	3	0.02
Other Pac. Isl., not spec.	3	0.02
Hispanic or Latino:	484	3.86
Central American:	11	0.09
Guatemalan	4	0.03
Panamanian	1	0.01
Salvadoran	6	0.05
Cuban	8	0.06
Mexican	311	2.48
Puerto Rican	88	0.70
South American:	11	0.09
Ecuadorian	10	0.08
Peruvian	1	0.01
Other Hispanic or Latino	55	0.44
Hungarian	97	0.78
Irish	950	7.66
Italian	416	3.35
Lithuanian	44	0.35
Norwegian	154	1.24
Pennsylvania German	6	0.05
Polish	597	4.81
Romanian	36	0.29
Russian	47	0.38
Scandinavian	7	0.06
Scotch-Irish	43	0.35
Scottish	127	1.02
Slovak	47	0.38
Slovene	9	0.07
Swedish	101	0.81
Swiss	19	0.15
Ukrainian	10	0.08
United States or American	169	1.36
Welsh	22	0.18
West Indian, excl. Hispanic:	111	0.89
Haitian	23	0.19
Jamaican	75	0.60
Trinidadian and Tobagonian	6	0.05
West Indian	7	0.06
White:	4,653	37.13
Not Hispanic (4,232)	4,374	34.90
Hispanic (242)	279	2.23

River Forest

Place Type: Village
County: Cook
Population: 11,635

Ancestry/Race	Number	%
African American/Black:	602	5.17
Not Hispanic (553)	588	5.05
Hispanic (7)	14	0.12
African, sub-Saharan:	71	0.61
African	6	0.05
Ghanian	65	0.56
Alaska Native tribes, specified:	1	0.01
Aleut	1	0.01
Am. Ind. or Alaska Nat., not spec.	17	0.15
Alsatian	12	0.10
American Indian tribes, specified:	22	0.19
Blackfeet	1	0.01
Cherokee	9	0.08
Chippewa (1)	1	0.01
Iroquois	2	0.02
Latin American Indians (2)	5	0.04
Osage	1	0.01
All other tribes	3	0.03
American Indian tribes, not spec.	1	0.01
Arab:	133	1.14
Egyptian	52	0.45
Lebanese	60	0.52
Palestinian	9	0.08
Syrian	12	0.10
Armenian	57	0.49
Asian:	442	3.80
Bangladeshi (2)	2	0.02
Cambodian (1)	5	0.04
Chinese, ex. Taiwanese (89)	115	0.99
Filipino (88)	100	0.86
Indian (107)	115	0.99
Japanese (22)	36	0.31
Korean (27)	33	0.28
Laotian (1)	2	0.02
Sri Lankan (8)	8	0.07
Taiwanese (2)	2	0.02
Thai (8)	9	0.08
Other Asian, specified (2)	4	0.03
Other Asian, not specified (3)	11	0.09
Australian	17	0.15
Austrian	78	0.67
Belgian	57	0.49
British	70	0.60
Canadian	93	0.80
Celtic	6	0.05
Croatian	111	0.95
Czech	92	0.79
Czechoslovakian	17	0.15
Danish	41	0.35
Dutch	249	2.14
English	1,248	10.73
European	120	1.03
Finnish	7	0.06
French, except Basque	247	2.12
French Canadian	32	0.28
German	2,897	24.90
Greek	222	1.91
Hawaii Native/Pacific Islander:	6	0.05
Micronesian: (2)	2	0.02
Guamanian/Chamorro (2)	2	0.02
Polynesian:	1	0.01
Native Hawaiian	1	0.01
Other Pac. Isl., not spec. (3)	3	0.03
Hispanic or Latino:	466	4.01
Central American:	20	0.17
Costa Rican	1	0.01
Guatemalan	6	0.05
Honduran	1	0.01
Nicaraguan	8	0.07
Panamanian	3	0.03
Salvadoran	1	0.01
Cuban	29	0.25
Dominican Republic	10	0.09
Mexican	213	1.83
Puerto Rican	50	0.43
South American:	67	0.58
Argentinean	5	0.04
Bolivian	13	0.11
Chilean	7	0.06
Colombian	9	0.08
Ecuadorian	8	0.07
Peruvian	18	0.15
Venezuelan	5	0.04
Other South American	2	0.02
Other Hispanic or Latino	77	0.66
Hungarian	120	1.03
Icelander	8	0.07
Iranian	27	0.23
Irish	3,586	30.82
Italian	1,224	10.52
Latvian	4	0.03
Lithuanian	119	1.02
Luxemburger	8	0.07
Norwegian	334	2.87
Polish	708	6.09
Portuguese	16	0.14
Romanian	9	0.08
Russian	325	2.79
Scandinavian	12	0.10
Scotch-Irish	202	1.74
Scottish	314	2.70
Serbian	11	0.09
Slavic	10	0.09
Slovak	23	0.20
Slovene	31	0.27
Swedish	320	2.75
Swiss	120	1.03
Turkish	9	0.08
Ukrainian	4	0.03
United States or American	408	3.51
Welsh	52	0.45
West Indian, excl. Hispanic:	31	0.27
Jamaican	20	0.17
Trinidadian and Tobagonian	11	0.09
White:	10,554	90.71
Not Hispanic (10,084)	10,202	87.68
Hispanic (312)	352	3.03
Yugoslavian	33	0.28

River Grove

Place Type: Village
County: Cook
Population: 10,668

Ancestry/Race	Number	%
African American/Black:	49	0.46
Not Hispanic (34)	45	0.42
Hispanic (4)	4	0.04
Am. Ind. or Alaska Nat., not spec.	29	0.27
American Indian tribes, specified:	30	0.28
Blackfeet	3	0.03
Cherokee (2)	15	0.14
Chippewa (6)	6	0.06
Cree (1)	1	0.01
Pueblo (3)	3	0.03
All other tribes (2)	2	0.02
American Indian tribes, not spec.	3	0.03
Arab:	20	0.19
Jordanian	9	0.08
Moroccan	11	0.10
Asian:	263	2.47
Chinese, ex. Taiwanese (19)	30	0.28
Filipino (130)	148	1.39
Indian (42)	43	0.40
Japanese (2)	3	0.03
Korean (12)	12	0.11
Thai (3)	3	0.03
Vietnamese (5)	7	0.07
Other Asian, not specified	17	0.16
Assyrian/Chaldean/Syriac	20	0.19
Austrian	92	0.87
Belgian	9	0.08
British	30	0.28
Bulgarian	82	0.77
Croatian	69	0.65
Czech	109	1.03
Czechoslovakian	32	0.30
Danish	49	0.46
Dutch	118	1.11
English	243	2.29
European	27	0.25
Finnish	25	0.24
French, except Basque	187	1.76
French Canadian	22	0.21
German	1,812	17.07
Greek	111	1.05
Guyanese	12	0.11
Hawaii Native/Pacific Islander:	7	0.07
Micronesian: (1)	1	0.01
Other Micronesian (1)	1	0.01
Polynesian: (1)	1	0.01
Native Hawaiian (1)	1	0.01
Other Pac. Isl., not spec. (4)	5	0.05
Hispanic or Latino:	1,043	9.78
Central American:	31	0.29
Guatemalan	21	0.20
Salvadoran	10	0.09
Cuban	51	0.48
Dominican Republic	1	0.01
Mexican	591	5.54
Puerto Rican	216	2.02
South American:	44	0.41
Argentinean	5	0.05
Chilean	2	0.02

Notes: 1. Figures in the "Number" column do not add up to the total population due to: a) Ancestry/Race overlap — e.g. persons can report being both White and Irish, b) persons of Hispanic origin can report being any race, c) persons reporting two ancestries are counted in both categories. 2. Numbers in parentheses indicate the number of persons reporting this ancestry/race alone, not in combination with any other ancestry/race. 3. Refer to the Explanation of Data in the front of the book for more detailed information.

Ancestry/Race	Number	%
Colombian	18	0.17
Ecuadorian	6	0.06
Peruvian	9	0.08
Uruguayan	1	0.01
Other South American	3	0.03
Other Hispanic or Latino	109	1.02
Hungarian	13	0.12
Icelander	8	0.08
Irish	1,527	14.38
Italian	1,864	17.56
Lithuanian	52	0.49
Luxemburger	5	0.05
Norwegian	270	2.54
Polish	3,375	31.79
Russian	69	0.65
Scandinavian	19	0.18
Scotch-Irish	66	0.62
Scottish	33	0.31
Slovak	6	0.06
Slovene	20	0.19
Swedish	187	1.76
Swiss	7	0.07
Ukrainian	114	1.07
United States or American	325	3.06
Welsh	20	0.19
West Indian, excl. Hispanic:	6	0.06
Jamaican	6	0.06
White:	9,981	93.56
Not Hispanic (9,258)	9,344	87.59
Hispanic (583)	637	5.97
Yugoslavian	9	0.08

Riverdale

Place Type: Village
County: Cook
Population: 15,055

Ancestry/Race	Number	%
African American/Black:	13,151	87.35
Not Hispanic (12,942)	13,066	86.79
Hispanic (62)	85	0.56
African, sub-Saharan:	406	2.71
African	264	1.76
Liberian	120	0.80
Other sub-Saharan African	22	0.15
Alaska Native tribes, specified:	1	0.01
Eskimo	1	0.01
Am. Ind. or Alaska Nat., not spec.	31	0.21
American Indian tribes, specified:	24	0.16
Blackfeet (1)	5	0.03
Cherokee (2)	5	0.03
Choctaw	6	0.04
Cree	3	0.02
Crow	1	0.01
Lumbee	3	0.02
Sioux	1	0.01
American Indian tribes, not spec.	4	0.03
Arab:	33	0.22
Arab/Arabic	6	0.04
Iraqi	21	0.14
Other Arab	6	0.04
Asian:	56	0.37
Cambodian (6)	6	0.04
Chinese, ex. Taiwanese (1)	2	0.01
Filipino (9)	14	0.09
Indian (3)	8	0.05
Japanese (1)	5	0.03
Korean	3	0.02
Pakistani (3)	5	0.03
Vietnamese (2)	3	0.02
Other Asian, specified	6	0.04
Other Asian, not specified (2)	4	0.03
Assyrian/Chaldean/Syriac	21	0.14
Austrian	17	0.11
Canadian	12	0.08
Croatian	8	0.05
Czech	46	0.31
Czechoslovakian	32	0.21
Danish	21	0.14
Dutch	34	0.23
English	159	1.06
French, except Basque	26	0.17
German	410	2.73
Hawaii Native/Pacific Islander:	10	0.07
Micronesian: (6)	6	0.04
Guamanian/Chamorro (6)	6	0.04
Polynesian:	3	0.02
Native Hawaiian	3	0.02
Other Pac. Isl., not spec. (1)	1	0.01
Hispanic or Latino:	366	2.43
Central American:	1	0.01
Panamanian	1	0.01
Cuban	20	0.13
Dominican Republic	2	0.01
Mexican	253	1.68
Puerto Rican	53	0.35
South American:	11	0.07
Colombian	11	0.07
Other Hispanic or Latino	26	0.17
Hungarian	26	0.17
Irish	220	1.47
Israeli	19	0.13
Italian	156	1.04
Lithuanian	69	0.46
Norwegian	8	0.05
Polish	343	2.29
Scotch-Irish	20	0.13
Scottish	16	0.11
Slovak	16	0.11
Swedish	118	0.79
Swiss	9	0.06
Ukrainian	20	0.13
United States or American	78	0.52
Welsh	6	0.04
West Indian, excl. Hispanic:	80	0.53
Jamaican	80	0.53
White:	1,749	11.62
Not Hispanic (1,539)	1,613	10.71
Hispanic (128)	136	0.90

Rock Island

Place Type: City
County: Rock Island
Population: 39,684

Ancestry/Race	Number	%
African American/Black:	7,328	18.47
Not Hispanic (6,741)	7,200	18.14
Hispanic (73)	128	0.32
African, sub-Saharan:	221	0.56
African	184	0.46
Liberian	15	0.04
Nigerian	6	0.02
Sierra Leonean	16	0.04
Alaska Native tribes, specified:	2	0.01
Alaska Athabascan	1	0.00
Aleut (1)	1	0.00
Am. Ind. or Alaska Nat., not spec.	111	0.28
Albanian	14	0.04
American Indian tribes, specified:	177	0.45
Apache (7)	10	0.03
Blackfeet	21	0.05
Cherokee (12)	49	0.12
Cheyenne	1	0.00
Chickasaw (1)	3	0.01
Chippewa (3)	8	0.02
Choctaw (1)	6	0.02
Comanche (1)	5	0.01
Cree	3	0.01
Creek	1	0.00
Iroquois (2)	3	0.01
Kiowa	1	0.00
Latin American Indians (4)	5	0.01
Menominee	7	0.02
Potawatomi (5)	6	0.02
Seminole	4	0.01
Sioux (16)	32	0.08
Yaqui	1	0.00
All other tribes (2)	11	0.03
American Indian tribes, not spec.	6	0.02
Arab:	49	0.12
Lebanese	10	0.03
Moroccan	24	0.06
Other Arab	15	0.04
Armenian	5	0.01
Asian:	427	1.08
Cambodian (3)	4	0.01
Chinese, ex. Taiwanese (37)	56	0.14
Filipino (30)	52	0.13
Indian (79)	90	0.23
Japanese (23)	46	0.12
Korean (40)	52	0.13
Laotian (14)	20	0.05
Taiwanese	3	0.01
Thai	5	0.01
Vietnamese (56)	75	0.19
Other Asian, specified (2)	4	0.01
Other Asian, not specified (6)	20	0.05
Australian	14	0.04
Austrian	35	0.09
Basque	8	0.02
Belgian	1,480	3.73
Brazilian	7	0.02
British	114	0.29
Canadian	56	0.14
Celtic	7	0.02
Croatian	55	0.14
Czech	203	0.51
Czechoslovakian	77	0.19
Danish	305	0.77
Dutch	735	1.85
Eastern European	5	0.01
English	3,257	8.20
European	149	0.38
Finnish	34	0.09
French, except Basque	735	1.85
French Canadian	124	0.31
German	9,282	23.37
Greek	182	0.46
Hawaii Native/Pacific Islander:	33	0.08
Micronesian: (1)	1	0.00
Guamanian/Chamorro (1)	1	0.00
Polynesian: (15)	20	0.05
Native Hawaiian (3)	7	0.02
Samoan (11)	12	0.03
Tongan (1)	1	0.00
Other Pac. Isl., specified	1	0.00
Other Pac. Isl., not spec. (10)	11	0.03
Hispanic or Latino:	2,341	5.90
Central American:	20	0.05
Costa Rican	1	0.00
Guatemalan	2	0.01
Honduran	9	0.02
Nicaraguan	1	0.00
Panamanian	3	0.01
Salvadoran	2	0.01
Other Central American	2	0.01
Cuban	14	0.04
Dominican Republic	3	0.01
Mexican	1,998	5.03
Puerto Rican	55	0.14
South American:	30	0.08
Argentinean	8	0.02
Chilean	1	0.00
Colombian	7	0.02
Ecuadorian	9	0.02
Peruvian	1	0.00
Venezuelan	3	0.01
Other South American	1	0.00
Other Hispanic or Latino	221	0.56
Hungarian	127	0.32
Irish	5,259	13.24
Italian	1,178	2.97
Lithuanian	89	0.22
Luxemburger	17	0.04
Norwegian	633	1.59
Pennsylvania German	40	0.10
Polish	711	1.79

Notes: 1. Figures in the "Number" column do not add up to the total population due to: a) Ancestry/Race overlap — e.g. persons can report being both White and Irish, b) persons of Hispanic origin can report being any race, c) persons reporting two ancestries are counted in both categories. 2. Numbers in parentheses indicate the number of persons reporting this ancestry/race alone, not in combination with any other ancestry/race. 3. Refer to the Explanation of Data in the front of the book for more detailed information.

Ancestry/Race	Number	%
Portuguese	16	0.04
Romanian	51	0.13
Russian	129	0.32
Scandinavian	116	0.29
Scotch-Irish	465	1.17
Scottish	667	1.68
Serbian	11	0.03
Slavic	5	0.01
Slovak	35	0.09
Slovene	26	0.07
Swedish	2,309	5.81
Swiss	95	0.24
Ukrainian	52	0.13
United States or American	2,702	6.80
Welsh	314	0.79
West Indian, excl. Hispanic:	17	0.04
Haitian	17	0.04
White:	31,382	79.08
Not Hispanic (29,485)	30,098	75.84
Hispanic (1,124)	1,284	3.24
Yugoslavian	83	0.21

Rockford

Place Type: City
County: Winnebago
Population: 150,115

Ancestry/Race	Number	%
Acadian/Cajun	18	0.01
Afghan	5	0.00
African American/Black:	27,596	18.38
Not Hispanic (25,822)	27,162	18.09
Hispanic (250)	434	0.29
African, sub-Saharan:	1,481	0.99
African	1,432	0.96
Ethiopian	7	0.00
Ghanian	12	0.01
Nigerian	14	0.01
Other sub-Saharan African	16	0.01
Alaska Native tribes, specified:	1	0.00
Eskimo	1	0.00
Am. Ind. or Alaska Nat., not spec.	432	0.29
Albanian	81	0.05
American Indian tribes, specified:	793	0.53
Apache (8)	30	0.02
Blackfeet (8)	62	0.04
Cherokee (100)	346	0.23
Cheyenne	6	0.00
Chickasaw (1)	3	0.00
Chippewa (14)	31	0.02
Choctaw (4)	19	0.01
Comanche (2)	5	0.00
Cree (1)	5	0.00
Creek	2	0.00
Crow (2)	5	0.00
Delaware (2)	3	0.00
Iroquois (17)	25	0.02
Latin American Indians (66)	107	0.07
Lumbee	3	0.00
Menominee (7)	7	0.00
Navajo (8)	21	0.01
Osage (4)	4	0.00
Ottawa (3)	5	0.00
Paiute (2)	4	0.00
Pima (1)	1	0.00
Potawatomi	1	0.00
Pueblo (2)	2	0.00
Seminole (2)	9	0.01
Sioux (7)	41	0.03
Tohono O'Odham	1	0.00
Ute	4	0.00
Yaqui (1)	1	0.00
All other tribes (7)	40	0.03
American Indian tribes, not spec.	75	0.05
Arab:	315	0.21
Arab/Arabic	100	0.07
Egyptian	33	0.02
Iraqi	13	0.01
Lebanese	42	0.03
Palestinian	41	0.03
Syrian	86	0.06
Armenian	14	0.01
Asian:	3,930	2.62
Bangladeshi (2)	2	0.00
Cambodian	1	0.00
Chinese, ex. Taiwanese (257)	323	0.22
Filipino (433)	527	0.35
Hmong (11)	12	0.01
Indian (507)	583	0.39
Indonesian (10)	14	0.01
Japanese (120)	180	0.12
Korean (233)	265	0.18
Laotian (958)	1,085	0.72
Malaysian (5)	5	0.00
Pakistani (71)	88	0.06
Sri Lankan (9)	9	0.01
Taiwanese (4)	7	0.00
Thai (47)	78	0.05
Vietnamese (460)	531	0.35
Other Asian, specified (12)	16	0.01
Other Asian, not specified (114)	204	0.14
Assyrian/Chaldean/Syriac	8	0.01
Australian	29	0.02
Austrian	247	0.16
Belgian	325	0.22
Brazilian	11	0.01
British	491	0.33
Bulgarian	33	0.02
Canadian	181	0.12
Celtic	32	0.02
Croatian	173	0.12
Czech	514	0.34
Czechoslovakian	252	0.17
Danish	847	0.57
Dutch	2,264	1.51
Eastern European	6	0.00
English	11,885	7.94
Estonian	5	0.00
European	376	0.25
Finnish	271	0.18
French, except Basque	3,501	2.34
French Canadian	546	0.36
German	29,443	19.67
Greek	357	0.24
Guyanese	41	0.03
Hawaii Native/Pacific Islander:	131	0.09
Micronesian: (4)	8	0.01
Guamanian/Chamorro (4)	8	0.01
Polynesian: (48)	71	0.05
Native Hawaiian (15)	33	0.02
Samoan (32)	36	0.02
Tongan	1	0.00
Other Polynesian (1)	1	0.00
Other Pac. Isl., specified	2	0.00
Other Pac. Isl., not spec. (15)	50	0.03
Hispanic or Latino:	15,278	10.18
Central American:	220	0.15
Costa Rican	42	0.03
Guatemalan	75	0.05
Honduran	49	0.03
Nicaraguan	2	0.00
Panamanian	13	0.01
Salvadoran	33	0.02
Other Central American	6	0.00
Cuban	310	0.21
Dominican Republic	30	0.02
Mexican	12,508	8.33
Puerto Rican	451	0.30
South American:	303	0.20
Argentinean	13	0.01
Bolivian	13	0.01
Chilean	15	0.01
Colombian	174	0.12
Ecuadorian	15	0.01
Paraguayan	1	0.00
Peruvian	29	0.02
Uruguayan	19	0.01
Venezuelan	7	0.00
Other South American	17	0.01
Other Hispanic or Latino	1,456	0.97
Hungarian	238	0.16
Icelander	6	0.00
Iranian	96	0.06
Irish	16,786	11.21
Italian	10,571	7.06
Latvian	75	0.05
Lithuanian	829	0.55
Luxemburger	22	0.01
Macedonian	18	0.01
Northern European	63	0.04
Norwegian	5,394	3.60
Pennsylvania German	232	0.15
Polish	4,948	3.31
Portuguese	45	0.03
Romanian	90	0.06
Russian	321	0.21
Scandinavian	217	0.14
Scotch-Irish	1,614	1.08
Scottish	1,811	1.21
Serbian	151	0.10
Slavic	48	0.03
Slovak	118	0.08
Slovene	66	0.04
Swedish	14,720	9.83
Swiss	642	0.43
Ukrainian	304	0.20
United States or American	6,352	4.24
Welsh	693	0.46
West Indian, excl. Hispanic:	94	0.06
Dutch West Indian	4	0.00
Jamaican	90	0.06
White:	112,487	74.93
Not Hispanic (102,678)	104,846	69.84
Hispanic (6,625)	7,641	5.09
Yugoslavian	590	0.39

Rolling Meadows

Place Type: City
County: Cook
Population: 24,604

Ancestry/Race	Number	%
African American/Black:	790	3.21
Not Hispanic (662)	730	2.97
Hispanic (34)	60	0.24
African, sub-Saharan:	62	0.25
African	45	0.18
Kenyan	17	0.07
Am. Ind. or Alaska Nat., not spec.	71	0.29
Albanian	8	0.03
American Indian tribes, specified:	59	0.24
Apache (2)	5	0.02
Blackfeet	2	0.01
Cherokee (3)	13	0.05
Chippewa (1)	2	0.01
Choctaw (1)	1	0.00
Comanche (1)	1	0.00
Iroquois (1)	1	0.00
Latin American Indians (10)	16	0.07
Seminole	1	0.00
Shoshone	2	0.01
Sioux (3)	5	0.02
Tohono O'Odham (2)	2	0.01
All other tribes	8	0.03
American Indian tribes, not spec.	6	0.02
Arab:	86	0.35
Arab/Arabic	28	0.11
Syrian	58	0.24
Armenian	32	0.13
Asian:	1,816	7.38
Chinese, ex. Taiwanese (238)	287	1.17
Filipino (259)	313	1.27
Hmong (10)	10	0.04
Indian (499)	512	2.08
Indonesian (2)	2	0.01
Japanese (175)	214	0.87
Korean (295)	327	1.33
Laotian (9)	9	0.04

Notes: 1. Figures in the "Number" column do not add up to the total population due to: a) Ancestry/Race overlap — e.g. persons can report being both White and Irish, b) persons of Hispanic origin can report being any race, c) persons reporting two ancestries are counted in both categories. 2. Numbers in parentheses indicate the number of persons reporting this ancestry/race alone, not in combination with any other ancestry/race. 3. Refer to the Explanation of Data in the front of the book for more detailed information.

Malaysian (9)	9	0.04
Pakistani (26)	38	0.15
Sri Lankan (4)	4	0.02
Taiwanese (16)	27	0.11
Thai (8)	8	0.03
Vietnamese (18)	19	0.08
Other Asian, specified (3)	7	0.03
Other Asian, not specified (17)	30	0.12
Assyrian/Chaldean/Syriac	66	0.27
Austrian	139	0.56
Belgian	170	0.69
Brazilian	16	0.06
British	59	0.24
Bulgarian	7	0.03
Canadian	30	0.12
Croatian	82	0.33
Czech	306	1.24
Czechoslovakian	102	0.41
Danish	175	0.71
Dutch	320	1.30
Eastern European	14	0.06
English	1,568	6.37
European	117	0.48
Finnish	41	0.17
French, except Basque	513	2.08
French Canadian	194	0.79
German	6,533	26.54
Greek	459	1.86
Hawaii Native/Pacific Islander:	18	0.07
Micronesian: (2)	2	0.01
Guamanian/Chamorro (2)	2	0.01
Polynesian: (3)	5	0.02
Native Hawaiian (3)	5	0.02
Other Pac. Isl., not spec. (2)	11	0.04
Hispanic or Latino:	4,725	19.20
Central American:	214	0.87
Costa Rican	1	0.00
Guatemalan	22	0.09
Honduran	6	0.02
Nicaraguan	3	0.01
Panamanian	3	0.01
Salvadoran	170	0.69
Other Central American	9	0.04
Cuban	40	0.16
Dominican Republic	6	0.02
Mexican	3,905	15.87
Puerto Rican	137	0.56
South American:	94	0.38
Argentinean	6	0.02
Bolivian	4	0.02
Chilean	10	0.04
Colombian	34	0.14
Ecuadorian	18	0.07
Paraguayan	2	0.01
Peruvian	14	0.06
Venezuelan	2	0.01
Other South American	4	0.02
Other Hispanic or Latino	329	1.34
Hungarian	136	0.55
Iranian	5	0.02
Irish	3,675	14.93
Israeli	25	0.10
Italian	2,319	9.42
Latvian	6	0.02
Lithuanian	79	0.32
Luxemburger	81	0.33
Norwegian	572	2.32
Pennsylvania German	7	0.03
Polish	2,886	11.72
Portuguese	23	0.09
Romanian	34	0.14
Russian	178	0.72
Scandinavian	44	0.18
Scotch-Irish	332	1.35
Scottish	384	1.56
Serbian	32	0.13
Slavic	7	0.03
Slovak	76	0.31
Slovene	19	0.08
Swedish	931	3.78
Swiss	103	0.42
Ukrainian	64	0.26
United States or American	525	2.13
Welsh	107	0.43
West Indian, excl. Hispanic:	9	0.04
Jamaican	9	0.04
White:	20,685	84.07
Not Hispanic (17,282)	17,504	71.14
Hispanic (2,974)	3,181	12.93
Yugoslavian	30	0.12

Romeoville

Place Type: Village
County: Will
Population: 21,153

Ancestry/Race	Number	%
African American/Black:	1,265	5.98
Not Hispanic (1,121)	1,229	5.81
Hispanic (16)	36	0.17
African, sub-Saharan:	224	1.06
African	140	0.66
Ethiopian	33	0.16
Ghanian	46	0.22
Kenyan	5	0.02
Alaska Native tribes, specified:	1	0.00
Eskimo	1	0.00
Am. Ind. or Alaska Nat., not spec.	74	0.35
American Indian tribes, specified:	121	0.57
Apache (5)	10	0.05
Blackfeet	6	0.03
Cherokee (10)	49	0.23
Chippewa (5)	8	0.04
Choctaw (2)	2	0.01
Delaware (5)	6	0.03
Latin American Indians (4)	7	0.03
Lumbee (1)	4	0.02
Navajo (2)	5	0.02
Seminole	1	0.00
Sioux (1)	3	0.01
All other tribes (10)	20	0.09
American Indian tribes, not spec.	10	0.05
Arab:	50	0.24
Iraqi	39	0.18
Lebanese	11	0.05
Asian:	627	2.96
Cambodian (2)	8	0.04
Chinese, ex. Taiwanese (31)	39	0.18
Filipino (256)	294	1.39
Indian (108)	116	0.55
Indonesian (6)	9	0.04
Japanese (8)	26	0.12
Korean (30)	36	0.17
Laotian (16)	23	0.11
Malaysian (2)	3	0.01
Pakistani (13)	15	0.07
Sri Lankan (4)	4	0.02
Taiwanese (1)	1	0.00
Thai (10)	12	0.06
Vietnamese (22)	31	0.15
Other Asian, not specified (3)	10	0.05
Assyrian/Chaldean/Syriac	14	0.07
Austrian	48	0.23
Brazilian	25	0.12
British	51	0.24
Canadian	29	0.14
Croatian	86	0.41
Czech	744	3.52
Czechoslovakian	105	0.50
Danish	106	0.50
Dutch	498	2.36
Eastern European	8	0.04
English	1,061	5.02
European	87	0.41
Finnish	17	0.08
French, except Basque	577	2.73
French Canadian	56	0.26
German	4,826	22.83
Greek	132	0.62
Hawaii Native/Pacific Islander:	11	0.05
Polynesian: (5)	6	0.03
Native Hawaiian (4)	5	0.02
Samoan (1)	1	0.00
Other Pac. Isl., not spec.	5	0.02
Hispanic or Latino:	2,781	13.15
Central American:	45	0.21
Costa Rican	8	0.04
Guatemalan	22	0.10
Honduran	12	0.06
Salvadoran	2	0.01
Other Central American	1	0.00
Cuban	15	0.07
Dominican Republic	8	0.04
Mexican	2,079	9.83
Puerto Rican	328	1.55
South American:	51	0.24
Argentinean	2	0.01
Bolivian	5	0.02
Colombian	14	0.07
Ecuadorian	14	0.07
Peruvian	7	0.03
Uruguayan	1	0.00
Venezuelan	4	0.02
Other South American	4	0.02
Other Hispanic or Latino	255	1.21
Hungarian	110	0.52
Icelander	12	0.06
Irish	4,087	19.33
Italian	2,078	9.83
Lithuanian	301	1.42
Norwegian	225	1.06
Polish	3,312	15.67
Portuguese	7	0.03
Romanian	17	0.08
Russian	171	0.81
Scandinavian	46	0.22
Scotch-Irish	325	1.54
Scottish	244	1.15
Serbian	27	0.13
Slavic	29	0.14
Slovak	221	1.05
Slovene	11	0.05
Swedish	547	2.59
Swiss	21	0.10
Ukrainian	26	0.12
United States or American	729	3.45
Welsh	111	0.53
White:	18,324	86.63
Not Hispanic (16,336)	16,631	78.62
Hispanic (1,536)	1,693	8.00
Yugoslavian	122	0.58

Roselle

Place Type: Village
County: Du Page
Population: 23,115

Ancestry/Race	Number	%
African American/Black:	434	1.88
Not Hispanic (377)	419	1.81
Hispanic (6)	15	0.06
Am. Ind. or Alaska Nat., not spec.	34	0.15
Albanian	28	0.12
American Indian tribes, specified:	63	0.27
Apache	1	0.00
Cherokee (6)	16	0.07
Cheyenne	1	0.00
Chippewa (3)	4	0.02
Comanche	1	0.00
Creek (1)	1	0.00
Iroquois (4)	5	0.02
Latin American Indians (5)	5	0.02
Menominee (1)	1	0.00
Navajo	3	0.01
Osage	2	0.01
Ottawa (1)	1	0.00
Pima (1)	1	0.00
Potawatomi (1)	2	0.01

Notes: 1. Figures in the "Number" column do not add up to the total population due to: a) Ancestry/Race overlap — e.g. persons can report being both White and Irish, b) persons of Hispanic origin can report being any race, c) persons reporting two ancestries are counted in both categories. 2. Numbers in parentheses indicate the number of persons reporting this ancestry/race alone, not in combination with any other ancestry/race. 3. Refer to the Explanation of Data in the front of the book for more detailed information.

Sioux (2)	5	0.02
All other tribes (6)	14	0.06
American Indian tribes, not spec.	5	0.02
Arab:	206	0.88
Arab/Arabic	138	0.59
Egyptian	26	0.11
Iraqi	10	0.04
Palestinian	7	0.03
Syrian	25	0.11
Asian:	1,862	8.06
Bangladeshi (8)	8	0.03
Cambodian (1)	1	0.00
Chinese, ex. Taiwanese (170)	183	0.79
Filipino (335)	390	1.69
Indian (695)	732	3.17
Japanese (113)	153	0.66
Korean (193)	204	0.88
Laotian (5)	5	0.02
Malaysian (1)	1	0.00
Pakistani (73)	98	0.42
Taiwanese (19)	22	0.10
Thai (12)	15	0.06
Vietnamese (21)	27	0.12
Other Asian, specified	1	0.00
Other Asian, not specified (14)	22	0.10
Assyrian/Chaldean/Syriac	16	0.07
Austrian	237	1.02
Belgian	76	0.33
British	12	0.05
Bulgarian	89	0.38
Canadian	28	0.12
Croatian	96	0.41
Czech	322	1.38
Czechoslovakian	113	0.49
Danish	169	0.73
Dutch	274	1.18
English	1,725	7.41
European	38	0.16
Finnish	65	0.28
French, except Basque	778	3.34
French Canadian	96	0.41
German	6,577	28.25
Greek	336	1.44
Hawaii Native/Pacific Islander:	26	0.11
Micronesian: (5)	5	0.02
Guamanian/Chamorro (5)	5	0.02
Polynesian: (4)	11	0.05
Native Hawaiian (2)	9	0.04
Samoan (2)	2	0.01
Other Pac. Isl., not spec. (2)	10	0.04
Hispanic or Latino:	1,197	5.18
Central American:	29	0.13
Costa Rican	1	0.00
Guatemalan	24	0.10
Panamanian	3	0.01
Other Central American	1	0.00
Cuban	65	0.28
Dominican Republic	8	0.03
Mexican	736	3.18
Puerto Rican	125	0.54
South American:	100	0.43
Argentinean	14	0.06
Chilean	8	0.03
Colombian	35	0.15
Ecuadorian	25	0.11
Peruvian	6	0.03
Uruguayan	5	0.02
Venezuelan	4	0.02
Other South American	3	0.01
Other Hispanic or Latino	134	0.58
Hungarian	171	0.73
Iranian	55	0.24
Irish	3,968	17.04
Italian	3,722	15.99
Lithuanian	226	0.97
Luxemburger	39	0.17
Norwegian	501	2.15
Pennsylvania German	20	0.09
Polish	3,980	17.10
Portuguese	22	0.09
Romanian	104	0.45
Russian	351	1.51
Scandinavian	52	0.22
Scotch-Irish	345	1.48
Scottish	218	0.94
Serbian	4	0.02
Slovak	112	0.48
Slovene	28	0.12
Swedish	776	3.33
Swiss	10	0.04
Turkish	83	0.36
Ukrainian	164	0.70
United States or American	545	2.34
Welsh	129	0.55
West Indian, excl. Hispanic:	29	0.12
Haitian	29	0.12
White:	20,608	89.15
Not Hispanic (19,578)	19,780	85.57
Hispanic (737)	828	3.58
Yugoslavian	76	0.33

Round Lake Beach

Place Type: Village
County: Lake
Population: 25,859

Ancestry/Race	Number	%
African American/Black:	933	3.61
Not Hispanic (740)	851	3.29
Hispanic (52)	82	0.32
African, sub-Saharan:	35	0.14
African	35	0.14
Am. Ind. or Alaska Nat., not spec.	146	0.56
American Indian tribes, specified:	157	0.61
Apache	5	0.02
Blackfeet	13	0.05
Cherokee (4)	37	0.14
Cheyenne (1)	1	0.00
Chickasaw (1)	1	0.00
Chippewa (16)	29	0.11
Choctaw (2)	4	0.02
Comanche (1)	7	0.03
Cree (1)	1	0.00
Iroquois (4)	4	0.02
Latin American Indians (19)	20	0.08
Lumbee (1)	1	0.00
Menominee (3)	3	0.01
Navajo	2	0.01
Ottawa (5)	5	0.02
Seminole (4)	4	0.02
Shoshone (4)	4	0.02
Sioux (1)	8	0.03
Yaqui (1)	1	0.00
All other tribes (2)	7	0.03
American Indian tribes, not spec.	19	0.07
Armenian	63	0.25
Asian:	690	2.67
Chinese, ex. Taiwanese (41)	60	0.23
Filipino (210)	272	1.05
Indian (121)	134	0.52
Japanese (22)	57	0.22
Korean (51)	57	0.22
Laotian	1	0.00
Pakistani (17)	17	0.07
Sri Lankan (1)	3	0.01
Taiwanese (1)	1	0.00
Thai (13)	17	0.07
Vietnamese (48)	60	0.23
Other Asian, not specified (4)	11	0.04
Assyrian/Chaldean/Syriac	27	0.11
Austrian	48	0.19
Belgian	51	0.20
Brazilian	7	0.03
British	120	0.47
Bulgarian	16	0.06
Canadian	54	0.21
Croatian	56	0.22
Czech	159	0.62
Czechoslovakian	42	0.16
Danish	131	0.51
Dutch	226	0.88
Eastern European	6	0.02
English	1,580	6.16
European	60	0.23
Finnish	78	0.30
French, except Basque	503	1.96
French Canadian	51	0.20
German	6,079	23.69
Greek	102	0.40
Hawaii Native/Pacific Islander:	27	0.10
Micronesian:	4	0.02
Guamanian/Chamorro	3	0.01
Other Micronesian	1	0.00
Polynesian: (5)	13	0.05
Native Hawaiian (5)	11	0.04
Samoan	2	0.01
Other Pac. Isl., not spec. (6)	10	0.04
Hispanic or Latino:	8,084	31.26
Central American:	182	0.70
Costa Rican	1	0.00
Guatemalan	35	0.14
Honduran	21	0.08
Nicaraguan	6	0.02
Panamanian	1	0.00
Salvadoran	113	0.44
Other Central American	5	0.02
Cuban	46	0.18
Dominican Republic	1	0.00
Mexican	6,880	26.61
Puerto Rican	318	1.23
South American:	131	0.51
Argentinean	17	0.07
Bolivian	13	0.05
Chilean	5	0.02
Colombian	47	0.18
Ecuadorian	27	0.10
Paraguayan	1	0.00
Peruvian	14	0.05
Other South American	7	0.03
Other Hispanic or Latino	526	2.03
Hungarian	132	0.51
Iranian	8	0.03
Irish	3,532	13.77
Italian	1,235	4.81
Latvian	49	0.19
Lithuanian	123	0.48
Macedonian	8	0.03
Northern European	39	0.15
Norwegian	638	2.49
Pennsylvania German	9	0.04
Polish	2,619	10.21
Portuguese	19	0.07
Romanian	45	0.18
Russian	181	0.71
Scandinavian	59	0.23
Scotch-Irish	185	0.72
Scottish	205	0.80
Serbian	21	0.08
Slavic	12	0.05
Slovak	60	0.23
Slovene	37	0.14
Swedish	492	1.92
Swiss	65	0.25
Ukrainian	183	0.71
United States or American	1,310	5.11
Welsh	74	0.29
West Indian, excl. Hispanic:	32	0.12
Haitian	5	0.02
Jamaican	27	0.11
White:	19,907	76.98
Not Hispanic (16,057)	16,387	63.37
Hispanic (3,170)	3,520	13.61
Yugoslavian	83	0.32

Notes: 1. Figures in the "Number" column do not add up to the total population due to: a) Ancestry/Race overlap — e.g. persons can report being both White and Irish, b) persons of Hispanic origin can report being any race, c) persons reporting two ancestries are counted in both categories. 2. Numbers in parentheses indicate the number of persons reporting this ancestry/race alone, not in combination with any other ancestry/race. 3. Refer to the Explanation of Data in the front of the book for more detailed information.

Saint Charles

Place Type: City
County: Kane
Population: 27,896

Ancestry/Race	Number	%
African American/Black:	518	1.86
Not Hispanic (450)	495	1.77
Hispanic (12)	23	0.08
African, sub-Saharan:	47	0.17
African	47	0.17
Am. Ind. or Alaska Nat., not spec.	28	0.10
Albanian	5	0.02
Alsatian	13	0.05
American Indian tribes, specified:	78	0.28
Apache (2)	2	0.01
Blackfeet	1	0.00
Cherokee (11)	29	0.10
Chippewa (1)	3	0.01
Choctaw (1)	3	0.01
Delaware	1	0.00
Iroquois	1	0.00
Latin American Indians (12)	24	0.09
Navajo (1)	1	0.00
Seminole	2	0.01
Shoshone	2	0.01
Sioux (1)	4	0.01
All other tribes (2)	5	0.02
Arab:	65	0.23
Lebanese	51	0.18
Moroccan	9	0.03
Syrian	5	0.02
Armenian	16	0.06
Asian:	604	2.17
Cambodian (10)	10	0.04
Chinese, ex. Taiwanese (68)	83	0.30
Filipino (106)	128	0.46
Indian (140)	151	0.54
Indonesian (3)	8	0.03
Japanese (25)	46	0.16
Korean (69)	81	0.29
Laotian (19)	19	0.07
Malaysian (1)	1	0.00
Pakistani (20)	24	0.09
Taiwanese (4)	4	0.01
Thai (3)	6	0.02
Vietnamese (12)	16	0.06
Other Asian, specified (2)	2	0.01
Other Asian, not specified (10)	25	0.09
Austrian	165	0.59
Belgian	229	0.82
British	92	0.33
Canadian	91	0.33
Croatian	81	0.29
Czech	535	1.91
Czechoslovakian	88	0.31
Danish	302	1.08
Dutch	577	2.06
English	3,412	12.21
European	181	0.65
Finnish	83	0.30
French, except Basque	1,011	3.62
French Canadian	224	0.80
German	8,298	29.68
Greek	212	0.76
Hawaii Native/Pacific Islander:	13	0.05
Melanesian:	1	0.00
Fijian	1	0.00
Polynesian:	5	0.02
Native Hawaiian	4	0.01
Samoan	1	0.00
Other Pac. Isl., not spec. (1)	7	0.03
Hispanic or Latino:	1,535	5.50
Central American:	22	0.08
Costa Rican	1	0.00
Guatemalan	9	0.03
Honduran	7	0.03
Nicaraguan	1	0.00
Panamanian	3	0.01
Salvadoran	1	0.00
Cuban	22	0.08
Dominican Republic	1	0.00
Mexican	1,127	4.04
Puerto Rican	105	0.38
South American:	64	0.23
Argentinean	9	0.03
Bolivian	8	0.03
Chilean	4	0.01
Colombian	25	0.09
Ecuadorian	3	0.01
Peruvian	9	0.03
Uruguayan	5	0.02
Venezuelan	1	0.00
Other Hispanic or Latino	194	0.70
Hungarian	147	0.53
Irish	5,003	17.90
Italian	2,692	9.63
Latvian	48	0.17
Lithuanian	290	1.04
Luxemburger	25	0.09
Macedonian	38	0.14
Northern European	31	0.11
Norwegian	740	2.65
Pennsylvania German	8	0.03
Polish	2,955	10.57
Portuguese	30	0.11
Romanian	37	0.13
Russian	201	0.72
Scandinavian	55	0.20
Scotch-Irish	420	1.50
Scottish	722	2.58
Serbian	31	0.11
Slavic	29	0.10
Slovak	195	0.70
Slovene	52	0.19
Swedish	1,631	5.83
Swiss	109	0.39
Ukrainian	295	1.06
United States or American	1,001	3.58
Welsh	266	0.95
West Indian, excl. Hispanic:	22	0.08
Haitian	11	0.04
Jamaican	4	0.01
West Indian	7	0.03
White:	26,384	94.58
Not Hispanic (25,212)	25,359	90.91
Hispanic (957)	1,025	3.67
Yugoslavian	138	0.49

Sauk Village

Place Type: Village
County: Cook
Population: 10,411

Ancestry/Race	Number	%
African American/Black:	3,563	34.22
Not Hispanic (3,338)	3,469	33.32
Hispanic (44)	94	0.90
African, sub-Saharan:	58	0.56
African	51	0.49
Nigerian	7	0.07
Am. Ind. or Alaska Nat., not spec.	45	0.43
American Indian tribes, specified:	64	0.61
Blackfeet	2	0.02
Cherokee (3)	24	0.23
Chippewa (4)	6	0.06
Choctaw	1	0.01
Comanche	1	0.01
Creek (1)	4	0.04
Iroquois (1)	4	0.04
Latin American Indians	6	0.06
Pueblo (1)	4	0.04
Seminole	3	0.03
Sioux (1)	2	0.02
All other tribes (2)	7	0.07
American Indian tribes, not spec.	4	0.04
Asian:	110	1.06
Chinese, ex. Taiwanese (1)	6	0.06
Filipino (30)	50	0.48
Indian (10)	22	0.21
Japanese (3)	3	0.03
Korean (11)	14	0.13
Laotian (6)	6	0.06
Pakistani	1	0.01
Thai (1)	1	0.01
Vietnamese (7)	7	0.07
Austrian	19	0.18
Belgian	31	0.30
British	44	0.42
Canadian	33	0.32
Croatian	175	1.68
Czech	47	0.45
Czechoslovakian	12	0.12
Danish	38	0.36
Dutch	294	2.82
English	575	5.52
European	27	0.26
Finnish	13	0.12
French, except Basque	263	2.52
French Canadian	12	0.12
German	1,882	18.07
Greek	60	0.58
Hawaii Native/Pacific Islander:	11	0.11
Melanesian: (4)	4	0.04
Fijian (4)	4	0.04
Micronesian:	1	0.01
Guamanian/Chamorro	1	0.01
Polynesian:	2	0.02
Native Hawaiian	2	0.02
Other Pac. Isl., not spec.	4	0.04
Hispanic or Latino:	1,224	11.76
Central American:	30	0.29
Guatemalan	3	0.03
Honduran	10	0.10
Panamanian	8	0.08
Salvadoran	8	0.08
Other Central American	1	0.01
Cuban	9	0.09
Mexican	951	9.13
Puerto Rican	81	0.78
South American:	5	0.05
Chilean	2	0.02
Colombian	1	0.01
Ecuadorian	1	0.01
Other South American	1	0.01
Other Hispanic or Latino	148	1.42
Hungarian	88	0.84
Irish	1,331	12.78
Italian	524	5.03
Latvian	7	0.07
Lithuanian	108	1.04
Norwegian	72	0.69
Polish	841	8.07
Russian	38	0.36
Scotch-Irish	107	1.03
Scottish	94	0.90
Serbian	6	0.06
Slovak	29	0.28
Swedish	180	1.73
Swiss	6	0.06
Ukrainian	16	0.15
United States or American	338	3.24
Welsh	18	0.17
West Indian, excl. Hispanic:	69	0.66
Belizean	46	0.44
Jamaican	23	0.22
White:	6,518	62.61
Not Hispanic (5,540)	5,702	54.77
Hispanic (681)	816	7.84
Yugoslavian	5	0.05

Schaumburg

Place Type: Village
County: Cook
Population: 75,386

Ancestry/Race	Number	%

Notes: 1. Figures in the "Number" column do not add up to the total population due to: a) Ancestry/Race overlap — e.g. persons can report being both White and Irish, b) persons of Hispanic origin can report being any race, c) persons reporting two ancestries are counted in both categories. 2. Numbers in parentheses indicate the number of persons reporting this ancestry/race alone, not in combination with any other ancestry/race. 3. Refer to the Explanation of Data in the front of the book for more detailed information.

African American/Black:	2,790	3.70
Not Hispanic (2,479)	2,716	3.60
Hispanic (47)	74	0.10
African, sub-Saharan:	362	0.49
African	237	0.32
Ghanian	7	0.01
Kenyan	19	0.03
South African	84	0.11
Other sub-Saharan African	15	0.02
Alaska Native tribes, specified:	1	0.00
Eskimo	1	0.00
Am. Ind. or Alaska Nat., not spec.	108	0.14
Albanian	94	0.13
Alsatian	8	0.01
American Indian tribes, specified:	183	0.24
Apache	6	0.01
Blackfeet	9	0.01
Cherokee (7)	63	0.08
Chickasaw	1	0.00
Chippewa (4)	12	0.02
Choctaw (3)	11	0.01
Comanche	5	0.01
Cree	6	0.01
Creek	1	0.00
Iroquois (4)	8	0.01
Latin American Indians (2)	11	0.01
Lumbee (1)	1	0.00
Menominee	1	0.00
Navajo (1)	9	0.01
Osage	1	0.00
Ottawa (3)	4	0.01
Potawatomi (2)	3	0.00
Seminole (1)	2	0.00
Shoshone (1)	1	0.00
Sioux (3)	9	0.01
All other tribes (8)	19	0.03
American Indian tribes, not spec.	13	0.02
Arab:	555	0.74
Arab/Arabic	84	0.11
Egyptian	23	0.03
Iraqi	21	0.03
Jordanian	42	0.06
Lebanese	160	0.21
Palestinian	67	0.09
Syrian	92	0.12
Other Arab	66	0.09
Armenian	130	0.17
Asian:	11,373	15.09
Bangladeshi (10)	13	0.02
Cambodian (12)	12	0.02
Chinese, ex. Taiwanese (1,296)	1,403	1.86
Filipino (1,037)	1,196	1.59
Indian (4,864)	5,006	6.64
Indonesian (26)	36	0.05
Japanese (1,106)	1,214	1.61
Korean (1,575)	1,641	2.18
Laotian (16)	16	0.02
Malaysian (13)	20	0.03
Pakistani (279)	326	0.43
Sri Lankan (7)	7	0.01
Taiwanese (92)	109	0.14
Thai (49)	65	0.09
Vietnamese (85)	104	0.14
Other Asian, specified (18)	23	0.03
Other Asian, not specified (116)	182	0.24
Assyrian/Chaldean/Syriac	272	0.37
Australian	48	0.06
Austrian	640	0.86
Belgian	226	0.30
Brazilian	27	0.04
British	253	0.34
Bulgarian	103	0.14
Canadian	68	0.09
Croatian	221	0.30
Czech	1,356	1.82
Czechoslovakian	250	0.34
Danish	617	0.83
Dutch	789	1.06
Eastern European	77	0.10
English	4,038	5.42
Estonian	31	0.04
European	350	0.47
Finnish	198	0.27
French, except Basque	1,662	2.23
French Canadian	373	0.50
German	18,501	24.83
Greek	1,152	1.55
Hawaii Native/Pacific Islander:	88	0.12
Micronesian: (3)	4	0.01
Guamanian/Chamorro (1)	2	0.00
Other Micronesian (2)	2	0.00
Polynesian: (23)	41	0.05
Native Hawaiian (12)	20	0.03
Samoan (10)	18	0.02
Other Polynesian (1)	3	0.00
Other Pac. Isl., specified	4	0.01
Other Pac. Isl., not spec. (17)	39	0.05
Hispanic or Latino:	3,988	5.29
Central American:	125	0.17
Costa Rican	9	0.01
Guatemalan	58	0.08
Honduran	10	0.01
Nicaraguan	5	0.01
Panamanian	7	0.01
Salvadoran	26	0.03
Other Central American	10	0.01
Cuban	142	0.19
Dominican Republic	16	0.02
Mexican	2,449	3.25
Puerto Rican	409	0.54
South American:	331	0.44
Argentinean	33	0.04
Bolivian	8	0.01
Chilean	25	0.03
Colombian	127	0.17
Ecuadorian	62	0.08
Paraguayan	2	0.00
Peruvian	48	0.06
Uruguayan	3	0.00
Venezuelan	11	0.01
Other South American	12	0.02
Other Hispanic or Latino	516	0.68
Hungarian	597	0.80
Icelander	14	0.02
Iranian	175	0.23
Irish	11,176	15.00
Israeli	7	0.01
Italian	9,392	12.60
Latvian	41	0.06
Lithuanian	514	0.69
Luxemburger	154	0.21
Macedonian	18	0.02
Maltese	19	0.03
Northern European	17	0.02
Norwegian	1,800	2.42
Pennsylvania German	17	0.02
Polish	11,109	14.91
Portuguese	80	0.11
Romanian	114	0.15
Russian	874	1.17
Scandinavian	156	0.21
Scotch-Irish	545	0.73
Scottish	1,092	1.47
Serbian	59	0.08
Slavic	49	0.07
Slovak	414	0.56
Slovene	31	0.04
Swedish	2,380	3.19
Swiss	190	0.25
Turkish	141	0.19
Ukrainian	626	0.84
United States or American	1,633	2.19
Welsh	391	0.52
West Indian, excl. Hispanic:	118	0.16
Bahamian	8	0.01
Belizean	12	0.02
British West Indian	11	0.01
Haitian	27	0.04
Jamaican	43	0.06
Trinidadian and Tobagonian	12	0.02
West Indian	5	0.01
White:	60,492	80.24
Not Hispanic (56,953)	57,832	76.71
Hispanic (2,438)	2,660	3.53
Yugoslavian	228	0.31

Schiller Park

Place Type: Village
County: Cook
Population: 11,850

Ancestry/Race	Number	%
African American/Black:	270	2.28
Not Hispanic (211)	236	1.99
Hispanic (24)	34	0.29
Am. Ind. or Alaska Nat., not spec.	33	0.28
American Indian tribes, specified:	55	0.46
Blackfeet	2	0.02
Cherokee (5)	15	0.13
Chippewa (1)	5	0.04
Choctaw	3	0.03
Iroquois (1)	5	0.04
Latin American Indians (10)	13	0.11
Menominee	4	0.03
Navajo (2)	2	0.02
Sioux	2	0.02
All other tribes	4	0.03
American Indian tribes, not spec.	6	0.05
Arab:	234	1.99
Arab/Arabic	91	0.77
Jordanian	33	0.28
Palestinian	75	0.64
Syrian	35	0.30
Asian:	699	5.90
Cambodian (2)	4	0.03
Chinese, ex. Taiwanese (20)	22	0.19
Filipino (169)	195	1.65
Indian (309)	333	2.81
Japanese (7)	13	0.11
Korean (13)	14	0.12
Pakistani (29)	34	0.29
Taiwanese (11)	11	0.09
Thai (13)	13	0.11
Vietnamese (14)	14	0.12
Other Asian, specified (7)	7	0.06
Other Asian, not specified (10)	39	0.33
Austrian	15	0.13
Belgian	7	0.06
Brazilian	21	0.18
British	10	0.08
Bulgarian	244	2.07
Croatian	9	0.08
Czech	60	0.51
Czechoslovakian	44	0.37
Danish	58	0.49
Dutch	45	0.38
English	234	1.99
European	24	0.20
French, except Basque	127	1.08
French Canadian	7	0.06
German	1,527	12.96
Greek	152	1.29
Hawaii Native/Pacific Islander:	9	0.08
Micronesian:	1	0.01
Guamanian/Chamorro	1	0.01
Polynesian: (1)	4	0.03
Native Hawaiian (1)	4	0.03
Other Pac. Isl., not spec. (1)	4	0.03
Hispanic or Latino:	2,598	21.92
Central American:	80	0.68
Costa Rican	5	0.04
Guatemalan	43	0.36
Honduran	8	0.07
Panamanian	2	0.02
Salvadoran	17	0.14
Other Central American	5	0.04
Cuban	37	0.31
Dominican Republic	1	0.01
Mexican	1,901	16.04

Notes: 1. Figures in the "Number" column do not add up to the total population due to: a) Ancestry/Race overlap — e.g. persons can report being both White and Irish, b) persons of Hispanic origin can report being any race, c) persons reporting two ancestries are counted in both categories. 2. Numbers in parentheses indicate the number of persons reporting this ancestry/race alone, not in combination with any other ancestry/race. 3. Refer to the Explanation of Data in the front of the book for more detailed information.

Ancestry/Race	Number	%
Puerto Rican	330	2.78
South American:	100	0.84
Argentinean	10	0.08
Chilean	1	0.01
Colombian	25	0.21
Ecuadorian	31	0.26
Paraguayan	1	0.01
Peruvian	22	0.19
Venezuelan	5	0.04
Other South American	5	0.04
Other Hispanic or Latino	149	1.26
Hungarian	45	0.38
Iranian	32	0.27
Irish	1,097	9.31
Italian	2,206	18.72
Lithuanian	37	0.31
Luxemburger	6	0.05
Norwegian	76	0.64
Polish	2,616	22.20
Romanian	46	0.39
Russian	20	0.17
Scotch-Irish	41	0.35
Scottish	27	0.23
Serbian	6	0.05
Slavic	6	0.05
Slovak	19	0.16
Slovene	6	0.05
Swedish	268	2.27
Turkish	48	0.41
Ukrainian	48	0.41
United States or American	200	1.70
Welsh	8	0.07
White:	9,965	84.09
Not Hispanic (8,169)	8,378	70.70
Hispanic (1,427)	1,587	13.39
Yugoslavian	187	1.59

Skokie

Place Type: Village
County: Cook
Population: 63,348

Ancestry/Race	Number	%
Afghan	14	0.02
African American/Black:	3,172	5.01
Not Hispanic (2,798)	3,067	4.84
Hispanic (56)	105	0.17
African, sub-Saharan:	224	0.35
African	26	0.04
Ethiopian	7	0.01
Nigerian	148	0.23
South African	43	0.07
Am. Ind. or Alaska Nat., not spec.	120	0.19
American Indian tribes, specified:	113	0.18
Apache (1)	2	0.00
Blackfeet	7	0.01
Cherokee (8)	41	0.06
Cheyenne	2	0.00
Chippewa (5)	5	0.01
Choctaw (6)	8	0.01
Creek (3)	3	0.00
Iroquois (1)	1	0.00
Latin American Indians (10)	22	0.03
Menominee (1)	1	0.00
Navajo (1)	1	0.00
Potawatomi	1	0.00
Pueblo	4	0.01
Seminole (1)	1	0.00
Sioux (3)	4	0.01
All other tribes (6)	10	0.02
American Indian tribes, not spec.	13	0.02
Arab:	592	0.93
Arab/Arabic	82	0.13
Iraqi	244	0.39
Lebanese	38	0.06
Moroccan	67	0.11
Palestinian	80	0.13
Syrian	37	0.06
Other Arab	44	0.07
Armenian	301	0.48
Asian:	14,565	22.99
Bangladeshi (31)	32	0.05
Cambodian (61)	73	0.12
Chinese, ex. Taiwanese (1,509)	1,702	2.69
Filipino (3,372)	3,594	5.67
Hmong (8)	9	0.01
Indian (3,944)	4,142	6.54
Indonesian (42)	47	0.07
Japanese (363)	494	0.78
Korean (2,465)	2,557	4.04
Laotian (22)	27	0.04
Malaysian (13)	17	0.03
Pakistani (697)	804	1.27
Sri Lankan (25)	26	0.04
Taiwanese (65)	81	0.13
Thai (210)	243	0.38
Vietnamese (290)	326	0.51
Other Asian, specified (15)	19	0.03
Other Asian, not specified (148)	372	0.59
Assyrian/Chaldean/Syriac	2,381	3.76
Austrian	397	0.63
Belgian	121	0.19
British	109	0.17
Bulgarian	208	0.33
Canadian	134	0.21
Celtic	16	0.03
Croatian	277	0.44
Czech	338	0.53
Czechoslovakian	134	0.21
Danish	115	0.18
Dutch	407	0.64
Eastern European	603	0.95
English	1,728	2.73
European	552	0.87
Finnish	94	0.15
French, except Basque	533	0.84
French Canadian	197	0.31
German	5,903	9.32
Greek	1,706	2.69
Guyanese	16	0.03
Hawaii Native/Pacific Islander:	94	0.15
Micronesian:	4	0.01
Guamanian/Chamorro	4	0.01
Polynesian: (3)	20	0.03
Native Hawaiian (2)	15	0.02
Samoan	3	0.00
Other Polynesian (1)	2	0.00
Other Pac. Isl., specified	2	0.00
Other Pac. Isl., not spec. (13)	68	0.11
Hispanic or Latino:	3,620	5.71
Central American:	271	0.43
Costa Rican	1	0.00
Guatemalan	127	0.20
Honduran	50	0.08
Nicaraguan	17	0.03
Panamanian	21	0.03
Salvadoran	31	0.05
Other Central American	24	0.04
Cuban	428	0.68
Dominican Republic	31	0.05
Mexican	1,373	2.17
Puerto Rican	381	0.60
South American:	583	0.92
Argentinean	43	0.07
Bolivian	69	0.11
Chilean	25	0.04
Colombian	144	0.23
Ecuadorian	127	0.20
Paraguayan	1	0.00
Peruvian	115	0.18
Uruguayan	7	0.01
Venezuelan	21	0.03
Other South American	31	0.05
Other Hispanic or Latino	553	0.87
Hungarian	716	1.13
Iranian	307	0.48
Irish	3,852	6.08
Israeli	251	0.40
Italian	1,756	2.77
Latvian	73	0.12
Lithuanian	517	0.82
Luxemburger	138	0.22
Macedonian	4	0.01
Norwegian	526	0.83
Pennsylvania German	5	0.01
Polish	4,232	6.68
Portuguese	5	0.01
Romanian	822	1.30
Russian	5,609	8.86
Scandinavian	19	0.03
Scotch-Irish	421	0.66
Scottish	367	0.58
Serbian	159	0.25
Slavic	29	0.05
Slovak	92	0.15
Slovene	16	0.03
Swedish	743	1.17
Swiss	81	0.13
Turkish	22	0.03
Ukrainian	1,206	1.90
United States or American	2,682	4.24
Welsh	95	0.15
West Indian, excl. Hispanic:	640	1.01
Barbadian	6	0.01
Belizean	62	0.10
Haitian	264	0.42
Jamaican	299	0.47
West Indian	9	0.01
White:	45,343	71.58
Not Hispanic (41,549)	42,982	67.85
Hispanic (2,112)	2,361	3.73
Yugoslavian	345	0.54

South Elgin

Place Type: Village
County: Kane
Population: 16,100

Ancestry/Race	Number	%
African American/Black:	469	2.91
Not Hispanic (412)	462	2.87
Hispanic (3)	7	0.04
African, sub-Saharan:	29	0.19
African	29	0.19
Am. Ind. or Alaska Nat., not spec.	34	0.21
American Indian tribes, specified:	53	0.33
Apache (1)	1	0.01
Blackfeet	1	0.01
Cherokee (4)	21	0.13
Chippewa (2)	2	0.01
Choctaw	5	0.03
Iroquois (2)	7	0.04
Latin American Indians (2)	5	0.03
Osage	1	0.01
Potawatomi	6	0.04
All other tribes	4	0.02
American Indian tribes, not spec.	4	0.02
Arab:	74	0.47
Jordanian	7	0.04
Palestinian	49	0.31
Syrian	18	0.11
Asian:	1,041	6.47
Cambodian (6)	7	0.04
Chinese, ex. Taiwanese (54)	79	0.49
Filipino (200)	262	1.63
Hmong (5)	5	0.03
Indian (110)	117	0.73
Indonesian (4)	5	0.03
Japanese (9)	24	0.15
Korean (43)	54	0.34
Laotian (335)	380	2.36
Malaysian (2)	3	0.02
Pakistani (26)	30	0.19
Thai (4)	5	0.03
Vietnamese (20)	28	0.17
Other Asian, specified (1)	1	0.01
Other Asian, not specified (23)	41	0.25
Assyrian/Chaldean/Syriac	25	0.16

Notes: 1. Figures in the "Number" column do not add up to the total population due to: a) Ancestry/Race overlap — e.g. persons can report being both White and Irish, b) persons of Hispanic origin can report being any race, c) persons reporting two ancestries are counted in both categories. 2. Numbers in parentheses indicate the number of persons reporting this ancestry/race alone, not in combination with any other ancestry/race. 3. Refer to the Explanation of Data in the front of the book for more detailed information.

Ancestry/Race	Number	%
Austrian	56	0.36
Belgian	63	0.40
British	27	0.17
Canadian	14	0.09
Croatian	15	0.10
Czech	257	1.64
Czechoslovakian	8	0.05
Danish	122	0.78
Dutch	289	1.84
Eastern European	8	0.05
English	1,294	8.26
European	97	0.62
Finnish	35	0.22
French, except Basque	551	3.52
French Canadian	79	0.50
German	4,647	29.65
Greek	182	1.16
Hawaii Native/Pacific Islander:	21	0.13
Micronesian:	4	0.02
Guamanian/Chamorro	4	0.02
Polynesian: (2)	6	0.04
Native Hawaiian	4	0.02
Samoan (1)	1	0.01
Other Polynesian (1)	1	0.01
Other Pac. Isl., not spec.	11	0.07
Hispanic or Latino:	1,664	10.34
Central American:	34	0.21
Costa Rican	5	0.03
Guatemalan	19	0.12
Honduran	2	0.01
Nicaraguan	1	0.01
Panamanian	4	0.02
Salvadoran	2	0.01
Other Central American	1	0.01
Cuban	18	0.11
Mexican	1,202	7.47
Puerto Rican	222	1.38
South American:	58	0.36
Argentinean	3	0.02
Chilean	5	0.03
Colombian	36	0.22
Peruvian	2	0.01
Uruguayan	1	0.01
Venezuelan	2	0.01
Other South American	9	0.06
Other Hispanic or Latino	130	0.81
Hungarian	168	1.07
Iranian	17	0.11
Irish	2,231	14.23
Italian	1,847	11.78
Latvian	8	0.05
Lithuanian	57	0.36
Norwegian	440	2.81
Pennsylvania German	21	0.13
Polish	1,686	10.76
Portuguese	8	0.05
Russian	77	0.49
Scandinavian	31	0.20
Scotch-Irish	133	0.85
Scottish	205	1.31
Serbian	9	0.06
Slavic	20	0.13
Slovak	18	0.11
Slovene	24	0.15
Swedish	509	3.25
Swiss	40	0.26
Ukrainian	54	0.34
United States or American	464	2.96
Welsh	54	0.34
West Indian, excl. Hispanic:	52	0.33
Jamaican	52	0.33
White:	14,103	87.60
Not Hispanic (12,894)	13,072	81.19
Hispanic (956)	1,031	6.40
Yugoslavian	19	0.12

South Holland

Place Type: Village
County: Cook
Population: 22,147

Ancestry/Race	Number	%
African American/Black:	11,416	51.55
Not Hispanic (11,195)	11,345	51.23
Hispanic (58)	71	0.32
African, sub-Saharan:	543	2.44
African	420	1.89
Ethiopian	19	0.09
Ghanian	12	0.05
Nigerian	53	0.24
Sierra Leonean	30	0.13
Other sub-Saharan African	9	0.04
Alaska Native tribes, specified:	1	0.00
Tlingit-Haida	1	0.00
Am. Ind. or Alaska Nat., not spec.	66	0.30
American Indian tribes, specified:	51	0.23
Blackfeet	9	0.04
Cherokee (6)	18	0.08
Chippewa (1)	4	0.02
Choctaw	2	0.01
Comanche (1)	1	0.00
Creek	1	0.00
Latin American Indians (1)	7	0.03
Ottawa	1	0.00
Seminole	1	0.00
Sioux (1)	1	0.00
All other tribes (4)	6	0.03
American Indian tribes, not spec.	3	0.01
Arab:	33	0.15
Arab/Arabic	4	0.02
Lebanese	17	0.08
Other Arab	12	0.05
Asian:	265	1.20
Chinese, ex. Taiwanese (42)	55	0.25
Filipino (53)	72	0.33
Indian (51)	60	0.27
Indonesian	3	0.01
Japanese (12)	25	0.11
Korean (12)	22	0.10
Pakistani	2	0.01
Taiwanese	3	0.01
Thai (6)	12	0.05
Vietnamese (8)	8	0.04
Other Asian, specified	1	0.00
Other Asian, not specified (1)	2	0.01
Austrian	50	0.22
Brazilian	8	0.04
British	27	0.12
Canadian	5	0.02
Croatian	160	0.72
Czech	97	0.44
Czechoslovakian	18	0.08
Danish	98	0.44
Dutch	2,718	12.20
Eastern European	5	0.02
English	642	2.88
European	43	0.19
Finnish	12	0.05
French, except Basque	186	0.83
French Canadian	103	0.46
German	1,927	8.65
Greek	65	0.29
Hawaii Native/Pacific Islander:	22	0.10
Polynesian: (2)	7	0.03
Native Hawaiian (1)	6	0.03
Samoan (1)	1	0.00
Other Pac. Isl., not spec.	15	0.07
Hispanic or Latino:	836	3.77
Central American:	10	0.05
Guatemalan	2	0.01
Honduran	3	0.01
Panamanian	2	0.01
Salvadoran	2	0.01
Other Central American	1	0.00
Cuban	13	0.06
Mexican	707	3.19
Puerto Rican	54	0.24
South American:	5	0.02
Colombian	3	0.01
Peruvian	1	0.00
Other South American	1	0.00
Other Hispanic or Latino	47	0.21
Hungarian	147	0.66
Irish	1,417	6.36
Israeli	6	0.03
Italian	906	4.07
Latvian	8	0.04
Lithuanian	122	0.55
Northern European	11	0.05
Norwegian	89	0.40
Polish	1,403	6.30
Portuguese	5	0.02
Romanian	8	0.04
Russian	72	0.32
Scandinavian	5	0.02
Scotch-Irish	120	0.54
Scottish	127	0.57
Serbian	157	0.70
Slovak	76	0.34
Slovene	18	0.08
Swedish	510	2.29
Swiss	9	0.04
Ukrainian	70	0.31
United States or American	117	0.53
Welsh	40	0.18
West Indian, excl. Hispanic:	237	1.06
Bahamian	5	0.02
Belizean	11	0.05
Haitian	58	0.26
Jamaican	159	0.71
Trinidadian and Tobagonian	4	0.02
White:	10,120	45.69
Not Hispanic (9,664)	9,776	44.14
Hispanic (311)	344	1.55
Yugoslavian	5	0.02

Springfield

Place Type: City
County: Sangamon
Population: 111,454

Ancestry/Race	Number	%
Acadian/Cajun	41	0.04
African American/Black:	18,072	16.21
Not Hispanic (17,007)	17,932	16.09
Hispanic (89)	140	0.13
African, sub-Saharan:	996	0.89
African	653	0.58
Ethiopian	73	0.07
Ghanian	48	0.04
Liberian	57	0.05
Nigerian	137	0.12
Somalian	7	0.01
South African	6	0.01
Other sub-Saharan African	15	0.01
Am. Ind. or Alaska Nat., not spec.	268	0.24
Alsatian	16	0.01
American Indian tribes, specified:	377	0.34
Apache (1)	13	0.01
Blackfeet (6)	16	0.01
Cherokee (58)	207	0.19
Cheyenne (1)	3	0.00
Chickasaw	4	0.00
Chippewa (4)	7	0.01
Choctaw (8)	18	0.02
Colville (1)	1	0.00
Creek (3)	7	0.01
Crow	3	0.00
Delaware	1	0.00
Iroquois (2)	5	0.00
Latin American Indians (2)	9	0.01
Menominee (9)	9	0.01
Navajo (1)	2	0.00
Osage (1)	3	0.00

Notes: 1. Figures in the "Number" column do not add up to the total population due to: a) Ancestry/Race overlap — e.g. persons can report being both White and Irish, b) persons of Hispanic origin can report being any race, c) persons reporting two ancestries are counted in both categories. 2. Numbers in parentheses indicate the number of persons reporting this ancestry/race alone, not in combination with any other ancestry/race. 3. Refer to the Explanation of Data in the front of the book for more detailed information.

Ottawa	1	0.00
Pima (1)	1	0.00
Potawatomi (4)	5	0.00
Puget Sound Salish (1)	1	0.00
Seminole (2)	6	0.01
Shoshone (1)	1	0.00
Sioux (19)	33	0.03
All other tribes (8)	21	0.02
American Indian tribes, not spec.	41	0.04
Arab:	315	0.28
Arab/Arabic	38	0.03
Egyptian	19	0.02
Iraqi	68	0.06
Lebanese	115	0.10
Moroccan	9	0.01
Palestinian	16	0.01
Syrian	43	0.04
Other Arab	7	0.01
Asian:	1,951	1.75
Bangladeshi (20)	25	0.02
Cambodian (11)	11	0.01
Chinese, ex. Taiwanese (295)	331	0.30
Filipino (171)	240	0.22
Indian (579)	646	0.58
Indonesian (6)	6	0.01
Japanese (47)	78	0.07
Korean (165)	205	0.18
Laotian (20)	25	0.02
Malaysian (4)	7	0.01
Pakistani (62)	74	0.07
Sri Lankan (1)	1	0.00
Taiwanese (41)	46	0.04
Thai (30)	43	0.04
Vietnamese (114)	123	0.11
Other Asian, specified (3)	6	0.01
Other Asian, not specified (39)	84	0.08
Assyrian/Chaldean/Syriac	9	0.01
Australian	20	0.02
Austrian	376	0.34
Belgian	204	0.18
Brazilian	15	0.01
British	282	0.25
Bulgarian	7	0.01
Canadian	71	0.06
Celtic	42	0.04
Croatian	161	0.14
Czech	343	0.31
Czechoslovakian	110	0.10
Danish	362	0.32
Dutch	2,001	1.78
Eastern European	30	0.03
English	13,288	11.84
Estonian	28	0.02
European	1,134	1.01
Finnish	86	0.08
French, except Basque	2,959	2.64
French Canadian	328	0.29
German	27,385	24.41
Greek	229	0.20
Hawaii Native/Pacific Islander:	92	0.08
Melanesian: (1)	2	0.00
Fijian (1)	2	0.00
Micronesian: (4)	8	0.01
Guamanian/Chamorro (4)	7	0.01
Other Micronesian	1	0.00
Polynesian: (22)	41	0.04
Native Hawaiian (7)	23	0.02
Samoan (14)	17	0.02
Tongan (1)	1	0.00
Other Pac. Isl., specified	1	0.00
Other Pac. Isl., not spec. (7)	40	0.04
Hispanic or Latino:	1,337	1.20
Central American:	39	0.03
Costa Rican	7	0.01
Guatemalan	2	0.00
Honduran	10	0.01
Nicaraguan	2	0.00
Panamanian	9	0.01
Salvadoran	3	0.00
Other Central American	6	0.01
Cuban	54	0.05
Dominican Republic	6	0.01
Mexican	630	0.57
Puerto Rican	172	0.15
South American:	111	0.10
Argentinean	6	0.01
Bolivian	7	0.01
Chilean	4	0.00
Colombian	26	0.02
Ecuadorian	8	0.01
Peruvian	37	0.03
Venezuelan	15	0.01
Other South American	8	0.01
Other Hispanic or Latino	325	0.29
Hungarian	543	0.48
Iranian	85	0.08
Irish	17,457	15.56
Italian	6,736	6.00
Latvian	14	0.01
Lithuanian	1,091	0.97
Luxemburger	20	0.02
New Zealander	9	0.01
Northern European	81	0.07
Norwegian	962	0.86
Pennsylvania German	39	0.03
Polish	2,188	1.95
Portuguese	455	0.41
Romanian	76	0.07
Russian	226	0.20
Scandinavian	100	0.09
Scotch-Irish	1,951	1.74
Scottish	2,199	1.96
Serbian	30	0.03
Slavic	50	0.04
Slovak	448	0.40
Slovene	143	0.13
Swedish	1,397	1.25
Swiss	184	0.16
Turkish	30	0.03
Ukrainian	70	0.06
United States or American	7,965	7.10
Welsh	847	0.75
West Indian, excl. Hispanic:	29	0.03
Dutch West Indian	6	0.01
Jamaican	13	0.01
West Indian	10	0.01
White:	91,715	82.29
Not Hispanic (89,510)	90,850	81.51
Hispanic (777)	865	0.78
Yugoslavian	45	0.04

Sterling

Place Type: City
County: Whiteside
Population: 15,451

Ancestry/Race	Number	%
African American/Black:	445	2.88
Not Hispanic (325)	395	2.56
Hispanic (22)	50	0.32
African, sub-Saharan:	12	0.08
African	12	0.08
Am. Ind. or Alaska Nat., not spec.	52	0.34
American Indian tribes, specified:	72	0.47
Apache (3)	4	0.03
Blackfeet (1)	3	0.02
Cherokee (7)	18	0.12
Cheyenne	2	0.01
Chippewa (1)	2	0.01
Choctaw	2	0.01
Cree (1)	2	0.01
Creek	3	0.02
Latin American Indians (12)	20	0.13
Lumbee (1)	1	0.01
Navajo	1	0.01
Pueblo (1)	1	0.01
Sioux (1)	7	0.05
All other tribes (2)	6	0.04
American Indian tribes, not spec.	10	0.06
Arab:	36	0.23
Arab/Arabic	17	0.11
Egyptian	12	0.08
Other Arab	7	0.05
Asian:	162	1.05
Chinese, ex. Taiwanese (8)	20	0.13
Filipino (32)	35	0.23
Indian (37)	40	0.26
Indonesian (1)	3	0.02
Japanese (1)	4	0.03
Korean (8)	14	0.09
Laotian (3)	3	0.02
Pakistani (3)	4	0.03
Taiwanese (1)	1	0.01
Thai (4)	7	0.05
Vietnamese (9)	21	0.14
Other Asian, specified (4)	4	0.03
Other Asian, not specified (2)	6	0.04
Belgian	57	0.37
British	15	0.10
Canadian	6	0.04
Carpatho Rusyn	9	0.06
Croatian	8	0.05
Czech	50	0.32
Czechoslovakian	12	0.08
Danish	63	0.41
Dutch	381	2.47
English	1,190	7.73
European	6	0.04
Finnish	36	0.23
French, except Basque	353	2.29
French Canadian	94	0.61
German	3,969	25.77
Greek	4	0.03
Hawaii Native/Pacific Islander:	4	0.03
Polynesian:	1	0.01
Native Hawaiian	1	0.01
Other Pac. Isl., not spec. (1)	3	0.02
Hispanic or Latino:	2,973	19.24
Central American:	7	0.05
Guatemalan	3	0.02
Honduran	3	0.02
Salvadoran	1	0.01
Cuban	3	0.02
Mexican	2,474	16.01
Puerto Rican	104	0.67
South American:	15	0.10
Argentinean	6	0.04
Bolivian	3	0.02
Peruvian	5	0.03
Venezuelan	1	0.01
Other Hispanic or Latino	370	2.39
Hungarian	23	0.15
Irish	2,270	14.74
Italian	420	2.73
Lithuanian	12	0.08
Luxemburger	6	0.04
Norwegian	324	2.10
Pennsylvania German	51	0.33
Polish	221	1.43
Russian	9	0.06
Scotch-Irish	164	1.06
Scottish	178	1.16
Serbian	14	0.09
Slovene	8	0.05
Swedish	258	1.67
Swiss	22	0.14
Ukrainian	5	0.03
United States or American	1,006	6.53
Welsh	134	0.87
West Indian, excl. Hispanic:	47	0.31
Haitian	47	0.31
White:	13,367	86.51
Not Hispanic (11,848)	11,981	77.54
Hispanic (1,187)	1,386	8.97
Yugoslavian	6	0.04

Notes: 1. Figures in the "Number" column do not add up to the total population due to: a) Ancestry/Race overlap — e.g. persons can report being both White and Irish, b) persons of Hispanic origin can report being any race, c) persons reporting two ancestries are counted in both categories. 2. Numbers in parentheses indicate the number of persons reporting this ancestry/race alone, not in combination with any other ancestry/race. 3. Refer to the Explanation of Data in the front of the book for more detailed information.

Streamwood

Place Type: Village
County: Cook
Population: 36,407

Ancestry/Race	Number	%
Acadian/Cajun	6	0.02
African American/Black:	1,548	4.25
Not Hispanic (1,352)	1,471	4.04
Hispanic (46)	77	0.21
African, sub-Saharan:	181	0.49
African	172	0.47
Nigerian	9	0.02
Alaska Native tribes, specified:	1	0.00
Alaska Athabascan	1	0.00
Am. Ind. or Alaska Nat., not spec.	114	0.31
American Indian tribes, specified:	136	0.37
Apache (1)	9	0.02
Blackfeet (1)	10	0.03
Cherokee (7)	54	0.15
Chippewa (4)	5	0.01
Choctaw (1)	6	0.02
Creek	1	0.00
Iroquois (1)	2	0.01
Latin American Indians (20)	24	0.07
Menominee (1)	5	0.01
Navajo	1	0.00
Osage	1	0.00
Potawatomi	1	0.00
Sioux (5)	13	0.04
All other tribes (2)	4	0.01
American Indian tribes, not spec.	15	0.04
Arab:	114	0.31
Arab/Arabic	11	0.03
Egyptian	7	0.02
Iraqi	30	0.08
Jordanian	25	0.07
Lebanese	16	0.04
Palestinian	6	0.02
Syrian	19	0.05
Armenian	94	0.26
Asian:	3,475	9.54
Cambodian (22)	22	0.06
Chinese, ex. Taiwanese (225)	258	0.71
Filipino (991)	1,109	3.05
Indian (1,144)	1,183	3.25
Indonesian (2)	5	0.01
Japanese (137)	196	0.54
Korean (223)	253	0.69
Laotian (60)	67	0.18
Malaysian (1)	1	0.00
Pakistani (116)	131	0.36
Taiwanese (4)	4	0.01
Thai (31)	37	0.10
Vietnamese (92)	101	0.28
Other Asian, specified (1)	1	0.00
Other Asian, not specified (64)	107	0.29
Assyrian/Chaldean/Syriac	161	0.44
Austrian	116	0.32
Belgian	189	0.51
Brazilian	39	0.11
British	51	0.14
Bulgarian	35	0.10
Canadian	117	0.32
Croatian	31	0.08
Czech	613	1.67
Czechoslovakian	50	0.14
Danish	400	1.09
Dutch	324	0.88
Eastern European	8	0.02
English	1,709	4.65
European	80	0.22
Finnish	211	0.57
French, except Basque	822	2.24
French Canadian	149	0.41
German	7,802	21.24
Greek	441	1.20
Hawaii Native/Pacific Islander:	57	0.16
Micronesian: (2)	3	0.01
Guamanian/Chamorro (2)	3	0.01
Polynesian: (3)	14	0.04
Native Hawaiian (3)	9	0.02
Samoan	5	0.01
Other Pac. Isl., not spec. (7)	40	0.11
Hispanic or Latino:	6,108	16.78
Central American:	179	0.49
Guatemalan	97	0.27
Honduran	17	0.05
Nicaraguan	12	0.03
Panamanian	1	0.00
Salvadoran	45	0.12
Other Central American	7	0.02
Cuban	42	0.12
Dominican Republic	15	0.04
Mexican	4,699	12.91
Puerto Rican	382	1.05
South American:	236	0.65
Argentinean	12	0.03
Bolivian	7	0.02
Chilean	21	0.06
Colombian	107	0.29
Ecuadorian	50	0.14
Peruvian	25	0.07
Venezuelan	9	0.02
Other South American	5	0.01
Other Hispanic or Latino	555	1.52
Hungarian	252	0.69
Iranian	37	0.10
Irish	5,025	13.68
Italian	3,856	10.50
Latvian	28	0.08
Lithuanian	109	0.30
Luxemburger	8	0.02
Macedonian	43	0.12
New Zealander	30	0.08
Northern European	11	0.03
Norwegian	766	2.09
Polish	5,371	14.62
Portuguese	49	0.13
Romanian	106	0.29
Russian	321	0.87
Scandinavian	56	0.15
Scotch-Irish	440	1.20
Scottish	332	0.90
Serbian	151	0.41
Slavic	10	0.03
Slovak	153	0.42
Slovene	8	0.02
Swedish	1,024	2.79
Swiss	61	0.17
Ukrainian	149	0.41
United States or American	1,055	2.87
Welsh	78	0.21
West Indian, excl. Hispanic:	28	0.08
Belizean	11	0.03
British West Indian	6	0.02
Jamaican	11	0.03
White:	29,015	79.70
Not Hispanic (25,130)	25,611	70.35
Hispanic (3,095)	3,404	9.35
Yugoslavian	227	0.62

Streator

Place Type: City
County: La Salle
Population: 14,190

Ancestry/Race	Number	%
African American/Black:	394	2.78
Not Hispanic (274)	352	2.48
Hispanic (18)	42	0.30
Am. Ind. or Alaska Nat., not spec.	22	0.16
American Indian tribes, specified:	40	0.28
Apache (1)	1	0.01
Blackfeet (2)	2	0.01
Cherokee (13)	24	0.17
Choctaw	1	0.01
Latin American Indians (4)	5	0.04
Potawatomi	1	0.01
Shoshone (1)	1	0.01
Sioux	2	0.01
All other tribes (2)	3	0.02
Arab:	85	0.60
Egyptian	7	0.05
Lebanese	78	0.55
Asian:	93	0.66
Chinese, ex. Taiwanese (12)	13	0.09
Filipino (7)	16	0.11
Indian (31)	33	0.23
Japanese (3)	3	0.02
Korean (6)	8	0.06
Pakistani (6)	6	0.04
Vietnamese (4)	12	0.08
Other Asian, not specified (1)	2	0.01
Austrian	10	0.07
British	6	0.04
Canadian	8	0.06
Celtic	8	0.06
Croatian	27	0.19
Czech	62	0.44
Czechoslovakian	89	0.63
Danish	135	0.96
Dutch	302	2.14
English	1,104	7.81
European	34	0.24
Finnish	3	0.02
French, except Basque	471	3.33
French Canadian	15	0.11
German	3,110	22.01
Greek	14	0.10
Hawaii Native/Pacific Islander:	3	0.02
Micronesian: (1)	2	0.01
Guamanian/Chamorro (1)	2	0.01
Polynesian:	1	0.01
Native Hawaiian	1	0.01
Hispanic or Latino:	942	6.64
Central American:	5	0.04
Guatemalan	3	0.02
Honduran	2	0.01
Cuban	5	0.04
Mexican	789	5.56
Puerto Rican	54	0.38
Other Hispanic or Latino	89	0.63
Hungarian	68	0.48
Irish	2,087	14.77
Italian	600	4.25
Lithuanian	11	0.08
Norwegian	176	1.25
Polish	479	3.39
Portuguese	6	0.04
Romanian	3	0.02
Russian	34	0.24
Scandinavian	25	0.18
Scotch-Irish	115	0.81
Scottish	168	1.19
Slavic	7	0.05
Slovak	1,653	11.70
Slovene	19	0.13
Swedish	114	0.81
Swiss	15	0.11
Ukrainian	11	0.08
United States or American	1,444	10.22
Welsh	79	0.56
White:	13,578	95.69
Not Hispanic (12,753)	12,882	90.78
Hispanic (625)	696	4.90
Yugoslavian	10	0.07

Summit

Place Type: Village
County: Cook
Population: 10,637

Ancestry/Race	Number	%
African American/Black:	1,320	12.41
Not Hispanic (1,261)	1,285	12.08
Hispanic (21)	35	0.33

Notes: 1. Figures in the "Number" column do not add up to the total population due to: a) Ancestry/Race overlap — e.g. persons can report being both White and Irish, b) persons of Hispanic origin can report being any race, c) persons reporting two ancestries are counted in both categories. 2. Numbers in parentheses indicate the number of persons reporting this ancestry/race alone, not in combination with any other ancestry/race. 3. Refer to the Explanation of Data in the front of the book for more detailed information.

African, sub-Saharan:	43	0.40
African	43	0.40
Am. Ind. or Alaska Nat., not spec.	40	0.38
Albanian	144	1.35
American Indian tribes, specified:	27	0.25
Apache	2	0.02
Blackfeet	1	0.01
Cherokee	3	0.03
Chippewa (1)	1	0.01
Creek	1	0.01
Iroquois (1)	1	0.01
Latin American Indians (9)	17	0.16
All other tribes (1)	1	0.01
American Indian tribes, not spec.	4	0.04
Arab:	160	1.50
Arab/Arabic	27	0.25
Jordanian	27	0.25
Palestinian	106	1.00
Asian:	197	1.85
Chinese, ex. Taiwanese	5	0.05
Filipino (11)	22	0.21
Indian (72)	78	0.73
Indonesian	2	0.02
Japanese (1)	4	0.04
Pakistani (38)	43	0.40
Thai (1)	1	0.01
Vietnamese (19)	19	0.18
Other Asian, not specified (7)	23	0.22
Austrian	6	0.06
British	7	0.07
Croatian	59	0.55
Czech	147	1.38
Czechoslovakian	12	0.11
Dutch	56	0.53
English	126	1.18
French, except Basque	57	0.54
German	548	5.15
Greek	55	0.52
Hawaii Native/Pacific Islander:	6	0.06
Micronesian: (1)	1	0.01
Guamanian/Chamorro (1)	1	0.01
Polynesian:	2	0.02
Native Hawaiian	2	0.02
Other Pac. Isl., not spec. (1)	3	0.03
Hispanic or Latino:	5,156	48.47
Central American:	75	0.71
Costa Rican	5	0.05
Guatemalan	32	0.30
Nicaraguan	4	0.04
Salvadoran	27	0.25
Other Central American	7	0.07
Cuban	7	0.07
Dominican Republic	1	0.01
Mexican	4,717	44.35
Puerto Rican	114	1.07
South American:	23	0.22
Colombian	9	0.08
Ecuadorian	12	0.11
Peruvian	2	0.02
Other Hispanic or Latino	219	2.06
Hungarian	24	0.23
Irish	473	4.45
Italian	318	2.99
Lithuanian	146	1.37
Macedonian	60	0.56
Norwegian	14	0.13
Polish	1,241	11.67
Romanian	22	0.21
Russian	51	0.48
Scotch-Irish	6	0.06
Scottish	15	0.14
Serbian	26	0.24
Slovak	56	0.53
Slovene	29	0.27
Swedish	71	0.67
Swiss	6	0.06
Turkish	112	1.05
Ukrainian	18	0.17
United States or American	179	1.68
White:	7,046	66.24
Not Hispanic (3,912)	4,028	37.87
Hispanic (2,822)	3,018	28.37
Yugoslavian	70	0.66

Swansea

Place Type: Village
County: Saint Clair
Population: 10,579

Ancestry/Race	Number	%
Acadian/Cajun	15	0.14
African American/Black:	955	9.03
Not Hispanic (909)	953	9.01
Hispanic	2	0.02
African, sub-Saharan:	42	0.40
African	42	0.40
Am. Ind. or Alaska Nat., not spec.	16	0.15
American Indian tribes, specified:	46	0.43
Apache	6	0.06
Cherokee (6)	22	0.21
Chippewa (3)	3	0.03
Choctaw (1)	1	0.01
Comanche (1)	1	0.01
Latin American Indians	1	0.01
Lumbee (3)	3	0.03
Osage (2)	3	0.03
Sioux (1)	5	0.05
All other tribes	1	0.01
American Indian tribes, not spec.	2	0.02
Arab:	17	0.16
Lebanese	9	0.09
Palestinian	8	0.08
Armenian	10	0.10
Asian:	213	2.01
Chinese, ex. Taiwanese (32)	45	0.43
Filipino (18)	26	0.25
Indian (28)	31	0.29
Japanese (6)	11	0.10
Korean (30)	33	0.31
Laotian	1	0.01
Pakistani (21)	23	0.22
Taiwanese (2)	3	0.03
Thai (6)	9	0.09
Vietnamese (18)	20	0.19
Other Asian, not specified (6)	11	0.10
Austrian	20	0.19
Belgian	7	0.07
British	35	0.34
Canadian	27	0.26
Croatian	62	0.60
Czech	76	0.73
Czechoslovakian	33	0.32
Danish	25	0.24
Dutch	182	1.75
English	1,091	10.48
European	37	0.36
French, except Basque	425	4.08
French Canadian	14	0.13
German	4,089	39.27
Greek	6	0.06
Hawaii Native/Pacific Islander:	10	0.09
Micronesian: (4)	4	0.04
Guamanian/Chamorro (4)	4	0.04
Polynesian: (3)	4	0.04
Native Hawaiian (2)	3	0.03
Samoan (1)	1	0.01
Other Pac. Isl., not spec. (1)	2	0.02
Hispanic or Latino:	163	1.54
Central American:	2	0.02
Costa Rican	1	0.01
Panamanian	1	0.01
Cuban	7	0.07
Mexican	87	0.82
Puerto Rican	16	0.15
South American:	7	0.07
Argentinean	1	0.01
Colombian	1	0.01
Ecuadorian	4	0.04
Venezuelan	1	0.01
Other Hispanic or Latino	44	0.42
Hungarian	25	0.24
Iranian	16	0.15
Irish	1,464	14.06
Italian	240	2.30
Lithuanian	69	0.66
Norwegian	109	1.05
Polish	481	4.62
Portuguese	32	0.31
Russian	60	0.58
Scotch-Irish	176	1.69
Scottish	178	1.71
Slavic	8	0.08
Slovak	52	0.50
Swedish	82	0.79
Swiss	17	0.16
Ukrainian	44	0.42
United States or American	665	6.39
Welsh	41	0.39
West Indian, excl. Hispanic:	8	0.08
Jamaican	8	0.08
White:	9,419	89.03
Not Hispanic (9,201)	9,294	87.85
Hispanic (112)	125	1.18
Yugoslavian	5	0.05

Sycamore

Place Type: City
County: De Kalb
Population: 12,020

Ancestry/Race	Number	%
African American/Black:	392	3.26
Not Hispanic (323)	379	3.15
Hispanic (6)	13	0.11
African, sub-Saharan:	20	0.16
African	14	0.12
South African	6	0.05
Am. Ind. or Alaska Nat., not spec.	23	0.19
American Indian tribes, specified:	33	0.27
Apache	2	0.02
Cherokee (6)	11	0.09
Chippewa (7)	10	0.08
Choctaw	1	0.01
Comanche (1)	1	0.01
Latin American Indians	1	0.01
Navajo (2)	2	0.02
Sioux (3)	3	0.02
All other tribes (1)	2	0.02
American Indian tribes, not spec.	1	0.01
Arab:	55	0.45
Egyptian	11	0.09
Jordanian	9	0.07
Lebanese	35	0.29
Asian:	131	1.09
Chinese, ex. Taiwanese (19)	27	0.22
Filipino (9)	12	0.10
Indian (26)	30	0.25
Japanese (4)	8	0.07
Korean (18)	21	0.17
Laotian (9)	12	0.10
Malaysian	1	0.01
Taiwanese (4)	5	0.04
Vietnamese (2)	2	0.02
Other Asian, specified (1)	1	0.01
Other Asian, not specified (6)	12	0.10
Austrian	71	0.59
Belgian	18	0.15
British	45	0.37
Bulgarian	8	0.07
Canadian	51	0.42
Croatian	19	0.16
Czech	85	0.70
Czechoslovakian	16	0.13
Danish	152	1.25
Dutch	262	2.16
English	1,263	10.41
European	215	1.77
Finnish	34	0.28

Notes: 1. Figures in the "Number" column do not add up to the total population due to: a) Ancestry/Race overlap — e.g. persons can report being both White and Irish, b) persons of Hispanic origin can report being any race, c) persons reporting two ancestries are counted in both categories. 2. Numbers in parentheses indicate the number of persons reporting this ancestry/race alone, not in combination with any other ancestry/race. 3. Refer to the Explanation of Data in the front of the book for more detailed information.

Ancestry/Race	Number	%
French, except Basque	370	3.05
French Canadian	81	0.67
German	3,744	30.86
Greek	91	0.75
Hawaii Native/Pacific Islander:	6	0.05
Other Pac. Isl., not spec. (2)	6	0.05
Hispanic or Latino:	513	4.27
Cuban	8	0.07
Mexican	405	3.37
Puerto Rican	24	0.20
South American:	13	0.11
Argentinean	1	0.01
Bolivian	3	0.02
Chilean	2	0.02
Colombian	3	0.02
Peruvian	1	0.01
Other South American	3	0.02
Other Hispanic or Latino	63	0.52
Hungarian	20	0.16
Icelander	10	0.08
Irish	1,947	16.05
Italian	564	4.65
Lithuanian	39	0.32
Macedonian	23	0.19
Northern European	5	0.04
Norwegian	701	5.78
Pennsylvania German	7	0.06
Polish	541	4.46
Portuguese	11	0.09
Russian	63	0.52
Scandinavian	98	0.81
Scotch-Irish	264	2.18
Scottish	181	1.49
Serbian	27	0.22
Slavic	17	0.14
Slovak	35	0.29
Slovene	6	0.05
Swedish	1,030	8.49
Swiss	58	0.48
Turkish	6	0.05
Ukrainian	39	0.32
United States or American	853	7.03
Welsh	73	0.60
White:	11,357	94.48
Not Hispanic (10,937)	11,029	91.76
Hispanic (288)	328	2.73
Yugoslavian	5	0.04

Taylorville

Place Type: City
County: Christian
Population: 11,427

Ancestry/Race	Number	%
African American/Black:	107	0.94
Not Hispanic (81)	107	0.94
African, sub-Saharan:	20	0.18
African	20	0.18
Am. Ind. or Alaska Nat., not spec.	15	0.13
American Indian tribes, specified:	29	0.25
Blackfeet	2	0.02
Cherokee (9)	19	0.17
Comanche	1	0.01
Potawatomi	1	0.01
Sioux (3)	4	0.04
All other tribes (1)	2	0.02
American Indian tribes, not spec.	1	0.01
Asian:	66	0.58
Chinese, ex. Taiwanese (15)	15	0.13
Filipino (20)	24	0.21
Indian (9)	10	0.09
Indonesian (1)	1	0.01
Korean (1)	1	0.01
Taiwanese (4)	4	0.04
Vietnamese (8)	9	0.08
Other Asian, not specified	2	0.02
Australian	10	0.09
Austrian	29	0.26
Belgian	20	0.18
British	34	0.30
Bulgarian	4	0.04
Canadian	16	0.14
Croatian	24	0.21
Czech	26	0.23
Czechoslovakian	36	0.32
Danish	25	0.22
Dutch	280	2.47
English	1,270	11.22
European	31	0.27
French, except Basque	339	2.99
French Canadian	30	0.26
German	2,316	20.46
Greek	7	0.06
Hawaii Native/Pacific Islander:	12	0.11
Micronesian: (3)	3	0.03
Guamanian/Chamorro (3)	3	0.03
Polynesian: (1)	3	0.03
Samoan (1)	3	0.03
Other Pac. Isl., not spec. (3)	6	0.05
Hispanic or Latino:	80	0.70
Central American:	3	0.03
Salvadoran	1	0.01
Other Central American	2	0.02
Dominican Republic	1	0.01
Mexican	49	0.43
Puerto Rican	7	0.06
Other Hispanic or Latino	20	0.18
Hungarian	60	0.53
Irish	1,300	11.48
Italian	778	6.87
Lithuanian	89	0.79
Norwegian	76	0.67
Polish	71	0.63
Portuguese	6	0.05
Romanian	6	0.05
Russian	49	0.43
Scotch-Irish	165	1.46
Scottish	197	1.74
Slavic	6	0.05
Slovak	13	0.11
Slovene	17	0.15
Swedish	114	1.01
Swiss	62	0.55
United States or American	1,353	11.95
Welsh	100	0.88
White:	11,221	98.20
Not Hispanic (11,122)	11,178	97.82
Hispanic (39)	43	0.38

Tinley Park

Place Type: Village
County: Cook
Population: 48,401

Ancestry/Race	Number	%
Acadian/Cajun	9	0.02
African American/Black:	1,013	2.09
Not Hispanic (923)	993	2.05
Hispanic (8)	20	0.04
African, sub-Saharan:	57	0.12
African	57	0.12
Am. Ind. or Alaska Nat., not spec.	63	0.13
Albanian	8	0.02
Alsatian	9	0.02
American Indian tribes, specified:	92	0.19
Apache	2	0.00
Blackfeet	4	0.01
Cherokee (6)	31	0.06
Chippewa (4)	5	0.01
Choctaw	14	0.03
Iroquois (4)	4	0.01
Latin American Indians (7)	10	0.02
Lumbee (1)	1	0.00
Menominee	2	0.00
Potawatomi	4	0.01
Sioux	4	0.01
All other tribes (4)	11	0.02
American Indian tribes, not spec.	10	0.02
Arab:	503	1.04
Arab/Arabic	324	0.67
Jordanian	8	0.02
Lebanese	32	0.07
Moroccan	6	0.01
Palestinian	97	0.20
Syrian	10	0.02
Other Arab	26	0.05
Armenian	35	0.07
Asian:	1,316	2.72
Chinese, ex. Taiwanese (105)	116	0.24
Filipino (348)	381	0.79
Indian (382)	415	0.86
Indonesian	2	0.00
Japanese (25)	43	0.09
Korean (51)	61	0.13
Laotian (5)	6	0.01
Malaysian (1)	1	0.00
Pakistani (50)	61	0.13
Sri Lankan (14)	14	0.03
Thai (71)	79	0.16
Vietnamese (62)	67	0.14
Other Asian, specified (8)	8	0.02
Other Asian, not specified (13)	62	0.13
Australian	4	0.01
Austrian	420	0.87
Belgian	68	0.14
Brazilian	8	0.02
British	90	0.19
Canadian	57	0.12
Celtic	6	0.01
Croatian	543	1.12
Czech	1,038	2.15
Czechoslovakian	235	0.49
Danish	298	0.62
Dutch	2,566	5.31
Eastern European	6	0.01
English	2,387	4.94
European	86	0.18
Finnish	105	0.22
French, except Basque	1,206	2.50
French Canadian	358	0.74
German	11,144	23.06
Greek	598	1.24
Hawaii Native/Pacific Islander:	24	0.05
Polynesian: (2)	7	0.01
Native Hawaiian (1)	5	0.01
Samoan (1)	2	0.00
Other Pac. Isl., not spec. (7)	17	0.04
Hispanic or Latino:	1,998	4.13
Central American:	24	0.05
Guatemalan	12	0.02
Honduran	4	0.01
Nicaraguan	3	0.01
Panamanian	3	0.01
Other Central American	2	0.00
Cuban	25	0.05
Mexican	1,582	3.27
Puerto Rican	100	0.21
South American:	40	0.08
Argentinean	14	0.03
Colombian	14	0.03
Ecuadorian	4	0.01
Paraguayan	2	0.00
Uruguayan	3	0.01
Other South American	3	0.01
Other Hispanic or Latino	227	0.47
Hungarian	350	0.72
Iranian	22	0.05
Irish	12,299	25.45
Israeli	9	0.02
Italian	6,926	14.33
Latvian	56	0.12
Lithuanian	1,250	2.59
Luxemburger	35	0.07
Macedonian	12	0.02
Norwegian	402	0.83
Polish	9,540	19.74
Portuguese	6	0.01
Romanian	21	0.04

Notes: 1. Figures in the "Number" column do not add up to the total population due to: a) Ancestry/Race overlap — e.g. persons can report being both White and Irish, b) persons of Hispanic origin can report being any race, c) persons reporting two ancestries are counted in both categories. 2. Numbers in parentheses indicate the number of persons reporting this ancestry/race alone, not in combination with any other ancestry/race. 3. Refer to the Explanation of Data in the front of the book for more detailed information.

Ancestry/Race	Number	%
Russian	141	0.29
Scandinavian	36	0.07
Scotch-Irish	533	1.10
Scottish	488	1.01
Serbian	95	0.20
Slavic	47	0.10
Slovak	454	0.94
Slovene	12	0.02
Swedish	1,617	3.35
Swiss	27	0.06
Ukrainian	378	0.78
United States or American	1,146	2.37
Welsh	197	0.41
White:	45,652	94.32
Not Hispanic (43,787)	44,211	91.34
Hispanic (1,305)	1,441	2.98
Yugoslavian	83	0.17

Urbana

Place Type: City
County: Champaign
Population: 36,395

Ancestry/Race	Number	%
Afghan	11	0.03
African American/Black:	5,535	15.21
Not Hispanic (5,181)	5,465	15.02
Hispanic (37)	70	0.19
African, sub-Saharan:	434	1.20
African	188	0.52
Ghanian	17	0.05
Kenyan	32	0.09
Nigerian	119	0.33
South African	59	0.16
Ugandan	6	0.02
Other sub-Saharan African	13	0.04
Alaska Native tribes, specified:	2	0.01
Alaska Athabascan (1)	1	0.00
Eskimo (1)	1	0.00
Am. Ind. or Alaska Nat., not spec.	80	0.22
Albanian	69	0.19
American Indian tribes, specified:	134	0.37
Apache (1)	3	0.01
Blackfeet (2)	8	0.02
Cherokee (18)	60	0.16
Cheyenne	2	0.01
Chippewa (2)	8	0.02
Choctaw (2)	4	0.01
Creek (4)	5	0.01
Crow (1)	1	0.00
Iroquois	5	0.01
Latin American Indians (4)	9	0.02
Navajo	1	0.00
Osage	1	0.00
Pueblo (2)	2	0.01
Seminole (1)	2	0.01
Sioux (3)	6	0.02
Yuman (1)	1	0.00
All other tribes (6)	16	0.04
American Indian tribes, not spec.	12	0.03
Arab:	247	0.68
Arab/Arabic	34	0.09
Egyptian	111	0.31
Iraqi	9	0.02
Lebanese	13	0.04
Moroccan	13	0.04
Palestinian	24	0.07
Syrian	12	0.03
Other Arab	31	0.09
Armenian	7	0.02
Asian:	5,661	15.55
Bangladeshi (1)	4	0.01
Cambodian (16)	18	0.05
Chinese, ex. Taiwanese (1,890)	2,034	5.59
Filipino (168)	212	0.58
Hmong (2)	2	0.01
Indian (949)	1,014	2.79
Indonesian (70)	77	0.21
Japanese (241)	316	0.87
Korean (1,091)	1,139	3.13
Laotian (40)	50	0.14
Malaysian (12)	33	0.09
Pakistani (38)	46	0.13
Sri Lankan (43)	46	0.13
Taiwanese (228)	260	0.71
Thai (81)	92	0.25
Vietnamese (171)	196	0.54
Other Asian, specified (16)	21	0.06
Other Asian, not specified (40)	101	0.28
Assyrian/Chaldean/Syriac	17	0.05
Australian	14	0.04
Austrian	100	0.28
Belgian	84	0.23
Brazilian	101	0.28
British	309	0.85
Bulgarian	4	0.01
Canadian	83	0.23
Celtic	14	0.04
Croatian	52	0.14
Cypriot	8	0.02
Czech	206	0.57
Czechoslovakian	61	0.17
Danish	160	0.44
Dutch	504	1.39
Eastern European	38	0.10
English	3,538	9.77
Estonian	9	0.02
European	447	1.23
Finnish	61	0.17
French, except Basque	776	2.14
French Canadian	178	0.49
German	7,413	20.48
Greek	165	0.46
Hawaii Native/Pacific Islander:	67	0.18
Micronesian: (6)	9	0.02
Guamanian/Chamorro (5)	8	0.02
Other Micronesian (1)	1	0.00
Polynesian: (6)	22	0.06
Native Hawaiian (4)	17	0.05
Samoan (2)	4	0.01
Other Polynesian	1	0.00
Other Pac. Isl., specified	3	0.01
Other Pac. Isl., not spec. (2)	33	0.09
Hispanic or Latino:	1,288	3.54
Central American:	66	0.18
Costa Rican	6	0.02
Guatemalan	25	0.07
Honduran	10	0.03
Nicaraguan	2	0.01
Panamanian	8	0.02
Salvadoran	14	0.04
Other Central American	1	0.00
Cuban	42	0.12
Dominican Republic	8	0.02
Mexican	673	1.85
Puerto Rican	135	0.37
South American:	183	0.50
Argentinean	48	0.13
Bolivian	13	0.04
Chilean	14	0.04
Colombian	46	0.13
Ecuadorian	14	0.04
Paraguayan	3	0.01
Peruvian	23	0.06
Venezuelan	17	0.05
Other South American	5	0.01
Other Hispanic or Latino	181	0.50
Hungarian	198	0.55
Icelander	31	0.09
Iranian	65	0.18
Irish	3,954	10.92
Israeli	113	0.31
Italian	1,199	3.31
Latvian	26	0.07
Lithuanian	194	0.54
Luxemburger	17	0.05
Macedonian	9	0.02
New Zealander	5	0.01
Northern European	12	0.03
Norwegian	588	1.62
Pennsylvania German	19	0.05
Polish	1,502	4.15
Portuguese	72	0.20
Romanian	77	0.21
Russian	542	1.50
Scandinavian	47	0.13
Scotch-Irish	716	1.98
Scottish	658	1.82
Serbian	32	0.09
Slavic	6	0.02
Slovak	97	0.27
Slovene	39	0.11
Swedish	806	2.23
Swiss	207	0.57
Turkish	65	0.18
Ukrainian	172	0.48
United States or American	1,259	3.48
Welsh	322	0.89
West Indian, excl. Hispanic:	52	0.14
Barbadian	6	0.02
Belizean	9	0.02
Haitian	14	0.04
Jamaican	23	0.06
White:	25,109	68.99
Not Hispanic (23,811)	24,437	67.14
Hispanic (578)	672	1.85
Yugoslavian	56	0.15

Vernon Hills

Place Type: Village
County: Lake
Population: 20,120

Ancestry/Race	Number	%
African American/Black:	393	1.95
Not Hispanic (336)	387	1.92
Hispanic (4)	6	0.03
African, sub-Saharan:	9	0.04
African	9	0.04
Am. Ind. or Alaska Nat., not spec.	25	0.12
American Indian tribes, specified:	27	0.13
Cherokee (1)	11	0.05
Iroquois (2)	2	0.01
Latin American Indians (4)	4	0.02
Pueblo	1	0.00
All other tribes (3)	9	0.04
Arab:	84	0.41
Arab/Arabic	38	0.18
Egyptian	14	0.07
Iraqi	2	0.01
Lebanese	8	0.04
Moroccan	2	0.01
Syrian	20	0.10
Armenian	41	0.20
Asian:	2,579	12.82
Cambodian (3)	3	0.01
Chinese, ex. Taiwanese (604)	649	3.23
Filipino (326)	407	2.02
Hmong (1)	1	0.00
Indian (506)	536	2.66
Indonesian (2)	4	0.02
Japanese (110)	144	0.72
Korean (605)	626	3.11
Laotian (2)	3	0.01
Pakistani (54)	58	0.29
Sri Lankan (5)	5	0.02
Taiwanese (31)	36	0.18
Thai (11)	14	0.07
Vietnamese (32)	43	0.21
Other Asian, specified (5)	5	0.02
Other Asian, not specified (14)	45	0.22
Assyrian/Chaldean/Syriac	8	0.04
Austrian	132	0.64
Belgian	29	0.14
Brazilian	29	0.14
British	155	0.75
Bulgarian	9	0.04
Canadian	89	0.43

Notes: 1. Figures in the "Number" column do not add up to the total population due to: a) Ancestry/Race overlap — e.g. persons can report being both White and Irish, b) persons of Hispanic origin can report being any race, c) persons reporting two ancestries are counted in both categories. 2. Numbers in parentheses indicate the number of persons reporting this ancestry/race alone, not in combination with any other ancestry/race. 3. Refer to the Explanation of Data in the front of the book for more detailed information.

Ancestry/Race	Number	%
Croatian	56	0.27
Czech	188	0.91
Czechoslovakian	111	0.54
Danish	116	0.56
Dutch	211	1.02
Eastern European	86	0.42
English	1,328	6.44
European	79	0.38
Finnish	36	0.17
French, except Basque	426	2.07
French Canadian	109	0.53
German	3,864	18.75
Greek	218	1.06
Hawaii Native/Pacific Islander:	30	0.15
Micronesian:	1	0.00
Guamanian/Chamorro	1	0.00
Polynesian: (5)	10	0.05
Native Hawaiian	4	0.02
Samoan (5)	6	0.03
Other Pac. Isl., not spec. (1)	19	0.09
Hispanic or Latino:	1,446	7.19
Central American:	65	0.32
Costa Rican	2	0.01
Guatemalan	18	0.09
Honduran	4	0.02
Nicaraguan	4	0.02
Panamanian	9	0.04
Salvadoran	28	0.14
Cuban	25	0.12
Dominican Republic	7	0.03
Mexican	1,007	5.00
Puerto Rican	91	0.45
South American:	90	0.45
Argentinean	6	0.03
Chilean	2	0.01
Colombian	33	0.16
Ecuadorian	15	0.07
Paraguayan	2	0.01
Peruvian	14	0.07
Venezuelan	10	0.05
Other South American	8	0.04
Other Hispanic or Latino	161	0.80
Hungarian	173	0.84
Icelander	7	0.03
Irish	2,868	13.92
Israeli	50	0.24
Italian	1,904	9.24
Latvian	38	0.18
Lithuanian	182	0.88
Luxemburger	11	0.05
New Zealander	6	0.03
Norwegian	408	1.98
Polish	2,082	10.10
Portuguese	5	0.02
Romanian	193	0.94
Russian	1,214	5.89
Scandinavian	13	0.06
Scotch-Irish	217	1.05
Scottish	240	1.16
Serbian	73	0.35
Slavic	7	0.03
Slovak	131	0.64
Slovene	15	0.07
Swedish	972	4.72
Swiss	61	0.30
Ukrainian	437	2.12
United States or American	624	3.03
Welsh	71	0.34
West Indian, excl. Hispanic:	15	0.07
Belizean	9	0.04
Haitian	6	0.03
White:	16,762	83.31
Not Hispanic (15,691)	15,906	79.06
Hispanic (779)	856	4.25
Yugoslavian	64	0.31

Villa Park

Place Type: Village
County: Du Page
Population: 22,075

Ancestry/Race	Number	%
Acadian/Cajun	18	0.08
African American/Black:	445	2.02
Not Hispanic (368)	429	1.94
Hispanic (1)	16	0.07
African, sub-Saharan:	14	0.06
African	14	0.06
Alaska Native tribes, specified:	1	0.00
All other tribes	1	0.00
Am. Ind. or Alaska Nat., not spec.	39	0.18
Albanian	71	0.32
Alsatian	8	0.04
American Indian tribes, specified:	74	0.34
Apache (1)	3	0.01
Blackfeet	2	0.01
Cherokee (7)	23	0.10
Chippewa (3)	4	0.02
Choctaw	1	0.00
Creek (1)	1	0.00
Iroquois (7)	11	0.05
Latin American Indians (2)	16	0.07
Ottawa	3	0.01
Potawatomi	2	0.01
Pueblo	1	0.00
Sioux (1)	1	0.00
Ute (1)	1	0.00
All other tribes	5	0.02
American Indian tribes, not spec.	3	0.01
Arab:	142	0.64
Lebanese	82	0.37
Palestinian	60	0.27
Armenian	18	0.08
Asian:	923	4.18
Bangladeshi (5)	5	0.02
Cambodian (1)	1	0.00
Chinese, ex. Taiwanese (62)	74	0.34
Filipino (148)	182	0.82
Hmong (1)	1	0.00
Indian (415)	442	2.00
Indonesian	4	0.02
Japanese (17)	28	0.13
Korean (34)	40	0.18
Laotian (6)	6	0.03
Pakistani (51)	66	0.30
Sri Lankan (3)	3	0.01
Taiwanese (9)	10	0.05
Thai (14)	14	0.06
Vietnamese (13)	13	0.06
Other Asian, specified (1)	1	0.00
Other Asian, not specified (14)	33	0.15
Australian	7	0.03
Austrian	94	0.42
Belgian	28	0.13
Brazilian	11	0.05
British	33	0.15
Bulgarian	9	0.04
Canadian	15	0.07
Croatian	95	0.43
Czech	661	2.97
Czechoslovakian	197	0.88
Danish	264	1.18
Dutch	586	2.63
English	1,611	7.23
Estonian	7	0.03
European	75	0.34
Finnish	55	0.25
French, except Basque	491	2.20
French Canadian	139	0.62
German	6,066	27.21
Greek	182	0.82
Hawaii Native/Pacific Islander:	27	0.12
Micronesian:	1	0.00
Guamanian/Chamorro	1	0.00
Polynesian: (2)	9	0.04
Native Hawaiian (2)	8	0.04
Samoan	1	0.00
Other Pac. Isl., not spec. (5)	17	0.08
Hispanic or Latino:	2,770	12.55
Central American:	56	0.25
Guatemalan	40	0.18
Honduran	5	0.02
Nicaraguan	2	0.01
Panamanian	2	0.01
Salvadoran	4	0.02
Other Central American	3	0.01
Cuban	67	0.30
Mexican	2,321	10.51
Puerto Rican	131	0.59
South American:	25	0.11
Argentinean	5	0.02
Chilean	5	0.02
Colombian	5	0.02
Ecuadorian	4	0.02
Peruvian	5	0.02
Venezuelan	1	0.00
Other Hispanic or Latino	170	0.77
Hungarian	66	0.30
Irish	4,278	19.19
Italian	2,878	12.91
Latvian	22	0.10
Lithuanian	291	1.31
Luxemburger	40	0.18
Norwegian	691	3.10
Polish	2,634	11.82
Portuguese	9	0.04
Romanian	18	0.08
Russian	125	0.56
Scandinavian	7	0.03
Scotch-Irish	271	1.22
Scottish	264	1.18
Serbian	147	0.66
Slavic	56	0.25
Slovak	96	0.43
Slovene	44	0.20
Swedish	742	3.33
Swiss	32	0.14
Ukrainian	230	1.03
United States or American	566	2.54
Welsh	118	0.53
White:	20,001	90.60
Not Hispanic (17,820)	18,048	81.76
Hispanic (1,859)	1,953	8.85
Yugoslavian	65	0.29

Warrenville

Place Type: City
County: Du Page
Population: 13,363

Ancestry/Race	Number	%
African American/Black:	368	2.75
Not Hispanic (304)	350	2.62
Hispanic (15)	18	0.13
African, sub-Saharan:	27	0.20
African	27	0.20
Alaska Native tribes, specified:	2	0.01
Alaska Athabascan	1	0.01
Eskimo	1	0.01
Am. Ind. or Alaska Nat., not spec.	29	0.22
Albanian	21	0.16
American Indian tribes, specified:	42	0.31
Cherokee (3)	13	0.10
Chippewa	3	0.02
Choctaw	1	0.01
Cree	1	0.01
Iroquois (2)	5	0.04
Latin American Indians (9)	12	0.09
Puget Sound Salish	1	0.01
Yaqui (4)	4	0.03
All other tribes (1)	2	0.01
American Indian tribes, not spec.	5	0.04
Arab:	86	0.65
Jordanian	14	0.11

Notes: 1. Figures in the "Number" column do not add up to the total population due to: a) Ancestry/Race overlap — e.g. persons can report being both White and Irish, b) persons of Hispanic origin can report being any race, c) persons reporting two ancestries are counted in both categories. 2. Numbers in parentheses indicate the number of persons reporting this ancestry/race alone, not in combination with any other ancestry/race. 3. Refer to the Explanation of Data in the front of the book for more detailed information.

Lebanese	72	0.55
Asian:	494	3.70
Cambodian (32)	32	0.24
Chinese, ex. Taiwanese (81)	85	0.64
Filipino (70)	83	0.62
Hmong (5)	7	0.05
Indian (111)	117	0.88
Indonesian (2)	2	0.01
Japanese (17)	24	0.18
Korean (58)	58	0.43
Laotian (9)	10	0.07
Malaysian (3)	3	0.02
Pakistani (4)	4	0.03
Taiwanese (2)	2	0.01
Thai (10)	12	0.09
Vietnamese (46)	46	0.34
Other Asian, specified (3)	3	0.02
Other Asian, not specified (6)	6	0.04
Austrian	151	1.14
British	68	0.52
Bulgarian	31	0.23
Canadian	23	0.17
Croatian	89	0.67
Czech	335	2.54
Czechoslovakian	64	0.49
Danish	157	1.19
Dutch	262	1.99
English	1,327	10.06
European	75	0.57
Finnish	35	0.27
French, except Basque	381	2.89
French Canadian	66	0.50
German	3,608	27.35
Greek	134	1.02
Hawaii Native/Pacific Islander:	6	0.04
Micronesian: (3)	3	0.02
Other Micronesian (3)	3	0.02
Polynesian: (2)	2	0.01
Native Hawaiian (2)	2	0.01
Other Pac. Isl., not spec.	1	0.01
Hispanic or Latino:	1,349	10.10
Central American:	9	0.07
Guatemalan	1	0.01
Honduran	4	0.03
Nicaraguan	1	0.01
Panamanian	1	0.01
Salvadoran	1	0.01
Other Central American	1	0.01
Cuban	24	0.18
Mexican	1,079	8.07
Puerto Rican	78	0.58
South American:	43	0.32
Argentinean	12	0.09
Bolivian	5	0.04
Chilean	3	0.02
Colombian	9	0.07
Ecuadorian	3	0.02
Peruvian	8	0.06
Venezuelan	3	0.02
Other Hispanic or Latino	116	0.87
Hungarian	152	1.15
Irish	2,210	16.75
Italian	1,274	9.66
Lithuanian	226	1.71
Luxemburger	11	0.08
Northern European	18	0.14
Norwegian	303	2.30
Pennsylvania German	8	0.06
Polish	1,175	8.91
Romanian	15	0.11
Russian	177	1.34
Scandinavian	26	0.20
Scotch-Irish	183	1.39
Scottish	344	2.61
Serbian	7	0.05
Slovak	84	0.64
Swedish	332	2.52
Swiss	33	0.25
Turkish	14	0.11
Ukrainian	55	0.42
United States or American	417	3.16
Welsh	110	0.83
West Indian, excl. Hispanic:	15	0.11
Trinidadian and Tobagonian	15	0.11
White:	12,067	90.30
Not Hispanic (11,106)	11,210	83.89
Hispanic (804)	857	6.41
Yugoslavian	78	0.59

Washington

Place Type: City
County: Tazewell
Population: 10,841

Ancestry/Race	Number	%
African American/Black:	45	0.42
Not Hispanic (28)	45	0.42
Alaska Native tribes, specified:	1	0.01
Alaska Athabascan (1)	1	0.01
Am. Ind. or Alaska Nat., not spec.	11	0.10
American Indian tribes, specified:	17	0.16
Cherokee (7)	12	0.11
Creek (1)	1	0.01
Ottawa	2	0.02
Seminole	1	0.01
All other tribes	1	0.01
American Indian tribes, not spec.	3	0.03
Arab:	40	0.37
Arab/Arabic	14	0.13
Lebanese	26	0.24
Asian:	58	0.54
Cambodian (1)	1	0.01
Chinese, ex. Taiwanese (14)	16	0.15
Filipino (5)	8	0.07
Indian (8)	9	0.08
Japanese (5)	8	0.07
Korean (5)	7	0.06
Malaysian (1)	1	0.01
Vietnamese (1)	1	0.01
Other Asian, specified (1)	2	0.02
Other Asian, not specified (5)	5	0.05
Australian	50	0.46
Austrian	40	0.37
Belgian	14	0.13
British	13	0.12
Croatian	8	0.07
Czech	33	0.30
Czechoslovakian	10	0.09
Danish	63	0.58
Dutch	199	1.83
English	1,713	15.73
European	144	1.32
French, except Basque	426	3.91
French Canadian	27	0.25
German	4,330	39.76
Greek	17	0.16
Hawaii Native/Pacific Islander:	1	0.01
Other Pac. Isl., not spec.	1	0.01
Hispanic or Latino:	73	0.67
Central American:	1	0.01
Panamanian	1	0.01
Mexican	58	0.54
Puerto Rican	1	0.01
South American:	3	0.03
Argentinean	1	0.01
Ecuadorian	1	0.01
Venezuelan	1	0.01
Other Hispanic or Latino	10	0.09
Hungarian	74	0.68
Iranian	11	0.10
Irish	1,611	14.79
Italian	601	5.52
Latvian	16	0.15
Lithuanian	43	0.39
Northern European	22	0.20
Norwegian	153	1.40
Polish	105	0.96
Portuguese	56	0.51
Romanian	10	0.09
Russian	31	0.28
Scandinavian	31	0.28
Scotch-Irish	166	1.52
Scottish	330	3.03
Slovak	5	0.05
Slovene	8	0.07
Swedish	230	2.11
Swiss	107	0.98
Ukrainian	16	0.15
United States or American	787	7.23
Welsh	76	0.70
White:	10,728	98.96
Not Hispanic (10,620)	10,678	98.50
Hispanic (43)	50	0.46
Yugoslavian	13	0.12

Waukegan

Place Type: City
County: Lake
Population: 87,901

Ancestry/Race	Number	%
African American/Black:	17,864	20.32
Not Hispanic (16,354)	17,042	19.39
Hispanic (536)	822	0.94
African, sub-Saharan:	827	0.94
African	609	0.69
Ghanian	155	0.18
Nigerian	10	0.01
Other sub-Saharan African	53	0.06
Alaska Native tribes, specified:	3	0.00
Aleut	1	0.00
Eskimo	2	0.00
Am. Ind. or Alaska Nat., not spec.	442	0.50
Albanian	9	0.01
American Indian tribes, specified:	396	0.45
Apache (3)	5	0.01
Blackfeet (1)	17	0.02
Cherokee (20)	113	0.13
Cheyenne (1)	5	0.01
Chickasaw (2)	2	0.00
Chippewa (24)	33	0.04
Choctaw (6)	16	0.02
Comanche (2)	3	0.00
Cree	3	0.00
Creek (1)	7	0.01
Iroquois (2)	4	0.00
Kiowa (1)	1	0.00
Latin American Indians (97)	125	0.14
Lumbee (4)	4	0.00
Navajo (1)	1	0.00
Osage (2)	2	0.00
Ottawa (1)	2	0.00
Potawatomi (1)	3	0.00
Pueblo (2)	2	0.00
Seminole	1	0.00
Sioux (6)	21	0.02
Tohono O'Odham (1)	1	0.00
All other tribes (9)	25	0.03
American Indian tribes, not spec.	38	0.04
Arab:	181	0.21
Arab/Arabic	35	0.04
Iraqi	16	0.02
Jordanian	47	0.05
Lebanese	8	0.01
Palestinian	32	0.04
Syrian	37	0.04
Other Arab	6	0.01
Armenian	252	0.29
Asian:	3,606	4.10
Bangladeshi (1)	1	0.00
Cambodian (22)	30	0.03
Chinese, ex. Taiwanese (287)	337	0.38
Filipino (1,802)	2,008	2.28
Hmong (1)	1	0.00
Indian (567)	613	0.70
Indonesian (5)	9	0.01
Japanese (61)	106	0.12
Korean (177)	221	0.25

Notes: 1. Figures in the "Number" column do not add up to the total population due to: a) Ancestry/Race overlap — e.g. persons can report being both White and Irish, b) persons of Hispanic origin can report being any race, c) persons reporting two ancestries are counted in both categories. 2. Numbers in parentheses indicate the number of persons reporting this ancestry/race alone, not in combination with any other ancestry/race. 3. Refer to the Explanation of Data in the front of the book for more detailed information.

Ancestry/Race	Number	%
Malaysian (3)	7	0.01
Pakistani (27)	47	0.05
Sri Lankan (4)	4	0.00
Taiwanese (21)	23	0.03
Thai (20)	29	0.03
Vietnamese (64)	71	0.08
Other Asian, specified (2)	5	0.01
Other Asian, not specified (51)	94	0.11
Assyrian/Chaldean/Syriac	18	0.02
Australian	13	0.01
Austrian	163	0.19
Basque	35	0.04
Belgian	76	0.09
Brazilian	32	0.04
British	275	0.31
Bulgarian	20	0.02
Canadian	150	0.17
Celtic	3	0.00
Croatian	317	0.36
Czech	170	0.19
Czechoslovakian	100	0.11
Danish	370	0.42
Dutch	447	0.51
Eastern European	20	0.02
English	2,885	3.28
Estonian	7	0.01
European	122	0.14
Finnish	635	0.72
French, except Basque	1,204	1.37
French Canadian	206	0.23
German	7,568	8.60
German Russian	7	0.01
Greek	456	0.52
Hawaii Native/Pacific Islander:	119	0.14
Micronesian: (11)	15	0.02
Guamanian/Chamorro (11)	15	0.02
Polynesian: (24)	47	0.05
Native Hawaiian (15)	34	0.04
Samoan (9)	13	0.01
Other Pac. Isl., specified	1	0.00
Other Pac. Isl., not spec. (22)	56	0.06
Hispanic or Latino:	39,396	44.82
Central American:	2,082	2.37
Costa Rican	5	0.01
Guatemalan	189	0.22
Honduran	1,287	1.46
Nicaraguan	26	0.03
Panamanian	24	0.03
Salvadoran	428	0.49
Other Central American	123	0.14
Cuban	103	0.12
Dominican Republic	69	0.08
Mexican	30,717	34.94
Puerto Rican	2,976	3.39
South American:	378	0.43
Argentinean	7	0.01
Bolivian	5	0.01
Chilean	14	0.02
Colombian	285	0.32
Ecuadorian	33	0.04
Peruvian	17	0.02
Uruguayan	2	0.00
Venezuelan	9	0.01
Other South American	6	0.01
Other Hispanic or Latino	3,071	3.49
Hungarian	210	0.24
Iranian	23	0.03
Irish	4,504	5.12
Israeli	76	0.09
Italian	2,113	2.40
Lithuanian	525	0.60
Luxemburger	33	0.04
Macedonian	50	0.06
Norwegian	838	0.95
Pennsylvania German	9	0.01
Polish	2,841	3.23
Portuguese	79	0.09
Romanian	50	0.06
Russian	205	0.23
Scandinavian	51	0.06
Scotch-Irish	400	0.45
Scottish	619	0.70
Serbian	93	0.11
Slavic	52	0.06
Slovak	93	0.11
Slovene	444	0.50
Swedish	1,287	1.46
Swiss	94	0.11
Ukrainian	78	0.09
United States or American	1,805	2.05
Welsh	197	0.22
West Indian, excl. Hispanic:	722	0.82
Belizean	366	0.42
Haitian	75	0.09
Jamaican	241	0.27
Trinidadian and Tobagonian	19	0.02
West Indian	21	0.02
White:	46,562	52.97
Not Hispanic (27,186)	28,094	31.96
Hispanic (16,887)	18,468	21.01
Yugoslavian	120	0.14

West Chicago

Place Type: City
County: Du Page
Population: 23,469

Ancestry/Race	Number	%
African American/Black:	466	1.99
Not Hispanic (326)	358	1.53
Hispanic (69)	108	0.46
African, sub-Saharan:	14	0.06
African	6	0.03
South African	8	0.03
Alaska Native tribes, not specified	1	0.00
Am. Ind. or Alaska Nat., not spec.	74	0.32
American Indian tribes, specified:	69	0.29
Apache	1	0.00
Cherokee (6)	18	0.08
Chippewa (5)	6	0.03
Iroquois (4)	5	0.02
Latin American Indians (11)	29	0.12
Sioux (1)	7	0.03
All other tribes (2)	3	0.01
American Indian tribes, not spec.	13	0.06
Armenian	10	0.04
Asian:	559	2.38
Cambodian (17)	18	0.08
Chinese, ex. Taiwanese (28)	51	0.22
Filipino (170)	206	0.88
Hmong (3)	3	0.01
Indian (115)	134	0.57
Indonesian	3	0.01
Japanese (17)	26	0.11
Korean (14)	24	0.10
Laotian (12)	13	0.06
Malaysian	2	0.01
Pakistani (14)	14	0.06
Thai (7)	7	0.03
Vietnamese (39)	44	0.19
Other Asian, not specified (6)	14	0.06
Austrian	83	0.35
Belgian	26	0.11
Brazilian	8	0.03
British	28	0.12
Bulgarian	23	0.10
Canadian	18	0.08
Celtic	31	0.13
Croatian	41	0.17
Czech	247	1.03
Czechoslovakian	56	0.23
Danish	113	0.47
Dutch	291	1.22
English	1,211	5.06
European	126	0.53
Finnish	17	0.07
French, except Basque	432	1.81
French Canadian	52	0.22
German	4,123	17.24
German Russian	7	0.03
Greek	119	0.50
Hawaii Native/Pacific Islander:	14	0.06
Micronesian: (1)	2	0.01
Guamanian/Chamorro (1)	2	0.01
Polynesian: (6)	9	0.04
Native Hawaiian (1)	2	0.01
Tongan (5)	7	0.03
Other Pac. Isl., not spec.	3	0.01
Hispanic or Latino:	11,405	48.60
Central American:	42	0.18
Guatemalan	20	0.09
Honduran	7	0.03
Nicaraguan	1	0.00
Salvadoran	14	0.06
Cuban	55	0.23
Dominican Republic	4	0.02
Mexican	10,550	44.95
Puerto Rican	150	0.64
South American:	42	0.18
Argentinean	3	0.01
Bolivian	7	0.03
Chilean	3	0.01
Colombian	13	0.06
Ecuadorian	8	0.03
Peruvian	5	0.02
Uruguayan	1	0.00
Venezuelan	2	0.01
Other Hispanic or Latino	562	2.39
Hungarian	56	0.23
Irish	2,315	9.68
Italian	1,536	6.42
Latvian	36	0.15
Lithuanian	150	0.63
Luxemburger	8	0.03
Northern European	34	0.14
Norwegian	214	0.89
Pennsylvania German	43	0.18
Polish	1,524	6.37
Russian	170	0.71
Scandinavian	30	0.13
Scotch-Irish	140	0.59
Scottish	335	1.40
Serbian	18	0.08
Slavic	29	0.12
Slovak	85	0.36
Slovene	23	0.10
Swedish	357	1.49
Swiss	17	0.07
Turkish	7	0.03
Ukrainian	66	0.28
United States or American	625	2.61
Welsh	63	0.26
West Indian, excl. Hispanic:	16	0.07
Belizean	16	0.07
White:	18,918	80.61
Not Hispanic (11,052)	11,223	47.82
Hispanic (7,219)	7,695	32.79
Yugoslavian	27	0.11

Westchester

Place Type: Village
County: Cook
Population: 16,824

Ancestry/Race	Number	%
African American/Black:	1,252	7.44
Not Hispanic (1,207)	1,243	7.39
Hispanic (5)	9	0.05
Am. Ind. or Alaska Nat., not spec.	22	0.13
American Indian tribes, specified:	31	0.18
Blackfeet	4	0.02
Cherokee (1)	9	0.05
Chippewa	4	0.02
Choctaw	4	0.02
Latin American Indians	1	0.01
Ottawa	3	0.02
Shoshone	1	0.01
All other tribes (1)	5	0.03

Notes: 1. Figures in the "Number" column do not add up to the total population due to: a) Ancestry/Race overlap — e.g. persons can report being both White and Irish, b) persons of Hispanic origin can report being any race, c) persons reporting two ancestries are counted in both categories. 2. Numbers in parentheses indicate the number of persons reporting this ancestry/race alone, not in combination with any other ancestry/race. 3. Refer to the Explanation of Data in the front of the book for more detailed information.

Ancestry/Race	Number	%
Arab:	13	0.08
Lebanese	13	0.08
Asian:	649	3.86
Cambodian (2)	2	0.01
Chinese, ex. Taiwanese (74)	90	0.53
Filipino (274)	301	1.79
Hmong	2	0.01
Indian (95)	102	0.61
Japanese (14)	26	0.15
Korean (36)	41	0.24
Laotian (1)	1	0.01
Pakistani (19)	25	0.15
Sri Lankan (1)	1	0.01
Taiwanese (3)	3	0.02
Thai (14)	14	0.08
Vietnamese (37)	39	0.23
Other Asian, not specified	2	0.01
Austrian	74	0.44
Belgian	22	0.13
British	13	0.08
Canadian	25	0.15
Carpatho Rusyn	15	0.09
Croatian	191	1.15
Czech	1,194	7.17
Czechoslovakian	260	1.56
Danish	42	0.25
Dutch	219	1.31
English	693	4.16
European	50	0.30
Finnish	19	0.11
French, except Basque	282	1.69
French Canadian	93	0.56
German	3,316	19.90
Greek	491	2.95
Hawaii Native/Pacific Islander:	4	0.02
Micronesian: (1)	1	0.01
Guamanian/Chamorro (1)	1	0.01
Polynesian:	1	0.01
Native Hawaiian	1	0.01
Other Pac. Isl., not spec.	2	0.01
Hispanic or Latino:	956	5.68
Central American:	13	0.08
Guatemalan	4	0.02
Honduran	3	0.02
Panamanian	1	0.01
Salvadoran	1	0.01
Other Central American	4	0.02
Cuban	36	0.21
Dominican Republic	4	0.02
Mexican	705	4.19
Puerto Rican	91	0.54
South American:	42	0.25
Argentinean	7	0.04
Chilean	1	0.01
Colombian	9	0.05
Ecuadorian	8	0.05
Peruvian	2	0.01
Uruguayan	3	0.02
Venezuelan	5	0.03
Other South American	7	0.04
Other Hispanic or Latino	65	0.39
Hungarian	34	0.20
Icelander	7	0.04
Irish	2,847	17.08
Italian	3,483	20.90
Latvian	44	0.26
Lithuanian	422	2.53
Luxemburger	15	0.09
Macedonian	35	0.21
New Zealander	7	0.04
Norwegian	250	1.50
Polish	2,500	15.00
Portuguese	10	0.06
Russian	45	0.27
Scandinavian	10	0.06
Scotch-Irish	150	0.90
Scottish	168	1.01
Serbian	11	0.07
Slavic	12	0.07
Slovak	214	1.28
Slovene	62	0.37
Swedish	324	1.94
Swiss	67	0.40
Turkish	8	0.05
Ukrainian	111	0.67
United States or American	152	0.91
Welsh	29	0.17
West Indian, excl. Hispanic:	10	0.06
Jamaican	10	0.06
White:	14,656	87.11
Not Hispanic (13,919)	14,044	83.48
Hispanic (575)	612	3.64
Yugoslavian	78	0.47

Western Springs

Place Type: Village
County: Cook
Population: 12,493

Ancestry/Race	Number	%
African American/Black:	32	0.26
Not Hispanic (23)	28	0.22
Hispanic	4	0.03
Am. Ind. or Alaska Nat., not spec.	9	0.07
American Indian tribes, specified:	11	0.09
Blackfeet (1)	1	0.01
Cherokee	3	0.02
Chippewa (3)	4	0.03
Delaware	1	0.01
Latin American Indians (1)	1	0.01
Sioux	1	0.01
Arab:	57	0.45
Lebanese	57	0.45
Armenian	48	0.38
Asian:	120	0.96
Cambodian (2)	2	0.02
Chinese, ex. Taiwanese (18)	20	0.16
Filipino (12)	20	0.16
Indian (29)	32	0.26
Japanese (7)	16	0.13
Korean (16)	18	0.14
Taiwanese	1	0.01
Thai (2)	2	0.02
Vietnamese (2)	4	0.03
Other Asian, not specified	5	0.04
Assyrian/Chaldean/Syriac	6	0.05
Austrian	81	0.64
Belgian	20	0.16
British	50	0.40
Canadian	8	0.06
Croatian	167	1.32
Czech	518	4.10
Czechoslovakian	131	1.04
Danish	138	1.09
Dutch	330	2.61
Eastern European	5	0.04
English	1,135	8.99
Estonian	11	0.09
European	84	0.67
French, except Basque	336	2.66
French Canadian	17	0.13
German	3,504	27.76
Greek	171	1.35
Hawaii Native/Pacific Islander:	3	0.02
Micronesian:	1	0.01
Guamanian/Chamorro	1	0.01
Polynesian:	1	0.01
Samoan	1	0.01
Other Pac. Isl., not spec.	1	0.01
Hispanic or Latino:	212	1.70
Central American:	5	0.04
Costa Rican	1	0.01
Guatemalan	4	0.03
Cuban	16	0.13
Mexican	131	1.05
Puerto Rican	15	0.12
South American:	9	0.07
Argentinean	1	0.01
Chilean	1	0.01
Colombian	4	0.03
Ecuadorian	3	0.02
Other Hispanic or Latino	36	0.29
Hungarian	39	0.31
Iranian	22	0.17
Irish	3,770	29.87
Italian	1,698	13.45
Latvian	42	0.33
Lithuanian	313	2.48
Luxemburger	13	0.10
Northern European	8	0.06
Norwegian	238	1.89
Polish	1,746	13.83
Portuguese	12	0.10
Romanian	8	0.06
Russian	112	0.89
Scotch-Irish	209	1.66
Scottish	319	2.53
Serbian	76	0.60
Slovak	144	1.14
Slovene	11	0.09
Swedish	663	5.25
Swiss	61	0.48
Turkish	25	0.20
Ukrainian	57	0.45
United States or American	341	2.70
Welsh	53	0.42
West Indian, excl. Hispanic:	22	0.17
Jamaican	5	0.04
West Indian	17	0.13
White:	12,345	98.82
Not Hispanic (12,118)	12,159	97.33
Hispanic (165)	186	1.49
Yugoslavian	64	0.51

Westmont

Place Type: Village
County: Du Page
Population: 24,554

Ancestry/Race	Number	%
African American/Black:	1,434	5.84
Not Hispanic (1,309)	1,406	5.73
Hispanic (12)	28	0.11
African, sub-Saharan:	250	1.03
African	208	0.85
South African	42	0.17
Alaska Native tribes, specified:	1	0.00
Eskimo	1	0.00
Am. Ind. or Alaska Nat., not spec.	41	0.17
Albanian	62	0.25
American Indian tribes, specified:	92	0.37
Apache (2)	4	0.02
Blackfeet	5	0.02
Cherokee (2)	34	0.14
Chickasaw	3	0.01
Choctaw (7)	7	0.03
Creek	2	0.01
Delaware	1	0.00
Iroquois	2	0.01
Latin American Indians (4)	7	0.03
Navajo (1)	1	0.00
Ottawa	2	0.01
Seminole	2	0.01
Sioux (1)	3	0.01
All other tribes (5)	19	0.08
American Indian tribes, not spec.	6	0.02
Arab:	195	0.80
Arab/Arabic	59	0.24
Egyptian	34	0.14
Jordanian	24	0.10
Lebanese	78	0.32
Asian:	3,126	12.73
Chinese, ex. Taiwanese (657)	710	2.89
Filipino (575)	617	2.51
Indian (1,274)	1,317	5.36
Indonesian (1)	4	0.02
Japanese (38)	58	0.24
Korean (152)	163	0.66

Notes: 1. Figures in the "Number" column do not add up to the total population due to: a) Ancestry/Race overlap — e.g. persons can report being both White and Irish, b) persons of Hispanic origin can report being any race, c) persons reporting two ancestries are counted in both categories. 2. Numbers in parentheses indicate the number of persons reporting this ancestry/race alone, not in combination with any other ancestry/race. 3. Refer to the Explanation of Data in the front of the book for more detailed information.

Ancestry/Race	Number	%
Laotian (1)	1	0.00
Malaysian (1)	6	0.02
Pakistani (92)	101	0.41
Sri Lankan (3)	3	0.01
Taiwanese (48)	54	0.22
Thai (23)	30	0.12
Vietnamese (12)	13	0.05
Other Asian, specified (1)	2	0.01
Other Asian, not specified (22)	47	0.19
Austrian	157	0.64
Belgian	109	0.45
British	61	0.25
Bulgarian	13	0.05
Canadian	6	0.02
Croatian	119	0.49
Czech	1,085	4.46
Czechoslovakian	164	0.67
Danish	190	0.78
Dutch	463	1.90
English	1,590	6.53
European	86	0.35
Finnish	46	0.19
French, except Basque	586	2.41
French Canadian	132	0.54
German	4,290	17.62
Greek	338	1.39
Hawaii Native/Pacific Islander:	14	0.06
Micronesian:	4	0.02
Guamanian/Chamorro	4	0.02
Polynesian:	1	0.00
Native Hawaiian	1	0.00
Other Pac. Isl., not spec.	9	0.04
Hispanic or Latino:	1,714	6.98
Central American:	28	0.11
Guatemalan	17	0.07
Honduran	1	0.00
Nicaraguan	1	0.00
Panamanian	1	0.00
Salvadoran	8	0.03
Cuban	25	0.10
Dominican Republic	5	0.02
Mexican	1,328	5.41
Puerto Rican	123	0.50
South American:	45	0.18
Argentinean	11	0.04
Bolivian	1	0.00
Colombian	19	0.08
Ecuadorian	8	0.03
Peruvian	5	0.02
Venezuelan	1	0.00
Other Hispanic or Latino	160	0.65
Hungarian	103	0.42
Iranian	6	0.02
Irish	3,716	15.27
Italian	2,121	8.71
Latvian	20	0.08
Lithuanian	727	2.99
Luxemburger	19	0.08
Macedonian	36	0.15
Norwegian	207	0.85
Polish	3,325	13.66
Romanian	71	0.29
Russian	199	0.82
Scotch-Irish	166	0.68
Scottish	270	1.11
Serbian	167	0.69
Slavic	25	0.10
Slovak	256	1.05
Slovene	35	0.14
Swedish	558	2.29
Swiss	17	0.07
Turkish	18	0.07
Ukrainian	138	0.57
United States or American	810	3.33
Welsh	90	0.37
West Indian, excl. Hispanic:	66	0.27
Bahamian	12	0.05
Haitian	6	0.02
Jamaican	48	0.20
White:	19,577	79.73
Not Hispanic (18,193)	18,480	75.26
Hispanic (963)	1,097	4.47
Yugoslavian	49	0.20

Wheaton

Place Type: City
County: Du Page
Population: 55,416

Ancestry/Race	Number	%
Afghan	16	0.03
African American/Black:	1,735	3.13
Not Hispanic (1,525)	1,682	3.04
Hispanic (40)	53	0.10
African, sub-Saharan:	282	0.51
African	146	0.26
Ethiopian	8	0.01
Kenyan	24	0.04
Sierra Leonean	20	0.04
South African	65	0.12
Other sub-Saharan African	19	0.03
Alaska Native tribes, specified:	1	0.00
All other tribes	1	0.00
Am. Ind. or Alaska Nat., not spec.	63	0.11
Albanian	9	0.02
American Indian tribes, specified:	103	0.19
Blackfeet	1	0.00
Cherokee (15)	39	0.07
Chickasaw (1)	1	0.00
Chippewa (6)	14	0.03
Choctaw (1)	1	0.00
Creek	2	0.00
Houma (4)	4	0.01
Iroquois (3)	4	0.01
Latin American Indians (5)	13	0.02
Menominee	3	0.01
Navajo	3	0.01
Potawatomi (4)	4	0.01
Pueblo	5	0.01
Sioux (2)	5	0.01
All other tribes (1)	4	0.01
American Indian tribes, not spec.	12	0.02
Arab:	314	0.57
Arab/Arabic	41	0.07
Egyptian	34	0.06
Iraqi	9	0.02
Jordanian	37	0.07
Lebanese	135	0.24
Palestinian	14	0.03
Syrian	37	0.07
Other Arab	7	0.01
Armenian	52	0.09
Asian:	3,072	5.54
Cambodian (69)	70	0.13
Chinese, ex. Taiwanese (453)	534	0.96
Filipino (235)	300	0.54
Hmong (20)	20	0.04
Indian (786)	847	1.53
Indonesian (4)	7	0.01
Japanese (102)	162	0.29
Korean (330)	355	0.64
Laotian (12)	15	0.03
Malaysian (1)	2	0.00
Pakistani (79)	97	0.18
Sri Lankan (3)	3	0.01
Taiwanese (54)	67	0.12
Thai (24)	27	0.05
Vietnamese (430)	462	0.83
Other Asian, specified (10)	13	0.02
Other Asian, not specified (24)	91	0.16
Assyrian/Chaldean/Syriac	5	0.01
Australian	53	0.10
Austrian	282	0.51
Belgian	141	0.25
Brazilian	32	0.06
British	515	0.93
Bulgarian	7	0.01
Canadian	190	0.34
Croatian	377	0.68
Czech	1,366	2.46
Czechoslovakian	288	0.52
Danish	466	0.84
Dutch	1,498	2.70
Eastern European	18	0.03
English	7,150	12.90
European	768	1.39
Finnish	135	0.24
French, except Basque	1,473	2.66
French Canadian	311	0.56
German	15,590	28.12
Greek	602	1.09
Hawaii Native/Pacific Islander:	38	0.07
Melanesian:	1	0.00
Other Melanesian	1	0.00
Micronesian: (1)	1	0.00
Guamanian/Chamorro (1)	1	0.00
Polynesian: (9)	22	0.04
Native Hawaiian (5)	9	0.02
Samoan (3)	8	0.01
Other Polynesian (1)	5	0.01
Other Pac. Isl., not spec. (1)	14	0.03
Hispanic or Latino:	2,023	3.65
Central American:	69	0.12
Costa Rican	15	0.03
Guatemalan	23	0.04
Honduran	12	0.02
Nicaraguan	2	0.00
Panamanian	5	0.01
Salvadoran	10	0.02
Other Central American	2	0.00
Cuban	108	0.19
Dominican Republic	8	0.01
Mexican	1,225	2.21
Puerto Rican	169	0.30
South American:	223	0.40
Argentinean	21	0.04
Bolivian	26	0.05
Chilean	16	0.03
Colombian	74	0.13
Ecuadorian	26	0.05
Paraguayan	2	0.00
Peruvian	28	0.05
Uruguayan	1	0.00
Venezuelan	16	0.03
Other South American	13	0.02
Other Hispanic or Latino	221	0.40
Hungarian	394	0.71
Icelander	22	0.04
Iranian	30	0.05
Irish	10,224	18.44
Italian	5,212	9.40
Latvian	75	0.14
Lithuanian	431	0.78
Luxemburger	81	0.15
Macedonian	42	0.08
Maltese	8	0.01
Northern European	16	0.03
Norwegian	1,834	3.31
Pennsylvania German	24	0.04
Polish	4,622	8.34
Romanian	115	0.21
Russian	687	1.24
Scandinavian	159	0.29
Scotch-Irish	994	1.79
Scottish	1,581	2.85
Serbian	153	0.28
Slavic	63	0.11
Slovak	300	0.54
Slovene	123	0.22
Swedish	3,197	5.77
Swiss	345	0.62
Turkish	28	0.05
Ukrainian	158	0.28
United States or American	1,567	2.83
Welsh	453	0.82
West Indian, excl. Hispanic:	47	0.08
Haitian	9	0.02
Jamaican	26	0.05
West Indian	12	0.02

Notes: 1. Figures in the "Number" column do not add up to the total population due to: a) Ancestry/Race overlap — e.g. persons can report being both White and Irish, b) persons of Hispanic origin can report being any race, c) persons reporting two ancestries are counted in both categories. 2. Numbers in parentheses indicate the number of persons reporting this ancestry/race alone, not in combination with any other ancestry/race. 3. Refer to the Explanation of Data in the front of the book for more detailed information.

White:	50,431	91.00
Not Hispanic (48,494)	49,006	88.43
Hispanic (1,297)	1,425	2.57
Yugoslavian	305	0.55

Wheeling

Place Type: Village
County: Cook
Population: 34,496

Ancestry/Race	Number	%
African American/Black:	926	2.68
Not Hispanic (799)	865	2.51
Hispanic (44)	61	0.18
African, sub-Saharan:	25	0.07
African	13	0.04
Ghanian	12	0.03
Alaska Native tribes, specified:	1	0.00
Eskimo	1	0.00
Am. Ind. or Alaska Nat., not spec.	80	0.23
American Indian tribes, specified:	89	0.26
Apache (4)	4	0.01
Blackfeet	5	0.01
Cherokee (7)	28	0.08
Chippewa (9)	11	0.03
Choctaw (2)	4	0.01
Iroquois (5)	11	0.03
Latin American Indians (13)	14	0.04
Lumbee	1	0.00
Menominee (2)	2	0.01
Sioux (2)	2	0.01
All other tribes	7	0.02
American Indian tribes, not spec.	7	0.02
Arab:	40	0.12
Egyptian	11	0.03
Jordanian	10	0.03
Lebanese	19	0.06
Armenian	165	0.48
Asian:	3,410	9.89
Bangladeshi (3)	3	0.01
Cambodian (39)	50	0.14
Chinese, ex. Taiwanese (321)	352	1.02
Filipino (577)	629	1.82
Indian (1,428)	1,472	4.27
Indonesian (7)	12	0.03
Japanese (146)	167	0.48
Korean (375)	387	1.12
Laotian (12)	12	0.03
Pakistani (86)	100	0.29
Sri Lankan (8)	11	0.03
Taiwanese (9)	11	0.03
Thai (31)	37	0.11
Vietnamese (87)	92	0.27
Other Asian, specified (16)	16	0.05
Other Asian, not specified (23)	59	0.17
Assyrian/Chaldean/Syriac	18	0.05
Austrian	138	0.40
Belgian	53	0.15
Brazilian	7	0.02
British	48	0.14
Bulgarian	67	0.19
Canadian	101	0.29
Celtic	5	0.01
Croatian	38	0.11
Czech	332	0.96
Czechoslovakian	56	0.16
Danish	221	0.64
Dutch	305	0.89
Eastern European	17	0.05
English	1,589	4.62
Estonian	10	0.03
European	56	0.16
Finnish	106	0.31
French, except Basque	632	1.84
French Canadian	53	0.15
German	5,731	16.65
Greek	375	1.09
Hawaii Native/Pacific Islander:	40	0.12
Micronesian: (1)	1	0.00
Guamanian/Chamorro (1)	1	0.00
Polynesian: (14)	19	0.06
Native Hawaiian (9)	10	0.03
Samoan (2)	4	0.01
Tongan (3)	3	0.01
Other Polynesian	2	0.01
Other Pac. Isl., not spec. (8)	20	0.06
Hispanic or Latino:	7,135	20.68
Central American:	191	0.55
Costa Rican	4	0.01
Guatemalan	52	0.15
Honduran	12	0.03
Nicaraguan	2	0.01
Panamanian	14	0.04
Salvadoran	86	0.25
Other Central American	21	0.06
Cuban	59	0.17
Dominican Republic	8	0.02
Mexican	6,086	17.64
Puerto Rican	183	0.53
South American:	177	0.51
Argentinean	28	0.08
Bolivian	2	0.01
Chilean	7	0.02
Colombian	64	0.19
Ecuadorian	23	0.07
Paraguayan	2	0.01
Peruvian	9	0.03
Venezuelan	33	0.10
Other South American	9	0.03
Other Hispanic or Latino	431	1.25
Hungarian	323	0.94
Iranian	100	0.29
Irish	3,332	9.68
Israeli	44	0.13
Italian	1,913	5.56
Latvian	52	0.15
Lithuanian	172	0.50
Luxemburger	38	0.11
Macedonian	14	0.04
Maltese	9	0.03
New Zealander	7	0.02
Norwegian	448	1.30
Pennsylvania German	15	0.04
Polish	3,709	10.78
Portuguese	22	0.06
Romanian	207	0.60
Russian	2,334	6.78
Scandinavian	7	0.02
Scotch-Irish	223	0.65
Scottish	327	0.95
Slavic	10	0.03
Slovak	97	0.28
Slovene	8	0.02
Swedish	846	2.46
Swiss	80	0.23
Turkish	92	0.27
Ukrainian	608	1.77
United States or American	1,207	3.51
Welsh	113	0.33
West Indian, excl. Hispanic:	207	0.60
Belizean	83	0.24
Haitian	56	0.16
Jamaican	48	0.14
Trinidadian and Tobagonian	12	0.03
West Indian	8	0.02
White:	27,087	78.52
Not Hispanic (22,892)	23,213	67.29
Hispanic (3,560)	3,874	11.23
Yugoslavian	90	0.26

Wilmette

Place Type: Village
County: Cook
Population: 27,651

Ancestry/Race	Number	%
Afghan	8	0.03
African American/Black:	191	0.69
Not Hispanic (147)	181	0.65
Hispanic (9)	10	0.04
African, sub-Saharan:	5	0.02
South African	5	0.02
Alaska Native tribes, specified:	1	0.00
Alaska Athabascan (1)	1	0.00
Am. Ind. or Alaska Nat., not spec.	18	0.07
Alsatian	14	0.05
American Indian tribes, specified:	25	0.09
Blackfeet (3)	5	0.02
Cherokee	6	0.02
Creek	1	0.00
Iroquois (1)	1	0.00
Latin American Indians (2)	3	0.01
Lumbee	2	0.01
Potawatomi (1)	1	0.00
Sioux (1)	1	0.00
All other tribes	5	0.02
American Indian tribes, not spec.	3	0.01
Arab:	60	0.22
Arab/Arabic	12	0.04
Lebanese	41	0.15
Moroccan	7	0.03
Asian:	2,522	9.12
Bangladeshi (1)	1	0.00
Cambodian (2)	10	0.04
Chinese, ex. Taiwanese (648)	734	2.65
Filipino (164)	205	0.74
Indian (226)	254	0.92
Indonesian	1	0.00
Japanese (284)	348	1.26
Korean (663)	701	2.54
Malaysian (6)	7	0.03
Pakistani (34)	39	0.14
Sri Lankan (5)	5	0.02
Taiwanese (57)	68	0.25
Thai (86)	91	0.33
Vietnamese (19)	25	0.09
Other Asian, specified (3)	3	0.01
Other Asian, not specified (12)	30	0.11
Assyrian/Chaldean/Syriac	54	0.20
Austrian	278	1.00
Belgian	119	0.43
Brazilian	7	0.03
British	176	0.64
Bulgarian	37	0.13
Canadian	64	0.23
Celtic	7	0.03
Croatian	98	0.35
Czech	228	0.82
Czechoslovakian	65	0.23
Danish	154	0.56
Dutch	403	1.46
Eastern European	338	1.22
English	3,193	11.53
Estonian	10	0.04
European	298	1.08
Finnish	68	0.25
French, except Basque	683	2.47
French Canadian	132	0.48
German	5,599	20.22
Greek	606	2.19
Hawaii Native/Pacific Islander:	15	0.05
Polynesian: (4)	15	0.05
Native Hawaiian (3)	14	0.05
Samoan (1)	1	0.00
Hispanic or Latino:	574	2.08
Central American:	35	0.13
Guatemalan	26	0.09
Honduran	6	0.02
Nicaraguan	1	0.00
Panamanian	1	0.00
Other Central American	1	0.00
Cuban	69	0.25
Dominican Republic	5	0.02
Mexican	206	0.75
Puerto Rican	41	0.15
South American:	120	0.43
Argentinean	33	0.12
Bolivian	11	0.04

Notes: 1. Figures in the "Number" column do not add up to the total population due to: a) Ancestry/Race overlap — e.g. persons can report being both White and Irish, b) persons of Hispanic origin can report being any race, c) persons reporting two ancestries are counted in both categories. 2. Numbers in parentheses indicate the number of persons reporting this ancestry/race alone, not in combination with any other ancestry/race. 3. Refer to the Explanation of Data in the front of the book for more detailed information.

Chilean	17	0.06
Colombian	29	0.10
Ecuadorian	7	0.03
Paraguayan	3	0.01
Peruvian	14	0.05
Uruguayan	1	0.00
Venezuelan	2	0.01
Other South American	3	0.01
Other Hispanic or Latino	98	0.35
Hungarian	241	0.87
Icelander	27	0.10
Iranian	77	0.28
Irish	5,369	19.39
Israeli	118	0.43
Italian	1,910	6.90
Latvian	37	0.13
Lithuanian	281	1.02
Luxemburger	80	0.29
Northern European	81	0.29
Norwegian	783	2.83
Polish	1,984	7.17
Portuguese	9	0.03
Romanian	133	0.48
Russian	1,631	5.89
Scandinavian	105	0.38
Scotch-Irish	471	1.70
Scottish	720	2.60
Serbian	86	0.31
Slavic	6	0.02
Slovak	34	0.12
Slovene	40	0.14
Swedish	1,129	4.08
Swiss	121	0.44
Turkish	44	0.16
Ukrainian	76	0.27
United States or American	1,630	5.89
Welsh	221	0.80
West Indian, excl. Hispanic:	3	0.01
Jamaican	3	0.01
White:	25,083	90.71
Not Hispanic (24,343)	24,601	88.97
Hispanic (448)	482	1.74
Yugoslavian	41	0.15

Winnetka

Place Type: Village
County: Cook
Population: 12,419

Ancestry/Race	Number	%
African American/Black:	36	0.29
Not Hispanic (31)	36	0.29
African, sub-Saharan:	13	0.10
African	7	0.06
Other sub-Saharan African	6	0.05
Alaska Native tribes, specified:	1	0.01
Tlingit-Haida	1	0.01
Am. Ind. or Alaska Nat., not spec.	3	0.02
Alsatian	5	0.04
American Indian tribes, specified:	6	0.05
Cherokee	3	0.02
Choctaw (1)	1	0.01
Latin American Indians	1	0.01
All other tribes	1	0.01
Arab:	41	0.33
Lebanese	31	0.25
Syrian	10	0.08
Armenian	14	0.11
Asian:	376	3.03
Chinese, ex. Taiwanese (70)	86	0.69
Filipino (27)	51	0.41
Indian (49)	59	0.48
Japanese (48)	66	0.53
Korean (75)	79	0.64
Pakistani (1)	1	0.01
Sri Lankan (3)	3	0.02
Taiwanese (9)	9	0.07
Thai (1)	8	0.06
Vietnamese (4)	5	0.04
Other Asian, specified	2	0.02
Other Asian, not specified (6)	7	0.06
Assyrian/Chaldean/Syriac	5	0.04
Austrian	75	0.61
Belgian	92	0.74
British	144	1.16
Canadian	68	0.55
Croatian	74	0.60
Czech	135	1.09
Czechoslovakian	14	0.11
Danish	143	1.15
Dutch	285	2.30
Eastern European	115	0.93
English	2,271	18.33
European	321	2.59
Finnish	28	0.23
French, except Basque	389	3.14
French Canadian	41	0.33
German	2,859	23.08
Greek	207	1.67
Hawaii Native/Pacific Islander:	2	0.02
Other Pac. Isl., specified	2	0.02
Hispanic or Latino:	156	1.26
Central American:	9	0.07
Guatemalan	6	0.05
Panamanian	3	0.02
Cuban	13	0.10
Dominican Republic	5	0.04
Mexican	54	0.43
Puerto Rican	13	0.10
South American:	32	0.26
Argentinean	4	0.03
Bolivian	5	0.04
Chilean	1	0.01
Colombian	10	0.08
Ecuadorian	1	0.01
Peruvian	3	0.02
Venezuelan	1	0.01
Other South American	7	0.06
Other Hispanic or Latino	30	0.24
Hungarian	60	0.48
Icelander	6	0.05
Iranian	16	0.13
Irish	2,769	22.35
Israeli	32	0.26
Italian	705	5.69
Latvian	34	0.27
Lithuanian	126	1.02
Luxemburger	33	0.27
Northern European	77	0.62
Norwegian	249	2.01
Pennsylvania German	7	0.06
Polish	667	5.38
Romanian	57	0.46
Russian	459	3.71
Scandinavian	41	0.33
Scotch-Irish	271	2.19
Scottish	495	4.00
Serbian	6	0.05
Slavic	6	0.05
Slovak	41	0.33
Slovene	49	0.40
Swedish	435	3.51
Swiss	120	0.97
Turkish	6	0.05
Ukrainian	41	0.33
United States or American	400	3.23
Welsh	144	1.16
West Indian, excl. Hispanic:	5	0.04
Jamaican	5	0.04
White:	12,045	96.99
Not Hispanic (11,848)	11,919	95.97
Hispanic (110)	126	1.01
Yugoslavian	29	0.23

Wood Dale

Place Type: City
County: Du Page
Population: 13,535

Ancestry/Race	Number	%
African American/Black:	91	0.67
Not Hispanic (71)	82	0.61
Hispanic (7)	9	0.07
African, sub-Saharan:	11	0.08
African	11	0.08
Alaska Native tribes, specified:	1	0.01
Alaska Athabascan (1)	1	0.01
Am. Ind. or Alaska Nat., not spec.	11	0.08
Albanian	9	0.06
American Indian tribes, specified:	36	0.27
Apache (1)	1	0.01
Cherokee (2)	15	0.11
Chippewa (1)	2	0.01
Choctaw (4)	4	0.03
Latin American Indians (7)	12	0.09
Seminole	1	0.01
All other tribes (1)	1	0.01
American Indian tribes, not spec.	12	0.09
Armenian	8	0.06
Asian:	500	3.69
Cambodian	3	0.02
Chinese, ex. Taiwanese (22)	25	0.18
Filipino (82)	91	0.67
Indian (198)	211	1.56
Japanese (18)	27	0.20
Korean (57)	63	0.47
Pakistani (37)	48	0.35
Thai (5)	6	0.04
Vietnamese (11)	12	0.09
Other Asian, not specified (6)	14	0.10
Austrian	173	1.24
Belgian	38	0.27
British	59	0.42
Bulgarian	39	0.28
Canadian	16	0.11
Croatian	69	0.49
Czech	186	1.33
Czechoslovakian	14	0.10
Danish	36	0.26
Dutch	41	0.29
English	690	4.93
Finnish	45	0.32
French, except Basque	250	1.79
French Canadian	56	0.40
German	2,698	19.28
Greek	326	2.33
Hawaii Native/Pacific Islander:	16	0.12
Melanesian: (1)	1	0.01
Fijian (1)	1	0.01
Micronesian: (5)	5	0.04
Guamanian/Chamorro (5)	5	0.04
Polynesian: (1)	1	0.01
Native Hawaiian (1)	1	0.01
Other Pac. Isl., not spec. (3)	9	0.07
Hispanic or Latino:	1,768	13.06
Central American:	39	0.29
Costa Rican	3	0.02
Guatemalan	19	0.14
Honduran	3	0.02
Nicaraguan	1	0.01
Panamanian	1	0.01
Salvadoran	6	0.04
Other Central American	6	0.04
Cuban	52	0.38
Dominican Republic	4	0.03
Mexican	1,399	10.34
Puerto Rican	93	0.69
South American:	65	0.48
Argentinean	7	0.05
Chilean	4	0.03
Colombian	14	0.10
Ecuadorian	19	0.14
Peruvian	12	0.09

Notes: 1. Figures in the "Number" column do not add up to the total population due to: a) Ancestry/Race overlap — e.g. persons can report being both White and Irish, b) persons of Hispanic origin can report being any race, c) persons reporting two ancestries are counted in both categories. 2. Numbers in parentheses indicate the number of persons reporting this ancestry/race alone, not in combination with any other ancestry/race. 3. Refer to the Explanation of Data in the front of the book for more detailed information.

Ancestry/Race	Number	%
Venezuelan	8	0.06
Other South American	1	0.01
Other Hispanic or Latino	116	0.86
Hungarian	80	0.57
Irish	1,683	12.03
Italian	2,637	18.85
Latvian	8	0.06
Lithuanian	168	1.20
Luxemburger	12	0.09
Norwegian	187	1.34
Polish	2,886	20.63
Portuguese	6	0.04
Romanian	29	0.21
Russian	150	1.07
Scandinavian	15	0.11
Scotch-Irish	148	1.06
Scottish	100	0.71
Serbian	45	0.32
Slavic	31	0.22
Slovak	44	0.31
Swedish	359	2.57
Ukrainian	108	0.77
United States or American	456	3.26
Welsh	25	0.18
White:	12,299	90.87
Not Hispanic (11,048)	11,198	82.73
Hispanic (1,028)	1,101	8.13
Yugoslavian	19	0.14

Wood River

Place Type: City
County: Madison
Population: 11,296

Ancestry/Race	Number	%
African American/Black:	85	0.75
Not Hispanic (71)	85	0.75
African, sub-Saharan:	5	0.04
African	5	0.04
Am. Ind. or Alaska Nat., not spec.	31	0.27
American Indian tribes, specified:	36	0.32
Apache	3	0.03
Blackfeet (6)	6	0.05
Cherokee (5)	15	0.13
Cheyenne	4	0.04
Choctaw (2)	2	0.02
Comanche (1)	1	0.01
Iroquois (2)	2	0.02
Latin American Indians (1)	2	0.02
All other tribes	1	0.01
American Indian tribes, not spec.	3	0.03
Arab:	6	0.05
Other Arab	6	0.05
Asian:	82	0.73
Chinese, ex. Taiwanese (11)	16	0.14
Filipino (16)	22	0.19
Indian (3)	4	0.04
Japanese (6)	16	0.14
Korean (1)	1	0.01
Laotian (4)	6	0.05
Malaysian	1	0.01
Taiwanese (3)	3	0.03
Thai	4	0.04
Vietnamese (2)	2	0.02
Other Asian, not specified (4)	7	0.06
Austrian	71	0.63
British	66	0.59
Bulgarian	9	0.08
Canadian	9	0.08
Croatian	73	0.65
Czech	6	0.05
Czechoslovakian	17	0.15
Danish	8	0.07
Dutch	274	2.45
English	1,151	10.28
European	299	2.67
Finnish	35	0.31
French, except Basque	367	3.28
French Canadian	21	0.19
German	2,404	21.47
Greek	8	0.07
Hawaii Native/Pacific Islander:	3	0.03
Micronesian:	1	0.01
Guamanian/Chamorro	1	0.01
Polynesian:	2	0.02
Native Hawaiian	2	0.02
Hispanic or Latino:	137	1.21
Central American:	1	0.01
Guatemalan	1	0.01
Cuban	2	0.02
Mexican	88	0.78
Puerto Rican	5	0.04
South American:	1	0.01
Ecuadorian	1	0.01
Other Hispanic or Latino	40	0.35
Hungarian	97	0.87
Irish	1,512	13.50
Italian	501	4.47
Polish	131	1.17
Russian	73	0.65
Scandinavian	7	0.06
Scotch-Irish	125	1.12
Scottish	137	1.22
Serbian	37	0.33
Slovak	16	0.14
Swedish	30	0.27
Swiss	45	0.40
Ukrainian	25	0.22
United States or American	1,426	12.73
Welsh	27	0.24
West Indian, excl. Hispanic:	21	0.19
Haitian	21	0.19
White:	11,096	98.23
Not Hispanic (10,928)	10,999	97.37
Hispanic (93)	97	0.86
Yugoslavian	20	0.18

Woodridge

Place Type: Village
County: Du Page
Population: 30,934

Ancestry/Race	Number	%
African American/Black:	2,680	8.66
Not Hispanic (2,440)	2,607	8.43
Hispanic (42)	73	0.24
African, sub-Saharan:	226	0.73
African	153	0.49
Ethiopian	8	0.03
Liberian	20	0.06
Nigerian	37	0.12
Zimbabwean	8	0.03
Alaska Native tribes, specified:	2	0.01
Aleut (2)	2	0.01
Am. Ind. or Alaska Nat., not spec.	76	0.25
American Indian tribes, specified:	84	0.27
Blackfeet	3	0.01
Cherokee (1)	31	0.10
Chippewa (5)	10	0.03
Choctaw	6	0.02
Creek (1)	8	0.03
Iroquois (2)	2	0.01
Kiowa (1)	1	0.00
Latin American Indians (2)	13	0.04
Navajo	1	0.00
Potawatomi	1	0.00
Seminole (1)	1	0.00
Sioux (2)	2	0.01
All other tribes (1)	5	0.02
American Indian tribes, not spec.	7	0.02
Arab:	220	0.71
Arab/Arabic	13	0.04
Egyptian	38	0.12
Jordanian	7	0.02
Lebanese	87	0.28
Palestinian	37	0.12
Syrian	6	0.02
Other Arab	32	0.10
Asian:	3,734	12.07
Cambodian (7)	7	0.02
Chinese, ex. Taiwanese (499)	542	1.75
Filipino (730)	819	2.65
Hmong (5)	5	0.02
Indian (1,705)	1,769	5.72
Indonesian (4)	5	0.02
Japanese (44)	62	0.20
Korean (161)	164	0.53
Laotian (14)	14	0.05
Pakistani (116)	150	0.48
Sri Lankan (4)	10	0.03
Taiwanese (30)	36	0.12
Thai (29)	32	0.10
Vietnamese (49)	58	0.19
Other Asian, specified (2)	2	0.01
Other Asian, not specified (42)	59	0.19
Assyrian/Chaldean/Syriac	30	0.10
Australian	19	0.06
Austrian	112	0.36
Basque	89	0.29
Belgian	31	0.10
Brazilian	18	0.06
British	185	0.60
Bulgarian	16	0.05
Croatian	294	0.95
Czech	1,396	4.49
Czechoslovakian	143	0.46
Danish	133	0.43
Dutch	487	1.57
English	1,980	6.37
Estonian	9	0.03
European	151	0.49
Finnish	71	0.23
French, except Basque	712	2.29
French Canadian	146	0.47
German	6,718	21.62
Greek	223	0.72
Guyanese	7	0.02
Hawaii Native/Pacific Islander:	42	0.14
Micronesian: (2)	13	0.04
Guamanian/Chamorro (2)	12	0.04
Other Micronesian	1	0.00
Polynesian:	13	0.04
Native Hawaiian	12	0.04
Samoan	1	0.00
Other Pac. Isl., not spec. (4)	16	0.05
Hispanic or Latino:	2,839	9.18
Central American:	33	0.11
Costa Rican	6	0.02
Guatemalan	9	0.03
Honduran	2	0.01
Nicaraguan	1	0.00
Panamanian	5	0.02
Salvadoran	9	0.03
Other Central American	1	0.00
Cuban	40	0.13
Dominican Republic	3	0.01
Mexican	2,314	7.48
Puerto Rican	145	0.47
South American:	64	0.21
Argentinean	6	0.02
Chilean	3	0.01
Colombian	20	0.06
Ecuadorian	10	0.03
Peruvian	20	0.06
Venezuelan	4	0.01
Other South American	1	0.00
Other Hispanic or Latino	240	0.78
Hungarian	233	0.75
Iranian	21	0.07
Irish	5,402	17.38
Italian	3,114	10.02
Latvian	26	0.08
Lithuanian	654	2.10
Luxemburger	33	0.11
Maltese	8	0.03
Northern European	29	0.09
Norwegian	497	1.60
Pennsylvania German	48	0.15

Notes: 1. Figures in the "Number" column do not add up to the total population due to: a) Ancestry/Race overlap — e.g. persons can report being both White and Irish, b) persons of Hispanic origin can report being any race, c) persons reporting two ancestries are counted in both categories. 2. Numbers in parentheses indicate the number of persons reporting this ancestry/race alone, not in combination with any other ancestry/race. 3. Refer to the Explanation of Data in the front of the book for more detailed information.

Polish	3,743	12.05
Portuguese	38	0.12
Romanian	6	0.02
Russian	169	0.54
Scandinavian	104	0.33
Scotch-Irish	312	1.00
Scottish	272	0.88
Serbian	26	0.08
Slavic	10	0.03
Slovak	298	0.96
Slovene	47	0.15
Swedish	749	2.41
Swiss	93	0.30
Turkish	12	0.04
Ukrainian	138	0.44
United States or American	573	1.84
Welsh	146	0.47
West Indian, excl. Hispanic:	28	0.09
Jamaican	28	0.09
White:	23,831	77.04
Not Hispanic (21,671)	22,023	71.19
Hispanic (1,618)	1,808	5.84
Yugoslavian	61	0.20

Woodstock

Place Type: City
County: McHenry
Population: 20,151

Ancestry/Race	Number	%
African American/Black:	263	1.31
Not Hispanic (195)	232	1.15
Hispanic (19)	31	0.15
African, sub-Saharan:	11	0.05
African	11	0.05
Am. Ind. or Alaska Nat., not spec.	43	0.21
Albanian	27	0.13
American Indian tribes, specified:	61	0.30
Apache (5)	7	0.03
Cherokee (5)	17	0.08
Chippewa (2)	8	0.04
Iroquois	1	0.00
Latin American Indians (6)	8	0.04
Lumbee (1)	1	0.00
Ottawa	1	0.00
Potawatomi (3)	7	0.03
Sioux (1)	1	0.00
Yaqui (1)	1	0.00
All other tribes (5)	9	0.04
American Indian tribes, not spec.	6	0.03
Arab:	9	0.04
Lebanese	9	0.04
Asian:	466	2.31
Chinese, ex. Taiwanese (56)	60	0.30
Filipino (113)	126	0.63
Indian (173)	185	0.92
Indonesian (2)	2	0.01
Japanese (9)	19	0.09
Korean (36)	43	0.21
Laotian (2)	4	0.02
Pakistani (1)	5	0.02
Sri Lankan (8)	8	0.04
Thai (4)	6	0.03
Vietnamese	1	0.00
Other Asian, specified	1	0.00
Other Asian, not specified (2)	6	0.03
Austrian	82	0.40
Belgian	43	0.21
British	60	0.29
Canadian	42	0.21
Celtic	42	0.21
Croatian	38	0.19
Czech	286	1.40
Czechoslovakian	35	0.17
Danish	230	1.13
Dutch	270	1.33
Eastern European	41	0.20
English	1,707	8.38
Estonian	23	0.11
European	166	0.82
Finnish	98	0.48
French, except Basque	582	2.86
French Canadian	100	0.49
German	6,369	31.27
Greek	25	0.12
Hawaii Native/Pacific Islander:	4	0.02
Polynesian:	3	0.01
Native Hawaiian	3	0.01
Other Pac. Isl., not spec.	1	0.00
Hispanic or Latino:	3,830	19.01
Central American:	34	0.17
Costa Rican	4	0.02
Guatemalan	14	0.07
Honduran	4	0.02
Nicaraguan	3	0.01
Salvadoran	9	0.04
Cuban	33	0.16
Dominican Republic	1	0.00
Mexican	3,346	16.60
Puerto Rican	63	0.31
South American:	11	0.05
Colombian	2	0.01
Ecuadorian	1	0.00
Peruvian	7	0.03
Other South American	1	0.00
Other Hispanic or Latino	342	1.70
Hungarian	53	0.26
Irish	2,793	13.71
Italian	1,098	5.39
Lithuanian	43	0.21
Luxemburger	23	0.11
Macedonian	55	0.27
Northern European	8	0.04
Norwegian	558	2.74
Pennsylvania German	9	0.04
Polish	1,367	6.71
Portuguese	24	0.12
Romanian	7	0.03
Russian	167	0.82
Scandinavian	21	0.10
Scotch-Irish	124	0.61
Scottish	344	1.69
Serbian	33	0.16
Slavic	18	0.09
Slovak	24	0.12
Slovene	19	0.09
Swedish	747	3.67
Swiss	64	0.31
Ukrainian	78	0.38
United States or American	808	3.97
Welsh	80	0.39
White:	17,900	88.83
Not Hispanic (15,511)	15,657	77.70
Hispanic (2,117)	2,243	11.13
Yugoslavian	11	0.05

Worth

Place Type: Village
County: Cook
Population: 11,047

Ancestry/Race	Number	%
African American/Black:	199	1.80
Not Hispanic (175)	189	1.71
Hispanic (1)	10	0.09
Am. Ind. or Alaska Nat., not spec.	26	0.24
American Indian tribes, specified:	43	0.39
Apache	4	0.04
Cherokee (3)	17	0.15
Chippewa (5)	7	0.06
Comanche	1	0.01
Cree	3	0.03
Iroquois (1)	1	0.01
Latin American Indians (1)	4	0.04
Menominee	2	0.02
Osage	2	0.02
All other tribes	2	0.02
Arab:	288	2.58
Arab/Arabic	201	1.80
Egyptian	20	0.18
Lebanese	15	0.13
Palestinian	52	0.47
Armenian	26	0.23
Asian:	162	1.47
Chinese, ex. Taiwanese (8)	11	0.10
Filipino (71)	76	0.69
Indian (17)	17	0.15
Japanese (4)	5	0.05
Korean (13)	18	0.16
Pakistani (11)	11	0.10
Thai (3)	3	0.03
Vietnamese (7)	7	0.06
Other Asian, not specified (1)	14	0.13
Austrian	54	0.48
Belgian	5	0.04
British	19	0.17
Bulgarian	21	0.19
Canadian	27	0.24
Croatian	132	1.18
Czech	350	3.14
Czechoslovakian	58	0.52
Danish	31	0.28
Dutch	500	4.48
English	488	4.38
European	5	0.04
Finnish	7	0.06
French, except Basque	249	2.23
French Canadian	29	0.26
German	2,615	23.45
Greek	89	0.80
Hawaii Native/Pacific Islander:	6	0.05
Polynesian: (1)	1	0.01
Native Hawaiian (1)	1	0.01
Other Pac. Isl., not spec. (1)	5	0.05
Hispanic or Latino:	669	6.06
Central American:	8	0.07
Costa Rican	1	0.01
Guatemalan	6	0.05
Salvadoran	1	0.01
Cuban	1	0.01
Mexican	530	4.80
Puerto Rican	39	0.35
South American:	8	0.07
Colombian	4	0.04
Ecuadorian	4	0.04
Other Hispanic or Latino	83	0.75
Hungarian	38	0.34
Irish	2,530	22.68
Italian	1,128	10.11
Lithuanian	433	3.88
Macedonian	5	0.04
Norwegian	50	0.45
Polish	2,264	20.30
Romanian	8	0.07
Russian	75	0.67
Scotch-Irish	103	0.92
Scottish	60	0.54
Serbian	6	0.05
Slavic	17	0.15
Slovak	88	0.79
Swedish	267	2.39
Swiss	15	0.13
Ukrainian	45	0.40
United States or American	207	1.86
Welsh	103	0.92
White:	10,456	94.65
Not Hispanic (9,850)	10,037	90.86
Hispanic (361)	419	3.79

Zion

Place Type: City
County: Lake
Population: 22,866

Ancestry/Race	Number	%
African American/Black:	6,591	28.82
Not Hispanic (6,051)	6,393	27.96

Notes: 1. Figures in the "Number" column do not add up to the total population due to: a) Ancestry/Race overlap — e.g. persons can report being both White and Irish, b) persons of Hispanic origin can report being any race, c) persons reporting two ancestries are counted in both categories. 2. Numbers in parentheses indicate the number of persons reporting this ancestry/race alone, not in combination with any other ancestry/race. 3. Refer to the Explanation of Data in the front of the book for more detailed information.

Ancestry/Race	Number	%
Hispanic (145)	198	0.87
African, sub-Saharan:	309	1.34
African	264	1.15
South African	11	0.05
Other sub-Saharan African	34	0.15
Alaska Native tribes, specified:	1	0.00
Tlingit-Haida	1	0.00
Am. Ind. or Alaska Nat., not spec.	91	0.40
American Indian tribes, specified:	212	0.93
Apache (2)	2	0.01
Blackfeet (1)	18	0.08
Cherokee (12)	89	0.39
Cheyenne	3	0.01
Chickasaw (1)	2	0.01
Chippewa (18)	29	0.13
Choctaw (2)	8	0.03
Comanche	5	0.02
Creek (2)	6	0.03
Iroquois (2)	7	0.03
Latin American Indians (1)	2	0.01
Menominee (1)	1	0.00
Navajo (2)	9	0.04
Pima (1)	1	0.00
Shoshone	1	0.00
Sioux (1)	9	0.04
All other tribes (9)	20	0.09
American Indian tribes, not spec.	20	0.09
Arab:	35	0.15
Arab/Arabic	17	0.07
Lebanese	9	0.04
Moroccan	9	0.04
Asian:	618	2.70
Cambodian (1)	1	0.00
Chinese, ex. Taiwanese (14)	37	0.16
Filipino (270)	349	1.53
Indian (52)	72	0.31
Indonesian	2	0.01
Japanese (25)	65	0.28
Korean (22)	29	0.13
Pakistani	10	0.04
Thai (1)	3	0.01
Vietnamese (24)	33	0.14
Other Asian, not specified (8)	17	0.07
Austrian	5	0.02
Belgian	34	0.15
British	103	0.45
Canadian	37	0.16
Celtic	19	0.08
Croatian	65	0.28
Czech	78	0.34
Czechoslovakian	37	0.16
Danish	198	0.86
Dutch	298	1.29
English	1,552	6.73
European	44	0.19
Finnish	423	1.84
French, except Basque	440	1.91
French Canadian	120	0.52
German	3,688	16.00
Greek	23	0.10
Hawaii Native/Pacific Islander:	30	0.13
Micronesian: (6)	9	0.04
Guamanian/Chamorro (6)	9	0.04
Polynesian: (5)	9	0.04
Native Hawaiian (5)	8	0.03
Samoan	1	0.00
Other Pac. Isl., not spec. (5)	12	0.05
Hispanic or Latino:	3,487	15.25
Central American:	107	0.47
Costa Rican	2	0.01
Guatemalan	9	0.04
Honduran	53	0.23
Nicaraguan	10	0.04
Panamanian	9	0.04
Salvadoran	17	0.07
Other Central American	7	0.03
Cuban	19	0.08
Dominican Republic	13	0.06
Mexican	2,279	9.97
Puerto Rican	616	2.69
South American:	71	0.31
Argentinean	4	0.02
Chilean	12	0.05
Colombian	32	0.14
Ecuadorian	11	0.05
Peruvian	2	0.01
Venezuelan	5	0.02
Other South American	5	0.02
Other Hispanic or Latino	382	1.67
Hungarian	35	0.15
Irish	1,810	7.85
Israeli	9	0.04
Italian	728	3.16
Lithuanian	94	0.41
Luxemburger	8	0.03
Macedonian	26	0.11
Norwegian	496	2.15
Pennsylvania German	20	0.09
Polish	995	4.32
Portuguese	13	0.06
Russian	69	0.30
Scandinavian	25	0.11
Scotch-Irish	222	0.96
Scottish	244	1.06
Serbian	4	0.02
Slavic	11	0.05
Slovak	20	0.09
Slovene	71	0.31
Swedish	424	1.84
Swiss	73	0.32
United States or American	1,062	4.61
Welsh	99	0.43
West Indian, excl. Hispanic:	205	0.89
Belizean	84	0.36
British West Indian	7	0.03
Haitian	24	0.10
Jamaican	83	0.36
Trinidadian and Tobagonian	7	0.03
White:	14,192	62.07
Not Hispanic (12,120)	12,658	55.36
Hispanic (1,315)	1,534	6.71
Yugoslavian	7	0.03

Anderson

Place Type: City
County: Madison
Population: 59,734

Ancestry/Race	Number	%
African American/Black:	9,366	15.68
Not Hispanic (8,833)	9,294	15.56
Hispanic (53)	72	0.12
African, sub-Saharan:	438	0.73
African	350	0.59
Kenyan	24	0.04
Liberian	45	0.08
Nigerian	9	0.02
Other sub-Saharan African	10	0.02
Alaska Native tribes, specified:	1	0.00
Alaska Athabascan (1)	1	0.00
Am. Ind. or Alaska Nat., not spec.	195	0.33
Albanian	14	0.02
American Indian tribes, specified:	275	0.46
Apache (7)	17	0.03
Blackfeet (8)	25	0.04
Cherokee (52)	147	0.25
Cheyenne (1)	1	0.00
Chickasaw (2)	7	0.01
Chippewa	1	0.00
Choctaw (2)	7	0.01
Cree	1	0.00
Crow	1	0.00
Delaware (1)	7	0.01
Iroquois (2)	3	0.01
Kiowa (1)	1	0.00
Latin American Indians (1)	8	0.01
Navajo (1)	4	0.01
Osage	1	0.00
Ottawa (1)	1	0.00
Potawatomi (1)	4	0.01
Seminole	1	0.00
Sioux (11)	21	0.04
All other tribes (7)	17	0.03
American Indian tribes, not spec.	48	0.08
Arab:	72	0.12
Egyptian	21	0.04
Lebanese	45	0.08
Syrian	6	0.01
Asian:	410	0.69
Bangladeshi (6)	6	0.01
Chinese, ex. Taiwanese (55)	61	0.10
Filipino (29)	39	0.07
Indian (70)	103	0.17
Japanese (17)	40	0.07
Korean (59)	79	0.13
Laotian	1	0.00
Pakistani (1)	1	0.00
Thai (3)	5	0.01
Vietnamese (44)	49	0.08
Other Asian, specified	11	0.02
Other Asian, not specified (5)	15	0.03
Australian	9	0.02
Austrian	27	0.05
Basque	17	0.03
Belgian	59	0.10
British	278	0.47
Bulgarian	7	0.01
Canadian	21	0.04
Celtic	13	0.02
Czech	60	0.10
Czechoslovakian	72	0.12
Danish	21	0.04
Dutch	1,080	1.81
English	5,363	8.99
European	325	0.54
Finnish	41	0.07
French, except Basque	1,020	1.71
French Canadian	101	0.17
German	8,844	14.83
Greek	127	0.21
Hawaii Native/Pacific Islander:	31	0.05
Micronesian: (3)	3	0.01
Guamanian/Chamorro (3)	3	0.01
Polynesian: (4)	12	0.02
Native Hawaiian (4)	12	0.02
Other Pac. Isl., specified	11	0.02
Other Pac. Isl., not spec. (2)	5	0.01
Hispanic or Latino:	1,235	2.07
Central American:	14	0.02
Costa Rican	1	0.00
Guatemalan	3	0.01
Honduran	5	0.01
Nicaraguan	2	0.00
Panamanian	2	0.00
Salvadoran	1	0.00
Cuban	23	0.04
Dominican Republic	7	0.01
Mexican	914	1.53
Puerto Rican	81	0.14
South American:	27	0.05
Argentinean	3	0.01
Bolivian	14	0.02
Chilean	1	0.00
Colombian	3	0.01
Ecuadorian	2	0.00
Paraguayan	1	0.00
Peruvian	1	0.00
Venezuelan	2	0.00
Other Hispanic or Latino	169	0.28
Hungarian	80	0.13
Iranian	6	0.01
Irish	4,672	7.83
Italian	873	1.46
Lithuanian	45	0.08
Norwegian	151	0.25
Pennsylvania German	21	0.04
Polish	483	0.81
Portuguese	14	0.02
Romanian	31	0.05

Notes: 1. Figures in the "Number" column do not add up to the total population due to: a) Ancestry/Race overlap — e.g. persons can report being both White and Irish, b) persons of Hispanic origin can report being any race, c) persons reporting two ancestries are counted in both categories. 2. Numbers in parentheses indicate the number of persons reporting this ancestry/race alone, not in combination with any other ancestry/race. 3. Refer to the Explanation of Data in the front of the book for more detailed information.

Russian	76	0.13
Scandinavian	39	0.07
Scotch-Irish	902	1.51
Scottish	813	1.36
Slovak	11	0.02
Swedish	235	0.39
Swiss	117	0.20
Turkish	38	0.06
Ukrainian	8	0.01
United States or American	9,501	15.93
Welsh	462	0.77
West Indian, excl. Hispanic:	28	0.05
Bermudan	9	0.02
Dutch West Indian	13	0.02
Jamaican	6	0.01
White:	49,736	83.26
Not Hispanic (48,340)	48,998	82.03
Hispanic (638)	738	1.24
Yugoslavian	9	0.02

Auburn

Place Type: City
County: De Kalb
Population: 12,074

Ancestry/Race	Number	%
African American/Black:	59	0.49
Not Hispanic (42)	59	0.49
African, sub-Saharan:	8	0.07
African	8	0.07
Alaska Native tribes, specified:	1	0.01
Aleut	1	0.01
Am. Ind. or Alaska Nat., not spec.	14	0.12
American Indian tribes, specified:	41	0.34
Cherokee (3)	31	0.26
Iroquois	1	0.01
Latin American Indians (1)	1	0.01
Navajo	1	0.01
Potawatomi	2	0.02
Sioux	3	0.02
All other tribes (1)	2	0.02
American Indian tribes, not spec.	11	0.09
Arab:	27	0.22
Arab/Arabic	10	0.08
Syrian	17	0.14
Asian:	62	0.51
Cambodian (3)	3	0.02
Chinese, ex. Taiwanese (17)	19	0.16
Filipino (4)	7	0.06
Indian (8)	8	0.07
Japanese (2)	9	0.07
Korean (3)	3	0.02
Pakistani (3)	3	0.02
Vietnamese (5)	5	0.04
Other Asian, specified (3)	3	0.02
Other Asian, not specified (2)	2	0.02
Austrian	16	0.13
Belgian	15	0.12
British	55	0.46
Canadian	32	0.27
Czechoslovakian	10	0.08
Danish	27	0.22
Dutch	223	1.85
English	1,128	9.35
European	72	0.60
Finnish	34	0.28
French, except Basque	387	3.21
French Canadian	8	0.07
German	4,246	35.18
Hawaii Native/Pacific Islander:	4	0.03
Polynesian: (3)	4	0.03
Native Hawaiian (3)	4	0.03
Hispanic or Latino:	211	1.75
Central American:	1	0.01
Panamanian	1	0.01
Cuban	2	0.02
Mexican	145	1.20
Puerto Rican	7	0.06
South American:	6	0.05
Ecuadorian	1	0.01
Peruvian	2	0.02
Venezuelan	3	0.02
Other Hispanic or Latino	50	0.41
Hungarian	23	0.19
Irish	1,156	9.58
Italian	160	1.33
Norwegian	57	0.47
Pennsylvania German	25	0.21
Polish	156	1.29
Romanian	6	0.05
Russian	17	0.14
Scotch-Irish	216	1.79
Scottish	147	1.22
Slavic	8	0.07
Swedish	150	1.24
Swiss	96	0.80
United States or American	1,759	14.58
Welsh	68	0.56
West Indian, excl. Hispanic:	8	0.07
West Indian	8	0.07
White:	11,892	98.49
Not Hispanic (11,673)	11,752	97.33
Hispanic (124)	140	1.16

Bedford

Place Type: City
County: Lawrence
Population: 13,768

Ancestry/Race	Number	%
African American/Black:	123	0.89
Not Hispanic (109)	122	0.89
Hispanic	1	0.01
African, sub-Saharan:	27	0.19
African	17	0.12
Nigerian	10	0.07
Am. Ind. or Alaska Nat., not spec.	25	0.18
American Indian tribes, specified:	59	0.43
Apache (3)	4	0.03
Blackfeet (1)	1	0.01
Cherokee (17)	38	0.28
Chippewa	1	0.01
Choctaw (1)	2	0.01
Delaware (1)	1	0.01
Iroquois (2)	2	0.01
Latin American Indians	1	0.01
Lumbee	2	0.01
Seminole	1	0.01
Sioux (2)	2	0.01
All other tribes (4)	4	0.03
American Indian tribes, not spec.	5	0.04
Arab:	7	0.05
Arab/Arabic	7	0.05
Asian:	94	0.68
Chinese, ex. Taiwanese (17)	19	0.14
Filipino (12)	28	0.20
Indian (16)	18	0.13
Japanese (1)	7	0.05
Korean (5)	6	0.04
Pakistani (5)	5	0.04
Vietnamese (8)	8	0.06
Other Asian, specified	1	0.01
Other Asian, not specified	2	0.01
Austrian	9	0.06
Belgian	23	0.17
British	52	0.37
Canadian	13	0.09
Croatian	16	0.12
Czech	5	0.04
Czechoslovakian	10	0.07
Danish	10	0.07
Dutch	188	1.35
English	1,267	9.13
European	62	0.45
Finnish	9	0.06
French, except Basque	213	1.53
French Canadian	87	0.63
German	1,753	12.63
Greek	10	0.07
Hawaii Native/Pacific Islander:	6	0.04
Polynesian: (1)	4	0.03
Native Hawaiian (1)	4	0.03
Other Pac. Isl., not spec.	2	0.01
Hispanic or Latino:	173	1.26
Central American:	4	0.03
Honduran	3	0.02
Other Central American	1	0.01
Mexican	112	0.81
Puerto Rican	6	0.04
South American:	6	0.04
Bolivian	3	0.02
Colombian	3	0.02
Other Hispanic or Latino	45	0.33
Hungarian	6	0.04
Irish	1,364	9.83
Italian	370	2.67
Norwegian	31	0.22
Polish	57	0.41
Russian	15	0.11
Scandinavian	16	0.12
Scotch-Irish	244	1.76
Scottish	218	1.57
Slovak	7	0.05
Swedish	62	0.45
United States or American	2,541	18.31
Welsh	66	0.48
White:	13,451	97.70
Not Hispanic (13,261)	13,359	97.03
Hispanic (76)	92	0.67
Yugoslavian	11	0.08

Beech Grove

Place Type: City
County: Marion
Population: 14,880

Ancestry/Race	Number	%
African American/Black:	173	1.16
Not Hispanic (124)	162	1.09
Hispanic (9)	11	0.07
Am. Ind. or Alaska Nat., not spec.	24	0.16
Alsatian	9	0.06
American Indian tribes, specified:	59	0.40
Apache	5	0.03
Cherokee (13)	26	0.17
Chippewa (1)	2	0.01
Comanche	1	0.01
Cree (1)	3	0.02
Creek (1)	2	0.01
Navajo	5	0.03
Potawatomi (1)	4	0.03
Sioux (5)	9	0.06
All other tribes (2)	2	0.01
Asian:	159	1.07
Chinese, ex. Taiwanese (22)	24	0.16
Filipino (21)	36	0.24
Indian (45)	50	0.34
Japanese (7)	15	0.10
Korean (9)	13	0.09
Pakistani (1)	3	0.02
Sri Lankan (5)	5	0.03
Thai (4)	4	0.03
Vietnamese (1)	2	0.01
Other Asian, not specified (5)	7	0.05
Austrian	15	0.11
British	34	0.24
Canadian	8	0.06
Czech	12	0.08
Danish	14	0.10
Dutch	296	2.08
English	1,670	11.76
European	90	0.63
French, except Basque	350	2.46
French Canadian	11	0.08
German	3,961	27.89
Greek	61	0.43
Hawaii Native/Pacific Islander:	7	0.05

Notes: 1. Figures in the "Number" column do not add up to the total population due to: a) Ancestry/Race overlap — e.g. persons can report being both White and Irish, b) persons of Hispanic origin can report being any race, c) persons reporting two ancestries are counted in both categories. 2. Numbers in parentheses indicate the number of persons reporting this ancestry/race alone, not in combination with any other ancestry/race. 3. Refer to the Explanation of Data in the front of the book for more detailed information.

Ancestry/Race	Number	%
Polynesian: (2)	2	0.01
Samoan (2)	2	0.01
Other Pac. Isl., not spec. (5)	5	0.03
Hispanic or Latino:	308	2.07
Central American:	6	0.04
Guatemalan	3	0.02
Panamanian	2	0.01
Salvadoran	1	0.01
Cuban	3	0.02
Dominican Republic	8	0.05
Mexican	231	1.55
Puerto Rican	11	0.07
South American:	5	0.03
Argentinean	1	0.01
Colombian	1	0.01
Peruvian	3	0.02
Other Hispanic or Latino	44	0.30
Hungarian	73	0.51
Irish	2,673	18.82
Italian	288	2.03
Norwegian	54	0.38
Polish	73	0.51
Scotch-Irish	275	1.94
Scottish	317	2.23
Slavic	18	0.13
Slovene	16	0.11
Swedish	100	0.70
Swiss	30	0.21
United States or American	2,865	20.18
Welsh	64	0.45
White:	14,469	97.24
Not Hispanic (14,161)	14,281	95.97
Hispanic (160)	188	1.26

Bloomington

Place Type: City
County: Monroe
Population: 69,291

Ancestry/Race	Number	%
Afghan	107	0.15
African American/Black:	3,371	4.86
Not Hispanic (2,897)	3,304	4.77
Hispanic (43)	67	0.10
African, sub-Saharan:	424	0.61
African	203	0.29
Ethiopian	75	0.11
Ghanian	11	0.02
Kenyan	12	0.02
Nigerian	32	0.05
Senegalese	7	0.01
Somalian	12	0.02
South African	45	0.07
Other sub-Saharan African	27	0.04
Alaska Native tribes, specified:	4	0.01
Alaska Athabascan	1	0.00
Eskimo	3	0.00
Am. Ind. or Alaska Nat., not spec.	214	0.31
Albanian	88	0.13
Alsatian	10	0.01
American Indian tribes, specified:	304	0.44
Apache (6)	12	0.02
Blackfeet (5)	20	0.03
Cherokee (32)	142	0.20
Cheyenne (1)	1	0.00
Chickasaw (2)	3	0.00
Chippewa (2)	2	0.00
Choctaw (7)	10	0.01
Creek (1)	2	0.00
Delaware	1	0.00
Iroquois (9)	13	0.02
Latin American Indians (6)	17	0.02
Lumbee (4)	6	0.01
Navajo (7)	9	0.01
Osage	2	0.00
Pima	1	0.00
Potawatomi (2)	2	0.00
Pueblo (1)	3	0.00
Puget Sound Salish (1)	1	0.00
Seminole (1)	4	0.01
Shoshone	1	0.00
Sioux (11)	16	0.02
Yaqui (1)	1	0.00
All other tribes (23)	35	0.05
American Indian tribes, not spec.	30	0.04
Arab:	403	0.58
Arab/Arabic	50	0.07
Egyptian	58	0.08
Iraqi	7	0.01
Jordanian	33	0.05
Lebanese	131	0.19
Palestinian	27	0.04
Syrian	48	0.07
Other Arab	49	0.07
Armenian	25	0.04
Asian:	4,258	6.15
Bangladeshi (3)	4	0.01
Cambodian (1)	1	0.00
Chinese, ex. Taiwanese (875)	998	1.44
Filipino (121)	205	0.30
Hmong (5)	5	0.01
Indian (623)	703	1.01
Indonesian (66)	105	0.15
Japanese (352)	422	0.61
Korean (1,008)	1,061	1.53
Laotian (8)	9	0.01
Malaysian (20)	28	0.04
Pakistani (48)	57	0.08
Sri Lankan (4)	6	0.01
Taiwanese (97)	113	0.16
Thai (75)	92	0.13
Vietnamese (93)	121	0.17
Other Asian, specified (25)	32	0.05
Other Asian, not specified (158)	296	0.43
Assyrian/Chaldean/Syriac	34	0.05
Australian	38	0.05
Austrian	219	0.32
Basque	7	0.01
Belgian	195	0.28
Brazilian	95	0.14
British	798	1.15
Bulgarian	56	0.08
Canadian	145	0.21
Carpatho Rusyn	8	0.01
Celtic	6	0.01
Croatian	225	0.33
Cypriot	7	0.01
Czech	347	0.50
Czechoslovakian	131	0.19
Danish	263	0.38
Dutch	1,331	1.92
Eastern European	188	0.27
English	7,525	10.87
Estonian	6	0.01
European	1,085	1.57
Finnish	178	0.26
French, except Basque	1,926	2.78
French Canadian	339	0.49
German	17,244	24.91
Greek	447	0.65
Hawaii Native/Pacific Islander:	113	0.16
Melanesian: (1)	1	0.00
Other Melanesian (1)	1	0.00
Micronesian: (7)	13	0.02
Guamanian/Chamorro (7)	13	0.02
Polynesian: (33)	53	0.08
Native Hawaiian (11)	25	0.04
Samoan (12)	16	0.02
Other Polynesian (10)	12	0.02
Other Pac. Isl., specified	1	0.00
Other Pac. Isl., not spec. (7)	45	0.06
Hispanic or Latino:	1,722	2.49
Central American:	74	0.11
Costa Rican	17	0.02
Guatemalan	15	0.02
Honduran	4	0.01
Nicaraguan	11	0.02
Panamanian	11	0.02
Salvadoran	11	0.02
Other Central American	5	0.01
Cuban	79	0.11
Dominican Republic	20	0.03
Mexican	765	1.10
Puerto Rican	213	0.31
South American:	210	0.30
Argentinean	23	0.03
Bolivian	5	0.01
Chilean	13	0.02
Colombian	47	0.07
Ecuadorian	27	0.04
Paraguayan	1	0.00
Peruvian	28	0.04
Uruguayan	9	0.01
Venezuelan	47	0.07
Other South American	10	0.01
Other Hispanic or Latino	361	0.52
Hungarian	488	0.70
Icelander	17	0.02
Iranian	23	0.03
Irish	9,185	13.27
Israeli	107	0.15
Italian	2,880	4.16
Latvian	20	0.03
Lithuanian	173	0.25
Luxemburger	16	0.02
Macedonian	16	0.02
New Zealander	20	0.03
Northern European	83	0.12
Norwegian	817	1.18
Pennsylvania German	19	0.03
Polish	2,760	3.99
Portuguese	81	0.12
Romanian	175	0.25
Russian	1,054	1.52
Scandinavian	164	0.24
Scotch-Irish	1,556	2.25
Scottish	2,107	3.04
Serbian	96	0.14
Slavic	41	0.06
Slovak	184	0.27
Slovene	60	0.09
Swedish	989	1.43
Swiss	331	0.48
Turkish	121	0.17
Ukrainian	272	0.39
United States or American	4,607	6.65
Welsh	653	0.94
West Indian, excl. Hispanic:	81	0.12
Haitian	48	0.07
Jamaican	27	0.04
Trinidadian and Tobagonian	6	0.01
White:	61,524	88.79
Not Hispanic (59,398)	60,477	87.28
Hispanic (903)	1,047	1.51
Yugoslavian	57	0.08

Brownsburg

Place Type: Town
County: Hendricks
Population: 14,520

Ancestry/Race	Number	%
African American/Black:	64	0.44
Not Hispanic (42)	57	0.39
Hispanic (5)	7	0.05
Am. Ind. or Alaska Nat., not spec.	29	0.20
American Indian tribes, specified:	38	0.26
Blackfeet	2	0.01
Cherokee (2)	18	0.12
Chickasaw (4)	4	0.03
Chippewa (1)	2	0.01
Delaware (1)	1	0.01
Latin American Indians (1)	2	0.01
Potawatomi	1	0.01
Sioux (2)	2	0.01
All other tribes (3)	6	0.04
Arab:	12	0.08
Egyptian	12	0.08

Notes: 1. Figures in the "Number" column do not add up to the total population due to: a) Ancestry/Race overlap — e.g. persons can report being both White and Irish, b) persons of Hispanic origin can report being any race, c) persons reporting two ancestries are counted in both categories. 2. Numbers in parentheses indicate the number of persons reporting this ancestry/race alone, not in combination with any other ancestry/race. 3. Refer to the Explanation of Data in the front of the book for more detailed information.

Ancestry/Race	Number	%
Asian:	170	1.17
Cambodian	4	0.03
Chinese, ex. Taiwanese (26)	32	0.22
Filipino (9)	21	0.14
Indian (19)	24	0.17
Indonesian (1)	1	0.01
Japanese (3)	14	0.10
Korean (7)	14	0.10
Thai	4	0.03
Vietnamese (43)	45	0.31
Other Asian, specified	4	0.03
Other Asian, not specified (1)	7	0.05
Austrian	15	0.10
Belgian	17	0.12
British	53	0.37
Czech	34	0.24
Czechoslovakian	33	0.23
Danish	19	0.13
Dutch	441	3.07
English	1,800	12.55
European	237	1.65
Finnish	24	0.17
French, except Basque	476	3.32
German	3,694	25.75
Greek	10	0.07
Hawaii Native/Pacific Islander:	14	0.10
Micronesian: (3)	3	0.02
Guamanian/Chamorro (3)	3	0.02
Polynesian: (6)	9	0.06
Native Hawaiian (6)	9	0.06
Other Pac. Isl., not spec. (1)	2	0.01
Hispanic or Latino:	172	1.18
Central American:	3	0.02
Costa Rican	2	0.01
Nicaraguan	1	0.01
Cuban	5	0.03
Dominican Republic	1	0.01
Mexican	104	0.72
Puerto Rican	18	0.12
South American:	8	0.06
Argentinean	1	0.01
Colombian	5	0.03
Peruvian	2	0.01
Other Hispanic or Latino	33	0.23
Hungarian	29	0.20
Irish	1,919	13.38
Italian	163	1.14
Lithuanian	27	0.19
Northern European	16	0.11
Norwegian	10	0.07
Pennsylvania German	26	0.18
Polish	232	1.62
Portuguese	33	0.23
Romanian	62	0.43
Russian	98	0.68
Scandinavian	19	0.13
Scotch-Irish	101	0.70
Scottish	148	1.03
Slovak	27	0.19
Slovene	58	0.40
Swedish	170	1.19
Swiss	23	0.16
Turkish	9	0.06
Ukrainian	8	0.06
United States or American	2,565	17.88
Welsh	108	0.75
White:	14,263	98.23
Not Hispanic (14,049)	14,150	97.45
Hispanic (99)	113	0.78
Yugoslavian	123	0.86

Carmel

Place Type: City
County: Hamilton
Population: 37,733

Ancestry/Race	Number	%
African American/Black:	634	1.68
Not Hispanic (550)	629	1.67
Hispanic (5)	5	0.01
African, sub-Saharan:	60	0.16
African	16	0.04
Ethiopian	12	0.03
Somalian	32	0.08
Am. Ind. or Alaska Nat., not spec.	32	0.08
American Indian tribes, specified:	99	0.26
Apache (2)	3	0.01
Blackfeet (1)	3	0.01
Cherokee (20)	50	0.13
Chippewa (1)	5	0.01
Choctaw	3	0.01
Crow (1)	1	0.00
Iroquois	4	0.01
Kiowa (2)	2	0.01
Latin American Indians (2)	5	0.01
Navajo (1)	1	0.00
Potawatomi (1)	1	0.00
Pueblo (2)	2	0.01
Shoshone	1	0.00
Sioux (2)	4	0.01
All other tribes (3)	14	0.04
American Indian tribes, not spec.	6	0.02
Arab:	235	0.62
Arab/Arabic	32	0.08
Lebanese	129	0.34
Palestinian	58	0.15
Syrian	16	0.04
Armenian	45	0.12
Asian:	1,813	4.80
Cambodian (1)	1	0.00
Chinese, ex. Taiwanese (649)	691	1.83
Filipino (65)	93	0.25
Hmong (23)	23	0.06
Indian (437)	459	1.22
Indonesian (4)	9	0.02
Japanese (80)	114	0.30
Korean (207)	224	0.59
Laotian (1)	1	0.00
Malaysian (1)	3	0.01
Pakistani (16)	19	0.05
Sri Lankan (3)	3	0.01
Taiwanese (42)	47	0.12
Thai (6)	8	0.02
Vietnamese (76)	80	0.21
Other Asian, specified	1	0.00
Other Asian, not specified (20)	37	0.10
Australian	16	0.04
Austrian	164	0.43
Belgian	67	0.18
British	344	0.91
Bulgarian	10	0.03
Canadian	155	0.41
Celtic	33	0.09
Croatian	65	0.17
Czech	158	0.42
Czechoslovakian	69	0.18
Danish	246	0.65
Dutch	804	2.13
Eastern European	117	0.31
English	5,656	14.96
European	553	1.46
Finnish	63	0.17
French, except Basque	1,010	2.67
French Canadian	207	0.55
German	10,610	28.07
Greek	314	0.83
Hawaii Native/Pacific Islander:	32	0.08
Micronesian: (2)	3	0.01
Guamanian/Chamorro (2)	3	0.01
Polynesian: (10)	14	0.04
Native Hawaiian (7)	11	0.03
Samoan (3)	3	0.01
Other Pac. Isl., not spec. (5)	15	0.04
Hispanic or Latino:	649	1.72
Central American:	24	0.06
Costa Rican	5	0.01
Guatemalan	2	0.01
Honduran	6	0.02
Nicaraguan	3	0.01
Panamanian	6	0.02
Salvadoran	1	0.00
Other Central American	1	0.00
Cuban	31	0.08
Dominican Republic	8	0.02
Mexican	313	0.83
Puerto Rican	53	0.14
South American:	52	0.14
Argentinean	13	0.03
Bolivian	3	0.01
Colombian	22	0.06
Ecuadorian	1	0.00
Paraguayan	1	0.00
Peruvian	5	0.01
Uruguayan	2	0.01
Venezuelan	4	0.01
Other South American	1	0.00
Other Hispanic or Latino	168	0.45
Hungarian	320	0.85
Icelander	6	0.02
Iranian	72	0.19
Irish	5,692	15.06
Italian	1,676	4.43
Latvian	23	0.06
Lithuanian	86	0.23
Macedonian	38	0.10
Northern European	126	0.33
Norwegian	588	1.56
Pennsylvania German	22	0.06
Polish	1,463	3.87
Portuguese	41	0.11
Romanian	93	0.25
Russian	541	1.43
Scandinavian	70	0.19
Scotch-Irish	781	2.07
Scottish	1,065	2.82
Serbian	47	0.12
Slovak	113	0.30
Slovene	12	0.03
Swedish	497	1.31
Swiss	294	0.78
Turkish	46	0.12
Ukrainian	176	0.47
United States or American	2,918	7.72
Welsh	302	0.80
West Indian, excl. Hispanic:	48	0.13
Jamaican	48	0.13
White:	35,250	93.42
Not Hispanic (34,467)	34,749	92.09
Hispanic (484)	501	1.33
Yugoslavian	14	0.04

Chesterton

Place Type: Town
County: Porter
Population: 10,488

Ancestry/Race	Number	%
African American/Black:	62	0.59
Not Hispanic (44)	60	0.57
Hispanic (2)	2	0.02
African, sub-Saharan:	35	0.34
Nigerian	35	0.34
Alaska Native tribes, not specified	1	0.01
Am. Ind. or Alaska Nat., not spec.	13	0.12
American Indian tribes, specified:	50	0.48
Apache (1)	1	0.01
Cherokee (4)	27	0.26
Chippewa (5)	7	0.07
Choctaw	1	0.01
Iroquois (3)	7	0.07
Latin American Indians	3	0.03
Seminole	1	0.01
Sioux (1)	3	0.03
American Indian tribes, not spec.	2	0.02
Asian:	173	1.65
Cambodian (1)	1	0.01
Chinese, ex. Taiwanese (13)	15	0.14
Filipino (12)	20	0.19

Notes: 1. Figures in the "Number" column do not add up to the total population due to: a) Ancestry/Race overlap — e.g. persons can report being both White and Irish, b) persons of Hispanic origin can report being any race, c) persons reporting two ancestries are counted in both categories. 2. Numbers in parentheses indicate the number of persons reporting this ancestry/race alone, not in combination with any other ancestry/race. 3. Refer to the Explanation of Data in the front of the book for more detailed information.

Ancestry/Race	Number	%
Indian (78)	79	0.75
Indonesian	1	0.01
Japanese (6)	13	0.12
Korean (20)	25	0.24
Laotian (1)	2	0.02
Pakistani (10)	10	0.10
Thai (3)	3	0.03
Vietnamese	2	0.02
Other Asian, not specified	2	0.02
Australian	9	0.09
Austrian	17	0.16
Belgian	23	0.22
British	74	0.71
Canadian	44	0.42
Carpatho Rusyn	7	0.07
Croatian	119	1.14
Czech	23	0.22
Czechoslovakian	100	0.96
Danish	29	0.28
Dutch	349	3.34
Eastern European	13	0.12
English	1,248	11.96
European	39	0.37
Finnish	23	0.22
French, except Basque	276	2.65
French Canadian	66	0.63
German	2,676	25.65
Greek	213	2.04
Hawaii Native/Pacific Islander:	2	0.02
Polynesian: (2)	2	0.02
Native Hawaiian (1)	1	0.01
Samoan (1)	1	0.01
Hispanic or Latino:	347	3.31
Central American:	6	0.06
Guatemalan	6	0.06
Cuban	2	0.02
Mexican	244	2.33
Puerto Rican	56	0.53
South American:	2	0.02
Peruvian	2	0.02
Other Hispanic or Latino	37	0.35
Hungarian	191	1.83
Irish	2,025	19.41
Italian	580	5.56
Lithuanian	151	1.45
Norwegian	126	1.21
Polish	1,060	10.16
Portuguese	31	0.30
Romanian	31	0.30
Russian	86	0.82
Scotch-Irish	264	2.53
Scottish	173	1.66
Serbian	73	0.70
Slavic	19	0.18
Slovak	282	2.70
Slovene	13	0.12
Swedish	653	6.26
Swiss	18	0.17
Turkish	7	0.07
Ukrainian	7	0.07
United States or American	304	2.91
Welsh	192	1.84
West Indian, excl. Hispanic:	34	0.33
Barbadian	34	0.33
White:	10,214	97.39
Not Hispanic (9,831)	9,925	94.63
Hispanic (268)	289	2.76
Yugoslavian	56	0.54

Clarksville

Place Type: Town
County: Clark
Population: 21,400

Ancestry/Race	Number	%
African American/Black:	1,345	6.29
Not Hispanic (1,177)	1,310	6.12
Hispanic (20)	35	0.16
African, sub-Saharan:	37	0.17
African	13	0.06
Nigerian	18	0.08
South African	6	0.03
Am. Ind. or Alaska Nat., not spec.	53	0.25
American Indian tribes, specified:	90	0.42
Blackfeet	3	0.01
Cherokee (18)	51	0.24
Chickasaw	1	0.00
Chippewa (3)	3	0.01
Choctaw (4)	5	0.02
Comanche (1)	1	0.00
Cree	2	0.01
Creek (1)	2	0.01
Iroquois (1)	4	0.02
Latin American Indians (9)	9	0.04
Pima	3	0.01
Seminole (1)	1	0.00
Sioux	3	0.01
All other tribes (1)	2	0.01
American Indian tribes, not spec.	4	0.02
Arab:	62	0.29
Arab/Arabic	8	0.04
Egyptian	6	0.03
Lebanese	48	0.22
Asian:	267	1.25
Chinese, ex. Taiwanese (22)	28	0.13
Filipino (24)	48	0.22
Indian (54)	61	0.29
Indonesian (2)	2	0.01
Japanese (12)	27	0.13
Korean (22)	28	0.13
Pakistani (15)	15	0.07
Taiwanese (4)	8	0.04
Thai (4)	9	0.04
Vietnamese (20)	20	0.09
Other Asian, specified	1	0.00
Other Asian, not specified (17)	20	0.09
Austrian	13	0.06
British	85	0.40
Canadian	16	0.07
Celtic	7	0.03
Croatian	9	0.04
Czech	23	0.11
Czechoslovakian	9	0.04
Dutch	284	1.32
English	1,902	8.85
European	127	0.59
French, except Basque	541	2.52
French Canadian	39	0.18
German	4,308	20.04
Greek	13	0.06
Hawaii Native/Pacific Islander:	18	0.08
Polynesian: (6)	11	0.05
Native Hawaiian (6)	11	0.05
Other Pac. Isl., not spec.	7	0.03
Hispanic or Latino:	599	2.80
Central American:	9	0.04
Costa Rican	1	0.00
Guatemalan	4	0.02
Nicaraguan	1	0.00
Panamanian	3	0.01
Cuban	20	0.09
Dominican Republic	1	0.00
Mexican	483	2.26
Puerto Rican	37	0.17
South American:	2	0.01
Ecuadorian	2	0.01
Other Hispanic or Latino	47	0.22
Hungarian	34	0.16
Irish	2,904	13.51
Italian	628	2.92
Lithuanian	6	0.03
Norwegian	112	0.52
Pennsylvania German	11	0.05
Polish	213	0.99
Portuguese	9	0.04
Russian	20	0.09
Scandinavian	10	0.05
Scotch-Irish	300	1.40
Scottish	330	1.54
Swedish	101	0.47
Swiss	74	0.34
Ukrainian	5	0.02
United States or American	2,745	12.77
Welsh	59	0.27
White:	19,668	91.91
Not Hispanic (19,059)	19,321	90.29
Hispanic (321)	347	1.62

Columbus

Place Type: City
County: Bartholomew
Population: 39,059

Ancestry/Race	Number	%
African American/Black:	1,240	3.17
Not Hispanic (1,034)	1,207	3.09
Hispanic (23)	33	0.08
African, sub-Saharan:	93	0.24
African	25	0.06
Nigerian	24	0.06
South African	44	0.11
Alaska Native tribes, specified:	2	0.01
Alaska Athabascan (1)	1	0.00
Aleut	1	0.00
Am. Ind. or Alaska Nat., not spec.	83	0.21
American Indian tribes, specified:	76	0.19
Apache	8	0.02
Blackfeet (4)	8	0.02
Cherokee (14)	41	0.10
Chippewa	1	0.00
Choctaw	4	0.01
Crow	1	0.00
Delaware (1)	2	0.01
Iroquois	1	0.00
Navajo (1)	1	0.00
Ottawa (1)	2	0.01
Potawatomi (1)	1	0.00
Shoshone	1	0.00
Sioux (3)	3	0.01
All other tribes (1)	2	0.01
American Indian tribes, not spec.	8	0.02
Arab:	27	0.07
Arab/Arabic	11	0.03
Lebanese	11	0.03
Syrian	5	0.01
Armenian	13	0.03
Asian:	1,369	3.50
Bangladeshi (2)	2	0.01
Chinese, ex. Taiwanese (231)	261	0.67
Filipino (47)	61	0.16
Indian (461)	480	1.23
Japanese (311)	327	0.84
Korean (55)	69	0.18
Laotian (1)	1	0.00
Malaysian (1)	1	0.00
Pakistani (4)	4	0.01
Sri Lankan (3)	3	0.01
Taiwanese (15)	29	0.07
Thai (4)	6	0.02
Vietnamese (92)	93	0.24
Other Asian, specified (1)	2	0.01
Other Asian, not specified (20)	30	0.08
Australian	8	0.02
Austrian	5	0.01
Belgian	33	0.08
Brazilian	18	0.05
British	345	0.88
Bulgarian	46	0.12
Canadian	77	0.20
Celtic	27	0.07
Croatian	38	0.10
Czech	49	0.13
Danish	66	0.17
Dutch	669	1.71
English	4,435	11.33
European	322	0.82
Finnish	63	0.16
French, except Basque	900	2.30

Notes: 1. Figures in the "Number" column do not add up to the total population due to: a) Ancestry/Race overlap — e.g. persons can report being both White and Irish, b) persons of Hispanic origin can report being any race, c) persons reporting two ancestries are counted in both categories. 2. Numbers in parentheses indicate the number of persons reporting this ancestry/race alone, not in combination with any other ancestry/race. 3. Refer to the Explanation of Data in the front of the book for more detailed information.

Ancestry/Race	Number	%
French Canadian	67	0.17
German	8,564	21.88
Greek	34	0.09
Hawaii Native/Pacific Islander:	33	0.08
Micronesian: (4)	4	0.01
Guamanian/Chamorro (4)	4	0.01
Polynesian: (14)	18	0.05
Native Hawaiian (4)	8	0.02
Samoan (10)	10	0.03
Other Pac. Isl., not spec. (1)	11	0.03
Hispanic or Latino:	1,096	2.81
Central American:	28	0.07
Costa Rican	1	0.00
Guatemalan	12	0.03
Honduran	7	0.02
Panamanian	4	0.01
Salvadoran	3	0.01
Other Central American	1	0.00
Cuban	14	0.04
Dominican Republic	4	0.01
Mexican	787	2.01
Puerto Rican	93	0.24
South American:	29	0.07
Bolivian	5	0.01
Chilean	3	0.01
Colombian	4	0.01
Ecuadorian	1	0.00
Uruguayan	5	0.01
Venezuelan	8	0.02
Other South American	3	0.01
Other Hispanic or Latino	141	0.36
Hungarian	155	0.40
Irish	4,042	10.33
Italian	820	2.10
Latvian	21	0.05
Lithuanian	28	0.07
Northern European	51	0.13
Norwegian	181	0.46
Polish	482	1.23
Portuguese	16	0.04
Russian	47	0.12
Scandinavian	71	0.18
Scotch-Irish	664	1.70
Scottish	717	1.83
Serbian	8	0.02
Slovak	23	0.06
Slovene	8	0.02
Swedish	332	0.85
Swiss	207	0.53
Ukrainian	77	0.20
United States or American	6,173	15.77
Welsh	171	0.44
West Indian, excl. Hispanic:	36	0.09
Jamaican	12	0.03
West Indian	24	0.06
White:	36,083	92.38
Not Hispanic (35,161)	35,513	90.92
Hispanic (507)	570	1.46
Yugoslavian	16	0.04

Connersville

Place Type: City
County: Fayette
Population: 15,411

Ancestry/Race	Number	%
African American/Black:	434	2.82
Not Hispanic (382)	432	2.80
Hispanic	2	0.01
African, sub-Saharan:	11	0.07
African	11	0.07
Am. Ind. or Alaska Nat., not spec.	27	0.18
American Indian tribes, specified:	38	0.25
Apache	5	0.03
Blackfeet	2	0.01
Cherokee (2)	14	0.09
Choctaw	1	0.01
Iroquois (2)	4	0.03
Latin American Indians	7	0.05
Pueblo (1)	3	0.02
Sioux	2	0.01
American Indian tribes, not spec.	4	0.03
Arab:	9	0.06
Lebanese	9	0.06
Asian:	66	0.43
Cambodian (1)	1	0.01
Chinese, ex. Taiwanese (11)	16	0.10
Filipino (12)	16	0.10
Indian (6)	9	0.06
Indonesian (2)	6	0.04
Japanese (2)	2	0.01
Korean (4)	8	0.05
Vietnamese (5)	5	0.03
Other Asian, not specified (1)	3	0.02
Austrian	13	0.08
Belgian	29	0.19
British	23	0.15
Canadian	5	0.03
Czech	18	0.12
Dutch	97	0.63
English	1,334	8.66
European	31	0.20
Finnish	18	0.12
French, except Basque	344	2.23
German	1,962	12.73
Greek	6	0.04
Hawaii Native/Pacific Islander:	6	0.04
Micronesian: (3)	3	0.02
Guamanian/Chamorro (3)	3	0.02
Polynesian: (2)	3	0.02
Native Hawaiian (1)	2	0.01
Samoan (1)	1	0.01
Hispanic or Latino:	100	0.65
Central American:	7	0.05
Guatemalan	6	0.04
Panamanian	1	0.01
Cuban	1	0.01
Mexican	48	0.31
Puerto Rican	7	0.05
South American:	1	0.01
Ecuadorian	1	0.01
Other Hispanic or Latino	36	0.23
Irish	1,561	10.13
Italian	149	0.97
Norwegian	82	0.53
Polish	54	0.35
Scandinavian	31	0.20
Scotch-Irish	163	1.06
Scottish	284	1.84
Slovak	7	0.05
Swedish	82	0.53
Swiss	30	0.19
United States or American	3,191	20.70
Welsh	74	0.48
White:	14,939	96.94
Not Hispanic (14,740)	14,858	96.41
Hispanic (70)	81	0.53

Crawfordsville

Place Type: City
County: Montgomery
Population: 15,243

Ancestry/Race	Number	%
African American/Black:	295	1.94
Not Hispanic (241)	290	1.90
Hispanic (5)	5	0.03
African, sub-Saharan:	43	0.28
African	28	0.18
Other sub-Saharan African	15	0.10
Alaska Native tribes, specified:	1	0.01
Eskimo (1)	1	0.01
Am. Ind. or Alaska Nat., not spec.	39	0.26
American Indian tribes, specified:	55	0.36
Apache	1	0.01
Blackfeet	6	0.04
Cherokee (11)	28	0.18
Cheyenne	1	0.01
Chickasaw	1	0.01
Chippewa	1	0.01
Iroquois (5)	6	0.04
Pueblo (4)	4	0.03
Seminole	1	0.01
Sioux (2)	3	0.02
All other tribes (2)	3	0.02
American Indian tribes, not spec.	9	0.06
Arab:	23	0.15
Lebanese	23	0.15
Asian:	141	0.93
Bangladeshi (1)	1	0.01
Cambodian	1	0.01
Chinese, ex. Taiwanese (23)	26	0.17
Filipino (9)	19	0.12
Indian (31)	36	0.24
Indonesian (1)	1	0.01
Japanese (22)	27	0.18
Korean (6)	11	0.07
Pakistani (3)	3	0.02
Taiwanese (4)	4	0.03
Thai (3)	4	0.03
Vietnamese	2	0.01
Other Asian, not specified (1)	6	0.04
Austrian	8	0.05
British	24	0.16
Bulgarian	16	0.10
Celtic	29	0.19
Czechoslovakian	5	0.03
Danish	51	0.33
Dutch	264	1.73
Eastern European	7	0.05
English	1,382	9.06
European	77	0.50
Finnish	8	0.05
French, except Basque	301	1.97
French Canadian	58	0.38
German	2,658	17.43
Greek	6	0.04
Hawaii Native/Pacific Islander:	15	0.10
Melanesian: (1)	1	0.01
Other Melanesian (1)	1	0.01
Micronesian:	2	0.01
Guamanian/Chamorro	2	0.01
Polynesian: (6)	9	0.06
Native Hawaiian (1)	3	0.02
Samoan (5)	6	0.04
Other Pac. Isl., not spec. (3)	3	0.02
Hispanic or Latino:	495	3.25
Central American:	18	0.12
Guatemalan	13	0.09
Nicaraguan	1	0.01
Salvadoran	4	0.03
Cuban	9	0.06
Dominican Republic	1	0.01
Mexican	404	2.65
Puerto Rican	6	0.04
South American:	17	0.11
Argentinean	3	0.02
Bolivian	1	0.01
Chilean	4	0.03
Colombian	6	0.04
Peruvian	1	0.01
Venezuelan	2	0.01
Other Hispanic or Latino	40	0.26
Irish	1,910	12.52
Italian	220	1.44
Lithuanian	25	0.16
Norwegian	121	0.79
Pennsylvania German	20	0.13
Polish	190	1.25
Portuguese	12	0.08
Russian	13	0.09
Scandinavian	14	0.09
Scotch-Irish	311	2.04
Scottish	279	1.83
Serbian	5	0.03
Swedish	198	1.30
Swiss	96	0.63
Ukrainian	4	0.03

Notes: 1. Figures in the "Number" column do not add up to the total population due to: a) Ancestry/Race overlap — e.g. persons can report being both White and Irish, b) persons of Hispanic origin can report being any race, c) persons reporting two ancestries are counted in both categories. 2. Numbers in parentheses indicate the number of persons reporting this ancestry/race alone, not in combination with any other ancestry/race. 3. Refer to the Explanation of Data in the front of the book for more detailed information.

United States or American	1,625	10.65
Welsh	179	1.17
White:	14,460	94.86
Not Hispanic (14,209)	14,317	93.93
Hispanic (122)	143	0.94

Crown Point

Place Type: City
County: Lake
Population: 19,806

Ancestry/Race	Number	%
African American/Black:	300	1.51
Not Hispanic (275)	295	1.49
Hispanic (5)	5	0.03
African, sub-Saharan:	9	0.05
Nigerian	9	0.05
Alaska Native tribes, specified:	1	0.01
Tlingit-Haida	1	0.01
Am. Ind. or Alaska Nat., not spec.	29	0.15
American Indian tribes, specified:	57	0.29
Apache	4	0.02
Blackfeet	2	0.01
Cherokee (5)	27	0.14
Chippewa (2)	2	0.01
Crow (1)	1	0.01
Delaware	2	0.01
Iroquois	3	0.02
Latin American Indians (1)	5	0.03
Navajo (4)	4	0.02
Potawatomi (1)	1	0.01
Sioux (2)	4	0.02
All other tribes	2	0.01
American Indian tribes, not spec.	1	0.01
Arab:	77	0.39
Arab/Arabic	7	0.04
Egyptian	16	0.08
Lebanese	27	0.14
Other Arab	27	0.14
Armenian	47	0.24
Asian:	256	1.29
Chinese, ex. Taiwanese (19)	29	0.15
Filipino (42)	55	0.28
Indian (47)	59	0.30
Indonesian	1	0.01
Japanese (2)	2	0.01
Korean (16)	21	0.11
Pakistani (14)	26	0.13
Thai (26)	31	0.16
Vietnamese (8)	11	0.06
Other Asian, specified (3)	6	0.03
Other Asian, not specified (8)	15	0.08
Assyrian/Chaldean/Syriac	6	0.03
Austrian	70	0.36
Belgian	52	0.27
British	72	0.37
Bulgarian	18	0.09
Canadian	27	0.14
Croatian	497	2.54
Czech	181	0.93
Czechoslovakian	56	0.29
Danish	137	0.70
Dutch	752	3.84
Eastern European	12	0.06
English	1,774	9.07
European	18	0.09
Finnish	35	0.18
French, except Basque	406	2.07
French Canadian	219	1.12
German	5,204	26.60
German Russian	9	0.05
Greek	509	2.60
Hawaii Native/Pacific Islander:	27	0.14
Micronesian: (4)	8	0.04
Guamanian/Chamorro (4)	8	0.04
Polynesian: (2)	10	0.05
Native Hawaiian	7	0.04
Samoan (2)	2	0.01
Other Polynesian	1	0.01
Other Pac. Isl., specified	1	0.01
Other Pac. Isl., not spec.	8	0.04
Hispanic or Latino:	793	4.00
Central American:	10	0.05
Costa Rican	2	0.01
Guatemalan	1	0.01
Nicaraguan	2	0.01
Panamanian	4	0.02
Salvadoran	1	0.01
Cuban	10	0.05
Mexican	576	2.91
Puerto Rican	85	0.43
South American:	13	0.07
Argentinean	4	0.02
Chilean	4	0.02
Colombian	1	0.01
Venezuelan	4	0.02
Other Hispanic or Latino	99	0.50
Hungarian	280	1.43
Irish	3,006	15.36
Italian	1,465	7.49
Latvian	31	0.16
Lithuanian	175	0.89
Macedonian	613	3.13
Norwegian	177	0.90
Pennsylvania German	9	0.05
Polish	2,280	11.65
Portuguese	11	0.06
Romanian	80	0.41
Russian	162	0.83
Scandinavian	5	0.03
Scotch-Irish	328	1.68
Scottish	353	1.80
Serbian	458	2.34
Slavic	9	0.05
Slovak	668	3.41
Swedish	478	2.44
Swiss	51	0.26
Ukrainian	49	0.25
United States or American	704	3.60
Welsh	152	0.78
White:	19,074	96.30
Not Hispanic (18,354)	18,489	93.35
Hispanic (525)	585	2.95
Yugoslavian	103	0.53

Dyer

Place Type: Town
County: Lake
Population: 13,895

Ancestry/Race	Number	%
Afghan	21	0.15
African American/Black:	113	0.81
Not Hispanic (91)	113	0.81
African, sub-Saharan:	54	0.39
African	5	0.04
Nigerian	49	0.35
Am. Ind. or Alaska Nat., not spec.	16	0.12
American Indian tribes, specified:	38	0.27
Apache (2)	3	0.02
Cherokee (2)	15	0.11
Cheyenne	1	0.01
Cree	2	0.01
Creek (1)	1	0.01
Crow	1	0.01
Delaware	1	0.01
Iroquois (1)	1	0.01
Latin American Indians (1)	1	0.01
Navajo (5)	8	0.06
Sioux (1)	1	0.01
All other tribes (1)	3	0.02
American Indian tribes, not spec.	2	0.01
Arab:	58	0.42
Egyptian	23	0.17
Other Arab	35	0.25
Asian:	267	1.92
Chinese, ex. Taiwanese (19)	22	0.16
Filipino (36)	45	0.32
Indian (94)	109	0.78
Indonesian	4	0.03
Japanese (6)	9	0.06
Korean (21)	24	0.17
Laotian (5)	5	0.04
Malaysian (1)	1	0.01
Thai (19)	19	0.14
Vietnamese (6)	6	0.04
Other Asian, not specified (9)	23	0.17
Austrian	105	0.76
Belgian	6	0.04
British	5	0.04
Bulgarian	8	0.06
Canadian	25	0.18
Celtic	9	0.06
Croatian	218	1.57
Czech	65	0.47
Czechoslovakian	35	0.25
Danish	10	0.07
Dutch	1,004	7.25
Eastern European	44	0.32
English	843	6.08
European	12	0.09
French, except Basque	420	3.03
French Canadian	146	1.05
German	3,077	22.21
Greek	326	2.35
Hawaii Native/Pacific Islander:	12	0.09
Polynesian: (4)	6	0.04
Native Hawaiian (4)	4	0.03
Samoan	1	0.01
Other Polynesian	1	0.01
Other Pac. Isl., not spec.	6	0.04
Hispanic or Latino:	696	5.01
Central American:	10	0.07
Guatemalan	5	0.04
Honduran	5	0.04
Cuban	4	0.03
Dominican Republic	1	0.01
Mexican	529	3.81
Puerto Rican	62	0.45
South American:	15	0.11
Argentinean	9	0.06
Chilean	1	0.01
Ecuadorian	1	0.01
Peruvian	4	0.03
Other Hispanic or Latino	75	0.54
Hungarian	287	2.07
Irish	2,440	17.61
Italian	1,384	9.99
Lithuanian	174	1.26
Macedonian	22	0.16
Norwegian	110	0.79
Polish	2,903	20.95
Romanian	67	0.48
Russian	45	0.32
Scandinavian	50	0.36
Scotch-Irish	128	0.92
Scottish	241	1.74
Serbian	180	1.30
Slavic	26	0.19
Slovak	311	2.24
Slovene	9	0.06
Swedish	377	2.72
Swiss	7	0.05
Ukrainian	39	0.28
United States or American	453	3.27
Welsh	72	0.52
White:	13,364	96.18
Not Hispanic (12,763)	12,844	92.44
Hispanic (495)	520	3.74
Yugoslavian	44	0.32

East Chicago

Place Type: City
County: Lake
Population: 32,414

Ancestry/Race	Number	%

Notes: 1. Figures in the "Number" column do not add up to the total population due to: a) Ancestry/Race overlap — e.g. persons can report being both White and Irish, b) persons of Hispanic origin can report being any race, c) persons reporting two ancestries are counted in both categories. 2. Numbers in parentheses indicate the number of persons reporting this ancestry/race alone, not in combination with any other ancestry/race. 3. Refer to the Explanation of Data in the front of the book for more detailed information.

Ancestry/Race	Number	%
African American/Black:	11,942	36.84
Not Hispanic (11,405)	11,531	35.57
Hispanic (290)	411	1.27
African, sub-Saharan:	234	0.72
African	234	0.72
Am. Ind. or Alaska Nat., not spec.	151	0.47
American Indian tribes, specified:	94	0.29
Apache	4	0.01
Blackfeet	8	0.02
Cherokee (4)	17	0.05
Chippewa (1)	1	0.00
Choctaw	7	0.02
Iroquois (3)	4	0.01
Latin American Indians (35)	41	0.13
Pueblo	1	0.00
Seminole	1	0.00
Sioux	4	0.01
All other tribes (1)	6	0.02
American Indian tribes, not spec.	13	0.04
Arab:	66	0.20
Arab/Arabic	40	0.12
Jordanian	16	0.05
Lebanese	10	0.03
Armenian	15	0.05
Asian:	111	0.34
Chinese, ex. Taiwanese (3)	7	0.02
Filipino (17)	29	0.09
Indian (26)	30	0.09
Japanese (2)	2	0.01
Korean (16)	20	0.06
Vietnamese (1)	4	0.01
Other Asian, not specified (1)	19	0.06
Austrian	11	0.03
Brazilian	11	0.03
Croatian	216	0.67
Czech	33	0.10
Czechoslovakian	83	0.26
Dutch	62	0.19
English	130	0.40
French, except Basque	79	0.24
French Canadian	14	0.04
German	492	1.52
Greek	40	0.12
Hawaii Native/Pacific Islander:	37	0.11
Micronesian: (3)	4	0.01
Guamanian/Chamorro (3)	4	0.01
Polynesian: (16)	25	0.08
Native Hawaiian (5)	7	0.02
Samoan (11)	18	0.06
Other Pac. Isl., not spec. (7)	8	0.02
Hispanic or Latino:	16,728	51.61
Central American:	70	0.22
Guatemalan	21	0.06
Honduran	29	0.09
Panamanian	2	0.01
Salvadoran	9	0.03
Other Central American	9	0.03
Cuban	30	0.09
Dominican Republic	10	0.03
Mexican	12,245	37.78
Puerto Rican	3,088	9.53
South American:	45	0.14
Argentinean	6	0.02
Bolivian	9	0.03
Chilean	4	0.01
Colombian	10	0.03
Peruvian	13	0.04
Uruguayan	1	0.00
Venezuelan	1	0.00
Other South American	1	0.00
Other Hispanic or Latino	1,240	3.83
Hungarian	212	0.65
Irish	379	1.17
Italian	252	0.78
Lithuanian	61	0.19
Norwegian	6	0.02
Polish	1,562	4.82
Romanian	128	0.39
Russian	26	0.08
Scotch-Irish	34	0.10
Scottish	62	0.19
Serbian	220	0.68
Slovak	213	0.66
Slovene	7	0.02
Swedish	82	0.25
Turkish	35	0.11
Ukrainian	7	0.02
United States or American	169	0.52
Welsh	6	0.02
West Indian, excl. Hispanic:	11	0.03
Belizean	11	0.03
White:	12,484	38.51
Not Hispanic (3,922)	4,056	12.51
Hispanic (7,921)	8,428	26.00
Yugoslavian	6	0.02

Elkhart

Place Type: City
County: Elkhart
Population: 51,874

Ancestry/Race	Number	%
African American/Black:	8,295	15.99
Not Hispanic (7,561)	8,166	15.74
Hispanic (88)	129	0.25
African, sub-Saharan:	656	1.27
African	586	1.13
Ghanian	7	0.01
Kenyan	22	0.04
Nigerian	32	0.06
Other sub-Saharan African	9	0.02
Alaska Native tribes, specified:	3	0.01
Alaska Athabascan (1)	1	0.00
Eskimo (1)	2	0.00
Alaska Native tribes, not specified	1	0.00
Am. Ind. or Alaska Nat., not spec.	175	0.34
American Indian tribes, specified:	372	0.72
Apache (5)	14	0.03
Blackfeet (3)	33	0.06
Cherokee (38)	143	0.28
Cheyenne	1	0.00
Chickasaw	2	0.00
Chippewa (4)	12	0.02
Choctaw (3)	5	0.01
Comanche (1)	3	0.01
Creek	1	0.00
Iroquois (1)	9	0.02
Latin American Indians (19)	38	0.07
Lumbee (2)	3	0.01
Menominee (1)	1	0.00
Navajo (6)	9	0.02
Osage	1	0.00
Ottawa (5)	8	0.02
Potawatomi (3)	7	0.01
Seminole (3)	3	0.01
Shoshone (4)	4	0.01
Sioux (8)	16	0.03
All other tribes (32)	59	0.11
American Indian tribes, not spec.	31	0.06
Arab:	138	0.27
Arab/Arabic	39	0.08
Iraqi	13	0.03
Lebanese	22	0.04
Syrian	64	0.12
Asian:	800	1.54
Bangladeshi	1	0.00
Cambodian (80)	84	0.16
Chinese, ex. Taiwanese (69)	77	0.15
Filipino (30)	51	0.10
Indian (123)	163	0.31
Indonesian (3)	8	0.02
Japanese (20)	31	0.06
Korean (63)	71	0.14
Laotian (97)	124	0.24
Malaysian	1	0.00
Pakistani (19)	23	0.04
Sri Lankan (1)	1	0.00
Taiwanese (8)	8	0.02
Thai (23)	28	0.05
Vietnamese (29)	35	0.07
Other Asian, not specified (33)	94	0.18
Austrian	42	0.08
Belgian	174	0.34
British	78	0.15
Canadian	88	0.17
Croatian	8	0.02
Czech	98	0.19
Czechoslovakian	55	0.11
Danish	128	0.25
Dutch	1,414	2.73
English	3,403	6.58
European	350	0.68
Finnish	103	0.20
French, except Basque	1,194	2.31
French Canadian	278	0.54
German	9,681	18.72
Greek	94	0.18
Hawaii Native/Pacific Islander:	71	0.14
Micronesian: (16)	28	0.05
Guamanian/Chamorro (9)	16	0.03
Other Micronesian (7)	12	0.02
Polynesian: (10)	22	0.04
Native Hawaiian (9)	14	0.03
Samoan	4	0.01
Tongan (1)	4	0.01
Other Pac. Isl., not spec. (4)	21	0.04
Hispanic or Latino:	7,678	14.80
Central American:	413	0.80
Costa Rican	1	0.00
Guatemalan	66	0.13
Honduran	167	0.32
Nicaraguan	10	0.02
Panamanian	7	0.01
Salvadoran	137	0.26
Other Central American	25	0.05
Cuban	17	0.03
Dominican Republic	15	0.03
Mexican	6,174	11.90
Puerto Rican	333	0.64
South American:	64	0.12
Argentinean	2	0.00
Bolivian	3	0.01
Colombian	12	0.02
Ecuadorian	6	0.01
Paraguayan	1	0.00
Peruvian	4	0.01
Uruguayan	1	0.00
Venezuelan	33	0.06
Other South American	2	0.00
Other Hispanic or Latino	662	1.28
Hungarian	248	0.48
Irish	4,263	8.25
Italian	1,664	3.22
Latvian	44	0.09
Lithuanian	42	0.08
Norwegian	474	0.92
Pennsylvania German	160	0.31
Polish	1,152	2.23
Russian	109	0.21
Scotch-Irish	567	1.10
Scottish	701	1.36
Serbian	66	0.13
Slavic	6	0.01
Slovak	39	0.08
Slovene	8	0.02
Swedish	570	1.10
Swiss	454	0.88
Ukrainian	99	0.19
United States or American	3,641	7.04
Welsh	347	0.67
West Indian, excl. Hispanic:	30	0.06
Belizean	7	0.01
Jamaican	23	0.04
White:	38,450	74.12
Not Hispanic (34,655)	35,635	68.70
Hispanic (2,422)	2,815	5.43

Notes: 1. Figures in the "Number" column do not add up to the total population due to: a) Ancestry/Race overlap — e.g. persons can report being both White and Irish, b) persons of Hispanic origin can report being any race, c) persons reporting two ancestries are counted in both categories. 2. Numbers in parentheses indicate the number of persons reporting this ancestry/race alone, not in combination with any other ancestry/race. 3. Refer to the Explanation of Data in the front of the book for more detailed information.

Evansville

Place Type: City
County: Vanderburgh
Population: 121,582

Ancestry/Race	Number	%
African American/Black:	14,192	11.67
Not Hispanic (13,209)	14,092	11.59
Hispanic (66)	100	0.08
African, sub-Saharan:	230	0.19
African	214	0.18
Nigerian	8	0.01
Sudanese	8	0.01
Am. Ind. or Alaska Nat., not spec.	253	0.21
Albanian	7	0.01
Alsatian	19	0.02
American Indian tribes, specified:	467	0.38
Apache (7)	15	0.01
Blackfeet (1)	28	0.02
Cherokee (70)	259	0.21
Cheyenne (2)	4	0.00
Chickasaw (1)	4	0.00
Chippewa (6)	16	0.01
Choctaw (4)	9	0.01
Comanche	3	0.00
Cree (1)	7	0.01
Creek	3	0.00
Crow	1	0.00
Delaware (1)	1	0.00
Iroquois (4)	9	0.01
Kiowa	1	0.00
Latin American Indians (6)	11	0.01
Lumbee (5)	10	0.01
Navajo (3)	6	0.00
Osage (2)	3	0.00
Ottawa	1	0.00
Paiute	1	0.00
Potawatomi (4)	5	0.00
Pueblo	3	0.00
Seminole	3	0.00
Shoshone	3	0.00
Sioux (18)	30	0.02
All other tribes (14)	31	0.03
American Indian tribes, not spec.	44	0.04
Arab:	365	0.30
Arab/Arabic	127	0.10
Egyptian	12	0.01
Lebanese	59	0.05
Moroccan	10	0.01
Palestinian	60	0.05
Syrian	80	0.07
Other Arab	17	0.01
Armenian	35	0.03
Asian:	1,167	0.96
Chinese, ex. Taiwanese (172)	219	0.18
Filipino (95)	136	0.11
Hmong	1	0.00
Indian (190)	231	0.19
Indonesian (7)	8	0.01
Japanese (81)	128	0.11
Korean (111)	158	0.13
Malaysian (7)	7	0.01
Pakistani (19)	22	0.02
Taiwanese (9)	11	0.01
Thai (24)	27	0.02
Vietnamese (115)	140	0.12
Other Asian, specified (1)	13	0.01
Other Asian, not specified (22)	66	0.05
Australian	28	0.02
Austrian	88	0.07
Belgian	100	0.08
Brazilian	25	0.02
British	594	0.49
Bulgarian	7	0.01
Canadian	60	0.05
Croatian	62	0.05
Czech	204	0.17
Czechoslovakian	119	0.10
Danish	112	0.09
Dutch	1,700	1.39
Eastern European	9	0.01
English	11,096	9.10
European	788	0.65
Finnish	19	0.02
French, except Basque	2,883	2.37
French Canadian	294	0.24
German	29,976	24.60
Greek	185	0.15
Guyanese	2	0.00
Hawaii Native/Pacific Islander:	111	0.09
Micronesian: (14)	23	0.02
Guamanian/Chamorro (8)	14	0.01
Other Micronesian (6)	9	0.01
Polynesian: (26)	57	0.05
Native Hawaiian (13)	37	0.03
Samoan (13)	15	0.01
Other Polynesian	5	0.00
Other Pac. Isl., specified	9	0.01
Other Pac. Isl., not spec. (15)	22	0.02
Hispanic or Latino:	1,392	1.14
Central American:	47	0.04
Costa Rican	5	0.00
Guatemalan	10	0.01
Honduran	9	0.01
Nicaraguan	10	0.01
Panamanian	9	0.01
Salvadoran	4	0.00
Cuban	79	0.06
Dominican Republic	2	0.00
Mexican	788	0.65
Puerto Rican	122	0.10
South American:	56	0.05
Argentinean	5	0.00
Bolivian	1	0.00
Chilean	7	0.01
Colombian	12	0.01
Ecuadorian	2	0.00
Peruvian	8	0.01
Venezuelan	20	0.02
Other South American	1	0.00
Other Hispanic or Latino	298	0.25
Hungarian	95	0.08
Icelander	4	0.00
Irish	12,659	10.39
Italian	1,740	1.43
Latvian	6	0.00
Lithuanian	115	0.09
Macedonian	7	0.01
Northern European	7	0.01
Norwegian	479	0.39
Pennsylvania German	15	0.01
Polish	1,006	0.83
Portuguese	7	0.01
Romanian	63	0.05
Russian	374	0.31
Scandinavian	31	0.03
Scotch-Irish	1,674	1.37
Scottish	1,678	1.38
Serbian	9	0.01
Slavic	7	0.01
Slovak	36	0.03
Swedish	453	0.37
Swiss	304	0.25
Turkish	7	0.01
Ukrainian	50	0.04
United States or American	13,067	10.72
Welsh	810	0.66
West Indian, excl. Hispanic:	44	0.04
Jamaican	44	0.04
White:	106,366	87.48
Not Hispanic (104,066)	105,476	86.75
Hispanic (792)	890	0.73
Yugoslavian	65	0.05

Fishers

Place Type: Town
County: Hamilton
Population: 37,835

Ancestry/Race	Number	%
African American/Black:	1,221	3.23
Not Hispanic (1,096)	1,197	3.16
Hispanic (14)	24	0.06
African, sub-Saharan:	31	0.08
African	17	0.04
Nigerian	14	0.04
Am. Ind. or Alaska Nat., not spec.	48	0.13
American Indian tribes, specified:	59	0.16
Blackfeet	3	0.01
Cherokee (5)	18	0.05
Chippewa (2)	4	0.01
Choctaw	1	0.00
Creek	1	0.00
Crow	1	0.00
Iroquois	1	0.00
Latin American Indians	2	0.01
Lumbee (5)	5	0.01
Navajo (1)	1	0.00
Ottawa	1	0.00
Paiute (2)	2	0.01
Potawatomi (3)	4	0.01
Sioux (1)	2	0.01
Ute	1	0.00
All other tribes (5)	12	0.03
American Indian tribes, not spec.	4	0.01
Arab:	152	0.39
Arab/Arabic	10	0.03
Egyptian	53	0.14
Lebanese	26	0.07
Palestinian	31	0.08
Syrian	32	0.08
Armenian	55	0.14
Asian:	1,383	3.66
Bangladeshi (7)	7	0.02
Cambodian (9)	9	0.02
Chinese, ex. Taiwanese (292)	329	0.87
Filipino (69)	120	0.32
Indian (305)	316	0.84
Indonesian (1)	4	0.01
Japanese (136)	173	0.46
Korean (160)	194	0.51
Laotian (2)	2	0.01
Malaysian (2)	3	0.01
Pakistani (13)	20	0.05
Sri Lankan (5)	5	0.01
Taiwanese (7)	7	0.02
Thai (2)	10	0.03
Vietnamese (106)	115	0.30
Other Asian, specified (6)	6	0.02
Other Asian, not specified (27)	63	0.17
Australian	13	0.03
Austrian	101	0.26
Belgian	110	0.28
Brazilian	16	0.04
British	238	0.61
Canadian	201	0.52
Celtic	9	0.02
Croatian	31	0.08
Czech	190	0.49
Czechoslovakian	128	0.33
Danish	157	0.40
Dutch	794	2.04
English	5,197	13.35
European	413	1.06
Finnish	36	0.09
French, except Basque	1,420	3.65
French Canadian	168	0.43
German	11,383	29.23
Greek	179	0.46
Hawaii Native/Pacific Islander:	20	0.05
Polynesian: (7)	17	0.04
Native Hawaiian (5)	13	0.03
Samoan (1)	1	0.00

Notes: 1. Figures in the "Number" column do not add up to the total population due to: a) Ancestry/Race overlap — e.g. persons can report being both White and Irish, b) persons of Hispanic origin can report being any race, c) persons reporting two ancestries are counted in both categories. 2. Numbers in parentheses indicate the number of persons reporting this ancestry/race alone, not in combination with any other ancestry/race. 3. Refer to the Explanation of Data in the front of the book for more detailed information.

Ancestry/Race	Number	%
Tongan (1)	3	0.01
Other Pac. Isl., not spec.	3	0.01
Hispanic or Latino:	764	2.02
Central American:	19	0.05
Costa Rican	3	0.01
Guatemalan	1	0.00
Honduran	2	0.01
Nicaraguan	2	0.01
Panamanian	10	0.03
Salvadoran	1	0.00
Cuban	32	0.08
Dominican Republic	14	0.04
Mexican	376	0.99
Puerto Rican	104	0.27
South American:	95	0.25
Argentinean	13	0.03
Chilean	7	0.02
Colombian	39	0.10
Ecuadorian	6	0.02
Paraguayan	1	0.00
Peruvian	8	0.02
Uruguayan	1	0.00
Venezuelan	18	0.05
Other South American	2	0.01
Other Hispanic or Latino	124	0.33
Hungarian	367	0.94
Icelander	9	0.02
Iranian	25	0.06
Irish	5,195	13.34
Italian	1,966	5.05
Latvian	43	0.11
Lithuanian	91	0.23
Macedonian	9	0.02
Northern European	30	0.08
Norwegian	509	1.31
Pennsylvania German	8	0.02
Polish	1,567	4.02
Portuguese	48	0.12
Romanian	41	0.11
Russian	276	0.71
Scandinavian	44	0.11
Scotch-Irish	694	1.78
Scottish	1,223	3.14
Serbian	16	0.04
Slavic	26	0.07
Slovak	146	0.37
Slovene	27	0.07
Swedish	567	1.46
Swiss	255	0.65
Turkish	30	0.08
Ukrainian	61	0.16
United States or American	2,817	7.23
Welsh	395	1.01
West Indian, excl. Hispanic:	25	0.06
Jamaican	25	0.06
White:	35,252	93.17
Not Hispanic (34,400)	34,696	91.70
Hispanic (510)	556	1.47
Yugoslavian	17	0.04

Fort Wayne

Place Type: City
County: Allen
Population: 205,727

Ancestry/Race	Number	%
Acadian/Cajun	20	0.01
African American/Black:	38,079	18.51
Not Hispanic (35,391)	37,523	18.24
Hispanic (361)	556	0.27
African, sub-Saharan:	1,379	0.67
African	1,111	0.54
Ethiopian	54	0.03
Nigerian	81	0.04
Somalian	16	0.01
South African	7	0.00
Sudanese	36	0.02
Zimbabwean	10	0.00
Other sub-Saharan African	64	0.03
Alaska Native tribes, specified:	6	0.00
Alaska Athabascan	1	0.00
Aleut (1)	1	0.00
Eskimo (1)	2	0.00
Tlingit-Haida (1)	2	0.00
Am. Ind. or Alaska Nat., not spec.	590	0.29
Albanian	19	0.01
Alsatian	24	0.01
American Indian tribes, specified:	1,159	0.56
Apache (9)	27	0.01
Blackfeet (11)	70	0.03
Cherokee (122)	418	0.20
Cheyenne	6	0.00
Chickasaw	2	0.00
Chippewa (34)	67	0.03
Choctaw (6)	25	0.01
Comanche (3)	7	0.00
Cree (5)	12	0.01
Creek (5)	8	0.00
Delaware	1	0.00
Iroquois (19)	26	0.01
Kiowa (1)	2	0.00
Latin American Indians (44)	78	0.04
Lumbee	2	0.00
Menominee	1	0.00
Navajo (6)	14	0.01
Osage (2)	3	0.00
Ottawa (1)	3	0.00
Pima (6)	6	0.00
Potawatomi (15)	23	0.01
Pueblo (1)	6	0.00
Seminole (2)	12	0.01
Shoshone (1)	1	0.00
Sioux (11)	32	0.02
Ute (2)	2	0.00
Yaqui (3)	3	0.00
Yuman (1)	1	0.00
All other tribes (190)	301	0.15
American Indian tribes, not spec.	96	0.05
Arab:	369	0.18
Arab/Arabic	65	0.03
Iraqi	20	0.01
Jordanian	21	0.01
Lebanese	122	0.06
Moroccan	48	0.02
Palestinian	18	0.01
Syrian	57	0.03
Other Arab	18	0.01
Armenian	148	0.07
Asian:	4,003	1.95
Bangladeshi (21)	22	0.01
Cambodian (16)	24	0.01
Chinese, ex. Taiwanese (311)	397	0.19
Filipino (240)	380	0.18
Hmong (2)	2	0.00
Indian (575)	661	0.32
Indonesian (21)	28	0.01
Japanese (109)	169	0.08
Korean (161)	258	0.13
Laotian (273)	335	0.16
Malaysian (67)	77	0.04
Pakistani (61)	87	0.04
Sri Lankan (14)	17	0.01
Taiwanese (21)	31	0.02
Thai (47)	78	0.04
Vietnamese (633)	682	0.33
Other Asian, specified (395)	476	0.23
Other Asian, not specified (166)	279	0.14
Australian	34	0.02
Austrian	292	0.14
Basque	8	0.00
Belgian	163	0.08
Brazilian	21	0.01
British	585	0.28
Bulgarian	56	0.03
Canadian	428	0.21
Celtic	9	0.00
Croatian	158	0.08
Czech	341	0.17
Czechoslovakian	135	0.07
Danish	509	0.25
Dutch	3,576	1.74
English	15,638	7.59
Estonian	25	0.01
European	1,212	0.59
Finnish	156	0.08
French, except Basque	7,836	3.80
French Canadian	751	0.36
German	56,716	27.54
German Russian	4	0.00
Greek	678	0.33
Hawaii Native/Pacific Islander:	195	0.09
Melanesian: (1)	1	0.00
Other Melanesian (1)	1	0.00
Micronesian: (33)	57	0.03
Guamanian/Chamorro (30)	49	0.02
Other Micronesian (3)	8	0.00
Polynesian: (37)	81	0.04
Native Hawaiian (19)	52	0.03
Samoan (18)	28	0.01
Other Polynesian	1	0.00
Other Pac. Isl., specified	5	0.00
Other Pac. Isl., not spec. (13)	51	0.02
Hispanic or Latino:	11,884	5.78
Central American:	471	0.23
Costa Rican	8	0.00
Guatemalan	255	0.12
Honduran	28	0.01
Nicaraguan	6	0.00
Panamanian	30	0.01
Salvadoran	115	0.06
Other Central American	29	0.01
Cuban	136	0.07
Dominican Republic	23	0.01
Mexican	8,619	4.19
Puerto Rican	533	0.26
South American:	282	0.14
Argentinean	6	0.00
Bolivian	10	0.00
Chilean	12	0.01
Colombian	116	0.06
Ecuadorian	81	0.04
Paraguayan	2	0.00
Peruvian	24	0.01
Uruguayan	3	0.00
Venezuelan	21	0.01
Other South American	7	0.00
Other Hispanic or Latino	1,820	0.88
Hungarian	803	0.39
Iranian	75	0.04
Irish	21,601	10.49
Israeli	6	0.00
Italian	4,784	2.32
Latvian	22	0.01
Lithuanian	245	0.12
Luxemburger	23	0.01
Macedonian	432	0.21
Maltese	10	0.00
Northern European	50	0.02
Norwegian	1,214	0.59
Pennsylvania German	149	0.07
Polish	4,107	1.99
Portuguese	201	0.10
Romanian	344	0.17
Russian	636	0.31
Scandinavian	166	0.08
Scotch-Irish	2,167	1.05
Scottish	3,423	1.66
Serbian	73	0.04
Slavic	93	0.05
Slovak	263	0.13
Slovene	78	0.04
Swedish	1,779	0.86
Swiss	1,905	0.93
Turkish	65	0.03
Ukrainian	341	0.17
United States or American	14,422	7.00
Welsh	1,073	0.52
West Indian, excl. Hispanic:	383	0.19
Bahamian	7	0.00

Notes: 1. Figures in the "Number" column do not add up to the total population due to: a) Ancestry/Race overlap — e.g. persons can report being both White and Irish, b) persons of Hispanic origin can report being any race, c) persons reporting two ancestries are counted in both categories. 2. Numbers in parentheses indicate the number of persons reporting this ancestry/race alone, not in combination with any other ancestry/race. 3. Refer to the Explanation of Data in the front of the book for more detailed information.

Ancestry/Race	Number	%
Barbadian	11	0.01
Belizean	5	0.00
British West Indian	35	0.02
Haitian	94	0.05
Jamaican	179	0.09
Trinidadian and Tobagonian	39	0.02
West Indian	13	0.01
White:	159,264	77.42
Not Hispanic (150,368)	153,635	74.68
Hispanic (4,863)	5,629	2.74
Yugoslavian	683	0.33

Frankfort

Place Type: City
County: Clinton
Population: 16,662

Ancestry/Race	Number	%
African American/Black:	103	0.62
Not Hispanic (48)	66	0.40
Hispanic (31)	37	0.22
African, sub-Saharan:	8	0.05
African	8	0.05
Am. Ind. or Alaska Nat., not spec.	37	0.22
American Indian tribes, specified:	55	0.33
Apache (1)	1	0.01
Blackfeet	4	0.02
Cherokee (4)	24	0.14
Chippewa	2	0.01
Comanche (1)	1	0.01
Cree	3	0.02
Iroquois	5	0.03
Latin American Indians (5)	6	0.04
Sioux (2)	2	0.01
Yakama	1	0.01
All other tribes	6	0.04
American Indian tribes, not spec.	1	0.01
Arab:	9	0.05
Lebanese	9	0.05
Asian:	52	0.31
Chinese, ex. Taiwanese (10)	10	0.06
Filipino (5)	5	0.03
Indian (11)	12	0.07
Japanese (8)	9	0.05
Korean (8)	9	0.05
Pakistani	1	0.01
Vietnamese (4)	4	0.02
Other Asian, not specified	2	0.01
British	217	1.30
Canadian	35	0.21
Czechoslovakian	10	0.06
Danish	10	0.06
Dutch	486	2.92
English	1,268	7.61
European	270	1.62
French, except Basque	305	1.83
German	2,663	15.98
Greek	30	0.18
Hawaii Native/Pacific Islander:	12	0.07
Polynesian: (4)	8	0.05
Native Hawaiian (1)	1	0.01
Samoan (3)	7	0.04
Other Pac. Isl., not spec. (1)	4	0.02
Hispanic or Latino:	2,255	13.53
Central American:	49	0.29
Costa Rican	1	0.01
Guatemalan	19	0.11
Honduran	5	0.03
Nicaraguan	5	0.03
Salvadoran	18	0.11
Other Central American	1	0.01
Cuban	1	0.01
Mexican	1,907	11.45
Puerto Rican	40	0.24
South American:	4	0.02
Argentinean	1	0.01
Chilean	1	0.01
Colombian	1	0.01
Ecuadorian	1	0.01
Other Hispanic or Latino	254	1.52
Hungarian	13	0.08
Irish	1,821	10.93
Italian	107	0.64
Lithuanian	26	0.16
Northern European	17	0.10
Norwegian	29	0.17
Polish	111	0.67
Romanian	22	0.13
Scotch-Irish	151	0.91
Scottish	241	1.45
Swedish	68	0.41
Swiss	54	0.32
United States or American	2,494	14.97
Welsh	67	0.40
White:	15,197	91.21
Not Hispanic (14,195)	14,293	85.78
Hispanic (814)	904	5.43

Franklin

Place Type: City
County: Johnson
Population: 19,463

Ancestry/Race	Number	%
African American/Black:	280	1.44
Not Hispanic (228)	277	1.42
Hispanic (1)	3	0.02
African, sub-Saharan:	51	0.26
Kenyan	51	0.26
Alaska Native tribes, specified:	2	0.01
Alaska Athabascan (1)	1	0.01
Eskimo (1)	1	0.01
Am. Ind. or Alaska Nat., not spec.	28	0.14
American Indian tribes, specified:	62	0.32
Apache (1)	6	0.03
Blackfeet (5)	8	0.04
Cherokee (5)	29	0.15
Cheyenne (1)	1	0.01
Chickasaw (1)	1	0.01
Chippewa (1)	2	0.01
Comanche	1	0.01
Cree	1	0.01
Iroquois	2	0.01
Puget Sound Salish (1)	1	0.01
Sioux (1)	1	0.01
Tohono O'Odham	3	0.02
All other tribes (5)	6	0.03
American Indian tribes, not spec.	7	0.04
Asian:	141	0.72
Chinese, ex. Taiwanese (24)	33	0.17
Filipino (11)	21	0.11
Indian (21)	23	0.12
Japanese (18)	23	0.12
Korean (11)	15	0.08
Pakistani (4)	4	0.02
Taiwanese (1)	4	0.02
Vietnamese (6)	9	0.05
Other Asian, not specified (2)	9	0.05
Australian	4	0.02
Austrian	11	0.06
British	10	0.05
Canadian	11	0.06
Czech	37	0.19
Danish	29	0.15
Dutch	501	2.53
English	1,933	9.75
European	231	1.17
French, except Basque	343	1.73
French Canadian	50	0.25
German	3,794	19.14
Greek	76	0.38
Hawaii Native/Pacific Islander:	19	0.10
Micronesian: (7)	7	0.04
Guamanian/Chamorro (7)	7	0.04
Polynesian: (3)	4	0.02
Native Hawaiian (1)	2	0.01
Samoan (2)	2	0.01
Other Pac. Isl., not spec.	8	0.04
Hispanic or Latino:	254	1.31
Central American:	9	0.05
Costa Rican	7	0.04
Guatemalan	2	0.01
Cuban	6	0.03
Dominican Republic	3	0.02
Mexican	147	0.76
Puerto Rican	28	0.14
South American:	12	0.06
Colombian	1	0.01
Peruvian	11	0.06
Other Hispanic or Latino	49	0.25
Irish	2,430	12.26
Italian	322	1.62
Latvian	13	0.07
Northern European	4	0.02
Norwegian	107	0.54
Pennsylvania German	19	0.10
Polish	297	1.50
Russian	63	0.32
Scandinavian	9	0.05
Scotch-Irish	370	1.87
Scottish	427	2.15
Serbian	7	0.04
Slavic	8	0.04
Slovak	31	0.16
Swedish	182	0.92
Swiss	41	0.21
Ukrainian	13	0.07
United States or American	2,729	13.77
Welsh	106	0.53
White:	18,964	97.44
Not Hispanic (18,680)	18,812	96.66
Hispanic (138)	152	0.78
Yugoslavian	18	0.09

Gary

Place Type: City
County: Lake
Population: 102,746

Ancestry/Race	Number	%
African American/Black:	87,604	85.26
Not Hispanic (85,704)	86,704	84.39
Hispanic (636)	900	0.88
African, sub-Saharan:	1,517	1.48
African	1,372	1.34
Ghanian	71	0.07
Liberian	30	0.03
Nigerian	43	0.04
South African	1	0.00
Alaska Native tribes, specified:	1	0.00
Aleut (1)	1	0.00
Am. Ind. or Alaska Nat., not spec.	342	0.33
American Indian tribes, specified:	342	0.33
Apache (1)	8	0.01
Blackfeet (4)	29	0.03
Cherokee (25)	168	0.16
Cheyenne	6	0.01
Chippewa (1)	6	0.01
Choctaw	13	0.01
Comanche (3)	3	0.00
Cree (1)	6	0.01
Creek	10	0.01
Crow	1	0.00
Delaware (3)	4	0.00
Iroquois	8	0.01
Latin American Indians (11)	19	0.02
Lumbee (1)	2	0.00
Navajo (2)	7	0.01
Ottawa (6)	6	0.01
Pueblo	1	0.00
Seminole	7	0.01
Sioux (9)	18	0.02
Yaqui	2	0.00
All other tribes (3)	18	0.02
American Indian tribes, not spec.	54	0.05
Arab:	40	0.04
Arab/Arabic	28	0.03

Notes: 1. Figures in the "Number" column do not add up to the total population due to: a) Ancestry/Race overlap — e.g. persons can report being both White and Irish, b) persons of Hispanic origin can report being any race, c) persons reporting two ancestries are counted in both categories. 2. Numbers in parentheses indicate the number of persons reporting this ancestry/race alone, not in combination with any other ancestry/race. 3. Refer to the Explanation of Data in the front of the book for more detailed information.

Ancestry/Race	Number	%
Egyptian	5	0.00
Lebanese	7	0.01
Asian:	313	0.30
Chinese, ex. Taiwanese (18)	41	0.04
Filipino (39)	77	0.07
Indian (32)	65	0.06
Japanese (10)	18	0.02
Korean (18)	45	0.04
Laotian (1)	3	0.00
Thai (4)	8	0.01
Vietnamese (11)	24	0.02
Other Asian, specified	1	0.00
Other Asian, not specified (7)	31	0.03
Assyrian/Chaldean/Syriac	10	0.01
Austrian	23	0.02
Belgian	49	0.05
British	33	0.03
Canadian	24	0.02
Croatian	172	0.17
Czech	65	0.06
Czechoslovakian	86	0.08
Danish	102	0.10
Dutch	339	0.33
English	970	0.94
European	77	0.07
Finnish	18	0.02
French, except Basque	272	0.26
French Canadian	38	0.04
German	1,957	1.90
Greek	207	0.20
Hawaii Native/Pacific Islander:	53	0.05
Melanesian:	1	0.00
Other Melanesian	1	0.00
Micronesian: (12)	15	0.01
Guamanian/Chamorro (12)	15	0.01
Polynesian: (11)	22	0.02
Native Hawaiian (6)	12	0.01
Samoan (5)	9	0.01
Other Polynesian	1	0.00
Other Pac. Isl., specified	1	0.00
Other Pac. Isl., not spec. (1)	14	0.01
Hispanic or Latino:	5,065	4.93
Central American:	28	0.03
Guatemalan	7	0.01
Honduran	8	0.01
Nicaraguan	1	0.00
Panamanian	8	0.01
Salvadoran	3	0.00
Other Central American	1	0.00
Cuban	83	0.08
Dominican Republic	9	0.01
Mexican	2,958	2.88
Puerto Rican	1,453	1.41
South American:	8	0.01
Argentinean	1	0.00
Bolivian	1	0.00
Colombian	1	0.00
Ecuadorian	3	0.00
Peruvian	1	0.00
Other South American	1	0.00
Other Hispanic or Latino	526	0.51
Hungarian	134	0.13
Icelander	7	0.01
Iranian	6	0.01
Irish	1,793	1.75
Israeli	9	0.01
Italian	519	0.51
Lithuanian	69	0.07
Macedonian	53	0.05
Maltese	6	0.01
Norwegian	77	0.07
Pennsylvania German	17	0.02
Polish	891	0.87
Romanian	182	0.18
Russian	96	0.09
Scotch-Irish	173	0.17
Scottish	192	0.19
Serbian	152	0.15
Slavic	5	0.00
Slovak	395	0.38
Swedish	96	0.09
Swiss	14	0.01
Ukrainian	46	0.04
United States or American	2,046	1.99
Welsh	36	0.04
West Indian, excl. Hispanic:	288	0.28
Bahamian	41	0.04
Belizean	4	0.00
British West Indian	6	0.01
Haitian	55	0.05
Jamaican	152	0.15
Trinidadian and Tobagonian	17	0.02
West Indian	13	0.01
White:	13,317	12.96
Not Hispanic (10,338)	11,078	10.78
Hispanic (1,907)	2,239	2.18
Yugoslavian	78	0.08

Goshen

Place Type: City
County: Elkhart
Population: 29,383

Ancestry/Race	Number	%
African American/Black:	613	2.09
Not Hispanic (428)	567	1.93
Hispanic (21)	46	0.16
African, sub-Saharan:	93	0.32
African	93	0.32
Am. Ind. or Alaska Nat., not spec.	63	0.21
Albanian	3	0.01
Alsatian	31	0.11
American Indian tribes, specified:	101	0.34
Blackfeet (1)	2	0.01
Cherokee (10)	44	0.15
Chippewa (9)	13	0.04
Comanche	3	0.01
Creek	2	0.01
Iroquois (1)	2	0.01
Kiowa	1	0.00
Latin American Indians (8)	9	0.03
Navajo (1)	1	0.00
Potawatomi (2)	3	0.01
Pueblo (2)	2	0.01
Seminole	1	0.00
Sioux (1)	3	0.01
All other tribes (11)	15	0.05
American Indian tribes, not spec.	6	0.02
Arab:	5	0.02
Palestinian	5	0.02
Armenian	8	0.03
Asian:	417	1.42
Bangladeshi (2)	2	0.01
Cambodian (31)	50	0.17
Chinese, ex. Taiwanese (64)	83	0.28
Filipino (21)	32	0.11
Indian (45)	48	0.16
Indonesian (8)	17	0.06
Japanese (37)	39	0.13
Korean (30)	35	0.12
Laotian (6)	10	0.03
Pakistani (1)	8	0.03
Sri Lankan (3)	3	0.01
Taiwanese (1)	3	0.01
Vietnamese (49)	59	0.20
Other Asian, specified (9)	10	0.03
Other Asian, not specified (4)	18	0.06
Austrian	66	0.23
Belgian	8	0.03
British	32	0.11
Canadian	122	0.42
Celtic	7	0.02
Croatian	21	0.07
Czech	47	0.16
Czechoslovakian	5	0.02
Danish	35	0.12
Dutch	887	3.03
English	1,334	4.55
European	223	0.76
Finnish	21	0.07
French, except Basque	689	2.35
French Canadian	113	0.39
German	7,429	25.37
Greek	12	0.04
Hawaii Native/Pacific Islander:	14	0.05
Micronesian: (6)	6	0.02
Guamanian/Chamorro (3)	3	0.01
Other Micronesian (3)	3	0.01
Polynesian: (1)	2	0.01
Native Hawaiian (1)	2	0.01
Other Pac. Isl., not spec.	6	0.02
Hispanic or Latino:	5,679	19.33
Central American:	101	0.34
Costa Rican	9	0.03
Guatemalan	34	0.12
Honduran	17	0.06
Nicaraguan	2	0.01
Salvadoran	33	0.11
Other Central American	6	0.02
Cuban	9	0.03
Dominican Republic	11	0.04
Mexican	4,912	16.72
Puerto Rican	231	0.79
South American:	42	0.14
Argentinean	2	0.01
Bolivian	12	0.04
Chilean	6	0.02
Colombian	16	0.05
Ecuadorian	2	0.01
Peruvian	2	0.01
Venezuelan	2	0.01
Other Hispanic or Latino	373	1.27
Hungarian	90	0.31
Irish	2,097	7.16
Italian	332	1.13
Lithuanian	5	0.02
Northern European	20	0.07
Norwegian	155	0.53
Pennsylvania German	252	0.86
Polish	452	1.54
Portuguese	15	0.05
Russian	87	0.30
Scotch-Irish	234	0.80
Scottish	189	0.65
Slavic	35	0.12
Slovak	30	0.10
Swedish	211	0.72
Swiss	1,577	5.38
Ukrainian	52	0.18
United States or American	3,268	11.16
Welsh	124	0.42
White:	24,943	84.89
Not Hispanic (22,525)	22,822	77.67
Hispanic (1,906)	2,121	7.22

Granger

Place Type: Census Designated Place
County: Saint Joseph
Population: 28,284

Ancestry/Race	Number	%
African American/Black:	573	2.03
Not Hispanic (493)	569	2.01
Hispanic	4	0.01
African, sub-Saharan:	88	0.31
African	34	0.12
Nigerian	54	0.19
Am. Ind. or Alaska Nat., not spec.	29	0.10
American Indian tribes, specified:	83	0.29
Apache (1)	2	0.01
Blackfeet	1	0.00
Cherokee (8)	32	0.11
Chippewa	2	0.01
Choctaw (2)	2	0.01
Creek	5	0.02
Delaware	3	0.01
Latin American Indians (1)	3	0.01
Potawatomi (8)	12	0.04

Notes: 1. Figures in the "Number" column do not add up to the total population due to: a) Ancestry/Race overlap — e.g. persons can report being both White and Irish, b) persons of Hispanic origin can report being any race, c) persons reporting two ancestries are counted in both categories. 2. Numbers in parentheses indicate the number of persons reporting this ancestry/race alone, not in combination with any other ancestry/race. 3. Refer to the Explanation of Data in the front of the book for more detailed information.

Ancestry/Race	Number	%
Sioux	2	0.01
All other tribes (11)	19	0.07
American Indian tribes, not spec.	3	0.01
Arab:	152	0.54
Arab/Arabic	16	0.06
Egyptian	23	0.08
Jordanian	9	0.03
Lebanese	80	0.28
Syrian	24	0.09
Armenian	7	0.02
Asian:	876	3.10
Chinese, ex. Taiwanese (188)	220	0.78
Filipino (28)	55	0.19
Hmong (11)	11	0.04
Indian (270)	283	1.00
Japanese (67)	98	0.35
Korean (92)	107	0.38
Laotian (1)	1	0.00
Pakistani (19)	30	0.11
Sri Lankan (7)	12	0.04
Taiwanese (17)	19	0.07
Thai (6)	7	0.02
Vietnamese (19)	21	0.07
Other Asian, not specified (8)	12	0.04
Australian	7	0.02
Austrian	84	0.30
Belgian	607	2.15
Brazilian	7	0.02
British	84	0.30
Canadian	87	0.31
Croatian	47	0.17
Cypriot	28	0.10
Czech	156	0.55
Czechoslovakian	57	0.20
Danish	178	0.63
Dutch	930	3.29
Eastern European	6	0.02
English	3,216	11.39
European	209	0.74
Finnish	69	0.24
French, except Basque	897	3.18
French Canadian	204	0.72
German	7,927	28.09
German Russian	7	0.02
Greek	134	0.47
Hawaii Native/Pacific Islander:	15	0.05
Micronesian: (1)	2	0.01
Guamanian/Chamorro	1	0.00
Other Micronesian (1)	1	0.00
Polynesian: (3)	9	0.03
Native Hawaiian (3)	8	0.03
Samoan	1	0.00
Other Pac. Isl., not spec. (3)	4	0.01
Hispanic or Latino:	341	1.21
Central American:	12	0.04
Guatemalan	4	0.01
Honduran	1	0.00
Nicaraguan	1	0.00
Panamanian	4	0.01
Salvadoran	2	0.01
Cuban	15	0.05
Dominican Republic	4	0.01
Mexican	130	0.46
Puerto Rican	54	0.19
South American:	42	0.15
Argentinean	2	0.01
Chilean	8	0.03
Colombian	13	0.05
Ecuadorian	4	0.01
Paraguayan	1	0.00
Peruvian	8	0.03
Venezuelan	4	0.01
Other South American	2	0.01
Other Hispanic or Latino	84	0.30
Hungarian	1,343	4.76
Icelander	12	0.04
Iranian	47	0.17
Irish	4,768	16.89
Italian	1,679	5.95
Latvian	17	0.06
Lithuanian	189	0.67
Macedonian	7	0.02
Northern European	8	0.03
Norwegian	467	1.65
Pennsylvania German	131	0.46
Polish	3,064	10.86
Portuguese	6	0.02
Romanian	42	0.15
Russian	440	1.56
Scandinavian	17	0.06
Scotch-Irish	522	1.85
Scottish	839	2.97
Serbian	68	0.24
Slavic	20	0.07
Slovak	187	0.66
Slovene	43	0.15
Swedish	693	2.46
Swiss	149	0.53
Ukrainian	143	0.51
United States or American	1,164	4.12
Welsh	280	0.99
West Indian, excl. Hispanic:	15	0.05
Barbadian	15	0.05
White:	26,903	95.12
Not Hispanic (26,376)	26,631	94.16
Hispanic (253)	272	0.96
Yugoslavian	24	0.09

Greenfield

Place Type: City
County: Hancock
Population: 14,600

Ancestry/Race	Number	%
African American/Black:	24	0.16
Not Hispanic (8)	24	0.16
Am. Ind. or Alaska Nat., not spec.	26	0.18
American Indian tribes, specified:	44	0.30
Apache (5)	5	0.03
Blackfeet	3	0.02
Cherokee (7)	24	0.16
Choctaw (1)	2	0.01
Osage	1	0.01
Pima (1)	1	0.01
Sioux (1)	1	0.01
All other tribes (6)	7	0.05
American Indian tribes, not spec.	7	0.05
Arab:	9	0.06
Egyptian	9	0.06
Asian:	98	0.67
Chinese, ex. Taiwanese (16)	18	0.12
Filipino (19)	22	0.15
Indian (17)	19	0.13
Indonesian (2)	3	0.02
Japanese (6)	12	0.08
Korean (10)	15	0.10
Laotian (3)	3	0.02
Taiwanese	1	0.01
Vietnamese (1)	1	0.01
Other Asian, not specified (3)	4	0.03
Belgian	38	0.26
British	27	0.19
Canadian	54	0.37
Croatian	37	0.25
Czech	19	0.13
Danish	27	0.19
Dutch	307	2.11
English	1,848	12.71
European	71	0.49
French, except Basque	246	1.69
French Canadian	32	0.22
German	3,287	22.60
Greek	29	0.20
Hawaii Native/Pacific Islander:	10	0.07
Polynesian: (1)	6	0.04
Native Hawaiian (1)	6	0.04
Other Pac. Isl., not spec. (1)	4	0.03
Hispanic or Latino:	186	1.27
Cuban	2	0.01
Dominican Republic	3	0.02
Mexican	145	0.99
Puerto Rican	4	0.03
South American:	3	0.02
Chilean	1	0.01
Colombian	1	0.01
Ecuadorian	1	0.01
Other Hispanic or Latino	29	0.20
Hungarian	5	0.03
Irish	1,557	10.70
Italian	259	1.78
Luxemburger	22	0.15
Northern European	26	0.18
Norwegian	125	0.86
Polish	145	1.00
Portuguese	9	0.06
Russian	40	0.28
Scotch-Irish	274	1.88
Scottish	207	1.42
Serbian	33	0.23
Slovak	33	0.23
Slovene	6	0.04
Swedish	82	0.56
Swiss	50	0.34
United States or American	2,009	13.81
Welsh	168	1.16
White:	14,431	98.84
Not Hispanic (14,215)	14,295	97.91
Hispanic (126)	136	0.93

Greensburg

Place Type: City
County: Decatur
Population: 10,260

Ancestry/Race	Number	%
African American/Black:	15	0.15
Not Hispanic (8)	13	0.13
Hispanic	2	0.02
Am. Ind. or Alaska Nat., not spec.	23	0.22
American Indian tribes, specified:	25	0.24
Apache (1)	3	0.03
Blackfeet (1)	2	0.02
Cherokee (3)	15	0.15
Crow	1	0.01
Iroquois	1	0.01
Potawatomi (2)	2	0.02
All other tribes (1)	1	0.01
Asian:	165	1.61
Chinese, ex. Taiwanese (15)	22	0.21
Filipino (24)	28	0.27
Indian (15)	24	0.23
Japanese (54)	56	0.55
Korean (7)	7	0.07
Vietnamese (23)	23	0.22
Other Asian, specified	1	0.01
Other Asian, not specified (2)	4	0.04
Austrian	22	0.21
British	32	0.31
Canadian	15	0.15
Danish	8	0.08
Dutch	89	0.86
English	935	9.06
European	136	1.32
French, except Basque	228	2.21
French Canadian	5	0.05
German	2,167	21.00
Greek	50	0.48
Hawaii Native/Pacific Islander:	5	0.05
Polynesian: (1)	1	0.01
Native Hawaiian (1)	1	0.01
Other Pac. Isl., specified	1	0.01
Other Pac. Isl., not spec.	3	0.03
Hispanic or Latino:	64	0.62
Dominican Republic	4	0.04
Mexican	44	0.43
Puerto Rican	3	0.03
South American:	1	0.01
Other South American	1	0.01

Notes: 1. Figures in the "Number" column do not add up to the total population due to: a) Ancestry/Race overlap — e.g. persons can report being both White and Irish, b) persons of Hispanic origin can report being any race, c) persons reporting two ancestries are counted in both categories. 2. Numbers in parentheses indicate the number of persons reporting this ancestry/race alone, not in combination with any other ancestry/race. 3. Refer to the Explanation of Data in the front of the book for more detailed information.

Other Hispanic or Latino	12	0.12
Hungarian	26	0.25
Irish	856	8.29
Italian	187	1.81
Norwegian	26	0.25
Polish	115	1.11
Scotch-Irish	122	1.18
Scottish	116	1.12
Slovene	6	0.06
Swedish	28	0.27
United States or American	1,306	12.65
Welsh	16	0.16
White:	10,080	98.25
Not Hispanic (9,965)	10,030	97.76
Hispanic (46)	50	0.49

Greenwood

Place Type: City
County: Johnson
Population: 36,037

Ancestry/Race	Number	%
African American/Black:	233	0.65
Not Hispanic (154)	224	0.62
Hispanic (5)	9	0.02
African, sub-Saharan:	46	0.13
African	46	0.13
Am. Ind. or Alaska Nat., not spec.	41	0.11
Albanian	21	0.06
American Indian tribes, specified:	102	0.28
Apache (2)	2	0.01
Blackfeet (2)	8	0.02
Cherokee (21)	41	0.11
Chickasaw (1)	1	0.00
Chippewa (4)	9	0.02
Choctaw	2	0.01
Creek	1	0.00
Delaware	1	0.00
Iroquois	1	0.00
Latin American Indians (2)	5	0.01
Navajo (3)	3	0.01
Osage (1)	1	0.00
Paiute (1)	1	0.00
Puget Sound Salish (1)	1	0.00
Sioux	6	0.02
All other tribes (13)	19	0.05
American Indian tribes, not spec.	9	0.02
Arab:	49	0.14
Arab/Arabic	7	0.02
Lebanese	20	0.06
Palestinian	10	0.03
Syrian	12	0.03
Armenian	8	0.02
Asian:	589	1.63
Chinese, ex. Taiwanese (147)	174	0.48
Filipino (70)	91	0.25
Indian (111)	125	0.35
Indonesian (1)	5	0.01
Japanese (69)	81	0.22
Korean (28)	41	0.11
Laotian (2)	2	0.01
Taiwanese (8)	9	0.02
Thai (7)	7	0.02
Vietnamese (28)	34	0.09
Other Asian, specified (4)	5	0.01
Other Asian, not specified (11)	15	0.04
Austrian	10	0.03
Belgian	62	0.17
British	225	0.63
Bulgarian	23	0.06
Canadian	32	0.09
Croatian	37	0.10
Cypriot	15	0.04
Czech	16	0.04
Czechoslovakian	24	0.07
Danish	77	0.22
Dutch	817	2.28
Eastern European	22	0.06
English	3,840	10.74
European	379	1.06
Finnish	84	0.23
French, except Basque	891	2.49
French Canadian	140	0.39
German	8,885	24.84
Greek	115	0.32
Hawaii Native/Pacific Islander:	28	0.08
Micronesian: (2)	9	0.02
Guamanian/Chamorro (2)	9	0.02
Polynesian: (8)	10	0.03
Native Hawaiian (6)	8	0.02
Samoan (2)	2	0.01
Other Pac. Isl., specified	1	0.00
Other Pac. Isl., not spec. (5)	8	0.02
Hispanic or Latino:	687	1.91
Central American:	20	0.06
Guatemalan	2	0.01
Honduran	4	0.01
Nicaraguan	1	0.00
Panamanian	3	0.01
Salvadoran	10	0.03
Cuban	16	0.04
Dominican Republic	1	0.00
Mexican	475	1.32
Puerto Rican	75	0.21
South American:	16	0.04
Argentinean	3	0.01
Chilean	1	0.00
Colombian	7	0.02
Peruvian	3	0.01
Venezuelan	1	0.00
Other South American	1	0.00
Other Hispanic or Latino	84	0.23
Hungarian	86	0.24
Irish	4,659	13.03
Italian	1,029	2.88
Lithuanian	7	0.02
Northern European	8	0.02
Norwegian	194	0.54
Pennsylvania German	17	0.05
Polish	605	1.69
Portuguese	16	0.04
Romanian	53	0.15
Russian	71	0.20
Scotch-Irish	529	1.48
Scottish	794	2.22
Serbian	14	0.04
Slavic	7	0.02
Slovak	51	0.14
Slovene	16	0.04
Swedish	345	0.96
Swiss	187	0.52
Ukrainian	17	0.05
United States or American	5,222	14.60
Welsh	264	0.74
West Indian, excl. Hispanic:	19	0.05
Dutch West Indian	8	0.02
Jamaican	11	0.03
White:	35,040	97.23
Not Hispanic (34,373)	34,600	96.01
Hispanic (417)	440	1.22
Yugoslavian	8	0.02

Griffith

Place Type: Town
County: Lake
Population: 17,334

Ancestry/Race	Number	%
African American/Black:	1,818	10.49
Not Hispanic (1,734)	1,787	10.31
Hispanic (19)	31	0.18
African, sub-Saharan:	11	0.06
African	11	0.06
Alaska Native tribes, specified:	1	0.01
Tlingit-Haida	1	0.01
Am. Ind. or Alaska Nat., not spec.	62	0.36
American Indian tribes, specified:	93	0.54
Blackfeet (2)	6	0.03
Cherokee (8)	41	0.24
Cheyenne	1	0.01
Choctaw (1)	6	0.03
Creek	2	0.01
Iroquois (1)	1	0.01
Latin American Indians (1)	1	0.01
Navajo	3	0.02
Ottawa (1)	1	0.01
Potawatomi (1)	5	0.03
Seminole	3	0.02
Shoshone	1	0.01
Sioux (10)	11	0.06
All other tribes (5)	11	0.06
American Indian tribes, not spec.	2	0.01
Armenian	9	0.05
Asian:	196	1.13
Chinese, ex. Taiwanese (21)	24	0.14
Filipino (31)	43	0.25
Indian (46)	53	0.31
Indonesian (1)	1	0.01
Japanese (6)	23	0.13
Korean (11)	22	0.13
Pakistani (2)	4	0.02
Vietnamese (19)	21	0.12
Other Asian, not specified (1)	5	0.03
Austrian	76	0.44
Belgian	38	0.22
British	126	0.73
Bulgarian	17	0.10
Canadian	52	0.30
Croatian	400	2.31
Czech	82	0.47
Czechoslovakian	54	0.31
Danish	66	0.38
Dutch	873	5.04
Eastern European	7	0.04
English	1,092	6.30
European	62	0.36
Finnish	31	0.18
French, except Basque	415	2.39
French Canadian	102	0.59
German	4,067	23.47
Greek	142	0.82
Hawaii Native/Pacific Islander:	10	0.06
Micronesian: (1)	1	0.01
Guamanian/Chamorro (1)	1	0.01
Polynesian: (6)	7	0.04
Native Hawaiian (1)	2	0.01
Samoan (5)	5	0.03
Other Pac. Isl., not spec.	2	0.01
Hispanic or Latino:	1,461	8.43
Central American:	17	0.10
Guatemalan	8	0.05
Nicaraguan	8	0.05
Panamanian	1	0.01
Cuban	7	0.04
Dominican Republic	1	0.01
Mexican	1,110	6.40
Puerto Rican	180	1.04
South American:	14	0.08
Argentinean	3	0.02
Bolivian	1	0.01
Chilean	1	0.01
Colombian	6	0.03
Ecuadorian	2	0.01
Venezuelan	1	0.01
Other Hispanic or Latino	132	0.76
Hungarian	519	2.99
Irish	2,310	13.33
Italian	759	4.38
Lithuanian	34	0.20
Macedonian	21	0.12
Northern European	46	0.27
Norwegian	153	0.88
Pennsylvania German	8	0.05
Polish	2,377	13.71
Romanian	105	0.61
Russian	82	0.47
Scotch-Irish	233	1.34
Scottish	235	1.36

Notes: 1. Figures in the "Number" column do not add up to the total population due to: a) Ancestry/Race overlap — e.g. persons can report being both White and Irish, b) persons of Hispanic origin can report being any race, c) persons reporting two ancestries are counted in both categories. 2. Numbers in parentheses indicate the number of persons reporting this ancestry/race alone, not in combination with any other ancestry/race. 3. Refer to the Explanation of Data in the front of the book for more detailed information.

Serbian	91	0.53
Slovak	499	2.88
Swedish	371	2.14
Swiss	24	0.14
Turkish	58	0.33
Ukrainian	30	0.17
United States or American	742	4.28
Welsh	125	0.72
White:	14,848	85.66
Not Hispanic (13,738)	13,925	80.33
Hispanic (824)	923	5.32
Yugoslavian	27	0.16

Hammond

Place Type: City
County: Lake
Population: 83,048

Ancestry/Race	Number	%
African American/Black:	12,699	15.29
Not Hispanic (11,876)	12,326	14.84
Hispanic (226)	373	0.45
African, sub-Saharan:	194	0.23
African	157	0.19
Nigerian	37	0.04
Alaska Native tribes, specified:	1	0.00
Tlingit-Haida (1)	1	0.00
Am. Ind. or Alaska Nat., not spec.	289	0.35
American Indian tribes, specified:	459	0.55
Apache (5)	13	0.02
Blackfeet (2)	16	0.02
Cherokee (41)	205	0.25
Cheyenne	5	0.01
Chickasaw	1	0.00
Chippewa (6)	19	0.02
Choctaw (5)	19	0.02
Comanche	2	0.00
Creek (8)	11	0.01
Iroquois (2)	16	0.02
Latin American Indians (60)	84	0.10
Menominee (4)	5	0.01
Navajo (4)	8	0.01
Osage	2	0.00
Potawatomi (4)	7	0.01
Seminole	1	0.00
Sioux (8)	21	0.03
All other tribes (15)	24	0.03
American Indian tribes, not spec.	71	0.09
Arab:	369	0.44
Arab/Arabic	152	0.18
Egyptian	42	0.05
Iraqi	16	0.02
Jordanian	63	0.08
Lebanese	41	0.05
Palestinian	39	0.05
Syrian	8	0.01
Other Arab	8	0.01
Armenian	55	0.07
Asian:	562	0.68
Chinese, ex. Taiwanese (50)	72	0.09
Filipino (93)	141	0.17
Indian (92)	113	0.14
Indonesian (1)	2	0.00
Japanese (19)	38	0.05
Korean (43)	56	0.07
Laotian (2)	2	0.00
Pakistani (14)	20	0.02
Sri Lankan (1)	1	0.00
Taiwanese (5)	6	0.01
Thai (11)	17	0.02
Vietnamese (34)	47	0.06
Other Asian, not specified (16)	47	0.06
Assyrian/Chaldean/Syriac	11	0.01
Australian	6	0.01
Austrian	141	0.17
Belgian	35	0.04
Brazilian	28	0.03
British	157	0.19
Bulgarian	47	0.06
Canadian	126	0.15
Carpatho Rusyn	5	0.01
Celtic	20	0.02
Croatian	1,221	1.47
Cypriot	35	0.04
Czech	205	0.25
Czechoslovakian	193	0.23
Danish	127	0.15
Dutch	1,780	2.14
English	3,905	4.70
European	80	0.10
Finnish	189	0.23
French, except Basque	1,799	2.17
French Canadian	190	0.23
German	11,586	13.95
Greek	577	0.69
Guyanese	11	0.01
Hawaii Native/Pacific Islander:	104	0.13
Micronesian: (6)	11	0.01
Guamanian/Chamorro (6)	11	0.01
Polynesian: (36)	51	0.06
Native Hawaiian (12)	17	0.02
Samoan (24)	32	0.04
Other Polynesian	2	0.00
Other Pac. Isl., not spec. (22)	42	0.05
Hispanic or Latino:	17,473	21.04
Central American:	208	0.25
Costa Rican	8	0.01
Guatemalan	83	0.10
Honduran	57	0.07
Nicaraguan	8	0.01
Panamanian	10	0.01
Salvadoran	34	0.04
Other Central American	8	0.01
Cuban	120	0.14
Dominican Republic	6	0.01
Mexican	13,583	16.36
Puerto Rican	2,012	2.42
South American:	53	0.06
Argentinean	7	0.01
Bolivian	5	0.01
Chilean	1	0.00
Colombian	15	0.02
Ecuadorian	4	0.00
Peruvian	18	0.02
Venezuelan	1	0.00
Other South American	2	0.00
Other Hispanic or Latino	1,491	1.80
Hungarian	1,436	1.73
Irish	9,590	11.55
Italian	3,016	3.63
Latvian	9	0.01
Lithuanian	248	0.30
Luxemburger	10	0.01
Macedonian	12	0.01
Northern European	7	0.01
Norwegian	258	0.31
Pennsylvania German	13	0.02
Polish	10,190	12.27
Portuguese	21	0.03
Romanian	412	0.50
Russian	612	0.74
Scandinavian	60	0.07
Scotch-Irish	763	0.92
Scottish	757	0.91
Serbian	567	0.68
Slavic	115	0.14
Slovak	3,259	3.92
Slovene	125	0.15
Swedish	1,020	1.23
Swiss	67	0.08
Turkish	6	0.01
Ukrainian	307	0.37
United States or American	3,254	3.92
Welsh	287	0.35
West Indian, excl. Hispanic:	115	0.14
Bermudan	13	0.02
British West Indian	7	0.01
Haitian	8	0.01
Jamaican	87	0.10
White:	62,135	74.82
Not Hispanic (51,822)	52,917	63.72
Hispanic (8,267)	9,218	11.10
Yugoslavian	206	0.25

Highland

Place Type: Town
County: Lake
Population: 23,546

Ancestry/Race	Number	%
African American/Black:	326	1.38
Not Hispanic (280)	306	1.30
Hispanic (16)	20	0.08
Alaska Native tribes, specified:	3	0.01
Aleut (3)	3	0.01
Am. Ind. or Alaska Nat., not spec.	26	0.11
American Indian tribes, specified:	76	0.32
Blackfeet (2)	3	0.01
Cherokee (4)	39	0.17
Chickasaw (2)	4	0.02
Chippewa (1)	9	0.04
Creek	3	0.01
Iroquois (1)	1	0.00
Latin American Indians (2)	4	0.02
Menominee	2	0.01
Potawatomi (1)	5	0.02
Sioux (5)	6	0.03
American Indian tribes, not spec.	3	0.01
Arab:	124	0.53
Arab/Arabic	80	0.34
Jordanian	6	0.03
Palestinian	23	0.10
Syrian	15	0.06
Armenian	24	0.10
Asian:	330	1.40
Chinese, ex. Taiwanese (26)	32	0.14
Filipino (48)	74	0.31
Indian (96)	103	0.44
Japanese (19)	31	0.13
Korean (45)	55	0.23
Laotian (5)	5	0.02
Thai (6)	6	0.03
Vietnamese (6)	6	0.03
Other Asian, specified	2	0.01
Other Asian, not specified (4)	16	0.07
Austrian	82	0.35
Basque	6	0.03
Belgian	7	0.03
British	12	0.05
Bulgarian	23	0.10
Canadian	7	0.03
Croatian	509	2.16
Czech	135	0.57
Czechoslovakian	95	0.40
Danish	101	0.43
Dutch	1,598	6.79
English	2,161	9.18
European	47	0.20
Finnish	28	0.12
French, except Basque	692	2.94
French Canadian	171	0.73
German	5,294	22.48
Greek	273	1.16
Hawaii Native/Pacific Islander:	9	0.04
Micronesian: (1)	1	0.00
Guamanian/Chamorro (1)	1	0.00
Polynesian: (1)	2	0.01
Native Hawaiian (1)	2	0.01
Other Pac. Isl., specified	2	0.01
Other Pac. Isl., not spec. (3)	4	0.02
Hispanic or Latino:	1,557	6.61
Central American:	8	0.03
Costa Rican	4	0.02
Guatemalan	2	0.01
Salvadoran	2	0.01
Cuban	11	0.05
Dominican Republic	1	0.00
Mexican	1,133	4.81

Notes: 1. Figures in the "Number" column do not add up to the total population due to: a) Ancestry/Race overlap — e.g. persons can report being both White and Irish, b) persons of Hispanic origin can report being any race, c) persons reporting two ancestries are counted in both categories. 2. Numbers in parentheses indicate the number of persons reporting this ancestry/race alone, not in combination with any other ancestry/race. 3. Refer to the Explanation of Data in the front of the book for more detailed information.

Ancestry/Race	Number	%
Puerto Rican	214	0.91
South American:	17	0.07
Argentinean	2	0.01
Bolivian	3	0.01
Chilean	1	0.00
Colombian	6	0.03
Ecuadorian	2	0.01
Peruvian	2	0.01
Uruguayan	1	0.00
Other Hispanic or Latino	173	0.73
Hungarian	846	3.59
Iranian	14	0.06
Irish	3,503	14.88
Italian	1,509	6.41
Lithuanian	219	0.93
Macedonian	65	0.28
Northern European	16	0.07
Norwegian	239	1.02
Pennsylvania German	10	0.04
Polish	4,141	17.59
Romanian	197	0.84
Russian	99	0.42
Scandinavian	18	0.08
Scotch-Irish	438	1.86
Scottish	459	1.95
Serbian	298	1.27
Slavic	24	0.10
Slovak	969	4.12
Slovene	30	0.13
Swedish	495	2.10
Swiss	66	0.28
Ukrainian	95	0.40
United States or American	1,041	4.42
Welsh	211	0.90
White:	22,513	95.61
Not Hispanic (21,231)	21,415	90.95
Hispanic (1,009)	1,098	4.66
Yugoslavian	79	0.34

Hobart

Place Type: City
County: Lake
Population: 25,363

Ancestry/Race	Number	%
African American/Black:	416	1.64
Not Hispanic (347)	398	1.57
Hispanic (6)	18	0.07
African, sub-Saharan:	6	0.02
African	6	0.02
Am. Ind. or Alaska Nat., not spec.	40	0.16
Albanian	9	0.04
Alsatian	6	0.02
American Indian tribes, specified:	118	0.47
Apache (1)	2	0.01
Blackfeet (1)	5	0.02
Cherokee (17)	61	0.24
Chippewa (1)	2	0.01
Choctaw	1	0.00
Comanche (1)	1	0.00
Creek	2	0.01
Crow	2	0.01
Delaware (1)	1	0.00
Iroquois	4	0.02
Latin American Indians (3)	7	0.03
Navajo	2	0.01
Potawatomi (4)	4	0.02
Pueblo (5)	5	0.02
Seminole (1)	1	0.00
Sioux (2)	5	0.02
All other tribes (3)	13	0.05
Arab:	54	0.21
Arab/Arabic	9	0.04
Lebanese	7	0.03
Syrian	38	0.15
Armenian	22	0.09
Asian:	200	0.79
Chinese, ex. Taiwanese (5)	7	0.03
Filipino (51)	75	0.30
Indian (48)	55	0.22
Indonesian	1	0.00
Japanese (4)	9	0.04
Korean (12)	23	0.09
Laotian (3)	3	0.01
Thai (2)	2	0.01
Vietnamese (9)	15	0.06
Other Asian, not specified (2)	10	0.04
Assyrian/Chaldean/Syriac	49	0.19
Austrian	10	0.04
Belgian	10	0.04
British	79	0.31
Bulgarian	9	0.04
Canadian	25	0.10
Croatian	630	2.48
Czech	91	0.36
Czechoslovakian	103	0.41
Danish	45	0.18
Dutch	685	2.70
English	2,536	9.98
European	187	0.74
Finnish	61	0.24
French, except Basque	741	2.92
French Canadian	305	1.20
German	6,009	23.66
Greek	331	1.30
Hawaii Native/Pacific Islander:	10	0.04
Polynesian: (4)	6	0.02
Native Hawaiian (2)	4	0.02
Other Polynesian (2)	2	0.01
Other Pac. Isl., not spec.	4	0.02
Hispanic or Latino:	2,042	8.05
Central American:	18	0.07
Costa Rican	1	0.00
Guatemalan	3	0.01
Nicaraguan	9	0.04
Panamanian	4	0.02
Other Central American	1	0.00
Cuban	11	0.04
Dominican Republic	5	0.02
Mexican	1,386	5.46
Puerto Rican	383	1.51
South American:	13	0.05
Colombian	6	0.02
Ecuadorian	2	0.01
Peruvian	4	0.02
Other South American	1	0.00
Other Hispanic or Latino	226	0.89
Hungarian	481	1.89
Irish	3,941	15.52
Italian	1,630	6.42
Lithuanian	225	0.89
Macedonian	230	0.91
Norwegian	321	1.26
Pennsylvania German	10	0.04
Polish	2,862	11.27
Romanian	216	0.85
Russian	264	1.04
Scandinavian	9	0.04
Scotch-Irish	520	2.05
Scottish	485	1.91
Serbian	415	1.63
Slavic	24	0.09
Slovak	680	2.68
Swedish	597	2.35
Swiss	31	0.12
Ukrainian	92	0.36
United States or American	1,649	6.49
Welsh	268	1.06
West Indian, excl. Hispanic:	7	0.03
Trinidadian and Tobagonian	7	0.03
White:	24,123	95.11
Not Hispanic (22,561)	22,771	89.78
Hispanic (1,212)	1,352	5.33
Yugoslavian	132	0.52

Huntington

Place Type: City
County: Huntington
Population: 17,450

Ancestry/Race	Number	%
African American/Black:	66	0.38
Not Hispanic (34)	59	0.34
Hispanic (3)	7	0.04
African, sub-Saharan:	26	0.15
African	4	0.02
Kenyan	22	0.13
Alaska Native tribes, specified:	1	0.01
Tlingit-Haida (1)	1	0.01
Am. Ind. or Alaska Nat., not spec.	31	0.18
American Indian tribes, specified:	107	0.61
Apache (1)	7	0.04
Blackfeet	3	0.02
Cherokee (3)	27	0.15
Chippewa (1)	2	0.01
Choctaw (1)	2	0.01
Iroquois	5	0.03
Kiowa (1)	3	0.02
Latin American Indians (3)	3	0.02
Navajo (1)	1	0.01
Osage (1)	1	0.01
Sioux	5	0.03
Ute	1	0.01
All other tribes (43)	47	0.27
American Indian tribes, not spec.	4	0.02
Asian:	104	0.60
Cambodian (3)	3	0.02
Chinese, ex. Taiwanese (21)	23	0.13
Filipino (10)	16	0.09
Indian (34)	46	0.26
Japanese (2)	4	0.02
Korean (5)	7	0.04
Vietnamese (1)	1	0.01
Other Asian, not specified (1)	4	0.02
British	68	0.39
Bulgarian	5	0.03
Canadian	44	0.25
Czech	29	0.16
Danish	34	0.19
Dutch	244	1.39
English	1,155	6.57
European	21	0.12
French, except Basque	447	2.54
French Canadian	57	0.32
German	5,017	28.52
Greek	28	0.16
Hawaii Native/Pacific Islander:	11	0.06
Micronesian: (2)	2	0.01
Guamanian/Chamorro (2)	2	0.01
Polynesian: (1)	7	0.04
Native Hawaiian	4	0.02
Samoan (1)	3	0.02
Other Pac. Isl., not spec. (1)	2	0.01
Hispanic or Latino:	196	1.12
Central American:	5	0.03
Guatemalan	4	0.02
Panamanian	1	0.01
Cuban	1	0.01
Mexican	131	0.75
Puerto Rican	17	0.10
South American:	2	0.01
Ecuadorian	1	0.01
Peruvian	1	0.01
Other Hispanic or Latino	40	0.23
Hungarian	97	0.55
Icelander	8	0.05
Irish	1,720	9.78
Italian	284	1.61
Latvian	10	0.06
Lithuanian	5	0.03
Macedonian	9	0.05
New Zealander	5	0.03
Norwegian	87	0.49
Pennsylvania German	20	0.11

Notes: 1. Figures in the "Number" column do not add up to the total population due to: a) Ancestry/Race overlap — e.g. persons can report being both White and Irish, b) persons of Hispanic origin can report being any race, c) persons reporting two ancestries are counted in both categories. 2. Numbers in parentheses indicate the number of persons reporting this ancestry/race alone, not in combination with any other ancestry/race. 3. Refer to the Explanation of Data in the front of the book for more detailed information.

Ancestry/Race	Number	%
Polish	190	1.08
Russian	36	0.20
Scandinavian	22	0.13
Scotch-Irish	237	1.35
Scottish	241	1.37
Slovak	24	0.14
Swedish	99	0.56
Swiss	75	0.43
Turkish	23	0.13
Ukrainian	9	0.05
United States or American	2,392	13.60
Welsh	125	0.71
White:	17,187	98.49
Not Hispanic (16,950)	17,045	97.68
Hispanic (122)	142	0.81

Indianapolis

Place Type: Special City
County: Marion
Population: 781,870

Ancestry/Race	Number	%
Acadian/Cajun	31	0.00
Afghan	22	0.00
African American/Black:	206,148	26.37
Not Hispanic (198,252)	204,455	26.15
Hispanic (1,160)	1,693	0.22
African, sub-Saharan:	8,665	1.11
African	6,845	0.87
Cape Verdean	74	0.01
Ethiopian	493	0.06
Ghanian	34	0.00
Kenyan	36	0.00
Liberian	213	0.03
Nigerian	524	0.07
Senegalese	8	0.00
Sierra Leonean	89	0.01
Somalian	6	0.00
South African	106	0.01
Sudanese	22	0.00
Ugandan	19	0.00
Zimbabwean	35	0.00
Other sub-Saharan African	161	0.02
Alaska Native tribes, specified:	38	0.00
Alaska Athabascan (4)	5	0.00
Aleut (5)	8	0.00
Eskimo (8)	16	0.00
Tlingit-Haida (1)	7	0.00
All other tribes (1)	2	0.00
Alaska Native tribes, not specified	3	0.00
Am. Ind. or Alaska Nat., not spec.	2,039	0.26
Albanian	37	0.00
Alsatian	50	0.01
American Indian tribes, specified:	2,995	0.38
Apache (43)	104	0.01
Blackfeet (46)	224	0.03
Cherokee (345)	1,375	0.18
Cheyenne (5)	11	0.00
Chickasaw (4)	11	0.00
Chippewa (40)	84	0.01
Choctaw (28)	72	0.01
Comanche (9)	18	0.00
Cree (3)	7	0.00
Creek (11)	31	0.00
Crow (5)	12	0.00
Delaware (14)	24	0.00
Houma (4)	4	0.00
Iroquois (26)	65	0.01
Kiowa (4)	7	0.00
Latin American Indians (106)	165	0.02
Lumbee (9)	15	0.00
Menominee (2)	7	0.00
Navajo (28)	66	0.01
Osage (15)	20	0.00
Ottawa (2)	6	0.00
Paiute (1)	3	0.00
Potawatomi (36)	56	0.01
Pueblo (14)	31	0.00
Puget Sound Salish (1)	2	0.00
Seminole (4)	20	0.00
Shoshone	3	0.00
Sioux (82)	192	0.02
Tohono O'Odham (2)	2	0.00
Ute	2	0.00
Yakama	3	0.00
Yaqui (2)	4	0.00
Yuman (2)	6	0.00
All other tribes (157)	343	0.04
American Indian tribes, not spec.	365	0.05
Arab:	1,973	0.25
Arab/Arabic	151	0.02
Egyptian	519	0.07
Iraqi	10	0.00
Jordanian	26	0.00
Lebanese	563	0.07
Moroccan	197	0.03
Palestinian	33	0.00
Syrian	346	0.04
Other Arab	128	0.02
Armenian	123	0.02
Asian:	13,902	1.78
Bangladeshi (55)	79	0.01
Cambodian (113)	122	0.02
Chinese, ex. Taiwanese (2,108)	2,461	0.31
Filipino (1,452)	2,043	0.26
Hmong (33)	35	0.00
Indian (3,325)	3,728	0.48
Indonesian (29)	70	0.01
Japanese (637)	1,043	0.13
Korean (1,107)	1,385	0.18
Laotian (87)	89	0.01
Malaysian (35)	41	0.01
Pakistani (296)	389	0.05
Sri Lankan (33)	37	0.00
Taiwanese (74)	105	0.01
Thai (149)	213	0.03
Vietnamese (1,101)	1,227	0.16
Other Asian, specified (52)	119	0.02
Other Asian, not specified (349)	716	0.09
Australian	221	0.03
Austrian	1,127	0.14
Basque	12	0.00
Belgian	576	0.07
Brazilian	208	0.03
British	3,585	0.46
Bulgarian	175	0.02
Canadian	873	0.11
Celtic	139	0.02
Croatian	545	0.07
Cypriot	26	0.00
Czech	1,332	0.17
Czechoslovakian	759	0.10
Danish	1,573	0.20
Dutch	12,223	1.56
Eastern European	228	0.03
English	60,562	7.74
Estonian	69	0.01
European	6,617	0.85
Finnish	610	0.08
French, except Basque	15,444	1.97
French Canadian	2,041	0.26
German	130,045	16.62
German Russian	26	0.00
Greek	2,074	0.27
Guyanese	17	0.00
Hawaii Native/Pacific Islander:	818	0.10
Melanesian: (3)	3	0.00
Fijian (3)	3	0.00
Micronesian: (93)	136	0.02
Guamanian/Chamorro (88)	125	0.02
Other Micronesian (5)	11	0.00
Polynesian: (147)	323	0.04
Native Hawaiian (98)	219	0.03
Samoan (45)	96	0.01
Tongan (1)	5	0.00
Other Polynesian (3)	3	0.00
Other Pac. Isl., specified	53	0.01
Other Pac. Isl., not spec. (76)	303	0.04
Hispanic or Latino:	30,636	3.92
Central American:	1,770	0.23
Costa Rican	56	0.01
Guatemalan	250	0.03
Honduran	495	0.06
Nicaraguan	247	0.03
Panamanian	138	0.02
Salvadoran	509	0.07
Other Central American	75	0.01
Cuban	457	0.06
Dominican Republic	262	0.03
Mexican	21,053	2.69
Puerto Rican	1,904	0.24
South American:	758	0.10
Argentinean	57	0.01
Bolivian	9	0.00
Chilean	36	0.00
Colombian	222	0.03
Ecuadorian	55	0.01
Paraguayan	6	0.00
Peruvian	177	0.02
Uruguayan	9	0.00
Venezuelan	152	0.02
Other South American	35	0.00
Other Hispanic or Latino	4,432	0.57
Hungarian	2,281	0.29
Icelander	79	0.01
Iranian	399	0.05
Irish	79,838	10.20
Israeli	93	0.01
Italian	17,442	2.23
Latvian	392	0.05
Lithuanian	875	0.11
Luxemburger	99	0.01
Macedonian	233	0.03
Maltese	23	0.00
New Zealander	21	0.00
Northern European	422	0.05
Norwegian	3,756	0.48
Pennsylvania German	241	0.03
Polish	10,643	1.36
Portuguese	402	0.05
Romanian	1,122	0.14
Russian	2,954	0.38
Scandinavian	621	0.08
Scotch-Irish	10,322	1.32
Scottish	13,190	1.69
Serbian	332	0.04
Slavic	361	0.05
Slovak	743	0.09
Slovene	734	0.09
Soviet Union	6	0.00
Swedish	5,192	0.66
Swiss	1,939	0.25
Turkish	192	0.02
Ukrainian	924	0.12
United States or American	72,698	9.29
Welsh	5,008	0.64
West Indian, excl. Hispanic:	1,306	0.17
Bahamian	17	0.00
Barbadian	15	0.00
Belizean	37	0.00
British West Indian	19	0.00
Dutch West Indian	21	0.00
Haitian	127	0.02
Jamaican	711	0.09
Trinidadian and Tobagonian	170	0.02
U.S. Virgin Islander	41	0.01
West Indian	148	0.02
White:	550,768	70.44
Not Hispanic (527,675)	536,689	68.64
Hispanic (12,537)	14,079	1.80
Yugoslavian	757	0.10

Jasper

Place Type: City
County: Dubois
Population: 12,100

Ancestry/Race	Number	%

Notes: 1. Figures in the "Number" column do not add up to the total population due to: a) Ancestry/Race overlap — e.g. persons can report being both White and Irish, b) persons of Hispanic origin can report being any race, c) persons reporting two ancestries are counted in both categories. 2. Numbers in parentheses indicate the number of persons reporting this ancestry/race alone, not in combination with any other ancestry/race. 3. Refer to the Explanation of Data in the front of the book for more detailed information.

African American/Black:	41	0.34
Not Hispanic (27)	38	0.31
Hispanic (3)	3	0.02
Am. Ind. or Alaska Nat., not spec.	13	0.11
American Indian tribes, specified:	22	0.18
Apache	4	0.03
Blackfeet	1	0.01
Cherokee	7	0.06
Chippewa (3)	3	0.02
Choctaw	1	0.01
Iroquois (1)	1	0.01
Latin American Indians	1	0.01
Navajo	1	0.01
Seminole	1	0.01
All other tribes (1)	2	0.02
Asian:	70	0.58
Chinese, ex. Taiwanese (11)	16	0.13
Filipino (5)	10	0.08
Indian (11)	13	0.11
Indonesian	4	0.03
Japanese (1)	4	0.03
Korean (3)	3	0.02
Thai (1)	2	0.02
Vietnamese (8)	8	0.07
Other Asian, specified (7)	7	0.06
Other Asian, not specified (2)	3	0.02
Austrian	15	0.13
British	43	0.36
Czechoslovakian	8	0.07
Danish	8	0.07
Dutch	121	1.01
English	799	6.68
European	8	0.07
Finnish	9	0.08
French, except Basque	221	1.85
French Canadian	12	0.10
German	6,497	54.30
Greek	6	0.05
Hawaii Native/Pacific Islander:	4	0.03
Micronesian: (1)	1	0.01
Guamanian/Chamorro (1)	1	0.01
Other Pac. Isl., not spec. (2)	3	0.02
Hispanic or Latino:	408	3.37
Central American:	65	0.54
Guatemalan	7	0.06
Honduran	11	0.09
Salvadoran	46	0.38
Other Central American	1	0.01
Cuban	2	0.02
Mexican	251	2.07
Puerto Rican	9	0.07
South American:	20	0.17
Argentinean	1	0.01
Bolivian	1	0.01
Chilean	1	0.01
Colombian	12	0.10
Ecuadorian	1	0.01
Peruvian	3	0.02
Other South American	1	0.01
Other Hispanic or Latino	61	0.50
Hungarian	16	0.13
Irish	1,002	8.37
Italian	189	1.58
Lithuanian	8	0.07
Norwegian	32	0.27
Polish	94	0.79
Romanian	7	0.06
Russian	5	0.04
Scandinavian	10	0.08
Scotch-Irish	102	0.85
Scottish	70	0.58
Slovak	26	0.22
Swedish	14	0.12
Swiss	23	0.19
Turkish	30	0.25
United States or American	1,315	10.99
Welsh	19	0.16
White:	11,816	97.65
Not Hispanic (11,556)	11,602	95.88
Hispanic (181)	214	1.77

Jeffersonville

Place Type: City
County: Clark
Population: 27,362

Ancestry/Race	Number	%
African American/Black:	4,069	14.87
Not Hispanic (3,720)	4,037	14.75
Hispanic (22)	32	0.12
African, sub-Saharan:	278	1.01
African	221	0.80
Ethiopian	25	0.09
Liberian	19	0.07
South African	8	0.03
Zimbabwean	5	0.02
Alaska Native tribes, specified:	3	0.01
Eskimo (1)	2	0.01
All other tribes (1)	1	0.00
Am. Ind. or Alaska Nat., not spec.	82	0.30
American Indian tribes, specified:	132	0.48
Apache (2)	2	0.01
Blackfeet (3)	14	0.05
Cherokee (19)	72	0.26
Chippewa (2)	7	0.03
Choctaw (1)	8	0.03
Iroquois (1)	3	0.01
Latin American Indians (4)	5	0.02
Lumbee (2)	2	0.01
Navajo (1)	3	0.01
Pima (1)	1	0.00
Pueblo	1	0.00
Seminole	1	0.00
Sioux (2)	2	0.01
Yaqui (1)	1	0.00
All other tribes (5)	10	0.04
American Indian tribes, not spec.	10	0.04
Arab:	25	0.09
Egyptian	6	0.02
Lebanese	19	0.07
Armenian	6	0.02
Asian:	296	1.08
Chinese, ex. Taiwanese (21)	28	0.10
Filipino (43)	60	0.22
Indian (61)	74	0.27
Indonesian	1	0.00
Japanese (14)	21	0.08
Korean (22)	34	0.12
Pakistani (17)	22	0.08
Taiwanese (3)	3	0.01
Thai (3)	6	0.02
Vietnamese (24)	26	0.10
Other Asian, not specified (16)	21	0.08
Austrian	12	0.04
Belgian	64	0.23
British	89	0.32
Canadian	6	0.02
Celtic	5	0.02
Czech	27	0.10
Czechoslovakian	8	0.03
Danish	13	0.05
Dutch	377	1.37
English	2,224	8.10
European	80	0.29
French, except Basque	703	2.56
French Canadian	39	0.14
German	5,184	18.88
Greek	13	0.05
Hawaii Native/Pacific Islander:	36	0.13
Melanesian: (1)	1	0.00
Fijian (1)	1	0.00
Micronesian: (7)	8	0.03
Guamanian/Chamorro (7)	8	0.03
Polynesian: (12)	17	0.06
Native Hawaiian (10)	14	0.05
Samoan (2)	2	0.01
Other Polynesian	1	0.00
Other Pac. Isl., not spec. (2)	10	0.04
Hispanic or Latino:	493	1.80
Central American:	7	0.03
Costa Rican	2	0.01
Guatemalan	1	0.00
Honduran	1	0.00
Panamanian	3	0.01
Cuban	19	0.07
Dominican Republic	3	0.01
Mexican	252	0.92
Puerto Rican	93	0.34
South American:	15	0.05
Colombian	4	0.01
Ecuadorian	2	0.01
Peruvian	5	0.02
Venezuelan	3	0.01
Other South American	1	0.00
Other Hispanic or Latino	104	0.38
Hungarian	62	0.23
Icelander	14	0.05
Irish	3,524	12.83
Italian	438	1.59
Lithuanian	6	0.02
Northern European	19	0.07
Norwegian	124	0.45
Pennsylvania German	14	0.05
Polish	270	0.98
Portuguese	27	0.10
Russian	51	0.19
Scandinavian	6	0.02
Scotch-Irish	481	1.75
Scottish	520	1.89
Serbian	16	0.06
Swedish	67	0.24
Swiss	26	0.09
Ukrainian	15	0.05
United States or American	3,539	12.89
Welsh	127	0.46
West Indian, excl. Hispanic:	26	0.09
Jamaican	22	0.08
U.S. Virgin Islander	4	0.01
White:	23,062	84.28
Not Hispanic (22,301)	22,762	83.19
Hispanic (274)	300	1.10
Yugoslavian	33	0.12

Kokomo

Place Type: City
County: Howard
Population: 46,113

Ancestry/Race	Number	%
Afghan	5	0.01
African American/Black:	5,215	11.31
Not Hispanic (4,737)	5,157	11.18
Hispanic (33)	58	0.13
African, sub-Saharan:	185	0.40
African	168	0.37
Other sub-Saharan African	17	0.04
Am. Ind. or Alaska Nat., not spec.	125	0.27
Albanian	6	0.01
American Indian tribes, specified:	284	0.62
Apache (1)	4	0.01
Blackfeet (11)	27	0.06
Cherokee (47)	133	0.29
Cheyenne (1)	6	0.01
Chippewa (2)	3	0.01
Choctaw (7)	15	0.03
Colville (2)	2	0.00
Comanche (2)	5	0.01
Cree (1)	2	0.00
Creek (1)	1	0.00
Crow (1)	1	0.00
Delaware (1)	1	0.00
Iroquois	1	0.00
Latin American Indians (5)	6	0.01
Menominee (1)	1	0.00
Navajo (2)	3	0.01
Osage	3	0.01
Seminole (1)	1	0.00
Sioux (7)	15	0.03
Yakama	1	0.00

Notes: 1. Figures in the "Number" column do not add up to the total population due to: a) Ancestry/Race overlap — e.g. persons can report being both White and Irish, b) persons of Hispanic origin can report being any race, c) persons reporting two ancestries are counted in both categories. 2. Numbers in parentheses indicate the number of persons reporting this ancestry/race alone, not in combination with any other ancestry/race. 3. Refer to the Explanation of Data in the front of the book for more detailed information.

Ancestry/Race	Number	%
All other tribes (36)	53	0.11
American Indian tribes, not spec.	26	0.06
Arab:	27	0.06
Lebanese	9	0.02
Moroccan	8	0.02
Syrian	10	0.02
Armenian	7	0.02
Asian:	621	1.35
Bangladeshi (1)	1	0.00
Chinese, ex. Taiwanese (156)	164	0.36
Filipino (49)	68	0.15
Hmong (9)	9	0.02
Indian (132)	156	0.34
Indonesian (1)	1	0.00
Japanese (25)	37	0.08
Korean (57)	81	0.18
Laotian (3)	3	0.01
Malaysian	1	0.00
Pakistani (3)	3	0.01
Sri Lankan (3)	3	0.01
Taiwanese (1)	5	0.01
Thai (2)	4	0.01
Vietnamese (60)	63	0.14
Other Asian, specified (1)	2	0.00
Other Asian, not specified (16)	20	0.04
Austrian	46	0.10
Basque	23	0.05
Belgian	13	0.03
British	94	0.20
Canadian	12	0.03
Celtic	24	0.05
Croatian	8	0.02
Czech	38	0.08
Danish	75	0.16
Dutch	854	1.86
English	3,557	7.74
European	336	0.73
Finnish	8	0.02
French, except Basque	872	1.90
French Canadian	162	0.35
German	7,246	15.76
Greek	50	0.11
Hawaii Native/Pacific Islander:	28	0.06
Micronesian: (2)	6	0.01
Guamanian/Chamorro (2)	6	0.01
Polynesian: (10)	20	0.04
Native Hawaiian (7)	10	0.02
Samoan (1)	5	0.01
Tongan (2)	3	0.01
Other Polynesian	2	0.00
Other Pac. Isl., not spec.	2	0.00
Hispanic or Latino:	1,204	2.61
Central American:	24	0.05
Costa Rican	1	0.00
Guatemalan	3	0.01
Honduran	8	0.02
Panamanian	1	0.00
Salvadoran	9	0.02
Other Central American	2	0.00
Cuban	16	0.03
Dominican Republic	1	0.00
Mexican	877	1.90
Puerto Rican	70	0.15
South American:	18	0.04
Argentinean	4	0.01
Bolivian	1	0.00
Chilean	3	0.01
Colombian	5	0.01
Peruvian	3	0.01
Venezuelan	1	0.00
Other South American	1	0.00
Other Hispanic or Latino	198	0.43
Hungarian	116	0.25
Icelander	6	0.01
Iranian	23	0.05
Irish	4,029	8.76
Italian	875	1.90
Lithuanian	23	0.05
Northern European	7	0.02
Norwegian	232	0.50
Pennsylvania German	45	0.10
Polish	627	1.36
Portuguese	20	0.04
Romanian	81	0.18
Russian	70	0.15
Scandinavian	23	0.05
Scotch-Irish	599	1.30
Scottish	622	1.35
Serbian	12	0.03
Slovak	34	0.07
Slovene	15	0.03
Swedish	310	0.67
Swiss	125	0.27
Turkish	11	0.02
Ukrainian	23	0.05
United States or American	6,941	15.10
Welsh	213	0.46
West Indian, excl. Hispanic:	18	0.04
British West Indian	6	0.01
Haitian	5	0.01
Jamaican	7	0.02
White:	40,032	86.81
Not Hispanic (38,655)	39,342	85.32
Hispanic (587)	690	1.50
Yugoslavian	16	0.03

La Porte

Place Type: City
County: La Porte
Population: 21,621

Ancestry/Race	Number	%
Acadian/Cajun	10	0.05
African American/Black:	504	2.33
Not Hispanic (411)	491	2.27
Hispanic (5)	13	0.06
African, sub-Saharan:	54	0.25
African	54	0.25
Alaska Native tribes, specified:	3	0.01
Aleut (2)	3	0.01
Am. Ind. or Alaska Nat., not spec.	72	0.33
American Indian tribes, specified:	70	0.32
Apache (1)	1	0.00
Blackfeet (3)	5	0.02
Cherokee (9)	29	0.13
Cheyenne (1)	1	0.00
Chickasaw (1)	1	0.00
Chippewa (4)	4	0.02
Choctaw	2	0.01
Cree	1	0.00
Crow	1	0.00
Iroquois (2)	3	0.01
Latin American Indians (10)	10	0.05
Potawatomi (2)	5	0.02
Seminole (1)	1	0.00
Sioux (1)	3	0.01
All other tribes (2)	3	0.01
American Indian tribes, not spec.	7	0.03
Arab:	68	0.31
Arab/Arabic	9	0.04
Lebanese	16	0.07
Syrian	43	0.20
Asian:	110	0.51
Chinese, ex. Taiwanese (13)	13	0.06
Filipino (16)	26	0.12
Indian (29)	33	0.15
Indonesian (2)	2	0.01
Japanese (4)	9	0.04
Korean (8)	13	0.06
Laotian (3)	3	0.01
Pakistani (3)	3	0.01
Thai (1)	1	0.00
Vietnamese (3)	3	0.01
Other Asian, specified	1	0.00
Other Asian, not specified	3	0.01
Australian	20	0.09
Austrian	50	0.23
Belgian	42	0.19
Brazilian	18	0.08
British	109	0.50
Bulgarian	11	0.05
Canadian	36	0.17
Croatian	32	0.15
Czech	75	0.35
Czechoslovakian	44	0.20
Danish	30	0.14
Dutch	467	2.16
Eastern European	16	0.07
English	1,772	8.20
European	120	0.56
Finnish	9	0.04
French, except Basque	301	1.39
French Canadian	183	0.85
German	6,417	29.71
Greek	91	0.42
Hawaii Native/Pacific Islander:	10	0.05
Polynesian: (1)	3	0.01
Native Hawaiian	2	0.01
Samoan (1)	1	0.00
Other Pac. Isl., specified	1	0.00
Other Pac. Isl., not spec.	6	0.03
Hispanic or Latino:	1,410	6.52
Central American:	7	0.03
Guatemalan	1	0.00
Nicaraguan	2	0.01
Panamanian	2	0.01
Salvadoran	2	0.01
Cuban	4	0.02
Mexican	1,236	5.72
Puerto Rican	41	0.19
South American:	4	0.02
Ecuadorian	4	0.02
Other Hispanic or Latino	118	0.55
Hungarian	157	0.73
Irish	2,541	11.77
Italian	603	2.79
Lithuanian	35	0.16
New Zealander	7	0.03
Norwegian	341	1.58
Pennsylvania German	38	0.18
Polish	2,353	10.90
Romanian	21	0.10
Russian	97	0.45
Scandinavian	28	0.13
Scotch-Irish	265	1.23
Scottish	309	1.43
Serbian	57	0.26
Slavic	7	0.03
Slovak	17	0.08
Swedish	640	2.96
Swiss	45	0.21
Ukrainian	46	0.21
United States or American	2,014	9.33
Welsh	152	0.70
White:	20,292	93.85
Not Hispanic (19,448)	19,643	90.85
Hispanic (573)	649	3.00
Yugoslavian	20	0.09

Lafayette

Place Type: City
County: Tippecanoe
Population: 56,397

Ancestry/Race	Number	%
African American/Black:	2,053	3.64
Not Hispanic (1,790)	2,007	3.56
Hispanic (26)	46	0.08
African, sub-Saharan:	105	0.19
African	90	0.16
Ethiopian	15	0.03
Alaska Native tribes, specified:	6	0.01
Eskimo	1	0.00
Tlingit-Haida (1)	5	0.01
Alaska Native tribes, not specified	1	0.00
Am. Ind. or Alaska Nat., not spec.	168	0.30
American Indian tribes, specified:	312	0.55
Apache (2)	8	0.01

Notes: 1. Figures in the "Number" column do not add up to the total population due to: a) Ancestry/Race overlap — e.g. persons can report being both White and Irish, b) persons of Hispanic origin can report being any race, c) persons reporting two ancestries are counted in both categories. 2. Numbers in parentheses indicate the number of persons reporting this ancestry/race alone, not in combination with any other ancestry/race. 3. Refer to the Explanation of Data in the front of the book for more detailed information.

Ancestry/Race	Number	%
Blackfeet (4)	11	0.02
Cherokee (39)	163	0.29
Cheyenne (1)	2	0.00
Chippewa (2)	12	0.02
Choctaw (7)	13	0.02
Comanche (1)	1	0.00
Creek (1)	3	0.01
Crow (2)	2	0.00
Delaware (1)	2	0.00
Iroquois (1)	5	0.01
Latin American Indians (5)	15	0.03
Lumbee	1	0.00
Ottawa (3)	5	0.01
Potawatomi (9)	11	0.02
Pueblo (1)	1	0.00
Seminole	4	0.01
Sioux (2)	12	0.02
All other tribes (24)	41	0.07
American Indian tribes, not spec.	46	0.08
Arab:	66	0.12
Lebanese	41	0.07
Syrian	25	0.04
Armenian	14	0.02
Asian:	827	1.47
Cambodian (1)	1	0.00
Chinese, ex. Taiwanese (174)	208	0.37
Filipino (76)	107	0.19
Hmong	1	0.00
Indian (88)	103	0.18
Indonesian (9)	16	0.03
Japanese (102)	121	0.21
Korean (96)	108	0.19
Laotian (13)	13	0.02
Malaysian (1)	1	0.00
Pakistani	4	0.01
Sri Lankan (2)	2	0.00
Taiwanese (5)	6	0.01
Thai (9)	17	0.03
Vietnamese (89)	96	0.17
Other Asian, specified (2)	2	0.00
Other Asian, not specified (11)	21	0.04
Australian	17	0.03
Austrian	90	0.16
Belgian	101	0.18
Brazilian	4	0.01
British	281	0.50
Canadian	106	0.19
Celtic	29	0.05
Croatian	21	0.04
Cypriot	8	0.01
Czech	137	0.24
Czechoslovakian	91	0.16
Danish	109	0.19
Dutch	1,874	3.33
Eastern European	11	0.02
English	5,235	9.31
European	530	0.94
Finnish	159	0.28
French, except Basque	1,706	3.03
French Canadian	273	0.49
German	12,226	21.74
Greek	153	0.27
Hawaii Native/Pacific Islander:	49	0.09
Micronesian: (8)	8	0.01
Guamanian/Chamorro (8)	8	0.01
Polynesian: (16)	33	0.06
Native Hawaiian (10)	20	0.04
Samoan (6)	12	0.02
Other Polynesian	1	0.00
Other Pac. Isl., not spec.	8	0.01
Hispanic or Latino:	5,136	9.11
Central American:	101	0.18
Costa Rican	2	0.00
Guatemalan	18	0.03
Honduran	4	0.01
Nicaraguan	7	0.01
Panamanian	13	0.02
Salvadoran	50	0.09
Other Central American	7	0.01
Cuban	51	0.09
Dominican Republic	4	0.01
Mexican	4,249	7.53
Puerto Rican	195	0.35
South American:	70	0.12
Argentinean	22	0.04
Bolivian	2	0.00
Chilean	2	0.00
Colombian	20	0.04
Ecuadorian	7	0.01
Peruvian	10	0.02
Venezuelan	5	0.01
Other South American	2	0.00
Other Hispanic or Latino	466	0.83
Hungarian	132	0.23
Iranian	26	0.05
Irish	6,492	11.54
Italian	1,294	2.30
Latvian	26	0.05
Lithuanian	52	0.09
Luxemburger	50	0.09
Maltese	5	0.01
Northern European	23	0.04
Norwegian	388	0.69
Pennsylvania German	51	0.09
Polish	1,070	1.90
Portuguese	33	0.06
Romanian	64	0.11
Russian	171	0.30
Scandinavian	50	0.09
Scotch-Irish	862	1.53
Scottish	1,030	1.83
Serbian	14	0.02
Slavic	25	0.04
Slovak	128	0.23
Slovene	15	0.03
Swedish	608	1.08
Swiss	131	0.23
Turkish	9	0.02
Ukrainian	134	0.24
United States or American	6,586	11.71
Welsh	295	0.52
West Indian, excl. Hispanic:	46	0.08
Haitian	11	0.02
Trinidadian and Tobagonian	28	0.05
U.S. Virgin Islander	7	0.01
White:	50,999	90.43
Not Hispanic (47,896)	48,481	85.96
Hispanic (2,247)	2,518	4.46
Yugoslavian	32	0.06

Lake Station

Place Type: City
County: Lake
Population: 13,948

Ancestry/Race	Number	%
African American/Black:	150	1.08
Not Hispanic (82)	111	0.80
Hispanic (25)	39	0.28
Am. Ind. or Alaska Nat., not spec.	55	0.39
American Indian tribes, specified:	99	0.71
Apache (5)	5	0.04
Blackfeet (7)	11	0.08
Cherokee (19)	45	0.32
Chippewa (1)	3	0.02
Choctaw	2	0.01
Comanche (1)	1	0.01
Iroquois (4)	4	0.03
Latin American Indians (7)	8	0.06
Potawatomi	1	0.01
Pueblo (3)	3	0.02
Seminole (1)	4	0.03
Sioux (4)	10	0.07
All other tribes (1)	2	0.01
American Indian tribes, not spec.	5	0.04
Arab:	14	0.10
Arab/Arabic	5	0.04
Lebanese	9	0.06
Armenian	34	0.24
Asian:	77	0.55
Chinese, ex. Taiwanese (6)	6	0.04
Filipino (7)	10	0.07
Indian (5)	11	0.08
Japanese (3)	6	0.04
Korean (4)	7	0.05
Laotian (1)	4	0.03
Pakistani	5	0.04
Thai (6)	8	0.06
Vietnamese (6)	10	0.07
Other Asian, not specified (2)	10	0.07
Australian	4	0.03
Austrian	22	0.16
British	23	0.16
Canadian	45	0.32
Croatian	77	0.55
Czech	97	0.69
Czechoslovakian	51	0.36
Danish	18	0.13
Dutch	419	3.00
English	763	5.46
Finnish	35	0.25
French, except Basque	378	2.70
French Canadian	87	0.62
German	2,222	15.90
Greek	189	1.35
Hawaii Native/Pacific Islander:	7	0.05
Micronesian: (4)	4	0.03
Guamanian/Chamorro (4)	4	0.03
Polynesian: (2)	2	0.01
Native Hawaiian (2)	2	0.01
Other Pac. Isl., not spec. (1)	1	0.01
Hispanic or Latino:	2,875	20.61
Central American:	16	0.11
Guatemalan	6	0.04
Honduran	1	0.01
Nicaraguan	6	0.04
Panamanian	1	0.01
Salvadoran	2	0.01
Cuban	6	0.04
Mexican	1,771	12.70
Puerto Rican	798	5.72
South American:	2	0.01
Argentinean	1	0.01
Other South American	1	0.01
Other Hispanic or Latino	282	2.02
Hungarian	106	0.76
Irish	2,038	14.58
Italian	516	3.69
Lithuanian	74	0.53
Macedonian	82	0.59
Norwegian	85	0.61
Pennsylvania German	22	0.16
Polish	740	5.30
Portuguese	6	0.04
Romanian	27	0.19
Russian	66	0.47
Scotch-Irish	192	1.37
Scottish	111	0.79
Serbian	118	0.84
Slovak	184	1.32
Swedish	230	1.65
Swiss	28	0.20
Ukrainian	52	0.37
United States or American	805	5.76
Welsh	98	0.70
White:	12,408	88.96
Not Hispanic (10,695)	10,896	78.12
Hispanic (1,332)	1,512	10.84
Yugoslavian	34	0.24

Lawrence

Place Type: City
County: Marion
Population: 38,915

Ancestry/Race	Number	%
African American/Black:	6,387	16.41
Not Hispanic (5,964)	6,296	16.18

Notes: 1. Figures in the "Number" column do not add up to the total population due to: a) Ancestry/Race overlap — e.g. persons can report being both White and Irish, b) persons of Hispanic origin can report being any race, c) persons reporting two ancestries are counted in both categories. 2. Numbers in parentheses indicate the number of persons reporting this ancestry/race alone, not in combination with any other ancestry/race. 3. Refer to the Explanation of Data in the front of the book for more detailed information.

Hispanic (72)	91	0.23
African, sub-Saharan:	245	0.62
African	112	0.29
Ethiopian	58	0.15
Ghanian	6	0.02
Kenyan	6	0.02
Nigerian	19	0.05
South African	12	0.03
Other sub-Saharan African	32	0.08
Am. Ind. or Alaska Nat., not spec.	86	0.22
Albanian	5	0.01
American Indian tribes, specified:	186	0.48
Apache	5	0.01
Blackfeet (5)	11	0.03
Cherokee (16)	90	0.23
Cheyenne	1	0.00
Chippewa (4)	9	0.02
Choctaw (4)	6	0.02
Creek	1	0.00
Delaware	1	0.00
Iroquois (2)	2	0.01
Latin American Indians (1)	7	0.02
Lumbee (1)	1	0.00
Navajo	1	0.00
Potawatomi (4)	6	0.02
Seminole	1	0.00
Sioux (1)	5	0.01
All other tribes (25)	39	0.10
American Indian tribes, not spec.	17	0.04
Arab:	137	0.35
Arab/Arabic	58	0.15
Lebanese	69	0.18
Other Arab	10	0.03
Asian:	882	2.27
Cambodian (6)	7	0.02
Chinese, ex. Taiwanese (78)	104	0.27
Filipino (88)	131	0.34
Hmong (11)	14	0.04
Indian (71)	80	0.21
Japanese (56)	93	0.24
Korean (279)	315	0.81
Laotian (6)	8	0.02
Pakistani (3)	3	0.01
Taiwanese	1	0.00
Thai (12)	20	0.05
Vietnamese (68)	80	0.21
Other Asian, not specified (7)	26	0.07
Australian	11	0.03
Austrian	72	0.18
Belgian	116	0.30
Brazilian	55	0.14
British	218	0.56
Canadian	91	0.23
Croatian	30	0.08
Czech	84	0.21
Czechoslovakian	55	0.14
Danish	223	0.57
Dutch	682	1.74
English	3,346	8.53
European	253	0.64
French, except Basque	1,033	2.63
French Canadian	172	0.44
German	7,851	20.01
Greek	119	0.30
Hawaii Native/Pacific Islander:	58	0.15
Micronesian: (7)	8	0.02
Guamanian/Chamorro (7)	8	0.02
Polynesian: (21)	35	0.09
Native Hawaiian (13)	23	0.06
Samoan (8)	12	0.03
Other Pac. Isl., not spec. (2)	15	0.04
Hispanic or Latino:	1,840	4.73
Central American:	113	0.29
Costa Rican	3	0.01
Guatemalan	41	0.11
Honduran	28	0.07
Nicaraguan	15	0.04
Panamanian	13	0.03
Salvadoran	9	0.02
Other Central American	4	0.01
Cuban	32	0.08
Dominican Republic	3	0.01
Mexican	1,213	3.12
Puerto Rican	164	0.42
South American:	69	0.18
Argentinean	1	0.00
Bolivian	1	0.00
Chilean	1	0.00
Colombian	20	0.05
Ecuadorian	10	0.03
Peruvian	12	0.03
Venezuelan	22	0.06
Other South American	2	0.01
Other Hispanic or Latino	246	0.63
Hungarian	157	0.40
Iranian	26	0.07
Irish	4,986	12.71
Italian	837	2.13
Latvian	9	0.02
Lithuanian	23	0.06
Macedonian	9	0.02
Northern European	7	0.02
Norwegian	265	0.68
Pennsylvania German	38	0.10
Polish	779	1.99
Portuguese	40	0.10
Romanian	19	0.05
Russian	149	0.38
Scandinavian	40	0.10
Scotch-Irish	537	1.37
Scottish	764	1.95
Serbian	6	0.02
Slovak	105	0.27
Swedish	410	1.04
Swiss	123	0.31
Turkish	8	0.02
Ukrainian	59	0.15
United States or American	3,944	10.05
Welsh	163	0.42
West Indian, excl. Hispanic:	102	0.26
British West Indian	10	0.03
Haitian	9	0.02
Jamaican	32	0.08
Trinidadian and Tobagonian	51	0.13
White:	31,214	80.21
Not Hispanic (29,559)	30,111	77.38
Hispanic (1,022)	1,103	2.83
Yugoslavian	6	0.02

Lebanon

Place Type: City
County: Boone
Population: 14,222

Ancestry/Race	Number	%
African American/Black:	74	0.52
Not Hispanic (44)	71	0.50
Hispanic (3)	3	0.02
African, sub-Saharan:	23	0.16
African	23	0.16
Alaska Native tribes, specified:	1	0.01
Alaska Athabascan (1)	1	0.01
Am. Ind. or Alaska Nat., not spec.	24	0.17
American Indian tribes, specified:	59	0.41
Apache (1)	1	0.01
Blackfeet (4)	4	0.03
Cherokee (13)	22	0.15
Cheyenne	1	0.01
Chippewa (1)	4	0.03
Delaware (1)	1	0.01
Kiowa (1)	2	0.01
Latin American Indians	2	0.01
Ottawa (1)	1	0.01
Sioux (3)	4	0.03
All other tribes (17)	17	0.12
American Indian tribes, not spec.	2	0.01
Arab:	18	0.13
Lebanese	11	0.08
Palestinian	7	0.05
Asian:	73	0.51
Chinese, ex. Taiwanese (16)	16	0.11
Filipino (14)	19	0.13
Indian (7)	9	0.06
Indonesian (1)	2	0.01
Japanese (3)	6	0.04
Korean (6)	7	0.05
Pakistani (2)	2	0.01
Vietnamese (3)	5	0.04
Other Asian, not specified (1)	7	0.05
Australian	15	0.11
Belgian	26	0.18
British	49	0.34
Canadian	11	0.08
Danish	10	0.07
Dutch	372	2.62
English	1,561	10.98
European	81	0.57
Finnish	7	0.05
French, except Basque	277	1.95
German	3,260	22.93
Greek	13	0.09
Hawaii Native/Pacific Islander:	5	0.04
Micronesian:	4	0.03
Guamanian/Chamorro	4	0.03
Other Pac. Isl., not spec.	1	0.01
Hispanic or Latino:	229	1.61
Cuban	2	0.01
Mexican	170	1.20
Puerto Rican	8	0.06
South American:	3	0.02
Peruvian	3	0.02
Other Hispanic or Latino	46	0.32
Irish	1,699	11.95
Italian	284	2.00
Lithuanian	28	0.20
Northern European	12	0.08
Norwegian	49	0.34
Polish	141	0.99
Portuguese	9	0.06
Romanian	11	0.08
Russian	30	0.21
Scandinavian	92	0.65
Scotch-Irish	181	1.27
Scottish	310	2.18
Slovak	8	0.06
Swedish	45	0.32
Swiss	39	0.27
Ukrainian	6	0.04
United States or American	2,071	14.57
Welsh	184	1.29
White:	13,982	98.31
Not Hispanic (13,763)	13,843	97.34
Hispanic (128)	139	0.98

Logansport

Place Type: City
County: Cass
Population: 19,684

Ancestry/Race	Number	%
African American/Black:	482	2.45
Not Hispanic (383)	447	2.27
Hispanic (26)	35	0.18
African, sub-Saharan:	12	0.06
African	12	0.06
Am. Ind. or Alaska Nat., not spec.	41	0.21
American Indian tribes, specified:	84	0.43
Apache	1	0.01
Cherokee (5)	15	0.08
Choctaw	4	0.02
Creek (1)	1	0.01
Latin American Indians (26)	27	0.14
Osage	5	0.03
Potawatomi	4	0.02
Seminole (1)	1	0.01
Sioux (3)	4	0.02
All other tribes (15)	22	0.11
American Indian tribes, not spec.	4	0.02

Notes: 1. Figures in the "Number" column do not add up to the total population due to: a) Ancestry/Race overlap — e.g. persons can report being both White and Irish, b) persons of Hispanic origin can report being any race, c) persons reporting two ancestries are counted in both categories. 2. Numbers in parentheses indicate the number of persons reporting this ancestry/race alone, not in combination with any other ancestry/race. 3. Refer to the Explanation of Data in the front of the book for more detailed information.

Ancestry/Race	Number	%
Armenian	6	0.03
Asian:	215	1.09
Chinese, ex. Taiwanese (32)	32	0.16
Filipino (23)	26	0.13
Indian (23)	23	0.12
Japanese (7)	14	0.07
Korean (2)	6	0.03
Laotian (22)	29	0.15
Thai (2)	4	0.02
Vietnamese (48)	55	0.28
Other Asian, specified	1	0.01
Other Asian, not specified (18)	25	0.13
Australian	6	0.03
Belgian	9	0.05
British	58	0.29
Canadian	14	0.07
Czech	14	0.07
Danish	49	0.25
Dutch	384	1.95
English	1,026	5.20
European	159	0.81
French, except Basque	276	1.40
French Canadian	46	0.23
German	4,104	20.80
Greek	58	0.29
Hawaii Native/Pacific Islander:	29	0.15
Micronesian: (12)	19	0.10
Guamanian/Chamorro (12)	19	0.10
Polynesian:	5	0.03
Samoan	1	0.01
Tongan	3	0.02
Other Polynesian	1	0.01
Other Pac. Isl., specified	1	0.01
Other Pac. Isl., not spec.	4	0.02
Hispanic or Latino:	2,476	12.58
Central American:	175	0.89
Guatemalan	84	0.43
Honduran	12	0.06
Nicaraguan	6	0.03
Salvadoran	69	0.35
Other Central American	4	0.02
Cuban	47	0.24
Mexican	1,998	10.15
Puerto Rican	33	0.17
South American:	13	0.07
Colombian	2	0.01
Ecuadorian	4	0.02
Peruvian	7	0.04
Other Hispanic or Latino	210	1.07
Hungarian	6	0.03
Irish	1,664	8.43
Italian	466	2.36
Lithuanian	8	0.04
Norwegian	77	0.39
Pennsylvania German	14	0.07
Polish	207	1.05
Russian	37	0.19
Scotch-Irish	107	0.54
Scottish	282	1.43
Serbian	8	0.04
Swedish	39	0.20
Swiss	29	0.15
Ukrainian	7	0.04
United States or American	2,533	12.84
Welsh	82	0.42
West Indian, excl. Hispanic:	9	0.05
West Indian	9	0.05
White:	17,884	90.86
Not Hispanic (16,442)	16,588	84.27
Hispanic (1,232)	1,296	6.58
Yugoslavian	37	0.19

Madison

Place Type: City
County: Jefferson
Population: 12,004

Ancestry/Race	Number	%
African American/Black:	340	2.83
Not Hispanic (287)	330	2.75
Hispanic (5)	10	0.08
African, sub-Saharan:	47	0.39
African	47	0.39
Am. Ind. or Alaska Nat., not spec.	24	0.20
American Indian tribes, specified:	66	0.55
Apache	1	0.01
Blackfeet	11	0.09
Cherokee (1)	31	0.26
Cheyenne	1	0.01
Chippewa	4	0.03
Cree	2	0.02
Crow	1	0.01
Iroquois (1)	2	0.02
Latin American Indians (2)	2	0.02
Potawatomi (1)	1	0.01
Sioux (5)	7	0.06
All other tribes (2)	3	0.02
American Indian tribes, not spec.	4	0.03
Asian:	124	1.03
Chinese, ex. Taiwanese (21)	26	0.22
Filipino (7)	19	0.16
Indian (28)	32	0.27
Japanese (37)	37	0.31
Korean (1)	2	0.02
Pakistani (4)	4	0.03
Vietnamese (1)	1	0.01
Other Asian, not specified (1)	3	0.02
Austrian	6	0.05
Belgian	56	0.46
British	41	0.34
Canadian	35	0.29
Croatian	15	0.12
Czechoslovakian	23	0.19
Danish	21	0.17
Dutch	180	1.49
English	1,364	11.31
European	243	2.01
French, except Basque	324	2.69
French Canadian	19	0.16
German	2,590	21.47
Greek	9	0.07
Hawaii Native/Pacific Islander:	6	0.05
Polynesian: (1)	5	0.04
Native Hawaiian	1	0.01
Samoan (1)	4	0.03
Other Pac. Isl., not spec.	1	0.01
Hispanic or Latino:	163	1.36
Central American:	1	0.01
Honduran	1	0.01
Cuban	6	0.05
Dominican Republic	3	0.02
Mexican	93	0.77
Puerto Rican	23	0.19
South American:	3	0.02
Argentinean	1	0.01
Chilean	1	0.01
Colombian	1	0.01
Other Hispanic or Latino	34	0.28
Hungarian	29	0.24
Iranian	29	0.24
Irish	1,273	10.55
Italian	207	1.72
Norwegian	29	0.24
Polish	117	0.97
Russian	14	0.12
Scandinavian	8	0.07
Scotch-Irish	243	2.01
Scottish	233	1.93
Swedish	135	1.12
Swiss	26	0.22
United States or American	1,740	14.42
Welsh	112	0.93
White:	11,516	95.93
Not Hispanic (11,278)	11,415	95.09
Hispanic (79)	101	0.84

Marion

Place Type: City
County: Grant
Population: 31,320

Ancestry/Race	Number	%
African American/Black:	5,266	16.81
Not Hispanic (4,830)	5,195	16.59
Hispanic (48)	71	0.23
African, sub-Saharan:	164	0.53
African	164	0.53
Alaska Native tribes, not specified	1	0.00
Am. Ind. or Alaska Nat., not spec.	108	0.34
American Indian tribes, specified:	222	0.71
Apache (3)	8	0.03
Blackfeet (3)	15	0.05
Cherokee (21)	92	0.29
Cheyenne	1	0.00
Chippewa (2)	3	0.01
Choctaw (1)	5	0.02
Comanche (2)	4	0.01
Creek (2)	4	0.01
Delaware	1	0.00
Iroquois (5)	8	0.03
Latin American Indians (5)	7	0.02
Lumbee (1)	1	0.00
Navajo (1)	1	0.00
Ottawa (1)	1	0.00
Seminole (3)	7	0.02
Sioux (1)	9	0.03
All other tribes (39)	55	0.18
American Indian tribes, not spec.	15	0.05
Arab:	18	0.06
Egyptian	10	0.03
Lebanese	8	0.03
Asian:	282	0.90
Chinese, ex. Taiwanese (40)	50	0.16
Filipino (35)	44	0.14
Indian (79)	88	0.28
Japanese (5)	15	0.05
Korean (14)	22	0.07
Pakistani (6)	6	0.02
Thai (7)	16	0.05
Vietnamese (17)	20	0.06
Other Asian, specified	3	0.01
Other Asian, not specified (8)	18	0.06
Austrian	7	0.02
Belgian	34	0.11
British	136	0.44
Canadian	100	0.32
Celtic	8	0.03
Croatian	15	0.05
Czech	32	0.10
Czechoslovakian	9	0.03
Danish	3	0.01
Dutch	642	2.06
English	2,389	7.68
European	102	0.33
French, except Basque	496	1.59
French Canadian	70	0.22
German	4,321	13.88
Greek	61	0.20
Hawaii Native/Pacific Islander:	24	0.08
Micronesian: (1)	1	0.00
Guamanian/Chamorro (1)	1	0.00
Polynesian: (4)	12	0.04
Native Hawaiian (1)	9	0.03
Samoan (3)	3	0.01
Other Pac. Isl., not spec. (2)	11	0.04
Hispanic or Latino:	1,128	3.60
Central American:	15	0.05
Costa Rican	1	0.00
Guatemalan	3	0.01
Honduran	10	0.03
Salvadoran	1	0.00
Cuban	25	0.08
Mexican	780	2.49
Puerto Rican	57	0.18
South American:	5	0.02

Notes: 1. Figures in the "Number" column do not add up to the total population due to: a) Ancestry/Race overlap — e.g. persons can report being both White and Irish, b) persons of Hispanic origin can report being any race, c) persons reporting two ancestries are counted in both categories. 2. Numbers in parentheses indicate the number of persons reporting this ancestry/race alone, not in combination with any other ancestry/race. 3. Refer to the Explanation of Data in the front of the book for more detailed information.

Colombian	1	0.00
Peruvian	2	0.01
Other South American	2	0.01
Other Hispanic or Latino	246	0.79
Hungarian	133	0.43
Irish	2,169	6.97
Italian	334	1.07
Latvian	9	0.03
Lithuanian	41	0.13
Norwegian	131	0.42
Pennsylvania German	15	0.05
Polish	256	0.82
Portuguese	28	0.09
Russian	34	0.11
Scandinavian	21	0.07
Scotch-Irish	407	1.31
Scottish	527	1.69
Slovak	10	0.03
Swedish	185	0.59
Swiss	119	0.38
Ukrainian	36	0.12
United States or American	4,231	13.59
Welsh	179	0.58
West Indian, excl. Hispanic:	7	0.02
Other West Indian	7	0.02
White:	25,550	81.58
Not Hispanic (24,381)	24,894	79.48
Hispanic (561)	656	2.09

Martinsville

Place Type: City
County: Morgan
Population: 11,698

Ancestry/Race	Number	%
African American/Black:	27	0.23
Not Hispanic (11)	27	0.23
Alaska Native tribes, specified:	1	0.01
Aleut (1)	1	0.01
Am. Ind. or Alaska Nat., not spec.	20	0.17
American Indian tribes, specified:	32	0.27
Apache	1	0.01
Blackfeet (2)	5	0.04
Cherokee (10)	14	0.12
Chickasaw (1)	3	0.03
Chippewa (1)	2	0.02
Creek	1	0.01
Pueblo (4)	4	0.03
Sioux (2)	2	0.02
American Indian tribes, not spec.	5	0.04
Asian:	38	0.32
Chinese, ex. Taiwanese (5)	8	0.07
Filipino (9)	11	0.09
Indian (1)	4	0.03
Japanese (3)	9	0.08
Korean (1)	3	0.03
Pakistani (1)	1	0.01
Thai (1)	1	0.01
Other Asian, specified	1	0.01
Belgian	15	0.13
British	21	0.18
Danish	12	0.10
Dutch	199	1.69
English	799	6.80
European	22	0.19
French, except Basque	150	1.28
French Canadian	30	0.26
German	1,825	15.53
Hawaii Native/Pacific Islander:	9	0.08
Micronesian: (1)	1	0.01
Guamanian/Chamorro (1)	1	0.01
Polynesian: (3)	5	0.04
Native Hawaiian	2	0.02
Samoan (3)	3	0.03
Other Pac. Isl., specified	1	0.01
Other Pac. Isl., not spec. (1)	2	0.02
Hispanic or Latino:	116	0.99
Cuban	1	0.01
Mexican	61	0.52
Puerto Rican	6	0.05
Other Hispanic or Latino	48	0.41
Hungarian	53	0.45
Irish	1,298	11.04
Italian	64	0.54
Polish	60	0.51
Scandinavian	7	0.06
Scotch-Irish	109	0.93
Scottish	161	1.37
Swedish	46	0.39
Swiss	29	0.25
United States or American	3,287	27.96
Welsh	39	0.33
White:	11,600	99.16
Not Hispanic (11,460)	11,515	98.44
Hispanic (76)	85	0.73
Yugoslavian	15	0.13

Merrillville

Place Type: Town
County: Lake
Population: 30,560

Ancestry/Race	Number	%
Acadian/Cajun	8	0.03
Afghan	30	0.10
African American/Black:	7,202	23.57
Not Hispanic (6,908)	7,086	23.19
Hispanic (79)	116	0.38
African, sub-Saharan:	342	1.11
African	151	0.49
Ethiopian	25	0.08
Ghanian	101	0.33
Nigerian	65	0.21
Alaska Native tribes, specified:	1	0.00
Tlingit-Haida	1	0.00
Am. Ind. or Alaska Nat., not spec.	101	0.33
Albanian	8	0.03
American Indian tribes, specified:	130	0.43
Apache (1)	6	0.02
Blackfeet (2)	10	0.03
Cherokee (11)	48	0.16
Cheyenne	4	0.01
Chippewa (3)	3	0.01
Choctaw (1)	4	0.01
Creek	3	0.01
Crow (1)	1	0.00
Iroquois (1)	8	0.03
Latin American Indians (2)	5	0.02
Navajo (7)	8	0.03
Osage (1)	1	0.00
Potawatomi (1)	6	0.02
Pueblo	1	0.00
Sioux (4)	6	0.02
Yaqui	2	0.01
All other tribes (9)	14	0.05
American Indian tribes, not spec.	17	0.06
Arab:	119	0.39
Arab/Arabic	32	0.10
Lebanese	60	0.20
Palestinian	12	0.04
Syrian	6	0.02
Other Arab	9	0.03
Armenian	33	0.11
Asian:	553	1.81
Bangladeshi (3)	3	0.01
Cambodian (5)	5	0.02
Chinese, ex. Taiwanese (51)	61	0.20
Filipino (113)	139	0.45
Indian (129)	144	0.47
Japanese (17)	23	0.08
Korean (36)	47	0.15
Laotian (5)	5	0.02
Pakistani (28)	30	0.10
Sri Lankan (6)	6	0.02
Taiwanese (4)	4	0.01
Thai (5)	10	0.03
Vietnamese (46)	52	0.17
Other Asian, not specified (12)	24	0.08
Assyrian/Chaldean/Syriac	55	0.18
Australian	7	0.02
Austrian	55	0.18
Belgian	24	0.08
Brazilian	15	0.05
British	43	0.14
Bulgarian	55	0.18
Canadian	22	0.07
Croatian	514	1.67
Czech	100	0.33
Czechoslovakian	73	0.24
Danish	79	0.26
Dutch	533	1.74
English	1,684	5.48
European	30	0.10
Finnish	40	0.13
French, except Basque	509	1.66
French Canadian	127	0.41
German	4,912	15.99
Greek	729	2.37
Guyanese	25	0.08
Hawaii Native/Pacific Islander:	19	0.06
Micronesian: (2)	2	0.01
Guamanian/Chamorro (2)	2	0.01
Polynesian: (2)	8	0.03
Native Hawaiian (1)	7	0.02
Samoan (1)	1	0.00
Other Pac. Isl., not spec. (2)	9	0.03
Hispanic or Latino:	2,950	9.65
Central American:	24	0.08
Costa Rican	2	0.01
Guatemalan	2	0.01
Honduran	1	0.00
Nicaraguan	4	0.01
Panamanian	8	0.03
Salvadoran	7	0.02
Cuban	23	0.08
Dominican Republic	6	0.02
Mexican	2,041	6.68
Puerto Rican	492	1.61
South American:	30	0.10
Argentinean	9	0.03
Bolivian	6	0.02
Chilean	1	0.00
Colombian	13	0.04
Ecuadorian	1	0.00
Other Hispanic or Latino	334	1.09
Hungarian	512	1.67
Irish	3,268	10.64
Italian	1,392	4.53
Lithuanian	197	0.64
Macedonian	466	1.52
Norwegian	227	0.74
Polish	3,013	9.81
Portuguese	10	0.03
Romanian	138	0.45
Russian	262	0.85
Scandinavian	10	0.03
Scotch-Irish	237	0.77
Scottish	287	0.93
Serbian	462	1.50
Slavic	39	0.13
Slovak	1,025	3.34
Slovene	34	0.11
Swedish	278	0.91
Swiss	87	0.28
Turkish	16	0.05
Ukrainian	48	0.16
United States or American	1,473	4.80
Welsh	145	0.47
West Indian, excl. Hispanic:	34	0.11
Barbadian	6	0.02
Bermudan	11	0.04
British West Indian	8	0.03
Jamaican	9	0.03
White:	21,885	71.61
Not Hispanic (19,701)	20,088	65.73
Hispanic (1,585)	1,797	5.88
Yugoslavian	122	0.40

Notes: 1. Figures in the "Number" column do not add up to the total population due to: a) Ancestry/Race overlap — e.g. persons can report being both White and Irish, b) persons of Hispanic origin can report being any race, c) persons reporting two ancestries are counted in both categories. 2. Numbers in parentheses indicate the number of persons reporting this ancestry/race alone, not in combination with any other ancestry/race. 3. Refer to the Explanation of Data in the front of the book for more detailed information.

Michigan City

Place Type: City
County: La Porte
Population: 32,900

Ancestry/Race	Number	%
African American/Black:	9,122	27.73
Not Hispanic (8,576)	8,999	27.35
Hispanic (81)	123	0.37
African, sub-Saharan:	253	0.77
African	204	0.62
Nigerian	44	0.13
South African	5	0.02
Alaska Native tribes, specified:	1	0.00
Tlingit-Haida (1)	1	0.00
Alaska Native tribes, not specified	1	0.00
Am. Ind. or Alaska Nat., not spec.	128	0.39
American Indian tribes, specified:	154	0.47
Apache (3)	5	0.02
Blackfeet (7)	21	0.06
Cherokee (16)	73	0.22
Cheyenne	1	0.00
Chickasaw	2	0.01
Chippewa (7)	12	0.04
Choctaw	9	0.03
Creek (1)	2	0.01
Iroquois	3	0.01
Kiowa (1)	1	0.00
Latin American Indians (3)	4	0.01
Navajo	1	0.00
Potawatomi	2	0.01
Sioux (1)	10	0.03
All other tribes (5)	8	0.02
American Indian tribes, not spec.	19	0.06
Arab:	525	1.60
Arab/Arabic	9	0.03
Jordanian	14	0.04
Lebanese	444	1.35
Palestinian	28	0.09
Syrian	7	0.02
Other Arab	23	0.07
Asian:	246	0.75
Cambodian (7)	7	0.02
Chinese, ex. Taiwanese (27)	31	0.09
Filipino (22)	43	0.13
Indian (31)	46	0.14
Japanese (10)	19	0.06
Korean (19)	32	0.10
Laotian (1)	1	0.00
Malaysian (2)	3	0.01
Pakistani (8)	10	0.03
Taiwanese	2	0.01
Thai (3)	3	0.01
Vietnamese (22)	25	0.08
Other Asian, not specified (15)	24	0.07
Australian	14	0.04
Austrian	65	0.20
Belgian	42	0.13
British	53	0.16
Bulgarian	13	0.04
Canadian	32	0.10
Celtic	13	0.04
Croatian	38	0.12
Czech	109	0.33
Czechoslovakian	22	0.07
Danish	82	0.25
Dutch	614	1.87
Eastern European	7	0.02
English	1,828	5.57
Estonian	10	0.03
European	148	0.45
Finnish	22	0.07
French, except Basque	710	2.16
French Canadian	79	0.24
German	6,619	20.17
Greek	126	0.38
Hawaii Native/Pacific Islander:	18	0.05
Polynesian: (4)	7	0.02
Native Hawaiian (3)	6	0.02
Samoan (1)	1	0.00
Other Pac. Isl., not spec. (2)	11	0.03
Hispanic or Latino:	1,035	3.15
Central American:	21	0.06
Guatemalan	2	0.01
Honduran	5	0.02
Nicaraguan	12	0.04
Panamanian	1	0.00
Other Central American	1	0.00
Cuban	18	0.05
Dominican Republic	10	0.03
Mexican	695	2.11
Puerto Rican	143	0.43
South American:	11	0.03
Argentinean	3	0.01
Colombian	1	0.00
Peruvian	6	0.02
Venezuelan	1	0.00
Other Hispanic or Latino	137	0.42
Hungarian	303	0.92
Irish	3,216	9.80
Italian	695	2.12
Lithuanian	149	0.45
Norwegian	230	0.70
Pennsylvania German	33	0.10
Polish	3,631	11.06
Portuguese	13	0.04
Romanian	12	0.04
Russian	160	0.49
Scandinavian	30	0.09
Scotch-Irish	294	0.90
Scottish	213	0.65
Serbian	30	0.09
Slavic	13	0.04
Slovak	81	0.25
Swedish	558	1.70
Swiss	78	0.24
Ukrainian	78	0.24
United States or American	2,350	7.16
Welsh	46	0.14
West Indian, excl. Hispanic:	48	0.15
Haitian	16	0.05
Jamaican	12	0.04
West Indian	20	0.06
White:	23,495	71.41
Not Hispanic (22,309)	22,871	69.52
Hispanic (539)	624	1.90
Yugoslavian	7	0.02

Mishawaka

Place Type: City
County: Saint Joseph
Population: 46,557

Ancestry/Race	Number	%
African American/Black:	1,987	4.27
Not Hispanic (1,620)	1,937	4.16
Hispanic (39)	50	0.11
African, sub-Saharan:	320	0.68
African	237	0.51
Ghanian	39	0.08
Kenyan	13	0.03
Zimbabwean	8	0.02
Other sub-Saharan African	23	0.05
Alaska Native tribes, specified:	1	0.00
Aleut (1)	1	0.00
Am. Ind. or Alaska Nat., not spec.	133	0.29
Alsatian	5	0.01
American Indian tribes, specified:	337	0.72
Apache (3)	7	0.02
Blackfeet (3)	21	0.05
Cherokee (25)	123	0.26
Cheyenne	3	0.01
Chickasaw	2	0.00
Chippewa (5)	13	0.03
Choctaw (7)	15	0.03
Cree	5	0.01
Creek (2)	2	0.00
Delaware (1)	1	0.00
Iroquois (1)	6	0.01
Latin American Indians (2)	4	0.01
Lumbee (1)	1	0.00
Menominee (1)	2	0.00
Navajo	2	0.00
Ottawa (2)	2	0.00
Paiute (1)	1	0.00
Pima (2)	2	0.00
Potawatomi (19)	30	0.06
Puget Sound Salish (3)	3	0.01
Seminole (1)	2	0.00
Shoshone (1)	2	0.00
Sioux (1)	6	0.01
Ute (1)	1	0.00
All other tribes (53)	81	0.17
American Indian tribes, not spec.	17	0.04
Arab:	229	0.49
Arab/Arabic	38	0.08
Egyptian	6	0.01
Iraqi	93	0.20
Lebanese	46	0.10
Palestinian	26	0.06
Syrian	20	0.04
Armenian	9	0.02
Asian:	811	1.74
Bangladeshi (8)	8	0.02
Cambodian (6)	8	0.02
Chinese, ex. Taiwanese (121)	144	0.31
Filipino (35)	51	0.11
Indian (193)	208	0.45
Indonesian (11)	12	0.03
Japanese (45)	75	0.16
Korean (104)	132	0.28
Laotian (7)	7	0.02
Malaysian (1)	4	0.01
Pakistani (7)	16	0.03
Taiwanese (4)	10	0.02
Thai (10)	14	0.03
Vietnamese (79)	89	0.19
Other Asian, specified	1	0.00
Other Asian, not specified (11)	32	0.07
Australian	46	0.10
Austrian	102	0.22
Belgian	1,595	3.41
British	178	0.38
Canadian	173	0.37
Celtic	7	0.01
Croatian	65	0.14
Czech	103	0.22
Czechoslovakian	65	0.14
Danish	127	0.27
Dutch	1,156	2.47
Eastern European	4	0.01
English	3,801	8.12
European	220	0.47
Finnish	24	0.05
French, except Basque	1,405	3.00
French Canadian	433	0.93
German	12,725	27.19
Greek	105	0.22
Hawaii Native/Pacific Islander:	43	0.09
Micronesian: (7)	9	0.02
Guamanian/Chamorro (7)	8	0.02
Other Micronesian	1	0.00
Polynesian: (7)	22	0.05
Native Hawaiian (6)	20	0.04
Samoan (1)	2	0.00
Other Pac. Isl., specified	1	0.00
Other Pac. Isl., not spec. (7)	11	0.02
Hispanic or Latino:	1,297	2.79
Central American:	66	0.14
Costa Rican	8	0.02
Guatemalan	13	0.03
Honduran	9	0.02
Nicaraguan	3	0.01
Panamanian	9	0.02
Salvadoran	23	0.05
Other Central American	1	0.00
Cuban	22	0.05
Dominican Republic	5	0.01

Notes: 1. Figures in the "Number" column do not add up to the total population due to: a) Ancestry/Race overlap — e.g. persons can report being both White and Irish, b) persons of Hispanic origin can report being any race, c) persons reporting two ancestries are counted in both categories. 2. Numbers in parentheses indicate the number of persons reporting this ancestry/race alone, not in combination with any other ancestry/race. 3. Refer to the Explanation of Data in the front of the book for more detailed information.

Ancestry/Race	Number	%
Mexican	835	1.79
Puerto Rican	105	0.23
South American:	66	0.14
Argentinean	8	0.02
Chilean	4	0.01
Colombian	7	0.02
Ecuadorian	15	0.03
Peruvian	3	0.01
Venezuelan	29	0.06
Other Hispanic or Latino	198	0.43
Hungarian	1,428	3.05
Iranian	13	0.03
Irish	6,552	14.00
Israeli	24	0.05
Italian	2,352	5.03
Lithuanian	151	0.32
Luxemburger	21	0.04
Maltese	26	0.06
Norwegian	370	0.79
Pennsylvania German	197	0.42
Polish	4,403	9.41
Portuguese	47	0.10
Romanian	5	0.01
Russian	160	0.34
Scandinavian	20	0.04
Scotch-Irish	715	1.53
Scottish	709	1.52
Serbian	69	0.15
Slavic	40	0.09
Slovak	46	0.10
Swedish	773	1.65
Swiss	279	0.60
Turkish	15	0.03
Ukrainian	238	0.51
United States or American	3,534	7.55
Welsh	247	0.53
West Indian, excl. Hispanic:	4	0.01
Jamaican	4	0.01
White:	43,441	93.31
Not Hispanic (41,979)	42,659	91.63
Hispanic (657)	782	1.68
Yugoslavian	27	0.06

Muncie

Place Type: City
County: Delaware
Population: 67,430

Ancestry/Race	Number	%
African American/Black:	7,880	11.69
Not Hispanic (7,334)	7,794	11.56
Hispanic (63)	86	0.13
African, sub-Saharan:	205	0.30
African	175	0.26
Kenyan	21	0.03
Nigerian	9	0.01
Alaska Native tribes, specified:	2	0.00
Alaska Athabascan (2)	2	0.00
Am. Ind. or Alaska Nat., not spec.	148	0.22
Albanian	12	0.02
American Indian tribes, specified:	299	0.44
Apache (4)	6	0.01
Blackfeet (2)	12	0.02
Cherokee (47)	158	0.23
Chippewa (4)	6	0.01
Choctaw (3)	5	0.01
Comanche	1	0.00
Creek	2	0.00
Crow	2	0.00
Delaware (4)	11	0.02
Iroquois (5)	9	0.01
Kiowa	3	0.00
Latin American Indians (3)	6	0.01
Navajo (5)	8	0.01
Osage	2	0.00
Potawatomi (6)	6	0.01
Pueblo	1	0.00
Shoshone (1)	1	0.00
Sioux (11)	16	0.02
All other tribes (16)	44	0.07
American Indian tribes, not spec.	32	0.05
Arab:	246	0.36
Arab/Arabic	90	0.13
Egyptian	24	0.04
Jordanian	9	0.01
Lebanese	6	0.01
Moroccan	57	0.08
Palestinian	6	0.01
Syrian	49	0.07
Other Arab	5	0.01
Armenian	24	0.04
Asian:	736	1.09
Cambodian (1)	2	0.00
Chinese, ex. Taiwanese (125)	148	0.22
Filipino (60)	118	0.17
Indian (79)	100	0.15
Indonesian (2)	2	0.00
Japanese (60)	81	0.12
Korean (118)	142	0.21
Laotian (1)	1	0.00
Malaysian (3)	3	0.00
Pakistani (1)	1	0.00
Sri Lankan (1)	1	0.00
Taiwanese (9)	10	0.01
Thai (20)	25	0.04
Vietnamese (16)	26	0.04
Other Asian, specified (21)	31	0.05
Other Asian, not specified (12)	45	0.07
Australian	19	0.03
Austrian	85	0.13
Belgian	86	0.13
Brazilian	7	0.01
British	276	0.41
Canadian	80	0.12
Croatian	81	0.12
Czech	51	0.08
Czechoslovakian	55	0.08
Danish	115	0.17
Dutch	1,282	1.90
Eastern European	25	0.04
English	6,095	9.03
European	555	0.82
Finnish	39	0.06
French, except Basque	1,308	1.94
French Canadian	227	0.34
German	11,825	17.53
German Russian	10	0.01
Greek	130	0.19
Hawaii Native/Pacific Islander:	117	0.17
Melanesian: (3)	3	0.00
Other Melanesian (3)	3	0.00
Micronesian: (6)	9	0.01
Guamanian/Chamorro (5)	8	0.01
Other Micronesian (1)	1	0.00
Polynesian: (33)	72	0.11
Native Hawaiian (21)	42	0.06
Samoan (10)	28	0.04
Other Polynesian (2)	2	0.00
Other Pac. Isl., specified	5	0.01
Other Pac. Isl., not spec. (20)	28	0.04
Hispanic or Latino:	971	1.44
Central American:	19	0.03
Guatemalan	1	0.00
Honduran	5	0.01
Panamanian	5	0.01
Salvadoran	8	0.01
Cuban	17	0.03
Dominican Republic	21	0.03
Mexican	551	0.82
Puerto Rican	91	0.13
South American:	30	0.04
Argentinean	10	0.01
Bolivian	5	0.01
Chilean	1	0.00
Colombian	6	0.01
Ecuadorian	1	0.00
Peruvian	1	0.00
Venezuelan	6	0.01
Other Hispanic or Latino	242	0.36
Hungarian	216	0.32
Iranian	23	0.03
Irish	6,260	9.28
Italian	1,637	2.43
Latvian	22	0.03
Lithuanian	38	0.06
Norwegian	336	0.50
Pennsylvania German	29	0.04
Polish	948	1.41
Portuguese	72	0.11
Romanian	41	0.06
Russian	114	0.17
Scandinavian	52	0.08
Scotch-Irish	830	1.23
Scottish	1,167	1.73
Serbian	32	0.05
Slavic	29	0.04
Slovak	125	0.19
Slovene	92	0.14
Swedish	385	0.57
Swiss	216	0.32
Turkish	39	0.06
Ukrainian	118	0.17
United States or American	8,603	12.75
Welsh	438	0.65
West Indian, excl. Hispanic:	52	0.08
Belizean	21	0.03
Jamaican	31	0.05
White:	58,719	87.08
Not Hispanic (57,313)	58,167	86.26
Hispanic (486)	552	0.82
Yugoslavian	35	0.05

Munster

Place Type: Town
County: Lake
Population: 21,511

Ancestry/Race	Number	%
African American/Black:	246	1.14
Not Hispanic (216)	236	1.10
Hispanic (6)	10	0.05
African, sub-Saharan:	5	0.02
Other sub-Saharan African	5	0.02
Am. Ind. or Alaska Nat., not spec.	21	0.10
Albanian	16	0.07
American Indian tribes, specified:	36	0.17
Apache (1)	6	0.03
Cherokee	13	0.06
Chippewa (2)	2	0.01
Choctaw	2	0.01
Iroquois (1)	1	0.00
Latin American Indians (1)	1	0.00
Menominee (1)	1	0.00
Osage	1	0.00
Sioux (1)	6	0.03
Tohono O'Odham (1)	1	0.00
All other tribes	2	0.01
Arab:	14	0.07
Moroccan	9	0.04
Palestinian	5	0.02
Armenian	24	0.11
Asian:	1,063	4.94
Bangladeshi (4)	4	0.02
Chinese, ex. Taiwanese (121)	132	0.61
Filipino (146)	178	0.83
Indian (487)	510	2.37
Japanese (25)	40	0.19
Korean (113)	116	0.54
Laotian (1)	1	0.00
Pakistani (30)	30	0.14
Taiwanese	7	0.03
Thai (6)	6	0.03
Vietnamese (8)	11	0.05
Other Asian, not specified (16)	28	0.13
Assyrian/Chaldean/Syriac	7	0.03
Austrian	88	0.41
Belgian	46	0.21
British	56	0.26

Notes: 1. Figures in the "Number" column do not add up to the total population due to: a) Ancestry/Race overlap — e.g. persons can report being both White and Irish, b) persons of Hispanic origin can report being any race, c) persons reporting two ancestries are counted in both categories. 2. Numbers in parentheses indicate the number of persons reporting this ancestry/race alone, not in combination with any other ancestry/race. 3. Refer to the Explanation of Data in the front of the book for more detailed information.

Ancestry/Race	Number	%
Bulgarian	23	0.11
Canadian	62	0.29
Croatian	446	2.07
Czech	150	0.70
Czechoslovakian	72	0.33
Danish	119	0.55
Dutch	1,083	5.03
Eastern European	100	0.46
English	1,523	7.08
European	84	0.39
French, except Basque	563	2.62
French Canadian	86	0.40
German	4,202	19.53
Greek	318	1.48
Hawaii Native/Pacific Islander:	10	0.05
Polynesian: (2)	2	0.01
Native Hawaiian (2)	2	0.01
Other Pac. Isl., not spec. (2)	8	0.04
Hispanic or Latino:	1,050	4.88
Central American:	7	0.03
Costa Rican	1	0.00
Guatemalan	5	0.02
Honduran	1	0.00
Cuban	17	0.08
Mexican	814	3.78
Puerto Rican	94	0.44
South American:	34	0.16
Argentinean	5	0.02
Bolivian	5	0.02
Colombian	6	0.03
Ecuadorian	8	0.04
Peruvian	9	0.04
Venezuelan	1	0.00
Other Hispanic or Latino	84	0.39
Hungarian	541	2.51
Iranian	19	0.09
Irish	3,024	14.06
Italian	1,725	8.02
Latvian	14	0.07
Lithuanian	215	1.00
Luxemburger	41	0.19
Macedonian	7	0.03
Norwegian	182	0.85
Polish	4,173	19.40
Romanian	215	1.00
Russian	294	1.37
Scotch-Irish	284	1.32
Scottish	244	1.13
Serbian	479	2.23
Slavic	13	0.06
Slovak	883	4.10
Swedish	674	3.13
Swiss	107	0.50
Turkish	7	0.03
Ukrainian	157	0.73
United States or American	561	2.61
Welsh	142	0.66
West Indian, excl. Hispanic:	16	0.07
Haitian	11	0.05
West Indian	5	0.02
White:	20,053	93.22
Not Hispanic (19,098)	19,246	89.47
Hispanic (753)	807	3.75
Yugoslavian	115	0.53

New Albany

Place Type: City
County: Floyd
Population: 37,603

Ancestry/Race	Number	%
African American/Black:	2,953	7.85
Not Hispanic (2,580)	2,910	7.74
Hispanic (27)	43	0.11
African, sub-Saharan:	127	0.34
African	98	0.26
Cape Verdean	29	0.08
Am. Ind. or Alaska Nat., not spec.	103	0.27
American Indian tribes, specified:	174	0.46
Apache (7)	9	0.02
Blackfeet (6)	11	0.03
Cherokee (39)	96	0.26
Chippewa (1)	1	0.00
Choctaw	1	0.00
Comanche (2)	2	0.01
Iroquois (6)	12	0.03
Latin American Indians (6)	11	0.03
Navajo (2)	2	0.01
Osage	3	0.01
Pima (2)	2	0.01
Potawatomi (1)	5	0.01
Pueblo (1)	6	0.02
Seminole	1	0.00
Shoshone	1	0.00
Sioux (2)	4	0.01
All other tribes (1)	7	0.02
American Indian tribes, not spec.	12	0.03
Arab:	61	0.16
Egyptian	25	0.07
Lebanese	24	0.06
Syrian	12	0.03
Asian:	260	0.69
Cambodian	1	0.00
Chinese, ex. Taiwanese (23)	33	0.09
Filipino (30)	44	0.12
Indian (32)	55	0.15
Indonesian	1	0.00
Japanese (12)	24	0.06
Korean (13)	25	0.07
Laotian (6)	7	0.02
Pakistani (24)	25	0.07
Taiwanese (6)	7	0.02
Thai (2)	2	0.01
Vietnamese (6)	14	0.04
Other Asian, specified	5	0.01
Other Asian, not specified (2)	17	0.05
Austrian	9	0.02
Basque	12	0.03
Belgian	8	0.02
British	121	0.32
Canadian	21	0.06
Celtic	8	0.02
Czech	59	0.16
Czechoslovakian	16	0.04
Danish	23	0.06
Dutch	554	1.48
English	3,399	9.10
European	263	0.70
Finnish	23	0.06
French, except Basque	1,161	3.11
French Canadian	48	0.13
German	8,120	21.73
Greek	17	0.05
Hawaii Native/Pacific Islander:	34	0.09
Micronesian: (3)	7	0.02
Guamanian/Chamorro (3)	7	0.02
Polynesian: (9)	18	0.05
Native Hawaiian (8)	15	0.04
Samoan (1)	3	0.01
Other Pac. Isl., specified	5	0.01
Other Pac. Isl., not spec. (2)	4	0.01
Hispanic or Latino:	512	1.36
Central American:	9	0.02
Guatemalan	1	0.00
Honduran	1	0.00
Panamanian	3	0.01
Salvadoran	4	0.01
Cuban	9	0.02
Mexican	311	0.83
Puerto Rican	76	0.20
South American:	8	0.02
Ecuadorian	2	0.01
Peruvian	5	0.01
Other South American	1	0.00
Other Hispanic or Latino	99	0.26
Hungarian	32	0.09
Irish	4,373	11.70
Italian	469	1.26
Norwegian	192	0.51
Pennsylvania German	6	0.02
Polish	234	0.63
Portuguese	45	0.12
Romanian	10	0.03
Russian	56	0.15
Scandinavian	14	0.04
Scotch-Irish	503	1.35
Scottish	544	1.46
Slovak	25	0.07
Swedish	163	0.44
Swiss	107	0.29
Turkish	13	0.03
Ukrainian	28	0.07
United States or American	5,572	14.91
Welsh	249	0.67
West Indian, excl. Hispanic:	7	0.02
Dutch West Indian	7	0.02
White:	34,404	91.49
Not Hispanic (33,622)	34,142	90.80
Hispanic (222)	262	0.70

New Castle

Place Type: City
County: Henry
Population: 17,780

Ancestry/Race	Number	%
African American/Black:	389	2.19
Not Hispanic (327)	387	2.18
Hispanic (2)	2	0.01
Alaska Native tribes, specified:	1	0.01
Alaska Athabascan	1	0.01
Am. Ind. or Alaska Nat., not spec.	46	0.26
American Indian tribes, specified:	63	0.35
Apache (1)	1	0.01
Blackfeet	2	0.01
Cherokee (7)	30	0.17
Chippewa	3	0.02
Comanche	2	0.01
Crow	2	0.01
Iroquois	1	0.01
Latin American Indians	3	0.02
Navajo (1)	3	0.02
Ottawa (2)	2	0.01
Seminole	1	0.01
Shoshone	1	0.01
All other tribes (5)	12	0.07
American Indian tribes, not spec.	4	0.02
Arab:	10	0.06
Lebanese	10	0.06
Asian:	59	0.33
Cambodian	1	0.01
Chinese, ex. Taiwanese (12)	17	0.10
Filipino (3)	6	0.03
Indian (12)	16	0.09
Japanese (1)	3	0.02
Korean (3)	5	0.03
Pakistani (3)	3	0.02
Vietnamese (4)	6	0.03
Other Asian, not specified	2	0.01
British	64	0.36
Croatian	24	0.13
Danish	9	0.05
Dutch	282	1.58
English	1,648	9.25
European	139	0.78
French, except Basque	161	0.90
French Canadian	13	0.07
German	2,081	11.68
Greek	21	0.12
Hawaii Native/Pacific Islander:	10	0.06
Polynesian: (3)	8	0.04
Native Hawaiian	4	0.02
Samoan (3)	3	0.02
Other Polynesian	1	0.01
Other Pac. Isl., not spec.	2	0.01
Hispanic or Latino:	193	1.09
Central American:	4	0.02
Guatemalan	1	0.01

Notes: 1. Figures in the "Number" column do not add up to the total population due to: a) Ancestry/Race overlap — e.g. persons can report being both White and Irish, b) persons of Hispanic origin can report being any race, c) persons reporting two ancestries are counted in both categories. 2. Numbers in parentheses indicate the number of persons reporting this ancestry/race alone, not in combination with any other ancestry/race. 3. Refer to the Explanation of Data in the front of the book for more detailed information.

Ancestry/Race	Number	%
Honduran	2	0.01
Salvadoran	1	0.01
Cuban	9	0.05
Dominican Republic	2	0.01
Mexican	95	0.53
Puerto Rican	23	0.13
South American:	6	0.03
Chilean	3	0.02
Peruvian	1	0.01
Venezuelan	2	0.01
Other Hispanic or Latino	54	0.30
Hungarian	6	0.03
Irish	1,361	7.64
Italian	140	0.79
Norwegian	66	0.37
Polish	91	0.51
Scandinavian	9	0.05
Scotch-Irish	90	0.51
Scottish	352	1.98
Swedish	30	0.17
Swiss	4	0.02
United States or American	3,900	21.90
Welsh	72	0.40
White:	17,283	97.20
Not Hispanic (17,021)	17,156	96.49
Hispanic (114)	127	0.71

New Haven

Place Type: City
County: Allen
Population: 12,406

Ancestry/Race	Number	%
African American/Black:	117	0.94
Not Hispanic (80)	113	0.91
Hispanic (3)	4	0.03
Am. Ind. or Alaska Nat., not spec.	20	0.16
American Indian tribes, specified:	78	0.63
Apache (2)	4	0.03
Blackfeet (2)	4	0.03
Cherokee (7)	35	0.28
Chippewa (1)	6	0.05
Choctaw (1)	1	0.01
Cree	5	0.04
Iroquois (1)	1	0.01
Latin American Indians (1)	1	0.01
Navajo (2)	2	0.02
Ottawa (1)	1	0.01
Pueblo	1	0.01
Sioux (1)	1	0.01
All other tribes (9)	16	0.13
American Indian tribes, not spec.	5	0.04
Arab:	35	0.28
Egyptian	22	0.18
Lebanese	6	0.05
Other Arab	7	0.06
Asian:	63	0.51
Chinese, ex. Taiwanese (9)	12	0.10
Filipino (7)	14	0.11
Indian (13)	16	0.13
Korean (2)	3	0.02
Laotian (4)	5	0.04
Thai	3	0.02
Vietnamese (1)	5	0.04
Other Asian, not specified	5	0.04
Austrian	17	0.14
Belgian	29	0.23
British	73	0.59
Canadian	26	0.21
Czechoslovakian	4	0.03
Danish	9	0.07
Dutch	251	2.03
English	1,261	10.19
European	44	0.36
Finnish	36	0.29
French, except Basque	817	6.60
French Canadian	45	0.36
German	4,658	37.65
Greek	16	0.13
Hawaii Native/Pacific Islander:	9	0.07
Micronesian:	1	0.01
Guamanian/Chamorro	1	0.01
Polynesian: (1)	2	0.02
Native Hawaiian	1	0.01
Samoan (1)	1	0.01
Other Pac. Isl., not spec.	6	0.05
Hispanic or Latino:	242	1.95
Central American:	4	0.03
Honduran	1	0.01
Salvadoran	3	0.02
Cuban	2	0.02
Mexican	159	1.28
Puerto Rican	13	0.10
South American:	4	0.03
Colombian	4	0.03
Other Hispanic or Latino	60	0.48
Hungarian	50	0.40
Iranian	5	0.04
Irish	1,452	11.74
Italian	293	2.37
Macedonian	11	0.09
Norwegian	29	0.23
Pennsylvania German	13	0.11
Polish	321	2.59
Portuguese	13	0.11
Romanian	6	0.05
Scandinavian	4	0.03
Scotch-Irish	118	0.95
Scottish	216	1.75
Slavic	7	0.06
Slovak	22	0.18
Swedish	104	0.84
Swiss	138	1.12
Ukrainian	6	0.05
United States or American	1,381	11.16
Welsh	41	0.33
White:	12,181	98.19
Not Hispanic (11,883)	11,998	96.71
Hispanic (154)	183	1.48
Yugoslavian	5	0.04

Noblesville

Place Type: City
County: Hamilton
Population: 28,590

Ancestry/Race	Number	%
African American/Black:	396	1.39
Not Hispanic (318)	383	1.34
Hispanic (8)	13	0.05
African, sub-Saharan:	20	0.07
African	8	0.03
Nigerian	12	0.04
Am. Ind. or Alaska Nat., not spec.	54	0.19
American Indian tribes, specified:	73	0.26
Blackfeet (2)	3	0.01
Cherokee (10)	33	0.12
Chippewa (9)	11	0.04
Choctaw (1)	1	0.00
Comanche	2	0.01
Creek (7)	7	0.02
Crow (1)	1	0.00
Iroquois	2	0.01
Latin American Indians (1)	1	0.00
Osage (1)	1	0.00
Sioux (1)	3	0.01
All other tribes (7)	8	0.03
American Indian tribes, not spec.	11	0.04
Arab:	167	0.58
Arab/Arabic	9	0.03
Jordanian	14	0.05
Lebanese	62	0.21
Palestinian	46	0.16
Syrian	36	0.12
Armenian	24	0.08
Asian:	315	1.10
Chinese, ex. Taiwanese (32)	40	0.14
Filipino (38)	58	0.20
Hmong (12)	12	0.04
Indian (53)	55	0.19
Indonesian (1)	1	0.00
Japanese (25)	46	0.16
Korean (20)	41	0.14
Laotian (2)	8	0.03
Malaysian (1)	1	0.00
Pakistani (1)	1	0.00
Thai (1)	1	0.00
Vietnamese (18)	26	0.09
Other Asian, specified (1)	2	0.01
Other Asian, not specified (21)	23	0.08
Australian	52	0.18
Austrian	31	0.11
Basque	12	0.04
Belgian	24	0.08
British	318	1.10
Canadian	113	0.39
Croatian	38	0.13
Czech	94	0.32
Czechoslovakian	54	0.19
Danish	118	0.41
Dutch	580	2.00
English	3,883	13.41
European	275	0.95
Finnish	13	0.04
French, except Basque	756	2.61
French Canadian	79	0.27
German	8,061	27.84
Greek	69	0.24
Hawaii Native/Pacific Islander:	31	0.11
Micronesian: (1)	6	0.02
Guamanian/Chamorro	5	0.02
Other Micronesian (1)	1	0.00
Polynesian: (14)	24	0.08
Native Hawaiian (10)	15	0.05
Samoan (4)	9	0.03
Other Pac. Isl., specified	1	0.00
Hispanic or Latino:	398	1.39
Central American:	6	0.02
Guatemalan	1	0.00
Honduran	2	0.01
Nicaraguan	2	0.01
Panamanian	1	0.00
Cuban	31	0.11
Mexican	247	0.86
Puerto Rican	27	0.09
South American:	17	0.06
Bolivian	1	0.00
Colombian	13	0.05
Peruvian	2	0.01
Venezuelan	1	0.00
Other Hispanic or Latino	70	0.24
Hungarian	217	0.75
Irish	3,986	13.77
Italian	1,020	3.52
Lithuanian	29	0.10
Macedonian	31	0.11
Norwegian	262	0.90
Polish	641	2.21
Portuguese	7	0.02
Romanian	48	0.17
Russian	83	0.29
Scandinavian	63	0.22
Scotch-Irish	375	1.30
Scottish	865	2.99
Serbian	25	0.09
Slavic	10	0.03
Slovak	56	0.19
Slovene	19	0.07
Swedish	362	1.25
Swiss	93	0.32
Ukrainian	16	0.06
United States or American	3,209	11.08
Welsh	248	0.86
West Indian, excl. Hispanic:	8	0.03
Jamaican	8	0.03
White:	27,779	97.16
Not Hispanic (27,350)	27,548	96.36
Hispanic (195)	231	0.81

Notes: 1. Figures in the "Number" column do not add up to the total population due to: a) Ancestry/Race overlap — e.g. persons can report being both White and Irish, b) persons of Hispanic origin can report being any race, c) persons reporting two ancestries are counted in both categories. 2. Numbers in parentheses indicate the number of persons reporting this ancestry/race alone, not in combination with any other ancestry/race. 3. Refer to the Explanation of Data in the front of the book for more detailed information.

Peru

Place Type: City
County: Miami
Population: 12,994

Ancestry/Race	Number	%
African American/Black:	439	3.38
Not Hispanic (379)	435	3.35
Hispanic (4)	4	0.03
African, sub-Saharan:	23	0.18
African	23	0.18
Am. Ind. or Alaska Nat., not spec.	48	0.37
American Indian tribes, specified:	261	2.01
Apache (1)	6	0.05
Blackfeet	12	0.09
Cherokee (6)	33	0.25
Cheyenne	1	0.01
Chickasaw	1	0.01
Chippewa (1)	5	0.04
Choctaw (3)	3	0.02
Delaware	1	0.01
Latin American Indians (1)	1	0.01
Navajo	1	0.01
Paiute	1	0.01
Potawatomi (1)	1	0.01
Pueblo (4)	4	0.03
Shoshone (1)	2	0.02
Sioux (1)	4	0.03
Ute (1)	1	0.01
All other tribes (142)	184	1.42
American Indian tribes, not spec.	23	0.18
Arab:	6	0.05
Egyptian	6	0.05
Asian:	91	0.70
Chinese, ex. Taiwanese (13)	14	0.11
Filipino (13)	18	0.14
Indian (13)	14	0.11
Japanese (5)	16	0.12
Korean (5)	9	0.07
Taiwanese (1)	1	0.01
Thai (4)	7	0.05
Vietnamese	1	0.01
Other Asian, not specified (2)	11	0.08
Austrian	13	0.10
Brazilian	23	0.18
British	76	0.59
Celtic	6	0.05
Czech	14	0.11
Czechoslovakian	5	0.04
Danish	14	0.11
Dutch	326	2.53
English	999	7.77
European	46	0.36
French, except Basque	313	2.43
French Canadian	23	0.18
German	2,688	20.90
Hawaii Native/Pacific Islander:	3	0.02
Polynesian: (1)	3	0.02
Native Hawaiian (1)	3	0.02
Hispanic or Latino:	172	1.32
Central American:	6	0.05
Costa Rican	1	0.01
Guatemalan	1	0.01
Honduran	3	0.02
Salvadoran	1	0.01
Cuban	7	0.05
Mexican	107	0.82
Puerto Rican	18	0.14
South American:	1	0.01
Peruvian	1	0.01
Other Hispanic or Latino	33	0.25
Hungarian	26	0.20
Irish	1,508	11.72
Italian	297	2.31
Lithuanian	20	0.16
Norwegian	55	0.43
Pennsylvania German	13	0.10
Polish	237	1.84
Portuguese	5	0.04
Russian	10	0.08
Scotch-Irish	177	1.38
Scottish	177	1.38
Slovene	9	0.07
Swedish	13	0.10
Swiss	17	0.13
Ukrainian	9	0.07
United States or American	1,693	13.16
Welsh	75	0.58
West Indian, excl. Hispanic:	16	0.12
West Indian	16	0.12
White:	12,268	94.41
Not Hispanic (11,972)	12,172	93.67
Hispanic (75)	96	0.74

Plainfield

Place Type: Town
County: Hendricks
Population: 18,396

Ancestry/Race	Number	%
African American/Black:	455	2.47
Not Hispanic (403)	445	2.42
Hispanic (7)	10	0.05
African, sub-Saharan:	58	0.31
African	58	0.31
Am. Ind. or Alaska Nat., not spec.	55	0.30
American Indian tribes, specified:	93	0.51
Apache (2)	2	0.01
Blackfeet (3)	5	0.03
Cherokee (9)	42	0.23
Chickasaw	3	0.02
Chippewa (4)	4	0.02
Choctaw (2)	3	0.02
Creek (1)	1	0.01
Delaware (1)	1	0.01
Iroquois	1	0.01
Latin American Indians (1)	1	0.01
Menominee (4)	4	0.02
Pima (3)	3	0.02
Potawatomi	5	0.03
Sioux	2	0.01
Ute (2)	2	0.01
All other tribes (9)	13	0.07
American Indian tribes, not spec.	5	0.03
Arab:	14	0.07
Moroccan	14	0.07
Asian:	218	1.19
Chinese, ex. Taiwanese (18)	24	0.13
Filipino (22)	42	0.23
Indian (63)	70	0.38
Indonesian (2)	2	0.01
Japanese (3)	5	0.03
Korean (9)	20	0.11
Laotian (3)	3	0.02
Pakistani (33)	33	0.18
Sri Lankan (3)	3	0.02
Thai (3)	4	0.02
Vietnamese (6)	7	0.04
Other Asian, not specified (2)	5	0.03
Australian	16	0.08
Austrian	37	0.20
Belgian	75	0.40
British	10	0.05
Canadian	59	0.31
Czech	15	0.08
Dutch	576	3.05
English	2,238	11.85
European	87	0.46
Finnish	54	0.29
French, except Basque	430	2.28
French Canadian	56	0.30
German	4,474	23.69
Greek	57	0.30
Hawaii Native/Pacific Islander:	8	0.04
Micronesian:	1	0.01
Guamanian/Chamorro	1	0.01
Polynesian: (1)	5	0.03
Native Hawaiian (1)	4	0.02
Samoan	1	0.01
Other Pac. Isl., not spec. (2)	2	0.01
Hispanic or Latino:	251	1.36
Central American:	8	0.04
Costa Rican	2	0.01
Guatemalan	3	0.02
Salvadoran	3	0.02
Cuban	11	0.06
Mexican	153	0.83
Puerto Rican	24	0.13
South American:	4	0.02
Colombian	2	0.01
Venezuelan	2	0.01
Other Hispanic or Latino	51	0.28
Hungarian	64	0.34
Irish	2,259	11.96
Italian	252	1.33
Lithuanian	8	0.04
Northern European	11	0.06
Norwegian	85	0.45
Polish	404	2.14
Portuguese	30	0.16
Russian	21	0.11
Scotch-Irish	253	1.34
Scottish	368	1.95
Serbian	37	0.20
Slovene	63	0.33
Swedish	51	0.27
Swiss	37	0.20
Ukrainian	7	0.04
United States or American	3,248	17.20
Welsh	135	0.71
White:	17,677	96.09
Not Hispanic (17,351)	17,500	95.13
Hispanic (145)	177	0.96
Yugoslavian	9	0.05

Portage

Place Type: City
County: Porter
Population: 33,496

Ancestry/Race	Number	%
African American/Black:	601	1.79
Not Hispanic (468)	545	1.63
Hispanic (17)	56	0.17
African, sub-Saharan:	41	0.12
African	41	0.12
Alaska Native tribes, specified:	2	0.01
Eskimo	2	0.01
Am. Ind. or Alaska Nat., not spec.	95	0.28
American Indian tribes, specified:	148	0.44
Apache (4)	10	0.03
Blackfeet	7	0.02
Cherokee (19)	77	0.23
Chippewa (5)	12	0.04
Choctaw (2)	2	0.01
Creek	1	0.00
Iroquois (1)	2	0.01
Latin American Indians (10)	12	0.04
Lumbee	2	0.01
Navajo	1	0.00
Ottawa	1	0.00
Potawatomi (1)	4	0.01
Pueblo (1)	1	0.00
Sioux (3)	7	0.02
Tohono O'Odham (1)	1	0.00
All other tribes (4)	8	0.02
American Indian tribes, not spec.	23	0.07
Arab:	136	0.41
Arab/Arabic	23	0.07
Lebanese	55	0.16
Palestinian	50	0.15
Syrian	8	0.02
Asian:	304	0.91
Chinese, ex. Taiwanese (31)	38	0.11
Filipino (54)	81	0.24
Indian (50)	63	0.19
Japanese (8)	17	0.05

Notes: 1. Figures in the "Number" column do not add up to the total population due to: a) Ancestry/Race overlap — e.g. persons can report being both White and Irish, b) persons of Hispanic origin can report being any race, c) persons reporting two ancestries are counted in both categories. 2. Numbers in parentheses indicate the number of persons reporting this ancestry/race alone, not in combination with any other ancestry/race. 3. Refer to the Explanation of Data in the front of the book for more detailed information.

Korean (20)	38	0.11
Pakistani (15)	16	0.05
Thai (9)	12	0.04
Vietnamese (21)	28	0.08
Other Asian, not specified (4)	11	0.03
Australian	10	0.03
Austrian	59	0.18
Belgian	38	0.11
Brazilian	9	0.03
British	78	0.23
Bulgarian	9	0.03
Canadian	52	0.16
Croatian	445	1.33
Czech	294	0.88
Czechoslovakian	131	0.39
Danish	86	0.26
Dutch	723	2.16
English	2,959	8.82
European	109	0.32
Finnish	75	0.22
French, except Basque	845	2.52
French Canadian	216	0.64
German	7,390	22.03
Greek	379	1.13
Hawaii Native/Pacific Islander:	48	0.14
Micronesian: (8)	9	0.03
Guamanian/Chamorro (8)	9	0.03
Polynesian: (6)	17	0.05
Native Hawaiian (1)	9	0.03
Samoan (5)	8	0.02
Other Pac. Isl., not spec. (5)	22	0.07
Hispanic or Latino:	3,330	9.94
Central American:	19	0.06
Guatemalan	2	0.01
Honduran	1	0.00
Nicaraguan	9	0.03
Panamanian	13	0.04
Salvadoran	2	0.01
Cuban	17	0.05
Dominican Republic	7	0.02
Mexican	1,915	5.72
Puerto Rican	987	2.95
South American:	16	0.05
Argentinean	5	0.01
Bolivian	1	0.00
Chilean	1	0.00
Colombian	3	0.01
Ecuadorian	1	0.00
Peruvian	3	0.01
Venezuelan	1	0.00
Other South American	1	0.00
Other Hispanic or Latino	369	1.10
Hungarian	301	0.90
Icelander	9	0.03
Irish	5,132	15.30
Italian	1,379	4.11
Lithuanian	280	0.83
Luxemburger	37	0.11
Macedonian	107	0.32
Norwegian	208	0.62
Pennsylvania German	66	0.20
Polish	2,875	8.57
Portuguese	29	0.09
Romanian	90	0.27
Russian	220	0.66
Scandinavian	46	0.14
Scotch-Irish	704	2.10
Scottish	510	1.52
Serbian	231	0.69
Slavic	44	0.13
Slovak	727	2.17
Slovene	15	0.04
Swedish	883	2.63
Swiss	28	0.08
Turkish	12	0.04
Ukrainian	74	0.22
United States or American	2,148	6.40
Welsh	264	0.79
White:	31,557	94.21
Not Hispanic (29,041)	29,367	87.67
Hispanic (1,951)	2,190	6.54
Yugoslavian	69	0.21

Richmond

Place Type: City
County: Wayne
Population: 39,124

Ancestry/Race	Number	%
African American/Black:	3,974	10.16
Not Hispanic (3,444)	3,934	10.06
Hispanic (25)	40	0.10
African, sub-Saharan:	157	0.40
African	140	0.36
Kenyan	8	0.02
Nigerian	9	0.02
Alaska Native tribes, specified:	3	0.01
Alaska Athabascan (2)	2	0.01
Eskimo	1	0.00
Am. Ind. or Alaska Nat., not spec.	118	0.30
American Indian tribes, specified:	198	0.51
Apache	4	0.01
Blackfeet (1)	11	0.03
Cherokee (21)	106	0.27
Cheyenne (1)	1	0.00
Chippewa (5)	7	0.02
Choctaw (4)	14	0.04
Cree	1	0.00
Creek (3)	4	0.01
Houma	1	0.00
Iroquois	8	0.02
Latin American Indians (2)	4	0.01
Lumbee	1	0.00
Navajo (3)	6	0.02
Seminole (2)	2	0.01
Shoshone	1	0.00
Sioux (8)	11	0.03
All other tribes (1)	16	0.04
American Indian tribes, not spec.	21	0.05
Arab:	39	0.10
Egyptian	7	0.02
Lebanese	19	0.05
Palestinian	7	0.02
Syrian	6	0.02
Asian:	417	1.07
Cambodian (3)	3	0.01
Chinese, ex. Taiwanese (38)	49	0.13
Filipino (56)	84	0.21
Indian (95)	108	0.28
Japanese (48)	72	0.18
Korean (24)	30	0.08
Laotian (8)	10	0.03
Pakistani (1)	1	0.00
Thai	1	0.00
Vietnamese (30)	32	0.08
Other Asian, specified (2)	5	0.01
Other Asian, not specified (3)	22	0.06
Austrian	48	0.12
Belgian	27	0.07
British	209	0.53
Canadian	30	0.08
Czech	28	0.07
Czechoslovakian	4	0.01
Danish	49	0.13
Dutch	769	1.96
Eastern European	7	0.02
English	3,408	8.71
European	661	1.69
Finnish	11	0.03
French, except Basque	620	1.58
French Canadian	78	0.20
German	7,009	17.91
Greek	42	0.11
Hawaii Native/Pacific Islander:	46	0.12
Micronesian: (4)	10	0.03
Guamanian/Chamorro (4)	5	0.01
Other Micronesian	5	0.01
Polynesian: (16)	29	0.07
Native Hawaiian (9)	21	0.05
Samoan (7)	8	0.02
Other Pac. Isl., specified	2	0.01
Other Pac. Isl., not spec. (2)	5	0.01
Hispanic or Latino:	796	2.03
Central American:	18	0.05
Costa Rican	3	0.01
Guatemalan	2	0.01
Honduran	3	0.01
Panamanian	2	0.01
Salvadoran	8	0.02
Cuban	13	0.03
Dominican Republic	5	0.01
Mexican	552	1.41
Puerto Rican	63	0.16
South American:	41	0.10
Bolivian	3	0.01
Colombian	13	0.03
Ecuadorian	10	0.03
Peruvian	14	0.04
Other South American	1	0.00
Other Hispanic or Latino	104	0.27
Hungarian	266	0.68
Irish	3,954	10.10
Italian	971	2.48
Latvian	10	0.03
Lithuanian	15	0.04
Maltese	8	0.02
Northern European	14	0.04
Norwegian	161	0.41
Pennsylvania German	56	0.14
Polish	294	0.75
Portuguese	32	0.08
Romanian	29	0.07
Russian	52	0.13
Scandinavian	29	0.07
Scotch-Irish	374	0.96
Scottish	555	1.42
Slovak	39	0.10
Swedish	180	0.46
Swiss	46	0.12
Ukrainian	62	0.16
United States or American	5,323	13.60
Welsh	209	0.53
West Indian, excl. Hispanic:	10	0.03
Barbadian	7	0.02
Jamaican	3	0.01
White:	34,725	88.76
Not Hispanic (33,588)	34,298	87.66
Hispanic (363)	427	1.09

Schererville

Place Type: Town
County: Lake
Population: 24,851

Ancestry/Race	Number	%
African American/Black:	582	2.34
Not Hispanic (520)	559	2.25
Hispanic (13)	23	0.09
African, sub-Saharan:	59	0.24
African	24	0.10
Nigerian	15	0.06
South African	13	0.05
Other sub-Saharan African	7	0.03
Alaska Native tribes, specified:	2	0.01
Alaska Athabascan (1)	1	0.00
Tlingit-Haida (1)	1	0.00
Am. Ind. or Alaska Nat., not spec.	22	0.09
American Indian tribes, specified:	67	0.27
Apache (1)	2	0.01
Blackfeet (1)	4	0.02
Cherokee (1)	24	0.10
Chippewa (2)	3	0.01
Choctaw (2)	8	0.03
Creek	3	0.01
Iroquois (2)	4	0.02
Latin American Indians (1)	3	0.01
Navajo (5)	6	0.02
Potawatomi	1	0.00

Notes: 1. Figures in the "Number" column do not add up to the total population due to: a) Ancestry/Race overlap — e.g. persons can report being both White and Irish, b) persons of Hispanic origin can report being any race, c) persons reporting two ancestries are counted in both categories. 2. Numbers in parentheses indicate the number of persons reporting this ancestry/race alone, not in combination with any other ancestry/race. 3. Refer to the Explanation of Data in the front of the book for more detailed information.

Pueblo (1)	1	0.00
Sioux	8	0.03
American Indian tribes, not spec.	3	0.01
Arab:	41	0.17
Lebanese	30	0.12
Palestinian	11	0.04
Armenian	12	0.05
Asian:	742	2.99
Cambodian (3)	3	0.01
Chinese, ex. Taiwanese (36)	49	0.20
Filipino (103)	130	0.52
Indian (295)	312	1.26
Indonesian (1)	1	0.00
Japanese (10)	17	0.07
Korean (78)	95	0.38
Laotian (2)	2	0.01
Malaysian	1	0.00
Pakistani (32)	35	0.14
Taiwanese	5	0.02
Thai (7)	9	0.04
Vietnamese (40)	46	0.19
Other Asian, not specified (18)	37	0.15
Assyrian/Chaldean/Syriac	7	0.03
Austrian	126	0.51
Belgian	35	0.14
Brazilian	24	0.10
British	42	0.17
Bulgarian	31	0.12
Canadian	37	0.15
Croatian	683	2.75
Czech	211	0.85
Czechoslovakian	88	0.35
Danish	91	0.37
Dutch	1,445	5.82
English	1,680	6.77
European	95	0.38
Finnish	52	0.21
French, except Basque	581	2.34
French Canadian	196	0.79
German	5,697	22.95
Greek	418	1.68
Hawaii Native/Pacific Islander:	13	0.05
Polynesian: (11)	11	0.04
Native Hawaiian (2)	2	0.01
Samoan (9)	9	0.04
Other Pac. Isl., not spec.	2	0.01
Hispanic or Latino:	1,576	6.34
Central American:	10	0.04
Guatemalan	2	0.01
Honduran	4	0.02
Nicaraguan	1	0.00
Salvadoran	3	0.01
Cuban	10	0.04
Mexican	1,200	4.83
Puerto Rican	171	0.69
South American:	25	0.10
Argentinean	4	0.02
Bolivian	1	0.00
Chilean	2	0.01
Colombian	3	0.01
Ecuadorian	4	0.02
Peruvian	7	0.03
Other South American	4	0.02
Other Hispanic or Latino	160	0.64
Hungarian	694	2.80
Irish	3,744	15.08
Italian	1,557	6.27
Latvian	8	0.03
Lithuanian	256	1.03
Luxemburger	8	0.03
Macedonian	384	1.55
Norwegian	373	1.50
Pennsylvania German	26	0.10
Polish	4,296	17.31
Portuguese	6	0.02
Romanian	181	0.73
Russian	259	1.04
Scandinavian	30	0.12
Scotch-Irish	260	1.05
Scottish	271	1.09
Serbian	1,137	4.58
Slavic	14	0.06
Slovak	775	3.12
Slovene	19	0.08
Swedish	700	2.82
Swiss	24	0.10
Ukrainian	160	0.64
United States or American	1,007	4.06
Welsh	165	0.66
White:	23,103	92.97
Not Hispanic (21,752)	22,044	88.70
Hispanic (974)	1,059	4.26
Yugoslavian	40	0.16

Seymour

Place Type: City
County: Jackson
Population: 18,101

Ancestry/Race	Number	%
African American/Black:	233	1.29
Not Hispanic (174)	219	1.21
Hispanic (10)	14	0.08
African, sub-Saharan:	15	0.08
African	8	0.04
Ethiopian	7	0.04
Alaska Native tribes, specified:	3	0.02
Alaska Athabascan (2)	2	0.01
Aleut	1	0.01
Alaska Native tribes, not specified	1	0.01
Am. Ind. or Alaska Nat., not spec.	41	0.23
American Indian tribes, specified:	57	0.31
Apache (1)	3	0.02
Blackfeet (1)	3	0.02
Cherokee (15)	29	0.16
Chippewa	1	0.01
Choctaw (1)	1	0.01
Crow	4	0.02
Iroquois (3)	3	0.02
Potawatomi (3)	3	0.02
Sioux (2)	3	0.02
Ute (1)	1	0.01
All other tribes (1)	6	0.03
American Indian tribes, not spec.	7	0.04
Asian:	289	1.60
Chinese, ex. Taiwanese (8)	14	0.08
Filipino (14)	28	0.15
Indian (9)	9	0.05
Japanese (166)	168	0.93
Korean (9)	12	0.07
Malaysian	1	0.01
Pakistani (4)	4	0.02
Taiwanese (1)	4	0.02
Thai (3)	4	0.02
Vietnamese (38)	40	0.22
Other Asian, not specified (4)	5	0.03
Australian	7	0.04
Austrian	5	0.03
British	53	0.29
Canadian	44	0.24
Celtic	14	0.08
Croatian	15	0.08
Czech	30	0.17
Czechoslovakian	13	0.07
Danish	18	0.10
Dutch	402	2.23
English	1,134	6.30
European	59	0.33
Finnish	24	0.13
French, except Basque	527	2.93
French Canadian	48	0.27
German	4,300	23.88
Greek	53	0.29
Hawaii Native/Pacific Islander:	15	0.08
Micronesian: (4)	4	0.02
Guamanian/Chamorro (4)	4	0.02
Polynesian: (5)	11	0.06
Native Hawaiian	6	0.03
Samoan (5)	5	0.03
Hispanic or Latino:	877	4.85
Central American:	30	0.17
Costa Rican	1	0.01
Guatemalan	3	0.02
Honduran	22	0.12
Panamanian	4	0.02
Cuban	10	0.06
Dominican Republic	2	0.01
Mexican	721	3.98
Puerto Rican	17	0.09
South American:	4	0.02
Argentinean	3	0.02
Peruvian	1	0.01
Other Hispanic or Latino	93	0.51
Hungarian	21	0.12
Irish	1,599	8.88
Italian	265	1.47
Lithuanian	12	0.07
Northern European	15	0.08
Norwegian	104	0.58
Pennsylvania German	7	0.04
Polish	137	0.76
Russian	6	0.03
Scandinavian	9	0.05
Scotch-Irish	227	1.26
Scottish	178	0.99
Slovak	64	0.36
Swedish	17	0.09
Swiss	11	0.06
United States or American	3,612	20.06
Welsh	46	0.26
White:	17,056	94.23
Not Hispanic (16,608)	16,726	92.40
Hispanic (299)	330	1.82

Shelbyville

Place Type: City
County: Shelby
Population: 17,951

Ancestry/Race	Number	%
African American/Black:	333	1.86
Not Hispanic (279)	326	1.82
Hispanic (4)	7	0.04
African, sub-Saharan:	48	0.27
African	48	0.27
Alaska Native tribes, specified:	6	0.03
Eskimo (2)	6	0.03
Am. Ind. or Alaska Nat., not spec.	22	0.12
American Indian tribes, specified:	68	0.38
Apache (1)	3	0.02
Blackfeet	2	0.01
Cherokee (7)	28	0.16
Cheyenne	1	0.01
Chippewa (1)	1	0.01
Creek (1)	2	0.01
Iroquois	5	0.03
Latin American Indians	15	0.08
Menominee (1)	1	0.01
Pueblo	2	0.01
Puget Sound Salish (1)	1	0.01
Sioux (1)	4	0.02
All other tribes (1)	3	0.02
American Indian tribes, not spec.	2	0.01
Asian:	234	1.30
Chinese, ex. Taiwanese (22)	22	0.12
Filipino (14)	21	0.12
Indian (14)	15	0.08
Japanese (139)	142	0.79
Korean (16)	26	0.14
Malaysian (1)	1	0.01
Vietnamese (2)	2	0.01
Other Asian, specified	2	0.01
Other Asian, not specified	3	0.02
Australian	13	0.07
Belgian	12	0.07
British	18	0.10
Celtic	7	0.04
Czechoslovakian	13	0.07

Notes: 1. Figures in the "Number" column do not add up to the total population due to: a) Ancestry/Race overlap — e.g. persons can report being both White and Irish, b) persons of Hispanic origin can report being any race, c) persons reporting two ancestries are counted in both categories. 2. Numbers in parentheses indicate the number of persons reporting this ancestry/race alone, not in combination with any other ancestry/race. 3. Refer to the Explanation of Data in the front of the book for more detailed information.

Danish	39	0.22
Dutch	426	2.41
English	1,122	6.34
European	78	0.44
French, except Basque	504	2.85
French Canadian	16	0.09
German	4,516	25.52
Greek	9	0.05
Hawaii Native/Pacific Islander:	13	0.07
Polynesian: (4)	11	0.06
Samoan (4)	11	0.06
Other Pac. Isl., specified	2	0.01
Hispanic or Latino:	343	1.91
Central American:	7	0.04
Guatemalan	7	0.04
Cuban	2	0.01
Dominican Republic	6	0.03
Mexican	258	1.44
Puerto Rican	11	0.06
South American:	10	0.06
Peruvian	7	0.04
Venezuelan	1	0.01
Other South American	2	0.01
Other Hispanic or Latino	49	0.27
Irish	1,892	10.69
Italian	101	0.57
Norwegian	18	0.10
Pennsylvania German	6	0.03
Polish	43	0.24
Portuguese	8	0.05
Scandinavian	6	0.03
Scotch-Irish	221	1.25
Scottish	239	1.35
Slovak	9	0.05
Slovene	6	0.03
Swedish	108	0.61
Swiss	48	0.27
United States or American	4,092	23.13
Welsh	80	0.45
White:	17,244	96.06
Not Hispanic (16,946)	17,071	95.10
Hispanic (158)	173	0.96

South Bend

Place Type: City
County: Saint Joseph
Population: 107,789

Ancestry/Race	Number	%
Acadian/Cajun	23	0.02
African American/Black:	28,114	26.08
Not Hispanic (26,259)	27,670	25.67
Hispanic (263)	444	0.41
African, sub-Saharan:	1,284	1.20
African	994	0.93
Ghanian	8	0.01
Kenyan	84	0.08
Liberian	46	0.04
Nigerian	11	0.01
South African	15	0.01
Zimbabwean	14	0.01
Other sub-Saharan African	112	0.10
Alaska Native tribes, specified:	5	0.00
Alaska Athabascan (3)	4	0.00
Eskimo	1	0.00
Am. Ind. or Alaska Nat., not spec.	394	0.37
Alsatian	2	0.00
American Indian tribes, specified:	736	0.68
Apache (4)	15	0.01
Blackfeet (7)	47	0.04
Cherokee (63)	274	0.25
Cheyenne	1	0.00
Chickasaw (3)	7	0.01
Chippewa (10)	28	0.03
Choctaw (6)	43	0.04
Comanche (1)	2	0.00
Cree	5	0.00
Creek	6	0.01
Crow	1	0.00
Delaware	1	0.00
Iroquois (4)	9	0.01
Kiowa	3	0.00
Latin American Indians (17)	36	0.03
Lumbee (3)	5	0.00
Menominee (7)	7	0.01
Navajo	1	0.00
Osage	1	0.00
Ottawa (1)	2	0.00
Paiute (1)	3	0.00
Pima	2	0.00
Potawatomi (54)	95	0.09
Pueblo	3	0.00
Seminole	12	0.01
Shoshone	1	0.00
Sioux (8)	24	0.02
Tohono O'Odham (1)	1	0.00
Ute	4	0.00
Yaqui	2	0.00
All other tribes (53)	95	0.09
American Indian tribes, not spec.	56	0.05
Arab:	377	0.35
Arab/Arabic	62	0.06
Egyptian	15	0.01
Iraqi	7	0.01
Jordanian	27	0.03
Lebanese	147	0.14
Palestinian	5	0.00
Syrian	30	0.03
Other Arab	84	0.08
Armenian	7	0.01
Asian:	1,722	1.60
Bangladeshi (1)	1	0.00
Cambodian (71)	88	0.08
Chinese, ex. Taiwanese (263)	322	0.30
Filipino (148)	231	0.21
Indian (251)	326	0.30
Indonesian (6)	19	0.02
Japanese (50)	98	0.09
Korean (89)	116	0.11
Laotian (51)	54	0.05
Malaysian (21)	39	0.04
Pakistani (5)	9	0.01
Sri Lankan (2)	3	0.00
Taiwanese (6)	16	0.01
Thai (21)	29	0.03
Vietnamese (241)	262	0.24
Other Asian, specified (6)	7	0.01
Other Asian, not specified (43)	102	0.09
Australian	27	0.03
Austrian	416	0.39
Belgian	1,423	1.33
Brazilian	31	0.03
British	396	0.37
Bulgarian	57	0.05
Canadian	251	0.23
Celtic	20	0.02
Croatian	210	0.20
Czech	180	0.17
Czechoslovakian	101	0.09
Danish	230	0.21
Dutch	1,933	1.81
Eastern European	104	0.10
English	6,274	5.86
European	542	0.51
Finnish	125	0.12
French, except Basque	2,288	2.14
French Canadian	542	0.51
German	18,800	17.56
Greek	347	0.32
Hawaii Native/Pacific Islander:	171	0.16
Micronesian: (16)	30	0.03
Guamanian/Chamorro (15)	29	0.03
Other Micronesian (1)	1	0.00
Polynesian: (39)	88	0.08
Native Hawaiian (19)	45	0.04
Samoan (14)	34	0.03
Tongan (5)	7	0.01
Other Polynesian (1)	2	0.00
Other Pac. Isl., not spec. (10)	53	0.05
Hispanic or Latino:	9,110	8.45
Central American:	165	0.15
Costa Rican	12	0.01
Guatemalan	26	0.02
Honduran	17	0.02
Nicaraguan	15	0.01
Panamanian	18	0.02
Salvadoran	66	0.06
Other Central American	11	0.01
Cuban	76	0.07
Dominican Republic	22	0.02
Mexican	7,063	6.55
Puerto Rican	322	0.30
South American:	187	0.17
Argentinean	24	0.02
Bolivian	6	0.01
Chilean	19	0.02
Colombian	42	0.04
Ecuadorian	6	0.01
Paraguayan	6	0.01
Peruvian	23	0.02
Uruguayan	3	0.00
Venezuelan	54	0.05
Other South American	4	0.00
Other Hispanic or Latino	1,275	1.18
Hungarian	3,605	3.37
Iranian	28	0.03
Irish	11,246	10.51
Italian	3,400	3.18
Latvian	20	0.02
Lithuanian	215	0.20
Macedonian	7	0.01
Maltese	18	0.02
Northern European	43	0.04
Norwegian	653	0.61
Pennsylvania German	91	0.09
Polish	11,417	10.67
Portuguese	97	0.09
Romanian	35	0.03
Russian	402	0.38
Scandinavian	108	0.10
Scotch-Irish	1,305	1.22
Scottish	1,224	1.14
Serbian	217	0.20
Slavic	151	0.14
Slovak	159	0.15
Slovene	24	0.02
Swedish	1,364	1.27
Swiss	414	0.39
Turkish	13	0.01
Ukrainian	196	0.18
United States or American	4,194	3.92
Welsh	468	0.44
West Indian, excl. Hispanic:	102	0.10
Bermudan	6	0.01
Jamaican	85	0.08
Trinidadian and Tobagonian	4	0.00
West Indian	7	0.01
White:	73,709	68.38
Not Hispanic (68,202)	70,206	65.13
Hispanic (2,993)	3,503	3.25
Yugoslavian	224	0.21

Speedway

Place Type: Town
County: Marion
Population: 12,881

Ancestry/Race	Number	%
African American/Black:	1,643	12.76
Not Hispanic (1,525)	1,630	12.65
Hispanic (6)	13	0.10
African, sub-Saharan:	31	0.24
African	22	0.17
Ethiopian	9	0.07
Am. Ind. or Alaska Nat., not spec.	18	0.14
American Indian tribes, specified:	51	0.40
Apache (1)	1	0.01
Blackfeet (1)	7	0.05

Notes: 1. Figures in the "Number" column do not add up to the total population due to: a) Ancestry/Race overlap — e.g. persons can report being both White and Irish, b) persons of Hispanic origin can report being any race, c) persons reporting two ancestries are counted in both categories. 2. Numbers in parentheses indicate the number of persons reporting this ancestry/race alone, not in combination with any other ancestry/race. 3. Refer to the Explanation of Data in the front of the book for more detailed information.

Ancestry/Race	Number	%
Cherokee (11)	25	0.19
Chippewa (1)	1	0.01
Colville (2)	2	0.02
Creek	1	0.01
Latin American Indians (1)	1	0.01
Navajo (2)	2	0.02
Osage	1	0.01
Pima	1	0.01
Potawatomi (1)	2	0.02
Sioux (1)	3	0.02
All other tribes (3)	4	0.03
American Indian tribes, not spec.	10	0.08
Arab:	57	0.44
Arab/Arabic	14	0.11
Egyptian	34	0.26
Lebanese	9	0.07
Armenian	16	0.12
Asian:	289	2.24
Chinese, ex. Taiwanese (14)	24	0.19
Filipino (23)	31	0.24
Hmong	1	0.01
Indian (82)	92	0.71
Japanese (8)	18	0.14
Korean (15)	21	0.16
Malaysian (17)	31	0.24
Pakistani (7)	15	0.12
Sri Lankan (1)	1	0.01
Thai (5)	6	0.05
Vietnamese (18)	20	0.16
Other Asian, specified (4)	10	0.08
Other Asian, not specified (9)	19	0.15
Belgian	24	0.19
British	117	0.91
Croatian	9	0.07
Danish	27	0.21
Dutch	278	2.16
Eastern European	11	0.09
English	1,468	11.42
European	71	0.55
Finnish	11	0.09
French, except Basque	417	3.24
French Canadian	97	0.75
German	2,919	22.71
Greek	49	0.38
Hawaii Native/Pacific Islander:	12	0.09
Micronesian: (1)	1	0.01
Guamanian/Chamorro (1)	1	0.01
Polynesian: (1)	9	0.07
Native Hawaiian	8	0.06
Samoan (1)	1	0.01
Other Pac. Isl., specified	1	0.01
Other Pac. Isl., not spec.	1	0.01
Hispanic or Latino:	339	2.63
Central American:	37	0.29
Guatemalan	7	0.05
Honduran	21	0.16
Nicaraguan	1	0.01
Panamanian	2	0.02
Salvadoran	6	0.05
Cuban	3	0.02
Dominican Republic	3	0.02
Mexican	208	1.61
Puerto Rican	26	0.20
South American:	18	0.14
Colombian	6	0.05
Peruvian	2	0.02
Venezuelan	10	0.08
Other Hispanic or Latino	44	0.34
Hungarian	46	0.36
Irish	1,639	12.75
Italian	293	2.28
Lithuanian	23	0.18
Macedonian	33	0.26
Northern European	18	0.14
Norwegian	33	0.26
Polish	161	1.25
Portuguese	20	0.16
Romanian	18	0.14
Russian	5	0.04
Scandinavian	5	0.04
Scotch-Irish	164	1.28
Scottish	262	2.04
Serbian	39	0.30
Slavic	9	0.07
Slovak	59	0.46
Slovene	59	0.46
Swedish	110	0.86
Swiss	71	0.55
Ukrainian	6	0.05
United States or American	1,299	10.11
Welsh	67	0.52
West Indian, excl. Hispanic:	18	0.14
Belizean	4	0.03
Haitian	14	0.11
White:	10,908	84.68
Not Hispanic (10,552)	10,728	83.29
Hispanic (160)	180	1.40

Terre Haute

Place Type: City
County: Vigo
Population: 59,614

Ancestry/Race	Number	%
African American/Black:	6,405	10.74
Not Hispanic (5,771)	6,321	10.60
Hispanic (56)	84	0.14
African, sub-Saharan:	464	0.78
African	333	0.56
Ethiopian	6	0.01
Liberian	10	0.02
Nigerian	92	0.15
Sierra Leonean	5	0.01
Zairian	18	0.03
Alaska Native tribes, specified:	4	0.01
Alaska Athabascan (1)	1	0.00
Eskimo (1)	1	0.00
Tlingit-Haida	2	0.00
Am. Ind. or Alaska Nat., not spec.	255	0.43
Alsatian	16	0.03
American Indian tribes, specified:	289	0.48
Apache	4	0.01
Blackfeet (6)	26	0.04
Cherokee (37)	132	0.22
Cheyenne (2)	6	0.01
Chickasaw	1	0.00
Chippewa (6)	7	0.01
Choctaw (1)	3	0.01
Comanche (1)	2	0.00
Cree (8)	10	0.02
Creek (1)	2	0.00
Crow	1	0.00
Delaware	3	0.01
Iroquois (1)	1	0.00
Latin American Indians (4)	7	0.01
Menominee (1)	1	0.00
Navajo (2)	10	0.02
Osage (1)	4	0.01
Pima (1)	2	0.00
Potawatomi	1	0.00
Pueblo (2)	2	0.00
Seminole (1)	5	0.01
Sioux (4)	30	0.05
Ute (1)	1	0.00
All other tribes (13)	28	0.05
American Indian tribes, not spec.	35	0.06
Arab:	291	0.49
Arab/Arabic	53	0.09
Lebanese	34	0.06
Palestinian	16	0.03
Syrian	188	0.32
Armenian	41	0.07
Asian:	899	1.51
Cambodian	3	0.01
Chinese, ex. Taiwanese (149)	166	0.28
Filipino (68)	96	0.16
Indian (123)	160	0.27
Indonesian (1)	3	0.01
Japanese (111)	145	0.24
Korean (126)	142	0.24
Laotian (1)	1	0.00
Malaysian (19)	27	0.05
Pakistani (4)	6	0.01
Sri Lankan (3)	3	0.01
Taiwanese (20)	24	0.04
Thai (9)	14	0.02
Vietnamese (19)	25	0.04
Other Asian, specified (3)	8	0.01
Other Asian, not specified (28)	76	0.13
Australian	8	0.01
Austrian	131	0.22
Belgian	40	0.07
Brazilian	9	0.02
British	201	0.34
Bulgarian	20	0.03
Canadian	39	0.07
Croatian	44	0.07
Czech	157	0.26
Czechoslovakian	67	0.11
Danish	115	0.19
Dutch	1,280	2.15
English	5,739	9.64
European	339	0.57
Finnish	32	0.05
French, except Basque	1,440	2.42
French Canadian	141	0.24
German	11,152	18.72
Greek	118	0.20
Hawaii Native/Pacific Islander:	55	0.09
Melanesian: (1)	1	0.00
Fijian (1)	1	0.00
Micronesian: (3)	8	0.01
Guamanian/Chamorro (3)	7	0.01
Other Micronesian	1	0.00
Polynesian: (17)	24	0.04
Native Hawaiian (5)	7	0.01
Samoan (6)	10	0.02
Tongan (6)	7	0.01
Other Pac. Isl., specified	2	0.00
Other Pac. Isl., not spec. (3)	20	0.03
Hispanic or Latino:	942	1.58
Central American:	21	0.04
Costa Rican	3	0.01
Guatemalan	5	0.01
Honduran	5	0.01
Nicaraguan	1	0.00
Panamanian	3	0.01
Salvadoran	3	0.01
Other Central American	1	0.00
Cuban	108	0.18
Dominican Republic	12	0.02
Mexican	413	0.69
Puerto Rican	93	0.16
South American:	45	0.08
Argentinean	3	0.01
Bolivian	1	0.00
Chilean	5	0.01
Colombian	17	0.03
Ecuadorian	4	0.01
Paraguayan	1	0.00
Peruvian	5	0.01
Venezuelan	8	0.01
Other South American	1	0.00
Other Hispanic or Latino	250	0.42
Hungarian	312	0.52
Icelander	17	0.03
Iranian	15	0.03
Irish	6,303	10.58
Italian	1,579	2.65
Latvian	12	0.02
Lithuanian	93	0.16
Northern European	21	0.04
Norwegian	290	0.49
Pennsylvania German	13	0.02
Polish	852	1.43
Portuguese	23	0.04
Romanian	83	0.14
Russian	140	0.24
Scandinavian	51	0.09

Notes: 1. Figures in the "Number" column do not add up to the total population due to: a) Ancestry/Race overlap — e.g. persons can report being both White and Irish, b) persons of Hispanic origin can report being any race, c) persons reporting two ancestries are counted in both categories. 2. Numbers in parentheses indicate the number of persons reporting this ancestry/race alone, not in combination with any other ancestry/race. 3. Refer to the Explanation of Data in the front of the book for more detailed information.

Ancestry/Race	Number	%
Scotch-Irish	716	1.20
Scottish	1,145	1.92
Serbian	23	0.04
Slavic	49	0.08
Slovak	52	0.09
Slovene	7	0.01
Swedish	329	0.55
Swiss	73	0.12
Turkish	7	0.01
Ukrainian	89	0.15
United States or American	7,800	13.10
Welsh	558	0.94
West Indian, excl. Hispanic:	55	0.09
Barbadian	7	0.01
Haitian	6	0.01
Jamaican	37	0.06
West Indian	5	0.01
White:	52,448	87.98
Not Hispanic (50,867)	51,799	86.89
Hispanic (555)	649	1.09
Yugoslavian	57	0.10

Valparaiso

Place Type: City
County: Porter
Population: 27,428

Ancestry/Race	Number	%
African American/Black:	517	1.88
Not Hispanic (435)	499	1.82
Hispanic (5)	18	0.07
African, sub-Saharan:	49	0.18
African	21	0.08
Nigerian	23	0.08
Ugandan	5	0.02
Am. Ind. or Alaska Nat., not spec.	45	0.16
American Indian tribes, specified:	148	0.54
Apache (4)	11	0.04
Blackfeet (1)	14	0.05
Cherokee (17)	70	0.26
Chippewa (1)	1	0.00
Creek (1)	1	0.00
Crow	1	0.00
Iroquois (6)	7	0.03
Latin American Indians (3)	13	0.05
Navajo (2)	3	0.01
Potawatomi	5	0.02
Sioux (3)	8	0.03
Tohono O'Odham	4	0.01
Yaqui	1	0.00
All other tribes (4)	9	0.03
American Indian tribes, not spec.	6	0.02
Arab:	79	0.29
Arab/Arabic	26	0.09
Lebanese	10	0.04
Palestinian	9	0.03
Syrian	27	0.10
Other Arab	7	0.03
Armenian	17	0.06
Asian:	512	1.87
Bangladeshi (2)	2	0.01
Cambodian (4)	4	0.01
Chinese, ex. Taiwanese (63)	71	0.26
Filipino (71)	92	0.34
Indian (111)	119	0.43
Indonesian (3)	4	0.01
Japanese (44)	64	0.23
Korean (36)	53	0.19
Laotian (5)	6	0.02
Pakistani	2	0.01
Sri Lankan (6)	7	0.03
Taiwanese (1)	1	0.00
Thai (11)	12	0.04
Vietnamese (41)	42	0.15
Other Asian, specified	3	0.01
Other Asian, not specified (11)	30	0.11
Assyrian/Chaldean/Syriac	16	0.06
Australian	10	0.04
Austrian	169	0.61
Belgian	56	0.20
Brazilian	8	0.03
British	151	0.55
Canadian	100	0.36
Celtic	24	0.09
Croatian	182	0.66
Czech	155	0.56
Czechoslovakian	88	0.32
Danish	152	0.55
Dutch	663	2.41
Eastern European	37	0.13
English	3,265	11.87
European	59	0.21
Finnish	61	0.22
French, except Basque	769	2.80
French Canadian	105	0.38
German	9,042	32.88
Greek	204	0.74
Hawaii Native/Pacific Islander:	24	0.09
Melanesian:	1	0.00
Fijian	1	0.00
Micronesian: (3)	3	0.01
Guamanian/Chamorro (2)	2	0.01
Other Micronesian (1)	1	0.00
Polynesian: (1)	15	0.05
Native Hawaiian (1)	12	0.04
Samoan	3	0.01
Other Pac. Isl., specified	3	0.01
Other Pac. Isl., not spec. (1)	2	0.01
Hispanic or Latino:	917	3.34
Central American:	20	0.07
Costa Rican	1	0.00
Guatemalan	10	0.04
Honduran	3	0.01
Nicaraguan	1	0.00
Salvadoran	5	0.02
Cuban	13	0.05
Mexican	586	2.14
Puerto Rican	128	0.47
South American:	43	0.16
Argentinean	7	0.03
Bolivian	1	0.00
Chilean	6	0.02
Colombian	4	0.01
Peruvian	17	0.06
Uruguayan	1	0.00
Venezuelan	6	0.02
Other South American	1	0.00
Other Hispanic or Latino	127	0.46
Hungarian	484	1.76
Iranian	62	0.23
Irish	4,453	16.19
Italian	1,527	5.55
Lithuanian	118	0.43
Macedonian	76	0.28
Northern European	40	0.15
Norwegian	485	1.76
Pennsylvania German	28	0.10
Polish	2,526	9.19
Portuguese	18	0.07
Romanian	79	0.29
Russian	261	0.95
Scandinavian	76	0.28
Scotch-Irish	441	1.60
Scottish	815	2.96
Serbian	158	0.57
Slavic	23	0.08
Slovak	436	1.59
Slovene	29	0.11
Swedish	983	3.57
Swiss	104	0.38
Turkish	5	0.02
Ukrainian	56	0.20
United States or American	1,444	5.25
Welsh	281	1.02
White:	26,255	95.72
Not Hispanic (25,271)	25,557	93.18
Hispanic (608)	698	2.54
Yugoslavian	60	0.22

Vincennes

Place Type: City
County: Knox
Population: 18,701

Ancestry/Race	Number	%
African American/Black:	681	3.64
Not Hispanic (612)	673	3.60
Hispanic (1)	8	0.04
African, sub-Saharan:	20	0.11
African	4	0.02
South African	16	0.09
Alaska Native tribes, not specified	1	0.01
Am. Ind. or Alaska Nat., not spec.	33	0.18
American Indian tribes, specified:	80	0.43
Blackfeet (2)	5	0.03
Cherokee (11)	41	0.22
Cheyenne (1)	1	0.01
Chippewa (6)	7	0.04
Choctaw	1	0.01
Iroquois	3	0.02
Navajo	1	0.01
Osage	2	0.01
Shoshone	3	0.02
Sioux (4)	9	0.05
All other tribes	7	0.04
American Indian tribes, not spec.	10	0.05
Arab:	27	0.15
Arab/Arabic	13	0.07
Jordanian	5	0.03
Lebanese	9	0.05
Asian:	155	0.83
Chinese, ex. Taiwanese (19)	22	0.12
Filipino (26)	34	0.18
Indian (10)	10	0.05
Indonesian (1)	1	0.01
Japanese (57)	60	0.32
Korean (15)	17	0.09
Pakistani (2)	3	0.02
Taiwanese (1)	1	0.01
Vietnamese (1)	2	0.01
Other Asian, not specified (1)	5	0.03
Austrian	7	0.04
Belgian	24	0.13
British	23	0.12
Canadian	6	0.03
Celtic	10	0.05
Croatian	14	0.08
Czech	25	0.13
Czechoslovakian	6	0.03
Danish	10	0.05
Dutch	234	1.26
English	1,551	8.35
European	211	1.14
French, except Basque	773	4.16
French Canadian	101	0.54
German	3,688	19.85
Hawaii Native/Pacific Islander:	27	0.14
Micronesian: (1)	8	0.04
Guamanian/Chamorro (1)	8	0.04
Polynesian: (5)	14	0.07
Native Hawaiian (4)	6	0.03
Samoan (1)	8	0.04
Other Pac. Isl., not spec. (5)	5	0.03
Hispanic or Latino:	191	1.02
Central American:	7	0.04
Guatemalan	4	0.02
Panamanian	2	0.01
Salvadoran	1	0.01
Cuban	1	0.01
Dominican Republic	4	0.02
Mexican	98	0.52
Puerto Rican	18	0.10
South American:	15	0.08
Argentinean	1	0.01
Colombian	7	0.04
Peruvian	4	0.02
Uruguayan	1	0.01
Venezuelan	2	0.01

Notes: 1. Figures in the "Number" column do not add up to the total population due to: a) Ancestry/Race overlap — e.g. persons can report being both White and Irish, b) persons of Hispanic origin can report being any race, c) persons reporting two ancestries are counted in both categories. 2. Numbers in parentheses indicate the number of persons reporting this ancestry/race alone, not in combination with any other ancestry/race. 3. Refer to the Explanation of Data in the front of the book for more detailed information.

Ancestry/Race	Number	%
Other Hispanic or Latino	48	0.26
Icelander	11	0.06
Irish	1,620	8.72
Italian	190	1.02
Norwegian	17	0.09
Pennsylvania German	8	0.04
Polish	156	0.84
Romanian	5	0.03
Russian	7	0.04
Scandinavian	28	0.15
Scotch-Irish	241	1.30
Scottish	263	1.42
Slovak	8	0.04
Swedish	32	0.17
Swiss	13	0.07
Turkish	8	0.04
Ukrainian	10	0.05
United States or American	3,242	17.45
Welsh	52	0.28
White:	17,781	95.08
Not Hispanic (17,564)	17,689	94.59
Hispanic (78)	92	0.49
Yugoslavian	6	0.03

Wabash

Place Type: City
County: Wabash
Population: 11,743

Ancestry/Race	Number	%
African American/Black:	59	0.50
Not Hispanic (44)	59	0.50
African, sub-Saharan:	14	0.12
African	14	0.12
Am. Ind. or Alaska Nat., not spec.	37	0.32
Alsatian	6	0.05
American Indian tribes, specified:	142	1.21
Blackfeet (1)	4	0.03
Cherokee (14)	24	0.20
Choctaw	2	0.02
Iroquois (1)	1	0.01
Menominee (1)	1	0.01
Potawatomi	1	0.01
Puget Sound Salish (1)	2	0.02
Seminole	2	0.02
All other tribes (84)	105	0.89
American Indian tribes, not spec.	4	0.03
Arab:	8	0.07
Other Arab	8	0.07
Asian:	71	0.60
Cambodian (4)	4	0.03
Chinese, ex. Taiwanese (18)	19	0.16
Filipino (3)	7	0.06
Indian (4)	5	0.04
Japanese (4)	5	0.04
Korean (3)	5	0.04
Laotian (12)	13	0.11
Pakistani (3)	3	0.03
Thai	1	0.01
Vietnamese (4)	4	0.03
Other Asian, not specified (5)	5	0.04
Belgian	4	0.03
British	5	0.04
Czech	12	0.10
Czechoslovakian	9	0.08
Danish	31	0.26
Dutch	293	2.50
English	1,419	12.09
European	66	0.56
Finnish	4	0.03
French, except Basque	318	2.71
French Canadian	15	0.13
German	2,678	22.82
Greek	61	0.52
Hawaii Native/Pacific Islander:	6	0.05
Micronesian: (2)	2	0.02
Guamanian/Chamorro (2)	2	0.02
Polynesian: (1)	2	0.02
Native Hawaiian (1)	2	0.02
Other Pac. Isl., not spec.	2	0.02
Hispanic or Latino:	172	1.46
Central American:	1	0.01
Salvadoran	1	0.01
Cuban	1	0.01
Mexican	119	1.01
Puerto Rican	9	0.08
South American:	4	0.03
Argentinean	1	0.01
Colombian	2	0.02
Other South American	1	0.01
Other Hispanic or Latino	38	0.32
Hungarian	11	0.09
Iranian	20	0.17
Irish	1,227	10.46
Italian	121	1.03
Norwegian	17	0.14
Pennsylvania German	35	0.30
Polish	95	0.81
Scotch-Irish	71	0.61
Scottish	162	1.38
Slovak	43	0.37
Swedish	34	0.29
Swiss	55	0.47
United States or American	1,450	12.36
Welsh	33	0.28
White:	11,464	97.62
Not Hispanic (11,254)	11,337	96.54
Hispanic (119)	127	1.08

Warsaw

Place Type: City
County: Kosciusko
Population: 12,415

Ancestry/Race	Number	%
African American/Black:	211	1.70
Not Hispanic (170)	206	1.66
Hispanic (5)	5	0.04
African, sub-Saharan:	11	0.09
African	11	0.09
Alaska Native tribes, specified:	2	0.02
Aleut (1)	1	0.01
Tlingit-Haida	1	0.01
Am. Ind. or Alaska Nat., not spec.	48	0.39
American Indian tribes, specified:	35	0.28
Apache	1	0.01
Blackfeet (2)	2	0.02
Cherokee (1)	12	0.10
Chippewa	1	0.01
Latin American Indians (8)	8	0.06
Lumbee (3)	4	0.03
Osage	1	0.01
Potawatomi (1)	2	0.02
Puget Sound Salish	1	0.01
Seminole	1	0.01
All other tribes	2	0.02
American Indian tribes, not spec.	12	0.10
Arab:	22	0.18
Lebanese	7	0.06
Syrian	15	0.12
Asian:	152	1.22
Cambodian (1)	1	0.01
Chinese, ex. Taiwanese (37)	37	0.30
Filipino (20)	21	0.17
Indian (33)	35	0.28
Indonesian (1)	1	0.01
Japanese (5)	7	0.06
Korean (12)	14	0.11
Pakistani (5)	5	0.04
Taiwanese (2)	2	0.02
Thai (3)	6	0.05
Vietnamese (9)	13	0.10
Other Asian, not specified (5)	10	0.08
Austrian	47	0.38
Belgian	6	0.05
Brazilian	15	0.12
British	46	0.37
Canadian	13	0.11
Celtic	6	0.05
Czech	27	0.22
Czechoslovakian	5	0.04
Danish	6	0.05
Dutch	260	2.12
English	1,261	10.27
European	58	0.47
French, except Basque	217	1.77
French Canadian	36	0.29
German	2,828	23.02
Greek	33	0.27
Hawaii Native/Pacific Islander:	4	0.03
Polynesian: (1)	3	0.02
Native Hawaiian	1	0.01
Samoan (1)	1	0.01
Other Polynesian	1	0.01
Other Pac. Isl., not spec. (1)	1	0.01
Hispanic or Latino:	1,144	9.21
Central American:	17	0.14
Guatemalan	11	0.09
Honduran	2	0.02
Salvadoran	4	0.03
Cuban	3	0.02
Dominican Republic	2	0.02
Mexican	966	7.78
Puerto Rican	30	0.24
South American:	14	0.11
Argentinean	5	0.04
Colombian	4	0.03
Ecuadorian	3	0.02
Peruvian	2	0.02
Other Hispanic or Latino	112	0.90
Hungarian	86	0.70
Irish	1,257	10.23
Italian	172	1.40
Norwegian	159	1.29
Pennsylvania German	11	0.09
Polish	190	1.55
Portuguese	8	0.07
Romanian	8	0.07
Russian	71	0.58
Scandinavian	7	0.06
Scotch-Irish	130	1.06
Scottish	225	1.83
Slavic	15	0.12
Slovak	13	0.11
Swedish	93	0.76
Swiss	53	0.43
Ukrainian	41	0.33
United States or American	1,525	12.41
Welsh	69	0.56
White:	11,394	91.78
Not Hispanic (10,821)	10,924	87.99
Hispanic (414)	470	3.79
Yugoslavian	6	0.05

Washington

Place Type: City
County: Daviess
Population: 11,380

Ancestry/Race	Number	%
African American/Black:	135	1.19
Not Hispanic (93)	120	1.05
Hispanic (11)	15	0.13
African, sub-Saharan:	11	0.10
African	11	0.10
Am. Ind. or Alaska Nat., not spec.	28	0.25
American Indian tribes, specified:	41	0.36
Blackfeet (5)	5	0.04
Cherokee (4)	20	0.18
Chippewa (1)	1	0.01
Choctaw	5	0.04
Cree (1)	1	0.01
Iroquois	1	0.01
Sioux (1)	2	0.02
All other tribes (4)	6	0.05
Asian:	60	0.53
Chinese, ex. Taiwanese (13)	14	0.12

Notes: 1. Figures in the "Number" column do not add up to the total population due to: a) Ancestry/Race overlap — e.g. persons can report being both White and Irish, b) persons of Hispanic origin can report being any race, c) persons reporting two ancestries are counted in both categories. 2. Numbers in parentheses indicate the number of persons reporting this ancestry/race alone, not in combination with any other ancestry/race. 3. Refer to the Explanation of Data in the front of the book for more detailed information.

Filipino (16)	22	0.19
Indian (1)	1	0.01
Japanese (2)	7	0.06
Korean (3)	7	0.06
Thai (4)	4	0.04
Vietnamese (5)	5	0.04
Belgian	5	0.04
British	23	0.20
Danish	12	0.11
Dutch	175	1.55
English	801	7.10
European	5	0.04
French, except Basque	358	3.17
French Canadian	33	0.29
German	2,276	20.18
Greek	34	0.30
Hawaii Native/Pacific Islander:	16	0.14
Micronesian: (4)	6	0.05
Guamanian/Chamorro (4)	6	0.05
Polynesian: (2)	10	0.09
Native Hawaiian (1)	9	0.08
Samoan (1)	1	0.01
Hispanic or Latino:	472	4.15
Central American:	74	0.65
Guatemalan	20	0.18
Honduran	8	0.07
Salvadoran	38	0.33
Other Central American	8	0.07
Cuban	2	0.02
Mexican	330	2.90
Puerto Rican	19	0.17
Other Hispanic or Latino	47	0.41
Hungarian	22	0.20
Irish	1,389	12.32
Italian	212	1.88
Lithuanian	21	0.19
Polish	98	0.87
Romanian	7	0.06
Scotch-Irish	159	1.41
Scottish	165	1.46
Swedish	54	0.48
Swiss	12	0.11
United States or American	2,510	22.26
Welsh	37	0.33
White:	10,938	96.12
Not Hispanic (10,660)	10,733	94.31
Hispanic (185)	205	1.80

West Lafayette

Place Type: City
County: Tippecanoe
Population: 28,778

Ancestry/Race	Number	%
Acadian/Cajun	15	0.05
Afghan	18	0.06
African American/Black:	765	2.66
Not Hispanic (675)	749	2.60
Hispanic (9)	16	0.06
African, sub-Saharan:	161	0.56
African	97	0.34
Cape Verdean	10	0.03
Ethiopian	7	0.02
Nigerian	20	0.07
Sierra Leonean	5	0.02
Other sub-Saharan African	22	0.08
Alaska Native tribes, specified:	3	0.01
Eskimo (2)	3	0.01
Am. Ind. or Alaska Nat., not spec.	28	0.10
Alsatian	10	0.03
American Indian tribes, specified:	70	0.24
Blackfeet	4	0.01
Cherokee (5)	19	0.07
Cheyenne (1)	1	0.00
Chickasaw	1	0.00
Chippewa	1	0.00
Choctaw (4)	5	0.02
Creek	1	0.00
Iroquois	2	0.01
Latin American Indians (1)	4	0.01
Ottawa	1	0.00
Pima	1	0.00
Potawatomi (2)	3	0.01
Pueblo	6	0.02
Puget Sound Salish (1)	1	0.00
Sioux (1)	3	0.01
Ute (4)	4	0.01
All other tribes (9)	13	0.05
American Indian tribes, not spec.	4	0.01
Arab:	286	0.99
Arab/Arabic	35	0.12
Egyptian	66	0.23
Jordanian	28	0.10
Lebanese	59	0.20
Palestinian	81	0.28
Syrian	8	0.03
Other Arab	9	0.03
Armenian	15	0.05
Asian:	3,565	12.39
Bangladeshi (12)	13	0.05
Cambodian (3)	3	0.01
Chinese, ex. Taiwanese (953)	1,027	3.57
Filipino (102)	137	0.48
Indian (990)	1,027	3.57
Indonesian (104)	139	0.48
Japanese (261)	294	1.02
Korean (401)	419	1.46
Laotian (5)	5	0.02
Malaysian (52)	60	0.21
Pakistani (73)	79	0.27
Sri Lankan (19)	19	0.07
Taiwanese (88)	105	0.36
Thai (48)	59	0.21
Vietnamese (58)	72	0.25
Other Asian, specified (5)	9	0.03
Other Asian, not specified (38)	98	0.34
Austrian	91	0.31
Basque	17	0.06
Belgian	73	0.25
Brazilian	7	0.02
British	211	0.73
Bulgarian	30	0.10
Canadian	28	0.10
Carpatho Rusyn	8	0.03
Celtic	6	0.02
Croatian	39	0.13
Cypriot	4	0.01
Czech	215	0.74
Czechoslovakian	66	0.23
Danish	163	0.56
Dutch	744	2.57
Eastern European	8	0.03
English	3,317	11.46
European	369	1.27
Finnish	106	0.37
French, except Basque	823	2.84
French Canadian	143	0.49
German	7,716	26.65
German Russian	6	0.02
Greek	138	0.48
Guyanese	11	0.04
Hawaii Native/Pacific Islander:	51	0.18
Micronesian: (2)	7	0.02
Guamanian/Chamorro (2)	5	0.02
Other Micronesian	2	0.01
Polynesian: (6)	21	0.07
Native Hawaiian (4)	16	0.06
Samoan (1)	4	0.01
Tongan (1)	1	0.00
Other Pac. Isl., not spec. (1)	23	0.08
Hispanic or Latino:	920	3.20
Central American:	80	0.28
Costa Rican	10	0.03
Guatemalan	20	0.07
Honduran	6	0.02
Nicaraguan	9	0.03
Panamanian	16	0.06
Salvadoran	11	0.04
Other Central American	8	0.03
Cuban	17	0.06
Dominican Republic	4	0.01
Mexican	381	1.32
Puerto Rican	150	0.52
South American:	146	0.51
Argentinean	33	0.11
Bolivian	3	0.01
Chilean	5	0.02
Colombian	43	0.15
Ecuadorian	10	0.03
Peruvian	23	0.08
Uruguayan	4	0.01
Venezuelan	10	0.03
Other South American	15	0.05
Other Hispanic or Latino	142	0.49
Hungarian	203	0.70
Iranian	61	0.21
Irish	3,535	12.21
Italian	1,143	3.95
Latvian	9	0.03
Lithuanian	147	0.51
Luxemburger	7	0.02
Macedonian	26	0.09
Maltese	12	0.04
New Zealander	7	0.02
Northern European	64	0.22
Norwegian	376	1.30
Pennsylvania German	14	0.05
Polish	1,696	5.86
Portuguese	29	0.10
Romanian	50	0.17
Russian	302	1.04
Scandinavian	57	0.20
Scotch-Irish	403	1.39
Scottish	824	2.85
Serbian	91	0.31
Slavic	38	0.13
Slovak	153	0.53
Slovene	54	0.19
Swedish	616	2.13
Swiss	226	0.78
Turkish	36	0.12
Ukrainian	129	0.45
United States or American	1,149	3.97
Welsh	212	0.73
West Indian, excl. Hispanic:	47	0.16
Haitian	11	0.04
Jamaican	16	0.06
Trinidadian and Tobagonian	5	0.02
West Indian	15	0.05
White:	24,352	84.62
Not Hispanic (23,454)	23,756	82.55
Hispanic (531)	596	2.07
Yugoslavian	34	0.12

Altoona

Place Type: City
County: Polk
Population: 10,345

Ancestry/Race	Number	%
African American/Black:	154	1.49
Not Hispanic (94)	148	1.43
Hispanic (1)	6	0.06
African, sub-Saharan:	15	0.15
African	15	0.15
Am. Ind. or Alaska Nat., not spec.	23	0.22
American Indian tribes, specified:	39	0.38
Apache (4)	5	0.05
Blackfeet	1	0.01
Cherokee (5)	8	0.08
Chippewa (2)	5	0.05
Choctaw (2)	2	0.02
Comanche (4)	5	0.05
Iroquois (1)	1	0.01
Sioux (4)	4	0.04
All other tribes (4)	8	0.08
Armenian	8	0.08
Asian:	75	0.72

Notes: 1. Figures in the "Number" column do not add up to the total population due to: a) Ancestry/Race overlap — e.g. persons can report being both White and Irish, b) persons of Hispanic origin can report being any race, c) persons reporting two ancestries are counted in both categories. 2. Numbers in parentheses indicate the number of persons reporting this ancestry/race alone, not in combination with any other ancestry/race. 3. Refer to the Explanation of Data in the front of the book for more detailed information.

Ancestry/Race	Number	%
Cambodian (8)	8	0.08
Chinese, ex. Taiwanese (5)	12	0.12
Filipino (3)	7	0.07
Indian (2)	8	0.08
Japanese (2)	3	0.03
Korean (11)	18	0.17
Laotian (12)	13	0.13
Thai (2)	3	0.03
Vietnamese (2)	2	0.02
Other Asian, not specified (1)	1	0.01
Belgian	56	0.55
British	22	0.21
Croatian	36	0.35
Czech	75	0.73
Czechoslovakian	9	0.09
Danish	193	1.88
Dutch	544	5.29
English	984	9.58
European	232	2.26
French, except Basque	252	2.45
French Canadian	16	0.16
German	3,024	29.43
Greek	13	0.13
Hawaii Native/Pacific Islander:	50	0.48
Micronesian: (37)	43	0.42
Other Micronesian (37)	43	0.42
Polynesian: (4)	5	0.05
Native Hawaiian (2)	3	0.03
Samoan (2)	2	0.02
Other Pac. Isl., not spec.	2	0.02
Hispanic or Latino:	171	1.65
Central American:	4	0.04
Costa Rican	1	0.01
Salvadoran	3	0.03
Cuban	3	0.03
Mexican	104	1.01
Puerto Rican	17	0.16
South American:	6	0.06
Colombian	1	0.01
Ecuadorian	1	0.01
Peruvian	4	0.04
Other Hispanic or Latino	37	0.36
Irish	1,376	13.39
Italian	224	2.18
Luxemburger	29	0.28
Norwegian	383	3.73
Pennsylvania German	43	0.42
Polish	178	1.73
Scandinavian	33	0.32
Scotch-Irish	133	1.29
Scottish	217	2.11
Serbian	41	0.40
Swedish	427	4.16
Swiss	49	0.48
United States or American	743	7.23
Welsh	124	1.21
White:	10,034	96.99
Not Hispanic (9,848)	9,945	96.13
Hispanic (74)	89	0.86

Ames

Place Type: City
County: Story
Population: 50,731

Ancestry/Race	Number	%
African American/Black:	1,541	3.04
Not Hispanic (1,323)	1,499	2.95
Hispanic (20)	42	0.08
African, sub-Saharan:	638	1.26
African	244	0.48
Ethiopian	18	0.04
Ghanian	24	0.05
Kenyan	30	0.06
Liberian	11	0.02
Nigerian	101	0.20
South African	28	0.06
Sudanese	147	0.29
Ugandan	5	0.01
Zairian	6	0.01
Zimbabwean	5	0.01
Other sub-Saharan African	19	0.04
Alaska Native tribes, specified:	4	0.01
Aleut (1)	1	0.00
Eskimo (2)	2	0.00
Tlingit-Haida (1)	1	0.00
Am. Ind. or Alaska Nat., not spec.	74	0.15
American Indian tribes, specified:	125	0.25
Apache (1)	8	0.02
Blackfeet (1)	5	0.01
Cherokee (14)	49	0.10
Cheyenne (1)	2	0.00
Chickasaw (2)	3	0.01
Chippewa (2)	5	0.01
Choctaw	2	0.00
Creek	1	0.00
Iroquois (1)	2	0.00
Kiowa (2)	2	0.00
Latin American Indians (6)	9	0.02
Lumbee	1	0.00
Menominee (1)	1	0.00
Potawatomi (1)	1	0.00
Seminole	2	0.00
Sioux (10)	18	0.04
Ute (1)	1	0.00
All other tribes (6)	13	0.03
American Indian tribes, not spec.	10	0.02
Arab:	314	0.62
Arab/Arabic	117	0.23
Egyptian	11	0.02
Iraqi	7	0.01
Jordanian	18	0.04
Lebanese	65	0.13
Palestinian	11	0.02
Syrian	51	0.10
Other Arab	34	0.07
Armenian	17	0.03
Asian:	4,281	8.44
Bangladeshi (20)	20	0.04
Cambodian (9)	10	0.02
Chinese, ex. Taiwanese (1,455)	1,545	3.05
Filipino (82)	110	0.22
Hmong (5)	5	0.01
Indian (629)	670	1.32
Indonesian (171)	195	0.38
Japanese (119)	158	0.31
Korean (728)	764	1.51
Laotian (71)	83	0.16
Malaysian (87)	102	0.20
Pakistani (40)	44	0.09
Sri Lankan (27)	33	0.07
Taiwanese (130)	143	0.28
Thai (80)	88	0.17
Vietnamese (139)	163	0.32
Other Asian, specified (11)	12	0.02
Other Asian, not specified (47)	136	0.27
Australian	40	0.08
Austrian	106	0.21
Basque	9	0.02
Belgian	67	0.13
Brazilian	7	0.01
British	385	0.76
Canadian	50	0.10
Croatian	42	0.08
Czech	774	1.53
Czechoslovakian	262	0.52
Danish	1,076	2.12
Dutch	1,683	3.32
Eastern European	32	0.06
English	5,180	10.23
Estonian	8	0.02
European	703	1.39
Finnish	104	0.21
French, except Basque	1,044	2.06
French Canadian	126	0.25
German	16,961	33.48
Greek	184	0.36
Guyanese	20	0.04
Hawaii Native/Pacific Islander:	64	0.13
Micronesian: (2)	6	0.01
Guamanian/Chamorro (2)	6	0.01
Polynesian: (15)	26	0.05
Native Hawaiian (8)	16	0.03
Samoan (6)	9	0.02
Tongan (1)	1	0.00
Other Pac. Isl., not spec. (5)	32	0.06
Hispanic or Latino:	1,002	1.98
Central American:	71	0.14
Costa Rican	5	0.01
Guatemalan	19	0.04
Honduran	23	0.05
Nicaraguan	2	0.00
Panamanian	6	0.01
Salvadoran	12	0.02
Other Central American	4	0.01
Cuban	23	0.05
Dominican Republic	5	0.01
Mexican	449	0.89
Puerto Rican	154	0.30
South American:	143	0.28
Argentinean	18	0.04
Bolivian	2	0.00
Chilean	13	0.03
Colombian	31	0.06
Ecuadorian	5	0.01
Paraguayan	2	0.00
Peruvian	23	0.05
Uruguayan	8	0.02
Venezuelan	32	0.06
Other South American	9	0.02
Other Hispanic or Latino	157	0.31
Hungarian	53	0.10
Icelander	23	0.05
Iranian	37	0.07
Irish	5,793	11.44
Italian	1,072	2.12
Latvian	13	0.03
Lithuanian	156	0.31
Luxemburger	72	0.14
Maltese	12	0.02
Northern European	141	0.28
Norwegian	4,365	8.62
Pennsylvania German	27	0.05
Polish	1,065	2.10
Portuguese	46	0.09
Romanian	52	0.10
Russian	314	0.62
Scandinavian	358	0.71
Scotch-Irish	612	1.21
Scottish	1,207	2.38
Serbian	48	0.09
Slavic	15	0.03
Slovak	104	0.21
Swedish	2,096	4.14
Swiss	301	0.59
Turkish	77	0.15
Ukrainian	69	0.14
United States or American	1,573	3.11
Welsh	342	0.68
West Indian, excl. Hispanic:	38	0.08
Bahamian	8	0.02
British West Indian	10	0.02
Haitian	14	0.03
Jamaican	6	0.01
White:	44,866	88.44
Not Hispanic (43,762)	44,233	87.19
Hispanic (546)	633	1.25
Yugoslavian	51	0.10

Ankeny

Place Type: City
County: Polk
Population: 27,117

Ancestry/Race	Number	%
African American/Black:	272	1.00
Not Hispanic (199)	258	0.95
Hispanic (7)	14	0.05

Notes: 1. Figures in the "Number" column do not add up to the total population due to: a) Ancestry/Race overlap — e.g. persons can report being both White and Irish, b) persons of Hispanic origin can report being any race, c) persons reporting two ancestries are counted in both categories. 2. Numbers in parentheses indicate the number of persons reporting this ancestry/race alone, not in combination with any other ancestry/race. 3. Refer to the Explanation of Data in the front of the book for more detailed information.

Ancestry/Race	Number	%
African, sub-Saharan:	33	0.12
African	7	0.03
Kenyan	26	0.10
Alaska Native tribes, specified:	2	0.01
Alaska Athabascan (1)	1	0.00
Aleut	1	0.00
Am. Ind. or Alaska Nat., not spec.	32	0.12
American Indian tribes, specified:	46	0.17
Blackfeet	3	0.01
Cherokee (3)	8	0.03
Chippewa (3)	7	0.03
Choctaw (2)	2	0.01
Delaware (5)	5	0.02
Kiowa	2	0.01
Latin American Indians	3	0.01
Seminole (1)	2	0.01
Sioux (3)	5	0.02
All other tribes (5)	9	0.03
American Indian tribes, not spec.	14	0.05
Arab:	40	0.15
Arab/Arabic	13	0.05
Egyptian	27	0.10
Asian:	320	1.18
Cambodian (1)	1	0.00
Chinese, ex. Taiwanese (52)	63	0.23
Filipino (21)	34	0.13
Indian (59)	64	0.24
Indonesian (2)	6	0.02
Japanese (19)	26	0.10
Korean (48)	64	0.24
Laotian (13)	15	0.06
Pakistani (3)	3	0.01
Taiwanese (1)	1	0.00
Thai (5)	6	0.02
Vietnamese (8)	8	0.03
Other Asian, not specified (17)	29	0.11
Austrian	23	0.09
Belgian	156	0.58
Brazilian	7	0.03
British	138	0.51
Canadian	11	0.04
Croatian	55	0.20
Czech	362	1.34
Czechoslovakian	17	0.06
Danish	571	2.12
Dutch	1,185	4.40
Eastern European	21	0.08
English	3,183	11.82
European	229	0.85
Finnish	37	0.14
French, except Basque	874	3.25
French Canadian	123	0.46
German	9,413	34.96
Greek	95	0.35
Hawaii Native/Pacific Islander:	17	0.06
Micronesian: (1)	1	0.00
Guamanian/Chamorro (1)	1	0.00
Polynesian: (3)	8	0.03
Native Hawaiian (3)	8	0.03
Other Pac. Isl., not spec. (3)	8	0.03
Hispanic or Latino:	293	1.08
Central American:	5	0.02
Guatemalan	1	0.00
Nicaraguan	1	0.00
Panamanian	2	0.01
Salvadoran	1	0.00
Cuban	4	0.01
Mexican	158	0.58
Puerto Rican	30	0.11
South American:	27	0.10
Bolivian	1	0.00
Chilean	3	0.01
Colombian	7	0.03
Ecuadorian	1	0.00
Paraguayan	1	0.00
Peruvian	5	0.02
Uruguayan	1	0.00
Venezuelan	6	0.02
Other South American	2	0.01
Other Hispanic or Latino	69	0.25
Hungarian	15	0.06
Irish	3,918	14.55
Italian	668	2.48
Latvian	41	0.15
Luxemburger	52	0.19
Northern European	46	0.17
Norwegian	1,964	7.29
Pennsylvania German	26	0.10
Polish	393	1.46
Romanian	4	0.01
Russian	61	0.23
Scandinavian	69	0.26
Scotch-Irish	429	1.59
Scottish	324	1.20
Serbian	33	0.12
Slavic	21	0.08
Slovak	7	0.03
Slovene	64	0.24
Swedish	1,346	5.00
Swiss	84	0.31
Turkish	7	0.03
United States or American	1,698	6.31
Welsh	189	0.70
West Indian, excl. Hispanic:	32	0.12
Jamaican	17	0.06
Other West Indian	15	0.06
White:	26,498	97.72
Not Hispanic (26,137)	26,310	97.02
Hispanic (150)	188	0.69
Yugoslavian	368	1.37

Bettendorf

Place Type: City
County: Scott
Population: 31,275

Ancestry/Race	Number	%
African American/Black:	601	1.92
Not Hispanic (483)	584	1.87
Hispanic (11)	17	0.05
African, sub-Saharan:	26	0.08
African	26	0.08
Am. Ind. or Alaska Nat., not spec.	74	0.24
American Indian tribes, specified:	99	0.32
Apache	2	0.01
Blackfeet (1)	4	0.01
Cherokee (14)	36	0.12
Cheyenne (1)	1	0.00
Chickasaw	3	0.01
Chippewa (6)	8	0.03
Choctaw (7)	8	0.03
Crow	1	0.00
Iroquois (3)	3	0.01
Latin American Indians (2)	3	0.01
Lumbee (5)	5	0.02
Navajo (1)	3	0.01
Osage (1)	1	0.00
Potawatomi (2)	2	0.01
Pueblo (1)	1	0.00
Sioux (8)	10	0.03
All other tribes	8	0.03
American Indian tribes, not spec.	3	0.01
Arab:	158	0.50
Arab/Arabic	9	0.03
Iraqi	12	0.04
Lebanese	48	0.15
Palestinian	38	0.12
Syrian	12	0.04
Other Arab	39	0.12
Armenian	28	0.09
Asian:	543	1.74
Chinese, ex. Taiwanese (63)	73	0.23
Filipino (22)	37	0.12
Indian (136)	149	0.48
Japanese (24)	40	0.13
Korean (100)	123	0.39
Laotian (4)	4	0.01
Pakistani (8)	9	0.03
Taiwanese (6)	6	0.02
Thai (14)	17	0.05
Vietnamese (46)	51	0.16
Other Asian, specified (6)	6	0.02
Other Asian, not specified (7)	28	0.09
Australian	7	0.02
Austrian	63	0.20
Belgian	392	1.25
Brazilian	7	0.02
British	115	0.37
Canadian	50	0.16
Celtic	19	0.06
Croatian	41	0.13
Czech	413	1.32
Czechoslovakian	85	0.27
Danish	489	1.56
Dutch	859	2.74
Eastern European	11	0.04
English	3,324	10.61
European	242	0.77
Finnish	48	0.15
French, except Basque	771	2.46
French Canadian	127	0.41
German	11,708	37.38
Greek	94	0.30
Hawaii Native/Pacific Islander:	19	0.06
Micronesian: (1)	3	0.01
Guamanian/Chamorro (1)	3	0.01
Polynesian: (1)	6	0.02
Native Hawaiian (1)	6	0.02
Other Pac. Isl., not spec. (2)	10	0.03
Hispanic or Latino:	772	2.47
Central American:	13	0.04
Costa Rican	2	0.01
Guatemalan	5	0.02
Honduran	1	0.00
Nicaraguan	3	0.01
Panamanian	1	0.00
Salvadoran	1	0.00
Cuban	9	0.03
Dominican Republic	1	0.00
Mexican	557	1.78
Puerto Rican	32	0.10
South American:	52	0.17
Argentinean	1	0.00
Colombian	6	0.02
Ecuadorian	7	0.02
Peruvian	12	0.04
Uruguayan	1	0.00
Venezuelan	13	0.04
Other South American	12	0.04
Other Hispanic or Latino	108	0.35
Hungarian	130	0.42
Icelander	7	0.02
Iranian	15	0.05
Irish	5,596	17.87
Italian	633	2.02
Latvian	4	0.01
Lithuanian	80	0.26
Luxemburger	32	0.10
New Zealander	6	0.02
Northern European	7	0.02
Norwegian	947	3.02
Pennsylvania German	13	0.04
Polish	760	2.43
Portuguese	6	0.02
Romanian	22	0.07
Russian	144	0.46
Scandinavian	57	0.18
Scotch-Irish	582	1.86
Scottish	759	2.42
Serbian	22	0.07
Slavic	7	0.02
Slovak	24	0.08
Swedish	1,338	4.27
Swiss	143	0.46
Turkish	19	0.06
Ukrainian	29	0.09
United States or American	2,033	6.49
Welsh	278	0.89
West Indian, excl. Hispanic:	4	0.01

Notes: 1. Figures in the "Number" column do not add up to the total population due to: a) Ancestry/Race overlap — e.g. persons can report being both White and Irish, b) persons of Hispanic origin can report being any race, c) persons reporting two ancestries are counted in both categories. 2. Numbers in parentheses indicate the number of persons reporting this ancestry/race alone, not in combination with any other ancestry/race. 3. Refer to the Explanation of Data in the front of the book for more detailed information.

Ancestry/Race	Number	%
Haitian	4	0.01
White:	30,017	95.98
Not Hispanic (29,228)	29,472	94.24
Hispanic (487)	545	1.74
Yugoslavian	25	0.08

Boone

Place Type: City
County: Boone
Population: 12,803

Ancestry/Race	Number	%
African American/Black:	64	0.50
Not Hispanic (35)	50	0.39
Hispanic (6)	14	0.11
African, sub-Saharan:	16	0.12
African	16	0.12
Am. Ind. or Alaska Nat., not spec.	19	0.15
American Indian tribes, specified:	36	0.28
Apache	2	0.02
Cherokee (8)	11	0.09
Chippewa (1)	1	0.01
Houma (1)	1	0.01
Latin American Indians (2)	7	0.05
Potawatomi	1	0.01
Sioux (3)	8	0.06
All other tribes	5	0.04
American Indian tribes, not spec.	6	0.05
Asian:	39	0.30
Chinese, ex. Taiwanese (6)	6	0.05
Filipino	4	0.03
Indian (2)	2	0.02
Japanese	1	0.01
Korean (7)	8	0.06
Laotian (1)	1	0.01
Thai (1)	1	0.01
Vietnamese (10)	15	0.12
Other Asian, not specified	1	0.01
Austrian	9	0.07
Belgian	13	0.10
British	29	0.23
Canadian	25	0.20
Czech	162	1.26
Czechoslovakian	10	0.08
Danish	316	2.47
Dutch	253	1.97
English	1,388	10.83
European	77	0.60
Finnish	5	0.04
French, except Basque	401	3.13
French Canadian	66	0.52
German	4,194	32.74
Greek	7	0.05
Hawaii Native/Pacific Islander:	6	0.05
Micronesian:	3	0.02
Guamanian/Chamorro	3	0.02
Polynesian:	2	0.02
Native Hawaiian	2	0.02
Other Pac. Isl., not spec.	1	0.01
Hispanic or Latino:	112	0.87
Central American:	5	0.04
Panamanian	2	0.02
Salvadoran	1	0.01
Other Central American	2	0.02
Cuban	2	0.02
Mexican	68	0.53
Puerto Rican	6	0.05
South American:	2	0.02
Argentinean	1	0.01
Chilean	1	0.01
Other Hispanic or Latino	29	0.23
Hungarian	43	0.34
Iranian	13	0.10
Irish	1,606	12.54
Italian	188	1.47
Latvian	14	0.11
Northern European	29	0.23
Norwegian	879	6.86
Pennsylvania German	6	0.05
Polish	112	0.87
Russian	30	0.23
Scandinavian	59	0.46
Scotch-Irish	216	1.69
Scottish	233	1.82
Slovak	8	0.06
Swedish	1,204	9.40
Swiss	46	0.36
United States or American	735	5.74
Welsh	82	0.64
White:	12,651	98.81
Not Hispanic (12,542)	12,596	98.38
Hispanic (48)	55	0.43

Burlington

Place Type: City
County: Des Moines
Population: 26,839

Ancestry/Race	Number	%
African American/Black:	1,575	5.87
Not Hispanic (1,332)	1,540	5.74
Hispanic (22)	35	0.13
African, sub-Saharan:	40	0.15
African	40	0.15
Alaska Native tribes, specified:	1	0.00
Aleut (1)	1	0.00
Am. Ind. or Alaska Nat., not spec.	70	0.26
American Indian tribes, specified:	111	0.41
Apache (1)	5	0.02
Blackfeet (2)	8	0.03
Cherokee (19)	41	0.15
Cheyenne (1)	1	0.00
Chippewa (3)	4	0.01
Cree	1	0.00
Creek (1)	4	0.01
Iroquois (3)	8	0.03
Kiowa (6)	7	0.03
Latin American Indians	2	0.01
Sioux (9)	16	0.06
All other tribes (8)	14	0.05
American Indian tribes, not spec.	13	0.05
Arab:	54	0.20
Arab/Arabic	22	0.08
Egyptian	6	0.02
Lebanese	6	0.02
Syrian	20	0.07
Asian:	234	0.87
Chinese, ex. Taiwanese (29)	39	0.15
Filipino (36)	51	0.19
Indian (57)	60	0.22
Japanese (3)	11	0.04
Korean (29)	42	0.16
Laotian (12)	12	0.04
Taiwanese (2)	2	0.01
Thai (3)	4	0.01
Vietnamese (4)	6	0.02
Other Asian, specified	2	0.01
Other Asian, not specified (1)	5	0.02
Australian	50	0.19
Austrian	38	0.14
Belgian	6	0.02
British	93	0.35
Canadian	17	0.06
Croatian	24	0.09
Czech	185	0.69
Czechoslovakian	27	0.10
Danish	247	0.92
Dutch	694	2.59
English	2,521	9.40
European	130	0.48
Finnish	14	0.05
French, except Basque	838	3.12
French Canadian	121	0.45
German	8,700	32.44
German Russian	3	0.01
Greek	32	0.12
Hawaii Native/Pacific Islander:	23	0.09
Micronesian: (4)	5	0.02
Guamanian/Chamorro (4)	5	0.02
Polynesian: (6)	14	0.05
Native Hawaiian (3)	9	0.03
Samoan (3)	5	0.02
Other Pac. Isl., specified	2	0.01
Other Pac. Isl., not spec.	2	0.01
Hispanic or Latino:	554	2.06
Central American:	5	0.02
Guatemalan	3	0.01
Panamanian	2	0.01
Cuban	3	0.01
Dominican Republic	2	0.01
Mexican	422	1.57
Puerto Rican	21	0.08
South American:	12	0.04
Argentinean	3	0.01
Bolivian	1	0.00
Colombian	3	0.01
Ecuadorian	3	0.01
Peruvian	2	0.01
Other Hispanic or Latino	89	0.33
Hungarian	64	0.24
Iranian	16	0.06
Irish	3,680	13.72
Italian	433	1.61
Lithuanian	25	0.09
Luxemburger	14	0.05
Norwegian	333	1.24
Pennsylvania German	30	0.11
Polish	195	0.73
Romanian	5	0.02
Russian	83	0.31
Scandinavian	11	0.04
Scotch-Irish	492	1.83
Scottish	408	1.52
Slovak	17	0.06
Swedish	1,231	4.59
Swiss	134	0.50
United States or American	2,408	8.98
Welsh	167	0.62
White:	24,938	92.92
Not Hispanic (24,328)	24,636	91.79
Hispanic (253)	302	1.13
Yugoslavian	26	0.10

Carroll

Place Type: City
County: Carroll
Population: 10,106

Ancestry/Race	Number	%
Acadian/Cajun	6	0.06
African American/Black:	30	0.30
Not Hispanic (16)	28	0.28
Hispanic (2)	2	0.02
Am. Ind. or Alaska Nat., not spec.	5	0.05
American Indian tribes, specified:	12	0.12
Cherokee	2	0.02
Chippewa (1)	1	0.01
Latin American Indians (2)	3	0.03
Sioux (1)	5	0.05
Yaqui	1	0.01
American Indian tribes, not spec.	2	0.02
Asian:	67	0.66
Chinese, ex. Taiwanese (18)	22	0.22
Filipino (10)	16	0.16
Indian (1)	3	0.03
Japanese (2)	4	0.04
Korean (8)	9	0.09
Thai (2)	3	0.03
Vietnamese (6)	9	0.09
Other Asian, not specified	1	0.01
Austrian	7	0.07
Belgian	33	0.33
British	16	0.16
Czech	55	0.55
Danish	262	2.61
Dutch	242	2.41
English	691	6.88

Notes: 1. Figures in the "Number" column do not add up to the total population due to: a) Ancestry/Race overlap — e.g. persons can report being both White and Irish, b) persons of Hispanic origin can report being any race, c) persons reporting two ancestries are counted in both categories. 2. Numbers in parentheses indicate the number of persons reporting this ancestry/race alone, not in combination with any other ancestry/race. 3. Refer to the Explanation of Data in the front of the book for more detailed information.

Ancestry/Race	Number	%
European	45	0.45
Finnish	6	0.06
French, except Basque	264	2.63
French Canadian	9	0.09
German	6,151	61.28
Hawaii Native/Pacific Islander:	1	0.01
Other Pac. Isl., not spec.	1	0.01
Hispanic or Latino:	58	0.57
Central American:	5	0.05
Costa Rican	2	0.02
Salvadoran	3	0.03
Mexican	38	0.38
Puerto Rican	3	0.03
South American:	1	0.01
Peruvian	1	0.01
Other Hispanic or Latino	11	0.11
Hungarian	42	0.42
Irish	1,286	12.81
Italian	91	0.91
Lithuanian	14	0.14
Luxemburger	21	0.21
Northern European	20	0.20
Norwegian	226	2.25
Polish	134	1.33
Scotch-Irish	68	0.68
Scottish	26	0.26
Swedish	233	2.32
Swiss	12	0.12
United States or American	475	4.73
Welsh	11	0.11
White:	9,996	98.91
Not Hispanic (9,939)	9,967	98.62
Hispanic (22)	29	0.29

Cedar Falls

Place Type: City
County: Black Hawk
Population: 36,145

Ancestry/Race	Number	%
African American/Black:	738	2.04
Not Hispanic (558)	723	2.00
Hispanic (10)	15	0.04
African, sub-Saharan:	41	0.11
African	41	0.11
Alaska Native tribes, specified:	1	0.00
Tlingit-Haida	1	0.00
Alaska Native tribes, not specified	1	0.00
Am. Ind. or Alaska Nat., not spec.	48	0.13
American Indian tribes, specified:	80	0.22
Apache	5	0.01
Blackfeet (1)	5	0.01
Cherokee (9)	29	0.08
Chippewa (5)	6	0.02
Cree	1	0.00
Delaware (1)	1	0.00
Latin American Indians	1	0.00
Navajo	1	0.00
Potawatomi (1)	1	0.00
Pueblo	1	0.00
Sioux (3)	10	0.03
Tohono O'Odham (1)	1	0.00
All other tribes (15)	18	0.05
American Indian tribes, not spec.	5	0.01
Arab:	73	0.20
Arab/Arabic	37	0.10
Lebanese	8	0.02
Moroccan	7	0.02
Syrian	6	0.02
Other Arab	15	0.04
Asian:	708	1.96
Bangladeshi (6)	6	0.02
Chinese, ex. Taiwanese (131)	170	0.47
Filipino (23)	40	0.11
Indian (152)	159	0.44
Indonesian (1)	1	0.00
Japanese (65)	80	0.22
Korean (118)	136	0.38
Laotian (23)	26	0.07
Malaysian (2)	4	0.01
Pakistani (4)	5	0.01
Taiwanese (4)	7	0.02
Thai (8)	11	0.03
Vietnamese (16)	21	0.06
Other Asian, specified	3	0.01
Other Asian, not specified (19)	39	0.11
Australian	22	0.06
Austrian	110	0.30
Belgian	61	0.17
British	191	0.53
Bulgarian	32	0.09
Canadian	26	0.07
Croatian	33	0.09
Czech	682	1.88
Czechoslovakian	93	0.26
Danish	1,702	4.69
Dutch	1,141	3.15
English	3,800	10.48
European	251	0.69
Finnish	100	0.28
French, except Basque	1,149	3.17
French Canadian	137	0.38
German	15,740	43.41
Greek	50	0.14
Hawaii Native/Pacific Islander:	23	0.06
Micronesian: (1)	3	0.01
Guamanian/Chamorro (1)	3	0.01
Polynesian: (7)	8	0.02
Native Hawaiian (3)	4	0.01
Samoan (3)	3	0.01
Other Polynesian (1)	1	0.00
Other Pac. Isl., specified	2	0.01
Other Pac. Isl., not spec.	10	0.03
Hispanic or Latino:	389	1.08
Central American:	15	0.04
Costa Rican	1	0.00
Guatemalan	2	0.01
Nicaraguan	3	0.01
Panamanian	5	0.01
Salvadoran	4	0.01
Cuban	16	0.04
Mexican	181	0.50
Puerto Rican	39	0.11
South American:	49	0.14
Argentinean	8	0.02
Chilean	18	0.05
Colombian	3	0.01
Ecuadorian	2	0.01
Peruvian	5	0.01
Venezuelan	12	0.03
Other South American	1	0.00
Other Hispanic or Latino	89	0.25
Hungarian	79	0.22
Iranian	6	0.02
Irish	4,694	12.95
Italian	512	1.41
Latvian	12	0.03
Lithuanian	8	0.02
Luxemburger	41	0.11
Northern European	76	0.21
Norwegian	3,167	8.73
Pennsylvania German	37	0.10
Polish	313	0.86
Romanian	13	0.04
Russian	139	0.38
Scandinavian	115	0.32
Scotch-Irish	396	1.09
Scottish	692	1.91
Serbian	11	0.03
Slavic	11	0.03
Slovak	51	0.14
Slovene	31	0.09
Swedish	889	2.45
Swiss	365	1.01
Ukrainian	29	0.08
United States or American	1,404	3.87
Welsh	423	1.17
West Indian, excl. Hispanic:	13	0.04
British West Indian	5	0.01
Trinidadian and Tobagonian	8	0.02
White:	34,739	96.11
Not Hispanic (34,207)	34,498	95.44
Hispanic (182)	241	0.67
Yugoslavian	14	0.04

Cedar Rapids

Place Type: City
County: Linn
Population: 120,758

Ancestry/Race	Number	%
African American/Black:	5,614	4.65
Not Hispanic (4,425)	5,505	4.56
Hispanic (56)	109	0.09
African, sub-Saharan:	429	0.36
African	237	0.20
Ethiopian	7	0.01
Ghanian	14	0.01
Kenyan	11	0.01
South African	31	0.03
Sudanese	129	0.11
Alaska Native tribes, specified:	4	0.00
Aleut	1	0.00
Tlingit-Haida (3)	3	0.00
Alaska Native tribes, not specified	4	0.00
Am. Ind. or Alaska Nat., not spec.	258	0.21
American Indian tribes, specified:	494	0.41
Apache (2)	10	0.01
Blackfeet (5)	20	0.02
Cherokee (28)	139	0.12
Cheyenne (1)	3	0.00
Chickasaw	1	0.00
Chippewa (17)	34	0.03
Choctaw (4)	14	0.01
Comanche (2)	6	0.00
Cree (1)	5	0.00
Creek (7)	12	0.01
Crow (1)	1	0.00
Houma	3	0.00
Iroquois (1)	7	0.01
Latin American Indians (9)	16	0.01
Lumbee (4)	4	0.00
Menominee (4)	8	0.01
Navajo (6)	6	0.00
Osage	4	0.00
Ottawa (1)	1	0.00
Pima	2	0.00
Pueblo	3	0.00
Puget Sound Salish	1	0.00
Seminole	3	0.00
Sioux (35)	78	0.06
Tohono O'Odham (2)	2	0.00
Ute (1)	1	0.00
Yuman (1)	1	0.00
All other tribes (65)	109	0.09
American Indian tribes, not spec.	52	0.04
Arab:	818	0.68
Arab/Arabic	22	0.02
Iraqi	105	0.09
Jordanian	9	0.01
Lebanese	637	0.53
Syrian	23	0.02
Other Arab	22	0.02
Armenian	8	0.01
Asian:	2,623	2.17
Bangladeshi (11)	12	0.01
Cambodian (6)	10	0.01
Chinese, ex. Taiwanese (249)	327	0.27
Filipino (139)	234	0.19
Hmong (1)	2	0.00
Indian (788)	828	0.69
Indonesian (7)	12	0.01
Japanese (79)	128	0.11
Korean (252)	317	0.26
Laotian (120)	144	0.12
Malaysian (2)	2	0.00
Pakistani (42)	51	0.04
Sri Lankan (4)	7	0.01

Notes: 1. Figures in the "Number" column do not add up to the total population due to: a) Ancestry/Race overlap — e.g. persons can report being both White and Irish, b) persons of Hispanic origin can report being any race, c) persons reporting two ancestries are counted in both categories. 2. Numbers in parentheses indicate the number of persons reporting this ancestry/race alone, not in combination with any other ancestry/race. 3. Refer to the Explanation of Data in the front of the book for more detailed information.

Ancestry/Race	Number	%
Taiwanese (2)	2	0.00
Thai (17)	33	0.03
Vietnamese (326)	372	0.31
Other Asian, specified (4)	6	0.00
Other Asian, not specified (44)	136	0.11
Australian	29	0.02
Austrian	255	0.21
Belgian	340	0.28
Brazilian	7	0.01
British	342	0.28
Bulgarian	11	0.01
Canadian	104	0.09
Croatian	103	0.09
Czech	7,934	6.58
Czechoslovakian	1,448	1.20
Danish	1,714	1.42
Dutch	3,345	2.77
Eastern European	11	0.01
English	11,379	9.44
European	1,042	0.86
Finnish	143	0.12
French, except Basque	3,527	2.93
French Canadian	408	0.34
German	42,747	35.46
Greek	405	0.34
Guyanese	13	0.01
Hawaii Native/Pacific Islander:	121	0.10
Micronesian: (32)	39	0.03
Guamanian/Chamorro (3)	7	0.01
Other Micronesian (29)	32	0.03
Polynesian: (23)	54	0.04
Native Hawaiian (11)	25	0.02
Samoan (10)	15	0.01
Tongan	6	0.00
Other Polynesian (2)	8	0.01
Other Pac. Isl., specified	1	0.00
Other Pac. Isl., not spec. (18)	27	0.02
Hispanic or Latino:	2,065	1.71
Central American:	85	0.07
Costa Rican	2	0.00
Guatemalan	12	0.01
Honduran	17	0.01
Nicaraguan	3	0.00
Panamanian	19	0.02
Salvadoran	23	0.02
Other Central American	9	0.01
Cuban	37	0.03
Dominican Republic	8	0.01
Mexican	1,315	1.09
Puerto Rican	143	0.12
South American:	80	0.07
Argentinean	4	0.00
Bolivian	4	0.00
Chilean	8	0.01
Colombian	18	0.01
Ecuadorian	20	0.02
Paraguayan	1	0.00
Peruvian	10	0.01
Venezuelan	11	0.01
Other South American	4	0.00
Other Hispanic or Latino	397	0.33
Hungarian	260	0.22
Icelander	11	0.01
Iranian	18	0.01
Irish	20,591	17.08
Israeli	16	0.01
Italian	2,265	1.88
Latvian	1	0.00
Lithuanian	86	0.07
Luxemburger	68	0.06
Northern European	128	0.11
Norwegian	6,145	5.10
Pennsylvania German	175	0.15
Polish	1,796	1.49
Portuguese	69	0.06
Romanian	31	0.03
Russian	204	0.17
Scandinavian	315	0.26
Scotch-Irish	1,927	1.60
Scottish	2,329	1.93
Serbian	7	0.01
Slavic	16	0.01
Slovak	164	0.14
Slovene	23	0.02
Swedish	3,179	2.64
Swiss	566	0.47
Turkish	37	0.03
Ukrainian	60	0.05
United States or American	6,605	5.48
Welsh	816	0.68
West Indian, excl. Hispanic:	74	0.06
Bahamian	36	0.03
British West Indian	24	0.02
Jamaican	11	0.01
West Indian	3	0.00
White:	112,874	93.47
Not Hispanic (109,759)	111,470	92.31
Hispanic (1,172)	1,404	1.16
Yugoslavian	93	0.08

Clinton

Place Type: City
County: Clinton
Population: 27,772

Ancestry/Race	Number	%
African American/Black:	1,060	3.82
Not Hispanic (878)	1,043	3.76
Hispanic (15)	17	0.06
African, sub-Saharan:	30	0.11
African	30	0.11
Am. Ind. or Alaska Nat., not spec.	72	0.26
American Indian tribes, specified:	149	0.54
Apache	4	0.01
Blackfeet (3)	5	0.02
Cherokee (21)	71	0.26
Cheyenne (6)	9	0.03
Chickasaw	1	0.00
Chippewa (13)	25	0.09
Choctaw (2)	2	0.01
Comanche	1	0.00
Delaware (2)	3	0.01
Iroquois	1	0.00
Latin American Indians (2)	3	0.01
Navajo	1	0.00
Ottawa (1)	4	0.01
Shoshone (3)	3	0.01
Sioux (5)	8	0.03
All other tribes (3)	8	0.03
American Indian tribes, not sp[illegible]	3	0.01
Arab:	27	0.10
Egyptian	22	0.08
Lebanese	5	0.02
Asian:	258	0.93
Chinese, ex. Taiwanese (23)	25	0.09
Filipino (30)	35	0.13
Indian (70)	74	0.27
Japanese (12)	20	0.07
Korean (47)	50	0.18
Laotian (12)	12	0.04
Pakistani (4)	6	0.02
Taiwanese	4	0.01
Thai	2	0.01
Vietnamese (14)	16	0.06
Other Asian, not specified (8)	14	0.05
Austrian	56	0.20
Belgian	132	0.47
British	67	0.24
Bulgarian	25	0.09
Canadian	40	0.14
Croatian	20	0.07
Czech	118	0.42
Czechoslovakian	51	0.18
Danish	804	2.89
Dutch	1,600	5.75
English	2,368	8.52
European	37	0.13
Finnish	5	0.02
French, except Basque	855	3.07
French Canadian	68	0.24
German	10,218	36.75
Greek	57	0.20
Hawaii Native/Pacific Islander:	11	0.04
Micronesian:	1	0.00
Guamanian/Chamorro	1	0.00
Polynesian: (2)	2	0.01
Native Hawaiian (1)	1	0.00
Samoan (1)	1	0.00
Other Pac. Isl., not spec. (1)	8	0.03
Hispanic or Latino:	466	1.68
Central American:	7	0.03
Guatemalan	2	0.01
Honduran	3	0.01
Other Central American	2	0.01
Cuban	12	0.04
Mexican	342	1.23
Puerto Rican	28	0.10
South American:	12	0.04
Argentinean	6	0.02
Chilean	4	0.01
Ecuadorian	2	0.01
Other Hispanic or Latino	65	0.23
Hungarian	34	0.12
Irish	4,260	15.32
Italian	435	1.56
Latvian	15	0.05
Lithuanian	28	0.10
Luxemburger	29	0.10
Northern European	35	0.13
Norwegian	567	2.04
Pennsylvania German	22	0.08
Polish	398	1.43
Portuguese	12	0.04
Romanian	27	0.10
Russian	32	0.12
Scandinavian	49	0.18
Scotch-Irish	389	1.40
Scottish	424	1.52
Serbian	6	0.02
Slavic	13	0.05
Slovak	11	0.04
Swedish	815	2.93
Swiss	126	0.45
United States or American	1,914	6.88
Welsh	128	0.46
West Indian, excl. Hispanic:	40	0.14
Bahamian	12	0.04
Belizean	28	0.10
White:	26,408	95.09
Not Hispanic (25,791)	26,108	94.01
Hispanic (258)	300	1.08
Yugoslavian	22	0.08

Clive

Place Type: City
County: Polk
Population: 12,855

Ancestry/Race	Number	%
African American/Black:	189	1.47
Not Hispanic (160)	184	1.43
Hispanic	5	0.04
African, sub-Saharan:	22	0.17
Kenyan	22	0.17
Am. Ind. or Alaska Nat., not spec.	15	0.12
American Indian tribes, specified:	23	0.18
Blackfeet	1	0.01
Cherokee (1)	10	0.08
Latin American Indians (2)	2	0.02
Pueblo	1	0.01
Sioux	3	0.02
All other tribes (2)	6	0.05
American Indian tribes, not spec.	2	0.02
Arab:	52	0.40
Egyptian	33	0.26
Lebanese	19	0.15
Asian:	431	3.35
Cambodian (2)	2	0.02

Notes: 1. Figures in the "Number" column do not add up to the total population due to: a) Ancestry/Race overlap — e.g. persons can report being both White and Irish, b) persons of Hispanic origin can report being any race, c) persons reporting two ancestries are counted in both categories. 2. Numbers in parentheses indicate the number of persons reporting this ancestry/race alone, not in combination with any other ancestry/race. 3. Refer to the Explanation of Data in the front of the book for more detailed information.

Ancestry/Race	Number	%
Other Asian, not specified (21)	26	0.14
British	22	0.12
Canadian	43	0.23
Czechoslovakian	15	0.08
Dutch	93	0.50
Eastern European	23	0.12
English	633	3.38
European	53	0.28
French, except Basque	302	1.61
French Canadian	60	0.32
German	783	4.18
Greek	19	0.10
Hawaii Native/Pacific Islander:	11	0.06
Micronesian: (4)	4	0.02
Guamanian/Chamorro (4)	4	0.02
Polynesian: (3)	5	0.03
Native Hawaiian (2)	2	0.01
Samoan (1)	3	0.02
Other Pac. Isl., specified	1	0.01
Other Pac. Isl., not spec.	1	0.01
Hispanic or Latino:	338	1.81
Central American:	52	0.28
Guatemalan	9	0.05
Honduran	1	0.01
Nicaraguan	1	0.01
Panamanian	34	0.18
Salvadoran	7	0.04
Cuban	19	0.10
Dominican Republic	2	0.01
Mexican	68	0.36
Puerto Rican	88	0.47
South American:	27	0.14
Argentinean	1	0.01
Bolivian	2	0.01
Chilean	1	0.01
Colombian	2	0.01
Ecuadorian	5	0.03
Peruvian	7	0.04
Venezuelan	9	0.05
Other Hispanic or Latino	82	0.44
Iranian	9	0.05
Irish	783	4.18
Italian	415	2.22
Lithuanian	8	0.04
Norwegian	33	0.18
Polish	146	0.78
Russian	24	0.13
Scotch-Irish	144	0.77
Scottish	169	0.90
Slovak	34	0.18
Swedish	56	0.30
Swiss	6	0.03
Ukrainian	32	0.17
United States or American	312	1.67
Welsh	43	0.23
West Indian, excl. Hispanic:	223	1.19
Barbadian	15	0.08
Bermudan	11	0.06
British West Indian	43	0.23
Dutch West Indian	12	0.06
Jamaican	106	0.57
Trinidadian and Tobagonian	36	0.19
White:	4,009	21.42
Not Hispanic (3,766)	3,909	20.88
Hispanic (90)	100	0.53

Green Haven

Place Type: Census Designated Place
County: Anne Arundel
Population: 17,415

Ancestry/Race	Number	%
African American/Black:	831	4.77
Not Hispanic (752)	823	4.73
Hispanic (8)	8	0.05
African, sub-Saharan:	43	0.25
African	38	0.22
Cape Verdean	5	0.03
Am. Ind. or Alaska Nat., not spec.	43	0.25
American Indian tribes, specified:	99	0.57
Blackfeet (4)	5	0.03
Cherokee (17)	44	0.25
Chippewa (3)	4	0.02
Choctaw (1)	4	0.02
Creek	1	0.01
Delaware	2	0.01
Houma (1)	1	0.01
Iroquois (1)	1	0.01
Latin American Indians (1)	1	0.01
Lumbee (8)	9	0.05
Navajo	2	0.01
Sioux	7	0.04
All other tribes (13)	18	0.10
American Indian tribes, not spec.	8	0.05
Arab:	35	0.20
Egyptian	13	0.07
Lebanese	8	0.05
Moroccan	7	0.04
Syrian	7	0.04
Asian:	320	1.84
Chinese, ex. Taiwanese (68)	72	0.41
Filipino (73)	100	0.57
Indian (10)	18	0.10
Japanese (18)	43	0.25
Korean (41)	58	0.33
Pakistani (5)	5	0.03
Thai (1)	1	0.01
Vietnamese (6)	6	0.03
Other Asian, specified	3	0.02
Other Asian, not specified (7)	14	0.08
Austrian	51	0.29
Belgian	17	0.10
Brazilian	32	0.18
Canadian	10	0.06
Croatian	11	0.06
Cypriot	8	0.05
Czech	63	0.36
Czechoslovakian	179	1.03
Dutch	291	1.68
English	1,616	9.30
Estonian	8	0.05
European	39	0.22
French, except Basque	494	2.84
French Canadian	141	0.81
German	4,828	27.79
German Russian	24	0.14
Greek	138	0.79
Hawaii Native/Pacific Islander:	13	0.07
Micronesian: (1)	2	0.01
Guamanian/Chamorro (1)	2	0.01
Polynesian: (3)	9	0.05
Native Hawaiian (3)	9	0.05
Other Pac. Isl., not spec.	2	0.01
Hispanic or Latino:	256	1.47
Central American:	11	0.06
Costa Rican	2	0.01
Guatemalan	4	0.02
Honduran	5	0.03
Cuban	18	0.10
Dominican Republic	4	0.02
Mexican	53	0.30
Puerto Rican	86	0.49
South American:	31	0.18
Argentinean	3	0.02
Bolivian	1	0.01
Colombian	3	0.02
Ecuadorian	6	0.03
Peruvian	9	0.05
Venezuelan	5	0.03
Other South American	4	0.02
Other Hispanic or Latino	53	0.30
Hungarian	159	0.92
Irish	3,541	20.38
Italian	1,490	8.58
Lithuanian	72	0.41
Maltese	86	0.50
Norwegian	95	0.55
Pennsylvania German	41	0.24
Polish	1,129	6.50
Romanian	29	0.17
Russian	98	0.56
Scotch-Irish	241	1.39
Scottish	240	1.38
Slavic	54	0.31
Slovak	54	0.31
Swedish	80	0.46
Swiss	33	0.19
Ukrainian	59	0.34
United States or American	1,662	9.57
Welsh	184	1.06
West Indian, excl. Hispanic:	20	0.12
British West Indian	6	0.03
Jamaican	14	0.08
White:	16,243	93.27
Not Hispanic (15,863)	16,072	92.29
Hispanic (151)	171	0.98

Green Valley

Place Type: Census Designated Place
County: Frederick
Population: 12,262

Ancestry/Race	Number	%
African American/Black:	194	1.58
Not Hispanic (151)	190	1.55
Hispanic (1)	4	0.03
African, sub-Saharan:	14	0.11
South African	14	0.11
Alaska Native tribes, specified:	3	0.02
Alaska Athabascan (3)	3	0.02
Am. Ind. or Alaska Nat., not spec.	19	0.15
American Indian tribes, specified:	45	0.37
Blackfeet	6	0.05
Cherokee (8)	25	0.20
Chickasaw	1	0.01
Delaware	1	0.01
Iroquois	1	0.01
Osage (1)	1	0.01
Pueblo (1)	1	0.01
Sioux (1)	1	0.01
All other tribes (3)	8	0.07
American Indian tribes, not spec.	1	0.01
Arab:	25	0.21
Arab/Arabic	12	0.10
Lebanese	8	0.07
Syrian	5	0.04
Asian:	162	1.32
Cambodian (1)	2	0.02
Chinese, ex. Taiwanese (25)	33	0.27
Filipino (13)	20	0.16
Indian (28)	28	0.23
Indonesian	1	0.01
Japanese (9)	19	0.15
Korean (14)	15	0.12
Pakistani (7)	9	0.07
Thai (2)	3	0.02
Vietnamese (11)	18	0.15
Other Asian, specified	3	0.02
Other Asian, not specified (6)	11	0.09
Austrian	5	0.04
Belgian	21	0.17
Brazilian	36	0.30
British	91	0.75
Canadian	71	0.58
Celtic	22	0.18
Czech	42	0.34
Czechoslovakian	56	0.46
Danish	15	0.12
Dutch	186	1.53
Eastern European	8	0.07
English	1,973	16.18
European	234	1.92
Finnish	7	0.06
French, except Basque	454	3.72
French Canadian	96	0.79
German	3,092	25.36
Greek	165	1.35
Hawaii Native/Pacific Islander:	6	0.05

Notes: 1. Figures in the "Number" column do not add up to the total population due to: a) Ancestry/Race overlap — e.g. persons can report being both White and Irish, b) persons of Hispanic origin can report being any race, c) persons reporting two ancestries are counted in both categories. 2. Numbers in parentheses indicate the number of persons reporting this ancestry/race alone, not in combination with any other ancestry/race. 3. Refer to the Explanation of Data in the front of the book for more detailed information.

Ancestry/Race	Number	%
Polynesian: (5)	5	0.04
Native Hawaiian (4)	4	0.03
Samoan (1)	1	0.01
Other Pac. Isl., not spec.	1	0.01
Hispanic or Latino:	207	1.69
Central American:	34	0.28
Costa Rican	2	0.02
Guatemalan	11	0.09
Honduran	2	0.02
Salvadoran	19	0.15
Cuban	16	0.13
Dominican Republic	1	0.01
Mexican	39	0.32
Puerto Rican	34	0.28
South American:	33	0.27
Argentinean	1	0.01
Bolivian	2	0.02
Chilean	3	0.02
Colombian	18	0.15
Ecuadorian	5	0.04
Paraguayan	1	0.01
Peruvian	3	0.02
Other Hispanic or Latino	50	0.41
Hungarian	124	1.02
Iranian	18	0.15
Irish	2,449	20.09
Italian	927	7.60
Lithuanian	25	0.21
Norwegian	117	0.96
Pennsylvania German	5	0.04
Polish	530	4.35
Portuguese	41	0.34
Romanian	32	0.26
Russian	200	1.64
Scandinavian	19	0.16
Scotch-Irish	203	1.67
Scottish	343	2.81
Slovak	151	1.24
Slovene	17	0.14
Swedish	201	1.65
Swiss	71	0.58
Ukrainian	37	0.30
United States or American	986	8.09
Welsh	103	0.84
White:	11,902	97.06
Not Hispanic (11,613)	11,736	95.71
Hispanic (148)	166	1.35
Yugoslavian	30	0.25

Greenbelt

Place Type: City
County: Prince George's
Population: 21,456

Ancestry/Race	Number	%
Acadian/Cajun	15	0.07
African American/Black:	9,254	43.13
Not Hispanic (8,746)	9,104	42.43
Hispanic (125)	150	0.70
African, sub-Saharan:	1,981	9.26
African	668	3.12
Cape Verdean	9	0.04
Ethiopian	79	0.37
Ghanian	154	0.72
Kenyan	28	0.13
Nigerian	599	2.80
Sierra Leonean	201	0.94
South African	6	0.03
Sudanese	37	0.17
Ugandan	11	0.05
Other sub-Saharan African	189	0.88
Am. Ind. or Alaska Nat., not spec.	105	0.49
American Indian tribes, specified:	97	0.45
Apache (1)	4	0.02
Blackfeet	5	0.02
Cherokee (2)	34	0.16
Chippewa (1)	1	0.00
Choctaw	1	0.00
Creek (2)	3	0.01
Iroquois (1)	4	0.02
Latin American Indians (2)	10	0.05
Lumbee (2)	2	0.01
Navajo (1)	1	0.00
Pueblo	8	0.04
Shoshone (2)	2	0.01
Sioux	8	0.04
Ute	1	0.00
All other tribes (8)	13	0.06
American Indian tribes, not spec.	13	0.06
Arab:	185	0.86
Arab/Arabic	36	0.17
Egyptian	18	0.08
Jordanian	23	0.11
Palestinian	48	0.22
Syrian	50	0.23
Other Arab	10	0.05
Armenian	9	0.04
Asian:	2,827	13.18
Bangladeshi (14)	15	0.07
Cambodian (16)	16	0.07
Chinese, ex. Taiwanese (557)	597	2.78
Filipino (125)	153	0.71
Indian (733)	807	3.76
Indonesian (12)	12	0.06
Japanese (70)	85	0.40
Korean (686)	706	3.29
Laotian (3)	3	0.01
Malaysian (4)	10	0.05
Pakistani (74)	94	0.44
Sri Lankan (2)	4	0.02
Taiwanese (32)	38	0.18
Thai (16)	23	0.11
Vietnamese (177)	187	0.87
Other Asian, specified (9)	17	0.08
Other Asian, not specified (36)	60	0.28
Austrian	7	0.03
Brazilian	65	0.30
British	93	0.43
Bulgarian	22	0.10
Canadian	27	0.13
Carpatho Rusyn	9	0.04
Croatian	6	0.03
Czech	12	0.06
Czechoslovakian	31	0.14
Danish	106	0.50
Dutch	225	1.05
English	1,401	6.55
Estonian	4	0.02
European	176	0.82
Finnish	31	0.14
French, except Basque	226	1.06
French Canadian	74	0.35
German	1,824	8.53
Greek	31	0.14
Guyanese	80	0.37
Hawaii Native/Pacific Islander:	36	0.17
Micronesian: (6)	6	0.03
Guamanian/Chamorro (6)	6	0.03
Polynesian: (2)	8	0.04
Native Hawaiian (2)	5	0.02
Samoan	2	0.01
Tongan	1	0.00
Other Pac. Isl., specified	5	0.02
Other Pac. Isl., not spec. (3)	16	0.07
Hispanic or Latino:	1,383	6.45
Central American:	325	1.51
Costa Rican	3	0.01
Guatemalan	57	0.27
Honduran	9	0.04
Nicaraguan	19	0.09
Panamanian	17	0.08
Salvadoran	199	0.93
Other Central American	21	0.10
Cuban	33	0.15
Dominican Republic	50	0.23
Mexican	261	1.22
Puerto Rican	167	0.78
South American:	166	0.77
Argentinean	15	0.07
Bolivian	16	0.07
Chilean	11	0.05
Colombian	31	0.14
Ecuadorian	20	0.09
Peruvian	40	0.19
Uruguayan	3	0.01
Venezuelan	8	0.04
Other South American	22	0.10
Other Hispanic or Latino	381	1.78
Hungarian	104	0.49
Iranian	57	0.27
Irish	1,640	7.67
Israeli	18	0.08
Italian	538	2.52
Latvian	11	0.05
Lithuanian	90	0.42
Northern European	20	0.09
Norwegian	105	0.49
Polish	432	2.02
Portuguese	60	0.28
Romanian	58	0.27
Russian	325	1.52
Scandinavian	7	0.03
Scotch-Irish	289	1.35
Scottish	216	1.01
Serbian	6	0.03
Slovak	53	0.25
Slovene	13	0.06
Swedish	120	0.56
Swiss	58	0.27
Turkish	35	0.16
Ukrainian	45	0.21
United States or American	814	3.81
Welsh	204	0.95
West Indian, excl. Hispanic:	680	3.18
Barbadian	31	0.14
British West Indian	25	0.12
Haitian	26	0.12
Jamaican	514	2.40
Trinidadian and Tobagonian	17	0.08
West Indian	67	0.31
White:	8,995	41.92
Not Hispanic (7,986)	8,376	39.04
Hispanic (540)	619	2.88

Hagerstown

Place Type: City
County: Washington
Population: 36,687

Ancestry/Race	Number	%
African American/Black:	4,125	11.24
Not Hispanic (3,661)	4,049	11.04
Hispanic (61)	76	0.21
African, sub-Saharan:	357	0.97
African	357	0.97
Am. Ind. or Alaska Nat., not spec.	112	0.31
American Indian tribes, specified:	132	0.36
Apache (6)	14	0.04
Blackfeet	3	0.01
Cherokee (22)	60	0.16
Chippewa (1)	3	0.01
Choctaw	6	0.02
Comanche (1)	1	0.00
Cree (1)	1	0.00
Creek (1)	2	0.01
Delaware	3	0.01
Iroquois (6)	14	0.04
Latin American Indians (2)	4	0.01
Lumbee (1)	3	0.01
Navajo	1	0.00
Pima	1	0.00
Sioux (4)	8	0.02
Yaqui (1)	1	0.00
All other tribes (3)	7	0.02
American Indian tribes, not spec.	11	0.03
Arab:	30	0.08
Arab/Arabic	1	0.00
Lebanese	14	0.04

Notes: 1. Figures in the "Number" column do not add up to the total population due to: a) Ancestry/Race overlap — e.g. persons can report being both White and Irish, b) persons of Hispanic origin can report being any race, c) persons reporting two ancestries are counted in both categories. 2. Numbers in parentheses indicate the number of persons reporting this ancestry/race alone, not in combination with any other ancestry/race. 3. Refer to the Explanation of Data in the front of the book for more detailed information.

Syrian	7	0.02
Other Arab	8	0.02
Armenian	9	0.02
Asian:	437	1.19
Cambodian (4)	6	0.02
Chinese, ex. Taiwanese (68)	72	0.20
Filipino (56)	76	0.21
Indian (112)	126	0.34
Indonesian (4)	5	0.01
Japanese (7)	10	0.03
Korean (39)	53	0.14
Pakistani (3)	3	0.01
Taiwanese (1)	2	0.01
Thai (6)	10	0.03
Vietnamese (45)	49	0.13
Other Asian, specified (1)	1	0.00
Other Asian, not specified (4)	24	0.07
Australian	23	0.06
Austrian	32	0.09
Belgian	6	0.02
British	124	0.34
Canadian	37	0.10
Celtic	5	0.01
Croatian	15	0.04
Czech	65	0.18
Czechoslovakian	14	0.04
Danish	29	0.08
Dutch	602	1.64
English	2,462	6.70
European	179	0.49
Finnish	48	0.13
French, except Basque	714	1.94
French Canadian	87	0.24
German	8,105	22.06
Greek	62	0.17
Hawaii Native/Pacific Islander:	38	0.10
Micronesian: (3)	4	0.01
Guamanian/Chamorro (3)	4	0.01
Polynesian: (8)	21	0.06
Native Hawaiian (8)	17	0.05
Samoan	4	0.01
Other Pac. Isl., not spec. (4)	13	0.04
Hispanic or Latino:	649	1.77
Central American:	28	0.08
Costa Rican	2	0.01
Guatemalan	2	0.01
Honduran	6	0.02
Nicaraguan	1	0.00
Panamanian	8	0.02
Salvadoran	9	0.02
Cuban	13	0.04
Dominican Republic	41	0.11
Mexican	195	0.53
Puerto Rican	210	0.57
South American:	27	0.07
Colombian	5	0.01
Ecuadorian	7	0.02
Peruvian	12	0.03
Other South American	3	0.01
Other Hispanic or Latino	135	0.37
Hungarian	92	0.25
Irish	3,999	10.88
Italian	1,322	3.60
Latvian	29	0.08
Lithuanian	69	0.19
Norwegian	132	0.36
Pennsylvania German	33	0.09
Polish	489	1.33
Portuguese	47	0.13
Romanian	75	0.20
Russian	155	0.42
Scandinavian	35	0.10
Scotch-Irish	449	1.22
Scottish	397	1.08
Serbian	5	0.01
Slavic	15	0.04
Slovak	65	0.18
Swedish	141	0.38
Swiss	63	0.17
Ukrainian	52	0.14
United States or American	5,166	14.06
Welsh	180	0.49
West Indian, excl. Hispanic:	81	0.22
Dutch West Indian	4	0.01
Haitian	24	0.07
Jamaican	46	0.13
West Indian	7	0.02
White:	32,136	87.60
Not Hispanic (31,244)	31,799	86.68
Hispanic (288)	337	0.92
Yugoslavian	16	0.04

Halfway

Place Type: Census Designated Place
County: Washington
Population: 10,065

Ancestry/Race	Number	%
African American/Black:	259	2.57
Not Hispanic (210)	247	2.45
Hispanic (4)	12	0.12
African, sub-Saharan:	10	0.10
Cape Verdean	6	0.06
Ethiopian	4	0.04
Am. Ind. or Alaska Nat., not spec.	8	0.08
American Indian tribes, specified:	19	0.19
Cherokee (4)	12	0.12
Latin American Indians	2	0.02
Sioux (2)	2	0.02
All other tribes	3	0.03
American Indian tribes, not spec.	1	0.01
Arab:	6	0.06
Moroccan	6	0.06
Asian:	128	1.27
Bangladeshi	1	0.01
Chinese, ex. Taiwanese (25)	28	0.28
Filipino (11)	16	0.16
Indian (8)	9	0.09
Indonesian (3)	4	0.04
Japanese (4)	13	0.13
Korean (10)	16	0.16
Pakistani (6)	6	0.06
Taiwanese	1	0.01
Thai (1)	1	0.01
Vietnamese (19)	19	0.19
Other Asian, specified (2)	2	0.02
Other Asian, not specified (8)	12	0.12
Austrian	49	0.49
British	18	0.18
Canadian	11	0.11
Czech	7	0.07
Czechoslovakian	35	0.35
Danish	7	0.07
Dutch	223	2.23
Eastern European	7	0.07
English	1,069	10.68
European	54	0.54
French, except Basque	191	1.91
French Canadian	25	0.25
German	2,936	29.32
Greek	16	0.16
Hawaii Native/Pacific Islander:	17	0.17
Micronesian: (10)	10	0.10
Guamanian/Chamorro (2)	2	0.02
Other Micronesian (8)	8	0.08
Polynesian:	2	0.02
Native Hawaiian	2	0.02
Other Pac. Isl., not spec. (2)	5	0.05
Hispanic or Latino:	110	1.09
Central American:	1	0.01
Guatemalan	1	0.01
Dominican Republic	8	0.08
Mexican	17	0.17
Puerto Rican	31	0.31
South American:	16	0.16
Chilean	1	0.01
Colombian	7	0.07
Peruvian	7	0.07
Uruguayan	1	0.01
Other Hispanic or Latino	37	0.37
Hungarian	21	0.21
Iranian	6	0.06
Irish	1,107	11.06
Italian	413	4.13
Norwegian	40	0.40
Pennsylvania German	8	0.08
Polish	115	1.15
Portuguese	19	0.19
Russian	45	0.45
Scotch-Irish	100	1.00
Scottish	361	3.61
Serbian	8	0.08
Slavic	28	0.28
Swedish	121	1.21
Swiss	49	0.49
United States or American	1,090	10.89
Welsh	46	0.46
West Indian, excl. Hispanic:	29	0.29
Trinidadian and Tobagonian	29	0.29
White:	9,702	96.39
Not Hispanic (9,544)	9,620	95.58
Hispanic (65)	82	0.81
Yugoslavian	19	0.19

Havre de Grace

Place Type: City
County: Harford
Population: 11,331

Ancestry/Race	Number	%
African American/Black:	1,942	17.14
Not Hispanic (1,816)	1,919	16.94
Hispanic (14)	23	0.20
African, sub-Saharan:	70	0.62
African	70	0.62
Alaska Native tribes, specified:	1	0.01
Alaska Athabascan (1)	1	0.01
Am. Ind. or Alaska Nat., not spec.	29	0.26
American Indian tribes, specified:	55	0.49
Apache (1)	2	0.02
Blackfeet (1)	5	0.04
Cherokee (9)	31	0.27
Choctaw	1	0.01
Iroquois	2	0.02
Latin American Indians	3	0.03
Navajo (1)	1	0.01
Osage (1)	1	0.01
Sioux	1	0.01
All other tribes (1)	8	0.07
American Indian tribes, not spec.	1	0.01
Arab:	20	0.18
Lebanese	20	0.18
Asian:	217	1.92
Chinese, ex. Taiwanese (14)	23	0.20
Filipino (35)	60	0.53
Indian (28)	31	0.27
Japanese (11)	32	0.28
Korean (33)	39	0.34
Pakistani (5)	5	0.04
Thai (2)	2	0.02
Vietnamese (4)	6	0.05
Other Asian, not specified (11)	19	0.17
Austrian	29	0.26
Belgian	18	0.16
British	67	0.59
Bulgarian	13	0.11
Canadian	31	0.27
Celtic	9	0.08
Czech	14	0.12
Czechoslovakian	42	0.37
Danish	19	0.17
Dutch	81	0.71
Eastern European	20	0.18
English	1,041	9.18
European	106	0.93
Finnish	7	0.06
French, except Basque	293	2.58
French Canadian	22	0.19

Notes: 1. Figures in the "Number" column do not add up to the total population due to: a) Ancestry/Race overlap — e.g. persons can report being both White and Irish, b) persons of Hispanic origin can report being any race, c) persons reporting two ancestries are counted in both categories. 2. Numbers in parentheses indicate the number of persons reporting this ancestry/race alone, not in combination with any other ancestry/race. 3. Refer to the Explanation of Data in the front of the book for more detailed information.

German	1,886	16.63
Greek	96	0.85
Hawaii Native/Pacific Islander:	18	0.16
Micronesian: (9)	10	0.09
Guamanian/Chamorro (9)	10	0.09
Polynesian: (3)	7	0.06
Native Hawaiian (3)	7	0.06
Other Pac. Isl., not spec. (1)	1	0.01
Hispanic or Latino:	241	2.13
Central American:	6	0.05
Guatemalan	2	0.02
Honduran	1	0.01
Panamanian	1	0.01
Salvadoran	2	0.02
Cuban	5	0.04
Dominican Republic	1	0.01
Mexican	59	0.52
Puerto Rican	111	0.98
South American:	10	0.09
Argentinean	3	0.03
Chilean	2	0.02
Colombian	1	0.01
Ecuadorian	1	0.01
Peruvian	1	0.01
Uruguayan	1	0.01
Other South American	1	0.01
Other Hispanic or Latino	49	0.43
Hungarian	54	0.48
Icelander	62	0.55
Irish	1,631	14.38
Italian	783	6.90
Lithuanian	23	0.20
Norwegian	87	0.77
Pennsylvania German	25	0.22
Polish	323	2.85
Portuguese	8	0.07
Russian	75	0.66
Scandinavian	39	0.34
Scotch-Irish	197	1.74
Scottish	276	2.43
Slavic	8	0.07
Swedish	145	1.28
Ukrainian	26	0.23
United States or American	982	8.66
Welsh	111	0.98
White:	9,204	81.23
Not Hispanic (8,875)	9,064	79.99
Hispanic (104)	140	1.24
Yugoslavian	8	0.07

Hillcrest Heights

Place Type: Census Designated Place
County: Prince George's
Population: 16,359

Ancestry/Race	Number	%
African American/Black:	15,451	94.45
Not Hispanic (15,174)	15,357	93.87
Hispanic (69)	94	0.57
African, sub-Saharan:	351	2.17
African	196	1.21
Ethiopian	41	0.25
Liberian	98	0.61
Sierra Leonean	7	0.04
Other sub-Saharan African	9	0.06
Am. Ind. or Alaska Nat., not spec.	64	0.39
American Indian tribes, specified:	73	0.45
Apache (1)	1	0.01
Blackfeet	21	0.13
Cherokee (4)	38	0.23
Comanche (1)	1	0.01
Iroquois	3	0.02
Latin American Indians	1	0.01
All other tribes (2)	8	0.05
American Indian tribes, not spec.	1	0.01
Asian:	100	0.61
Chinese, ex. Taiwanese (16)	22	0.13
Filipino (20)	36	0.22
Indian (9)	15	0.09
Indonesian	1	0.01
Japanese (4)	6	0.04
Korean (2)	6	0.04
Taiwanese	1	0.01
Thai	3	0.02
Vietnamese (2)	5	0.03
Other Asian, not specified (4)	5	0.03
Belgian	4	0.02
British	6	0.04
Czech	5	0.03
Czechoslovakian	10	0.06
Danish	7	0.04
Dutch	31	0.19
English	110	0.68
French, except Basque	25	0.15
German	154	0.95
Greek	26	0.16
Guyanese	12	0.07
Hawaii Native/Pacific Islander:	7	0.04
Polynesian: (1)	2	0.01
Native Hawaiian	1	0.01
Samoan (1)	1	0.01
Other Pac. Isl., not spec.	5	0.03
Hispanic or Latino:	182	1.11
Central American:	29	0.18
Guatemalan	8	0.05
Panamanian	17	0.10
Salvadoran	3	0.02
Other Central American	1	0.01
Cuban	5	0.03
Dominican Republic	11	0.07
Mexican	37	0.23
Puerto Rican	42	0.26
South American:	7	0.04
Chilean	1	0.01
Colombian	1	0.01
Paraguayan	2	0.01
Other South American	3	0.02
Other Hispanic or Latino	51	0.31
Hungarian	7	0.04
Irish	192	1.19
Italian	113	0.70
Lithuanian	11	0.07
Polish	26	0.16
Portuguese	15	0.09
Scottish	19	0.12
Ukrainian	24	0.15
United States or American	130	0.80
Welsh	6	0.04
West Indian, excl. Hispanic:	196	1.21
Barbadian	29	0.18
British West Indian	15	0.09
Haitian	11	0.07
Jamaican	67	0.41
Trinidadian and Tobagonian	62	0.38
West Indian	12	0.07
White:	858	5.24
Not Hispanic (711)	807	4.93
Hispanic (39)	51	0.31

Hyattsville

Place Type: City
County: Prince George's
Population: 14,733

Ancestry/Race	Number	%
African American/Black:	6,339	43.03
Not Hispanic (5,918)	6,158	41.80
Hispanic (127)	181	1.23
African, sub-Saharan:	816	5.50
African	279	1.88
Cape Verdean	12	0.08
Ethiopian	74	0.50
Kenyan	26	0.18
Liberian	49	0.33
Nigerian	192	1.29
Sierra Leonean	68	0.46
South African	28	0.19
Zimbabwean	4	0.03
Other sub-Saharan African	84	0.57
Am. Ind. or Alaska Nat., not spec.	74	0.50
Albanian	24	0.16
American Indian tribes, specified:	112	0.76
Apache (3)	3	0.02
Blackfeet (1)	5	0.03
Cherokee (9)	30	0.20
Cheyenne (1)	2	0.01
Chippewa	1	0.01
Choctaw (3)	3	0.02
Comanche	1	0.01
Iroquois (2)	5	0.03
Latin American Indians (22)	27	0.18
Lumbee (4)	4	0.03
Navajo (1)	3	0.02
Pueblo	1	0.01
Seminole	3	0.02
All other tribes (8)	24	0.16
American Indian tribes, not spec.	12	0.08
Arab:	63	0.42
Lebanese	19	0.13
Moroccan	19	0.13
Palestinian	6	0.04
Syrian	10	0.07
Other Arab	9	0.06
Armenian	8	0.05
Asian:	704	4.78
Bangladeshi (40)	49	0.33
Cambodian (11)	15	0.10
Chinese, ex. Taiwanese (103)	126	0.86
Filipino (82)	90	0.61
Indian (168)	198	1.34
Indonesian (10)	10	0.07
Japanese (16)	25	0.17
Korean (49)	53	0.36
Laotian (6)	10	0.07
Pakistani (9)	11	0.07
Taiwanese (4)	5	0.03
Thai (7)	12	0.08
Vietnamese (45)	54	0.37
Other Asian, specified (17)	19	0.13
Other Asian, not specified (5)	27	0.18
Austrian	31	0.21
Belgian	7	0.05
Brazilian	6	0.04
British	52	0.35
Canadian	8	0.05
Croatian	17	0.11
Czech	21	0.14
Czechoslovakian	7	0.05
Danish	28	0.19
Dutch	93	0.63
Eastern European	6	0.04
English	769	5.18
European	137	0.92
Finnish	6	0.04
French, except Basque	200	1.35
French Canadian	102	0.69
German	1,038	7.00
Greek	33	0.22
Guyanese	49	0.33
Hawaii Native/Pacific Islander:	23	0.16
Micronesian: (1)	3	0.02
Guamanian/Chamorro (1)	2	0.01
Other Micronesian	1	0.01
Polynesian: (2)	3	0.02
Native Hawaiian (2)	2	0.01
Other Polynesian	1	0.01
Other Pac. Isl., specified	2	0.01
Other Pac. Isl., not spec. (3)	15	0.10
Hispanic or Latino:	2,673	18.14
Central American:	960	6.52
Costa Rican	6	0.04
Guatemalan	108	0.73
Honduran	50	0.34
Nicaraguan	59	0.40
Panamanian	15	0.10
Salvadoran	678	4.60
Other Central American	44	0.30
Cuban	21	0.14

Notes: 1. Figures in the "Number" column do not add up to the total population due to: a) Ancestry/Race overlap — e.g. persons can report being both White and Irish, b) persons of Hispanic origin can report being any race, c) persons reporting two ancestries are counted in both categories. 2. Numbers in parentheses indicate the number of persons reporting this ancestry/race alone, not in combination with any other ancestry/race. 3. Refer to the Explanation of Data in the front of the book for more detailed information.

Dominican Republic	96	0.65
Mexican	496	3.37
Puerto Rican	140	0.95
South American:	149	1.01
Argentinean	7	0.05
Bolivian	11	0.07
Chilean	1	0.01
Colombian	18	0.12
Ecuadorian	24	0.16
Peruvian	76	0.52
Venezuelan	5	0.03
Other South American	7	0.05
Other Hispanic or Latino	811	5.50
Hungarian	33	0.22
Irish	1,420	9.57
Italian	448	3.02
Lithuanian	76	0.51
Northern European	21	0.14
Norwegian	54	0.36
Pennsylvania German	7	0.05
Polish	192	1.29
Portuguese	22	0.15
Romanian	21	0.14
Russian	107	0.72
Scotch-Irish	270	1.82
Scottish	214	1.44
Serbian	14	0.09
Slovak	25	0.17
Swedish	84	0.57
Swiss	47	0.32
Ukrainian	37	0.25
United States or American	569	3.84
Welsh	116	0.78
West Indian, excl. Hispanic:	605	4.08
Bahamian	7	0.05
Barbadian	6	0.04
Bermudan	10	0.07
British West Indian	59	0.40
Haitian	48	0.32
Jamaican	352	2.37
Trinidadian and Tobagonian	32	0.22
West Indian	72	0.49
Other West Indian	19	0.13
White:	6,192	42.03
Not Hispanic (5,095)	5,297	35.95
Hispanic (729)	895	6.07
Yugoslavian	70	0.47

Joppatowne

Place Type: Census Designated Place
County: Harford
Population: 11,391

Ancestry/Race	Number	%
African American/Black:	1,249	10.96
Not Hispanic (1,174)	1,247	10.95
Hispanic	2	0.02
African, sub-Saharan:	28	0.25
African	28	0.25
Am. Ind. or Alaska Nat., not spec.	24	0.21
Albanian	7	0.06
American Indian tribes, specified:	45	0.40
Blackfeet	1	0.01
Cherokee (10)	19	0.17
Creek	1	0.01
Iroquois	1	0.01
Lumbee (7)	16	0.14
Seminole	2	0.02
Sioux	2	0.02
All other tribes (3)	3	0.03
American Indian tribes, not spec.	4	0.04
Arab:	45	0.40
Egyptian	28	0.25
Lebanese	17	0.15
Armenian	22	0.19
Asian:	192	1.69
Chinese, ex. Taiwanese (35)	38	0.33
Filipino (31)	43	0.38
Indian (48)	54	0.47
Indonesian (1)	1	0.01
Japanese (8)	12	0.11
Korean (15)	26	0.23
Pakistani (4)	4	0.04
Thai (5)	6	0.05
Vietnamese (1)	1	0.01
Other Asian, specified	3	0.03
Other Asian, not specified (1)	4	0.04
Austrian	66	0.58
British	25	0.22
Canadian	35	0.31
Croatian	7	0.06
Czech	83	0.73
Czechoslovakian	79	0.70
Danish	17	0.15
Dutch	154	1.36
Eastern European	8	0.07
English	1,458	12.88
European	96	0.85
Finnish	6	0.05
French, except Basque	299	2.64
French Canadian	15	0.13
German	3,008	26.58
Greek	143	1.26
Hawaii Native/Pacific Islander:	26	0.23
Micronesian:	1	0.01
Other Micronesian	1	0.01
Polynesian:	12	0.11
Native Hawaiian	6	0.05
Samoan	6	0.05
Other Pac. Isl., specified	3	0.03
Other Pac. Isl., not spec. (4)	10	0.09
Hispanic or Latino:	236	2.07
Central American:	20	0.18
Costa Rican	5	0.04
Guatemalan	11	0.10
Honduran	2	0.02
Nicaraguan	1	0.01
Panamanian	1	0.01
Cuban	14	0.12
Mexican	50	0.44
Puerto Rican	68	0.60
South American:	12	0.11
Colombian	5	0.04
Peruvian	7	0.06
Other Hispanic or Latino	72	0.63
Hungarian	36	0.32
Icelander	30	0.27
Irish	1,981	17.51
Italian	862	7.62
Latvian	84	0.74
Lithuanian	9	0.08
Norwegian	111	0.98
Polish	984	8.70
Portuguese	14	0.12
Romanian	80	0.71
Russian	98	0.87
Scotch-Irish	190	1.68
Scottish	156	1.38
Slavic	14	0.12
Swedish	18	0.16
Swiss	38	0.34
Ukrainian	43	0.38
United States or American	375	3.31
Welsh	113	1.00
West Indian, excl. Hispanic:	54	0.48
Belizean	37	0.33
Jamaican	17	0.15
White:	9,902	86.93
Not Hispanic (9,628)	9,765	85.73
Hispanic (111)	137	1.20

Kettering

Place Type: Census Designated Place
County: Prince George's
Population: 11,008

Ancestry/Race	Number	%
African American/Black:	10,146	92.17
Not Hispanic (9,935)	10,095	91.71
Hispanic (40)	51	0.46
African, sub-Saharan:	364	3.28
African	265	2.39
Kenyan	16	0.14
Nigerian	83	0.75
Am. Ind. or Alaska Nat., not spec.	40	0.36
American Indian tribes, specified:	49	0.45
Blackfeet	2	0.02
Cherokee (3)	28	0.25
Choctaw	2	0.02
Iroquois	1	0.01
Navajo	3	0.03
Sioux	3	0.03
All other tribes (7)	10	0.09
Asian:	170	1.54
Chinese, ex. Taiwanese (30)	40	0.36
Filipino (49)	53	0.48
Indian (12)	22	0.20
Japanese (1)	8	0.07
Korean (23)	27	0.25
Pakistani (5)	5	0.05
Thai	3	0.03
Vietnamese (5)	5	0.05
Other Asian, specified	5	0.05
Other Asian, not specified (2)	2	0.02
Eastern European	22	0.20
English	125	1.13
European	109	0.98
French, except Basque	29	0.26
German	84	0.76
Guyanese	56	0.50
Hawaii Native/Pacific Islander:	8	0.07
Melanesian:	2	0.02
Fijian	2	0.02
Other Pac. Isl., not spec.	6	0.05
Hispanic or Latino:	105	0.95
Central American:	17	0.15
Panamanian	8	0.07
Salvadoran	9	0.08
Cuban	10	0.09
Mexican	15	0.14
Puerto Rican	26	0.24
South American:	2	0.02
Bolivian	1	0.01
Other South American	1	0.01
Other Hispanic or Latino	35	0.32
Irish	143	1.29
Italian	14	0.13
Lithuanian	6	0.05
Polish	17	0.15
Scandinavian	26	0.23
Slavic	8	0.07
Swedish	17	0.15
United States or American	119	1.07
West Indian, excl. Hispanic:	314	2.83
Bahamian	7	0.06
Barbadian	7	0.06
Belizean	19	0.17
British West Indian	42	0.38
Haitian	17	0.15
Jamaican	89	0.80
Trinidadian and Tobagonian	45	0.41
West Indian	75	0.68
Other West Indian	13	0.12
White:	714	6.49
Not Hispanic (611)	688	6.25
Hispanic (25)	26	0.24

Lake Shore

Place Type: Census Designated Place
County: Anne Arundel
Population: 13,065

Ancestry/Race	Number	%
African American/Black:	231	1.77
Not Hispanic (217)	230	1.76
Hispanic (1)	1	0.01
African, sub-Saharan:	7	0.05

Notes: 1. Figures in the "Number" column do not add up to the total population due to: a) Ancestry/Race overlap — e.g. persons can report being both White and Irish, b) persons of Hispanic origin can report being any race, c) persons reporting two ancestries are counted in both categories. 2. Numbers in parentheses indicate the number of persons reporting this ancestry/race alone, not in combination with any other ancestry/race. 3. Refer to the Explanation of Data in the front of the book for more detailed information.

African	7	0.05
Am. Ind. or Alaska Nat., not spec.	31	0.24
American Indian tribes, specified:	83	0.64
Apache	1	0.01
Blackfeet (2)	8	0.06
Cherokee (3)	43	0.33
Cheyenne	1	0.01
Iroquois	1	0.01
Lumbee (14)	17	0.13
Navajo (1)	1	0.01
Seminole	1	0.01
Sioux (1)	1	0.01
All other tribes (4)	9	0.07
American Indian tribes, not spec.	3	0.02
Arab:	40	0.30
Jordanian	40	0.30
Armenian	8	0.06
Asian:	134	1.03
Chinese, ex. Taiwanese (16)	24	0.18
Filipino (17)	28	0.21
Indian (2)	10	0.08
Japanese (15)	24	0.18
Korean (34)	37	0.28
Pakistani (4)	5	0.04
Thai (4)	4	0.03
Other Asian, not specified (1)	2	0.02
Australian	48	0.37
Austrian	18	0.14
Belgian	14	0.11
British	35	0.27
Canadian	26	0.20
Croatian	11	0.08
Czech	61	0.46
Czechoslovakian	30	0.23
Danish	59	0.45
Dutch	155	1.18
English	2,127	16.19
European	27	0.21
Finnish	4	0.03
French, except Basque	404	3.08
French Canadian	97	0.74
German	4,169	31.73
Greek	25	0.19
Hawaii Native/Pacific Islander:	13	0.10
Micronesian: (3)	4	0.03
Guamanian/Chamorro (3)	4	0.03
Polynesian: (2)	8	0.06
Native Hawaiian (2)	8	0.06
Other Pac. Isl., not spec. (1)	1	0.01
Hispanic or Latino:	109	0.83
Central American:	1	0.01
Guatemalan	1	0.01
Cuban	7	0.05
Mexican	25	0.19
Puerto Rican	30	0.23
South American:	12	0.09
Bolivian	1	0.01
Chilean	2	0.02
Colombian	1	0.01
Ecuadorian	2	0.02
Peruvian	3	0.02
Venezuelan	3	0.02
Other Hispanic or Latino	34	0.26
Hungarian	65	0.49
Irish	2,417	18.40
Italian	892	6.79
Latvian	7	0.05
Lithuanian	158	1.20
Northern European	21	0.16
Norwegian	49	0.37
Pennsylvania German	8	0.06
Polish	1,087	8.27
Portuguese	11	0.08
Romanian	8	0.06
Russian	23	0.18
Scotch-Irish	264	2.01
Scottish	288	2.19
Slovak	41	0.31
Swedish	108	0.82
Swiss	30	0.23
Ukrainian	60	0.46
United States or American	684	5.21
Welsh	81	0.62
West Indian, excl. Hispanic:	7	0.05
Trinidadian and Tobagonian	7	0.05
White:	12,678	97.04
Not Hispanic (12,477)	12,589	96.36
Hispanic (82)	89	0.68
Yugoslavian	8	0.06

Langley Park

Place Type: Census Designated Place
County: Prince George's
Population: 16,214

Ancestry/Race	Number	%
African American/Black:	4,620	28.49
Not Hispanic (4,074)	4,323	26.66
Hispanic (216)	297	1.83
African, sub-Saharan:	928	5.72
African	191	1.18
Ethiopian	60	0.37
Ghanian	14	0.09
Kenyan	14	0.09
Liberian	12	0.07
Nigerian	292	1.80
Sierra Leonean	212	1.31
Somalian	8	0.05
Sudanese	27	0.17
Zairian	26	0.16
Other sub-Saharan African	72	0.44
Am. Ind. or Alaska Nat., not spec.	88	0.54
American Indian tribes, specified:	109	0.67
Cherokee (1)	6	0.04
Houma (2)	2	0.01
Iroquois	2	0.01
Latin American Indians (48)	81	0.50
Navajo (3)	3	0.02
Potawatomi (1)	1	0.01
All other tribes (8)	14	0.09
American Indian tribes, not spec.	31	0.19
Arab:	28	0.17
Lebanese	28	0.17
Asian:	649	4.00
Bangladeshi (17)	17	0.10
Cambodian (32)	32	0.20
Chinese, ex. Taiwanese (53)	72	0.44
Filipino (32)	41	0.25
Indian (203)	235	1.45
Japanese (3)	8	0.05
Korean (16)	17	0.10
Laotian (4)	8	0.05
Pakistani (12)	13	0.08
Sri Lankan (4)	4	0.02
Thai (7)	7	0.04
Vietnamese (149)	152	0.94
Other Asian, not specified (14)	43	0.27
Canadian	5	0.03
Czech	6	0.04
Danish	13	0.08
Dutch	13	0.08
English	102	0.63
European	45	0.28
French, except Basque	38	0.23
French Canadian	26	0.16
German	128	0.79
Guyanese	145	0.89
Hawaii Native/Pacific Islander:	73	0.45
Micronesian: (16)	19	0.12
Guamanian/Chamorro (16)	19	0.12
Polynesian: (12)	12	0.07
Native Hawaiian (8)	8	0.05
Samoan (4)	4	0.02
Other Pac. Isl., not spec. (3)	42	0.26
Hispanic or Latino:	10,294	63.49
Central American:	5,970	36.82
Costa Rican	5	0.03
Guatemalan	1,825	11.26
Honduran	328	2.02
Nicaraguan	177	1.09
Panamanian	26	0.16
Salvadoran	3,483	21.48
Other Central American	126	0.78
Cuban	23	0.14
Dominican Republic	202	1.25
Mexican	866	5.34
Puerto Rican	125	0.77
South American:	185	1.14
Argentinean	4	0.02
Bolivian	16	0.10
Chilean	11	0.07
Colombian	50	0.31
Ecuadorian	7	0.04
Paraguayan	3	0.02
Peruvian	67	0.41
Venezuelan	11	0.07
Other South American	16	0.10
Other Hispanic or Latino	2,923	18.03
Irish	74	0.46
Italian	59	0.36
Polish	37	0.23
Russian	31	0.19
Scotch-Irish	23	0.14
Scottish	21	0.13
Slovak	15	0.09
Swiss	6	0.04
United States or American	521	3.21
West Indian, excl. Hispanic:	1,070	6.60
Barbadian	17	0.10
British West Indian	5	0.03
Haitian	164	1.01
Jamaican	654	4.03
Trinidadian and Tobagonian	208	1.28
West Indian	22	0.14
White:	7,358	45.38
Not Hispanic (881)	953	5.88
Hispanic (5,877)	6,405	39.50

Lanham-Seabrook

Place Type: Census Designated Place
County: Prince George's
Population: 18,190

Ancestry/Race	Number	%
African American/Black:	11,899	65.42
Not Hispanic (11,491)	11,793	64.83
Hispanic (68)	106	0.58
African, sub-Saharan:	1,605	8.87
African	668	3.69
Cape Verdean	56	0.31
Ethiopian	44	0.24
Ghanian	47	0.26
Kenyan	13	0.07
Liberian	73	0.40
Nigerian	627	3.47
Senegalese	8	0.04
Sierra Leonean	43	0.24
Other sub-Saharan African	26	0.14
Alaska Native tribes, specified:	1	0.01
Eskimo	1	0.01
Am. Ind. or Alaska Nat., not spec.	62	0.34
American Indian tribes, specified:	78	0.43
Blackfeet	5	0.03
Cherokee (11)	32	0.18
Chickasaw (2)	2	0.01
Chippewa	3	0.02
Comanche	1	0.01
Creek	1	0.01
Delaware (1)	1	0.01
Iroquois	4	0.02
Latin American Indians (2)	10	0.05
Navajo	1	0.01
Seminole	1	0.01
All other tribes (10)	17	0.09
American Indian tribes, not spec.	11	0.06
Arab:	26	0.14
Moroccan	26	0.14
Asian:	1,003	5.51

Notes: 1. Figures in the "Number" column do not add up to the total population due to: a) Ancestry/Race overlap — e.g. persons can report being both White and Irish, b) persons of Hispanic origin can report being any race, c) persons reporting two ancestries are counted in both categories. 2. Numbers in parentheses indicate the number of persons reporting this ancestry/race alone, not in combination with any other ancestry/race. 3. Refer to the Explanation of Data in the front of the book for more detailed information.

Ancestry/Race	Number	%
Bangladeshi (4)	4	0.02
Cambodian (5)	8	0.04
Chinese, ex. Taiwanese (124)	125	0.69
Filipino (163)	185	1.02
Indian (239)	268	1.47
Indonesian (2)	5	0.03
Japanese (19)	30	0.16
Korean (161)	168	0.92
Malaysian	2	0.01
Pakistani (7)	12	0.07
Sri Lankan (5)	5	0.03
Taiwanese (6)	13	0.07
Thai (5)	6	0.03
Vietnamese (141)	142	0.78
Other Asian, specified (3)	4	0.02
Other Asian, not specified (7)	26	0.14
Australian	7	0.04
Austrian	56	0.31
Belgian	15	0.08
Brazilian	9	0.05
British	163	0.90
Canadian	11	0.06
Celtic	7	0.04
Czech	39	0.22
Czechoslovakian	14	0.08
Danish	14	0.08
Dutch	62	0.34
English	603	3.33
European	115	0.64
Finnish	14	0.08
French, except Basque	206	1.14
French Canadian	81	0.45
German	931	5.15
Greek	58	0.32
Guyanese	170	0.94
Hawaii Native/Pacific Islander:	26	0.14
Micronesian:	2	0.01
Guamanian/Chamorro	2	0.01
Polynesian: (5)	9	0.05
Native Hawaiian	3	0.02
Samoan (5)	6	0.03
Other Pac. Isl., not spec.	15	0.08
Hispanic or Latino:	841	4.62
Central American:	136	0.75
Costa Rican	1	0.01
Guatemalan	15	0.08
Honduran	1	0.01
Nicaraguan	14	0.08
Panamanian	15	0.08
Salvadoran	84	0.46
Other Central American	6	0.03
Cuban	23	0.13
Dominican Republic	20	0.11
Mexican	281	1.54
Puerto Rican	75	0.41
South American:	82	0.45
Argentinean	4	0.02
Bolivian	27	0.15
Chilean	5	0.03
Colombian	8	0.04
Ecuadorian	2	0.01
Peruvian	21	0.12
Uruguayan	1	0.01
Venezuelan	3	0.02
Other South American	11	0.06
Other Hispanic or Latino	224	1.23
Hungarian	117	0.65
Irish	960	5.31
Italian	564	3.12
Lithuanian	8	0.04
Norwegian	36	0.20
Polish	209	1.16
Portuguese	19	0.11
Romanian	39	0.22
Russian	123	0.68
Scotch-Irish	100	0.55
Scottish	101	0.56
Serbian	24	0.13
Slavic	13	0.07
Slovak	38	0.21
Swedish	31	0.17
Swiss	12	0.07
Turkish	5	0.03
Ukrainian	49	0.27
United States or American	518	2.86
Welsh	36	0.20
West Indian, excl. Hispanic:	701	3.88
Bahamian	9	0.05
Barbadian	10	0.06
British West Indian	39	0.22
Haitian	173	0.96
Jamaican	340	1.88
Trinidadian and Tobagonian	122	0.67
West Indian	8	0.04
White:	5,075	27.90
Not Hispanic (4,478)	4,673	25.69
Hispanic (367)	402	2.21
Yugoslavian	5	0.03

Lansdowne-Baltimore Highlands

Place Type: Census Designated Place
County: Baltimore
Population: 15,724

Ancestry/Race	Number	%
African American/Black:	3,029	19.26
Not Hispanic (2,867)	2,994	19.04
Hispanic (21)	35	0.22
African, sub-Saharan:	120	0.76
African	111	0.71
Cape Verdean	9	0.06
Alaska Native tribes, not specified	2	0.01
Am. Ind. or Alaska Nat., not spec.	47	0.30
American Indian tribes, specified:	81	0.52
Apache (3)	4	0.03
Blackfeet (1)	6	0.04
Cherokee (12)	30	0.19
Cheyenne (2)	2	0.01
Chippewa (1)	1	0.01
Comanche (2)	6	0.04
Cree (1)	1	0.01
Creek (2)	2	0.01
Delaware (3)	3	0.02
Iroquois (1)	3	0.02
Lumbee (3)	4	0.03
Navajo	1	0.01
Pueblo (1)	1	0.01
Sioux (1)	9	0.06
All other tribes (4)	8	0.05
American Indian tribes, not spec.	3	0.02
Arab:	37	0.24
Egyptian	14	0.09
Lebanese	6	0.04
Syrian	17	0.11
Asian:	355	2.26
Chinese, ex. Taiwanese (69)	76	0.48
Filipino (80)	101	0.64
Indian (33)	38	0.24
Japanese (4)	4	0.03
Korean (36)	40	0.25
Pakistani (29)	46	0.29
Taiwanese (1)	1	0.01
Thai	1	0.01
Vietnamese (22)	24	0.15
Other Asian, specified (4)	4	0.03
Other Asian, not specified (14)	20	0.13
British	41	0.26
Canadian	19	0.12
Czech	67	0.43
Czechoslovakian	25	0.16
Dutch	121	0.77
English	1,332	8.47
European	58	0.37
French, except Basque	322	2.05
French Canadian	15	0.10
German	3,784	24.07
Greek	61	0.39
Hawaii Native/Pacific Islander:	23	0.15
Micronesian: (5)	10	0.06
Guamanian/Chamorro (5)	10	0.06
Polynesian:	9	0.06
Native Hawaiian	6	0.04
Samoan	3	0.02
Other Pac. Isl., not spec.	4	0.03
Hispanic or Latino:	557	3.54
Central American:	71	0.45
Guatemalan	16	0.10
Honduran	20	0.13
Nicaraguan	1	0.01
Panamanian	1	0.01
Salvadoran	15	0.10
Other Central American	18	0.11
Cuban	8	0.05
Dominican Republic	4	0.03
Mexican	210	1.34
Puerto Rican	74	0.47
South American:	33	0.21
Argentinean	3	0.02
Colombian	9	0.06
Ecuadorian	8	0.05
Peruvian	10	0.06
Venezuelan	2	0.01
Other South American	1	0.01
Other Hispanic or Latino	157	1.00
Hungarian	72	0.46
Irish	2,638	16.78
Italian	918	5.84
Lithuanian	129	0.82
Norwegian	43	0.27
Polish	464	2.95
Russian	18	0.11
Scotch-Irish	101	0.64
Scottish	147	0.93
Serbian	14	0.09
Slavic	8	0.05
Slovak	12	0.08
Swedish	49	0.31
Swiss	7	0.04
Ukrainian	27	0.17
United States or American	953	6.06
Welsh	52	0.33
West Indian, excl. Hispanic:	47	0.30
Haitian	38	0.24
Jamaican	9	0.06
White:	12,145	77.24
Not Hispanic (11,689)	11,884	75.58
Hispanic (214)	261	1.66
Yugoslavian	13	0.08

Laurel

Place Type: City
County: Prince George's
Population: 19,960

Ancestry/Race	Number	%
African American/Black:	7,243	36.29
Not Hispanic (6,783)	7,086	35.50
Hispanic (104)	157	0.79
African, sub-Saharan:	754	3.76
African	358	1.79
Ghanian	77	0.38
Liberian	21	0.10
Nigerian	245	1.22
Sierra Leonean	41	0.20
Other sub-Saharan African	12	0.06
Alaska Native tribes, specified:	1	0.01
Eskimo	1	0.01
Am. Ind. or Alaska Nat., not spec.	86	0.43
Alsatian	12	0.06
American Indian tribes, specified:	125	0.63
Apache (1)	2	0.01
Blackfeet	15	0.08
Cherokee (13)	49	0.25
Chickasaw (1)	1	0.01
Chippewa (1)	1	0.01
Comanche (1)	1	0.01
Creek	2	0.01

Notes: 1. Figures in the "Number" column do not add up to the total population due to: a) Ancestry/Race overlap — e.g. persons can report being both White and Irish, b) persons of Hispanic origin can report being any race, c) persons reporting two ancestries are counted in both categories. 2. Numbers in parentheses indicate the number of persons reporting this ancestry/race alone, not in combination with any other ancestry/race. 3. Refer to the Explanation of Data in the front of the book for more detailed information.

Ancestry/Race	Number	%
Iroquois (2)	7	0.04
Latin American Indians (3)	11	0.06
Lumbee (3)	3	0.02
Navajo (4)	6	0.03
Sioux	3	0.02
Yaqui (1)	1	0.01
All other tribes (7)	23	0.12
American Indian tribes, not spec.	7	0.04
Arab:	144	0.72
Arab/Arabic	12	0.06
Egyptian	35	0.17
Lebanese	64	0.32
Syrian	33	0.16
Armenian	20	0.10
Asian:	1,588	7.96
Cambodian (2)	2	0.01
Chinese, ex. Taiwanese (116)	133	0.67
Filipino (212)	245	1.23
Indian (487)	528	2.65
Indonesian	3	0.02
Japanese (23)	46	0.23
Korean (251)	281	1.41
Laotian (3)	4	0.02
Malaysian (1)	1	0.01
Pakistani (118)	146	0.73
Taiwanese (3)	5	0.03
Thai (7)	11	0.06
Vietnamese (87)	93	0.47
Other Asian, specified	4	0.02
Other Asian, not specified (38)	86	0.43
Australian	12	0.06
Austrian	37	0.18
Belgian	13	0.06
Brazilian	23	0.11
British	77	0.38
Canadian	12	0.06
Celtic	9	0.04
Croatian	10	0.05
Czech	37	0.18
Czechoslovakian	31	0.15
Danish	27	0.13
Dutch	209	1.04
Eastern European	10	0.05
English	1,530	7.63
European	161	0.80
Finnish	29	0.14
French, except Basque	487	2.43
French Canadian	195	0.97
German	2,354	11.74
German Russian	8	0.04
Greek	34	0.17
Guyanese	62	0.31
Hawaii Native/Pacific Islander:	64	0.32
Micronesian: (16)	20	0.10
Guamanian/Chamorro (16)	20	0.10
Polynesian: (16)	17	0.09
Native Hawaiian (12)	13	0.07
Samoan (4)	4	0.02
Other Pac. Isl., specified	4	0.02
Other Pac. Isl., not spec. (10)	24	0.12
Hispanic or Latino:	1,245	6.24
Central American:	271	1.36
Costa Rican	3	0.02
Guatemalan	116	0.58
Honduran	17	0.09
Nicaraguan	14	0.07
Panamanian	25	0.13
Salvadoran	84	0.42
Other Central American	12	0.06
Cuban	38	0.19
Dominican Republic	21	0.11
Mexican	261	1.31
Puerto Rican	231	1.16
South American:	89	0.45
Argentinean	5	0.03
Bolivian	4	0.02
Chilean	10	0.05
Colombian	22	0.11
Ecuadorian	6	0.03
Paraguayan	3	0.02
Peruvian	24	0.12
Venezuelan	7	0.04
Other South American	8	0.04
Other Hispanic or Latino	334	1.67
Hungarian	81	0.40
Iranian	24	0.12
Irish	2,015	10.05
Italian	750	3.74
Lithuanian	27	0.13
Northern European	18	0.09
Norwegian	160	0.80
Pennsylvania German	18	0.09
Polish	561	2.80
Portuguese	21	0.10
Russian	102	0.51
Scandinavian	25	0.12
Scotch-Irish	322	1.61
Scottish	304	1.52
Slavic	11	0.05
Slovak	45	0.22
Swedish	119	0.59
Swiss	57	0.28
Turkish	12	0.06
Ukrainian	30	0.15
United States or American	1,101	5.49
Welsh	263	1.31
West Indian, excl. Hispanic:	514	2.56
Belizean	15	0.07
Bermudan	14	0.07
British West Indian	81	0.40
Haitian	42	0.21
Jamaican	202	1.01
Trinidadian and Tobagonian	128	0.64
West Indian	32	0.16
White:	10,919	54.70
Not Hispanic (9,894)	10,272	51.46
Hispanic (534)	647	3.24

Lexington Park

Place Type: Census Designated Place
County: Saint Mary's
Population: 11,021

Ancestry/Race	Number	%
African American/Black:	3,484	31.61
Not Hispanic (3,273)	3,432	31.14
Hispanic (33)	52	0.47
African, sub-Saharan:	190	1.75
African	190	1.75
Am. Ind. or Alaska Nat., not spec.	52	0.47
American Indian tribes, specified:	105	0.95
Apache	2	0.02
Blackfeet	17	0.15
Cherokee (8)	53	0.48
Cheyenne (1)	1	0.01
Choctaw (3)	3	0.03
Comanche (1)	5	0.05
Creek (1)	1	0.01
Latin American Indians (2)	2	0.02
Lumbee (1)	1	0.01
Seminole	6	0.05
Sioux (1)	1	0.01
Ute (1)	2	0.02
All other tribes (4)	11	0.10
American Indian tribes, not spec.	28	0.25
Arab:	11	0.10
Syrian	11	0.10
Asian:	632	5.73
Chinese, ex. Taiwanese (69)	78	0.71
Filipino (232)	309	2.80
Hmong (4)	5	0.05
Indian (45)	46	0.42
Indonesian (1)	3	0.03
Japanese (30)	77	0.70
Korean (20)	25	0.23
Laotian (4)	4	0.04
Thai (3)	4	0.04
Vietnamese (37)	42	0.38
Other Asian, specified (3)	9	0.08
Other Asian, not specified (12)	30	0.27
Austrian	31	0.29
British	101	0.93
Canadian	14	0.13
Czech	7	0.06
Danish	17	0.16
Dutch	178	1.64
English	954	8.80
European	95	0.88
Finnish	23	0.21
French, except Basque	449	4.14
French Canadian	97	0.89
German	1,304	12.02
Greek	7	0.06
Hawaii Native/Pacific Islander:	26	0.24
Micronesian: (9)	13	0.12
Guamanian/Chamorro (8)	9	0.08
Other Micronesian (1)	4	0.04
Polynesian: (4)	6	0.05
Native Hawaiian (2)	4	0.04
Samoan (2)	2	0.02
Other Pac. Isl., specified	4	0.04
Other Pac. Isl., not spec.	3	0.03
Hispanic or Latino:	527	4.78
Central American:	22	0.20
Guatemalan	7	0.06
Honduran	1	0.01
Panamanian	4	0.04
Salvadoran	8	0.07
Other Central American	2	0.02
Cuban	18	0.16
Dominican Republic	15	0.14
Mexican	184	1.67
Puerto Rican	152	1.38
South American:	36	0.33
Bolivian	4	0.04
Chilean	1	0.01
Colombian	12	0.11
Ecuadorian	12	0.11
Peruvian	3	0.03
Other South American	4	0.04
Other Hispanic or Latino	100	0.91
Hungarian	73	0.67
Irish	1,283	11.83
Israeli	15	0.14
Italian	434	4.00
Northern European	8	0.07
Norwegian	95	0.88
Pennsylvania German	9	0.08
Polish	175	1.61
Russian	39	0.36
Scandinavian	7	0.06
Scotch-Irish	126	1.16
Scottish	181	1.67
Slovak	7	0.06
Swedish	138	1.27
Ukrainian	29	0.27
United States or American	529	4.88
Welsh	72	0.66
West Indian, excl. Hispanic:	66	0.61
Belizean	27	0.25
Haitian	19	0.18
Jamaican	20	0.18
White:	6,913	62.73
Not Hispanic (6,332)	6,596	59.85
Hispanic (280)	317	2.88

Linganore-Bartonsville

Place Type: Census Designated Place
County: Frederick
Population: 12,529

Ancestry/Race	Number	%
African American/Black:	460	3.67
Not Hispanic (404)	450	3.59
Hispanic (7)	10	0.08
African, sub-Saharan:	46	0.37
African	11	0.09
South African	35	0.28

Notes: 1. Figures in the "Number" column do not add up to the total population due to: a) Ancestry/Race overlap — e.g. persons can report being both White and Irish, b) persons of Hispanic origin can report being any race, c) persons reporting two ancestries are counted in both categories. 2. Numbers in parentheses indicate the number of persons reporting this ancestry/race alone, not in combination with any other ancestry/race. 3. Refer to the Explanation of Data in the front of the book for more detailed information.

Ancestry/Race	Number	%
Alaska Native tribes, specified:	1	0.01
Alaska Athabascan (1)	1	0.01
Am. Ind. or Alaska Nat., not spec.	18	0.14
Albanian	45	0.36
American Indian tribes, specified:	43	0.34
Blackfeet	1	0.01
Cherokee (4)	19	0.15
Chippewa (1)	1	0.01
Choctaw (1)	1	0.01
Lumbee (3)	6	0.05
Pueblo (4)	4	0.03
All other tribes (3)	11	0.09
American Indian tribes, not spec.	2	0.02
Arab:	65	0.52
Lebanese	8	0.06
Palestinian	23	0.19
Syrian	25	0.20
Other Arab	9	0.07
Asian:	231	1.84
Bangladeshi (5)	5	0.04
Chinese, ex. Taiwanese (42)	54	0.43
Filipino (27)	41	0.33
Indian (39)	42	0.34
Japanese (8)	22	0.18
Korean (19)	24	0.19
Pakistani (1)	1	0.01
Sri Lankan (2)	2	0.02
Thai (1)	4	0.03
Vietnamese (14)	15	0.12
Other Asian, not specified (11)	21	0.17
Austrian	33	0.27
British	108	0.87
Canadian	47	0.38
Czech	152	1.22
Czechoslovakian	9	0.07
Danish	81	0.65
Dutch	151	1.21
Eastern European	26	0.21
English	1,890	15.21
European	171	1.38
Finnish	34	0.27
French, except Basque	476	3.83
French Canadian	62	0.50
German	3,139	25.26
Greek	69	0.56
Hawaii Native/Pacific Islander:	16	0.13
Micronesian: (2)	6	0.05
Guamanian/Chamorro (2)	6	0.05
Polynesian: (2)	5	0.04
Native Hawaiian (1)	3	0.02
Samoan (1)	2	0.02
Other Pac. Isl., not spec. (2)	5	0.04
Hispanic or Latino:	270	2.16
Central American:	22	0.18
Guatemalan	11	0.09
Honduran	2	0.02
Nicaraguan	1	0.01
Panamanian	1	0.01
Salvadoran	6	0.05
Other Central American	1	0.01
Cuban	16	0.13
Dominican Republic	1	0.01
Mexican	72	0.57
Puerto Rican	46	0.37
South American:	43	0.34
Argentinean	5	0.04
Bolivian	2	0.02
Chilean	3	0.02
Colombian	13	0.10
Ecuadorian	4	0.03
Peruvian	6	0.05
Venezuelan	3	0.02
Other South American	7	0.06
Other Hispanic or Latino	70	0.56
Hungarian	145	1.17
Irish	2,160	17.38
Italian	914	7.35
Lithuanian	11	0.09
Macedonian	9	0.07
Northern European	21	0.17
Norwegian	218	1.75
Pennsylvania German	10	0.08
Polish	585	4.71
Portuguese	66	0.53
Romanian	17	0.14
Russian	158	1.27
Scotch-Irish	326	2.62
Scottish	406	3.27
Slavic	38	0.31
Slovak	79	0.64
Slovene	32	0.26
Swedish	319	2.57
Swiss	22	0.18
Turkish	21	0.17
Ukrainian	8	0.06
United States or American	862	6.94
Welsh	126	1.01
White:	11,840	94.50
Not Hispanic (11,503)	11,645	92.94
Hispanic (164)	195	1.56
Yugoslavian	16	0.13

Lochearn

Place Type: Census Designated Place
County: Baltimore
Population: 25,269

Ancestry/Race	Number	%
African American/Black:	20,131	79.67
Not Hispanic (19,721)	20,003	79.16
Hispanic (91)	128	0.51
African, sub-Saharan:	565	2.23
African	366	1.45
Cape Verdean	26	0.10
Ghanian	30	0.12
Nigerian	98	0.39
Other sub-Saharan African	45	0.18
Am. Ind. or Alaska Nat., not spec.	104	0.41
American Indian tribes, specified:	74	0.29
Blackfeet (6)	22	0.09
Cherokee (11)	31	0.12
Iroquois (1)	2	0.01
Lumbee (4)	7	0.03
Pueblo (4)	5	0.02
All other tribes (4)	7	0.03
American Indian tribes, not spec.	13	0.05
Arab:	11	0.04
Egyptian	6	0.02
Moroccan	5	0.02
Asian:	272	1.08
Chinese, ex. Taiwanese (16)	24	0.09
Filipino (28)	50	0.20
Indian (59)	68	0.27
Japanese (13)	20	0.08
Korean (31)	36	0.14
Pakistani (9)	9	0.04
Taiwanese (2)	2	0.01
Thai (11)	11	0.04
Vietnamese (19)	22	0.09
Other Asian, specified	10	0.04
Other Asian, not specified (16)	20	0.08
Austrian	34	0.13
Belgian	5	0.02
British	70	0.28
Croatian	23	0.09
Czech	31	0.12
Czechoslovakian	7	0.03
Danish	15	0.06
Dutch	34	0.13
Eastern European	6	0.02
English	544	2.15
European	36	0.14
French, except Basque	168	0.66
German	1,231	4.87
Greek	64	0.25
Guyanese	6	0.02
Hawaii Native/Pacific Islander:	30	0.12
Micronesian: (2)	4	0.02
Guamanian/Chamorro (2)	4	0.02
Polynesian:	8	0.03
Native Hawaiian	7	0.03
Samoan	1	0.00
Other Pac. Isl., specified	8	0.03
Other Pac. Isl., not spec. (7)	10	0.04
Hispanic or Latino:	378	1.50
Central American:	30	0.12
Costa Rican	2	0.01
Guatemalan	4	0.02
Honduran	5	0.02
Panamanian	4	0.02
Salvadoran	15	0.06
Cuban	18	0.07
Dominican Republic	2	0.01
Mexican	138	0.55
Puerto Rican	77	0.30
South American:	32	0.13
Argentinean	5	0.02
Chilean	2	0.01
Colombian	8	0.03
Ecuadorian	2	0.01
Paraguayan	4	0.02
Peruvian	6	0.02
Venezuelan	1	0.00
Other South American	4	0.02
Other Hispanic or Latino	81	0.32
Hungarian	43	0.17
Irish	842	3.33
Israeli	6	0.02
Italian	321	1.27
Latvian	11	0.04
Lithuanian	36	0.14
Norwegian	68	0.27
Polish	186	0.74
Portuguese	11	0.04
Romanian	30	0.12
Russian	246	0.97
Scotch-Irish	70	0.28
Scottish	70	0.28
Swedish	17	0.07
Swiss	22	0.09
Ukrainian	45	0.18
United States or American	460	1.82
Welsh	41	0.16
West Indian, excl. Hispanic:	689	2.72
Bahamian	5	0.02
Barbadian	15	0.06
Bermudan	6	0.02
Haitian	38	0.15
Jamaican	419	1.66
Trinidadian and Tobagonian	103	0.41
West Indian	103	0.41
White:	4,848	19.19
Not Hispanic (4,558)	4,714	18.66
Hispanic (116)	134	0.53
Yugoslavian	7	0.03

Lutherville-Timonium

Place Type: Census Designated Place
County: Baltimore
Population: 15,814

Ancestry/Race	Number	%
African American/Black:	538	3.40
Not Hispanic (507)	534	3.38
Hispanic (2)	4	0.03
African, sub-Saharan:	16	0.10
African	6	0.04
Nigerian	10	0.06
Am. Ind. or Alaska Nat., not spec.	18	0.11
American Indian tribes, specified:	14	0.09
Blackfeet (2)	2	0.01
Cherokee (2)	3	0.02
Chickasaw	1	0.01
Choctaw	3	0.02
Latin American Indians (3)	3	0.02
Navajo (1)	1	0.01
Sioux (1)	1	0.01
American Indian tribes, not spec.	10	0.06

Notes: 1. Figures in the "Number" column do not add up to the total population due to: a) Ancestry/Race overlap — e.g. persons can report being both White and Irish, b) persons of Hispanic origin can report being any race, c) persons reporting two ancestries are counted in both categories. 2. Numbers in parentheses indicate the number of persons reporting this ancestry/race alone, not in combination with any other ancestry/race. 3. Refer to the Explanation of Data in the front of the book for more detailed information.

Arab:	96	0.62
Arab/Arabic	6	0.04
Egyptian	6	0.04
Lebanese	77	0.49
Palestinian	7	0.04
Armenian	18	0.12
Asian:	915	5.79
Bangladeshi (4)	4	0.03
Cambodian (4)	4	0.03
Chinese, ex. Taiwanese (196)	206	1.30
Filipino (118)	140	0.89
Indian (114)	122	0.77
Indonesian (1)	1	0.01
Japanese (24)	31	0.20
Korean (301)	307	1.94
Sri Lankan (7)	8	0.05
Taiwanese (17)	19	0.12
Thai (4)	5	0.03
Vietnamese (17)	17	0.11
Other Asian, specified (4)	5	0.03
Other Asian, not specified (16)	46	0.29
Austrian	78	0.50
British	148	0.95
Canadian	59	0.38
Cypriot	22	0.14
Czech	153	0.98
Czechoslovakian	50	0.32
Danish	54	0.35
Dutch	241	1.55
Eastern European	13	0.08
English	2,579	16.54
Estonian	15	0.10
European	105	0.67
Finnish	5	0.03
French, except Basque	295	1.89
French Canadian	119	0.76
German	4,325	27.74
Greek	404	2.59
Hawaii Native/Pacific Islander:	5	0.03
Polynesian: (1)	2	0.01
Native Hawaiian (1)	2	0.01
Other Pac. Isl., not spec.	3	0.02
Hispanic or Latino:	193	1.22
Central American:	13	0.08
Guatemalan	8	0.05
Panamanian	1	0.01
Salvadoran	4	0.03
Cuban	8	0.05
Dominican Republic	9	0.06
Mexican	37	0.23
Puerto Rican	28	0.18
South American:	35	0.22
Argentinean	10	0.06
Bolivian	4	0.03
Chilean	3	0.02
Colombian	12	0.08
Ecuadorian	2	0.01
Paraguayan	2	0.01
Peruvian	1	0.01
Venezuelan	1	0.01
Other Hispanic or Latino	63	0.40
Hungarian	49	0.31
Icelander	26	0.17
Iranian	83	0.53
Irish	2,900	18.60
Italian	1,473	9.45
Latvian	6	0.04
Lithuanian	103	0.66
New Zealander	16	0.10
Norwegian	112	0.72
Pennsylvania German	8	0.05
Polish	954	6.12
Portuguese	34	0.22
Romanian	6	0.04
Russian	176	1.13
Scotch-Irish	244	1.57
Scottish	567	3.64
Serbian	7	0.04
Slavic	6	0.04
Slovak	59	0.38
Slovene	3	0.02
Swedish	141	0.90
Swiss	72	0.46
Turkish	17	0.11
Ukrainian	87	0.56
United States or American	520	3.34
Welsh	225	1.44
West Indian, excl. Hispanic:	37	0.24
Haitian	9	0.06
Trinidadian and Tobagonian	16	0.10
U.S. Virgin Islander	5	0.03
West Indian	7	0.04
White:	14,395	91.03
Not Hispanic (14,097)	14,234	90.01
Hispanic (152)	161	1.02
Yugoslavian	6	0.04

Mays Chapel

Place Type: Census Designated Place
County: Baltimore
Population: 11,427

Ancestry/Race	Number	%
African American/Black:	123	1.08
Not Hispanic (98)	123	1.08
African, sub-Saharan:	106	0.93
African	9	0.08
Ethiopian	51	0.45
Nigerian	46	0.40
Am. Ind. or Alaska Nat., not spec.	3	0.03
Albanian	9	0.08
American Indian tribes, specified:	9	0.08
Blackfeet	1	0.01
Cherokee (2)	6	0.05
Latin American Indians	1	0.01
All other tribes	1	0.01
American Indian tribes, not spec.	1	0.01
Arab:	295	2.58
Egyptian	8	0.07
Lebanese	94	0.82
Palestinian	34	0.30
Syrian	133	1.16
Other Arab	26	0.23
Armenian	12	0.11
Asian:	862	7.54
Cambodian (4)	4	0.04
Chinese, ex. Taiwanese (174)	192	1.68
Filipino (69)	87	0.76
Indian (98)	111	0.97
Japanese (11)	16	0.14
Korean (361)	373	3.26
Pakistani (15)	17	0.15
Taiwanese (19)	19	0.17
Thai (9)	13	0.11
Vietnamese (8)	8	0.07
Other Asian, specified (9)	9	0.08
Other Asian, not specified (3)	13	0.11
Austrian	88	0.77
British	25	0.22
Celtic	8	0.07
Czech	86	0.75
Czechoslovakian	7	0.06
Danish	53	0.46
Dutch	84	0.74
Eastern European	48	0.42
English	1,793	15.70
European	85	0.74
Finnish	12	0.11
French, except Basque	269	2.36
French Canadian	24	0.21
German	2,767	24.23
Greek	134	1.17
Hawaii Native/Pacific Islander:	1	0.01
Micronesian: (1)	1	0.01
Guamanian/Chamorro (1)	1	0.01
Hispanic or Latino:	151	1.32
Central American:	10	0.09
Costa Rican	3	0.03
Guatemalan	3	0.03
Honduran	1	0.01
Nicaraguan	1	0.01
Salvadoran	2	0.02
Cuban	17	0.15
Dominican Republic	2	0.02
Mexican	17	0.15
Puerto Rican	21	0.18
South American:	34	0.30
Argentinean	9	0.08
Bolivian	1	0.01
Chilean	2	0.02
Ecuadorian	15	0.13
Paraguayan	1	0.01
Peruvian	4	0.04
Other South American	2	0.02
Other Hispanic or Latino	50	0.44
Hungarian	74	0.65
Iranian	59	0.52
Irish	2,811	24.61
Italian	1,306	11.43
Latvian	8	0.07
Lithuanian	89	0.78
Northern European	7	0.06
Norwegian	67	0.59
Polish	609	5.33
Portuguese	11	0.10
Romanian	70	0.61
Russian	286	2.50
Scandinavian	10	0.09
Scotch-Irish	166	1.45
Scottish	322	2.82
Slavic	24	0.21
Slovak	10	0.09
Swedish	103	0.90
Swiss	21	0.18
Turkish	26	0.23
Ukrainian	26	0.23
United States or American	534	4.68
Welsh	154	1.35
West Indian, excl. Hispanic:	5	0.04
Jamaican	5	0.04
White:	10,475	91.67
Not Hispanic (10,277)	10,365	90.71
Hispanic (105)	110	0.96

Middle River

Place Type: Census Designated Place
County: Baltimore
Population: 23,958

Ancestry/Race	Number	%
Acadian/Cajun	10	0.04
African American/Black:	3,366	14.05
Not Hispanic (3,139)	3,327	13.89
Hispanic (26)	39	0.16
African, sub-Saharan:	486	2.03
African	270	1.13
Ghanian	15	0.06
Kenyan	33	0.14
Nigerian	164	0.69
Other sub-Saharan African	4	0.02
Am. Ind. or Alaska Nat., not spec.	100	0.42
American Indian tribes, specified:	106	0.44
Apache	2	0.01
Blackfeet (2)	2	0.01
Cherokee (35)	59	0.25
Cheyenne (1)	1	0.00
Chippewa (1)	1	0.00
Iroquois (1)	2	0.01
Latin American Indians (1)	3	0.01
Lumbee (22)	26	0.11
Navajo	2	0.01
Osage (1)	1	0.00
Sioux (1)	2	0.01
All other tribes (3)	5	0.02
American Indian tribes, not spec.	22	0.09
Arab:	44	0.18
Arab/Arabic	29	0.12
Palestinian	15	0.06

Notes: 1. Figures in the "Number" column do not add up to the total population due to: a) Ancestry/Race overlap — e.g. persons can report being both White and Irish, b) persons of Hispanic origin can report being any race, c) persons reporting two ancestries are counted in both categories. 2. Numbers in parentheses indicate the number of persons reporting this ancestry/race alone, not in combination with any other ancestry/race. 3. Refer to the Explanation of Data in the front of the book for more detailed information.

Asian:	366	1.53
Chinese, ex. Taiwanese (21)	21	0.09
Filipino (48)	66	0.28
Indian (79)	93	0.39
Indonesian (1)	6	0.03
Japanese (7)	12	0.05
Korean (68)	74	0.31
Laotian (4)	6	0.03
Pakistani (16)	18	0.08
Taiwanese (1)	1	0.00
Thai (7)	8	0.03
Vietnamese (25)	30	0.13
Other Asian, specified (1)	5	0.02
Other Asian, not specified (15)	26	0.11
Austrian	33	0.14
Belgian	28	0.12
British	59	0.25
Canadian	16	0.07
Celtic	6	0.03
Croatian	7	0.03
Czech	267	1.12
Czechoslovakian	89	0.37
Danish	45	0.19
Dutch	439	1.84
English	2,081	8.70
European	34	0.14
Finnish	11	0.05
French, except Basque	410	1.71
French Canadian	106	0.44
German	6,319	26.43
Greek	62	0.26
Guyanese	14	0.06
Hawaii Native/Pacific Islander:	22	0.09
Micronesian: (2)	4	0.02
Guamanian/Chamorro (2)	4	0.02
Polynesian: (4)	4	0.02
Native Hawaiian (2)	2	0.01
Samoan (2)	2	0.01
Other Pac. Isl., specified	4	0.02
Other Pac. Isl., not spec. (2)	10	0.04
Hispanic or Latino:	461	1.92
Central American:	55	0.23
Guatemalan	3	0.01
Honduran	10	0.04
Panamanian	5	0.02
Salvadoran	30	0.13
Other Central American	7	0.03
Cuban	6	0.03
Dominican Republic	16	0.07
Mexican	93	0.39
Puerto Rican	116	0.48
South American:	34	0.14
Argentinean	1	0.00
Bolivian	1	0.00
Chilean	1	0.00
Colombian	4	0.02
Ecuadorian	7	0.03
Peruvian	17	0.07
Venezuelan	3	0.01
Other Hispanic or Latino	141	0.59
Hungarian	62	0.26
Iranian	8	0.03
Irish	3,719	15.56
Italian	1,699	7.11
Lithuanian	42	0.18
Norwegian	15	0.06
Pennsylvania German	5	0.02
Polish	1,597	6.68
Portuguese	72	0.30
Romanian	31	0.13
Russian	44	0.18
Scandinavian	13	0.05
Scotch-Irish	283	1.18
Scottish	250	1.05
Slavic	10	0.04
Slovak	35	0.15
Swedish	108	0.45
Swiss	23	0.10
Turkish	8	0.03
Ukrainian	78	0.33
United States or American	1,420	5.94
Welsh	215	0.90
West Indian, excl. Hispanic:	62	0.26
British West Indian	8	0.03
Jamaican	38	0.16
Trinidadian and Tobagonian	10	0.04
West Indian	6	0.03
White:	20,081	83.82
Not Hispanic (19,585)	19,837	82.80
Hispanic (205)	244	1.02
Yugoslavian	7	0.03

Milford Mill

Place Type: Census Designated Place
County: Baltimore
Population: 26,527

Ancestry/Race	Number	%
African American/Black:	21,353	80.50
Not Hispanic (20,870)	21,214	79.97
Hispanic (101)	139	0.52
African, sub-Saharan:	914	3.45
African	701	2.64
Cape Verdean	16	0.06
Ghanian	28	0.11
Kenyan	13	0.05
Liberian	17	0.06
Nigerian	139	0.52
Alaska Native tribes, specified:	2	0.01
Alaska Athabascan (2)	2	0.01
Am. Ind. or Alaska Nat., not spec.	100	0.38
American Indian tribes, specified:	65	0.25
Blackfeet (2)	4	0.02
Cherokee (2)	34	0.13
Chickasaw (1)	1	0.00
Choctaw	1	0.00
Iroquois (2)	2	0.01
Latin American Indians (6)	7	0.03
Lumbee (1)	2	0.01
Pima (1)	1	0.00
Seminole	1	0.00
Sioux	3	0.01
All other tribes (7)	9	0.03
American Indian tribes, not spec.	23	0.09
Arab:	114	0.43
Arab/Arabic	7	0.03
Egyptian	44	0.17
Lebanese	40	0.15
Other Arab	23	0.09
Asian:	596	2.25
Bangladeshi (1)	1	0.00
Chinese, ex. Taiwanese (41)	51	0.19
Filipino (38)	55	0.21
Indian (144)	194	0.73
Indonesian	1	0.00
Japanese (11)	25	0.09
Korean (32)	45	0.17
Pakistani (83)	100	0.38
Taiwanese (2)	2	0.01
Thai (1)	2	0.01
Vietnamese (50)	52	0.20
Other Asian, specified (4)	4	0.02
Other Asian, not specified (28)	64	0.24
Austrian	12	0.05
Belgian	4	0.02
British	25	0.09
Croatian	10	0.04
Czech	11	0.04
Czechoslovakian	14	0.05
Danish	33	0.12
Dutch	81	0.31
Eastern European	4	0.02
English	425	1.60
European	44	0.17
French, except Basque	58	0.22
French Canadian	32	0.12
German	928	3.50
Greek	67	0.25
Guyanese	49	0.18
Hawaii Native/Pacific Islander:	21	0.08
Polynesian: (1)	8	0.03
Native Hawaiian (1)	7	0.03
Samoan	1	0.00
Other Pac. Isl., not spec. (3)	13	0.05
Hispanic or Latino:	483	1.82
Central American:	43	0.16
Guatemalan	1	0.00
Honduran	8	0.03
Nicaraguan	7	0.03
Panamanian	11	0.04
Salvadoran	16	0.06
Cuban	20	0.08
Dominican Republic	12	0.05
Mexican	151	0.57
Puerto Rican	75	0.28
South American:	21	0.08
Argentinean	2	0.01
Chilean	5	0.02
Colombian	3	0.01
Ecuadorian	1	0.00
Peruvian	9	0.03
Venezuelan	1	0.00
Other Hispanic or Latino	161	0.61
Hungarian	27	0.10
Iranian	8	0.03
Irish	498	1.88
Israeli	13	0.05
Italian	470	1.77
Lithuanian	33	0.12
Norwegian	64	0.24
Polish	236	0.89
Portuguese	7	0.03
Romanian	15	0.06
Russian	268	1.01
Scotch-Irish	72	0.27
Scottish	61	0.23
Slavic	14	0.05
Slovene	7	0.03
Swedish	35	0.13
Swiss	5	0.02
Turkish	13	0.05
Ukrainian	48	0.18
United States or American	466	1.76
Welsh	26	0.10
West Indian, excl. Hispanic:	838	3.16
Barbadian	22	0.08
British West Indian	8	0.03
Haitian	31	0.12
Jamaican	549	2.07
Trinidadian and Tobagonian	130	0.49
U.S. Virgin Islander	44	0.17
West Indian	54	0.20
White:	4,591	17.31
Not Hispanic (4,115)	4,378	16.50
Hispanic (179)	213	0.80
Yugoslavian	22	0.08

Montgomery Village

Place Type: Census Designated Place
County: Montgomery
Population: 38,051

Ancestry/Race	Number	%
Afghan	98	0.26
African American/Black:	6,964	18.30
Not Hispanic (6,297)	6,727	17.68
Hispanic (135)	237	0.62
African, sub-Saharan:	1,216	3.21
African	518	1.37
Cape Verdean	40	0.11
Ethiopian	105	0.28
Ghanian	142	0.37
Kenyan	7	0.02
Liberian	56	0.15
Nigerian	210	0.55
Senegalese	8	0.02
Sierra Leonean	5	0.01
Zairian	22	0.06

Notes: 1. Figures in the "Number" column do not add up to the total population due to: a) Ancestry/Race overlap — e.g. persons can report being both White and Irish, b) persons of Hispanic origin can report being any race, c) persons reporting two ancestries are counted in both categories. 2. Numbers in parentheses indicate the number of persons reporting this ancestry/race alone, not in combination with any other ancestry/race. 3. Refer to the Explanation of Data in the front of the book for more detailed information.

Ancestry/Race	Number	%
Zimbabwean	23	0.06
Other sub-Saharan African	80	0.21
Alaska Native tribes, specified:	1	0.00
Aleut	1	0.00
Am. Ind. or Alaska Nat., not spec.	146	0.38
Albanian	46	0.12
American Indian tribes, specified:	196	0.52
Apache (2)	8	0.02
Blackfeet (7)	10	0.03
Cherokee (9)	51	0.13
Chickasaw (3)	3	0.01
Chippewa	2	0.01
Choctaw	4	0.01
Creek	5	0.01
Delaware (1)	1	0.00
Iroquois (7)	12	0.03
Kiowa (1)	1	0.00
Latin American Indians (32)	55	0.14
Lumbee (1)	2	0.01
Navajo (7)	8	0.02
Pueblo	3	0.01
Puget Sound Salish (1)	1	0.00
Seminole	3	0.01
Sioux (1)	6	0.02
Yaqui (4)	4	0.01
All other tribes (12)	17	0.04
American Indian tribes, not spec.	22	0.06
Arab:	522	1.38
Arab/Arabic	73	0.19
Egyptian	87	0.23
Lebanese	88	0.23
Moroccan	25	0.07
Palestinian	147	0.39
Syrian	9	0.02
Other Arab	93	0.25
Armenian	87	0.23
Asian:	5,053	13.28
Bangladeshi (36)	44	0.12
Cambodian (72)	79	0.21
Chinese, ex. Taiwanese (811)	896	2.35
Filipino (558)	632	1.66
Indian (1,785)	1,889	4.96
Indonesian (7)	11	0.03
Japanese (72)	119	0.31
Korean (336)	368	0.97
Laotian (26)	32	0.08
Malaysian (2)	3	0.01
Pakistani (159)	191	0.50
Sri Lankan (59)	63	0.17
Taiwanese (20)	21	0.06
Thai (38)	50	0.13
Vietnamese (391)	420	1.10
Other Asian, specified (15)	21	0.06
Other Asian, not specified (81)	214	0.56
Assyrian/Chaldean/Syriac	8	0.02
Australian	22	0.06
Austrian	163	0.43
Basque	9	0.02
Belgian	24	0.06
Brazilian	120	0.32
British	229	0.60
Bulgarian	13	0.03
Canadian	100	0.26
Carpatho Rusyn	12	0.03
Celtic	16	0.04
Croatian	17	0.04
Czech	93	0.25
Czechoslovakian	78	0.21
Danish	120	0.32
Dutch	303	0.80
Eastern European	205	0.54
English	3,386	8.94
Estonian	5	0.01
European	593	1.57
Finnish	42	0.11
French, except Basque	819	2.16
French Canadian	199	0.53
German	4,361	11.51
Greek	212	0.56
Guyanese	89	0.23
Hawaii Native/Pacific Islander:	87	0.23
Melanesian:	1	0.00
Other Melanesian	1	0.00
Micronesian: (5)	9	0.02
Guamanian/Chamorro (2)	6	0.02
Other Micronesian (3)	3	0.01
Polynesian: (13)	32	0.08
Native Hawaiian (8)	26	0.07
Samoan (3)	4	0.01
Other Polynesian (2)	2	0.01
Other Pac. Isl., specified	1	0.00
Other Pac. Isl., not spec. (8)	44	0.12
Hispanic or Latino:	4,458	11.72
Central American:	1,016	2.67
Costa Rican	21	0.06
Guatemalan	151	0.40
Honduran	50	0.13
Nicaraguan	112	0.29
Panamanian	39	0.10
Salvadoran	592	1.56
Other Central American	51	0.13
Cuban	93	0.24
Dominican Republic	93	0.24
Mexican	393	1.03
Puerto Rican	338	0.89
South American:	1,034	2.72
Argentinean	34	0.09
Bolivian	122	0.32
Chilean	69	0.18
Colombian	229	0.60
Ecuadorian	112	0.29
Paraguayan	8	0.02
Peruvian	308	0.81
Uruguayan	9	0.02
Venezuelan	74	0.19
Other South American	69	0.18
Other Hispanic or Latino	1,491	3.92
Hungarian	177	0.47
Icelander	9	0.02
Iranian	705	1.86
Irish	4,284	11.31
Israeli	18	0.05
Italian	1,978	5.22
Latvian	15	0.04
Lithuanian	170	0.45
Luxemburger	6	0.02
Northern European	52	0.14
Norwegian	212	0.56
Pennsylvania German	14	0.04
Polish	980	2.59
Portuguese	69	0.18
Romanian	119	0.31
Russian	1,095	2.89
Scandinavian	66	0.17
Scotch-Irish	557	1.47
Scottish	776	2.05
Serbian	41	0.11
Slavic	28	0.07
Slovak	131	0.35
Swedish	363	0.96
Swiss	76	0.20
Turkish	89	0.23
Ukrainian	224	0.59
United States or American	1,440	3.80
Welsh	303	0.80
West Indian, excl. Hispanic:	733	1.93
Belizean	10	0.03
British West Indian	23	0.06
Haitian	174	0.46
Jamaican	296	0.78
Trinidadian and Tobagonian	99	0.26
West Indian	131	0.35
White:	24,775	65.11
Not Hispanic (21,433)	22,224	58.41
Hispanic (2,251)	2,551	6.70
Yugoslavian	54	0.14

New Carrollton

Place Type: City
County: Prince George's
Population: 12,589

Ancestry/Race	Number	%
African American/Black:	8,680	68.95
Not Hispanic (8,416)	8,576	68.12
Hispanic (82)	104	0.83
African, sub-Saharan:	1,117	8.70
African	521	4.06
Ethiopian	36	0.28
Ghanian	85	0.66
Liberian	9	0.07
Nigerian	203	1.58
Sierra Leonean	77	0.60
South African	49	0.38
Other sub-Saharan African	137	1.07
Am. Ind. or Alaska Nat., not spec.	37	0.29
American Indian tribes, specified:	37	0.29
Apache (1)	1	0.01
Blackfeet	1	0.01
Cherokee	8	0.06
Choctaw	1	0.01
Creek	6	0.05
Iroquois (1)	1	0.01
Latin American Indians (10)	10	0.08
Lumbee (1)	1	0.01
Seminole (1)	2	0.02
All other tribes (6)	6	0.05
American Indian tribes, not spec.	7	0.06
Arab:	17	0.13
Arab/Arabic	17	0.13
Asian:	695	5.52
Bangladeshi (5)	10	0.08
Cambodian (36)	42	0.33
Chinese, ex. Taiwanese (58)	68	0.54
Filipino (79)	86	0.68
Indian (217)	238	1.89
Indonesian	6	0.05
Japanese (11)	18	0.14
Korean (53)	63	0.50
Laotian (2)	2	0.02
Pakistani (48)	50	0.40
Sri Lankan (2)	2	0.02
Taiwanese (3)	3	0.02
Thai (3)	6	0.05
Vietnamese (55)	61	0.48
Other Asian, specified (6)	6	0.05
Other Asian, not specified (12)	34	0.27
Austrian	12	0.09
Czechoslovakian	13	0.10
Danish	20	0.16
Dutch	44	0.34
English	466	3.63
European	11	0.09
French, except Basque	113	0.88
French Canadian	27	0.21
German	695	5.41
Greek	42	0.33
Guyanese	151	1.18
Hawaii Native/Pacific Islander:	26	0.21
Melanesian:	2	0.02
Other Melanesian	2	0.02
Polynesian: (3)	8	0.06
Native Hawaiian (3)	8	0.06
Other Pac. Isl., not spec. (5)	16	0.13
Hispanic or Latino:	827	6.57
Central American:	98	0.78
Costa Rican	1	0.01
Guatemalan	32	0.25
Honduran	4	0.03
Nicaraguan	9	0.07
Panamanian	13	0.10
Salvadoran	39	0.31
Cuban	19	0.15
Dominican Republic	32	0.25
Mexican	403	3.20
Puerto Rican	62	0.49

Notes: 1. Figures in the "Number" column do not add up to the total population due to: a) Ancestry/Race overlap — e.g. persons can report being both White and Irish, b) persons of Hispanic origin can report being any race, c) persons reporting two ancestries are counted in both categories. 2. Numbers in parentheses indicate the number of persons reporting this ancestry/race alone, not in combination with any other ancestry/race. 3. Refer to the Explanation of Data in the front of the book for more detailed information.

South American:	50	0.40
Argentinean	1	0.01
Bolivian	4	0.03
Chilean	3	0.02
Colombian	9	0.07
Ecuadorian	15	0.12
Paraguayan	7	0.06
Peruvian	4	0.03
Other South American	7	0.06
Other Hispanic or Latino	163	1.29
Hungarian	6	0.05
Irish	623	4.85
Italian	299	2.33
Latvian	21	0.16
Lithuanian	20	0.16
Northern European	12	0.09
Norwegian	11	0.09
Polish	164	1.28
Portuguese	41	0.32
Russian	13	0.10
Scandinavian	15	0.12
Scotch-Irish	63	0.49
Scottish	57	0.44
Slovak	14	0.11
Slovene	11	0.09
Swedish	37	0.29
Turkish	18	0.14
Ukrainian	14	0.11
United States or American	369	2.87
Welsh	55	0.43
West Indian, excl. Hispanic:	627	4.88
Haitian	19	0.15
Jamaican	496	3.86
Trinidadian and Tobagonian	77	0.60
U.S. Virgin Islander	15	0.12
West Indian	20	0.16
White:	2,910	23.12
Not Hispanic (2,452)	2,573	20.44
Hispanic (294)	337	2.68

North Bethesda

Place Type: Census Designated Place
County: Montgomery
Population: 38,610

Ancestry/Race	Number	%
Afghan	32	0.08
African American/Black:	2,114	5.48
Not Hispanic (1,877)	2,040	5.28
Hispanic (39)	74	0.19
African, sub-Saharan:	632	1.64
African	329	0.85
Ethiopian	28	0.07
Kenyan	65	0.17
Nigerian	22	0.06
Senegalese	3	0.01
South African	48	0.12
Sudanese	4	0.01
Ugandan	8	0.02
Other sub-Saharan African	125	0.32
Alaska Native tribes, specified:	1	0.00
Alaska Athabascan (1)	1	0.00
Am. Ind. or Alaska Nat., not spec.	92	0.24
Alsatian	8	0.02
American Indian tribes, specified:	154	0.40
Apache (1)	3	0.01
Blackfeet	3	0.01
Cherokee (14)	45	0.12
Chickasaw (1)	3	0.01
Chippewa (1)	1	0.00
Choctaw (5)	5	0.01
Creek (1)	3	0.01
Crow	1	0.00
Delaware	1	0.00
Houma (1)	1	0.00
Iroquois (2)	7	0.02
Kiowa (1)	1	0.00
Latin American Indians (23)	46	0.12
Lumbee (3)	7	0.02
Menominee (1)	2	0.01
Navajo (1)	1	0.00
Osage (1)	3	0.01
Pueblo (1)	1	0.00
Seminole	1	0.00
Shoshone (1)	1	0.00
Sioux (1)	2	0.01
All other tribes (11)	16	0.04
American Indian tribes, not spec.	11	0.03
Arab:	546	1.41
Arab/Arabic	52	0.13
Egyptian	53	0.14
Iraqi	7	0.02
Jordanian	2	0.01
Lebanese	185	0.48
Moroccan	35	0.09
Palestinian	64	0.17
Syrian	88	0.23
Other Arab	60	0.16
Armenian	85	0.22
Asian:	5,101	13.21
Bangladeshi (32)	38	0.10
Cambodian (17)	19	0.05
Chinese, ex. Taiwanese (1,515)	1,603	4.15
Filipino (314)	369	0.96
Indian (895)	976	2.53
Indonesian (67)	82	0.21
Japanese (548)	596	1.54
Korean (639)	691	1.79
Laotian (5)	6	0.02
Malaysian (11)	14	0.04
Pakistani (63)	72	0.19
Sri Lankan (58)	61	0.16
Taiwanese (39)	51	0.13
Thai (69)	78	0.20
Vietnamese (194)	216	0.56
Other Asian, specified (39)	45	0.12
Other Asian, not specified (49)	184	0.48
Assyrian/Chaldean/Syriac	24	0.06
Australian	6	0.02
Austrian	354	0.92
Belgian	105	0.27
Brazilian	187	0.48
British	331	0.86
Bulgarian	30	0.08
Canadian	249	0.64
Croatian	43	0.11
Czech	203	0.53
Czechoslovakian	45	0.12
Danish	182	0.47
Dutch	293	0.76
Eastern European	679	1.76
English	3,492	9.04
Estonian	4	0.01
European	451	1.17
Finnish	47	0.12
French, except Basque	1,147	2.97
French Canadian	158	0.41
German	4,411	11.41
Greek	438	1.13
Guyanese	3	0.01
Hawaii Native/Pacific Islander:	50	0.13
Melanesian: (8)	8	0.02
Fijian (5)	5	0.01
Other Melanesian (3)	3	0.01
Micronesian: (2)	6	0.02
Guamanian/Chamorro (2)	6	0.02
Polynesian: (1)	9	0.02
Native Hawaiian (1)	5	0.01
Samoan	4	0.01
Other Pac. Isl., not spec. (6)	27	0.07
Hispanic or Latino:	3,680	9.53
Central American:	659	1.71
Costa Rican	32	0.08
Guatemalan	51	0.13
Honduran	98	0.25
Nicaraguan	50	0.13
Panamanian	4	0.01
Salvadoran	386	1.00
Other Central American	38	0.10
Cuban	134	0.35
Dominican Republic	43	0.11
Mexican	325	0.84
Puerto Rican	149	0.39
South American:	1,114	2.89
Argentinean	128	0.33
Bolivian	164	0.42
Chilean	138	0.36
Colombian	199	0.52
Ecuadorian	110	0.28
Paraguayan	13	0.03
Peruvian	219	0.57
Uruguayan	23	0.06
Venezuelan	55	0.14
Other South American	65	0.17
Other Hispanic or Latino	1,256	3.25
Hungarian	394	1.02
Icelander	10	0.03
Iranian	688	1.78
Irish	4,009	10.37
Israeli	389	1.01
Italian	1,723	4.46
Latvian	82	0.21
Lithuanian	202	0.52
Luxemburger	7	0.02
Maltese	2	0.01
New Zealander	4	0.01
Northern European	62	0.16
Norwegian	352	0.91
Polish	1,571	4.07
Portuguese	103	0.27
Romanian	179	0.46
Russian	2,758	7.14
Scandinavian	23	0.06
Scotch-Irish	528	1.37
Scottish	892	2.31
Serbian	63	0.16
Slavic	19	0.05
Slovak	250	0.65
Slovene	26	0.07
Soviet Union	13	0.03
Swedish	306	0.79
Swiss	63	0.16
Turkish	240	0.62
Ukrainian	302	0.78
United States or American	1,354	3.50
Welsh	206	0.53
West Indian, excl. Hispanic:	223	0.58
British West Indian	10	0.03
Haitian	44	0.11
Jamaican	102	0.26
Trinidadian and Tobagonian	42	0.11
West Indian	23	0.06
Other West Indian	2	0.01
White:	30,760	79.67
Not Hispanic (27,444)	28,118	72.83
Hispanic (2,378)	2,642	6.84
Yugoslavian	18	0.05

North Laurel

Place Type: Census Designated Place
County: Howard
Population: 20,468

Ancestry/Race	Number	%
African American/Black:	3,759	18.37
Not Hispanic (3,470)	3,704	18.10
Hispanic (30)	55	0.27
African, sub-Saharan:	483	2.34
African	259	1.26
Ghanian	51	0.25
Kenyan	15	0.07
Liberian	32	0.16
Nigerian	110	0.53
Sierra Leonean	8	0.04
Other sub-Saharan African	8	0.04
Alaska Native tribes, specified:	1	0.00
Eskimo (1)	1	0.00
Am. Ind. or Alaska Nat., not spec.	42	0.21

Notes: 1. Figures in the "Number" column do not add up to the total population due to: a) Ancestry/Race overlap — e.g. persons can report being both White and Irish, b) persons of Hispanic origin can report being any race, c) persons reporting two ancestries are counted in both categories. 2. Numbers in parentheses indicate the number of persons reporting this ancestry/race alone, not in combination with any other ancestry/race. 3. Refer to the Explanation of Data in the front of the book for more detailed information.

Ancestry/Race	Number	%
American Indian tribes, specified:	138	0.67
Blackfeet	8	0.04
Cherokee (16)	67	0.33
Choctaw (4)	6	0.03
Creek	1	0.00
Delaware (1)	1	0.00
Iroquois (3)	11	0.05
Latin American Indians (2)	5	0.02
Lumbee (1)	4	0.02
Sioux (3)	5	0.02
Tohono O'Odham (1)	1	0.00
Yuman (2)	2	0.01
All other tribes (14)	27	0.13
American Indian tribes, not spec.	9	0.04
Arab:	99	0.48
Arab/Arabic	32	0.16
Jordanian	18	0.09
Lebanese	10	0.05
Palestinian	32	0.16
Syrian	7	0.03
Armenian	24	0.12
Asian:	1,636	7.99
Bangladeshi (4)	4	0.02
Cambodian (11)	12	0.06
Chinese, ex. Taiwanese (200)	256	1.25
Filipino (124)	146	0.71
Indian (393)	436	2.13
Indonesian (2)	4	0.02
Japanese (22)	56	0.27
Korean (419)	455	2.22
Laotian (1)	1	0.00
Malaysian (1)	1	0.00
Pakistani (54)	57	0.28
Sri Lankan (2)	2	0.01
Taiwanese (7)	7	0.03
Thai (5)	9	0.04
Vietnamese (135)	138	0.67
Other Asian, specified (11)	12	0.06
Other Asian, not specified (22)	40	0.20
Assyrian/Chaldean/Syriac	6	0.03
Austrian	61	0.30
Basque	19	0.09
Brazilian	39	0.19
British	44	0.21
Bulgarian	6	0.03
Canadian	7	0.03
Carpatho Rusyn	35	0.17
Celtic	8	0.04
Czech	84	0.41
Czechoslovakian	82	0.40
Danish	58	0.28
Dutch	307	1.49
Eastern European	57	0.28
English	2,423	11.74
European	314	1.52
Finnish	15	0.07
French, except Basque	418	2.03
French Canadian	125	0.61
German	3,973	19.26
Greek	178	0.86
Guyanese	51	0.25
Hawaii Native/Pacific Islander:	27	0.13
Micronesian: (4)	4	0.02
Guamanian/Chamorro (4)	4	0.02
Polynesian: (10)	12	0.06
Native Hawaiian (10)	11	0.05
Samoan	1	0.00
Other Pac. Isl., not spec. (2)	11	0.05
Hispanic or Latino:	818	4.00
Central American:	121	0.59
Costa Rican	4	0.02
Guatemalan	34	0.17
Honduran	7	0.03
Nicaraguan	4	0.02
Panamanian	19	0.09
Salvadoran	48	0.23
Other Central American	5	0.02
Cuban	39	0.19
Dominican Republic	12	0.06
Mexican	190	0.93
Puerto Rican	146	0.71
South American:	112	0.55
Bolivian	11	0.05
Chilean	29	0.14
Colombian	16	0.08
Ecuadorian	13	0.06
Peruvian	23	0.11
Uruguayan	5	0.02
Venezuelan	8	0.04
Other South American	7	0.03
Other Hispanic or Latino	198	0.97
Hungarian	102	0.49
Iranian	45	0.22
Irish	3,112	15.08
Italian	1,471	7.13
Lithuanian	66	0.32
Luxemburger	7	0.03
Maltese	10	0.05
Norwegian	69	0.33
Pennsylvania German	27	0.13
Polish	691	3.35
Portuguese	28	0.14
Romanian	16	0.08
Russian	376	1.82
Scandinavian	7	0.03
Scotch-Irish	376	1.82
Scottish	281	1.36
Serbian	34	0.16
Slavic	8	0.04
Slovak	58	0.28
Slovene	9	0.04
Swedish	166	0.80
Swiss	36	0.17
Ukrainian	60	0.29
United States or American	1,230	5.96
Welsh	217	1.05
West Indian, excl. Hispanic:	455	2.21
Bahamian	6	0.03
Barbadian	40	0.19
Belizean	7	0.03
Haitian	45	0.22
Jamaican	314	1.52
Trinidadian and Tobagonian	18	0.09
West Indian	25	0.12
White:	15,022	73.39
Not Hispanic (14,160)	14,519	70.94
Hispanic (459)	503	2.46

North Potomac

Place Type: Census Designated Place
County: Montgomery
Population: 23,044

Ancestry/Race	Number	%
Acadian/Cajun	8	0.03
African American/Black:	1,080	4.69
Not Hispanic (951)	1,047	4.54
Hispanic (19)	33	0.14
African, sub-Saharan:	187	0.81
African	81	0.35
Ethiopian	24	0.10
Ghanian	8	0.03
Senegalese	33	0.14
South African	16	0.07
Other sub-Saharan African	25	0.11
Am. Ind. or Alaska Nat., not spec.	23	0.10
Albanian	9	0.04
American Indian tribes, specified:	42	0.18
Blackfeet	3	0.01
Cherokee (2)	9	0.04
Chickasaw (2)	2	0.01
Creek	1	0.00
Iroquois (1)	1	0.00
Latin American Indians (2)	5	0.02
Lumbee (4)	4	0.02
Navajo (2)	2	0.01
Osage (3)	3	0.01
Sioux (1)	1	0.00
All other tribes (8)	11	0.05
American Indian tribes, not spec.	1	0.00
Arab:	198	0.86
Lebanese	58	0.25
Moroccan	8	0.03
Syrian	57	0.25
Other Arab	75	0.33
Armenian	42	0.18
Asian:	6,793	29.48
Bangladeshi (16)	18	0.08
Cambodian (13)	15	0.07
Chinese, ex. Taiwanese (3,025)	3,186	13.83
Filipino (91)	123	0.53
Indian (1,242)	1,339	5.81
Indonesian (23)	29	0.13
Japanese (74)	110	0.48
Korean (1,098)	1,130	4.90
Laotian (4)	4	0.02
Malaysian (4)	4	0.02
Pakistani (79)	89	0.39
Sri Lankan (7)	8	0.03
Taiwanese (313)	374	1.62
Thai (24)	25	0.11
Vietnamese (184)	198	0.86
Other Asian, specified (15)	17	0.07
Other Asian, not specified (31)	124	0.54
Australian	41	0.18
Austrian	123	0.54
Belgian	13	0.06
Brazilian	71	0.31
British	155	0.68
Canadian	87	0.38
Croatian	25	0.11
Czech	56	0.24
Czechoslovakian	50	0.22
Danish	68	0.30
Dutch	217	0.95
Eastern European	555	2.42
English	1,663	7.25
Estonian	18	0.08
European	314	1.37
Finnish	8	0.03
French, except Basque	333	1.45
French Canadian	204	0.89
German	2,189	9.54
Greek	278	1.21
Hawaii Native/Pacific Islander:	41	0.18
Polynesian: (8)	12	0.05
Native Hawaiian (7)	11	0.05
Samoan (1)	1	0.00
Other Pac. Isl., not spec. (2)	29	0.13
Hispanic or Latino:	908	3.94
Central American:	111	0.48
Costa Rican	9	0.04
Guatemalan	9	0.04
Nicaraguan	19	0.08
Panamanian	13	0.06
Salvadoran	53	0.23
Other Central American	8	0.03
Cuban	46	0.20
Dominican Republic	9	0.04
Mexican	86	0.37
Puerto Rican	61	0.26
South American:	291	1.26
Argentinean	43	0.19
Bolivian	34	0.15
Chilean	26	0.11
Colombian	56	0.24
Ecuadorian	30	0.13
Paraguayan	7	0.03
Peruvian	58	0.25
Uruguayan	4	0.02
Venezuelan	8	0.03
Other South American	25	0.11
Other Hispanic or Latino	304	1.32
Hungarian	79	0.34
Icelander	7	0.03
Iranian	487	2.12
Irish	1,955	8.52
Israeli	54	0.24
Italian	1,084	4.72

Notes: 1. Figures in the "Number" column do not add up to the total population due to: a) Ancestry/Race overlap — e.g. persons can report being both White and Irish, b) persons of Hispanic origin can report being any race, c) persons reporting two ancestries are counted in both categories. 2. Numbers in parentheses indicate the number of persons reporting this ancestry/race alone, not in combination with any other ancestry/race. 3. Refer to the Explanation of Data in the front of the book for more detailed information.

Latvian	75	0.33
Lithuanian	164	0.71
Northern European	71	0.31
Norwegian	129	0.56
Polish	1,013	4.41
Portuguese	71	0.31
Romanian	102	0.44
Russian	1,281	5.58
Scandinavian	64	0.28
Scotch-Irish	330	1.44
Scottish	406	1.77
Slavic	12	0.05
Slovak	74	0.32
Slovene	7	0.03
Swedish	142	0.62
Swiss	104	0.45
Turkish	22	0.10
Ukrainian	102	0.44
United States or American	1,206	5.26
Welsh	168	0.73
West Indian, excl. Hispanic:	111	0.48
Haitian	8	0.03
Jamaican	67	0.29
Trinidadian and Tobagonian	16	0.07
U.S. Virgin Islander	20	0.09
White:	15,318	66.47
Not Hispanic (14,276)	14,651	63.58
Hispanic (620)	667	2.89
Yugoslavian	18	0.08

Ocean Pines

Place Type: Census Designated Place
County: Worcester
Population: 10,496

Ancestry/Race	Number	%
African American/Black:	258	2.46
Not Hispanic (213)	256	2.44
Hispanic (2)	2	0.02
Am. Ind. or Alaska Nat., not spec.	9	0.09
Albanian	14	0.13
Alsatian	13	0.12
American Indian tribes, specified:	33	0.31
Blackfeet	2	0.02
Cherokee (3)	11	0.10
Choctaw	1	0.01
Creek	2	0.02
Iroquois (6)	6	0.06
Navajo (1)	1	0.01
Osage	1	0.01
Seminole	1	0.01
Sioux	1	0.01
All other tribes	7	0.07
Asian:	77	0.73
Cambodian (1)	1	0.01
Chinese, ex. Taiwanese (11)	15	0.14
Filipino (28)	29	0.28
Indian (2)	5	0.05
Indonesian	1	0.01
Japanese (1)	2	0.02
Korean (11)	14	0.13
Laotian (1)	1	0.01
Taiwanese	1	0.01
Thai	1	0.01
Vietnamese (2)	2	0.02
Other Asian, not specified (1)	5	0.05
Austrian	54	0.51
Brazilian	6	0.06
British	47	0.45
Canadian	11	0.10
Croatian	20	0.19
Czech	49	0.46
Czechoslovakian	11	0.10
Danish	26	0.25
Dutch	222	2.10
Eastern European	21	0.20
English	1,668	15.79
European	25	0.24
Finnish	21	0.20
French, except Basque	319	3.02
French Canadian	89	0.84
German	3,089	29.25
Greek	159	1.51
Hawaii Native/Pacific Islander:	8	0.08
Polynesian:	7	0.07
Native Hawaiian	5	0.05
Samoan	2	0.02
Other Pac. Isl., not spec.	1	0.01
Hispanic or Latino:	96	0.91
Central American:	3	0.03
Costa Rican	3	0.03
Cuban	4	0.04
Mexican	26	0.25
Puerto Rican	23	0.22
South American:	7	0.07
Bolivian	2	0.02
Chilean	1	0.01
Colombian	2	0.02
Peruvian	2	0.02
Other Hispanic or Latino	33	0.31
Hungarian	56	0.53
Irish	2,719	25.75
Israeli	7	0.07
Italian	1,072	10.15
Latvian	19	0.18
Lithuanian	127	1.20
Maltese	7	0.07
Norwegian	112	1.06
Pennsylvania German	40	0.38
Polish	623	5.90
Portuguese	10	0.09
Russian	124	1.17
Scandinavian	13	0.12
Scotch-Irish	191	1.81
Scottish	354	3.35
Slavic	5	0.05
Slovak	74	0.70
Slovene	12	0.11
Swedish	145	1.37
Swiss	30	0.28
Ukrainian	69	0.65
United States or American	502	4.75
Welsh	130	1.23
White:	10,173	96.92
Not Hispanic (10,023)	10,095	96.18
Hispanic (72)	78	0.74

Odenton

Place Type: Census Designated Place
County: Anne Arundel
Population: 20,534

Ancestry/Race	Number	%
African American/Black:	2,843	13.85
Not Hispanic (2,582)	2,786	13.57
Hispanic (38)	57	0.28
African, sub-Saharan:	63	0.31
African	56	0.27
Cape Verdean	7	0.03
Alaska Native tribes, specified:	1	0.00
Alaska Athabascan (1)	1	0.00
Am. Ind. or Alaska Nat., not spec.	68	0.33
American Indian tribes, specified:	132	0.64
Apache (3)	4	0.02
Blackfeet (5)	14	0.07
Cherokee (13)	67	0.33
Choctaw	1	0.00
Creek (1)	1	0.00
Iroquois (4)	11	0.05
Latin American Indians (4)	7	0.03
Lumbee (1)	1	0.00
Potawatomi	1	0.00
Seminole (1)	1	0.00
Sioux (2)	4	0.02
All other tribes (16)	20	0.10
American Indian tribes, not spec.	11	0.05
Arab:	27	0.13
Lebanese	27	0.13
Armenian	11	0.05
Asian:	830	4.04
Cambodian (10)	11	0.05
Chinese, ex. Taiwanese (51)	86	0.42
Filipino (99)	148	0.72
Indian (100)	104	0.51
Indonesian (2)	2	0.01
Japanese (40)	77	0.37
Korean (152)	199	0.97
Laotian (1)	3	0.01
Pakistani (4)	4	0.02
Taiwanese (2)	2	0.01
Thai (21)	32	0.16
Vietnamese (101)	112	0.55
Other Asian, specified	4	0.02
Other Asian, not specified (31)	46	0.22
Austrian	36	0.17
Belgian	16	0.08
British	90	0.44
Bulgarian	9	0.04
Canadian	31	0.15
Croatian	12	0.06
Czech	65	0.31
Czechoslovakian	56	0.27
Danish	29	0.14
Dutch	223	1.08
Eastern European	7	0.03
English	2,658	12.88
Estonian	6	0.03
European	211	1.02
Finnish	84	0.41
French, except Basque	585	2.83
French Canadian	231	1.12
German	4,124	19.98
Greek	35	0.17
Guyanese	13	0.06
Hawaii Native/Pacific Islander:	47	0.23
Micronesian: (12)	22	0.11
Guamanian/Chamorro (11)	21	0.10
Other Micronesian (1)	1	0.00
Polynesian: (2)	12	0.06
Native Hawaiian (2)	12	0.06
Other Pac. Isl., not spec. (2)	13	0.06
Hispanic or Latino:	568	2.77
Central American:	53	0.26
Guatemalan	4	0.02
Honduran	6	0.03
Nicaraguan	2	0.01
Panamanian	26	0.13
Salvadoran	8	0.04
Other Central American	7	0.03
Cuban	16	0.08
Dominican Republic	16	0.08
Mexican	130	0.63
Puerto Rican	201	0.98
South American:	38	0.19
Bolivian	8	0.04
Chilean	1	0.00
Colombian	10	0.05
Ecuadorian	1	0.00
Peruvian	10	0.05
Venezuelan	7	0.03
Other South American	1	0.00
Other Hispanic or Latino	114	0.56
Hungarian	156	0.76
Irish	3,351	16.24
Italian	1,322	6.41
Latvian	12	0.06
Lithuanian	94	0.46
Luxemburger	7	0.03
Northern European	23	0.11
Norwegian	145	0.70
Pennsylvania German	10	0.05
Polish	880	4.26
Portuguese	74	0.36
Romanian	15	0.07
Russian	208	1.01
Scandinavian	34	0.16
Scotch-Irish	416	2.02
Scottish	486	2.36

Notes: 1. Figures in the "Number" column do not add up to the total population due to: a) Ancestry/Race overlap — e.g. persons can report being both White and Irish, b) persons of Hispanic origin can report being any race, c) persons reporting two ancestries are counted in both categories. 2. Numbers in parentheses indicate the number of persons reporting this ancestry/race alone, not in combination with any other ancestry/race. 3. Refer to the Explanation of Data in the front of the book for more detailed information.

Ancestry/Race	Number	%
Slavic	10	0.05
Slovak	55	0.27
Swedish	176	0.85
Swiss	49	0.24
Ukrainian	120	0.58
United States or American	1,386	6.72
Welsh	289	1.40
West Indian, excl. Hispanic:	237	1.15
Haitian	16	0.08
Jamaican	30	0.15
Trinidadian and Tobagonian	13	0.06
U.S. Virgin Islander	170	0.82
West Indian	8	0.04
White:	16,912	82.36
Not Hispanic (16,167)	16,548	80.59
Hispanic (291)	364	1.77

Olney

Place Type: Census Designated Place
County: Montgomery
Population: 31,438

Ancestry/Race	Number	%
African American/Black:	2,968	9.44
Not Hispanic (2,734)	2,919	9.28
Hispanic (27)	49	0.16
African, sub-Saharan:	436	1.38
African	202	0.64
Ethiopian	6	0.02
Ghanian	3	0.01
Liberian	72	0.23
Nigerian	34	0.11
Sierra Leonean	46	0.15
Ugandan	7	0.02
Other sub-Saharan African	66	0.21
Am. Ind. or Alaska Nat., not spec.	49	0.16
Albanian	42	0.13
American Indian tribes, specified:	116	0.37
Blackfeet (1)	2	0.01
Cherokee (19)	42	0.13
Cheyenne	1	0.00
Chickasaw	1	0.00
Chippewa (4)	4	0.01
Choctaw (4)	7	0.02
Delaware	4	0.01
Iroquois (4)	4	0.01
Latin American Indians (6)	11	0.03
Lumbee (5)	5	0.02
Menominee (1)	1	0.00
Osage (4)	7	0.02
Pima (1)	1	0.00
Pueblo (5)	9	0.03
Sioux	3	0.01
All other tribes (8)	14	0.04
American Indian tribes, not spec.	7	0.02
Arab:	323	1.02
Arab/Arabic	13	0.04
Egyptian	62	0.20
Lebanese	141	0.45
Syrian	59	0.19
Other Arab	48	0.15
Armenian	115	0.36
Asian:	2,824	8.98
Bangladeshi (3)	3	0.01
Cambodian (49)	54	0.17
Chinese, ex. Taiwanese (670)	736	2.34
Filipino (192)	238	0.76
Indian (569)	638	2.03
Indonesian (13)	13	0.04
Japanese (47)	77	0.24
Korean (529)	562	1.79
Laotian (9)	18	0.06
Pakistani (32)	35	0.11
Sri Lankan (41)	47	0.15
Taiwanese (13)	18	0.06
Thai (59)	74	0.24
Vietnamese (231)	244	0.78
Other Asian, specified (3)	3	0.01
Other Asian, not specified (26)	64	0.20
Austrian	320	1.01
Belgian	41	0.13
Brazilian	81	0.26
British	231	0.73
Canadian	60	0.19
Carpatho Rusyn	10	0.03
Celtic	8	0.03
Croatian	17	0.05
Czech	95	0.30
Czechoslovakian	121	0.38
Danish	76	0.24
Dutch	437	1.38
Eastern European	302	0.95
English	3,412	10.78
Estonian	20	0.06
European	518	1.64
Finnish	47	0.15
French, except Basque	867	2.74
French Canadian	200	0.63
German	4,173	13.18
Greek	584	1.85
Guyanese	111	0.35
Hawaii Native/Pacific Islander:	30	0.10
Micronesian: (3)	3	0.01
Guamanian/Chamorro (3)	3	0.01
Polynesian: (5)	11	0.03
Native Hawaiian (5)	8	0.03
Other Polynesian	3	0.01
Other Pac. Isl., not spec. (6)	16	0.05
Hispanic or Latino:	1,576	5.01
Central American:	224	0.71
Costa Rican	4	0.01
Guatemalan	39	0.12
Honduran	22	0.07
Nicaraguan	36	0.11
Panamanian	9	0.03
Salvadoran	111	0.35
Other Central American	3	0.01
Cuban	98	0.31
Dominican Republic	33	0.10
Mexican	155	0.49
Puerto Rican	147	0.47
South American:	350	1.11
Argentinean	19	0.06
Bolivian	66	0.21
Chilean	27	0.09
Colombian	95	0.30
Ecuadorian	35	0.11
Paraguayan	6	0.02
Peruvian	56	0.18
Uruguayan	1	0.00
Venezuelan	17	0.05
Other South American	28	0.09
Other Hispanic or Latino	569	1.81
Hungarian	212	0.67
Iranian	198	0.63
Irish	5,432	17.16
Israeli	40	0.13
Italian	2,544	8.04
Latvian	21	0.07
Lithuanian	236	0.75
Maltese	8	0.03
Northern European	27	0.09
Norwegian	293	0.93
Pennsylvania German	6	0.02
Polish	1,358	4.29
Portuguese	101	0.32
Romanian	44	0.14
Russian	1,240	3.92
Scotch-Irish	540	1.71
Scottish	717	2.27
Serbian	10	0.03
Slovak	128	0.40
Slovene	6	0.02
Swedish	392	1.24
Swiss	191	0.60
Turkish	15	0.05
Ukrainian	236	0.75
United States or American	2,088	6.60
Welsh	226	0.71
West Indian, excl. Hispanic:	475	1.50
Barbadian	6	0.02
British West Indian	40	0.13
Haitian	13	0.04
Jamaican	241	0.76
Trinidadian and Tobagonian	99	0.31
West Indian	71	0.22
Other West Indian	5	0.02
White:	25,423	80.87
Not Hispanic (23,949)	24,370	77.52
Hispanic (900)	1,053	3.35
Yugoslavian	9	0.03

Overlea

Place Type: Census Designated Place
County: Baltimore
Population: 12,148

Ancestry/Race	Number	%
Acadian/Cajun	10	0.08
African American/Black:	1,126	9.27
Not Hispanic (1,066)	1,118	9.20
Hispanic (1)	8	0.07
African, sub-Saharan:	99	0.83
African	99	0.83
Am. Ind. or Alaska Nat., not spec.	18	0.15
American Indian tribes, specified:	42	0.35
Blackfeet (1)	4	0.03
Cherokee (8)	22	0.18
Cheyenne	1	0.01
Chippewa (1)	1	0.01
Choctaw (3)	4	0.03
Iroquois (1)	1	0.01
Lumbee (2)	2	0.02
Menominee (1)	1	0.01
Sioux (1)	1	0.01
All other tribes (3)	5	0.04
American Indian tribes, not spec.	3	0.02
Asian:	273	2.25
Chinese, ex. Taiwanese (25)	38	0.31
Filipino (40)	63	0.52
Indian (27)	32	0.26
Japanese (10)	14	0.12
Korean (45)	47	0.39
Laotian (4)	4	0.03
Malaysian (2)	2	0.02
Pakistani (12)	12	0.10
Taiwanese (7)	8	0.07
Thai (1)	3	0.02
Vietnamese (26)	26	0.21
Other Asian, not specified (10)	24	0.20
Austrian	69	0.58
British	15	0.13
Celtic	10	0.08
Croatian	63	0.53
Czech	248	2.07
Czechoslovakian	26	0.22
Danish	16	0.13
Dutch	182	1.52
English	1,222	10.19
European	71	0.59
French, except Basque	243	2.03
French Canadian	59	0.49
German	4,301	35.85
Greek	91	0.76
Hawaii Native/Pacific Islander:	4	0.03
Micronesian: (2)	2	0.02
Guamanian/Chamorro (2)	2	0.02
Polynesian:	1	0.01
Native Hawaiian	1	0.01
Other Pac. Isl., not spec.	1	0.01
Hispanic or Latino:	169	1.39
Central American:	10	0.08
Costa Rican	1	0.01
Guatemalan	1	0.01
Honduran	2	0.02
Salvadoran	6	0.05
Cuban	11	0.09
Dominican Republic	5	0.04

Notes: 1. Figures in the "Number" column do not add up to the total population due to: a) Ancestry/Race overlap — e.g. persons can report being both White and Irish, b) persons of Hispanic origin can report being any race, c) persons reporting two ancestries are counted in both categories. 2. Numbers in parentheses indicate the number of persons reporting this ancestry/race alone, not in combination with any other ancestry/race. 3. Refer to the Explanation of Data in the front of the book for more detailed information.

Ancestry/Race	Number	%
Mexican	40	0.33
Puerto Rican	50	0.41
South American:	24	0.20
Argentinean	1	0.01
Bolivian	4	0.03
Chilean	3	0.02
Colombian	1	0.01
Ecuadorian	7	0.06
Peruvian	6	0.05
Venezuelan	2	0.02
Other Hispanic or Latino	29	0.24
Hungarian	92	0.77
Iranian	7	0.06
Irish	2,245	18.71
Italian	1,111	9.26
Latvian	5	0.04
Lithuanian	31	0.26
Norwegian	43	0.36
Polish	1,184	9.87
Portuguese	105	0.88
Russian	188	1.57
Scandinavian	33	0.28
Scotch-Irish	99	0.83
Scottish	113	0.94
Serbian	8	0.07
Slovak	24	0.20
Swedish	50	0.42
Ukrainian	44	0.37
United States or American	481	4.01
Welsh	163	1.36
West Indian, excl. Hispanic:	12	0.10
West Indian	12	0.10
White:	10,775	88.70
Not Hispanic (10,538)	10,645	87.63
Hispanic (121)	130	1.07
Yugoslavian	20	0.17

Owings Mills

Place Type: Census Designated Place
County: Baltimore
Population: 20,193

Ancestry/Race	Number	%
African American/Black:	7,637	37.82
Not Hispanic (7,301)	7,540	37.34
Hispanic (58)	97	0.48
African, sub-Saharan:	493	2.44
African	219	1.08
Cape Verdean	3	0.01
Ghanian	16	0.08
Nigerian	229	1.13
Ugandan	10	0.05
Other sub-Saharan African	16	0.08
Am. Ind. or Alaska Nat., not spec.	65	0.32
American Indian tribes, specified:	65	0.32
Apache (1)	2	0.01
Blackfeet (3)	5	0.02
Cherokee (8)	21	0.10
Comanche	4	0.02
Delaware (1)	1	0.00
Iroquois	2	0.01
Latin American Indians	5	0.02
Lumbee (5)	5	0.02
Seminole	3	0.01
Sioux (1)	3	0.01
All other tribes (3)	14	0.07
American Indian tribes, not spec.	8	0.04
Arab:	143	0.71
Egyptian	63	0.31
Lebanese	22	0.11
Syrian	30	0.15
Other Arab	28	0.14
Armenian	21	0.10
Asian:	930	4.61
Cambodian (1)	1	0.00
Chinese, ex. Taiwanese (125)	146	0.72
Filipino (103)	134	0.66
Indian (310)	337	1.67
Indonesian (2)	2	0.01
Japanese (13)	22	0.11
Korean (104)	121	0.60
Laotian (5)	5	0.02
Pakistani (41)	59	0.29
Sri Lankan (5)	5	0.02
Taiwanese (3)	4	0.02
Thai (11)	12	0.06
Vietnamese (29)	41	0.20
Other Asian, specified (8)	14	0.07
Other Asian, not specified (10)	27	0.13
Austrian	47	0.23
Basque	5	0.02
British	66	0.33
Canadian	13	0.06
Croatian	7	0.03
Czech	69	0.34
Czechoslovakian	7	0.03
Danish	16	0.08
Dutch	182	0.90
Eastern European	20	0.10
English	1,062	5.25
Estonian	8	0.04
European	95	0.47
Finnish	10	0.05
French, except Basque	222	1.10
French Canadian	41	0.20
German	2,462	12.18
Greek	77	0.38
Hawaii Native/Pacific Islander:	27	0.13
Polynesian: (6)	11	0.05
Native Hawaiian (2)	3	0.01
Samoan (2)	4	0.02
Tongan (2)	4	0.02
Other Pac. Isl., specified	3	0.01
Other Pac. Isl., not spec. (2)	13	0.06
Hispanic or Latino:	647	3.20
Central American:	108	0.53
Costa Rican	1	0.00
Guatemalan	27	0.13
Honduran	20	0.10
Panamanian	11	0.05
Salvadoran	43	0.21
Other Central American	6	0.03
Cuban	22	0.11
Dominican Republic	11	0.05
Mexican	95	0.47
Puerto Rican	146	0.72
South American:	77	0.38
Argentinean	9	0.04
Bolivian	5	0.02
Chilean	13	0.06
Colombian	11	0.05
Ecuadorian	1	0.00
Peruvian	27	0.13
Venezuelan	10	0.05
Other South American	1	0.00
Other Hispanic or Latino	188	0.93
Hungarian	107	0.53
Iranian	61	0.30
Irish	1,741	8.61
Israeli	9	0.04
Italian	1,144	5.66
Latvian	7	0.03
Lithuanian	98	0.48
Maltese	22	0.11
Northern European	14	0.07
Norwegian	40	0.20
Pennsylvania German	8	0.04
Polish	715	3.54
Portuguese	32	0.16
Romanian	19	0.09
Russian	815	4.03
Scandinavian	10	0.05
Scotch-Irish	215	1.06
Scottish	233	1.15
Serbian	20	0.10
Slovak	65	0.32
Swedish	114	0.56
Swiss	17	0.08
Turkish	36	0.18
Ukrainian	116	0.57
United States or American	888	4.39
Welsh	94	0.47
West Indian, excl. Hispanic:	270	1.34
Barbadian	7	0.03
British West Indian	14	0.07
Haitian	33	0.16
Jamaican	129	0.64
Trinidadian and Tobagonian	31	0.15
West Indian	56	0.28
White:	11,615	57.52
Not Hispanic (10,998)	11,257	55.75
Hispanic (270)	358	1.77
Yugoslavian	25	0.12

Oxon Hill-Glassmanor

Place Type: Census Designated Place
County: Prince George's
Population: 35,355

Ancestry/Race	Number	%
African American/Black:	31,149	88.10
Not Hispanic (30,463)	30,900	87.40
Hispanic (183)	249	0.70
African, sub-Saharan:	814	2.32
African	625	1.78
Cape Verdean	30	0.09
Ethiopian	53	0.15
Ghanian	7	0.02
Nigerian	88	0.25
Other sub-Saharan African	11	0.03
Am. Ind. or Alaska Nat., not spec.	165	0.47
American Indian tribes, specified:	171	0.48
Apache	1	0.00
Blackfeet (4)	22	0.06
Cherokee (9)	72	0.20
Chickasaw	3	0.01
Choctaw	1	0.00
Crow	1	0.00
Iroquois (2)	9	0.03
Latin American Indians (5)	9	0.03
Lumbee (1)	1	0.00
Potawatomi (3)	3	0.01
Seminole (3)	10	0.03
Sioux (2)	4	0.01
All other tribes (28)	35	0.10
American Indian tribes, not spec.	8	0.02
Arab:	25	0.07
Moroccan	25	0.07
Asian:	1,173	3.32
Cambodian (7)	7	0.02
Chinese, ex. Taiwanese (53)	73	0.21
Filipino (765)	857	2.42
Indian (53)	81	0.23
Japanese (17)	28	0.08
Korean (37)	44	0.12
Pakistani (12)	22	0.06
Sri Lankan	3	0.01
Thai (5)	11	0.03
Vietnamese (8)	9	0.03
Other Asian, specified (5)	5	0.01
Other Asian, not specified (13)	33	0.09
Austrian	7	0.02
British	40	0.11
Canadian	6	0.02
Czech	5	0.01
Danish	13	0.04
Dutch	76	0.22
English	411	1.17
European	64	0.18
French, except Basque	25	0.07
French Canadian	30	0.09
German	602	1.71
Greek	16	0.05
Guyanese	21	0.06
Hawaii Native/Pacific Islander:	59	0.17
Micronesian: (14)	22	0.06
Guamanian/Chamorro (13)	21	0.06
Other Micronesian (1)	1	0.00

Notes: 1. Figures in the "Number" column do not add up to the total population due to: a) Ancestry/Race overlap — e.g. persons can report being both White and Irish, b) persons of Hispanic origin can report being any race, c) persons reporting two ancestries are counted in both categories. 2. Numbers in parentheses indicate the number of persons reporting this ancestry/race alone, not in combination with any other ancestry/race. 3. Refer to the Explanation of Data in the front of the book for more detailed information.

Polynesian: (8)	15	0.04
Native Hawaiian (6)	12	0.03
Samoan (2)	3	0.01
Other Pac. Isl., not spec. (8)	22	0.06
Hispanic or Latino:	593	1.68
Central American:	113	0.32
Guatemalan	14	0.04
Honduran	9	0.03
Nicaraguan	1	0.00
Panamanian	41	0.12
Salvadoran	47	0.13
Other Central American	1	0.00
Cuban	18	0.05
Dominican Republic	16	0.05
Mexican	79	0.22
Puerto Rican	120	0.34
South American:	36	0.10
Argentinean	4	0.01
Bolivian	3	0.01
Colombian	6	0.02
Ecuadorian	1	0.00
Peruvian	19	0.05
Venezuelan	3	0.01
Other Hispanic or Latino	211	0.60
Hungarian	12	0.03
Irish	435	1.24
Italian	312	0.89
Latvian	10	0.03
Polish	69	0.20
Portuguese	19	0.05
Russian	18	0.05
Scandinavian	14	0.04
Scotch-Irish	25	0.07
Scottish	30	0.09
Slavic	9	0.03
Slovene	9	0.03
Swedish	20	0.06
Swiss	12	0.03
Ukrainian	19	0.05
United States or American	676	1.92
Welsh	19	0.05
West Indian, excl. Hispanic:	559	1.59
British West Indian	16	0.05
Dutch West Indian	18	0.05
Haitian	35	0.10
Jamaican	305	0.87
Trinidadian and Tobagonian	78	0.22
U.S. Virgin Islander	15	0.04
West Indian	92	0.26
White:	2,951	8.35
Not Hispanic (2,602)	2,828	8.00
Hispanic (98)	123	0.35
Yugoslavian	6	0.02

Parkville

Place Type: Census Designated Place
County: Baltimore
Population: 31,118

Ancestry/Race	Number	%
African American/Black:	7,232	23.24
Not Hispanic (6,938)	7,144	22.96
Hispanic (57)	88	0.28
African, sub-Saharan:	795	2.56
African	369	1.19
Ethiopian	10	0.03
Ghanian	64	0.21
Kenyan	107	0.34
Nigerian	245	0.79
Alaska Native tribes, specified:	1	0.00
Eskimo	1	0.00
Am. Ind. or Alaska Nat., not spec.	71	0.23
American Indian tribes, specified:	114	0.37
Blackfeet	14	0.04
Cherokee (16)	61	0.20
Cheyenne	2	0.01
Chippewa	1	0.00
Choctaw	1	0.00
Creek	2	0.01
Iroquois (1)	6	0.02
Latin American Indians (3)	3	0.01
Lumbee	5	0.02
Pima (2)	4	0.01
Pueblo	1	0.00
Seminole	1	0.00
Shoshone	1	0.00
Sioux	1	0.00
Yaqui (1)	1	0.00
All other tribes (5)	10	0.03
American Indian tribes, not spec.	11	0.04
Arab:	54	0.17
Egyptian	19	0.06
Lebanese	11	0.04
Palestinian	24	0.08
Asian:	689	2.21
Cambodian (6)	7	0.02
Chinese, ex. Taiwanese (167)	188	0.60
Filipino (120)	147	0.47
Indian (83)	95	0.31
Indonesian (5)	5	0.02
Japanese (16)	24	0.08
Korean (101)	115	0.37
Laotian (13)	13	0.04
Malaysian	1	0.00
Pakistani (8)	25	0.08
Thai (6)	9	0.03
Vietnamese (36)	41	0.13
Other Asian, specified (5)	6	0.02
Other Asian, not specified (10)	13	0.04
Austrian	66	0.21
Belgian	21	0.07
British	85	0.27
Canadian	52	0.17
Celtic	37	0.12
Croatian	22	0.07
Czech	244	0.79
Czechoslovakian	79	0.25
Danish	47	0.15
Dutch	273	0.88
Eastern European	8	0.03
English	3,008	9.69
Estonian	26	0.08
European	70	0.23
Finnish	27	0.09
French, except Basque	614	1.98
French Canadian	93	0.30
German	8,263	26.62
Greek	218	0.70
Guyanese	9	0.03
Hawaii Native/Pacific Islander:	13	0.04
Micronesian: (1)	3	0.01
Guamanian/Chamorro (1)	3	0.01
Polynesian: (2)	7	0.02
Native Hawaiian (2)	4	0.01
Samoan	3	0.01
Other Pac. Isl., not spec. (3)	3	0.01
Hispanic or Latino:	515	1.65
Central American:	30	0.10
Guatemalan	9	0.03
Honduran	7	0.02
Panamanian	6	0.02
Salvadoran	6	0.02
Other Central American	2	0.01
Cuban	31	0.10
Dominican Republic	7	0.02
Mexican	96	0.31
Puerto Rican	125	0.40
South American:	101	0.32
Argentinean	3	0.01
Bolivian	11	0.04
Chilean	2	0.01
Colombian	28	0.09
Ecuadorian	26	0.08
Peruvian	18	0.06
Venezuelan	11	0.04
Other South American	2	0.01
Other Hispanic or Latino	125	0.40
Hungarian	118	0.38
Iranian	14	0.05
Irish	5,386	17.35
Italian	2,627	8.46
Latvian	46	0.15
Lithuanian	105	0.34
Norwegian	50	0.16
Pennsylvania German	21	0.07
Polish	1,651	5.32
Portuguese	48	0.15
Romanian	8	0.03
Russian	159	0.51
Scandinavian	39	0.13
Scotch-Irish	345	1.11
Scottish	434	1.40
Serbian	14	0.05
Slavic	7	0.02
Slovak	49	0.16
Swedish	122	0.39
Swiss	57	0.18
Turkish	18	0.06
Ukrainian	101	0.33
United States or American	1,324	4.27
Welsh	354	1.14
West Indian, excl. Hispanic:	269	0.87
Belizean	10	0.03
Bermudan	9	0.03
British West Indian	34	0.11
Haitian	34	0.11
Jamaican	111	0.36
Trinidadian and Tobagonian	59	0.19
West Indian	12	0.04
White:	23,212	74.59
Not Hispanic (22,630)	22,888	73.55
Hispanic (286)	324	1.04
Yugoslavian	13	0.04

Parole

Place Type: Census Designated Place
County: Anne Arundel
Population: 14,031

Ancestry/Race	Number	%
African American/Black:	952	6.78
Not Hispanic (899)	937	6.68
Hispanic (11)	15	0.11
African, sub-Saharan:	10	0.07
African	10	0.07
Alaska Native tribes, specified:	1	0.01
Aleut (1)	1	0.01
Am. Ind. or Alaska Nat., not spec.	27	0.19
Albanian	7	0.05
American Indian tribes, specified:	36	0.26
Cherokee (10)	22	0.16
Chippewa (1)	1	0.01
Choctaw	1	0.01
Crow (1)	1	0.01
Iroquois	1	0.01
Latin American Indians (1)	3	0.02
Navajo	1	0.01
Puget Sound Salish (1)	1	0.01
Seminole	1	0.01
Sioux (1)	1	0.01
All other tribes (2)	3	0.02
American Indian tribes, not spec.	5	0.04
Arab:	57	0.41
Lebanese	48	0.34
Syrian	9	0.06
Asian:	255	1.82
Chinese, ex. Taiwanese (41)	43	0.31
Filipino (39)	52	0.37
Indian (36)	38	0.27
Indonesian (1)	4	0.03
Japanese (14)	22	0.16
Korean (40)	42	0.30
Pakistani (9)	10	0.07
Taiwanese (2)	2	0.01
Thai (6)	6	0.04
Vietnamese (17)	20	0.14
Other Asian, specified (1)	1	0.01
Other Asian, not specified (6)	15	0.11

Notes: 1. Figures in the "Number" column do not add up to the total population due to: a) Ancestry/Race overlap — e.g. persons can report being both White and Irish, b) persons of Hispanic origin can report being any race, c) persons reporting two ancestries are counted in both categories. 2. Numbers in parentheses indicate the number of persons reporting this ancestry/race alone, not in combination with any other ancestry/race. 3. Refer to the Explanation of Data in the front of the book for more detailed information.

Australian	19	0.14
Austrian	128	0.92
Belgian	29	0.21
Brazilian	7	0.05
British	142	1.02
Canadian	70	0.50
Celtic	44	0.32
Croatian	14	0.10
Cypriot	37	0.27
Czech	51	0.37
Czechoslovakian	29	0.21
Danish	169	1.21
Dutch	134	0.96
Eastern European	77	0.55
English	2,571	18.43
Estonian	8	0.06
European	88	0.63
Finnish	34	0.24
French, except Basque	401	2.87
French Canadian	77	0.55
German	2,808	20.13
Greek	107	0.77
Hawaii Native/Pacific Islander:	21	0.15
Micronesian: (1)	2	0.01
Guamanian/Chamorro	1	0.01
Other Micronesian (1)	1	0.01
Polynesian: (8)	14	0.10
Native Hawaiian (8)	12	0.09
Other Polynesian	2	0.01
Other Pac. Isl., not spec. (2)	5	0.04
Hispanic or Latino:	219	1.56
Central American:	30	0.21
Costa Rican	1	0.01
Guatemalan	3	0.02
Honduran	2	0.01
Nicaraguan	3	0.02
Panamanian	2	0.01
Salvadoran	16	0.11
Other Central American	3	0.02
Cuban	16	0.11
Mexican	35	0.25
Puerto Rican	43	0.31
South American:	38	0.27
Argentinean	2	0.01
Bolivian	6	0.04
Chilean	7	0.05
Colombian	7	0.05
Ecuadorian	1	0.01
Paraguayan	1	0.01
Peruvian	5	0.04
Uruguayan	1	0.01
Venezuelan	2	0.01
Other South American	6	0.04
Other Hispanic or Latino	57	0.41
Hungarian	126	0.90
Irish	2,494	17.88
Israeli	8	0.06
Italian	1,210	8.67
Lithuanian	51	0.37
Northern European	20	0.14
Norwegian	206	1.48
Pennsylvania German	12	0.09
Polish	732	5.25
Portuguese	64	0.46
Romanian	87	0.62
Russian	258	1.85
Scotch-Irish	387	2.77
Scottish	489	3.51
Slavic	21	0.15
Slovak	34	0.24
Swedish	253	1.81
Swiss	79	0.57
Ukrainian	64	0.46
United States or American	794	5.69
Welsh	185	1.33
West Indian, excl. Hispanic:	34	0.24
British West Indian	11	0.08
Jamaican	5	0.04
Trinidadian and Tobagonian	10	0.07
West Indian	8	0.06
White:	12,792	91.17
Not Hispanic (12,546)	12,643	90.11
Hispanic (133)	149	1.06
Yugoslavian	7	0.05

Pasadena

Place Type: Census Designated Place
County: Anne Arundel
Population: 12,093

Ancestry/Race	Number	%
Acadian/Cajun	21	0.17
African American/Black:	866	7.16
Not Hispanic (820)	861	7.12
Hispanic (3)	5	0.04
African, sub-Saharan:	22	0.18
African	22	0.18
Alaska Native tribes, specified:	2	0.02
Eskimo	2	0.02
Am. Ind. or Alaska Nat., not spec.	24	0.20
American Indian tribes, specified:	46	0.38
Blackfeet (3)	4	0.03
Cherokee (8)	16	0.13
Chickasaw	1	0.01
Latin American Indians	2	0.02
Lumbee (3)	4	0.03
Potawatomi (1)	1	0.01
Seminole	1	0.01
Sioux (1)	10	0.08
All other tribes (4)	7	0.06
American Indian tribes, not spec.	6	0.05
Arab:	19	0.16
Lebanese	19	0.16
Asian:	227	1.88
Chinese, ex. Taiwanese (19)	22	0.18
Filipino (32)	55	0.45
Indian (12)	16	0.13
Indonesian	1	0.01
Japanese (8)	18	0.15
Korean (74)	78	0.65
Pakistani (8)	8	0.07
Thai (2)	2	0.02
Vietnamese (15)	16	0.13
Other Asian, not specified (6)	11	0.09
Austrian	5	0.04
British	107	0.89
Czech	62	0.52
Czechoslovakian	130	1.08
Danish	15	0.12
Dutch	193	1.61
Eastern European	6	0.05
English	1,825	15.21
European	138	1.15
Finnish	8	0.07
French, except Basque	406	3.38
French Canadian	113	0.94
German	3,564	29.70
Greek	70	0.58
Hawaii Native/Pacific Islander:	8	0.07
Micronesian: (1)	1	0.01
Guamanian/Chamorro (1)	1	0.01
Polynesian: (4)	6	0.05
Native Hawaiian (1)	2	0.02
Samoan (3)	4	0.03
Other Pac. Isl., not spec.	1	0.01
Hispanic or Latino:	161	1.33
Central American:	4	0.03
Guatemalan	3	0.02
Salvadoran	1	0.01
Cuban	9	0.07
Dominican Republic	2	0.02
Mexican	53	0.44
Puerto Rican	42	0.35
South American:	21	0.17
Argentinean	4	0.03
Bolivian	1	0.01
Colombian	6	0.05
Ecuadorian	1	0.01
Paraguayan	1	0.01
Peruvian	7	0.06
Other South American	1	0.01
Other Hispanic or Latino	30	0.25
Hungarian	154	1.28
Iranian	10	0.08
Irish	2,447	20.39
Italian	826	6.88
Lithuanian	64	0.53
Northern European	7	0.06
Norwegian	135	1.12
Pennsylvania German	10	0.08
Polish	780	6.50
Portuguese	54	0.45
Romanian	19	0.16
Russian	66	0.55
Scotch-Irish	215	1.79
Scottish	264	2.20
Slovak	72	0.60
Slovene	17	0.14
Swedish	103	0.86
Swiss	31	0.26
United States or American	900	7.50
Welsh	106	0.88
White:	10,999	90.95
Not Hispanic (10,773)	10,877	89.94
Hispanic (117)	122	1.01

Perry Hall

Place Type: Census Designated Place
County: Baltimore
Population: 28,705

Ancestry/Race	Number	%
Afghan	25	0.09
African American/Black:	1,391	4.85
Not Hispanic (1,282)	1,363	4.75
Hispanic (17)	28	0.10
African, sub-Saharan:	109	0.38
African	90	0.31
Nigerian	7	0.02
Other sub-Saharan African	12	0.04
Am. Ind. or Alaska Nat., not spec.	27	0.09
American Indian tribes, specified:	57	0.20
Blackfeet	1	0.00
Cherokee (7)	28	0.10
Chickasaw (1)	1	0.00
Chippewa	1	0.00
Choctaw (1)	3	0.01
Delaware (1)	5	0.02
Iroquois	1	0.00
Lumbee (7)	10	0.03
Pueblo	2	0.01
Sioux (1)	1	0.00
All other tribes (4)	4	0.01
American Indian tribes, not spec.	6	0.02
Arab:	82	0.29
Egyptian	26	0.09
Lebanese	31	0.11
Palestinian	11	0.04
Syrian	4	0.01
Other Arab	10	0.03
Asian:	1,590	5.54
Cambodian (1)	1	0.00
Chinese, ex. Taiwanese (338)	366	1.28
Filipino (317)	363	1.26
Indian (253)	263	0.92
Japanese (20)	25	0.09
Korean (396)	415	1.45
Laotian (2)	4	0.01
Pakistani (21)	25	0.09
Sri Lankan (2)	2	0.01
Taiwanese (2)	2	0.01
Thai (9)	12	0.04
Vietnamese (69)	75	0.26
Other Asian, specified (1)	2	0.01
Other Asian, not specified (16)	35	0.12
Austrian	102	0.36
Belgian	41	0.14
British	103	0.36

Notes: 1. Figures in the "Number" column do not add up to the total population due to: a) Ancestry/Race overlap — e.g. persons can report being both White and Irish, b) persons of Hispanic origin can report being any race, c) persons reporting two ancestries are counted in both categories. 2. Numbers in parentheses indicate the number of persons reporting this ancestry/race alone, not in combination with any other ancestry/race. 3. Refer to the Explanation of Data in the front of the book for more detailed information.

Ancestry/Race	Number	%
Canadian	18	0.06
Celtic	18	0.06
Croatian	39	0.14
Czech	407	1.42
Czechoslovakian	143	0.50
Danish	25	0.09
Dutch	306	1.07
Eastern European	61	0.21
English	2,970	10.38
Estonian	4	0.01
European	148	0.52
French, except Basque	582	2.03
French Canadian	118	0.41
German	8,866	31.00
Greek	546	1.91
Hawaii Native/Pacific Islander:	20	0.07
Micronesian: (4)	4	0.01
Guamanian/Chamorro (4)	4	0.01
Polynesian: (1)	4	0.01
Native Hawaiian	3	0.01
Samoan (1)	1	0.00
Other Pac. Isl., not spec. (3)	12	0.04
Hispanic or Latino:	430	1.50
Central American:	22	0.08
Guatemalan	6	0.02
Honduran	1	0.00
Nicaraguan	2	0.01
Panamanian	6	0.02
Salvadoran	7	0.02
Cuban	27	0.09
Dominican Republic	10	0.03
Mexican	84	0.29
Puerto Rican	83	0.29
South American:	63	0.22
Argentinean	9	0.03
Chilean	2	0.01
Colombian	16	0.06
Ecuadorian	8	0.03
Peruvian	15	0.05
Uruguayan	3	0.01
Venezuelan	2	0.01
Other South American	8	0.03
Other Hispanic or Latino	141	0.49
Hungarian	84	0.29
Iranian	92	0.32
Irish	5,494	19.21
Italian	3,962	13.85
Latvian	9	0.03
Lithuanian	197	0.69
Northern European	7	0.02
Norwegian	113	0.40
Pennsylvania German	39	0.14
Polish	2,989	10.45
Portuguese	28	0.10
Romanian	24	0.08
Russian	251	0.88
Scandinavian	9	0.03
Scotch-Irish	331	1.16
Scottish	426	1.49
Serbian	21	0.07
Slovak	123	0.43
Slovene	7	0.02
Swedish	141	0.49
Swiss	48	0.17
Ukrainian	99	0.35
United States or American	941	3.29
Welsh	341	1.19
West Indian, excl. Hispanic:	15	0.05
Haitian	10	0.03
Jamaican	5	0.02
White:	25,756	89.73
Not Hispanic (25,197)	25,446	88.65
Hispanic (289)	310	1.08
Yugoslavian	13	0.05

Pikesville

Place Type: Census Designated Place
County: Baltimore
Population: 29,123

Ancestry/Race	Number	%
African American/Black:	2,577	8.85
Not Hispanic (2,455)	2,536	8.71
Hispanic (27)	41	0.14
African, sub-Saharan:	272	0.94
African	109	0.38
Nigerian	20	0.07
Senegalese	23	0.08
South African	109	0.38
Other sub-Saharan African	11	0.04
Am. Ind. or Alaska Nat., not spec.	30	0.10
American Indian tribes, specified:	32	0.11
Apache	1	0.00
Blackfeet	4	0.01
Cherokee (4)	13	0.04
Choctaw	1	0.00
Cree (1)	1	0.00
Creek (1)	1	0.00
Iroquois (1)	1	0.00
Latin American Indians (2)	5	0.02
Lumbee (1)	1	0.00
Navajo (1)	1	0.00
Sioux	1	0.00
Yaqui	1	0.00
All other tribes	1	0.00
American Indian tribes, not spec.	6	0.02
Arab:	89	0.31
Egyptian	25	0.09
Jordanian	13	0.04
Lebanese	21	0.07
Moroccan	6	0.02
Palestinian	13	0.04
Other Arab	11	0.04
Asian:	1,134	3.89
Cambodian (1)	1	0.00
Chinese, ex. Taiwanese (149)	164	0.56
Filipino (42)	51	0.18
Indian (243)	252	0.87
Indonesian	1	0.00
Japanese (220)	228	0.78
Korean (219)	229	0.79
Laotian (2)	2	0.01
Pakistani (18)	24	0.08
Taiwanese (37)	41	0.14
Thai (31)	38	0.13
Vietnamese (36)	39	0.13
Other Asian, specified (2)	3	0.01
Other Asian, not specified (13)	61	0.21
Australian	24	0.08
Austrian	235	0.81
Basque	8	0.03
Belgian	8	0.03
Brazilian	9	0.03
British	150	0.52
Bulgarian	45	0.16
Canadian	85	0.29
Croatian	17	0.06
Czech	7	0.02
Czechoslovakian	49	0.17
Danish	30	0.10
Dutch	63	0.22
Eastern European	599	2.07
English	926	3.20
European	537	1.86
Finnish	18	0.06
French, except Basque	169	0.58
French Canadian	7	0.02
German	2,224	7.69
Greek	85	0.29
Hawaii Native/Pacific Islander:	21	0.07
Micronesian:	2	0.01
Guamanian/Chamorro	2	0.01
Polynesian: (1)	5	0.02
Native Hawaiian	4	0.01
Samoan (1)	1	0.00
Other Pac. Isl., not spec. (2)	14	0.05
Hispanic or Latino:	438	1.50
Central American:	33	0.11
Costa Rican	3	0.01
Guatemalan	9	0.03
Honduran	3	0.01
Nicaraguan	2	0.01
Panamanian	7	0.02
Salvadoran	4	0.01
Other Central American	5	0.02
Cuban	22	0.08
Dominican Republic	17	0.06
Mexican	77	0.26
Puerto Rican	79	0.27
South American:	129	0.44
Argentinean	41	0.14
Bolivian	1	0.00
Chilean	14	0.05
Colombian	20	0.07
Ecuadorian	12	0.04
Paraguayan	5	0.02
Peruvian	20	0.07
Uruguayan	4	0.01
Venezuelan	8	0.03
Other South American	4	0.01
Other Hispanic or Latino	81	0.28
Hungarian	334	1.15
Iranian	26	0.09
Irish	1,043	3.60
Israeli	120	0.41
Italian	500	1.73
Latvian	101	0.35
Lithuanian	404	1.40
Norwegian	71	0.25
Pennsylvania German	10	0.03
Polish	1,828	6.32
Portuguese	11	0.04
Romanian	185	0.64
Russian	5,365	18.54
Scotch-Irish	145	0.50
Scottish	168	0.58
Slovak	21	0.07
Soviet Union	13	0.04
Swedish	45	0.16
Swiss	9	0.03
Turkish	7	0.02
Ukrainian	1,026	3.55
United States or American	2,682	9.27
Welsh	100	0.35
West Indian, excl. Hispanic:	66	0.23
Jamaican	38	0.13
West Indian	28	0.10
White:	25,382	87.15
Not Hispanic (24,874)	25,076	86.10
Hispanic (284)	306	1.05
Yugoslavian	18	0.06

Potomac

Place Type: Census Designated Place
County: Montgomery
Population: 44,822

Ancestry/Race	Number	%
Afghan	20	0.04
African American/Black:	1,957	4.37
Not Hispanic (1,713)	1,895	4.23
Hispanic (50)	62	0.14
African, sub-Saharan:	642	1.43
African	234	0.52
Ethiopian	58	0.13
Ghanian	7	0.02
Kenyan	49	0.11
Liberian	46	0.10
Senegalese	44	0.10
South African	55	0.12
Zimbabwean	9	0.02
Other sub-Saharan African	140	0.31
Am. Ind. or Alaska Nat., not spec.	59	0.13

Notes: 1. Figures in the "Number" column do not add up to the total population due to: a) Ancestry/Race overlap — e.g. persons can report being both White and Irish, b) persons of Hispanic origin can report being any race, c) persons reporting two ancestries are counted in both categories. 2. Numbers in parentheses indicate the number of persons reporting this ancestry/race alone, not in combination with any other ancestry/race. 3. Refer to the Explanation of Data in the front of the book for more detailed information.

Albanian	6	0.01
Alsatian	7	0.02
American Indian tribes, specified:	80	0.18
Cherokee (3)	20	0.04
Chickasaw (3)	4	0.01
Choctaw	5	0.01
Comanche	1	0.00
Delaware (4)	5	0.01
Iroquois	2	0.00
Kiowa (1)	1	0.00
Latin American Indians (13)	18	0.04
Lumbee	1	0.00
Ottawa	1	0.00
Sioux	1	0.00
All other tribes (14)	21	0.05
American Indian tribes, not spec.	4	0.01
Arab:	629	1.40
Arab/Arabic	79	0.18
Egyptian	85	0.19
Lebanese	235	0.52
Moroccan	52	0.12
Syrian	53	0.12
Other Arab	125	0.28
Armenian	53	0.12
Asian:	6,582	14.68
Bangladeshi (33)	38	0.08
Cambodian (14)	14	0.03
Chinese, ex. Taiwanese (2,277)	2,458	5.48
Filipino (296)	327	0.73
Indian (1,268)	1,371	3.06
Indonesian (24)	33	0.07
Japanese (279)	338	0.75
Korean (1,015)	1,060	2.36
Laotian (4)	5	0.01
Malaysian (10)	11	0.02
Pakistani (116)	144	0.32
Sri Lankan (25)	25	0.06
Taiwanese (239)	287	0.64
Thai (61)	72	0.16
Vietnamese (173)	185	0.41
Other Asian, specified (35)	41	0.09
Other Asian, not specified (50)	173	0.39
Assyrian/Chaldean/Syriac	7	0.02
Australian	48	0.11
Austrian	345	0.77
Belgian	37	0.08
Brazilian	55	0.12
British	391	0.87
Canadian	109	0.24
Celtic	14	0.03
Croatian	55	0.12
Czech	231	0.52
Czechoslovakian	60	0.13
Danish	154	0.34
Dutch	408	0.91
Eastern European	1,306	2.91
English	4,348	9.70
Estonian	32	0.07
European	836	1.87
Finnish	56	0.12
French, except Basque	1,046	2.33
French Canadian	154	0.34
German	4,704	10.50
Greek	609	1.36
Hawaii Native/Pacific Islander:	35	0.08
Melanesian:	1	0.00
Fijian	1	0.00
Micronesian:	1	0.00
Other Micronesian	1	0.00
Polynesian: (3)	14	0.03
Native Hawaiian (3)	7	0.02
Other Polynesian	7	0.02
Other Pac. Isl., not spec. (1)	19	0.04
Hispanic or Latino:	2,411	5.38
Central American:	251	0.56
Costa Rican	25	0.06
Guatemalan	55	0.12
Honduran	23	0.05
Nicaraguan	37	0.08
Panamanian	14	0.03
Salvadoran	83	0.19
Other Central American	14	0.03
Cuban	148	0.33
Dominican Republic	62	0.14
Mexican	204	0.46
Puerto Rican	117	0.26
South American:	900	2.01
Argentinean	164	0.37
Bolivian	39	0.09
Chilean	110	0.25
Colombian	169	0.38
Ecuadorian	52	0.12
Paraguayan	10	0.02
Peruvian	199	0.44
Uruguayan	58	0.13
Venezuelan	42	0.09
Other South American	57	0.13
Other Hispanic or Latino	729	1.63
Hungarian	566	1.26
Icelander	8	0.02
Iranian	1,116	2.49
Irish	4,295	9.58
Israeli	217	0.48
Italian	2,074	4.63
Latvian	61	0.14
Lithuanian	419	0.93
Northern European	23	0.05
Norwegian	304	0.68
Pennsylvania German	7	0.02
Polish	2,451	5.47
Portuguese	208	0.46
Romanian	212	0.47
Russian	3,824	8.53
Scandinavian	33	0.07
Scotch-Irish	501	1.12
Scottish	688	1.53
Serbian	13	0.03
Slavic	25	0.06
Slovak	75	0.17
Slovene	34	0.08
Swedish	543	1.21
Swiss	327	0.73
Turkish	148	0.33
Ukrainian	418	0.93
United States or American	2,324	5.19
Welsh	213	0.48
West Indian, excl. Hispanic:	215	0.48
Barbadian	13	0.03
British West Indian	14	0.03
Haitian	9	0.02
Jamaican	153	0.34
Trinidadian and Tobagonian	4	0.01
West Indian	22	0.05
White:	36,418	81.25
Not Hispanic (33,724)	34,432	76.82
Hispanic (1,891)	1,986	4.43
Yugoslavian	47	0.10

Randallstown

Place Type: Census Designated Place
County: Baltimore
Population: 30,870

Ancestry/Race	Number	%
African American/Black:	22,679	73.47
Not Hispanic (22,112)	22,493	72.86
Hispanic (147)	186	0.60
African, sub-Saharan:	1,618	5.23
African	930	3.01
Cape Verdean	5	0.02
Ethiopian	41	0.13
Ghanian	68	0.22
Kenyan	10	0.03
Nigerian	550	1.78
Sierra Leonean	7	0.02
Zimbabwean	7	0.02
Am. Ind. or Alaska Nat., not spec.	111	0.36
American Indian tribes, specified:	119	0.39
Apache	2	0.01
Blackfeet	14	0.05
Cherokee (8)	58	0.19
Cheyenne	2	0.01
Choctaw (2)	2	0.01
Crow	2	0.01
Iroquois (2)	5	0.02
Kiowa	1	0.00
Latin American Indians	5	0.02
Lumbee (1)	5	0.02
Pueblo	1	0.00
Seminole	5	0.02
Sioux (1)	1	0.00
All other tribes (1)	16	0.05
American Indian tribes, not spec.	14	0.05
Arab:	15	0.05
Moroccan	15	0.05
Asian:	799	2.59
Cambodian (3)	6	0.02
Chinese, ex. Taiwanese (142)	151	0.49
Filipino (83)	115	0.37
Indian (269)	290	0.94
Japanese (8)	23	0.07
Korean (71)	77	0.25
Pakistani (2)	14	0.05
Taiwanese (1)	1	0.00
Thai (21)	22	0.07
Vietnamese (51)	59	0.19
Other Asian, specified (1)	4	0.01
Other Asian, not specified (20)	37	0.12
Austrian	63	0.20
Brazilian	13	0.04
British	43	0.14
Canadian	20	0.06
Czech	6	0.02
Czechoslovakian	9	0.03
Danish	9	0.03
Dutch	69	0.22
Eastern European	51	0.16
English	563	1.82
Estonian	8	0.03
European	199	0.64
Finnish	5	0.02
French, except Basque	79	0.26
French Canadian	19	0.06
German	1,304	4.21
Greek	8	0.03
Guyanese	18	0.06
Hawaii Native/Pacific Islander:	17	0.06
Micronesian: (1)	3	0.01
Other Micronesian (1)	3	0.01
Polynesian: (5)	8	0.03
Native Hawaiian (3)	4	0.01
Samoan (2)	4	0.01
Other Pac. Isl., specified	3	0.01
Other Pac. Isl., not spec.	3	0.01
Hispanic or Latino:	476	1.54
Central American:	38	0.12
Guatemalan	8	0.03
Panamanian	18	0.06
Salvadoran	10	0.03
Other Central American	2	0.01
Cuban	30	0.10
Dominican Republic	14	0.05
Mexican	84	0.27
Puerto Rican	115	0.37
South American:	53	0.17
Argentinean	5	0.02
Chilean	4	0.01
Colombian	12	0.04
Ecuadorian	4	0.01
Peruvian	23	0.07
Venezuelan	3	0.01
Other South American	2	0.01
Other Hispanic or Latino	142	0.46
Hungarian	83	0.27
Iranian	31	0.10
Irish	732	2.37
Italian	452	1.46
Latvian	39	0.13
Lithuanian	115	0.37

Notes: 1. Figures in the "Number" column do not add up to the total population due to: a) Ancestry/Race overlap — e.g. persons can report being both White and Irish, b) persons of Hispanic origin can report being any race, c) persons reporting two ancestries are counted in both categories. 2. Numbers in parentheses indicate the number of persons reporting this ancestry/race alone, not in combination with any other ancestry/race. 3. Refer to the Explanation of Data in the front of the book for more detailed information.

Ancestry/Race	Number	%
New Zealander	16	0.05
Norwegian	44	0.14
Polish	493	1.59
Romanian	43	0.14
Russian	708	2.29
Scandinavian	27	0.09
Scotch-Irish	111	0.36
Scottish	54	0.17
Slavic	26	0.08
Slovak	36	0.12
Swedish	41	0.13
Swiss	17	0.05
Ukrainian	110	0.36
United States or American	771	2.49
Welsh	26	0.08
West Indian, excl. Hispanic:	767	2.48
Bahamian	27	0.09
Barbadian	6	0.02
Bermudan	6	0.02
British West Indian	6	0.02
Haitian	80	0.26
Jamaican	447	1.44
Trinidadian and Tobagonian	170	0.55
West Indian	25	0.08
White:	7,432	24.08
Not Hispanic (7,017)	7,261	23.52
Hispanic (139)	171	0.55

Redland

Place Type: Census Designated Place
County: Montgomery
Population: 16,998

Ancestry/Race	Number	%
Acadian/Cajun	4	0.02
Afghan	27	0.16
African American/Black:	2,890	17.00
Not Hispanic (2,613)	2,790	16.41
Hispanic (64)	100	0.59
African, sub-Saharan:	696	4.03
African	301	1.74
Ethiopian	49	0.28
Ghanian	82	0.48
Liberian	165	0.96
Nigerian	38	0.22
Senegalese	4	0.02
Sierra Leonean	7	0.04
Ugandan	36	0.21
Other sub-Saharan African	14	0.08
Am. Ind. or Alaska Nat., not spec.	50	0.29
Alsatian	16	0.09
American Indian tribes, specified:	69	0.41
Apache (1)	1	0.01
Cherokee (4)	15	0.09
Chippewa (2)	2	0.01
Choctaw (1)	1	0.01
Comanche (1)	1	0.01
Creek	2	0.01
Iroquois (2)	3	0.02
Latin American Indians (11)	23	0.14
Lumbee (3)	4	0.02
Navajo	3	0.02
Pueblo	2	0.01
Seminole	1	0.01
Sioux (1)	1	0.01
Yuman	2	0.01
All other tribes (1)	8	0.05
American Indian tribes, not spec.	12	0.07
Arab:	107	0.62
Arab/Arabic	17	0.10
Egyptian	23	0.13
Lebanese	40	0.23
Moroccan	2	0.01
Syrian	23	0.13
Other Arab	2	0.01
Armenian	36	0.21
Asian:	2,962	17.43
Bangladeshi (11)	12	0.07
Cambodian (82)	94	0.55
Chinese, ex. Taiwanese (733)	773	4.55
Filipino (251)	287	1.69
Indian (702)	758	4.46
Indonesian (19)	22	0.13
Japanese (41)	70	0.41
Korean (347)	375	2.21
Laotian (7)	7	0.04
Malaysian (9)	13	0.08
Pakistani (85)	97	0.57
Sri Lankan (20)	22	0.13
Taiwanese (28)	30	0.18
Thai (22)	31	0.18
Vietnamese (252)	265	1.56
Other Asian, specified (22)	31	0.18
Other Asian, not specified (33)	75	0.44
Assyrian/Chaldean/Syriac	14	0.08
Australian	24	0.14
Austrian	92	0.53
Belgian	14	0.08
Brazilian	54	0.31
British	162	0.94
Canadian	57	0.33
Carpatho Rusyn	6	0.03
Celtic	20	0.12
Croatian	12	0.07
Czech	49	0.28
Czechoslovakian	2	0.01
Danish	29	0.17
Dutch	135	0.78
Eastern European	32	0.19
English	1,325	7.68
European	227	1.32
Finnish	8	0.05
French, except Basque	287	1.66
French Canadian	108	0.63
German	1,888	10.94
Greek	97	0.56
Guyanese	8	0.05
Hawaii Native/Pacific Islander:	51	0.30
Micronesian: (2)	15	0.09
Guamanian/Chamorro (1)	14	0.08
Other Micronesian (1)	1	0.01
Polynesian: (5)	11	0.06
Native Hawaiian (5)	9	0.05
Other Polynesian	2	0.01
Other Pac. Isl., not spec. (1)	25	0.15
Hispanic or Latino:	2,566	15.10
Central American:	821	4.83
Costa Rican	5	0.03
Guatemalan	59	0.35
Honduran	37	0.22
Nicaraguan	52	0.31
Panamanian	15	0.09
Salvadoran	621	3.65
Other Central American	32	0.19
Cuban	37	0.22
Dominican Republic	115	0.68
Mexican	180	1.06
Puerto Rican	136	0.80
South American:	371	2.18
Argentinean	15	0.09
Bolivian	57	0.34
Chilean	19	0.11
Colombian	51	0.30
Ecuadorian	54	0.32
Paraguayan	4	0.02
Peruvian	123	0.72
Uruguayan	6	0.04
Venezuelan	23	0.14
Other South American	19	0.11
Other Hispanic or Latino	906	5.33
Hungarian	84	0.49
Iranian	231	1.34
Irish	1,469	8.52
Israeli	35	0.20
Italian	793	4.60
Latvian	19	0.11
Lithuanian	33	0.19
Northern European	5	0.03
Norwegian	43	0.25
Pennsylvania German	3	0.02
Polish	642	3.72
Portuguese	120	0.70
Romanian	11	0.06
Russian	347	2.01
Scandinavian	40	0.23
Scotch-Irish	238	1.38
Scottish	251	1.45
Slavic	22	0.13
Slovak	48	0.28
Slovene	5	0.03
Swedish	135	0.78
Swiss	72	0.42
Turkish	12	0.07
Ukrainian	49	0.28
United States or American	715	4.14
Welsh	118	0.68
West Indian, excl. Hispanic:	409	2.37
Barbadian	28	0.16
Bermudan	10	0.06
British West Indian	7	0.04
Haitian	137	0.79
Jamaican	204	1.18
Trinidadian and Tobagonian	14	0.08
West Indian	9	0.05
White:	9,898	58.23
Not Hispanic (8,521)	8,865	52.15
Hispanic (834)	1,033	6.08

Reisterstown

Place Type: Census Designated Place
County: Baltimore
Population: 22,438

Ancestry/Race	Number	%
African American/Black:	4,350	19.39
Not Hispanic (4,067)	4,270	19.03
Hispanic (60)	80	0.36
African, sub-Saharan:	176	0.78
African	69	0.31
Ethiopian	45	0.20
Liberian	5	0.02
Nigerian	48	0.21
Other sub-Saharan African	9	0.04
Am. Ind. or Alaska Nat., not spec.	56	0.25
American Indian tribes, specified:	74	0.33
Apache	4	0.02
Blackfeet (1)	5	0.02
Cherokee (6)	32	0.14
Comanche	1	0.00
Creek (1)	1	0.00
Delaware (1)	1	0.00
Iroquois (3)	3	0.01
Latin American Indians (7)	10	0.04
Lumbee	4	0.02
Navajo (1)	3	0.01
Seminole	1	0.00
Tohono O'Odham (1)	1	0.00
All other tribes (1)	8	0.04
American Indian tribes, not spec.	9	0.04
Arab:	149	0.66
Arab/Arabic	65	0.29
Lebanese	58	0.26
Moroccan	15	0.07
Syrian	11	0.05
Armenian	88	0.39
Asian:	1,053	4.69
Bangladeshi (9)	9	0.04
Cambodian (9)	9	0.04
Chinese, ex. Taiwanese (181)	190	0.85
Filipino (76)	97	0.43
Indian (355)	413	1.84
Japanese (10)	24	0.11
Korean (76)	84	0.37
Laotian (2)	2	0.01
Pakistani (53)	81	0.36
Sri Lankan (2)	3	0.01
Taiwanese (9)	9	0.04
Thai (12)	17	0.08

Notes: 1. Figures in the "Number" column do not add up to the total population due to: a) Ancestry/Race overlap — e.g. persons can report being both White and Irish, b) persons of Hispanic origin can report being any race, c) persons reporting two ancestries are counted in both categories. 2. Numbers in parentheses indicate the number of persons reporting this ancestry/race alone, not in combination with any other ancestry/race. 3. Refer to the Explanation of Data in the front of the book for more detailed information.

Vietnamese (52)	57	0.25
Other Asian, specified (9)	11	0.05
Other Asian, not specified (31)	47	0.21
Australian	8	0.04
Austrian	107	0.48
British	95	0.42
Canadian	48	0.21
Croatian	8	0.04
Czech	111	0.49
Czechoslovakian	28	0.12
Danish	33	0.15
Dutch	265	1.18
Eastern European	139	0.62
English	1,999	8.89
European	285	1.27
French, except Basque	353	1.57
French Canadian	105	0.47
German	4,039	17.96
Greek	67	0.30
Hawaii Native/Pacific Islander:	24	0.11
Micronesian: (6)	6	0.03
Guamanian/Chamorro (6)	6	0.03
Polynesian: (3)	4	0.02
Samoan (3)	4	0.02
Other Pac. Isl., specified	2	0.01
Other Pac. Isl., not spec. (7)	12	0.05
Hispanic or Latino:	986	4.39
Central American:	206	0.92
Costa Rican	9	0.04
Guatemalan	74	0.33
Honduran	45	0.20
Nicaraguan	2	0.01
Panamanian	20	0.09
Salvadoran	35	0.16
Other Central American	21	0.09
Cuban	39	0.17
Dominican Republic	19	0.08
Mexican	132	0.59
Puerto Rican	143	0.64
South American:	155	0.69
Argentinean	22	0.10
Chilean	7	0.03
Colombian	42	0.19
Ecuadorian	3	0.01
Peruvian	66	0.29
Uruguayan	2	0.01
Venezuelan	9	0.04
Other South American	4	0.02
Other Hispanic or Latino	292	1.30
Hungarian	184	0.82
Irish	2,326	10.35
Italian	1,230	5.47
Latvian	19	0.08
Lithuanian	88	0.39
Northern European	15	0.07
Norwegian	37	0.16
Polish	1,095	4.87
Portuguese	7	0.03
Romanian	50	0.22
Russian	1,413	6.28
Scandinavian	6	0.03
Scotch-Irish	251	1.12
Scottish	281	1.25
Serbian	8	0.04
Slovak	82	0.36
Slovene	8	0.04
Soviet Union	7	0.03
Swedish	74	0.33
Swiss	27	0.12
Turkish	8	0.04
Ukrainian	469	2.09
United States or American	1,422	6.32
Welsh	171	0.76
West Indian, excl. Hispanic:	312	1.39
British West Indian	31	0.14
Haitian	54	0.24
Jamaican	210	0.93
Trinidadian and Tobagonian	17	0.08
White:	16,827	74.99
Not Hispanic (15,976)	16,259	72.46
Hispanic (491)	568	2.53
Yugoslavian	7	0.03

Riviera Beach

Place Type: Census Designated Place
County: Anne Arundel
Population: 12,695

Ancestry/Race	Number	%
African American/Black:	312	2.46
Not Hispanic (269)	307	2.42
Hispanic (5)	5	0.04
Am. Ind. or Alaska Nat., not spec.	14	0.11
American Indian tribes, specified:	55	0.43
Apache (1)	1	0.01
Blackfeet (1)	4	0.03
Cherokee (10)	24	0.19
Cheyenne (1)	1	0.01
Choctaw (2)	2	0.02
Crow	1	0.01
Iroquois	1	0.01
Lumbee (4)	5	0.04
Pueblo (3)	3	0.02
Sioux (5)	7	0.06
All other tribes (4)	6	0.05
American Indian tribes, not spec.	6	0.05
Armenian	7	0.06
Asian:	170	1.34
Chinese, ex. Taiwanese (25)	28	0.22
Filipino (43)	58	0.46
Indian (10)	16	0.13
Indonesian (1)	1	0.01
Japanese (7)	14	0.11
Korean (33)	38	0.30
Pakistani	4	0.03
Vietnamese (4)	5	0.04
Other Asian, not specified (4)	6	0.05
Austrian	8	0.06
Belgian	8	0.06
British	29	0.23
Canadian	13	0.10
Croatian	27	0.21
Czech	16	0.13
Czechoslovakian	26	0.21
Dutch	238	1.88
Eastern European	15	0.12
English	1,499	11.83
Estonian	12	0.09
European	72	0.57
Finnish	10	0.08
French, except Basque	212	1.67
French Canadian	91	0.72
German	3,666	28.93
Greek	24	0.19
Hawaii Native/Pacific Islander:	21	0.17
Micronesian: (9)	14	0.11
Guamanian/Chamorro (9)	13	0.10
Other Micronesian	1	0.01
Polynesian: (5)	6	0.05
Native Hawaiian (5)	6	0.05
Other Pac. Isl., not spec.	1	0.01
Hispanic or Latino:	175	1.38
Central American:	7	0.06
Guatemalan	3	0.02
Salvadoran	4	0.03
Cuban	4	0.03
Dominican Republic	5	0.04
Mexican	27	0.21
Puerto Rican	60	0.47
South American:	12	0.09
Argentinean	2	0.02
Colombian	5	0.04
Ecuadorian	1	0.01
Peruvian	2	0.02
Other South American	2	0.02
Other Hispanic or Latino	60	0.47
Hungarian	107	0.84
Irish	2,459	19.41
Italian	959	7.57
Latvian	9	0.07
Lithuanian	85	0.67
Norwegian	139	1.10
Pennsylvania German	19	0.15
Polish	1,018	8.03
Romanian	21	0.17
Russian	36	0.28
Scandinavian	8	0.06
Scotch-Irish	267	2.11
Scottish	351	2.77
Slavic	10	0.08
Slovak	9	0.07
Swedish	43	0.34
Swiss	79	0.62
Ukrainian	44	0.35
United States or American	994	7.85
Welsh	110	0.87
White:	12,182	95.96
Not Hispanic (11,955)	12,053	94.94
Hispanic (121)	129	1.02

Rockville

Place Type: City
County: Montgomery
Population: 47,388

Ancestry/Race	Number	%
Acadian/Cajun	9	0.02
African American/Black:	4,675	9.87
Not Hispanic (4,200)	4,495	9.49
Hispanic (117)	180	0.38
African, sub-Saharan:	669	1.42
African	213	0.45
Cape Verdean	19	0.04
Ethiopian	45	0.10
Ghanian	36	0.08
Kenyan	34	0.07
Liberian	4	0.01
Nigerian	105	0.22
Senegalese	8	0.02
Sierra Leonean	28	0.06
South African	17	0.04
Ugandan	29	0.06
Zairian	8	0.02
Other sub-Saharan African	123	0.26
Am. Ind. or Alaska Nat., not spec.	161	0.34
American Indian tribes, specified:	223	0.47
Apache (1)	3	0.01
Blackfeet	8	0.02
Cherokee (12)	57	0.12
Chippewa (3)	5	0.01
Choctaw (9)	15	0.03
Comanche (5)	8	0.02
Cree	1	0.00
Creek (2)	3	0.01
Crow (3)	3	0.01
Delaware	1	0.00
Houma	1	0.00
Iroquois	3	0.01
Kiowa (1)	1	0.00
Latin American Indians (16)	46	0.10
Lumbee (5)	11	0.02
Menominee (1)	2	0.00
Navajo (8)	11	0.02
Osage (3)	3	0.01
Pueblo (5)	5	0.01
Seminole	1	0.00
Shoshone	1	0.00
Sioux (9)	11	0.02
Yaqui (2)	3	0.01
All other tribes (12)	20	0.04
American Indian tribes, not spec.	27	0.06
Arab:	395	0.84
Arab/Arabic	48	0.10
Egyptian	40	0.08
Iraqi	5	0.01
Jordanian	26	0.06
Lebanese	105	0.22
Moroccan	53	0.11

Notes: 1. Figures in the "Number" column do not add up to the total population due to: a) Ancestry/Race overlap — e.g. persons can report being both White and Irish, b) persons of Hispanic origin can report being any race, c) persons reporting two ancestries are counted in both categories. 2. Numbers in parentheses indicate the number of persons reporting this ancestry/race alone, not in combination with any other ancestry/race. 3. Refer to the Explanation of Data in the front of the book for more detailed information.

Palestinian	27	0.06
Syrian	17	0.04
Other Arab	74	0.16
Armenian	154	0.33
Asian:	7,723	16.30
Bangladeshi (67)	71	0.15
Cambodian (32)	34	0.07
Chinese, ex. Taiwanese (2,770)	2,963	6.25
Filipino (592)	684	1.44
Indian (984)	1,074	2.27
Indonesian (59)	72	0.15
Japanese (565)	635	1.34
Korean (971)	1,015	2.14
Laotian (7)	10	0.02
Malaysian (3)	6	0.01
Pakistani (116)	145	0.31
Sri Lankan (88)	97	0.20
Taiwanese (118)	166	0.35
Thai (95)	111	0.23
Vietnamese (316)	348	0.73
Other Asian, specified (65)	81	0.17
Other Asian, not specified (80)	211	0.45
Australian	48	0.10
Austrian	259	0.55
Belgian	72	0.15
Brazilian	221	0.47
British	438	0.93
Bulgarian	41	0.09
Canadian	127	0.27
Carpatho Rusyn	9	0.02
Celtic	34	0.07
Croatian	34	0.07
Cypriot	7	0.01
Czech	196	0.41
Czechoslovakian	110	0.23
Danish	201	0.43
Dutch	331	0.70
Eastern European	422	0.89
English	3,866	8.18
Estonian	6	0.01
European	799	1.69
Finnish	30	0.06
French, except Basque	922	1.95
French Canadian	255	0.54
German	5,416	11.46
Greek	352	0.74
Guyanese	39	0.08
Hawaii Native/Pacific Islander:	80	0.17
Micronesian: (1)	10	0.02
Guamanian/Chamorro	7	0.01
Other Micronesian (1)	3	0.01
Polynesian: (11)	25	0.05
Native Hawaiian (11)	18	0.04
Samoan	6	0.01
Other Polynesian	1	0.00
Other Pac. Isl., specified	1	0.00
Other Pac. Isl., not spec.	44	0.09
Hispanic or Latino:	5,529	11.67
Central American:	1,577	3.33
Costa Rican	37	0.08
Guatemalan	123	0.26
Honduran	197	0.42
Nicaraguan	95	0.20
Panamanian	23	0.05
Salvadoran	1,046	2.21
Other Central American	56	0.12
Cuban	145	0.31
Dominican Republic	63	0.13
Mexican	426	0.90
Puerto Rican	225	0.47
South American:	1,137	2.40
Argentinean	104	0.22
Bolivian	160	0.34
Chilean	125	0.26
Colombian	147	0.31
Ecuadorian	83	0.18
Paraguayan	53	0.11
Peruvian	336	0.71
Uruguayan	30	0.06
Venezuelan	45	0.09
Other South American	54	0.11
Other Hispanic or Latino	1,956	4.13
Hungarian	279	0.59
Iranian	858	1.82
Irish	5,165	10.93
Israeli	383	0.81
Italian	1,930	4.08
Latvian	83	0.18
Lithuanian	157	0.33
Luxemburger	8	0.02
Macedonian	20	0.04
Northern European	116	0.25
Norwegian	358	0.76
Pennsylvania German	15	0.03
Polish	1,398	2.96
Portuguese	130	0.28
Romanian	145	0.31
Russian	1,999	4.23
Scandinavian	51	0.11
Scotch-Irish	837	1.77
Scottish	984	2.08
Serbian	37	0.08
Slavic	31	0.07
Slovak	120	0.25
Slovene	11	0.02
Soviet Union	31	0.07
Swedish	366	0.77
Swiss	88	0.19
Turkish	82	0.17
Ukrainian	342	0.72
United States or American	2,444	5.17
Welsh	355	0.75
West Indian, excl. Hispanic:	485	1.03
Bahamian	7	0.01
British West Indian	7	0.01
Haitian	42	0.09
Jamaican	297	0.63
Trinidadian and Tobagonian	68	0.14
West Indian	32	0.07
Other West Indian	32	0.07
White:	33,262	70.19
Not Hispanic (29,342)	30,105	63.53
Hispanic (2,778)	3,157	6.66
Yugoslavian	10	0.02

Rosaryville

Place Type: Census Designated Place
County: Prince George's
Population: 12,322

Ancestry/Race	Number	%
African American/Black:	7,530	61.11
Not Hispanic (7,297)	7,476	60.67
Hispanic (43)	54	0.44
African, sub-Saharan:	107	0.88
African	65	0.53
Cape Verdean	8	0.07
Liberian	3	0.02
Nigerian	22	0.18
South African	9	0.07
Am. Ind. or Alaska Nat., not spec.	62	0.50
American Indian tribes, specified:	89	0.72
Blackfeet	2	0.02
Cherokee (7)	32	0.26
Choctaw (2)	2	0.02
Delaware (2)	5	0.04
Iroquois (1)	3	0.02
Latin American Indians	2	0.02
Lumbee (2)	2	0.02
Potawatomi (2)	2	0.02
Pueblo (1)	1	0.01
Seminole (1)	2	0.02
All other tribes (28)	36	0.29
American Indian tribes, not spec.	5	0.04
Arab:	38	0.31
Arab/Arabic	28	0.23
Lebanese	10	0.08
Asian:	414	3.36
Chinese, ex. Taiwanese (50)	62	0.50
Filipino (178)	216	1.75
Indian (30)	38	0.31
Indonesian	1	0.01
Japanese (11)	15	0.12
Korean (24)	30	0.24
Laotian (3)	3	0.02
Thai (9)	16	0.13
Vietnamese (14)	15	0.12
Other Asian, specified (1)	1	0.01
Other Asian, not specified (3)	17	0.14
Austrian	20	0.16
Basque	7	0.06
Belgian	43	0.35
British	79	0.65
Celtic	9	0.07
Croatian	9	0.07
Czech	29	0.24
Czechoslovakian	8	0.07
Danish	13	0.11
Dutch	116	0.95
English	600	4.93
European	92	0.76
Finnish	13	0.11
French, except Basque	79	0.65
French Canadian	33	0.27
German	816	6.71
Greek	28	0.23
Guyanese	70	0.58
Hawaii Native/Pacific Islander:	21	0.17
Micronesian: (11)	18	0.15
Guamanian/Chamorro (11)	18	0.15
Polynesian: (1)	2	0.02
Native Hawaiian (1)	2	0.02
Other Pac. Isl., not spec. (1)	1	0.01
Hispanic or Latino:	261	2.12
Central American:	35	0.28
Costa Rican	2	0.02
Guatemalan	1	0.01
Honduran	11	0.09
Panamanian	8	0.06
Salvadoran	13	0.11
Cuban	14	0.11
Dominican Republic	12	0.10
Mexican	59	0.48
Puerto Rican	73	0.59
South American:	14	0.11
Chilean	2	0.02
Colombian	11	0.09
Peruvian	1	0.01
Other Hispanic or Latino	54	0.44
Hungarian	38	0.31
Iranian	25	0.21
Irish	714	5.87
Italian	318	2.61
Lithuanian	24	0.20
Macedonian	9	0.07
Norwegian	26	0.21
Pennsylvania German	8	0.07
Polish	144	1.18
Portuguese	34	0.28
Russian	11	0.09
Scandinavian	9	0.07
Scotch-Irish	46	0.38
Scottish	100	0.82
Slavic	9	0.07
Slovak	29	0.24
Slovene	5	0.04
Swedish	20	0.16
Swiss	6	0.05
United States or American	382	3.14
Welsh	34	0.28
West Indian, excl. Hispanic:	141	1.16
Jamaican	93	0.76
Trinidadian and Tobagonian	28	0.23
U.S. Virgin Islander	4	0.03
West Indian	16	0.13
White:	4,383	35.57
Not Hispanic (4,105)	4,264	34.60
Hispanic (101)	119	0.97
Yugoslavian	8	0.07

Notes: 1. Figures in the "Number" column do not add up to the total population due to: a) Ancestry/Race overlap — e.g. persons can report being both White and Irish, b) persons of Hispanic origin can report being any race, c) persons reporting two ancestries are counted in both categories. 2. Numbers in parentheses indicate the number of persons reporting this ancestry/race alone, not in combination with any other ancestry/race. 3. Refer to the Explanation of Data in the front of the book for more detailed information.

Rosedale

Place Type: Census Designated Place
County: Baltimore
Population: 19,199

Ancestry/Race	Number	%
African American/Black:	4,190	21.82
Not Hispanic (4,050)	4,164	21.69
Hispanic (20)	26	0.14
African, sub-Saharan:	299	1.56
African	161	0.84
Ethiopian	25	0.13
Nigerian	92	0.48
Other sub-Saharan African	21	0.11
Am. Ind. or Alaska Nat., not spec.	45	0.23
Albanian	33	0.17
American Indian tribes, specified:	68	0.35
Apache (1)	1	0.01
Cherokee (12)	39	0.20
Cree	1	0.01
Iroquois (2)	3	0.02
Latin American Indians (1)	1	0.01
Lumbee (14)	20	0.10
Sioux	2	0.01
All other tribes (1)	1	0.01
American Indian tribes, not spec.	10	0.05
Asian:	430	2.24
Chinese, ex. Taiwanese (22)	34	0.18
Filipino (146)	163	0.85
Indian (73)	79	0.41
Japanese (2)	11	0.06
Korean (58)	65	0.34
Laotian (5)	5	0.03
Pakistani (11)	12	0.06
Thai (3)	6	0.03
Vietnamese (38)	41	0.21
Other Asian, specified	1	0.01
Other Asian, not specified (3)	13	0.07
Australian	8	0.04
Austrian	35	0.18
British	48	0.25
Cypriot	8	0.04
Czech	339	1.77
Czechoslovakian	87	0.45
Dutch	288	1.50
English	1,525	7.94
Estonian	23	0.12
European	47	0.24
French, except Basque	450	2.34
French Canadian	101	0.53
German	4,558	23.73
Greek	560	2.92
Hawaii Native/Pacific Islander:	21	0.11
Micronesian: (7)	7	0.04
Guamanian/Chamorro (7)	7	0.04
Polynesian: (1)	6	0.03
Native Hawaiian (1)	5	0.03
Other Polynesian	1	0.01
Other Pac. Isl., not spec. (4)	8	0.04
Hispanic or Latino:	266	1.39
Central American:	21	0.11
Guatemalan	9	0.05
Honduran	4	0.02
Salvadoran	8	0.04
Cuban	11	0.06
Dominican Republic	16	0.08
Mexican	40	0.21
Puerto Rican	65	0.34
South American:	21	0.11
Colombian	13	0.07
Ecuadorian	1	0.01
Peruvian	7	0.04
Other Hispanic or Latino	92	0.48
Hungarian	83	0.43
Irish	2,696	14.04
Italian	1,728	9.00
Lithuanian	72	0.37
Norwegian	45	0.23
Pennsylvania German	31	0.16
Polish	2,014	10.49
Portuguese	41	0.21
Romanian	7	0.04
Russian	83	0.43
Scotch-Irish	186	0.97
Scottish	210	1.09
Slovak	74	0.39
Swedish	89	0.46
Swiss	18	0.09
Turkish	8	0.04
Ukrainian	132	0.69
United States or American	632	3.29
Welsh	148	0.77
West Indian, excl. Hispanic:	93	0.48
Jamaican	47	0.24
Trinidadian and Tobagonian	17	0.09
U.S. Virgin Islander	20	0.10
West Indian	9	0.05
White:	14,558	75.83
Not Hispanic (14,210)	14,403	75.02
Hispanic (133)	155	0.81

Rossville

Place Type: Census Designated Place
County: Baltimore
Population: 11,515

Ancestry/Race	Number	%
African American/Black:	2,631	22.85
Not Hispanic (2,497)	2,602	22.60
Hispanic (23)	29	0.25
African, sub-Saharan:	217	1.86
African	47	0.40
Ethiopian	31	0.27
Kenyan	34	0.29
Nigerian	95	0.82
Ugandan	10	0.09
Am. Ind. or Alaska Nat., not spec.	28	0.24
American Indian tribes, specified:	46	0.40
Blackfeet	1	0.01
Cherokee (6)	20	0.17
Choctaw	1	0.01
Iroquois (1)	1	0.01
Latin American Indians	2	0.02
Lumbee (7)	8	0.07
Seminole	4	0.03
Sioux	1	0.01
All other tribes (6)	8	0.07
American Indian tribes, not spec.	5	0.04
Arab:	50	0.43
Lebanese	18	0.15
Moroccan	32	0.27
Asian:	533	4.63
Cambodian (2)	2	0.02
Chinese, ex. Taiwanese (28)	35	0.30
Filipino (110)	120	1.04
Indian (172)	181	1.57
Japanese (2)	3	0.03
Korean (94)	100	0.87
Laotian (2)	2	0.02
Pakistani	2	0.02
Sri Lankan (5)	5	0.04
Taiwanese (3)	3	0.03
Thai (15)	17	0.15
Vietnamese (35)	36	0.31
Other Asian, specified (14)	16	0.14
Other Asian, not specified (5)	11	0.10
Austrian	8	0.07
Brazilian	19	0.16
British	114	0.98
Bulgarian	7	0.06
Celtic	7	0.06
Croatian	8	0.07
Czech	120	1.03
Czechoslovakian	21	0.18
Danish	16	0.14
Dutch	84	0.72
English	907	7.78
Estonian	11	0.09
European	107	0.92
Finnish	42	0.36
French, except Basque	285	2.45
French Canadian	52	0.45
German	2,883	24.74
Greek	90	0.77
Hawaii Native/Pacific Islander:	10	0.09
Micronesian: (1)	1	0.01
Guamanian/Chamorro (1)	1	0.01
Polynesian:	5	0.04
Native Hawaiian	4	0.03
Samoan	1	0.01
Other Pac. Isl., not spec.	4	0.03
Hispanic or Latino:	329	2.86
Central American:	55	0.48
Guatemalan	3	0.03
Honduran	2	0.02
Nicaraguan	2	0.02
Panamanian	6	0.05
Salvadoran	39	0.34
Other Central American	3	0.03
Cuban	16	0.14
Dominican Republic	13	0.11
Mexican	55	0.48
Puerto Rican	49	0.43
South American:	31	0.27
Chilean	1	0.01
Colombian	8	0.07
Ecuadorian	7	0.06
Peruvian	13	0.11
Venezuelan	2	0.02
Other Hispanic or Latino	110	0.96
Hungarian	64	0.55
Irish	1,810	15.53
Italian	1,167	10.01
Latvian	10	0.09
Lithuanian	19	0.16
Norwegian	24	0.21
Pennsylvania German	9	0.08
Polish	909	7.80
Portuguese	4	0.03
Russian	57	0.49
Scandinavian	8	0.07
Scotch-Irish	107	0.92
Scottish	157	1.35
Slovak	43	0.37
Swedish	47	0.40
Swiss	6	0.05
Ukrainian	30	0.26
United States or American	300	2.57
Welsh	53	0.45
West Indian, excl. Hispanic:	139	1.19
Barbadian	11	0.09
British West Indian	8	0.07
Jamaican	51	0.44
Trinidadian and Tobagonian	11	0.09
West Indian	58	0.50
White:	8,279	71.90
Not Hispanic (7,969)	8,091	70.26
Hispanic (161)	188	1.63

Saint Charles

Place Type: Census Designated Place
County: Charles
Population: 33,379

Ancestry/Race	Number	%
African American/Black:	10,102	30.26
Not Hispanic (9,489)	9,966	29.86
Hispanic (82)	136	0.41
African, sub-Saharan:	452	1.35
African	395	1.18
Nigerian	57	0.17
Alaska Native tribes, specified:	1	0.00
Tlingit-Haida (1)	1	0.00
Am. Ind. or Alaska Nat., not spec.	169	0.51
American Indian tribes, specified:	327	0.98
Apache	3	0.01
Blackfeet (3)	14	0.04

Notes: 1. Figures in the "Number" column do not add up to the total population due to: a) Ancestry/Race overlap — e.g. persons can report being both White and Irish, b) persons of Hispanic origin can report being any race, c) persons reporting two ancestries are counted in both categories. 2. Numbers in parentheses indicate the number of persons reporting this ancestry/race alone, not in combination with any other ancestry/race. 3. Refer to the Explanation of Data in the front of the book for more detailed information.

Ancestry/Race	Number	%
Cherokee (20)	69	0.21
Cheyenne (1)	3	0.01
Chickasaw (2)	5	0.01
Chippewa (4)	6	0.02
Choctaw (1)	2	0.01
Comanche (1)	3	0.01
Creek (2)	8	0.02
Crow (1)	5	0.01
Iroquois (10)	29	0.09
Latin American Indians (6)	10	0.03
Lumbee (3)	5	0.01
Menominee (1)	1	0.00
Navajo (1)	3	0.01
Osage (1)	1	0.00
Potawatomi	4	0.01
Sioux (8)	14	0.04
All other tribes (88)	142	0.43
American Indian tribes, not spec.	26	0.08
Arab:	156	0.47
Arab/Arabic	5	0.01
Egyptian	36	0.11
Lebanese	64	0.19
Palestinian	7	0.02
Syrian	19	0.06
Other Arab	25	0.07
Armenian	6	0.02
Asian:	1,087	3.26
Bangladeshi (14)	16	0.05
Cambodian (1)	2	0.01
Chinese, ex. Taiwanese (90)	123	0.37
Filipino (282)	427	1.28
Indian (86)	103	0.31
Japanese (33)	58	0.17
Korean (152)	180	0.54
Laotian	1	0.00
Malaysian (3)	3	0.01
Pakistani (32)	35	0.10
Sri Lankan (1)	1	0.00
Taiwanese (3)	3	0.01
Thai (22)	27	0.08
Vietnamese (44)	51	0.15
Other Asian, specified (3)	5	0.01
Other Asian, not specified (23)	52	0.16
Austrian	12	0.04
Belgian	20	0.06
Brazilian	36	0.11
British	174	0.52
Canadian	93	0.28
Celtic	27	0.08
Croatian	40	0.12
Czech	89	0.27
Czechoslovakian	16	0.05
Danish	20	0.06
Dutch	322	0.96
English	3,552	10.62
European	219	0.66
Finnish	7	0.02
French, except Basque	844	2.52
French Canadian	121	0.36
German	4,850	14.51
Greek	200	0.60
Guyanese	15	0.04
Hawaii Native/Pacific Islander:	51	0.15
Micronesian: (5)	14	0.04
Guamanian/Chamorro (4)	10	0.03
Other Micronesian (1)	4	0.01
Polynesian: (12)	26	0.08
Native Hawaiian (9)	21	0.06
Samoan (3)	5	0.01
Other Pac. Isl., not spec. (5)	11	0.03
Hispanic or Latino:	1,114	3.34
Central American:	72	0.22
Costa Rican	3	0.01
Guatemalan	4	0.01
Honduran	3	0.01
Nicaraguan	3	0.01
Panamanian	16	0.05
Salvadoran	41	0.12
Other Central American	2	0.01
Cuban	66	0.20
Dominican Republic	14	0.04
Mexican	275	0.82
Puerto Rican	417	1.25
South American:	43	0.13
Argentinean	6	0.02
Bolivian	4	0.01
Chilean	5	0.01
Colombian	8	0.02
Ecuadorian	7	0.02
Peruvian	9	0.03
Venezuelan	4	0.01
Other Hispanic or Latino	227	0.68
Hungarian	174	0.52
Irish	4,765	14.25
Italian	2,157	6.45
Latvian	15	0.04
Lithuanian	96	0.29
Macedonian	9	0.03
Maltese	4	0.01
Northern European	85	0.25
Norwegian	326	0.98
Pennsylvania German	19	0.06
Polish	972	2.91
Portuguese	79	0.24
Romanian	14	0.04
Russian	126	0.38
Scandinavian	20	0.06
Scotch-Irish	642	1.92
Scottish	577	1.73
Serbian	51	0.15
Slavic	59	0.18
Slovak	116	0.35
Swedish	289	0.86
Swiss	7	0.02
Turkish	10	0.03
Ukrainian	87	0.26
United States or American	1,739	5.20
Welsh	123	0.37
West Indian, excl. Hispanic:	176	0.53
British West Indian	15	0.04
Haitian	9	0.03
Jamaican	97	0.29
Trinidadian and Tobagonian	9	0.03
West Indian	46	0.14
White:	22,177	66.44
Not Hispanic (20,869)	21,494	64.39
Hispanic (584)	683	2.05
Yugoslavian	24	0.07

Salisbury

Place Type: City
County: Wicomico
Population: 23,743

Ancestry/Race	Number	%
African American/Black:	7,956	33.51
Not Hispanic (7,612)	7,864	33.12
Hispanic (61)	92	0.39
African, sub-Saharan:	484	2.00
African	476	1.97
Other sub-Saharan African	8	0.03
Am. Ind. or Alaska Nat., not spec.	60	0.25
Albanian	31	0.13
American Indian tribes, specified:	70	0.29
Apache	6	0.03
Blackfeet	3	0.01
Cherokee (9)	26	0.11
Cheyenne	1	0.00
Chippewa (1)	1	0.00
Choctaw (1)	4	0.02
Crow	1	0.00
Delaware	1	0.00
Iroquois (3)	5	0.02
Latin American Indians (3)	3	0.01
Lumbee	2	0.01
Pima (1)	1	0.00
Pueblo (1)	1	0.00
Sioux	1	0.00
All other tribes (7)	14	0.06
American Indian tribes, not spec.	14	0.06
Arab:	72	0.30
Arab/Arabic	6	0.02
Lebanese	21	0.09
Moroccan	21	0.09
Syrian	16	0.07
Other Arab	8	0.03
Armenian	16	0.07
Asian:	854	3.60
Bangladeshi (2)	3	0.01
Chinese, ex. Taiwanese (89)	98	0.41
Filipino (30)	38	0.16
Indian (212)	231	0.97
Japanese (12)	24	0.10
Korean (293)	303	1.28
Malaysian (1)	1	0.00
Pakistani (53)	61	0.26
Sri Lankan	1	0.00
Taiwanese (2)	2	0.01
Thai (7)	8	0.03
Vietnamese (17)	19	0.08
Other Asian, not specified (35)	66	0.28
Austrian	16	0.07
Basque	7	0.03
Belgian	25	0.10
British	117	0.48
Canadian	25	0.10
Celtic	10	0.04
Croatian	8	0.03
Czech	35	0.14
Czechoslovakian	33	0.14
Danish	30	0.12
Dutch	156	0.65
Eastern European	10	0.04
English	2,487	10.29
Estonian	8	0.03
European	105	0.43
French, except Basque	425	1.76
French Canadian	87	0.36
German	2,639	10.92
Greek	87	0.36
Guyanese	9	0.04
Hawaii Native/Pacific Islander:	26	0.11
Polynesian: (2)	5	0.02
Native Hawaiian (2)	3	0.01
Samoan	1	0.00
Tongan	1	0.00
Other Pac. Isl., not spec. (4)	21	0.09
Hispanic or Latino:	806	3.39
Central American:	47	0.20
Guatemalan	20	0.08
Honduran	14	0.06
Nicaraguan	2	0.01
Panamanian	1	0.00
Salvadoran	9	0.04
Other Central American	1	0.00
Cuban	28	0.12
Dominican Republic	25	0.11
Mexican	251	1.06
Puerto Rican	222	0.94
South American:	44	0.19
Bolivian	4	0.02
Chilean	7	0.03
Colombian	4	0.02
Ecuadorian	4	0.02
Paraguayan	2	0.01
Peruvian	15	0.06
Venezuelan	5	0.02
Other South American	3	0.01
Other Hispanic or Latino	189	0.80
Hungarian	15	0.06
Icelander	5	0.02
Irish	2,589	10.72
Italian	1,108	4.59
Lithuanian	3	0.01
Northern European	4	0.02
Norwegian	89	0.37
Pennsylvania German	27	0.11
Polish	378	1.56
Portuguese	7	0.03

Notes: 1. Figures in the "Number" column do not add up to the total population due to: a) Ancestry/Race overlap — e.g. persons can report being both White and Irish, b) persons of Hispanic origin can report being any race, c) persons reporting two ancestries are counted in both categories. 2. Numbers in parentheses indicate the number of persons reporting this ancestry/race alone, not in combination with any other ancestry/race. 3. Refer to the Explanation of Data in the front of the book for more detailed information.

Romanian	17	0.07
Russian	112	0.46
Scandinavian	7	0.03
Scotch-Irish	337	1.39
Scottish	427	1.77
Slovak	57	0.24
Swedish	145	0.60
Swiss	104	0.43
Ukrainian	57	0.24
United States or American	2,123	8.79
Welsh	132	0.55
West Indian, excl. Hispanic:	349	1.44
Haitian	319	1.32
Trinidadian and Tobagonian	14	0.06
U.S. Virgin Islander	16	0.07
White:	14,740	62.08
Not Hispanic (14,111)	14,366	60.51
Hispanic (303)	374	1.58
Yugoslavian	8	0.03

Savage-Guilford

Place Type: Census Designated Place
County: Howard
Population: 12,918

Ancestry/Race	Number	%
African American/Black:	3,258	25.22
Not Hispanic (2,995)	3,200	24.77
Hispanic (20)	58	0.45
African, sub-Saharan:	479	3.80
African	364	2.89
Cape Verdean	8	0.06
Ghanian	8	0.06
Liberian	6	0.05
Nigerian	87	0.69
Sierra Leonean	6	0.05
Alaska Native tribes, specified:	3	0.02
Tlingit-Haida (1)	3	0.02
Am. Ind. or Alaska Nat., not spec.	48	0.37
Albanian	15	0.12
American Indian tribes, specified:	59	0.46
Apache (3)	5	0.04
Blackfeet (1)	5	0.04
Cherokee (10)	26	0.20
Chippewa	1	0.01
Choctaw	2	0.02
Iroquois (4)	4	0.03
Latin American Indians	1	0.01
Lumbee (3)	6	0.05
Navajo (1)	1	0.01
Ottawa	1	0.01
Seminole	1	0.01
All other tribes (4)	6	0.05
American Indian tribes, not spec.	5	0.04
Arab:	116	0.92
Arab/Arabic	18	0.14
Egyptian	13	0.10
Lebanese	34	0.27
Syrian	27	0.21
Other Arab	24	0.19
Asian:	904	7.00
Bangladeshi	7	0.05
Cambodian (12)	13	0.10
Chinese, ex. Taiwanese (107)	132	1.02
Filipino (47)	69	0.53
Indian (223)	247	1.91
Indonesian	1	0.01
Japanese (24)	41	0.32
Korean (241)	261	2.02
Pakistani (31)	37	0.29
Taiwanese (3)	3	0.02
Thai (7)	13	0.10
Vietnamese (42)	47	0.36
Other Asian, specified (2)	2	0.02
Other Asian, not specified (14)	31	0.24
Austrian	34	0.27
Belgian	9	0.07
Brazilian	25	0.20
British	131	1.04
Canadian	14	0.11
Celtic	6	0.05
Croatian	13	0.10
Czech	15	0.12
Czechoslovakian	9	0.07
Danish	15	0.12
Dutch	173	1.37
Eastern European	33	0.26
English	1,390	11.02
European	229	1.82
Finnish	61	0.48
French, except Basque	231	1.83
French Canadian	36	0.29
German	2,101	16.66
Greek	77	0.61
Guyanese	17	0.13
Hawaii Native/Pacific Islander:	13	0.10
Micronesian: (2)	4	0.03
Guamanian/Chamorro (2)	4	0.03
Polynesian:	3	0.02
Native Hawaiian	3	0.02
Other Pac. Isl., not spec.	6	0.05
Hispanic or Latino:	468	3.62
Central American:	80	0.62
Costa Rican	1	0.01
Guatemalan	6	0.05
Honduran	8	0.06
Nicaraguan	4	0.03
Panamanian	24	0.19
Salvadoran	36	0.28
Other Central American	1	0.01
Cuban	38	0.29
Dominican Republic	5	0.04
Mexican	107	0.83
Puerto Rican	76	0.59
South American:	46	0.36
Argentinean	5	0.04
Chilean	5	0.04
Colombian	11	0.09
Ecuadorian	5	0.04
Peruvian	15	0.12
Uruguayan	2	0.02
Venezuelan	3	0.02
Other Hispanic or Latino	116	0.90
Hungarian	64	0.51
Icelander	6	0.05
Irish	1,593	12.63
Italian	698	5.54
Latvian	19	0.15
Lithuanian	55	0.44
Norwegian	89	0.71
Pennsylvania German	7	0.06
Polish	436	3.46
Portuguese	45	0.36
Romanian	19	0.15
Russian	178	1.41
Scandinavian	7	0.06
Scotch-Irish	260	2.06
Scottish	235	1.86
Slovak	47	0.37
Slovene	10	0.08
Swedish	83	0.66
Swiss	49	0.39
Turkish	13	0.10
Ukrainian	35	0.28
United States or American	701	5.56
Welsh	103	0.82
West Indian, excl. Hispanic:	113	0.90
British West Indian	8	0.06
Haitian	6	0.05
Jamaican	75	0.59
Trinidadian and Tobagonian	10	0.08
U.S. Virgin Islander	14	0.11
White:	8,801	68.13
Not Hispanic (8,256)	8,502	65.82
Hispanic (249)	299	2.31
Yugoslavian	59	0.47

Severn

Place Type: Census Designated Place
County: Anne Arundel
Population: 35,076

Ancestry/Race	Number	%
African American/Black:	12,663	36.10
Not Hispanic (11,943)	12,404	35.36
Hispanic (181)	259	0.74
African, sub-Saharan:	578	1.64
African	447	1.27
Cape Verdean	5	0.01
Ethiopian	8	0.02
Ghanian	31	0.09
Kenyan	7	0.02
Nigerian	56	0.16
Sierra Leonean	9	0.03
Other sub-Saharan African	15	0.04
Am. Ind. or Alaska Nat., not spec.	114	0.33
Albanian	11	0.03
American Indian tribes, specified:	237	0.68
Apache (1)	10	0.03
Blackfeet (7)	20	0.06
Cherokee (29)	95	0.27
Cheyenne	2	0.01
Chickasaw (1)	2	0.01
Chippewa (4)	10	0.03
Choctaw (1)	5	0.01
Cree	1	0.00
Creek (1)	2	0.01
Crow	2	0.01
Delaware (1)	2	0.01
Iroquois (5)	7	0.02
Latin American Indians (5)	12	0.03
Lumbee (17)	22	0.06
Navajo	1	0.00
Potawatomi (1)	1	0.00
Seminole (1)	1	0.00
Sioux (2)	6	0.02
All other tribes (19)	36	0.10
American Indian tribes, not spec.	11	0.03
Arab:	15	0.04
Egyptian	9	0.03
Other Arab	6	0.02
Asian:	1,891	5.39
Bangladeshi (2)	2	0.01
Cambodian (1)	2	0.01
Chinese, ex. Taiwanese (134)	160	0.46
Filipino (218)	331	0.94
Indian (147)	166	0.47
Indonesian	1	0.00
Japanese (82)	132	0.38
Korean (707)	824	2.35
Laotian (5)	7	0.02
Pakistani (31)	31	0.09
Taiwanese (6)	7	0.02
Thai (54)	79	0.23
Vietnamese (93)	103	0.29
Other Asian, specified	3	0.01
Other Asian, not specified (14)	43	0.12
Australian	23	0.07
Austrian	15	0.04
Basque	8	0.02
Belgian	14	0.04
British	281	0.80
Canadian	33	0.09
Celtic	9	0.03
Croatian	22	0.06
Czech	127	0.36
Czechoslovakian	54	0.15
Danish	82	0.23
Dutch	330	0.94
English	2,591	7.37
European	240	0.68
Finnish	76	0.22
French, except Basque	672	1.91
French Canadian	293	0.83
German	5,546	15.77
Greek	138	0.39

Notes: 1. Figures in the "Number" column do not add up to the total population due to: a) Ancestry/Race overlap — e.g. persons can report being both White and Irish, b) persons of Hispanic origin can report being any race, c) persons reporting two ancestries are counted in both categories. 2. Numbers in parentheses indicate the number of persons reporting this ancestry/race alone, not in combination with any other ancestry/race. 3. Refer to the Explanation of Data in the front of the book for more detailed information.

Ancestry/Race	Number	%
Guyanese	49	0.14
Hawaii Native/Pacific Islander:	76	0.22
Melanesian: (1)	1	0.00
Fijian (1)	1	0.00
Micronesian: (7)	13	0.04
Guamanian/Chamorro (7)	13	0.04
Polynesian: (17)	31	0.09
Native Hawaiian (15)	28	0.08
Samoan (2)	3	0.01
Other Pac. Isl., specified	1	0.00
Other Pac. Isl., not spec. (9)	30	0.09
Hispanic or Latino:	1,390	3.96
Central American:	132	0.38
Costa Rican	7	0.02
Guatemalan	20	0.06
Honduran	11	0.03
Nicaraguan	5	0.01
Panamanian	52	0.15
Salvadoran	37	0.11
Cuban	27	0.08
Dominican Republic	37	0.11
Mexican	292	0.83
Puerto Rican	596	1.70
South American:	80	0.23
Argentinean	4	0.01
Chilean	8	0.02
Colombian	34	0.10
Ecuadorian	7	0.02
Peruvian	24	0.07
Venezuelan	3	0.01
Other Hispanic or Latino	226	0.64
Hungarian	153	0.43
Irish	3,941	11.20
Italian	1,751	4.98
Lithuanian	131	0.37
Northern European	18	0.05
Norwegian	408	1.16
Polish	1,027	2.92
Portuguese	97	0.28
Romanian	37	0.11
Russian	164	0.47
Scotch-Irish	378	1.07
Scottish	565	1.61
Slavic	15	0.04
Slovak	56	0.16
Swedish	195	0.55
Swiss	31	0.09
Turkish	20	0.06
Ukrainian	51	0.14
United States or American	1,724	4.90
Welsh	162	0.46
West Indian, excl. Hispanic:	470	1.34
Belizean	6	0.02
British West Indian	75	0.21
Dutch West Indian	7	0.02
Jamaican	169	0.48
Trinidadian and Tobagonian	147	0.42
U.S. Virgin Islander	5	0.01
West Indian	53	0.15
Other West Indian	8	0.02
White:	20,553	58.60
Not Hispanic (19,106)	19,794	56.43
Hispanic (624)	759	2.16

Severna Park

Place Type: Census Designated Place
County: Anne Arundel
Population: 28,507

Ancestry/Race	Number	%
African American/Black:	994	3.49
Not Hispanic (932)	984	3.45
Hispanic (7)	10	0.04
African, sub-Saharan:	20	0.07
South African	20	0.07
Am. Ind. or Alaska Nat., not spec.	41	0.14
American Indian tribes, specified:	86	0.30
Blackfeet (1)	6	0.02
Cherokee (6)	26	0.09
Chickasaw (2)	2	0.01
Chippewa	4	0.01
Choctaw	1	0.00
Creek (1)	3	0.01
Crow	3	0.01
Delaware (1)	1	0.00
Iroquois (2)	3	0.01
Kiowa (1)	1	0.00
Latin American Indians (4)	6	0.02
Lumbee (1)	3	0.01
Ottawa (1)	1	0.00
Seminole	1	0.00
Sioux (1)	6	0.02
All other tribes (12)	19	0.07
American Indian tribes, not spec.	11	0.04
Arab:	75	0.26
Egyptian	6	0.02
Iraqi	20	0.07
Lebanese	25	0.09
Syrian	24	0.08
Armenian	27	0.09
Asian:	912	3.20
Cambodian (6)	6	0.02
Chinese, ex. Taiwanese (151)	170	0.60
Filipino (94)	139	0.49
Indian (152)	159	0.56
Indonesian (4)	4	0.01
Japanese (28)	45	0.16
Korean (297)	312	1.09
Laotian (1)	1	0.00
Pakistani (6)	11	0.04
Taiwanese (4)	6	0.02
Thai (7)	7	0.02
Vietnamese (15)	15	0.05
Other Asian, specified (6)	6	0.02
Other Asian, not specified (18)	31	0.11
Australian	16	0.06
Austrian	67	0.23
Belgian	22	0.08
Brazilian	22	0.08
British	229	0.80
Bulgarian	21	0.07
Canadian	53	0.19
Carpatho Rusyn	10	0.03
Celtic	33	0.12
Croatian	16	0.06
Czech	136	0.48
Czechoslovakian	56	0.20
Danish	181	0.63
Dutch	654	2.29
Eastern European	7	0.02
English	4,981	17.42
Estonian	6	0.02
European	397	1.39
Finnish	61	0.21
French, except Basque	1,096	3.83
French Canadian	203	0.71
German	7,490	26.19
Greek	79	0.28
Hawaii Native/Pacific Islander:	34	0.12
Micronesian: (5)	8	0.03
Guamanian/Chamorro (5)	8	0.03
Polynesian: (5)	18	0.06
Native Hawaiian (3)	16	0.06
Samoan (2)	2	0.01
Other Pac. Isl., not spec. (2)	8	0.03
Hispanic or Latino:	338	1.19
Central American:	28	0.10
Costa Rican	7	0.02
Guatemalan	9	0.03
Nicaraguan	5	0.02
Panamanian	1	0.00
Salvadoran	6	0.02
Cuban	29	0.10
Mexican	73	0.26
Puerto Rican	86	0.30
South American:	37	0.13
Argentinean	1	0.00
Bolivian	1	0.00
Chilean	10	0.04
Colombian	4	0.01
Ecuadorian	4	0.01
Peruvian	13	0.05
Venezuelan	4	0.01
Other Hispanic or Latino	85	0.30
Hungarian	264	0.92
Icelander	7	0.02
Iranian	29	0.10
Irish	5,680	19.86
Israeli	62	0.22
Italian	2,355	8.23
Latvian	13	0.05
Lithuanian	97	0.34
Northern European	18	0.06
Norwegian	295	1.03
Pennsylvania German	20	0.07
Polish	1,758	6.15
Portuguese	37	0.13
Romanian	31	0.11
Russian	441	1.54
Scandinavian	23	0.08
Scotch-Irish	774	2.71
Scottish	992	3.47
Slavic	102	0.36
Slovak	109	0.38
Swedish	439	1.54
Swiss	262	0.92
Turkish	24	0.08
Ukrainian	117	0.41
United States or American	1,429	5.00
Welsh	352	1.23
West Indian, excl. Hispanic:	30	0.10
Jamaican	26	0.09
West Indian	4	0.01
White:	26,578	93.23
Not Hispanic (26,108)	26,315	92.31
Hispanic (247)	263	0.92
Yugoslavian	18	0.06

Silver Spring

Place Type: Census Designated Place
County: Montgomery
Population: 76,540

Ancestry/Race	Number	%
Afghan	14	0.02
African American/Black:	23,284	30.42
Not Hispanic (20,901)	22,416	29.29
Hispanic (581)	868	1.13
African, sub-Saharan:	6,076	7.92
African	2,128	2.77
Cape Verdean	43	0.06
Ethiopian	1,680	2.19
Ghanian	180	0.23
Kenyan	133	0.17
Liberian	151	0.20
Nigerian	843	1.10
Senegalese	108	0.14
Sierra Leonean	152	0.20
Somalian	26	0.03
South African	14	0.02
Sudanese	85	0.11
Ugandan	24	0.03
Zairian	17	0.02
Other sub-Saharan African	492	0.64
Alaska Native tribes, specified:	8	0.01
Aleut	4	0.01
Tlingit-Haida (2)	4	0.01
Alaska Native tribes, not specified	2	0.00
Am. Ind. or Alaska Nat., not spec.	344	0.45
Albanian	56	0.07
Alsatian	20	0.03
American Indian tribes, specified:	471	0.62
Apache (3)	5	0.01
Blackfeet (3)	17	0.02
Cherokee (20)	110	0.14
Chickasaw	3	0.00
Chippewa (3)	9	0.01
Choctaw (3)	12	0.02

Notes: 1. Figures in the "Number" column do not add up to the total population due to: a) Ancestry/Race overlap — e.g. persons can report being both White and Irish, b) persons of Hispanic origin can report being any race, c) persons reporting two ancestries are counted in both categories. 2. Numbers in parentheses indicate the number of persons reporting this ancestry/race alone, not in combination with any other ancestry/race. 3. Refer to the Explanation of Data in the front of the book for more detailed information.

Ancestry/Race	Number	%
Colville (1)	1	0.00
Comanche	1	0.00
Cree	1	0.00
Creek (3)	15	0.02
Crow (1)	1	0.00
Delaware (4)	5	0.01
Iroquois (6)	17	0.02
Kiowa	3	0.00
Latin American Indians (81)	168	0.22
Lumbee (1)	3	0.00
Menominee (1)	2	0.00
Navajo (5)	6	0.01
Osage (1)	1	0.00
Pima (2)	2	0.00
Pueblo (2)	7	0.01
Seminole (1)	6	0.01
Sioux (7)	16	0.02
Tohono O'Odham	1	0.00
Ute (1)	2	0.00
Yuman	3	0.00
All other tribes (23)	54	0.07
American Indian tribes, not spec.	51	0.07
Arab:	537	0.70
Arab/Arabic	67	0.09
Egyptian	87	0.11
Iraqi	12	0.02
Jordanian	12	0.02
Lebanese	98	0.13
Moroccan	116	0.15
Palestinian	12	0.02
Syrian	20	0.03
Other Arab	113	0.15
Armenian	117	0.15
Asian:	7,191	9.40
Bangladeshi (111)	130	0.17
Cambodian (244)	304	0.40
Chinese, ex. Taiwanese (818)	960	1.25
Filipino (528)	649	0.85
Hmong (2)	2	0.00
Indian (1,365)	1,580	2.06
Indonesian (88)	97	0.13
Japanese (158)	243	0.32
Korean (397)	441	0.58
Laotian (44)	51	0.07
Malaysian (2)	9	0.01
Pakistani (122)	142	0.19
Sri Lankan (39)	46	0.06
Taiwanese (19)	24	0.03
Thai (142)	162	0.21
Vietnamese (1,966)	2,023	2.64
Other Asian, specified (34)	57	0.07
Other Asian, not specified (122)	271	0.35
Assyrian/Chaldean/Syriac	11	0.01
Australian	11	0.01
Austrian	378	0.49
Belgian	96	0.13
Brazilian	110	0.14
British	459	0.60
Bulgarian	7	0.01
Canadian	134	0.17
Carpatho Rusyn	19	0.02
Celtic	29	0.04
Croatian	76	0.10
Czech	177	0.23
Czechoslovakian	67	0.09
Danish	313	0.41
Dutch	430	0.56
Eastern European	576	0.75
English	4,974	6.48
Estonian	11	0.01
European	1,064	1.39
Finnish	46	0.06
French, except Basque	1,109	1.45
French Canadian	336	0.44
German	6,503	8.48
German Russian	7	0.01
Greek	413	0.54
Guyanese	293	0.38
Hawaii Native/Pacific Islander:	204	0.27
Melanesian: (7)	9	0.01
Fijian (1)	3	0.00
Other Melanesian (6)	6	0.01
Micronesian: (4)	9	0.01
Guamanian/Chamorro (3)	4	0.01
Other Micronesian (1)	5	0.01
Polynesian: (14)	41	0.05
Native Hawaiian (10)	30	0.04
Samoan (3)	10	0.01
Other Polynesian (1)	1	0.00
Other Pac. Isl., specified	9	0.01
Other Pac. Isl., not spec. (22)	136	0.18
Hispanic or Latino:	17,004	22.22
Central American:	6,973	9.11
Costa Rican	44	0.06
Guatemalan	852	1.11
Honduran	397	0.52
Nicaraguan	500	0.65
Panamanian	123	0.16
Salvadoran	4,764	6.22
Other Central American	293	0.38
Cuban	315	0.41
Dominican Republic	669	0.87
Mexican	1,364	1.78
Puerto Rican	593	0.77
South American:	1,242	1.62
Argentinean	70	0.09
Bolivian	287	0.37
Chilean	69	0.09
Colombian	232	0.30
Ecuadorian	146	0.19
Paraguayan	21	0.03
Peruvian	286	0.37
Uruguayan	8	0.01
Venezuelan	38	0.05
Other South American	85	0.11
Other Hispanic or Latino	5,848	7.64
Hungarian	281	0.37
Icelander	25	0.03
Iranian	133	0.17
Irish	6,377	8.31
Israeli	44	0.06
Italian	2,335	3.04
Latvian	89	0.12
Lithuanian	254	0.33
New Zealander	5	0.01
Northern European	126	0.16
Norwegian	526	0.69
Polish	1,776	2.31
Portuguese	125	0.16
Romanian	161	0.21
Russian	1,651	2.15
Scandinavian	91	0.12
Scotch-Irish	736	0.96
Scottish	1,362	1.78
Serbian	28	0.04
Slavic	21	0.03
Slovak	138	0.18
Slovene	21	0.03
Swedish	512	0.67
Swiss	218	0.28
Turkish	251	0.33
Ukrainian	376	0.49
United States or American	1,785	2.33
Welsh	431	0.56
West Indian, excl. Hispanic:	2,862	3.73
Bahamian	7	0.01
Barbadian	61	0.08
Belizean	15	0.02
Bermudan	17	0.02
British West Indian	126	0.16
Haitian	766	1.00
Jamaican	1,185	1.54
Trinidadian and Tobagonian	455	0.59
U.S. Virgin Islander	29	0.04
West Indian	194	0.25
Other West Indian	7	0.01
White:	37,982	49.62
Not Hispanic (29,617)	30,668	40.07
Hispanic (6,061)	7,314	9.56
Yugoslavian	79	0.10

South Gate

Place Type: Census Designated Place
County: Anne Arundel
Population: 28,672

Ancestry/Race	Number	%
Acadian/Cajun	9	0.03
African American/Black:	5,984	20.87
Not Hispanic (5,589)	5,901	20.58
Hispanic (42)	83	0.29
African, sub-Saharan:	255	0.89
African	189	0.66
Cape Verdean	16	0.06
Nigerian	37	0.13
South African	13	0.05
Alaska Native tribes, specified:	2	0.01
Alaska Athabascan (1)	1	0.00
Tlingit-Haida	1	0.00
Am. Ind. or Alaska Nat., not spec.	116	0.40
Albanian	11	0.04
American Indian tribes, specified:	137	0.48
Apache	2	0.01
Blackfeet	6	0.02
Cherokee (21)	63	0.22
Chickasaw (2)	2	0.01
Chippewa (1)	1	0.00
Choctaw (2)	2	0.01
Creek	1	0.00
Crow	2	0.01
Iroquois (9)	18	0.06
Lumbee (10)	13	0.05
Potawatomi (1)	1	0.00
Seminole	4	0.01
Sioux (2)	3	0.01
All other tribes (12)	19	0.07
American Indian tribes, not spec.	19	0.07
Arab:	44	0.15
Egyptian	34	0.12
Lebanese	10	0.03
Asian:	1,749	6.10
Cambodian (1)	3	0.01
Chinese, ex. Taiwanese (122)	139	0.48
Filipino (204)	260	0.91
Indian (240)	259	0.90
Japanese (26)	64	0.22
Korean (797)	836	2.92
Malaysian	1	0.00
Pakistani (27)	55	0.19
Sri Lankan (6)	6	0.02
Taiwanese (1)	2	0.01
Thai (12)	20	0.07
Vietnamese (34)	45	0.16
Other Asian, specified	3	0.01
Other Asian, not specified (27)	56	0.20
Australian	8	0.03
Austrian	51	0.18
Belgian	19	0.07
Brazilian	47	0.16
British	189	0.66
Canadian	73	0.25
Croatian	18	0.06
Czech	168	0.58
Czechoslovakian	16	0.06
Danish	111	0.39
Dutch	361	1.26
Eastern European	9	0.03
English	2,766	9.63
European	285	0.99
Finnish	45	0.16
French, except Basque	575	2.00
French Canadian	185	0.64
German	5,552	19.32
Greek	107	0.37
Guyanese	29	0.10
Hawaii Native/Pacific Islander:	53	0.18
Micronesian: (7)	11	0.04
Guamanian/Chamorro (7)	11	0.04
Polynesian: (15)	31	0.11
Native Hawaiian (3)	19	0.07

Notes: 1. Figures in the "Number" column do not add up to the total population due to: a) Ancestry/Race overlap — e.g. persons can report being both White and Irish, b) persons of Hispanic origin can report being any race, c) persons reporting two ancestries are counted in both categories. 2. Numbers in parentheses indicate the number of persons reporting this ancestry/race alone, not in combination with any other ancestry/race. 3. Refer to the Explanation of Data in the front of the book for more detailed information.

Ancestry/Race	Number	%
Samoan (12)	12	0.04
Other Pac. Isl., specified	1	0.00
Other Pac. Isl., not spec. (4)	10	0.03
Hispanic or Latino:	899	3.14
Central American:	101	0.35
Costa Rican	8	0.03
Guatemalan	20	0.07
Honduran	9	0.03
Nicaraguan	9	0.03
Panamanian	26	0.09
Salvadoran	27	0.09
Other Central American	2	0.01
Cuban	20	0.07
Dominican Republic	6	0.02
Mexican	223	0.78
Puerto Rican	271	0.95
South American:	68	0.24
Argentinean	6	0.02
Bolivian	3	0.01
Chilean	15	0.05
Colombian	20	0.07
Ecuadorian	9	0.03
Paraguayan	1	0.00
Peruvian	11	0.04
Venezuelan	3	0.01
Other Hispanic or Latino	210	0.73
Hungarian	171	0.60
Iranian	37	0.13
Irish	4,161	14.48
Italian	1,959	6.82
Latvian	20	0.07
Lithuanian	141	0.49
Norwegian	102	0.36
Pennsylvania German	25	0.09
Polish	1,316	4.58
Portuguese	79	0.27
Romanian	8	0.03
Russian	245	0.85
Scandinavian	8	0.03
Scotch-Irish	457	1.59
Scottish	617	2.15
Slovak	67	0.23
Swedish	142	0.49
Swiss	39	0.14
Ukrainian	132	0.46
United States or American	1,665	5.79
Welsh	252	0.88
West Indian, excl. Hispanic:	119	0.41
Barbadian	23	0.08
British West Indian	11	0.04
Jamaican	56	0.19
Trinidadian and Tobagonian	19	0.07
West Indian	10	0.03
White:	20,854	72.73
Not Hispanic (19,907)	20,357	71.00
Hispanic (434)	497	1.73
Yugoslavian	16	0.06

South Laurel

Place Type: Census Designated Place
County: Prince George's
Population: 20,479

Ancestry/Race	Number	%
Afghan	65	0.31
African American/Black:	10,609	51.80
Not Hispanic (10,090)	10,480	51.17
Hispanic (88)	129	0.63
African, sub-Saharan:	1,543	7.42
African	452	2.17
Ethiopian	37	0.18
Ghanian	186	0.89
Kenyan	16	0.08
Liberian	80	0.38
Nigerian	661	3.18
Sierra Leonean	11	0.05
Other sub-Saharan African	100	0.48
Alaska Native tribes, specified:	2	0.01
Tlingit-Haida (2)	2	0.01
Am. Ind. or Alaska Nat., not spec.	85	0.42
American Indian tribes, specified:	76	0.37
Apache	5	0.02
Blackfeet (2)	4	0.02
Cherokee	24	0.12
Chippewa (1)	1	0.00
Choctaw (2)	4	0.02
Crow	1	0.00
Delaware	1	0.00
Iroquois (1)	2	0.01
Latin American Indians	2	0.01
Lumbee	5	0.02
Navajo	2	0.01
Pueblo	2	0.01
Shoshone	6	0.03
All other tribes (7)	17	0.08
American Indian tribes, not spec.	9	0.04
Arab:	104	0.50
Arab/Arabic	90	0.43
Lebanese	7	0.03
Syrian	7	0.03
Armenian	40	0.19
Asian:	1,347	6.58
Bangladeshi (3)	3	0.01
Cambodian (2)	2	0.01
Chinese, ex. Taiwanese (113)	149	0.73
Filipino (144)	181	0.88
Indian (398)	437	2.13
Indonesian (2)	4	0.02
Japanese (23)	39	0.19
Korean (249)	272	1.33
Laotian	1	0.00
Pakistani (97)	113	0.55
Taiwanese (12)	17	0.08
Thai (10)	16	0.08
Vietnamese (52)	64	0.31
Other Asian, specified (3)	4	0.02
Other Asian, not specified (17)	45	0.22
Austrian	56	0.27
Basque	7	0.03
Belgian	25	0.12
Brazilian	120	0.58
British	86	0.41
Canadian	22	0.11
Croatian	14	0.07
Czech	28	0.13
Czechoslovakian	10	0.05
Danish	41	0.20
Dutch	135	0.65
Eastern European	5	0.02
English	1,083	5.21
European	140	0.67
Finnish	15	0.07
French, except Basque	261	1.26
French Canadian	11	0.05
German	1,696	8.16
Greek	98	0.47
Guyanese	97	0.47
Hawaii Native/Pacific Islander:	23	0.11
Melanesian: (1)	1	0.00
Fijian (1)	1	0.00
Micronesian: (1)	1	0.00
Guamanian/Chamorro (1)	1	0.00
Polynesian: (3)	11	0.05
Native Hawaiian (1)	9	0.04
Samoan (1)	1	0.00
Tongan (1)	1	0.00
Other Pac. Isl., specified	1	0.00
Other Pac. Isl., not spec. (2)	9	0.04
Hispanic or Latino:	1,077	5.26
Central American:	203	0.99
Costa Rican	3	0.01
Guatemalan	36	0.18
Honduran	25	0.12
Nicaraguan	5	0.02
Panamanian	40	0.20
Salvadoran	90	0.44
Other Central American	4	0.02
Cuban	47	0.23
Dominican Republic	29	0.14
Mexican	181	0.88
Puerto Rican	196	0.96
South American:	94	0.46
Argentinean	9	0.04
Bolivian	3	0.01
Chilean	30	0.15
Colombian	13	0.06
Ecuadorian	3	0.01
Peruvian	24	0.12
Venezuelan	5	0.02
Other South American	7	0.03
Other Hispanic or Latino	327	1.60
Hungarian	79	0.38
Iranian	25	0.12
Irish	1,521	7.32
Israeli	13	0.06
Italian	771	3.71
Lithuanian	45	0.22
Luxemburger	16	0.08
Northern European	9	0.04
Norwegian	27	0.13
Polish	428	2.06
Portuguese	69	0.33
Romanian	24	0.12
Russian	168	0.81
Scotch-Irish	148	0.71
Scottish	244	1.17
Slavic	10	0.05
Slovak	79	0.38
Swedish	48	0.23
Swiss	7	0.03
Turkish	21	0.10
Ukrainian	61	0.29
United States or American	821	3.95
Welsh	138	0.66
West Indian, excl. Hispanic:	680	3.27
Barbadian	51	0.25
British West Indian	36	0.17
Haitian	60	0.29
Jamaican	210	1.01
Trinidadian and Tobagonian	235	1.13
U.S. Virgin Islander	27	0.13
West Indian	61	0.29
White:	8,340	40.72
Not Hispanic (7,470)	7,836	38.26
Hispanic (452)	504	2.46

Suitland-Silver Hill

Place Type: Census Designated Place
County: Prince George's
Population: 33,515

Ancestry/Race	Number	%
African American/Black:	31,625	94.36
Not Hispanic (30,994)	31,413	93.73
Hispanic (178)	212	0.63
African, sub-Saharan:	475	1.42
African	359	1.07
Cape Verdean	19	0.06
Ethiopian	14	0.04
Ghanian	21	0.06
Liberian	8	0.02
Nigerian	34	0.10
Sudanese	20	0.06
Am. Ind. or Alaska Nat., not spec.	164	0.49
American Indian tribes, specified:	140	0.42
Blackfeet (2)	30	0.09
Cherokee (14)	69	0.21
Choctaw	4	0.01
Creek	1	0.00
Crow	1	0.00
Iroquois	1	0.00
Latin American Indians (2)	4	0.01
Lumbee	1	0.00
Navajo (2)	2	0.01
Seminole	1	0.00
All other tribes (18)	26	0.08
American Indian tribes, not spec.	18	0.05
Arab:	49	0.15

Notes: 1. Figures in the "Number" column do not add up to the total population due to: a) Ancestry/Race overlap — e.g. persons can report being both White and Irish, b) persons of Hispanic origin can report being any race, c) persons reporting two ancestries are counted in both categories. 2. Numbers in parentheses indicate the number of persons reporting this ancestry/race alone, not in combination with any other ancestry/race. 3. Refer to the Explanation of Data in the front of the book for more detailed information.

Ancestry/Race	Number	%
Moroccan	40	0.12
Other Arab	9	0.03
Asian:	261	0.78
Bangladeshi (1)	1	0.00
Chinese, ex. Taiwanese (59)	65	0.19
Filipino (46)	62	0.18
Indian (22)	33	0.10
Indonesian (5)	5	0.01
Japanese (5)	5	0.01
Korean (22)	31	0.09
Laotian (7)	7	0.02
Pakistani (4)	5	0.01
Sri Lankan (1)	1	0.00
Thai (9)	13	0.04
Vietnamese (6)	6	0.02
Other Asian, specified	2	0.01
Other Asian, not specified (12)	25	0.07
British	21	0.06
Canadian	10	0.03
Dutch	78	0.23
English	110	0.33
European	24	0.07
Finnish	12	0.04
French, except Basque	55	0.16
German	314	0.94
Greek	7	0.02
Guyanese	28	0.08
Hawaii Native/Pacific Islander:	36	0.11
Micronesian: (1)	3	0.01
Guamanian/Chamorro (1)	3	0.01
Polynesian: (5)	12	0.04
Native Hawaiian (3)	6	0.02
Samoan (2)	6	0.02
Other Pac. Isl., not spec. (2)	21	0.06
Hispanic or Latino:	625	1.86
Central American:	188	0.56
Costa Rican	1	0.00
Guatemalan	11	0.03
Honduran	6	0.02
Nicaraguan	2	0.01
Panamanian	27	0.08
Salvadoran	131	0.39
Other Central American	10	0.03
Cuban	20	0.06
Dominican Republic	16	0.05
Mexican	116	0.35
Puerto Rican	78	0.23
South American:	8	0.02
Argentinean	2	0.01
Colombian	3	0.01
Uruguayan	3	0.01
Other Hispanic or Latino	199	0.59
Hungarian	8	0.02
Irish	262	0.78
Italian	118	0.35
Polish	35	0.10
Scotch-Irish	49	0.15
Scottish	11	0.03
Slovak	11	0.03
United States or American	397	1.19
West Indian, excl. Hispanic:	381	1.14
Barbadian	16	0.05
British West Indian	39	0.12
Haitian	31	0.09
Jamaican	194	0.58
Trinidadian and Tobagonian	58	0.17
U.S. Virgin Islander	18	0.05
West Indian	25	0.07
White:	1,537	4.59
Not Hispanic (1,104)	1,317	3.93
Hispanic (191)	220	0.66

Takoma Park

Place Type: City
County: Montgomery
Population: 17,299

Ancestry/Race	Number	%
Acadian/Cajun	7	0.04
African American/Black:	6,375	36.85
Not Hispanic (5,697)	6,119	35.37
Hispanic (179)	256	1.48
African, sub-Saharan:	1,765	10.27
African	421	2.45
Ethiopian	539	3.14
Ghanian	55	0.32
Kenyan	55	0.32
Liberian	74	0.43
Nigerian	230	1.34
Senegalese	8	0.05
Sierra Leonean	58	0.34
Somalian	77	0.45
South African	13	0.08
Zimbabwean	8	0.05
Other sub-Saharan African	227	1.32
Alaska Native tribes, specified:	1	0.01
Eskimo (1)	1	0.01
Am. Ind. or Alaska Nat., not spec.	74	0.43
American Indian tribes, specified:	129	0.75
Blackfeet (2)	3	0.02
Cherokee (5)	21	0.12
Chippewa	2	0.01
Choctaw	1	0.01
Delaware (1)	2	0.01
Iroquois	2	0.01
Latin American Indians (30)	80	0.46
Lumbee (1)	1	0.01
Navajo (1)	2	0.01
Osage	1	0.01
Seminole	2	0.01
Sioux	2	0.01
Yaqui (1)	1	0.01
All other tribes (3)	9	0.05
American Indian tribes, not spec.	14	0.08
Arab:	78	0.45
Arab/Arabic	14	0.08
Jordanian	17	0.10
Lebanese	23	0.13
Palestinian	10	0.06
Syrian	8	0.05
Other Arab	6	0.03
Armenian	19	0.11
Asian:	898	5.19
Bangladeshi	2	0.01
Cambodian (10)	15	0.09
Chinese, ex. Taiwanese (88)	107	0.62
Filipino (107)	123	0.71
Indian (333)	384	2.22
Indonesian (5)	7	0.04
Japanese (26)	39	0.23
Korean (29)	37	0.21
Pakistani (11)	16	0.09
Sri Lankan (2)	4	0.02
Thai (7)	7	0.04
Vietnamese (103)	107	0.62
Other Asian, specified (3)	5	0.03
Other Asian, not specified (20)	45	0.26
Austrian	74	0.43
Belgian	34	0.20
Brazilian	58	0.34
British	207	1.20
Bulgarian	6	0.03
Canadian	29	0.17
Celtic	20	0.12
Croatian	16	0.09
Czech	36	0.21
Czechoslovakian	15	0.09
Danish	60	0.35
Dutch	161	0.94
Eastern European	163	0.95
English	1,186	6.90
European	323	1.88
Finnish	59	0.34
French, except Basque	265	1.54
French Canadian	52	0.30
German	1,418	8.25
Greek	41	0.24
Guyanese	99	0.58
Hawaii Native/Pacific Islander:	33	0.19
Micronesian: (2)	3	0.02
Guamanian/Chamorro	1	0.01
Other Micronesian (2)	2	0.01
Polynesian: (3)	6	0.03
Native Hawaiian (3)	6	0.03
Other Pac. Isl., specified	2	0.01
Other Pac. Isl., not spec. (1)	22	0.13
Hispanic or Latino:	2,494	14.42
Central American:	895	5.17
Costa Rican	3	0.02
Guatemalan	134	0.77
Honduran	35	0.20
Nicaraguan	88	0.51
Panamanian	32	0.18
Salvadoran	561	3.24
Other Central American	42	0.24
Cuban	82	0.47
Dominican Republic	163	0.94
Mexican	236	1.36
Puerto Rican	128	0.74
South American:	196	1.13
Argentinean	25	0.14
Bolivian	17	0.10
Chilean	15	0.09
Colombian	47	0.27
Ecuadorian	35	0.20
Paraguayan	2	0.01
Peruvian	40	0.23
Uruguayan	1	0.01
Venezuelan	7	0.04
Other South American	7	0.04
Other Hispanic or Latino	794	4.59
Hungarian	73	0.42
Iranian	10	0.06
Irish	1,290	7.51
Israeli	6	0.03
Italian	616	3.59
Latvian	20	0.12
Lithuanian	52	0.30
Northern European	81	0.47
Norwegian	86	0.50
Polish	367	2.14
Portuguese	52	0.30
Romanian	84	0.49
Russian	434	2.53
Scandinavian	11	0.06
Scotch-Irish	250	1.46
Scottish	361	2.10
Slavic	6	0.03
Slovak	26	0.15
Slovene	8	0.05
Swedish	176	1.02
Swiss	68	0.40
Turkish	15	0.09
Ukrainian	137	0.80
United States or American	426	2.48
Welsh	135	0.79
West Indian, excl. Hispanic:	763	4.44
Bahamian	6	0.03
Bermudan	6	0.03
British West Indian	41	0.24
Haitian	209	1.22
Jamaican	267	1.55
Trinidadian and Tobagonian	171	1.00
West Indian	48	0.28
Other West Indian	15	0.09
White:	8,910	51.51
Not Hispanic (7,638)	7,888	45.60
Hispanic (802)	1,022	5.91

Towson

Place Type: Census Designated Place
County: Baltimore
Population: 51,793

Ancestry/Race	Number	%
African American/Black:	4,089	7.89
Not Hispanic (3,848)	4,012	7.75
Hispanic (53)	77	0.15

Notes: 1. Figures in the "Number" column do not add up to the total population due to: a) Ancestry/Race overlap — e.g. persons can report being both White and Irish, b) persons of Hispanic origin can report being any race, c) persons reporting two ancestries are counted in both categories. 2. Numbers in parentheses indicate the number of persons reporting this ancestry/race alone, not in combination with any other ancestry/race. 3. Refer to the Explanation of Data in the front of the book for more detailed information.

Ancestry/Race	Number	%
African, sub-Saharan:	542	1.05
African	224	0.43
Ethiopian	37	0.07
Ghanian	15	0.03
Liberian	15	0.03
Nigerian	171	0.33
South African	38	0.07
Other sub-Saharan African	42	0.08
Alaska Native tribes, specified:	1	0.00
Eskimo	1	0.00
Am. Ind. or Alaska Nat., not spec.	66	0.13
Albanian	5	0.01
Alsatian	7	0.01
American Indian tribes, specified:	106	0.20
Apache	3	0.01
Blackfeet	5	0.01
Cherokee (8)	44	0.08
Chippewa	4	0.01
Choctaw	2	0.00
Comanche	1	0.00
Creek	1	0.00
Delaware (1)	2	0.00
Iroquois (1)	4	0.01
Latin American Indians (2)	8	0.02
Lumbee (3)	6	0.01
Ottawa	2	0.00
Seminole (1)	1	0.00
Sioux	6	0.01
All other tribes (10)	17	0.03
American Indian tribes, not spec.	17	0.03
Arab:	387	0.75
Arab/Arabic	86	0.17
Egyptian	149	0.29
Jordanian	9	0.02
Lebanese	62	0.12
Moroccan	5	0.01
Palestinian	4	0.01
Syrian	24	0.05
Other Arab	48	0.09
Armenian	35	0.07
Asian:	2,183	4.21
Bangladeshi (2)	6	0.01
Cambodian (4)	7	0.01
Chinese, ex. Taiwanese (741)	778	1.50
Filipino (211)	257	0.50
Indian (313)	347	0.67
Indonesian (4)	6	0.01
Japanese (125)	158	0.31
Korean (251)	275	0.53
Malaysian (8)	10	0.02
Pakistani (19)	26	0.05
Sri Lankan (7)	7	0.01
Taiwanese (40)	44	0.08
Thai (25)	29	0.06
Vietnamese (62)	65	0.13
Other Asian, specified (15)	22	0.04
Other Asian, not specified (98)	146	0.28
Australian	26	0.05
Austrian	267	0.52
Belgian	14	0.03
Brazilian	28	0.05
British	748	1.44
Bulgarian	19	0.04
Canadian	109	0.21
Celtic	5	0.01
Croatian	13	0.03
Czech	469	0.90
Czechoslovakian	138	0.27
Danish	215	0.41
Dutch	552	1.06
Eastern European	138	0.27
English	8,609	16.61
Estonian	55	0.11
European	345	0.67
Finnish	53	0.10
French, except Basque	1,503	2.90
French Canadian	219	0.42
German	11,996	23.14
Greek	638	1.23
Hawaii Native/Pacific Islander:	30	0.06
Melanesian: (1)	3	0.01
Fijian (1)	3	0.01
Micronesian: (1)	3	0.01
Guamanian/Chamorro (1)	3	0.01
Polynesian: (5)	13	0.03
Native Hawaiian (3)	8	0.02
Samoan (2)	4	0.01
Other Polynesian	1	0.00
Other Pac. Isl., specified	1	0.00
Other Pac. Isl., not spec. (4)	10	0.02
Hispanic or Latino:	985	1.90
Central American:	127	0.25
Costa Rican	7	0.01
Guatemalan	15	0.03
Honduran	15	0.03
Nicaraguan	7	0.01
Panamanian	9	0.02
Salvadoran	70	0.14
Other Central American	4	0.01
Cuban	63	0.12
Dominican Republic	15	0.03
Mexican	156	0.30
Puerto Rican	164	0.32
South American:	157	0.30
Argentinean	20	0.04
Bolivian	7	0.01
Chilean	27	0.05
Colombian	40	0.08
Ecuadorian	10	0.02
Paraguayan	3	0.01
Peruvian	33	0.06
Venezuelan	12	0.02
Other South American	5	0.01
Other Hispanic or Latino	303	0.59
Hungarian	388	0.75
Icelander	14	0.03
Iranian	111	0.21
Irish	10,665	20.57
Italian	3,962	7.64
Latvian	76	0.15
Lithuanian	253	0.49
Luxemburger	5	0.01
Northern European	41	0.08
Norwegian	433	0.84
Pennsylvania German	34	0.07
Polish	2,398	4.63
Portuguese	48	0.09
Romanian	122	0.24
Russian	974	1.88
Scandinavian	50	0.10
Scotch-Irish	1,059	2.04
Scottish	1,727	3.33
Serbian	11	0.02
Slavic	21	0.04
Slovak	148	0.29
Slovene	33	0.06
Swedish	420	0.81
Swiss	252	0.49
Turkish	69	0.13
Ukrainian	377	0.73
United States or American	1,976	3.81
Welsh	644	1.24
West Indian, excl. Hispanic:	197	0.38
Bahamian	5	0.01
Bermudan	17	0.03
British West Indian	5	0.01
Haitian	23	0.04
Jamaican	79	0.15
Trinidadian and Tobagonian	12	0.02
West Indian	56	0.11
White:	45,514	87.88
Not Hispanic (44,376)	44,806	86.51
Hispanic (652)	708	1.37
Yugoslavian	26	0.05

Waldorf

Place Type: Census Designated Place
County: Charles
Population: 22,312

Ancestry/Race	Number	%
African American/Black:	7,446	33.37
Not Hispanic (7,076)	7,370	33.03
Hispanic (60)	76	0.34
African, sub-Saharan:	151	0.67
African	151	0.67
Alaska Native tribes, specified:	1	0.00
Eskimo (1)	1	0.00
Am. Ind. or Alaska Nat., not spec.	80	0.36
American Indian tribes, specified:	223	1.00
Blackfeet	5	0.02
Cherokee (16)	79	0.35
Chippewa (7)	12	0.05
Choctaw	1	0.00
Creek	2	0.01
Crow	4	0.02
Delaware (1)	1	0.00
Iroquois (8)	14	0.06
Latin American Indians	5	0.02
Lumbee	2	0.01
Navajo (1)	6	0.03
Seminole (1)	4	0.02
Shoshone (1)	2	0.01
Sioux (1)	5	0.02
Yakama (1)	1	0.00
All other tribes (57)	80	0.36
American Indian tribes, not spec.	12	0.05
Arab:	156	0.70
Arab/Arabic	66	0.29
Egyptian	10	0.04
Lebanese	68	0.30
Palestinian	4	0.02
Other Arab	8	0.04
Armenian	32	0.14
Asian:	795	3.56
Bangladeshi (6)	6	0.03
Chinese, ex. Taiwanese (88)	105	0.47
Filipino (199)	292	1.31
Indian (53)	75	0.34
Japanese (25)	63	0.28
Korean (80)	110	0.49
Malaysian (1)	2	0.01
Pakistani (14)	16	0.07
Taiwanese (3)	3	0.01
Thai (22)	27	0.12
Vietnamese (70)	71	0.32
Other Asian, specified	5	0.02
Other Asian, not specified (10)	20	0.09
Austrian	58	0.26
Belgian	14	0.06
British	66	0.29
Bulgarian	11	0.05
Canadian	37	0.17
Carpatho Rusyn	11	0.05
Croatian	16	0.07
Czech	83	0.37
Czechoslovakian	34	0.15
Danish	26	0.12
Dutch	278	1.24
English	2,160	9.64
European	169	0.75
Finnish	14	0.06
French, except Basque	828	3.70
French Canadian	161	0.72
German	2,906	12.97
Greek	118	0.53
Hawaii Native/Pacific Islander:	26	0.12
Micronesian: (5)	9	0.04
Guamanian/Chamorro (5)	9	0.04
Polynesian:	9	0.04
Native Hawaiian	9	0.04
Other Pac. Isl., specified	2	0.01
Other Pac. Isl., not spec.	6	0.03
Hispanic or Latino:	650	2.91

Notes: 1. Figures in the "Number" column do not add up to the total population due to: a) Ancestry/Race overlap — e.g. persons can report being both White and Irish, b) persons of Hispanic origin can report being any race, c) persons reporting two ancestries are counted in both categories. 2. Numbers in parentheses indicate the number of persons reporting this ancestry/race alone, not in combination with any other ancestry/race. 3. Refer to the Explanation of Data in the front of the book for more detailed information.

Central American:	70	0.31
Costa Rican	6	0.03
Guatemalan	21	0.09
Honduran	3	0.01
Nicaraguan	5	0.02
Panamanian	20	0.09
Salvadoran	15	0.07
Cuban	23	0.10
Dominican Republic	15	0.07
Mexican	199	0.89
Puerto Rican	175	0.78
South American:	27	0.12
Argentinean	3	0.01
Bolivian	5	0.02
Chilean	2	0.01
Colombian	7	0.03
Ecuadorian	1	0.00
Peruvian	5	0.02
Other South American	4	0.02
Other Hispanic or Latino	141	0.63
Hungarian	135	0.60
Icelander	4	0.02
Irish	2,813	12.56
Italian	1,145	5.11
Latvian	8	0.04
Lithuanian	57	0.25
Northern European	28	0.13
Norwegian	263	1.17
Pennsylvania German	36	0.16
Polish	499	2.23
Portuguese	20	0.09
Romanian	7	0.03
Russian	69	0.31
Scandinavian	23	0.10
Scotch-Irish	355	1.59
Scottish	336	1.50
Slavic	24	0.11
Slovak	92	0.41
Slovene	6	0.03
Swedish	181	0.81
Swiss	56	0.25
Ukrainian	53	0.24
United States or American	1,426	6.37
Welsh	51	0.23
West Indian, excl. Hispanic:	78	0.35
Belizean	13	0.06
Jamaican	47	0.21
West Indian	18	0.08
White:	14,167	63.49
Not Hispanic (13,268)	13,757	61.66
Hispanic (366)	410	1.84

Walker Mill

Place Type: Census Designated Place
County: Prince George's
Population: 11,104

Ancestry/Race	Number	%
African American/Black:	10,709	96.44
Not Hispanic (10,508)	10,648	95.89
Hispanic (40)	61	0.55
African, sub-Saharan:	133	1.18
African	111	0.98
Ghanian	6	0.05
Nigerian	12	0.11
Other sub-Saharan African	4	0.04
Am. Ind. or Alaska Nat., not spec.	60	0.54
American Indian tribes, specified:	52	0.47
Blackfeet	10	0.09
Cherokee (4)	19	0.17
Chippewa (1)	1	0.01
Navajo	2	0.02
Seminole	2	0.02
Sioux	1	0.01
Yuman (2)	2	0.02
All other tribes (7)	15	0.14
American Indian tribes, not spec.	10	0.09
Asian:	60	0.54
Chinese, ex. Taiwanese (1)	5	0.05
Filipino (18)	31	0.28
Indian (7)	14	0.13
Japanese (1)	7	0.06
Korean (1)	1	0.01
Thai (1)	1	0.01
Other Asian, not specified	1	0.01
Czechoslovakian	5	0.04
English	25	0.22
French, except Basque	7	0.06
French Canadian	17	0.15
German	83	0.74
Guyanese	51	0.45
Hawaii Native/Pacific Islander:	7	0.06
Micronesian: (1)	2	0.02
Guamanian/Chamorro (1)	2	0.02
Polynesian:	2	0.02
Native Hawaiian	2	0.02
Other Pac. Isl., not spec.	3	0.03
Hispanic or Latino:	100	0.90
Central American:	14	0.13
Costa Rican	3	0.03
Guatemalan	4	0.04
Panamanian	5	0.05
Salvadoran	2	0.02
Cuban	6	0.05
Dominican Republic	2	0.02
Mexican	24	0.22
Puerto Rican	26	0.23
South American:	3	0.03
Chilean	1	0.01
Peruvian	2	0.02
Other Hispanic or Latino	25	0.23
Irish	141	1.25
Israeli	15	0.13
Italian	67	0.59
Polish	27	0.24
Romanian	43	0.38
United States or American	123	1.09
Welsh	5	0.04
West Indian, excl. Hispanic:	109	0.97
Jamaican	37	0.33
Trinidadian and Tobagonian	63	0.56
West Indian	9	0.08
White:	343	3.09
Not Hispanic (255)	321	2.89
Hispanic (19)	22	0.20

Westminster

Place Type: City
County: Carroll
Population: 16,731

Ancestry/Race	Number	%
African American/Black:	994	5.94
Not Hispanic (911)	979	5.85
Hispanic (8)	15	0.09
African, sub-Saharan:	37	0.23
African	31	0.19
Ethiopian	6	0.04
Am. Ind. or Alaska Nat., not spec.	39	0.23
American Indian tribes, specified:	42	0.25
Apache (1)	2	0.01
Blackfeet	2	0.01
Cherokee (6)	17	0.10
Chippewa (1)	1	0.01
Choctaw (1)	4	0.02
Delaware	6	0.04
Iroquois	1	0.01
Latin American Indians	1	0.01
Lumbee (1)	1	0.01
Navajo	1	0.01
Seminole	1	0.01
All other tribes (2)	5	0.03
American Indian tribes, not spec.	3	0.02
Arab:	30	0.18
Lebanese	24	0.15
Palestinian	6	0.04
Armenian	19	0.12
Asian:	246	1.47
Cambodian (7)	7	0.04
Chinese, ex. Taiwanese (40)	47	0.28
Filipino (43)	59	0.35
Indian (31)	39	0.23
Indonesian (1)	1	0.01
Japanese (7)	11	0.07
Korean (33)	41	0.25
Malaysian (1)	1	0.01
Pakistani (13)	13	0.08
Sri Lankan (2)	3	0.02
Taiwanese (1)	1	0.01
Thai (2)	3	0.02
Vietnamese (14)	15	0.09
Other Asian, specified	1	0.01
Other Asian, not specified (1)	4	0.02
Austrian	33	0.20
British	64	0.39
Canadian	9	0.05
Croatian	8	0.05
Czech	32	0.19
Czechoslovakian	16	0.10
Danish	28	0.17
Dutch	223	1.36
Eastern European	21	0.13
English	2,244	13.65
European	35	0.21
Finnish	7	0.04
French, except Basque	410	2.49
French Canadian	64	0.39
German	4,678	28.45
Greek	163	0.99
Guyanese	7	0.04
Hawaii Native/Pacific Islander:	18	0.11
Micronesian: (1)	5	0.03
Guamanian/Chamorro (1)	5	0.03
Polynesian: (3)	8	0.05
Native Hawaiian (2)	7	0.04
Samoan (1)	1	0.01
Other Pac. Isl., not spec. (2)	5	0.03
Hispanic or Latino:	297	1.78
Central American:	23	0.14
Costa Rican	2	0.01
Guatemalan	3	0.02
Honduran	4	0.02
Panamanian	2	0.01
Salvadoran	10	0.06
Other Central American	2	0.01
Cuban	10	0.06
Dominican Republic	8	0.05
Mexican	49	0.29
Puerto Rican	105	0.63
South American:	25	0.15
Argentinean	1	0.01
Chilean	2	0.01
Colombian	4	0.02
Ecuadorian	1	0.01
Peruvian	14	0.08
Venezuelan	3	0.02
Other Hispanic or Latino	77	0.46
Hungarian	106	0.64
Irish	2,451	14.91
Italian	1,032	6.28
Latvian	7	0.04
Lithuanian	25	0.15
Northern European	19	0.12
Norwegian	115	0.70
Pennsylvania German	6	0.04
Polish	760	4.62
Romanian	11	0.07
Russian	111	0.68
Scotch-Irish	215	1.31
Scottish	283	1.72
Serbian	14	0.09
Slovak	12	0.07
Swedish	84	0.51
Swiss	65	0.40
Turkish	7	0.04
Ukrainian	27	0.16
United States or American	1,147	6.98
Welsh	126	0.77

Notes: 1. Figures in the "Number" column do not add up to the total population due to: a) Ancestry/Race overlap — e.g. persons can report being both White and Irish, b) persons of Hispanic origin can report being any race, c) persons reporting two ancestries are counted in both categories. 2. Numbers in parentheses indicate the number of persons reporting this ancestry/race alone, not in combination with any other ancestry/race. 3. Refer to the Explanation of Data in the front of the book for more detailed information.

West Indian, excl. Hispanic:	48	0.29
Dutch West Indian	8	0.05
Jamaican	21	0.13
Trinidadian and Tobagonian	19	0.12
White:	15,442	92.30
Not Hispanic (15,114)	15,261	91.21
Hispanic (158)	181	1.08

Wheaton-Glenmont

Place Type: Census Designated Place
County: Montgomery
Population: 57,694

Ancestry/Race	Number	%
Acadian/Cajun	5	0.01
African American/Black:	11,851	20.54
Not Hispanic (10,564)	11,353	19.68
Hispanic (298)	498	0.86
African, sub-Saharan:	2,223	3.85
African	566	0.98
Cape Verdean	83	0.14
Ethiopian	660	1.14
Ghanian	141	0.24
Kenyan	19	0.03
Liberian	5	0.01
Nigerian	273	0.47
Senegalese	32	0.06
Sierra Leonean	168	0.29
Somalian	8	0.01
Other sub-Saharan African	268	0.46
Alaska Native tribes, specified:	2	0.00
Aleut	1	0.00
All other tribes	1	0.00
Am. Ind. or Alaska Nat., not spec.	292	0.51
Albanian	8	0.01
Alsatian	28	0.05
American Indian tribes, specified:	321	0.56
Apache (2)	3	0.01
Blackfeet (2)	8	0.01
Cherokee (25)	108	0.19
Chippewa (1)	2	0.00
Choctaw (4)	5	0.01
Cree	3	0.01
Creek (2)	4	0.01
Iroquois (2)	6	0.01
Latin American Indians (45)	104	0.18
Lumbee (1)	3	0.01
Menominee	2	0.00
Navajo (5)	8	0.01
Osage (1)	1	0.00
Pueblo (2)	8	0.01
Seminole	1	0.00
Sioux (2)	6	0.01
All other tribes (17)	49	0.08
American Indian tribes, not spec.	25	0.04
Arab:	456	0.79
Arab/Arabic	113	0.20
Egyptian	25	0.04
Jordanian	46	0.08
Lebanese	81	0.14
Moroccan	39	0.07
Palestinian	21	0.04
Syrian	18	0.03
Other Arab	113	0.20
Armenian	117	0.20
Asian:	7,877	13.65
Bangladeshi (33)	38	0.07
Cambodian (160)	213	0.37
Chinese, ex. Taiwanese (1,892)	2,059	3.57
Filipino (821)	962	1.67
Indian (969)	1,106	1.92
Indonesian (176)	196	0.34
Japanese (82)	140	0.24
Korean (836)	888	1.54
Laotian (25)	28	0.05
Malaysian (11)	15	0.03
Pakistani (79)	98	0.17
Sri Lankan (149)	184	0.32
Taiwanese (33)	47	0.08
Thai (269)	309	0.54
Vietnamese (1,148)	1,237	2.14
Other Asian, specified (93)	113	0.20
Other Asian, not specified (135)	244	0.42
Australian	6	0.01
Austrian	119	0.21
Belgian	67	0.12
Brazilian	244	0.42
British	391	0.68
Bulgarian	27	0.05
Canadian	29	0.05
Celtic	16	0.03
Croatian	61	0.11
Czech	137	0.24
Czechoslovakian	142	0.25
Danish	73	0.13
Dutch	232	0.40
Eastern European	150	0.26
English	2,994	5.19
European	445	0.77
Finnish	27	0.05
French, except Basque	815	1.41
French Canadian	169	0.29
German	4,122	7.14
Greek	778	1.35
Guyanese	280	0.49
Hawaii Native/Pacific Islander:	141	0.24
Micronesian: (11)	14	0.02
Guamanian/Chamorro (10)	13	0.02
Other Micronesian (1)	1	0.00
Polynesian: (11)	21	0.04
Native Hawaiian (6)	15	0.03
Samoan (4)	5	0.01
Other Polynesian (1)	1	0.00
Other Pac. Isl., specified	12	0.02
Other Pac. Isl., not spec. (13)	94	0.16
Hispanic or Latino:	14,956	25.92
Central American:	5,350	9.27
Costa Rican	66	0.11
Guatemalan	626	1.09
Honduran	216	0.37
Nicaraguan	371	0.64
Panamanian	64	0.11
Salvadoran	3,770	6.53
Other Central American	237	0.41
Cuban	213	0.37
Dominican Republic	285	0.49
Mexican	1,066	1.85
Puerto Rican	481	0.83
South American:	1,784	3.09
Argentinean	84	0.15
Bolivian	349	0.60
Chilean	121	0.21
Colombian	325	0.56
Ecuadorian	175	0.30
Paraguayan	38	0.07
Peruvian	499	0.86
Uruguayan	8	0.01
Venezuelan	62	0.11
Other South American	123	0.21
Other Hispanic or Latino	5,777	10.01
Hungarian	216	0.37
Icelander	26	0.05
Iranian	254	0.44
Irish	3,973	6.88
Israeli	75	0.13
Italian	1,861	3.22
Latvian	35	0.06
Lithuanian	154	0.27
Luxemburger	9	0.02
Norwegian	73	0.13
Pennsylvania German	13	0.02
Polish	1,023	1.77
Portuguese	476	0.82
Romanian	18	0.03
Russian	1,125	1.95
Scandinavian	28	0.05
Scotch-Irish	587	1.02
Scottish	599	1.04
Serbian	4	0.01
Slavic	46	0.08
Slovak	200	0.35
Swedish	257	0.45
Swiss	193	0.33
Turkish	23	0.04
Ukrainian	226	0.39
United States or American	2,348	4.07
Welsh	224	0.39
West Indian, excl. Hispanic:	1,747	3.03
Bahamian	17	0.03
Barbadian	46	0.08
Belizean	7	0.01
Bermudan	6	0.01
British West Indian	19	0.03
Haitian	448	0.78
Jamaican	889	1.54
Trinidadian and Tobagonian	232	0.40
West Indian	83	0.14
White:	31,036	53.79
Not Hispanic (23,093)	24,116	41.80
Hispanic (5,709)	6,920	11.99
Yugoslavian	55	0.10

White Oak

Place Type: Census Designated Place
County: Montgomery
Population: 20,973

Ancestry/Race	Number	%
African American/Black:	8,229	39.24
Not Hispanic (7,606)	7,998	38.13
Hispanic (165)	231	1.10
African, sub-Saharan:	2,375	11.37
African	743	3.56
Ethiopian	247	1.18
Ghanian	267	1.28
Kenyan	21	0.10
Liberian	46	0.22
Nigerian	181	0.87
Senegalese	19	0.09
Sierra Leonean	115	0.55
Sudanese	146	0.70
Ugandan	83	0.40
Zimbabwean	60	0.29
Other sub-Saharan African	447	2.14
Am. Ind. or Alaska Nat., not spec.	72	0.34
American Indian tribes, specified:	96	0.46
Blackfeet (2)	3	0.01
Cherokee (4)	27	0.13
Chippewa	1	0.00
Choctaw	3	0.01
Delaware	1	0.00
Iroquois	1	0.00
Latin American Indians (18)	26	0.12
Lumbee	1	0.00
Osage (3)	4	0.02
Puget Sound Salish	2	0.01
Seminole	1	0.00
Sioux (5)	7	0.03
All other tribes (9)	19	0.09
American Indian tribes, not spec.	10	0.05
Arab:	133	0.64
Arab/Arabic	18	0.09
Lebanese	74	0.35
Palestinian	5	0.02
Syrian	36	0.17
Armenian	15	0.07
Asian:	2,564	12.23
Bangladeshi (9)	19	0.09
Cambodian (20)	26	0.12
Chinese, ex. Taiwanese (387)	429	2.05
Filipino (85)	104	0.50
Indian (512)	571	2.72
Indonesian (3)	4	0.02
Japanese (25)	37	0.18
Korean (651)	678	3.23
Laotian (8)	10	0.05
Malaysian (6)	6	0.03
Pakistani (23)	29	0.14

Notes: 1. Figures in the "Number" column do not add up to the total population due to: a) Ancestry/Race overlap — e.g. persons can report being both White and Irish, b) persons of Hispanic origin can report being any race, c) persons reporting two ancestries are counted in both categories. 2. Numbers in parentheses indicate the number of persons reporting this ancestry/race alone, not in combination with any other ancestry/race. 3. Refer to the Explanation of Data in the front of the book for more detailed information.

Sri Lankan (17)	20	0.10
Taiwanese (20)	22	0.10
Thai (22)	28	0.13
Vietnamese (485)	501	2.39
Other Asian, specified (14)	15	0.07
Other Asian, not specified (32)	65	0.31
Australian	5	0.02
Austrian	110	0.53
Belgian	9	0.04
Brazilian	107	0.51
British	128	0.61
Canadian	51	0.24
Croatian	69	0.33
Cypriot	9	0.04
Czech	27	0.13
Czechoslovakian	52	0.25
Danish	54	0.26
Dutch	154	0.74
Eastern European	80	0.38
English	1,039	4.97
European	176	0.84
Finnish	27	0.13
French, except Basque	333	1.59
French Canadian	25	0.12
German	1,356	6.49
Greek	97	0.46
Guyanese	79	0.38
Hawaii Native/Pacific Islander:	33	0.16
Micronesian: (6)	6	0.03
Guamanian/Chamorro (6)	6	0.03
Polynesian: (6)	12	0.06
Native Hawaiian (1)	6	0.03
Samoan (5)	6	0.03
Other Pac. Isl., not spec. (8)	15	0.07
Hispanic or Latino:	2,722	12.98
Central American:	827	3.94
Costa Rican	6	0.03
Guatemalan	90	0.43
Honduran	80	0.38
Nicaraguan	76	0.36
Panamanian	25	0.12
Salvadoran	493	2.35
Other Central American	57	0.27
Cuban	67	0.32
Dominican Republic	94	0.45
Mexican	195	0.93
Puerto Rican	203	0.97
South American:	344	1.64
Argentinean	35	0.17
Bolivian	76	0.36
Chilean	14	0.07
Colombian	69	0.33
Ecuadorian	17	0.08
Paraguayan	5	0.02
Peruvian	91	0.43
Uruguayan	4	0.02
Venezuelan	10	0.05
Other South American	23	0.11
Other Hispanic or Latino	992	4.73
Hungarian	67	0.32
Iranian	92	0.44
Irish	1,109	5.31
Israeli	63	0.30
Italian	636	3.04
Lithuanian	132	0.63
Norwegian	80	0.38
Pennsylvania German	22	0.11
Polish	515	2.46
Portuguese	24	0.11
Romanian	40	0.19
Russian	581	2.78
Scotch-Irish	143	0.68
Scottish	232	1.11
Slovak	21	0.10
Slovene	10	0.05
Swedish	139	0.67
Swiss	18	0.09
Turkish	6	0.03
Ukrainian	103	0.49
United States or American	688	3.29
Welsh	130	0.62
West Indian, excl. Hispanic:	746	3.57
Barbadian	14	0.07
British West Indian	28	0.13
Haitian	119	0.57
Jamaican	366	1.75
Trinidadian and Tobagonian	93	0.45
U.S. Virgin Islander	7	0.03
West Indian	119	0.57
White:	9,037	43.09
Not Hispanic (7,538)	7,829	37.33
Hispanic (971)	1,208	5.76

Woodlawn

Place Type: Census Designated Place
County: Baltimore
Population: 36,079

Ancestry/Race	Number	%
African American/Black:	19,112	52.97
Not Hispanic (18,465)	18,939	52.49
Hispanic (116)	173	0.48
African, sub-Saharan:	1,527	4.23
African	1,160	3.21
Ethiopian	41	0.11
Liberian	57	0.16
Nigerian	232	0.64
Sierra Leonean	24	0.07
Other sub-Saharan African	13	0.04
Am. Ind. or Alaska Nat., not spec.	131	0.36
Albanian	23	0.06
American Indian tribes, specified:	170	0.47
Apache	5	0.01
Blackfeet (12)	25	0.07
Cherokee (20)	81	0.22
Chippewa (1)	1	0.00
Choctaw (4)	7	0.02
Comanche (1)	1	0.00
Creek (1)	1	0.00
Delaware (3)	4	0.01
Iroquois (1)	3	0.01
Latin American Indians (3)	11	0.03
Lumbee (6)	9	0.02
Seminole (2)	2	0.01
Shoshone	3	0.01
Sioux (3)	4	0.01
All other tribes (7)	13	0.04
American Indian tribes, not spec.	14	0.04
Arab:	140	0.39
Arab/Arabic	52	0.14
Egyptian	15	0.04
Moroccan	45	0.12
Palestinian	20	0.06
Syrian	8	0.02
Armenian	8	0.02
Asian:	2,548	7.06
Bangladeshi (53)	61	0.17
Cambodian (4)	4	0.01
Chinese, ex. Taiwanese (134)	164	0.45
Filipino (167)	207	0.57
Hmong (1)	3	0.01
Indian (1,079)	1,159	3.21
Indonesian (1)	1	0.00
Japanese (21)	47	0.13
Korean (168)	181	0.50
Laotian (1)	1	0.00
Malaysian (1)	3	0.01
Pakistani (243)	306	0.85
Sri Lankan (9)	14	0.04
Taiwanese (3)	4	0.01
Thai (62)	69	0.19
Vietnamese (182)	193	0.53
Other Asian, specified (3)	11	0.03
Other Asian, not specified (77)	120	0.33
Australian	12	0.03
Austrian	47	0.13
Belgian	6	0.02
Brazilian	33	0.09
British	26	0.07
Canadian	33	0.09
Celtic	8	0.02
Czech	63	0.17
Czechoslovakian	51	0.14
Danish	25	0.07
Dutch	161	0.45
Eastern European	8	0.02
English	2,050	5.67
European	211	0.58
Finnish	19	0.05
French, except Basque	523	1.45
French Canadian	75	0.21
German	4,147	11.48
Greek	140	0.39
Hawaii Native/Pacific Islander:	47	0.13
Micronesian: (3)	4	0.01
Guamanian/Chamorro (3)	4	0.01
Polynesian: (11)	16	0.04
Native Hawaiian (10)	14	0.04
Samoan (1)	2	0.01
Other Pac. Isl., not spec. (4)	27	0.07
Hispanic or Latino:	849	2.35
Central American:	108	0.30
Guatemalan	8	0.02
Honduran	11	0.03
Nicaraguan	4	0.01
Panamanian	13	0.04
Salvadoran	56	0.16
Other Central American	16	0.04
Cuban	45	0.12
Dominican Republic	15	0.04
Mexican	242	0.67
Puerto Rican	192	0.53
South American:	61	0.17
Argentinean	7	0.02
Chilean	5	0.01
Colombian	8	0.02
Ecuadorian	5	0.01
Paraguayan	1	0.00
Peruvian	17	0.05
Uruguayan	5	0.01
Venezuelan	9	0.02
Other South American	4	0.01
Other Hispanic or Latino	186	0.52
Hungarian	67	0.19
Iranian	9	0.02
Irish	2,736	7.57
Israeli	27	0.07
Italian	1,448	4.01
Latvian	13	0.04
Lithuanian	129	0.36
Northern European	37	0.10
Norwegian	59	0.16
Pennsylvania German	37	0.10
Polish	725	2.01
Portuguese	61	0.17
Romanian	36	0.10
Russian	135	0.37
Scandinavian	11	0.03
Scotch-Irish	348	0.96
Scottish	300	0.83
Serbian	23	0.06
Slovak	50	0.14
Swedish	80	0.22
Swiss	4	0.01
Ukrainian	63	0.17
United States or American	1,069	2.96
Welsh	179	0.50
West Indian, excl. Hispanic:	554	1.53
Barbadian	13	0.04
British West Indian	4	0.01
Haitian	30	0.08
Jamaican	332	0.92
Trinidadian and Tobagonian	167	0.46
West Indian	8	0.02
White:	14,349	39.77
Not Hispanic (13,532)	13,956	38.68
Hispanic (317)	393	1.09

Notes: 1. Figures in the "Number" column do not add up to the total population due to: a) Ancestry/Race overlap — e.g. persons can report being both White and Irish, b) persons of Hispanic origin can report being any race, c) persons reporting two ancestries are counted in both categories. 2. Numbers in parentheses indicate the number of persons reporting this ancestry/race alone, not in combination with any other ancestry/race. 3. Refer to the Explanation of Data in the front of the book for more detailed information.

Abington

Place Type: Census Designated Place
County: Plymouth
Population: 14,605

Ancestry/Race	Number	%
African American/Black:	143	0.98
Not Hispanic (107)	137	0.94
Hispanic (4)	6	0.04
African, sub-Saharan:	55	0.38
Cape Verdean	55	0.38
Alaska Native tribes, specified:	4	0.03
Alaska Athabascan	3	0.02
Tlingit-Haida	1	0.01
Am. Ind. or Alaska Nat., not spec.	23	0.16
American Indian tribes, specified:	16	0.11
Cherokee (2)	4	0.03
Iroquois (3)	6	0.04
Latin American Indians	2	0.01
Pueblo	1	0.01
All other tribes (1)	3	0.02
American Indian tribes, not spec.	2	0.01
Arab:	139	0.95
Egyptian	7	0.05
Lebanese	112	0.77
Syrian	20	0.14
Armenian	89	0.61
Asian:	104	0.71
Cambodian	1	0.01
Chinese, ex. Taiwanese (9)	14	0.10
Filipino (11)	26	0.18
Indian (15)	18	0.12
Indonesian (1)	2	0.01
Japanese (8)	10	0.07
Korean (10)	15	0.10
Thai (3)	3	0.02
Vietnamese (10)	10	0.07
Other Asian, not specified (2)	5	0.03
Austrian	6	0.04
Belgian	38	0.26
Brazilian	17	0.12
British	9	0.06
Canadian	189	1.29
Celtic	17	0.12
Croatian	8	0.05
Czech	19	0.13
Czechoslovakian	8	0.05
Danish	16	0.11
Dutch	126	0.86
Eastern European	44	0.30
English	2,179	14.92
European	13	0.09
Finnish	87	0.60
French, except Basque	775	5.31
French Canadian	624	4.27
German	1,106	7.57
Greek	147	1.01
Hawaii Native/Pacific Islander:	4	0.03
Micronesian: (1)	2	0.01
Guamanian/Chamorro (1)	2	0.01
Polynesian:	1	0.01
Native Hawaiian	1	0.01
Other Pac. Isl., not spec.	1	0.01
Hispanic or Latino:	103	0.71
Central American:	3	0.02
Guatemalan	1	0.01
Salvadoran	2	0.01
Cuban	8	0.05
Dominican Republic	2	0.01
Mexican	13	0.09
Puerto Rican	44	0.30
South American:	9	0.06
Bolivian	1	0.01
Colombian	8	0.05
Other Hispanic or Latino	24	0.16
Hungarian	16	0.11
Irish	5,741	39.31
Italian	2,263	15.49
Latvian	6	0.04
Lithuanian	168	1.15
Norwegian	82	0.56
Polish	558	3.82
Portuguese	322	2.20
Russian	56	0.38
Scotch-Irish	516	3.53
Scottish	403	2.76
Slavic	7	0.05
Slovak	9	0.06
Swedish	444	3.04
Swiss	14	0.10
Ukrainian	18	0.12
United States or American	505	3.46
Welsh	42	0.29
White:	14,346	98.23
Not Hispanic (14,163)	14,262	97.65
Hispanic (74)	84	0.58

Acton

Place Type: Town
County: Middlesex
Population: 20,331

Ancestry/Race	Number	%
African American/Black:	196	0.96
Not Hispanic (139)	181	0.89
Hispanic (3)	15	0.07
African, sub-Saharan:	30	0.15
Cape Verdean	23	0.11
South African	7	0.03
Am. Ind. or Alaska Nat., not spec.	16	0.08
Alsatian	15	0.07
American Indian tribes, specified:	38	0.19
Blackfeet	3	0.01
Cherokee (3)	11	0.05
Chippewa	1	0.00
Comanche	1	0.00
Iroquois (2)	5	0.02
Latin American Indians (3)	5	0.02
Seminole	3	0.01
Sioux (1)	2	0.01
All other tribes (2)	7	0.03
Arab:	164	0.81
Arab/Arabic	9	0.04
Egyptian	8	0.04
Iraqi	31	0.15
Lebanese	61	0.30
Syrian	32	0.16
Other Arab	23	0.11
Armenian	54	0.27
Asian:	1,943	9.56
Bangladeshi (3)	7	0.03
Cambodian (8)	8	0.04
Chinese, ex. Taiwanese (769)	838	4.12
Filipino (43)	59	0.29
Indian (617)	651	3.20
Indonesian (3)	5	0.02
Japanese (35)	87	0.43
Korean (152)	168	0.83
Malaysian (1)	4	0.02
Sri Lankan (5)	5	0.02
Taiwanese (43)	49	0.24
Thai (10)	10	0.05
Vietnamese (31)	33	0.16
Other Asian, specified (6)	8	0.04
Other Asian, not specified (8)	11	0.05
Australian	30	0.15
Austrian	108	0.53
Belgian	34	0.17
Brazilian	90	0.44
British	200	0.98
Canadian	227	1.12
Celtic	5	0.02
Croatian	47	0.23
Czech	78	0.38
Czechoslovakian	43	0.21
Danish	117	0.58
Dutch	247	1.21
Eastern European	119	0.59
English	3,222	15.85
European	422	2.08
Finnish	111	0.55
French, except Basque	1,145	5.63
French Canadian	566	2.78
German	2,254	11.09
Greek	248	1.22
Hawaii Native/Pacific Islander:	8	0.04
Polynesian: (1)	4	0.02
Native Hawaiian	2	0.01
Samoan (1)	2	0.01
Other Pac. Isl., not spec. (4)	4	0.02
Hispanic or Latino:	360	1.77
Central American:	58	0.29
Costa Rican	12	0.06
Guatemalan	19	0.09
Honduran	1	0.00
Nicaraguan	1	0.00
Panamanian	3	0.01
Salvadoran	5	0.02
Other Central American	17	0.08
Cuban	24	0.12
Dominican Republic	1	0.00
Mexican	56	0.28
Puerto Rican	54	0.27
South American:	69	0.34
Argentinean	3	0.01
Bolivian	1	0.00
Chilean	3	0.01
Colombian	33	0.16
Ecuadorian	4	0.02
Paraguayan	5	0.02
Peruvian	4	0.02
Venezuelan	13	0.06
Other South American	3	0.01
Other Hispanic or Latino	98	0.48
Hungarian	224	1.10
Iranian	33	0.16
Irish	4,159	20.46
Italian	2,682	13.19
Lithuanian	169	0.83
New Zealander	5	0.02
Northern European	11	0.05
Norwegian	269	1.32
Polish	1,094	5.38
Portuguese	241	1.19
Romanian	32	0.16
Russian	697	3.43
Scandinavian	9	0.04
Scotch-Irish	477	2.35
Scottish	864	4.25
Serbian	11	0.05
Slavic	23	0.11
Slovak	54	0.27
Swedish	540	2.66
Swiss	92	0.45
Turkish	36	0.18
Ukrainian	139	0.68
United States or American	821	4.04
Welsh	166	0.82
West Indian, excl. Hispanic:	24	0.12
Bahamian	6	0.03
Haitian	14	0.07
Jamaican	4	0.02
White:	18,270	89.86
Not Hispanic (17,730)	17,991	88.49
Hispanic (252)	279	1.37
Yugoslavian	9	0.04

Acushnet

Place Type: Town
County: Bristol
Population: 10,161

Ancestry/Race	Number	%
African American/Black:	80	0.79
Not Hispanic (42)	76	0.75
Hispanic (1)	4	0.04
African, sub-Saharan:	111	1.09

Notes: 1. Figures in the "Number" column do not add up to the total population due to: a) Ancestry/Race overlap — e.g. persons can report being both White and Irish, b) persons of Hispanic origin can report being any race, c) persons reporting two ancestries are counted in both categories. 2. Numbers in parentheses indicate the number of persons reporting this ancestry/race alone, not in combination with any other ancestry/race. 3. Refer to the Explanation of Data in the front of the book for more detailed information.

Cape Verdean	111	1.09
Am. Ind. or Alaska Nat., not spec.	16	0.16
American Indian tribes, specified:	26	0.26
Cherokee (1)	5	0.05
Comanche (1)	1	0.01
All other tribes (8)	20	0.20
American Indian tribes, not spec.	3	0.03
Arab:	97	0.95
Lebanese	97	0.95
Asian:	27	0.27
Chinese, ex. Taiwanese (3)	5	0.05
Filipino (3)	3	0.03
Indian	2	0.02
Japanese (2)	4	0.04
Korean (8)	9	0.09
Vietnamese (1)	1	0.01
Other Asian, not specified	3	0.03
Austrian	6	0.06
Belgian	34	0.33
Brazilian	23	0.23
British	9	0.09
Canadian	64	0.63
Czech	13	0.13
Czechoslovakian	7	0.07
Danish	11	0.11
Dutch	33	0.32
English	1,189	11.70
Estonian	5	0.05
Finnish	8	0.08
French, except Basque	1,791	17.63
French Canadian	1,492	14.68
German	240	2.36
Greek	45	0.44
Hawaii Native/Pacific Islander:	11	0.11
Micronesian: (1)	1	0.01
Guamanian/Chamorro (1)	1	0.01
Polynesian: (1)	2	0.02
Native Hawaiian (1)	1	0.01
Samoan	1	0.01
Other Pac. Isl., not spec.	8	0.08
Hispanic or Latino:	80	0.79
Central American:	12	0.12
Guatemalan	4	0.04
Salvadoran	8	0.08
Cuban	2	0.02
Mexican	9	0.09
Puerto Rican	34	0.33
South American:	1	0.01
Bolivian	1	0.01
Other Hispanic or Latino	22	0.22
Hungarian	5	0.05
Irish	812	7.99
Italian	397	3.91
Northern European	22	0.22
Norwegian	42	0.41
Polish	733	7.21
Portuguese	3,827	37.66
Romanian	7	0.07
Russian	26	0.26
Scotch-Irish	36	0.35
Scottish	64	0.63
Slovak	19	0.19
Swedish	85	0.84
Ukrainian	8	0.08
United States or American	487	4.79
Welsh	27	0.27
West Indian, excl. Hispanic:	23	0.23
Jamaican	23	0.23
White:	9,988	98.30
Not Hispanic (9,842)	9,936	97.79
Hispanic (34)	52	0.51

Agawam

Place Type: City
County: Hampden
Population: 28,144

Ancestry/Race	Number	%
African American/Black:	307	1.09
Not Hispanic (249)	295	1.05
Hispanic (8)	12	0.04
African, sub-Saharan:	23	0.08
Cape Verdean	23	0.08
Am. Ind. or Alaska Nat., not spec.	55	0.20
American Indian tribes, specified:	54	0.19
Blackfeet (2)	6	0.02
Cherokee	4	0.01
Chippewa (1)	2	0.01
Cree (2)	3	0.01
Iroquois (2)	5	0.02
Latin American Indians (1)	2	0.01
Pueblo	1	0.00
Sioux	1	0.00
All other tribes (12)	30	0.11
American Indian tribes, not spec.	8	0.03
Arab:	356	1.26
Egyptian	17	0.06
Lebanese	314	1.12
Other Arab	25	0.09
Armenian	8	0.03
Asian:	310	1.10
Chinese, ex. Taiwanese (53)	60	0.21
Filipino (10)	13	0.05
Indian (89)	90	0.32
Indonesian (4)	10	0.04
Japanese (27)	30	0.11
Korean (47)	56	0.20
Laotian (7)	7	0.02
Pakistani (7)	7	0.02
Thai (1)	1	0.00
Vietnamese (23)	24	0.09
Other Asian, specified	1	0.00
Other Asian, not specified (5)	11	0.04
Assyrian/Chaldean/Syriac	9	0.03
Austrian	120	0.43
Belgian	23	0.08
British	117	0.42
Canadian	246	0.87
Croatian	31	0.11
Czech	41	0.15
Czechoslovakian	65	0.23
Danish	88	0.31
Dutch	200	0.71
Eastern European	8	0.03
English	2,984	10.60
European	72	0.26
Finnish	79	0.28
French, except Basque	4,839	17.19
French Canadian	2,909	10.34
German	2,143	7.61
Greek	323	1.15
Hawaii Native/Pacific Islander:	16	0.06
Micronesian:	1	0.00
Guamanian/Chamorro	1	0.00
Polynesian: (3)	7	0.02
Native Hawaiian (1)	5	0.02
Samoan (2)	2	0.01
Other Pac. Isl., specified	1	0.00
Other Pac. Isl., not spec.	7	0.02
Hispanic or Latino:	514	1.83
Central American:	26	0.09
Costa Rican	15	0.05
Guatemalan	4	0.01
Honduran	3	0.01
Nicaraguan	1	0.00
Salvadoran	3	0.01
Cuban	19	0.07
Dominican Republic	6	0.02
Mexican	47	0.17
Puerto Rican	266	0.95
South American:	61	0.22
Bolivian	1	0.00
Chilean	1	0.00
Colombian	37	0.13
Ecuadorian	5	0.02
Paraguayan	1	0.00
Peruvian	13	0.05
Venezuelan	1	0.00
Other South American	2	0.01
Other Hispanic or Latino	89	0.32
Hungarian	41	0.15
Iranian	15	0.05
Irish	5,752	20.44
Italian	6,633	23.57
Lithuanian	149	0.53
Northern European	8	0.03
Norwegian	147	0.52
Pennsylvania German	7	0.02
Polish	3,614	12.84
Portuguese	180	0.64
Russian	523	1.86
Scandinavian	16	0.06
Scotch-Irish	369	1.31
Scottish	680	2.42
Slovak	48	0.17
Swedish	495	1.76
Swiss	51	0.18
Ukrainian	152	0.54
United States or American	1,161	4.13
Welsh	121	0.43
West Indian, excl. Hispanic:	60	0.21
Jamaican	60	0.21
White:	27,424	97.44
Not Hispanic (26,871)	27,040	96.08
Hispanic (346)	384	1.36

Amesbury

Place Type: Town
County: Essex
Population: 16,450

Ancestry/Race	Number	%
African American/Black:	157	0.95
Not Hispanic (92)	137	0.83
Hispanic (13)	20	0.12
African, sub-Saharan:	10	0.06
African	4	0.02
Ethiopian	6	0.04
Am. Ind. or Alaska Nat., not spec.	49	0.30
American Indian tribes, specified:	87	0.53
Apache	1	0.01
Blackfeet	8	0.05
Cherokee (2)	21	0.13
Chippewa (1)	1	0.01
Delaware (2)	2	0.01
Iroquois	6	0.04
Latin American Indians (3)	6	0.04
Sioux (1)	1	0.01
Yaqui (3)	3	0.02
All other tribes (13)	38	0.23
American Indian tribes, not spec.	2	0.01
Arab:	65	0.40
Lebanese	56	0.34
Syrian	9	0.05
Armenian	82	0.50
Asian:	126	0.77
Cambodian (4)	4	0.02
Chinese, ex. Taiwanese (39)	41	0.25
Filipino (10)	14	0.09
Indian (10)	13	0.08
Indonesian	2	0.01
Japanese (8)	16	0.10
Korean (8)	9	0.05
Taiwanese (1)	1	0.01
Thai (3)	4	0.02
Vietnamese (9)	18	0.11
Other Asian, not specified (2)	4	0.02
Austrian	28	0.17
Belgian	37	0.23
Brazilian	38	0.23
British	44	0.27
Canadian	105	0.64
Celtic	23	0.14
Croatian	7	0.04
Czech	45	0.27
Czechoslovakian	13	0.08
Danish	20	0.12
Dutch	194	1.18

Notes: 1. Figures in the "Number" column do not add up to the total population due to: a) Ancestry/Race overlap — e.g. persons can report being both White and Irish, b) persons of Hispanic origin can report being any race, c) persons reporting two ancestries are counted in both categories. 2. Numbers in parentheses indicate the number of persons reporting this ancestry/race alone, not in combination with any other ancestry/race. 3. Refer to the Explanation of Data in the front of the book for more detailed information.

Ancestry/Race	Number	%
English	3,030	18.48
European	189	1.15
Finnish	166	1.01
French, except Basque	2,426	14.80
French Canadian	1,553	9.47
German	1,280	7.81
Greek	236	1.44
Hawaii Native/Pacific Islander:	5	0.03
Polynesian: (4)	4	0.02
Native Hawaiian (2)	2	0.01
Samoan (2)	2	0.01
Other Pac. Isl., not spec.	1	0.01
Hispanic or Latino:	156	0.95
Central American:	23	0.14
Guatemalan	3	0.02
Honduran	6	0.04
Nicaraguan	3	0.02
Panamanian	4	0.02
Salvadoran	4	0.02
Other Central American	3	0.02
Cuban	19	0.12
Dominican Republic	8	0.05
Mexican	33	0.20
Puerto Rican	37	0.22
South American:	10	0.06
Chilean	2	0.01
Colombian	4	0.02
Ecuadorian	2	0.01
Peruvian	1	0.01
Other South American	1	0.01
Other Hispanic or Latino	26	0.16
Hungarian	35	0.21
Irish	4,066	24.80
Italian	2,174	13.26
Latvian	10	0.06
Lithuanian	118	0.72
Northern European	17	0.10
Norwegian	99	0.60
Polish	673	4.10
Portuguese	87	0.53
Romanian	10	0.06
Russian	186	1.13
Scandinavian	16	0.10
Scotch-Irish	370	2.26
Scottish	848	5.17
Slovene	7	0.04
Swedish	225	1.37
Swiss	93	0.57
Turkish	8	0.05
Ukrainian	11	0.07
United States or American	655	3.99
Welsh	67	0.41
West Indian, excl. Hispanic:	30	0.18
British West Indian	16	0.10
Jamaican	9	0.05
West Indian	5	0.03
White:	16,157	98.22
Not Hispanic (15,889)	16,043	97.53
Hispanic (99)	114	0.69
Yugoslavian	8	0.05

Amherst Center

Place Type: Census Designated Place
County: Hampshire
Population: 17,050

Ancestry/Race	Number	%
African American/Black:	1,076	6.31
Not Hispanic (824)	992	5.82
Hispanic (54)	84	0.49
African, sub-Saharan:	301	1.75
African	107	0.62
Cape Verdean	79	0.46
Ghanian	12	0.07
Liberian	11	0.06
Nigerian	16	0.09
South African	11	0.06
Sudanese	42	0.24
Other sub-Saharan African	23	0.13
Am. Ind. or Alaska Nat., not spec.	40	0.23
Albanian	19	0.11
Alsatian	11	0.06
American Indian tribes, specified:	90	0.53
Blackfeet	3	0.02
Cherokee (4)	23	0.13
Chippewa (1)	2	0.01
Choctaw	2	0.01
Cree	1	0.01
Creek (1)	1	0.01
Delaware	5	0.03
Iroquois (2)	8	0.05
Latin American Indians (3)	8	0.05
Navajo (1)	1	0.01
Pueblo (2)	2	0.01
Puget Sound Salish (1)	1	0.01
Seminole	1	0.01
Sioux	3	0.02
All other tribes (12)	29	0.17
American Indian tribes, not spec.	17	0.10
Arab:	131	0.76
Egyptian	19	0.11
Jordanian	9	0.05
Lebanese	84	0.49
Palestinian	9	0.05
Syrian	10	0.06
Armenian	57	0.33
Asian:	1,618	9.49
Bangladeshi (4)	4	0.02
Cambodian (81)	82	0.48
Chinese, ex. Taiwanese (448)	534	3.13
Filipino (34)	59	0.35
Hmong (2)	2	0.01
Indian (208)	238	1.40
Indonesian (4)	5	0.03
Japanese (99)	145	0.85
Korean (209)	239	1.40
Laotian (11)	13	0.08
Malaysian	1	0.01
Pakistani (20)	22	0.13
Sri Lankan (12)	12	0.07
Taiwanese (26)	29	0.17
Thai (15)	20	0.12
Vietnamese (119)	132	0.77
Other Asian, specified (6)	13	0.08
Other Asian, not specified (24)	68	0.40
Australian	35	0.20
Austrian	106	0.62
Belgian	30	0.17
Brazilian	25	0.15
British	123	0.72
Canadian	64	0.37
Croatian	10	0.06
Czech	20	0.12
Czechoslovakian	17	0.10
Danish	81	0.47
Dutch	215	1.25
Eastern European	130	0.76
English	2,063	12.03
Estonian	20	0.12
European	264	1.54
Finnish	51	0.30
French, except Basque	885	5.16
French Canadian	560	3.26
German	1,664	9.70
Greek	113	0.66
Hawaii Native/Pacific Islander:	33	0.19
Micronesian: (3)	4	0.02
Guamanian/Chamorro (3)	4	0.02
Polynesian: (6)	14	0.08
Native Hawaiian (3)	7	0.04
Samoan (3)	7	0.04
Other Pac. Isl., not spec. (2)	15	0.09
Hispanic or Latino:	916	5.37
Central American:	58	0.34
Costa Rican	7	0.04
Guatemalan	8	0.05
Honduran	7	0.04
Nicaraguan	2	0.01
Panamanian	8	0.05
Salvadoran	17	0.10
Other Central American	9	0.05
Cuban	55	0.32
Dominican Republic	67	0.39
Mexican	88	0.52
Puerto Rican	374	2.19
South American:	112	0.66
Argentinean	17	0.10
Bolivian	1	0.01
Chilean	20	0.12
Colombian	39	0.23
Ecuadorian	7	0.04
Paraguayan	1	0.01
Peruvian	14	0.08
Uruguayan	4	0.02
Venezuelan	6	0.04
Other South American	3	0.02
Other Hispanic or Latino	162	0.95
Hungarian	145	0.85
Iranian	64	0.37
Irish	3,726	21.72
Israeli	64	0.37
Italian	1,997	11.64
Latvian	31	0.18
Lithuanian	136	0.79
Luxemburger	4	0.02
Northern European	16	0.09
Norwegian	166	0.97
Polish	1,206	7.03
Portuguese	258	1.50
Romanian	23	0.13
Russian	755	4.40
Scandinavian	81	0.47
Scotch-Irish	264	1.54
Scottish	591	3.45
Slavic	18	0.10
Slovak	5	0.03
Swedish	499	2.91
Swiss	48	0.28
Turkish	36	0.21
Ukrainian	80	0.47
United States or American	246	1.43
Welsh	150	0.87
West Indian, excl. Hispanic:	149	0.87
Barbadian	12	0.07
British West Indian	10	0.06
Haitian	42	0.24
Jamaican	49	0.29
Trinidadian and Tobagonian	10	0.06
U.S. Virgin Islander	11	0.06
West Indian	15	0.09
White:	14,216	83.38
Not Hispanic (13,400)	13,727	80.51
Hispanic (410)	489	2.87
Yugoslavian	25	0.15

Amherst

Place Type: Town
County: Hampshire
Population: 34,874

Ancestry/Race	Number	%
African American/Black:	2,233	6.40
Not Hispanic (1,648)	2,024	5.80
Hispanic (132)	209	0.60
African, sub-Saharan:	469	1.34
African	162	0.46
Cape Verdean	89	0.26
Ghanian	32	0.09
Liberian	11	0.03
Nigerian	87	0.25
South African	16	0.05
Sudanese	42	0.12
Other sub-Saharan African	30	0.09
Alaska Native tribes, specified:	1	0.00
Eskimo (1)	1	0.00
Am. Ind. or Alaska Nat., not spec.	89	0.26
Albanian	19	0.05
Alsatian	11	0.03

Notes: 1. Figures in the "Number" column do not add up to the total population due to: a) Ancestry/Race overlap — e.g. persons can report being both White and Irish, b) persons of Hispanic origin can report being any race, c) persons reporting two ancestries are counted in both categories. 2. Numbers in parentheses indicate the number of persons reporting this ancestry/race alone, not in combination with any other ancestry/race. 3. Refer to the Explanation of Data in the front of the book for more detailed information.

American Indian tribes, specified:	192	0.55
Apache (1)	2	0.01
Blackfeet (2)	11	0.03
Cherokee (5)	45	0.13
Cheyenne	1	0.00
Chickasaw	1	0.00
Chippewa (3)	6	0.02
Choctaw	3	0.01
Cree	1	0.00
Creek (1)	1	0.00
Delaware	7	0.02
Iroquois (4)	13	0.04
Latin American Indians (7)	28	0.08
Navajo (2)	2	0.01
Pueblo (2)	3	0.01
Puget Sound Salish (1)	1	0.00
Seminole	1	0.00
Shoshone (5)	5	0.01
Sioux (1)	4	0.01
All other tribes (14)	57	0.16
American Indian tribes, not spec.	30	0.09
Arab:	259	0.74
Arab/Arabic	30	0.09
Egyptian	25	0.07
Iraqi	75	0.22
Jordanian	9	0.03
Lebanese	89	0.26
Palestinian	21	0.06
Syrian	10	0.03
Armenian	141	0.40
Asian:	3,665	10.51
Bangladeshi (10)	10	0.03
Cambodian (212)	249	0.71
Chinese, ex. Taiwanese (1,125)	1,280	3.67
Filipino (73)	118	0.34
Hmong (2)	2	0.01
Indian (556)	621	1.78
Indonesian (14)	15	0.04
Japanese (205)	292	0.84
Korean (448)	501	1.44
Laotian (11)	13	0.04
Malaysian (4)	11	0.03
Pakistani (40)	49	0.14
Sri Lankan (19)	21	0.06
Taiwanese (63)	67	0.19
Thai (22)	27	0.08
Vietnamese (188)	220	0.63
Other Asian, specified (11)	27	0.08
Other Asian, not specified (62)	142	0.41
Australian	35	0.10
Austrian	240	0.69
Basque	12	0.03
Belgian	40	0.11
Brazilian	54	0.15
British	309	0.89
Canadian	193	0.55
Celtic	50	0.14
Croatian	16	0.05
Czech	88	0.25
Czechoslovakian	47	0.13
Danish	111	0.32
Dutch	409	1.17
Eastern European	263	0.75
English	4,325	12.40
Estonian	32	0.09
European	574	1.65
Finnish	122	0.35
French, except Basque	1,812	5.20
French Canadian	1,404	4.03
German	3,522	10.10
Greek	172	0.49
Hawaii Native/Pacific Islander:	74	0.21
Melanesian: (7)	7	0.02
Other Melanesian (7)	7	0.02
Micronesian: (3)	4	0.01
Guamanian/Chamorro (3)	4	0.01
Polynesian: (17)	34	0.10
Native Hawaiian (3)	15	0.04
Samoan (13)	17	0.05
Other Polynesian (1)	2	0.01
Other Pac. Isl., specified	2	0.01
Other Pac. Isl., not spec. (6)	27	0.08
Hispanic or Latino:	2,159	6.19
Central American:	189	0.54
Costa Rican	9	0.03
Guatemalan	30	0.09
Honduran	14	0.04
Nicaraguan	2	0.01
Panamanian	18	0.05
Salvadoran	90	0.26
Other Central American	26	0.07
Cuban	92	0.26
Dominican Republic	97	0.28
Mexican	189	0.54
Puerto Rican	983	2.82
South American:	231	0.66
Argentinean	39	0.11
Bolivian	7	0.02
Chilean	30	0.09
Colombian	83	0.24
Ecuadorian	18	0.05
Paraguayan	1	0.00
Peruvian	24	0.07
Uruguayan	4	0.01
Venezuelan	13	0.04
Other South American	12	0.03
Other Hispanic or Latino	378	1.08
Hungarian	265	0.76
Iranian	103	0.30
Irish	6,784	19.45
Israeli	85	0.24
Italian	3,394	9.73
Latvian	31	0.09
Lithuanian	376	1.08
Luxemburger	10	0.03
New Zealander	9	0.03
Northern European	30	0.09
Norwegian	270	0.77
Polish	2,304	6.61
Portuguese	491	1.41
Romanian	51	0.15
Russian	1,368	3.92
Scandinavian	81	0.23
Scotch-Irish	682	1.96
Scottish	1,076	3.09
Slavic	27	0.08
Slovak	72	0.21
Slovene	23	0.07
Swedish	891	2.55
Swiss	78	0.22
Turkish	141	0.40
Ukrainian	123	0.35
United States or American	578	1.66
Welsh	266	0.76
West Indian, excl. Hispanic:	230	0.66
Barbadian	12	0.03
British West Indian	10	0.03
Dutch West Indian	8	0.02
Haitian	94	0.27
Jamaican	63	0.18
Trinidadian and Tobagonian	10	0.03
U.S. Virgin Islander	11	0.03
West Indian	22	0.06
White:	28,608	82.03
Not Hispanic (26,740)	27,506	78.87
Hispanic (925)	1,102	3.16
Yugoslavian	67	0.19

Andover

Place Type: Town
County: Essex
Population: 31,247

Ancestry/Race	Number	%
Acadian/Cajun	7	0.02
African American/Black:	283	0.91
Not Hispanic (221)	270	0.86
Hispanic (13)	13	0.04
African, sub-Saharan:	90	0.29
African	16	0.05
Cape Verdean	74	0.24
Alaska Native tribes, specified:	3	0.01
Aleut	3	0.01
Am. Ind. or Alaska Nat., not spec.	29	0.09
Albanian	14	0.04
Alsatian	23	0.07
American Indian tribes, specified:	27	0.09
Cherokee	6	0.02
Chippewa (1)	1	0.00
Iroquois (3)	3	0.01
Latin American Indians (2)	2	0.01
Menominee	1	0.00
Navajo	1	0.00
Potawatomi	1	0.00
All other tribes	12	0.04
American Indian tribes, not spec.	3	0.01
Arab:	433	1.39
Arab/Arabic	17	0.05
Egyptian	49	0.16
Iraqi	8	0.03
Lebanese	301	0.96
Syrian	58	0.19
Armenian	292	0.93
Asian:	1,996	6.39
Bangladeshi (3)	3	0.01
Cambodian	1	0.00
Chinese, ex. Taiwanese (726)	785	2.51
Filipino (33)	49	0.16
Indian (485)	535	1.71
Indonesian (2)	2	0.01
Japanese (96)	132	0.42
Korean (286)	306	0.98
Laotian (5)	5	0.02
Malaysian (1)	4	0.01
Pakistani (19)	23	0.07
Sri Lankan (11)	12	0.04
Taiwanese (51)	57	0.18
Thai (6)	6	0.02
Vietnamese (38)	41	0.13
Other Asian, not specified (9)	35	0.11
Australian	23	0.07
Austrian	131	0.42
Belgian	120	0.38
Brazilian	8	0.03
British	232	0.74
Canadian	262	0.84
Celtic	9	0.03
Croatian	6	0.02
Czech	62	0.20
Danish	128	0.41
Dutch	342	1.09
Eastern European	206	0.66
English	4,705	15.06
Estonian	26	0.08
European	300	0.96
Finnish	124	0.40
French, except Basque	1,778	5.69
French Canadian	1,231	3.94
German	2,714	8.69
Greek	548	1.75
Hawaii Native/Pacific Islander:	34	0.11
Micronesian:	2	0.01
Guamanian/Chamorro	1	0.00
Other Micronesian	1	0.00
Polynesian: (10)	19	0.06
Native Hawaiian (3)	11	0.04
Samoan (7)	8	0.03
Other Pac. Isl., not spec. (1)	13	0.04
Hispanic or Latino:	567	1.81
Central American:	15	0.05
Costa Rican	3	0.01
Guatemalan	2	0.01
Nicaraguan	1	0.00
Panamanian	2	0.01
Salvadoran	6	0.02
Other Central American	1	0.00
Cuban	59	0.19
Dominican Republic	72	0.23
Mexican	65	0.21

Notes: 1. Figures in the "Number" column do not add up to the total population due to: a) Ancestry/Race overlap — e.g. persons can report being both White and Irish, b) persons of Hispanic origin can report being any race, c) persons reporting two ancestries are counted in both categories. 2. Numbers in parentheses indicate the number of persons reporting this ancestry/race alone, not in combination with any other ancestry/race. 3. Refer to the Explanation of Data in the front of the book for more detailed information.

Puerto Rican	169	0.54
South American:	62	0.20
Argentinean	5	0.02
Bolivian	2	0.01
Chilean	4	0.01
Colombian	29	0.09
Ecuadorian	3	0.01
Paraguayan	1	0.00
Peruvian	7	0.02
Venezuelan	7	0.02
Other South American	4	0.01
Other Hispanic or Latino	125	0.40
Hungarian	210	0.67
Icelander	11	0.04
Iranian	52	0.17
Irish	7,094	22.70
Israeli	21	0.07
Italian	4,777	15.29
Latvian	8	0.03
Lithuanian	362	1.16
Luxemburger	8	0.03
Northern European	15	0.05
Norwegian	175	0.56
Polish	1,457	4.66
Portuguese	358	1.15
Romanian	29	0.09
Russian	1,059	3.39
Scandinavian	63	0.20
Scotch-Irish	697	2.23
Scottish	1,074	3.44
Slavic	7	0.02
Slovak	28	0.09
Swedish	776	2.48
Swiss	62	0.20
Turkish	28	0.09
Ukrainian	181	0.58
United States or American	1,124	3.60
Welsh	322	1.03
West Indian, excl. Hispanic:	55	0.18
Bahamian	5	0.02
Haitian	7	0.02
Jamaican	43	0.14
White:	28,882	92.43
Not Hispanic (28,326)	28,568	91.43
Hispanic (295)	314	1.00
Yugoslavian	5	0.02

Arlington

Place Type: Census Designated Place
County: Middlesex
Population: 42,389

Ancestry/Race	Number	%
African American/Black:	935	2.21
Not Hispanic (690)	885	2.09
Hispanic (29)	50	0.12
African, sub-Saharan:	247	0.58
African	46	0.11
Cape Verdean	45	0.11
Ethiopian	27	0.06
Liberian	9	0.02
Nigerian	17	0.04
South African	30	0.07
Ugandan	73	0.17
Am. Ind. or Alaska Nat., not spec.	41	0.10
Albanian	106	0.25
American Indian tribes, specified:	83	0.20
Apache (1)	4	0.01
Blackfeet	4	0.01
Cherokee (7)	19	0.04
Cree	1	0.00
Creek (2)	2	0.00
Crow	1	0.00
Delaware (1)	1	0.00
Iroquois (5)	7	0.02
Latin American Indians (7)	12	0.03
Navajo	4	0.01
Sioux (1)	2	0.00
All other tribes (9)	26	0.06
American Indian tribes, not spec.	10	0.02
Arab:	379	0.89
Arab/Arabic	46	0.11
Egyptian	53	0.13
Lebanese	109	0.26
Palestinian	11	0.03
Syrian	120	0.28
Other Arab	40	0.09
Armenian	763	1.80
Asian:	2,416	5.70
Bangladeshi (10)	11	0.03
Cambodian (16)	18	0.04
Chinese, ex. Taiwanese (842)	947	2.23
Filipino (94)	132	0.31
Indian (470)	520	1.23
Indonesian (8)	11	0.03
Japanese (246)	291	0.69
Korean (223)	238	0.56
Laotian (1)	1	0.00
Malaysian (3)	5	0.01
Pakistani (26)	31	0.07
Sri Lankan (9)	9	0.02
Taiwanese (18)	28	0.07
Thai (23)	33	0.08
Vietnamese (52)	61	0.14
Other Asian, specified (22)	28	0.07
Other Asian, not specified (20)	52	0.12
Assyrian/Chaldean/Syriac	30	0.07
Australian	10	0.02
Austrian	284	0.67
Belgian	55	0.13
Brazilian	52	0.12
British	318	0.75
Bulgarian	9	0.02
Canadian	529	1.25
Celtic	30	0.07
Croatian	24	0.06
Cypriot	24	0.06
Czech	193	0.46
Czechoslovakian	73	0.17
Danish	248	0.59
Dutch	412	0.97
Eastern European	248	0.59
English	5,075	11.97
European	287	0.68
Finnish	94	0.22
French, except Basque	1,655	3.90
French Canadian	1,478	3.49
German	3,499	8.25
Greek	1,418	3.35
Guyanese	20	0.05
Hawaii Native/Pacific Islander:	25	0.06
Micronesian: (2)	3	0.01
Guamanian/Chamorro (2)	3	0.01
Polynesian: (3)	10	0.02
Native Hawaiian (1)	6	0.01
Samoan (2)	3	0.01
Tongan	1	0.00
Other Pac. Isl., not spec. (1)	12	0.03
Hispanic or Latino:	787	1.86
Central American:	77	0.18
Costa Rican	4	0.01
Guatemalan	28	0.07
Honduran	10	0.02
Nicaraguan	6	0.01
Panamanian	12	0.03
Salvadoran	7	0.02
Other Central American	10	0.02
Cuban	49	0.12
Dominican Republic	23	0.05
Mexican	121	0.29
Puerto Rican	125	0.29
South American:	207	0.49
Argentinean	38	0.09
Bolivian	12	0.03
Chilean	31	0.07
Colombian	51	0.12
Ecuadorian	11	0.03
Paraguayan	5	0.01
Peruvian	16	0.04
Uruguayan	2	0.00
Venezuelan	8	0.02
Other South American	33	0.08
Other Hispanic or Latino	185	0.44
Hungarian	177	0.42
Iranian	48	0.11
Irish	12,394	29.24
Israeli	26	0.06
Italian	6,622	15.62
Latvian	56	0.13
Lithuanian	328	0.77
Maltese	2	0.00
Northern European	49	0.12
Norwegian	285	0.67
Pennsylvania German	18	0.04
Polish	1,307	3.08
Portuguese	1,177	2.78
Romanian	103	0.24
Russian	975	2.30
Scandinavian	77	0.18
Scotch-Irish	1,075	2.54
Scottish	1,081	2.55
Serbian	37	0.09
Slavic	17	0.04
Slovak	114	0.27
Slovene	21	0.05
Swedish	782	1.84
Swiss	189	0.45
Ukrainian	144	0.34
United States or American	1,611	3.80
Welsh	338	0.80
West Indian, excl. Hispanic:	164	0.39
Barbadian	6	0.01
Dutch West Indian	14	0.03
Haitian	79	0.19
Jamaican	24	0.06
Trinidadian and Tobagonian	24	0.06
West Indian	17	0.04
White:	39,115	92.28
Not Hispanic (38,058)	38,556	90.96
Hispanic (503)	559	1.32
Yugoslavian	40	0.09

Ashland

Place Type: Town
County: Middlesex
Population: 14,674

Ancestry/Race	Number	%
African American/Black:	347	2.36
Not Hispanic (250)	327	2.23
Hispanic (12)	20	0.14
African, sub-Saharan:	15	0.10
Ghanian	15	0.10
Am. Ind. or Alaska Nat., not spec.	27	0.18
Albanian	48	0.33
American Indian tribes, specified:	25	0.17
Apache	2	0.01
Blackfeet	4	0.03
Cherokee (4)	5	0.03
Choctaw	1	0.01
Cree	1	0.01
Iroquois (2)	2	0.01
Paiute	1	0.01
Potawatomi (1)	1	0.01
All other tribes (4)	8	0.05
American Indian tribes, not spec.	3	0.02
Arab:	72	0.49
Lebanese	72	0.49
Armenian	141	0.96
Asian:	436	2.97
Chinese, ex. Taiwanese (113)	134	0.91
Filipino (25)	34	0.23
Indian (157)	178	1.21
Indonesian (3)	6	0.04
Japanese (16)	21	0.14
Korean (24)	29	0.20
Malaysian (1)	2	0.01
Pakistani (4)	4	0.03

Notes: 1. Figures in the "Number" column do not add up to the total population due to: a) Ancestry/Race overlap — e.g. persons can report being both White and Irish, b) persons of Hispanic origin can report being any race, c) persons reporting two ancestries are counted in both categories. 2. Numbers in parentheses indicate the number of persons reporting this ancestry/race alone, not in combination with any other ancestry/race. 3. Refer to the Explanation of Data in the front of the book for more detailed information.

Ancestry/Race	Number	%
Taiwanese (4)	4	0.03
Vietnamese (11)	12	0.08
Other Asian, specified (2)	4	0.03
Other Asian, not specified (1)	8	0.05
Austrian	50	0.34
Belgian	3	0.02
Brazilian	207	1.41
British	63	0.43
Canadian	185	1.26
Celtic	8	0.05
Croatian	16	0.11
Czech	18	0.12
Czechoslovakian	4	0.03
Danish	93	0.63
Dutch	162	1.10
Eastern European	62	0.42
English	2,293	15.63
European	128	0.87
Finnish	32	0.22
French, except Basque	827	5.64
French Canadian	469	3.20
German	945	6.44
Greek	286	1.95
Hawaii Native/Pacific Islander:	4	0.03
Polynesian: (1)	1	0.01
Native Hawaiian (1)	1	0.01
Other Pac. Isl., not spec. (3)	3	0.02
Hispanic or Latino:	428	2.92
Central American:	28	0.19
Costa Rican	1	0.01
Guatemalan	16	0.11
Nicaraguan	1	0.01
Salvadoran	9	0.06
Other Central American	1	0.01
Cuban	16	0.11
Dominican Republic	10	0.07
Mexican	34	0.23
Puerto Rican	132	0.90
South American:	74	0.50
Argentinean	5	0.03
Bolivian	8	0.05
Chilean	8	0.05
Colombian	25	0.17
Paraguayan	1	0.01
Peruvian	9	0.06
Uruguayan	6	0.04
Venezuelan	4	0.03
Other South American	8	0.05
Other Hispanic or Latino	134	0.91
Hungarian	49	0.33
Iranian	41	0.28
Irish	3,626	24.71
Italian	2,979	20.30
Lithuanian	72	0.49
Norwegian	111	0.76
Pennsylvania German	23	0.16
Polish	548	3.73
Portuguese	261	1.78
Romanian	27	0.18
Russian	601	4.10
Scandinavian	7	0.05
Scotch-Irish	248	1.69
Scottish	416	2.83
Serbian	11	0.07
Slavic	17	0.12
Slovak	15	0.10
Swedish	317	2.16
Swiss	21	0.14
Ukrainian	59	0.40
United States or American	792	5.40
Welsh	25	0.17
West Indian, excl. Hispanic:	32	0.22
Jamaican	32	0.22
White:	13,748	93.69
Not Hispanic (13,226)	13,458	91.71
Hispanic (256)	290	1.98
Yugoslavian	22	0.15

Athol

Place Type: Town
County: Worcester
Population: 11,299

Ancestry/Race	Number	%
Acadian/Cajun	11	0.10
African American/Black:	103	0.91
Not Hispanic (72)	93	0.82
Hispanic (2)	10	0.09
African, sub-Saharan:	31	0.27
African	6	0.05
Cape Verdean	25	0.22
Am. Ind. or Alaska Nat., not spec.	50	0.44
American Indian tribes, specified:	59	0.52
Apache (5)	5	0.04
Blackfeet	3	0.03
Cherokee (5)	15	0.13
Cree	1	0.01
Crow	9	0.08
Iroquois (3)	5	0.04
Seminole	1	0.01
All other tribes (10)	20	0.18
American Indian tribes, not spec.	5	0.04
Arab:	33	0.29
Lebanese	33	0.29
Asian:	71	0.63
Cambodian (1)	1	0.01
Chinese, ex. Taiwanese (9)	11	0.10
Filipino (13)	23	0.20
Indian (5)	6	0.05
Japanese (5)	5	0.04
Korean (6)	11	0.10
Laotian (1)	2	0.02
Thai	2	0.02
Vietnamese	4	0.04
Other Asian, not specified (6)	6	0.05
Austrian	57	0.50
British	15	0.13
Canadian	161	1.42
Celtic	5	0.04
Croatian	5	0.04
Danish	13	0.12
Dutch	69	0.61
English	1,825	16.15
Finnish	171	1.51
French, except Basque	2,331	20.63
French Canadian	1,419	12.56
German	580	5.13
Greek	116	1.03
Guyanese	5	0.04
Hawaii Native/Pacific Islander:	10	0.09
Micronesian: (1)	2	0.02
Guamanian/Chamorro (1)	2	0.02
Polynesian: (1)	2	0.02
Native Hawaiian (1)	1	0.01
Samoan	1	0.01
Other Pac. Isl., not spec. (1)	6	0.05
Hispanic or Latino:	222	1.96
Central American:	6	0.05
Honduran	1	0.01
Nicaraguan	1	0.01
Panamanian	3	0.03
Salvadoran	1	0.01
Cuban	2	0.02
Dominican Republic	14	0.12
Mexican	23	0.20
Puerto Rican	143	1.27
South American:	6	0.05
Colombian	4	0.04
Peruvian	1	0.01
Venezuelan	1	0.01
Other Hispanic or Latino	28	0.25
Irish	1,464	12.96
Italian	1,320	11.68
Lithuanian	399	3.53
Norwegian	59	0.52
Polish	574	5.08
Portuguese	55	0.49
Russian	26	0.23
Scandinavian	3	0.03
Scotch-Irish	143	1.27
Scottish	355	3.14
Swedish	192	1.70
Swiss	12	0.11
Ukrainian	33	0.29
United States or American	484	4.28
Welsh	27	0.24
West Indian, excl. Hispanic:	6	0.05
Barbadian	6	0.05
White:	11,042	97.73
Not Hispanic (10,771)	10,912	96.57
Hispanic (113)	130	1.15
Yugoslavian	6	0.05

Attleboro

Place Type: City
County: Bristol
Population: 42,068

Ancestry/Race	Number	%
African American/Black:	861	2.05
Not Hispanic (665)	814	1.93
Hispanic (26)	47	0.11
African, sub-Saharan:	346	0.82
African	107	0.25
Cape Verdean	239	0.57
Alaska Native tribes, specified:	4	0.01
Eskimo	2	0.00
Tlingit-Haida	2	0.00
Am. Ind. or Alaska Nat., not spec.	81	0.19
Albanian	30	0.07
American Indian tribes, specified:	162	0.39
Apache	4	0.01
Blackfeet (1)	25	0.06
Cherokee (5)	23	0.05
Cheyenne (1)	1	0.00
Chippewa (2)	4	0.01
Choctaw (1)	1	0.00
Iroquois (3)	14	0.03
Latin American Indians	3	0.01
Navajo	4	0.01
Pueblo (3)	3	0.01
Seminole	4	0.01
Sioux (1)	2	0.00
Ute	1	0.00
All other tribes (23)	73	0.17
American Indian tribes, not spec.	14	0.03
Arab:	320	0.76
Arab/Arabic	16	0.04
Egyptian	6	0.01
Lebanese	197	0.47
Moroccan	5	0.01
Palestinian	8	0.02
Syrian	88	0.21
Armenian	214	0.51
Asian:	1,659	3.94
Cambodian (541)	643	1.53
Chinese, ex. Taiwanese (120)	147	0.35
Filipino (48)	70	0.17
Hmong (3)	3	0.01
Indian (359)	415	0.99
Indonesian	2	0.00
Japanese (28)	41	0.10
Korean (47)	69	0.16
Laotian (6)	13	0.03
Malaysian (1)	1	0.00
Pakistani (12)	12	0.03
Taiwanese (1)	1	0.00
Thai (15)	25	0.06
Vietnamese (103)	117	0.28
Other Asian, specified	8	0.02
Other Asian, not specified (44)	92	0.22
Assyrian/Chaldean/Syriac	26	0.06
Australian	12	0.03
Austrian	29	0.07
Belgian	21	0.05
Brazilian	39	0.09

Notes: 1. Figures in the "Number" column do not add up to the total population due to: a) Ancestry/Race overlap — e.g. persons can report being both White and Irish, b) persons of Hispanic origin can report being any race, c) persons reporting two ancestries are counted in both categories. 2. Numbers in parentheses indicate the number of persons reporting this ancestry/race alone, not in combination with any other ancestry/race. 3. Refer to the Explanation of Data in the front of the book for more detailed information.

Ancestry/Race	Number	%
British	148	0.35
Canadian	270	0.64
Celtic	20	0.05
Croatian	102	0.24
Czech	11	0.03
Czechoslovakian	12	0.03
Danish	108	0.26
Dutch	208	0.49
English	6,084	14.46
European	169	0.40
Finnish	86	0.20
French, except Basque	6,310	15.00
French Canadian	3,627	8.62
German	2,115	5.03
Greek	242	0.58
Hawaii Native/Pacific Islander:	67	0.16
Melanesian:	2	0.00
Fijian	2	0.00
Micronesian: (7)	10	0.02
Guamanian/Chamorro (6)	8	0.02
Other Micronesian (1)	2	0.00
Polynesian: (8)	12	0.03
Native Hawaiian (3)	7	0.02
Samoan (2)	2	0.00
Tongan (3)	3	0.01
Other Pac. Isl., specified	8	0.02
Other Pac. Isl., not spec.	35	0.08
Hispanic or Latino:	1,805	4.29
Central American:	559	1.33
Costa Rican	4	0.01
Guatemalan	489	1.16
Honduran	4	0.01
Panamanian	1	0.00
Salvadoran	43	0.10
Other Central American	18	0.04
Cuban	16	0.04
Dominican Republic	38	0.09
Mexican	144	0.34
Puerto Rican	593	1.41
South American:	80	0.19
Argentinean	3	0.01
Chilean	2	0.00
Colombian	38	0.09
Ecuadorian	15	0.04
Peruvian	3	0.01
Venezuelan	11	0.03
Other South American	8	0.02
Other Hispanic or Latino	375	0.89
Hungarian	125	0.30
Iranian	7	0.02
Irish	8,933	21.23
Italian	4,356	10.35
Latvian	25	0.06
Lithuanian	67	0.16
New Zealander	11	0.03
Northern European	37	0.09
Norwegian	211	0.50
Pennsylvania German	7	0.02
Polish	1,716	4.08
Portuguese	3,851	9.15
Romanian	24	0.06
Russian	344	0.82
Scandinavian	58	0.14
Scotch-Irish	543	1.29
Scottish	1,136	2.70
Slovak	42	0.10
Swedish	903	2.15
Swiss	60	0.14
Turkish	21	0.05
Ukrainian	15	0.04
United States or American	1,855	4.41
Welsh	122	0.29
West Indian, excl. Hispanic:	23	0.05
Haitian	12	0.03
Trinidadian and Tobagonian	11	0.03
White:	38,987	92.68
Not Hispanic (37,467)	37,928	90.16
Hispanic (943)	1,059	2.52
Yugoslavian	13	0.03

Auburn

Place Type: Town
County: Worcester
Population: 15,901

Ancestry/Race	Number	%
African American/Black:	116	0.73
Not Hispanic (89)	111	0.70
Hispanic (3)	5	0.03
African, sub-Saharan:	35	0.22
African	35	0.22
Alaska Native tribes, specified:	1	0.01
Tlingit-Haida (1)	1	0.01
Am. Ind. or Alaska Nat., not spec.	23	0.14
Albanian	67	0.42
American Indian tribes, specified:	18	0.11
Blackfeet	2	0.01
Cherokee (1)	2	0.01
Cree	2	0.01
Navajo	2	0.01
Sioux	1	0.01
All other tribes (4)	9	0.06
Arab:	134	0.84
Arab/Arabic	28	0.18
Lebanese	81	0.51
Other Arab	25	0.16
Armenian	169	1.06
Asian:	168	1.06
Chinese, ex. Taiwanese (19)	21	0.13
Filipino (6)	8	0.05
Indian (11)	16	0.10
Indonesian	1	0.01
Japanese (2)	3	0.02
Korean (20)	23	0.14
Laotian (1)	1	0.01
Pakistani (13)	13	0.08
Taiwanese (1)	1	0.01
Thai (1)	1	0.01
Vietnamese (68)	68	0.43
Other Asian, not specified	12	0.08
Austrian	22	0.14
Brazilian	8	0.05
British	47	0.30
Canadian	117	0.74
Czech	4	0.03
Czechoslovakian	29	0.18
Danish	72	0.45
Dutch	119	0.75
English	2,138	13.45
European	27	0.17
Finnish	115	0.72
French, except Basque	3,000	18.87
French Canadian	1,330	8.36
German	850	5.35
Greek	95	0.60
Hawaii Native/Pacific Islander:	12	0.08
Polynesian: (3)	9	0.06
Native Hawaiian (2)	6	0.04
Samoan (1)	1	0.01
Other Polynesian	2	0.01
Other Pac. Isl., not spec. (1)	3	0.02
Hispanic or Latino:	166	1.04
Central American:	14	0.09
Honduran	4	0.03
Salvadoran	6	0.04
Other Central American	4	0.03
Cuban	8	0.05
Dominican Republic	7	0.04
Mexican	18	0.11
Puerto Rican	66	0.42
South American:	23	0.14
Argentinean	3	0.02
Colombian	13	0.08
Ecuadorian	1	0.01
Peruvian	1	0.01
Other South American	5	0.03
Other Hispanic or Latino	30	0.19
Hungarian	41	0.26
Iranian	6	0.04
Irish	4,146	26.07
Italian	2,411	15.16
Latvian	6	0.04
Lithuanian	464	2.92
Norwegian	73	0.46
Polish	1,260	7.92
Portuguese	56	0.35
Romanian	41	0.26
Russian	146	0.92
Scandinavian	8	0.05
Scotch-Irish	181	1.14
Scottish	265	1.67
Slovak	7	0.04
Slovene	5	0.03
Swedish	1,299	8.17
Ukrainian	32	0.20
United States or American	635	3.99
Welsh	13	0.08
White:	15,600	98.11
Not Hispanic (15,395)	15,469	97.28
Hispanic (115)	131	0.82
Yugoslavian	5	0.03

Barnstable Town

Place Type: City
County: Barnstable
Population: 47,821

Ancestry/Race	Number	%
Acadian/Cajun	22	0.05
African American/Black:	1,695	3.54
Not Hispanic (1,271)	1,634	3.42
Hispanic (38)	61	0.13
African, sub-Saharan:	954	1.99
African	47	0.10
Cape Verdean	857	1.79
South African	50	0.10
Alaska Native tribes, specified:	3	0.01
Aleut (1)	1	0.00
Eskimo	1	0.00
Tlingit-Haida (1)	1	0.00
Am. Ind. or Alaska Nat., not spec.	157	0.33
Albanian	62	0.13
American Indian tribes, specified:	341	0.71
Apache (1)	7	0.01
Blackfeet (1)	17	0.04
Cherokee (20)	42	0.09
Chickasaw (4)	5	0.01
Chippewa (1)	2	0.00
Choctaw	1	0.00
Creek	1	0.00
Iroquois (1)	10	0.02
Latin American Indians (8)	10	0.02
Lumbee (1)	1	0.00
Navajo (4)	4	0.01
Osage	1	0.00
Paiute (1)	1	0.00
Puget Sound Salish (1)	1	0.00
Seminole (1)	1	0.00
Shoshone	1	0.00
Sioux (1)	2	0.00
Yuman (1)	1	0.00
All other tribes (149)	233	0.49
American Indian tribes, not spec.	21	0.04
Arab:	200	0.42
Arab/Arabic	5	0.01
Lebanese	97	0.20
Palestinian	25	0.05
Syrian	42	0.09
Other Arab	31	0.06
Armenian	189	0.40
Asian:	513	1.07
Cambodian (2)	2	0.00
Chinese, ex. Taiwanese (101)	112	0.23
Filipino (32)	50	0.10
Indian (81)	101	0.21
Japanese (21)	37	0.08
Korean (42)	60	0.13
Laotian (8)	16	0.03

Notes: 1. Figures in the "Number" column do not add up to the total population due to: a) Ancestry/Race overlap — e.g. persons can report being both White and Irish, b) persons of Hispanic origin can report being any race, c) persons reporting two ancestries are counted in both categories. 2. Numbers in parentheses indicate the number of persons reporting this ancestry/race alone, not in combination with any other ancestry/race. 3. Refer to the Explanation of Data in the front of the book for more detailed information.

Ancestry/Race	Number	%
Malaysian (1)	1	0.00
Pakistani (28)	38	0.08
Thai (4)	18	0.04
Vietnamese (31)	31	0.06
Other Asian, specified (22)	23	0.05
Other Asian, not specified (11)	24	0.05
Assyrian/Chaldean/Syriac	3	0.01
Austrian	166	0.35
Belgian	39	0.08
Brazilian	930	1.94
British	289	0.60
Bulgarian	6	0.01
Canadian	366	0.77
Celtic	19	0.04
Croatian	57	0.12
Czech	75	0.16
Czechoslovakian	80	0.17
Danish	168	0.35
Dutch	365	0.76
Eastern European	96	0.20
English	8,449	17.67
Estonian	9	0.02
European	170	0.36
Finnish	688	1.44
French, except Basque	3,055	6.39
French Canadian	1,937	4.05
German	3,766	7.88
Greek	619	1.29
Guyanese	20	0.04
Hawaii Native/Pacific Islander:	37	0.08
Micronesian: (5)	6	0.01
Guamanian/Chamorro (5)	6	0.01
Polynesian: (9)	16	0.03
Native Hawaiian (3)	9	0.02
Samoan (2)	2	0.00
Other Polynesian (4)	5	0.01
Other Pac. Isl., specified	1	0.00
Other Pac. Isl., not spec. (4)	14	0.03
Hispanic or Latino:	812	1.70
Central American:	52	0.11
Costa Rican	4	0.01
Guatemalan	4	0.01
Honduran	11	0.02
Nicaraguan	1	0.00
Salvadoran	29	0.06
Other Central American	3	0.01
Cuban	38	0.08
Dominican Republic	46	0.10
Mexican	105	0.22
Puerto Rican	257	0.54
South American:	64	0.13
Argentinean	5	0.01
Bolivian	2	0.00
Chilean	5	0.01
Colombian	16	0.03
Ecuadorian	20	0.04
Peruvian	5	0.01
Venezuelan	1	0.00
Other South American	10	0.02
Other Hispanic or Latino	250	0.52
Hungarian	101	0.21
Iranian	7	0.01
Irish	13,450	28.13
Italian	5,297	11.08
Latvian	68	0.14
Lithuanian	389	0.81
Northern European	30	0.06
Norwegian	393	0.82
Pennsylvania German	8	0.02
Polish	1,844	3.86
Portuguese	2,183	4.56
Romanian	20	0.04
Russian	548	1.15
Scandinavian	44	0.09
Scotch-Irish	997	2.08
Scottish	2,114	4.42
Serbian	16	0.03
Slavic	17	0.04
Slovak	42	0.09
Slovene	12	0.03
Swedish	1,392	2.91
Swiss	93	0.19
Ukrainian	169	0.35
United States or American	2,252	4.71
Welsh	319	0.67
West Indian, excl. Hispanic:	143	0.30
Barbadian	19	0.04
Haitian	17	0.04
Jamaican	55	0.12
Trinidadian and Tobagonian	11	0.02
West Indian	41	0.09
White:	44,834	93.75
Not Hispanic (43,443)	44,305	92.65
Hispanic (482)	529	1.11
Yugoslavian	33	0.07

Bedford

Place Type: Town
County: Middlesex
Population: 12,595

Ancestry/Race	Number	%
African American/Black:	253	2.01
Not Hispanic (204)	239	1.90
Hispanic (4)	14	0.11
African, sub-Saharan:	21	0.17
African	21	0.17
Am. Ind. or Alaska Nat., not spec.	15	0.12
Albanian	22	0.17
American Indian tribes, specified:	34	0.27
Apache (2)	2	0.02
Cherokee (3)	4	0.03
Choctaw (1)	1	0.01
Creek	4	0.03
Latin American Indians (12)	15	0.12
Seminole (1)	1	0.01
Sioux (1)	1	0.01
All other tribes (1)	6	0.05
American Indian tribes, not spec.	1	0.01
Arab:	120	0.95
Lebanese	24	0.19
Syrian	96	0.76
Armenian	83	0.66
Asian:	773	6.14
Bangladeshi (2)	2	0.02
Cambodian (8)	8	0.06
Chinese, ex. Taiwanese (387)	427	3.39
Filipino (19)	23	0.18
Indian (144)	164	1.30
Japanese (17)	33	0.26
Korean (33)	45	0.36
Pakistani (2)	2	0.02
Sri Lankan (3)	3	0.02
Taiwanese (22)	32	0.25
Thai (6)	6	0.05
Vietnamese (16)	16	0.13
Other Asian, not specified (7)	12	0.10
Austrian	56	0.44
Belgian	15	0.12
Brazilian	17	0.13
British	152	1.21
Canadian	225	1.79
Croatian	23	0.18
Czech	25	0.20
Danish	74	0.59
Dutch	125	0.99
Eastern European	27	0.21
English	1,692	13.43
European	109	0.87
Finnish	9	0.07
French, except Basque	603	4.79
French Canadian	422	3.35
German	1,439	11.43
Greek	170	1.35
Hawaii Native/Pacific Islander:	4	0.03
Micronesian:	2	0.02
Guamanian/Chamorro	2	0.02
Polynesian:	2	0.02
Native Hawaiian	1	0.01
Samoan	1	0.01
Hispanic or Latino:	227	1.80
Central American:	19	0.15
Guatemalan	6	0.05
Honduran	1	0.01
Nicaraguan	4	0.03
Panamanian	2	0.02
Salvadoran	4	0.03
Other Central American	2	0.02
Cuban	29	0.23
Dominican Republic	5	0.04
Mexican	33	0.26
Puerto Rican	42	0.33
South American:	43	0.34
Argentinean	8	0.06
Chilean	3	0.02
Colombian	8	0.06
Ecuadorian	3	0.02
Paraguayan	2	0.02
Peruvian	1	0.01
Venezuelan	15	0.12
Other South American	3	0.02
Other Hispanic or Latino	56	0.44
Hungarian	135	1.07
Iranian	28	0.22
Irish	2,918	23.17
Italian	1,755	13.93
Latvian	9	0.07
Lithuanian	94	0.75
Northern European	55	0.44
Norwegian	142	1.13
Polish	457	3.63
Portuguese	176	1.40
Romanian	24	0.19
Russian	307	2.44
Scandinavian	46	0.37
Scotch-Irish	305	2.42
Scottish	430	3.41
Swedish	229	1.82
Swiss	61	0.48
Turkish	32	0.25
Ukrainian	55	0.44
United States or American	637	5.06
Welsh	269	2.14
West Indian, excl. Hispanic:	12	0.10
West Indian	12	0.10
White:	11,615	92.22
Not Hispanic (11,324)	11,434	90.78
Hispanic (162)	181	1.44

Belchertown

Place Type: Town
County: Hampshire
Population: 12,968

Ancestry/Race	Number	%
Acadian/Cajun	6	0.05
African American/Black:	157	1.21
Not Hispanic (91)	138	1.06
Hispanic (14)	19	0.15
African, sub-Saharan:	36	0.28
African	27	0.21
Cape Verdean	9	0.07
Am. Ind. or Alaska Nat., not spec.	32	0.25
American Indian tribes, specified:	73	0.56
Blackfeet	8	0.06
Cherokee (1)	19	0.15
Chickasaw (1)	1	0.01
Chippewa	1	0.01
Choctaw	1	0.01
Iroquois (2)	4	0.03
Latin American Indians (2)	7	0.05
Navajo (3)	4	0.03
Potawatomi (2)	2	0.02
Pueblo (1)	1	0.01
Sioux (2)	4	0.03
All other tribes (5)	21	0.16
American Indian tribes, not spec.	1	0.01
Arab:	59	0.45

Notes: 1. Figures in the "Number" column do not add up to the total population due to: a) Ancestry/Race overlap — e.g. persons can report being both White and Irish, b) persons of Hispanic origin can report being any race, c) persons reporting two ancestries are counted in both categories. 2. Numbers in parentheses indicate the number of persons reporting this ancestry/race alone, not in combination with any other ancestry/race. 3. Refer to the Explanation of Data in the front of the book for more detailed information.

Ancestry/Race	Number	%
Arab/Arabic	7	0.05
Lebanese	52	0.40
Armenian	58	0.45
Asian:	158	1.22
Cambodian (12)	13	0.10
Chinese, ex. Taiwanese (30)	33	0.25
Filipino (3)	6	0.05
Indian (21)	36	0.28
Indonesian (4)	5	0.04
Japanese (5)	10	0.08
Korean (18)	20	0.15
Laotian (3)	3	0.02
Pakistani (2)	2	0.02
Sri Lankan (1)	1	0.01
Taiwanese (4)	4	0.03
Thai (1)	1	0.01
Vietnamese (9)	9	0.07
Other Asian, not specified (9)	15	0.12
Assyrian/Chaldean/Syriac	8	0.06
Austrian	37	0.29
Belgian	24	0.19
Brazilian	18	0.14
British	7	0.05
Canadian	61	0.47
Czech	17	0.13
Danish	69	0.53
Dutch	158	1.22
English	1,828	14.10
European	111	0.86
Finnish	56	0.43
French, except Basque	2,337	18.02
French Canadian	1,715	13.22
German	1,222	9.42
Greek	114	0.88
Hawaii Native/Pacific Islander:	7	0.05
Polynesian: (5)	5	0.04
Native Hawaiian (5)	5	0.04
Other Pac. Isl., not spec. (1)	2	0.02
Hispanic or Latino:	204	1.57
Central American:	7	0.05
Costa Rican	1	0.01
Honduran	2	0.02
Panamanian	3	0.02
Salvadoran	1	0.01
Cuban	12	0.09
Dominican Republic	1	0.01
Mexican	27	0.21
Puerto Rican	118	0.91
South American:	11	0.08
Argentinean	3	0.02
Colombian	3	0.02
Ecuadorian	2	0.02
Peruvian	1	0.01
Other South American	2	0.02
Other Hispanic or Latino	28	0.22
Hungarian	69	0.53
Iranian	18	0.14
Irish	2,747	21.18
Italian	1,264	9.75
Latvian	11	0.08
Lithuanian	80	0.62
New Zealander	15	0.12
Northern European	8	0.06
Norwegian	47	0.36
Pennsylvania German	11	0.08
Polish	1,794	13.83
Portuguese	216	1.67
Russian	283	2.18
Scandinavian	34	0.26
Scotch-Irish	187	1.44
Scottish	365	2.81
Slovak	13	0.10
Swedish	271	2.09
Swiss	14	0.11
Ukrainian	99	0.76
United States or American	637	4.91
Welsh	16	0.12
West Indian, excl. Hispanic:	10	0.08
West Indian	10	0.08
White:	12,623	97.34
Not Hispanic (12,357)	12,492	96.33
Hispanic (110)	131	1.01
Yugoslavian	7	0.05

Bellingham

Place Type: Town
County: Norfolk
Population: 15,314

Ancestry/Race	Number	%
African American/Black:	172	1.12
Not Hispanic (136)	167	1.09
Hispanic (4)	5	0.03
African, sub-Saharan:	26	0.17
Cape Verdean	26	0.17
Am. Ind. or Alaska Nat., not spec.	25	0.16
American Indian tribes, specified:	32	0.21
Blackfeet (1)	3	0.02
Cherokee (2)	5	0.03
Cree	1	0.01
Delaware	2	0.01
Iroquois (1)	1	0.01
All other tribes (4)	20	0.13
American Indian tribes, not spec.	6	0.04
Arab:	144	0.94
Lebanese	122	0.80
Syrian	22	0.14
Armenian	46	0.30
Asian:	177	1.16
Bangladeshi (1)	1	0.01
Cambodian (4)	4	0.03
Chinese, ex. Taiwanese (38)	43	0.28
Filipino (13)	23	0.15
Indian (34)	40	0.26
Indonesian	7	0.05
Japanese (12)	17	0.11
Korean (15)	18	0.12
Laotian (1)	1	0.01
Pakistani	2	0.01
Thai (3)	3	0.02
Vietnamese (9)	10	0.07
Other Asian, specified	2	0.01
Other Asian, not specified	6	0.04
Austrian	24	0.16
British	95	0.62
Canadian	209	1.36
Croatian	8	0.05
Czech	13	0.08
Czechoslovakian	24	0.16
Danish	12	0.08
Dutch	106	0.69
English	1,891	12.35
Estonian	7	0.05
European	5	0.03
Finnish	35	0.23
French, except Basque	2,198	14.35
French Canadian	1,615	10.55
German	1,189	7.76
Greek	96	0.63
Hawaii Native/Pacific Islander:	17	0.11
Polynesian: (4)	5	0.03
Native Hawaiian (4)	5	0.03
Other Pac. Isl., not spec. (1)	12	0.08
Hispanic or Latino:	184	1.20
Central American:	8	0.05
Guatemalan	2	0.01
Honduran	4	0.03
Panamanian	2	0.01
Cuban	10	0.07
Dominican Republic	6	0.04
Mexican	23	0.15
Puerto Rican	84	0.55
South American:	29	0.19
Argentinean	9	0.06
Chilean	1	0.01
Colombian	8	0.05
Ecuadorian	5	0.03
Peruvian	4	0.03
Other South American	2	0.01
Other Hispanic or Latino	24	0.16
Hungarian	75	0.49
Irish	4,428	28.91
Italian	2,561	16.72
Latvian	18	0.12
Lithuanian	27	0.18
Luxemburger	22	0.14
Norwegian	100	0.65
Polish	986	6.44
Portuguese	210	1.37
Romanian	9	0.06
Russian	143	0.93
Scandinavian	6	0.04
Scotch-Irish	215	1.40
Scottish	470	3.07
Slovak	24	0.16
Swedish	386	2.52
Swiss	12	0.08
Ukrainian	38	0.25
United States or American	709	4.63
Welsh	99	0.65
West Indian, excl. Hispanic:	33	0.22
Jamaican	10	0.07
West Indian	23	0.15
White:	14,958	97.68
Not Hispanic (14,717)	14,823	96.79
Hispanic (127)	135	0.88

Belmont

Place Type: Census Designated Place
County: Middlesex
Population: 24,194

Ancestry/Race	Number	%
African American/Black:	331	1.37
Not Hispanic (260)	319	1.32
Hispanic (6)	12	0.05
African, sub-Saharan:	26	0.11
African	19	0.08
Other sub-Saharan African	7	0.03
Am. Ind. or Alaska Nat., not spec.	29	0.12
Albanian	100	0.41
Alsatian	18	0.07
American Indian tribes, specified:	52	0.21
Apache (1)	1	0.00
Cherokee (4)	11	0.05
Chickasaw (1)	1	0.00
Choctaw	5	0.02
Crow	1	0.00
Delaware (1)	1	0.00
Iroquois (2)	5	0.02
Latin American Indians	4	0.02
Navajo (2)	3	0.01
Pueblo (1)	1	0.00
Sioux	1	0.00
Ute (2)	2	0.01
All other tribes (4)	16	0.07
American Indian tribes, not spec.	6	0.02
Arab:	370	1.53
Arab/Arabic	48	0.20
Egyptian	37	0.15
Jordanian	4	0.02
Lebanese	152	0.63
Palestinian	45	0.19
Syrian	44	0.18
Other Arab	40	0.17
Armenian	1,165	4.82
Asian:	1,617	6.68
Bangladeshi (2)	2	0.01
Cambodian (2)	2	0.01
Chinese, ex. Taiwanese (669)	743	3.07
Filipino (32)	49	0.20
Indian (183)	214	0.88
Indonesian	12	0.05
Japanese (212)	246	1.02
Korean (205)	235	0.97
Laotian (2)	2	0.01
Malaysian	1	0.00
Pakistani (16)	16	0.07

Notes: 1. Figures in the "Number" column do not add up to the total population due to: a) Ancestry/Race overlap — e.g. persons can report being both White and Irish, b) persons of Hispanic origin can report being any race, c) persons reporting two ancestries are counted in both categories. 2. Numbers in parentheses indicate the number of persons reporting this ancestry/race alone, not in combination with any other ancestry/race. 3. Refer to the Explanation of Data in the front of the book for more detailed information.

Ancestry/Race	Number	%
Taiwanese (16)	18	0.07
Thai (5)	6	0.02
Vietnamese (11)	12	0.05
Other Asian, specified (2)	6	0.02
Other Asian, not specified (16)	53	0.22
Australian	82	0.34
Austrian	171	0.71
Belgian	34	0.14
Brazilian	46	0.19
British	168	0.69
Bulgarian	19	0.08
Canadian	184	0.76
Celtic	12	0.05
Croatian	6	0.02
Czech	54	0.22
Czechoslovakian	16	0.07
Danish	92	0.38
Dutch	283	1.17
Eastern European	210	0.87
English	2,712	11.21
European	327	1.35
Finnish	45	0.19
French, except Basque	846	3.50
French Canadian	719	2.97
German	1,965	8.12
Greek	752	3.11
Hawaii Native/Pacific Islander:	10	0.04
Micronesian: (1)	1	0.00
Guamanian/Chamorro (1)	1	0.00
Polynesian: (1)	1	0.00
Other Polynesian (1)	1	0.00
Other Pac. Isl., specified	2	0.01
Other Pac. Isl., not spec.	6	0.02
Hispanic or Latino:	440	1.82
Central American:	28	0.12
Costa Rican	1	0.00
Guatemalan	15	0.06
Honduran	1	0.00
Nicaraguan	1	0.00
Panamanian	1	0.00
Salvadoran	7	0.03
Other Central American	2	0.01
Cuban	47	0.19
Dominican Republic	12	0.05
Mexican	67	0.28
Puerto Rican	86	0.36
South American:	117	0.48
Argentinean	10	0.04
Bolivian	1	0.00
Chilean	14	0.06
Colombian	28	0.12
Ecuadorian	17	0.07
Paraguayan	1	0.00
Peruvian	10	0.04
Uruguayan	5	0.02
Venezuelan	13	0.05
Other South American	18	0.07
Other Hispanic or Latino	83	0.34
Hungarian	156	0.64
Iranian	49	0.20
Irish	5,979	24.71
Israeli	53	0.22
Italian	3,966	16.39
Latvian	33	0.14
Lithuanian	85	0.35
Macedonian	21	0.09
Northern European	17	0.07
Norwegian	149	0.62
Pennsylvania German	9	0.04
Polish	736	3.04
Portuguese	131	0.54
Romanian	76	0.31
Russian	834	3.45
Scandinavian	19	0.08
Scotch-Irish	517	2.14
Scottish	760	3.14
Slavic	13	0.05
Slovak	39	0.16
Swedish	382	1.58
Swiss	150	0.62
Turkish	12	0.05
Ukrainian	121	0.50
United States or American	592	2.45
Welsh	192	0.79
West Indian, excl. Hispanic:	92	0.38
Barbadian	18	0.07
Haitian	48	0.20
Jamaican	22	0.09
West Indian	4	0.02
White:	22,368	92.45
Not Hispanic (21,726)	22,004	90.95
Hispanic (336)	364	1.50
Yugoslavian	6	0.02

Beverly

Place Type: City
County: Essex
Population: 39,862

Ancestry/Race	Number	%
African American/Black:	573	1.44
Not Hispanic (391)	537	1.35
Hispanic (22)	36	0.09
African, sub-Saharan:	64	0.16
African	59	0.15
South African	5	0.01
Alaska Native tribes, not specified	1	0.00
Am. Ind. or Alaska Nat., not spec.	57	0.14
Albanian	61	0.15
American Indian tribes, specified:	108	0.27
Apache	2	0.01
Blackfeet (1)	11	0.03
Cherokee (9)	26	0.07
Cheyenne	1	0.00
Comanche	1	0.00
Cree	4	0.01
Creek	1	0.00
Iroquois (2)	5	0.01
Latin American Indians (4)	13	0.03
Navajo (1)	1	0.00
Osage	1	0.00
Paiute (2)	2	0.01
Puget Sound Salish (1)	1	0.00
Sioux (2)	3	0.01
All other tribes (12)	36	0.09
American Indian tribes, not spec.	6	0.02
Arab:	97	0.24
Arab/Arabic	7	0.02
Egyptian	16	0.04
Jordanian	7	0.02
Lebanese	32	0.08
Moroccan	13	0.03
Palestinian	22	0.06
Armenian	37	0.09
Asian:	618	1.55
Cambodian (5)	5	0.01
Chinese, ex. Taiwanese (132)	150	0.38
Filipino (34)	51	0.13
Indian (146)	161	0.40
Indonesian (2)	3	0.01
Japanese (57)	71	0.18
Korean (72)	84	0.21
Laotian (7)	13	0.03
Pakistani (9)	12	0.03
Sri Lankan (1)	1	0.00
Taiwanese (3)	3	0.01
Thai (3)	9	0.02
Vietnamese (17)	18	0.05
Other Asian, specified (8)	10	0.03
Other Asian, not specified (13)	27	0.07
Australian	23	0.06
Austrian	72	0.18
Belgian	15	0.04
Brazilian	72	0.18
British	189	0.47
Bulgarian	19	0.05
Canadian	363	0.91
Celtic	28	0.07
Czech	73	0.18
Czechoslovakian	18	0.05
Danish	71	0.18
Dutch	315	0.79
Eastern European	61	0.15
English	7,429	18.64
European	202	0.51
Finnish	155	0.39
French, except Basque	3,369	8.45
French Canadian	1,837	4.61
German	2,516	6.31
Greek	741	1.86
Hawaii Native/Pacific Islander:	22	0.06
Micronesian: (5)	7	0.02
Guamanian/Chamorro (5)	7	0.02
Polynesian: (5)	10	0.03
Native Hawaiian (3)	8	0.02
Samoan (2)	2	0.01
Other Pac. Isl., specified	2	0.01
Other Pac. Isl., not spec. (2)	3	0.01
Hispanic or Latino:	720	1.81
Central American:	76	0.19
Costa Rican	16	0.04
Guatemalan	33	0.08
Honduran	14	0.04
Nicaraguan	1	0.00
Panamanian	4	0.01
Salvadoran	4	0.01
Other Central American	4	0.01
Cuban	16	0.04
Dominican Republic	78	0.20
Mexican	93	0.23
Puerto Rican	178	0.45
South American:	69	0.17
Argentinean	15	0.04
Bolivian	1	0.00
Chilean	2	0.01
Colombian	15	0.04
Ecuadorian	5	0.01
Peruvian	10	0.03
Uruguayan	12	0.03
Venezuelan	8	0.02
Other South American	1	0.00
Other Hispanic or Latino	210	0.53
Hungarian	148	0.37
Iranian	7	0.02
Irish	10,904	27.35
Israeli	30	0.08
Italian	6,694	16.79
Latvian	20	0.05
Lithuanian	268	0.67
Northern European	32	0.08
Norwegian	391	0.98
Polish	1,828	4.59
Portuguese	708	1.78
Romanian	51	0.13
Russian	735	1.84
Scandinavian	40	0.10
Scotch-Irish	1,094	2.74
Scottish	1,706	4.28
Serbian	16	0.04
Slavic	17	0.04
Slovak	32	0.08
Swedish	986	2.47
Swiss	78	0.20
Turkish	19	0.05
Ukrainian	70	0.18
United States or American	1,452	3.64
Welsh	226	0.57
West Indian, excl. Hispanic:	94	0.24
Haitian	56	0.14
Jamaican	19	0.05
West Indian	19	0.05
White:	38,626	96.90
Not Hispanic (37,781)	38,115	95.62
Hispanic (476)	511	1.28

Notes: 1. Figures in the "Number" column do not add up to the total population due to: a) Ancestry/Race overlap — e.g. persons can report being both White and Irish, b) persons of Hispanic origin can report being any race, c) persons reporting two ancestries are counted in both categories. 2. Numbers in parentheses indicate the number of persons reporting this ancestry/race alone, not in combination with any other ancestry/race. 3. Refer to the Explanation of Data in the front of the book for more detailed information.

Billerica

Place Type: Town
County: Middlesex
Population: 38,981

Ancestry/Race	Number	%
African American/Black:	534	1.37
Not Hispanic (418)	514	1.32
Hispanic (14)	20	0.05
African, sub-Saharan:	68	0.17
African	40	0.10
Cape Verdean	28	0.07
Alaska Native tribes, specified:	1	0.00
Eskimo	1	0.00
Am. Ind. or Alaska Nat., not spec.	84	0.22
Albanian	18	0.05
American Indian tribes, specified:	70	0.18
Apache (1)	2	0.01
Blackfeet (1)	7	0.02
Cherokee (2)	6	0.02
Chippewa (2)	5	0.01
Cree	3	0.01
Iroquois (1)	8	0.02
Latin American Indians (1)	7	0.02
Navajo	3	0.01
Sioux (2)	4	0.01
All other tribes (8)	25	0.06
American Indian tribes, not spec.	3	0.01
Arab:	282	0.72
Arab/Arabic	25	0.06
Lebanese	154	0.40
Other Arab	103	0.26
Armenian	373	0.96
Asian:	1,182	3.03
Bangladeshi (9)	10	0.03
Cambodian (56)	58	0.15
Chinese, ex. Taiwanese (267)	280	0.72
Filipino (90)	116	0.30
Indian (412)	434	1.11
Indonesian (2)	3	0.01
Japanese (25)	43	0.11
Korean (62)	76	0.19
Laotian (14)	16	0.04
Malaysian	1	0.00
Pakistani (28)	29	0.07
Sri Lankan (6)	6	0.02
Taiwanese (10)	10	0.03
Thai (14)	15	0.04
Vietnamese (57)	61	0.16
Other Asian, specified (1)	2	0.01
Other Asian, not specified (16)	22	0.06
Austrian	66	0.17
Belgian	100	0.26
Brazilian	18	0.05
British	66	0.17
Canadian	574	1.47
Czech	45	0.12
Czechoslovakian	8	0.02
Danish	120	0.31
Dutch	188	0.48
Eastern European	4	0.01
English	5,238	13.45
European	63	0.16
Finnish	112	0.29
French, except Basque	3,256	8.36
French Canadian	2,323	5.96
German	2,342	6.01
Greek	448	1.15
Hawaii Native/Pacific Islander:	25	0.06
Melanesian:	1	0.00
Fijian	1	0.00
Micronesian: (12)	12	0.03
Guamanian/Chamorro (10)	10	0.03
Other Micronesian (2)	2	0.01
Polynesian: (4)	9	0.02
Native Hawaiian	3	0.01
Samoan (4)	6	0.02
Other Pac. Isl., not spec.	3	0.01
Hispanic or Latino:	600	1.54
Central American:	39	0.10
Costa Rican	1	0.00
Guatemalan	22	0.06
Honduran	2	0.01
Nicaraguan	1	0.00
Panamanian	6	0.02
Salvadoran	5	0.01
Other Central American	2	0.01
Cuban	36	0.09
Dominican Republic	14	0.04
Mexican	84	0.22
Puerto Rican	178	0.46
South American:	87	0.22
Argentinean	8	0.02
Bolivian	1	0.00
Colombian	34	0.09
Ecuadorian	2	0.01
Peruvian	15	0.04
Uruguayan	1	0.00
Venezuelan	11	0.03
Other South American	15	0.04
Other Hispanic or Latino	162	0.42
Hungarian	68	0.17
Icelander	10	0.03
Iranian	24	0.06
Irish	13,157	33.78
Israeli	14	0.04
Italian	9,403	24.14
Latvian	10	0.03
Lithuanian	261	0.67
Northern European	23	0.06
Norwegian	257	0.66
Polish	1,506	3.87
Portuguese	1,383	3.55
Romanian	15	0.04
Russian	229	0.59
Scandinavian	7	0.02
Scotch-Irish	924	2.37
Scottish	1,235	3.17
Serbian	10	0.03
Slovak	51	0.13
Swedish	868	2.23
Swiss	24	0.06
Ukrainian	34	0.09
United States or American	1,165	2.99
Welsh	97	0.25
West Indian, excl. Hispanic:	20	0.05
Barbadian	3	0.01
Dutch West Indian	7	0.02
Jamaican	10	0.03
White:	37,257	95.58
Not Hispanic (36,487)	36,769	94.33
Hispanic (419)	488	1.25

Boston

Place Type: City
County: Suffolk
Population: 589,141

Ancestry/Race	Number	%
Acadian/Cajun	41	0.01
Afghan	20	0.00
African American/Black:	163,006	27.67
Not Hispanic (140,305)	151,246	25.67
Hispanic (8,897)	11,760	2.00
African, sub-Saharan:	21,176	3.59
African	5,962	1.01
Cape Verdean	11,060	1.88
Ethiopian	658	0.11
Ghanian	201	0.03
Kenyan	95	0.02
Liberian	171	0.03
Nigerian	1,702	0.29
Senegalese	18	0.00
Sierra Leonean	199	0.03
Somalian	614	0.10
South African	125	0.02
Sudanese	31	0.01
Ugandan	38	0.01
Zairian	10	0.00
Zimbabwean	7	0.00
Other sub-Saharan African	285	0.05
Alaska Native tribes, specified:	33	0.01
Alaska Athabascan (1)	2	0.00
Aleut (1)	3	0.00
Eskimo (4)	7	0.00
Tlingit-Haida (5)	17	0.00
All other tribes	4	0.00
Alaska Native tribes, not specified	10	0.00
Am. Ind. or Alaska Nat., not spec.	2,611	0.44
Albanian	1,420	0.24
Alsatian	57	0.01
American Indian tribes, specified:	2,510	0.43
Apache (9)	26	0.00
Blackfeet (44)	209	0.04
Cherokee (126)	609	0.10
Cheyenne	6	0.00
Chickasaw (1)	2	0.00
Chippewa (8)	27	0.00
Choctaw (8)	37	0.01
Colville (1)	1	0.00
Comanche (1)	3	0.00
Cree (2)	14	0.00
Creek (9)	37	0.01
Delaware (3)	7	0.00
Iroquois (39)	118	0.02
Kiowa	1	0.00
Latin American Indians (274)	541	0.09
Lumbee (1)	2	0.00
Menominee (2)	2	0.00
Navajo (20)	42	0.01
Osage	2	0.00
Ottawa	1	0.00
Paiute (2)	4	0.00
Pima (1)	1	0.00
Potawatomi (1)	5	0.00
Pueblo (32)	65	0.01
Puget Sound Salish (4)	6	0.00
Seminole (3)	30	0.01
Shoshone	1	0.00
Sioux (20)	53	0.01
Tohono O'Odham (4)	5	0.00
Ute	1	0.00
Yaqui (1)	2	0.00
All other tribes (312)	650	0.11
American Indian tribes, not spec.	321	0.05
Arab:	5,955	1.01
Arab/Arabic	871	0.15
Egyptian	363	0.06
Iraqi	77	0.01
Jordanian	87	0.01
Lebanese	2,901	0.49
Moroccan	321	0.05
Palestinian	118	0.02
Syrian	709	0.12
Other Arab	508	0.09
Armenian	1,080	0.18
Asian:	48,469	8.23
Bangladeshi (63)	113	0.02
Cambodian (528)	651	0.11
Chinese, ex. Taiwanese (19,282)	20,370	3.46
Filipino (1,405)	1,835	0.31
Hmong (10)	10	0.00
Indian (4,442)	5,154	0.87
Indonesian (198)	255	0.04
Japanese (2,384)	2,817	0.48
Korean (2,564)	2,753	0.47
Laotian (114)	149	0.03
Malaysian (55)	79	0.01
Pakistani (267)	390	0.07
Sri Lankan (60)	80	0.01
Taiwanese (356)	430	0.07
Thai (378)	454	0.08
Vietnamese (10,818)	11,376	1.93
Other Asian, specified (91)	186	0.03
Other Asian, not specified (643)	1,367	0.23
Assyrian/Chaldean/Syriac	38	0.01
Australian	246	0.04
Austrian	1,346	0.23

Notes: 1. Figures in the "Number" column do not add up to the total population due to: a) Ancestry/Race overlap — e.g. persons can report being both White and Irish, b) persons of Hispanic origin can report being any race, c) persons reporting two ancestries are counted in both categories. 2. Numbers in parentheses indicate the number of persons reporting this ancestry/race alone, not in combination with any other ancestry/race. 3. Refer to the Explanation of Data in the front of the book for more detailed information.

Basque	69	0.01
Belgian	342	0.06
Brazilian	3,594	0.61
British	2,405	0.41
Bulgarian	159	0.03
Canadian	3,178	0.54
Carpatho Rusyn	17	0.00
Celtic	162	0.03
Croatian	220	0.04
Cypriot	22	0.00
Czech	866	0.15
Czechoslovakian	355	0.06
Danish	931	0.16
Dutch	2,495	0.42
Eastern European	1,398	0.24
English	26,384	4.48
Estonian	112	0.02
European	2,588	0.44
Finnish	756	0.13
French, except Basque	10,903	1.85
French Canadian	7,145	1.21
German	24,426	4.15
German Russian	6	0.00
Greek	5,325	0.90
Guyanese	381	0.06
Hawaii Native/Pacific Islander:	1,576	0.27
Melanesian: (1)	3	0.00
Fijian (1)	2	0.00
Other Melanesian	1	0.00
Micronesian: (46)	92	0.02
Guamanian/Chamorro (44)	86	0.01
Other Micronesian (2)	6	0.00
Polynesian: (168)	299	0.05
Native Hawaiian (84)	164	0.03
Samoan (77)	121	0.02
Tongan (3)	4	0.00
Other Polynesian (4)	10	0.00
Other Pac. Isl., specified	58	0.01
Other Pac. Isl., not spec. (148)	1,124	0.19
Hispanic or Latino:	85,089	14.44
Central American:	11,532	1.96
Costa Rican	437	0.07
Guatemalan	2,554	0.43
Honduran	1,822	0.31
Nicaraguan	247	0.04
Panamanian	527	0.09
Salvadoran	5,333	0.91
Other Central American	612	0.10
Cuban	2,221	0.38
Dominican Republic	12,981	2.20
Mexican	4,126	0.70
Puerto Rican	27,442	4.66
South American:	7,004	1.19
Argentinean	421	0.07
Bolivian	115	0.02
Chilean	315	0.05
Colombian	4,065	0.69
Ecuadorian	385	0.07
Paraguayan	24	0.00
Peruvian	759	0.13
Uruguayan	54	0.01
Venezuelan	638	0.11
Other South American	228	0.04
Other Hispanic or Latino	19,783	3.36
Hungarian	1,236	0.21
Icelander	52	0.01
Iranian	649	0.11
Irish	93,198	15.82
Israeli	483	0.08
Italian	49,017	8.32
Latvian	428	0.07
Lithuanian	2,778	0.47
Luxemburger	15	0.00
Macedonian	14	0.00
Maltese	12	0.00
New Zealander	78	0.01
Northern European	406	0.07
Norwegian	2,213	0.38
Pennsylvania German	25	0.00
Polish	13,704	2.33
Portuguese	4,513	0.77
Romanian	743	0.13
Russian	10,267	1.74
Scandinavian	403	0.07
Scotch-Irish	5,138	0.87
Scottish	7,340	1.25
Serbian	181	0.03
Slavic	136	0.02
Slovak	348	0.06
Slovene	123	0.02
Soviet Union	37	0.01
Swedish	4,211	0.71
Swiss	824	0.14
Turkish	612	0.10
Ukrainian	2,337	0.40
United States or American	19,387	3.29
Welsh	1,544	0.26
West Indian, excl. Hispanic:	37,614	6.38
Bahamian	47	0.01
Barbadian	2,165	0.37
Belizean	33	0.01
Bermudan	105	0.02
British West Indian	1,359	0.23
Dutch West Indian	48	0.01
Haitian	18,979	3.22
Jamaican	8,226	1.40
Trinidadian and Tobagonian	3,309	0.56
U.S. Virgin Islander	232	0.04
West Indian	3,101	0.53
Other West Indian	10	0.00
White:	334,684	56.81
Not Hispanic (291,561)	300,117	50.94
Hispanic (29,383)	34,567	5.87
Yugoslavian	345	0.06

Bourne

Place Type: Town
County: Barnstable
Population: 18,721

Ancestry/Race	Number	%
African American/Black:	373	1.99
Not Hispanic (249)	356	1.90
Hispanic (12)	17	0.09
African, sub-Saharan:	196	1.05
African	18	0.10
Cape Verdean	178	0.95
Alaska Native tribes, specified:	1	0.01
Eskimo	1	0.01
Am. Ind. or Alaska Nat., not spec.	60	0.32
American Indian tribes, specified:	138	0.74
Apache (2)	2	0.01
Blackfeet	6	0.03
Cherokee (5)	16	0.09
Chickasaw	4	0.02
Comanche	3	0.02
Cree	1	0.01
Iroquois (4)	8	0.04
Potawatomi	1	0.01
Seminole (1)	1	0.01
Sioux (2)	3	0.02
All other tribes (59)	93	0.50
American Indian tribes, not spec.	16	0.09
Arab:	76	0.41
Egyptian	7	0.04
Lebanese	33	0.18
Syrian	36	0.19
Armenian	27	0.14
Asian:	187	1.00
Cambodian (6)	6	0.03
Chinese, ex. Taiwanese (21)	24	0.13
Filipino (26)	41	0.22
Indian (16)	29	0.15
Japanese (10)	20	0.11
Korean (22)	31	0.17
Pakistani (1)	7	0.04
Sri Lankan	2	0.01
Taiwanese (1)	1	0.01
Thai (2)	3	0.02
Vietnamese (13)	13	0.07
Other Asian, not specified (5)	10	0.05
Austrian	34	0.18
Belgian	7	0.04
Brazilian	8	0.04
British	108	0.58
Bulgarian	6	0.03
Canadian	151	0.81
Celtic	26	0.14
Croatian	13	0.07
Czech	9	0.05
Czechoslovakian	27	0.14
Danish	90	0.48
Dutch	215	1.15
English	3,326	17.77
Estonian	5	0.03
European	89	0.48
Finnish	168	0.90
French, except Basque	1,106	5.91
French Canadian	742	3.97
German	1,544	8.25
Greek	195	1.04
Hawaii Native/Pacific Islander:	24	0.13
Micronesian:	9	0.05
Guamanian/Chamorro	9	0.05
Polynesian: (2)	10	0.05
Native Hawaiian	4	0.02
Samoan (2)	6	0.03
Other Pac. Isl., not spec.	5	0.03
Hispanic or Latino:	273	1.46
Central American:	29	0.15
Costa Rican	4	0.02
Guatemalan	2	0.01
Honduran	8	0.04
Panamanian	9	0.05
Salvadoran	6	0.03
Cuban	13	0.07
Dominican Republic	8	0.04
Mexican	60	0.32
Puerto Rican	101	0.54
South American:	8	0.04
Chilean	1	0.01
Colombian	2	0.01
Peruvian	5	0.03
Other Hispanic or Latino	54	0.29
Hungarian	19	0.10
Irish	5,683	30.37
Italian	2,446	13.07
Latvian	30	0.16
Lithuanian	229	1.22
Northern European	7	0.04
Norwegian	141	0.75
Pennsylvania German	13	0.07
Polish	589	3.15
Portuguese	531	2.84
Romanian	10	0.05
Russian	113	0.60
Scandinavian	23	0.12
Scotch-Irish	507	2.71
Scottish	716	3.83
Serbian	6	0.03
Slavic	33	0.18
Slovak	18	0.10
Swedish	674	3.60
Swiss	36	0.19
Ukrainian	45	0.24
United States or American	840	4.49
Welsh	156	0.83
West Indian, excl. Hispanic:	58	0.31
Jamaican	46	0.25
U.S. Virgin Islander	12	0.06
White:	17,986	96.07
Not Hispanic (17,583)	17,810	95.13
Hispanic (149)	176	0.94

Notes: 1. Figures in the "Number" column do not add up to the total population due to: a) Ancestry/Race overlap — e.g. persons can report being both White and Irish, b) persons of Hispanic origin can report being any race, c) persons reporting two ancestries are counted in both categories. 2. Numbers in parentheses indicate the number of persons reporting this ancestry/race alone, not in combination with any other ancestry/race. 3. Refer to the Explanation of Data in the front of the book for more detailed information.

Braintree

Place Type: Town
County: Norfolk
Population: 33,828

Ancestry/Race	Number	%
African American/Black:	497	1.47
Not Hispanic (384)	470	1.39
Hispanic (14)	27	0.08
African, sub-Saharan:	210	0.62
African	50	0.15
Cape Verdean	160	0.47
Am. Ind. or Alaska Nat., not spec.	39	0.12
Albanian	46	0.14
Alsatian	23	0.07
American Indian tribes, specified:	54	0.16
Blackfeet	1	0.00
Cherokee (7)	13	0.04
Chickasaw	1	0.00
Iroquois	4	0.01
Ottawa	1	0.00
Sioux	2	0.01
All other tribes (16)	32	0.09
American Indian tribes, not spec.	12	0.04
Arab:	309	0.91
Arab/Arabic	35	0.10
Egyptian	63	0.19
Lebanese	151	0.45
Palestinian	30	0.09
Syrian	30	0.09
Armenian	98	0.29
Asian:	1,178	3.48
Bangladeshi (1)	1	0.00
Cambodian (12)	18	0.05
Chinese, ex. Taiwanese (538)	567	1.68
Filipino (79)	92	0.27
Indian (131)	152	0.45
Japanese (16)	25	0.07
Korean (56)	74	0.22
Malaysian (2)	2	0.01
Pakistani (25)	32	0.09
Sri Lankan (7)	7	0.02
Taiwanese (4)	5	0.01
Thai (3)	4	0.01
Vietnamese (141)	148	0.44
Other Asian, specified (9)	10	0.03
Other Asian, not specified (24)	41	0.12
Australian	25	0.07
Austrian	103	0.30
Belgian	74	0.22
Brazilian	13	0.04
British	112	0.33
Canadian	431	1.27
Celtic	15	0.04
Croatian	31	0.09
Czech	16	0.05
Czechoslovakian	50	0.15
Danish	29	0.09
Dutch	127	0.38
Eastern European	5	0.01
English	3,470	10.26
European	146	0.43
Finnish	130	0.38
French, except Basque	1,003	2.96
French Canadian	938	2.77
German	1,414	4.18
Greek	443	1.31
Hawaii Native/Pacific Islander:	24	0.07
Micronesian: (5)	9	0.03
Guamanian/Chamorro (5)	9	0.03
Polynesian: (4)	6	0.02
Native Hawaiian (4)	6	0.02
Other Pac. Isl., not spec. (2)	9	0.03
Hispanic or Latino:	394	1.16
Central American:	29	0.09
Costa Rican	4	0.01
Guatemalan	11	0.03
Honduran	2	0.01
Panamanian	1	0.00
Salvadoran	9	0.03
Other Central American	2	0.01
Cuban	28	0.08
Dominican Republic	8	0.02
Mexican	46	0.14
Puerto Rican	138	0.41
South American:	57	0.17
Argentinean	8	0.02
Chilean	3	0.01
Colombian	23	0.07
Ecuadorian	5	0.01
Peruvian	9	0.03
Uruguayan	3	0.01
Venezuelan	4	0.01
Other South American	2	0.01
Other Hispanic or Latino	88	0.26
Hungarian	80	0.24
Irish	13,869	41.00
Italian	6,776	20.03
Latvian	25	0.07
Lithuanian	417	1.23
Northern European	8	0.02
Norwegian	176	0.52
Polish	991	2.93
Portuguese	578	1.71
Romanian	10	0.03
Russian	319	0.94
Scandinavian	41	0.12
Scotch-Irish	922	2.73
Scottish	1,077	3.18
Slovak	21	0.06
Swedish	652	1.93
Turkish	55	0.16
Ukrainian	28	0.08
United States or American	1,398	4.13
Welsh	58	0.17
West Indian, excl. Hispanic:	59	0.17
British West Indian	15	0.04
Jamaican	35	0.10
West Indian	9	0.03
White:	32,065	94.79
Not Hispanic (31,545)	31,795	93.99
Hispanic (239)	270	0.80

Brewster

Place Type: Town
County: Barnstable
Population: 10,094

Ancestry/Race	Number	%
African American/Black:	89	0.88
Not Hispanic (71)	82	0.81
Hispanic (6)	7	0.07
African, sub-Saharan:	16	0.16
African	8	0.08
Cape Verdean	8	0.08
Am. Ind. or Alaska Nat., not spec.	23	0.23
American Indian tribes, specified:	24	0.24
Blackfeet	2	0.02
Cherokee (5)	6	0.06
Comanche (1)	1	0.01
Creek	3	0.03
Iroquois	2	0.02
Latin American Indians	1	0.01
All other tribes (3)	9	0.09
American Indian tribes, not spec.	1	0.01
Arab:	39	0.39
Lebanese	39	0.39
Armenian	12	0.12
Asian:	91	0.90
Chinese, ex. Taiwanese (17)	21	0.21
Filipino (14)	16	0.16
Indian (17)	17	0.17
Japanese (9)	16	0.16
Korean (6)	6	0.06
Pakistani (1)	1	0.01
Vietnamese (10)	11	0.11
Other Asian, not specified (3)	3	0.03
Austrian	27	0.27
Basque	9	0.09
Belgian	27	0.27
British	66	0.65
Canadian	80	0.79
Czech	26	0.26
Czechoslovakian	15	0.15
Danish	65	0.64
Dutch	130	1.29
English	2,594	25.70
European	58	0.57
Finnish	49	0.49
French, except Basque	929	9.20
French Canadian	176	1.74
German	1,410	13.97
Greek	53	0.53
Hawaii Native/Pacific Islander:	4	0.04
Micronesian: (3)	3	0.03
Guamanian/Chamorro (3)	3	0.03
Polynesian:	1	0.01
Samoan	1	0.01
Hispanic or Latino:	107	1.06
Central American:	5	0.05
Guatemalan	3	0.03
Salvadoran	2	0.02
Cuban	11	0.11
Mexican	25	0.25
Puerto Rican	37	0.37
South American:	13	0.13
Colombian	7	0.07
Ecuadorian	1	0.01
Other South American	5	0.05
Other Hispanic or Latino	16	0.16
Hungarian	22	0.22
Irish	3,056	30.28
Italian	877	8.69
Lithuanian	159	1.58
Norwegian	115	1.14
Pennsylvania German	7	0.07
Polish	382	3.78
Portuguese	170	1.68
Russian	145	1.44
Scandinavian	41	0.41
Scotch-Irish	223	2.21
Scottish	612	6.06
Slovak	21	0.21
Slovene	15	0.15
Swedish	424	4.20
Swiss	36	0.36
Ukrainian	18	0.18
United States or American	283	2.80
Welsh	40	0.40
White:	9,875	97.83
Not Hispanic (9,731)	9,791	97.00
Hispanic (84)	84	0.83

Bridgewater

Place Type: Town
County: Plymouth
Population: 25,185

Ancestry/Race	Number	%
African American/Black:	1,137	4.51
Not Hispanic (959)	1,065	4.23
Hispanic (58)	72	0.29
African, sub-Saharan:	385	1.53
African	113	0.45
Cape Verdean	272	1.08
Alaska Native tribes, specified:	3	0.01
Aleut (1)	1	0.00
Tlingit-Haida	2	0.01
Am. Ind. or Alaska Nat., not spec.	56	0.22
Albanian	39	0.15
American Indian tribes, specified:	74	0.29
Apache (1)	1	0.00
Blackfeet (3)	7	0.03
Cherokee (3)	12	0.05
Chickasaw	1	0.00
Chippewa (1)	2	0.01
Choctaw (3)	4	0.02

Notes: 1. Figures in the "Number" column do not add up to the total population due to: a) Ancestry/Race overlap — e.g. persons can report being both White and Irish, b) persons of Hispanic origin can report being any race, c) persons reporting two ancestries are counted in both categories. 2. Numbers in parentheses indicate the number of persons reporting this ancestry/race alone, not in combination with any other ancestry/race. 3. Refer to the Explanation of Data in the front of the book for more detailed information.

Crow	1	0.00
Iroquois (3)	4	0.02
Latin American Indians (1)	1	0.00
Lumbee (1)	1	0.00
Navajo (1)	1	0.00
Pueblo (2)	2	0.01
Puget Sound Salish (1)	1	0.00
Seminole	1	0.00
Sioux	2	0.01
All other tribes (17)	33	0.13
American Indian tribes, not spec.	10	0.04
Arab:	283	1.12
Egyptian	22	0.09
Jordanian	6	0.02
Lebanese	229	0.91
Syrian	26	0.10
Armenian	44	0.17
Asian:	339	1.35
Cambodian (8)	8	0.03
Chinese, ex. Taiwanese (79)	97	0.39
Filipino (15)	32	0.13
Indian (67)	75	0.30
Japanese (42)	53	0.21
Korean (21)	26	0.10
Malaysian (1)	2	0.01
Pakistani (7)	7	0.03
Taiwanese (3)	3	0.01
Thai (6)	8	0.03
Vietnamese (14)	17	0.07
Other Asian, specified	1	0.00
Other Asian, not specified (2)	10	0.04
Australian	6	0.02
Austrian	18	0.07
Belgian	36	0.14
Brazilian	39	0.15
British	92	0.37
Canadian	241	0.96
Celtic	19	0.08
Croatian	13	0.05
Czech	29	0.12
Czechoslovakian	25	0.10
Danish	89	0.35
Dutch	205	0.81
Eastern European	6	0.02
English	3,491	13.87
European	20	0.08
Finnish	65	0.26
French, except Basque	1,463	5.81
French Canadian	1,259	5.00
German	1,402	5.57
Greek	177	0.70
Hawaii Native/Pacific Islander:	7	0.03
Polynesian: (2)	2	0.01
Native Hawaiian (1)	1	0.00
Samoan (1)	1	0.00
Other Pac. Isl., not spec. (3)	5	0.02
Hispanic or Latino:	693	2.75
Central American:	42	0.17
Costa Rican	2	0.01
Guatemalan	15	0.06
Honduran	2	0.01
Nicaraguan	1	0.00
Panamanian	7	0.03
Salvadoran	13	0.05
Other Central American	2	0.01
Cuban	16	0.06
Dominican Republic	25	0.10
Mexican	72	0.29
Puerto Rican	325	1.29
South American:	70	0.28
Argentinean	4	0.02
Chilean	7	0.03
Colombian	22	0.09
Ecuadorian	10	0.04
Peruvian	9	0.04
Venezuelan	13	0.05
Other South American	5	0.02
Other Hispanic or Latino	143	0.57
Hungarian	75	0.30
Irish	7,734	30.73
Italian	4,451	17.69
Lithuanian	490	1.95
Norwegian	140	0.56
Polish	918	3.65
Portuguese	1,485	5.90
Russian	182	0.72
Scandinavian	28	0.11
Scotch-Irish	555	2.21
Scottish	904	3.59
Slavic	18	0.07
Slovak	69	0.27
Slovene	27	0.11
Swedish	771	3.06
Swiss	14	0.06
Turkish	14	0.06
Ukrainian	30	0.12
United States or American	1,086	4.32
Welsh	22	0.09
West Indian, excl. Hispanic:	151	0.60
Barbadian	7	0.03
Bermudan	6	0.02
Haitian	48	0.19
Jamaican	65	0.26
Trinidadian and Tobagonian	18	0.07
West Indian	7	0.03
White:	22,214	88.20
Not Hispanic (21,775)	21,975	87.25
Hispanic (207)	239	0.95

Brockton

Place Type: City
County: Plymouth
Population: 94,304

Ancestry/Race	Number	%
African American/Black:	21,970	23.30
Not Hispanic (15,913)	20,764	22.02
Hispanic (898)	1,206	1.28
African, sub-Saharan:	10,010	10.61
African	684	0.73
Cape Verdean	8,844	9.38
Ethiopian	39	0.04
Ghanian	81	0.09
Kenyan	22	0.02
Liberian	14	0.01
Nigerian	74	0.08
Somalian	31	0.03
South African	13	0.01
Other sub-Saharan African	208	0.22
Alaska Native tribes, specified:	3	0.00
Aleut (1)	1	0.00
Tlingit-Haida (1)	2	0.00
Am. Ind. or Alaska Nat., not spec.	406	0.43
Albanian	126	0.13
American Indian tribes, specified:	433	0.46
Apache (8)	12	0.01
Blackfeet (11)	47	0.05
Cherokee (26)	125	0.13
Chippewa (1)	3	0.00
Choctaw (1)	4	0.00
Cree (1)	2	0.00
Creek	1	0.00
Crow	1	0.00
Iroquois (3)	12	0.01
Kiowa	4	0.00
Latin American Indians (8)	20	0.02
Navajo (2)	7	0.01
Pueblo (1)	2	0.00
Seminole	2	0.00
Shoshone	1	0.00
Sioux (2)	13	0.01
Yuman (1)	1	0.00
All other tribes (79)	176	0.19
American Indian tribes, not spec.	60	0.06
Arab:	727	0.77
Arab/Arabic	74	0.08
Egyptian	47	0.05
Lebanese	569	0.60
Moroccan	13	0.01
Palestinian	11	0.01
Syrian	6	0.01
Other Arab	7	0.01
Armenian	194	0.21
Asian:	2,665	2.83
Bangladeshi (6)	6	0.01
Cambodian (162)	220	0.23
Chinese, ex. Taiwanese (530)	645	0.68
Filipino (249)	326	0.35
Hmong (197)	259	0.27
Indian (220)	300	0.32
Indonesian (6)	13	0.01
Japanese (34)	46	0.05
Korean (66)	88	0.09
Laotian (84)	118	0.13
Malaysian	2	0.00
Pakistani (47)	54	0.06
Sri Lankan (2)	2	0.00
Taiwanese	4	0.00
Thai (20)	31	0.03
Vietnamese (283)	387	0.41
Other Asian, not specified (45)	164	0.17
Australian	11	0.01
Austrian	74	0.08
Belgian	23	0.02
Brazilian	441	0.47
British	202	0.21
Bulgarian	9	0.01
Canadian	405	0.43
Celtic	10	0.01
Czech	79	0.08
Czechoslovakian	27	0.03
Danish	113	0.12
Dutch	327	0.35
Eastern European	84	0.09
English	6,442	6.83
European	369	0.39
Finnish	223	0.24
French, except Basque	4,180	4.43
French Canadian	2,376	2.52
German	3,231	3.43
Greek	1,061	1.13
Guyanese	31	0.03
Hawaii Native/Pacific Islander:	239	0.25
Melanesian: (1)	1	0.00
Other Melanesian (1)	1	0.00
Micronesian: (5)	14	0.01
Guamanian/Chamorro (5)	14	0.01
Polynesian: (10)	33	0.03
Native Hawaiian (4)	23	0.02
Samoan (6)	9	0.01
Other Polynesian	1	0.00
Other Pac. Isl., not spec. (13)	191	0.20
Hispanic or Latino:	7,552	8.01
Central American:	481	0.51
Costa Rican	49	0.05
Guatemalan	147	0.16
Honduran	91	0.10
Nicaraguan	18	0.02
Panamanian	43	0.05
Salvadoran	109	0.12
Other Central American	24	0.03
Cuban	152	0.16
Dominican Republic	403	0.43
Mexican	404	0.43
Puerto Rican	4,545	4.82
South American:	370	0.39
Argentinean	22	0.02
Bolivian	12	0.01
Chilean	52	0.06
Colombian	86	0.09
Ecuadorian	30	0.03
Paraguayan	2	0.00
Peruvian	125	0.13
Venezuelan	30	0.03
Other South American	11	0.01
Other Hispanic or Latino	1,197	1.27
Hungarian	83	0.09
Icelander	6	0.01
Irish	16,690	17.70

Notes: 1. Figures in the "Number" column do not add up to the total population due to: a) Ancestry/Race overlap — e.g. persons can report being both White and Irish, b) persons of Hispanic origin can report being any race, c) persons reporting two ancestries are counted in both categories. 2. Numbers in parentheses indicate the number of persons reporting this ancestry/race alone, not in combination with any other ancestry/race. 3. Refer to the Explanation of Data in the front of the book for more detailed information.

Italian	9,565	10.14
Latvian	79	0.08
Lithuanian	1,370	1.45
Norwegian	193	0.20
Polish	2,074	2.20
Portuguese	2,789	2.96
Romanian	36	0.04
Russian	562	0.60
Scandinavian	34	0.04
Scotch-Irish	1,167	1.24
Scottish	1,961	2.08
Slavic	21	0.02
Slovak	17	0.02
Swedish	2,025	2.15
Swiss	47	0.05
Turkish	78	0.08
Ukrainian	50	0.05
United States or American	4,064	4.31
Welsh	196	0.21
West Indian, excl. Hispanic:	5,732	6.08
Bahamian	8	0.01
Barbadian	173	0.18
Belizean	15	0.02
British West Indian	34	0.04
Dutch West Indian	10	0.01
Haitian	4,720	5.01
Jamaican	408	0.43
Trinidadian and Tobagonian	165	0.17
West Indian	199	0.21
White:	60,758	64.43
Not Hispanic (54,902)	57,194	60.65
Hispanic (3,087)	3,564	3.78

Brookline

Place Type: Census Designated Place
County: Norfolk
Population: 57,107

Ancestry/Race	Number	%
Acadian/Cajun	9	0.02
African American/Black:	1,873	3.28
Not Hispanic (1,501)	1,776	3.11
Hispanic (65)	97	0.17
African, sub-Saharan:	416	0.73
African	157	0.28
Cape Verdean	137	0.24
Ethiopian	39	0.07
Ghanian	8	0.01
Kenyan	22	0.04
Senegalese	8	0.01
South African	40	0.07
Other sub-Saharan African	5	0.01
Alaska Native tribes, specified:	1	0.00
Eskimo (1)	1	0.00
Am. Ind. or Alaska Nat., not spec.	105	0.18
Albanian	8	0.01
Alsatian	10	0.02
American Indian tribes, specified:	148	0.26
Apache (1)	2	0.00
Blackfeet	2	0.00
Cherokee (8)	49	0.09
Chippewa (1)	2	0.00
Choctaw	1	0.00
Cree	1	0.00
Creek	4	0.01
Iroquois (2)	4	0.01
Kiowa	1	0.00
Latin American Indians (26)	46	0.08
Osage (1)	1	0.00
Ottawa	1	0.00
Pueblo	1	0.00
Seminole	4	0.01
Sioux	1	0.00
Ute	1	0.00
All other tribes (6)	27	0.05
American Indian tribes, not spec.	15	0.03
Arab:	819	1.44
Arab/Arabic	176	0.31
Egyptian	134	0.23
Iraqi	26	0.05
Jordanian	9	0.02
Lebanese	196	0.34
Moroccan	98	0.17
Palestinian	28	0.05
Syrian	83	0.15
Other Arab	69	0.12
Armenian	132	0.23
Asian:	7,984	13.98
Bangladeshi (7)	13	0.02
Cambodian (26)	30	0.05
Chinese, ex. Taiwanese (3,362)	3,579	6.27
Filipino (143)	195	0.34
Hmong (1)	1	0.00
Indian (932)	1,036	1.81
Indonesian (50)	57	0.10
Japanese (1,302)	1,406	2.46
Korean (861)	907	1.59
Laotian (4)	4	0.01
Malaysian (4)	11	0.02
Pakistani (63)	74	0.13
Sri Lankan (13)	14	0.02
Taiwanese (147)	177	0.31
Thai (83)	94	0.16
Vietnamese (109)	121	0.21
Other Asian, specified (20)	31	0.05
Other Asian, not specified (109)	234	0.41
Assyrian/Chaldean/Syriac	14	0.02
Australian	136	0.24
Austrian	554	0.97
Basque	11	0.02
Belgian	101	0.18
Brazilian	177	0.31
British	593	1.04
Bulgarian	64	0.11
Canadian	549	0.96
Celtic	18	0.03
Croatian	33	0.06
Czech	235	0.41
Czechoslovakian	97	0.17
Danish	150	0.26
Dutch	401	0.70
Eastern European	1,184	2.07
English	4,190	7.34
European	987	1.73
Finnish	135	0.24
French, except Basque	1,138	1.99
French Canadian	538	0.94
German	4,106	7.20
Greek	854	1.50
Hawaii Native/Pacific Islander:	45	0.08
Micronesian: (4)	7	0.01
Guamanian/Chamorro (4)	7	0.01
Polynesian: (10)	19	0.03
Native Hawaiian (9)	15	0.03
Samoan (1)	2	0.00
Other Polynesian	2	0.00
Other Pac. Isl., specified	3	0.01
Other Pac. Isl., not spec. (2)	16	0.03
Hispanic or Latino:	2,018	3.53
Central American:	152	0.27
Costa Rican	24	0.04
Guatemalan	45	0.08
Honduran	25	0.04
Nicaraguan	5	0.01
Panamanian	13	0.02
Salvadoran	34	0.06
Other Central American	7	0.01
Cuban	115	0.20
Dominican Republic	51	0.09
Mexican	361	0.63
Puerto Rican	309	0.54
South American:	552	0.97
Argentinean	80	0.14
Bolivian	9	0.02
Chilean	65	0.11
Colombian	162	0.28
Ecuadorian	28	0.05
Paraguayan	9	0.02
Peruvian	50	0.09
Venezuelan	116	0.20
Other South American	33	0.06
Other Hispanic or Latino	478	0.84
Hungarian	834	1.46
Icelander	19	0.03
Iranian	369	0.65
Irish	6,905	12.10
Israeli	605	1.06
Italian	3,290	5.77
Latvian	183	0.32
Lithuanian	403	0.71
Northern European	76	0.13
Norwegian	411	0.72
Polish	2,629	4.61
Portuguese	357	0.63
Romanian	391	0.69
Russian	5,338	9.35
Scandinavian	60	0.11
Scotch-Irish	479	0.84
Scottish	1,091	1.91
Serbian	33	0.06
Slavic	38	0.07
Slovak	111	0.19
Slovene	10	0.02
Soviet Union	59	0.10
Swedish	525	0.92
Swiss	173	0.30
Turkish	133	0.23
Ukrainian	435	0.76
United States or American	2,772	4.86
Welsh	304	0.53
West Indian, excl. Hispanic:	437	0.77
Barbadian	28	0.05
British West Indian	8	0.01
Haitian	243	0.43
Jamaican	121	0.21
Trinidadian and Tobagonian	18	0.03
West Indian	19	0.03
White:	47,340	82.90
Not Hispanic (44,922)	45,825	80.24
Hispanic (1,382)	1,515	2.65
Yugoslavian	45	0.08

Burlington

Place Type: Census Designated Place
County: Middlesex
Population: 22,876

Ancestry/Race	Number	%
African American/Black:	364	1.59
Not Hispanic (307)	350	1.53
Hispanic (5)	14	0.06
African, sub-Saharan:	100	0.44
African	51	0.22
South African	9	0.04
Sudanese	30	0.13
Other sub-Saharan African	10	0.04
Am. Ind. or Alaska Nat., not spec.	18	0.08
Albanian	57	0.25
American Indian tribes, specified:	36	0.16
Cherokee (4)	12	0.05
Creek (1)	1	0.00
Crow (1)	1	0.00
Iroquois (1)	6	0.03
Latin American Indians	1	0.00
Navajo	1	0.00
Pueblo	1	0.00
All other tribes (3)	13	0.06
American Indian tribes, not spec.	7	0.03
Arab:	214	0.94
Arab/Arabic	17	0.07
Jordanian	9	0.04
Lebanese	73	0.32
Moroccan	42	0.18
Syrian	73	0.32
Armenian	389	1.70
Asian:	2,532	11.07
Bangladeshi (24)	26	0.11
Cambodian (8)	9	0.04

Notes: 1. Figures in the "Number" column do not add up to the total population due to: a) Ancestry/Race overlap — e.g. persons can report being both White and Irish, b) persons of Hispanic origin can report being any race, c) persons reporting two ancestries are counted in both categories. 2. Numbers in parentheses indicate the number of persons reporting this ancestry/race alone, not in combination with any other ancestry/race. 3. Refer to the Explanation of Data in the front of the book for more detailed information.

Ancestry/Race	Number	%
Chinese, ex. Taiwanese (513)	544	2.38
Filipino (22)	33	0.14
Indian (1,570)	1,608	7.03
Indonesian (4)	4	0.02
Japanese (68)	72	0.31
Korean (56)	60	0.26
Pakistani (18)	19	0.08
Sri Lankan (27)	27	0.12
Taiwanese (16)	20	0.09
Thai (16)	16	0.07
Vietnamese (65)	69	0.30
Other Asian, not specified (12)	25	0.11
Austrian	37	0.16
Belgian	18	0.08
Brazilian	51	0.22
British	33	0.14
Canadian	190	0.83
Croatian	18	0.08
Czech	20	0.09
Czechoslovakian	4	0.02
Danish	47	0.21
Dutch	169	0.74
Eastern European	7	0.03
English	2,380	10.40
Estonian	22	0.10
European	117	0.51
Finnish	85	0.37
French, except Basque	819	3.58
French Canadian	919	4.02
German	1,006	4.40
Greek	416	1.82
Hawaii Native/Pacific Islander:	11	0.05
Micronesian: (1)	1	0.00
Guamanian/Chamorro (1)	1	0.00
Polynesian: (4)	9	0.04
Native Hawaiian	5	0.02
Tongan (4)	4	0.02
Other Pac. Isl., not spec.	1	0.00
Hispanic or Latino:	296	1.29
Central American:	13	0.06
Costa Rican	1	0.00
Guatemalan	2	0.01
Honduran	3	0.01
Salvadoran	6	0.03
Other Central American	1	0.00
Cuban	22	0.10
Dominican Republic	4	0.02
Mexican	40	0.17
Puerto Rican	65	0.28
South American:	73	0.32
Bolivian	4	0.02
Chilean	5	0.02
Colombian	36	0.16
Ecuadorian	14	0.06
Peruvian	3	0.01
Venezuelan	7	0.03
Other South American	4	0.02
Other Hispanic or Latino	79	0.35
Hungarian	55	0.24
Icelander	8	0.03
Iranian	48	0.21
Irish	6,604	28.87
Italian	5,367	23.46
Lithuanian	174	0.76
Northern European	14	0.06
Norwegian	120	0.52
Polish	540	2.36
Portuguese	480	2.10
Romanian	38	0.17
Russian	394	1.72
Scandinavian	6	0.03
Scotch-Irish	441	1.93
Scottish	835	3.65
Slavic	11	0.05
Slovene	9	0.04
Swedish	444	1.94
Swiss	16	0.07
Turkish	6	0.03
Ukrainian	41	0.18
United States or American	889	3.89
Welsh	47	0.21
West Indian, excl. Hispanic:	357	1.56
Belizean	18	0.08
Haitian	299	1.31
Jamaican	40	0.17
White:	19,982	87.35
Not Hispanic (19,626)	19,751	86.34
Hispanic (210)	231	1.01

Cambridge

Place Type: City
County: Middlesex
Population: 101,355

Ancestry/Race	Number	%
Acadian/Cajun	40	0.04
Afghan	6	0.01
African American/Black:	13,959	13.77
Not Hispanic (11,627)	13,238	13.06
Hispanic (452)	721	0.71
African, sub-Saharan:	2,190	2.16
African	656	0.65
Cape Verdean	394	0.39
Ethiopian	499	0.49
Ghanian	60	0.06
Kenyan	30	0.03
Liberian	82	0.08
Nigerian	171	0.17
Senegalese	6	0.01
Somalian	26	0.03
South African	146	0.14
Ugandan	19	0.02
Zairian	9	0.01
Zimbabwean	16	0.02
Other sub-Saharan African	76	0.07
Alaska Native tribes, specified:	9	0.01
Alaska Athabascan (1)	3	0.00
Aleut (1)	3	0.00
Eskimo (1)	2	0.00
Tlingit-Haida	1	0.00
Am. Ind. or Alaska Nat., not spec.	327	0.32
Albanian	70	0.07
Alsatian	55	0.05
American Indian tribes, specified:	467	0.46
Apache (1)	10	0.01
Blackfeet (6)	23	0.02
Cherokee (28)	131	0.13
Cheyenne (1)	2	0.00
Chickasaw (5)	5	0.00
Chippewa (4)	7	0.01
Choctaw (5)	19	0.02
Comanche	2	0.00
Cree	7	0.01
Creek (1)	5	0.00
Crow (1)	2	0.00
Delaware (3)	3	0.00
Iroquois (4)	18	0.02
Kiowa (1)	1	0.00
Latin American Indians (44)	79	0.08
Lumbee (1)	3	0.00
Navajo (7)	9	0.01
Osage (1)	2	0.00
Ottawa (1)	1	0.00
Pima (1)	1	0.00
Pueblo (6)	17	0.02
Seminole	4	0.00
Shoshone	7	0.01
Sioux (9)	14	0.01
All other tribes (34)	95	0.09
American Indian tribes, not spec.	66	0.07
Arab:	1,374	1.36
Arab/Arabic	342	0.34
Egyptian	85	0.08
Iraqi	24	0.02
Jordanian	51	0.05
Lebanese	438	0.43
Moroccan	72	0.07
Palestinian	109	0.11
Syrian	98	0.10
Other Arab	155	0.15
Armenian	342	0.34
Asian:	13,516	13.34
Bangladeshi (120)	152	0.15
Cambodian (51)	54	0.05
Chinese, ex. Taiwanese (4,514)	4,969	4.90
Filipino (265)	384	0.38
Hmong (6)	6	0.01
Indian (2,720)	3,001	2.96
Indonesian (66)	80	0.08
Japanese (943)	1,155	1.14
Korean (1,901)	1,993	1.97
Laotian (11)	18	0.02
Malaysian (30)	43	0.04
Pakistani (125)	161	0.16
Sri Lankan (49)	54	0.05
Taiwanese (340)	397	0.39
Thai (156)	178	0.18
Vietnamese (235)	276	0.27
Other Asian, specified (61)	83	0.08
Other Asian, not specified (246)	512	0.51
Australian	149	0.15
Austrian	580	0.57
Basque	47	0.05
Belgian	138	0.14
Brazilian	694	0.68
British	1,251	1.23
Bulgarian	84	0.08
Canadian	880	0.87
Celtic	57	0.06
Croatian	72	0.07
Cypriot	21	0.02
Czech	415	0.41
Czechoslovakian	83	0.08
Danish	470	0.46
Dutch	905	0.89
Eastern European	942	0.93
English	9,366	9.24
Estonian	38	0.04
European	1,346	1.33
Finnish	252	0.25
French, except Basque	2,872	2.83
French Canadian	1,613	1.59
German	8,016	7.91
Greek	1,069	1.05
Guyanese	58	0.06
Hawaii Native/Pacific Islander:	252	0.25
Melanesian: (1)	1	0.00
Fijian (1)	1	0.00
Micronesian: (17)	27	0.03
Guamanian/Chamorro (16)	23	0.02
Other Micronesian (1)	4	0.00
Polynesian: (37)	63	0.06
Native Hawaiian (28)	48	0.05
Samoan (9)	15	0.01
Other Pac. Isl., specified	10	0.01
Other Pac. Isl., not spec. (22)	151	0.15
Hispanic or Latino:	7,455	7.36
Central American:	928	0.92
Costa Rican	49	0.05
Guatemalan	129	0.13
Honduran	66	0.07
Nicaraguan	39	0.04
Panamanian	43	0.04
Salvadoran	567	0.56
Other Central American	35	0.03
Cuban	270	0.27
Dominican Republic	424	0.42
Mexican	1,175	1.16
Puerto Rican	1,637	1.62
South American:	1,251	1.23
Argentinean	243	0.24
Bolivian	46	0.05
Chilean	133	0.13
Colombian	378	0.37
Ecuadorian	68	0.07
Paraguayan	12	0.01
Peruvian	163	0.16
Uruguayan	37	0.04
Venezuelan	112	0.11

Notes: 1. Figures in the "Number" column do not add up to the total population due to: a) Ancestry/Race overlap — e.g. persons can report being both White and Irish, b) persons of Hispanic origin can report being any race, c) persons reporting two ancestries are counted in both categories. 2. Numbers in parentheses indicate the number of persons reporting this ancestry/race alone, not in combination with any other ancestry/race. 3. Refer to the Explanation of Data in the front of the book for more detailed information.

Ancestry/Race	Number	%
Other South American	59	0.06
Other Hispanic or Latino	1,770	1.75
Hungarian	683	0.67
Icelander	14	0.01
Iranian	239	0.24
Irish	13,440	13.26
Israeli	353	0.35
Italian	7,620	7.52
Latvian	114	0.11
Lithuanian	614	0.61
New Zealander	25	0.02
Northern European	348	0.34
Norwegian	888	0.88
Pennsylvania German	31	0.03
Polish	3,464	3.42
Portuguese	3,128	3.09
Romanian	330	0.33
Russian	3,870	3.82
Scandinavian	227	0.22
Scotch-Irish	1,410	1.39
Scottish	2,442	2.41
Serbian	78	0.08
Slavic	43	0.04
Slovak	192	0.19
Slovene	25	0.02
Soviet Union	8	0.01
Swedish	1,351	1.33
Swiss	468	0.46
Turkish	238	0.23
Ukrainian	650	0.64
United States or American	2,556	2.52
Welsh	561	0.55
West Indian, excl. Hispanic:	5,164	5.09
Barbadian	374	0.37
Belizean	10	0.01
Bermudan	45	0.04
British West Indian	51	0.05
Haitian	3,265	3.22
Jamaican	939	0.93
Trinidadian and Tobagonian	204	0.20
U.S. Virgin Islander	4	0.00
West Indian	265	0.26
Other West Indian	7	0.01
White:	72,213	71.25
Not Hispanic (65,425)	68,080	67.17
Hispanic (3,597)	4,133	4.08
Yugoslavian	100	0.10

Canton

Place Type: Town
County: Norfolk
Population: 20,775

Ancestry/Race	Number	%
African American/Black:	666	3.21
Not Hispanic (581)	638	3.07
Hispanic (17)	28	0.13
African, sub-Saharan:	171	0.82
African	32	0.15
Cape Verdean	123	0.59
Nigerian	16	0.08
Am. Ind. or Alaska Nat., not spec.	32	0.15
Albanian	14	0.07
American Indian tribes, specified:	37	0.18
Apache	3	0.01
Blackfeet (1)	1	0.00
Cherokee	6	0.03
Choctaw	2	0.01
Creek	1	0.00
Iroquois (3)	4	0.02
Latin American Indians (1)	2	0.01
Sioux	1	0.00
All other tribes (9)	17	0.08
American Indian tribes, not spec.	2	0.01
Arab:	244	1.17
Lebanese	217	1.04
Palestinian	8	0.04
Syrian	13	0.06
Other Arab	6	0.03
Armenian	110	0.53
Asian:	707	3.40
Cambodian (2)	2	0.01
Chinese, ex. Taiwanese (315)	347	1.67
Filipino (15)	21	0.10
Indian (154)	168	0.81
Indonesian (1)	3	0.01
Japanese (11)	19	0.09
Korean (54)	62	0.30
Malaysian (1)	1	0.00
Pakistani (1)	3	0.01
Sri Lankan (3)	4	0.02
Taiwanese (3)	9	0.04
Thai (7)	9	0.04
Vietnamese (43)	47	0.23
Other Asian, specified (1)	3	0.01
Other Asian, not specified (2)	9	0.04
Austrian	22	0.11
Belgian	73	0.35
Brazilian	14	0.07
British	88	0.42
Canadian	183	0.88
Celtic	22	0.11
Czech	9	0.04
Czechoslovakian	6	0.03
Danish	77	0.37
Dutch	121	0.58
Eastern European	39	0.19
English	2,063	9.93
European	41	0.20
Finnish	70	0.34
French, except Basque	563	2.71
French Canadian	510	2.45
German	1,291	6.21
Greek	536	2.58
Hawaii Native/Pacific Islander:	11	0.05
Polynesian: (3)	3	0.01
Native Hawaiian (3)	3	0.01
Other Pac. Isl., specified	1	0.00
Other Pac. Isl., not spec. (2)	7	0.03
Hispanic or Latino:	296	1.42
Central American:	14	0.07
Costa Rican	5	0.02
Guatemalan	1	0.00
Honduran	5	0.02
Nicaraguan	1	0.00
Salvadoran	2	0.01
Cuban	22	0.11
Dominican Republic	30	0.14
Mexican	19	0.09
Puerto Rican	102	0.49
South American:	38	0.18
Argentinean	5	0.02
Chilean	3	0.01
Colombian	15	0.07
Ecuadorian	3	0.01
Peruvian	3	0.01
Uruguayan	1	0.00
Venezuelan	3	0.01
Other South American	5	0.02
Other Hispanic or Latino	71	0.34
Hungarian	30	0.14
Icelander	14	0.07
Iranian	34	0.16
Irish	6,862	33.03
Israeli	28	0.13
Italian	3,585	17.26
Latvian	12	0.06
Lithuanian	271	1.30
Northern European	14	0.07
Norwegian	119	0.57
Polish	892	4.29
Portuguese	284	1.37
Romanian	20	0.10
Russian	815	3.92
Scandinavian	33	0.16
Scotch-Irish	265	1.28
Scottish	502	2.42
Serbian	4	0.02
Slovak	18	0.09
Swedish	245	1.18
Swiss	55	0.26
Turkish	12	0.06
Ukrainian	67	0.32
United States or American	835	4.02
Welsh	103	0.50
West Indian, excl. Hispanic:	67	0.32
Haitian	53	0.26
Jamaican	6	0.03
Trinidadian and Tobagonian	8	0.04
White:	19,374	93.26
Not Hispanic (19,025)	19,160	92.23
Hispanic (195)	214	1.03

Carver

Place Type: Town
County: Plymouth
Population: 11,163

Ancestry/Race	Number	%
African American/Black:	205	1.84
Not Hispanic (135)	202	1.81
Hispanic (1)	3	0.03
African, sub-Saharan:	261	2.34
Cape Verdean	261	2.34
Am. Ind. or Alaska Nat., not spec.	40	0.36
Albanian	5	0.04
American Indian tribes, specified:	31	0.28
Cherokee (2)	6	0.05
Chippewa	1	0.01
Latin American Indians (1)	3	0.03
Pueblo	3	0.03
Sioux	5	0.04
All other tribes (2)	13	0.12
American Indian tribes, not spec.	2	0.02
Arab:	32	0.29
Lebanese	24	0.21
Syrian	8	0.07
Armenian	14	0.13
Asian:	63	0.56
Cambodian (9)	9	0.08
Chinese, ex. Taiwanese (6)	17	0.15
Filipino (5)	6	0.05
Indian (3)	5	0.04
Indonesian	1	0.01
Japanese	2	0.02
Korean (4)	13	0.12
Thai	3	0.03
Other Asian, not specified (6)	7	0.06
Austrian	7	0.06
Brazilian	9	0.08
British	37	0.33
Canadian	123	1.10
Czech	44	0.39
Dutch	111	0.99
English	2,092	18.74
European	16	0.14
Finnish	170	1.52
French, except Basque	1,037	9.29
French Canadian	500	4.48
German	859	7.70
Greek	31	0.28
Hawaii Native/Pacific Islander:	7	0.06
Micronesian:	1	0.01
Guamanian/Chamorro	1	0.01
Polynesian:	4	0.04
Native Hawaiian	4	0.04
Other Pac. Isl., not spec.	2	0.02
Hispanic or Latino:	91	0.82
Central American:	3	0.03
Costa Rican	1	0.01
Guatemalan	1	0.01
Salvadoran	1	0.01
Cuban	6	0.05
Mexican	18	0.16
Puerto Rican	34	0.30
South American:	14	0.13
Colombian	4	0.04
Peruvian	9	0.08

Notes: 1. Figures in the "Number" column do not add up to the total population due to: a) Ancestry/Race overlap — e.g. persons can report being both White and Irish, b) persons of Hispanic origin can report being any race, c) persons reporting two ancestries are counted in both categories. 2. Numbers in parentheses indicate the number of persons reporting this ancestry/race alone, not in combination with any other ancestry/race. 3. Refer to the Explanation of Data in the front of the book for more detailed information.

Venezuelan	1	0.01
Other Hispanic or Latino	16	0.14
Hungarian	8	0.07
Iranian	22	0.20
Irish	3,414	30.58
Italian	2,363	21.17
Lithuanian	116	1.04
Norwegian	97	0.87
Polish	233	2.09
Portuguese	662	5.93
Russian	83	0.74
Scandinavian	10	0.09
Scotch-Irish	280	2.51
Scottish	756	6.77
Slovak	21	0.19
Swedish	215	1.93
United States or American	517	4.63
Welsh	85	0.76
West Indian, excl. Hispanic:	42	0.38
Jamaican	6	0.05
West Indian	36	0.32
White:	10,847	97.17
Not Hispanic (10,636)	10,783	96.60
Hispanic (56)	64	0.57

Charlton

Place Type: Town
County: Worcester
Population: 11,263

Ancestry/Race	Number	%
African American/Black:	37	0.33
Not Hispanic (24)	35	0.31
Hispanic (2)	2	0.02
African, sub-Saharan:	42	0.37
African	8	0.07
Cape Verdean	15	0.13
Ghanian	19	0.17
Am. Ind. or Alaska Nat., not spec.	14	0.12
Albanian	37	0.33
American Indian tribes, specified:	35	0.31
Apache (2)	2	0.02
Blackfeet	1	0.01
Cherokee	4	0.04
Chippewa (2)	2	0.02
Iroquois (2)	4	0.04
Sioux (1)	1	0.01
All other tribes (12)	21	0.19
American Indian tribes, not spec.	4	0.04
Arab:	27	0.24
Lebanese	27	0.24
Armenian	37	0.33
Asian:	77	0.68
Chinese, ex. Taiwanese (18)	23	0.20
Filipino (9)	12	0.11
Indian (5)	9	0.08
Japanese (1)	2	0.02
Korean (12)	20	0.18
Laotian (2)	3	0.03
Vietnamese (4)	7	0.06
Other Asian, not specified (1)	1	0.01
Austrian	36	0.32
Belgian	18	0.16
Brazilian	40	0.36
Canadian	47	0.42
Czechoslovakian	13	0.12
Danish	19	0.17
Dutch	83	0.74
English	1,987	17.64
Finnish	36	0.32
French, except Basque	2,520	22.37
French Canadian	811	7.20
German	693	6.15
Greek	124	1.10
Hawaii Native/Pacific Islander:	11	0.10
Melanesian: (1)	2	0.02
Fijian (1)	2	0.02
Micronesian: (1)	1	0.01
Guamanian/Chamorro (1)	1	0.01
Polynesian: (5)	5	0.04
Native Hawaiian (5)	5	0.04
Other Pac. Isl., not spec.	3	0.03
Hispanic or Latino:	110	0.98
Central American:	8	0.07
Guatemalan	2	0.02
Honduran	3	0.03
Salvadoran	3	0.03
Cuban	1	0.01
Mexican	11	0.10
Puerto Rican	81	0.72
South American:	4	0.04
Bolivian	1	0.01
Colombian	1	0.01
Ecuadorian	2	0.02
Other Hispanic or Latino	5	0.04
Hungarian	11	0.10
Irish	2,180	19.36
Italian	1,171	10.40
Lithuanian	229	2.03
Norwegian	108	0.96
Pennsylvania German	9	0.08
Polish	1,248	11.08
Portuguese	63	0.56
Russian	28	0.25
Scotch-Irish	133	1.18
Scottish	386	3.43
Swedish	487	4.32
Swiss	18	0.16
Ukrainian	26	0.23
United States or American	735	6.53
Welsh	40	0.36
White:	11,104	98.59
Not Hispanic (10,980)	11,028	97.91
Hispanic (67)	76	0.67
Yugoslavian	9	0.08

Chelmsford

Place Type: Town
County: Middlesex
Population: 33,858

Ancestry/Race	Number	%
African American/Black:	327	0.97
Not Hispanic (257)	313	0.92
Hispanic (9)	14	0.04
African, sub-Saharan:	58	0.17
African	36	0.11
Cape Verdean	14	0.04
Other sub-Saharan African	8	0.02
Am. Ind. or Alaska Nat., not spec.	26	0.08
Albanian	13	0.04
American Indian tribes, specified:	76	0.22
Apache	1	0.00
Blackfeet (2)	12	0.04
Cherokee (4)	15	0.04
Chippewa	1	0.00
Choctaw	4	0.01
Cree	1	0.00
Crow	2	0.01
Iroquois	6	0.02
Latin American Indians (1)	2	0.01
Sioux (2)	2	0.01
All other tribes (9)	30	0.09
American Indian tribes, not spec.	4	0.01
Arab:	293	0.87
Arab/Arabic	64	0.19
Egyptian	32	0.09
Lebanese	131	0.39
Syrian	58	0.17
Other Arab	8	0.02
Armenian	168	0.50
Asian:	1,696	5.01
Cambodian (101)	119	0.35
Chinese, ex. Taiwanese (664)	709	2.09
Filipino (15)	28	0.08
Indian (460)	474	1.40
Indonesian (1)	2	0.01
Japanese (38)	55	0.16
Korean (136)	147	0.43
Laotian (1)	1	0.00
Malaysian (1)	1	0.00
Pakistani (8)	15	0.04
Taiwanese (26)	33	0.10
Thai (6)	8	0.02
Vietnamese (62)	63	0.19
Other Asian, specified (5)	8	0.02
Other Asian, not specified (26)	33	0.10
Australian	25	0.07
Austrian	97	0.29
Belgian	24	0.07
Brazilian	19	0.06
British	289	0.85
Bulgarian	8	0.02
Canadian	429	1.27
Celtic	49	0.14
Croatian	8	0.02
Czech	37	0.11
Czechoslovakian	33	0.10
Danish	174	0.51
Dutch	336	0.99
Eastern European	20	0.06
English	5,726	16.91
Estonian	13	0.04
European	69	0.20
Finnish	124	0.37
French, except Basque	2,813	8.31
French Canadian	2,268	6.70
German	2,309	6.82
Greek	872	2.58
Hawaii Native/Pacific Islander:	12	0.04
Micronesian: (2)	2	0.01
Guamanian/Chamorro (2)	2	0.01
Polynesian: (1)	2	0.01
Native Hawaiian (1)	2	0.01
Other Pac. Isl., specified	3	0.01
Other Pac. Isl., not spec.	5	0.01
Hispanic or Latino:	418	1.23
Central American:	9	0.03
Costa Rican	2	0.01
Guatemalan	1	0.00
Nicaraguan	1	0.00
Panamanian	1	0.00
Salvadoran	4	0.01
Cuban	25	0.07
Dominican Republic	8	0.02
Mexican	63	0.19
Puerto Rican	181	0.53
South American:	54	0.16
Argentinean	4	0.01
Bolivian	2	0.01
Chilean	2	0.01
Colombian	26	0.08
Ecuadorian	6	0.02
Paraguayan	1	0.00
Peruvian	6	0.02
Venezuelan	5	0.01
Other South American	2	0.01
Other Hispanic or Latino	78	0.23
Hungarian	83	0.25
Iranian	76	0.22
Irish	10,803	31.91
Israeli	10	0.03
Italian	4,752	14.04
Latvian	20	0.06
Lithuanian	272	0.80
Northern European	22	0.06
Norwegian	449	1.33
Pennsylvania German	43	0.13
Polish	1,569	4.63
Portuguese	942	2.78
Russian	486	1.44
Scandinavian	15	0.04
Scotch-Irish	721	2.13
Scottish	1,211	3.58
Slavic	4	0.01
Slovak	121	0.36
Slovene	7	0.02
Swedish	821	2.42

Notes: 1. Figures in the "Number" column do not add up to the total population due to: a) Ancestry/Race overlap — e.g. persons can report being both White and Irish, b) persons of Hispanic origin can report being any race, c) persons reporting two ancestries are counted in both categories. 2. Numbers in parentheses indicate the number of persons reporting this ancestry/race alone, not in combination with any other ancestry/race. 3. Refer to the Explanation of Data in the front of the book for more detailed information.

Ancestry/Race	Number	%
Swiss	31	0.09
Ukrainian	105	0.31
United States or American	974	2.88
Welsh	176	0.52
West Indian, excl. Hispanic:	27	0.08
Jamaican	10	0.03
Trinidadian and Tobagonian	9	0.03
West Indian	8	0.02
White:	31,800	93.92
Not Hispanic (31,291)	31,542	93.16
Hispanic (229)	258	0.76
Yugoslavian	8	0.02

Chelsea

Place Type: City
County: Suffolk
Population: 35,080

Ancestry/Race	Number	%
African American/Black:	3,037	8.66
Not Hispanic (1,971)	2,282	6.51
Hispanic (573)	755	2.15
African, sub-Saharan:	835	2.38
African	397	1.13
Cape Verdean	212	0.60
Ethiopian	69	0.20
Kenyan	15	0.04
Nigerian	38	0.11
Sierra Leonean	9	0.03
Somalian	42	0.12
Ugandan	46	0.13
Other sub-Saharan African	7	0.02
Alaska Native tribes, specified:	1	0.00
Tlingit-Haida (1)	1	0.00
Alaska Native tribes, not specified	1	0.00
Am. Ind. or Alaska Nat., not spec.	156	0.44
Albanian	179	0.51
American Indian tribes, specified:	150	0.43
Apache	1	0.00
Blackfeet	3	0.01
Cherokee (4)	20	0.06
Chippewa (1)	1	0.00
Comanche	6	0.02
Iroquois (1)	5	0.01
Latin American Indians (27)	60	0.17
Navajo	1	0.00
Pima (6)	6	0.02
Pueblo	4	0.01
Seminole	2	0.01
Sioux (1)	4	0.01
All other tribes (18)	37	0.11
American Indian tribes, not spec.	30	0.09
Arab:	190	0.54
Arab/Arabic	21	0.06
Egyptian	27	0.08
Iraqi	8	0.02
Lebanese	20	0.06
Moroccan	52	0.15
Syrian	7	0.02
Other Arab	55	0.16
Armenian	179	0.51
Asian:	1,818	5.18
Bangladeshi (2)	2	0.01
Cambodian (250)	299	0.85
Chinese, ex. Taiwanese (213)	240	0.68
Filipino (75)	90	0.26
Indian (121)	130	0.37
Indonesian	3	0.01
Japanese (13)	24	0.07
Korean (37)	46	0.13
Laotian (4)	4	0.01
Malaysian (2)	2	0.01
Sri Lankan (1)	1	0.00
Thai (7)	10	0.03
Vietnamese (870)	901	2.57
Other Asian, specified (3)	3	0.01
Other Asian, not specified (31)	63	0.18
Austrian	41	0.12
Belgian	9	0.03
Brazilian	415	1.18
British	25	0.07
Canadian	142	0.40
Croatian	62	0.18
Czech	7	0.02
Czechoslovakian	17	0.05
Danish	30	0.09
Dutch	29	0.08
Eastern European	25	0.07
English	992	2.83
European	17	0.05
Finnish	49	0.14
French, except Basque	749	2.14
French Canadian	525	1.50
German	492	1.40
Greek	50	0.14
Hawaii Native/Pacific Islander:	113	0.32
Micronesian: (18)	20	0.06
Guamanian/Chamorro (17)	19	0.05
Other Micronesian (1)	1	0.00
Polynesian: (5)	26	0.07
Native Hawaiian	11	0.03
Samoan (5)	12	0.03
Other Polynesian	3	0.01
Other Pac. Isl., not spec. (9)	67	0.19
Hispanic or Latino:	16,984	48.42
Central American:	6,010	17.13
Costa Rican	156	0.44
Guatemalan	1,177	3.36
Honduran	1,582	4.51
Nicaraguan	68	0.19
Panamanian	8	0.02
Salvadoran	2,711	7.73
Other Central American	308	0.88
Cuban	227	0.65
Dominican Republic	533	1.52
Mexican	660	1.88
Puerto Rican	5,363	15.29
South American:	905	2.58
Argentinean	32	0.09
Bolivian	1	0.00
Chilean	24	0.07
Colombian	658	1.88
Ecuadorian	33	0.09
Peruvian	112	0.32
Venezuelan	27	0.08
Other South American	18	0.05
Other Hispanic or Latino	3,286	9.37
Iranian	36	0.10
Irish	2,973	8.47
Italian	3,161	9.01
Latvian	18	0.05
Lithuanian	54	0.15
Norwegian	53	0.15
Polish	1,279	3.65
Portuguese	354	1.01
Russian	320	0.91
Scotch-Irish	184	0.52
Scottish	154	0.44
Serbian	24	0.07
Slavic	22	0.06
Slovak	7	0.02
Swedish	137	0.39
Swiss	30	0.09
Turkish	11	0.03
Ukrainian	37	0.11
United States or American	1,445	4.12
Welsh	22	0.06
West Indian, excl. Hispanic:	540	1.54
Bahamian	10	0.03
British West Indian	10	0.03
Haitian	256	0.73
Jamaican	72	0.21
Trinidadian and Tobagonian	154	0.44
West Indian	38	0.11
White:	22,201	63.29
Not Hispanic (13,424)	13,987	39.87
Hispanic (6,904)	8,214	23.42
Yugoslavian	573	1.63

Chicopee

Place Type: City
County: Hampden
Population: 54,653

Ancestry/Race	Number	%
African American/Black:	1,553	2.84
Not Hispanic (1,078)	1,305	2.39
Hispanic (166)	248	0.45
African, sub-Saharan:	55	0.10
African	48	0.09
Cape Verdean	7	0.01
Am. Ind. or Alaska Nat., not spec.	134	0.25
Albanian	24	0.04
American Indian tribes, specified:	107	0.20
Apache (1)	2	0.00
Blackfeet (2)	18	0.03
Cherokee (3)	16	0.03
Chickasaw (1)	1	0.00
Chippewa (3)	5	0.01
Creek (1)	1	0.00
Iroquois (6)	19	0.03
Latin American Indians (4)	12	0.02
Shoshone	7	0.01
Sioux	3	0.01
All other tribes (8)	23	0.04
American Indian tribes, not spec.	31	0.06
Arab:	88	0.16
Arab/Arabic	13	0.02
Lebanese	75	0.14
Armenian	7	0.01
Asian:	631	1.15
Bangladeshi	3	0.01
Cambodian (32)	36	0.07
Chinese, ex. Taiwanese (116)	129	0.24
Filipino (36)	67	0.12
Hmong (3)	4	0.01
Indian (59)	75	0.14
Indonesian (5)	9	0.02
Japanese (41)	60	0.11
Korean (70)	84	0.15
Laotian (1)	2	0.00
Pakistani (13)	20	0.04
Taiwanese (1)	2	0.00
Thai (12)	16	0.03
Vietnamese (73)	81	0.15
Other Asian, specified	1	0.00
Other Asian, not specified (7)	42	0.08
Assyrian/Chaldean/Syriac	15	0.03
Austrian	132	0.24
Basque	8	0.01
Belgian	42	0.08
Brazilian	6	0.01
British	124	0.23
Canadian	366	0.67
Croatian	13	0.02
Czech	85	0.16
Czechoslovakian	16	0.03
Danish	70	0.13
Dutch	232	0.42
English	3,131	5.73
Estonian	10	0.02
European	36	0.07
Finnish	38	0.07
French, except Basque	10,946	20.03
French Canadian	7,827	14.32
German	2,742	5.02
Greek	531	0.97
Hawaii Native/Pacific Islander:	86	0.16
Micronesian: (3)	5	0.01
Guamanian/Chamorro (3)	5	0.01
Polynesian: (49)	60	0.11
Native Hawaiian (11)	17	0.03
Samoan (34)	38	0.07
Tongan (4)	4	0.01
Other Polynesian	1	0.00
Other Pac. Isl., specified	1	0.00
Other Pac. Isl., not spec. (5)	20	0.04
Hispanic or Latino:	4,790	8.76

Notes: 1. Figures in the "Number" column do not add up to the total population due to: a) Ancestry/Race overlap — e.g. persons can report being both White and Irish, b) persons of Hispanic origin can report being any race, c) persons reporting two ancestries are counted in both categories. 2. Numbers in parentheses indicate the number of persons reporting this ancestry/race alone, not in combination with any other ancestry/race. 3. Refer to the Explanation of Data in the front of the book for more detailed information.

Ancestry/Race	Number	%
Central American:	26	0.05
Costa Rican	2	0.00
Guatemalan	5	0.01
Honduran	10	0.02
Panamanian	5	0.01
Salvadoran	4	0.01
Cuban	32	0.06
Dominican Republic	97	0.18
Mexican	93	0.17
Puerto Rican	3,932	7.19
South American:	79	0.14
Argentinean	1	0.00
Chilean	1	0.00
Colombian	39	0.07
Ecuadorian	24	0.04
Peruvian	6	0.01
Uruguayan	2	0.00
Venezuelan	3	0.01
Other South American	3	0.01
Other Hispanic or Latino	531	0.97
Hungarian	46	0.08
Irish	8,255	15.10
Italian	3,116	5.70
Latvian	7	0.01
Lithuanian	252	0.46
Northern European	12	0.02
Norwegian	84	0.15
Pennsylvania German	15	0.03
Polish	12,448	22.78
Portuguese	1,289	2.36
Russian	660	1.21
Scandinavian	43	0.08
Scotch-Irish	658	1.20
Scottish	851	1.56
Serbian	18	0.03
Slavic	18	0.03
Slovak	67	0.12
Swedish	431	0.79
Swiss	12	0.02
Turkish	50	0.09
Ukrainian	355	0.65
United States or American	1,608	2.94
Welsh	130	0.24
West Indian, excl. Hispanic:	133	0.24
Barbadian	9	0.02
Belizean	6	0.01
Haitian	9	0.02
Jamaican	87	0.16
Trinidadian and Tobagonian	17	0.03
Other West Indian	5	0.01
White:	49,962	91.42
Not Hispanic (47,478)	48,086	87.98
Hispanic (1,611)	1,876	3.43
Yugoslavian	35	0.06

Clinton

Place Type: Town
County: Worcester
Population: 13,435

Ancestry/Race	Number	%
African American/Black:	422	3.14
Not Hispanic (239)	300	2.23
Hispanic (107)	122	0.91
African, sub-Saharan:	60	0.45
African	27	0.20
Ethiopian	28	0.21
Liberian	5	0.04
Am. Ind. or Alaska Nat., not spec.	41	0.31
Albanian	34	0.25
American Indian tribes, specified:	43	0.32
Blackfeet	5	0.04
Cherokee (1)	3	0.02
Chippewa	3	0.02
Comanche (1)	1	0.01
Delaware (2)	2	0.01
Houma (2)	2	0.01
Iroquois (5)	6	0.04
Latin American Indians (2)	3	0.02
Pima	3	0.02
Shoshone (1)	1	0.01
Sioux (1)	2	0.01
All other tribes (5)	12	0.09
American Indian tribes, not spec.	5	0.04
Arab:	14	0.10
Arab/Arabic	8	0.06
Lebanese	6	0.04
Armenian	45	0.33
Asian:	160	1.19
Cambodian (1)	1	0.01
Chinese, ex. Taiwanese (25)	29	0.22
Filipino (10)	13	0.10
Indian (42)	53	0.39
Japanese (7)	26	0.19
Korean (12)	14	0.10
Laotian (8)	8	0.06
Pakistani (1)	1	0.01
Thai (9)	9	0.07
Other Asian, specified (1)	1	0.01
Other Asian, not specified (3)	5	0.04
Assyrian/Chaldean/Syriac	21	0.16
Austrian	7	0.05
Belgian	3	0.02
Brazilian	90	0.67
British	46	0.34
Canadian	115	0.86
Croatian	12	0.09
Czechoslovakian	26	0.19
Danish	39	0.29
Dutch	103	0.77
English	1,125	8.37
European	23	0.17
Finnish	38	0.28
French, except Basque	1,301	9.68
French Canadian	517	3.85
German	1,048	7.80
Greek	161	1.20
Hawaii Native/Pacific Islander:	14	0.10
Polynesian: (2)	2	0.01
Native Hawaiian (2)	2	0.01
Other Pac. Isl., not spec. (4)	12	0.09
Hispanic or Latino:	1,558	11.60
Central American:	131	0.98
Costa Rican	8	0.06
Guatemalan	62	0.46
Honduran	26	0.19
Nicaraguan	1	0.01
Panamanian	18	0.13
Salvadoran	10	0.07
Other Central American	6	0.04
Cuban	3	0.02
Dominican Republic	221	1.64
Mexican	53	0.39
Puerto Rican	757	5.63
South American:	90	0.67
Argentinean	5	0.04
Bolivian	7	0.05
Colombian	23	0.17
Ecuadorian	9	0.07
Peruvian	15	0.11
Uruguayan	2	0.01
Venezuelan	28	0.21
Other South American	1	0.01
Other Hispanic or Latino	303	2.26
Hungarian	37	0.28
Irish	3,567	26.55
Italian	1,806	13.44
Lithuanian	43	0.32
Norwegian	46	0.34
Polish	1,088	8.10
Portuguese	139	1.03
Russian	23	0.17
Scandinavian	5	0.04
Scotch-Irish	149	1.11
Scottish	292	2.17
Slovak	28	0.21
Swedish	223	1.66
Swiss	12	0.09
Ukrainian	31	0.23
United States or American	1,012	7.53
Welsh	34	0.25
West Indian, excl. Hispanic:	153	1.14
Haitian	113	0.84
Jamaican	31	0.23
West Indian	9	0.07
White:	12,089	89.98
Not Hispanic (11,249)	11,398	84.84
Hispanic (600)	691	5.14
Yugoslavian	14	0.10

Concord

Place Type: Town
County: Middlesex
Population: 16,993

Ancestry/Race	Number	%
African American/Black:	440	2.59
Not Hispanic (378)	429	2.52
Hispanic (2)	11	0.06
African, sub-Saharan:	62	0.36
African	24	0.14
Cape Verdean	16	0.09
Nigerian	6	0.04
South African	16	0.09
Am. Ind. or Alaska Nat., not spec.	12	0.07
Albanian	6	0.04
Alsatian	6	0.04
American Indian tribes, specified:	21	0.12
Blackfeet (1)	3	0.02
Cherokee (2)	4	0.02
Choctaw	4	0.02
Latin American Indians (3)	3	0.02
Navajo	1	0.01
Sioux (1)	1	0.01
All other tribes (3)	5	0.03
American Indian tribes, not spec.	5	0.03
Arab:	95	0.56
Egyptian	6	0.04
Lebanese	51	0.30
Syrian	29	0.17
Other Arab	9	0.05
Armenian	126	0.74
Asian:	569	3.35
Cambodian (4)	4	0.02
Chinese, ex. Taiwanese (248)	292	1.72
Filipino (12)	14	0.08
Indian (97)	107	0.63
Indonesian (1)	2	0.01
Japanese (54)	64	0.38
Korean (60)	65	0.38
Malaysian	1	0.01
Pakistani	1	0.01
Taiwanese (5)	5	0.03
Thai (1)	1	0.01
Vietnamese (2)	2	0.01
Other Asian, not specified (6)	11	0.06
Australian	6	0.04
Austrian	158	0.93
Belgian	12	0.07
Brazilian	21	0.12
British	285	1.68
Bulgarian	12	0.07
Canadian	108	0.64
Celtic	45	0.26
Croatian	15	0.09
Czech	71	0.42
Danish	108	0.64
Dutch	269	1.58
Eastern European	116	0.68
English	4,016	23.63
European	430	2.53
Finnish	89	0.52
French, except Basque	766	4.51
French Canadian	348	2.05
German	1,479	8.70
Greek	113	0.66
Hawaii Native/Pacific Islander:	5	0.03
Polynesian: (3)	4	0.02

Notes: 1. Figures in the "Number" column do not add up to the total population due to: a) Ancestry/Race overlap — e.g. persons can report being both White and Irish, b) persons of Hispanic origin can report being any race, c) persons reporting two ancestries are counted in both categories. 2. Numbers in parentheses indicate the number of persons reporting this ancestry/race alone, not in combination with any other ancestry/race. 3. Refer to the Explanation of Data in the front of the book for more detailed information.

Native Hawaiian (1)	1	0.01
Samoan (2)	3	0.02
Other Pac. Isl., not spec. (1)	1	0.01
Hispanic or Latino:	475	2.80
Central American:	17	0.10
Guatemalan	8	0.05
Honduran	2	0.01
Nicaraguan	2	0.01
Salvadoran	5	0.03
Cuban	38	0.22
Dominican Republic	26	0.15
Mexican	35	0.21
Puerto Rican	210	1.24
South American:	37	0.22
Argentinean	3	0.02
Chilean	2	0.01
Colombian	21	0.12
Peruvian	1	0.01
Venezuelan	7	0.04
Other South American	3	0.02
Other Hispanic or Latino	112	0.66
Hungarian	108	0.64
Icelander	18	0.11
Iranian	37	0.22
Irish	3,532	20.79
Israeli	23	0.14
Italian	1,856	10.92
Latvian	11	0.06
Lithuanian	82	0.48
Macedonian	5	0.03
Northern European	47	0.28
Norwegian	165	0.97
Polish	382	2.25
Portuguese	112	0.66
Romanian	18	0.11
Russian	382	2.25
Scandinavian	60	0.35
Scotch-Irish	267	1.57
Scottish	756	4.45
Serbian	9	0.05
Slovak	7	0.04
Swedish	401	2.36
Swiss	65	0.38
Ukrainian	83	0.49
United States or American	650	3.83
Welsh	139	0.82
West Indian, excl. Hispanic:	46	0.27
Haitian	21	0.12
Jamaican	11	0.06
Trinidadian and Tobagonian	14	0.08
White:	15,718	92.50
Not Hispanic (15,432)	15,562	91.58
Hispanic (140)	156	0.92

Danvers

Place Type: Census Designated Place
County: Essex
Population: 25,212

Ancestry/Race	Number	%
African American/Black:	128	0.51
Not Hispanic (81)	121	0.48
Hispanic (6)	7	0.03
African, sub-Saharan:	39	0.15
African	9	0.04
Nigerian	8	0.03
Senegalese	10	0.04
Other sub-Saharan African	12	0.05
Alaska Native tribes, specified:	1	0.00
Eskimo (1)	1	0.00
Am. Ind. or Alaska Nat., not spec.	16	0.06
Albanian	75	0.30
American Indian tribes, specified:	35	0.14
Apache (1)	1	0.00
Blackfeet	9	0.04
Cherokee (4)	8	0.03
Chippewa (1)	1	0.00
Cree	2	0.01
Latin American Indians (2)	2	0.01
Lumbee (2)	2	0.01
Navajo (1)	1	0.00
All other tribes (6)	9	0.04
American Indian tribes, not spec.	3	0.01
Arab:	77	0.31
Lebanese	62	0.25
Syrian	15	0.06
Armenian	62	0.25
Asian:	313	1.24
Cambodian (8)	8	0.03
Chinese, ex. Taiwanese (72)	79	0.31
Filipino (11)	13	0.05
Indian (75)	83	0.33
Japanese (23)	29	0.12
Korean (38)	42	0.17
Laotian (6)	6	0.02
Sri Lankan (3)	3	0.01
Taiwanese (5)	5	0.02
Thai (1)	1	0.00
Vietnamese (32)	37	0.15
Other Asian, not specified (4)	7	0.03
Australian	6	0.02
Austrian	47	0.19
Belgian	10	0.04
Brazilian	10	0.04
British	107	0.42
Canadian	286	1.13
Czech	42	0.17
Czechoslovakian	28	0.11
Danish	80	0.32
Dutch	97	0.38
Eastern European	9	0.04
English	3,722	14.76
European	24	0.10
Finnish	104	0.41
French, except Basque	2,371	9.40
French Canadian	1,578	6.26
German	1,045	4.14
Greek	827	3.28
Hawaii Native/Pacific Islander:	7	0.03
Micronesian: (1)	1	0.00
Guamanian/Chamorro (1)	1	0.00
Polynesian: (1)	3	0.01
Native Hawaiian (1)	2	0.01
Samoan	1	0.00
Other Pac. Isl., not spec. (2)	3	0.01
Hispanic or Latino:	210	0.83
Central American:	11	0.04
Costa Rican	2	0.01
Guatemalan	2	0.01
Honduran	2	0.01
Panamanian	1	0.00
Salvadoran	4	0.02
Cuban	13	0.05
Dominican Republic	37	0.15
Mexican	34	0.13
Puerto Rican	43	0.17
South American:	27	0.11
Argentinean	3	0.01
Chilean	1	0.00
Colombian	6	0.02
Ecuadorian	6	0.02
Paraguayan	4	0.02
Peruvian	4	0.02
Venezuelan	3	0.01
Other Hispanic or Latino	45	0.18
Hungarian	25	0.10
Irish	7,163	28.41
Italian	4,637	18.39
Latvian	15	0.06
Lithuanian	109	0.43
Northern European	6	0.02
Norwegian	159	0.63
Polish	1,730	6.86
Portuguese	536	2.13
Romanian	41	0.16
Russian	286	1.13
Scandinavian	8	0.03
Scotch-Irish	394	1.56
Scottish	956	3.79
Serbian	8	0.03
Slavic	11	0.04
Slovak	8	0.03
Slovene	9	0.04
Swedish	548	2.17
Swiss	29	0.12
Ukrainian	68	0.27
United States or American	1,479	5.87
Welsh	84	0.33
West Indian, excl. Hispanic:	9	0.04
West Indian	9	0.04
White:	24,744	98.14
Not Hispanic (24,498)	24,596	97.56
Hispanic (140)	148	0.59

Dartmouth

Place Type: Town
County: Bristol
Population: 30,666

Ancestry/Race	Number	%
African American/Black:	466	1.52
Not Hispanic (291)	424	1.38
Hispanic (34)	42	0.14
African, sub-Saharan:	679	2.21
Cape Verdean	679	2.21
Alaska Native tribes, specified:	4	0.01
Eskimo	2	0.01
Tlingit-Haida (2)	2	0.01
Am. Ind. or Alaska Nat., not spec.	53	0.17
Albanian	61	0.20
American Indian tribes, specified:	71	0.23
Blackfeet	3	0.01
Cherokee (1)	7	0.02
Chippewa (1)	3	0.01
Cree	1	0.00
Iroquois (2)	6	0.02
Latin American Indians (3)	3	0.01
Paiute	2	0.01
Seminole	1	0.00
All other tribes (31)	45	0.15
American Indian tribes, not spec.	4	0.01
Arab:	156	0.51
Egyptian	10	0.03
Iraqi	18	0.06
Lebanese	123	0.40
Syrian	5	0.02
Armenian	7	0.02
Asian:	442	1.44
Cambodian (14)	14	0.05
Chinese, ex. Taiwanese (117)	127	0.41
Filipino (33)	43	0.14
Indian (105)	113	0.37
Japanese (19)	34	0.11
Korean (26)	33	0.11
Malaysian (1)	1	0.00
Pakistani	1	0.00
Taiwanese (5)	8	0.03
Thai (6)	9	0.03
Vietnamese (25)	26	0.08
Other Asian, specified	1	0.00
Other Asian, not specified (8)	32	0.10
Austrian	82	0.27
Belgian	9	0.03
Brazilian	69	0.23
British	186	0.61
Canadian	101	0.33
Czech	15	0.05
Czechoslovakian	8	0.03
Danish	60	0.20
Dutch	80	0.26
Eastern European	23	0.08
English	3,412	11.13
European	59	0.19
Finnish	15	0.05
French, except Basque	2,826	9.22
French Canadian	1,522	4.96
German	1,004	3.27
Greek	80	0.26

Notes: 1. Figures in the "Number" column do not add up to the total population due to: a) Ancestry/Race overlap — e.g. persons can report being both White and Irish, b) persons of Hispanic origin can report being any race, c) persons reporting two ancestries are counted in both categories. 2. Numbers in parentheses indicate the number of persons reporting this ancestry/race alone, not in combination with any other ancestry/race. 3. Refer to the Explanation of Data in the front of the book for more detailed information.

Ancestry/Race	Number	%
Hawaii Native/Pacific Islander:	51	0.17
Micronesian: (5)	6	0.02
Guamanian/Chamorro (5)	6	0.02
Polynesian: (3)	4	0.01
Native Hawaiian (2)	3	0.01
Samoan (1)	1	0.00
Other Pac. Isl., not spec. (2)	41	0.13
Hispanic or Latino:	461	1.50
Central American:	20	0.07
Costa Rican	7	0.02
Guatemalan	3	0.01
Nicaraguan	3	0.01
Panamanian	1	0.00
Salvadoran	6	0.02
Cuban	9	0.03
Dominican Republic	22	0.07
Mexican	47	0.15
Puerto Rican	213	0.69
South American:	60	0.20
Argentinean	5	0.02
Chilean	2	0.01
Colombian	37	0.12
Ecuadorian	5	0.02
Peruvian	9	0.03
Venezuelan	2	0.01
Other Hispanic or Latino	90	0.29
Hungarian	46	0.15
Irish	3,750	12.23
Israeli	8	0.03
Italian	1,437	4.69
Latvian	7	0.02
Lithuanian	95	0.31
Northern European	10	0.03
Norwegian	300	0.98
Polish	1,274	4.15
Portuguese	12,408	40.46
Romanian	8	0.03
Russian	398	1.30
Scotch-Irish	292	0.95
Scottish	401	1.31
Slovene	15	0.05
Swedish	296	0.97
Swiss	7	0.02
Ukrainian	51	0.17
United States or American	889	2.90
Welsh	80	0.26
West Indian, excl. Hispanic:	7	0.02
Haitian	7	0.02
White:	28,234	92.07
Not Hispanic (27,629)	27,998	91.30
Hispanic (207)	236	0.77

Dedham

Place Type: Census Designated Place
County: Norfolk
Population: 23,464

Ancestry/Race	Number	%
African American/Black:	418	1.78
Not Hispanic (335)	382	1.63
Hispanic (27)	36	0.15
African, sub-Saharan:	4	0.02
Ethiopian	4	0.02
Am. Ind. or Alaska Nat., not spec.	37	0.16
Albanian	12	0.05
American Indian tribes, specified:	52	0.22
Blackfeet (1)	6	0.03
Cherokee (1)	6	0.03
Chippewa (1)	2	0.01
Creek	2	0.01
Iroquois (4)	4	0.02
Latin American Indians	2	0.01
Menominee	1	0.00
Sioux (1)	1	0.00
All other tribes (17)	28	0.12
American Indian tribes, not spec.	3	0.01
Arab:	965	4.10
Arab/Arabic	22	0.09
Egyptian	9	0.04
Lebanese	763	3.25
Moroccan	14	0.06
Syrian	126	0.54
Other Arab	31	0.13
Armenian	61	0.26
Asian:	517	2.20
Cambodian (4)	4	0.02
Chinese, ex. Taiwanese (158)	175	0.75
Filipino (88)	105	0.45
Indian (72)	83	0.35
Indonesian (1)	2	0.01
Japanese (12)	25	0.11
Korean (18)	23	0.10
Laotian (12)	13	0.06
Pakistani	1	0.00
Sri Lankan (4)	4	0.02
Taiwanese (2)	2	0.01
Thai (9)	11	0.05
Vietnamese (45)	47	0.20
Other Asian, specified (2)	2	0.01
Other Asian, not specified (5)	20	0.09
Australian	9	0.04
Austrian	20	0.09
Belgian	36	0.15
Brazilian	59	0.25
British	88	0.37
Canadian	321	1.37
Croatian	6	0.03
Czech	38	0.16
Czechoslovakian	11	0.05
Danish	71	0.30
Dutch	110	0.47
Eastern European	29	0.12
English	2,593	11.03
European	51	0.22
Finnish	10	0.04
French, except Basque	770	3.28
French Canadian	629	2.68
German	1,621	6.89
Greek	600	2.55
Hawaii Native/Pacific Islander:	25	0.11
Polynesian: (10)	12	0.05
Native Hawaiian (4)	5	0.02
Samoan (6)	6	0.03
Other Polynesian	1	0.00
Other Pac. Isl., not spec.	13	0.06
Hispanic or Latino:	567	2.42
Central American:	55	0.23
Costa Rican	3	0.01
Guatemalan	8	0.03
Honduran	24	0.10
Nicaraguan	2	0.01
Panamanian	1	0.00
Salvadoran	17	0.07
Cuban	38	0.16
Dominican Republic	42	0.18
Mexican	42	0.18
Puerto Rican	174	0.74
South American:	47	0.20
Argentinean	6	0.03
Chilean	4	0.02
Colombian	20	0.09
Ecuadorian	3	0.01
Peruvian	6	0.03
Venezuelan	1	0.00
Other South American	7	0.03
Other Hispanic or Latino	169	0.72
Hungarian	42	0.18
Icelander	6	0.03
Iranian	26	0.11
Irish	8,661	36.84
Italian	4,685	19.93
Latvian	95	0.40
Lithuanian	148	0.63
Norwegian	145	0.62
Polish	719	3.06
Portuguese	200	0.85
Romanian	13	0.06
Russian	227	0.97
Scandinavian	8	0.03
Scotch-Irish	638	2.71
Scottish	740	3.15
Slavic	7	0.03
Slovak	24	0.10
Swedish	460	1.96
Swiss	21	0.09
Turkish	37	0.16
Ukrainian	90	0.38
United States or American	1,297	5.52
Welsh	98	0.42
West Indian, excl. Hispanic:	93	0.40
Bermudan	4	0.02
Haitian	13	0.06
Jamaican	58	0.25
West Indian	18	0.08
White:	22,395	95.44
Not Hispanic (21,873)	22,051	93.98
Hispanic (302)	344	1.47

Dennis

Place Type: Town
County: Barnstable
Population: 15,973

Ancestry/Race	Number	%
African American/Black:	413	2.59
Not Hispanic (296)	401	2.51
Hispanic (12)	12	0.08
African, sub-Saharan:	104	0.65
Cape Verdean	98	0.61
Nigerian	6	0.04
Alaska Native tribes, specified:	2	0.01
Tlingit-Haida (2)	2	0.01
Am. Ind. or Alaska Nat., not spec.	31	0.19
American Indian tribes, specified:	77	0.48
Apache	5	0.03
Blackfeet	4	0.03
Cherokee (6)	14	0.09
Iroquois	1	0.01
Latin American Indians (1)	1	0.01
All other tribes (36)	52	0.33
American Indian tribes, not spec.	8	0.05
Arab:	85	0.53
Lebanese	70	0.44
Syrian	15	0.09
Armenian	79	0.49
Asian:	76	0.48
Chinese, ex. Taiwanese (17)	18	0.11
Filipino (4)	7	0.04
Indian (17)	17	0.11
Japanese (3)	7	0.04
Korean (9)	13	0.08
Pakistani (1)	1	0.01
Thai (1)	3	0.02
Vietnamese (2)	2	0.01
Other Asian, specified (5)	5	0.03
Other Asian, not specified	3	0.02
Austrian	38	0.24
Belgian	19	0.12
Brazilian	91	0.57
British	68	0.43
Bulgarian	6	0.04
Canadian	120	0.75
Czech	10	0.06
Czechoslovakian	37	0.23
Danish	43	0.27
Dutch	220	1.38
Eastern European	15	0.09
English	3,133	19.61
Estonian	5	0.03
European	49	0.31
Finnish	84	0.53
French, except Basque	1,263	7.91
French Canadian	506	3.17
German	1,213	7.59
Greek	156	0.98
Hawaii Native/Pacific Islander:	6	0.04
Polynesian:	5	0.03
Native Hawaiian	4	0.03

Notes: 1. Figures in the "Number" column do not add up to the total population due to: a) Ancestry/Race overlap — e.g. persons can report being both White and Irish, b) persons of Hispanic origin can report being any race, c) persons reporting two ancestries are counted in both categories. 2. Numbers in parentheses indicate the number of persons reporting this ancestry/race alone, not in combination with any other ancestry/race. 3. Refer to the Explanation of Data in the front of the book for more detailed information.

Samoan	1	0.01
Other Pac. Isl., not spec.	1	0.01
Hispanic or Latino:	264	1.65
Central American:	3	0.02
Nicaraguan	2	0.01
Panamanian	1	0.01
Cuban	6	0.04
Dominican Republic	19	0.12
Mexican	55	0.34
Puerto Rican	102	0.64
South American:	18	0.11
Chilean	5	0.03
Colombian	4	0.03
Ecuadorian	5	0.03
Peruvian	4	0.03
Other Hispanic or Latino	61	0.38
Hungarian	85	0.53
Irish	4,693	29.38
Italian	1,901	11.90
Latvian	11	0.07
Lithuanian	117	0.73
Northern European	8	0.05
Norwegian	153	0.96
Pennsylvania German	6	0.04
Polish	714	4.47
Portuguese	469	2.94
Romanian	16	0.10
Russian	128	0.80
Scandinavian	33	0.21
Scotch-Irish	284	1.78
Scottish	674	4.22
Slovak	10	0.06
Swedish	587	3.67
Swiss	27	0.17
Ukrainian	38	0.24
United States or American	800	5.01
Welsh	82	0.51
West Indian, excl. Hispanic:	131	0.82
Haitian	92	0.58
Jamaican	34	0.21
Trinidadian and Tobagonian	5	0.03
White:	15,358	96.15
Not Hispanic (14,999)	15,171	94.98
Hispanic (174)	187	1.17
Yugoslavian	22	0.14

Dracut

Place Type: Town
County: Middlesex
Population: 28,562

Ancestry/Race	Number	%
African American/Black:	284	0.99
Not Hispanic (213)	268	0.94
Hispanic (9)	16	0.06
African, sub-Saharan:	56	0.20
African	56	0.20
Am. Ind. or Alaska Nat., not spec.	50	0.18
Albanian	6	0.02
American Indian tribes, specified:	57	0.20
Apache	1	0.00
Blackfeet	1	0.00
Cherokee	10	0.04
Chippewa	3	0.01
Iroquois (5)	10	0.04
Latin American Indians (1)	2	0.01
Navajo (1)	1	0.00
All other tribes (11)	29	0.10
American Indian tribes, not spec.	8	0.03
Arab:	219	0.77
Lebanese	206	0.72
Palestinian	13	0.05
Armenian	115	0.40
Asian:	818	2.86
Cambodian (148)	166	0.58
Chinese, ex. Taiwanese (135)	149	0.52
Filipino (15)	29	0.10
Indian (268)	271	0.95
Indonesian	1	0.00
Japanese (6)	12	0.04
Korean (64)	70	0.25
Laotian (24)	25	0.09
Pakistani (1)	4	0.01
Taiwanese	1	0.00
Thai (5)	5	0.02
Vietnamese (53)	58	0.20
Other Asian, not specified (10)	27	0.09
Australian	6	0.02
Austrian	41	0.14
Belgian	31	0.11
Brazilian	9	0.03
British	7	0.02
Canadian	351	1.23
Czech	6	0.02
Czechoslovakian	6	0.02
Danish	28	0.10
Dutch	110	0.39
English	2,870	10.05
European	57	0.20
French, except Basque	5,165	18.08
French Canadian	4,522	15.83
German	1,102	3.86
Greek	1,401	4.91
Hawaii Native/Pacific Islander:	21	0.07
Micronesian:	1	0.00
Guamanian/Chamorro	1	0.00
Polynesian: (8)	14	0.05
Native Hawaiian (4)	10	0.04
Samoan (4)	4	0.01
Other Pac. Isl., not spec. (1)	6	0.02
Hispanic or Latino:	443	1.55
Central American:	6	0.02
Honduran	2	0.01
Panamanian	1	0.00
Salvadoran	3	0.01
Cuban	12	0.04
Dominican Republic	11	0.04
Mexican	32	0.11
Puerto Rican	224	0.78
South American:	85	0.30
Argentinean	6	0.02
Chilean	1	0.00
Colombian	58	0.20
Ecuadorian	6	0.02
Peruvian	1	0.00
Venezuelan	5	0.02
Other South American	8	0.03
Other Hispanic or Latino	73	0.26
Hungarian	55	0.19
Iranian	8	0.03
Irish	8,299	29.06
Italian	3,202	11.21
Lithuanian	223	0.78
Norwegian	92	0.32
Polish	2,104	7.37
Portuguese	1,360	4.76
Russian	205	0.72
Scandinavian	12	0.04
Scotch-Irish	535	1.87
Scottish	547	1.92
Slovak	20	0.07
Swedish	283	0.99
Turkish	8	0.03
Ukrainian	55	0.19
United States or American	940	3.29
Welsh	49	0.17
White:	27,421	96.01
Not Hispanic (26,864)	27,095	94.86
Hispanic (306)	326	1.14

Dudley

Place Type: Town
County: Worcester
Population: 10,036

Ancestry/Race	Number	%
African American/Black:	79	0.79
Not Hispanic (45)	69	0.69
Hispanic (4)	10	0.10
African, sub-Saharan:	73	0.73
African	64	0.64
Nigerian	9	0.09
Alaska Native tribes, specified:	1	0.01
All other tribes (1)	1	0.01
Am. Ind. or Alaska Nat., not spec.	18	0.18
Albanian	75	0.75
American Indian tribes, specified:	40	0.40
Blackfeet (1)	3	0.03
Cherokee (1)	2	0.02
Chippewa (1)	1	0.01
Iroquois (2)	3	0.03
Sioux (1)	4	0.04
All other tribes (10)	27	0.27
American Indian tribes, not spec.	1	0.01
Arab:	22	0.22
Egyptian	8	0.08
Lebanese	14	0.14
Armenian	79	0.79
Asian:	94	0.94
Cambodian (7)	7	0.07
Chinese, ex. Taiwanese (10)	14	0.14
Filipino (3)	10	0.10
Indian (23)	23	0.23
Indonesian	1	0.01
Japanese (5)	5	0.05
Korean (5)	12	0.12
Laotian (7)	7	0.07
Malaysian (1)	1	0.01
Pakistani (3)	3	0.03
Thai (4)	4	0.04
Vietnamese (2)	2	0.02
Other Asian, specified	1	0.01
Other Asian, not specified (1)	4	0.04
Belgian	6	0.06
Bulgarian	7	0.07
Canadian	28	0.28
Celtic	4	0.04
Czech	27	0.27
Czechoslovakian	7	0.07
Danish	7	0.07
Dutch	36	0.36
English	996	9.92
Finnish	70	0.70
French, except Basque	2,565	25.56
French Canadian	957	9.54
German	648	6.46
Greek	104	1.04
Hawaii Native/Pacific Islander:	10	0.10
Micronesian:	2	0.02
Guamanian/Chamorro	2	0.02
Polynesian:	7	0.07
Native Hawaiian	7	0.07
Other Pac. Isl., not spec.	1	0.01
Hispanic or Latino:	202	2.01
Central American:	3	0.03
Nicaraguan	3	0.03
Cuban	13	0.13
Dominican Republic	2	0.02
Mexican	31	0.31
Puerto Rican	109	1.09
South American:	12	0.12
Bolivian	1	0.01
Colombian	2	0.02
Ecuadorian	1	0.01
Venezuelan	3	0.03
Other South American	5	0.05
Other Hispanic or Latino	32	0.32
Irish	1,792	17.86
Italian	975	9.72
Lithuanian	198	1.97
Northern European	7	0.07
Norwegian	5	0.05
Polish	2,542	25.33
Portuguese	49	0.49
Romanian	28	0.28
Russian	47	0.47
Scotch-Irish	166	1.65
Scottish	184	1.83

Notes: 1. Figures in the "Number" column do not add up to the total population due to: a) Ancestry/Race overlap — e.g. persons can report being both White and Irish, b) persons of Hispanic origin can report being any race, c) persons reporting two ancestries are counted in both categories. 2. Numbers in parentheses indicate the number of persons reporting this ancestry/race alone, not in combination with any other ancestry/race. 3. Refer to the Explanation of Data in the front of the book for more detailed information.

	Number	%
Slovak	94	0.94
Swedish	252	2.51
Ukrainian	14	0.14
United States or American	245	2.44
Welsh	7	0.07
White:	9,809	97.74
Not Hispanic (9,615)	9,691	96.56
Hispanic (103)	118	1.18

Duxbury

Place Type: Town
County: Plymouth
Population: 14,248

Ancestry/Race	Number	%
African American/Black:	104	0.73
Not Hispanic (91)	101	0.71
Hispanic	3	0.02
African, sub-Saharan:	27	0.19
Cape Verdean	27	0.19
Am. Ind. or Alaska Nat., not spec.	16	0.11
Albanian	50	0.35
American Indian tribes, specified:	18	0.13
Blackfeet	2	0.01
Cherokee (1)	7	0.05
Latin American Indians (1)	1	0.01
All other tribes (5)	8	0.06
Arab:	128	0.90
Lebanese	117	0.82
Moroccan	11	0.08
Armenian	22	0.15
Asian:	115	0.81
Chinese, ex. Taiwanese (36)	47	0.33
Filipino (6)	8	0.06
Indian (2)	2	0.01
Japanese (3)	7	0.05
Korean (29)	30	0.21
Vietnamese (1)	1	0.01
Other Asian, not specified (14)	20	0.14
Assyrian/Chaldean/Syriac	24	0.17
Austrian	45	0.32
Belgian	22	0.15
British	66	0.46
Canadian	49	0.34
Croatian	7	0.05
Czech	42	0.29
Czechoslovakian	7	0.05
Danish	107	0.75
Dutch	102	0.72
Eastern European	8	0.06
English	3,063	21.50
European	60	0.42
Finnish	43	0.30
French, except Basque	699	4.91
French Canadian	403	2.83
German	1,452	10.19
Greek	99	0.69
Hawaii Native/Pacific Islander:	1	0.01
Polynesian: (1)	1	0.01
Samoan (1)	1	0.01
Hispanic or Latino:	102	0.72
Central American:	10	0.07
Costa Rican	1	0.01
Guatemalan	1	0.01
Panamanian	4	0.03
Salvadoran	4	0.03
Cuban	16	0.11
Mexican	24	0.17
Puerto Rican	11	0.08
South American:	18	0.13
Argentinean	1	0.01
Bolivian	1	0.01
Colombian	10	0.07
Venezuelan	2	0.01
Other South American	4	0.03
Other Hispanic or Latino	23	0.16
Hungarian	24	0.17
Irish	5,566	39.07
Italian	1,771	12.43
Latvian	48	0.34
Lithuanian	176	1.24
New Zealander	7	0.05
Northern European	19	0.13
Norwegian	156	1.09
Polish	743	5.21
Portuguese	231	1.62
Russian	158	1.11
Scandinavian	38	0.27
Scotch-Irish	439	3.08
Scottish	594	4.17
Slovak	22	0.15
Swedish	600	4.21
Swiss	68	0.48
Ukrainian	142	1.00
United States or American	367	2.58
Welsh	101	0.71
West Indian, excl. Hispanic:	3	0.02
Jamaican	3	0.02
White:	14,003	98.28
Not Hispanic (13,850)	13,909	97.62
Hispanic (84)	94	0.66
Yugoslavian	26	0.18

East Bridgewater

Place Type: Town
County: Plymouth
Population: 12,974

Ancestry/Race	Number	%
African American/Black:	171	1.32
Not Hispanic (122)	161	1.24
Hispanic (7)	10	0.08
African, sub-Saharan:	255	1.97
Cape Verdean	232	1.79
Ghanian	23	0.18
Am. Ind. or Alaska Nat., not spec.	23	0.18
Albanian	20	0.15
American Indian tribes, specified:	33	0.25
Blackfeet	1	0.01
Cherokee	7	0.05
Iroquois	1	0.01
Latin American Indians (1)	1	0.01
Shoshone (1)	1	0.01
Sioux (2)	2	0.02
Yuman	1	0.01
All other tribes (7)	19	0.15
American Indian tribes, not spec.	3	0.02
Arab:	158	1.22
Lebanese	97	0.75
Syrian	61	0.47
Armenian	19	0.15
Asian:	79	0.61
Chinese, ex. Taiwanese (12)	16	0.12
Filipino (4)	5	0.04
Indian (6)	7	0.05
Japanese (6)	12	0.09
Korean (7)	9	0.07
Pakistani (6)	6	0.05
Vietnamese (16)	16	0.12
Other Asian, not specified (5)	8	0.06
Australian	4	0.03
Austrian	23	0.18
Belgian	16	0.12
Brazilian	18	0.14
British	90	0.69
Canadian	149	1.15
Czech	9	0.07
Danish	6	0.05
Dutch	70	0.54
English	2,011	15.50
European	13	0.10
Finnish	40	0.31
French, except Basque	833	6.42
French Canadian	542	4.18
German	818	6.30
Greek	66	0.51
Hawaii Native/Pacific Islander:	6	0.05
Polynesian: (2)	4	0.03
Native Hawaiian (1)	3	0.02
Samoan (1)	1	0.01
Other Pac. Isl., not spec. (2)	2	0.02
Hispanic or Latino:	97	0.75
Central American:	8	0.06
Honduran	7	0.05
Panamanian	1	0.01
Cuban	14	0.11
Mexican	11	0.08
Puerto Rican	29	0.22
South American:	12	0.09
Argentinean	3	0.02
Chilean	4	0.03
Colombian	1	0.01
Peruvian	3	0.02
Venezuelan	1	0.01
Other Hispanic or Latino	23	0.18
Irish	4,210	32.45
Italian	2,214	17.06
Lithuanian	168	1.29
Norwegian	161	1.24
Polish	435	3.35
Portuguese	437	3.37
Russian	216	1.66
Scandinavian	14	0.11
Scotch-Irish	367	2.83
Scottish	461	3.55
Slavic	37	0.29
Slovak	23	0.18
Swedish	470	3.62
Swiss	14	0.11
Ukrainian	14	0.11
United States or American	793	6.11
Welsh	7	0.05
West Indian, excl. Hispanic:	72	0.55
Haitian	45	0.35
Jamaican	20	0.15
Trinidadian and Tobagonian	7	0.05
White:	12,695	97.85
Not Hispanic (12,503)	12,614	97.23
Hispanic (70)	81	0.62

East Longmeadow

Place Type: Town
County: Hampden
Population: 14,100

Ancestry/Race	Number	%
African American/Black:	127	0.90
Not Hispanic (103)	125	0.89
Hispanic (2)	2	0.01
African, sub-Saharan:	29	0.21
African	11	0.08
Nigerian	11	0.08
South African	7	0.05
Am. Ind. or Alaska Nat., not spec.	6	0.04
Albanian	9	0.06
Alsatian	33	0.23
American Indian tribes, specified:	27	0.19
Blackfeet	3	0.02
Cherokee (2)	11	0.08
Latin American Indians	5	0.04
Potawatomi	1	0.01
Sioux (1)	2	0.01
All other tribes (3)	5	0.04
American Indian tribes, not spec.	1	0.01
Arab:	78	0.55
Lebanese	15	0.11
Syrian	57	0.40
Other Arab	6	0.04
Armenian	30	0.21
Asian:	155	1.10
Chinese, ex. Taiwanese (61)	73	0.52
Filipino (4)	11	0.08
Indian (27)	36	0.26
Indonesian (1)	2	0.01
Japanese (2)	3	0.02
Korean (3)	3	0.02
Pakistani (4)	4	0.03

Notes: 1. Figures in the "Number" column do not add up to the total population due to: a) Ancestry/Race overlap — e.g. persons can report being both White and Irish, b) persons of Hispanic origin can report being any race, c) persons reporting two ancestries are counted in both categories. 2. Numbers in parentheses indicate the number of persons reporting this ancestry/race alone, not in combination with any other ancestry/race. 3. Refer to the Explanation of Data in the front of the book for more detailed information.

Ancestry/Race	Number	%
Taiwanese (1)	6	0.04
Vietnamese (10)	11	0.08
Other Asian, not specified (4)	6	0.04
Austrian	47	0.33
British	58	0.41
Canadian	118	0.84
Czech	10	0.07
Czechoslovakian	26	0.18
Danish	36	0.26
Dutch	106	0.75
English	1,976	14.01
European	86	0.61
Finnish	50	0.35
French, except Basque	1,647	11.68
French Canadian	956	6.78
German	1,282	9.09
Greek	247	1.75
Hawaii Native/Pacific Islander:	10	0.07
Polynesian: (5)	7	0.05
Native Hawaiian (4)	5	0.04
Samoan	1	0.01
Other Polynesian (1)	1	0.01
Other Pac. Isl., not spec. (1)	3	0.02
Hispanic or Latino:	130	0.92
Central American:	5	0.04
Costa Rican	2	0.01
Panamanian	3	0.02
Cuban	6	0.04
Dominican Republic	1	0.01
Mexican	10	0.07
Puerto Rican	70	0.50
South American:	11	0.08
Argentinean	1	0.01
Bolivian	1	0.01
Chilean	1	0.01
Colombian	7	0.05
Venezuelan	1	0.01
Other Hispanic or Latino	27	0.19
Hungarian	98	0.70
Iranian	35	0.25
Irish	3,626	25.72
Italian	3,165	22.45
Lithuanian	54	0.38
Northern European	29	0.21
Norwegian	8	0.06
Pennsylvania German	11	0.08
Polish	1,364	9.67
Portuguese	221	1.57
Russian	190	1.35
Scotch-Irish	309	2.19
Scottish	450	3.19
Slovak	9	0.06
Slovene	6	0.04
Swedish	230	1.63
Swiss	24	0.17
Ukrainian	106	0.75
United States or American	520	3.69
Welsh	13	0.09
West Indian, excl. Hispanic:	24	0.17
Jamaican	24	0.17
White:	13,809	97.94
Not Hispanic (13,662)	13,717	97.28
Hispanic (88)	92	0.65

Easthampton

Place Type: City
County: Hampshire
Population: 15,994

Ancestry/Race	Number	%
Acadian/Cajun	8	0.05
African American/Black:	128	0.80
Not Hispanic (86)	109	0.68
Hispanic (16)	19	0.12
African, sub-Saharan:	6	0.04
African	6	0.04
Alaska Native tribes, specified:	1	0.01
Aleut (1)	1	0.01
Alaska Native tribes, not specified	1	0.01
Am. Ind. or Alaska Nat., not spec.	31	0.19
American Indian tribes, specified:	50	0.31
Blackfeet	3	0.02
Cherokee (3)	15	0.09
Cree	3	0.02
Creek (2)	2	0.01
Iroquois	3	0.02
Kiowa	1	0.01
Yaqui (1)	1	0.01
All other tribes (3)	22	0.14
American Indian tribes, not spec.	12	0.08
Arab:	18	0.11
Lebanese	11	0.07
Palestinian	7	0.04
Asian:	315	1.97
Cambodian (130)	133	0.83
Chinese, ex. Taiwanese (46)	51	0.32
Filipino (7)	12	0.08
Indian (27)	28	0.18
Japanese (5)	19	0.12
Korean (25)	31	0.19
Malaysian (1)	1	0.01
Pakistani (4)	4	0.03
Taiwanese (1)	1	0.01
Thai (6)	7	0.04
Vietnamese (15)	17	0.11
Other Asian, not specified (2)	11	0.07
Austrian	21	0.13
Basque	10	0.06
Belgian	28	0.18
British	68	0.43
Canadian	185	1.16
Celtic	6	0.04
Croatian	5	0.03
Czech	36	0.23
Czechoslovakian	68	0.43
Danish	53	0.33
Dutch	212	1.33
Eastern European	8	0.05
English	1,504	9.40
European	62	0.39
Finnish	45	0.28
French, except Basque	3,096	19.36
French Canadian	2,005	12.54
German	1,506	9.42
Greek	30	0.19
Hawaii Native/Pacific Islander:	7	0.04
Micronesian:	1	0.01
Guamanian/Chamorro	1	0.01
Polynesian: (1)	3	0.02
Native Hawaiian	2	0.01
Samoan (1)	1	0.01
Other Pac. Isl., not spec.	3	0.02
Hispanic or Latino:	336	2.10
Central American:	7	0.04
Honduran	2	0.01
Nicaraguan	3	0.02
Salvadoran	2	0.01
Cuban	3	0.02
Dominican Republic	1	0.01
Mexican	29	0.18
Puerto Rican	226	1.41
South American:	18	0.11
Argentinean	2	0.01
Colombian	7	0.04
Ecuadorian	3	0.02
Peruvian	5	0.03
Venezuelan	1	0.01
Other Hispanic or Latino	52	0.33
Hungarian	32	0.20
Irish	2,911	18.20
Italian	1,122	7.02
Latvian	9	0.06
Lithuanian	183	1.14
Northern European	7	0.04
Norwegian	32	0.20
Polish	3,591	22.45
Portuguese	63	0.39
Romanian	6	0.04
Russian	112	0.70
Scandinavian	5	0.03
Scotch-Irish	267	1.67
Scottish	374	2.34
Slovak	11	0.07
Swedish	228	1.43
Swiss	25	0.16
Ukrainian	109	0.68
United States or American	855	5.35
Welsh	54	0.34
West Indian, excl. Hispanic:	34	0.21
Jamaican	16	0.10
Trinidadian and Tobagonian	8	0.05
West Indian	10	0.06
White:	15,400	96.29
Not Hispanic (15,125)	15,241	95.29
Hispanic (135)	159	0.99

Easton

Place Type: Town
County: Bristol
Population: 22,299

Ancestry/Race	Number	%
African American/Black:	418	1.87
Not Hispanic (351)	408	1.83
Hispanic (3)	10	0.04
African, sub-Saharan:	92	0.41
African	13	0.06
Cape Verdean	79	0.35
Am. Ind. or Alaska Nat., not spec.	18	0.08
Albanian	16	0.07
American Indian tribes, specified:	35	0.16
Cherokee	12	0.05
Choctaw (1)	1	0.00
Iroquois	1	0.00
Latin American Indians (2)	6	0.03
All other tribes (2)	15	0.07
American Indian tribes, not spec.	5	0.02
Arab:	237	1.06
Arab/Arabic	21	0.09
Egyptian	7	0.03
Lebanese	183	0.82
Syrian	26	0.12
Armenian	82	0.37
Asian:	369	1.65
Bangladeshi (10)	10	0.04
Cambodian (2)	4	0.02
Chinese, ex. Taiwanese (70)	84	0.38
Filipino (46)	55	0.25
Hmong (12)	14	0.06
Indian (61)	67	0.30
Indonesian (6)	10	0.04
Japanese (11)	18	0.08
Korean (53)	64	0.29
Sri Lankan	1	0.00
Taiwanese (1)	1	0.00
Thai (19)	22	0.10
Vietnamese (10)	14	0.06
Other Asian, not specified (2)	5	0.02
Austrian	112	0.50
Belgian	15	0.07
Brazilian	68	0.30
British	78	0.35
Canadian	292	1.31
Celtic	12	0.05
Croatian	11	0.05
Czech	58	0.26
Czechoslovakian	23	0.10
Danish	122	0.55
Dutch	206	0.92
Eastern European	58	0.26
English	3,160	14.17
European	94	0.42
Finnish	47	0.21
French, except Basque	1,082	4.85
French Canadian	663	2.97
German	1,681	7.54
Greek	429	1.92
Hawaii Native/Pacific Islander:	10	0.04

Notes: 1. Figures in the "Number" column do not add up to the total population due to: a) Ancestry/Race overlap — e.g. persons can report being both White and Irish, b) persons of Hispanic origin can report being any race, c) persons reporting two ancestries are counted in both categories. 2. Numbers in parentheses indicate the number of persons reporting this ancestry/race alone, not in combination with any other ancestry/race. 3. Refer to the Explanation of Data in the front of the book for more detailed information.

Ancestry/Race	Number	%
Micronesian:	3	0.01
Guamanian/Chamorro	3	0.01
Polynesian: (2)	2	0.01
Native Hawaiian (2)	2	0.01
Other Pac. Isl., not spec.	5	0.02
Hispanic or Latino:	352	1.58
Central American:	28	0.13
Guatemalan	4	0.02
Nicaraguan	2	0.01
Panamanian	5	0.02
Salvadoran	12	0.05
Other Central American	5	0.02
Cuban	29	0.13
Dominican Republic	12	0.05
Mexican	73	0.33
Puerto Rican	95	0.43
South American:	79	0.35
Argentinean	7	0.03
Bolivian	2	0.01
Chilean	8	0.04
Colombian	29	0.13
Ecuadorian	6	0.03
Peruvian	10	0.04
Venezuelan	12	0.05
Other South American	5	0.02
Other Hispanic or Latino	36	0.16
Hungarian	132	0.59
Irish	7,310	32.78
Israeli	5	0.02
Italian	3,875	17.38
Latvian	14	0.06
Lithuanian	286	1.28
Norwegian	138	0.62
Polish	1,062	4.76
Portuguese	904	4.05
Romanian	23	0.10
Russian	561	2.52
Scandinavian	8	0.04
Scotch-Irish	592	2.65
Scottish	772	3.46
Slovene	4	0.02
Swedish	968	4.34
Swiss	48	0.22
Turkish	6	0.03
Ukrainian	75	0.34
United States or American	871	3.91
Welsh	48	0.22
West Indian, excl. Hispanic:	68	0.30
Haitian	30	0.13
Jamaican	15	0.07
Trinidadian and Tobagonian	18	0.08
West Indian	5	0.02
White:	20,671	92.70
Not Hispanic (20,335)	20,480	91.84
Hispanic (166)	191	0.86

Everett

Place Type: City
County: Middlesex
Population: 38,037

Ancestry/Race	Number	%
Acadian/Cajun	8	0.02
African American/Black:	2,835	7.45
Not Hispanic (2,269)	2,675	7.03
Hispanic (117)	160	0.42
African, sub-Saharan:	407	1.07
African	184	0.48
Cape Verdean	150	0.39
Ethiopian	65	0.17
Other sub-Saharan African	8	0.02
Alaska Native tribes, specified:	2	0.01
Tlingit-Haida	2	0.01
Am. Ind. or Alaska Nat., not spec.	151	0.40
Albanian	36	0.09
American Indian tribes, specified:	115	0.30
Apache (2)	3	0.01
Blackfeet	3	0.01
Cherokee (2)	27	0.07
Chickasaw (1)	1	0.00
Choctaw (1)	1	0.00
Comanche	1	0.00
Iroquois (5)	6	0.02
Latin American Indians (4)	15	0.04
Pueblo	2	0.01
Sioux	8	0.02
Ute (1)	1	0.00
All other tribes (23)	47	0.12
American Indian tribes, not spec.	22	0.06
Arab:	490	1.29
Arab/Arabic	50	0.13
Egyptian	32	0.08
Iraqi	14	0.04
Jordanian	27	0.07
Lebanese	78	0.21
Moroccan	166	0.44
Palestinian	42	0.11
Syrian	37	0.10
Other Arab	44	0.12
Armenian	139	0.37
Asian:	1,457	3.83
Bangladeshi (4)	7	0.02
Cambodian (28)	48	0.13
Chinese, ex. Taiwanese (207)	241	0.63
Filipino (44)	60	0.16
Indian (126)	187	0.49
Indonesian (2)	3	0.01
Japanese (15)	22	0.06
Korean (25)	33	0.09
Laotian (2)	3	0.01
Malaysian (5)	5	0.01
Pakistani (15)	23	0.06
Sri Lankan (5)	9	0.02
Taiwanese (4)	4	0.01
Thai (6)	10	0.03
Vietnamese (674)	736	1.93
Other Asian, specified (3)	5	0.01
Other Asian, not specified (29)	61	0.16
Austrian	8	0.02
Belgian	31	0.08
Brazilian	1,278	3.36
British	69	0.18
Bulgarian	22	0.06
Canadian	505	1.33
Czech	35	0.09
Danish	76	0.20
Dutch	84	0.22
Eastern European	13	0.03
English	2,072	5.45
European	25	0.07
Finnish	39	0.10
French, except Basque	1,419	3.73
French Canadian	854	2.25
German	1,042	2.74
Greek	225	0.59
Hawaii Native/Pacific Islander:	67	0.18
Micronesian: (17)	24	0.06
Guamanian/Chamorro (17)	23	0.06
Other Micronesian	1	0.00
Polynesian: (7)	16	0.04
Native Hawaiian (6)	12	0.03
Samoan (1)	4	0.01
Other Pac. Isl., specified	1	0.00
Other Pac. Isl., not spec. (2)	26	0.07
Hispanic or Latino:	3,617	9.51
Central American:	1,201	3.16
Costa Rican	22	0.06
Guatemalan	127	0.33
Honduran	90	0.24
Nicaraguan	10	0.03
Panamanian	4	0.01
Salvadoran	888	2.33
Other Central American	60	0.16
Cuban	50	0.13
Dominican Republic	79	0.21
Mexican	186	0.49
Puerto Rican	542	1.42
South American:	463	1.22
Argentinean	15	0.04
Bolivian	16	0.04
Chilean	8	0.02
Colombian	290	0.76
Ecuadorian	14	0.04
Peruvian	81	0.21
Uruguayan	3	0.01
Venezuelan	14	0.04
Other South American	22	0.06
Other Hispanic or Latino	1,096	2.88
Hungarian	55	0.14
Iranian	12	0.03
Irish	8,123	21.36
Italian	11,963	31.45
Lithuanian	86	0.23
Luxemburger	6	0.02
Norwegian	76	0.20
Pennsylvania German	12	0.03
Polish	917	2.41
Portuguese	921	2.42
Romanian	36	0.09
Russian	259	0.68
Scandinavian	8	0.02
Scotch-Irish	444	1.17
Scottish	624	1.64
Swedish	214	0.56
Swiss	27	0.07
Turkish	21	0.06
Ukrainian	136	0.36
United States or American	1,509	3.97
Welsh	26	0.07
West Indian, excl. Hispanic:	1,354	3.56
Barbadian	7	0.02
Haitian	1,208	3.18
Jamaican	70	0.18
U.S. Virgin Islander	55	0.14
West Indian	14	0.04
White:	31,977	84.07
Not Hispanic (28,587)	29,905	78.62
Hispanic (1,734)	2,072	5.45
Yugoslavian	134	0.35

Fairhaven

Place Type: Town
County: Bristol
Population: 16,159

Ancestry/Race	Number	%
African American/Black:	143	0.88
Not Hispanic (94)	139	0.86
Hispanic (3)	4	0.02
African, sub-Saharan:	229	1.42
Cape Verdean	218	1.35
Nigerian	4	0.02
Senegalese	7	0.04
Am. Ind. or Alaska Nat., not spec.	29	0.18
American Indian tribes, specified:	62	0.38
Blackfeet	2	0.01
Cherokee	4	0.02
Chippewa (3)	4	0.02
Kiowa (3)	3	0.02
Latin American Indians (2)	4	0.02
Navajo (1)	1	0.01
Sioux (1)	1	0.01
Yaqui (1)	1	0.01
All other tribes (22)	42	0.26
American Indian tribes, not spec.	1	0.01
Arab:	147	0.91
Arab/Arabic	15	0.09
Egyptian	38	0.24
Lebanese	94	0.58
Asian:	91	0.56
Cambodian (1)	1	0.01
Chinese, ex. Taiwanese (45)	48	0.30
Filipino (9)	11	0.07
Indian	3	0.02
Japanese (2)	5	0.03
Korean (3)	5	0.03
Thai (4)	7	0.04
Vietnamese (6)	6	0.04

Notes: 1. Figures in the "Number" column do not add up to the total population due to: a) Ancestry/Race overlap — e.g. persons can report being both White and Irish, b) persons of Hispanic origin can report being any race, c) persons reporting two ancestries are counted in both categories. 2. Numbers in parentheses indicate the number of persons reporting this ancestry/race alone, not in combination with any other ancestry/race. 3. Refer to the Explanation of Data in the front of the book for more detailed information.

Other Asian, specified	1	0.01
Other Asian, not specified (1)	4	0.02
Belgian	13	0.08
Brazilian	47	0.29
British	54	0.33
Canadian	84	0.52
Czech	55	0.34
Czechoslovakian	28	0.17
Danish	30	0.19
Dutch	35	0.22
English	2,756	17.06
European	10	0.06
Finnish	10	0.06
French, except Basque	2,514	15.56
French Canadian	1,372	8.49
German	476	2.95
Greek	129	0.80
Hawaii Native/Pacific Islander:	14	0.09
Micronesian:	2	0.01
Guamanian/Chamorro	2	0.01
Polynesian: (2)	3	0.02
Native Hawaiian (2)	3	0.02
Other Pac. Isl., specified	1	0.01
Other Pac. Isl., not spec. (1)	8	0.05
Hispanic or Latino:	135	0.84
Central American:	13	0.08
Guatemalan	7	0.04
Honduran	3	0.02
Nicaraguan	1	0.01
Panamanian	2	0.01
Cuban	6	0.04
Dominican Republic	6	0.04
Mexican	9	0.06
Puerto Rican	64	0.40
South American:	6	0.04
Colombian	3	0.02
Peruvian	2	0.01
Other South American	1	0.01
Other Hispanic or Latino	31	0.19
Hungarian	17	0.11
Irish	2,382	14.74
Italian	921	5.70
Latvian	12	0.07
Lithuanian	66	0.41
Norwegian	321	1.99
Polish	1,064	6.58
Portuguese	5,384	33.32
Russian	59	0.37
Scotch-Irish	117	0.72
Scottish	263	1.63
Slovak	6	0.04
Swedish	149	0.92
Swiss	13	0.08
United States or American	449	2.78
Welsh	30	0.19
West Indian, excl. Hispanic:	6	0.04
Jamaican	6	0.04
White:	15,729	97.34
Not Hispanic (15,489)	15,645	96.82
Hispanic (76)	84	0.52

Fall River

Place Type: City
County: Bristol
Population: 91,938

Ancestry/Race	Number	%
Acadian/Cajun	13	0.01
African American/Black:	2,947	3.21
Not Hispanic (2,097)	2,665	2.90
Hispanic (186)	282	0.31
African, sub-Saharan:	635	0.69
African	64	0.07
Cape Verdean	571	0.62
Alaska Native tribes, specified:	13	0.01
Eskimo (1)	12	0.01
All other tribes	1	0.00
Alaska Native tribes, not specified	1	0.00
Am. Ind. or Alaska Nat., not spec.	265	0.29
Albanian	7	0.01
American Indian tribes, specified:	295	0.32
Apache (1)	11	0.01
Blackfeet (9)	43	0.05
Cherokee (27)	77	0.08
Cheyenne	1	0.00
Chippewa (1)	5	0.01
Choctaw	1	0.00
Cree	1	0.00
Creek	2	0.00
Iroquois (4)	15	0.02
Latin American Indians (2)	2	0.00
Lumbee	1	0.00
Menominee (2)	2	0.00
Navajo (1)	6	0.01
Pueblo	1	0.00
Sioux (6)	7	0.01
All other tribes (41)	120	0.13
American Indian tribes, not spec.	27	0.03
Arab:	920	1.00
Egyptian	40	0.04
Lebanese	820	0.89
Syrian	60	0.07
Armenian	6	0.01
Asian:	2,370	2.58
Bangladeshi (8)	24	0.03
Cambodian (1,225)	1,344	1.46
Chinese, ex. Taiwanese (213)	260	0.28
Filipino (69)	107	0.12
Indian (154)	205	0.22
Indonesian	1	0.00
Japanese (26)	46	0.05
Korean (31)	44	0.05
Laotian (22)	28	0.03
Malaysian	1	0.00
Pakistani (4)	16	0.02
Taiwanese (3)	5	0.01
Thai (13)	27	0.03
Vietnamese (99)	110	0.12
Other Asian, not specified (61)	152	0.17
Austrian	67	0.07
Belgian	16	0.02
Brazilian	595	0.65
British	78	0.08
Canadian	238	0.26
Celtic	6	0.01
Czech	28	0.03
Danish	44	0.05
Dutch	161	0.18
Eastern European	17	0.02
English	6,085	6.62
European	77	0.08
Finnish	22	0.02
French, except Basque	12,343	13.43
French Canadian	5,445	5.92
German	1,386	1.51
Greek	170	0.18
Hawaii Native/Pacific Islander:	276	0.30
Micronesian: (3)	7	0.01
Guamanian/Chamorro (3)	7	0.01
Polynesian: (6)	27	0.03
Native Hawaiian (5)	14	0.02
Samoan (1)	12	0.01
Other Polynesian	1	0.00
Other Pac. Isl., not spec. (16)	242	0.26
Hispanic or Latino:	3,040	3.31
Central American:	68	0.07
Costa Rican	4	0.00
Guatemalan	23	0.03
Honduran	34	0.04
Panamanian	4	0.00
Salvadoran	3	0.00
Cuban	38	0.04
Dominican Republic	112	0.12
Mexican	179	0.19
Puerto Rican	1,946	2.12
South American:	89	0.10
Argentinean	6	0.01
Bolivian	1	0.00
Chilean	4	0.00
Colombian	25	0.03
Ecuadorian	28	0.03
Peruvian	9	0.01
Venezuelan	11	0.01
Other South American	5	0.01
Other Hispanic or Latino	608	0.66
Hungarian	32	0.03
Iranian	32	0.03
Irish	9,023	9.81
Italian	3,293	3.58
Latvian	54	0.06
Lithuanian	51	0.06
Norwegian	122	0.13
Polish	3,148	3.42
Portuguese	43,253	47.05
Romanian	15	0.02
Russian	215	0.23
Scandinavian	19	0.02
Scotch-Irish	246	0.27
Scottish	604	0.66
Slovak	4	0.00
Swedish	244	0.27
Swiss	32	0.03
Turkish	18	0.02
Ukrainian	230	0.25
United States or American	2,197	2.39
Welsh	106	0.12
West Indian, excl. Hispanic:	149	0.16
British West Indian	10	0.01
Haitian	76	0.08
Jamaican	35	0.04
West Indian	28	0.03
White:	85,786	93.31
Not Hispanic (82,274)	84,043	91.41
Hispanic (1,541)	1,743	1.90
Yugoslavian	12	0.01

Falmouth

Place Type: Town
County: Barnstable
Population: 32,660

Ancestry/Race	Number	%
African American/Black:	836	2.56
Not Hispanic (573)	808	2.47
Hispanic (20)	28	0.09
African, sub-Saharan:	839	2.57
African	8	0.02
Cape Verdean	831	2.54
Am. Ind. or Alaska Nat., not spec.	124	0.38
Albanian	45	0.14
Alsatian	22	0.07
American Indian tribes, specified:	195	0.60
Apache	1	0.00
Blackfeet (1)	2	0.01
Cherokee (3)	29	0.09
Cheyenne (1)	1	0.00
Chickasaw	1	0.00
Chippewa (1)	2	0.01
Choctaw (4)	4	0.01
Cree	1	0.00
Creek	1	0.00
Delaware (2)	2	0.01
Iroquois (2)	9	0.03
Latin American Indians	3	0.01
Lumbee	1	0.00
Navajo (2)	2	0.01
Osage	2	0.01
Seminole	1	0.00
Sioux (1)	1	0.00
All other tribes (88)	132	0.40
American Indian tribes, not spec.	13	0.04
Arab:	283	0.87
Arab/Arabic	11	0.03
Egyptian	6	0.02
Lebanese	231	0.71
Syrian	35	0.11
Armenian	163	0.50
Asian:	384	1.18

Notes: 1. Figures in the "Number" column do not add up to the total population due to: a) Ancestry/Race overlap — e.g. persons can report being both White and Irish, b) persons of Hispanic origin can report being any race, c) persons reporting two ancestries are counted in both categories. 2. Numbers in parentheses indicate the number of persons reporting this ancestry/race alone, not in combination with any other ancestry/race. 3. Refer to the Explanation of Data in the front of the book for more detailed information.

Chinese, ex. Taiwanese (112)	125	0.38
Filipino (28)	45	0.14
Indian (32)	35	0.11
Indonesian (1)	3	0.01
Japanese (43)	69	0.21
Korean (39)	42	0.13
Pakistani (3)	3	0.01
Sri Lankan (3)	3	0.01
Taiwanese (13)	13	0.04
Thai (1)	3	0.01
Vietnamese (14)	18	0.06
Other Asian, not specified (10)	25	0.08
Australian	58	0.18
Austrian	98	0.30
Basque	8	0.02
Belgian	8	0.02
Brazilian	98	0.30
British	143	0.44
Canadian	298	0.91
Celtic	44	0.13
Croatian	22	0.07
Czech	97	0.30
Czechoslovakian	26	0.08
Danish	77	0.24
Dutch	580	1.78
Eastern European	53	0.16
English	5,835	17.87
Estonian	8	0.02
European	135	0.41
Finnish	134	0.41
French, except Basque	1,950	5.97
French Canadian	1,095	3.35
German	2,808	8.60
Greek	402	1.23
Hawaii Native/Pacific Islander:	27	0.08
Micronesian: (3)	4	0.01
Guamanian/Chamorro (2)	2	0.01
Other Micronesian (1)	2	0.01
Polynesian: (2)	7	0.02
Native Hawaiian (1)	6	0.02
Samoan (1)	1	0.00
Other Pac. Isl., not spec.	16	0.05
Hispanic or Latino:	417	1.28
Central American:	6	0.02
Costa Rican	1	0.00
Guatemalan	1	0.00
Nicaraguan	1	0.00
Panamanian	2	0.01
Other Central American	1	0.00
Cuban	20	0.06
Dominican Republic	6	0.02
Mexican	58	0.18
Puerto Rican	204	0.62
South American:	31	0.09
Argentinean	2	0.01
Chilean	10	0.03
Colombian	4	0.01
Ecuadorian	3	0.01
Paraguayan	6	0.02
Peruvian	3	0.01
Uruguayan	1	0.00
Venezuelan	1	0.00
Other South American	1	0.00
Other Hispanic or Latino	92	0.28
Hungarian	85	0.26
Iranian	14	0.04
Irish	8,367	25.62
Italian	2,994	9.17
Latvian	26	0.08
Lithuanian	202	0.62
Northern European	8	0.02
Norwegian	285	0.87
Pennsylvania German	11	0.03
Polish	1,117	3.42
Portuguese	3,247	9.94
Romanian	20	0.06
Russian	493	1.51
Scandinavian	33	0.10
Scotch-Irish	562	1.72
Scottish	1,016	3.11
Slovak	25	0.08
Slovene	6	0.02
Swedish	966	2.96
Swiss	140	0.43
Ukrainian	101	0.31
United States or American	1,201	3.68
Welsh	245	0.75
West Indian, excl. Hispanic:	8	0.02
Trinidadian and Tobagonian	8	0.02
White:	30,994	94.90
Not Hispanic (30,207)	30,671	93.91
Hispanic (295)	323	0.99
Yugoslavian	19	0.06

Fitchburg

Place Type: City
County: Worcester
Population: 39,102

Ancestry/Race	Number	%
African American/Black:	1,829	4.68
Not Hispanic (1,209)	1,515	3.87
Hispanic (217)	314	0.80
African, sub-Saharan:	293	0.75
African	182	0.47
Cape Verdean	33	0.08
Ethiopian	2	0.01
Kenyan	6	0.02
South African	7	0.02
Zairian	8	0.02
Other sub-Saharan African	55	0.14
Alaska Native tribes, specified:	5	0.01
Eskimo (1)	5	0.01
Alaska Native tribes, not specified	4	0.01
Am. Ind. or Alaska Nat., not spec.	118	0.30
Albanian	11	0.03
American Indian tribes, specified:	219	0.56
Apache (1)	4	0.01
Blackfeet (5)	24	0.06
Cherokee (17)	56	0.14
Chippewa (3)	4	0.01
Comanche	1	0.00
Crow	3	0.01
Iroquois (8)	20	0.05
Latin American Indians (8)	31	0.08
Navajo (2)	3	0.01
Seminole (1)	5	0.01
Sioux (9)	11	0.03
Yakama	1	0.00
All other tribes (23)	56	0.14
American Indian tribes, not spec.	21	0.05
Arab:	132	0.34
Egyptian	42	0.11
Lebanese	69	0.18
Syrian	21	0.05
Armenian	124	0.32
Asian:	1,957	5.00
Cambodian (52)	64	0.16
Chinese, ex. Taiwanese (87)	106	0.27
Filipino (24)	39	0.10
Hmong (629)	688	1.76
Indian (79)	101	0.26
Indonesian (2)	2	0.01
Japanese (33)	54	0.14
Korean (58)	77	0.20
Laotian (368)	463	1.18
Pakistani (34)	47	0.12
Taiwanese	4	0.01
Thai (14)	20	0.05
Vietnamese (206)	228	0.58
Other Asian, specified (3)	4	0.01
Other Asian, not specified (41)	60	0.15
Australian	11	0.03
Austrian	10	0.03
Belgian	15	0.04
British	56	0.14
Canadian	362	0.93
Celtic	7	0.02
Croatian	7	0.02
Czech	38	0.10
Czechoslovakian	2	0.01
Danish	24	0.06
Dutch	167	0.43
Eastern European	19	0.05
English	3,218	8.23
Estonian	5	0.01
European	110	0.28
Finnish	1,593	4.07
French, except Basque	7,289	18.64
French Canadian	4,702	12.02
German	1,850	4.73
German Russian	5	0.01
Greek	467	1.19
Guyanese	7	0.02
Hawaii Native/Pacific Islander:	53	0.14
Micronesian: (2)	6	0.02
Guamanian/Chamorro (2)	6	0.02
Polynesian: (6)	18	0.05
Native Hawaiian (6)	17	0.04
Samoan	1	0.00
Other Pac. Isl., specified	1	0.00
Other Pac. Isl., not spec. (5)	28	0.07
Hispanic or Latino:	5,852	14.97
Central American:	69	0.18
Costa Rican	4	0.01
Guatemalan	25	0.06
Honduran	25	0.06
Nicaraguan	2	0.01
Panamanian	8	0.02
Salvadoran	4	0.01
Other Central American	1	0.00
Cuban	28	0.07
Dominican Republic	288	0.74
Mexican	391	1.00
Puerto Rican	4,199	10.74
South American:	278	0.71
Argentinean	10	0.03
Bolivian	4	0.01
Chilean	3	0.01
Colombian	29	0.07
Ecuadorian	57	0.15
Paraguayan	1	0.00
Peruvian	12	0.03
Uruguayan	142	0.36
Venezuelan	7	0.02
Other South American	13	0.03
Other Hispanic or Latino	599	1.53
Hungarian	19	0.05
Icelander	37	0.09
Irish	5,563	14.23
Italian	4,649	11.89
Lithuanian	228	0.58
Luxemburger	6	0.02
Northern European	7	0.02
Norwegian	78	0.20
Polish	988	2.53
Portuguese	406	1.04
Romanian	4	0.01
Russian	134	0.34
Scandinavian	53	0.14
Scotch-Irish	536	1.37
Scottish	794	2.03
Slavic	7	0.02
Slovak	57	0.15
Swedish	507	1.30
Swiss	33	0.08
United States or American	1,436	3.67
Welsh	72	0.18
West Indian, excl. Hispanic:	164	0.42
Haitian	124	0.32
Jamaican	24	0.06
West Indian	16	0.04
White:	32,921	84.19
Not Hispanic (29,414)	29,995	76.71
Hispanic (2,593)	2,926	7.48

Notes: 1. Figures in the "Number" column do not add up to the total population due to: a) Ancestry/Race overlap — e.g. persons can report being both White and Irish, b) persons of Hispanic origin can report being any race, c) persons reporting two ancestries are counted in both categories. 2. Numbers in parentheses indicate the number of persons reporting this ancestry/race alone, not in combination with any other ancestry/race. 3. Refer to the Explanation of Data in the front of the book for more detailed information.

Foxborough

Place Type: Town
County: Norfolk
Population: 16,246

Ancestry/Race	Number	%
African American/Black:	158	0.97
Not Hispanic (114)	138	0.85
Hispanic (20)	20	0.12
African, sub-Saharan:	11	0.07
African	4	0.02
Cape Verdean	7	0.04
Am. Ind. or Alaska Nat., not spec.	12	0.07
Albanian	13	0.08
American Indian tribes, specified:	29	0.18
Blackfeet	2	0.01
Cherokee (2)	3	0.02
Iroquois (6)	6	0.04
Navajo (2)	2	0.01
Potawatomi (1)	1	0.01
Sioux	3	0.02
All other tribes (5)	12	0.07
Arab:	438	2.70
Egyptian	33	0.20
Lebanese	326	2.01
Syrian	30	0.18
Other Arab	49	0.30
Armenian	45	0.28
Asian:	225	1.38
Bangladeshi (3)	3	0.02
Cambodian (4)	4	0.02
Chinese, ex. Taiwanese (69)	74	0.46
Filipino (16)	23	0.14
Indian (36)	40	0.25
Indonesian (2)	2	0.01
Japanese (5)	5	0.03
Korean (16)	18	0.11
Pakistani (12)	15	0.09
Sri Lankan (2)	2	0.01
Thai (3)	3	0.02
Vietnamese (23)	23	0.14
Other Asian, not specified (8)	13	0.08
Austrian	31	0.19
British	81	0.50
Canadian	175	1.08
Czech	62	0.38
Czechoslovakian	20	0.12
Danish	62	0.38
Dutch	182	1.12
Eastern European	75	0.46
English	2,618	16.11
European	53	0.33
Finnish	116	0.71
French, except Basque	971	5.98
French Canadian	576	3.55
German	1,368	8.42
Greek	65	0.40
Hawaii Native/Pacific Islander:	11	0.07
Polynesian: (2)	7	0.04
Native Hawaiian (1)	6	0.04
Other Polynesian (1)	1	0.01
Other Pac. Isl., not spec.	4	0.02
Hispanic or Latino:	172	1.06
Central American:	15	0.09
Costa Rican	3	0.02
Guatemalan	5	0.03
Honduran	6	0.04
Panamanian	1	0.01
Cuban	17	0.10
Dominican Republic	4	0.02
Mexican	28	0.17
Puerto Rican	43	0.26
South American:	27	0.17
Argentinean	8	0.05
Chilean	1	0.01
Colombian	7	0.04
Peruvian	7	0.04
Venezuelan	4	0.02
Other Hispanic or Latino	38	0.23
Hungarian	43	0.26
Irish	5,316	32.72
Italian	2,679	16.49
Latvian	6	0.04
Lithuanian	239	1.47
Maltese	10	0.06
Norwegian	167	1.03
Pennsylvania German	7	0.04
Polish	508	3.13
Portuguese	470	2.89
Russian	246	1.51
Scotch-Irish	469	2.89
Scottish	593	3.65
Slovak	17	0.10
Swedish	382	2.35
Swiss	48	0.30
Ukrainian	122	0.75
United States or American	754	4.64
Welsh	79	0.49
West Indian, excl. Hispanic:	32	0.20
Jamaican	6	0.04
Trinidadian and Tobagonian	26	0.16
White:	15,854	97.59
Not Hispanic (15,659)	15,727	96.81
Hispanic (115)	127	0.78
Yugoslavian	10	0.06

Framingham

Place Type: Census Designated Place
County: Middlesex
Population: 66,910

Ancestry/Race	Number	%
Afghan	35	0.05
African American/Black:	3,925	5.87
Not Hispanic (2,991)	3,338	4.99
Hispanic (418)	587	0.88
African, sub-Saharan:	803	1.20
African	325	0.49
Cape Verdean	70	0.10
Ghanian	44	0.07
Liberian	7	0.01
Nigerian	118	0.18
Sierra Leonean	11	0.02
Somalian	110	0.16
Ugandan	19	0.03
Other sub-Saharan African	99	0.15
Alaska Native tribes, specified:	2	0.00
Alaska Athabascan (1)	1	0.00
Tlingit-Haida	1	0.00
Am. Ind. or Alaska Nat., not spec.	172	0.26
Albanian	129	0.19
American Indian tribes, specified:	169	0.25
Apache	4	0.01
Blackfeet (1)	10	0.01
Cherokee (2)	34	0.05
Chickasaw	1	0.00
Chippewa (1)	2	0.00
Choctaw	6	0.01
Comanche	3	0.00
Cree	2	0.00
Crow	4	0.01
Delaware	1	0.00
Iroquois (2)	12	0.02
Latin American Indians (18)	37	0.06
Navajo	1	0.00
Ottawa (1)	1	0.00
Potawatomi (1)	1	0.00
Pueblo (1)	1	0.00
Sioux (2)	2	0.00
Tohono O'Odham (1)	1	0.00
All other tribes (18)	46	0.07
American Indian tribes, not spec.	17	0.03
Arab:	471	0.70
Arab/Arabic	7	0.01
Egyptian	164	0.25
Lebanese	151	0.23
Syrian	120	0.18
Other Arab	29	0.04
Armenian	287	0.43
Asian:	3,926	5.87
Bangladeshi (1)	1	0.00
Cambodian (24)	34	0.05
Chinese, ex. Taiwanese (1,182)	1,273	1.90
Filipino (101)	135	0.20
Hmong (1)	1	0.00
Indian (1,488)	1,564	2.34
Indonesian (13)	14	0.02
Japanese (152)	198	0.30
Korean (208)	230	0.34
Laotian (1)	1	0.00
Malaysian (3)	9	0.01
Pakistani (56)	88	0.13
Sri Lankan (38)	46	0.07
Taiwanese (33)	42	0.06
Thai (18)	25	0.04
Vietnamese (137)	169	0.25
Other Asian, specified (3)	10	0.01
Other Asian, not specified (21)	86	0.13
Assyrian/Chaldean/Syriac	9	0.01
Australian	21	0.03
Austrian	195	0.29
Basque	16	0.02
Belgian	20	0.03
Brazilian	3,500	5.23
British	385	0.58
Canadian	539	0.81
Celtic	42	0.06
Croatian	43	0.06
Czech	67	0.10
Czechoslovakian	90	0.13
Danish	115	0.17
Dutch	358	0.54
Eastern European	453	0.68
English	5,859	8.76
European	518	0.77
Finnish	86	0.13
French, except Basque	2,146	3.21
French Canadian	1,973	2.95
German	3,930	5.87
Greek	731	1.09
Hawaii Native/Pacific Islander:	91	0.14
Micronesian: (3)	6	0.01
Guamanian/Chamorro (3)	6	0.01
Polynesian: (4)	25	0.04
Native Hawaiian (3)	17	0.03
Samoan	4	0.01
Tongan	2	0.00
Other Polynesian (1)	2	0.00
Other Pac. Isl., specified	7	0.01
Other Pac. Isl., not spec. (19)	53	0.08
Hispanic or Latino:	7,265	10.86
Central American:	1,129	1.69
Costa Rican	34	0.05
Guatemalan	454	0.68
Honduran	34	0.05
Nicaraguan	3	0.00
Panamanian	36	0.05
Salvadoran	518	0.77
Other Central American	50	0.07
Cuban	110	0.16
Dominican Republic	402	0.60
Mexican	345	0.52
Puerto Rican	2,903	4.34
South American:	556	0.83
Argentinean	28	0.04
Bolivian	54	0.08
Chilean	38	0.06
Colombian	265	0.40
Ecuadorian	24	0.04
Paraguayan	4	0.01
Peruvian	65	0.10
Uruguayan	1	0.00
Venezuelan	45	0.07
Other South American	32	0.05
Other Hispanic or Latino	1,820	2.72
Hungarian	150	0.22
Iranian	224	0.33
Irish	12,577	18.80

Notes: 1. Figures in the "Number" column do not add up to the total population due to: a) Ancestry/Race overlap — e.g. persons can report being both White and Irish, b) persons of Hispanic origin can report being any race, c) persons reporting two ancestries are counted in both categories. 2. Numbers in parentheses indicate the number of persons reporting this ancestry/race alone, not in combination with any other ancestry/race. 3. Refer to the Explanation of Data in the front of the book for more detailed information.

Israeli	70	0.10
Italian	9,060	13.54
Latvian	67	0.10
Lithuanian	488	0.73
Maltese	14	0.02
Northern European	31	0.05
Norwegian	298	0.45
Pennsylvania German	12	0.02
Polish	2,109	3.15
Portuguese	1,469	2.20
Romanian	143	0.21
Russian	2,753	4.11
Scandinavian	75	0.11
Scotch-Irish	966	1.44
Scottish	1,125	1.68
Serbian	41	0.06
Slavic	21	0.03
Slovak	91	0.14
Slovene	14	0.02
Soviet Union	12	0.02
Swedish	866	1.29
Swiss	97	0.14
Turkish	13	0.02
Ukrainian	233	0.35
United States or American	2,804	4.19
Welsh	188	0.28
West Indian, excl. Hispanic:	532	0.80
Barbadian	6	0.01
Haitian	202	0.30
Jamaican	150	0.22
Trinidadian and Tobagonian	6	0.01
West Indian	168	0.25
White:	55,285	82.63
Not Hispanic (50,293)	51,652	77.20
Hispanic (3,080)	3,633	5.43

Franklin

Place Type: City
County: Norfolk
Population: 29,560

Ancestry/Race	Number	%
Acadian/Cajun	15	0.05
African American/Black:	390	1.32
Not Hispanic (305)	368	1.24
Hispanic (13)	22	0.07
African, sub-Saharan:	72	0.24
African	12	0.04
Cape Verdean	49	0.17
Ugandan	11	0.04
Alaska Native tribes, specified:	4	0.01
Alaska Athabascan (4)	4	0.01
Am. Ind. or Alaska Nat., not spec.	30	0.10
Albanian	6	0.02
American Indian tribes, specified:	69	0.23
Apache (1)	1	0.00
Blackfeet (3)	6	0.02
Cherokee (2)	8	0.03
Chickasaw	1	0.00
Chippewa (1)	3	0.01
Choctaw (1)	3	0.01
Crow	2	0.01
Delaware	2	0.01
Iroquois (3)	13	0.04
Latin American Indians (4)	5	0.02
Navajo (1)	1	0.00
Potawatomi (1)	2	0.01
Pueblo (1)	1	0.00
Sioux (1)	1	0.00
All other tribes (12)	20	0.07
American Indian tribes, not spec.	1	0.00
Arab:	216	0.73
Arab/Arabic	7	0.02
Lebanese	184	0.62
Syrian	25	0.08
Armenian	247	0.84
Asian:	593	2.01
Cambodian (1)	2	0.01
Chinese, ex. Taiwanese (200)	239	0.81
Filipino (13)	20	0.07
Indian (123)	134	0.45
Indonesian (2)	3	0.01
Japanese (31)	43	0.15
Korean (45)	51	0.17
Laotian (15)	21	0.07
Pakistani (10)	13	0.04
Taiwanese (3)	6	0.02
Thai (9)	11	0.04
Vietnamese (29)	30	0.10
Other Asian, specified (1)	1	0.00
Other Asian, not specified (6)	19	0.06
Austrian	99	0.33
Basque	6	0.02
Belgian	22	0.07
Brazilian	23	0.08
British	195	0.66
Canadian	355	1.20
Celtic	26	0.09
Croatian	24	0.08
Czech	111	0.38
Czechoslovakian	82	0.28
Danish	139	0.47
Dutch	302	1.02
Eastern European	30	0.10
English	4,303	14.56
Estonian	37	0.13
European	142	0.48
Finnish	79	0.27
French, except Basque	1,938	6.56
French Canadian	1,348	4.56
German	2,677	9.06
Greek	258	0.87
Hawaii Native/Pacific Islander:	16	0.05
Micronesian: (2)	4	0.01
Guamanian/Chamorro (2)	3	0.01
Other Micronesian	1	0.00
Polynesian: (4)	6	0.02
Native Hawaiian (3)	5	0.02
Samoan (1)	1	0.00
Other Pac. Isl., not spec. (3)	6	0.02
Hispanic or Latino:	318	1.08
Central American:	24	0.08
Costa Rican	2	0.01
Guatemalan	13	0.04
Honduran	4	0.01
Panamanian	1	0.00
Salvadoran	1	0.00
Other Central American	3	0.01
Cuban	42	0.14
Dominican Republic	13	0.04
Mexican	40	0.14
Puerto Rican	92	0.31
South American:	44	0.15
Argentinean	3	0.01
Bolivian	1	0.00
Chilean	6	0.02
Colombian	14	0.05
Ecuadorian	6	0.02
Paraguayan	1	0.00
Peruvian	11	0.04
Venezuelan	1	0.00
Other South American	1	0.00
Other Hispanic or Latino	63	0.21
Hungarian	90	0.30
Irish	9,496	32.12
Italian	7,320	24.76
Latvian	79	0.27
Lithuanian	220	0.74
Norwegian	223	0.75
Polish	1,298	4.39
Portuguese	368	1.24
Romanian	39	0.13
Russian	394	1.33
Scandinavian	14	0.05
Scotch-Irish	614	2.08
Scottish	905	3.06
Slovak	77	0.26
Slovene	33	0.11
Swedish	704	2.38
Swiss	54	0.18
Turkish	58	0.20
Ukrainian	220	0.74
United States or American	1,045	3.54
Welsh	129	0.44
West Indian, excl. Hispanic:	24	0.08
Haitian	12	0.04
Jamaican	6	0.02
Trinidadian and Tobagonian	6	0.02
White:	28,580	96.68
Not Hispanic (28,165)	28,351	95.91
Hispanic (199)	229	0.77
Yugoslavian	9	0.03

Gardner

Place Type: City
County: Worcester
Population: 20,770

Ancestry/Race	Number	%
Acadian/Cajun	27	0.13
African American/Black:	593	2.86
Not Hispanic (436)	530	2.55
Hispanic (40)	63	0.30
African, sub-Saharan:	122	0.59
African	97	0.47
Cape Verdean	8	0.04
Ghanian	17	0.08
Alaska Native tribes, specified:	13	0.06
Aleut (5)	9	0.04
Eskimo (4)	4	0.02
Am. Ind. or Alaska Nat., not spec.	52	0.25
Albanian	6	0.03
American Indian tribes, specified:	82	0.39
Apache (1)	2	0.01
Blackfeet	4	0.02
Cherokee (4)	14	0.07
Chickasaw (3)	3	0.01
Chippewa	1	0.00
Choctaw	2	0.01
Iroquois (4)	6	0.03
Latin American Indians (2)	2	0.01
Lumbee	3	0.01
Navajo (4)	7	0.03
Seminole (2)	2	0.01
Sioux (3)	7	0.03
All other tribes (10)	29	0.14
American Indian tribes, not spec.	10	0.05
Arab:	113	0.54
Egyptian	9	0.04
Lebanese	75	0.36
Palestinian	20	0.10
Syrian	9	0.04
Armenian	50	0.24
Asian:	341	1.64
Bangladeshi	1	0.00
Cambodian (9)	12	0.06
Chinese, ex. Taiwanese (51)	54	0.26
Filipino (20)	31	0.15
Indian (21)	28	0.13
Japanese (11)	19	0.09
Korean (29)	35	0.17
Laotian (89)	103	0.50
Pakistani (1)	1	0.00
Thai	1	0.00
Vietnamese (45)	45	0.22
Other Asian, specified	1	0.00
Other Asian, not specified (5)	10	0.05
Austrian	41	0.20
Belgian	14	0.07
Brazilian	11	0.05
British	44	0.21
Canadian	237	1.14
Czech	12	0.06
Czechoslovakian	10	0.05
Danish	51	0.25
Dutch	57	0.27
Eastern European	6	0.03
English	1,922	9.25

Notes: 1. Figures in the "Number" column do not add up to the total population due to: a) Ancestry/Race overlap — e.g. persons can report being both White and Irish, b) persons of Hispanic origin can report being any race, c) persons reporting two ancestries are counted in both categories. 2. Numbers in parentheses indicate the number of persons reporting this ancestry/race alone, not in combination with any other ancestry/race. 3. Refer to the Explanation of Data in the front of the book for more detailed information.

Ancestry/Race	Number	%
Estonian	7	0.03
European	13	0.06
Finnish	964	4.64
French, except Basque	3,915	18.85
French Canadian	3,734	17.98
German	1,005	4.84
Greek	110	0.53
Hawaii Native/Pacific Islander:	32	0.15
Micronesian: (6)	6	0.03
Guamanian/Chamorro (6)	6	0.03
Polynesian: (9)	14	0.07
Native Hawaiian (9)	14	0.07
Other Pac. Isl., not spec. (1)	12	0.06
Hispanic or Latino:	848	4.08
Central American:	22	0.11
Guatemalan	6	0.03
Honduran	1	0.00
Nicaraguan	6	0.03
Panamanian	4	0.02
Salvadoran	2	0.01
Other Central American	3	0.01
Cuban	18	0.09
Dominican Republic	49	0.24
Mexican	119	0.57
Puerto Rican	506	2.44
South American:	39	0.19
Argentinean	4	0.02
Chilean	15	0.07
Colombian	8	0.04
Peruvian	4	0.02
Uruguayan	7	0.03
Venezuelan	1	0.00
Other Hispanic or Latino	95	0.46
Hungarian	16	0.08
Irish	3,534	17.01
Italian	1,591	7.66
Lithuanian	311	1.50
Northern European	18	0.09
Norwegian	111	0.53
Pennsylvania German	5	0.02
Polish	1,365	6.57
Portuguese	141	0.68
Russian	63	0.30
Scandinavian	12	0.06
Scotch-Irish	210	1.01
Scottish	414	1.99
Slovak	4	0.02
Swedish	562	2.71
Swiss	46	0.22
Ukrainian	26	0.13
United States or American	823	3.96
Welsh	47	0.23
West Indian, excl. Hispanic:	18	0.09
Bermudan	11	0.05
Jamaican	7	0.03
White:	19,619	94.46
Not Hispanic (18,882)	19,072	91.82
Hispanic (461)	547	2.63
Yugoslavian	6	0.03

Gloucester

Place Type: City
County: Essex
Population: 30,273

Ancestry/Race	Number	%
Afghan	7	0.02
African American/Black:	283	0.93
Not Hispanic (159)	231	0.76
Hispanic (27)	52	0.17
African, sub-Saharan:	43	0.14
Cape Verdean	7	0.02
Kenyan	27	0.09
South African	9	0.03
Alaska Native tribes, specified:	6	0.02
Aleut (4)	6	0.02
Am. Ind. or Alaska Nat., not spec.	51	0.17
Albanian	26	0.09
Alsatian	5	0.02
American Indian tribes, specified:	51	0.17
Apache	1	0.00
Blackfeet	3	0.01
Cherokee (2)	7	0.02
Cheyenne	1	0.00
Chickasaw	1	0.00
Chippewa	1	0.00
Choctaw	2	0.01
Iroquois (5)	8	0.03
Latin American Indians (2)	3	0.01
Pueblo (1)	1	0.00
All other tribes (8)	23	0.08
American Indian tribes, not spec.	10	0.03
Arab:	331	1.09
Arab/Arabic	6	0.02
Egyptian	5	0.02
Lebanese	260	0.86
Syrian	52	0.17
Other Arab	8	0.03
Armenian	123	0.41
Asian:	288	0.95
Cambodian (12)	20	0.07
Chinese, ex. Taiwanese (37)	51	0.17
Filipino (30)	44	0.15
Indian (46)	51	0.17
Japanese (27)	39	0.13
Korean (38)	45	0.15
Laotian (3)	4	0.01
Pakistani (6)	6	0.02
Thai (2)	4	0.01
Vietnamese (12)	13	0.04
Other Asian, specified	2	0.01
Other Asian, not specified (3)	9	0.03
Austrian	64	0.21
Belgian	7	0.02
Brazilian	60	0.20
British	201	0.66
Canadian	419	1.38
Czech	45	0.15
Czechoslovakian	11	0.04
Danish	151	0.50
Dutch	257	0.85
Eastern European	18	0.06
English	4,564	15.08
European	178	0.59
Finnish	830	2.74
French, except Basque	1,784	5.89
French Canadian	1,316	4.35
German	1,424	4.70
Greek	363	1.20
Hawaii Native/Pacific Islander:	18	0.06
Micronesian: (2)	4	0.01
Guamanian/Chamorro (2)	4	0.01
Polynesian: (5)	10	0.03
Native Hawaiian (3)	8	0.03
Samoan (2)	2	0.01
Other Pac. Isl., specified	2	0.01
Other Pac. Isl., not spec.	2	0.01
Hispanic or Latino:	449	1.48
Central American:	23	0.08
Costa Rican	1	0.00
Guatemalan	9	0.03
Honduran	9	0.03
Panamanian	1	0.00
Salvadoran	3	0.01
Cuban	13	0.04
Dominican Republic	74	0.24
Mexican	77	0.25
Puerto Rican	122	0.40
South American:	33	0.11
Argentinean	5	0.02
Chilean	6	0.02
Colombian	12	0.04
Ecuadorian	5	0.02
Peruvian	2	0.01
Venezuelan	2	0.01
Other South American	1	0.00
Other Hispanic or Latino	107	0.35
Hungarian	61	0.20
Icelander	14	0.05
Irish	6,085	20.10
Italian	6,624	21.88
Latvian	53	0.18
Lithuanian	106	0.35
Northern European	101	0.33
Norwegian	298	0.98
Polish	763	2.52
Portuguese	2,977	9.83
Romanian	11	0.04
Russian	168	0.55
Scandinavian	26	0.09
Scotch-Irish	673	2.22
Scottish	1,156	3.82
Slovak	32	0.11
Swedish	913	3.02
Swiss	47	0.16
Ukrainian	76	0.25
United States or American	1,804	5.96
Welsh	108	0.36
West Indian, excl. Hispanic:	31	0.10
Barbadian	26	0.09
West Indian	5	0.02
White:	29,646	97.93
Not Hispanic (29,117)	29,367	97.01
Hispanic (244)	279	0.92
Yugoslavian	25	0.08

Grafton

Place Type: Town
County: Worcester
Population: 14,894

Ancestry/Race	Number	%
African American/Black:	222	1.49
Not Hispanic (177)	211	1.42
Hispanic (9)	11	0.07
African, sub-Saharan:	23	0.15
African	5	0.03
Cape Verdean	18	0.12
Alaska Native tribes, specified:	1	0.01
Eskimo (1)	1	0.01
Am. Ind. or Alaska Nat., not spec.	28	0.19
Albanian	56	0.38
American Indian tribes, specified:	37	0.25
Blackfeet	4	0.03
Cherokee (1)	6	0.04
Chippewa (1)	2	0.01
Iroquois	5	0.03
Latin American Indians	4	0.03
Navajo (1)	1	0.01
Sioux (1)	1	0.01
All other tribes (9)	14	0.09
American Indian tribes, not spec.	3	0.02
Arab:	144	0.97
Egyptian	15	0.10
Lebanese	102	0.68
Syrian	23	0.15
Other Arab	4	0.03
Armenian	66	0.44
Asian:	254	1.71
Cambodian (3)	3	0.02
Chinese, ex. Taiwanese (68)	77	0.52
Filipino (17)	24	0.16
Indian (64)	66	0.44
Indonesian (2)	2	0.01
Japanese (5)	11	0.07
Korean (29)	35	0.23
Laotian (1)	1	0.01
Pakistani (4)	10	0.07
Thai (8)	8	0.05
Vietnamese (11)	13	0.09
Other Asian, specified (1)	1	0.01
Other Asian, not specified (1)	3	0.02
Assyrian/Chaldean/Syriac	40	0.27
Austrian	16	0.11
Belgian	21	0.14
British	29	0.19
Canadian	154	1.03
Czechoslovakian	5	0.03

Notes: 1. Figures in the "Number" column do not add up to the total population due to: a) Ancestry/Race overlap — e.g. persons can report being both White and Irish, b) persons of Hispanic origin can report being any race, c) persons reporting two ancestries are counted in both categories. 2. Numbers in parentheses indicate the number of persons reporting this ancestry/race alone, not in combination with any other ancestry/race. 3. Refer to the Explanation of Data in the front of the book for more detailed information.

Ancestry/Race	Number	%
Danish	26	0.17
Dutch	235	1.58
English	2,141	14.37
European	83	0.56
Finnish	72	0.48
French, except Basque	2,129	14.29
French Canadian	1,662	11.16
German	1,045	7.02
Greek	189	1.27
Hawaii Native/Pacific Islander:	3	0.02
Micronesian:	2	0.01
Guamanian/Chamorro	2	0.01
Other Pac. Isl., not spec.	1	0.01
Hispanic or Latino:	285	1.91
Central American:	13	0.09
Guatemalan	7	0.05
Panamanian	1	0.01
Salvadoran	5	0.03
Cuban	22	0.15
Dominican Republic	5	0.03
Mexican	23	0.15
Puerto Rican	174	1.17
South American:	20	0.13
Argentinean	3	0.02
Chilean	2	0.01
Colombian	9	0.06
Ecuadorian	2	0.01
Peruvian	2	0.01
Uruguayan	1	0.01
Other South American	1	0.01
Other Hispanic or Latino	28	0.19
Hungarian	20	0.13
Iranian	13	0.09
Irish	4,014	26.95
Italian	2,459	16.51
Latvian	13	0.09
Lithuanian	217	1.46
Northern European	7	0.05
Norwegian	80	0.54
Polish	1,211	8.13
Portuguese	146	0.98
Russian	247	1.66
Scandinavian	6	0.04
Scotch-Irish	194	1.30
Scottish	491	3.30
Slovene	7	0.05
Swedish	468	3.14
Swiss	16	0.11
Ukrainian	16	0.11
United States or American	511	3.43
Welsh	28	0.19
West Indian, excl. Hispanic:	12	0.08
Jamaican	12	0.08
White:	14,425	96.85
Not Hispanic (14,068)	14,186	95.25
Hispanic (218)	239	1.60

Greenfield

Place Type: Town
County: Franklin
Population: 18,168

Ancestry/Race	Number	%
African American/Black:	364	2.00
Not Hispanic (233)	326	1.79
Hispanic (11)	38	0.21
African, sub-Saharan:	50	0.28
African	39	0.21
Nigerian	5	0.03
South African	6	0.03
Am. Ind. or Alaska Nat., not spec.	99	0.54
Albanian	22	0.12
American Indian tribes, specified:	133	0.73
Apache	5	0.03
Blackfeet (5)	21	0.12
Cherokee (6)	25	0.14
Cheyenne	1	0.01
Cree	5	0.03
Crow	1	0.01
Delaware	1	0.01
Iroquois (4)	25	0.14
Latin American Indians (1)	1	0.01
Navajo	1	0.01
Seminole	1	0.01
Shoshone	1	0.01
Sioux (2)	7	0.04
All other tribes (10)	38	0.21
American Indian tribes, not spec.	7	0.04
Arab:	27	0.15
Lebanese	16	0.09
Syrian	4	0.02
Other Arab	7	0.04
Armenian	22	0.12
Asian:	286	1.57
Cambodian (6)	7	0.04
Chinese, ex. Taiwanese (55)	65	0.36
Filipino (29)	34	0.19
Indian (17)	23	0.13
Japanese (11)	21	0.12
Korean (43)	57	0.31
Laotian (5)	12	0.07
Pakistani	4	0.02
Taiwanese (3)	3	0.02
Thai (14)	14	0.08
Vietnamese (11)	15	0.08
Other Asian, not specified (5)	31	0.17
Austrian	89	0.49
Belgian	8	0.04
British	111	0.61
Canadian	44	0.24
Celtic	6	0.03
Croatian	4	0.02
Czech	30	0.17
Czechoslovakian	10	0.06
Danish	33	0.18
Dutch	154	0.85
Eastern European	10	0.06
English	3,338	18.37
Estonian	4	0.02
European	106	0.58
Finnish	85	0.47
French, except Basque	2,606	14.34
French Canadian	1,441	7.93
German	1,587	8.74
Greek	78	0.43
Hawaii Native/Pacific Islander:	17	0.09
Polynesian: (3)	14	0.08
Native Hawaiian	11	0.06
Samoan (3)	3	0.02
Other Pac. Isl., not spec.	3	0.02
Hispanic or Latino:	644	3.54
Central American:	13	0.07
Costa Rican	1	0.01
Nicaraguan	4	0.02
Panamanian	2	0.01
Salvadoran	6	0.03
Cuban	15	0.08
Dominican Republic	5	0.03
Mexican	73	0.40
Puerto Rican	441	2.43
South American:	14	0.08
Chilean	3	0.02
Colombian	6	0.03
Ecuadorian	1	0.01
Peruvian	3	0.02
Other South American	1	0.01
Other Hispanic or Latino	83	0.46
Hungarian	49	0.27
Icelander	5	0.03
Irish	3,256	17.92
Italian	1,210	6.66
Latvian	7	0.04
Lithuanian	135	0.74
Northern European	30	0.17
Norwegian	188	1.03
Polish	1,891	10.41
Portuguese	87	0.48
Romanian	48	0.26
Russian	329	1.81
Scandinavian	6	0.03
Scotch-Irish	329	1.81
Scottish	620	3.41
Slavic	23	0.13
Slovak	4	0.02
Slovene	5	0.03
Swedish	342	1.88
Swiss	13	0.07
Turkish	12	0.07
Ukrainian	179	0.99
United States or American	1,022	5.63
Welsh	95	0.52
West Indian, excl. Hispanic:	30	0.17
Jamaican	30	0.17
White:	17,352	95.51
Not Hispanic (16,695)	16,987	93.50
Hispanic (272)	365	2.01
Yugoslavian	7	0.04

Hanover

Place Type: Town
County: Plymouth
Population: 13,164

Ancestry/Race	Number	%
African American/Black:	98	0.74
Not Hispanic (65)	89	0.68
Hispanic (8)	9	0.07
African, sub-Saharan:	54	0.41
African	12	0.09
Cape Verdean	42	0.32
Am. Ind. or Alaska Nat., not spec.	14	0.11
Albanian	25	0.19
American Indian tribes, specified:	15	0.11
Blackfeet	1	0.01
Latin American Indians	1	0.01
Lumbee (1)	1	0.01
Navajo (4)	4	0.03
Seminole	1	0.01
All other tribes	7	0.05
American Indian tribes, not spec.	1	0.01
Arab:	137	1.04
Arab/Arabic	34	0.26
Lebanese	85	0.65
Syrian	18	0.14
Armenian	108	0.82
Asian:	123	0.93
Chinese, ex. Taiwanese (25)	29	0.22
Filipino (3)	5	0.04
Indian (23)	24	0.18
Japanese (2)	4	0.03
Korean (22)	24	0.18
Thai (6)	6	0.05
Vietnamese (19)	21	0.16
Other Asian, specified	1	0.01
Other Asian, not specified (1)	9	0.07
Austrian	34	0.26
Belgian	23	0.17
British	31	0.24
Canadian	175	1.33
Czech	20	0.15
Czechoslovakian	16	0.12
Danish	31	0.24
Dutch	102	0.77
Eastern European	9	0.07
English	2,225	16.90
European	75	0.57
Finnish	74	0.56
French, except Basque	734	5.58
French Canadian	601	4.57
German	811	6.16
Greek	184	1.40
Hawaii Native/Pacific Islander:	4	0.03
Micronesian:	1	0.01
Guamanian/Chamorro	1	0.01
Polynesian: (1)	2	0.02
Native Hawaiian (1)	2	0.02
Other Pac. Isl., specified	1	0.01
Hispanic or Latino:	90	0.68

Notes: 1. Figures in the "Number" column do not add up to the total population due to: a) Ancestry/Race overlap — e.g. persons can report being both White and Irish, b) persons of Hispanic origin can report being any race, c) persons reporting two ancestries are counted in both categories. 2. Numbers in parentheses indicate the number of persons reporting this ancestry/race alone, not in combination with any other ancestry/race. 3. Refer to the Explanation of Data in the front of the book for more detailed information.

Ancestry/Race	Number	%
Central American:	2	0.02
Guatemalan	2	0.02
Cuban	10	0.08
Mexican	20	0.15
Puerto Rican	20	0.15
South American:	19	0.14
Argentinean	3	0.02
Chilean	2	0.02
Colombian	6	0.05
Paraguayan	4	0.03
Peruvian	1	0.01
Venezuelan	1	0.01
Other South American	2	0.02
Other Hispanic or Latino	19	0.14
Hungarian	11	0.08
Irish	5,208	39.56
Italian	2,370	18.00
Latvian	28	0.21
Lithuanian	340	2.58
Norwegian	141	1.07
Polish	298	2.26
Portuguese	191	1.45
Russian	70	0.53
Scandinavian	7	0.05
Scotch-Irish	504	3.83
Scottish	490	3.72
Slovak	20	0.15
Swedish	519	3.94
Swiss	30	0.23
Turkish	26	0.20
Ukrainian	34	0.26
United States or American	671	5.10
Welsh	31	0.24
West Indian, excl. Hispanic:	29	0.22
Trinidadian and Tobagonian	29	0.22
White:	12,927	98.20
Not Hispanic (12,798)	12,862	97.71
Hispanic (60)	65	0.49

Harwich

Place Type: Town
County: Barnstable
Population: 12,386

Ancestry/Race	Number	%
African American/Black:	150	1.21
Not Hispanic (85)	145	1.17
Hispanic (3)	5	0.04
African, sub-Saharan:	224	1.81
African	10	0.08
Cape Verdean	214	1.73
Alaska Native tribes, not specified	1	0.01
Am. Ind. or Alaska Nat., not spec.	26	0.21
Albanian	14	0.11
Alsatian	7	0.06
American Indian tribes, specified:	41	0.33
Apache	3	0.02
Blackfeet	2	0.02
Cherokee (4)	12	0.10
Latin American Indians (1)	4	0.03
Shoshone	3	0.02
All other tribes (4)	17	0.14
American Indian tribes, not spec.	3	0.02
Arab:	64	0.52
Arab/Arabic	9	0.07
Lebanese	34	0.27
Syrian	14	0.11
Other Arab	7	0.06
Armenian	36	0.29
Asian:	44	0.36
Chinese, ex. Taiwanese (11)	11	0.09
Filipino (3)	10	0.08
Indian (3)	4	0.03
Japanese (3)	8	0.06
Korean (3)	5	0.04
Vietnamese (1)	1	0.01
Other Asian, not specified (3)	5	0.04
Austrian	35	0.28
Brazilian	7	0.06
British	57	0.46
Canadian	70	0.57
Czech	25	0.20
Czechoslovakian	25	0.20
Danish	89	0.72
Dutch	184	1.49
English	3,159	25.50
European	17	0.14
Finnish	85	0.69
French, except Basque	810	6.54
French Canadian	259	2.09
German	1,315	10.62
Greek	182	1.47
Hawaii Native/Pacific Islander:	7	0.06
Micronesian: (4)	4	0.03
Guamanian/Chamorro (4)	4	0.03
Polynesian: (1)	2	0.02
Native Hawaiian (1)	2	0.02
Other Pac. Isl., not spec. (1)	1	0.01
Hispanic or Latino:	119	0.96
Central American:	3	0.02
Nicaraguan	1	0.01
Salvadoran	2	0.02
Cuban	17	0.14
Dominican Republic	1	0.01
Mexican	47	0.38
Puerto Rican	26	0.21
South American:	11	0.09
Argentinean	1	0.01
Chilean	3	0.02
Colombian	2	0.02
Peruvian	5	0.04
Other Hispanic or Latino	14	0.11
Hungarian	53	0.43
Irish	3,609	29.14
Italian	1,118	9.03
Lithuanian	89	0.72
Norwegian	145	1.17
Polish	393	3.17
Portuguese	538	4.34
Romanian	7	0.06
Russian	153	1.24
Scandinavian	6	0.05
Scotch-Irish	286	2.31
Scottish	668	5.39
Slovak	14	0.11
Swedish	524	4.23
Swiss	12	0.10
Ukrainian	9	0.07
United States or American	570	4.60
Welsh	152	1.23
West Indian, excl. Hispanic:	51	0.41
Haitian	10	0.08
Jamaican	21	0.17
West Indian	20	0.16
White:	11,949	96.47
Not Hispanic (11,738)	11,856	95.72
Hispanic (79)	93	0.75
Yugoslavian	39	0.31

Haverhill

Place Type: City
County: Essex
Population: 58,969

Ancestry/Race	Number	%
Acadian/Cajun	9	0.02
African American/Black:	1,794	3.04
Not Hispanic (1,110)	1,388	2.35
Hispanic (309)	406	0.69
African, sub-Saharan:	233	0.40
African	104	0.18
Cape Verdean	35	0.06
Ghanian	7	0.01
Nigerian	8	0.01
South African	15	0.03
Zairian	18	0.03
Zimbabwean	17	0.03
Other sub-Saharan African	29	0.05
Alaska Native tribes, specified:	3	0.01
Aleut (2)	2	0.00
Eskimo (1)	1	0.00
Alaska Native tribes, not specified	1	0.00
Am. Ind. or Alaska Nat., not spec.	148	0.25
Albanian	74	0.13
American Indian tribes, specified:	202	0.34
Apache (1)	1	0.00
Blackfeet (3)	19	0.03
Cherokee (17)	43	0.07
Cheyenne (1)	2	0.00
Chippewa (1)	10	0.02
Choctaw (1)	4	0.01
Cree	4	0.01
Creek (1)	4	0.01
Iroquois (4)	16	0.03
Latin American Indians (2)	8	0.01
Lumbee (1)	1	0.00
Potawatomi	5	0.01
Pueblo (2)	4	0.01
Seminole	5	0.01
Shoshone	1	0.00
Sioux (4)	6	0.01
All other tribes (24)	69	0.12
American Indian tribes, not spec.	21	0.04
Arab:	657	1.11
Arab/Arabic	5	0.01
Egyptian	72	0.12
Jordanian	58	0.10
Lebanese	452	0.77
Moroccan	9	0.02
Palestinian	10	0.02
Syrian	51	0.09
Armenian	607	1.03
Asian:	1,008	1.71
Cambodian (44)	49	0.08
Chinese, ex. Taiwanese (149)	169	0.29
Filipino (46)	89	0.15
Indian (179)	201	0.34
Indonesian (6)	8	0.01
Japanese (53)	77	0.13
Korean (100)	128	0.22
Laotian	1	0.00
Pakistani (4)	4	0.01
Sri Lankan (5)	5	0.01
Taiwanese (4)	4	0.01
Thai (8)	11	0.02
Vietnamese (190)	205	0.35
Other Asian, specified	6	0.01
Other Asian, not specified (9)	51	0.09
Austrian	57	0.10
Belgian	52	0.09
Brazilian	14	0.02
British	67	0.11
Canadian	357	0.61
Celtic	21	0.04
Cypriot	5	0.01
Czech	24	0.04
Czechoslovakian	15	0.03
Danish	79	0.13
Dutch	371	0.63
Eastern European	13	0.02
English	7,649	12.97
Estonian	14	0.02
European	122	0.21
Finnish	111	0.19
French, except Basque	7,842	13.30
French Canadian	4,657	7.90
German	2,865	4.86
Greek	1,549	2.63
Hawaii Native/Pacific Islander:	50	0.08
Micronesian: (5)	7	0.01
Guamanian/Chamorro (5)	7	0.01
Polynesian: (9)	18	0.03
Native Hawaiian (2)	9	0.02
Samoan (5)	6	0.01
Tongan (2)	3	0.01
Other Pac. Isl., specified	6	0.01
Other Pac. Isl., not spec. (4)	19	0.03
Hispanic or Latino:	5,174	8.77

Notes: 1. Figures in the "Number" column do not add up to the total population due to: a) Ancestry/Race overlap — e.g. persons can report being both White and Irish, b) persons of Hispanic origin can report being any race, c) persons reporting two ancestries are counted in both categories. 2. Numbers in parentheses indicate the number of persons reporting this ancestry/race alone, not in combination with any other ancestry/race. 3. Refer to the Explanation of Data in the front of the book for more detailed information.

Ancestry/Race	Number	%
Central American:	189	0.32
Costa Rican	17	0.03
Guatemalan	93	0.16
Honduran	23	0.04
Nicaraguan	4	0.01
Panamanian	7	0.01
Salvadoran	36	0.06
Other Central American	9	0.02
Cuban	84	0.14
Dominican Republic	1,179	2.00
Mexican	340	0.58
Puerto Rican	2,242	3.80
South American:	114	0.19
Argentinean	9	0.02
Chilean	9	0.02
Colombian	56	0.09
Ecuadorian	11	0.02
Peruvian	16	0.03
Uruguayan	1	0.00
Venezuelan	11	0.02
Other South American	1	0.00
Other Hispanic or Latino	1,026	1.74
Hungarian	107	0.18
Icelander	20	0.03
Iranian	29	0.05
Irish	12,407	21.04
Israeli	8	0.01
Italian	9,294	15.76
Latvian	28	0.05
Lithuanian	459	0.78
Northern European	31	0.05
Norwegian	311	0.53
Pennsylvania German	7	0.01
Polish	2,655	4.50
Portuguese	765	1.30
Romanian	40	0.07
Russian	448	0.76
Scandinavian	50	0.08
Scotch-Irish	1,025	1.74
Scottish	1,887	3.20
Slovak	14	0.02
Slovene	5	0.01
Swedish	403	0.68
Turkish	11	0.02
Ukrainian	106	0.18
United States or American	3,161	5.36
Welsh	184	0.31
West Indian, excl. Hispanic:	330	0.56
Barbadian	15	0.03
British West Indian	14	0.02
Haitian	168	0.28
Jamaican	105	0.18
West Indian	28	0.05
White:	53,915	91.43
Not Hispanic (50,912)	51,611	87.52
Hispanic (1,966)	2,304	3.91
Yugoslavian	20	0.03

Hingham

Place Type: Town
County: Plymouth
Population: 19,882

Ancestry/Race	Number	%
African American/Black:	128	0.64
Not Hispanic (79)	123	0.62
Hispanic	5	0.03
African, sub-Saharan:	28	0.14
Cape Verdean	28	0.14
Am. Ind. or Alaska Nat., not spec.	28	0.14
Albanian	40	0.20
American Indian tribes, specified:	50	0.25
Apache	2	0.01
Blackfeet	1	0.01
Cherokee	11	0.06
Choctaw	7	0.04
Delaware	1	0.01
Iroquois	2	0.01
Latin American Indians (2)	3	0.02
Pueblo	1	0.01
Sioux	5	0.03
All other tribes (1)	17	0.09
American Indian tribes, not spec.	2	0.01
Arab:	158	0.79
Lebanese	149	0.75
Syrian	9	0.05
Armenian	90	0.45
Asian:	252	1.27
Chinese, ex. Taiwanese (73)	103	0.52
Filipino (17)	31	0.16
Indian (26)	38	0.19
Indonesian (1)	1	0.01
Japanese (10)	16	0.08
Korean (31)	36	0.18
Pakistani (1)	6	0.03
Taiwanese (4)	4	0.02
Thai (1)	4	0.02
Vietnamese (3)	4	0.02
Other Asian, specified	1	0.01
Other Asian, not specified (7)	8	0.04
Austrian	48	0.24
Belgian	20	0.10
British	164	0.82
Canadian	168	0.84
Czech	62	0.31
Czechoslovakian	30	0.15
Danish	120	0.60
Dutch	178	0.90
Eastern European	45	0.23
English	3,523	17.72
European	107	0.54
Finnish	95	0.48
French, except Basque	731	3.68
French Canadian	398	2.00
German	1,540	7.75
Greek	333	1.67
Hawaii Native/Pacific Islander:	6	0.03
Micronesian: (1)	1	0.01
Guamanian/Chamorro (1)	1	0.01
Polynesian: (1)	4	0.02
Native Hawaiian	3	0.02
Samoan (1)	1	0.01
Other Pac. Isl., not spec. (1)	1	0.01
Hispanic or Latino:	149	0.75
Central American:	16	0.08
Costa Rican	1	0.01
Guatemalan	6	0.03
Honduran	4	0.02
Nicaraguan	1	0.01
Salvadoran	3	0.02
Other Central American	1	0.01
Cuban	10	0.05
Mexican	14	0.07
Puerto Rican	30	0.15
South American:	36	0.18
Argentinean	10	0.05
Chilean	5	0.03
Colombian	7	0.04
Ecuadorian	1	0.01
Paraguayan	2	0.01
Peruvian	5	0.03
Venezuelan	3	0.02
Other South American	3	0.02
Other Hispanic or Latino	43	0.22
Hungarian	56	0.28
Iranian	6	0.03
Irish	7,406	37.25
Italian	3,348	16.84
Lithuanian	138	0.69
Norwegian	215	1.08
Polish	573	2.88
Portuguese	138	0.69
Russian	259	1.30
Scandinavian	28	0.14
Scotch-Irish	558	2.81
Scottish	816	4.10
Slavic	7	0.04
Slovak	45	0.23
Slovene	16	0.08
Swedish	691	3.48
Swiss	46	0.23
Ukrainian	53	0.27
United States or American	1,486	7.47
Welsh	41	0.21
West Indian, excl. Hispanic:	15	0.08
Haitian	10	0.05
West Indian	5	0.03
White:	19,549	98.33
Not Hispanic (19,274)	19,429	97.72
Hispanic (112)	120	0.60

Holbrook

Place Type: Census Designated Place
County: Norfolk
Population: 10,785

Ancestry/Race	Number	%
African American/Black:	505	4.68
Not Hispanic (420)	480	4.45
Hispanic (10)	25	0.23
African, sub-Saharan:	87	0.81
African	7	0.07
Cape Verdean	52	0.48
Ethiopian	28	0.26
Alaska Native tribes, specified:	4	0.04
Eskimo	4	0.04
Am. Ind. or Alaska Nat., not spec.	22	0.20
Albanian	19	0.18
American Indian tribes, specified:	31	0.29
Apache (1)	1	0.01
Cherokee (1)	8	0.07
Chippewa	1	0.01
Comanche (1)	1	0.01
Iroquois (2)	3	0.03
Pima	1	0.01
All other tribes (9)	16	0.15
American Indian tribes, not spec.	3	0.03
Arab:	80	0.74
Lebanese	66	0.61
Syrian	14	0.13
Asian:	184	1.71
Bangladeshi (5)	5	0.05
Chinese, ex. Taiwanese (31)	41	0.38
Filipino (34)	36	0.33
Indian (26)	27	0.25
Indonesian (1)	1	0.01
Japanese (11)	19	0.18
Korean (15)	15	0.14
Vietnamese (33)	37	0.34
Other Asian, specified	2	0.02
Other Asian, not specified	1	0.01
Austrian	49	0.46
British	74	0.69
Canadian	89	0.83
Celtic	7	0.07
Danish	8	0.07
Dutch	24	0.22
English	1,292	12.02
European	10	0.09
Finnish	28	0.26
French, except Basque	345	3.21
French Canadian	357	3.32
German	461	4.29
Greek	96	0.89
Hawaii Native/Pacific Islander:	8	0.07
Polynesian: (1)	1	0.01
Samoan (1)	1	0.01
Other Pac. Isl., specified	2	0.02
Other Pac. Isl., not spec.	5	0.05
Hispanic or Latino:	257	2.38
Central American:	19	0.18
Costa Rican	6	0.06
Guatemalan	2	0.02
Honduran	6	0.06
Panamanian	4	0.04
Salvadoran	1	0.01
Cuban	19	0.18
Dominican Republic	4	0.04

Notes: 1. Figures in the "Number" column do not add up to the total population due to: a) Ancestry/Race overlap — e.g. persons can report being both White and Irish, b) persons of Hispanic origin can report being any race, c) persons reporting two ancestries are counted in both categories. 2. Numbers in parentheses indicate the number of persons reporting this ancestry/race alone, not in combination with any other ancestry/race. 3. Refer to the Explanation of Data in the front of the book for more detailed information.

Mexican	22	0.20
Puerto Rican	80	0.74
South American:	38	0.35
Argentinean	1	0.01
Chilean	4	0.04
Colombian	7	0.06
Ecuadorian	4	0.04
Peruvian	15	0.14
Uruguayan	1	0.01
Venezuelan	3	0.03
Other South American	3	0.03
Other Hispanic or Latino	75	0.70
Hungarian	13	0.12
Irish	3,787	35.22
Italian	1,796	16.71
Latvian	25	0.23
Lithuanian	147	1.37
Norwegian	67	0.62
Polish	324	3.01
Portuguese	129	1.20
Russian	118	1.10
Scandinavian	8	0.07
Scotch-Irish	285	2.65
Scottish	468	4.35
Serbian	10	0.09
Swedish	333	3.10
Turkish	11	0.10
Ukrainian	67	0.62
United States or American	654	6.08
Welsh	49	0.46
West Indian, excl. Hispanic:	64	0.60
Bermudan	6	0.06
Haitian	39	0.36
Jamaican	19	0.18
White:	10,009	92.80
Not Hispanic (9,754)	9,833	91.17
Hispanic (154)	176	1.63

Holden

Place Type: Town
County: Worcester
Population: 15,621

Ancestry/Race	Number	%
African American/Black:	103	0.66
Not Hispanic (75)	92	0.59
Hispanic (1)	11	0.07
Am. Ind. or Alaska Nat., not spec.	13	0.08
Albanian	94	0.60
American Indian tribes, specified:	26	0.17
Blackfeet (2)	2	0.01
Cherokee (4)	14	0.09
Iroquois	6	0.04
Sioux	1	0.01
All other tribes (1)	3	0.02
American Indian tribes, not spec.	4	0.03
Arab:	165	1.06
Egyptian	16	0.10
Lebanese	127	0.81
Syrian	10	0.06
Other Arab	12	0.08
Armenian	208	1.33
Asian:	209	1.34
Cambodian (6)	6	0.04
Chinese, ex. Taiwanese (35)	59	0.38
Filipino (5)	9	0.06
Indian (35)	45	0.29
Indonesian (2)	2	0.01
Japanese (15)	21	0.13
Korean (36)	38	0.24
Pakistani (3)	7	0.04
Taiwanese (1)	1	0.01
Thai (1)	1	0.01
Vietnamese (13)	15	0.10
Other Asian, not specified (1)	5	0.03
Assyrian/Chaldean/Syriac	43	0.28
Austrian	23	0.15
British	46	0.29
Canadian	60	0.38
Celtic	6	0.04
Czech	12	0.08
Czechoslovakian	56	0.36
Danish	93	0.60
Dutch	313	2.00
Eastern European	22	0.14
English	2,825	18.08
Estonian	29	0.19
European	66	0.42
Finnish	154	0.99
French, except Basque	2,024	12.96
French Canadian	935	5.99
German	1,204	7.71
Greek	180	1.15
Hawaii Native/Pacific Islander:	7	0.04
Polynesian: (1)	3	0.02
Native Hawaiian (1)	2	0.01
Samoan	1	0.01
Other Pac. Isl., not spec.	4	0.03
Hispanic or Latino:	150	0.96
Central American:	12	0.08
Costa Rican	4	0.03
Guatemalan	3	0.02
Honduran	2	0.01
Salvadoran	3	0.02
Cuban	10	0.06
Dominican Republic	3	0.02
Mexican	16	0.10
Puerto Rican	42	0.27
South American:	21	0.13
Chilean	5	0.03
Colombian	6	0.04
Ecuadorian	5	0.03
Peruvian	2	0.01
Uruguayan	1	0.01
Venezuelan	2	0.01
Other Hispanic or Latino	46	0.29
Hungarian	49	0.31
Iranian	11	0.07
Irish	4,591	29.39
Italian	1,929	12.35
Lithuanian	334	2.14
Northern European	13	0.08
Norwegian	101	0.65
Polish	1,061	6.79
Portuguese	69	0.44
Romanian	32	0.20
Russian	267	1.71
Scandinavian	44	0.28
Scotch-Irish	396	2.54
Scottish	499	3.19
Slovak	24	0.15
Swedish	1,316	8.42
Swiss	43	0.28
Turkish	30	0.19
Ukrainian	8	0.05
United States or American	524	3.35
Welsh	107	0.68
White:	15,323	98.09
Not Hispanic (15,125)	15,213	97.39
Hispanic (89)	110	0.70
Yugoslavian	5	0.03

Holliston

Place Type: Town
County: Middlesex
Population: 13,801

Ancestry/Race	Number	%
African American/Black:	145	1.05
Not Hispanic (119)	139	1.01
Hispanic (4)	6	0.04
Am. Ind. or Alaska Nat., not spec.	11	0.08
Albanian	45	0.33
American Indian tribes, specified:	30	0.22
Blackfeet	1	0.01
Cherokee (1)	4	0.03
Iroquois	2	0.01
Latin American Indians (2)	2	0.01
Lumbee (2)	2	0.01
Navajo	2	0.01
All other tribes (9)	17	0.12
American Indian tribes, not spec.	1	0.01
Arab:	60	0.43
Arab/Arabic	15	0.11
Lebanese	22	0.16
Syrian	16	0.12
Other Arab	7	0.05
Armenian	57	0.41
Asian:	199	1.44
Cambodian	1	0.01
Chinese, ex. Taiwanese (57)	61	0.44
Filipino (19)	19	0.14
Indian (46)	51	0.37
Indonesian (1)	2	0.01
Japanese (9)	22	0.16
Korean (16)	22	0.16
Laotian (3)	3	0.02
Taiwanese (1)	1	0.01
Thai (3)	3	0.02
Vietnamese (4)	6	0.04
Other Asian, specified (4)	5	0.04
Other Asian, not specified	3	0.02
Australian	5	0.04
Austrian	15	0.11
Belgian	48	0.35
Brazilian	19	0.14
British	56	0.41
Canadian	118	0.86
Croatian	6	0.04
Czech	39	0.28
Czechoslovakian	3	0.02
Danish	68	0.49
Dutch	87	0.63
Eastern European	58	0.42
English	2,459	17.82
European	109	0.79
Finnish	73	0.53
French, except Basque	775	5.62
French Canadian	491	3.56
German	1,340	9.71
Greek	141	1.02
Hawaii Native/Pacific Islander:	1	0.01
Polynesian: (1)	1	0.01
Samoan (1)	1	0.01
Hispanic or Latino:	190	1.38
Central American:	15	0.11
Costa Rican	3	0.02
Guatemalan	4	0.03
Honduran	1	0.01
Nicaraguan	1	0.01
Panamanian	1	0.01
Salvadoran	4	0.03
Other Central American	1	0.01
Cuban	8	0.06
Dominican Republic	3	0.02
Mexican	17	0.12
Puerto Rican	60	0.43
South American:	26	0.19
Bolivian	4	0.03
Colombian	17	0.12
Ecuadorian	1	0.01
Paraguayan	1	0.01
Peruvian	1	0.01
Venezuelan	1	0.01
Other South American	1	0.01
Other Hispanic or Latino	61	0.44
Hungarian	118	0.86
Iranian	36	0.26
Irish	4,055	29.38
Italian	2,521	18.27
Latvian	10	0.07
Lithuanian	116	0.84
Northern European	35	0.25
Norwegian	163	1.18
Polish	772	5.59
Portuguese	205	1.49
Romanian	3	0.02
Russian	518	3.75

Notes: 1. Figures in the "Number" column do not add up to the total population due to: a) Ancestry/Race overlap — e.g. persons can report being both White and Irish, b) persons of Hispanic origin can report being any race, c) persons reporting two ancestries are counted in both categories. 2. Numbers in parentheses indicate the number of persons reporting this ancestry/race alone, not in combination with any other ancestry/race. 3. Refer to the Explanation of Data in the front of the book for more detailed information.

Ancestry/Race	Number	%
Scandinavian	57	0.41
Scotch-Irish	222	1.61
Scottish	498	3.61
Serbian	8	0.06
Slovak	30	0.22
Swedish	369	2.67
Swiss	79	0.57
Ukrainian	57	0.41
United States or American	730	5.29
Welsh	122	0.88
West Indian, excl. Hispanic:	83	0.60
Haitian	78	0.57
Trinidadian and Tobagonian	5	0.04
White:	13,436	97.36
Not Hispanic (13,208)	13,281	96.23
Hispanic (138)	155	1.12

Holyoke

Place Type: City
County: Hampden
Population: 39,838

Ancestry/Race	Number	%
African American/Black:	1,828	4.59
Not Hispanic (1,016)	1,187	2.98
Hispanic (460)	641	1.61
African, sub-Saharan:	142	0.36
African	103	0.26
Cape Verdean	8	0.02
Nigerian	31	0.08
Alaska Native tribes, not specified	1	0.00
Am. Ind. or Alaska Nat., not spec.	185	0.46
Alsatian	33	0.08
American Indian tribes, specified:	102	0.26
Apache	1	0.00
Blackfeet (1)	13	0.03
Cherokee (4)	11	0.03
Chippewa (2)	6	0.02
Cree	1	0.00
Creek (1)	1	0.00
Iroquois (1)	18	0.05
Latin American Indians (4)	15	0.04
Navajo (2)	2	0.01
Seminole	3	0.01
Sioux (2)	4	0.01
All other tribes (7)	27	0.07
American Indian tribes, not spec.	18	0.05
Arab:	114	0.29
Arab/Arabic	28	0.07
Jordanian	29	0.07
Lebanese	57	0.14
Asian:	406	1.02
Cambodian (75)	91	0.23
Chinese, ex. Taiwanese (62)	70	0.18
Filipino (30)	37	0.09
Indian (83)	104	0.26
Indonesian (3)	3	0.01
Japanese (7)	14	0.04
Korean (25)	31	0.08
Pakistani (6)	7	0.02
Taiwanese (2)	2	0.01
Thai (3)	3	0.01
Vietnamese (14)	21	0.05
Other Asian, specified	2	0.01
Other Asian, not specified (7)	21	0.05
Austrian	131	0.33
Belgian	41	0.10
British	25	0.06
Bulgarian	18	0.05
Canadian	195	0.49
Czech	72	0.18
Czechoslovakian	35	0.09
Danish	21	0.05
Dutch	78	0.20
Eastern European	31	0.08
English	1,609	4.04
Estonian	7	0.02
European	42	0.11
Finnish	8	0.02
French, except Basque	3,880	9.74
French Canadian	2,397	6.02
German	1,868	4.69
Greek	92	0.23
Guyanese	18	0.05
Hawaii Native/Pacific Islander:	97	0.24
Micronesian: (7)	9	0.02
Guamanian/Chamorro (7)	9	0.02
Polynesian: (11)	17	0.04
Native Hawaiian (5)	9	0.02
Samoan (6)	7	0.02
Other Polynesian	1	0.00
Other Pac. Isl., specified	2	0.01
Other Pac. Isl., not spec. (30)	69	0.17
Hispanic or Latino:	16,485	41.38
Central American:	57	0.14
Costa Rican	12	0.03
Guatemalan	5	0.01
Honduran	9	0.02
Nicaraguan	3	0.01
Panamanian	11	0.03
Salvadoran	13	0.03
Other Central American	4	0.01
Cuban	58	0.15
Dominican Republic	168	0.42
Mexican	85	0.21
Puerto Rican	14,539	36.50
South American:	234	0.59
Argentinean	3	0.01
Chilean	4	0.01
Colombian	190	0.48
Ecuadorian	16	0.04
Peruvian	7	0.02
Uruguayan	2	0.01
Venezuelan	4	0.01
Other South American	8	0.02
Other Hispanic or Latino	1,344	3.37
Hungarian	59	0.15
Irish	6,834	17.15
Italian	1,589	3.99
Lithuanian	108	0.27
Norwegian	79	0.20
Polish	4,041	10.14
Portuguese	287	0.72
Russian	120	0.30
Scandinavian	14	0.04
Scotch-Irish	228	0.57
Scottish	424	1.06
Slavic	7	0.02
Slovak	31	0.08
Slovene	5	0.01
Swedish	131	0.33
Swiss	35	0.09
Ukrainian	37	0.09
United States or American	722	1.81
Welsh	41	0.10
West Indian, excl. Hispanic:	81	0.20
Barbadian	6	0.02
British West Indian	6	0.02
Haitian	11	0.03
Jamaican	13	0.03
West Indian	36	0.09
Other West Indian	9	0.02
White:	27,088	68.00
Not Hispanic (21,508)	21,845	54.83
Hispanic (4,689)	5,243	13.16
Yugoslavian	35	0.09

Hopkinton

Place Type: Town
County: Middlesex
Population: 13,346

Ancestry/Race	Number	%
African American/Black:	116	0.87
Not Hispanic (84)	108	0.81
Hispanic (8)	8	0.06
African, sub-Saharan:	110	0.82
African	38	0.28
Cape Verdean	8	0.06
Somalian	47	0.35
South African	17	0.13
Am. Ind. or Alaska Nat., not spec.	16	0.12
Albanian	38	0.28
American Indian tribes, specified:	19	0.14
Blackfeet	4	0.03
Cherokee	5	0.04
Iroquois (1)	1	0.01
Latin American Indians (1)	2	0.01
All other tribes (2)	7	0.05
American Indian tribes, not spec.	8	0.06
Arab:	92	0.69
Lebanese	84	0.63
Other Arab	8	0.06
Armenian	88	0.66
Asian:	277	2.08
Cambodian (1)	1	0.01
Chinese, ex. Taiwanese (90)	111	0.83
Filipino (10)	15	0.11
Indian (67)	78	0.58
Japanese (7)	18	0.13
Korean (29)	34	0.25
Pakistani (1)	3	0.02
Taiwanese (5)	5	0.04
Thai (1)	1	0.01
Vietnamese (5)	5	0.04
Other Asian, not specified (3)	6	0.04
Austrian	8	0.06
British	133	1.00
Canadian	97	0.73
Celtic	13	0.10
Czech	48	0.36
Czechoslovakian	11	0.08
Danish	65	0.49
Dutch	201	1.51
Eastern European	56	0.42
English	2,155	16.15
European	67	0.50
Finnish	152	1.14
French, except Basque	1,124	8.42
French Canadian	477	3.57
German	1,391	10.42
Greek	46	0.34
Hawaii Native/Pacific Islander:	10	0.07
Micronesian: (1)	4	0.03
Guamanian/Chamorro (1)	4	0.03
Polynesian: (5)	6	0.04
Native Hawaiian (3)	4	0.03
Samoan (2)	2	0.01
Hispanic or Latino:	177	1.33
Central American:	4	0.03
Guatemalan	4	0.03
Cuban	22	0.16
Dominican Republic	2	0.01
Mexican	30	0.22
Puerto Rican	66	0.49
South American:	27	0.20
Argentinean	1	0.01
Bolivian	1	0.01
Chilean	3	0.02
Colombian	16	0.12
Ecuadorian	2	0.01
Peruvian	2	0.01
Venezuelan	1	0.01
Other South American	1	0.01
Other Hispanic or Latino	26	0.19
Hungarian	81	0.61
Iranian	10	0.07
Irish	4,253	31.87
Italian	2,110	15.81
Latvian	18	0.13
Lithuanian	117	0.88
Northern European	6	0.04
Norwegian	167	1.25
Pennsylvania German	8	0.06
Polish	749	5.61
Portuguese	55	0.41
Romanian	8	0.06
Russian	170	1.27

Notes: 1. Figures in the "Number" column do not add up to the total population due to: a) Ancestry/Race overlap — e.g. persons can report being both White and Irish, b) persons of Hispanic origin can report being any race, c) persons reporting two ancestries are counted in both categories. 2. Numbers in parentheses indicate the number of persons reporting this ancestry/race alone, not in combination with any other ancestry/race. 3. Refer to the Explanation of Data in the front of the book for more detailed information.

Scandinavian	23	0.17
Scotch-Irish	244	1.83
Scottish	392	2.94
Serbian	9	0.07
Slavic	11	0.08
Slovak	31	0.23
Slovene	6	0.04
Swedish	437	3.27
Swiss	68	0.51
Turkish	19	0.14
Ukrainian	27	0.20
United States or American	430	3.22
Welsh	72	0.54
West Indian, excl. Hispanic:	53	0.40
Haitian	47	0.35
Jamaican	6	0.04
White:	12,960	97.11
Not Hispanic (12,723)	12,818	96.04
Hispanic (133)	142	1.06
Yugoslavian	10	0.07

Hudson

Place Type: Town
County: Middlesex
Population: 18,113

Ancestry/Race	Number	%
African American/Black:	217	1.20
Not Hispanic (153)	203	1.12
Hispanic (12)	14	0.08
African, sub-Saharan:	107	0.59
African	27	0.15
Cape Verdean	27	0.15
Nigerian	26	0.14
South African	23	0.13
Other sub-Saharan African	4	0.02
Am. Ind. or Alaska Nat., not spec.	47	0.26
Albanian	57	0.31
Alsatian	10	0.06
American Indian tribes, specified:	34	0.19
Blackfeet (1)	3	0.02
Cherokee	5	0.03
Choctaw (2)	4	0.02
Iroquois	2	0.01
Latin American Indians (2)	4	0.02
Pueblo	1	0.01
Sioux	2	0.01
All other tribes (4)	13	0.07
American Indian tribes, not spec.	3	0.02
Arab:	25	0.14
Lebanese	25	0.14
Armenian	97	0.54
Asian:	301	1.66
Chinese, ex. Taiwanese (74)	80	0.44
Filipino (11)	18	0.10
Indian (126)	131	0.72
Japanese (4)	13	0.07
Korean (18)	26	0.14
Pakistani (4)	4	0.02
Thai (1)	1	0.01
Vietnamese (11)	15	0.08
Other Asian, not specified (2)	13	0.07
Austrian	22	0.12
Belgian	24	0.13
Brazilian	487	2.69
British	86	0.47
Bulgarian	12	0.07
Canadian	131	0.72
Celtic	3	0.02
Croatian	5	0.03
Czech	23	0.13
Czechoslovakian	6	0.03
Danish	121	0.67
Dutch	105	0.58
Eastern European	30	0.17
English	2,481	13.70
European	154	0.85
Finnish	182	1.00
French, except Basque	1,875	10.35
French Canadian	1,091	6.02
German	1,366	7.54
Greek	154	0.85
Hawaii Native/Pacific Islander:	40	0.22
Micronesian: (1)	1	0.01
Guamanian/Chamorro (1)	1	0.01
Polynesian: (9)	11	0.06
Native Hawaiian (9)	11	0.06
Other Pac. Isl., not spec.	28	0.15
Hispanic or Latino:	554	3.06
Central American:	61	0.34
Costa Rican	6	0.03
Guatemalan	45	0.25
Nicaraguan	3	0.02
Salvadoran	1	0.01
Other Central American	6	0.03
Cuban	16	0.09
Dominican Republic	16	0.09
Mexican	108	0.60
Puerto Rican	154	0.85
South American:	67	0.37
Argentinean	4	0.02
Bolivian	3	0.02
Chilean	20	0.11
Colombian	18	0.10
Ecuadorian	6	0.03
Peruvian	11	0.06
Venezuelan	4	0.02
Other South American	1	0.01
Other Hispanic or Latino	132	0.73
Hungarian	63	0.35
Icelander	6	0.03
Iranian	41	0.23
Irish	4,175	23.05
Italian	2,609	14.40
Lithuanian	152	0.84
Northern European	39	0.22
Norwegian	245	1.35
Polish	715	3.95
Portuguese	2,290	12.64
Romanian	18	0.10
Russian	130	0.72
Scandinavian	66	0.36
Scotch-Irish	278	1.53
Scottish	539	2.98
Serbian	5	0.03
Slavic	9	0.05
Slovak	5	0.03
Swedish	287	1.58
Swiss	22	0.12
Ukrainian	5	0.03
United States or American	697	3.85
Welsh	97	0.54
West Indian, excl. Hispanic:	77	0.43
British West Indian	3	0.02
Haitian	64	0.35
Jamaican	5	0.03
West Indian	5	0.03
White:	17,386	95.99
Not Hispanic (16,715)	17,011	93.92
Hispanic (333)	375	2.07

Hull

Place Type: Census Designated Place
County: Plymouth
Population: 11,050

Ancestry/Race	Number	%
African American/Black:	70	0.63
Not Hispanic (39)	58	0.52
Hispanic (12)	12	0.11
African, sub-Saharan:	83	0.75
Cape Verdean	83	0.75
Alaska Native tribes, specified:	1	0.01
Tlingit-Haida (1)	1	0.01
Am. Ind. or Alaska Nat., not spec.	20	0.18
Albanian	9	0.08
American Indian tribes, specified:	49	0.44
Blackfeet (1)	4	0.04
Cherokee (2)	5	0.05
Chickasaw	1	0.01
Chippewa (1)	1	0.01
Cree	1	0.01
Creek (4)	5	0.05
Iroquois	1	0.01
Potawatomi (1)	1	0.01
Seminole	2	0.02
Shoshone	1	0.01
Sioux	1	0.01
All other tribes (16)	26	0.24
American Indian tribes, not spec.	1	0.01
Arab:	64	0.58
Arab/Arabic	8	0.07
Egyptian	11	0.10
Lebanese	27	0.24
Syrian	18	0.16
Armenian	23	0.21
Asian:	126	1.14
Cambodian (26)	26	0.24
Chinese, ex. Taiwanese (20)	24	0.22
Filipino (1)	13	0.12
Indian (9)	13	0.12
Japanese (7)	12	0.11
Korean (9)	14	0.13
Thai (3)	3	0.03
Vietnamese (13)	14	0.13
Other Asian, not specified (6)	7	0.06
Australian	7	0.06
Austrian	15	0.14
Basque	14	0.13
Belgian	5	0.05
British	7	0.06
Canadian	84	0.76
Celtic	6	0.05
Czech	29	0.26
Czechoslovakian	37	0.33
Danish	71	0.64
Dutch	79	0.71
Eastern European	51	0.46
English	1,414	12.80
European	21	0.19
Finnish	50	0.45
French, except Basque	525	4.75
French Canadian	574	5.19
German	776	7.02
Greek	163	1.48
Hawaii Native/Pacific Islander:	9	0.08
Polynesian: (5)	9	0.08
Native Hawaiian (1)	1	0.01
Samoan (4)	8	0.07
Hispanic or Latino:	120	1.09
Central American:	7	0.06
Costa Rican	1	0.01
Honduran	1	0.01
Salvadoran	5	0.05
Cuban	12	0.11
Dominican Republic	7	0.06
Mexican	23	0.21
Puerto Rican	38	0.34
South American:	4	0.04
Argentinean	3	0.03
Chilean	1	0.01
Other Hispanic or Latino	29	0.26
Hungarian	12	0.11
Irish	3,986	36.07
Israeli	7	0.06
Italian	1,835	16.61
Lithuanian	109	0.99
Northern European	20	0.18
Norwegian	130	1.18
Polish	347	3.14
Portuguese	206	1.86
Romanian	39	0.35
Russian	291	2.63
Scandinavian	16	0.14
Scotch-Irish	308	2.79
Scottish	392	3.55
Serbian	14	0.13
Slavic	11	0.10

Notes: 1. Figures in the "Number" column do not add up to the total population due to: a) Ancestry/Race overlap — e.g. persons can report being both White and Irish, b) persons of Hispanic origin can report being any race, c) persons reporting two ancestries are counted in both categories. 2. Numbers in parentheses indicate the number of persons reporting this ancestry/race alone, not in combination with any other ancestry/race. 3. Refer to the Explanation of Data in the front of the book for more detailed information.

Slovak	9	0.08
Swedish	200	1.81
Swiss	37	0.33
Turkish	4	0.04
Ukrainian	29	0.26
United States or American	450	4.07
Welsh	52	0.47
White:	10,807	97.80
Not Hispanic (10,642)	10,728	97.09
Hispanic (71)	79	0.71

Ipswich

Place Type: Town
County: Essex
Population: 12,987

Ancestry/Race	Number	%
African American/Black:	82	0.63
Not Hispanic (43)	74	0.57
Hispanic (8)	8	0.06
African, sub-Saharan:	25	0.19
African	15	0.12
South African	10	0.08
Am. Ind. or Alaska Nat., not spec.	10	0.08
Albanian	5	0.04
American Indian tribes, specified:	30	0.23
Cherokee (4)	5	0.04
Chickasaw (1)	1	0.01
Chippewa	2	0.02
Choctaw	1	0.01
Cree	1	0.01
Delaware	1	0.01
Iroquois	1	0.01
Latin American Indians (2)	3	0.02
Navajo (1)	2	0.02
Sioux	2	0.02
Yaqui	1	0.01
All other tribes (1)	10	0.08
Arab:	45	0.35
Arab/Arabic	6	0.05
Egyptian	10	0.08
Lebanese	29	0.22
Armenian	4	0.03
Asian:	131	1.01
Cambodian (2)	2	0.02
Chinese, ex. Taiwanese (38)	50	0.39
Filipino (4)	8	0.06
Indian (12)	12	0.09
Japanese (12)	20	0.15
Korean (22)	23	0.18
Taiwanese (1)	3	0.02
Thai (2)	2	0.02
Vietnamese (10)	10	0.08
Other Asian, not specified	1	0.01
Austrian	24	0.18
Belgian	14	0.11
British	157	1.21
Canadian	185	1.42
Celtic	11	0.08
Czech	20	0.15
Czechoslovakian	9	0.07
Danish	40	0.31
Dutch	142	1.09
Eastern European	9	0.07
English	2,956	22.76
European	90	0.69
Finnish	55	0.42
French, except Basque	1,039	8.00
French Canadian	753	5.80
German	791	6.09
Greek	583	4.49
Hawaii Native/Pacific Islander:	5	0.04
Polynesian: (1)	4	0.03
Native Hawaiian (1)	4	0.03
Other Pac. Isl., not spec.	1	0.01
Hispanic or Latino:	135	1.04
Central American:	9	0.07
Costa Rican	1	0.01
Guatemalan	6	0.05
Honduran	1	0.01
Panamanian	1	0.01
Cuban	8	0.06
Dominican Republic	15	0.12
Mexican	23	0.18
Puerto Rican	39	0.30
South American:	14	0.11
Argentinean	1	0.01
Chilean	2	0.02
Ecuadorian	7	0.05
Peruvian	3	0.02
Venezuelan	1	0.01
Other Hispanic or Latino	27	0.21
Hungarian	46	0.35
Irish	3,417	26.31
Italian	1,643	12.65
Latvian	35	0.27
Lithuanian	38	0.29
New Zealander	5	0.04
Northern European	14	0.11
Norwegian	95	0.73
Pennsylvania German	8	0.06
Polish	990	7.62
Portuguese	95	0.73
Romanian	13	0.10
Russian	173	1.33
Scandinavian	9	0.07
Scotch-Irish	263	2.03
Scottish	532	4.10
Serbian	20	0.15
Swedish	414	3.19
Swiss	20	0.15
Turkish	8	0.06
Ukrainian	49	0.38
United States or American	553	4.26
Welsh	94	0.72
West Indian, excl. Hispanic:	4	0.03
Trinidadian and Tobagonian	4	0.03
White:	12,774	98.36
Not Hispanic (12,591)	12,682	97.65
Hispanic (84)	92	0.71

Kingston

Place Type: Town
County: Plymouth
Population: 11,780

Ancestry/Race	Number	%
African American/Black:	161	1.37
Not Hispanic (112)	158	1.34
Hispanic (1)	3	0.03
African, sub-Saharan:	249	2.11
African	9	0.08
Cape Verdean	240	2.04
Am. Ind. or Alaska Nat., not spec.	28	0.24
Albanian	5	0.04
American Indian tribes, specified:	24	0.20
Cherokee	6	0.05
Iroquois	1	0.01
Latin American Indians (1)	1	0.01
Lumbee (1)	1	0.01
Osage (1)	1	0.01
Sioux	1	0.01
All other tribes (7)	13	0.11
Arab:	132	1.12
Egyptian	6	0.05
Lebanese	96	0.81
Syrian	30	0.25
Armenian	114	0.97
Asian:	70	0.59
Cambodian (1)	5	0.04
Chinese, ex. Taiwanese (27)	31	0.26
Filipino (6)	9	0.08
Indian (1)	5	0.04
Japanese (1)	1	0.01
Korean (3)	4	0.03
Taiwanese (2)	2	0.02
Thai (3)	3	0.03
Vietnamese (6)	6	0.05
Other Asian, not specified (1)	4	0.03
Austrian	27	0.23
Basque	6	0.05
Belgian	18	0.15
British	57	0.48
Canadian	72	0.61
Czech	27	0.23
Danish	43	0.37
Dutch	48	0.41
English	1,859	15.78
European	18	0.15
Finnish	17	0.14
French, except Basque	920	7.81
French Canadian	419	3.56
German	1,139	9.67
Greek	169	1.43
Hawaii Native/Pacific Islander:	1	0.01
Polynesian: (1)	1	0.01
Native Hawaiian (1)	1	0.01
Hispanic or Latino:	88	0.75
Central American:	4	0.03
Costa Rican	1	0.01
Guatemalan	2	0.02
Honduran	1	0.01
Cuban	10	0.08
Mexican	23	0.20
Puerto Rican	20	0.17
South American:	15	0.13
Argentinean	9	0.08
Peruvian	2	0.02
Uruguayan	1	0.01
Venezuelan	1	0.01
Other South American	2	0.02
Other Hispanic or Latino	16	0.14
Hungarian	15	0.13
Irish	4,147	35.20
Italian	1,853	15.73
Latvian	20	0.17
Lithuanian	66	0.56
Norwegian	65	0.55
Polish	463	3.93
Portuguese	660	5.60
Russian	99	0.84
Scandinavian	30	0.25
Scotch-Irish	310	2.63
Scottish	510	4.33
Slovak	8	0.07
Swedish	327	2.78
Swiss	8	0.07
Ukrainian	10	0.08
United States or American	262	2.22
Welsh	91	0.77
West Indian, excl. Hispanic:	24	0.20
Barbadian	14	0.12
Jamaican	10	0.08
White:	11,522	97.81
Not Hispanic (11,370)	11,457	97.26
Hispanic (57)	65	0.55
Yugoslavian	7	0.06

Lawrence

Place Type: City
County: Essex
Population: 72,043

Ancestry/Race	Number	%
African American/Black:	5,444	7.56
Not Hispanic (1,412)	1,658	2.30
Hispanic (2,104)	3,786	5.26
African, sub-Saharan:	249	0.35
African	164	0.23
Cape Verdean	56	0.08
Ethiopian	7	0.01
Kenyan	22	0.03
Alaska Native tribes, specified:	2	0.00
Eskimo	1	0.00
Tlingit-Haida (1)	1	0.00
Alaska Native tribes, not specified	1	0.00
Am. Ind. or Alaska Nat., not spec.	606	0.84

Notes: 1. Figures in the "Number" column do not add up to the total population due to: a) Ancestry/Race overlap — e.g. persons can report being both White and Irish, b) persons of Hispanic origin can report being any race, c) persons reporting two ancestries are counted in both categories. 2. Numbers in parentheses indicate the number of persons reporting this ancestry/race alone, not in combination with any other ancestry/race. 3. Refer to the Explanation of Data in the front of the book for more detailed information.

Ancestry/Race	Number	%
American Indian tribes, specified:	287	0.40
Apache	1	0.00
Blackfeet (4)	9	0.01
Cherokee (4)	25	0.03
Chickasaw	2	0.00
Choctaw	3	0.00
Comanche	3	0.00
Cree	2	0.00
Iroquois	5	0.01
Latin American Indians (55)	146	0.20
Lumbee (3)	3	0.00
Navajo	3	0.00
Potawatomi	1	0.00
Pueblo (11)	32	0.04
Sioux	5	0.01
All other tribes (22)	47	0.07
American Indian tribes, not spec.	42	0.06
Arab:	1,290	1.79
Arab/Arabic	27	0.04
Lebanese	1,133	1.57
Moroccan	18	0.02
Syrian	75	0.10
Other Arab	37	0.05
Armenian	149	0.21
Asian:	2,238	3.11
Cambodian (497)	570	0.79
Chinese, ex. Taiwanese (263)	313	0.43
Filipino (9)	23	0.03
Indian (184)	251	0.35
Japanese (18)	30	0.04
Korean (104)	110	0.15
Laotian (1)	7	0.01
Malaysian (1)	1	0.00
Pakistani (2)	3	0.00
Taiwanese (2)	3	0.00
Thai (8)	9	0.01
Vietnamese (722)	779	1.08
Other Asian, specified (3)	4	0.01
Other Asian, not specified (55)	135	0.19
Australian	6	0.01
Austrian	34	0.05
Basque	5	0.01
Belgian	74	0.10
Brazilian	57	0.08
British	23	0.03
Bulgarian	19	0.03
Canadian	318	0.44
Celtic	6	0.01
Croatian	7	0.01
Czechoslovakian	7	0.01
Danish	5	0.01
Dutch	13	0.02
Eastern European	11	0.02
English	2,306	3.20
European	33	0.05
Finnish	10	0.01
French, except Basque	3,381	4.69
French Canadian	3,175	4.41
German	1,174	1.63
Greek	145	0.20
Hawaii Native/Pacific Islander:	196	0.27
Melanesian: (1)	2	0.00
Fijian (1)	1	0.00
Other Melanesian	1	0.00
Micronesian: (6)	8	0.01
Guamanian/Chamorro (6)	7	0.01
Other Micronesian	1	0.00
Polynesian: (15)	27	0.04
Native Hawaiian (6)	15	0.02
Samoan (9)	11	0.02
Other Polynesian	1	0.00
Other Pac. Isl., specified	1	0.00
Other Pac. Isl., not spec. (49)	158	0.22
Hispanic or Latino:	43,019	59.71
Central American:	1,001	1.39
Costa Rican	53	0.07
Guatemalan	794	1.10
Honduran	60	0.08
Nicaraguan	13	0.02
Panamanian	3	0.00
Salvadoran	53	0.07
Other Central American	25	0.03
Cuban	408	0.57
Dominican Republic	16,186	22.47
Mexican	316	0.44
Puerto Rican	15,816	21.95
South American:	725	1.01
Argentinean	24	0.03
Bolivian	7	0.01
Chilean	5	0.01
Colombian	198	0.27
Ecuadorian	372	0.52
Paraguayan	3	0.00
Peruvian	50	0.07
Venezuelan	44	0.06
Other South American	22	0.03
Other Hispanic or Latino	8,567	11.89
Hungarian	6	0.01
Iranian	6	0.01
Irish	4,716	6.55
Israeli	6	0.01
Italian	4,646	6.45
Lithuanian	327	0.45
Maltese	6	0.01
Norwegian	67	0.09
Pennsylvania German	5	0.01
Polish	921	1.28
Portuguese	805	1.12
Romanian	8	0.01
Russian	177	0.25
Scandinavian	24	0.03
Scotch-Irish	362	0.50
Scottish	412	0.57
Swedish	109	0.15
Swiss	19	0.03
Turkish	41	0.06
Ukrainian	39	0.05
United States or American	1,975	2.74
Welsh	23	0.03
West Indian, excl. Hispanic:	335	0.47
Belizean	7	0.01
British West Indian	36	0.05
Haitian	151	0.21
Jamaican	58	0.08
U.S. Virgin Islander	60	0.08
West Indian	23	0.03
White:	38,553	53.51
Not Hispanic (24,569)	25,184	34.96
Hispanic (10,475)	13,369	18.56

Leicester

Place Type: Town
County: Worcester
Population: 10,471

Ancestry/Race	Number	%
African American/Black:	167	1.59
Not Hispanic (130)	160	1.53
Hispanic (4)	7	0.07
African, sub-Saharan:	184	1.76
African	38	0.36
Cape Verdean	19	0.18
Ghanian	37	0.35
Kenyan	90	0.86
Am. Ind. or Alaska Nat., not spec.	19	0.18
Albanian	55	0.53
American Indian tribes, specified:	51	0.49
Apache	2	0.02
Blackfeet	1	0.01
Cherokee	9	0.09
Iroquois	2	0.02
Navajo (1)	1	0.01
All other tribes (23)	36	0.34
American Indian tribes, not spec.	2	0.02
Arab:	19	0.18
Iraqi	19	0.18
Armenian	202	1.93
Asian:	97	0.93
Chinese, ex. Taiwanese (5)	6	0.06
Filipino (10)	10	0.10
Indian (8)	9	0.09
Indonesian (1)	1	0.01
Japanese (6)	8	0.08
Korean (10)	15	0.14
Malaysian (1)	1	0.01
Pakistani (5)	5	0.05
Vietnamese (30)	30	0.29
Other Asian, specified	6	0.06
Other Asian, not specified (2)	6	0.06
Assyrian/Chaldean/Syriac	6	0.06
Austrian	8	0.08
Belgian	24	0.23
British	40	0.38
Canadian	63	0.60
Czech	12	0.11
Czechoslovakian	9	0.09
Danish	14	0.13
Dutch	124	1.18
English	1,355	12.94
European	39	0.37
Finnish	155	1.48
French, except Basque	2,164	20.67
French Canadian	766	7.32
German	460	4.39
Greek	24	0.23
Hawaii Native/Pacific Islander:	14	0.13
Micronesian: (2)	2	0.02
Guamanian/Chamorro (2)	2	0.02
Polynesian: (4)	5	0.05
Native Hawaiian	1	0.01
Samoan (4)	4	0.04
Other Pac. Isl., specified	6	0.06
Other Pac. Isl., not spec.	1	0.01
Hispanic or Latino:	183	1.75
Central American:	6	0.06
Costa Rican	4	0.04
Salvadoran	2	0.02
Cuban	9	0.09
Dominican Republic	1	0.01
Mexican	21	0.20
Puerto Rican	103	0.98
South American:	12	0.11
Colombian	5	0.05
Ecuadorian	6	0.06
Peruvian	1	0.01
Other Hispanic or Latino	31	0.30
Hungarian	34	0.32
Icelander	14	0.13
Irish	2,575	24.59
Italian	1,169	11.16
Lithuanian	370	3.53
Norwegian	7	0.07
Pennsylvania German	28	0.27
Polish	587	5.61
Portuguese	53	0.51
Russian	47	0.45
Scandinavian	7	0.07
Scotch-Irish	170	1.62
Scottish	306	2.92
Slovak	15	0.14
Swedish	657	6.27
Swiss	14	0.13
Turkish	16	0.15
United States or American	328	3.13
Welsh	36	0.34
White:	10,175	97.17
Not Hispanic (9,952)	10,032	95.81
Hispanic (131)	143	1.37

Leominster

Place Type: City
County: Worcester
Population: 41,303

Ancestry/Race	Number	%
African American/Black:	1,803	4.37
Not Hispanic (1,255)	1,476	3.57
Hispanic (274)	327	0.79

Notes: 1. Figures in the "Number" column do not add up to the total population due to: a) Ancestry/Race overlap — e.g. persons can report being both White and Irish, b) persons of Hispanic origin can report being any race, c) persons reporting two ancestries are counted in both categories. 2. Numbers in parentheses indicate the number of persons reporting this ancestry/race alone, not in combination with any other ancestry/race. 3. Refer to the Explanation of Data in the front of the book for more detailed information.

Ancestry/Race	Number	%
African, sub-Saharan:	373	0.90
African	248	0.60
Cape Verdean	17	0.04
Ethiopian	12	0.03
Ghanian	37	0.09
Kenyan	28	0.07
South African	14	0.03
Zimbabwean	17	0.04
Am. Ind. or Alaska Nat., not spec.	78	0.19
Albanian	9	0.02
American Indian tribes, specified:	119	0.29
Blackfeet (4)	10	0.02
Cherokee (10)	24	0.06
Chippewa (3)	4	0.01
Choctaw	4	0.01
Creek	5	0.01
Crow	2	0.00
Iroquois (2)	9	0.02
Latin American Indians (5)	18	0.04
Navajo (1)	3	0.01
Potawatomi	1	0.00
Pueblo	1	0.00
Seminole	1	0.00
Sioux	2	0.00
Tohono O'Odham	1	0.00
All other tribes (15)	34	0.08
American Indian tribes, not spec.	7	0.02
Arab:	243	0.59
Arab/Arabic	30	0.07
Egyptian	12	0.03
Jordanian	44	0.11
Lebanese	132	0.32
Palestinian	10	0.02
Syrian	15	0.04
Armenian	84	0.20
Asian:	1,239	3.00
Bangladeshi (12)	13	0.03
Cambodian (22)	35	0.08
Chinese, ex. Taiwanese (94)	118	0.29
Filipino (33)	48	0.12
Hmong (100)	120	0.29
Indian (147)	177	0.43
Japanese (27)	48	0.12
Korean (160)	195	0.47
Laotian (194)	209	0.51
Pakistani (17)	39	0.09
Taiwanese (2)	2	0.00
Thai (23)	29	0.07
Vietnamese (101)	122	0.30
Other Asian, specified (6)	9	0.02
Other Asian, not specified (34)	75	0.18
Austrian	31	0.08
Basque	8	0.02
Belgian	5	0.01
Brazilian	289	0.70
British	40	0.10
Canadian	437	1.06
Czech	54	0.13
Czechoslovakian	28	0.07
Danish	57	0.14
Dutch	130	0.31
Eastern European	34	0.08
English	3,589	8.69
European	61	0.15
Finnish	572	1.38
French, except Basque	6,803	16.47
French Canadian	4,627	11.20
German	2,275	5.51
Greek	498	1.21
Guyanese	8	0.02
Hawaii Native/Pacific Islander:	42	0.10
Melanesian:	1	0.00
Fijian	1	0.00
Micronesian: (3)	6	0.01
Guamanian/Chamorro (3)	6	0.01
Polynesian: (5)	8	0.02
Native Hawaiian (4)	6	0.01
Samoan (1)	2	0.00
Other Pac. Isl., specified	3	0.01
Other Pac. Isl., not spec. (16)	24	0.06
Hispanic or Latino:	4,544	11.00
Central American:	108	0.26
Costa Rican	3	0.01
Guatemalan	38	0.09
Honduran	15	0.04
Nicaraguan	3	0.01
Panamanian	24	0.06
Salvadoran	19	0.05
Other Central American	6	0.01
Cuban	34	0.08
Dominican Republic	190	0.46
Mexican	246	0.60
Puerto Rican	2,843	6.88
South American:	486	1.18
Argentinean	16	0.04
Bolivian	8	0.02
Chilean	1	0.00
Colombian	79	0.19
Ecuadorian	51	0.12
Paraguayan	1	0.00
Peruvian	12	0.03
Uruguayan	265	0.64
Venezuelan	21	0.05
Other South American	32	0.08
Other Hispanic or Latino	637	1.54
Hungarian	82	0.20
Iranian	8	0.02
Irish	7,563	18.31
Italian	7,924	19.19
Lithuanian	213	0.52
Norwegian	168	0.41
Pennsylvania German	12	0.03
Polish	1,283	3.11
Portuguese	460	1.11
Romanian	7	0.02
Russian	111	0.27
Scandinavian	36	0.09
Scotch-Irish	476	1.15
Scottish	920	2.23
Serbian	21	0.05
Slavic	5	0.01
Slovak	8	0.02
Swedish	623	1.51
Swiss	12	0.03
Ukrainian	71	0.17
United States or American	1,342	3.25
Welsh	160	0.39
West Indian, excl. Hispanic:	258	0.62
Barbadian	25	0.06
Haitian	148	0.36
Jamaican	73	0.18
Trinidadian and Tobagonian	12	0.03
White:	36,712	88.88
Not Hispanic (33,673)	34,181	82.76
Hispanic (2,309)	2,531	6.13
Yugoslavian	5	0.01

Lexington

Place Type: Census Designated Place
County: Middlesex
Population: 30,355

Ancestry/Race	Number	%
African American/Black:	450	1.48
Not Hispanic (337)	428	1.41
Hispanic (6)	22	0.07
African, sub-Saharan:	138	0.45
African	32	0.11
Cape Verdean	15	0.05
South African	58	0.19
Other sub-Saharan African	33	0.11
Am. Ind. or Alaska Nat., not spec.	21	0.07
Albanian	10	0.03
Alsatian	9	0.03
American Indian tribes, specified:	47	0.15
Blackfeet (2)	4	0.01
Cherokee (2)	13	0.04
Comanche	1	0.00
Cree	1	0.00
Iroquois	2	0.01
Latin American Indians (1)	5	0.02
Sioux (6)	6	0.02
All other tribes (9)	15	0.05
American Indian tribes, not spec.	9	0.03
Arab:	223	0.73
Arab/Arabic	33	0.11
Egyptian	52	0.17
Lebanese	111	0.37
Syrian	21	0.07
Other Arab	6	0.02
Armenian	457	1.51
Asian:	3,634	11.97
Bangladeshi (24)	25	0.08
Cambodian (47)	49	0.16
Chinese, ex. Taiwanese (1,532)	1,670	5.50
Filipino (45)	69	0.23
Indian (672)	726	2.39
Indonesian (6)	10	0.03
Japanese (214)	262	0.86
Korean (431)	466	1.54
Pakistani (30)	32	0.11
Sri Lankan (11)	12	0.04
Taiwanese (160)	182	0.60
Thai (17)	18	0.06
Vietnamese (27)	30	0.10
Other Asian, specified (2)	5	0.02
Other Asian, not specified (39)	78	0.26
Assyrian/Chaldean/Syriac	18	0.06
Australian	8	0.03
Austrian	205	0.68
Basque	30	0.10
Belgian	57	0.19
Brazilian	22	0.07
British	375	1.24
Canadian	295	0.97
Celtic	5	0.02
Croatian	6	0.02
Cypriot	7	0.02
Czech	99	0.33
Czechoslovakian	12	0.04
Danish	116	0.38
Dutch	281	0.93
Eastern European	307	1.01
English	4,466	14.71
Estonian	7	0.02
European	283	0.93
Finnish	120	0.40
French, except Basque	1,167	3.84
French Canadian	532	1.75
German	2,759	9.09
Greek	430	1.42
Guyanese	30	0.10
Hawaii Native/Pacific Islander:	15	0.05
Polynesian: (1)	2	0.01
Native Hawaiian	1	0.00
Samoan (1)	1	0.00
Other Pac. Isl., not spec. (1)	13	0.04
Hispanic or Latino:	428	1.41
Central American:	16	0.05
Costa Rican	3	0.01
Guatemalan	5	0.02
Salvadoran	8	0.03
Cuban	31	0.10
Dominican Republic	17	0.06
Mexican	70	0.23
Puerto Rican	71	0.23
South American:	121	0.40
Argentinean	24	0.08
Bolivian	3	0.01
Chilean	32	0.11
Colombian	14	0.05
Ecuadorian	5	0.02
Paraguayan	4	0.01
Peruvian	9	0.03
Uruguayan	2	0.01
Venezuelan	18	0.06
Other South American	10	0.03
Other Hispanic or Latino	102	0.34
Hungarian	301	0.99

Notes: 1. Figures in the "Number" column do not add up to the total population due to: a) Ancestry/Race overlap — e.g. persons can report being both White and Irish, b) persons of Hispanic origin can report being any race, c) persons reporting two ancestries are counted in both categories. 2. Numbers in parentheses indicate the number of persons reporting this ancestry/race alone, not in combination with any other ancestry/race. 3. Refer to the Explanation of Data in the front of the book for more detailed information.

Iranian	208	0.69
Irish	5,457	17.98
Israeli	124	0.41
Italian	3,518	11.59
Latvian	57	0.19
Lithuanian	172	0.57
Northern European	82	0.27
Norwegian	204	0.67
Polish	1,338	4.41
Portuguese	284	0.94
Romanian	125	0.41
Russian	1,481	4.88
Scandinavian	17	0.06
Scotch-Irish	381	1.26
Scottish	1,061	3.50
Slavic	18	0.06
Slovak	61	0.20
Slovene	29	0.10
Swedish	748	2.46
Swiss	229	0.75
Ukrainian	192	0.63
United States or American	1,239	4.08
Welsh	84	0.28
West Indian, excl. Hispanic:	62	0.20
Barbadian	7	0.02
Haitian	43	0.14
Jamaican	6	0.02
West Indian	6	0.02
White:	26,527	87.39
Not Hispanic (25,822)	26,156	86.17
Hispanic (324)	371	1.22

Longmeadow

Place Type: Census Designated Place
County: Hampden
Population: 15,633

Ancestry/Race	Number	%
African American/Black:	128	0.82
Not Hispanic (104)	117	0.75
Hispanic (4)	11	0.07
African, sub-Saharan:	10	0.06
African	3	0.02
Cape Verdean	7	0.04
Am. Ind. or Alaska Nat., not spec.	15	0.10
Albanian	8	0.05
Alsatian	7	0.04
American Indian tribes, specified:	18	0.12
Blackfeet	3	0.02
Chippewa (1)	2	0.01
Cree (1)	1	0.01
Delaware (1)	1	0.01
Iroquois (1)	4	0.03
Latin American Indians	2	0.01
Tohono O'Odham	1	0.01
All other tribes (1)	4	0.03
American Indian tribes, not spec.	1	0.01
Arab:	102	0.65
Iraqi	7	0.04
Lebanese	64	0.41
Syrian	23	0.15
Other Arab	8	0.05
Armenian	89	0.57
Asian:	507	3.24
Cambodian	1	0.01
Chinese, ex. Taiwanese (140)	146	0.93
Filipino (34)	52	0.33
Indian (115)	118	0.75
Indonesian (3)	4	0.03
Japanese (23)	33	0.21
Korean (69)	71	0.45
Pakistani (13)	13	0.08
Taiwanese (21)	21	0.13
Thai (5)	5	0.03
Vietnamese (23)	25	0.16
Other Asian, not specified (7)	18	0.12
Assyrian/Chaldean/Syriac	9	0.06
Austrian	149	0.95
Belgian	7	0.04
British	95	0.61
Canadian	113	0.72
Czech	58	0.37
Czechoslovakian	22	0.14
Danish	17	0.11
Dutch	130	0.83
Eastern European	139	0.89
English	1,686	10.78
European	55	0.35
Finnish	38	0.24
French, except Basque	909	5.81
French Canadian	950	6.08
German	1,172	7.50
Greek	379	2.42
Hawaii Native/Pacific Islander:	12	0.08
Micronesian: (2)	2	0.01
Guamanian/Chamorro (2)	2	0.01
Polynesian: (3)	4	0.03
Native Hawaiian (3)	3	0.02
Samoan	1	0.01
Other Pac. Isl., not spec. (4)	6	0.04
Hispanic or Latino:	170	1.09
Central American:	10	0.06
Costa Rican	1	0.01
Guatemalan	4	0.03
Honduran	1	0.01
Nicaraguan	1	0.01
Panamanian	1	0.01
Salvadoran	2	0.01
Cuban	11	0.07
Dominican Republic	6	0.04
Mexican	18	0.12
Puerto Rican	48	0.31
South American:	21	0.13
Argentinean	1	0.01
Chilean	5	0.03
Colombian	2	0.01
Ecuadorian	6	0.04
Peruvian	7	0.04
Other Hispanic or Latino	56	0.36
Hungarian	121	0.77
Iranian	74	0.47
Irish	3,555	22.74
Israeli	37	0.24
Italian	2,402	15.36
Latvian	8	0.05
Lithuanian	90	0.58
Northern European	7	0.04
Norwegian	39	0.25
Polish	1,873	11.98
Portuguese	198	1.27
Romanian	77	0.49
Russian	1,007	6.44
Scandinavian	37	0.24
Scotch-Irish	223	1.43
Scottish	450	2.88
Serbian	7	0.04
Slavic	7	0.04
Slovak	8	0.05
Swedish	276	1.77
Swiss	14	0.09
Turkish	45	0.29
Ukrainian	92	0.59
United States or American	451	2.88
Welsh	99	0.63
West Indian, excl. Hispanic:	10	0.06
Jamaican	10	0.06
White:	15,003	95.97
Not Hispanic (14,793)	14,869	95.11
Hispanic (124)	134	0.86
Yugoslavian	8	0.05

Lowell

Place Type: City
County: Middlesex
Population: 105,167

Ancestry/Race	Number	%
African American/Black:	5,209	4.95
Not Hispanic (3,644)	4,196	3.99
Hispanic (779)	1,013	0.96
African, sub-Saharan:	1,605	1.53
African	810	0.77
Cape Verdean	44	0.04
Ethiopian	9	0.01
Ghanian	133	0.13
Kenyan	80	0.08
Liberian	111	0.11
Nigerian	169	0.16
Sierra Leonean	73	0.07
South African	34	0.03
Ugandan	20	0.02
Zimbabwean	30	0.03
Other sub-Saharan African	92	0.09
Alaska Native tribes, specified:	1	0.00
Eskimo	1	0.00
Alaska Native tribes, not specified	1	0.00
Am. Ind. or Alaska Nat., not spec.	361	0.34
Albanian	23	0.02
American Indian tribes, specified:	277	0.26
Apache (3)	6	0.01
Blackfeet (3)	31	0.03
Cherokee (18)	65	0.06
Chippewa	7	0.01
Choctaw (1)	3	0.00
Cree	5	0.00
Creek	1	0.00
Delaware (2)	2	0.00
Iroquois (9)	25	0.02
Latin American Indians (9)	31	0.03
Navajo (1)	5	0.00
Pueblo (1)	2	0.00
Seminole	2	0.00
Sioux (7)	8	0.01
All other tribes (23)	84	0.08
American Indian tribes, not spec.	51	0.05
Arab:	526	0.50
Arab/Arabic	123	0.12
Egyptian	11	0.01
Jordanian	21	0.02
Lebanese	269	0.26
Moroccan	6	0.01
Palestinian	9	0.01
Syrian	69	0.07
Other Arab	18	0.02
Armenian	317	0.30
Asian:	19,238	18.29
Bangladeshi (16)	16	0.02
Cambodian (9,850)	10,904	10.37
Chinese, ex. Taiwanese (640)	852	0.81
Filipino (106)	181	0.17
Hmong (1)	2	0.00
Indian (2,424)	2,616	2.49
Indonesian (28)	35	0.03
Japanese (48)	66	0.06
Korean (147)	168	0.16
Laotian (1,541)	1,750	1.66
Pakistani (32)	37	0.04
Sri Lankan (8)	8	0.01
Taiwanese (21)	24	0.02
Thai (108)	155	0.15
Vietnamese (1,598)	1,769	1.68
Other Asian, specified (9)	19	0.02
Other Asian, not specified (393)	636	0.60
Assyrian/Chaldean/Syriac	17	0.02
Australian	11	0.01
Austrian	48	0.05
Belgian	24	0.02
Brazilian	1,820	1.73
British	181	0.17
Canadian	468	0.45
Croatian	8	0.01
Czech	24	0.02
Czechoslovakian	22	0.02
Danish	88	0.08
Dutch	345	0.33
Eastern European	6	0.01
English	6,252	5.94
European	73	0.07

Notes: 1. Figures in the "Number" column do not add up to the total population due to: a) Ancestry/Race overlap — e.g. persons can report being both White and Irish, b) persons of Hispanic origin can report being any race, c) persons reporting two ancestries are counted in both categories. 2. Numbers in parentheses indicate the number of persons reporting this ancestry/race alone, not in combination with any other ancestry/race. 3. Refer to the Explanation of Data in the front of the book for more detailed information.

Finnish	92	0.09
French, except Basque	11,607	11.04
French Canadian	8,846	8.41
German	2,403	2.28
Greek	2,815	2.68
Hawaii Native/Pacific Islander:	276	0.26
Micronesian: (9)	9	0.01
Guamanian/Chamorro (8)	8	0.01
Other Micronesian (1)	1	0.00
Polynesian: (9)	19	0.02
Native Hawaiian (5)	9	0.01
Samoan (4)	9	0.01
Other Polynesian	1	0.00
Other Pac. Isl., specified	7	0.01
Other Pac. Isl., not spec. (20)	241	0.23
Hispanic or Latino:	14,734	14.01
Central American:	229	0.22
Costa Rican	10	0.01
Guatemalan	86	0.08
Honduran	44	0.04
Nicaraguan	4	0.00
Panamanian	33	0.03
Salvadoran	47	0.04
Other Central American	5	0.00
Cuban	121	0.12
Dominican Republic	1,024	0.97
Mexican	282	0.27
Puerto Rican	9,604	9.13
South American:	1,336	1.27
Argentinean	31	0.03
Bolivian	2	0.00
Chilean	22	0.02
Colombian	1,167	1.11
Ecuadorian	20	0.02
Paraguayan	4	0.00
Peruvian	31	0.03
Venezuelan	34	0.03
Other South American	25	0.02
Other Hispanic or Latino	2,138	2.03
Hungarian	74	0.07
Iranian	104	0.10
Irish	20,467	19.46
Israeli	13	0.01
Italian	5,972	5.68
Latvian	22	0.02
Lithuanian	397	0.38
Northern European	10	0.01
Norwegian	172	0.16
Pennsylvania German	10	0.01
Polish	3,304	3.14
Portuguese	6,067	5.77
Romanian	25	0.02
Russian	416	0.40
Scandinavian	52	0.05
Scotch-Irish	895	0.85
Scottish	1,296	1.23
Serbian	7	0.01
Slavic	6	0.01
Slovak	9	0.01
Soviet Union	7	0.01
Swedish	586	0.56
Swiss	6	0.01
Turkish	16	0.02
Ukrainian	55	0.05
United States or American	2,644	2.51
Welsh	83	0.08
West Indian, excl. Hispanic:	437	0.42
Barbadian	34	0.03
Haitian	261	0.25
Jamaican	119	0.11
Trinidadian and Tobagonian	14	0.01
U.S. Virgin Islander	6	0.01
West Indian	3	0.00
White:	75,049	71.36
Not Hispanic (65,760)	67,775	64.45
Hispanic (6,385)	7,274	6.92

Ludlow

Place Type: Town
County: Hampden
Population: 21,209

Ancestry/Race	Number	%
African American/Black:	464	2.19
Not Hispanic (423)	453	2.14
Hispanic (9)	11	0.05
African, sub-Saharan:	9	0.04
Cape Verdean	9	0.04
Am. Ind. or Alaska Nat., not spec.	32	0.15
Albanian	9	0.04
American Indian tribes, specified:	24	0.11
Cherokee	3	0.01
Cheyenne	1	0.00
Chippewa (1)	2	0.01
Iroquois	4	0.02
Latin American Indians	2	0.01
Lumbee (1)	1	0.00
Ottawa	1	0.00
Sioux (1)	1	0.00
All other tribes (3)	9	0.04
American Indian tribes, not spec.	3	0.01
Arab:	46	0.22
Lebanese	46	0.22
Armenian	28	0.13
Asian:	145	0.68
Cambodian (1)	1	0.00
Chinese, ex. Taiwanese (26)	26	0.12
Filipino (34)	41	0.19
Indian (20)	20	0.09
Japanese (6)	7	0.03
Korean (16)	19	0.09
Thai (2)	2	0.01
Vietnamese (17)	21	0.10
Other Asian, not specified (3)	8	0.04
Austrian	49	0.23
Brazilian	28	0.13
British	27	0.13
Canadian	94	0.44
Czech	24	0.11
Czechoslovakian	9	0.04
Danish	52	0.25
Dutch	171	0.81
English	1,396	6.58
European	65	0.31
Finnish	9	0.04
French, except Basque	3,068	14.47
French Canadian	1,799	8.48
German	849	4.00
Greek	140	0.66
Hawaii Native/Pacific Islander:	7	0.03
Polynesian: (1)	2	0.01
Native Hawaiian (1)	1	0.00
Samoan	1	0.00
Other Pac. Isl., not spec. (1)	5	0.02
Hispanic or Latino:	1,372	6.47
Central American:	20	0.09
Guatemalan	3	0.01
Honduran	4	0.02
Nicaraguan	6	0.03
Panamanian	7	0.03
Cuban	15	0.07
Dominican Republic	37	0.17
Mexican	18	0.08
Puerto Rican	1,182	5.57
South American:	37	0.17
Argentinean	5	0.02
Bolivian	1	0.00
Colombian	14	0.07
Ecuadorian	3	0.01
Peruvian	4	0.02
Venezuelan	8	0.04
Other South American	2	0.01
Other Hispanic or Latino	63	0.30
Hungarian	6	0.03
Iranian	21	0.10
Irish	2,701	12.74
Italian	1,939	9.14
Lithuanian	36	0.17
Macedonian	21	0.10
Norwegian	22	0.10
Polish	3,572	16.84
Portuguese	4,506	21.25
Russian	140	0.66
Scotch-Irish	240	1.13
Scottish	515	2.43
Slovak	22	0.10
Swedish	129	0.61
Swiss	13	0.06
Ukrainian	135	0.64
United States or American	500	2.36
Welsh	6	0.03
West Indian, excl. Hispanic:	25	0.12
Jamaican	25	0.12
White:	20,558	96.93
Not Hispanic (19,028)	19,257	90.80
Hispanic (1,287)	1,301	6.13

Lynn

Place Type: City
County: Essex
Population: 89,050

Ancestry/Race	Number	%
Acadian/Cajun	33	0.04
African American/Black:	11,196	12.57
Not Hispanic (8,165)	9,229	10.36
Hispanic (1,229)	1,967	2.21
African, sub-Saharan:	1,026	1.15
African	433	0.49
Cape Verdean	42	0.05
Ethiopian	5	0.01
Ghanian	6	0.01
Kenyan	15	0.02
Liberian	85	0.10
Nigerian	305	0.34
Sierra Leonean	12	0.01
Somalian	9	0.01
Sudanese	55	0.06
Ugandan	36	0.04
Other sub-Saharan African	23	0.03
Alaska Native tribes, specified:	3	0.00
Aleut	2	0.00
Tlingit-Haida	1	0.00
Alaska Native tribes, not specified	3	0.00
Am. Ind. or Alaska Nat., not spec.	389	0.44
Albanian	221	0.25
American Indian tribes, specified:	340	0.38
Apache (2)	10	0.01
Blackfeet (9)	37	0.04
Cherokee (11)	68	0.08
Chippewa (1)	3	0.00
Choctaw	1	0.00
Cree (1)	1	0.00
Creek	5	0.01
Crow	2	0.00
Delaware (2)	2	0.00
Iroquois (13)	31	0.03
Latin American Indians (32)	66	0.07
Navajo (9)	9	0.01
Paiute	1	0.00
Pueblo	7	0.01
Shoshone (1)	1	0.00
Sioux (4)	9	0.01
All other tribes (19)	87	0.10
American Indian tribes, not spec.	72	0.08
Arab:	362	0.41
Arab/Arabic	83	0.09
Egyptian	92	0.10
Iraqi	26	0.03
Jordanian	50	0.06
Lebanese	21	0.02
Moroccan	10	0.01
Palestinian	22	0.02
Syrian	21	0.02
Other Arab	37	0.04

Notes: 1. Figures in the "Number" column do not add up to the total population due to: a) Ancestry/Race overlap — e.g. persons can report being both White and Irish, b) persons of Hispanic origin can report being any race, c) persons reporting two ancestries are counted in both categories. 2. Numbers in parentheses indicate the number of persons reporting this ancestry/race alone, not in combination with any other ancestry/race. 3. Refer to the Explanation of Data in the front of the book for more detailed information.

Ancestry/Race	Number	%
Armenian	239	0.27
Asian:	6,976	7.83
Bangladeshi (11)	40	0.04
Cambodian (3,050)	3,748	4.21
Chinese, ex. Taiwanese (199)	306	0.34
Filipino (77)	123	0.14
Hmong (1)	1	0.00
Indian (353)	500	0.56
Indonesian (7)	10	0.01
Japanese (27)	59	0.07
Korean (68)	89	0.10
Laotian (262)	310	0.35
Malaysian (13)	13	0.01
Pakistani (35)	43	0.05
Taiwanese (5)	5	0.01
Thai (30)	37	0.04
Vietnamese (1,112)	1,255	1.41
Other Asian, specified	2	0.00
Other Asian, not specified (253)	435	0.49
Australian	4	0.00
Austrian	65	0.07
Belgian	40	0.04
Brazilian	163	0.18
British	179	0.20
Canadian	622	0.70
Croatian	40	0.04
Czech	22	0.02
Czechoslovakian	26	0.03
Danish	62	0.07
Dutch	219	0.25
Eastern European	27	0.03
English	6,406	7.19
Estonian	26	0.03
European	81	0.09
Finnish	98	0.11
French, except Basque	5,112	5.74
French Canadian	3,826	4.29
German	2,163	2.43
Greek	2,527	2.84
Hawaii Native/Pacific Islander:	221	0.25
Micronesian: (53)	70	0.08
Guamanian/Chamorro (53)	70	0.08
Polynesian: (14)	31	0.03
Native Hawaiian (5)	19	0.02
Samoan (8)	11	0.01
Tongan (1)	1	0.00
Other Pac. Isl., specified	2	0.00
Other Pac. Isl., not spec. (12)	118	0.13
Hispanic or Latino:	16,383	18.40
Central American:	1,963	2.20
Costa Rican	47	0.05
Guatemalan	1,442	1.62
Honduran	104	0.12
Nicaraguan	15	0.02
Panamanian	18	0.02
Salvadoran	269	0.30
Other Central American	68	0.08
Cuban	148	0.17
Dominican Republic	5,517	6.20
Mexican	853	0.96
Puerto Rican	3,769	4.23
South American:	316	0.35
Argentinean	20	0.02
Chilean	33	0.04
Colombian	144	0.16
Ecuadorian	14	0.02
Paraguayan	1	0.00
Peruvian	71	0.08
Uruguayan	1	0.00
Venezuelan	22	0.02
Other South American	10	0.01
Other Hispanic or Latino	3,817	4.29
Hungarian	125	0.14
Iranian	14	0.02
Irish	16,252	18.24
Italian	9,372	10.52
Latvian	33	0.04
Lithuanian	459	0.52
Luxemburger	9	0.01
Northern European	3	0.00
Norwegian	227	0.25
Pennsylvania German	18	0.02
Polish	2,444	2.74
Portuguese	1,099	1.23
Romanian	57	0.06
Russian	1,425	1.60
Scandinavian	43	0.05
Scotch-Irish	818	0.92
Scottish	1,283	1.44
Serbian	6	0.01
Slovak	7	0.01
Swedish	911	1.02
Swiss	77	0.09
Turkish	19	0.02
Ukrainian	363	0.41
United States or American	4,060	4.56
Welsh	244	0.27
West Indian, excl. Hispanic:	1,573	1.76
Bahamian	16	0.02
Barbadian	86	0.10
Belizean	17	0.02
British West Indian	11	0.01
Haitian	926	1.04
Jamaican	202	0.23
Trinidadian and Tobagonian	90	0.10
West Indian	225	0.25
White:	63,262	71.04
Not Hispanic (55,630)	57,207	64.24
Hispanic (4,822)	6,055	6.80
Yugoslavian	297	0.33

Lynnfield

Place Type: Census Designated Place
County: Essex
Population: 11,542

Ancestry/Race	Number	%
African American/Black:	54	0.47
Not Hispanic (49)	53	0.46
Hispanic (1)	1	0.01
African, sub-Saharan:	61	0.53
Cape Verdean	61	0.53
Am. Ind. or Alaska Nat., not spec.	4	0.03
Albanian	6	0.05
American Indian tribes, specified:	5	0.04
Blackfeet	2	0.02
Creek	1	0.01
Seminole	1	0.01
All other tribes	1	0.01
Arab:	10	0.09
Egyptian	6	0.05
Lebanese	4	0.03
Armenian	87	0.75
Asian:	274	2.37
Cambodian (1)	1	0.01
Chinese, ex. Taiwanese (76)	98	0.85
Filipino (11)	17	0.15
Indian (71)	77	0.67
Japanese (5)	15	0.13
Korean (33)	35	0.30
Malaysian	1	0.01
Pakistani	2	0.02
Taiwanese (3)	5	0.04
Thai (1)	5	0.04
Vietnamese (16)	18	0.16
Austrian	39	0.34
Basque	9	0.08
Belgian	6	0.05
British	73	0.63
Canadian	149	1.29
Czech	6	0.05
Danish	24	0.21
Dutch	40	0.35
English	1,655	14.34
European	24	0.21
Finnish	44	0.38
French, except Basque	522	4.52
French Canadian	430	3.73
German	565	4.90
Greek	405	3.51
Hawaii Native/Pacific Islander:	11	0.10
Micronesian:	1	0.01
Guamanian/Chamorro	1	0.01
Polynesian: (4)	8	0.07
Native Hawaiian (1)	2	0.02
Samoan (3)	6	0.05
Other Pac. Isl., not spec.	2	0.02
Hispanic or Latino:	77	0.67
Central American:	7	0.06
Costa Rican	1	0.01
Guatemalan	3	0.03
Nicaraguan	1	0.01
Salvadoran	2	0.02
Cuban	3	0.03
Dominican Republic	4	0.03
Mexican	11	0.10
Puerto Rican	17	0.15
South American:	16	0.14
Argentinean	4	0.03
Chilean	1	0.01
Colombian	3	0.03
Ecuadorian	5	0.04
Paraguayan	1	0.01
Peruvian	1	0.01
Other South American	1	0.01
Other Hispanic or Latino	19	0.16
Hungarian	22	0.19
Iranian	41	0.36
Irish	3,185	27.59
Italian	3,243	28.10
Latvian	6	0.05
Lithuanian	87	0.75
Northern European	9	0.08
Norwegian	86	0.75
Pennsylvania German	9	0.08
Polish	536	4.64
Portuguese	94	0.81
Romanian	9	0.08
Russian	348	3.02
Scandinavian	20	0.17
Scotch-Irish	209	1.81
Scottish	308	2.67
Slavic	8	0.07
Swedish	290	2.51
Swiss	6	0.05
Turkish	45	0.39
Ukrainian	23	0.20
United States or American	453	3.92
Welsh	43	0.37
West Indian, excl. Hispanic:	24	0.21
Trinidadian and Tobagonian	9	0.08
West Indian	15	0.13
White:	11,234	97.33
Not Hispanic (11,107)	11,172	96.79
Hispanic (58)	62	0.54

Malden

Place Type: City
County: Middlesex
Population: 56,340

Ancestry/Race	Number	%
African American/Black:	5,438	9.65
Not Hispanic (4,468)	5,259	9.33
Hispanic (124)	179	0.32
African, sub-Saharan:	906	1.61
African	313	0.56
Cape Verdean	211	0.37
Ethiopian	166	0.29
Kenyan	27	0.05
Nigerian	108	0.19
Senegalese	7	0.01
South African	10	0.02
Sudanese	13	0.02
Ugandan	51	0.09
Alaska Native tribes, specified:	1	0.00
Tlingit-Haida	1	0.00
Am. Ind. or Alaska Nat., not spec.	137	0.24

Notes: 1. Figures in the "Number" column do not add up to the total population due to: a) Ancestry/Race overlap — e.g. persons can report being both White and Irish, b) persons of Hispanic origin can report being any race, c) persons reporting two ancestries are counted in both categories. 2. Numbers in parentheses indicate the number of persons reporting this ancestry/race alone, not in combination with any other ancestry/race. 3. Refer to the Explanation of Data in the front of the book for more detailed information.

Albanian	37	0.07
American Indian tribes, specified:	137	0.24
Blackfeet (2)	3	0.01
Cherokee (6)	33	0.06
Chippewa	2	0.00
Choctaw	2	0.00
Comanche (1)	1	0.00
Cree	1	0.00
Creek	2	0.00
Crow	1	0.00
Iroquois (6)	9	0.02
Latin American Indians (5)	25	0.04
Navajo (1)	3	0.01
Pueblo	1	0.00
Seminole	4	0.01
Shoshone	1	0.00
Sioux (2)	2	0.00
Yaqui	5	0.01
All other tribes (19)	42	0.07
American Indian tribes, not spec.	17	0.03
Arab:	750	1.33
Arab/Arabic	113	0.20
Egyptian	120	0.21
Jordanian	9	0.02
Lebanese	136	0.24
Moroccan	175	0.31
Syrian	64	0.11
Other Arab	133	0.24
Armenian	121	0.21
Asian:	8,401	14.91
Bangladeshi (16)	22	0.04
Cambodian (144)	180	0.32
Chinese, ex. Taiwanese (4,471)	4,660	8.27
Filipino (157)	204	0.36
Indian (962)	1,048	1.86
Indonesian (29)	31	0.06
Japanese (80)	110	0.20
Korean (249)	262	0.47
Laotian (14)	18	0.03
Malaysian (4)	9	0.02
Pakistani (57)	96	0.17
Sri Lankan (26)	32	0.06
Taiwanese (33)	39	0.07
Thai (44)	54	0.10
Vietnamese (1,343)	1,434	2.55
Other Asian, specified (21)	24	0.04
Other Asian, not specified (66)	178	0.32
Australian	17	0.03
Austrian	72	0.13
Belgian	100	0.18
Brazilian	1,027	1.82
British	151	0.27
Bulgarian	18	0.03
Canadian	646	1.15
Celtic	24	0.04
Croatian	16	0.03
Czech	69	0.12
Czechoslovakian	16	0.03
Danish	148	0.26
Dutch	233	0.41
Eastern European	10	0.02
English	3,497	6.21
Estonian	7	0.01
European	93	0.17
Finnish	34	0.06
French, except Basque	1,971	3.50
French Canadian	1,708	3.03
German	1,543	2.74
Greek	348	0.62
Guyanese	55	0.10
Hawaii Native/Pacific Islander:	98	0.17
Melanesian:	2	0.00
Fijian	2	0.00
Micronesian: (9)	11	0.02
Guamanian/Chamorro (9)	11	0.02
Polynesian: (14)	27	0.05
Native Hawaiian (7)	17	0.03
Samoan (7)	10	0.02
Other Pac. Isl., not spec. (9)	58	0.10
Hispanic or Latino:	2,696	4.79
Central American:	329	0.58
Costa Rican	39	0.07
Guatemalan	62	0.11
Honduran	26	0.05
Nicaraguan	3	0.01
Panamanian	7	0.01
Salvadoran	178	0.32
Other Central American	14	0.02
Cuban	83	0.15
Dominican Republic	65	0.12
Mexican	172	0.31
Puerto Rican	486	0.86
South American:	580	1.03
Argentinean	54	0.10
Bolivian	7	0.01
Chilean	84	0.15
Colombian	285	0.51
Ecuadorian	23	0.04
Peruvian	82	0.15
Uruguayan	1	0.00
Venezuelan	23	0.04
Other South American	21	0.04
Other Hispanic or Latino	981	1.74
Hungarian	63	0.11
Iranian	129	0.23
Irish	11,799	20.94
Italian	11,828	20.99
Latvian	45	0.08
Lithuanian	151	0.27
Northern European	29	0.05
Norwegian	169	0.30
Polish	1,503	2.67
Portuguese	1,298	2.30
Romanian	145	0.26
Russian	900	1.60
Scotch-Irish	672	1.19
Scottish	1,130	2.01
Slovak	40	0.07
Swedish	674	1.20
Swiss	22	0.04
Turkish	32	0.06
Ukrainian	176	0.31
United States or American	1,493	2.65
Welsh	68	0.12
West Indian, excl. Hispanic:	1,810	3.21
Barbadian	30	0.05
British West Indian	6	0.01
Haitian	1,508	2.68
Jamaican	136	0.24
Trinidadian and Tobagonian	36	0.06
West Indian	94	0.17
White:	41,812	74.21
Not Hispanic (39,230)	40,200	71.35
Hispanic (1,388)	1,612	2.86
Yugoslavian	64	0.11

Mansfield

Place Type: Town
County: Bristol
Population: 22,414

Ancestry/Race	Number	%
African American/Black:	578	2.58
Not Hispanic (482)	566	2.53
Hispanic (7)	12	0.05
African, sub-Saharan:	209	0.93
African	39	0.17
Cape Verdean	114	0.51
Ghanian	10	0.04
Nigerian	26	0.12
Sierra Leonean	14	0.06
Zimbabwean	6	0.03
Am. Ind. or Alaska Nat., not spec.	50	0.22
American Indian tribes, specified:	52	0.23
Apache	3	0.01
Blackfeet (2)	2	0.01
Cherokee (3)	15	0.07
Chippewa (4)	4	0.02
Choctaw	2	0.01
Iroquois	3	0.01
Latin American Indians (2)	3	0.01
Seminole	1	0.00
All other tribes (6)	19	0.08
American Indian tribes, not spec.	8	0.04
Arab:	307	1.37
Lebanese	192	0.86
Palestinian	20	0.09
Syrian	73	0.33
Other Arab	22	0.10
Armenian	35	0.16
Asian:	494	2.20
Cambodian (7)	7	0.03
Chinese, ex. Taiwanese (117)	132	0.59
Filipino (10)	15	0.07
Hmong (2)	2	0.01
Indian (225)	235	1.05
Indonesian	3	0.01
Japanese (8)	20	0.09
Korean (22)	32	0.14
Laotian (2)	2	0.01
Sri Lankan (4)	6	0.03
Thai (12)	12	0.05
Vietnamese (13)	14	0.06
Other Asian, specified (2)	4	0.02
Other Asian, not specified (7)	10	0.04
Australian	8	0.04
Austrian	68	0.30
Belgian	50	0.22
Brazilian	22	0.10
British	36	0.16
Bulgarian	23	0.10
Canadian	173	0.77
Celtic	20	0.09
Croatian	15	0.07
Czech	41	0.18
Danish	122	0.54
Dutch	156	0.70
Eastern European	29	0.13
English	3,252	14.51
European	186	0.83
Finnish	50	0.22
French, except Basque	1,658	7.40
French Canadian	842	3.76
German	2,153	9.61
Greek	169	0.75
Hawaii Native/Pacific Islander:	11	0.05
Micronesian: (4)	5	0.02
Guamanian/Chamorro (4)	5	0.02
Other Pac. Isl., specified	2	0.01
Other Pac. Isl., not spec.	4	0.02
Hispanic or Latino:	317	1.41
Central American:	14	0.06
Costa Rican	2	0.01
Guatemalan	4	0.02
Honduran	2	0.01
Salvadoran	1	0.00
Other Central American	5	0.02
Cuban	37	0.17
Dominican Republic	3	0.01
Mexican	56	0.25
Puerto Rican	107	0.48
South American:	51	0.23
Argentinean	11	0.05
Bolivian	7	0.03
Colombian	8	0.04
Ecuadorian	2	0.01
Peruvian	14	0.06
Venezuelan	3	0.01
Other South American	6	0.03
Other Hispanic or Latino	49	0.22
Hungarian	36	0.16
Irish	7,233	32.27
Israeli	11	0.05
Italian	4,551	20.30
Latvian	12	0.05
Lithuanian	456	2.03
Norwegian	127	0.57
Pennsylvania German	7	0.03
Polish	1,249	5.57

Notes: 1. Figures in the "Number" column do not add up to the total population due to: a) Ancestry/Race overlap — e.g. persons can report being both White and Irish, b) persons of Hispanic origin can report being any race, c) persons reporting two ancestries are counted in both categories. 2. Numbers in parentheses indicate the number of persons reporting this ancestry/race alone, not in combination with any other ancestry/race. 3. Refer to the Explanation of Data in the front of the book for more detailed information.

Portuguese	695	3.10
Romanian	11	0.05
Russian	422	1.88
Scotch-Irish	477	2.13
Scottish	525	2.34
Slavic	6	0.03
Swedish	517	2.31
Swiss	21	0.09
Turkish	7	0.03
Ukrainian	75	0.33
United States or American	1,120	5.00
Welsh	124	0.55
West Indian, excl. Hispanic:	85	0.38
Barbadian	17	0.08
British West Indian	12	0.05
Haitian	17	0.08
West Indian	39	0.17
White:	21,308	95.07
Not Hispanic (20,894)	21,055	93.94
Hispanic (243)	253	1.13
Yugoslavian	24	0.11

Marblehead

Place Type: Census Designated Place
County: Essex
Population: 20,377

Ancestry/Race	Number	%
African American/Black:	125	0.61
Not Hispanic (88)	120	0.59
Hispanic (1)	5	0.02
African, sub-Saharan:	35	0.17
African	16	0.08
Cape Verdean	19	0.09
Am. Ind. or Alaska Nat., not spec.	15	0.07
Albanian	30	0.15
American Indian tribes, specified:	29	0.14
Apache (2)	2	0.01
Cherokee (2)	8	0.04
Chippewa	1	0.00
Iroquois	2	0.01
Latin American Indians (1)	2	0.01
Osage	3	0.01
All other tribes (4)	11	0.05
Arab:	35	0.17
Arab/Arabic	8	0.04
Lebanese	10	0.05
Syrian	17	0.08
Armenian	42	0.21
Asian:	269	1.32
Cambodian (4)	4	0.02
Chinese, ex. Taiwanese (41)	51	0.25
Filipino (17)	36	0.18
Indian (33)	46	0.23
Indonesian (1)	3	0.01
Japanese (16)	29	0.14
Korean (40)	45	0.22
Malaysian (1)	1	0.00
Pakistani (1)	2	0.01
Taiwanese (7)	9	0.04
Thai (7)	9	0.04
Vietnamese (17)	19	0.09
Other Asian, not specified (7)	15	0.07
Australian	24	0.12
Austrian	83	0.41
Belgian	32	0.16
Brazilian	15	0.07
British	315	1.55
Bulgarian	14	0.07
Canadian	163	0.80
Croatian	33	0.16
Czech	74	0.36
Czechoslovakian	23	0.11
Danish	156	0.77
Dutch	218	1.07
Eastern European	254	1.25
English	4,326	21.23
European	263	1.29
Finnish	51	0.25
French, except Basque	1,005	4.93
French Canadian	767	3.76
German	1,832	8.99
Greek	255	1.25
Hawaii Native/Pacific Islander:	16	0.08
Micronesian:	4	0.02
Guamanian/Chamorro	2	0.01
Other Micronesian	2	0.01
Polynesian: (6)	11	0.05
Native Hawaiian (1)	6	0.03
Samoan (5)	5	0.02
Other Pac. Isl., not spec.	1	0.00
Hispanic or Latino:	179	0.88
Central American:	17	0.08
Costa Rican	1	0.00
Guatemalan	4	0.02
Honduran	4	0.02
Nicaraguan	1	0.00
Salvadoran	6	0.03
Other Central American	1	0.00
Cuban	12	0.06
Dominican Republic	12	0.06
Mexican	25	0.12
Puerto Rican	39	0.19
South American:	43	0.21
Argentinean	2	0.01
Bolivian	1	0.00
Chilean	2	0.01
Colombian	28	0.14
Peruvian	8	0.04
Other South American	2	0.01
Other Hispanic or Latino	31	0.15
Hungarian	83	0.41
Irish	4,932	24.20
Italian	1,951	9.57
Latvian	29	0.14
Lithuanian	103	0.51
Northern European	9	0.04
Norwegian	199	0.98
Polish	819	4.02
Portuguese	228	1.12
Romanian	50	0.25
Russian	1,273	6.25
Scandinavian	63	0.31
Scotch-Irish	544	2.67
Scottish	873	4.28
Slovak	13	0.06
Swedish	406	1.99
Swiss	144	0.71
Ukrainian	100	0.49
United States or American	1,037	5.09
Welsh	123	0.60
West Indian, excl. Hispanic:	25	0.12
Haitian	13	0.06
West Indian	12	0.06
White:	20,015	98.22
Not Hispanic (19,747)	19,868	97.50
Hispanic (132)	147	0.72
Yugoslavian	40	0.20

Marlborough

Place Type: City
County: Middlesex
Population: 36,255

Ancestry/Race	Number	%
African American/Black:	952	2.63
Not Hispanic (724)	861	2.37
Hispanic (63)	91	0.25
African, sub-Saharan:	234	0.65
African	70	0.19
Cape Verdean	10	0.03
Ghanian	22	0.06
Kenyan	11	0.03
South African	76	0.21
Ugandan	27	0.07
Other sub-Saharan African	18	0.05
Am. Ind. or Alaska Nat., not spec.	128	0.35
Albanian	164	0.45
American Indian tribes, specified:	102	0.28
Blackfeet	9	0.02
Cherokee	13	0.04
Chippewa (2)	2	0.01
Comanche	1	0.00
Cree	3	0.01
Iroquois	7	0.02
Latin American Indians (16)	20	0.06
Navajo (1)	1	0.00
Shoshone	1	0.00
Sioux	3	0.01
All other tribes (17)	42	0.12
American Indian tribes, not spec.	6	0.02
Arab:	198	0.55
Arab/Arabic	12	0.03
Egyptian	31	0.09
Iraqi	20	0.06
Lebanese	66	0.18
Syrian	69	0.19
Armenian	230	0.63
Asian:	1,548	4.27
Bangladeshi (7)	8	0.02
Cambodian (2)	13	0.04
Chinese, ex. Taiwanese (332)	377	1.04
Filipino (42)	65	0.18
Indian (638)	670	1.85
Indonesian (4)	10	0.03
Japanese (58)	76	0.21
Korean (65)	76	0.21
Laotian (8)	10	0.03
Malaysian (3)	4	0.01
Pakistani (8)	8	0.02
Sri Lankan (2)	2	0.01
Taiwanese (13)	22	0.06
Thai (23)	28	0.08
Vietnamese (125)	134	0.37
Other Asian, not specified (14)	45	0.12
Australian	15	0.04
Austrian	37	0.10
Basque	6	0.02
Belgian	26	0.07
Brazilian	1,388	3.83
British	168	0.46
Canadian	406	1.12
Croatian	61	0.17
Czech	64	0.18
Czechoslovakian	59	0.16
Danish	131	0.36
Dutch	313	0.86
Eastern European	42	0.12
English	4,576	12.62
European	104	0.29
Finnish	115	0.32
French, except Basque	3,333	9.19
French Canadian	2,252	6.21
German	2,638	7.28
Greek	748	2.06
Hawaii Native/Pacific Islander:	45	0.12
Melanesian:	2	0.01
Other Melanesian	2	0.01
Micronesian: (4)	7	0.02
Guamanian/Chamorro (4)	7	0.02
Polynesian: (9)	17	0.05
Native Hawaiian (3)	7	0.02
Samoan (5)	6	0.02
Tongan (1)	4	0.01
Other Pac. Isl., not spec.	19	0.05
Hispanic or Latino:	2,196	6.06
Central American:	502	1.38
Costa Rican	6	0.02
Guatemalan	384	1.06
Honduran	18	0.05
Nicaraguan	1	0.00
Panamanian	8	0.02
Salvadoran	44	0.12
Other Central American	41	0.11
Cuban	25	0.07
Dominican Republic	68	0.19
Mexican	372	1.03
Puerto Rican	567	1.56

Notes: 1. Figures in the "Number" column do not add up to the total population due to: a) Ancestry/Race overlap — e.g. persons can report being both White and Irish, b) persons of Hispanic origin can report being any race, c) persons reporting two ancestries are counted in both categories. 2. Numbers in parentheses indicate the number of persons reporting this ancestry/race alone, not in combination with any other ancestry/race. 3. Refer to the Explanation of Data in the front of the book for more detailed information.

Ancestry/Race	Number	%
South American:	168	0.46
Argentinean	6	0.02
Bolivian	2	0.01
Chilean	6	0.02
Colombian	67	0.18
Ecuadorian	10	0.03
Peruvian	36	0.10
Venezuelan	24	0.07
Other South American	17	0.05
Other Hispanic or Latino	494	1.36
Hungarian	45	0.12
Irish	8,431	23.25
Israeli	10	0.03
Italian	5,944	16.39
Latvian	50	0.14
Lithuanian	227	0.63
Northern European	9	0.02
Norwegian	247	0.68
Polish	1,525	4.21
Portuguese	858	2.37
Romanian	22	0.06
Russian	421	1.16
Scandinavian	27	0.07
Scotch-Irish	553	1.53
Scottish	924	2.55
Slovak	77	0.21
Swedish	582	1.61
Swiss	53	0.15
Turkish	34	0.09
Ukrainian	137	0.38
United States or American	1,664	4.59
Welsh	106	0.29
West Indian, excl. Hispanic:	138	0.38
British West Indian	8	0.02
Haitian	29	0.08
Jamaican	93	0.26
West Indian	8	0.02
White:	32,750	90.33
Not Hispanic (30,778)	31,444	86.73
Hispanic (1,018)	1,306	3.60
Yugoslavian	12	0.03

Marshfield

Place Type: Town
County: Plymouth
Population: 24,324

Ancestry/Race	Number	%
African American/Black:	201	0.83
Not Hispanic (124)	189	0.78
Hispanic (7)	12	0.05
African, sub-Saharan:	104	0.43
African	5	0.02
Cape Verdean	99	0.41
Alaska Native tribes, specified:	1	0.00
Aleut (1)	1	0.00
Am. Ind. or Alaska Nat., not spec.	22	0.09
American Indian tribes, specified:	59	0.24
Apache (1)	1	0.00
Blackfeet	5	0.02
Cherokee (4)	12	0.05
Chippewa	6	0.02
Cree	3	0.01
Delaware	1	0.00
Iroquois	1	0.00
Latin American Indians (5)	6	0.02
Lumbee (3)	3	0.01
Navajo (2)	3	0.01
Seminole (1)	1	0.00
Sioux (1)	1	0.00
All other tribes (3)	16	0.07
American Indian tribes, not spec.	3	0.01
Arab:	180	0.74
Lebanese	133	0.55
Syrian	47	0.19
Armenian	45	0.19
Asian:	137	0.56
Cambodian (3)	5	0.02
Chinese, ex. Taiwanese (24)	41	0.17
Filipino (3)	8	0.03
Indian (9)	14	0.06
Japanese (10)	16	0.07
Korean (25)	27	0.11
Laotian	2	0.01
Sri Lankan (1)	1	0.00
Taiwanese (2)	2	0.01
Thai (3)	5	0.02
Vietnamese (7)	7	0.03
Other Asian, specified	3	0.01
Other Asian, not specified (4)	6	0.02
Austrian	42	0.17
Belgian	37	0.15
Brazilian	108	0.44
British	44	0.18
Canadian	262	1.08
Celtic	38	0.16
Czech	56	0.23
Czechoslovakian	40	0.16
Danish	159	0.65
Dutch	237	0.97
Eastern European	31	0.13
English	4,373	17.98
Estonian	9	0.04
European	29	0.12
Finnish	82	0.34
French, except Basque	1,475	6.06
French Canadian	729	3.00
German	1,788	7.35
Greek	121	0.50
Hawaii Native/Pacific Islander:	21	0.09
Micronesian: (2)	2	0.01
Guamanian/Chamorro (2)	2	0.01
Polynesian:	4	0.02
Native Hawaiian	4	0.02
Other Pac. Isl., specified	3	0.01
Other Pac. Isl., not spec. (2)	12	0.05
Hispanic or Latino:	163	0.67
Central American:	14	0.06
Costa Rican	2	0.01
Guatemalan	7	0.03
Salvadoran	2	0.01
Other Central American	3	0.01
Cuban	5	0.02
Dominican Republic	5	0.02
Mexican	30	0.12
Puerto Rican	54	0.22
South American:	13	0.05
Bolivian	1	0.00
Chilean	3	0.01
Colombian	5	0.02
Paraguayan	1	0.00
Peruvian	1	0.00
Venezuelan	2	0.01
Other Hispanic or Latino	42	0.17
Hungarian	63	0.26
Irish	10,932	44.94
Italian	3,884	15.97
Latvian	6	0.02
Lithuanian	161	0.66
Northern European	7	0.03
Norwegian	173	0.71
Polish	990	4.07
Portuguese	401	1.65
Romanian	10	0.04
Russian	176	0.72
Scandinavian	43	0.18
Scotch-Irish	810	3.33
Scottish	955	3.93
Slovak	34	0.14
Swedish	649	2.67
Swiss	52	0.21
Ukrainian	64	0.26
United States or American	773	3.18
Welsh	118	0.49
West Indian, excl. Hispanic:	21	0.09
Jamaican	13	0.05
West Indian	8	0.03
White:	23,911	98.30
Not Hispanic (23,650)	23,793	97.82
Hispanic (111)	118	0.49

Mashpee

Place Type: Town
County: Barnstable
Population: 12,946

Ancestry/Race	Number	%
African American/Black:	524	4.05
Not Hispanic (355)	503	3.89
Hispanic (10)	21	0.16
African, sub-Saharan:	304	2.35
African	14	0.11
Cape Verdean	290	2.24
Alaska Native tribes, specified:	2	0.02
Aleut	1	0.01
Eskimo	1	0.01
Am. Ind. or Alaska Nat., not spec.	59	0.46
Albanian	6	0.05
American Indian tribes, specified:	434	3.35
Apache	3	0.02
Blackfeet (3)	9	0.07
Cherokee (4)	25	0.19
Chippewa (1)	4	0.03
Delaware	1	0.01
Iroquois (1)	5	0.04
Lumbee (1)	1	0.01
Navajo	1	0.01
Seminole	2	0.02
Sioux (2)	3	0.02
Tohono O'Odham	1	0.01
Ute (1)	1	0.01
All other tribes (312)	378	2.92
American Indian tribes, not spec.	17	0.13
Arab:	42	0.32
Lebanese	27	0.21
Other Arab	15	0.12
Armenian	21	0.16
Asian:	117	0.90
Chinese, ex. Taiwanese (13)	15	0.12
Filipino (14)	27	0.21
Indian (12)	18	0.14
Indonesian	3	0.02
Japanese (7)	8	0.06
Korean (7)	11	0.08
Pakistani (7)	7	0.05
Thai (1)	5	0.04
Vietnamese (12)	12	0.09
Other Asian, specified	2	0.02
Other Asian, not specified (1)	9	0.07
Austrian	18	0.14
Belgian	6	0.05
Brazilian	5	0.04
British	66	0.51
Canadian	64	0.49
Celtic	5	0.04
Czech	16	0.12
Czechoslovakian	8	0.06
Danish	20	0.15
Dutch	119	0.92
English	1,851	14.30
European	65	0.50
Finnish	69	0.53
French, except Basque	914	7.06
French Canadian	319	2.46
German	1,083	8.37
Greek	223	1.72
Guyanese	20	0.15
Hawaii Native/Pacific Islander:	12	0.09
Polynesian: (2)	4	0.03
Native Hawaiian (1)	3	0.02
Samoan (1)	1	0.01
Other Pac. Isl., specified	2	0.02
Other Pac. Isl., not spec. (1)	6	0.05
Hispanic or Latino:	212	1.64
Central American:	10	0.08
Honduran	2	0.02
Panamanian	4	0.03
Salvadoran	4	0.03

Notes: 1. Figures in the "Number" column do not add up to the total population due to: a) Ancestry/Race overlap — e.g. persons can report being both White and Irish, b) persons of Hispanic origin can report being any race, c) persons reporting two ancestries are counted in both categories. 2. Numbers in parentheses indicate the number of persons reporting this ancestry/race alone, not in combination with any other ancestry/race. 3. Refer to the Explanation of Data in the front of the book for more detailed information.

Ancestry/Race	Number	%
Cuban	14	0.11
Dominican Republic	2	0.02
Mexican	28	0.22
Puerto Rican	86	0.66
South American:	20	0.15
Chilean	1	0.01
Colombian	9	0.07
Paraguayan	1	0.01
Venezuelan	2	0.02
Other South American	7	0.05
Other Hispanic or Latino	52	0.40
Hungarian	25	0.19
Irish	3,531	27.27
Italian	1,627	12.57
Latvian	44	0.34
Lithuanian	123	0.95
Northern European	15	0.12
Norwegian	161	1.24
Polish	596	4.60
Portuguese	487	3.76
Romanian	7	0.05
Russian	200	1.54
Scotch-Irish	194	1.50
Scottish	479	3.70
Slovak	6	0.05
Swedish	391	3.02
Swiss	31	0.24
Ukrainian	41	0.32
United States or American	516	3.99
Welsh	138	1.07
West Indian, excl. Hispanic:	41	0.32
Bahamian	8	0.06
Barbadian	10	0.08
Haitian	9	0.07
Jamaican	5	0.04
West Indian	9	0.07
White:	11,906	91.97
Not Hispanic (11,573)	11,778	90.98
Hispanic (110)	128	0.99

Maynard

Place Type: Census Designated Place
County: Middlesex
Population: 10,433

Ancestry/Race	Number	%
African American/Black:	150	1.44
Not Hispanic (102)	137	1.31
Hispanic (6)	13	0.12
African, sub-Saharan:	88	0.84
African	88	0.84
Alaska Native tribes, specified:	1	0.01
Eskimo (1)	1	0.01
Am. Ind. or Alaska Nat., not spec.	16	0.15
American Indian tribes, specified:	33	0.32
Blackfeet	1	0.01
Cherokee (6)	11	0.11
Iroquois	1	0.01
Navajo	3	0.03
Ottawa	1	0.01
Pueblo	1	0.01
Puget Sound Salish	1	0.01
Sioux (1)	2	0.02
All other tribes (10)	12	0.12
American Indian tribes, not spec.	5	0.05
Arab:	29	0.28
Lebanese	11	0.11
Syrian	18	0.17
Armenian	31	0.30
Asian:	201	1.93
Cambodian (3)	3	0.03
Chinese, ex. Taiwanese (65)	68	0.65
Filipino (17)	26	0.25
Indian (25)	28	0.27
Indonesian (1)	1	0.01
Japanese (6)	7	0.07
Korean (14)	20	0.19
Laotian (6)	6	0.06
Malaysian (2)	2	0.02
Pakistani (1)	2	0.02
Taiwanese (1)	2	0.02
Thai (9)	11	0.11
Vietnamese (9)	9	0.09
Other Asian, not specified (10)	16	0.15
Austrian	39	0.37
Belgian	7	0.07
Brazilian	67	0.64
British	28	0.27
Canadian	213	2.04
Celtic	32	0.31
Czech	8	0.08
Danish	58	0.56
Dutch	99	0.95
Eastern European	43	0.41
English	1,587	15.21
Estonian	6	0.06
European	44	0.42
Finnish	391	3.75
French, except Basque	784	7.51
French Canadian	437	4.19
German	932	8.93
Greek	120	1.15
Hawaii Native/Pacific Islander:	2	0.02
Polynesian:	2	0.02
Native Hawaiian	1	0.01
Samoan	1	0.01
Hispanic or Latino:	290	2.78
Central American:	30	0.29
Guatemalan	21	0.20
Honduran	3	0.03
Nicaraguan	1	0.01
Panamanian	1	0.01
Salvadoran	3	0.03
Other Central American	1	0.01
Cuban	3	0.03
Dominican Republic	8	0.08
Mexican	34	0.33
Puerto Rican	88	0.84
South American:	14	0.13
Bolivian	2	0.02
Chilean	3	0.03
Colombian	6	0.06
Ecuadorian	3	0.03
Other Hispanic or Latino	113	1.08
Hungarian	6	0.06
Irish	3,045	29.19
Italian	1,918	18.38
Latvian	7	0.07
Lithuanian	105	1.01
Norwegian	151	1.45
Polish	664	6.36
Portuguese	218	2.09
Russian	160	1.53
Scandinavian	16	0.15
Scotch-Irish	206	1.97
Scottish	345	3.31
Slovene	11	0.11
Swedish	285	2.73
Swiss	18	0.17
Ukrainian	35	0.34
United States or American	422	4.04
Welsh	30	0.29
West Indian, excl. Hispanic:	26	0.25
Jamaican	26	0.25
White:	9,988	95.73
Not Hispanic (9,734)	9,823	94.15
Hispanic (140)	165	1.58
Yugoslavian	12	0.12

Medfield

Place Type: Town
County: Norfolk
Population: 12,273

Ancestry/Race	Number	%
African American/Black:	90	0.73
Not Hispanic (62)	87	0.71
Hispanic	3	0.02
African, sub-Saharan:	39	0.32
Nigerian	17	0.14
South African	22	0.18
Am. Ind. or Alaska Nat., not spec.	4	0.03
Albanian	9	0.07
American Indian tribes, specified:	8	0.07
Cherokee (2)	2	0.02
Cree	1	0.01
Seminole	1	0.01
Shoshone (1)	1	0.01
All other tribes (1)	3	0.02
American Indian tribes, not spec.	1	0.01
Arab:	93	0.76
Lebanese	82	0.67
Syrian	11	0.09
Armenian	135	1.10
Asian:	256	2.09
Chinese, ex. Taiwanese (115)	129	1.05
Filipino (14)	20	0.16
Indian (41)	46	0.37
Japanese (9)	17	0.14
Korean (18)	19	0.15
Sri Lankan	1	0.01
Taiwanese (5)	7	0.06
Thai (5)	6	0.05
Vietnamese (6)	8	0.07
Other Asian, specified	1	0.01
Other Asian, not specified (1)	2	0.02
Austrian	64	0.52
Belgian	5	0.04
Brazilian	17	0.14
British	49	0.40
Canadian	154	1.25
Celtic	25	0.20
Croatian	12	0.10
Czech	40	0.33
Czechoslovakian	12	0.10
Danish	59	0.48
Dutch	124	1.01
Eastern European	15	0.12
English	1,745	14.22
European	125	1.02
Finnish	7	0.06
French, except Basque	613	4.99
French Canadian	410	3.34
German	1,163	9.48
Greek	147	1.20
Hawaii Native/Pacific Islander:	5	0.04
Polynesian: (1)	2	0.02
Native Hawaiian (1)	2	0.02
Other Pac. Isl., not spec.	3	0.02
Hispanic or Latino:	110	0.90
Central American:	6	0.05
Costa Rican	1	0.01
Guatemalan	3	0.02
Panamanian	1	0.01
Salvadoran	1	0.01
Cuban	15	0.12
Dominican Republic	1	0.01
Mexican	12	0.10
Puerto Rican	22	0.18
South American:	25	0.20
Argentinean	5	0.04
Colombian	11	0.09
Ecuadorian	4	0.03
Paraguayan	1	0.01
Peruvian	3	0.02
Venezuelan	1	0.01
Other Hispanic or Latino	29	0.24
Hungarian	75	0.61
Icelander	9	0.07
Irish	4,527	36.89
Italian	2,128	17.34
Latvian	61	0.50
Lithuanian	99	0.81
Northern European	17	0.14
Norwegian	106	0.86
Polish	524	4.27
Portuguese	61	0.50
Russian	405	3.30

Notes: 1. Figures in the "Number" column do not add up to the total population due to: a) Ancestry/Race overlap — e.g. persons can report being both White and Irish, b) persons of Hispanic origin can report being any race, c) persons reporting two ancestries are counted in both categories. 2. Numbers in parentheses indicate the number of persons reporting this ancestry/race alone, not in combination with any other ancestry/race. 3. Refer to the Explanation of Data in the front of the book for more detailed information.

Scotch-Irish	178	1.45
Scottish	438	3.57
Slovak	7	0.06
Slovene	26	0.21
Swedish	297	2.42
Swiss	9	0.07
Turkish	6	0.05
Ukrainian	17	0.14
United States or American	627	5.11
Welsh	82	0.67
White:	11,953	97.39
Not Hispanic (11,794)	11,860	96.63
Hispanic (84)	93	0.76

Medford

Place Type: City
County: Middlesex
Population: 55,765

Ancestry/Race	Number	%
Acadian/Cajun	6	0.01
African American/Black:	3,947	7.08
Not Hispanic (3,324)	3,828	6.86
Hispanic (77)	119	0.21
African, sub-Saharan:	463	0.83
African	194	0.35
Cape Verdean	66	0.12
Ethiopian	4	0.01
Ghanian	42	0.08
Kenyan	13	0.02
Nigerian	47	0.08
South African	14	0.03
Ugandan	32	0.06
Zairian	7	0.01
Other sub-Saharan African	44	0.08
Alaska Native tribes, specified:	1	0.00
Eskimo (1)	1	0.00
Am. Ind. or Alaska Nat., not spec.	102	0.18
Albanian	90	0.16
Alsatian	5	0.01
American Indian tribes, specified:	133	0.24
Blackfeet (7)	13	0.02
Cherokee (4)	24	0.04
Chickasaw	1	0.00
Choctaw	1	0.00
Cree	1	0.00
Creek	1	0.00
Crow	1	0.00
Houma (1)	1	0.00
Iroquois (5)	14	0.03
Latin American Indians (12)	21	0.04
Navajo (1)	3	0.01
Pueblo	1	0.00
Sioux (1)	4	0.01
All other tribes (19)	47	0.08
American Indian tribes, not spec.	10	0.02
Arab:	409	0.73
Arab/Arabic	76	0.14
Egyptian	32	0.06
Jordanian	7	0.01
Lebanese	113	0.20
Moroccan	69	0.12
Palestinian	18	0.03
Syrian	68	0.12
Other Arab	26	0.05
Armenian	405	0.73
Asian:	2,441	4.38
Bangladeshi (16)	23	0.04
Cambodian (5)	5	0.01
Chinese, ex. Taiwanese (863)	940	1.69
Filipino (89)	117	0.21
Indian (411)	467	0.84
Indonesian (7)	11	0.02
Japanese (91)	135	0.24
Korean (159)	177	0.32
Laotian (3)	5	0.01
Malaysian (1)	1	0.00
Pakistani (13)	26	0.05
Sri Lankan (27)	27	0.05
Taiwanese (23)	24	0.04
Thai (34)	38	0.07
Vietnamese (319)	342	0.61
Other Asian, specified (20)	27	0.05
Other Asian, not specified (40)	76	0.14
Austrian	126	0.23
Basque	7	0.01
Belgian	140	0.25
Brazilian	520	0.93
British	179	0.32
Bulgarian	4	0.01
Canadian	584	1.05
Celtic	19	0.03
Croatian	17	0.03
Czech	43	0.08
Czechoslovakian	12	0.02
Danish	168	0.30
Dutch	286	0.51
Eastern European	118	0.21
English	4,352	7.80
Estonian	57	0.10
European	323	0.58
Finnish	111	0.20
French, except Basque	1,573	2.82
French Canadian	1,613	2.89
German	2,144	3.84
Greek	940	1.69
Guyanese	10	0.02
Hawaii Native/Pacific Islander:	52	0.09
Micronesian: (6)	10	0.02
Guamanian/Chamorro (6)	10	0.02
Polynesian: (7)	13	0.02
Native Hawaiian (4)	10	0.02
Samoan (3)	3	0.01
Other Pac. Isl., specified	2	0.00
Other Pac. Isl., not spec. (3)	27	0.05
Hispanic or Latino:	1,443	2.59
Central American:	220	0.39
Costa Rican	16	0.03
Guatemalan	48	0.09
Honduran	10	0.02
Nicaraguan	9	0.02
Panamanian	22	0.04
Salvadoran	101	0.18
Other Central American	14	0.03
Cuban	82	0.15
Dominican Republic	45	0.08
Mexican	148	0.27
Puerto Rican	311	0.56
South American:	290	0.52
Argentinean	29	0.05
Bolivian	16	0.03
Chilean	40	0.07
Colombian	95	0.17
Ecuadorian	28	0.05
Paraguayan	4	0.01
Peruvian	28	0.05
Uruguayan	10	0.02
Venezuelan	21	0.04
Other South American	19	0.03
Other Hispanic or Latino	347	0.62
Hungarian	122	0.22
Iranian	57	0.10
Irish	14,249	25.55
Israeli	18	0.03
Italian	17,390	31.18
Latvian	24	0.04
Lithuanian	452	0.81
Macedonian	8	0.01
Northern European	4	0.01
Norwegian	214	0.38
Polish	1,568	2.81
Portuguese	1,639	2.94
Romanian	19	0.03
Russian	847	1.52
Scandinavian	21	0.04
Scotch-Irish	826	1.48
Scottish	1,084	1.94
Serbian	9	0.02
Slovak	53	0.10
Slovene	18	0.03
Swedish	600	1.08
Swiss	59	0.11
Turkish	28	0.05
Ukrainian	328	0.59
United States or American	1,775	3.18
Welsh	107	0.19
West Indian, excl. Hispanic:	1,679	3.01
Barbadian	116	0.21
British West Indian	28	0.05
Dutch West Indian	9	0.02
Haitian	1,112	1.99
Jamaican	210	0.38
Trinidadian and Tobagonian	104	0.19
West Indian	100	0.18
White:	49,161	88.16
Not Hispanic (47,403)	48,236	86.50
Hispanic (806)	925	1.66
Yugoslavian	71	0.13

Medway

Place Type: Town
County: Norfolk
Population: 12,448

Ancestry/Race	Number	%
African American/Black:	88	0.71
Not Hispanic (70)	86	0.69
Hispanic (1)	2	0.02
Am. Ind. or Alaska Nat., not spec.	13	0.10
Albanian	18	0.14
American Indian tribes, specified:	22	0.18
Blackfeet (5)	5	0.04
Cherokee	1	0.01
Choctaw (1)	1	0.01
Crow	1	0.01
Iroquois	1	0.01
Ottawa (1)	1	0.01
Shoshone	1	0.01
All other tribes (3)	11	0.09
American Indian tribes, not spec.	6	0.05
Arab:	156	1.25
Egyptian	18	0.14
Lebanese	127	1.02
Syrian	11	0.09
Armenian	41	0.33
Asian:	155	1.25
Bangladeshi (1)	3	0.02
Chinese, ex. Taiwanese (30)	35	0.28
Filipino (10)	18	0.14
Indian (45)	53	0.43
Japanese (5)	9	0.07
Korean (13)	16	0.13
Pakistani (2)	4	0.03
Vietnamese (8)	8	0.06
Other Asian, specified (2)	6	0.05
Other Asian, not specified	3	0.02
Australian	4	0.03
Austrian	25	0.20
Belgian	3	0.02
Brazilian	21	0.17
British	76	0.61
Canadian	108	0.87
Czech	9	0.07
Czechoslovakian	35	0.28
Danish	88	0.71
Dutch	111	0.89
Eastern European	20	0.16
English	2,108	16.93
European	38	0.31
Finnish	45	0.36
French, except Basque	746	5.99
French Canadian	652	5.24
German	1,208	9.70
Greek	101	0.81
Hawaii Native/Pacific Islander:	7	0.06
Micronesian: (2)	4	0.03
Guamanian/Chamorro (2)	4	0.03
Polynesian:	1	0.01

Notes: 1. Figures in the "Number" column do not add up to the total population due to: a) Ancestry/Race overlap — e.g. persons can report being both White and Irish, b) persons of Hispanic origin can report being any race, c) persons reporting two ancestries are counted in both categories. 2. Numbers in parentheses indicate the number of persons reporting this ancestry/race alone, not in combination with any other ancestry/race. 3. Refer to the Explanation of Data in the front of the book for more detailed information.

Ancestry/Race	Number	%
Samoan	1	0.01
Other Pac. Isl., specified	2	0.02
Hispanic or Latino:	105	0.84
Central American:	2	0.02
Salvadoran	2	0.02
Cuban	15	0.12
Dominican Republic	2	0.02
Mexican	29	0.23
Puerto Rican	23	0.18
South American:	14	0.11
Argentinean	2	0.02
Colombian	5	0.04
Ecuadorian	7	0.06
Other Hispanic or Latino	20	0.16
Hungarian	30	0.24
Iranian	8	0.06
Irish	4,341	34.87
Italian	2,401	19.29
Latvian	37	0.30
Lithuanian	138	1.11
Northern European	16	0.13
Norwegian	157	1.26
Polish	662	5.32
Portuguese	274	2.20
Romanian	25	0.20
Russian	260	2.09
Scandinavian	38	0.31
Scotch-Irish	260	2.09
Scottish	465	3.74
Serbian	9	0.07
Slovak	7	0.06
Swedish	429	3.45
Swiss	8	0.06
Ukrainian	47	0.38
United States or American	557	4.47
Welsh	68	0.55
West Indian, excl. Hispanic:	15	0.12
Bermudan	8	0.06
Haitian	7	0.06
White:	12,214	98.12
Not Hispanic (12,052)	12,126	97.41
Hispanic (87)	88	0.71
Yugoslavian	30	0.24

Melrose

Place Type: City
County: Middlesex
Population: 27,134

Ancestry/Race	Number	%
African American/Black:	342	1.26
Not Hispanic (246)	329	1.21
Hispanic (9)	13	0.05
African, sub-Saharan:	81	0.30
African	20	0.07
Cape Verdean	8	0.03
Nigerian	15	0.06
Sierra Leonean	5	0.02
Ugandan	33	0.12
Alaska Native tribes, specified:	2	0.01
Alaska Athabascan (1)	2	0.01
Am. Ind. or Alaska Nat., not spec.	49	0.18
American Indian tribes, specified:	39	0.14
Blackfeet	4	0.01
Cherokee (3)	15	0.06
Chippewa (1)	1	0.00
Choctaw (1)	2	0.01
Iroquois	1	0.00
Latin American Indians (1)	1	0.00
Potawatomi	1	0.00
Pueblo (1)	2	0.01
Puget Sound Salish	1	0.00
All other tribes (4)	11	0.04
American Indian tribes, not spec.	10	0.04
Arab:	114	0.42
Arab/Arabic	5	0.02
Lebanese	60	0.22
Moroccan	8	0.03
Palestinian	36	0.13
Other Arab	5	0.02
Armenian	33	0.12
Asian:	666	2.45
Chinese, ex. Taiwanese (253)	287	1.06
Filipino (76)	104	0.38
Indian (97)	116	0.43
Indonesian (2)	7	0.03
Japanese (17)	27	0.10
Korean (22)	29	0.11
Pakistani (2)	7	0.03
Sri Lankan (5)	5	0.02
Thai (5)	8	0.03
Vietnamese (48)	55	0.20
Other Asian, specified	1	0.00
Other Asian, not specified (11)	20	0.07
Austrian	59	0.22
Belgian	47	0.17
Brazilian	7	0.03
British	133	0.49
Bulgarian	37	0.14
Canadian	465	1.71
Czech	27	0.10
Czechoslovakian	7	0.03
Danish	23	0.08
Dutch	87	0.32
Eastern European	51	0.19
English	3,563	13.13
Estonian	20	0.07
European	293	1.08
Finnish	218	0.80
French, except Basque	1,315	4.85
French Canadian	1,038	3.83
German	1,516	5.59
Greek	314	1.16
Hawaii Native/Pacific Islander:	14	0.05
Polynesian: (4)	8	0.03
Native Hawaiian (1)	2	0.01
Samoan (3)	3	0.01
Tongan	3	0.01
Other Pac. Isl., specified	1	0.00
Other Pac. Isl., not spec. (2)	5	0.02
Hispanic or Latino:	283	1.04
Central American:	42	0.15
Costa Rican	2	0.01
Guatemalan	19	0.07
Honduran	4	0.01
Nicaraguan	3	0.01
Salvadoran	13	0.05
Other Central American	1	0.00
Cuban	19	0.07
Dominican Republic	5	0.02
Mexican	36	0.13
Puerto Rican	60	0.22
South American:	50	0.18
Argentinean	8	0.03
Bolivian	1	0.00
Chilean	8	0.03
Colombian	17	0.06
Ecuadorian	6	0.02
Peruvian	5	0.02
Venezuelan	4	0.01
Other South American	1	0.00
Other Hispanic or Latino	71	0.26
Hungarian	125	0.46
Iranian	58	0.21
Irish	9,588	35.34
Italian	6,090	22.44
Latvian	17	0.06
Lithuanian	110	0.41
Norwegian	168	0.62
Polish	838	3.09
Portuguese	469	1.73
Romanian	29	0.11
Russian	484	1.78
Scandinavian	19	0.07
Scotch-Irish	884	3.26
Scottish	865	3.19
Slovak	17	0.06
Swedish	723	2.66
Swiss	23	0.08
Turkish	9	0.03
Ukrainian	133	0.49
United States or American	996	3.67
Welsh	90	0.33
West Indian, excl. Hispanic:	62	0.23
Dutch West Indian	6	0.02
Haitian	42	0.15
West Indian	14	0.05
White:	26,156	96.40
Not Hispanic (25,640)	25,953	95.65
Hispanic (180)	203	0.75
Yugoslavian	29	0.11

Methuen

Place Type: City
County: Essex
Population: 43,789

Ancestry/Race	Number	%
Acadian/Cajun	7	0.02
African American/Black:	770	1.76
Not Hispanic (406)	489	1.12
Hispanic (185)	281	0.64
African, sub-Saharan:	47	0.11
African	18	0.04
Cape Verdean	26	0.06
Nigerian	3	0.01
Alaska Native tribes, specified:	3	0.01
Eskimo (3)	3	0.01
Am. Ind. or Alaska Nat., not spec.	115	0.26
Albanian	38	0.09
Alsatian	3	0.01
American Indian tribes, specified:	69	0.16
Apache (1)	3	0.01
Blackfeet (1)	2	0.00
Cherokee	9	0.02
Chippewa	2	0.00
Choctaw	1	0.00
Delaware	1	0.00
Iroquois (3)	4	0.01
Latin American Indians (4)	6	0.01
Potawatomi (1)	1	0.00
Pueblo	4	0.01
Sioux (1)	1	0.00
All other tribes (15)	35	0.08
American Indian tribes, not spec.	6	0.01
Arab:	1,936	4.42
Arab/Arabic	73	0.17
Egyptian	50	0.11
Lebanese	1,751	4.00
Palestinian	10	0.02
Syrian	44	0.10
Other Arab	8	0.02
Armenian	384	0.88
Asian:	1,189	2.72
Bangladeshi (4)	4	0.01
Cambodian (59)	77	0.18
Chinese, ex. Taiwanese (154)	170	0.39
Filipino (32)	49	0.11
Indian (265)	293	0.67
Japanese (19)	22	0.05
Korean (177)	204	0.47
Laotian (7)	9	0.02
Pakistani (10)	14	0.03
Thai (12)	16	0.04
Vietnamese (277)	292	0.67
Other Asian, not specified (5)	39	0.09
Assyrian/Chaldean/Syriac	8	0.02
Australian	8	0.02
Austrian	30	0.07
Belgian	79	0.18
British	114	0.26
Canadian	332	0.76
Celtic	13	0.03
Croatian	8	0.02
Czech	39	0.09
Czechoslovakian	21	0.05
Danish	81	0.18
Dutch	110	0.25

Notes: 1. Figures in the "Number" column do not add up to the total population due to: a) Ancestry/Race overlap — e.g. persons can report being both White and Irish, b) persons of Hispanic origin can report being any race, c) persons reporting two ancestries are counted in both categories. 2. Numbers in parentheses indicate the number of persons reporting this ancestry/race alone, not in combination with any other ancestry/race. 3. Refer to the Explanation of Data in the front of the book for more detailed information.

Ancestry/Race	Number	%
English	4,302	9.82
European	54	0.12
Finnish	34	0.08
French, except Basque	4,615	10.54
French Canadian	3,833	8.75
German	2,096	4.79
Greek	497	1.13
Hawaii Native/Pacific Islander:	31	0.07
Micronesian: (2)	2	0.00
Guamanian/Chamorro (2)	2	0.00
Polynesian: (3)	4	0.01
Samoan (3)	4	0.01
Other Pac. Isl., not spec.	25	0.06
Hispanic or Latino:	4,221	9.64
Central American:	116	0.26
Costa Rican	1	0.00
Guatemalan	83	0.19
Honduran	5	0.01
Nicaraguan	1	0.00
Panamanian	1	0.00
Salvadoran	24	0.05
Other Central American	1	0.00
Cuban	73	0.17
Dominican Republic	1,308	2.99
Mexican	70	0.16
Puerto Rican	1,691	3.86
South American:	115	0.26
Argentinean	4	0.01
Colombian	28	0.06
Ecuadorian	55	0.13
Peruvian	13	0.03
Venezuelan	9	0.02
Other South American	6	0.01
Other Hispanic or Latino	848	1.94
Hungarian	110	0.25
Iranian	12	0.03
Irish	9,069	20.71
Israeli	22	0.05
Italian	9,580	21.88
Lithuanian	453	1.03
Norwegian	129	0.29
Polish	1,683	3.84
Portuguese	823	1.88
Romanian	6	0.01
Russian	175	0.40
Scandinavian	12	0.03
Scotch-Irish	587	1.34
Scottish	889	2.03
Slavic	9	0.02
Slovak	57	0.13
Swedish	384	0.88
Swiss	19	0.04
Turkish	170	0.39
Ukrainian	74	0.17
United States or American	1,809	4.13
Welsh	62	0.14
West Indian, excl. Hispanic:	123	0.28
British West Indian	6	0.01
Haitian	46	0.11
Jamaican	71	0.16
White:	39,819	90.93
Not Hispanic (37,561)	37,951	86.67
Hispanic (1,565)	1,868	4.27

Middleborough

Place Type: Town
County: Plymouth
Population: 19,941

Ancestry/Race	Number	%
Acadian/Cajun	7	0.04
African American/Black:	343	1.72
Not Hispanic (248)	333	1.67
Hispanic (4)	10	0.05
African, sub-Saharan:	198	0.99
Cape Verdean	198	0.99
Am. Ind. or Alaska Nat., not spec.	48	0.24
American Indian tribes, specified:	84	0.42
Blackfeet (1)	11	0.06
Cherokee (5)	20	0.10
Chippewa (1)	1	0.01
Choctaw (1)	1	0.01
Iroquois	1	0.01
Latin American Indians (5)	6	0.03
Sioux (1)	4	0.02
All other tribes (13)	40	0.20
American Indian tribes, not spec.	8	0.04
Arab:	132	0.66
Lebanese	132	0.66
Armenian	94	0.47
Asian:	120	0.60
Cambodian (2)	2	0.01
Chinese, ex. Taiwanese (9)	15	0.08
Filipino (28)	38	0.19
Indian (23)	25	0.13
Indonesian	1	0.01
Japanese (5)	6	0.03
Korean (8)	9	0.05
Laotian (6)	6	0.03
Pakistani	4	0.02
Taiwanese	1	0.01
Thai (1)	1	0.01
Vietnamese (4)	5	0.03
Other Asian, specified (1)	2	0.01
Other Asian, not specified	5	0.03
Austrian	79	0.40
British	39	0.20
Canadian	172	0.86
Celtic	70	0.35
Czech	8	0.04
Danish	62	0.31
Dutch	67	0.34
English	4,037	20.24
European	138	0.69
Finnish	84	0.42
French, except Basque	2,444	12.26
French Canadian	717	3.60
German	1,136	5.70
Greek	110	0.55
Hawaii Native/Pacific Islander:	22	0.11
Melanesian: (1)	3	0.02
Fijian (1)	3	0.02
Micronesian: (1)	1	0.01
Guamanian/Chamorro (1)	1	0.01
Polynesian: (2)	5	0.03
Native Hawaiian (2)	5	0.03
Other Pac. Isl., specified	1	0.01
Other Pac. Isl., not spec. (3)	12	0.06
Hispanic or Latino:	156	0.78
Central American:	13	0.07
Costa Rican	4	0.02
Guatemalan	5	0.03
Honduran	2	0.01
Salvadoran	1	0.01
Other Central American	1	0.01
Cuban	14	0.07
Mexican	27	0.14
Puerto Rican	67	0.34
South American:	10	0.05
Chilean	1	0.01
Colombian	5	0.03
Ecuadorian	4	0.02
Other Hispanic or Latino	25	0.13
Hungarian	50	0.25
Iranian	10	0.05
Irish	5,370	26.93
Israeli	5	0.03
Italian	2,298	11.52
Latvian	53	0.27
Lithuanian	275	1.38
Northern European	33	0.17
Norwegian	154	0.77
Polish	755	3.79
Portuguese	1,634	8.19
Russian	191	0.96
Scandinavian	19	0.10
Scotch-Irish	646	3.24
Scottish	614	3.08
Slavic	8	0.04
Slovak	6	0.03
Swedish	738	3.70
Swiss	24	0.12
Turkish	28	0.14
Ukrainian	6	0.03
United States or American	927	4.65
Welsh	68	0.34
West Indian, excl. Hispanic:	33	0.17
Haitian	13	0.07
West Indian	20	0.10
White:	19,363	97.10
Not Hispanic (19,057)	19,243	96.50
Hispanic (111)	120	0.60
Yugoslavian	13	0.07

Milford

Place Type: Town
County: Worcester
Population: 26,799

Ancestry/Race	Number	%
African American/Black:	459	1.71
Not Hispanic (346)	441	1.65
Hispanic (16)	18	0.07
African, sub-Saharan:	63	0.24
African	38	0.14
Cape Verdean	25	0.09
Am. Ind. or Alaska Nat., not spec.	42	0.16
Albanian	66	0.25
Alsatian	6	0.02
American Indian tribes, specified:	44	0.16
Blackfeet (1)	2	0.01
Cherokee (3)	9	0.03
Chippewa	3	0.01
Choctaw	1	0.00
Iroquois (1)	5	0.02
Latin American Indians (4)	5	0.02
Seminole	1	0.00
Sioux	1	0.00
All other tribes (6)	17	0.06
Arab:	188	0.70
Arab/Arabic	13	0.05
Egyptian	48	0.18
Lebanese	88	0.33
Syrian	39	0.15
Armenian	171	0.64
Asian:	541	2.02
Bangladeshi (6)	6	0.02
Chinese, ex. Taiwanese (100)	106	0.40
Filipino (23)	33	0.12
Indian (234)	248	0.93
Indonesian (1)	1	0.00
Japanese (18)	26	0.10
Korean (45)	49	0.18
Laotian (1)	1	0.00
Pakistani (2)	9	0.03
Sri Lankan (1)	2	0.01
Taiwanese (4)	4	0.01
Thai (2)	3	0.01
Vietnamese (27)	30	0.11
Other Asian, not specified (7)	23	0.09
Austrian	88	0.33
Belgian	26	0.10
Brazilian	495	1.85
British	138	0.51
Canadian	256	0.96
Celtic	13	0.05
Czech	98	0.37
Czechoslovakian	6	0.02
Danish	42	0.16
Dutch	146	0.54
Eastern European	25	0.09
English	2,850	10.63
European	35	0.13
Finnish	32	0.12
French, except Basque	2,126	7.93
French Canadian	935	3.49
German	1,918	7.16
Greek	294	1.10

Notes: 1. Figures in the "Number" column do not add up to the total population due to: a) Ancestry/Race overlap — e.g. persons can report being both White and Irish, b) persons of Hispanic origin can report being any race, c) persons reporting two ancestries are counted in both categories. 2. Numbers in parentheses indicate the number of persons reporting this ancestry/race alone, not in combination with any other ancestry/race. 3. Refer to the Explanation of Data in the front of the book for more detailed information.

Ancestry/Race	Number	%
Hawaii Native/Pacific Islander:	37	0.14
Micronesian: (5)	5	0.02
Guamanian/Chamorro (5)	5	0.02
Polynesian: (2)	4	0.01
Native Hawaiian (1)	3	0.01
Samoan (1)	1	0.00
Other Pac. Isl., not spec. (10)	28	0.10
Hispanic or Latino:	1,168	4.36
Central American:	36	0.13
Costa Rican	3	0.01
Guatemalan	11	0.04
Honduran	1	0.00
Salvadoran	17	0.06
Other Central American	4	0.01
Cuban	38	0.14
Dominican Republic	43	0.16
Mexican	84	0.31
Puerto Rican	608	2.27
South American:	84	0.31
Argentinean	3	0.01
Chilean	3	0.01
Colombian	33	0.12
Ecuadorian	15	0.06
Paraguayan	1	0.00
Peruvian	11	0.04
Uruguayan	1	0.00
Venezuelan	9	0.03
Other South American	8	0.03
Other Hispanic or Latino	275	1.03
Hungarian	78	0.29
Iranian	5	0.02
Irish	6,098	22.75
Italian	8,025	29.95
Latvian	16	0.06
Lithuanian	87	0.32
Maltese	9	0.03
Northern European	38	0.14
Norwegian	147	0.55
Polish	1,138	4.25
Portuguese	2,087	7.79
Romanian	5	0.02
Russian	173	0.65
Scandinavian	17	0.06
Scotch-Irish	327	1.22
Scottish	494	1.84
Slavic	6	0.02
Slovak	65	0.24
Slovene	4	0.01
Swedish	450	1.68
Turkish	5	0.02
Ukrainian	71	0.26
United States or American	677	2.53
Welsh	83	0.31
West Indian, excl. Hispanic:	36	0.13
Haitian	15	0.06
Jamaican	21	0.08
White:	25,345	94.57
Not Hispanic (24,264)	24,622	91.88
Hispanic (645)	723	2.70

Millbury

Place Type: Town
County: Worcester
Population: 12,784

Ancestry/Race	Number	%
African American/Black:	109	0.85
Not Hispanic (63)	102	0.80
Hispanic (5)	7	0.05
Am. Ind. or Alaska Nat., not spec.	18	0.14
Albanian	16	0.13
American Indian tribes, specified:	32	0.25
Blackfeet (1)	2	0.02
Cherokee (1)	2	0.02
Choctaw (2)	2	0.02
Iroquois	2	0.02
Shoshone	3	0.02
Sioux	1	0.01
All other tribes (8)	20	0.16
Arab:	154	1.20
Lebanese	79	0.62
Syrian	75	0.59
Armenian	81	0.63
Asian:	168	1.31
Cambodian (1)	1	0.01
Chinese, ex. Taiwanese (14)	29	0.23
Filipino (13)	14	0.11
Indian (45)	45	0.35
Indonesian (1)	1	0.01
Japanese (3)	13	0.10
Korean (13)	14	0.11
Laotian (4)	4	0.03
Pakistani (3)	9	0.07
Thai (3)	7	0.05
Vietnamese (17)	21	0.16
Other Asian, specified	1	0.01
Other Asian, not specified (7)	9	0.07
Austrian	6	0.05
British	41	0.32
Canadian	36	0.28
Czech	6	0.05
Danish	38	0.30
Dutch	82	0.64
English	1,558	12.19
European	19	0.15
Finnish	150	1.17
French, except Basque	2,768	21.65
French Canadian	1,403	10.97
German	528	4.13
Greek	42	0.33
Hawaii Native/Pacific Islander:	9	0.07
Micronesian: (1)	1	0.01
Other Micronesian (1)	1	0.01
Polynesian: (2)	6	0.05
Native Hawaiian (2)	6	0.05
Other Pac. Isl., specified	1	0.01
Other Pac. Isl., not spec. (1)	1	0.01
Hispanic or Latino:	131	1.02
Central American:	2	0.02
Honduran	2	0.02
Cuban	9	0.07
Dominican Republic	1	0.01
Mexican	21	0.16
Puerto Rican	62	0.48
South American:	12	0.09
Argentinean	1	0.01
Chilean	2	0.02
Colombian	5	0.04
Peruvian	1	0.01
Venezuelan	2	0.02
Other South American	1	0.01
Other Hispanic or Latino	24	0.19
Hungarian	6	0.05
Irish	2,849	22.29
Italian	1,689	13.21
Lithuanian	541	4.23
Macedonian	14	0.11
Norwegian	69	0.54
Polish	1,174	9.18
Portuguese	80	0.63
Romanian	40	0.31
Russian	41	0.32
Scandinavian	17	0.13
Scotch-Irish	125	0.98
Scottish	355	2.78
Slovak	7	0.05
Swedish	993	7.77
Swiss	5	0.04
Ukrainian	50	0.39
United States or American	705	5.51
Welsh	45	0.35
White:	12,515	97.90
Not Hispanic (12,334)	12,418	97.14
Hispanic (91)	97	0.76

Milton

Place Type: Census Designated Place
County: Norfolk
Population: 26,062

Ancestry/Race	Number	%
African American/Black:	2,910	11.17
Not Hispanic (2,614)	2,837	10.89
Hispanic (52)	73	0.28
African, sub-Saharan:	330	1.27
African	6	0.02
Cape Verdean	160	0.61
Ethiopian	42	0.16
Nigerian	116	0.45
Other sub-Saharan African	6	0.02
Am. Ind. or Alaska Nat., not spec.	48	0.18
Albanian	45	0.17
American Indian tribes, specified:	65	0.25
Blackfeet	2	0.01
Cherokee (2)	26	0.10
Chickasaw	2	0.01
Chippewa	1	0.00
Choctaw	4	0.02
Latin American Indians (1)	8	0.03
Navajo (1)	2	0.01
Sioux	1	0.00
All other tribes (6)	19	0.07
American Indian tribes, not spec.	1	0.00
Arab:	191	0.73
Arab/Arabic	16	0.06
Egyptian	21	0.08
Lebanese	144	0.55
Syrian	10	0.04
Armenian	22	0.08
Asian:	643	2.47
Cambodian (7)	8	0.03
Chinese, ex. Taiwanese (330)	377	1.45
Filipino (17)	21	0.08
Indian (46)	57	0.22
Japanese (14)	31	0.12
Korean (29)	35	0.13
Laotian (2)	2	0.01
Taiwanese (1)	1	0.00
Thai (12)	13	0.05
Vietnamese (66)	71	0.27
Other Asian, specified (1)	6	0.02
Other Asian, not specified	21	0.08
Austrian	29	0.11
Belgian	86	0.33
British	83	0.32
Canadian	254	0.97
Celtic	19	0.07
Croatian	36	0.14
Czech	17	0.07
Czechoslovakian	12	0.05
Danish	37	0.14
Dutch	148	0.57
Eastern European	72	0.28
English	2,229	8.55
European	83	0.32
Finnish	64	0.25
French, except Basque	690	2.65
French Canadian	675	2.59
German	1,232	4.73
Greek	266	1.02
Guyanese	16	0.06
Hawaii Native/Pacific Islander:	23	0.09
Micronesian: (3)	3	0.01
Guamanian/Chamorro (3)	3	0.01
Polynesian: (1)	6	0.02
Native Hawaiian (1)	5	0.02
Other Polynesian	1	0.00
Other Pac. Isl., not spec. (6)	14	0.05
Hispanic or Latino:	450	1.73
Central American:	46	0.18
Costa Rican	10	0.04
Guatemalan	9	0.03
Honduran	10	0.04
Panamanian	6	0.02

Notes: 1. Figures in the "Number" column do not add up to the total population due to: a) Ancestry/Race overlap — e.g. persons can report being both White and Irish, b) persons of Hispanic origin can report being any race, c) persons reporting two ancestries are counted in both categories. 2. Numbers in parentheses indicate the number of persons reporting this ancestry/race alone, not in combination with any other ancestry/race. 3. Refer to the Explanation of Data in the front of the book for more detailed information.

Salvadoran	8	0.03
Other Central American	3	0.01
Cuban	24	0.09
Dominican Republic	35	0.13
Mexican	56	0.21
Puerto Rican	122	0.47
South American:	53	0.20
Argentinean	4	0.02
Bolivian	2	0.01
Chilean	5	0.02
Colombian	16	0.06
Ecuadorian	5	0.02
Paraguayan	2	0.01
Peruvian	8	0.03
Venezuelan	7	0.03
Other South American	4	0.02
Other Hispanic or Latino	114	0.44
Hungarian	80	0.31
Irish	11,198	42.97
Italian	2,937	11.27
Latvian	29	0.11
Lithuanian	316	1.21
Maltese	21	0.08
Northern European	20	0.08
Norwegian	145	0.56
Polish	779	2.99
Portuguese	327	1.25
Romanian	27	0.10
Russian	382	1.47
Scandinavian	34	0.13
Scotch-Irish	484	1.86
Scottish	452	1.73
Slovak	5	0.02
Slovene	9	0.03
Swedish	503	1.93
Swiss	53	0.20
Turkish	8	0.03
Ukrainian	76	0.29
United States or American	875	3.36
Welsh	49	0.19
West Indian, excl. Hispanic:	1,240	4.76
Barbadian	25	0.10
Bermudan	19	0.07
British West Indian	93	0.36
Haitian	574	2.20
Jamaican	346	1.33
Trinidadian and Tobagonian	43	0.16
West Indian	140	0.54
White:	22,537	86.47
Not Hispanic (21,985)	22,239	85.33
Hispanic (267)	298	1.14

Natick

Place Type: Town
County: Middlesex
Population: 32,170

Ancestry/Race	Number	%
African American/Black:	660	2.05
Not Hispanic (510)	632	1.96
Hispanic (15)	28	0.09
African, sub-Saharan:	13	0.04
African	13	0.04
Alaska Native tribes, specified:	1	0.00
Tlingit-Haida	1	0.00
Alaska Native tribes, not specified	1	0.00
Am. Ind. or Alaska Nat., not spec.	51	0.16
Albanian	212	0.66
Alsatian	8	0.02
American Indian tribes, specified:	73	0.23
Apache (1)	2	0.01
Blackfeet (1)	3	0.01
Cherokee (8)	15	0.05
Chippewa	1	0.00
Choctaw (1)	2	0.01
Creek	1	0.00
Delaware	1	0.00
Iroquois (1)	2	0.01
Latin American Indians (2)	8	0.02
Osage	4	0.01
Sioux (1)	1	0.00
Tohono O'Odham	1	0.00
All other tribes (6)	32	0.10
American Indian tribes, not spec.	8	0.02
Arab:	182	0.57
Arab/Arabic	8	0.02
Egyptian	9	0.03
Jordanian	17	0.05
Lebanese	95	0.30
Syrian	46	0.14
Other Arab	7	0.02
Armenian	169	0.53
Asian:	1,433	4.45
Bangladeshi (4)	4	0.01
Cambodian (9)	11	0.03
Chinese, ex. Taiwanese (525)	594	1.85
Filipino (46)	67	0.21
Indian (378)	416	1.29
Indonesian (6)	12	0.04
Japanese (65)	81	0.25
Korean (66)	84	0.26
Laotian (2)	2	0.01
Malaysian (1)	5	0.02
Pakistani (10)	11	0.03
Sri Lankan (1)	1	0.00
Taiwanese (21)	24	0.07
Thai (15)	19	0.06
Vietnamese (53)	57	0.18
Other Asian, specified (1)	4	0.01
Other Asian, not specified (18)	41	0.13
Australian	39	0.12
Austrian	129	0.40
Belgian	32	0.10
Brazilian	229	0.71
British	147	0.46
Canadian	507	1.58
Croatian	8	0.02
Czech	93	0.29
Czechoslovakian	30	0.09
Danish	177	0.55
Dutch	239	0.74
Eastern European	224	0.70
English	4,730	14.70
European	276	0.86
Finnish	76	0.24
French, except Basque	1,438	4.47
French Canadian	1,055	3.28
German	2,605	8.10
Greek	251	0.78
Guyanese	5	0.02
Hawaii Native/Pacific Islander:	29	0.09
Micronesian: (4)	4	0.01
Guamanian/Chamorro (4)	4	0.01
Polynesian: (6)	9	0.03
Native Hawaiian (4)	7	0.02
Samoan (2)	2	0.01
Other Pac. Isl., not spec. (7)	16	0.05
Hispanic or Latino:	635	1.97
Central American:	43	0.13
Costa Rican	15	0.05
Guatemalan	16	0.05
Honduran	2	0.01
Panamanian	1	0.00
Salvadoran	9	0.03
Cuban	47	0.15
Dominican Republic	11	0.03
Mexican	103	0.32
Puerto Rican	159	0.49
South American:	114	0.35
Argentinean	13	0.04
Bolivian	3	0.01
Chilean	4	0.01
Colombian	26	0.08
Ecuadorian	8	0.02
Peruvian	35	0.11
Venezuelan	16	0.05
Other South American	9	0.03
Other Hispanic or Latino	158	0.49
Hungarian	99	0.31
Iranian	30	0.09
Irish	8,409	26.14
Israeli	9	0.03
Italian	5,238	16.28
Latvian	87	0.27
Lithuanian	251	0.78
Northern European	31	0.10
Norwegian	342	1.06
Pennsylvania German	6	0.02
Polish	1,514	4.71
Portuguese	299	0.93
Romanian	35	0.11
Russian	1,363	4.24
Scandinavian	22	0.07
Scotch-Irish	722	2.24
Scottish	947	2.94
Slovak	46	0.14
Slovene	27	0.08
Swedish	629	1.96
Swiss	99	0.31
Turkish	20	0.06
Ukrainian	104	0.32
United States or American	1,384	4.30
Welsh	141	0.44
West Indian, excl. Hispanic:	75	0.23
Haitian	4	0.01
Jamaican	52	0.16
Trinidadian and Tobagonian	11	0.03
U.S. Virgin Islander	4	0.01
Other West Indian	4	0.01
White:	30,046	93.40
Not Hispanic (29,208)	29,603	92.02
Hispanic (394)	443	1.38
Yugoslavian	10	0.03

Needham

Place Type: Census Designated Place
County: Norfolk
Population: 28,911

Ancestry/Race	Number	%
African American/Black:	246	0.85
Not Hispanic (187)	227	0.79
Hispanic (14)	19	0.07
African, sub-Saharan:	45	0.16
African	13	0.04
Cape Verdean	7	0.02
South African	25	0.09
Am. Ind. or Alaska Nat., not spec.	10	0.03
Albanian	7	0.02
American Indian tribes, specified:	21	0.07
Apache	1	0.00
Blackfeet (1)	2	0.01
Cherokee	4	0.01
Chippewa (1)	1	0.00
Iroquois (1)	1	0.00
Latin American Indians (1)	3	0.01
Navajo	1	0.00
All other tribes (1)	8	0.03
American Indian tribes, not spec.	4	0.01
Arab:	136	0.47
Lebanese	87	0.30
Syrian	49	0.17
Armenian	242	0.84
Asian:	1,147	3.97
Bangladeshi (7)	7	0.02
Cambodian (5)	6	0.02
Chinese, ex. Taiwanese (488)	525	1.82
Filipino (34)	57	0.20
Indian (200)	213	0.74
Indonesian (7)	9	0.03
Japanese (61)	78	0.27
Korean (91)	102	0.35
Laotian (8)	8	0.03
Pakistani (11)	11	0.04
Sri Lankan (1)	1	0.00
Taiwanese (45)	55	0.19
Thai (11)	13	0.04
Vietnamese (33)	35	0.12

Notes: 1. Figures in the "Number" column do not add up to the total population due to: a) Ancestry/Race overlap — e.g. persons can report being both White and Irish, b) persons of Hispanic origin can report being any race, c) persons reporting two ancestries are counted in both categories. 2. Numbers in parentheses indicate the number of persons reporting this ancestry/race alone, not in combination with any other ancestry/race. 3. Refer to the Explanation of Data in the front of the book for more detailed information.

Ancestry/Race	Number	%
Other Asian, specified (5)	6	0.02
Other Asian, not specified (8)	21	0.07
Australian	18	0.06
Austrian	123	0.43
Belgian	21	0.07
Brazilian	33	0.11
British	170	0.59
Canadian	207	0.72
Croatian	32	0.11
Czech	20	0.07
Czechoslovakian	28	0.10
Danish	153	0.53
Dutch	252	0.87
Eastern European	596	2.06
English	3,547	12.27
European	269	0.93
Finnish	67	0.23
French, except Basque	854	2.95
French Canadian	584	2.02
German	2,302	7.96
Greek	523	1.81
Hawaii Native/Pacific Islander:	12	0.04
Polynesian:	5	0.02
Native Hawaiian	5	0.02
Other Pac. Isl., not spec.	7	0.02
Hispanic or Latino:	341	1.18
Central American:	16	0.06
Costa Rican	1	0.00
Guatemalan	6	0.02
Honduran	1	0.00
Nicaraguan	1	0.00
Salvadoran	5	0.02
Other Central American	2	0.01
Cuban	16	0.06
Dominican Republic	15	0.05
Mexican	56	0.19
Puerto Rican	51	0.18
South American:	113	0.39
Argentinean	19	0.07
Bolivian	1	0.00
Chilean	14	0.05
Colombian	34	0.12
Ecuadorian	9	0.03
Paraguayan	1	0.00
Peruvian	14	0.05
Venezuelan	16	0.06
Other South American	5	0.02
Other Hispanic or Latino	74	0.26
Hungarian	202	0.70
Iranian	108	0.37
Irish	8,020	27.74
Israeli	127	0.44
Italian	3,255	11.26
Latvian	7	0.02
Lithuanian	426	1.47
Luxemburger	30	0.10
Macedonian	14	0.05
Northern European	26	0.09
Norwegian	244	0.84
Polish	1,339	4.63
Portuguese	139	0.48
Romanian	76	0.26
Russian	1,979	6.85
Scandinavian	42	0.15
Scotch-Irish	590	2.04
Scottish	763	2.64
Slovak	64	0.22
Slovene	8	0.03
Swedish	393	1.36
Swiss	109	0.38
Turkish	35	0.12
Ukrainian	192	0.66
United States or American	1,460	5.05
Welsh	192	0.66
West Indian, excl. Hispanic:	7	0.02
Jamaican	7	0.02
White:	27,575	95.38
Not Hispanic (27,140)	27,291	94.40
Hispanic (272)	284	0.98
Yugoslavian	21	0.07

New Bedford

Place Type: City
County: Bristol
Population: 93,768

Ancestry/Race	Number	%
Acadian/Cajun	4	0.00
African American/Black:	6,382	6.81
Not Hispanic (3,503)	5,486	5.85
Hispanic (609)	896	0.96
African, sub-Saharan:	7,726	8.24
African	156	0.17
Cape Verdean	7,508	8.01
Kenyan	34	0.04
Liberian	4	0.00
Senegalese	11	0.01
Other sub-Saharan African	13	0.01
Alaska Native tribes, specified:	6	0.01
Eskimo	4	0.00
Tlingit-Haida (2)	2	0.00
Am. Ind. or Alaska Nat., not spec.	462	0.49
Albanian	72	0.08
American Indian tribes, specified:	796	0.85
Apache (1)	12	0.01
Blackfeet (8)	26	0.03
Cherokee (25)	99	0.11
Chippewa (6)	6	0.01
Comanche	1	0.00
Cree	3	0.00
Creek (1)	1	0.00
Crow	1	0.00
Delaware (1)	4	0.00
Iroquois (8)	32	0.03
Latin American Indians (110)	203	0.22
Navajo (4)	5	0.01
Potawatomi (1)	2	0.00
Pueblo (2)	3	0.00
Seminole	1	0.00
Shoshone	2	0.00
Sioux (6)	13	0.01
All other tribes (183)	382	0.41
American Indian tribes, not spec.	49	0.05
Arab:	528	0.56
Arab/Arabic	29	0.03
Egyptian	12	0.01
Jordanian	22	0.02
Lebanese	429	0.46
Moroccan	26	0.03
Syrian	10	0.01
Armenian	69	0.07
Asian:	867	0.92
Cambodian (6)	10	0.01
Chinese, ex. Taiwanese (183)	213	0.23
Filipino (66)	119	0.13
Indian (68)	103	0.11
Indonesian (1)	2	0.00
Japanese (27)	51	0.05
Korean (71)	82	0.09
Laotian (7)	7	0.01
Malaysian (1)	3	0.00
Pakistani (9)	9	0.01
Sri Lankan	2	0.00
Taiwanese (4)	4	0.00
Thai (11)	20	0.02
Vietnamese (138)	147	0.16
Other Asian, specified (1)	2	0.00
Other Asian, not specified (14)	93	0.10
Austrian	54	0.06
Basque	6	0.01
Belgian	54	0.06
Brazilian	377	0.40
British	56	0.06
Bulgarian	14	0.01
Canadian	282	0.30
Celtic	7	0.01
Czech	85	0.09
Czechoslovakian	5	0.01
Danish	32	0.03
Dutch	227	0.24
Eastern European	13	0.01
English	6,863	7.32
European	50	0.05
Finnish	30	0.03
French, except Basque	8,529	9.10
French Canadian	5,557	5.93
German	1,541	1.64
Greek	352	0.38
Hawaii Native/Pacific Islander:	287	0.31
Micronesian: (22)	29	0.03
Guamanian/Chamorro (22)	29	0.03
Polynesian: (15)	44	0.05
Native Hawaiian (7)	33	0.04
Samoan (8)	11	0.01
Other Pac. Isl., specified	1	0.00
Other Pac. Isl., not spec. (6)	213	0.23
Hispanic or Latino:	9,576	10.21
Central American:	531	0.57
Costa Rican	11	0.01
Guatemalan	303	0.32
Honduran	43	0.05
Nicaraguan	1	0.00
Panamanian	17	0.02
Salvadoran	128	0.14
Other Central American	28	0.03
Cuban	59	0.06
Dominican Republic	430	0.46
Mexican	322	0.34
Puerto Rican	6,657	7.10
South American:	101	0.11
Argentinean	10	0.01
Bolivian	1	0.00
Chilean	3	0.00
Colombian	45	0.05
Ecuadorian	3	0.00
Paraguayan	2	0.00
Peruvian	11	0.01
Uruguayan	6	0.01
Venezuelan	10	0.01
Other South American	10	0.01
Other Hispanic or Latino	1,476	1.57
Hungarian	52	0.06
Iranian	15	0.02
Irish	7,405	7.90
Italian	2,707	2.89
Latvian	5	0.01
Lithuanian	126	0.13
Maltese	8	0.01
Norwegian	395	0.42
Pennsylvania German	5	0.01
Polish	3,134	3.34
Portuguese	36,239	38.65
Romanian	12	0.01
Russian	183	0.20
Scandinavian	21	0.02
Scotch-Irish	448	0.48
Scottish	403	0.43
Serbian	10	0.01
Slovak	27	0.03
Swedish	293	0.31
Swiss	12	0.01
Turkish	7	0.01
Ukrainian	32	0.03
United States or American	2,752	2.93
Welsh	64	0.07
West Indian, excl. Hispanic:	261	0.28
Barbadian	4	0.00
Bermudan	7	0.01
British West Indian	4	0.00
Haitian	12	0.01
Jamaican	69	0.07
U.S. Virgin Islander	7	0.01
West Indian	158	0.17
White:	77,695	82.86
Not Hispanic (70,520)	73,633	78.53
Hispanic (3,430)	4,062	4.33

Notes: 1. Figures in the "Number" column do not add up to the total population due to: a) Ancestry/Race overlap — e.g. persons can report being both White and Irish, b) persons of Hispanic origin can report being any race, c) persons reporting two ancestries are counted in both categories. 2. Numbers in parentheses indicate the number of persons reporting this ancestry/race alone, not in combination with any other ancestry/race. 3. Refer to the Explanation of Data in the front of the book for more detailed information.

Newburyport

Place Type: City
County: Essex
Population: 17,189

Ancestry/Race	Number	%
African American/Black:	105	0.61
Not Hispanic (70)	100	0.58
Hispanic (3)	5	0.03
African, sub-Saharan:	8	0.05
South African	8	0.05
Am. Ind. or Alaska Nat., not spec.	19	0.11
Albanian	14	0.08
Alsatian	9	0.05
American Indian tribes, specified:	34	0.20
Blackfeet	1	0.01
Cherokee	2	0.01
Chippewa (2)	3	0.02
Iroquois (1)	3	0.02
Latin American Indians (2)	2	0.01
Paiute (1)	1	0.01
All other tribes (10)	22	0.13
American Indian tribes, not spec.	2	0.01
Arab:	91	0.53
Lebanese	80	0.46
Syrian	11	0.06
Armenian	80	0.46
Asian:	136	0.79
Cambodian (5)	5	0.03
Chinese, ex. Taiwanese (39)	46	0.27
Filipino (9)	16	0.09
Indian (13)	13	0.08
Indonesian	5	0.03
Japanese (8)	12	0.07
Korean (24)	25	0.15
Laotian (1)	2	0.01
Taiwanese	1	0.01
Vietnamese	1	0.01
Other Asian, specified (1)	1	0.01
Other Asian, not specified (4)	9	0.05
Australian	6	0.03
Austrian	69	0.40
Belgian	18	0.10
British	139	0.81
Bulgarian	6	0.03
Canadian	179	1.04
Celtic	11	0.06
Croatian	37	0.21
Czech	34	0.20
Czechoslovakian	40	0.23
Danish	45	0.26
Dutch	129	0.75
Eastern European	56	0.32
English	3,291	19.09
Estonian	8	0.05
European	101	0.59
Finnish	109	0.63
French, except Basque	1,533	8.89
French Canadian	828	4.80
German	1,262	7.32
Greek	399	2.31
Hawaii Native/Pacific Islander:	8	0.05
Polynesian: (2)	2	0.01
Native Hawaiian (1)	1	0.01
Samoan (1)	1	0.01
Other Pac. Isl., not spec.	6	0.03
Hispanic or Latino:	151	0.88
Central American:	4	0.02
Honduran	1	0.01
Other Central American	3	0.02
Cuban	13	0.08
Dominican Republic	13	0.08
Mexican	28	0.16
Puerto Rican	38	0.22
South American:	20	0.12
Argentinean	4	0.02
Colombian	7	0.04
Peruvian	4	0.02
Venezuelan	5	0.03
Other Hispanic or Latino	35	0.20
Hungarian	73	0.42
Iranian	72	0.42
Irish	5,256	30.48
Italian	2,232	12.95
Latvian	13	0.08
Lithuanian	89	0.52
Norwegian	232	1.35
Polish	1,137	6.59
Portuguese	105	0.61
Romanian	27	0.16
Russian	390	2.26
Scandinavian	18	0.10
Scotch-Irish	387	2.24
Scottish	758	4.40
Serbian	28	0.16
Slavic	9	0.05
Slovak	30	0.17
Slovene	14	0.08
Swedish	387	2.24
Swiss	24	0.14
Ukrainian	103	0.60
United States or American	499	2.89
Welsh	59	0.34
White:	16,959	98.66
Not Hispanic (16,753)	16,838	97.96
Hispanic (111)	121	0.70

Newton

Place Type: City
County: Middlesex
Population: 83,829

Ancestry/Race	Number	%
Acadian/Cajun	13	0.02
Afghan	5	0.01
African American/Black:	1,997	2.38
Not Hispanic (1,584)	1,894	2.26
Hispanic (69)	103	0.12
African, sub-Saharan:	583	0.70
African	123	0.15
Cape Verdean	148	0.18
Ethiopian	21	0.03
Kenyan	10	0.01
Liberian	10	0.01
Somalian	5	0.01
South African	189	0.23
Ugandan	7	0.01
Zimbabwean	7	0.01
Other sub-Saharan African	63	0.08
Am. Ind. or Alaska Nat., not spec.	105	0.13
Albanian	135	0.16
Alsatian	6	0.01
American Indian tribes, specified:	147	0.18
Apache (1)	2	0.00
Blackfeet (1)	10	0.01
Cherokee (8)	46	0.05
Chickasaw	1	0.00
Chippewa	2	0.00
Choctaw	1	0.00
Cree	1	0.00
Creek (3)	5	0.01
Iroquois (1)	4	0.00
Latin American Indians (14)	24	0.03
Lumbee	2	0.00
Menominee	1	0.00
Navajo	1	0.00
Osage	2	0.00
Pima (1)	2	0.00
Pueblo (1)	2	0.00
Seminole	4	0.00
Sioux (2)	9	0.01
All other tribes (4)	28	0.03
American Indian tribes, not spec.	22	0.03
Arab:	669	0.80
Arab/Arabic	72	0.09
Egyptian	82	0.10
Iraqi	46	0.05
Lebanese	275	0.33
Moroccan	9	0.01
Palestinian	25	0.03
Syrian	90	0.11
Other Arab	70	0.08
Armenian	640	0.76
Asian:	7,120	8.49
Bangladeshi (5)	11	0.01
Cambodian (34)	56	0.07
Chinese, ex. Taiwanese (3,912)	4,164	4.97
Filipino (161)	232	0.28
Hmong (4)	4	0.00
Indian (769)	874	1.04
Indonesian (35)	47	0.06
Japanese (352)	439	0.52
Korean (530)	567	0.68
Laotian (4)	5	0.01
Malaysian (6)	8	0.01
Pakistani (28)	29	0.03
Sri Lankan (20)	24	0.03
Taiwanese (135)	169	0.20
Thai (49)	55	0.07
Vietnamese (181)	233	0.28
Other Asian, specified (8)	19	0.02
Other Asian, not specified (82)	184	0.22
Assyrian/Chaldean/Syriac	6	0.01
Australian	63	0.08
Austrian	549	0.65
Basque	14	0.02
Belgian	93	0.11
Brazilian	117	0.14
British	705	0.84
Bulgarian	72	0.09
Canadian	845	1.01
Celtic	46	0.05
Croatian	27	0.03
Cypriot	7	0.01
Czech	230	0.27
Czechoslovakian	105	0.13
Danish	171	0.20
Dutch	646	0.77
Eastern European	1,817	2.17
English	7,441	8.88
Estonian	7	0.01
European	958	1.14
Finnish	171	0.20
French, except Basque	2,300	2.74
French Canadian	1,535	1.83
German	6,276	7.49
Greek	1,244	1.48
Guyanese	23	0.03
Hawaii Native/Pacific Islander:	108	0.13
Micronesian: (14)	16	0.02
Guamanian/Chamorro (11)	13	0.02
Other Micronesian (3)	3	0.00
Polynesian: (6)	31	0.04
Native Hawaiian (4)	22	0.03
Samoan (2)	9	0.01
Other Pac. Isl., specified	10	0.01
Other Pac. Isl., not spec. (9)	51	0.06
Hispanic or Latino:	2,111	2.52
Central American:	184	0.22
Costa Rican	9	0.01
Guatemalan	75	0.09
Honduran	18	0.02
Nicaraguan	13	0.02
Panamanian	15	0.02
Salvadoran	31	0.04
Other Central American	23	0.03
Cuban	167	0.20
Dominican Republic	79	0.09
Mexican	305	0.36
Puerto Rican	334	0.40
South American:	548	0.65
Argentinean	99	0.12
Bolivian	17	0.02
Chilean	37	0.04
Colombian	161	0.19
Ecuadorian	48	0.06
Paraguayan	7	0.01
Peruvian	71	0.08

Notes: 1. Figures in the "Number" column do not add up to the total population due to: a) Ancestry/Race overlap — e.g. persons can report being both White and Irish, b) persons of Hispanic origin can report being any race, c) persons reporting two ancestries are counted in both categories. 2. Numbers in parentheses indicate the number of persons reporting this ancestry/race alone, not in combination with any other ancestry/race. 3. Refer to the Explanation of Data in the front of the book for more detailed information.

Ancestry/Race	Number	%
Uruguayan	8	0.01
Venezuelan	62	0.07
Other South American	38	0.05
Other Hispanic or Latino	494	0.59
Hungarian	547	0.65
Iranian	336	0.40
Irish	13,949	16.64
Israeli	483	0.58
Italian	10,256	12.23
Latvian	177	0.21
Lithuanian	853	1.02
New Zealander	19	0.02
Northern European	73	0.09
Norwegian	479	0.57
Pennsylvania German	9	0.01
Polish	3,821	4.56
Portuguese	493	0.59
Romanian	318	0.38
Russian	8,055	9.61
Scandinavian	130	0.16
Scotch-Irish	877	1.05
Scottish	1,650	1.97
Slavic	9	0.01
Slovak	123	0.15
Slovene	70	0.08
Soviet Union	6	0.01
Swedish	1,224	1.46
Swiss	151	0.18
Turkish	112	0.13
Ukrainian	939	1.12
United States or American	4,060	4.84
Welsh	429	0.51
West Indian, excl. Hispanic:	448	0.53
Bahamian	15	0.02
Barbadian	14	0.02
Bermudan	7	0.01
British West Indian	50	0.06
Dutch West Indian	23	0.03
Haitian	226	0.27
Jamaican	44	0.05
Trinidadian and Tobagonian	41	0.05
West Indian	28	0.03
White:	74,862	89.30
Not Hispanic (72,388)	73,279	87.41
Hispanic (1,443)	1,583	1.89
Yugoslavian	25	0.03

Norfolk

Place Type: Town
County: Norfolk
Population: 10,460

Ancestry/Race	Number	%
African American/Black:	569	5.44
Not Hispanic (493)	533	5.10
Hispanic (20)	36	0.34
African, sub-Saharan:	104	0.99
African	84	0.80
Cape Verdean	20	0.19
Am. Ind. or Alaska Nat., not spec.	29	0.28
Albanian	20	0.19
American Indian tribes, specified:	33	0.32
Blackfeet (2)	3	0.03
Cherokee (6)	11	0.11
Iroquois (1)	2	0.02
Latin American Indians (6)	8	0.08
Osage	1	0.01
Ute	1	0.01
All other tribes (3)	7	0.07
American Indian tribes, not spec.	7	0.07
Arab:	96	0.92
Lebanese	79	0.76
Syrian	17	0.16
Armenian	54	0.52
Asian:	163	1.56
Cambodian (8)	11	0.11
Chinese, ex. Taiwanese (24)	40	0.38
Filipino (6)	9	0.09
Indian (28)	31	0.30
Japanese (3)	8	0.08
Korean (12)	13	0.12
Laotian (5)	5	0.05
Pakistani (4)	6	0.06
Taiwanese (4)	4	0.04
Vietnamese (16)	20	0.19
Other Asian, specified (1)	1	0.01
Other Asian, not specified (8)	15	0.14
Austrian	15	0.14
Belgian	45	0.43
British	67	0.64
Canadian	152	1.45
Danish	17	0.16
Dutch	190	1.82
Eastern European	6	0.06
English	1,583	15.13
European	84	0.80
Finnish	11	0.11
French, except Basque	598	5.72
French Canadian	239	2.28
German	878	8.39
Greek	143	1.37
Hawaii Native/Pacific Islander:	13	0.12
Micronesian: (2)	2	0.02
Guamanian/Chamorro (2)	2	0.02
Polynesian:	1	0.01
Native Hawaiian	1	0.01
Other Pac. Isl., not spec.	10	0.10
Hispanic or Latino:	510	4.88
Central American:	16	0.15
Guatemalan	5	0.05
Honduran	3	0.03
Panamanian	2	0.02
Salvadoran	6	0.06
Cuban	18	0.17
Dominican Republic	125	1.20
Mexican	29	0.28
Puerto Rican	175	1.67
South American:	46	0.44
Argentinean	6	0.06
Colombian	30	0.29
Ecuadorian	4	0.04
Paraguayan	2	0.02
Peruvian	2	0.02
Venezuelan	1	0.01
Other South American	1	0.01
Other Hispanic or Latino	101	0.97
Hungarian	43	0.41
Irish	3,552	33.96
Italian	1,834	17.53
Latvian	13	0.12
Lithuanian	80	0.76
Northern European	11	0.11
Norwegian	94	0.90
Polish	449	4.29
Portuguese	201	1.92
Romanian	11	0.11
Russian	84	0.80
Scandinavian	48	0.46
Scotch-Irish	142	1.36
Scottish	444	4.24
Slavic	6	0.06
Swedish	461	4.41
Swiss	18	0.17
Ukrainian	16	0.15
United States or American	276	2.64
Welsh	50	0.48
West Indian, excl. Hispanic:	22	0.21
Haitian	8	0.08
Jamaican	14	0.13
White:	9,390	89.77
Not Hispanic (9,199)	9,264	88.57
Hispanic (107)	126	1.20

North Adams

Place Type: City
County: Berkshire
Population: 14,681

Ancestry/Race	Number	%
African American/Black:	356	2.42
Not Hispanic (230)	331	2.25
Hispanic (15)	25	0.17
African, sub-Saharan:	51	0.35
African	24	0.16
Cape Verdean	13	0.09
Liberian	9	0.06
Sudanese	5	0.03
Am. Ind. or Alaska Nat., not spec.	41	0.28
Alsatian	8	0.05
American Indian tribes, specified:	66	0.45
Blackfeet	10	0.07
Cherokee (1)	9	0.06
Chippewa (2)	3	0.02
Choctaw (4)	4	0.03
Cree	3	0.02
Creek	2	0.01
Crow	1	0.01
Houma (1)	1	0.01
Iroquois (5)	10	0.07
Latin American Indians (2)	2	0.01
Navajo (1)	1	0.01
Sioux (1)	2	0.01
Ute (1)	1	0.01
All other tribes (5)	19	0.13
American Indian tribes, not spec.	6	0.04
Arab:	208	1.42
Arab/Arabic	9	0.06
Lebanese	193	1.31
Syrian	6	0.04
Armenian	31	0.21
Asian:	135	0.92
Bangladeshi	1	0.01
Cambodian (8)	8	0.05
Chinese, ex. Taiwanese (25)	30	0.20
Filipino (1)	2	0.01
Indian (34)	36	0.25
Indonesian (1)	1	0.01
Japanese (6)	8	0.05
Korean (10)	13	0.09
Laotian (4)	4	0.03
Malaysian (3)	3	0.02
Thai (1)	1	0.01
Vietnamese (16)	16	0.11
Other Asian, specified (1)	1	0.01
Other Asian, not specified (6)	11	0.07
Austrian	103	0.70
British	48	0.33
Canadian	25	0.17
Celtic	8	0.05
Czech	20	0.14
Dutch	82	0.56
English	1,514	10.32
European	52	0.35
Finnish	14	0.10
French, except Basque	3,706	25.25
French Canadian	1,198	8.16
German	1,206	8.22
Greek	127	0.87
Guyanese	9	0.06
Hawaii Native/Pacific Islander:	12	0.08
Micronesian: (4)	4	0.03
Guamanian/Chamorro (4)	4	0.03
Polynesian: (1)	5	0.03
Native Hawaiian (1)	4	0.03
Samoan	1	0.01
Other Pac. Isl., not spec.	3	0.02
Hispanic or Latino:	298	2.03
Central American:	42	0.29
Costa Rican	2	0.01
Guatemalan	3	0.02
Honduran	29	0.20
Panamanian	1	0.01

Notes: 1. Figures in the "Number" column do not add up to the total population due to: a) Ancestry/Race overlap — e.g. persons can report being both White and Irish, b) persons of Hispanic origin can report being any race, c) persons reporting two ancestries are counted in both categories. 2. Numbers in parentheses indicate the number of persons reporting this ancestry/race alone, not in combination with any other ancestry/race. 3. Refer to the Explanation of Data in the front of the book for more detailed information.

Ancestry/Race	Number	%
Salvadoran	2	0.01
Other Central American	5	0.03
Cuban	17	0.12
Dominican Republic	12	0.08
Mexican	39	0.27
Puerto Rican	111	0.76
South American:	15	0.10
Argentinean	2	0.01
Bolivian	1	0.01
Colombian	9	0.06
Peruvian	2	0.01
Other South American	1	0.01
Other Hispanic or Latino	62	0.42
Hungarian	41	0.28
Irish	2,625	17.89
Italian	3,125	21.29
Lithuanian	50	0.34
Northern European	15	0.10
Norwegian	37	0.25
Polish	990	6.75
Portuguese	125	0.85
Romanian	6	0.04
Russian	73	0.50
Scotch-Irish	126	0.86
Scottish	366	2.49
Swedish	131	0.89
Swiss	17	0.12
Turkish	23	0.16
United States or American	625	4.26
Welsh	80	0.55
White:	14,150	96.38
Not Hispanic (13,800)	13,970	95.16
Hispanic (146)	180	1.23

North Andover

Place Type: Town
County: Essex
Population: 27,202

Ancestry/Race	Number	%
African American/Black:	222	0.82
Not Hispanic (184)	207	0.76
Hispanic (12)	15	0.06
African, sub-Saharan:	6	0.02
Cape Verdean	6	0.02
Am. Ind. or Alaska Nat., not spec.	20	0.07
American Indian tribes, specified:	33	0.12
Cherokee (3)	11	0.04
Choctaw	1	0.00
Creek (3)	4	0.01
Iroquois (1)	1	0.00
Latin American Indians	6	0.02
Navajo	1	0.00
Seminole	1	0.00
All other tribes (3)	8	0.03
American Indian tribes, not spec.	4	0.01
Arab:	366	1.35
Arab/Arabic	10	0.04
Egyptian	5	0.02
Lebanese	276	1.01
Moroccan	25	0.09
Syrian	32	0.12
Other Arab	18	0.07
Armenian	258	0.95
Asian:	1,198	4.40
Bangladeshi (7)	7	0.03
Cambodian (2)	6	0.02
Chinese, ex. Taiwanese (352)	385	1.42
Filipino (53)	65	0.24
Indian (333)	345	1.27
Japanese (57)	71	0.26
Korean (157)	172	0.63
Pakistani (9)	9	0.03
Sri Lankan	1	0.00
Taiwanese (16)	31	0.11
Thai (6)	6	0.02
Vietnamese (51)	71	0.26
Other Asian, not specified (19)	29	0.11
Australian	26	0.10
Austrian	64	0.24
Belgian	37	0.14
British	55	0.20
Canadian	193	0.71
Celtic	10	0.04
Croatian	25	0.09
Czech	16	0.06
Czechoslovakian	45	0.17
Danish	66	0.24
Dutch	262	0.96
Eastern European	19	0.07
English	4,464	16.41
European	100	0.37
Finnish	49	0.18
French, except Basque	2,109	7.75
French Canadian	1,149	4.22
German	2,266	8.33
Greek	344	1.26
Hawaii Native/Pacific Islander:	10	0.04
Micronesian: (1)	1	0.00
Guamanian/Chamorro (1)	1	0.00
Polynesian: (1)	3	0.01
Native Hawaiian (1)	3	0.01
Other Pac. Isl., not spec.	6	0.02
Hispanic or Latino:	541	1.99
Central American:	20	0.07
Costa Rican	5	0.02
Guatemalan	3	0.01
Honduran	2	0.01
Nicaraguan	3	0.01
Panamanian	1	0.00
Salvadoran	4	0.01
Other Central American	2	0.01
Cuban	51	0.19
Dominican Republic	92	0.34
Mexican	52	0.19
Puerto Rican	133	0.49
South American:	91	0.33
Argentinean	12	0.04
Chilean	2	0.01
Colombian	41	0.15
Ecuadorian	10	0.04
Paraguayan	1	0.00
Peruvian	7	0.03
Venezuelan	10	0.04
Other South American	8	0.03
Other Hispanic or Latino	102	0.37
Hungarian	141	0.52
Iranian	47	0.17
Irish	8,266	30.39
Israeli	80	0.29
Italian	5,386	19.80
Lithuanian	222	0.82
Maltese	7	0.03
Northern European	6	0.02
Norwegian	173	0.64
Polish	1,222	4.49
Portuguese	357	1.31
Romanian	7	0.03
Russian	481	1.77
Scandinavian	45	0.17
Scotch-Irish	459	1.69
Scottish	914	3.36
Serbian	19	0.07
Slavic	21	0.08
Slovak	50	0.18
Swedish	400	1.47
Swiss	21	0.08
Turkish	44	0.16
Ukrainian	124	0.46
United States or American	697	2.56
Welsh	89	0.33
West Indian, excl. Hispanic:	85	0.31
Haitian	6	0.02
Jamaican	68	0.25
West Indian	11	0.04
White:	25,681	94.41
Not Hispanic (25,172)	25,344	93.17
Hispanic (309)	337	1.24

North Attleborough Center

Place Type: Census Designated Place
County: Bristol
Population: 16,796

Ancestry/Race	Number	%
African American/Black:	232	1.38
Not Hispanic (178)	219	1.30
Hispanic (11)	13	0.08
African, sub-Saharan:	24	0.14
African	8	0.05
Cape Verdean	16	0.10
Alaska Native tribes, specified:	4	0.02
Eskimo	4	0.02
Am. Ind. or Alaska Nat., not spec.	23	0.14
Albanian	16	0.10
American Indian tribes, specified:	60	0.36
Blackfeet (3)	4	0.02
Cherokee (1)	6	0.04
Chippewa (1)	2	0.01
Comanche (2)	2	0.01
Cree	2	0.01
Creek	3	0.02
Iroquois	11	0.07
Navajo (1)	2	0.01
All other tribes (6)	28	0.17
American Indian tribes, not spec.	4	0.02
Arab:	245	1.46
Lebanese	228	1.35
Syrian	9	0.05
Other Arab	8	0.05
Armenian	47	0.28
Asian:	343	2.04
Cambodian (25)	25	0.15
Chinese, ex. Taiwanese (55)	60	0.36
Filipino (13)	19	0.11
Indian (128)	145	0.86
Indonesian	1	0.01
Japanese (5)	16	0.10
Korean (14)	16	0.10
Pakistani (4)	5	0.03
Taiwanese (2)	2	0.01
Thai (4)	5	0.03
Vietnamese (36)	38	0.23
Other Asian, not specified (6)	11	0.07
Austrian	18	0.11
Belgian	21	0.12
Brazilian	10	0.06
British	59	0.35
Canadian	130	0.77
Czech	8	0.05
Czechoslovakian	36	0.21
Danish	71	0.42
Dutch	67	0.40
English	2,297	13.64
European	29	0.17
Finnish	30	0.18
French, except Basque	2,515	14.94
French Canadian	1,634	9.71
German	1,284	7.63
Greek	110	0.65
Hawaii Native/Pacific Islander:	9	0.05
Polynesian: (4)	9	0.05
Native Hawaiian (1)	6	0.04
Samoan (3)	3	0.02
Hispanic or Latino:	284	1.69
Central American:	35	0.21
Costa Rican	2	0.01
Guatemalan	10	0.06
Honduran	3	0.02
Nicaraguan	4	0.02
Panamanian	4	0.02
Salvadoran	7	0.04
Other Central American	5	0.03
Cuban	11	0.07
Dominican Republic	7	0.04
Mexican	33	0.20

Notes: 1. Figures in the "Number" column do not add up to the total population due to: a) Ancestry/Race overlap — e.g. persons can report being both White and Irish, b) persons of Hispanic origin can report being any race, c) persons reporting two ancestries are counted in both categories. 2. Numbers in parentheses indicate the number of persons reporting this ancestry/race alone, not in combination with any other ancestry/race. 3. Refer to the Explanation of Data in the front of the book for more detailed information.

Ancestry/Race	Number	%
Puerto Rican	94	0.56
South American:	31	0.18
Argentinean	2	0.01
Bolivian	2	0.01
Chilean	1	0.01
Colombian	13	0.08
Ecuadorian	8	0.05
Peruvian	4	0.02
Other South American	1	0.01
Other Hispanic or Latino	73	0.43
Hungarian	42	0.25
Irish	4,589	27.26
Italian	2,645	15.71
Latvian	6	0.04
Lithuanian	114	0.68
Northern European	45	0.27
Norwegian	120	0.71
Polish	721	4.28
Portuguese	560	3.33
Romanian	8	0.05
Russian	154	0.91
Scandinavian	45	0.27
Scotch-Irish	296	1.76
Scottish	608	3.61
Swedish	514	3.05
Swiss	39	0.23
Ukrainian	69	0.41
United States or American	654	3.88
Welsh	69	0.41
West Indian, excl. Hispanic:	73	0.43
Haitian	68	0.40
Trinidadian and Tobagonian	5	0.03
White:	16,153	96.17
Not Hispanic (15,865)	15,976	95.12
Hispanic (164)	177	1.05

North Attleborough

Place Type: Town
County: Bristol
Population: 27,143

Ancestry/Race	Number	%
African American/Black:	305	1.12
Not Hispanic (238)	287	1.06
Hispanic (13)	18	0.07
African, sub-Saharan:	188	0.69
African	28	0.10
Cape Verdean	104	0.38
South African	56	0.21
Alaska Native tribes, specified:	4	0.01
Eskimo	4	0.01
Am. Ind. or Alaska Nat., not spec.	29	0.11
Albanian	16	0.06
American Indian tribes, specified:	70	0.26
Blackfeet (3)	5	0.02
Cherokee (1)	9	0.03
Chippewa (1)	3	0.01
Choctaw	1	0.00
Comanche (2)	2	0.01
Cree	2	0.01
Creek (1)	4	0.01
Iroquois (1)	12	0.04
Navajo (1)	2	0.01
All other tribes (7)	30	0.11
American Indian tribes, not spec.	4	0.01
Arab:	311	1.15
Lebanese	237	0.87
Syrian	66	0.24
Other Arab	8	0.03
Armenian	47	0.17
Asian:	549	2.02
Cambodian (33)	36	0.13
Chinese, ex. Taiwanese (105)	120	0.44
Filipino (24)	31	0.11
Indian (171)	194	0.71
Indonesian	1	0.00
Japanese (12)	29	0.11
Korean (28)	35	0.13
Pakistani (7)	8	0.03
Sri Lankan (5)	7	0.03
Taiwanese (7)	7	0.03
Thai (5)	9	0.03
Vietnamese (55)	59	0.22
Other Asian, not specified (7)	13	0.05
Austrian	27	0.10
Belgian	38	0.14
Brazilian	10	0.04
British	105	0.39
Canadian	227	0.84
Celtic	6	0.02
Czech	22	0.08
Czechoslovakian	45	0.17
Danish	161	0.59
Dutch	195	0.72
Eastern European	8	0.03
English	3,724	13.72
Estonian	26	0.10
European	33	0.12
Finnish	58	0.21
French, except Basque	3,579	13.19
French Canadian	2,602	9.59
German	2,085	7.68
Greek	119	0.44
Hawaii Native/Pacific Islander:	13	0.05
Polynesian: (4)	9	0.03
Native Hawaiian (1)	6	0.02
Samoan (3)	3	0.01
Other Pac. Isl., not spec. (1)	4	0.01
Hispanic or Latino:	358	1.32
Central American:	43	0.16
Costa Rican	5	0.02
Guatemalan	13	0.05
Honduran	5	0.02
Nicaraguan	4	0.01
Panamanian	4	0.01
Salvadoran	7	0.03
Other Central American	5	0.02
Cuban	19	0.07
Dominican Republic	7	0.03
Mexican	51	0.19
Puerto Rican	109	0.40
South American:	36	0.13
Argentinean	2	0.01
Bolivian	2	0.01
Chilean	2	0.01
Colombian	16	0.06
Ecuadorian	8	0.03
Peruvian	4	0.01
Venezuelan	1	0.00
Other South American	1	0.00
Other Hispanic or Latino	93	0.34
Hungarian	50	0.18
Irish	7,262	26.75
Italian	4,276	15.75
Latvian	25	0.09
Lithuanian	222	0.82
Northern European	45	0.17
Norwegian	185	0.68
Polish	1,261	4.65
Portuguese	931	3.43
Romanian	8	0.03
Russian	203	0.75
Scandinavian	53	0.20
Scotch-Irish	498	1.83
Scottish	1,017	3.75
Swedish	777	2.86
Swiss	50	0.18
Ukrainian	120	0.44
United States or American	1,504	5.54
Welsh	138	0.51
West Indian, excl. Hispanic:	80	0.29
Haitian	68	0.25
Trinidadian and Tobagonian	5	0.02
West Indian	7	0.03
White:	26,237	96.66
Not Hispanic (25,839)	26,004	95.80
Hispanic (209)	233	0.86

North Reading

Place Type: Town
County: Middlesex
Population: 13,837

Ancestry/Race	Number	%
African American/Black:	77	0.56
Not Hispanic (54)	74	0.53
Hispanic (1)	3	0.02
African, sub-Saharan:	10	0.07
African	10	0.07
Am. Ind. or Alaska Nat., not spec.	7	0.05
Albanian	37	0.27
American Indian tribes, specified:	7	0.05
Creek	1	0.01
Iroquois	1	0.01
Navajo (1)	1	0.01
All other tribes (4)	4	0.03
American Indian tribes, not spec.	3	0.02
Arab:	144	1.04
Lebanese	80	0.58
Moroccan	25	0.18
Palestinian	14	0.10
Syrian	8	0.06
Other Arab	17	0.12
Armenian	51	0.37
Asian:	206	1.49
Bangladeshi (7)	8	0.06
Cambodian (2)	2	0.01
Chinese, ex. Taiwanese (74)	84	0.61
Filipino (14)	18	0.13
Indian (38)	45	0.33
Japanese (6)	6	0.04
Korean (18)	19	0.14
Malaysian	1	0.01
Sri Lankan (1)	1	0.01
Taiwanese (7)	9	0.07
Thai (2)	2	0.01
Vietnamese (8)	9	0.07
Other Asian, not specified (1)	2	0.01
Austrian	17	0.12
Brazilian	54	0.39
British	6	0.04
Canadian	229	1.65
Czech	42	0.30
Czechoslovakian	8	0.06
Danish	15	0.11
Dutch	37	0.27
Eastern European	14	0.10
English	2,243	16.21
European	88	0.64
Finnish	24	0.17
French, except Basque	861	6.22
French Canadian	774	5.59
German	878	6.35
Greek	174	1.26
Hawaii Native/Pacific Islander:	1	0.01
Polynesian: (1)	1	0.01
Samoan (1)	1	0.01
Hispanic or Latino:	102	0.74
Central American:	9	0.07
Costa Rican	3	0.02
Guatemalan	3	0.02
Honduran	2	0.01
Salvadoran	1	0.01
Cuban	6	0.04
Dominican Republic	5	0.04
Mexican	15	0.11
Puerto Rican	17	0.12
South American:	32	0.23
Argentinean	4	0.03
Bolivian	1	0.01
Chilean	2	0.01
Colombian	15	0.11
Ecuadorian	3	0.02
Peruvian	1	0.01
Uruguayan	1	0.01
Venezuelan	4	0.03
Other South American	1	0.01

Notes: 1. Figures in the "Number" column do not add up to the total population due to: a) Ancestry/Race overlap — e.g. persons can report being both White and Irish, b) persons of Hispanic origin can report being any race, c) persons reporting two ancestries are counted in both categories. 2. Numbers in parentheses indicate the number of persons reporting this ancestry/race alone, not in combination with any other ancestry/race. 3. Refer to the Explanation of Data in the front of the book for more detailed information.

Ancestry/Race	Number	%
Other Hispanic or Latino	18	0.13
Hungarian	38	0.27
Irish	4,155	30.03
Italian	3,406	24.62
Latvian	7	0.05
Lithuanian	100	0.72
Northern European	21	0.15
Norwegian	58	0.42
Polish	582	4.21
Portuguese	367	2.65
Russian	160	1.16
Scotch-Irish	352	2.54
Scottish	427	3.09
Slovak	9	0.07
Swedish	433	3.13
Swiss	38	0.27
Ukrainian	30	0.22
United States or American	787	5.69
Welsh	52	0.38
West Indian, excl. Hispanic:	13	0.09
Trinidadian and Tobagonian	13	0.09
White:	13,554	97.95
Not Hispanic (13,420)	13,471	97.35
Hispanic (75)	83	0.60
Yugoslavian	27	0.20

Northampton

Place Type: City
County: Hampshire
Population: 28,978

Ancestry/Race	Number	%
African American/Black:	800	2.76
Not Hispanic (544)	691	2.38
Hispanic (58)	109	0.38
African, sub-Saharan:	212	0.73
African	65	0.22
Cape Verdean	17	0.06
Ghanian	8	0.03
Kenyan	39	0.13
Nigerian	70	0.24
South African	7	0.02
Other sub-Saharan African	6	0.02
Alaska Native tribes, specified:	3	0.01
Eskimo (1)	1	0.00
Tlingit-Haida (1)	2	0.01
Am. Ind. or Alaska Nat., not spec.	89	0.31
Albanian	6	0.02
American Indian tribes, specified:	170	0.59
Apache (2)	4	0.01
Blackfeet (2)	18	0.06
Cherokee (10)	34	0.12
Cheyenne	1	0.00
Chippewa (4)	6	0.02
Choctaw (1)	3	0.01
Cree (1)	3	0.01
Creek (2)	2	0.01
Iroquois (8)	16	0.06
Kiowa	1	0.00
Latin American Indians (13)	24	0.08
Pueblo (1)	3	0.01
Puget Sound Salish (2)	2	0.01
Seminole (1)	4	0.01
Sioux (3)	6	0.02
Yaqui	2	0.01
All other tribes (18)	41	0.14
American Indian tribes, not spec.	8	0.03
Arab:	132	0.46
Arab/Arabic	7	0.02
Egyptian	43	0.15
Lebanese	37	0.13
Moroccan	12	0.04
Syrian	20	0.07
Other Arab	13	0.04
Armenian	63	0.22
Asian:	1,103	3.81
Bangladeshi (6)	6	0.02
Cambodian (75)	90	0.31
Chinese, ex. Taiwanese (211)	248	0.86
Filipino (38)	60	0.21
Hmong (1)	1	0.00
Indian (225)	260	0.90
Indonesian (1)	2	0.01
Japanese (55)	97	0.33
Korean (155)	166	0.57
Laotian (2)	4	0.01
Malaysian	3	0.01
Pakistani (20)	20	0.07
Sri Lankan (5)	7	0.02
Taiwanese (6)	6	0.02
Thai (7)	11	0.04
Vietnamese (56)	63	0.22
Other Asian, specified (4)	12	0.04
Other Asian, not specified (29)	47	0.16
Assyrian/Chaldean/Syriac	22	0.08
Austrian	196	0.68
Basque	12	0.04
Belgian	14	0.05
Brazilian	21	0.07
British	291	1.00
Bulgarian	15	0.05
Canadian	157	0.54
Celtic	5	0.02
Croatian	31	0.11
Czech	108	0.37
Czechoslovakian	50	0.17
Danish	128	0.44
Dutch	322	1.11
Eastern European	188	0.65
English	4,016	13.86
Estonian	19	0.07
European	350	1.21
Finnish	77	0.27
French, except Basque	2,811	9.70
French Canadian	1,791	6.18
German	2,975	10.27
German Russian	6	0.02
Greek	150	0.52
Guyanese	9	0.03
Hawaii Native/Pacific Islander:	41	0.14
Micronesian: (4)	8	0.03
Guamanian/Chamorro (4)	6	0.02
Other Micronesian	2	0.01
Polynesian: (11)	22	0.08
Native Hawaiian (3)	10	0.03
Samoan (8)	12	0.04
Other Pac. Isl., specified	3	0.01
Other Pac. Isl., not spec.	8	0.03
Hispanic or Latino:	1,518	5.24
Central American:	49	0.17
Costa Rican	4	0.01
Guatemalan	18	0.06
Honduran	3	0.01
Nicaraguan	1	0.00
Panamanian	4	0.01
Salvadoran	15	0.05
Other Central American	4	0.01
Cuban	37	0.13
Dominican Republic	16	0.06
Mexican	106	0.37
Puerto Rican	1,011	3.49
South American:	87	0.30
Argentinean	16	0.06
Bolivian	3	0.01
Chilean	12	0.04
Colombian	30	0.10
Ecuadorian	7	0.02
Peruvian	13	0.04
Venezuelan	2	0.01
Other South American	4	0.01
Other Hispanic or Latino	212	0.73
Hungarian	202	0.70
Icelander	13	0.04
Iranian	40	0.14
Irish	6,089	21.01
Israeli	34	0.12
Italian	2,270	7.83
Latvian	13	0.04
Lithuanian	246	0.85
Macedonian	11	0.04
Northern European	56	0.19
Norwegian	198	0.68
Polish	3,540	12.22
Portuguese	170	0.59
Romanian	118	0.41
Russian	1,002	3.46
Scandinavian	50	0.17
Scotch-Irish	544	1.88
Scottish	872	3.01
Serbian	6	0.02
Slavic	10	0.03
Slovak	69	0.24
Slovene	6	0.02
Swedish	426	1.47
Swiss	107	0.37
Turkish	7	0.02
Ukrainian	207	0.71
United States or American	818	2.82
Welsh	219	0.76
West Indian, excl. Hispanic:	101	0.35
Barbadian	10	0.03
British West Indian	6	0.02
Haitian	47	0.16
Jamaican	38	0.13
White:	26,573	91.70
Not Hispanic (25,433)	25,822	89.11
Hispanic (650)	751	2.59
Yugoslavian	11	0.04

Northborough

Place Type: Town
County: Worcester
Population: 14,013

Ancestry/Race	Number	%
African American/Black:	111	0.79
Not Hispanic (89)	109	0.78
Hispanic (2)	2	0.01
Am. Ind. or Alaska Nat., not spec.	6	0.04
Albanian	36	0.26
American Indian tribes, specified:	23	0.16
Blackfeet (1)	1	0.01
Cherokee (1)	2	0.01
Creek (1)	1	0.01
Iroquois	2	0.01
Latin American Indians (1)	1	0.01
Navajo	1	0.01
Seminole (1)	1	0.01
Sioux	1	0.01
All other tribes (2)	13	0.09
American Indian tribes, not spec.	1	0.01
Arab:	84	0.60
Lebanese	63	0.45
Syrian	21	0.15
Armenian	54	0.39
Asian:	768	5.48
Bangladeshi (3)	3	0.02
Cambodian (5)	5	0.04
Chinese, ex. Taiwanese (276)	303	2.16
Filipino (9)	15	0.11
Indian (257)	268	1.91
Indonesian (4)	4	0.03
Japanese (6)	12	0.09
Korean (86)	95	0.68
Laotian (4)	5	0.04
Pakistani (4)	4	0.03
Taiwanese (20)	20	0.14
Vietnamese (21)	23	0.16
Other Asian, not specified (4)	11	0.08
Australian	18	0.13
Austrian	31	0.22
Belgian	6	0.04
British	39	0.28
Canadian	220	1.57
Croatian	7	0.05
Czech	20	0.14
Czechoslovakian	46	0.33
Danish	34	0.24

Notes: 1. Figures in the "Number" column do not add up to the total population due to: a) Ancestry/Race overlap — e.g. persons can report being both White and Irish, b) persons of Hispanic origin can report being any race, c) persons reporting two ancestries are counted in both categories. 2. Numbers in parentheses indicate the number of persons reporting this ancestry/race alone, not in combination with any other ancestry/race. 3. Refer to the Explanation of Data in the front of the book for more detailed information.

Dutch	149	1.06
Eastern European	21	0.15
English	2,163	15.44
European	83	0.59
Finnish	74	0.53
French, except Basque	1,420	10.13
French Canadian	948	6.77
German	1,209	8.63
Greek	218	1.56
Hawaii Native/Pacific Islander:	11	0.08
Micronesian: (2)	2	0.01
Guamanian/Chamorro (2)	2	0.01
Other Pac. Isl., not spec. (8)	9	0.06
Hispanic or Latino:	179	1.28
Central American:	14	0.10
Guatemalan	6	0.04
Salvadoran	8	0.06
Cuban	8	0.06
Dominican Republic	8	0.06
Mexican	46	0.33
Puerto Rican	40	0.29
South American:	27	0.19
Argentinean	10	0.07
Colombian	8	0.06
Ecuadorian	2	0.01
Peruvian	3	0.02
Venezuelan	4	0.03
Other Hispanic or Latino	36	0.26
Hungarian	85	0.61
Iranian	7	0.05
Irish	3,581	25.55
Italian	1,914	13.66
Latvian	5	0.04
Lithuanian	184	1.31
Luxemburger	9	0.06
Norwegian	155	1.11
Polish	613	4.37
Portuguese	144	1.03
Russian	180	1.28
Scandinavian	23	0.16
Scotch-Irish	228	1.63
Scottish	319	2.28
Slovak	14	0.10
Swedish	683	4.87
Swiss	29	0.21
Ukrainian	61	0.44
United States or American	732	5.22
Welsh	124	0.88
West Indian, excl. Hispanic:	69	0.49
Bahamian	9	0.06
Haitian	12	0.09
Jamaican	34	0.24
Trinidadian and Tobagonian	14	0.10
White:	13,132	93.71
Not Hispanic (12,903)	12,995	92.74
Hispanic (130)	137	0.98
Yugoslavian	23	0.16

Northbridge

Place Type: Town
County: Worcester
Population: 13,182

Ancestry/Race	Number	%
African American/Black:	141	1.07
Not Hispanic (77)	129	0.98
Hispanic (2)	12	0.09
Am. Ind. or Alaska Nat., not spec.	33	0.25
Albanian	31	0.23
American Indian tribes, specified:	46	0.35
Blackfeet (3)	8	0.06
Cherokee (4)	9	0.07
Iroquois	2	0.02
Latin American Indians	3	0.02
Sioux (1)	5	0.04
All other tribes (7)	19	0.14
American Indian tribes, not spec.	4	0.03
Arab:	82	0.62
Egyptian	18	0.14
Lebanese	46	0.35
Syrian	18	0.14
Armenian	309	2.34
Asian:	74	0.56
Cambodian (2)	2	0.02
Chinese, ex. Taiwanese (4)	7	0.05
Filipino (5)	18	0.14
Indian (1)	2	0.02
Japanese (1)	2	0.02
Korean (9)	14	0.11
Laotian (10)	10	0.08
Pakistani (1)	1	0.01
Thai (5)	5	0.04
Vietnamese (1)	1	0.01
Other Asian, not specified (3)	12	0.09
Austrian	56	0.42
Belgian	4	0.03
Brazilian	6	0.05
British	18	0.14
Canadian	42	0.32
Croatian	5	0.04
Czech	25	0.19
Danish	20	0.15
Dutch	861	6.52
Eastern European	7	0.05
English	1,785	13.52
European	52	0.39
Finnish	38	0.29
French, except Basque	2,050	15.53
French Canadian	1,294	9.80
German	636	4.82
Greek	174	1.32
Hawaii Native/Pacific Islander:	25	0.19
Micronesian:	3	0.02
Guamanian/Chamorro	3	0.02
Polynesian: (4)	13	0.10
Native Hawaiian (1)	10	0.08
Samoan (2)	2	0.02
Other Polynesian (1)	1	0.01
Other Pac. Isl., not spec.	9	0.07
Hispanic or Latino:	241	1.83
Central American:	11	0.08
Guatemalan	3	0.02
Panamanian	3	0.02
Salvadoran	5	0.04
Cuban	6	0.05
Dominican Republic	16	0.12
Mexican	28	0.21
Puerto Rican	104	0.79
South American:	13	0.10
Argentinean	1	0.01
Chilean	2	0.02
Colombian	3	0.02
Venezuelan	4	0.03
Other South American	3	0.02
Other Hispanic or Latino	63	0.48
Hungarian	47	0.36
Icelander	5	0.04
Irish	2,919	22.11
Italian	1,355	10.26
Latvian	6	0.05
Lithuanian	84	0.64
Norwegian	55	0.42
Polish	1,025	7.76
Portuguese	170	1.29
Romanian	8	0.06
Russian	32	0.24
Scandinavian	15	0.11
Scotch-Irish	250	1.89
Scottish	342	2.59
Slovak	65	0.49
Slovene	6	0.05
Swedish	400	3.03
Ukrainian	23	0.17
United States or American	564	4.27
Welsh	56	0.42
West Indian, excl. Hispanic:	39	0.30
West Indian	39	0.30
White:	12,880	97.71
Not Hispanic (12,587)	12,754	96.75
Hispanic (101)	126	0.96

Norton

Place Type: Town
County: Bristol
Population: 18,036

Ancestry/Race	Number	%
African American/Black:	268	1.49
Not Hispanic (205)	256	1.42
Hispanic (4)	12	0.07
African, sub-Saharan:	98	0.54
African	7	0.04
Cape Verdean	81	0.45
South African	10	0.06
Am. Ind. or Alaska Nat., not spec.	16	0.09
American Indian tribes, specified:	49	0.27
Blackfeet (1)	2	0.01
Cherokee (11)	21	0.12
Cheyenne	1	0.01
Chippewa	3	0.02
Iroquois (2)	2	0.01
Latin American Indians (1)	1	0.01
Menominee (1)	1	0.01
Sioux	3	0.02
All other tribes (4)	15	0.08
American Indian tribes, not spec.	1	0.01
Arab:	142	0.79
Lebanese	101	0.56
Palestinian	8	0.04
Syrian	26	0.14
Other Arab	7	0.04
Armenian	34	0.19
Asian:	239	1.33
Cambodian (4)	4	0.02
Chinese, ex. Taiwanese (34)	47	0.26
Filipino (15)	19	0.11
Indian (53)	58	0.32
Indonesian (1)	2	0.01
Japanese (13)	27	0.15
Korean (19)	24	0.13
Pakistani	4	0.02
Sri Lankan (1)	1	0.01
Taiwanese	1	0.01
Thai (2)	9	0.05
Vietnamese (31)	32	0.18
Other Asian, not specified (4)	11	0.06
Australian	29	0.16
Austrian	38	0.21
Belgian	40	0.22
British	42	0.23
Canadian	121	0.67
Czech	66	0.37
Czechoslovakian	31	0.17
Danish	70	0.39
Dutch	300	1.66
English	2,865	15.88
European	100	0.55
Finnish	92	0.51
French, except Basque	1,709	9.48
French Canadian	1,191	6.60
German	1,391	7.71
Greek	227	1.26
Hawaii Native/Pacific Islander:	9	0.05
Melanesian:	1	0.01
Fijian	1	0.01
Polynesian: (1)	6	0.03
Native Hawaiian (1)	4	0.02
Samoan	2	0.01
Other Pac. Isl., not spec.	2	0.01
Hispanic or Latino:	206	1.14
Central American:	24	0.13
Costa Rican	6	0.03
Guatemalan	10	0.06
Panamanian	1	0.01
Salvadoran	6	0.03
Other Central American	1	0.01
Cuban	18	0.10
Dominican Republic	8	0.04

Notes: 1. Figures in the "Number" column do not add up to the total population due to: a) Ancestry/Race overlap — e.g. persons can report being both White and Irish, b) persons of Hispanic origin can report being any race, c) persons reporting two ancestries are counted in both categories. 2. Numbers in parentheses indicate the number of persons reporting this ancestry/race alone, not in combination with any other ancestry/race. 3. Refer to the Explanation of Data in the front of the book for more detailed information.

Mexican	25	0.14
Puerto Rican	56	0.31
South American:	34	0.19
Argentinean	2	0.01
Colombian	15	0.08
Ecuadorian	2	0.01
Paraguayan	2	0.01
Peruvian	8	0.04
Venezuelan	4	0.02
Other South American	1	0.01
Other Hispanic or Latino	41	0.23
Hungarian	15	0.08
Irish	5,162	28.62
Italian	2,781	15.42
Latvian	7	0.04
Lithuanian	189	1.05
Northern European	13	0.07
Norwegian	100	0.55
Polish	942	5.22
Portuguese	1,219	6.76
Russian	97	0.54
Scandinavian	26	0.14
Scotch-Irish	315	1.75
Scottish	592	3.28
Swedish	488	2.71
Swiss	27	0.15
Ukrainian	31	0.17
United States or American	659	3.65
Welsh	47	0.26
West Indian, excl. Hispanic:	30	0.17
Barbadian	9	0.05
British West Indian	9	0.05
Haitian	6	0.03
Trinidadian and Tobagonian	6	0.03
White:	16,794	93.11
Not Hispanic (16,527)	16,683	92.50
Hispanic (94)	111	0.62

Norwood

Place Type: Census Designated Place
County: Norfolk
Population: 28,587

Ancestry/Race	Number	%
African American/Black:	761	2.66
Not Hispanic (643)	727	2.54
Hispanic (16)	34	0.12
African, sub-Saharan:	99	0.35
African	31	0.11
Cape Verdean	10	0.03
Ghanian	34	0.12
Liberian	14	0.05
Nigerian	10	0.03
Am. Ind. or Alaska Nat., not spec.	28	0.10
Albanian	53	0.19
American Indian tribes, specified:	39	0.14
Apache (1)	1	0.00
Cherokee (3)	5	0.02
Cheyenne	1	0.00
Creek	1	0.00
Iroquois (2)	2	0.01
Latin American Indians (4)	9	0.03
Pima (1)	1	0.00
Seminole	2	0.01
Sioux	2	0.01
All other tribes (4)	15	0.05
American Indian tribes, not spec.	4	0.01
Arab:	1,070	3.74
Arab/Arabic	28	0.10
Egyptian	37	0.13
Iraqi	23	0.08
Jordanian	8	0.03
Lebanese	725	2.54
Syrian	245	0.86
Other Arab	4	0.01
Armenian	60	0.21
Asian:	1,567	5.48
Bangladeshi (10)	10	0.03
Cambodian (4)	4	0.01
Chinese, ex. Taiwanese (225)	248	0.87
Filipino (60)	71	0.25
Indian (921)	934	3.27
Indonesian	7	0.02
Japanese (18)	29	0.10
Korean (104)	114	0.40
Malaysian (5)	5	0.02
Pakistani (11)	14	0.05
Sri Lankan (5)	5	0.02
Taiwanese (7)	12	0.04
Thai (3)	5	0.02
Vietnamese (47)	58	0.20
Other Asian, specified (5)	9	0.03
Other Asian, not specified (11)	42	0.15
Assyrian/Chaldean/Syriac	9	0.03
Austrian	84	0.29
Belgian	6	0.02
Brazilian	86	0.30
British	39	0.14
Bulgarian	26	0.09
Canadian	424	1.48
Celtic	4	0.01
Croatian	21	0.07
Czech	36	0.13
Czechoslovakian	7	0.02
Danish	55	0.19
Dutch	130	0.45
Eastern European	74	0.26
English	2,561	8.96
European	33	0.12
Finnish	165	0.58
French, except Basque	814	2.85
French Canadian	734	2.57
German	1,781	6.23
German Russian	5	0.02
Greek	473	1.65
Hawaii Native/Pacific Islander:	14	0.05
Micronesian: (2)	2	0.01
Other Micronesian (2)	2	0.01
Polynesian: (1)	4	0.01
Native Hawaiian (1)	3	0.01
Samoan	1	0.00
Other Pac. Isl., not spec. (1)	8	0.03
Hispanic or Latino:	473	1.65
Central American:	57	0.20
Costa Rican	12	0.04
Guatemalan	15	0.05
Honduran	9	0.03
Nicaraguan	6	0.02
Panamanian	2	0.01
Salvadoran	6	0.02
Other Central American	7	0.02
Cuban	36	0.13
Dominican Republic	21	0.07
Mexican	45	0.16
Puerto Rican	106	0.37
South American:	78	0.27
Bolivian	10	0.03
Chilean	13	0.05
Colombian	17	0.06
Ecuadorian	10	0.03
Peruvian	18	0.06
Venezuelan	8	0.03
Other South American	2	0.01
Other Hispanic or Latino	130	0.45
Hungarian	119	0.42
Icelander	16	0.06
Iranian	16	0.06
Irish	10,680	37.36
Italian	4,906	17.16
Latvian	15	0.05
Lithuanian	568	1.99
Northern European	16	0.06
Norwegian	183	0.64
Polish	945	3.31
Portuguese	401	1.40
Romanian	37	0.13
Russian	400	1.40
Scandinavian	14	0.05
Scotch-Irish	555	1.94
Scottish	595	2.08
Slavic	22	0.08
Swedish	570	1.99
Swiss	46	0.16
Turkish	26	0.09
Ukrainian	136	0.48
United States or American	1,370	4.79
Welsh	47	0.16
West Indian, excl. Hispanic:	211	0.74
Haitian	72	0.25
Jamaican	81	0.28
Trinidadian and Tobagonian	30	0.10
West Indian	28	0.10
White:	26,164	91.52
Not Hispanic (25,606)	25,862	90.47
Hispanic (267)	302	1.06
Yugoslavian	41	0.14

Oxford

Place Type: Town
County: Worcester
Population: 13,352

Ancestry/Race	Number	%
African American/Black:	152	1.14
Not Hispanic (105)	139	1.04
Hispanic (11)	13	0.10
African, sub-Saharan:	12	0.09
Other sub-Saharan African	12	0.09
Am. Ind. or Alaska Nat., not spec.	23	0.17
Albanian	63	0.47
American Indian tribes, specified:	56	0.42
Blackfeet (4)	8	0.06
Cherokee (3)	9	0.07
Choctaw	3	0.02
Comanche	1	0.01
Cree	1	0.01
Iroquois (1)	1	0.01
Lumbee	1	0.01
Shoshone	1	0.01
Sioux	4	0.03
Yaqui (1)	1	0.01
All other tribes (20)	26	0.19
Arab:	79	0.59
Lebanese	79	0.59
Armenian	112	0.84
Asian:	140	1.05
Cambodian (3)	4	0.03
Chinese, ex. Taiwanese (11)	15	0.11
Filipino (6)	14	0.10
Indian (49)	56	0.42
Japanese (4)	5	0.04
Korean (7)	9	0.07
Laotian (4)	4	0.03
Thai (3)	5	0.04
Vietnamese (23)	24	0.18
Other Asian, not specified (2)	4	0.03
Austrian	8	0.06
British	12	0.09
Canadian	78	0.58
Czechoslovakian	28	0.21
Danish	31	0.23
Dutch	134	1.00
English	1,945	14.57
European	9	0.07
Finnish	82	0.61
French, except Basque	3,195	23.93
French Canadian	976	7.31
German	946	7.09
Greek	193	1.45
Hawaii Native/Pacific Islander:	3	0.02
Polynesian: (2)	2	0.01
Native Hawaiian (2)	2	0.01
Other Pac. Isl., not spec. (1)	1	0.01
Hispanic or Latino:	263	1.97
Central American:	9	0.07
Costa Rican	6	0.04
Guatemalan	3	0.02
Cuban	13	0.10

Notes: 1. Figures in the "Number" column do not add up to the total population due to: a) Ancestry/Race overlap — e.g. persons can report being both White and Irish, b) persons of Hispanic origin can report being any race, c) persons reporting two ancestries are counted in both categories. 2. Numbers in parentheses indicate the number of persons reporting this ancestry/race alone, not in combination with any other ancestry/race. 3. Refer to the Explanation of Data in the front of the book for more detailed information.

Ancestry/Race	Number	%
Dominican Republic	5	0.04
Mexican	21	0.16
Puerto Rican	162	1.21
South American:	16	0.12
Chilean	4	0.03
Colombian	8	0.06
Peruvian	2	0.01
Venezuelan	2	0.01
Other Hispanic or Latino	37	0.28
Irish	2,943	22.04
Italian	1,691	12.66
Lithuanian	268	2.01
Norwegian	73	0.55
Polish	1,391	10.42
Portuguese	84	0.63
Romanian	10	0.07
Russian	101	0.76
Scandinavian	11	0.08
Scotch-Irish	130	0.97
Scottish	342	2.56
Slavic	12	0.09
Slovak	71	0.53
Swedish	1,069	8.01
Turkish	33	0.25
Ukrainian	20	0.15
United States or American	582	4.36
Welsh	15	0.11
West Indian, excl. Hispanic:	14	0.10
Haitian	14	0.10
White:	13,036	97.63
Not Hispanic (12,719)	12,825	96.05
Hispanic (182)	211	1.58

Palmer

Place Type: Town
County: Hampden
Population: 12,497

Ancestry/Race	Number	%
African American/Black:	123	0.98
Not Hispanic (89)	115	0.92
Hispanic (5)	8	0.06
African, sub-Saharan:	66	0.53
African	66	0.53
Am. Ind. or Alaska Nat., not spec.	40	0.32
American Indian tribes, specified:	49	0.39
Blackfeet	7	0.06
Cherokee (1)	3	0.02
Cree (2)	3	0.02
Delaware (1)	1	0.01
Iroquois (4)	8	0.06
Latin American Indians (2)	7	0.06
Pueblo	1	0.01
All other tribes (9)	19	0.15
Arab:	22	0.18
Lebanese	12	0.10
Other Arab	10	0.08
Armenian	27	0.22
Asian:	108	0.86
Chinese, ex. Taiwanese (38)	47	0.38
Filipino (7)	10	0.08
Indian (15)	15	0.12
Japanese (2)	8	0.06
Korean (4)	7	0.06
Laotian	3	0.02
Pakistani	8	0.06
Thai	3	0.02
Vietnamese (1)	1	0.01
Other Asian, not specified	6	0.05
Austrian	30	0.24
Belgian	6	0.05
British	31	0.25
Canadian	155	1.24
Czech	6	0.05
Czechoslovakian	9	0.07
Danish	78	0.62
Dutch	68	0.54
English	1,080	8.64
European	13	0.10
Finnish	26	0.21
French, except Basque	3,043	24.35
French Canadian	1,235	9.88
German	576	4.61
Greek	128	1.02
Hawaii Native/Pacific Islander:	7	0.06
Polynesian:	7	0.06
Native Hawaiian	6	0.05
Samoan	1	0.01
Hispanic or Latino:	154	1.23
Central American:	1	0.01
Honduran	1	0.01
Cuban	8	0.06
Dominican Republic	3	0.02
Mexican	15	0.12
Puerto Rican	96	0.77
South American:	8	0.06
Colombian	3	0.02
Ecuadorian	5	0.04
Other Hispanic or Latino	23	0.18
Hungarian	13	0.10
Iranian	9	0.07
Irish	2,365	18.92
Italian	1,190	9.52
Latvian	17	0.14
Lithuanian	136	1.09
Norwegian	59	0.47
Polish	3,132	25.06
Portuguese	231	1.85
Russian	140	1.12
Scandinavian	35	0.28
Scotch-Irish	177	1.42
Scottish	451	3.61
Swedish	159	1.27
Swiss	55	0.44
Turkish	7	0.06
Ukrainian	42	0.34
United States or American	373	2.98
Welsh	23	0.18
White:	12,228	97.85
Not Hispanic (12,024)	12,138	97.13
Hispanic (76)	90	0.72

Peabody

Place Type: City
County: Essex
Population: 48,129

Ancestry/Race	Number	%
African American/Black:	623	1.29
Not Hispanic (396)	513	1.07
Hispanic (70)	110	0.23
African, sub-Saharan:	71	0.15
African	28	0.06
Cape Verdean	35	0.07
South African	8	0.02
Alaska Native tribes, specified:	1	0.00
Eskimo (1)	1	0.00
Am. Ind. or Alaska Nat., not spec.	89	0.18
Albanian	214	0.44
American Indian tribes, specified:	61	0.13
Apache	1	0.00
Blackfeet	3	0.01
Cherokee (3)	9	0.02
Chippewa	2	0.00
Choctaw	2	0.00
Creek	4	0.01
Iroquois (4)	6	0.01
Latin American Indians (4)	9	0.02
Pueblo	1	0.00
Seminole (1)	1	0.00
Sioux	1	0.00
All other tribes (5)	22	0.05
American Indian tribes, not spec.	16	0.03
Arab:	176	0.37
Arab/Arabic	40	0.08
Jordanian	14	0.03
Lebanese	103	0.21
Syrian	11	0.02
Other Arab	8	0.02
Armenian	193	0.40
Asian:	785	1.63
Cambodian (24)	36	0.07
Chinese, ex. Taiwanese (178)	214	0.44
Filipino (39)	49	0.10
Indian (119)	131	0.27
Indonesian (2)	5	0.01
Japanese (30)	41	0.09
Korean (102)	119	0.25
Laotian (7)	7	0.01
Malaysian (1)	2	0.00
Pakistani (1)	1	0.00
Sri Lankan (4)	4	0.01
Taiwanese (8)	8	0.02
Thai (7)	11	0.02
Vietnamese (128)	134	0.28
Other Asian, specified (1)	1	0.00
Other Asian, not specified (6)	22	0.05
Assyrian/Chaldean/Syriac	7	0.01
Austrian	72	0.15
Brazilian	270	0.56
British	122	0.25
Canadian	514	1.07
Celtic	11	0.02
Czech	25	0.05
Czechoslovakian	14	0.03
Danish	43	0.09
Dutch	239	0.50
Eastern European	50	0.10
English	4,762	9.89
European	163	0.34
Finnish	179	0.37
French, except Basque	3,323	6.90
French Canadian	2,153	4.47
German	1,450	3.01
Greek	2,391	4.97
Hawaii Native/Pacific Islander:	60	0.12
Micronesian: (1)	1	0.00
Guamanian/Chamorro (1)	1	0.00
Polynesian: (5)	16	0.03
Native Hawaiian (1)	10	0.02
Samoan (4)	6	0.01
Other Pac. Isl., not spec. (1)	43	0.09
Hispanic or Latino:	1,651	3.43
Central American:	71	0.15
Costa Rican	21	0.04
Guatemalan	16	0.03
Honduran	8	0.02
Panamanian	5	0.01
Salvadoran	19	0.04
Other Central American	2	0.00
Cuban	38	0.08
Dominican Republic	639	1.33
Mexican	70	0.15
Puerto Rican	280	0.58
South American:	68	0.14
Argentinean	6	0.01
Chilean	10	0.02
Colombian	18	0.04
Ecuadorian	10	0.02
Paraguayan	1	0.00
Peruvian	14	0.03
Venezuelan	7	0.01
Other South American	2	0.00
Other Hispanic or Latino	485	1.01
Hungarian	114	0.24
Iranian	40	0.08
Irish	11,807	24.53
Italian	10,283	21.37
Latvian	21	0.04
Lithuanian	284	0.59
Luxemburger	11	0.02
Macedonian	9	0.02
Maltese	7	0.01
Norwegian	163	0.34
Polish	2,668	5.54
Portuguese	3,816	7.93
Romanian	40	0.08
Russian	1,178	2.45

Notes: 1. Figures in the "Number" column do not add up to the total population due to: a) Ancestry/Race overlap — e.g. persons can report being both White and Irish, b) persons of Hispanic origin can report being any race, c) persons reporting two ancestries are counted in both categories. 2. Numbers in parentheses indicate the number of persons reporting this ancestry/race alone, not in combination with any other ancestry/race. 3. Refer to the Explanation of Data in the front of the book for more detailed information.

Ancestry/Race	Number	%
Scandinavian	25	0.05
Scotch-Irish	473	0.98
Scottish	1,066	2.21
Slovak	15	0.03
Swedish	604	1.25
Swiss	41	0.09
Turkish	26	0.05
Ukrainian	260	0.54
United States or American	2,248	4.67
Welsh	98	0.20
West Indian, excl. Hispanic:	86	0.18
Belizean	13	0.03
Bermudan	6	0.01
British West Indian	1	0.00
Haitian	49	0.10
Jamaican	17	0.04
White:	45,963	95.50
Not Hispanic (44,466)	45,154	93.82
Hispanic (738)	809	1.68
Yugoslavian	14	0.03

Pembroke

Place Type: Town
County: Plymouth
Population: 16,927

Ancestry/Race	Number	%
Acadian/Cajun	2	0.01
African American/Black:	114	0.67
Not Hispanic (82)	110	0.65
Hispanic (3)	4	0.02
African, sub-Saharan:	58	0.34
Cape Verdean	58	0.34
Am. Ind. or Alaska Nat., not spec.	17	0.10
Albanian	7	0.04
American Indian tribes, specified:	23	0.14
Blackfeet	1	0.01
Cherokee (1)	4	0.02
Creek	1	0.01
Iroquois (1)	1	0.01
Osage	1	0.01
Sioux	2	0.01
All other tribes (3)	13	0.08
American Indian tribes, not spec.	1	0.01
Arab:	46	0.27
Lebanese	33	0.19
Syrian	13	0.08
Armenian	39	0.23
Asian:	129	0.76
Chinese, ex. Taiwanese (24)	31	0.18
Filipino (4)	11	0.06
Indian (19)	29	0.17
Japanese (3)	4	0.02
Korean (5)	10	0.06
Thai (3)	3	0.02
Vietnamese (23)	35	0.21
Other Asian, specified	1	0.01
Other Asian, not specified (4)	5	0.03
Australian	8	0.05
Austrian	14	0.08
Belgian	20	0.12
British	17	0.10
Canadian	302	1.78
Celtic	15	0.09
Czechoslovakian	20	0.12
Danish	32	0.19
Dutch	153	0.90
Eastern European	12	0.07
English	2,522	14.90
Estonian	15	0.09
European	28	0.17
Finnish	173	1.02
French, except Basque	897	5.30
French Canadian	641	3.79
German	1,146	6.77
Greek	61	0.36
Hawaii Native/Pacific Islander:	10	0.06
Micronesian: (1)	2	0.01
Guamanian/Chamorro (1)	2	0.01
Polynesian:	5	0.03
Native Hawaiian	2	0.01
Samoan	3	0.02
Other Pac. Isl., not spec. (1)	3	0.02
Hispanic or Latino:	90	0.53
Central American:	3	0.02
Costa Rican	1	0.01
Honduran	2	0.01
Cuban	5	0.03
Dominican Republic	2	0.01
Mexican	27	0.16
Puerto Rican	19	0.11
South American:	16	0.09
Argentinean	1	0.01
Colombian	1	0.01
Ecuadorian	4	0.02
Paraguayan	2	0.01
Peruvian	1	0.01
Uruguayan	1	0.01
Venezuelan	4	0.02
Other South American	2	0.01
Other Hispanic or Latino	18	0.11
Hungarian	12	0.07
Irish	6,971	41.18
Italian	3,020	17.84
Latvian	21	0.12
Lithuanian	231	1.36
Norwegian	122	0.72
Polish	537	3.17
Portuguese	315	1.86
Romanian	10	0.06
Russian	184	1.09
Scotch-Irish	387	2.29
Scottish	703	4.15
Slovak	29	0.17
Swedish	569	3.36
Swiss	30	0.18
Ukrainian	74	0.44
United States or American	678	4.01
Welsh	99	0.58
West Indian, excl. Hispanic:	11	0.06
West Indian	11	0.06
White:	16,686	98.58
Not Hispanic (16,514)	16,626	98.22
Hispanic (55)	60	0.35
Yugoslavian	6	0.04

Pepperell

Place Type: Town
County: Middlesex
Population: 11,142

Ancestry/Race	Number	%
African American/Black:	70	0.63
Not Hispanic (50)	68	0.61
Hispanic (2)	2	0.02
Alaska Native tribes, specified:	1	0.01
Alaska Athabascan	1	0.01
Am. Ind. or Alaska Nat., not spec.	26	0.23
Albanian	7	0.06
American Indian tribes, specified:	47	0.42
Blackfeet	2	0.02
Cherokee (1)	4	0.04
Cheyenne (1)	1	0.01
Choctaw	1	0.01
Cree	2	0.02
Iroquois (1)	6	0.05
Latin American Indians (1)	1	0.01
Navajo	4	0.04
Paiute	1	0.01
Pueblo (1)	1	0.01
Seminole (1)	1	0.01
Sioux (1)	5	0.04
All other tribes (3)	18	0.16
American Indian tribes, not spec.	2	0.02
Armenian	37	0.33
Asian:	123	1.10
Cambodian (5)	5	0.04
Chinese, ex. Taiwanese (13)	20	0.18
Filipino (6)	15	0.13
Indian (6)	10	0.09
Japanese (13)	26	0.23
Korean (21)	25	0.22
Laotian (1)	1	0.01
Pakistani (2)	2	0.02
Thai (4)	9	0.08
Vietnamese (3)	6	0.05
Other Asian, not specified (3)	4	0.04
British	30	0.27
Canadian	156	1.40
Czech	8	0.07
Czechoslovakian	7	0.06
Danish	44	0.39
Dutch	109	0.98
Eastern European	12	0.11
English	2,128	19.10
European	96	0.86
Finnish	98	0.88
French, except Basque	1,259	11.30
French Canadian	639	5.74
German	944	8.47
Greek	91	0.82
Hawaii Native/Pacific Islander:	4	0.04
Polynesian:	3	0.03
Native Hawaiian	3	0.03
Other Pac. Isl., not spec.	1	0.01
Hispanic or Latino:	114	1.02
Central American:	5	0.04
Honduran	2	0.02
Salvadoran	2	0.02
Other Central American	1	0.01
Cuban	8	0.07
Dominican Republic	3	0.03
Mexican	18	0.16
Puerto Rican	38	0.34
South American:	16	0.14
Bolivian	5	0.04
Colombian	6	0.05
Venezuelan	1	0.01
Other South American	4	0.04
Other Hispanic or Latino	26	0.23
Hungarian	88	0.79
Iranian	32	0.29
Irish	2,674	24.00
Italian	1,230	11.04
Latvian	22	0.20
Lithuanian	85	0.76
Norwegian	168	1.51
Polish	431	3.87
Portuguese	276	2.48
Romanian	3	0.03
Russian	121	1.09
Scandinavian	13	0.12
Scotch-Irish	289	2.59
Scottish	415	3.72
Slovak	13	0.12
Swedish	227	2.04
Swiss	21	0.19
Ukrainian	74	0.66
United States or American	799	7.17
Welsh	60	0.54
West Indian, excl. Hispanic:	20	0.18
Jamaican	20	0.18
White:	10,954	98.31
Not Hispanic (10,763)	10,881	97.66
Hispanic (63)	73	0.66
Yugoslavian	34	0.31

Pittsfield

Place Type: City
County: Berkshire
Population: 45,793

Ancestry/Race	Number	%
Acadian/Cajun	6	0.01
African American/Black:	2,105	4.60
Not Hispanic (1,592)	1,970	4.30
Hispanic (82)	135	0.29

Notes: 1. Figures in the "Number" column do not add up to the total population due to: a) Ancestry/Race overlap — e.g. persons can report being both White and Irish, b) persons of Hispanic origin can report being any race, c) persons reporting two ancestries are counted in both categories. 2. Numbers in parentheses indicate the number of persons reporting this ancestry/race alone, not in combination with any other ancestry/race. 3. Refer to the Explanation of Data in the front of the book for more detailed information.

Ancestry/Race	Number	%
African, sub-Saharan:	197	0.43
African	136	0.30
Cape Verdean	24	0.05
Ghanian	30	0.07
Sierra Leonean	7	0.02
Am. Ind. or Alaska Nat., not spec.	106	0.23
American Indian tribes, specified:	139	0.30
Apache (2)	2	0.00
Blackfeet (3)	16	0.03
Cherokee (3)	25	0.05
Chippewa	1	0.00
Choctaw (1)	9	0.02
Cree	2	0.00
Iroquois (3)	23	0.05
Latin American Indians (4)	5	0.01
Navajo (1)	1	0.00
Ottawa	1	0.00
Pima (2)	2	0.00
Pueblo	4	0.01
Seminole	1	0.00
Sioux (1)	11	0.02
All other tribes (13)	36	0.08
American Indian tribes, not spec.	16	0.03
Arab:	395	0.86
Arab/Arabic	6	0.01
Egyptian	4	0.01
Lebanese	356	0.78
Moroccan	29	0.06
Armenian	25	0.05
Asian:	666	1.45
Cambodian (12)	18	0.04
Chinese, ex. Taiwanese (72)	103	0.22
Filipino (21)	40	0.09
Indian (233)	252	0.55
Indonesian (5)	8	0.02
Japanese (33)	39	0.09
Korean (38)	45	0.10
Malaysian (3)	5	0.01
Pakistani (6)	6	0.01
Sri Lankan (5)	5	0.01
Taiwanese (4)	8	0.02
Thai (6)	16	0.03
Vietnamese (66)	73	0.16
Other Asian, specified	9	0.02
Other Asian, not specified (17)	39	0.09
Austrian	117	0.26
Basque	10	0.02
Belgian	23	0.05
Brazilian	31	0.07
British	112	0.24
Canadian	112	0.24
Celtic	7	0.02
Croatian	7	0.02
Czech	95	0.21
Czechoslovakian	33	0.07
Danish	87	0.19
Dutch	807	1.76
Eastern European	33	0.07
English	5,155	11.26
European	166	0.36
Finnish	37	0.08
French, except Basque	6,083	13.28
French Canadian	2,025	4.42
German	4,316	9.43
Greek	389	0.85
Hawaii Native/Pacific Islander:	38	0.08
Melanesian: (1)	1	0.00
Fijian (1)	1	0.00
Micronesian: (2)	2	0.00
Guamanian/Chamorro (2)	2	0.00
Polynesian: (5)	14	0.03
Native Hawaiian	3	0.01
Samoan (5)	11	0.02
Other Pac. Isl., specified	7	0.02
Other Pac. Isl., not spec. (12)	14	0.03
Hispanic or Latino:	934	2.04
Central American:	58	0.13
Guatemalan	13	0.03
Honduran	5	0.01
Nicaraguan	2	0.00
Panamanian	2	0.00
Salvadoran	35	0.08
Other Central American	1	0.00
Cuban	17	0.04
Dominican Republic	6	0.01
Mexican	115	0.25
Puerto Rican	421	0.92
South American:	93	0.20
Argentinean	5	0.01
Bolivian	2	0.00
Chilean	3	0.01
Colombian	23	0.05
Ecuadorian	40	0.09
Peruvian	14	0.03
Venezuelan	3	0.01
Other South American	3	0.01
Other Hispanic or Latino	224	0.49
Hungarian	134	0.29
Iranian	17	0.04
Irish	10,697	23.36
Israeli	11	0.02
Italian	8,979	19.61
Lithuanian	167	0.36
Maltese	5	0.01
Norwegian	174	0.38
Pennsylvania German	14	0.03
Polish	3,597	7.85
Portuguese	350	0.76
Romanian	6	0.01
Russian	495	1.08
Scandinavian	11	0.02
Scotch-Irish	632	1.38
Scottish	1,004	2.19
Slavic	33	0.07
Slovak	15	0.03
Swedish	281	0.61
Swiss	117	0.26
Ukrainian	357	0.78
United States or American	1,942	4.24
Welsh	193	0.42
West Indian, excl. Hispanic:	143	0.31
Barbadian	16	0.03
Haitian	20	0.04
Jamaican	107	0.23
White:	43,059	94.03
Not Hispanic (41,951)	42,524	92.86
Hispanic (444)	535	1.17

Plymouth

Place Type: Town
County: Plymouth
Population: 51,701

Ancestry/Race	Number	%
African American/Black:	1,294	2.50
Not Hispanic (924)	1,197	2.32
Hispanic (64)	97	0.19
African, sub-Saharan:	476	0.92
African	65	0.13
Cape Verdean	389	0.75
Liberian	11	0.02
Nigerian	11	0.02
Alaska Native tribes, specified:	1	0.00
Aleut	1	0.00
Am. Ind. or Alaska Nat., not spec.	131	0.25
Albanian	8	0.02
Alsatian	10	0.02
American Indian tribes, specified:	238	0.46
Apache (3)	4	0.01
Blackfeet (6)	14	0.03
Cherokee (4)	42	0.08
Chippewa (4)	5	0.01
Choctaw (1)	6	0.01
Comanche (1)	1	0.00
Cree	2	0.00
Creek (1)	1	0.00
Delaware (1)	1	0.00
Iroquois (7)	16	0.03
Latin American Indians (6)	10	0.02
Navajo (2)	2	0.00
Ottawa (1)	1	0.00
Pueblo (1)	1	0.00
Seminole (4)	7	0.01
Shoshone (2)	2	0.00
Sioux (2)	4	0.01
Ute	3	0.01
All other tribes (50)	116	0.22
American Indian tribes, not spec.	9	0.02
Arab:	198	0.38
Egyptian	26	0.05
Lebanese	141	0.27
Syrian	8	0.02
Other Arab	23	0.04
Armenian	81	0.16
Asian:	421	0.81
Cambodian (5)	5	0.01
Chinese, ex. Taiwanese (58)	75	0.15
Filipino (29)	60	0.12
Indian (27)	42	0.08
Indonesian (1)	1	0.00
Japanese (13)	26	0.05
Korean (60)	73	0.14
Laotian (32)	34	0.07
Pakistani (1)	10	0.02
Taiwanese (1)	3	0.01
Thai (3)	6	0.01
Vietnamese (41)	48	0.09
Other Asian, specified (1)	5	0.01
Other Asian, not specified (16)	33	0.06
Assyrian/Chaldean/Syriac	11	0.02
Austrian	55	0.11
Basque	7	0.01
Belgian	66	0.13
Brazilian	70	0.14
British	170	0.33
Bulgarian	15	0.03
Canadian	488	0.94
Celtic	6	0.01
Czech	24	0.05
Czechoslovakian	38	0.07
Danish	78	0.15
Dutch	480	0.93
Eastern European	27	0.05
English	8,617	16.67
Estonian	47	0.09
European	294	0.57
Finnish	525	1.02
French, except Basque	3,090	5.98
French Canadian	1,659	3.21
German	3,791	7.33
Greek	502	0.97
Hawaii Native/Pacific Islander:	52	0.10
Micronesian: (5)	12	0.02
Guamanian/Chamorro (2)	9	0.02
Other Micronesian (3)	3	0.01
Polynesian: (5)	12	0.02
Native Hawaiian (5)	10	0.02
Samoan	2	0.00
Other Pac. Isl., not spec. (10)	28	0.05
Hispanic or Latino:	870	1.68
Central American:	40	0.08
Costa Rican	6	0.01
Guatemalan	13	0.03
Honduran	4	0.01
Nicaraguan	2	0.00
Panamanian	2	0.00
Salvadoran	13	0.03
Cuban	20	0.04
Dominican Republic	98	0.19
Mexican	126	0.24
Puerto Rican	323	0.62
South American:	71	0.14
Argentinean	3	0.01
Bolivian	2	0.00
Chilean	2	0.00
Colombian	38	0.07
Ecuadorian	3	0.01
Paraguayan	3	0.01
Peruvian	7	0.01

Notes: 1. Figures in the "Number" column do not add up to the total population due to: a) Ancestry/Race overlap — e.g. persons can report being both White and Irish, b) persons of Hispanic origin can report being any race, c) persons reporting two ancestries are counted in both categories. 2. Numbers in parentheses indicate the number of persons reporting this ancestry/race alone, not in combination with any other ancestry/race. 3. Refer to the Explanation of Data in the front of the book for more detailed information.

Venezuelan	5	0.01
Other South American	8	0.02
Other Hispanic or Latino	192	0.37
Hungarian	191	0.37
Icelander	16	0.03
Iranian	41	0.08
Irish	17,701	34.24
Israeli	7	0.01
Italian	9,337	18.06
Latvian	74	0.14
Lithuanian	463	0.90
Macedonian	7	0.01
Maltese	7	0.01
Northern European	7	0.01
Norwegian	401	0.78
Polish	1,470	2.84
Portuguese	3,239	6.26
Romanian	18	0.03
Russian	383	0.74
Scandinavian	30	0.06
Scotch-Irish	1,409	2.73
Scottish	1,911	3.70
Serbian	38	0.07
Slavic	8	0.02
Slovak	10	0.02
Swedish	1,350	2.61
Swiss	71	0.14
Turkish	9	0.02
Ukrainian	128	0.25
United States or American	1,859	3.60
Welsh	175	0.34
West Indian, excl. Hispanic:	175	0.34
Dutch West Indian	6	0.01
Haitian	88	0.17
Jamaican	66	0.13
West Indian	15	0.03
White:	49,618	95.97
Not Hispanic (48,599)	49,114	95.00
Hispanic (423)	504	0.97
Yugoslavian	16	0.03

Quincy

Place Type: City
County: Norfolk
Population: 88,025

Ancestry/Race	Number	%
African American/Black:	2,322	2.64
Not Hispanic (1,846)	2,187	2.48
Hispanic (101)	135	0.15
African, sub-Saharan:	481	0.55
African	130	0.15
Cape Verdean	113	0.13
Ethiopian	11	0.01
Ghanian	9	0.01
Kenyan	54	0.06
Nigerian	22	0.02
Senegalese	8	0.01
Sierra Leonean	33	0.04
Somalian	8	0.01
South African	10	0.01
Other sub-Saharan African	83	0.09
Alaska Native tribes, specified:	2	0.00
Eskimo (2)	2	0.00
Am. Ind. or Alaska Nat., not spec.	156	0.18
Albanian	402	0.46
American Indian tribes, specified:	197	0.22
Apache (3)	12	0.01
Blackfeet (2)	13	0.01
Cherokee (8)	39	0.04
Chippewa (2)	2	0.00
Choctaw	1	0.00
Creek (1)	5	0.01
Crow	1	0.00
Delaware (1)	1	0.00
Iroquois (2)	10	0.01
Latin American Indians (9)	19	0.02
Lumbee (1)	1	0.00
Ottawa (1)	1	0.00
Puget Sound Salish (1)	1	0.00
Seminole	1	0.00
Shoshone (1)	1	0.00
Sioux (3)	4	0.00
All other tribes (42)	85	0.10
American Indian tribes, not spec.	23	0.03
Arab:	1,388	1.58
Arab/Arabic	130	0.15
Egyptian	39	0.04
Iraqi	23	0.03
Jordanian	26	0.03
Lebanese	821	0.93
Moroccan	52	0.06
Palestinian	26	0.03
Syrian	162	0.18
Other Arab	109	0.12
Armenian	147	0.17
Asian:	14,195	16.13
Bangladeshi (3)	3	0.00
Cambodian (69)	87	0.10
Chinese, ex. Taiwanese (9,161)	9,511	10.80
Filipino (517)	576	0.65
Hmong (15)	17	0.02
Indian (1,127)	1,202	1.37
Indonesian (21)	21	0.02
Japanese (146)	180	0.20
Korean (241)	254	0.29
Laotian (12)	14	0.02
Malaysian (15)	18	0.02
Pakistani (51)	71	0.08
Sri Lankan (13)	14	0.02
Taiwanese (23)	31	0.04
Thai (102)	118	0.13
Vietnamese (1,679)	1,850	2.10
Other Asian, specified (24)	34	0.04
Other Asian, not specified (97)	194	0.22
Australian	12	0.01
Austrian	149	0.17
Basque	5	0.01
Belgian	88	0.10
Brazilian	375	0.43
British	218	0.25
Bulgarian	30	0.03
Canadian	1,191	1.35
Celtic	30	0.03
Croatian	75	0.09
Czech	108	0.12
Czechoslovakian	48	0.05
Danish	231	0.26
Dutch	407	0.46
Eastern European	35	0.04
English	6,604	7.50
European	117	0.13
Finnish	513	0.58
French, except Basque	2,924	3.32
French Canadian	2,264	2.57
German	4,202	4.77
Greek	919	1.04
Guyanese	12	0.01
Hawaii Native/Pacific Islander:	72	0.08
Micronesian: (5)	6	0.01
Guamanian/Chamorro (5)	5	0.01
Other Micronesian	1	0.00
Polynesian: (7)	22	0.02
Native Hawaiian (4)	13	0.01
Samoan (1)	6	0.01
Tongan (2)	2	0.00
Other Polynesian	1	0.00
Other Pac. Isl., specified	5	0.01
Other Pac. Isl., not spec. (8)	39	0.04
Hispanic or Latino:	1,835	2.08
Central American:	115	0.13
Costa Rican	5	0.01
Guatemalan	59	0.07
Honduran	20	0.02
Nicaraguan	5	0.01
Panamanian	7	0.01
Salvadoran	13	0.01
Other Central American	6	0.01
Cuban	111	0.13
Dominican Republic	79	0.09
Mexican	163	0.19
Puerto Rican	548	0.62
South American:	293	0.33
Argentinean	29	0.03
Bolivian	1	0.00
Chilean	52	0.06
Colombian	100	0.11
Ecuadorian	18	0.02
Paraguayan	1	0.00
Peruvian	57	0.06
Uruguayan	6	0.01
Venezuelan	15	0.02
Other South American	14	0.02
Other Hispanic or Latino	526	0.60
Hungarian	138	0.16
Icelander	30	0.03
Iranian	29	0.03
Irish	30,036	34.12
Italian	11,919	13.54
Latvian	87	0.10
Lithuanian	630	0.72
Macedonian	6	0.01
Northern European	31	0.04
Norwegian	506	0.57
Pennsylvania German	9	0.01
Polish	2,581	2.93
Portuguese	777	0.88
Romanian	87	0.10
Russian	796	0.90
Scandinavian	26	0.03
Scotch-Irish	1,865	2.12
Scottish	1,947	2.21
Serbian	6	0.01
Slavic	18	0.02
Slovak	30	0.03
Slovene	21	0.02
Swedish	1,522	1.73
Swiss	69	0.08
Turkish	110	0.12
Ukrainian	211	0.24
United States or American	2,437	2.77
Welsh	242	0.27
West Indian, excl. Hispanic:	345	0.39
Barbadian	33	0.04
British West Indian	7	0.01
Haitian	128	0.15
Jamaican	116	0.13
Trinidadian and Tobagonian	8	0.01
U.S. Virgin Islander	10	0.01
West Indian	43	0.05
White:	71,325	81.03
Not Hispanic (68,980)	70,123	79.66
Hispanic (1,086)	1,202	1.37
Yugoslavian	74	0.08

Randolph

Place Type: Census Designated Place
County: Norfolk
Population: 30,963

Ancestry/Race	Number	%
African American/Black:	7,171	23.16
Not Hispanic (6,357)	6,997	22.60
Hispanic (99)	174	0.56
African, sub-Saharan:	1,214	3.92
African	362	1.17
Cape Verdean	451	1.45
Ethiopian	88	0.28
Kenyan	12	0.04
Liberian	53	0.17
Nigerian	201	0.65
Other sub-Saharan African	47	0.15
Am. Ind. or Alaska Nat., not spec.	118	0.38
Albanian	6	0.02
American Indian tribes, specified:	110	0.36
Apache	2	0.01
Blackfeet (1)	13	0.04
Cherokee (4)	37	0.12

Notes: 1. Figures in the "Number" column do not add up to the total population due to: a) Ancestry/Race overlap — e.g. persons can report being both White and Irish, b) persons of Hispanic origin can report being any race, c) persons reporting two ancestries are counted in both categories. 2. Numbers in parentheses indicate the number of persons reporting this ancestry/race alone, not in combination with any other ancestry/race. 3. Refer to the Explanation of Data in the front of the book for more detailed information.

Creek	1	0.00
Houma (1)	1	0.00
Iroquois (6)	6	0.02
Latin American Indians (3)	7	0.02
Navajo (1)	1	0.00
Potawatomi	2	0.01
Shoshone	1	0.00
Sioux	6	0.02
All other tribes (13)	33	0.11
American Indian tribes, not spec.	27	0.09
Arab:	237	0.76
Lebanese	142	0.46
Palestinian	6	0.02
Syrian	71	0.23
Other Arab	18	0.06
Armenian	102	0.33
Asian:	3,399	10.98
Bangladeshi (6)	6	0.02
Cambodian (21)	31	0.10
Chinese, ex. Taiwanese (1,495)	1,592	5.14
Filipino (232)	267	0.86
Hmong (1)	1	0.00
Indian (439)	497	1.61
Indonesian	2	0.01
Japanese (12)	15	0.05
Korean (43)	57	0.18
Laotian (12)	12	0.04
Pakistani (32)	33	0.11
Sri Lankan (1)	2	0.01
Taiwanese (21)	27	0.09
Thai (14)	18	0.06
Vietnamese (718)	762	2.46
Other Asian, specified (10)	26	0.08
Other Asian, not specified (24)	51	0.16
Australian	21	0.07
Austrian	69	0.22
Belgian	8	0.03
Brazilian	24	0.08
British	135	0.44
Canadian	227	0.73
Croatian	23	0.07
Czech	9	0.03
Danish	15	0.05
Dutch	97	0.31
Eastern European	142	0.46
English	1,756	5.67
European	85	0.27
Finnish	103	0.33
French, except Basque	707	2.28
French Canadian	767	2.47
German	1,159	3.74
Greek	201	0.65
Hawaii Native/Pacific Islander:	58	0.19
Micronesian:	1	0.00
Guamanian/Chamorro	1	0.00
Polynesian: (2)	4	0.01
Native Hawaiian	2	0.01
Samoan (2)	2	0.01
Other Pac. Isl., specified	16	0.05
Other Pac. Isl., not spec. (9)	37	0.12
Hispanic or Latino:	1,006	3.25
Central American:	143	0.46
Costa Rican	6	0.02
Guatemalan	66	0.21
Honduran	23	0.07
Nicaraguan	4	0.01
Panamanian	26	0.08
Salvadoran	6	0.02
Other Central American	12	0.04
Cuban	32	0.10
Dominican Republic	82	0.26
Mexican	49	0.16
Puerto Rican	317	1.02
South American:	140	0.45
Argentinean	12	0.04
Bolivian	2	0.01
Chilean	7	0.02
Colombian	46	0.15
Ecuadorian	6	0.02
Peruvian	59	0.19
Venezuelan	2	0.01
Other South American	6	0.02
Other Hispanic or Latino	243	0.78
Hungarian	61	0.20
Iranian	20	0.06
Irish	6,664	21.50
Italian	3,566	11.50
Latvian	53	0.17
Lithuanian	211	0.68
Northern European	12	0.04
Norwegian	192	0.62
Pennsylvania German	7	0.02
Polish	776	2.50
Portuguese	326	1.05
Romanian	35	0.11
Russian	796	2.57
Scotch-Irish	315	1.02
Scottish	471	1.52
Slovak	17	0.05
Swedish	380	1.23
Swiss	31	0.10
Turkish	28	0.09
Ukrainian	35	0.11
United States or American	1,398	4.51
Welsh	44	0.14
West Indian, excl. Hispanic:	3,111	10.04
Barbadian	65	0.21
British West Indian	136	0.44
Haitian	2,060	6.65
Jamaican	515	1.66
Trinidadian and Tobagonian	87	0.28
West Indian	238	0.77
Other West Indian	10	0.03
White:	19,914	64.32
Not Hispanic (19,038)	19,433	62.76
Hispanic (417)	481	1.55
Yugoslavian	9	0.03

Raynham

Place Type: Town
County: Bristol
Population: 11,739

Ancestry/Race	Number	%
African American/Black:	150	1.28
Not Hispanic (119)	144	1.23
Hispanic (3)	6	0.05
African, sub-Saharan:	136	1.16
Cape Verdean	136	1.16
Am. Ind. or Alaska Nat., not spec.	15	0.13
Albanian	12	0.10
American Indian tribes, specified:	16	0.14
Blackfeet	1	0.01
Cherokee (2)	2	0.02
Iroquois (1)	1	0.01
All other tribes (4)	12	0.10
American Indian tribes, not spec.	2	0.02
Arab:	116	0.99
Lebanese	116	0.99
Armenian	19	0.16
Asian:	100	0.85
Cambodian	6	0.05
Chinese, ex. Taiwanese (18)	27	0.23
Filipino (6)	6	0.05
Indian (28)	29	0.25
Japanese (5)	5	0.04
Korean (12)	12	0.10
Thai (2)	7	0.06
Vietnamese (6)	6	0.05
Other Asian, not specified (2)	2	0.02
Austrian	33	0.28
Brazilian	26	0.22
British	48	0.41
Canadian	80	0.68
Danish	64	0.55
Dutch	51	0.43
Eastern European	10	0.09
English	1,735	14.78
Finnish	42	0.36
French, except Basque	1,227	10.45
French Canadian	564	4.80
German	685	5.84
Greek	118	1.01
Hawaii Native/Pacific Islander:	9	0.08
Micronesian:	3	0.03
Guamanian/Chamorro	3	0.03
Other Pac. Isl., not spec. (3)	6	0.05
Hispanic or Latino:	97	0.83
Central American:	3	0.03
Guatemalan	3	0.03
Cuban	13	0.11
Dominican Republic	3	0.03
Mexican	4	0.03
Puerto Rican	35	0.30
South American:	5	0.04
Peruvian	2	0.02
Venezuelan	3	0.03
Other Hispanic or Latino	34	0.29
Hungarian	18	0.15
Iranian	9	0.08
Irish	3,338	28.44
Italian	1,832	15.61
Latvian	30	0.26
Lithuanian	231	1.97
Norwegian	151	1.29
Polish	599	5.10
Portuguese	1,573	13.40
Russian	192	1.64
Scandinavian	25	0.21
Scotch-Irish	200	1.70
Scottish	296	2.52
Swedish	293	2.50
Swiss	20	0.17
Ukrainian	9	0.08
United States or American	575	4.90
Welsh	27	0.23
White:	11,431	97.38
Not Hispanic (11,271)	11,362	96.79
Hispanic (62)	69	0.59

Reading

Place Type: Census Designated Place
County: Middlesex
Population: 23,708

Ancestry/Race	Number	%
African American/Black:	135	0.57
Not Hispanic (81)	128	0.54
Hispanic (5)	7	0.03
African, sub-Saharan:	7	0.03
Nigerian	7	0.03
Am. Ind. or Alaska Nat., not spec.	17	0.07
Albanian	6	0.03
American Indian tribes, specified:	33	0.14
Blackfeet (1)	1	0.00
Cherokee	3	0.01
Creek	1	0.00
Iroquois (1)	1	0.00
Latin American Indians (2)	3	0.01
Osage	1	0.00
Sioux	3	0.01
All other tribes (7)	20	0.08
American Indian tribes, not spec.	4	0.02
Arab:	90	0.38
Lebanese	82	0.35
Syrian	8	0.03
Armenian	190	0.80
Asian:	599	2.53
Cambodian (1)	1	0.00
Chinese, ex. Taiwanese (203)	215	0.91
Filipino (9)	18	0.08
Indian (126)	140	0.59
Japanese (42)	58	0.24
Korean (75)	78	0.33
Pakistani (11)	14	0.06
Sri Lankan (15)	27	0.11
Taiwanese (5)	5	0.02
Thai (2)	4	0.02

Notes: 1. Figures in the "Number" column do not add up to the total population due to: a) Ancestry/Race overlap — e.g. persons can report being both White and Irish, b) persons of Hispanic origin can report being any race, c) persons reporting two ancestries are counted in both categories. 2. Numbers in parentheses indicate the number of persons reporting this ancestry/race alone, not in combination with any other ancestry/race. 3. Refer to the Explanation of Data in the front of the book for more detailed information.

Vietnamese (20)	23	0.10
Other Asian, not specified (5)	16	0.07
Austrian	122	0.51
Belgian	44	0.19
Brazilian	64	0.27
British	97	0.41
Bulgarian	6	0.03
Canadian	463	1.95
Croatian	19	0.08
Czech	61	0.26
Czechoslovakian	10	0.04
Danish	67	0.28
Dutch	139	0.59
Eastern European	41	0.17
English	3,886	16.39
Estonian	5	0.02
European	47	0.20
Finnish	28	0.12
French, except Basque	1,203	5.07
French Canadian	1,177	4.96
German	1,422	6.00
Greek	321	1.35
Hawaii Native/Pacific Islander:	8	0.03
Micronesian: (1)	1	0.00
Other Micronesian (1)	1	0.00
Polynesian: (5)	7	0.03
Native Hawaiian (2)	2	0.01
Samoan (3)	5	0.02
Hispanic or Latino:	200	0.84
Central American:	16	0.07
Costa Rican	3	0.01
Guatemalan	7	0.03
Honduran	4	0.02
Salvadoran	2	0.01
Cuban	15	0.06
Dominican Republic	9	0.04
Mexican	44	0.19
Puerto Rican	35	0.15
South American:	37	0.16
Argentinean	2	0.01
Bolivian	1	0.00
Chilean	1	0.00
Colombian	16	0.07
Ecuadorian	5	0.02
Paraguayan	1	0.00
Peruvian	4	0.02
Uruguayan	3	0.01
Venezuelan	2	0.01
Other South American	2	0.01
Other Hispanic or Latino	44	0.19
Hungarian	74	0.31
Iranian	34	0.14
Irish	7,776	32.80
Italian	5,986	25.25
Latvian	7	0.03
Lithuanian	198	0.84
Luxemburger	5	0.02
Northern European	15	0.06
Norwegian	179	0.76
Polish	737	3.11
Portuguese	265	1.12
Romanian	20	0.08
Russian	413	1.74
Scandinavian	19	0.08
Scotch-Irish	654	2.76
Scottish	828	3.49
Swedish	634	2.67
Swiss	34	0.14
Turkish	9	0.04
Ukrainian	40	0.17
United States or American	848	3.58
Welsh	103	0.43
West Indian, excl. Hispanic:	57	0.24
Barbadian	17	0.07
British West Indian	7	0.03
Haitian	33	0.14
White:	23,012	97.06
Not Hispanic (22,721)	22,854	96.40
Hispanic (150)	158	0.67
Yugoslavian	10	0.04

Rehoboth

Place Type: Town
County: Bristol
Population: 10,172

Ancestry/Race	Number	%
African American/Black:	47	0.46
Not Hispanic (36)	46	0.45
Hispanic	1	0.01
African, sub-Saharan:	6	0.06
Cape Verdean	6	0.06
Am. Ind. or Alaska Nat., not spec.	9	0.09
Albanian	35	0.34
American Indian tribes, specified:	41	0.40
Apache (1)	1	0.01
Blackfeet (2)	2	0.02
Cherokee (4)	11	0.11
Comanche	4	0.04
Cree (1)	1	0.01
Delaware	1	0.01
All other tribes (20)	21	0.21
American Indian tribes, not spec.	2	0.02
Arab:	78	0.77
Lebanese	43	0.42
Syrian	35	0.34
Armenian	74	0.73
Asian:	90	0.88
Cambodian (1)	3	0.03
Chinese, ex. Taiwanese (12)	22	0.22
Filipino (6)	10	0.10
Indian (12)	13	0.13
Japanese (1)	6	0.06
Korean (15)	23	0.23
Laotian (1)	1	0.01
Vietnamese (2)	4	0.04
Other Asian, not specified	8	0.08
Assyrian/Chaldean/Syriac	9	0.09
Austrian	9	0.09
Brazilian	6	0.06
British	52	0.51
Canadian	61	0.60
Czechoslovakian	40	0.39
Danish	28	0.28
Dutch	41	0.40
Eastern European	56	0.55
English	2,257	22.19
European	32	0.31
Finnish	41	0.40
French, except Basque	1,447	14.23
French Canadian	851	8.37
German	593	5.83
Greek	101	0.99
Hawaii Native/Pacific Islander:	5	0.05
Micronesian: (1)	1	0.01
Guamanian/Chamorro (1)	1	0.01
Other Pac. Isl., not spec.	4	0.04
Hispanic or Latino:	51	0.50
Central American:	8	0.08
Guatemalan	8	0.08
Cuban	1	0.01
Dominican Republic	2	0.02
Mexican	6	0.06
Puerto Rican	18	0.18
South American:	5	0.05
Chilean	1	0.01
Colombian	3	0.03
Ecuadorian	1	0.01
Other Hispanic or Latino	11	0.11
Hungarian	28	0.28
Irish	2,292	22.53
Italian	1,197	11.77
Latvian	6	0.06
Lithuanian	50	0.49
Norwegian	44	0.43
Pennsylvania German	6	0.06
Polish	492	4.84
Portuguese	2,205	21.68
Romanian	25	0.25
Russian	37	0.36
Scandinavian	7	0.07
Scotch-Irish	87	0.86
Scottish	297	2.92
Slovene	6	0.06
Swedish	196	1.93
Swiss	32	0.31
Turkish	27	0.27
Ukrainian	8	0.08
United States or American	376	3.70
Welsh	24	0.24
White:	10,024	98.55
Not Hispanic (9,899)	9,983	98.14
Hispanic (39)	41	0.40
Yugoslavian	30	0.29

Revere

Place Type: City
County: Suffolk
Population: 47,283

Ancestry/Race	Number	%
African American/Black:	1,706	3.61
Not Hispanic (1,248)	1,540	3.26
Hispanic (116)	166	0.35
African, sub-Saharan:	347	0.73
African	146	0.31
Cape Verdean	9	0.02
Ethiopian	45	0.10
Nigerian	94	0.20
Somalian	46	0.10
Ugandan	7	0.01
Alaska Native tribes, specified:	2	0.00
Eskimo	1	0.00
Tlingit-Haida	1	0.00
Am. Ind. or Alaska Nat., not spec.	115	0.24
Albanian	158	0.33
American Indian tribes, specified:	145	0.31
Apache (1)	3	0.01
Blackfeet (1)	5	0.01
Cherokee (10)	25	0.05
Chickasaw	1	0.00
Chippewa (1)	9	0.02
Choctaw	3	0.01
Iroquois (5)	7	0.01
Latin American Indians (9)	13	0.03
Navajo (1)	8	0.02
Pueblo (1)	4	0.01
Seminole (3)	4	0.01
Sioux (1)	1	0.00
All other tribes (24)	62	0.13
American Indian tribes, not spec.	7	0.01
Arab:	791	1.67
Arab/Arabic	185	0.39
Egyptian	147	0.31
Lebanese	137	0.29
Moroccan	289	0.61
Syrian	27	0.06
Other Arab	6	0.01
Armenian	105	0.22
Asian:	2,739	5.79
Bangladeshi	2	0.00
Cambodian (847)	1,214	2.57
Chinese, ex. Taiwanese (264)	306	0.65
Filipino (36)	66	0.14
Hmong (14)	14	0.03
Indian (251)	299	0.63
Indonesian (2)	2	0.00
Japanese (46)	59	0.12
Korean (72)	86	0.18
Laotian (1)	1	0.00
Malaysian (3)	3	0.01
Pakistani (47)	62	0.13
Sri Lankan (2)	2	0.00
Taiwanese (7)	7	0.01
Thai (13)	24	0.05
Vietnamese (397)	437	0.92
Other Asian, specified (4)	4	0.01
Other Asian, not specified (99)	151	0.32
Australian	28	0.06

Notes: 1. Figures in the "Number" column do not add up to the total population due to: a) Ancestry/Race overlap — e.g. persons can report being both White and Irish, b) persons of Hispanic origin can report being any race, c) persons reporting two ancestries are counted in both categories. 2. Numbers in parentheses indicate the number of persons reporting this ancestry/race alone, not in combination with any other ancestry/race. 3. Refer to the Explanation of Data in the front of the book for more detailed information.

Ancestry/Race	Number	%
Belgian	15	0.03
Brazilian	846	1.79
British	81	0.17
Bulgarian	7	0.01
Canadian	432	0.91
Croatian	81	0.17
Czech	9	0.02
Czechoslovakian	5	0.01
Danish	25	0.05
Dutch	53	0.11
English	1,986	4.20
European	76	0.16
Finnish	45	0.10
French, except Basque	1,370	2.90
French Canadian	1,029	2.18
German	1,197	2.53
Greek	334	0.71
Hawaii Native/Pacific Islander:	164	0.35
Micronesian: (8)	9	0.02
Guamanian/Chamorro (8)	9	0.02
Polynesian: (16)	27	0.06
Native Hawaiian (9)	19	0.04
Samoan (7)	8	0.02
Other Pac. Isl., not spec. (11)	128	0.27
Hispanic or Latino:	4,465	9.44
Central American:	753	1.59
Costa Rican	27	0.06
Guatemalan	131	0.28
Honduran	93	0.20
Nicaraguan	9	0.02
Panamanian	7	0.01
Salvadoran	440	0.93
Other Central American	46	0.10
Cuban	74	0.16
Dominican Republic	127	0.27
Mexican	473	1.00
Puerto Rican	802	1.70
South American:	857	1.81
Argentinean	42	0.09
Bolivian	5	0.01
Chilean	47	0.10
Colombian	622	1.32
Ecuadorian	34	0.07
Paraguayan	1	0.00
Peruvian	72	0.15
Uruguayan	2	0.00
Venezuelan	19	0.04
Other South American	13	0.03
Other Hispanic or Latino	1,379	2.92
Hungarian	15	0.03
Icelander	5	0.01
Iranian	33	0.07
Irish	7,713	16.31
Italian	17,662	37.35
Latvian	31	0.07
Lithuanian	241	0.51
Maltese	9	0.02
Norwegian	173	0.37
Pennsylvania German	8	0.02
Polish	980	2.07
Portuguese	750	1.59
Romanian	40	0.08
Russian	465	0.98
Scandinavian	21	0.04
Scotch-Irish	446	0.94
Scottish	691	1.46
Serbian	15	0.03
Swedish	260	0.55
Swiss	56	0.12
Turkish	40	0.08
Ukrainian	99	0.21
United States or American	1,486	3.14
Welsh	102	0.22
West Indian, excl. Hispanic:	305	0.65
Haitian	161	0.34
Jamaican	39	0.08
Trinidadian and Tobagonian	105	0.22
White:	41,070	86.86
Not Hispanic (37,530)	38,484	81.39
Hispanic (2,354)	2,586	5.47
Yugoslavian	414	0.88

Rockland

Place Type: Town
County: Plymouth
Population: 17,670

Ancestry/Race	Number	%
African American/Black:	386	2.18
Not Hispanic (292)	371	2.10
Hispanic (10)	15	0.08
African, sub-Saharan:	119	0.67
African	10	0.06
Cape Verdean	109	0.62
Am. Ind. or Alaska Nat., not spec.	44	0.25
Albanian	15	0.08
Alsatian	8	0.05
American Indian tribes, specified:	68	0.38
Apache	4	0.02
Blackfeet	2	0.01
Cherokee (4)	15	0.08
Comanche	5	0.03
Cree	3	0.02
Iroquois (1)	7	0.04
Seminole	3	0.02
All other tribes (14)	29	0.16
American Indian tribes, not spec.	1	0.01
Arab:	30	0.17
Lebanese	20	0.11
Syrian	10	0.06
Armenian	108	0.61
Asian:	246	1.39
Bangladeshi	3	0.02
Cambodian (4)	4	0.02
Chinese, ex. Taiwanese (23)	41	0.23
Filipino (18)	36	0.20
Indian (17)	27	0.15
Japanese (2)	4	0.02
Korean (11)	13	0.07
Pakistani (3)	5	0.03
Vietnamese (103)	110	0.62
Other Asian, specified	1	0.01
Other Asian, not specified	2	0.01
Assyrian/Chaldean/Syriac	9	0.05
Austrian	11	0.06
Belgian	29	0.16
Brazilian	79	0.45
British	71	0.40
Canadian	277	1.57
Czech	11	0.06
Dutch	99	0.56
English	2,663	15.07
European	60	0.34
Finnish	83	0.47
French, except Basque	1,121	6.34
French Canadian	739	4.18
German	838	4.74
Greek	178	1.01
Hawaii Native/Pacific Islander:	6	0.03
Polynesian:	2	0.01
Native Hawaiian	2	0.01
Other Pac. Isl., specified	1	0.01
Other Pac. Isl., not spec.	3	0.02
Hispanic or Latino:	180	1.02
Central American:	8	0.05
Costa Rican	3	0.02
Guatemalan	2	0.01
Honduran	3	0.02
Salvadoran	1	0.01
Cuban	10	0.06
Dominican Republic	6	0.03
Mexican	19	0.11
Puerto Rican	54	0.31
South American:	14	0.08
Chilean	5	0.03
Colombian	7	0.04
Other South American	2	0.01
Other Hispanic or Latino	69	0.39
Hungarian	7	0.04
Iranian	6	0.03
Irish	6,525	36.93
Italian	2,824	15.98
Latvian	58	0.33
Lithuanian	162	0.92
Norwegian	64	0.36
Pennsylvania German	22	0.12
Polish	431	2.44
Portuguese	318	1.80
Russian	52	0.29
Scandinavian	5	0.03
Scotch-Irish	409	2.31
Scottish	631	3.57
Serbian	14	0.08
Slavic	8	0.05
Swedish	344	1.95
Swiss	13	0.07
Turkish	7	0.04
Ukrainian	13	0.07
United States or American	1,042	5.90
Welsh	60	0.34
West Indian, excl. Hispanic:	59	0.33
Barbadian	7	0.04
Haitian	52	0.29
White:	16,993	96.17
Not Hispanic (16,641)	16,870	95.47
Hispanic (112)	123	0.70

Salem

Place Type: City
County: Essex
Population: 40,407

Ancestry/Race	Number	%
Afghan	9	0.02
African American/Black:	1,562	3.87
Not Hispanic (966)	1,143	2.83
Hispanic (308)	419	1.04
African, sub-Saharan:	192	0.48
African	29	0.07
Cape Verdean	116	0.29
Somalian	30	0.07
Sudanese	17	0.04
Am. Ind. or Alaska Nat., not spec.	109	0.27
Albanian	46	0.11
American Indian tribes, specified:	123	0.30
Apache (1)	2	0.00
Blackfeet (4)	12	0.03
Cherokee (4)	14	0.03
Chickasaw (1)	1	0.00
Chippewa	1	0.00
Choctaw (1)	2	0.00
Creek	3	0.01
Crow	3	0.01
Iroquois (4)	16	0.04
Latin American Indians (5)	14	0.03
Navajo (1)	1	0.00
Osage	1	0.00
Ottawa	1	0.00
Sioux (2)	7	0.02
All other tribes (13)	45	0.11
American Indian tribes, not spec.	8	0.02
Arab:	202	0.50
Arab/Arabic	19	0.05
Egyptian	9	0.02
Jordanian	15	0.04
Lebanese	123	0.30
Palestinian	6	0.01
Syrian	7	0.02
Other Arab	23	0.06
Armenian	192	0.48
Asian:	978	2.42
Cambodian (5)	7	0.02
Chinese, ex. Taiwanese (157)	189	0.47
Filipino (91)	113	0.28
Indian (120)	134	0.33
Indonesian (2)	8	0.02
Japanese (117)	145	0.36
Korean (52)	61	0.15

Notes: 1. Figures in the "Number" column do not add up to the total population due to: a) Ancestry/Race overlap — e.g. persons can report being both White and Irish, b) persons of Hispanic origin can report being any race, c) persons reporting two ancestries are counted in both categories. 2. Numbers in parentheses indicate the number of persons reporting this ancestry/race alone, not in combination with any other ancestry/race. 3. Refer to the Explanation of Data in the front of the book for more detailed information.

Laotian (8)	11	0.03
Malaysian (2)	2	0.00
Pakistani (4)	13	0.03
Sri Lankan (1)	1	0.00
Taiwanese (1)	2	0.00
Thai (14)	16	0.04
Vietnamese (200)	233	0.58
Other Asian, specified (1)	1	0.00
Other Asian, not specified (14)	42	0.10
Austrian	122	0.30
Belgian	42	0.10
Brazilian	83	0.21
British	136	0.34
Canadian	261	0.65
Celtic	10	0.02
Croatian	6	0.01
Cypriot	8	0.02
Czech	31	0.08
Danish	71	0.18
Dutch	128	0.32
Eastern European	107	0.26
English	4,244	10.50
European	140	0.35
Finnish	126	0.31
French, except Basque	4,468	11.06
French Canadian	3,309	8.19
German	1,621	4.01
Greek	1,188	2.94
Hawaii Native/Pacific Islander:	74	0.18
Micronesian: (3)	3	0.01
Guamanian/Chamorro (3)	3	0.01
Polynesian: (8)	17	0.04
Native Hawaiian (7)	14	0.03
Samoan (1)	3	0.01
Other Pac. Isl., not spec. (8)	54	0.13
Hispanic or Latino:	4,541	11.24
Central American:	163	0.40
Costa Rican	15	0.04
Guatemalan	24	0.06
Honduran	87	0.22
Nicaraguan	3	0.01
Panamanian	8	0.02
Salvadoran	18	0.04
Other Central American	8	0.02
Cuban	44	0.11
Dominican Republic	2,176	5.39
Mexican	131	0.32
Puerto Rican	759	1.88
South American:	81	0.20
Argentinean	9	0.02
Chilean	12	0.03
Colombian	23	0.06
Ecuadorian	7	0.02
Paraguayan	1	0.00
Peruvian	11	0.03
Uruguayan	6	0.01
Venezuelan	9	0.02
Other South American	3	0.01
Other Hispanic or Latino	1,187	2.94
Hungarian	120	0.30
Icelander	24	0.06
Iranian	22	0.05
Irish	9,632	23.84
Italian	5,035	12.46
Latvian	38	0.09
Lithuanian	296	0.73
Maltese	7	0.02
Northern European	5	0.01
Norwegian	113	0.28
Polish	2,856	7.07
Portuguese	914	2.26
Romanian	25	0.06
Russian	605	1.50
Scandinavian	52	0.13
Scotch-Irish	575	1.42
Scottish	758	1.88
Slovak	40	0.10
Swedish	468	1.16
Swiss	59	0.15
Turkish	47	0.12
Ukrainian	182	0.45
United States or American	1,220	3.02
Welsh	199	0.49
West Indian, excl. Hispanic:	252	0.62
British West Indian	7	0.02
Haitian	109	0.27
Jamaican	115	0.28
Trinidadian and Tobagonian	7	0.02
West Indian	14	0.03
White:	35,303	87.37
Not Hispanic (33,277)	33,812	83.68
Hispanic (1,220)	1,491	3.69

Sandwich

Place Type: Town
County: Barnstable
Population: 20,136

Ancestry/Race	Number	%
African American/Black:	116	0.58
Not Hispanic (70)	108	0.54
Hispanic (7)	8	0.04
African, sub-Saharan:	117	0.58
Cape Verdean	106	0.53
Other sub-Saharan African	11	0.05
Am. Ind. or Alaska Nat., not spec.	36	0.18
Alsatian	5	0.02
American Indian tribes, specified:	63	0.31
Blackfeet (3)	3	0.01
Cherokee (4)	17	0.08
Cheyenne	1	0.00
Chippewa	1	0.00
Comanche	1	0.00
Cree (1)	1	0.00
Iroquois (1)	1	0.00
Latin American Indians (3)	3	0.01
Paiute	1	0.00
Sioux	1	0.00
All other tribes (27)	33	0.16
American Indian tribes, not spec.	8	0.04
Arab:	124	0.62
Lebanese	46	0.23
Syrian	78	0.39
Armenian	91	0.45
Asian:	148	0.74
Cambodian (1)	1	0.00
Chinese, ex. Taiwanese (26)	38	0.19
Filipino (11)	17	0.08
Indian (14)	14	0.07
Indonesian	4	0.02
Japanese (13)	17	0.08
Korean (24)	34	0.17
Laotian (1)	1	0.00
Malaysian (4)	5	0.02
Sri Lankan (1)	2	0.01
Thai (2)	4	0.02
Vietnamese (3)	3	0.01
Other Asian, specified (3)	3	0.01
Other Asian, not specified (4)	5	0.02
Austrian	31	0.15
Belgian	32	0.16
British	103	0.51
Canadian	234	1.16
Croatian	5	0.02
Czech	36	0.18
Czechoslovakian	31	0.15
Danish	95	0.47
Dutch	220	1.09
Eastern European	11	0.05
English	4,029	20.00
European	33	0.16
Finnish	168	0.83
French, except Basque	1,349	6.70
French Canadian	834	4.14
German	1,719	8.53
Greek	145	0.72
Hawaii Native/Pacific Islander:	19	0.09
Micronesian:	5	0.02
Guamanian/Chamorro	5	0.02
Polynesian: (2)	11	0.05
Native Hawaiian (2)	10	0.05
Samoan	1	0.00
Other Pac. Isl., not spec.	3	0.01
Hispanic or Latino:	161	0.80
Central American:	11	0.05
Costa Rican	1	0.00
Guatemalan	2	0.01
Honduran	1	0.00
Salvadoran	7	0.03
Cuban	5	0.02
Dominican Republic	1	0.00
Mexican	39	0.19
Puerto Rican	61	0.30
South American:	8	0.04
Colombian	2	0.01
Peruvian	1	0.00
Venezuelan	4	0.02
Other South American	1	0.00
Other Hispanic or Latino	36	0.18
Hungarian	59	0.29
Irish	6,400	31.77
Israeli	5	0.02
Italian	2,606	12.94
Latvian	32	0.16
Lithuanian	153	0.76
Northern European	18	0.09
Norwegian	205	1.02
Pennsylvania German	11	0.05
Polish	916	4.55
Portuguese	662	3.29
Romanian	20	0.10
Russian	180	0.89
Scandinavian	11	0.05
Scotch-Irish	439	2.18
Scottish	937	4.65
Serbian	8	0.04
Slavic	8	0.04
Slovak	18	0.09
Swedish	530	2.63
Swiss	29	0.14
Ukrainian	35	0.17
United States or American	988	4.90
Welsh	128	0.64
White:	19,803	98.35
Not Hispanic (19,569)	19,686	97.77
Hispanic (114)	117	0.58
Yugoslavian	8	0.04

Saugus

Place Type: Census Designated Place
County: Essex
Population: 26,078

Ancestry/Race	Number	%
Afghan	46	0.18
African American/Black:	162	0.62
Not Hispanic (107)	153	0.59
Hispanic (7)	9	0.03
Alaska Native tribes, specified:	2	0.01
Aleut (2)	2	0.01
Am. Ind. or Alaska Nat., not spec.	35	0.13
American Indian tribes, specified:	33	0.13
Blackfeet	4	0.02
Cherokee	1	0.00
Cheyenne	1	0.00
Chippewa	1	0.00
Choctaw	2	0.01
Latin American Indians (1)	3	0.01
Sioux	4	0.02
All other tribes (1)	17	0.07
American Indian tribes, not spec.	2	0.01
Arab:	93	0.36
Arab/Arabic	9	0.03
Lebanese	36	0.14
Moroccan	10	0.04
Syrian	38	0.15
Armenian	185	0.71
Asian:	358	1.37

Notes: 1. Figures in the "Number" column do not add up to the total population due to: a) Ancestry/Race overlap — e.g. persons can report being both White and Irish, b) persons of Hispanic origin can report being any race, c) persons reporting two ancestries are counted in both categories. 2. Numbers in parentheses indicate the number of persons reporting this ancestry/race alone, not in combination with any other ancestry/race. 3. Refer to the Explanation of Data in the front of the book for more detailed information.

Ancestry/Race	Number	%
Cambodian (19)	30	0.12
Chinese, ex. Taiwanese (105)	114	0.44
Filipino (25)	32	0.12
Indian (50)	53	0.20
Japanese (9)	15	0.06
Korean (14)	14	0.05
Laotian (7)	7	0.03
Pakistani (3)	4	0.02
Sri Lankan (4)	4	0.02
Taiwanese (1)	1	0.00
Thai (12)	14	0.05
Vietnamese (47)	48	0.18
Other Asian, not specified (14)	22	0.08
Australian	6	0.02
Austrian	65	0.25
Belgian	10	0.04
British	60	0.23
Canadian	241	0.93
Czech	9	0.03
Czechoslovakian	19	0.07
Danish	26	0.10
Dutch	103	0.40
English	2,846	10.94
European	83	0.32
Finnish	16	0.06
French, except Basque	1,272	4.89
French Canadian	1,234	4.75
German	705	2.71
Greek	368	1.42
Hawaii Native/Pacific Islander:	10	0.04
Micronesian: (1)	1	0.00
Guamanian/Chamorro (1)	1	0.00
Polynesian: (7)	7	0.03
Native Hawaiian (5)	5	0.02
Samoan (1)	1	0.00
Other Polynesian (1)	1	0.00
Other Pac. Isl., not spec. (2)	2	0.01
Hispanic or Latino:	254	0.97
Central American:	24	0.09
Costa Rican	5	0.02
Guatemalan	13	0.05
Honduran	1	0.00
Salvadoran	5	0.02
Cuban	19	0.07
Dominican Republic	14	0.05
Mexican	48	0.18
Puerto Rican	52	0.20
South American:	26	0.10
Argentinean	8	0.03
Chilean	1	0.00
Colombian	10	0.04
Ecuadorian	1	0.00
Peruvian	5	0.02
Venezuelan	1	0.00
Other Hispanic or Latino	71	0.27
Hungarian	25	0.10
Iranian	30	0.12
Irish	6,461	24.84
Italian	9,518	36.60
Latvian	5	0.02
Lithuanian	109	0.42
Norwegian	144	0.55
Polish	1,053	4.05
Portuguese	315	1.21
Russian	223	0.86
Scandinavian	33	0.13
Scotch-Irish	475	1.83
Scottish	701	2.70
Slovak	25	0.10
Swedish	433	1.67
Swiss	18	0.07
Ukrainian	58	0.22
United States or American	692	2.66
Welsh	21	0.08
West Indian, excl. Hispanic:	32	0.12
Haitian	7	0.03
Jamaican	17	0.07
West Indian	8	0.03
White:	25,518	97.85
Not Hispanic (25,207)	25,336	97.15
Hispanic (172)	182	0.70
Yugoslavian	57	0.22

Scituate

Place Type: Town
County: Plymouth
Population: 17,863

Ancestry/Race	Number	%
African American/Black:	140	0.78
Not Hispanic (80)	130	0.73
Hispanic (8)	10	0.06
African, sub-Saharan:	344	1.93
Cape Verdean	344	1.93
Am. Ind. or Alaska Nat., not spec.	13	0.07
American Indian tribes, specified:	42	0.24
Blackfeet	5	0.03
Cherokee (1)	10	0.06
Choctaw (1)	1	0.01
Cree	1	0.01
Iroquois	6	0.03
Latin American Indians	1	0.01
Potawatomi	3	0.02
All other tribes (1)	15	0.08
American Indian tribes, not spec.	5	0.03
Arab:	27	0.15
Lebanese	19	0.11
Syrian	8	0.04
Armenian	97	0.54
Asian:	119	0.67
Chinese, ex. Taiwanese (33)	42	0.24
Filipino (12)	23	0.13
Indian (10)	18	0.10
Indonesian (1)	1	0.01
Japanese (5)	8	0.04
Korean (15)	17	0.10
Thai (1)	1	0.01
Vietnamese (3)	3	0.02
Other Asian, not specified	6	0.03
Australian	20	0.11
Austrian	53	0.30
Belgian	26	0.15
British	57	0.32
Canadian	156	0.87
Celtic	14	0.08
Czech	5	0.03
Czechoslovakian	27	0.15
Danish	89	0.50
Dutch	104	0.58
Eastern European	7	0.04
English	3,194	17.88
European	103	0.58
Finnish	90	0.50
French, except Basque	869	4.86
French Canadian	447	2.50
German	1,542	8.63
Greek	146	0.82
Hawaii Native/Pacific Islander:	7	0.04
Micronesian: (2)	2	0.01
Other Micronesian (2)	2	0.01
Polynesian:	1	0.01
Native Hawaiian	1	0.01
Other Pac. Isl., not spec.	4	0.02
Hispanic or Latino:	148	0.83
Central American:	12	0.07
Costa Rican	4	0.02
Guatemalan	3	0.02
Honduran	1	0.01
Panamanian	1	0.01
Salvadoran	3	0.02
Cuban	17	0.10
Dominican Republic	8	0.04
Mexican	18	0.10
Puerto Rican	28	0.16
South American:	34	0.19
Argentinean	1	0.01
Chilean	1	0.01
Colombian	20	0.11
Ecuadorian	4	0.02
Peruvian	2	0.01
Other South American	6	0.03
Other Hispanic or Latino	31	0.17
Hungarian	37	0.21
Irish	7,877	44.10
Israeli	8	0.04
Italian	2,576	14.42
Lithuanian	227	1.27
Northern European	15	0.08
Norwegian	107	0.60
Polish	445	2.49
Portuguese	333	1.86
Romanian	8	0.04
Russian	84	0.47
Scandinavian	23	0.13
Scotch-Irish	487	2.73
Scottish	742	4.15
Slavic	7	0.04
Slovak	17	0.10
Swedish	386	2.16
Swiss	7	0.04
Ukrainian	5	0.03
United States or American	883	4.94
Welsh	125	0.70
West Indian, excl. Hispanic:	15	0.08
West Indian	15	0.08
White:	17,431	97.58
Not Hispanic (17,182)	17,328	97.00
Hispanic (94)	103	0.58
Yugoslavian	5	0.03

Seekonk

Place Type: Town
County: Bristol
Population: 13,425

Ancestry/Race	Number	%
African American/Black:	120	0.89
Not Hispanic (67)	117	0.87
Hispanic (3)	3	0.02
African, sub-Saharan:	113	0.84
African	29	0.22
Cape Verdean	84	0.63
Am. Ind. or Alaska Nat., not spec.	23	0.17
American Indian tribes, specified:	66	0.49
Blackfeet	3	0.02
Cherokee (8)	9	0.07
Osage (3)	3	0.02
Potawatomi (1)	3	0.02
Seminole	3	0.02
Sioux	2	0.01
All other tribes (19)	43	0.32
American Indian tribes, not spec.	6	0.04
Arab:	226	1.68
Lebanese	155	1.15
Syrian	71	0.53
Armenian	91	0.68
Asian:	147	1.09
Chinese, ex. Taiwanese (76)	87	0.65
Filipino (6)	7	0.05
Indian (20)	23	0.17
Japanese (3)	7	0.05
Korean (12)	13	0.10
Pakistani (4)	4	0.03
Vietnamese (5)	5	0.04
Other Asian, not specified	1	0.01
British	10	0.07
Canadian	83	0.62
Czechoslovakian	50	0.37
Danish	27	0.20
Dutch	38	0.28
English	2,241	16.69
European	51	0.38
French, except Basque	1,928	14.36
French Canadian	854	6.36
German	649	4.83
Greek	149	1.11
Hawaii Native/Pacific Islander:	15	0.11
Micronesian:	4	0.03

Notes: 1. Figures in the "Number" column do not add up to the total population due to: a) Ancestry/Race overlap — e.g. persons can report being both White and Irish, b) persons of Hispanic origin can report being any race, c) persons reporting two ancestries are counted in both categories. 2. Numbers in parentheses indicate the number of persons reporting this ancestry/race alone, not in combination with any other ancestry/race. 3. Refer to the Explanation of Data in the front of the book for more detailed information.

Ancestry/Race	Number	%
Guamanian/Chamorro	4	0.03
Polynesian:	1	0.01
Native Hawaiian	1	0.01
Other Pac. Isl., not spec.	10	0.07
Hispanic or Latino:	99	0.74
Central American:	2	0.01
Guatemalan	1	0.01
Salvadoran	1	0.01
Cuban	4	0.03
Dominican Republic	5	0.04
Mexican	20	0.15
Puerto Rican	29	0.22
South American:	8	0.06
Colombian	3	0.02
Peruvian	4	0.03
Venezuelan	1	0.01
Other Hispanic or Latino	31	0.23
Hungarian	17	0.13
Irish	2,873	21.40
Italian	1,598	11.90
Latvian	8	0.06
Lithuanian	42	0.31
Northern European	23	0.17
Norwegian	101	0.75
Polish	686	5.11
Portuguese	2,947	21.95
Romanian	17	0.13
Russian	74	0.55
Scotch-Irish	203	1.51
Scottish	277	2.06
Slovak	8	0.06
Swedish	377	2.81
Ukrainian	30	0.22
United States or American	511	3.81
Welsh	8	0.06
West Indian, excl. Hispanic:	30	0.22
West Indian	17	0.13
Other West Indian	13	0.10
White:	13,097	97.56
Not Hispanic (12,897)	13,023	97.01
Hispanic (67)	74	0.55
Yugoslavian	38	0.28

Sharon

Place Type: Town
County: Norfolk
Population: 17,408

Ancestry/Race	Number	%
African American/Black:	661	3.80
Not Hispanic (578)	640	3.68
Hispanic (13)	21	0.12
African, sub-Saharan:	89	0.51
African	40	0.23
Cape Verdean	49	0.28
Alaska Native tribes, specified:	1	0.01
Eskimo (1)	1	0.01
Am. Ind. or Alaska Nat., not spec.	16	0.09
Albanian	25	0.14
American Indian tribes, specified:	44	0.25
Blackfeet (1)	1	0.01
Cherokee	2	0.01
Chickasaw	1	0.01
Choctaw	1	0.01
Comanche	1	0.01
Creek	4	0.02
Iroquois	3	0.02
Latin American Indians (3)	4	0.02
Shoshone	5	0.03
All other tribes (14)	22	0.13
Arab:	356	2.05
Egyptian	31	0.18
Jordanian	5	0.03
Lebanese	200	1.15
Moroccan	14	0.08
Palestinian	38	0.22
Syrian	39	0.22
Other Arab	29	0.17
Armenian	33	0.19
Asian:	957	5.50
Bangladeshi (3)	3	0.02
Cambodian (1)	1	0.01
Chinese, ex. Taiwanese (317)	360	2.07
Filipino (28)	41	0.24
Indian (315)	325	1.87
Indonesian	1	0.01
Japanese (11)	23	0.13
Korean (71)	80	0.46
Malaysian	1	0.01
Pakistani (17)	18	0.10
Sri Lankan (1)	3	0.02
Taiwanese (10)	14	0.08
Thai (4)	4	0.02
Vietnamese (27)	33	0.19
Other Asian, specified (1)	3	0.02
Other Asian, not specified (26)	47	0.27
Austrian	102	0.59
Basque	7	0.04
Belgian	8	0.05
Brazilian	9	0.05
British	125	0.72
Bulgarian	7	0.04
Canadian	125	0.72
Czech	27	0.16
Czechoslovakian	12	0.07
Danish	35	0.20
Dutch	143	0.82
Eastern European	498	2.86
English	1,230	7.07
European	263	1.51
Finnish	35	0.20
French, except Basque	407	2.34
French Canadian	208	1.19
German	1,058	6.08
Greek	98	0.56
Hawaii Native/Pacific Islander:	8	0.05
Polynesian: (1)	2	0.01
Native Hawaiian (1)	1	0.01
Other Polynesian	1	0.01
Other Pac. Isl., not spec.	6	0.03
Hispanic or Latino:	194	1.11
Central American:	18	0.10
Costa Rican	4	0.02
Guatemalan	7	0.04
Honduran	5	0.03
Panamanian	1	0.01
Salvadoran	1	0.01
Cuban	19	0.11
Dominican Republic	4	0.02
Mexican	17	0.10
Puerto Rican	46	0.26
South American:	36	0.21
Argentinean	5	0.03
Chilean	3	0.02
Colombian	22	0.13
Ecuadorian	2	0.01
Paraguayan	1	0.01
Peruvian	1	0.01
Venezuelan	2	0.01
Other Hispanic or Latino	54	0.31
Hungarian	87	0.50
Iranian	8	0.05
Irish	2,177	12.51
Israeli	56	0.32
Italian	1,377	7.91
Latvian	43	0.25
Lithuanian	406	2.33
Norwegian	103	0.59
Polish	955	5.49
Portuguese	106	0.61
Romanian	109	0.63
Russian	2,490	14.30
Scandinavian	48	0.28
Scotch-Irish	219	1.26
Scottish	326	1.87
Slovak	7	0.04
Slovene	6	0.03
Swedish	261	1.50
Swiss	4	0.02
Turkish	29	0.17
Ukrainian	215	1.24
United States or American	1,489	8.55
Welsh	47	0.27
West Indian, excl. Hispanic:	171	0.98
Barbadian	19	0.11
Haitian	101	0.58
Jamaican	36	0.21
West Indian	15	0.09
White:	15,833	90.95
Not Hispanic (15,541)	15,696	90.17
Hispanic (118)	137	0.79

Shrewsbury

Place Type: Town
County: Worcester
Population: 31,640

Ancestry/Race	Number	%
Afghan	10	0.03
African American/Black:	510	1.61
Not Hispanic (426)	473	1.49
Hispanic (33)	37	0.12
African, sub-Saharan:	113	0.36
African	6	0.02
Ghanian	33	0.10
Nigerian	33	0.10
South African	41	0.13
Am. Ind. or Alaska Nat., not spec.	45	0.14
Albanian	87	0.27
Alsatian	8	0.03
American Indian tribes, specified:	47	0.15
Blackfeet	4	0.01
Cherokee	5	0.02
Chippewa (1)	1	0.00
Choctaw (1)	1	0.00
Creek	1	0.00
Delaware (3)	3	0.01
Iroquois (2)	7	0.02
Latin American Indians (4)	4	0.01
Shoshone	1	0.00
Sioux	1	0.00
All other tribes (7)	19	0.06
American Indian tribes, not spec.	5	0.02
Arab:	524	1.66
Arab/Arabic	48	0.15
Egyptian	40	0.13
Lebanese	378	1.19
Syrian	42	0.13
Other Arab	16	0.05
Armenian	235	0.74
Asian:	2,579	8.15
Bangladeshi (11)	11	0.03
Cambodian (20)	24	0.08
Chinese, ex. Taiwanese (707)	753	2.38
Filipino (36)	53	0.17
Indian (1,148)	1,204	3.81
Indonesian (2)	2	0.01
Japanese (66)	78	0.25
Korean (97)	113	0.36
Laotian (4)	4	0.01
Pakistani (28)	31	0.10
Sri Lankan (21)	21	0.07
Taiwanese (13)	16	0.05
Thai (7)	7	0.02
Vietnamese (212)	221	0.70
Other Asian, specified (10)	11	0.03
Other Asian, not specified (15)	30	0.09
Assyrian/Chaldean/Syriac	40	0.13
Australian	25	0.08
Austrian	111	0.35
Basque	8	0.03
Belgian	24	0.08
Brazilian	203	0.64
British	158	0.50
Bulgarian	12	0.04
Canadian	108	0.34
Croatian	12	0.04
Czech	34	0.11

Notes: 1. Figures in the "Number" column do not add up to the total population due to: a) Ancestry/Race overlap — e.g. persons can report being both White and Irish, b) persons of Hispanic origin can report being any race, c) persons reporting two ancestries are counted in both categories. 2. Numbers in parentheses indicate the number of persons reporting this ancestry/race alone, not in combination with any other ancestry/race. 3. Refer to the Explanation of Data in the front of the book for more detailed information.

Ancestry/Race	Number	%
Czechoslovakian	5	0.02
Danish	74	0.23
Dutch	180	0.57
Eastern European	64	0.20
English	3,739	11.82
Estonian	33	0.10
European	126	0.40
Finnish	202	0.64
French, except Basque	2,768	8.75
French Canadian	1,413	4.47
German	2,244	7.09
Greek	477	1.51
Hawaii Native/Pacific Islander:	10	0.03
Micronesian: (1)	1	0.00
Other Micronesian (1)	1	0.00
Polynesian: (2)	6	0.02
Native Hawaiian (2)	5	0.02
Samoan	1	0.00
Other Pac. Isl., not spec. (1)	3	0.01
Hispanic or Latino:	504	1.59
Central American:	32	0.10
Costa Rican	6	0.02
Guatemalan	10	0.03
Honduran	1	0.00
Panamanian	10	0.03
Salvadoran	5	0.02
Cuban	27	0.09
Dominican Republic	12	0.04
Mexican	46	0.15
Puerto Rican	204	0.64
South American:	63	0.20
Argentinean	8	0.03
Chilean	2	0.01
Colombian	22	0.07
Ecuadorian	15	0.05
Peruvian	8	0.03
Venezuelan	1	0.00
Other South American	7	0.02
Other Hispanic or Latino	120	0.38
Hungarian	62	0.20
Iranian	19	0.06
Irish	7,414	23.43
Italian	5,903	18.66
Latvian	22	0.07
Lithuanian	611	1.93
Northern European	51	0.16
Norwegian	292	0.92
Pennsylvania German	7	0.02
Polish	1,604	5.07
Portuguese	308	0.97
Romanian	21	0.07
Russian	340	1.07
Scandinavian	52	0.16
Scotch-Irish	519	1.64
Scottish	862	2.72
Serbian	9	0.03
Slovak	51	0.16
Swedish	1,187	3.75
Swiss	35	0.11
Turkish	18	0.06
Ukrainian	102	0.32
United States or American	2,030	6.42
Welsh	187	0.59
West Indian, excl. Hispanic:	74	0.23
Bahamian	10	0.03
British West Indian	6	0.02
Haitian	9	0.03
Jamaican	17	0.05
U.S. Virgin Islander	26	0.08
West Indian	6	0.02
White:	28,454	89.93
Not Hispanic (27,875)	28,110	88.84
Hispanic (324)	344	1.09
Yugoslavian	8	0.03

Somerset

Place Type: Census Designated Place
County: Bristol
Population: 18,234

Ancestry/Race	Number	%
Acadian/Cajun	16	0.09
African American/Black:	60	0.33
Not Hispanic (29)	59	0.32
Hispanic (1)	1	0.01
African, sub-Saharan:	40	0.22
African	9	0.05
Cape Verdean	31	0.17
Am. Ind. or Alaska Nat., not spec.	15	0.08
American Indian tribes, specified:	46	0.25
Blackfeet	6	0.03
Cherokee (1)	3	0.02
Chippewa	1	0.01
Cree	4	0.02
Creek (3)	3	0.02
Iroquois (1)	2	0.01
Navajo	1	0.01
All other tribes (14)	26	0.14
American Indian tribes, not spec.	2	0.01
Arab:	263	1.44
Lebanese	239	1.31
Syrian	24	0.13
Asian:	125	0.69
Chinese, ex. Taiwanese (33)	36	0.20
Filipino (12)	18	0.10
Indian (22)	27	0.15
Japanese (3)	4	0.02
Korean (10)	11	0.06
Thai (5)	5	0.03
Vietnamese (11)	11	0.06
Other Asian, specified	1	0.01
Other Asian, not specified	12	0.07
Australian	6	0.03
Brazilian	24	0.13
British	10	0.05
Canadian	40	0.22
Croatian	15	0.08
Czech	1	0.01
Czechoslovakian	6	0.03
Danish	16	0.09
Dutch	70	0.38
English	2,493	13.67
European	31	0.17
Finnish	64	0.35
French, except Basque	2,835	15.55
French Canadian	1,706	9.36
German	433	2.37
Greek	109	0.60
Hawaii Native/Pacific Islander:	12	0.07
Micronesian: (1)	1	0.01
Guamanian/Chamorro (1)	1	0.01
Polynesian: (3)	6	0.03
Native Hawaiian (3)	4	0.02
Samoan	2	0.01
Other Pac. Isl., specified	1	0.01
Other Pac. Isl., not spec.	4	0.02
Hispanic or Latino:	90	0.49
Central American:	4	0.02
Honduran	3	0.02
Salvadoran	1	0.01
Cuban	1	0.01
Dominican Republic	2	0.01
Mexican	31	0.17
Puerto Rican	16	0.09
South American:	10	0.05
Bolivian	1	0.01
Chilean	1	0.01
Paraguayan	1	0.01
Peruvian	6	0.03
Uruguayan	1	0.01
Other Hispanic or Latino	26	0.14
Irish	2,971	16.29
Italian	1,198	6.57
Latvian	28	0.15
Lithuanian	38	0.21
Maltese	10	0.05
Norwegian	28	0.15
Polish	799	4.38
Portuguese	7,578	41.56
Romanian	9	0.05
Russian	75	0.41
Scotch-Irish	198	1.09
Scottish	262	1.44
Slovak	26	0.14
Swedish	66	0.36
Ukrainian	36	0.20
United States or American	512	2.81
Welsh	15	0.08
West Indian, excl. Hispanic:	9	0.05
Haitian	9	0.05
White:	18,046	98.97
Not Hispanic (17,834)	17,969	98.55
Hispanic (75)	77	0.42
Yugoslavian	15	0.08

Somerville

Place Type: City
County: Middlesex
Population: 77,478

Ancestry/Race	Number	%
African American/Black:	6,122	7.90
Not Hispanic (4,868)	5,854	7.56
Hispanic (167)	268	0.35
African, sub-Saharan:	950	1.23
African	297	0.38
Cape Verdean	398	0.51
Ethiopian	70	0.09
Ghanian	39	0.05
Kenyan	16	0.02
Nigerian	19	0.02
Sierra Leonean	7	0.01
Somalian	17	0.02
South African	32	0.04
Ugandan	19	0.02
Other sub-Saharan African	36	0.05
Alaska Native tribes, specified:	4	0.01
Aleut	1	0.00
Eskimo (1)	2	0.00
Tlingit-Haida (1)	1	0.00
Alaska Native tribes, not specified	1	0.00
Am. Ind. or Alaska Nat., not spec.	203	0.26
Albanian	287	0.37
Alsatian	42	0.05
American Indian tribes, specified:	230	0.30
Apache (4)	6	0.01
Blackfeet	5	0.01
Cherokee (10)	49	0.06
Cheyenne	1	0.00
Chickasaw	1	0.00
Chippewa (2)	4	0.01
Choctaw	2	0.00
Cree	4	0.01
Creek	6	0.01
Delaware	1	0.00
Iroquois (10)	14	0.02
Latin American Indians (23)	58	0.07
Navajo (4)	8	0.01
Osage (1)	1	0.00
Pueblo (2)	5	0.01
Seminole (1)	1	0.00
Shoshone	2	0.00
Sioux (1)	6	0.01
Yaqui (1)	2	0.00
Yuman (1)	1	0.00
All other tribes (24)	53	0.07
American Indian tribes, not spec.	12	0.02
Arab:	701	0.90
Arab/Arabic	139	0.18
Egyptian	76	0.10
Lebanese	237	0.31
Moroccan	100	0.13
Palestinian	7	0.01

Notes: 1. Figures in the "Number" column do not add up to the total population due to: a) Ancestry/Race overlap — e.g. persons can report being both White and Irish, b) persons of Hispanic origin can report being any race, c) persons reporting two ancestries are counted in both categories. 2. Numbers in parentheses indicate the number of persons reporting this ancestry/race alone, not in combination with any other ancestry/race. 3. Refer to the Explanation of Data in the front of the book for more detailed information.

Ancestry/Race	Number	%
Syrian	81	0.10
Other Arab	61	0.08
Armenian	125	0.16
Asian:	5,649	7.29
Bangladeshi (28)	35	0.05
Cambodian (37)	41	0.05
Chinese, ex. Taiwanese (1,798)	1,954	2.52
Filipino (161)	218	0.28
Hmong (5)	6	0.01
Indian (1,363)	1,521	1.96
Indonesian (19)	22	0.03
Japanese (289)	380	0.49
Korean (462)	499	0.64
Laotian (19)	19	0.02
Malaysian (7)	12	0.02
Pakistani (92)	116	0.15
Sri Lankan (20)	26	0.03
Taiwanese (64)	73	0.09
Thai (45)	58	0.07
Vietnamese (329)	362	0.47
Other Asian, specified (90)	113	0.15
Other Asian, not specified (87)	194	0.25
Australian	29	0.04
Austrian	165	0.21
Basque	6	0.01
Belgian	74	0.10
Brazilian	3,870	4.99
British	518	0.67
Bulgarian	23	0.03
Canadian	779	1.01
Celtic	49	0.06
Croatian	35	0.05
Cypriot	9	0.01
Czech	184	0.24
Czechoslovakian	41	0.05
Danish	253	0.33
Dutch	511	0.66
Eastern European	393	0.51
English	5,278	6.81
Estonian	30	0.04
European	582	0.75
Finnish	210	0.27
French, except Basque	2,203	2.84
French Canadian	1,858	2.40
German	4,336	5.60
Greek	1,252	1.62
Guyanese	11	0.01
Hawaii Native/Pacific Islander:	139	0.18
Micronesian: (15)	16	0.02
Guamanian/Chamorro (15)	16	0.02
Polynesian: (22)	43	0.06
Native Hawaiian (6)	21	0.03
Samoan (14)	19	0.02
Tongan (2)	3	0.00
Other Pac. Isl., specified	2	0.00
Other Pac. Isl., not spec. (13)	78	0.10
Hispanic or Latino:	6,786	8.76
Central American:	2,636	3.40
Costa Rican	60	0.08
Guatemalan	202	0.26
Honduran	102	0.13
Nicaraguan	28	0.04
Panamanian	15	0.02
Salvadoran	2,075	2.68
Other Central American	154	0.20
Cuban	173	0.22
Dominican Republic	173	0.22
Mexican	464	0.60
Puerto Rican	776	1.00
South American:	598	0.77
Argentinean	75	0.10
Bolivian	14	0.02
Chilean	31	0.04
Colombian	219	0.28
Ecuadorian	52	0.07
Paraguayan	5	0.01
Peruvian	71	0.09
Uruguayan	15	0.02
Venezuelan	47	0.06
Other South American	69	0.09
Other Hispanic or Latino	1,966	2.54
Hungarian	442	0.57
Icelander	106	0.14
Iranian	61	0.08
Irish	14,568	18.80
Israeli	91	0.12
Italian	11,213	14.47
Latvian	88	0.11
Lithuanian	486	0.63
Maltese	18	0.02
New Zealander	30	0.04
Northern European	74	0.10
Norwegian	382	0.49
Polish	2,137	2.76
Portuguese	5,815	7.51
Romanian	204	0.26
Russian	1,516	1.96
Scandinavian	171	0.22
Scotch-Irish	965	1.25
Scottish	1,360	1.76
Serbian	38	0.05
Slavic	25	0.03
Slovak	91	0.12
Slovene	20	0.03
Soviet Union	15	0.02
Swedish	629	0.81
Swiss	140	0.18
Turkish	202	0.26
Ukrainian	280	0.36
United States or American	1,996	2.58
Welsh	351	0.45
West Indian, excl. Hispanic:	2,844	3.67
Barbadian	135	0.17
Belizean	9	0.01
Bermudan	20	0.03
British West Indian	10	0.01
Dutch West Indian	13	0.02
Haitian	2,168	2.80
Jamaican	292	0.38
Trinidadian and Tobagonian	26	0.03
U.S. Virgin Islander	23	0.03
West Indian	148	0.19
White:	62,447	80.60
Not Hispanic (56,320)	58,668	75.72
Hispanic (3,315)	3,779	4.88
Yugoslavian	32	0.04

South Hadley

Place Type: Town
County: Hampshire
Population: 17,196

Ancestry/Race	Number	%
African American/Black:	290	1.69
Not Hispanic (198)	276	1.61
Hispanic (9)	14	0.08
African, sub-Saharan:	53	0.31
African	23	0.13
Kenyan	10	0.06
South African	20	0.12
Am. Ind. or Alaska Nat., not spec.	33	0.19
Alsatian	7	0.04
American Indian tribes, specified:	48	0.28
Blackfeet	8	0.05
Cherokee (2)	5	0.03
Chippewa	5	0.03
Choctaw	2	0.01
Iroquois	1	0.01
Latin American Indians	1	0.01
Navajo (8)	8	0.05
Osage	1	0.01
Ottawa	3	0.02
Pueblo (1)	2	0.01
Seminole (1)	1	0.01
Sioux	3	0.02
All other tribes (2)	8	0.05
American Indian tribes, not spec.	6	0.03
Arab:	56	0.33
Arab/Arabic	43	0.25
Moroccan	5	0.03
Syrian	8	0.05
Asian:	512	2.98
Bangladeshi (7)	7	0.04
Cambodian (23)	23	0.13
Chinese, ex. Taiwanese (79)	102	0.59
Filipino (37)	50	0.29
Hmong (1)	1	0.01
Indian (99)	109	0.63
Japanese (30)	47	0.27
Korean (53)	57	0.33
Laotian (2)	2	0.01
Malaysian (1)	1	0.01
Pakistani (37)	37	0.22
Sri Lankan (7)	7	0.04
Taiwanese (3)	4	0.02
Thai (10)	10	0.06
Vietnamese (20)	28	0.16
Other Asian, specified (11)	11	0.06
Other Asian, not specified (8)	16	0.09
Australian	5	0.03
Austrian	79	0.46
Belgian	16	0.09
British	187	1.09
Bulgarian	18	0.10
Canadian	189	1.10
Czech	92	0.54
Czechoslovakian	12	0.07
Danish	44	0.26
Dutch	151	0.88
Eastern European	38	0.22
English	2,355	13.70
Estonian	7	0.04
European	124	0.72
Finnish	67	0.39
French, except Basque	2,678	15.57
French Canadian	2,058	11.97
German	1,965	11.43
Greek	217	1.26
Guyanese	7	0.04
Hawaii Native/Pacific Islander:	15	0.09
Melanesian: (1)	1	0.01
Other Melanesian (1)	1	0.01
Polynesian: (5)	10	0.06
Native Hawaiian (1)	4	0.02
Samoan (4)	6	0.03
Other Pac. Isl., not spec. (4)	4	0.02
Hispanic or Latino:	405	2.36
Central American:	17	0.10
Costa Rican	2	0.01
Guatemalan	2	0.01
Honduran	1	0.01
Panamanian	2	0.01
Salvadoran	9	0.05
Other Central American	1	0.01
Cuban	6	0.03
Dominican Republic	16	0.09
Mexican	54	0.31
Puerto Rican	207	1.20
South American:	33	0.19
Bolivian	3	0.02
Chilean	3	0.02
Colombian	11	0.06
Ecuadorian	2	0.01
Peruvian	6	0.03
Uruguayan	2	0.01
Venezuelan	3	0.02
Other South American	3	0.02
Other Hispanic or Latino	72	0.42
Hungarian	52	0.30
Icelander	7	0.04
Iranian	14	0.08
Irish	3,390	19.71
Italian	1,164	6.77
Lithuanian	120	0.70
New Zealander	10	0.06
Northern European	9	0.05
Norwegian	73	0.42
Pennsylvania German	21	0.12
Polish	2,553	14.85

Notes: 1. Figures in the "Number" column do not add up to the total population due to: a) Ancestry/Race overlap — e.g. persons can report being both White and Irish, b) persons of Hispanic origin can report being any race, c) persons reporting two ancestries are counted in both categories. 2. Numbers in parentheses indicate the number of persons reporting this ancestry/race alone, not in combination with any other ancestry/race. 3. Refer to the Explanation of Data in the front of the book for more detailed information.

Portuguese	236	1.37
Russian	169	0.98
Scandinavian	23	0.13
Scotch-Irish	330	1.92
Scottish	502	2.92
Slavic	26	0.15
Slovak	9	0.05
Slovene	15	0.09
Swedish	171	0.99
Swiss	33	0.19
Ukrainian	96	0.56
United States or American	330	1.92
Welsh	108	0.63
West Indian, excl. Hispanic:	64	0.37
Bahamian	10	0.06
Jamaican	18	0.10
Trinidadian and Tobagonian	23	0.13
West Indian	13	0.08
White:	16,376	95.23
Not Hispanic (15,942)	16,111	93.69
Hispanic (230)	265	1.54

South Yarmouth

Place Type: Census Designated Place
County: Barnstable
Population: 11,603

Ancestry/Race	Number	%
African American/Black:	233	2.01
Not Hispanic (171)	221	1.90
Hispanic (6)	12	0.10
African, sub-Saharan:	72	0.61
African	5	0.04
Cape Verdean	67	0.57
Alaska Native tribes, specified:	1	0.01
Eskimo (1)	1	0.01
Am. Ind. or Alaska Nat., not spec.	26	0.22
Albanian	26	0.22
American Indian tribes, specified:	61	0.53
Apache	1	0.01
Blackfeet	4	0.03
Cherokee (2)	9	0.08
Chippewa	1	0.01
Choctaw (2)	4	0.03
Comanche	2	0.02
Iroquois (2)	3	0.03
Latin American Indians	1	0.01
Seminole (1)	1	0.01
Sioux (2)	6	0.05
All other tribes (16)	29	0.25
American Indian tribes, not spec.	1	0.01
Arab:	178	1.51
Egyptian	7	0.06
Lebanese	95	0.81
Moroccan	69	0.59
Syrian	7	0.06
Armenian	81	0.69
Asian:	100	0.86
Cambodian (12)	13	0.11
Chinese, ex. Taiwanese (26)	27	0.23
Filipino (7)	14	0.12
Indian (8)	12	0.10
Japanese (2)	5	0.04
Korean (4)	4	0.03
Laotian	1	0.01
Pakistani (8)	8	0.07
Thai (2)	2	0.02
Vietnamese (1)	2	0.02
Other Asian, specified (1)	3	0.03
Other Asian, not specified (1)	9	0.08
Australian	14	0.12
Austrian	32	0.27
Brazilian	106	0.90
British	110	0.94
Canadian	160	1.36
Celtic	21	0.18
Czechoslovakian	18	0.15
Danish	59	0.50
Dutch	138	1.17
English	2,056	17.48
European	14	0.12
Finnish	36	0.31
French, except Basque	861	7.32
French Canadian	437	3.72
German	1,039	8.84
Greek	139	1.18
Hawaii Native/Pacific Islander:	14	0.12
Polynesian: (7)	11	0.09
Native Hawaiian (6)	7	0.06
Samoan (1)	4	0.03
Other Pac. Isl., specified	2	0.02
Other Pac. Isl., not spec.	1	0.01
Hispanic or Latino:	189	1.63
Central American:	12	0.10
Guatemalan	3	0.03
Honduran	5	0.04
Nicaraguan	1	0.01
Salvadoran	3	0.03
Cuban	1	0.01
Dominican Republic	4	0.03
Mexican	24	0.21
Puerto Rican	84	0.72
South American:	15	0.13
Chilean	2	0.02
Colombian	2	0.02
Ecuadorian	2	0.02
Peruvian	3	0.03
Uruguayan	1	0.01
Other South American	5	0.04
Other Hispanic or Latino	49	0.42
Hungarian	52	0.44
Icelander	5	0.04
Irish	3,266	27.77
Italian	1,187	10.09
Latvian	26	0.22
Lithuanian	101	0.86
Norwegian	87	0.74
Polish	319	2.71
Portuguese	482	4.10
Romanian	9	0.08
Russian	55	0.47
Scandinavian	27	0.23
Scotch-Irish	258	2.19
Scottish	573	4.87
Swedish	507	4.31
Swiss	29	0.25
Ukrainian	17	0.14
United States or American	428	3.64
Welsh	82	0.70
White:	11,164	96.22
Not Hispanic (10,903)	11,052	95.25
Hispanic (90)	112	0.97

Southbridge

Place Type: Town
County: Worcester
Population: 17,214

Ancestry/Race	Number	%
African American/Black:	322	1.87
Not Hispanic (123)	157	0.91
Hispanic (123)	165	0.96
African, sub-Saharan:	18	0.10
African	11	0.06
Other sub-Saharan African	7	0.04
Alaska Native tribes, specified:	4	0.02
Alaska Athabascan (2)	3	0.02
Eskimo	1	0.01
Am. Ind. or Alaska Nat., not spec.	79	0.46
Albanian	55	0.32
American Indian tribes, specified:	66	0.38
Apache	1	0.01
Blackfeet	4	0.02
Cherokee (2)	9	0.05
Iroquois (3)	5	0.03
Latin American Indians (1)	9	0.05
Pueblo	2	0.01
Sioux	2	0.01
All other tribes (23)	34	0.20
American Indian tribes, not spec.	4	0.02
Arab:	57	0.33
Lebanese	49	0.28
Palestinian	8	0.05
Armenian	22	0.13
Asian:	347	2.02
Chinese, ex. Taiwanese (26)	35	0.20
Filipino (16)	26	0.15
Indian (35)	41	0.24
Indonesian (2)	3	0.02
Japanese (8)	15	0.09
Korean (7)	8	0.05
Laotian (130)	165	0.96
Pakistani (2)	2	0.01
Taiwanese (1)	1	0.01
Thai (3)	3	0.02
Vietnamese (6)	10	0.06
Other Asian, not specified (22)	38	0.22
Australian	6	0.03
Austrian	15	0.09
British	46	0.27
Canadian	276	1.60
Croatian	6	0.03
Czech	6	0.03
Czechoslovakian	11	0.06
Danish	17	0.10
Dutch	29	0.17
English	1,194	6.94
European	7	0.04
Finnish	18	0.10
French, except Basque	4,103	23.84
French Canadian	2,385	13.86
German	627	3.64
Greek	111	0.64
Hawaii Native/Pacific Islander:	37	0.21
Polynesian: (4)	14	0.08
Native Hawaiian (3)	13	0.08
Other Polynesian (1)	1	0.01
Other Pac. Isl., not spec. (7)	23	0.13
Hispanic or Latino:	3,472	20.17
Central American:	14	0.08
Costa Rican	4	0.02
Guatemalan	1	0.01
Honduran	3	0.02
Panamanian	1	0.01
Salvadoran	5	0.03
Cuban	26	0.15
Dominican Republic	56	0.33
Mexican	62	0.36
Puerto Rican	3,033	17.62
South American:	29	0.17
Argentinean	2	0.01
Chilean	1	0.01
Colombian	6	0.03
Ecuadorian	14	0.08
Venezuelan	4	0.02
Other South American	2	0.01
Other Hispanic or Latino	252	1.46
Hungarian	13	0.08
Iranian	7	0.04
Irish	2,251	13.08
Italian	1,482	8.61
Lithuanian	79	0.46
Norwegian	11	0.06
Polish	1,367	7.94
Portuguese	119	0.69
Romanian	47	0.27
Russian	69	0.40
Scotch-Irish	140	0.81
Scottish	296	1.72
Slovak	21	0.12
Swedish	220	1.28
Ukrainian	22	0.13
United States or American	604	3.51
Welsh	46	0.27
West Indian, excl. Hispanic:	8	0.05
Haitian	8	0.05
White:	15,035	87.34
Not Hispanic (13,028)	13,241	76.92

Notes: 1. Figures in the "Number" column do not add up to the total population due to: a) Ancestry/Race overlap — e.g. persons can report being both White and Irish, b) persons of Hispanic origin can report being any race, c) persons reporting two ancestries are counted in both categories. 2. Numbers in parentheses indicate the number of persons reporting this ancestry/race alone, not in combination with any other ancestry/race. 3. Refer to the Explanation of Data in the front of the book for more detailed information.

Hispanic (1,644)	1,794	10.42
Yugoslavian	8	0.05

Spencer

Place Type: Town
County: Worcester
Population: 11,691

Ancestry/Race	Number	%
African American/Black:	92	0.79
Not Hispanic (65)	85	0.73
Hispanic (4)	7	0.06
African, sub-Saharan:	4	0.03
African	4	0.03
Am. Ind. or Alaska Nat., not spec.	19	0.16
Albanian	7	0.06
American Indian tribes, specified:	41	0.35
Blackfeet (1)	2	0.02
Cherokee (1)	3	0.03
Choctaw	3	0.03
Iroquois (8)	13	0.11
Ute (2)	2	0.02
All other tribes (3)	18	0.15
American Indian tribes, not spec.	6	0.05
Arab:	6	0.05
Lebanese	6	0.05
Armenian	30	0.26
Asian:	52	0.44
Chinese, ex. Taiwanese (10)	13	0.11
Filipino (4)	7	0.06
Hmong (3)	3	0.03
Indian (4)	4	0.03
Japanese (1)	3	0.03
Korean (7)	9	0.08
Vietnamese (4)	11	0.09
Other Asian, not specified (2)	2	0.02
Austrian	12	0.10
British	65	0.56
Canadian	49	0.42
Czech	7	0.06
Czechoslovakian	13	0.11
Danish	12	0.10
Dutch	87	0.74
English	1,243	10.63
Estonian	7	0.06
European	25	0.21
Finnish	174	1.49
French, except Basque	2,796	23.92
French Canadian	1,581	13.52
German	526	4.50
German Russian	10	0.09
Greek	28	0.24
Hawaii Native/Pacific Islander:	5	0.04
Polynesian: (2)	3	0.03
Native Hawaiian (2)	3	0.03
Other Pac. Isl., not spec.	2	0.02
Hispanic or Latino:	156	1.33
Central American:	8	0.07
Costa Rican	1	0.01
Honduran	1	0.01
Salvadoran	6	0.05
Cuban	1	0.01
Dominican Republic	2	0.02
Mexican	7	0.06
Puerto Rican	106	0.91
South American:	8	0.07
Argentinean	2	0.02
Chilean	2	0.02
Ecuadorian	1	0.01
Venezuelan	3	0.03
Other Hispanic or Latino	24	0.21
Hungarian	18	0.15
Irish	2,272	19.43
Italian	1,087	9.30
Lithuanian	275	2.35
Norwegian	31	0.27
Polish	830	7.10
Portuguese	47	0.40
Russian	57	0.49
Scandinavian	16	0.14
Scotch-Irish	38	0.33
Scottish	221	1.89
Swedish	499	4.27
Swiss	8	0.07
Ukrainian	21	0.18
United States or American	702	6.00
Welsh	12	0.10
West Indian, excl. Hispanic:	17	0.15
Haitian	17	0.15
White:	11,513	98.48
Not Hispanic (11,347)	11,395	97.47
Hispanic (102)	118	1.01

Springfield

Place Type: City
County: Hampden
Population: 152,082

Ancestry/Race	Number	%
African American/Black:	34,863	22.92
Not Hispanic (29,831)	31,806	20.91
Hispanic (2,129)	3,057	2.01
African, sub-Saharan:	1,858	1.22
African	1,273	0.84
Cape Verdean	365	0.24
Ethiopian	17	0.01
Ghanian	10	0.01
Kenyan	4	0.00
Nigerian	34	0.02
Senegalese	6	0.00
Sierra Leonean	12	0.01
Sudanese	9	0.01
Other sub-Saharan African	128	0.08
Alaska Native tribes, specified:	6	0.00
Alaska Athabascan (2)	2	0.00
Aleut (2)	2	0.00
Eskimo (2)	2	0.00
Am. Ind. or Alaska Nat., not spec.	742	0.49
Albanian	13	0.01
American Indian tribes, specified:	688	0.45
Apache (3)	11	0.01
Blackfeet (7)	82	0.05
Cherokee (40)	196	0.13
Cheyenne	7	0.00
Chickasaw (1)	2	0.00
Chippewa (2)	2	0.00
Choctaw (3)	14	0.01
Cree (2)	2	0.00
Creek	4	0.00
Crow (1)	1	0.00
Delaware	1	0.00
Iroquois (13)	68	0.04
Latin American Indians (20)	62	0.04
Lumbee	2	0.00
Menominee	4	0.00
Navajo	3	0.00
Paiute (2)	2	0.00
Pima (1)	1	0.00
Potawatomi (1)	1	0.00
Pueblo (3)	5	0.00
Seminole (5)	17	0.01
Shoshone (1)	4	0.00
Sioux (2)	16	0.01
Yaqui	1	0.00
All other tribes (63)	180	0.12
American Indian tribes, not spec.	103	0.07
Arab:	828	0.54
Arab/Arabic	64	0.04
Lebanese	575	0.38
Moroccan	7	0.00
Palestinian	10	0.01
Syrian	131	0.09
Other Arab	41	0.03
Armenian	311	0.20
Asian:	3,528	2.32
Cambodian (114)	131	0.09
Chinese, ex. Taiwanese (398)	463	0.30
Filipino (115)	183	0.12
Hmong (78)	93	0.06
Indian (205)	285	0.19
Indonesian (7)	17	0.01
Japanese (73)	133	0.09
Korean (104)	142	0.09
Laotian (145)	155	0.10
Malaysian (2)	6	0.00
Pakistani (47)	65	0.04
Sri Lankan (1)	2	0.00
Taiwanese (6)	6	0.00
Thai (21)	29	0.02
Vietnamese (1,501)	1,601	1.05
Other Asian, specified (1)	4	0.00
Other Asian, not specified (51)	213	0.14
Assyrian/Chaldean/Syriac	6	0.00
Australian	43	0.03
Austrian	141	0.09
Belgian	46	0.03
Brazilian	6	0.00
British	328	0.22
Canadian	688	0.45
Cypriot	6	0.00
Czech	190	0.12
Czechoslovakian	45	0.03
Danish	181	0.12
Dutch	424	0.28
Eastern European	30	0.02
English	7,236	4.76
Estonian	19	0.01
European	225	0.15
Finnish	104	0.07
French, except Basque	12,437	8.18
French Canadian	6,656	4.38
German	5,392	3.55
Greek	1,026	0.67
Guyanese	37	0.02
Hawaii Native/Pacific Islander:	766	0.50
Micronesian: (19)	28	0.02
Guamanian/Chamorro (19)	27	0.02
Other Micronesian	1	0.00
Polynesian: (58)	103	0.07
Native Hawaiian (17)	47	0.03
Samoan (41)	55	0.04
Tongan	1	0.00
Other Pac. Isl., specified	2	0.00
Other Pac. Isl., not spec. (65)	633	0.42
Hispanic or Latino:	41,343	27.18
Central American:	381	0.25
Costa Rican	72	0.05
Guatemalan	78	0.05
Honduran	33	0.02
Nicaraguan	9	0.01
Panamanian	110	0.07
Salvadoran	66	0.04
Other Central American	13	0.01
Cuban	232	0.15
Dominican Republic	614	0.40
Mexican	630	0.41
Puerto Rican	35,251	23.18
South American:	418	0.27
Argentinean	12	0.01
Bolivian	2	0.00
Chilean	7	0.00
Colombian	173	0.11
Ecuadorian	68	0.04
Paraguayan	7	0.00
Peruvian	91	0.06
Uruguayan	5	0.00
Venezuelan	23	0.02
Other South American	30	0.02
Other Hispanic or Latino	3,817	2.51
Hungarian	136	0.09
Icelander	6	0.00
Iranian	49	0.03
Irish	19,143	12.59
Israeli	162	0.11
Italian	14,093	9.27
Latvian	12	0.01
Lithuanian	294	0.19
Northern European	26	0.02

Notes: 1. Figures in the "Number" column do not add up to the total population due to: a) Ancestry/Race overlap — e.g. persons can report being both White and Irish, b) persons of Hispanic origin can report being any race, c) persons reporting two ancestries are counted in both categories. 2. Numbers in parentheses indicate the number of persons reporting this ancestry/race alone, not in combination with any other ancestry/race. 3. Refer to the Explanation of Data in the front of the book for more detailed information.

Ancestry/Race	Number	%
Norwegian	251	0.17
Pennsylvania German	14	0.01
Polish	9,094	5.98
Portuguese	1,892	1.24
Romanian	69	0.05
Russian	1,443	0.95
Scandinavian	45	0.03
Scotch-Irish	1,056	0.69
Scottish	1,891	1.24
Serbian	10	0.01
Slavic	11	0.01
Slovak	41	0.03
Swedish	1,159	0.76
Swiss	58	0.04
Turkish	64	0.04
Ukrainian	489	0.32
United States or American	3,770	2.48
Welsh	299	0.20
West Indian, excl. Hispanic:	3,198	2.10
Barbadian	292	0.19
Bermudan	39	0.03
British West Indian	28	0.02
Haitian	123	0.08
Jamaican	2,314	1.52
Trinidadian and Tobagonian	139	0.09
U.S. Virgin Islander	26	0.02
West Indian	237	0.16
White:	89,328	58.74
Not Hispanic (74,291)	76,507	50.31
Hispanic (11,038)	12,821	8.43
Yugoslavian	6	0.00

Stoneham

Place Type: Town
County: Middlesex
Population: 22,219

Ancestry/Race	Number	%
African American/Black:	247	1.11
Not Hispanic (181)	230	1.04
Hispanic (16)	17	0.08
African, sub-Saharan:	80	0.36
African	26	0.12
Cape Verdean	45	0.20
Other sub-Saharan African	9	0.04
Am. Ind. or Alaska Nat., not spec.	25	0.11
Albanian	141	0.63
American Indian tribes, specified:	23	0.10
Cherokee	6	0.03
Chippewa (1)	1	0.00
Choctaw	7	0.03
Delaware	1	0.00
Iroquois (1)	1	0.00
Seminole	1	0.00
All other tribes (2)	6	0.03
American Indian tribes, not spec.	2	0.01
Arab:	186	0.84
Arab/Arabic	5	0.02
Egyptian	35	0.16
Lebanese	78	0.35
Syrian	57	0.26
Other Arab	11	0.05
Armenian	182	0.82
Asian:	619	2.79
Bangladeshi (2)	2	0.01
Cambodian (13)	13	0.06
Chinese, ex. Taiwanese (270)	290	1.31
Filipino (24)	39	0.18
Indian (113)	116	0.52
Indonesian (2)	4	0.02
Japanese (16)	20	0.09
Korean (74)	77	0.35
Pakistani (6)	7	0.03
Sri Lankan (4)	11	0.05
Taiwanese (1)	2	0.01
Thai (4)	4	0.02
Vietnamese (22)	22	0.10
Other Asian, not specified (5)	12	0.05
Australian	10	0.05
Austrian	45	0.20
Belgian	17	0.08
Brazilian	20	0.09
British	68	0.31
Canadian	289	1.30
Czech	23	0.10
Danish	68	0.31
Dutch	109	0.49
Eastern European	23	0.10
English	2,569	11.56
European	34	0.15
Finnish	35	0.16
French, except Basque	1,102	4.96
French Canadian	865	3.89
German	885	3.98
Greek	221	0.99
Hawaii Native/Pacific Islander:	16	0.07
Micronesian: (1)	1	0.00
Guamanian/Chamorro (1)	1	0.00
Polynesian: (4)	6	0.03
Native Hawaiian (3)	4	0.02
Other Polynesian (1)	2	0.01
Other Pac. Isl., not spec. (4)	9	0.04
Hispanic or Latino:	397	1.79
Central American:	53	0.24
Costa Rican	15	0.07
Guatemalan	13	0.06
Honduran	2	0.01
Nicaraguan	2	0.01
Salvadoran	21	0.09
Cuban	20	0.09
Dominican Republic	22	0.10
Mexican	42	0.19
Puerto Rican	100	0.45
South American:	47	0.21
Argentinean	5	0.02
Chilean	4	0.02
Colombian	6	0.03
Ecuadorian	5	0.02
Peruvian	18	0.08
Venezuelan	3	0.01
Other South American	6	0.03
Other Hispanic or Latino	113	0.51
Hungarian	26	0.12
Iranian	17	0.08
Irish	6,871	30.92
Italian	7,350	33.08
Latvian	9	0.04
Lithuanian	196	0.88
Norwegian	93	0.42
Polish	633	2.85
Portuguese	574	2.58
Romanian	20	0.09
Russian	165	0.74
Scotch-Irish	421	1.89
Scottish	612	2.75
Slavic	6	0.03
Slovak	17	0.08
Swedish	394	1.77
Swiss	18	0.08
Ukrainian	55	0.25
United States or American	641	2.88
Welsh	99	0.45
West Indian, excl. Hispanic:	19	0.09
Belizean	12	0.05
Jamaican	7	0.03
White:	21,287	95.81
Not Hispanic (20,875)	21,022	94.61
Hispanic (235)	265	1.19
Yugoslavian	6	0.03

Stoughton

Place Type: Town
County: Norfolk
Population: 27,149

Ancestry/Race	Number	%
African American/Black:	1,772	6.53
Not Hispanic (1,534)	1,752	6.45
Hispanic (14)	20	0.07
African, sub-Saharan:	542	2.00
African	160	0.59
Cape Verdean	244	0.90
Ghanian	8	0.03
Nigerian	97	0.36
Other sub-Saharan African	33	0.12
Alaska Native tribes, specified:	1	0.00
Tlingit-Haida	1	0.00
Am. Ind. or Alaska Nat., not spec.	41	0.15
Albanian	75	0.28
American Indian tribes, specified:	51	0.19
Apache (1)	1	0.00
Cherokee	15	0.06
Cheyenne	1	0.00
Chippewa (2)	2	0.01
Iroquois (1)	3	0.01
Latin American Indians (3)	3	0.01
Paiute	1	0.00
Sioux (2)	6	0.02
All other tribes (8)	19	0.07
American Indian tribes, not spec.	7	0.03
Arab:	318	1.17
Arab/Arabic	97	0.36
Egyptian	6	0.02
Lebanese	159	0.59
Syrian	56	0.21
Armenian	109	0.40
Asian:	714	2.63
Bangladeshi (1)	2	0.01
Cambodian (2)	2	0.01
Chinese, ex. Taiwanese (185)	212	0.78
Filipino (60)	82	0.30
Hmong (1)	1	0.00
Indian (152)	179	0.66
Indonesian (3)	3	0.01
Japanese (12)	25	0.09
Korean (54)	63	0.23
Laotian (1)	2	0.01
Malaysian (2)	4	0.01
Pakistani (12)	12	0.04
Taiwanese (7)	7	0.03
Thai (17)	19	0.07
Vietnamese (53)	60	0.22
Other Asian, not specified (6)	41	0.15
Austrian	62	0.23
Belgian	11	0.04
Brazilian	85	0.31
British	49	0.18
Bulgarian	26	0.10
Canadian	287	1.06
Croatian	26	0.10
Czech	59	0.22
Czechoslovakian	33	0.12
Danish	74	0.27
Dutch	110	0.41
Eastern European	84	0.31
English	2,323	8.56
Estonian	7	0.03
European	139	0.51
Finnish	77	0.28
French, except Basque	1,010	3.72
French Canadian	609	2.24
German	1,485	5.47
Greek	349	1.29
Hawaii Native/Pacific Islander:	20	0.07
Micronesian: (3)	3	0.01
Guamanian/Chamorro (3)	3	0.01
Polynesian: (2)	6	0.02
Native Hawaiian (1)	5	0.02
Samoan (1)	1	0.00
Other Pac. Isl., not spec. (8)	11	0.04
Hispanic or Latino:	419	1.54
Central American:	41	0.15
Costa Rican	12	0.04
Guatemalan	20	0.07
Honduran	1	0.00
Panamanian	2	0.01
Salvadoran	1	0.00
Other Central American	5	0.02

Notes: 1. Figures in the "Number" column do not add up to the total population due to: a) Ancestry/Race overlap — e.g. persons can report being both White and Irish, b) persons of Hispanic origin can report being any race, c) persons reporting two ancestries are counted in both categories. 2. Numbers in parentheses indicate the number of persons reporting this ancestry/race alone, not in combination with any other ancestry/race. 3. Refer to the Explanation of Data in the front of the book for more detailed information.

Cuban	25	0.09
Dominican Republic	14	0.05
Mexican	44	0.16
Puerto Rican	128	0.47
South American:	50	0.18
Argentinean	11	0.04
Chilean	7	0.03
Colombian	19	0.07
Peruvian	9	0.03
Venezuelan	3	0.01
Other South American	1	0.00
Other Hispanic or Latino	117	0.43
Hungarian	64	0.24
Irish	6,778	24.97
Israeli	23	0.08
Italian	3,744	13.79
Latvian	57	0.21
Lithuanian	412	1.52
Northern European	5	0.02
Norwegian	151	0.56
Polish	1,360	5.01
Portuguese	2,794	10.29
Romanian	27	0.10
Russian	1,366	5.03
Scandinavian	10	0.04
Scotch-Irish	462	1.70
Scottish	507	1.87
Slovak	12	0.04
Swedish	446	1.64
Swiss	17	0.06
Ukrainian	185	0.68
United States or American	1,314	4.84
Welsh	61	0.22
West Indian, excl. Hispanic:	599	2.21
Barbadian	8	0.03
British West Indian	17	0.06
Haitian	281	1.04
Jamaican	143	0.53
Trinidadian and Tobagonian	77	0.28
West Indian	73	0.27
White:	24,513	90.29
Not Hispanic (23,751)	24,228	89.24
Hispanic (266)	285	1.05
Yugoslavian	19	0.07

Sudbury

Place Type: Town
County: Middlesex
Population: 16,841

Ancestry/Race	Number	%
African American/Black:	164	0.97
Not Hispanic (134)	162	0.96
Hispanic	2	0.01
African, sub-Saharan:	31	0.18
South African	31	0.18
Am. Ind. or Alaska Nat., not spec.	14	0.08
Albanian	12	0.07
American Indian tribes, specified:	22	0.13
Chippewa	2	0.01
Creek	3	0.02
Iroquois	2	0.01
Latin American Indians	1	0.01
Lumbee	1	0.01
Navajo (1)	1	0.01
Osage	1	0.01
Seminole	1	0.01
Sioux	4	0.02
All other tribes (1)	6	0.04
American Indian tribes, not spec.	1	0.01
Arab:	33	0.20
Egyptian	18	0.11
Lebanese	4	0.02
Syrian	6	0.04
Other Arab	5	0.03
Armenian	92	0.55
Asian:	727	4.32
Cambodian (3)	3	0.02
Chinese, ex. Taiwanese (293)	341	2.02
Filipino (19)	31	0.18
Indian (182)	200	1.19
Indonesian (2)	2	0.01
Japanese (23)	38	0.23
Korean (50)	54	0.32
Pakistani (1)	11	0.07
Sri Lankan (2)	2	0.01
Taiwanese (29)	29	0.17
Thai (4)	4	0.02
Vietnamese (3)	3	0.02
Other Asian, not specified (5)	9	0.05
Australian	12	0.07
Austrian	217	1.29
Belgian	47	0.28
Brazilian	32	0.19
British	297	1.76
Canadian	206	1.22
Czech	42	0.25
Czechoslovakian	28	0.17
Danish	99	0.59
Dutch	413	2.45
Eastern European	184	1.09
English	2,786	16.54
European	277	1.64
Finnish	167	0.99
French, except Basque	518	3.08
French Canadian	357	2.12
German	2,058	12.22
Greek	207	1.23
Hawaii Native/Pacific Islander:	10	0.06
Micronesian: (3)	3	0.02
Guamanian/Chamorro (3)	3	0.02
Polynesian: (1)	4	0.02
Native Hawaiian	3	0.02
Samoan (1)	1	0.01
Other Pac. Isl., not spec. (1)	3	0.02
Hispanic or Latino:	208	1.24
Central American:	18	0.11
Costa Rican	2	0.01
Guatemalan	10	0.06
Honduran	1	0.01
Panamanian	1	0.01
Salvadoran	4	0.02
Cuban	27	0.16
Dominican Republic	2	0.01
Mexican	34	0.20
Puerto Rican	37	0.22
South American:	40	0.24
Chilean	6	0.04
Colombian	16	0.10
Ecuadorian	3	0.02
Peruvian	10	0.06
Venezuelan	3	0.02
Other South American	2	0.01
Other Hispanic or Latino	50	0.30
Hungarian	59	0.35
Iranian	6	0.04
Irish	4,130	24.52
Israeli	31	0.18
Italian	2,331	13.84
Latvian	30	0.18
Lithuanian	148	0.88
Northern European	21	0.12
Norwegian	276	1.64
Polish	647	3.84
Portuguese	94	0.56
Romanian	22	0.13
Russian	752	4.47
Scandinavian	26	0.15
Scotch-Irish	238	1.41
Scottish	671	3.98
Slavic	7	0.04
Slovak	42	0.25
Slovene	7	0.04
Swedish	441	2.62
Swiss	159	0.94
Turkish	15	0.09
Ukrainian	149	0.88
United States or American	774	4.60
Welsh	106	0.63
White:	16,023	95.14
Not Hispanic (15,711)	15,849	94.11
Hispanic (159)	174	1.03

Swampscott

Place Type: Census Designated Place
County: Essex
Population: 14,412

Ancestry/Race	Number	%
Afghan	11	0.08
African American/Black:	141	0.98
Not Hispanic (98)	126	0.87
Hispanic (8)	15	0.10
African, sub-Saharan:	21	0.15
African	15	0.10
South African	6	0.04
Am. Ind. or Alaska Nat., not spec.	6	0.04
Albanian	8	0.06
Alsatian	11	0.08
American Indian tribes, specified:	11	0.08
Blackfeet	1	0.01
Cherokee (1)	4	0.03
Creek	1	0.01
Latin American Indians (1)	1	0.01
Sioux	1	0.01
All other tribes (2)	3	0.02
American Indian tribes, not spec.	2	0.01
Arab:	69	0.48
Lebanese	35	0.24
Palestinian	34	0.24
Armenian	19	0.13
Asian:	142	0.99
Cambodian (1)	2	0.01
Chinese, ex. Taiwanese (31)	39	0.27
Filipino (9)	17	0.12
Indian (15)	29	0.20
Japanese (16)	24	0.17
Korean (7)	9	0.06
Thai (3)	3	0.02
Vietnamese (15)	18	0.12
Other Asian, specified	1	0.01
Australian	10	0.07
Austrian	53	0.37
Brazilian	17	0.12
British	35	0.24
Canadian	196	1.36
Czech	47	0.33
Danish	42	0.29
Dutch	73	0.51
Eastern European	79	0.55
English	1,566	10.87
European	70	0.49
Finnish	22	0.15
French, except Basque	726	5.04
French Canadian	531	3.68
German	686	4.76
Greek	350	2.43
Hawaii Native/Pacific Islander:	10	0.07
Micronesian: (1)	4	0.03
Other Micronesian (1)	4	0.03
Polynesian: (2)	6	0.04
Native Hawaiian (1)	1	0.01
Samoan (1)	4	0.03
Other Polynesian	1	0.01
Hispanic or Latino:	183	1.27
Central American:	9	0.06
Costa Rican	2	0.01
Guatemalan	4	0.03
Other Central American	3	0.02
Cuban	7	0.05
Dominican Republic	15	0.10
Mexican	26	0.18
Puerto Rican	32	0.22
South American:	36	0.25
Argentinean	9	0.06
Chilean	5	0.03
Colombian	11	0.08
Ecuadorian	3	0.02

Notes: 1. Figures in the "Number" column do not add up to the total population due to: a) Ancestry/Race overlap — e.g. persons can report being both White and Irish, b) persons of Hispanic origin can report being any race, c) persons reporting two ancestries are counted in both categories. 2. Numbers in parentheses indicate the number of persons reporting this ancestry/race alone, not in combination with any other ancestry/race. 3. Refer to the Explanation of Data in the front of the book for more detailed information.

Ancestry/Race	Number	%
Peruvian	5	0.03
Venezuelan	1	0.01
Other South American	2	0.01
Other Hispanic or Latino	58	0.40
Hungarian	66	0.46
Iranian	54	0.37
Irish	3,516	24.40
Italian	2,161	14.99
Latvian	27	0.19
Lithuanian	132	0.92
Norwegian	143	0.99
Polish	804	5.58
Portuguese	53	0.37
Romanian	56	0.39
Russian	1,280	8.88
Scotch-Irish	153	1.06
Scottish	313	2.17
Slovak	18	0.12
Soviet Union	28	0.19
Swedish	272	1.89
Swiss	32	0.22
Ukrainian	88	0.61
United States or American	756	5.25
Welsh	116	0.80
West Indian, excl. Hispanic:	5	0.03
Other West Indian	5	0.03
White:	14,145	98.15
Not Hispanic (13,916)	14,007	97.19
Hispanic (131)	138	0.96

Swansea

Place Type: Town
County: Bristol
Population: 15,901

Ancestry/Race	Number	%
African American/Black:	85	0.53
Not Hispanic (59)	83	0.52
Hispanic (1)	2	0.01
African, sub-Saharan:	89	0.56
African	6	0.04
Cape Verdean	83	0.52
Am. Ind. or Alaska Nat., not spec.	16	0.10
American Indian tribes, specified:	37	0.23
Apache (1)	2	0.01
Blackfeet	2	0.01
Cherokee	3	0.02
Chippewa (2)	2	0.01
Iroquois	6	0.04
Latin American Indians	3	0.02
Seminole	4	0.03
All other tribes (3)	15	0.09
American Indian tribes, not spec.	1	0.01
Arab:	183	1.15
Egyptian	36	0.23
Lebanese	133	0.84
Syrian	14	0.09
Armenian	10	0.06
Asian:	97	0.61
Cambodian (12)	16	0.10
Chinese, ex. Taiwanese (9)	12	0.08
Filipino (11)	24	0.15
Indian (5)	6	0.04
Japanese (5)	19	0.12
Korean (7)	8	0.05
Pakistani (2)	2	0.01
Thai (3)	3	0.02
Vietnamese (1)	4	0.03
Other Asian, not specified (1)	3	0.02
Austrian	25	0.16
Brazilian	13	0.08
British	12	0.08
Canadian	67	0.42
Czech	7	0.04
Danish	30	0.19
Dutch	66	0.42
English	2,259	14.21
European	14	0.09
Finnish	29	0.18
French, except Basque	2,956	18.59
French Canadian	1,299	8.17
German	618	3.89
Hawaii Native/Pacific Islander:	13	0.08
Polynesian:	1	0.01
Native Hawaiian	1	0.01
Other Pac. Isl., not spec. (1)	12	0.08
Hispanic or Latino:	96	0.60
Central American:	4	0.03
Guatemalan	2	0.01
Honduran	2	0.01
Cuban	5	0.03
Dominican Republic	2	0.01
Mexican	10	0.06
Puerto Rican	26	0.16
South American:	5	0.03
Colombian	3	0.02
Peruvian	2	0.01
Other Hispanic or Latino	44	0.28
Irish	2,980	18.74
Italian	956	6.01
Norwegian	59	0.37
Polish	540	3.40
Portuguese	5,922	37.24
Russian	23	0.14
Scotch-Irish	144	0.91
Scottish	240	1.51
Swedish	127	0.80
Swiss	8	0.05
Ukrainian	35	0.22
United States or American	620	3.90
Welsh	31	0.19
West Indian, excl. Hispanic:	12	0.08
West Indian	12	0.08
White:	15,715	98.83
Not Hispanic (15,494)	15,632	98.31
Hispanic (75)	83	0.52

Taunton

Place Type: City
County: Bristol
Population: 55,976

Ancestry/Race	Number	%
African American/Black:	1,965	3.51
Not Hispanic (1,366)	1,747	3.12
Hispanic (168)	218	0.39
African, sub-Saharan:	1,425	2.55
Cape Verdean	1,425	2.55
Alaska Native tribes, specified:	4	0.01
Eskimo	4	0.01
Am. Ind. or Alaska Nat., not spec.	127	0.23
Albanian	65	0.12
American Indian tribes, specified:	170	0.30
Apache	6	0.01
Blackfeet (1)	15	0.03
Cherokee (6)	35	0.06
Chippewa (4)	6	0.01
Choctaw (2)	4	0.01
Creek	1	0.00
Crow	1	0.00
Delaware	4	0.01
Iroquois (5)	6	0.01
Latin American Indians	5	0.01
Navajo	4	0.01
Seminole (1)	5	0.01
Shoshone	1	0.00
Sioux (2)	6	0.01
All other tribes (25)	71	0.13
American Indian tribes, not spec.	8	0.01
Arab:	359	0.64
Egyptian	37	0.07
Lebanese	270	0.48
Syrian	52	0.09
Armenian	57	0.10
Asian:	494	0.88
Cambodian (5)	7	0.01
Chinese, ex. Taiwanese (69)	87	0.16
Filipino (53)	85	0.15
Indian (63)	80	0.14
Indonesian (3)	4	0.01
Japanese (10)	35	0.06
Korean (34)	49	0.09
Laotian (13)	13	0.02
Pakistani (18)	20	0.04
Thai (7)	15	0.03
Vietnamese (34)	38	0.07
Other Asian, not specified (20)	61	0.11
Austrian	45	0.08
Brazilian	137	0.24
British	42	0.08
Bulgarian	9	0.02
Canadian	205	0.37
Czech	57	0.10
Czechoslovakian	20	0.04
Danish	17	0.03
Dutch	140	0.25
Eastern European	22	0.04
English	6,263	11.19
European	52	0.09
Finnish	37	0.07
French, except Basque	5,851	10.45
French Canadian	2,836	5.07
German	1,891	3.38
Greek	400	0.71
Hawaii Native/Pacific Islander:	87	0.16
Micronesian: (5)	12	0.02
Guamanian/Chamorro (4)	9	0.02
Other Micronesian (1)	3	0.01
Polynesian: (5)	16	0.03
Native Hawaiian (5)	9	0.02
Samoan	7	0.01
Other Pac. Isl., not spec. (8)	59	0.11
Hispanic or Latino:	2,198	3.93
Central American:	58	0.10
Costa Rican	6	0.01
Guatemalan	24	0.04
Honduran	7	0.01
Panamanian	7	0.01
Salvadoran	8	0.01
Other Central American	6	0.01
Cuban	30	0.05
Dominican Republic	72	0.13
Mexican	86	0.15
Puerto Rican	1,518	2.71
South American:	60	0.11
Argentinean	6	0.01
Bolivian	6	0.01
Colombian	28	0.05
Ecuadorian	4	0.01
Peruvian	10	0.02
Venezuelan	5	0.01
Other South American	1	0.00
Other Hispanic or Latino	374	0.67
Hungarian	75	0.13
Icelander	32	0.06
Irish	11,947	21.34
Italian	4,636	8.28
Lithuanian	340	0.61
Northern European	21	0.04
Norwegian	274	0.49
Polish	2,543	4.54
Portuguese	15,370	27.46
Russian	229	0.41
Scotch-Irish	638	1.14
Scottish	1,064	1.90
Slavic	8	0.01
Slovak	19	0.03
Swedish	939	1.68
Swiss	40	0.07
Turkish	7	0.01
Ukrainian	27	0.05
United States or American	1,730	3.09
Welsh	63	0.11
West Indian, excl. Hispanic:	97	0.17
Haitian	67	0.12
Jamaican	30	0.05
White:	52,289	93.41
Not Hispanic (50,272)	51,106	91.30

Notes: 1. Figures in the "Number" column do not add up to the total population due to: a) Ancestry/Race overlap — e.g. persons can report being both White and Irish, b) persons of Hispanic origin can report being any race, c) persons reporting two ancestries are counted in both categories. 2. Numbers in parentheses indicate the number of persons reporting this ancestry/race alone, not in combination with any other ancestry/race. 3. Refer to the Explanation of Data in the front of the book for more detailed information.

Hispanic (1,043)	1,183	2.11
Yugoslavian	9	0.02

Tewksbury

Place Type: Town
County: Middlesex
Population: 28,851

Ancestry/Race	Number	%
Afghan	10	0.03
African American/Black:	248	0.86
Not Hispanic (187)	240	0.83
Hispanic (7)	8	0.03
African, sub-Saharan:	53	0.18
African	33	0.11
Cape Verdean	20	0.07
Alaska Native tribes, specified:	3	0.01
Eskimo (3)	3	0.01
Am. Ind. or Alaska Nat., not spec.	32	0.11
Albanian	71	0.25
American Indian tribes, specified:	38	0.13
Blackfeet	5	0.02
Cherokee (4)	7	0.02
Choctaw	2	0.01
Iroquois (10)	14	0.05
Puget Sound Salish (1)	1	0.00
Sioux (1)	2	0.01
All other tribes (2)	7	0.02
American Indian tribes, not spec.	6	0.02
Arab:	70	0.24
Arab/Arabic	9	0.03
Lebanese	44	0.15
Syrian	17	0.06
Armenian	122	0.42
Asian:	531	1.84
Cambodian (26)	27	0.09
Chinese, ex. Taiwanese (126)	150	0.52
Filipino (33)	44	0.15
Indian (142)	149	0.52
Indonesian (1)	1	0.00
Japanese (10)	17	0.06
Korean (55)	68	0.24
Laotian (3)	3	0.01
Pakistani (5)	6	0.02
Taiwanese	3	0.01
Thai (1)	1	0.00
Vietnamese (46)	47	0.16
Other Asian, not specified (7)	15	0.05
Austrian	90	0.31
Belgian	67	0.23
Brazilian	56	0.19
British	84	0.29
Bulgarian	9	0.03
Canadian	454	1.57
Croatian	7	0.02
Czech	64	0.22
Czechoslovakian	34	0.12
Danish	57	0.20
Dutch	82	0.28
English	3,605	12.48
Estonian	8	0.03
European	70	0.24
Finnish	38	0.13
French, except Basque	2,287	7.92
French Canadian	1,771	6.13
German	1,889	6.54
Greek	398	1.38
Hawaii Native/Pacific Islander:	26	0.09
Micronesian: (1)	4	0.01
Guamanian/Chamorro (1)	4	0.01
Polynesian: (1)	5	0.02
Native Hawaiian	4	0.01
Samoan (1)	1	0.00
Other Pac. Isl., not spec.	17	0.06
Hispanic or Latino:	352	1.22
Central American:	16	0.06
Costa Rican	3	0.01
Guatemalan	2	0.01
Honduran	1	0.00
Panamanian	1	0.00
Salvadoran	6	0.02
Other Central American	3	0.01
Cuban	26	0.09
Dominican Republic	28	0.10
Mexican	27	0.09
Puerto Rican	123	0.43
South American:	46	0.16
Argentinean	1	0.00
Chilean	2	0.01
Colombian	33	0.11
Ecuadorian	3	0.01
Peruvian	2	0.01
Venezuelan	1	0.00
Other South American	4	0.01
Other Hispanic or Latino	86	0.30
Hungarian	80	0.28
Irish	10,158	35.16
Italian	6,967	24.12
Latvian	16	0.06
Lithuanian	155	0.54
Norwegian	147	0.51
Pennsylvania German	8	0.03
Polish	1,355	4.69
Portuguese	962	3.33
Romanian	11	0.04
Russian	305	1.06
Scandinavian	22	0.08
Scotch-Irish	712	2.46
Scottish	1,010	3.50
Slovak	17	0.06
Swedish	523	1.81
Swiss	8	0.03
Ukrainian	96	0.33
United States or American	974	3.37
Welsh	71	0.25
West Indian, excl. Hispanic:	37	0.13
Bermudan	5	0.02
Jamaican	26	0.09
West Indian	6	0.02
White:	28,019	97.12
Not Hispanic (27,608)	27,783	96.30
Hispanic (216)	236	0.82
Yugoslavian	12	0.04

Tyngsborough

Place Type: Town
County: Middlesex
Population: 11,081

Ancestry/Race	Number	%
African American/Black:	89	0.80
Not Hispanic (54)	85	0.77
Hispanic (1)	4	0.04
African, sub-Saharan:	32	0.29
South African	20	0.18
Other sub-Saharan African	12	0.11
Am. Ind. or Alaska Nat., not spec.	18	0.16
Albanian	28	0.25
American Indian tribes, specified:	44	0.40
Blackfeet	6	0.05
Cherokee	10	0.09
Choctaw (1)	1	0.01
Iroquois	2	0.02
Lumbee	4	0.04
Sioux	1	0.01
All other tribes (13)	20	0.18
American Indian tribes, not spec.	1	0.01
Arab:	96	0.87
Arab/Arabic	74	0.67
Lebanese	22	0.20
Armenian	15	0.14
Asian:	342	3.09
Cambodian (38)	55	0.50
Chinese, ex. Taiwanese (35)	59	0.53
Filipino (5)	13	0.12
Indian (95)	103	0.93
Japanese	1	0.01
Korean (28)	29	0.26
Laotian (7)	10	0.09
Pakistani (1)	1	0.01
Thai (5)	9	0.08
Vietnamese (37)	45	0.41
Other Asian, specified	4	0.04
Other Asian, not specified (4)	13	0.12
Austrian	40	0.36
Belgian	6	0.05
Brazilian	29	0.26
British	23	0.21
Canadian	93	0.84
Czechoslovakian	8	0.07
Danish	10	0.09
Dutch	58	0.52
English	1,728	15.59
European	67	0.60
Finnish	7	0.06
French, except Basque	1,857	16.76
French Canadian	1,122	10.13
German	743	6.71
Greek	329	2.97
Hawaii Native/Pacific Islander:	9	0.08
Micronesian: (1)	1	0.01
Guamanian/Chamorro (1)	1	0.01
Polynesian: (3)	3	0.03
Samoan (3)	3	0.03
Other Pac. Isl., specified	4	0.04
Other Pac. Isl., not spec.	1	0.01
Hispanic or Latino:	123	1.11
Central American:	11	0.10
Guatemalan	6	0.05
Honduran	2	0.02
Panamanian	2	0.02
Other Central American	1	0.01
Cuban	7	0.06
Dominican Republic	5	0.05
Mexican	11	0.10
Puerto Rican	34	0.31
South American:	26	0.23
Chilean	3	0.03
Colombian	15	0.14
Ecuadorian	2	0.02
Peruvian	3	0.03
Venezuelan	3	0.03
Other Hispanic or Latino	29	0.26
Hungarian	9	0.08
Irish	3,409	30.76
Israeli	5	0.05
Italian	1,271	11.47
Lithuanian	112	1.01
Northern European	23	0.21
Norwegian	104	0.94
Polish	481	4.34
Portuguese	369	3.33
Russian	57	0.51
Scandinavian	9	0.08
Scotch-Irish	179	1.62
Scottish	367	3.31
Slovak	25	0.23
Swedish	131	1.18
Ukrainian	7	0.06
United States or American	365	3.29
Welsh	41	0.37
West Indian, excl. Hispanic:	14	0.13
Barbadian	14	0.13
White:	10,695	96.52
Not Hispanic (10,499)	10,591	95.58
Hispanic (98)	104	0.94

Uxbridge

Place Type: Town
County: Worcester
Population: 11,156

Ancestry/Race	Number	%
African American/Black:	32	0.29
Not Hispanic (16)	31	0.28
Hispanic (1)	1	0.01
African, sub-Saharan:	5	0.04

Notes: 1. Figures in the "Number" column do not add up to the total population due to: a) Ancestry/Race overlap — e.g. persons can report being both White and Irish, b) persons of Hispanic origin can report being any race, c) persons reporting two ancestries are counted in both categories. 2. Numbers in parentheses indicate the number of persons reporting this ancestry/race alone, not in combination with any other ancestry/race. 3. Refer to the Explanation of Data in the front of the book for more detailed information.

Cape Verdean	5	0.04
Am. Ind. or Alaska Nat., not spec.	19	0.17
Albanian	15	0.13
American Indian tribes, specified:	22	0.20
Apache (1)	2	0.02
Blackfeet (4)	6	0.05
Cherokee	2	0.02
Chippewa (1)	4	0.04
Delaware	1	0.01
Iroquois	2	0.02
All other tribes (5)	5	0.04
Arab:	83	0.75
Arab/Arabic	12	0.11
Egyptian	27	0.24
Lebanese	44	0.40
Armenian	37	0.33
Asian:	87	0.78
Chinese, ex. Taiwanese (17)	22	0.20
Filipino (5)	9	0.08
Indian (30)	34	0.30
Indonesian (1)	5	0.04
Japanese (1)	3	0.03
Korean (6)	7	0.06
Malaysian (1)	1	0.01
Taiwanese (2)	2	0.02
Vietnamese (1)	2	0.02
Other Asian, not specified (2)	2	0.02
Austrian	28	0.25
Belgian	15	0.13
British	68	0.61
Canadian	103	0.92
Czech	41	0.37
Czechoslovakian	31	0.28
Dutch	212	1.90
English	1,543	13.86
European	42	0.38
Finnish	50	0.45
French, except Basque	1,951	17.52
French Canadian	1,255	11.27
German	629	5.65
Greek	84	0.75
Hawaii Native/Pacific Islander:	12	0.11
Micronesian: (3)	3	0.03
Guamanian/Chamorro (1)	1	0.01
Other Micronesian (2)	2	0.02
Polynesian: (1)	1	0.01
Native Hawaiian (1)	1	0.01
Other Pac. Isl., not spec. (4)	8	0.07
Hispanic or Latino:	106	0.95
Central American:	4	0.04
Guatemalan	3	0.03
Salvadoran	1	0.01
Cuban	4	0.04
Dominican Republic	2	0.02
Mexican	18	0.16
Puerto Rican	34	0.30
South American:	13	0.12
Argentinean	2	0.02
Colombian	5	0.04
Peruvian	2	0.02
Other South American	4	0.04
Other Hispanic or Latino	31	0.28
Hungarian	5	0.04
Irish	2,864	25.72
Italian	1,964	17.64
Lithuanian	61	0.55
Norwegian	35	0.31
Polish	693	6.22
Portuguese	246	2.21
Romanian	6	0.05
Russian	45	0.40
Scandinavian	13	0.12
Scotch-Irish	365	3.28
Scottish	513	4.61
Slovak	59	0.53
Swedish	276	2.48
Swiss	7	0.06
Ukrainian	13	0.12
United States or American	438	3.93
Welsh	6	0.05
West Indian, excl. Hispanic:	5	0.04
Jamaican	5	0.04
White:	11,011	98.70
Not Hispanic (10,855)	10,922	97.90
Hispanic (82)	89	0.80
Yugoslavian	25	0.22

Wakefield

Place Type: Census Designated Place
County: Middlesex
Population: 24,804

Ancestry/Race	Number	%
Acadian/Cajun	5	0.02
African American/Black:	172	0.69
Not Hispanic (106)	162	0.65
Hispanic (5)	10	0.04
African, sub-Saharan:	65	0.26
Cape Verdean	12	0.05
Nigerian	53	0.21
Alaska Native tribes, not specified	1	0.00
Am. Ind. or Alaska Nat., not spec.	32	0.13
Albanian	10	0.04
American Indian tribes, specified:	43	0.17
Blackfeet	1	0.00
Cherokee (2)	8	0.03
Cheyenne	1	0.00
Chippewa (1)	1	0.00
Choctaw	3	0.01
Cree (3)	3	0.01
Iroquois	3	0.01
Latin American Indians (4)	5	0.02
Sioux	1	0.00
All other tribes (7)	17	0.07
Arab:	98	0.40
Lebanese	79	0.32
Syrian	19	0.08
Armenian	99	0.40
Asian:	432	1.74
Cambodian (6)	7	0.03
Chinese, ex. Taiwanese (179)	207	0.83
Filipino (20)	35	0.14
Indian (77)	90	0.36
Japanese (7)	13	0.05
Korean (44)	45	0.18
Pakistani	2	0.01
Sri Lankan	4	0.02
Taiwanese (5)	5	0.02
Thai (2)	2	0.01
Vietnamese (8)	8	0.03
Other Asian, specified	1	0.00
Other Asian, not specified (2)	13	0.05
Austrian	26	0.10
Belgian	36	0.15
Brazilian	50	0.20
British	83	0.33
Canadian	274	1.10
Celtic	11	0.04
Czech	30	0.12
Czechoslovakian	36	0.15
Danish	44	0.18
Dutch	138	0.56
Eastern European	7	0.03
English	3,314	13.36
European	13	0.05
Finnish	63	0.25
French, except Basque	1,560	6.29
French Canadian	1,197	4.83
German	1,369	5.52
Greek	385	1.55
Hawaii Native/Pacific Islander:	4	0.02
Polynesian:	1	0.00
Native Hawaiian	1	0.00
Other Pac. Isl., specified	1	0.00
Other Pac. Isl., not spec. (2)	2	0.01
Hispanic or Latino:	204	0.82
Central American:	20	0.08
Costa Rican	6	0.02
Guatemalan	1	0.00
Honduran	1	0.00
Panamanian	1	0.00
Salvadoran	11	0.04
Cuban	7	0.03
Dominican Republic	12	0.05
Mexican	23	0.09
Puerto Rican	58	0.23
South American:	25	0.10
Argentinean	1	0.00
Colombian	12	0.05
Paraguayan	2	0.01
Venezuelan	4	0.02
Other South American	6	0.02
Other Hispanic or Latino	59	0.24
Hungarian	19	0.08
Iranian	30	0.12
Irish	8,185	33.00
Israeli	10	0.04
Italian	7,069	28.50
Latvian	7	0.03
Lithuanian	68	0.27
Northern European	30	0.12
Norwegian	140	0.56
Polish	799	3.22
Portuguese	443	1.79
Romanian	15	0.06
Russian	249	1.00
Scandinavian	22	0.09
Scotch-Irish	593	2.39
Scottish	1,058	4.27
Slovak	19	0.08
Swedish	440	1.77
Swiss	107	0.43
Turkish	32	0.13
Ukrainian	90	0.36
United States or American	1,033	4.16
Welsh	61	0.25
West Indian, excl. Hispanic:	30	0.12
Trinidadian and Tobagonian	30	0.12
White:	24,246	97.75
Not Hispanic (23,902)	24,081	97.09
Hispanic (143)	165	0.67

Walpole

Place Type: Town
County: Norfolk
Population: 22,824

Ancestry/Race	Number	%
Acadian/Cajun	20	0.09
African American/Black:	397	1.74
Not Hispanic (353)	382	1.67
Hispanic (10)	15	0.07
African, sub-Saharan:	109	0.48
African	44	0.19
Cape Verdean	37	0.16
Liberian	28	0.12
Am. Ind. or Alaska Nat., not spec.	18	0.08
Albanian	55	0.24
American Indian tribes, specified:	31	0.14
Blackfeet (1)	4	0.02
Cherokee (3)	10	0.04
Chippewa (2)	2	0.01
Iroquois (1)	2	0.01
Latin American Indians (5)	5	0.02
Lumbee	1	0.00
All other tribes (2)	7	0.03
American Indian tribes, not spec.	4	0.02
Arab:	370	1.62
Lebanese	218	0.96
Syrian	152	0.67
Armenian	140	0.61
Asian:	314	1.38
Cambodian (3)	3	0.01
Chinese, ex. Taiwanese (104)	126	0.55
Filipino (6)	12	0.05
Indian (67)	71	0.31
Japanese (12)	22	0.10
Korean (27)	31	0.14

Notes: 1. Figures in the "Number" column do not add up to the total population due to: a) Ancestry/Race overlap — e.g. persons can report being both White and Irish, b) persons of Hispanic origin can report being any race, c) persons reporting two ancestries are counted in both categories. 2. Numbers in parentheses indicate the number of persons reporting this ancestry/race alone, not in combination with any other ancestry/race. 3. Refer to the Explanation of Data in the front of the book for more detailed information.

Ancestry/Race	Number	%
Laotian (8)	8	0.04
Sri Lankan (2)	2	0.01
Taiwanese (5)	6	0.03
Vietnamese (20)	23	0.10
Other Asian, not specified	10	0.04
Australian	10	0.04
Austrian	54	0.24
Brazilian	25	0.11
British	84	0.37
Bulgarian	9	0.04
Canadian	299	1.31
Czech	39	0.17
Czechoslovakian	7	0.03
Danish	54	0.24
Dutch	75	0.33
Eastern European	18	0.08
English	3,328	14.58
European	90	0.39
Finnish	96	0.42
French, except Basque	951	4.17
French Canadian	700	3.07
German	2,183	9.56
Greek	306	1.34
Hawaii Native/Pacific Islander:	6	0.03
Polynesian: (2)	3	0.01
Native Hawaiian (1)	2	0.01
Samoan (1)	1	0.00
Other Pac. Isl., not spec.	3	0.01
Hispanic or Latino:	461	2.02
Central American:	18	0.08
Costa Rican	6	0.03
Guatemalan	4	0.02
Panamanian	2	0.01
Salvadoran	5	0.02
Other Central American	1	0.00
Cuban	33	0.14
Dominican Republic	14	0.06
Mexican	42	0.18
Puerto Rican	202	0.89
South American:	52	0.23
Argentinean	3	0.01
Chilean	1	0.00
Colombian	34	0.15
Ecuadorian	1	0.00
Peruvian	10	0.04
Venezuelan	1	0.00
Other South American	2	0.01
Other Hispanic or Latino	100	0.44
Hungarian	26	0.11
Iranian	7	0.03
Irish	9,097	39.86
Italian	4,660	20.42
Latvian	50	0.22
Lithuanian	284	1.24
Norwegian	204	0.89
Polish	981	4.30
Portuguese	252	1.10
Russian	361	1.58
Scotch-Irish	451	1.98
Scottish	642	2.81
Slovak	27	0.12
Swedish	490	2.15
Swiss	32	0.14
Turkish	29	0.13
Ukrainian	59	0.26
United States or American	654	2.87
Welsh	62	0.27
West Indian, excl. Hispanic:	27	0.12
Jamaican	18	0.08
Trinidadian and Tobagonian	9	0.04
White:	21,895	95.93
Not Hispanic (21,582)	21,687	95.02
Hispanic (195)	208	0.91
Yugoslavian	23	0.10

Waltham

Place Type: City
County: Middlesex
Population: 59,226

Ancestry/Race	Number	%
Afghan	20	0.03
African American/Black:	2,953	4.99
Not Hispanic (2,484)	2,780	4.69
Hispanic (130)	173	0.29
African, sub-Saharan:	642	1.08
African	314	0.53
Cape Verdean	103	0.17
Ethiopian	5	0.01
Ghanian	50	0.08
Nigerian	32	0.05
South African	6	0.01
Ugandan	61	0.10
Other sub-Saharan African	71	0.12
Alaska Native tribes, specified:	2	0.00
Alaska Athabascan (1)	1	0.00
All other tribes	1	0.00
Am. Ind. or Alaska Nat., not spec.	103	0.17
Albanian	55	0.09
American Indian tribes, specified:	117	0.20
Apache (3)	4	0.01
Blackfeet (1)	8	0.01
Cherokee (6)	20	0.03
Chippewa (3)	4	0.01
Choctaw	1	0.00
Creek (2)	3	0.01
Delaware (1)	4	0.01
Iroquois (1)	2	0.00
Latin American Indians (15)	32	0.05
Potawatomi (1)	1	0.00
Pueblo (1)	3	0.01
Seminole (1)	1	0.00
Sioux (9)	10	0.02
All other tribes (8)	24	0.04
American Indian tribes, not spec.	13	0.02
Arab:	558	0.94
Arab/Arabic	8	0.01
Egyptian	49	0.08
Iraqi	31	0.05
Lebanese	256	0.43
Moroccan	74	0.12
Syrian	94	0.16
Other Arab	46	0.08
Armenian	1,091	1.84
Asian:	4,659	7.87
Bangladeshi (15)	24	0.04
Cambodian (40)	46	0.08
Chinese, ex. Taiwanese (1,433)	1,525	2.57
Filipino (115)	156	0.26
Indian (1,580)	1,642	2.77
Indonesian (9)	13	0.02
Japanese (129)	156	0.26
Korean (355)	369	0.62
Laotian (95)	104	0.18
Malaysian (1)	2	0.00
Pakistani (33)	42	0.07
Sri Lankan (12)	13	0.02
Taiwanese (39)	45	0.08
Thai (54)	62	0.10
Vietnamese (301)	318	0.54
Other Asian, specified (3)	7	0.01
Other Asian, not specified (54)	135	0.23
Assyrian/Chaldean/Syriac	16	0.03
Australian	20	0.03
Austrian	146	0.25
Belgian	42	0.07
Brazilian	117	0.20
British	255	0.43
Bulgarian	56	0.09
Canadian	1,086	1.83
Celtic	9	0.02
Croatian	18	0.03
Czech	100	0.17
Czechoslovakian	105	0.18
Danish	181	0.31
Dutch	251	0.42
Eastern European	179	0.30
English	4,902	8.28
European	273	0.46
Finnish	129	0.22
French, except Basque	2,712	4.58
French Canadian	3,395	5.73
German	2,903	4.90
Greek	802	1.35
Guyanese	6	0.01
Hawaii Native/Pacific Islander:	69	0.12
Micronesian: (12)	15	0.03
Guamanian/Chamorro (10)	11	0.02
Other Micronesian (2)	4	0.01
Polynesian: (18)	24	0.04
Native Hawaiian (12)	17	0.03
Samoan (6)	7	0.01
Other Pac. Isl., specified	1	0.00
Other Pac. Isl., not spec. (8)	29	0.05
Hispanic or Latino:	5,031	8.49
Central American:	1,167	1.97
Costa Rican	15	0.03
Guatemalan	928	1.57
Honduran	38	0.06
Nicaraguan	12	0.02
Panamanian	10	0.02
Salvadoran	113	0.19
Other Central American	51	0.09
Cuban	95	0.16
Dominican Republic	86	0.15
Mexican	609	1.03
Puerto Rican	1,360	2.30
South American:	609	1.03
Argentinean	47	0.08
Bolivian	89	0.15
Chilean	29	0.05
Colombian	110	0.19
Ecuadorian	140	0.24
Paraguayan	2	0.00
Peruvian	104	0.18
Uruguayan	8	0.01
Venezuelan	44	0.07
Other South American	36	0.06
Other Hispanic or Latino	1,105	1.87
Hungarian	252	0.43
Iranian	75	0.13
Irish	12,561	21.21
Israeli	103	0.17
Italian	10,938	18.47
Latvian	37	0.06
Lithuanian	325	0.55
Northern European	6	0.01
Norwegian	362	0.61
Polish	1,773	2.99
Portuguese	534	0.90
Romanian	106	0.18
Russian	1,412	2.38
Scandinavian	25	0.04
Scotch-Irish	869	1.47
Scottish	1,330	2.25
Serbian	10	0.02
Slovak	29	0.05
Slovene	7	0.01
Swedish	858	1.45
Swiss	105	0.18
Turkish	81	0.14
Ukrainian	295	0.50
United States or American	1,788	3.02
Welsh	198	0.33
West Indian, excl. Hispanic:	1,114	1.88
Barbadian	11	0.02
British West Indian	16	0.03
Haitian	977	1.65
Jamaican	93	0.16
Trinidadian and Tobagonian	6	0.01
U.S. Virgin Islander	4	0.01
Other West Indian	7	0.01
White:	49,963	84.36
Not Hispanic (46,416)	46,947	79.27

Notes: 1. Figures in the "Number" column do not add up to the total population due to: a) Ancestry/Race overlap — e.g. persons can report being both White and Irish, b) persons of Hispanic origin can report being any race, c) persons reporting two ancestries are counted in both categories. 2. Numbers in parentheses indicate the number of persons reporting this ancestry/race alone, not in combination with any other ancestry/race. 3. Refer to the Explanation of Data in the front of the book for more detailed information.

Ancestry/Race	Number	%
Hispanic (2,729)	3,016	5.09
Yugoslavian	24	0.04

Wareham

Place Type: Town
County: Plymouth
Population: 20,335

Ancestry/Race	Number	%
African American/Black:	910	4.48
Not Hispanic (566)	857	4.21
Hispanic (28)	53	0.26
African, sub-Saharan:	1,556	7.65
Cape Verdean	1,556	7.65
Alaska Native tribes, not specified	2	0.01
Am. Ind. or Alaska Nat., not spec.	81	0.40
American Indian tribes, specified:	127	0.62
Blackfeet (2)	9	0.04
Cherokee (8)	25	0.12
Creek	1	0.00
Delaware (1)	1	0.00
Iroquois (4)	9	0.04
Latin American Indians (1)	2	0.01
Pueblo (1)	1	0.00
Seminole	1	0.00
Shoshone	2	0.01
Sioux (2)	2	0.01
Yuman (1)	1	0.00
All other tribes (55)	73	0.36
American Indian tribes, not spec.	18	0.09
Arab:	167	0.82
Arab/Arabic	6	0.03
Lebanese	144	0.71
Syrian	17	0.08
Armenian	25	0.12
Asian:	148	0.73
Cambodian (12)	12	0.06
Chinese, ex. Taiwanese (15)	26	0.13
Filipino (9)	12	0.06
Indian (5)	7	0.03
Japanese (17)	36	0.18
Korean (6)	11	0.05
Laotian (8)	9	0.04
Thai (3)	5	0.02
Vietnamese (5)	8	0.04
Other Asian, specified	1	0.00
Other Asian, not specified (8)	21	0.10
Austrian	83	0.41
Brazilian	25	0.12
British	34	0.17
Canadian	225	1.11
Czechoslovakian	8	0.04
Danish	70	0.34
Dutch	123	0.60
English	3,255	16.01
European	38	0.19
Finnish	131	0.64
French, except Basque	1,757	8.64
French Canadian	914	4.49
German	1,134	5.58
Greek	84	0.41
Hawaii Native/Pacific Islander:	24	0.12
Micronesian: (2)	5	0.02
Guamanian/Chamorro (2)	5	0.02
Polynesian: (8)	14	0.07
Native Hawaiian (6)	11	0.05
Samoan (2)	3	0.01
Other Pac. Isl., not spec.	5	0.02
Hispanic or Latino:	292	1.44
Central American:	16	0.08
Costa Rican	1	0.00
Guatemalan	4	0.02
Honduran	4	0.02
Salvadoran	6	0.03
Other Central American	1	0.00
Cuban	3	0.01
Dominican Republic	6	0.03
Mexican	23	0.11
Puerto Rican	166	0.82
South American:	11	0.05
Colombian	5	0.02
Ecuadorian	2	0.01
Peruvian	4	0.02
Other Hispanic or Latino	67	0.33
Hungarian	33	0.16
Irish	4,555	22.40
Italian	2,548	12.53
Latvian	34	0.17
Lithuanian	127	0.62
Luxemburger	10	0.05
Norwegian	45	0.22
Polish	792	3.89
Portuguese	1,820	8.95
Romanian	19	0.09
Russian	158	0.78
Scandinavian	56	0.28
Scotch-Irish	401	1.97
Scottish	429	2.11
Slovene	7	0.03
Swedish	581	2.86
Swiss	18	0.09
Ukrainian	28	0.14
United States or American	892	4.39
Welsh	106	0.52
West Indian, excl. Hispanic:	21	0.10
Haitian	11	0.05
Trinidadian and Tobagonian	10	0.05
White:	18,272	89.85
Not Hispanic (17,646)	18,114	89.08
Hispanic (130)	158	0.78
Yugoslavian	36	0.18

Watertown

Place Type: City
County: Middlesex
Population: 32,986

Ancestry/Race	Number	%
African American/Black:	682	2.07
Not Hispanic (556)	658	1.99
Hispanic (16)	24	0.07
African, sub-Saharan:	152	0.46
African	65	0.20
Cape Verdean	30	0.09
South African	25	0.08
Ugandan	24	0.07
Other sub-Saharan African	8	0.02
Alaska Native tribes, specified:	1	0.00
Alaska Athabascan (1)	1	0.00
Am. Ind. or Alaska Nat., not spec.	56	0.17
Albanian	27	0.08
American Indian tribes, specified:	54	0.16
Blackfeet	1	0.00
Cherokee (2)	12	0.04
Choctaw (2)	2	0.01
Cree	1	0.00
Creek (3)	3	0.01
Iroquois (1)	3	0.01
Latin American Indians (7)	8	0.02
Lumbee	1	0.00
Navajo (1)	1	0.00
Ottawa	1	0.00
Yakama	2	0.01
Yaqui	1	0.00
All other tribes (3)	18	0.05
American Indian tribes, not spec.	7	0.02
Arab:	708	2.15
Arab/Arabic	86	0.26
Egyptian	50	0.15
Jordanian	53	0.16
Lebanese	387	1.17
Moroccan	11	0.03
Syrian	51	0.15
Other Arab	70	0.21
Armenian	2,708	8.21
Asian:	1,501	4.55
Bangladeshi	10	0.03
Cambodian (7)	7	0.02
Chinese, ex. Taiwanese (472)	516	1.56
Filipino (60)	76	0.23
Indian (257)	283	0.86
Indonesian (19)	25	0.08
Japanese (82)	110	0.33
Korean (131)	149	0.45
Laotian (4)	4	0.01
Pakistani (16)	20	0.06
Sri Lankan (6)	10	0.03
Taiwanese (14)	17	0.05
Thai (41)	48	0.15
Vietnamese (106)	106	0.32
Other Asian, specified (15)	15	0.05
Other Asian, not specified (22)	105	0.32
Austrian	61	0.18
Belgian	35	0.11
Brazilian	97	0.29
British	183	0.55
Bulgarian	16	0.05
Canadian	477	1.45
Croatian	10	0.03
Czech	47	0.14
Czechoslovakian	37	0.11
Danish	81	0.25
Dutch	161	0.49
Eastern European	100	0.30
English	2,893	8.77
Estonian	9	0.03
European	237	0.72
Finnish	89	0.27
French, except Basque	1,204	3.65
French Canadian	1,058	3.21
German	1,952	5.92
Greek	1,257	3.81
Hawaii Native/Pacific Islander:	29	0.09
Micronesian:	7	0.02
Guamanian/Chamorro	4	0.01
Other Micronesian	3	0.01
Polynesian: (5)	8	0.02
Native Hawaiian (1)	3	0.01
Samoan (3)	3	0.01
Other Polynesian (1)	2	0.01
Other Pac. Isl., not spec. (1)	14	0.04
Hispanic or Latino:	883	2.68
Central American:	108	0.33
Costa Rican	8	0.02
Guatemalan	70	0.21
Honduran	8	0.02
Nicaraguan	4	0.01
Panamanian	7	0.02
Salvadoran	9	0.03
Other Central American	2	0.01
Cuban	53	0.16
Dominican Republic	24	0.07
Mexican	89	0.27
Puerto Rican	115	0.35
South American:	250	0.76
Argentinean	49	0.15
Bolivian	10	0.03
Chilean	27	0.08
Colombian	58	0.18
Ecuadorian	33	0.10
Paraguayan	1	0.00
Peruvian	27	0.08
Uruguayan	4	0.01
Venezuelan	31	0.09
Other South American	10	0.03
Other Hispanic or Latino	244	0.74
Hungarian	167	0.51
Icelander	23	0.07
Iranian	245	0.74
Irish	7,606	23.06
Israeli	10	0.03
Italian	6,498	19.70
Latvian	80	0.24
Lithuanian	237	0.72
Luxemburger	15	0.05
Northern European	16	0.05
Norwegian	174	0.53
Pennsylvania German	5	0.02

Notes: 1. Figures in the "Number" column do not add up to the total population due to: a) Ancestry/Race overlap — e.g. persons can report being both White and Irish, b) persons of Hispanic origin can report being any race, c) persons reporting two ancestries are counted in both categories. 2. Numbers in parentheses indicate the number of persons reporting this ancestry/race alone, not in combination with any other ancestry/race. 3. Refer to the Explanation of Data in the front of the book for more detailed information.

Polish	1,093	3.31
Portuguese	206	0.62
Romanian	119	0.36
Russian	961	2.91
Scandinavian	33	0.10
Scotch-Irish	505	1.53
Scottish	931	2.82
Serbian	20	0.06
Slovak	23	0.07
Swedish	516	1.56
Swiss	67	0.20
Turkish	72	0.22
Ukrainian	191	0.58
United States or American	784	2.38
Welsh	244	0.74
West Indian, excl. Hispanic:	255	0.77
Barbadian	18	0.05
Bermudan	14	0.04
Haitian	136	0.41
Jamaican	66	0.20
Trinidadian and Tobagonian	13	0.04
West Indian	8	0.02
White:	30,727	93.15
Not Hispanic (29,591)	30,101	91.25
Hispanic (564)	626	1.90
Yugoslavian	77	0.23

Wayland

Place Type: Town
County: Middlesex
Population: 13,100

Ancestry/Race	Number	%
African American/Black:	136	1.04
Not Hispanic (97)	129	0.98
Hispanic (1)	7	0.05
African, sub-Saharan:	24	0.18
African	13	0.10
Cape Verdean	6	0.05
South African	5	0.04
Am. Ind. or Alaska Nat., not spec.	14	0.11
Albanian	34	0.26
American Indian tribes, specified:	17	0.13
Blackfeet	3	0.02
Cherokee (1)	2	0.02
Chippewa (1)	1	0.01
Delaware	1	0.01
Latin American Indians	3	0.02
Navajo (1)	1	0.01
Sioux	1	0.01
All other tribes	5	0.04
American Indian tribes, not spec.	6	0.05
Arab:	44	0.34
Lebanese	6	0.05
Moroccan	14	0.11
Syrian	24	0.18
Armenian	96	0.73
Asian:	789	6.02
Chinese, ex. Taiwanese (373)	411	3.14
Filipino (19)	25	0.19
Indian (134)	148	1.13
Indonesian (1)	1	0.01
Japanese (33)	49	0.37
Korean (69)	81	0.62
Malaysian (2)	2	0.02
Taiwanese (27)	34	0.26
Thai (15)	20	0.15
Vietnamese (9)	11	0.08
Other Asian, not specified (1)	7	0.05
Assyrian/Chaldean/Syriac	6	0.05
Australian	9	0.07
Austrian	61	0.47
Belgian	32	0.24
Brazilian	25	0.19
British	211	1.61
Canadian	248	1.89
Czech	109	0.83
Czechoslovakian	6	0.05
Danish	73	0.56
Dutch	182	1.39
Eastern European	193	1.47
English	2,053	15.67
Estonian	9	0.07
European	333	2.54
Finnish	14	0.11
French, except Basque	582	4.44
French Canadian	360	2.75
German	1,434	10.95
Greek	107	0.82
Hawaii Native/Pacific Islander:	10	0.08
Micronesian: (3)	3	0.02
Guamanian/Chamorro (3)	3	0.02
Polynesian:	4	0.03
Native Hawaiian	4	0.03
Other Pac. Isl., not spec. (1)	3	0.02
Hispanic or Latino:	151	1.15
Central American:	12	0.09
Costa Rican	1	0.01
Guatemalan	5	0.04
Honduran	3	0.02
Nicaraguan	1	0.01
Salvadoran	2	0.02
Cuban	13	0.10
Dominican Republic	11	0.08
Mexican	24	0.18
Puerto Rican	24	0.18
South American:	29	0.22
Argentinean	3	0.02
Bolivian	2	0.02
Chilean	1	0.01
Colombian	9	0.07
Ecuadorian	1	0.01
Paraguayan	2	0.02
Peruvian	2	0.02
Venezuelan	1	0.01
Other South American	8	0.06
Other Hispanic or Latino	38	0.29
Hungarian	103	0.79
Iranian	20	0.15
Irish	2,531	19.32
Italian	1,962	14.98
Latvian	39	0.30
Lithuanian	154	1.18
Northern European	15	0.11
Norwegian	197	1.50
Polish	706	5.39
Portuguese	45	0.34
Romanian	21	0.16
Russian	919	7.02
Scotch-Irish	282	2.15
Scottish	437	3.34
Serbian	24	0.18
Slavic	23	0.18
Slovak	13	0.10
Slovene	6	0.05
Swedish	196	1.50
Swiss	47	0.36
Turkish	13	0.10
Ukrainian	162	1.24
United States or American	423	3.23
Welsh	88	0.67
White:	12,225	93.32
Not Hispanic (11,971)	12,106	92.41
Hispanic (109)	119	0.91

Webster

Place Type: Town
County: Worcester
Population: 16,415

Ancestry/Race	Number	%
African American/Black:	231	1.41
Not Hispanic (159)	190	1.16
Hispanic (24)	41	0.25
African, sub-Saharan:	64	0.39
African	4	0.02
Cape Verdean	60	0.37
Am. Ind. or Alaska Nat., not spec.	34	0.21
Albanian	60	0.37
American Indian tribes, specified:	95	0.58
Blackfeet (2)	11	0.07
Cherokee (1)	13	0.08
Chickasaw (1)	1	0.01
Choctaw	1	0.01
Iroquois	6	0.04
Navajo	2	0.01
Pueblo	2	0.01
Sioux (1)	5	0.03
All other tribes (35)	54	0.33
American Indian tribes, not spec.	3	0.02
Arab:	22	0.13
Lebanese	22	0.13
Armenian	34	0.21
Asian:	194	1.18
Cambodian (4)	4	0.02
Chinese, ex. Taiwanese (16)	18	0.11
Filipino (7)	15	0.09
Indian (37)	42	0.26
Indonesian (2)	2	0.01
Japanese (7)	12	0.07
Korean (11)	12	0.07
Laotian (28)	33	0.20
Pakistani (21)	21	0.13
Thai (2)	2	0.01
Vietnamese (18)	20	0.12
Other Asian, not specified (3)	13	0.08
Austrian	18	0.11
British	31	0.19
Canadian	32	0.19
Celtic	5	0.03
Czechoslovakian	23	0.14
Danish	40	0.24
Dutch	109	0.66
English	1,385	8.44
European	18	0.11
Finnish	29	0.18
French, except Basque	3,308	20.15
French Canadian	1,461	8.90
German	921	5.61
Greek	235	1.43
Hawaii Native/Pacific Islander:	6	0.04
Polynesian:	5	0.03
Native Hawaiian	4	0.02
Samoan	1	0.01
Other Pac. Isl., not spec.	1	0.01
Hispanic or Latino:	649	3.95
Central American:	24	0.15
Costa Rican	3	0.02
Guatemalan	2	0.01
Honduran	1	0.01
Nicaraguan	2	0.01
Panamanian	5	0.03
Salvadoran	11	0.07
Cuban	9	0.05
Dominican Republic	13	0.08
Mexican	26	0.16
Puerto Rican	454	2.77
South American:	39	0.24
Argentinean	1	0.01
Bolivian	9	0.05
Chilean	1	0.01
Colombian	18	0.11
Ecuadorian	7	0.04
Peruvian	1	0.01
Venezuelan	1	0.01
Other South American	1	0.01
Other Hispanic or Latino	84	0.51
Hungarian	21	0.13
Irish	2,492	15.18
Italian	1,529	9.31
Lithuanian	141	0.86
Macedonian	6	0.04
Northern European	6	0.04
Norwegian	25	0.15
Polish	3,744	22.81
Portuguese	172	1.05
Romanian	69	0.42
Russian	123	0.75

Notes: 1. Figures in the "Number" column do not add up to the total population due to: a) Ancestry/Race overlap — e.g. persons can report being both White and Irish, b) persons of Hispanic origin can report being any race, c) persons reporting two ancestries are counted in both categories. 2. Numbers in parentheses indicate the number of persons reporting this ancestry/race alone, not in combination with any other ancestry/race. 3. Refer to the Explanation of Data in the front of the book for more detailed information.

Ancestry/Race	Number	%
Scandinavian	23	0.14
Scotch-Irish	139	0.85
Scottish	119	0.72
Serbian	9	0.05
Slavic	12	0.07
Slovak	258	1.57
Swedish	342	2.08
Swiss	7	0.04
Ukrainian	42	0.26
United States or American	549	3.34
Welsh	30	0.18
West Indian, excl. Hispanic:	25	0.15
Jamaican	11	0.07
U.S. Virgin Islander	14	0.09
White:	15,755	95.98
Not Hispanic (15,246)	15,378	93.68
Hispanic (318)	377	2.30

Wellesley

Place Type: Census Designated Place
County: Norfolk
Population: 26,613

Ancestry/Race	Number	%
African American/Black:	517	1.94
Not Hispanic (409)	488	1.83
Hispanic (17)	29	0.11
African, sub-Saharan:	90	0.34
African	20	0.08
Cape Verdean	6	0.02
Ethiopian	6	0.02
Ghanian	8	0.03
Nigerian	6	0.02
South African	25	0.09
Ugandan	19	0.07
Am. Ind. or Alaska Nat., not spec.	33	0.12
Albanian	43	0.16
Alsatian	9	0.03
American Indian tribes, specified:	54	0.20
Cherokee	13	0.05
Chippewa	1	0.00
Choctaw	8	0.03
Comanche	1	0.00
Cree	1	0.00
Creek (1)	2	0.01
Delaware	1	0.00
Latin American Indians (7)	12	0.05
Lumbee	1	0.00
Potawatomi	1	0.00
Pueblo (1)	1	0.00
Sioux	1	0.00
All other tribes (3)	11	0.04
American Indian tribes, not spec.	4	0.02
Arab:	208	0.78
Arab/Arabic	31	0.12
Egyptian	40	0.15
Jordanian	7	0.03
Lebanese	83	0.31
Palestinian	15	0.06
Syrian	32	0.12
Armenian	166	0.62
Asian:	1,948	7.32
Bangladeshi (3)	3	0.01
Cambodian (3)	4	0.02
Chinese, ex. Taiwanese (792)	867	3.26
Filipino (43)	65	0.24
Hmong	2	0.01
Indian (300)	345	1.30
Indonesian (1)	3	0.01
Japanese (120)	182	0.68
Korean (266)	290	1.09
Laotian	2	0.01
Malaysian (1)	2	0.01
Pakistani (9)	13	0.05
Sri Lankan (4)	7	0.03
Taiwanese (62)	74	0.28
Thai (12)	13	0.05
Vietnamese (22)	27	0.10
Other Asian, specified (4)	4	0.02
Other Asian, not specified (11)	45	0.17
Australian	39	0.15
Austrian	176	0.66
Belgian	92	0.35
British	451	1.69
Bulgarian	13	0.05
Canadian	290	1.09
Celtic	10	0.04
Croatian	11	0.04
Czech	132	0.50
Czechoslovakian	72	0.27
Danish	120	0.45
Dutch	323	1.21
Eastern European	200	0.75
English	4,394	16.51
Estonian	23	0.09
European	414	1.56
Finnish	63	0.24
French, except Basque	963	3.62
French Canadian	355	1.33
German	2,610	9.81
Greek	426	1.60
Hawaii Native/Pacific Islander:	19	0.07
Micronesian: (2)	3	0.01
Guamanian/Chamorro (2)	3	0.01
Polynesian: (1)	10	0.04
Native Hawaiian (1)	9	0.03
Samoan	1	0.00
Other Pac. Isl., not spec.	6	0.02
Hispanic or Latino:	617	2.32
Central American:	36	0.14
Costa Rican	4	0.02
Guatemalan	7	0.03
Honduran	1	0.00
Nicaraguan	1	0.00
Panamanian	9	0.03
Salvadoran	6	0.02
Other Central American	8	0.03
Cuban	56	0.21
Dominican Republic	14	0.05
Mexican	125	0.47
Puerto Rican	80	0.30
South American:	202	0.76
Argentinean	30	0.11
Bolivian	9	0.03
Chilean	24	0.09
Colombian	72	0.27
Ecuadorian	15	0.06
Paraguayan	2	0.01
Peruvian	12	0.05
Uruguayan	2	0.01
Venezuelan	34	0.13
Other South American	2	0.01
Other Hispanic or Latino	104	0.39
Hungarian	207	0.78
Icelander	46	0.17
Iranian	27	0.10
Irish	6,223	23.38
Israeli	8	0.03
Italian	2,951	11.09
Latvian	16	0.06
Lithuanian	276	1.04
New Zealander	7	0.03
Northern European	66	0.25
Norwegian	388	1.46
Polish	917	3.45
Portuguese	121	0.45
Romanian	159	0.60
Russian	1,059	3.98
Scandinavian	52	0.20
Scotch-Irish	613	2.30
Scottish	1,066	4.01
Slovak	34	0.13
Slovene	36	0.14
Swedish	541	2.03
Swiss	113	0.42
Turkish	40	0.15
Ukrainian	140	0.53
United States or American	1,073	4.03
Welsh	194	0.73
West Indian, excl. Hispanic:	138	0.52
Barbadian	16	0.06
Belizean	5	0.02
British West Indian	12	0.05
Haitian	28	0.11
Jamaican	47	0.18
Trinidadian and Tobagonian	11	0.04
West Indian	19	0.07
White:	24,286	91.26
Not Hispanic (23,509)	23,807	89.46
Hispanic (438)	479	1.80
Yugoslavian	54	0.20

West Springfield

Place Type: Census Designated Place
County: Hampden
Population: 27,899

Ancestry/Race	Number	%
African American/Black:	706	2.53
Not Hispanic (519)	628	2.25
Hispanic (53)	78	0.28
African, sub-Saharan:	79	0.28
Cape Verdean	22	0.08
Kenyan	14	0.05
Nigerian	34	0.12
Zimbabwean	9	0.03
Am. Ind. or Alaska Nat., not spec.	84	0.30
Albanian	67	0.24
American Indian tribes, specified:	77	0.28
Apache	1	0.00
Blackfeet (1)	2	0.01
Cherokee (1)	11	0.04
Chippewa	2	0.01
Creek (1)	1	0.00
Iroquois (11)	26	0.09
Latin American Indians (4)	8	0.03
Ottawa	1	0.00
All other tribes (12)	25	0.09
American Indian tribes, not spec.	6	0.02
Arab:	331	1.19
Arab/Arabic	34	0.12
Lebanese	213	0.76
Palestinian	39	0.14
Syrian	45	0.16
Armenian	22	0.08
Asian:	653	2.34
Cambodian (5)	5	0.02
Chinese, ex. Taiwanese (112)	133	0.48
Filipino (38)	44	0.16
Hmong (1)	1	0.00
Indian (74)	90	0.32
Indonesian	1	0.00
Japanese (12)	20	0.07
Korean (37)	39	0.14
Laotian (2)	2	0.01
Pakistani (25)	38	0.14
Sri Lankan (1)	1	0.00
Taiwanese (1)	1	0.00
Thai (6)	7	0.03
Vietnamese (202)	220	0.79
Other Asian, specified	2	0.01
Other Asian, not specified (25)	49	0.18
Austrian	88	0.32
Belgian	29	0.10
Brazilian	19	0.07
British	31	0.11
Canadian	137	0.49
Croatian	12	0.04
Cypriot	40	0.14
Czech	76	0.27
Czechoslovakian	27	0.10
Danish	52	0.19
Dutch	137	0.49
English	2,880	10.32
European	64	0.23
Finnish	29	0.10
French, except Basque	3,877	13.90
French Canadian	2,137	7.66

Notes: 1. Figures in the "Number" column do not add up to the total population due to: a) Ancestry/Race overlap — e.g. persons can report being both White and Irish, b) persons of Hispanic origin can report being any race, c) persons reporting two ancestries are counted in both categories. 2. Numbers in parentheses indicate the number of persons reporting this ancestry/race alone, not in combination with any other ancestry/race. 3. Refer to the Explanation of Data in the front of the book for more detailed information.

German	1,846	6.62
Greek	262	0.94
Hawaii Native/Pacific Islander:	25	0.09
Micronesian:	1	0.00
Guamanian/Chamorro	1	0.00
Polynesian: (3)	8	0.03
Native Hawaiian (2)	6	0.02
Samoan (1)	2	0.01
Other Pac. Isl., not spec. (7)	16	0.06
Hispanic or Latino:	1,605	5.75
Central American:	34	0.12
Costa Rican	1	0.00
Guatemalan	9	0.03
Honduran	4	0.01
Panamanian	5	0.02
Salvadoran	14	0.05
Other Central American	1	0.00
Cuban	15	0.05
Dominican Republic	20	0.07
Mexican	70	0.25
Puerto Rican	1,155	4.14
South American:	77	0.28
Argentinean	2	0.01
Chilean	2	0.01
Colombian	35	0.13
Ecuadorian	19	0.07
Peruvian	10	0.04
Venezuelan	9	0.03
Other Hispanic or Latino	234	0.84
Hungarian	122	0.44
Irish	6,177	22.14
Italian	5,000	17.92
Latvian	20	0.07
Lithuanian	164	0.59
Norwegian	96	0.34
Pennsylvania German	19	0.07
Polish	3,036	10.88
Portuguese	139	0.50
Romanian	48	0.17
Russian	1,163	4.17
Scandinavian	5	0.02
Scotch-Irish	282	1.01
Scottish	791	2.84
Slavic	5	0.02
Slovak	29	0.10
Swedish	235	0.84
Swiss	69	0.25
Turkish	29	0.10
Ukrainian	379	1.36
United States or American	681	2.44
Welsh	143	0.51
West Indian, excl. Hispanic:	13	0.05
Jamaican	13	0.05
White:	25,832	92.59
Not Hispanic (24,673)	25,088	89.92
Hispanic (627)	744	2.67
Yugoslavian	32	0.11

Westborough

Place Type: Town
County: Worcester
Population: 17,997

Ancestry/Race	Number	%
African American/Black:	320	1.78
Not Hispanic (252)	308	1.71
Hispanic (7)	12	0.07
African, sub-Saharan:	146	0.81
African	12	0.07
Cape Verdean	16	0.09
South African	84	0.47
Sudanese	30	0.17
Other sub-Saharan African	4	0.02
Am. Ind. or Alaska Nat., not spec.	28	0.16
Albanian	39	0.22
American Indian tribes, specified:	37	0.21
Blackfeet (2)	5	0.03
Cherokee (2)	5	0.03
Choctaw	3	0.02
Iroquois	1	0.01
Latin American Indians (2)	8	0.04
Potawatomi (1)	1	0.01
Seminole (1)	1	0.01
All other tribes (7)	13	0.07
American Indian tribes, not spec.	4	0.02
Arab:	263	1.46
Arab/Arabic	8	0.04
Egyptian	10	0.06
Lebanese	56	0.31
Palestinian	8	0.04
Syrian	110	0.61
Other Arab	71	0.39
Armenian	101	0.56
Asian:	1,559	8.66
Cambodian (4)	4	0.02
Chinese, ex. Taiwanese (406)	443	2.46
Filipino (21)	25	0.14
Indian (740)	764	4.25
Indonesian (2)	2	0.01
Japanese (19)	25	0.14
Korean (143)	160	0.89
Laotian (4)	4	0.02
Malaysian	1	0.01
Pakistani (48)	60	0.33
Sri Lankan (22)	22	0.12
Taiwanese (14)	16	0.09
Thai (2)	2	0.01
Vietnamese (10)	10	0.06
Other Asian, not specified (14)	21	0.12
Australian	10	0.06
Austrian	53	0.29
Belgian	39	0.22
Brazilian	141	0.78
British	141	0.78
Canadian	140	0.78
Czech	42	0.23
Czechoslovakian	29	0.16
Danish	115	0.64
Dutch	152	0.84
Eastern European	83	0.46
English	2,362	13.12
Estonian	20	0.11
European	297	1.65
Finnish	100	0.56
French, except Basque	1,006	5.59
French Canadian	606	3.37
German	1,423	7.91
Greek	180	1.00
Guyanese	6	0.03
Hawaii Native/Pacific Islander:	6	0.03
Polynesian: (3)	3	0.02
Samoan (3)	3	0.02
Other Pac. Isl., not spec. (1)	3	0.02
Hispanic or Latino:	587	3.26
Central American:	65	0.36
Guatemalan	47	0.26
Panamanian	2	0.01
Salvadoran	9	0.05
Other Central American	7	0.04
Cuban	17	0.09
Dominican Republic	17	0.09
Mexican	100	0.56
Puerto Rican	91	0.51
South American:	78	0.43
Argentinean	8	0.04
Bolivian	3	0.02
Chilean	4	0.02
Colombian	11	0.06
Ecuadorian	33	0.18
Paraguayan	1	0.01
Peruvian	7	0.04
Venezuelan	4	0.02
Other South American	7	0.04
Other Hispanic or Latino	219	1.22
Hungarian	87	0.48
Iranian	80	0.44
Irish	3,946	21.93
Israeli	4	0.02
Italian	2,019	11.22
Latvian	10	0.06
Lithuanian	173	0.96
Macedonian	19	0.11
Northern European	9	0.05
Norwegian	141	0.78
Polish	686	3.81
Portuguese	274	1.52
Romanian	20	0.11
Russian	519	2.88
Scandinavian	12	0.07
Scotch-Irish	354	1.97
Scottish	539	2.99
Serbian	31	0.17
Slavic	24	0.13
Slovak	28	0.16
Slovene	7	0.04
Swedish	344	1.91
Swiss	13	0.07
Turkish	15	0.08
Ukrainian	104	0.58
United States or American	699	3.88
Welsh	147	0.82
West Indian, excl. Hispanic:	60	0.33
British West Indian	19	0.11
Haitian	23	0.13
Jamaican	18	0.10
White:	16,082	89.36
Not Hispanic (15,444)	15,628	86.84
Hispanic (425)	454	2.52
Yugoslavian	5	0.03

Westfield

Place Type: City
County: Hampden
Population: 40,072

Ancestry/Race	Number	%
African American/Black:	497	1.24
Not Hispanic (323)	427	1.07
Hispanic (42)	70	0.17
African, sub-Saharan:	31	0.08
African	26	0.06
Cape Verdean	5	0.01
Am. Ind. or Alaska Nat., not spec.	99	0.25
American Indian tribes, specified:	121	0.30
Apache (1)	1	0.00
Blackfeet (7)	14	0.03
Cherokee (10)	22	0.05
Cheyenne (1)	1	0.00
Chickasaw	4	0.01
Choctaw	4	0.01
Cree	2	0.00
Creek	3	0.01
Delaware	1	0.00
Iroquois (6)	15	0.04
Latin American Indians	1	0.00
Pueblo	3	0.01
Seminole (1)	1	0.00
Sioux (8)	17	0.04
All other tribes (17)	32	0.08
American Indian tribes, not spec.	6	0.01
Arab:	193	0.48
Egyptian	27	0.07
Lebanese	108	0.27
Syrian	58	0.14
Armenian	84	0.21
Asian:	473	1.18
Cambodian (6)	7	0.02
Chinese, ex. Taiwanese (75)	92	0.23
Filipino (55)	81	0.20
Indian (59)	81	0.20
Indonesian	2	0.00
Japanese (10)	27	0.07
Korean (77)	94	0.23
Laotian (1)	1	0.00
Pakistani (15)	16	0.04
Taiwanese	1	0.00
Thai (2)	3	0.01
Vietnamese (23)	27	0.07

Notes: 1. Figures in the "Number" column do not add up to the total population due to: a) Ancestry/Race overlap — e.g. persons can report being both White and Irish, b) persons of Hispanic origin can report being any race, c) persons reporting two ancestries are counted in both categories. 2. Numbers in parentheses indicate the number of persons reporting this ancestry/race alone, not in combination with any other ancestry/race. 3. Refer to the Explanation of Data in the front of the book for more detailed information.

Other Asian, specified	5	0.01
Other Asian, not specified	36	0.09
Australian	8	0.02
Austrian	139	0.35
Belgian	19	0.05
British	96	0.24
Canadian	196	0.49
Celtic	18	0.04
Croatian	8	0.02
Czech	148	0.37
Czechoslovakian	126	0.31
Danish	92	0.23
Dutch	242	0.60
Eastern European	7	0.02
English	4,507	11.25
European	197	0.49
Finnish	110	0.27
French, except Basque	5,813	14.51
French Canadian	3,078	7.68
German	3,592	8.96
Greek	477	1.19
Hawaii Native/Pacific Islander:	47	0.12
Micronesian: (4)	4	0.01
Guamanian/Chamorro (4)	4	0.01
Polynesian: (14)	17	0.04
Native Hawaiian (10)	13	0.03
Samoan (4)	4	0.01
Other Pac. Isl., specified	5	0.01
Other Pac. Isl., not spec. (1)	21	0.05
Hispanic or Latino:	2,008	5.01
Central American:	16	0.04
Costa Rican	2	0.00
Guatemalan	3	0.01
Honduran	2	0.00
Nicaraguan	2	0.00
Panamanian	2	0.00
Salvadoran	4	0.01
Other Central American	1	0.00
Cuban	11	0.03
Dominican Republic	7	0.02
Mexican	58	0.14
Puerto Rican	1,671	4.17
South American:	34	0.08
Argentinean	1	0.00
Chilean	8	0.02
Colombian	14	0.03
Ecuadorian	2	0.00
Paraguayan	2	0.00
Peruvian	5	0.01
Venezuelan	1	0.00
Other South American	1	0.00
Other Hispanic or Latino	211	0.53
Hungarian	67	0.17
Iranian	28	0.07
Irish	8,964	22.37
Italian	5,077	12.67
Lithuanian	522	1.30
New Zealander	6	0.01
Norwegian	140	0.35
Polish	6,290	15.70
Portuguese	444	1.11
Romanian	42	0.10
Russian	776	1.94
Scandinavian	29	0.07
Scotch-Irish	483	1.21
Scottish	1,132	2.82
Serbian	72	0.18
Slavic	10	0.02
Slovak	384	0.96
Slovene	6	0.01
Soviet Union	7	0.02
Swedish	687	1.71
Swiss	58	0.14
Ukrainian	881	2.20
United States or American	1,621	4.05
Welsh	68	0.17
West Indian, excl. Hispanic:	64	0.16
Barbadian	13	0.03
Haitian	8	0.02
Jamaican	24	0.06
West Indian	19	0.05
White:	38,371	95.76
Not Hispanic (36,893)	37,275	93.02
Hispanic (988)	1,096	2.74
Yugoslavian	38	0.09

Westford

Place Type: Town
County: Middlesex
Population: 20,754

Ancestry/Race	Number	%
African American/Black:	95	0.46
Not Hispanic (61)	89	0.43
Hispanic (1)	6	0.03
African, sub-Saharan:	44	0.21
Cape Verdean	13	0.06
Nigerian	31	0.15
Am. Ind. or Alaska Nat., not spec.	8	0.04
Albanian	19	0.09
American Indian tribes, specified:	39	0.19
Blackfeet (1)	3	0.01
Cherokee	6	0.03
Chippewa	3	0.01
Choctaw (1)	1	0.00
Iroquois	2	0.01
Latin American Indians (2)	6	0.03
Menominee	1	0.00
Osage (3)	3	0.01
All other tribes (3)	14	0.07
American Indian tribes, not spec.	2	0.01
Arab:	193	0.93
Arab/Arabic	26	0.13
Egyptian	18	0.09
Lebanese	116	0.56
Moroccan	16	0.08
Syrian	17	0.08
Armenian	94	0.45
Asian:	1,085	5.23
Bangladeshi (4)	4	0.02
Cambodian (18)	18	0.09
Chinese, ex. Taiwanese (462)	508	2.45
Filipino (15)	17	0.08
Indian (386)	403	1.94
Indonesian	4	0.02
Japanese (16)	29	0.14
Korean (47)	52	0.25
Pakistani (1)	1	0.00
Taiwanese (10)	14	0.07
Thai (2)	3	0.01
Vietnamese (18)	18	0.09
Other Asian, not specified (6)	14	0.07
Australian	5	0.02
Austrian	84	0.40
Belgian	4	0.02
Brazilian	25	0.12
British	100	0.48
Canadian	127	0.61
Celtic	19	0.09
Croatian	7	0.03
Czech	74	0.36
Czechoslovakian	18	0.09
Danish	83	0.40
Dutch	319	1.54
Eastern European	26	0.13
English	3,544	17.08
European	190	0.92
Finnish	160	0.77
French, except Basque	1,528	7.36
French Canadian	1,334	6.43
German	2,051	9.88
Greek	452	2.18
Hawaii Native/Pacific Islander:	12	0.06
Polynesian: (3)	5	0.02
Native Hawaiian (3)	5	0.02
Other Pac. Isl., not spec.	7	0.03
Hispanic or Latino:	229	1.10
Central American:	11	0.05
Costa Rican	2	0.01
Guatemalan	4	0.02
Honduran	2	0.01
Panamanian	2	0.01
Salvadoran	1	0.00
Cuban	17	0.08
Dominican Republic	2	0.01
Mexican	51	0.25
Puerto Rican	50	0.24
South American:	35	0.17
Argentinean	2	0.01
Bolivian	1	0.00
Chilean	5	0.02
Colombian	16	0.08
Ecuadorian	4	0.02
Paraguayan	2	0.01
Peruvian	2	0.01
Venezuelan	2	0.01
Other South American	1	0.00
Other Hispanic or Latino	63	0.30
Hungarian	169	0.81
Iranian	20	0.10
Irish	5,785	27.87
Israeli	9	0.04
Italian	2,829	13.63
Latvian	13	0.06
Lithuanian	195	0.94
Northern European	37	0.18
Norwegian	322	1.55
Polish	1,071	5.16
Portuguese	362	1.74
Russian	192	0.93
Scandinavian	67	0.32
Scotch-Irish	424	2.04
Scottish	796	3.84
Serbian	8	0.04
Slavic	9	0.04
Slovak	53	0.26
Slovene	9	0.04
Swedish	560	2.70
Swiss	102	0.49
Ukrainian	110	0.53
United States or American	887	4.27
Welsh	41	0.20
West Indian, excl. Hispanic:	19	0.09
Haitian	19	0.09
White:	19,605	94.46
Not Hispanic (19,267)	19,418	93.56
Hispanic (177)	187	0.90

Weston

Place Type: Town
County: Middlesex
Population: 11,469

Ancestry/Race	Number	%
African American/Black:	151	1.32
Not Hispanic (132)	148	1.29
Hispanic (3)	3	0.03
African, sub-Saharan:	23	0.20
Cape Verdean	18	0.16
South African	5	0.04
Am. Ind. or Alaska Nat., not spec.	12	0.10
Albanian	7	0.06
American Indian tribes, specified:	13	0.11
Cherokee	8	0.07
Iroquois	1	0.01
Latin American Indians (1)	1	0.01
All other tribes (1)	3	0.03
American Indian tribes, not spec.	1	0.01
Arab:	34	0.30
Lebanese	34	0.30
Armenian	47	0.41
Asian:	885	7.72
Chinese, ex. Taiwanese (354)	404	3.52
Filipino (24)	38	0.33
Hmong (2)	2	0.02
Indian (204)	230	2.01
Indonesian (2)	2	0.02
Japanese (26)	30	0.26

Notes: 1. Figures in the "Number" column do not add up to the total population due to: a) Ancestry/Race overlap — e.g. persons can report being both White and Irish, b) persons of Hispanic origin can report being any race, c) persons reporting two ancestries are counted in both categories. 2. Numbers in parentheses indicate the number of persons reporting this ancestry/race alone, not in combination with any other ancestry/race. 3. Refer to the Explanation of Data in the front of the book for more detailed information.

Korean (85)	96	0.84
Laotian (4)	4	0.03
Pakistani (9)	9	0.08
Taiwanese (13)	19	0.17
Thai (2)	3	0.03
Vietnamese (31)	32	0.28
Other Asian, not specified (9)	16	0.14
Australian	10	0.09
Austrian	95	0.83
Belgian	15	0.13
Brazilian	45	0.39
British	129	1.12
Canadian	85	0.74
Celtic	17	0.15
Czech	51	0.44
Czechoslovakian	7	0.06
Danish	99	0.86
Dutch	125	1.09
Eastern European	165	1.44
English	1,875	16.35
Estonian	7	0.06
European	336	2.93
Finnish	18	0.16
French, except Basque	488	4.25
French Canadian	105	0.92
German	815	7.11
Greek	218	1.90
Hawaii Native/Pacific Islander:	10	0.09
Polynesian: (5)	6	0.05
Native Hawaiian (1)	2	0.02
Tongan (4)	4	0.03
Other Pac. Isl., not spec. (1)	4	0.03
Hispanic or Latino:	218	1.90
Central American:	5	0.04
Guatemalan	4	0.03
Salvadoran	1	0.01
Cuban	19	0.17
Dominican Republic	7	0.06
Mexican	38	0.33
Puerto Rican	16	0.14
South American:	76	0.66
Argentinean	18	0.16
Bolivian	2	0.02
Chilean	4	0.03
Colombian	33	0.29
Ecuadorian	3	0.03
Peruvian	3	0.03
Uruguayan	1	0.01
Venezuelan	5	0.04
Other South American	7	0.06
Other Hispanic or Latino	57	0.50
Hungarian	77	0.67
Iranian	66	0.58
Irish	1,902	16.58
Israeli	17	0.15
Italian	1,019	8.88
Lithuanian	94	0.82
Northern European	30	0.26
Norwegian	51	0.44
Polish	457	3.98
Portuguese	68	0.59
Romanian	27	0.24
Russian	652	5.68
Scandinavian	8	0.07
Scotch-Irish	284	2.48
Scottish	341	2.97
Slovak	8	0.07
Swedish	229	2.00
Swiss	45	0.39
Ukrainian	20	0.17
United States or American	569	4.96
Welsh	94	0.82
West Indian, excl. Hispanic:	74	0.65
British West Indian	16	0.14
Haitian	16	0.14
Jamaican	35	0.31
Trinidadian and Tobagonian	7	0.06
White:	10,472	91.31
Not Hispanic (10,167)	10,284	89.67
Hispanic (185)	188	1.64
Yugoslavian	7	0.06

Westport

Place Type: Town
County: Bristol
Population: 14,183

Ancestry/Race	Number	%
African American/Black:	52	0.37
Not Hispanic (23)	49	0.35
Hispanic (1)	3	0.02
African, sub-Saharan:	29	0.20
Cape Verdean	29	0.20
Alaska Native tribes, specified:	1	0.01
Eskimo	1	0.01
Am. Ind. or Alaska Nat., not spec.	23	0.16
Albanian	11	0.08
American Indian tribes, specified:	22	0.16
Cherokee (4)	4	0.03
Iroquois (1)	1	0.01
Sioux (1)	4	0.03
All other tribes (6)	13	0.09
American Indian tribes, not spec.	4	0.03
Arab:	62	0.44
Egyptian	12	0.08
Lebanese	50	0.35
Asian:	84	0.59
Chinese, ex. Taiwanese (18)	21	0.15
Filipino (11)	13	0.09
Indian (13)	13	0.09
Japanese (5)	5	0.04
Korean (15)	16	0.11
Pakistani (4)	4	0.03
Sri Lankan (2)	2	0.01
Taiwanese (1)	1	0.01
Vietnamese	1	0.01
Other Asian, not specified (1)	8	0.06
Austrian	16	0.11
British	26	0.18
Canadian	76	0.54
Croatian	7	0.05
Czech	35	0.25
Danish	9	0.06
Dutch	64	0.45
English	2,423	17.08
Estonian	26	0.18
European	51	0.36
Finnish	23	0.16
French, except Basque	2,247	15.84
French Canadian	1,339	9.44
German	299	2.11
Greek	63	0.44
Hawaii Native/Pacific Islander:	18	0.13
Micronesian: (1)	1	0.01
Guamanian/Chamorro (1)	1	0.01
Polynesian: (1)	2	0.01
Native Hawaiian (1)	1	0.01
Samoan	1	0.01
Other Pac. Isl., not spec. (1)	15	0.11
Hispanic or Latino:	98	0.69
Central American:	11	0.08
Guatemalan	6	0.04
Salvadoran	4	0.03
Other Central American	1	0.01
Cuban	3	0.02
Dominican Republic	3	0.02
Mexican	11	0.08
Puerto Rican	25	0.18
South American:	9	0.06
Argentinean	1	0.01
Chilean	1	0.01
Colombian	1	0.01
Ecuadorian	1	0.01
Venezuelan	4	0.03
Other South American	1	0.01
Other Hispanic or Latino	36	0.25
Hungarian	19	0.13
Irish	1,802	12.71
Italian	657	4.63
Lithuanian	6	0.04
Northern European	32	0.23
Norwegian	50	0.35
Polish	654	4.61
Portuguese	4,918	34.68
Russian	9	0.06
Scandinavian	33	0.23
Scotch-Irish	143	1.01
Scottish	260	1.83
Slavic	9	0.06
Swedish	60	0.42
Swiss	11	0.08
United States or American	447	3.15
Welsh	20	0.14
West Indian, excl. Hispanic:	5	0.04
West Indian	5	0.04
White:	14,009	98.77
Not Hispanic (13,836)	13,939	98.28
Hispanic (65)	70	0.49

Westwood

Place Type: Town
County: Norfolk
Population: 14,117

Ancestry/Race	Number	%
African American/Black:	99	0.70
Not Hispanic (63)	89	0.63
Hispanic (7)	10	0.07
African, sub-Saharan:	19	0.13
South African	19	0.13
Am. Ind. or Alaska Nat., not spec.	21	0.15
Albanian	5	0.04
American Indian tribes, specified:	16	0.11
Cherokee	3	0.02
Latin American Indians	5	0.04
All other tribes (5)	8	0.06
Arab:	436	3.09
Arab/Arabic	12	0.09
Lebanese	365	2.59
Syrian	59	0.42
Armenian	130	0.92
Asian:	401	2.84
Chinese, ex. Taiwanese (139)	160	1.13
Filipino (15)	23	0.16
Indian (74)	85	0.60
Indonesian (1)	1	0.01
Japanese (11)	15	0.11
Korean (59)	59	0.42
Pakistani (21)	23	0.16
Taiwanese (5)	5	0.04
Thai (1)	1	0.01
Vietnamese (14)	15	0.11
Other Asian, not specified (9)	14	0.10
Austrian	32	0.23
British	79	0.56
Bulgarian	7	0.05
Canadian	116	0.82
Czech	20	0.14
Czechoslovakian	5	0.04
Dutch	91	0.64
Eastern European	84	0.60
English	1,941	13.75
European	130	0.92
Finnish	32	0.23
French, except Basque	362	2.56
French Canadian	359	2.54
German	1,191	8.44
Greek	341	2.42
Hawaii Native/Pacific Islander:	1	0.01
Other Pac. Isl., not spec.	1	0.01
Hispanic or Latino:	132	0.94
Central American:	17	0.12
Guatemalan	5	0.04
Honduran	9	0.06
Salvadoran	3	0.02
Cuban	18	0.13
Dominican Republic	5	0.04
Mexican	23	0.16

Notes: 1. Figures in the "Number" column do not add up to the total population due to: a) Ancestry/Race overlap — e.g. persons can report being both White and Irish, b) persons of Hispanic origin can report being any race, c) persons reporting two ancestries are counted in both categories. 2. Numbers in parentheses indicate the number of persons reporting this ancestry/race alone, not in combination with any other ancestry/race. 3. Refer to the Explanation of Data in the front of the book for more detailed information.

Puerto Rican	9	0.06
South American:	36	0.26
Argentinean	2	0.01
Chilean	1	0.01
Colombian	8	0.06
Ecuadorian	2	0.01
Peruvian	6	0.04
Uruguayan	1	0.01
Venezuelan	16	0.11
Other Hispanic or Latino	24	0.17
Hungarian	36	0.26
Icelander	29	0.21
Iranian	119	0.84
Irish	4,744	33.60
Israeli	6	0.04
Italian	2,290	16.22
Latvian	29	0.21
Lithuanian	182	1.29
Northern European	49	0.35
Norwegian	105	0.74
Polish	563	3.99
Portuguese	107	0.76
Romanian	5	0.04
Russian	294	2.08
Scandinavian	19	0.13
Scotch-Irish	294	2.08
Scottish	470	3.33
Swedish	327	2.32
Swiss	34	0.24
Ukrainian	82	0.58
United States or American	527	3.73
Welsh	59	0.42
West Indian, excl. Hispanic:	16	0.11
Jamaican	16	0.11
White:	13,651	96.70
Not Hispanic (13,460)	13,544	95.94
Hispanic (89)	107	0.76

Weymouth

Place Type: Census Designated Place
County: Norfolk
Population: 53,988

Ancestry/Race	Number	%
African American/Black:	944	1.75
Not Hispanic (759)	907	1.68
Hispanic (20)	37	0.07
African, sub-Saharan:	310	0.57
African	22	0.04
Cape Verdean	231	0.43
Ethiopian	31	0.06
Kenyan	19	0.04
South African	7	0.01
Am. Ind. or Alaska Nat., not spec.	99	0.18
Albanian	92	0.17
American Indian tribes, specified:	154	0.29
Apache	1	0.00
Blackfeet (10)	23	0.04
Cherokee (3)	21	0.04
Chippewa	1	0.00
Creek	3	0.01
Crow (1)	1	0.00
Iroquois (8)	14	0.03
Latin American Indians (1)	5	0.01
Lumbee	1	0.00
Navajo (1)	2	0.00
Osage	1	0.00
Potawatomi (4)	5	0.01
Seminole	1	0.00
Sioux (1)	1	0.00
Ute	1	0.00
All other tribes (34)	73	0.14
American Indian tribes, not spec.	19	0.04
Arab:	543	1.01
Arab/Arabic	29	0.05
Egyptian	48	0.09
Jordanian	21	0.04
Lebanese	294	0.54
Moroccan	48	0.09
Syrian	84	0.16
Other Arab	19	0.04
Armenian	103	0.19
Asian:	1,026	1.90
Cambodian (4)	5	0.01
Chinese, ex. Taiwanese (238)	261	0.48
Filipino (59)	85	0.16
Indian (288)	340	0.63
Indonesian (3)	4	0.01
Japanese (22)	43	0.08
Korean (54)	77	0.14
Laotian (11)	11	0.02
Pakistani (16)	24	0.04
Sri Lankan (6)	9	0.02
Taiwanese (6)	11	0.02
Thai (9)	17	0.03
Vietnamese (114)	115	0.21
Other Asian, specified (1)	3	0.01
Other Asian, not specified (6)	21	0.04
Assyrian/Chaldean/Syriac	22	0.04
Austrian	156	0.29
Belgian	48	0.09
Brazilian	253	0.47
British	153	0.28
Bulgarian	17	0.03
Canadian	781	1.45
Celtic	111	0.21
Croatian	9	0.02
Czech	100	0.19
Czechoslovakian	32	0.06
Danish	144	0.27
Dutch	556	1.03
English	6,957	12.89
Estonian	22	0.04
European	103	0.19
Finnish	349	0.65
French, except Basque	2,203	4.08
French Canadian	1,866	3.46
German	2,867	5.31
Greek	532	0.99
Hawaii Native/Pacific Islander:	57	0.11
Melanesian: (4)	4	0.01
Fijian (4)	4	0.01
Micronesian: (6)	9	0.02
Guamanian/Chamorro (6)	9	0.02
Polynesian: (11)	20	0.04
Native Hawaiian (4)	6	0.01
Samoan (7)	14	0.03
Other Pac. Isl., specified	2	0.00
Other Pac. Isl., not spec. (7)	22	0.04
Hispanic or Latino:	721	1.34
Central American:	48	0.09
Costa Rican	13	0.02
Guatemalan	20	0.04
Honduran	4	0.01
Nicaraguan	1	0.00
Panamanian	5	0.01
Salvadoran	4	0.01
Other Central American	1	0.00
Cuban	42	0.08
Dominican Republic	13	0.02
Mexican	99	0.18
Puerto Rican	238	0.44
South American:	83	0.15
Argentinean	14	0.03
Bolivian	4	0.01
Chilean	3	0.01
Colombian	37	0.07
Ecuadorian	10	0.02
Peruvian	3	0.01
Venezuelan	10	0.02
Other South American	2	0.00
Other Hispanic or Latino	198	0.37
Hungarian	77	0.14
Icelander	18	0.03
Iranian	27	0.05
Irish	21,420	39.68
Italian	9,537	17.67
Latvian	6	0.01
Lithuanian	465	0.86
Northern European	29	0.05
Norwegian	460	0.85
Polish	1,919	3.55
Portuguese	767	1.42
Russian	372	0.69
Scandinavian	58	0.11
Scotch-Irish	1,486	2.75
Scottish	2,014	3.73
Slovak	23	0.04
Swedish	1,572	2.91
Swiss	66	0.12
Ukrainian	53	0.10
United States or American	2,636	4.88
Welsh	180	0.33
West Indian, excl. Hispanic:	180	0.33
Haitian	90	0.17
Jamaican	33	0.06
Trinidadian and Tobagonian	23	0.04
U.S. Virgin Islander	15	0.03
West Indian	19	0.04
White:	51,767	95.89
Not Hispanic (50,758)	51,236	94.90
Hispanic (471)	531	0.98
Yugoslavian	6	0.01

Whitman

Place Type: Town
County: Plymouth
Population: 13,882

Ancestry/Race	Number	%
African American/Black:	128	0.92
Not Hispanic (87)	125	0.90
Hispanic (3)	3	0.02
African, sub-Saharan:	40	0.29
Cape Verdean	40	0.29
Alaska Native tribes, specified:	1	0.01
Tlingit-Haida	1	0.01
Am. Ind. or Alaska Nat., not spec.	22	0.16
Albanian	15	0.11
American Indian tribes, specified:	50	0.36
Apache	1	0.01
Cherokee (6)	9	0.06
Chippewa	1	0.01
Comanche (2)	2	0.01
Creek	1	0.01
Iroquois (1)	8	0.06
Latin American Indians	1	0.01
Navajo (1)	1	0.01
Pueblo	2	0.01
Sioux (1)	1	0.01
All other tribes (9)	23	0.17
American Indian tribes, not spec.	7	0.05
Arab:	109	0.79
Egyptian	7	0.05
Lebanese	91	0.66
Syrian	11	0.08
Asian:	79	0.57
Chinese, ex. Taiwanese (10)	10	0.07
Filipino (21)	30	0.22
Indian (3)	3	0.02
Indonesian	2	0.01
Japanese (5)	8	0.06
Korean (9)	12	0.09
Vietnamese (6)	6	0.04
Other Asian, specified (3)	3	0.02
Other Asian, not specified (2)	5	0.04
Austrian	8	0.06
Brazilian	5	0.04
British	66	0.48
Canadian	166	1.20
Celtic	11	0.08
Croatian	5	0.04
Czech	10	0.07
Czechoslovakian	45	0.32
Danish	37	0.27
Dutch	93	0.67
English	2,170	15.63
European	63	0.45

Notes: 1. Figures in the "Number" column do not add up to the total population due to: a) Ancestry/Race overlap — e.g. persons can report being both White and Irish, b) persons of Hispanic origin can report being any race, c) persons reporting two ancestries are counted in both categories. 2. Numbers in parentheses indicate the number of persons reporting this ancestry/race alone, not in combination with any other ancestry/race. 3. Refer to the Explanation of Data in the front of the book for more detailed information.

Finnish	117	0.84
French, except Basque	858	6.18
French Canadian	815	5.87
German	830	5.98
Greek	75	0.54
Hawaii Native/Pacific Islander:	9	0.06
Micronesian:	1	0.01
Guamanian/Chamorro	1	0.01
Polynesian: (1)	6	0.04
Native Hawaiian	3	0.02
Samoan (1)	2	0.01
Other Polynesian	1	0.01
Other Pac. Isl., not spec. (1)	2	0.01
Hispanic or Latino:	122	0.88
Central American:	3	0.02
Guatemalan	3	0.02
Cuban	3	0.02
Dominican Republic	3	0.02
Mexican	15	0.11
Puerto Rican	62	0.45
South American:	16	0.12
Argentinean	1	0.01
Colombian	3	0.02
Peruvian	9	0.06
Venezuelan	2	0.01
Other South American	1	0.01
Other Hispanic or Latino	20	0.14
Hungarian	16	0.12
Irish	5,470	39.40
Italian	2,293	16.52
Lithuanian	200	1.44
Norwegian	96	0.69
Polish	532	3.83
Portuguese	317	2.28
Russian	17	0.12
Scandinavian	31	0.22
Scotch-Irish	437	3.15
Scottish	621	4.47
Slovak	12	0.09
Swedish	406	2.92
United States or American	459	3.31
Welsh	50	0.36
West Indian, excl. Hispanic:	17	0.12
Jamaican	17	0.12
White:	13,627	98.16
Not Hispanic (13,434)	13,559	97.67
Hispanic (53)	68	0.49

Wilbraham

Place Type: Town
County: Hampden
Population: 13,473

Ancestry/Race	Number	%
African American/Black:	203	1.51
Not Hispanic (154)	190	1.41
Hispanic (7)	13	0.10
African, sub-Saharan:	51	0.38
African	18	0.13
Cape Verdean	33	0.24
Am. Ind. or Alaska Nat., not spec.	14	0.10
Albanian	21	0.16
American Indian tribes, specified:	12	0.09
Cherokee (1)	6	0.04
Pueblo	1	0.01
Sioux (2)	2	0.01
All other tribes	3	0.02
Arab:	148	1.10
Jordanian	10	0.07
Lebanese	122	0.91
Syrian	16	0.12
Armenian	76	0.56
Asian:	200	1.48
Bangladeshi (4)	4	0.03
Cambodian (4)	4	0.03
Chinese, ex. Taiwanese (35)	40	0.30
Filipino (7)	20	0.15
Hmong (1)	1	0.01
Indian (39)	45	0.33
Japanese	1	0.01
Korean (36)	38	0.28
Pakistani (8)	8	0.06
Sri Lankan (4)	4	0.03
Taiwanese (6)	6	0.04
Vietnamese (22)	22	0.16
Other Asian, not specified (4)	7	0.05
Assyrian/Chaldean/Syriac	6	0.04
Australian	7	0.05
Austrian	35	0.26
Belgian	20	0.15
Brazilian	8	0.06
British	116	0.86
Canadian	120	0.89
Croatian	22	0.16
Czech	29	0.22
Czechoslovakian	9	0.07
Danish	24	0.18
Dutch	99	0.73
English	2,033	15.09
European	69	0.51
Finnish	21	0.16
French, except Basque	1,678	12.45
French Canadian	988	7.33
German	1,575	11.69
Greek	115	0.85
Hawaii Native/Pacific Islander:	9	0.07
Micronesian: (2)	2	0.01
Guamanian/Chamorro (2)	2	0.01
Polynesian: (6)	6	0.04
Native Hawaiian (4)	4	0.03
Samoan (2)	2	0.01
Other Pac. Isl., not spec.	1	0.01
Hispanic or Latino:	189	1.40
Central American:	4	0.03
Guatemalan	1	0.01
Nicaraguan	2	0.01
Panamanian	1	0.01
Cuban	7	0.05
Dominican Republic	3	0.02
Mexican	29	0.22
Puerto Rican	88	0.65
South American:	21	0.16
Argentinean	3	0.02
Colombian	11	0.08
Ecuadorian	3	0.02
Peruvian	4	0.03
Other Hispanic or Latino	37	0.27
Hungarian	40	0.30
Irish	2,897	21.50
Italian	1,898	14.09
Lithuanian	62	0.46
Northern European	47	0.35
Norwegian	81	0.60
Polish	2,094	15.54
Portuguese	203	1.51
Romanian	35	0.26
Russian	191	1.42
Scandinavian	18	0.13
Scotch-Irish	214	1.59
Scottish	562	4.17
Slavic	11	0.08
Slovak	7	0.05
Swedish	342	2.54
Swiss	36	0.27
Turkish	7	0.05
Ukrainian	105	0.78
United States or American	361	2.68
Welsh	111	0.82
White:	13,080	97.08
Not Hispanic (12,873)	12,941	96.05
Hispanic (115)	139	1.03

Wilmington

Place Type: Census Designated Place
County: Middlesex
Population: 21,363

Ancestry/Race	Number	%
African American/Black:	130	0.61
Not Hispanic (85)	126	0.59
Hispanic (3)	4	0.02
African, sub-Saharan:	15	0.07
African	4	0.02
Ugandan	11	0.05
Am. Ind. or Alaska Nat., not spec.	37	0.17
Albanian	24	0.11
American Indian tribes, specified:	30	0.14
Blackfeet	2	0.01
Cherokee (5)	12	0.06
Latin American Indians	1	0.00
Seminole	1	0.00
All other tribes (2)	14	0.07
American Indian tribes, not spec.	2	0.01
Arab:	95	0.44
Arab/Arabic	16	0.07
Lebanese	39	0.18
Syrian	31	0.15
Other Arab	9	0.04
Armenian	79	0.37
Asian:	506	2.37
Cambodian (5)	5	0.02
Chinese, ex. Taiwanese (147)	171	0.80
Filipino (13)	22	0.10
Indian (133)	144	0.67
Japanese (15)	32	0.15
Korean (48)	48	0.22
Laotian (1)	2	0.01
Pakistani	4	0.02
Sri Lankan (4)	4	0.02
Taiwanese (8)	8	0.04
Thai (2)	4	0.02
Vietnamese (47)	56	0.26
Other Asian, not specified (4)	6	0.03
Australian	5	0.02
Austrian	39	0.18
Belgian	35	0.16
British	79	0.37
Canadian	345	1.61
Czech	24	0.11
Czechoslovakian	17	0.08
Danish	99	0.46
Dutch	144	0.67
English	2,964	13.87
European	30	0.14
Finnish	44	0.21
French, except Basque	1,524	7.13
French Canadian	1,265	5.92
German	1,082	5.06
Greek	218	1.02
Hawaii Native/Pacific Islander:	6	0.03
Micronesian: (1)	2	0.01
Guamanian/Chamorro (1)	2	0.01
Polynesian:	1	0.00
Native Hawaiian	1	0.00
Other Pac. Isl., not spec.	3	0.01
Hispanic or Latino:	203	0.95
Central American:	23	0.11
Costa Rican	2	0.01
Guatemalan	11	0.05
Honduran	2	0.01
Salvadoran	8	0.04
Cuban	3	0.01
Dominican Republic	8	0.04
Mexican	36	0.17
Puerto Rican	64	0.30
South American:	28	0.13
Argentinean	2	0.01
Chilean	5	0.02
Colombian	7	0.03
Peruvian	3	0.01
Venezuelan	6	0.03
Other South American	5	0.02
Other Hispanic or Latino	41	0.19
Hungarian	30	0.14
Icelander	7	0.03
Irish	7,201	33.71
Italian	5,625	26.33
Lithuanian	181	0.85

Notes: 1. Figures in the "Number" column do not add up to the total population due to: a) Ancestry/Race overlap — e.g. persons can report being both White and Irish, b) persons of Hispanic origin can report being any race, c) persons reporting two ancestries are counted in both categories. 2. Numbers in parentheses indicate the number of persons reporting this ancestry/race alone, not in combination with any other ancestry/race. 3. Refer to the Explanation of Data in the front of the book for more detailed information.

Ancestry/Race	Number	%
Northern European	4	0.02
Norwegian	86	0.40
Pennsylvania German	7	0.03
Polish	598	2.80
Portuguese	716	3.35
Russian	281	1.32
Scotch-Irish	633	2.96
Scottish	720	3.37
Swedish	411	1.92
Turkish	12	0.06
Ukrainian	22	0.10
United States or American	747	3.50
Welsh	86	0.40
West Indian, excl. Hispanic:	15	0.07
Barbadian	5	0.02
British West Indian	6	0.03
Trinidadian and Tobagonian	4	0.02
White:	20,724	97.01
Not Hispanic (20,463)	20,596	96.41
Hispanic (112)	128	0.60

Winchester

Place Type: Census Designated Place
County: Middlesex
Population: 20,810

Ancestry/Race	Number	%
African American/Black:	198	0.95
Not Hispanic (135)	183	0.88
Hispanic (7)	15	0.07
African, sub-Saharan:	51	0.25
African	28	0.13
Nigerian	11	0.05
South African	12	0.06
Alaska Native tribes, specified:	1	0.00
Eskimo (1)	1	0.00
Am. Ind. or Alaska Nat., not spec.	33	0.16
Albanian	67	0.32
American Indian tribes, specified:	30	0.14
Apache (4)	4	0.02
Cherokee (4)	15	0.07
Chickasaw	1	0.00
Chippewa	2	0.01
Creek	1	0.00
Latin American Indians (3)	3	0.01
Menominee (1)	1	0.00
Potawatomi (1)	1	0.00
Pueblo	1	0.00
All other tribes (1)	1	0.00
American Indian tribes, not spec.	2	0.01
Arab:	88	0.42
Egyptian	33	0.16
Jordanian	8	0.04
Lebanese	30	0.14
Palestinian	6	0.03
Syrian	11	0.05
Armenian	339	1.63
Asian:	1,105	5.31
Bangladeshi (3)	3	0.01
Cambodian (2)	5	0.02
Chinese, ex. Taiwanese (383)	434	2.09
Filipino (27)	47	0.23
Indian (256)	274	1.32
Indonesian	1	0.00
Japanese (99)	128	0.62
Korean (109)	114	0.55
Pakistani (1)	6	0.03
Sri Lankan (22)	25	0.12
Taiwanese (16)	21	0.10
Thai (6)	7	0.03
Vietnamese (13)	14	0.07
Other Asian, specified (3)	4	0.02
Other Asian, not specified (6)	22	0.11
Australian	74	0.36
Austrian	94	0.45
Belgian	75	0.36
Brazilian	20	0.10
British	226	1.09
Canadian	174	0.84
Croatian	13	0.06
Czech	32	0.15
Czechoslovakian	15	0.07
Danish	87	0.42
Dutch	227	1.09
Eastern European	52	0.25
English	3,101	14.90
European	240	1.15
Finnish	14	0.07
French, except Basque	856	4.11
French Canadian	419	2.01
German	1,809	8.69
Greek	340	1.63
Hawaii Native/Pacific Islander:	15	0.07
Polynesian: (2)	4	0.02
Native Hawaiian (2)	4	0.02
Other Pac. Isl., not spec. (1)	11	0.05
Hispanic or Latino:	211	1.01
Central American:	13	0.06
Costa Rican	1	0.00
Guatemalan	4	0.02
Honduran	1	0.00
Nicaraguan	1	0.00
Salvadoran	4	0.02
Other Central American	2	0.01
Cuban	11	0.05
Dominican Republic	3	0.01
Mexican	25	0.12
Puerto Rican	40	0.19
South American:	49	0.24
Argentinean	15	0.07
Bolivian	3	0.01
Chilean	7	0.03
Colombian	10	0.05
Peruvian	6	0.03
Uruguayan	1	0.00
Venezuelan	3	0.01
Other South American	4	0.02
Other Hispanic or Latino	70	0.34
Hungarian	124	0.60
Iranian	57	0.27
Irish	5,916	28.43
Israeli	57	0.27
Italian	4,239	20.37
Latvian	25	0.12
Lithuanian	136	0.65
Maltese	5	0.02
Northern European	83	0.40
Norwegian	160	0.77
Pennsylvania German	5	0.02
Polish	697	3.35
Portuguese	172	0.83
Romanian	50	0.24
Russian	474	2.28
Scandinavian	16	0.08
Scotch-Irish	319	1.53
Scottish	627	3.01
Slovak	51	0.25
Slovene	23	0.11
Swedish	453	2.18
Swiss	40	0.19
Turkish	6	0.03
Ukrainian	98	0.47
United States or American	807	3.88
Welsh	133	0.64
West Indian, excl. Hispanic:	40	0.19
British West Indian	11	0.05
Haitian	29	0.14
White:	19,599	94.18
Not Hispanic (19,222)	19,427	93.35
Hispanic (153)	172	0.83

Winthrop

Place Type: Census Designated Place
County: Suffolk
Population: 18,303

Ancestry/Race	Number	%
African American/Black:	358	1.96
Not Hispanic (293)	339	1.85
Hispanic (15)	19	0.10
African, sub-Saharan:	55	0.30
African	39	0.21
Cape Verdean	16	0.09
Alaska Native tribes, specified:	3	0.02
Tlingit-Haida	3	0.02
Am. Ind. or Alaska Nat., not spec.	27	0.15
Albanian	140	0.76
American Indian tribes, specified:	49	0.27
Apache (1)	2	0.01
Blackfeet	1	0.01
Cherokee (2)	11	0.06
Chippewa (1)	1	0.01
Iroquois	4	0.02
Latin American Indians (2)	3	0.02
Navajo (1)	2	0.01
Seminole	1	0.01
Shoshone	1	0.01
Sioux (1)	1	0.01
All other tribes (11)	22	0.12
Arab:	183	1.00
Egyptian	14	0.08
Lebanese	131	0.72
Moroccan	15	0.08
Syrian	13	0.07
Other Arab	10	0.05
Armenian	17	0.09
Asian:	268	1.46
Cambodian (11)	11	0.06
Chinese, ex. Taiwanese (61)	62	0.34
Filipino (26)	45	0.25
Indian (28)	39	0.21
Indonesian (2)	2	0.01
Japanese (6)	22	0.12
Korean (13)	15	0.08
Laotian (1)	1	0.01
Malaysian (1)	1	0.01
Pakistani (5)	6	0.03
Thai (2)	2	0.01
Vietnamese (29)	33	0.18
Other Asian, not specified (17)	29	0.16
Austrian	31	0.17
Belgian	5	0.03
Brazilian	196	1.07
British	39	0.21
Canadian	216	1.18
Danish	67	0.37
Dutch	126	0.69
Eastern European	36	0.20
English	1,974	10.79
European	27	0.15
Finnish	11	0.06
French, except Basque	595	3.25
French Canadian	603	3.29
German	845	4.62
Greek	290	1.58
Hawaii Native/Pacific Islander:	12	0.07
Micronesian: (1)	1	0.01
Guamanian/Chamorro (1)	1	0.01
Polynesian: (4)	6	0.03
Native Hawaiian (4)	5	0.03
Tongan	1	0.01
Other Pac. Isl., not spec. (3)	5	0.03
Hispanic or Latino:	493	2.69
Central American:	36	0.20
Costa Rican	2	0.01
Guatemalan	13	0.07
Honduran	3	0.02
Panamanian	3	0.02
Salvadoran	9	0.05
Other Central American	6	0.03
Cuban	24	0.13
Dominican Republic	15	0.08
Mexican	66	0.36
Puerto Rican	110	0.60
South American:	105	0.57
Argentinean	14	0.08
Chilean	8	0.04
Colombian	44	0.24

Notes: 1. Figures in the "Number" column do not add up to the total population due to: a) Ancestry/Race overlap — e.g. persons can report being both White and Irish, b) persons of Hispanic origin can report being any race, c) persons reporting two ancestries are counted in both categories. 2. Numbers in parentheses indicate the number of persons reporting this ancestry/race alone, not in combination with any other ancestry/race. 3. Refer to the Explanation of Data in the front of the book for more detailed information.

Ancestry/Race	Number	%
Ecuadorian	3	0.02
Paraguayan	1	0.01
Peruvian	10	0.05
Uruguayan	1	0.01
Venezuelan	10	0.05
Other South American	14	0.08
Other Hispanic or Latino	137	0.75
Hungarian	48	0.26
Irish	6,117	33.42
Italian	5,439	29.72
Latvian	12	0.07
Lithuanian	104	0.57
Norwegian	59	0.32
Pennsylvania German	8	0.04
Polish	482	2.63
Portuguese	233	1.27
Romanian	7	0.04
Russian	173	0.95
Scandinavian	13	0.07
Scotch-Irish	347	1.90
Scottish	397	2.17
Slovak	19	0.10
Swedish	211	1.15
Swiss	36	0.20
Ukrainian	39	0.21
United States or American	767	4.19
Welsh	21	0.11
West Indian, excl. Hispanic:	64	0.35
British West Indian	19	0.10
Haitian	17	0.09
Trinidadian and Tobagonian	14	0.08
U.S. Virgin Islander	14	0.08
White:	17,483	95.52
Not Hispanic (17,020)	17,189	93.91
Hispanic (266)	294	1.61
Yugoslavian	15	0.08

Woburn

Place Type: City
County: Middlesex
Population: 37,258

Ancestry/Race	Number	%
African American/Black:	811	2.18
Not Hispanic (644)	744	2.00
Hispanic (53)	67	0.18
African, sub-Saharan:	105	0.28
African	22	0.06
Cape Verdean	65	0.17
Somalian	9	0.02
Ugandan	9	0.02
Alaska Native tribes, specified:	1	0.00
Aleut (1)	1	0.00
Am. Ind. or Alaska Nat., not spec.	66	0.18
Albanian	16	0.04
Alsatian	8	0.02
American Indian tribes, specified:	45	0.12
Cherokee	8	0.02
Chippewa (3)	4	0.01
Iroquois (1)	6	0.02
Latin American Indians (6)	9	0.02
All other tribes (4)	18	0.05
American Indian tribes, not spec.	3	0.01
Arab:	119	0.32
Arab/Arabic	5	0.01
Lebanese	67	0.18
Moroccan	13	0.03
Palestinian	9	0.02
Syrian	19	0.05
Other Arab	6	0.02
Armenian	224	0.60
Asian:	1,973	5.30
Bangladeshi	3	0.01
Cambodian (14)	17	0.05
Chinese, ex. Taiwanese (346)	365	0.98
Filipino (79)	99	0.27
Indian (932)	979	2.63
Indonesian (5)	14	0.04
Japanese (46)	52	0.14
Korean (96)	102	0.27
Laotian (16)	16	0.04
Pakistani (26)	29	0.08
Sri Lankan (22)	24	0.06
Taiwanese (12)	16	0.04
Thai (10)	15	0.04
Vietnamese (165)	177	0.48
Other Asian, not specified (17)	65	0.17
Austrian	33	0.09
Belgian	36	0.10
Brazilian	207	0.56
British	119	0.32
Bulgarian	56	0.15
Canadian	382	1.03
Celtic	4	0.01
Croatian	8	0.02
Czechoslovakian	27	0.07
Danish	174	0.47
Dutch	183	0.49
Eastern European	6	0.02
English	3,726	10.00
European	58	0.16
Finnish	44	0.12
French, except Basque	1,771	4.75
French Canadian	1,258	3.38
German	1,806	4.85
Greek	592	1.59
Hawaii Native/Pacific Islander:	39	0.10
Micronesian: (11)	12	0.03
Guamanian/Chamorro (11)	12	0.03
Polynesian: (3)	5	0.01
Native Hawaiian (2)	2	0.01
Samoan (1)	3	0.01
Other Pac. Isl., not spec. (5)	22	0.06
Hispanic or Latino:	1,152	3.09
Central American:	91	0.24
Costa Rican	6	0.02
Guatemalan	28	0.08
Honduran	12	0.03
Nicaraguan	3	0.01
Panamanian	5	0.01
Salvadoran	26	0.07
Other Central American	11	0.03
Cuban	29	0.08
Dominican Republic	59	0.16
Mexican	75	0.20
Puerto Rican	537	1.44
South American:	145	0.39
Argentinean	28	0.08
Bolivian	3	0.01
Chilean	17	0.05
Colombian	37	0.10
Ecuadorian	23	0.06
Peruvian	9	0.02
Venezuelan	20	0.05
Other South American	8	0.02
Other Hispanic or Latino	216	0.58
Hungarian	79	0.21
Iranian	9	0.02
Irish	13,434	36.06
Italian	9,532	25.58
Latvian	9	0.02
Lithuanian	202	0.54
Northern European	28	0.08
Norwegian	303	0.81
Pennsylvania German	9	0.02
Polish	1,013	2.72
Portuguese	1,009	2.71
Romanian	11	0.03
Russian	318	0.85
Scandinavian	20	0.05
Scotch-Irish	868	2.33
Scottish	867	2.33
Slavic	20	0.05
Slovak	27	0.07
Swedish	999	2.68
Swiss	53	0.14
Turkish	38	0.10
Ukrainian	107	0.29
United States or American	1,072	2.88
Welsh	35	0.09
West Indian, excl. Hispanic:	121	0.32
Barbadian	7	0.02
Haitian	80	0.21
Jamaican	24	0.06
West Indian	10	0.03
White:	34,075	91.46
Not Hispanic (33,176)	33,449	89.78
Hispanic (568)	626	1.68
Yugoslavian	2	0.01

Worcester

Place Type: City
County: Worcester
Population: 172,648

Ancestry/Race	Number	%
African American/Black:	13,786	7.99
Not Hispanic (10,762)	12,178	7.05
Hispanic (1,130)	1,608	0.93
African, sub-Saharan:	3,878	2.25
African	2,001	1.16
Cape Verdean	218	0.13
Ghanian	983	0.57
Kenyan	312	0.18
Liberian	110	0.06
Nigerian	118	0.07
Ugandan	9	0.01
Zimbabwean	17	0.01
Other sub-Saharan African	110	0.06
Alaska Native tribes, specified:	10	0.01
Alaska Athabascan	1	0.00
Aleut	1	0.00
Eskimo (3)	4	0.00
Tlingit-Haida	4	0.00
Alaska Native tribes, not specified	3	0.00
Am. Ind. or Alaska Nat., not spec.	714	0.41
Albanian	2,029	1.18
American Indian tribes, specified:	899	0.52
Apache (4)	9	0.01
Blackfeet (5)	66	0.04
Cherokee (31)	120	0.07
Cheyenne (1)	2	0.00
Chickasaw	2	0.00
Chippewa (8)	18	0.01
Choctaw (2)	14	0.01
Comanche	1	0.00
Cree	1	0.00
Crow	1	0.00
Delaware	3	0.00
Iroquois (43)	98	0.06
Kiowa (1)	2	0.00
Latin American Indians (73)	104	0.06
Lumbee	2	0.00
Navajo	4	0.00
Pima (4)	4	0.00
Potawatomi (2)	3	0.00
Pueblo (1)	13	0.01
Puget Sound Salish	1	0.00
Seminole (2)	5	0.00
Shoshone	1	0.00
Sioux (6)	24	0.01
Tohono O'Odham (2)	3	0.00
Yakama	1	0.00
Yaqui	1	0.00
All other tribes (185)	396	0.23
American Indian tribes, not spec.	115	0.07
Arab:	2,292	1.33
Arab/Arabic	120	0.07
Egyptian	76	0.04
Jordanian	71	0.04
Lebanese	1,373	0.80
Moroccan	18	0.01
Palestinian	58	0.03
Syrian	559	0.32
Other Arab	17	0.01
Armenian	1,306	0.76
Asian:	9,377	5.43
Bangladeshi (18)	20	0.01

Notes: 1. Figures in the "Number" column do not add up to the total population due to: a) Ancestry/Race overlap — e.g. persons can report being both White and Irish, b) persons of Hispanic origin can report being any race, c) persons reporting two ancestries are counted in both categories. 2. Numbers in parentheses indicate the number of persons reporting this ancestry/race alone, not in combination with any other ancestry/race. 3. Refer to the Explanation of Data in the front of the book for more detailed information.

Cambodian (250)	313	0.18
Chinese, ex. Taiwanese (1,163)	1,347	0.78
Filipino (147)	221	0.13
Hmong (22)	24	0.01
Indian (1,021)	1,153	0.67
Indonesian (12)	21	0.01
Japanese (191)	259	0.15
Korean (224)	265	0.15
Laotian (120)	144	0.08
Malaysian (4)	10	0.01
Pakistani (46)	71	0.04
Sri Lankan (11)	11	0.01
Taiwanese (18)	20	0.01
Thai (38)	68	0.04
Vietnamese (4,764)	5,061	2.93
Other Asian, specified (15)	22	0.01
Other Asian, not specified (148)	347	0.20
Assyrian/Chaldean/Syriac	45	0.03
Australian	11	0.01
Austrian	175	0.10
Belgian	82	0.05
Brazilian	1,099	0.64
British	493	0.29
Bulgarian	37	0.02
Canadian	619	0.36
Celtic	51	0.03
Croatian	52	0.03
Cypriot	15	0.01
Czech	104	0.06
Czechoslovakian	97	0.06
Danish	171	0.10
Dutch	633	0.37
Eastern European	109	0.06
English	10,633	6.16
Estonian	32	0.02
European	493	0.29
Finnish	1,012	0.59
French, except Basque	17,719	10.26
French Canadian	7,394	4.28
German	5,894	3.41
Greek	2,431	1.41
Guyanese	105	0.06
Hawaii Native/Pacific Islander:	410	0.24
Melanesian: (1)	4	0.00
Fijian (1)	4	0.00
Micronesian: (21)	35	0.02
Guamanian/Chamorro (18)	32	0.02
Other Micronesian (3)	3	0.00
Polynesian: (29)	90	0.05
Native Hawaiian (16)	53	0.03
Samoan (12)	32	0.02
Tongan	1	0.00
Other Polynesian (1)	4	0.00
Other Pac. Isl., not spec. (45)	281	0.16
Hispanic or Latino:	26,155	15.15
Central American:	1,407	0.81
Costa Rican	70	0.04
Guatemalan	132	0.08
Honduran	61	0.04
Nicaraguan	31	0.02
Panamanian	47	0.03
Salvadoran	1,000	0.58
Other Central American	66	0.04
Cuban	399	0.23
Dominican Republic	1,611	0.93
Mexican	706	0.41
Puerto Rican	17,091	9.90
South American:	1,136	0.66
Argentinean	38	0.02
Bolivian	3	0.00
Chilean	61	0.04
Colombian	383	0.22
Ecuadorian	413	0.24
Paraguayan	1	0.00
Peruvian	94	0.05
Uruguayan	13	0.01
Venezuelan	56	0.03
Other South American	74	0.04
Other Hispanic or Latino	3,805	2.20
Hungarian	272	0.16
Iranian	183	0.11
Irish	32,733	18.96
Israeli	155	0.09
Italian	19,950	11.56
Latvian	78	0.05
Lithuanian	3,812	2.21
Macedonian	36	0.02
Northern European	51	0.03
Norwegian	526	0.30
Pennsylvania German	7	0.00
Polish	10,482	6.07
Portuguese	1,247	0.72
Romanian	262	0.15
Russian	2,174	1.26
Scandinavian	137	0.08
Scotch-Irish	1,521	0.88
Scottish	2,156	1.25
Serbian	14	0.01
Slavic	38	0.02
Slovak	156	0.09
Slovene	10	0.01
Swedish	5,535	3.21
Swiss	77	0.04
Turkish	133	0.08
Ukrainian	228	0.13
United States or American	6,054	3.51
Welsh	288	0.17
West Indian, excl. Hispanic:	1,121	0.65
Bahamian	15	0.01
Barbadian	50	0.03
Bermudan	9	0.01
British West Indian	86	0.05
Haitian	313	0.18
Jamaican	427	0.25
Trinidadian and Tobagonian	45	0.03
U.S. Virgin Islander	12	0.01
West Indian	164	0.09
White:	137,758	79.79
Not Hispanic (122,211)	125,264	72.55
Hispanic (10,913)	12,494	7.24
Yugoslavian	161	0.09

Wrentham

Place Type: Town
County: Norfolk
Population: 10,554

Ancestry/Race	Number	%
African American/Black:	84	0.80
Not Hispanic (60)	78	0.74
Hispanic (4)	6	0.06
African, sub-Saharan:	79	0.75
African	36	0.34
Cape Verdean	12	0.11
South African	31	0.29
Am. Ind. or Alaska Nat., not spec.	7	0.07
American Indian tribes, specified:	20	0.19
Apache (4)	4	0.04
Blackfeet	1	0.01
Cherokee	2	0.02
Latin American Indians (1)	1	0.01
All other tribes (6)	12	0.11
American Indian tribes, not spec.	2	0.02
Arab:	43	0.41
Lebanese	18	0.17
Syrian	25	0.24
Armenian	27	0.26
Asian:	99	0.94
Cambodian (1)	1	0.01
Chinese, ex. Taiwanese (18)	20	0.19
Filipino (8)	8	0.08
Indian (18)	19	0.18
Indonesian (2)	2	0.02
Japanese (6)	13	0.12
Korean (15)	17	0.16
Malaysian (1)	1	0.01
Sri Lankan (2)	2	0.02
Taiwanese (1)	2	0.02
Thai (4)	4	0.04
Vietnamese (6)	6	0.06
Other Asian, not specified	4	0.04
Austrian	18	0.17
Belgian	7	0.07
British	10	0.09
Canadian	77	0.73
Czech	27	0.26
Czechoslovakian	8	0.08
Danish	9	0.09
Dutch	62	0.59
Eastern European	10	0.09
English	1,432	13.57
European	51	0.48
Finnish	50	0.47
French, except Basque	564	5.34
French Canadian	906	8.58
German	863	8.18
Greek	28	0.27
Hawaii Native/Pacific Islander:	3	0.03
Other Pac. Isl., not spec. (1)	3	0.03
Hispanic or Latino:	83	0.79
Central American:	14	0.13
Costa Rican	1	0.01
Honduran	1	0.01
Nicaraguan	4	0.04
Salvadoran	8	0.08
Cuban	1	0.01
Mexican	11	0.10
Puerto Rican	24	0.23
South American:	16	0.15
Colombian	7	0.07
Ecuadorian	2	0.02
Peruvian	5	0.05
Other South American	2	0.02
Other Hispanic or Latino	17	0.16
Hungarian	95	0.90
Iranian	13	0.12
Irish	3,686	34.93
Italian	1,778	16.85
Latvian	62	0.59
Lithuanian	146	1.38
New Zealander	10	0.09
Norwegian	39	0.37
Polish	413	3.91
Portuguese	219	2.08
Romanian	9	0.09
Russian	64	0.61
Scandinavian	10	0.09
Scotch-Irish	285	2.70
Scottish	475	4.50
Swedish	542	5.14
Turkish	7	0.07
United States or American	492	4.66
Welsh	59	0.56
West Indian, excl. Hispanic:	25	0.24
Jamaican	25	0.24
White:	10,356	98.12
Not Hispanic (10,248)	10,295	97.55
Hispanic (57)	61	0.58

Yarmouth

Place Type: Town
County: Barnstable
Population: 24,807

Ancestry/Race	Number	%
African American/Black:	446	1.80
Not Hispanic (326)	433	1.75
Hispanic (7)	13	0.05
African, sub-Saharan:	105	0.42
African	5	0.02
Cape Verdean	100	0.40
Alaska Native tribes, specified:	4	0.02
Eskimo (1)	1	0.00
Tlingit-Haida (2)	3	0.01
Am. Ind. or Alaska Nat., not spec.	39	0.16
Albanian	64	0.26
American Indian tribes, specified:	115	0.46
Apache	1	0.00

Notes: 1. Figures in the "Number" column do not add up to the total population due to: a) Ancestry/Race overlap — e.g. persons can report being both White and Irish, b) persons of Hispanic origin can report being any race, c) persons reporting two ancestries are counted in both categories. 2. Numbers in parentheses indicate the number of persons reporting this ancestry/race alone, not in combination with any other ancestry/race. 3. Refer to the Explanation of Data in the front of the book for more detailed information.

Ancestry/Race	Number	%
Blackfeet	6	0.02
Cherokee (4)	22	0.09
Chippewa (1)	2	0.01
Choctaw (3)	5	0.02
Comanche	2	0.01
Creek (1)	1	0.00
Iroquois (2)	6	0.02
Latin American Indians (1)	2	0.01
Seminole (1)	1	0.00
Sioux (2)	6	0.02
All other tribes (37)	61	0.25
American Indian tribes, not spec.	3	0.01
Arab:	266	1.07
Egyptian	7	0.03
Lebanese	157	0.63
Moroccan	69	0.28
Syrian	33	0.13
Armenian	103	0.42
Asian:	188	0.76
Cambodian (12)	13	0.05
Chinese, ex. Taiwanese (38)	42	0.17
Filipino (11)	21	0.08
Indian (16)	28	0.11
Indonesian (1)	1	0.00
Japanese (7)	13	0.05
Korean (10)	15	0.06
Laotian	1	0.00
Pakistani (13)	15	0.06
Taiwanese (7)	7	0.03
Thai (4)	4	0.02
Vietnamese (5)	8	0.03
Other Asian, specified (1)	3	0.01
Other Asian, not specified (5)	17	0.07
Australian	14	0.06
Austrian	57	0.23
Belgian	18	0.07
Brazilian	352	1.42
British	192	0.77
Canadian	261	1.05
Celtic	30	0.12
Czech	18	0.07
Czechoslovakian	75	0.30
Danish	145	0.58
Dutch	321	1.29
Eastern European	13	0.05
English	4,759	19.18
European	104	0.42
Finnish	102	0.41
French, except Basque	1,454	5.86
French Canadian	854	3.44
German	2,063	8.32
Greek	330	1.33
Hawaii Native/Pacific Islander:	18	0.07
Polynesian: (10)	15	0.06
Native Hawaiian (9)	11	0.04
Samoan (1)	4	0.02
Other Pac. Isl., specified	2	0.01
Other Pac. Isl., not spec.	1	0.00
Hispanic or Latino:	358	1.44
Central American:	19	0.08
Costa Rican	2	0.01
Guatemalan	4	0.02
Honduran	7	0.03
Nicaraguan	1	0.00
Salvadoran	5	0.02
Cuban	5	0.02
Dominican Republic	9	0.04
Mexican	43	0.17
Puerto Rican	140	0.56
South American:	32	0.13
Argentinean	4	0.02
Bolivian	2	0.01
Chilean	3	0.01
Colombian	4	0.02
Ecuadorian	8	0.03
Peruvian	3	0.01
Uruguayan	1	0.00
Venezuelan	2	0.01
Other South American	5	0.02
Other Hispanic or Latino	110	0.44
Hungarian	131	0.53
Icelander	5	0.02
Iranian	7	0.03
Irish	6,666	26.87
Italian	2,638	10.63
Latvian	35	0.14
Lithuanian	227	0.92
Northern European	8	0.03
Norwegian	173	0.70
Polish	734	2.96
Portuguese	889	3.58
Romanian	9	0.04
Russian	219	0.88
Scandinavian	48	0.19
Scotch-Irish	496	2.00
Scottish	1,231	4.96
Serbian	11	0.04
Slavic	7	0.03
Swedish	944	3.81
Swiss	74	0.30
Ukrainian	67	0.27
United States or American	996	4.01
Welsh	116	0.47
West Indian, excl. Hispanic:	5	0.02
West Indian	5	0.02
White:	23,969	96.62
Not Hispanic (23,428)	23,737	95.69
Hispanic (195)	232	0.94

Adrian

Place Type: City
County: Lenawee
Population: 21,574

Ancestry/Race	Number	%
African American/Black:	1,009	4.68
Not Hispanic (722)	899	4.17
Hispanic (38)	110	0.51
African, sub-Saharan:	19	0.09
African	19	0.09
Alaska Native tribes, specified:	2	0.01
Eskimo (1)	1	0.00
Tlingit-Haida	1	0.00
Am. Ind. or Alaska Nat., not spec.	86	0.40
American Indian tribes, specified:	153	0.71
Apache (3)	4	0.02
Blackfeet (1)	4	0.02
Cherokee (27)	48	0.22
Cheyenne (1)	3	0.01
Chickasaw	3	0.01
Chippewa (20)	41	0.19
Choctaw (7)	7	0.03
Comanche	1	0.00
Creek	1	0.00
Iroquois (4)	5	0.02
Latin American Indians (5)	12	0.06
Navajo (1)	3	0.01
Ottawa (3)	7	0.03
Potawatomi	3	0.01
Seminole	1	0.00
Sioux (1)	4	0.02
All other tribes (6)	6	0.03
American Indian tribes, not spec.	16	0.07
Arab:	34	0.16
Arab/Arabic	20	0.09
Syrian	10	0.05
Other Arab	4	0.02
Armenian	10	0.05
Asian:	226	1.05
Bangladeshi (1)	1	0.00
Chinese, ex. Taiwanese (31)	38	0.18
Filipino (21)	31	0.14
Hmong (13)	13	0.06
Indian (46)	52	0.24
Japanese (9)	18	0.08
Korean (21)	31	0.14
Pakistani (8)	8	0.04
Thai (1)	1	0.00
Vietnamese (22)	24	0.11
Other Asian, not specified (5)	9	0.04
Assyrian/Chaldean/Syriac	37	0.17
Austrian	10	0.05
Belgian	36	0.17
British	59	0.27
Canadian	79	0.37
Czech	80	0.37
Czechoslovakian	48	0.22
Danish	7	0.03
Dutch	411	1.91
English	2,485	11.56
European	17	0.08
Finnish	79	0.37
French, except Basque	870	4.05
French Canadian	224	1.04
German	5,295	24.63
Greek	60	0.28
Hawaii Native/Pacific Islander:	14	0.06
Micronesian: (1)	1	0.00
Guamanian/Chamorro (1)	1	0.00
Polynesian: (2)	9	0.04
Native Hawaiian (1)	6	0.03
Samoan (1)	2	0.01
Tongan	1	0.00
Other Pac. Isl., not spec. (1)	4	0.02
Hispanic or Latino:	3,665	16.99
Central American:	13	0.06
Costa Rican	2	0.01
Guatemalan	7	0.03
Honduran	1	0.00
Nicaraguan	3	0.01
Cuban	1	0.00
Dominican Republic	2	0.01
Mexican	2,691	12.47
Puerto Rican	213	0.99
South American:	13	0.06
Colombian	4	0.02
Ecuadorian	5	0.02
Peruvian	4	0.02
Other Hispanic or Latino	732	3.39
Hungarian	130	0.60
Irish	2,027	9.43
Italian	655	3.05
Northern European	81	0.38
Norwegian	42	0.20
Pennsylvania German	7	0.03
Polish	738	3.43
Portuguese	12	0.06
Romanian	10	0.05
Russian	48	0.22
Scandinavian	7	0.03
Scotch-Irish	197	0.92
Scottish	307	1.43
Serbian	8	0.04
Slavic	7	0.03
Slovak	14	0.07
Swedish	87	0.40
Swiss	67	0.31
Ukrainian	25	0.12
United States or American	1,503	6.99
Welsh	135	0.63
West Indian, excl. Hispanic:	29	0.13
Jamaican	14	0.07
West Indian	15	0.07
White:	18,755	86.93
Not Hispanic (16,582)	16,868	78.19
Hispanic (1,641)	1,887	8.75
Yugoslavian	13	0.06

Allen Park

Place Type: City
County: Wayne
Population: 29,376

Ancestry/Race	Number	%
African American/Black:	246	0.84
Not Hispanic (211)	241	0.82
Hispanic (3)	5	0.02
African, sub-Saharan:	19	0.06

Notes: 1. Figures in the "Number" column do not add up to the total population due to: a) Ancestry/Race overlap — e.g. persons can report being both White and Irish, b) persons of Hispanic origin can report being any race, c) persons reporting two ancestries are counted in both categories. 2. Numbers in parentheses indicate the number of persons reporting this ancestry/race alone, not in combination with any other ancestry/race. 3. Refer to the Explanation of Data in the front of the book for more detailed information.

Ancestry/Race	Number	%
African	19	0.06
Alaska Native tribes, specified:	1	0.00
All other tribes (1)	1	0.00
Am. Ind. or Alaska Nat., not spec.	74	0.25
Albanian	9	0.03
American Indian tribes, specified:	196	0.67
Apache (1)	1	0.00
Blackfeet (7)	11	0.04
Cherokee (14)	56	0.19
Cheyenne	4	0.01
Chickasaw	1	0.00
Chippewa (25)	48	0.16
Choctaw (1)	2	0.01
Comanche	1	0.00
Cree	1	0.00
Crow	1	0.00
Delaware (3)	3	0.01
Iroquois (13)	14	0.05
Latin American Indians (4)	17	0.06
Lumbee (2)	8	0.03
Menominee (1)	4	0.01
Navajo (3)	4	0.01
Ottawa (2)	3	0.01
Potawatomi	1	0.00
Seminole	4	0.01
Shoshone	2	0.01
Sioux	4	0.01
All other tribes (1)	6	0.02
American Indian tribes, not spec.	6	0.02
Arab:	302	1.03
Arab/Arabic	49	0.17
Jordanian	5	0.02
Lebanese	161	0.55
Palestinian	28	0.10
Syrian	29	0.10
Other Arab	30	0.10
Armenian	226	0.77
Asian:	312	1.06
Chinese, ex. Taiwanese (23)	39	0.13
Filipino (58)	76	0.26
Indian (60)	63	0.21
Japanese (23)	45	0.15
Korean (20)	25	0.09
Pakistani (8)	8	0.03
Thai (2)	3	0.01
Vietnamese (27)	28	0.10
Other Asian, specified	1	0.00
Other Asian, not specified (9)	24	0.08
Assyrian/Chaldean/Syriac	31	0.11
Australian	14	0.05
Austrian	62	0.21
Belgian	107	0.36
Brazilian	36	0.12
British	96	0.33
Bulgarian	6	0.02
Canadian	166	0.57
Croatian	72	0.25
Czech	145	0.49
Czechoslovakian	106	0.36
Danish	67	0.23
Dutch	572	1.95
Eastern European	8	0.03
English	3,062	10.42
European	134	0.46
Finnish	171	0.58
French, except Basque	1,950	6.64
French Canadian	833	2.84
German	5,768	19.64
Greek	253	0.86
Hawaii Native/Pacific Islander:	21	0.07
Micronesian: (1)	7	0.02
Guamanian/Chamorro (1)	7	0.02
Polynesian: (5)	10	0.03
Native Hawaiian (2)	7	0.02
Samoan (3)	3	0.01
Other Pac. Isl., specified	1	0.00
Other Pac. Isl., not spec. (1)	3	0.01
Hispanic or Latino:	1,389	4.73
Central American:	3	0.01
Costa Rican	1	0.00
Guatemalan	1	0.00
Panamanian	1	0.00
Cuban	22	0.07
Mexican	1,113	3.79
Puerto Rican	77	0.26
South American:	7	0.02
Argentinean	3	0.01
Colombian	1	0.00
Peruvian	2	0.01
Other South American	1	0.00
Other Hispanic or Latino	167	0.57
Hungarian	2,020	6.88
Irish	4,427	15.07
Italian	3,001	10.22
Lithuanian	254	0.86
Macedonian	36	0.12
Maltese	265	0.90
Norwegian	164	0.56
Pennsylvania German	9	0.03
Polish	4,939	16.81
Portuguese	15	0.05
Romanian	275	0.94
Russian	236	0.80
Scandinavian	49	0.17
Scotch-Irish	570	1.94
Scottish	846	2.88
Serbian	52	0.18
Slavic	33	0.11
Slovak	302	1.03
Slovene	55	0.19
Swedish	242	0.82
Swiss	62	0.21
Ukrainian	181	0.62
United States or American	918	3.13
Welsh	164	0.56
West Indian, excl. Hispanic:	7	0.02
Barbadian	7	0.02
White:	28,436	96.80
Not Hispanic (27,174)	27,417	93.33
Hispanic (909)	1,019	3.47
Yugoslavian	90	0.31

Allendale

Place Type: Township
County: Ottawa
Population: 13,042

Ancestry/Race	Number	%
African American/Black:	392	3.01
Not Hispanic (346)	387	2.97
Hispanic (4)	5	0.04
Am. Ind. or Alaska Nat., not spec.	32	0.25
American Indian tribes, specified:	63	0.48
Cherokee (3)	7	0.05
Chippewa (11)	27	0.21
Choctaw	3	0.02
Iroquois (3)	3	0.02
Latin American Indians (1)	1	0.01
Ottawa (3)	8	0.06
Potawatomi (1)	2	0.02
Sioux	6	0.05
All other tribes (5)	6	0.05
American Indian tribes, not spec.	5	0.04
Arab:	38	0.29
Lebanese	7	0.05
Syrian	31	0.24
Armenian	16	0.12
Asian:	142	1.09
Bangladeshi (1)	1	0.01
Chinese, ex. Taiwanese (11)	14	0.11
Filipino (12)	21	0.16
Indian (16)	19	0.15
Indonesian (1)	4	0.03
Japanese (5)	7	0.05
Korean (46)	49	0.38
Laotian (2)	2	0.02
Pakistani (1)	1	0.01
Taiwanese (1)	1	0.01
Thai (1)	3	0.02
Vietnamese (11)	13	0.10
Other Asian, not specified (1)	7	0.05
Australian	15	0.11
Austrian	26	0.20
Belgian	44	0.33
Brazilian	10	0.08
British	25	0.19
Canadian	52	0.40
Czech	41	0.31
Czechoslovakian	8	0.06
Danish	30	0.23
Dutch	3,719	28.30
English	999	7.60
European	76	0.58
Finnish	79	0.60
French, except Basque	377	2.87
French Canadian	148	1.13
German	2,898	22.05
Greek	57	0.43
Hawaii Native/Pacific Islander:	13	0.10
Melanesian:	3	0.02
Fijian	3	0.02
Micronesian: (4)	4	0.03
Guamanian/Chamorro (4)	4	0.03
Polynesian: (1)	2	0.02
Native Hawaiian	1	0.01
Samoan (1)	1	0.01
Other Pac. Isl., not spec. (4)	4	0.03
Hispanic or Latino:	376	2.88
Central American:	6	0.05
Costa Rican	4	0.03
Guatemalan	1	0.01
Honduran	1	0.01
Cuban	18	0.14
Dominican Republic	2	0.02
Mexican	252	1.93
Puerto Rican	14	0.11
South American:	9	0.07
Argentinean	1	0.01
Bolivian	4	0.03
Chilean	1	0.01
Colombian	3	0.02
Other Hispanic or Latino	75	0.58
Hungarian	53	0.40
Irish	1,100	8.37
Italian	385	2.93
Lithuanian	30	0.23
Maltese	17	0.13
Northern European	4	0.03
Norwegian	125	0.95
Polish	991	7.54
Romanian	8	0.06
Russian	52	0.40
Scandinavian	7	0.05
Scotch-Irish	157	1.19
Scottish	199	1.51
Slavic	26	0.20
Slovak	7	0.05
Swedish	239	1.82
Swiss	20	0.15
Ukrainian	26	0.20
United States or American	694	5.28
Welsh	35	0.27
West Indian, excl. Hispanic:	15	0.11
Haitian	8	0.06
Jamaican	7	0.05
White:	12,338	94.60
Not Hispanic (12,044)	12,156	93.21
Hispanic (165)	182	1.40

Alpena

Place Type: City
County: Alpena
Population: 11,304

Ancestry/Race	Number	%
African American/Black:	65	0.58
Not Hispanic (45)	63	0.56
Hispanic (2)	2	0.02

Notes: 1. Figures in the "Number" column do not add up to the total population due to: a) Ancestry/Race overlap — e.g. persons can report being both White and Irish, b) persons of Hispanic origin can report being any race, c) persons reporting two ancestries are counted in both categories. 2. Numbers in parentheses indicate the number of persons reporting this ancestry/race alone, not in combination with any other ancestry/race. 3. Refer to the Explanation of Data in the front of the book for more detailed information.

Ancestry/Race	Number	%
African, sub-Saharan:	25	0.22
African	6	0.05
Nigerian	19	0.17
Am. Ind. or Alaska Nat., not spec.	32	0.28
American Indian tribes, specified:	71	0.63
Apache	1	0.01
Blackfeet (1)	3	0.03
Cherokee (1)	10	0.09
Chippewa (30)	40	0.35
Latin American Indians (1)	1	0.01
Ottawa (2)	4	0.04
Potawatomi	9	0.08
Sioux	1	0.01
All other tribes	2	0.02
American Indian tribes, not spec.	8	0.07
Arab:	127	1.14
Arab/Arabic	51	0.46
Lebanese	23	0.21
Other Arab	53	0.48
Armenian	22	0.20
Asian:	66	0.58
Chinese, ex. Taiwanese (11)	17	0.15
Filipino (11)	12	0.11
Indian (10)	10	0.09
Indonesian (1)	1	0.01
Japanese (7)	10	0.09
Korean (2)	3	0.03
Pakistani (3)	3	0.03
Vietnamese (1)	1	0.01
Other Asian, not specified (8)	9	0.08
Austrian	4	0.04
British	7	0.06
Canadian	20	0.18
Croatian	6	0.05
Czech	4	0.04
Czechoslovakian	21	0.19
Danish	22	0.20
Dutch	149	1.34
Eastern European	28	0.25
English	1,062	9.52
European	16	0.14
Finnish	32	0.29
French, except Basque	1,588	14.23
French Canadian	546	4.89
German	2,789	25.00
Greek	6	0.05
Hawaii Native/Pacific Islander:	12	0.11
Micronesian: (1)	7	0.06
Other Micronesian (1)	7	0.06
Polynesian:	3	0.03
Native Hawaiian	3	0.03
Other Pac. Isl., not spec.	2	0.02
Hispanic or Latino:	67	0.59
Central American:	1	0.01
Costa Rican	1	0.01
Mexican	37	0.33
Puerto Rican	3	0.03
Other Hispanic or Latino	26	0.23
Hungarian	48	0.43
Irish	860	7.71
Italian	246	2.21
Lithuanian	26	0.23
Norwegian	276	2.47
Pennsylvania German	8	0.07
Polish	2,963	26.56
Romanian	6	0.05
Russian	87	0.78
Scandinavian	6	0.05
Scotch-Irish	128	1.15
Scottish	330	2.96
Slovak	5	0.04
Slovene	6	0.05
Swedish	125	1.12
Swiss	13	0.12
Ukrainian	23	0.21
United States or American	466	4.18
Welsh	128	1.15
West Indian, excl. Hispanic:	9	0.08
Jamaican	9	0.08
White:	11,138	98.53
Not Hispanic (10,993)	11,084	98.05
Hispanic (47)	54	0.48
Yugoslavian	6	0.05

Alpine

Place Type: Township
County: Kent
Population: 13,976

Ancestry/Race	Number	%
African American/Black:	552	3.95
Not Hispanic (424)	523	3.74
Hispanic (11)	29	0.21
African, sub-Saharan:	99	0.70
African	91	0.65
Nigerian	8	0.06
Am. Ind. or Alaska Nat., not spec.	50	0.36
American Indian tribes, specified:	134	0.96
Apache (4)	5	0.04
Blackfeet (1)	3	0.02
Cherokee (17)	27	0.19
Chickasaw (1)	1	0.01
Chippewa (24)	36	0.26
Iroquois	3	0.02
Latin American Indians (1)	1	0.01
Ottawa (20)	34	0.24
Potawatomi (2)	15	0.11
All other tribes (6)	9	0.06
American Indian tribes, not spec.	10	0.07
Arab:	19	0.13
Lebanese	19	0.13
Asian:	258	1.85
Chinese, ex. Taiwanese (9)	10	0.07
Filipino (28)	52	0.37
Indian (77)	80	0.57
Japanese (4)	6	0.04
Korean (26)	36	0.26
Malaysian	3	0.02
Pakistani (8)	9	0.06
Thai (2)	2	0.01
Vietnamese (55)	56	0.40
Other Asian, not specified (1)	4	0.03
Australian	11	0.08
Austrian	19	0.13
Belgian	87	0.62
Brazilian	7	0.05
British	30	0.21
Canadian	26	0.18
Croatian	7	0.05
Czech	79	0.56
Czechoslovakian	13	0.09
Danish	66	0.47
Dutch	2,156	15.30
English	1,574	11.17
Estonian	9	0.06
European	63	0.45
Finnish	94	0.67
French, except Basque	562	3.99
French Canadian	103	0.73
German	3,421	24.28
Greek	73	0.52
Hawaii Native/Pacific Islander:	18	0.13
Melanesian:	2	0.01
Fijian	2	0.01
Micronesian: (1)	2	0.01
Guamanian/Chamorro (1)	2	0.01
Polynesian: (4)	10	0.07
Native Hawaiian (4)	8	0.06
Samoan	2	0.01
Other Pac. Isl., not spec.	4	0.03
Hispanic or Latino:	916	6.55
Central American:	53	0.38
Guatemalan	20	0.14
Honduran	9	0.06
Nicaraguan	1	0.01
Panamanian	3	0.02
Salvadoran	19	0.14
Other Central American	1	0.01
Cuban	20	0.14
Dominican Republic	6	0.04
Mexican	666	4.77
Puerto Rican	53	0.38
South American:	4	0.03
Argentinean	3	0.02
Peruvian	1	0.01
Other Hispanic or Latino	114	0.82
Hungarian	47	0.33
Irish	1,485	10.54
Italian	363	2.58
Latvian	6	0.04
Lithuanian	164	1.16
Northern European	6	0.04
Norwegian	187	1.33
Pennsylvania German	7	0.05
Polish	1,384	9.82
Portuguese	19	0.13
Romanian	10	0.07
Russian	51	0.36
Scandinavian	16	0.11
Scotch-Irish	241	1.71
Scottish	277	1.97
Serbian	10	0.07
Slavic	25	0.18
Slovene	12	0.09
Swedish	257	1.82
Ukrainian	33	0.23
United States or American	474	3.36
Welsh	52	0.37
West Indian, excl. Hispanic:	14	0.10
Haitian	14	0.10
White:	12,779	91.44
Not Hispanic (12,119)	12,303	88.03
Hispanic (396)	476	3.41

Ann Arbor

Place Type: City
County: Washtenaw
Population: 114,024

Ancestry/Race	Number	%
Acadian/Cajun	7	0.01
African American/Black:	11,333	9.94
Not Hispanic (9,906)	11,068	9.71
Hispanic (164)	265	0.23
African, sub-Saharan:	1,007	0.88
African	547	0.48
Ethiopian	51	0.04
Ghanian	51	0.04
Kenyan	21	0.02
Liberian	10	0.01
Nigerian	138	0.12
Senegalese	30	0.03
Somalian	12	0.01
South African	72	0.06
Ugandan	12	0.01
Zimbabwean	16	0.01
Other sub-Saharan African	47	0.04
Alaska Native tribes, specified:	11	0.01
Alaska Athabascan	1	0.00
Eskimo (4)	5	0.00
Tlingit-Haida (4)	5	0.00
Alaska Native tribes, not specified	1	0.00
Am. Ind. or Alaska Nat., not spec.	313	0.27
Albanian	13	0.01
American Indian tribes, specified:	638	0.56
Apache (4)	5	0.00
Blackfeet (6)	36	0.03
Cherokee (36)	210	0.18
Chickasaw (3)	6	0.01
Chippewa (54)	99	0.09
Choctaw (6)	18	0.02
Colville	1	0.00
Cree	1	0.00
Creek (5)	11	0.01
Delaware (2)	4	0.00
Iroquois (17)	37	0.03
Latin American Indians (28)	63	0.06
Lumbee (6)	6	0.01

Notes: 1. Figures in the "Number" column do not add up to the total population due to: a) Ancestry/Race overlap — e.g. persons can report being both White and Irish, b) persons of Hispanic origin can report being any race, c) persons reporting two ancestries are counted in both categories. 2. Numbers in parentheses indicate the number of persons reporting this ancestry/race alone, not in combination with any other ancestry/race. 3. Refer to the Explanation of Data in the front of the book for more detailed information.

Ancestry/Race	Number	%
Menominee (5)	9	0.01
Navajo (5)	17	0.01
Osage	4	0.00
Ottawa (11)	23	0.02
Paiute (1)	3	0.00
Potawatomi (9)	16	0.01
Pueblo (1)	5	0.00
Puget Sound Salish	1	0.00
Seminole	5	0.00
Shoshone (4)	4	0.00
Sioux (3)	12	0.01
Yakama (1)	2	0.00
Yaqui	4	0.00
All other tribes (18)	36	0.03
American Indian tribes, not spec.	57	0.05
Arab:	1,795	1.57
Arab/Arabic	235	0.21
Egyptian	299	0.26
Iraqi	195	0.17
Jordanian	44	0.04
Lebanese	446	0.39
Moroccan	16	0.01
Palestinian	107	0.09
Syrian	132	0.12
Other Arab	321	0.28
Armenian	316	0.28
Asian:	15,128	13.27
Bangladeshi (20)	23	0.02
Cambodian (16)	18	0.02
Chinese, ex. Taiwanese (4,621)	5,021	4.40
Filipino (419)	614	0.54
Hmong (4)	7	0.01
Indian (3,292)	3,527	3.09
Indonesian (65)	92	0.08
Japanese (1,204)	1,450	1.27
Korean (2,432)	2,581	2.26
Laotian (10)	10	0.01
Malaysian (24)	35	0.03
Pakistani (160)	216	0.19
Sri Lankan (19)	30	0.03
Taiwanese (439)	523	0.46
Thai (186)	225	0.20
Vietnamese (268)	314	0.28
Other Asian, specified (32)	47	0.04
Other Asian, not specified (138)	395	0.35
Assyrian/Chaldean/Syriac	61	0.05
Australian	61	0.05
Austrian	569	0.50
Basque	9	0.01
Belgian	340	0.30
Brazilian	226	0.20
British	1,277	1.12
Bulgarian	56	0.05
Canadian	682	0.60
Carpatho Rusyn	8	0.01
Celtic	17	0.01
Croatian	206	0.18
Cypriot	23	0.02
Czech	655	0.57
Czechoslovakian	235	0.21
Danish	822	0.72
Dutch	2,661	2.33
Eastern European	635	0.56
English	13,521	11.85
Estonian	32	0.03
European	2,104	1.84
Finnish	1,012	0.89
French, except Basque	4,081	3.58
French Canadian	1,215	1.06
German	22,546	19.76
Greek	934	0.82
Guyanese	10	0.01
Hawaii Native/Pacific Islander:	156	0.14
Melanesian:	1	0.00
Other Melanesian	1	0.00
Micronesian: (10)	15	0.01
Guamanian/Chamorro (8)	13	0.01
Other Micronesian (2)	2	0.00
Polynesian: (26)	61	0.05
Native Hawaiian (13)	43	0.04
Samoan (10)	13	0.01
Tongan (3)	4	0.00
Other Polynesian	1	0.00
Other Pac. Isl., specified	3	0.00
Other Pac. Isl., not spec. (5)	76	0.07
Hispanic or Latino:	3,814	3.34
Central American:	255	0.22
Costa Rican	30	0.03
Guatemalan	38	0.03
Honduran	59	0.05
Nicaraguan	35	0.03
Panamanian	38	0.03
Salvadoran	41	0.04
Other Central American	14	0.01
Cuban	180	0.16
Dominican Republic	38	0.03
Mexican	1,538	1.35
Puerto Rican	434	0.38
South American:	636	0.56
Argentinean	80	0.07
Bolivian	23	0.02
Chilean	77	0.07
Colombian	187	0.16
Ecuadorian	35	0.03
Paraguayan	12	0.01
Peruvian	100	0.09
Uruguayan	15	0.01
Venezuelan	88	0.08
Other South American	19	0.02
Other Hispanic or Latino	733	0.64
Hungarian	1,401	1.23
Icelander	11	0.01
Iranian	380	0.33
Irish	12,703	11.13
Israeli	311	0.27
Italian	5,347	4.69
Latvian	144	0.13
Lithuanian	510	0.45
Luxemburger	44	0.04
Macedonian	91	0.08
Maltese	55	0.05
Northern European	297	0.26
Norwegian	1,624	1.42
Pennsylvania German	66	0.06
Polish	7,288	6.39
Portuguese	115	0.10
Romanian	482	0.42
Russian	3,149	2.76
Scandinavian	270	0.24
Scotch-Irish	2,018	1.77
Scottish	3,770	3.30
Serbian	219	0.19
Slavic	69	0.06
Slovak	372	0.33
Slovene	146	0.13
Swedish	2,360	2.07
Swiss	827	0.72
Turkish	248	0.22
Ukrainian	755	0.66
United States or American	2,950	2.59
Welsh	1,048	0.92
West Indian, excl. Hispanic:	591	0.52
Bahamian	15	0.01
Barbadian	4	0.00
British West Indian	19	0.02
Haitian	177	0.16
Jamaican	263	0.23
Trinidadian and Tobagonian	47	0.04
West Indian	66	0.06
White:	88,113	77.28
Not Hispanic (82,975)	85,613	75.08
Hispanic (2,176)	2,500	2.19
Yugoslavian	131	0.11

Antwerp

Place Type: Township
County: Van Buren
Population: 10,813

Ancestry/Race	Number	%
African American/Black:	197	1.82
Not Hispanic (133)	185	1.71
Hispanic (7)	12	0.11
African, sub-Saharan:	4	0.04
African	4	0.04
Am. Ind. or Alaska Nat., not spec.	38	0.35
American Indian tribes, specified:	92	0.85
Apache	1	0.01
Blackfeet	6	0.06
Cherokee (3)	32	0.30
Chippewa (15)	24	0.22
Choctaw	3	0.03
Lumbee (1)	1	0.01
Osage	1	0.01
Ottawa	3	0.03
Potawatomi (7)	7	0.06
Seminole	3	0.03
Sioux (1)	8	0.07
All other tribes	3	0.03
American Indian tribes, not spec.	9	0.08
Asian:	90	0.83
Chinese, ex. Taiwanese (6)	12	0.11
Filipino (7)	15	0.14
Indian (15)	17	0.16
Japanese (1)	9	0.08
Korean (17)	24	0.22
Thai (2)	2	0.02
Vietnamese (2)	2	0.02
Other Asian, specified (1)	1	0.01
Other Asian, not specified (5)	8	0.07
Austrian	17	0.16
Belgian	10	0.09
British	52	0.49
Canadian	16	0.15
Celtic	8	0.08
Croatian	57	0.53
Czech	53	0.50
Czechoslovakian	72	0.68
Danish	49	0.46
Dutch	1,194	11.21
English	1,247	11.70
European	147	1.38
Finnish	17	0.16
French, except Basque	402	3.77
French Canadian	87	0.82
German	2,622	24.61
German Russian	9	0.08
Greek	20	0.19
Hawaii Native/Pacific Islander:	2	0.02
Polynesian:	2	0.02
Native Hawaiian	2	0.02
Hispanic or Latino:	548	5.07
Central American:	2	0.02
Panamanian	2	0.02
Cuban	5	0.05
Mexican	424	3.92
Puerto Rican	7	0.06
South American:	7	0.06
Bolivian	2	0.02
Colombian	2	0.02
Other South American	3	0.03
Other Hispanic or Latino	103	0.95
Hungarian	138	1.30
Irish	1,428	13.40
Italian	279	2.62
Latvian	5	0.05
Lithuanian	24	0.23
Norwegian	118	1.11
Polish	852	8.00
Portuguese	10	0.09
Romanian	23	0.22
Russian	46	0.43
Scandinavian	20	0.19

Notes: 1. Figures in the "Number" column do not add up to the total population due to: a) Ancestry/Race overlap — e.g. persons can report being both White and Irish, b) persons of Hispanic origin can report being any race, c) persons reporting two ancestries are counted in both categories. 2. Numbers in parentheses indicate the number of persons reporting this ancestry/race alone, not in combination with any other ancestry/race. 3. Refer to the Explanation of Data in the front of the book for more detailed information.

Ancestry/Race	Number	%
Scotch-Irish	94	0.88
Scottish	192	1.80
Slavic	3	0.03
Slovak	43	0.40
Swedish	250	2.35
Swiss	15	0.14
Ukrainian	33	0.31
United States or American	993	9.32
Welsh	33	0.31
West Indian, excl. Hispanic:	7	0.07
Jamaican	7	0.07
White:	10,334	95.57
Not Hispanic (9,875)	10,025	92.71
Hispanic (240)	309	2.86
Yugoslavian	9	0.08

Auburn Hills

Place Type: City
County: Oakland
Population: 19,837

Ancestry/Race	Number	%
African American/Black:	2,789	14.06
Not Hispanic (2,593)	2,742	13.82
Hispanic (30)	47	0.24
African, sub-Saharan:	114	0.58
African	114	0.58
Alaska Native tribes, specified:	1	0.01
Eskimo	1	0.01
Am. Ind. or Alaska Nat., not spec.	89	0.45
Albanian	16	0.08
American Indian tribes, specified:	124	0.63
Apache	4	0.02
Blackfeet (5)	6	0.03
Cherokee (4)	42	0.21
Cheyenne	2	0.01
Chippewa (19)	31	0.16
Choctaw	3	0.02
Comanche	1	0.01
Creek	6	0.03
Iroquois (2)	5	0.03
Latin American Indians (1)	3	0.02
Navajo (1)	2	0.01
Osage	1	0.01
Ottawa (3)	3	0.02
Potawatomi (1)	1	0.01
Seminole	1	0.01
Shoshone	1	0.01
Sioux	6	0.03
Yaqui (1)	1	0.01
All other tribes (4)	5	0.03
American Indian tribes, not spec.	15	0.08
Arab:	171	0.86
Arab/Arabic	14	0.07
Egyptian	11	0.06
Lebanese	74	0.37
Palestinian	11	0.06
Syrian	21	0.11
Other Arab	40	0.20
Armenian	33	0.17
Asian:	1,420	7.16
Bangladeshi (8)	8	0.04
Cambodian (7)	7	0.04
Chinese, ex. Taiwanese (146)	171	0.86
Filipino (98)	135	0.68
Hmong (2)	9	0.05
Indian (703)	734	3.70
Indonesian (6)	10	0.05
Japanese (88)	112	0.56
Korean (58)	78	0.39
Laotian (10)	17	0.09
Pakistani (40)	45	0.23
Sri Lankan (5)	5	0.03
Taiwanese (3)	10	0.05
Thai (3)	4	0.02
Vietnamese (49)	52	0.26
Other Asian, specified (1)	1	0.01
Other Asian, not specified (12)	22	0.11
Assyrian/Chaldean/Syriac	10	0.05
Australian	5	0.03
Austrian	28	0.14
Belgian	56	0.28
Brazilian	22	0.11
British	130	0.66
Bulgarian	35	0.18
Canadian	142	0.72
Celtic	16	0.08
Croatian	32	0.16
Czech	100	0.51
Czechoslovakian	55	0.28
Danish	94	0.47
Dutch	415	2.10
English	2,065	10.43
European	105	0.53
Finnish	106	0.54
French, except Basque	812	4.10
French Canadian	497	2.51
German	3,323	16.78
Greek	57	0.29
Hawaii Native/Pacific Islander:	22	0.11
Micronesian: (1)	1	0.01
Guamanian/Chamorro (1)	1	0.01
Polynesian: (3)	12	0.06
Native Hawaiian	7	0.04
Samoan (3)	3	0.02
Tongan	1	0.01
Other Polynesian	1	0.01
Other Pac. Isl., not spec. (3)	9	0.05
Hispanic or Latino:	892	4.50
Central American:	8	0.04
Costa Rican	2	0.01
Honduran	2	0.01
Panamanian	3	0.02
Other Central American	1	0.01
Cuban	17	0.09
Dominican Republic	2	0.01
Mexican	584	2.94
Puerto Rican	149	0.75
South American:	32	0.16
Argentinean	9	0.05
Chilean	3	0.02
Colombian	9	0.05
Ecuadorian	2	0.01
Venezuelan	7	0.04
Other South American	2	0.01
Other Hispanic or Latino	100	0.50
Hungarian	176	0.89
Icelander	10	0.05
Iranian	43	0.22
Irish	1,900	9.60
Israeli	22	0.11
Italian	892	4.50
Lithuanian	95	0.48
Maltese	24	0.12
Norwegian	180	0.91
Pennsylvania German	30	0.15
Polish	1,412	7.13
Portuguese	8	0.04
Romanian	35	0.18
Russian	151	0.76
Scandinavian	13	0.07
Scotch-Irish	261	1.32
Scottish	685	3.46
Slavic	8	0.04
Slovak	44	0.22
Slovene	13	0.07
Swedish	201	1.02
Swiss	66	0.33
Ukrainian	85	0.43
United States or American	972	4.91
Welsh	117	0.59
West Indian, excl. Hispanic:	46	0.23
Haitian	18	0.09
Jamaican	28	0.14
White:	15,506	78.17
Not Hispanic (14,579)	14,957	75.40
Hispanic (482)	549	2.77

Bangor

Place Type: Township
County: Bay
Population: 15,547

Ancestry/Race	Number	%
African American/Black:	145	0.93
Not Hispanic (84)	133	0.86
Hispanic (12)	12	0.08
African, sub-Saharan:	12	0.08
African	12	0.08
Alaska Native tribes, specified:	1	0.01
Eskimo (1)	1	0.01
Am. Ind. or Alaska Nat., not spec.	40	0.26
American Indian tribes, specified:	102	0.66
Cherokee (2)	13	0.08
Chippewa (40)	67	0.43
Latin American Indians	1	0.01
Navajo (1)	1	0.01
Ottawa (7)	10	0.06
Potawatomi	1	0.01
Pueblo (1)	5	0.03
Yaqui (1)	1	0.01
All other tribes (1)	3	0.02
American Indian tribes, not spec.	6	0.04
Arab:	69	0.44
Lebanese	32	0.21
Palestinian	17	0.11
Syrian	4	0.03
Other Arab	16	0.10
Asian:	109	0.70
Chinese, ex. Taiwanese (16)	19	0.12
Filipino (17)	22	0.14
Hmong (7)	7	0.05
Indian (19)	24	0.15
Japanese (2)	4	0.03
Korean (17)	23	0.15
Pakistani (3)	3	0.02
Thai (1)	1	0.01
Vietnamese (1)	3	0.02
Other Asian, specified (1)	1	0.01
Other Asian, not specified (2)	2	0.01
Austrian	45	0.29
Belgian	73	0.47
British	16	0.10
Bulgarian	9	0.06
Canadian	111	0.71
Czech	22	0.14
Danish	84	0.54
Dutch	378	2.43
English	1,359	8.74
European	53	0.34
Finnish	23	0.15
French, except Basque	2,516	16.18
French Canadian	569	3.66
German	4,973	31.99
Greek	45	0.29
Hawaii Native/Pacific Islander:	4	0.03
Polynesian: (3)	4	0.03
Native Hawaiian (2)	2	0.01
Samoan (1)	2	0.01
Hispanic or Latino:	414	2.66
Central American:	7	0.05
Costa Rican	6	0.04
Salvadoran	1	0.01
Cuban	2	0.01
Mexican	298	1.92
Puerto Rican	4	0.03
South American:	4	0.03
Argentinean	1	0.01
Chilean	3	0.02
Other Hispanic or Latino	99	0.64
Hungarian	195	1.25
Iranian	29	0.19
Irish	1,714	11.02
Italian	295	1.90
Macedonian	11	0.07
Northern European	14	0.09
Norwegian	102	0.66

Notes: 1. Figures in the "Number" column do not add up to the total population due to: a) Ancestry/Race overlap — e.g. persons can report being both White and Irish, b) persons of Hispanic origin can report being any race, c) persons reporting two ancestries are counted in both categories. 2. Numbers in parentheses indicate the number of persons reporting this ancestry/race alone, not in combination with any other ancestry/race. 3. Refer to the Explanation of Data in the front of the book for more detailed information.

Ancestry/Race	Number	%
Polish	2,986	19.21
Russian	31	0.20
Scandinavian	7	0.05
Scotch-Irish	206	1.33
Scottish	435	2.80
Slovak	48	0.31
Slovene	17	0.11
Swedish	205	1.32
Swiss	32	0.21
Ukrainian	73	0.47
United States or American	996	6.41
Welsh	23	0.15
White:	15,172	97.59
Not Hispanic (14,740)	14,875	95.68
Hispanic (259)	297	1.91
Yugoslavian	15	0.10

Battle Creek

Place Type: City
County: Calhoun
Population: 53,364

Ancestry/Race	Number	%
African American/Black:	10,345	19.39
Not Hispanic (9,440)	10,216	19.14
Hispanic (61)	129	0.24
African, sub-Saharan:	496	0.93
African	482	0.91
Nigerian	14	0.03
Alaska Native tribes, specified:	11	0.02
Alaska Athabascan (7)	8	0.01
Eskimo (1)	1	0.00
Tlingit-Haida	2	0.00
Am. Ind. or Alaska Nat., not spec.	274	0.51
Albanian	8	0.02
American Indian tribes, specified:	632	1.18
Apache (8)	21	0.04
Blackfeet (19)	71	0.13
Cherokee (48)	192	0.36
Cheyenne (1)	2	0.00
Chippewa (44)	73	0.14
Choctaw (1)	8	0.01
Comanche (1)	4	0.01
Cree	3	0.01
Creek (2)	4	0.01
Crow	3	0.01
Delaware	1	0.00
Iroquois (3)	8	0.01
Kiowa (1)	5	0.01
Latin American Indians (11)	19	0.04
Lumbee (2)	2	0.00
Navajo (5)	7	0.01
Ottawa (32)	37	0.07
Potawatomi (61)	97	0.18
Pueblo (6)	7	0.01
Puget Sound Salish (4)	4	0.01
Seminole	4	0.01
Shoshone	2	0.00
Sioux (8)	24	0.04
All other tribes (25)	34	0.06
American Indian tribes, not spec.	36	0.07
Arab:	98	0.18
Arab/Arabic	23	0.04
Egyptian	11	0.02
Lebanese	13	0.02
Moroccan	27	0.05
Syrian	24	0.05
Armenian	7	0.01
Asian:	1,177	2.21
Chinese, ex. Taiwanese (84)	105	0.20
Filipino (78)	104	0.19
Indian (258)	273	0.51
Indonesian (5)	8	0.01
Japanese (392)	420	0.79
Korean (112)	131	0.25
Laotian (1)	2	0.00
Pakistani (3)	3	0.01
Sri Lankan (1)	1	0.00
Taiwanese (1)	1	0.00
Thai (5)	11	0.02
Vietnamese (42)	52	0.10
Other Asian, specified (36)	50	0.09
Other Asian, not specified (8)	16	0.03
Australian	5	0.01
Austrian	75	0.14
Belgian	40	0.08
British	190	0.36
Bulgarian	7	0.01
Canadian	160	0.30
Croatian	119	0.22
Czech	83	0.16
Czechoslovakian	22	0.04
Danish	227	0.43
Dutch	2,111	3.96
English	6,128	11.51
European	239	0.45
Finnish	132	0.25
French, except Basque	1,737	3.26
French Canadian	349	0.66
German	8,375	15.73
Greek	122	0.23
Hawaii Native/Pacific Islander:	38	0.07
Micronesian:	6	0.01
Guamanian/Chamorro	6	0.01
Polynesian: (3)	18	0.03
Native Hawaiian (2)	16	0.03
Samoan (1)	1	0.00
Other Polynesian	1	0.00
Other Pac. Isl., not spec. (3)	14	0.03
Hispanic or Latino:	2,475	4.64
Central American:	21	0.04
Costa Rican	7	0.01
Guatemalan	4	0.01
Honduran	2	0.00
Panamanian	3	0.01
Other Central American	5	0.01
Cuban	15	0.03
Dominican Republic	19	0.04
Mexican	1,945	3.64
Puerto Rican	173	0.32
South American:	28	0.05
Argentinean	1	0.00
Chilean	1	0.00
Colombian	11	0.02
Ecuadorian	1	0.00
Peruvian	14	0.03
Other Hispanic or Latino	274	0.51
Hungarian	130	0.24
Iranian	12	0.02
Irish	4,648	8.73
Italian	1,356	2.55
Latvian	26	0.05
Lithuanian	59	0.11
Macedonian	37	0.07
Maltese	6	0.01
Northern European	44	0.08
Norwegian	252	0.47
Pennsylvania German	46	0.09
Polish	1,420	2.67
Portuguese	29	0.05
Romanian	10	0.02
Russian	86	0.16
Scandinavian	128	0.24
Scotch-Irish	563	1.06
Scottish	931	1.75
Serbian	49	0.09
Slavic	46	0.09
Slovak	11	0.02
Slovene	11	0.02
Swedish	531	1.00
Swiss	80	0.15
Turkish	5	0.01
Ukrainian	94	0.18
United States or American	4,717	8.86
Welsh	306	0.57
West Indian, excl. Hispanic:	145	0.27
Bahamian	20	0.04
British West Indian	8	0.02
Haitian	4	0.01
Jamaican	94	0.18
Trinidadian and Tobagonian	13	0.02
West Indian	6	0.01
White:	41,060	76.94
Not Hispanic (38,761)	39,803	74.59
Hispanic (1,077)	1,257	2.36
Yugoslavian	16	0.03

Bay City

Place Type: City
County: Bay
Population: 36,817

Ancestry/Race	Number	%
African American/Black:	1,298	3.53
Not Hispanic (972)	1,236	3.36
Hispanic (31)	62	0.17
African, sub-Saharan:	53	0.14
African	53	0.14
Am. Ind. or Alaska Nat., not spec.	206	0.56
American Indian tribes, specified:	417	1.13
Apache (10)	24	0.07
Blackfeet (2)	23	0.06
Cherokee (16)	53	0.14
Cheyenne (2)	2	0.01
Chickasaw	3	0.01
Chippewa (101)	206	0.56
Choctaw (1)	3	0.01
Cree (3)	7	0.02
Creek (1)	1	0.00
Iroquois (10)	16	0.04
Latin American Indians (8)	15	0.04
Lumbee	3	0.01
Navajo (4)	4	0.01
Ottawa (2)	15	0.04
Pima	1	0.00
Potawatomi (1)	7	0.02
Pueblo (1)	4	0.01
Sioux (3)	6	0.02
Yaqui	1	0.00
All other tribes (6)	23	0.06
American Indian tribes, not spec.	24	0.07
Arab:	70	0.19
Lebanese	47	0.13
Syrian	23	0.06
Armenian	7	0.02
Asian:	269	0.73
Chinese, ex. Taiwanese (10)	17	0.05
Filipino (19)	37	0.10
Hmong (70)	78	0.21
Indian (8)	22	0.06
Japanese (9)	21	0.06
Korean (21)	29	0.08
Laotian (15)	16	0.04
Thai (3)	3	0.01
Vietnamese (19)	22	0.06
Other Asian, specified (5)	8	0.02
Other Asian, not specified (8)	16	0.04
Austrian	38	0.10
Belgian	150	0.41
British	35	0.10
Bulgarian	12	0.03
Canadian	142	0.39
Celtic	10	0.03
Croatian	39	0.11
Czech	99	0.27
Czechoslovakian	26	0.07
Danish	14	0.04
Dutch	707	1.92
Eastern European	12	0.03
English	3,052	8.29
Estonian	5	0.01
European	105	0.29
Finnish	91	0.25
French, except Basque	4,414	11.99
French Canadian	1,403	3.81
German	10,135	27.53
Greek	92	0.25
Hawaii Native/Pacific Islander:	13	0.04

Notes: 1. Figures in the "Number" column do not add up to the total population due to: a) Ancestry/Race overlap — e.g. persons can report being both White and Irish, b) persons of Hispanic origin can report being any race, c) persons reporting two ancestries are counted in both categories. 2. Numbers in parentheses indicate the number of persons reporting this ancestry/race alone, not in combination with any other ancestry/race. 3. Refer to the Explanation of Data in the front of the book for more detailed information.

Micronesian: (1)	2	0.01
Guamanian/Chamorro	1	0.00
Other Micronesian (1)	1	0.00
Polynesian:	3	0.01
Native Hawaiian	3	0.01
Other Pac. Isl., specified	1	0.00
Other Pac. Isl., not spec. (2)	7	0.02
Hispanic or Latino:	2,473	6.72
Central American:	4	0.01
Costa Rican	1	0.00
Guatemalan	1	0.00
Panamanian	2	0.01
Cuban	9	0.02
Dominican Republic	1	0.00
Mexican	1,922	5.22
Puerto Rican	32	0.09
South American:	10	0.03
Argentinean	1	0.00
Colombian	6	0.02
Ecuadorian	1	0.00
Paraguayan	1	0.00
Venezuelan	1	0.00
Other Hispanic or Latino	495	1.34
Hungarian	306	0.83
Iranian	15	0.04
Irish	4,603	12.50
Italian	806	2.19
Lithuanian	46	0.12
Northern European	6	0.02
Norwegian	158	0.43
Pennsylvania German	14	0.04
Polish	7,968	21.64
Portuguese	10	0.03
Romanian	6	0.02
Russian	173	0.47
Scandinavian	23	0.06
Scotch-Irish	445	1.21
Scottish	809	2.20
Serbian	6	0.02
Slavic	5	0.01
Slovak	19	0.05
Swedish	402	1.09
Swiss	83	0.23
Ukrainian	139	0.38
United States or American	1,242	3.37
Welsh	127	0.34
White:	34,373	93.36
Not Hispanic (32,333)	32,888	89.33
Hispanic (1,242)	1,485	4.03
Yugoslavian	13	0.04

Bedford

Place Type: Township
County: Monroe
Population: 28,606

Ancestry/Race	Number	%
African American/Black:	143	0.50
Not Hispanic (113)	141	0.49
Hispanic (1)	2	0.01
Am. Ind. or Alaska Nat., not spec.	50	0.17
American Indian tribes, specified:	123	0.43
Apache	3	0.01
Blackfeet (1)	3	0.01
Cherokee (12)	60	0.21
Chickasaw (5)	5	0.02
Chippewa (9)	20	0.07
Choctaw	2	0.01
Cree	1	0.00
Creek	2	0.01
Delaware	1	0.00
Iroquois	2	0.01
Latin American Indians (1)	2	0.01
Lumbee (3)	3	0.01
Menominee	1	0.00
Navajo	1	0.00
Ottawa (1)	3	0.01
Pueblo	1	0.00
Seminole	1	0.00
All other tribes (6)	12	0.04
American Indian tribes, not spec.	11	0.04
Arab:	256	0.89
Arab/Arabic	101	0.35
Iraqi	28	0.10
Lebanese	118	0.41
Syrian	9	0.03
Armenian	29	0.10
Asian:	192	0.67
Bangladeshi (3)	3	0.01
Cambodian	1	0.00
Chinese, ex. Taiwanese (20)	22	0.08
Filipino (28)	36	0.13
Indian (29)	32	0.11
Japanese (17)	25	0.09
Korean (44)	49	0.17
Laotian (1)	2	0.01
Thai (2)	2	0.01
Vietnamese (2)	3	0.01
Other Asian, not specified	17	0.06
Assyrian/Chaldean/Syriac	85	0.30
Australian	6	0.02
Austrian	45	0.16
Belgian	203	0.71
British	110	0.38
Bulgarian	70	0.24
Canadian	178	0.62
Croatian	20	0.07
Czech	126	0.44
Czechoslovakian	48	0.17
Danish	74	0.26
Dutch	667	2.33
Eastern European	7	0.02
English	3,454	12.07
Estonian	5	0.02
European	240	0.84
Finnish	46	0.16
French, except Basque	2,369	8.28
French Canadian	536	1.87
German	10,062	35.17
Greek	98	0.34
Hawaii Native/Pacific Islander:	6	0.02
Polynesian: (1)	2	0.01
Native Hawaiian (1)	2	0.01
Other Pac. Isl., not spec. (1)	4	0.01
Hispanic or Latino:	552	1.93
Central American:	3	0.01
Panamanian	3	0.01
Cuban	8	0.03
Mexican	394	1.38
Puerto Rican	25	0.09
South American:	12	0.04
Argentinean	1	0.00
Ecuadorian	1	0.00
Paraguayan	2	0.01
Peruvian	5	0.02
Venezuelan	1	0.00
Other South American	2	0.01
Other Hispanic or Latino	110	0.38
Hungarian	533	1.86
Icelander	4	0.01
Iranian	36	0.13
Irish	3,743	13.08
Italian	1,313	4.59
Latvian	5	0.02
Lithuanian	35	0.12
Macedonian	10	0.03
Maltese	11	0.04
Norwegian	210	0.73
Pennsylvania German	39	0.14
Polish	3,844	13.44
Romanian	70	0.24
Russian	108	0.38
Scandinavian	15	0.05
Scotch-Irish	545	1.91
Scottish	554	1.94
Serbian	23	0.08
Slavic	24	0.08
Slovak	172	0.60
Slovene	5	0.02
Swedish	302	1.06
Swiss	187	0.65
Ukrainian	115	0.40
United States or American	1,348	4.71
Welsh	173	0.60
West Indian, excl. Hispanic:	6	0.02
Jamaican	6	0.02
White:	28,165	98.46
Not Hispanic (27,532)	27,735	96.96
Hispanic (375)	430	1.50
Yugoslavian	18	0.06

Beecher

Place Type: Census Designated Place
County: Genesee
Population: 12,793

Ancestry/Race	Number	%
African American/Black:	8,728	68.22
Not Hispanic (8,394)	8,660	67.69
Hispanic (44)	68	0.53
African, sub-Saharan:	309	2.39
African	309	2.39
Alaska Native tribes, specified:	1	0.01
Tlingit-Haida (1)	1	0.01
Am. Ind. or Alaska Nat., not spec.	103	0.81
American Indian tribes, specified:	154	1.20
Apache (3)	15	0.12
Blackfeet (1)	15	0.12
Cherokee (11)	54	0.42
Chickasaw	5	0.04
Chippewa (17)	36	0.28
Choctaw	2	0.02
Comanche	2	0.02
Creek (2)	2	0.02
Delaware (1)	1	0.01
Latin American Indians (5)	6	0.05
Ottawa	2	0.02
Potawatomi	1	0.01
Pueblo	1	0.01
Seminole	1	0.01
Shoshone	1	0.01
All other tribes (4)	10	0.08
American Indian tribes, not spec.	12	0.09
Arab:	49	0.38
Syrian	49	0.38
Asian:	32	0.25
Chinese, ex. Taiwanese	2	0.02
Filipino (1)	10	0.08
Indian (5)	7	0.05
Japanese	1	0.01
Korean	1	0.01
Thai (3)	3	0.02
Vietnamese (1)	1	0.01
Other Asian, not specified	7	0.05
Assyrian/Chaldean/Syriac	7	0.05
Canadian	44	0.34
Croatian	5	0.04
Danish	5	0.04
Dutch	48	0.37
English	401	3.10
European	66	0.51
French, except Basque	149	1.15
French Canadian	51	0.39
German	416	3.21
Hawaii Native/Pacific Islander:	13	0.10
Micronesian:	1	0.01
Guamanian/Chamorro	1	0.01
Polynesian: (5)	7	0.05
Native Hawaiian (3)	5	0.04
Samoan (2)	2	0.02
Other Pac. Isl., not spec.	5	0.04
Hispanic or Latino:	506	3.96
Central American:	1	0.01
Salvadoran	1	0.01
Cuban	3	0.02
Mexican	406	3.17
Puerto Rican	28	0.22
South American:	1	0.01

Notes: 1. Figures in the "Number" column do not add up to the total population due to: a) Ancestry/Race overlap — e.g. persons can report being both White and Irish, b) persons of Hispanic origin can report being any race, c) persons reporting two ancestries are counted in both categories. 2. Numbers in parentheses indicate the number of persons reporting this ancestry/race alone, not in combination with any other ancestry/race. 3. Refer to the Explanation of Data in the front of the book for more detailed information.

Peruvian	1	0.01
Other Hispanic or Latino	67	0.52
Hungarian	13	0.10
Irish	291	2.25
Italian	140	1.08
Norwegian	8	0.06
Pennsylvania German	6	0.05
Polish	133	1.03
Russian	10	0.08
Scotch-Irish	10	0.08
Scottish	69	0.53
Swedish	68	0.53
United States or American	392	3.03
West Indian, excl. Hispanic:	46	0.36
Jamaican	46	0.36
White:	3,910	30.56
Not Hispanic (3,422)	3,695	28.88
Hispanic (161)	215	1.68
Yugoslavian	5	0.04

Benton Harbor

Place Type: City
County: Berrien
Population: 11,182

Ancestry/Race	Number	%
African American/Black:	10,493	93.84
Not Hispanic (10,303)	10,457	93.52
Hispanic (29)	36	0.32
African, sub-Saharan:	483	4.30
African	474	4.22
Nigerian	9	0.08
Am. Ind. or Alaska Nat., not spec.	58	0.52
American Indian tribes, specified:	32	0.29
Apache	1	0.01
Blackfeet (3)	8	0.07
Cherokee (2)	12	0.11
Chippewa	2	0.02
Choctaw	5	0.04
Creek	2	0.02
Iroquois	1	0.01
All other tribes (1)	1	0.01
American Indian tribes, not spec.	1	0.01
Arab:	8	0.07
Moroccan	8	0.07
Asian:	30	0.27
Chinese, ex. Taiwanese	1	0.01
Filipino (2)	2	0.02
Indian (4)	11	0.10
Japanese	2	0.02
Laotian (9)	9	0.08
Other Asian, specified	3	0.03
Other Asian, not specified	2	0.02
Canadian	7	0.06
Dutch	21	0.19
English	45	0.40
European	7	0.06
French, except Basque	24	0.21
French Canadian	14	0.12
German	190	1.69
Greek	18	0.16
Hawaii Native/Pacific Islander:	9	0.08
Polynesian: (4)	6	0.05
Native Hawaiian	1	0.01
Samoan (2)	3	0.03
Tongan (2)	2	0.02
Other Pac. Isl., specified	3	0.03
Hispanic or Latino:	65	0.58
Central American:	3	0.03
Nicaraguan	1	0.01
Panamanian	2	0.02
Cuban	1	0.01
Mexican	35	0.31
Puerto Rican	5	0.04
Other Hispanic or Latino	21	0.19
Irish	103	0.92
Italian	103	0.92
Polish	62	0.55
Russian	16	0.14
Scotch-Irish	17	0.15
Scottish	17	0.15
Slavic	17	0.15
United States or American	212	1.89
West Indian, excl. Hispanic:	32	0.28
Jamaican	7	0.06
U.S. Virgin Islander	19	0.17
West Indian	6	0.05
White:	720	6.44
Not Hispanic (600)	697	6.23
Hispanic (13)	23	0.21
Yugoslavian	6	0.05

Benton charter

Place Type: Township
County: Berrien
Population: 16,404

Ancestry/Race	Number	%
African American/Black:	8,705	53.07
Not Hispanic (8,478)	8,671	52.86
Hispanic (29)	34	0.21
African, sub-Saharan:	482	2.94
African	472	2.88
Kenyan	5	0.03
Nigerian	5	0.03
Am. Ind. or Alaska Nat., not spec.	70	0.43
American Indian tribes, specified:	72	0.44
Apache (2)	3	0.02
Blackfeet (1)	11	0.07
Cherokee (4)	21	0.13
Chippewa (4)	5	0.03
Choctaw	2	0.01
Iroquois	1	0.01
Latin American Indians	1	0.01
Ottawa	1	0.01
Potawatomi (17)	23	0.14
Seminole	1	0.01
Sioux (2)	2	0.01
All other tribes	1	0.01
American Indian tribes, not spec.	3	0.02
Arab:	6	0.04
Syrian	6	0.04
Asian:	70	0.43
Chinese, ex. Taiwanese (7)	7	0.04
Filipino (13)	17	0.10
Indian (27)	27	0.16
Japanese (1)	2	0.01
Korean (5)	9	0.05
Vietnamese (3)	3	0.02
Other Asian, not specified (3)	5	0.03
Austrian	12	0.07
Belgian	3	0.02
British	43	0.26
Canadian	20	0.12
Czech	95	0.58
Czechoslovakian	15	0.09
Danish	6	0.04
Dutch	136	0.83
English	522	3.19
European	41	0.25
Finnish	6	0.04
French, except Basque	261	1.59
French Canadian	42	0.26
German	1,736	10.60
Greek	24	0.15
Hawaii Native/Pacific Islander:	3	0.02
Polynesian: (2)	3	0.02
Native Hawaiian (2)	3	0.02
Hispanic or Latino:	515	3.14
Central American:	2	0.01
Panamanian	2	0.01
Cuban	4	0.02
Mexican	400	2.44
Puerto Rican	16	0.10
South American:	2	0.01
Argentinean	1	0.01
Other South American	1	0.01
Other Hispanic or Latino	91	0.55
Hungarian	56	0.34
Irish	981	5.99
Italian	357	2.18
Latvian	4	0.02
Norwegian	18	0.11
Polish	233	1.42
Russian	63	0.38
Scotch-Irish	84	0.51
Scottish	104	0.63
Swedish	135	0.82
Ukrainian	16	0.10
United States or American	710	4.33
Welsh	33	0.20
West Indian, excl. Hispanic:	61	0.37
Jamaican	50	0.31
Trinidadian and Tobagonian	11	0.07
White:	7,484	45.62
Not Hispanic (6,989)	7,213	43.97
Hispanic (246)	271	1.65
Yugoslavian	7	0.04

Berkley

Place Type: City
County: Oakland
Population: 15,531

Ancestry/Race	Number	%
Acadian/Cajun	6	0.04
African American/Black:	145	0.93
Not Hispanic (102)	137	0.88
Hispanic (6)	8	0.05
African, sub-Saharan:	18	0.12
African	18	0.12
Am. Ind. or Alaska Nat., not spec.	40	0.26
Albanian	29	0.19
Alsatian	14	0.09
American Indian tribes, specified:	73	0.47
Apache	1	0.01
Blackfeet	3	0.02
Cherokee (1)	12	0.08
Cheyenne	1	0.01
Chippewa (15)	18	0.12
Choctaw	2	0.01
Comanche (1)	2	0.01
Iroquois (3)	9	0.06
Latin American Indians (1)	3	0.02
Navajo (1)	3	0.02
Ottawa (8)	10	0.06
Potawatomi	3	0.02
Ute (1)	1	0.01
All other tribes (4)	5	0.03
American Indian tribes, not spec.	6	0.04
Arab:	78	0.50
Arab/Arabic	26	0.17
Lebanese	52	0.33
Armenian	59	0.38
Asian:	233	1.50
Cambodian (5)	5	0.03
Chinese, ex. Taiwanese (18)	28	0.18
Filipino (37)	56	0.36
Indian (16)	33	0.21
Indonesian	1	0.01
Japanese (8)	16	0.10
Korean (26)	29	0.19
Pakistani	9	0.06
Thai (2)	2	0.01
Vietnamese (18)	24	0.15
Other Asian, not specified (19)	30	0.19
Assyrian/Chaldean/Syriac	74	0.48
Austrian	44	0.28
Belgian	108	0.70
Brazilian	7	0.05
British	123	0.79
Canadian	152	0.98
Celtic	12	0.08
Croatian	64	0.41
Czech	110	0.71
Czechoslovakian	29	0.19
Danish	32	0.21

Notes: 1. Figures in the "Number" column do not add up to the total population due to: a) Ancestry/Race overlap — e.g. persons can report being both White and Irish, b) persons of Hispanic origin can report being any race, c) persons reporting two ancestries are counted in both categories. 2. Numbers in parentheses indicate the number of persons reporting this ancestry/race alone, not in combination with any other ancestry/race. 3. Refer to the Explanation of Data in the front of the book for more detailed information.

Ancestry/Race	Number	%
Dutch	366	2.36
Eastern European	6	0.04
English	2,093	13.48
Estonian	15	0.10
European	100	0.64
Finnish	312	2.01
French, except Basque	849	5.47
French Canadian	427	2.75
German	4,337	27.92
Greek	195	1.26
Hawaii Native/Pacific Islander:	8	0.05
Polynesian: (2)	7	0.05
Native Hawaiian (1)	6	0.04
Samoan (1)	1	0.01
Other Pac. Isl., not spec.	1	0.01
Hispanic or Latino:	204	1.31
Central American:	10	0.06
Costa Rican	5	0.03
Guatemalan	2	0.01
Nicaraguan	2	0.01
Other Central American	1	0.01
Cuban	6	0.04
Mexican	101	0.65
Puerto Rican	28	0.18
South American:	19	0.12
Argentinean	5	0.03
Colombian	5	0.03
Ecuadorian	5	0.03
Paraguayan	2	0.01
Peruvian	2	0.01
Uruguayan	1	0.01
Other Hispanic or Latino	40	0.26
Hungarian	197	1.27
Irish	3,030	19.51
Israeli	11	0.07
Italian	1,231	7.93
Latvian	41	0.26
Lithuanian	31	0.20
Macedonian	12	0.08
Maltese	40	0.26
Northern European	13	0.08
Norwegian	154	0.99
Pennsylvania German	7	0.05
Polish	2,207	14.21
Portuguese	26	0.17
Romanian	55	0.35
Russian	183	1.18
Scandinavian	26	0.17
Scotch-Irish	295	1.90
Scottish	768	4.94
Serbian	16	0.10
Slavic	54	0.35
Slovak	62	0.40
Slovene	12	0.08
Swedish	247	1.59
Swiss	39	0.25
Ukrainian	128	0.82
United States or American	601	3.87
Welsh	196	1.26
West Indian, excl. Hispanic:	14	0.09
Jamaican	14	0.09
White:	15,154	97.57
Not Hispanic (14,784)	14,994	96.54
Hispanic (139)	160	1.03
Yugoslavian	42	0.27

Beverly Hills

Place Type: Village
County: Oakland
Population: 10,437

Ancestry/Race	Number	%
African American/Black:	356	3.41
Not Hispanic (315)	352	3.37
Hispanic (3)	4	0.04
African, sub-Saharan:	16	0.15
African	16	0.15
Am. Ind. or Alaska Nat., not spec.	15	0.14
Albanian	24	0.23
American Indian tribes, specified:	29	0.28
Apache (1)	1	0.01
Blackfeet	2	0.02
Cherokee (4)	11	0.11
Chippewa	4	0.04
Choctaw	1	0.01
Iroquois (2)	2	0.02
Latin American Indians (1)	1	0.01
Lumbee (1)	1	0.01
Ottawa	2	0.02
Seminole	2	0.02
Sioux	1	0.01
All other tribes	1	0.01
American Indian tribes, not spec.	1	0.01
Arab:	204	1.95
Arab/Arabic	34	0.33
Egyptian	17	0.16
Iraqi	45	0.43
Lebanese	84	0.80
Palestinian	19	0.18
Syrian	5	0.05
Armenian	101	0.97
Asian:	238	2.28
Chinese, ex. Taiwanese (61)	71	0.68
Filipino (14)	19	0.18
Indian (62)	74	0.71
Japanese (23)	30	0.29
Korean (18)	26	0.25
Pakistani (4)	5	0.05
Taiwanese	3	0.03
Vietnamese (1)	4	0.04
Other Asian, not specified (3)	6	0.06
Assyrian/Chaldean/Syriac	242	2.32
Australian	4	0.04
Austrian	19	0.18
Belgian	55	0.53
British	54	0.52
Canadian	86	0.82
Croatian	16	0.15
Czech	52	0.50
Czechoslovakian	21	0.20
Danish	39	0.37
Dutch	308	2.95
Eastern European	33	0.32
English	1,626	15.57
European	86	0.82
Finnish	81	0.78
French, except Basque	396	3.79
French Canadian	165	1.58
German	2,693	25.79
Greek	156	1.49
Hawaii Native/Pacific Islander:	11	0.11
Other Pac. Isl., not spec. (2)	11	0.11
Hispanic or Latino:	147	1.41
Central American:	3	0.03
Guatemalan	2	0.02
Panamanian	1	0.01
Cuban	1	0.01
Dominican Republic	2	0.02
Mexican	84	0.80
Puerto Rican	17	0.16
South American:	13	0.12
Argentinean	3	0.03
Bolivian	1	0.01
Colombian	2	0.02
Ecuadorian	4	0.04
Paraguayan	1	0.01
Venezuelan	2	0.02
Other Hispanic or Latino	27	0.26
Hungarian	123	1.18
Iranian	42	0.40
Irish	2,220	21.26
Italian	801	7.67
Latvian	7	0.07
Lithuanian	104	1.00
Luxemburger	2	0.02
Macedonian	10	0.10
Norwegian	87	0.83
Pennsylvania German	4	0.04
Polish	1,173	11.23
Portuguese	4	0.04
Romanian	52	0.50
Russian	312	2.99
Scandinavian	9	0.09
Scotch-Irish	171	1.64
Scottish	404	3.87
Slovak	43	0.41
Slovene	14	0.13
Swedish	182	1.74
Swiss	58	0.56
Ukrainian	54	0.52
United States or American	507	4.86
Welsh	153	1.47
West Indian, excl. Hispanic:	5	0.05
Jamaican	5	0.05
White:	9,862	94.49
Not Hispanic (9,631)	9,745	93.37
Hispanic (97)	117	1.12
Yugoslavian	19	0.18

Big Rapids

Place Type: City
County: Mecosta
Population: 10,849

Ancestry/Race	Number	%
African American/Black:	1,268	11.69
Not Hispanic (1,147)	1,255	11.57
Hispanic (6)	13	0.12
African, sub-Saharan:	63	0.59
African	30	0.28
Ethiopian	19	0.18
Nigerian	14	0.13
Am. Ind. or Alaska Nat., not spec.	57	0.53
Albanian	21	0.20
American Indian tribes, specified:	79	0.73
Blackfeet (4)	13	0.12
Cherokee (7)	15	0.14
Chippewa (23)	32	0.29
Creek	1	0.01
Iroquois (2)	2	0.02
Latin American Indians (2)	3	0.03
Navajo (2)	2	0.02
Ottawa (2)	6	0.06
Potawatomi (1)	1	0.01
Sioux (1)	1	0.01
All other tribes (2)	3	0.03
American Indian tribes, not spec.	2	0.02
Arab:	70	0.66
Arab/Arabic	45	0.42
Iraqi	5	0.05
Lebanese	5	0.05
Palestinian	8	0.08
Other Arab	7	0.07
Asian:	310	2.86
Chinese, ex. Taiwanese (25)	31	0.29
Filipino (13)	27	0.25
Hmong (12)	13	0.12
Indian (56)	64	0.59
Indonesian (1)	1	0.01
Japanese (23)	35	0.32
Korean (45)	45	0.41
Laotian (5)	5	0.05
Pakistani (3)	5	0.05
Thai (5)	8	0.07
Vietnamese (43)	46	0.42
Other Asian, specified (5)	5	0.05
Other Asian, not specified (5)	25	0.23
Assyrian/Chaldean/Syriac	6	0.06
Austrian	25	0.24
Belgian	36	0.34
British	5	0.05
Canadian	52	0.49
Celtic	8	0.08
Croatian	15	0.14
Czech	45	0.42
Czechoslovakian	21	0.20
Danish	49	0.46
Dutch	502	4.73

Notes: 1. Figures in the "Number" column do not add up to the total population due to: a) Ancestry/Race overlap — e.g. persons can report being both White and Irish, b) persons of Hispanic origin can report being any race, c) persons reporting two ancestries are counted in both categories. 2. Numbers in parentheses indicate the number of persons reporting this ancestry/race alone, not in combination with any other ancestry/race. 3. Refer to the Explanation of Data in the front of the book for more detailed information.

Ancestry/Race	Number	%
English	883	8.32
European	70	0.66
Finnish	130	1.22
French, except Basque	462	4.35
French Canadian	219	2.06
German	2,573	24.24
Greek	30	0.28
Hawaii Native/Pacific Islander:	15	0.14
Micronesian:	1	0.01
Guamanian/Chamorro	1	0.01
Polynesian: (4)	9	0.08
Native Hawaiian (2)	3	0.03
Samoan (2)	4	0.04
Other Polynesian	2	0.02
Other Pac. Isl., not spec.	5	0.05
Hispanic or Latino:	199	1.83
Central American:	9	0.08
Costa Rican	7	0.06
Guatemalan	2	0.02
Cuban	6	0.06
Dominican Republic	1	0.01
Mexican	116	1.07
Puerto Rican	13	0.12
South American:	9	0.08
Chilean	1	0.01
Colombian	5	0.05
Venezuelan	3	0.03
Other Hispanic or Latino	45	0.41
Hungarian	49	0.46
Irish	1,217	11.46
Italian	452	4.26
Latvian	7	0.07
Lithuanian	20	0.19
Maltese	6	0.06
Norwegian	116	1.09
Polish	693	6.53
Portuguese	10	0.09
Romanian	7	0.07
Russian	38	0.36
Scandinavian	35	0.33
Scotch-Irish	128	1.21
Scottish	262	2.47
Serbian	14	0.13
Slovak	5	0.05
Swedish	263	2.48
Swiss	39	0.37
Turkish	9	0.08
Ukrainian	7	0.07
United States or American	279	2.63
Welsh	30	0.28
White:	9,263	85.38
Not Hispanic (8,939)	9,126	84.12
Hispanic (127)	137	1.26
Yugoslavian	14	0.13

Birmingham

Place Type: City
County: Oakland
Population: 19,291

Ancestry/Race	Number	%
African American/Black:	216	1.12
Not Hispanic (168)	208	1.08
Hispanic (7)	8	0.04
African, sub-Saharan:	30	0.15
African	6	0.03
Nigerian	11	0.06
South African	13	0.07
Am. Ind. or Alaska Nat., not spec.	19	0.10
Albanian	137	0.71
Alsatian	8	0.04
American Indian tribes, specified:	65	0.34
Blackfeet (1)	1	0.01
Cherokee (3)	25	0.13
Cheyenne (1)	1	0.01
Chippewa (4)	7	0.04
Choctaw (1)	5	0.03
Creek (2)	2	0.01
Iroquois	3	0.02
Latin American Indians	3	0.02
Lumbee (1)	1	0.01
Ottawa (3)	3	0.02
Potawatomi (1)	1	0.01
Seminole	1	0.01
Sioux	4	0.02
Ute (1)	2	0.01
All other tribes (4)	6	0.03
American Indian tribes, not spec.	2	0.01
Arab:	250	1.29
Arab/Arabic	17	0.09
Jordanian	5	0.03
Lebanese	202	1.04
Syrian	20	0.10
Other Arab	6	0.03
Armenian	231	1.19
Asian:	395	2.05
Chinese, ex. Taiwanese (78)	99	0.51
Filipino (50)	68	0.35
Indian (44)	61	0.32
Indonesian (2)	4	0.02
Japanese (38)	50	0.26
Korean (43)	53	0.27
Laotian	2	0.01
Taiwanese (3)	7	0.04
Thai (7)	10	0.05
Vietnamese (8)	11	0.06
Other Asian, specified	2	0.01
Other Asian, not specified (7)	28	0.15
Assyrian/Chaldean/Syriac	15	0.08
Australian	66	0.34
Austrian	70	0.36
Basque	9	0.05
Belgian	75	0.39
Brazilian	6	0.03
British	220	1.14
Bulgarian	4	0.02
Canadian	206	1.06
Croatian	102	0.53
Czech	90	0.46
Czechoslovakian	119	0.61
Danish	72	0.37
Dutch	513	2.65
Eastern European	224	1.16
English	3,166	16.34
European	201	1.04
Finnish	133	0.69
French, except Basque	969	5.00
French Canadian	230	1.19
German	4,189	21.62
Greek	268	1.38
Hawaii Native/Pacific Islander:	16	0.08
Polynesian: (6)	9	0.05
Native Hawaiian (5)	7	0.04
Samoan (1)	1	0.01
Other Polynesian	1	0.01
Other Pac. Isl., specified	2	0.01
Other Pac. Isl., not spec. (1)	5	0.03
Hispanic or Latino:	230	1.19
Central American:	3	0.02
Guatemalan	1	0.01
Nicaraguan	1	0.01
Salvadoran	1	0.01
Cuban	5	0.03
Dominican Republic	6	0.03
Mexican	104	0.54
Puerto Rican	15	0.08
South American:	49	0.25
Argentinean	16	0.08
Bolivian	1	0.01
Chilean	5	0.03
Colombian	11	0.06
Ecuadorian	1	0.01
Peruvian	7	0.04
Venezuelan	6	0.03
Other South American	2	0.01
Other Hispanic or Latino	47	0.24
Hungarian	291	1.50
Iranian	7	0.04
Irish	3,151	16.26
Israeli	9	0.05
Italian	1,331	6.87
Latvian	48	0.25
Lithuanian	121	0.62
Maltese	67	0.35
Northern European	30	0.15
Norwegian	332	1.71
Pennsylvania German	14	0.07
Polish	1,749	9.03
Portuguese	16	0.08
Romanian	77	0.40
Russian	800	4.13
Scandinavian	41	0.21
Scotch-Irish	520	2.68
Scottish	1,202	6.20
Serbian	10	0.05
Slavic	60	0.31
Slovak	68	0.35
Slovene	36	0.19
Swedish	268	1.38
Swiss	91	0.47
Ukrainian	115	0.59
United States or American	818	4.22
Welsh	256	1.32
West Indian, excl. Hispanic:	11	0.06
Jamaican	11	0.06
White:	18,736	97.12
Not Hispanic (18,375)	18,538	96.10
Hispanic (170)	198	1.03
Yugoslavian	110	0.57

Blackman

Place Type: Township
County: Jackson
Population: 22,800

Ancestry/Race	Number	%
African American/Black:	4,035	17.70
Not Hispanic (3,901)	3,997	17.53
Hispanic (30)	38	0.17
African, sub-Saharan:	32	0.14
African	32	0.14
Alaska Native tribes, specified:	1	0.00
Aleut	1	0.00
Am. Ind. or Alaska Nat., not spec.	87	0.38
American Indian tribes, specified:	117	0.51
Apache (3)	5	0.02
Blackfeet (1)	8	0.04
Cherokee (12)	58	0.25
Chippewa (14)	20	0.09
Choctaw (1)	1	0.00
Comanche (1)	1	0.00
Iroquois	2	0.01
Lumbee (3)	4	0.02
Menominee	1	0.00
Navajo	1	0.00
Osage	1	0.00
Ottawa (2)	2	0.01
Potawatomi (1)	3	0.01
Pueblo	1	0.00
Sioux	2	0.01
All other tribes (2)	7	0.03
American Indian tribes, not spec.	4	0.02
Arab:	72	0.32
Arab/Arabic	24	0.11
Lebanese	14	0.06
Palestinian	18	0.08
Syrian	16	0.07
Asian:	161	0.71
Chinese, ex. Taiwanese (13)	15	0.07
Filipino (7)	10	0.04
Indian (46)	50	0.22
Japanese (24)	29	0.13
Korean (22)	29	0.13
Laotian	2	0.01
Pakistani (2)	3	0.01
Taiwanese (1)	2	0.01
Thai (2)	3	0.01
Vietnamese (10)	10	0.04

Notes: 1. Figures in the "Number" column do not add up to the total population due to: a) Ancestry/Race overlap — e.g. persons can report being both White and Irish, b) persons of Hispanic origin can report being any race, c) persons reporting two ancestries are counted in both categories. 2. Numbers in parentheses indicate the number of persons reporting this ancestry/race alone, not in combination with any other ancestry/race. 3. Refer to the Explanation of Data in the front of the book for more detailed information.

Ancestry/Race	Number	%
Other Asian, specified	1	0.00
Other Asian, not specified (4)	7	0.03
Austrian	34	0.15
Belgian	38	0.17
British	51	0.22
Bulgarian	11	0.05
Canadian	63	0.28
Croatian	15	0.07
Czech	24	0.11
Czechoslovakian	16	0.07
Danish	58	0.26
Dutch	613	2.70
English	2,459	10.81
European	135	0.59
Finnish	115	0.51
French, except Basque	775	3.41
French Canadian	124	0.55
German	3,864	16.99
Greek	44	0.19
Hawaii Native/Pacific Islander:	8	0.04
Micronesian: (1)	1	0.00
Guamanian/Chamorro (1)	1	0.00
Polynesian: (4)	4	0.02
Native Hawaiian (1)	1	0.00
Samoan (2)	2	0.01
Tongan (1)	1	0.00
Other Pac. Isl., specified	1	0.00
Other Pac. Isl., not spec.	2	0.01
Hispanic or Latino:	563	2.47
Central American:	2	0.01
Honduran	1	0.00
Other Central American	1	0.00
Cuban	5	0.02
Mexican	443	1.94
Puerto Rican	52	0.23
South American:	3	0.01
Chilean	1	0.00
Colombian	1	0.00
Peruvian	1	0.00
Other Hispanic or Latino	58	0.25
Hungarian	51	0.22
Irish	2,065	9.08
Italian	443	1.95
Lithuanian	45	0.20
Macedonian	58	0.26
Norwegian	67	0.29
Polish	1,313	5.77
Portuguese	15	0.07
Romanian	54	0.24
Russian	125	0.55
Scandinavian	15	0.07
Scotch-Irish	204	0.90
Scottish	361	1.59
Slavic	9	0.04
Slovak	45	0.20
Slovene	15	0.07
Swedish	113	0.50
Swiss	74	0.33
Ukrainian	25	0.11
United States or American	1,393	6.12
Welsh	51	0.22
West Indian, excl. Hispanic:	14	0.06
Jamaican	14	0.06
White:	18,374	80.59
Not Hispanic (17,875)	18,088	79.33
Hispanic (241)	286	1.25

Bloomfield

Place Type: Township
County: Oakland
Population: 43,023

Ancestry/Race	Number	%
Afghan	26	0.06
African American/Black:	1,949	4.53
Not Hispanic (1,835)	1,935	4.50
Hispanic (14)	14	0.03
African, sub-Saharan:	85	0.20
African	33	0.08
Nigerian	25	0.06
Sierra Leonean	6	0.01
South African	13	0.03
Other sub-Saharan African	8	0.02
Alaska Native tribes, specified:	1	0.00
Eskimo	1	0.00
Am. Ind. or Alaska Nat., not spec.	40	0.09
Albanian	132	0.31
American Indian tribes, specified:	78	0.18
Apache (1)	1	0.00
Blackfeet	6	0.01
Cherokee (6)	24	0.06
Chippewa (6)	16	0.04
Choctaw	4	0.01
Crow	1	0.00
Delaware	1	0.00
Iroquois	1	0.00
Lumbee (6)	7	0.02
Osage	1	0.00
Pueblo	1	0.00
Seminole	3	0.01
Sioux	1	0.00
All other tribes (4)	11	0.03
American Indian tribes, not spec.	4	0.01
Arab:	1,272	2.96
Arab/Arabic	176	0.41
Egyptian	126	0.29
Iraqi	209	0.49
Jordanian	11	0.03
Lebanese	413	0.96
Palestinian	151	0.35
Syrian	156	0.36
Other Arab	30	0.07
Armenian	479	1.11
Asian:	3,047	7.08
Bangladeshi (5)	5	0.01
Chinese, ex. Taiwanese (321)	349	0.81
Filipino (239)	279	0.65
Hmong (10)	10	0.02
Indian (1,262)	1,352	3.14
Japanese (156)	192	0.45
Korean (479)	492	1.14
Laotian (1)	1	0.00
Malaysian (1)	1	0.00
Pakistani (119)	134	0.31
Sri Lankan (25)	25	0.06
Taiwanese (59)	65	0.15
Thai (25)	26	0.06
Vietnamese (28)	32	0.07
Other Asian, specified (5)	5	0.01
Other Asian, not specified (30)	79	0.18
Assyrian/Chaldean/Syriac	513	1.19
Australian	107	0.25
Austrian	261	0.61
Belgian	247	0.57
Brazilian	57	0.13
British	400	0.93
Bulgarian	21	0.05
Canadian	444	1.03
Celtic	22	0.05
Croatian	179	0.42
Czech	309	0.72
Czechoslovakian	141	0.33
Danish	239	0.56
Dutch	645	1.50
Eastern European	213	0.50
English	5,858	13.61
Estonian	29	0.07
European	482	1.12
Finnish	347	0.81
French, except Basque	1,800	4.18
French Canadian	666	1.55
German	8,307	19.31
Greek	634	1.47
Hawaii Native/Pacific Islander:	36	0.08
Micronesian: (9)	9	0.02
Guamanian/Chamorro (2)	2	0.00
Other Micronesian (7)	7	0.02
Polynesian: (8)	11	0.03
Native Hawaiian (4)	4	0.01
Samoan (3)	3	0.01
Other Polynesian (1)	4	0.01
Other Pac. Isl., not spec. (6)	16	0.04
Hispanic or Latino:	595	1.38
Central American:	27	0.06
Guatemalan	8	0.02
Honduran	6	0.01
Nicaraguan	6	0.01
Panamanian	4	0.01
Salvadoran	1	0.00
Other Central American	2	0.00
Cuban	43	0.10
Mexican	235	0.55
Puerto Rican	47	0.11
South American:	102	0.24
Argentinean	33	0.08
Bolivian	3	0.01
Chilean	7	0.02
Colombian	34	0.08
Ecuadorian	2	0.00
Paraguayan	3	0.01
Peruvian	12	0.03
Venezuelan	5	0.01
Other South American	3	0.01
Other Hispanic or Latino	141	0.33
Hungarian	425	0.99
Iranian	152	0.35
Irish	6,009	13.97
Israeli	23	0.05
Italian	2,419	5.62
Latvian	80	0.19
Lithuanian	287	0.67
Luxemburger	38	0.09
Macedonian	93	0.22
Maltese	70	0.16
Northern European	59	0.14
Norwegian	284	0.66
Pennsylvania German	6	0.01
Polish	3,556	8.26
Portuguese	47	0.11
Romanian	271	0.63
Russian	1,676	3.90
Scandinavian	90	0.21
Scotch-Irish	776	1.80
Scottish	1,337	3.11
Serbian	76	0.18
Slavic	43	0.10
Slovak	152	0.35
Slovene	52	0.12
Swedish	900	2.09
Swiss	208	0.48
Turkish	94	0.22
Ukrainian	418	0.97
United States or American	1,615	3.75
Welsh	306	0.71
West Indian, excl. Hispanic:	39	0.09
Jamaican	34	0.08
West Indian	5	0.01
White:	38,134	88.64
Not Hispanic (37,249)	37,627	87.46
Hispanic (483)	507	1.18
Yugoslavian	93	0.22

Brandon

Place Type: Township
County: Oakland
Population: 14,765

Ancestry/Race	Number	%
African American/Black:	85	0.58
Not Hispanic (57)	81	0.55
Hispanic (2)	4	0.03
Am. Ind. or Alaska Nat., not spec.	24	0.16
American Indian tribes, specified:	72	0.49
Blackfeet	7	0.05
Cherokee (3)	17	0.12
Chippewa (13)	20	0.14
Choctaw	5	0.03
Comanche	2	0.01

Notes: 1. Figures in the "Number" column do not add up to the total population due to: a) Ancestry/Race overlap — e.g. persons can report being both White and Irish, b) persons of Hispanic origin can report being any race, c) persons reporting two ancestries are counted in both categories. 2. Numbers in parentheses indicate the number of persons reporting this ancestry/race alone, not in combination with any other ancestry/race. 3. Refer to the Explanation of Data in the front of the book for more detailed information.

Ancestry/Race	Number	%
Cree	2	0.01
Iroquois	2	0.01
Latin American Indians (2)	2	0.01
Navajo	1	0.01
Potawatomi (4)	4	0.03
Sioux (2)	6	0.04
All other tribes (1)	4	0.03
American Indian tribes, not spec.	10	0.07
Arab:	59	0.40
Arab/Arabic	8	0.05
Iraqi	6	0.04
Lebanese	8	0.05
Syrian	37	0.25
Armenian	2	0.01
Asian:	85	0.58
Chinese, ex. Taiwanese (7)	10	0.07
Filipino (10)	17	0.12
Hmong	5	0.03
Indian (6)	10	0.07
Japanese (1)	3	0.02
Korean (17)	25	0.17
Laotian (1)	6	0.04
Thai (1)	3	0.02
Vietnamese (3)	5	0.03
Other Asian, not specified	1	0.01
Assyrian/Chaldean/Syriac	17	0.12
Australian	5	0.03
Austrian	22	0.15
Belgian	120	0.81
Brazilian	3	0.02
British	31	0.21
Bulgarian	2	0.01
Canadian	143	0.97
Croatian	10	0.07
Czech	91	0.62
Czechoslovakian	37	0.25
Danish	71	0.48
Dutch	298	2.02
Eastern European	6	0.04
English	1,910	12.94
European	134	0.91
Finnish	125	0.85
French, except Basque	1,100	7.45
French Canadian	367	2.49
German	3,647	24.70
Greek	103	0.70
Hawaii Native/Pacific Islander:	9	0.06
Polynesian: (2)	7	0.05
Samoan (2)	7	0.05
Other Pac. Isl., not spec.	2	0.01
Hispanic or Latino:	235	1.59
Cuban	5	0.03
Dominican Republic	2	0.01
Mexican	179	1.21
Puerto Rican	5	0.03
South American:	12	0.08
Chilean	1	0.01
Colombian	10	0.07
Other South American	1	0.01
Other Hispanic or Latino	32	0.22
Hungarian	145	0.98
Irish	1,950	13.21
Italian	1,187	8.04
Latvian	10	0.07
Lithuanian	46	0.31
Macedonian	5	0.03
Maltese	15	0.10
Norwegian	127	0.86
Polish	1,587	10.75
Romanian	25	0.17
Russian	67	0.45
Scandinavian	52	0.35
Scotch-Irish	308	2.09
Scottish	568	3.85
Slavic	16	0.11
Slovak	61	0.41
Slovene	17	0.12
Swedish	295	2.00
Swiss	5	0.03
Ukrainian	65	0.44
United States or American	705	4.78
Welsh	74	0.50
White:	14,556	98.58
Not Hispanic (14,258)	14,385	97.43
Hispanic (150)	171	1.16
Yugoslavian	19	0.13

Bridgeport charter

Place Type: Township
County: Saginaw
Population: 11,709

Ancestry/Race	Number	%
African American/Black:	2,555	21.82
Not Hispanic (2,403)	2,512	21.45
Hispanic (15)	43	0.37
African, sub-Saharan:	50	0.43
African	50	0.43
Alaska Native tribes, specified:	1	0.01
Aleut (1)	1	0.01
Am. Ind. or Alaska Nat., not spec.	55	0.47
American Indian tribes, specified:	101	0.86
Apache (1)	1	0.01
Cherokee (1)	17	0.15
Cheyenne (1)	1	0.01
Chippewa (40)	55	0.47
Creek	2	0.02
Iroquois	6	0.05
Latin American Indians	9	0.08
Navajo (6)	6	0.05
Potawatomi	2	0.02
Seminole	2	0.02
American Indian tribes, not spec.	2	0.02
Asian:	55	0.47
Chinese, ex. Taiwanese (3)	5	0.04
Filipino (10)	13	0.11
Hmong (5)	5	0.04
Indian (4)	5	0.04
Japanese (3)	8	0.07
Korean (4)	6	0.05
Laotian (6)	6	0.05
Pakistani (1)	1	0.01
Taiwanese	1	0.01
Thai	1	0.01
Other Asian, not specified	4	0.03
Australian	7	0.06
Austrian	6	0.05
Belgian	38	0.33
British	23	0.20
Canadian	23	0.20
Croatian	15	0.13
Czech	32	0.27
Czechoslovakian	34	0.29
Danish	59	0.51
Dutch	146	1.25
English	698	5.98
European	31	0.27
Finnish	16	0.14
French, except Basque	722	6.19
French Canadian	213	1.82
German	3,254	27.88
Greek	20	0.17
Hawaii Native/Pacific Islander:	6	0.05
Micronesian: (1)	3	0.03
Guamanian/Chamorro (1)	3	0.03
Polynesian:	1	0.01
Samoan	1	0.01
Other Pac. Isl., not spec.	2	0.02
Hispanic or Latino:	1,060	9.05
Central American:	1	0.01
Guatemalan	1	0.01
Mexican	870	7.43
Puerto Rican	24	0.20
South American:	1	0.01
Colombian	1	0.01
Other Hispanic or Latino	164	1.40
Hungarian	92	0.79
Irish	908	7.78
Italian	278	2.38
Lithuanian	78	0.67
Norwegian	77	0.66
Polish	1,076	9.22
Portuguese	6	0.05
Romanian	26	0.22
Russian	63	0.54
Scandinavian	4	0.03
Scotch-Irish	121	1.04
Scottish	195	1.67
Slavic	13	0.11
Slovak	14	0.12
Swedish	70	0.60
Swiss	20	0.17
Ukrainian	10	0.09
United States or American	485	4.16
Welsh	49	0.42
White:	8,732	74.58
Not Hispanic (7,943)	8,089	69.08
Hispanic (555)	643	5.49
Yugoslavian	14	0.12

Brighton

Place Type: Township
County: Livingston
Population: 17,673

Ancestry/Race	Number	%
African American/Black:	91	0.51
Not Hispanic (76)	90	0.51
Hispanic	1	0.01
Alaska Native tribes, specified:	2	0.01
Eskimo	2	0.01
Am. Ind. or Alaska Nat., not spec.	29	0.16
Albanian	24	0.14
American Indian tribes, specified:	91	0.51
Apache (1)	2	0.01
Blackfeet (1)	4	0.02
Cherokee (5)	21	0.12
Cheyenne	5	0.03
Chippewa (23)	33	0.19
Choctaw (1)	1	0.01
Creek (4)	4	0.02
Iroquois (2)	8	0.05
Lumbee (3)	3	0.02
Ottawa	3	0.02
Potawatomi (1)	1	0.01
Sioux (2)	3	0.02
All other tribes (1)	3	0.02
American Indian tribes, not spec.	2	0.01
Arab:	90	0.51
Arab/Arabic	30	0.17
Lebanese	42	0.24
Syrian	18	0.10
Armenian	90	0.51
Asian:	190	1.08
Chinese, ex. Taiwanese (24)	28	0.16
Filipino (12)	24	0.14
Hmong (1)	5	0.03
Indian (33)	40	0.23
Japanese (7)	11	0.06
Korean (36)	38	0.22
Taiwanese (3)	3	0.02
Thai (10)	13	0.07
Vietnamese (15)	15	0.08
Other Asian, not specified (4)	13	0.07
Australian	9	0.05
Austrian	6	0.03
Basque	17	0.10
Belgian	154	0.87
British	135	0.76
Bulgarian	10	0.06
Canadian	278	1.57
Croatian	79	0.45
Czech	90	0.51
Czechoslovakian	89	0.50
Danish	57	0.32
Dutch	289	1.63
English	2,291	12.95
European	135	0.76

Notes: 1. Figures in the "Number" column do not add up to the total population due to: a) Ancestry/Race overlap — e.g. persons can report being both White and Irish, b) persons of Hispanic origin can report being any race, c) persons reporting two ancestries are counted in both categories. 2. Numbers in parentheses indicate the number of persons reporting this ancestry/race alone, not in combination with any other ancestry/race. 3. Refer to the Explanation of Data in the front of the book for more detailed information.

Finnish	567	3.20
French, except Basque	937	5.30
French Canadian	418	2.36
German	4,560	25.77
Greek	96	0.54
Hawaii Native/Pacific Islander:	12	0.07
Micronesian: (7)	7	0.04
Guamanian/Chamorro (6)	6	0.03
Other Micronesian (1)	1	0.01
Polynesian:	5	0.03
Native Hawaiian	5	0.03
Hispanic or Latino:	215	1.22
Central American:	2	0.01
Costa Rican	1	0.01
Nicaraguan	1	0.01
Cuban	8	0.05
Mexican	156	0.88
Puerto Rican	7	0.04
South American:	10	0.06
Chilean	2	0.01
Colombian	2	0.01
Peruvian	2	0.01
Venezuelan	4	0.02
Other Hispanic or Latino	32	0.18
Hungarian	335	1.89
Iranian	71	0.40
Irish	2,666	15.07
Italian	1,523	8.61
Lithuanian	199	1.12
Macedonian	18	0.10
Maltese	92	0.52
Northern European	19	0.11
Norwegian	275	1.55
Pennsylvania German	18	0.10
Polish	2,445	13.82
Romanian	8	0.05
Russian	140	0.79
Scandinavian	8	0.05
Scotch-Irish	322	1.82
Scottish	544	3.07
Serbian	41	0.23
Slavic	52	0.29
Slovak	98	0.55
Slovene	10	0.06
Swedish	366	2.07
Swiss	30	0.17
Ukrainian	162	0.92
United States or American	746	4.22
Welsh	116	0.66
White:	17,332	98.07
Not Hispanic (17,049)	17,175	97.18
Hispanic (145)	157	0.89
Yugoslavian	20	0.11

Brownstown

Place Type: Township
County: Wayne
Population: 22,989

Ancestry/Race	Number	%
African American/Black:	991	4.31
Not Hispanic (867)	971	4.22
Hispanic (11)	20	0.09
African, sub-Saharan:	93	0.40
African	87	0.38
Sudanese	6	0.03
Alaska Native tribes, specified:	4	0.02
Eskimo (4)	4	0.02
Am. Ind. or Alaska Nat., not spec.	77	0.33
Albanian	95	0.41
American Indian tribes, specified:	203	0.88
Apache	2	0.01
Blackfeet (2)	11	0.05
Cherokee (29)	76	0.33
Cheyenne	1	0.00
Chippewa (21)	43	0.19
Choctaw (6)	9	0.04
Creek	4	0.02
Crow	1	0.00
Delaware	2	0.01
Iroquois (14)	19	0.08
Latin American Indians (5)	8	0.03
Lumbee (3)	7	0.03
Navajo (3)	3	0.01
Ottawa (5)	8	0.03
Pueblo (2)	2	0.01
Sioux	2	0.01
All other tribes (1)	5	0.02
American Indian tribes, not spec.	4	0.02
Arab:	193	0.84
Arab/Arabic	72	0.31
Lebanese	64	0.28
Moroccan	7	0.03
Syrian	28	0.12
Other Arab	22	0.10
Armenian	67	0.29
Asian:	1,002	4.36
Bangladeshi (1)	1	0.00
Chinese, ex. Taiwanese (68)	75	0.33
Filipino (129)	144	0.63
Indian (293)	316	1.37
Japanese (9)	22	0.10
Korean (42)	56	0.24
Malaysian	4	0.02
Pakistani (233)	277	1.20
Thai (5)	8	0.03
Vietnamese (45)	45	0.20
Other Asian, not specified (42)	54	0.23
Assyrian/Chaldean/Syriac	41	0.18
Austrian	26	0.11
Belgian	31	0.13
Brazilian	14	0.06
British	96	0.42
Canadian	104	0.45
Croatian	6	0.03
Czech	46	0.20
Czechoslovakian	43	0.19
Danish	13	0.06
Dutch	362	1.57
English	2,016	8.77
European	106	0.46
Finnish	167	0.73
French, except Basque	1,566	6.81
French Canadian	705	3.07
German	4,401	19.14
Greek	189	0.82
Hawaii Native/Pacific Islander:	9	0.04
Polynesian:	1	0.00
Native Hawaiian	1	0.00
Other Pac. Isl., not spec.	8	0.03
Hispanic or Latino:	824	3.58
Central American:	1	0.00
Guatemalan	1	0.00
Cuban	17	0.07
Dominican Republic	1	0.00
Mexican	630	2.74
Puerto Rican	70	0.30
South American:	5	0.02
Ecuadorian	4	0.02
Peruvian	1	0.00
Other Hispanic or Latino	100	0.43
Hungarian	1,026	4.46
Irish	3,101	13.49
Italian	1,803	7.84
Lithuanian	65	0.28
Macedonian	14	0.06
Maltese	100	0.43
Norwegian	72	0.31
Pennsylvania German	19	0.08
Polish	2,904	12.63
Portuguese	45	0.20
Romanian	18	0.08
Russian	161	0.70
Scandinavian	21	0.09
Scotch-Irish	371	1.61
Scottish	529	2.30
Serbian	19	0.08
Slovak	136	0.59
Swedish	94	0.41
Swiss	42	0.18
Ukrainian	128	0.56
United States or American	1,593	6.93
Welsh	133	0.58
White:	20,852	90.70
Not Hispanic (19,915)	20,227	87.99
Hispanic (549)	625	2.72
Yugoslavian	9	0.04

Buena Vista charter

Place Type: Township
County: Saginaw
Population: 10,318

Ancestry/Race	Number	%
African American/Black:	5,900	57.18
Not Hispanic (5,678)	5,787	56.09
Hispanic (56)	113	1.10
African, sub-Saharan:	324	3.14
African	324	3.14
Am. Ind. or Alaska Nat., not spec.	47	0.46
American Indian tribes, specified:	77	0.75
Apache	3	0.03
Blackfeet	10	0.10
Cherokee (1)	15	0.15
Chippewa (17)	37	0.36
Choctaw	1	0.01
Creek	1	0.01
Iroquois	1	0.01
Latin American Indians	2	0.02
Navajo	1	0.01
Yaqui (1)	2	0.02
All other tribes (3)	4	0.04
American Indian tribes, not spec.	8	0.08
Arab:	10	0.10
Moroccan	10	0.10
Asian:	23	0.22
Chinese, ex. Taiwanese (3)	5	0.05
Filipino (4)	8	0.08
Indian (4)	5	0.05
Korean (1)	3	0.03
Thai (1)	1	0.01
Other Asian, not specified	1	0.01
Belgian	13	0.13
Canadian	6	0.06
Croatian	10	0.10
Czech	4	0.04
Czechoslovakian	21	0.20
Dutch	111	1.08
English	393	3.81
Finnish	21	0.20
French, except Basque	267	2.59
French Canadian	79	0.77
German	1,511	14.65
Greek	5	0.05
Hawaii Native/Pacific Islander:	3	0.03
Polynesian:	1	0.01
Samoan	1	0.01
Other Pac. Isl., not spec. (1)	2	0.02
Hispanic or Latino:	940	9.11
Central American:	8	0.08
Panamanian	8	0.08
Dominican Republic	1	0.01
Mexican	791	7.67
Puerto Rican	8	0.08
South American:	1	0.01
Peruvian	1	0.01
Other Hispanic or Latino	131	1.27
Hungarian	28	0.27
Irish	340	3.30
Italian	99	0.96
Norwegian	8	0.08
Polish	409	3.97
Scotch-Irish	24	0.23
Scottish	45	0.44
Swedish	26	0.25
Swiss	6	0.06
United States or American	308	2.99
Welsh	6	0.06

Notes: 1. Figures in the "Number" column do not add up to the total population due to: a) Ancestry/Race overlap — e.g. persons can report being both White and Irish, b) persons of Hispanic origin can report being any race, c) persons reporting two ancestries are counted in both categories. 2. Numbers in parentheses indicate the number of persons reporting this ancestry/race alone, not in combination with any other ancestry/race. 3. Refer to the Explanation of Data in the front of the book for more detailed information.

White:	3,982	38.59
Not Hispanic (3,484)	3,599	34.88
Hispanic (334)	383	3.71

Burton

Place Type: City
County: Genesee
Population: 30,308

Ancestry/Race	Number	%
Acadian/Cajun	22	0.07
African American/Black:	1,229	4.06
Not Hispanic (1,073)	1,221	4.03
Hispanic (2)	8	0.03
African, sub-Saharan:	72	0.24
African	55	0.18
Nigerian	10	0.03
Other sub-Saharan African	7	0.02
Alaska Native tribes, specified:	4	0.01
Aleut (3)	3	0.01
Eskimo	1	0.00
Alaska Native tribes, not specified	1	0.00
Am. Ind. or Alaska Nat., not spec.	175	0.58
American Indian tribes, specified:	355	1.17
Apache (6)	11	0.04
Blackfeet (2)	14	0.05
Cherokee (50)	152	0.50
Chippewa (42)	81	0.27
Choctaw (2)	5	0.02
Cree	1	0.00
Creek	1	0.00
Crow	2	0.01
Iroquois (4)	5	0.02
Latin American Indians (9)	13	0.04
Navajo (1)	4	0.01
Osage	3	0.01
Ottawa (5)	13	0.04
Potawatomi (5)	11	0.04
Pueblo (1)	1	0.00
Seminole	1	0.00
Sioux (2)	11	0.04
All other tribes (18)	26	0.09
American Indian tribes, not spec.	23	0.08
Arab:	123	0.41
Arab/Arabic	35	0.12
Lebanese	62	0.20
Moroccan	5	0.02
Palestinian	6	0.02
Syrian	15	0.05
Asian:	302	1.00
Chinese, ex. Taiwanese (70)	85	0.28
Filipino (31)	55	0.18
Indian (32)	41	0.14
Japanese (9)	21	0.07
Korean (20)	22	0.07
Pakistani (2)	5	0.02
Taiwanese (15)	18	0.06
Thai (7)	10	0.03
Vietnamese (24)	31	0.10
Other Asian, specified (3)	5	0.02
Other Asian, not specified (1)	9	0.03
Assyrian/Chaldean/Syriac	109	0.36
Australian	8	0.03
Austrian	46	0.15
British	154	0.51
Bulgarian	4	0.01
Canadian	139	0.46
Czech	139	0.46
Czechoslovakian	167	0.55
Danish	92	0.30
Dutch	734	2.42
English	3,541	11.68
European	181	0.60
Finnish	156	0.51
French, except Basque	1,736	5.73
French Canadian	992	3.27
German	5,428	17.91
Greek	196	0.65
Hawaii Native/Pacific Islander:	18	0.06
Micronesian: (1)	1	0.00
Guamanian/Chamorro (1)	1	0.00
Polynesian: (6)	12	0.04
Native Hawaiian (6)	12	0.04
Other Pac. Isl., not spec. (1)	5	0.02
Hispanic or Latino:	705	2.33
Central American:	10	0.03
Guatemalan	1	0.00
Honduran	5	0.02
Panamanian	3	0.01
Other Central American	1	0.00
Cuban	10	0.03
Dominican Republic	3	0.01
Mexican	521	1.72
Puerto Rican	31	0.10
South American:	13	0.04
Chilean	2	0.01
Colombian	5	0.02
Ecuadorian	2	0.01
Peruvian	2	0.01
Venezuelan	2	0.01
Other Hispanic or Latino	117	0.39
Hungarian	515	1.70
Irish	3,699	12.20
Italian	720	2.38
Lithuanian	38	0.13
Luxemburger	3	0.01
Macedonian	6	0.02
Maltese	6	0.02
Norwegian	211	0.70
Polish	1,314	4.34
Portuguese	13	0.04
Romanian	40	0.13
Russian	114	0.38
Scandinavian	48	0.16
Scotch-Irish	455	1.50
Scottish	569	1.88
Serbian	27	0.09
Slavic	22	0.07
Slovak	41	0.14
Slovene	7	0.02
Swedish	459	1.51
Swiss	14	0.05
Ukrainian	139	0.46
United States or American	3,401	11.22
Welsh	153	0.50
West Indian, excl. Hispanic:	35	0.12
Jamaican	35	0.12
White:	28,495	94.02
Not Hispanic (27,538)	28,045	92.53
Hispanic (372)	450	1.48
Yugoslavian	21	0.07

Byron

Place Type: Township
County: Kent
Population: 17,553

Ancestry/Race	Number	%
African American/Black:	310	1.77
Not Hispanic (199)	281	1.60
Hispanic (14)	29	0.17
African, sub-Saharan:	12	0.07
African	12	0.07
Alaska Native tribes, specified:	1	0.01
Eskimo (1)	1	0.01
Am. Ind. or Alaska Nat., not spec.	29	0.17
American Indian tribes, specified:	85	0.48
Apache (4)	4	0.02
Blackfeet	5	0.03
Cherokee (6)	11	0.06
Chippewa (19)	31	0.18
Creek (3)	3	0.02
Iroquois (2)	2	0.01
Latin American Indians	2	0.01
Ottawa (4)	14	0.08
Potawatomi (8)	11	0.06
Sioux	1	0.01
All other tribes	1	0.01
American Indian tribes, not spec.	7	0.04
Arab:	101	0.57
Arab/Arabic	39	0.22
Lebanese	39	0.22
Syrian	23	0.13
Asian:	252	1.44
Cambodian	4	0.02
Chinese, ex. Taiwanese (18)	23	0.13
Filipino (16)	23	0.13
Indian (10)	14	0.08
Indonesian (3)	10	0.06
Japanese (3)	15	0.09
Korean (50)	58	0.33
Laotian	1	0.01
Malaysian (1)	1	0.01
Thai (1)	1	0.01
Vietnamese (77)	79	0.45
Other Asian, not specified (5)	23	0.13
Austrian	17	0.10
Belgian	7	0.04
British	8	0.05
Canadian	38	0.22
Croatian	42	0.24
Czech	47	0.27
Danish	110	0.62
Dutch	6,469	36.73
English	1,464	8.31
European	115	0.65
Finnish	10	0.06
French, except Basque	642	3.65
French Canadian	112	0.64
German	3,329	18.90
Greek	13	0.07
Hawaii Native/Pacific Islander:	16	0.09
Polynesian: (3)	9	0.05
Native Hawaiian (3)	8	0.05
Samoan	1	0.01
Other Pac. Isl., not spec.	7	0.04
Hispanic or Latino:	487	2.77
Central American:	11	0.06
Costa Rican	1	0.01
Guatemalan	8	0.05
Panamanian	1	0.01
Salvadoran	1	0.01
Cuban	27	0.15
Dominican Republic	5	0.03
Mexican	303	1.73
Puerto Rican	48	0.27
South American:	10	0.06
Bolivian	6	0.03
Colombian	2	0.01
Venezuelan	2	0.01
Other Hispanic or Latino	83	0.47
Hungarian	95	0.54
Iranian	13	0.07
Irish	1,576	8.95
Italian	460	2.61
Lithuanian	50	0.28
Norwegian	115	0.65
Polish	824	4.68
Russian	26	0.15
Scandinavian	17	0.10
Scotch-Irish	111	0.63
Scottish	206	1.17
Serbian	11	0.06
Swedish	242	1.37
Swiss	36	0.20
United States or American	825	4.68
Welsh	20	0.11
White:	16,865	96.08
Not Hispanic (16,397)	16,597	94.55
Hispanic (241)	268	1.53
Yugoslavian	18	0.10

Notes: 1. Figures in the "Number" column do not add up to the total population due to: a) Ancestry/Race overlap — e.g. persons can report being both White and Irish, b) persons of Hispanic origin can report being any race, c) persons reporting two ancestries are counted in both categories. 2. Numbers in parentheses indicate the number of persons reporting this ancestry/race alone, not in combination with any other ancestry/race. 3. Refer to the Explanation of Data in the front of the book for more detailed information.

Cadillac

Place Type: City
County: Wexford
Population: 10,000

Ancestry/Race	Number	%
African American/Black:	49	0.49
Not Hispanic (19)	44	0.44
Hispanic (2)	5	0.05
Alaska Native tribes, specified:	2	0.02
Alaska Athabascan (1)	1	0.01
Eskimo (1)	1	0.01
Alaska Native tribes, not specified	1	0.01
Am. Ind. or Alaska Nat., not spec.	45	0.45
American Indian tribes, specified:	106	1.06
Apache (1)	1	0.01
Blackfeet (1)	1	0.01
Cherokee (11)	24	0.24
Chippewa (27)	38	0.38
Choctaw (3)	5	0.05
Comanche	1	0.01
Cree (1)	1	0.01
Iroquois (3)	8	0.08
Latin American Indians	5	0.05
Ottawa (6)	9	0.09
Potawatomi (4)	9	0.09
Sioux	1	0.01
All other tribes	3	0.03
American Indian tribes, not spec.	12	0.12
Arab:	85	0.85
Arab/Arabic	7	0.07
Egyptian	21	0.21
Lebanese	28	0.28
Syrian	29	0.29
Asian:	80	0.80
Chinese, ex. Taiwanese (16)	16	0.16
Filipino (8)	14	0.14
Indian (8)	12	0.12
Japanese (3)	4	0.04
Korean (8)	11	0.11
Laotian (11)	12	0.12
Taiwanese (1)	1	0.01
Vietnamese (6)	7	0.07
Other Asian, not specified (2)	3	0.03
Austrian	6	0.06
Belgian	10	0.10
British	30	0.30
Canadian	10	0.10
Czech	44	0.44
Czechoslovakian	22	0.22
Danish	72	0.72
Dutch	886	8.89
English	1,372	13.77
Estonian	5	0.05
European	47	0.47
Finnish	59	0.59
French, except Basque	589	5.91
French Canadian	190	1.91
German	2,213	22.21
Greek	15	0.15
Hawaii Native/Pacific Islander:	4	0.04
Micronesian:	1	0.01
Guamanian/Chamorro	1	0.01
Polynesian: (3)	3	0.03
Samoan (3)	3	0.03
Hispanic or Latino:	118	1.18
Central American:	1	0.01
Costa Rican	1	0.01
Cuban	3	0.03
Mexican	70	0.70
Puerto Rican	9	0.09
Other Hispanic or Latino	35	0.35
Hungarian	39	0.39
Irish	1,124	11.28
Italian	278	2.79
Norwegian	196	1.97
Pennsylvania German	19	0.19
Polish	690	6.92
Russian	77	0.77
Scandinavian	50	0.50
Scotch-Irish	124	1.24
Scottish	370	3.71
Slavic	33	0.33
Slovak	15	0.15
Swedish	678	6.80
Swiss	19	0.19
Turkish	16	0.16
Ukrainian	71	0.71
United States or American	605	6.07
Welsh	81	0.81
White:	9,790	97.90
Not Hispanic (9,593)	9,707	97.07
Hispanic (62)	83	0.83
Yugoslavian	9	0.09

Cannon

Place Type: Township
County: Kent
Population: 12,075

Ancestry/Race	Number	%
African American/Black:	82	0.68
Not Hispanic (57)	82	0.68
Am. Ind. or Alaska Nat., not spec.	18	0.15
American Indian tribes, specified:	49	0.41
Apache	1	0.01
Blackfeet	2	0.02
Cherokee (2)	12	0.10
Chippewa (7)	8	0.07
Choctaw	6	0.05
Iroquois	1	0.01
Ottawa	10	0.08
Potawatomi	4	0.03
Pueblo (1)	1	0.01
Sioux (1)	1	0.01
All other tribes (2)	3	0.02
American Indian tribes, not spec.	3	0.02
Arab:	66	0.55
Lebanese	59	0.49
Syrian	7	0.06
Asian:	75	0.62
Cambodian (1)	1	0.01
Chinese, ex. Taiwanese (17)	20	0.17
Filipino (1)	10	0.08
Indian (1)	2	0.02
Indonesian (1)	5	0.04
Japanese (5)	8	0.07
Korean (12)	14	0.12
Thai (1)	1	0.01
Vietnamese (2)	6	0.05
Other Asian, not specified	8	0.07
Austrian	51	0.42
Belgian	13	0.11
British	8	0.07
Canadian	10	0.08
Croatian	6	0.05
Czech	17	0.14
Czechoslovakian	18	0.15
Danish	192	1.59
Dutch	2,281	18.87
English	1,730	14.31
Estonian	5	0.04
European	68	0.56
Finnish	66	0.55
French, except Basque	540	4.47
French Canadian	211	1.75
German	3,801	31.45
Greek	67	0.55
Hawaii Native/Pacific Islander:	15	0.12
Melanesian: (6)	6	0.05
Fijian (6)	6	0.05
Micronesian: (1)	2	0.02
Guamanian/Chamorro (1)	2	0.02
Other Pac. Isl., not spec. (3)	7	0.06
Hispanic or Latino:	122	1.01
Central American:	4	0.03
Costa Rican	1	0.01
Guatemalan	2	0.02
Other Central American	1	0.01
Cuban	6	0.05
Mexican	81	0.67
South American:	12	0.10
Argentinean	2	0.02
Chilean	1	0.01
Colombian	9	0.07
Other Hispanic or Latino	19	0.16
Hungarian	52	0.43
Irish	2,023	16.74
Italian	298	2.47
Latvian	22	0.18
Lithuanian	108	0.89
Northern European	13	0.11
Norwegian	241	1.99
Pennsylvania German	25	0.21
Polish	1,117	9.24
Romanian	44	0.36
Russian	34	0.28
Scandinavian	17	0.14
Scotch-Irish	174	1.44
Scottish	238	1.97
Slovak	41	0.34
Slovene	8	0.07
Swedish	321	2.66
Swiss	64	0.53
Ukrainian	71	0.59
United States or American	653	5.40
Welsh	67	0.55
White:	11,891	98.48
Not Hispanic (11,724)	11,805	97.76
Hispanic (70)	86	0.71
Yugoslavian	23	0.19

Canton

Place Type: Census Designated Place
County: Wayne
Population: 76,366

Ancestry/Race	Number	%
African American/Black:	3,830	5.02
Not Hispanic (3,434)	3,774	4.94
Hispanic (32)	56	0.07
African, sub-Saharan:	190	0.25
African	83	0.11
Ethiopian	37	0.05
Ghanian	27	0.04
Kenyan	12	0.02
Nigerian	31	0.04
Am. Ind. or Alaska Nat., not spec.	147	0.19
Albanian	133	0.17
American Indian tribes, specified:	421	0.55
Apache (4)	4	0.01
Blackfeet (1)	26	0.03
Cherokee (23)	126	0.16
Cheyenne	1	0.00
Chickasaw	1	0.00
Chippewa (76)	115	0.15
Choctaw	7	0.01
Cree (2)	3	0.00
Creek (1)	2	0.00
Delaware (5)	9	0.01
Iroquois (20)	35	0.05
Latin American Indians (3)	8	0.01
Lumbee (7)	18	0.02
Menominee (5)	5	0.01
Navajo	3	0.00
Ottawa (5)	11	0.01
Potawatomi (5)	5	0.01
Pueblo (2)	3	0.00
Seminole (1)	1	0.00
Sioux (3)	14	0.02
All other tribes (6)	24	0.03
American Indian tribes, not spec.	40	0.05
Arab:	1,448	1.90
Arab/Arabic	313	0.41
Egyptian	20	0.03
Iraqi	62	0.08
Jordanian	7	0.01

Notes: 1. Figures in the "Number" column do not add up to the total population due to: a) Ancestry/Race overlap — e.g. persons can report being both White and Irish, b) persons of Hispanic origin can report being any race, c) persons reporting two ancestries are counted in both categories. 2. Numbers in parentheses indicate the number of persons reporting this ancestry/race alone, not in combination with any other ancestry/race. 3. Refer to the Explanation of Data in the front of the book for more detailed information.

Ancestry/Race	Number	%
Lebanese	570	0.75
Moroccan	11	0.01
Palestinian	170	0.22
Syrian	158	0.21
Other Arab	137	0.18
Armenian	330	0.43
Asian:	7,350	9.62
Bangladeshi (24)	25	0.03
Cambodian	1	0.00
Chinese, ex. Taiwanese (1,404)	1,509	1.98
Filipino (621)	749	0.98
Hmong (3)	3	0.00
Indian (3,405)	3,523	4.61
Indonesian (2)	3	0.00
Japanese (195)	302	0.40
Korean (382)	435	0.57
Laotian (5)	9	0.01
Malaysian (1)	3	0.00
Pakistani (272)	312	0.41
Sri Lankan (14)	14	0.02
Taiwanese (53)	60	0.08
Thai (28)	35	0.05
Vietnamese (157)	196	0.26
Other Asian, specified (7)	10	0.01
Other Asian, not specified (48)	161	0.21
Assyrian/Chaldean/Syriac	55	0.07
Australian	11	0.01
Austrian	379	0.50
Belgian	274	0.36
Brazilian	7	0.01
British	431	0.56
Bulgarian	10	0.01
Canadian	721	0.94
Celtic	7	0.01
Croatian	200	0.26
Cypriot	26	0.03
Czech	458	0.60
Czechoslovakian	171	0.22
Danish	396	0.52
Dutch	1,472	1.93
English	8,271	10.84
Estonian	11	0.01
European	519	0.68
Finnish	900	1.18
French, except Basque	3,470	4.55
French Canadian	1,390	1.82
German	16,947	22.21
German Russian	6	0.01
Greek	506	0.66
Hawaii Native/Pacific Islander:	60	0.08
Micronesian: (9)	15	0.02
Guamanian/Chamorro (7)	11	0.01
Other Micronesian (2)	4	0.01
Polynesian: (7)	25	0.03
Native Hawaiian (6)	22	0.03
Samoan (1)	3	0.00
Other Pac. Isl., specified	3	0.00
Other Pac. Isl., not spec.	17	0.02
Hispanic or Latino:	1,788	2.34
Central American:	31	0.04
Costa Rican	1	0.00
Guatemalan	4	0.01
Honduran	3	0.00
Nicaraguan	1	0.00
Panamanian	13	0.02
Salvadoran	9	0.01
Cuban	55	0.07
Dominican Republic	15	0.02
Mexican	1,099	1.44
Puerto Rican	147	0.19
South American:	99	0.13
Argentinean	22	0.03
Bolivian	1	0.00
Chilean	5	0.01
Colombian	26	0.03
Ecuadorian	8	0.01
Paraguayan	4	0.01
Peruvian	8	0.01
Venezuelan	16	0.02
Other South American	9	0.01
Other Hispanic or Latino	342	0.45
Hungarian	1,236	1.62
Iranian	60	0.08
Irish	10,985	14.40
Israeli	7	0.01
Italian	5,813	7.62
Latvian	69	0.09
Lithuanian	406	0.53
Macedonian	257	0.34
Maltese	592	0.78
Northern European	70	0.09
Norwegian	792	1.04
Pennsylvania German	64	0.08
Polish	10,506	13.77
Portuguese	46	0.06
Romanian	335	0.44
Russian	612	0.80
Scandinavian	54	0.07
Scotch-Irish	1,423	1.86
Scottish	2,793	3.66
Serbian	125	0.16
Slavic	110	0.14
Slovak	306	0.40
Slovene	78	0.10
Swedish	976	1.28
Swiss	206	0.27
Turkish	24	0.03
Ukrainian	863	1.13
United States or American	2,759	3.62
Welsh	570	0.75
West Indian, excl. Hispanic:	97	0.13
Bahamian	5	0.01
Bermudan	21	0.03
British West Indian	6	0.01
Haitian	9	0.01
Jamaican	44	0.06
Trinidadian and Tobagonian	12	0.02
White:	65,282	85.49
Not Hispanic (62,846)	63,943	83.73
Hispanic (1,199)	1,339	1.75
Yugoslavian	187	0.25

Cascade

Place Type: Township
County: Kent
Population: 15,107

Ancestry/Race	Number	%
African American/Black:	182	1.20
Not Hispanic (146)	176	1.17
Hispanic (5)	6	0.04
African, sub-Saharan:	5	0.03
African	5	0.03
Am. Ind. or Alaska Nat., not spec.	13	0.09
American Indian tribes, specified:	43	0.28
Blackfeet	1	0.01
Cherokee (5)	7	0.05
Chippewa (15)	17	0.11
Iroquois (4)	4	0.03
Latin American Indians (1)	1	0.01
Ottawa (5)	6	0.04
Potawatomi (1)	2	0.01
Seminole (1)	1	0.01
Sioux	1	0.01
All other tribes	3	0.02
American Indian tribes, not spec.	8	0.05
Arab:	99	0.66
Lebanese	67	0.44
Syrian	32	0.21
Armenian	17	0.11
Asian:	531	3.51
Chinese, ex. Taiwanese (94)	111	0.73
Filipino (41)	55	0.36
Indian (142)	143	0.95
Indonesian (3)	8	0.05
Japanese (13)	26	0.17
Korean (86)	97	0.64
Laotian (5)	5	0.03
Malaysian (4)	5	0.03
Pakistani (21)	21	0.14
Sri Lankan (1)	1	0.01
Taiwanese (2)	6	0.04
Thai (2)	3	0.02
Vietnamese (36)	42	0.28
Other Asian, not specified (5)	8	0.05
Austrian	29	0.19
Belgian	53	0.35
British	113	0.75
Canadian	119	0.79
Croatian	58	0.38
Czech	55	0.36
Czechoslovakian	43	0.28
Danish	180	1.19
Dutch	2,768	18.32
Eastern European	32	0.21
English	2,498	16.54
European	224	1.48
Finnish	168	1.11
French, except Basque	549	3.63
French Canadian	71	0.47
German	3,528	23.35
Greek	107	0.71
Hawaii Native/Pacific Islander:	2	0.01
Polynesian:	1	0.01
Native Hawaiian	1	0.01
Other Pac. Isl., not spec.	1	0.01
Hispanic or Latino:	131	0.87
Central American:	12	0.08
Guatemalan	8	0.05
Honduran	1	0.01
Nicaraguan	2	0.01
Panamanian	1	0.01
Cuban	4	0.03
Dominican Republic	2	0.01
Mexican	59	0.39
Puerto Rican	17	0.11
South American:	14	0.09
Argentinean	1	0.01
Chilean	1	0.01
Colombian	7	0.05
Peruvian	1	0.01
Venezuelan	4	0.03
Other Hispanic or Latino	23	0.15
Hungarian	59	0.39
Irish	2,074	13.73
Italian	819	5.42
Latvian	25	0.17
Lithuanian	64	0.42
Macedonian	15	0.10
Northern European	5	0.03
Norwegian	162	1.07
Polish	1,068	7.07
Romanian	23	0.15
Russian	134	0.89
Scandinavian	17	0.11
Scotch-Irish	363	2.40
Scottish	650	4.30
Serbian	6	0.04
Slavic	10	0.07
Slovak	32	0.21
Slovene	16	0.11
Swedish	508	3.36
Swiss	58	0.38
Ukrainian	66	0.44
United States or American	764	5.06
Welsh	190	1.26
White:	14,404	95.35
Not Hispanic (14,198)	14,304	94.68
Hispanic (86)	100	0.66
Yugoslavian	25	0.17

Chesterfield

Place Type: Township
County: Macomb
Population: 37,405

Ancestry/Race	Number	%
African American/Black:	1,321	3.53

Notes: 1. Figures in the "Number" column do not add up to the total population due to: a) Ancestry/Race overlap — e.g. persons can report being both White and Irish, b) persons of Hispanic origin can report being any race, c) persons reporting two ancestries are counted in both categories. 2. Numbers in parentheses indicate the number of persons reporting this ancestry/race alone, not in combination with any other ancestry/race. 3. Refer to the Explanation of Data in the front of the book for more detailed information.

Ancestry/Race	Number	%
Not Hispanic (1,093)	1,286	3.44
Hispanic (17)	35	0.09
Alaska Native tribes, specified:	6	0.02
Aleut (3)	3	0.01
Tlingit-Haida (3)	3	0.01
Am. Ind. or Alaska Nat., not spec.	95	0.25
Albanian	91	0.24
American Indian tribes, specified:	260	0.70
Apache (3)	3	0.01
Blackfeet (1)	15	0.04
Cherokee (28)	91	0.24
Cheyenne	3	0.01
Chippewa (32)	58	0.16
Choctaw (1)	4	0.01
Cree (1)	4	0.01
Crow	6	0.02
Iroquois (8)	20	0.05
Latin American Indians (1)	5	0.01
Lumbee (7)	15	0.04
Osage	1	0.00
Ottawa	2	0.01
Potawatomi	9	0.02
Pueblo	3	0.01
Sioux	2	0.01
Yuman (1)	1	0.00
All other tribes (15)	18	0.05
American Indian tribes, not spec.	13	0.03
Arab:	432	1.15
Arab/Arabic	95	0.25
Jordanian	45	0.12
Lebanese	212	0.57
Syrian	71	0.19
Other Arab	9	0.02
Armenian	68	0.18
Asian:	388	1.04
Chinese, ex. Taiwanese (46)	56	0.15
Filipino (55)	79	0.21
Indian (39)	58	0.16
Indonesian (1)	1	0.00
Japanese (15)	28	0.07
Korean (77)	101	0.27
Laotian (2)	2	0.01
Pakistani (4)	10	0.03
Thai (5)	7	0.02
Vietnamese (30)	35	0.09
Other Asian, specified (1)	1	0.00
Other Asian, not specified (1)	10	0.03
Assyrian/Chaldean/Syriac	6	0.02
Australian	24	0.06
Austrian	52	0.14
Belgian	844	2.25
British	144	0.38
Bulgarian	7	0.02
Canadian	314	0.84
Croatian	111	0.30
Czech	148	0.39
Czechoslovakian	104	0.28
Danish	67	0.18
Dutch	583	1.55
English	2,902	7.74
European	33	0.09
Finnish	216	0.58
French, except Basque	2,740	7.31
French Canadian	1,184	3.16
German	10,350	27.60
Greek	286	0.76
Guyanese	19	0.05
Hawaii Native/Pacific Islander:	22	0.06
Polynesian: (4)	14	0.04
Native Hawaiian (3)	11	0.03
Samoan (1)	3	0.01
Other Pac. Isl., not spec. (2)	8	0.02
Hispanic or Latino:	941	2.52
Central American:	10	0.03
Costa Rican	1	0.00
Guatemalan	1	0.00
Panamanian	5	0.01
Salvadoran	3	0.01
Cuban	20	0.05
Dominican Republic	4	0.01
Mexican	663	1.77
Puerto Rican	92	0.25
South American:	9	0.02
Chilean	1	0.00
Ecuadorian	1	0.00
Peruvian	4	0.01
Venezuelan	3	0.01
Other Hispanic or Latino	143	0.38
Hungarian	481	1.28
Iranian	26	0.07
Irish	4,574	12.20
Israeli	11	0.03
Italian	4,936	13.16
Latvian	26	0.07
Lithuanian	87	0.23
Macedonian	77	0.21
Maltese	72	0.19
Northern European	22	0.06
Norwegian	327	0.87
Pennsylvania German	7	0.02
Polish	6,877	18.34
Romanian	261	0.70
Russian	356	0.95
Scandinavian	25	0.07
Scotch-Irish	564	1.50
Scottish	944	2.52
Serbian	107	0.29
Slavic	57	0.15
Slovak	245	0.65
Slovene	8	0.02
Swedish	349	0.93
Swiss	47	0.13
Ukrainian	151	0.40
United States or American	1,797	4.79
Welsh	269	0.72
White:	35,485	94.87
Not Hispanic (34,406)	34,881	93.25
Hispanic (542)	604	1.61
Yugoslavian	129	0.34

Clawson

Place Type: City
County: Oakland
Population: 12,732

Ancestry/Race	Number	%
African American/Black:	131	1.03
Not Hispanic (100)	129	1.01
Hispanic (2)	2	0.02
Alaska Native tribes, specified:	2	0.02
Tlingit-Haida	2	0.02
Am. Ind. or Alaska Nat., not spec.	19	0.15
Albanian	172	1.35
American Indian tribes, specified:	74	0.58
Apache	3	0.02
Blackfeet (1)	1	0.01
Cherokee (5)	25	0.20
Chippewa (15)	21	0.16
Crow (1)	1	0.01
Delaware	1	0.01
Iroquois (5)	5	0.04
Navajo (1)	1	0.01
Ottawa (3)	5	0.04
Potawatomi (4)	6	0.05
Pueblo	1	0.01
Sioux	2	0.02
All other tribes (1)	2	0.02
American Indian tribes, not spec.	3	0.02
Arab:	131	1.03
Arab/Arabic	21	0.16
Egyptian	18	0.14
Lebanese	87	0.68
Syrian	5	0.04
Armenian	7	0.05
Asian:	214	1.68
Chinese, ex. Taiwanese (31)	40	0.31
Filipino (33)	50	0.39
Indian (35)	37	0.29
Japanese (32)	38	0.30
Korean (20)	23	0.18
Laotian (5)	5	0.04
Pakistani	2	0.02
Thai (1)	2	0.02
Vietnamese (9)	9	0.07
Other Asian, not specified	8	0.06
Assyrian/Chaldean/Syriac	6	0.05
Austrian	26	0.20
Belgian	58	0.46
British	64	0.50
Bulgarian	30	0.24
Canadian	109	0.86
Croatian	6	0.05
Czech	31	0.24
Czechoslovakian	22	0.17
Danish	103	0.81
Dutch	288	2.26
Eastern European	4	0.03
English	1,971	15.48
European	36	0.28
Finnish	206	1.62
French, except Basque	824	6.47
French Canadian	266	2.09
German	3,153	24.76
Greek	122	0.96
Hawaii Native/Pacific Islander:	2	0.02
Polynesian:	2	0.02
Native Hawaiian	1	0.01
Other Polynesian	1	0.01
Hispanic or Latino:	145	1.14
Central American:	1	0.01
Guatemalan	1	0.01
Cuban	5	0.04
Mexican	85	0.67
Puerto Rican	12	0.09
South American:	9	0.07
Argentinean	3	0.02
Chilean	2	0.02
Colombian	2	0.02
Ecuadorian	1	0.01
Venezuelan	1	0.01
Other Hispanic or Latino	33	0.26
Hungarian	87	0.68
Irish	2,262	17.77
Italian	1,034	8.12
Lithuanian	46	0.36
Maltese	53	0.42
Northern European	6	0.05
Norwegian	162	1.27
Polish	1,580	12.41
Portuguese	16	0.13
Romanian	174	1.37
Russian	143	1.12
Scotch-Irish	335	2.63
Scottish	668	5.25
Slavic	23	0.18
Slovak	67	0.53
Slovene	14	0.11
Swedish	258	2.03
Swiss	66	0.52
Ukrainian	77	0.60
United States or American	643	5.05
Welsh	179	1.41
White:	12,381	97.24
Not Hispanic (12,124)	12,260	96.29
Hispanic (111)	121	0.95
Yugoslavian	36	0.28

Clinton

Place Type: Census Designated Place
County: Macomb
Population: 95,648

Ancestry/Race	Number	%
African American/Black:	5,011	5.24
Not Hispanic (4,424)	4,938	5.16
Hispanic (37)	73	0.08
African, sub-Saharan:	62	0.06
African	58	0.06

Notes: 1. Figures in the "Number" column do not add up to the total population due to: a) Ancestry/Race overlap — e.g. persons can report being both White and Irish, b) persons of Hispanic origin can report being any race, c) persons reporting two ancestries are counted in both categories. 2. Numbers in parentheses indicate the number of persons reporting this ancestry/race alone, not in combination with any other ancestry/race. 3. Refer to the Explanation of Data in the front of the book for more detailed information.

Ancestry/Race	Number	%
Nigerian	4	0.00
Alaska Native tribes, specified:	4	0.00
Alaska Athabascan (2)	2	0.00
Eskimo (1)	1	0.00
Tlingit-Haida	1	0.00
Alaska Native tribes, not specified	1	0.00
Am. Ind. or Alaska Nat., not spec.	278	0.29
Albanian	994	1.04
Alsatian	8	0.01
American Indian tribes, specified:	527	0.55
Apache (7)	15	0.02
Blackfeet (2)	34	0.04
Cherokee (51)	226	0.24
Cheyenne	2	0.00
Chickasaw	2	0.00
Chippewa (50)	96	0.10
Choctaw	6	0.01
Comanche	3	0.00
Creek	1	0.00
Delaware (1)	3	0.00
Iroquois (7)	28	0.03
Kiowa (1)	1	0.00
Latin American Indians (11)	21	0.02
Lumbee (18)	31	0.03
Menominee	1	0.00
Navajo (1)	1	0.00
Osage	1	0.00
Ottawa (1)	5	0.01
Paiute (1)	3	0.00
Potawatomi (1)	1	0.00
Pueblo (1)	1	0.00
Sioux (6)	10	0.01
Ute (3)	3	0.00
All other tribes (8)	32	0.03
American Indian tribes, not spec.	39	0.04
Arab:	1,869	1.95
Arab/Arabic	203	0.21
Egyptian	31	0.03
Iraqi	18	0.02
Jordanian	38	0.04
Lebanese	1,284	1.34
Palestinian	9	0.01
Syrian	255	0.27
Other Arab	31	0.03
Armenian	188	0.20
Asian:	1,999	2.09
Cambodian (10)	18	0.02
Chinese, ex. Taiwanese (293)	341	0.36
Filipino (280)	385	0.40
Hmong (58)	80	0.08
Indian (448)	482	0.50
Indonesian	1	0.00
Japanese (50)	98	0.10
Korean (197)	244	0.26
Laotian (28)	37	0.04
Pakistani (41)	54	0.06
Sri Lankan (1)	1	0.00
Thai (7)	11	0.01
Vietnamese (149)	164	0.17
Other Asian, not specified (24)	83	0.09
Assyrian/Chaldean/Syriac	225	0.24
Australian	4	0.00
Austrian	359	0.38
Belgian	2,337	2.44
Brazilian	41	0.04
British	209	0.22
Bulgarian	38	0.04
Canadian	581	0.61
Carpatho Rusyn	6	0.01
Croatian	249	0.26
Czech	363	0.38
Czechoslovakian	174	0.18
Danish	172	0.18
Dutch	1,255	1.31
Eastern European	11	0.01
English	7,323	7.66
Estonian	10	0.01
European	309	0.32
Finnish	591	0.62
French, except Basque	5,707	5.97
French Canadian	2,258	2.36
German	22,997	24.04
Greek	867	0.91
Hawaii Native/Pacific Islander:	61	0.06
Micronesian: (4)	8	0.01
Guamanian/Chamorro (4)	8	0.01
Polynesian: (10)	33	0.03
Native Hawaiian (3)	18	0.02
Samoan (7)	14	0.01
Other Polynesian	1	0.00
Other Pac. Isl., not spec.	20	0.02
Hispanic or Latino:	1,664	1.74
Central American:	25	0.03
Costa Rican	5	0.01
Guatemalan	8	0.01
Honduran	9	0.01
Nicaraguan	1	0.00
Panamanian	2	0.00
Cuban	44	0.05
Dominican Republic	1	0.00
Mexican	1,128	1.18
Puerto Rican	111	0.12
South American:	72	0.08
Argentinean	14	0.01
Colombian	30	0.03
Ecuadorian	13	0.01
Paraguayan	1	0.00
Peruvian	5	0.01
Uruguayan	2	0.00
Venezuelan	4	0.00
Other South American	3	0.00
Other Hispanic or Latino	283	0.30
Hungarian	903	0.94
Iranian	12	0.01
Irish	11,162	11.67
Italian	15,285	15.98
Latvian	4	0.00
Lithuanian	415	0.43
Luxemburger	12	0.01
Macedonian	147	0.15
Maltese	210	0.22
Norwegian	436	0.46
Pennsylvania German	6	0.01
Polish	17,532	18.33
Portuguese	56	0.06
Romanian	430	0.45
Russian	717	0.75
Scandinavian	22	0.02
Scotch-Irish	1,090	1.14
Scottish	2,060	2.15
Serbian	201	0.21
Slavic	62	0.06
Slovak	736	0.77
Slovene	33	0.03
Swedish	821	0.86
Swiss	168	0.18
Turkish	10	0.01
Ukrainian	1,007	1.05
United States or American	3,058	3.20
Welsh	408	0.43
West Indian, excl. Hispanic:	54	0.06
Belizean	26	0.03
Haitian	7	0.01
Jamaican	21	0.02
White:	88,716	92.75
Not Hispanic (86,042)	87,486	91.47
Hispanic (1,109)	1,230	1.29
Yugoslavian	902	0.94

Coldwater

Place Type: City
County: Branch
Population: 12,697

Ancestry/Race	Number	%
African American/Black:	1,127	8.88
Not Hispanic (1,054)	1,102	8.68
Hispanic (15)	25	0.20
African, sub-Saharan:	56	0.44
African	56	0.44
Am. Ind. or Alaska Nat., not spec.	61	0.48
American Indian tribes, specified:	134	1.06
Apache (3)	6	0.05
Blackfeet (2)	10	0.08
Cherokee (15)	37	0.29
Cheyenne (2)	5	0.04
Chippewa (11)	23	0.18
Choctaw	4	0.03
Comanche (3)	3	0.02
Cree (1)	2	0.02
Creek	1	0.01
Iroquois (1)	3	0.02
Latin American Indians (4)	4	0.03
Navajo (3)	6	0.05
Ottawa (4)	5	0.04
Potawatomi (6)	9	0.07
Seminole (1)	2	0.02
Sioux (2)	4	0.03
Yakama (4)	4	0.03
All other tribes (2)	6	0.05
American Indian tribes, not spec.	14	0.11
Arab:	292	2.30
Arab/Arabic	185	1.46
Lebanese	19	0.15
Moroccan	32	0.25
Other Arab	56	0.44
Armenian	12	0.09
Asian:	173	1.36
Cambodian (2)	4	0.03
Chinese, ex. Taiwanese (8)	14	0.11
Filipino (5)	15	0.12
Indian (30)	34	0.27
Japanese (41)	42	0.33
Korean (3)	7	0.06
Laotian	1	0.01
Pakistani (3)	4	0.03
Thai	1	0.01
Vietnamese (6)	6	0.05
Other Asian, specified (2)	2	0.02
Other Asian, not specified (12)	43	0.34
Austrian	15	0.12
Belgian	24	0.19
British	43	0.34
Canadian	50	0.39
Croatian	7	0.06
Czech	20	0.16
Czechoslovakian	17	0.13
Danish	32	0.25
Dutch	492	3.87
English	1,234	9.71
European	45	0.35
Finnish	43	0.34
French, except Basque	505	3.97
French Canadian	212	1.67
German	2,471	19.44
Greek	17	0.13
Hawaii Native/Pacific Islander:	12	0.09
Micronesian:	5	0.04
Guamanian/Chamorro	5	0.04
Polynesian: (2)	3	0.02
Native Hawaiian (1)	2	0.02
Samoan (1)	1	0.01
Other Pac. Isl., not spec.	4	0.03
Hispanic or Latino:	574	4.52
Central American:	5	0.04
Honduran	1	0.01
Panamanian	4	0.03
Cuban	14	0.11
Mexican	425	3.35
Puerto Rican	49	0.39
Other Hispanic or Latino	81	0.64
Hungarian	63	0.50
Irish	1,100	8.65
Italian	323	2.54
Lithuanian	17	0.13
Norwegian	69	0.54
Pennsylvania German	17	0.13
Polish	582	4.58
Portuguese	6	0.05

Notes: 1. Figures in the "Number" column do not add up to the total population due to: a) Ancestry/Race overlap — e.g. persons can report being both White and Irish, b) persons of Hispanic origin can report being any race, c) persons reporting two ancestries are counted in both categories. 2. Numbers in parentheses indicate the number of persons reporting this ancestry/race alone, not in combination with any other ancestry/race. 3. Refer to the Explanation of Data in the front of the book for more detailed information.

Russian	5	0.04
Scandinavian	9	0.07
Scotch-Irish	144	1.13
Scottish	135	1.06
Slavic	21	0.17
Slovak	28	0.22
Swedish	113	0.89
Swiss	19	0.15
Turkish	11	0.09
United States or American	938	7.38
Welsh	58	0.46
West Indian, excl. Hispanic:	6	0.05
Jamaican	6	0.05
White:	11,180	88.05
Not Hispanic (10,514)	10,829	85.29
Hispanic (323)	351	2.76

Commerce

Place Type: Township
County: Oakland
Population: 34,764

Ancestry/Race	Number	%
Acadian/Cajun	6	0.02
African American/Black:	215	0.62
Not Hispanic (173)	211	0.61
Hispanic (2)	4	0.01
African, sub-Saharan:	48	0.14
African	48	0.14
Am. Ind. or Alaska Nat., not spec.	64	0.18
Albanian	34	0.10
American Indian tribes, specified:	143	0.41
Apache (1)	2	0.01
Blackfeet (1)	1	0.00
Cherokee (1)	41	0.12
Cheyenne	1	0.00
Chippewa (17)	42	0.12
Choctaw (3)	16	0.05
Iroquois (8)	16	0.05
Lumbee (3)	8	0.02
Navajo	1	0.00
Osage	1	0.00
Ottawa (1)	4	0.01
Seminole	1	0.00
Sioux (2)	3	0.01
All other tribes (3)	6	0.02
American Indian tribes, not spec.	9	0.03
Arab:	402	1.15
Arab/Arabic	19	0.05
Egyptian	29	0.08
Iraqi	15	0.04
Lebanese	249	0.71
Syrian	83	0.24
Other Arab	7	0.02
Armenian	211	0.60
Asian:	549	1.58
Cambodian (2)	3	0.01
Chinese, ex. Taiwanese (55)	70	0.20
Filipino (38)	54	0.16
Indian (94)	100	0.29
Indonesian	3	0.01
Japanese (151)	180	0.52
Korean (74)	88	0.25
Pakistani (5)	5	0.01
Taiwanese	1	0.00
Thai (1)	1	0.00
Vietnamese (18)	19	0.05
Other Asian, not specified (11)	25	0.07
Assyrian/Chaldean/Syriac	298	0.85
Australian	6	0.02
Austrian	117	0.33
Belgian	168	0.48
Brazilian	6	0.02
British	301	0.86
Bulgarian	36	0.10
Canadian	333	0.95
Celtic	28	0.08
Croatian	135	0.39
Czech	172	0.49
Czechoslovakian	90	0.26
Danish	188	0.54
Dutch	545	1.56
Eastern European	61	0.17
English	4,603	13.16
European	261	0.75
Finnish	549	1.57
French, except Basque	2,200	6.29
French Canadian	1,019	2.91
German	8,555	24.45
Greek	194	0.55
Hawaii Native/Pacific Islander:	15	0.04
Micronesian: (3)	3	0.01
Guamanian/Chamorro (3)	3	0.01
Polynesian: (1)	1	0.00
Samoan (1)	1	0.00
Other Pac. Isl., not spec.	11	0.03
Hispanic or Latino:	404	1.16
Central American:	13	0.04
Guatemalan	5	0.01
Honduran	3	0.01
Panamanian	4	0.01
Salvadoran	1	0.00
Cuban	12	0.03
Dominican Republic	4	0.01
Mexican	237	0.68
Puerto Rican	27	0.08
South American:	38	0.11
Argentinean	5	0.01
Bolivian	4	0.01
Chilean	4	0.01
Colombian	14	0.04
Ecuadorian	4	0.01
Peruvian	6	0.02
Other South American	1	0.00
Other Hispanic or Latino	73	0.21
Hungarian	365	1.04
Iranian	15	0.04
Irish	5,784	16.53
Italian	2,935	8.39
Lithuanian	184	0.53
Macedonian	31	0.09
Maltese	230	0.66
Norwegian	385	1.10
Pennsylvania German	30	0.09
Polish	4,718	13.49
Portuguese	4	0.01
Romanian	157	0.45
Russian	627	1.79
Scandinavian	23	0.07
Scotch-Irish	662	1.89
Scottish	1,682	4.81
Serbian	23	0.07
Slavic	31	0.09
Slovak	105	0.30
Slovene	27	0.08
Swedish	595	1.70
Swiss	165	0.47
Turkish	6	0.02
Ukrainian	361	1.03
United States or American	2,016	5.76
Welsh	302	0.86
White:	33,945	97.64
Not Hispanic (33,343)	33,636	96.76
Hispanic (283)	309	0.89
Yugoslavian	103	0.29

Comstock Park

Place Type: Census Designated Place
County: Kent
Population: 10,674

Ancestry/Race	Number	%
African American/Black:	531	4.97
Not Hispanic (405)	502	4.70
Hispanic (12)	29	0.27
African, sub-Saharan:	99	0.93
African	91	0.86
Nigerian	8	0.08
Am. Ind. or Alaska Nat., not spec.	47	0.44
American Indian tribes, specified:	108	1.01
Apache	1	0.01
Blackfeet (1)	1	0.01
Cherokee (11)	21	0.20
Chickasaw (1)	1	0.01
Chippewa (25)	33	0.31
Crow	1	0.01
Iroquois	2	0.02
Latin American Indians (1)	1	0.01
Ottawa (11)	24	0.22
Potawatomi (2)	14	0.13
Pueblo (1)	1	0.01
Shoshone (1)	1	0.01
All other tribes (5)	7	0.07
American Indian tribes, not spec.	9	0.08
Arab:	29	0.27
Lebanese	29	0.27
Asian:	249	2.33
Chinese, ex. Taiwanese (12)	13	0.12
Filipino (28)	49	0.46
Indian (77)	80	0.75
Indonesian (1)	4	0.04
Japanese (3)	5	0.05
Korean (18)	24	0.22
Malaysian	3	0.03
Pakistani (8)	9	0.08
Thai (2)	2	0.02
Vietnamese (54)	55	0.52
Other Asian, not specified (1)	5	0.05
Australian	11	0.10
Austrian	28	0.26
Belgian	87	0.82
Brazilian	7	0.07
British	30	0.28
Canadian	26	0.24
Czech	40	0.38
Czechoslovakian	10	0.09
Danish	25	0.24
Dutch	1,519	14.30
English	1,364	12.84
Estonian	9	0.08
European	52	0.49
Finnish	32	0.30
French, except Basque	406	3.82
French Canadian	87	0.82
German	2,257	21.25
Greek	65	0.61
Hawaii Native/Pacific Islander:	18	0.17
Melanesian:	2	0.02
Fijian	2	0.02
Polynesian: (4)	10	0.09
Native Hawaiian (4)	8	0.07
Samoan	2	0.02
Other Pac. Isl., not spec.	6	0.06
Hispanic or Latino:	771	7.22
Central American:	50	0.47
Guatemalan	20	0.19
Honduran	9	0.08
Nicaraguan	1	0.01
Panamanian	3	0.03
Salvadoran	16	0.15
Other Central American	1	0.01
Cuban	14	0.13
Dominican Republic	6	0.06
Mexican	556	5.21
Puerto Rican	44	0.41
South American:	4	0.04
Argentinean	3	0.03
Peruvian	1	0.01
Other Hispanic or Latino	97	0.91
Hungarian	54	0.51
Irish	1,111	10.46
Italian	239	2.25
Latvian	6	0.06
Lithuanian	107	1.01
Norwegian	122	1.15
Polish	876	8.25
Portuguese	10	0.09
Romanian	10	0.09

Notes: 1. Figures in the "Number" column do not add up to the total population due to: a) Ancestry/Race overlap — e.g. persons can report being both White and Irish, b) persons of Hispanic origin can report being any race, c) persons reporting two ancestries are counted in both categories. 2. Numbers in parentheses indicate the number of persons reporting this ancestry/race alone, not in combination with any other ancestry/race. 3. Refer to the Explanation of Data in the front of the book for more detailed information.

Russian	51	0.48
Scandinavian	16	0.15
Scotch-Irish	153	1.44
Scottish	235	2.21
Serbian	10	0.09
Swedish	212	2.00
Ukrainian	19	0.18
United States or American	391	3.68
Welsh	58	0.55
West Indian, excl. Hispanic:	14	0.13
Haitian	14	0.13
White:	9,567	89.63
Not Hispanic (9,021)	9,192	86.12
Hispanic (297)	375	3.51

Comstock

Place Type: Township
County: Kalamazoo
Population: 13,851

Ancestry/Race	Number	%
African American/Black:	628	4.53
Not Hispanic (553)	623	4.50
Hispanic (3)	5	0.04
African, sub-Saharan:	128	0.93
African	98	0.71
Ethiopian	8	0.06
Nigerian	9	0.07
Other sub-Saharan African	13	0.09
Alaska Native tribes, specified:	1	0.01
Eskimo	1	0.01
Am. Ind. or Alaska Nat., not spec.	67	0.48
American Indian tribes, specified:	115	0.83
Apache	1	0.01
Blackfeet (1)	11	0.08
Cherokee (15)	54	0.39
Chippewa (12)	15	0.11
Choctaw (1)	1	0.01
Cree	3	0.02
Iroquois	3	0.02
Latin American Indians (2)	4	0.03
Ottawa (1)	4	0.03
Potawatomi (4)	12	0.09
Pueblo (1)	2	0.01
Seminole	1	0.01
Sioux (4)	4	0.03
American Indian tribes, not spec.	4	0.03
Arab:	8	0.06
Arab/Arabic	8	0.06
Asian:	199	1.44
Bangladeshi (1)	1	0.01
Cambodian	1	0.01
Chinese, ex. Taiwanese (18)	25	0.18
Filipino (27)	32	0.23
Indian (65)	72	0.52
Japanese (12)	24	0.17
Korean (21)	23	0.17
Malaysian (3)	3	0.02
Pakistani (3)	6	0.04
Thai (2)	2	0.01
Vietnamese (2)	3	0.02
Other Asian, not specified (4)	7	0.05
Austrian	17	0.12
Belgian	25	0.18
British	26	0.19
Canadian	26	0.19
Croatian	33	0.24
Czech	29	0.21
Czechoslovakian	9	0.07
Danish	71	0.51
Dutch	1,967	14.23
English	1,900	13.75
European	121	0.88
Finnish	35	0.25
French, except Basque	494	3.57
French Canadian	73	0.53
German	2,822	20.42
Greek	58	0.42
Hawaii Native/Pacific Islander:	3	0.02
Polynesian: (1)	3	0.02
Samoan (1)	3	0.02
Hispanic or Latino:	232	1.67
Central American:	13	0.09
Guatemalan	11	0.08
Panamanian	2	0.01
Cuban	2	0.01
Dominican Republic	2	0.01
Mexican	148	1.07
Puerto Rican	19	0.14
South American:	18	0.13
Colombian	11	0.08
Ecuadorian	2	0.01
Uruguayan	1	0.01
Venezuelan	4	0.03
Other Hispanic or Latino	30	0.22
Hungarian	141	1.02
Iranian	5	0.04
Irish	1,760	12.73
Italian	360	2.60
Latvian	7	0.05
Lithuanian	30	0.22
Maltese	7	0.05
Norwegian	147	1.06
Polish	613	4.43
Romanian	12	0.09
Russian	55	0.40
Scandinavian	25	0.18
Scotch-Irish	186	1.35
Scottish	344	2.49
Serbian	7	0.05
Slovak	20	0.14
Slovene	24	0.17
Swedish	207	1.50
Swiss	30	0.22
Ukrainian	38	0.27
United States or American	1,536	11.11
Welsh	208	1.50
West Indian, excl. Hispanic:	6	0.04
Jamaican	6	0.04
White:	12,949	93.49
Not Hispanic (12,613)	12,799	92.40
Hispanic (127)	150	1.08
Yugoslavian	14	0.10

Cutlerville

Place Type: Census Designated Place
County: Kent
Population: 15,114

Ancestry/Race	Number	%
African American/Black:	833	5.51
Not Hispanic (671)	790	5.23
Hispanic (25)	43	0.28
African, sub-Saharan:	102	0.67
African	55	0.36
Ethiopian	37	0.24
Zimbabwean	10	0.07
Alaska Native tribes, specified:	1	0.01
Eskimo (1)	1	0.01
Am. Ind. or Alaska Nat., not spec.	54	0.36
American Indian tribes, specified:	119	0.79
Apache (4)	4	0.03
Blackfeet	10	0.07
Cherokee (11)	33	0.22
Chickasaw	1	0.01
Chippewa (17)	22	0.15
Choctaw	3	0.02
Iroquois (2)	2	0.01
Latin American Indians (9)	11	0.07
Ottawa	10	0.07
Potawatomi (16)	19	0.13
Seminole (1)	1	0.01
Sioux	1	0.01
All other tribes	2	0.01
American Indian tribes, not spec.	5	0.03
Arab:	48	0.32
Arab/Arabic	39	0.26
Other Arab	9	0.06
Asian:	317	2.10
Cambodian	4	0.03
Chinese, ex. Taiwanese (13)	21	0.14
Filipino (27)	37	0.24
Hmong (1)	1	0.01
Indian (12)	17	0.11
Indonesian (2)	3	0.02
Japanese (6)	27	0.18
Korean (35)	39	0.26
Laotian	1	0.01
Malaysian (1)	1	0.01
Thai (1)	1	0.01
Vietnamese (134)	142	0.94
Other Asian, not specified (5)	23	0.15
Austrian	17	0.11
Belgian	7	0.05
British	7	0.05
Canadian	48	0.32
Croatian	17	0.11
Czech	32	0.21
Czechoslovakian	7	0.05
Danish	102	0.67
Dutch	4,219	27.87
English	1,550	10.24
European	70	0.46
Finnish	59	0.39
French, except Basque	779	5.15
French Canadian	162	1.07
German	2,796	18.47
Greek	24	0.16
Hawaii Native/Pacific Islander:	13	0.09
Polynesian: (3)	8	0.05
Native Hawaiian (3)	7	0.05
Samoan	1	0.01
Other Pac. Isl., not spec.	5	0.03
Hispanic or Latino:	679	4.49
Central American:	20	0.13
Guatemalan	8	0.05
Honduran	1	0.01
Panamanian	1	0.01
Salvadoran	10	0.07
Cuban	31	0.21
Dominican Republic	8	0.05
Mexican	385	2.55
Puerto Rican	87	0.58
South American:	11	0.07
Peruvian	8	0.05
Venezuelan	3	0.02
Other Hispanic or Latino	137	0.91
Hungarian	92	0.61
Iranian	13	0.09
Irish	1,440	9.51
Israeli	37	0.24
Italian	350	2.31
Lithuanian	43	0.28
Norwegian	125	0.83
Polish	652	4.31
Russian	60	0.40
Scandinavian	17	0.11
Scotch-Irish	142	0.94
Scottish	198	1.31
Slovak	8	0.05
Swedish	188	1.24
Swiss	48	0.32
United States or American	696	4.60
Welsh	35	0.23
White:	13,750	90.98
Not Hispanic (13,133)	13,403	88.68
Hispanic (308)	347	2.30
Yugoslavian	200	1.32

Davison

Place Type: Township
County: Genesee
Population: 17,722

Ancestry/Race	Number	%
African American/Black:	452	2.55
Not Hispanic (362)	447	2.52

Notes: 1. Figures in the "Number" column do not add up to the total population due to: a) Ancestry/Race overlap — e.g. persons can report being both White and Irish, b) persons of Hispanic origin can report being any race, c) persons reporting two ancestries are counted in both categories. 2. Numbers in parentheses indicate the number of persons reporting this ancestry/race alone, not in combination with any other ancestry/race. 3. Refer to the Explanation of Data in the front of the book for more detailed information.

Ancestry/Race	Number	%
Hispanic (2)	5	0.03
African, sub-Saharan:	67	0.38
African	59	0.33
Other sub-Saharan African	8	0.05
Alaska Native tribes, not specified	1	0.01
Am. Ind. or Alaska Nat., not spec.	75	0.42
American Indian tribes, specified:	161	0.91
Apache	6	0.03
Blackfeet	13	0.07
Cherokee (13)	60	0.34
Chickasaw	4	0.02
Chippewa (19)	50	0.28
Choctaw (2)	4	0.02
Iroquois (1)	5	0.03
Latin American Indians (1)	2	0.01
Lumbee (2)	5	0.03
Ottawa (4)	4	0.02
Potawatomi	3	0.02
Pueblo	2	0.01
All other tribes (3)	3	0.02
American Indian tribes, not spec.	1	0.01
Arab:	139	0.78
Arab/Arabic	18	0.10
Lebanese	97	0.55
Other Arab	24	0.14
Armenian	19	0.11
Asian:	211	1.19
Chinese, ex. Taiwanese (27)	33	0.19
Filipino (23)	33	0.19
Hmong (12)	12	0.07
Indian (27)	29	0.16
Indonesian (1)	1	0.01
Japanese (10)	21	0.12
Korean (30)	44	0.25
Pakistani (4)	4	0.02
Sri Lankan (1)	1	0.01
Thai	1	0.01
Vietnamese (16)	21	0.12
Other Asian, not specified (4)	11	0.06
Assyrian/Chaldean/Syriac	44	0.25
Australian	16	0.09
Austrian	40	0.23
Belgian	50	0.28
British	107	0.60
Canadian	182	1.03
Croatian	16	0.09
Czech	89	0.50
Czechoslovakian	68	0.38
Danish	36	0.20
Dutch	408	2.30
English	2,481	13.99
European	127	0.72
Finnish	94	0.53
French, except Basque	1,239	6.98
French Canadian	589	3.32
German	4,213	23.75
Greek	43	0.24
Hawaii Native/Pacific Islander:	7	0.04
Polynesian:	6	0.03
Native Hawaiian	6	0.03
Other Pac. Isl., not spec. (1)	1	0.01
Hispanic or Latino:	370	2.09
Central American:	4	0.02
Guatemalan	1	0.01
Honduran	1	0.01
Panamanian	2	0.01
Cuban	10	0.06
Mexican	262	1.48
Puerto Rican	24	0.14
South American:	8	0.05
Colombian	3	0.02
Ecuadorian	2	0.01
Peruvian	2	0.01
Venezuelan	1	0.01
Other Hispanic or Latino	62	0.35
Hungarian	432	2.44
Icelander	5	0.03
Iranian	9	0.05
Irish	2,765	15.59
Italian	670	3.78
Macedonian	5	0.03
Maltese	10	0.06
Norwegian	228	1.29
Polish	1,227	6.92
Portuguese	37	0.21
Romanian	8	0.05
Russian	111	0.63
Scandinavian	28	0.16
Scotch-Irish	323	1.82
Scottish	386	2.18
Serbian	19	0.11
Slavic	25	0.14
Slovak	80	0.45
Swedish	298	1.68
Swiss	74	0.42
Ukrainian	72	0.41
United States or American	1,440	8.12
Welsh	70	0.39
White:	17,035	96.12
Not Hispanic (16,475)	16,757	94.55
Hispanic (237)	278	1.57
Yugoslavian	4	0.02

De Witt

Place Type: Township
County: Clinton
Population: 12,143

Ancestry/Race	Number	%
African American/Black:	216	1.78
Not Hispanic (162)	214	1.76
Hispanic (1)	2	0.02
African, sub-Saharan:	10	0.08
African	10	0.08
Am. Ind. or Alaska Nat., not spec.	60	0.49
American Indian tribes, specified:	124	1.02
Blackfeet (1)	1	0.01
Cherokee (20)	31	0.26
Chippewa (27)	43	0.35
Iroquois (4)	5	0.04
Latin American Indians	5	0.04
Ottawa (12)	22	0.18
Potawatomi (1)	6	0.05
Shoshone	1	0.01
Sioux	1	0.01
All other tribes (6)	9	0.07
American Indian tribes, not spec.	2	0.02
Arab:	29	0.24
Lebanese	29	0.24
Armenian	8	0.07
Asian:	137	1.13
Chinese, ex. Taiwanese (8)	14	0.12
Filipino (12)	12	0.10
Hmong (19)	24	0.20
Indian (18)	20	0.16
Japanese (9)	19	0.16
Korean (19)	24	0.20
Laotian (10)	15	0.12
Thai (2)	2	0.02
Vietnamese (2)	5	0.04
Other Asian, specified	1	0.01
Other Asian, not specified (1)	1	0.01
Australian	9	0.07
Austrian	35	0.29
Belgian	32	0.27
British	32	0.27
Bulgarian	7	0.06
Canadian	52	0.43
Croatian	61	0.51
Czech	48	0.40
Czechoslovakian	38	0.32
Danish	65	0.54
Dutch	556	4.62
English	1,794	14.90
European	173	1.44
Finnish	93	0.77
French, except Basque	531	4.41
French Canadian	208	1.73
German	3,683	30.58
Greek	15	0.12
Hawaii Native/Pacific Islander:	7	0.06
Micronesian: (2)	2	0.02
Guamanian/Chamorro (2)	2	0.02
Polynesian: (1)	4	0.03
Native Hawaiian (1)	1	0.01
Samoan	3	0.02
Other Pac. Isl., specified	1	0.01
Hispanic or Latino:	488	4.02
Central American:	6	0.05
Costa Rican	1	0.01
Guatemalan	2	0.02
Nicaraguan	2	0.02
Panamanian	1	0.01
Cuban	23	0.19
Mexican	325	2.68
Puerto Rican	17	0.14
South American:	8	0.07
Peruvian	4	0.03
Venezuelan	3	0.02
Other South American	1	0.01
Other Hispanic or Latino	109	0.90
Hungarian	91	0.76
Irish	1,753	14.55
Italian	292	2.42
Lithuanian	15	0.12
Northern European	4	0.03
Norwegian	163	1.35
Pennsylvania German	25	0.21
Polish	536	4.45
Portuguese	21	0.17
Romanian	9	0.07
Russian	26	0.22
Scandinavian	15	0.12
Scotch-Irish	124	1.03
Scottish	299	2.48
Slovak	27	0.22
Swedish	174	1.44
Swiss	53	0.44
Ukrainian	28	0.23
United States or American	1,001	8.31
Welsh	57	0.47
White:	11,620	95.69
Not Hispanic (11,157)	11,290	92.98
Hispanic (277)	330	2.72
Yugoslavian	14	0.12

Dearborn Heights

Place Type: City
County: Wayne
Population: 58,264

Ancestry/Race	Number	%
Afghan	5	0.01
African American/Black:	1,376	2.36
Not Hispanic (1,224)	1,358	2.33
Hispanic (12)	18	0.03
African, sub-Saharan:	66	0.11
African	45	0.08
Ethiopian	13	0.02
Nigerian	8	0.01
Alaska Native tribes, specified:	2	0.00
Eskimo (1)	1	0.00
Tlingit-Haida (1)	1	0.00
Am. Ind. or Alaska Nat., not spec.	149	0.26
Albanian	67	0.11
Alsatian	3	0.01
American Indian tribes, specified:	343	0.59
Apache (1)	4	0.01
Blackfeet (4)	16	0.03
Cherokee (28)	109	0.19
Chickasaw (2)	3	0.01
Chippewa (26)	61	0.10
Choctaw	8	0.01
Comanche	1	0.00
Cree (2)	4	0.01
Creek (2)	3	0.01
Delaware (5)	9	0.02
Iroquois (43)	53	0.09

Notes: 1. Figures in the "Number" column do not add up to the total population due to: a) Ancestry/Race overlap — e.g. persons can report being both White and Irish, b) persons of Hispanic origin can report being any race, c) persons reporting two ancestries are counted in both categories. 2. Numbers in parentheses indicate the number of persons reporting this ancestry/race alone, not in combination with any other ancestry/race. 3. Refer to the Explanation of Data in the front of the book for more detailed information.

Latin American Indians (2)	3	0.01
Lumbee (7)	9	0.02
Menominee (2)	3	0.01
Navajo (2)	3	0.01
Osage (2)	5	0.01
Ottawa (8)	16	0.03
Potawatomi (5)	5	0.01
Seminole	1	0.00
Sioux (6)	11	0.02
Yaqui	2	0.00
All other tribes (3)	14	0.02
American Indian tribes, not spec.	19	0.03
Arab:	4,578	7.86
Arab/Arabic	826	1.42
Egyptian	85	0.15
Iraqi	55	0.09
Jordanian	110	0.19
Lebanese	3,136	5.38
Palestinian	220	0.38
Syrian	111	0.19
Other Arab	35	0.06
Armenian	333	0.57
Asian:	1,667	2.86
Cambodian (6)	6	0.01
Chinese, ex. Taiwanese (267)	284	0.49
Filipino (149)	198	0.34
Indian (558)	597	1.02
Indonesian (2)	4	0.01
Japanese (26)	39	0.07
Korean (54)	73	0.13
Malaysian (1)	2	0.00
Pakistani (41)	58	0.10
Sri Lankan (4)	4	0.01
Taiwanese (3)	4	0.01
Thai (10)	11	0.02
Vietnamese (141)	155	0.27
Other Asian, specified	1	0.00
Other Asian, not specified (36)	231	0.40
Assyrian/Chaldean/Syriac	31	0.05
Austrian	184	0.32
Belgian	176	0.30
Brazilian	14	0.02
British	118	0.20
Bulgarian	6	0.01
Canadian	381	0.65
Croatian	153	0.26
Czech	121	0.21
Czechoslovakian	217	0.37
Danish	128	0.22
Dutch	700	1.20
Eastern European	10	0.02
English	4,130	7.09
European	312	0.54
Finnish	341	0.59
French, except Basque	2,460	4.22
French Canadian	1,276	2.19
German	9,206	15.80
Greek	601	1.03
Hawaii Native/Pacific Islander:	65	0.11
Micronesian:	5	0.01
Guamanian/Chamorro	5	0.01
Polynesian: (3)	10	0.02
Native Hawaiian (3)	7	0.01
Samoan	3	0.01
Other Pac. Isl., not spec. (1)	50	0.09
Hispanic or Latino:	1,974	3.39
Central American:	22	0.04
Costa Rican	4	0.01
Guatemalan	2	0.00
Honduran	6	0.01
Nicaraguan	5	0.01
Panamanian	4	0.01
Salvadoran	1	0.00
Cuban	31	0.05
Dominican Republic	9	0.02
Mexican	1,299	2.23
Puerto Rican	164	0.28
South American:	79	0.14
Argentinean	17	0.03
Chilean	2	0.00
Colombian	23	0.04
Ecuadorian	11	0.02
Paraguayan	2	0.00
Peruvian	6	0.01
Venezuelan	12	0.02
Other South American	6	0.01
Other Hispanic or Latino	370	0.64
Hungarian	1,060	1.82
Iranian	19	0.03
Irish	7,147	12.27
Israeli	31	0.05
Italian	4,922	8.45
Latvian	7	0.01
Lithuanian	460	0.79
Macedonian	705	1.21
Maltese	656	1.13
Northern European	14	0.02
Norwegian	225	0.39
Pennsylvania German	21	0.04
Polish	12,058	20.70
Portuguese	16	0.03
Romanian	520	0.89
Russian	440	0.76
Scotch-Irish	923	1.58
Scottish	1,301	2.23
Serbian	62	0.11
Slavic	38	0.07
Slovak	275	0.47
Slovene	9	0.02
Soviet Union	7	0.01
Swedish	501	0.86
Swiss	22	0.04
Turkish	84	0.14
Ukrainian	916	1.57
United States or American	2,017	3.46
Welsh	304	0.52
West Indian, excl. Hispanic:	8	0.01
West Indian	8	0.01
White:	54,939	94.29
Not Hispanic (52,032)	53,439	91.72
Hispanic (1,363)	1,500	2.57
Yugoslavian	395	0.68

Dearborn

Place Type: City
County: Wayne
Population: 97,775

Ancestry/Race	Number	%
African American/Black:	1,435	1.47
Not Hispanic (1,225)	1,390	1.42
Hispanic (23)	45	0.05
African, sub-Saharan:	70	0.07
African	48	0.05
Cape Verdean	9	0.01
Ethiopian	5	0.01
Nigerian	8	0.01
Alaska Native tribes, specified:	5	0.01
Alaska Athabascan	4	0.00
Aleut	1	0.00
Alaska Native tribes, not specified	1	0.00
Am. Ind. or Alaska Nat., not spec.	185	0.19
Albanian	694	0.71
Alsatian	25	0.03
American Indian tribes, specified:	390	0.40
Apache (1)	7	0.01
Blackfeet (2)	21	0.02
Cherokee (31)	96	0.10
Cheyenne (1)	2	0.00
Chickasaw	2	0.00
Chippewa (62)	97	0.10
Choctaw (4)	11	0.01
Comanche (1)	1	0.00
Cree	1	0.00
Creek	2	0.00
Delaware (1)	4	0.00
Houma	1	0.00
Iroquois (28)	38	0.04
Latin American Indians (11)	22	0.02
Lumbee (6)	8	0.01
Menominee (3)	5	0.01
Navajo	1	0.00
Osage	2	0.00
Ottawa (6)	11	0.01
Potawatomi (11)	16	0.02
Pueblo (1)	1	0.00
Seminole	1	0.00
Shoshone (1)	1	0.00
Sioux (1)	4	0.00
Yaqui (1)	1	0.00
All other tribes (17)	34	0.03
American Indian tribes, not spec.	16	0.02
Arab:	29,344	30.01
Arab/Arabic	5,027	5.14
Egyptian	206	0.21
Iraqi	2,042	2.09
Jordanian	501	0.51
Lebanese	17,305	17.70
Moroccan	42	0.04
Palestinian	953	0.97
Syrian	567	0.58
Other Arab	2,701	2.76
Armenian	895	0.92
Asian:	2,545	2.60
Bangladeshi (4)	9	0.01
Cambodian (2)	2	0.00
Chinese, ex. Taiwanese (220)	288	0.29
Filipino (141)	195	0.20
Indian (494)	646	0.66
Indonesian (8)	10	0.01
Japanese (42)	83	0.08
Korean (86)	108	0.11
Laotian (5)	5	0.01
Malaysian (13)	14	0.01
Pakistani (117)	188	0.19
Sri Lankan (1)	1	0.00
Taiwanese (13)	14	0.01
Thai (6)	13	0.01
Vietnamese (116)	138	0.14
Other Asian, specified (2)	7	0.01
Other Asian, not specified (148)	824	0.84
Assyrian/Chaldean/Syriac	96	0.10
Australian	58	0.06
Austrian	360	0.37
Belgian	244	0.25
Brazilian	92	0.09
British	362	0.37
Bulgarian	52	0.05
Canadian	480	0.49
Carpatho Rusyn	11	0.01
Celtic	25	0.03
Croatian	178	0.18
Czech	489	0.50
Czechoslovakian	191	0.20
Danish	224	0.23
Dutch	970	0.99
Eastern European	12	0.01
English	6,515	6.66
European	378	0.39
Finnish	413	0.42
French, except Basque	2,976	3.04
French Canadian	1,158	1.18
German	13,363	13.67
German Russian	10	0.01
Greek	577	0.59
Hawaii Native/Pacific Islander:	78	0.08
Micronesian: (3)	5	0.01
Guamanian/Chamorro (3)	4	0.00
Other Micronesian	1	0.00
Polynesian: (6)	17	0.02
Native Hawaiian (4)	11	0.01
Samoan (2)	6	0.01
Other Pac. Isl., specified	5	0.01
Other Pac. Isl., not spec. (5)	51	0.05
Hispanic or Latino:	2,931	3.00
Central American:	31	0.03
Guatemalan	8	0.01
Honduran	3	0.00
Nicaraguan	2	0.00

Notes: 1. Figures in the "Number" column do not add up to the total population due to: a) Ancestry/Race overlap — e.g. persons can report being both White and Irish, b) persons of Hispanic origin can report being any race, c) persons reporting two ancestries are counted in both categories. 2. Numbers in parentheses indicate the number of persons reporting this ancestry/race alone, not in combination with any other ancestry/race. 3. Refer to the Explanation of Data in the front of the book for more detailed information.

Panamanian	7	0.01
Salvadoran	11	0.01
Cuban	82	0.08
Dominican Republic	8	0.01
Mexican	1,875	1.92
Puerto Rican	273	0.28
South American:	124	0.13
Argentinean	18	0.02
Bolivian	4	0.00
Chilean	3	0.00
Colombian	24	0.02
Ecuadorian	8	0.01
Paraguayan	1	0.00
Peruvian	4	0.00
Venezuelan	55	0.06
Other South American	7	0.01
Other Hispanic or Latino	538	0.55
Hungarian	2,232	2.28
Iranian	97	0.10
Irish	9,146	9.35
Israeli	28	0.03
Italian	6,248	6.39
Latvian	27	0.03
Lithuanian	590	0.60
Luxemburger	17	0.02
Macedonian	193	0.20
Maltese	626	0.64
Northern European	24	0.02
Norwegian	480	0.49
Pennsylvania German	31	0.03
Polish	11,555	11.82
Portuguese	84	0.09
Romanian	939	0.96
Russian	681	0.70
Scandinavian	51	0.05
Scotch-Irish	1,468	1.50
Scottish	2,155	2.20
Serbian	136	0.14
Slavic	113	0.12
Slovak	400	0.41
Slovene	104	0.11
Swedish	824	0.84
Swiss	244	0.25
Turkish	154	0.16
Ukrainian	958	0.98
United States or American	2,416	2.47
Welsh	406	0.42
West Indian, excl. Hispanic:	34	0.03
Barbadian	8	0.01
Jamaican	21	0.02
West Indian	5	0.01
White:	93,961	96.10
Not Hispanic (82,893)	91,715	93.80
Hispanic (2,038)	2,246	2.30
Yugoslavian	272	0.28

Delhi charter

Place Type: Township
County: Ingham
Population: 22,569

Ancestry/Race	Number	%
African American/Black:	697	3.09
Not Hispanic (526)	682	3.02
Hispanic (6)	15	0.07
African, sub-Saharan:	34	0.15
African	34	0.15
Am. Ind. or Alaska Nat., not spec.	86	0.38
American Indian tribes, specified:	189	0.84
Apache	1	0.00
Blackfeet (2)	8	0.04
Cherokee (10)	51	0.23
Cheyenne	1	0.00
Chickasaw	1	0.00
Chippewa (33)	68	0.30
Choctaw (1)	1	0.00
Cree	2	0.01
Iroquois (1)	8	0.04
Latin American Indians (3)	5	0.02
Navajo	2	0.01
Ottawa (10)	17	0.08
Potawatomi (6)	11	0.05
Sioux (1)	1	0.00
All other tribes (4)	12	0.05
American Indian tribes, not spec.	10	0.04
Arab:	126	0.56
Lebanese	94	0.41
Syrian	32	0.14
Armenian	81	0.36
Asian:	341	1.51
Cambodian (2)	3	0.01
Chinese, ex. Taiwanese (33)	44	0.19
Filipino (18)	35	0.16
Indian (26)	31	0.14
Indonesian	1	0.00
Japanese (16)	44	0.19
Korean (70)	83	0.37
Pakistani (4)	4	0.02
Thai (4)	4	0.02
Vietnamese (79)	88	0.39
Other Asian, specified (1)	1	0.00
Other Asian, not specified (3)	3	0.01
Australian	9	0.04
Austrian	56	0.25
Belgian	59	0.26
British	57	0.25
Canadian	105	0.46
Croatian	20	0.09
Czech	105	0.46
Czechoslovakian	57	0.25
Danish	141	0.62
Dutch	1,088	4.80
English	3,523	15.55
European	178	0.79
Finnish	144	0.64
French, except Basque	1,071	4.73
French Canadian	493	2.18
German	5,935	26.20
Greek	65	0.29
Hawaii Native/Pacific Islander:	18	0.08
Micronesian: (1)	1	0.00
Guamanian/Chamorro (1)	1	0.00
Polynesian: (4)	8	0.04
Native Hawaiian (2)	6	0.03
Samoan (2)	2	0.01
Other Pac. Isl., not spec. (5)	9	0.04
Hispanic or Latino:	804	3.56
Central American:	13	0.06
Costa Rican	2	0.01
Guatemalan	3	0.01
Honduran	5	0.02
Panamanian	2	0.01
Salvadoran	1	0.00
Cuban	43	0.19
Dominican Republic	1	0.00
Mexican	536	2.37
Puerto Rican	38	0.17
South American:	8	0.04
Argentinean	1	0.00
Colombian	3	0.01
Peruvian	1	0.00
Venezuelan	2	0.01
Other South American	1	0.00
Other Hispanic or Latino	165	0.73
Hungarian	156	0.69
Irish	3,003	13.26
Italian	880	3.88
Lithuanian	64	0.28
Macedonian	4	0.02
Northern European	48	0.21
Norwegian	214	0.94
Pennsylvania German	57	0.25
Polish	1,175	5.19
Portuguese	30	0.13
Romanian	21	0.09
Russian	163	0.72
Scandinavian	52	0.23
Scotch-Irish	321	1.42
Scottish	650	2.87
Serbian	65	0.29
Slavic	8	0.04
Slovak	45	0.20
Slovene	18	0.08
Swedish	455	2.01
Swiss	80	0.35
Ukrainian	45	0.20
United States or American	1,514	6.68
Welsh	152	0.67
White:	21,427	94.94
Not Hispanic (20,474)	20,850	92.38
Hispanic (504)	577	2.56
Yugoslavian	49	0.22

Delta charter

Place Type: Township
County: Eaton
Population: 29,682

Ancestry/Race	Number	%
African American/Black:	2,640	8.89
Not Hispanic (2,341)	2,573	8.67
Hispanic (34)	67	0.23
African, sub-Saharan:	106	0.36
African	101	0.34
Nigerian	5	0.02
Alaska Native tribes, not specified	1	0.00
Am. Ind. or Alaska Nat., not spec.	103	0.35
American Indian tribes, specified:	189	0.64
Apache	8	0.03
Blackfeet (3)	8	0.03
Cherokee (16)	54	0.18
Cheyenne (1)	1	0.00
Chickasaw	1	0.00
Chippewa (44)	61	0.21
Choctaw (1)	2	0.01
Comanche (3)	3	0.01
Cree	1	0.00
Creek	1	0.00
Delaware	1	0.00
Iroquois (1)	6	0.02
Latin American Indians (1)	2	0.01
Osage	1	0.00
Ottawa (7)	14	0.05
Potawatomi (3)	6	0.02
Shoshone	2	0.01
Sioux (3)	8	0.03
Tohono O'Odham (1)	1	0.00
All other tribes (1)	8	0.03
American Indian tribes, not spec.	9	0.03
Arab:	405	1.36
Arab/Arabic	54	0.18
Lebanese	291	0.98
Palestinian	26	0.09
Syrian	14	0.05
Other Arab	20	0.07
Armenian	17	0.06
Asian:	860	2.90
Bangladeshi (1)	1	0.00
Cambodian (3)	5	0.02
Chinese, ex. Taiwanese (65)	76	0.26
Filipino (25)	36	0.12
Hmong (10)	10	0.03
Indian (334)	356	1.20
Indonesian (2)	2	0.01
Japanese (20)	32	0.11
Korean (74)	84	0.28
Laotian (1)	4	0.01
Malaysian (3)	3	0.01
Pakistani (19)	25	0.08
Sri Lankan (1)	5	0.02
Taiwanese (1)	1	0.00
Thai (8)	14	0.05
Vietnamese (167)	178	0.60
Other Asian, specified	4	0.01
Other Asian, not specified (18)	24	0.08
Austrian	75	0.25
Belgian	153	0.51
Brazilian	7	0.02

Notes: 1. Figures in the "Number" column do not add up to the total population due to: a) Ancestry/Race overlap — e.g. persons can report being both White and Irish, b) persons of Hispanic origin can report being any race, c) persons reporting two ancestries are counted in both categories. 2. Numbers in parentheses indicate the number of persons reporting this ancestry/race alone, not in combination with any other ancestry/race. 3. Refer to the Explanation of Data in the front of the book for more detailed information.

Ancestry/Race	Number	%
British	129	0.43
Bulgarian	30	0.10
Canadian	149	0.50
Celtic	14	0.05
Croatian	98	0.33
Czech	216	0.73
Czechoslovakian	42	0.14
Danish	171	0.57
Dutch	1,475	4.96
Eastern European	4	0.01
English	4,590	15.42
Estonian	6	0.02
European	380	1.28
Finnish	293	0.98
French, except Basque	1,288	4.33
French Canadian	473	1.59
German	8,042	27.03
Greek	124	0.42
Hawaii Native/Pacific Islander:	24	0.08
Melanesian: (1)	2	0.01
Fijian (1)	2	0.01
Micronesian: (2)	2	0.01
Guamanian/Chamorro (2)	2	0.01
Polynesian: (7)	10	0.03
Native Hawaiian (4)	6	0.02
Samoan (3)	4	0.01
Other Pac. Isl., specified	3	0.01
Other Pac. Isl., not spec. (1)	7	0.02
Hispanic or Latino:	1,105	3.72
Central American:	8	0.03
Costa Rican	1	0.00
Guatemalan	1	0.00
Honduran	4	0.01
Panamanian	2	0.01
Cuban	66	0.22
Dominican Republic	7	0.02
Mexican	771	2.60
Puerto Rican	34	0.11
South American:	25	0.08
Bolivian	2	0.01
Colombian	7	0.02
Ecuadorian	2	0.01
Paraguayan	1	0.00
Peruvian	5	0.02
Venezuelan	8	0.03
Other Hispanic or Latino	194	0.65
Hungarian	91	0.31
Iranian	28	0.09
Irish	4,187	14.07
Italian	1,374	4.62
Latvian	25	0.08
Lithuanian	58	0.19
Maltese	6	0.02
Norwegian	427	1.43
Pennsylvania German	16	0.05
Polish	1,617	5.43
Portuguese	36	0.12
Romanian	41	0.14
Russian	166	0.56
Scandinavian	49	0.16
Scotch-Irish	386	1.30
Scottish	762	2.56
Slavic	8	0.03
Slovak	175	0.59
Slovene	12	0.04
Swedish	821	2.76
Swiss	100	0.34
Ukrainian	55	0.18
United States or American	1,432	4.81
Welsh	199	0.67
West Indian, excl. Hispanic:	40	0.13
Haitian	8	0.03
Trinidadian and Tobagonian	27	0.09
West Indian	5	0.02
White:	25,959	87.46
Not Hispanic (24,807)	25,260	85.10
Hispanic (598)	699	2.35
Yugoslavian	6	0.02

Detroit

Place Type: City
County: Wayne
Population: 951,270

Ancestry/Race	Number	%
Acadian/Cajun	5	0.00
Afghan	62	0.01
African American/Black:	787,687	82.80
Not Hispanic (771,966)	782,837	82.29
Hispanic (3,806)	4,850	0.51
African, sub-Saharan:	16,870	1.77
African	14,175	1.49
Cape Verdean	50	0.01
Ethiopian	300	0.03
Ghanian	147	0.02
Kenyan	7	0.00
Liberian	216	0.02
Nigerian	1,459	0.15
Senegalese	83	0.01
Sierra Leonean	9	0.00
Somalian	52	0.01
South African	39	0.00
Sudanese	35	0.00
Zairian	15	0.00
Other sub-Saharan African	283	0.03
Alaska Native tribes, specified:	18	0.00
Alaska Athabascan	4	0.00
Aleut	1	0.00
Eskimo	6	0.00
Tlingit-Haida (4)	7	0.00
Alaska Native tribes, not specified	6	0.00
Am. Ind. or Alaska Nat., not spec.	4,419	0.46
Albanian	334	0.04
Alsatian	10	0.00
American Indian tribes, specified:	4,215	0.44
Apache (26)	76	0.01
Blackfeet (101)	565	0.06
Cherokee (304)	1,599	0.17
Cheyenne (3)	10	0.00
Chickasaw (11)	43	0.00
Chippewa (214)	407	0.04
Choctaw (14)	192	0.02
Colville	1	0.00
Comanche (4)	11	0.00
Cree (4)	18	0.00
Creek (18)	98	0.01
Crow (1)	22	0.00
Delaware (23)	31	0.00
Houma (1)	1	0.00
Iroquois (159)	272	0.03
Kiowa (1)	2	0.00
Latin American Indians (106)	191	0.02
Lumbee (55)	71	0.01
Menominee (4)	6	0.00
Navajo (15)	40	0.00
Ottawa (42)	83	0.01
Paiute (1)	1	0.00
Potawatomi (15)	38	0.00
Pueblo (16)	30	0.00
Puget Sound Salish (1)	1	0.00
Seminole (9)	58	0.01
Shoshone (3)	6	0.00
Sioux (26)	95	0.01
Ute	1	0.00
Yakama (3)	3	0.00
Yaqui (1)	4	0.00
Yuman (1)	1	0.00
All other tribes (66)	238	0.03
American Indian tribes, not spec.	555	0.06
Arab:	8,300	0.87
Arab/Arabic	3,614	0.38
Egyptian	110	0.01
Iraqi	966	0.10
Jordanian	92	0.01
Lebanese	1,925	0.20
Moroccan	156	0.02
Palestinian	234	0.02
Syrian	193	0.02
Other Arab	1,010	0.11
Armenian	247	0.03
Asian:	12,733	1.34
Bangladeshi (632)	1,131	0.12
Cambodian (30)	49	0.01
Chinese, ex. Taiwanese (885)	1,114	0.12
Filipino (951)	1,286	0.14
Hmong (1,715)	1,882	0.20
Indian (2,827)	3,700	0.39
Indonesian (4)	18	0.00
Japanese (188)	382	0.04
Korean (217)	347	0.04
Laotian (421)	504	0.05
Malaysian (1)	9	0.00
Pakistani (179)	255	0.03
Sri Lankan (32)	36	0.00
Taiwanese (27)	28	0.00
Thai (47)	70	0.01
Vietnamese (393)	444	0.05
Other Asian, specified (7)	108	0.01
Other Asian, not specified (484)	1,370	0.14
Assyrian/Chaldean/Syriac	1,963	0.21
Australian	8	0.00
Austrian	370	0.04
Basque	5	0.00
Belgian	727	0.08
Brazilian	45	0.00
British	205	0.02
Bulgarian	82	0.01
Canadian	1,094	0.12
Carpatho Rusyn	17	0.00
Celtic	9	0.00
Croatian	249	0.03
Czech	429	0.05
Czechoslovakian	235	0.02
Danish	405	0.04
Dutch	1,609	0.17
Eastern European	43	0.00
English	7,188	0.76
European	715	0.08
Finnish	720	0.08
French, except Basque	5,130	0.54
French Canadian	2,181	0.23
German	16,891	1.78
German Russian	69	0.01
Greek	653	0.07
Guyanese	117	0.01
Hawaii Native/Pacific Islander:	846	0.09
Melanesian:	2	0.00
Fijian	1	0.00
Other Melanesian	1	0.00
Micronesian: (48)	103	0.01
Guamanian/Chamorro (45)	100	0.01
Other Micronesian (3)	3	0.00
Polynesian: (111)	265	0.03
Native Hawaiian (46)	149	0.02
Samoan (64)	110	0.01
Tongan (1)	2	0.00
Other Polynesian	4	0.00
Other Pac. Isl., specified	96	0.01
Other Pac. Isl., not spec. (89)	380	0.04
Hispanic or Latino:	47,167	4.96
Central American:	869	0.09
Costa Rican	41	0.00
Guatemalan	184	0.02
Honduran	207	0.02
Nicaraguan	98	0.01
Panamanian	78	0.01
Salvadoran	231	0.02
Other Central American	30	0.00
Cuban	871	0.09
Dominican Republic	386	0.04
Mexican	33,143	3.48
Puerto Rican	6,615	0.70
South American:	288	0.03
Argentinean	16	0.00
Bolivian	1	0.00
Chilean	39	0.00
Colombian	131	0.01
Ecuadorian	34	0.00

Notes: 1. Figures in the "Number" column do not add up to the total population due to: a) Ancestry/Race overlap — e.g. persons can report being both White and Irish, b) persons of Hispanic origin can report being any race, c) persons reporting two ancestries are counted in both categories. 2. Numbers in parentheses indicate the number of persons reporting this ancestry/race alone, not in combination with any other ancestry/race. 3. Refer to the Explanation of Data in the front of the book for more detailed information.

Ancestry/Race	Number	%
Peruvian	31	0.00
Venezuelan	21	0.00
Other South American	15	0.00
Other Hispanic or Latino	4,995	0.53
Hungarian	1,527	0.16
Icelander	29	0.00
Iranian	130	0.01
Irish	14,421	1.52
Israeli	54	0.01
Italian	7,443	0.78
Latvian	43	0.00
Lithuanian	597	0.06
Macedonian	124	0.01
Maltese	473	0.05
Northern European	32	0.00
Norwegian	667	0.07
Pennsylvania German	28	0.00
Polish	18,992	2.00
Portuguese	128	0.01
Romanian	1,510	0.16
Russian	1,139	0.12
Scandinavian	110	0.01
Scotch-Irish	1,526	0.16
Scottish	2,274	0.24
Serbian	198	0.02
Slavic	48	0.01
Slovak	455	0.05
Slovene	52	0.01
Swedish	833	0.09
Swiss	98	0.01
Turkish	76	0.01
Ukrainian	1,346	0.14
United States or American	11,574	1.22
Welsh	428	0.04
West Indian, excl. Hispanic:	3,413	0.36
Bahamian	102	0.01
Barbadian	86	0.01
Belizean	32	0.00
Bermudan	17	0.00
British West Indian	127	0.01
Dutch West Indian	6	0.00
Haitian	264	0.03
Jamaican	2,260	0.24
Trinidadian and Tobagonian	213	0.02
U.S. Virgin Islander	12	0.00
West Indian	294	0.03
White:	131,691	13.84
Not Hispanic (99,921)	112,574	11.83
Hispanic (16,678)	19,117	2.01
Yugoslavian	264	0.03

East Grand Rapids

Place Type: City
County: Kent
Population: 10,764

Ancestry/Race	Number	%
African American/Black:	127	1.18
Not Hispanic (105)	127	1.18
African, sub-Saharan:	8	0.07
Nigerian	8	0.07
Am. Ind. or Alaska Nat., not spec.	12	0.11
American Indian tribes, specified:	24	0.22
Cherokee	5	0.05
Chippewa (9)	11	0.10
Latin American Indians (1)	1	0.01
Ottawa	2	0.02
Potawatomi	3	0.03
Sioux (2)	2	0.02
Arab:	202	1.87
Egyptian	5	0.05
Lebanese	184	1.71
Syrian	13	0.12
Armenian	20	0.19
Asian:	122	1.13
Chinese, ex. Taiwanese (33)	36	0.33
Filipino (3)	3	0.03
Indian (15)	15	0.14
Indonesian	1	0.01
Japanese (10)	17	0.16
Korean (44)	48	0.45
Vietnamese (1)	1	0.01
Other Asian, not specified (1)	1	0.01
Austrian	23	0.21
Belgian	15	0.14
British	74	0.69
Canadian	36	0.33
Celtic	10	0.09
Croatian	24	0.22
Czech	26	0.24
Czechoslovakian	24	0.22
Danish	90	0.83
Dutch	1,787	16.57
Eastern European	20	0.19
English	2,051	19.02
European	152	1.41
Finnish	29	0.27
French, except Basque	527	4.89
French Canadian	113	1.05
German	2,827	26.22
Greek	71	0.66
Hawaii Native/Pacific Islander:	2	0.02
Micronesian:	1	0.01
Guamanian/Chamorro	1	0.01
Other Pac. Isl., not spec.	1	0.01
Hispanic or Latino:	92	0.85
Central American:	2	0.02
Honduran	1	0.01
Other Central American	1	0.01
Cuban	4	0.04
Mexican	49	0.46
Puerto Rican	9	0.08
South American:	17	0.16
Argentinean	5	0.05
Chilean	1	0.01
Colombian	1	0.01
Ecuadorian	2	0.02
Paraguayan	2	0.02
Peruvian	6	0.06
Other Hispanic or Latino	11	0.10
Hungarian	88	0.82
Irish	2,153	19.97
Italian	418	3.88
Latvian	9	0.08
Lithuanian	71	0.66
Macedonian	15	0.14
Maltese	12	0.11
Northern European	23	0.21
Norwegian	193	1.79
Pennsylvania German	11	0.10
Polish	718	6.66
Portuguese	5	0.05
Romanian	30	0.28
Russian	120	1.11
Scandinavian	53	0.49
Scotch-Irish	297	2.75
Scottish	436	4.04
Serbian	4	0.04
Slovak	10	0.09
Slovene	8	0.07
Swedish	469	4.35
Swiss	78	0.72
Ukrainian	60	0.56
United States or American	386	3.58
Welsh	140	1.30
White:	10,499	97.54
Not Hispanic (10,384)	10,435	96.94
Hispanic (56)	64	0.59
Yugoslavian	22	0.20

East Lansing

Place Type: City
County: Ingham
Population: 46,525

Ancestry/Race	Number	%
African American/Black:	3,772	8.11
Not Hispanic (3,410)	3,717	7.99
Hispanic (31)	55	0.12
African, sub-Saharan:	511	1.09
African	181	0.39
Ethiopian	112	0.24
Kenyan	22	0.05
Nigerian	71	0.15
Somalian	13	0.03
South African	43	0.09
Other sub-Saharan African	69	0.15
Alaska Native tribes, specified:	1	0.00
Aleut (1)	1	0.00
Alaska Native tribes, not specified	1	0.00
Am. Ind. or Alaska Nat., not spec.	105	0.23
Albanian	14	0.03
Alsatian	14	0.03
American Indian tribes, specified:	218	0.47
Apache	3	0.01
Blackfeet (1)	8	0.02
Cherokee (12)	50	0.11
Chickasaw (3)	4	0.01
Chippewa (50)	72	0.15
Choctaw	2	0.00
Cree	1	0.00
Creek	1	0.00
Iroquois (4)	5	0.01
Kiowa (1)	1	0.00
Latin American Indians (3)	13	0.03
Lumbee (2)	2	0.00
Navajo (2)	4	0.01
Ottawa (10)	15	0.03
Potawatomi (6)	9	0.02
Pueblo (3)	3	0.01
Seminole (1)	1	0.00
Sioux (6)	9	0.02
Yaqui (3)	4	0.01
All other tribes (3)	11	0.02
American Indian tribes, not spec.	24	0.05
Arab:	528	1.13
Arab/Arabic	54	0.12
Egyptian	85	0.18
Iraqi	13	0.03
Jordanian	6	0.01
Lebanese	179	0.38
Palestinian	8	0.02
Syrian	104	0.22
Other Arab	79	0.17
Armenian	149	0.32
Asian:	4,215	9.06
Bangladeshi (8)	11	0.02
Cambodian (13)	24	0.05
Chinese, ex. Taiwanese (1,014)	1,091	2.34
Filipino (190)	252	0.54
Hmong (39)	39	0.08
Indian (651)	712	1.53
Indonesian (63)	73	0.16
Japanese (240)	291	0.63
Korean (996)	1,051	2.26
Laotian (10)	10	0.02
Malaysian (32)	35	0.08
Pakistani (80)	92	0.20
Sri Lankan (6)	6	0.01
Taiwanese (139)	157	0.34
Thai (98)	104	0.22
Vietnamese (100)	111	0.24
Other Asian, specified (24)	25	0.05
Other Asian, not specified (63)	131	0.28
Assyrian/Chaldean/Syriac	17	0.04
Australian	30	0.06
Austrian	220	0.47
Belgian	234	0.50
Brazilian	74	0.16
British	318	0.68
Bulgarian	12	0.03
Canadian	313	0.67
Croatian	102	0.22
Czech	250	0.54
Czechoslovakian	95	0.20
Danish	230	0.49
Dutch	1,484	3.18
Eastern European	100	0.21

Notes: 1. Figures in the "Number" column do not add up to the total population due to: a) Ancestry/Race overlap — e.g. persons can report being both White and Irish, b) persons of Hispanic origin can report being any race, c) persons reporting two ancestries are counted in both categories. 2. Numbers in parentheses indicate the number of persons reporting this ancestry/race alone, not in combination with any other ancestry/race. 3. Refer to the Explanation of Data in the front of the book for more detailed information.

English	4,711	10.09
European	487	1.04
Finnish	398	0.85
French, except Basque	1,628	3.49
French Canadian	641	1.37
German	9,679	20.72
Greek	440	0.94
Hawaii Native/Pacific Islander:	83	0.18
Micronesian: (7)	11	0.02
Guamanian/Chamorro (6)	10	0.02
Other Micronesian (1)	1	0.00
Polynesian: (22)	36	0.08
Native Hawaiian (11)	19	0.04
Samoan (11)	12	0.03
Other Polynesian	5	0.01
Other Pac. Isl., not spec. (9)	36	0.08
Hispanic or Latino:	1,252	2.69
Central American:	61	0.13
Costa Rican	9	0.02
Guatemalan	13	0.03
Honduran	8	0.02
Nicaraguan	9	0.02
Panamanian	12	0.03
Salvadoran	5	0.01
Other Central American	5	0.01
Cuban	57	0.12
Dominican Republic	12	0.03
Mexican	626	1.35
Puerto Rican	130	0.28
South American:	140	0.30
Argentinean	22	0.05
Bolivian	2	0.00
Chilean	11	0.02
Colombian	34	0.07
Ecuadorian	21	0.05
Paraguayan	5	0.01
Peruvian	12	0.03
Uruguayan	1	0.00
Venezuelan	20	0.04
Other South American	12	0.03
Other Hispanic or Latino	226	0.49
Hungarian	446	0.95
Icelander	6	0.01
Iranian	132	0.28
Irish	5,721	12.25
Israeli	32	0.07
Italian	2,911	6.23
Latvian	38	0.08
Lithuanian	154	0.33
Macedonian	54	0.12
Maltese	47	0.10
New Zealander	15	0.03
Northern European	78	0.17
Norwegian	543	1.16
Pennsylvania German	7	0.01
Polish	3,943	8.44
Portuguese	16	0.03
Romanian	130	0.28
Russian	736	1.58
Scandinavian	84	0.18
Scotch-Irish	816	1.75
Scottish	1,314	2.81
Serbian	11	0.02
Slavic	57	0.12
Slovak	110	0.24
Slovene	44	0.09
Swedish	927	1.98
Swiss	127	0.27
Turkish	43	0.09
Ukrainian	299	0.64
United States or American	953	2.04
Welsh	437	0.94
West Indian, excl. Hispanic:	129	0.28
Barbadian	14	0.03
Haitian	39	0.08
Jamaican	43	0.09
Trinidadian and Tobagonian	14	0.03
U.S. Virgin Islander	19	0.04
White:	38,465	82.68
Not Hispanic (36,919)	37,622	80.86
Hispanic (726)	843	1.81
Yugoslavian	86	0.18

Eastpointe

Place Type: City
County: Macomb
Population: 34,077

Ancestry/Race	Number	%
African American/Black:	1,740	5.11
Not Hispanic (1,594)	1,725	5.06
Hispanic (7)	15	0.04
African, sub-Saharan:	124	0.36
African	108	0.32
Nigerian	16	0.05
Am. Ind. or Alaska Nat., not spec.	124	0.36
Albanian	89	0.26
American Indian tribes, specified:	294	0.86
Apache (2)	9	0.03
Blackfeet (5)	14	0.04
Cherokee (24)	118	0.35
Chickasaw	2	0.01
Chippewa (33)	55	0.16
Choctaw	2	0.01
Cree	1	0.00
Delaware (2)	2	0.01
Iroquois (11)	19	0.06
Latin American Indians (1)	8	0.02
Lumbee (12)	24	0.07
Navajo (1)	2	0.01
Osage (1)	1	0.00
Ottawa (6)	7	0.02
Paiute (1)	1	0.00
Potawatomi	1	0.00
Seminole (2)	2	0.01
Shoshone (1)	1	0.00
Sioux (3)	4	0.01
All other tribes (7)	21	0.06
American Indian tribes, not spec.	3	0.01
Arab:	631	1.85
Arab/Arabic	85	0.25
Egyptian	13	0.04
Jordanian	13	0.04
Lebanese	421	1.24
Palestinian	6	0.02
Syrian	69	0.20
Other Arab	24	0.07
Armenian	47	0.14
Asian:	394	1.16
Cambodian (34)	39	0.11
Chinese, ex. Taiwanese (21)	30	0.09
Filipino (58)	98	0.29
Hmong (52)	52	0.15
Indian (10)	19	0.06
Indonesian (1)	2	0.01
Japanese (12)	22	0.06
Korean (24)	34	0.10
Laotian (27)	29	0.09
Pakistani (2)	9	0.03
Thai (3)	4	0.01
Vietnamese (35)	37	0.11
Other Asian, specified	3	0.01
Other Asian, not specified (12)	16	0.05
Assyrian/Chaldean/Syriac	61	0.18
Austrian	98	0.29
Belgian	852	2.50
British	41	0.12
Bulgarian	5	0.01
Canadian	146	0.43
Croatian	72	0.21
Cypriot	13	0.04
Czech	187	0.55
Czechoslovakian	108	0.32
Danish	56	0.16
Dutch	437	1.28
Eastern European	5	0.01
English	2,778	8.15
European	70	0.21
Finnish	203	0.60
French, except Basque	2,142	6.29
French Canadian	950	2.79
German	9,238	27.11
Greek	427	1.25
Hawaii Native/Pacific Islander:	23	0.07
Micronesian:	5	0.01
Guamanian/Chamorro	5	0.01
Polynesian: (1)	3	0.01
Native Hawaiian	2	0.01
Samoan (1)	1	0.00
Other Pac. Isl., specified	3	0.01
Other Pac. Isl., not spec. (1)	12	0.04
Hispanic or Latino:	453	1.33
Central American:	9	0.03
Costa Rican	1	0.00
Guatemalan	1	0.00
Honduran	2	0.01
Nicaraguan	2	0.01
Panamanian	3	0.01
Cuban	16	0.05
Dominican Republic	1	0.00
Mexican	283	0.83
Puerto Rican	39	0.11
South American:	14	0.04
Chilean	4	0.01
Colombian	6	0.02
Ecuadorian	1	0.00
Venezuelan	3	0.01
Other Hispanic or Latino	91	0.27
Hungarian	308	0.90
Irish	4,743	13.92
Italian	5,707	16.75
Latvian	12	0.04
Lithuanian	161	0.47
Macedonian	7	0.02
Maltese	24	0.07
Northern European	4	0.01
Norwegian	148	0.43
Pennsylvania German	26	0.08
Polish	6,278	18.42
Portuguese	31	0.09
Romanian	124	0.36
Russian	299	0.88
Scandinavian	13	0.04
Scotch-Irish	600	1.76
Scottish	780	2.29
Serbian	63	0.18
Slavic	16	0.05
Slovak	156	0.46
Slovene	12	0.04
Swedish	277	0.81
Swiss	21	0.06
Ukrainian	253	0.74
United States or American	1,200	3.52
Welsh	177	0.52
West Indian, excl. Hispanic:	16	0.05
Jamaican	7	0.02
West Indian	9	0.03
White:	31,920	93.67
Not Hispanic (31,094)	31,562	92.62
Hispanic (301)	358	1.05
Yugoslavian	103	0.30

Ecorse

Place Type: City
County: Wayne
Population: 11,229

Ancestry/Race	Number	%
African American/Black:	4,686	41.73
Not Hispanic (4,533)	4,652	41.43
Hispanic (22)	34	0.30
African, sub-Saharan:	66	0.59
African	66	0.59
Alaska Native tribes, specified:	3	0.03
Tlingit-Haida (3)	3	0.03
Am. Ind. or Alaska Nat., not spec.	85	0.76
American Indian tribes, specified:	119	1.06
Apache	2	0.02

Notes: 1. Figures in the "Number" column do not add up to the total population due to: a) Ancestry/Race overlap — e.g. persons can report being both White and Irish, b) persons of Hispanic origin can report being any race, c) persons reporting two ancestries are counted in both categories. 2. Numbers in parentheses indicate the number of persons reporting this ancestry/race alone, not in combination with any other ancestry/race. 3. Refer to the Explanation of Data in the front of the book for more detailed information.

Ancestry/Race	Number	%
Blackfeet (2)	5	0.04
Cherokee (11)	62	0.55
Chippewa (7)	10	0.09
Choctaw (1)	4	0.04
Crow (1)	1	0.01
Iroquois (2)	2	0.02
Latin American Indians (1)	7	0.06
Lumbee (1)	4	0.04
Navajo	1	0.01
Osage	4	0.04
Paiute	1	0.01
Pueblo (2)	8	0.07
Seminole	3	0.03
Sioux (1)	1	0.01
All other tribes (2)	4	0.04
American Indian tribes, not spec.	8	0.07
Arab:	82	0.73
Arab/Arabic	27	0.24
Lebanese	37	0.33
Moroccan	7	0.06
Other Arab	11	0.10
Armenian	7	0.06
Asian:	44	0.39
Chinese, ex. Taiwanese	2	0.02
Filipino (5)	6	0.05
Indian (2)	9	0.08
Japanese (2)	2	0.02
Korean (2)	5	0.04
Pakistani (10)	10	0.09
Other Asian, specified	5	0.04
Other Asian, not specified	5	0.04
Austrian	4	0.04
British	21	0.19
Canadian	18	0.16
Croatian	7	0.06
Czech	7	0.06
Czechoslovakian	6	0.05
Danish	4	0.04
Dutch	45	0.40
English	315	2.81
European	58	0.52
Finnish	24	0.21
French, except Basque	476	4.24
French Canadian	236	2.10
German	796	7.09
Greek	131	1.17
Hawaii Native/Pacific Islander:	22	0.20
Micronesian:	5	0.04
Guamanian/Chamorro	5	0.04
Polynesian: (2)	8	0.07
Native Hawaiian (1)	4	0.04
Samoan (1)	4	0.04
Other Pac. Isl., specified	5	0.04
Other Pac. Isl., not spec.	4	0.04
Hispanic or Latino:	1,004	8.94
Central American:	1	0.01
Salvadoran	1	0.01
Cuban	5	0.04
Mexican	789	7.03
Puerto Rican	58	0.52
South American:	1	0.01
Colombian	1	0.01
Other Hispanic or Latino	150	1.34
Hungarian	159	1.42
Irish	811	7.22
Italian	243	2.16
Lithuanian	12	0.11
Maltese	7	0.06
Norwegian	66	0.59
Pennsylvania German	14	0.12
Polish	450	4.01
Portuguese	7	0.06
Romanian	75	0.67
Russian	11	0.10
Scotch-Irish	58	0.52
Scottish	146	1.30
Slovak	13	0.12
Swedish	12	0.11
Swiss	24	0.21
Ukrainian	47	0.42
United States or American	787	7.01
Welsh	24	0.21
West Indian, excl. Hispanic:	5	0.04
British West Indian	5	0.04
White:	6,144	54.72
Not Hispanic (5,313)	5,538	49.32
Hispanic (546)	606	5.40

Emmett

Place Type: Township
County: Calhoun
Population: 11,979

Ancestry/Race	Number	%
African American/Black:	317	2.65
Not Hispanic (248)	303	2.53
Hispanic (5)	14	0.12
African, sub-Saharan:	20	0.17
African	20	0.17
Alaska Native tribes, specified:	1	0.01
Alaska Athabascan	1	0.01
Am. Ind. or Alaska Nat., not spec.	60	0.50
American Indian tribes, specified:	107	0.89
Blackfeet (7)	15	0.13
Cherokee (6)	39	0.33
Chickasaw (3)	3	0.03
Chippewa (14)	16	0.13
Crow	1	0.01
Iroquois	3	0.03
Latin American Indians (3)	5	0.04
Menominee	1	0.01
Ottawa (4)	4	0.03
Potawatomi (3)	13	0.11
Sioux (2)	5	0.04
All other tribes (2)	2	0.02
American Indian tribes, not spec.	6	0.05
Arab:	5	0.04
Arab/Arabic	5	0.04
Armenian	11	0.09
Asian:	176	1.47
Chinese, ex. Taiwanese (11)	13	0.11
Filipino (18)	23	0.19
Indian (71)	74	0.62
Japanese (18)	18	0.15
Korean (32)	38	0.32
Pakistani	1	0.01
Vietnamese (2)	2	0.02
Other Asian, not specified (1)	7	0.06
Austrian	17	0.14
Belgian	4	0.03
British	14	0.12
Canadian	30	0.25
Croatian	67	0.56
Czech	28	0.23
Czechoslovakian	22	0.18
Danish	86	0.71
Dutch	490	4.07
English	1,438	11.95
European	142	1.18
Finnish	120	1.00
French, except Basque	500	4.15
French Canadian	103	0.86
German	2,512	20.87
Greek	51	0.42
Hawaii Native/Pacific Islander:	11	0.09
Micronesian: (1)	1	0.01
Guamanian/Chamorro (1)	1	0.01
Polynesian: (2)	8	0.07
Native Hawaiian (2)	5	0.04
Samoan	3	0.03
Other Pac. Isl., not spec.	2	0.02
Hispanic or Latino:	277	2.31
Central American:	10	0.08
Costa Rican	7	0.06
Honduran	1	0.01
Panamanian	2	0.02
Cuban	9	0.08
Mexican	187	1.56
Puerto Rican	17	0.14
South American:	3	0.03
Chilean	1	0.01
Ecuadorian	2	0.02
Other Hispanic or Latino	51	0.43
Hungarian	50	0.42
Icelander	5	0.04
Irish	1,308	10.87
Italian	289	2.40
Lithuanian	64	0.53
Macedonian	4	0.03
Norwegian	119	0.99
Pennsylvania German	31	0.26
Polish	314	2.61
Portuguese	8	0.07
Romanian	16	0.13
Russian	41	0.34
Scotch-Irish	142	1.18
Scottish	189	1.57
Slovak	5	0.04
Swedish	145	1.20
Swiss	6	0.05
Turkish	5	0.04
Ukrainian	53	0.44
United States or American	1,177	9.78
Welsh	96	0.80
White:	11,371	94.92
Not Hispanic (11,062)	11,209	93.57
Hispanic (139)	162	1.35
Yugoslavian	28	0.23

Escanaba

Place Type: City
County: Delta
Population: 13,140

Ancestry/Race	Number	%
African American/Black:	29	0.22
Not Hispanic (14)	27	0.21
Hispanic	2	0.02
African, sub-Saharan:	4	0.03
Nigerian	4	0.03
Alaska Native tribes, specified:	3	0.02
Tlingit-Haida (3)	3	0.02
Alaska Native tribes, not specified	2	0.02
Am. Ind. or Alaska Nat., not spec.	86	0.65
American Indian tribes, specified:	369	2.81
Blackfeet	1	0.01
Cherokee (11)	17	0.13
Cheyenne (2)	2	0.02
Chippewa (166)	222	1.69
Choctaw	3	0.02
Creek	1	0.01
Kiowa (1)	1	0.01
Latin American Indians	2	0.02
Menominee (1)	1	0.01
Navajo (1)	4	0.03
Ottawa (22)	28	0.21
Paiute (1)	1	0.01
Pima	1	0.01
Potawatomi (55)	70	0.53
Sioux (4)	6	0.05
All other tribes (7)	9	0.07
American Indian tribes, not spec.	6	0.05
Arab:	40	0.30
Lebanese	40	0.30
Asian:	54	0.41
Chinese, ex. Taiwanese (6)	6	0.05
Filipino (7)	7	0.05
Indian (12)	12	0.09
Japanese (1)	4	0.03
Korean (11)	16	0.12
Vietnamese (5)	5	0.04
Other Asian, specified (1)	1	0.01
Other Asian, not specified	3	0.02
Australian	19	0.14
Austrian	23	0.18
Belgian	392	2.98
Brazilian	10	0.08
British	29	0.22

Notes: 1. Figures in the "Number" column do not add up to the total population due to: a) Ancestry/Race overlap — e.g. persons can report being both White and Irish, b) persons of Hispanic origin can report being any race, c) persons reporting two ancestries are counted in both categories. 2. Numbers in parentheses indicate the number of persons reporting this ancestry/race alone, not in combination with any other ancestry/race. 3. Refer to the Explanation of Data in the front of the book for more detailed information.

Ancestry/Race	Number	%
Canadian	31	0.24
Croatian	330	2.51
Czech	48	0.37
Czechoslovakian	12	0.09
Danish	136	1.04
Dutch	273	2.08
English	1,018	7.75
European	61	0.46
Finnish	549	4.18
French, except Basque	2,659	20.25
French Canadian	1,386	10.55
German	2,810	21.40
Greek	50	0.38
Hawaii Native/Pacific Islander:	4	0.03
Polynesian: (3)	4	0.03
Native Hawaiian (3)	4	0.03
Hispanic or Latino:	87	0.66
Cuban	6	0.05
Mexican	51	0.39
Puerto Rican	15	0.11
South American:	2	0.02
Colombian	1	0.01
Venezuelan	1	0.01
Other Hispanic or Latino	13	0.10
Hungarian	17	0.13
Iranian	23	0.18
Irish	1,207	9.19
Italian	469	3.57
Lithuanian	34	0.26
Luxemburger	37	0.28
Norwegian	634	4.83
Polish	600	4.57
Portuguese	16	0.12
Russian	36	0.27
Scandinavian	30	0.23
Scotch-Irish	155	1.18
Scottish	170	1.29
Serbian	12	0.09
Slavic	13	0.10
Slovene	17	0.13
Swedish	1,457	11.09
Swiss	34	0.26
Ukrainian	7	0.05
United States or American	371	2.82
Welsh	22	0.17
West Indian, excl. Hispanic:	7	0.05
Haitian	4	0.03
Jamaican	3	0.02
White:	12,709	96.72
Not Hispanic (12,521)	12,651	96.28
Hispanic (49)	58	0.44
Yugoslavian	18	0.14

Farmington Hills

Place Type: City
County: Oakland
Population: 82,111

Ancestry/Race	Number	%
African American/Black:	6,079	7.40
Not Hispanic (5,681)	6,040	7.36
Hispanic (18)	39	0.05
African, sub-Saharan:	350	0.43
African	229	0.28
Cape Verdean	25	0.03
Ethiopian	8	0.01
Liberian	18	0.02
Nigerian	28	0.03
Ugandan	42	0.05
Alaska Native tribes, specified:	2	0.00
Aleut (1)	2	0.00
Am. Ind. or Alaska Nat., not spec.	146	0.18
Albanian	509	0.62
American Indian tribes, specified:	305	0.37
Apache (2)	5	0.01
Blackfeet (3)	22	0.03
Cherokee (25)	115	0.14
Chippewa (38)	82	0.10
Choctaw	7	0.01
Cree (1)	1	0.00
Creek	7	0.01
Delaware	4	0.00
Iroquois (6)	13	0.02
Latin American Indians (4)	7	0.01
Lumbee	2	0.00
Ottawa (2)	5	0.01
Pueblo	1	0.00
Seminole (1)	12	0.01
Sioux (3)	5	0.01
Yuman (1)	1	0.00
All other tribes (9)	16	0.02
American Indian tribes, not spec.	19	0.02
Arab:	2,082	2.54
Arab/Arabic	366	0.45
Egyptian	12	0.01
Iraqi	499	0.61
Jordanian	63	0.08
Lebanese	716	0.87
Palestinian	107	0.13
Syrian	245	0.30
Other Arab	74	0.09
Armenian	1,009	1.23
Asian:	6,780	8.26
Bangladeshi (3)	5	0.01
Cambodian (1)	1	0.00
Chinese, ex. Taiwanese (852)	936	1.14
Filipino (394)	479	0.58
Hmong (10)	10	0.01
Indian (3,364)	3,482	4.24
Indonesian (6)	8	0.01
Japanese (610)	679	0.83
Korean (523)	560	0.68
Laotian (9)	11	0.01
Malaysian (6)	6	0.01
Pakistani (184)	223	0.27
Sri Lankan (21)	27	0.03
Taiwanese (32)	56	0.07
Thai (18)	22	0.03
Vietnamese (46)	55	0.07
Other Asian, specified (7)	8	0.01
Other Asian, not specified (45)	212	0.26
Assyrian/Chaldean/Syriac	2,499	3.04
Australian	31	0.04
Austrian	603	0.73
Belgian	237	0.29
Brazilian	9	0.01
British	441	0.54
Bulgarian	11	0.01
Canadian	739	0.90
Celtic	6	0.01
Croatian	169	0.21
Czech	374	0.46
Czechoslovakian	208	0.25
Danish	234	0.28
Dutch	1,085	1.32
Eastern European	433	0.53
English	8,258	10.06
Estonian	40	0.05
European	645	0.79
Finnish	1,044	1.27
French, except Basque	2,722	3.32
French Canadian	1,227	1.49
German	14,187	17.28
German Russian	9	0.01
Greek	770	0.94
Guyanese	26	0.03
Hawaii Native/Pacific Islander:	48	0.06
Micronesian: (7)	11	0.01
Guamanian/Chamorro (4)	5	0.01
Other Micronesian (3)	6	0.01
Polynesian: (6)	12	0.01
Native Hawaiian (5)	11	0.01
Other Polynesian (1)	1	0.00
Other Pac. Isl., specified	1	0.00
Other Pac. Isl., not spec. (2)	24	0.03
Hispanic or Latino:	1,211	1.47
Central American:	26	0.03
Costa Rican	2	0.00
Guatemalan	8	0.01
Honduran	4	0.00
Nicaraguan	5	0.01
Panamanian	4	0.00
Salvadoran	3	0.00
Cuban	58	0.07
Dominican Republic	7	0.01
Mexican	593	0.72
Puerto Rican	108	0.13
South American:	130	0.16
Argentinean	23	0.03
Bolivian	1	0.00
Chilean	9	0.01
Colombian	41	0.05
Ecuadorian	13	0.02
Paraguayan	3	0.00
Peruvian	15	0.02
Uruguayan	7	0.01
Venezuelan	12	0.01
Other South American	6	0.01
Other Hispanic or Latino	289	0.35
Hungarian	1,490	1.81
Iranian	127	0.15
Irish	9,966	12.14
Israeli	82	0.10
Italian	4,909	5.98
Latvian	86	0.10
Lithuanian	649	0.79
Luxemburger	18	0.02
Macedonian	69	0.08
Maltese	145	0.18
Northern European	37	0.05
Norwegian	621	0.76
Pennsylvania German	31	0.04
Polish	9,011	10.97
Portuguese	83	0.10
Romanian	508	0.62
Russian	3,773	4.59
Scandinavian	136	0.17
Scotch-Irish	1,303	1.59
Scottish	2,409	2.93
Serbian	97	0.12
Slavic	103	0.13
Slovak	357	0.43
Slovene	97	0.12
Swedish	1,228	1.50
Swiss	284	0.35
Turkish	78	0.09
Ukrainian	672	0.82
United States or American	3,049	3.71
Welsh	534	0.65
West Indian, excl. Hispanic:	107	0.13
Bahamian	9	0.01
Haitian	32	0.04
Jamaican	66	0.08
White:	69,510	84.65
Not Hispanic (67,250)	68,579	83.52
Hispanic (857)	931	1.13
Yugoslavian	265	0.32

Farmington

Place Type: City
County: Oakland
Population: 10,423

Ancestry/Race	Number	%
African American/Black:	303	2.91
Not Hispanic (280)	298	2.86
Hispanic (5)	5	0.05
African, sub-Saharan:	18	0.17
Somalian	18	0.17
Am. Ind. or Alaska Nat., not spec.	20	0.19
Albanian	22	0.21
American Indian tribes, specified:	19	0.18
Blackfeet	1	0.01
Cherokee (2)	4	0.04
Chippewa (6)	8	0.08
Choctaw (1)	1	0.01
Iroquois (1)	1	0.01
Latin American Indians	1	0.01

Notes: 1. Figures in the "Number" column do not add up to the total population due to: a) Ancestry/Race overlap — e.g. persons can report being both White and Irish, b) persons of Hispanic origin can report being any race, c) persons reporting two ancestries are counted in both categories. 2. Numbers in parentheses indicate the number of persons reporting this ancestry/race alone, not in combination with any other ancestry/race. 3. Refer to the Explanation of Data in the front of the book for more detailed information.

Ancestry/Race	Number	%
Ottawa (1)	1	0.01
All other tribes (1)	2	0.02
American Indian tribes, not spec.	4	0.04
Arab:	181	1.74
Arab/Arabic	24	0.23
Egyptian	29	0.28
Lebanese	84	0.81
Palestinian	20	0.19
Syrian	24	0.23
Armenian	45	0.43
Asian:	1,101	10.56
Bangladeshi (5)	5	0.05
Chinese, ex. Taiwanese (73)	85	0.82
Filipino (37)	43	0.41
Indian (800)	813	7.80
Japanese (32)	38	0.36
Korean (32)	34	0.33
Malaysian	1	0.01
Pakistani (40)	47	0.45
Sri Lankan (15)	15	0.14
Taiwanese	3	0.03
Vietnamese (4)	5	0.05
Other Asian, specified (4)	4	0.04
Other Asian, not specified (3)	8	0.08
Assyrian/Chaldean/Syriac	72	0.69
Austrian	29	0.28
Belgian	61	0.59
British	33	0.32
Bulgarian	25	0.24
Canadian	71	0.68
Carpatho Rusyn	9	0.09
Croatian	50	0.48
Czech	44	0.42
Czechoslovakian	15	0.14
Danish	93	0.89
Dutch	283	2.72
Eastern European	9	0.09
English	1,468	14.08
European	101	0.97
Finnish	175	1.68
French, except Basque	574	5.51
French Canadian	103	0.99
German	2,519	24.17
Greek	35	0.34
Hawaii Native/Pacific Islander:	2	0.02
Polynesian: (2)	2	0.02
Native Hawaiian (1)	1	0.01
Samoan (1)	1	0.01
Hispanic or Latino:	125	1.20
Central American:	1	0.01
Salvadoran	1	0.01
Cuban	3	0.03
Dominican Republic	1	0.01
Mexican	59	0.57
Puerto Rican	13	0.12
South American:	21	0.20
Argentinean	4	0.04
Chilean	4	0.04
Colombian	9	0.09
Ecuadorian	2	0.02
Peruvian	2	0.02
Other Hispanic or Latino	27	0.26
Hungarian	98	0.94
Irish	1,895	18.18
Israeli	9	0.09
Italian	501	4.81
Latvian	13	0.12
Lithuanian	106	1.02
Macedonian	7	0.07
Maltese	46	0.44
Northern European	10	0.10
Norwegian	196	1.88
Polish	951	9.12
Portuguese	6	0.06
Romanian	91	0.87
Russian	110	1.06
Scandinavian	31	0.30
Scotch-Irish	232	2.23
Scottish	482	4.62
Slavic	23	0.22
Slovak	40	0.38
Slovene	21	0.20
Swedish	216	2.07
Swiss	50	0.48
Ukrainian	62	0.59
United States or American	362	3.47
Welsh	128	1.23
White:	9,016	86.50
Not Hispanic (8,839)	8,918	85.56
Hispanic (90)	98	0.94
Yugoslavian	47	0.45

Fenton

Place Type: City
County: Genesee
Population: 10,582

Ancestry/Race	Number	%
African American/Black:	97	0.92
Not Hispanic (62)	95	0.90
Hispanic (1)	2	0.02
African, sub-Saharan:	10	0.09
Sudanese	10	0.09
Am. Ind. or Alaska Nat., not spec.	23	0.22
Albanian	14	0.13
American Indian tribes, specified:	50	0.47
Blackfeet (2)	3	0.03
Cherokee (6)	14	0.13
Chippewa (18)	24	0.23
Iroquois (1)	1	0.01
Lumbee (2)	2	0.02
Menominee (3)	3	0.03
Shoshone	1	0.01
Sioux	1	0.01
All other tribes (1)	1	0.01
American Indian tribes, not spec.	4	0.04
Arab:	135	1.28
Arab/Arabic	8	0.08
Lebanese	91	0.86
Palestinian	36	0.34
Asian:	129	1.22
Chinese, ex. Taiwanese (18)	24	0.23
Filipino (10)	14	0.13
Hmong (5)	5	0.05
Indian (34)	36	0.34
Japanese (4)	7	0.07
Korean (17)	23	0.22
Laotian (8)	8	0.08
Malaysian (1)	3	0.03
Sri Lankan (1)	1	0.01
Thai (1)	1	0.01
Other Asian, not specified (1)	7	0.07
Austrian	26	0.25
Belgian	14	0.13
British	68	0.64
Canadian	51	0.48
Croatian	9	0.09
Czech	66	0.62
Czechoslovakian	28	0.26
Danish	89	0.84
Dutch	315	2.98
English	1,555	14.69
European	114	1.08
Finnish	121	1.14
French, except Basque	744	7.03
French Canadian	388	3.67
German	2,111	19.95
Greek	74	0.70
Hawaii Native/Pacific Islander:	10	0.09
Micronesian:	2	0.02
Guamanian/Chamorro	2	0.02
Polynesian:	8	0.08
Native Hawaiian	8	0.08
Hispanic or Latino:	191	1.80
Central American:	3	0.03
Guatemalan	1	0.01
Panamanian	2	0.02
Cuban	8	0.08
Mexican	125	1.18
Puerto Rican	15	0.14
South American:	10	0.09
Colombian	9	0.09
Ecuadorian	1	0.01
Other Hispanic or Latino	30	0.28
Hungarian	139	1.31
Iranian	10	0.09
Irish	1,461	13.81
Italian	470	4.44
Lithuanian	60	0.57
Maltese	20	0.19
Norwegian	99	0.94
Pennsylvania German	10	0.09
Polish	705	6.66
Romanian	14	0.13
Russian	17	0.16
Scandinavian	41	0.39
Scotch-Irish	346	3.27
Scottish	376	3.55
Serbian	5	0.05
Slavic	24	0.23
Slovak	29	0.27
Slovene	7	0.07
Swedish	213	2.01
Swiss	22	0.21
Ukrainian	20	0.19
United States or American	736	6.96
Welsh	51	0.48
West Indian, excl. Hispanic:	29	0.27
Jamaican	29	0.27
White:	10,304	97.37
Not Hispanic (10,071)	10,163	96.04
Hispanic (114)	141	1.33
Yugoslavian	5	0.05

Fenton

Place Type: Township
County: Genesee
Population: 12,968

Ancestry/Race	Number	%
African American/Black:	56	0.43
Not Hispanic (33)	53	0.41
Hispanic (3)	3	0.02
Am. Ind. or Alaska Nat., not spec.	30	0.23
American Indian tribes, specified:	107	0.83
Apache (3)	3	0.02
Blackfeet	3	0.02
Cherokee (9)	27	0.21
Chippewa (16)	33	0.25
Choctaw	4	0.03
Comanche	7	0.05
Cree	1	0.01
Crow	3	0.02
Iroquois (1)	2	0.02
Menominee	5	0.04
Osage	1	0.01
Ottawa (3)	4	0.03
Sioux	8	0.06
Yaqui	1	0.01
All other tribes (4)	5	0.04
American Indian tribes, not spec.	1	0.01
Arab:	72	0.56
Arab/Arabic	39	0.30
Lebanese	33	0.26
Armenian	43	0.33
Asian:	126	0.97
Chinese, ex. Taiwanese (21)	21	0.16
Filipino (12)	16	0.12
Indian (28)	30	0.23
Japanese (10)	17	0.13
Korean (19)	29	0.22
Taiwanese (5)	5	0.04
Vietnamese (2)	3	0.02
Other Asian, not specified (3)	5	0.04
Assyrian/Chaldean/Syriac	23	0.18
Belgian	86	0.67
British	24	0.19
Canadian	134	1.04

Notes: 1. Figures in the "Number" column do not add up to the total population due to: a) Ancestry/Race overlap — e.g. persons can report being both White and Irish, b) persons of Hispanic origin can report being any race, c) persons reporting two ancestries are counted in both categories. 2. Numbers in parentheses indicate the number of persons reporting this ancestry/race alone, not in combination with any other ancestry/race. 3. Refer to the Explanation of Data in the front of the book for more detailed information.

Croatian	39	0.30
Czech	94	0.73
Czechoslovakian	31	0.24
Danish	82	0.63
Dutch	402	3.11
English	1,957	15.13
European	164	1.27
Finnish	97	0.75
French, except Basque	902	6.97
French Canadian	248	1.92
German	2,969	22.96
Greek	16	0.12
Hawaii Native/Pacific Islander:	9	0.07
Polynesian: (4)	9	0.07
Native Hawaiian (3)	8	0.06
Samoan (1)	1	0.01
Hispanic or Latino:	153	1.18
Central American:	3	0.02
Guatemalan	2	0.02
Honduran	1	0.01
Cuban	6	0.05
Mexican	107	0.83
Puerto Rican	3	0.02
South American:	6	0.05
Argentinean	1	0.01
Chilean	3	0.02
Colombian	1	0.01
Peruvian	1	0.01
Other Hispanic or Latino	28	0.22
Hungarian	229	1.77
Irish	2,069	16.00
Italian	535	4.14
Latvian	7	0.05
Lithuanian	34	0.26
Macedonian	12	0.09
Maltese	38	0.29
Norwegian	227	1.76
Polish	1,163	8.99
Romanian	50	0.39
Russian	46	0.36
Scandinavian	5	0.04
Scotch-Irish	210	1.62
Scottish	444	3.43
Serbian	26	0.20
Slavic	28	0.22
Slovak	75	0.58
Swedish	325	2.51
Swiss	32	0.25
Ukrainian	38	0.29
United States or American	1,192	9.22
Welsh	88	0.68
White:	12,729	98.16
Not Hispanic (12,500)	12,626	97.36
Hispanic (82)	103	0.79
Yugoslavian	24	0.19

Ferndale

Place Type: City
County: Oakland
Population: 22,105

Ancestry/Race	Number	%
Acadian/Cajun	12	0.05
African American/Black:	942	4.26
Not Hispanic (754)	930	4.21
Hispanic (3)	12	0.05
African, sub-Saharan:	47	0.21
African	47	0.21
Am. Ind. or Alaska Nat., not spec.	113	0.51
Albanian	29	0.13
American Indian tribes, specified:	251	1.14
Apache	3	0.01
Blackfeet (2)	15	0.07
Cherokee (26)	113	0.51
Cheyenne	1	0.00
Chippewa (25)	58	0.26
Choctaw	2	0.01
Comanche (1)	2	0.01
Cree	1	0.00
Creek	2	0.01
Crow	1	0.00
Iroquois (10)	14	0.06
Latin American Indians (2)	4	0.02
Lumbee (1)	5	0.02
Ottawa (9)	13	0.06
Potawatomi (1)	3	0.01
Pueblo (1)	1	0.00
Seminole (1)	1	0.00
Sioux	4	0.02
All other tribes (5)	8	0.04
American Indian tribes, not spec.	4	0.02
Arab:	290	1.31
Arab/Arabic	94	0.43
Egyptian	12	0.05
Jordanian	7	0.03
Lebanese	129	0.58
Syrian	37	0.17
Other Arab	11	0.05
Armenian	30	0.14
Asian:	387	1.75
Chinese, ex. Taiwanese (92)	110	0.50
Filipino (62)	83	0.38
Hmong (5)	5	0.02
Indian (26)	33	0.15
Japanese (8)	24	0.11
Korean (27)	38	0.17
Laotian	5	0.02
Pakistani (7)	8	0.04
Taiwanese (2)	2	0.01
Thai (8)	17	0.08
Vietnamese (27)	35	0.16
Other Asian, specified (2)	2	0.01
Other Asian, not specified (9)	25	0.11
Assyrian/Chaldean/Syriac	182	0.82
Australian	32	0.14
Austrian	34	0.15
Belgian	81	0.37
Brazilian	5	0.02
British	114	0.52
Canadian	189	0.86
Carpatho Rusyn	18	0.08
Celtic	20	0.09
Croatian	32	0.14
Czech	116	0.52
Czechoslovakian	25	0.11
Danish	43	0.19
Dutch	395	1.79
Eastern European	7	0.03
English	2,667	12.07
European	323	1.46
Finnish	363	1.64
French, except Basque	1,396	6.32
French Canadian	697	3.15
German	4,423	20.01
Greek	203	0.92
Hawaii Native/Pacific Islander:	19	0.09
Micronesian: (3)	5	0.02
Guamanian/Chamorro (3)	5	0.02
Polynesian: (2)	4	0.02
Native Hawaiian (2)	3	0.01
Samoan	1	0.00
Other Pac. Isl., not spec.	10	0.05
Hispanic or Latino:	399	1.81
Central American:	9	0.04
Costa Rican	1	0.00
Guatemalan	2	0.01
Honduran	1	0.00
Nicaraguan	2	0.01
Salvadoran	1	0.00
Other Central American	2	0.01
Cuban	14	0.06
Dominican Republic	3	0.01
Mexican	247	1.12
Puerto Rican	33	0.15
South American:	16	0.07
Argentinean	3	0.01
Chilean	1	0.00
Colombian	5	0.02
Ecuadorian	4	0.02
Peruvian	1	0.00
Venezuelan	1	0.00
Other South American	1	0.00
Other Hispanic or Latino	77	0.35
Hungarian	324	1.47
Icelander	6	0.03
Iranian	11	0.05
Irish	3,533	15.98
Israeli	6	0.03
Italian	1,207	5.46
Lithuanian	117	0.53
Macedonian	35	0.16
Maltese	35	0.16
Norwegian	175	0.79
Pennsylvania German	6	0.03
Polish	2,451	11.09
Portuguese	3	0.01
Romanian	111	0.50
Russian	278	1.26
Scandinavian	6	0.03
Scotch-Irish	461	2.09
Scottish	762	3.45
Serbian	67	0.30
Slavic	42	0.19
Slovak	81	0.37
Slovene	23	0.10
Swedish	204	0.92
Swiss	44	0.20
Ukrainian	186	0.84
United States or American	1,193	5.40
Welsh	109	0.49
West Indian, excl. Hispanic:	26	0.12
Jamaican	26	0.12
White:	20,750	93.87
Not Hispanic (19,971)	20,462	92.57
Hispanic (247)	288	1.30
Yugoslavian	34	0.15

Flint

Place Type: City
County: Genesee
Population: 124,943

Ancestry/Race	Number	%
Acadian/Cajun	5	0.00
African American/Black:	69,102	55.31
Not Hispanic (66,231)	68,602	54.91
Hispanic (329)	500	0.40
African, sub-Saharan:	3,131	2.51
African	3,081	2.47
Cape Verdean	7	0.01
Ethiopian	11	0.01
Kenyan	17	0.01
South African	11	0.01
Other sub-Saharan African	4	0.00
Alaska Native tribes, specified:	5	0.00
Eskimo (1)	5	0.00
Alaska Native tribes, not specified	3	0.00
Am. Ind. or Alaska Nat., not spec.	1,111	0.89
American Indian tribes, specified:	1,615	1.29
Apache (15)	48	0.04
Blackfeet (11)	160	0.13
Cherokee (152)	660	0.53
Cheyenne	11	0.01
Chickasaw (10)	20	0.02
Chippewa (191)	355	0.28
Choctaw (7)	52	0.04
Comanche (2)	5	0.00
Creek	9	0.01
Crow (1)	7	0.01
Delaware	3	0.00
Iroquois (10)	33	0.03
Latin American Indians (11)	38	0.03
Lumbee (4)	9	0.01
Navajo (9)	12	0.01
Osage (1)	4	0.00
Ottawa (30)	55	0.04
Paiute (1)	1	0.00
Pima (8)	8	0.01

Notes: 1. Figures in the "Number" column do not add up to the total population due to: a) Ancestry/Race overlap — e.g. persons can report being both White and Irish, b) persons of Hispanic origin can report being any race, c) persons reporting two ancestries are counted in both categories. 2. Numbers in parentheses indicate the number of persons reporting this ancestry/race alone, not in combination with any other ancestry/race. 3. Refer to the Explanation of Data in the front of the book for more detailed information.

Ancestry/Race	Number	%
Potawatomi (10)	18	0.01
Pueblo (1)	3	0.00
Seminole	18	0.01
Sioux (4)	30	0.02
Tohono O'Odham	1	0.00
Ute	2	0.00
Yaqui (3)	8	0.01
All other tribes (17)	45	0.04
American Indian tribes, not spec.	94	0.08
Arab:	417	0.33
Arab/Arabic	87	0.07
Egyptian	7	0.01
Iraqi	29	0.02
Lebanese	212	0.17
Moroccan	51	0.04
Palestinian	31	0.02
Armenian	25	0.02
Asian:	837	0.67
Cambodian (1)	1	0.00
Chinese, ex. Taiwanese (118)	152	0.12
Filipino (91)	152	0.12
Hmong (11)	11	0.01
Indian (120)	192	0.15
Indonesian (1)	1	0.00
Japanese (37)	63	0.05
Korean (50)	87	0.07
Laotian (8)	8	0.01
Malaysian (4)	4	0.00
Pakistani (7)	7	0.01
Thai (3)	12	0.01
Vietnamese (43)	58	0.05
Other Asian, specified (21)	30	0.02
Other Asian, not specified (25)	59	0.05
Assyrian/Chaldean/Syriac	123	0.10
Australian	10	0.01
Austrian	87	0.07
Belgian	106	0.08
British	230	0.18
Canadian	329	0.26
Croatian	57	0.05
Czech	222	0.18
Czechoslovakian	174	0.14
Danish	169	0.14
Dutch	1,133	0.91
Eastern European	6	0.00
English	6,125	4.90
Estonian	5	0.00
European	580	0.46
Finnish	178	0.14
French, except Basque	3,212	2.57
French Canadian	1,512	1.21
German	9,928	7.95
Greek	381	0.30
Hawaii Native/Pacific Islander:	95	0.08
Micronesian: (1)	8	0.01
Guamanian/Chamorro (1)	8	0.01
Polynesian: (7)	38	0.03
Native Hawaiian (6)	26	0.02
Samoan (1)	11	0.01
Tongan	1	0.00
Other Pac. Isl., specified	3	0.00
Other Pac. Isl., not spec. (11)	46	0.04
Hispanic or Latino:	3,742	2.99
Central American:	42	0.03
Costa Rican	4	0.00
Guatemalan	1	0.00
Honduran	12	0.01
Nicaraguan	2	0.00
Panamanian	17	0.01
Salvadoran	1	0.00
Other Central American	5	0.00
Cuban	50	0.04
Dominican Republic	3	0.00
Mexican	2,633	2.11
Puerto Rican	247	0.20
South American:	41	0.03
Argentinean	13	0.01
Bolivian	3	0.00
Colombian	12	0.01
Ecuadorian	4	0.00
Peruvian	5	0.00
Venezuelan	4	0.00
Other Hispanic or Latino	726	0.58
Hungarian	780	0.62
Iranian	15	0.01
Irish	7,005	5.61
Israeli	15	0.01
Italian	1,584	1.27
Lithuanian	74	0.06
Luxemburger	20	0.02
Macedonian	90	0.07
Maltese	6	0.00
Northern European	21	0.02
Norwegian	589	0.47
Pennsylvania German	38	0.03
Polish	2,959	2.37
Portuguese	48	0.04
Romanian	60	0.05
Russian	334	0.27
Scandinavian	81	0.06
Scotch-Irish	687	0.55
Scottish	1,315	1.05
Serbian	22	0.02
Slavic	33	0.03
Slovak	145	0.12
Slovene	10	0.01
Swedish	799	0.64
Swiss	50	0.04
Turkish	7	0.01
Ukrainian	211	0.17
United States or American	5,421	4.34
Welsh	316	0.25
West Indian, excl. Hispanic:	198	0.16
Bahamian	9	0.01
Jamaican	123	0.10
Trinidadian and Tobagonian	7	0.01
West Indian	59	0.05
White:	54,614	43.71
Not Hispanic (50,020)	52,568	42.07
Hispanic (1,690)	2,046	1.64
Yugoslavian	76	0.06

Flint

Place Type: Township
County: Genesee
Population: 33,691

Ancestry/Race	Number	%
Acadian/Cajun	6	0.02
African American/Black:	5,707	16.94
Not Hispanic (5,367)	5,622	16.69
Hispanic (63)	85	0.25
African, sub-Saharan:	250	0.74
African	208	0.62
Ghanian	30	0.09
Nigerian	12	0.04
Alaska Native tribes, specified:	7	0.02
Alaska Athabascan (2)	2	0.01
Eskimo	3	0.01
Tlingit-Haida (2)	2	0.01
Am. Ind. or Alaska Nat., not spec.	191	0.57
American Indian tribes, specified:	382	1.13
Apache (1)	9	0.03
Blackfeet (1)	27	0.08
Cherokee (39)	146	0.43
Chickasaw	2	0.01
Chippewa (54)	104	0.31
Choctaw	3	0.01
Cree (3)	7	0.02
Creek	3	0.01
Crow	5	0.01
Iroquois	12	0.04
Latin American Indians (6)	11	0.03
Navajo (2)	2	0.01
Osage	1	0.00
Ottawa (5)	11	0.03
Paiute	4	0.01
Potawatomi	6	0.02
Pueblo (2)	2	0.01
Seminole	5	0.01
Sioux (1)	7	0.02
All other tribes (4)	15	0.04
American Indian tribes, not spec.	13	0.04
Arab:	638	1.89
Arab/Arabic	176	0.52
Egyptian	84	0.25
Jordanian	34	0.10
Lebanese	252	0.75
Palestinian	22	0.07
Syrian	70	0.21
Armenian	5	0.01
Asian:	887	2.63
Bangladeshi (7)	9	0.03
Chinese, ex. Taiwanese (98)	106	0.31
Filipino (63)	86	0.26
Hmong (3)	3	0.01
Indian (390)	417	1.24
Indonesian	1	0.00
Japanese (10)	26	0.08
Korean (72)	83	0.25
Pakistani (25)	31	0.09
Sri Lankan (11)	13	0.04
Taiwanese (5)	10	0.03
Thai (7)	9	0.03
Vietnamese (25)	27	0.08
Other Asian, specified (1)	1	0.00
Other Asian, not specified (15)	65	0.19
Assyrian/Chaldean/Syriac	36	0.11
Austrian	32	0.09
Belgian	85	0.25
British	130	0.39
Canadian	151	0.45
Croatian	19	0.06
Czech	80	0.24
Czechoslovakian	169	0.50
Danish	47	0.14
Dutch	829	2.46
Eastern European	13	0.04
English	4,191	12.44
European	237	0.70
Finnish	81	0.24
French, except Basque	1,664	4.94
French Canadian	789	2.34
German	5,558	16.50
Greek	127	0.38
Guyanese	7	0.02
Hawaii Native/Pacific Islander:	25	0.07
Micronesian:	2	0.01
Guamanian/Chamorro	2	0.01
Polynesian: (6)	15	0.04
Native Hawaiian (5)	12	0.04
Samoan (1)	3	0.01
Other Pac. Isl., not spec.	8	0.02
Hispanic or Latino:	784	2.33
Central American:	19	0.06
Costa Rican	1	0.00
Guatemalan	3	0.01
Honduran	2	0.01
Nicaraguan	6	0.02
Panamanian	5	0.01
Salvadoran	2	0.01
Cuban	23	0.07
Dominican Republic	6	0.02
Mexican	537	1.59
Puerto Rican	45	0.13
South American:	8	0.02
Bolivian	2	0.01
Colombian	3	0.01
Peruvian	2	0.01
Other South American	1	0.00
Other Hispanic or Latino	146	0.43
Hungarian	295	0.88
Irish	3,600	10.69
Israeli	5	0.01
Italian	716	2.13
Latvian	16	0.05
Lithuanian	34	0.10
Luxemburger	6	0.02
Macedonian	13	0.04

Notes: 1. Figures in the "Number" column do not add up to the total population due to: a) Ancestry/Race overlap — e.g. persons can report being both White and Irish, b) persons of Hispanic origin can report being any race, c) persons reporting two ancestries are counted in both categories. 2. Numbers in parentheses indicate the number of persons reporting this ancestry/race alone, not in combination with any other ancestry/race. 3. Refer to the Explanation of Data in the front of the book for more detailed information.

Maltese	65	0.19
Norwegian	262	0.78
Pennsylvania German	62	0.18
Polish	1,526	4.53
Portuguese	14	0.04
Romanian	22	0.07
Russian	210	0.62
Scandinavian	21	0.06
Scotch-Irish	495	1.47
Scottish	707	2.10
Serbian	30	0.09
Slavic	52	0.15
Slovak	113	0.34
Slovene	9	0.03
Swedish	315	0.93
Swiss	71	0.21
Ukrainian	139	0.41
United States or American	2,135	6.34
Welsh	118	0.35
West Indian, excl. Hispanic:	83	0.25
Bermudan	27	0.08
Jamaican	41	0.12
West Indian	15	0.04
White:	26,949	79.99
Not Hispanic (25,819)	26,478	78.59
Hispanic (381)	471	1.40
Yugoslavian	69	0.20

Flushing

Place Type: Township
County: Genesee
Population: 10,230

Ancestry/Race	Number	%
African American/Black:	139	1.36
Not Hispanic (109)	136	1.33
Hispanic (3)	3	0.03
Am. Ind. or Alaska Nat., not spec.	35	0.34
American Indian tribes, specified:	63	0.62
Apache (2)	2	0.02
Blackfeet (1)	3	0.03
Cherokee (2)	13	0.13
Chippewa (20)	29	0.28
Iroquois (1)	2	0.02
Latin American Indians (1)	1	0.01
Ottawa (4)	5	0.05
Potawatomi	2	0.02
Sioux (5)	5	0.05
All other tribes (1)	1	0.01
American Indian tribes, not spec.	1	0.01
Arab:	109	1.07
Arab/Arabic	41	0.40
Lebanese	33	0.32
Palestinian	9	0.09
Syrian	26	0.25
Armenian	45	0.44
Asian:	79	0.77
Cambodian	1	0.01
Chinese, ex. Taiwanese (19)	22	0.22
Filipino (4)	5	0.05
Indian (8)	12	0.12
Japanese (5)	5	0.05
Korean (22)	31	0.30
Thai (1)	1	0.01
Other Asian, not specified	2	0.02
Assyrian/Chaldean/Syriac	66	0.65
Austrian	32	0.31
Basque	6	0.06
British	42	0.41
Canadian	69	0.67
Croatian	31	0.30
Czech	94	0.92
Czechoslovakian	84	0.82
Danish	106	1.04
Dutch	144	1.41
English	1,474	14.41
European	136	1.33
Finnish	112	1.09
French, except Basque	581	5.68
French Canadian	413	4.04
German	2,343	22.90
Greek	115	1.12
Hawaii Native/Pacific Islander:	16	0.16
Micronesian: (1)	7	0.07
Guamanian/Chamorro (1)	7	0.07
Polynesian: (5)	5	0.05
Samoan (5)	5	0.05
Other Pac. Isl., not spec. (4)	4	0.04
Hispanic or Latino:	201	1.96
Central American:	6	0.06
Costa Rican	1	0.01
Nicaraguan	1	0.01
Salvadoran	4	0.04
Cuban	12	0.12
Mexican	151	1.48
Puerto Rican	5	0.05
South American:	4	0.04
Colombian	1	0.01
Paraguayan	2	0.02
Peruvian	1	0.01
Other Hispanic or Latino	23	0.22
Hungarian	278	2.72
Iranian	14	0.14
Irish	1,368	13.37
Italian	410	4.01
Latvian	11	0.11
Lithuanian	20	0.20
Maltese	9	0.09
Norwegian	92	0.90
Pennsylvania German	7	0.07
Polish	1,290	12.61
Russian	40	0.39
Scandinavian	15	0.15
Scotch-Irish	208	2.03
Scottish	281	2.75
Serbian	22	0.22
Slavic	6	0.06
Slovak	111	1.09
Swedish	215	2.10
Swiss	56	0.55
Ukrainian	37	0.36
United States or American	698	6.82
Welsh	62	0.61
White:	9,933	97.10
Not Hispanic (9,699)	9,800	95.80
Hispanic (114)	133	1.30

Forest Hills

Place Type: Census Designated Place
County: Kent
Population: 20,942

Ancestry/Race	Number	%
African American/Black:	169	0.81
Not Hispanic (130)	162	0.77
Hispanic (3)	7	0.03
African, sub-Saharan:	5	0.02
African	5	0.02
Am. Ind. or Alaska Nat., not spec.	12	0.06
American Indian tribes, specified:	64	0.31
Blackfeet	7	0.03
Cherokee (9)	15	0.07
Chippewa (16)	20	0.10
Iroquois (4)	4	0.02
Latin American Indians (1)	1	0.00
Ottawa (6)	8	0.04
Potawatomi (1)	2	0.01
Seminole	1	0.00
Sioux	1	0.00
All other tribes (1)	5	0.02
American Indian tribes, not spec.	3	0.01
Arab:	177	0.85
Arab/Arabic	38	0.18
Lebanese	101	0.48
Syrian	38	0.18
Armenian	17	0.08
Asian:	638	3.05
Chinese, ex. Taiwanese (71)	86	0.41
Filipino (58)	80	0.38
Indian (188)	190	0.91
Indonesian (1)	8	0.04
Japanese (25)	41	0.20
Korean (114)	127	0.61
Laotian (5)	5	0.02
Malaysian (4)	5	0.02
Pakistani (21)	23	0.11
Sri Lankan (1)	1	0.00
Taiwanese (2)	6	0.03
Thai (5)	5	0.02
Vietnamese (36)	43	0.21
Other Asian, not specified (10)	18	0.09
Assyrian/Chaldean/Syriac	6	0.03
Austrian	51	0.24
Belgian	45	0.21
British	168	0.80
Canadian	153	0.73
Croatian	77	0.37
Cypriot	5	0.02
Czech	93	0.44
Danish	203	0.97
Dutch	4,256	20.33
Eastern European	40	0.19
English	3,413	16.31
European	310	1.48
Finnish	195	0.93
French, except Basque	758	3.62
French Canadian	169	0.81
German	5,231	24.99
Greek	113	0.54
Hawaii Native/Pacific Islander:	7	0.03
Polynesian: (1)	4	0.02
Native Hawaiian (1)	4	0.02
Other Pac. Isl., not spec.	3	0.01
Hispanic or Latino:	198	0.95
Central American:	6	0.03
Costa Rican	1	0.00
Guatemalan	1	0.00
Honduran	1	0.00
Nicaraguan	2	0.01
Panamanian	1	0.00
Cuban	12	0.06
Dominican Republic	2	0.01
Mexican	105	0.50
Puerto Rican	18	0.09
South American:	14	0.07
Chilean	2	0.01
Colombian	7	0.03
Peruvian	1	0.00
Venezuelan	4	0.02
Other Hispanic or Latino	41	0.20
Hungarian	165	0.79
Irish	2,991	14.29
Italian	1,007	4.81
Latvian	16	0.08
Lithuanian	128	0.61
Macedonian	15	0.07
Maltese	8	0.04
Northern European	17	0.08
Norwegian	310	1.48
Polish	1,653	7.90
Romanian	18	0.09
Russian	130	0.62
Scandinavian	31	0.15
Scotch-Irish	460	2.20
Scottish	716	3.42
Serbian	41	0.20
Slavic	22	0.11
Slovak	36	0.17
Slovene	42	0.20
Swedish	655	3.13
Swiss	98	0.47
Ukrainian	112	0.54
United States or American	837	4.00
Welsh	281	1.34
White:	20,133	96.14
Not Hispanic (19,832)	19,991	95.46
Hispanic (122)	142	0.68
Yugoslavian	77	0.37

Notes: 1. Figures in the "Number" column do not add up to the total population due to: a) Ancestry/Race overlap — e.g. persons can report being both White and Irish, b) persons of Hispanic origin can report being any race, c) persons reporting two ancestries are counted in both categories. 2. Numbers in parentheses indicate the number of persons reporting this ancestry/race alone, not in combination with any other ancestry/race. 3. Refer to the Explanation of Data in the front of the book for more detailed information.

Fort Gratiot

Place Type: Township
County: Saint Clair
Population: 10,691

Ancestry/Race	Number	%
African American/Black:	195	1.82
Not Hispanic (154)	192	1.80
Hispanic (2)	3	0.03
African, sub-Saharan:	48	0.45
African	48	0.45
Am. Ind. or Alaska Nat., not spec.	43	0.40
American Indian tribes, specified:	21	0.20
Apache (2)	2	0.02
Cherokee (1)	1	0.01
Chippewa (4)	5	0.05
Cree	1	0.01
Creek (1)	1	0.01
Iroquois (3)	3	0.03
Latin American Indians (5)	5	0.05
Pueblo	1	0.01
All other tribes	2	0.02
American Indian tribes, not spec.	3	0.03
Arab:	104	0.98
Lebanese	32	0.30
Palestinian	47	0.44
Syrian	25	0.23
Asian:	172	1.61
Bangladeshi (4)	4	0.04
Chinese, ex. Taiwanese (11)	18	0.17
Filipino (16)	18	0.17
Indian (71)	78	0.73
Japanese (10)	14	0.13
Korean (12)	12	0.11
Pakistani (9)	12	0.11
Thai	1	0.01
Vietnamese (9)	9	0.08
Other Asian, specified	6	0.06
Austrian	14	0.13
Belgian	98	0.92
British	41	0.38
Canadian	193	1.81
Czech	11	0.10
Czechoslovakian	11	0.10
Danish	7	0.07
Dutch	304	2.85
English	1,581	14.82
European	63	0.59
Finnish	22	0.21
French, except Basque	767	7.19
French Canadian	274	2.57
German	2,966	27.81
Greek	34	0.32
Hawaii Native/Pacific Islander:	8	0.07
Other Pac. Isl., specified	6	0.06
Other Pac. Isl., not spec. (1)	2	0.02
Hispanic or Latino:	187	1.75
Central American:	7	0.07
Guatemalan	1	0.01
Honduran	5	0.05
Nicaraguan	1	0.01
Cuban	2	0.02
Mexican	144	1.35
Puerto Rican	9	0.08
South American:	1	0.01
Ecuadorian	1	0.01
Other Hispanic or Latino	24	0.22
Hungarian	87	0.82
Irish	1,813	17.00
Italian	417	3.91
Latvian	19	0.18
Lithuanian	26	0.24
Norwegian	47	0.44
Polish	787	7.38
Portuguese	8	0.08
Romanian	8	0.08
Russian	55	0.52
Scandinavian	15	0.14
Scotch-Irish	265	2.48
Scottish	537	5.03
Slovak	22	0.21
Swedish	106	0.99
Swiss	26	0.24
Ukrainian	40	0.38
United States or American	486	4.56
Welsh	172	1.61
White:	10,296	96.31
Not Hispanic (10,091)	10,165	95.08
Hispanic (111)	131	1.23
Yugoslavian	24	0.23

Fraser

Place Type: City
County: Macomb
Population: 15,297

Ancestry/Race	Number	%
African American/Black:	178	1.16
Not Hispanic (136)	175	1.14
Hispanic (3)	3	0.02
Am. Ind. or Alaska Nat., not spec.	20	0.13
Albanian	190	1.24
American Indian tribes, specified:	84	0.55
Apache (1)	1	0.01
Blackfeet	1	0.01
Cherokee (8)	32	0.21
Chippewa (8)	25	0.16
Comanche (4)	4	0.03
Cree	2	0.01
Iroquois (4)	5	0.03
Latin American Indians	1	0.01
Lumbee (3)	5	0.03
Menominee	1	0.01
Potawatomi	1	0.01
All other tribes (2)	6	0.04
American Indian tribes, not spec.	1	0.01
Arab:	369	2.41
Arab/Arabic	31	0.20
Egyptian	8	0.05
Lebanese	237	1.55
Palestinian	22	0.14
Syrian	45	0.29
Other Arab	26	0.17
Armenian	35	0.23
Asian:	170	1.11
Cambodian (3)	3	0.02
Chinese, ex. Taiwanese (49)	56	0.37
Filipino (21)	32	0.21
Hmong (7)	7	0.05
Indian (28)	29	0.19
Japanese (7)	9	0.06
Korean (11)	15	0.10
Pakistani (7)	7	0.05
Thai (1)	1	0.01
Vietnamese (8)	10	0.07
Other Asian, not specified	1	0.01
Austrian	39	0.25
Belgian	407	2.66
British	100	0.65
Canadian	84	0.55
Croatian	57	0.37
Czech	32	0.21
Czechoslovakian	58	0.38
Danish	26	0.17
Dutch	134	0.88
English	1,286	8.41
European	13	0.08
Finnish	141	0.92
French, except Basque	1,068	6.98
French Canadian	454	2.97
German	3,929	25.68
Greek	191	1.25
Hawaii Native/Pacific Islander:	5	0.03
Polynesian: (2)	2	0.01
Native Hawaiian (1)	1	0.01
Samoan (1)	1	0.01
Other Pac. Isl., not spec.	3	0.02
Hispanic or Latino:	203	1.33
Central American:	2	0.01
Salvadoran	2	0.01
Cuban	8	0.05
Mexican	127	0.83
Puerto Rican	18	0.12
South American:	1	0.01
Argentinean	1	0.01
Other Hispanic or Latino	47	0.31
Hungarian	169	1.10
Irish	2,148	14.04
Italian	2,433	15.91
Lithuanian	29	0.19
Macedonian	6	0.04
Maltese	28	0.18
Norwegian	49	0.32
Polish	3,203	20.94
Romanian	73	0.48
Russian	110	0.72
Scandinavian	14	0.09
Scotch-Irish	145	0.95
Scottish	295	1.93
Serbian	36	0.24
Slavic	27	0.18
Slovak	64	0.42
Slovene	5	0.03
Swedish	114	0.75
Swiss	33	0.22
Turkish	6	0.04
Ukrainian	151	0.99
United States or American	422	2.76
Welsh	56	0.37
West Indian, excl. Hispanic:	14	0.09
Jamaican	14	0.09
White:	14,935	97.63
Not Hispanic (14,628)	14,764	96.52
Hispanic (159)	171	1.12
Yugoslavian	61	0.40

Frenchtown

Place Type: Township
County: Monroe
Population: 20,777

Ancestry/Race	Number	%
African American/Black:	402	1.93
Not Hispanic (326)	386	1.86
Hispanic (5)	16	0.08
African, sub-Saharan:	12	0.06
African	12	0.06
Alaska Native tribes, specified:	4	0.02
Eskimo	1	0.00
Tlingit-Haida	3	0.01
Am. Ind. or Alaska Nat., not spec.	79	0.38
American Indian tribes, specified:	179	0.86
Apache	3	0.01
Blackfeet (1)	11	0.05
Cherokee (14)	83	0.40
Chippewa (22)	30	0.14
Comanche (1)	1	0.00
Crow	1	0.00
Delaware	1	0.00
Iroquois (4)	9	0.04
Latin American Indians (8)	10	0.05
Menominee (1)	1	0.00
Navajo	2	0.01
Ottawa	2	0.01
Seminole	5	0.02
Sioux (3)	5	0.02
All other tribes (4)	15	0.07
American Indian tribes, not spec.	11	0.05
Arab:	37	0.18
Arab/Arabic	21	0.10
Lebanese	16	0.08
Armenian	42	0.20
Asian:	146	0.70
Cambodian (1)	1	0.00
Chinese, ex. Taiwanese (7)	12	0.06
Filipino (11)	19	0.09
Indian (49)	52	0.25

Notes: 1. Figures in the "Number" column do not add up to the total population due to: a) Ancestry/Race overlap — e.g. persons can report being both White and Irish, b) persons of Hispanic origin can report being any race, c) persons reporting two ancestries are counted in both categories. 2. Numbers in parentheses indicate the number of persons reporting this ancestry/race alone, not in combination with any other ancestry/race. 3. Refer to the Explanation of Data in the front of the book for more detailed information.

Japanese (8)	10	0.05
Korean (8)	11	0.05
Malaysian	1	0.00
Pakistani (9)	9	0.04
Thai (4)	4	0.02
Vietnamese (4)	4	0.02
Other Asian, not specified (7)	23	0.11
Australian	6	0.03
Austrian	6	0.03
Belgian	184	0.89
British	26	0.13
Canadian	98	0.47
Croatian	58	0.28
Czech	59	0.29
Czechoslovakian	56	0.27
Danish	16	0.08
Dutch	499	2.41
English	1,704	8.24
European	57	0.28
Finnish	72	0.35
French, except Basque	2,443	11.81
French Canadian	564	2.73
German	4,983	24.08
Greek	18	0.09
Hawaii Native/Pacific Islander:	9	0.04
Polynesian: (1)	7	0.03
Native Hawaiian (1)	5	0.02
Samoan	2	0.01
Other Pac. Isl., not spec. (2)	2	0.01
Hispanic or Latino:	510	2.45
Central American:	2	0.01
Nicaraguan	1	0.00
Salvadoran	1	0.00
Cuban	4	0.02
Mexican	364	1.75
Puerto Rican	44	0.21
South American:	5	0.02
Colombian	1	0.00
Peruvian	4	0.02
Other Hispanic or Latino	91	0.44
Hungarian	482	2.33
Irish	2,429	11.74
Italian	1,449	7.00
Lithuanian	29	0.14
Northern European	16	0.08
Norwegian	116	0.56
Polish	1,277	6.17
Portuguese	13	0.06
Romanian	17	0.08
Russian	77	0.37
Scotch-Irish	248	1.20
Scottish	416	2.01
Serbian	78	0.38
Slavic	10	0.05
Slovak	54	0.26
Swedish	124	0.60
Swiss	18	0.09
Ukrainian	35	0.17
United States or American	1,599	7.73
Welsh	154	0.74
West Indian, excl. Hispanic:	6	0.03
Belizean	6	0.03
White:	20,132	96.90
Not Hispanic (19,475)	19,731	94.97
Hispanic (370)	401	1.93
Yugoslavian	5	0.02

Fruitport charter

Place Type: Township
County: Muskegon
Population: 12,533

Ancestry/Race	Number	%
African American/Black:	103	0.82
Not Hispanic (75)	96	0.77
Hispanic (7)	7	0.06
Am. Ind. or Alaska Nat., not spec.	20	0.16
American Indian tribes, specified:	119	0.95
Blackfeet	2	0.02
Cherokee (7)	14	0.11
Chippewa (15)	26	0.21
Iroquois	1	0.01
Ottawa (40)	57	0.45
Potawatomi	2	0.02
Sioux (5)	11	0.09
All other tribes (5)	6	0.05
American Indian tribes, not spec.	9	0.07
Arab:	9	0.07
Arab/Arabic	2	0.02
Lebanese	7	0.06
Asian:	67	0.53
Cambodian (2)	2	0.02
Chinese, ex. Taiwanese (3)	6	0.05
Filipino (21)	21	0.17
Indian (4)	6	0.05
Japanese (2)	4	0.03
Korean (20)	27	0.22
Thai (1)	1	0.01
Austrian	42	0.34
Belgian	7	0.06
British	18	0.14
Canadian	9	0.07
Croatian	27	0.22
Czech	80	0.64
Czechoslovakian	18	0.14
Danish	120	0.96
Dutch	2,202	17.57
English	1,543	12.31
European	120	0.96
Finnish	92	0.73
French, except Basque	811	6.47
French Canadian	269	2.15
German	2,740	21.86
Greek	80	0.64
Hawaii Native/Pacific Islander:	3	0.02
Polynesian:	3	0.02
Native Hawaiian	3	0.02
Hispanic or Latino:	211	1.68
Central American:	3	0.02
Guatemalan	1	0.01
Honduran	1	0.01
Panamanian	1	0.01
Cuban	3	0.02
Mexican	160	1.28
Puerto Rican	13	0.10
South American:	1	0.01
Peruvian	1	0.01
Other Hispanic or Latino	31	0.25
Hungarian	230	1.84
Irish	1,441	11.50
Italian	268	2.14
Lithuanian	89	0.71
Maltese	4	0.03
Norwegian	307	2.45
Pennsylvania German	17	0.14
Polish	1,087	8.67
Portuguese	3	0.02
Romanian	2	0.02
Russian	79	0.63
Scandinavian	14	0.11
Scotch-Irish	102	0.81
Scottish	155	1.24
Slavic	11	0.09
Slovak	25	0.20
Slovene	5	0.04
Swedish	567	4.52
Swiss	70	0.56
Ukrainian	48	0.38
United States or American	933	7.44
Welsh	87	0.69
West Indian, excl. Hispanic:	2	0.02
Dutch West Indian	2	0.02
White:	12,248	97.73
Not Hispanic (12,002)	12,096	96.51
Hispanic (143)	152	1.21
Yugoslavian	10	0.08

Gaines

Place Type: Township
County: Kent
Population: 20,112

Ancestry/Race	Number	%
African American/Black:	1,198	5.96
Not Hispanic (1,038)	1,168	5.81
Hispanic (20)	30	0.15
African, sub-Saharan:	138	0.69
African	77	0.38
Ethiopian	37	0.18
Ugandan	14	0.07
Zimbabwean	10	0.05
Am. Ind. or Alaska Nat., not spec.	59	0.29
American Indian tribes, specified:	137	0.68
Apache	1	0.00
Blackfeet	6	0.03
Cherokee (9)	32	0.16
Chickasaw	1	0.00
Chippewa (21)	33	0.16
Choctaw	3	0.01
Creek	1	0.00
Iroquois	1	0.00
Latin American Indians (11)	12	0.06
Lumbee	1	0.00
Ottawa (10)	16	0.08
Potawatomi (12)	21	0.10
Seminole (1)	1	0.00
Sioux	4	0.02
All other tribes	3	0.01
American Indian tribes, not spec.	6	0.03
Arab:	37	0.18
Lebanese	20	0.10
Syrian	8	0.04
Other Arab	9	0.04
Asian:	509	2.53
Cambodian (1)	1	0.00
Chinese, ex. Taiwanese (18)	30	0.15
Filipino (21)	30	0.15
Hmong (1)	1	0.00
Indian (36)	51	0.25
Indonesian	4	0.02
Japanese (11)	32	0.16
Korean (92)	113	0.56
Laotian	1	0.00
Pakistani (3)	3	0.01
Sri Lankan (1)	1	0.00
Thai (2)	2	0.01
Vietnamese (207)	220	1.09
Other Asian, not specified (6)	20	0.10
Austrian	20	0.10
Belgian	27	0.13
British	13	0.06
Canadian	40	0.20
Czech	70	0.35
Czechoslovakian	31	0.15
Danish	114	0.57
Dutch	6,410	31.96
English	2,045	10.20
European	126	0.63
Finnish	105	0.52
French, except Basque	963	4.80
French Canadian	224	1.12
German	3,532	17.61
Greek	28	0.14
Hawaii Native/Pacific Islander:	12	0.06
Polynesian: (4)	5	0.02
Native Hawaiian (4)	4	0.02
Other Polynesian	1	0.00
Other Pac. Isl., not spec. (1)	7	0.03
Hispanic or Latino:	567	2.82
Central American:	17	0.08
Guatemalan	6	0.03
Honduran	1	0.00
Salvadoran	10	0.05
Cuban	37	0.18
Dominican Republic	13	0.06
Mexican	290	1.44

Notes: 1. Figures in the "Number" column do not add up to the total population due to: a) Ancestry/Race overlap — e.g. persons can report being both White and Irish, b) persons of Hispanic origin can report being any race, c) persons reporting two ancestries are counted in both categories. 2. Numbers in parentheses indicate the number of persons reporting this ancestry/race alone, not in combination with any other ancestry/race. 3. Refer to the Explanation of Data in the front of the book for more detailed information.

Puerto Rican	76	0.38
South American:	17	0.08
Chilean	3	0.01
Colombian	1	0.00
Peruvian	8	0.04
Venezuelan	1	0.00
Other South American	4	0.02
Other Hispanic or Latino	117	0.58
Hungarian	47	0.23
Irish	1,775	8.85
Israeli	37	0.18
Italian	481	2.40
Latvian	7	0.03
Lithuanian	61	0.30
Northern European	6	0.03
Norwegian	190	0.95
Pennsylvania German	17	0.08
Polish	1,032	5.15
Romanian	31	0.15
Russian	49	0.24
Scotch-Irish	211	1.05
Scottish	249	1.24
Slavic	21	0.10
Slovak	8	0.04
Swedish	382	1.90
Swiss	27	0.13
Ukrainian	14	0.07
United States or American	933	4.65
Welsh	78	0.39
West Indian, excl. Hispanic:	3	0.01
Jamaican	3	0.01
White:	18,298	90.98
Not Hispanic (17,662)	17,958	89.29
Hispanic (298)	340	1.69
Yugoslavian	182	0.91

Garden City

Place Type: City
County: Wayne
Population: 30,047

Ancestry/Race	Number	%
African American/Black:	397	1.32
Not Hispanic (330)	389	1.29
Hispanic (2)	8	0.03
African, sub-Saharan:	30	0.10
African	12	0.04
Ethiopian	18	0.06
Am. Ind. or Alaska Nat., not spec.	71	0.24
Albanian	44	0.15
American Indian tribes, specified:	201	0.67
Apache (1)	1	0.00
Blackfeet	17	0.06
Cherokee (11)	47	0.16
Chickasaw (1)	1	0.00
Chippewa (30)	43	0.14
Delaware (3)	4	0.01
Iroquois (23)	31	0.10
Latin American Indians (1)	3	0.01
Lumbee (1)	1	0.00
Menominee (3)	3	0.01
Osage (3)	6	0.02
Ottawa (5)	13	0.04
Potawatomi	6	0.02
Pueblo (1)	1	0.00
Sioux (2)	12	0.04
All other tribes (5)	12	0.04
American Indian tribes, not spec.	10	0.03
Arab:	239	0.80
Arab/Arabic	44	0.15
Jordanian	41	0.14
Lebanese	120	0.40
Palestinian	27	0.09
Syrian	7	0.02
Armenian	63	0.21
Asian:	298	0.99
Chinese, ex. Taiwanese (39)	50	0.17
Filipino (54)	73	0.24
Indian (46)	57	0.19
Indonesian (1)	1	0.00
Japanese (19)	36	0.12
Korean (18)	24	0.08
Pakistani (9)	13	0.04
Sri Lankan	1	0.00
Taiwanese (4)	4	0.01
Thai (1)	2	0.01
Vietnamese (17)	20	0.07
Other Asian, not specified (5)	17	0.06
Assyrian/Chaldean/Syriac	10	0.03
Austrian	62	0.21
Basque	8	0.03
Belgian	58	0.19
British	169	0.56
Canadian	239	0.80
Croatian	114	0.38
Czech	112	0.37
Czechoslovakian	33	0.11
Danish	97	0.32
Dutch	508	1.69
English	3,545	11.80
European	4	0.01
Finnish	612	2.04
French, except Basque	2,186	7.28
French Canadian	868	2.89
German	6,915	23.01
Greek	145	0.48
Hawaii Native/Pacific Islander:	6	0.02
Polynesian: (2)	5	0.02
Native Hawaiian (2)	4	0.01
Other Polynesian	1	0.00
Other Pac. Isl., not spec.	1	0.00
Hispanic or Latino:	611	2.03
Central American:	5	0.02
Honduran	4	0.01
Salvadoran	1	0.00
Cuban	10	0.03
Mexican	403	1.34
Puerto Rican	55	0.18
South American:	8	0.03
Argentinean	4	0.01
Colombian	1	0.00
Ecuadorian	3	0.01
Other Hispanic or Latino	130	0.43
Hungarian	512	1.70
Irish	5,150	17.14
Israeli	9	0.03
Italian	1,723	5.73
Latvian	5	0.02
Lithuanian	132	0.44
Luxemburger	6	0.02
Macedonian	40	0.13
Maltese	211	0.70
Northern European	8	0.03
Norwegian	250	0.83
Polish	5,027	16.73
Portuguese	19	0.06
Romanian	156	0.52
Russian	229	0.76
Scandinavian	86	0.29
Scotch-Irish	802	2.67
Scottish	927	3.09
Serbian	99	0.33
Slavic	27	0.09
Slovak	174	0.58
Slovene	7	0.02
Swedish	415	1.38
Swiss	52	0.17
Ukrainian	343	1.14
United States or American	2,187	7.28
Welsh	180	0.60
White:	29,270	97.41
Not Hispanic (28,438)	28,758	95.71
Hispanic (466)	512	1.70
Yugoslavian	90	0.30

Garfield

Place Type: Township
County: Grand Traverse
Population: 13,840

Ancestry/Race	Number	%
African American/Black:	95	0.69
Not Hispanic (44)	92	0.66
Hispanic (2)	3	0.02
African, sub-Saharan:	31	0.23
Nigerian	10	0.07
Other sub-Saharan African	21	0.16
Am. Ind. or Alaska Nat., not spec.	34	0.25
American Indian tribes, specified:	178	1.29
Blackfeet (1)	1	0.01
Cherokee (1)	14	0.10
Chickasaw	1	0.01
Chippewa (93)	118	0.85
Creek	1	0.01
Iroquois	2	0.01
Menominee (1)	1	0.01
Navajo (1)	1	0.01
Ottawa (14)	23	0.17
Pima (1)	1	0.01
Potawatomi (3)	3	0.02
Sioux (2)	4	0.03
All other tribes (3)	8	0.06
American Indian tribes, not spec.	8	0.06
Arab:	47	0.35
Arab/Arabic	16	0.12
Lebanese	15	0.11
Syrian	16	0.12
Armenian	9	0.07
Asian:	143	1.03
Chinese, ex. Taiwanese (24)	31	0.22
Filipino (11)	22	0.16
Hmong (4)	4	0.03
Indian (8)	12	0.09
Japanese (2)	15	0.11
Korean (10)	18	0.13
Laotian (7)	7	0.05
Malaysian (2)	2	0.01
Vietnamese (23)	23	0.17
Other Asian, not specified (7)	9	0.07
Austrian	24	0.18
Belgian	48	0.36
British	79	0.59
Canadian	70	0.52
Croatian	7	0.05
Czech	185	1.37
Czechoslovakian	15	0.11
Danish	59	0.44
Dutch	648	4.80
English	2,098	15.54
European	39	0.29
Finnish	109	0.81
French, except Basque	792	5.86
French Canadian	294	2.18
German	3,504	25.95
Greek	58	0.43
Hawaii Native/Pacific Islander:	11	0.08
Micronesian: (2)	2	0.01
Guamanian/Chamorro (1)	1	0.01
Other Micronesian (1)	1	0.01
Polynesian: (2)	9	0.07
Native Hawaiian	7	0.05
Samoan (2)	2	0.01
Hispanic or Latino:	207	1.50
Central American:	3	0.02
Costa Rican	1	0.01
Nicaraguan	1	0.01
Salvadoran	1	0.01
Cuban	3	0.02
Mexican	110	0.79
Puerto Rican	29	0.21
South American:	8	0.06
Argentinean	1	0.01
Colombian	6	0.04
Venezuelan	1	0.01

Notes: 1. Figures in the "Number" column do not add up to the total population due to: a) Ancestry/Race overlap — e.g. persons can report being both White and Irish, b) persons of Hispanic origin can report being any race, c) persons reporting two ancestries are counted in both categories. 2. Numbers in parentheses indicate the number of persons reporting this ancestry/race alone, not in combination with any other ancestry/race. 3. Refer to the Explanation of Data in the front of the book for more detailed information.

Other Hispanic or Latino	54	0.39
Hungarian	140	1.04
Irish	1,936	14.34
Italian	432	3.20
Lithuanian	39	0.29
Macedonian	9	0.07
Northern European	17	0.13
Norwegian	275	2.04
Pennsylvania German	20	0.15
Polish	1,042	7.72
Russian	37	0.27
Scandinavian	60	0.44
Scotch-Irish	157	1.16
Scottish	506	3.75
Slavic	14	0.10
Slovak	20	0.15
Swedish	247	1.83
Swiss	91	0.67
Ukrainian	28	0.21
United States or American	982	7.27
Welsh	165	1.22
White:	13,486	97.44
Not Hispanic (13,193)	13,328	96.30
Hispanic (141)	158	1.14
Yugoslavian	6	0.04

Genesee

Place Type: Township
County: Genesee
Population: 24,125

Ancestry/Race	Number	%
African American/Black:	2,131	8.83
Not Hispanic (1,961)	2,110	8.75
Hispanic (12)	21	0.09
African, sub-Saharan:	73	0.30
African	73	0.30
Alaska Native tribes, specified:	5	0.02
Tlingit-Haida (4)	5	0.02
Am. Ind. or Alaska Nat., not spec.	128	0.53
American Indian tribes, specified:	323	1.34
Apache (11)	21	0.09
Blackfeet (7)	20	0.08
Cherokee (32)	118	0.49
Cheyenne	2	0.01
Chippewa (43)	90	0.37
Choctaw (2)	2	0.01
Comanche	1	0.00
Cree	3	0.01
Iroquois	3	0.01
Latin American Indians (1)	2	0.01
Lumbee	1	0.00
Menominee (1)	1	0.00
Ottawa (9)	16	0.07
Potawatomi (1)	2	0.01
Pueblo	1	0.00
Seminole (1)	1	0.00
Sioux (4)	14	0.06
Tohono O'Odham	1	0.00
All other tribes (8)	24	0.10
American Indian tribes, not spec.	21	0.09
Arab:	144	0.60
Arab/Arabic	103	0.43
Jordanian	18	0.07
Lebanese	23	0.10
Armenian	4	0.02
Asian:	118	0.49
Chinese, ex. Taiwanese (13)	29	0.12
Filipino (7)	21	0.09
Indian (9)	13	0.05
Japanese (8)	11	0.05
Korean (18)	22	0.09
Thai (2)	6	0.02
Vietnamese (8)	9	0.04
Other Asian, not specified (6)	7	0.03
Assyrian/Chaldean/Syriac	24	0.10
Australian	7	0.03
Austrian	29	0.12
Basque	30	0.12
Belgian	33	0.14
British	22	0.09
Canadian	151	0.63
Croatian	20	0.08
Czech	64	0.27
Czechoslovakian	93	0.39
Danish	70	0.29
Dutch	622	2.59
Eastern European	5	0.02
English	2,578	10.72
European	161	0.67
Finnish	79	0.33
French, except Basque	1,749	7.27
French Canadian	824	3.43
German	4,632	19.26
Greek	12	0.05
Hawaii Native/Pacific Islander:	15	0.06
Micronesian:		0.00
Guamanian/Chamorro	1	0.00
Polynesian: (3)	9	0.04
Native Hawaiian (2)	8	0.03
Samoan (1)	1	0.00
Other Pac. Isl., not spec.	5	0.02
Hispanic or Latino:	651	2.70
Central American:	15	0.06
Costa Rican	3	0.01
Honduran	3	0.01
Panamanian	8	0.03
Salvadoran	1	0.00
Cuban	2	0.01
Mexican	488	2.02
Puerto Rican	29	0.12
South American:	3	0.01
Peruvian	3	0.01
Other Hispanic or Latino	114	0.47
Hungarian	374	1.55
Irish	3,107	12.92
Israeli	15	0.06
Italian	624	2.59
Lithuanian	10	0.04
Luxemburger	7	0.03
Macedonian	36	0.15
Norwegian	186	0.77
Pennsylvania German	11	0.05
Polish	1,123	4.67
Portuguese	4	0.02
Romanian	25	0.10
Russian	100	0.42
Scandinavian	15	0.06
Scotch-Irish	224	0.93
Scottish	398	1.65
Slavic	12	0.05
Slovak	42	0.17
Swedish	241	1.00
Swiss	17	0.07
Ukrainian	40	0.17
United States or American	1,942	8.07
Welsh	129	0.54
West Indian, excl. Hispanic:	7	0.03
Jamaican	7	0.03
White:	21,680	89.87
Not Hispanic (20,837)	21,252	88.09
Hispanic (369)	428	1.77
Yugoslavian	70	0.29

Genoa

Place Type: Township
County: Livingston
Population: 15,901

Ancestry/Race	Number	%
African American/Black:	58	0.36
Not Hispanic (30)	55	0.35
Hispanic	3	0.02
Am. Ind. or Alaska Nat., not spec.	66	0.42
American Indian tribes, specified:	121	0.76
Blackfeet	2	0.01
Cherokee (11)	51	0.32
Chippewa (17)	27	0.17
Choctaw	3	0.02
Delaware (1)	4	0.03
Iroquois (13)	17	0.11
Latin American Indians	4	0.03
Ottawa (3)	4	0.03
Potawatomi	2	0.01
Sioux	2	0.01
Tohono O'Odham (1)	1	0.01
All other tribes (1)	4	0.03
American Indian tribes, not spec.	6	0.04
Arab:	119	0.74
Arab/Arabic	25	0.16
Jordanian	17	0.11
Lebanese	54	0.34
Syrian	23	0.14
Armenian	49	0.31
Asian:	147	0.92
Chinese, ex. Taiwanese (13)	21	0.13
Filipino (12)	20	0.13
Hmong (7)	7	0.04
Indian (11)	12	0.08
Indonesian (1)	1	0.01
Japanese (15)	23	0.14
Korean (33)	38	0.24
Laotian (5)	5	0.03
Malaysian (1)	1	0.01
Taiwanese (1)	5	0.03
Thai (1)	2	0.01
Vietnamese (6)	8	0.05
Other Asian, specified (3)	4	0.03
Austrian	75	0.47
Belgian	71	0.44
British	143	0.89
Canadian	94	0.59
Czech	43	0.27
Czechoslovakian	48	0.30
Danish	58	0.36
Dutch	442	2.76
English	2,139	13.36
European	53	0.33
Finnish	330	2.06
French, except Basque	1,195	7.47
French Canadian	550	3.44
German	3,610	22.56
Greek	59	0.37
Hawaii Native/Pacific Islander:	3	0.02
Micronesian: (1)	1	0.01
Guamanian/Chamorro (1)	1	0.01
Polynesian: (1)	2	0.01
Native Hawaiian	1	0.01
Samoan (1)	1	0.01
Hispanic or Latino:	159	1.00
Central American:	1	0.01
Salvadoran	1	0.01
Cuban	7	0.04
Mexican	89	0.56
Puerto Rican	12	0.08
South American:	9	0.06
Argentinean	2	0.01
Chilean	1	0.01
Colombian	3	0.02
Ecuadorian	2	0.01
Venezuelan	1	0.01
Other Hispanic or Latino	41	0.26
Hungarian	311	1.94
Irish	2,356	14.72
Italian	1,392	8.70
Latvian	12	0.07
Lithuanian	190	1.19
Luxemburger	9	0.06
Macedonian	20	0.12
Maltese	38	0.24
Northern European	8	0.05
Norwegian	111	0.69
Pennsylvania German	17	0.11
Polish	1,927	12.04
Portuguese	6	0.04
Romanian	39	0.24
Russian	183	1.14
Scandinavian	61	0.38

Notes: 1. Figures in the "Number" column do not add up to the total population due to: a) Ancestry/Race overlap — e.g. persons can report being both White and Irish, b) persons of Hispanic origin can report being any race, c) persons reporting two ancestries are counted in both categories. 2. Numbers in parentheses indicate the number of persons reporting this ancestry/race alone, not in combination with any other ancestry/race. 3. Refer to the Explanation of Data in the front of the book for more detailed information.

Ancestry/Race	Number	%
Scotch-Irish	359	2.24
Scottish	616	3.85
Serbian	8	0.05
Slavic	7	0.04
Slovak	39	0.24
Slovene	17	0.11
Swedish	332	2.07
Swiss	40	0.25
Ukrainian	62	0.39
United States or American	823	5.14
Welsh	257	1.61
White:	15,652	98.43
Not Hispanic (15,361)	15,520	97.60
Hispanic (111)	132	0.83

Georgetown

Place Type: Township
County: Ottawa
Population: 41,658

Ancestry/Race	Number	%
African American/Black:	319	0.77
Not Hispanic (233)	307	0.74
Hispanic (7)	12	0.03
Alaska Native tribes, specified:	1	0.00
All other tribes (1)	1	0.00
Am. Ind. or Alaska Nat., not spec.	49	0.12
Albanian	8	0.02
American Indian tribes, specified:	139	0.33
Apache	4	0.01
Blackfeet (2)	4	0.01
Cherokee (4)	16	0.04
Cheyenne	3	0.01
Chippewa (18)	40	0.10
Choctaw (1)	4	0.01
Creek	1	0.00
Iroquois	5	0.01
Latin American Indians (2)	5	0.01
Ottawa (13)	24	0.06
Potawatomi (10)	22	0.05
Sioux	4	0.01
All other tribes (4)	7	0.02
American Indian tribes, not spec.	9	0.02
Arab:	31	0.07
Lebanese	23	0.06
Syrian	8	0.02
Asian:	486	1.17
Bangladeshi (4)	4	0.01
Cambodian (9)	13	0.03
Chinese, ex. Taiwanese (55)	72	0.17
Filipino (11)	22	0.05
Hmong (2)	2	0.00
Indian (20)	26	0.06
Indonesian (4)	15	0.04
Japanese (22)	30	0.07
Korean (140)	163	0.39
Laotian (2)	5	0.01
Thai (2)	2	0.00
Vietnamese (87)	104	0.25
Other Asian, specified	3	0.01
Other Asian, not specified (13)	25	0.06
Australian	8	0.02
Austrian	96	0.23
Belgian	73	0.18
Brazilian	6	0.01
British	75	0.18
Canadian	71	0.17
Croatian	8	0.02
Czech	121	0.29
Czechoslovakian	100	0.24
Danish	278	0.67
Dutch	17,780	42.68
Eastern European	6	0.01
English	3,794	9.11
Estonian	8	0.02
European	261	0.63
Finnish	156	0.37
French, except Basque	1,337	3.21
French Canadian	545	1.31
German	8,395	20.15
Greek	38	0.09
Hawaii Native/Pacific Islander:	23	0.06
Micronesian: (1)	1	0.00
Guamanian/Chamorro (1)	1	0.00
Polynesian: (5)	12	0.03
Native Hawaiian (2)	8	0.02
Samoan (3)	4	0.01
Other Pac. Isl., specified	3	0.01
Other Pac. Isl., not spec. (1)	7	0.02
Hispanic or Latino:	694	1.67
Central American:	30	0.07
Costa Rican	2	0.00
Guatemalan	16	0.04
Honduran	6	0.01
Nicaraguan	2	0.00
Panamanian	1	0.00
Salvadoran	2	0.00
Other Central American	1	0.00
Cuban	55	0.13
Dominican Republic	10	0.02
Mexican	407	0.98
Puerto Rican	61	0.15
South American:	25	0.06
Argentinean	2	0.00
Chilean	3	0.01
Colombian	10	0.02
Paraguayan	1	0.00
Peruvian	9	0.02
Other Hispanic or Latino	106	0.25
Hungarian	165	0.40
Irish	3,447	8.27
Italian	1,175	2.82
Latvian	23	0.06
Lithuanian	78	0.19
Macedonian	11	0.03
Maltese	5	0.01
Norwegian	396	0.95
Pennsylvania German	16	0.04
Polish	2,495	5.99
Portuguese	15	0.04
Romanian	38	0.09
Russian	104	0.25
Scandinavian	68	0.16
Scotch-Irish	375	0.90
Scottish	566	1.36
Slovak	45	0.11
Slovene	5	0.01
Swedish	970	2.33
Swiss	100	0.24
Ukrainian	93	0.22
United States or American	1,732	4.16
Welsh	192	0.46
West Indian, excl. Hispanic:	14	0.03
Jamaican	14	0.03
White:	40,722	97.75
Not Hispanic (39,990)	40,257	96.64
Hispanic (413)	465	1.12
Yugoslavian	45	0.11

Grand Blanc

Place Type: Township
County: Genesee
Population: 29,827

Ancestry/Race	Number	%
African American/Black:	2,129	7.14
Not Hispanic (1,992)	2,119	7.10
Hispanic (6)	10	0.03
African, sub-Saharan:	120	0.40
African	103	0.34
Nigerian	17	0.06
Alaska Native tribes, specified:	1	0.00
Tlingit-Haida (1)	1	0.00
Am. Ind. or Alaska Nat., not spec.	73	0.24
American Indian tribes, specified:	185	0.62
Apache (2)	4	0.01
Blackfeet (3)	12	0.04
Cherokee (20)	75	0.25
Chippewa (30)	57	0.19
Choctaw (3)	3	0.01
Cree	2	0.01
Crow	1	0.00
Delaware	1	0.00
Kiowa (1)	3	0.01
Latin American Indians (5)	6	0.02
Navajo (1)	3	0.01
Osage	1	0.00
Ottawa	2	0.01
Potawatomi	1	0.00
Sioux (5)	8	0.03
All other tribes (5)	6	0.02
American Indian tribes, not spec.	14	0.05
Arab:	432	1.45
Arab/Arabic	123	0.41
Iraqi	47	0.16
Lebanese	219	0.73
Palestinian	25	0.08
Syrian	6	0.02
Other Arab	12	0.04
Armenian	16	0.05
Asian:	884	2.96
Bangladeshi (5)	6	0.02
Cambodian (1)	1	0.00
Chinese, ex. Taiwanese (109)	124	0.42
Filipino (89)	105	0.35
Hmong (2)	2	0.01
Indian (277)	289	0.97
Indonesian (2)	3	0.01
Japanese (10)	23	0.08
Korean (112)	134	0.45
Laotian (5)	16	0.05
Pakistani (33)	35	0.12
Taiwanese (12)	16	0.05
Thai (9)	12	0.04
Vietnamese (50)	54	0.18
Other Asian, specified (5)	6	0.02
Other Asian, not specified (20)	58	0.19
Assyrian/Chaldean/Syriac	76	0.25
Austrian	52	0.17
Belgian	124	0.42
British	73	0.24
Bulgarian	20	0.07
Canadian	136	0.46
Celtic	8	0.03
Croatian	44	0.15
Czech	128	0.43
Czechoslovakian	99	0.33
Danish	80	0.27
Dutch	780	2.61
English	4,348	14.55
European	205	0.69
Finnish	290	0.97
French, except Basque	1,699	5.69
French Canadian	756	2.53
German	6,727	22.52
Greek	223	0.75
Hawaii Native/Pacific Islander:	16	0.05
Micronesian: (4)	5	0.02
Guamanian/Chamorro (4)	5	0.02
Polynesian: (3)	4	0.01
Native Hawaiian (3)	4	0.01
Other Pac. Isl., not spec.	7	0.02
Hispanic or Latino:	622	2.09
Central American:	4	0.01
Guatemalan	2	0.01
Panamanian	2	0.01
Cuban	17	0.06
Dominican Republic	4	0.01
Mexican	422	1.41
Puerto Rican	45	0.15
South American:	30	0.10
Argentinean	1	0.00
Bolivian	2	0.01
Chilean	4	0.01
Colombian	9	0.03
Peruvian	13	0.04
Venezuelan	1	0.00
Other Hispanic or Latino	100	0.34

Notes: 1. Figures in the "Number" column do not add up to the total population due to: a) Ancestry/Race overlap — e.g. persons can report being both White and Irish, b) persons of Hispanic origin can report being any race, c) persons reporting two ancestries are counted in both categories. 2. Numbers in parentheses indicate the number of persons reporting this ancestry/race alone, not in combination with any other ancestry/race. 3. Refer to the Explanation of Data in the front of the book for more detailed information.

Ancestry/Race	Number	%
Hungarian	399	1.34
Iranian	49	0.16
Irish	4,262	14.27
Italian	896	3.00
Lithuanian	110	0.37
Macedonian	64	0.21
Maltese	32	0.11
Norwegian	315	1.05
Pennsylvania German	9	0.03
Polish	2,063	6.90
Portuguese	11	0.04
Romanian	87	0.29
Russian	197	0.66
Scandinavian	29	0.10
Scotch-Irish	427	1.43
Scottish	786	2.63
Serbian	17	0.06
Slavic	45	0.15
Slovak	91	0.30
Slovene	22	0.07
Swedish	250	0.84
Swiss	97	0.32
Ukrainian	95	0.32
United States or American	2,381	7.97
Welsh	211	0.71
West Indian, excl. Hispanic:	24	0.08
Jamaican	10	0.03
Trinidadian and Tobagonian	14	0.05
White:	26,732	89.62
Not Hispanic (25,886)	26,288	88.13
Hispanic (399)	444	1.49
Yugoslavian	16	0.05

Grand Haven

Place Type: City
County: Ottawa
Population: 11,168

Ancestry/Race	Number	%
African American/Black:	89	0.80
Not Hispanic (49)	87	0.78
Hispanic (1)	2	0.02
African, sub-Saharan:	53	0.47
African	53	0.47
Alaska Native tribes, specified:	2	0.02
All other tribes (2)	2	0.02
Am. Ind. or Alaska Nat., not spec.	56	0.50
American Indian tribes, specified:	74	0.66
Apache (3)	3	0.03
Blackfeet (1)	1	0.01
Cherokee (3)	11	0.10
Chippewa (8)	17	0.15
Choctaw (1)	2	0.02
Latin American Indians (1)	2	0.02
Lumbee (1)	1	0.01
Navajo (1)	1	0.01
Osage (1)	1	0.01
Ottawa (14)	18	0.16
Potawatomi (7)	13	0.12
All other tribes (2)	4	0.04
American Indian tribes, not spec.	2	0.02
Asian:	142	1.27
Cambodian (1)	1	0.01
Chinese, ex. Taiwanese (19)	23	0.21
Filipino (5)	17	0.15
Indian (6)	13	0.12
Japanese (2)	8	0.07
Korean (22)	27	0.24
Thai (2)	2	0.02
Vietnamese (39)	42	0.38
Other Asian, specified (1)	1	0.01
Other Asian, not specified	8	0.07
Australian	11	0.10
Austrian	5	0.04
Belgian	80	0.72
British	20	0.18
Canadian	14	0.13
Czech	87	0.78
Czechoslovakian	38	0.34
Danish	93	0.83
Dutch	2,586	23.17
English	1,432	12.83
European	65	0.58
Finnish	69	0.62
French, except Basque	578	5.18
French Canadian	215	1.93
German	2,686	24.07
Greek	8	0.07
Hawaii Native/Pacific Islander:	4	0.04
Micronesian:	1	0.01
Guamanian/Chamorro	1	0.01
Polynesian:	1	0.01
Native Hawaiian	1	0.01
Other Pac. Isl., not spec. (2)	2	0.02
Hispanic or Latino:	177	1.58
Central American:	7	0.06
Guatemalan	1	0.01
Honduran	2	0.02
Panamanian	1	0.01
Salvadoran	3	0.03
Cuban	4	0.04
Dominican Republic	2	0.02
Mexican	102	0.91
Puerto Rican	13	0.12
South American:	4	0.04
Colombian	2	0.02
Peruvian	2	0.02
Other Hispanic or Latino	45	0.40
Hungarian	41	0.37
Irish	1,451	13.00
Italian	479	4.29
Latvian	33	0.30
Lithuanian	40	0.36
Norwegian	152	1.36
Polish	770	6.90
Russian	59	0.53
Scandinavian	52	0.47
Scotch-Irish	154	1.38
Scottish	321	2.88
Slavic	27	0.24
Slovak	75	0.67
Slovene	32	0.29
Swedish	372	3.33
Swiss	22	0.20
Ukrainian	39	0.35
United States or American	394	3.53
Welsh	47	0.42
White:	10,905	97.65
Not Hispanic (10,654)	10,776	96.49
Hispanic (106)	129	1.16
Yugoslavian	16	0.14

Grand Haven

Place Type: Township
County: Ottawa
Population: 13,278

Ancestry/Race	Number	%
African American/Black:	37	0.28
Not Hispanic (16)	35	0.26
Hispanic	2	0.02
Am. Ind. or Alaska Nat., not spec.	18	0.14
American Indian tribes, specified:	105	0.79
Apache (1)	3	0.02
Blackfeet	1	0.01
Cherokee (2)	6	0.05
Chippewa (23)	40	0.30
Creek	2	0.02
Crow	4	0.03
Ottawa (8)	12	0.09
Potawatomi (5)	28	0.21
Pueblo	1	0.01
Seminole	1	0.01
All other tribes (1)	7	0.05
American Indian tribes, not spec.	4	0.03
Asian:	107	0.81
Chinese, ex. Taiwanese (8)	10	0.08
Filipino (12)	17	0.13
Indian (2)	5	0.04
Indonesian	1	0.01
Japanese (1)	10	0.08
Korean (28)	36	0.27
Laotian (6)	8	0.06
Sri Lankan	4	0.03
Thai (1)	1	0.01
Vietnamese (7)	8	0.06
Other Asian, not specified (7)	7	0.05
Austrian	25	0.19
Belgian	97	0.72
Brazilian	7	0.05
British	40	0.30
Canadian	83	0.62
Croatian	21	0.16
Czech	82	0.61
Czechoslovakian	17	0.13
Danish	213	1.59
Dutch	3,397	25.28
English	1,763	13.12
European	49	0.36
Finnish	26	0.19
French, except Basque	841	6.26
French Canadian	389	2.89
German	4,114	30.61
Greek	23	0.17
Hawaii Native/Pacific Islander:	8	0.06
Other Pac. Isl., not spec. (1)	8	0.06
Hispanic or Latino:	252	1.90
Central American:	2	0.02
Costa Rican	2	0.02
Cuban	1	0.01
Mexican	183	1.38
Puerto Rican	7	0.05
South American:	8	0.06
Colombian	3	0.02
Venezuelan	5	0.04
Other Hispanic or Latino	51	0.38
Hungarian	124	0.92
Irish	1,248	9.29
Italian	557	4.14
Lithuanian	6	0.04
Northern European	22	0.16
Norwegian	234	1.74
Pennsylvania German	9	0.07
Polish	916	6.82
Portuguese	28	0.21
Russian	63	0.47
Scandinavian	9	0.07
Scotch-Irish	105	0.78
Scottish	553	4.12
Serbian	7	0.05
Slavic	7	0.05
Slovak	81	0.60
Slovene	29	0.22
Swedish	498	3.71
Swiss	18	0.13
Ukrainian	57	0.42
United States or American	557	4.14
Welsh	47	0.35
West Indian, excl. Hispanic:	9	0.07
Haitian	2	0.01
Trinidadian and Tobagonian	7	0.05
White:	13,044	98.24
Not Hispanic (12,762)	12,872	96.94
Hispanic (138)	172	1.30
Yugoslavian	9	0.07

Grand Rapids charter

Place Type: Township
County: Kent
Population: 14,056

Ancestry/Race	Number	%
African American/Black:	186	1.32
Not Hispanic (138)	183	1.30
Hispanic (1)	3	0.02
African, sub-Saharan:	27	0.19
Ethiopian	27	0.19

Notes: 1. Figures in the "Number" column do not add up to the total population due to: a) Ancestry/Race overlap — e.g. persons can report being both White and Irish, b) persons of Hispanic origin can report being any race, c) persons reporting two ancestries are counted in both categories. 2. Numbers in parentheses indicate the number of persons reporting this ancestry/race alone, not in combination with any other ancestry/race. 3. Refer to the Explanation of Data in the front of the book for more detailed information.

Ancestry/Race	Number	%
Am. Ind. or Alaska Nat., not spec.	19	0.14
Albanian	9	0.06
American Indian tribes, specified:	41	0.29
Blackfeet	1	0.01
Cherokee (1)	12	0.09
Chippewa (12)	14	0.10
Iroquois	3	0.02
Latin American Indians (1)	2	0.01
Ottawa (2)	7	0.05
All other tribes (2)	2	0.01
American Indian tribes, not spec.	1	0.01
Arab:	149	1.06
Iraqi	6	0.04
Lebanese	115	0.82
Palestinian	8	0.06
Syrian	20	0.14
Asian:	245	1.74
Cambodian (1)	1	0.01
Chinese, ex. Taiwanese (39)	55	0.39
Filipino (7)	12	0.09
Indian (66)	70	0.50
Indonesian (3)	3	0.02
Japanese (15)	20	0.14
Korean (55)	66	0.47
Malaysian (1)	1	0.01
Pakistani (1)	2	0.01
Thai (1)	1	0.01
Vietnamese (12)	12	0.09
Other Asian, specified (1)	1	0.01
Other Asian, not specified	1	0.01
Austrian	38	0.27
Belgian	24	0.17
British	48	0.34
Canadian	57	0.41
Croatian	8	0.06
Czech	130	0.93
Czechoslovakian	38	0.27
Danish	145	1.03
Dutch	2,972	21.18
Eastern European	30	0.21
English	2,331	16.61
European	167	1.19
Finnish	59	0.42
French, except Basque	638	4.55
French Canadian	208	1.48
German	3,553	25.32
Greek	153	1.09
Hawaii Native/Pacific Islander:	6	0.04
Micronesian: (1)	1	0.01
Guamanian/Chamorro (1)	1	0.01
Polynesian:	5	0.04
Native Hawaiian	5	0.04
Hispanic or Latino:	183	1.30
Central American:	7	0.05
Costa Rican	1	0.01
Guatemalan	4	0.03
Honduran	2	0.01
Cuban	11	0.08
Dominican Republic	3	0.02
Mexican	98	0.70
Puerto Rican	26	0.18
South American:	3	0.02
Chilean	1	0.01
Colombian	1	0.01
Paraguayan	1	0.01
Other Hispanic or Latino	35	0.25
Hungarian	102	0.73
Irish	1,760	12.54
Italian	415	2.96
Latvian	38	0.27
Lithuanian	109	0.78
Norwegian	224	1.60
Pennsylvania German	11	0.08
Polish	1,136	8.09
Portuguese	27	0.19
Romanian	5	0.04
Russian	107	0.76
Scandinavian	51	0.36
Scotch-Irish	501	3.57
Scottish	371	2.64
Slavic	7	0.05
Slovak	18	0.13
Swedish	421	3.00
Swiss	42	0.30
United States or American	445	3.17
Welsh	97	0.69
West Indian, excl. Hispanic:	30	0.21
Belizean	7	0.05
Haitian	10	0.07
Jamaican	13	0.09
White:	13,602	96.77
Not Hispanic (13,375)	13,486	95.94
Hispanic (91)	116	0.83
Yugoslavian	34	0.24

Grand Rapids

Place Type: City
County: Kent
Population: 197,800

Ancestry/Race	Number	%
African American/Black:	43,463	21.97
Not Hispanic (39,401)	41,954	21.21
Hispanic (972)	1,509	0.76
African, sub-Saharan:	2,645	1.34
African	2,025	1.02
Ethiopian	388	0.20
Ghanian	24	0.01
Kenyan	11	0.01
Liberian	58	0.03
Nigerian	77	0.04
South African	7	0.00
Sudanese	25	0.01
Ugandan	11	0.01
Other sub-Saharan African	19	0.01
Alaska Native tribes, specified:	5	0.00
Eskimo	2	0.00
Tlingit-Haida (2)	3	0.00
Alaska Native tribes, not specified	1	0.00
Am. Ind. or Alaska Nat., not spec.	1,058	0.53
Albanian	152	0.08
American Indian tribes, specified:	1,878	0.95
Apache (8)	28	0.01
Blackfeet (22)	113	0.06
Cherokee (63)	327	0.17
Cheyenne (6)	9	0.00
Chickasaw (3)	5	0.00
Chippewa (251)	422	0.21
Choctaw (2)	18	0.01
Cree (3)	17	0.01
Creek (4)	15	0.01
Crow (2)	10	0.01
Delaware (1)	3	0.00
Iroquois (4)	29	0.01
Latin American Indians (121)	182	0.09
Lumbee (1)	4	0.00
Navajo (18)	28	0.01
Osage	1	0.00
Ottawa (234)	357	0.18
Paiute (1)	1	0.00
Pima (2)	3	0.00
Potawatomi (76)	155	0.08
Pueblo (2)	8	0.00
Puget Sound Salish	1	0.00
Seminole (1)	8	0.00
Sioux (15)	55	0.03
Tohono O'Odham (1)	1	0.00
Ute	1	0.00
Yuman (1)	1	0.00
All other tribes (44)	76	0.04
American Indian tribes, not spec.	149	0.08
Arab:	1,248	0.63
Arab/Arabic	186	0.09
Egyptian	6	0.00
Jordanian	182	0.09
Lebanese	561	0.28
Moroccan	38	0.02
Palestinian	23	0.01
Syrian	207	0.10
Other Arab	45	0.02
Armenian	121	0.06
Asian:	3,966	2.01
Bangladeshi (12)	16	0.01
Cambodian (10)	19	0.01
Chinese, ex. Taiwanese (344)	485	0.25
Filipino (210)	351	0.18
Hmong (5)	5	0.00
Indian (322)	416	0.21
Indonesian (25)	57	0.03
Japanese (64)	138	0.07
Korean (445)	531	0.27
Laotian (17)	32	0.02
Malaysian (7)	12	0.01
Pakistani (22)	27	0.01
Sri Lankan (10)	10	0.01
Taiwanese (4)	8	0.00
Thai (21)	45	0.02
Vietnamese (1,558)	1,651	0.83
Other Asian, specified (9)	27	0.01
Other Asian, not specified (34)	136	0.07
Assyrian/Chaldean/Syriac	13	0.01
Australian	43	0.02
Austrian	349	0.18
Belgian	262	0.13
Brazilian	63	0.03
British	368	0.19
Bulgarian	37	0.02
Canadian	580	0.29
Celtic	32	0.02
Croatian	164	0.08
Czech	473	0.24
Czechoslovakian	152	0.08
Danish	958	0.48
Dutch	31,050	15.69
Eastern European	40	0.02
English	13,683	6.92
European	924	0.47
Finnish	453	0.23
French, except Basque	5,217	2.64
French Canadian	1,657	0.84
German	27,296	13.80
German Russian	28	0.01
Greek	584	0.30
Hawaii Native/Pacific Islander:	381	0.19
Micronesian: (171)	193	0.10
Guamanian/Chamorro (169)	188	0.10
Other Micronesian (2)	5	0.00
Polynesian: (42)	84	0.04
Native Hawaiian (16)	54	0.03
Samoan (22)	25	0.01
Tongan (3)	3	0.00
Other Polynesian (1)	2	0.00
Other Pac. Isl., specified	14	0.01
Other Pac. Isl., not spec. (24)	90	0.05
Hispanic or Latino:	25,818	13.05
Central American:	2,191	1.11
Costa Rican	21	0.01
Guatemalan	1,762	0.89
Honduran	123	0.06
Nicaraguan	21	0.01
Panamanian	30	0.02
Salvadoran	198	0.10
Other Central American	36	0.02
Cuban	425	0.21
Dominican Republic	863	0.44
Mexican	16,600	8.39
Puerto Rican	2,331	1.18
South American:	175	0.09
Argentinean	24	0.01
Bolivian	9	0.00
Chilean	21	0.01
Colombian	50	0.03
Ecuadorian	9	0.00
Paraguayan	2	0.00
Peruvian	30	0.02
Venezuelan	19	0.01
Other South American	11	0.01
Other Hispanic or Latino	3,233	1.63
Hungarian	640	0.32

Notes: 1. Figures in the "Number" column do not add up to the total population due to: a) Ancestry/Race overlap — e.g. persons can report being both White and Irish, b) persons of Hispanic origin can report being any race, c) persons reporting two ancestries are counted in both categories. 2. Numbers in parentheses indicate the number of persons reporting this ancestry/race alone, not in combination with any other ancestry/race. 3. Refer to the Explanation of Data in the front of the book for more detailed information.

Ancestry/Race	Number	%
Iranian	92	0.05
Irish	16,984	8.58
Israeli	3	0.00
Italian	4,119	2.08
Latvian	378	0.19
Lithuanian	1,509	0.76
Luxemburger	6	0.00
Macedonian	7	0.00
Maltese	27	0.01
Northern European	223	0.11
Norwegian	1,326	0.67
Pennsylvania German	188	0.10
Polish	15,442	7.81
Portuguese	103	0.05
Romanian	181	0.09
Russian	856	0.43
Scandinavian	212	0.11
Scotch-Irish	2,170	1.10
Scottish	2,361	1.19
Serbian	74	0.04
Slavic	49	0.02
Slovak	121	0.06
Slovene	41	0.02
Swedish	2,966	1.50
Swiss	475	0.24
Turkish	29	0.01
Ukrainian	313	0.16
United States or American	5,996	3.03
Welsh	811	0.41
West Indian, excl. Hispanic:	156	0.08
Belizean	8	0.00
British West Indian	8	0.00
Dutch West Indian	15	0.01
Haitian	4	0.00
Jamaican	47	0.02
Trinidadian and Tobagonian	40	0.02
U.S. Virgin Islander	5	0.00
West Indian	29	0.01
White:	138,222	69.88
Not Hispanic (123,537)	127,058	64.24
Hispanic (9,579)	11,164	5.64
Yugoslavian	1,215	0.61

Grandville

Place Type: City
County: Kent
Population: 16,263

Ancestry/Race	Number	%
African American/Black:	304	1.87
Not Hispanic (217)	292	1.80
Hispanic (10)	12	0.07
African, sub-Saharan:	23	0.14
African	23	0.14
Alaska Native tribes, specified:	1	0.01
Alaska Athabascan (1)	1	0.01
Am. Ind. or Alaska Nat., not spec.	18	0.11
American Indian tribes, specified:	63	0.39
Cherokee (1)	5	0.03
Chippewa (11)	21	0.13
Crow	1	0.01
Iroquois (2)	2	0.01
Latin American Indians (1)	3	0.02
Navajo	6	0.04
Ottawa (7)	9	0.06
Potawatomi (8)	10	0.06
Pueblo	2	0.01
Sioux	1	0.01
Yuman	1	0.01
All other tribes (2)	2	0.01
American Indian tribes, not spec.	5	0.03
Arab:	79	0.49
Arab/Arabic	11	0.07
Lebanese	42	0.26
Syrian	26	0.16
Asian:	244	1.50
Chinese, ex. Taiwanese (25)	32	0.20
Filipino (14)	28	0.17
Indian (12)	18	0.11
Indonesian (3)	7	0.04
Japanese (7)	13	0.08
Korean (55)	71	0.44
Vietnamese (64)	73	0.45
Other Asian, not specified (1)	2	0.01
Austrian	27	0.17
Belgian	9	0.06
Brazilian	25	0.15
British	23	0.14
Canadian	48	0.30
Czech	93	0.57
Czechoslovakian	9	0.06
Danish	74	0.46
Dutch	6,073	37.34
English	1,747	10.74
European	78	0.48
Finnish	43	0.26
French, except Basque	671	4.13
French Canadian	90	0.55
German	3,021	18.58
Greek	27	0.17
Hawaii Native/Pacific Islander:	13	0.08
Polynesian: (2)	6	0.04
Native Hawaiian (1)	4	0.02
Samoan (1)	2	0.01
Other Pac. Isl., not spec. (2)	7	0.04
Hispanic or Latino:	501	3.08
Central American:	9	0.06
Costa Rican	1	0.01
Guatemalan	2	0.01
Honduran	2	0.01
Panamanian	1	0.01
Salvadoran	2	0.01
Other Central American	1	0.01
Cuban	75	0.46
Dominican Republic	7	0.04
Mexican	282	1.73
Puerto Rican	54	0.33
South American:	14	0.09
Argentinean	3	0.02
Bolivian	4	0.02
Colombian	1	0.01
Uruguayan	4	0.02
Venezuelan	2	0.01
Other Hispanic or Latino	60	0.37
Hungarian	59	0.36
Irish	1,200	7.38
Italian	545	3.35
Lithuanian	96	0.59
Norwegian	122	0.75
Polish	976	6.00
Romanian	7	0.04
Russian	20	0.12
Scandinavian	12	0.07
Scotch-Irish	114	0.70
Scottish	180	1.11
Slovak	15	0.09
Swedish	466	2.87
Swiss	45	0.28
Ukrainian	33	0.20
United States or American	915	5.63
Welsh	61	0.38
West Indian, excl. Hispanic:	20	0.12
Haitian	20	0.12
White:	15,643	96.19
Not Hispanic (15,113)	15,281	93.96
Hispanic (327)	362	2.23

Green Oak

Place Type: Township
County: Livingston
Population: 15,618

Ancestry/Race	Number	%
African American/Black:	280	1.79
Not Hispanic (245)	274	1.75
Hispanic (2)	6	0.04
Alaska Native tribes, not specified	1	0.01
Am. Ind. or Alaska Nat., not spec.	54	0.35
American Indian tribes, specified:	131	0.84
Apache (1)	6	0.04
Blackfeet (1)	4	0.03
Cherokee (4)	30	0.19
Cheyenne	2	0.01
Chippewa (25)	49	0.31
Choctaw (2)	3	0.02
Cree (1)	1	0.01
Iroquois (4)	6	0.04
Lumbee (5)	6	0.04
Navajo	6	0.04
Ottawa (5)	9	0.06
Potawatomi	4	0.03
Pueblo	1	0.01
Sioux	1	0.01
All other tribes (1)	3	0.02
American Indian tribes, not spec.	2	0.01
Arab:	56	0.36
Lebanese	56	0.36
Armenian	19	0.12
Asian:	110	0.70
Chinese, ex. Taiwanese (23)	23	0.15
Filipino (8)	13	0.08
Indian (12)	14	0.09
Indonesian	1	0.01
Japanese (10)	23	0.15
Korean (17)	22	0.14
Malaysian (1)	1	0.01
Thai (1)	5	0.03
Vietnamese (3)	3	0.02
Other Asian, not specified (2)	5	0.03
Austrian	27	0.17
Belgian	30	0.19
British	83	0.53
Canadian	81	0.52
Croatian	43	0.27
Czech	43	0.27
Czechoslovakian	55	0.35
Danish	116	0.74
Dutch	367	2.35
English	2,114	13.51
European	170	1.09
Finnish	296	1.89
French, except Basque	831	5.31
French Canadian	370	2.36
German	4,265	27.26
Greek	42	0.27
Hawaii Native/Pacific Islander:	10	0.06
Micronesian: (2)	2	0.01
Guamanian/Chamorro (2)	2	0.01
Polynesian:	6	0.04
Native Hawaiian	6	0.04
Other Pac. Isl., not spec.	2	0.01
Hispanic or Latino:	200	1.28
Central American:	5	0.03
Guatemalan	1	0.01
Honduran	1	0.01
Nicaraguan	1	0.01
Salvadoran	2	0.01
Cuban	18	0.12
Mexican	106	0.68
Puerto Rican	15	0.10
South American:	15	0.10
Argentinean	3	0.02
Colombian	3	0.02
Peruvian	3	0.02
Venezuelan	1	0.01
Other South American	5	0.03
Other Hispanic or Latino	41	0.26
Hungarian	225	1.44
Irish	2,422	15.48
Italian	1,055	6.74
Lithuanian	81	0.52
Maltese	45	0.29
Norwegian	176	1.12
Polish	2,232	14.27
Romanian	41	0.26
Russian	124	0.79
Scandinavian	9	0.06
Scotch-Irish	426	2.72

Notes: 1. Figures in the "Number" column do not add up to the total population due to: a) Ancestry/Race overlap — e.g. persons can report being both White and Irish, b) persons of Hispanic origin can report being any race, c) persons reporting two ancestries are counted in both categories. 2. Numbers in parentheses indicate the number of persons reporting this ancestry/race alone, not in combination with any other ancestry/race. 3. Refer to the Explanation of Data in the front of the book for more detailed information.

Scottish	617	3.94
Serbian	21	0.13
Slovak	81	0.52
Slovene	11	0.07
Swedish	220	1.41
Swiss	56	0.36
Ukrainian	128	0.82
United States or American	1,013	6.47
Welsh	119	0.76
White:	15,181	97.20
Not Hispanic (14,834)	15,007	96.09
Hispanic (147)	174	1.11
Yugoslavian	6	0.04

Grosse Ile

Place Type: Census Designated Place
County: Wayne
Population: 10,894

Ancestry/Race	Number	%
African American/Black:	49	0.45
Not Hispanic (39)	47	0.43
Hispanic	2	0.02
Am. Ind. or Alaska Nat., not spec.	25	0.23
Albanian	8	0.07
American Indian tribes, specified:	66	0.61
Blackfeet	1	0.01
Cherokee (6)	19	0.17
Chippewa (2)	6	0.06
Choctaw (2)	5	0.05
Iroquois (15)	24	0.22
Latin American Indians (1)	2	0.02
Lumbee (1)	5	0.05
Menominee (3)	3	0.03
Sioux (1)	1	0.01
Arab:	138	1.27
Lebanese	26	0.24
Palestinian	5	0.05
Syrian	107	0.98
Armenian	23	0.21
Asian:	340	3.12
Chinese, ex. Taiwanese (54)	59	0.54
Filipino (27)	35	0.32
Indian (101)	103	0.95
Indonesian (1)	8	0.07
Japanese (27)	31	0.28
Korean (62)	73	0.67
Pakistani (13)	17	0.16
Thai (11)	11	0.10
Vietnamese	1	0.01
Other Asian, not specified	2	0.02
Austrian	47	0.43
Belgian	24	0.22
British	38	0.35
Canadian	95	0.87
Celtic	9	0.08
Croatian	11	0.10
Czech	43	0.39
Czechoslovakian	39	0.36
Danish	17	0.16
Dutch	271	2.49
English	1,282	11.77
European	61	0.56
Finnish	37	0.34
French, except Basque	826	7.58
French Canadian	229	2.10
German	2,849	26.15
Greek	74	0.68
Hawaii Native/Pacific Islander:	4	0.04
Micronesian: (3)	3	0.03
Guamanian/Chamorro (3)	3	0.03
Polynesian: (1)	1	0.01
Native Hawaiian (1)	1	0.01
Hispanic or Latino:	175	1.61
Central American:	2	0.02
Guatemalan	1	0.01
Honduran	1	0.01
Cuban	10	0.09
Mexican	96	0.88
Puerto Rican	5	0.05
South American:	19	0.17
Argentinean	4	0.04
Chilean	3	0.03
Colombian	8	0.07
Ecuadorian	2	0.02
Peruvian	1	0.01
Venezuelan	1	0.01
Other Hispanic or Latino	43	0.39
Hungarian	508	4.66
Irish	1,785	16.39
Italian	1,068	9.80
Latvian	16	0.15
Lithuanian	82	0.75
Macedonian	9	0.08
Maltese	131	1.20
Northern European	13	0.12
Norwegian	64	0.59
Pennsylvania German	7	0.06
Polish	1,883	17.28
Romanian	34	0.31
Russian	107	0.98
Scandinavian	10	0.09
Scotch-Irish	214	1.96
Scottish	249	2.29
Serbian	119	1.09
Slovak	37	0.34
Swedish	153	1.40
Swiss	20	0.18
Turkish	29	0.27
Ukrainian	78	0.72
United States or American	465	4.27
Welsh	156	1.43
White:	10,474	96.14
Not Hispanic (10,241)	10,333	94.85
Hispanic (133)	141	1.29
Yugoslavian	48	0.44

Grosse Pointe Park

Place Type: City
County: Wayne
Population: 12,443

Ancestry/Race	Number	%
African American/Black:	437	3.51
Not Hispanic (362)	430	3.46
Hispanic (5)	7	0.06
African, sub-Saharan:	29	0.23
Ghanian	29	0.23
Am. Ind. or Alaska Nat., not spec.	31	0.25
Albanian	219	1.76
American Indian tribes, specified:	50	0.40
Apache (1)	1	0.01
Blackfeet (1)	2	0.02
Cherokee (2)	14	0.11
Chippewa (3)	11	0.09
Choctaw	1	0.01
Creek	1	0.01
Iroquois (1)	4	0.03
Latin American Indians (4)	4	0.03
Lumbee (2)	2	0.02
Ottawa	1	0.01
Potawatomi	1	0.01
All other tribes (6)	8	0.06
American Indian tribes, not spec.	5	0.04
Arab:	385	3.09
Arab/Arabic	33	0.27
Iraqi	8	0.06
Lebanese	272	2.19
Palestinian	25	0.20
Syrian	20	0.16
Other Arab	27	0.22
Armenian	70	0.56
Asian:	275	2.21
Bangladeshi (5)	5	0.04
Chinese, ex. Taiwanese (45)	59	0.47
Filipino (54)	62	0.50
Indian (56)	62	0.50
Indonesian (1)	1	0.01
Japanese (17)	31	0.25
Korean (25)	27	0.22
Pakistani (2)	2	0.02
Sri Lankan (4)	4	0.03
Taiwanese (2)	2	0.02
Thai (2)	2	0.02
Vietnamese (8)	10	0.08
Other Asian, specified (1)	1	0.01
Other Asian, not specified (3)	7	0.06
Assyrian/Chaldean/Syriac	13	0.10
Australian	38	0.31
Austrian	84	0.68
Belgian	141	1.13
British	115	0.92
Canadian	107	0.86
Croatian	57	0.46
Cypriot	9	0.07
Czech	83	0.67
Czechoslovakian	19	0.15
Danish	74	0.59
Dutch	374	3.01
Eastern European	7	0.06
English	1,561	12.55
European	60	0.48
Finnish	58	0.47
French, except Basque	575	4.62
French Canadian	254	2.04
German	3,092	24.85
Greek	370	2.97
Hawaii Native/Pacific Islander:	7	0.06
Polynesian: (3)	5	0.04
Native Hawaiian (1)	2	0.02
Samoan (1)	2	0.02
Other Polynesian (1)	1	0.01
Other Pac. Isl., not spec. (1)	2	0.02
Hispanic or Latino:	217	1.74
Central American:	6	0.05
Costa Rican	1	0.01
Guatemalan	1	0.01
Honduran	4	0.03
Cuban	14	0.11
Mexican	99	0.80
Puerto Rican	3	0.02
South American:	34	0.27
Argentinean	5	0.04
Chilean	3	0.02
Colombian	9	0.07
Ecuadorian	2	0.02
Paraguayan	1	0.01
Peruvian	2	0.02
Venezuelan	4	0.03
Other South American	8	0.06
Other Hispanic or Latino	61	0.49
Hungarian	81	0.65
Iranian	11	0.09
Irish	2,500	20.09
Italian	1,070	8.60
Lithuanian	60	0.48
Maltese	5	0.04
Northern European	4	0.03
Norwegian	152	1.22
Polish	1,320	10.61
Portuguese	6	0.05
Romanian	53	0.43
Russian	105	0.84
Scandinavian	23	0.18
Scotch-Irish	305	2.45
Scottish	575	4.62
Serbian	19	0.15
Slavic	7	0.06
Slovak	44	0.35
Slovene	26	0.21
Swedish	238	1.91
Swiss	107	0.86
Ukrainian	38	0.31
United States or American	414	3.33
Welsh	105	0.84
West Indian, excl. Hispanic:	30	0.24
Jamaican	23	0.18
West Indian	7	0.06

Notes: 1. Figures in the "Number" column do not add up to the total population due to: a) Ancestry/Race overlap — e.g. persons can report being both White and Irish, b) persons of Hispanic origin can report being any race, c) persons reporting two ancestries are counted in both categories. 2. Numbers in parentheses indicate the number of persons reporting this ancestry/race alone, not in combination with any other ancestry/race. 3. Refer to the Explanation of Data in the front of the book for more detailed information.

Ancestry/Race	Number	%
White:	11,735	94.31
Not Hispanic (11,345)	11,560	92.90
Hispanic (162)	175	1.41
Yugoslavian	33	0.27

Grosse Pointe Woods

Place Type: City
County: Wayne
Population: 17,080

Ancestry/Race	Number	%
African American/Black:	134	0.78
Not Hispanic (106)	132	0.77
Hispanic (2)	2	0.01
Am. Ind. or Alaska Nat., not spec.	23	0.13
American Indian tribes, specified:	18	0.11
Cherokee	5	0.03
Chippewa (2)	2	0.01
Cree	1	0.01
Delaware	1	0.01
Iroquois (5)	7	0.04
Seminole	1	0.01
Sioux (1)	1	0.01
American Indian tribes, not spec.	2	0.01
Arab:	912	5.34
Arab/Arabic	124	0.73
Lebanese	649	3.80
Syrian	131	0.77
Other Arab	8	0.05
Armenian	58	0.34
Asian:	421	2.46
Bangladeshi (11)	11	0.06
Chinese, ex. Taiwanese (46)	61	0.36
Filipino (75)	96	0.56
Indian (148)	155	0.91
Indonesian	1	0.01
Japanese (7)	11	0.06
Korean (51)	57	0.33
Laotian (1)	1	0.01
Pakistani (5)	9	0.05
Taiwanese (2)	2	0.01
Thai (2)	2	0.01
Vietnamese (5)	5	0.03
Other Asian, specified	3	0.02
Other Asian, not specified	7	0.04
Assyrian/Chaldean/Syriac	4	0.02
Australian	20	0.12
Austrian	101	0.59
Belgian	630	3.69
British	85	0.50
Bulgarian	27	0.16
Canadian	75	0.44
Celtic	13	0.08
Croatian	60	0.35
Czech	61	0.36
Czechoslovakian	11	0.06
Danish	45	0.26
Dutch	307	1.80
Eastern European	5	0.03
English	1,810	10.60
European	58	0.34
Finnish	72	0.42
French, except Basque	889	5.20
French Canadian	319	1.87
German	4,463	26.13
Greek	586	3.43
Hawaii Native/Pacific Islander:	7	0.04
Micronesian:	4	0.02
Guamanian/Chamorro	4	0.02
Polynesian:	1	0.01
Native Hawaiian	1	0.01
Other Pac. Isl., not spec.	2	0.01
Hispanic or Latino:	167	0.98
Central American:	2	0.01
Guatemalan	1	0.01
Honduran	1	0.01
Cuban	5	0.03
Dominican Republic	8	0.05
Mexican	64	0.37
Puerto Rican	16	0.09
South American:	23	0.13
Argentinean	5	0.03
Chilean	1	0.01
Colombian	4	0.02
Ecuadorian	6	0.04
Venezuelan	4	0.02
Other South American	3	0.02
Other Hispanic or Latino	49	0.29
Hungarian	147	0.86
Iranian	31	0.18
Irish	2,544	14.89
Italian	2,597	15.20
Lithuanian	33	0.19
Macedonian	23	0.13
Maltese	36	0.21
Northern European	28	0.16
Norwegian	188	1.10
Pennsylvania German	9	0.05
Polish	2,058	12.05
Portuguese	3	0.02
Romanian	97	0.57
Russian	132	0.77
Scandinavian	15	0.09
Scotch-Irish	261	1.53
Scottish	885	5.18
Serbian	62	0.36
Slavic	24	0.14
Slovak	88	0.52
Slovene	4	0.02
Swedish	284	1.66
Swiss	94	0.55
Ukrainian	180	1.05
United States or American	441	2.58
Welsh	103	0.60
White:	16,562	96.97
Not Hispanic (16,310)	16,414	96.10
Hispanic (138)	148	0.87
Yugoslavian	29	0.17

Hamburg

Place Type: Township
County: Livingston
Population: 20,627

Ancestry/Race	Number	%
African American/Black:	237	1.15
Not Hispanic (210)	233	1.13
Hispanic (1)	4	0.02
African, sub-Saharan:	30	0.15
African	30	0.15
Am. Ind. or Alaska Nat., not spec.	39	0.19
American Indian tribes, specified:	97	0.47
Apache	5	0.02
Blackfeet	3	0.01
Cherokee (8)	24	0.12
Chippewa (11)	28	0.14
Choctaw	2	0.01
Delaware (6)	6	0.03
Iroquois (5)	7	0.03
Latin American Indians (1)	1	0.00
Menominee (1)	1	0.00
Ottawa (4)	8	0.04
Shoshone (1)	1	0.00
Sioux (1)	5	0.02
Yaqui (3)	3	0.01
All other tribes (1)	3	0.01
American Indian tribes, not spec.	2	0.01
Arab:	94	0.46
Arab/Arabic	5	0.02
Jordanian	10	0.05
Lebanese	79	0.39
Armenian	108	0.53
Asian:	147	0.71
Chinese, ex. Taiwanese (23)	31	0.15
Filipino (13)	36	0.17
Indian (6)	11	0.05
Indonesian	1	0.00
Japanese (17)	28	0.14
Korean (20)	21	0.10
Vietnamese (5)	7	0.03
Other Asian, specified	2	0.01
Other Asian, not specified (4)	10	0.05
Assyrian/Chaldean/Syriac	10	0.05
Austrian	65	0.32
Basque	6	0.03
Belgian	85	0.41
British	62	0.30
Canadian	219	1.07
Croatian	82	0.40
Czech	47	0.23
Czechoslovakian	105	0.51
Danish	97	0.47
Dutch	539	2.63
Eastern European	10	0.05
English	2,826	13.79
Estonian	6	0.03
European	166	0.81
Finnish	209	1.02
French, except Basque	1,340	6.54
French Canadian	498	2.43
German	5,656	27.61
Greek	146	0.71
Hawaii Native/Pacific Islander:	15	0.07
Micronesian: (4)	4	0.02
Guamanian/Chamorro (4)	4	0.02
Polynesian: (2)	8	0.04
Native Hawaiian (2)	8	0.04
Other Pac. Isl., specified	2	0.01
Other Pac. Isl., not spec.	1	0.00
Hispanic or Latino:	236	1.14
Central American:	6	0.03
Costa Rican	1	0.00
Guatemalan	2	0.01
Panamanian	3	0.01
Cuban	7	0.03
Mexican	142	0.69
Puerto Rican	9	0.04
South American:	13	0.06
Chilean	3	0.01
Colombian	7	0.03
Ecuadorian	2	0.01
Peruvian	1	0.00
Other Hispanic or Latino	59	0.29
Hungarian	241	1.18
Iranian	35	0.17
Irish	3,607	17.61
Italian	1,294	6.32
Lithuanian	83	0.41
Macedonian	31	0.15
Maltese	96	0.47
Northern European	7	0.03
Norwegian	251	1.23
Polish	2,717	13.26
Romanian	35	0.17
Russian	94	0.46
Scandinavian	79	0.39
Scotch-Irish	372	1.82
Scottish	755	3.69
Serbian	8	0.04
Slavic	7	0.03
Slovak	66	0.32
Slovene	9	0.04
Swedish	429	2.09
Swiss	62	0.30
Ukrainian	141	0.69
United States or American	1,468	7.17
Welsh	245	1.20
West Indian, excl. Hispanic:	9	0.04
Jamaican	9	0.04
White:	20,209	97.97
Not Hispanic (19,902)	20,018	97.05
Hispanic (152)	191	0.93
Yugoslavian	19	0.09

Notes: 1. Figures in the "Number" column do not add up to the total population due to: a) Ancestry/Race overlap — e.g. persons can report being both White and Irish, b) persons of Hispanic origin can report being any race, c) persons reporting two ancestries are counted in both categories. 2. Numbers in parentheses indicate the number of persons reporting this ancestry/race alone, not in combination with any other ancestry/race. 3. Refer to the Explanation of Data in the front of the book for more detailed information.

Hamtramck

Place Type: City
County: Wayne
Population: 22,976

Ancestry/Race	Number	%
African American/Black:	3,690	16.06
Not Hispanic (3,430)	3,630	15.80
Hispanic (43)	60	0.26
African, sub-Saharan:	79	0.34
African	73	0.32
Other sub-Saharan African	6	0.03
Alaska Native tribes, specified:	4	0.02
Eskimo	4	0.02
Alaska Native tribes, not specified	5	0.02
Am. Ind. or Alaska Nat., not spec.	129	0.56
Albanian	635	2.76
American Indian tribes, specified:	94	0.41
Blackfeet (3)	6	0.03
Cherokee (13)	30	0.13
Cheyenne	8	0.03
Chippewa (4)	9	0.04
Creek	1	0.00
Iroquois (13)	19	0.08
Latin American Indians (1)	1	0.00
Lumbee (2)	3	0.01
Ottawa	3	0.01
Potawatomi (1)	2	0.01
Pueblo	1	0.00
Seminole	1	0.00
All other tribes (5)	10	0.04
American Indian tribes, not spec.	18	0.08
Arab:	2,158	9.39
Arab/Arabic	1,285	5.59
Egyptian	13	0.06
Iraqi	111	0.48
Jordanian	17	0.07
Lebanese	172	0.75
Palestinian	14	0.06
Syrian	5	0.02
Other Arab	541	2.35
Armenian	15	0.07
Asian:	3,209	13.97
Bangladeshi (609)	1,034	4.50
Chinese, ex. Taiwanese (39)	46	0.20
Filipino (55)	62	0.27
Indian (1,245)	1,537	6.69
Japanese (4)	8	0.03
Korean (18)	24	0.10
Laotian (2)	2	0.01
Pakistani (134)	181	0.79
Vietnamese (2)	3	0.01
Other Asian, not specified (118)	312	1.36
Australian	9	0.04
Austrian	7	0.03
Belgian	19	0.08
British	20	0.09
Bulgarian	15	0.07
Canadian	55	0.24
Croatian	27	0.12
Czech	33	0.14
Czechoslovakian	17	0.07
Danish	16	0.07
Dutch	61	0.27
English	245	1.07
European	48	0.21
Finnish	23	0.10
French, except Basque	186	0.81
French Canadian	64	0.28
German	661	2.88
Greek	11	0.05
Hawaii Native/Pacific Islander:	69	0.30
Micronesian: (13)	17	0.07
Guamanian/Chamorro (13)	17	0.07
Polynesian: (9)	13	0.06
Native Hawaiian	4	0.02
Samoan (9)	9	0.04
Other Pac. Isl., not spec. (1)	39	0.17
Hispanic or Latino:	300	1.31
Central American:	3	0.01
Nicaraguan	3	0.01
Cuban	9	0.04
Dominican Republic	3	0.01
Mexican	140	0.61
Puerto Rican	44	0.19
South American:	7	0.03
Chilean	1	0.00
Colombian	3	0.01
Ecuadorian	2	0.01
Peruvian	1	0.00
Other Hispanic or Latino	94	0.41
Hungarian	28	0.12
Irish	497	2.16
Italian	424	1.85
Lithuanian	35	0.15
Macedonian	125	0.54
Maltese	8	0.03
Norwegian	29	0.13
Polish	5,263	22.91
Romanian	33	0.14
Russian	315	1.37
Scotch-Irish	49	0.21
Scottish	158	0.69
Serbian	5	0.02
Slavic	20	0.09
Slovak	94	0.41
Slovene	7	0.03
Swedish	25	0.11
Swiss	5	0.02
Ukrainian	738	3.21
United States or American	412	1.79
Welsh	21	0.09
West Indian, excl. Hispanic:	16	0.07
Jamaican	16	0.07
White:	16,305	70.97
Not Hispanic (13,872)	16,142	70.26
Hispanic (135)	163	0.71
Yugoslavian	2,403	10.46

Harper Woods

Place Type: City
County: Wayne
Population: 14,254

Ancestry/Race	Number	%
African American/Black:	1,539	10.80
Not Hispanic (1,449)	1,523	10.68
Hispanic (11)	16	0.11
African, sub-Saharan:	65	0.46
African	65	0.46
Am. Ind. or Alaska Nat., not spec.	35	0.25
Albanian	6	0.04
American Indian tribes, specified:	94	0.66
Apache	2	0.01
Blackfeet	1	0.01
Cherokee (5)	25	0.18
Chippewa (11)	18	0.13
Choctaw	2	0.01
Comanche	1	0.01
Creek	2	0.01
Iroquois (2)	5	0.04
Latin American Indians (4)	5	0.04
Lumbee (8)	11	0.08
Ottawa (6)	17	0.12
All other tribes (3)	5	0.04
American Indian tribes, not spec.	2	0.01
Arab:	328	2.30
Arab/Arabic	25	0.18
Lebanese	214	1.50
Moroccan	15	0.11
Syrian	68	0.48
Other Arab	6	0.04
Armenian	101	0.71
Asian:	282	1.98
Chinese, ex. Taiwanese (35)	43	0.30
Filipino (94)	108	0.76
Hmong (13)	13	0.09
Indian (51)	54	0.38
Indonesian	1	0.01
Japanese (7)	15	0.11
Korean (12)	17	0.12
Pakistani (8)	8	0.06
Vietnamese (21)	21	0.15
Other Asian, not specified (1)	2	0.01
Austrian	102	0.72
Belgian	343	2.41
Brazilian	9	0.06
British	24	0.17
Bulgarian	32	0.22
Canadian	122	0.86
Carpatho Rusyn	5	0.04
Celtic	7	0.05
Croatian	56	0.39
Czech	5	0.04
Czechoslovakian	69	0.48
Danish	11	0.08
Dutch	201	1.41
Eastern European	30	0.21
English	1,110	7.79
European	129	0.91
Finnish	44	0.31
French, except Basque	871	6.11
French Canadian	427	3.00
German	2,835	19.89
Greek	252	1.77
Hawaii Native/Pacific Islander:	1	0.01
Micronesian: (1)	1	0.01
Guamanian/Chamorro (1)	1	0.01
Hispanic or Latino:	224	1.57
Central American:	4	0.03
Honduran	1	0.01
Panamanian	1	0.01
Other Central American	2	0.01
Cuban	16	0.11
Dominican Republic	1	0.01
Mexican	118	0.83
Puerto Rican	23	0.16
South American:	12	0.08
Argentinean	4	0.03
Bolivian	2	0.01
Chilean	2	0.01
Colombian	2	0.01
Peruvian	2	0.01
Other Hispanic or Latino	50	0.35
Hungarian	147	1.03
Irish	2,295	16.10
Israeli	5	0.04
Italian	2,031	14.25
Lithuanian	95	0.67
Macedonian	12	0.08
Maltese	31	0.22
Northern European	40	0.28
Norwegian	69	0.48
Pennsylvania German	11	0.08
Polish	2,133	14.96
Romanian	34	0.24
Russian	78	0.55
Scandinavian	10	0.07
Scotch-Irish	269	1.89
Scottish	369	2.59
Serbian	44	0.31
Slavic	11	0.08
Slovak	54	0.38
Slovene	7	0.05
Swedish	152	1.07
Swiss	27	0.19
Turkish	5	0.04
Ukrainian	87	0.61
United States or American	403	2.83
Welsh	88	0.62
West Indian, excl. Hispanic:	19	0.13
Haitian	12	0.08
West Indian	7	0.05
White:	12,423	87.15
Not Hispanic (12,099)	12,252	85.95
Hispanic (148)	171	1.20
Yugoslavian	32	0.22

Notes: 1. Figures in the "Number" column do not add up to the total population due to: a) Ancestry/Race overlap — e.g. persons can report being both White and Irish, b) persons of Hispanic origin can report being any race, c) persons reporting two ancestries are counted in both categories. 2. Numbers in parentheses indicate the number of persons reporting this ancestry/race alone, not in combination with any other ancestry/race. 3. Refer to the Explanation of Data in the front of the book for more detailed information.

Harrison

Place Type: Census Designated Place
County: Macomb
Population: 24,461

Ancestry/Race	Number	%
African American/Black:	694	2.84
Not Hispanic (586)	674	2.76
Hispanic (18)	20	0.08
African, sub-Saharan:	35	0.14
African	35	0.14
Am. Ind. or Alaska Nat., not spec.	82	0.34
Albanian	43	0.18
American Indian tribes, specified:	153	0.63
Apache (1)	1	0.00
Blackfeet (2)	10	0.04
Cherokee (20)	53	0.22
Chippewa (17)	38	0.16
Cree	3	0.01
Creek	1	0.00
Crow	1	0.00
Delaware (2)	2	0.01
Iroquois (1)	6	0.02
Lumbee (10)	15	0.06
Ottawa (1)	2	0.01
Potawatomi (1)	11	0.04
Pueblo (1)	1	0.00
All other tribes (3)	9	0.04
American Indian tribes, not spec.	7	0.03
Arab:	453	1.85
Arab/Arabic	77	0.31
Lebanese	273	1.12
Moroccan	5	0.02
Syrian	98	0.40
Armenian	8	0.03
Asian:	215	0.88
Chinese, ex. Taiwanese (16)	30	0.12
Filipino (29)	48	0.20
Indian (31)	41	0.17
Indonesian	1	0.00
Japanese (11)	28	0.11
Korean (34)	39	0.16
Laotian (1)	1	0.00
Taiwanese (2)	2	0.01
Vietnamese (12)	15	0.06
Other Asian, not specified (5)	10	0.04
Assyrian/Chaldean/Syriac	72	0.29
Australian	16	0.07
Austrian	151	0.62
Belgian	637	2.60
British	134	0.55
Bulgarian	9	0.04
Canadian	159	0.65
Celtic	14	0.06
Croatian	79	0.32
Czech	147	0.60
Czechoslovakian	50	0.20
Danish	116	0.47
Dutch	247	1.01
English	2,515	10.28
European	25	0.10
Finnish	188	0.77
French, except Basque	1,807	7.39
French Canadian	777	3.18
German	6,838	27.96
German Russian	7	0.03
Greek	303	1.24
Hawaii Native/Pacific Islander:	22	0.09
Micronesian: (3)	8	0.03
Guamanian/Chamorro (2)	7	0.03
Other Micronesian (1)	1	0.00
Polynesian: (7)	9	0.04
Native Hawaiian (2)	4	0.02
Samoan (5)	5	0.02
Other Pac. Isl., not spec.	5	0.02
Hispanic or Latino:	362	1.48
Central American:	7	0.03
Costa Rican	2	0.01
Guatemalan	5	0.02
Cuban	14	0.06
Dominican Republic	1	0.00
Mexican	206	0.84
Puerto Rican	39	0.16
South American:	20	0.08
Argentinean	5	0.02
Chilean	2	0.01
Colombian	5	0.02
Peruvian	2	0.01
Venezuelan	5	0.02
Other South American	1	0.00
Other Hispanic or Latino	75	0.31
Hungarian	278	1.14
Irish	3,009	12.30
Italian	3,164	12.94
Latvian	14	0.06
Lithuanian	69	0.28
Maltese	60	0.25
Northern European	9	0.04
Norwegian	245	1.00
Pennsylvania German	7	0.03
Polish	4,073	16.65
Romanian	66	0.27
Russian	236	0.96
Scandinavian	17	0.07
Scotch-Irish	267	1.09
Scottish	708	2.89
Serbian	21	0.09
Slovak	120	0.49
Slovene	9	0.04
Swedish	148	0.61
Swiss	77	0.31
Turkish	7	0.03
Ukrainian	126	0.52
United States or American	1,019	4.17
Welsh	59	0.24
West Indian, excl. Hispanic:	13	0.05
Haitian	13	0.05
White:	23,474	95.97
Not Hispanic (22,902)	23,226	94.95
Hispanic (221)	248	1.01
Yugoslavian	113	0.46

Hartland

Place Type: Township
County: Livingston
Population: 10,996

Ancestry/Race	Number	%
African American/Black:	45	0.41
Not Hispanic (29)	44	0.40
Hispanic (1)	1	0.01
Alaska Native tribes, specified:	5	0.05
Eskimo	3	0.03
Tlingit-Haida (2)	2	0.02
Am. Ind. or Alaska Nat., not spec.	19	0.17
American Indian tribes, specified:	53	0.48
Apache	3	0.03
Blackfeet	1	0.01
Cherokee (2)	19	0.17
Chippewa (8)	11	0.10
Colville (1)	5	0.05
Crow	2	0.02
Iroquois (1)	3	0.03
Latin American Indians (2)	3	0.03
All other tribes (3)	6	0.05
American Indian tribes, not spec.	3	0.03
Arab:	128	1.17
Arab/Arabic	6	0.05
Iraqi	14	0.13
Lebanese	70	0.64
Syrian	38	0.35
Asian:	69	0.63
Chinese, ex. Taiwanese (9)	10	0.09
Filipino (4)	13	0.12
Indian (4)	9	0.08
Japanese (7)	16	0.15
Korean (12)	17	0.15
Taiwanese (3)	3	0.03
Vietnamese (1)	1	0.01
Austrian	23	0.21
Belgian	35	0.32
British	63	0.58
Canadian	48	0.44
Carpatho Rusyn	6	0.05
Croatian	13	0.12
Czech	122	1.11
Czechoslovakian	52	0.48
Danish	156	1.43
Dutch	206	1.88
English	1,939	17.71
European	36	0.33
Finnish	191	1.74
French, except Basque	650	5.94
French Canadian	267	2.44
German	3,124	28.54
Greek	88	0.80
Hawaii Native/Pacific Islander:	1	0.01
Other Pac. Isl., not spec.	1	0.01
Hispanic or Latino:	122	1.11
Central American:	6	0.05
Guatemalan	6	0.05
Cuban	3	0.03
Mexican	62	0.56
Puerto Rican	13	0.12
South American:	4	0.04
Chilean	3	0.03
Colombian	1	0.01
Other Hispanic or Latino	34	0.31
Hungarian	178	1.63
Irish	2,031	18.55
Israeli	8	0.07
Italian	569	5.20
Lithuanian	57	0.52
Luxemburger	12	0.11
Macedonian	34	0.31
Maltese	40	0.37
Norwegian	298	2.72
Polish	1,141	10.42
Romanian	15	0.14
Russian	80	0.73
Scotch-Irish	212	1.94
Scottish	247	2.26
Slovak	48	0.44
Slovene	26	0.24
Swedish	236	2.16
Ukrainian	59	0.54
United States or American	502	4.59
Welsh	111	1.01
West Indian, excl. Hispanic:	10	0.09
Other West Indian	10	0.09
White:	10,861	98.77
Not Hispanic (10,691)	10,770	97.94
Hispanic (78)	91	0.83
Yugoslavian	8	0.07

Haslett

Place Type: Census Designated Place
County: Ingham
Population: 11,283

Ancestry/Race	Number	%
African American/Black:	319	2.83
Not Hispanic (270)	317	2.81
Hispanic	2	0.02
African, sub-Saharan:	23	0.20
African	15	0.13
Cape Verdean	8	0.07
Am. Ind. or Alaska Nat., not spec.	19	0.17
American Indian tribes, specified:	51	0.45
Apache (1)	3	0.03
Blackfeet	1	0.01
Cherokee (5)	12	0.11
Chippewa (16)	26	0.23
Choctaw	1	0.01
Iroquois (1)	1	0.01
Latin American Indians (1)	1	0.01
Ottawa (1)	2	0.02

Notes: 1. Figures in the "Number" column do not add up to the total population due to: a) Ancestry/Race overlap — e.g. persons can report being both White and Irish, b) persons of Hispanic origin can report being any race, c) persons reporting two ancestries are counted in both categories. 2. Numbers in parentheses indicate the number of persons reporting this ancestry/race alone, not in combination with any other ancestry/race. 3. Refer to the Explanation of Data in the front of the book for more detailed information.

Ancestry/Race	Number	%
Pueblo	1	0.01
Sioux (1)	1	0.01
Yaqui	1	0.01
All other tribes (1)	1	0.01
American Indian tribes, not spec.	5	0.04
Arab:	54	0.48
Lebanese	47	0.42
Palestinian	7	0.06
Armenian	9	0.08
Asian:	352	3.12
Chinese, ex. Taiwanese (92)	106	0.94
Filipino (19)	30	0.27
Hmong (4)	4	0.04
Indian (62)	67	0.59
Indonesian	1	0.01
Japanese (13)	16	0.14
Korean (54)	58	0.51
Pakistani (10)	10	0.09
Taiwanese (15)	17	0.15
Thai (1)	1	0.01
Vietnamese (22)	22	0.19
Other Asian, specified (7)	8	0.07
Other Asian, not specified (3)	12	0.11
Austrian	16	0.14
Belgian	60	0.53
British	84	0.75
Canadian	72	0.64
Celtic	6	0.05
Croatian	31	0.27
Czech	67	0.59
Czechoslovakian	25	0.22
Danish	70	0.62
Dutch	493	4.37
Eastern European	18	0.16
English	1,612	14.30
European	155	1.37
Finnish	89	0.79
French, except Basque	406	3.60
French Canadian	120	1.06
German	3,232	28.67
Greek	69	0.61
Hawaii Native/Pacific Islander:	12	0.11
Polynesian: (2)	2	0.02
Native Hawaiian (1)	1	0.01
Samoan (1)	1	0.01
Other Pac. Isl., not spec. (1)	10	0.09
Hispanic or Latino:	280	2.48
Central American:	8	0.07
Costa Rican	2	0.02
Guatemalan	2	0.02
Honduran	1	0.01
Nicaraguan	1	0.01
Panamanian	2	0.02
Cuban	12	0.11
Dominican Republic	2	0.02
Mexican	172	1.52
Puerto Rican	14	0.12
South American:	29	0.26
Argentinean	1	0.01
Bolivian	2	0.02
Chilean	2	0.02
Colombian	13	0.12
Paraguayan	1	0.01
Peruvian	6	0.05
Venezuelan	4	0.04
Other Hispanic or Latino	43	0.38
Hungarian	93	0.82
Iranian	21	0.19
Irish	1,746	15.49
Israeli	16	0.14
Italian	543	4.82
Lithuanian	29	0.26
Macedonian	9	0.08
Northern European	59	0.52
Norwegian	172	1.53
Pennsylvania German	20	0.18
Polish	898	7.97
Portuguese	13	0.12
Romanian	38	0.34
Russian	98	0.87
Scandinavian	15	0.13
Scotch-Irish	239	2.12
Scottish	446	3.96
Serbian	14	0.12
Slavic	19	0.17
Slovak	40	0.35
Swedish	326	2.89
Swiss	53	0.47
Turkish	12	0.11
Ukrainian	70	0.62
United States or American	551	4.89
Welsh	135	1.20
West Indian, excl. Hispanic:	8	0.07
Haitian	8	0.07
White:	10,570	93.68
Not Hispanic (10,246)	10,357	91.79
Hispanic (176)	213	1.89
Yugoslavian	21	0.19

Hazel Park

Place Type: City
County: Oakland
Population: 18,963

Ancestry/Race	Number	%
African American/Black:	457	2.41
Not Hispanic (301)	443	2.34
Hispanic (7)	14	0.07
African, sub-Saharan:	2	0.01
African	2	0.01
Am. Ind. or Alaska Nat., not spec.	144	0.76
Albanian	28	0.15
American Indian tribes, specified:	322	1.70
Apache (2)	3	0.02
Blackfeet (2)	14	0.07
Cherokee (20)	117	0.62
Chickasaw (1)	1	0.01
Chippewa (29)	66	0.35
Choctaw (3)	11	0.06
Cree	1	0.01
Iroquois (24)	31	0.16
Latin American Indians (8)	8	0.04
Lumbee (12)	14	0.07
Navajo	3	0.02
Ottawa (5)	14	0.07
Potawatomi (3)	6	0.03
Seminole	1	0.01
Sioux (1)	11	0.06
All other tribes (12)	21	0.11
American Indian tribes, not spec.	8	0.04
Arab:	482	2.54
Arab/Arabic	114	0.60
Egyptian	45	0.24
Iraqi	188	0.99
Lebanese	114	0.60
Syrian	6	0.03
Other Arab	15	0.08
Armenian	34	0.18
Asian:	461	2.43
Bangladeshi	1	0.01
Cambodian (7)	7	0.04
Chinese, ex. Taiwanese (18)	20	0.11
Filipino (62)	82	0.43
Hmong (72)	82	0.43
Indian (40)	56	0.30
Japanese (7)	17	0.09
Korean (9)	18	0.09
Laotian (11)	19	0.10
Pakistani (14)	16	0.08
Taiwanese (2)	2	0.01
Thai (18)	21	0.11
Vietnamese (54)	61	0.32
Other Asian, not specified (17)	59	0.31
Assyrian/Chaldean/Syriac	512	2.70
Austrian	26	0.14
Belgian	26	0.14
Brazilian	30	0.16
British	55	0.29
Bulgarian	18	0.09
Canadian	163	0.86
Croatian	51	0.27
Czech	54	0.28
Czechoslovakian	10	0.05
Danish	49	0.26
Dutch	302	1.59
English	1,846	9.73
European	150	0.79
Finnish	258	1.36
French, except Basque	1,134	5.98
French Canadian	683	3.60
German	3,531	18.62
Greek	106	0.56
Hawaii Native/Pacific Islander:	22	0.12
Micronesian: (1)	6	0.03
Guamanian/Chamorro (1)	6	0.03
Polynesian: (3)	5	0.03
Native Hawaiian (3)	4	0.02
Other Polynesian	1	0.01
Other Pac. Isl., not spec.	11	0.06
Hispanic or Latino:	395	2.08
Central American:	3	0.02
Honduran	1	0.01
Panamanian	2	0.01
Cuban	4	0.02
Mexican	220	1.16
Puerto Rican	64	0.34
South American:	7	0.04
Argentinean	1	0.01
Chilean	1	0.01
Colombian	2	0.01
Peruvian	3	0.02
Other Hispanic or Latino	97	0.51
Hungarian	215	1.13
Irish	2,802	14.78
Italian	787	4.15
Lithuanian	30	0.16
Macedonian	8	0.04
Maltese	108	0.57
Norwegian	147	0.78
Polish	1,953	10.30
Portuguese	33	0.17
Romanian	153	0.81
Russian	93	0.49
Scandinavian	13	0.07
Scotch-Irish	271	1.43
Scottish	563	2.97
Serbian	30	0.16
Slavic	22	0.12
Slovak	20	0.11
Swedish	167	0.88
Ukrainian	75	0.40
United States or American	1,145	6.04
Welsh	119	0.63
West Indian, excl. Hispanic:	9	0.05
Jamaican	9	0.05
White:	17,997	94.91
Not Hispanic (17,143)	17,734	93.52
Hispanic (231)	263	1.39
Yugoslavian	8	0.04

Highland Park

Place Type: City
County: Wayne
Population: 16,746

Ancestry/Race	Number	%
African American/Black:	15,903	94.97
Not Hispanic (15,598)	15,850	94.65
Hispanic (50)	53	0.32
African, sub-Saharan:	287	1.71
African	287	1.71
Am. Ind. or Alaska Nat., not spec.	108	0.64
American Indian tribes, specified:	78	0.47
Apache	2	0.01
Blackfeet (5)	14	0.08
Cherokee (3)	27	0.16
Chickasaw	1	0.01
Chippewa (5)	9	0.05

Notes: 1. Figures in the "Number" column do not add up to the total population due to: a) Ancestry/Race overlap — e.g. persons can report being both White and Irish, b) persons of Hispanic origin can report being any race, c) persons reporting two ancestries are counted in both categories. 2. Numbers in parentheses indicate the number of persons reporting this ancestry/race alone, not in combination with any other ancestry/race. 3. Refer to the Explanation of Data in the front of the book for more detailed information.

Ancestry/Race	Number	%
Choctaw	3	0.02
Comanche (1)	1	0.01
Creek	4	0.02
Iroquois	3	0.02
Latin American Indians	1	0.01
All other tribes (4)	13	0.08
American Indian tribes, not spec.	4	0.02
Arab:	16	0.10
Arab/Arabic	7	0.04
Lebanese	9	0.05
Asian:	80	0.48
Bangladeshi (2)	5	0.03
Cambodian (4)	4	0.02
Chinese, ex. Taiwanese (4)	6	0.04
Filipino (10)	21	0.13
Indian (12)	21	0.13
Japanese (2)	6	0.04
Korean (1)	1	0.01
Vietnamese (1)	2	0.01
Other Asian, specified	3	0.02
Other Asian, not specified (2)	11	0.07
Canadian	25	0.15
English	49	0.29
German	241	1.44
Greek	7	0.04
Hawaii Native/Pacific Islander:	14	0.08
Polynesian: (3)	11	0.07
Native Hawaiian (2)	8	0.05
Samoan (1)	3	0.02
Other Pac. Isl., specified	3	0.02
Hispanic or Latino:	95	0.57
Central American:	1	0.01
Panamanian	1	0.01
Cuban	8	0.05
Dominican Republic	2	0.01
Mexican	38	0.23
Puerto Rican	12	0.07
South American:	1	0.01
Bolivian	1	0.01
Other Hispanic or Latino	33	0.20
Hungarian	2	0.01
Icelander	6	0.04
Irish	94	0.56
Israeli	26	0.16
Italian	20	0.12
Lithuanian	8	0.05
Norwegian	20	0.12
Polish	125	0.75
Russian	5	0.03
Scotch-Irish	7	0.04
Scottish	14	0.08
Swedish	22	0.13
Swiss	5	0.03
United States or American	121	0.72
West Indian, excl. Hispanic:	54	0.32
Haitian	14	0.08
Jamaican	40	0.24
White:	819	4.89
Not Hispanic (668)	796	4.75
Hispanic (20)	23	0.14
Yugoslavian	15	0.09

Highland

Place Type: Township
County: Oakland
Population: 19,169

Ancestry/Race	Number	%
African American/Black:	87	0.45
Not Hispanic (58)	86	0.45
Hispanic	1	0.01
African, sub-Saharan:	33	0.17
African	33	0.17
Alaska Native tribes, specified:	4	0.02
Alaska Athabascan (2)	2	0.01
Aleut (1)	2	0.01
Am. Ind. or Alaska Nat., not spec.	68	0.35
Albanian	49	0.26
American Indian tribes, specified:	152	0.79
Apache	2	0.01
Blackfeet (1)	3	0.02
Cherokee (10)	61	0.32
Chippewa (16)	37	0.19
Comanche	2	0.01
Cree	1	0.01
Iroquois (3)	5	0.03
Menominee	1	0.01
Navajo (3)	3	0.02
Ottawa (4)	11	0.06
Potawatomi	3	0.02
Pueblo	2	0.01
Seminole (3)	6	0.03
Sioux (1)	3	0.02
All other tribes (6)	12	0.06
American Indian tribes, not spec.	9	0.05
Arab:	163	0.85
Arab/Arabic	82	0.43
Egyptian	24	0.13
Iraqi	12	0.06
Lebanese	29	0.15
Syrian	16	0.08
Armenian	46	0.24
Asian:	111	0.58
Chinese, ex. Taiwanese (17)	22	0.11
Filipino (8)	19	0.10
Indian (6)	7	0.04
Japanese (3)	14	0.07
Korean (25)	31	0.16
Taiwanese (1)	1	0.01
Thai (3)	5	0.03
Vietnamese (6)	7	0.04
Other Asian, specified	2	0.01
Other Asian, not specified (1)	3	0.02
Assyrian/Chaldean/Syriac	40	0.21
Australian	18	0.09
Austrian	40	0.21
Belgian	27	0.14
Brazilian	22	0.11
British	92	0.48
Canadian	186	0.97
Croatian	33	0.17
Czech	75	0.39
Czechoslovakian	6	0.03
Danish	115	0.60
Dutch	395	2.06
English	2,698	14.06
European	102	0.53
Finnish	337	1.76
French, except Basque	1,005	5.24
French Canadian	703	3.66
German	4,677	24.37
Greek	162	0.84
Hawaii Native/Pacific Islander:	8	0.04
Micronesian: (1)	2	0.01
Guamanian/Chamorro (1)	2	0.01
Polynesian:	2	0.01
Native Hawaiian	2	0.01
Other Pac. Isl., specified	2	0.01
Other Pac. Isl., not spec. (2)	2	0.01
Hispanic or Latino:	244	1.27
Central American:	5	0.03
Honduran	1	0.01
Salvadoran	4	0.02
Cuban	8	0.04
Mexican	153	0.80
Puerto Rican	28	0.15
South American:	6	0.03
Argentinean	1	0.01
Chilean	1	0.01
Ecuadorian	1	0.01
Peruvian	3	0.02
Other Hispanic or Latino	44	0.23
Hungarian	316	1.65
Irish	3,225	16.80
Italian	1,046	5.45
Lithuanian	160	0.83
Maltese	80	0.42
Northern European	41	0.21
Norwegian	158	0.82
Polish	2,199	11.46
Romanian	41	0.21
Russian	173	0.90
Scandinavian	63	0.33
Scotch-Irish	387	2.02
Scottish	805	4.19
Serbian	16	0.08
Slavic	18	0.09
Slovak	104	0.54
Slovene	8	0.04
Swedish	352	1.83
Swiss	35	0.18
Ukrainian	130	0.68
United States or American	1,194	6.22
Welsh	158	0.82
White:	18,897	98.58
Not Hispanic (18,497)	18,698	97.54
Hispanic (178)	199	1.04
Yugoslavian	21	0.11

Holland

Place Type: City
County: Ottawa
Population: 35,048

Ancestry/Race	Number	%
Acadian/Cajun	8	0.02
African American/Black:	1,125	3.21
Not Hispanic (819)	977	2.79
Hispanic (69)	148	0.42
African, sub-Saharan:	64	0.18
African	41	0.12
Ethiopian	16	0.05
Kenyan	7	0.02
Am. Ind. or Alaska Nat., not spec.	166	0.47
American Indian tribes, specified:	199	0.57
Apache (8)	12	0.03
Blackfeet (2)	6	0.02
Cherokee (13)	38	0.11
Chippewa (28)	45	0.13
Choctaw (1)	1	0.00
Cree	1	0.00
Creek (1)	4	0.01
Iroquois (2)	2	0.01
Latin American Indians (9)	27	0.08
Navajo (1)	3	0.01
Ottawa (12)	24	0.07
Potawatomi (3)	9	0.03
Pueblo	2	0.01
Sioux (8)	9	0.03
All other tribes (2)	16	0.05
American Indian tribes, not spec.	26	0.07
Arab:	147	0.42
Arab/Arabic	10	0.03
Jordanian	70	0.20
Lebanese	21	0.06
Moroccan	38	0.11
Syrian	8	0.02
Armenian	11	0.03
Asian:	1,486	4.24
Bangladeshi	3	0.01
Cambodian (328)	387	1.10
Chinese, ex. Taiwanese (124)	163	0.47
Filipino (52)	73	0.21
Hmong (4)	4	0.01
Indian (67)	82	0.23
Indonesian (2)	4	0.01
Japanese (27)	47	0.13
Korean (141)	158	0.45
Laotian (177)	210	0.60
Malaysian (3)	4	0.01
Pakistani (7)	8	0.02
Taiwanese (5)	6	0.02
Thai (5)	14	0.04
Vietnamese (220)	233	0.66
Other Asian, specified (3)	3	0.01
Other Asian, not specified (43)	87	0.25
Austrian	53	0.15
Belgian	39	0.11

Notes: 1. Figures in the "Number" column do not add up to the total population due to: a) Ancestry/Race overlap — e.g. persons can report being both White and Irish, b) persons of Hispanic origin can report being any race, c) persons reporting two ancestries are counted in both categories. 2. Numbers in parentheses indicate the number of persons reporting this ancestry/race alone, not in combination with any other ancestry/race. 3. Refer to the Explanation of Data in the front of the book for more detailed information.

Brazilian	6	0.02
British	105	0.30
Canadian	58	0.16
Croatian	16	0.05
Czech	45	0.13
Czechoslovakian	62	0.18
Danish	149	0.42
Dutch	10,564	30.00
English	2,636	7.49
European	209	0.59
Finnish	88	0.25
French, except Basque	870	2.47
French Canadian	292	0.83
German	5,317	15.10
Greek	19	0.05
Hawaii Native/Pacific Islander:	17	0.05
Micronesian: (1)	3	0.01
Guamanian/Chamorro (1)	3	0.01
Polynesian: (1)	3	0.01
Native Hawaiian (1)	3	0.01
Other Pac. Isl., not spec. (8)	11	0.03
Hispanic or Latino:	7,783	22.21
Central American:	72	0.21
Costa Rican	1	0.00
Guatemalan	13	0.04
Honduran	21	0.06
Nicaraguan	15	0.04
Panamanian	2	0.01
Salvadoran	18	0.05
Other Central American	2	0.01
Cuban	66	0.19
Dominican Republic	12	0.03
Mexican	5,859	16.72
Puerto Rican	326	0.93
South American:	73	0.21
Argentinean	6	0.02
Chilean	43	0.12
Colombian	14	0.04
Ecuadorian	3	0.01
Peruvian	6	0.02
Other South American	1	0.00
Other Hispanic or Latino	1,375	3.92
Hungarian	195	0.55
Icelander	7	0.02
Iranian	19	0.05
Irish	2,542	7.22
Italian	569	1.62
Latvian	9	0.03
Lithuanian	30	0.09
Macedonian	6	0.02
Northern European	26	0.07
Norwegian	267	0.76
Pennsylvania German	19	0.05
Polish	894	2.54
Portuguese	18	0.05
Romanian	14	0.04
Russian	80	0.23
Scandinavian	14	0.04
Scotch-Irish	318	0.90
Scottish	736	2.09
Serbian	7	0.02
Slavic	9	0.03
Slovak	7	0.02
Swedish	567	1.61
Swiss	91	0.26
Ukrainian	57	0.16
United States or American	934	2.65
Welsh	137	0.39
West Indian, excl. Hispanic:	12	0.03
Jamaican	12	0.03
White:	28,183	80.41
Not Hispanic (24,543)	24,992	71.31
Hispanic (2,856)	3,191	9.10
Yugoslavian	17	0.05

Holland

Place Type: Township
County: Ottawa
Population: 28,911

Ancestry/Race	Number	%
African American/Black:	818	2.83
Not Hispanic (609)	755	2.61
Hispanic (33)	63	0.22
African, sub-Saharan:	32	0.11
African	32	0.11
Am. Ind. or Alaska Nat., not spec.	85	0.29
American Indian tribes, specified:	163	0.56
Apache	2	0.01
Blackfeet (2)	5	0.02
Cherokee	30	0.10
Cheyenne	3	0.01
Chippewa (27)	37	0.13
Choctaw	1	0.00
Comanche (1)	1	0.00
Iroquois (1)	4	0.01
Latin American Indians (19)	36	0.12
Navajo (5)	5	0.02
Ottawa (10)	18	0.06
Potawatomi	9	0.03
Sioux	4	0.01
Yaqui (4)	4	0.01
All other tribes (2)	4	0.01
American Indian tribes, not spec.	17	0.06
Arab:	87	0.30
Egyptian	87	0.30
Armenian	14	0.05
Asian:	2,538	8.78
Bangladeshi (9)	9	0.03
Cambodian (384)	439	1.52
Chinese, ex. Taiwanese (146)	179	0.62
Filipino (48)	69	0.24
Indian (141)	178	0.62
Indonesian (1)	3	0.01
Japanese (21)	38	0.13
Korean (74)	89	0.31
Laotian (863)	932	3.22
Malaysian	1	0.00
Sri Lankan	1	0.00
Taiwanese (8)	8	0.03
Thai (24)	35	0.12
Vietnamese (419)	439	1.52
Other Asian, specified (4)	4	0.01
Other Asian, not specified (82)	114	0.39
Australian	22	0.08
Austrian	60	0.21
Belgian	45	0.16
Brazilian	19	0.07
British	26	0.09
Canadian	56	0.20
Croatian	8	0.03
Czech	102	0.36
Czechoslovakian	31	0.11
Danish	44	0.15
Dutch	9,446	33.01
English	1,869	6.53
European	79	0.28
Finnish	82	0.29
French, except Basque	768	2.68
French Canadian	253	0.88
German	3,964	13.85
Greek	47	0.16
Hawaii Native/Pacific Islander:	47	0.16
Micronesian: (1)	2	0.01
Guamanian/Chamorro (1)	2	0.01
Polynesian: (6)	7	0.02
Native Hawaiian (3)	4	0.01
Samoan (3)	3	0.01
Other Pac. Isl., not spec. (1)	38	0.13
Hispanic or Latino:	4,574	15.82
Central American:	57	0.20
Guatemalan	12	0.04
Honduran	18	0.06
Nicaraguan	4	0.01
Panamanian	1	0.00
Salvadoran	14	0.05
Other Central American	8	0.03
Cuban	37	0.13
Dominican Republic	2	0.01
Mexican	3,667	12.68
Puerto Rican	125	0.43
South American:	35	0.12
Chilean	6	0.02
Colombian	3	0.01
Ecuadorian	1	0.00
Peruvian	5	0.02
Venezuelan	14	0.05
Other South American	6	0.02
Other Hispanic or Latino	651	2.25
Hungarian	68	0.24
Iranian	53	0.19
Irish	2,152	7.52
Italian	554	1.94
Lithuanian	23	0.08
Norwegian	265	0.93
Pennsylvania German	13	0.05
Polish	822	2.87
Portuguese	7	0.02
Russian	19	0.07
Scotch-Irish	132	0.46
Scottish	107	0.37
Slovak	5	0.02
Swedish	373	1.30
Swiss	102	0.36
Turkish	18	0.06
Ukrainian	37	0.13
United States or American	1,439	5.03
Welsh	51	0.18
White:	23,548	81.45
Not Hispanic (20,897)	21,258	73.53
Hispanic (2,005)	2,290	7.92
Yugoslavian	39	0.14

Holly

Place Type: Township
County: Oakland
Population: 10,037

Ancestry/Race	Number	%
African American/Black:	261	2.60
Not Hispanic (212)	250	2.49
Hispanic (9)	11	0.11
Am. Ind. or Alaska Nat., not spec.	39	0.39
Albanian	10	0.10
American Indian tribes, specified:	81	0.81
Apache (1)	4	0.04
Blackfeet (1)	3	0.03
Cherokee (10)	37	0.37
Cheyenne	2	0.02
Chippewa (8)	11	0.11
Iroquois (3)	3	0.03
Latin American Indians (1)	6	0.06
Osage (3)	3	0.03
Ottawa (3)	3	0.03
Seminole (5)	5	0.05
Sioux	1	0.01
All other tribes (2)	3	0.03
American Indian tribes, not spec.	3	0.03
Arab:	84	0.84
Arab/Arabic	39	0.39
Iraqi	45	0.45
Armenian	16	0.16
Asian:	57	0.57
Chinese, ex. Taiwanese (3)	3	0.03
Filipino (10)	12	0.12
Indian (5)	8	0.08
Japanese (2)	5	0.05
Korean (9)	15	0.15
Vietnamese (3)	3	0.03
Other Asian, not specified (10)	11	0.11
Austrian	84	0.84
Belgian	36	0.36
British	84	0.84

Notes: 1. Figures in the "Number" column do not add up to the total population due to: a) Ancestry/Race overlap — e.g. persons can report being both White and Irish, b) persons of Hispanic origin can report being any race, c) persons reporting two ancestries are counted in both categories. 2. Numbers in parentheses indicate the number of persons reporting this ancestry/race alone, not in combination with any other ancestry/race. 3. Refer to the Explanation of Data in the front of the book for more detailed information.

Ancestry/Race	Number	%
Bulgarian	8	0.08
Canadian	9	0.09
Celtic	19	0.19
Czech	38	0.38
Czechoslovakian	43	0.43
Danish	23	0.23
Dutch	302	3.01
English	1,499	14.93
European	86	0.86
Finnish	86	0.86
French, except Basque	583	5.81
French Canadian	290	2.89
German	2,162	21.54
Greek	32	0.32
Hawaii Native/Pacific Islander:	12	0.12
Melanesian:	1	0.01
Other Melanesian	1	0.01
Micronesian: (1)	5	0.05
Guamanian/Chamorro (1)	5	0.05
Polynesian: (3)	4	0.04
Native Hawaiian (2)	3	0.03
Samoan (1)	1	0.01
Other Pac. Isl., not spec.	2	0.02
Hispanic or Latino:	289	2.88
Central American:	2	0.02
Honduran	1	0.01
Salvadoran	1	0.01
Cuban	4	0.04
Mexican	206	2.05
Puerto Rican	22	0.22
South American:	2	0.02
Argentinean	1	0.01
Peruvian	1	0.01
Other Hispanic or Latino	53	0.53
Hungarian	164	1.63
Irish	1,468	14.63
Italian	351	3.50
Lithuanian	38	0.38
Northern European	17	0.17
Norwegian	119	1.19
Polish	719	7.16
Romanian	20	0.20
Russian	93	0.93
Scotch-Irish	227	2.26
Scottish	355	3.54
Serbian	7	0.07
Slavic	6	0.06
Slovak	25	0.25
Swedish	206	2.05
Swiss	51	0.51
Ukrainian	48	0.48
United States or American	691	6.88
Welsh	34	0.34
White:	9,630	95.95
Not Hispanic (9,317)	9,438	94.03
Hispanic (169)	192	1.91
Yugoslavian	17	0.17

Holt

Place Type: Census Designated Place
County: Ingham
Population: 11,315

Ancestry/Race	Number	%
African American/Black:	356	3.15
Not Hispanic (272)	347	3.07
Hispanic (3)	9	0.08
African, sub-Saharan:	19	0.17
African	19	0.17
Am. Ind. or Alaska Nat., not spec.	36	0.32
American Indian tribes, specified:	111	0.98
Apache	1	0.01
Blackfeet (2)	8	0.07
Cherokee (7)	33	0.29
Chickasaw	1	0.01
Chippewa (16)	38	0.34
Choctaw (1)	1	0.01
Cree	2	0.02
Iroquois	2	0.02
Latin American Indians (2)	2	0.02
Navajo	2	0.02
Ottawa (6)	9	0.08
Potawatomi (2)	3	0.03
Sioux (1)	1	0.01
All other tribes (4)	8	0.07
American Indian tribes, not spec.	6	0.05
Arab:	70	0.62
Lebanese	53	0.47
Syrian	17	0.15
Armenian	25	0.22
Asian:	159	1.41
Cambodian (2)	3	0.03
Chinese, ex. Taiwanese (9)	13	0.11
Filipino (13)	23	0.20
Indian (5)	7	0.06
Indonesian	1	0.01
Japanese (8)	21	0.19
Korean (43)	53	0.47
Vietnamese (30)	35	0.31
Other Asian, specified (1)	1	0.01
Other Asian, not specified (2)	2	0.02
Australian	9	0.08
Austrian	27	0.24
Belgian	10	0.09
British	20	0.18
Canadian	79	0.70
Czech	72	0.64
Czechoslovakian	12	0.11
Danish	37	0.33
Dutch	460	4.08
English	1,760	15.60
European	86	0.76
Finnish	72	0.64
French, except Basque	642	5.69
French Canadian	305	2.70
German	2,775	24.59
Greek	28	0.25
Hawaii Native/Pacific Islander:	7	0.06
Polynesian: (2)	3	0.03
Native Hawaiian	1	0.01
Samoan (2)	2	0.02
Other Pac. Isl., not spec. (3)	4	0.04
Hispanic or Latino:	411	3.63
Central American:	5	0.04
Costa Rican	2	0.02
Guatemalan	1	0.01
Panamanian	1	0.01
Salvadoran	1	0.01
Cuban	17	0.15
Dominican Republic	1	0.01
Mexican	275	2.43
Puerto Rican	21	0.19
South American:	5	0.04
Colombian	2	0.02
Peruvian	1	0.01
Venezuelan	2	0.02
Other Hispanic or Latino	87	0.77
Hungarian	109	0.97
Irish	1,549	13.73
Italian	392	3.47
Lithuanian	29	0.26
Macedonian	4	0.04
Norwegian	139	1.23
Polish	622	5.51
Portuguese	7	0.06
Romanian	11	0.10
Russian	98	0.87
Scandinavian	19	0.17
Scotch-Irish	206	1.83
Scottish	365	3.23
Serbian	65	0.58
Slavic	8	0.07
Slovak	8	0.07
Slovene	6	0.05
Swedish	199	1.76
Swiss	27	0.24
Ukrainian	24	0.21
United States or American	770	6.82
Welsh	90	0.80
White:	10,748	94.99
Not Hispanic (10,245)	10,443	92.29
Hispanic (265)	305	2.70
Yugoslavian	35	0.31

Huron charter

Place Type: Township
County: Wayne
Population: 13,737

Ancestry/Race	Number	%
African American/Black:	171	1.24
Not Hispanic (140)	162	1.18
Hispanic (8)	9	0.07
African, sub-Saharan:	9	0.07
Nigerian	9	0.07
Alaska Native tribes, not specified	4	0.03
Am. Ind. or Alaska Nat., not spec.	48	0.35
American Indian tribes, specified:	145	1.06
Apache (5)	8	0.06
Blackfeet (2)	13	0.09
Cherokee (16)	54	0.39
Chickasaw (3)	3	0.02
Chippewa (19)	33	0.24
Choctaw (1)	1	0.01
Comanche (3)	3	0.02
Iroquois (9)	10	0.07
Latin American Indians (1)	2	0.01
Lumbee (5)	8	0.06
Osage	2	0.01
Pueblo	1	0.01
Sioux	1	0.01
All other tribes (4)	6	0.04
American Indian tribes, not spec.	4	0.03
Arab:	72	0.52
Egyptian	10	0.07
Lebanese	53	0.39
Palestinian	9	0.07
Armenian	10	0.07
Asian:	75	0.55
Chinese, ex. Taiwanese (5)	13	0.09
Filipino (9)	17	0.12
Indian (13)	15	0.11
Japanese (6)	9	0.07
Korean (10)	12	0.09
Vietnamese (4)	6	0.04
Other Asian, not specified (2)	3	0.02
British	63	0.46
Canadian	91	0.66
Croatian	73	0.53
Czech	70	0.51
Czechoslovakian	80	0.58
Danish	7	0.05
Dutch	244	1.78
English	1,322	9.62
Finnish	46	0.33
French, except Basque	1,087	7.91
French Canadian	372	2.71
German	3,436	25.01
Greek	70	0.51
Hawaii Native/Pacific Islander:	1	0.01
Polynesian: (1)	1	0.01
Native Hawaiian (1)	1	0.01
Hispanic or Latino:	344	2.50
Cuban	11	0.08
Mexican	242	1.76
Puerto Rican	16	0.12
South American:	5	0.04
Argentinean	1	0.01
Colombian	2	0.01
Paraguayan	2	0.01
Other Hispanic or Latino	70	0.51
Hungarian	401	2.92
Icelander	7	0.05
Irish	1,909	13.90
Italian	1,020	7.43
Lithuanian	78	0.57
Macedonian	7	0.05
Maltese	27	0.20

Notes: 1. Figures in the "Number" column do not add up to the total population due to: a) Ancestry/Race overlap — e.g. persons can report being both White and Irish, b) persons of Hispanic origin can report being any race, c) persons reporting two ancestries are counted in both categories. 2. Numbers in parentheses indicate the number of persons reporting this ancestry/race alone, not in combination with any other ancestry/race. 3. Refer to the Explanation of Data in the front of the book for more detailed information.

Ancestry/Race	Number	%
Norwegian	66	0.48
Pennsylvania German	6	0.04
Polish	1,954	14.22
Portuguese	55	0.40
Romanian	29	0.21
Russian	143	1.04
Scotch-Irish	199	1.45
Scottish	300	2.18
Slovak	117	0.85
Slovene	17	0.12
Swedish	82	0.60
Ukrainian	40	0.29
United States or American	939	6.84
Welsh	86	0.63
White:	13,374	97.36
Not Hispanic (12,958)	13,116	95.48
Hispanic (224)	258	1.88
Yugoslavian	63	0.46

Independence

Place Type: Township
County: Oakland
Population: 32,581

Ancestry/Race	Number	%
Acadian/Cajun	8	0.02
African American/Black:	352	1.08
Not Hispanic (264)	337	1.03
Hispanic (10)	15	0.05
African, sub-Saharan:	32	0.10
African	32	0.10
Am. Ind. or Alaska Nat., not spec.	44	0.14
Albanian	31	0.10
American Indian tribes, specified:	178	0.55
Apache	5	0.02
Blackfeet (2)	6	0.02
Cherokee (16)	64	0.20
Chippewa (26)	59	0.18
Choctaw	2	0.01
Cree	1	0.00
Crow	3	0.01
Iroquois	1	0.00
Latin American Indians	1	0.00
Osage	1	0.00
Ottawa (3)	9	0.03
Potawatomi (7)	12	0.04
Pueblo (3)	3	0.01
Sioux (1)	2	0.01
All other tribes (3)	9	0.03
American Indian tribes, not spec.	8	0.02
Arab:	268	0.82
Arab/Arabic	30	0.09
Jordanian	39	0.12
Lebanese	102	0.31
Syrian	90	0.28
Other Arab	7	0.02
Armenian	128	0.39
Asian:	490	1.50
Chinese, ex. Taiwanese (79)	86	0.26
Filipino (76)	99	0.30
Hmong (2)	2	0.01
Indian (89)	101	0.31
Indonesian (2)	2	0.01
Japanese (15)	37	0.11
Korean (82)	90	0.28
Laotian (5)	5	0.02
Pakistani (4)	4	0.01
Sri Lankan	4	0.01
Taiwanese (2)	2	0.01
Thai (9)	10	0.03
Vietnamese (11)	17	0.05
Other Asian, not specified (20)	31	0.10
Austrian	43	0.13
Belgian	157	0.48
Brazilian	24	0.07
British	139	0.43
Bulgarian	32	0.10
Canadian	211	0.65
Celtic	7	0.02
Croatian	29	0.09
Czech	109	0.33
Czechoslovakian	97	0.30
Danish	193	0.59
Dutch	865	2.66
English	4,890	15.03
European	241	0.74
Finnish	472	1.45
French, except Basque	1,882	5.78
French Canadian	930	2.86
German	8,207	25.22
Greek	221	0.68
Hawaii Native/Pacific Islander:	11	0.03
Polynesian: (2)	8	0.02
Native Hawaiian (2)	8	0.02
Other Pac. Isl., not spec. (1)	3	0.01
Hispanic or Latino:	818	2.51
Central American:	18	0.06
Costa Rican	7	0.02
Guatemalan	3	0.01
Honduran	3	0.01
Panamanian	3	0.01
Salvadoran	2	0.01
Cuban	11	0.03
Dominican Republic	4	0.01
Mexican	580	1.78
Puerto Rican	57	0.17
South American:	27	0.08
Argentinean	7	0.02
Bolivian	2	0.01
Chilean	1	0.00
Colombian	7	0.02
Peruvian	4	0.01
Other South American	6	0.02
Other Hispanic or Latino	121	0.37
Hungarian	323	0.99
Iranian	36	0.11
Irish	5,170	15.89
Italian	2,175	6.68
Lithuanian	63	0.19
Luxemburger	5	0.02
Macedonian	23	0.07
Maltese	24	0.07
Northern European	7	0.02
Norwegian	401	1.23
Pennsylvania German	7	0.02
Polish	3,150	9.68
Portuguese	13	0.04
Romanian	84	0.26
Russian	260	0.80
Scandinavian	45	0.14
Scotch-Irish	611	1.88
Scottish	1,359	4.18
Serbian	31	0.10
Slavic	57	0.18
Slovak	82	0.25
Slovene	1	0.00
Swedish	725	2.23
Swiss	65	0.20
Ukrainian	208	0.64
United States or American	2,148	6.60
Welsh	172	0.53
White:	31,611	97.02
Not Hispanic (30,683)	31,000	95.15
Hispanic (543)	611	1.88
Yugoslavian	12	0.04

Inkster

Place Type: City
County: Wayne
Population: 30,115

Ancestry/Race	Number	%
African American/Black:	20,937	69.52
Not Hispanic (20,267)	20,841	69.20
Hispanic (63)	96	0.32
African, sub-Saharan:	350	1.16
African	310	1.03
Ghanian	8	0.03
Nigerian	12	0.04
Sudanese	20	0.07
Am. Ind. or Alaska Nat., not spec.	195	0.65
American Indian tribes, specified:	207	0.69
Apache	8	0.03
Blackfeet (2)	23	0.08
Cherokee (14)	89	0.30
Chippewa (8)	20	0.07
Choctaw (3)	5	0.02
Cree	3	0.01
Crow	3	0.01
Delaware (5)	6	0.02
Iroquois (9)	16	0.05
Latin American Indians (4)	6	0.02
Lumbee	1	0.00
Ottawa (1)	6	0.02
Seminole	2	0.01
Sioux (1)	3	0.01
All other tribes (2)	16	0.05
American Indian tribes, not spec.	16	0.05
Arab:	156	0.52
Arab/Arabic	30	0.10
Egyptian	33	0.11
Lebanese	85	0.28
Palestinian	8	0.03
Armenian	6	0.02
Asian:	1,131	3.76
Bangladeshi (3)	4	0.01
Cambodian (4)	4	0.01
Chinese, ex. Taiwanese (62)	69	0.23
Filipino (86)	112	0.37
Indian (779)	814	2.70
Japanese (9)	19	0.06
Korean (24)	30	0.10
Pakistani (41)	45	0.15
Taiwanese (6)	6	0.02
Thai (1)	3	0.01
Vietnamese (2)	2	0.01
Other Asian, specified (2)	8	0.03
Other Asian, not specified (6)	15	0.05
Austrian	6	0.02
British	35	0.12
Canadian	102	0.34
Croatian	16	0.05
Czech	22	0.07
Czechoslovakian	32	0.11
Danish	22	0.07
Dutch	175	0.58
English	744	2.47
European	70	0.23
Finnish	48	0.16
French, except Basque	487	1.62
French Canadian	263	0.87
German	1,442	4.79
Greek	66	0.22
Hawaii Native/Pacific Islander:	23	0.08
Micronesian:	4	0.01
Guamanian/Chamorro	4	0.01
Polynesian: (3)	9	0.03
Native Hawaiian	4	0.01
Samoan (3)	5	0.02
Other Pac. Isl., specified	6	0.02
Other Pac. Isl., not spec.	4	0.01
Hispanic or Latino:	482	1.60
Central American:	8	0.03
Panamanian	2	0.01
Other Central American	6	0.02
Cuban	7	0.02
Mexican	275	0.91
Puerto Rican	87	0.29
South American:	9	0.03
Argentinean	6	0.02
Colombian	1	0.00
Ecuadorian	1	0.00
Peruvian	1	0.00
Other Hispanic or Latino	96	0.32
Hungarian	77	0.26
Iranian	11	0.04
Irish	1,248	4.14
Italian	387	1.29

Notes: 1. Figures in the "Number" column do not add up to the total population due to: a) Ancestry/Race overlap — e.g. persons can report being both White and Irish, b) persons of Hispanic origin can report being any race, c) persons reporting two ancestries are counted in both categories. 2. Numbers in parentheses indicate the number of persons reporting this ancestry/race alone, not in combination with any other ancestry/race. 3. Refer to the Explanation of Data in the front of the book for more detailed information.

Lithuanian	23	0.08
Maltese	53	0.18
Norwegian	67	0.22
Pennsylvania German	10	0.03
Polish	1,136	3.77
Portuguese	5	0.02
Romanian	8	0.03
Russian	42	0.14
Scandinavian	3	0.01
Scotch-Irish	65	0.22
Scottish	204	0.68
Serbian	11	0.04
Slavic	13	0.04
Slovak	72	0.24
Swedish	81	0.27
Swiss	14	0.05
Turkish	21	0.07
Ukrainian	95	0.32
United States or American	650	2.16
Welsh	49	0.16
West Indian, excl. Hispanic:	112	0.37
British West Indian	6	0.02
Haitian	11	0.04
Jamaican	70	0.23
Trinidadian and Tobagonian	21	0.07
West Indian	4	0.01
White:	8,160	27.10
Not Hispanic (7,379)	7,926	26.32
Hispanic (192)	234	0.78

Ionia

Place Type: City
County: Ionia
Population: 10,569

Ancestry/Race	Number	%
African American/Black:	2,496	23.62
Not Hispanic (2,283)	2,440	23.09
Hispanic (36)	56	0.53
African, sub-Saharan:	226	2.12
African	211	1.98
Ethiopian	7	0.07
Nigerian	8	0.08
Alaska Native tribes, specified:	1	0.01
Eskimo	1	0.01
Am. Ind. or Alaska Nat., not spec.	79	0.75
Albanian	13	0.12
American Indian tribes, specified:	170	1.61
Apache (3)	7	0.07
Blackfeet	15	0.14
Cherokee (8)	45	0.43
Cheyenne	1	0.01
Chippewa (24)	37	0.35
Comanche	1	0.01
Iroquois (1)	2	0.02
Latin American Indians (17)	22	0.21
Lumbee (1)	1	0.01
Navajo	2	0.02
Osage	2	0.02
Ottawa (7)	9	0.09
Potawatomi (8)	13	0.12
Seminole	2	0.02
Sioux (1)	2	0.02
All other tribes (3)	9	0.09
American Indian tribes, not spec.	18	0.17
Arab:	60	0.56
Arab/Arabic	6	0.06
Lebanese	5	0.05
Moroccan	49	0.46
Asian:	155	1.47
Cambodian (2)	3	0.03
Chinese, ex. Taiwanese (3)	6	0.06
Filipino (5)	11	0.10
Hmong (5)	6	0.06
Indian (12)	23	0.22
Japanese (2)	7	0.07
Korean (11)	15	0.14
Laotian (3)	3	0.03
Thai	1	0.01
Vietnamese (2)	3	0.03
Other Asian, specified	2	0.02
Other Asian, not specified (22)	75	0.71
Austrian	3	0.03
British	28	0.26
Canadian	17	0.16
Celtic	4	0.04
Czech	54	0.51
Czechoslovakian	29	0.27
Danish	73	0.69
Dutch	306	2.87
English	819	7.69
European	53	0.50
Finnish	17	0.16
French, except Basque	232	2.18
French Canadian	134	1.26
German	1,683	15.80
Greek	10	0.09
Guyanese	8	0.08
Hawaii Native/Pacific Islander:	22	0.21
Micronesian:	3	0.03
Guamanian/Chamorro	3	0.03
Polynesian:	11	0.10
Native Hawaiian	5	0.05
Samoan	5	0.05
Other Polynesian	1	0.01
Other Pac. Isl., specified	1	0.01
Other Pac. Isl., not spec.	7	0.07
Hispanic or Latino:	537	5.08
Central American:	5	0.05
Guatemalan	5	0.05
Cuban	18	0.17
Dominican Republic	3	0.03
Mexican	372	3.52
Puerto Rican	44	0.42
South American:	3	0.03
Chilean	1	0.01
Colombian	1	0.01
Peruvian	1	0.01
Other Hispanic or Latino	92	0.87
Hungarian	50	0.47
Icelander	6	0.06
Irish	925	8.68
Israeli	7	0.07
Italian	232	2.18
Latvian	2	0.02
Norwegian	79	0.74
Pennsylvania German	3	0.03
Polish	213	2.00
Russian	30	0.28
Scandinavian	50	0.47
Scotch-Irish	118	1.11
Scottish	208	1.95
Slavic	10	0.09
Slovak	2	0.02
Swedish	124	1.16
Swiss	6	0.06
Turkish	6	0.06
Ukrainian	17	0.16
United States or American	626	5.88
Welsh	35	0.33
West Indian, excl. Hispanic:	8	0.08
Jamaican	8	0.08
White:	7,709	72.94
Not Hispanic (7,328)	7,480	70.77
Hispanic (184)	229	2.17
Yugoslavian	5	0.05

Jackson

Place Type: City
County: Jackson
Population: 36,316

Ancestry/Race	Number	%
African American/Black:	8,005	22.04
Not Hispanic (7,069)	7,854	21.63
Hispanic (85)	151	0.42
African, sub-Saharan:	249	0.69
African	204	0.56
Nigerian	45	0.12
Alaska Native tribes, specified:	9	0.02
Alaska Athabascan	5	0.01
Eskimo (2)	4	0.01
Am. Ind. or Alaska Nat., not spec.	248	0.68
American Indian tribes, specified:	367	1.01
Apache (7)	16	0.04
Blackfeet (5)	29	0.08
Cherokee (21)	114	0.31
Cheyenne	2	0.01
Chickasaw	3	0.01
Chippewa (41)	70	0.19
Choctaw	6	0.02
Cree (1)	2	0.01
Creek	8	0.02
Crow	1	0.00
Iroquois (1)	4	0.01
Latin American Indians (1)	6	0.02
Lumbee (3)	6	0.02
Menominee	1	0.00
Navajo	2	0.01
Ottawa (3)	4	0.01
Paiute	1	0.00
Potawatomi (14)	41	0.11
Puget Sound Salish (3)	3	0.01
Seminole	8	0.02
Sioux (3)	12	0.03
All other tribes (4)	28	0.08
American Indian tribes, not spec.	32	0.09
Arab:	11	0.03
Egyptian	6	0.02
Jordanian	5	0.01
Armenian	12	0.03
Asian:	279	0.77
Chinese, ex. Taiwanese (18)	24	0.07
Filipino (33)	55	0.15
Indian (32)	51	0.14
Japanese (16)	47	0.13
Korean (27)	35	0.10
Laotian (1)	1	0.00
Pakistani (10)	13	0.04
Vietnamese (38)	39	0.11
Other Asian, specified	2	0.01
Other Asian, not specified (7)	12	0.03
Assyrian/Chaldean/Syriac	17	0.05
Australian	3	0.01
Belgian	91	0.25
Brazilian	8	0.02
British	68	0.19
Bulgarian	8	0.02
Canadian	79	0.22
Croatian	5	0.01
Czech	63	0.17
Czechoslovakian	10	0.03
Danish	52	0.14
Dutch	1,267	3.49
Eastern European	6	0.02
English	3,581	9.86
European	245	0.67
Finnish	91	0.25
French, except Basque	1,125	3.10
French Canadian	527	1.45
German	5,955	16.40
German Russian	9	0.02
Greek	84	0.23
Hawaii Native/Pacific Islander:	27	0.07
Melanesian: (1)	1	0.00
Other Melanesian (1)	1	0.00
Micronesian:	1	0.00
Guamanian/Chamorro	1	0.00
Polynesian: (8)	19	0.05
Native Hawaiian (2)	4	0.01
Samoan (5)	10	0.03
Tongan (1)	5	0.01
Other Pac. Isl., specified	2	0.01
Other Pac. Isl., not spec. (1)	4	0.01
Hispanic or Latino:	1,469	4.05
Central American:	19	0.05
Costa Rican	2	0.01
Honduran	10	0.03

Notes: 1. Figures in the "Number" column do not add up to the total population due to: a) Ancestry/Race overlap — e.g. persons can report being both White and Irish, b) persons of Hispanic origin can report being any race, c) persons reporting two ancestries are counted in both categories. 2. Numbers in parentheses indicate the number of persons reporting this ancestry/race alone, not in combination with any other ancestry/race. 3. Refer to the Explanation of Data in the front of the book for more detailed information.

Ancestry/Race	Number	%
Nicaraguan	1	0.00
Panamanian	2	0.01
Other Central American	4	0.01
Cuban	17	0.05
Mexican	1,108	3.05
Puerto Rican	124	0.34
South American:	12	0.03
Bolivian	1	0.00
Colombian	5	0.01
Peruvian	3	0.01
Uruguayan	1	0.00
Other South American	2	0.01
Other Hispanic or Latino	189	0.52
Hungarian	122	0.34
Irish	4,078	11.23
Italian	878	2.42
Latvian	13	0.04
Lithuanian	82	0.23
Macedonian	46	0.13
Norwegian	253	0.70
Pennsylvania German	30	0.08
Polish	2,577	7.10
Portuguese	19	0.05
Romanian	9	0.02
Russian	86	0.24
Scandinavian	29	0.08
Scotch-Irish	546	1.50
Scottish	697	1.92
Serbian	8	0.02
Slavic	58	0.16
Slovak	16	0.04
Slovene	7	0.02
Swedish	211	0.58
Swiss	39	0.11
Ukrainian	57	0.16
United States or American	2,036	5.61
Welsh	117	0.32
West Indian, excl. Hispanic:	21	0.06
Barbadian	5	0.01
Jamaican	9	0.02
Trinidadian and Tobagonian	7	0.02
White:	27,962	77.00
Not Hispanic (26,204)	27,177	74.83
Hispanic (621)	785	2.16

Jenison

Place Type: Census Designated Place
County: Ottawa
Population: 17,211

Ancestry/Race	Number	%
African American/Black:	118	0.69
Not Hispanic (83)	116	0.67
Hispanic (1)	2	0.01
Am. Ind. or Alaska Nat., not spec.	20	0.12
Albanian	8	0.05
American Indian tribes, specified:	83	0.48
Apache	4	0.02
Blackfeet	2	0.01
Cherokee (1)	5	0.03
Cheyenne	3	0.02
Chippewa (10)	25	0.15
Creek	1	0.01
Iroquois	4	0.02
Latin American Indians	1	0.01
Ottawa (9)	17	0.10
Potawatomi (7)	13	0.08
Sioux	3	0.02
All other tribes (4)	5	0.03
American Indian tribes, not spec.	7	0.04
Arab:	8	0.05
Syrian	8	0.05
Asian:	190	1.10
Bangladeshi (2)	2	0.01
Cambodian (5)	7	0.04
Chinese, ex. Taiwanese (24)	32	0.19
Filipino (5)	14	0.08
Indian (4)	6	0.03
Indonesian	2	0.01
Japanese (4)	4	0.02
Korean (50)	59	0.34
Laotian (2)	5	0.03
Vietnamese (41)	49	0.28
Other Asian, not specified (4)	10	0.06
Austrian	76	0.44
Belgian	19	0.11
British	13	0.08
Canadian	32	0.19
Czech	60	0.35
Czechoslovakian	45	0.26
Danish	90	0.52
Dutch	7,218	41.88
Eastern European	6	0.03
English	1,731	10.04
European	154	0.89
Finnish	82	0.48
French, except Basque	618	3.59
French Canadian	325	1.89
German	3,440	19.96
Greek	14	0.08
Hawaii Native/Pacific Islander:	4	0.02
Polynesian: (1)	3	0.02
Native Hawaiian (1)	3	0.02
Other Pac. Isl., not spec.	1	0.01
Hispanic or Latino:	305	1.77
Central American:	7	0.04
Guatemalan	6	0.03
Panamanian	1	0.01
Cuban	31	0.18
Mexican	190	1.10
Puerto Rican	25	0.15
South American:	11	0.06
Argentinean	2	0.01
Chilean	2	0.01
Colombian	5	0.03
Paraguayan	1	0.01
Peruvian	1	0.01
Other Hispanic or Latino	41	0.24
Hungarian	61	0.35
Irish	1,559	9.05
Italian	508	2.95
Latvian	7	0.04
Lithuanian	13	0.08
Macedonian	11	0.06
Maltese	5	0.03
Norwegian	190	1.10
Polish	986	5.72
Russian	52	0.30
Scandinavian	50	0.29
Scotch-Irish	187	1.08
Scottish	334	1.94
Slovak	34	0.20
Slovene	5	0.03
Swedish	297	1.72
Swiss	53	0.31
Ukrainian	30	0.17
United States or American	671	3.89
Welsh	44	0.26
White:	16,845	97.87
Not Hispanic (16,511)	16,633	96.64
Hispanic (190)	212	1.23
Yugoslavian	45	0.26

Kalamazoo

Place Type: City
County: Kalamazoo
Population: 77,145

Ancestry/Race	Number	%
Acadian/Cajun	20	0.03
Afghan	19	0.02
African American/Black:	17,264	22.38
Not Hispanic (15,757)	16,974	22.00
Hispanic (167)	290	0.38
African, sub-Saharan:	1,043	1.35
African	845	1.10
Ghanian	99	0.13
Kenyan	9	0.01
Nigerian	60	0.08
South African	25	0.03
Sudanese	5	0.01
Alaska Native tribes, specified:	4	0.01
Alaska Athabascan (3)	4	0.01
Alaska Native tribes, not specified	5	0.01
Am. Ind. or Alaska Nat., not spec.	487	0.63
Albanian	15	0.02
American Indian tribes, specified:	674	0.87
Apache (8)	27	0.03
Blackfeet (3)	32	0.04
Cherokee (84)	293	0.38
Cheyenne (1)	2	0.00
Chippewa (57)	97	0.13
Choctaw	13	0.02
Cree	4	0.01
Creek (1)	2	0.00
Delaware	1	0.00
Iroquois (6)	18	0.02
Latin American Indians (17)	27	0.03
Lumbee (5)	5	0.01
Navajo (1)	3	0.00
Ottawa (23)	35	0.05
Pima (1)	1	0.00
Potawatomi (33)	67	0.09
Pueblo	1	0.00
Shoshone	2	0.00
Sioux (10)	24	0.03
All other tribes (7)	20	0.03
American Indian tribes, not spec.	65	0.08
Arab:	471	0.61
Arab/Arabic	98	0.13
Egyptian	14	0.02
Iraqi	5	0.01
Lebanese	221	0.29
Palestinian	18	0.02
Syrian	22	0.03
Other Arab	93	0.12
Armenian	39	0.05
Asian:	2,270	2.94
Bangladeshi (11)	11	0.01
Cambodian (10)	11	0.01
Chinese, ex. Taiwanese (436)	485	0.63
Filipino (104)	186	0.24
Hmong (1)	3	0.00
Indian (552)	628	0.81
Indonesian (16)	20	0.03
Japanese (130)	178	0.23
Korean (197)	229	0.30
Laotian (13)	19	0.02
Malaysian (72)	91	0.12
Pakistani (48)	52	0.07
Sri Lankan (6)	7	0.01
Taiwanese (8)	8	0.01
Thai (62)	80	0.10
Vietnamese (92)	103	0.13
Other Asian, specified (10)	25	0.03
Other Asian, not specified (54)	134	0.17
Assyrian/Chaldean/Syriac	32	0.04
Australian	9	0.01
Austrian	137	0.18
Basque	11	0.01
Belgian	162	0.21
Brazilian	33	0.04
British	394	0.51
Bulgarian	15	0.02
Canadian	229	0.30
Celtic	6	0.01
Croatian	169	0.22
Czech	295	0.38
Czechoslovakian	129	0.17
Danish	286	0.37
Dutch	5,969	7.74
English	7,556	9.80
Estonian	5	0.01
European	572	0.74
Finnish	225	0.29
French, except Basque	2,371	3.08
French Canadian	900	1.17
German	13,319	17.28

Notes: 1. Figures in the "Number" column do not add up to the total population due to: a) Ancestry/Race overlap — e.g. persons can report being both White and Irish, b) persons of Hispanic origin can report being any race, c) persons reporting two ancestries are counted in both categories. 2. Numbers in parentheses indicate the number of persons reporting this ancestry/race alone, not in combination with any other ancestry/race. 3. Refer to the Explanation of Data in the front of the book for more detailed information.

Ancestry/Race	Number	%
Greek	307	0.40
Hawaii Native/Pacific Islander:	124	0.16
Micronesian: (10)	13	0.02
Guamanian/Chamorro (10)	11	0.01
Other Micronesian	2	0.00
Polynesian: (33)	76	0.10
Native Hawaiian (19)	47	0.06
Samoan (14)	29	0.04
Other Pac. Isl., specified	10	0.01
Other Pac. Isl., not spec. (7)	25	0.03
Hispanic or Latino:	3,304	4.28
Central American:	76	0.10
Costa Rican	3	0.00
Guatemalan	26	0.03
Honduran	13	0.02
Nicaraguan	1	0.00
Panamanian	21	0.03
Salvadoran	9	0.01
Other Central American	3	0.00
Cuban	102	0.13
Dominican Republic	17	0.02
Mexican	2,281	2.96
Puerto Rican	184	0.24
South American:	83	0.11
Argentinean	13	0.02
Bolivian	3	0.00
Chilean	4	0.01
Colombian	29	0.04
Ecuadorian	9	0.01
Peruvian	8	0.01
Venezuelan	15	0.02
Other South American	2	0.00
Other Hispanic or Latino	561	0.73
Hungarian	536	0.70
Iranian	48	0.06
Irish	7,721	10.02
Israeli	6	0.01
Italian	2,731	3.54
Latvian	228	0.30
Lithuanian	98	0.13
Luxemburger	18	0.02
Macedonian	16	0.02
Maltese	21	0.03
Northern European	48	0.06
Norwegian	762	0.99
Pennsylvania German	45	0.06
Polish	3,762	4.88
Portuguese	60	0.08
Romanian	154	0.20
Russian	380	0.49
Scandinavian	99	0.13
Scotch-Irish	1,215	1.58
Scottish	1,702	2.21
Serbian	47	0.06
Slavic	56	0.07
Slovak	144	0.19
Slovene	26	0.03
Swedish	1,319	1.71
Swiss	189	0.25
Turkish	45	0.06
Ukrainian	260	0.34
United States or American	3,068	3.98
Welsh	433	0.56
West Indian, excl. Hispanic:	112	0.15
Bahamian	9	0.01
British West Indian	19	0.02
Jamaican	61	0.08
West Indian	23	0.03
White:	56,672	73.46
Not Hispanic (53,589)	55,307	71.69
Hispanic (1,004)	1,365	1.77
Yugoslavian	110	0.14

Kalamazoo

Place Type: Township
County: Kalamazoo
Population: 21,675

Ancestry/Race	Number	%
African American/Black:	2,917	13.46
Not Hispanic (2,643)	2,878	13.28
Hispanic (25)	39	0.18
African, sub-Saharan:	88	0.41
African	63	0.29
Other sub-Saharan African	25	0.12
Am. Ind. or Alaska Nat., not spec.	81	0.37
American Indian tribes, specified:	153	0.71
Apache (4)	5	0.02
Blackfeet (1)	17	0.08
Cherokee (12)	55	0.25
Chippewa (6)	15	0.07
Choctaw (1)	3	0.01
Comanche	1	0.00
Creek	1	0.00
Iroquois (1)	1	0.00
Kiowa	1	0.00
Latin American Indians (1)	5	0.02
Menominee	1	0.00
Ottawa (3)	13	0.06
Potawatomi (4)	15	0.07
Shoshone	4	0.02
Sioux (6)	12	0.06
All other tribes (1)	4	0.02
American Indian tribes, not spec.	8	0.04
Arab:	112	0.52
Arab/Arabic	4	0.02
Egyptian	72	0.33
Lebanese	29	0.13
Syrian	7	0.03
Armenian	5	0.02
Asian:	328	1.51
Chinese, ex. Taiwanese (47)	60	0.28
Filipino (38)	47	0.22
Indian (50)	64	0.30
Indonesian (2)	3	0.01
Japanese (19)	30	0.14
Korean (52)	63	0.29
Laotian (3)	3	0.01
Malaysian (9)	12	0.06
Taiwanese (2)	3	0.01
Thai (6)	8	0.04
Vietnamese (21)	25	0.12
Other Asian, not specified (3)	10	0.05
Australian	11	0.05
Austrian	32	0.15
Basque	5	0.02
Belgian	32	0.15
Brazilian	21	0.10
British	195	0.90
Canadian	56	0.26
Croatian	24	0.11
Czech	100	0.46
Czechoslovakian	38	0.17
Danish	142	0.65
Dutch	3,068	14.12
English	2,646	12.18
European	154	0.71
Finnish	35	0.16
French, except Basque	846	3.89
French Canadian	204	0.94
German	3,812	17.55
Greek	27	0.12
Hawaii Native/Pacific Islander:	19	0.09
Micronesian: (1)	4	0.02
Guamanian/Chamorro (1)	4	0.02
Polynesian: (3)	8	0.04
Native Hawaiian (2)	5	0.02
Samoan (1)	3	0.01
Other Pac. Isl., not spec. (1)	7	0.03
Hispanic or Latino:	666	3.07
Central American:	9	0.04
Guatemalan	5	0.02
Honduran	1	0.01
Nicaraguan	1	0.00
Panamanian	1	0.00
Cuban	16	0.07
Dominican Republic	1	0.00
Mexican	473	2.18
Puerto Rican	37	0.17
South American:	11	0.05
Chilean	1	0.00
Colombian	4	0.02
Ecuadorian	2	0.01
Peruvian	2	0.01
Venezuelan	2	0.01
Other Hispanic or Latino	119	0.55
Hungarian	191	0.88
Irish	2,303	10.60
Italian	536	2.47
Latvian	103	0.47
Lithuanian	32	0.15
Luxemburger	6	0.03
Northern European	6	0.03
Norwegian	227	1.04
Pennsylvania German	26	0.12
Polish	947	4.36
Portuguese	31	0.14
Romanian	38	0.17
Russian	86	0.40
Scandinavian	25	0.12
Scotch-Irish	500	2.30
Scottish	537	2.47
Slovak	95	0.44
Slovene	11	0.05
Swedish	369	1.70
Swiss	67	0.31
Turkish	4	0.02
Ukrainian	14	0.06
United States or American	1,188	5.47
Welsh	98	0.45
West Indian, excl. Hispanic:	16	0.07
Jamaican	7	0.03
Trinidadian and Tobagonian	9	0.04
White:	18,286	84.36
Not Hispanic (17,602)	17,955	82.84
Hispanic (272)	331	1.53

Kentwood

Place Type: City
County: Kent
Population: 45,255

Ancestry/Race	Number	%
Acadian/Cajun	6	0.01
African American/Black:	4,596	10.16
Not Hispanic (4,040)	4,458	9.85
Hispanic (75)	138	0.30
African, sub-Saharan:	282	0.62
African	233	0.52
Somalian	32	0.07
South African	17	0.04
Alaska Native tribes, specified:	4	0.01
Eskimo (4)	4	0.01
Am. Ind. or Alaska Nat., not spec.	149	0.33
Albanian	50	0.11
Alsatian	12	0.03
American Indian tribes, specified:	301	0.67
Apache	5	0.01
Blackfeet (4)	16	0.04
Cherokee (19)	72	0.16
Cheyenne	1	0.00
Chickasaw	3	0.01
Chippewa (38)	58	0.13
Choctaw (2)	3	0.01
Comanche	4	0.01
Cree	2	0.00
Creek (3)	5	0.01
Delaware	1	0.00
Iroquois	2	0.00
Latin American Indians (8)	14	0.03
Navajo (2)	6	0.01
Ottawa (26)	42	0.09
Potawatomi (19)	32	0.07
Seminole (1)	5	0.01
Shoshone	3	0.01
Sioux (3)	13	0.03
All other tribes (3)	14	0.03
American Indian tribes, not spec.	20	0.04

Notes: 1. Figures in the "Number" column do not add up to the total population due to: a) Ancestry/Race overlap — e.g. persons can report being both White and Irish, b) persons of Hispanic origin can report being any race, c) persons reporting two ancestries are counted in both categories. 2. Numbers in parentheses indicate the number of persons reporting this ancestry/race alone, not in combination with any other ancestry/race. 3. Refer to the Explanation of Data in the front of the book for more detailed information.

Ancestry/Race	Number	%
Arab:	624	1.38
Arab/Arabic	199	0.44
Iraqi	25	0.06
Jordanian	23	0.05
Lebanese	225	0.50
Palestinian	16	0.04
Syrian	84	0.19
Other Arab	52	0.11
Asian:	2,876	6.36
Bangladeshi (4)	5	0.01
Cambodian (3)	3	0.01
Chinese, ex. Taiwanese (296)	363	0.80
Filipino (104)	147	0.32
Hmong (6)	6	0.01
Indian (436)	467	1.03
Indonesian (3)	8	0.02
Japanese (91)	126	0.28
Korean (290)	325	0.72
Laotian (7)	8	0.02
Malaysian (1)	2	0.00
Pakistani (31)	50	0.11
Sri Lankan (11)	15	0.03
Taiwanese (16)	20	0.04
Thai (8)	11	0.02
Vietnamese (1,160)	1,240	2.74
Other Asian, specified (2)	8	0.02
Other Asian, not specified (25)	72	0.16
Australian	9	0.02
Austrian	55	0.12
Basque	26	0.06
Belgian	62	0.14
Brazilian	3	0.01
British	235	0.52
Bulgarian	7	0.02
Canadian	156	0.34
Carpatho Rusyn	9	0.02
Celtic	20	0.04
Croatian	88	0.19
Czech	78	0.17
Czechoslovakian	143	0.32
Danish	307	0.68
Dutch	8,098	17.90
English	4,460	9.86
European	407	0.90
Finnish	187	0.41
French, except Basque	1,733	3.83
French Canadian	552	1.22
German	8,289	18.32
Greek	133	0.29
Hawaii Native/Pacific Islander:	53	0.12
Micronesian: (5)	6	0.01
Guamanian/Chamorro (5)	5	0.01
Other Micronesian	1	0.00
Polynesian: (12)	23	0.05
Native Hawaiian (4)	9	0.02
Samoan (7)	13	0.03
Other Polynesian (1)	1	0.00
Other Pac. Isl., specified	6	0.01
Other Pac. Isl., not spec. (1)	18	0.04
Hispanic or Latino:	1,757	3.88
Central American:	51	0.11
Costa Rican	4	0.01
Guatemalan	26	0.06
Honduran	2	0.00
Nicaraguan	2	0.00
Panamanian	2	0.00
Salvadoran	12	0.03
Other Central American	3	0.01
Cuban	79	0.17
Dominican Republic	72	0.16
Mexican	930	2.06
Puerto Rican	276	0.61
South American:	54	0.12
Argentinean	6	0.01
Bolivian	3	0.01
Colombian	7	0.02
Ecuadorian	2	0.00
Peruvian	18	0.04
Venezuelan	15	0.03
Other South American	3	0.01
Other Hispanic or Latino	295	0.65
Hungarian	153	0.34
Iranian	56	0.12
Irish	4,402	9.73
Israeli	4	0.01
Italian	1,494	3.30
Latvian	47	0.10
Lithuanian	153	0.34
Luxemburger	10	0.02
Macedonian	12	0.03
Maltese	32	0.07
Northern European	30	0.07
Norwegian	581	1.28
Pennsylvania German	9	0.02
Polish	2,821	6.24
Portuguese	18	0.04
Romanian	52	0.11
Russian	135	0.30
Scandinavian	38	0.08
Scotch-Irish	540	1.19
Scottish	709	1.57
Serbian	41	0.09
Slavic	24	0.05
Slovak	58	0.13
Slovene	47	0.10
Swedish	1,067	2.36
Swiss	85	0.19
Ukrainian	101	0.22
United States or American	2,448	5.41
Welsh	205	0.45
West Indian, excl. Hispanic:	60	0.13
Haitian	32	0.07
Jamaican	28	0.06
White:	37,547	82.97
Not Hispanic (35,740)	36,526	80.71
Hispanic (859)	1,021	2.26
Yugoslavian	443	0.98

Lansing

Place Type: City
County: Ingham
Population: 119,128

Ancestry/Race	Number	%
African American/Black:	29,078	24.41
Not Hispanic (25,498)	28,058	23.55
Hispanic (597)	1,020	0.86
African, sub-Saharan:	1,806	1.52
African	1,344	1.13
Ethiopian	5	0.00
Ghanian	17	0.01
Kenyan	12	0.01
Liberian	15	0.01
Nigerian	73	0.06
Sierra Leonean	8	0.01
Somalian	203	0.17
Sudanese	38	0.03
Zimbabwean	33	0.03
Other sub-Saharan African	58	0.05
Alaska Native tribes, specified:	11	0.01
Aleut	1	0.00
Eskimo (3)	3	0.00
Tlingit-Haida (3)	3	0.00
All other tribes (3)	4	0.00
Am. Ind. or Alaska Nat., not spec.	883	0.74
Albanian	84	0.07
American Indian tribes, specified:	1,448	1.22
Apache (13)	42	0.04
Blackfeet (20)	84	0.07
Cherokee (85)	327	0.27
Cheyenne (2)	7	0.01
Chickasaw	9	0.01
Chippewa (200)	399	0.33
Choctaw (10)	29	0.02
Comanche	8	0.01
Cree	3	0.00
Creek	10	0.01
Crow	3	0.00
Delaware (6)	8	0.01
Iroquois (37)	68	0.06
Latin American Indians (34)	66	0.06
Lumbee (1)	9	0.01
Menominee (3)	4	0.00
Navajo (6)	16	0.01
Ottawa (131)	192	0.16
Pima (2)	2	0.00
Potawatomi (22)	44	0.04
Pueblo	11	0.01
Seminole (1)	12	0.01
Shoshone	4	0.00
Sioux (10)	28	0.02
Tohono O'Odham	1	0.00
Ute (1)	4	0.00
Yaqui (1)	1	0.00
All other tribes (25)	57	0.05
American Indian tribes, not spec.	112	0.09
Arab:	975	0.82
Arab/Arabic	138	0.12
Egyptian	19	0.02
Iraqi	75	0.06
Lebanese	615	0.52
Moroccan	3	0.00
Palestinian	15	0.01
Syrian	25	0.02
Other Arab	85	0.07
Armenian	81	0.07
Asian:	4,031	3.38
Cambodian (15)	16	0.01
Chinese, ex. Taiwanese (268)	349	0.29
Filipino (145)	214	0.18
Hmong (692)	798	0.67
Indian (214)	277	0.23
Indonesian (13)	17	0.01
Japanese (90)	160	0.13
Korean (301)	357	0.30
Laotian (138)	213	0.18
Malaysian (1)	3	0.00
Pakistani (14)	21	0.02
Sri Lankan (2)	6	0.01
Taiwanese (17)	29	0.02
Thai (36)	53	0.04
Vietnamese (1,275)	1,324	1.11
Other Asian, specified (1)	10	0.01
Other Asian, not specified (77)	184	0.15
Australian	11	0.01
Austrian	192	0.16
Belgian	162	0.14
Brazilian	46	0.04
British	459	0.39
Bulgarian	23	0.02
Canadian	438	0.37
Celtic	29	0.02
Croatian	146	0.12
Czech	472	0.40
Czechoslovakian	247	0.21
Danish	370	0.31
Dutch	3,248	2.73
Eastern European	58	0.05
English	11,010	9.26
Estonian	10	0.01
European	1,254	1.05
Finnish	592	0.50
French, except Basque	3,678	3.09
French Canadian	1,618	1.36
German	20,168	16.96
German Russian	8	0.01
Greek	318	0.27
Hawaii Native/Pacific Islander:	174	0.15
Melanesian:	1	0.00
Fijian	1	0.00
Micronesian: (17)	24	0.02
Guamanian/Chamorro (5)	10	0.01
Other Micronesian (12)	14	0.01
Polynesian: (25)	71	0.06
Native Hawaiian (19)	56	0.05
Samoan (6)	12	0.01
Other Polynesian	3	0.00
Other Pac. Isl., specified	6	0.01
Other Pac. Isl., not spec. (19)	72	0.06

Notes: 1. Figures in the "Number" column do not add up to the total population due to: a) Ancestry/Race overlap — e.g. persons can report being both White and Irish, b) persons of Hispanic origin can report being any race, c) persons reporting two ancestries are counted in both categories. 2. Numbers in parentheses indicate the number of persons reporting this ancestry/race alone, not in combination with any other ancestry/race. 3. Refer to the Explanation of Data in the front of the book for more detailed information.

Ancestry/Race	Number	%
Hispanic or Latino:	11,886	9.98
Central American:	112	0.09
Costa Rican	8	0.01
Guatemalan	42	0.04
Honduran	17	0.01
Nicaraguan	1	0.00
Panamanian	24	0.02
Salvadoran	14	0.01
Other Central American	6	0.01
Cuban	793	0.67
Dominican Republic	17	0.01
Mexican	8,113	6.81
Puerto Rican	491	0.41
South American:	111	0.09
Argentinean	25	0.02
Bolivian	3	0.00
Chilean	8	0.01
Colombian	28	0.02
Ecuadorian	13	0.01
Peruvian	6	0.01
Uruguayan	1	0.00
Venezuelan	24	0.02
Other South American	3	0.00
Other Hispanic or Latino	2,249	1.89
Hungarian	508	0.43
Icelander	5	0.00
Iranian	18	0.02
Irish	10,926	9.19
Israeli	13	0.01
Italian	2,850	2.40
Latvian	42	0.04
Lithuanian	253	0.21
Macedonian	29	0.02
Maltese	23	0.02
New Zealander	2	0.00
Northern European	187	0.16
Norwegian	1,104	0.93
Pennsylvania German	71	0.06
Polish	3,940	3.31
Portuguese	125	0.11
Romanian	171	0.14
Russian	422	0.35
Scandinavian	150	0.13
Scotch-Irish	1,384	1.16
Scottish	2,092	1.76
Serbian	104	0.09
Slavic	57	0.05
Slovak	224	0.19
Slovene	15	0.01
Swedish	1,422	1.20
Swiss	176	0.15
Turkish	55	0.05
Ukrainian	307	0.26
United States or American	5,812	4.89
Welsh	448	0.38
West Indian, excl. Hispanic:	457	0.38
Belizean	28	0.02
Dutch West Indian	10	0.01
Haitian	181	0.15
Jamaican	178	0.15
Trinidadian and Tobagonian	5	0.00
U.S. Virgin Islander	11	0.01
West Indian	44	0.04
White:	82,215	69.01
Not Hispanic (73,105)	76,554	64.26
Hispanic (4,661)	5,661	4.75
Yugoslavian	258	0.22

Leoni

Place Type: Township
County: Jackson
Population: 13,459

Ancestry/Race	Number	%
African American/Black:	159	1.18
Not Hispanic (103)	151	1.12
Hispanic (7)	8	0.06
African, sub-Saharan:	7	0.05
African	7	0.05
Am. Ind. or Alaska Nat., not spec.	39	0.29
American Indian tribes, specified:	76	0.56
Apache (1)	1	0.01
Blackfeet (1)	3	0.02
Cherokee (4)	32	0.24
Chippewa (17)	20	0.15
Choctaw	1	0.01
Comanche	3	0.02
Creek (1)	1	0.01
Iroquois (1)	2	0.01
Potawatomi (1)	5	0.04
Sioux	4	0.03
Yaqui (1)	1	0.01
All other tribes (1)	3	0.02
American Indian tribes, not spec.	3	0.02
Arab:	62	0.46
Egyptian	6	0.04
Lebanese	33	0.25
Syrian	23	0.17
Asian:	56	0.42
Chinese, ex. Taiwanese (1)	5	0.04
Filipino (12)	14	0.10
Indian (10)	10	0.07
Japanese (4)	8	0.06
Korean (5)	5	0.04
Thai (1)	1	0.01
Vietnamese (7)	8	0.06
Other Asian, not specified (4)	5	0.04
Austrian	8	0.06
Belgian	8	0.06
British	65	0.48
Croatian	20	0.15
Czech	17	0.13
Czechoslovakian	6	0.04
Danish	33	0.25
Dutch	446	3.32
Eastern European	9	0.07
English	2,023	15.08
European	117	0.87
Finnish	65	0.48
French, except Basque	661	4.93
French Canadian	208	1.55
German	3,234	24.11
Greek	51	0.38
Hawaii Native/Pacific Islander:	4	0.03
Micronesian: (3)	4	0.03
Guamanian/Chamorro	1	0.01
Other Micronesian (3)	3	0.02
Hispanic or Latino:	218	1.62
Central American:	2	0.01
Costa Rican	1	0.01
Honduran	1	0.01
Cuban	11	0.08
Mexican	135	1.00
Puerto Rican	16	0.12
South American:	3	0.02
Colombian	1	0.01
Paraguayan	1	0.01
Venezuelan	1	0.01
Other Hispanic or Latino	51	0.38
Hungarian	77	0.57
Iranian	11	0.08
Irish	1,594	11.88
Italian	244	1.82
Lithuanian	6	0.04
Maltese	17	0.13
Norwegian	101	0.75
Pennsylvania German	14	0.10
Polish	1,420	10.59
Romanian	17	0.13
Russian	66	0.49
Scotch-Irish	244	1.82
Scottish	352	2.62
Serbian	34	0.25
Slovak	36	0.27
Swedish	144	1.07
Swiss	15	0.11
Ukrainian	43	0.32
United States or American	1,377	10.27
Welsh	47	0.35
West Indian, excl. Hispanic:	13	0.10
Haitian	13	0.10
White:	13,218	98.21
Not Hispanic (12,913)	13,052	96.98
Hispanic (147)	166	1.23

Lincoln Park

Place Type: City
County: Wayne
Population: 40,008

Ancestry/Race	Number	%
African American/Black:	949	2.37
Not Hispanic (810)	926	2.31
Hispanic (14)	23	0.06
African, sub-Saharan:	58	0.14
African	58	0.14
Alaska Native tribes, specified:	1	0.00
Eskimo (1)	1	0.00
Am. Ind. or Alaska Nat., not spec.	149	0.37
Albanian	90	0.22
American Indian tribes, specified:	356	0.89
Apache (3)	14	0.03
Blackfeet (1)	12	0.03
Cherokee (40)	134	0.33
Chippewa (43)	76	0.19
Choctaw (1)	6	0.01
Comanche (1)	2	0.00
Cree	2	0.00
Creek (2)	2	0.00
Delaware (1)	1	0.00
Iroquois (16)	28	0.07
Latin American Indians (8)	15	0.04
Lumbee (15)	28	0.07
Menominee (2)	2	0.00
Navajo	1	0.00
Osage	2	0.00
Ottawa (6)	8	0.02
Pueblo (2)	2	0.00
Seminole (1)	1	0.00
Sioux (1)	2	0.00
All other tribes (15)	18	0.04
American Indian tribes, not spec.	22	0.05
Arab:	264	0.66
Arab/Arabic	51	0.13
Iraqi	5	0.01
Jordanian	5	0.01
Lebanese	180	0.45
Moroccan	5	0.01
Syrian	12	0.03
Other Arab	6	0.01
Armenian	105	0.26
Asian:	291	0.73
Chinese, ex. Taiwanese (27)	35	0.09
Filipino (67)	104	0.26
Hmong (4)	5	0.01
Indian (49)	55	0.14
Japanese (3)	15	0.04
Korean (23)	32	0.08
Laotian (5)	5	0.01
Pakistani (6)	13	0.03
Thai (6)	7	0.02
Vietnamese (9)	10	0.02
Other Asian, not specified (1)	10	0.02
Assyrian/Chaldean/Syriac	7	0.02
Australian	12	0.03
Austrian	64	0.16
Belgian	84	0.21
British	120	0.30
Bulgarian	23	0.06
Canadian	248	0.62
Celtic	7	0.02
Croatian	31	0.08
Czech	112	0.28
Czechoslovakian	103	0.26
Danish	28	0.07
Dutch	609	1.52
Eastern European	12	0.03
English	3,226	8.06

Notes: 1. Figures in the "Number" column do not add up to the total population due to: a) Ancestry/Race overlap — e.g. persons can report being both White and Irish, b) persons of Hispanic origin can report being any race, c) persons reporting two ancestries are counted in both categories. 2. Numbers in parentheses indicate the number of persons reporting this ancestry/race alone, not in combination with any other ancestry/race. 3. Refer to the Explanation of Data in the front of the book for more detailed information.

European	108	0.27
Finnish	171	0.43
French, except Basque	2,609	6.52
French Canadian	1,081	2.70
German	7,792	19.48
Greek	354	0.88
Hawaii Native/Pacific Islander:	18	0.04
Micronesian:	1	0.00
Guamanian/Chamorro	1	0.00
Polynesian: (2)	13	0.03
Native Hawaiian (2)	10	0.02
Samoan	2	0.00
Other Polynesian	1	0.00
Other Pac. Isl., not spec.	4	0.01
Hispanic or Latino:	2,556	6.39
Central American:	18	0.04
Costa Rican	2	0.00
Guatemalan	1	0.00
Honduran	2	0.00
Panamanian	1	0.00
Salvadoran	12	0.03
Cuban	32	0.08
Dominican Republic	3	0.01
Mexican	1,985	4.96
Puerto Rican	208	0.52
South American:	11	0.03
Argentinean	2	0.00
Chilean	1	0.00
Colombian	5	0.01
Ecuadorian	1	0.00
Peruvian	1	0.00
Other South American	1	0.00
Other Hispanic or Latino	299	0.75
Hungarian	2,225	5.56
Irish	5,926	14.81
Italian	3,107	7.77
Lithuanian	68	0.17
Macedonian	66	0.16
Maltese	110	0.27
Norwegian	266	0.66
Pennsylvania German	13	0.03
Polish	5,637	14.09
Portuguese	55	0.14
Romanian	129	0.32
Russian	219	0.55
Scandinavian	5	0.01
Scotch-Irish	706	1.76
Scottish	1,064	2.66
Serbian	30	0.07
Slavic	51	0.13
Slovak	198	0.49
Slovene	6	0.01
Swedish	284	0.71
Swiss	36	0.09
Ukrainian	224	0.56
United States or American	2,354	5.88
Welsh	157	0.39
White:	37,983	94.94
Not Hispanic (35,701)	36,200	90.48
Hispanic (1,611)	1,783	4.46
Yugoslavian	58	0.14

Lincoln charter

Place Type: Township
County: Berrien
Population: 13,952

Ancestry/Race	Number	%
African American/Black:	190	1.36
Not Hispanic (147)	189	1.35
Hispanic (1)	1	0.01
African, sub-Saharan:	44	0.32
African	27	0.19
Nigerian	1	0.01
South African	6	0.04
Other sub-Saharan African	10	0.07
Alaska Native tribes, specified:	1	0.01
Tlingit-Haida	1	0.01
Am. Ind. or Alaska Nat., not spec.	33	0.24
American Indian tribes, specified:	50	0.36
Blackfeet (1)	1	0.01
Cherokee (5)	16	0.11
Chippewa (5)	8	0.06
Delaware	1	0.01
Iroquois	2	0.01
Latin American Indians	1	0.01
Ottawa (1)	1	0.01
Potawatomi (11)	17	0.12
Seminole	1	0.01
Sioux	1	0.01
Yaqui (1)	1	0.01
American Indian tribes, not spec.	4	0.03
Arab:	27	0.19
Arab/Arabic	7	0.05
Lebanese	13	0.09
Syrian	7	0.05
Armenian	2	0.01
Asian:	234	1.68
Chinese, ex. Taiwanese (37)	44	0.32
Filipino (19)	30	0.22
Indian (64)	68	0.49
Indonesian	1	0.01
Japanese (11)	21	0.15
Korean (43)	47	0.34
Laotian (2)	2	0.01
Malaysian (1)	1	0.01
Thai (2)	3	0.02
Vietnamese (10)	10	0.07
Other Asian, not specified (3)	7	0.05
Austrian	41	0.29
Belgian	50	0.36
Brazilian	4	0.03
British	52	0.37
Canadian	25	0.18
Croatian	49	0.35
Czech	246	1.77
Czechoslovakian	55	0.39
Danish	127	0.91
Dutch	553	3.97
English	1,867	13.41
European	84	0.60
Finnish	47	0.34
French, except Basque	609	4.37
French Canadian	150	1.08
German	5,556	39.89
Greek	58	0.42
Hawaii Native/Pacific Islander:	3	0.02
Micronesian: (1)	1	0.01
Guamanian/Chamorro (1)	1	0.01
Polynesian: (1)	1	0.01
Samoan (1)	1	0.01
Other Pac. Isl., not spec. (1)	1	0.01
Hispanic or Latino:	182	1.30
Central American:	2	0.01
Guatemalan	1	0.01
Salvadoran	1	0.01
Cuban	6	0.04
Mexican	126	0.90
Puerto Rican	13	0.09
South American:	7	0.05
Argentinean	1	0.01
Colombian	1	0.01
Peruvian	3	0.02
Venezuelan	2	0.01
Other Hispanic or Latino	28	0.20
Hungarian	138	0.99
Iranian	2	0.01
Irish	1,605	11.52
Italian	574	4.12
Latvian	25	0.18
Lithuanian	17	0.12
Northern European	40	0.29
Norwegian	210	1.51
Pennsylvania German	7	0.05
Polish	814	5.84
Romanian	2	0.01
Russian	126	0.90
Scandinavian	18	0.13
Scotch-Irish	194	1.39
Scottish	270	1.94
Serbian	8	0.06
Slavic	4	0.03
Slovak	84	0.60
Slovene	8	0.06
Swedish	335	2.41
Swiss	83	0.60
Ukrainian	117	0.84
United States or American	871	6.25
Welsh	201	1.44
White:	13,471	96.55
Not Hispanic (13,251)	13,363	95.78
Hispanic (90)	108	0.77

Livonia

Place Type: City
County: Wayne
Population: 100,545

Ancestry/Race	Number	%
Acadian/Cajun	13	0.01
African American/Black:	1,123	1.12
Not Hispanic (945)	1,105	1.10
Hispanic (6)	18	0.02
African, sub-Saharan:	101	0.10
African	81	0.08
Ethiopian	15	0.01
Liberian	5	0.00
Alaska Native tribes, specified:	4	0.00
Aleut	1	0.00
Eskimo (3)	3	0.00
Alaska Native tribes, not specified	3	0.00
Am. Ind. or Alaska Nat., not spec.	170	0.17
Albanian	272	0.27
American Indian tribes, specified:	402	0.40
Apache (1)	1	0.00
Blackfeet	10	0.01
Cherokee (15)	99	0.10
Cheyenne	3	0.00
Chippewa (66)	116	0.12
Choctaw (1)	7	0.01
Cree (1)	2	0.00
Delaware (4)	5	0.00
Iroquois (18)	52	0.05
Latin American Indians (11)	19	0.02
Lumbee (16)	22	0.02
Navajo (2)	4	0.00
Osage	1	0.00
Ottawa (1)	10	0.01
Paiute (1)	4	0.00
Potawatomi (2)	8	0.01
Pueblo	2	0.00
Seminole	3	0.00
Sioux	3	0.00
Ute	3	0.00
Yaqui	2	0.00
All other tribes (16)	28	0.03
American Indian tribes, not spec.	19	0.02
Arab:	1,972	1.96
Arab/Arabic	396	0.39
Iraqi	7	0.01
Jordanian	147	0.15
Lebanese	897	0.89
Palestinian	325	0.32
Syrian	176	0.18
Other Arab	24	0.02
Armenian	928	0.92
Asian:	2,320	2.31
Bangladeshi (3)	3	0.00
Cambodian	3	0.00
Chinese, ex. Taiwanese (498)	555	0.55
Filipino (340)	438	0.44
Hmong (1)	1	0.00
Indian (620)	667	0.66
Indonesian (5)	12	0.01
Japanese (115)	189	0.19
Korean (160)	184	0.18
Laotian (4)	5	0.00
Malaysian (2)	2	0.00

Notes: 1. Figures in the "Number" column do not add up to the total population due to: a) Ancestry/Race overlap — e.g. persons can report being both White and Irish, b) persons of Hispanic origin can report being any race, c) persons reporting two ancestries are counted in both categories. 2. Numbers in parentheses indicate the number of persons reporting this ancestry/race alone, not in combination with any other ancestry/race. 3. Refer to the Explanation of Data in the front of the book for more detailed information.

Ancestry/Race	Number	%
Pakistani (30)	33	0.03
Sri Lankan (8)	8	0.01
Taiwanese (11)	22	0.02
Thai (8)	15	0.01
Vietnamese (100)	107	0.11
Other Asian, specified	6	0.01
Other Asian, not specified (26)	70	0.07
Assyrian/Chaldean/Syriac	115	0.11
Austrian	485	0.48
Basque	5	0.00
Belgian	460	0.46
Brazilian	7	0.01
British	409	0.41
Bulgarian	30	0.03
Canadian	910	0.91
Carpatho Rusyn	5	0.00
Celtic	15	0.01
Croatian	322	0.32
Czech	476	0.47
Czechoslovakian	263	0.26
Danish	503	0.50
Dutch	1,439	1.43
Eastern European	32	0.03
English	11,989	11.92
Estonian	10	0.01
European	503	0.50
Finnish	1,323	1.32
French, except Basque	5,485	5.46
French Canadian	2,637	2.62
German	22,822	22.70
Greek	1,079	1.07
Hawaii Native/Pacific Islander:	43	0.04
Micronesian: (1)	1	0.00
Guamanian/Chamorro (1)	1	0.00
Polynesian: (7)	12	0.01
Native Hawaiian (4)	7	0.01
Samoan (3)	5	0.00
Other Pac. Isl., specified	6	0.01
Other Pac. Isl., not spec. (6)	24	0.02
Hispanic or Latino:	1,731	1.72
Central American:	41	0.04
Costa Rican	7	0.01
Guatemalan	12	0.01
Honduran	8	0.01
Nicaraguan	2	0.00
Panamanian	4	0.00
Salvadoran	8	0.01
Cuban	63	0.06
Dominican Republic	6	0.01
Mexican	1,105	1.10
Puerto Rican	109	0.11
South American:	95	0.09
Argentinean	22	0.02
Bolivian	7	0.01
Chilean	7	0.01
Colombian	41	0.04
Ecuadorian	3	0.00
Paraguayan	3	0.00
Peruvian	5	0.00
Uruguayan	4	0.00
Venezuelan	3	0.00
Other Hispanic or Latino	312	0.31
Hungarian	1,839	1.83
Icelander	17	0.02
Iranian	42	0.04
Irish	16,435	16.35
Italian	9,251	9.20
Latvian	39	0.04
Lithuanian	728	0.72
Macedonian	421	0.42
Maltese	942	0.94
Northern European	77	0.08
Norwegian	1,104	1.10
Pennsylvania German	41	0.04
Polish	18,131	18.03
Portuguese	57	0.06
Romanian	719	0.72
Russian	913	0.91
Scandinavian	66	0.07
Scotch-Irish	2,386	2.37
Scottish	4,245	4.22
Serbian	161	0.16
Slavic	178	0.18
Slovak	387	0.38
Slovene	138	0.14
Swedish	1,515	1.51
Swiss	288	0.29
Turkish	14	0.01
Ukrainian	1,402	1.39
United States or American	3,387	3.37
Welsh	668	0.66
West Indian, excl. Hispanic:	34	0.03
Bahamian	17	0.02
Haitian	14	0.01
Jamaican	3	0.00
White:	97,018	96.49
Not Hispanic (94,651)	95,576	95.06
Hispanic (1,324)	1,442	1.43
Yugoslavian	403	0.40

Lyon

Place Type: Township
County: Oakland
Population: 11,041

Ancestry/Race	Number	%
African American/Black:	59	0.53
Not Hispanic (39)	59	0.53
Am. Ind. or Alaska Nat., not spec.	35	0.32
Albanian	22	0.20
American Indian tribes, specified:	74	0.67
Cherokee (6)	23	0.21
Cheyenne	4	0.04
Chippewa (14)	25	0.23
Choctaw	1	0.01
Delaware (1)	3	0.03
Iroquois (4)	5	0.05
Lumbee (5)	9	0.08
All other tribes (1)	4	0.04
American Indian tribes, not spec.	3	0.03
Arab:	66	0.60
Arab/Arabic	32	0.29
Lebanese	13	0.12
Syrian	21	0.19
Armenian	27	0.24
Asian:	89	0.81
Chinese, ex. Taiwanese (15)	15	0.14
Filipino (4)	7	0.06
Indian (22)	29	0.26
Indonesian	1	0.01
Japanese (9)	15	0.14
Korean (8)	10	0.09
Taiwanese (1)	1	0.01
Thai (1)	1	0.01
Vietnamese (3)	5	0.05
Other Asian, not specified (4)	5	0.05
Assyrian/Chaldean/Syriac	59	0.54
Austrian	11	0.10
Belgian	31	0.28
British	68	0.62
Bulgarian	14	0.13
Canadian	122	1.11
Croatian	49	0.44
Czech	22	0.20
Czechoslovakian	21	0.19
Danish	104	0.94
Dutch	237	2.15
Eastern European	7	0.06
English	1,508	13.68
European	109	0.99
Finnish	362	3.28
French, except Basque	690	6.26
French Canadian	424	3.85
German	3,033	27.52
Greek	108	0.98
Hawaii Native/Pacific Islander:	6	0.05
Polynesian: (1)	2	0.02
Native Hawaiian (1)	2	0.02
Other Pac. Isl., not spec. (3)	4	0.04
Hispanic or Latino:	162	1.47
Central American:	2	0.02
Guatemalan	1	0.01
Salvadoran	1	0.01
Mexican	112	1.01
Puerto Rican	10	0.09
South American:	9	0.08
Argentinean	6	0.05
Colombian	2	0.02
Ecuadorian	1	0.01
Other Hispanic or Latino	29	0.26
Hungarian	79	0.72
Irish	1,737	15.76
Italian	945	8.57
Latvian	16	0.15
Maltese	13	0.12
Norwegian	127	1.15
Polish	1,499	13.60
Romanian	25	0.23
Russian	91	0.83
Scandinavian	7	0.06
Scotch-Irish	215	1.95
Scottish	448	4.06
Slavic	8	0.07
Slovak	8	0.07
Slovene	23	0.21
Swedish	147	1.33
Swiss	72	0.65
Turkish	5	0.05
Ukrainian	38	0.34
United States or American	624	5.66
Welsh	125	1.13
White:	10,834	98.13
Not Hispanic (10,611)	10,721	97.10
Hispanic (110)	113	1.02
Yugoslavian	6	0.05

Macomb

Place Type: Township
County: Macomb
Population: 50,478

Ancestry/Race	Number	%
African American/Black:	527	1.04
Not Hispanic (420)	516	1.02
Hispanic (6)	11	0.02
African, sub-Saharan:	85	0.17
African	44	0.09
Ghanian	32	0.06
Other sub-Saharan African	9	0.02
Alaska Native tribes, specified:	7	0.01
Alaska Athabascan (1)	1	0.00
Eskimo (3)	6	0.01
Am. Ind. or Alaska Nat., not spec.	65	0.13
Albanian	652	1.29
American Indian tribes, specified:	163	0.32
Apache (1)	2	0.00
Blackfeet	3	0.01
Cherokee (9)	49	0.10
Cheyenne	3	0.01
Chippewa (20)	43	0.09
Choctaw	2	0.00
Creek	2	0.00
Delaware	1	0.00
Iroquois (10)	19	0.04
Kiowa (2)	2	0.00
Latin American Indians (4)	4	0.01
Lumbee (9)	13	0.03
Navajo (2)	5	0.01
Ottawa (1)	2	0.00
Paiute (1)	1	0.00
Potawatomi (5)	5	0.01
Seminole	1	0.00
All other tribes (4)	6	0.01
American Indian tribes, not spec.	1	0.00
Arab:	846	1.68
Arab/Arabic	112	0.22
Iraqi	69	0.14
Lebanese	500	0.99

Notes: 1. Figures in the "Number" column do not add up to the total population due to: a) Ancestry/Race overlap — e.g. persons can report being both White and Irish, b) persons of Hispanic origin can report being any race, c) persons reporting two ancestries are counted in both categories. 2. Numbers in parentheses indicate the number of persons reporting this ancestry/race alone, not in combination with any other ancestry/race. 3. Refer to the Explanation of Data in the front of the book for more detailed information.

Syrian	144	0.29
Other Arab	21	0.04
Armenian	137	0.27
Asian:	874	1.73
Bangladeshi (3)	3	0.01
Cambodian (7)	9	0.02
Chinese, ex. Taiwanese (140)	162	0.32
Filipino (107)	159	0.31
Hmong (28)	29	0.06
Indian (193)	207	0.41
Indonesian	2	0.00
Japanese (11)	29	0.06
Korean (101)	126	0.25
Laotian (7)	7	0.01
Pakistani (23)	25	0.05
Taiwanese (7)	8	0.02
Thai (6)	10	0.02
Vietnamese (69)	74	0.15
Other Asian, not specified (8)	24	0.05
Assyrian/Chaldean/Syriac	196	0.39
Australian	15	0.03
Austrian	114	0.23
Belgian	1,322	2.62
British	135	0.27
Bulgarian	33	0.07
Canadian	327	0.65
Croatian	173	0.34
Czech	141	0.28
Czechoslovakian	57	0.11
Danish	206	0.41
Dutch	696	1.38
Eastern European	20	0.04
English	4,113	8.15
European	116	0.23
Finnish	114	0.23
French, except Basque	2,958	5.86
French Canadian	1,193	2.36
German	13,746	27.23
Greek	555	1.10
Hawaii Native/Pacific Islander:	15	0.03
Micronesian: (1)	1	0.00
Guamanian/Chamorro (1)	1	0.00
Polynesian: (1)	2	0.00
Native Hawaiian (1)	1	0.00
Samoan	1	0.00
Other Pac. Isl., not spec. (2)	12	0.02
Hispanic or Latino:	735	1.46
Central American:	14	0.03
Costa Rican	3	0.01
Guatemalan	5	0.01
Panamanian	6	0.01
Cuban	34	0.07
Dominican Republic	3	0.01
Mexican	441	0.87
Puerto Rican	76	0.15
South American:	27	0.05
Argentinean	3	0.01
Chilean	2	0.00
Colombian	9	0.02
Peruvian	4	0.01
Uruguayan	6	0.01
Venezuelan	2	0.00
Other South American	1	0.00
Other Hispanic or Latino	140	0.28
Hungarian	370	0.73
Irish	5,834	11.56
Italian	10,716	21.23
Latvian	9	0.02
Lithuanian	116	0.23
Macedonian	454	0.90
Maltese	207	0.41
Norwegian	220	0.44
Pennsylvania German	8	0.02
Polish	9,909	19.63
Portuguese	43	0.09
Romanian	303	0.60
Russian	366	0.73
Scandinavian	4	0.01
Scotch-Irish	510	1.01
Scottish	1,292	2.56
Serbian	127	0.25
Slavic	65	0.13
Slovak	408	0.81
Slovene	10	0.02
Swedish	329	0.65
Swiss	33	0.07
Turkish	5	0.01
Ukrainian	526	1.04
United States or American	2,104	4.17
Welsh	288	0.57
White:	49,065	97.20
Not Hispanic (47,968)	48,476	96.03
Hispanic (550)	589	1.17
Yugoslavian	428	0.85

Madison Heights

Place Type: City
County: Oakland
Population: 31,101

Ancestry/Race	Number	%
African American/Black:	652	2.10
Not Hispanic (559)	638	2.05
Hispanic (8)	14	0.05
African, sub-Saharan:	30	0.10
African	20	0.06
Other sub-Saharan African	10	0.03
Am. Ind. or Alaska Nat., not spec.	118	0.38
Albanian	158	0.51
American Indian tribes, specified:	203	0.65
Apache (1)	3	0.01
Blackfeet (1)	4	0.01
Cherokee (12)	76	0.24
Chippewa (24)	45	0.14
Choctaw (1)	6	0.02
Cree (1)	1	0.00
Creek (6)	10	0.03
Delaware (3)	3	0.01
Iroquois (9)	12	0.04
Latin American Indians (1)	2	0.01
Lumbee (10)	12	0.04
Navajo (1)	1	0.00
Ottawa	5	0.02
Potawatomi	1	0.00
Pueblo	1	0.00
Seminole	1	0.00
Sioux (3)	5	0.02
All other tribes (9)	15	0.05
American Indian tribes, not spec.	17	0.05
Arab:	609	1.96
Arab/Arabic	70	0.23
Egyptian	28	0.09
Iraqi	237	0.76
Jordanian	51	0.16
Lebanese	122	0.39
Palestinian	41	0.13
Syrian	52	0.17
Other Arab	8	0.03
Armenian	77	0.25
Asian:	1,780	5.72
Bangladeshi (21)	23	0.07
Cambodian (3)	3	0.01
Chinese, ex. Taiwanese (415)	446	1.43
Filipino (248)	293	0.94
Indian (481)	500	1.61
Indonesian (1)	1	0.00
Japanese (25)	49	0.16
Korean (80)	101	0.32
Laotian (21)	22	0.07
Pakistani (55)	63	0.20
Sri Lankan (2)	3	0.01
Taiwanese (9)	14	0.05
Thai (7)	8	0.03
Vietnamese (131)	148	0.48
Other Asian, specified (4)	4	0.01
Other Asian, not specified (19)	102	0.33
Assyrian/Chaldean/Syriac	1,428	4.59
Austrian	55	0.18
Belgian	154	0.50
British	120	0.39
Bulgarian	32	0.10
Canadian	344	1.11
Celtic	9	0.03
Croatian	138	0.44
Czech	172	0.55
Czechoslovakian	67	0.22
Danish	79	0.25
Dutch	449	1.44
Eastern European	10	0.03
English	3,321	10.68
European	174	0.56
Finnish	408	1.31
French, except Basque	1,436	4.62
French Canadian	656	2.11
German	5,679	18.26
Greek	324	1.04
Hawaii Native/Pacific Islander:	19	0.06
Polynesian: (5)	7	0.02
Native Hawaiian (4)	6	0.02
Samoan (1)	1	0.00
Other Pac. Isl., not spec. (3)	12	0.04
Hispanic or Latino:	502	1.61
Central American:	12	0.04
Costa Rican	4	0.01
Guatemalan	2	0.01
Honduran	1	0.00
Panamanian	5	0.02
Cuban	21	0.07
Dominican Republic	1	0.00
Mexican	266	0.86
Puerto Rican	55	0.18
South American:	13	0.04
Argentinean	3	0.01
Bolivian	2	0.01
Chilean	1	0.00
Colombian	5	0.02
Peruvian	2	0.01
Other Hispanic or Latino	134	0.43
Hungarian	251	0.81
Iranian	8	0.03
Irish	3,625	11.66
Italian	1,997	6.42
Latvian	19	0.06
Lithuanian	83	0.27
Luxemburger	9	0.03
Macedonian	16	0.05
Maltese	15	0.05
Northern European	7	0.02
Norwegian	194	0.62
Pennsylvania German	4	0.01
Polish	4,264	13.71
Portuguese	12	0.04
Romanian	577	1.86
Russian	184	0.59
Scandinavian	56	0.18
Scotch-Irish	546	1.76
Scottish	881	2.83
Serbian	54	0.17
Slavic	62	0.20
Slovak	105	0.34
Slovene	7	0.02
Swedish	295	0.95
Turkish	7	0.02
Ukrainian	354	1.14
United States or American	1,857	5.97
Welsh	120	0.39
West Indian, excl. Hispanic:	20	0.06
Jamaican	20	0.06
White:	28,651	92.12
Not Hispanic (27,516)	28,274	90.91
Hispanic (350)	377	1.21
Yugoslavian	265	0.85

Notes: 1. Figures in the "Number" column do not add up to the total population due to: a) Ancestry/Race overlap — e.g. persons can report being both White and Irish, b) persons of Hispanic origin can report being any race, c) persons reporting two ancestries are counted in both categories. 2. Numbers in parentheses indicate the number of persons reporting this ancestry/race alone, not in combination with any other ancestry/race. 3. Refer to the Explanation of Data in the front of the book for more detailed information.

Marquette

Place Type: City
County: Marquette
Population: 19,661

Ancestry/Race	Number	%
African American/Black:	224	1.14
Not Hispanic (161)	220	1.12
Hispanic (1)	4	0.02
African, sub-Saharan:	47	0.24
African	41	0.21
Nigerian	6	0.03
Alaska Native tribes, specified:	1	0.01
Eskimo	1	0.01
Am. Ind. or Alaska Nat., not spec.	100	0.51
American Indian tribes, specified:	386	1.96
Apache (1)	1	0.01
Blackfeet	7	0.04
Cherokee (3)	13	0.07
Chippewa (223)	306	1.56
Choctaw	1	0.01
Cree (1)	1	0.01
Delaware	2	0.01
Iroquois (1)	3	0.02
Latin American Indians	3	0.02
Menominee (3)	3	0.02
Navajo (1)	1	0.01
Ottawa (6)	11	0.06
Potawatomi (7)	12	0.06
Sioux (4)	12	0.06
All other tribes (5)	10	0.05
American Indian tribes, not spec.	22	0.11
Arab:	3	0.02
Syrian	3	0.02
Asian:	204	1.04
Chinese, ex. Taiwanese (39)	57	0.29
Filipino (20)	29	0.15
Hmong (15)	15	0.08
Indian (14)	15	0.08
Indonesian	1	0.01
Japanese (23)	34	0.17
Korean (28)	30	0.15
Pakistani (2)	2	0.01
Taiwanese (4)	4	0.02
Thai (3)	6	0.03
Vietnamese (4)	4	0.02
Other Asian, not specified (2)	7	0.04
Assyrian/Chaldean/Syriac	30	0.15
Austrian	93	0.47
Belgian	338	1.72
British	70	0.36
Bulgarian	10	0.05
Canadian	106	0.54
Celtic	7	0.04
Croatian	110	0.56
Czech	92	0.47
Czechoslovakian	132	0.67
Danish	158	0.81
Dutch	392	2.00
Eastern European	6	0.03
English	2,479	12.65
Estonian	6	0.03
European	179	0.91
Finnish	2,654	13.54
French, except Basque	2,539	12.96
French Canadian	916	4.67
German	3,999	20.41
Greek	63	0.32
Hawaii Native/Pacific Islander:	13	0.07
Micronesian: (3)	4	0.02
Other Micronesian (3)	4	0.02
Polynesian: (1)	6	0.03
Native Hawaiian (1)	6	0.03
Other Pac. Isl., not spec.	3	0.02
Hispanic or Latino:	152	0.77
Central American:	4	0.02
Guatemalan	3	0.02
Honduran	1	0.01
Cuban	9	0.05
Dominican Republic	2	0.01
Mexican	73	0.37
Puerto Rican	19	0.10
South American:	12	0.06
Argentinean	2	0.01
Chilean	2	0.01
Colombian	3	0.02
Peruvian	1	0.01
Venezuelan	4	0.02
Other Hispanic or Latino	33	0.17
Hungarian	93	0.47
Irish	2,291	11.69
Italian	1,367	6.98
Latvian	7	0.04
Lithuanian	34	0.17
Luxemburger	6	0.03
Maltese	5	0.03
Northern European	28	0.14
Norwegian	591	3.02
Polish	1,095	5.59
Portuguese	27	0.14
Russian	81	0.41
Scandinavian	144	0.73
Scotch-Irish	335	1.71
Scottish	470	2.40
Serbian	6	0.03
Slavic	30	0.15
Slovak	31	0.16
Slovene	31	0.16
Swedish	1,690	8.62
Swiss	70	0.36
Ukrainian	48	0.24
United States or American	492	2.51
Welsh	108	0.55
West Indian, excl. Hispanic:	12	0.06
Jamaican	7	0.04
West Indian	5	0.03
White:	18,936	96.31
Not Hispanic (18,579)	18,818	95.71
Hispanic (106)	118	0.60
Yugoslavian	31	0.16

Melvindale

Place Type: City
County: Wayne
Population: 10,735

Ancestry/Race	Number	%
African American/Black:	617	5.75
Not Hispanic (556)	603	5.62
Hispanic (9)	14	0.13
African, sub-Saharan:	29	0.27
African	29	0.27
Am. Ind. or Alaska Nat., not spec.	44	0.41
Albanian	40	0.37
American Indian tribes, specified:	140	1.30
Blackfeet (3)	9	0.08
Cherokee (23)	63	0.59
Chippewa (14)	21	0.20
Choctaw (2)	3	0.03
Comanche (2)	2	0.02
Iroquois (10)	18	0.17
Latin American Indians (2)	7	0.07
Lumbee (1)	2	0.02
Navajo (2)	2	0.02
Ottawa (1)	1	0.01
Seminole	1	0.01
Sioux	4	0.04
All other tribes (4)	7	0.07
American Indian tribes, not spec.	9	0.08
Arab:	268	2.50
Arab/Arabic	124	1.16
Iraqi	19	0.18
Jordanian	9	0.08
Lebanese	110	1.02
Other Arab	6	0.06
Armenian	84	0.78
Asian:	185	1.72
Chinese, ex. Taiwanese (5)	6	0.06
Filipino (36)	55	0.51
Hmong (7)	9	0.08
Indian (66)	67	0.62
Japanese (3)	8	0.07
Korean (3)	9	0.08
Laotian (1)	2	0.02
Pakistani (3)	3	0.03
Sri Lankan (1)	1	0.01
Vietnamese (11)	11	0.10
Other Asian, not specified (2)	14	0.13
Assyrian/Chaldean/Syriac	18	0.17
Australian	23	0.21
Austrian	57	0.53
Belgian	19	0.18
British	25	0.23
Canadian	40	0.37
Croatian	8	0.07
Czech	39	0.36
Czechoslovakian	31	0.29
Danish	8	0.07
Dutch	154	1.43
English	713	6.64
European	5	0.05
Finnish	61	0.57
French, except Basque	560	5.22
French Canadian	233	2.17
German	1,712	15.95
Greek	13	0.12
Hawaii Native/Pacific Islander:	7	0.07
Polynesian: (4)	5	0.05
Native Hawaiian (2)	3	0.03
Samoan (2)	2	0.02
Other Pac. Isl., not spec.	2	0.02
Hispanic or Latino:	955	8.90
Central American:	10	0.09
Honduran	7	0.07
Salvadoran	3	0.03
Cuban	10	0.09
Dominican Republic	7	0.07
Mexican	682	6.35
Puerto Rican	107	1.00
South American:	10	0.09
Argentinean	5	0.05
Chilean	1	0.01
Peruvian	4	0.04
Other Hispanic or Latino	129	1.20
Hungarian	412	3.84
Irish	1,284	11.96
Italian	711	6.62
Latvian	16	0.15
Lithuanian	55	0.51
Macedonian	28	0.26
Maltese	26	0.24
Norwegian	48	0.45
Polish	1,111	10.35
Romanian	52	0.48
Russian	61	0.57
Scandinavian	6	0.06
Scotch-Irish	91	0.85
Scottish	291	2.71
Slovak	37	0.34
Swedish	137	1.28
Ukrainian	109	1.02
United States or American	519	4.83
Welsh	84	0.78
White:	9,670	90.08
Not Hispanic (8,773)	8,990	83.74
Hispanic (609)	680	6.33
Yugoslavian	24	0.22

Meridian charter

Place Type: Township
County: Ingham
Population: 39,116

Ancestry/Race	Number	%
Afghan	24	0.06
African American/Black:	1,822	4.66
Not Hispanic (1,578)	1,802	4.61

Notes: 1. Figures in the "Number" column do not add up to the total population due to: a) Ancestry/Race overlap — e.g. persons can report being both White and Irish, b) persons of Hispanic origin can report being any race, c) persons reporting two ancestries are counted in both categories. 2. Numbers in parentheses indicate the number of persons reporting this ancestry/race alone, not in combination with any other ancestry/race. 3. Refer to the Explanation of Data in the front of the book for more detailed information.

Ancestry/Race	Number	%
Hispanic (6)	20	0.05
African, sub-Saharan:	305	0.78
African	146	0.37
Cape Verdean	8	0.02
Nigerian	66	0.17
Somalian	18	0.05
South African	33	0.08
Other sub-Saharan African	34	0.09
Alaska Native tribes, specified:	6	0.02
Aleut	1	0.00
Eskimo (5)	5	0.01
Am. Ind. or Alaska Nat., not spec.	81	0.21
American Indian tribes, specified:	221	0.56
Apache (4)	13	0.03
Blackfeet	7	0.02
Cherokee (11)	60	0.15
Chippewa (41)	70	0.18
Choctaw (3)	9	0.02
Comanche	2	0.01
Creek	1	0.00
Iroquois (5)	9	0.02
Latin American Indians (3)	6	0.02
Ottawa (21)	23	0.06
Pueblo (3)	5	0.01
Sioux (1)	3	0.01
Yaqui	1	0.00
All other tribes (5)	12	0.03
American Indian tribes, not spec.	16	0.04
Arab:	445	1.14
Arab/Arabic	71	0.18
Egyptian	20	0.05
Iraqi	21	0.05
Jordanian	5	0.01
Lebanese	230	0.59
Palestinian	45	0.12
Syrian	43	0.11
Other Arab	10	0.03
Armenian	70	0.18
Asian:	2,882	7.37
Bangladeshi (8)	13	0.03
Cambodian (1)	1	0.00
Chinese, ex. Taiwanese (604)	672	1.72
Filipino (88)	136	0.35
Hmong (14)	19	0.05
Indian (865)	937	2.40
Indonesian (9)	11	0.03
Japanese (123)	152	0.39
Korean (445)	481	1.23
Laotian (5)	10	0.03
Malaysian (3)	3	0.01
Pakistani (58)	73	0.19
Sri Lankan (5)	6	0.02
Taiwanese (81)	94	0.24
Thai (23)	27	0.07
Vietnamese (132)	137	0.35
Other Asian, specified (7)	10	0.03
Other Asian, not specified (41)	100	0.26
Assyrian/Chaldean/Syriac	7	0.02
Austrian	100	0.26
Belgian	220	0.56
Brazilian	35	0.09
British	314	0.81
Canadian	190	0.49
Celtic	6	0.02
Croatian	75	0.19
Czech	187	0.48
Czechoslovakian	86	0.22
Danish	196	0.50
Dutch	1,291	3.31
Eastern European	40	0.10
English	6,019	15.44
European	409	1.05
Finnish	294	0.75
French, except Basque	1,411	3.62
French Canadian	539	1.38
German	10,047	25.77
Greek	269	0.69
Hawaii Native/Pacific Islander:	49	0.13
Micronesian: (2)	3	0.01
Guamanian/Chamorro (2)	3	0.01
Polynesian: (10)	14	0.04
Native Hawaiian (6)	8	0.02
Samoan (4)	6	0.02
Other Pac. Isl., not spec. (9)	32	0.08
Hispanic or Latino:	990	2.53
Central American:	27	0.07
Costa Rican	4	0.01
Guatemalan	10	0.03
Honduran	2	0.01
Nicaraguan	4	0.01
Panamanian	6	0.02
Salvadoran	1	0.00
Cuban	44	0.11
Dominican Republic	9	0.02
Mexican	570	1.46
Puerto Rican	70	0.18
South American:	87	0.22
Argentinean	6	0.02
Bolivian	3	0.01
Chilean	7	0.02
Colombian	27	0.07
Ecuadorian	3	0.01
Paraguayan	1	0.00
Peruvian	15	0.04
Uruguayan	2	0.01
Venezuelan	5	0.01
Other South American	18	0.05
Other Hispanic or Latino	183	0.47
Hungarian	384	0.98
Icelander	6	0.02
Iranian	125	0.32
Irish	5,086	13.05
Israeli	49	0.13
Italian	1,886	4.84
Latvian	99	0.25
Lithuanian	167	0.43
Luxemburger	34	0.09
Macedonian	51	0.13
Maltese	15	0.04
Northern European	70	0.18
Norwegian	666	1.71
Pennsylvania German	26	0.07
Polish	2,681	6.88
Portuguese	34	0.09
Romanian	47	0.12
Russian	593	1.52
Scandinavian	41	0.11
Scotch-Irish	736	1.89
Scottish	1,477	3.79
Serbian	37	0.09
Slavic	35	0.09
Slovak	112	0.29
Slovene	36	0.09
Swedish	1,116	2.86
Swiss	267	0.68
Turkish	20	0.05
Ukrainian	189	0.48
United States or American	1,540	3.95
Welsh	371	0.95
West Indian, excl. Hispanic:	32	0.08
Bahamian	15	0.04
Haitian	8	0.02
West Indian	9	0.02
White:	34,474	88.13
Not Hispanic (33,157)	33,737	86.25
Hispanic (624)	737	1.88
Yugoslavian	21	0.05

Midland

Place Type: City
County: Midland
Population: 41,685

Ancestry/Race	Number	%
African American/Black:	895	2.15
Not Hispanic (749)	863	2.07
Hispanic (11)	32	0.08
African, sub-Saharan:	42	0.10
African	17	0.04
Nigerian	25	0.06
Alaska Native tribes, specified:	1	0.00
Eskimo	1	0.00
Alaska Native tribes, not specified	3	0.01
Am. Ind. or Alaska Nat., not spec.	65	0.16
American Indian tribes, specified:	226	0.54
Apache (1)	1	0.00
Blackfeet (1)	10	0.02
Cherokee (6)	38	0.09
Chickasaw	2	0.00
Chippewa (57)	118	0.28
Choctaw (1)	2	0.00
Comanche	1	0.00
Cree (2)	2	0.00
Creek	1	0.00
Iroquois (4)	8	0.02
Latin American Indians (4)	13	0.03
Lumbee (1)	1	0.00
Osage	2	0.00
Ottawa (5)	12	0.03
Potawatomi (1)	2	0.00
Shoshone	1	0.00
Sioux (1)	5	0.01
All other tribes (4)	7	0.02
American Indian tribes, not spec.	10	0.02
Arab:	33	0.08
Arab/Arabic	19	0.05
Lebanese	8	0.02
Syrian	6	0.01
Armenian	84	0.20
Asian:	1,267	3.04
Bangladeshi (2)	3	0.01
Cambodian (1)	1	0.00
Chinese, ex. Taiwanese (374)	412	0.99
Filipino (61)	90	0.22
Hmong (6)	6	0.01
Indian (334)	349	0.84
Japanese (71)	105	0.25
Korean (119)	131	0.31
Laotian (3)	4	0.01
Malaysian (25)	29	0.07
Pakistani (12)	12	0.03
Sri Lankan (1)	2	0.00
Taiwanese (17)	21	0.05
Thai (16)	19	0.05
Vietnamese (51)	57	0.14
Other Asian, not specified (15)	26	0.06
Australian	19	0.05
Austrian	135	0.32
Belgian	239	0.57
Brazilian	38	0.09
British	309	0.74
Canadian	495	1.19
Carpatho Rusyn	7	0.02
Celtic	6	0.01
Croatian	61	0.15
Czech	282	0.68
Czechoslovakian	102	0.24
Danish	234	0.56
Dutch	1,589	3.81
English	5,723	13.74
European	450	1.08
Finnish	292	0.70
French, except Basque	2,546	6.11
French Canadian	832	2.00
German	12,939	31.06
Greek	219	0.53
Hawaii Native/Pacific Islander:	33	0.08
Micronesian: (3)	4	0.01
Guamanian/Chamorro (3)	4	0.01
Polynesian: (16)	17	0.04
Native Hawaiian (9)	9	0.02
Samoan (3)	3	0.01
Tongan (4)	5	0.01
Other Pac. Isl., not spec. (5)	12	0.03
Hispanic or Latino:	802	1.92
Central American:	25	0.06
Costa Rican	8	0.02
Guatemalan	5	0.01
Panamanian	8	0.02

Notes: 1. Figures in the "Number" column do not add up to the total population due to: a) Ancestry/Race overlap — e.g. persons can report being both White and Irish, b) persons of Hispanic origin can report being any race, c) persons reporting two ancestries are counted in both categories. 2. Numbers in parentheses indicate the number of persons reporting this ancestry/race alone, not in combination with any other ancestry/race. 3. Refer to the Explanation of Data in the front of the book for more detailed information.

Ancestry/Race	Number	%
Salvadoran	4	0.01
Cuban	30	0.07
Dominican Republic	2	0.00
Mexican	488	1.17
Puerto Rican	51	0.12
South American:	75	0.18
Argentinean	25	0.06
Bolivian	4	0.01
Chilean	7	0.02
Colombian	28	0.07
Ecuadorian	3	0.01
Peruvian	1	0.00
Uruguayan	4	0.01
Venezuelan	3	0.01
Other Hispanic or Latino	131	0.31
Hungarian	322	0.77
Iranian	46	0.11
Irish	5,590	13.42
Italian	1,143	2.74
Latvian	33	0.08
Lithuanian	98	0.24
Luxemburger	6	0.01
Maltese	6	0.01
Northern European	21	0.05
Norwegian	668	1.60
Pennsylvania German	48	0.12
Polish	3,098	7.44
Portuguese	29	0.07
Romanian	37	0.09
Russian	133	0.32
Scandinavian	104	0.25
Scotch-Irish	663	1.59
Scottish	1,499	3.60
Serbian	5	0.01
Slavic	33	0.08
Slovak	146	0.35
Slovene	46	0.11
Swedish	784	1.88
Swiss	180	0.43
Turkish	27	0.06
Ukrainian	248	0.60
United States or American	2,384	5.72
Welsh	345	0.83
West Indian, excl. Hispanic:	38	0.09
British West Indian	6	0.01
Haitian	9	0.02
Jamaican	23	0.06
White:	39,387	94.49
Not Hispanic (38,416)	38,807	93.10
Hispanic (508)	580	1.39
Yugoslavian	23	0.06

Milford

Place Type: Township
County: Oakland
Population: 15,271

Ancestry/Race	Number	%
African American/Black:	83	0.54
Not Hispanic (65)	83	0.54
African, sub-Saharan:	21	0.14
African	21	0.14
Am. Ind. or Alaska Nat., not spec.	31	0.20
Albanian	4	0.03
American Indian tribes, specified:	89	0.58
Apache (1)	3	0.02
Blackfeet	11	0.07
Cherokee (5)	24	0.16
Chippewa (12)	24	0.16
Choctaw	1	0.01
Iroquois (2)	11	0.07
Kiowa (1)	1	0.01
Latin American Indians (5)	5	0.03
Lumbee (2)	2	0.01
Menominee (1)	1	0.01
Potawatomi (1)	2	0.01
Sioux	3	0.02
All other tribes	1	0.01
American Indian tribes, not spec.	6	0.04
Arab:	157	1.03
Arab/Arabic	100	0.65
Jordanian	42	0.28
Lebanese	15	0.10
Armenian	63	0.41
Asian:	105	0.69
Chinese, ex. Taiwanese (13)	16	0.10
Filipino (8)	19	0.12
Indian (7)	10	0.07
Japanese (3)	12	0.08
Korean (25)	28	0.18
Laotian (8)	11	0.07
Thai	1	0.01
Vietnamese (1)	1	0.01
Other Asian, specified (3)	3	0.02
Other Asian, not specified (2)	4	0.03
Assyrian/Chaldean/Syriac	82	0.54
Austrian	55	0.36
Belgian	116	0.76
Brazilian	22	0.14
British	76	0.50
Canadian	141	0.92
Celtic	5	0.03
Croatian	64	0.42
Czech	50	0.33
Czechoslovakian	15	0.10
Danish	89	0.58
Dutch	429	2.81
English	2,123	13.90
European	187	1.22
Finnish	345	2.26
French, except Basque	1,021	6.69
French Canadian	351	2.30
German	3,778	24.74
Greek	101	0.66
Hawaii Native/Pacific Islander:	3	0.02
Polynesian:	1	0.01
Native Hawaiian	1	0.01
Other Pac. Isl., not spec.	2	0.01
Hispanic or Latino:	182	1.19
Central American:	1	0.01
Panamanian	1	0.01
Cuban	15	0.10
Mexican	116	0.76
Puerto Rican	8	0.05
South American:	7	0.05
Chilean	6	0.04
Colombian	1	0.01
Other Hispanic or Latino	35	0.23
Hungarian	229	1.50
Icelander	8	0.05
Iranian	31	0.20
Irish	2,183	14.30
Italian	1,196	7.83
Latvian	54	0.35
Lithuanian	90	0.59
Maltese	144	0.94
Northern European	30	0.20
Norwegian	191	1.25
Polish	2,033	13.31
Portuguese	66	0.43
Romanian	64	0.42
Russian	114	0.75
Scandinavian	20	0.13
Scotch-Irish	394	2.58
Scottish	621	4.07
Slavic	17	0.11
Slovak	72	0.47
Slovene	5	0.03
Swedish	475	3.11
Swiss	63	0.41
Ukrainian	148	0.97
United States or American	723	4.73
Welsh	210	1.38
White:	15,046	98.53
Not Hispanic (14,749)	14,897	97.55
Hispanic (135)	149	0.98
Yugoslavian	58	0.38

Monitor

Place Type: Township
County: Bay
Population: 10,037

Ancestry/Race	Number	%
African American/Black:	40	0.40
Not Hispanic (21)	36	0.36
Hispanic (1)	4	0.04
Alaska Native tribes, specified:	1	0.01
Eskimo (1)	1	0.01
Am. Ind. or Alaska Nat., not spec.	19	0.19
American Indian tribes, specified:	41	0.41
Cherokee (2)	5	0.05
Chickasaw	1	0.01
Chippewa (14)	33	0.33
Ottawa	1	0.01
All other tribes (1)	1	0.01
American Indian tribes, not spec.	4	0.04
Armenian	6	0.06
Asian:	47	0.47
Chinese, ex. Taiwanese (4)	4	0.04
Filipino	1	0.01
Hmong (1)	1	0.01
Indian (5)	5	0.05
Japanese (2)	7	0.07
Korean (8)	10	0.10
Laotian (8)	8	0.08
Pakistani (5)	5	0.05
Vietnamese (2)	4	0.04
Other Asian, specified (1)	1	0.01
Other Asian, not specified (1)	1	0.01
Austrian	16	0.16
Belgian	29	0.29
British	13	0.13
Canadian	47	0.47
Czech	50	0.50
Czechoslovakian	13	0.13
Danish	8	0.08
Dutch	266	2.65
English	914	9.11
European	37	0.37
Finnish	49	0.49
French, except Basque	1,253	12.48
French Canadian	383	3.82
German	3,938	39.23
Hawaii Native/Pacific Islander:	3	0.03
Micronesian:	2	0.02
Other Micronesian	2	0.02
Other Pac. Isl., not spec.	1	0.01
Hispanic or Latino:	169	1.68
Mexican	134	1.34
Puerto Rican	2	0.02
Other Hispanic or Latino	33	0.33
Hungarian	71	0.71
Irish	1,011	10.07
Italian	193	1.92
Lithuanian	21	0.21
Norwegian	63	0.63
Polish	2,246	22.38
Romanian	5	0.05
Russian	109	1.09
Scandinavian	16	0.16
Scotch-Irish	112	1.12
Scottish	250	2.49
Serbian	10	0.10
Slavic	27	0.27
Slovak	8	0.08
Swedish	71	0.71
Swiss	48	0.48
Ukrainian	7	0.07
United States or American	342	3.41
Welsh	67	0.67
White:	9,902	98.65
Not Hispanic (9,717)	9,786	97.50
Hispanic (102)	116	1.16
Yugoslavian	6	0.06

Notes: 1. Figures in the "Number" column do not add up to the total population due to: a) Ancestry/Race overlap — e.g. persons can report being both White and Irish, b) persons of Hispanic origin can report being any race, c) persons reporting two ancestries are counted in both categories. 2. Numbers in parentheses indicate the number of persons reporting this ancestry/race alone, not in combination with any other ancestry/race. 3. Refer to the Explanation of Data in the front of the book for more detailed information.

Monroe charter

Place Type: Township
County: Monroe
Population: 13,491

Ancestry/Race	Number	%
African American/Black:	327	2.42
Not Hispanic (244)	313	2.32
Hispanic (8)	14	0.10
Am. Ind. or Alaska Nat., not spec.	32	0.24
American Indian tribes, specified:	46	0.34
Apache	3	0.02
Blackfeet (1)	3	0.02
Cherokee (1)	18	0.13
Cheyenne (3)	3	0.02
Chippewa (1)	2	0.01
Iroquois	2	0.01
Latin American Indians	1	0.01
Ottawa (1)	5	0.04
Seminole	1	0.01
Sioux (5)	5	0.04
All other tribes (3)	4	0.03
American Indian tribes, not spec.	1	0.01
Arab:	45	0.34
Arab/Arabic	15	0.11
Iraqi	5	0.04
Lebanese	25	0.19
Asian:	134	0.99
Bangladeshi (8)	8	0.06
Chinese, ex. Taiwanese (19)	22	0.16
Filipino (8)	13	0.10
Indian (48)	49	0.36
Japanese (5)	6	0.04
Korean (5)	11	0.08
Pakistani (12)	12	0.09
Taiwanese (2)	2	0.01
Thai (3)	6	0.04
Vietnamese (1)	1	0.01
Other Asian, not specified	4	0.03
Assyrian/Chaldean/Syriac	32	0.24
Austrian	12	0.09
Belgian	147	1.10
British	8	0.06
Canadian	42	0.32
Croatian	6	0.05
Czech	26	0.20
Czechoslovakian	59	0.44
Dutch	273	2.05
English	1,353	10.15
European	56	0.42
Finnish	13	0.10
French, except Basque	1,655	12.41
French Canadian	317	2.38
German	3,383	25.38
Greek	19	0.14
Hawaii Native/Pacific Islander:	4	0.03
Micronesian:	1	0.01
Guamanian/Chamorro	1	0.01
Other Pac. Isl., not spec. (1)	3	0.02
Hispanic or Latino:	266	1.97
Central American:	3	0.02
Guatemalan	1	0.01
Nicaraguan	2	0.01
Cuban	2	0.01
Mexican	171	1.27
Puerto Rican	43	0.32
South American:	6	0.04
Bolivian	3	0.02
Chilean	1	0.01
Ecuadorian	1	0.01
Peruvian	1	0.01
Other Hispanic or Latino	41	0.30
Hungarian	306	2.30
Iranian	50	0.38
Irish	1,236	9.27
Italian	966	7.25
Lithuanian	24	0.18
Macedonian	13	0.10
Norwegian	43	0.32
Pennsylvania German	7	0.05
Polish	627	4.70
Romanian	26	0.20
Russian	65	0.49
Scotch-Irish	231	1.73
Scottish	204	1.53
Serbian	75	0.56
Slovak	18	0.14
Slovene	10	0.08
Swedish	28	0.21
Swiss	35	0.26
Ukrainian	31	0.23
United States or American	1,084	8.13
Welsh	65	0.49
White:	12,990	96.29
Not Hispanic (12,659)	12,828	95.09
Hispanic (148)	162	1.20

Monroe

Place Type: City
County: Monroe
Population: 22,076

Ancestry/Race	Number	%
African American/Black:	1,338	6.06
Not Hispanic (1,092)	1,297	5.88
Hispanic (28)	41	0.19
African, sub-Saharan:	78	0.35
African	78	0.35
Alaska Native tribes, specified:	4	0.02
Aleut (3)	3	0.01
Tlingit-Haida	1	0.00
Am. Ind. or Alaska Nat., not spec.	60	0.27
Alsatian	10	0.04
American Indian tribes, specified:	121	0.55
Blackfeet	3	0.01
Cherokee (11)	57	0.26
Chippewa (10)	10	0.05
Choctaw	6	0.03
Creek	1	0.00
Iroquois (1)	8	0.04
Latin American Indians (4)	7	0.03
Ottawa (1)	1	0.00
Potawatomi (3)	6	0.03
Pueblo	2	0.01
Seminole (1)	3	0.01
Sioux (1)	9	0.04
All other tribes	10	0.05
American Indian tribes, not spec.	3	0.01
Arab:	67	0.30
Arab/Arabic	15	0.07
Iraqi	12	0.05
Lebanese	34	0.15
Syrian	6	0.03
Armenian	20	0.09
Asian:	238	1.08
Cambodian (3)	3	0.01
Chinese, ex. Taiwanese (21)	23	0.10
Filipino (16)	28	0.13
Indian (36)	39	0.18
Japanese (54)	70	0.32
Korean (15)	27	0.12
Pakistani (8)	8	0.04
Thai (5)	6	0.03
Vietnamese (8)	9	0.04
Other Asian, not specified (18)	25	0.11
Assyrian/Chaldean/Syriac	24	0.11
Austrian	20	0.09
Belgian	201	0.90
British	107	0.48
Bulgarian	7	0.03
Canadian	87	0.39
Croatian	47	0.21
Czech	35	0.16
Czechoslovakian	102	0.46
Danish	31	0.14
Dutch	497	2.22
English	1,806	8.08
European	104	0.47
Finnish	29	0.13
French, except Basque	2,295	10.27
French Canadian	493	2.21
German	5,798	25.94
Greek	77	0.34
Hawaii Native/Pacific Islander:	8	0.04
Polynesian: (1)	4	0.02
Native Hawaiian (1)	2	0.01
Other Polynesian	2	0.01
Other Pac. Isl., not spec. (3)	4	0.02
Hispanic or Latino:	610	2.76
Central American:	7	0.03
Nicaraguan	3	0.01
Panamanian	3	0.01
Salvadoran	1	0.00
Cuban	5	0.02
Mexican	447	2.02
Puerto Rican	60	0.27
South American:	7	0.03
Colombian	4	0.02
Peruvian	2	0.01
Venezuelan	1	0.00
Other Hispanic or Latino	84	0.38
Hungarian	325	1.45
Irish	2,815	12.60
Italian	1,633	7.31
Lithuanian	39	0.17
Norwegian	189	0.85
Pennsylvania German	23	0.10
Polish	1,269	5.68
Portuguese	4	0.02
Romanian	33	0.15
Russian	34	0.15
Scandinavian	7	0.03
Scotch-Irish	288	1.29
Scottish	300	1.34
Serbian	100	0.45
Slavic	61	0.27
Slovak	98	0.44
Swedish	193	0.86
Swiss	31	0.14
Ukrainian	30	0.13
United States or American	1,733	7.75
Welsh	100	0.45
West Indian, excl. Hispanic:	18	0.08
Jamaican	18	0.08
White:	20,461	92.68
Not Hispanic (19,748)	20,076	90.94
Hispanic (312)	385	1.74
Yugoslavian	52	0.23

Mount Clemens

Place Type: City
County: Macomb
Population: 17,312

Ancestry/Race	Number	%
African American/Black:	3,647	21.07
Not Hispanic (3,375)	3,610	20.85
Hispanic (20)	37	0.21
African, sub-Saharan:	67	0.39
African	50	0.29
Senegalese	17	0.10
Alaska Native tribes, specified:	1	0.01
Tlingit-Haida (1)	1	0.01
Am. Ind. or Alaska Nat., not spec.	92	0.53
Albanian	14	0.08
American Indian tribes, specified:	206	1.19
Apache (1)	7	0.04
Blackfeet	20	0.12
Cherokee (19)	68	0.39
Cheyenne	2	0.01
Chippewa (26)	50	0.29
Choctaw	3	0.02
Comanche (1)	2	0.01
Creek	1	0.01
Delaware	2	0.01
Iroquois (2)	5	0.03
Latin American Indians (7)	9	0.05

Notes: 1. Figures in the "Number" column do not add up to the total population due to: a) Ancestry/Race overlap — e.g. persons can report being both White and Irish, b) persons of Hispanic origin can report being any race, c) persons reporting two ancestries are counted in both categories. 2. Numbers in parentheses indicate the number of persons reporting this ancestry/race alone, not in combination with any other ancestry/race. 3. Refer to the Explanation of Data in the front of the book for more detailed information.

Navajo (5)	5	0.03
Ottawa (1)	4	0.02
Paiute (1)	1	0.01
Potawatomi (2)	7	0.04
Pueblo (1)	2	0.01
Seminole	1	0.01
Shoshone (1)	1	0.01
Sioux (1)	5	0.03
All other tribes (6)	11	0.06
American Indian tribes, not spec.	11	0.06
Arab:	192	1.11
Arab/Arabic	21	0.12
Lebanese	89	0.51
Moroccan	7	0.04
Syrian	68	0.39
Other Arab	7	0.04
Armenian	45	0.26
Asian:	146	0.84
Cambodian	1	0.01
Chinese, ex. Taiwanese (10)	13	0.08
Filipino (32)	49	0.28
Hmong (3)	7	0.04
Indian (14)	26	0.15
Japanese (4)	17	0.10
Korean (14)	17	0.10
Laotian (1)	1	0.01
Malaysian	1	0.01
Thai (1)	1	0.01
Vietnamese (1)	2	0.01
Other Asian, specified	1	0.01
Other Asian, not specified (4)	10	0.06
Assyrian/Chaldean/Syriac	6	0.03
Austrian	56	0.32
Belgian	337	1.95
Brazilian	2	0.01
British	21	0.12
Bulgarian	14	0.08
Canadian	140	0.81
Croatian	13	0.08
Czech	87	0.50
Czechoslovakian	53	0.31
Danish	7	0.04
Dutch	254	1.47
English	1,329	7.68
European	165	0.95
Finnish	37	0.21
French, except Basque	1,023	5.91
French Canadian	425	2.45
German	3,912	22.60
Greek	85	0.49
Hawaii Native/Pacific Islander:	24	0.14
Micronesian: (1)	1	0.01
Guamanian/Chamorro (1)	1	0.01
Polynesian: (2)	11	0.06
Native Hawaiian (2)	11	0.06
Other Pac. Isl., specified	1	0.01
Other Pac. Isl., not spec.	11	0.06
Hispanic or Latino:	404	2.33
Central American:	12	0.07
Guatemalan	3	0.02
Honduran	6	0.03
Panamanian	2	0.01
Salvadoran	1	0.01
Cuban	5	0.03
Dominican Republic	2	0.01
Mexican	279	1.61
Puerto Rican	29	0.17
South American:	4	0.02
Colombian	1	0.01
Ecuadorian	1	0.01
Peruvian	1	0.01
Other South American	1	0.01
Other Hispanic or Latino	73	0.42
Hungarian	93	0.54
Iranian	5	0.03
Irish	1,883	10.88
Italian	1,321	7.63
Latvian	32	0.18
Lithuanian	39	0.23
Luxemburger	6	0.03
Maltese	24	0.14
Norwegian	39	0.23
Polish	1,680	9.70
Portuguese	4	0.02
Romanian	60	0.35
Russian	132	0.76
Scandinavian	10	0.06
Scotch-Irish	334	1.93
Scottish	362	2.09
Serbian	51	0.29
Slavic	10	0.06
Slovak	59	0.34
Swedish	158	0.91
Swiss	18	0.10
Ukrainian	92	0.53
United States or American	561	3.24
Welsh	103	0.59
White:	13,496	77.96
Not Hispanic (12,897)	13,226	76.40
Hispanic (224)	270	1.56
Yugoslavian	46	0.27

Mount Morris

Place Type: Township
County: Genesee
Population: 23,725

Ancestry/Race	Number	%
African American/Black:	9,891	41.69
Not Hispanic (9,476)	9,816	41.37
Hispanic (50)	75	0.32
African, sub-Saharan:	298	1.25
African	298	1.25
Alaska Native tribes, specified:	1	0.00
Tlingit-Haida (1)	1	0.00
Am. Ind. or Alaska Nat., not spec.	195	0.82
American Indian tribes, specified:	274	1.15
Apache (5)	17	0.07
Blackfeet (2)	25	0.11
Cherokee (17)	98	0.41
Chickasaw	6	0.03
Chippewa (39)	68	0.29
Choctaw	8	0.03
Comanche	2	0.01
Creek (2)	3	0.01
Delaware (1)	1	0.00
Iroquois	1	0.00
Latin American Indians (5)	7	0.03
Lumbee (2)	5	0.02
Navajo	2	0.01
Osage (1)	5	0.02
Ottawa (3)	6	0.03
Potawatomi (1)	3	0.01
Pueblo	2	0.01
Seminole	1	0.00
Shoshone	1	0.00
Sioux (1)	3	0.01
All other tribes (4)	10	0.04
American Indian tribes, not spec.	16	0.07
Arab:	277	1.16
Arab/Arabic	42	0.18
Iraqi	70	0.29
Lebanese	22	0.09
Palestinian	94	0.39
Syrian	49	0.21
Asian:	105	0.44
Chinese, ex. Taiwanese (12)	15	0.06
Filipino (13)	26	0.11
Indian (9)	11	0.05
Japanese (9)	19	0.08
Korean (10)	12	0.05
Pakistani	1	0.00
Thai (3)	3	0.01
Vietnamese (2)	3	0.01
Other Asian, not specified (2)	15	0.06
Assyrian/Chaldean/Syriac	14	0.06
Austrian	23	0.10
Belgian	23	0.10
British	25	0.10
Canadian	41	0.17
Croatian	16	0.07
Czech	37	0.16
Czechoslovakian	81	0.34
Danish	22	0.09
Dutch	260	1.09
English	1,672	7.02
European	76	0.32
Finnish	54	0.23
French, except Basque	1,016	4.26
French Canadian	468	1.96
German	2,384	10.00
Greek	45	0.19
Hawaii Native/Pacific Islander:	19	0.08
Micronesian: (1)	5	0.02
Guamanian/Chamorro (1)	5	0.02
Polynesian: (5)	8	0.03
Native Hawaiian (2)	5	0.02
Samoan (3)	3	0.01
Other Pac. Isl., not spec. (3)	6	0.03
Hispanic or Latino:	722	3.04
Central American:	11	0.05
Guatemalan	3	0.01
Honduran	8	0.03
Cuban	4	0.02
Mexican	541	2.28
Puerto Rican	46	0.19
South American:	1	0.00
Colombian	1	0.00
Other Hispanic or Latino	119	0.50
Hungarian	139	0.58
Irish	1,604	6.73
Italian	524	2.20
Lithuanian	6	0.03
Norwegian	60	0.25
Pennsylvania German	6	0.03
Polish	940	3.94
Romanian	26	0.11
Russian	73	0.31
Scandinavian	15	0.06
Scotch-Irish	171	0.72
Scottish	363	1.52
Serbian	16	0.07
Slavic	27	0.11
Slovak	16	0.07
Swedish	211	0.89
Swiss	13	0.05
Ukrainian	79	0.33
United States or American	1,335	5.60
Welsh	28	0.12
West Indian, excl. Hispanic:	54	0.23
Haitian	9	0.04
Jamaican	45	0.19
White:	13,550	57.11
Not Hispanic (12,663)	13,175	55.53
Hispanic (277)	375	1.58
Yugoslavian	12	0.05

Mount Pleasant

Place Type: City
County: Isabella
Population: 25,946

Ancestry/Race	Number	%
African American/Black:	1,115	4.30
Not Hispanic (946)	1,099	4.24
Hispanic (5)	16	0.06
African, sub-Saharan:	103	0.39
African	77	0.30
Liberian	16	0.06
South African	2	0.01
Zimbabwean	8	0.03
Alaska Native tribes, specified:	2	0.01
Alaska Athabascan (1)	1	0.00
Tlingit-Haida	1	0.00
Alaska Native tribes, not specified	1	0.00
Am. Ind. or Alaska Nat., not spec.	94	0.36
Albanian	6	0.02
American Indian tribes, specified:	435	1.68

Notes: 1. Figures in the "Number" column do not add up to the total population due to: a) Ancestry/Race overlap — e.g. persons can report being both White and Irish, b) persons of Hispanic origin can report being any race, c) persons reporting two ancestries are counted in both categories. 2. Numbers in parentheses indicate the number of persons reporting this ancestry/race alone, not in combination with any other ancestry/race. 3. Refer to the Explanation of Data in the front of the book for more detailed information.

Apache (2)	4	0.02
Blackfeet (1)	4	0.02
Cherokee (12)	35	0.13
Chippewa (234)	283	1.09
Choctaw	1	0.00
Cree (2)	2	0.01
Iroquois (6)	13	0.05
Kiowa (1)	1	0.00
Latin American Indians (6)	9	0.03
Lumbee (1)	2	0.01
Menominee (6)	7	0.03
Navajo (3)	3	0.01
Ottawa (27)	38	0.15
Potawatomi (5)	10	0.04
Seminole (1)	2	0.01
Sioux (3)	6	0.02
Yakama (2)	2	0.01
All other tribes (9)	13	0.05
American Indian tribes, not spec.	32	0.12
Arab:	206	0.79
Arab/Arabic	26	0.10
Lebanese	26	0.10
Moroccan	9	0.03
Palestinian	108	0.41
Syrian	11	0.04
Other Arab	26	0.10
Armenian	10	0.04
Asian:	849	3.27
Bangladeshi (10)	10	0.04
Cambodian (11)	12	0.05
Chinese, ex. Taiwanese (152)	170	0.66
Filipino (40)	56	0.22
Hmong (7)	9	0.03
Indian (182)	199	0.77
Indonesian (1)	4	0.02
Japanese (72)	84	0.32
Korean (103)	116	0.45
Laotian (6)	6	0.02
Malaysian (8)	9	0.03
Pakistani (3)	4	0.02
Sri Lankan (6)	6	0.02
Taiwanese (19)	20	0.08
Thai (40)	47	0.18
Vietnamese (30)	32	0.12
Other Asian, specified (3)	8	0.03
Other Asian, not specified (37)	57	0.22
Assyrian/Chaldean/Syriac	8	0.03
Austrian	88	0.34
Basque	1	0.00
Belgian	141	0.54
British	154	0.59
Bulgarian	30	0.11
Canadian	95	0.36
Croatian	73	0.28
Czech	155	0.59
Czechoslovakian	40	0.15
Danish	109	0.42
Dutch	842	3.23
Eastern European	11	0.04
English	2,750	10.54
Estonian	8	0.03
European	289	1.11
Finnish	206	0.79
French, except Basque	1,316	5.04
French Canadian	532	2.04
German	6,758	25.89
Greek	144	0.55
Guyanese	6	0.02
Hawaii Native/Pacific Islander:	34	0.13
Micronesian: (6)	6	0.02
Guamanian/Chamorro (5)	5	0.02
Other Micronesian (1)	1	0.00
Polynesian: (8)	14	0.05
Native Hawaiian (5)	8	0.03
Samoan (3)	4	0.02
Tongan	2	0.01
Other Pac. Isl., specified	3	0.01
Other Pac. Isl., not spec. (3)	11	0.04
Hispanic or Latino:	646	2.49
Central American:	6	0.02
Costa Rican	3	0.01
Guatemalan	1	0.00
Honduran	1	0.00
Salvadoran	1	0.00
Cuban	21	0.08
Dominican Republic	3	0.01
Mexican	413	1.59
Puerto Rican	33	0.13
South American:	33	0.13
Argentinean	3	0.01
Bolivian	2	0.01
Chilean	3	0.01
Colombian	3	0.01
Venezuelan	19	0.07
Other South American	3	0.01
Other Hispanic or Latino	137	0.53
Hungarian	239	0.92
Iranian	2	0.01
Irish	3,220	12.34
Israeli	11	0.04
Italian	1,169	4.48
Latvian	31	0.12
Lithuanian	70	0.27
Luxemburger	3	0.01
Macedonian	6	0.02
Maltese	14	0.05
Northern European	7	0.03
Norwegian	304	1.16
Polish	2,294	8.79
Portuguese	38	0.15
Romanian	55	0.21
Russian	165	0.63
Scandinavian	34	0.13
Scotch-Irish	350	1.34
Scottish	684	2.62
Serbian	3	0.01
Slavic	7	0.03
Slovak	67	0.26
Slovene	7	0.03
Swedish	568	2.18
Swiss	49	0.19
Turkish	19	0.07
Ukrainian	123	0.47
United States or American	710	2.72
Welsh	213	0.82
West Indian, excl. Hispanic:	1	0.00
Haitian	1	0.00
White:	23,534	90.70
Not Hispanic (22,822)	23,158	89.25
Hispanic (302)	376	1.45
Yugoslavian	41	0.16

Mundy

Place Type: Township
County: Genesee
Population: 12,191

Ancestry/Race	Number	%
African American/Black:	185	1.52
Not Hispanic (169)	181	1.48
Hispanic (3)	4	0.03
African, sub-Saharan:	7	0.06
African	7	0.06
Am. Ind. or Alaska Nat., not spec.	18	0.15
American Indian tribes, specified:	63	0.52
Blackfeet (1)	3	0.02
Cherokee (5)	26	0.21
Chippewa (9)	19	0.16
Choctaw	1	0.01
Crow	1	0.01
Iroquois	2	0.02
Latin American Indians	1	0.01
Potawatomi (1)	1	0.01
Pueblo (4)	4	0.03
Sioux	1	0.01
All other tribes	4	0.03
American Indian tribes, not spec.	5	0.04
Arab:	8	0.07
Arab/Arabic	8	0.07
Asian:	126	1.03
Chinese, ex. Taiwanese (5)	6	0.05
Filipino (13)	19	0.16
Indian (34)	34	0.28
Japanese (5)	9	0.07
Korean (26)	35	0.29
Pakistani (4)	5	0.04
Taiwanese (5)	6	0.05
Thai (1)	5	0.04
Vietnamese (7)	7	0.06
Assyrian/Chaldean/Syriac	7	0.06
Austrian	31	0.25
Belgian	7	0.06
Brazilian	7	0.06
British	43	0.35
Canadian	65	0.53
Croatian	7	0.06
Czech	37	0.30
Czechoslovakian	119	0.98
Danish	73	0.60
Dutch	333	2.73
English	1,719	14.10
European	97	0.80
Finnish	135	1.11
French, except Basque	619	5.08
French Canadian	405	3.32
German	2,682	21.99
Greek	64	0.52
Hawaii Native/Pacific Islander:	2	0.02
Polynesian: (1)	1	0.01
Samoan (1)	1	0.01
Other Pac. Isl., not spec.	1	0.01
Hispanic or Latino:	225	1.85
Cuban	15	0.12
Dominican Republic	1	0.01
Mexican	154	1.26
Puerto Rican	15	0.12
South American:	7	0.06
Bolivian	2	0.02
Venezuelan	5	0.04
Other Hispanic or Latino	33	0.27
Hungarian	220	1.80
Irish	1,776	14.56
Italian	421	3.45
Latvian	6	0.05
Lithuanian	28	0.23
Macedonian	37	0.30
Maltese	17	0.14
Norwegian	138	1.13
Pennsylvania German	8	0.07
Polish	760	6.23
Portuguese	11	0.09
Romanian	50	0.41
Russian	48	0.39
Scandinavian	17	0.14
Scotch-Irish	254	2.08
Scottish	353	2.89
Slavic	14	0.11
Slovak	96	0.79
Swedish	160	1.31
Swiss	35	0.29
Ukrainian	23	0.19
United States or American	996	8.17
Welsh	75	0.62
White:	11,833	97.06
Not Hispanic (11,577)	11,668	95.71
Hispanic (131)	165	1.35

Muskegon Heights

Place Type: City
County: Muskegon
Population: 12,049

Ancestry/Race	Number	%
African American/Black:	9,568	79.41
Not Hispanic (9,315)	9,503	78.87
Hispanic (55)	65	0.54
African, sub-Saharan:	384	3.20
African	375	3.13

Notes: 1. Figures in the "Number" column do not add up to the total population due to: a) Ancestry/Race overlap — e.g. persons can report being both White and Irish, b) persons of Hispanic origin can report being any race, c) persons reporting two ancestries are counted in both categories. 2. Numbers in parentheses indicate the number of persons reporting this ancestry/race alone, not in combination with any other ancestry/race. 3. Refer to the Explanation of Data in the front of the book for more detailed information.

Ethiopian	9	0.08
Alaska Native tribes, not specified	1	0.01
Am. Ind. or Alaska Nat., not spec.	80	0.66
American Indian tribes, specified:	102	0.85
Blackfeet	14	0.12
Cherokee (2)	28	0.23
Cheyenne	1	0.01
Chippewa (9)	28	0.23
Choctaw	1	0.01
Cree	1	0.01
Creek	1	0.01
Latin American Indians (1)	1	0.01
Osage	1	0.01
Ottawa (18)	22	0.18
Potawatomi (1)	1	0.01
Sioux	1	0.01
All other tribes	2	0.02
American Indian tribes, not spec.	4	0.03
Arab:	11	0.09
Arab/Arabic	11	0.09
Asian:	40	0.33
Chinese, ex. Taiwanese (16)	16	0.13
Filipino (1)	1	0.01
Indian (7)	11	0.09
Japanese (1)	1	0.01
Korean	2	0.02
Sri Lankan	1	0.01
Thai (1)	3	0.02
Vietnamese (4)	4	0.03
Other Asian, not specified	1	0.01
Austrian	5	0.04
Croatian	5	0.04
Czech	27	0.23
Danish	14	0.12
Dutch	122	1.02
English	211	1.76
European	33	0.28
French, except Basque	196	1.63
French Canadian	11	0.09
German	429	3.58
Greek	14	0.12
Hawaii Native/Pacific Islander:	5	0.04
Polynesian: (2)	4	0.03
Native Hawaiian (2)	2	0.02
Samoan	2	0.02
Other Pac. Isl., not spec. (1)	1	0.01
Hispanic or Latino:	424	3.52
Central American:	2	0.02
Honduran	1	0.01
Panamanian	1	0.01
Cuban	4	0.03
Mexican	277	2.30
Puerto Rican	34	0.28
Other Hispanic or Latino	107	0.89
Hungarian	46	0.38
Irish	229	1.91
Italian	38	0.32
Lithuanian	8	0.07
Norwegian	45	0.38
Pennsylvania German	9	0.08
Polish	110	0.92
Russian	6	0.05
Scotch-Irish	21	0.18
Scottish	5	0.04
Slovak	37	0.31
Slovene	14	0.12
Swedish	103	0.86
Swiss	6	0.05
United States or American	424	3.53
Welsh	6	0.05
West Indian, excl. Hispanic:	51	0.43
Barbadian	8	0.07
Jamaican	43	0.36
White:	2,328	19.32
Not Hispanic (1,982)	2,162	17.94
Hispanic (149)	166	1.38
Yugoslavian	12	0.10

Muskegon

Place Type: City
County: Muskegon
Population: 40,105

Ancestry/Race	Number	%
African American/Black:	13,405	33.42
Not Hispanic (12,582)	13,240	33.01
Hispanic (119)	165	0.41
African, sub-Saharan:	391	0.97
African	391	0.97
Alaska Native tribes, specified:	1	0.00
Eskimo	1	0.00
Am. Ind. or Alaska Nat., not spec.	319	0.80
American Indian tribes, specified:	587	1.46
Apache (3)	11	0.03
Blackfeet (6)	30	0.07
Cherokee (23)	106	0.26
Cheyenne (1)	1	0.00
Chickasaw	1	0.00
Chippewa (58)	94	0.23
Choctaw (1)	8	0.02
Comanche (1)	1	0.00
Cree	8	0.02
Creek (1)	1	0.00
Crow	1	0.00
Delaware (1)	1	0.00
Iroquois	6	0.01
Latin American Indians (14)	22	0.05
Lumbee	3	0.01
Navajo (1)	4	0.01
Ottawa (119)	212	0.53
Pima (3)	3	0.01
Potawatomi (26)	33	0.08
Pueblo	1	0.00
Seminole (1)	1	0.00
Sioux (4)	13	0.03
All other tribes (10)	26	0.06
American Indian tribes, not spec.	38	0.09
Arab:	94	0.23
Arab/Arabic	4	0.01
Jordanian	7	0.02
Lebanese	14	0.03
Moroccan	69	0.17
Armenian	8	0.02
Asian:	336	0.84
Cambodian (6)	6	0.01
Chinese, ex. Taiwanese (41)	61	0.15
Filipino (23)	41	0.10
Hmong (6)	6	0.01
Indian (29)	40	0.10
Japanese (14)	38	0.09
Korean (27)	51	0.13
Laotian (4)	4	0.01
Thai (3)	8	0.02
Vietnamese (11)	13	0.03
Other Asian, specified	3	0.01
Other Asian, not specified (12)	65	0.16
Austrian	44	0.11
Belgian	65	0.16
British	119	0.30
Canadian	42	0.10
Celtic	14	0.03
Croatian	7	0.02
Czech	106	0.26
Czechoslovakian	58	0.14
Danish	246	0.61
Dutch	2,669	6.65
Eastern European	11	0.03
English	2,594	6.46
European	171	0.43
Finnish	177	0.44
French, except Basque	1,711	4.26
French Canadian	593	1.48
German	5,661	14.10
Greek	86	0.21
Hawaii Native/Pacific Islander:	55	0.14
Micronesian:	8	0.02
Guamanian/Chamorro	7	0.02
Other Micronesian	1	0.00
Polynesian: (10)	30	0.07
Native Hawaiian (5)	17	0.04
Samoan (2)	9	0.02
Other Polynesian (3)	4	0.01
Other Pac. Isl., specified	1	0.00
Other Pac. Isl., not spec. (2)	16	0.04
Hispanic or Latino:	2,560	6.38
Central American:	10	0.02
Costa Rican	1	0.00
Guatemalan	7	0.02
Honduran	1	0.00
Panamanian	1	0.00
Cuban	25	0.06
Mexican	1,942	4.84
Puerto Rican	193	0.48
South American:	10	0.02
Chilean	1	0.00
Colombian	3	0.01
Peruvian	1	0.00
Venezuelan	5	0.01
Other Hispanic or Latino	380	0.95
Hungarian	245	0.61
Irish	2,877	7.17
Italian	731	1.82
Lithuanian	68	0.17
Norwegian	617	1.54
Pennsylvania German	37	0.09
Polish	1,519	3.78
Romanian	6	0.01
Russian	142	0.35
Scandinavian	61	0.15
Scotch-Irish	463	1.15
Scottish	312	0.78
Slavic	10	0.02
Slovak	52	0.13
Slovene	14	0.03
Swedish	1,448	3.61
Swiss	22	0.05
Turkish	7	0.02
Ukrainian	29	0.07
United States or American	1,671	4.16
Welsh	111	0.28
West Indian, excl. Hispanic:	10	0.02
Jamaican	10	0.02
White:	25,483	63.54
Not Hispanic (23,231)	24,155	60.23
Hispanic (1,078)	1,328	3.31
Yugoslavian	7	0.02

Muskegon

Place Type: Township
County: Muskegon
Population: 17,737

Ancestry/Race	Number	%
African American/Black:	920	5.19
Not Hispanic (816)	906	5.11
Hispanic (6)	14	0.08
African, sub-Saharan:	68	0.38
African	60	0.34
South African	8	0.05
Am. Ind. or Alaska Nat., not spec.	116	0.65
American Indian tribes, specified:	216	1.22
Blackfeet	4	0.02
Cherokee (7)	21	0.12
Chippewa (20)	41	0.23
Choctaw	7	0.04
Cree	2	0.01
Iroquois (1)	5	0.03
Latin American Indians (2)	3	0.02
Ottawa (73)	112	0.63
Potawatomi (5)	8	0.05
Sioux (2)	9	0.05
All other tribes (2)	4	0.02
American Indian tribes, not spec.	7	0.04
Arab:	10	0.06
Lebanese	10	0.06
Asian:	93	0.52

Notes: 1. Figures in the "Number" column do not add up to the total population due to: a) Ancestry/Race overlap — e.g. persons can report being both White and Irish, b) persons of Hispanic origin can report being any race, c) persons reporting two ancestries are counted in both categories. 2. Numbers in parentheses indicate the number of persons reporting this ancestry/race alone, not in combination with any other ancestry/race. 3. Refer to the Explanation of Data in the front of the book for more detailed information.

Ancestry/Race	Number	%
Chinese, ex. Taiwanese (5)	5	0.03
Filipino (4)	7	0.04
Indian (5)	6	0.03
Indonesian (1)	3	0.02
Japanese (2)	9	0.05
Korean (22)	33	0.19
Laotian (2)	4	0.02
Thai	6	0.03
Vietnamese (7)	17	0.10
Other Asian, not specified (2)	3	0.02
Austrian	52	0.29
Basque	6	0.03
Belgian	51	0.29
British	12	0.07
Canadian	10	0.06
Czech	27	0.15
Czechoslovakian	29	0.16
Danish	175	0.99
Dutch	2,410	13.62
English	1,956	11.06
European	61	0.34
Finnish	76	0.43
French, except Basque	1,245	7.04
French Canadian	397	2.24
German	3,808	21.53
Greek	24	0.14
Hawaii Native/Pacific Islander:	6	0.03
Micronesian:	1	0.01
Guamanian/Chamorro	1	0.01
Polynesian: (1)	1	0.01
Native Hawaiian (1)	1	0.01
Other Pac. Isl., not spec.	4	0.02
Hispanic or Latino:	569	3.21
Central American:	5	0.03
Costa Rican	2	0.01
Honduran	1	0.01
Panamanian	2	0.01
Cuban	5	0.03
Mexican	424	2.39
Puerto Rican	34	0.19
South American:	7	0.04
Colombian	2	0.01
Peruvian	3	0.02
Venezuelan	2	0.01
Other Hispanic or Latino	94	0.53
Hungarian	128	0.72
Irish	2,392	13.52
Italian	577	3.26
Latvian	6	0.03
Lithuanian	51	0.29
Norwegian	409	2.31
Pennsylvania German	33	0.19
Polish	1,054	5.96
Romanian	21	0.12
Russian	54	0.31
Scandinavian	21	0.12
Scotch-Irish	202	1.14
Scottish	188	1.06
Slovak	26	0.15
Slovene	6	0.03
Swedish	688	3.89
Swiss	26	0.15
Ukrainian	110	0.62
United States or American	952	5.38
Welsh	52	0.29
West Indian, excl. Hispanic:	19	0.11
Jamaican	19	0.11
White:	16,530	93.20
Not Hispanic (15,878)	16,131	90.95
Hispanic (345)	399	2.25

Niles

Place Type: City
County: Berrien
Population: 12,204

Ancestry/Race	Number	%
African American/Black:	1,720	14.09
Not Hispanic (1,498)	1,697	13.91
Hispanic (11)	23	0.19
African, sub-Saharan:	133	1.10
African	123	1.02
Other sub-Saharan African	10	0.08
Am. Ind. or Alaska Nat., not spec.	72	0.59
American Indian tribes, specified:	116	0.95
Apache (2)	4	0.03
Blackfeet (1)	10	0.08
Cherokee (11)	43	0.35
Cheyenne (1)	1	0.01
Chickasaw	1	0.01
Chippewa (11)	12	0.10
Choctaw	1	0.01
Iroquois (3)	4	0.03
Potawatomi (19)	25	0.20
Puget Sound Salish	1	0.01
Shoshone	1	0.01
Sioux	2	0.02
All other tribes (6)	11	0.09
American Indian tribes, not spec.	6	0.05
Arab:	31	0.26
Egyptian	23	0.19
Palestinian	8	0.07
Asian:	96	0.79
Bangladeshi (1)	6	0.05
Chinese, ex. Taiwanese (14)	19	0.16
Filipino (6)	9	0.07
Indian (9)	18	0.15
Japanese (7)	16	0.13
Korean (12)	16	0.13
Laotian (5)	5	0.04
Thai (1)	1	0.01
Vietnamese (3)	3	0.02
Other Asian, not specified	3	0.02
Austrian	12	0.10
Belgian	32	0.26
British	57	0.47
Canadian	39	0.32
Czech	32	0.26
Czechoslovakian	15	0.12
Danish	91	0.75
Dutch	507	4.19
English	1,120	9.25
Estonian	6	0.05
European	93	0.77
Finnish	59	0.49
French, except Basque	535	4.42
French Canadian	55	0.45
German	2,867	23.68
Greek	3	0.02
Hawaii Native/Pacific Islander:	17	0.14
Micronesian: (2)	2	0.02
Other Micronesian (2)	2	0.02
Polynesian: (4)	7	0.06
Native Hawaiian (4)	5	0.04
Samoan	2	0.02
Other Pac. Isl., not spec. (4)	8	0.07
Hispanic or Latino:	485	3.97
Central American:	8	0.07
Guatemalan	3	0.02
Honduran	2	0.02
Nicaraguan	1	0.01
Panamanian	1	0.01
Salvadoran	1	0.01
Cuban	9	0.07
Mexican	230	1.88
Puerto Rican	153	1.25
South American:	14	0.11
Argentinean	8	0.07
Colombian	5	0.04
Ecuadorian	1	0.01
Other Hispanic or Latino	71	0.58
Hungarian	71	0.59
Irish	1,517	12.53
Italian	403	3.33
Lithuanian	39	0.32
Norwegian	109	0.90
Pennsylvania German	75	0.62
Polish	353	2.92
Portuguese	15	0.12
Romanian	14	0.12
Russian	7	0.06
Scandinavian	8	0.07
Scotch-Irish	179	1.48
Scottish	148	1.22
Slovak	40	0.33
Swedish	252	2.08
Swiss	26	0.21
United States or American	922	7.62
Welsh	57	0.47
West Indian, excl. Hispanic:	36	0.30
Belizean	6	0.05
Jamaican	30	0.25
White:	10,346	84.78
Not Hispanic (9,782)	10,037	82.24
Hispanic (248)	309	2.53

Niles

Place Type: Township
County: Berrien
Population: 13,325

Ancestry/Race	Number	%
African American/Black:	488	3.66
Not Hispanic (399)	481	3.61
Hispanic (5)	7	0.05
African, sub-Saharan:	63	0.47
African	20	0.15
Liberian	4	0.03
South African	39	0.29
Am. Ind. or Alaska Nat., not spec.	38	0.29
American Indian tribes, specified:	173	1.30
Apache (1)	4	0.03
Blackfeet (1)	13	0.10
Cherokee (12)	62	0.47
Cheyenne	2	0.02
Chippewa (8)	23	0.17
Choctaw (1)	2	0.02
Comanche	1	0.01
Cree (1)	1	0.01
Creek	4	0.03
Delaware (1)	1	0.01
Iroquois	4	0.03
Ottawa (2)	3	0.02
Potawatomi (24)	40	0.30
Sioux	1	0.01
All other tribes (5)	12	0.09
American Indian tribes, not spec.	3	0.02
Arab:	17	0.13
Arab/Arabic	9	0.07
Lebanese	8	0.06
Asian:	100	0.75
Chinese, ex. Taiwanese (6)	10	0.08
Filipino (23)	33	0.25
Indian (5)	13	0.10
Japanese (7)	13	0.10
Korean (10)	12	0.09
Taiwanese (1)	2	0.02
Thai (2)	4	0.03
Vietnamese (11)	11	0.08
Other Asian, not specified (1)	2	0.02
Austrian	49	0.37
Belgian	84	0.63
Brazilian	18	0.13
British	17	0.13
Canadian	53	0.39
Croatian	7	0.05
Czech	17	0.13
Czechoslovakian	23	0.17
Danish	20	0.15
Dutch	602	4.49
English	1,393	10.38
European	12	0.09
Finnish	32	0.24
French, except Basque	479	3.57
French Canadian	104	0.78
German	4,052	30.20
Hawaii Native/Pacific Islander:	13	0.10
Polynesian: (2)	11	0.08

Notes: 1. Figures in the "Number" column do not add up to the total population due to: a) Ancestry/Race overlap — e.g. persons can report being both White and Irish, b) persons of Hispanic origin can report being any race, c) persons reporting two ancestries are counted in both categories. 2. Numbers in parentheses indicate the number of persons reporting this ancestry/race alone, not in combination with any other ancestry/race. 3. Refer to the Explanation of Data in the front of the book for more detailed information.

Ancestry/Race	Number	%
Native Hawaiian (2)	7	0.05
Tongan	4	0.03
Other Pac. Isl., not spec.	2	0.02
Hispanic or Latino:	256	1.92
Central American:	3	0.02
Costa Rican	1	0.01
Panamanian	1	0.01
Salvadoran	1	0.01
Cuban	6	0.05
Mexican	139	1.04
Puerto Rican	72	0.54
South American:	3	0.02
Chilean	3	0.02
Other Hispanic or Latino	33	0.25
Hungarian	395	2.94
Irish	1,754	13.07
Italian	569	4.24
Latvian	13	0.10
Lithuanian	40	0.30
Norwegian	100	0.75
Pennsylvania German	73	0.54
Polish	929	6.92
Portuguese	27	0.20
Romanian	6	0.04
Russian	35	0.26
Scandinavian	8	0.06
Scotch-Irish	200	1.49
Scottish	241	1.80
Serbian	35	0.26
Slavic	16	0.12
Slovak	43	0.32
Slovene	8	0.06
Swedish	235	1.75
Swiss	34	0.25
Turkish	8	0.06
Ukrainian	41	0.31
United States or American	1,320	9.84
Welsh	43	0.32
West Indian, excl. Hispanic:	22	0.16
Barbadian	22	0.16
White:	12,623	94.73
Not Hispanic (12,300)	12,473	93.61
Hispanic (132)	150	1.13
Yugoslavian	4	0.03

Northview

Place Type: Census Designated Place
County: Kent
Population: 14,730

Ancestry/Race	Number	%
African American/Black:	368	2.50
Not Hispanic (284)	356	2.42
Hispanic (2)	12	0.08
African, sub-Saharan:	24	0.16
Sudanese	24	0.16
Am. Ind. or Alaska Nat., not spec.	34	0.23
American Indian tribes, specified:	72	0.49
Cherokee (2)	9	0.06
Chippewa (12)	15	0.10
Choctaw	2	0.01
Latin American Indians (1)	1	0.01
Lumbee (1)	1	0.01
Navajo (1)	1	0.01
Ottawa (9)	14	0.10
Potawatomi (10)	12	0.08
Pueblo	1	0.01
Sioux (1)	2	0.01
Yaqui	1	0.01
All other tribes (4)	13	0.09
American Indian tribes, not spec.	3	0.02
Arab:	20	0.14
Syrian	20	0.14
Armenian	17	0.12
Asian:	196	1.33
Cambodian (1)	1	0.01
Chinese, ex. Taiwanese (17)	19	0.13
Filipino (10)	14	0.10
Hmong (5)	5	0.03
Indian (36)	42	0.29
Japanese (8)	13	0.09
Korean (52)	64	0.43
Pakistani (8)	13	0.09
Thai (2)	2	0.01
Vietnamese (15)	16	0.11
Other Asian, not specified (5)	7	0.05
Austrian	34	0.23
Belgian	42	0.29
Brazilian	5	0.03
British	62	0.42
Bulgarian	18	0.12
Canadian	27	0.18
Croatian	24	0.16
Czech	12	0.08
Czechoslovakian	38	0.26
Danish	139	0.95
Dutch	2,977	20.29
English	1,918	13.07
European	221	1.51
Finnish	107	0.73
French, except Basque	579	3.95
French Canadian	159	1.08
German	3,487	23.76
Greek	30	0.20
Hawaii Native/Pacific Islander:	12	0.08
Melanesian: (1)	1	0.01
Fijian (1)	1	0.01
Micronesian: (5)	5	0.03
Guamanian/Chamorro (5)	5	0.03
Polynesian: (2)	2	0.01
Native Hawaiian (1)	1	0.01
Samoan (1)	1	0.01
Other Pac. Isl., not spec. (4)	4	0.03
Hispanic or Latino:	313	2.12
Central American:	12	0.08
Costa Rican	1	0.01
Guatemalan	4	0.03
Honduran	1	0.01
Salvadoran	6	0.04
Cuban	6	0.04
Dominican Republic	3	0.02
Mexican	188	1.28
Puerto Rican	23	0.16
South American:	8	0.05
Colombian	5	0.03
Venezuelan	2	0.01
Other South American	1	0.01
Other Hispanic or Latino	73	0.50
Hungarian	40	0.27
Irish	1,892	12.89
Italian	415	2.83
Latvian	13	0.09
Lithuanian	164	1.12
Norwegian	217	1.48
Pennsylvania German	4	0.03
Polish	1,605	10.94
Portuguese	27	0.18
Romanian	22	0.15
Russian	73	0.50
Scandinavian	13	0.09
Scotch-Irish	306	2.09
Scottish	295	2.01
Serbian	25	0.17
Slavic	34	0.23
Slovak	14	0.10
Swedish	577	3.93
Ukrainian	11	0.07
United States or American	1,137	7.75
Welsh	145	0.99
White:	14,089	95.65
Not Hispanic (13,755)	13,899	94.36
Hispanic (147)	190	1.29
Yugoslavian	10	0.07

Northville

Place Type: Township
County: Wayne
Population: 21,036

Ancestry/Race	Number	%
African American/Black:	991	4.71
Not Hispanic (914)	978	4.65
Hispanic (9)	13	0.06
African, sub-Saharan:	115	0.55
African	73	0.35
Nigerian	27	0.13
South African	9	0.04
Other sub-Saharan African	6	0.03
Alaska Native tribes, specified:	2	0.01
Eskimo (1)	2	0.01
Am. Ind. or Alaska Nat., not spec.	47	0.22
Albanian	58	0.28
American Indian tribes, specified:	90	0.43
Apache (1)	4	0.02
Blackfeet	3	0.01
Cherokee (5)	30	0.14
Chickasaw (1)	1	0.00
Chippewa (14)	26	0.12
Choctaw	1	0.00
Delaware (1)	1	0.00
Iroquois (2)	5	0.02
Latin American Indians (1)	1	0.00
Navajo	1	0.00
Ottawa (3)	3	0.01
Potawatomi	2	0.01
Seminole (1)	4	0.02
Sioux	3	0.01
All other tribes (4)	5	0.02
American Indian tribes, not spec.	4	0.02
Arab:	367	1.74
Arab/Arabic	71	0.34
Egyptian	10	0.05
Iraqi	8	0.04
Jordanian	7	0.03
Lebanese	185	0.88
Palestinian	71	0.34
Syrian	15	0.07
Armenian	172	0.82
Asian:	1,009	4.80
Cambodian (2)	2	0.01
Chinese, ex. Taiwanese (198)	222	1.06
Filipino (61)	76	0.36
Indian (342)	349	1.66
Japanese (158)	187	0.89
Korean (82)	94	0.45
Pakistani (4)	4	0.02
Sri Lankan (1)	2	0.01
Taiwanese (15)	16	0.08
Thai (4)	6	0.03
Vietnamese (28)	33	0.16
Other Asian, specified	1	0.00
Other Asian, not specified (4)	17	0.08
Assyrian/Chaldean/Syriac	36	0.17
Austrian	90	0.43
Belgian	114	0.54
British	78	0.37
Bulgarian	9	0.04
Canadian	262	1.25
Croatian	35	0.17
Czech	73	0.35
Czechoslovakian	25	0.12
Danish	151	0.72
Dutch	262	1.25
Eastern European	37	0.18
English	2,895	13.76
European	125	0.59
Finnish	220	1.05
French, except Basque	866	4.12
French Canadian	340	1.62
German	4,699	22.34
Greek	352	1.67
Hawaii Native/Pacific Islander:	17	0.08
Melanesian: (1)	1	0.00

Notes: 1. Figures in the "Number" column do not add up to the total population due to: a) Ancestry/Race overlap — e.g. persons can report being both White and Irish, b) persons of Hispanic origin can report being any race, c) persons reporting two ancestries are counted in both categories. 2. Numbers in parentheses indicate the number of persons reporting this ancestry/race alone, not in combination with any other ancestry/race. 3. Refer to the Explanation of Data in the front of the book for more detailed information.

Other Melanesian (1)	1	0.00
Micronesian:	1	0.00
Guamanian/Chamorro	1	0.00
Polynesian:	2	0.01
Native Hawaiian	1	0.00
Samoan	1	0.00
Other Pac. Isl., specified	1	0.00
Other Pac. Isl., not spec. (6)	12	0.06
Hispanic or Latino:	372	1.77
Central American:	9	0.04
Costa Rican	1	0.00
Guatemalan	4	0.02
Honduran	1	0.00
Nicaraguan	2	0.01
Salvadoran	1	0.00
Cuban	11	0.05
Mexican	206	0.98
Puerto Rican	39	0.19
South American:	43	0.20
Argentinean	7	0.03
Chilean	6	0.03
Colombian	14	0.07
Ecuadorian	3	0.01
Paraguayan	2	0.01
Peruvian	2	0.01
Venezuelan	6	0.03
Other South American	3	0.01
Other Hispanic or Latino	64	0.30
Hungarian	290	1.38
Iranian	108	0.51
Irish	3,434	16.32
Israeli	14	0.07
Italian	1,733	8.24
Lithuanian	139	0.66
Luxemburger	25	0.12
Macedonian	70	0.33
Maltese	89	0.42
Northern European	20	0.10
Norwegian	247	1.17
Pennsylvania German	17	0.08
Polish	3,031	14.41
Portuguese	15	0.07
Romanian	70	0.33
Russian	239	1.14
Scandinavian	14	0.07
Scotch-Irish	341	1.62
Scottish	913	4.34
Serbian	49	0.23
Slovak	106	0.50
Slovene	14	0.07
Swedish	336	1.60
Swiss	77	0.37
Ukrainian	161	0.77
United States or American	666	3.17
Welsh	207	0.98
West Indian, excl. Hispanic:	7	0.03
Jamaican	7	0.03
White:	19,016	90.40
Not Hispanic (18,538)	18,755	89.16
Hispanic (249)	261	1.24
Yugoslavian	40	0.19

Norton Shores

Place Type: City
County: Muskegon
Population: 22,527

Ancestry/Race	Number	%
African American/Black:	449	1.99
Not Hispanic (362)	437	1.94
Hispanic (6)	12	0.05
African, sub-Saharan:	39	0.17
African	39	0.17
Am. Ind. or Alaska Nat., not spec.	71	0.32
American Indian tribes, specified:	230	1.02
Apache (2)	2	0.01
Blackfeet	10	0.04
Cherokee (9)	31	0.14
Chippewa (31)	53	0.24
Iroquois (1)	1	0.00
Latin American Indians (2)	15	0.07
Menominee (4)	4	0.02
Ottawa (61)	93	0.41
Potawatomi (8)	15	0.07
Shoshone (1)	1	0.00
Sioux	2	0.01
All other tribes (3)	3	0.01
American Indian tribes, not spec.	14	0.06
Arab:	14	0.06
Lebanese	14	0.06
Asian:	257	1.14
Cambodian (1)	1	0.00
Chinese, ex. Taiwanese (34)	43	0.19
Filipino (13)	30	0.13
Indian (47)	56	0.25
Indonesian	1	0.00
Japanese (10)	19	0.08
Korean (68)	76	0.34
Pakistani (2)	2	0.01
Taiwanese	3	0.01
Thai (5)	13	0.06
Vietnamese (7)	10	0.04
Other Asian, not specified	3	0.01
Assyrian/Chaldean/Syriac	76	0.34
Austrian	89	0.40
Belgian	52	0.23
British	53	0.24
Bulgarian	6	0.03
Canadian	89	0.40
Croatian	14	0.06
Czech	110	0.49
Czechoslovakian	89	0.40
Danish	330	1.47
Dutch	3,253	14.44
English	2,584	11.47
European	97	0.43
Finnish	213	0.95
French, except Basque	1,685	7.48
French Canadian	353	1.57
German	5,347	23.74
Greek	156	0.69
Hawaii Native/Pacific Islander:	19	0.08
Micronesian: (1)	3	0.01
Guamanian/Chamorro (1)	3	0.01
Polynesian:	5	0.02
Native Hawaiian	1	0.00
Samoan	1	0.00
Other Polynesian	3	0.01
Other Pac. Isl., not spec. (1)	11	0.05
Hispanic or Latino:	606	2.69
Central American:	12	0.05
Costa Rican	1	0.00
Guatemalan	4	0.02
Honduran	3	0.01
Panamanian	3	0.01
Other Central American	1	0.00
Cuban	19	0.08
Mexican	411	1.82
Puerto Rican	35	0.16
South American:	11	0.05
Argentinean	1	0.00
Bolivian	2	0.01
Chilean	2	0.01
Colombian	2	0.01
Ecuadorian	3	0.01
Paraguayan	1	0.00
Other Hispanic or Latino	118	0.52
Hungarian	333	1.48
Irish	3,062	13.59
Italian	841	3.73
Latvian	8	0.04
Lithuanian	46	0.20
Maltese	3	0.01
Northern European	53	0.24
Norwegian	591	2.62
Polish	1,784	7.92
Portuguese	9	0.04
Romanian	13	0.06
Russian	102	0.45
Scandinavian	30	0.13
Scotch-Irish	264	1.17
Scottish	378	1.68
Serbian	11	0.05
Slavic	14	0.06
Slovak	199	0.88
Slovene	15	0.07
Swedish	1,961	8.71
Swiss	61	0.27
Turkish	6	0.03
Ukrainian	137	0.61
United States or American	869	3.86
Welsh	128	0.57
West Indian, excl. Hispanic:	16	0.07
West Indian	16	0.07
White:	21,634	96.04
Not Hispanic (20,948)	21,192	94.07
Hispanic (369)	442	1.96
Yugoslavian	14	0.06

Novi

Place Type: City
County: Oakland
Population: 47,386

Ancestry/Race	Number	%
African American/Black:	1,051	2.22
Not Hispanic (899)	1,036	2.19
Hispanic (9)	15	0.03
African, sub-Saharan:	89	0.19
African	41	0.09
Ethiopian	9	0.02
Nigerian	39	0.08
Alaska Native tribes, specified:	1	0.00
Eskimo	1	0.00
Am. Ind. or Alaska Nat., not spec.	84	0.18
Albanian	105	0.22
American Indian tribes, specified:	150	0.32
Apache	4	0.01
Blackfeet (1)	5	0.01
Cherokee (14)	59	0.12
Chickasaw	1	0.00
Chippewa (19)	37	0.08
Choctaw (1)	2	0.00
Comanche	1	0.00
Cree	2	0.00
Iroquois (6)	13	0.03
Latin American Indians (1)	1	0.00
Navajo (3)	3	0.01
Ottawa (2)	4	0.01
Potawatomi	2	0.00
Sioux (1)	3	0.01
All other tribes (5)	13	0.03
American Indian tribes, not spec.	7	0.01
Arab:	678	1.43
Arab/Arabic	126	0.27
Egyptian	38	0.08
Iraqi	19	0.04
Jordanian	22	0.05
Lebanese	363	0.76
Moroccan	10	0.02
Palestinian	6	0.01
Syrian	84	0.18
Other Arab	10	0.02
Armenian	374	0.79
Asian:	4,423	9.33
Bangladeshi (7)	7	0.01
Chinese, ex. Taiwanese (897)	951	2.01
Filipino (175)	212	0.45
Hmong (3)	4	0.01
Indian (1,269)	1,326	2.80
Indonesian (11)	15	0.03
Japanese (1,109)	1,185	2.50
Korean (344)	366	0.77
Laotian (3)	4	0.01
Malaysian (1)	1	0.00
Pakistani (52)	61	0.13
Sri Lankan (3)	3	0.01
Taiwanese (92)	99	0.21

Notes: 1. Figures in the "Number" column do not add up to the total population due to: a) Ancestry/Race overlap — e.g. persons can report being both White and Irish, b) persons of Hispanic origin can report being any race, c) persons reporting two ancestries are counted in both categories. 2. Numbers in parentheses indicate the number of persons reporting this ancestry/race alone, not in combination with any other ancestry/race. 3. Refer to the Explanation of Data in the front of the book for more detailed information.

Ancestry/Race	Number	%
Thai (9)	12	0.03
Vietnamese (84)	96	0.20
Other Asian, specified (4)	5	0.01
Other Asian, not specified (20)	76	0.16
Assyrian/Chaldean/Syriac	164	0.35
Australian	15	0.03
Austrian	247	0.52
Belgian	265	0.56
Brazilian	92	0.19
British	264	0.56
Bulgarian	17	0.04
Canadian	494	1.04
Croatian	162	0.34
Czech	174	0.37
Czechoslovakian	182	0.38
Danish	81	0.17
Dutch	900	1.90
English	6,141	12.94
European	455	0.96
Finnish	693	1.46
French, except Basque	2,053	4.33
French Canadian	1,008	2.12
German	10,775	22.70
Greek	576	1.21
Hawaii Native/Pacific Islander:	31	0.07
Micronesian: (2)	5	0.01
Guamanian/Chamorro (2)	5	0.01
Polynesian: (6)	13	0.03
Native Hawaiian (6)	10	0.02
Samoan	3	0.01
Other Pac. Isl., specified	1	0.00
Other Pac. Isl., not spec.	12	0.03
Hispanic or Latino:	855	1.80
Central American:	35	0.07
Costa Rican	4	0.01
Guatemalan	8	0.02
Honduran	8	0.02
Nicaraguan	2	0.00
Panamanian	8	0.02
Salvadoran	5	0.01
Cuban	22	0.05
Dominican Republic	10	0.02
Mexican	453	0.96
Puerto Rican	56	0.12
South American:	66	0.14
Argentinean	6	0.01
Chilean	2	0.00
Colombian	24	0.05
Ecuadorian	1	0.00
Paraguayan	1	0.00
Peruvian	16	0.03
Venezuelan	10	0.02
Other South American	6	0.01
Other Hispanic or Latino	213	0.45
Hungarian	703	1.48
Iranian	100	0.21
Irish	7,044	14.84
Italian	4,284	9.03
Lithuanian	256	0.54
Luxemburger	6	0.01
Macedonian	81	0.17
Maltese	171	0.36
Northern European	63	0.13
Norwegian	429	0.90
Pennsylvania German	8	0.02
Polish	5,940	12.52
Portuguese	80	0.17
Romanian	332	0.70
Russian	724	1.53
Scandinavian	81	0.17
Scotch-Irish	693	1.46
Scottish	1,556	3.28
Serbian	58	0.12
Slavic	21	0.04
Slovak	201	0.42
Slovene	52	0.11
Soviet Union	9	0.02
Swedish	837	1.76
Swiss	164	0.35
Turkish	16	0.03
Ukrainian	394	0.83
United States or American	1,887	3.98
Welsh	440	0.93
West Indian, excl. Hispanic:	39	0.08
Dutch West Indian	8	0.02
Jamaican	24	0.05
West Indian	7	0.01
White:	41,994	88.62
Not Hispanic (40,777)	41,361	87.29
Hispanic (572)	633	1.34
Yugoslavian	179	0.38

Oak Park

Place Type: City
County: Oakland
Population: 29,793

Ancestry/Race	Number	%
Afghan	22	0.07
African American/Black:	14,090	47.29
Not Hispanic (13,622)	14,004	47.00
Hispanic (68)	86	0.29
African, sub-Saharan:	502	1.68
African	295	0.99
Nigerian	74	0.25
Somalian	8	0.03
Ugandan	41	0.14
Other sub-Saharan African	84	0.28
Alaska Native tribes, not specified	1	0.00
Am. Ind. or Alaska Nat., not spec.	112	0.38
Alsatian	7	0.02
American Indian tribes, specified:	106	0.36
Blackfeet	14	0.05
Cherokee (5)	38	0.13
Chippewa (8)	19	0.06
Choctaw	8	0.03
Cree	1	0.00
Creek (3)	4	0.01
Iroquois (1)	2	0.01
Latin American Indians (1)	1	0.00
Seminole	2	0.01
Sioux (7)	7	0.02
All other tribes (2)	10	0.03
American Indian tribes, not spec.	11	0.04
Arab:	780	2.62
Arab/Arabic	233	0.78
Egyptian	14	0.05
Iraqi	412	1.38
Jordanian	8	0.03
Moroccan	12	0.04
Palestinian	7	0.02
Syrian	82	0.28
Other Arab	12	0.04
Armenian	63	0.21
Asian:	839	2.82
Bangladeshi	2	0.01
Cambodian (1)	1	0.00
Chinese, ex. Taiwanese (99)	129	0.43
Filipino (220)	270	0.91
Indian (67)	91	0.31
Indonesian	2	0.01
Japanese (13)	22	0.07
Korean (25)	35	0.12
Laotian (2)	3	0.01
Malaysian	1	0.00
Pakistani (6)	10	0.03
Sri Lankan (8)	8	0.03
Thai (2)	9	0.03
Vietnamese (177)	199	0.67
Other Asian, specified (1)	3	0.01
Other Asian, not specified (6)	54	0.18
Assyrian/Chaldean/Syriac	1,864	6.26
Australian	6	0.02
Austrian	79	0.27
Belgian	35	0.12
British	15	0.05
Bulgarian	4	0.01
Canadian	115	0.39
Celtic	5	0.02
Croatian	6	0.02
Czech	35	0.12
Czechoslovakian	40	0.13
Danish	45	0.15
Dutch	115	0.39
Eastern European	112	0.38
English	861	2.89
Estonian	13	0.04
European	224	0.75
Finnish	95	0.32
French, except Basque	480	1.61
French Canadian	315	1.06
German	1,524	5.12
Greek	43	0.14
Hawaii Native/Pacific Islander:	27	0.09
Micronesian:	1	0.00
Guamanian/Chamorro	1	0.00
Polynesian: (4)	9	0.03
Native Hawaiian (4)	9	0.03
Other Pac. Isl., specified	2	0.01
Other Pac. Isl., not spec. (1)	15	0.05
Hispanic or Latino:	381	1.28
Central American:	14	0.05
Guatemalan	2	0.01
Honduran	4	0.01
Panamanian	6	0.02
Salvadoran	1	0.00
Other Central American	1	0.00
Cuban	22	0.07
Dominican Republic	9	0.03
Mexican	131	0.44
Puerto Rican	74	0.25
South American:	17	0.06
Chilean	6	0.02
Colombian	6	0.02
Ecuadorian	2	0.01
Peruvian	1	0.00
Uruguayan	1	0.00
Venezuelan	1	0.00
Other Hispanic or Latino	114	0.38
Hungarian	191	0.64
Iranian	5	0.02
Irish	1,026	3.44
Israeli	62	0.21
Italian	659	2.21
Lithuanian	85	0.29
Macedonian	11	0.04
Norwegian	154	0.52
Pennsylvania German	4	0.01
Polish	1,710	5.74
Romanian	139	0.47
Russian	1,445	4.85
Scotch-Irish	169	0.57
Scottish	367	1.23
Serbian	28	0.09
Slovak	51	0.17
Slovene	12	0.04
Swedish	99	0.33
Swiss	27	0.09
Ukrainian	255	0.86
United States or American	1,184	3.97
Welsh	59	0.20
West Indian, excl. Hispanic:	214	0.72
Bahamian	10	0.03
Barbadian	15	0.05
Belizean	21	0.07
Jamaican	160	0.54
West Indian	8	0.03
White:	15,036	50.47
Not Hispanic (13,813)	14,825	49.76
Hispanic (176)	211	0.71
Yugoslavian	41	0.14

Oakland charter

Place Type: Township
County: Oakland
Population: 13,071

Ancestry/Race	Number	%

Notes: 1. Figures in the "Number" column do not add up to the total population due to: a) Ancestry/Race overlap — e.g. persons can report being both White and Irish, b) persons of Hispanic origin can report being any race, c) persons reporting two ancestries are counted in both categories. 2. Numbers in parentheses indicate the number of persons reporting this ancestry/race alone, not in combination with any other ancestry/race. 3. Refer to the Explanation of Data in the front of the book for more detailed information.

African American/Black:	291	2.23
Not Hispanic (255)	279	2.13
Hispanic (7)	12	0.09
African, sub-Saharan:	24	0.18
African	24	0.18
Alaska Native tribes, specified:	3	0.02
Aleut	3	0.02
Am. Ind. or Alaska Nat., not spec.	16	0.12
American Indian tribes, specified:	37	0.28
Blackfeet	3	0.02
Cherokee (1)	14	0.11
Chippewa (2)	6	0.05
Cree (3)	3	0.02
Iroquois	3	0.02
Ottawa	4	0.03
Potawatomi (1)	2	0.02
Puget Sound Salish	1	0.01
All other tribes	1	0.01
American Indian tribes, not spec.	2	0.02
Arab:	52	0.40
Lebanese	47	0.36
Syrian	5	0.04
Armenian	116	0.89
Asian:	393	3.01
Bangladeshi (6)	6	0.05
Chinese, ex. Taiwanese (77)	82	0.63
Filipino (22)	42	0.32
Indian (129)	144	1.10
Japanese (13)	24	0.18
Korean (69)	70	0.54
Pakistani (6)	6	0.05
Sri Lankan (4)	4	0.03
Taiwanese (7)	8	0.06
Thai	1	0.01
Vietnamese (4)	5	0.04
Other Asian, not specified (1)	1	0.01
Assyrian/Chaldean/Syriac	93	0.71
Austrian	67	0.51
Belgian	119	0.91
Brazilian	23	0.18
British	76	0.58
Bulgarian	10	0.08
Canadian	209	1.60
Croatian	43	0.33
Czech	33	0.25
Czechoslovakian	8	0.06
Danish	41	0.31
Dutch	259	1.98
English	2,036	15.58
European	36	0.28
Finnish	103	0.79
French, except Basque	635	4.86
French Canadian	201	1.54
German	3,377	25.84
Greek	30	0.23
Hawaii Native/Pacific Islander:	6	0.05
Polynesian:	6	0.05
Samoan	6	0.05
Hispanic or Latino:	155	1.19
Central American:	5	0.04
Honduran	3	0.02
Panamanian	1	0.01
Salvadoran	1	0.01
Cuban	17	0.13
Mexican	58	0.44
Puerto Rican	21	0.16
South American:	21	0.16
Argentinean	3	0.02
Colombian	10	0.08
Peruvian	8	0.06
Other Hispanic or Latino	33	0.25
Hungarian	256	1.96
Iranian	77	0.59
Irish	1,407	10.76
Italian	1,316	10.07
Lithuanian	23	0.18
Macedonian	25	0.19
Norwegian	143	1.09
Polish	1,809	13.84
Romanian	91	0.70
Russian	262	2.00
Scandinavian	11	0.08
Scotch-Irish	293	2.24
Scottish	597	4.57
Slavic	8	0.06
Slovak	110	0.84
Swedish	250	1.91
Swiss	58	0.44
Turkish	31	0.24
Ukrainian	287	2.20
United States or American	760	5.81
Welsh	115	0.88
West Indian, excl. Hispanic:	8	0.06
Jamaican	8	0.06
White:	12,413	94.97
Not Hispanic (12,189)	12,290	94.02
Hispanic (116)	123	0.94
Yugoslavian	8	0.06

Okemos

Place Type: Census Designated Place
County: Ingham
Population: 22,805

Ancestry/Race	Number	%
Afghan	24	0.11
African American/Black:	1,086	4.76
Not Hispanic (954)	1,075	4.71
Hispanic (4)	11	0.05
African, sub-Saharan:	210	0.93
African	109	0.48
Nigerian	66	0.29
South African	25	0.11
Other sub-Saharan African	10	0.04
Alaska Native tribes, specified:	6	0.03
Aleut	1	0.00
Eskimo (5)	5	0.02
Am. Ind. or Alaska Nat., not spec.	38	0.17
American Indian tribes, specified:	143	0.63
Apache (3)	8	0.04
Blackfeet	6	0.03
Cherokee (6)	48	0.21
Chippewa (20)	36	0.16
Choctaw (3)	6	0.03
Comanche	2	0.01
Creek	1	0.00
Iroquois (4)	8	0.04
Latin American Indians (2)	2	0.01
Ottawa (13)	14	0.06
Pueblo (1)	2	0.01
Sioux	2	0.01
All other tribes (4)	8	0.04
American Indian tribes, not spec.	10	0.04
Arab:	339	1.49
Arab/Arabic	44	0.19
Egyptian	8	0.04
Iraqi	21	0.09
Jordanian	5	0.02
Lebanese	170	0.75
Palestinian	38	0.17
Syrian	43	0.19
Other Arab	10	0.04
Armenian	39	0.17
Asian:	2,221	9.74
Bangladeshi (8)	13	0.06
Cambodian (1)	1	0.00
Chinese, ex. Taiwanese (441)	489	2.14
Filipino (63)	90	0.39
Hmong (6)	6	0.03
Indian (733)	788	3.46
Indonesian (9)	10	0.04
Japanese (93)	117	0.51
Korean (347)	371	1.63
Laotian (5)	5	0.02
Malaysian (3)	3	0.01
Pakistani (39)	53	0.23
Sri Lankan (4)	4	0.02
Taiwanese (61)	72	0.32
Thai (22)	26	0.11
Vietnamese (89)	91	0.40
Other Asian, specified	1	0.00
Other Asian, not specified (34)	81	0.36
Assyrian/Chaldean/Syriac	7	0.03
Austrian	84	0.37
Belgian	155	0.68
Brazilian	35	0.15
British	208	0.92
Canadian	118	0.52
Croatian	44	0.19
Czech	80	0.35
Czechoslovakian	56	0.25
Danish	94	0.41
Dutch	680	3.00
Eastern European	22	0.10
English	3,696	16.29
European	181	0.80
Finnish	183	0.81
French, except Basque	802	3.54
French Canadian	391	1.72
German	5,678	25.03
Greek	162	0.71
Hawaii Native/Pacific Islander:	27	0.12
Micronesian:	1	0.00
Guamanian/Chamorro	1	0.00
Polynesian: (3)	7	0.03
Native Hawaiian (2)	4	0.02
Samoan (1)	3	0.01
Other Pac. Isl., not spec. (6)	19	0.08
Hispanic or Latino:	509	2.23
Central American:	14	0.06
Costa Rican	1	0.00
Guatemalan	8	0.04
Honduran	1	0.00
Nicaraguan	3	0.01
Panamanian	1	0.00
Cuban	21	0.09
Dominican Republic	7	0.03
Mexican	286	1.25
Puerto Rican	43	0.19
South American:	51	0.22
Argentinean	5	0.02
Bolivian	1	0.00
Chilean	4	0.02
Colombian	13	0.06
Ecuadorian	3	0.01
Peruvian	5	0.02
Uruguayan	2	0.01
Venezuelan	1	0.00
Other South American	17	0.07
Other Hispanic or Latino	87	0.38
Hungarian	244	1.08
Iranian	65	0.29
Irish	2,650	11.68
Israeli	33	0.15
Italian	1,129	4.98
Latvian	94	0.41
Lithuanian	105	0.46
Luxemburger	34	0.15
Macedonian	34	0.15
Maltese	15	0.07
Northern European	11	0.05
Norwegian	446	1.97
Pennsylvania German	6	0.03
Polish	1,510	6.66
Portuguese	21	0.09
Romanian	9	0.04
Russian	380	1.68
Scandinavian	18	0.08
Scotch-Irish	428	1.89
Scottish	837	3.69
Serbian	8	0.04
Slavic	16	0.07
Slovak	53	0.23
Slovene	36	0.16
Swedish	663	2.92
Swiss	199	0.88
Turkish	8	0.04
Ukrainian	105	0.46
United States or American	779	3.43

Notes: 1. Figures in the "Number" column do not add up to the total population due to: a) Ancestry/Race overlap — e.g. persons can report being both White and Irish, b) persons of Hispanic origin can report being any race, c) persons reporting two ancestries are counted in both categories. 2. Numbers in parentheses indicate the number of persons reporting this ancestry/race alone, not in combination with any other ancestry/race. 3. Refer to the Explanation of Data in the front of the book for more detailed information.

Welsh	209	0.92
West Indian, excl. Hispanic:	18	0.08
Bahamian	9	0.04
West Indian	9	0.04
White:	19,580	85.86
Not Hispanic (18,836)	19,204	84.21
Hispanic (323)	376	1.65

Orion

Place Type: Township
County: Oakland
Population: 33,463

Ancestry/Race	Number	%
African American/Black:	490	1.46
Not Hispanic (413)	470	1.40
Hispanic (10)	20	0.06
African, sub-Saharan:	35	0.10
African	10	0.03
Nigerian	16	0.05
South African	9	0.03
Am. Ind. or Alaska Nat., not spec.	73	0.22
Albanian	47	0.14
American Indian tribes, specified:	178	0.53
Apache	4	0.01
Blackfeet (2)	7	0.02
Cherokee (6)	55	0.16
Chippewa (23)	51	0.15
Choctaw	1	0.00
Cree	1	0.00
Iroquois (6)	20	0.06
Latin American Indians (1)	1	0.00
Lumbee (3)	4	0.01
Navajo	1	0.00
Ottawa (1)	2	0.01
Potawatomi (1)	5	0.01
Seminole (3)	4	0.01
Sioux (3)	8	0.02
All other tribes (6)	14	0.04
American Indian tribes, not spec.	12	0.04
Arab:	215	0.64
Arab/Arabic	14	0.04
Iraqi	23	0.07
Lebanese	95	0.28
Moroccan	7	0.02
Syrian	30	0.09
Other Arab	46	0.14
Armenian	86	0.26
Asian:	516	1.54
Chinese, ex. Taiwanese (76)	95	0.28
Filipino (40)	69	0.21
Hmong (37)	38	0.11
Indian (101)	116	0.35
Indonesian (1)	2	0.01
Japanese (34)	67	0.20
Korean (68)	79	0.24
Laotian (12)	14	0.04
Pakistani	1	0.00
Sri Lankan (3)	3	0.01
Thai (1)	2	0.01
Vietnamese (11)	18	0.05
Other Asian, not specified (6)	12	0.04
Assyrian/Chaldean/Syriac	41	0.12
Austrian	134	0.40
Belgian	323	0.96
Brazilian	34	0.10
British	184	0.55
Bulgarian	15	0.04
Canadian	216	0.64
Croatian	163	0.49
Czech	234	0.70
Czechoslovakian	82	0.24
Danish	330	0.98
Dutch	882	2.63
Eastern European	10	0.03
English	4,314	12.88
European	312	0.93
Finnish	218	0.65
French, except Basque	2,049	6.12
French Canadian	962	2.87
German	8,957	26.73
Greek	174	0.52
Hawaii Native/Pacific Islander:	12	0.04
Micronesian: (2)	2	0.01
Guamanian/Chamorro (2)	2	0.01
Polynesian: (3)	5	0.01
Native Hawaiian	2	0.01
Samoan (2)	2	0.01
Tongan (1)	1	0.00
Other Pac. Isl., not spec. (3)	5	0.01
Hispanic or Latino:	858	2.56
Central American:	7	0.02
Costa Rican	1	0.00
Panamanian	5	0.01
Salvadoran	1	0.00
Cuban	20	0.06
Dominican Republic	2	0.01
Mexican	546	1.63
Puerto Rican	101	0.30
South American:	34	0.10
Argentinean	5	0.01
Chilean	4	0.01
Colombian	10	0.03
Ecuadorian	1	0.00
Paraguayan	2	0.01
Peruvian	9	0.03
Venezuelan	2	0.01
Other South American	1	0.00
Other Hispanic or Latino	148	0.44
Hungarian	408	1.22
Icelander	23	0.07
Iranian	33	0.10
Irish	5,267	15.72
Italian	2,481	7.40
Latvian	29	0.09
Lithuanian	196	0.58
Macedonian	9	0.03
Maltese	118	0.35
Northern European	21	0.06
Norwegian	348	1.04
Polish	3,995	11.92
Portuguese	15	0.04
Romanian	227	0.68
Russian	153	0.46
Scandinavian	73	0.22
Scotch-Irish	503	1.50
Scottish	1,232	3.68
Serbian	65	0.19
Slavic	19	0.06
Slovak	237	0.71
Swedish	600	1.79
Swiss	162	0.48
Turkish	27	0.08
Ukrainian	245	0.73
United States or American	1,836	5.48
Welsh	278	0.83
West Indian, excl. Hispanic:	24	0.07
West Indian	6	0.02
Other West Indian	18	0.05
White:	32,323	96.59
Not Hispanic (31,370)	31,673	94.65
Hispanic (561)	650	1.94
Yugoslavian	17	0.05

Oshtemo

Place Type: Township
County: Kalamazoo
Population: 17,003

Ancestry/Race	Number	%
African American/Black:	1,798	10.57
Not Hispanic (1,580)	1,766	10.39
Hispanic (17)	32	0.19
African, sub-Saharan:	170	1.00
African	64	0.38
Ghanian	34	0.20
Kenyan	10	0.06
Nigerian	27	0.16
Other sub-Saharan African	35	0.21
Am. Ind. or Alaska Nat., not spec.	57	0.34
American Indian tribes, specified:	114	0.67
Apache (1)	7	0.04
Blackfeet (2)	13	0.08
Cherokee (4)	31	0.18
Chippewa (10)	14	0.08
Choctaw	4	0.02
Creek (1)	4	0.02
Iroquois (1)	1	0.01
Latin American Indians (2)	3	0.02
Ottawa (5)	7	0.04
Potawatomi (9)	16	0.09
Seminole (1)	3	0.02
Sioux (5)	5	0.03
All other tribes	6	0.04
American Indian tribes, not spec.	11	0.06
Arab:	154	0.91
Arab/Arabic	10	0.06
Lebanese	107	0.63
Syrian	32	0.19
Other Arab	5	0.03
Asian:	447	2.63
Bangladeshi (3)	3	0.02
Chinese, ex. Taiwanese (99)	105	0.62
Filipino (23)	30	0.18
Hmong (2)	2	0.01
Indian (114)	135	0.79
Indonesian (3)	3	0.02
Japanese (22)	28	0.16
Korean (58)	64	0.38
Laotian (2)	2	0.01
Malaysian (16)	18	0.11
Pakistani (6)	7	0.04
Taiwanese (3)	3	0.02
Thai (1)	2	0.01
Vietnamese (19)	25	0.15
Other Asian, specified (5)	7	0.04
Other Asian, not specified (3)	13	0.08
Australian	9	0.05
Austrian	32	0.19
Belgian	51	0.30
British	163	0.96
Canadian	97	0.57
Celtic	19	0.11
Croatian	26	0.15
Czech	72	0.42
Czechoslovakian	27	0.16
Danish	167	0.98
Dutch	2,212	13.01
English	2,409	14.17
European	110	0.65
Finnish	88	0.52
French, except Basque	665	3.91
French Canadian	154	0.91
German	3,805	22.38
Greek	59	0.35
Hawaii Native/Pacific Islander:	7	0.04
Micronesian: (2)	3	0.02
Guamanian/Chamorro (2)	3	0.02
Polynesian: (2)	3	0.02
Native Hawaiian (2)	3	0.02
Other Pac. Isl., specified	1	0.01
Hispanic or Latino:	397	2.33
Central American:	10	0.06
Guatemalan	2	0.01
Honduran	2	0.01
Nicaraguan	1	0.01
Panamanian	5	0.03
Cuban	18	0.11
Dominican Republic	5	0.03
Mexican	229	1.35
Puerto Rican	42	0.25
South American:	22	0.13
Argentinean	1	0.01
Bolivian	3	0.02
Chilean	2	0.01
Colombian	5	0.03
Uruguayan	1	0.01
Venezuelan	10	0.06

Notes: 1. Figures in the "Number" column do not add up to the total population due to: a) Ancestry/Race overlap — e.g. persons can report being both White and Irish, b) persons of Hispanic origin can report being any race, c) persons reporting two ancestries are counted in both categories. 2. Numbers in parentheses indicate the number of persons reporting this ancestry/race alone, not in combination with any other ancestry/race. 3. Refer to the Explanation of Data in the front of the book for more detailed information.

Ancestry/Race	Number	%
Other Hispanic or Latino	71	0.42
Hungarian	65	0.38
Icelander	32	0.19
Iranian	23	0.14
Irish	1,935	11.38
Italian	557	3.28
Latvian	55	0.32
Lithuanian	55	0.32
Maltese	8	0.05
Northern European	30	0.18
Norwegian	161	0.95
Pennsylvania German	22	0.13
Polish	804	4.73
Portuguese	8	0.05
Romanian	10	0.06
Russian	55	0.32
Scandinavian	17	0.10
Scotch-Irish	291	1.71
Scottish	482	2.83
Serbian	9	0.05
Slovak	53	0.31
Swedish	287	1.69
Swiss	31	0.18
Turkish	23	0.14
Ukrainian	87	0.51
United States or American	849	4.99
Welsh	59	0.35
West Indian, excl. Hispanic:	12	0.07
Dutch West Indian	6	0.04
Jamaican	6	0.04
White:	14,725	86.60
Not Hispanic (14,249)	14,494	85.24
Hispanic (198)	231	1.36
Yugoslavian	19	0.11

Owosso

Place Type: City
County: Shiawassee
Population: 15,713

Ancestry/Race	Number	%
African American/Black:	65	0.41
Not Hispanic (26)	62	0.39
Hispanic (1)	3	0.02
Alaska Native tribes, specified:	1	0.01
Alaska Athabascan (1)	1	0.01
Am. Ind. or Alaska Nat., not spec.	66	0.42
Albanian	5	0.03
American Indian tribes, specified:	122	0.78
Apache (1)	9	0.06
Blackfeet (2)	9	0.06
Cherokee (17)	34	0.22
Chippewa (23)	33	0.21
Choctaw	1	0.01
Comanche	1	0.01
Iroquois (1)	5	0.03
Latin American Indians (3)	4	0.03
Lumbee	3	0.02
Navajo (1)	5	0.03
Ottawa (2)	8	0.05
Potawatomi	1	0.01
Seminole	1	0.01
Sioux (1)	1	0.01
All other tribes (5)	7	0.04
American Indian tribes, not spec.	3	0.02
Arab:	16	0.10
Lebanese	16	0.10
Asian:	82	0.52
Chinese, ex. Taiwanese (23)	25	0.16
Filipino (6)	11	0.07
Indian (10)	12	0.08
Japanese (5)	10	0.06
Korean (9)	12	0.08
Taiwanese	1	0.01
Thai (2)	3	0.02
Vietnamese (3)	3	0.02
Other Asian, not specified	5	0.03
Assyrian/Chaldean/Syriac	10	0.06
Australian	11	0.07
Austrian	38	0.24
Belgian	11	0.07
British	55	0.35
Canadian	94	0.60
Croatian	19	0.12
Czech	335	2.14
Czechoslovakian	189	1.21
Danish	36	0.23
Dutch	377	2.41
Eastern European	7	0.04
English	2,240	14.30
European	45	0.29
Finnish	21	0.13
French, except Basque	692	4.42
French Canadian	252	1.61
German	4,253	27.15
Greek	33	0.21
Hawaii Native/Pacific Islander:	1	0.01
Polynesian:	1	0.01
Native Hawaiian	1	0.01
Hispanic or Latino:	465	2.96
Central American:	3	0.02
Salvadoran	3	0.02
Cuban	3	0.02
Dominican Republic	1	0.01
Mexican	332	2.11
Puerto Rican	22	0.14
South American:	6	0.04
Argentinean	3	0.02
Peruvian	2	0.01
Uruguayan	1	0.01
Other Hispanic or Latino	98	0.62
Hungarian	158	1.01
Irish	2,233	14.26
Italian	423	2.70
Lithuanian	6	0.04
Macedonian	39	0.25
Maltese	9	0.06
New Zealander	6	0.04
Norwegian	74	0.47
Polish	672	4.29
Romanian	21	0.13
Russian	57	0.36
Scotch-Irish	186	1.19
Scottish	401	2.56
Serbian	14	0.09
Slavic	41	0.26
Slovak	121	0.77
Swedish	143	0.91
Swiss	14	0.09
Ukrainian	20	0.13
United States or American	1,427	9.11
Welsh	100	0.64
White:	15,407	98.05
Not Hispanic (14,944)	15,084	96.00
Hispanic (300)	323	2.06
Yugoslavian	13	0.08

Oxford charter

Place Type: Township
County: Oakland
Population: 16,025

Ancestry/Race	Number	%
African American/Black:	96	0.60
Not Hispanic (72)	95	0.59
Hispanic	1	0.01
African, sub-Saharan:	7	0.04
African	7	0.04
Am. Ind. or Alaska Nat., not spec.	42	0.26
American Indian tribes, specified:	116	0.72
Apache	5	0.03
Blackfeet	3	0.02
Cherokee (7)	39	0.24
Chippewa (10)	39	0.24
Choctaw (1)	4	0.02
Creek	3	0.02
Crow	1	0.01
Delaware (1)	1	0.01
Iroquois	3	0.02
Latin American Indians (1)	2	0.01
Navajo	1	0.01
Ottawa	6	0.04
Potawatomi (2)	2	0.01
Sioux (1)	1	0.01
All other tribes (5)	6	0.04
American Indian tribes, not spec.	2	0.01
Arab:	64	0.40
Iraqi	9	0.06
Lebanese	50	0.31
Syrian	5	0.03
Armenian	75	0.47
Asian:	129	0.80
Cambodian (1)	2	0.01
Chinese, ex. Taiwanese (5)	13	0.08
Filipino (15)	30	0.19
Hmong (9)	10	0.06
Indian (12)	16	0.10
Indonesian	2	0.01
Japanese (3)	12	0.07
Korean (20)	27	0.17
Malaysian (1)	1	0.01
Pakistani (3)	4	0.02
Thai (1)	2	0.01
Vietnamese (3)	3	0.02
Other Asian, not specified (4)	7	0.04
Assyrian/Chaldean/Syriac	9	0.06
Austrian	22	0.14
Belgian	160	1.00
British	101	0.63
Canadian	142	0.89
Croatian	39	0.24
Czech	21	0.13
Czechoslovakian	54	0.34
Danish	84	0.52
Dutch	333	2.08
Eastern European	20	0.12
English	2,545	15.88
European	110	0.69
Finnish	81	0.51
French, except Basque	914	5.70
French Canadian	473	2.95
German	3,811	23.78
Greek	19	0.12
Hawaii Native/Pacific Islander:	10	0.06
Micronesian: (3)	5	0.03
Guamanian/Chamorro (3)	5	0.03
Polynesian:	3	0.02
Native Hawaiian	3	0.02
Other Pac. Isl., not spec.	2	0.01
Hispanic or Latino:	351	2.19
Central American:	6	0.04
Costa Rican	2	0.01
Guatemalan	1	0.01
Nicaraguan	3	0.02
Cuban	5	0.03
Mexican	240	1.50
Puerto Rican	41	0.26
South American:	8	0.05
Argentinean	6	0.04
Chilean	1	0.01
Colombian	1	0.01
Other Hispanic or Latino	51	0.32
Hungarian	148	0.92
Icelander	45	0.28
Irish	2,690	16.79
Italian	970	6.05
Latvian	50	0.31
Lithuanian	39	0.24
Maltese	50	0.31
Northern European	19	0.12
Norwegian	168	1.05
Pennsylvania German	32	0.20
Polish	1,630	10.17
Romanian	79	0.49
Russian	214	1.34
Scandinavian	30	0.19
Scotch-Irish	169	1.05
Scottish	491	3.06

Notes: 1. Figures in the "Number" column do not add up to the total population due to: a) Ancestry/Race overlap — e.g. persons can report being both White and Irish, b) persons of Hispanic origin can report being any race, c) persons reporting two ancestries are counted in both categories. 2. Numbers in parentheses indicate the number of persons reporting this ancestry/race alone, not in combination with any other ancestry/race. 3. Refer to the Explanation of Data in the front of the book for more detailed information.

Serbian	4	0.02
Slavic	7	0.04
Slovak	44	0.27
Slovene	24	0.15
Swedish	330	2.06
Swiss	49	0.31
Ukrainian	78	0.49
United States or American	1,166	7.28
Welsh	75	0.47
West Indian, excl. Hispanic:	49	0.31
Jamaican	49	0.31
White:	15,714	98.06
Not Hispanic (15,311)	15,463	96.49
Hispanic (206)	251	1.57
Yugoslavian	5	0.03

Park

Place Type: Township
County: Ottawa
Population: 17,579

Ancestry/Race	Number	%
African American/Black:	136	0.77
Not Hispanic (70)	117	0.67
Hispanic (9)	19	0.11
African, sub-Saharan:	3	0.02
Somalian	3	0.02
Alaska Native tribes, specified:	4	0.02
Tlingit-Haida (1)	4	0.02
Am. Ind. or Alaska Nat., not spec.	28	0.16
Alsatian	9	0.05
American Indian tribes, specified:	73	0.42
Apache	1	0.01
Blackfeet	5	0.03
Cherokee (3)	20	0.11
Chickasaw	1	0.01
Chippewa (8)	18	0.10
Choctaw (1)	4	0.02
Iroquois (5)	5	0.03
Latin American Indians (5)	6	0.03
Ottawa (2)	3	0.02
Potawatomi	2	0.01
Sioux	2	0.01
Ute	1	0.01
All other tribes (2)	5	0.03
American Indian tribes, not spec.	2	0.01
Arab:	24	0.14
Egyptian	8	0.05
Lebanese	16	0.09
Armenian	23	0.13
Asian:	447	2.54
Bangladeshi (1)	1	0.01
Cambodian (38)	40	0.23
Chinese, ex. Taiwanese (25)	34	0.19
Filipino (10)	19	0.11
Indian (31)	37	0.21
Indonesian (1)	7	0.04
Japanese (11)	19	0.11
Korean (58)	69	0.39
Laotian (138)	151	0.86
Sri Lankan (4)	4	0.02
Taiwanese (5)	7	0.04
Thai (2)	5	0.03
Vietnamese (36)	41	0.23
Other Asian, specified (1)	2	0.01
Other Asian, not specified (8)	11	0.06
Australian	10	0.06
Austrian	42	0.24
Belgian	42	0.24
British	48	0.27
Canadian	32	0.18
Celtic	23	0.13
Croatian	36	0.20
Czech	54	0.31
Czechoslovakian	21	0.12
Danish	139	0.79
Dutch	6,249	35.57
English	1,979	11.26
European	122	0.69
Finnish	70	0.40
French, except Basque	564	3.21
French Canadian	352	2.00
German	3,687	20.99
Greek	57	0.32
Hawaii Native/Pacific Islander:	19	0.11
Polynesian: (3)	9	0.05
Native Hawaiian (1)	3	0.02
Samoan (2)	6	0.03
Other Pac. Isl., not spec.	10	0.06
Hispanic or Latino:	959	5.46
Central American:	15	0.09
Costa Rican	4	0.02
Guatemalan	2	0.01
Honduran	4	0.02
Panamanian	2	0.01
Salvadoran	3	0.02
Cuban	24	0.14
Dominican Republic	2	0.01
Mexican	660	3.75
Puerto Rican	34	0.19
South American:	21	0.12
Bolivian	1	0.01
Chilean	9	0.05
Colombian	2	0.01
Peruvian	5	0.03
Venezuelan	4	0.02
Other Hispanic or Latino	203	1.15
Hungarian	91	0.52
Irish	1,701	9.68
Italian	489	2.78
Lithuanian	24	0.14
Luxemburger	8	0.05
Northern European	27	0.15
Norwegian	189	1.08
Polish	663	3.77
Portuguese	10	0.06
Romanian	43	0.24
Russian	40	0.23
Scotch-Irish	163	0.93
Scottish	594	3.38
Slavic	8	0.05
Slovak	38	0.22
Swedish	548	3.12
Swiss	60	0.34
Ukrainian	37	0.21
United States or American	924	5.26
Welsh	71	0.40
West Indian, excl. Hispanic:	4	0.02
Dutch West Indian	4	0.02
White:	16,676	94.86
Not Hispanic (15,961)	16,118	91.69
Hispanic (485)	558	3.17
Yugoslavian	16	0.09

Pittsfield charter

Place Type: Township
County: Washtenaw
Population: 30,167

Ancestry/Race	Number	%
African American/Black:	4,664	15.46
Not Hispanic (4,261)	4,570	15.15
Hispanic (50)	94	0.31
African, sub-Saharan:	403	1.34
African	156	0.52
Ethiopian	18	0.06
Kenyan	16	0.05
Liberian	6	0.02
Nigerian	101	0.34
Senegalese	28	0.09
South African	26	0.09
Zimbabwean	5	0.02
Other sub-Saharan African	47	0.16
Alaska Native tribes, specified:	2	0.01
Alaska Athabascan (1)	1	0.00
Tlingit-Haida (1)	1	0.00
Am. Ind. or Alaska Nat., not spec.	128	0.42
American Indian tribes, specified:	192	0.64
Apache (1)	7	0.02
Blackfeet (2)	8	0.03
Cherokee (20)	57	0.19
Cheyenne	1	0.00
Chippewa (16)	38	0.13
Choctaw	3	0.01
Cree (3)	3	0.01
Creek	7	0.02
Crow	1	0.00
Delaware	4	0.01
Iroquois (3)	9	0.03
Latin American Indians (6)	11	0.04
Navajo (2)	2	0.01
Ottawa (10)	21	0.07
Potawatomi	2	0.01
Sioux (6)	8	0.03
Yaqui (1)	1	0.00
Yuman (1)	1	0.00
All other tribes (3)	8	0.03
American Indian tribes, not spec.	13	0.04
Arab:	902	2.99
Arab/Arabic	224	0.74
Egyptian	155	0.51
Iraqi	42	0.14
Jordanian	29	0.10
Lebanese	170	0.56
Moroccan	33	0.11
Palestinian	98	0.33
Syrian	60	0.20
Other Arab	91	0.30
Armenian	78	0.26
Asian:	3,332	11.05
Bangladeshi (15)	18	0.06
Cambodian (18)	19	0.06
Chinese, ex. Taiwanese (903)	971	3.22
Filipino (145)	191	0.63
Hmong (5)	6	0.02
Indian (956)	1,004	3.33
Indonesian (21)	25	0.08
Japanese (128)	162	0.54
Korean (407)	445	1.48
Laotian (16)	17	0.06
Malaysian (6)	7	0.02
Pakistani (64)	66	0.22
Sri Lankan (5)	6	0.02
Taiwanese (55)	65	0.22
Thai (75)	79	0.26
Vietnamese (81)	104	0.34
Other Asian, specified (1)	3	0.01
Other Asian, not specified (59)	144	0.48
Assyrian/Chaldean/Syriac	53	0.18
Australian	10	0.03
Austrian	135	0.45
Basque	18	0.06
Belgian	61	0.20
Brazilian	32	0.11
British	247	0.82
Bulgarian	20	0.07
Canadian	190	0.63
Carpatho Rusyn	11	0.04
Croatian	42	0.14
Cypriot	5	0.02
Czech	189	0.63
Czechoslovakian	82	0.27
Danish	95	0.32
Dutch	698	2.32
Eastern European	23	0.08
English	2,948	9.79
European	399	1.32
Finnish	400	1.33
French, except Basque	1,107	3.67
French Canadian	616	2.04
German	5,148	17.09
Greek	313	1.04
Hawaii Native/Pacific Islander:	59	0.20
Micronesian: (2)	6	0.02
Guamanian/Chamorro (1)	1	0.00
Other Micronesian (1)	5	0.02
Polynesian: (6)	21	0.07
Native Hawaiian (5)	14	0.05

Notes: 1. Figures in the "Number" column do not add up to the total population due to: a) Ancestry/Race overlap — e.g. persons can report being both White and Irish, b) persons of Hispanic origin can report being any race, c) persons reporting two ancestries are counted in both categories. 2. Numbers in parentheses indicate the number of persons reporting this ancestry/race alone, not in combination with any other ancestry/race. 3. Refer to the Explanation of Data in the front of the book for more detailed information.

Samoan (1)	7	0.02
Other Pac. Isl., specified	2	0.01
Other Pac. Isl., not spec. (6)	30	0.10
Hispanic or Latino:	1,199	3.97
Central American:	160	0.53
Costa Rican	11	0.04
Guatemalan	25	0.08
Honduran	34	0.11
Nicaraguan	12	0.04
Panamanian	21	0.07
Salvadoran	47	0.16
Other Central American	10	0.03
Cuban	58	0.19
Dominican Republic	17	0.06
Mexican	534	1.77
Puerto Rican	103	0.34
South American:	70	0.23
Argentinean	6	0.02
Bolivian	3	0.01
Chilean	6	0.02
Colombian	27	0.09
Ecuadorian	1	0.00
Peruvian	6	0.02
Uruguayan	2	0.01
Venezuelan	19	0.06
Other Hispanic or Latino	257	0.85
Hungarian	257	0.85
Iranian	100	0.33
Irish	3,109	10.32
Israeli	12	0.04
Italian	1,274	4.23
Latvian	29	0.10
Lithuanian	51	0.17
Macedonian	7	0.02
Maltese	6	0.02
Northern European	6	0.02
Norwegian	372	1.23
Pennsylvania German	6	0.02
Polish	1,751	5.81
Portuguese	39	0.13
Romanian	157	0.52
Russian	411	1.36
Scandinavian	78	0.26
Scotch-Irish	344	1.14
Scottish	924	3.07
Serbian	24	0.08
Slavic	39	0.13
Slovak	138	0.46
Slovene	47	0.16
Swedish	361	1.20
Swiss	174	0.58
Turkish	40	0.13
Ukrainian	234	0.78
United States or American	1,244	4.13
Welsh	200	0.66
West Indian, excl. Hispanic:	72	0.24
Jamaican	53	0.18
Trinidadian and Tobagonian	10	0.03
West Indian	9	0.03
White:	22,038	73.05
Not Hispanic (20,612)	21,325	70.69
Hispanic (617)	713	2.36
Yugoslavian	12	0.04

Plainfield

Place Type: Township
County: Kent
Population: 30,195

Ancestry/Race	Number	%
African American/Black:	482	1.60
Not Hispanic (364)	467	1.55
Hispanic (5)	15	0.05
African, sub-Saharan:	33	0.11
African	9	0.03
Sudanese	24	0.08
Am. Ind. or Alaska Nat., not spec.	71	0.24
American Indian tribes, specified:	158	0.52
Apache (1)	5	0.02
Cherokee (8)	30	0.10
Chippewa (31)	46	0.15
Choctaw	2	0.01
Crow	1	0.00
Iroquois	2	0.01
Latin American Indians (2)	6	0.02
Lumbee (1)	1	0.00
Navajo (1)	1	0.00
Ottawa (12)	21	0.07
Potawatomi (14)	18	0.06
Pueblo (1)	2	0.01
Shoshone (1)	1	0.00
Sioux (1)	7	0.02
Yaqui	1	0.00
All other tribes (4)	14	0.05
American Indian tribes, not spec.	8	0.03
Arab:	88	0.29
Arab/Arabic	21	0.07
Lebanese	40	0.13
Syrian	27	0.09
Armenian	17	0.06
Asian:	352	1.17
Bangladeshi (3)	3	0.01
Cambodian (1)	1	0.00
Chinese, ex. Taiwanese (40)	43	0.14
Filipino (29)	43	0.14
Hmong (14)	14	0.05
Indian (38)	45	0.15
Indonesian (1)	5	0.02
Japanese (27)	39	0.13
Korean (82)	95	0.31
Pakistani (8)	13	0.04
Sri Lankan	1	0.00
Thai (4)	6	0.02
Vietnamese (28)	29	0.10
Other Asian, not specified (7)	15	0.05
Austrian	52	0.17
Belgian	74	0.25
Brazilian	5	0.02
British	184	0.61
Bulgarian	18	0.06
Canadian	52	0.17
Croatian	78	0.26
Czech	83	0.28
Czechoslovakian	62	0.21
Danish	284	0.94
Dutch	5,800	19.27
English	4,057	13.48
European	308	1.02
Finnish	178	0.59
French, except Basque	1,348	4.48
French Canadian	430	1.43
German	7,151	23.75
Greek	38	0.13
Hawaii Native/Pacific Islander:	20	0.07
Melanesian: (1)	1	0.00
Fijian (1)	1	0.00
Micronesian: (6)	7	0.02
Guamanian/Chamorro (5)	5	0.02
Other Micronesian (1)	2	0.01
Polynesian: (2)	4	0.01
Native Hawaiian (1)	3	0.01
Samoan (1)	1	0.00
Other Pac. Isl., not spec. (4)	8	0.03
Hispanic or Latino:	529	1.75
Central American:	19	0.06
Costa Rican	3	0.01
Guatemalan	8	0.03
Honduran	1	0.00
Panamanian	1	0.00
Salvadoran	6	0.02
Cuban	14	0.05
Dominican Republic	5	0.02
Mexican	333	1.10
Puerto Rican	37	0.12
South American:	17	0.06
Argentinean	1	0.00
Bolivian	4	0.01
Chilean	2	0.01
Colombian	6	0.02
Uruguayan	1	0.00
Venezuelan	2	0.01
Other South American	1	0.00
Other Hispanic or Latino	104	0.34
Hungarian	159	0.53
Irish	4,704	15.63
Italian	873	2.90
Latvian	41	0.14
Lithuanian	260	0.86
Norwegian	428	1.42
Pennsylvania German	20	0.07
Polish	3,386	11.25
Romanian	45	0.15
Russian	180	0.60
Scandinavian	28	0.09
Scotch-Irish	547	1.82
Scottish	640	2.13
Serbian	31	0.10
Slavic	34	0.11
Slovak	66	0.22
Swedish	960	3.19
Swiss	17	0.06
Ukrainian	88	0.29
United States or American	1,863	6.19
Welsh	263	0.87
White:	29,233	96.81
Not Hispanic (28,626)	28,898	95.70
Hispanic (266)	335	1.11
Yugoslavian	24	0.08

Plymouth Township

Place Type: Census Designated Place
County: Wayne
Population: 27,798

Ancestry/Race	Number	%
African American/Black:	900	3.24
Not Hispanic (809)	882	3.17
Hispanic (13)	18	0.06
African, sub-Saharan:	124	0.45
African	107	0.39
Ethiopian	9	0.03
Nigerian	8	0.03
Alaska Native tribes, specified:	2	0.01
Eskimo	2	0.01
Am. Ind. or Alaska Nat., not spec.	55	0.20
Albanian	83	0.30
Alsatian	8	0.03
American Indian tribes, specified:	139	0.50
Blackfeet (1)	8	0.03
Cherokee (16)	51	0.18
Chippewa (22)	34	0.12
Choctaw	2	0.01
Cree (1)	2	0.01
Creek	1	0.00
Iroquois (8)	11	0.04
Latin American Indians (2)	5	0.02
Lumbee (4)	4	0.01
Ottawa (1)	1	0.00
Pima	2	0.01
Potawatomi	2	0.01
Pueblo (1)	3	0.01
Seminole	2	0.01
Sioux (1)	4	0.01
All other tribes	7	0.03
American Indian tribes, not spec.	5	0.02
Arab:	494	1.79
Arab/Arabic	78	0.28
Egyptian	36	0.13
Jordanian	43	0.16
Lebanese	252	0.91
Moroccan	44	0.16
Palestinian	24	0.09
Syrian	17	0.06
Armenian	133	0.48
Asian:	886	3.19
Bangladeshi (1)	1	0.00
Chinese, ex. Taiwanese (170)	186	0.67
Filipino (71)	81	0.29

Notes: 1. Figures in the "Number" column do not add up to the total population due to: a) Ancestry/Race overlap — e.g. persons can report being both White and Irish, b) persons of Hispanic origin can report being any race, c) persons reporting two ancestries are counted in both categories. 2. Numbers in parentheses indicate the number of persons reporting this ancestry/race alone, not in combination with any other ancestry/race. 3. Refer to the Explanation of Data in the front of the book for more detailed information.

Ancestry/Race	Number	%
Indian (309)	334	1.20
Indonesian (4)	7	0.03
Japanese (37)	59	0.21
Korean (82)	102	0.37
Malaysian (2)	2	0.01
Pakistani (10)	10	0.04
Taiwanese (17)	22	0.08
Thai (1)	4	0.01
Vietnamese (39)	48	0.17
Other Asian, specified (2)	2	0.01
Other Asian, not specified (6)	28	0.10
Assyrian/Chaldean/Syriac	52	0.19
Australian	33	0.12
Austrian	48	0.17
Belgian	140	0.51
Brazilian	37	0.13
British	218	0.79
Canadian	146	0.53
Croatian	163	0.59
Czech	143	0.52
Czechoslovakian	73	0.26
Danish	96	0.35
Dutch	690	2.50
Eastern European	6	0.02
English	3,651	13.20
Estonian	8	0.03
European	158	0.57
Finnish	365	1.32
French, except Basque	1,633	5.91
French Canadian	399	1.44
German	6,812	24.64
Greek	358	1.29
Hawaii Native/Pacific Islander:	12	0.04
Micronesian:	1	0.00
Other Micronesian	1	0.00
Polynesian: (1)	2	0.01
Samoan (1)	2	0.01
Other Pac. Isl., not spec. (3)	9	0.03
Hispanic or Latino:	455	1.64
Central American:	13	0.05
Costa Rican	1	0.00
Guatemalan	7	0.03
Salvadoran	5	0.02
Cuban	25	0.09
Dominican Republic	1	0.00
Mexican	258	0.93
Puerto Rican	35	0.13
South American:	14	0.05
Argentinean	3	0.01
Bolivian	1	0.00
Chilean	2	0.01
Colombian	2	0.01
Peruvian	3	0.01
Venezuelan	2	0.01
Other South American	1	0.00
Other Hispanic or Latino	109	0.39
Hungarian	347	1.25
Icelander	6	0.02
Iranian	23	0.08
Irish	5,288	19.12
Israeli	12	0.04
Italian	2,057	7.44
Latvian	29	0.10
Lithuanian	149	0.54
Luxemburger	10	0.04
Macedonian	153	0.55
Maltese	108	0.39
Northern European	10	0.04
Norwegian	192	0.69
Pennsylvania German	24	0.09
Polish	4,279	15.48
Portuguese	9	0.03
Romanian	147	0.53
Russian	216	0.78
Scandinavian	60	0.22
Scotch-Irish	588	2.13
Scottish	1,010	3.65
Serbian	53	0.19
Slavic	55	0.20
Slovak	93	0.34
Slovene	32	0.12
Swedish	403	1.46
Swiss	143	0.52
Ukrainian	292	1.06
United States or American	911	3.29
Welsh	205	0.74
West Indian, excl. Hispanic:	9	0.03
Belizean	9	0.03
White:	25,996	93.52
Not Hispanic (25,365)	25,644	92.25
Hispanic (315)	352	1.27
Yugoslavian	86	0.31

Pontiac

Place Type: City
County: Oakland
Population: 66,337

Ancestry/Race	Number	%
African American/Black:	33,098	49.89
Not Hispanic (31,416)	32,484	48.97
Hispanic (375)	614	0.93
African, sub-Saharan:	1,294	1.95
African	1,218	1.84
Ethiopian	23	0.03
Ghanian	10	0.02
Liberian	14	0.02
Nigerian	29	0.04
Alaska Native tribes, specified:	1	0.00
Alaska Athabascan	1	0.00
Alaska Native tribes, not specified	3	0.00
Am. Ind. or Alaska Nat., not spec.	466	0.70
Albanian	44	0.07
American Indian tribes, specified:	534	0.80
Apache (10)	13	0.02
Blackfeet (2)	25	0.04
Cherokee (54)	201	0.30
Cheyenne (1)	1	0.00
Chickasaw	1	0.00
Chippewa (39)	88	0.13
Choctaw (6)	14	0.02
Comanche	2	0.00
Crow	2	0.00
Iroquois (11)	23	0.03
Kiowa	2	0.00
Latin American Indians (31)	44	0.07
Lumbee (1)	1	0.00
Navajo (7)	13	0.02
Ottawa (8)	18	0.03
Potawatomi (3)	17	0.03
Pueblo (2)	3	0.00
Seminole (1)	7	0.01
Shoshone	3	0.00
Sioux (1)	21	0.03
Ute	3	0.00
All other tribes (12)	32	0.05
American Indian tribes, not spec.	49	0.07
Arab:	360	0.54
Arab/Arabic	34	0.05
Jordanian	33	0.05
Lebanese	92	0.14
Moroccan	29	0.04
Palestinian	14	0.02
Syrian	145	0.22
Other Arab	13	0.02
Armenian	32	0.05
Asian:	1,947	2.94
Cambodian (7)	12	0.02
Chinese, ex. Taiwanese (164)	189	0.28
Filipino (111)	157	0.24
Hmong (787)	884	1.33
Indian (145)	201	0.30
Japanese (20)	41	0.06
Korean (27)	46	0.07
Laotian (90)	144	0.22
Malaysian	1	0.00
Pakistani (6)	8	0.01
Sri Lankan	1	0.00
Taiwanese	1	0.00
Thai (16)	26	0.04
Vietnamese (106)	132	0.20
Other Asian, specified	6	0.01
Other Asian, not specified (50)	98	0.15
Assyrian/Chaldean/Syriac	143	0.22
Austrian	20	0.03
Belgian	59	0.09
British	80	0.12
Canadian	200	0.30
Croatian	21	0.03
Czech	70	0.11
Czechoslovakian	7	0.01
Danish	60	0.09
Dutch	714	1.08
English	2,602	3.92
European	176	0.27
Finnish	128	0.19
French, except Basque	1,097	1.65
French Canadian	654	0.99
German	4,571	6.89
German Russian	6	0.01
Greek	62	0.09
Hawaii Native/Pacific Islander:	101	0.15
Micronesian: (10)	13	0.02
Guamanian/Chamorro (9)	12	0.02
Other Micronesian (1)	1	0.00
Polynesian: (9)	45	0.07
Native Hawaiian (3)	29	0.04
Samoan (6)	16	0.02
Other Pac. Isl., specified	4	0.01
Other Pac. Isl., not spec. (7)	39	0.06
Hispanic or Latino:	8,463	12.76
Central American:	136	0.21
Costa Rican	8	0.01
Guatemalan	8	0.01
Honduran	30	0.05
Nicaraguan	1	0.00
Panamanian	5	0.01
Salvadoran	73	0.11
Other Central American	11	0.02
Cuban	43	0.06
Dominican Republic	13	0.02
Mexican	5,141	7.75
Puerto Rican	2,273	3.43
South American:	29	0.04
Argentinean	2	0.00
Bolivian	3	0.00
Chilean	2	0.00
Colombian	6	0.01
Ecuadorian	9	0.01
Peruvian	4	0.01
Venezuelan	2	0.00
Other South American	1	0.00
Other Hispanic or Latino	828	1.25
Hungarian	199	0.30
Iranian	12	0.02
Irish	3,319	5.00
Italian	889	1.34
Latvian	22	0.03
Lithuanian	25	0.04
Maltese	9	0.01
Northern European	28	0.04
Norwegian	193	0.29
Pennsylvania German	20	0.03
Polish	1,437	2.17
Portuguese	14	0.02
Romanian	120	0.18
Russian	221	0.33
Scandinavian	24	0.04
Scotch-Irish	382	0.58
Scottish	661	1.00
Serbian	57	0.09
Slavic	25	0.04
Slovak	18	0.03
Slovene	34	0.05
Swedish	239	0.36
Swiss	31	0.05
Ukrainian	87	0.13
United States or American	2,550	3.84
Welsh	195	0.29

Notes: 1. Figures in the "Number" column do not add up to the total population due to: a) Ancestry/Race overlap — e.g. persons can report being both White and Irish, b) persons of Hispanic origin can report being any race, c) persons reporting two ancestries are counted in both categories. 2. Numbers in parentheses indicate the number of persons reporting this ancestry/race alone, not in combination with any other ancestry/race. 3. Refer to the Explanation of Data in the front of the book for more detailed information.

Ancestry/Race	Number	%
West Indian, excl. Hispanic:	151	0.23
Barbadian	15	0.02
British West Indian	9	0.01
Jamaican	110	0.17
West Indian	17	0.03
White:	27,733	41.81
Not Hispanic (22,875)	24,139	36.39
Hispanic (3,059)	3,594	5.42
Yugoslavian	7	0.01

Port Huron

Place Type: City
County: Saint Clair
Population: 32,338

Ancestry/Race	Number	%
African American/Black:	2,959	9.15
Not Hispanic (2,451)	2,840	8.78
Hispanic (53)	119	0.37
African, sub-Saharan:	181	0.56
African	181	0.56
Am. Ind. or Alaska Nat., not spec.	197	0.61
American Indian tribes, specified:	389	1.20
Apache (10)	12	0.04
Blackfeet (6)	23	0.07
Cherokee (26)	74	0.23
Chickasaw (1)	5	0.02
Chippewa (87)	143	0.44
Choctaw	4	0.01
Comanche (1)	6	0.02
Cree	3	0.01
Delaware (2)	2	0.01
Iroquois (8)	24	0.07
Latin American Indians (11)	18	0.06
Lumbee (1)	1	0.00
Navajo (3)	3	0.01
Ottawa (10)	14	0.04
Pima (8)	13	0.04
Potawatomi (2)	5	0.02
Seminole	2	0.01
Shoshone	1	0.00
Sioux (6)	8	0.02
All other tribes (18)	28	0.09
American Indian tribes, not spec.	17	0.05
Arab:	208	0.64
Arab/Arabic	16	0.05
Egyptian	3	0.01
Iraqi	4	0.01
Lebanese	90	0.28
Syrian	75	0.23
Other Arab	20	0.06
Asian:	251	0.78
Cambodian (3)	7	0.02
Chinese, ex. Taiwanese (46)	57	0.18
Filipino (41)	56	0.17
Indian (29)	44	0.14
Japanese (6)	12	0.04
Korean (13)	16	0.05
Laotian (15)	17	0.05
Pakistani (11)	11	0.03
Thai (3)	9	0.03
Vietnamese (11)	11	0.03
Other Asian, specified	2	0.01
Other Asian, not specified (1)	9	0.03
Austrian	67	0.21
Belgian	186	0.57
British	85	0.26
Bulgarian	15	0.05
Canadian	320	0.99
Croatian	89	0.28
Czech	107	0.33
Czechoslovakian	51	0.16
Danish	106	0.33
Dutch	560	1.73
Eastern European	13	0.04
English	3,419	10.56
European	103	0.32
Finnish	87	0.27
French, except Basque	1,731	5.35
French Canadian	879	2.72
German	7,894	24.39
Greek	68	0.21
Hawaii Native/Pacific Islander:	11	0.03
Polynesian: (1)	2	0.01
Native Hawaiian (1)	2	0.01
Other Pac. Isl., specified	1	0.00
Other Pac. Isl., not spec. (3)	8	0.02
Hispanic or Latino:	1,383	4.28
Central American:	7	0.02
Guatemalan	2	0.01
Nicaraguan	4	0.01
Panamanian	1	0.00
Cuban	14	0.04
Mexican	1,023	3.16
Puerto Rican	82	0.25
South American:	3	0.01
Argentinean	1	0.00
Bolivian	2	0.01
Other Hispanic or Latino	254	0.79
Hungarian	278	0.86
Irish	4,070	12.58
Italian	786	2.43
Lithuanian	19	0.06
Maltese	6	0.02
Northern European	13	0.04
Norwegian	186	0.57
Pennsylvania German	5	0.02
Polish	2,074	6.41
Romanian	110	0.34
Russian	186	0.57
Scandinavian	28	0.09
Scotch-Irish	664	2.05
Scottish	976	3.02
Serbian	17	0.05
Slavic	4	0.01
Slovak	47	0.15
Swedish	159	0.49
Swiss	68	0.21
Turkish	7	0.02
Ukrainian	115	0.36
United States or American	2,042	6.31
Welsh	118	0.36
West Indian, excl. Hispanic:	13	0.04
Jamaican	13	0.04
White:	28,856	89.23
Not Hispanic (27,326)	28,005	86.60
Hispanic (708)	851	2.63
Yugoslavian	58	0.18

Portage

Place Type: City
County: Kalamazoo
Population: 44,897

Ancestry/Race	Number	%
African American/Black:	1,999	4.45
Not Hispanic (1,649)	1,963	4.37
Hispanic (27)	36	0.08
African, sub-Saharan:	142	0.32
African	81	0.18
Ethiopian	20	0.04
Ghanian	15	0.03
Sudanese	20	0.04
Zimbabwean	6	0.01
Alaska Native tribes, specified:	1	0.00
Eskimo (1)	1	0.00
Am. Ind. or Alaska Nat., not spec.	122	0.27
Albanian	7	0.02
American Indian tribes, specified:	314	0.70
Apache (1)	9	0.02
Blackfeet (1)	22	0.05
Cherokee (16)	103	0.23
Chickasaw	2	0.00
Chippewa (29)	65	0.14
Choctaw	2	0.00
Comanche	5	0.01
Creek (2)	4	0.01
Delaware (1)	1	0.00
Iroquois (3)	8	0.02
Latin American Indians (2)	4	0.01
Lumbee	1	0.00
Navajo	5	0.01
Osage	2	0.00
Ottawa (12)	17	0.04
Potawatomi (22)	36	0.08
Pueblo	1	0.00
Seminole	1	0.00
Shoshone (1)	1	0.00
Sioux (2)	11	0.02
All other tribes (4)	14	0.03
American Indian tribes, not spec.	13	0.03
Arab:	160	0.36
Arab/Arabic	21	0.05
Lebanese	74	0.16
Palestinian	10	0.02
Syrian	46	0.10
Other Arab	9	0.02
Armenian	21	0.05
Asian:	1,385	3.08
Cambodian (5)	5	0.01
Chinese, ex. Taiwanese (314)	352	0.78
Filipino (63)	86	0.19
Indian (403)	435	0.97
Indonesian (3)	11	0.02
Japanese (48)	71	0.16
Korean (143)	175	0.39
Malaysian (2)	2	0.00
Pakistani (27)	35	0.08
Sri Lankan (7)	7	0.02
Taiwanese (18)	18	0.04
Thai (9)	18	0.04
Vietnamese (101)	111	0.25
Other Asian, specified (2)	3	0.01
Other Asian, not specified (25)	56	0.12
Assyrian/Chaldean/Syriac	5	0.01
Australian	42	0.09
Austrian	199	0.44
Belgian	95	0.21
Brazilian	6	0.01
British	264	0.59
Bulgarian	19	0.04
Canadian	274	0.61
Celtic	7	0.02
Croatian	180	0.40
Cypriot	5	0.01
Czech	157	0.35
Czechoslovakian	177	0.39
Danish	283	0.63
Dutch	5,388	11.99
Eastern European	58	0.13
English	6,420	14.29
European	478	1.06
Finnish	294	0.65
French, except Basque	1,926	4.29
French Canadian	825	1.84
German	11,566	25.74
Greek	286	0.64
Guyanese	17	0.04
Hawaii Native/Pacific Islander:	26	0.06
Micronesian: (3)	5	0.01
Guamanian/Chamorro (1)	1	0.00
Other Micronesian (2)	4	0.01
Polynesian: (6)	13	0.03
Native Hawaiian (5)	7	0.02
Samoan	5	0.01
Tongan (1)	1	0.00
Other Pac. Isl., not spec.	8	0.02
Hispanic or Latino:	868	1.93
Central American:	25	0.06
Costa Rican	2	0.00
Guatemalan	8	0.02
Honduran	1	0.00
Nicaraguan	3	0.01
Panamanian	9	0.02
Salvadoran	2	0.00
Cuban	26	0.06
Dominican Republic	15	0.03
Mexican	496	1.10

Notes: 1. Figures in the "Number" column do not add up to the total population due to: a) Ancestry/Race overlap — e.g. persons can report being both White and Irish, b) persons of Hispanic origin can report being any race, c) persons reporting two ancestries are counted in both categories. 2. Numbers in parentheses indicate the number of persons reporting this ancestry/race alone, not in combination with any other ancestry/race. 3. Refer to the Explanation of Data in the front of the book for more detailed information.

Puerto Rican	63	0.14
South American:	61	0.14
Argentinean	7	0.02
Bolivian	1	0.00
Chilean	5	0.01
Colombian	15	0.03
Ecuadorian	5	0.01
Peruvian	7	0.02
Venezuelan	14	0.03
Other South American	7	0.02
Other Hispanic or Latino	182	0.41
Hungarian	321	0.71
Iranian	10	0.02
Irish	5,796	12.90
Italian	1,876	4.18
Latvian	54	0.12
Lithuanian	94	0.21
Macedonian	87	0.19
Maltese	4	0.01
Northern European	19	0.04
Norwegian	737	1.64
Pennsylvania German	45	0.10
Polish	2,842	6.33
Portuguese	65	0.14
Romanian	53	0.12
Russian	300	0.67
Scandinavian	62	0.14
Scotch-Irish	813	1.81
Scottish	1,169	2.60
Serbian	18	0.04
Slavic	46	0.10
Slovak	191	0.43
Slovene	23	0.05
Swedish	954	2.12
Swiss	103	0.23
Turkish	15	0.03
Ukrainian	89	0.20
United States or American	2,411	5.37
Welsh	189	0.42
West Indian, excl. Hispanic:	64	0.14
Bahamian	56	0.12
Trinidadian and Tobagonian	8	0.02
White:	41,507	92.45
Not Hispanic (40,220)	40,918	91.14
Hispanic (526)	589	1.31
Yugoslavian	52	0.12

Redford

Place Type: Census Designated Place
County: Wayne
Population: 51,622

Ancestry/Race	Number	%
African American/Black:	4,692	9.09
Not Hispanic (4,383)	4,655	9.02
Hispanic (27)	37	0.07
African, sub-Saharan:	210	0.41
African	192	0.37
Liberian	18	0.03
Alaska Native tribes, specified:	5	0.01
Aleut	1	0.00
Eskimo (4)	4	0.01
Am. Ind. or Alaska Nat., not spec.	151	0.29
Albanian	26	0.05
Alsatian	37	0.07
American Indian tribes, specified:	334	0.65
Apache (3)	7	0.01
Blackfeet (6)	18	0.03
Cherokee (19)	105	0.20
Chippewa (63)	100	0.19
Choctaw	6	0.01
Crow (1)	1	0.00
Iroquois (32)	53	0.10
Latin American Indians (5)	7	0.01
Lumbee	3	0.01
Menominee	1	0.00
Navajo	2	0.00
Ottawa (2)	5	0.01
Potawatomi (2)	4	0.01
Shoshone	1	0.00
Sioux (1)	4	0.01
All other tribes (7)	17	0.03
American Indian tribes, not spec.	20	0.04
Arab:	578	1.12
Arab/Arabic	137	0.27
Egyptian	10	0.02
Iraqi	7	0.01
Jordanian	8	0.02
Lebanese	226	0.44
Palestinian	29	0.06
Syrian	102	0.20
Other Arab	59	0.11
Armenian	235	0.46
Asian:	580	1.12
Bangladeshi	3	0.01
Cambodian (4)	4	0.01
Chinese, ex. Taiwanese (31)	57	0.11
Filipino (83)	137	0.27
Indian (132)	146	0.28
Indonesian	4	0.01
Japanese (29)	45	0.09
Korean (41)	75	0.15
Laotian (5)	7	0.01
Malaysian (1)	1	0.00
Pakistani (11)	12	0.02
Thai (2)	4	0.01
Vietnamese (41)	51	0.10
Other Asian, specified	5	0.01
Other Asian, not specified (3)	29	0.06
Assyrian/Chaldean/Syriac	20	0.04
Austrian	202	0.39
Belgian	245	0.47
British	181	0.35
Canadian	487	0.94
Celtic	18	0.03
Croatian	158	0.31
Czech	182	0.35
Czechoslovakian	93	0.18
Danish	272	0.53
Dutch	1,047	2.03
English	5,506	10.67
European	195	0.38
Finnish	963	1.87
French, except Basque	2,720	5.27
French Canadian	1,609	3.12
German	11,031	21.37
Greek	514	1.00
Hawaii Native/Pacific Islander:	35	0.07
Micronesian: (1)	3	0.01
Guamanian/Chamorro (1)	3	0.01
Polynesian: (6)	16	0.03
Native Hawaiian (3)	11	0.02
Samoan (2)	2	0.00
Tongan (1)	3	0.01
Other Pac. Isl., specified	5	0.01
Other Pac. Isl., not spec. (3)	11	0.02
Hispanic or Latino:	1,044	2.02
Central American:	21	0.04
Costa Rican	1	0.00
Guatemalan	5	0.01
Honduran	1	0.00
Nicaraguan	6	0.01
Panamanian	3	0.01
Salvadoran	4	0.01
Other Central American	1	0.00
Cuban	19	0.04
Dominican Republic	7	0.01
Mexican	721	1.40
Puerto Rican	93	0.18
South American:	29	0.06
Argentinean	1	0.00
Chilean	8	0.02
Colombian	16	0.03
Ecuadorian	1	0.00
Peruvian	2	0.00
Other South American	1	0.00
Other Hispanic or Latino	154	0.30
Hungarian	886	1.72
Icelander	8	0.02
Irish	8,452	16.37
Italian	3,606	6.99
Latvian	81	0.16
Lithuanian	340	0.66
Macedonian	40	0.08
Maltese	251	0.49
Northern European	15	0.03
Norwegian	355	0.69
Pennsylvania German	36	0.07
Polish	7,787	15.08
Portuguese	30	0.06
Romanian	221	0.43
Russian	463	0.90
Scandinavian	107	0.21
Scotch-Irish	1,342	2.60
Scottish	2,040	3.95
Serbian	55	0.11
Slavic	57	0.11
Slovak	176	0.34
Slovene	54	0.10
Swedish	691	1.34
Swiss	69	0.13
Turkish	12	0.02
Ukrainian	410	0.79
United States or American	2,533	4.91
Welsh	413	0.80
West Indian, excl. Hispanic:	22	0.04
Jamaican	10	0.02
Trinidadian and Tobagonian	5	0.01
West Indian	7	0.01
White:	46,231	89.56
Not Hispanic (44,731)	45,469	88.08
Hispanic (687)	762	1.48
Yugoslavian	69	0.13

Riverview

Place Type: City
County: Wayne
Population: 13,272

Ancestry/Race	Number	%
African American/Black:	314	2.37
Not Hispanic (275)	311	2.34
Hispanic (1)	3	0.02
African, sub-Saharan:	21	0.16
African	21	0.16
Am. Ind. or Alaska Nat., not spec.	17	0.13
Albanian	22	0.17
American Indian tribes, specified:	94	0.71
Blackfeet (1)	4	0.03
Cherokee (14)	34	0.26
Chippewa (14)	22	0.17
Choctaw	1	0.01
Cree	1	0.01
Delaware	1	0.01
Iroquois (5)	8	0.06
Lumbee (4)	4	0.03
Navajo (1)	1	0.01
Osage (1)	1	0.01
Ottawa (1)	1	0.01
Potawatomi	3	0.02
Sioux (5)	7	0.05
All other tribes	6	0.05
American Indian tribes, not spec.	5	0.04
Arab:	54	0.41
Arab/Arabic	27	0.20
Egyptian	13	0.10
Lebanese	6	0.05
Syrian	8	0.06
Armenian	49	0.37
Asian:	290	2.19
Chinese, ex. Taiwanese (32)	34	0.26
Filipino (35)	41	0.31
Indian (91)	100	0.75
Japanese (31)	35	0.26
Korean (24)	30	0.23
Pakistani (18)	29	0.22
Vietnamese (6)	6	0.05
Other Asian, not specified (4)	15	0.11

Notes: 1. Figures in the "Number" column do not add up to the total population due to: a) Ancestry/Race overlap — e.g. persons can report being both White and Irish, b) persons of Hispanic origin can report being any race, c) persons reporting two ancestries are counted in both categories. 2. Numbers in parentheses indicate the number of persons reporting this ancestry/race alone, not in combination with any other ancestry/race. 3. Refer to the Explanation of Data in the front of the book for more detailed information.

Ancestry/Race	Number	%
Austrian	13	0.10
Belgian	54	0.41
Brazilian	5	0.04
British	87	0.66
Canadian	87	0.66
Croatian	49	0.37
Czech	33	0.25
Czechoslovakian	34	0.26
Danish	10	0.08
Dutch	142	1.07
English	1,411	10.63
European	16	0.12
Finnish	41	0.31
French, except Basque	1,048	7.90
French Canadian	281	2.12
German	2,767	20.85
Greek	240	1.81
Hawaii Native/Pacific Islander:	6	0.05
Polynesian: (2)	4	0.03
Native Hawaiian (2)	4	0.03
Other Pac. Isl., not spec.	2	0.02
Hispanic or Latino:	327	2.46
Cuban	4	0.03
Mexican	251	1.89
Puerto Rican	20	0.15
South American:	11	0.08
Argentinean	1	0.01
Chilean	2	0.02
Colombian	8	0.06
Other Hispanic or Latino	41	0.31
Hungarian	770	5.80
Iranian	4	0.03
Irish	1,994	15.02
Italian	1,241	9.35
Lithuanian	114	0.86
Maltese	77	0.58
Norwegian	205	1.54
Pennsylvania German	20	0.15
Polish	1,767	13.31
Romanian	87	0.66
Russian	115	0.87
Scotch-Irish	225	1.70
Scottish	335	2.52
Serbian	45	0.34
Slavic	9	0.07
Slovak	79	0.60
Slovene	19	0.14
Swedish	64	0.48
Swiss	22	0.17
Ukrainian	67	0.50
United States or American	705	5.31
Welsh	71	0.53
White:	12,638	95.22
Not Hispanic (12,227)	12,349	93.05
Hispanic (270)	289	2.18
Yugoslavian	7	0.05

Rochester Hills

Place Type: City
County: Oakland
Population: 68,825

Ancestry/Race	Number	%
African American/Black:	1,850	2.69
Not Hispanic (1,650)	1,819	2.64
Hispanic (17)	31	0.05
African, sub-Saharan:	164	0.24
African	72	0.10
Kenyan	28	0.04
Nigerian	14	0.02
South African	33	0.05
Other sub-Saharan African	17	0.02
Am. Ind. or Alaska Nat., not spec.	124	0.18
Albanian	302	0.44
American Indian tribes, specified:	264	0.38
Apache (1)	2	0.00
Blackfeet (2)	5	0.01
Cherokee (22)	87	0.13
Chickasaw (2)	4	0.01
Chippewa (27)	56	0.08
Choctaw (2)	6	0.01
Comanche (1)	1	0.00
Cree	4	0.01
Creek (1)	1	0.00
Crow (1)	1	0.00
Delaware (1)	1	0.00
Iroquois (6)	16	0.02
Latin American Indians (6)	9	0.01
Lumbee (2)	8	0.01
Navajo (2)	2	0.00
Ottawa (2)	6	0.01
Potawatomi (4)	10	0.01
Pueblo	1	0.00
Seminole (1)	2	0.00
Sioux	7	0.01
Tohono O'Odham (1)	1	0.00
All other tribes (13)	34	0.05
American Indian tribes, not spec.	25	0.04
Arab:	1,137	1.65
Arab/Arabic	126	0.18
Egyptian	77	0.11
Iraqi	125	0.18
Jordanian	49	0.07
Lebanese	619	0.90
Syrian	124	0.18
Other Arab	17	0.02
Armenian	93	0.14
Asian:	5,063	7.36
Bangladeshi (9)	12	0.02
Cambodian (4)	4	0.01
Chinese, ex. Taiwanese (1,122)	1,223	1.78
Filipino (260)	326	0.47
Hmong (11)	24	0.03
Indian (2,087)	2,169	3.15
Indonesian (5)	9	0.01
Japanese (232)	303	0.44
Korean (401)	441	0.64
Laotian (11)	13	0.02
Malaysian (6)	10	0.01
Pakistani (141)	154	0.22
Sri Lankan (23)	29	0.04
Taiwanese (121)	145	0.21
Thai (32)	38	0.06
Vietnamese (90)	99	0.14
Other Asian, specified (7)	8	0.01
Other Asian, not specified (25)	56	0.08
Assyrian/Chaldean/Syriac	265	0.38
Australian	14	0.02
Austrian	429	0.62
Belgian	603	0.88
Brazilian	15	0.02
British	429	0.62
Bulgarian	45	0.07
Canadian	593	0.86
Celtic	5	0.01
Croatian	372	0.54
Czech	247	0.36
Czechoslovakian	287	0.42
Danish	397	0.58
Dutch	1,359	1.97
Eastern European	40	0.06
English	9,322	13.54
Estonian	10	0.01
European	507	0.74
Finnish	486	0.71
French, except Basque	3,587	5.21
French Canadian	1,355	1.97
German	15,852	23.03
Greek	461	0.67
Guyanese	4	0.01
Hawaii Native/Pacific Islander:	53	0.08
Melanesian:	1	0.00
Other Melanesian	1	0.00
Micronesian: (4)	9	0.01
Guamanian/Chamorro (4)	8	0.01
Other Micronesian	1	0.00
Polynesian: (8)	21	0.03
Native Hawaiian (4)	16	0.02
Samoan (3)	4	0.01
Other Polynesian (1)	1	0.00
Other Pac. Isl., not spec. (8)	22	0.03
Hispanic or Latino:	1,576	2.29
Central American:	38	0.06
Costa Rican	5	0.01
Guatemalan	9	0.01
Honduran	5	0.01
Nicaraguan	2	0.00
Panamanian	12	0.02
Salvadoran	5	0.01
Cuban	47	0.07
Dominican Republic	5	0.01
Mexican	925	1.34
Puerto Rican	157	0.23
South American:	163	0.24
Argentinean	87	0.13
Bolivian	4	0.01
Chilean	13	0.02
Colombian	32	0.05
Ecuadorian	6	0.01
Peruvian	5	0.01
Venezuelan	15	0.02
Other South American	1	0.00
Other Hispanic or Latino	241	0.35
Hungarian	611	0.89
Icelander	24	0.03
Iranian	82	0.12
Irish	9,712	14.11
Israeli	7	0.01
Italian	6,217	9.03
Latvian	13	0.02
Lithuanian	257	0.37
Macedonian	89	0.13
Maltese	129	0.19
Northern European	20	0.03
Norwegian	899	1.31
Pennsylvania German	6	0.01
Polish	8,482	12.32
Portuguese	32	0.05
Romanian	393	0.57
Russian	618	0.90
Scandinavian	67	0.10
Scotch-Irish	1,128	1.64
Scottish	2,251	3.27
Serbian	108	0.16
Slavic	51	0.07
Slovak	336	0.49
Slovene	56	0.08
Swedish	1,079	1.57
Swiss	416	0.60
Turkish	52	0.08
Ukrainian	697	1.01
United States or American	2,625	3.81
Welsh	625	0.91
West Indian, excl. Hispanic:	20	0.03
Haitian	17	0.02
Jamaican	3	0.00
White:	61,957	90.02
Not Hispanic (59,917)	60,699	88.19
Hispanic (1,167)	1,258	1.83
Yugoslavian	184	0.27

Rochester

Place Type: City
County: Oakland
Population: 10,467

Ancestry/Race	Number	%
African American/Black:	253	2.42
Not Hispanic (231)	247	2.36
Hispanic (3)	6	0.06
African, sub-Saharan:	9	0.09
Other sub-Saharan African	9	0.09
Am. Ind. or Alaska Nat., not spec.	11	0.11
Albanian	27	0.26
American Indian tribes, specified:	37	0.35
Cherokee (9)	18	0.17
Cheyenne	1	0.01
Chippewa (10)	11	0.11

Notes: 1. Figures in the "Number" column do not add up to the total population due to: a) Ancestry/Race overlap — e.g. persons can report being both White and Irish, b) persons of Hispanic origin can report being any race, c) persons reporting two ancestries are counted in both categories. 2. Numbers in parentheses indicate the number of persons reporting this ancestry/race alone, not in combination with any other ancestry/race. 3. Refer to the Explanation of Data in the front of the book for more detailed information.

Ancestry/Race	Number	%
Comanche	3	0.03
Cree	1	0.01
Creek	1	0.01
Latin American Indians (1)	2	0.02
American Indian tribes, not spec.	6	0.06
Arab:	204	1.95
Arab/Arabic	5	0.05
Egyptian	23	0.22
Iraqi	48	0.46
Jordanian	21	0.20
Lebanese	64	0.61
Moroccan	6	0.06
Palestinian	6	0.06
Syrian	31	0.30
Armenian	21	0.20
Asian:	451	4.31
Chinese, ex. Taiwanese (72)	81	0.77
Filipino (35)	49	0.47
Indian (148)	157	1.50
Japanese (15)	22	0.21
Korean (71)	75	0.72
Pakistani (14)	14	0.13
Sri Lankan (1)	1	0.01
Taiwanese (6)	6	0.06
Thai (1)	1	0.01
Vietnamese (13)	19	0.18
Other Asian, specified (1)	4	0.04
Other Asian, not specified (7)	22	0.21
Assyrian/Chaldean/Syriac	8	0.08
Austrian	43	0.41
Belgian	163	1.56
British	85	0.81
Canadian	109	1.04
Croatian	29	0.28
Czech	68	0.65
Czechoslovakian	51	0.49
Danish	89	0.85
Dutch	316	3.02
English	1,578	15.08
Estonian	26	0.25
European	17	0.16
Finnish	104	0.99
French, except Basque	613	5.86
French Canadian	209	2.00
German	2,640	25.22
Greek	96	0.92
Hawaii Native/Pacific Islander:	7	0.07
Polynesian:	4	0.04
Native Hawaiian	2	0.02
Samoan	2	0.02
Other Pac. Isl., specified	2	0.02
Other Pac. Isl., not spec. (1)	1	0.01
Hispanic or Latino:	176	1.68
Central American:	4	0.04
Nicaraguan	3	0.03
Panamanian	1	0.01
Cuban	3	0.03
Mexican	101	0.96
Puerto Rican	10	0.10
South American:	20	0.19
Argentinean	2	0.02
Chilean	2	0.02
Colombian	5	0.05
Peruvian	3	0.03
Venezuelan	8	0.08
Other Hispanic or Latino	38	0.36
Hungarian	199	1.90
Iranian	10	0.10
Irish	1,511	14.44
Italian	748	7.15
Latvian	13	0.12
Lithuanian	48	0.46
Macedonian	12	0.11
Maltese	53	0.51
Northern European	13	0.12
Norwegian	131	1.25
Polish	1,391	13.29
Romanian	32	0.31
Russian	135	1.29
Scandinavian	16	0.15
Scotch-Irish	122	1.17
Scottish	599	5.72
Serbian	13	0.12
Slavic	8	0.08
Slovak	100	0.96
Swedish	352	3.36
Swiss	59	0.56
Ukrainian	65	0.62
United States or American	336	3.21
Welsh	98	0.94
White:	9,791	93.54
Not Hispanic (9,537)	9,643	92.13
Hispanic (133)	148	1.41
Yugoslavian	39	0.37

Romulus

Place Type: City
County: Wayne
Population: 22,979

Ancestry/Race	Number	%
Acadian/Cajun	5	0.02
African American/Black:	7,249	31.55
Not Hispanic (6,854)	7,197	31.32
Hispanic (37)	52	0.23
African, sub-Saharan:	286	1.24
African	235	1.02
Nigerian	46	0.20
Other sub-Saharan African	5	0.02
Am. Ind. or Alaska Nat., not spec.	146	0.64
Albanian	28	0.12
American Indian tribes, specified:	191	0.83
Apache (1)	2	0.01
Blackfeet (5)	19	0.08
Cherokee (23)	82	0.36
Chickasaw	2	0.01
Chippewa (18)	33	0.14
Choctaw	8	0.03
Cree (1)	1	0.00
Creek (4)	5	0.02
Crow	1	0.00
Iroquois (4)	7	0.03
Latin American Indians (1)	1	0.00
Lumbee (4)	5	0.02
Osage	1	0.00
Ottawa (2)	3	0.01
Potawatomi (2)	7	0.03
Pueblo (1)	1	0.00
Seminole (2)	2	0.01
Sioux	3	0.01
All other tribes (3)	8	0.03
American Indian tribes, not spec.	13	0.06
Arab:	47	0.20
Arab/Arabic	12	0.05
Lebanese	28	0.12
Syrian	7	0.03
Armenian	9	0.04
Asian:	205	0.89
Chinese, ex. Taiwanese (5)	15	0.07
Filipino (53)	65	0.28
Indian (17)	24	0.10
Indonesian	1	0.00
Japanese (9)	27	0.12
Korean (7)	10	0.04
Malaysian (1)	1	0.00
Pakistani (33)	33	0.14
Taiwanese (1)	1	0.00
Thai (3)	9	0.04
Vietnamese (4)	8	0.03
Other Asian, specified	5	0.02
Other Asian, not specified	6	0.03
Austrian	41	0.18
Basque	6	0.03
Belgian	27	0.12
British	52	0.23
Canadian	110	0.48
Croatian	26	0.11
Czech	15	0.07
Czechoslovakian	29	0.13
Danish	19	0.08
Dutch	308	1.34
Eastern European	5	0.02
English	1,192	5.19
European	47	0.20
Finnish	158	0.69
French, except Basque	873	3.80
French Canadian	565	2.46
German	3,742	16.28
Greek	63	0.27
Hawaii Native/Pacific Islander:	39	0.17
Micronesian:	2	0.01
Guamanian/Chamorro	2	0.01
Polynesian: (16)	27	0.12
Native Hawaiian (12)	19	0.08
Samoan (4)	8	0.03
Other Pac. Isl., specified	5	0.02
Other Pac. Isl., not spec. (1)	5	0.02
Hispanic or Latino:	463	2.01
Central American:	13	0.06
Costa Rican	1	0.00
Guatemalan	7	0.03
Panamanian	2	0.01
Salvadoran	3	0.01
Cuban	8	0.03
Dominican Republic	2	0.01
Mexican	297	1.29
Puerto Rican	56	0.24
South American:	6	0.03
Bolivian	5	0.02
Colombian	1	0.00
Other Hispanic or Latino	81	0.35
Hungarian	292	1.27
Irish	2,037	8.86
Italian	660	2.87
Lithuanian	50	0.22
Macedonian	11	0.05
Maltese	19	0.08
Northern European	7	0.03
Norwegian	117	0.51
Pennsylvania German	14	0.06
Polish	2,060	8.96
Portuguese	59	0.26
Romanian	32	0.14
Russian	37	0.16
Scandinavian	5	0.02
Scotch-Irish	319	1.39
Scottish	307	1.34
Slavic	17	0.07
Slovak	10	0.04
Swedish	116	0.50
Swiss	6	0.03
Ukrainian	97	0.42
United States or American	1,241	5.40
Welsh	96	0.42
West Indian, excl. Hispanic:	44	0.19
Haitian	19	0.08
Jamaican	18	0.08
West Indian	7	0.03
White:	15,542	67.64
Not Hispanic (14,773)	15,256	66.39
Hispanic (246)	286	1.24
Yugoslavian	20	0.09

Roseville

Place Type: City
County: Macomb
Population: 48,129

Ancestry/Race	Number	%
African American/Black:	1,426	2.96
Not Hispanic (1,247)	1,413	2.94
Hispanic (5)	13	0.03
African, sub-Saharan:	59	0.12
African	59	0.12
Alaska Native tribes, specified:	2	0.00
Aleut	1	0.00
Eskimo (1)	1	0.00
Am. Ind. or Alaska Nat., not spec.	148	0.31

Notes: 1. Figures in the "Number" column do not add up to the total population due to: a) Ancestry/Race overlap — e.g. persons can report being both White and Irish, b) persons of Hispanic origin can report being any race, c) persons reporting two ancestries are counted in both categories. 2. Numbers in parentheses indicate the number of persons reporting this ancestry/race alone, not in combination with any other ancestry/race. 3. Refer to the Explanation of Data in the front of the book for more detailed information.

Albanian	262	0.54
American Indian tribes, specified:	395	0.82
Apache (8)	11	0.02
Blackfeet (1)	33	0.07
Cherokee (33)	151	0.31
Chippewa (42)	81	0.17
Choctaw (2)	5	0.01
Comanche (1)	2	0.00
Creek (1)	4	0.01
Iroquois (11)	23	0.05
Latin American Indians (1)	3	0.01
Lumbee (16)	24	0.05
Menominee	1	0.00
Navajo (2)	3	0.01
Ottawa (7)	15	0.03
Pima	2	0.00
Potawatomi (1)	8	0.02
Pueblo (2)	2	0.00
Seminole (2)	3	0.01
Sioux	6	0.01
Tohono O'Odham	2	0.00
All other tribes (5)	16	0.03
American Indian tribes, not spec.	11	0.02
Arab:	626	1.30
Arab/Arabic	63	0.13
Iraqi	6	0.01
Jordanian	5	0.01
Lebanese	406	0.84
Palestinian	24	0.05
Syrian	122	0.25
Armenian	36	0.07
Asian:	932	1.94
Cambodian (10)	10	0.02
Chinese, ex. Taiwanese (97)	112	0.23
Filipino (118)	151	0.31
Hmong (41)	50	0.10
Indian (300)	317	0.66
Japanese (15)	42	0.09
Korean (33)	58	0.12
Laotian (35)	38	0.08
Pakistani (34)	37	0.08
Taiwanese (2)	4	0.01
Thai (15)	20	0.04
Vietnamese (57)	63	0.13
Other Asian, specified (4)	6	0.01
Other Asian, not specified (15)	24	0.05
Assyrian/Chaldean/Syriac	22	0.05
Australian	6	0.01
Austrian	150	0.31
Belgian	1,002	2.08
Brazilian	11	0.02
British	128	0.27
Bulgarian	4	0.01
Canadian	239	0.50
Croatian	95	0.20
Czech	82	0.17
Czechoslovakian	115	0.24
Danish	138	0.29
Dutch	512	1.06
Eastern European	4	0.01
English	3,652	7.59
European	64	0.13
Finnish	185	0.38
French, except Basque	3,422	7.11
French Canadian	1,527	3.17
German	11,792	24.50
Greek	395	0.82
Guyanese	6	0.01
Hawaii Native/Pacific Islander:	35	0.07
Micronesian: (6)	7	0.01
Guamanian/Chamorro (6)	7	0.01
Polynesian: (3)	20	0.04
Native Hawaiian (2)	16	0.03
Samoan (1)	4	0.01
Other Pac. Isl., specified	1	0.00
Other Pac. Isl., not spec. (6)	7	0.01
Hispanic or Latino:	722	1.50
Central American:	11	0.02
Guatemalan	2	0.00
Nicaraguan	1	0.00
Panamanian	4	0.01
Salvadoran	3	0.01
Other Central American	1	0.00
Cuban	41	0.09
Dominican Republic	8	0.02
Mexican	462	0.96
Puerto Rican	61	0.13
South American:	24	0.05
Argentinean	3	0.01
Colombian	4	0.01
Ecuadorian	7	0.01
Peruvian	6	0.01
Venezuelan	4	0.01
Other Hispanic or Latino	115	0.24
Hungarian	483	1.00
Iranian	10	0.02
Irish	6,443	13.39
Italian	6,930	14.40
Lithuanian	180	0.37
Macedonian	12	0.02
Maltese	103	0.21
Northern European	10	0.02
Norwegian	153	0.32
Pennsylvania German	20	0.04
Polish	9,549	19.84
Portuguese	9	0.02
Romanian	285	0.59
Russian	405	0.84
Scandinavian	17	0.04
Scotch-Irish	584	1.21
Scottish	1,113	2.31
Serbian	78	0.16
Slavic	38	0.08
Slovak	209	0.43
Swedish	404	0.84
Swiss	38	0.08
Turkish	9	0.02
Ukrainian	284	0.59
United States or American	1,785	3.71
Welsh	234	0.49
West Indian, excl. Hispanic:	52	0.11
Bahamian	15	0.03
British West Indian	5	0.01
Jamaican	10	0.02
Trinidadian and Tobagonian	22	0.05
White:	45,679	94.91
Not Hispanic (44,477)	45,110	93.73
Hispanic (491)	569	1.18
Yugoslavian	164	0.34

Royal Oak

Place Type: City
County: Oakland
Population: 60,062

Ancestry/Race	Number	%
African American/Black:	1,076	1.79
Not Hispanic (910)	1,045	1.74
Hispanic (17)	31	0.05
African, sub-Saharan:	171	0.28
African	126	0.21
Nigerian	11	0.02
South African	34	0.06
Am. Ind. or Alaska Nat., not spec.	138	0.23
Albanian	370	0.62
Alsatian	9	0.01
American Indian tribes, specified:	276	0.46
Apache (2)	2	0.00
Blackfeet	11	0.02
Cherokee (25)	102	0.17
Cheyenne (1)	1	0.00
Chippewa (37)	67	0.11
Choctaw (1)	3	0.00
Comanche (1)	2	0.00
Cree	2	0.00
Creek	2	0.00
Delaware	2	0.00
Iroquois (6)	13	0.02
Latin American Indians (8)	15	0.02
Lumbee (1)	2	0.00
Menominee	1	0.00
Navajo (1)	4	0.01
Osage	1	0.00
Ottawa (4)	10	0.02
Potawatomi	6	0.01
Seminole (1)	4	0.01
Sioux (5)	11	0.02
All other tribes (5)	15	0.02
American Indian tribes, not spec.	23	0.04
Arab:	792	1.32
Arab/Arabic	156	0.26
Egyptian	54	0.09
Iraqi	109	0.18
Jordanian	10	0.02
Lebanese	293	0.49
Moroccan	21	0.03
Palestinian	26	0.04
Syrian	104	0.17
Other Arab	19	0.03
Armenian	259	0.43
Asian:	1,185	1.97
Bangladeshi (6)	6	0.01
Cambodian (9)	12	0.02
Chinese, ex. Taiwanese (184)	212	0.35
Filipino (175)	235	0.39
Hmong (2)	2	0.00
Indian (259)	291	0.48
Indonesian (2)	3	0.00
Japanese (60)	102	0.17
Korean (108)	137	0.23
Laotian (3)	3	0.00
Pakistani (20)	26	0.04
Sri Lankan (5)	6	0.01
Taiwanese (4)	5	0.01
Thai (5)	6	0.01
Vietnamese (63)	70	0.12
Other Asian, specified (5)	5	0.01
Other Asian, not specified (18)	64	0.11
Assyrian/Chaldean/Syriac	206	0.34
Australian	31	0.05
Austrian	219	0.36
Belgian	364	0.61
Brazilian	21	0.03
British	464	0.77
Bulgarian	42	0.07
Canadian	604	1.01
Celtic	38	0.06
Croatian	276	0.46
Czech	229	0.38
Czechoslovakian	133	0.22
Danish	367	0.61
Dutch	1,479	2.46
Eastern European	50	0.08
English	8,773	14.61
Estonian	15	0.02
European	552	0.92
Finnish	802	1.34
French, except Basque	3,083	5.13
French Canadian	1,456	2.42
German	13,754	22.90
German Russian	9	0.01
Greek	443	0.74
Hawaii Native/Pacific Islander:	67	0.11
Micronesian: (14)	14	0.02
Guamanian/Chamorro (10)	10	0.02
Other Micronesian (4)	4	0.01
Polynesian: (12)	27	0.04
Native Hawaiian (3)	18	0.03
Samoan (8)	8	0.01
Other Polynesian (1)	1	0.00
Other Pac. Isl., not spec. (6)	26	0.04
Hispanic or Latino:	781	1.30
Central American:	33	0.05
Costa Rican	2	0.00
Guatemalan	4	0.01
Honduran	2	0.00
Nicaraguan	5	0.01
Panamanian	12	0.02
Salvadoran	6	0.01

Notes: 1. Figures in the "Number" column do not add up to the total population due to: a) Ancestry/Race overlap — e.g. persons can report being both White and Irish, b) persons of Hispanic origin can report being any race, c) persons reporting two ancestries are counted in both categories. 2. Numbers in parentheses indicate the number of persons reporting this ancestry/race alone, not in combination with any other ancestry/race. 3. Refer to the Explanation of Data in the front of the book for more detailed information.

Ancestry/Race	Number	%
Other Central American	2	0.00
Cuban	32	0.05
Dominican Republic	1	0.00
Mexican	429	0.71
Puerto Rican	65	0.11
South American:	80	0.13
Argentinean	14	0.02
Bolivian	5	0.01
Chilean	7	0.01
Colombian	25	0.04
Ecuadorian	9	0.01
Paraguayan	1	0.00
Peruvian	10	0.02
Venezuelan	6	0.01
Other South American	3	0.00
Other Hispanic or Latino	141	0.23
Hungarian	678	1.13
Iranian	50	0.08
Irish	10,256	17.08
Israeli	9	0.01
Italian	4,565	7.60
Latvian	40	0.07
Lithuanian	372	0.62
Macedonian	70	0.12
Maltese	166	0.28
Northern European	60	0.10
Norwegian	579	0.96
Pennsylvania German	23	0.04
Polish	6,987	11.63
Portuguese	64	0.11
Romanian	338	0.56
Russian	936	1.56
Scandinavian	156	0.26
Scotch-Irish	1,533	2.55
Scottish	2,738	4.56
Serbian	150	0.25
Slavic	15	0.02
Slovak	333	0.55
Slovene	47	0.08
Swedish	1,334	2.22
Swiss	200	0.33
Turkish	39	0.06
Ukrainian	638	1.06
United States or American	2,374	3.95
Welsh	517	0.86
West Indian, excl. Hispanic:	23	0.04
Jamaican	8	0.01
West Indian	15	0.02
White:	57,720	96.10
Not Hispanic (56,421)	57,132	95.12
Hispanic (520)	588	0.98
Yugoslavian	191	0.32

Saginaw Township North

Place Type: Census Designated Place
County: Saginaw
Population: 24,994

Ancestry/Race	Number	%
African American/Black:	1,450	5.80
Not Hispanic (1,319)	1,419	5.68
Hispanic (19)	31	0.12
African, sub-Saharan:	31	0.12
African	17	0.07
Ethiopian	7	0.03
Nigerian	7	0.03
Alaska Native tribes, specified:	3	0.01
Eskimo	2	0.01
Tlingit-Haida (1)	1	0.00
Am. Ind. or Alaska Nat., not spec.	48	0.19
American Indian tribes, specified:	98	0.39
Blackfeet (1)	5	0.02
Cherokee (2)	11	0.04
Chickasaw (1)	1	0.00
Chippewa (26)	54	0.22
Comanche	1	0.00
Delaware	1	0.00
Iroquois (2)	8	0.03
Latin American Indians (3)	5	0.02
Lumbee (1)	1	0.00
Navajo (2)	2	0.01
Ottawa (1)	1	0.00
Potawatomi (1)	2	0.01
Pueblo (1)	1	0.00
Sioux	1	0.00
All other tribes (3)	4	0.02
American Indian tribes, not spec.	6	0.02
Arab:	65	0.26
Arab/Arabic	26	0.10
Jordanian	4	0.02
Lebanese	35	0.14
Armenian	21	0.08
Asian:	868	3.47
Chinese, ex. Taiwanese (146)	169	0.68
Filipino (89)	104	0.42
Indian (274)	289	1.16
Indonesian (6)	9	0.04
Japanese (25)	28	0.11
Korean (105)	109	0.44
Laotian	1	0.00
Pakistani (34)	36	0.14
Sri Lankan (2)	2	0.01
Taiwanese (10)	15	0.06
Thai (13)	17	0.07
Vietnamese (38)	43	0.17
Other Asian, specified (6)	6	0.02
Other Asian, not specified (16)	40	0.16
Assyrian/Chaldean/Syriac	75	0.30
Australian	22	0.09
Austrian	79	0.32
Belgian	86	0.34
Brazilian	13	0.05
British	77	0.31
Canadian	139	0.55
Carpatho Rusyn	2	0.01
Celtic	9	0.04
Croatian	19	0.08
Czech	189	0.75
Czechoslovakian	112	0.45
Danish	79	0.32
Dutch	486	1.94
English	2,633	10.51
European	92	0.37
Finnish	150	0.60
French, except Basque	2,076	8.28
French Canadian	548	2.19
German	8,689	34.67
Greek	227	0.91
Hawaii Native/Pacific Islander:	6	0.02
Polynesian:	2	0.01
Native Hawaiian	2	0.01
Other Pac. Isl., not spec.	4	0.02
Hispanic or Latino:	1,023	4.09
Central American:	1	0.00
Honduran	1	0.00
Cuban	11	0.04
Mexican	768	3.07
Puerto Rican	37	0.15
South American:	16	0.06
Bolivian	2	0.01
Chilean	2	0.01
Colombian	9	0.04
Paraguayan	1	0.00
Venezuelan	1	0.00
Other South American	1	0.00
Other Hispanic or Latino	190	0.76
Hungarian	225	0.90
Iranian	14	0.06
Irish	2,685	10.71
Italian	972	3.88
Latvian	7	0.03
Lithuanian	34	0.14
Maltese	27	0.11
Northern European	36	0.14
Norwegian	168	0.67
Pennsylvania German	17	0.07
Polish	2,851	11.38
Romanian	24	0.10
Russian	211	0.84
Scandinavian	11	0.04
Scotch-Irish	433	1.73
Scottish	781	3.12
Slavic	30	0.12
Slovak	77	0.31
Slovene	13	0.05
Swedish	280	1.12
Swiss	91	0.36
Ukrainian	75	0.30
United States or American	987	3.94
Welsh	243	0.97
West Indian, excl. Hispanic:	8	0.03
Bahamian	8	0.03
White:	22,375	89.52
Not Hispanic (21,501)	21,784	87.16
Hispanic (512)	591	2.36
Yugoslavian	96	0.38

Saginaw Township South

Place Type: Census Designated Place
County: Saginaw
Population: 13,801

Ancestry/Race	Number	%
African American/Black:	799	5.79
Not Hispanic (730)	782	5.67
Hispanic (10)	17	0.12
African, sub-Saharan:	8	0.06
African	8	0.06
Alaska Native tribes, specified:	1	0.01
Tlingit-Haida	1	0.01
Am. Ind. or Alaska Nat., not spec.	22	0.16
American Indian tribes, specified:	41	0.30
Cherokee (1)	6	0.04
Chippewa (12)	15	0.11
Choctaw (2)	6	0.04
Iroquois (4)	5	0.04
Lumbee (1)	2	0.01
Menominee (3)	3	0.02
Ottawa (1)	2	0.01
All other tribes (2)	2	0.01
American Indian tribes, not spec.	4	0.03
Arab:	181	1.31
Egyptian	12	0.09
Iraqi	37	0.27
Lebanese	132	0.96
Asian:	318	2.30
Cambodian (1)	1	0.01
Chinese, ex. Taiwanese (34)	42	0.30
Filipino (25)	34	0.25
Hmong (16)	16	0.12
Indian (97)	101	0.73
Japanese (9)	11	0.08
Korean (55)	59	0.43
Laotian	1	0.01
Pakistani (4)	7	0.05
Taiwanese (6)	8	0.06
Thai (7)	8	0.06
Vietnamese (4)	5	0.04
Other Asian, not specified (12)	25	0.18
Austrian	49	0.36
Belgian	16	0.12
British	51	0.37
Canadian	61	0.44
Croatian	6	0.04
Czech	88	0.64
Czechoslovakian	68	0.49
Danish	58	0.42
Dutch	242	1.76
Eastern European	10	0.07
English	1,439	10.44
European	18	0.13
Finnish	23	0.17
French, except Basque	1,064	7.72
French Canadian	193	1.40
German	4,926	35.73
Greek	165	1.20
Hawaii Native/Pacific Islander:	12	0.09
Micronesian:	1	0.01

Notes: 1. Figures in the "Number" column do not add up to the total population due to: a) Ancestry/Race overlap — e.g. persons can report being both White and Irish, b) persons of Hispanic origin can report being any race, c) persons reporting two ancestries are counted in both categories. 2. Numbers in parentheses indicate the number of persons reporting this ancestry/race alone, not in combination with any other ancestry/race. 3. Refer to the Explanation of Data in the front of the book for more detailed information.

Ancestry/Race	Number	%
Guamanian/Chamorro	1	0.01
Polynesian: (1)	8	0.06
Native Hawaiian (1)	8	0.06
Other Pac. Isl., not spec. (1)	3	0.02
Hispanic or Latino:	609	4.41
Central American:	4	0.03
Costa Rican	3	0.02
Salvadoran	1	0.01
Cuban	6	0.04
Dominican Republic	3	0.02
Mexican	485	3.51
Puerto Rican	16	0.12
South American:	5	0.04
Colombian	2	0.01
Paraguayan	1	0.01
Peruvian	1	0.01
Venezuelan	1	0.01
Other Hispanic or Latino	90	0.65
Hungarian	113	0.82
Iranian	27	0.20
Irish	1,814	13.16
Italian	573	4.16
Latvian	15	0.11
Lithuanian	105	0.76
Norwegian	68	0.49
Pennsylvania German	10	0.07
Polish	1,430	10.37
Romanian	30	0.22
Russian	96	0.70
Scotch-Irish	292	2.12
Scottish	519	3.76
Serbian	9	0.07
Slavic	13	0.09
Slovak	41	0.30
Swedish	145	1.05
Swiss	42	0.30
Ukrainian	5	0.04
United States or American	580	4.21
Welsh	56	0.41
White:	12,566	91.05
Not Hispanic (12,003)	12,142	87.98
Hispanic (398)	424	3.07
Yugoslavian	12	0.09

Saginaw charter

Place Type: Township
County: Saginaw
Population: 39,657

Ancestry/Race	Number	%
African American/Black:	2,267	5.72
Not Hispanic (2,066)	2,219	5.60
Hispanic (29)	48	0.12
African, sub-Saharan:	39	0.10
African	25	0.06
Ethiopian	7	0.02
Nigerian	7	0.02
Alaska Native tribes, specified:	4	0.01
Eskimo	2	0.01
Tlingit-Haida (1)	2	0.01
Am. Ind. or Alaska Nat., not spec.	70	0.18
American Indian tribes, specified:	150	0.38
Blackfeet (1)	5	0.01
Cherokee (3)	19	0.05
Chickasaw (1)	1	0.00
Chippewa (38)	69	0.17
Choctaw (2)	6	0.02
Comanche	1	0.00
Delaware	1	0.00
Iroquois (6)	15	0.04
Latin American Indians (3)	5	0.01
Lumbee (2)	3	0.01
Menominee (3)	3	0.01
Navajo (2)	2	0.01
Ottawa (8)	9	0.02
Potawatomi (1)	2	0.01
Pueblo (1)	1	0.00
Sioux	1	0.00
All other tribes (5)	7	0.02
American Indian tribes, not spec.	10	0.03
Arab:	246	0.62
Arab/Arabic	26	0.07
Egyptian	12	0.03
Iraqi	37	0.09
Jordanian	4	0.01
Lebanese	167	0.42
Armenian	21	0.05
Asian:	1,221	3.08
Cambodian (1)	1	0.00
Chinese, ex. Taiwanese (181)	214	0.54
Filipino (124)	153	0.39
Hmong (16)	16	0.04
Indian (375)	394	0.99
Indonesian (6)	9	0.02
Japanese (34)	39	0.10
Korean (165)	173	0.44
Laotian	2	0.01
Pakistani (38)	43	0.11
Sri Lankan (2)	2	0.01
Taiwanese (16)	23	0.06
Thai (21)	26	0.07
Vietnamese (42)	48	0.12
Other Asian, specified (6)	6	0.02
Other Asian, not specified (28)	72	0.18
Assyrian/Chaldean/Syriac	75	0.19
Australian	22	0.06
Austrian	128	0.32
Belgian	102	0.26
Brazilian	13	0.03
British	128	0.32
Canadian	210	0.53
Carpatho Rusyn	2	0.01
Celtic	9	0.02
Croatian	34	0.09
Czech	277	0.70
Czechoslovakian	180	0.45
Danish	137	0.35
Dutch	743	1.87
Eastern European	10	0.03
English	4,100	10.34
European	110	0.28
Finnish	173	0.44
French, except Basque	3,247	8.19
French Canadian	780	1.97
German	13,834	34.89
Greek	392	0.99
Hawaii Native/Pacific Islander:	18	0.05
Micronesian:	1	0.00
Guamanian/Chamorro	1	0.00
Polynesian: (1)	10	0.03
Native Hawaiian (1)	10	0.03
Other Pac. Isl., not spec. (1)	7	0.02
Hispanic or Latino:	1,652	4.17
Central American:	6	0.02
Costa Rican	3	0.01
Guatemalan	1	0.00
Honduran	1	0.00
Salvadoran	1	0.00
Cuban	18	0.05
Dominican Republic	3	0.01
Mexican	1,265	3.19
Puerto Rican	53	0.13
South American:	21	0.05
Bolivian	2	0.01
Chilean	2	0.01
Colombian	11	0.03
Paraguayan	2	0.01
Peruvian	1	0.00
Venezuelan	2	0.01
Other South American	1	0.00
Other Hispanic or Latino	286	0.72
Hungarian	338	0.85
Iranian	41	0.10
Irish	4,567	11.52
Italian	1,576	3.97
Latvian	22	0.06
Lithuanian	139	0.35
Maltese	27	0.07
Northern European	36	0.09
Norwegian	249	0.63
Pennsylvania German	27	0.07
Polish	4,433	11.18
Romanian	54	0.14
Russian	317	0.80
Scandinavian	11	0.03
Scotch-Irish	725	1.83
Scottish	1,320	3.33
Serbian	9	0.02
Slavic	43	0.11
Slovak	118	0.30
Slovene	13	0.03
Swedish	430	1.08
Swiss	133	0.34
Ukrainian	80	0.20
United States or American	1,582	3.99
Welsh	299	0.75
West Indian, excl. Hispanic:	8	0.02
Bahamian	8	0.02
White:	35,744	90.13
Not Hispanic (34,281)	34,713	87.53
Hispanic (924)	1,031	2.60
Yugoslavian	108	0.27

Saginaw

Place Type: City
County: Saginaw
Population: 61,799

Ancestry/Race	Number	%
African American/Black:	27,718	44.85
Not Hispanic (26,440)	27,201	44.02
Hispanic (295)	517	0.84
African, sub-Saharan:	782	1.26
African	722	1.17
Ethiopian	20	0.03
Nigerian	11	0.02
Sierra Leonean	10	0.02
South African	9	0.01
Other sub-Saharan African	10	0.02
Alaska Native tribes, not specified	3	0.00
Am. Ind. or Alaska Nat., not spec.	328	0.53
American Indian tribes, specified:	402	0.65
Apache (7)	7	0.01
Blackfeet (8)	45	0.07
Cherokee (14)	72	0.12
Cheyenne	4	0.01
Chippewa (93)	182	0.29
Choctaw	4	0.01
Comanche (1)	1	0.00
Cree (3)	3	0.00
Creek	6	0.01
Delaware	1	0.00
Iroquois	7	0.01
Latin American Indians (12)	25	0.04
Navajo (3)	3	0.00
Ottawa (6)	12	0.02
Paiute	1	0.00
Pima (1)	1	0.00
Potawatomi	1	0.00
Pueblo	3	0.00
Seminole	1	0.00
Sioux (4)	7	0.01
Yaqui	3	0.00
Yuman	1	0.00
All other tribes (1)	12	0.02
American Indian tribes, not spec.	36	0.06
Arab:	61	0.10
Arab/Arabic	11	0.02
Lebanese	43	0.07
Syrian	7	0.01
Armenian	8	0.01
Asian:	366	0.59
Bangladeshi (2)	2	0.00
Chinese, ex. Taiwanese (28)	33	0.05
Filipino (24)	49	0.08
Hmong (39)	40	0.06
Indian (26)	65	0.11
Japanese (11)	35	0.06

Notes: 1. Figures in the "Number" column do not add up to the total population due to: a) Ancestry/Race overlap — e.g. persons can report being both White and Irish, b) persons of Hispanic origin can report being any race, c) persons reporting two ancestries are counted in both categories. 2. Numbers in parentheses indicate the number of persons reporting this ancestry/race alone, not in combination with any other ancestry/race. 3. Refer to the Explanation of Data in the front of the book for more detailed information.

Korean (29)	53	0.09
Laotian (13)	17	0.03
Malaysian (1)	1	0.00
Pakistani (1)	2	0.00
Taiwanese	1	0.00
Thai (15)	20	0.03
Vietnamese (9)	16	0.03
Other Asian, specified	5	0.01
Other Asian, not specified (4)	27	0.04
Assyrian/Chaldean/Syriac	24	0.04
Australian	8	0.01
Austrian	46	0.07
Belgian	112	0.18
Brazilian	4	0.01
British	68	0.11
Canadian	93	0.15
Celtic	12	0.02
Croatian	3	0.00
Czech	153	0.25
Czechoslovakian	67	0.11
Danish	89	0.14
Dutch	499	0.81
English	2,960	4.79
European	153	0.25
Finnish	60	0.10
French, except Basque	2,896	4.68
French Canadian	894	1.45
German	9,821	15.88
German Russian	5	0.01
Greek	131	0.21
Guyanese	8	0.01
Hawaii Native/Pacific Islander:	50	0.08
Micronesian: (5)	9	0.01
Guamanian/Chamorro (5)	9	0.01
Polynesian: (4)	6	0.01
Native Hawaiian (4)	5	0.01
Samoan	1	0.00
Other Pac. Isl., specified	5	0.01
Other Pac. Isl., not spec. (1)	30	0.05
Hispanic or Latino:	7,259	11.75
Central American:	12	0.02
Guatemalan	3	0.00
Honduran	4	0.01
Nicaraguan	1	0.00
Panamanian	1	0.00
Salvadoran	3	0.00
Cuban	19	0.03
Mexican	5,780	9.35
Puerto Rican	132	0.21
South American:	11	0.02
Bolivian	1	0.00
Colombian	4	0.01
Peruvian	2	0.00
Other South American	4	0.01
Other Hispanic or Latino	1,305	2.11
Hungarian	257	0.42
Iranian	20	0.03
Irish	3,169	5.12
Italian	1,139	1.84
Latvian	33	0.05
Lithuanian	91	0.15
Norwegian	151	0.24
Pennsylvania German	30	0.05
Polish	3,104	5.02
Portuguese	9	0.01
Romanian	80	0.13
Russian	293	0.47
Scandinavian	21	0.03
Scotch-Irish	432	0.70
Scottish	825	1.33
Serbian	11	0.02
Slavic	27	0.04
Slovak	44	0.07
Slovene	11	0.02
Swedish	360	0.58
Swiss	65	0.11
Ukrainian	85	0.14
United States or American	1,229	1.99
Welsh	130	0.21
West Indian, excl. Hispanic:	29	0.05
Jamaican	29	0.05
White:	30,541	49.42
Not Hispanic (26,372)	27,343	44.25
Hispanic (2,684)	3,198	5.17

Saint Clair Shores

Place Type: City
County: Macomb
Population: 63,096

Ancestry/Race	Number	%
African American/Black:	526	0.83
Not Hispanic (434)	522	0.83
Hispanic (1)	4	0.01
African, sub-Saharan:	35	0.06
African	32	0.05
Sierra Leonean	3	0.00
Am. Ind. or Alaska Nat., not spec.	123	0.19
Albanian	122	0.19
American Indian tribes, specified:	435	0.69
Apache (4)	12	0.02
Blackfeet (7)	26	0.04
Cherokee (16)	150	0.24
Chippewa (49)	124	0.20
Choctaw	6	0.01
Comanche	4	0.01
Creek	2	0.00
Delaware (2)	3	0.00
Iroquois (9)	14	0.02
Latin American Indians (5)	6	0.01
Lumbee (8)	17	0.03
Menominee	1	0.00
Navajo	2	0.00
Osage (2)	2	0.00
Ottawa (3)	13	0.02
Paiute (2)	2	0.00
Potawatomi	7	0.01
Seminole (1)	3	0.00
Shoshone (3)	3	0.00
Sioux (1)	16	0.03
All other tribes (12)	22	0.03
American Indian tribes, not spec.	15	0.02
Arab:	1,677	2.66
Arab/Arabic	167	0.26
Egyptian	11	0.02
Iraqi	11	0.02
Lebanese	1,182	1.87
Moroccan	7	0.01
Palestinian	27	0.04
Syrian	264	0.42
Other Arab	8	0.01
Armenian	70	0.11
Asian:	726	1.15
Cambodian	2	0.00
Chinese, ex. Taiwanese (110)	136	0.22
Filipino (206)	269	0.43
Indian (59)	72	0.11
Japanese (24)	60	0.10
Korean (69)	97	0.15
Pakistani (12)	16	0.03
Taiwanese (1)	1	0.00
Thai (5)	7	0.01
Vietnamese (19)	23	0.04
Other Asian, specified (1)	1	0.00
Other Asian, not specified (15)	42	0.07
Assyrian/Chaldean/Syriac	84	0.13
Austrian	320	0.51
Belgian	2,150	3.41
Brazilian	28	0.04
British	199	0.32
Bulgarian	17	0.03
Canadian	522	0.83
Celtic	14	0.02
Croatian	210	0.33
Czech	230	0.36
Czechoslovakian	169	0.27
Danish	205	0.32
Dutch	1,029	1.63
English	5,901	9.35
European	150	0.24
Finnish	366	0.58
French, except Basque	4,201	6.66
French Canadian	1,888	2.99
German	16,345	25.89
Greek	935	1.48
Guyanese	7	0.01
Hawaii Native/Pacific Islander:	24	0.04
Micronesian: (4)	7	0.01
Guamanian/Chamorro (4)	7	0.01
Polynesian: (7)	10	0.02
Native Hawaiian (5)	7	0.01
Samoan (2)	3	0.00
Other Pac. Isl., not spec. (3)	7	0.01
Hispanic or Latino:	745	1.18
Central American:	6	0.01
Costa Rican	1	0.00
Guatemalan	1	0.00
Panamanian	3	0.00
Salvadoran	1	0.00
Cuban	30	0.05
Dominican Republic	4	0.01
Mexican	408	0.65
Puerto Rican	74	0.12
South American:	35	0.06
Argentinean	4	0.01
Colombian	10	0.02
Ecuadorian	5	0.01
Peruvian	6	0.01
Venezuelan	4	0.01
Other South American	6	0.01
Other Hispanic or Latino	188	0.30
Hungarian	712	1.13
Iranian	19	0.03
Irish	9,978	15.81
Israeli	7	0.01
Italian	10,492	16.62
Latvian	21	0.03
Lithuanian	437	0.69
Luxemburger	9	0.01
Macedonian	7	0.01
Maltese	151	0.24
Norwegian	369	0.58
Pennsylvania German	23	0.04
Polish	10,776	17.07
Portuguese	50	0.08
Romanian	372	0.59
Russian	612	0.97
Scandinavian	23	0.04
Scotch-Irish	1,159	1.84
Scottish	1,860	2.95
Serbian	206	0.33
Slavic	87	0.14
Slovak	409	0.65
Slovene	29	0.05
Swedish	656	1.04
Swiss	172	0.27
Ukrainian	601	0.95
United States or American	1,740	2.76
Welsh	479	0.76
West Indian, excl. Hispanic:	5	0.01
U.S. Virgin Islander	5	0.01
White:	61,787	97.93
Not Hispanic (60,544)	61,155	96.92
Hispanic (591)	632	1.00
Yugoslavian	198	0.31

Saint Joseph charter

Place Type: Township
County: Berrien
Population: 10,042

Ancestry/Race	Number	%
African American/Black:	1,183	11.78
Not Hispanic (1,150)	1,181	11.76
Hispanic (2)	2	0.02
African, sub-Saharan:	56	0.55
African	39	0.38
South African	8	0.08

Notes: 1. Figures in the "Number" column do not add up to the total population due to: a) Ancestry/Race overlap — e.g. persons can report being both White and Irish, b) persons of Hispanic origin can report being any race, c) persons reporting two ancestries are counted in both categories. 2. Numbers in parentheses indicate the number of persons reporting this ancestry/race alone, not in combination with any other ancestry/race. 3. Refer to the Explanation of Data in the front of the book for more detailed information.

Zimbabwean	9	0.09
Am. Ind. or Alaska Nat., not spec.	9	0.09
American Indian tribes, specified:	45	0.45
Apache (1)	1	0.01
Blackfeet	3	0.03
Cherokee (2)	13	0.13
Chippewa (5)	8	0.08
Potawatomi (12)	14	0.14
Shoshone (2)	2	0.02
Tohono O'Odham (1)	1	0.01
All other tribes	3	0.03
American Indian tribes, not spec.	3	0.03
Arab:	10	0.10
Lebanese	10	0.10
Armenian	5	0.05
Asian:	200	1.99
Chinese, ex. Taiwanese (29)	32	0.32
Filipino (30)	33	0.33
Indian (66)	68	0.68
Japanese (7)	11	0.11
Korean (23)	25	0.25
Laotian (6)	6	0.06
Pakistani (5)	5	0.05
Vietnamese (5)	5	0.05
Other Asian, specified (1)	2	0.02
Other Asian, not specified (1)	13	0.13
Austrian	59	0.58
Belgian	22	0.22
British	16	0.16
Canadian	22	0.22
Croatian	7	0.07
Czech	104	1.02
Czechoslovakian	40	0.39
Danish	46	0.45
Dutch	449	4.41
Eastern European	21	0.21
English	1,175	11.55
European	92	0.90
Finnish	25	0.25
French, except Basque	409	4.02
French Canadian	92	0.90
German	3,136	30.82
Greek	72	0.71
Hawaii Native/Pacific Islander:	9	0.09
Polynesian: (3)	6	0.06
Native Hawaiian	1	0.01
Samoan (3)	3	0.03
Other Polynesian	2	0.02
Other Pac. Isl., not spec.	3	0.03
Hispanic or Latino:	105	1.05
Cuban	7	0.07
Mexican	59	0.59
Puerto Rican	6	0.06
South American:	14	0.14
Chilean	1	0.01
Colombian	3	0.03
Ecuadorian	9	0.09
Venezuelan	1	0.01
Other Hispanic or Latino	19	0.19
Hungarian	104	1.02
Iranian	23	0.23
Irish	1,088	10.69
Italian	572	5.62
Latvian	8	0.08
Lithuanian	32	0.31
Macedonian	5	0.05
Maltese	6	0.06
Northern European	7	0.07
Norwegian	102	1.00
Pennsylvania German	5	0.05
Polish	503	4.94
Portuguese	6	0.06
Romanian	29	0.28
Russian	108	1.06
Scotch-Irish	222	2.18
Scottish	150	1.47
Serbian	20	0.20
Slovak	4	0.04
Swedish	295	2.90
Swiss	40	0.39
Turkish	12	0.12
Ukrainian	25	0.25
United States or American	520	5.11
Welsh	104	1.02
White:	8,625	85.89
Not Hispanic (8,485)	8,548	85.12
Hispanic (72)	77	0.77
Yugoslavian	5	0.05

Sault Sainte Marie

Place Type: City
County: Chippewa
Population: 16,542

Ancestry/Race	Number	%
African American/Black:	1,208	7.30
Not Hispanic (1,054)	1,176	7.11
Hispanic (23)	32	0.19
African, sub-Saharan:	200	1.21
African	188	1.14
Sudanese	6	0.04
Other sub-Saharan African	6	0.04
Alaska Native tribes, specified:	6	0.04
Aleut (1)	1	0.01
Eskimo (1)	2	0.01
Tlingit-Haida (3)	3	0.02
Am. Ind. or Alaska Nat., not spec.	376	2.27
American Indian tribes, specified:	2,440	14.75
Apache (3)	6	0.04
Blackfeet	3	0.02
Cherokee (11)	34	0.21
Cheyenne (3)	4	0.02
Chippewa (1,859)	2,257	13.64
Choctaw	5	0.03
Comanche	2	0.01
Cree (1)	1	0.01
Creek (1)	1	0.01
Crow (1)	1	0.01
Iroquois (3)	4	0.02
Latin American Indians (7)	8	0.05
Lumbee	1	0.01
Ottawa (14)	28	0.17
Pima (1)	1	0.01
Potawatomi (14)	17	0.10
Seminole	1	0.01
Sioux (4)	5	0.03
Yuman (1)	1	0.01
All other tribes (37)	60	0.36
American Indian tribes, not spec.	64	0.39
Arab:	108	0.65
Arab/Arabic	14	0.08
Lebanese	58	0.35
Moroccan	36	0.22
Asian:	175	1.06
Bangladeshi (3)	3	0.02
Chinese, ex. Taiwanese (6)	8	0.05
Filipino (18)	30	0.18
Hmong (15)	15	0.09
Indian (22)	33	0.20
Japanese (4)	12	0.07
Korean (3)	8	0.05
Laotian (1)	1	0.01
Pakistani (3)	3	0.02
Vietnamese (2)	2	0.01
Other Asian, specified	2	0.01
Other Asian, not specified (30)	58	0.35
Austrian	28	0.17
Belgian	127	0.77
British	9	0.05
Canadian	128	0.77
Celtic	8	0.05
Croatian	24	0.15
Czech	110	0.67
Czechoslovakian	7	0.04
Danish	32	0.19
Dutch	357	2.16
Eastern European	7	0.04
English	1,633	9.88
Estonian	7	0.04
European	145	0.88
Finnish	444	2.69
French, except Basque	1,528	9.24
French Canadian	379	2.29
German	2,756	16.67
Greek	40	0.24
Hawaii Native/Pacific Islander:	29	0.18
Micronesian: (1)	4	0.02
Guamanian/Chamorro (1)	2	0.01
Other Micronesian	2	0.01
Polynesian: (2)	12	0.07
Native Hawaiian (1)	8	0.05
Samoan (1)	4	0.02
Other Pac. Isl., specified	2	0.01
Other Pac. Isl., not spec. (6)	11	0.07
Hispanic or Latino:	308	1.86
Cuban	20	0.12
Dominican Republic	1	0.01
Mexican	158	0.96
Puerto Rican	55	0.33
South American:	3	0.02
Chilean	1	0.01
Colombian	2	0.01
Other Hispanic or Latino	71	0.43
Hungarian	89	0.54
Irish	2,232	13.50
Italian	935	5.66
Lithuanian	6	0.04
Macedonian	8	0.05
New Zealander	5	0.03
Norwegian	172	1.04
Polish	1,044	6.31
Portuguese	41	0.25
Romanian	8	0.05
Russian	80	0.48
Scandinavian	37	0.22
Scotch-Irish	308	1.86
Scottish	687	4.16
Serbian	15	0.09
Slovak	28	0.17
Slovene	8	0.05
Swedish	309	1.87
Swiss	13	0.08
Ukrainian	54	0.33
United States or American	541	3.27
Welsh	66	0.40
White:	12,910	78.04
Not Hispanic (12,102)	12,742	77.03
Hispanic (137)	168	1.02
Yugoslavian	10	0.06

Scio

Place Type: Township
County: Washtenaw
Population: 15,759

Ancestry/Race	Number	%
African American/Black:	765	4.85
Not Hispanic (647)	752	4.77
Hispanic (4)	13	0.08
African, sub-Saharan:	18	0.11
African	18	0.11
Alaska Native tribes, specified:	2	0.01
Aleut	2	0.01
Am. Ind. or Alaska Nat., not spec.	34	0.22
American Indian tribes, specified:	96	0.61
Apache	2	0.01
Blackfeet	9	0.06
Cherokee (7)	32	0.20
Chippewa (12)	19	0.12
Choctaw	1	0.01
Creek (1)	1	0.01
Iroquois (1)	3	0.02
Latin American Indians (6)	10	0.06
Lumbee (1)	1	0.01
Navajo	2	0.01
Ottawa (2)	6	0.04
Potawatomi (1)	2	0.01
Sioux	4	0.03

Notes: 1. Figures in the "Number" column do not add up to the total population due to: a) Ancestry/Race overlap — e.g. persons can report being both White and Irish, b) persons of Hispanic origin can report being any race, c) persons reporting two ancestries are counted in both categories. 2. Numbers in parentheses indicate the number of persons reporting this ancestry/race alone, not in combination with any other ancestry/race. 3. Refer to the Explanation of Data in the front of the book for more detailed information.

Ancestry/Race	Number	%
Yuman (1)	1	0.01
All other tribes (1)	3	0.02
American Indian tribes, not spec.	5	0.03
Arab:	102	0.65
Arab/Arabic	10	0.06
Jordanian	19	0.12
Lebanese	61	0.39
Moroccan	9	0.06
Syrian	3	0.02
Armenian	38	0.24
Asian:	704	4.47
Bangladeshi (4)	4	0.03
Chinese, ex. Taiwanese (154)	187	1.19
Filipino (13)	27	0.17
Indian (151)	165	1.05
Indonesian (3)	3	0.02
Japanese (52)	81	0.51
Korean (154)	171	1.09
Pakistani (5)	5	0.03
Sri Lankan (4)	8	0.05
Taiwanese (7)	12	0.08
Thai (3)	7	0.04
Vietnamese (15)	19	0.12
Other Asian, specified (2)	2	0.01
Other Asian, not specified (5)	13	0.08
Assyrian/Chaldean/Syriac	15	0.10
Australian	29	0.19
Austrian	68	0.43
Belgian	80	0.51
Brazilian	11	0.07
British	183	1.17
Canadian	141	0.90
Croatian	30	0.19
Cypriot	7	0.04
Czech	71	0.45
Czechoslovakian	84	0.54
Danish	65	0.41
Dutch	546	3.48
Eastern European	65	0.41
English	2,595	16.56
Estonian	30	0.19
European	254	1.62
Finnish	103	0.66
French, except Basque	611	3.90
French Canadian	197	1.26
German	4,493	28.67
Greek	122	0.78
Guyanese	9	0.06
Hawaii Native/Pacific Islander:	8	0.05
Polynesian: (5)	7	0.04
Native Hawaiian (5)	6	0.04
Other Polynesian	1	0.01
Other Pac. Isl., not spec.	1	0.01
Hispanic or Latino:	241	1.53
Central American:	14	0.09
Costa Rican	4	0.03
Guatemalan	3	0.02
Honduran	3	0.02
Panamanian	1	0.01
Salvadoran	2	0.01
Other Central American	1	0.01
Cuban	8	0.05
Dominican Republic	1	0.01
Mexican	97	0.62
Puerto Rican	23	0.15
South American:	40	0.25
Argentinean	6	0.04
Chilean	2	0.01
Colombian	10	0.06
Ecuadorian	8	0.05
Peruvian	5	0.03
Venezuelan	8	0.05
Other South American	1	0.01
Other Hispanic or Latino	58	0.37
Hungarian	247	1.58
Iranian	8	0.05
Irish	2,128	13.58
Israeli	3	0.02
Italian	777	4.96
Latvian	29	0.19
Lithuanian	44	0.28
Macedonian	5	0.03
Maltese	10	0.06
Northern European	40	0.26
Norwegian	248	1.58
Polish	1,316	8.40
Romanian	80	0.51
Russian	189	1.21
Scandinavian	52	0.33
Scotch-Irish	279	1.78
Scottish	669	4.27
Serbian	17	0.11
Slavic	9	0.06
Slovak	48	0.31
Swedish	308	1.97
Swiss	92	0.59
Turkish	4	0.03
Ukrainian	86	0.55
United States or American	545	3.48
Welsh	202	1.29
West Indian, excl. Hispanic:	20	0.13
Jamaican	20	0.13
White:	14,392	91.33
Not Hispanic (13,953)	14,206	90.15
Hispanic (156)	186	1.18
Yugoslavian	56	0.36

Shelby

Place Type: Census Designated Place
County: Macomb
Population: 65,159

Ancestry/Race	Number	%
African American/Black:	649	1.00
Not Hispanic (547)	631	0.97
Hispanic (6)	18	0.03
African, sub-Saharan:	51	0.08
African	28	0.04
Kenyan	7	0.01
Nigerian	10	0.02
Other sub-Saharan African	6	0.01
Am. Ind. or Alaska Nat., not spec.	92	0.14
Albanian	1,180	1.81
American Indian tribes, specified:	318	0.49
Blackfeet (1)	13	0.02
Cherokee (17)	89	0.14
Cheyenne (1)	4	0.01
Chippewa (35)	65	0.10
Choctaw (2)	11	0.02
Comanche (1)	1	0.00
Cree (1)	2	0.00
Creek	1	0.00
Delaware (1)	2	0.00
Iroquois (17)	27	0.04
Latin American Indians (8)	12	0.02
Lumbee (12)	23	0.04
Menominee	3	0.00
Osage	2	0.00
Ottawa (10)	17	0.03
Potawatomi (2)	16	0.02
Pueblo (2)	2	0.00
Seminole (1)	6	0.01
Sioux (1)	6	0.01
All other tribes (7)	17	0.03
American Indian tribes, not spec.	22	0.03
Arab:	1,147	1.76
Arab/Arabic	230	0.35
Egyptian	47	0.07
Iraqi	79	0.12
Jordanian	62	0.10
Lebanese	544	0.84
Syrian	179	0.28
Other Arab	6	0.01
Armenian	95	0.15
Asian:	1,600	2.46
Bangladeshi (9)	13	0.02
Cambodian (1)	4	0.01
Chinese, ex. Taiwanese (160)	197	0.30
Filipino (160)	207	0.32
Hmong (24)	29	0.04
Indian (545)	598	0.92
Indonesian (1)	1	0.00
Japanese (63)	78	0.12
Korean (241)	263	0.40
Laotian (8)	10	0.02
Pakistani (39)	49	0.08
Taiwanese (6)	7	0.01
Thai (12)	25	0.04
Vietnamese (67)	70	0.11
Other Asian, specified (3)	4	0.01
Other Asian, not specified (23)	45	0.07
Assyrian/Chaldean/Syriac	493	0.76
Austrian	229	0.35
Belgian	1,525	2.34
British	290	0.45
Bulgarian	39	0.06
Canadian	303	0.47
Croatian	321	0.49
Cypriot	36	0.06
Czech	264	0.41
Czechoslovakian	271	0.42
Danish	204	0.31
Dutch	970	1.49
Eastern European	12	0.02
English	6,121	9.41
European	271	0.42
Finnish	390	0.60
French, except Basque	3,178	4.88
French Canadian	1,456	2.24
German	16,131	24.79
Greek	726	1.12
Hawaii Native/Pacific Islander:	25	0.04
Micronesian: (3)	3	0.00
Guamanian/Chamorro (3)	3	0.00
Polynesian: (6)	14	0.02
Native Hawaiian (2)	7	0.01
Samoan (4)	7	0.01
Other Pac. Isl., specified	1	0.00
Other Pac. Isl., not spec. (3)	7	0.01
Hispanic or Latino:	1,112	1.71
Central American:	28	0.04
Costa Rican	3	0.00
Guatemalan	5	0.01
Honduran	9	0.01
Panamanian	6	0.01
Other Central American	5	0.01
Cuban	40	0.06
Dominican Republic	4	0.01
Mexican	629	0.97
Puerto Rican	97	0.15
South American:	70	0.11
Argentinean	21	0.03
Bolivian	1	0.00
Chilean	4	0.01
Colombian	16	0.02
Ecuadorian	3	0.00
Peruvian	19	0.03
Venezuelan	6	0.01
Other Hispanic or Latino	244	0.37
Hungarian	727	1.12
Icelander	25	0.04
Iranian	76	0.12
Irish	7,170	11.02
Italian	9,430	14.49
Latvian	23	0.04
Lithuanian	165	0.25
Luxemburger	8	0.01
Macedonian	486	0.75
Maltese	162	0.25
Northern European	35	0.05
Norwegian	364	0.56
Polish	12,462	19.15
Portuguese	29	0.04
Romanian	464	0.71
Russian	637	0.98
Scandinavian	61	0.09
Scotch-Irish	1,077	1.66
Scottish	1,702	2.62
Serbian	130	0.20

Notes: 1. Figures in the "Number" column do not add up to the total population due to: a) Ancestry/Race overlap — e.g. persons can report being both White and Irish, b) persons of Hispanic origin can report being any race, c) persons reporting two ancestries are counted in both categories. 2. Numbers in parentheses indicate the number of persons reporting this ancestry/race alone, not in combination with any other ancestry/race. 3. Refer to the Explanation of Data in the front of the book for more detailed information.

Slavic	65	0.10
Slovak	367	0.56
Slovene	44	0.07
Swedish	783	1.20
Swiss	72	0.11
Ukrainian	619	0.95
United States or American	2,408	3.70
Welsh	329	0.51
West Indian, excl. Hispanic:	54	0.08
British West Indian	20	0.03
Haitian	34	0.05
White:	62,695	96.22
Not Hispanic (61,122)	61,879	94.97
Hispanic (748)	816	1.25
Yugoslavian	495	0.76

South Lyon

Place Type: City
County: Oakland
Population: 10,036

Ancestry/Race	Number	%
African American/Black:	53	0.53
Not Hispanic (39)	53	0.53
Am. Ind. or Alaska Nat., not spec.	8	0.08
American Indian tribes, specified:	53	0.53
Blackfeet	1	0.01
Cherokee (1)	18	0.18
Chippewa (10)	23	0.23
Iroquois (3)	4	0.04
Latin American Indians (1)	2	0.02
Lumbee (2)	2	0.02
All other tribes	3	0.03
American Indian tribes, not spec.	1	0.01
Arab:	10	0.10
Lebanese	10	0.10
Asian:	139	1.39
Chinese, ex. Taiwanese (40)	43	0.43
Filipino (17)	19	0.19
Indian (9)	14	0.14
Japanese (17)	31	0.31
Korean (16)	16	0.16
Taiwanese (1)	1	0.01
Thai (2)	2	0.02
Vietnamese (7)	10	0.10
Other Asian, not specified	3	0.03
Australian	15	0.15
Austrian	72	0.72
Belgian	70	0.70
British	33	0.33
Canadian	48	0.48
Croatian	13	0.13
Czech	24	0.24
Czechoslovakian	31	0.31
Danish	172	1.71
Dutch	269	2.68
Eastern European	5	0.05
English	1,424	14.18
European	13	0.13
Finnish	181	1.80
French, except Basque	592	5.90
French Canadian	340	3.39
German	2,553	25.43
Greek	29	0.29
Hawaii Native/Pacific Islander:	15	0.15
Micronesian: (5)	5	0.05
Other Micronesian (5)	5	0.05
Polynesian: (2)	5	0.05
Native Hawaiian (1)	2	0.02
Other Polynesian (1)	3	0.03
Other Pac. Isl., not spec. (5)	5	0.05
Hispanic or Latino:	161	1.60
Central American:	1	0.01
Costa Rican	1	0.01
Cuban	5	0.05
Mexican	108	1.08
Puerto Rican	18	0.18
South American:	7	0.07
Chilean	1	0.01
Peruvian	2	0.02
Venezuelan	4	0.04
Other Hispanic or Latino	22	0.22
Hungarian	188	1.87
Irish	1,524	15.18
Italian	658	6.55
Latvian	9	0.09
Lithuanian	32	0.32
Macedonian	8	0.08
Maltese	100	1.00
Northern European	15	0.15
Norwegian	56	0.56
Pennsylvania German	27	0.27
Polish	1,054	10.50
Portuguese	19	0.19
Romanian	41	0.41
Russian	58	0.58
Scotch-Irish	300	2.99
Scottish	581	5.79
Serbian	25	0.25
Slovak	40	0.40
Slovene	10	0.10
Swedish	198	1.97
Swiss	23	0.23
Ukrainian	53	0.53
United States or American	528	5.26
Welsh	78	0.78
White:	9,816	97.81
Not Hispanic (9,591)	9,695	96.60
Hispanic (112)	121	1.21
Yugoslavian	20	0.20

Southfield

Place Type: City
County: Oakland
Population: 78,296

Ancestry/Race	Number	%
African American/Black:	43,711	55.83
Not Hispanic (42,259)	43,412	55.45
Hispanic (195)	299	0.38
African, sub-Saharan:	2,044	2.61
African	1,308	1.67
Ethiopian	50	0.06
Ghanian	55	0.07
Kenyan	6	0.01
Liberian	102	0.13
Nigerian	392	0.50
Sierra Leonean	20	0.03
South African	13	0.02
Ugandan	5	0.01
Other sub-Saharan African	93	0.12
Alaska Native tribes, specified:	1	0.00
Tlingit-Haida (1)	1	0.00
Alaska Native tribes, not specified	2	0.00
Am. Ind. or Alaska Nat., not spec.	335	0.43
Albanian	95	0.12
American Indian tribes, specified:	313	0.40
Apache (1)	13	0.02
Blackfeet	30	0.04
Cherokee (22)	134	0.17
Chickasaw	1	0.00
Chippewa (24)	40	0.05
Choctaw (1)	10	0.01
Cree	5	0.01
Creek (1)	1	0.00
Crow	4	0.01
Delaware (1)	1	0.00
Houma (3)	3	0.00
Iroquois (8)	17	0.02
Latin American Indians (8)	16	0.02
Lumbee (2)	2	0.00
Navajo	2	0.00
Ottawa (2)	3	0.00
Pueblo	1	0.00
Seminole	2	0.00
Sioux (1)	4	0.01
All other tribes (7)	24	0.03
American Indian tribes, not spec.	35	0.04
Arab:	1,607	2.05
Arab/Arabic	479	0.61
Egyptian	61	0.08
Iraqi	753	0.96
Lebanese	159	0.20
Moroccan	32	0.04
Palestinian	20	0.03
Syrian	79	0.10
Other Arab	24	0.03
Armenian	468	0.60
Asian:	2,848	3.64
Bangladeshi (7)	10	0.01
Cambodian (4)	7	0.01
Chinese, ex. Taiwanese (375)	429	0.55
Filipino (341)	400	0.51
Hmong (16)	18	0.02
Indian (1,088)	1,202	1.54
Indonesian (7)	8	0.01
Japanese (68)	100	0.13
Korean (143)	170	0.22
Laotian (1)	6	0.01
Malaysian (1)	2	0.00
Pakistani (86)	96	0.12
Sri Lankan (28)	28	0.04
Taiwanese (20)	21	0.03
Thai (11)	23	0.03
Vietnamese (147)	165	0.21
Other Asian, specified (14)	22	0.03
Other Asian, not specified (35)	141	0.18
Assyrian/Chaldean/Syriac	3,684	4.71
Australian	24	0.03
Austrian	213	0.27
Basque	7	0.01
Belgian	101	0.13
Brazilian	8	0.01
British	87	0.11
Bulgarian	5	0.01
Canadian	338	0.43
Celtic	28	0.04
Croatian	68	0.09
Czech	94	0.12
Czechoslovakian	106	0.14
Danish	139	0.18
Dutch	476	0.61
Eastern European	194	0.25
English	2,490	3.18
Estonian	9	0.01
European	255	0.33
Finnish	265	0.34
French, except Basque	1,087	1.39
French Canadian	549	0.70
German	4,029	5.15
Greek	222	0.28
Guyanese	66	0.08
Hawaii Native/Pacific Islander:	73	0.09
Melanesian:	1	0.00
Fijian	1	0.00
Micronesian:	1	0.00
Guamanian/Chamorro	1	0.00
Polynesian: (16)	27	0.03
Native Hawaiian (4)	11	0.01
Samoan (12)	16	0.02
Other Pac. Isl., specified	1	0.00
Other Pac. Isl., not spec. (8)	43	0.05
Hispanic or Latino:	934	1.19
Central American:	20	0.03
Costa Rican	1	0.00
Guatemalan	2	0.00
Honduran	3	0.00
Nicaraguan	3	0.00
Panamanian	7	0.01
Salvadoran	4	0.01
Cuban	57	0.07
Dominican Republic	13	0.02
Mexican	381	0.49
Puerto Rican	182	0.23
South American:	55	0.07
Argentinean	11	0.01
Bolivian	1	0.00
Chilean	4	0.01

Notes: 1. Figures in the "Number" column do not add up to the total population due to: a) Ancestry/Race overlap — e.g. persons can report being both White and Irish, b) persons of Hispanic origin can report being any race, c) persons reporting two ancestries are counted in both categories. 2. Numbers in parentheses indicate the number of persons reporting this ancestry/race alone, not in combination with any other ancestry/race. 3. Refer to the Explanation of Data in the front of the book for more detailed information.

Ancestry/Race	Number	%
Colombian	25	0.03
Ecuadorian	1	0.00
Paraguayan	2	0.00
Peruvian	5	0.01
Venezuelan	5	0.01
Other South American	1	0.00
Other Hispanic or Latino	226	0.29
Hungarian	616	0.79
Icelander	5	0.01
Iranian	133	0.17
Irish	2,691	3.44
Israeli	124	0.16
Italian	1,252	1.60
Latvian	65	0.08
Lithuanian	199	0.25
Maltese	38	0.05
Northern European	20	0.03
Norwegian	186	0.24
Pennsylvania German	25	0.03
Polish	3,114	3.98
Portuguese	21	0.03
Romanian	276	0.35
Russian	2,514	3.21
Scandinavian	39	0.05
Scotch-Irish	408	0.52
Scottish	614	0.78
Serbian	25	0.03
Slovak	116	0.15
Slovene	10	0.01
Soviet Union	27	0.03
Swedish	268	0.34
Swiss	37	0.05
Turkish	47	0.06
Ukrainian	488	0.62
United States or American	1,890	2.41
Welsh	187	0.24
West Indian, excl. Hispanic:	499	0.64
Bahamian	15	0.02
Barbadian	31	0.04
Bermudan	6	0.01
British West Indian	2	0.00
Haitian	35	0.04
Jamaican	375	0.48
Trinidadian and Tobagonian	12	0.02
West Indian	23	0.03
White:	32,129	41.04
Not Hispanic (30,025)	31,686	40.47
Hispanic (381)	443	0.57
Yugoslavian	18	0.02

Southfield

Place Type: Township
County: Oakland
Population: 14,430

Ancestry/Race	Number	%
African American/Black:	572	3.96
Not Hispanic (519)	567	3.93
Hispanic (4)	5	0.03
African, sub-Saharan:	27	0.19
African	27	0.19
Am. Ind. or Alaska Nat., not spec.	22	0.15
Albanian	41	0.28
American Indian tribes, specified:	36	0.25
Apache (1)	1	0.01
Blackfeet	2	0.01
Cherokee (6)	16	0.11
Cheyenne	1	0.01
Chippewa (1)	5	0.03
Choctaw	1	0.01
Iroquois (2)	2	0.01
Latin American Indians (1)	1	0.01
Lumbee (1)	1	0.01
Ottawa	2	0.01
Seminole	2	0.01
Sioux	1	0.01
All other tribes	1	0.01
American Indian tribes, not spec.	1	0.01
Arab:	284	1.97
Arab/Arabic	36	0.25
Egyptian	17	0.12
Iraqi	51	0.35
Lebanese	133	0.92
Palestinian	28	0.19
Syrian	9	0.06
Other Arab	10	0.07
Armenian	145	1.00
Asian:	392	2.72
Chinese, ex. Taiwanese (86)	100	0.69
Filipino (27)	38	0.26
Indian (117)	138	0.96
Japanese (25)	32	0.22
Korean (35)	45	0.31
Pakistani (4)	8	0.06
Sri Lankan (1)	3	0.02
Taiwanese (2)	5	0.03
Thai (1)	1	0.01
Vietnamese (3)	6	0.04
Other Asian, specified	6	0.04
Other Asian, not specified (3)	10	0.07
Assyrian/Chaldean/Syriac	264	1.83
Australian	4	0.03
Austrian	55	0.38
Belgian	103	0.71
British	69	0.48
Canadian	122	0.85
Croatian	26	0.18
Czech	62	0.43
Czechoslovakian	35	0.24
Danish	62	0.43
Dutch	390	2.70
Eastern European	112	0.78
English	2,188	15.16
European	114	0.79
Finnish	106	0.73
French, except Basque	559	3.87
French Canadian	199	1.38
German	3,307	22.92
Greek	236	1.64
Hawaii Native/Pacific Islander:	18	0.12
Other Pac. Isl., specified	6	0.04
Other Pac. Isl., not spec. (2)	12	0.08
Hispanic or Latino:	177	1.23
Central American:	4	0.03
Guatemalan	3	0.02
Panamanian	1	0.01
Cuban	1	0.01
Dominican Republic	2	0.01
Mexican	95	0.66
Puerto Rican	17	0.12
South American:	19	0.13
Argentinean	5	0.03
Bolivian	1	0.01
Chilean	2	0.01
Colombian	3	0.02
Ecuadorian	4	0.03
Paraguayan	1	0.01
Peruvian	1	0.01
Venezuelan	2	0.01
Other Hispanic or Latino	39	0.27
Hungarian	193	1.34
Iranian	51	0.35
Irish	2,636	18.27
Italian	995	6.90
Latvian	15	0.10
Lithuanian	144	1.00
Luxemburger	2	0.01
Macedonian	20	0.14
Maltese	16	0.11
Northern European	2	0.01
Norwegian	129	0.89
Pennsylvania German	4	0.03
Polish	1,610	11.16
Portuguese	4	0.03
Romanian	65	0.45
Russian	660	4.57
Scandinavian	18	0.12
Scotch-Irish	239	1.66
Scottish	516	3.58
Serbian	5	0.03
Slavic	2	0.01
Slovak	57	0.40
Slovene	14	0.10
Swedish	255	1.77
Swiss	81	0.56
Turkish	18	0.12
Ukrainian	108	0.75
United States or American	708	4.91
Welsh	188	1.30
West Indian, excl. Hispanic:	9	0.06
Jamaican	9	0.06
White:	13,513	93.65
Not Hispanic (13,207)	13,368	92.64
Hispanic (125)	145	1.00
Yugoslavian	24	0.17

Southgate

Place Type: City
County: Wayne
Population: 30,136

Ancestry/Race	Number	%
African American/Black:	698	2.32
Not Hispanic (624)	685	2.27
Hispanic (11)	13	0.04
African, sub-Saharan:	51	0.17
African	38	0.13
Sudanese	13	0.04
Am. Ind. or Alaska Nat., not spec.	75	0.25
American Indian tribes, specified:	197	0.65
Apache	2	0.01
Blackfeet (4)	4	0.01
Cherokee (20)	63	0.21
Chippewa (29)	45	0.15
Choctaw (2)	5	0.02
Cree (1)	1	0.00
Delaware	1	0.00
Iroquois (18)	23	0.08
Latin American Indians (7)	7	0.02
Lumbee (13)	19	0.06
Menominee (3)	3	0.01
Navajo (5)	5	0.02
Osage	1	0.00
Ottawa (1)	2	0.01
Potawatomi (2)	2	0.01
Puget Sound Salish (1)	1	0.00
Yakama (1)	1	0.00
All other tribes (5)	12	0.04
American Indian tribes, not spec.	8	0.03
Arab:	109	0.36
Arab/Arabic	24	0.08
Lebanese	49	0.16
Syrian	36	0.12
Armenian	69	0.23
Asian:	585	1.94
Cambodian (5)	5	0.02
Chinese, ex. Taiwanese (101)	113	0.37
Filipino (80)	103	0.34
Hmong (2)	2	0.01
Indian (209)	218	0.72
Indonesian (4)	5	0.02
Japanese (13)	22	0.07
Korean (23)	31	0.10
Pakistani (28)	36	0.12
Taiwanese	1	0.00
Thai (2)	3	0.01
Vietnamese (24)	33	0.11
Other Asian, specified (1)	2	0.01
Other Asian, not specified (5)	11	0.04
Assyrian/Chaldean/Syriac	30	0.10
Australian	7	0.02
Austrian	57	0.19
Basque	20	0.07
Belgian	87	0.29
Brazilian	41	0.14
British	45	0.15
Canadian	236	0.78
Croatian	90	0.30

Notes: 1. Figures in the "Number" column do not add up to the total population due to: a) Ancestry/Race overlap — e.g. persons can report being both White and Irish, b) persons of Hispanic origin can report being any race, c) persons reporting two ancestries are counted in both categories. 2. Numbers in parentheses indicate the number of persons reporting this ancestry/race alone, not in combination with any other ancestry/race. 3. Refer to the Explanation of Data in the front of the book for more detailed information.

Czech	34	0.11
Czechoslovakian	90	0.30
Danish	79	0.26
Dutch	417	1.38
Eastern European	8	0.03
English	2,641	8.76
European	165	0.55
Finnish	168	0.56
French, except Basque	2,407	7.99
French Canadian	765	2.54
German	5,564	18.46
Greek	551	1.83
Hawaii Native/Pacific Islander:	20	0.07
Micronesian: (3)	4	0.01
Guamanian/Chamorro (2)	3	0.01
Other Micronesian (1)	1	0.00
Polynesian: (6)	10	0.03
Native Hawaiian (4)	7	0.02
Samoan (2)	3	0.01
Other Pac. Isl., specified	1	0.00
Other Pac. Isl., not spec. (4)	5	0.02
Hispanic or Latino:	1,198	3.98
Central American:	6	0.02
Guatemalan	2	0.01
Panamanian	2	0.01
Salvadoran	2	0.01
Cuban	10	0.03
Dominican Republic	1	0.00
Mexican	913	3.03
Puerto Rican	75	0.25
South American:	26	0.09
Argentinean	5	0.02
Colombian	16	0.05
Ecuadorian	1	0.00
Venezuelan	3	0.01
Other South American	1	0.00
Other Hispanic or Latino	167	0.55
Hungarian	1,691	5.61
Iranian	19	0.06
Irish	4,514	14.98
Italian	2,499	8.29
Lithuanian	61	0.20
Macedonian	109	0.36
Maltese	184	0.61
Norwegian	115	0.38
Polish	4,591	15.23
Portuguese	19	0.06
Romanian	80	0.27
Russian	169	0.56
Scotch-Irish	465	1.54
Scottish	813	2.70
Serbian	36	0.12
Slavic	41	0.14
Slovak	186	0.62
Slovene	36	0.12
Swedish	220	0.73
Swiss	5	0.02
Turkish	8	0.03
Ukrainian	247	0.82
United States or American	1,525	5.06
Welsh	177	0.59
West Indian, excl. Hispanic:	22	0.07
Bahamian	8	0.03
Jamaican	14	0.05
White:	28,559	94.77
Not Hispanic (27,382)	27,645	91.73
Hispanic (842)	914	3.03
Yugoslavian	58	0.19

Spring Lake

Place Type: Township
County: Ottawa
Population: 13,140

Ancestry/Race	Number	%
African American/Black:	66	0.50
Not Hispanic (42)	64	0.49
Hispanic (1)	2	0.02
Alaska Native tribes, not specified	1	0.01
Am. Ind. or Alaska Nat., not spec.	23	0.18
American Indian tribes, specified:	81	0.62
Apache	1	0.01
Cherokee (7)	17	0.13
Chickasaw	1	0.01
Chippewa (26)	33	0.25
Choctaw (1)	3	0.02
Latin American Indians	2	0.02
Ottawa (8)	11	0.08
Potawatomi (1)	4	0.03
Pueblo (1)	1	0.01
Shoshone (1)	1	0.01
Sioux (2)	3	0.02
All other tribes (2)	4	0.03
American Indian tribes, not spec.	3	0.02
Arab:	15	0.11
Lebanese	15	0.11
Asian:	94	0.72
Chinese, ex. Taiwanese (11)	12	0.09
Filipino (7)	17	0.13
Indian (12)	13	0.10
Japanese (3)	6	0.05
Korean (29)	31	0.24
Laotian (1)	1	0.01
Thai (2)	3	0.02
Vietnamese (2)	3	0.02
Other Asian, not specified (1)	8	0.06
Austrian	46	0.35
Belgian	61	0.46
British	53	0.40
Canadian	47	0.36
Czech	164	1.25
Czechoslovakian	62	0.47
Danish	106	0.81
Dutch	2,922	22.23
English	1,970	14.99
European	161	1.22
Finnish	207	1.57
French, except Basque	526	4.00
French Canadian	222	1.69
German	2,981	22.68
Greek	8	0.06
Hawaii Native/Pacific Islander:	5	0.04
Polynesian:	5	0.04
Native Hawaiian	5	0.04
Hispanic or Latino:	206	1.57
Central American:	3	0.02
Costa Rican	1	0.01
Honduran	1	0.01
Salvadoran	1	0.01
Cuban	4	0.03
Mexican	137	1.04
Puerto Rican	12	0.09
South American:	9	0.07
Argentinean	1	0.01
Chilean	3	0.02
Colombian	4	0.03
Uruguayan	1	0.01
Other Hispanic or Latino	41	0.31
Hungarian	96	0.73
Irish	1,508	11.47
Italian	414	3.15
Lithuanian	51	0.39
Northern European	22	0.17
Norwegian	278	2.11
Pennsylvania German	16	0.12
Polish	739	5.62
Portuguese	55	0.42
Romanian	32	0.24
Russian	108	0.82
Scotch-Irish	225	1.71
Scottish	329	2.50
Slovak	25	0.19
Swedish	478	3.64
Swiss	38	0.29
Ukrainian	73	0.56
United States or American	772	5.87
Welsh	136	1.03
White:	12,909	98.24
Not Hispanic (12,678)	12,769	97.18
Hispanic (114)	140	1.07
Yugoslavian	43	0.33

Springfield

Place Type: Township
County: Oakland
Population: 13,338

Ancestry/Race	Number	%
Afghan	9	0.07
African American/Black:	162	1.21
Not Hispanic (139)	155	1.16
Hispanic (7)	7	0.05
Am. Ind. or Alaska Nat., not spec.	26	0.19
American Indian tribes, specified:	95	0.71
Apache (1)	6	0.04
Blackfeet	3	0.02
Cherokee (23)	33	0.25
Chippewa (13)	36	0.27
Creek (1)	2	0.01
Latin American Indians (2)	2	0.01
Menominee (1)	1	0.01
Navajo	2	0.01
Osage	1	0.01
Pima (1)	1	0.01
Sioux (2)	2	0.01
All other tribes (3)	6	0.04
American Indian tribes, not spec.	13	0.10
Arab:	52	0.39
Arab/Arabic	13	0.10
Lebanese	39	0.29
Armenian	34	0.26
Asian:	104	0.78
Chinese, ex. Taiwanese (12)	16	0.12
Filipino (20)	29	0.22
Indian (4)	9	0.07
Japanese (7)	14	0.10
Korean (21)	27	0.20
Laotian	3	0.02
Pakistani (1)	1	0.01
Thai (1)	1	0.01
Vietnamese (3)	3	0.02
Other Asian, not specified (1)	1	0.01
Assyrian/Chaldean/Syriac	7	0.05
Austrian	18	0.14
Belgian	108	0.81
British	64	0.48
Bulgarian	8	0.06
Canadian	109	0.82
Celtic	20	0.15
Croatian	23	0.17
Czech	16	0.12
Czechoslovakian	49	0.37
Danish	55	0.41
Dutch	481	3.62
English	2,311	17.38
European	61	0.46
Finnish	111	0.83
French, except Basque	946	7.12
French Canadian	525	3.95
German	2,993	22.51
Greek	48	0.36
Hawaii Native/Pacific Islander:	5	0.04
Micronesian: (1)	3	0.02
Guamanian/Chamorro (1)	3	0.02
Polynesian:	1	0.01
Native Hawaiian	1	0.01
Other Pac. Isl., not spec.	1	0.01
Hispanic or Latino:	264	1.98
Cuban	1	0.01
Dominican Republic	1	0.01
Mexican	201	1.51
Puerto Rican	10	0.07
South American:	5	0.04
Colombian	3	0.02
Peruvian	2	0.01
Other Hispanic or Latino	46	0.34
Hungarian	216	1.62
Iranian	27	0.20

Notes: 1. Figures in the "Number" column do not add up to the total population due to: a) Ancestry/Race overlap — e.g. persons can report being both White and Irish, b) persons of Hispanic origin can report being any race, c) persons reporting two ancestries are counted in both categories. 2. Numbers in parentheses indicate the number of persons reporting this ancestry/race alone, not in combination with any other ancestry/race. 3. Refer to the Explanation of Data in the front of the book for more detailed information.

Ancestry/Race	Number	%
Irish	1,769	13.31
Italian	983	7.39
Latvian	10	0.08
Lithuanian	13	0.10
Maltese	46	0.35
Norwegian	135	1.02
Pennsylvania German	16	0.12
Polish	1,332	10.02
Romanian	100	0.75
Russian	125	0.94
Scandinavian	39	0.29
Scotch-Irish	202	1.52
Scottish	482	3.63
Serbian	42	0.32
Slavic	19	0.14
Slovak	53	0.40
Swedish	175	1.32
Swiss	20	0.15
Ukrainian	73	0.55
United States or American	680	5.11
Welsh	86	0.65
White:	13,014	97.57
Not Hispanic (12,703)	12,795	95.93
Hispanic (194)	219	1.64
Yugoslavian	35	0.26

Sterling Heights

Place Type: City
County: Macomb
Population: 124,471

Ancestry/Race	Number	%
Afghan	11	0.01
African American/Black:	1,895	1.52
Not Hispanic (1,602)	1,853	1.49
Hispanic (12)	42	0.03
African, sub-Saharan:	93	0.07
African	74	0.06
Other sub-Saharan African	19	0.02
Alaska Native tribes, specified:	1	0.00
Alaska Athabascan	1	0.00
Am. Ind. or Alaska Nat., not spec.	211	0.17
Albanian	2,295	1.84
American Indian tribes, specified:	473	0.38
Apache (7)	12	0.01
Blackfeet (1)	20	0.02
Cherokee (38)	176	0.14
Cheyenne	2	0.00
Chippewa (51)	100	0.08
Choctaw (2)	9	0.01
Comanche (1)	2	0.00
Cree (1)	1	0.00
Creek	1	0.00
Crow	3	0.00
Delaware	1	0.00
Iroquois (18)	35	0.03
Latin American Indians (2)	9	0.01
Lumbee (26)	38	0.03
Menominee	1	0.00
Navajo	4	0.00
Ottawa (8)	13	0.01
Potawatomi (5)	9	0.01
Seminole (2)	7	0.01
Sioux (3)	4	0.00
Yaqui	3	0.00
Yuman (1)	1	0.00
All other tribes (7)	22	0.02
American Indian tribes, not spec.	26	0.02
Arab:	4,598	3.69
Arab/Arabic	775	0.62
Egyptian	221	0.18
Iraqi	1,384	1.11
Jordanian	226	0.18
Lebanese	1,598	1.28
Palestinian	68	0.05
Syrian	265	0.21
Other Arab	61	0.05
Armenian	337	0.27
Asian:	6,880	5.53
Bangladeshi (9)	20	0.02
Cambodian (22)	22	0.02
Chinese, ex. Taiwanese (875)	931	0.75
Filipino (1,350)	1,495	1.20
Hmong (46)	59	0.05
Indian (2,410)	2,581	2.07
Indonesian (10)	14	0.01
Japanese (59)	101	0.08
Korean (488)	539	0.43
Laotian (26)	39	0.03
Malaysian (2)	3	0.00
Pakistani (194)	261	0.21
Sri Lankan (8)	10	0.01
Taiwanese (15)	20	0.02
Thai (26)	32	0.03
Vietnamese (435)	475	0.38
Other Asian, specified (6)	12	0.01
Other Asian, not specified (60)	266	0.21
Assyrian/Chaldean/Syriac	5,515	4.43
Australian	26	0.02
Austrian	464	0.37
Belgian	1,931	1.55
Brazilian	70	0.06
British	349	0.28
Bulgarian	55	0.04
Canadian	614	0.49
Celtic	6	0.00
Croatian	425	0.34
Cypriot	5	0.00
Czech	481	0.39
Czechoslovakian	286	0.23
Danish	223	0.18
Dutch	1,438	1.16
Eastern European	9	0.01
English	9,264	7.44
European	436	0.35
Finnish	816	0.66
French, except Basque	5,744	4.61
French Canadian	2,679	2.15
German	24,814	19.94
Greek	1,086	0.87
Hawaii Native/Pacific Islander:	102	0.08
Micronesian: (26)	28	0.02
Guamanian/Chamorro (9)	10	0.01
Other Micronesian (17)	18	0.01
Polynesian: (5)	16	0.01
Native Hawaiian (5)	14	0.01
Samoan	1	0.00
Other Pac. Isl., specified	5	0.00
Other Pac. Isl., not spec. (13)	53	0.04
Hispanic or Latino:	1,665	1.34
Central American:	32	0.03
Costa Rican	11	0.01
Guatemalan	5	0.00
Honduran	2	0.00
Nicaraguan	1	0.00
Panamanian	6	0.00
Salvadoran	5	0.00
Other Central American	2	0.00
Cuban	58	0.05
Dominican Republic	9	0.01
Mexican	890	0.72
Puerto Rican	152	0.12
South American:	137	0.11
Argentinean	37	0.03
Bolivian	2	0.00
Chilean	13	0.01
Colombian	21	0.02
Ecuadorian	10	0.01
Peruvian	16	0.01
Uruguayan	3	0.00
Venezuelan	22	0.02
Other South American	13	0.01
Other Hispanic or Latino	387	0.31
Hungarian	1,322	1.06
Icelander	13	0.01
Iranian	59	0.05
Irish	11,943	9.60
Italian	16,556	13.30
Latvian	43	0.03
Lithuanian	405	0.33
Macedonian	887	0.71
Maltese	418	0.34
Northern European	16	0.01
Norwegian	556	0.45
Polish	26,123	20.99
Portuguese	92	0.07
Romanian	1,282	1.03
Russian	886	0.71
Scandinavian	64	0.05
Scotch-Irish	1,654	1.33
Scottish	2,765	2.22
Serbian	476	0.38
Slavic	102	0.08
Slovak	937	0.75
Slovene	92	0.07
Swedish	758	0.61
Swiss	135	0.11
Turkish	29	0.02
Ukrainian	1,405	1.13
United States or American	4,357	3.50
Welsh	436	0.35
West Indian, excl. Hispanic:	29	0.02
Haitian	10	0.01
Jamaican	8	0.01
West Indian	11	0.01
White:	115,818	93.05
Not Hispanic (111,743)	114,532	92.02
Hispanic (1,156)	1,286	1.03
Yugoslavian	1,044	0.84

Sturgis

Place Type: City
County: Saint Joseph
Population: 11,285

Ancestry/Race	Number	%
African American/Black:	190	1.68
Not Hispanic (115)	161	1.43
Hispanic (24)	29	0.26
African, sub-Saharan:	13	0.11
African	13	0.11
Am. Ind. or Alaska Nat., not spec.	46	0.41
American Indian tribes, specified:	58	0.51
Apache	4	0.04
Blackfeet	3	0.03
Cherokee (5)	20	0.18
Chippewa (1)	7	0.06
Comanche	1	0.01
Creek (1)	1	0.01
Crow	2	0.02
Iroquois	1	0.01
Latin American Indians (2)	4	0.04
Navajo (2)	2	0.02
Ottawa	2	0.02
Potawatomi	1	0.01
Seminole (1)	1	0.01
Sioux	1	0.01
All other tribes (6)	8	0.07
American Indian tribes, not spec.	3	0.03
Arab:	33	0.29
Lebanese	10	0.09
Other Arab	23	0.20
Asian:	94	0.83
Cambodian (1)	1	0.01
Chinese, ex. Taiwanese (6)	7	0.06
Filipino (22)	28	0.25
Indian (26)	28	0.25
Japanese (5)	5	0.04
Korean (5)	6	0.05
Laotian (1)	1	0.01
Thai (1)	1	0.01
Vietnamese (10)	10	0.09
Other Asian, specified	1	0.01
Other Asian, not specified (1)	6	0.05
Belgian	15	0.13
British	35	0.31
Bulgarian	19	0.17
Canadian	2	0.02

Notes: 1. Figures in the "Number" column do not add up to the total population due to: a) Ancestry/Race overlap — e.g. persons can report being both White and Irish, b) persons of Hispanic origin can report being any race, c) persons reporting two ancestries are counted in both categories. 2. Numbers in parentheses indicate the number of persons reporting this ancestry/race alone, not in combination with any other ancestry/race. 3. Refer to the Explanation of Data in the front of the book for more detailed information.

Ancestry/Race	Number	%
Celtic	1	0.01
Croatian	5	0.04
Czech	5	0.04
Danish	35	0.31
Dutch	280	2.47
English	1,021	8.99
European	64	0.56
Finnish	28	0.25
French, except Basque	508	4.47
French Canadian	13	0.11
German	2,985	26.29
Greek	35	0.31
Hawaii Native/Pacific Islander:	3	0.03
Polynesian:	1	0.01
Native Hawaiian	1	0.01
Other Pac. Isl., specified	1	0.01
Other Pac. Isl., not spec.	1	0.01
Hispanic or Latino:	1,499	13.28
Central American:	4	0.04
Nicaraguan	2	0.02
Panamanian	1	0.01
Salvadoran	1	0.01
Cuban	6	0.05
Mexican	1,330	11.79
Puerto Rican	34	0.30
South American:	1	0.01
Colombian	1	0.01
Other Hispanic or Latino	124	1.10
Hungarian	49	0.43
Irish	1,071	9.43
Italian	239	2.10
Lithuanian	50	0.44
Luxemburger	6	0.05
Northern European	13	0.11
Norwegian	85	0.75
Pennsylvania German	51	0.45
Polish	428	3.77
Romanian	1	0.01
Russian	23	0.20
Scotch-Irish	309	2.72
Scottish	204	1.80
Slovak	20	0.18
Swedish	90	0.79
Swiss	118	1.04
Ukrainian	2	0.02
United States or American	1,116	9.83
Welsh	8	0.07
White:	10,484	92.90
Not Hispanic (9,424)	9,549	84.62
Hispanic (882)	935	8.29
Yugoslavian	8	0.07

Summit

Place Type: Township
County: Jackson
Population: 21,534

Ancestry/Race	Number	%
African American/Black:	1,056	4.90
Not Hispanic (894)	1,033	4.80
Hispanic (12)	23	0.11
African, sub-Saharan:	73	0.34
African	68	0.31
Ethiopian	5	0.02
Alaska Native tribes, specified:	1	0.00
Aleut (1)	1	0.00
Alaska Native tribes, not specified	1	0.00
Am. Ind. or Alaska Nat., not spec.	68	0.32
American Indian tribes, specified:	117	0.54
Apache (1)	5	0.02
Blackfeet (1)	7	0.03
Cherokee (7)	44	0.20
Chippewa (14)	22	0.10
Choctaw (1)	2	0.01
Cree	2	0.01
Delaware	1	0.00
Iroquois (3)	6	0.03
Latin American Indians (3)	3	0.01
Ottawa	5	0.02
Potawatomi	3	0.01
Pueblo (1)	3	0.01
Seminole	1	0.00
Sioux	1	0.00
Yaqui	1	0.00
All other tribes (2)	11	0.05
American Indian tribes, not spec.	6	0.03
Arab:	45	0.21
Arab/Arabic	19	0.09
Lebanese	16	0.07
Syrian	10	0.05
Asian:	374	1.74
Bangladeshi (2)	2	0.01
Cambodian (1)	1	0.00
Chinese, ex. Taiwanese (23)	26	0.12
Filipino (15)	23	0.11
Indian (107)	113	0.52
Indonesian	1	0.00
Japanese (87)	101	0.47
Korean (35)	44	0.20
Pakistani (24)	32	0.15
Thai (3)	4	0.02
Vietnamese (16)	21	0.10
Other Asian, not specified (1)	6	0.03
Australian	9	0.04
Austrian	26	0.12
Belgian	175	0.81
British	88	0.41
Bulgarian	29	0.13
Canadian	64	0.30
Celtic	6	0.03
Croatian	9	0.04
Czech	54	0.25
Czechoslovakian	18	0.08
Danish	72	0.33
Dutch	862	3.99
English	3,244	15.02
European	141	0.65
Finnish	97	0.45
French, except Basque	1,023	4.74
French Canadian	257	1.19
German	5,187	24.02
Greek	98	0.45
Guyanese	13	0.06
Hawaii Native/Pacific Islander:	27	0.13
Melanesian: (1)	1	0.00
Other Melanesian (1)	1	0.00
Micronesian: (1)	2	0.01
Guamanian/Chamorro	1	0.00
Other Micronesian (1)	1	0.00
Polynesian: (8)	16	0.07
Native Hawaiian (2)	7	0.03
Tongan (6)	9	0.04
Other Pac. Isl., not spec. (7)	8	0.04
Hispanic or Latino:	398	1.85
Central American:	6	0.03
Panamanian	4	0.02
Salvadoran	2	0.01
Cuban	1	0.00
Mexican	275	1.28
Puerto Rican	40	0.19
South American:	10	0.05
Bolivian	1	0.00
Colombian	5	0.02
Peruvian	1	0.00
Venezuelan	3	0.01
Other Hispanic or Latino	66	0.31
Hungarian	77	0.36
Irish	3,374	15.63
Italian	674	3.12
Latvian	8	0.04
Lithuanian	86	0.40
Macedonian	76	0.35
Northern European	37	0.17
Norwegian	189	0.88
Pennsylvania German	15	0.07
Polish	1,676	7.76
Portuguese	38	0.18
Romanian	33	0.15
Russian	188	0.87
Scandinavian	59	0.27
Scotch-Irish	234	1.08
Scottish	657	3.04
Serbian	9	0.04
Slavic	5	0.02
Slovak	26	0.12
Slovene	10	0.05
Swedish	294	1.36
Swiss	121	0.56
Ukrainian	44	0.20
United States or American	1,650	7.64
Welsh	143	0.66
West Indian, excl. Hispanic:	10	0.05
Belizean	10	0.05
White:	20,068	93.19
Not Hispanic (19,514)	19,792	91.91
Hispanic (238)	276	1.28
Yugoslavian	23	0.11

Sumpter

Place Type: Township
County: Wayne
Population: 11,856

Ancestry/Race	Number	%
African American/Black:	1,541	13.00
Not Hispanic (1,456)	1,534	12.94
Hispanic (6)	7	0.06
African, sub-Saharan:	64	0.54
African	64	0.54
Am. Ind. or Alaska Nat., not spec.	45	0.38
American Indian tribes, specified:	121	1.02
Apache (1)	5	0.04
Blackfeet	2	0.02
Cherokee (13)	52	0.44
Chippewa (16)	24	0.20
Choctaw (1)	4	0.03
Iroquois (2)	12	0.10
Latin American Indians	2	0.02
Lumbee	1	0.01
Navajo (2)	5	0.04
Ottawa (2)	2	0.02
Potawatomi (3)	6	0.05
Sioux (2)	6	0.05
American Indian tribes, not spec.	6	0.05
Arab:	48	0.40
Lebanese	48	0.40
Armenian	49	0.41
Asian:	49	0.41
Chinese, ex. Taiwanese (1)	1	0.01
Filipino (5)	9	0.08
Indian (1)	2	0.02
Japanese (1)	4	0.03
Korean (7)	7	0.06
Vietnamese (4)	5	0.04
Other Asian, not specified (2)	21	0.18
Australian	42	0.35
Austrian	16	0.13
Belgian	15	0.13
Canadian	69	0.58
Croatian	8	0.07
Czech	15	0.13
Czechoslovakian	14	0.12
Danish	8	0.07
Dutch	156	1.32
English	1,006	8.49
European	88	0.74
Finnish	47	0.40
French, except Basque	424	3.58
French Canadian	272	2.29
German	2,328	19.64
Greek	76	0.64
Hawaii Native/Pacific Islander:	1	0.01
Other Pac. Isl., not spec.	1	0.01
Hispanic or Latino:	211	1.78
Central American:	3	0.03
Panamanian	3	0.03
Cuban	3	0.03
Mexican	140	1.18

Notes: 1. Figures in the "Number" column do not add up to the total population due to: a) Ancestry/Race overlap — e.g. persons can report being both White and Irish, b) persons of Hispanic origin can report being any race, c) persons reporting two ancestries are counted in both categories. 2. Numbers in parentheses indicate the number of persons reporting this ancestry/race alone, not in combination with any other ancestry/race. 3. Refer to the Explanation of Data in the front of the book for more detailed information.

Ancestry/Race	Number	%
Puerto Rican	23	0.19
South American:	2	0.02
Argentinean	1	0.01
Other South American	1	0.01
Other Hispanic or Latino	40	0.34
Hungarian	299	2.52
Icelander	6	0.05
Irish	1,810	15.27
Italian	348	2.94
Lithuanian	28	0.24
Macedonian	7	0.06
Maltese	5	0.04
Norwegian	109	0.92
Polish	1,068	9.01
Portuguese	9	0.08
Russian	42	0.35
Scotch-Irish	134	1.13
Scottish	236	1.99
Serbian	5	0.04
Slovak	18	0.15
Swedish	97	0.82
Swiss	11	0.09
Ukrainian	22	0.19
United States or American	513	4.33
Welsh	53	0.45
West Indian, excl. Hispanic:	21	0.18
Haitian	14	0.12
Jamaican	7	0.06
White:	10,236	86.34
Not Hispanic (9,895)	10,075	84.98
Hispanic (145)	161	1.36
Yugoslavian	47	0.40

Superior

Place Type: Township
County: Washtenaw
Population: 10,740

Ancestry/Race	Number	%
African American/Black:	3,485	32.45
Not Hispanic (3,294)	3,465	32.26
Hispanic (15)	20	0.19
African, sub-Saharan:	101	0.94
African	74	0.69
Ghanian	27	0.25
Am. Ind. or Alaska Nat., not spec.	46	0.43
Alsatian	7	0.07
American Indian tribes, specified:	90	0.84
Apache	1	0.01
Blackfeet (4)	13	0.12
Cherokee (11)	23	0.21
Chickasaw	1	0.01
Chippewa (6)	14	0.13
Choctaw	5	0.05
Creek	4	0.04
Iroquois	3	0.03
Latin American Indians (1)	1	0.01
Ottawa (5)	6	0.06
Potawatomi	3	0.03
Pueblo (2)	2	0.02
Sioux	3	0.03
All other tribes (5)	11	0.10
American Indian tribes, not spec.	6	0.06
Arab:	71	0.66
Arab/Arabic	44	0.41
Lebanese	18	0.17
Syrian	9	0.08
Asian:	312	2.91
Chinese, ex. Taiwanese (62)	78	0.73
Filipino (29)	37	0.34
Indian (56)	69	0.64
Indonesian (2)	2	0.02
Japanese (6)	16	0.15
Korean (33)	42	0.39
Laotian (17)	19	0.18
Malaysian (1)	1	0.01
Pakistani (12)	12	0.11
Taiwanese (3)	3	0.03
Thai	2	0.02
Vietnamese (17)	21	0.20
Other Asian, not specified (3)	10	0.09
Austrian	41	0.38
Belgian	23	0.21
British	65	0.61
Canadian	11	0.10
Croatian	6	0.06
Czech	25	0.23
Czechoslovakian	10	0.09
Danish	41	0.38
Dutch	135	1.26
English	1,107	10.31
Estonian	16	0.15
European	149	1.39
Finnish	10	0.09
French, except Basque	339	3.16
French Canadian	67	0.62
German	1,762	16.41
Greek	25	0.23
Hawaii Native/Pacific Islander:	7	0.07
Micronesian:	2	0.02
Other Micronesian	2	0.02
Polynesian: (3)	5	0.05
Native Hawaiian (3)	5	0.05
Hispanic or Latino:	197	1.83
Central American:	12	0.11
Costa Rican	10	0.09
Guatemalan	1	0.01
Honduran	1	0.01
Cuban	12	0.11
Dominican Republic	4	0.04
Mexican	100	0.93
Puerto Rican	38	0.35
South American:	3	0.03
Chilean	1	0.01
Colombian	2	0.02
Other Hispanic or Latino	28	0.26
Hungarian	84	0.78
Icelander	4	0.04
Iranian	8	0.07
Irish	1,160	10.80
Italian	509	4.74
Latvian	6	0.06
Lithuanian	52	0.48
Northern European	24	0.22
Norwegian	71	0.66
Polish	672	6.26
Romanian	14	0.13
Russian	152	1.42
Scandinavian	21	0.20
Scotch-Irish	93	0.87
Scottish	207	1.93
Slavic	33	0.31
Slovak	8	0.07
Slovene	12	0.11
Swedish	188	1.75
Swiss	26	0.24
Ukrainian	98	0.91
United States or American	291	2.71
Welsh	46	0.43
West Indian, excl. Hispanic:	41	0.38
Bahamian	35	0.33
Barbadian	6	0.06
White:	6,996	65.14
Not Hispanic (6,674)	6,888	64.13
Hispanic (93)	108	1.01

Taylor

Place Type: City
County: Wayne
Population: 65,868

Ancestry/Race	Number	%
African American/Black:	6,270	9.52
Not Hispanic (5,721)	6,181	9.38
Hispanic (42)	89	0.14
African, sub-Saharan:	333	0.51
African	294	0.45
Nigerian	39	0.06
Alaska Native tribes, specified:	3	0.00
Alaska Athabascan (1)	1	0.00
Tlingit-Haida (1)	2	0.00
Am. Ind. or Alaska Nat., not spec.	293	0.44
Albanian	143	0.22
American Indian tribes, specified:	707	1.07
Apache (4)	19	0.03
Blackfeet (6)	33	0.05
Cherokee (98)	306	0.46
Cheyenne (1)	3	0.00
Chickasaw	1	0.00
Chippewa (81)	127	0.19
Choctaw (2)	3	0.00
Comanche (3)	5	0.01
Cree (2)	4	0.01
Creek (1)	14	0.02
Delaware (13)	16	0.02
Iroquois (45)	59	0.09
Latin American Indians (13)	21	0.03
Lumbee (20)	26	0.04
Menominee	1	0.00
Navajo (1)	2	0.00
Osage (1)	3	0.00
Ottawa (14)	16	0.02
Potawatomi	2	0.00
Pueblo (1)	1	0.00
Seminole	2	0.00
Sioux (2)	13	0.02
Yaqui (1)	1	0.00
All other tribes (16)	29	0.04
American Indian tribes, not spec.	38	0.06
Arab:	402	0.61
Arab/Arabic	164	0.25
Jordanian	20	0.03
Lebanese	142	0.22
Palestinian	31	0.05
Syrian	45	0.07
Armenian	158	0.24
Asian:	1,249	1.90
Cambodian (10)	14	0.02
Chinese, ex. Taiwanese (69)	78	0.12
Filipino (169)	212	0.32
Indian (466)	495	0.75
Indonesian (15)	16	0.02
Japanese (40)	69	0.10
Korean (47)	59	0.09
Laotian (1)	1	0.00
Pakistani (132)	146	0.22
Taiwanese (3)	3	0.00
Thai (8)	8	0.01
Vietnamese (75)	84	0.13
Other Asian, specified (4)	5	0.01
Other Asian, not specified (28)	59	0.09
Assyrian/Chaldean/Syriac	18	0.03
Australian	6	0.01
Austrian	202	0.31
Belgian	158	0.24
Brazilian	66	0.10
British	170	0.26
Bulgarian	30	0.05
Canadian	388	0.59
Celtic	40	0.06
Croatian	76	0.12
Czech	135	0.20
Czechoslovakian	92	0.14
Danish	55	0.08
Dutch	1,125	1.71
Eastern European	6	0.01
English	5,378	8.16
European	264	0.40
Finnish	355	0.54
French, except Basque	3,992	6.06
French Canadian	1,962	2.98
German	12,110	18.39
Greek	261	0.40
Hawaii Native/Pacific Islander:	47	0.07
Micronesian: (6)	8	0.01
Guamanian/Chamorro (5)	7	0.01
Other Micronesian (1)	1	0.00
Polynesian: (9)	17	0.03

Notes: 1. Figures in the "Number" column do not add up to the total population due to: a) Ancestry/Race overlap — e.g. persons can report being both White and Irish, b) persons of Hispanic origin can report being any race, c) persons reporting two ancestries are counted in both categories. 2. Numbers in parentheses indicate the number of persons reporting this ancestry/race alone, not in combination with any other ancestry/race. 3. Refer to the Explanation of Data in the front of the book for more detailed information.

Ancestry/Race	Number	%
Native Hawaiian (8)	13	0.02
Samoan	3	0.00
Other Polynesian (1)	1	0.00
Other Pac. Isl., specified	1	0.00
Other Pac. Isl., not spec. (6)	21	0.03
Hispanic or Latino:	2,131	3.24
Central American:	30	0.05
Costa Rican	6	0.01
Guatemalan	10	0.02
Nicaraguan	11	0.02
Panamanian	1	0.00
Salvadoran	2	0.00
Cuban	60	0.09
Dominican Republic	4	0.01
Mexican	1,482	2.25
Puerto Rican	178	0.27
South American:	27	0.04
Argentinean	16	0.02
Chilean	1	0.00
Colombian	3	0.00
Ecuadorian	3	0.00
Peruvian	1	0.00
Venezuelan	2	0.00
Other South American	1	0.00
Other Hispanic or Latino	350	0.53
Hungarian	2,146	3.26
Irish	8,955	13.60
Italian	3,230	4.90
Lithuanian	234	0.36
Macedonian	51	0.08
Maltese	296	0.45
Northern European	4	0.01
Norwegian	318	0.48
Pennsylvania German	25	0.04
Polish	7,143	10.84
Portuguese	49	0.07
Romanian	119	0.18
Russian	303	0.46
Scandinavian	22	0.03
Scotch-Irish	882	1.34
Scottish	1,739	2.64
Serbian	40	0.06
Slavic	60	0.09
Slovak	312	0.47
Slovene	66	0.10
Swedish	552	0.84
Swiss	68	0.10
Turkish	15	0.02
Ukrainian	204	0.31
United States or American	4,411	6.70
Welsh	238	0.36
West Indian, excl. Hispanic:	87	0.13
Bahamian	18	0.03
Haitian	11	0.02
Jamaican	31	0.05
Trinidadian and Tobagonian	10	0.02
West Indian	17	0.03
White:	57,896	87.90
Not Hispanic (55,338)	56,316	85.50
Hispanic (1,393)	1,580	2.40
Yugoslavian	77	0.12

Texas

Place Type: Township
County: Kalamazoo
Population: 10,919

Ancestry/Race	Number	%
African American/Black:	214	1.96
Not Hispanic (163)	212	1.94
Hispanic (2)	2	0.02
African, sub-Saharan:	6	0.05
Ethiopian	6	0.05
Am. Ind. or Alaska Nat., not spec.	22	0.20
Albanian	6	0.05
American Indian tribes, specified:	35	0.32
Apache	1	0.01
Blackfeet	3	0.03
Cherokee (2)	7	0.06
Chippewa (2)	6	0.05
Choctaw (1)	1	0.01
Comanche	1	0.01
Creek	1	0.01
Kiowa	1	0.01
Latin American Indians (2)	2	0.02
Ottawa (3)	3	0.03
Potawatomi (1)	8	0.07
Sioux	1	0.01
American Indian tribes, not spec.	1	0.01
Arab:	44	0.40
Lebanese	12	0.11
Palestinian	32	0.29
Armenian	5	0.05
Asian:	293	2.68
Chinese, ex. Taiwanese (52)	53	0.49
Filipino (11)	15	0.14
Indian (117)	124	1.14
Japanese (11)	15	0.14
Korean (46)	48	0.44
Malaysian (1)	1	0.01
Pakistani (12)	17	0.16
Taiwanese (1)	1	0.01
Thai (3)	5	0.05
Vietnamese (8)	8	0.07
Other Asian, not specified (1)	6	0.05
Austrian	17	0.16
Belgian	19	0.17
British	73	0.67
Canadian	24	0.22
Croatian	165	1.51
Czech	55	0.50
Czechoslovakian	9	0.08
Danish	74	0.68
Dutch	1,463	13.40
English	1,715	15.71
European	50	0.46
Finnish	82	0.75
French, except Basque	393	3.60
French Canadian	162	1.48
German	3,191	29.22
Greek	39	0.36
Hawaii Native/Pacific Islander:	3	0.03
Micronesian: (2)	2	0.02
Guamanian/Chamorro (2)	2	0.02
Polynesian: (1)	1	0.01
Native Hawaiian (1)	1	0.01
Hispanic or Latino:	170	1.56
Central American:	3	0.03
Guatemalan	1	0.01
Honduran	1	0.01
Panamanian	1	0.01
Cuban	7	0.06
Dominican Republic	4	0.04
Mexican	90	0.82
Puerto Rican	24	0.22
South American:	12	0.11
Bolivian	1	0.01
Chilean	5	0.05
Colombian	1	0.01
Peruvian	1	0.01
Venezuelan	2	0.02
Other South American	2	0.02
Other Hispanic or Latino	30	0.27
Hungarian	60	0.55
Irish	1,570	14.38
Israeli	6	0.05
Italian	477	4.37
Latvian	73	0.67
Lithuanian	75	0.69
New Zealander	20	0.18
Northern European	54	0.49
Norwegian	130	1.19
Polish	738	6.76
Portuguese	6	0.05
Russian	68	0.62
Scandinavian	8	0.07
Scotch-Irish	132	1.21
Scottish	387	3.54
Serbian	13	0.12
Slavic	12	0.11
Slovak	16	0.15
Slovene	14	0.13
Swedish	273	2.50
Swiss	106	0.97
Ukrainian	36	0.33
United States or American	361	3.31
Welsh	73	0.67
White:	10,410	95.34
Not Hispanic (10,184)	10,282	94.17
Hispanic (113)	128	1.17
Yugoslavian	13	0.12

Thomas

Place Type: Township
County: Saginaw
Population: 11,877

Ancestry/Race	Number	%
African American/Black:	93	0.78
Not Hispanic (71)	86	0.72
Hispanic (3)	7	0.06
Am. Ind. or Alaska Nat., not spec.	9	0.08
American Indian tribes, specified:	40	0.34
Blackfeet (1)	1	0.01
Cherokee	3	0.03
Chippewa (11)	19	0.16
Choctaw (1)	1	0.01
Iroquois	1	0.01
Latin American Indians (6)	6	0.05
Osage	1	0.01
Potawatomi (1)	1	0.01
All other tribes (1)	7	0.06
American Indian tribes, not spec.	1	0.01
Arab:	47	0.40
Lebanese	6	0.05
Syrian	11	0.09
Other Arab	30	0.25
Asian:	94	0.79
Bangladeshi (1)	1	0.01
Chinese, ex. Taiwanese (9)	10	0.08
Filipino (12)	15	0.13
Indian (35)	38	0.32
Japanese (2)	2	0.02
Korean (20)	22	0.19
Pakistani (2)	2	0.02
Other Asian, not specified	4	0.03
Austrian	45	0.38
Belgian	49	0.41
Brazilian	11	0.09
British	37	0.31
Canadian	77	0.65
Croatian	6	0.05
Czech	65	0.55
Czechoslovakian	27	0.23
Danish	33	0.28
Dutch	238	2.00
English	1,291	10.87
European	28	0.24
Finnish	10	0.08
French, except Basque	900	7.58
French Canadian	368	3.10
German	4,648	39.13
Greek	21	0.18
Hispanic or Latino:	314	2.64
Central American:	4	0.03
Honduran	1	0.01
Panamanian	2	0.02
Salvadoran	1	0.01
Cuban	2	0.02
Mexican	228	1.92
Puerto Rican	6	0.05
South American:	7	0.06
Colombian	3	0.03
Venezuelan	1	0.01
Other South American	3	0.03
Other Hispanic or Latino	67	0.56
Hungarian	197	1.66
Iranian	14	0.12

Notes: 1. Figures in the "Number" column do not add up to the total population due to: a) Ancestry/Race overlap — e.g. persons can report being both White and Irish, b) persons of Hispanic origin can report being any race, c) persons reporting two ancestries are counted in both categories. 2. Numbers in parentheses indicate the number of persons reporting this ancestry/race alone, not in combination with any other ancestry/race. 3. Refer to the Explanation of Data in the front of the book for more detailed information.

Ancestry/Race	Number	%
Irish	1,512	12.73
Italian	367	3.09
Latvian	16	0.13
Lithuanian	91	0.77
Norwegian	67	0.56
Pennsylvania German	30	0.25
Polish	1,274	10.73
Russian	106	0.89
Scandinavian	32	0.27
Scotch-Irish	149	1.25
Scottish	327	2.75
Serbian	28	0.24
Slavic	36	0.30
Slovak	104	0.88
Slovene	10	0.08
Swedish	160	1.35
Swiss	34	0.29
Ukrainian	12	0.10
United States or American	654	5.51
Welsh	84	0.71
White:	11,621	97.84
Not Hispanic (11,332)	11,391	95.91
Hispanic (201)	230	1.94
Yugoslavian	5	0.04

Traverse City

Place Type: City
County: Grand Traverse
Population: 14,532

Ancestry/Race	Number	%
African American/Black:	138	0.95
Not Hispanic (91)	132	0.91
Hispanic (4)	6	0.04
Alaska Native tribes, specified:	1	0.01
Alaska Athabascan (1)	1	0.01
Am. Ind. or Alaska Nat., not spec.	67	0.46
American Indian tribes, specified:	175	1.20
Apache	3	0.02
Blackfeet (1)	1	0.01
Cherokee (8)	22	0.15
Chippewa (85)	111	0.76
Choctaw	1	0.01
Crow (1)	1	0.01
Iroquois (1)	2	0.01
Latin American Indians	1	0.01
Menominee	1	0.01
Navajo (1)	1	0.01
Ottawa (4)	16	0.11
Potawatomi	3	0.02
Seminole (2)	3	0.02
Sioux	5	0.03
All other tribes (1)	4	0.03
American Indian tribes, not spec.	12	0.08
Arab:	57	0.39
Arab/Arabic	29	0.20
Jordanian	7	0.05
Lebanese	16	0.11
Syrian	5	0.03
Armenian	29	0.20
Asian:	120	0.83
Chinese, ex. Taiwanese (15)	17	0.12
Filipino (7)	9	0.06
Hmong (8)	8	0.06
Indian (11)	12	0.08
Indonesian (1)	3	0.02
Japanese (5)	6	0.04
Korean (11)	21	0.14
Laotian (3)	3	0.02
Malaysian (1)	1	0.01
Taiwanese	2	0.01
Thai (2)	4	0.03
Vietnamese (6)	12	0.08
Other Asian, specified	2	0.01
Other Asian, not specified	20	0.14
Australian	22	0.15
Austrian	42	0.29
Belgian	49	0.34
British	70	0.48
Canadian	108	0.74
Celtic	9	0.06
Croatian	13	0.09
Czech	269	1.85
Czechoslovakian	80	0.55
Danish	132	0.91
Dutch	685	4.71
English	2,329	16.01
European	148	1.02
Finnish	226	1.55
French, except Basque	803	5.52
French Canadian	392	2.69
German	3,747	25.75
Greek	70	0.48
Hawaii Native/Pacific Islander:	17	0.12
Micronesian: (5)	6	0.04
Guamanian/Chamorro (4)	4	0.03
Other Micronesian (1)	2	0.01
Polynesian:	4	0.03
Native Hawaiian	3	0.02
Samoan	1	0.01
Other Pac. Isl., not spec.	7	0.05
Hispanic or Latino:	242	1.67
Central American:	12	0.08
Guatemalan	2	0.01
Honduran	1	0.01
Panamanian	2	0.01
Salvadoran	4	0.03
Other Central American	3	0.02
Cuban	3	0.02
Dominican Republic	1	0.01
Mexican	135	0.93
Puerto Rican	17	0.12
South American:	3	0.02
Colombian	2	0.01
Ecuadorian	1	0.01
Other Hispanic or Latino	71	0.49
Hungarian	50	0.34
Irish	2,383	16.38
Italian	549	3.77
Lithuanian	62	0.43
Luxemburger	7	0.05
Maltese	3	0.02
New Zealander	7	0.05
Northern European	16	0.11
Norwegian	338	2.32
Pennsylvania German	6	0.04
Polish	1,298	8.92
Romanian	8	0.05
Russian	107	0.74
Scandinavian	88	0.60
Scotch-Irish	214	1.47
Scottish	576	3.96
Serbian	6	0.04
Slavic	10	0.07
Slovak	24	0.16
Slovene	8	0.05
Swedish	509	3.50
Swiss	56	0.38
Turkish	16	0.11
Ukrainian	87	0.60
United States or American	624	4.29
Welsh	168	1.15
White:	14,130	97.23
Not Hispanic (13,803)	13,969	96.13
Hispanic (147)	161	1.11
Yugoslavian	9	0.06

Trenton

Place Type: City
County: Wayne
Population: 19,584

Ancestry/Race	Number	%
African American/Black:	107	0.55
Not Hispanic (73)	106	0.54
Hispanic	1	0.01
African, sub-Saharan:	6	0.03
African	6	0.03
Am. Ind. or Alaska Nat., not spec.	37	0.19
Albanian	17	0.09
Alsatian	6	0.03
American Indian tribes, specified:	156	0.80
Apache (1)	3	0.02
Blackfeet	2	0.01
Cherokee (12)	50	0.26
Chickasaw	1	0.01
Chippewa (23)	41	0.21
Choctaw (2)	2	0.01
Comanche	1	0.01
Crow	2	0.01
Iroquois	9	0.05
Latin American Indians	6	0.03
Lumbee (4)	5	0.03
Menominee (4)	6	0.03
Navajo (4)	5	0.03
Osage (3)	3	0.02
Ottawa (3)	3	0.02
Potawatomi (1)	2	0.01
Sioux (1)	9	0.05
All other tribes (5)	6	0.03
American Indian tribes, not spec.	3	0.02
Arab:	151	0.77
Egyptian	17	0.09
Jordanian	25	0.13
Lebanese	103	0.53
Syrian	6	0.03
Armenian	32	0.16
Asian:	224	1.14
Chinese, ex. Taiwanese (18)	23	0.12
Filipino (28)	54	0.28
Indian (33)	39	0.20
Japanese (21)	37	0.19
Korean (32)	41	0.21
Pakistani (8)	8	0.04
Sri Lankan (2)	2	0.01
Thai (7)	12	0.06
Vietnamese (1)	4	0.02
Other Asian, not specified (1)	4	0.02
Austrian	84	0.43
Belgian	114	0.58
Brazilian	6	0.03
British	83	0.42
Bulgarian	6	0.03
Canadian	64	0.33
Croatian	30	0.15
Czech	182	0.93
Czechoslovakian	67	0.34
Danish	47	0.24
Dutch	325	1.66
Eastern European	7	0.04
English	2,521	12.87
European	70	0.36
Finnish	81	0.41
French, except Basque	1,858	9.49
French Canadian	802	4.10
German	4,295	21.93
Greek	232	1.18
Hawaii Native/Pacific Islander:	6	0.03
Polynesian: (4)	5	0.03
Native Hawaiian (4)	5	0.03
Other Pac. Isl., not spec. (1)	1	0.01
Hispanic or Latino:	390	1.99
Cuban	3	0.02
Mexican	267	1.36
Puerto Rican	26	0.13
South American:	9	0.05
Argentinean	6	0.03
Colombian	3	0.02
Other Hispanic or Latino	85	0.43
Hungarian	990	5.06
Irish	3,076	15.71
Italian	1,799	9.19
Latvian	21	0.11
Lithuanian	80	0.41
Macedonian	9	0.05
Maltese	103	0.53
Norwegian	156	0.80
Polish	3,126	15.96

Notes: 1. Figures in the "Number" column do not add up to the total population due to: a) Ancestry/Race overlap — e.g. persons can report being both White and Irish, b) persons of Hispanic origin can report being any race, c) persons reporting two ancestries are counted in both categories. 2. Numbers in parentheses indicate the number of persons reporting this ancestry/race alone, not in combination with any other ancestry/race. 3. Refer to the Explanation of Data in the front of the book for more detailed information.

Ancestry/Race	Number	%
Portuguese	21	0.11
Romanian	34	0.17
Russian	86	0.44
Scandinavian	7	0.04
Scotch-Irish	442	2.26
Scottish	738	3.77
Serbian	63	0.32
Slavic	28	0.14
Slovak	106	0.54
Slovene	13	0.07
Swedish	197	1.01
Swiss	64	0.33
Ukrainian	217	1.11
United States or American	914	4.67
Welsh	94	0.48
White:	19,215	98.12
Not Hispanic (18,688)	18,875	96.38
Hispanic (293)	340	1.74
Yugoslavian	59	0.30

Troy

Place Type: City
County: Oakland
Population: 80,959

Ancestry/Race	Number	%
Afghan	11	0.01
African American/Black:	1,883	2.33
Not Hispanic (1,678)	1,850	2.29
Hispanic (16)	33	0.04
African, sub-Saharan:	118	0.15
African	54	0.07
Ghanian	40	0.05
Liberian	10	0.01
Nigerian	6	0.01
South African	8	0.01
Am. Ind. or Alaska Nat., not spec.	140	0.17
Albanian	410	0.51
Alsatian	12	0.01
American Indian tribes, specified:	237	0.29
Apache (4)	13	0.02
Blackfeet (6)	7	0.01
Cherokee (22)	81	0.10
Cheyenne	2	0.00
Chippewa (15)	41	0.05
Choctaw (2)	4	0.00
Cree (1)	1	0.00
Iroquois (11)	19	0.02
Latin American Indians (7)	9	0.01
Lumbee (1)	3	0.00
Navajo	1	0.00
Ottawa (3)	12	0.01
Potawatomi (4)	6	0.01
Pueblo (1)	5	0.01
Seminole	2	0.00
Sioux	7	0.01
Ute	2	0.00
All other tribes (14)	22	0.03
American Indian tribes, not spec.	12	0.01
Arab:	2,570	3.17
Arab/Arabic	236	0.29
Egyptian	355	0.44
Iraqi	438	0.54
Jordanian	60	0.07
Lebanese	1,036	1.28
Palestinian	114	0.14
Syrian	294	0.36
Other Arab	37	0.05
Armenian	307	0.38
Asian:	11,419	14.10
Bangladeshi (41)	41	0.05
Cambodian (6)	6	0.01
Chinese, ex. Taiwanese (2,680)	2,821	3.48
Filipino (798)	923	1.14
Hmong (5)	5	0.01
Indian (4,655)	4,789	5.92
Indonesian (3)	3	0.00
Japanese (269)	339	0.42
Korean (1,213)	1,283	1.58
Laotian (9)	9	0.01
Malaysian (5)	6	0.01
Pakistani (264)	306	0.38
Sri Lankan (20)	20	0.02
Taiwanese (381)	419	0.52
Thai (40)	55	0.07
Vietnamese (162)	172	0.21
Other Asian, specified (7)	12	0.01
Other Asian, not specified (66)	210	0.26
Assyrian/Chaldean/Syriac	2,047	2.53
Australian	42	0.05
Austrian	481	0.59
Belgian	669	0.83
Brazilian	57	0.07
British	455	0.56
Bulgarian	56	0.07
Canadian	771	0.95
Celtic	22	0.03
Croatian	355	0.44
Czech	329	0.41
Czechoslovakian	292	0.36
Danish	439	0.54
Dutch	1,312	1.62
Eastern European	36	0.04
English	9,313	11.50
Estonian	7	0.01
European	622	0.77
Finnish	810	1.00
French, except Basque	3,395	4.19
French Canadian	1,431	1.77
German	15,646	19.33
Greek	1,003	1.24
Hawaii Native/Pacific Islander:	59	0.07
Polynesian: (16)	25	0.03
Native Hawaiian (11)	19	0.02
Samoan (4)	5	0.01
Tongan (1)	1	0.00
Other Pac. Isl., specified	1	0.00
Other Pac. Isl., not spec. (2)	33	0.04
Hispanic or Latino:	1,184	1.46
Central American:	43	0.05
Guatemalan	4	0.00
Honduran	10	0.01
Nicaraguan	3	0.00
Panamanian	2	0.00
Salvadoran	24	0.03
Cuban	30	0.04
Dominican Republic	3	0.00
Mexican	578	0.71
Puerto Rican	87	0.11
South American:	160	0.20
Argentinean	32	0.04
Chilean	10	0.01
Colombian	47	0.06
Ecuadorian	9	0.01
Paraguayan	5	0.01
Peruvian	20	0.02
Venezuelan	21	0.03
Other South American	16	0.02
Other Hispanic or Latino	283	0.35
Hungarian	1,019	1.26
Icelander	36	0.04
Iranian	169	0.21
Irish	10,233	12.64
Israeli	49	0.06
Italian	5,862	7.24
Latvian	29	0.04
Lithuanian	482	0.60
Macedonian	211	0.26
Maltese	104	0.13
New Zealander	8	0.01
Northern European	46	0.06
Norwegian	853	1.05
Pennsylvania German	6	0.01
Polish	8,928	11.03
Portuguese	57	0.07
Romanian	1,111	1.37
Russian	895	1.11
Scandinavian	108	0.13
Scotch-Irish	1,068	1.32
Scottish	2,497	3.08
Serbian	177	0.22
Slavic	25	0.03
Slovak	465	0.57
Slovene	86	0.11
Swedish	1,077	1.33
Swiss	181	0.22
Turkish	54	0.07
Ukrainian	1,179	1.46
United States or American	2,618	3.23
Welsh	680	0.84
West Indian, excl. Hispanic:	69	0.09
Barbadian	10	0.01
Belizean	9	0.01
Dutch West Indian	4	0.00
Haitian	30	0.04
Jamaican	10	0.01
Trinidadian and Tobagonian	6	0.01
White:	67,910	83.88
Not Hispanic (65,809)	67,002	82.76
Hispanic (818)	908	1.12
Yugoslavian	161	0.20

Van Buren

Place Type: Township
County: Wayne
Population: 23,559

Ancestry/Race	Number	%
African American/Black:	3,097	13.15
Not Hispanic (2,820)	3,064	13.01
Hispanic (15)	33	0.14
African, sub-Saharan:	134	0.57
African	97	0.41
Ethiopian	18	0.08
Kenyan	11	0.05
Nigerian	8	0.03
Alaska Native tribes, specified:	2	0.01
Eskimo (2)	2	0.01
Alaska Native tribes, not specified	1	0.00
Am. Ind. or Alaska Nat., not spec.	86	0.37
Albanian	7	0.03
American Indian tribes, specified:	221	0.94
Apache (1)	5	0.02
Blackfeet (1)	10	0.04
Cherokee (12)	68	0.29
Chickasaw (1)	1	0.00
Chippewa (31)	42	0.18
Choctaw	5	0.02
Creek (4)	4	0.02
Iroquois (9)	14	0.06
Latin American Indians (6)	10	0.04
Lumbee (1)	1	0.00
Navajo (1)	5	0.02
Ottawa (6)	10	0.04
Potawatomi (8)	9	0.04
Pueblo (2)	2	0.01
Seminole	1	0.00
Shoshone	6	0.03
Sioux	12	0.05
All other tribes (7)	16	0.07
American Indian tribes, not spec.	14	0.06
Arab:	199	0.84
Arab/Arabic	53	0.22
Lebanese	73	0.31
Syrian	51	0.22
Other Arab	22	0.09
Armenian	31	0.13
Asian:	552	2.34
Bangladeshi (1)	1	0.00
Chinese, ex. Taiwanese (63)	83	0.35
Filipino (57)	91	0.39
Indian (176)	194	0.82
Japanese (28)	46	0.20
Korean (38)	46	0.20
Pakistani (20)	21	0.09
Taiwanese (9)	9	0.04
Thai (4)	7	0.03
Vietnamese (22)	24	0.10

Notes: 1. Figures in the "Number" column do not add up to the total population due to: a) Ancestry/Race overlap — e.g. persons can report being both White and Irish, b) persons of Hispanic origin can report being any race, c) persons reporting two ancestries are counted in both categories. 2. Numbers in parentheses indicate the number of persons reporting this ancestry/race alone, not in combination with any other ancestry/race. 3. Refer to the Explanation of Data in the front of the book for more detailed information.

Other Asian, specified	1	0.00
Other Asian, not specified (16)	29	0.12
Assyrian/Chaldean/Syriac	16	0.07
Australian	6	0.03
Austrian	86	0.36
Belgian	72	0.31
British	49	0.21
Canadian	72	0.31
Croatian	88	0.37
Czech	86	0.36
Czechoslovakian	32	0.14
Danish	97	0.41
Dutch	607	2.58
English	2,373	10.07
European	127	0.54
Finnish	181	0.77
French, except Basque	1,112	4.72
French Canadian	473	2.01
German	4,532	19.23
Greek	133	0.56
Hawaii Native/Pacific Islander:	38	0.16
Polynesian: (10)	29	0.12
Native Hawaiian (10)	28	0.12
Samoan	1	0.00
Other Pac. Isl., specified	1	0.00
Other Pac. Isl., not spec.	8	0.03
Hispanic or Latino:	529	2.25
Central American:	18	0.08
Costa Rican	1	0.00
Guatemalan	2	0.01
Honduran	3	0.01
Panamanian	8	0.03
Salvadoran	4	0.02
Cuban	23	0.10
Dominican Republic	4	0.02
Mexican	332	1.41
Puerto Rican	52	0.22
South American:	10	0.04
Bolivian	1	0.00
Chilean	1	0.00
Colombian	5	0.02
Peruvian	2	0.01
Venezuelan	1	0.00
Other Hispanic or Latino	90	0.38
Hungarian	602	2.55
Iranian	56	0.24
Irish	2,837	12.04
Italian	875	3.71
Lithuanian	72	0.31
Macedonian	7	0.03
Maltese	55	0.23
Norwegian	136	0.58
Pennsylvania German	17	0.07
Polish	2,413	10.24
Portuguese	10	0.04
Romanian	133	0.56
Russian	97	0.41
Scandinavian	5	0.02
Scotch-Irish	458	1.94
Scottish	628	2.67
Serbian	20	0.08
Slavic	18	0.08
Slovak	70	0.30
Swedish	143	0.61
Swiss	73	0.31
Ukrainian	70	0.30
United States or American	1,575	6.68
Welsh	70	0.30
West Indian, excl. Hispanic:	45	0.19
Barbadian	9	0.04
Bermudan	18	0.08
Jamaican	8	0.03
West Indian	10	0.04
White:	19,930	84.60
Not Hispanic (19,135)	19,549	82.98
Hispanic (333)	381	1.62
Yugoslavian	7	0.03

Vienna

Place Type: Township
County: Genesee
Population: 13,108

Ancestry/Race	Number	%
African American/Black:	174	1.33
Not Hispanic (147)	173	1.32
Hispanic	1	0.01
Am. Ind. or Alaska Nat., not spec.	52	0.40
American Indian tribes, specified:	94	0.72
Apache	2	0.02
Blackfeet	6	0.05
Cherokee (4)	21	0.16
Chickasaw (6)	6	0.05
Chippewa (21)	37	0.28
Choctaw (2)	3	0.02
Iroquois (2)	4	0.03
Kiowa	1	0.01
Latin American Indians	2	0.02
Osage	1	0.01
Potawatomi (1)	1	0.01
Sioux	2	0.02
All other tribes (4)	8	0.06
American Indian tribes, not spec.	9	0.07
Arab:	100	0.77
Arab/Arabic	73	0.56
Lebanese	27	0.21
Armenian	11	0.08
Asian:	71	0.54
Chinese, ex. Taiwanese (5)	5	0.04
Filipino (5)	7	0.05
Hmong (6)	6	0.05
Indian (5)	5	0.04
Japanese (2)	6	0.05
Korean (15)	25	0.19
Vietnamese (2)	5	0.04
Other Asian, specified (1)	3	0.02
Other Asian, not specified (4)	9	0.07
Assyrian/Chaldean/Syriac	26	0.20
Austrian	6	0.05
Belgian	19	0.15
British	10	0.08
Canadian	122	0.94
Croatian	21	0.16
Czech	81	0.62
Czechoslovakian	67	0.51
Danish	30	0.23
Dutch	451	3.46
English	1,620	12.43
European	48	0.37
Finnish	38	0.29
French, except Basque	1,101	8.44
French Canadian	406	3.11
German	2,700	20.71
Greek	6	0.05
Hawaii Native/Pacific Islander:	2	0.02
Micronesian: (1)	1	0.01
Guamanian/Chamorro (1)	1	0.01
Other Pac. Isl., specified	1	0.01
Hispanic or Latino:	258	1.97
Central American:	3	0.02
Guatemalan	1	0.01
Panamanian	1	0.01
Salvadoran	1	0.01
Cuban	3	0.02
Mexican	193	1.47
Puerto Rican	11	0.08
Other Hispanic or Latino	48	0.37
Hungarian	260	1.99
Irish	1,923	14.75
Italian	478	3.67
Luxemburger	14	0.11
Macedonian	4	0.03
Norwegian	53	0.41
Pennsylvania German	5	0.04
Polish	994	7.62
Romanian	9	0.07
Russian	66	0.51
Scandinavian	2	0.02
Scotch-Irish	161	1.23
Scottish	262	2.01
Slavic	4	0.03
Slovak	49	0.38
Swedish	267	2.05
Swiss	25	0.19
Ukrainian	46	0.35
United States or American	1,311	10.06
Welsh	132	1.01
White:	12,741	97.20
Not Hispanic (12,444)	12,575	95.93
Hispanic (139)	166	1.27

Walker

Place Type: City
County: Kent
Population: 21,842

Ancestry/Race	Number	%
African American/Black:	415	1.90
Not Hispanic (312)	398	1.82
Hispanic (10)	17	0.08
African, sub-Saharan:	71	0.33
African	57	0.26
Kenyan	14	0.06
Alaska Native tribes, specified:	3	0.01
Eskimo (3)	3	0.01
Am. Ind. or Alaska Nat., not spec.	83	0.38
American Indian tribes, specified:	130	0.60
Apache (1)	1	0.00
Blackfeet	6	0.03
Cherokee (7)	22	0.10
Chippewa (30)	44	0.20
Choctaw (1)	1	0.00
Cree	1	0.00
Iroquois	1	0.00
Latin American Indians	1	0.00
Navajo	2	0.01
Ottawa (22)	34	0.16
Potawatomi (2)	12	0.05
Sioux (1)	2	0.01
All other tribes	3	0.01
American Indian tribes, not spec.	5	0.02
Arab:	128	0.59
Lebanese	119	0.55
Palestinian	9	0.04
Asian:	285	1.30
Bangladeshi (7)	8	0.04
Cambodian (1)	1	0.00
Chinese, ex. Taiwanese (27)	31	0.14
Filipino (15)	27	0.12
Indian (55)	68	0.31
Indonesian (1)	2	0.01
Japanese (6)	14	0.06
Korean (34)	37	0.17
Pakistani (4)	17	0.08
Thai	1	0.00
Vietnamese (57)	62	0.28
Other Asian, specified	1	0.00
Other Asian, not specified	16	0.07
Austrian	27	0.12
Belgian	18	0.08
Brazilian	7	0.03
British	25	0.11
Canadian	54	0.25
Croatian	29	0.13
Czech	63	0.29
Czechoslovakian	18	0.08
Danish	109	0.50
Dutch	5,470	25.10
English	1,759	8.07
European	33	0.15
Finnish	114	0.52
French, except Basque	1,032	4.74
French Canadian	330	1.51
German	4,922	22.58
Greek	29	0.13
Hawaii Native/Pacific Islander:	16	0.07

Notes: 1. Figures in the "Number" column do not add up to the total population due to: a) Ancestry/Race overlap — e.g. persons can report being both White and Irish, b) persons of Hispanic origin can report being any race, c) persons reporting two ancestries are counted in both categories. 2. Numbers in parentheses indicate the number of persons reporting this ancestry/race alone, not in combination with any other ancestry/race. 3. Refer to the Explanation of Data in the front of the book for more detailed information.

Micronesian: (3)	3	0.01
Guamanian/Chamorro (1)	1	0.00
Other Micronesian (2)	2	0.01
Polynesian: (6)	9	0.04
Native Hawaiian (2)	5	0.02
Samoan (4)	4	0.02
Other Pac. Isl., specified	1	0.00
Other Pac. Isl., not spec.	3	0.01
Hispanic or Latino:	601	2.75
Central American:	28	0.13
Guatemalan	6	0.03
Honduran	10	0.05
Nicaraguan	6	0.03
Panamanian	2	0.01
Salvadoran	2	0.01
Other Central American	2	0.01
Cuban	26	0.12
Dominican Republic	3	0.01
Mexican	350	1.60
Puerto Rican	76	0.35
South American:	15	0.07
Chilean	1	0.00
Colombian	7	0.03
Peruvian	3	0.01
Uruguayan	2	0.01
Venezuelan	1	0.00
Other South American	1	0.00
Other Hispanic or Latino	103	0.47
Hungarian	84	0.39
Iranian	30	0.14
Irish	2,636	12.09
Italian	716	3.29
Latvian	34	0.16
Lithuanian	354	1.62
Macedonian	9	0.04
Maltese	15	0.07
Norwegian	207	0.95
Polish	3,354	15.39
Portuguese	15	0.07
Romanian	6	0.03
Russian	117	0.54
Scotch-Irish	232	1.06
Scottish	251	1.15
Slavic	7	0.03
Slovak	25	0.11
Slovene	6	0.03
Swedish	410	1.88
Swiss	28	0.13
Ukrainian	27	0.12
United States or American	968	4.44
Welsh	79	0.36
West Indian, excl. Hispanic:	19	0.09
Jamaican	19	0.09
White:	20,931	95.83
Not Hispanic (20,350)	20,571	94.18
Hispanic (293)	360	1.65

Warren

Place Type: City
County: Macomb
Population: 138,247

Ancestry/Race	Number	%
African American/Black:	4,240	3.07
Not Hispanic (3,676)	4,204	3.04
Hispanic (21)	36	0.03
African, sub-Saharan:	213	0.15
African	158	0.11
Nigerian	27	0.02
South African	28	0.02
Alaska Native tribes, specified:	4	0.00
Aleut	1	0.00
Eskimo (2)	2	0.00
Tlingit-Haida (1)	1	0.00
Am. Ind. or Alaska Nat., not spec.	496	0.36
Albanian	1,053	0.76
American Indian tribes, specified:	1,001	0.72
Apache (10)	25	0.02
Blackfeet (8)	46	0.03
Cherokee (98)	429	0.31
Cheyenne	1	0.00
Chickasaw	2	0.00
Chippewa (93)	193	0.14
Choctaw (6)	18	0.01
Comanche (1)	5	0.00
Cree (1)	5	0.00
Creek	1	0.00
Crow	3	0.00
Delaware (8)	11	0.01
Iroquois (21)	61	0.04
Latin American Indians (7)	16	0.01
Lumbee (53)	66	0.05
Menominee (1)	1	0.00
Osage (1)	5	0.00
Ottawa (14)	32	0.02
Paiute (1)	1	0.00
Potawatomi (2)	12	0.01
Pueblo (5)	5	0.00
Seminole	3	0.00
Sioux (7)	17	0.01
Ute (1)	1	0.00
All other tribes (16)	42	0.03
American Indian tribes, not spec.	58	0.04
Arab:	3,478	2.52
Arab/Arabic	753	0.54
Egyptian	101	0.07
Iraqi	906	0.66
Jordanian	114	0.08
Lebanese	1,152	0.83
Palestinian	174	0.13
Syrian	266	0.19
Other Arab	12	0.01
Armenian	165	0.12
Asian:	5,100	3.69
Bangladeshi (41)	56	0.04
Cambodian (29)	42	0.03
Chinese, ex. Taiwanese (306)	367	0.27
Filipino (839)	1,026	0.74
Hmong (733)	780	0.56
Indian (1,013)	1,145	0.83
Indonesian (4)	7	0.01
Japanese (62)	107	0.08
Korean (168)	203	0.15
Laotian (206)	258	0.19
Malaysian (2)	2	0.00
Pakistani (138)	177	0.13
Sri Lankan (1)	6	0.00
Taiwanese (6)	6	0.00
Thai (26)	38	0.03
Vietnamese (512)	551	0.40
Other Asian, specified	1	0.00
Other Asian, not specified (95)	328	0.24
Assyrian/Chaldean/Syriac	2,625	1.90
Australian	18	0.01
Austrian	507	0.37
Belgian	1,825	1.32
Brazilian	32	0.02
British	428	0.31
Bulgarian	34	0.02
Canadian	861	0.62
Carpatho Rusyn	35	0.03
Celtic	22	0.02
Croatian	398	0.29
Czech	446	0.32
Czechoslovakian	370	0.27
Danish	291	0.21
Dutch	1,771	1.28
Eastern European	13	0.01
English	10,088	7.30
Estonian	32	0.02
European	442	0.32
Finnish	820	0.59
French, except Basque	7,314	5.29
French Canadian	3,469	2.51
German	28,146	20.35
German Russian	6	0.00
Greek	977	0.71
Guyanese	18	0.01
Hawaii Native/Pacific Islander:	117	0.08
Micronesian: (6)	19	0.01
Guamanian/Chamorro (6)	18	0.01
Other Micronesian	1	0.00
Polynesian: (15)	29	0.02
Native Hawaiian (9)	20	0.01
Samoan (4)	5	0.00
Other Polynesian (2)	4	0.00
Other Pac. Isl., specified	1	0.00
Other Pac. Isl., not spec. (8)	68	0.05
Hispanic or Latino:	1,868	1.35
Central American:	26	0.02
Costa Rican	3	0.00
Guatemalan	7	0.01
Honduran	1	0.00
Panamanian	13	0.01
Salvadoran	2	0.00
Cuban	46	0.03
Dominican Republic	8	0.01
Mexican	1,094	0.79
Puerto Rican	175	0.13
South American:	62	0.04
Argentinean	22	0.02
Bolivian	1	0.00
Chilean	3	0.00
Colombian	5	0.00
Ecuadorian	9	0.01
Peruvian	8	0.01
Uruguayan	3	0.00
Venezuelan	3	0.00
Other South American	8	0.01
Other Hispanic or Latino	457	0.33
Hungarian	1,129	0.82
Icelander	15	0.01
Irish	15,820	11.44
Israeli	34	0.02
Italian	14,700	10.63
Latvian	48	0.03
Lithuanian	581	0.42
Luxemburger	6	0.00
Macedonian	191	0.14
Maltese	258	0.19
New Zealander	7	0.01
Northern European	8	0.01
Norwegian	723	0.52
Pennsylvania German	35	0.03
Polish	29,075	21.03
Portuguese	62	0.04
Romanian	753	0.54
Russian	1,375	0.99
Scandinavian	87	0.06
Scotch-Irish	1,739	1.26
Scottish	2,481	1.79
Serbian	287	0.21
Slavic	98	0.07
Slovak	1,002	0.72
Slovene	129	0.09
Swedish	1,175	0.85
Swiss	208	0.15
Turkish	25	0.02
Ukrainian	2,397	1.73
United States or American	6,176	4.47
Welsh	545	0.39
West Indian, excl. Hispanic:	36	0.03
Jamaican	14	0.01
Trinidadian and Tobagonian	22	0.02
White:	128,997	93.31
Not Hispanic (124,936)	127,532	92.25
Hispanic (1,269)	1,465	1.06
Yugoslavian	628	0.45

Washington

Place Type: Township
County: Macomb
Population: 19,080

Ancestry/Race	Number	%
African American/Black:	137	0.72
Not Hispanic (91)	132	0.69
Hispanic (3)	5	0.03

Notes: 1. Figures in the "Number" column do not add up to the total population due to: a) Ancestry/Race overlap — e.g. persons can report being both White and Irish, b) persons of Hispanic origin can report being any race, c) persons reporting two ancestries are counted in both categories. 2. Numbers in parentheses indicate the number of persons reporting this ancestry/race alone, not in combination with any other ancestry/race. 3. Refer to the Explanation of Data in the front of the book for more detailed information.

African, sub-Saharan:	6	0.03
African	6	0.03
Am. Ind. or Alaska Nat., not spec.	33	0.17
Albanian	70	0.37
American Indian tribes, specified:	64	0.34
Apache (2)	2	0.01
Cherokee (11)	18	0.09
Chickasaw	1	0.01
Chippewa (7)	14	0.07
Choctaw (1)	1	0.01
Cree	1	0.01
Iroquois (1)	1	0.01
Latin American Indians	2	0.01
Lumbee (6)	11	0.06
Navajo (1)	1	0.01
Ottawa (4)	4	0.02
Seminole (1)	2	0.01
Sioux	1	0.01
All other tribes (5)	5	0.03
American Indian tribes, not spec.	1	0.01
Arab:	128	0.67
Arab/Arabic	4	0.02
Lebanese	124	0.65
Armenian	26	0.14
Asian:	151	0.79
Cambodian (4)	5	0.03
Chinese, ex. Taiwanese (12)	17	0.09
Filipino (22)	31	0.16
Hmong (9)	9	0.05
Indian (10)	12	0.06
Indonesian	1	0.01
Japanese (11)	11	0.06
Korean (37)	41	0.21
Pakistani (5)	10	0.05
Taiwanese	2	0.01
Vietnamese (3)	7	0.04
Other Asian, not specified (4)	5	0.03
Austrian	143	0.75
Belgian	507	2.65
Brazilian	33	0.17
British	80	0.42
Canadian	133	0.70
Croatian	82	0.43
Czech	114	0.60
Czechoslovakian	7	0.04
Danish	96	0.50
Dutch	198	1.04
English	1,983	10.37
European	100	0.52
Finnish	40	0.21
French, except Basque	1,289	6.74
French Canadian	578	3.02
German	5,552	29.03
Greek	221	1.16
Hawaii Native/Pacific Islander:	9	0.05
Micronesian: (2)	3	0.02
Guamanian/Chamorro (2)	3	0.02
Other Pac. Isl., not spec. (2)	6	0.03
Hispanic or Latino:	458	2.40
Cuban	11	0.06
Mexican	364	1.91
Puerto Rican	26	0.14
South American:	9	0.05
Argentinean	2	0.01
Chilean	3	0.02
Peruvian	1	0.01
Venezuelan	2	0.01
Other South American	1	0.01
Other Hispanic or Latino	48	0.25
Hungarian	213	1.11
Iranian	12	0.06
Irish	2,461	12.87
Italian	2,445	12.78
Lithuanian	71	0.37
Luxemburger	22	0.12
Macedonian	60	0.31
Maltese	71	0.37
Northern European	8	0.04
Norwegian	126	0.66
Pennsylvania German	8	0.04
Polish	3,796	19.85
Portuguese	5	0.03
Romanian	145	0.76
Russian	113	0.59
Scandinavian	55	0.29
Scotch-Irish	327	1.71
Scottish	698	3.65
Serbian	14	0.07
Slavic	18	0.09
Slovak	68	0.36
Slovene	18	0.09
Swedish	172	0.90
Swiss	58	0.30
Turkish	7	0.04
Ukrainian	192	1.00
United States or American	703	3.68
Welsh	55	0.29
West Indian, excl. Hispanic:	9	0.05
Jamaican	9	0.05
White:	18,694	97.98
Not Hispanic (18,216)	18,346	96.15
Hispanic (336)	348	1.82

Waterford

Place Type: Census Designated Place
County: Oakland
Population: 73,150

Ancestry/Race	Number	%
Afghan	15	0.02
African American/Black:	2,342	3.20
Not Hispanic (2,047)	2,254	3.08
Hispanic (67)	88	0.12
African, sub-Saharan:	156	0.21
African	128	0.17
South African	22	0.03
Other sub-Saharan African	6	0.01
Alaska Native tribes, specified:	4	0.01
Alaska Athabascan (1)	1	0.00
Eskimo (1)	2	0.00
Tlingit-Haida (1)	1	0.00
Am. Ind. or Alaska Nat., not spec.	183	0.25
Albanian	373	0.51
Alsatian	11	0.02
American Indian tribes, specified:	461	0.63
Apache (5)	18	0.02
Blackfeet (2)	25	0.03
Cherokee (32)	157	0.21
Cheyenne (1)	3	0.00
Chippewa (77)	145	0.20
Choctaw (5)	18	0.02
Comanche	1	0.00
Cree	3	0.00
Creek	2	0.00
Delaware (1)	2	0.00
Iroquois (8)	14	0.02
Latin American Indians (10)	17	0.02
Lumbee (4)	5	0.01
Navajo (5)	9	0.01
Ottawa (11)	13	0.02
Potawatomi (2)	9	0.01
Pueblo (2)	2	0.00
Seminole (1)	1	0.00
Shoshone (1)	1	0.00
Sioux (1)	7	0.01
All other tribes (4)	11	0.02
American Indian tribes, not spec.	25	0.03
Arab:	259	0.35
Arab/Arabic	82	0.11
Egyptian	10	0.01
Iraqi	17	0.02
Lebanese	97	0.13
Syrian	34	0.05
Other Arab	19	0.03
Armenian	223	0.30
Asian:	1,188	1.62
Cambodian (2)	6	0.01
Chinese, ex. Taiwanese (129)	164	0.22
Filipino (190)	282	0.39
Hmong (61)	73	0.10
Indian (208)	221	0.30
Indonesian (5)	6	0.01
Japanese (41)	68	0.09
Korean (104)	146	0.20
Laotian (16)	16	0.02
Malaysian (1)	1	0.00
Pakistani (14)	19	0.03
Taiwanese (6)	7	0.01
Thai (14)	17	0.02
Vietnamese (68)	80	0.11
Other Asian, specified (18)	24	0.03
Other Asian, not specified (39)	58	0.08
Assyrian/Chaldean/Syriac	413	0.56
Austrian	183	0.25
Belgian	262	0.36
Brazilian	24	0.03
British	428	0.59
Bulgarian	82	0.11
Canadian	635	0.87
Croatian	155	0.21
Czech	245	0.33
Czechoslovakian	138	0.19
Danish	348	0.48
Dutch	1,669	2.28
Eastern European	12	0.02
English	10,169	13.90
European	466	0.64
Finnish	660	0.90
French, except Basque	4,108	5.61
French Canadian	1,866	2.55
German	15,514	21.20
Greek	457	0.62
Hawaii Native/Pacific Islander:	32	0.04
Micronesian: (4)	4	0.01
Guamanian/Chamorro (4)	4	0.01
Polynesian: (3)	13	0.02
Native Hawaiian (3)	13	0.02
Other Pac. Isl., not spec. (2)	15	0.02
Hispanic or Latino:	2,863	3.91
Central American:	27	0.04
Costa Rican	5	0.01
Guatemalan	5	0.01
Honduran	2	0.00
Nicaraguan	1	0.00
Panamanian	8	0.01
Salvadoran	6	0.01
Cuban	20	0.03
Dominican Republic	7	0.01
Mexican	2,089	2.86
Puerto Rican	272	0.37
South American:	55	0.08
Argentinean	2	0.00
Chilean	7	0.01
Colombian	15	0.02
Ecuadorian	12	0.02
Paraguayan	1	0.00
Peruvian	13	0.02
Venezuelan	2	0.00
Other South American	3	0.00
Other Hispanic or Latino	393	0.54
Hungarian	593	0.81
Icelander	6	0.01
Iranian	23	0.03
Irish	10,595	14.48
Israeli	4	0.01
Italian	4,032	5.51
Latvian	10	0.01
Lithuanian	339	0.46
Luxemburger	21	0.03
Macedonian	41	0.06
Maltese	50	0.07
Northern European	13	0.02
Norwegian	568	0.78
Pennsylvania German	21	0.03
Polish	6,070	8.30
Romanian	357	0.49
Russian	710	0.97
Scandinavian	108	0.15
Scotch-Irish	1,237	1.69

Notes: 1. Figures in the "Number" column do not add up to the total population due to: a) Ancestry/Race overlap — e.g. persons can report being both White and Irish, b) persons of Hispanic origin can report being any race, c) persons reporting two ancestries are counted in both categories. 2. Numbers in parentheses indicate the number of persons reporting this ancestry/race alone, not in combination with any other ancestry/race. 3. Refer to the Explanation of Data in the front of the book for more detailed information.

Scottish	2,474	3.38
Serbian	114	0.16
Slavic	106	0.14
Slovak	161	0.22
Slovene	25	0.03
Swedish	1,015	1.39
Swiss	170	0.23
Ukrainian	370	0.51
United States or American	5,828	7.97
Welsh	477	0.65
West Indian, excl. Hispanic:	68	0.09
Dutch West Indian	9	0.01
Haitian	5	0.01
Jamaican	54	0.07
White:	68,936	94.24
Not Hispanic (66,062)	66,965	91.54
Hispanic (1,715)	1,971	2.69
Yugoslavian	121	0.17

Waverly

Place Type: Census Designated Place
County: Eaton
Population: 16,194

Ancestry/Race	Number	%
African American/Black:	1,924	11.88
Not Hispanic (1,709)	1,878	11.60
Hispanic (23)	46	0.28
African, sub-Saharan:	14	0.09
African	9	0.06
Nigerian	5	0.03
Am. Ind. or Alaska Nat., not spec.	74	0.46
American Indian tribes, specified:	112	0.69
Apache	8	0.05
Blackfeet (3)	8	0.05
Cherokee (2)	31	0.19
Cheyenne (1)	1	0.01
Chippewa (24)	33	0.20
Choctaw	1	0.01
Cree	1	0.01
Creek	1	0.01
Iroquois (1)	1	0.01
Ottawa (3)	9	0.06
Potawatomi (1)	4	0.02
Sioux (3)	8	0.05
Tohono O'Odham (1)	1	0.01
All other tribes	5	0.03
American Indian tribes, not spec.	4	0.02
Arab:	210	1.30
Arab/Arabic	36	0.22
Lebanese	135	0.84
Palestinian	20	0.12
Syrian	8	0.05
Other Arab	11	0.07
Armenian	17	0.11
Asian:	613	3.79
Bangladeshi (1)	1	0.01
Cambodian (3)	5	0.03
Chinese, ex. Taiwanese (55)	62	0.38
Filipino (11)	17	0.10
Hmong (5)	5	0.03
Indian (239)	256	1.58
Indonesian (1)	1	0.01
Japanese (14)	19	0.12
Korean (44)	52	0.32
Malaysian (3)	3	0.02
Pakistani (15)	21	0.13
Sri Lankan (1)	5	0.03
Thai (3)	4	0.02
Vietnamese (136)	147	0.91
Other Asian, specified	3	0.02
Other Asian, not specified (6)	12	0.07
Austrian	47	0.29
Belgian	45	0.28
Brazilian	7	0.04
British	49	0.30
Bulgarian	5	0.03
Canadian	106	0.66
Celtic	5	0.03
Croatian	37	0.23
Czech	86	0.53
Czechoslovakian	27	0.17
Danish	72	0.45
Dutch	717	4.44
Eastern European	4	0.02
English	2,445	15.14
European	162	1.00
Finnish	205	1.27
French, except Basque	744	4.61
French Canadian	163	1.01
German	4,036	24.99
Greek	44	0.27
Hawaii Native/Pacific Islander:	16	0.10
Melanesian: (1)	2	0.01
Fijian (1)	2	0.01
Polynesian: (6)	7	0.04
Native Hawaiian (4)	4	0.02
Samoan (2)	3	0.02
Other Pac. Isl., specified	3	0.02
Other Pac. Isl., not spec.	4	0.02
Hispanic or Latino:	739	4.56
Central American:	5	0.03
Guatemalan	1	0.01
Honduran	2	0.01
Panamanian	2	0.01
Cuban	53	0.33
Dominican Republic	5	0.03
Mexican	511	3.16
Puerto Rican	28	0.17
South American:	21	0.13
Bolivian	2	0.01
Colombian	5	0.03
Ecuadorian	2	0.01
Paraguayan	1	0.01
Peruvian	3	0.02
Venezuelan	8	0.05
Other Hispanic or Latino	116	0.72
Hungarian	43	0.27
Iranian	7	0.04
Irish	2,176	13.47
Italian	837	5.18
Latvian	20	0.12
Lithuanian	48	0.30
Maltese	6	0.04
Norwegian	186	1.15
Pennsylvania German	6	0.04
Polish	927	5.74
Portuguese	30	0.19
Romanian	10	0.06
Russian	77	0.48
Scandinavian	21	0.13
Scotch-Irish	228	1.41
Scottish	360	2.23
Slavic	8	0.05
Slovak	59	0.37
Slovene	12	0.07
Swedish	524	3.24
Swiss	56	0.35
Ukrainian	44	0.27
United States or American	672	4.16
Welsh	124	0.77
West Indian, excl. Hispanic:	17	0.11
Haitian	8	0.05
Trinidadian and Tobagonian	4	0.02
West Indian	5	0.03
White:	13,549	83.67
Not Hispanic (12,769)	13,076	80.75
Hispanic (401)	473	2.92
Yugoslavian	6	0.04

Wayne

Place Type: City
County: Wayne
Population: 19,051

Ancestry/Race	Number	%
African American/Black:	2,251	11.82
Not Hispanic (2,145)	2,242	11.77
Hispanic (6)	9	0.05
African, sub-Saharan:	112	0.59
African	95	0.50
Ethiopian	4	0.02
Liberian	13	0.07
Alaska Native tribes, specified:	1	0.01
Tlingit-Haida	1	0.01
Am. Ind. or Alaska Nat., not spec.	53	0.28
Albanian	44	0.23
American Indian tribes, specified:	191	1.00
Apache (1)	1	0.01
Blackfeet (5)	13	0.07
Cherokee (14)	65	0.34
Chippewa (30)	46	0.24
Creek	1	0.01
Delaware	1	0.01
Iroquois (21)	26	0.14
Latin American Indians (1)	1	0.01
Lumbee (6)	9	0.05
Navajo (3)	4	0.02
Ottawa (6)	7	0.04
Pueblo	3	0.02
Sioux (1)	2	0.01
All other tribes (8)	12	0.06
American Indian tribes, not spec.	6	0.03
Arab:	127	0.67
Arab/Arabic	41	0.22
Jordanian	6	0.03
Lebanese	61	0.32
Syrian	10	0.05
Other Arab	9	0.05
Armenian	40	0.21
Asian:	336	1.76
Chinese, ex. Taiwanese (9)	11	0.06
Filipino (43)	60	0.31
Indian (98)	108	0.57
Indonesian (1)	1	0.01
Japanese (3)	7	0.04
Korean (96)	109	0.57
Pakistani (14)	16	0.08
Thai (1)	1	0.01
Vietnamese (4)	4	0.02
Other Asian, not specified (4)	19	0.10
Assyrian/Chaldean/Syriac	7	0.04
Austrian	9	0.05
Belgian	17	0.09
British	40	0.21
Canadian	103	0.54
Croatian	23	0.12
Czech	53	0.28
Czechoslovakian	41	0.22
Danish	37	0.19
Dutch	299	1.57
English	1,962	10.30
European	63	0.33
Finnish	176	0.92
French, except Basque	1,150	6.04
French Canadian	371	1.95
German	3,722	19.54
Greek	82	0.43
Hawaii Native/Pacific Islander:	18	0.09
Micronesian: (2)	2	0.01
Guamanian/Chamorro (2)	2	0.01
Polynesian: (5)	10	0.05
Native Hawaiian (2)	7	0.04
Samoan (3)	3	0.02
Other Pac. Isl., not spec. (1)	6	0.03
Hispanic or Latino:	369	1.94
Central American:	2	0.01
Costa Rican	2	0.01
Cuban	12	0.06
Mexican	268	1.41
Puerto Rican	21	0.11
South American:	5	0.03
Paraguayan	1	0.01
Venezuelan	4	0.02
Other Hispanic or Latino	61	0.32
Hungarian	338	1.77
Irish	2,552	13.40
Italian	673	3.53

Notes: 1. Figures in the "Number" column do not add up to the total population due to: a) Ancestry/Race overlap — e.g. persons can report being both White and Irish, b) persons of Hispanic origin can report being any race, c) persons reporting two ancestries are counted in both categories. 2. Numbers in parentheses indicate the number of persons reporting this ancestry/race alone, not in combination with any other ancestry/race. 3. Refer to the Explanation of Data in the front of the book for more detailed information.

Lithuanian	82	0.43
Macedonian	28	0.15
Maltese	71	0.37
Norwegian	234	1.23
Pennsylvania German	7	0.04
Polish	1,771	9.30
Portuguese	11	0.06
Romanian	43	0.23
Russian	40	0.21
Scandinavian	32	0.17
Scotch-Irish	358	1.88
Scottish	580	3.04
Serbian	16	0.08
Slavic	21	0.11
Slovak	31	0.16
Swedish	136	0.71
Swiss	7	0.04
Ukrainian	57	0.30
United States or American	1,178	6.18
Welsh	86	0.45
West Indian, excl. Hispanic:	16	0.08
Haitian	16	0.08
White:	16,389	86.03
Not Hispanic (15,819)	16,104	84.53
Hispanic (253)	285	1.50
Yugoslavian	32	0.17

West Bloomfield

Place Type: Township
County: Oakland
Population: 64,860

Ancestry/Race	Number	%
African American/Black:	3,553	5.48
Not Hispanic (3,327)	3,510	5.41
Hispanic (33)	43	0.07
African, sub-Saharan:	155	0.24
African	98	0.15
Nigerian	18	0.03
South African	27	0.04
Other sub-Saharan African	12	0.02
Alaska Native tribes, specified:	1	0.00
Alaska Athabascan (1)	1	0.00
Am. Ind. or Alaska Nat., not spec.	86	0.13
Albanian	206	0.32
American Indian tribes, specified:	137	0.21
Apache (1)	3	0.00
Blackfeet (2)	11	0.02
Cherokee (17)	55	0.08
Chippewa (15)	22	0.03
Choctaw (1)	3	0.00
Cree (1)	1	0.00
Creek	2	0.00
Iroquois (2)	9	0.01
Latin American Indians (2)	8	0.01
Lumbee (1)	1	0.00
Ottawa	1	0.00
Pima	2	0.00
Pueblo	2	0.00
Sioux	4	0.01
All other tribes (10)	13	0.02
American Indian tribes, not spec.	9	0.01
Arab:	2,092	3.23
Arab/Arabic	392	0.60
Egyptian	24	0.04
Iraqi	973	1.50
Jordanian	20	0.03
Lebanese	346	0.53
Moroccan	7	0.01
Palestinian	119	0.18
Syrian	154	0.24
Other Arab	57	0.09
Armenian	564	0.87
Asian:	5,532	8.53
Bangladeshi (1)	4	0.01
Cambodian (1)	1	0.00
Chinese, ex. Taiwanese (636)	713	1.10
Filipino (270)	323	0.50
Hmong (6)	9	0.01
Indian (1,909)	2,000	3.08
Indonesian	2	0.00
Japanese (1,454)	1,511	2.33
Korean (432)	456	0.70
Malaysian (1)	1	0.00
Pakistani (139)	168	0.26
Sri Lankan (4)	9	0.01
Taiwanese (80)	98	0.15
Thai (6)	17	0.03
Vietnamese (33)	35	0.05
Other Asian, specified (3)	5	0.01
Other Asian, not specified (29)	180	0.28
Assyrian/Chaldean/Syriac	4,874	7.52
Australian	18	0.03
Austrian	374	0.58
Basque	9	0.01
Belgian	201	0.31
Brazilian	67	0.10
British	229	0.35
Bulgarian	54	0.08
Canadian	507	0.78
Croatian	147	0.23
Czech	319	0.49
Czechoslovakian	162	0.25
Danish	184	0.28
Dutch	815	1.26
Eastern European	630	0.97
English	4,846	7.48
European	477	0.74
Finnish	270	0.42
French, except Basque	1,677	2.59
French Canadian	685	1.06
German	7,252	11.19
Greek	543	0.84
Hawaii Native/Pacific Islander:	37	0.06
Melanesian: (1)	4	0.00
Fijian (1)	4	0.00
Micronesian: (3)	4	0.01
Guamanian/Chamorro (3)	4	0.01
Polynesian: (6)	10	0.02
Native Hawaiian (1)	4	0.01
Samoan (5)	6	0.01
Other Pac. Isl., specified	1	0.00
Other Pac. Isl., not spec. (1)	21	0.03
Hispanic or Latino:	905	1.40
Central American:	32	0.05
Costa Rican	2	0.00
Guatemalan	15	0.02
Honduran	5	0.01
Panamanian	1	0.00
Salvadoran	9	0.01
Cuban	38	0.06
Dominican Republic	6	0.01
Mexican	391	0.60
Puerto Rican	73	0.11
South American:	130	0.20
Argentinean	28	0.04
Chilean	22	0.03
Colombian	30	0.05
Ecuadorian	5	0.01
Paraguayan	2	0.00
Peruvian	13	0.02
Venezuelan	18	0.03
Other South American	12	0.02
Other Hispanic or Latino	235	0.36
Hungarian	1,271	1.96
Iranian	290	0.45
Irish	4,668	7.20
Israeli	314	0.48
Italian	2,707	4.18
Latvian	84	0.13
Lithuanian	451	0.70
Luxemburger	9	0.01
Macedonian	36	0.06
Maltese	115	0.18
Northern European	25	0.04
Norwegian	354	0.55
Pennsylvania German	17	0.03
Polish	5,964	9.20
Portuguese	103	0.16
Romanian	586	0.90
Russian	6,071	9.37
Scandinavian	80	0.12
Scotch-Irish	674	1.04
Scottish	1,009	1.56
Serbian	56	0.09
Slavic	38	0.06
Slovak	120	0.19
Slovene	51	0.08
Swedish	697	1.08
Swiss	113	0.17
Turkish	84	0.13
Ukrainian	737	1.14
United States or American	2,976	4.59
Welsh	347	0.54
West Indian, excl. Hispanic:	76	0.12
Bahamian	10	0.02
British West Indian	12	0.02
Jamaican	18	0.03
Trinidadian and Tobagonian	21	0.03
West Indian	3	0.00
Other West Indian	12	0.02
White:	55,983	86.31
Not Hispanic (53,958)	55,259	85.20
Hispanic (686)	724	1.12
Yugoslavian	51	0.08

Westland

Place Type: City
County: Wayne
Population: 86,602

Ancestry/Race	Number	%
African American/Black:	6,374	7.36
Not Hispanic (5,823)	6,302	7.28
Hispanic (44)	72	0.08
African, sub-Saharan:	228	0.26
African	141	0.16
Kenyan	18	0.02
Liberian	7	0.01
Nigerian	54	0.06
Other sub-Saharan African	8	0.01
Alaska Native tribes, specified:	2	0.00
Eskimo	2	0.00
Am. Ind. or Alaska Nat., not spec.	267	0.31
Albanian	301	0.35
Alsatian	17	0.02
American Indian tribes, specified:	676	0.78
Apache (3)	9	0.01
Blackfeet (4)	26	0.03
Cherokee (56)	221	0.26
Cheyenne	1	0.00
Chickasaw (2)	5	0.01
Chippewa (95)	176	0.20
Choctaw (2)	6	0.01
Comanche (2)	2	0.00
Cree (3)	5	0.01
Creek	3	0.00
Delaware (9)	13	0.02
Iroquois (34)	72	0.08
Latin American Indians (8)	18	0.02
Lumbee (12)	13	0.02
Navajo (8)	10	0.01
Osage (2)	5	0.01
Ottawa (9)	15	0.02
Potawatomi	3	0.00
Pueblo (2)	11	0.01
Seminole (1)	4	0.00
Sioux (4)	18	0.02
All other tribes (17)	40	0.05
American Indian tribes, not spec.	74	0.09
Arab:	1,099	1.27
Arab/Arabic	366	0.42
Egyptian	48	0.06
Iraqi	11	0.01
Jordanian	28	0.03
Lebanese	469	0.54
Palestinian	64	0.07
Syrian	69	0.08

Notes: 1. Figures in the "Number" column do not add up to the total population due to: a) Ancestry/Race overlap — e.g. persons can report being both White and Irish, b) persons of Hispanic origin can report being any race, c) persons reporting two ancestries are counted in both categories. 2. Numbers in parentheses indicate the number of persons reporting this ancestry/race alone, not in combination with any other ancestry/race. 3. Refer to the Explanation of Data in the front of the book for more detailed information.

Other Arab	44	0.05
Armenian	244	0.28
Asian:	2,820	3.26
Bangladeshi (5)	5	0.01
Chinese, ex. Taiwanese (509)	558	0.64
Filipino (361)	439	0.51
Hmong (9)	12	0.01
Indian (1,072)	1,143	1.32
Indonesian (3)	6	0.01
Japanese (63)	125	0.14
Korean (138)	166	0.19
Laotian (4)	7	0.01
Malaysian (4)	4	0.00
Pakistani (89)	107	0.12
Sri Lankan (3)	3	0.00
Taiwanese (9)	10	0.01
Thai (13)	18	0.02
Vietnamese (105)	125	0.14
Other Asian, specified	4	0.00
Other Asian, not specified (25)	88	0.10
Assyrian/Chaldean/Syriac	27	0.03
Australian	25	0.03
Austrian	187	0.22
Belgian	315	0.36
Brazilian	33	0.04
British	223	0.26
Canadian	705	0.81
Celtic	21	0.02
Croatian	183	0.21
Czech	377	0.44
Czechoslovakian	251	0.29
Danish	233	0.27
Dutch	1,394	1.61
Eastern European	50	0.06
English	8,444	9.74
European	454	0.52
Finnish	999	1.15
French, except Basque	4,722	5.45
French Canadian	1,998	2.31
German	17,519	20.22
Greek	535	0.62
Hawaii Native/Pacific Islander:	79	0.09
Micronesian: (8)	16	0.02
Guamanian/Chamorro (5)	13	0.02
Other Micronesian (3)	3	0.00
Polynesian: (12)	29	0.03
Native Hawaiian (8)	20	0.02
Samoan (4)	9	0.01
Other Pac. Isl., specified	2	0.00
Other Pac. Isl., not spec. (8)	32	0.04
Hispanic or Latino:	2,138	2.47
Central American:	47	0.05
Costa Rican	3	0.00
Guatemalan	10	0.01
Honduran	13	0.02
Nicaraguan	3	0.00
Panamanian	4	0.00
Salvadoran	5	0.01
Other Central American	9	0.01
Cuban	57	0.07
Mexican	1,378	1.59
Puerto Rican	166	0.19
South American:	85	0.10
Argentinean	13	0.02
Bolivian	2	0.00
Chilean	4	0.00
Colombian	29	0.03
Ecuadorian	9	0.01
Peruvian	25	0.03
Venezuelan	2	0.00
Other South American	1	0.00
Other Hispanic or Latino	405	0.47
Hungarian	1,351	1.56
Icelander	17	0.02
Iranian	12	0.01
Irish	12,793	14.76
Israeli	20	0.02
Italian	5,435	6.27
Latvian	7	0.01
Lithuanian	387	0.45
Macedonian	134	0.15
Maltese	519	0.60
Norwegian	607	0.70
Pennsylvania German	26	0.03
Polish	11,905	13.74
Portuguese	106	0.12
Romanian	504	0.58
Russian	654	0.75
Scandinavian	64	0.07
Scotch-Irish	1,481	1.71
Scottish	2,250	2.60
Serbian	138	0.16
Slavic	40	0.05
Slovak	296	0.34
Slovene	48	0.06
Swedish	1,021	1.18
Swiss	127	0.15
Turkish	46	0.05
Ukrainian	640	0.74
United States or American	3,800	4.38
Welsh	530	0.61
West Indian, excl. Hispanic:	51	0.06
Bahamian	6	0.01
Barbadian	7	0.01
Haitian	11	0.01
Jamaican	27	0.03
White:	77,090	89.02
Not Hispanic (74,116)	75,519	87.20
Hispanic (1,411)	1,571	1.81
Yugoslavian	195	0.23

White Lake

Place Type: Township
County: Oakland
Population: 28,219

Ancestry/Race	Number	%
African American/Black:	281	1.00
Not Hispanic (212)	263	0.93
Hispanic (7)	18	0.06
African, sub-Saharan:	24	0.09
African	24	0.09
Alaska Native tribes, specified:	5	0.02
Aleut (3)	3	0.01
Tlingit-Haida	1	0.00
All other tribes	1	0.00
Am. Ind. or Alaska Nat., not spec.	129	0.46
Albanian	44	0.16
American Indian tribes, specified:	200	0.71
Apache	3	0.01
Blackfeet	6	0.02
Cherokee (23)	56	0.20
Chippewa (56)	82	0.29
Choctaw (1)	4	0.01
Comanche (1)	1	0.00
Delaware	1	0.00
Iroquois (1)	7	0.02
Latin American Indians (2)	4	0.01
Navajo (4)	4	0.01
Ottawa	2	0.01
Paiute (1)	1	0.00
Seminole	1	0.00
Sioux	9	0.03
Yaqui (5)	5	0.02
All other tribes (8)	14	0.05
American Indian tribes, not spec.	11	0.04
Arab:	230	0.82
Arab/Arabic	7	0.02
Iraqi	20	0.07
Lebanese	129	0.46
Syrian	74	0.26
Armenian	124	0.44
Asian:	235	0.83
Chinese, ex. Taiwanese (26)	33	0.12
Filipino (29)	44	0.16
Indian (29)	32	0.11
Indonesian (1)	2	0.01
Japanese (22)	36	0.13
Korean (37)	43	0.15
Laotian (5)	5	0.02
Malaysian (2)	2	0.01
Thai (5)	12	0.04
Vietnamese (7)	12	0.04
Other Asian, specified	6	0.02
Other Asian, not specified (3)	8	0.03
Assyrian/Chaldean/Syriac	27	0.10
Australian	43	0.15
Austrian	106	0.38
Basque	13	0.05
Belgian	159	0.56
British	110	0.39
Bulgarian	30	0.11
Canadian	242	0.86
Croatian	75	0.27
Czech	74	0.26
Czechoslovakian	53	0.19
Danish	134	0.48
Dutch	783	2.78
Eastern European	10	0.04
English	3,805	13.49
European	85	0.30
Finnish	252	0.89
French, except Basque	1,941	6.88
French Canadian	816	2.89
German	7,143	25.33
Greek	110	0.39
Hawaii Native/Pacific Islander:	17	0.06
Micronesian: (3)	4	0.01
Guamanian/Chamorro (1)	2	0.01
Other Micronesian (2)	2	0.01
Polynesian:	1	0.00
Native Hawaiian	1	0.00
Other Pac. Isl., specified	6	0.02
Other Pac. Isl., not spec. (3)	6	0.02
Hispanic or Latino:	510	1.81
Central American:	8	0.03
Guatemalan	3	0.01
Honduran	3	0.01
Salvadoran	2	0.01
Cuban	20	0.07
Dominican Republic	1	0.00
Mexican	324	1.15
Puerto Rican	50	0.18
South American:	18	0.06
Argentinean	3	0.01
Bolivian	1	0.00
Chilean	3	0.01
Colombian	7	0.02
Ecuadorian	2	0.01
Peruvian	2	0.01
Other Hispanic or Latino	89	0.32
Hungarian	165	0.59
Irish	4,399	15.60
Italian	2,090	7.41
Latvian	10	0.04
Lithuanian	118	0.42
Macedonian	13	0.05
Maltese	170	0.60
Norwegian	327	1.16
Pennsylvania German	9	0.03
Polish	2,847	10.10
Portuguese	13	0.05
Romanian	78	0.28
Russian	215	0.76
Scandinavian	28	0.10
Scotch-Irish	684	2.43
Scottish	931	3.30
Serbian	43	0.15
Slavic	48	0.17
Slovak	33	0.12
Slovene	9	0.03
Swedish	614	2.18
Swiss	52	0.18
Turkish	36	0.13
Ukrainian	234	0.83
United States or American	1,823	6.47
Welsh	241	0.85
West Indian, excl. Hispanic:	14	0.05
Dutch West Indian	8	0.03

Notes: 1. Figures in the "Number" column do not add up to the total population due to: a) Ancestry/Race overlap — e.g. persons can report being both White and Irish, b) persons of Hispanic origin can report being any race, c) persons reporting two ancestries are counted in both categories. 2. Numbers in parentheses indicate the number of persons reporting this ancestry/race alone, not in combination with any other ancestry/race. 3. Refer to the Explanation of Data in the front of the book for more detailed information.

Jamaican	6	0.02
White:	27,591	97.77
Not Hispanic (26,907)	27,187	96.34
Hispanic (340)	404	1.43
Yugoslavian	30	0.11

Wixom

Place Type: City
County: Oakland
Population: 13,263

Ancestry/Race	Number	%
African American/Black:	381	2.87
Not Hispanic (327)	370	2.79
Hispanic (5)	11	0.08
African, sub-Saharan:	118	0.89
African	89	0.67
Ethiopian	13	0.10
South African	16	0.12
Am. Ind. or Alaska Nat., not spec.	37	0.28
Albanian	171	1.29
American Indian tribes, specified:	80	0.60
Apache (1)	1	0.01
Blackfeet (3)	5	0.04
Cherokee (9)	16	0.12
Cheyenne (1)	1	0.01
Chippewa (16)	33	0.25
Comanche (4)	4	0.03
Cree (1)	1	0.01
Iroquois (7)	8	0.06
Latin American Indians (1)	1	0.01
Ottawa	2	0.02
Sioux	1	0.01
All other tribes (4)	7	0.05
American Indian tribes, not spec.	14	0.11
Arab:	202	1.52
Arab/Arabic	70	0.53
Iraqi	48	0.36
Lebanese	57	0.43
Other Arab	27	0.20
Armenian	82	0.62
Asian:	441	3.33
Chinese, ex. Taiwanese (56)	62	0.47
Filipino (47)	57	0.43
Indian (138)	139	1.05
Japanese (39)	50	0.38
Korean (28)	32	0.24
Malaysian (2)	2	0.02
Pakistani (5)	5	0.04
Sri Lankan (3)	5	0.04
Taiwanese (4)	4	0.03
Thai (2)	2	0.02
Vietnamese (35)	37	0.28
Other Asian, specified (7)	8	0.06
Other Asian, not specified (11)	38	0.29
Assyrian/Chaldean/Syriac	52	0.39
Austrian	44	0.33
Belgian	91	0.69
British	99	0.75
Bulgarian	154	1.16
Canadian	70	0.53
Croatian	13	0.10
Czech	39	0.29
Czechoslovakian	47	0.35
Danish	112	0.84
Dutch	336	2.53
English	1,397	10.53
European	37	0.28
Finnish	203	1.53
French, except Basque	783	5.90
French Canadian	336	2.53
German	3,044	22.95
Greek	90	0.68
Hawaii Native/Pacific Islander:	5	0.04
Micronesian: (4)	4	0.03
Guamanian/Chamorro (4)	4	0.03
Polynesian: (1)	1	0.01
Samoan (1)	1	0.01
Hispanic or Latino:	424	3.20
Central American:	30	0.23
Guatemalan	22	0.17
Honduran	5	0.04
Salvadoran	1	0.01
Other Central American	2	0.02
Cuban	2	0.02
Dominican Republic	2	0.02
Mexican	259	1.95
Puerto Rican	43	0.32
South American:	15	0.11
Colombian	9	0.07
Ecuadorian	3	0.02
Paraguayan	1	0.01
Peruvian	1	0.01
Other South American	1	0.01
Other Hispanic or Latino	73	0.55
Hungarian	235	1.77
Irish	2,043	15.40
Italian	941	7.09
Lithuanian	18	0.14
Macedonian	18	0.14
Maltese	159	1.20
Norwegian	171	1.29
Polish	1,498	11.29
Portuguese	11	0.08
Romanian	12	0.09
Russian	313	2.36
Scandinavian	38	0.29
Scotch-Irish	243	1.83
Scottish	374	2.82
Slavic	21	0.16
Slovak	43	0.32
Slovene	10	0.08
Swedish	167	1.26
Swiss	63	0.48
Turkish	10	0.08
Ukrainian	81	0.61
United States or American	537	4.05
Welsh	163	1.23
White:	12,247	92.34
Not Hispanic (11,792)	12,031	90.71
Hispanic (198)	216	1.63
Yugoslavian	29	0.22

Woodhaven

Place Type: City
County: Wayne
Population: 12,530

Ancestry/Race	Number	%
African American/Black:	321	2.56
Not Hispanic (292)	319	2.55
Hispanic	2	0.02
African, sub-Saharan:	11	0.09
African	11	0.09
Am. Ind. or Alaska Nat., not spec.	29	0.23
American Indian tribes, specified:	92	0.73
Apache (1)	1	0.01
Blackfeet (1)	2	0.02
Cherokee (12)	30	0.24
Chippewa (9)	20	0.16
Choctaw (3)	3	0.02
Iroquois (5)	8	0.06
Latin American Indians	4	0.03
Lumbee (1)	1	0.01
Menominee	1	0.01
Navajo (3)	3	0.02
Ottawa (2)	2	0.02
Potawatomi (1)	1	0.01
Sioux (1)	1	0.01
Ute (2)	2	0.02
Yaqui (4)	4	0.03
All other tribes (6)	9	0.07
American Indian tribes, not spec.	10	0.08
Arab:	150	1.20
Arab/Arabic	4	0.03
Lebanese	146	1.17
Armenian	92	0.73
Asian:	240	1.92
Chinese, ex. Taiwanese (16)	19	0.15
Filipino (56)	66	0.53
Indian (48)	55	0.44
Japanese (14)	17	0.14
Korean (25)	25	0.20
Malaysian (1)	1	0.01
Pakistani (20)	25	0.20
Thai (2)	2	0.02
Vietnamese (13)	13	0.10
Other Asian, not specified (5)	17	0.14
Australian	11	0.09
Austrian	15	0.12
Belgian	25	0.20
British	29	0.23
Canadian	17	0.14
Croatian	17	0.14
Czech	134	1.07
Danish	26	0.21
Dutch	169	1.35
English	1,138	9.08
European	18	0.14
Finnish	49	0.39
French, except Basque	1,002	8.00
French Canadian	326	2.60
German	2,490	19.87
Greek	125	1.00
Hawaii Native/Pacific Islander:	4	0.03
Polynesian: (2)	3	0.02
Native Hawaiian (2)	3	0.02
Other Pac. Isl., not spec.	1	0.01
Hispanic or Latino:	433	3.46
Central American:	5	0.04
Guatemalan	5	0.04
Cuban	17	0.14
Dominican Republic	1	0.01
Mexican	321	2.56
Puerto Rican	23	0.18
South American:	6	0.05
Colombian	5	0.04
Peruvian	1	0.01
Other Hispanic or Latino	60	0.48
Hungarian	688	5.49
Irish	1,646	13.14
Italian	1,409	11.25
Lithuanian	29	0.23
Maltese	123	0.98
Norwegian	74	0.59
Polish	2,084	16.63
Romanian	61	0.49
Russian	97	0.77
Scotch-Irish	212	1.69
Scottish	278	2.22
Serbian	47	0.38
Slovak	123	0.98
Swedish	102	0.81
Swiss	9	0.07
Ukrainian	101	0.81
United States or American	802	6.40
Welsh	111	0.89
White:	11,850	94.57
Not Hispanic (11,381)	11,510	91.86
Hispanic (299)	340	2.71
Yugoslavian	36	0.29

Wyandotte

Place Type: City
County: Wayne
Population: 28,006

Ancestry/Race	Number	%
African American/Black:	219	0.78
Not Hispanic (144)	213	0.76
Hispanic (2)	6	0.02
African, sub-Saharan:	59	0.21
African	23	0.08
Ethiopian	12	0.04
Somalian	6	0.02
Other sub-Saharan African	18	0.06
Am. Ind. or Alaska Nat., not spec.	89	0.32

Notes: 1. Figures in the "Number" column do not add up to the total population due to: a) Ancestry/Race overlap — e.g. persons can report being both White and Irish, b) persons of Hispanic origin can report being any race, c) persons reporting two ancestries are counted in both categories. 2. Numbers in parentheses indicate the number of persons reporting this ancestry/race alone, not in combination with any other ancestry/race. 3. Refer to the Explanation of Data in the front of the book for more detailed information.

American Indian tribes, specified:	279	1.00
Apache (3)	4	0.01
Blackfeet	15	0.05
Cherokee (31)	101	0.36
Chickasaw (1)	2	0.01
Chippewa (39)	73	0.26
Choctaw (1)	2	0.01
Comanche (1)	1	0.00
Crow	1	0.00
Delaware (1)	7	0.02
Iroquois (5)	10	0.04
Latin American Indians (3)	14	0.05
Lumbee (6)	11	0.04
Menominee	2	0.01
Navajo	3	0.01
Ottawa (5)	8	0.03
Pueblo (1)	5	0.02
Shoshone	1	0.00
Sioux (1)	4	0.01
All other tribes (3)	15	0.05
American Indian tribes, not spec.	17	0.06
Arab:	205	0.73
Arab/Arabic	25	0.09
Jordanian	46	0.16
Lebanese	123	0.44
Syrian	11	0.04
Armenian	38	0.14
Asian:	147	0.52
Cambodian (1)	1	0.00
Chinese, ex. Taiwanese (25)	37	0.13
Filipino (13)	25	0.09
Indian (7)	11	0.04
Japanese (9)	23	0.08
Korean (22)	26	0.09
Laotian (6)	6	0.02
Taiwanese	1	0.00
Thai (3)	4	0.01
Vietnamese (3)	6	0.02
Other Asian, not specified (3)	7	0.02
Australian	6	0.02
Austrian	33	0.12
Belgian	11	0.04
British	54	0.19
Canadian	119	0.42
Croatian	86	0.31
Czech	69	0.25
Czechoslovakian	95	0.34
Danish	47	0.17
Dutch	442	1.58
Eastern European	7	0.02
English	2,525	9.02
European	138	0.49
Finnish	146	0.52
French, except Basque	2,387	8.52
French Canadian	908	3.24
German	6,135	21.91
Greek	195	0.70
Hawaii Native/Pacific Islander:	20	0.07
Melanesian:	1	0.00
Fijian	1	0.00
Micronesian: (2)	5	0.02
Guamanian/Chamorro (2)	5	0.02
Polynesian: (4)	9	0.03
Native Hawaiian (4)	9	0.03
Other Pac. Isl., not spec. (2)	5	0.02
Hispanic or Latino:	816	2.91
Central American:	9	0.03
Costa Rican	3	0.01
Guatemalan	2	0.01
Panamanian	3	0.01
Salvadoran	1	0.00
Cuban	13	0.05
Mexican	615	2.20
Puerto Rican	53	0.19
South American:	10	0.04
Chilean	2	0.01
Colombian	2	0.01
Ecuadorian	5	0.02
Venezuelan	1	0.00
Other Hispanic or Latino	116	0.41
Hungarian	1,204	4.30
Irish	4,894	17.47
Italian	2,360	8.43
Lithuanian	228	0.81
Maltese	111	0.40
Norwegian	80	0.29
Pennsylvania German	5	0.02
Polish	6,292	22.47
Portuguese	80	0.29
Romanian	122	0.44
Russian	173	0.62
Scandinavian	14	0.05
Scotch-Irish	484	1.73
Scottish	785	2.80
Serbian	93	0.33
Slavic	22	0.08
Slovak	123	0.44
Slovene	5	0.02
Swedish	210	0.75
Swiss	77	0.27
Ukrainian	217	0.77
United States or American	1,101	3.93
Welsh	205	0.73
West Indian, excl. Hispanic:	7	0.02
West Indian	7	0.02
White:	27,400	97.84
Not Hispanic (26,421)	26,791	95.66
Hispanic (555)	609	2.17
Yugoslavian	76	0.27

Wyoming

Place Type: City
County: Kent
Population: 69,368

Ancestry/Race	Number	%
African American/Black:	4,008	5.78
Not Hispanic (3,205)	3,756	5.41
Hispanic (157)	252	0.36
African, sub-Saharan:	265	0.38
African	211	0.30
Ethiopian	18	0.03
Somalian	11	0.02
Other sub-Saharan African	25	0.04
Alaska Native tribes, specified:	2	0.00
Alaska Athabascan (1)	1	0.00
Aleut (1)	1	0.00
Am. Ind. or Alaska Nat., not spec.	261	0.38
American Indian tribes, specified:	613	0.88
Apache (8)	10	0.01
Blackfeet (2)	22	0.03
Cherokee (32)	121	0.17
Cheyenne	1	0.00
Chickasaw (1)	1	0.00
Chippewa (89)	152	0.22
Choctaw (2)	9	0.01
Comanche	6	0.01
Cree (1)	3	0.00
Iroquois (4)	16	0.02
Kiowa	2	0.00
Latin American Indians (10)	17	0.02
Lumbee (1)	1	0.00
Navajo (4)	6	0.01
Ottawa (73)	111	0.16
Potawatomi (58)	84	0.12
Shoshone	1	0.00
Sioux (6)	16	0.02
Tohono O'Odham (1)	1	0.00
Yaqui (1)	1	0.00
Yuman (1)	1	0.00
All other tribes (5)	31	0.04
American Indian tribes, not spec.	37	0.05
Arab:	552	0.80
Arab/Arabic	173	0.25
Egyptian	22	0.03
Iraqi	13	0.02
Lebanese	232	0.33
Moroccan	12	0.02
Palestinian	11	0.02
Syrian	89	0.13
Armenian	76	0.11
Asian:	2,305	3.32
Cambodian (6)	9	0.01
Chinese, ex. Taiwanese (186)	235	0.34
Filipino (71)	119	0.17
Hmong (6)	6	0.01
Indian (108)	131	0.19
Indonesian	1	0.00
Japanese (16)	47	0.07
Korean (187)	214	0.31
Laotian (12)	14	0.02
Malaysian (1)	3	0.00
Pakistani (10)	11	0.02
Sri Lankan	1	0.00
Taiwanese (1)	4	0.01
Thai (9)	20	0.03
Vietnamese (1,357)	1,449	2.09
Other Asian, specified	2	0.00
Other Asian, not specified (20)	39	0.06
Australian	10	0.01
Austrian	97	0.14
Belgian	163	0.23
Brazilian	31	0.04
British	243	0.35
Canadian	125	0.18
Croatian	204	0.29
Czech	93	0.13
Czechoslovakian	86	0.12
Danish	493	0.71
Dutch	15,679	22.60
English	6,338	9.14
Estonian	6	0.01
European	386	0.56
Finnish	268	0.39
French, except Basque	2,663	3.84
French Canadian	608	0.88
German	13,041	18.80
Greek	35	0.05
Hawaii Native/Pacific Islander:	57	0.08
Micronesian: (7)	11	0.02
Guamanian/Chamorro (7)	11	0.02
Polynesian: (19)	27	0.04
Native Hawaiian (4)	11	0.02
Samoan (14)	15	0.02
Tongan (1)	1	0.00
Other Pac. Isl., specified	1	0.00
Other Pac. Isl., not spec. (1)	18	0.03
Hispanic or Latino:	6,704	9.66
Central American:	246	0.35
Costa Rican	3	0.00
Guatemalan	99	0.14
Honduran	45	0.06
Nicaraguan	15	0.02
Panamanian	5	0.01
Salvadoran	72	0.10
Other Central American	7	0.01
Cuban	484	0.70
Dominican Republic	192	0.28
Mexican	4,047	5.83
Puerto Rican	746	1.08
South American:	66	0.10
Argentinean	10	0.01
Bolivian	6	0.01
Chilean	2	0.00
Colombian	20	0.03
Ecuadorian	4	0.01
Paraguayan	1	0.00
Peruvian	10	0.01
Uruguayan	1	0.00
Venezuelan	11	0.02
Other South American	1	0.00
Other Hispanic or Latino	923	1.33
Hungarian	252	0.36
Iranian	7	0.01
Irish	7,058	10.18
Italian	2,062	2.97
Latvian	94	0.14
Lithuanian	329	0.47
Northern European	8	0.01

Notes: 1. Figures in the "Number" column do not add up to the total population due to: a) Ancestry/Race overlap — e.g. persons can report being both White and Irish, b) persons of Hispanic origin can report being any race, c) persons reporting two ancestries are counted in both categories. 2. Numbers in parentheses indicate the number of persons reporting this ancestry/race alone, not in combination with any other ancestry/race. 3. Refer to the Explanation of Data in the front of the book for more detailed information.

Norwegian	661	0.95
Pennsylvania German	18	0.03
Polish	5,053	7.28
Portuguese	62	0.09
Romanian	69	0.10
Russian	153	0.22
Scandinavian	113	0.16
Scotch-Irish	763	1.10
Scottish	889	1.28
Serbian	4	0.01
Slovak	84	0.12
Slovene	5	0.01
Swedish	1,299	1.87
Swiss	174	0.25
Ukrainian	122	0.18
United States or American	3,503	5.05
Welsh	206	0.30
West Indian, excl. Hispanic:	191	0.28
Bahamian	6	0.01
Belizean	6	0.01
Dutch West Indian	10	0.01
Haitian	81	0.12
Jamaican	79	0.11
West Indian	9	0.01
White:	60,100	86.64
Not Hispanic (55,801)	56,904	82.03
Hispanic (2,690)	3,196	4.61
Yugoslavian	309	0.45

Ypsilanti

Place Type: City
County: Washtenaw
Population: 22,362

Ancestry/Race	Number	%
African American/Black:	7,271	32.51
Not Hispanic (6,793)	7,201	32.20
Hispanic (45)	70	0.31
African, sub-Saharan:	274	1.22
African	242	1.08
Nigerian	7	0.03
Other sub-Saharan African	25	0.11
Alaska Native tribes, specified:	9	0.04
Eskimo (3)	3	0.01
Tlingit-Haida (1)	6	0.03
Am. Ind. or Alaska Nat., not spec.	115	0.51
Albanian	8	0.04
American Indian tribes, specified:	174	0.78
Apache (3)	4	0.02
Blackfeet (1)	9	0.04
Cherokee (12)	71	0.32
Chippewa (18)	34	0.15
Choctaw	5	0.02
Comanche (1)	2	0.01
Cree	1	0.00
Creek	3	0.01
Iroquois	6	0.03
Latin American Indians (1)	2	0.01
Lumbee (2)	3	0.01
Navajo (2)	3	0.01
Ottawa (2)	6	0.03
Potawatomi (1)	5	0.02
Puget Sound Salish	1	0.00
Seminole	1	0.00
Sioux (1)	6	0.03
Yuman	1	0.00
All other tribes (5)	11	0.05
American Indian tribes, not spec.	17	0.08
Arab:	139	0.62
Arab/Arabic	11	0.05
Egyptian	16	0.07
Lebanese	100	0.45
Palestinian	12	0.05
Armenian	42	0.19
Asian:	813	3.64
Bangladeshi (1)	1	0.00
Cambodian (1)	1	0.00
Chinese, ex. Taiwanese (226)	244	1.09
Filipino (32)	49	0.22
Hmong (3)	3	0.01
Indian (176)	187	0.84
Indonesian (2)	2	0.01
Japanese (39)	53	0.24
Korean (70)	87	0.39
Laotian (35)	37	0.17
Malaysian (7)	11	0.05
Pakistani (11)	14	0.06
Taiwanese (4)	8	0.04
Thai (27)	29	0.13
Vietnamese (20)	22	0.10
Other Asian, not specified (48)	65	0.29
Assyrian/Chaldean/Syriac	22	0.10
Austrian	87	0.39
Belgian	32	0.14
Brazilian	18	0.08
British	196	0.87
Canadian	84	0.37
Celtic	13	0.06
Croatian	17	0.08
Czech	67	0.30
Czechoslovakian	82	0.37
Danish	94	0.42
Dutch	275	1.23
Eastern European	32	0.14
English	1,796	8.02
European	322	1.44
Finnish	111	0.50
French, except Basque	724	3.23
French Canadian	315	1.41
German	3,639	16.24
German Russian	10	0.04
Greek	89	0.40
Guyanese	9	0.04
Hawaii Native/Pacific Islander:	41	0.18
Micronesian: (1)	1	0.00
Guamanian/Chamorro (1)	1	0.00
Polynesian: (12)	23	0.10
Native Hawaiian (11)	18	0.08
Samoan (1)	1	0.00
Other Polynesian	4	0.02
Other Pac. Isl., not spec. (2)	17	0.08
Hispanic or Latino:	552	2.47
Central American:	37	0.17
Costa Rican	4	0.02
Guatemalan	3	0.01
Honduran	8	0.04
Nicaraguan	1	0.00
Panamanian	7	0.03
Salvadoran	14	0.06
Cuban	14	0.06
Dominican Republic	6	0.03
Mexican	325	1.45
Puerto Rican	48	0.21
South American:	15	0.07
Argentinean	2	0.01
Chilean	2	0.01
Colombian	5	0.02
Ecuadorian	1	0.00
Peruvian	3	0.01
Venezuelan	2	0.01
Other Hispanic or Latino	107	0.48
Hungarian	230	1.03
Iranian	7	0.03
Irish	1,931	8.62
Italian	932	4.16
Latvian	12	0.05
Lithuanian	90	0.40
Luxemburger	8	0.04
Macedonian	16	0.07
Maltese	14	0.06
Northern European	49	0.22
Norwegian	185	0.83
Pennsylvania German	17	0.08
Polish	1,348	6.02
Portuguese	15	0.07
Romanian	44	0.20
Russian	177	0.79
Scandinavian	11	0.05
Scotch-Irish	221	0.99
Scottish	604	2.70
Serbian	20	0.09
Slavic	28	0.12
Slovak	45	0.20
Slovene	9	0.04
Swedish	232	1.04
Swiss	54	0.24
Turkish	26	0.12
Ukrainian	87	0.39
United States or American	558	2.49
Welsh	152	0.68
West Indian, excl. Hispanic:	135	0.60
Bahamian	13	0.06
Haitian	57	0.25
Jamaican	36	0.16
West Indian	29	0.13
White:	14,243	63.69
Not Hispanic (13,529)	13,993	62.57
Hispanic (202)	250	1.12
Yugoslavian	6	0.03

Ypsilanti

Place Type: Township
County: Washtenaw
Population: 49,182

Ancestry/Race	Number	%
African American/Black:	13,335	27.11
Not Hispanic (12,453)	13,213	26.87
Hispanic (72)	122	0.25
African, sub-Saharan:	753	1.53
African	491	1.00
Ethiopian	20	0.04
Ghanian	15	0.03
Nigerian	86	0.18
Somalian	60	0.12
Zimbabwean	6	0.01
Other sub-Saharan African	75	0.15
Alaska Native tribes, specified:	5	0.01
Aleut	1	0.00
Eskimo (1)	1	0.00
Tlingit-Haida (1)	3	0.01
Alaska Native tribes, not specified	1	0.00
Am. Ind. or Alaska Nat., not spec.	294	0.60
Albanian	4	0.01
American Indian tribes, specified:	400	0.81
Apache (2)	5	0.01
Blackfeet (5)	30	0.06
Cherokee (48)	178	0.36
Chickasaw (2)	2	0.00
Chippewa (50)	72	0.15
Choctaw	6	0.01
Comanche	1	0.00
Cree	2	0.00
Creek (4)	6	0.01
Crow	5	0.01
Delaware (1)	2	0.00
Iroquois (8)	20	0.04
Kiowa (1)	1	0.00
Latin American Indians (3)	7	0.01
Lumbee (1)	3	0.01
Navajo (2)	4	0.01
Osage	1	0.00
Ottawa (3)	7	0.01
Potawatomi (3)	5	0.01
Pueblo (2)	2	0.00
Seminole	6	0.01
Sioux (6)	20	0.04
Yuman	1	0.00
All other tribes (3)	14	0.03
American Indian tribes, not spec.	19	0.04
Arab:	759	1.54
Arab/Arabic	279	0.57
Egyptian	41	0.08
Iraqi	14	0.03
Jordanian	10	0.02
Lebanese	149	0.30
Moroccan	14	0.03
Palestinian	113	0.23

Notes: 1. Figures in the "Number" column do not add up to the total population due to: a) Ancestry/Race overlap — e.g. persons can report being both White and Irish, b) persons of Hispanic origin can report being any race, c) persons reporting two ancestries are counted in both categories. 2. Numbers in parentheses indicate the number of persons reporting this ancestry/race alone, not in combination with any other ancestry/race. 3. Refer to the Explanation of Data in the front of the book for more detailed information.

Syrian	30	0.06
Other Arab	109	0.22
Armenian	116	0.24
Asian:	1,266	2.57
Bangladeshi (6)	6	0.01
Cambodian (2)	2	0.00
Chinese, ex. Taiwanese (183)	249	0.51
Filipino (96)	136	0.28
Hmong (6)	7	0.01
Indian (269)	300	0.61
Indonesian (9)	10	0.02
Japanese (56)	87	0.18
Korean (112)	141	0.29
Laotian (21)	26	0.05
Malaysian (2)	7	0.01
Pakistani (62)	71	0.14
Sri Lankan (5)	6	0.01
Taiwanese (5)	5	0.01
Thai (17)	21	0.04
Vietnamese (78)	103	0.21
Other Asian, specified (7)	9	0.02
Other Asian, not specified (30)	80	0.16
Assyrian/Chaldean/Syriac	58	0.12
Australian	15	0.03
Austrian	58	0.12
Belgian	129	0.26
Brazilian	29	0.06
British	137	0.28
Bulgarian	30	0.06
Canadian	207	0.42
Celtic	22	0.04
Croatian	167	0.34
Cypriot	9	0.02
Czech	90	0.18
Czechoslovakian	76	0.15
Danish	155	0.32
Dutch	1,057	2.15
Eastern European	3	0.01
English	4,902	9.98
European	393	0.80
Finnish	317	0.65
French, except Basque	1,563	3.18
French Canadian	566	1.15
German	7,880	16.04
Greek	263	0.54
Hawaii Native/Pacific Islander:	52	0.11
Melanesian: (2)	2	0.00
Other Melanesian (2)	2	0.00
Micronesian: (2)	7	0.01
Guamanian/Chamorro (2)	7	0.01
Polynesian: (7)	26	0.05
Native Hawaiian (4)	17	0.03
Samoan (3)	8	0.02
Other Polynesian	1	0.00
Other Pac. Isl., specified	1	0.00
Other Pac. Isl., not spec. (5)	16	0.03
Hispanic or Latino:	1,379	2.80
Central American:	132	0.27
Costa Rican	56	0.11
Guatemalan	22	0.04
Honduran	22	0.04
Nicaraguan	11	0.02
Panamanian	10	0.02
Salvadoran	9	0.02
Other Central American	2	0.00
Cuban	56	0.11
Dominican Republic	5	0.01
Mexican	735	1.49
Puerto Rican	120	0.24
South American:	63	0.13
Argentinean	8	0.02
Bolivian	1	0.00
Chilean	3	0.01
Colombian	24	0.05
Ecuadorian	4	0.01
Peruvian	8	0.02
Uruguayan	4	0.01
Venezuelan	8	0.02
Other South American	3	0.01
Other Hispanic or Latino	268	0.54
Hungarian	426	0.87
Iranian	69	0.14
Irish	5,066	10.31
Italian	1,536	3.13
Latvian	11	0.02
Lithuanian	83	0.17
Maltese	18	0.04
Northern European	19	0.04
Norwegian	321	0.65
Pennsylvania German	11	0.02
Polish	2,341	4.76
Portuguese	19	0.04
Romanian	306	0.62
Russian	312	0.63
Scandinavian	80	0.16
Scotch-Irish	695	1.41
Scottish	1,128	2.30
Serbian	38	0.08
Slavic	22	0.04
Slovak	105	0.21
Slovene	5	0.01
Swedish	331	0.67
Swiss	120	0.24
Turkish	6	0.01
Ukrainian	198	0.40
United States or American	3,093	6.29
Welsh	198	0.40
West Indian, excl. Hispanic:	218	0.44
Haitian	18	0.04
Jamaican	147	0.30
Trinidadian and Tobagonian	27	0.05
West Indian	26	0.05
White:	34,586	70.32
Not Hispanic (32,497)	33,772	68.67
Hispanic (705)	814	1.66
Yugoslavian	31	0.06

Albert Lea

Place Type: City
County: Freeborn
Population: 18,356

Ancestry/Race	Number	%
African American/Black:	104	0.57
Not Hispanic (54)	88	0.48
Hispanic (14)	16	0.09
African, sub-Saharan:	5	0.03
African	5	0.03
Alaska Native tribes, specified:	1	0.01
Aleut (1)	1	0.01
Alaska Native tribes, not specified	1	0.01
Am. Ind. or Alaska Nat., not spec.	53	0.29
Albanian	14	0.08
American Indian tribes, specified:	51	0.28
Blackfeet (1)	2	0.01
Cherokee (1)	2	0.01
Chippewa (6)	16	0.09
Comanche (1)	3	0.02
Iroquois	3	0.02
Latin American Indians (4)	4	0.02
Osage (1)	1	0.01
Sioux (3)	9	0.05
All other tribes (7)	11	0.06
American Indian tribes, not spec.	5	0.03
Arab:	20	0.11
Egyptian	6	0.03
Lebanese	14	0.08
Asian:	192	1.05
Cambodian (1)	2	0.01
Chinese, ex. Taiwanese (12)	15	0.08
Filipino (10)	28	0.15
Hmong (12)	12	0.07
Indian (37)	40	0.22
Indonesian (2)	2	0.01
Japanese (4)	8	0.04
Korean (21)	28	0.15
Laotian (32)	36	0.20
Thai (3)	3	0.02
Vietnamese (11)	14	0.08
Other Asian, specified	1	0.01
Other Asian, not specified	3	0.02
Austrian	27	0.15
Belgian	11	0.06
British	54	0.29
Canadian	12	0.07
Croatian	22	0.12
Czech	433	2.36
Czechoslovakian	49	0.27
Danish	1,533	8.35
Dutch	466	2.54
English	1,175	6.40
Estonian	5	0.03
European	23	0.13
Finnish	47	0.26
French, except Basque	391	2.13
French Canadian	140	0.76
German	5,611	30.56
Greek	30	0.16
Hawaii Native/Pacific Islander:	6	0.03
Micronesian: (2)	2	0.01
Guamanian/Chamorro (2)	2	0.01
Polynesian: (2)	2	0.01
Samoan (2)	2	0.01
Other Pac. Isl., specified	1	0.01
Other Pac. Isl., not spec. (1)	1	0.01
Hispanic or Latino:	1,740	9.48
Central American:	36	0.20
Costa Rican	4	0.02
Guatemalan	6	0.03
Honduran	4	0.02
Nicaraguan	16	0.09
Salvadoran	6	0.03
Cuban	43	0.23
Mexican	1,326	7.22
Puerto Rican	43	0.23
South American:	6	0.03
Colombian	6	0.03
Other Hispanic or Latino	286	1.56
Hungarian	11	0.06
Irish	1,524	8.30
Israeli	6	0.03
Italian	100	0.54
Latvian	4	0.02
Lithuanian	1	0.01
Luxemburger	20	0.11
Norwegian	6,369	34.68
Polish	423	2.30
Portuguese	6	0.03
Russian	37	0.20
Scandinavian	132	0.72
Scotch-Irish	123	0.67
Scottish	154	0.84
Serbian	6	0.03
Slavic	6	0.03
Slovak	5	0.03
Slovene	5	0.03
Swedish	687	3.74
Swiss	27	0.15
Ukrainian	23	0.13
United States or American	458	2.49
Welsh	73	0.40
White:	17,239	93.91
Not Hispanic (16,237)	16,362	89.14
Hispanic (797)	877	4.78

Andover

Place Type: City
County: Anoka
Population: 26,588

Ancestry/Race	Number	%
Afghan	59	0.22
African American/Black:	232	0.87
Not Hispanic (135)	220	0.83
Hispanic (8)	12	0.05
African, sub-Saharan:	37	0.14
Ethiopian	23	0.09
Nigerian	14	0.05

Notes: 1. Figures in the "Number" column do not add up to the total population due to: a) Ancestry/Race overlap — e.g. persons can report being both White and Irish, b) persons of Hispanic origin can report being any race, c) persons reporting two ancestries are counted in both categories. 2. Numbers in parentheses indicate the number of persons reporting this ancestry/race alone, not in combination with any other ancestry/race. 3. Refer to the Explanation of Data in the front of the book for more detailed information.

Am. Ind. or Alaska Nat., not spec.	83	0.31
American Indian tribes, specified:	138	0.52
Blackfeet (1)	1	0.00
Cherokee (3)	11	0.04
Chippewa (47)	94	0.35
Choctaw (1)	1	0.00
Cree (1)	1	0.00
Creek (4)	4	0.02
Iroquois (1)	2	0.01
Kiowa	1	0.00
Latin American Indians (1)	1	0.00
Sioux (5)	12	0.05
All other tribes (4)	10	0.04
American Indian tribes, not spec.	2	0.01
Arab:	54	0.20
Lebanese	54	0.20
Armenian	49	0.18
Asian:	388	1.46
Bangladeshi	3	0.01
Cambodian (2)	7	0.03
Chinese, ex. Taiwanese (25)	28	0.11
Filipino (34)	61	0.23
Hmong (11)	11	0.04
Indian (62)	87	0.33
Japanese (17)	27	0.10
Korean (78)	97	0.36
Laotian (15)	20	0.08
Taiwanese (1)	2	0.01
Thai (4)	6	0.02
Vietnamese (20)	29	0.11
Other Asian, not specified (8)	10	0.04
Austrian	91	0.34
Belgian	48	0.18
British	55	0.21
Bulgarian	25	0.09
Canadian	17	0.06
Celtic	6	0.02
Croatian	49	0.18
Czech	406	1.53
Czechoslovakian	138	0.52
Danish	496	1.87
Dutch	396	1.49
English	1,699	6.39
Estonian	11	0.04
European	151	0.57
Finnish	716	2.69
French, except Basque	1,544	5.81
French Canadian	492	1.85
German	9,708	36.51
Greek	78	0.29
Hawaii Native/Pacific Islander:	9	0.03
Micronesian: (3)	3	0.01
Guamanian/Chamorro (3)	3	0.01
Polynesian:	2	0.01
Native Hawaiian	2	0.01
Other Pac. Isl., not spec. (1)	4	0.02
Hispanic or Latino:	278	1.05
Central American:	10	0.04
Costa Rican	4	0.02
Guatemalan	6	0.02
Cuban	3	0.01
Mexican	155	0.58
Puerto Rican	30	0.11
South American:	39	0.15
Bolivian	3	0.01
Chilean	1	0.00
Colombian	17	0.06
Ecuadorian	10	0.04
Paraguayan	3	0.01
Peruvian	2	0.01
Venezuelan	1	0.00
Other South American	2	0.01
Other Hispanic or Latino	41	0.15
Hungarian	84	0.32
Icelander	8	0.03
Iranian	7	0.03
Irish	3,429	12.90
Italian	1,076	4.05
Latvian	21	0.08
Lithuanian	57	0.21
Luxemburger	9	0.03
New Zealander	6	0.02
Northern European	18	0.07
Norwegian	4,656	17.51
Polish	2,246	8.45
Portuguese	10	0.04
Romanian	8	0.03
Russian	199	0.75
Scandinavian	284	1.07
Scotch-Irish	251	0.94
Scottish	342	1.29
Serbian	10	0.04
Slavic	20	0.08
Slovak	103	0.39
Slovene	32	0.12
Swedish	3,613	13.59
Swiss	158	0.59
Ukrainian	184	0.69
United States or American	861	3.24
Welsh	142	0.53
White:	25,953	97.61
Not Hispanic (25,477)	25,758	96.88
Hispanic (176)	195	0.73
Yugoslavian	51	0.19

Anoka

Place Type: City
County: Anoka
Population: 18,076

Ancestry/Race	Number	%
African American/Black:	563	3.11
Not Hispanic (442)	553	3.06
Hispanic (4)	10	0.06
African, sub-Saharan:	24	0.13
African	6	0.03
Sudanese	18	0.10
Am. Ind. or Alaska Nat., not spec.	96	0.53
American Indian tribes, specified:	188	1.04
Apache	2	0.01
Blackfeet	2	0.01
Cherokee (2)	12	0.07
Chippewa (72)	111	0.61
Delaware (1)	1	0.01
Iroquois (1)	4	0.02
Lumbee (6)	6	0.03
Navajo (4)	4	0.02
Potawatomi (1)	1	0.01
Seminole (1)	2	0.01
Sioux (11)	23	0.13
All other tribes (13)	20	0.11
American Indian tribes, not spec.	29	0.16
Arab:	31	0.17
Egyptian	13	0.07
Lebanese	18	0.10
Armenian	16	0.09
Asian:	245	1.36
Cambodian (11)	14	0.08
Chinese, ex. Taiwanese (19)	23	0.13
Filipino (24)	46	0.25
Hmong (2)	3	0.02
Indian (24)	29	0.16
Indonesian	2	0.01
Japanese (5)	16	0.09
Korean (35)	51	0.28
Laotian (2)	3	0.02
Malaysian (1)	2	0.01
Pakistani (5)	5	0.03
Thai (1)	1	0.01
Vietnamese (34)	42	0.23
Other Asian, not specified (3)	8	0.04
Austrian	38	0.21
Belgian	69	0.38
British	7	0.04
Canadian	34	0.19
Celtic	16	0.09
Croatian	20	0.11
Czech	218	1.21
Czechoslovakian	90	0.50
Danish	274	1.52
Dutch	263	1.45
Eastern European	5	0.03
English	1,094	6.05
European	204	1.13
Finnish	283	1.57
French, except Basque	860	4.76
French Canadian	251	1.39
German	5,958	32.96
Greek	46	0.25
Hawaii Native/Pacific Islander:	16	0.09
Micronesian: (1)	2	0.01
Guamanian/Chamorro (1)	2	0.01
Polynesian: (4)	12	0.07
Native Hawaiian (4)	10	0.06
Samoan	2	0.01
Other Pac. Isl., not spec.	2	0.01
Hispanic or Latino:	349	1.93
Central American:	13	0.07
Guatemalan	7	0.04
Honduran	3	0.02
Nicaraguan	2	0.01
Salvadoran	1	0.01
Cuban	7	0.04
Mexican	235	1.30
Puerto Rican	21	0.12
South American:	8	0.04
Bolivian	3	0.02
Colombian	3	0.02
Ecuadorian	1	0.01
Other South American	1	0.01
Other Hispanic or Latino	65	0.36
Hungarian	68	0.38
Icelander	9	0.05
Irish	2,025	11.20
Italian	427	2.36
Latvian	6	0.03
Northern European	59	0.33
Norwegian	3,084	17.06
Pennsylvania German	17	0.09
Polish	1,045	5.78
Portuguese	10	0.06
Russian	145	0.80
Scandinavian	307	1.70
Scotch-Irish	132	0.73
Scottish	251	1.39
Slovak	26	0.14
Slovene	7	0.04
Swedish	2,307	12.76
Swiss	110	0.61
Turkish	29	0.16
Ukrainian	88	0.49
United States or American	585	3.24
Welsh	77	0.43
West Indian, excl. Hispanic:	8	0.04
Jamaican	8	0.04
White:	17,143	94.84
Not Hispanic (16,629)	16,900	93.49
Hispanic (208)	243	1.34
Yugoslavian	8	0.04

Apple Valley

Place Type: City
County: Dakota
Population: 45,527

Ancestry/Race	Number	%
Afghan	39	0.09
African American/Black:	1,136	2.50
Not Hispanic (861)	1,103	2.42
Hispanic (9)	33	0.07
African, sub-Saharan:	237	0.52
African	100	0.22
Ethiopian	52	0.11
Ghanian	5	0.01
Nigerian	42	0.09
Somalian	38	0.08
Alaska Native tribes, specified:	4	0.01
All other tribes (4)	4	0.01

Notes: 1. Figures in the "Number" column do not add up to the total population due to: a) Ancestry/Race overlap — e.g. persons can report being both White and Irish, b) persons of Hispanic origin can report being any race, c) persons reporting two ancestries are counted in both categories. 2. Numbers in parentheses indicate the number of persons reporting this ancestry/race alone, not in combination with any other ancestry/race. 3. Refer to the Explanation of Data in the front of the book for more detailed information.

Am. Ind. or Alaska Nat., not spec.	93	0.20
American Indian tribes, specified:	196	0.43
Apache (1)	1	0.00
Blackfeet	5	0.01
Cherokee (9)	35	0.08
Chippewa (52)	78	0.17
Choctaw (3)	8	0.02
Colville	1	0.00
Cree (3)	4	0.01
Creek	5	0.01
Iroquois	2	0.00
Latin American Indians (3)	7	0.02
Potawatomi (5)	6	0.01
Pueblo	2	0.00
Seminole	1	0.00
Sioux (10)	18	0.04
Tohono O'Odham (1)	1	0.00
All other tribes (11)	22	0.05
American Indian tribes, not spec.	9	0.02
Arab:	274	0.60
Arab/Arabic	22	0.05
Egyptian	9	0.02
Iraqi	14	0.03
Jordanian	38	0.08
Lebanese	96	0.21
Moroccan	11	0.02
Syrian	57	0.13
Other Arab	27	0.06
Armenian	9	0.02
Asian:	1,880	4.13
Bangladeshi	4	0.01
Cambodian (73)	86	0.19
Chinese, ex. Taiwanese (287)	344	0.76
Filipino (76)	115	0.25
Hmong (34)	43	0.09
Indian (248)	289	0.63
Indonesian (2)	6	0.01
Japanese (56)	122	0.27
Korean (221)	253	0.56
Laotian (137)	149	0.33
Pakistani (11)	21	0.05
Sri Lankan (3)	3	0.01
Thai (19)	31	0.07
Vietnamese (287)	327	0.72
Other Asian, specified (2)	2	0.00
Other Asian, not specified (49)	85	0.19
Austrian	133	0.29
Belgian	120	0.26
British	127	0.28
Bulgarian	15	0.03
Canadian	161	0.35
Celtic	12	0.03
Croatian	42	0.09
Czech	968	2.13
Czechoslovakian	274	0.60
Danish	683	1.50
Dutch	944	2.07
English	3,400	7.47
European	558	1.23
Finnish	738	1.62
French, except Basque	1,987	4.36
French Canadian	543	1.19
German	17,157	37.69
Greek	226	0.50
Guyanese	22	0.05
Hawaii Native/Pacific Islander:	41	0.09
Micronesian: (2)	4	0.01
Guamanian/Chamorro (2)	4	0.01
Polynesian: (5)	18	0.04
Native Hawaiian (4)	15	0.03
Samoan (1)	3	0.01
Other Pac. Isl., not spec. (10)	19	0.04
Hispanic or Latino:	912	2.00
Central American:	11	0.02
Costa Rican	1	0.00
Guatemalan	3	0.01
Honduran	4	0.01
Nicaraguan	1	0.00
Salvadoran	2	0.00
Cuban	26	0.06
Dominican Republic	3	0.01
Mexican	586	1.29
Puerto Rican	89	0.20
South American:	62	0.14
Argentinean	5	0.01
Bolivian	1	0.00
Chilean	2	0.00
Colombian	31	0.07
Ecuadorian	14	0.03
Paraguayan	1	0.00
Peruvian	2	0.00
Uruguayan	2	0.00
Venezuelan	2	0.00
Other South American	2	0.00
Other Hispanic or Latino	135	0.30
Hungarian	86	0.19
Icelander	115	0.25
Iranian	51	0.11
Irish	6,508	14.29
Italian	1,491	3.27
Latvian	26	0.06
Lithuanian	51	0.11
Luxemburger	28	0.06
Northern European	198	0.43
Norwegian	7,828	17.19
Polish	2,217	4.87
Portuguese	7	0.02
Romanian	45	0.10
Russian	302	0.66
Scandinavian	508	1.12
Scotch-Irish	460	1.01
Scottish	683	1.50
Serbian	64	0.14
Slavic	97	0.21
Slovak	115	0.25
Slovene	93	0.20
Soviet Union	8	0.02
Swedish	4,476	9.83
Swiss	188	0.41
Turkish	28	0.06
Ukrainian	195	0.43
United States or American	1,022	2.24
Welsh	343	0.75
West Indian, excl. Hispanic:	14	0.03
Dutch West Indian	7	0.02
West Indian	7	0.02
White:	42,483	93.31
Not Hispanic (41,372)	41,975	92.20
Hispanic (426)	508	1.12
Yugoslavian	79	0.17

Austin

Place Type: City
County: Mower
Population: 23,314

Ancestry/Race	Number	%
African American/Black:	246	1.06
Not Hispanic (180)	231	0.99
Hispanic (8)	15	0.06
African, sub-Saharan:	36	0.15
African	25	0.11
Nigerian	5	0.02
Sudanese	6	0.03
Alaska Native tribes, specified:	5	0.02
Tlingit-Haida	5	0.02
Am. Ind. or Alaska Nat., not spec.	43	0.18
American Indian tribes, specified:	56	0.24
Blackfeet (4)	5	0.02
Cherokee	6	0.03
Chippewa (10)	12	0.05
Iroquois	1	0.00
Latin American Indians (6)	14	0.06
Menominee (1)	3	0.01
Pueblo	1	0.00
Seminole (1)	1	0.00
Sioux (2)	5	0.02
All other tribes (2)	8	0.03
American Indian tribes, not spec.	4	0.02
Arab:	24	0.10
Lebanese	24	0.10
Asian:	591	2.53
Cambodian (16)	17	0.07
Chinese, ex. Taiwanese (43)	49	0.21
Filipino (10)	16	0.07
Hmong (2)	2	0.01
Indian (38)	40	0.17
Japanese (19)	25	0.11
Korean (23)	33	0.14
Laotian (108)	130	0.56
Thai	6	0.03
Vietnamese (216)	240	1.03
Other Asian, not specified (31)	33	0.14
Austrian	64	0.27
Belgian	21	0.09
British	50	0.21
Canadian	34	0.15
Celtic	7	0.03
Croatian	5	0.02
Czech	756	3.25
Czechoslovakian	124	0.53
Danish	760	3.26
Dutch	614	2.64
English	1,665	7.15
European	40	0.17
Finnish	110	0.47
French, except Basque	969	4.16
French Canadian	121	0.52
German	8,646	37.13
Greek	105	0.45
Hawaii Native/Pacific Islander:	11	0.05
Polynesian: (4)	5	0.02
Native Hawaiian (4)	4	0.02
Samoan	1	0.00
Other Pac. Isl., not spec.	6	0.03
Hispanic or Latino:	1,426	6.12
Central American:	39	0.17
Costa Rican	1	0.00
Guatemalan	28	0.12
Honduran	6	0.03
Nicaraguan	1	0.00
Salvadoran	3	0.01
Cuban	52	0.22
Dominican Republic	5	0.02
Mexican	1,166	5.00
Puerto Rican	15	0.06
South American:	6	0.03
Argentinean	1	0.00
Chilean	1	0.00
Colombian	2	0.01
Venezuelan	2	0.01
Other Hispanic or Latino	143	0.61
Hungarian	24	0.10
Icelander	2	0.01
Irish	2,954	12.69
Italian	238	1.02
Luxemburger	20	0.09
Northern European	19	0.08
Norwegian	5,584	23.98
Pennsylvania German	11	0.05
Polish	369	1.58
Russian	67	0.29
Scandinavian	110	0.47
Scotch-Irish	298	1.28
Scottish	237	1.02
Slavic	6	0.03
Slovak	4	0.02
Slovene	56	0.24
Swedish	779	3.35
Swiss	39	0.17
United States or American	892	3.83
Welsh	114	0.49
West Indian, excl. Hispanic:	5	0.02
Jamaican	5	0.02
White:	21,806	93.53
Not Hispanic (20,998)	21,139	90.67
Hispanic (591)	667	2.86
Yugoslavian	104	0.45

Notes: 1. Figures in the "Number" column do not add up to the total population due to: a) Ancestry/Race overlap — e.g. persons can report being both White and Irish, b) persons of Hispanic origin can report being any race, c) persons reporting two ancestries are counted in both categories. 2. Numbers in parentheses indicate the number of persons reporting this ancestry/race alone, not in combination with any other ancestry/race. 3. Refer to the Explanation of Data in the front of the book for more detailed information.

Bemidji

Place Type: City
County: Beltrami
Population: 11,917

Ancestry/Race	Number	%
African American/Black:	123	1.03
Not Hispanic (89)	117	0.98
Hispanic (2)	6	0.05
African, sub-Saharan:	83	0.69
African	4	0.03
Ghanian	79	0.65
Alaska Native tribes, specified:	4	0.03
Eskimo (4)	4	0.03
Am. Ind. or Alaska Nat., not spec.	256	2.15
Albanian	9	0.07
American Indian tribes, specified:	1,243	10.43
Cherokee	8	0.07
Chickasaw (1)	2	0.02
Chippewa (1,002)	1,111	9.32
Choctaw (1)	2	0.02
Creek (5)	5	0.04
Iroquois (2)	2	0.02
Menominee (4)	5	0.04
Osage	1	0.01
Paiute (1)	1	0.01
Potawatomi (4)	4	0.03
Pueblo (5)	6	0.05
Shoshone (1)	1	0.01
Sioux (41)	55	0.46
All other tribes (33)	40	0.34
American Indian tribes, not spec.	59	0.50
Arab:	22	0.18
Iraqi	11	0.09
Lebanese	11	0.09
Asian:	171	1.43
Bangladeshi (2)	2	0.02
Chinese, ex. Taiwanese (56)	63	0.53
Filipino (9)	14	0.12
Indian (17)	20	0.17
Indonesian (2)	2	0.02
Japanese (10)	12	0.10
Korean (15)	23	0.19
Laotian (1)	2	0.02
Malaysian (5)	8	0.07
Pakistani (1)	2	0.02
Thai	2	0.02
Vietnamese (2)	4	0.03
Other Asian, specified (1)	2	0.02
Other Asian, not specified (8)	15	0.13
Austrian	27	0.22
British	48	0.40
Canadian	66	0.55
Celtic	8	0.07
Croatian	9	0.07
Czech	131	1.08
Czechoslovakian	47	0.39
Danish	164	1.36
Dutch	175	1.45
Eastern European	5	0.04
English	782	6.48
European	57	0.47
Finnish	277	2.29
French, except Basque	596	4.94
French Canadian	124	1.03
German	3,475	28.78
Greek	6	0.05
Hawaii Native/Pacific Islander:	9	0.08
Micronesian:	2	0.02
Guamanian/Chamorro	2	0.02
Polynesian: (3)	3	0.03
Native Hawaiian (3)	3	0.03
Other Pac. Isl., specified	1	0.01
Other Pac. Isl., not spec. (1)	3	0.03
Hispanic or Latino:	136	1.14
Central American:	3	0.03
Guatemalan	1	0.01
Honduran	1	0.01
Panamanian	1	0.01
Cuban	4	0.03
Mexican	74	0.62
Puerto Rican	14	0.12
South American:	10	0.08
Colombian	6	0.05
Peruvian	4	0.03
Other Hispanic or Latino	31	0.26
Hungarian	34	0.28
Icelander	15	0.12
Irish	1,037	8.59
Italian	358	2.97
Latvian	9	0.07
Luxemburger	6	0.05
Northern European	11	0.09
Norwegian	2,732	22.63
Polish	412	3.41
Romanian	6	0.05
Russian	44	0.36
Scandinavian	320	2.65
Scotch-Irish	168	1.39
Scottish	144	1.19
Slavic	16	0.13
Slovak	22	0.18
Slovene	2	0.02
Swedish	1,063	8.80
Swiss	36	0.30
Ukrainian	34	0.28
United States or American	401	3.32
Welsh	5	0.04
White:	10,275	86.22
Not Hispanic (9,974)	10,191	85.52
Hispanic (73)	84	0.70
Yugoslavian	18	0.15

Blaine

Place Type: City
County: Anoka
Population: 44,942

Ancestry/Race	Number	%
African American/Black:	619	1.38
Not Hispanic (385)	613	1.36
Hispanic (2)	6	0.01
African, sub-Saharan:	122	0.27
African	31	0.07
Ethiopian	36	0.08
Nigerian	43	0.10
Other sub-Saharan African	12	0.03
Alaska Native tribes, specified:	5	0.01
Alaska Athabascan (1)	2	0.00
Aleut (1)	1	0.00
Eskimo	2	0.00
Am. Ind. or Alaska Nat., not spec.	168	0.37
American Indian tribes, specified:	403	0.90
Apache	4	0.01
Blackfeet (5)	8	0.02
Cherokee (9)	21	0.05
Cheyenne (2)	2	0.00
Chippewa (156)	276	0.61
Choctaw (2)	3	0.01
Comanche (1)	1	0.00
Cree (1)	1	0.00
Iroquois (5)	8	0.02
Latin American Indians (2)	7	0.02
Lumbee	2	0.00
Ottawa (1)	2	0.00
Potawatomi (1)	1	0.00
Pueblo	1	0.00
Seminole	1	0.00
Sioux (22)	45	0.10
All other tribes (11)	20	0.04
American Indian tribes, not spec.	12	0.03
Arab:	159	0.35
Egyptian	17	0.04
Lebanese	142	0.32
Armenian	9	0.02
Asian:	1,377	3.06
Bangladeshi (2)	2	0.00
Cambodian (25)	33	0.07
Chinese, ex. Taiwanese (110)	133	0.30
Filipino (70)	123	0.27
Hmong (185)	188	0.42
Indian (171)	191	0.42
Indonesian (2)	2	0.00
Japanese (22)	45	0.10
Korean (126)	166	0.37
Laotian (17)	20	0.04
Pakistani (20)	22	0.05
Sri Lankan (2)	4	0.01
Taiwanese (7)	7	0.02
Thai (4)	18	0.04
Vietnamese (329)	358	0.80
Other Asian, specified (3)	10	0.02
Other Asian, not specified (32)	55	0.12
Australian	16	0.04
Austrian	203	0.45
Belgian	17	0.04
British	142	0.32
Bulgarian	12	0.03
Canadian	60	0.13
Celtic	6	0.01
Croatian	54	0.12
Czech	621	1.38
Czechoslovakian	89	0.20
Danish	674	1.50
Dutch	786	1.75
Eastern European	4	0.01
English	2,663	5.93
European	259	0.58
Finnish	1,119	2.49
French, except Basque	2,493	5.55
French Canadian	735	1.64
German	17,204	38.29
Greek	42	0.09
Guyanese	18	0.04
Hawaii Native/Pacific Islander:	39	0.09
Micronesian: (2)	7	0.02
Guamanian/Chamorro (2)	7	0.02
Polynesian: (5)	20	0.04
Native Hawaiian (4)	18	0.04
Samoan (1)	1	0.00
Other Polynesian	1	0.00
Other Pac. Isl., specified	5	0.01
Other Pac. Isl., not spec. (2)	7	0.02
Hispanic or Latino:	773	1.72
Central American:	53	0.12
Costa Rican	6	0.01
Guatemalan	8	0.02
Nicaraguan	12	0.03
Panamanian	17	0.04
Salvadoran	9	0.02
Other Central American	1	0.00
Cuban	12	0.03
Mexican	462	1.03
Puerto Rican	60	0.13
South American:	46	0.10
Argentinean	1	0.00
Bolivian	2	0.00
Chilean	3	0.01
Colombian	22	0.05
Peruvian	11	0.02
Venezuelan	5	0.01
Other South American	2	0.00
Other Hispanic or Latino	140	0.31
Hungarian	121	0.27
Icelander	18	0.04
Iranian	5	0.01
Irish	5,648	12.57
Israeli	14	0.03
Italian	975	2.17
Latvian	30	0.07
Lithuanian	18	0.04
Luxemburger	25	0.06
Maltese	17	0.04
Northern European	15	0.03
Norwegian	7,910	17.60
Pennsylvania German	50	0.11
Polish	2,953	6.57
Romanian	41	0.09

Notes: 1. Figures in the "Number" column do not add up to the total population due to: a) Ancestry/Race overlap — e.g. persons can report being both White and Irish, b) persons of Hispanic origin can report being any race, c) persons reporting two ancestries are counted in both categories. 2. Numbers in parentheses indicate the number of persons reporting this ancestry/race alone, not in combination with any other ancestry/race. 3. Refer to the Explanation of Data in the front of the book for more detailed information.

Russian	327	0.73
Scandinavian	494	1.10
Scotch-Irish	455	1.01
Scottish	581	1.29
Serbian	30	0.07
Slavic	8	0.02
Slovak	73	0.16
Slovene	50	0.11
Swedish	5,609	12.48
Swiss	122	0.27
Ukrainian	386	0.86
United States or American	1,591	3.54
Welsh	144	0.32
West Indian, excl. Hispanic:	41	0.09
Jamaican	41	0.09
White:	42,744	95.11
Not Hispanic (41,628)	42,302	94.13
Hispanic (374)	442	0.98
Yugoslavian	88	0.20

Bloomington

Place Type: City
County: Hennepin
Population: 85,172

Ancestry/Race	Number	%
African American/Black:	3,523	4.14
Not Hispanic (2,854)	3,433	4.03
Hispanic (63)	90	0.11
African, sub-Saharan:	750	0.88
African	263	0.31
Ethiopian	148	0.17
Ghanian	160	0.19
Kenyan	28	0.03
Liberian	51	0.06
Nigerian	89	0.10
Senegalese	5	0.01
South African	6	0.01
Alaska Native tribes, specified:	8	0.01
Alaska Athabascan (1)	1	0.00
Aleut (1)	1	0.00
Eskimo	2	0.00
Tlingit-Haida (1)	4	0.00
Am. Ind. or Alaska Nat., not spec.	213	0.25
Albanian	6	0.01
Alsatian	5	0.01
American Indian tribes, specified:	378	0.44
Apache	3	0.00
Blackfeet (2)	8	0.01
Cherokee (5)	30	0.04
Cheyenne	8	0.01
Chickasaw	1	0.00
Chippewa (116)	181	0.21
Choctaw	6	0.01
Comanche (1)	1	0.00
Cree (2)	4	0.00
Creek (1)	2	0.00
Iroquois (5)	13	0.02
Latin American Indians (14)	17	0.02
Navajo (1)	8	0.01
Potawatomi	1	0.00
Seminole	1	0.00
Shoshone	1	0.00
Sioux (31)	65	0.08
Yakama (2)	2	0.00
Yaqui (1)	1	0.00
All other tribes (10)	25	0.03
American Indian tribes, not spec.	22	0.03
Arab:	191	0.22
Arab/Arabic	5	0.01
Egyptian	47	0.06
Lebanese	112	0.13
Syrian	16	0.02
Other Arab	11	0.01
Armenian	41	0.05
Asian:	4,983	5.85
Bangladeshi (9)	11	0.01
Cambodian (497)	552	0.65
Chinese, ex. Taiwanese (668)	804	0.94
Filipino (168)	228	0.27
Hmong (55)	57	0.07
Indian (756)	835	0.98
Indonesian (8)	8	0.01
Japanese (129)	204	0.24
Korean (376)	440	0.52
Laotian (255)	283	0.33
Malaysian (3)	4	0.00
Pakistani (48)	59	0.07
Sri Lankan (44)	50	0.06
Taiwanese (13)	23	0.03
Thai (18)	32	0.04
Vietnamese (1,071)	1,149	1.35
Other Asian, specified (12)	21	0.02
Other Asian, not specified (104)	223	0.26
Australian	19	0.02
Austrian	401	0.47
Belgian	196	0.23
Brazilian	10	0.01
British	204	0.24
Bulgarian	35	0.04
Canadian	155	0.18
Croatian	113	0.13
Czech	1,650	1.94
Czechoslovakian	375	0.44
Danish	1,765	2.07
Dutch	1,825	2.14
Eastern European	9	0.01
English	7,257	8.52
Estonian	8	0.01
European	557	0.65
Finnish	896	1.05
French, except Basque	3,548	4.16
French Canadian	777	0.91
German	27,642	32.44
German Russian	17	0.02
Greek	334	0.39
Guyanese	7	0.01
Hawaii Native/Pacific Islander:	105	0.12
Micronesian: (6)	8	0.01
Guamanian/Chamorro (6)	8	0.01
Polynesian: (22)	57	0.07
Native Hawaiian (14)	36	0.04
Samoan (6)	13	0.02
Tongan (1)	6	0.01
Other Polynesian (1)	2	0.00
Other Pac. Isl., not spec. (1)	40	0.05
Hispanic or Latino:	2,290	2.69
Central American:	204	0.24
Costa Rican	22	0.03
Guatemalan	32	0.04
Honduran	11	0.01
Nicaraguan	10	0.01
Panamanian	12	0.01
Salvadoran	100	0.12
Other Central American	17	0.02
Cuban	45	0.05
Dominican Republic	11	0.01
Mexican	1,385	1.63
Puerto Rican	136	0.16
South American:	141	0.17
Argentinean	4	0.00
Bolivian	8	0.01
Chilean	12	0.01
Colombian	44	0.05
Ecuadorian	24	0.03
Paraguayan	9	0.01
Peruvian	20	0.02
Venezuelan	12	0.01
Other South American	8	0.01
Other Hispanic or Latino	368	0.43
Hungarian	197	0.23
Icelander	92	0.11
Iranian	170	0.20
Irish	11,002	12.91
Italian	2,197	2.58
Latvian	125	0.15
Lithuanian	109	0.13
Luxemburger	94	0.11
Macedonian	9	0.01
Northern European	178	0.21
Norwegian	15,600	18.31
Pennsylvania German	107	0.13
Polish	3,446	4.04
Portuguese	11	0.01
Romanian	86	0.10
Russian	613	0.72
Scandinavian	1,313	1.54
Scotch-Irish	1,215	1.43
Scottish	1,369	1.61
Serbian	30	0.04
Slavic	43	0.05
Slovak	147	0.17
Slovene	82	0.10
Swedish	10,368	12.17
Swiss	561	0.66
Turkish	46	0.05
Ukrainian	283	0.33
United States or American	1,768	2.08
Welsh	526	0.62
West Indian, excl. Hispanic:	68	0.08
Barbadian	11	0.01
Jamaican	43	0.05
West Indian	14	0.02
White:	76,240	89.51
Not Hispanic (74,008)	75,033	88.10
Hispanic (1,047)	1,207	1.42
Yugoslavian	106	0.12

Brainerd

Place Type: City
County: Crow Wing
Population: 13,178

Ancestry/Race	Number	%
African American/Black:	135	1.02
Not Hispanic (94)	132	1.00
Hispanic	3	0.02
African, sub-Saharan:	9	0.07
African	9	0.07
Am. Ind. or Alaska Nat., not spec.	60	0.46
American Indian tribes, specified:	209	1.59
Apache (1)	4	0.03
Cherokee	1	0.01
Chickasaw	2	0.02
Chippewa (125)	161	1.22
Iroquois (2)	2	0.02
Kiowa (1)	1	0.01
Latin American Indians (1)	2	0.02
Navajo (1)	2	0.02
Osage	1	0.01
Pueblo	2	0.02
Sioux (17)	20	0.15
All other tribes	11	0.08
American Indian tribes, not spec.	8	0.06
Arab:	24	0.18
Arab/Arabic	18	0.14
Lebanese	6	0.05
Asian:	100	0.76
Cambodian	1	0.01
Chinese, ex. Taiwanese (18)	24	0.18
Filipino (9)	14	0.11
Indian (10)	13	0.10
Japanese (3)	10	0.08
Korean (9)	19	0.14
Thai	2	0.02
Vietnamese (8)	12	0.09
Other Asian, not specified (2)	5	0.04
Austrian	40	0.31
Belgian	2	0.02
British	8	0.06
Canadian	24	0.18
Croatian	30	0.23
Czech	137	1.05
Czechoslovakian	18	0.14
Danish	272	2.09
Dutch	244	1.87
English	921	7.06
European	37	0.28

Notes: 1. Figures in the "Number" column do not add up to the total population due to: a) Ancestry/Race overlap — e.g. persons can report being both White and Irish, b) persons of Hispanic origin can report being any race, c) persons reporting two ancestries are counted in both categories. 2. Numbers in parentheses indicate the number of persons reporting this ancestry/race alone, not in combination with any other ancestry/race. 3. Refer to the Explanation of Data in the front of the book for more detailed information.

Finnish	348	2.67
French, except Basque	616	4.72
French Canadian	243	1.86
German	4,338	33.26
Greek	4	0.03
Hawaii Native/Pacific Islander:	4	0.03
Micronesian: (1)	3	0.02
Guamanian/Chamorro	1	0.01
Other Micronesian (1)	2	0.02
Polynesian:	1	0.01
Native Hawaiian	1	0.01
Hispanic or Latino:	113	0.86
Central American:	6	0.05
Guatemalan	6	0.05
Cuban	2	0.02
Mexican	60	0.46
Puerto Rican	6	0.05
South American:	9	0.07
Colombian	2	0.02
Peruvian	6	0.05
Other South American	1	0.01
Other Hispanic or Latino	30	0.23
Hungarian	28	0.21
Icelander	19	0.15
Irish	1,378	10.57
Italian	181	1.39
Latvian	6	0.05
Lithuanian	16	0.12
Luxemburger	11	0.08
Northern European	21	0.16
Norwegian	2,185	16.75
Polish	668	5.12
Portuguese	7	0.05
Russian	7	0.05
Scandinavian	98	0.75
Scotch-Irish	139	1.07
Scottish	124	0.95
Slavic	15	0.12
Slovak	22	0.17
Slovene	14	0.11
Swedish	1,327	10.18
Swiss	18	0.14
Ukrainian	13	0.10
United States or American	617	4.73
Welsh	51	0.39
West Indian, excl. Hispanic:	5	0.04
West Indian	5	0.04
White:	12,787	97.03
Not Hispanic (12,567)	12,714	96.48
Hispanic (62)	73	0.55
Yugoslavian	14	0.11

Brooklyn Center

Place Type: City
County: Hennepin
Population: 29,172

Ancestry/Race	Number	%
African American/Black:	4,639	15.90
Not Hispanic (4,088)	4,580	15.70
Hispanic (22)	59	0.20
African, sub-Saharan:	1,258	4.33
African	402	1.38
Ethiopian	195	0.67
Kenyan	116	0.40
Liberian	439	1.51
Nigerian	34	0.12
Zairian	54	0.19
Other sub-Saharan African	18	0.06
Alaska Native tribes, specified:	3	0.01
Aleut (1)	1	0.00
Tlingit-Haida (2)	2	0.01
Am. Ind. or Alaska Nat., not spec.	171	0.59
American Indian tribes, specified:	268	0.92
Blackfeet (1)	14	0.05
Cherokee (2)	17	0.06
Chippewa (110)	151	0.52
Choctaw	2	0.01
Comanche (1)	1	0.00
Creek (1)	1	0.00
Iroquois (5)	5	0.02
Latin American Indians (7)	12	0.04
Menominee (1)	1	0.00
Navajo (2)	2	0.01
Pima (1)	1	0.00
Pueblo (1)	1	0.00
Seminole (1)	3	0.01
Sioux (25)	39	0.13
All other tribes (10)	18	0.06
American Indian tribes, not spec.	8	0.03
Arab:	51	0.18
Egyptian	5	0.02
Lebanese	20	0.07
Syrian	11	0.04
Other Arab	15	0.05
Asian:	2,850	9.77
Bangladeshi (1)	1	0.00
Cambodian (15)	18	0.06
Chinese, ex. Taiwanese (85)	113	0.39
Filipino (69)	98	0.34
Hmong (1,346)	1,448	4.96
Indian (179)	214	0.73
Indonesian (2)	4	0.01
Japanese (30)	52	0.18
Korean (53)	72	0.25
Laotian (415)	462	1.58
Pakistani (3)	5	0.02
Taiwanese (2)	3	0.01
Thai (7)	8	0.03
Vietnamese (263)	274	0.94
Other Asian, specified	2	0.01
Other Asian, not specified (60)	76	0.26
Austrian	63	0.22
Belgian	23	0.08
British	45	0.15
Bulgarian	8	0.03
Canadian	18	0.06
Carpatho Rusyn	12	0.04
Croatian	44	0.15
Czech	306	1.05
Czechoslovakian	143	0.49
Danish	472	1.62
Dutch	375	1.29
Eastern European	10	0.03
English	1,622	5.58
European	110	0.38
Finnish	513	1.77
French, except Basque	1,215	4.18
French Canadian	389	1.34
German	8,020	27.60
German Russian	8	0.03
Greek	24	0.08
Guyanese	14	0.05
Hawaii Native/Pacific Islander:	63	0.22
Polynesian: (1)	5	0.02
Native Hawaiian (1)	4	0.01
Samoan	1	0.00
Other Pac. Isl., not spec. (3)	58	0.20
Hispanic or Latino:	823	2.82
Central American:	55	0.19
Costa Rican	7	0.02
Guatemalan	6	0.02
Honduran	4	0.01
Nicaraguan	18	0.06
Salvadoran	13	0.04
Other Central American	7	0.02
Cuban	13	0.04
Dominican Republic	6	0.02
Mexican	543	1.86
Puerto Rican	71	0.24
South American:	29	0.10
Bolivian	1	0.00
Chilean	9	0.03
Colombian	11	0.04
Ecuadorian	1	0.00
Peruvian	1	0.00
Venezuelan	2	0.01
Other South American	4	0.01
Other Hispanic or Latino	106	0.36
Hungarian	46	0.16
Irish	2,929	10.08
Italian	429	1.48
Latvian	6	0.02
Lithuanian	49	0.17
Luxemburger	7	0.02
Norwegian	4,009	13.80
Pennsylvania German	9	0.03
Polish	1,369	4.71
Russian	119	0.41
Scandinavian	346	1.19
Scotch-Irish	292	1.00
Scottish	288	0.99
Serbian	13	0.04
Slavic	3	0.01
Slovak	96	0.33
Slovene	55	0.19
Swedish	2,905	10.00
Swiss	130	0.45
Ukrainian	95	0.33
United States or American	684	2.35
Welsh	113	0.39
West Indian, excl. Hispanic:	56	0.19
Jamaican	29	0.10
West Indian	27	0.09
White:	21,536	73.82
Not Hispanic (20,530)	21,162	72.54
Hispanic (295)	374	1.28
Yugoslavian	105	0.36

Brooklyn Park

Place Type: City
County: Hennepin
Population: 67,388

Ancestry/Race	Number	%
African American/Black:	10,681	15.85
Not Hispanic (9,583)	10,565	15.68
Hispanic (76)	116	0.17
African, sub-Saharan:	3,232	4.80
African	1,396	2.07
Ethiopian	130	0.19
Ghanian	69	0.10
Kenyan	43	0.06
Liberian	1,079	1.60
Nigerian	319	0.47
Sierra Leonean	70	0.10
Somalian	13	0.02
Sudanese	23	0.03
Ugandan	9	0.01
Other sub-Saharan African	81	0.12
Alaska Native tribes, specified:	3	0.00
Eskimo (3)	3	0.00
Am. Ind. or Alaska Nat., not spec.	238	0.35
American Indian tribes, specified:	460	0.68
Apache (2)	4	0.01
Blackfeet (2)	7	0.01
Cherokee (2)	31	0.05
Chickasaw	5	0.01
Chippewa (186)	268	0.40
Choctaw (3)	6	0.01
Cree	2	0.00
Creek	2	0.00
Crow (1)	1	0.00
Delaware (1)	1	0.00
Iroquois (3)	3	0.00
Latin American Indians (10)	18	0.03
Menominee (1)	1	0.00
Navajo	3	0.00
Ottawa (4)	4	0.01
Pueblo (4)	4	0.01
Seminole (1)	1	0.00
Shoshone (4)	4	0.01
Sioux (40)	59	0.09
Yuman	1	0.00
All other tribes (13)	35	0.05
American Indian tribes, not spec.	23	0.03
Arab:	363	0.54
Arab/Arabic	6	0.01

Notes: 1. Figures in the "Number" column do not add up to the total population due to: a) Ancestry/Race overlap — e.g. persons can report being both White and Irish, b) persons of Hispanic origin can report being any race, c) persons reporting two ancestries are counted in both categories. 2. Numbers in parentheses indicate the number of persons reporting this ancestry/race alone, not in combination with any other ancestry/race. 3. Refer to the Explanation of Data in the front of the book for more detailed information.

Egyptian	88	0.13
Lebanese	87	0.13
Moroccan	27	0.04
Palestinian	34	0.05
Syrian	25	0.04
Other Arab	96	0.14
Armenian	25	0.04
Asian:	6,893	10.23
Bangladeshi (3)	3	0.00
Cambodian (133)	164	0.24
Chinese, ex. Taiwanese (237)	336	0.50
Filipino (123)	185	0.27
Hmong (1,226)	1,292	1.92
Indian (726)	850	1.26
Indonesian (8)	11	0.02
Japanese (42)	88	0.13
Korean (249)	310	0.46
Laotian (1,216)	1,299	1.93
Malaysian (2)	7	0.01
Pakistani (19)	30	0.04
Sri Lankan (6)	6	0.01
Taiwanese (4)	7	0.01
Thai (21)	36	0.05
Vietnamese (1,899)	1,989	2.95
Other Asian, specified (20)	28	0.04
Other Asian, not specified (159)	252	0.37
Assyrian/Chaldean/Syriac	5	0.01
Australian	45	0.07
Austrian	131	0.19
Belgian	162	0.24
British	140	0.21
Bulgarian	49	0.07
Canadian	80	0.12
Celtic	37	0.05
Croatian	27	0.04
Czech	669	0.99
Czechoslovakian	253	0.38
Danish	863	1.28
Dutch	1,082	1.61
Eastern European	37	0.05
English	3,659	5.43
European	552	0.82
Finnish	1,446	2.15
French, except Basque	2,633	3.91
French Canadian	760	1.13
German	19,113	28.36
German Russian	22	0.03
Greek	133	0.20
Guyanese	149	0.22
Hawaii Native/Pacific Islander:	150	0.22
Micronesian: (5)	12	0.02
Guamanian/Chamorro (5)	10	0.01
Other Micronesian	2	0.00
Polynesian: (26)	52	0.08
Native Hawaiian (4)	17	0.03
Samoan (16)	25	0.04
Tongan (5)	7	0.01
Other Polynesian (1)	3	0.00
Other Pac. Isl., specified	1	0.00
Other Pac. Isl., not spec. (13)	85	0.13
Hispanic or Latino:	1,944	2.88
Central American:	167	0.25
Costa Rican	8	0.01
Guatemalan	36	0.05
Honduran	45	0.07
Nicaraguan	2	0.00
Panamanian	9	0.01
Salvadoran	48	0.07
Other Central American	19	0.03
Cuban	33	0.05
Dominican Republic	14	0.02
Mexican	1,179	1.75
Puerto Rican	138	0.20
South American:	92	0.14
Argentinean	5	0.01
Bolivian	6	0.01
Chilean	2	0.00
Colombian	35	0.05
Ecuadorian	2	0.00
Peruvian	28	0.04
Venezuelan	3	0.00
Other South American	11	0.02
Other Hispanic or Latino	321	0.48
Hungarian	128	0.19
Icelander	15	0.02
Irish	6,952	10.32
Italian	1,329	1.97
Latvian	19	0.03
Lithuanian	61	0.09
Luxemburger	30	0.04
Northern European	22	0.03
Norwegian	9,712	14.41
Pennsylvania German	30	0.04
Polish	3,165	4.70
Portuguese	60	0.09
Romanian	62	0.09
Russian	672	1.00
Scandinavian	680	1.01
Scotch-Irish	763	1.13
Scottish	607	0.90
Serbian	22	0.03
Slavic	115	0.17
Slovak	81	0.12
Slovene	74	0.11
Swedish	6,371	9.45
Swiss	133	0.20
Turkish	16	0.02
Ukrainian	285	0.42
United States or American	1,883	2.79
Welsh	227	0.34
West Indian, excl. Hispanic:	174	0.26
Barbadian	14	0.02
Belizean	12	0.02
British West Indian	19	0.03
Haitian	12	0.02
Jamaican	95	0.14
West Indian	22	0.03
White:	49,569	73.56
Not Hispanic (47,365)	48,671	72.23
Hispanic (780)	898	1.33
Yugoslavian	82	0.12

Buffalo

Place Type: City
County: Wright
Population: 10,097

Ancestry/Race	Number	%
Acadian/Cajun	7	0.07
African American/Black:	97	0.96
Not Hispanic (53)	95	0.94
Hispanic	2	0.02
Alaska Native tribes, specified:	1	0.01
Eskimo (1)	1	0.01
Am. Ind. or Alaska Nat., not spec.	24	0.24
American Indian tribes, specified:	79	0.78
Apache (2)	2	0.02
Blackfeet	3	0.03
Cherokee (3)	4	0.04
Chippewa (21)	41	0.41
Iroquois	1	0.01
Potawatomi (2)	2	0.02
Sioux (4)	15	0.15
Tohono O'Odham (5)	5	0.05
All other tribes (2)	6	0.06
American Indian tribes, not spec.	2	0.02
Asian:	95	0.94
Chinese, ex. Taiwanese (12)	12	0.12
Filipino (6)	16	0.16
Hmong (10)	10	0.10
Indian (11)	14	0.14
Japanese (2)	8	0.08
Korean (23)	28	0.28
Thai (1)	2	0.02
Vietnamese (3)	3	0.03
Other Asian, not specified	2	0.02
Austrian	3	0.03
Belgian	15	0.15
British	39	0.38
Canadian	23	0.23
Czech	111	1.10
Czechoslovakian	14	0.14
Danish	171	1.69
Dutch	150	1.48
English	723	7.14
European	32	0.32
Finnish	282	2.78
French, except Basque	651	6.43
French Canadian	130	1.28
German	4,318	42.62
Greek	13	0.13
Hawaii Native/Pacific Islander:	1	0.01
Polynesian:	1	0.01
Native Hawaiian	1	0.01
Hispanic or Latino:	112	1.11
Central American:	1	0.01
Salvadoran	1	0.01
Mexican	65	0.64
Puerto Rican	15	0.15
South American:	5	0.05
Colombian	4	0.04
Paraguayan	1	0.01
Other Hispanic or Latino	26	0.26
Hungarian	8	0.08
Irish	1,102	10.88
Italian	133	1.31
Latvian	4	0.04
Lithuanian	3	0.03
Luxemburger	9	0.09
Norwegian	1,833	18.09
Polish	400	3.95
Portuguese	6	0.06
Russian	48	0.47
Scandinavian	208	2.05
Scotch-Irish	58	0.57
Scottish	114	1.13
Slavic	17	0.17
Slovak	3	0.03
Swedish	1,273	12.57
Swiss	45	0.44
United States or American	310	3.06
Welsh	19	0.19
White:	9,893	97.98
Not Hispanic (9,701)	9,809	97.15
Hispanic (67)	84	0.83
Yugoslavian	24	0.24

Burnsville

Place Type: City
County: Dakota
Population: 60,220

Ancestry/Race	Number	%
Afghan	53	0.09
African American/Black:	3,103	5.15
Not Hispanic (2,433)	3,056	5.07
Hispanic (19)	47	0.08
African, sub-Saharan:	707	1.18
African	235	0.39
Ethiopian	73	0.12
Ghanian	20	0.03
Liberian	42	0.07
Nigerian	113	0.19
Somalian	178	0.30
South African	46	0.08
Alaska Native tribes, specified:	3	0.00
Alaska Athabascan	1	0.00
Eskimo	1	0.00
Tlingit-Haida (1)	1	0.00
Alaska Native tribes, not specified	1	0.00
Am. Ind. or Alaska Nat., not spec.	175	0.29
Alsatian	10	0.02
American Indian tribes, specified:	357	0.59
Apache (1)	3	0.00
Blackfeet	9	0.01
Cherokee (14)	54	0.09
Cheyenne (1)	1	0.00
Chickasaw	3	0.00

Notes: 1. Figures in the "Number" column do not add up to the total population due to: a) Ancestry/Race overlap — e.g. persons can report being both White and Irish, b) persons of Hispanic origin can report being any race, c) persons reporting two ancestries are counted in both categories. 2. Numbers in parentheses indicate the number of persons reporting this ancestry/race alone, not in combination with any other ancestry/race. 3. Refer to the Explanation of Data in the front of the book for more detailed information.

Ancestry/Race	Number	%
Chippewa (97)	133	0.22
Choctaw (5)	10	0.02
Comanche	2	0.00
Cree (2)	3	0.00
Iroquois	5	0.01
Latin American Indians (19)	32	0.05
Lumbee	2	0.00
Menominee (1)	2	0.00
Navajo (4)	4	0.01
Seminole (4)	4	0.01
Shoshone	1	0.00
Sioux (44)	69	0.11
All other tribes (10)	20	0.03
American Indian tribes, not spec.	17	0.03
Arab:	230	0.38
Egyptian	60	0.10
Jordanian	35	0.06
Lebanese	124	0.21
Moroccan	11	0.02
Armenian	9	0.01
Asian:	2,990	4.97
Bangladeshi (1)	2	0.00
Cambodian (217)	277	0.46
Chinese, ex. Taiwanese (229)	290	0.48
Filipino (127)	189	0.31
Hmong (72)	80	0.13
Indian (446)	528	0.88
Indonesian (4)	7	0.01
Japanese (62)	127	0.21
Korean (257)	321	0.53
Laotian (183)	205	0.34
Malaysian (7)	14	0.02
Pakistani (30)	46	0.08
Sri Lankan (10)	10	0.02
Taiwanese (8)	8	0.01
Thai (29)	50	0.08
Vietnamese (641)	688	1.14
Other Asian, specified (4)	7	0.01
Other Asian, not specified (66)	141	0.23
Australian	44	0.07
Austrian	191	0.32
Belgian	91	0.15
British	247	0.41
Canadian	135	0.22
Celtic	44	0.07
Croatian	148	0.25
Czech	846	1.41
Czechoslovakian	299	0.50
Danish	1,029	1.71
Dutch	1,145	1.90
Eastern European	13	0.02
English	4,920	8.18
Estonian	10	0.02
European	421	0.70
Finnish	674	1.12
French, except Basque	2,197	3.65
French Canadian	610	1.01
German	21,199	35.24
Greek	221	0.37
Guyanese	36	0.06
Hawaii Native/Pacific Islander:	125	0.21
Micronesian: (10)	22	0.04
Guamanian/Chamorro (4)	13	0.02
Other Micronesian (6)	9	0.01
Polynesian: (22)	51	0.08
Native Hawaiian (10)	34	0.06
Samoan (10)	15	0.02
Other Polynesian (2)	2	0.00
Other Pac. Isl., specified	3	0.00
Other Pac. Isl., not spec. (14)	49	0.08
Hispanic or Latino:	1,725	2.86
Central American:	161	0.27
Costa Rican	8	0.01
Guatemalan	21	0.03
Honduran	12	0.02
Nicaraguan	3	0.00
Panamanian	12	0.02
Salvadoran	90	0.15
Other Central American	15	0.02
Cuban	22	0.04
Dominican Republic	6	0.01
Mexican	921	1.53
Puerto Rican	147	0.24
South American:	176	0.29
Argentinean	2	0.00
Bolivian	1	0.00
Chilean	10	0.02
Colombian	47	0.08
Ecuadorian	89	0.15
Paraguayan	3	0.00
Peruvian	5	0.01
Venezuelan	15	0.02
Other South American	4	0.01
Other Hispanic or Latino	292	0.48
Hungarian	158	0.26
Icelander	147	0.24
Iranian	76	0.13
Irish	9,133	15.18
Italian	1,609	2.68
Lithuanian	108	0.18
Luxemburger	54	0.09
Macedonian	10	0.02
Northern European	37	0.06
Norwegian	10,603	17.63
Pennsylvania German	6	0.01
Polish	2,412	4.01
Portuguese	5	0.01
Romanian	110	0.18
Russian	469	0.78
Scandinavian	693	1.15
Scotch-Irish	639	1.06
Scottish	782	1.30
Serbian	46	0.08
Slavic	30	0.05
Slovak	86	0.14
Slovene	60	0.10
Swedish	6,026	10.02
Swiss	275	0.46
Turkish	36	0.06
Ukrainian	209	0.35
United States or American	1,958	3.26
Welsh	326	0.54
West Indian, excl. Hispanic:	84	0.14
Jamaican	84	0.14
White:	53,867	89.45
Not Hispanic (51,952)	52,971	87.96
Hispanic (765)	896	1.49
Yugoslavian	134	0.22

Champlin

Place Type: City
County: Hennepin
Population: 22,193

Ancestry/Race	Number	%
Afghan	38	0.17
African American/Black:	380	1.71
Not Hispanic (308)	370	1.67
Hispanic (6)	10	0.05
African, sub-Saharan:	117	0.52
African	113	0.51
South African	4	0.02
Alaska Native tribes, specified:	4	0.02
Alaska Athabascan (1)	1	0.00
Tlingit-Haida	3	0.01
Am. Ind. or Alaska Nat., not spec.	53	0.24
American Indian tribes, specified:	112	0.50
Blackfeet	1	0.00
Cherokee	4	0.02
Chippewa (57)	80	0.36
Cree	1	0.00
Creek	1	0.00
Iroquois	1	0.00
Latin American Indians (1)	2	0.01
Shoshone (3)	4	0.02
Sioux (13)	15	0.07
Yuman (1)	1	0.00
All other tribes (2)	2	0.01
American Indian tribes, not spec.	4	0.02
Arab:	90	0.40
Lebanese	46	0.21
Palestinian	16	0.07
Syrian	28	0.13
Asian:	460	2.07
Chinese, ex. Taiwanese (45)	58	0.26
Filipino (30)	52	0.23
Hmong (28)	34	0.15
Indian (40)	50	0.23
Japanese (16)	30	0.14
Korean (64)	79	0.36
Laotian (50)	51	0.23
Thai (4)	9	0.04
Vietnamese (63)	73	0.33
Other Asian, specified (1)	1	0.00
Other Asian, not specified (15)	23	0.10
Austrian	72	0.32
British	32	0.14
Bulgarian	4	0.02
Canadian	66	0.30
Croatian	61	0.27
Czech	384	1.72
Czechoslovakian	76	0.34
Danish	317	1.42
Dutch	509	2.28
Eastern European	9	0.04
English	1,586	7.09
European	281	1.26
Finnish	715	3.20
French, except Basque	1,291	5.77
French Canadian	219	0.98
German	8,976	40.14
Greek	13	0.06
Hawaii Native/Pacific Islander:	15	0.07
Polynesian: (4)	13	0.06
Native Hawaiian (1)	10	0.05
Samoan (3)	3	0.01
Other Pac. Isl., not spec.	2	0.01
Hispanic or Latino:	250	1.13
Central American:	5	0.02
Costa Rican	2	0.01
Guatemalan	2	0.01
Other Central American	1	0.00
Cuban	4	0.02
Mexican	121	0.55
Puerto Rican	32	0.14
South American:	36	0.16
Chilean	4	0.02
Colombian	11	0.05
Ecuadorian	1	0.00
Paraguayan	1	0.00
Peruvian	6	0.03
Venezuelan	8	0.04
Other South American	5	0.02
Other Hispanic or Latino	52	0.23
Hungarian	99	0.44
Iranian	26	0.12
Irish	2,665	11.92
Italian	537	2.40
Latvian	24	0.11
Lithuanian	6	0.03
Luxemburger	3	0.01
New Zealander	40	0.18
Northern European	6	0.03
Norwegian	4,248	19.00
Polish	1,304	5.83
Portuguese	18	0.08
Romanian	9	0.04
Russian	124	0.55
Scandinavian	186	0.83
Scotch-Irish	229	1.02
Scottish	314	1.40
Slovak	46	0.21
Slovene	80	0.36
Swedish	2,451	10.96
Swiss	23	0.10
Ukrainian	122	0.55
United States or American	967	4.32
Welsh	79	0.35
West Indian, excl. Hispanic:	6	0.03

Notes: 1. Figures in the "Number" column do not add up to the total population due to: a) Ancestry/Race overlap — e.g. persons can report being both White and Irish, b) persons of Hispanic origin can report being any race, c) persons reporting two ancestries are counted in both categories. 2. Numbers in parentheses indicate the number of persons reporting this ancestry/race alone, not in combination with any other ancestry/race. 3. Refer to the Explanation of Data in the front of the book for more detailed information.

Jamaican	6	0.03
White:	21,309	96.02
Not Hispanic (20,948)	21,142	95.26
Hispanic (138)	167	0.75
Yugoslavian	68	0.30

Chanhassen

Place Type: City
County: Carver
Population: 20,321

Ancestry/Race	Number	%
Acadian/Cajun	17	0.08
African American/Black:	216	1.06
Not Hispanic (145)	209	1.03
Hispanic (7)	7	0.03
African, sub-Saharan:	52	0.26
Nigerian	52	0.26
Alaska Native tribes, specified:	1	0.00
Eskimo (1)	1	0.00
Am. Ind. or Alaska Nat., not spec.	23	0.11
Alsatian	6	0.03
American Indian tribes, specified:	44	0.22
Blackfeet (1)	3	0.01
Cherokee (4)	9	0.04
Chippewa (6)	16	0.08
Crow (1)	1	0.00
Iroquois (1)	1	0.00
Latin American Indians (1)	1	0.00
Menominee	1	0.00
Osage (1)	2	0.01
Shoshone (1)	2	0.01
Sioux (1)	6	0.03
All other tribes (1)	2	0.01
American Indian tribes, not spec.	4	0.02
Arab:	55	0.27
Egyptian	22	0.11
Lebanese	33	0.16
Armenian	6	0.03
Asian:	689	3.39
Cambodian (76)	77	0.38
Chinese, ex. Taiwanese (87)	110	0.54
Filipino (53)	81	0.40
Hmong (7)	7	0.03
Indian (41)	50	0.25
Japanese (8)	17	0.08
Korean (88)	98	0.48
Laotian (72)	93	0.46
Malaysian	1	0.00
Pakistani (4)	4	0.02
Thai (1)	5	0.02
Vietnamese (102)	113	0.56
Other Asian, specified (1)	1	0.00
Other Asian, not specified (18)	32	0.16
Austrian	19	0.09
Belgian	31	0.15
British	99	0.49
Canadian	85	0.42
Celtic	5	0.02
Croatian	7	0.03
Czech	439	2.16
Czechoslovakian	100	0.49
Danish	347	1.71
Dutch	394	1.94
English	1,824	8.97
European	127	0.62
Finnish	291	1.43
French, except Basque	893	4.39
French Canadian	331	1.63
German	8,422	41.43
Greek	64	0.31
Guyanese	33	0.16
Hawaii Native/Pacific Islander:	11	0.05
Polynesian: (1)	5	0.02
Native Hawaiian	4	0.02
Samoan (1)	1	0.00
Other Pac. Isl., not spec.	6	0.03
Hispanic or Latino:	402	1.98
Central American:	37	0.18
Costa Rican	1	0.00
Guatemalan	8	0.04
Honduran	20	0.10
Nicaraguan	4	0.02
Panamanian	2	0.01
Salvadoran	1	0.00
Other Central American	1	0.00
Cuban	13	0.06
Dominican Republic	7	0.03
Mexican	225	1.11
Puerto Rican	24	0.12
South American:	23	0.11
Argentinean	3	0.01
Colombian	15	0.07
Peruvian	4	0.02
Venezuelan	1	0.00
Other Hispanic or Latino	73	0.36
Hungarian	146	0.72
Icelander	14	0.07
Iranian	37	0.18
Irish	2,641	12.99
Israeli	25	0.12
Italian	702	3.45
Latvian	6	0.03
Lithuanian	41	0.20
Luxemburger	29	0.14
Northern European	123	0.61
Norwegian	3,671	18.06
Polish	969	4.77
Portuguese	31	0.15
Romanian	13	0.06
Russian	182	0.90
Scandinavian	204	1.00
Scotch-Irish	208	1.02
Scottish	271	1.33
Serbian	18	0.09
Slavic	42	0.21
Slovak	46	0.23
Slovene	19	0.09
Swedish	2,437	11.99
Swiss	128	0.63
Ukrainian	21	0.10
United States or American	392	1.93
Welsh	187	0.92
West Indian, excl. Hispanic:	7	0.03
Dutch West Indian	7	0.03
White:	19,445	95.69
Not Hispanic (18,979)	19,130	94.14
Hispanic (305)	315	1.55
Yugoslavian	46	0.23

Chaska

Place Type: City
County: Carver
Population: 17,449

Ancestry/Race	Number	%
African American/Black:	246	1.41
Not Hispanic (168)	219	1.26
Hispanic (10)	27	0.15
African, sub-Saharan:	86	0.49
African	66	0.38
Ghanian	18	0.10
Liberian	2	0.01
Am. Ind. or Alaska Nat., not spec.	33	0.19
Albanian	14	0.08
Alsatian	6	0.03
American Indian tribes, specified:	59	0.34
Apache	1	0.01
Blackfeet	1	0.01
Cherokee (3)	5	0.03
Chippewa (6)	12	0.07
Choctaw (1)	3	0.02
Creek	1	0.01
Iroquois	1	0.01
Latin American Indians (4)	5	0.03
Lumbee (2)	2	0.01
Paiute	1	0.01
Pueblo	1	0.01
Seminole	2	0.01
Shoshone	2	0.01
Sioux (5)	10	0.06
All other tribes (9)	12	0.07
American Indian tribes, not spec.	4	0.02
Arab:	14	0.08
Lebanese	5	0.03
Palestinian	9	0.05
Asian:	329	1.89
Cambodian (7)	9	0.05
Chinese, ex. Taiwanese (31)	35	0.20
Filipino (36)	42	0.24
Indian (24)	26	0.15
Japanese (8)	10	0.06
Korean (57)	65	0.37
Laotian (49)	57	0.33
Sri Lankan (2)	2	0.01
Taiwanese (4)	4	0.02
Thai (4)	4	0.02
Vietnamese (63)	67	0.38
Other Asian, specified (1)	1	0.01
Other Asian, not specified (4)	7	0.04
Austrian	116	0.67
Belgian	79	0.45
British	62	0.36
Canadian	6	0.03
Croatian	12	0.07
Czech	274	1.57
Czechoslovakian	81	0.46
Danish	259	1.48
Dutch	354	2.03
English	1,024	5.87
Estonian	5	0.03
European	121	0.69
Finnish	238	1.36
French, except Basque	803	4.60
French Canadian	277	1.59
German	7,830	44.89
Greek	34	0.19
Hawaii Native/Pacific Islander:	4	0.02
Polynesian:	3	0.02
Native Hawaiian	1	0.01
Samoan	2	0.01
Other Pac. Isl., not spec. (1)	1	0.01
Hispanic or Latino:	1,013	5.81
Central American:	56	0.32
Guatemalan	30	0.17
Honduran	10	0.06
Nicaraguan	4	0.02
Salvadoran	11	0.06
Other Central American	1	0.01
Cuban	4	0.02
Dominican Republic	1	0.01
Mexican	739	4.24
Puerto Rican	12	0.07
South American:	27	0.15
Argentinean	1	0.01
Chilean	2	0.01
Colombian	7	0.04
Ecuadorian	2	0.01
Paraguayan	3	0.02
Peruvian	12	0.07
Other Hispanic or Latino	174	1.00
Hungarian	120	0.69
Icelander	14	0.08
Irish	2,250	12.90
Italian	398	2.28
Latvian	28	0.16
Lithuanian	43	0.25
Luxemburger	27	0.15
Northern European	43	0.25
Norwegian	2,710	15.54
Polish	511	2.93
Portuguese	6	0.03
Romanian	25	0.14
Russian	129	0.74
Scandinavian	135	0.77
Scotch-Irish	217	1.24
Scottish	239	1.37
Serbian	2	0.01

Notes: 1. Figures in the "Number" column do not add up to the total population due to: a) Ancestry/Race overlap — e.g. persons can report being both White and Irish, b) persons of Hispanic origin can report being any race, c) persons reporting two ancestries are counted in both categories. 2. Numbers in parentheses indicate the number of persons reporting this ancestry/race alone, not in combination with any other ancestry/race. 3. Refer to the Explanation of Data in the front of the book for more detailed information.

Ancestry/Race	Number	%
Slovak	6	0.03
Slovene	10	0.06
Swedish	1,505	8.63
Swiss	76	0.44
Ukrainian	68	0.39
United States or American	695	3.98
Welsh	60	0.34
White:	16,517	94.66
Not Hispanic (15,786)	15,908	91.17
Hispanic (565)	609	3.49
Yugoslavian	35	0.20

Cloquet

Place Type: City
County: Carlton
Population: 11,201

Ancestry/Race	Number	%
African American/Black:	47	0.42
Not Hispanic (17)	46	0.41
Hispanic (1)	1	0.01
Alaska Native tribes, specified:	2	0.02
Eskimo (2)	2	0.02
Am. Ind. or Alaska Nat., not spec.	175	1.56
American Indian tribes, specified:	992	8.86
Apache	1	0.01
Blackfeet	1	0.01
Cherokee (1)	3	0.03
Chippewa (858)	954	8.52
Iroquois (1)	2	0.02
Latin American Indians (1)	1	0.01
Ottawa (1)	1	0.01
Potawatomi (2)	2	0.02
Sioux (17)	17	0.15
All other tribes (6)	10	0.09
American Indian tribes, not spec.	31	0.28
Arab:	22	0.20
Other Arab	22	0.20
Asian:	61	0.54
Chinese, ex. Taiwanese (11)	11	0.10
Filipino (9)	16	0.14
Indian (8)	9	0.08
Japanese (1)	4	0.04
Korean (11)	11	0.10
Thai (1)	3	0.03
Vietnamese (2)	4	0.04
Other Asian, not specified (1)	3	0.03
Australian	8	0.07
Austrian	21	0.19
Belgian	35	0.31
Brazilian	11	0.10
British	19	0.17
Croatian	15	0.13
Czech	161	1.44
Danish	49	0.44
Dutch	138	1.24
English	684	6.13
European	56	0.50
Finnish	1,755	15.73
French, except Basque	687	6.16
French Canadian	364	3.26
German	2,400	21.51
Greek	54	0.48
Hawaii Native/Pacific Islander:	6	0.05
Micronesian:	1	0.01
Guamanian/Chamorro	1	0.01
Polynesian: (1)	5	0.04
Native Hawaiian	2	0.02
Samoan (1)	3	0.03
Hispanic or Latino:	71	0.63
Central American:	3	0.03
Guatemalan	2	0.02
Honduran	1	0.01
Cuban	3	0.03
Mexican	40	0.36
Puerto Rican	6	0.05
South American:	3	0.03
Chilean	1	0.01
Colombian	1	0.01
Venezuelan	1	0.01
Other Hispanic or Latino	16	0.14
Hungarian	16	0.14
Irish	758	6.79
Italian	374	3.35
Lithuanian	13	0.12
Northern European	38	0.34
Norwegian	1,764	15.81
Polish	743	6.66
Romanian	29	0.26
Russian	17	0.15
Scandinavian	168	1.51
Scotch-Irish	168	1.51
Scottish	196	1.76
Slavic	4	0.04
Slovak	29	0.26
Slovene	68	0.61
Swedish	1,734	15.54
Ukrainian	43	0.39
United States or American	307	2.75
Welsh	30	0.27
White:	10,056	89.78
Not Hispanic (9,831)	10,001	89.29
Hispanic (49)	55	0.49
Yugoslavian	69	0.62

Columbia Heights

Place Type: City
County: Anoka
Population: 18,520

Ancestry/Race	Number	%
Afghan	86	0.46
African American/Black:	844	4.56
Not Hispanic (667)	828	4.47
Hispanic (4)	16	0.09
African, sub-Saharan:	240	1.30
African	23	0.12
Ethiopian	113	0.61
Liberian	7	0.04
Nigerian	42	0.23
Somalian	43	0.23
Sudanese	12	0.06
Alaska Native tribes, specified:	2	0.01
Tlingit-Haida (2)	2	0.01
Am. Ind. or Alaska Nat., not spec.	123	0.66
Albanian	23	0.12
American Indian tribes, specified:	359	1.94
Apache (1)	1	0.01
Blackfeet (1)	4	0.02
Cherokee (3)	13	0.07
Chippewa (174)	249	1.34
Choctaw	1	0.01
Cree (3)	4	0.02
Iroquois (1)	2	0.01
Latin American Indians (1)	4	0.02
Menominee (4)	4	0.02
Navajo	2	0.01
Ottawa (1)	2	0.01
Sioux (26)	35	0.19
All other tribes (23)	38	0.21
American Indian tribes, not spec.	9	0.05
Arab:	123	0.66
Egyptian	58	0.31
Lebanese	58	0.31
Syrian	7	0.04
Asian:	740	4.00
Cambodian (4)	6	0.03
Chinese, ex. Taiwanese (73)	81	0.44
Filipino (87)	112	0.60
Hmong (117)	119	0.64
Indian (131)	146	0.79
Japanese (14)	23	0.12
Korean (35)	44	0.24
Laotian (16)	20	0.11
Malaysian (1)	1	0.01
Pakistani (24)	25	0.13
Sri Lankan (1)	4	0.02
Thai (9)	13	0.07
Vietnamese (113)	124	0.67
Other Asian, not specified (8)	22	0.12
Austrian	56	0.30
Belgian	36	0.19
British	30	0.16
Bulgarian	12	0.06
Carpatho Rusyn	5	0.03
Celtic	7	0.04
Croatian	22	0.12
Czech	213	1.15
Czechoslovakian	53	0.29
Danish	219	1.18
Dutch	223	1.20
Eastern European	11	0.06
English	1,082	5.84
European	160	0.86
Finnish	243	1.31
French, except Basque	759	4.10
French Canadian	206	1.11
German	5,614	30.33
Greek	34	0.18
Guyanese	20	0.11
Hawaii Native/Pacific Islander:	12	0.06
Micronesian: (1)	1	0.01
Guamanian/Chamorro (1)	1	0.01
Polynesian: (1)	7	0.04
Native Hawaiian (1)	5	0.03
Samoan	2	0.01
Other Pac. Isl., not spec.	4	0.02
Hispanic or Latino:	583	3.15
Central American:	42	0.23
Costa Rican	2	0.01
Guatemalan	15	0.08
Honduran	8	0.04
Salvadoran	16	0.09
Other Central American	1	0.01
Cuban	6	0.03
Dominican Republic	2	0.01
Mexican	378	2.04
Puerto Rican	20	0.11
South American:	55	0.30
Argentinean	1	0.01
Chilean	3	0.02
Colombian	13	0.07
Ecuadorian	16	0.09
Peruvian	11	0.06
Venezuelan	1	0.01
Other South American	10	0.05
Other Hispanic or Latino	80	0.43
Hungarian	21	0.11
Icelander	13	0.07
Irish	2,289	12.36
Italian	381	2.06
Lithuanian	11	0.06
Luxemburger	30	0.16
Northern European	12	0.06
Norwegian	3,011	16.27
Pennsylvania German	7	0.04
Polish	2,084	11.26
Portuguese	8	0.04
Romanian	11	0.06
Russian	156	0.84
Scandinavian	238	1.29
Scotch-Irish	206	1.11
Scottish	166	0.90
Serbian	5	0.03
Slavic	12	0.06
Slovak	149	0.80
Slovene	23	0.12
Swedish	2,240	12.10
Swiss	89	0.48
Ukrainian	181	0.98
United States or American	690	3.73
Welsh	89	0.48
West Indian, excl. Hispanic:	72	0.39
Haitian	58	0.31
Jamaican	14	0.08
White:	16,611	89.69
Not Hispanic (15,893)	16,269	87.85
Hispanic (291)	342	1.85

Notes: 1. Figures in the "Number" column do not add up to the total population due to: a) Ancestry/Race overlap — e.g. persons can report being both White and Irish, b) persons of Hispanic origin can report being any race, c) persons reporting two ancestries are counted in both categories. 2. Numbers in parentheses indicate the number of persons reporting this ancestry/race alone, not in combination with any other ancestry/race. 3. Refer to the Explanation of Data in the front of the book for more detailed information.

Yugoslavian	171	0.92

Coon Rapids

Place Type: City
County: Anoka
Population: 61,607

Ancestry/Race	Number	%
Afghan	5	0.01
African American/Black:	1,688	2.74
Not Hispanic (1,327)	1,640	2.66
Hispanic (19)	48	0.08
African, sub-Saharan:	287	0.47
African	125	0.20
Ethiopian	16	0.03
Kenyan	35	0.06
Liberian	45	0.07
Nigerian	12	0.02
Sudanese	21	0.03
Other sub-Saharan African	33	0.05
Alaska Native tribes, specified:	6	0.01
Aleut (1)	1	0.00
Eskimo (5)	5	0.01
Am. Ind. or Alaska Nat., not spec.	178	0.29
Albanian	31	0.05
American Indian tribes, specified:	499	0.81
Apache (2)	2	0.00
Blackfeet	8	0.01
Cherokee (8)	31	0.05
Chippewa (249)	342	0.56
Choctaw (5)	6	0.01
Delaware (3)	3	0.00
Houma	1	0.00
Iroquois	8	0.01
Kiowa (1)	1	0.00
Latin American Indians (5)	7	0.01
Lumbee	3	0.00
Pima	3	0.00
Potawatomi (4)	6	0.01
Pueblo	4	0.01
Seminole	1	0.00
Sioux (29)	56	0.09
All other tribes (8)	17	0.03
American Indian tribes, not spec.	28	0.05
Arab:	390	0.63
Egyptian	97	0.16
Iraqi	58	0.09
Jordanian	12	0.02
Lebanese	159	0.26
Palestinian	6	0.01
Other Arab	58	0.09
Armenian	9	0.01
Asian:	1,313	2.13
Cambodian (15)	18	0.03
Chinese, ex. Taiwanese (112)	149	0.24
Filipino (57)	114	0.19
Hmong (97)	100	0.16
Indian (125)	151	0.25
Indonesian (1)	2	0.00
Japanese (18)	72	0.12
Korean (142)	197	0.32
Laotian (50)	54	0.09
Malaysian (1)	2	0.00
Pakistani (6)	11	0.02
Sri Lankan (8)	8	0.01
Taiwanese (4)	4	0.01
Thai (15)	23	0.04
Vietnamese (291)	342	0.56
Other Asian, specified (1)	2	0.00
Other Asian, not specified (18)	64	0.10
Australian	21	0.03
Austrian	201	0.33
Belgian	83	0.13
Brazilian	31	0.05
British	79	0.13
Bulgarian	23	0.04
Canadian	124	0.20
Carpatho Rusyn	5	0.01
Croatian	80	0.13
Czech	815	1.32
Czechoslovakian	236	0.38
Danish	1,187	1.93
Dutch	1,237	2.01
English	4,068	6.60
Estonian	7	0.01
European	330	0.54
Finnish	1,310	2.13
French, except Basque	3,353	5.44
French Canadian	989	1.60
German	22,440	36.41
Greek	146	0.24
Hawaii Native/Pacific Islander:	48	0.08
Micronesian:	1	0.00
Guamanian/Chamorro	1	0.00
Polynesian: (4)	14	0.02
Native Hawaiian (4)	14	0.02
Other Pac. Isl., specified	1	0.00
Other Pac. Isl., not spec. (4)	32	0.05
Hispanic or Latino:	933	1.51
Central American:	56	0.09
Costa Rican	4	0.01
Guatemalan	15	0.02
Honduran	2	0.00
Nicaraguan	6	0.01
Panamanian	9	0.01
Salvadoran	19	0.03
Other Central American	1	0.00
Cuban	28	0.05
Dominican Republic	14	0.02
Mexican	493	0.80
Puerto Rican	92	0.15
South American:	56	0.09
Argentinean	3	0.00
Bolivian	3	0.00
Chilean	3	0.00
Colombian	17	0.03
Ecuadorian	2	0.00
Paraguayan	1	0.00
Peruvian	12	0.02
Venezuelan	13	0.02
Other South American	2	0.00
Other Hispanic or Latino	194	0.31
Hungarian	150	0.24
Icelander	69	0.11
Irish	7,611	12.35
Italian	1,389	2.25
Latvian	61	0.10
Lithuanian	70	0.11
Luxemburger	27	0.04
Macedonian	6	0.01
Northern European	19	0.03
Norwegian	11,159	18.11
Pennsylvania German	35	0.06
Polish	4,368	7.09
Romanian	28	0.05
Russian	606	0.98
Scandinavian	796	1.29
Scotch-Irish	665	1.08
Scottish	668	1.08
Serbian	35	0.06
Slavic	51	0.08
Slovak	259	0.42
Slovene	70	0.11
Swedish	8,022	13.02
Swiss	138	0.22
Ukrainian	522	0.85
United States or American	1,858	3.01
Welsh	220	0.36
West Indian, excl. Hispanic:	143	0.23
Haitian	55	0.09
Jamaican	51	0.08
Trinidadian and Tobagonian	37	0.06
White:	58,394	94.78
Not Hispanic (56,955)	57,811	93.84
Hispanic (475)	583	0.95
Yugoslavian	144	0.23

Cottage Grove

Place Type: City
County: Washington
Population: 30,582

Ancestry/Race	Number	%
African American/Black:	855	2.80
Not Hispanic (699)	824	2.69
Hispanic (21)	31	0.10
African, sub-Saharan:	184	0.60
African	53	0.17
South African	119	0.39
Other sub-Saharan African	12	0.04
Am. Ind. or Alaska Nat., not spec.	68	0.22
American Indian tribes, specified:	163	0.53
Apache (1)	1	0.00
Blackfeet	4	0.01
Cherokee (1)	13	0.04
Cheyenne	2	0.01
Chippewa (57)	83	0.27
Choctaw (2)	7	0.02
Comanche (1)	1	0.00
Cree (1)	6	0.02
Iroquois	2	0.01
Latin American Indians (1)	4	0.01
Potawatomi (2)	4	0.01
Seminole (1)	1	0.00
Sioux (14)	26	0.09
All other tribes (5)	9	0.03
American Indian tribes, not spec.	6	0.02
Arab:	64	0.21
Egyptian	4	0.01
Lebanese	60	0.20
Asian:	575	1.88
Bangladeshi (6)	6	0.02
Cambodian (1)	2	0.01
Chinese, ex. Taiwanese (45)	55	0.18
Filipino (79)	138	0.45
Hmong (107)	122	0.40
Indian (16)	26	0.09
Indonesian	1	0.00
Japanese (21)	33	0.11
Korean (79)	96	0.31
Laotian (8)	11	0.04
Malaysian (1)	1	0.00
Pakistani (15)	15	0.05
Sri Lankan (5)	5	0.02
Thai (1)	4	0.01
Vietnamese (33)	46	0.15
Other Asian, not specified (8)	14	0.05
Austrian	110	0.36
Belgian	113	0.37
British	31	0.10
Canadian	78	0.26
Croatian	28	0.09
Czech	490	1.60
Czechoslovakian	94	0.31
Danish	506	1.66
Dutch	577	1.89
English	1,723	5.64
European	138	0.45
Finnish	398	1.30
French, except Basque	1,844	6.03
French Canadian	568	1.86
German	13,219	43.26
Greek	38	0.12
Hawaii Native/Pacific Islander:	44	0.14
Micronesian: (9)	14	0.05
Guamanian/Chamorro (9)	14	0.05
Polynesian: (1)	9	0.03
Native Hawaiian (1)	5	0.02
Samoan	4	0.01
Other Pac. Isl., not spec. (8)	21	0.07
Hispanic or Latino:	775	2.53
Central American:	31	0.10
Costa Rican	1	0.00
Guatemalan	9	0.03
Honduran	7	0.02
Nicaraguan	2	0.01

Notes: 1. Figures in the "Number" column do not add up to the total population due to: a) Ancestry/Race overlap — e.g. persons can report being both White and Irish, b) persons of Hispanic origin can report being any race, c) persons reporting two ancestries are counted in both categories. 2. Numbers in parentheses indicate the number of persons reporting this ancestry/race alone, not in combination with any other ancestry/race. 3. Refer to the Explanation of Data in the front of the book for more detailed information.

Ancestry/Race	Number	%
Panamanian	9	0.03
Salvadoran	1	0.00
Other Central American	2	0.01
Cuban	11	0.04
Dominican Republic	2	0.01
Mexican	491	1.61
Puerto Rican	68	0.22
South American:	50	0.16
Argentinean	7	0.02
Bolivian	2	0.01
Chilean	1	0.00
Colombian	18	0.06
Ecuadorian	13	0.04
Paraguayan	1	0.00
Peruvian	5	0.02
Venezuelan	3	0.01
Other Hispanic or Latino	122	0.40
Hungarian	156	0.51
Iranian	36	0.12
Irish	4,473	14.64
Italian	1,404	4.59
Latvian	19	0.06
Lithuanian	38	0.12
Luxemburger	25	0.08
Northern European	66	0.22
Norwegian	4,374	14.31
Pennsylvania German	20	0.07
Polish	1,619	5.30
Portuguese	2	0.01
Romanian	37	0.12
Russian	180	0.59
Scandinavian	341	1.12
Scotch-Irish	178	0.58
Scottish	203	0.66
Serbian	19	0.06
Slavic	39	0.13
Slovak	28	0.09
Swedish	2,662	8.71
Swiss	222	0.73
Turkish	8	0.03
Ukrainian	82	0.27
United States or American	763	2.50
Welsh	64	0.21
White:	28,956	94.68
Not Hispanic (28,196)	28,489	93.16
Hispanic (410)	467	1.53
Yugoslavian	23	0.08

Crystal

Place Type: City
County: Hennepin
Population: 22,698

Ancestry/Race	Number	%
African American/Black:	1,204	5.30
Not Hispanic (941)	1,174	5.17
Hispanic (12)	30	0.13
African, sub-Saharan:	158	0.69
African	29	0.13
Kenyan	5	0.02
Liberian	37	0.16
Nigerian	33	0.14
Somalian	6	0.03
Other sub-Saharan African	48	0.21
Alaska Native tribes, specified:	1	0.00
Aleut (1)	1	0.00
Am. Ind. or Alaska Nat., not spec.	89	0.39
American Indian tribes, specified:	208	0.92
Blackfeet	3	0.01
Cherokee	18	0.08
Chickasaw (1)	1	0.00
Chippewa (76)	133	0.59
Choctaw (3)	3	0.01
Creek (4)	4	0.02
Iroquois (1)	4	0.02
Latin American Indians (1)	2	0.01
Lumbee	1	0.00
Potawatomi	4	0.02
Pueblo	2	0.01
Seminole	5	0.02
Sioux (12)	21	0.09
All other tribes (3)	7	0.03
American Indian tribes, not spec.	3	0.01
Arab:	75	0.33
Egyptian	26	0.11
Lebanese	44	0.19
Moroccan	5	0.02
Asian:	910	4.01
Bangladeshi (4)	4	0.02
Cambodian (12)	16	0.07
Chinese, ex. Taiwanese (52)	68	0.30
Filipino (75)	98	0.43
Hmong (68)	74	0.33
Indian (174)	197	0.87
Japanese (7)	18	0.08
Korean (54)	72	0.32
Laotian (122)	131	0.58
Malaysian	1	0.00
Pakistani	1	0.00
Sri Lankan (5)	5	0.02
Thai (4)	5	0.02
Vietnamese (182)	190	0.84
Other Asian, specified (1)	4	0.02
Other Asian, not specified (13)	26	0.11
Austrian	75	0.33
Belgian	45	0.20
British	43	0.19
Canadian	31	0.14
Carpatho Rusyn	7	0.03
Croatian	25	0.11
Czech	302	1.32
Czechoslovakian	85	0.37
Danish	441	1.93
Dutch	446	1.95
English	1,567	6.86
European	184	0.81
Finnish	528	2.31
French, except Basque	928	4.06
French Canadian	370	1.62
German	7,906	34.60
Greek	76	0.33
Guyanese	7	0.03
Hawaii Native/Pacific Islander:	15	0.07
Polynesian: (3)	8	0.04
Native Hawaiian (3)	7	0.03
Tongan	1	0.00
Other Pac. Isl., specified	3	0.01
Other Pac. Isl., not spec. (1)	4	0.02
Hispanic or Latino:	570	2.51
Central American:	22	0.10
Costa Rican	6	0.03
Guatemalan	5	0.02
Honduran	3	0.01
Nicaraguan	2	0.01
Panamanian	1	0.00
Salvadoran	3	0.01
Other Central American	2	0.01
Cuban	19	0.08
Dominican Republic	2	0.01
Mexican	334	1.47
Puerto Rican	24	0.11
South American:	42	0.19
Argentinean	7	0.03
Chilean	1	0.00
Colombian	14	0.06
Ecuadorian	7	0.03
Paraguayan	2	0.01
Peruvian	6	0.03
Uruguayan	1	0.00
Venezuelan	1	0.00
Other South American	3	0.01
Other Hispanic or Latino	127	0.56
Hungarian	44	0.19
Icelander	8	0.04
Iranian	11	0.05
Irish	2,560	11.20
Italian	449	1.97
Latvian	43	0.19
Lithuanian	24	0.11
Luxemburger	38	0.17
New Zealander	4	0.02
Norwegian	3,952	17.30
Pennsylvania German	5	0.02
Polish	962	4.21
Romanian	52	0.23
Russian	157	0.69
Scandinavian	489	2.14
Scotch-Irish	300	1.31
Scottish	221	0.97
Slavic	20	0.09
Slovak	122	0.53
Swedish	2,741	12.00
Swiss	90	0.39
Ukrainian	87	0.38
United States or American	760	3.33
Welsh	43	0.19
West Indian, excl. Hispanic:	14	0.06
Haitian	8	0.04
Jamaican	6	0.03
White:	20,511	90.36
Not Hispanic (19,797)	20,198	88.99
Hispanic (255)	313	1.38
Yugoslavian	85	0.37

Duluth

Place Type: City
County: Saint Louis
Population: 86,918

Ancestry/Race	Number	%
African American/Black:	1,904	2.19
Not Hispanic (1,389)	1,840	2.12
Hispanic (26)	64	0.07
African, sub-Saharan:	191	0.22
African	129	0.15
Kenyan	38	0.04
Nigerian	5	0.01
Sudanese	9	0.01
Other sub-Saharan African	10	0.01
Alaska Native tribes, specified:	9	0.01
Aleut (1)	1	0.00
Eskimo (5)	6	0.01
Tlingit-Haida (2)	2	0.00
Am. Ind. or Alaska Nat., not spec.	899	1.03
American Indian tribes, specified:	1,955	2.25
Apache (7)	8	0.01
Blackfeet (3)	13	0.01
Cherokee (15)	42	0.05
Cheyenne (5)	8	0.01
Chippewa (1,264)	1,637	1.88
Choctaw (4)	7	0.01
Colville (1)	1	0.00
Cree (2)	3	0.00
Creek (4)	9	0.01
Delaware	1	0.00
Iroquois (10)	14	0.02
Latin American Indians (9)	19	0.02
Menominee (1)	3	0.00
Navajo (6)	6	0.01
Ottawa (1)	1	0.00
Potawatomi (8)	10	0.01
Pueblo (2)	2	0.00
Seminole	3	0.00
Shoshone (1)	1	0.00
Sioux (65)	90	0.10
Ute	2	0.00
Yaqui (1)	5	0.01
All other tribes (44)	70	0.08
American Indian tribes, not spec.	138	0.16
Arab:	154	0.18
Arab/Arabic	24	0.03
Egyptian	11	0.01
Lebanese	89	0.10
Moroccan	6	0.01
Syrian	24	0.03
Armenian	5	0.01
Asian:	1,268	1.46
Bangladeshi (1)	3	0.00

Notes: 1. Figures in the "Number" column do not add up to the total population due to: a) Ancestry/Race overlap — e.g. persons can report being both White and Irish, b) persons of Hispanic origin can report being any race, c) persons reporting two ancestries are counted in both categories. 2. Numbers in parentheses indicate the number of persons reporting this ancestry/race alone, not in combination with any other ancestry/race. 3. Refer to the Explanation of Data in the front of the book for more detailed information.

Ancestry/Race	Number	%
Cambodian (4)	4	0.00
Chinese, ex. Taiwanese (198)	243	0.28
Filipino (81)	138	0.16
Hmong (147)	157	0.18
Indian (124)	151	0.17
Indonesian (3)	3	0.00
Japanese (52)	92	0.11
Korean (182)	221	0.25
Laotian (14)	18	0.02
Malaysian (2)	2	0.00
Pakistani (8)	8	0.01
Sri Lankan (6)	6	0.01
Taiwanese (6)	6	0.01
Thai (2)	11	0.01
Vietnamese (115)	146	0.17
Other Asian, specified (4)	13	0.01
Other Asian, not specified (27)	46	0.05
Australian	7	0.01
Austrian	262	0.30
Belgian	218	0.25
British	246	0.28
Bulgarian	6	0.01
Canadian	153	0.18
Celtic	14	0.02
Croatian	469	0.54
Czech	621	0.72
Czechoslovakian	204	0.23
Danish	1,298	1.50
Dutch	1,107	1.28
Eastern European	25	0.03
English	6,076	7.00
Estonian	7	0.01
European	321	0.37
Finnish	6,593	7.59
French, except Basque	4,632	5.34
French Canadian	1,740	2.00
German	20,466	23.58
German Russian	7	0.01
Greek	370	0.43
Hawaii Native/Pacific Islander:	70	0.08
Micronesian: (5)	10	0.01
Guamanian/Chamorro (3)	7	0.01
Other Micronesian (2)	3	0.00
Polynesian: (18)	38	0.04
Native Hawaiian (9)	24	0.03
Samoan (7)	7	0.01
Tongan (1)	3	0.00
Other Polynesian (1)	4	0.00
Other Pac. Isl., specified	7	0.01
Other Pac. Isl., not spec. (2)	15	0.02
Hispanic or Latino:	921	1.06
Central American:	57	0.07
Costa Rican	4	0.00
Guatemalan	10	0.01
Honduran	6	0.01
Nicaraguan	2	0.00
Panamanian	16	0.02
Salvadoran	15	0.02
Other Central American	4	0.00
Cuban	54	0.06
Dominican Republic	1	0.00
Mexican	410	0.47
Puerto Rican	81	0.09
South American:	54	0.06
Argentinean	8	0.01
Bolivian	1	0.00
Chilean	5	0.01
Colombian	22	0.03
Ecuadorian	5	0.01
Paraguayan	3	0.00
Peruvian	9	0.01
Venezuelan	1	0.00
Other Hispanic or Latino	264	0.30
Hungarian	223	0.26
Icelander	11	0.01
Iranian	13	0.01
Irish	9,203	10.60
Italian	4,429	5.10
Latvian	47	0.05
Lithuanian	145	0.17
Luxemburger	14	0.02
Macedonian	15	0.02
Northern European	97	0.11
Norwegian	14,601	16.82
Pennsylvania German	42	0.05
Polish	6,128	7.06
Portuguese	35	0.04
Romanian	105	0.12
Russian	504	0.58
Scandinavian	1,146	1.32
Scotch-Irish	1,152	1.33
Scottish	1,653	1.90
Serbian	292	0.34
Slavic	271	0.31
Slovak	184	0.21
Slovene	558	0.64
Swedish	13,253	15.27
Swiss	246	0.28
Turkish	36	0.04
Ukrainian	296	0.34
United States or American	2,005	2.31
Welsh	338	0.39
West Indian, excl. Hispanic:	65	0.07
Bermudan	6	0.01
Haitian	59	0.07
White:	81,993	94.33
Not Hispanic (80,043)	81,367	93.61
Hispanic (489)	626	0.72
Yugoslavian	420	0.48

Eagan

Place Type: City
County: Dakota
Population: 63,557

Ancestry/Race	Number	%
Afghan	22	0.03
African American/Black:	2,607	4.10
Not Hispanic (2,147)	2,557	4.02
Hispanic (19)	50	0.08
African, sub-Saharan:	491	0.77
African	186	0.29
Ethiopian	30	0.05
Ghanian	11	0.02
Nigerian	53	0.08
Somalian	133	0.21
South African	78	0.12
Alaska Native tribes, specified:	3	0.00
Tlingit-Haida (1)	3	0.00
Am. Ind. or Alaska Nat., not spec.	156	0.25
Alsatian	19	0.03
American Indian tribes, specified:	264	0.42
Apache (2)	4	0.01
Blackfeet	1	0.00
Cherokee (9)	43	0.07
Chickasaw	3	0.00
Chippewa (54)	106	0.17
Choctaw (1)	4	0.01
Cree	1	0.00
Creek (1)	2	0.00
Houma	1	0.00
Iroquois (1)	6	0.01
Latin American Indians (1)	5	0.01
Menominee (7)	9	0.01
Navajo (3)	4	0.01
Potawatomi	5	0.01
Pueblo (1)	2	0.00
Puget Sound Salish	1	0.00
Seminole	1	0.00
Shoshone (4)	5	0.01
Sioux (21)	41	0.06
Ute	1	0.00
All other tribes (12)	19	0.03
American Indian tribes, not spec.	12	0.02
Arab:	341	0.54
Arab/Arabic	77	0.12
Egyptian	45	0.07
Iraqi	69	0.11
Lebanese	132	0.21
Moroccan	18	0.03
Asian:	3,841	6.04
Bangladeshi (3)	4	0.01
Cambodian (171)	191	0.30
Chinese, ex. Taiwanese (477)	560	0.88
Filipino (219)	287	0.45
Hmong (104)	107	0.17
Indian (858)	914	1.44
Indonesian (11)	14	0.02
Japanese (59)	137	0.22
Korean (330)	379	0.60
Laotian (334)	366	0.58
Malaysian (8)	10	0.02
Pakistani (34)	49	0.08
Sri Lankan (4)	8	0.01
Taiwanese (30)	42	0.07
Thai (16)	29	0.05
Vietnamese (578)	625	0.98
Other Asian, specified (11)	16	0.03
Other Asian, not specified (63)	103	0.16
Australian	114	0.18
Austrian	339	0.53
Basque	9	0.01
Belgian	139	0.22
Brazilian	15	0.02
British	298	0.47
Bulgarian	7	0.01
Canadian	35	0.06
Croatian	84	0.13
Czech	1,055	1.66
Czechoslovakian	307	0.48
Danish	936	1.47
Dutch	1,313	2.06
Eastern European	10	0.02
English	4,673	7.34
European	611	0.96
Finnish	531	0.83
French, except Basque	2,434	3.83
French Canadian	617	0.97
German	23,246	36.53
German Russian	9	0.01
Greek	208	0.33
Guyanese	17	0.03
Hawaii Native/Pacific Islander:	126	0.20
Micronesian: (4)	8	0.01
Guamanian/Chamorro (4)	7	0.01
Other Micronesian	1	0.00
Polynesian: (51)	78	0.12
Native Hawaiian (15)	36	0.06
Samoan (36)	42	0.07
Other Pac. Isl., not spec. (11)	40	0.06
Hispanic or Latino:	1,424	2.24
Central American:	91	0.14
Costa Rican	4	0.01
Guatemalan	20	0.03
Honduran	8	0.01
Nicaraguan	13	0.02
Panamanian	7	0.01
Salvadoran	34	0.05
Other Central American	5	0.01
Cuban	31	0.05
Dominican Republic	1	0.00
Mexican	793	1.25
Puerto Rican	131	0.21
South American:	134	0.21
Argentinean	3	0.00
Bolivian	9	0.01
Chilean	8	0.01
Colombian	49	0.08
Ecuadorian	18	0.03
Paraguayan	4	0.01
Peruvian	25	0.04
Venezuelan	12	0.02
Other South American	6	0.01
Other Hispanic or Latino	243	0.38
Hungarian	212	0.33
Icelander	53	0.08
Iranian	62	0.10
Irish	8,934	14.04
Israeli	41	0.06

Notes: 1. Figures in the "Number" column do not add up to the total population due to: a) Ancestry/Race overlap — e.g. persons can report being both White and Irish, b) persons of Hispanic origin can report being any race, c) persons reporting two ancestries are counted in both categories. 2. Numbers in parentheses indicate the number of persons reporting this ancestry/race alone, not in combination with any other ancestry/race. 3. Refer to the Explanation of Data in the front of the book for more detailed information.

Italian	2,328	3.66
Latvian	15	0.02
Lithuanian	112	0.18
Luxemburger	121	0.19
New Zealander	7	0.01
Northern European	255	0.40
Norwegian	9,558	15.02
Pennsylvania German	40	0.06
Polish	3,047	4.79
Portuguese	32	0.05
Romanian	34	0.05
Russian	851	1.34
Scandinavian	589	0.93
Scotch-Irish	730	1.15
Scottish	1,092	1.72
Serbian	97	0.15
Slavic	108	0.17
Slovak	160	0.25
Slovene	178	0.28
Swedish	6,179	9.71
Swiss	403	0.63
Ukrainian	372	0.58
United States or American	1,584	2.49
Welsh	205	0.32
West Indian, excl. Hispanic:	17	0.03
Bermudan	5	0.01
Haitian	7	0.01
Jamaican	5	0.01
White:	56,984	89.66
Not Hispanic (55,219)	56,128	88.31
Hispanic (730)	856	1.35
Yugoslavian	57	0.09

East Bethel

Place Type: City
County: Anoka
Population: 10,941

Ancestry/Race	Number	%
African American/Black:	42	0.38
Not Hispanic (21)	41	0.37
Hispanic	1	0.01
Alaska Native tribes, specified:	3	0.03
Aleut	1	0.01
Eskimo (1)	1	0.01
Tlingit-Haida (1)	1	0.01
Am. Ind. or Alaska Nat., not spec.	42	0.38
American Indian tribes, specified:	65	0.59
Cherokee (1)	7	0.06
Chippewa (24)	44	0.40
Choctaw (1)	1	0.01
Iroquois	1	0.01
Latin American Indians (1)	1	0.01
Paiute	2	0.02
Pima	2	0.02
Sioux (2)	7	0.06
American Indian tribes, not spec.	2	0.02
Arab:	81	0.74
Lebanese	81	0.74
Asian:	83	0.76
Cambodian (1)	2	0.02
Chinese, ex. Taiwanese (3)	7	0.06
Filipino (5)	15	0.14
Hmong (14)	14	0.13
Indian (2)	6	0.05
Japanese (2)	14	0.13
Korean (13)	16	0.15
Laotian (1)	2	0.02
Taiwanese	1	0.01
Vietnamese (5)	5	0.05
Other Asian, not specified (1)	1	0.01
Austrian	54	0.49
Belgian	3	0.03
Brazilian	8	0.07
British	28	0.26
Canadian	24	0.22
Czech	211	1.93
Czechoslovakian	16	0.15
Danish	111	1.01
Dutch	108	0.99
English	563	5.15
European	23	0.21
Finnish	226	2.07
French, except Basque	452	4.13
French Canadian	84	0.77
German	4,056	37.07
Greek	38	0.35
Hawaii Native/Pacific Islander:	6	0.05
Micronesian:	2	0.02
Other Micronesian	2	0.02
Polynesian:	4	0.04
Native Hawaiian	3	0.03
Tongan	1	0.01
Hispanic or Latino:	104	0.95
Central American:	6	0.05
Guatemalan	3	0.03
Nicaraguan	1	0.01
Panamanian	2	0.02
Mexican	81	0.74
Puerto Rican	1	0.01
South American:	2	0.02
Peruvian	1	0.01
Other South American	1	0.01
Other Hispanic or Latino	14	0.13
Hungarian	45	0.41
Irish	1,190	10.88
Italian	123	1.12
Latvian	3	0.03
Northern European	32	0.29
Norwegian	1,845	16.86
Polish	1,023	9.35
Romanian	13	0.12
Russian	56	0.51
Scandinavian	78	0.71
Scotch-Irish	113	1.03
Scottish	57	0.52
Slavic	2	0.02
Slovak	18	0.16
Slovene	7	0.06
Swedish	1,657	15.14
Swiss	7	0.06
Ukrainian	31	0.28
United States or American	759	6.94
Welsh	53	0.48
White:	10,778	98.51
Not Hispanic (10,610)	10,706	97.85
Hispanic (63)	72	0.66
Yugoslavian	7	0.06

Eden Prairie

Place Type: City
County: Hennepin
Population: 54,901

Ancestry/Race	Number	%
Afghan	56	0.10
African American/Black:	1,530	2.79
Not Hispanic (1,238)	1,505	2.74
Hispanic (15)	25	0.05
African, sub-Saharan:	509	0.93
African	53	0.10
Kenyan	15	0.03
Liberian	17	0.03
Nigerian	42	0.08
Somalian	382	0.70
Am. Ind. or Alaska Nat., not spec.	68	0.12
Albanian	20	0.04
American Indian tribes, specified:	165	0.30
Apache	1	0.00
Blackfeet	1	0.00
Cherokee (8)	26	0.05
Chippewa (37)	60	0.11
Choctaw (1)	5	0.01
Cree (1)	5	0.01
Creek	1	0.00
Iroquois (4)	6	0.01
Latin American Indians (4)	11	0.02
Potawatomi (3)	4	0.01
Pueblo (5)	6	0.01
Sioux (14)	21	0.04
All other tribes (5)	18	0.03
American Indian tribes, not spec.	16	0.03
Arab:	378	0.69
Arab/Arabic	11	0.02
Egyptian	134	0.24
Iraqi	23	0.04
Jordanian	8	0.01
Lebanese	182	0.33
Palestinian	16	0.03
Syrian	4	0.01
Armenian	49	0.09
Asian:	3,064	5.58
Bangladeshi (6)	6	0.01
Cambodian (163)	182	0.33
Chinese, ex. Taiwanese (579)	666	1.21
Filipino (112)	169	0.31
Hmong (4)	5	0.01
Indian (750)	817	1.49
Indonesian (12)	15	0.03
Japanese (82)	154	0.28
Korean (271)	302	0.55
Laotian (52)	59	0.11
Malaysian (2)	6	0.01
Pakistani (49)	57	0.10
Sri Lankan (12)	16	0.03
Taiwanese (7)	16	0.03
Thai (12)	22	0.04
Vietnamese (434)	469	0.85
Other Asian, specified (6)	7	0.01
Other Asian, not specified (25)	96	0.17
Australian	23	0.04
Austrian	184	0.34
Belgian	85	0.15
Brazilian	68	0.12
British	176	0.32
Bulgarian	25	0.05
Canadian	277	0.50
Carpatho Rusyn	4	0.01
Celtic	6	0.01
Croatian	90	0.16
Czech	860	1.57
Czechoslovakian	214	0.39
Danish	1,172	2.13
Dutch	1,045	1.90
Eastern European	37	0.07
English	5,238	9.54
European	529	0.96
Finnish	695	1.27
French, except Basque	2,340	4.26
French Canadian	609	1.11
German	19,191	34.96
German Russian	7	0.01
Greek	243	0.44
Hawaii Native/Pacific Islander:	64	0.12
Micronesian: (5)	15	0.03
Guamanian/Chamorro (5)	15	0.03
Polynesian: (5)	18	0.03
Native Hawaiian (5)	15	0.03
Samoan	3	0.01
Other Pac. Isl., specified	1	0.00
Other Pac. Isl., not spec. (7)	30	0.05
Hispanic or Latino:	862	1.57
Central American:	46	0.08
Costa Rican	9	0.02
Guatemalan	3	0.01
Honduran	13	0.02
Nicaraguan	7	0.01
Panamanian	7	0.01
Salvadoran	7	0.01
Cuban	28	0.05
Dominican Republic	12	0.02
Mexican	341	0.62
Puerto Rican	70	0.13
South American:	153	0.28
Argentinean	14	0.03
Bolivian	1	0.00
Chilean	11	0.02
Colombian	41	0.07

Notes: 1. Figures in the "Number" column do not add up to the total population due to: a) Ancestry/Race overlap — e.g. persons can report being both White and Irish, b) persons of Hispanic origin can report being any race, c) persons reporting two ancestries are counted in both categories. 2. Numbers in parentheses indicate the number of persons reporting this ancestry/race alone, not in combination with any other ancestry/race. 3. Refer to the Explanation of Data in the front of the book for more detailed information.

Ecuadorian	32	0.06
Paraguayan	8	0.01
Peruvian	14	0.03
Venezuelan	28	0.05
Other South American	4	0.01
Other Hispanic or Latino	212	0.39
Hungarian	171	0.31
Icelander	74	0.13
Iranian	100	0.18
Irish	7,177	13.07
Israeli	7	0.01
Italian	1,925	3.51
Lithuanian	67	0.12
Luxemburger	55	0.10
Northern European	105	0.19
Norwegian	9,185	16.73
Pennsylvania German	5	0.01
Polish	2,465	4.49
Portuguese	53	0.10
Romanian	87	0.16
Russian	775	1.41
Scandinavian	649	1.18
Scotch-Irish	643	1.17
Scottish	1,066	1.94
Serbian	69	0.13
Slavic	44	0.08
Slovak	248	0.45
Slovene	89	0.16
Swedish	5,735	10.45
Swiss	366	0.67
Turkish	31	0.06
Ukrainian	242	0.44
United States or American	1,577	2.87
Welsh	340	0.62
West Indian, excl. Hispanic:	35	0.06
Haitian	32	0.06
Jamaican	3	0.01
White:	50,442	91.88
Not Hispanic (49,230)	49,831	90.77
Hispanic (541)	611	1.11
Yugoslavian	54	0.10

Edina

Place Type: City
County: Hennepin
Population: 47,425

Ancestry/Race	Number	%
African American/Black:	696	1.47
Not Hispanic (527)	667	1.41
Hispanic (19)	29	0.06
African, sub-Saharan:	96	0.20
African	23	0.05
Ghanian	22	0.05
Somalian	19	0.04
South African	15	0.03
Other sub-Saharan African	17	0.04
Alaska Native tribes, specified:	1	0.00
Eskimo (1)	1	0.00
Am. Ind. or Alaska Nat., not spec.	54	0.11
Albanian	6	0.01
American Indian tribes, specified:	90	0.19
Blackfeet (1)	1	0.00
Cherokee (3)	12	0.03
Chickasaw (1)	2	0.00
Chippewa (18)	37	0.08
Choctaw	6	0.01
Iroquois (1)	1	0.00
Menominee	2	0.00
Navajo (2)	2	0.00
Paiute (1)	1	0.00
Potawatomi (2)	2	0.00
Pueblo (1)	1	0.00
Seminole	1	0.00
Sioux (10)	14	0.03
All other tribes (4)	8	0.02
American Indian tribes, not spec.	4	0.01
Arab:	227	0.48
Egyptian	66	0.14
Jordanian	32	0.07
Lebanese	34	0.07
Palestinian	41	0.09
Syrian	17	0.04
Other Arab	37	0.08
Armenian	20	0.04
Asian:	1,689	3.56
Cambodian (17)	17	0.04
Chinese, ex. Taiwanese (378)	452	0.95
Filipino (85)	128	0.27
Hmong (2)	2	0.00
Indian (415)	446	0.94
Indonesian (5)	5	0.01
Japanese (66)	113	0.24
Korean (227)	253	0.53
Laotian (23)	25	0.05
Malaysian (1)	1	0.00
Pakistani (36)	45	0.09
Sri Lankan (20)	20	0.04
Taiwanese (8)	13	0.03
Thai (14)	18	0.04
Vietnamese (76)	101	0.21
Other Asian, specified (5)	9	0.02
Other Asian, not specified (17)	41	0.09
Australian	18	0.04
Austrian	273	0.57
Belgian	122	0.26
Brazilian	21	0.04
British	224	0.47
Bulgarian	7	0.01
Canadian	168	0.35
Celtic	6	0.01
Croatian	102	0.21
Czech	708	1.49
Czechoslovakian	171	0.36
Danish	1,042	2.19
Dutch	839	1.77
Eastern European	75	0.16
English	6,023	12.68
Estonian	16	0.03
European	390	0.82
Finnish	473	1.00
French, except Basque	1,824	3.84
French Canadian	391	0.82
German	13,664	28.76
Greek	411	0.87
Guyanese	13	0.03
Hawaii Native/Pacific Islander:	33	0.07
Micronesian: (7)	10	0.02
Guamanian/Chamorro (6)	9	0.02
Other Micronesian (1)	1	0.00
Polynesian: (3)	11	0.02
Native Hawaiian (2)	8	0.02
Samoan	2	0.00
Other Polynesian (1)	1	0.00
Other Pac. Isl., not spec. (4)	12	0.03
Hispanic or Latino:	539	1.14
Central American:	34	0.07
Costa Rican	7	0.01
Guatemalan	10	0.02
Honduran	2	0.00
Nicaraguan	4	0.01
Panamanian	9	0.02
Salvadoran	2	0.00
Cuban	39	0.08
Dominican Republic	3	0.01
Mexican	177	0.37
Puerto Rican	57	0.12
South American:	97	0.20
Argentinean	4	0.01
Chilean	11	0.02
Colombian	37	0.08
Ecuadorian	16	0.03
Paraguayan	4	0.01
Peruvian	13	0.03
Venezuelan	8	0.02
Other South American	4	0.01
Other Hispanic or Latino	132	0.28
Hungarian	130	0.27
Icelander	8	0.02
Iranian	200	0.42
Irish	7,282	15.33
Italian	1,503	3.16
Latvian	45	0.09
Lithuanian	117	0.25
Luxemburger	52	0.11
New Zealander	21	0.04
Northern European	197	0.41
Norwegian	7,951	16.74
Pennsylvania German	6	0.01
Polish	1,638	3.45
Portuguese	8	0.02
Romanian	114	0.24
Russian	877	1.85
Scandinavian	669	1.41
Scotch-Irish	752	1.58
Scottish	1,075	2.26
Serbian	44	0.09
Slavic	34	0.07
Slovak	60	0.13
Slovene	76	0.16
Swedish	6,023	12.68
Swiss	372	0.78
Turkish	56	0.12
Ukrainian	286	0.60
United States or American	1,388	2.92
Welsh	473	1.00
West Indian, excl. Hispanic:	49	0.10
Bahamian	9	0.02
Jamaican	31	0.07
West Indian	9	0.02
White:	45,144	95.19
Not Hispanic (44,367)	44,762	94.38
Hispanic (345)	382	0.81
Yugoslavian	109	0.23

Elk River

Place Type: City
County: Sherburne
Population: 16,447

Ancestry/Race	Number	%
African American/Black:	130	0.79
Not Hispanic (70)	126	0.77
Hispanic (3)	4	0.02
Alaska Native tribes, specified:	6	0.04
Eskimo (6)	6	0.04
Am. Ind. or Alaska Nat., not spec.	46	0.28
American Indian tribes, specified:	71	0.43
Cherokee	1	0.01
Cheyenne	1	0.01
Chippewa (19)	52	0.32
Cree (1)	4	0.02
Creek (2)	2	0.01
Latin American Indians (1)	1	0.01
Lumbee (1)	1	0.01
Navajo (4)	4	0.02
Ottawa	1	0.01
Potawatomi (1)	1	0.01
Sioux (1)	1	0.01
All other tribes (1)	2	0.01
American Indian tribes, not spec.	3	0.02
Arab:	35	0.21
Lebanese	28	0.17
Syrian	7	0.04
Asian:	126	0.77
Chinese, ex. Taiwanese (3)	9	0.05
Filipino (13)	25	0.15
Hmong (6)	6	0.04
Indian (11)	14	0.09
Indonesian (1)	1	0.01
Japanese (2)	6	0.04
Korean (26)	36	0.22
Thai (8)	11	0.07
Vietnamese (5)	15	0.09
Other Asian, specified (1)	1	0.01
Other Asian, not specified (1)	2	0.01
Austrian	44	0.27
British	23	0.14

Notes: 1. Figures in the "Number" column do not add up to the total population due to: a) Ancestry/Race overlap — e.g. persons can report being both White and Irish, b) persons of Hispanic origin can report being any race, c) persons reporting two ancestries are counted in both categories. 2. Numbers in parentheses indicate the number of persons reporting this ancestry/race alone, not in combination with any other ancestry/race. 3. Refer to the Explanation of Data in the front of the book for more detailed information.

Canadian	16	0.10
Croatian	20	0.12
Czech	241	1.47
Czechoslovakian	60	0.36
Danish	242	1.47
Dutch	472	2.87
Eastern European	6	0.04
English	920	5.59
European	51	0.31
Finnish	332	2.02
French, except Basque	1,065	6.48
French Canadian	195	1.19
German	7,297	44.37
Greek	66	0.40
Hawaii Native/Pacific Islander:	7	0.04
Micronesian: (1)	3	0.02
Other Micronesian (1)	3	0.02
Polynesian: (1)	3	0.02
Native Hawaiian (1)	3	0.02
Other Pac. Isl., not spec.	1	0.01
Hispanic or Latino:	219	1.33
Central American:	5	0.03
Other Central American	5	0.03
Cuban	1	0.01
Dominican Republic	2	0.01
Mexican	145	0.88
Puerto Rican	17	0.10
South American:	5	0.03
Colombian	1	0.01
Peruvian	3	0.02
Venezuelan	1	0.01
Other Hispanic or Latino	44	0.27
Hungarian	212	1.29
Irish	2,233	13.58
Italian	336	2.04
Lithuanian	9	0.05
New Zealander	7	0.04
Northern European	16	0.10
Norwegian	2,828	17.19
Polish	1,020	6.20
Portuguese	13	0.08
Russian	33	0.20
Scandinavian	203	1.23
Scotch-Irish	115	0.70
Scottish	108	0.66
Slavic	9	0.05
Slovak	10	0.06
Slovene	48	0.29
Swedish	1,756	10.68
Swiss	79	0.48
Ukrainian	36	0.22
United States or American	577	3.51
Welsh	62	0.38
White:	16,139	98.13
Not Hispanic (15,857)	15,996	97.26
Hispanic (127)	143	0.87
Yugoslavian	33	0.20

Fairmont

Place Type: City
County: Martin
Population: 10,889

Ancestry/Race	Number	%
African American/Black:	62	0.57
Not Hispanic (46)	59	0.54
Hispanic (2)	3	0.03
Alaska Native tribes, specified:	3	0.03
Eskimo	1	0.01
Tlingit-Haida	2	0.02
Am. Ind. or Alaska Nat., not spec.	15	0.14
American Indian tribes, specified:	19	0.17
Cherokee	3	0.03
Chippewa (1)	4	0.04
Latin American Indians (2)	2	0.02
Sioux (4)	5	0.05
Yuman	1	0.01
All other tribes	4	0.04
Asian:	90	0.83
Bangladeshi (2)	2	0.02
Chinese, ex. Taiwanese (19)	20	0.18
Filipino (5)	7	0.06
Indian (7)	8	0.07
Indonesian (1)	1	0.01
Japanese (5)	10	0.09
Korean (10)	13	0.12
Laotian (9)	12	0.11
Thai	1	0.01
Vietnamese (13)	13	0.12
Other Asian, not specified (1)	3	0.03
Austrian	7	0.06
Belgian	7	0.06
Canadian	10	0.09
Czech	105	0.96
Czechoslovakian	10	0.09
Danish	195	1.79
Dutch	366	3.36
English	869	7.98
European	7	0.06
Finnish	49	0.45
French, except Basque	433	3.98
French Canadian	44	0.40
German	5,579	51.25
Hawaii Native/Pacific Islander:	6	0.06
Polynesian: (2)	3	0.03
Native Hawaiian (1)	2	0.02
Samoan (1)	1	0.01
Other Pac. Isl., not spec. (1)	3	0.03
Hispanic or Latino:	324	2.98
Central American:	7	0.06
Costa Rican	1	0.01
Guatemalan	4	0.04
Honduran	1	0.01
Panamanian	1	0.01
Cuban	2	0.02
Mexican	237	2.18
Puerto Rican	6	0.06
South American:	4	0.04
Chilean	1	0.01
Colombian	2	0.02
Ecuadorian	1	0.01
Other Hispanic or Latino	68	0.62
Irish	889	8.17
Italian	46	0.42
Norwegian	1,671	15.35
Pennsylvania German	16	0.15
Polish	580	5.33
Russian	14	0.13
Scandinavian	166	1.52
Scotch-Irish	113	1.04
Scottish	123	1.13
Slovak	6	0.06
Swedish	626	5.75
Swiss	59	0.54
Ukrainian	34	0.31
United States or American	262	2.41
Welsh	102	0.94
White:	10,504	96.46
Not Hispanic (10,363)	10,422	95.71
Hispanic (46)	82	0.75
Yugoslavian	18	0.17

Faribault

Place Type: City
County: Rice
Population: 20,818

Ancestry/Race	Number	%
African American/Black:	662	3.18
Not Hispanic (538)	633	3.04
Hispanic (23)	29	0.14
African, sub-Saharan:	143	0.69
African	61	0.29
Nigerian	1	0.00
Somalian	53	0.25
Sudanese	28	0.13
Am. Ind. or Alaska Nat., not spec.	65	0.31
American Indian tribes, specified:	127	0.61
Apache (1)	1	0.00
Blackfeet	4	0.02
Cherokee (2)	10	0.05
Chippewa (49)	62	0.30
Choctaw	1	0.00
Colville (9)	9	0.04
Iroquois (1)	1	0.00
Latin American Indians (7)	10	0.05
Pueblo (1)	1	0.00
Sioux (10)	19	0.09
All other tribes (6)	9	0.04
American Indian tribes, not spec.	12	0.06
Arab:	38	0.18
Jordanian	10	0.05
Moroccan	28	0.13
Asian:	461	2.21
Cambodian (148)	180	0.86
Chinese, ex. Taiwanese (34)	43	0.21
Filipino (15)	23	0.11
Hmong (42)	51	0.24
Indian (20)	35	0.17
Japanese (8)	13	0.06
Korean (27)	37	0.18
Laotian (8)	8	0.04
Taiwanese (1)	1	0.00
Vietnamese (37)	44	0.21
Other Asian, specified (6)	6	0.03
Other Asian, not specified (12)	20	0.10
Austrian	22	0.11
Belgian	88	0.42
British	7	0.03
Bulgarian	13	0.06
Canadian	40	0.19
Czech	973	4.67
Czechoslovakian	181	0.87
Danish	381	1.83
Dutch	608	2.92
English	1,077	5.17
European	210	1.01
Finnish	61	0.29
French, except Basque	1,269	6.09
French Canadian	362	1.74
German	7,373	35.39
Greek	22	0.11
Hawaii Native/Pacific Islander:	35	0.17
Micronesian: (4)	6	0.03
Guamanian/Chamorro (4)	6	0.03
Polynesian: (5)	10	0.05
Native Hawaiian (4)	7	0.03
Samoan (1)	3	0.01
Other Pac. Isl., not spec. (4)	19	0.09
Hispanic or Latino:	1,852	8.90
Central American:	106	0.51
Guatemalan	76	0.37
Honduran	9	0.04
Panamanian	2	0.01
Salvadoran	9	0.04
Other Central American	10	0.05
Cuban	12	0.06
Mexican	1,406	6.75
Puerto Rican	18	0.09
South American:	21	0.10
Argentinean	4	0.02
Bolivian	1	0.00
Chilean	2	0.01
Colombian	13	0.06
Paraguayan	1	0.00
Other Hispanic or Latino	289	1.39
Hungarian	37	0.18
Icelander	7	0.03
Irish	2,366	11.36
Italian	295	1.42
Latvian	16	0.08
Lithuanian	33	0.16
Northern European	18	0.09
Norwegian	3,079	14.78
Pennsylvania German	5	0.02
Polish	577	2.77
Portuguese	47	0.23
Romanian	13	0.06

Notes: 1. Figures in the "Number" column do not add up to the total population due to: a) Ancestry/Race overlap — e.g. persons can report being both White and Irish, b) persons of Hispanic origin can report being any race, c) persons reporting two ancestries are counted in both categories. 2. Numbers in parentheses indicate the number of persons reporting this ancestry/race alone, not in combination with any other ancestry/race. 3. Refer to the Explanation of Data in the front of the book for more detailed information.

Russian	61	0.29
Scandinavian	108	0.52
Scotch-Irish	161	0.77
Scottish	174	0.84
Serbian	13	0.06
Slovene	9	0.04
Swedish	919	4.41
Swiss	82	0.39
Ukrainian	11	0.05
United States or American	547	2.63
Welsh	101	0.48
West Indian, excl. Hispanic:	45	0.22
Jamaican	17	0.08
West Indian	28	0.13
White:	18,937	90.96
Not Hispanic (17,689)	17,820	85.60
Hispanic (1,021)	1,117	5.37
Yugoslavian	7	0.03

Farmington

Place Type: City
County: Dakota
Population: 12,365

Ancestry/Race	Number	%
African American/Black:	136	1.10
Not Hispanic (91)	134	1.08
Hispanic (1)	2	0.02
African, sub-Saharan:	32	0.26
African	32	0.26
Alaska Native tribes, specified:	1	0.01
Eskimo (1)	1	0.01
Am. Ind. or Alaska Nat., not spec.	14	0.11
American Indian tribes, specified:	37	0.30
Blackfeet	2	0.02
Cherokee	1	0.01
Chippewa (1)	6	0.05
Choctaw (2)	2	0.02
Creek	1	0.01
Iroquois (2)	2	0.02
Latin American Indians (2)	2	0.02
Sioux (10)	13	0.11
All other tribes (6)	8	0.06
American Indian tribes, not spec.	5	0.04
Arab:	10	0.08
Lebanese	10	0.08
Asian:	276	2.23
Cambodian (21)	24	0.19
Chinese, ex. Taiwanese (8)	13	0.11
Filipino (33)	61	0.49
Hmong (7)	7	0.06
Indian (17)	28	0.23
Indonesian	3	0.02
Japanese (12)	27	0.22
Korean (27)	42	0.34
Laotian (31)	37	0.30
Thai (1)	2	0.02
Vietnamese (13)	17	0.14
Other Asian, not specified (10)	15	0.12
Austrian	69	0.55
Belgian	29	0.23
British	54	0.43
Canadian	29	0.23
Croatian	20	0.16
Czech	158	1.27
Czechoslovakian	29	0.23
Danish	255	2.04
Dutch	420	3.37
English	763	6.12
European	103	0.83
Finnish	123	0.99
French, except Basque	628	5.03
French Canadian	153	1.23
German	5,256	42.14
Greek	15	0.12
Hawaii Native/Pacific Islander:	13	0.11
Micronesian: (1)	1	0.01
Guamanian/Chamorro (1)	1	0.01
Polynesian: (1)	5	0.04
Native Hawaiian	3	0.02
Samoan (1)	2	0.02
Other Pac. Isl., not spec. (1)	7	0.06
Hispanic or Latino:	232	1.88
Central American:	6	0.05
Costa Rican	1	0.01
Guatemalan	1	0.01
Honduran	1	0.01
Panamanian	1	0.01
Salvadoran	2	0.02
Cuban	2	0.02
Mexican	132	1.07
Puerto Rican	18	0.15
South American:	20	0.16
Argentinean	1	0.01
Bolivian	1	0.01
Colombian	3	0.02
Ecuadorian	12	0.10
Peruvian	1	0.01
Other South American	2	0.02
Other Hispanic or Latino	54	0.44
Hungarian	14	0.11
Irish	1,635	13.11
Italian	215	1.72
Luxemburger	34	0.27
Norwegian	2,076	16.64
Polish	469	3.76
Portuguese	9	0.07
Romanian	7	0.06
Russian	35	0.28
Scandinavian	98	0.79
Scotch-Irish	97	0.78
Scottish	241	1.93
Slovak	38	0.30
Swedish	926	7.42
Swiss	41	0.33
Ukrainian	84	0.67
United States or American	412	3.30
Welsh	33	0.26
West Indian, excl. Hispanic:	33	0.26
Jamaican	33	0.26
White:	11,953	96.67
Not Hispanic (11,677)	11,799	95.42
Hispanic (147)	154	1.25
Yugoslavian	18	0.14

Fergus Falls

Place Type: City
County: Otter Tail
Population: 13,471

Ancestry/Race	Number	%
African American/Black:	100	0.74
Not Hispanic (81)	97	0.72
Hispanic (2)	3	0.02
African, sub-Saharan:	2	0.01
South African	2	0.01
Alaska Native tribes, specified:	1	0.01
Tlingit-Haida (1)	1	0.01
Am. Ind. or Alaska Nat., not spec.	46	0.34
American Indian tribes, specified:	104	0.77
Blackfeet (1)	1	0.01
Cherokee (1)	11	0.08
Chippewa (56)	70	0.52
Choctaw (2)	3	0.02
Puget Sound Salish	1	0.01
Sioux (14)	17	0.13
All other tribes (1)	1	0.01
American Indian tribes, not spec.	2	0.01
Arab:	30	0.22
Lebanese	21	0.16
Moroccan	9	0.07
Asian:	107	0.79
Chinese, ex. Taiwanese (16)	19	0.14
Filipino (5)	11	0.08
Indian (9)	12	0.09
Japanese (4)	10	0.07
Korean (18)	25	0.19
Laotian (2)	4	0.03
Pakistani (2)	2	0.01
Thai (3)	4	0.03
Vietnamese (17)	19	0.14
Other Asian, not specified	1	0.01
Austrian	26	0.19
Belgian	11	0.08
British	24	0.18
Canadian	14	0.10
Croatian	2	0.01
Czech	97	0.72
Czechoslovakian	23	0.17
Danish	271	2.01
Dutch	253	1.88
English	674	5.00
European	16	0.12
Finnish	185	1.37
French, except Basque	372	2.76
French Canadian	86	0.64
German	4,533	33.63
Greek	9	0.07
Hawaii Native/Pacific Islander:	5	0.04
Micronesian: (1)	2	0.01
Guamanian/Chamorro	1	0.01
Other Micronesian (1)	1	0.01
Polynesian:	3	0.02
Native Hawaiian	1	0.01
Samoan	2	0.01
Hispanic or Latino:	122	0.91
Central American:	4	0.03
Guatemalan	3	0.02
Panamanian	1	0.01
Cuban	4	0.03
Mexican	77	0.57
Puerto Rican	5	0.04
South American:	2	0.01
Colombian	1	0.01
Venezuelan	1	0.01
Other Hispanic or Latino	30	0.22
Hungarian	5	0.04
Irish	724	5.37
Italian	87	0.65
Latvian	7	0.05
Lithuanian	10	0.07
Northern European	11	0.08
Norwegian	5,497	40.78
Polish	411	3.05
Portuguese	2	0.01
Romanian	3	0.02
Russian	69	0.51
Scandinavian	256	1.90
Scotch-Irish	65	0.48
Scottish	48	0.36
Slovak	8	0.06
Slovene	32	0.24
Swedish	1,436	10.65
Swiss	25	0.19
Ukrainian	65	0.48
United States or American	260	1.93
Welsh	63	0.47
White:	13,176	97.81
Not Hispanic (12,987)	13,082	97.11
Hispanic (82)	94	0.70
Yugoslavian	22	0.16

Fridley

Place Type: City
County: Anoka
Population: 27,449

Ancestry/Race	Number	%
Acadian/Cajun	6	0.02
Afghan	6	0.02
African American/Black:	1,203	4.38
Not Hispanic (931)	1,182	4.31
Hispanic (8)	21	0.08
African, sub-Saharan:	282	1.03
African	139	0.51
Ethiopian	7	0.03
Ghanian	17	0.06

Notes: 1. Figures in the "Number" column do not add up to the total population due to: a) Ancestry/Race overlap — e.g. persons can report being both White and Irish, b) persons of Hispanic origin can report being any race, c) persons reporting two ancestries are counted in both categories. 2. Numbers in parentheses indicate the number of persons reporting this ancestry/race alone, not in combination with any other ancestry/race. 3. Refer to the Explanation of Data in the front of the book for more detailed information.

Liberian	51	0.19
Sierra Leonean	16	0.06
Somalian	25	0.09
Sudanese	11	0.04
Ugandan	13	0.05
Other sub-Saharan African	3	0.01
Alaska Native tribes, specified:	1	0.00
Eskimo (1)	1	0.00
Am. Ind. or Alaska Nat., not spec.	87	0.32
Alsatian	4	0.01
American Indian tribes, specified:	320	1.17
Blackfeet (1)	6	0.02
Cherokee (8)	25	0.09
Chippewa (118)	195	0.71
Choctaw (1)	1	0.00
Cree (1)	1	0.00
Creek	3	0.01
Delaware	1	0.00
Iroquois (2)	8	0.03
Kiowa	1	0.00
Latin American Indians	1	0.00
Menominee (2)	2	0.01
Navajo (1)	4	0.01
Pueblo	1	0.00
Seminole (1)	4	0.01
Sioux (21)	51	0.19
All other tribes (11)	16	0.06
American Indian tribes, not spec.	20	0.07
Arab:	422	1.54
Arab/Arabic	39	0.14
Egyptian	212	0.77
Iraqi	10	0.04
Jordanian	8	0.03
Lebanese	37	0.13
Moroccan	41	0.15
Palestinian	55	0.20
Syrian	14	0.05
Other Arab	6	0.02
Armenian	52	0.19
Asian:	1,000	3.64
Bangladeshi	2	0.01
Cambodian (5)	5	0.02
Chinese, ex. Taiwanese (104)	119	0.43
Filipino (63)	100	0.36
Hmong (95)	110	0.40
Indian (137)	183	0.67
Indonesian (1)	1	0.00
Japanese (19)	38	0.14
Korean (124)	148	0.54
Laotian (17)	33	0.12
Malaysian (2)	2	0.01
Pakistani (18)	21	0.08
Sri Lankan (2)	3	0.01
Thai (9)	15	0.05
Vietnamese (158)	181	0.66
Other Asian, not specified (19)	39	0.14
Assyrian/Chaldean/Syriac	6	0.02
Australian	6	0.02
Austrian	105	0.38
Basque	4	0.01
Belgian	63	0.23
British	56	0.20
Canadian	27	0.10
Croatian	93	0.34
Czech	370	1.35
Czechoslovakian	101	0.37
Danish	346	1.26
Dutch	382	1.39
Eastern European	13	0.05
English	1,643	5.99
European	213	0.78
Finnish	631	2.30
French, except Basque	1,436	5.23
French Canadian	501	1.83
German	8,795	32.04
Greek	108	0.39
Guyanese	21	0.08
Hawaii Native/Pacific Islander:	42	0.15
Micronesian:	3	0.01
Guamanian/Chamorro	3	0.01
Polynesian: (14)	24	0.09
Native Hawaiian (10)	16	0.06
Samoan (4)	8	0.03
Other Pac. Isl., not spec. (4)	15	0.05
Hispanic or Latino:	704	2.56
Central American:	34	0.12
Costa Rican	1	0.00
Guatemalan	17	0.06
Honduran	8	0.03
Nicaraguan	1	0.00
Panamanian	3	0.01
Salvadoran	2	0.01
Other Central American	2	0.01
Cuban	13	0.05
Dominican Republic	11	0.04
Mexican	430	1.57
Puerto Rican	33	0.12
South American:	22	0.08
Argentinean	1	0.00
Bolivian	1	0.00
Colombian	13	0.05
Ecuadorian	2	0.01
Peruvian	4	0.01
Other South American	1	0.00
Other Hispanic or Latino	161	0.59
Hungarian	78	0.28
Iranian	33	0.12
Irish	3,047	11.10
Italian	700	2.55
Latvian	69	0.25
Lithuanian	11	0.04
Luxemburger	22	0.08
Macedonian	7	0.03
Northern European	26	0.09
Norwegian	4,428	16.13
Pennsylvania German	11	0.04
Polish	2,519	9.18
Romanian	50	0.18
Russian	275	1.00
Scandinavian	354	1.29
Scotch-Irish	264	0.96
Scottish	261	0.95
Serbian	32	0.12
Slavic	24	0.09
Slovak	138	0.50
Slovene	56	0.20
Swedish	3,472	12.65
Swiss	62	0.23
Ukrainian	217	0.79
United States or American	662	2.41
Welsh	114	0.42
West Indian, excl. Hispanic:	82	0.30
Jamaican	68	0.25
Trinidadian and Tobagonian	7	0.03
West Indian	7	0.03
White:	25,020	91.15
Not Hispanic (24,026)	24,630	89.73
Hispanic (308)	390	1.42
Yugoslavian	141	0.51

Golden Valley

Place Type: City
County: Hennepin
Population: 20,281

Ancestry/Race	Number	%
African American/Black:	864	4.26
Not Hispanic (720)	854	4.21
Hispanic (8)	10	0.05
African, sub-Saharan:	110	0.54
African	36	0.18
Ethiopian	55	0.27
Liberian	19	0.09
Am. Ind. or Alaska Nat., not spec.	54	0.27
Albanian	7	0.03
American Indian tribes, specified:	88	0.43
Cherokee	4	0.02
Chickasaw	1	0.00
Chippewa (21)	52	0.26
Choctaw	1	0.00
Creek	1	0.00
Delaware (1)	1	0.00
Iroquois (3)	7	0.03
Latin American Indians (1)	1	0.00
Menominee	1	0.00
Potawatomi	1	0.00
Puget Sound Salish	1	0.00
Seminole	1	0.00
Sioux (5)	6	0.03
All other tribes (4)	10	0.05
American Indian tribes, not spec.	1	0.00
Arab:	119	0.59
Egyptian	8	0.04
Iraqi	7	0.03
Lebanese	84	0.41
Syrian	8	0.04
Other Arab	12	0.06
Armenian	15	0.07
Asian:	711	3.51
Bangladeshi	3	0.01
Cambodian (4)	4	0.02
Chinese, ex. Taiwanese (106)	143	0.71
Filipino (31)	54	0.27
Hmong (57)	57	0.28
Indian (100)	124	0.61
Japanese (30)	46	0.23
Korean (84)	94	0.46
Laotian (52)	53	0.26
Pakistani (7)	10	0.05
Sri Lankan (3)	4	0.02
Taiwanese (1)	1	0.00
Thai (1)	1	0.00
Vietnamese (72)	78	0.38
Other Asian, specified	2	0.01
Other Asian, not specified (23)	37	0.18
Austrian	171	0.84
Belgian	29	0.14
British	100	0.49
Bulgarian	21	0.10
Canadian	137	0.68
Croatian	36	0.18
Czech	257	1.27
Czechoslovakian	39	0.19
Danish	357	1.76
Dutch	354	1.75
Eastern European	112	0.55
English	1,768	8.73
European	187	0.92
Finnish	349	1.72
French, except Basque	710	3.51
French Canadian	136	0.67
German	6,091	30.09
Greek	100	0.49
Hawaii Native/Pacific Islander:	32	0.16
Micronesian: (1)	1	0.00
Guamanian/Chamorro (1)	1	0.00
Polynesian: (5)	21	0.10
Native Hawaiian (2)	15	0.07
Samoan (1)	2	0.01
Tongan (2)	4	0.02
Other Pac. Isl., specified	2	0.01
Other Pac. Isl., not spec.	8	0.04
Hispanic or Latino:	357	1.76
Central American:	23	0.11
Costa Rican	2	0.01
Guatemalan	4	0.02
Honduran	8	0.04
Nicaraguan	5	0.02
Panamanian	1	0.00
Salvadoran	3	0.01
Cuban	9	0.04
Dominican Republic	2	0.01
Mexican	149	0.73
Puerto Rican	21	0.10
South American:	68	0.34
Argentinean	10	0.05
Bolivian	1	0.00
Chilean	3	0.01
Colombian	19	0.09

Notes: 1. Figures in the "Number" column do not add up to the total population due to: a) Ancestry/Race overlap — e.g. persons can report being both White and Irish, b) persons of Hispanic origin can report being any race, c) persons reporting two ancestries are counted in both categories. 2. Numbers in parentheses indicate the number of persons reporting this ancestry/race alone, not in combination with any other ancestry/race. 3. Refer to the Explanation of Data in the front of the book for more detailed information.

Ancestry/Race	Number	%
Ecuadorian	4	0.02
Paraguayan	3	0.01
Peruvian	23	0.11
Venezuelan	2	0.01
Other South American	3	0.01
Other Hispanic or Latino	85	0.42
Hungarian	100	0.49
Icelander	33	0.16
Iranian	50	0.25
Irish	2,180	10.77
Italian	461	2.28
Latvian	8	0.04
Lithuanian	74	0.37
Luxemburger	24	0.12
Northern European	67	0.33
Norwegian	3,457	17.08
Pennsylvania German	9	0.04
Polish	1,036	5.12
Romanian	156	0.77
Russian	789	3.90
Scandinavian	271	1.34
Scotch-Irish	200	0.99
Scottish	406	2.01
Slavic	7	0.03
Slovak	99	0.49
Slovene	58	0.29
Swedish	2,509	12.39
Swiss	59	0.29
Turkish	16	0.08
Ukrainian	143	0.71
United States or American	536	2.65
Welsh	152	0.75
West Indian, excl. Hispanic:	43	0.21
Bahamian	13	0.06
British West Indian	17	0.08
Jamaican	13	0.06
White:	18,752	92.46
Not Hispanic (18,236)	18,496	91.20
Hispanic (233)	256	1.26
Yugoslavian	47	0.23

Grand Rapids

Place Type: Township
County: Itasca
Population: 11,747

Ancestry/Race	Number	%
African American/Black:	45	0.38
Not Hispanic (25)	42	0.36
Hispanic (2)	3	0.03
African, sub-Saharan:	2	0.02
African	2	0.02
Alaska Native tribes, specified:	5	0.04
Aleut	1	0.01
Eskimo (3)	4	0.03
Am. Ind. or Alaska Nat., not spec.	101	0.86
American Indian tribes, specified:	177	1.51
Cherokee (2)	4	0.03
Chippewa (114)	157	1.34
Cree (1)	1	0.01
Creek	1	0.01
Pima (2)	2	0.02
Potawatomi (3)	3	0.03
Sioux (1)	3	0.03
All other tribes (4)	6	0.05
American Indian tribes, not spec.	6	0.05
Arab:	1	0.01
Syrian	1	0.01
Armenian	2	0.02
Asian:	85	0.72
Cambodian (1)	2	0.02
Chinese, ex. Taiwanese (21)	23	0.20
Filipino (8)	9	0.08
Hmong (2)	2	0.02
Indian (8)	9	0.08
Indonesian (1)	3	0.03
Japanese (3)	6	0.05
Korean (16)	23	0.20
Other Asian, specified (3)	3	0.03
Other Asian, not specified	5	0.04
Austrian	52	0.44
Belgian	18	0.15
British	8	0.07
Bulgarian	20	0.17
Canadian	83	0.71
Croatian	57	0.49
Czech	112	0.96
Czechoslovakian	60	0.51
Danish	109	0.93
Dutch	266	2.27
Eastern European	2	0.02
English	987	8.43
European	48	0.41
Finnish	886	7.57
French, except Basque	685	5.85
French Canadian	263	2.25
German	3,420	29.23
Hawaii Native/Pacific Islander:	5	0.04
Micronesian: (2)	2	0.02
Guamanian/Chamorro (2)	2	0.02
Polynesian:	2	0.02
Native Hawaiian	1	0.01
Samoan	1	0.01
Other Pac. Isl., not spec.	1	0.01
Hispanic or Latino:	86	0.73
Central American:	2	0.02
Guatemalan	1	0.01
Panamanian	1	0.01
Mexican	46	0.39
Puerto Rican	8	0.07
South American:	2	0.02
Peruvian	2	0.02
Other Hispanic or Latino	28	0.24
Irish	1,374	11.74
Israeli	2	0.02
Italian	532	4.55
Lithuanian	5	0.04
Norwegian	1,664	14.22
Pennsylvania German	13	0.11
Polish	388	3.32
Romanian	8	0.07
Russian	23	0.20
Scandinavian	114	0.97
Scotch-Irish	118	1.01
Scottish	149	1.27
Serbian	70	0.60
Slavic	19	0.16
Slovak	21	0.18
Slovene	53	0.45
Swedish	1,201	10.26
Swiss	41	0.35
Turkish	21	0.18
Ukrainian	8	0.07
United States or American	477	4.08
Welsh	49	0.42
White:	11,421	97.22
Not Hispanic (11,255)	11,369	96.78
Hispanic (45)	52	0.44
Yugoslavian	33	0.28

Ham Lake

Place Type: City
County: Anoka
Population: 12,710

Ancestry/Race	Number	%
African American/Black:	95	0.75
Not Hispanic (60)	90	0.71
Hispanic (4)	5	0.04
African, sub-Saharan:	5	0.04
African	5	0.04
Am. Ind. or Alaska Nat., not spec.	33	0.26
American Indian tribes, specified:	82	0.65
Blackfeet	3	0.02
Cherokee (4)	5	0.04
Chickasaw	1	0.01
Chippewa (21)	47	0.37
Choctaw	1	0.01
Iroquois	1	0.01
Latin American Indians	2	0.02
Navajo (1)	1	0.01
Potawatomi (5)	5	0.04
Seminole (1)	1	0.01
Sioux (4)	9	0.07
All other tribes (1)	6	0.05
American Indian tribes, not spec.	2	0.02
Arab:	34	0.27
Lebanese	34	0.27
Armenian	34	0.27
Asian:	136	1.07
Chinese, ex. Taiwanese	1	0.01
Filipino (9)	18	0.14
Hmong (22)	23	0.18
Indian (14)	21	0.17
Japanese (5)	9	0.07
Korean (29)	45	0.35
Laotian (1)	2	0.02
Thai (2)	2	0.02
Vietnamese (13)	13	0.10
Other Asian, not specified (1)	2	0.02
Australian	6	0.05
Austrian	23	0.18
British	24	0.19
Canadian	15	0.12
Croatian	7	0.05
Czech	238	1.87
Czechoslovakian	30	0.24
Danish	140	1.10
Dutch	221	1.73
English	639	5.02
European	39	0.31
Finnish	241	1.89
French, except Basque	654	5.13
French Canadian	202	1.59
German	4,764	37.39
Greek	7	0.05
Hawaii Native/Pacific Islander:	17	0.13
Polynesian: (1)	12	0.09
Native Hawaiian (1)	12	0.09
Other Pac. Isl., not spec. (4)	5	0.04
Hispanic or Latino:	145	1.14
Central American:	2	0.02
Guatemalan	2	0.02
Cuban	1	0.01
Mexican	89	0.70
Puerto Rican	15	0.12
South American:	8	0.06
Chilean	3	0.02
Colombian	1	0.01
Paraguayan	1	0.01
Peruvian	3	0.02
Other Hispanic or Latino	30	0.24
Hungarian	90	0.71
Icelander	5	0.04
Irish	1,716	13.47
Italian	257	2.02
Latvian	4	0.03
Lithuanian	5	0.04
Northern European	10	0.08
Norwegian	2,587	20.30
Pennsylvania German	17	0.13
Polish	1,055	8.28
Portuguese	18	0.14
Romanian	17	0.13
Russian	75	0.59
Scandinavian	208	1.63
Scotch-Irish	93	0.73
Scottish	123	0.97
Serbian	30	0.24
Slavic	16	0.13
Slovak	10	0.08
Swedish	2,040	16.01
Swiss	35	0.27
Ukrainian	100	0.78
United States or American	409	3.21
Welsh	15	0.12
White:	12,442	97.89
Not Hispanic (12,213)	12,347	97.14

Notes: 1. Figures in the "Number" column do not add up to the total population due to: a) Ancestry/Race overlap — e.g. persons can report being both White and Irish, b) persons of Hispanic origin can report being any race, c) persons reporting two ancestries are counted in both categories. 2. Numbers in parentheses indicate the number of persons reporting this ancestry/race alone, not in combination with any other ancestry/race. 3. Refer to the Explanation of Data in the front of the book for more detailed information.

Hispanic (77)	95	0.75
Yugoslavian	6	0.05

Hastings

Place Type: City
County: Dakota
Population: 18,204

Ancestry/Race	Number	%
African American/Black:	135	0.74
Not Hispanic (78)	130	0.71
Hispanic (1)	5	0.03
African, sub-Saharan:	4	0.02
African	4	0.02
Alaska Native tribes, specified:	2	0.01
Aleut	1	0.01
All other tribes	1	0.01
Alaska Native tribes, not specified	1	0.01
Am. Ind. or Alaska Nat., not spec.	49	0.27
American Indian tribes, specified:	100	0.55
Apache	3	0.02
Blackfeet	3	0.02
Cherokee (3)	15	0.08
Cheyenne	3	0.02
Chippewa (19)	34	0.19
Creek (1)	1	0.01
Delaware	1	0.01
Iroquois	3	0.02
Latin American Indians (1)	3	0.02
Navajo	1	0.01
Sioux (19)	29	0.16
Yaqui	1	0.01
All other tribes (1)	3	0.02
American Indian tribes, not spec.	5	0.03
Arab:	49	0.27
Egyptian	5	0.03
Lebanese	25	0.14
Syrian	19	0.10
Asian:	165	0.91
Chinese, ex. Taiwanese (12)	17	0.09
Filipino (23)	33	0.18
Hmong (10)	10	0.05
Indian (6)	12	0.07
Japanese (6)	17	0.09
Korean (38)	48	0.26
Laotian (2)	2	0.01
Sri Lankan (5)	6	0.03
Thai (5)	7	0.04
Vietnamese (5)	6	0.03
Other Asian, specified	3	0.02
Other Asian, not specified (2)	4	0.02
Australian	3	0.02
Austrian	48	0.26
Belgian	58	0.32
British	17	0.09
Canadian	30	0.16
Celtic	11	0.06
Croatian	18	0.10
Czech	304	1.67
Czechoslovakian	27	0.15
Danish	330	1.81
Dutch	223	1.22
Eastern European	31	0.17
English	940	5.16
European	131	0.72
Finnish	170	0.93
French, except Basque	645	3.54
French Canadian	216	1.19
German	8,512	46.75
Greek	2	0.01
Hawaii Native/Pacific Islander:	20	0.11
Polynesian: (7)	11	0.06
Native Hawaiian (2)	6	0.03
Samoan (5)	5	0.03
Other Pac. Isl., specified	3	0.02
Other Pac. Isl., not spec.	6	0.03
Hispanic or Latino:	207	1.14
Central American:	11	0.06
Guatemalan	5	0.03
Honduran	2	0.01
Salvadoran	4	0.02
Cuban	5	0.03
Mexican	132	0.73
Puerto Rican	14	0.08
South American:	6	0.03
Colombian	4	0.02
Ecuadorian	1	0.01
Other South American	1	0.01
Other Hispanic or Latino	39	0.21
Hungarian	37	0.20
Icelander	7	0.04
Irish	2,847	15.64
Italian	397	2.18
Lithuanian	8	0.04
Luxemburger	38	0.21
Norwegian	2,890	15.87
Pennsylvania German	11	0.06
Polish	770	4.23
Romanian	33	0.18
Russian	104	0.57
Scandinavian	153	0.84
Scotch-Irish	111	0.61
Scottish	209	1.15
Serbian	10	0.05
Slavic	7	0.04
Slovak	11	0.06
Slovene	9	0.05
Swedish	1,743	9.57
Swiss	83	0.46
Ukrainian	39	0.21
United States or American	743	4.08
Welsh	91	0.50
West Indian, excl. Hispanic:	4	0.02
Jamaican	4	0.02
White:	17,850	98.06
Not Hispanic (17,570)	17,715	97.31
Hispanic (117)	135	0.74
Yugoslavian	11	0.06

Hibbing

Place Type: City
County: Saint Louis
Population: 17,071

Ancestry/Race	Number	%
African American/Black:	116	0.68
Not Hispanic (79)	116	0.68
Alaska Native tribes, specified:	2	0.01
Eskimo (1)	1	0.01
Tlingit-Haida	1	0.01
Am. Ind. or Alaska Nat., not spec.	64	0.37
American Indian tribes, specified:	142	0.83
Cherokee (4)	14	0.08
Chippewa (79)	105	0.62
Choctaw (1)	2	0.01
Cree (1)	1	0.01
Crow	1	0.01
Iroquois (1)	3	0.02
Latin American Indians	1	0.01
Sioux (1)	6	0.04
All other tribes (4)	9	0.05
American Indian tribes, not spec.	16	0.09
Arab:	7	0.04
Arab/Arabic	7	0.04
Asian:	70	0.41
Chinese, ex. Taiwanese (13)	13	0.08
Filipino (11)	15	0.09
Indian (1)	7	0.04
Indonesian (1)	1	0.01
Japanese (1)	3	0.02
Korean (11)	20	0.12
Taiwanese (1)	1	0.01
Vietnamese (6)	6	0.04
Other Asian, specified	1	0.01
Other Asian, not specified (1)	3	0.02
Austrian	63	0.37
Belgian	24	0.14
British	46	0.27
Bulgarian	10	0.06
Canadian	35	0.21
Croatian	561	3.29
Czech	219	1.28
Czechoslovakian	48	0.28
Danish	141	0.83
Dutch	202	1.18
English	980	5.74
European	51	0.30
Finnish	2,350	13.77
French, except Basque	851	4.99
French Canadian	367	2.15
German	3,742	21.92
Greek	52	0.30
Hawaii Native/Pacific Islander:	5	0.03
Micronesian:	1	0.01
Guamanian/Chamorro	1	0.01
Polynesian: (1)	1	0.01
Native Hawaiian (1)	1	0.01
Other Pac. Isl., not spec.	3	0.02
Hispanic or Latino:	116	0.68
Central American:	1	0.01
Costa Rican	1	0.01
Cuban	3	0.02
Mexican	59	0.35
Puerto Rican	18	0.11
South American:	3	0.02
Chilean	1	0.01
Colombian	1	0.01
Ecuadorian	1	0.01
Other Hispanic or Latino	32	0.19
Hungarian	33	0.19
Icelander	9	0.05
Irish	1,740	10.19
Italian	1,672	9.79
Lithuanian	7	0.04
Macedonian	5	0.03
Northern European	16	0.09
Norwegian	2,192	12.84
Polish	610	3.57
Portuguese	6	0.04
Romanian	18	0.11
Russian	50	0.29
Scandinavian	248	1.45
Scotch-Irish	130	0.76
Scottish	155	0.91
Serbian	401	2.35
Slavic	198	1.16
Slovak	55	0.32
Slovene	544	3.19
Swedish	1,728	10.12
Swiss	28	0.16
Ukrainian	44	0.26
United States or American	668	3.91
Welsh	31	0.18
White:	16,786	98.33
Not Hispanic (16,541)	16,695	97.80
Hispanic (75)	91	0.53
Yugoslavian	467	2.74

Hopkins

Place Type: City
County: Hennepin
Population: 17,145

Ancestry/Race	Number	%
African American/Black:	1,116	6.51
Not Hispanic (874)	1,085	6.33
Hispanic (16)	31	0.18
African, sub-Saharan:	468	2.74
African	136	0.80
Ethiopian	85	0.50
Ghanian	19	0.11
Kenyan	13	0.08
Nigerian	20	0.12
Somalian	195	1.14
Am. Ind. or Alaska Nat., not spec.	86	0.50
American Indian tribes, specified:	158	0.92
Blackfeet (1)	5	0.03

Notes: 1. Figures in the "Number" column do not add up to the total population due to: a) Ancestry/Race overlap — e.g. persons can report being both White and Irish, b) persons of Hispanic origin can report being any race, c) persons reporting two ancestries are counted in both categories. 2. Numbers in parentheses indicate the number of persons reporting this ancestry/race alone, not in combination with any other ancestry/race. 3. Refer to the Explanation of Data in the front of the book for more detailed information.

Cherokee (6)	11	0.06
Chippewa (49)	77	0.45
Colville (1)	1	0.01
Cree (1)	1	0.01
Iroquois (1)	1	0.01
Kiowa	1	0.01
Latin American Indians (8)	12	0.07
Osage	1	0.01
Ottawa (4)	4	0.02
Potawatomi (2)	2	0.01
Pueblo (2)	2	0.01
Sioux (13)	21	0.12
Ute	3	0.02
All other tribes (5)	16	0.09
American Indian tribes, not spec.	4	0.02
Arab:	61	0.36
Arab/Arabic	10	0.06
Lebanese	19	0.11
Palestinian	32	0.19
Asian:	1,141	6.66
Bangladeshi (12)	16	0.09
Cambodian (51)	59	0.34
Chinese, ex. Taiwanese (121)	145	0.85
Filipino (44)	52	0.30
Hmong (6)	9	0.05
Indian (538)	559	3.26
Japanese (15)	34	0.20
Korean (46)	61	0.36
Laotian (50)	62	0.36
Malaysian (4)	4	0.02
Pakistani (11)	16	0.09
Sri Lankan (11)	11	0.06
Thai (1)	1	0.01
Vietnamese (70)	72	0.42
Other Asian, specified (9)	10	0.06
Other Asian, not specified (15)	30	0.17
Assyrian/Chaldean/Syriac	8	0.05
Austrian	18	0.11
Basque	30	0.18
Belgian	11	0.06
Brazilian	39	0.23
British	36	0.21
Bulgarian	60	0.35
Canadian	28	0.16
Celtic	8	0.05
Croatian	20	0.12
Czech	543	3.18
Czechoslovakian	80	0.47
Danish	179	1.05
Dutch	231	1.35
Eastern European	9	0.05
English	1,219	7.14
Estonian	12	0.07
European	175	1.03
Finnish	176	1.03
French, except Basque	692	4.06
French Canadian	218	1.28
German	5,032	29.49
Greek	82	0.48
Guyanese	16	0.09
Hawaii Native/Pacific Islander:	35	0.20
Micronesian:	4	0.02
Other Micronesian	4	0.02
Polynesian: (14)	26	0.15
Native Hawaiian (6)	14	0.08
Samoan (7)	11	0.06
Other Polynesian (1)	1	0.01
Other Pac. Isl., not spec. (1)	5	0.03
Hispanic or Latino:	949	5.54
Central American:	31	0.18
Costa Rican	1	0.01
Guatemalan	11	0.06
Honduran	3	0.02
Nicaraguan	2	0.01
Panamanian	4	0.02
Salvadoran	9	0.05
Other Central American	1	0.01
Cuban	24	0.14
Dominican Republic	4	0.02
Mexican	624	3.64
Puerto Rican	42	0.24
South American:	57	0.33
Bolivian	8	0.05
Chilean	3	0.02
Colombian	10	0.06
Ecuadorian	12	0.07
Paraguayan	2	0.01
Peruvian	19	0.11
Venezuelan	2	0.01
Other South American	1	0.01
Other Hispanic or Latino	167	0.97
Hungarian	8	0.05
Icelander	8	0.05
Iranian	16	0.09
Irish	1,984	11.63
Italian	370	2.17
Lithuanian	30	0.18
Luxemburger	58	0.34
Macedonian	10	0.06
Norwegian	2,659	15.59
Pennsylvania German	11	0.06
Polish	615	3.60
Romanian	38	0.22
Russian	187	1.10
Scandinavian	188	1.10
Scotch-Irish	216	1.27
Scottish	305	1.79
Serbian	11	0.06
Slavic	16	0.09
Slovak	28	0.16
Slovene	37	0.22
Swedish	1,710	10.02
Swiss	48	0.28
Turkish	10	0.06
Ukrainian	44	0.26
United States or American	324	1.90
Welsh	83	0.49
White:	14,541	84.81
Not Hispanic (13,755)	14,051	81.95
Hispanic (409)	490	2.86
Yugoslavian	59	0.35

Hutchinson

Place Type: City
County: McLeod
Population: 13,080

Ancestry/Race	Number	%
African American/Black:	76	0.58
Not Hispanic (46)	75	0.57
Hispanic (1)	1	0.01
African, sub-Saharan:	21	0.16
African	21	0.16
Am. Ind. or Alaska Nat., not spec.	24	0.18
American Indian tribes, specified:	57	0.44
Blackfeet (3)	7	0.05
Cherokee	2	0.02
Chippewa (17)	31	0.24
Cree (1)	1	0.01
Iroquois	1	0.01
Navajo (1)	1	0.01
Sioux (3)	12	0.09
All other tribes (2)	2	0.02
American Indian tribes, not spec.	3	0.02
Asian:	146	1.12
Chinese, ex. Taiwanese (27)	30	0.23
Filipino (11)	21	0.16
Indian (34)	34	0.26
Indonesian (1)	1	0.01
Japanese (8)	11	0.08
Korean (13)	20	0.15
Laotian (1)	2	0.02
Thai (2)	2	0.02
Vietnamese (16)	17	0.13
Other Asian, specified	2	0.02
Other Asian, not specified (6)	6	0.05
Austrian	13	0.10
Belgian	8	0.06
British	14	0.11
Canadian	42	0.32
Croatian	7	0.05
Czech	331	2.54
Czechoslovakian	80	0.61
Danish	427	3.27
Dutch	193	1.48
English	686	5.25
European	9	0.07
Finnish	124	0.95
French, except Basque	621	4.76
French Canadian	65	0.50
German	7,209	55.22
Hawaii Native/Pacific Islander:	10	0.08
Polynesian: (2)	5	0.04
Native Hawaiian (1)	4	0.03
Samoan (1)	1	0.01
Other Pac. Isl., not spec. (2)	5	0.04
Hispanic or Latino:	278	2.13
Central American:	8	0.06
Guatemalan	2	0.02
Panamanian	6	0.05
Cuban	2	0.02
Mexican	221	1.69
Puerto Rican	6	0.05
Other Hispanic or Latino	41	0.31
Icelander	15	0.11
Irish	1,173	8.98
Italian	162	1.24
Luxemburger	21	0.16
Macedonian	27	0.21
Norwegian	2,053	15.72
Polish	573	4.39
Romanian	35	0.27
Russian	88	0.67
Scandinavian	131	1.00
Scotch-Irish	39	0.30
Scottish	147	1.13
Slavic	11	0.08
Slovak	7	0.05
Swedish	1,355	10.38
Swiss	63	0.48
Ukrainian	14	0.11
United States or American	373	2.86
Welsh	20	0.15
West Indian, excl. Hispanic:	10	0.08
Jamaican	10	0.08
White:	12,697	97.07
Not Hispanic (12,499)	12,594	96.28
Hispanic (89)	103	0.79

Inver Grove Heights

Place Type: City
County: Dakota
Population: 29,751

Ancestry/Race	Number	%
African American/Black:	823	2.77
Not Hispanic (586)	766	2.57
Hispanic (39)	57	0.19
African, sub-Saharan:	192	0.65
African	183	0.62
Nigerian	9	0.03
Alaska Native tribes, specified:	1	0.00
Eskimo (1)	1	0.00
Alaska Native tribes, not specified	1	0.00
Am. Ind. or Alaska Nat., not spec.	71	0.24
Albanian	13	0.04
American Indian tribes, specified:	183	0.62
Apache (4)	8	0.03
Blackfeet	1	0.00
Cherokee (8)	21	0.07
Chippewa (57)	77	0.26
Choctaw	2	0.01
Delaware (1)	4	0.01
Iroquois (1)	2	0.01
Latin American Indians (9)	16	0.05
Menominee	1	0.00
Potawatomi	2	0.01
Pueblo (1)	1	0.00

Notes: 1. Figures in the "Number" column do not add up to the total population due to: a) Ancestry/Race overlap — e.g. persons can report being both White and Irish, b) persons of Hispanic origin can report being any race, c) persons reporting two ancestries are counted in both categories. 2. Numbers in parentheses indicate the number of persons reporting this ancestry/race alone, not in combination with any other ancestry/race. 3. Refer to the Explanation of Data in the front of the book for more detailed information.

Ancestry/Race	Number	%
Sioux (16)	33	0.11
All other tribes (9)	15	0.05
American Indian tribes, not spec.	8	0.03
Arab:	225	0.76
Arab/Arabic	15	0.05
Egyptian	25	0.08
Lebanese	185	0.62
Asian:	740	2.49
Cambodian (8)	14	0.05
Chinese, ex. Taiwanese (81)	101	0.34
Filipino (87)	122	0.41
Hmong (109)	115	0.39
Indian (115)	122	0.41
Indonesian (2)	2	0.01
Japanese (15)	36	0.12
Korean (71)	88	0.30
Laotian (19)	21	0.07
Malaysian	1	0.00
Pakistani (6)	9	0.03
Sri Lankan (8)	10	0.03
Taiwanese (2)	10	0.03
Thai (2)	4	0.01
Vietnamese (56)	71	0.24
Other Asian, not specified (7)	14	0.05
Austrian	189	0.64
Belgian	23	0.08
British	102	0.34
Canadian	54	0.18
Croatian	55	0.19
Czech	495	1.67
Czechoslovakian	64	0.22
Danish	531	1.79
Dutch	517	1.74
English	1,747	5.88
European	169	0.57
Finnish	216	0.73
French, except Basque	1,423	4.79
French Canadian	496	1.67
German	11,858	39.89
German Russian	9	0.03
Greek	74	0.25
Hawaii Native/Pacific Islander:	21	0.07
Polynesian: (5)	12	0.04
Native Hawaiian (2)	5	0.02
Samoan	1	0.00
Tongan (3)	6	0.02
Other Pac. Isl., not spec. (1)	9	0.03
Hispanic or Latino:	1,256	4.22
Central American:	46	0.15
Costa Rican	2	0.01
Guatemalan	8	0.03
Honduran	13	0.04
Panamanian	6	0.02
Salvadoran	13	0.04
Other Central American	4	0.01
Cuban	38	0.13
Dominican Republic	2	0.01
Mexican	922	3.10
Puerto Rican	85	0.29
South American:	27	0.09
Chilean	4	0.01
Colombian	12	0.04
Ecuadorian	3	0.01
Paraguayan	2	0.01
Peruvian	6	0.02
Other Hispanic or Latino	136	0.46
Hungarian	127	0.43
Icelander	12	0.04
Irish	4,548	15.30
Italian	976	3.28
Latvian	5	0.02
Lithuanian	52	0.17
Luxemburger	11	0.04
Macedonian	36	0.12
Northern European	27	0.09
Norwegian	4,541	15.28
Pennsylvania German	8	0.03
Polish	1,889	6.36
Portuguese	35	0.12
Romanian	33	0.11
Russian	221	0.74
Scandinavian	210	0.71
Scotch-Irish	411	1.38
Scottish	455	1.53
Serbian	49	0.16
Slavic	19	0.06
Slovak	25	0.08
Slovene	51	0.17
Swedish	2,359	7.94
Swiss	232	0.78
Ukrainian	228	0.77
United States or American	969	3.26
Welsh	225	0.76
White:	27,810	93.48
Not Hispanic (26,727)	27,107	91.11
Hispanic (585)	703	2.36
Yugoslavian	34	0.11

Lakeville

Place Type: City
County: Dakota
Population: 43,128

Ancestry/Race	Number	%
African American/Black:	735	1.70
Not Hispanic (544)	705	1.63
Hispanic (9)	30	0.07
African, sub-Saharan:	92	0.21
African	64	0.15
Kenyan	21	0.05
Liberian	7	0.02
Alaska Native tribes, specified:	8	0.02
Aleut (1)	1	0.00
Eskimo	1	0.00
Tlingit-Haida (3)	6	0.01
Alaska Native tribes, not specified	1	0.00
Am. Ind. or Alaska Nat., not spec.	80	0.19
American Indian tribes, specified:	195	0.45
Apache (2)	2	0.00
Blackfeet	4	0.01
Cherokee (5)	22	0.05
Chippewa (60)	89	0.21
Choctaw (5)	5	0.01
Comanche (1)	3	0.01
Cree (1)	1	0.00
Crow	1	0.00
Iroquois	5	0.01
Kiowa	3	0.01
Latin American Indians (7)	7	0.02
Lumbee (3)	5	0.01
Navajo (3)	7	0.02
Potawatomi (2)	2	0.00
Puget Sound Salish (1)	1	0.00
Seminole (3)	3	0.01
Sioux (4)	9	0.02
All other tribes (19)	24	0.06
American Indian tribes, not spec.	7	0.02
Arab:	119	0.28
Lebanese	50	0.12
Syrian	44	0.10
Other Arab	25	0.06
Asian:	1,100	2.55
Cambodian (128)	138	0.32
Chinese, ex. Taiwanese (125)	144	0.33
Filipino (51)	96	0.22
Hmong (12)	14	0.03
Indian (108)	147	0.34
Indonesian (4)	10	0.02
Japanese (30)	63	0.15
Korean (138)	170	0.39
Laotian (74)	83	0.19
Thai (9)	22	0.05
Vietnamese (134)	158	0.37
Other Asian, specified (4)	4	0.01
Other Asian, not specified (33)	51	0.12
Australian	33	0.08
Austrian	207	0.48
Belgian	114	0.26
British	114	0.26
Canadian	51	0.12
Croatian	39	0.09
Czech	1,183	2.74
Czechoslovakian	172	0.40
Danish	947	2.20
Dutch	986	2.29
English	3,406	7.90
Estonian	10	0.02
European	290	0.67
Finnish	556	1.29
French, except Basque	1,291	2.99
French Canadian	460	1.07
German	17,770	41.20
Greek	70	0.16
Hawaii Native/Pacific Islander:	38	0.09
Melanesian: (1)	1	0.00
Other Melanesian (1)	1	0.00
Micronesian:	5	0.01
Guamanian/Chamorro	5	0.01
Polynesian: (7)	19	0.04
Native Hawaiian (2)	11	0.03
Samoan (4)	4	0.01
Other Polynesian (1)	4	0.01
Other Pac. Isl., not spec. (2)	13	0.03
Hispanic or Latino:	835	1.94
Central American:	27	0.06
Costa Rican	1	0.00
Guatemalan	5	0.01
Honduran	5	0.01
Nicaraguan	4	0.01
Panamanian	5	0.01
Salvadoran	6	0.01
Other Central American	1	0.00
Cuban	24	0.06
Dominican Republic	1	0.00
Mexican	484	1.12
Puerto Rican	79	0.18
South American:	55	0.13
Argentinean	7	0.02
Bolivian	2	0.00
Chilean	1	0.00
Colombian	18	0.04
Ecuadorian	5	0.01
Paraguayan	3	0.01
Peruvian	11	0.03
Uruguayan	1	0.00
Venezuelan	2	0.00
Other South American	5	0.01
Other Hispanic or Latino	165	0.38
Hungarian	73	0.17
Iranian	16	0.04
Irish	6,602	15.31
Italian	1,167	2.71
Latvian	12	0.03
Lithuanian	208	0.48
Northern European	47	0.11
Norwegian	8,436	19.56
Pennsylvania German	16	0.04
Polish	1,827	4.24
Portuguese	9	0.02
Romanian	50	0.12
Russian	409	0.95
Scandinavian	523	1.21
Scotch-Irish	309	0.72
Scottish	750	1.74
Serbian	28	0.06
Slavic	55	0.13
Slovak	86	0.20
Slovene	95	0.22
Swedish	4,322	10.02
Swiss	211	0.49
Turkish	48	0.11
Ukrainian	176	0.41
United States or American	1,114	2.58
Welsh	283	0.66
White:	41,144	95.40
Not Hispanic (40,226)	40,620	94.18
Hispanic (428)	524	1.21
Yugoslavian	71	0.16

Notes: 1. Figures in the "Number" column do not add up to the total population due to: a) Ancestry/Race overlap — e.g. persons can report being both White and Irish, b) persons of Hispanic origin can report being any race, c) persons reporting two ancestries are counted in both categories. 2. Numbers in parentheses indicate the number of persons reporting this ancestry/race alone, not in combination with any other ancestry/race. 3. Refer to the Explanation of Data in the front of the book for more detailed information.

Lino Lakes

Place Type: City
County: Anoka
Population: 16,791

Ancestry/Race	Number	%
African American/Black:	472	2.81
Not Hispanic (405)	460	2.74
Hispanic (12)	12	0.07
African, sub-Saharan:	60	0.36
African	60	0.36
Alaska Native tribes, specified:	1	0.01
Tlingit-Haida (1)	1	0.01
Am. Ind. or Alaska Nat., not spec.	46	0.27
American Indian tribes, specified:	140	0.83
Apache (1)	4	0.02
Blackfeet (1)	1	0.01
Cherokee (2)	9	0.05
Chippewa (63)	87	0.52
Choctaw	1	0.01
Cree (1)	1	0.01
Kiowa (1)	1	0.01
Latin American Indians (2)	2	0.01
Pima (2)	2	0.01
Seminole	1	0.01
Sioux (11)	23	0.14
All other tribes (5)	8	0.05
American Indian tribes, not spec.	6	0.04
Arab:	5	0.03
Lebanese	5	0.03
Asian:	278	1.66
Cambodian (3)	3	0.02
Chinese, ex. Taiwanese (14)	21	0.13
Filipino (14)	34	0.20
Hmong (31)	32	0.19
Indian (41)	50	0.30
Japanese (7)	26	0.15
Korean (36)	53	0.32
Laotian (7)	12	0.07
Malaysian (3)	3	0.02
Pakistani (4)	4	0.02
Taiwanese (1)	1	0.01
Thai (3)	3	0.02
Vietnamese (23)	27	0.16
Other Asian, not specified (3)	9	0.05
Australian	10	0.06
Austrian	92	0.55
Belgian	6	0.04
British	60	0.36
Canadian	43	0.26
Celtic	5	0.03
Croatian	10	0.06
Czech	386	2.30
Czechoslovakian	37	0.22
Danish	353	2.10
Dutch	312	1.86
English	1,196	7.13
European	68	0.41
Finnish	448	2.67
French, except Basque	1,044	6.23
French Canadian	284	1.69
German	7,228	43.10
Greek	20	0.12
Hawaii Native/Pacific Islander:	7	0.04
Other Pac. Isl., not spec. (1)	7	0.04
Hispanic or Latino:	259	1.54
Central American:	12	0.07
Costa Rican	2	0.01
Guatemalan	5	0.03
Panamanian	3	0.02
Salvadoran	2	0.01
Cuban	1	0.01
Mexican	129	0.77
Puerto Rican	31	0.18
South American:	27	0.16
Argentinean	3	0.02
Chilean	1	0.01
Colombian	13	0.08
Ecuadorian	5	0.03
Peruvian	2	0.01
Uruguayan	1	0.01
Venezuelan	2	0.01
Other Hispanic or Latino	59	0.35
Hungarian	83	0.49
Icelander	6	0.04
Iranian	25	0.15
Irish	2,347	14.00
Israeli	12	0.07
Italian	788	4.70
Latvian	9	0.05
Lithuanian	38	0.23
Luxemburger	17	0.10
Northern European	10	0.06
Norwegian	2,727	16.26
Polish	999	5.96
Portuguese	33	0.20
Romanian	54	0.32
Russian	92	0.55
Scandinavian	159	0.95
Scotch-Irish	164	0.98
Scottish	127	0.76
Slavic	59	0.35
Slovak	32	0.19
Slovene	65	0.39
Swedish	1,902	11.34
Swiss	55	0.33
Ukrainian	52	0.31
United States or American	596	3.55
Welsh	58	0.35
West Indian, excl. Hispanic:	12	0.07
West Indian	12	0.07
White:	15,924	94.84
Not Hispanic (15,608)	15,789	94.03
Hispanic (118)	135	0.80
Yugoslavian	25	0.15

Mankato

Place Type: City
County: Blue Earth
Population: 32,427

Ancestry/Race	Number	%
African American/Black:	770	2.37
Not Hispanic (608)	755	2.33
Hispanic (8)	15	0.05
African, sub-Saharan:	239	0.74
African	91	0.28
Ethiopian	13	0.04
Nigerian	37	0.11
Somalian	78	0.24
Sudanese	13	0.04
Zimbabwean	7	0.02
Alaska Native tribes, specified:	2	0.01
Aleut	1	0.00
Eskimo	1	0.00
Am. Ind. or Alaska Nat., not spec.	82	0.25
Alsatian	5	0.02
American Indian tribes, specified:	131	0.40
Apache (1)	4	0.01
Blackfeet (1)	6	0.02
Cherokee (4)	19	0.06
Chippewa (25)	37	0.11
Iroquois (1)	2	0.01
Latin American Indians (1)	6	0.02
Osage (1)	2	0.01
Seminole	2	0.01
Sioux (20)	31	0.10
All other tribes (14)	22	0.07
American Indian tribes, not spec.	14	0.04
Arab:	106	0.33
Arab/Arabic	12	0.04
Egyptian	7	0.02
Jordanian	7	0.02
Lebanese	69	0.21
Other Arab	11	0.03
Asian:	1,049	3.23
Bangladeshi (13)	17	0.05
Cambodian (93)	107	0.33
Chinese, ex. Taiwanese (143)	164	0.51
Filipino (29)	53	0.16
Hmong (37)	43	0.13
Indian (146)	160	0.49
Indonesian (3)	4	0.01
Japanese (89)	97	0.30
Korean (89)	106	0.33
Laotian (18)	20	0.06
Pakistani (23)	29	0.09
Sri Lankan (3)	3	0.01
Taiwanese (10)	12	0.04
Thai (10)	14	0.04
Vietnamese (122)	134	0.41
Other Asian, specified (29)	33	0.10
Other Asian, not specified (38)	53	0.16
Australian	28	0.09
Austrian	100	0.31
Belgian	128	0.40
British	113	0.35
Canadian	37	0.11
Croatian	30	0.09
Czech	417	1.29
Czechoslovakian	72	0.22
Danish	526	1.63
Dutch	672	2.08
English	1,929	5.96
Estonian	6	0.02
European	287	0.89
Finnish	152	0.47
French, except Basque	913	2.82
French Canadian	420	1.30
German	14,801	45.74
Greek	26	0.08
Hawaii Native/Pacific Islander:	46	0.14
Melanesian: (1)	3	0.01
Other Melanesian (1)	3	0.01
Micronesian:	1	0.00
Guamanian/Chamorro	1	0.00
Polynesian: (27)	31	0.10
Native Hawaiian (2)	6	0.02
Samoan (25)	25	0.08
Other Pac. Isl., not spec. (3)	11	0.03
Hispanic or Latino:	719	2.22
Central American:	29	0.09
Costa Rican	10	0.03
Guatemalan	6	0.02
Honduran	6	0.02
Nicaraguan	1	0.00
Panamanian	2	0.01
Salvadoran	3	0.01
Other Central American	1	0.00
Cuban	7	0.02
Mexican	525	1.62
Puerto Rican	16	0.05
South American:	31	0.10
Argentinean	3	0.01
Bolivian	1	0.00
Chilean	3	0.01
Colombian	14	0.04
Paraguayan	2	0.01
Peruvian	4	0.01
Uruguayan	1	0.00
Venezuelan	3	0.01
Other Hispanic or Latino	111	0.34
Hungarian	43	0.13
Irish	3,578	11.06
Italian	336	1.04
Lithuanian	19	0.06
Luxemburger	23	0.07
Norwegian	5,646	17.45
Pennsylvania German	26	0.08
Polish	967	2.99
Portuguese	24	0.07
Romanian	27	0.08
Russian	71	0.22
Scandinavian	283	0.87
Scotch-Irish	371	1.15
Scottish	332	1.03
Serbian	4	0.01
Slavic	20	0.06

Notes: 1. Figures in the "Number" column do not add up to the total population due to: a) Ancestry/Race overlap — e.g. persons can report being both White and Irish, b) persons of Hispanic origin can report being any race, c) persons reporting two ancestries are counted in both categories. 2. Numbers in parentheses indicate the number of persons reporting this ancestry/race alone, not in combination with any other ancestry/race. 3. Refer to the Explanation of Data in the front of the book for more detailed information.

Slovak	15	0.05
Slovene	19	0.06
Swedish	1,701	5.26
Swiss	103	0.32
Turkish	9	0.03
Ukrainian	36	0.11
United States or American	928	2.87
Welsh	354	1.09
West Indian, excl. Hispanic:	37	0.11
Bahamian	7	0.02
West Indian	30	0.09
White:	30,362	93.63
Not Hispanic (29,670)	29,957	92.38
Hispanic (341)	405	1.25
Yugoslavian	78	0.24

Maple Grove

Place Type: City
County: Hennepin
Population: 50,365

Ancestry/Race	Number	%
Afghan	6	0.01
African American/Black:	708	1.41
Not Hispanic (519)	694	1.38
Hispanic (9)	14	0.03
African, sub-Saharan:	306	0.61
African	168	0.33
Ghanian	56	0.11
Liberian	42	0.08
Nigerian	31	0.06
South African	9	0.02
Alaska Native tribes, specified:	3	0.01
Alaska Athabascan	2	0.00
Aleut	1	0.00
Am. Ind. or Alaska Nat., not spec.	52	0.10
Albanian	10	0.02
American Indian tribes, specified:	193	0.38
Cherokee (7)	16	0.03
Chippewa (65)	120	0.24
Choctaw (2)	7	0.01
Comanche (2)	2	0.00
Cree	1	0.00
Creek	1	0.00
Iroquois (2)	3	0.01
Kiowa (1)	1	0.00
Latin American Indians (1)	13	0.03
Navajo	2	0.00
Pueblo	1	0.00
Seminole	2	0.00
Sioux (10)	16	0.03
All other tribes (5)	8	0.02
American Indian tribes, not spec.	10	0.02
Arab:	132	0.26
Egyptian	16	0.03
Lebanese	86	0.17
Syrian	15	0.03
Other Arab	15	0.03
Armenian	28	0.06
Asian:	1,476	2.93
Bangladeshi (4)	4	0.01
Cambodian (7)	13	0.03
Chinese, ex. Taiwanese (208)	234	0.46
Filipino (103)	166	0.33
Hmong (40)	44	0.09
Indian (291)	312	0.62
Indonesian (3)	4	0.01
Japanese (39)	72	0.14
Korean (280)	319	0.63
Laotian (29)	30	0.06
Malaysian (2)	5	0.01
Pakistani (12)	13	0.03
Sri Lankan (5)	5	0.01
Taiwanese (15)	16	0.03
Thai (12)	17	0.03
Vietnamese (183)	194	0.39
Other Asian, not specified (12)	28	0.06
Australian	30	0.06
Austrian	233	0.46
Basque	13	0.03
Belgian	120	0.24
British	140	0.28
Canadian	62	0.12
Croatian	65	0.13
Czech	650	1.29
Czechoslovakian	219	0.44
Danish	1,065	2.12
Dutch	1,078	2.14
Eastern European	26	0.05
English	4,007	7.96
European	508	1.01
Finnish	1,205	2.39
French, except Basque	2,006	3.98
French Canadian	680	1.35
German	19,965	39.66
German Russian	6	0.01
Greek	182	0.36
Hawaii Native/Pacific Islander:	34	0.07
Melanesian: (2)	2	0.00
Fijian (2)	2	0.00
Micronesian: (3)	7	0.01
Guamanian/Chamorro (1)	5	0.01
Other Micronesian (2)	2	0.00
Polynesian: (10)	18	0.04
Native Hawaiian (3)	10	0.02
Samoan (4)	5	0.01
Other Polynesian (3)	3	0.01
Other Pac. Isl., not spec. (1)	7	0.01
Hispanic or Latino:	534	1.06
Central American:	29	0.06
Costa Rican	4	0.01
Guatemalan	4	0.01
Honduran	10	0.02
Nicaraguan	2	0.00
Panamanian	2	0.00
Salvadoran	7	0.01
Cuban	17	0.03
Dominican Republic	1	0.00
Mexican	240	0.48
Puerto Rican	46	0.09
South American:	77	0.15
Argentinean	12	0.02
Bolivian	2	0.00
Chilean	6	0.01
Colombian	29	0.06
Ecuadorian	1	0.00
Paraguayan	3	0.01
Peruvian	13	0.03
Uruguayan	3	0.01
Venezuelan	7	0.01
Other South American	1	0.00
Other Hispanic or Latino	124	0.25
Hungarian	188	0.37
Icelander	53	0.11
Iranian	60	0.12
Irish	6,173	12.26
Italian	1,303	2.59
Latvian	35	0.07
Lithuanian	55	0.11
Luxemburger	45	0.09
Macedonian	4	0.01
Northern European	67	0.13
Norwegian	8,946	17.77
Pennsylvania German	6	0.01
Polish	3,029	6.02
Portuguese	25	0.05
Romanian	50	0.10
Russian	769	1.53
Scandinavian	800	1.59
Scotch-Irish	350	0.70
Scottish	667	1.32
Serbian	48	0.10
Slavic	43	0.09
Slovak	84	0.17
Slovene	155	0.31
Swedish	6,417	12.75
Swiss	200	0.40
Turkish	4	0.01
Ukrainian	196	0.39
United States or American	1,587	3.15
Welsh	169	0.34
West Indian, excl. Hispanic:	71	0.14
Dutch West Indian	10	0.02
Haitian	17	0.03
Jamaican	24	0.05
West Indian	20	0.04
White:	48,230	95.76
Not Hispanic (47,407)	47,858	95.02
Hispanic (310)	372	0.74
Yugoslavian	80	0.16

Maplewood

Place Type: City
County: Ramsey
Population: 34,947

Ancestry/Race	Number	%
African American/Black:	1,521	4.35
Not Hispanic (1,215)	1,466	4.19
Hispanic (21)	55	0.16
African, sub-Saharan:	208	0.60
African	112	0.32
Ghanian	27	0.08
Liberian	30	0.09
Nigerian	20	0.06
Somalian	11	0.03
Other sub-Saharan African	8	0.02
Alaska Native tribes, specified:	2	0.01
Aleut (1)	2	0.01
Am. Ind. or Alaska Nat., not spec.	108	0.31
American Indian tribes, specified:	223	0.64
Apache (1)	1	0.00
Blackfeet (1)	9	0.03
Cherokee (5)	11	0.03
Chippewa (70)	102	0.29
Choctaw	2	0.01
Comanche (2)	2	0.01
Cree	2	0.01
Iroquois (3)	3	0.01
Kiowa (2)	2	0.01
Latin American Indians (1)	6	0.02
Navajo (3)	3	0.01
Ottawa (2)	2	0.01
Potawatomi	4	0.01
Pueblo	1	0.00
Seminole (1)	4	0.01
Sioux (31)	52	0.15
All other tribes (13)	17	0.05
American Indian tribes, not spec.	14	0.04
Arab:	97	0.28
Lebanese	60	0.17
Syrian	37	0.11
Armenian	16	0.05
Asian:	1,772	5.07
Bangladeshi (3)	3	0.01
Cambodian (90)	103	0.29
Chinese, ex. Taiwanese (195)	223	0.64
Filipino (62)	85	0.24
Hmong (685)	714	2.04
Indian (123)	134	0.38
Japanese (20)	44	0.13
Korean (95)	118	0.34
Laotian (23)	32	0.09
Malaysian (1)	2	0.01
Pakistani (18)	19	0.05
Sri Lankan (3)	3	0.01
Taiwanese (6)	9	0.03
Thai (10)	11	0.03
Vietnamese (199)	209	0.60
Other Asian, specified (2)	2	0.01
Other Asian, not specified (31)	61	0.17
Austrian	342	0.98
Belgian	48	0.14
British	50	0.14
Bulgarian	10	0.03
Canadian	17	0.05
Celtic	5	0.01
Croatian	43	0.12

Notes: 1. Figures in the "Number" column do not add up to the total population due to: a) Ancestry/Race overlap — e.g. persons can report being both White and Irish, b) persons of Hispanic origin can report being any race, c) persons reporting two ancestries are counted in both categories. 2. Numbers in parentheses indicate the number of persons reporting this ancestry/race alone, not in combination with any other ancestry/race. 3. Refer to the Explanation of Data in the front of the book for more detailed information.

Ancestry/Race	Number	%
Czech	643	1.84
Czechoslovakian	85	0.24
Danish	508	1.45
Dutch	400	1.14
English	1,971	5.64
Estonian	7	0.02
European	315	0.90
Finnish	312	0.89
French, except Basque	1,960	5.61
French Canadian	603	1.73
German	13,534	38.73
Greek	86	0.25
Guyanese	8	0.02
Hawaii Native/Pacific Islander:	45	0.13
Micronesian: (4)	4	0.01
Guamanian/Chamorro (4)	4	0.01
Polynesian: (16)	22	0.06
Native Hawaiian (2)	3	0.01
Samoan (13)	16	0.05
Tongan (1)	3	0.01
Other Pac. Isl., not spec. (4)	19	0.05
Hispanic or Latino:	779	2.23
Central American:	16	0.05
Costa Rican	3	0.01
Guatemalan	1	0.00
Honduran	1	0.00
Panamanian	8	0.02
Salvadoran	3	0.01
Cuban	11	0.03
Dominican Republic	2	0.01
Mexican	565	1.62
Puerto Rican	38	0.11
South American:	31	0.09
Argentinean	2	0.01
Bolivian	2	0.01
Colombian	12	0.03
Ecuadorian	8	0.02
Paraguayan	3	0.01
Peruvian	1	0.00
Venezuelan	2	0.01
Other South American	1	0.00
Other Hispanic or Latino	116	0.33
Hungarian	180	0.52
Irish	5,496	15.73
Italian	1,444	4.13
Latvian	6	0.02
Lithuanian	43	0.12
Luxemburger	27	0.08
Maltese	6	0.02
New Zealander	9	0.03
Northern European	71	0.20
Norwegian	4,352	12.45
Pennsylvania German	16	0.05
Polish	2,146	6.14
Portuguese	12	0.03
Romanian	46	0.13
Russian	218	0.62
Scandinavian	271	0.78
Scotch-Irish	349	1.00
Scottish	351	1.00
Serbian	39	0.11
Slavic	7	0.02
Slovak	49	0.14
Slovene	65	0.19
Swedish	4,087	11.70
Swiss	222	0.64
Ukrainian	48	0.14
United States or American	763	2.18
Welsh	164	0.47
West Indian, excl. Hispanic:	28	0.08
British West Indian	11	0.03
Jamaican	11	0.03
West Indian	6	0.02
White:	31,561	90.31
Not Hispanic (30,602)	31,064	88.89
Hispanic (392)	497	1.42
Yugoslavian	59	0.17

Marshall

Place Type: City
County: Lyon
Population: 12,735

Ancestry/Race	Number	%
African American/Black:	432	3.39
Not Hispanic (341)	412	3.24
Hispanic (14)	20	0.16
African, sub-Saharan:	173	1.36
African	16	0.13
Kenyan	20	0.16
Nigerian	16	0.13
Somalian	112	0.88
Other sub-Saharan African	9	0.07
Am. Ind. or Alaska Nat., not spec.	24	0.19
American Indian tribes, specified:	44	0.35
Apache (1)	2	0.02
Blackfeet (3)	6	0.05
Cherokee (1)	3	0.02
Chickasaw (4)	4	0.03
Chippewa (6)	7	0.05
Iroquois (1)	2	0.02
Latin American Indians	1	0.01
Sioux (11)	18	0.14
All other tribes (1)	1	0.01
American Indian tribes, not spec.	5	0.04
Asian:	225	1.77
Bangladeshi (6)	6	0.05
Chinese, ex. Taiwanese (37)	48	0.38
Filipino (5)	9	0.07
Hmong (36)	36	0.28
Indian (39)	47	0.37
Indonesian (1)	1	0.01
Japanese (5)	7	0.05
Korean (15)	16	0.13
Laotian (17)	17	0.13
Malaysian	9	0.07
Pakistani (1)	1	0.01
Sri Lankan (2)	3	0.02
Thai (7)	7	0.05
Vietnamese (1)	3	0.02
Other Asian, specified (3)	6	0.05
Other Asian, not specified (6)	9	0.07
Austrian	18	0.14
Belgian	1,043	8.18
British	25	0.20
Bulgarian	9	0.07
Czech	119	0.93
Czechoslovakian	20	0.16
Danish	481	3.77
Dutch	626	4.91
English	713	5.59
European	32	0.25
French, except Basque	479	3.76
French Canadian	108	0.85
German	5,035	39.49
German Russian	12	0.09
Greek	5	0.04
Hawaii Native/Pacific Islander:	12	0.09
Micronesian:	1	0.01
Guamanian/Chamorro	1	0.01
Polynesian: (1)	4	0.03
Native Hawaiian	3	0.02
Samoan (1)	1	0.01
Other Pac. Isl., not spec. (3)	7	0.05
Hispanic or Latino:	755	5.93
Central American:	51	0.40
Costa Rican	1	0.01
Guatemalan	17	0.13
Honduran	11	0.09
Nicaraguan	7	0.05
Panamanian	9	0.07
Salvadoran	1	0.01
Other Central American	5	0.04
Cuban	2	0.02
Dominican Republic	1	0.01
Mexican	557	4.37
Puerto Rican	13	0.10
South American:	7	0.05
Colombian	6	0.05
Venezuelan	1	0.01
Other Hispanic or Latino	124	0.97
Hungarian	5	0.04
Icelander	18	0.14
Iranian	2	0.02
Irish	1,213	9.51
Italian	99	0.78
Lithuanian	5	0.04
Luxemburger	6	0.05
Northern European	17	0.13
Norwegian	2,260	17.72
Polish	519	4.07
Portuguese	5	0.04
Russian	76	0.60
Scandinavian	58	0.45
Scotch-Irish	126	0.99
Scottish	112	0.88
Slovene	14	0.11
Swedish	786	6.16
Swiss	29	0.23
Ukrainian	6	0.05
United States or American	467	3.66
Welsh	48	0.38
White:	11,754	92.30
Not Hispanic (11,290)	11,356	89.17
Hispanic (344)	398	3.13

Mendota Heights

Place Type: City
County: Dakota
Population: 11,434

Ancestry/Race	Number	%
African American/Black:	142	1.24
Not Hispanic (97)	132	1.15
Hispanic (4)	10	0.09
African, sub-Saharan:	2	0.02
Ghanian	2	0.02
Am. Ind. or Alaska Nat., not spec.	13	0.11
American Indian tribes, specified:	28	0.24
Cherokee (3)	4	0.03
Chippewa (6)	11	0.10
Latin American Indians (3)	4	0.03
Sioux (3)	6	0.05
All other tribes (2)	3	0.03
American Indian tribes, not spec.	1	0.01
Arab:	142	1.25
Arab/Arabic	5	0.04
Lebanese	137	1.21
Armenian	36	0.32
Asian:	270	2.36
Bangladeshi (7)	7	0.06
Cambodian (2)	2	0.02
Chinese, ex. Taiwanese (51)	67	0.59
Filipino (10)	32	0.28
Hmong (9)	9	0.08
Indian (51)	59	0.52
Japanese (9)	20	0.17
Korean (45)	50	0.44
Laotian	1	0.01
Malaysian	2	0.02
Thai (1)	1	0.01
Vietnamese (13)	19	0.17
Other Asian, not specified	1	0.01
Austrian	131	1.15
Belgian	21	0.18
British	65	0.57
Canadian	3	0.03
Croatian	41	0.36
Czech	144	1.27
Czechoslovakian	32	0.28
Danish	307	2.70
Dutch	161	1.42
Eastern European	125	1.10
English	1,143	10.07
European	136	1.20
Finnish	89	0.78

Notes: 1. Figures in the "Number" column do not add up to the total population due to: a) Ancestry/Race overlap — e.g. persons can report being both White and Irish, b) persons of Hispanic origin can report being any race, c) persons reporting two ancestries are counted in both categories. 2. Numbers in parentheses indicate the number of persons reporting this ancestry/race alone, not in combination with any other ancestry/race. 3. Refer to the Explanation of Data in the front of the book for more detailed information.

French, except Basque	656	5.78
French Canadian	108	0.95
German	4,124	36.32
Greek	9	0.08
Hawaii Native/Pacific Islander:	5	0.04
Polynesian:	4	0.03
Native Hawaiian	4	0.03
Other Pac. Isl., not spec.	1	0.01
Hispanic or Latino:	203	1.78
Central American:	6	0.05
Guatemalan	1	0.01
Honduran	3	0.03
Nicaraguan	1	0.01
Salvadoran	1	0.01
Cuban	4	0.03
Dominican Republic	3	0.03
Mexican	126	1.10
Puerto Rican	8	0.07
South American:	32	0.28
Argentinean	2	0.02
Bolivian	1	0.01
Chilean	5	0.04
Colombian	15	0.13
Paraguayan	2	0.02
Peruvian	5	0.04
Other South American	2	0.02
Other Hispanic or Latino	24	0.21
Hungarian	84	0.74
Iranian	25	0.22
Irish	2,464	21.70
Italian	493	4.34
Latvian	11	0.10
Lithuanian	81	0.71
Luxemburger	59	0.52
Norwegian	1,186	10.44
Polish	532	4.68
Portuguese	9	0.08
Romanian	75	0.66
Russian	330	2.91
Scandinavian	103	0.91
Scotch-Irish	246	2.17
Scottish	221	1.95
Serbian	36	0.32
Slavic	26	0.23
Slovak	28	0.25
Slovene	53	0.47
Swedish	862	7.59
Swiss	77	0.68
Ukrainian	86	0.76
United States or American	282	2.48
Welsh	87	0.77
West Indian, excl. Hispanic:	68	0.60
Bahamian	16	0.14
Jamaican	15	0.13
Trinidadian and Tobagonian	27	0.24
West Indian	10	0.09
White:	11,051	96.65
Not Hispanic (10,816)	10,913	95.44
Hispanic (122)	138	1.21
Yugoslavian	4	0.04

Minneapolis

Place Type: City
County: Hennepin
Population: 382,618

Ancestry/Race	Number	%
Acadian/Cajun	34	0.01
Afghan	41	0.01
African American/Black:	78,291	20.46
Not Hispanic (67,966)	76,672	20.04
Hispanic (852)	1,619	0.42
African, sub-Saharan:	16,262	4.25
African	5,198	1.36
Ethiopian	2,259	0.59
Ghanian	117	0.03
Kenyan	186	0.05
Liberian	484	0.13
Nigerian	467	0.12
Senegalese	40	0.01
Sierra Leonean	71	0.02
Somalian	6,537	1.71
South African	89	0.02
Sudanese	261	0.07
Ugandan	11	0.00
Zairian	77	0.02
Zimbabwean	19	0.00
Other sub-Saharan African	446	0.12
Alaska Native tribes, specified:	62	0.02
Alaska Athabascan (15)	20	0.01
Aleut (1)	9	0.00
Eskimo (10)	19	0.00
Tlingit-Haida (11)	13	0.00
All other tribes	1	0.00
Alaska Native tribes, not specified	9	0.00
Am. Ind. or Alaska Nat., not spec.	3,742	0.98
Albanian	53	0.01
Alsatian	21	0.01
American Indian tribes, specified:	8,586	2.24
Apache (28)	56	0.01
Blackfeet (16)	135	0.04
Cherokee (66)	453	0.12
Cheyenne (7)	16	0.00
Chickasaw (3)	8	0.00
Chippewa (4,197)	5,154	1.35
Choctaw (31)	76	0.02
Colville (1)	2	0.00
Comanche (4)	13	0.00
Cree (12)	38	0.01
Creek (15)	57	0.01
Crow (7)	9	0.00
Delaware (3)	6	0.00
Houma	1	0.00
Iroquois (52)	107	0.03
Kiowa (1)	2	0.00
Latin American Indians (207)	402	0.11
Lumbee (4)	6	0.00
Menominee (44)	47	0.01
Navajo (37)	48	0.01
Osage (1)	6	0.00
Ottawa (1)	6	0.00
Pima (5)	5	0.00
Potawatomi (32)	38	0.01
Pueblo (9)	27	0.01
Puget Sound Salish (1)	5	0.00
Seminole (5)	30	0.01
Shoshone (2)	14	0.00
Sioux (1,089)	1,395	0.36
Tohono O'Odham (1)	1	0.00
Ute	3	0.00
Yakama (1)	8	0.00
Yaqui	1	0.00
Yuman (4)	4	0.00
All other tribes (250)	407	0.11
American Indian tribes, not spec.	473	0.12
Arab:	2,192	0.57
Arab/Arabic	230	0.06
Egyptian	488	0.13
Iraqi	123	0.03
Jordanian	17	0.00
Lebanese	807	0.21
Moroccan	63	0.02
Palestinian	150	0.04
Syrian	80	0.02
Other Arab	234	0.06
Armenian	192	0.05
Asian:	27,217	7.11
Bangladeshi (19)	26	0.01
Cambodian (342)	404	0.11
Chinese, ex. Taiwanese (2,369)	2,822	0.74
Filipino (615)	945	0.25
Hmong (9,595)	10,489	2.74
Indian (1,816)	2,369	0.62
Indonesian (65)	102	0.03
Japanese (662)	1,032	0.27
Korean (1,637)	1,934	0.51
Laotian (2,212)	2,522	0.66
Malaysian (55)	78	0.02
Pakistani (82)	111	0.03
Sri Lankan (36)	43	0.01
Taiwanese (78)	99	0.03
Thai (220)	299	0.08
Vietnamese (2,395)	2,612	0.68
Other Asian, specified (42)	79	0.02
Other Asian, not specified (723)	1,251	0.33
Assyrian/Chaldean/Syriac	22	0.01
Australian	81	0.02
Austrian	1,250	0.33
Basque	9	0.00
Belgian	751	0.20
Brazilian	74	0.02
British	1,795	0.47
Bulgarian	136	0.04
Canadian	598	0.16
Carpatho Rusyn	48	0.01
Celtic	108	0.03
Croatian	661	0.17
Cypriot	11	0.00
Czech	4,522	1.18
Czechoslovakian	1,226	0.32
Danish	5,355	1.40
Dutch	5,083	1.33
Eastern European	513	0.13
English	23,356	6.11
Estonian	79	0.02
European	3,925	1.03
Finnish	4,069	1.06
French, except Basque	12,685	3.32
French Canadian	3,457	0.90
German	82,283	21.51
German Russian	48	0.01
Greek	1,107	0.29
Guyanese	373	0.10
Hawaii Native/Pacific Islander:	953	0.25
Melanesian:	5	0.00
Fijian	1	0.00
Other Melanesian	4	0.00
Micronesian: (49)	65	0.02
Guamanian/Chamorro (41)	49	0.01
Other Micronesian (8)	16	0.00
Polynesian: (174)	324	0.08
Native Hawaiian (49)	140	0.04
Samoan (111)	160	0.04
Tongan (6)	8	0.00
Other Polynesian (8)	16	0.00
Other Pac. Isl., specified	15	0.00
Other Pac. Isl., not spec. (66)	544	0.14
Hispanic or Latino:	29,175	7.63
Central American:	1,107	0.29
Costa Rican	54	0.01
Guatemalan	384	0.10
Honduran	125	0.03
Nicaraguan	65	0.02
Panamanian	93	0.02
Salvadoran	338	0.09
Other Central American	48	0.01
Cuban	490	0.13
Dominican Republic	126	0.03
Mexican	19,835	5.18
Puerto Rican	1,202	0.31
South American:	2,457	0.64
Argentinean	78	0.02
Bolivian	23	0.01
Chilean	112	0.03
Colombian	289	0.08
Ecuadorian	1,639	0.43
Paraguayan	21	0.01
Peruvian	122	0.03
Uruguayan	31	0.01
Venezuelan	70	0.02
Other South American	72	0.02
Other Hispanic or Latino	3,958	1.03
Hungarian	1,181	0.31
Icelander	245	0.06
Iranian	293	0.08
Irish	38,670	10.11
Israeli	80	0.02
Italian	8,566	2.24
Latvian	479	0.13

Notes: 1. Figures in the "Number" column do not add up to the total population due to: a) Ancestry/Race overlap — e.g. persons can report being both White and Irish, b) persons of Hispanic origin can report being any race, c) persons reporting two ancestries are counted in both categories. 2. Numbers in parentheses indicate the number of persons reporting this ancestry/race alone, not in combination with any other ancestry/race. 3. Refer to the Explanation of Data in the front of the book for more detailed information.

Lithuanian	606	0.16
Luxemburger	397	0.10
Macedonian	7	0.00
Maltese	10	0.00
New Zealander	8	0.00
Northern European	843	0.22
Norwegian	41,917	10.96
Pennsylvania German	82	0.02
Polish	15,785	4.13
Portuguese	298	0.08
Romanian	570	0.15
Russian	4,220	1.10
Scandinavian	4,239	1.11
Scotch-Irish	3,744	0.98
Scottish	6,354	1.66
Serbian	278	0.07
Slavic	354	0.09
Slovak	847	0.22
Slovene	447	0.12
Swedish	30,518	7.98
Swiss	1,557	0.41
Turkish	261	0.07
Ukrainian	1,510	0.39
United States or American	6,025	1.58
Welsh	2,270	0.59
West Indian, excl. Hispanic:	1,077	0.28
Bahamian	17	0.00
Barbadian	7	0.00
British West Indian	46	0.01
Haitian	68	0.02
Jamaican	673	0.18
Trinidadian and Tobagonian	121	0.03
U.S. Virgin Islander	16	0.00
West Indian	129	0.03
White:	260,089	67.98
Not Hispanic (239,080)	247,853	64.78
Hispanic (10,106)	12,236	3.20
Yugoslavian	691	0.18

Minnetonka

Place Type: City
County: Hennepin
Population: 51,301

Ancestry/Race	Number	%
Acadian/Cajun	16	0.03
African American/Black:	944	1.84
Not Hispanic (754)	924	1.80
Hispanic (13)	20	0.04
African, sub-Saharan:	131	0.26
African	73	0.14
Liberian	9	0.02
Nigerian	49	0.10
Alaska Native tribes, specified:	2	0.00
Alaska Athabascan (1)	1	0.00
Aleut (1)	1	0.00
Am. Ind. or Alaska Nat., not spec.	75	0.15
American Indian tribes, specified:	140	0.27
Apache (1)	4	0.01
Cherokee (2)	9	0.02
Chickasaw (4)	6	0.01
Chippewa (37)	60	0.12
Choctaw (1)	5	0.01
Cree (1)	4	0.01
Creek	1	0.00
Iroquois (1)	3	0.01
Latin American Indians (8)	14	0.03
Menominee (1)	1	0.00
Navajo (1)	1	0.00
Osage (1)	1	0.00
Pima	1	0.00
Seminole	1	0.00
Shoshone	1	0.00
Sioux (6)	15	0.03
All other tribes (7)	13	0.03
American Indian tribes, not spec.	6	0.01
Arab:	228	0.44
Arab/Arabic	7	0.01
Iraqi	10	0.02
Lebanese	115	0.22
Moroccan	32	0.06
Palestinian	40	0.08
Syrian	15	0.03
Other Arab	9	0.02
Asian:	1,401	2.73
Bangladeshi (3)	3	0.01
Cambodian (31)	43	0.08
Chinese, ex. Taiwanese (247)	291	0.57
Filipino (95)	126	0.25
Hmong (7)	8	0.02
Indian (298)	324	0.63
Indonesian (5)	7	0.01
Japanese (66)	102	0.20
Korean (222)	262	0.51
Laotian (10)	12	0.02
Malaysian	1	0.00
Pakistani (32)	35	0.07
Sri Lankan (3)	3	0.01
Taiwanese (3)	3	0.01
Thai (10)	12	0.02
Vietnamese (98)	113	0.22
Other Asian, specified	2	0.00
Other Asian, not specified (23)	54	0.11
Assyrian/Chaldean/Syriac	5	0.01
Australian	55	0.11
Austrian	280	0.55
Basque	16	0.03
Belgian	207	0.40
Brazilian	40	0.08
British	203	0.40
Canadian	98	0.19
Celtic	36	0.07
Croatian	56	0.11
Cypriot	11	0.02
Czech	799	1.56
Czechoslovakian	182	0.35
Danish	1,006	1.96
Dutch	1,149	2.24
Eastern European	234	0.46
English	6,038	11.77
European	705	1.37
Finnish	736	1.43
French, except Basque	1,794	3.50
French Canadian	533	1.04
German	16,247	31.67
Greek	159	0.31
Guyanese	28	0.05
Hawaii Native/Pacific Islander:	29	0.06
Melanesian:	3	0.01
Other Melanesian	3	0.01
Micronesian:	1	0.00
Guamanian/Chamorro	1	0.00
Polynesian: (7)	13	0.03
Native Hawaiian (6)	11	0.02
Samoan (1)	1	0.00
Other Polynesian	1	0.00
Other Pac. Isl., specified	1	0.00
Other Pac. Isl., not spec. (7)	11	0.02
Hispanic or Latino:	657	1.28
Central American:	29	0.06
Costa Rican	3	0.01
Guatemalan	11	0.02
Honduran	4	0.01
Nicaraguan	3	0.01
Panamanian	1	0.00
Salvadoran	5	0.01
Other Central American	2	0.00
Cuban	35	0.07
Dominican Republic	8	0.02
Mexican	301	0.59
Puerto Rican	32	0.06
South American:	109	0.21
Argentinean	6	0.01
Chilean	5	0.01
Colombian	57	0.11
Ecuadorian	3	0.01
Paraguayan	6	0.01
Peruvian	5	0.01
Uruguayan	2	0.00
Venezuelan	10	0.02
Other South American	15	0.03
Other Hispanic or Latino	143	0.28
Hungarian	261	0.51
Icelander	68	0.13
Iranian	78	0.15
Irish	6,991	13.63
Israeli	10	0.02
Italian	1,384	2.70
Latvian	93	0.18
Lithuanian	287	0.56
Luxemburger	117	0.23
New Zealander	29	0.06
Northern European	115	0.22
Norwegian	8,445	16.46
Pennsylvania German	5	0.01
Polish	2,213	4.31
Portuguese	73	0.14
Romanian	230	0.45
Russian	1,771	3.45
Scandinavian	541	1.05
Scotch-Irish	779	1.52
Scottish	1,160	2.26
Serbian	27	0.05
Slavic	15	0.03
Slovak	117	0.23
Slovene	143	0.28
Soviet Union	15	0.03
Swedish	5,746	11.20
Swiss	328	0.64
Ukrainian	207	0.40
United States or American	1,578	3.08
Welsh	267	0.52
West Indian, excl. Hispanic:	19	0.04
Bahamian	7	0.01
Jamaican	12	0.02
White:	48,891	95.30
Not Hispanic (48,067)	48,473	94.49
Hispanic (359)	418	0.81
Yugoslavian	75	0.15

Moorhead

Place Type: City
County: Clay
Population: 32,177

Ancestry/Race	Number	%
Acadian/Cajun	2	0.01
African American/Black:	347	1.08
Not Hispanic (240)	333	1.03
Hispanic (7)	14	0.04
African, sub-Saharan:	71	0.22
African	20	0.06
Ghanian	20	0.06
Nigerian	11	0.03
Sierra Leonean	10	0.03
Other sub-Saharan African	10	0.03
Alaska Native tribes, specified:	1	0.00
Tlingit-Haida	1	0.00
Alaska Native tribes, not specified	2	0.01
Am. Ind. or Alaska Nat., not spec.	211	0.66
American Indian tribes, specified:	599	1.86
Apache (1)	2	0.01
Blackfeet	2	0.01
Cherokee (1)	18	0.06
Cheyenne (3)	7	0.02
Chippewa (238)	317	0.99
Choctaw (2)	4	0.01
Comanche	1	0.00
Cree	2	0.01
Iroquois (1)	3	0.01
Latin American Indians (10)	11	0.03
Pima (1)	1	0.00
Pueblo	1	0.00
Puget Sound Salish	2	0.01
Sioux (177)	202	0.63
Yakama (1)	1	0.00
All other tribes (22)	25	0.08
American Indian tribes, not spec.	32	0.10

Notes: 1. Figures in the "Number" column do not add up to the total population due to: a) Ancestry/Race overlap — e.g. persons can report being both White and Irish, b) persons of Hispanic origin can report being any race, c) persons reporting two ancestries are counted in both categories. 2. Numbers in parentheses indicate the number of persons reporting this ancestry/race alone, not in combination with any other ancestry/race. 3. Refer to the Explanation of Data in the front of the book for more detailed information.

Arab:	276	0.86
Arab/Arabic	7	0.02
Egyptian	6	0.02
Iraqi	58	0.18
Lebanese	21	0.07
Other Arab	184	0.57
Asian:	584	1.81
Bangladeshi (7)	7	0.02
Cambodian (3)	5	0.02
Chinese, ex. Taiwanese (42)	48	0.15
Filipino (18)	32	0.10
Hmong	1	0.00
Indian (52)	62	0.19
Indonesian (2)	2	0.01
Japanese (35)	49	0.15
Korean (60)	81	0.25
Laotian (18)	20	0.06
Pakistani (4)	8	0.02
Sri Lankan (4)	4	0.01
Taiwanese (5)	5	0.02
Thai (5)	6	0.02
Vietnamese (127)	144	0.45
Other Asian, specified (5)	6	0.02
Other Asian, not specified (19)	104	0.32
Austrian	28	0.09
Belgian	137	0.43
Brazilian	6	0.02
British	83	0.26
Bulgarian	21	0.07
Canadian	18	0.06
Croatian	12	0.04
Czech	407	1.27
Czechoslovakian	70	0.22
Danish	597	1.86
Dutch	445	1.38
English	1,786	5.55
European	108	0.34
Finnish	400	1.24
French, except Basque	1,232	3.83
French Canadian	209	0.65
German	11,397	35.44
German Russian	10	0.03
Greek	41	0.13
Hawaii Native/Pacific Islander:	22	0.07
Micronesian: (3)	5	0.02
Guamanian/Chamorro (1)	1	0.00
Other Micronesian (2)	4	0.01
Polynesian: (10)	12	0.04
Native Hawaiian (6)	8	0.02
Samoan (4)	4	0.01
Other Pac. Isl., specified	1	0.00
Other Pac. Isl., not spec. (1)	4	0.01
Hispanic or Latino:	1,439	4.47
Central American:	31	0.10
Costa Rican	2	0.01
Guatemalan	7	0.02
Honduran	6	0.02
Nicaraguan	2	0.01
Panamanian	12	0.04
Salvadoran	2	0.01
Cuban	17	0.05
Mexican	885	2.75
Puerto Rican	26	0.08
South American:	15	0.05
Bolivian	3	0.01
Chilean	1	0.00
Colombian	9	0.03
Peruvian	1	0.00
Uruguayan	1	0.00
Other Hispanic or Latino	465	1.45
Hungarian	90	0.28
Icelander	41	0.13
Irish	2,454	7.63
Italian	505	1.57
Lithuanian	14	0.04
Luxemburger	12	0.04
Northern European	43	0.13
Norwegian	12,855	39.97
Pennsylvania German	2	0.01
Polish	869	2.70
Portuguese	4	0.01
Romanian	12	0.04
Russian	259	0.81
Scandinavian	376	1.17
Scotch-Irish	331	1.03
Scottish	312	0.97
Slavic	6	0.02
Slovak	28	0.09
Slovene	28	0.09
Swedish	2,966	9.22
Swiss	114	0.35
Ukrainian	99	0.31
United States or American	456	1.42
Welsh	105	0.33
West Indian, excl. Hispanic:	20	0.06
Haitian	12	0.04
Jamaican	8	0.02
White:	30,170	93.76
Not Hispanic (29,001)	29,467	91.58
Hispanic (627)	703	2.18
Yugoslavian	18	0.06

Mounds View

Place Type: City
County: Ramsey
Population: 12,738

Ancestry/Race	Number	%
African American/Black:	406	3.19
Not Hispanic (300)	389	3.05
Hispanic (6)	17	0.13
African, sub-Saharan:	52	0.41
African	21	0.17
Ethiopian	13	0.10
Other sub-Saharan African	18	0.14
Alaska Native tribes, specified:	2	0.02
Alaska Athabascan (1)	1	0.01
Tlingit-Haida (1)	1	0.01
Am. Ind. or Alaska Nat., not spec.	37	0.29
Alsatian	9	0.07
American Indian tribes, specified:	135	1.06
Blackfeet (1)	2	0.02
Cherokee	6	0.05
Chippewa (57)	87	0.68
Choctaw	4	0.03
Delaware	1	0.01
Iroquois	3	0.02
Latin American Indians (1)	3	0.02
Osage	1	0.01
Seminole	5	0.04
Sioux (5)	20	0.16
All other tribes (1)	3	0.02
American Indian tribes, not spec.	6	0.05
Arab:	54	0.42
Lebanese	18	0.14
Other Arab	36	0.28
Asian:	455	3.57
Cambodian (11)	14	0.11
Chinese, ex. Taiwanese (61)	70	0.55
Filipino (20)	32	0.25
Hmong (73)	73	0.57
Indian (70)	72	0.57
Japanese (5)	9	0.07
Korean (47)	61	0.48
Laotian (17)	17	0.13
Pakistani (8)	8	0.06
Taiwanese (4)	4	0.03
Thai (5)	7	0.05
Vietnamese (64)	73	0.57
Other Asian, not specified (11)	15	0.12
Austrian	35	0.28
Belgian	11	0.09
British	23	0.18
Canadian	7	0.06
Croatian	41	0.32
Cypriot	7	0.06
Czech	122	0.96
Czechoslovakian	55	0.43
Danish	244	1.92
Dutch	249	1.96
Eastern European	10	0.08
English	778	6.12
European	53	0.42
Finnish	264	2.08
French, except Basque	728	5.73
French Canadian	222	1.75
German	4,620	36.36
Greek	26	0.20
Hawaii Native/Pacific Islander:	16	0.13
Polynesian: (7)	7	0.05
Samoan (7)	7	0.05
Other Pac. Isl., not spec.	9	0.07
Hispanic or Latino:	334	2.62
Central American:	21	0.16
Costa Rican	1	0.01
Guatemalan	10	0.08
Nicaraguan	3	0.02
Salvadoran	2	0.02
Other Central American	5	0.04
Cuban	2	0.02
Dominican Republic	1	0.01
Mexican	202	1.59
Puerto Rican	16	0.13
South American:	24	0.19
Argentinean	1	0.01
Bolivian	1	0.01
Chilean	3	0.02
Colombian	8	0.06
Ecuadorian	4	0.03
Peruvian	4	0.03
Venezuelan	2	0.02
Other South American	1	0.01
Other Hispanic or Latino	68	0.53
Hungarian	30	0.24
Icelander	6	0.05
Irish	1,570	12.35
Italian	649	5.11
Latvian	10	0.08
Lithuanian	8	0.06
Norwegian	1,932	15.20
Pennsylvania German	5	0.04
Polish	841	6.62
Portuguese	6	0.05
Romanian	6	0.05
Russian	95	0.75
Scandinavian	189	1.49
Scotch-Irish	106	0.83
Scottish	151	1.19
Serbian	6	0.05
Slavic	20	0.16
Slovak	39	0.31
Slovene	38	0.30
Swedish	1,618	12.73
Swiss	64	0.50
Ukrainian	51	0.40
United States or American	257	2.02
Welsh	29	0.23
White:	11,793	92.58
Not Hispanic (11,390)	11,594	91.02
Hispanic (157)	199	1.56
Yugoslavian	67	0.53

New Brighton

Place Type: City
County: Ramsey
Population: 22,206

Ancestry/Race	Number	%
Afghan	15	0.07
African American/Black:	918	4.13
Not Hispanic (733)	900	4.05
Hispanic (5)	18	0.08
African, sub-Saharan:	234	1.05
African	132	0.59
Ethiopian	25	0.11
Ghanian	21	0.09
Liberian	23	0.10
Nigerian	9	0.04

Notes: 1. Figures in the "Number" column do not add up to the total population due to: a) Ancestry/Race overlap — e.g. persons can report being both White and Irish, b) persons of Hispanic origin can report being any race, c) persons reporting two ancestries are counted in both categories. 2. Numbers in parentheses indicate the number of persons reporting this ancestry/race alone, not in combination with any other ancestry/race. 3. Refer to the Explanation of Data in the front of the book for more detailed information.

Ancestry/Race	Number	%
Sudanese	5	0.02
Other sub-Saharan African	19	0.09
Alaska Native tribes, specified:	1	0.00
Alaska Athabascan (1)	1	0.00
Am. Ind. or Alaska Nat., not spec.	67	0.30
Albanian	108	0.49
American Indian tribes, specified:	159	0.72
Blackfeet	2	0.01
Cherokee (3)	12	0.05
Chippewa (68)	94	0.42
Choctaw	1	0.00
Comanche	2	0.01
Cree	2	0.01
Iroquois	4	0.02
Latin American Indians (1)	4	0.02
Osage	1	0.00
Potawatomi (1)	1	0.00
Pueblo (2)	2	0.01
Seminole	3	0.01
Sioux (13)	21	0.09
Tohono O'Odham	2	0.01
All other tribes (4)	8	0.04
American Indian tribes, not spec.	12	0.05
Arab:	109	0.49
Arab/Arabic	9	0.04
Lebanese	85	0.38
Syrian	5	0.02
Other Arab	10	0.04
Armenian	61	0.27
Asian:	1,113	5.01
Bangladeshi	2	0.01
Cambodian (11)	14	0.06
Chinese, ex. Taiwanese (193)	215	0.97
Filipino (34)	61	0.27
Hmong (16)	20	0.09
Indian (305)	318	1.43
Indonesian (1)	3	0.01
Japanese (14)	27	0.12
Korean (143)	165	0.74
Laotian (5)	5	0.02
Malaysian (2)	3	0.01
Pakistani (6)	10	0.05
Sri Lankan (3)	3	0.01
Taiwanese (32)	39	0.18
Thai (2)	2	0.01
Vietnamese (181)	185	0.83
Other Asian, specified (2)	3	0.01
Other Asian, not specified (14)	38	0.17
Austrian	98	0.44
Belgian	23	0.10
Brazilian	11	0.05
British	112	0.50
Bulgarian	6	0.03
Celtic	14	0.06
Croatian	13	0.06
Czech	252	1.13
Czechoslovakian	59	0.27
Danish	443	1.99
Dutch	363	1.63
Eastern European	11	0.05
English	1,546	6.95
European	306	1.38
Finnish	344	1.55
French, except Basque	1,275	5.73
French Canadian	318	1.43
German	7,462	33.54
Greek	40	0.18
Hawaii Native/Pacific Islander:	27	0.12
Micronesian:	4	0.02
Guamanian/Chamorro	4	0.02
Polynesian: (5)	16	0.07
Native Hawaiian (5)	11	0.05
Samoan	4	0.02
Other Polynesian	1	0.00
Other Pac. Isl., not spec. (5)	7	0.03
Hispanic or Latino:	393	1.77
Central American:	33	0.15
Guatemalan	8	0.04
Honduran	13	0.06
Nicaraguan	6	0.03
Salvadoran	2	0.01
Other Central American	4	0.02
Cuban	6	0.03
Dominican Republic	1	0.00
Mexican	209	0.94
Puerto Rican	17	0.08
South American:	48	0.22
Argentinean	3	0.01
Bolivian	1	0.00
Colombian	18	0.08
Ecuadorian	14	0.06
Peruvian	5	0.02
Venezuelan	7	0.03
Other Hispanic or Latino	79	0.36
Hungarian	31	0.14
Icelander	7	0.03
Iranian	61	0.27
Irish	3,045	13.69
Italian	863	3.88
Latvian	51	0.23
Lithuanian	37	0.17
Luxemburger	54	0.24
Northern European	81	0.36
Norwegian	3,293	14.80
Pennsylvania German	18	0.08
Polish	1,881	8.45
Romanian	41	0.18
Russian	158	0.71
Scandinavian	245	1.10
Scotch-Irish	197	0.89
Scottish	373	1.68
Slavic	32	0.14
Slovak	109	0.49
Slovene	23	0.10
Swedish	2,780	12.49
Swiss	93	0.42
Ukrainian	108	0.49
United States or American	475	2.13
Welsh	44	0.20
West Indian, excl. Hispanic:	20	0.09
West Indian	20	0.09
White:	20,063	90.35
Not Hispanic (19,487)	19,851	89.39
Hispanic (185)	212	0.95
Yugoslavian	140	0.63

New Hope

Place Type: City
County: Hennepin
Population: 20,873

Ancestry/Race	Number	%
African American/Black:	1,457	6.98
Not Hispanic (1,188)	1,425	6.83
Hispanic (19)	32	0.15
African, sub-Saharan:	440	2.11
African	189	0.91
Ethiopian	6	0.03
Ghanian	4	0.02
Kenyan	17	0.08
Liberian	98	0.47
Nigerian	23	0.11
Sierra Leonean	9	0.04
Somalian	41	0.20
South African	23	0.11
Sudanese	30	0.14
Alaska Native tribes, specified:	1	0.00
Alaska Athabascan (1)	1	0.00
Alaska Native tribes, not specified	2	0.01
Am. Ind. or Alaska Nat., not spec.	70	0.34
American Indian tribes, specified:	116	0.56
Apache (2)	2	0.01
Blackfeet	1	0.00
Cherokee (2)	21	0.10
Chippewa (44)	60	0.29
Choctaw (4)	11	0.05
Iroquois	1	0.00
Sioux (6)	15	0.07
All other tribes (2)	5	0.02
American Indian tribes, not spec.	6	0.03
Arab:	98	0.47
Egyptian	30	0.14
Lebanese	31	0.15
Moroccan	6	0.03
Other Arab	31	0.15
Asian:	781	3.74
Cambodian (18)	18	0.09
Chinese, ex. Taiwanese (71)	89	0.43
Filipino (46)	58	0.28
Hmong (21)	21	0.10
Indian (133)	141	0.68
Indonesian (1)	3	0.01
Japanese (7)	13	0.06
Korean (61)	82	0.39
Laotian (60)	81	0.39
Malaysian (1)	1	0.00
Pakistani (14)	15	0.07
Taiwanese (2)	2	0.01
Thai (5)	12	0.06
Vietnamese (191)	200	0.96
Other Asian, specified (7)	8	0.04
Other Asian, not specified (20)	37	0.18
Australian	8	0.04
Austrian	68	0.33
Belgian	27	0.13
British	29	0.14
Canadian	20	0.10
Croatian	39	0.19
Czech	246	1.18
Czechoslovakian	47	0.23
Danish	265	1.27
Dutch	405	1.94
Eastern European	38	0.18
English	1,502	7.20
European	192	0.92
Finnish	369	1.77
French, except Basque	842	4.04
French Canadian	253	1.21
German	6,395	30.67
Greek	62	0.30
Hawaii Native/Pacific Islander:	13	0.06
Polynesian: (8)	10	0.05
Native Hawaiian (2)	4	0.02
Samoan (6)	6	0.03
Other Pac. Isl., not spec.	3	0.01
Hispanic or Latino:	721	3.45
Central American:	10	0.05
Costa Rican	1	0.00
Honduran	4	0.02
Panamanian	4	0.02
Other Central American	1	0.00
Cuban	12	0.06
Mexican	524	2.51
Puerto Rican	35	0.17
South American:	39	0.19
Argentinean	2	0.01
Bolivian	4	0.02
Chilean	5	0.02
Colombian	11	0.05
Ecuadorian	2	0.01
Peruvian	12	0.06
Uruguayan	1	0.00
Venezuelan	1	0.00
Other South American	1	0.00
Other Hispanic or Latino	101	0.48
Hungarian	94	0.45
Icelander	18	0.09
Iranian	80	0.38
Irish	2,260	10.84
Italian	332	1.59
Latvian	17	0.08
Lithuanian	29	0.14
Luxemburger	6	0.03
Northern European	75	0.36
Norwegian	3,020	14.48
Polish	953	4.57
Romanian	56	0.27
Russian	357	1.71
Scandinavian	259	1.24

Notes: 1. Figures in the "Number" column do not add up to the total population due to: a) Ancestry/Race overlap — e.g. persons can report being both White and Irish, b) persons of Hispanic origin can report being any race, c) persons reporting two ancestries are counted in both categories. 2. Numbers in parentheses indicate the number of persons reporting this ancestry/race alone, not in combination with any other ancestry/race. 3. Refer to the Explanation of Data in the front of the book for more detailed information.

Ancestry/Race	Number	%
Scotch-Irish	193	0.93
Scottish	249	1.19
Serbian	11	0.05
Slavic	6	0.03
Slovak	22	0.11
Slovene	28	0.13
Swedish	2,067	9.91
Swiss	60	0.29
Ukrainian	157	0.75
United States or American	367	1.76
Welsh	153	0.73
West Indian, excl. Hispanic:	14	0.07
Jamaican	14	0.07
White:	18,428	88.29
Not Hispanic (17,748)	18,055	86.50
Hispanic (340)	373	1.79
Yugoslavian	38	0.18

New Ulm

Place Type: City
County: Brown
Population: 13,594

Ancestry/Race	Number	%
African American/Black:	30	0.22
Not Hispanic (13)	26	0.19
Hispanic (2)	4	0.03
Am. Ind. or Alaska Nat., not spec.	17	0.13
American Indian tribes, specified:	34	0.25
Apache (1)	1	0.01
Blackfeet	1	0.01
Cherokee (2)	5	0.04
Chippewa (5)	8	0.06
Cree	2	0.01
Iroquois (2)	3	0.02
Latin American Indians	1	0.01
Sioux (5)	11	0.08
All other tribes	2	0.01
American Indian tribes, not spec.	2	0.01
Asian:	85	0.63
Cambodian (4)	4	0.03
Chinese, ex. Taiwanese (11)	14	0.10
Filipino (5)	9	0.07
Indian (10)	15	0.11
Japanese (3)	6	0.04
Korean (20)	24	0.18
Vietnamese (9)	9	0.07
Other Asian, specified	1	0.01
Other Asian, not specified (1)	3	0.02
Austrian	76	0.56
Basque	6	0.04
Belgian	52	0.38
Brazilian	12	0.09
British	9	0.07
Bulgarian	7	0.05
Canadian	12	0.09
Croatian	2	0.01
Czech	332	2.45
Czechoslovakian	16	0.12
Danish	211	1.56
Dutch	199	1.47
English	422	3.11
European	71	0.52
Finnish	42	0.31
French, except Basque	308	2.27
French Canadian	95	0.70
German	8,926	65.86
Greek	10	0.07
Hawaii Native/Pacific Islander:	8	0.06
Micronesian: (3)	6	0.04
Guamanian/Chamorro (3)	6	0.04
Polynesian: (1)	1	0.01
Samoan (1)	1	0.01
Other Pac. Isl., specified	1	0.01
Hispanic or Latino:	171	1.26
Central American:	5	0.04
Guatemalan	3	0.02
Panamanian	2	0.01
Cuban	2	0.01
Mexican	96	0.71
Puerto Rican	17	0.13
South American:	2	0.01
Colombian	2	0.01
Other Hispanic or Latino	49	0.36
Hungarian	19	0.14
Irish	768	5.67
Italian	51	0.38
Lithuanian	5	0.04
Luxemburger	17	0.13
Northern European	4	0.03
Norwegian	1,602	11.82
Pennsylvania German	6	0.04
Polish	262	1.93
Portuguese	10	0.07
Russian	30	0.22
Scandinavian	53	0.39
Scotch-Irish	68	0.50
Scottish	55	0.41
Slovene	36	0.27
Swedish	680	5.02
Swiss	25	0.18
United States or American	513	3.79
Welsh	36	0.27
West Indian, excl. Hispanic:	8	0.06
British West Indian	8	0.06
White:	13,417	98.70
Not Hispanic (13,253)	13,325	98.02
Hispanic (83)	92	0.68
Yugoslavian	22	0.16

North Mankato

Place Type: City
County: Nicollet
Population: 11,798

Ancestry/Race	Number	%
Acadian/Cajun	8	0.07
African American/Black:	124	1.05
Not Hispanic (71)	118	1.00
Hispanic (6)	6	0.05
African, sub-Saharan:	47	0.40
African	5	0.04
Somalian	42	0.36
Alaska Native tribes, specified:	1	0.01
Eskimo (1)	1	0.01
Am. Ind. or Alaska Nat., not spec.	23	0.19
Albanian	7	0.06
American Indian tribes, specified:	33	0.28
Apache (1)	1	0.01
Cherokee (2)	7	0.06
Chippewa (10)	11	0.09
Cree (1)	2	0.02
Delaware (1)	1	0.01
Latin American Indians	1	0.01
Sioux (7)	8	0.07
All other tribes (2)	2	0.02
American Indian tribes, not spec.	1	0.01
Arab:	7	0.06
Lebanese	2	0.02
Syrian	5	0.04
Asian:	176	1.49
Chinese, ex. Taiwanese (29)	31	0.26
Filipino (15)	18	0.15
Hmong (9)	9	0.08
Indian (20)	21	0.18
Indonesian (1)	4	0.03
Japanese (6)	10	0.08
Korean (30)	30	0.25
Pakistani (4)	4	0.03
Thai (1)	1	0.01
Vietnamese (44)	44	0.37
Other Asian, specified (1)	1	0.01
Other Asian, not specified (3)	3	0.03
Austrian	49	0.41
Belgian	86	0.73
British	20	0.17
Canadian	28	0.24
Czech	222	1.88
Czechoslovakian	27	0.23
Danish	329	2.79
Dutch	171	1.45
English	817	6.92
European	45	0.38
Finnish	68	0.58
French, except Basque	342	2.90
French Canadian	105	0.89
German	6,446	54.59
Greek	6	0.05
Hawaii Native/Pacific Islander:	9	0.08
Micronesian: (1)	1	0.01
Guamanian/Chamorro (1)	1	0.01
Polynesian: (3)	5	0.04
Native Hawaiian (1)	2	0.02
Samoan (2)	3	0.03
Other Pac. Isl., not spec.	3	0.03
Hispanic or Latino:	188	1.59
Central American:	7	0.06
Guatemalan	3	0.03
Nicaraguan	3	0.03
Other Central American	1	0.01
Cuban	2	0.02
Mexican	125	1.06
Puerto Rican	12	0.10
South American:	3	0.03
Argentinean	1	0.01
Chilean	1	0.01
Colombian	1	0.01
Other Hispanic or Latino	39	0.33
Hungarian	1	0.01
Icelander	35	0.30
Iranian	9	0.08
Irish	1,241	10.51
Italian	155	1.31
Luxemburger	29	0.25
Norwegian	1,941	16.44
Pennsylvania German	9	0.08
Polish	346	2.93
Romanian	18	0.15
Russian	33	0.28
Scandinavian	66	0.56
Scotch-Irish	177	1.50
Scottish	127	1.08
Serbian	5	0.04
Swedish	929	7.87
Swiss	50	0.42
Ukrainian	13	0.11
United States or American	415	3.51
Welsh	151	1.28
West Indian, excl. Hispanic:	16	0.14
West Indian	16	0.14
White:	11,451	97.06
Not Hispanic (11,266)	11,325	95.99
Hispanic (115)	126	1.07
Yugoslavian	1	0.01

North Saint Paul

Place Type: City
County: Ramsey
Population: 11,929

Ancestry/Race	Number	%
African American/Black:	370	3.10
Not Hispanic (303)	357	2.99
Hispanic (10)	13	0.11
African, sub-Saharan:	157	1.32
African	68	0.57
Kenyan	11	0.09
Sudanese	48	0.40
Other sub-Saharan African	30	0.25
Am. Ind. or Alaska Nat., not spec.	31	0.26
Albanian	15	0.13
American Indian tribes, specified:	91	0.76
Cherokee (2)	5	0.04
Chippewa (29)	47	0.39
Comanche (1)	1	0.01
Cree (1)	1	0.01
Iroquois (2)	5	0.04

Notes: 1. Figures in the "Number" column do not add up to the total population due to: a) Ancestry/Race overlap — e.g. persons can report being both White and Irish, b) persons of Hispanic origin can report being any race, c) persons reporting two ancestries are counted in both categories. 2. Numbers in parentheses indicate the number of persons reporting this ancestry/race alone, not in combination with any other ancestry/race. 3. Refer to the Explanation of Data in the front of the book for more detailed information.

Ancestry/Race	Number	%
Navajo	1	0.01
Potawatomi (1)	1	0.01
Sioux (9)	24	0.20
All other tribes (1)	6	0.05
American Indian tribes, not spec.	6	0.05
Arab:	52	0.44
Jordanian	10	0.08
Lebanese	33	0.28
Syrian	9	0.08
Asian:	233	1.95
Cambodian (6)	11	0.09
Chinese, ex. Taiwanese (32)	36	0.30
Filipino (18)	26	0.22
Hmong (78)	79	0.66
Indian (15)	15	0.13
Japanese (3)	9	0.08
Korean (31)	35	0.29
Laotian (2)	2	0.02
Taiwanese	2	0.02
Thai (2)	3	0.03
Vietnamese (8)	9	0.08
Other Asian, not specified (6)	6	0.05
Australian	6	0.05
Austrian	68	0.57
Basque	4	0.03
British	18	0.15
Canadian	10	0.08
Croatian	35	0.29
Czech	206	1.73
Czechoslovakian	45	0.38
Danish	181	1.52
Dutch	144	1.21
English	733	6.14
European	58	0.49
Finnish	115	0.96
French, except Basque	772	6.47
French Canadian	268	2.25
German	4,758	39.87
Greek	6	0.05
Hawaii Native/Pacific Islander:	10	0.08
Micronesian: (3)	6	0.05
Guamanian/Chamorro (2)	2	0.02
Other Micronesian (1)	4	0.03
Polynesian:	3	0.03
Native Hawaiian	3	0.03
Other Pac. Isl., not spec. (1)	1	0.01
Hispanic or Latino:	281	2.36
Central American:	19	0.16
Guatemalan	12	0.10
Salvadoran	6	0.05
Other Central American	1	0.01
Cuban	5	0.04
Mexican	192	1.61
Puerto Rican	20	0.17
South American:	7	0.06
Colombian	6	0.05
Venezuelan	1	0.01
Other Hispanic or Latino	38	0.32
Hungarian	43	0.36
Irish	1,852	15.52
Italian	491	4.11
Latvian	5	0.04
Northern European	5	0.04
Norwegian	1,457	12.21
Pennsylvania German	7	0.06
Polish	727	6.09
Romanian	38	0.32
Russian	27	0.23
Scandinavian	142	1.19
Scotch-Irish	74	0.62
Scottish	156	1.31
Serbian	44	0.37
Slavic	5	0.04
Slovak	6	0.05
Slovene	6	0.05
Swedish	1,305	10.94
Swiss	124	1.04
Turkish	17	0.14
Ukrainian	6	0.05
United States or American	305	2.56
Welsh	35	0.29
White:	11,240	94.22
Not Hispanic (10,923)	11,064	92.75
Hispanic (154)	176	1.48
Yugoslavian	62	0.52

Northfield

Place Type: City
County: Rice
Population: 17,147

Ancestry/Race	Number	%
Acadian/Cajun	5	0.03
African American/Black:	233	1.36
Not Hispanic (149)	218	1.27
Hispanic (5)	15	0.09
African, sub-Saharan:	99	0.58
African	27	0.16
Nigerian	7	0.04
Other sub-Saharan African	65	0.38
Alaska Native tribes, specified:	1	0.01
Aleut (1)	1	0.01
Am. Ind. or Alaska Nat., not spec.	67	0.39
Albanian	6	0.04
American Indian tribes, specified:	81	0.47
Apache (1)	1	0.01
Blackfeet	1	0.01
Cherokee	13	0.08
Chippewa (9)	15	0.09
Choctaw (6)	7	0.04
Creek	1	0.01
Iroquois (2)	3	0.02
Latin American Indians (18)	24	0.14
Navajo (4)	4	0.02
Sioux (4)	8	0.05
All other tribes (1)	4	0.02
American Indian tribes, not spec.	5	0.03
Arab:	36	0.21
Egyptian	11	0.06
Lebanese	15	0.09
Palestinian	2	0.01
Syrian	8	0.05
Armenian	11	0.06
Asian:	532	3.10
Cambodian (3)	3	0.02
Chinese, ex. Taiwanese (92)	117	0.68
Filipino (17)	42	0.24
Hmong (24)	26	0.15
Indian (53)	75	0.44
Indonesian	2	0.01
Japanese (28)	57	0.33
Korean (84)	97	0.57
Malaysian	4	0.02
Pakistani (3)	4	0.02
Sri Lankan (6)	6	0.03
Taiwanese (2)	2	0.01
Thai (7)	12	0.07
Vietnamese (68)	68	0.40
Other Asian, specified (1)	2	0.01
Other Asian, not specified (12)	15	0.09
Australian	7	0.04
Austrian	29	0.17
Basque	6	0.04
Belgian	40	0.23
Brazilian	14	0.08
British	160	0.93
Canadian	20	0.12
Celtic	2	0.01
Croatian	40	0.23
Czech	514	3.00
Czechoslovakian	161	0.94
Danish	432	2.52
Dutch	385	2.25
Eastern European	22	0.13
English	1,792	10.47
Estonian	5	0.03
European	245	1.43
Finnish	205	1.20
French, except Basque	552	3.22
French Canadian	147	0.86
German	5,553	32.44
Greek	40	0.23
Hawaii Native/Pacific Islander:	24	0.14
Micronesian: (1)	2	0.01
Guamanian/Chamorro (1)	2	0.01
Polynesian: (7)	19	0.11
Native Hawaiian (6)	16	0.09
Samoan (1)	2	0.01
Other Polynesian	1	0.01
Other Pac. Isl., specified	1	0.01
Other Pac. Isl., not spec.	2	0.01
Hispanic or Latino:	982	5.73
Central American:	32	0.19
Costa Rican	6	0.03
Guatemalan	13	0.08
Nicaraguan	1	0.01
Panamanian	1	0.01
Salvadoran	11	0.06
Cuban	19	0.11
Mexican	767	4.47
Puerto Rican	23	0.13
South American:	39	0.23
Argentinean	9	0.05
Chilean	2	0.01
Colombian	17	0.10
Ecuadorian	1	0.01
Peruvian	8	0.05
Venezuelan	2	0.01
Other Hispanic or Latino	102	0.59
Hungarian	11	0.06
Icelander	21	0.12
Iranian	18	0.11
Irish	1,837	10.73
Italian	372	2.17
Latvian	22	0.13
Lithuanian	10	0.06
Northern European	32	0.19
Norwegian	3,425	20.01
Pennsylvania German	12	0.07
Polish	462	2.70
Portuguese	10	0.06
Russian	132	0.77
Scandinavian	162	0.95
Scotch-Irish	243	1.42
Scottish	450	2.63
Slavic	7	0.04
Slovak	28	0.16
Slovene	11	0.06
Swedish	1,533	8.96
Swiss	130	0.76
Ukrainian	33	0.19
United States or American	516	3.01
Welsh	82	0.48
White:	16,193	94.44
Not Hispanic (15,324)	15,537	90.61
Hispanic (549)	656	3.83
Yugoslavian	32	0.19

Oakdale

Place Type: City
County: Washington
Population: 26,653

Ancestry/Race	Number	%
African American/Black:	799	3.00
Not Hispanic (599)	770	2.89
Hispanic (12)	29	0.11
African, sub-Saharan:	143	0.54
African	78	0.29
Ethiopian	23	0.09
Ghanian	32	0.12
Nigerian	10	0.04
Am. Ind. or Alaska Nat., not spec.	76	0.29
Albanian	6	0.02
American Indian tribes, specified:	128	0.48
Blackfeet (1)	1	0.00
Cherokee (1)	3	0.01
Chippewa (36)	67	0.25

Notes: 1. Figures in the "Number" column do not add up to the total population due to: a) Ancestry/Race overlap — e.g. persons can report being both White and Irish, b) persons of Hispanic origin can report being any race, c) persons reporting two ancestries are counted in both categories. 2. Numbers in parentheses indicate the number of persons reporting this ancestry/race alone, not in combination with any other ancestry/race. 3. Refer to the Explanation of Data in the front of the book for more detailed information.

Ancestry/Race	Number	%
Choctaw (1)	1	0.00
Comanche	3	0.01
Cree (1)	1	0.00
Iroquois (3)	5	0.02
Latin American Indians	1	0.00
Lumbee (3)	3	0.01
Potawatomi (1)	1	0.00
Seminole	5	0.02
Sioux (6)	21	0.08
All other tribes (7)	16	0.06
American Indian tribes, not spec.	10	0.04
Arab:	66	0.25
Arab/Arabic	7	0.03
Lebanese	47	0.18
Syrian	12	0.04
Asian:	803	3.01
Cambodian (50)	55	0.21
Chinese, ex. Taiwanese (62)	90	0.34
Filipino (48)	76	0.29
Hmong (189)	219	0.82
Indian (93)	100	0.38
Indonesian (2)	4	0.02
Japanese (20)	40	0.15
Korean (50)	75	0.28
Laotian (15)	20	0.08
Malaysian (1)	1	0.00
Thai (6)	9	0.03
Vietnamese (69)	83	0.31
Other Asian, specified	1	0.00
Other Asian, not specified (20)	30	0.11
Austrian	136	0.51
Belgian	67	0.25
British	53	0.20
Bulgarian	6	0.02
Croatian	55	0.21
Czech	489	1.83
Czechoslovakian	116	0.43
Danish	354	1.33
Dutch	339	1.27
Eastern European	9	0.03
English	1,399	5.25
European	219	0.82
Finnish	260	0.97
French, except Basque	1,545	5.79
French Canadian	513	1.92
German	11,078	41.54
Greek	73	0.27
Hawaii Native/Pacific Islander:	23	0.09
Micronesian: (1)	8	0.03
Guamanian/Chamorro (1)	7	0.03
Other Micronesian	1	0.00
Polynesian:	4	0.02
Native Hawaiian	2	0.01
Samoan	1	0.00
Tongan	1	0.00
Other Pac. Isl., not spec. (1)	11	0.04
Hispanic or Latino:	732	2.75
Central American:	18	0.07
Costa Rican	2	0.01
Guatemalan	7	0.03
Honduran	1	0.00
Nicaraguan	5	0.02
Panamanian	3	0.01
Cuban	19	0.07
Dominican Republic	3	0.01
Mexican	539	2.02
Puerto Rican	38	0.14
South American:	11	0.04
Chilean	2	0.01
Colombian	6	0.02
Paraguayan	3	0.01
Other Hispanic or Latino	104	0.39
Hungarian	80	0.30
Irish	4,240	15.90
Italian	1,380	5.17
Latvian	23	0.09
Luxemburger	49	0.18
Northern European	12	0.04
Norwegian	3,804	14.26
Pennsylvania German	7	0.03
Polish	1,598	5.99
Romanian	55	0.21
Russian	165	0.62
Scandinavian	355	1.33
Scotch-Irish	198	0.74
Scottish	233	0.87
Serbian	8	0.03
Slovak	24	0.09
Slovene	40	0.15
Swedish	2,634	9.88
Swiss	144	0.54
Turkish	21	0.08
Ukrainian	35	0.13
United States or American	865	3.24
Welsh	120	0.45
West Indian, excl. Hispanic:	8	0.03
Jamaican	8	0.03
White:	25,016	93.86
Not Hispanic (24,168)	24,497	91.91
Hispanic (408)	519	1.95
Yugoslavian	17	0.06

Owatonna

Place Type: City
County: Steele
Population: 22,434

Ancestry/Race	Number	%
African American/Black:	518	2.31
Not Hispanic (348)	513	2.29
Hispanic (3)	5	0.02
African, sub-Saharan:	445	1.99
African	12	0.05
Somalian	433	1.93
Alaska Native tribes, specified:	4	0.02
Aleut	1	0.00
Eskimo (1)	3	0.01
Am. Ind. or Alaska Nat., not spec.	17	0.08
American Indian tribes, specified:	46	0.21
Cherokee (3)	11	0.05
Chippewa (8)	15	0.07
Choctaw (1)	1	0.00
Comanche	1	0.00
Latin American Indians (1)	1	0.00
Lumbee	1	0.00
Potawatomi	3	0.01
Pueblo	3	0.01
Sioux (3)	5	0.02
Ute (1)	1	0.00
All other tribes (3)	4	0.02
American Indian tribes, not spec.	5	0.02
Asian:	269	1.20
Bangladeshi (2)	2	0.01
Cambodian (1)	2	0.01
Chinese, ex. Taiwanese (26)	27	0.12
Filipino (16)	25	0.11
Hmong (44)	63	0.28
Indian (37)	40	0.18
Japanese (11)	19	0.08
Korean (21)	23	0.10
Laotian (15)	15	0.07
Pakistani (5)	6	0.03
Taiwanese (2)	2	0.01
Thai	1	0.00
Vietnamese (39)	40	0.18
Other Asian, not specified (3)	4	0.02
Austrian	66	0.29
Belgian	47	0.21
Brazilian	15	0.07
British	35	0.16
Canadian	37	0.17
Croatian	11	0.05
Czech	1,376	6.14
Czechoslovakian	146	0.65
Danish	606	2.70
Dutch	509	2.27
English	1,213	5.41
European	134	0.60
Finnish	146	0.65
French, except Basque	820	3.66
French Canadian	128	0.57
German	9,461	42.21
Greek	41	0.18
Hawaii Native/Pacific Islander:	16	0.07
Other Pac. Isl., not spec. (7)	16	0.07
Hispanic or Latino:	967	4.31
Central American:	1	0.00
Guatemalan	1	0.00
Cuban	11	0.05
Mexican	724	3.23
Puerto Rican	19	0.08
South American:	15	0.07
Colombian	8	0.04
Ecuadorian	3	0.01
Other South American	4	0.02
Other Hispanic or Latino	197	0.88
Hungarian	59	0.26
Icelander	16	0.07
Irish	1,944	8.67
Italian	161	0.72
Lithuanian	5	0.02
Luxemburger	53	0.24
Norwegian	4,384	19.56
Pennsylvania German	18	0.08
Polish	791	3.53
Portuguese	9	0.04
Russian	33	0.15
Scandinavian	156	0.70
Scotch-Irish	203	0.91
Scottish	261	1.16
Slovak	33	0.15
Slovene	32	0.14
Swedish	1,051	4.69
Swiss	120	0.54
Ukrainian	48	0.21
United States or American	766	3.42
Welsh	115	0.51
White:	21,252	94.73
Not Hispanic (20,604)	20,710	92.32
Hispanic (504)	542	2.42
Yugoslavian	28	0.12

Plymouth

Place Type: City
County: Hennepin
Population: 65,894

Ancestry/Race	Number	%
African American/Black:	2,118	3.21
Not Hispanic (1,751)	2,050	3.11
Hispanic (32)	68	0.10
African, sub-Saharan:	426	0.65
African	169	0.26
Cape Verdean	5	0.01
Ethiopian	10	0.02
Kenyan	11	0.02
Liberian	57	0.09
Nigerian	108	0.16
Somalian	9	0.01
South African	33	0.05
Other sub-Saharan African	24	0.04
Alaska Native tribes, specified:	6	0.01
Alaska Athabascan (2)	2	0.00
Aleut	1	0.00
Tlingit-Haida	2	0.00
All other tribes (1)	1	0.00
Am. Ind. or Alaska Nat., not spec.	149	0.23
Albanian	13	0.02
American Indian tribes, specified:	205	0.31
Blackfeet	5	0.01
Cherokee (3)	16	0.02
Chippewa (71)	111	0.17
Choctaw (1)	1	0.00
Creek (1)	1	0.00
Crow (1)	2	0.00
Delaware	2	0.00
Iroquois (1)	3	0.00
Latin American Indians (7)	12	0.02

Notes: 1. Figures in the "Number" column do not add up to the total population due to: a) Ancestry/Race overlap — e.g. persons can report being both White and Irish, b) persons of Hispanic origin can report being any race, c) persons reporting two ancestries are counted in both categories. 2. Numbers in parentheses indicate the number of persons reporting this ancestry/race alone, not in combination with any other ancestry/race. 3. Refer to the Explanation of Data in the front of the book for more detailed information.

Ancestry/Race	Number	%
Navajo	1	0.00
Potawatomi (2)	2	0.00
Pueblo	1	0.00
Sioux (19)	30	0.05
Yuman (1)	1	0.00
All other tribes (11)	17	0.03
American Indian tribes, not spec.	24	0.04
Arab:	293	0.44
Egyptian	88	0.13
Lebanese	138	0.21
Palestinian	8	0.01
Syrian	13	0.02
Other Arab	46	0.07
Armenian	17	0.03
Asian:	2,835	4.30
Bangladeshi (18)	18	0.03
Cambodian (17)	22	0.03
Chinese, ex. Taiwanese (594)	652	0.99
Filipino (103)	147	0.22
Hmong (8)	14	0.02
Indian (797)	858	1.30
Indonesian (7)	7	0.01
Japanese (73)	123	0.19
Korean (373)	421	0.64
Laotian (37)	45	0.07
Malaysian	5	0.01
Pakistani (31)	39	0.06
Sri Lankan (19)	21	0.03
Taiwanese (20)	25	0.04
Thai (24)	27	0.04
Vietnamese (283)	311	0.47
Other Asian, specified (12)	12	0.02
Other Asian, not specified (41)	88	0.13
Austrian	308	0.47
Basque	6	0.01
Belgian	221	0.34
Brazilian	21	0.03
British	282	0.43
Bulgarian	48	0.07
Canadian	209	0.32
Celtic	7	0.01
Croatian	126	0.19
Cypriot	5	0.01
Czech	879	1.33
Czechoslovakian	147	0.22
Danish	1,098	1.67
Dutch	1,089	1.65
Eastern European	230	0.35
English	5,274	8.00
Estonian	7	0.01
European	743	1.13
Finnish	1,428	2.17
French, except Basque	2,707	4.11
French Canadian	656	1.00
German	22,230	33.73
Greek	171	0.26
Hawaii Native/Pacific Islander:	41	0.06
Micronesian: (5)	5	0.01
Guamanian/Chamorro (5)	5	0.01
Polynesian: (2)	16	0.02
Native Hawaiian (2)	16	0.02
Other Pac. Isl., not spec. (2)	20	0.03
Hispanic or Latino:	1,079	1.64
Central American:	59	0.09
Costa Rican	4	0.01
Guatemalan	19	0.03
Honduran	7	0.01
Nicaraguan	3	0.00
Panamanian	13	0.02
Salvadoran	11	0.02
Other Central American	2	0.00
Cuban	46	0.07
Mexican	496	0.75
Puerto Rican	80	0.12
South American:	159	0.24
Argentinean	8	0.01
Bolivian	3	0.00
Chilean	13	0.02
Colombian	75	0.11
Ecuadorian	8	0.01
Paraguayan	6	0.01
Peruvian	20	0.03
Venezuelan	18	0.03
Other South American	8	0.01
Other Hispanic or Latino	239	0.36
Hungarian	324	0.49
Icelander	64	0.10
Iranian	108	0.16
Irish	8,497	12.89
Israeli	26	0.04
Italian	2,131	3.23
Latvian	79	0.12
Lithuanian	116	0.18
Luxemburger	114	0.17
Maltese	6	0.01
Northern European	93	0.14
Norwegian	10,577	16.05
Pennsylvania German	5	0.01
Polish	3,456	5.24
Portuguese	86	0.13
Romanian	174	0.26
Russian	1,715	2.60
Scandinavian	1,014	1.54
Scotch-Irish	666	1.01
Scottish	1,124	1.71
Serbian	88	0.13
Slavic	75	0.11
Slovak	144	0.22
Slovene	62	0.09
Swedish	7,222	10.96
Swiss	298	0.45
Turkish	27	0.04
Ukrainian	283	0.43
United States or American	2,179	3.31
Welsh	386	0.59
West Indian, excl. Hispanic:	62	0.09
Haitian	38	0.06
Jamaican	24	0.04
White:	60,969	92.53
Not Hispanic (59,565)	60,227	91.40
Hispanic (635)	742	1.13
Yugoslavian	106	0.16

Prior Lake

Place Type: City
County: Scott
Population: 15,917

Ancestry/Race	Number	%
African American/Black:	174	1.09
Not Hispanic (119)	167	1.05
Hispanic (3)	7	0.04
African, sub-Saharan:	7	0.04
African	7	0.04
Alaska Native tribes, specified:	3	0.02
Tlingit-Haida (3)	3	0.02
Am. Ind. or Alaska Nat., not spec.	78	0.49
American Indian tribes, specified:	342	2.15
Apache	4	0.03
Cherokee (2)	3	0.02
Chippewa (45)	70	0.44
Choctaw (1)	3	0.02
Creek (1)	1	0.01
Iroquois (2)	2	0.01
Latin American Indians	3	0.02
Navajo (3)	3	0.02
Sioux (216)	250	1.57
All other tribes (3)	3	0.02
American Indian tribes, not spec.	22	0.14
Arab:	18	0.11
Arab/Arabic	9	0.06
Lebanese	9	0.06
Asian:	196	1.23
Cambodian (8)	12	0.08
Chinese, ex. Taiwanese (33)	44	0.28
Filipino (10)	20	0.13
Indian (10)	15	0.09
Indonesian (1)	1	0.01
Japanese (9)	12	0.08
Korean (35)	46	0.29
Laotian (7)	9	0.06
Malaysian	1	0.01
Sri Lankan (4)	4	0.03
Thai (2)	2	0.01
Vietnamese (19)	20	0.13
Other Asian, not specified (9)	10	0.06
Austrian	31	0.19
Belgian	14	0.09
British	69	0.43
Canadian	18	0.11
Celtic	8	0.05
Croatian	9	0.06
Czech	561	3.52
Czechoslovakian	41	0.26
Danish	276	1.73
Dutch	305	1.91
Eastern European	18	0.11
English	948	5.95
Estonian	2	0.01
European	95	0.60
Finnish	286	1.79
French, except Basque	509	3.19
French Canadian	108	0.68
German	6,435	40.38
Greek	25	0.16
Hawaii Native/Pacific Islander:	13	0.08
Polynesian: (5)	7	0.04
Native Hawaiian (2)	4	0.03
Samoan (3)	3	0.02
Other Pac. Isl., not spec. (2)	6	0.04
Hispanic or Latino:	177	1.11
Central American:	5	0.03
Panamanian	1	0.01
Salvadoran	4	0.03
Cuban	5	0.03
Mexican	104	0.65
Puerto Rican	26	0.16
South American:	13	0.08
Argentinean	1	0.01
Chilean	3	0.02
Colombian	5	0.03
Peruvian	1	0.01
Venezuelan	3	0.02
Other Hispanic or Latino	24	0.15
Hungarian	8	0.05
Icelander	9	0.06
Iranian	45	0.28
Irish	2,484	15.59
Italian	375	2.35
Latvian	9	0.06
Lithuanian	7	0.04
Luxemburger	20	0.13
Northern European	34	0.21
Norwegian	2,808	17.62
Pennsylvania German	8	0.05
Polish	736	4.62
Portuguese	9	0.06
Romanian	42	0.26
Russian	156	0.98
Scandinavian	249	1.56
Scotch-Irish	190	1.19
Scottish	158	0.99
Serbian	32	0.20
Slovak	38	0.24
Slovene	11	0.07
Swedish	1,609	10.10
Swiss	86	0.54
Ukrainian	14	0.09
United States or American	613	3.85
Welsh	59	0.37
White:	15,238	95.73
Not Hispanic (14,951)	15,127	95.04
Hispanic (95)	111	0.70

Notes: 1. Figures in the "Number" column do not add up to the total population due to: a) Ancestry/Race overlap — e.g. persons can report being both White and Irish, b) persons of Hispanic origin can report being any race, c) persons reporting two ancestries are counted in both categories. 2. Numbers in parentheses indicate the number of persons reporting this ancestry/race alone, not in combination with any other ancestry/race. 3. Refer to the Explanation of Data in the front of the book for more detailed information.

Ramsey

Place Type: City
County: Anoka
Population: 18,510

Ancestry/Race	Number	%
African American/Black:	100	0.54
Not Hispanic (58)	100	0.54
Am. Ind. or Alaska Nat., not spec.	64	0.35
American Indian tribes, specified:	125	0.68
Cherokee (4)	9	0.05
Chippewa (46)	85	0.46
Choctaw	1	0.01
Creek (4)	4	0.02
Iroquois	4	0.02
Latin American Indians (2)	2	0.01
Navajo	3	0.02
Pima	2	0.01
Pueblo	1	0.01
Sioux (6)	10	0.05
All other tribes (1)	4	0.02
American Indian tribes, not spec.	7	0.04
Arab:	38	0.21
Lebanese	38	0.21
Asian:	234	1.26
Cambodian (2)	6	0.03
Chinese, ex. Taiwanese (33)	34	0.18
Filipino (17)	25	0.14
Hmong (32)	32	0.17
Indian (16)	19	0.10
Japanese (5)	15	0.08
Korean (47)	53	0.29
Laotian	1	0.01
Thai (4)	7	0.04
Vietnamese (14)	24	0.13
Other Asian, not specified (11)	18	0.10
Australian	9	0.05
Austrian	47	0.25
Belgian	54	0.29
British	35	0.19
Croatian	11	0.06
Czech	299	1.62
Czechoslovakian	57	0.31
Danish	467	2.53
Dutch	279	1.51
Eastern European	9	0.05
English	1,159	6.27
European	62	0.34
Finnish	504	2.73
French, except Basque	1,004	5.43
French Canadian	354	1.91
German	7,539	40.77
Greek	126	0.68
Hawaii Native/Pacific Islander:	5	0.03
Micronesian:	2	0.01
Guamanian/Chamorro	2	0.01
Polynesian: (1)	1	0.01
Samoan (1)	1	0.01
Other Pac. Isl., not spec.	2	0.01
Hispanic or Latino:	221	1.19
Central American:	5	0.03
Costa Rican	1	0.01
Guatemalan	3	0.02
Nicaraguan	1	0.01
Cuban	1	0.01
Mexican	147	0.79
Puerto Rican	16	0.09
South American:	19	0.10
Colombian	9	0.05
Paraguayan	1	0.01
Venezuelan	9	0.05
Other Hispanic or Latino	33	0.18
Hungarian	69	0.37
Icelander	24	0.13
Irish	2,235	12.09
Italian	285	1.54
Luxemburger	16	0.09
Northern European	34	0.18
Norwegian	3,586	19.39
Pennsylvania German	8	0.04
Polish	1,683	9.10
Russian	58	0.31
Scandinavian	382	2.07
Scotch-Irish	139	0.75
Scottish	107	0.58
Slavic	12	0.06
Slovak	17	0.09
Slovene	33	0.18
Swedish	2,406	13.01
Swiss	48	0.26
Ukrainian	52	0.28
United States or American	615	3.33
Welsh	80	0.43
White:	18,114	97.86
Not Hispanic (17,769)	17,942	96.93
Hispanic (149)	172	0.93
Yugoslavian	17	0.09

Red Wing

Place Type: City
County: Goodhue
Population: 16,116

Ancestry/Race	Number	%
African American/Black:	272	1.69
Not Hispanic (206)	260	1.61
Hispanic (7)	12	0.07
African, sub-Saharan:	11	0.07
African	2	0.01
Ghanian	9	0.06
Am. Ind. or Alaska Nat., not spec.	88	0.55
American Indian tribes, specified:	317	1.97
Cherokee	5	0.03
Chippewa (33)	45	0.28
Choctaw (1)	1	0.01
Comanche (1)	1	0.01
Cree (2)	3	0.02
Crow (4)	4	0.02
Delaware (1)	1	0.01
Iroquois (1)	1	0.01
Latin American Indians	5	0.03
Menominee	2	0.01
Potawatomi (2)	2	0.01
Sioux (218)	233	1.45
Yuman (1)	1	0.01
All other tribes (6)	13	0.08
American Indian tribes, not spec.	14	0.09
Arab:	9	0.06
Palestinian	9	0.06
Asian:	136	0.84
Chinese, ex. Taiwanese (17)	17	0.11
Filipino (9)	12	0.07
Hmong (4)	5	0.03
Indian (8)	12	0.07
Japanese (2)	2	0.01
Korean (26)	31	0.19
Malaysian (2)	2	0.01
Thai (1)	2	0.01
Vietnamese (44)	45	0.28
Other Asian, not specified (5)	8	0.05
Austrian	54	0.33
Belgian	10	0.06
British	44	0.27
Bulgarian	8	0.05
Canadian	17	0.11
Croatian	18	0.11
Czech	226	1.40
Czechoslovakian	70	0.43
Danish	271	1.68
Dutch	208	1.29
English	794	4.92
European	139	0.86
Finnish	178	1.10
French, except Basque	337	2.09
French Canadian	179	1.11
German	6,879	42.63
Greek	8	0.05
Hawaii Native/Pacific Islander:	17	0.11
Micronesian: (5)	8	0.05
Guamanian/Chamorro (4)	4	0.02
Other Micronesian (1)	4	0.02
Polynesian: (2)	4	0.02
Native Hawaiian (2)	4	0.02
Other Pac. Isl., not spec. (1)	5	0.03
Hispanic or Latino:	205	1.27
Central American:	10	0.06
Guatemalan	2	0.01
Panamanian	3	0.02
Salvadoran	5	0.03
Cuban	3	0.02
Dominican Republic	1	0.01
Mexican	144	0.89
Puerto Rican	14	0.09
South American:	3	0.02
Chilean	1	0.01
Colombian	1	0.01
Other South American	1	0.01
Other Hispanic or Latino	30	0.19
Hungarian	64	0.40
Icelander	10	0.06
Irish	1,882	11.66
Italian	146	0.90
Latvian	3	0.02
Lithuanian	9	0.06
Luxemburger	19	0.12
Northern European	16	0.10
Norwegian	3,241	20.09
Pennsylvania German	15	0.09
Polish	485	3.01
Portuguese	12	0.07
Russian	3	0.02
Scandinavian	222	1.38
Scotch-Irish	104	0.64
Scottish	205	1.27
Serbian	5	0.03
Slovak	24	0.15
Slovene	4	0.02
Swedish	2,047	12.69
Swiss	159	0.99
Ukrainian	32	0.20
United States or American	511	3.17
Welsh	89	0.55
West Indian, excl. Hispanic:	10	0.06
Haitian	8	0.05
West Indian	2	0.01
White:	15,318	95.05
Not Hispanic (15,121)	15,219	94.43
Hispanic (81)	99	0.61
Yugoslavian	10	0.06

Richfield

Place Type: City
County: Hennepin
Population: 34,439

Ancestry/Race	Number	%
African American/Black:	2,735	7.94
Not Hispanic (2,257)	2,668	7.75
Hispanic (32)	67	0.19
African, sub-Saharan:	539	1.56
African	306	0.89
Ethiopian	122	0.35
Ghanian	28	0.08
Liberian	28	0.08
Nigerian	14	0.04
Somalian	18	0.05
South African	16	0.05
Other sub-Saharan African	7	0.02
Alaska Native tribes, specified:	2	0.01
Aleut (1)	2	0.01
Am. Ind. or Alaska Nat., not spec.	147	0.43
American Indian tribes, specified:	289	0.84
Apache (2)	2	0.01
Blackfeet (1)	7	0.02
Cherokee (6)	19	0.06
Cheyenne	1	0.00
Chippewa (102)	145	0.42

Notes: 1. Figures in the "Number" column do not add up to the total population due to: a) Ancestry/Race overlap — e.g. persons can report being both White and Irish, b) persons of Hispanic origin can report being any race, c) persons reporting two ancestries are counted in both categories. 2. Numbers in parentheses indicate the number of persons reporting this ancestry/race alone, not in combination with any other ancestry/race. 3. Refer to the Explanation of Data in the front of the book for more detailed information.

Choctaw (1)	1	0.00
Comanche (1)	1	0.00
Creek	5	0.01
Crow (1)	1	0.00
Iroquois (2)	6	0.02
Latin American Indians (22)	27	0.08
Menominee (1)	1	0.00
Navajo	3	0.01
Shoshone (3)	3	0.01
Sioux (21)	38	0.11
All other tribes (13)	29	0.08
American Indian tribes, not spec.	15	0.04
Arab:	20	0.06
Egyptian	5	0.01
Lebanese	9	0.03
Palestinian	6	0.02
Armenian	15	0.04
Asian:	2,171	6.30
Bangladeshi (3)	8	0.02
Cambodian (135)	178	0.52
Chinese, ex. Taiwanese (249)	307	0.89
Filipino (91)	121	0.35
Hmong (19)	22	0.06
Indian (295)	380	1.10
Indonesian (2)	2	0.01
Japanese (33)	56	0.16
Korean (89)	106	0.31
Laotian (281)	320	0.93
Pakistani (16)	20	0.06
Sri Lankan (29)	33	0.10
Taiwanese (3)	5	0.01
Thai (9)	17	0.05
Vietnamese (459)	511	1.48
Other Asian, specified (9)	13	0.04
Other Asian, not specified (30)	72	0.21
Australian	32	0.09
Austrian	99	0.29
Belgian	96	0.28
Brazilian	9	0.03
British	95	0.28
Bulgarian	27	0.08
Canadian	94	0.27
Croatian	50	0.15
Czech	397	1.15
Czechoslovakian	122	0.35
Danish	561	1.63
Dutch	620	1.80
Eastern European	5	0.01
English	2,328	6.76
European	143	0.42
Finnish	477	1.38
French, except Basque	1,319	3.83
French Canadian	388	1.13
German	9,849	28.60
German Russian	31	0.09
Greek	197	0.57
Guyanese	50	0.15
Hawaii Native/Pacific Islander:	46	0.13
Melanesian: (2)	2	0.01
Fijian (2)	2	0.01
Micronesian: (3)	7	0.02
Guamanian/Chamorro (3)	5	0.01
Other Micronesian	2	0.01
Polynesian: (6)	14	0.04
Native Hawaiian (4)	10	0.03
Samoan (2)	3	0.01
Tongan	1	0.00
Other Pac. Isl., specified	3	0.01
Other Pac. Isl., not spec. (3)	20	0.06
Hispanic or Latino:	2,158	6.27
Central American:	185	0.54
Costa Rican	13	0.04
Guatemalan	14	0.04
Honduran	7	0.02
Nicaraguan	3	0.01
Panamanian	13	0.04
Salvadoran	132	0.38
Other Central American	3	0.01
Cuban	25	0.07
Dominican Republic	4	0.01
Mexican	1,546	4.49
Puerto Rican	70	0.20
South American:	71	0.21
Argentinean	3	0.01
Bolivian	2	0.01
Chilean	8	0.02
Colombian	23	0.07
Ecuadorian	8	0.02
Peruvian	7	0.02
Uruguayan	2	0.01
Venezuelan	6	0.02
Other South American	12	0.03
Other Hispanic or Latino	257	0.75
Hungarian	48	0.14
Icelander	24	0.07
Iranian	8	0.02
Irish	4,296	12.47
Italian	565	1.64
Latvian	54	0.16
Lithuanian	64	0.19
Luxemburger	41	0.12
Northern European	62	0.18
Norwegian	6,030	17.51
Polish	1,230	3.57
Portuguese	7	0.02
Romanian	33	0.10
Russian	236	0.69
Scandinavian	437	1.27
Scotch-Irish	476	1.38
Scottish	589	1.71
Serbian	6	0.02
Slavic	21	0.06
Slovak	102	0.30
Slovene	28	0.08
Swedish	4,758	13.81
Swiss	204	0.59
Ukrainian	100	0.29
United States or American	864	2.51
Welsh	127	0.37
West Indian, excl. Hispanic:	128	0.37
Bahamian	7	0.02
Jamaican	88	0.26
West Indian	33	0.10
White:	28,648	83.18
Not Hispanic (27,125)	27,669	80.34
Hispanic (856)	979	2.84
Yugoslavian	92	0.27

Robbinsdale

Place Type: City
County: Hennepin
Population: 14,123

Ancestry/Race	Number	%
African American/Black:	922	6.53
Not Hispanic (808)	911	6.45
Hispanic (3)	11	0.08
African, sub-Saharan:	173	1.23
African	115	0.81
Ethiopian	16	0.11
Kenyan	38	0.27
Other sub-Saharan African	4	0.03
Am. Ind. or Alaska Nat., not spec.	31	0.22
American Indian tribes, specified:	109	0.77
Apache (1)	1	0.01
Blackfeet	3	0.02
Cherokee (4)	11	0.08
Chickasaw	2	0.01
Chippewa (45)	63	0.45
Choctaw	1	0.01
Iroquois (1)	1	0.01
Latin American Indians (1)	2	0.01
Seminole	1	0.01
Sioux (12)	18	0.13
All other tribes (2)	6	0.04
American Indian tribes, not spec.	7	0.05
Arab:	6	0.04
Arab/Arabic	6	0.04
Asian:	354	2.51
Cambodian (6)	7	0.05
Chinese, ex. Taiwanese (18)	23	0.16
Filipino (24)	34	0.24
Hmong (44)	51	0.36
Indian (48)	54	0.38
Indonesian (1)	1	0.01
Japanese (6)	15	0.11
Korean (22)	33	0.23
Laotian (66)	66	0.47
Pakistani (2)	4	0.03
Thai (9)	9	0.06
Vietnamese (42)	50	0.35
Other Asian, not specified (3)	7	0.05
Austrian	27	0.19
Belgian	22	0.16
Brazilian	5	0.04
British	39	0.28
Bulgarian	10	0.07
Canadian	11	0.08
Croatian	11	0.08
Czech	147	1.04
Czechoslovakian	40	0.28
Danish	214	1.52
Dutch	109	0.77
Eastern European	11	0.08
English	1,163	8.24
European	150	1.06
Finnish	289	2.05
French, except Basque	590	4.18
French Canadian	199	1.41
German	4,500	31.88
German Russian	6	0.04
Greek	29	0.21
Guyanese	11	0.08
Hawaii Native/Pacific Islander:	4	0.03
Polynesian: (1)	4	0.03
Native Hawaiian (1)	4	0.03
Hispanic or Latino:	282	2.00
Central American:	20	0.14
Costa Rican	6	0.04
Guatemalan	3	0.02
Honduran	2	0.01
Panamanian	3	0.02
Salvadoran	5	0.04
Other Central American	1	0.01
Cuban	10	0.07
Dominican Republic	1	0.01
Mexican	184	1.30
Puerto Rican	10	0.07
South American:	10	0.07
Argentinean	1	0.01
Colombian	5	0.04
Ecuadorian	4	0.03
Other Hispanic or Latino	47	0.33
Hungarian	12	0.09
Irish	1,811	12.83
Italian	309	2.19
Lithuanian	15	0.11
Luxemburger	12	0.09
Northern European	13	0.09
Norwegian	2,605	18.45
Pennsylvania German	17	0.12
Polish	1,004	7.11
Portuguese	26	0.18
Romanian	5	0.04
Russian	119	0.84
Scandinavian	149	1.06
Scotch-Irish	153	1.08
Scottish	194	1.37
Serbian	5	0.04
Slovak	28	0.20
Slovene	7	0.05
Swedish	1,984	14.05
Swiss	67	0.47
Ukrainian	138	0.98
United States or American	230	1.63
Welsh	42	0.30
West Indian, excl. Hispanic:	76	0.54
Bahamian	13	0.09
Jamaican	34	0.24

Notes: 1. Figures in the "Number" column do not add up to the total population due to: a) Ancestry/Race overlap — e.g. persons can report being both White and Irish, b) persons of Hispanic origin can report being any race, c) persons reporting two ancestries are counted in both categories. 2. Numbers in parentheses indicate the number of persons reporting this ancestry/race alone, not in combination with any other ancestry/race. 3. Refer to the Explanation of Data in the front of the book for more detailed information.

U.S. Virgin Islander	8	0.06
West Indian	21	0.15
White:	12,757	90.33
Not Hispanic (12,435)	12,613	89.31
Hispanic (118)	144	1.02

Rochester

Place Type: City
County: Olmsted
Population: 85,806

Ancestry/Race	Number	%
Acadian/Cajun	10	0.01
African American/Black:	3,654	4.26
Not Hispanic (3,034)	3,600	4.20
Hispanic (30)	54	0.06
African, sub-Saharan:	1,811	2.12
African	357	0.42
Cape Verdean	13	0.02
Ethiopian	88	0.10
Ghanian	7	0.01
Nigerian	92	0.11
Somalian	1,131	1.32
South African	8	0.01
Sudanese	67	0.08
Other sub-Saharan African	48	0.06
Alaska Native tribes, specified:	5	0.01
Eskimo (1)	1	0.00
Tlingit-Haida (4)	4	0.00
Alaska Native tribes, not specified	2	0.00
Am. Ind. or Alaska Nat., not spec.	196	0.23
Alsatian	9	0.01
American Indian tribes, specified:	312	0.36
Apache (7)	10	0.01
Blackfeet (1)	4	0.00
Cherokee (16)	57	0.07
Cheyenne (4)	5	0.01
Chickasaw	1	0.00
Chippewa (42)	74	0.09
Choctaw (4)	8	0.01
Colville	1	0.00
Cree	1	0.00
Creek (1)	3	0.00
Delaware	2	0.00
Iroquois (2)	6	0.01
Kiowa	1	0.00
Latin American Indians (7)	24	0.03
Menominee (7)	7	0.01
Navajo (1)	7	0.01
Paiute (1)	1	0.00
Potawatomi (7)	7	0.01
Pueblo	3	0.00
Seminole	2	0.00
Shoshone (1)	1	0.00
Sioux (30)	66	0.08
All other tribes (11)	21	0.02
American Indian tribes, not spec.	15	0.02
Arab:	278	0.33
Arab/Arabic	78	0.09
Egyptian	57	0.07
Iraqi	14	0.02
Jordanian	13	0.02
Lebanese	62	0.07
Moroccan	13	0.02
Palestinian	22	0.03
Syrian	6	0.01
Other Arab	13	0.02
Armenian	13	0.02
Asian:	5,504	6.41
Bangladeshi (12)	12	0.01
Cambodian (808)	945	1.10
Chinese, ex. Taiwanese (689)	784	0.91
Filipino (221)	302	0.35
Hmong (211)	230	0.27
Indian (788)	858	1.00
Indonesian (13)	13	0.02
Japanese (230)	283	0.33
Korean (284)	353	0.41
Laotian (474)	522	0.61
Malaysian (9)	19	0.02
Pakistani (51)	58	0.07
Sri Lankan (9)	12	0.01
Taiwanese (27)	35	0.04
Thai (36)	44	0.05
Vietnamese (729)	782	0.91
Other Asian, specified (16)	26	0.03
Other Asian, not specified (140)	226	0.26
Australian	70	0.08
Austrian	204	0.24
Basque	12	0.01
Belgian	241	0.28
Brazilian	42	0.05
British	425	0.50
Canadian	142	0.17
Celtic	24	0.03
Croatian	144	0.17
Cypriot	19	0.02
Czech	1,252	1.47
Czechoslovakian	179	0.21
Danish	1,630	1.91
Dutch	1,954	2.29
Eastern European	48	0.06
English	7,069	8.28
Estonian	15	0.02
European	947	1.11
Finnish	549	0.64
French, except Basque	2,458	2.88
French Canadian	523	0.61
German	30,572	35.80
Greek	442	0.52
Hawaii Native/Pacific Islander:	91	0.11
Micronesian: (3)	8	0.01
Guamanian/Chamorro (2)	6	0.01
Other Micronesian (1)	2	0.00
Polynesian: (17)	39	0.05
Native Hawaiian (12)	22	0.03
Samoan (4)	15	0.02
Other Polynesian (1)	2	0.00
Other Pac. Isl., not spec. (13)	44	0.05
Hispanic or Latino:	2,565	2.99
Central American:	78	0.09
Costa Rican	9	0.01
Guatemalan	34	0.04
Honduran	1	0.00
Nicaraguan	3	0.00
Panamanian	6	0.01
Salvadoran	10	0.01
Other Central American	15	0.02
Cuban	55	0.06
Dominican Republic	21	0.02
Mexican	1,543	1.80
Puerto Rican	174	0.20
South American:	181	0.21
Argentinean	23	0.03
Bolivian	2	0.00
Chilean	26	0.03
Colombian	74	0.09
Ecuadorian	11	0.01
Paraguayan	2	0.00
Peruvian	22	0.03
Uruguayan	1	0.00
Venezuelan	16	0.02
Other South American	4	0.00
Other Hispanic or Latino	513	0.60
Hungarian	210	0.25
Icelander	48	0.06
Iranian	71	0.08
Irish	10,067	11.79
Italian	1,704	2.00
Latvian	22	0.03
Lithuanian	148	0.17
Luxemburger	149	0.17
Macedonian	18	0.02
Maltese	27	0.03
Northern European	171	0.20
Norwegian	14,772	17.30
Pennsylvania German	60	0.07
Polish	2,727	3.19
Portuguese	73	0.09
Romanian	134	0.16
Russian	530	0.62
Scandinavian	650	0.76
Scotch-Irish	853	1.00
Scottish	1,210	1.42
Slavic	22	0.03
Slovak	116	0.14
Slovene	9	0.01
Swedish	4,299	5.03
Swiss	804	0.94
Turkish	48	0.06
Ukrainian	181	0.21
United States or American	3,296	3.86
Welsh	465	0.54
West Indian, excl. Hispanic:	32	0.04
Bermudan	8	0.01
Jamaican	8	0.01
West Indian	16	0.02
White:	76,128	88.72
Not Hispanic (73,656)	74,568	86.90
Hispanic (1,432)	1,560	1.82
Yugoslavian	433	0.51

Rosemount

Place Type: City
County: Dakota
Population: 14,619

Ancestry/Race	Number	%
African American/Black:	395	2.70
Not Hispanic (279)	367	2.51
Hispanic (18)	28	0.19
African, sub-Saharan:	43	0.29
Ethiopian	22	0.15
Sudanese	21	0.14
Alaska Native tribes, specified:	3	0.02
Alaska Athabascan	1	0.01
Eskimo	2	0.01
Am. Ind. or Alaska Nat., not spec.	46	0.31
American Indian tribes, specified:	78	0.53
Cherokee (1)	22	0.15
Chickasaw (1)	1	0.01
Chippewa (14)	21	0.14
Choctaw	3	0.02
Latin American Indians	5	0.03
Sioux (9)	19	0.13
All other tribes (4)	7	0.05
American Indian tribes, not spec.	3	0.02
Arab:	42	0.29
Lebanese	42	0.29
Asian:	418	2.86
Cambodian (1)	2	0.01
Chinese, ex. Taiwanese (53)	62	0.42
Filipino (36)	55	0.38
Hmong (5)	5	0.03
Indian (57)	70	0.48
Japanese (11)	27	0.18
Korean (28)	43	0.29
Laotian (35)	42	0.29
Sri Lankan (4)	7	0.05
Thai (5)	5	0.03
Vietnamese (62)	68	0.47
Other Asian, specified (2)	7	0.05
Other Asian, not specified (9)	25	0.17
Austrian	58	0.40
Belgian	53	0.36
British	3	0.02
Canadian	31	0.21
Croatian	23	0.16
Czech	204	1.40
Czechoslovakian	101	0.69
Danish	270	1.85
Dutch	175	1.20
English	1,166	7.98
European	63	0.43
Finnish	146	1.00
French, except Basque	774	5.30
French Canadian	191	1.31
German	6,193	42.37

Notes: 1. Figures in the "Number" column do not add up to the total population due to: a) Ancestry/Race overlap — e.g. persons can report being both White and Irish, b) persons of Hispanic origin can report being any race, c) persons reporting two ancestries are counted in both categories. 2. Numbers in parentheses indicate the number of persons reporting this ancestry/race alone, not in combination with any other ancestry/race. 3. Refer to the Explanation of Data in the front of the book for more detailed information.

Ancestry/Race	Number	%
Greek	68	0.47
Guyanese	20	0.14
Hawaii Native/Pacific Islander:	6	0.04
Polynesian:	4	0.03
Native Hawaiian	3	0.02
Samoan	1	0.01
Other Pac. Isl., not spec.	2	0.01
Hispanic or Latino:	268	1.83
Central American:	9	0.06
Costa Rican	1	0.01
Guatemalan	3	0.02
Honduran	3	0.02
Panamanian	2	0.01
Cuban	2	0.01
Mexican	132	0.90
Puerto Rican	56	0.38
South American:	16	0.11
Chilean	1	0.01
Colombian	8	0.05
Uruguayan	1	0.01
Venezuelan	2	0.01
Other South American	4	0.03
Other Hispanic or Latino	53	0.36
Hungarian	29	0.20
Irish	2,329	15.94
Italian	289	1.98
Lithuanian	32	0.22
Luxemburger	6	0.04
Northern European	8	0.05
Norwegian	2,459	16.83
Polish	694	4.75
Romanian	30	0.21
Russian	39	0.27
Scandinavian	296	2.03
Scotch-Irish	118	0.81
Scottish	114	0.78
Slavic	46	0.31
Slovak	71	0.49
Swedish	1,135	7.77
Swiss	81	0.55
Ukrainian	86	0.59
United States or American	417	2.85
Welsh	92	0.63
White:	13,785	94.30
Not Hispanic (13,429)	13,623	93.19
Hispanic (135)	162	1.11
Yugoslavian	25	0.17

Roseville

Place Type: City
County: Ramsey
Population: 33,690

Ancestry/Race	Number	%
African American/Black:	1,168	3.47
Not Hispanic (928)	1,132	3.36
Hispanic (17)	36	0.11
African, sub-Saharan:	190	0.56
African	98	0.29
Ethiopian	44	0.13
Liberian	5	0.01
Nigerian	13	0.04
Somalian	21	0.06
Sudanese	5	0.01
Other sub-Saharan African	4	0.01
Alaska Native tribes, specified:	1	0.00
Tlingit-Haida (1)	1	0.00
Am. Ind. or Alaska Nat., not spec.	90	0.27
American Indian tribes, specified:	158	0.47
Apache	1	0.00
Blackfeet (2)	2	0.01
Cherokee (5)	22	0.07
Cheyenne (1)	3	0.01
Chickasaw	1	0.00
Chippewa (34)	64	0.19
Choctaw	1	0.00
Cree	4	0.01
Creek	2	0.01
Iroquois (3)	4	0.01
Latin American Indians (5)	5	0.01
Navajo (2)	2	0.01
Ottawa (1)	1	0.00
Seminole	3	0.01
Sioux (14)	35	0.10
Ute (2)	2	0.01
Yaqui (2)	2	0.01
All other tribes (4)	4	0.01
American Indian tribes, not spec.	5	0.01
Arab:	123	0.36
Arab/Arabic	47	0.14
Lebanese	76	0.23
Asian:	1,858	5.51
Bangladeshi (6)	10	0.03
Cambodian (15)	16	0.05
Chinese, ex. Taiwanese (548)	587	1.74
Filipino (56)	82	0.24
Hmong (117)	122	0.36
Indian (303)	336	1.00
Indonesian (2)	2	0.01
Japanese (78)	115	0.34
Korean (168)	199	0.59
Laotian (10)	13	0.04
Malaysian (3)	4	0.01
Pakistani (23)	29	0.09
Sri Lankan (6)	7	0.02
Taiwanese (24)	32	0.09
Thai (5)	8	0.02
Vietnamese (229)	243	0.72
Other Asian, specified (9)	14	0.04
Other Asian, not specified (18)	39	0.12
Australian	19	0.06
Austrian	326	0.97
Basque	5	0.01
Belgian	113	0.33
Brazilian	8	0.02
British	132	0.39
Canadian	42	0.12
Celtic	16	0.05
Croatian	42	0.12
Czech	433	1.28
Czechoslovakian	185	0.55
Danish	645	1.91
Dutch	520	1.54
Eastern European	18	0.05
English	2,790	8.26
European	253	0.75
Finnish	329	0.97
French, except Basque	1,445	4.28
French Canadian	429	1.27
German	12,665	37.52
Greek	57	0.17
Guyanese	6	0.02
Hawaii Native/Pacific Islander:	59	0.18
Melanesian: (6)	6	0.02
Other Melanesian (6)	6	0.02
Micronesian: (3)	5	0.01
Guamanian/Chamorro (3)	5	0.01
Polynesian: (17)	32	0.09
Native Hawaiian (4)	17	0.05
Samoan (4)	6	0.02
Other Polynesian (9)	9	0.03
Other Pac. Isl., specified	1	0.00
Other Pac. Isl., not spec. (1)	15	0.04
Hispanic or Latino:	664	1.97
Central American:	25	0.07
Costa Rican	2	0.01
Guatemalan	8	0.02
Honduran	6	0.02
Nicaraguan	1	0.00
Panamanian	7	0.02
Salvadoran	1	0.00
Cuban	8	0.02
Dominican Republic	1	0.00
Mexican	409	1.21
Puerto Rican	30	0.09
South American:	81	0.24
Argentinean	3	0.01
Bolivian	5	0.01
Chilean	14	0.04
Colombian	20	0.06
Ecuadorian	12	0.04
Paraguayan	3	0.01
Peruvian	16	0.05
Uruguayan	1	0.00
Venezuelan	7	0.02
Other Hispanic or Latino	110	0.33
Hungarian	124	0.37
Icelander	10	0.03
Iranian	34	0.10
Irish	4,466	13.23
Israeli	21	0.06
Italian	973	2.88
Latvian	29	0.09
Lithuanian	24	0.07
Luxemburger	36	0.11
Macedonian	34	0.10
Maltese	10	0.03
Northern European	103	0.31
Norwegian	5,026	14.89
Pennsylvania German	11	0.03
Polish	1,703	5.04
Portuguese	60	0.18
Romanian	73	0.22
Russian	233	0.69
Scandinavian	277	0.82
Scotch-Irish	440	1.30
Scottish	576	1.71
Serbian	43	0.13
Slavic	16	0.05
Slovak	72	0.21
Slovene	56	0.17
Swedish	4,045	11.98
Swiss	261	0.77
Turkish	56	0.17
Ukrainian	118	0.35
United States or American	821	2.43
Welsh	186	0.55
West Indian, excl. Hispanic:	32	0.09
Haitian	8	0.02
Jamaican	18	0.05
Trinidadian and Tobagonian	6	0.02
White:	30,622	90.89
Not Hispanic (29,831)	30,229	89.73
Hispanic (319)	393	1.17
Yugoslavian	16	0.05

Saint Cloud

Place Type: City
County: Stearns
Population: 59,107

Ancestry/Race	Number	%
Acadian/Cajun	2	0.00
African American/Black:	1,724	2.92
Not Hispanic (1,378)	1,688	2.86
Hispanic (24)	36	0.06
African, sub-Saharan:	189	0.32
African	124	0.21
Ethiopian	9	0.02
Nigerian	37	0.06
Other sub-Saharan African	19	0.03
Alaska Native tribes, specified:	4	0.01
Eskimo (3)	4	0.01
Alaska Native tribes, not specified	2	0.00
Am. Ind. or Alaska Nat., not spec.	214	0.36
Alsatian	6	0.01
American Indian tribes, specified:	474	0.80
Blackfeet (2)	12	0.02
Cherokee (9)	31	0.05
Cheyenne	4	0.01
Chippewa (175)	256	0.43
Choctaw (2)	7	0.01
Comanche	1	0.00
Cree (1)	3	0.01
Creek	4	0.01
Iroquois (2)	5	0.01
Latin American Indians (8)	11	0.02
Menominee (3)	4	0.01

Notes: 1. Figures in the "Number" column do not add up to the total population due to: a) Ancestry/Race overlap — e.g. persons can report being both White and Irish, b) persons of Hispanic origin can report being any race, c) persons reporting two ancestries are counted in both categories. 2. Numbers in parentheses indicate the number of persons reporting this ancestry/race alone, not in combination with any other ancestry/race. 3. Refer to the Explanation of Data in the front of the book for more detailed information.

Ancestry/Race	Number	%
Navajo (3)	3	0.01
Osage	1	0.00
Ottawa (2)	2	0.00
Potawatomi (1)	1	0.00
Seminole (1)	5	0.01
Sioux (58)	82	0.14
Ute	2	0.00
Yaqui (2)	2	0.00
All other tribes (14)	38	0.06
American Indian tribes, not spec.	31	0.05
Arab:	165	0.28
Arab/Arabic	10	0.02
Egyptian	14	0.02
Lebanese	84	0.14
Syrian	16	0.03
Other Arab	41	0.07
Asian:	2,137	3.62
Bangladeshi (44)	48	0.08
Cambodian (52)	61	0.10
Chinese, ex. Taiwanese (260)	306	0.52
Filipino (77)	113	0.19
Hmong (57)	72	0.12
Indian (217)	241	0.41
Indonesian (11)	16	0.03
Japanese (118)	144	0.24
Korean (123)	158	0.27
Laotian (304)	327	0.55
Malaysian (35)	50	0.08
Pakistani (26)	27	0.05
Sri Lankan (7)	9	0.02
Taiwanese (6)	8	0.01
Thai (24)	30	0.05
Vietnamese (368)	396	0.67
Other Asian, specified (26)	31	0.05
Other Asian, not specified (52)	100	0.17
Assyrian/Chaldean/Syriac	24	0.04
Australian	23	0.04
Austrian	210	0.36
Belgian	240	0.41
British	130	0.22
Bulgarian	5	0.01
Canadian	83	0.14
Croatian	79	0.13
Cypriot	8	0.01
Czech	814	1.38
Czechoslovakian	198	0.34
Danish	754	1.28
Dutch	928	1.57
Eastern European	7	0.01
English	2,682	4.55
European	342	0.58
Finnish	853	1.45
French, except Basque	2,295	3.89
French Canadian	511	0.87
German	28,762	48.77
Greek	150	0.25
Hawaii Native/Pacific Islander:	85	0.14
Micronesian: (1)	3	0.01
Guamanian/Chamorro	2	0.00
Other Micronesian (1)	1	0.00
Polynesian: (30)	49	0.08
Native Hawaiian (11)	26	0.04
Samoan (19)	20	0.03
Other Polynesian	3	0.01
Other Pac. Isl., not spec. (6)	33	0.06
Hispanic or Latino:	784	1.33
Central American:	37	0.06
Costa Rican	4	0.01
Guatemalan	12	0.02
Honduran	6	0.01
Nicaraguan	2	0.00
Panamanian	1	0.00
Salvadoran	12	0.02
Cuban	27	0.05
Dominican Republic	5	0.01
Mexican	407	0.69
Puerto Rican	73	0.12
South American:	38	0.06
Argentinean	1	0.00
Bolivian	1	0.00
Chilean	9	0.02
Colombian	12	0.02
Ecuadorian	4	0.01
Paraguayan	2	0.00
Peruvian	2	0.00
Venezuelan	3	0.01
Other South American	4	0.01
Other Hispanic or Latino	197	0.33
Hungarian	69	0.12
Icelander	28	0.05
Iranian	55	0.09
Irish	5,640	9.56
Israeli	7	0.01
Italian	1,015	1.72
Latvian	8	0.01
Lithuanian	5	0.01
Luxemburger	66	0.11
Maltese	7	0.01
New Zealander	8	0.01
Northern European	57	0.10
Norwegian	8,030	13.62
Pennsylvania German	10	0.02
Polish	4,117	6.98
Portuguese	56	0.09
Romanian	52	0.09
Russian	190	0.32
Scandinavian	517	0.88
Scotch-Irish	478	0.81
Scottish	638	1.08
Serbian	57	0.10
Slavic	117	0.20
Slovak	98	0.17
Slovene	164	0.28
Swedish	4,407	7.47
Swiss	322	0.55
Ukrainian	108	0.18
United States or American	1,974	3.35
Welsh	165	0.28
West Indian, excl. Hispanic:	17	0.03
Jamaican	17	0.03
White:	54,913	92.90
Not Hispanic (53,857)	54,491	92.19
Hispanic (372)	422	0.71
Yugoslavian	83	0.14

Saint Louis Park

Place Type: City
County: Hennepin
Population: 44,126

Ancestry/Race	Number	%
African American/Black:	2,314	5.24
Not Hispanic (1,893)	2,244	5.09
Hispanic (37)	70	0.16
African, sub-Saharan:	625	1.42
African	199	0.45
Ethiopian	185	0.42
Kenyan	29	0.07
Liberian	78	0.18
Nigerian	22	0.05
Somalian	96	0.22
South African	9	0.02
Other sub-Saharan African	7	0.02
Alaska Native tribes, specified:	6	0.01
Tlingit-Haida (3)	6	0.01
Alaska Native tribes, not specified	1	0.00
Am. Ind. or Alaska Nat., not spec.	125	0.28
American Indian tribes, specified:	240	0.54
Apache (3)	3	0.01
Blackfeet	2	0.00
Cherokee (8)	20	0.05
Cheyenne	1	0.00
Chippewa (104)	136	0.31
Choctaw	4	0.01
Comanche	1	0.00
Creek (1)	1	0.00
Iroquois	2	0.00
Latin American Indians (9)	13	0.03
Ottawa	1	0.00
Pueblo (1)	1	0.00
Shoshone (4)	4	0.01
Sioux (22)	40	0.09
All other tribes (3)	11	0.02
American Indian tribes, not spec.	6	0.01
Arab:	140	0.32
Arab/Arabic	13	0.03
Egyptian	8	0.02
Iraqi	6	0.01
Lebanese	53	0.12
Moroccan	7	0.02
Palestinian	23	0.05
Other Arab	30	0.07
Armenian	16	0.04
Asian:	1,667	3.78
Bangladeshi (5)	5	0.01
Cambodian (85)	100	0.23
Chinese, ex. Taiwanese (186)	238	0.54
Filipino (91)	124	0.28
Hmong (9)	9	0.02
Indian (456)	511	1.16
Indonesian (3)	3	0.01
Japanese (81)	117	0.27
Korean (152)	181	0.41
Laotian (13)	18	0.04
Malaysian (3)	4	0.01
Pakistani (18)	24	0.05
Sri Lankan (23)	23	0.05
Taiwanese (4)	4	0.01
Thai (10)	13	0.03
Vietnamese (199)	218	0.49
Other Asian, specified (16)	16	0.04
Other Asian, not specified (31)	59	0.13
Austrian	190	0.43
Basque	7	0.02
Belgian	95	0.22
Brazilian	5	0.01
British	198	0.45
Canadian	94	0.21
Celtic	27	0.06
Croatian	64	0.15
Czech	500	1.13
Czechoslovakian	186	0.42
Danish	784	1.78
Dutch	656	1.49
Eastern European	178	0.40
English	3,426	7.77
Estonian	40	0.09
European	430	0.97
Finnish	854	1.94
French, except Basque	1,698	3.85
French Canadian	383	0.87
German	12,028	27.26
Greek	160	0.36
Guyanese	47	0.11
Hawaii Native/Pacific Islander:	42	0.10
Melanesian: (4)	4	0.01
Fijian (4)	4	0.01
Micronesian: (3)	4	0.01
Guamanian/Chamorro (3)	4	0.01
Polynesian: (13)	21	0.05
Native Hawaiian (9)	16	0.04
Samoan (4)	5	0.01
Other Pac. Isl., not spec. (5)	13	0.03
Hispanic or Latino:	1,294	2.93
Central American:	46	0.10
Costa Rican	8	0.02
Guatemalan	5	0.01
Honduran	4	0.01
Nicaraguan	3	0.01
Panamanian	12	0.03
Salvadoran	9	0.02
Other Central American	5	0.01
Cuban	40	0.09
Mexican	854	1.94
Puerto Rican	67	0.15
South American:	101	0.23
Argentinean	10	0.02
Bolivian	3	0.01
Chilean	6	0.01

Notes: 1. Figures in the "Number" column do not add up to the total population due to: a) Ancestry/Race overlap — e.g. persons can report being both White and Irish, b) persons of Hispanic origin can report being any race, c) persons reporting two ancestries are counted in both categories. 2. Numbers in parentheses indicate the number of persons reporting this ancestry/race alone, not in combination with any other ancestry/race. 3. Refer to the Explanation of Data in the front of the book for more detailed information.

Ancestry/Race	Number	%
Colombian	30	0.07
Ecuadorian	12	0.03
Paraguayan	1	0.00
Peruvian	22	0.05
Venezuelan	6	0.01
Other South American	11	0.02
Other Hispanic or Latino	186	0.42
Hungarian	231	0.52
Icelander	62	0.14
Iranian	19	0.04
Irish	5,531	12.54
Israeli	75	0.17
Italian	899	2.04
Latvian	52	0.12
Lithuanian	249	0.56
Luxemburger	34	0.08
Northern European	116	0.26
Norwegian	7,082	16.05
Pennsylvania German	19	0.04
Polish	2,046	4.64
Portuguese	36	0.08
Romanian	405	0.92
Russian	1,937	4.39
Scandinavian	554	1.26
Scotch-Irish	484	1.10
Scottish	865	1.96
Serbian	45	0.10
Slavic	13	0.03
Slovak	100	0.23
Slovene	85	0.19
Swedish	4,177	9.47
Swiss	278	0.63
Turkish	24	0.05
Ukrainian	195	0.44
United States or American	1,320	2.99
Welsh	333	0.75
West Indian, excl. Hispanic:	54	0.12
Jamaican	31	0.07
Trinidadian and Tobagonian	20	0.05
West Indian	3	0.01
White:	39,842	90.29
Not Hispanic (38,599)	39,115	88.64
Hispanic (633)	727	1.65
Yugoslavian	147	0.33

Saint Paul

Place Type: City
County: Ramsey
Population: 287,151

Ancestry/Race	Number	%
Acadian/Cajun	73	0.03
Afghan	23	0.01
African American/Black:	38,402	13.37
Not Hispanic (32,818)	37,062	12.91
Hispanic (819)	1,340	0.47
African, sub-Saharan:	7,147	2.49
African	3,032	1.06
Ethiopian	1,279	0.45
Ghanian	105	0.04
Kenyan	77	0.03
Liberian	356	0.12
Nigerian	804	0.28
Senegalese	20	0.01
Sierra Leonean	45	0.02
Somalian	1,026	0.36
South African	49	0.02
Sudanese	71	0.02
Ugandan	35	0.01
Zimbabwean	6	0.00
Other sub-Saharan African	242	0.08
Alaska Native tribes, specified:	24	0.01
Alaska Athabascan	1	0.00
Aleut (1)	1	0.00
Eskimo (8)	16	0.01
Tlingit-Haida (3)	6	0.00
Alaska Native tribes, not specified	8	0.00
Am. Ind. or Alaska Nat., not spec.	2,104	0.73
Albanian	70	0.02
Alsatian	64	0.02
American Indian tribes, specified:	3,722	1.30
Apache (11)	28	0.01
Blackfeet (16)	51	0.02
Cherokee (51)	250	0.09
Cheyenne (6)	6	0.00
Chickasaw (1)	1	0.00
Chippewa (1,126)	1,675	0.58
Choctaw (13)	69	0.02
Comanche (1)	8	0.00
Cree (7)	20	0.01
Creek (9)	32	0.01
Crow (2)	2	0.00
Delaware (3)	10	0.00
Houma (1)	3	0.00
Iroquois (18)	46	0.02
Kiowa (9)	10	0.00
Latin American Indians (84)	199	0.07
Menominee (7)	9	0.00
Navajo (11)	24	0.01
Osage (1)	1	0.00
Ottawa (4)	6	0.00
Paiute (2)	3	0.00
Pima (3)	4	0.00
Potawatomi (5)	8	0.00
Pueblo (4)	11	0.00
Puget Sound Salish (4)	4	0.00
Seminole (3)	14	0.00
Shoshone (2)	2	0.00
Sioux (513)	827	0.29
Tohono O'Odham	1	0.00
Yakama (2)	5	0.00
Yaqui	2	0.00
All other tribes (273)	391	0.14
American Indian tribes, not spec.	224	0.08
Arab:	1,239	0.43
Arab/Arabic	214	0.07
Egyptian	98	0.03
Iraqi	30	0.01
Jordanian	7	0.00
Lebanese	666	0.23
Moroccan	10	0.00
Palestinian	44	0.02
Syrian	36	0.01
Other Arab	134	0.05
Armenian	82	0.03
Asian:	39,586	13.79
Bangladeshi (9)	15	0.01
Cambodian (1,138)	1,358	0.47
Chinese, ex. Taiwanese (1,059)	1,315	0.46
Filipino (655)	923	0.32
Hmong (24,389)	26,509	9.23
Indian (1,112)	1,681	0.59
Indonesian (39)	55	0.02
Japanese (326)	533	0.19
Korean (839)	1,026	0.36
Laotian (994)	1,426	0.50
Malaysian (11)	26	0.01
Pakistani (46)	61	0.02
Sri Lankan (26)	42	0.01
Taiwanese (41)	56	0.02
Thai (114)	147	0.05
Vietnamese (2,767)	2,915	1.02
Other Asian, specified (104)	130	0.05
Other Asian, not specified (997)	1,368	0.48
Assyrian/Chaldean/Syriac	9	0.00
Australian	78	0.03
Austrian	1,761	0.61
Basque	52	0.02
Belgian	456	0.16
Brazilian	37	0.01
British	812	0.28
Bulgarian	59	0.02
Canadian	448	0.16
Celtic	131	0.05
Croatian	309	0.11
Czech	3,310	1.15
Czechoslovakian	823	0.29
Danish	3,116	1.09
Dutch	3,499	1.22
Eastern European	208	0.07
English	15,261	5.31
Estonian	4	0.00
European	2,676	0.93
Finnish	2,206	0.77
French, except Basque	10,853	3.78
French Canadian	3,286	1.14
German	73,265	25.51
German Russian	6	0.00
Greek	730	0.25
Guyanese	13	0.00
Hawaii Native/Pacific Islander:	1,284	0.45
Melanesian: (1)	1	0.00
Fijian (1)	1	0.00
Micronesian: (34)	44	0.02
Guamanian/Chamorro (31)	41	0.01
Other Micronesian (3)	3	0.00
Polynesian: (83)	198	0.07
Native Hawaiian (25)	92	0.03
Samoan (55)	97	0.03
Tongan (3)	6	0.00
Other Polynesian	3	0.00
Other Pac. Isl., specified	18	0.01
Other Pac. Isl., not spec. (82)	1,023	0.36
Hispanic or Latino:	22,715	7.91
Central American:	1,137	0.40
Costa Rican	22	0.01
Guatemalan	204	0.07
Honduran	159	0.06
Nicaraguan	22	0.01
Panamanian	55	0.02
Salvadoran	593	0.21
Other Central American	82	0.03
Cuban	356	0.12
Dominican Republic	100	0.03
Mexican	16,565	5.77
Puerto Rican	1,037	0.36
South American:	585	0.20
Argentinean	57	0.02
Bolivian	12	0.00
Chilean	54	0.02
Colombian	178	0.06
Ecuadorian	49	0.02
Paraguayan	18	0.01
Peruvian	96	0.03
Uruguayan	13	0.00
Venezuelan	85	0.03
Other South American	23	0.01
Other Hispanic or Latino	2,935	1.02
Hungarian	1,130	0.39
Icelander	129	0.04
Iranian	95	0.03
Irish	36,699	12.78
Israeli	97	0.03
Italian	9,332	3.25
Latvian	172	0.06
Lithuanian	575	0.20
Luxemburger	389	0.14
Macedonian	5	0.00
Maltese	22	0.01
New Zealander	31	0.01
Northern European	528	0.18
Norwegian	24,035	8.37
Pennsylvania German	88	0.03
Polish	10,868	3.78
Portuguese	160	0.06
Romanian	459	0.16
Russian	2,651	0.92
Scandinavian	1,877	0.65
Scotch-Irish	2,757	0.96
Scottish	3,564	1.24
Serbian	130	0.05
Slavic	131	0.05
Slovak	254	0.09
Slovene	324	0.11
Swedish	18,394	6.41
Swiss	1,278	0.45
Turkish	91	0.03
Ukrainian	691	0.24
United States or American	5,297	1.84

Notes: 1. Figures in the "Number" column do not add up to the total population due to: a) Ancestry/Race overlap — e.g. persons can report being both White and Irish, b) persons of Hispanic origin can report being any race, c) persons reporting two ancestries are counted in both categories. 2. Numbers in parentheses indicate the number of persons reporting this ancestry/race alone, not in combination with any other ancestry/race. 3. Refer to the Explanation of Data in the front of the book for more detailed information.

Ancestry/Race	Number	%
Welsh	1,298	0.45
West Indian, excl. Hispanic:	533	0.19
Bahamian	24	0.01
Barbadian	21	0.01
Belizean	19	0.01
British West Indian	22	0.01
Dutch West Indian	9	0.00
Haitian	158	0.06
Jamaican	248	0.09
Trinidadian and Tobagonian	26	0.01
West Indian	6	0.00
White:	199,862	69.60
Not Hispanic (183,898)	189,419	65.96
Hispanic (8,546)	10,443	3.64
Yugoslavian	280	0.10

Sauk Rapids

Place Type: City
County: Benton
Population: 10,213

Ancestry/Race	Number	%
African American/Black:	90	0.88
Not Hispanic (58)	88	0.86
Hispanic	2	0.02
African, sub-Saharan:	22	0.22
African	8	0.08
Ghanian	14	0.14
Am. Ind. or Alaska Nat., not spec.	18	0.18
American Indian tribes, specified:	29	0.28
Cherokee (1)	3	0.03
Chippewa (15)	17	0.17
Delaware	1	0.01
Latin American Indians	1	0.01
Ottawa	1	0.01
Sioux (4)	4	0.04
All other tribes (1)	2	0.02
American Indian tribes, not spec.	5	0.05
Asian:	113	1.11
Cambodian (2)	5	0.05
Chinese, ex. Taiwanese (4)	7	0.07
Filipino (10)	14	0.14
Indian (11)	12	0.12
Japanese (3)	5	0.05
Korean (24)	35	0.34
Laotian (3)	6	0.06
Pakistani (4)	4	0.04
Thai	2	0.02
Vietnamese (14)	15	0.15
Other Asian, not specified (3)	8	0.08
Austrian	24	0.24
Belgian	17	0.17
British	10	0.10
Canadian	6	0.06
Czech	131	1.29
Czechoslovakian	11	0.11
Danish	174	1.71
Dutch	93	0.91
English	514	5.05
European	41	0.40
Finnish	102	1.00
French, except Basque	421	4.13
French Canadian	181	1.78
German	5,642	55.41
Greek	48	0.47
Hawaii Native/Pacific Islander:	5	0.05
Micronesian:	1	0.01
Guamanian/Chamorro	1	0.01
Polynesian: (3)	3	0.03
Samoan (3)	3	0.03
Other Pac. Isl., not spec. (1)	1	0.01
Hispanic or Latino:	110	1.08
Central American:	4	0.04
Guatemalan	2	0.02
Other Central American	2	0.02
Cuban	17	0.17
Mexican	58	0.57
Puerto Rican	7	0.07
South American:	4	0.04
Chilean	4	0.04
Other Hispanic or Latino	20	0.20
Hungarian	25	0.25
Irish	933	9.16
Italian	85	0.83
Lithuanian	7	0.07
Luxemburger	58	0.57
Norwegian	1,158	11.37
Pennsylvania German	10	0.10
Polish	1,286	12.63
Russian	28	0.27
Scandinavian	57	0.56
Scotch-Irish	56	0.55
Scottish	91	0.89
Serbian	9	0.09
Slovak	26	0.26
Slovene	56	0.55
Swedish	481	4.72
Swiss	28	0.27
Ukrainian	14	0.14
United States or American	453	4.45
Welsh	36	0.35
White:	10,014	98.05
Not Hispanic (9,848)	9,929	97.22
Hispanic (70)	85	0.83
Yugoslavian	26	0.26

Savage

Place Type: City
County: Scott
Population: 21,115

Ancestry/Race	Number	%
African American/Black:	404	1.91
Not Hispanic (330)	393	1.86
Hispanic (5)	11	0.05
African, sub-Saharan:	40	0.19
Nigerian	40	0.19
Am. Ind. or Alaska Nat., not spec.	54	0.26
American Indian tribes, specified:	94	0.45
Apache (1)	2	0.01
Blackfeet (1)	3	0.01
Cherokee (2)	9	0.04
Chippewa (16)	30	0.14
Creek	1	0.00
Delaware	1	0.00
Iroquois (1)	5	0.02
Latin American Indians (1)	1	0.00
Navajo (1)	1	0.00
Osage	1	0.00
Potawatomi (1)	2	0.01
Sioux (5)	16	0.08
All other tribes (9)	22	0.10
Arab:	132	0.62
Egyptian	56	0.26
Lebanese	60	0.28
Syrian	16	0.08
Asian:	1,312	6.21
Cambodian (212)	235	1.11
Chinese, ex. Taiwanese (176)	221	1.05
Filipino (52)	83	0.39
Hmong (29)	29	0.14
Indian (116)	131	0.62
Japanese (10)	27	0.13
Korean (69)	91	0.43
Laotian (122)	131	0.62
Malaysian (1)	1	0.00
Pakistani (2)	2	0.01
Sri Lankan (7)	9	0.04
Taiwanese (1)	1	0.00
Thai (18)	23	0.11
Vietnamese (261)	291	1.38
Other Asian, not specified (15)	37	0.18
Austrian	83	0.39
Belgian	83	0.39
British	30	0.14
Bulgarian	6	0.03
Canadian	48	0.23
Croatian	32	0.15
Czech	374	1.77
Czechoslovakian	137	0.65
Danish	448	2.11
Dutch	399	1.88
English	1,605	7.58
European	89	0.42
Finnish	384	1.81
French, except Basque	789	3.72
French Canadian	251	1.18
German	8,666	40.91
Greek	88	0.42
Guyanese	7	0.03
Hawaii Native/Pacific Islander:	23	0.11
Micronesian: (1)	2	0.01
Guamanian/Chamorro	1	0.00
Other Micronesian (1)	1	0.00
Polynesian: (2)	16	0.08
Native Hawaiian	8	0.04
Samoan (1)	1	0.00
Other Polynesian (1)	7	0.03
Other Pac. Isl., not spec. (2)	5	0.02
Hispanic or Latino:	345	1.63
Central American:	18	0.09
Costa Rican	1	0.00
Guatemalan	1	0.00
Honduran	6	0.03
Nicaraguan	5	0.02
Salvadoran	5	0.02
Cuban	13	0.06
Mexican	185	0.88
Puerto Rican	16	0.08
South American:	32	0.15
Bolivian	1	0.00
Chilean	2	0.01
Colombian	8	0.04
Ecuadorian	18	0.09
Peruvian	2	0.01
Other South American	1	0.00
Other Hispanic or Latino	81	0.38
Hungarian	48	0.23
Irish	3,221	15.20
Italian	543	2.56
Latvian	33	0.16
Lithuanian	22	0.10
Luxemburger	7	0.03
Northern European	27	0.13
Norwegian	4,075	19.24
Polish	905	4.27
Portuguese	42	0.20
Romanian	15	0.07
Russian	148	0.70
Scandinavian	319	1.51
Scotch-Irish	230	1.09
Scottish	481	2.27
Serbian	25	0.12
Slavic	8	0.04
Slovak	32	0.15
Slovene	13	0.06
Swedish	2,227	10.51
Swiss	36	0.17
Ukrainian	55	0.26
United States or American	420	1.98
Welsh	114	0.54
West Indian, excl. Hispanic:	4	0.02
West Indian	4	0.02
White:	19,415	91.95
Not Hispanic (18,978)	19,225	91.05
Hispanic (162)	190	0.90
Yugoslavian	39	0.18

Shakopee

Place Type: City
County: Scott
Population: 20,568

Ancestry/Race	Number	%
African American/Black:	370	1.80
Not Hispanic (264)	348	1.69
Hispanic (9)	22	0.11

Notes: 1. Figures in the "Number" column do not add up to the total population due to: a) Ancestry/Race overlap — e.g. persons can report being both White and Irish, b) persons of Hispanic origin can report being any race, c) persons reporting two ancestries are counted in both categories. 2. Numbers in parentheses indicate the number of persons reporting this ancestry/race alone, not in combination with any other ancestry/race. 3. Refer to the Explanation of Data in the front of the book for more detailed information.

Ancestry/Race	Number	%
African, sub-Saharan:	5	0.02
African	5	0.02
Am. Ind. or Alaska Nat., not spec.	90	0.44
American Indian tribes, specified:	207	1.01
Apache	1	0.00
Blackfeet	1	0.00
Cherokee (5)	19	0.09
Cheyenne (1)	1	0.00
Chippewa (48)	70	0.34
Cree (1)	1	0.00
Crow (1)	3	0.01
Iroquois (3)	3	0.01
Latin American Indians (2)	7	0.03
Menominee (1)	1	0.00
Navajo (4)	4	0.02
Osage (1)	1	0.00
Ottawa	1	0.00
Potawatomi (1)	1	0.00
Sioux (52)	74	0.36
Yakama (4)	4	0.02
All other tribes (10)	15	0.07
American Indian tribes, not spec.	6	0.03
Arab:	6	0.03
Syrian	6	0.03
Armenian	3	0.01
Asian:	616	2.99
Cambodian (81)	95	0.46
Chinese, ex. Taiwanese (63)	73	0.35
Filipino (27)	40	0.19
Hmong (2)	4	0.02
Indian (56)	59	0.29
Indonesian (2)	2	0.01
Japanese (9)	26	0.13
Korean (35)	66	0.32
Laotian (110)	120	0.58
Malaysian (1)	1	0.00
Taiwanese (2)	6	0.03
Thai (8)	9	0.04
Vietnamese (78)	89	0.43
Other Asian, specified	2	0.01
Other Asian, not specified (11)	24	0.12
Austrian	63	0.31
Belgian	67	0.33
British	61	0.30
Canadian	85	0.41
Croatian	7	0.03
Czech	814	3.97
Czechoslovakian	133	0.65
Danish	218	1.06
Dutch	432	2.11
English	1,250	6.10
European	110	0.54
Finnish	228	1.11
French, except Basque	686	3.35
French Canadian	201	0.98
German	9,784	47.73
German Russian	11	0.05
Guyanese	49	0.24
Hawaii Native/Pacific Islander:	35	0.17
Micronesian: (2)	3	0.01
Guamanian/Chamorro (2)	3	0.01
Polynesian: (1)	16	0.08
Native Hawaiian (1)	14	0.07
Samoan	1	0.00
Other Polynesian	1	0.00
Other Pac. Isl., specified	2	0.01
Other Pac. Isl., not spec. (5)	14	0.07
Hispanic or Latino:	906	4.40
Central American:	23	0.11
Costa Rican	1	0.00
Guatemalan	8	0.04
Honduran	2	0.01
Panamanian	2	0.01
Salvadoran	10	0.05
Cuban	11	0.05
Dominican Republic	4	0.02
Mexican	720	3.50
Puerto Rican	24	0.12
South American:	6	0.03
Chilean	1	0.00
Colombian	1	0.00
Paraguayan	2	0.01
Peruvian	1	0.00
Other South American	1	0.00
Other Hispanic or Latino	118	0.57
Hungarian	71	0.35
Icelander	8	0.04
Irish	2,695	13.15
Italian	253	1.23
Latvian	27	0.13
Lithuanian	6	0.03
Luxemburger	114	0.56
Norwegian	2,767	13.50
Pennsylvania German	16	0.08
Polish	685	3.34
Romanian	27	0.13
Russian	119	0.58
Scandinavian	193	0.94
Scotch-Irish	193	0.94
Scottish	243	1.19
Slavic	23	0.11
Slovak	7	0.03
Slovene	39	0.19
Swedish	1,459	7.12
Swiss	53	0.26
Ukrainian	34	0.17
United States or American	578	2.82
Welsh	54	0.26
West Indian, excl. Hispanic:	9	0.04
Belizean	9	0.04
White:	19,101	92.87
Not Hispanic (18,432)	18,643	90.64
Hispanic (410)	458	2.23
Yugoslavian	24	0.12

Shoreview

Place Type: City
County: Ramsey
Population: 25,924

Ancestry/Race	Number	%
African American/Black:	319	1.23
Not Hispanic (253)	308	1.19
Hispanic (8)	11	0.04
African, sub-Saharan:	127	0.49
African	41	0.16
Kenyan	64	0.25
Nigerian	7	0.03
South African	8	0.03
Ugandan	7	0.03
Alaska Native tribes, specified:	1	0.00
Eskimo	1	0.00
Am. Ind. or Alaska Nat., not spec.	42	0.16
Alsatian	8	0.03
American Indian tribes, specified:	100	0.39
Blackfeet	1	0.00
Cherokee	6	0.02
Chippewa (35)	65	0.25
Choctaw (1)	1	0.00
Cree	3	0.01
Latin American Indians (3)	4	0.02
Menominee	1	0.00
Osage	2	0.01
Sioux (4)	12	0.05
All other tribes (4)	5	0.02
American Indian tribes, not spec.	5	0.02
Arab:	92	0.35
Lebanese	85	0.33
Syrian	7	0.03
Armenian	21	0.08
Asian:	1,115	4.30
Bangladeshi (1)	1	0.00
Cambodian (5)	5	0.02
Chinese, ex. Taiwanese (199)	232	0.89
Filipino (21)	43	0.17
Hmong (50)	51	0.20
Indian (296)	318	1.23
Indonesian (5)	6	0.02
Japanese (34)	71	0.27
Korean (168)	187	0.72
Laotian (7)	7	0.03
Malaysian (1)	1	0.00
Pakistani (17)	20	0.08
Taiwanese (23)	34	0.13
Thai (9)	10	0.04
Vietnamese (81)	98	0.38
Other Asian, specified (1)	1	0.00
Other Asian, not specified (16)	30	0.12
Austrian	201	0.78
Belgian	98	0.38
Brazilian	26	0.10
British	54	0.21
Bulgarian	6	0.02
Canadian	55	0.21
Celtic	6	0.02
Croatian	83	0.32
Czech	435	1.68
Czechoslovakian	39	0.15
Danish	851	3.28
Dutch	402	1.55
Eastern European	7	0.03
English	2,159	8.33
European	329	1.27
Finnish	343	1.32
French, except Basque	1,082	4.17
French Canadian	435	1.68
German	9,934	38.32
German Russian	6	0.02
Greek	107	0.41
Hawaii Native/Pacific Islander:	23	0.09
Micronesian:	3	0.01
Guamanian/Chamorro	3	0.01
Polynesian: (13)	15	0.06
Native Hawaiian (2)	3	0.01
Samoan (1)	1	0.00
Tongan (10)	11	0.04
Other Pac. Isl., not spec. (1)	5	0.02
Hispanic or Latino:	346	1.33
Central American:	14	0.05
Costa Rican	1	0.00
Guatemalan	7	0.03
Honduran	2	0.01
Panamanian	2	0.01
Salvadoran	1	0.00
Other Central American	1	0.00
Cuban	9	0.03
Dominican Republic	5	0.02
Mexican	189	0.73
Puerto Rican	24	0.09
South American:	39	0.15
Argentinean	3	0.01
Bolivian	2	0.01
Chilean	3	0.01
Colombian	22	0.08
Paraguayan	1	0.00
Peruvian	6	0.02
Uruguayan	1	0.00
Venezuelan	1	0.00
Other Hispanic or Latino	66	0.25
Hungarian	108	0.42
Irish	3,590	13.85
Italian	1,058	4.08
Latvian	7	0.03
Lithuanian	27	0.10
Luxemburger	23	0.09
Northern European	35	0.14
Norwegian	4,119	15.89
Pennsylvania German	5	0.02
Polish	1,427	5.50
Portuguese	14	0.05
Romanian	37	0.14
Russian	315	1.22
Scandinavian	402	1.55
Scotch-Irish	235	0.91
Scottish	410	1.58
Serbian	16	0.06
Slavic	43	0.17
Slovak	52	0.20
Slovene	75	0.29

Notes: 1. Figures in the "Number" column do not add up to the total population due to: a) Ancestry/Race overlap — e.g. persons can report being both White and Irish, b) persons of Hispanic origin can report being any race, c) persons reporting two ancestries are counted in both categories. 2. Numbers in parentheses indicate the number of persons reporting this ancestry/race alone, not in combination with any other ancestry/race. 3. Refer to the Explanation of Data in the front of the book for more detailed information.

Ancestry/Race	Number	%
Swedish	3,614	13.94
Swiss	167	0.64
Turkish	13	0.05
Ukrainian	85	0.33
United States or American	535	2.06
Welsh	220	0.85
West Indian, excl. Hispanic:	18	0.07
Barbadian	9	0.03
Jamaican	9	0.03
White:	24,503	94.52
Not Hispanic (23,984)	24,269	93.62
Hispanic (199)	234	0.90
Yugoslavian	88	0.34

South Saint Paul

Place Type: City
County: Dakota
Population: 20,167

Ancestry/Race	Number	%
African American/Black:	372	1.84
Not Hispanic (243)	349	1.73
Hispanic (15)	23	0.11
African, sub-Saharan:	36	0.18
African	31	0.15
Nigerian	5	0.02
Am. Ind. or Alaska Nat., not spec.	75	0.37
Albanian	6	0.03
American Indian tribes, specified:	131	0.65
Blackfeet	1	0.00
Cherokee (2)	14	0.07
Chippewa (48)	71	0.35
Choctaw	3	0.01
Cree	4	0.02
Menominee (1)	1	0.00
Sioux (10)	25	0.12
All other tribes (8)	12	0.06
American Indian tribes, not spec.	24	0.12
Arab:	131	0.65
Egyptian	99	0.49
Lebanese	32	0.16
Asian:	202	1.00
Cambodian (7)	11	0.05
Chinese, ex. Taiwanese (24)	30	0.15
Filipino (30)	39	0.19
Hmong (38)	39	0.19
Indian (5)	5	0.02
Japanese (12)	16	0.08
Korean (24)	31	0.15
Sri Lankan	2	0.01
Vietnamese (10)	14	0.07
Other Asian, specified (1)	1	0.00
Other Asian, not specified (11)	14	0.07
Austrian	206	1.02
Belgian	44	0.22
British	12	0.06
Canadian	24	0.12
Celtic	34	0.17
Croatian	142	0.70
Czech	330	1.63
Czechoslovakian	34	0.17
Danish	274	1.36
Dutch	343	1.70
Eastern European	9	0.04
English	964	4.77
European	133	0.66
Finnish	248	1.23
French, except Basque	1,138	5.64
French Canadian	354	1.75
German	8,036	39.80
Greek	82	0.41
Hawaii Native/Pacific Islander:	8	0.04
Micronesian:	2	0.01
Guamanian/Chamorro	2	0.01
Polynesian: (1)	5	0.02
Native Hawaiian (1)	4	0.02
Samoan	1	0.00
Other Pac. Isl., not spec. (1)	1	0.00
Hispanic or Latino:	1,295	6.42
Central American:	49	0.24
Costa Rican	4	0.02
Guatemalan	5	0.02
Honduran	5	0.02
Nicaraguan	2	0.01
Salvadoran	30	0.15
Other Central American	3	0.01
Cuban	12	0.06
Dominican Republic	2	0.01
Mexican	977	4.84
Puerto Rican	114	0.57
South American:	11	0.05
Colombian	5	0.02
Ecuadorian	6	0.03
Other Hispanic or Latino	130	0.64
Hungarian	78	0.39
Irish	3,141	15.56
Italian	847	4.19
Lithuanian	14	0.07
Luxemburger	9	0.04
Macedonian	7	0.03
Northern European	16	0.08
Norwegian	2,360	11.69
Pennsylvania German	7	0.03
Polish	1,576	7.81
Portuguese	14	0.07
Romanian	160	0.79
Russian	146	0.72
Scandinavian	194	0.96
Scotch-Irish	153	0.76
Scottish	220	1.09
Serbian	152	0.75
Slovak	6	0.03
Slovene	8	0.04
Swedish	1,685	8.34
Swiss	94	0.47
Ukrainian	65	0.32
United States or American	489	2.42
Welsh	43	0.21
West Indian, excl. Hispanic:	4	0.02
Haitian	4	0.02
White:	19,049	94.46
Not Hispanic (18,089)	18,343	90.96
Hispanic (591)	706	3.50
Yugoslavian	19	0.09

Stillwater

Place Type: City
County: Washington
Population: 15,143

Ancestry/Race	Number	%
African American/Black:	85	0.56
Not Hispanic (48)	81	0.53
Hispanic	4	0.03
African, sub-Saharan:	10	0.07
African	10	0.07
Alaska Native tribes, specified:	3	0.02
Tlingit-Haida (3)	3	0.02
Am. Ind. or Alaska Nat., not spec.	20	0.13
Alsatian	8	0.05
American Indian tribes, specified:	66	0.44
Blackfeet	1	0.01
Cherokee (1)	6	0.04
Chippewa (17)	34	0.22
Cree	5	0.03
Sioux (7)	13	0.09
All other tribes (1)	7	0.05
American Indian tribes, not spec.	1	0.01
Arab:	7	0.05
Lebanese	7	0.05
Asian:	135	0.89
Chinese, ex. Taiwanese (21)	26	0.17
Filipino (8)	24	0.16
Indian (11)	21	0.14
Japanese (4)	7	0.05
Korean (35)	39	0.26
Malaysian	4	0.03
Pakistani (1)	1	0.01
Thai	1	0.01
Vietnamese	6	0.04
Other Asian, specified (1)	1	0.01
Other Asian, not specified (4)	5	0.03
Australian	15	0.10
Austrian	84	0.55
Belgian	48	0.32
British	92	0.61
Bulgarian	7	0.05
Canadian	13	0.09
Celtic	6	0.04
Croatian	34	0.22
Czech	165	1.09
Czechoslovakian	28	0.18
Danish	448	2.95
Dutch	180	1.19
English	1,046	6.89
European	85	0.56
Finnish	222	1.46
French, except Basque	978	6.44
French Canadian	295	1.94
German	5,997	39.49
Guyanese	12	0.08
Hawaii Native/Pacific Islander:	9	0.06
Polynesian: (3)	9	0.06
Native Hawaiian (2)	6	0.04
Samoan (1)	3	0.02
Hispanic or Latino:	148	0.98
Central American:	10	0.07
Costa Rican	1	0.01
Guatemalan	6	0.04
Honduran	1	0.01
Panamanian	1	0.01
Other Central American	1	0.01
Cuban	1	0.01
Dominican Republic	1	0.01
Mexican	94	0.62
Puerto Rican	4	0.03
South American:	5	0.03
Chilean	2	0.01
Colombian	1	0.01
Peruvian	1	0.01
Uruguayan	1	0.01
Other Hispanic or Latino	33	0.22
Hungarian	49	0.32
Icelander	13	0.09
Irish	2,880	18.97
Italian	805	5.30
Latvian	9	0.06
Lithuanian	11	0.07
Luxemburger	19	0.13
Northern European	31	0.20
Norwegian	2,238	14.74
Pennsylvania German	8	0.05
Polish	730	4.81
Portuguese	5	0.03
Romanian	7	0.05
Russian	33	0.22
Scandinavian	166	1.09
Scotch-Irish	200	1.32
Scottish	325	2.14
Serbian	5	0.03
Slavic	9	0.06
Slovak	7	0.05
Swedish	2,250	14.82
Swiss	189	1.24
United States or American	365	2.40
Welsh	184	1.21
West Indian, excl. Hispanic:	9	0.06
Jamaican	9	0.06
White:	14,901	98.40
Not Hispanic (14,685)	14,802	97.75
Hispanic (82)	99	0.65
Yugoslavian	7	0.05

Notes: 1. Figures in the "Number" column do not add up to the total population due to: a) Ancestry/Race overlap — e.g. persons can report being both White and Irish, b) persons of Hispanic origin can report being any race, c) persons reporting two ancestries are counted in both categories. 2. Numbers in parentheses indicate the number of persons reporting this ancestry/race alone, not in combination with any other ancestry/race. 3. Refer to the Explanation of Data in the front of the book for more detailed information.

Vadnais Heights

Place Type: City
County: Ramsey
Population: 13,069

Ancestry/Race	Number	%
African American/Black:	245	1.87
Not Hispanic (185)	235	1.80
Hispanic (9)	10	0.08
African, sub-Saharan:	45	0.34
African	31	0.24
Other sub-Saharan African	14	0.11
Am. Ind. or Alaska Nat., not spec.	30	0.23
American Indian tribes, specified:	72	0.55
Apache	1	0.01
Cherokee (1)	4	0.03
Cheyenne (1)	1	0.01
Chippewa (22)	32	0.24
Latin American Indians (9)	10	0.08
Potawatomi (1)	1	0.01
Pueblo	1	0.01
Sioux (7)	14	0.11
All other tribes (4)	8	0.06
American Indian tribes, not spec.	2	0.02
Arab:	10	0.08
Lebanese	10	0.08
Asian:	673	5.15
Bangladeshi (1)	1	0.01
Cambodian (15)	19	0.15
Chinese, ex. Taiwanese (64)	78	0.60
Filipino (11)	25	0.19
Hmong (219)	228	1.74
Indian (73)	81	0.62
Japanese (8)	16	0.12
Korean (50)	61	0.47
Laotian (17)	18	0.14
Pakistani (13)	13	0.10
Sri Lankan (3)	3	0.02
Taiwanese (19)	19	0.15
Thai (2)	2	0.02
Vietnamese (69)	86	0.66
Other Asian, not specified (17)	23	0.18
Austrian	111	0.85
Belgian	21	0.16
British	25	0.19
Canadian	25	0.19
Croatian	26	0.20
Czech	178	1.36
Czechoslovakian	113	0.87
Danish	227	1.74
Dutch	192	1.47
Eastern European	8	0.06
English	792	6.06
European	130	1.00
Finnish	211	1.62
French, except Basque	669	5.12
French Canadian	285	2.18
German	5,201	39.82
Greek	39	0.30
Hawaii Native/Pacific Islander:	9	0.07
Polynesian:	3	0.02
Native Hawaiian	3	0.02
Other Pac. Isl., not spec.	6	0.05
Hispanic or Latino:	210	1.61
Central American:	4	0.03
Guatemalan	2	0.02
Honduran	1	0.01
Salvadoran	1	0.01
Cuban	6	0.05
Mexican	150	1.15
Puerto Rican	9	0.07
South American:	13	0.10
Chilean	1	0.01
Colombian	10	0.08
Paraguayan	1	0.01
Peruvian	1	0.01
Other Hispanic or Latino	28	0.21
Hungarian	16	0.12
Icelander	21	0.16
Iranian	44	0.34
Irish	1,892	14.48
Italian	561	4.29
Latvian	23	0.18
Lithuanian	9	0.07
Northern European	6	0.05
Norwegian	1,860	14.24
Polish	760	5.82
Russian	80	0.61
Scandinavian	104	0.80
Scotch-Irish	55	0.42
Scottish	182	1.39
Serbian	36	0.28
Slovak	9	0.07
Slovene	24	0.18
Swedish	1,924	14.73
Swiss	52	0.40
Ukrainian	20	0.15
United States or American	452	3.46
Welsh	70	0.54
White:	12,144	92.92
Not Hispanic (11,891)	12,019	91.97
Hispanic (90)	125	0.96

West Saint Paul

Place Type: City
County: Dakota
Population: 19,405

Ancestry/Race	Number	%
African American/Black:	714	3.68
Not Hispanic (533)	676	3.48
Hispanic (16)	38	0.20
African, sub-Saharan:	170	0.88
African	43	0.22
Ethiopian	10	0.05
Ghanian	24	0.12
Nigerian	17	0.09
Other sub-Saharan African	76	0.39
Am. Ind. or Alaska Nat., not spec.	93	0.48
American Indian tribes, specified:	133	0.69
Blackfeet	4	0.02
Cherokee (2)	5	0.03
Chippewa (27)	47	0.24
Choctaw (1)	3	0.02
Comanche (1)	1	0.01
Cree (1)	3	0.02
Creek (1)	1	0.01
Delaware (1)	1	0.01
Iroquois (2)	3	0.02
Latin American Indians (6)	8	0.04
Navajo	2	0.01
Pueblo (3)	3	0.02
Sioux (21)	38	0.20
All other tribes (11)	14	0.07
American Indian tribes, not spec.	11	0.06
Arab:	290	1.49
Egyptian	4	0.02
Lebanese	251	1.29
Palestinian	19	0.10
Syrian	16	0.08
Asian:	433	2.23
Cambodian (10)	14	0.07
Chinese, ex. Taiwanese (51)	60	0.31
Filipino (109)	126	0.65
Hmong (56)	57	0.29
Indian (45)	62	0.32
Indonesian (4)	5	0.03
Japanese (10)	14	0.07
Korean (40)	42	0.22
Laotian (2)	3	0.02
Pakistani (1)	1	0.01
Thai (2)	2	0.01
Vietnamese (21)	25	0.13
Other Asian, specified (1)	4	0.02
Other Asian, not specified (8)	18	0.09
Austrian	176	0.91
Belgian	55	0.28
British	42	0.22
Canadian	14	0.07
Croatian	46	0.24
Czech	337	1.74
Czechoslovakian	98	0.51
Danish	245	1.26
Dutch	322	1.66
English	995	5.13
European	102	0.53
Finnish	144	0.74
French, except Basque	926	4.77
French Canadian	329	1.70
German	7,337	37.81
Greek	40	0.21
Hawaii Native/Pacific Islander:	15	0.08
Polynesian: (5)	11	0.06
Native Hawaiian	3	0.02
Samoan (5)	8	0.04
Other Pac. Isl., not spec.	4	0.02
Hispanic or Latino:	1,937	9.98
Central American:	104	0.54
Costa Rican	1	0.01
Guatemalan	13	0.07
Honduran	32	0.16
Nicaraguan	4	0.02
Panamanian	6	0.03
Salvadoran	45	0.23
Other Central American	3	0.02
Cuban	21	0.11
Dominican Republic	3	0.02
Mexican	1,440	7.42
Puerto Rican	132	0.68
South American:	32	0.16
Argentinean	2	0.01
Chilean	2	0.01
Colombian	11	0.06
Ecuadorian	5	0.03
Peruvian	5	0.03
Venezuelan	6	0.03
Other South American	1	0.01
Other Hispanic or Latino	205	1.06
Hungarian	78	0.40
Iranian	7	0.04
Irish	2,920	15.05
Italian	864	4.45
Lithuanian	32	0.16
Luxemburger	60	0.31
Northern European	34	0.18
Norwegian	1,866	9.62
Pennsylvania German	9	0.05
Polish	770	3.97
Romanian	55	0.28
Russian	93	0.48
Scandinavian	116	0.60
Scotch-Irish	196	1.01
Scottish	224	1.15
Serbian	7	0.04
Slavic	17	0.09
Slovak	37	0.19
Slovene	66	0.34
Swedish	1,403	7.23
Swiss	119	0.61
Ukrainian	103	0.53
United States or American	572	2.95
Welsh	53	0.27
White:	17,372	89.52
Not Hispanic (16,144)	16,425	84.64
Hispanic (790)	947	4.88
Yugoslavian	39	0.20

White Bear Lake

Place Type: City
County: Ramsey
Population: 24,325

Ancestry/Race	Number	%
African American/Black:	356	1.46
Not Hispanic (253)	338	1.39
Hispanic (9)	18	0.07
African, sub-Saharan:	84	0.34

Notes: 1. Figures in the "Number" column do not add up to the total population due to: a) Ancestry/Race overlap — e.g. persons can report being both White and Irish, b) persons of Hispanic origin can report being any race, c) persons reporting two ancestries are counted in both categories. 2. Numbers in parentheses indicate the number of persons reporting this ancestry/race alone, not in combination with any other ancestry/race. 3. Refer to the Explanation of Data in the front of the book for more detailed information.

African	8	0.03
Ghanian	13	0.05
Somalian	63	0.26
Alaska Native tribes, specified:	1	0.00
Alaska Athabascan (1)	1	0.00
Alaska Native tribes, not specified	1	0.00
Am. Ind. or Alaska Nat., not spec.	65	0.27
American Indian tribes, specified:	138	0.57
Apache	1	0.00
Blackfeet	1	0.00
Cherokee (3)	9	0.04
Chippewa (33)	59	0.24
Choctaw (1)	1	0.00
Comanche	1	0.00
Iroquois (1)	1	0.00
Latin American Indians (8)	12	0.05
Navajo (2)	5	0.02
Ottawa	8	0.03
Puget Sound Salish	1	0.00
Sioux (8)	28	0.12
All other tribes (2)	11	0.05
American Indian tribes, not spec.	9	0.04
Arab:	57	0.23
Egyptian	18	0.07
Lebanese	31	0.13
Syrian	8	0.03
Asian:	470	1.93
Cambodian (27)	28	0.12
Chinese, ex. Taiwanese (31)	45	0.18
Filipino (17)	32	0.13
Hmong (110)	118	0.49
Indian (35)	42	0.17
Indonesian (7)	7	0.03
Japanese (19)	35	0.14
Korean (68)	79	0.32
Laotian (5)	7	0.03
Pakistani (1)	3	0.01
Sri Lankan	1	0.00
Taiwanese	1	0.00
Thai	1	0.00
Vietnamese (44)	51	0.21
Other Asian, specified (2)	2	0.01
Other Asian, not specified (4)	18	0.07
Austrian	273	1.12
Belgian	108	0.44
Brazilian	15	0.06
British	38	0.16
Bulgarian	14	0.06
Canadian	26	0.11
Celtic	6	0.02
Croatian	88	0.36
Czech	288	1.18
Czechoslovakian	89	0.36
Danish	387	1.58
Dutch	406	1.66
Eastern European	5	0.02
English	1,713	7.01
Estonian	9	0.04
European	184	0.75
Finnish	513	2.10
French, except Basque	1,775	7.26
French Canadian	816	3.34
German	9,223	37.72
Greek	37	0.15
Hawaii Native/Pacific Islander:	20	0.08
Polynesian: (10)	15	0.06
Native Hawaiian (6)	6	0.02
Samoan (2)	4	0.02
Tongan (2)	5	0.02
Other Pac. Isl., not spec. (3)	5	0.02
Hispanic or Latino:	425	1.75
Central American:	15	0.06
Costa Rican	4	0.02
Guatemalan	3	0.01
Nicaraguan	3	0.01
Panamanian	2	0.01
Other Central American	3	0.01
Cuban	14	0.06
Mexican	291	1.20
Puerto Rican	11	0.05
South American:	17	0.07
Argentinean	3	0.01
Chilean	5	0.02
Colombian	7	0.03
Paraguayan	1	0.00
Other South American	1	0.00
Other Hispanic or Latino	77	0.32
Hungarian	122	0.50
Iranian	4	0.02
Irish	3,493	14.28
Italian	1,013	4.14
Latvian	76	0.31
Lithuanian	21	0.09
Luxemburger	13	0.05
Northern European	86	0.35
Norwegian	3,544	14.49
Polish	1,313	5.37
Portuguese	3	0.01
Romanian	11	0.04
Russian	161	0.66
Scandinavian	295	1.21
Scotch-Irish	150	0.61
Scottish	408	1.67
Serbian	22	0.09
Slavic	19	0.08
Slovak	83	0.34
Slovene	61	0.25
Swedish	2,918	11.93
Swiss	104	0.43
Ukrainian	20	0.08
United States or American	661	2.70
Welsh	110	0.45
White:	23,470	96.49
Not Hispanic (22,919)	23,157	95.20
Hispanic (264)	313	1.29

White Bear

Place Type: Township
County: Ramsey
Population: 11,293

Ancestry/Race	Number	%
African American/Black:	59	0.52
Not Hispanic (45)	57	0.50
Hispanic (1)	2	0.02
African, sub-Saharan:	19	0.17
African	6	0.05
South African	13	0.12
Alaska Native tribes, not specified	1	0.01
Am. Ind. or Alaska Nat., not spec.	10	0.09
American Indian tribes, specified:	35	0.31
Cherokee (1)	1	0.01
Cheyenne (1)	1	0.01
Chippewa (13)	17	0.15
Cree	3	0.03
Latin American Indians	2	0.02
Ottawa (1)	1	0.01
Sioux (4)	4	0.04
All other tribes	6	0.05
American Indian tribes, not spec.	1	0.01
Arab:	54	0.48
Egyptian	26	0.23
Lebanese	28	0.25
Asian:	167	1.48
Chinese, ex. Taiwanese (15)	22	0.19
Filipino (7)	12	0.11
Hmong (28)	29	0.26
Indian (13)	15	0.13
Japanese (15)	18	0.16
Korean (36)	46	0.41
Laotian (2)	2	0.02
Pakistani (4)	4	0.04
Thai (1)	1	0.01
Vietnamese (10)	11	0.10
Other Asian, not specified (5)	7	0.06
Austrian	50	0.45
Belgian	38	0.34
British	60	0.54
Canadian	9	0.08
Croatian	52	0.46
Czech	120	1.07
Czechoslovakian	19	0.17
Danish	189	1.69
Dutch	127	1.13
English	941	8.41
European	129	1.15
Finnish	292	2.61
French, except Basque	958	8.56
French Canadian	182	1.63
German	4,463	39.88
Hawaii Native/Pacific Islander:	6	0.05
Micronesian: (1)	3	0.03
Guamanian/Chamorro (1)	3	0.03
Polynesian:	2	0.02
Native Hawaiian	2	0.02
Other Pac. Isl., not spec. (1)	1	0.01
Hispanic or Latino:	134	1.19
Central American:	7	0.06
Guatemalan	4	0.04
Panamanian	3	0.03
Cuban	1	0.01
Mexican	77	0.68
Puerto Rican	9	0.08
South American:	15	0.13
Argentinean	1	0.01
Colombian	5	0.04
Ecuadorian	3	0.03
Peruvian	6	0.05
Other Hispanic or Latino	25	0.22
Hungarian	20	0.18
Icelander	6	0.05
Irish	1,755	15.68
Italian	528	4.72
Latvian	84	0.75
Lithuanian	7	0.06
Luxemburger	10	0.09
Northern European	25	0.22
Norwegian	1,594	14.24
Polish	794	7.09
Portuguese	39	0.35
Russian	64	0.57
Scandinavian	250	2.23
Scotch-Irish	79	0.71
Scottish	201	1.80
Serbian	30	0.27
Slavic	49	0.44
Slovak	44	0.39
Slovene	12	0.11
Swedish	1,318	11.78
Swiss	90	0.80
Turkish	6	0.05
Ukrainian	51	0.46
United States or American	311	2.78
Welsh	21	0.19
White:	11,045	97.80
Not Hispanic (10,882)	10,943	96.90
Hispanic (88)	102	0.90
Yugoslavian	7	0.06

Willmar

Place Type: City
County: Kandiyohi
Population: 18,351

Ancestry/Race	Number	%
Acadian/Cajun	6	0.03
African American/Black:	244	1.33
Not Hispanic (131)	207	1.13
Hispanic (34)	37	0.20
African, sub-Saharan:	133	0.72
African	24	0.13
Somalian	109	0.59
Am. Ind. or Alaska Nat., not spec.	41	0.22
American Indian tribes, specified:	73	0.40
Blackfeet	2	0.01
Cherokee (4)	9	0.05
Chippewa (15)	17	0.09
Choctaw (1)	3	0.02

Notes: 1. Figures in the "Number" column do not add up to the total population due to: a) Ancestry/Race overlap — e.g. persons can report being both White and Irish, b) persons of Hispanic origin can report being any race, c) persons reporting two ancestries are counted in both categories. 2. Numbers in parentheses indicate the number of persons reporting this ancestry/race alone, not in combination with any other ancestry/race. 3. Refer to the Explanation of Data in the front of the book for more detailed information.

Latin American Indians (6)	10	0.05
Lumbee	1	0.01
Paiute (1)	2	0.01
Sioux (16)	18	0.10
Yuman (1)	4	0.02
All other tribes (3)	7	0.04
American Indian tribes, not spec.	8	0.04
Arab:	2	0.01
Egyptian	2	0.01
Asian:	132	0.72
Cambodian (4)	4	0.02
Chinese, ex. Taiwanese (19)	20	0.11
Filipino (15)	27	0.15
Hmong (15)	21	0.11
Indian (8)	10	0.05
Indonesian (1)	3	0.02
Japanese (2)	3	0.02
Korean (14)	16	0.09
Pakistani (1)	1	0.01
Thai (1)	1	0.01
Vietnamese (10)	12	0.07
Other Asian, not specified (8)	14	0.08
Austrian	36	0.20
Belgian	76	0.41
Brazilian	21	0.11
British	12	0.07
Bulgarian	6	0.03
Canadian	11	0.06
Croatian	8	0.04
Czech	275	1.49
Czechoslovakian	38	0.21
Danish	396	2.15
Dutch	1,072	5.83
English	525	2.85
European	13	0.07
Finnish	73	0.40
French, except Basque	492	2.67
French Canadian	93	0.51
German	6,256	34.01
Greek	5	0.03
Hawaii Native/Pacific Islander:	23	0.13
Micronesian: (1)	1	0.01
Guamanian/Chamorro (1)	1	0.01
Polynesian: (17)	17	0.09
Native Hawaiian (1)	1	0.01
Samoan (16)	16	0.09
Other Pac. Isl., not spec. (2)	5	0.03
Hispanic or Latino:	2,911	15.86
Central American:	98	0.53
Guatemalan	12	0.07
Honduran	56	0.31
Nicaraguan	3	0.02
Panamanian	2	0.01
Salvadoran	23	0.13
Other Central American	2	0.01
Cuban	18	0.10
Dominican Republic	2	0.01
Mexican	1,806	9.84
Puerto Rican	29	0.16
South American:	29	0.16
Bolivian	4	0.02
Chilean	6	0.03
Colombian	12	0.07
Ecuadorian	1	0.01
Peruvian	2	0.01
Venezuelan	4	0.02
Other Hispanic or Latino	929	5.06
Hungarian	4	0.02
Icelander	25	0.14
Irish	1,173	6.38
Italian	108	0.59
Luxemburger	1	0.01
Northern European	41	0.22
Norwegian	4,631	25.18
Pennsylvania German	7	0.04
Polish	488	2.65
Portuguese	11	0.06
Russian	16	0.09
Scandinavian	102	0.55
Scotch-Irish	85	0.46
Scottish	147	0.80
Serbian	10	0.05
Swedish	2,487	13.52
Swiss	59	0.32
Ukrainian	20	0.11
United States or American	527	2.86
Welsh	21	0.11
White:	16,350	89.10
Not Hispanic (14,990)	15,061	82.07
Hispanic (1,181)	1,289	7.02
Yugoslavian	2	0.01

Winona

Place Type: City
County: Winona
Population: 27,069

Ancestry/Race	Number	%
African American/Black:	360	1.33
Not Hispanic (306)	354	1.31
Hispanic	6	0.02
African, sub-Saharan:	75	0.28
African	53	0.20
Cape Verdean	8	0.03
Ethiopian	7	0.03
Kenyan	7	0.03
Am. Ind. or Alaska Nat., not spec.	64	0.24
American Indian tribes, specified:	93	0.34
Apache (2)	2	0.01
Blackfeet	7	0.03
Cherokee (6)	20	0.07
Cheyenne	3	0.01
Chippewa (5)	14	0.05
Cree	1	0.00
Iroquois (2)	4	0.01
Latin American Indians	1	0.00
Menominee (1)	1	0.00
Navajo (1)	1	0.00
Ottawa	3	0.01
Paiute (1)	1	0.00
Sioux (11)	24	0.09
All other tribes (2)	11	0.04
American Indian tribes, not spec.	5	0.02
Arab:	62	0.23
Egyptian	6	0.02
Lebanese	12	0.04
Palestinian	8	0.03
Syrian	20	0.07
Other Arab	16	0.06
Asian:	847	3.13
Bangladeshi (12)	13	0.05
Cambodian (1)	2	0.01
Chinese, ex. Taiwanese (121)	133	0.49
Filipino (19)	31	0.11
Hmong (199)	227	0.84
Indian (94)	119	0.44
Indonesian (7)	9	0.03
Japanese (55)	66	0.24
Korean (73)	87	0.32
Laotian (3)	3	0.01
Malaysian (37)	45	0.17
Pakistani (13)	13	0.05
Sri Lankan (5)	5	0.02
Taiwanese (4)	5	0.02
Thai (6)	6	0.02
Vietnamese (33)	37	0.14
Other Asian, specified (4)	7	0.03
Other Asian, not specified (24)	39	0.14
Australian	9	0.03
Austrian	93	0.34
Belgian	53	0.20
Brazilian	5	0.02
British	49	0.18
Canadian	57	0.21
Croatian	26	0.10
Czech	563	2.09
Czechoslovakian	73	0.27
Danish	319	1.18
Dutch	397	1.47
English	1,494	5.54
European	219	0.81
Finnish	139	0.52
French, except Basque	985	3.65
French Canadian	167	0.62
German	11,693	43.33
Greek	32	0.12
Hawaii Native/Pacific Islander:	22	0.08
Micronesian:	4	0.01
Guamanian/Chamorro	4	0.01
Polynesian: (2)	7	0.03
Native Hawaiian (2)	6	0.02
Samoan	1	0.00
Other Pac. Isl., specified	2	0.01
Other Pac. Isl., not spec. (2)	9	0.03
Hispanic or Latino:	365	1.35
Central American:	4	0.01
Costa Rican	1	0.00
Panamanian	2	0.01
Salvadoran	1	0.00
Cuban	17	0.06
Dominican Republic	1	0.00
Mexican	231	0.85
Puerto Rican	17	0.06
South American:	19	0.07
Argentinean	2	0.01
Bolivian	1	0.00
Chilean	1	0.00
Colombian	9	0.03
Peruvian	2	0.01
Venezuelan	1	0.00
Other South American	3	0.01
Other Hispanic or Latino	76	0.28
Hungarian	99	0.37
Icelander	7	0.03
Iranian	6	0.02
Irish	3,525	13.06
Italian	565	2.09
Lithuanian	35	0.13
Luxemburger	174	0.64
Norwegian	4,192	15.53
Polish	4,010	14.86
Romanian	26	0.10
Russian	86	0.32
Scandinavian	152	0.56
Scotch-Irish	196	0.73
Scottish	239	0.89
Serbian	7	0.03
Slovak	15	0.06
Slovene	37	0.14
Swedish	904	3.35
Swiss	243	0.90
Ukrainian	54	0.20
United States or American	658	2.44
Welsh	110	0.41
White:	25,795	95.29
Not Hispanic (25,376)	25,554	94.40
Hispanic (197)	241	0.89
Yugoslavian	55	0.20

Woodbury

Place Type: City
County: Washington
Population: 46,463

Ancestry/Race	Number	%
African American/Black:	1,425	3.07
Not Hispanic (1,152)	1,378	2.97
Hispanic (16)	47	0.10
African, sub-Saharan:	274	0.59
African	102	0.22
Ethiopian	70	0.15
Liberian	6	0.01
Nigerian	66	0.14
Senegalese	8	0.02
Somalian	20	0.04
Ugandan	2	0.00
Alaska Native tribes, specified:	1	0.00
Alaska Athabascan (1)	1	0.00

Notes: 1. Figures in the "Number" column do not add up to the total population due to: a) Ancestry/Race overlap — e.g. persons can report being both White and Irish, b) persons of Hispanic origin can report being any race, c) persons reporting two ancestries are counted in both categories. 2. Numbers in parentheses indicate the number of persons reporting this ancestry/race alone, not in combination with any other ancestry/race. 3. Refer to the Explanation of Data in the front of the book for more detailed information.

Ancestry/Race	Number	%
Am. Ind. or Alaska Nat., not spec.	74	0.16
Alsatian	10	0.02
American Indian tribes, specified:	183	0.39
Blackfeet	1	0.00
Cherokee (8)	29	0.06
Cheyenne (2)	2	0.00
Chippewa (31)	73	0.16
Choctaw	4	0.01
Cree (1)	1	0.00
Creek (1)	1	0.00
Houma	1	0.00
Kiowa (1)	1	0.00
Latin American Indians (3)	8	0.02
Lumbee (1)	1	0.00
Navajo	4	0.01
Osage (3)	3	0.01
Potawatomi (1)	1	0.00
Pueblo (1)	1	0.00
Seminole (3)	8	0.02
Sioux (16)	28	0.06
All other tribes (12)	16	0.03
American Indian tribes, not spec.	12	0.03
Arab:	316	0.68
Arab/Arabic	20	0.04
Egyptian	78	0.17
Iraqi	8	0.02
Lebanese	163	0.35
Syrian	12	0.03
Other Arab	35	0.08
Asian:	2,643	5.69
Bangladeshi (5)	11	0.02
Cambodian (64)	74	0.16
Chinese, ex. Taiwanese (618)	694	1.49
Filipino (121)	162	0.35
Hmong (264)	291	0.63
Indian (438)	474	1.02
Japanese (103)	153	0.33
Korean (293)	334	0.72
Laotian (34)	35	0.08
Malaysian (1)	1	0.00
Pakistani (18)	24	0.05
Sri Lankan (15)	16	0.03
Taiwanese (47)	49	0.11
Thai (17)	25	0.05
Vietnamese (189)	217	0.47
Other Asian, specified (6)	6	0.01
Other Asian, not specified (58)	77	0.17
Assyrian/Chaldean/Syriac	8	0.02
Australian	10	0.02
Austrian	251	0.54
Belgian	108	0.23
British	229	0.49
Canadian	92	0.20
Croatian	171	0.37
Czech	956	2.06
Czechoslovakian	214	0.46
Danish	812	1.75
Dutch	784	1.69
English	3,444	7.41
European	369	0.79
Finnish	420	0.90
French, except Basque	1,877	4.04
French Canadian	788	1.70
German	17,457	37.57
German Russian	6	0.01
Greek	136	0.29
Hawaii Native/Pacific Islander:	35	0.08
Micronesian:	1	0.00
Guamanian/Chamorro	1	0.00
Polynesian: (6)	12	0.03
Native Hawaiian (2)	5	0.01
Samoan (1)	1	0.00
Tongan (1)	4	0.01
Other Polynesian (2)	2	0.00
Other Pac. Isl., not spec.	22	0.05
Hispanic or Latino:	996	2.14
Central American:	54	0.12
Costa Rican	4	0.01
Guatemalan	10	0.02
Honduran	8	0.02
Nicaraguan	6	0.01
Panamanian	6	0.01
Salvadoran	16	0.03
Other Central American	4	0.01
Cuban	25	0.05
Dominican Republic	6	0.01
Mexican	556	1.20
Puerto Rican	97	0.21
South American:	115	0.25
Argentinean	8	0.02
Bolivian	5	0.01
Chilean	4	0.01
Colombian	48	0.10
Ecuadorian	3	0.01
Paraguayan	5	0.01
Peruvian	14	0.03
Venezuelan	22	0.05
Other South American	6	0.01
Other Hispanic or Latino	143	0.31
Hungarian	137	0.29
Icelander	38	0.08
Iranian	95	0.20
Irish	7,332	15.78
Italian	2,279	4.90
Latvian	6	0.01
Lithuanian	164	0.35
Luxemburger	12	0.03
Macedonian	24	0.05
Northern European	79	0.17
Norwegian	6,359	13.69
Polish	2,734	5.88
Portuguese	86	0.19
Romanian	54	0.12
Russian	188	0.40
Scandinavian	537	1.16
Scotch-Irish	579	1.25
Scottish	605	1.30
Serbian	76	0.16
Slavic	11	0.02
Slovak	27	0.06
Slovene	27	0.06
Swedish	4,067	8.75
Swiss	257	0.55
Ukrainian	141	0.30
United States or American	1,301	2.80
Welsh	180	0.39
West Indian, excl. Hispanic:	38	0.08
British West Indian	16	0.03
Haitian	7	0.02
Trinidadian and Tobagonian	15	0.03
White:	42,475	91.42
Not Hispanic (41,238)	41,749	89.85
Hispanic (598)	726	1.56
Yugoslavian	86	0.19

Worthington

Place Type: City
County: Nobles
Population: 11,283

Ancestry/Race	Number	%
African American/Black:	249	2.21
Not Hispanic (205)	229	2.03
Hispanic (10)	20	0.18
African, sub-Saharan:	96	0.85
African	4	0.04
Ethiopian	67	0.59
Nigerian	10	0.09
Sudanese	15	0.13
Am. Ind. or Alaska Nat., not spec.	38	0.34
Alsatian	5	0.04
American Indian tribes, specified:	47	0.42
Blackfeet (1)	1	0.01
Chippewa	8	0.07
Latin American Indians (5)	5	0.04
Potawatomi	1	0.01
Sioux (13)	16	0.14
All other tribes (10)	16	0.14
American Indian tribes, not spec.	6	0.05
Arab:	13	0.12
Arab/Arabic	13	0.12
Asian:	917	8.13
Cambodian (1)	4	0.04
Chinese, ex. Taiwanese (22)	22	0.19
Filipino (6)	11	0.10
Hmong (1)	1	0.01
Indian (41)	55	0.49
Japanese (10)	20	0.18
Korean (19)	26	0.23
Laotian (443)	510	4.52
Malaysian (1)	1	0.01
Pakistani	1	0.01
Thai (27)	31	0.27
Vietnamese (182)	196	1.74
Other Asian, not specified (23)	39	0.35
Austrian	17	0.15
Belgian	14	0.12
British	14	0.12
Canadian	11	0.10
Carpatho Rusyn	8	0.07
Czech	77	0.68
Danish	181	1.60
Dutch	781	6.92
English	580	5.14
European	6	0.05
Finnish	8	0.07
French, except Basque	175	1.55
French Canadian	32	0.28
German	4,150	36.76
Hawaii Native/Pacific Islander:	30	0.27
Micronesian: (10)	10	0.09
Guamanian/Chamorro (10)	10	0.09
Other Pac. Isl., not spec. (5)	20	0.18
Hispanic or Latino:	2,175	19.28
Central American:	271	2.40
Guatemalan	124	1.10
Honduran	29	0.26
Nicaraguan	35	0.31
Panamanian	1	0.01
Salvadoran	69	0.61
Other Central American	13	0.12
Cuban	10	0.09
Mexican	1,554	13.77
Puerto Rican	27	0.24
South American:	7	0.06
Colombian	2	0.02
Uruguayan	1	0.01
Venezuelan	4	0.04
Other Hispanic or Latino	306	2.71
Irish	727	6.44
Italian	38	0.34
Latvian	8	0.07
Luxemburger	35	0.31
Northern European	7	0.06
Norwegian	1,305	11.56
Polish	107	0.95
Romanian	1	0.01
Russian	31	0.27
Scandinavian	51	0.45
Scotch-Irish	44	0.39
Scottish	66	0.58
Slovak	5	0.04
Swedish	575	5.09
Swiss	32	0.28
Turkish	2	0.02
Ukrainian	32	0.28
United States or American	256	2.27
Welsh	34	0.30
West Indian, excl. Hispanic:	7	0.06
Haitian	7	0.06
White:	8,834	78.29
Not Hispanic (7,934)	8,025	71.12
Hispanic (733)	809	7.17

Notes: 1. Figures in the "Number" column do not add up to the total population due to: a) Ancestry/Race overlap — e.g. persons can report being both White and Irish, b) persons of Hispanic origin can report being any race, c) persons reporting two ancestries are counted in both categories. 2. Numbers in parentheses indicate the number of persons reporting this ancestry/race alone, not in combination with any other ancestry/race. 3. Refer to the Explanation of Data in the front of the book for more detailed information.

Biloxi

Place Type: City
County: Harrison
Population: 50,644

Ancestry/Race	Number	%
Acadian/Cajun	117	0.23
Afghan	4	0.01
African American/Black:	10,037	19.82
Not Hispanic (9,569)	9,910	19.57
Hispanic (74)	127	0.25
African, sub-Saharan:	382	0.75
African	350	0.69
Cape Verdean	6	0.01
Zimbabwean	12	0.02
Other sub-Saharan African	14	0.03
Alaska Native tribes, specified:	3	0.01
Eskimo (1)	2	0.00
Tlingit-Haida (1)	1	0.00
Alaska Native tribes, not specified	1	0.00
Am. Ind. or Alaska Nat., not spec.	141	0.28
American Indian tribes, specified:	383	0.76
Apache (4)	10	0.02
Blackfeet (7)	22	0.04
Cherokee (59)	137	0.27
Cheyenne	1	0.00
Chickasaw	6	0.01
Chippewa (7)	11	0.02
Choctaw (19)	55	0.11
Comanche (4)	8	0.02
Cree (1)	1	0.00
Creek (12)	17	0.03
Houma (11)	13	0.03
Iroquois (3)	9	0.02
Latin American Indians (6)	18	0.04
Lumbee (1)	1	0.00
Navajo (2)	4	0.01
Osage (3)	3	0.01
Ottawa (2)	2	0.00
Paiute	1	0.00
Pima	1	0.00
Potawatomi (1)	4	0.01
Pueblo (2)	4	0.01
Seminole (8)	10	0.02
Shoshone (1)	1	0.00
Sioux (4)	4	0.01
Tohono O'Odham (1)	1	0.00
Ute (1)	1	0.00
Yaqui (1)	3	0.01
Yuman	1	0.00
All other tribes (15)	34	0.07
American Indian tribes, not spec.	33	0.07
Arab:	161	0.32
Arab/Arabic	14	0.03
Egyptian	10	0.02
Lebanese	64	0.13
Palestinian	6	0.01
Syrian	32	0.06
Other Arab	35	0.07
Armenian	8	0.02
Asian:	3,109	6.14
Bangladeshi (1)	1	0.00
Cambodian (1)	1	0.00
Chinese, ex. Taiwanese (79)	133	0.26
Filipino (339)	515	1.02
Indian (116)	129	0.25
Indonesian (1)	1	0.00
Japanese (82)	160	0.32
Korean (157)	231	0.46
Laotian (3)	3	0.01
Malaysian	3	0.01
Pakistani (1)	1	0.00
Sri Lankan (1)	1	0.00
Taiwanese (4)	9	0.02
Thai (35)	66	0.13
Vietnamese (1,707)	1,774	3.50
Other Asian, specified (1)	5	0.01
Other Asian, not specified (36)	76	0.15
Australian	8	0.02
Austrian	119	0.23
Belgian	55	0.11
British	248	0.49
Canadian	127	0.25
Celtic	42	0.08
Croatian	109	0.21
Cypriot	18	0.04
Czech	51	0.10
Czechoslovakian	79	0.16
Danish	114	0.22
Dutch	592	1.17
Eastern European	20	0.04
English	4,335	8.55
European	443	0.87
Finnish	39	0.08
French, except Basque	4,296	8.47
French Canadian	571	1.13
German	5,323	10.50
Greek	84	0.17
Guyanese	7	0.01
Hawaii Native/Pacific Islander:	153	0.30
Micronesian: (30)	54	0.11
Guamanian/Chamorro (29)	53	0.10
Other Micronesian (1)	1	0.00
Polynesian: (27)	79	0.16
Native Hawaiian (16)	58	0.11
Samoan (9)	17	0.03
Tongan (2)	4	0.01
Other Pac. Isl., specified	1	0.00
Other Pac. Isl., not spec.	19	0.04
Hispanic or Latino:	1,848	3.65
Central American:	115	0.23
Costa Rican	11	0.02
Guatemalan	9	0.02
Honduran	30	0.06
Nicaraguan	13	0.03
Panamanian	40	0.08
Salvadoran	11	0.02
Other Central American	1	0.00
Cuban	95	0.19
Dominican Republic	19	0.04
Mexican	749	1.48
Puerto Rican	362	0.71
South American:	95	0.19
Argentinean	2	0.00
Bolivian	2	0.00
Colombian	50	0.10
Ecuadorian	12	0.02
Peruvian	13	0.03
Venezuelan	13	0.03
Other South American	3	0.01
Other Hispanic or Latino	413	0.82
Hungarian	186	0.37
Irish	5,104	10.06
Italian	2,207	4.35
Lithuanian	43	0.08
Luxemburger	39	0.08
Northern European	24	0.05
Norwegian	360	0.71
Polish	717	1.41
Portuguese	101	0.20
Romanian	7	0.01
Russian	146	0.29
Scandinavian	39	0.08
Scotch-Irish	1,284	2.53
Scottish	1,094	2.16
Slavic	121	0.24
Slovak	40	0.08
Slovene	8	0.02
Swedish	301	0.59
Swiss	98	0.19
Turkish	5	0.01
Ukrainian	76	0.15
United States or American	4,229	8.34
Welsh	293	0.58
West Indian, excl. Hispanic:	119	0.23
Bahamian	7	0.01
Dutch West Indian	6	0.01
Haitian	23	0.05
Jamaican	57	0.11
U.S. Virgin Islander	7	0.01
West Indian	19	0.04
White:	37,154	73.36
Not Hispanic (35,292)	36,134	71.35
Hispanic (885)	1,020	2.01
Yugoslavian	377	0.74

Brandon

Place Type: City
County: Rankin
Population: 16,436

Ancestry/Race	Number	%
African American/Black:	1,982	12.06
Not Hispanic (1,943)	1,967	11.97
Hispanic (11)	15	0.09
African, sub-Saharan:	218	1.33
African	185	1.13
Nigerian	15	0.09
South African	18	0.11
Alaska Native tribes, specified:	2	0.01
Tlingit-Haida (1)	2	0.01
Am. Ind. or Alaska Nat., not spec.	13	0.08
American Indian tribes, specified:	28	0.17
Blackfeet	1	0.01
Cherokee (6)	15	0.09
Chickasaw (1)	1	0.01
Chippewa (4)	4	0.02
Choctaw (1)	2	0.01
Creek	1	0.01
Navajo	1	0.01
Seminole (1)	1	0.01
Sioux	1	0.01
All other tribes	1	0.01
Arab:	22	0.13
Lebanese	22	0.13
Asian:	131	0.80
Chinese, ex. Taiwanese (16)	19	0.12
Filipino (20)	24	0.15
Indian (26)	30	0.18
Japanese (5)	11	0.07
Korean (14)	16	0.10
Vietnamese (13)	14	0.09
Other Asian, specified	5	0.03
Other Asian, not specified	12	0.07
Australian	15	0.09
Austrian	7	0.04
British	139	0.85
Celtic	8	0.05
Czech	10	0.06
Czechoslovakian	7	0.04
Danish	19	0.12
Dutch	124	0.76
English	1,590	9.73
European	249	1.52
French, except Basque	452	2.77
French Canadian	77	0.47
German	1,214	7.43
Greek	22	0.13
Guyanese	37	0.23
Hawaii Native/Pacific Islander:	20	0.12
Micronesian: (8)	8	0.05
Guamanian/Chamorro (5)	5	0.03
Other Micronesian (3)	3	0.02
Polynesian: (1)	6	0.04
Native Hawaiian	5	0.03
Samoan (1)	1	0.01
Other Pac. Isl., specified	4	0.02
Other Pac. Isl., not spec. (1)	2	0.01
Hispanic or Latino:	213	1.30
Central American:	3	0.02
Guatemalan	2	0.01
Nicaraguan	1	0.01
Cuban	4	0.02
Mexican	111	0.68
Puerto Rican	26	0.16
South American:	19	0.12
Argentinean	2	0.01
Bolivian	1	0.01

Notes: 1. Figures in the "Number" column do not add up to the total population due to: a) Ancestry/Race overlap — e.g. persons can report being both White and Irish, b) persons of Hispanic origin can report being any race, c) persons reporting two ancestries are counted in both categories. 2. Numbers in parentheses indicate the number of persons reporting this ancestry/race alone, not in combination with any other ancestry/race. 3. Refer to the Explanation of Data in the front of the book for more detailed information.

Chilean	3	0.02
Colombian	4	0.02
Paraguayan	2	0.01
Venezuelan	7	0.04
Other Hispanic or Latino	50	0.30
Hungarian	6	0.04
Iranian	67	0.41
Irish	1,622	9.93
Italian	199	1.22
Lithuanian	8	0.05
Norwegian	70	0.43
Polish	33	0.20
Russian	11	0.07
Scotch-Irish	636	3.89
Scottish	318	1.95
Slovak	17	0.10
Swedish	32	0.20
Swiss	42	0.26
United States or American	3,017	18.47
Welsh	67	0.41
West Indian, excl. Hispanic:	31	0.19
Jamaican	31	0.19
White:	14,300	87.00
Not Hispanic (14,090)	14,146	86.07
Hispanic (145)	154	0.94

Canton

Place Type: City
County: Madison
Population: 12,911

Ancestry/Race	Number	%
African American/Black:	10,428	80.77
Not Hispanic (10,342)	10,402	80.57
Hispanic (26)	26	0.20
African, sub-Saharan:	91	0.69
African	91	0.69
Am. Ind. or Alaska Nat., not spec.	32	0.25
American Indian tribes, specified:	13	0.10
Blackfeet	1	0.01
Cherokee	2	0.02
Chickasaw	1	0.01
Choctaw (3)	7	0.05
Houma (1)	1	0.01
All other tribes	1	0.01
American Indian tribes, not spec.	1	0.01
Arab:	12	0.09
Arab/Arabic	5	0.04
Syrian	7	0.05
Asian:	66	0.51
Chinese, ex. Taiwanese (7)	17	0.13
Filipino (9)	9	0.07
Indian (10)	32	0.25
Japanese	4	0.03
Other Asian, not specified	4	0.03
British	9	0.07
Celtic	20	0.15
Danish	9	0.07
Dutch	27	0.21
English	391	2.98
European	12	0.09
French, except Basque	107	0.81
French Canadian	6	0.05
German	239	1.82
Hawaii Native/Pacific Islander:	4	0.03
Polynesian:	4	0.03
Native Hawaiian	4	0.03
Hispanic or Latino:	56	0.43
Cuban	1	0.01
Mexican	36	0.28
Puerto Rican	1	0.01
South American:	1	0.01
Colombian	1	0.01
Other Hispanic or Latino	17	0.13
Irish	341	2.60
Italian	17	0.13
Northern European	10	0.08
Scotch-Irish	181	1.38
Scottish	65	0.49
Swedish	8	0.06
United States or American	429	3.26
Welsh	5	0.04
White:	2,445	18.94
Not Hispanic (2,396)	2,432	18.84
Hispanic (10)	13	0.10

Clarksdale

Place Type: City
County: Coahoma
Population: 20,645

Ancestry/Race	Number	%
African American/Black:	14,223	68.89
Not Hispanic (14,105)	14,181	68.69
Hispanic (41)	42	0.20
African, sub-Saharan:	217	1.05
African	217	1.05
Am. Ind. or Alaska Nat., not spec.	44	0.21
American Indian tribes, specified:	23	0.11
Blackfeet	1	0.00
Cherokee (2)	9	0.04
Choctaw	8	0.04
Latin American Indians (1)	1	0.00
Pueblo (1)	1	0.00
Seminole	1	0.00
All other tribes	2	0.01
American Indian tribes, not spec.	4	0.02
Arab:	100	0.48
Lebanese	86	0.42
Syrian	12	0.06
Other Arab	2	0.01
Asian:	166	0.80
Chinese, ex. Taiwanese (60)	67	0.32
Filipino (13)	18	0.09
Indian (36)	42	0.20
Korean	3	0.01
Taiwanese (1)	1	0.00
Thai (1)	1	0.00
Vietnamese (5)	6	0.03
Other Asian, specified (1)	1	0.00
Other Asian, not specified	27	0.13
Belgian	13	0.06
British	2	0.01
Canadian	23	0.11
Dutch	75	0.36
English	745	3.61
European	146	0.71
French, except Basque	61	0.30
French Canadian	9	0.04
German	205	0.99
Greek	42	0.20
Hawaii Native/Pacific Islander:	12	0.06
Micronesian:	1	0.00
Other Micronesian	1	0.00
Polynesian: (3)	10	0.05
Native Hawaiian (2)	8	0.04
Samoan (1)	2	0.01
Other Pac. Isl., not spec.	1	0.00
Hispanic or Latino:	134	0.65
Central American:	5	0.02
Costa Rican	1	0.00
Nicaraguan	2	0.01
Panamanian	1	0.00
Salvadoran	1	0.00
Mexican	77	0.37
Puerto Rican	5	0.02
South American:	4	0.02
Argentinean	2	0.01
Colombian	2	0.01
Other Hispanic or Latino	43	0.21
Hungarian	8	0.04
Irish	662	3.21
Italian	348	1.69
Lithuanian	9	0.04
Norwegian	34	0.16
Polish	43	0.21
Romanian	5	0.02
Scotch-Irish	333	1.61
Scottish	54	0.26
Serbian	9	0.04
Swedish	80	0.39
United States or American	1,278	6.19
Welsh	43	0.21
White:	6,253	30.29
Not Hispanic (6,135)	6,203	30.05
Hispanic (49)	50	0.24
Yugoslavian	2	0.01

Cleveland

Place Type: City
County: Bolivar
Population: 13,841

Ancestry/Race	Number	%
African American/Black:	6,703	48.43
Not Hispanic (6,643)	6,661	48.13
Hispanic (36)	42	0.30
African, sub-Saharan:	40	0.29
African	34	0.25
Other sub-Saharan African	6	0.04
Am. Ind. or Alaska Nat., not spec.	14	0.10
American Indian tribes, specified:	9	0.07
Cherokee (5)	7	0.05
All other tribes	2	0.01
American Indian tribes, not spec.	3	0.02
Arab:	40	0.29
Lebanese	33	0.24
Moroccan	7	0.05
Asian:	162	1.17
Bangladeshi (6)	6	0.04
Chinese, ex. Taiwanese (42)	49	0.35
Filipino (34)	37	0.27
Indian (29)	35	0.25
Korean (4)	8	0.06
Sri Lankan (4)	4	0.03
Thai (2)	3	0.02
Vietnamese (10)	10	0.07
Other Asian, not specified (5)	10	0.07
British	33	0.24
Celtic	7	0.05
Danish	7	0.05
Dutch	93	0.68
English	614	4.48
French, except Basque	137	1.00
French Canadian	24	0.18
German	693	5.06
Hawaii Native/Pacific Islander:	16	0.12
Micronesian: (1)	7	0.05
Guamanian/Chamorro (1)	7	0.05
Polynesian: (2)	2	0.01
Native Hawaiian (2)	2	0.01
Other Pac. Isl., not spec.	7	0.05
Hispanic or Latino:	130	0.94
Central American:	4	0.03
Costa Rican	3	0.02
Panamanian	1	0.01
Cuban	3	0.02
Mexican	85	0.61
Puerto Rican	1	0.01
Other Hispanic or Latino	37	0.27
Irish	792	5.78
Italian	379	2.77
Lithuanian	17	0.12
Norwegian	72	0.53
Polish	10	0.07
Russian	10	0.07
Scotch-Irish	219	1.60
Scottish	191	1.39
Swedish	12	0.09
Swiss	7	0.05
United States or American	1,656	12.09
Welsh	17	0.12
White:	6,946	50.18
Not Hispanic (6,858)	6,895	49.82
Hispanic (49)	51	0.37

Notes: 1. Figures in the "Number" column do not add up to the total population due to: a) Ancestry/Race overlap — e.g. persons can report being both White and Irish, b) persons of Hispanic origin can report being any race, c) persons reporting two ancestries are counted in both categories. 2. Numbers in parentheses indicate the number of persons reporting this ancestry/race alone, not in combination with any other ancestry/race. 3. Refer to the Explanation of Data in the front of the book for more detailed information.

Clinton

Place Type: City
County: Hinds
Population: 23,347

Ancestry/Race	Number	%
Acadian/Cajun	16	0.07
African American/Black:	5,315	22.77
Not Hispanic (5,242)	5,297	22.69
Hispanic (17)	18	0.08
African, sub-Saharan:	138	0.59
African	138	0.59
Alaska Native tribes, specified:	1	0.00
Eskimo (1)	1	0.00
Am. Ind. or Alaska Nat., not spec.	25	0.11
American Indian tribes, specified:	48	0.21
Cherokee (8)	22	0.09
Chickasaw	2	0.01
Chippewa (1)	1	0.00
Choctaw (7)	17	0.07
Creek (2)	2	0.01
Iroquois (1)	1	0.00
Paiute (1)	1	0.00
Sioux	1	0.00
All other tribes	1	0.00
American Indian tribes, not spec.	4	0.02
Arab:	95	0.41
Arab/Arabic	37	0.16
Lebanese	30	0.13
Syrian	28	0.12
Asian:	417	1.79
Bangladeshi	6	0.03
Chinese, ex. Taiwanese (36)	46	0.20
Filipino (7)	13	0.06
Hmong (9)	9	0.04
Indian (198)	218	0.93
Japanese (12)	17	0.07
Korean (49)	52	0.22
Laotian (1)	1	0.00
Pakistani (3)	3	0.01
Sri Lankan (1)	1	0.00
Taiwanese	1	0.00
Vietnamese (16)	32	0.14
Other Asian, not specified (5)	18	0.08
Australian	14	0.06
Austrian	11	0.05
British	96	0.41
Canadian	22	0.09
Croatian	16	0.07
Czech	4	0.02
Danish	17	0.07
Dutch	379	1.62
English	2,272	9.71
European	346	1.48
Finnish	20	0.09
French, except Basque	562	2.40
French Canadian	67	0.29
German	1,721	7.35
Greek	25	0.11
Hawaii Native/Pacific Islander:	10	0.04
Micronesian: (1)	1	0.00
Guamanian/Chamorro (1)	1	0.00
Polynesian: (3)	6	0.03
Native Hawaiian (3)	6	0.03
Other Pac. Isl., not spec.	3	0.01
Hispanic or Latino:	203	0.87
Central American:	11	0.05
Guatemalan	4	0.02
Honduran	3	0.01
Nicaraguan	2	0.01
Salvadoran	2	0.01
Cuban	5	0.02
Mexican	105	0.45
Puerto Rican	13	0.06
South American:	11	0.05
Argentinean	4	0.02
Chilean	6	0.03
Peruvian	1	0.00
Other Hispanic or Latino	58	0.25
Hungarian	12	0.05
Iranian	29	0.12
Irish	2,086	8.91
Italian	293	1.25
Lithuanian	8	0.03
Northern European	115	0.49
Norwegian	101	0.43
Pennsylvania German	19	0.08
Polish	118	0.50
Scandinavian	19	0.08
Scotch-Irish	1,355	5.79
Scottish	620	2.65
Serbian	32	0.14
Slavic	9	0.04
Slovak	9	0.04
Slovene	12	0.05
Swedish	177	0.76
Swiss	20	0.09
Ukrainian	24	0.10
United States or American	2,629	11.23
Welsh	112	0.48
West Indian, excl. Hispanic:	6	0.03
Trinidadian and Tobagonian	6	0.03
White:	17,622	75.48
Not Hispanic (17,375)	17,492	74.92
Hispanic (117)	130	0.56

Columbus

Place Type: City
County: Lowndes
Population: 25,944

Ancestry/Race	Number	%
Acadian/Cajun	3	0.01
African American/Black:	14,235	54.87
Not Hispanic (14,075)	14,176	54.64
Hispanic (42)	59	0.23
African, sub-Saharan:	156	0.60
African	156	0.60
Alaska Native tribes, specified:	2	0.01
Eskimo	2	0.01
Am. Ind. or Alaska Nat., not spec.	38	0.15
American Indian tribes, specified:	41	0.16
Apache	1	0.00
Blackfeet	2	0.01
Cherokee (6)	16	0.06
Chickasaw (1)	2	0.01
Choctaw	6	0.02
Comanche	1	0.00
Creek (1)	3	0.01
Navajo (1)	1	0.00
Osage (1)	1	0.00
Puget Sound Salish	1	0.00
Seminole	2	0.01
Sioux	1	0.00
All other tribes (1)	4	0.02
American Indian tribes, not spec.	5	0.02
Arab:	63	0.24
Egyptian	6	0.02
Jordanian	11	0.04
Lebanese	38	0.15
Other Arab	8	0.03
Asian:	197	0.76
Chinese, ex. Taiwanese (38)	45	0.17
Filipino (21)	26	0.10
Indian (33)	50	0.19
Indonesian (3)	3	0.01
Japanese (9)	11	0.04
Korean (18)	23	0.09
Malaysian	1	0.00
Thai (9)	10	0.04
Vietnamese (7)	7	0.03
Other Asian, specified (1)	10	0.04
Other Asian, not specified (4)	11	0.04
Australian	6	0.02
Belgian	3	0.01
British	54	0.21
Canadian	18	0.07
Czech	20	0.08
Danish	56	0.22
Dutch	294	1.13
English	1,596	6.13
European	155	0.60
French, except Basque	242	0.93
French Canadian	22	0.08
German	869	3.34
Greek	12	0.05
Hawaii Native/Pacific Islander:	29	0.11
Micronesian: (2)	3	0.01
Guamanian/Chamorro (2)	3	0.01
Polynesian: (1)	7	0.03
Native Hawaiian	6	0.02
Samoan (1)	1	0.00
Other Pac. Isl., specified	9	0.03
Other Pac. Isl., not spec.	10	0.04
Hispanic or Latino:	292	1.13
Central American:	8	0.03
Costa Rican	4	0.02
Honduran	2	0.01
Panamanian	1	0.00
Other Central American	1	0.00
Cuban	8	0.03
Dominican Republic	5	0.02
Mexican	157	0.61
Puerto Rican	16	0.06
South American:	9	0.03
Argentinean	1	0.00
Colombian	4	0.02
Ecuadorian	1	0.00
Venezuelan	3	0.01
Other Hispanic or Latino	89	0.34
Hungarian	30	0.12
Irish	1,514	5.82
Italian	137	0.53
Latvian	9	0.03
Lithuanian	5	0.02
Northern European	6	0.02
Norwegian	62	0.24
Polish	110	0.42
Russian	36	0.14
Scandinavian	20	0.08
Scotch-Irish	438	1.68
Scottish	311	1.19
Swedish	67	0.26
Swiss	30	0.12
Turkish	21	0.08
Ukrainian	42	0.16
United States or American	2,369	9.10
Welsh	98	0.38
White:	11,449	44.13
Not Hispanic (11,224)	11,340	43.71
Hispanic (93)	109	0.42

Corinth

Place Type: City
County: Alcorn
Population: 14,054

Ancestry/Race	Number	%
African American/Black:	3,080	21.92
Not Hispanic (3,023)	3,061	21.78
Hispanic (12)	19	0.14
African, sub-Saharan:	52	0.37
African	52	0.37
Am. Ind. or Alaska Nat., not spec.	23	0.16
American Indian tribes, specified:	14	0.10
Blackfeet (1)	1	0.01
Cherokee (1)	5	0.04
Chickasaw (1)	1	0.01
Choctaw	2	0.01
Iroquois (2)	2	0.01
Latin American Indians (3)	3	0.02
American Indian tribes, not spec.	6	0.04
Arab:	8	0.06
Arab/Arabic	3	0.02
Egyptian	5	0.04
Asian:	72	0.51
Cambodian (4)	4	0.03

Notes: 1. Figures in the "Number" column do not add up to the total population due to: a) Ancestry/Race overlap — e.g. persons can report being both White and Irish, b) persons of Hispanic origin can report being any race, c) persons reporting two ancestries are counted in both categories. 2. Numbers in parentheses indicate the number of persons reporting this ancestry/race alone, not in combination with any other ancestry/race. 3. Refer to the Explanation of Data in the front of the book for more detailed information.

Chinese, ex. Taiwanese (12)	13	0.09
Filipino (11)	16	0.11
Indian (10)	15	0.11
Japanese (4)	4	0.03
Korean (2)	4	0.03
Thai (1)	4	0.03
Vietnamese (6)	6	0.04
Other Asian, not specified	6	0.04
Austrian	7	0.05
British	127	0.90
Canadian	37	0.26
Croatian	4	0.03
Czech	4	0.03
Dutch	86	0.61
English	1,211	8.62
European	136	0.97
French, except Basque	106	0.75
French Canadian	19	0.14
German	392	2.79
Greek	27	0.19
Hawaii Native/Pacific Islander:	21	0.15
Micronesian: (12)	13	0.09
Guamanian/Chamorro (12)	13	0.09
Polynesian: (4)	6	0.04
Native Hawaiian (4)	4	0.03
Samoan	2	0.01
Other Pac. Isl., not spec. (1)	2	0.01
Hispanic or Latino:	243	1.73
Central American:	1	0.01
Guatemalan	1	0.01
Cuban	10	0.07
Mexican	171	1.22
Puerto Rican	18	0.13
South American:	3	0.02
Colombian	3	0.02
Other Hispanic or Latino	40	0.28
Hungarian	7	0.05
Irish	870	6.19
Italian	104	0.74
Norwegian	27	0.19
Polish	28	0.20
Scandinavian	6	0.04
Scotch-Irish	190	1.35
Scottish	69	0.49
Swedish	11	0.08
United States or American	3,246	23.10
Welsh	19	0.14
White:	10,803	76.87
Not Hispanic (10,616)	10,689	76.06
Hispanic (104)	114	0.81

Gautier

Place Type: City
County: Jackson
Population: 11,681

Ancestry/Race	Number	%
Acadian/Cajun	31	0.26
African American/Black:	3,300	28.25
Not Hispanic (3,213)	3,279	28.07
Hispanic (17)	21	0.18
African, sub-Saharan:	28	0.24
African	28	0.24
Am. Ind. or Alaska Nat., not spec.	17	0.15
American Indian tribes, specified:	93	0.80
Apache (1)	1	0.01
Blackfeet (1)	5	0.04
Cherokee (17)	38	0.33
Chippewa	6	0.05
Choctaw (12)	19	0.16
Creek (5)	13	0.11
Iroquois (2)	3	0.03
Latin American Indians	2	0.02
Lumbee (2)	3	0.03
Navajo (1)	1	0.01
Sioux	1	0.01
All other tribes (1)	1	0.01
American Indian tribes, not spec.	7	0.06
Arab:	19	0.16
Lebanese	7	0.06
Other Arab	12	0.10
Asian:	210	1.80
Cambodian (1)	4	0.03
Chinese, ex. Taiwanese (20)	23	0.20
Filipino (24)	48	0.41
Indian (9)	21	0.18
Indonesian (2)	3	0.03
Japanese (7)	14	0.12
Korean (2)	3	0.03
Malaysian (2)	2	0.02
Thai (4)	4	0.03
Vietnamese (74)	81	0.69
Other Asian, not specified (5)	7	0.06
British	21	0.18
Celtic	8	0.07
Czech	8	0.07
Czechoslovakian	10	0.08
Danish	37	0.31
Dutch	115	0.98
English	979	8.32
European	102	0.87
French, except Basque	444	3.77
French Canadian	93	0.79
German	931	7.91
Greek	23	0.20
Hawaii Native/Pacific Islander:	13	0.11
Micronesian: (3)	3	0.03
Guamanian/Chamorro (3)	3	0.03
Polynesian: (2)	9	0.08
Native Hawaiian (2)	9	0.08
Other Pac. Isl., not spec.	1	0.01
Hispanic or Latino:	373	3.19
Central American:	18	0.15
Costa Rican	4	0.03
Guatemalan	6	0.05
Nicaraguan	1	0.01
Panamanian	7	0.06
Cuban	13	0.11
Dominican Republic	1	0.01
Mexican	245	2.10
Puerto Rican	26	0.22
South American:	22	0.19
Bolivian	3	0.03
Colombian	5	0.04
Peruvian	1	0.01
Venezuelan	13	0.11
Other Hispanic or Latino	48	0.41
Hungarian	23	0.20
Iranian	8	0.07
Irish	1,117	9.49
Italian	170	1.44
Lithuanian	9	0.08
Norwegian	81	0.69
Polish	164	1.39
Portuguese	29	0.25
Romanian	16	0.14
Russian	23	0.20
Scotch-Irish	193	1.64
Scottish	297	2.52
Slovak	9	0.08
Swedish	53	0.45
Swiss	42	0.36
Ukrainian	9	0.08
United States or American	1,549	13.16
White:	8,091	69.27
Not Hispanic (7,733)	7,839	67.11
Hispanic (232)	252	2.16

Greenville

Place Type: City
County: Washington
Population: 41,633

Ancestry/Race	Number	%
Acadian/Cajun	14	0.03
African American/Black:	29,093	69.88
Not Hispanic (28,871)	28,971	69.59
Hispanic (105)	122	0.29
African, sub-Saharan:	547	1.31
African	501	1.20
Ghanian	13	0.03
Kenyan	8	0.02
Nigerian	19	0.05
Ugandan	6	0.01
Am. Ind. or Alaska Nat., not spec.	48	0.12
American Indian tribes, specified:	43	0.10
Cherokee (3)	18	0.04
Choctaw (3)	13	0.03
Iroquois	3	0.01
Kiowa (1)	1	0.00
Latin American Indians	1	0.00
Pueblo	1	0.00
Sioux (1)	2	0.00
All other tribes (2)	4	0.01
American Indian tribes, not spec.	1	0.00
Arab:	163	0.39
Lebanese	163	0.39
Asian:	389	0.93
Chinese, ex. Taiwanese (147)	164	0.39
Filipino (24)	43	0.10
Indian (71)	92	0.22
Japanese (7)	14	0.03
Korean (9)	18	0.04
Malaysian (1)	1	0.00
Vietnamese (27)	39	0.09
Other Asian, specified	9	0.02
Other Asian, not specified (3)	9	0.02
Austrian	10	0.02
British	35	0.08
Canadian	6	0.01
Croatian	7	0.02
Danish	37	0.09
Dutch	120	0.29
English	1,293	3.11
European	97	0.23
French, except Basque	319	0.77
French Canadian	63	0.15
German	797	1.91
Greek	84	0.20
Hawaii Native/Pacific Islander:	34	0.08
Micronesian: (1)	2	0.00
Guamanian/Chamorro (1)	2	0.00
Polynesian: (3)	18	0.04
Native Hawaiian (2)	6	0.01
Samoan (1)	12	0.03
Other Pac. Isl., specified	9	0.02
Other Pac. Isl., not spec. (2)	5	0.01
Hispanic or Latino:	297	0.71
Central American:	5	0.01
Honduran	4	0.01
Panamanian	1	0.00
Cuban	10	0.02
Dominican Republic	1	0.00
Mexican	156	0.37
Puerto Rican	36	0.09
Other Hispanic or Latino	89	0.21
Hungarian	9	0.02
Irish	1,298	3.12
Italian	719	1.73
Latvian	7	0.02
Luxemburger	15	0.04
Norwegian	4	0.01
Polish	74	0.18
Portuguese	15	0.04
Russian	9	0.02
Scotch-Irish	535	1.29
Scottish	211	0.51
Swedish	40	0.10
Swiss	9	0.02
United States or American	1,992	4.79
Welsh	18	0.04
White:	12,165	29.22
Not Hispanic (11,963)	12,069	28.99
Hispanic (76)	96	0.23

Notes: 1. Figures in the "Number" column do not add up to the total population due to: a) Ancestry/Race overlap — e.g. persons can report being both White and Irish, b) persons of Hispanic origin can report being any race, c) persons reporting two ancestries are counted in both categories. 2. Numbers in parentheses indicate the number of persons reporting this ancestry/race alone, not in combination with any other ancestry/race. 3. Refer to the Explanation of Data in the front of the book for more detailed information.

Greenwood

Place Type: City
County: Leflore
Population: 18,425

Ancestry/Race	Number	%
African American/Black:	12,091	65.62
Not Hispanic (11,950)	11,997	65.11
Hispanic (92)	94	0.51
African, sub-Saharan:	153	0.83
African	153	0.83
Am. Ind. or Alaska Nat., not spec.	42	0.23
American Indian tribes, specified:	6	0.03
Cherokee	2	0.01
Creek (1)	1	0.01
Potawatomi (1)	1	0.01
Sioux (1)	2	0.01
American Indian tribes, not spec.	2	0.01
Arab:	41	0.22
Lebanese	41	0.22
Asian:	188	1.02
Bangladeshi (4)	4	0.02
Chinese, ex. Taiwanese (63)	68	0.37
Filipino (46)	49	0.27
Indian (33)	37	0.20
Japanese (1)	1	0.01
Korean (17)	18	0.10
Taiwanese	1	0.01
Vietnamese (4)	4	0.02
Other Asian, specified	2	0.01
Other Asian, not specified	4	0.02
British	41	0.22
Canadian	6	0.03
Danish	12	0.06
Dutch	84	0.45
English	763	4.13
European	69	0.37
French, except Basque	88	0.48
French Canadian	5	0.03
German	394	2.13
Hawaii Native/Pacific Islander:	31	0.17
Micronesian: (11)	11	0.06
Guamanian/Chamorro (11)	11	0.06
Polynesian: (3)	11	0.06
Native Hawaiian (1)	9	0.05
Samoan (2)	2	0.01
Other Pac. Isl., specified	2	0.01
Other Pac. Isl., not spec.	7	0.04
Hispanic or Latino:	189	1.03
Central American:	7	0.04
Guatemalan	7	0.04
Cuban	19	0.10
Mexican	78	0.42
Puerto Rican	3	0.02
South American:	2	0.01
Chilean	1	0.01
Peruvian	1	0.01
Other Hispanic or Latino	80	0.43
Irish	613	3.32
Israeli	24	0.13
Italian	193	1.05
Scandinavian	7	0.04
Scotch-Irish	342	1.85
Scottish	131	0.71
Slovene	6	0.03
Swedish	10	0.05
Turkish	16	0.09
Ukrainian	23	0.12
United States or American	1,065	5.77
Welsh	43	0.23
West Indian, excl. Hispanic:	13	0.07
Haitian	13	0.07
White:	6,093	33.07
Not Hispanic (6,008)	6,037	32.77
Hispanic (39)	56	0.30
Yugoslavian	33	0.18

Grenada

Place Type: City
County: Grenada
Population: 14,879

Ancestry/Race	Number	%
African American/Black:	7,373	49.55
Not Hispanic (7,303)	7,327	49.24
Hispanic (39)	46	0.31
African, sub-Saharan:	94	0.63
African	94	0.63
Am. Ind. or Alaska Nat., not spec.	23	0.15
American Indian tribes, specified:	19	0.13
Cherokee (2)	5	0.03
Choctaw (2)	6	0.04
Creek	2	0.01
Iroquois	1	0.01
Latin American Indians	1	0.01
Lumbee (1)	1	0.01
Seminole (1)	1	0.01
Sioux (2)	2	0.01
American Indian tribes, not spec.	6	0.04
Arab:	12	0.08
Lebanese	12	0.08
Asian:	105	0.71
Chinese, ex. Taiwanese (17)	21	0.14
Filipino (24)	25	0.17
Indian (18)	32	0.22
Japanese (3)	7	0.05
Vietnamese (11)	11	0.07
Other Asian, specified	2	0.01
Other Asian, not specified (2)	7	0.05
British	24	0.16
Bulgarian	7	0.05
Canadian	18	0.12
Czechoslovakian	6	0.04
Dutch	110	0.73
English	801	5.33
European	107	0.71
French, except Basque	91	0.61
French Canadian	34	0.23
German	480	3.20
Greek	7	0.05
Hawaii Native/Pacific Islander:	9	0.06
Micronesian:	1	0.01
Guamanian/Chamorro	1	0.01
Polynesian: (3)	6	0.04
Samoan (3)	6	0.04
Other Pac. Isl., specified	1	0.01
Other Pac. Isl., not spec.	1	0.01
Hispanic or Latino:	104	0.70
Central American:	2	0.01
Costa Rican	1	0.01
Honduran	1	0.01
Cuban	4	0.03
Mexican	44	0.30
Puerto Rican	9	0.06
South American:	1	0.01
Colombian	1	0.01
Other Hispanic or Latino	44	0.30
Hungarian	29	0.19
Iranian	8	0.05
Irish	692	4.61
Italian	240	1.60
Norwegian	23	0.15
Polish	21	0.14
Scandinavian	6	0.04
Scotch-Irish	206	1.37
Scottish	148	0.99
Swedish	9	0.06
United States or American	1,762	11.73
White:	7,393	49.69
Not Hispanic (7,298)	7,353	49.42
Hispanic (35)	40	0.27

Gulfport

Place Type: City
County: Harrison
Population: 71,127

Ancestry/Race	Number	%
Acadian/Cajun	108	0.15
African American/Black:	24,276	34.13
Not Hispanic (23,692)	24,075	33.85
Hispanic (156)	201	0.28
African, sub-Saharan:	850	1.20
African	807	1.14
Nigerian	10	0.01
South African	33	0.05
Alaska Native tribes, specified:	2	0.00
Eskimo (1)	2	0.00
Am. Ind. or Alaska Nat., not spec.	261	0.37
Alsatian	9	0.01
American Indian tribes, specified:	433	0.61
Apache (3)	11	0.02
Blackfeet (7)	18	0.03
Cherokee (62)	171	0.24
Cheyenne (2)	2	0.00
Chickasaw (12)	24	0.03
Chippewa (6)	13	0.02
Choctaw (19)	65	0.09
Colville (1)	1	0.00
Comanche (1)	6	0.01
Cree	1	0.00
Creek (4)	10	0.01
Crow	2	0.00
Delaware	1	0.00
Houma (12)	21	0.03
Iroquois	2	0.00
Latin American Indians (5)	9	0.01
Menominee (1)	1	0.00
Navajo (4)	8	0.01
Osage	2	0.00
Ottawa	1	0.00
Potawatomi (1)	2	0.00
Pueblo (1)	1	0.00
Puget Sound Salish	1	0.00
Seminole (4)	17	0.02
Sioux (4)	9	0.01
Tohono O'Odham (1)	1	0.00
Yaqui (2)	4	0.01
All other tribes (18)	29	0.04
American Indian tribes, not spec.	33	0.05
Arab:	252	0.35
Arab/Arabic	10	0.01
Egyptian	79	0.11
Lebanese	99	0.14
Syrian	64	0.09
Armenian	33	0.05
Asian:	1,246	1.75
Chinese, ex. Taiwanese (70)	105	0.15
Filipino (373)	526	0.74
Indian (47)	68	0.10
Indonesian (2)	2	0.00
Japanese (48)	103	0.14
Korean (39)	59	0.08
Laotian (2)	2	0.00
Malaysian (1)	5	0.01
Taiwanese (1)	5	0.01
Thai (21)	38	0.05
Vietnamese (258)	272	0.38
Other Asian, specified	4	0.01
Other Asian, not specified (19)	57	0.08
Assyrian/Chaldean/Syriac	8	0.01
Australian	12	0.02
Austrian	98	0.14
Belgian	25	0.04
British	274	0.39
Canadian	103	0.15
Celtic	19	0.03
Croatian	35	0.05
Czech	50	0.07
Czechoslovakian	32	0.05
Danish	261	0.37

Notes: 1. Figures in the "Number" column do not add up to the total population due to: a) Ancestry/Race overlap — e.g. persons can report being both White and Irish, b) persons of Hispanic origin can report being any race, c) persons reporting two ancestries are counted in both categories. 2. Numbers in parentheses indicate the number of persons reporting this ancestry/race alone, not in combination with any other ancestry/race. 3. Refer to the Explanation of Data in the front of the book for more detailed information.

Ancestry/Race	Number	%
Dutch	718	1.01
Eastern European	4	0.01
English	5,352	7.54
European	674	0.95
Finnish	91	0.13
French, except Basque	3,757	5.29
French Canadian	320	0.45
German	5,365	7.56
Greek	79	0.11
Guyanese	19	0.03
Hawaii Native/Pacific Islander:	149	0.21
Micronesian: (34)	52	0.07
Guamanian/Chamorro (33)	48	0.07
Other Micronesian (1)	4	0.01
Polynesian: (22)	47	0.07
Native Hawaiian (11)	29	0.04
Samoan (11)	18	0.03
Other Pac. Isl., specified	3	0.00
Other Pac. Isl., not spec. (8)	47	0.07
Hispanic or Latino:	1,814	2.55
Central American:	95	0.13
Costa Rican	9	0.01
Guatemalan	11	0.02
Honduran	19	0.03
Nicaraguan	6	0.01
Panamanian	42	0.06
Salvadoran	3	0.00
Other Central American	5	0.01
Cuban	75	0.11
Dominican Republic	16	0.02
Mexican	762	1.07
Puerto Rican	312	0.44
South American:	57	0.08
Argentinean	9	0.01
Chilean	3	0.00
Colombian	22	0.03
Ecuadorian	5	0.01
Peruvian	10	0.01
Venezuelan	2	0.00
Other South American	6	0.01
Other Hispanic or Latino	497	0.70
Hungarian	119	0.17
Iranian	120	0.17
Irish	6,067	8.55
Italian	2,181	3.07
Latvian	17	0.02
Lithuanian	66	0.09
Northern European	9	0.01
Norwegian	317	0.45
Polish	427	0.60
Portuguese	51	0.07
Romanian	26	0.04
Russian	192	0.27
Scandinavian	50	0.07
Scotch-Irish	1,356	1.91
Scottish	1,059	1.49
Slavic	29	0.04
Slovak	17	0.02
Swedish	350	0.49
Swiss	40	0.06
Turkish	7	0.01
Ukrainian	23	0.03
United States or American	7,467	10.52
Welsh	416	0.59
West Indian, excl. Hispanic:	167	0.24
Belizean	30	0.04
Bermudan	7	0.01
British West Indian	31	0.04
Dutch West Indian	24	0.03
Haitian	8	0.01
Jamaican	67	0.09
White:	45,132	63.45
Not Hispanic (43,337)	44,118	62.03
Hispanic (892)	1,014	1.43
Yugoslavian	90	0.13

Hattiesburg

Place Type: City
County: Forrest
Population: 44,779

Ancestry/Race	Number	%
Acadian/Cajun	43	0.10
African American/Black:	21,366	47.71
Not Hispanic (21,099)	21,260	47.48
Hispanic (101)	106	0.24
African, sub-Saharan:	565	1.26
African	531	1.19
Nigerian	22	0.05
Other sub-Saharan African	12	0.03
Alaska Native tribes, specified:	4	0.01
Alaska Athabascan (2)	2	0.00
Eskimo (2)	2	0.00
Alaska Native tribes, not specified	2	0.00
Am. Ind. or Alaska Nat., not spec.	96	0.21
Albanian	16	0.04
American Indian tribes, specified:	88	0.20
Apache (2)	2	0.00
Blackfeet	1	0.00
Cherokee (8)	33	0.07
Chickasaw	6	0.01
Choctaw (6)	24	0.05
Creek (2)	4	0.01
Houma (1)	1	0.00
Iroquois	4	0.01
Latin American Indians (1)	1	0.00
Lumbee (4)	5	0.01
Ottawa (1)	1	0.00
Sioux (1)	1	0.00
All other tribes (2)	5	0.01
American Indian tribes, not spec.	9	0.02
Arab:	169	0.38
Arab/Arabic	52	0.12
Egyptian	16	0.04
Lebanese	36	0.08
Palestinian	22	0.05
Syrian	21	0.05
Other Arab	22	0.05
Asian:	627	1.40
Bangladeshi (1)	1	0.00
Chinese, ex. Taiwanese (100)	113	0.25
Filipino (36)	53	0.12
Indian (126)	134	0.30
Indonesian (2)	3	0.01
Japanese (72)	79	0.18
Korean (97)	107	0.24
Malaysian (1)	2	0.00
Pakistani (28)	28	0.06
Sri Lankan	1	0.00
Taiwanese (5)	5	0.01
Thai (2)	4	0.01
Vietnamese (62)	63	0.14
Other Asian, specified (1)	4	0.01
Other Asian, not specified (9)	30	0.07
Australian	15	0.03
Austrian	5	0.01
Belgian	19	0.04
British	230	0.51
Canadian	6	0.01
Celtic	3	0.01
Croatian	19	0.04
Czech	28	0.06
Czechoslovakian	8	0.02
Danish	73	0.16
Dutch	312	0.70
Eastern European	13	0.03
English	2,755	6.16
European	335	0.75
Finnish	14	0.03
French, except Basque	1,112	2.49
French Canadian	210	0.47
German	2,366	5.29
Greek	73	0.16
Hawaii Native/Pacific Islander:	25	0.06
Micronesian: (2)	5	0.01
Guamanian/Chamorro (2)	5	0.01
Polynesian: (7)	10	0.02
Native Hawaiian (2)	5	0.01
Samoan (5)	5	0.01
Other Pac. Isl., specified	3	0.01
Other Pac. Isl., not spec.	7	0.02
Hispanic or Latino:	630	1.41
Central American:	56	0.13
Guatemalan	3	0.01
Honduran	32	0.07
Nicaraguan	5	0.01
Panamanian	4	0.01
Salvadoran	6	0.01
Other Central American	6	0.01
Cuban	17	0.04
Dominican Republic	2	0.00
Mexican	308	0.69
Puerto Rican	36	0.08
South American:	57	0.13
Argentinean	2	0.00
Bolivian	1	0.00
Chilean	5	0.01
Colombian	21	0.05
Ecuadorian	6	0.01
Peruvian	3	0.01
Venezuelan	16	0.04
Other South American	3	0.01
Other Hispanic or Latino	154	0.34
Hungarian	48	0.11
Iranian	6	0.01
Irish	2,953	6.61
Israeli	12	0.03
Italian	798	1.79
Lithuanian	7	0.02
Luxemburger	10	0.02
Northern European	12	0.03
Norwegian	172	0.38
Pennsylvania German	9	0.02
Polish	194	0.43
Portuguese	27	0.06
Romanian	6	0.01
Russian	125	0.28
Scandinavian	37	0.08
Scotch-Irish	1,408	3.15
Scottish	620	1.39
Slavic	8	0.02
Slovak	18	0.04
Swedish	161	0.36
Swiss	28	0.06
Turkish	29	0.06
Ukrainian	26	0.06
United States or American	4,241	9.49
Welsh	242	0.54
West Indian, excl. Hispanic:	34	0.08
Barbadian	7	0.02
Jamaican	16	0.04
West Indian	11	0.02
White:	22,658	50.60
Not Hispanic (22,060)	22,318	49.84
Hispanic (305)	340	0.76
Yugoslavian	37	0.08

Horn Lake

Place Type: City
County: De Soto
Population: 14,099

Ancestry/Race	Number	%
Acadian/Cajun	10	0.07
African American/Black:	1,763	12.50
Not Hispanic (1,728)	1,762	12.50
Hispanic (1)	1	0.01
African, sub-Saharan:	208	1.51
African	178	1.29
Liberian	30	0.22
Am. Ind. or Alaska Nat., not spec.	30	0.21
American Indian tribes, specified:	85	0.60
Apache	1	0.01
Cherokee (23)	33	0.23

Notes: 1. Figures in the "Number" column do not add up to the total population due to: a) Ancestry/Race overlap — e.g. persons can report being both White and Irish, b) persons of Hispanic origin can report being any race, c) persons reporting two ancestries are counted in both categories. 2. Numbers in parentheses indicate the number of persons reporting this ancestry/race alone, not in combination with any other ancestry/race. 3. Refer to the Explanation of Data in the front of the book for more detailed information.

Chippewa (2)	2	0.01
Choctaw (12)	18	0.13
Comanche	1	0.01
Cree	1	0.01
Creek (8)	9	0.06
Houma	2	0.01
Kiowa (1)	1	0.01
Latin American Indians	7	0.05
Navajo (4)	4	0.03
Shoshone (3)	3	0.02
All other tribes	3	0.02
American Indian tribes, not spec.	6	0.04
Arab:	6	0.04
Lebanese	6	0.04
Asian:	156	1.11
Cambodian (7)	9	0.06
Chinese, ex. Taiwanese (10)	12	0.09
Filipino (25)	30	0.21
Indian (53)	61	0.43
Japanese (3)	6	0.04
Korean (10)	17	0.12
Laotian (7)	7	0.05
Pakistani	2	0.01
Thai (1)	1	0.01
Vietnamese (2)	3	0.02
Other Asian, not specified (5)	8	0.06
Belgian	7	0.05
British	34	0.25
Canadian	18	0.13
Croatian	18	0.13
Czech	18	0.13
Czechoslovakian	9	0.07
Danish	8	0.06
Dutch	235	1.70
English	1,099	7.96
European	61	0.44
French, except Basque	296	2.14
French Canadian	7	0.05
German	1,244	9.01
Greek	70	0.51
Hawaii Native/Pacific Islander:	12	0.09
Micronesian:	1	0.01
Guamanian/Chamorro	1	0.01
Polynesian: (5)	7	0.05
Native Hawaiian (3)	4	0.03
Samoan (2)	3	0.02
Other Pac. Isl., not spec. (1)	4	0.03
Hispanic or Latino:	603	4.28
Central American:	17	0.12
Guatemalan	1	0.01
Honduran	2	0.01
Panamanian	14	0.10
Cuban	10	0.07
Mexican	452	3.21
Puerto Rican	18	0.13
South American:	6	0.04
Argentinean	1	0.01
Colombian	3	0.02
Ecuadorian	1	0.01
Peruvian	1	0.01
Other Hispanic or Latino	100	0.71
Iranian	21	0.15
Irish	1,909	13.82
Italian	493	3.57
Luxemburger	9	0.07
Norwegian	87	0.63
Polish	74	0.54
Scandinavian	27	0.20
Scotch-Irish	233	1.69
Scottish	146	1.06
Swedish	12	0.09
Ukrainian	10	0.07
United States or American	2,505	18.14
Welsh	46	0.33
West Indian, excl. Hispanic:	21	0.15
Bermudan	21	0.15
White:	11,830	83.91
Not Hispanic (11,463)	11,554	81.95
Hispanic (241)	276	1.96
Yugoslavian	19	0.14

Indianola

Place Type: City
County: Sunflower
Population: 12,066

Ancestry/Race	Number	%
Acadian/Cajun	7	0.06
African American/Black:	8,871	73.52
Not Hispanic (8,830)	8,842	73.28
Hispanic (24)	29	0.24
African, sub-Saharan:	99	0.81
African	65	0.53
Nigerian	34	0.28
Am. Ind. or Alaska Nat., not spec.	3	0.02
American Indian tribes, specified:	7	0.06
Cherokee	1	0.01
Choctaw	5	0.04
Sioux	1	0.01
Asian:	73	0.61
Chinese, ex. Taiwanese (27)	32	0.27
Filipino (11)	14	0.12
Indian (8)	13	0.11
Korean (6)	6	0.05
Vietnamese (2)	2	0.02
Other Asian, not specified	6	0.05
British	57	0.47
Czech	6	0.05
Dutch	60	0.49
English	384	3.15
French, except Basque	37	0.30
French Canadian	10	0.08
German	248	2.03
Hawaii Native/Pacific Islander:	1	0.01
Polynesian:	1	0.01
Native Hawaiian	1	0.01
Hispanic or Latino:	86	0.71
Cuban	2	0.02
Mexican	45	0.37
Puerto Rican	3	0.02
Other Hispanic or Latino	36	0.30
Irish	346	2.84
Italian	119	0.98
Polish	24	0.20
Scotch-Irish	154	1.26
Scottish	95	0.78
Swedish	59	0.48
United States or American	578	4.74
Welsh	31	0.25
West Indian, excl. Hispanic:	10	0.08
Haitian	10	0.08
White:	3,125	25.90
Not Hispanic (3,064)	3,084	25.56
Hispanic (41)	41	0.34

Jackson

Place Type: City
County: Hinds
Population: 184,256

Ancestry/Race	Number	%
Acadian/Cajun	128	0.07
Afghan	5	0.00
African American/Black:	131,005	71.10
Not Hispanic (129,609)	130,387	70.76
Hispanic (542)	618	0.34
African, sub-Saharan:	2,089	1.14
African	1,911	1.04
Ethiopian	13	0.01
Nigerian	165	0.09
Alaska Native tribes, specified:	3	0.00
Eskimo (1)	2	0.00
Tlingit-Haida (1)	1	0.00
Am. Ind. or Alaska Nat., not spec.	326	0.18
Albanian	7	0.00
American Indian tribes, specified:	299	0.16
Apache (5)	7	0.00
Blackfeet (1)	15	0.01
Cherokee (20)	71	0.04
Cheyenne	3	0.00
Chickasaw (6)	9	0.00
Chippewa (8)	10	0.01
Choctaw (35)	105	0.06
Comanche (1)	3	0.00
Cree	6	0.00
Creek (3)	13	0.01
Crow (2)	4	0.00
Iroquois (1)	1	0.00
Latin American Indians (5)	11	0.01
Navajo (1)	1	0.00
Osage (1)	1	0.00
Paiute	1	0.00
Pueblo (1)	3	0.00
Seminole (1)	3	0.00
Shoshone	1	0.00
Sioux (2)	10	0.01
Yakama (1)	1	0.00
All other tribes (4)	20	0.01
American Indian tribes, not spec.	36	0.02
Arab:	338	0.18
Arab/Arabic	40	0.02
Egyptian	29	0.02
Jordanian	10	0.01
Lebanese	246	0.13
Syrian	13	0.01
Armenian	18	0.01
Asian:	1,365	0.74
Chinese, ex. Taiwanese (214)	257	0.14
Filipino (61)	109	0.06
Indian (476)	561	0.30
Indonesian (2)	2	0.00
Japanese (26)	44	0.02
Korean (50)	68	0.04
Malaysian	1	0.00
Pakistani (18)	27	0.01
Taiwanese (8)	8	0.00
Thai (16)	18	0.01
Vietnamese (156)	166	0.09
Other Asian, specified (3)	32	0.02
Other Asian, not specified (16)	72	0.04
Australian	6	0.00
Austrian	104	0.06
Belgian	55	0.03
British	432	0.23
Canadian	102	0.06
Celtic	36	0.02
Croatian	6	0.00
Czech	127	0.07
Czechoslovakian	15	0.01
Danish	177	0.10
Dutch	698	0.38
Eastern European	25	0.01
English	8,164	4.44
Estonian	7	0.00
European	907	0.49
French, except Basque	1,797	0.98
French Canadian	217	0.12
German	4,563	2.48
Greek	163	0.09
Hawaii Native/Pacific Islander:	114	0.06
Melanesian: (1)	3	0.00
Fijian	1	0.00
Other Melanesian (1)	2	0.00
Micronesian: (1)	5	0.00
Guamanian/Chamorro (1)	5	0.00
Polynesian: (17)	42	0.02
Native Hawaiian (9)	26	0.01
Samoan (8)	16	0.01
Other Pac. Isl., specified	29	0.02
Other Pac. Isl., not spec. (5)	35	0.02
Hispanic or Latino:	1,451	0.79
Central American:	60	0.03
Costa Rican	6	0.00
Guatemalan	13	0.01
Honduran	5	0.00
Nicaraguan	11	0.01
Panamanian	20	0.01
Salvadoran	2	0.00
Other Central American	3	0.00

Notes: 1. Figures in the "Number" column do not add up to the total population due to: a) Ancestry/Race overlap — e.g. persons can report being both White and Irish, b) persons of Hispanic origin can report being any race, c) persons reporting two ancestries are counted in both categories. 2. Numbers in parentheses indicate the number of persons reporting this ancestry/race alone, not in combination with any other ancestry/race. 3. Refer to the Explanation of Data in the front of the book for more detailed information.

Cuban	71	0.04
Dominican Republic	1	0.00
Mexican	670	0.36
Puerto Rican	138	0.07
South American:	52	0.03
Argentinean	14	0.01
Bolivian	2	0.00
Chilean	3	0.00
Colombian	12	0.01
Ecuadorian	1	0.00
Peruvian	5	0.00
Uruguayan	2	0.00
Venezuelan	11	0.01
Other South American	2	0.00
Other Hispanic or Latino	459	0.25
Hungarian	19	0.01
Icelander	17	0.01
Iranian	116	0.06
Irish	5,981	3.25
Israeli	19	0.01
Italian	1,125	0.61
Lithuanian	61	0.03
Luxemburger	11	0.01
Norwegian	358	0.19
Pennsylvania German	4	0.00
Polish	371	0.20
Portuguese	4	0.00
Romanian	12	0.01
Russian	78	0.04
Scandinavian	41	0.02
Scotch-Irish	3,759	2.04
Scottish	2,114	1.15
Slavic	13	0.01
Slovak	5	0.00
Slovene	17	0.01
Swedish	159	0.09
Swiss	69	0.04
Ukrainian	19	0.01
United States or American	8,353	4.54
Welsh	404	0.22
West Indian, excl. Hispanic:	312	0.17
Barbadian	10	0.01
Belizean	10	0.01
Haitian	85	0.05
Jamaican	109	0.06
Trinidadian and Tobagonian	68	0.04
West Indian	30	0.02
White:	52,006	28.22
Not Hispanic (50,679)	51,415	27.90
Hispanic (529)	591	0.32
Yugoslavian	38	0.02

Laurel

Place Type: City
County: Jones
Population: 18,393

Ancestry/Race	Number	%
Acadian/Cajun	63	0.34
African American/Black:	10,208	55.50
Not Hispanic (10,091)	10,155	55.21
Hispanic (39)	53	0.29
African, sub-Saharan:	232	1.24
African	232	1.24
Am. Ind. or Alaska Nat., not spec.	30	0.16
American Indian tribes, specified:	28	0.15
Blackfeet	3	0.02
Cherokee (3)	9	0.05
Choctaw (7)	12	0.07
Creek (1)	2	0.01
All other tribes	2	0.01
Asian:	85	0.46
Chinese, ex. Taiwanese (11)	13	0.07
Filipino (1)	4	0.02
Indian (31)	32	0.17
Japanese (2)	5	0.03
Korean (3)	5	0.03
Vietnamese (12)	12	0.07
Other Asian, specified	3	0.02
Other Asian, not specified	11	0.06
Belgian	6	0.03
British	40	0.21
Canadian	5	0.03
Czech	19	0.10
Danish	13	0.07
Dutch	24	0.13
Eastern European	9	0.05
English	973	5.19
European	49	0.26
French, except Basque	235	1.25
French Canadian	32	0.17
German	404	2.15
Greek	5	0.03
Hawaii Native/Pacific Islander:	4	0.02
Polynesian: (1)	2	0.01
Native Hawaiian (1)	2	0.01
Other Pac. Isl., specified	1	0.01
Other Pac. Isl., not spec.	1	0.01
Hispanic or Latino:	712	3.87
Central American:	33	0.18
Guatemalan	12	0.07
Honduran	4	0.02
Panamanian	10	0.05
Salvadoran	7	0.04
Cuban	7	0.04
Mexican	568	3.09
Puerto Rican	9	0.05
South American:	9	0.05
Colombian	2	0.01
Peruvian	1	0.01
Venezuelan	6	0.03
Other Hispanic or Latino	86	0.47
Hungarian	7	0.04
Irish	751	4.00
Italian	132	0.70
Norwegian	47	0.25
Polish	48	0.26
Romanian	6	0.03
Russian	7	0.04
Scandinavian	4	0.02
Scotch-Irish	393	2.10
Scottish	240	1.28
Swedish	22	0.12
United States or American	1,616	8.62
Welsh	22	0.12
West Indian, excl. Hispanic:	14	0.07
Bermudan	10	0.05
Jamaican	4	0.02
White:	7,560	41.10
Not Hispanic (7,413)	7,480	40.67
Hispanic (61)	80	0.43
Yugoslavian	8	0.04

Long Beach

Place Type: City
County: Harrison
Population: 17,320

Ancestry/Race	Number	%
Acadian/Cajun	45	0.25
African American/Black:	1,332	7.69
Not Hispanic (1,271)	1,327	7.66
Hispanic (4)	5	0.03
Am. Ind. or Alaska Nat., not spec.	26	0.15
American Indian tribes, specified:	109	0.63
Blackfeet	1	0.01
Cherokee (18)	45	0.26
Cheyenne (1)	1	0.01
Chippewa (2)	4	0.02
Choctaw (6)	24	0.14
Creek (1)	6	0.03
Delaware (1)	1	0.01
Houma (1)	1	0.01
Iroquois (1)	2	0.01
Latin American Indians (4)	4	0.02
Navajo	1	0.01
Sioux (6)	12	0.07
All other tribes (5)	7	0.04
American Indian tribes, not spec.	22	0.13
Arab:	38	0.21
Arab/Arabic	7	0.04
Lebanese	31	0.17
Armenian	16	0.09
Asian:	525	3.03
Bangladeshi (10)	10	0.06
Chinese, ex. Taiwanese (27)	32	0.18
Filipino (125)	153	0.88
Indian (52)	58	0.33
Japanese (18)	36	0.21
Korean (11)	18	0.10
Malaysian	2	0.01
Pakistani (8)	8	0.05
Taiwanese	1	0.01
Thai (6)	9	0.05
Vietnamese (171)	177	1.02
Other Asian, not specified (12)	21	0.12
British	31	0.17
Canadian	96	0.54
Czech	20	0.11
Czechoslovakian	15	0.08
Danish	93	0.52
Dutch	258	1.45
English	1,816	10.23
European	135	0.76
Finnish	7	0.04
French, except Basque	1,554	8.76
French Canadian	100	0.56
German	2,478	13.96
Greek	49	0.28
Hawaii Native/Pacific Islander:	19	0.11
Micronesian: (9)	10	0.06
Guamanian/Chamorro (8)	9	0.05
Other Micronesian (1)	1	0.01
Polynesian: (3)	9	0.05
Native Hawaiian (2)	8	0.05
Samoan (1)	1	0.01
Hispanic or Latino:	397	2.29
Central American:	49	0.28
Costa Rican	1	0.01
Guatemalan	8	0.05
Honduran	16	0.09
Nicaraguan	8	0.05
Panamanian	5	0.03
Salvadoran	2	0.01
Other Central American	9	0.05
Cuban	13	0.08
Dominican Republic	5	0.03
Mexican	130	0.75
Puerto Rican	64	0.37
South American:	9	0.05
Colombian	3	0.02
Peruvian	1	0.01
Venezuelan	5	0.03
Other Hispanic or Latino	127	0.73
Hungarian	8	0.05
Irish	2,331	13.14
Italian	1,333	7.51
Lithuanian	20	0.11
Norwegian	134	0.76
Pennsylvania German	5	0.03
Polish	187	1.05
Portuguese	22	0.12
Romanian	15	0.08
Russian	20	0.11
Scandinavian	18	0.10
Scotch-Irish	483	2.72
Scottish	419	2.36
Slavic	36	0.20
Slovak	17	0.10
Swedish	142	0.80
Swiss	7	0.04
Ukrainian	32	0.18
United States or American	2,333	13.15
Welsh	105	0.59
West Indian, excl. Hispanic:	26	0.15
Belizean	5	0.03
Jamaican	10	0.06
West Indian	11	0.06

Notes: 1. Figures in the "Number" column do not add up to the total population due to: a) Ancestry/Race overlap — e.g. persons can report being both White and Irish, b) persons of Hispanic origin can report being any race, c) persons reporting two ancestries are counted in both categories. 2. Numbers in parentheses indicate the number of persons reporting this ancestry/race alone, not in combination with any other ancestry/race. 3. Refer to the Explanation of Data in the front of the book for more detailed information.

White:	15,374	88.76
Not Hispanic (14,905)	15,093	87.14
Hispanic (249)	281	1.62
Yugoslavian	23	0.13

Madison

Place Type: City
County: Madison
Population: 14,692

Ancestry/Race	Number	%
Acadian/Cajun	12	0.08
African American/Black:	726	4.94
Not Hispanic (717)	724	4.93
Hispanic (2)	2	0.01
African, sub-Saharan:	19	0.13
African	19	0.13
Am. Ind. or Alaska Nat., not spec.	8	0.05
American Indian tribes, specified:	12	0.08
Cherokee (1)	4	0.03
Chippewa (2)	5	0.03
Choctaw (1)	3	0.02
American Indian tribes, not spec.	6	0.04
Arab:	111	0.75
Lebanese	111	0.75
Armenian	13	0.09
Asian:	211	1.44
Chinese, ex. Taiwanese (42)	52	0.35
Filipino (5)	7	0.05
Indian (58)	61	0.42
Japanese (8)	8	0.05
Korean (7)	7	0.05
Pakistani (25)	30	0.20
Taiwanese (4)	4	0.03
Thai	2	0.01
Vietnamese (24)	26	0.18
Other Asian, not specified (3)	14	0.10
Belgian	19	0.13
British	149	1.01
Canadian	48	0.33
Czechoslovakian	10	0.07
Danish	19	0.13
Dutch	97	0.66
English	2,022	13.75
European	256	1.74
French, except Basque	501	3.41
French Canadian	72	0.49
German	1,271	8.64
Greek	58	0.39
Hawaii Native/Pacific Islander:	7	0.05
Micronesian:	1	0.01
Guamanian/Chamorro	1	0.01
Polynesian: (4)	5	0.03
Native Hawaiian	1	0.01
Samoan (4)	4	0.03
Other Pac. Isl., not spec.	1	0.01
Hispanic or Latino:	102	0.69
Central American:	4	0.03
Costa Rican	2	0.01
Nicaraguan	1	0.01
Salvadoran	1	0.01
Cuban	4	0.03
Mexican	41	0.28
Puerto Rican	6	0.04
South American:	14	0.10
Bolivian	1	0.01
Colombian	8	0.05
Ecuadorian	1	0.01
Peruvian	1	0.01
Other South American	3	0.02
Other Hispanic or Latino	33	0.22
Hungarian	52	0.35
Iranian	57	0.39
Irish	1,498	10.19
Italian	377	2.56
Lithuanian	15	0.10
Norwegian	37	0.25
Polish	88	0.60
Romanian	7	0.05
Russian	15	0.10
Scotch-Irish	769	5.23
Scottish	522	3.55
Serbian	12	0.08
Slovak	7	0.05
Slovene	6	0.04
Swedish	102	0.69
Swiss	26	0.18
Ukrainian	31	0.21
United States or American	2,339	15.91
Welsh	127	0.86
West Indian, excl. Hispanic:	24	0.16
Jamaican	24	0.16
White:	13,744	93.55
Not Hispanic (13,629)	13,670	93.04
Hispanic (68)	74	0.50

McComb

Place Type: City
County: Pike
Population: 13,337

Ancestry/Race	Number	%
African American/Black:	7,825	58.67
Not Hispanic (7,769)	7,805	58.52
Hispanic (20)	20	0.15
African, sub-Saharan:	109	0.81
African	109	0.81
Am. Ind. or Alaska Nat., not spec.	20	0.15
American Indian tribes, specified:	19	0.14
Apache	1	0.01
Blackfeet	1	0.01
Cherokee (2)	5	0.04
Choctaw	2	0.01
Houma	1	0.01
Latin American Indians	7	0.05
Sioux (1)	1	0.01
All other tribes (1)	1	0.01
American Indian tribes, not spec.	1	0.01
Arab:	7	0.05
Lebanese	7	0.05
Asian:	96	0.72
Cambodian (3)	3	0.02
Chinese, ex. Taiwanese (20)	22	0.16
Filipino (1)	2	0.01
Indian (23)	29	0.22
Japanese (3)	6	0.04
Korean (6)	9	0.07
Pakistani (4)	4	0.03
Thai (1)	1	0.01
Vietnamese (4)	4	0.03
Other Asian, specified	9	0.07
Other Asian, not specified	7	0.05
British	6	0.04
Canadian	8	0.06
Danish	7	0.05
Dutch	19	0.14
English	693	5.12
European	58	0.43
French, except Basque	193	1.43
French Canadian	15	0.11
German	451	3.33
Greek	13	0.10
Hawaii Native/Pacific Islander:	13	0.10
Polynesian: (3)	3	0.02
Native Hawaiian (3)	3	0.02
Other Pac. Isl., specified	9	0.07
Other Pac. Isl., not spec. (1)	1	0.01
Hispanic or Latino:	113	0.85
Central American:	11	0.08
Costa Rican	3	0.02
Guatemalan	1	0.01
Honduran	3	0.02
Salvadoran	4	0.03
Cuban	3	0.02
Mexican	67	0.50
Puerto Rican	1	0.01
South American:	8	0.06
Colombian	2	0.01
Ecuadorian	2	0.01
Venezuelan	3	0.02
Other South American	1	0.01
Other Hispanic or Latino	23	0.17
Hungarian	10	0.07
Irish	509	3.76
Italian	103	0.76
Norwegian	45	0.33
Polish	40	0.30
Scotch-Irish	230	1.70
Scottish	117	0.86
United States or American	1,499	11.08
Welsh	29	0.21
White:	5,379	40.33
Not Hispanic (5,323)	5,347	40.09
Hispanic (31)	32	0.24

Meridian

Place Type: City
County: Lauderdale
Population: 39,968

Ancestry/Race	Number	%
Acadian/Cajun	8	0.02
African American/Black:	21,855	54.68
Not Hispanic (21,637)	21,749	54.42
Hispanic (92)	106	0.27
African, sub-Saharan:	511	1.28
African	502	1.25
Nigerian	9	0.02
Alaska Native tribes, not specified	1	0.00
Am. Ind. or Alaska Nat., not spec.	57	0.14
American Indian tribes, specified:	72	0.18
Apache (1)	1	0.00
Blackfeet	1	0.00
Cherokee (9)	26	0.07
Chickasaw	1	0.00
Choctaw (11)	21	0.05
Creek (2)	3	0.01
Iroquois	1	0.00
Latin American Indians (3)	3	0.01
Navajo	2	0.01
Pueblo (1)	1	0.00
Shoshone (1)	1	0.00
Sioux (2)	3	0.01
All other tribes (6)	8	0.02
American Indian tribes, not spec.	19	0.05
Arab:	46	0.11
Lebanese	46	0.11
Asian:	320	0.80
Chinese, ex. Taiwanese (28)	41	0.10
Filipino (67)	77	0.19
Indian (53)	67	0.17
Japanese (9)	25	0.06
Korean (19)	33	0.08
Pakistani (17)	17	0.04
Taiwanese	1	0.00
Thai (7)	7	0.02
Vietnamese (26)	39	0.10
Other Asian, not specified (6)	13	0.03
Australian	14	0.03
Austrian	18	0.04
British	141	0.35
Canadian	15	0.04
Celtic	7	0.02
Croatian	41	0.10
Czech	62	0.15
Czechoslovakian	16	0.04
Danish	55	0.14
Dutch	143	0.36
English	2,127	5.31
European	163	0.41
French, except Basque	347	0.87
French Canadian	42	0.10
German	1,225	3.06
Greek	14	0.03
Hawaii Native/Pacific Islander:	24	0.06
Micronesian: (2)	5	0.01
Guamanian/Chamorro (2)	5	0.01

Notes: 1. Figures in the "Number" column do not add up to the total population due to: a) Ancestry/Race overlap — e.g. persons can report being both White and Irish, b) persons of Hispanic origin can report being any race, c) persons reporting two ancestries are counted in both categories. 2. Numbers in parentheses indicate the number of persons reporting this ancestry/race alone, not in combination with any other ancestry/race. 3. Refer to the Explanation of Data in the front of the book for more detailed information.

Polynesian: (7)	15	0.04
Native Hawaiian	4	0.01
Samoan (7)	11	0.03
Other Pac. Isl., not spec. (1)	4	0.01
Hispanic or Latino:	433	1.08
Central American:	9	0.02
Costa Rican	1	0.00
Guatemalan	3	0.01
Nicaraguan	3	0.01
Panamanian	2	0.01
Cuban	9	0.02
Dominican Republic	5	0.01
Mexican	216	0.54
Puerto Rican	54	0.14
South American:	12	0.03
Chilean	3	0.01
Colombian	4	0.01
Ecuadorian	1	0.00
Paraguayan	1	0.00
Venezuelan	3	0.01
Other Hispanic or Latino	128	0.32
Hungarian	17	0.04
Icelander	8	0.02
Irish	1,788	4.47
Italian	269	0.67
Norwegian	59	0.15
Polish	86	0.21
Portuguese	17	0.04
Russian	21	0.05
Scotch-Irish	844	2.11
Scottish	502	1.25
Slovak	9	0.02
Swedish	91	0.23
Swiss	18	0.04
Turkish	7	0.02
Ukrainian	15	0.04
United States or American	2,886	7.21
Welsh	57	0.14
West Indian, excl. Hispanic:	8	0.02
West Indian	8	0.02
White:	17,734	44.37
Not Hispanic (17,383)	17,510	43.81
Hispanic (197)	224	0.56

Moss Point

Place Type: City
County: Jackson
Population: 15,851

Ancestry/Race	Number	%
Acadian/Cajun	6	0.04
African American/Black:	11,249	70.97
Not Hispanic (11,136)	11,194	70.62
Hispanic (48)	55	0.35
African, sub-Saharan:	229	1.45
African	212	1.34
South African	9	0.06
Other sub-Saharan African	8	0.05
Am. Ind. or Alaska Nat., not spec.	16	0.10
American Indian tribes, specified:	39	0.25
Apache	1	0.01
Blackfeet (1)	3	0.02
Cherokee (2)	11	0.07
Chippewa (3)	3	0.02
Choctaw (1)	8	0.05
Cree	1	0.01
Creek (1)	1	0.01
Houma (3)	3	0.02
Iroquois (1)	1	0.01
Lumbee (3)	3	0.02
Pima (1)	1	0.01
Sioux (2)	2	0.01
All other tribes	1	0.01
American Indian tribes, not spec.	3	0.02
Arab:	44	0.28
Lebanese	7	0.04
Syrian	37	0.23
Asian:	59	0.37
Chinese, ex. Taiwanese	3	0.02
Filipino (12)	18	0.11
Indian (7)	11	0.07
Indonesian	1	0.01
Japanese (1)	2	0.01
Korean	1	0.01
Laotian (1)	1	0.01
Vietnamese (13)	13	0.08
Other Asian, not specified	9	0.06
British	17	0.11
Croatian	5	0.03
Danish	10	0.06
Dutch	78	0.49
English	396	2.50
European	64	0.40
Finnish	19	0.12
French, except Basque	209	1.32
French Canadian	15	0.09
German	338	2.13
Hawaii Native/Pacific Islander:	4	0.03
Micronesian: (3)	3	0.02
Other Micronesian (3)	3	0.02
Polynesian: (1)	1	0.01
Native Hawaiian (1)	1	0.01
Hispanic or Latino:	159	1.00
Central American:	10	0.06
Costa Rican	5	0.03
Nicaraguan	1	0.01
Panamanian	4	0.03
Cuban	6	0.04
Mexican	73	0.46
Puerto Rican	17	0.11
South American:	4	0.03
Argentinean	1	0.01
Venezuelan	3	0.02
Other Hispanic or Latino	49	0.31
Irish	461	2.91
Italian	58	0.37
Norwegian	16	0.10
Polish	6	0.04
Scotch-Irish	179	1.13
Scottish	40	0.25
Swedish	17	0.11
United States or American	873	5.51
Welsh	9	0.06
West Indian, excl. Hispanic:	10	0.06
Haitian	10	0.06
White:	4,496	28.36
Not Hispanic (4,402)	4,450	28.07
Hispanic (43)	46	0.29

Natchez

Place Type: City
County: Adams
Population: 18,464

Ancestry/Race	Number	%
Acadian/Cajun	4	0.02
African American/Black:	10,135	54.89
Not Hispanic (10,020)	10,086	54.63
Hispanic (41)	49	0.27
African, sub-Saharan:	78	0.42
African	78	0.42
Am. Ind. or Alaska Nat., not spec.	47	0.25
American Indian tribes, specified:	23	0.12
Blackfeet	1	0.01
Cherokee (2)	10	0.05
Choctaw (3)	7	0.04
Creek	2	0.01
Seminole	2	0.01
All other tribes (1)	1	0.01
American Indian tribes, not spec.	1	0.01
Arab:	10	0.05
Lebanese	5	0.03
Syrian	5	0.03
Asian:	121	0.66
Bangladeshi (2)	2	0.01
Cambodian (3)	4	0.02
Chinese, ex. Taiwanese (20)	24	0.13
Filipino (7)	15	0.08
Indian (28)	37	0.20
Japanese (1)	1	0.01
Korean (1)	2	0.01
Vietnamese (7)	8	0.04
Other Asian, specified (1)	8	0.04
Other Asian, not specified	20	0.11
Austrian	7	0.04
British	63	0.34
Canadian	12	0.06
Czech	8	0.04
Czechoslovakian	12	0.06
Danish	5	0.03
Dutch	118	0.64
English	1,248	6.73
European	119	0.64
French, except Basque	294	1.59
French Canadian	34	0.18
German	783	4.22
Greek	7	0.04
Hawaii Native/Pacific Islander:	25	0.14
Micronesian:	3	0.02
Guamanian/Chamorro	3	0.02
Polynesian: (2)	10	0.05
Native Hawaiian (1)	7	0.04
Samoan (1)	3	0.02
Other Pac. Isl., specified	7	0.04
Other Pac. Isl., not spec. (1)	5	0.03
Hispanic or Latino:	130	0.70
Central American:	6	0.03
Guatemalan	2	0.01
Honduran	1	0.01
Panamanian	2	0.01
Salvadoran	1	0.01
Cuban	2	0.01
Mexican	53	0.29
Puerto Rican	11	0.06
South American:	1	0.01
Colombian	1	0.01
Other Hispanic or Latino	57	0.31
Hungarian	6	0.03
Irish	1,118	6.03
Italian	410	2.21
Norwegian	40	0.22
Pennsylvania German	7	0.04
Polish	36	0.19
Portuguese	4	0.02
Russian	12	0.06
Scotch-Irish	461	2.49
Scottish	220	1.19
Swedish	15	0.08
United States or American	1,356	7.32
Welsh	35	0.19
White:	8,214	44.49
Not Hispanic (8,108)	8,163	44.21
Hispanic (50)	51	0.28

Ocean Springs

Place Type: City
County: Jackson
Population: 17,225

Ancestry/Race	Number	%
Acadian/Cajun	28	0.16
African American/Black:	1,254	7.28
Not Hispanic (1,203)	1,244	7.22
Hispanic (8)	10	0.06
African, sub-Saharan:	67	0.39
African	67	0.39
Am. Ind. or Alaska Nat., not spec.	43	0.25
American Indian tribes, specified:	125	0.73
Apache (1)	4	0.02
Blackfeet (1)	5	0.03
Cherokee (15)	49	0.28
Chickasaw (1)	1	0.01
Chippewa	2	0.01
Choctaw (5)	12	0.07
Creek (7)	10	0.06
Houma (4)	4	0.02
Iroquois (2)	6	0.03

Notes: 1. Figures in the "Number" column do not add up to the total population due to: a) Ancestry/Race overlap — e.g. persons can report being both White and Irish, b) persons of Hispanic origin can report being any race, c) persons reporting two ancestries are counted in both categories. 2. Numbers in parentheses indicate the number of persons reporting this ancestry/race alone, not in combination with any other ancestry/race. 3. Refer to the Explanation of Data in the front of the book for more detailed information.

Ancestry/Race	Number	%
Latin American Indians (2)	4	0.02
Ottawa	1	0.01
Potawatomi (1)	2	0.01
Seminole (1)	7	0.04
Shoshone (1)	2	0.01
Sioux (1)	1	0.01
Ute (2)	2	0.01
All other tribes (8)	13	0.08
American Indian tribes, not spec.	3	0.02
Arab:	63	0.37
Lebanese	56	0.33
Moroccan	7	0.04
Armenian	13	0.08
Asian:	522	3.03
Chinese, ex. Taiwanese (47)	59	0.34
Filipino (78)	102	0.59
Indian (41)	41	0.24
Indonesian	2	0.01
Japanese (13)	25	0.15
Korean (23)	30	0.17
Laotian (4)	4	0.02
Pakistani (16)	21	0.12
Sri Lankan (3)	3	0.02
Thai (6)	11	0.06
Vietnamese (215)	217	1.26
Other Asian, not specified (6)	7	0.04
Assyrian/Chaldean/Syriac	11	0.06
Austrian	14	0.08
Basque	16	0.09
Belgian	47	0.27
British	184	1.07
Canadian	28	0.16
Celtic	7	0.04
Croatian	40	0.23
Czech	87	0.51
Czechoslovakian	13	0.08
Danish	147	0.85
Dutch	167	0.97
Eastern European	14	0.08
English	2,475	14.38
European	248	1.44
Finnish	28	0.16
French, except Basque	1,520	8.83
French Canadian	214	1.24
German	2,562	14.88
Greek	87	0.51
Hawaii Native/Pacific Islander:	43	0.25
Micronesian: (2)	8	0.05
Guamanian/Chamorro (2)	8	0.05
Polynesian: (7)	25	0.15
Native Hawaiian (4)	12	0.07
Samoan (3)	8	0.05
Tongan	5	0.03
Other Pac. Isl., not spec. (4)	10	0.06
Hispanic or Latino:	430	2.50
Central American:	23	0.13
Costa Rican	1	0.01
Guatemalan	4	0.02
Honduran	10	0.06
Nicaraguan	3	0.02
Panamanian	5	0.03
Cuban	12	0.07
Mexican	171	0.99
Puerto Rican	70	0.41
South American:	33	0.19
Argentinean	6	0.03
Chilean	5	0.03
Colombian	9	0.05
Ecuadorian	2	0.01
Peruvian	3	0.02
Venezuelan	6	0.03
Other South American	2	0.01
Other Hispanic or Latino	121	0.70
Hungarian	24	0.14
Irish	2,053	11.92
Italian	859	4.99
Latvian	7	0.04
Lithuanian	30	0.17
Maltese	36	0.21
Northern European	50	0.29
Norwegian	194	1.13
Polish	250	1.45
Portuguese	10	0.06
Romanian	9	0.05
Russian	74	0.43
Scandinavian	14	0.08
Scotch-Irish	565	3.28
Scottish	517	3.00
Slavic	41	0.24
Swedish	171	0.99
Swiss	11	0.06
Turkish	15	0.09
Ukrainian	17	0.10
United States or American	1,651	9.59
Welsh	165	0.96
West Indian, excl. Hispanic:	6	0.03
Jamaican	6	0.03
White:	15,347	89.10
Not Hispanic (14,842)	15,025	87.23
Hispanic (271)	322	1.87
Yugoslavian	27	0.16

Olive Branch

Place Type: City
County: De Soto
Population: 21,054

Ancestry/Race	Number	%
African American/Black:	2,429	11.54
Not Hispanic (2,369)	2,415	11.47
Hispanic (10)	14	0.07
African, sub-Saharan:	57	0.27
African	57	0.27
Am. Ind. or Alaska Nat., not spec.	24	0.11
American Indian tribes, specified:	51	0.24
Blackfeet (2)	2	0.01
Cherokee (10)	18	0.09
Chippewa (2)	5	0.02
Choctaw (10)	13	0.06
Comanche	4	0.02
Delaware (1)	1	0.00
Iroquois	1	0.00
Sioux (2)	3	0.01
All other tribes (4)	4	0.02
American Indian tribes, not spec.	4	0.02
Arab:	52	0.24
Arab/Arabic	44	0.21
Lebanese	8	0.04
Asian:	124	0.59
Cambodian (2)	2	0.01
Chinese, ex. Taiwanese (23)	28	0.13
Filipino (16)	24	0.11
Indian (5)	7	0.03
Japanese (4)	12	0.06
Korean (19)	24	0.11
Pakistani (5)	5	0.02
Thai (4)	5	0.02
Vietnamese (4)	4	0.02
Other Asian, specified	1	0.00
Other Asian, not specified (2)	12	0.06
Belgian	6	0.03
Brazilian	17	0.08
British	49	0.23
Canadian	11	0.05
Celtic	37	0.17
Czech	54	0.25
Danish	62	0.29
Dutch	285	1.34
English	1,959	9.21
European	397	1.87
French, except Basque	503	2.36
French Canadian	71	0.33
German	1,969	9.26
Greek	17	0.08
Hawaii Native/Pacific Islander:	5	0.02
Micronesian:	2	0.01
Guamanian/Chamorro	2	0.01
Polynesian: (1)	2	0.01
Native Hawaiian	1	0.00
Samoan (1)	1	0.00
Other Pac. Isl., specified	1	0.00
Hispanic or Latino:	307	1.46
Central American:	19	0.09
Costa Rican	4	0.02
Guatemalan	1	0.00
Honduran	1	0.00
Nicaraguan	2	0.01
Panamanian	1	0.00
Salvadoran	10	0.05
Cuban	8	0.04
Dominican Republic	1	0.00
Mexican	193	0.92
Puerto Rican	23	0.11
South American:	18	0.09
Argentinean	1	0.00
Chilean	1	0.00
Colombian	7	0.03
Paraguayan	1	0.00
Peruvian	2	0.01
Venezuelan	5	0.02
Other South American	1	0.00
Other Hispanic or Latino	45	0.21
Hungarian	54	0.25
Irish	2,485	11.68
Italian	652	3.07
Lithuanian	10	0.05
Northern European	24	0.11
Norwegian	147	0.69
Polish	200	0.94
Portuguese	28	0.13
Romanian	22	0.10
Russian	34	0.16
Scotch-Irish	663	3.12
Scottish	352	1.65
Slavic	9	0.04
Slovak	14	0.07
Slovene	8	0.04
Swedish	171	0.80
Swiss	44	0.21
United States or American	3,144	14.78
Welsh	76	0.36
West Indian, excl. Hispanic:	7	0.03
West Indian	7	0.03
White:	18,372	87.26
Not Hispanic (18,105)	18,230	86.59
Hispanic (128)	142	0.67

Oxford

Place Type: City
County: Lafayette
Population: 11,756

Ancestry/Race	Number	%
African American/Black:	2,489	21.17
Not Hispanic (2,443)	2,469	21.00
Hispanic (20)	20	0.17
African, sub-Saharan:	112	0.95
African	91	0.77
Nigerian	13	0.11
Other sub-Saharan African	8	0.07
Alaska Native tribes, specified:	1	0.01
Tlingit-Haida (1)	1	0.01
Am. Ind. or Alaska Nat., not spec.	7	0.06
American Indian tribes, specified:	21	0.18
Blackfeet (1)	1	0.01
Cherokee (5)	6	0.05
Choctaw (2)	9	0.08
Delaware	1	0.01
Iroquois	1	0.01
Lumbee	1	0.01
Sioux (1)	1	0.01
All other tribes	1	0.01
American Indian tribes, not spec.	1	0.01
Arab:	38	0.32
Lebanese	38	0.32
Asian:	364	3.10
Chinese, ex. Taiwanese (84)	92	0.78
Filipino (9)	13	0.11

Notes: 1. Figures in the "Number" column do not add up to the total population due to: a) Ancestry/Race overlap — e.g. persons can report being both White and Irish, b) persons of Hispanic origin can report being any race, c) persons reporting two ancestries are counted in both categories. 2. Numbers in parentheses indicate the number of persons reporting this ancestry/race alone, not in combination with any other ancestry/race. 3. Refer to the Explanation of Data in the front of the book for more detailed information.

Ancestry/Race	Number	%
Indian (109)	119	1.01
Japanese (32)	38	0.32
Korean (23)	29	0.25
Malaysian (3)	4	0.03
Pakistani (11)	14	0.12
Sri Lankan (1)	1	0.01
Taiwanese (3)	3	0.03
Thai (6)	6	0.05
Vietnamese (18)	20	0.17
Other Asian, specified (8)	8	0.07
Other Asian, not specified (3)	17	0.14
Austrian	17	0.14
Basque	9	0.08
Belgian	14	0.12
British	99	0.84
Canadian	12	0.10
Czechoslovakian	6	0.05
Danish	13	0.11
Dutch	180	1.53
English	1,619	13.73
European	251	2.13
French, except Basque	298	2.53
French Canadian	79	0.67
German	1,122	9.51
Greek	27	0.23
Guyanese	6	0.05
Hawaii Native/Pacific Islander:	7	0.06
Micronesian: (1)	2	0.02
Guamanian/Chamorro (1)	2	0.02
Other Pac. Isl., not spec. (1)	5	0.04
Hispanic or Latino:	122	1.04
Central American:	11	0.09
Costa Rican	2	0.02
Honduran	2	0.02
Nicaraguan	1	0.01
Salvadoran	6	0.05
Cuban	7	0.06
Dominican Republic	2	0.02
Mexican	67	0.57
Puerto Rican	6	0.05
South American:	8	0.07
Argentinean	2	0.02
Chilean	1	0.01
Colombian	4	0.03
Ecuadorian	1	0.01
Other Hispanic or Latino	21	0.18
Icelander	9	0.08
Irish	1,173	9.95
Italian	284	2.41
Lithuanian	19	0.16
Norwegian	89	0.75
Polish	143	1.21
Portuguese	18	0.15
Romanian	17	0.14
Russian	35	0.30
Scandinavian	7	0.06
Scotch-Irish	330	2.80
Scottish	621	5.27
Swedish	56	0.47
Swiss	18	0.15
Turkish	8	0.07
Ukrainian	4	0.03
United States or American	898	7.62
Welsh	69	0.59
White:	8,900	75.71
Not Hispanic (8,760)	8,836	75.16
Hispanic (58)	64	0.54
Yugoslavian	8	0.07

Pascagoula

Place Type: City
County: Jackson
Population: 26,200

Ancestry/Race	Number	%
Acadian/Cajun	23	0.09
African American/Black:	7,679	29.31
Not Hispanic (7,557)	7,635	29.14
Hispanic (33)	44	0.17
African, sub-Saharan:	216	0.82
African	205	0.78
Nigerian	7	0.03
Other sub-Saharan African	4	0.02
Am. Ind. or Alaska Nat., not spec.	35	0.13
American Indian tribes, specified:	85	0.32
Apache (2)	6	0.02
Blackfeet	1	0.00
Cherokee (6)	38	0.15
Cheyenne	1	0.00
Chippewa (2)	2	0.01
Choctaw (7)	10	0.04
Creek	5	0.02
Houma (3)	3	0.01
Iroquois	1	0.00
Latin American Indians	4	0.02
Lumbee (1)	1	0.00
Navajo (8)	8	0.03
Pueblo (1)	1	0.00
Seminole (1)	2	0.01
Sioux	1	0.00
All other tribes (1)	1	0.00
American Indian tribes, not spec.	11	0.04
Arab:	20	0.08
Lebanese	20	0.08
Asian:	323	1.23
Chinese, ex. Taiwanese (18)	23	0.09
Filipino (34)	55	0.21
Indian (58)	66	0.25
Indonesian (1)	1	0.00
Japanese (3)	10	0.04
Korean (9)	18	0.07
Pakistani (3)	5	0.02
Thai (1)	2	0.01
Vietnamese (116)	125	0.48
Other Asian, specified (1)	3	0.01
Other Asian, not specified (7)	15	0.06
Austrian	31	0.12
British	125	0.48
Bulgarian	12	0.05
Canadian	13	0.05
Czech	79	0.30
Czechoslovakian	7	0.03
Danish	25	0.10
Dutch	142	0.54
English	2,066	7.88
European	227	0.87
Finnish	32	0.12
French, except Basque	1,066	4.07
French Canadian	173	0.66
German	1,502	5.73
Hawaii Native/Pacific Islander:	16	0.06
Micronesian: (1)	4	0.02
Guamanian/Chamorro (1)	4	0.02
Polynesian: (5)	9	0.03
Native Hawaiian (2)	6	0.02
Samoan (2)	2	0.01
Other Polynesian (1)	1	0.00
Other Pac. Isl., specified	2	0.01
Other Pac. Isl., not spec.	1	0.00
Hispanic or Latino:	1,019	3.89
Central American:	12	0.05
Costa Rican	1	0.00
Guatemalan	1	0.00
Honduran	2	0.01
Nicaraguan	1	0.00
Panamanian	2	0.01
Salvadoran	4	0.02
Other Central American	1	0.00
Cuban	8	0.03
Dominican Republic	7	0.03
Mexican	679	2.59
Puerto Rican	149	0.57
South American:	23	0.09
Chilean	3	0.01
Colombian	9	0.03
Ecuadorian	4	0.02
Peruvian	5	0.02
Venezuelan	1	0.00
Other South American	1	0.00
Other Hispanic or Latino	141	0.54
Hungarian	12	0.05
Irish	2,304	8.79
Italian	427	1.63
Lithuanian	14	0.05
Macedonian	9	0.03
Norwegian	79	0.30
Pennsylvania German	5	0.02
Polish	142	0.54
Portuguese	9	0.03
Russian	18	0.07
Scandinavian	6	0.02
Scotch-Irish	587	2.24
Scottish	285	1.09
Swedish	81	0.31
Swiss	36	0.14
United States or American	3,216	12.26
Welsh	109	0.42
West Indian, excl. Hispanic:	42	0.16
Jamaican	42	0.16
White:	17,828	68.05
Not Hispanic (17,084)	17,276	65.94
Hispanic (510)	552	2.11
Yugoslavian	5	0.02

Pearl

Place Type: City
County: Rankin
Population: 21,961

Ancestry/Race	Number	%
African American/Black:	3,610	16.44
Not Hispanic (3,557)	3,594	16.37
Hispanic (10)	16	0.07
African, sub-Saharan:	177	0.81
African	164	0.75
Nigerian	13	0.06
Alaska Native tribes, specified:	1	0.00
Aleut (1)	1	0.00
Am. Ind. or Alaska Nat., not spec.	24	0.11
American Indian tribes, specified:	74	0.34
Apache (2)	2	0.01
Blackfeet	1	0.00
Cherokee (9)	26	0.12
Cheyenne	2	0.01
Chickasaw	3	0.01
Chippewa (1)	1	0.00
Choctaw (10)	14	0.06
Comanche	1	0.00
Creek (4)	6	0.03
Crow	1	0.00
Houma (1)	1	0.00
Iroquois (1)	1	0.00
Latin American Indians (3)	3	0.01
Navajo	1	0.00
Puget Sound Salish (2)	2	0.01
Sioux	3	0.01
All other tribes (4)	6	0.03
American Indian tribes, not spec.	6	0.03
Arab:	74	0.34
Lebanese	28	0.13
Moroccan	33	0.15
Syrian	13	0.06
Asian:	207	0.94
Chinese, ex. Taiwanese (9)	13	0.06
Filipino (41)	54	0.25
Indian (61)	64	0.29
Japanese (4)	13	0.06
Korean (6)	6	0.03
Pakistani (1)	1	0.00
Thai (7)	7	0.03
Vietnamese (41)	42	0.19
Other Asian, not specified (3)	7	0.03
Austrian	36	0.16
British	109	0.50
Celtic	6	0.03
Dutch	224	1.02
English	1,749	7.96
European	112	0.51

Notes: 1. Figures in the "Number" column do not add up to the total population due to: a) Ancestry/Race overlap — e.g. persons can report being both White and Irish, b) persons of Hispanic origin can report being any race, c) persons reporting two ancestries are counted in both categories. 2. Numbers in parentheses indicate the number of persons reporting this ancestry/race alone, not in combination with any other ancestry/race. 3. Refer to the Explanation of Data in the front of the book for more detailed information.

Ancestry/Race	Number	%
Finnish	21	0.10
French, except Basque	424	1.93
French Canadian	42	0.19
German	1,551	7.06
Greek	14	0.06
Hawaii Native/Pacific Islander:	11	0.05
Melanesian:	2	0.01
Fijian	2	0.01
Micronesian:	2	0.01
Guamanian/Chamorro	2	0.01
Polynesian: (2)	4	0.02
Native Hawaiian (1)	1	0.00
Samoan (1)	3	0.01
Other Pac. Isl., not spec. (3)	3	0.01
Hispanic or Latino:	446	2.03
Central American:	44	0.20
Guatemalan	6	0.03
Honduran	32	0.15
Nicaraguan	3	0.01
Panamanian	3	0.01
Cuban	15	0.07
Mexican	210	0.96
Puerto Rican	33	0.15
South American:	16	0.07
Colombian	14	0.06
Paraguayan	1	0.00
Other South American	1	0.00
Other Hispanic or Latino	128	0.58
Hungarian	7	0.03
Irish	2,276	10.36
Italian	137	0.62
Norwegian	32	0.15
Polish	28	0.13
Romanian	8	0.04
Russian	32	0.15
Scotch-Irish	494	2.25
Scottish	469	2.14
Swedish	41	0.19
Swiss	15	0.07
Ukrainian	8	0.04
United States or American	4,941	22.50
Welsh	50	0.23
West Indian, excl. Hispanic:	8	0.04
Jamaican	8	0.04
White:	17,977	81.86
Not Hispanic (17,603)	17,712	80.65
Hispanic (225)	265	1.21

Picayune

Place Type: City
County: Pearl River
Population: 10,535

Ancestry/Race	Number	%
Acadian/Cajun	7	0.07
African American/Black:	3,840	36.45
Not Hispanic (3,769)	3,820	36.26
Hispanic (15)	20	0.19
African, sub-Saharan:	81	0.78
African	81	0.78
Alaska Native tribes, specified:	4	0.04
Aleut (4)	4	0.04
Am. Ind. or Alaska Nat., not spec.	27	0.26
American Indian tribes, specified:	67	0.64
Apache	4	0.04
Blackfeet	5	0.05
Cherokee (8)	19	0.18
Chickasaw (1)	1	0.01
Chippewa	1	0.01
Choctaw (6)	23	0.22
Creek (1)	1	0.01
Crow	2	0.02
Houma (1)	1	0.01
Latin American Indians (1)	1	0.01
Lumbee	1	0.01
Pueblo (5)	5	0.05
All other tribes (2)	3	0.03
American Indian tribes, not spec.	4	0.04
Arab:	70	0.68
Lebanese	70	0.68
Asian:	53	0.50
Chinese, ex. Taiwanese (10)	10	0.09
Filipino (2)	10	0.09
Indian (5)	10	0.09
Japanese (4)	12	0.11
Korean (4)	4	0.04
Vietnamese (7)	7	0.07
Austrian	7	0.07
British	78	0.75
Czech	7	0.07
Danish	7	0.07
Dutch	48	0.46
English	750	7.24
European	104	1.00
Finnish	20	0.19
French, except Basque	673	6.49
French Canadian	19	0.18
German	847	8.17
Greek	48	0.46
Hawaii Native/Pacific Islander:	12	0.11
Micronesian: (1)	2	0.02
Guamanian/Chamorro (1)	2	0.02
Polynesian: (3)	4	0.04
Native Hawaiian (1)	2	0.02
Samoan (2)	2	0.02
Other Pac. Isl., not spec. (1)	6	0.06
Hispanic or Latino:	121	1.15
Central American:	17	0.16
Costa Rican	6	0.06
Honduran	2	0.02
Nicaraguan	1	0.01
Panamanian	8	0.08
Cuban	3	0.03
Dominican Republic	2	0.02
Mexican	53	0.50
Puerto Rican	7	0.07
South American:	1	0.01
Colombian	1	0.01
Other Hispanic or Latino	38	0.36
Hungarian	9	0.09
Iranian	32	0.31
Irish	841	8.11
Italian	304	2.93
Northern European	6	0.06
Norwegian	20	0.19
Polish	53	0.51
Portuguese	7	0.07
Russian	25	0.24
Scandinavian	15	0.14
Scotch-Irish	190	1.83
Scottish	149	1.44
Swedish	15	0.14
Ukrainian	11	0.11
United States or American	1,521	14.68
Welsh	27	0.26
West Indian, excl. Hispanic:	5	0.05
Haitian	5	0.05
White:	6,631	62.94
Not Hispanic (6,471)	6,547	62.15
Hispanic (63)	84	0.80

Ridgeland

Place Type: City
County: Madison
Population: 20,173

Ancestry/Race	Number	%
African American/Black:	3,770	18.69
Not Hispanic (3,703)	3,745	18.56
Hispanic (16)	25	0.12
African, sub-Saharan:	169	0.84
African	143	0.71
Nigerian	26	0.13
Am. Ind. or Alaska Nat., not spec.	36	0.18
American Indian tribes, specified:	37	0.18
Apache (2)	3	0.01
Cherokee (3)	15	0.07
Chickasaw	1	0.00
Choctaw (6)	14	0.07
Cree (1)	1	0.00
Houma (1)	1	0.00
All other tribes (2)	2	0.01
American Indian tribes, not spec.	4	0.02
Arab:	195	0.97
Arab/Arabic	50	0.25
Egyptian	15	0.07
Lebanese	105	0.52
Palestinian	25	0.12
Armenian	5	0.02
Asian:	645	3.20
Bangladeshi (2)	2	0.01
Chinese, ex. Taiwanese (153)	167	0.83
Filipino (19)	28	0.14
Indian (292)	306	1.52
Indonesian (1)	1	0.00
Japanese (21)	25	0.12
Korean (10)	14	0.07
Laotian (1)	1	0.00
Pakistani (23)	25	0.12
Sri Lankan (3)	3	0.01
Taiwanese (6)	6	0.03
Thai (4)	4	0.02
Vietnamese (47)	47	0.23
Other Asian, specified (4)	4	0.02
Other Asian, not specified (9)	12	0.06
Austrian	64	0.32
Belgian	14	0.07
British	127	0.63
Bulgarian	21	0.10
Canadian	23	0.11
Czech	34	0.17
Danish	67	0.33
Dutch	145	0.72
English	2,191	10.89
European	333	1.66
French, except Basque	554	2.75
French Canadian	194	0.96
German	1,426	7.09
Greek	44	0.22
Hawaii Native/Pacific Islander:	15	0.07
Polynesian: (5)	11	0.05
Native Hawaiian (3)	4	0.02
Samoan (2)	7	0.03
Other Pac. Isl., not spec. (2)	4	0.02
Hispanic or Latino:	313	1.55
Central American:	16	0.08
Guatemalan	4	0.02
Honduran	7	0.03
Nicaraguan	1	0.00
Panamanian	2	0.01
Salvadoran	2	0.01
Cuban	17	0.08
Dominican Republic	1	0.00
Mexican	160	0.79
Puerto Rican	7	0.03
South American:	33	0.16
Argentinean	3	0.01
Chilean	15	0.07
Colombian	7	0.03
Peruvian	5	0.02
Venezuelan	3	0.01
Other Hispanic or Latino	79	0.39
Hungarian	35	0.17
Iranian	23	0.11
Irish	2,051	10.20
Italian	510	2.54
Northern European	33	0.16
Norwegian	101	0.50
Polish	129	0.64
Portuguese	12	0.06
Russian	48	0.24
Scotch-Irish	803	3.99
Scottish	696	3.46
Swedish	162	0.81
Swiss	18	0.09
Turkish	10	0.05
Ukrainian	16	0.08
United States or American	2,084	10.36

Notes: 1. Figures in the "Number" column do not add up to the total population due to: a) Ancestry/Race overlap — e.g. persons can report being both White and Irish, b) persons of Hispanic origin can report being any race, c) persons reporting two ancestries are counted in both categories. 2. Numbers in parentheses indicate the number of persons reporting this ancestry/race alone, not in combination with any other ancestry/race. 3. Refer to the Explanation of Data in the front of the book for more detailed information.

Ancestry/Race	Number	%
Welsh	137	0.68
West Indian, excl. Hispanic:	56	0.28
British West Indian	11	0.05
Haitian	8	0.04
Jamaican	37	0.18
White:	15,679	77.72
Not Hispanic (15,382)	15,492	76.80
Hispanic (162)	187	0.93

Southaven

Place Type: City
County: De Soto
Population: 28,977

Ancestry/Race	Number	%
Acadian/Cajun	4	0.01
African American/Black:	1,977	6.82
Not Hispanic (1,920)	1,965	6.78
Hispanic (8)	12	0.04
African, sub-Saharan:	85	0.29
African	85	0.29
Alaska Native tribes, specified:	2	0.01
Eskimo	2	0.01
Am. Ind. or Alaska Nat., not spec.	40	0.14
American Indian tribes, specified:	124	0.43
Blackfeet	8	0.03
Cherokee (21)	62	0.21
Chippewa (2)	6	0.02
Choctaw (13)	14	0.05
Comanche (3)	3	0.01
Creek (5)	7	0.02
Crow	1	0.00
Delaware (4)	4	0.01
Houma (1)	1	0.00
Iroquois (1)	1	0.00
Latin American Indians (3)	4	0.01
Osage (1)	1	0.00
Pima (1)	1	0.00
Potawatomi (4)	4	0.01
Shoshone (4)	4	0.01
Sioux (1)	1	0.00
All other tribes (2)	2	0.01
American Indian tribes, not spec.	10	0.03
Arab:	56	0.19
Arab/Arabic	5	0.02
Lebanese	51	0.18
Asian:	264	0.91
Cambodian (18)	26	0.09
Chinese, ex. Taiwanese (17)	18	0.06
Filipino (31)	44	0.15
Indian (78)	80	0.28
Indonesian (2)	2	0.01
Japanese (14)	19	0.07
Korean (22)	30	0.10
Laotian (6)	6	0.02
Pakistani (2)	2	0.01
Thai (1)	1	0.00
Vietnamese (10)	12	0.04
Other Asian, not specified (12)	24	0.08
British	141	0.48
Canadian	49	0.17
Celtic	10	0.03
Czech	16	0.06
Czechoslovakian	11	0.04
Danish	68	0.23
Dutch	507	1.74
Eastern European	4	0.01
English	2,652	9.12
European	296	1.02
French, except Basque	539	1.85
French Canadian	22	0.08
German	2,373	8.16
Greek	31	0.11
Hawaii Native/Pacific Islander:	24	0.08
Micronesian: (4)	5	0.02
Other Micronesian (4)	5	0.02
Polynesian: (4)	12	0.04
Native Hawaiian (4)	7	0.02
Samoan	5	0.02
Other Pac. Isl., not spec.	7	0.02
Hispanic or Latino:	654	2.26
Central American:	16	0.06
Costa Rican	1	0.00
Honduran	9	0.03
Salvadoran	6	0.02
Cuban	23	0.08
Mexican	481	1.66
Puerto Rican	23	0.08
South American:	9	0.03
Argentinean	2	0.01
Bolivian	1	0.00
Colombian	4	0.01
Ecuadorian	1	0.00
Venezuelan	1	0.00
Other Hispanic or Latino	102	0.35
Hungarian	88	0.30
Irish	4,206	14.46
Italian	1,082	3.72
Latvian	10	0.03
Lithuanian	7	0.02
Norwegian	120	0.41
Pennsylvania German	6	0.02
Polish	185	0.64
Portuguese	10	0.03
Russian	37	0.13
Scandinavian	33	0.11
Scotch-Irish	720	2.48
Scottish	480	1.65
Serbian	7	0.02
Swedish	207	0.71
Swiss	13	0.04
United States or American	5,312	18.26
Welsh	61	0.21
White:	26,372	91.01
Not Hispanic (25,883)	26,053	89.91
Hispanic (292)	319	1.10

Starkville

Place Type: City
County: Oktibbeha
Population: 21,869

Ancestry/Race	Number	%
Acadian/Cajun	26	0.12
Afghan	2	0.01
African American/Black:	6,621	30.28
Not Hispanic (6,538)	6,588	30.12
Hispanic (27)	33	0.15
African, sub-Saharan:	253	1.15
African	227	1.03
Kenyan	18	0.08
Nigerian	8	0.04
Alaska Native tribes, not specified	1	0.00
Am. Ind. or Alaska Nat., not spec.	21	0.10
American Indian tribes, specified:	37	0.17
Apache (3)	3	0.01
Cherokee (10)	12	0.05
Chickasaw	2	0.01
Chippewa (1)	1	0.00
Choctaw (7)	12	0.05
Creek (1)	1	0.00
Lumbee (1)	1	0.00
Pueblo	1	0.00
Seminole (3)	3	0.01
All other tribes (1)	1	0.00
American Indian tribes, not spec.	2	0.01
Arab:	86	0.39
Arab/Arabic	28	0.13
Lebanese	32	0.15
Other Arab	26	0.12
Asian:	898	4.11
Bangladeshi (8)	8	0.04
Cambodian (1)	1	0.00
Chinese, ex. Taiwanese (399)	415	1.90
Filipino (25)	36	0.16
Indian (140)	153	0.70
Indonesian (28)	30	0.14
Japanese (13)	18	0.08
Korean (94)	98	0.45
Malaysian (14)	14	0.06
Pakistani (20)	21	0.10
Sri Lankan (9)	9	0.04
Taiwanese (22)	29	0.13
Thai (23)	25	0.11
Vietnamese (8)	8	0.04
Other Asian, specified	3	0.01
Other Asian, not specified (10)	30	0.14
Australian	14	0.06
Austrian	37	0.17
Belgian	6	0.03
British	132	0.60
Canadian	20	0.09
Celtic	43	0.20
Croatian	23	0.10
Czech	56	0.25
Czechoslovakian	30	0.14
Danish	38	0.17
Dutch	231	1.05
English	1,891	8.58
European	275	1.25
French, except Basque	392	1.78
French Canadian	61	0.28
German	1,753	7.95
Greek	41	0.19
Hawaii Native/Pacific Islander:	21	0.10
Micronesian:	1	0.00
Guamanian/Chamorro	1	0.00
Polynesian: (7)	9	0.04
Native Hawaiian (2)	3	0.01
Samoan (5)	6	0.03
Other Pac. Isl., specified	3	0.01
Other Pac. Isl., not spec. (1)	8	0.04
Hispanic or Latino:	294	1.34
Central American:	27	0.12
Costa Rican	2	0.01
Guatemalan	5	0.02
Honduran	14	0.06
Nicaraguan	3	0.01
Panamanian	2	0.01
Salvadoran	1	0.00
Cuban	5	0.02
Mexican	112	0.51
Puerto Rican	25	0.11
South American:	34	0.16
Argentinean	1	0.00
Chilean	3	0.01
Ecuadorian	1	0.00
Peruvian	4	0.02
Venezuelan	25	0.11
Other Hispanic or Latino	91	0.42
Hungarian	19	0.09
Iranian	29	0.13
Irish	1,952	8.86
Italian	337	1.53
Lithuanian	8	0.04
Macedonian	9	0.04
Norwegian	84	0.38
Polish	144	0.65
Portuguese	25	0.11
Romanian	6	0.03
Russian	54	0.25
Scandinavian	23	0.10
Scotch-Irish	894	4.06
Scottish	601	2.73
Serbian	9	0.04
Slavic	9	0.04
Slovak	17	0.08
Swedish	114	0.52
Swiss	77	0.35
Ukrainian	43	0.20
United States or American	2,003	9.09
Welsh	105	0.48
West Indian, excl. Hispanic:	36	0.16
Jamaican	36	0.16
White:	14,251	65.17
Not Hispanic (14,005)	14,111	64.53
Hispanic (123)	140	0.64
Yugoslavian	12	0.05

Notes: 1. Figures in the "Number" column do not add up to the total population due to: a) Ancestry/Race overlap — e.g. persons can report being both White and Irish, b) persons of Hispanic origin can report being any race, c) persons reporting two ancestries are counted in both categories. 2. Numbers in parentheses indicate the number of persons reporting this ancestry/race alone, not in combination with any other ancestry/race. 3. Refer to the Explanation of Data in the front of the book for more detailed information.

Tupelo

Place Type: City
County: Lee
Population: 34,211

Ancestry/Race	Number	%
African American/Black:	9,805	28.66
Not Hispanic (9,630)	9,753	28.51
Hispanic (46)	52	0.15
African, sub-Saharan:	386	1.12
African	386	1.12
Am. Ind. or Alaska Nat., not spec.	49	0.14
American Indian tribes, specified:	58	0.17
Apache (1)	2	0.01
Blackfeet	1	0.00
Cherokee (7)	22	0.06
Cheyenne	1	0.00
Chickasaw	3	0.01
Choctaw (5)	14	0.04
Creek (1)	1	0.00
Iroquois (1)	2	0.01
Latin American Indians	4	0.01
Lumbee (2)	2	0.01
Osage	1	0.00
Potawatomi (1)	1	0.00
Ute	1	0.00
All other tribes	3	0.01
American Indian tribes, not spec.	8	0.02
Arab:	38	0.11
Lebanese	24	0.07
Syrian	14	0.04
Asian:	358	1.05
Cambodian (3)	3	0.01
Chinese, ex. Taiwanese (44)	52	0.15
Filipino (9)	15	0.04
Indian (89)	102	0.30
Indonesian (1)	2	0.01
Japanese (13)	19	0.06
Korean (32)	34	0.10
Laotian (29)	35	0.10
Sri Lankan	2	0.01
Taiwanese (1)	1	0.00
Thai (4)	8	0.02
Vietnamese (45)	51	0.15
Other Asian, specified (1)	2	0.01
Other Asian, not specified (28)	32	0.09
Austrian	8	0.02
Belgian	6	0.02
British	141	0.41
Canadian	38	0.11
Celtic	9	0.03
Croatian	22	0.06
Czech	57	0.17
Czechoslovakian	7	0.02
Danish	20	0.06
Dutch	323	0.94
English	3,414	9.92
European	278	0.81
Finnish	8	0.02
French, except Basque	501	1.46
French Canadian	48	0.14
German	1,828	5.31
Greek	38	0.11
Hawaii Native/Pacific Islander:	15	0.04
Micronesian: (1)	1	0.00
Guamanian/Chamorro (1)	1	0.00
Polynesian: (4)	7	0.02
Native Hawaiian (4)	6	0.02
Other Polynesian	1	0.00
Other Pac. Isl., specified	1	0.00
Other Pac. Isl., not spec.	6	0.02
Hispanic or Latino:	484	1.41
Central American:	19	0.06
Costa Rican	1	0.00
Guatemalan	2	0.01
Honduran	5	0.01
Nicaraguan	2	0.01
Panamanian	5	0.01
Salvadoran	4	0.01
Cuban	5	0.01
Mexican	316	0.92
Puerto Rican	41	0.12
South American:	11	0.03
Bolivian	1	0.00
Colombian	2	0.01
Ecuadorian	6	0.02
Venezuelan	2	0.01
Other Hispanic or Latino	92	0.27
Hungarian	53	0.15
Irish	3,006	8.73
Italian	312	0.91
Latvian	32	0.09
Northern European	6	0.02
Norwegian	167	0.49
Pennsylvania German	10	0.03
Polish	119	0.35
Portuguese	10	0.03
Russian	28	0.08
Scotch-Irish	836	2.43
Scottish	806	2.34
Slovak	20	0.06
Slovene	7	0.02
Swedish	112	0.33
Swiss	32	0.09
Ukrainian	14	0.04
United States or American	6,066	17.62
Welsh	171	0.50
White:	23,980	70.09
Not Hispanic (23,500)	23,704	69.29
Hispanic (244)	276	0.81

Vicksburg

Place Type: City
County: Warren
Population: 26,407

Ancestry/Race	Number	%
Acadian/Cajun	8	0.03
African American/Black:	16,043	60.75
Not Hispanic (15,892)	15,970	60.48
Hispanic (65)	73	0.28
African, sub-Saharan:	234	0.89
African	219	0.84
Nigerian	15	0.06
Am. Ind. or Alaska Nat., not spec.	43	0.16
American Indian tribes, specified:	47	0.18
Blackfeet	1	0.00
Cherokee (6)	25	0.09
Choctaw (8)	11	0.04
Comanche	1	0.00
Iroquois (1)	1	0.00
Ottawa (1)	1	0.00
Sioux (1)	1	0.00
All other tribes (3)	6	0.02
American Indian tribes, not spec.	4	0.02
Arab:	145	0.55
Arab/Arabic	8	0.03
Lebanese	122	0.47
Palestinian	8	0.03
Syrian	7	0.03
Armenian	6	0.02
Asian:	199	0.75
Bangladeshi (2)	2	0.01
Chinese, ex. Taiwanese (15)	18	0.07
Filipino (53)	55	0.21
Indian (59)	75	0.28
Japanese (4)	9	0.03
Korean (12)	15	0.06
Pakistani (3)	6	0.02
Thai (2)	2	0.01
Vietnamese (6)	6	0.02
Other Asian, not specified (3)	11	0.04
Austrian	28	0.11
Belgian	11	0.04
British	67	0.26
Bulgarian	12	0.05
Canadian	18	0.07
Czech	7	0.03
Danish	31	0.12
Dutch	113	0.43
English	1,363	5.21
European	163	0.62
French, except Basque	282	1.08
French Canadian	63	0.24
German	1,123	4.29
Greek	38	0.15
Hawaii Native/Pacific Islander:	11	0.04
Micronesian: (1)	2	0.01
Guamanian/Chamorro (1)	2	0.01
Polynesian: (2)	2	0.01
Native Hawaiian (2)	2	0.01
Other Pac. Isl., not spec. (1)	7	0.03
Hispanic or Latino:	274	1.04
Central American:	3	0.01
Honduran	1	0.00
Other Central American	2	0.01
Cuban	14	0.05
Mexican	170	0.64
Puerto Rican	18	0.07
South American:	1	0.00
Ecuadorian	1	0.00
Other Hispanic or Latino	68	0.26
Hungarian	3	0.01
Irish	1,427	5.45
Italian	406	1.55
Norwegian	42	0.16
Polish	94	0.36
Romanian	5	0.02
Russian	18	0.07
Scotch-Irish	620	2.37
Scottish	199	0.76
Slavic	10	0.04
Slovak	5	0.02
Slovene	5	0.02
Swedish	34	0.13
Swiss	23	0.09
United States or American	1,613	6.16
Welsh	49	0.19
White:	10,071	38.14
Not Hispanic (9,873)	9,956	37.70
Hispanic (109)	115	0.44

West Point

Place Type: City
County: Clay
Population: 12,145

Ancestry/Race	Number	%
Acadian/Cajun	10	0.08
African American/Black:	6,850	56.40
Not Hispanic (6,785)	6,810	56.07
Hispanic (38)	40	0.33
African, sub-Saharan:	43	0.35
African	43	0.35
Am. Ind. or Alaska Nat., not spec.	17	0.14
American Indian tribes, specified:	9	0.07
Cherokee (1)	6	0.05
Choctaw	1	0.01
Latin American Indians (2)	2	0.02
American Indian tribes, not spec.	1	0.01
Asian:	44	0.36
Indian (22)	22	0.18
Korean (3)	4	0.03
Thai (1)	1	0.01
Vietnamese	2	0.02
Other Asian, specified	12	0.10
Other Asian, not specified (1)	3	0.02
Australian	5	0.04
Austrian	22	0.18
British	18	0.15
Canadian	6	0.05
Czech	8	0.07
Dutch	56	0.46
Eastern European	6	0.05
English	599	4.93
European	48	0.39
French, except Basque	136	1.12

Notes: 1. Figures in the "Number" column do not add up to the total population due to: a) Ancestry/Race overlap — e.g. persons can report being both White and Irish, b) persons of Hispanic origin can report being any race, c) persons reporting two ancestries are counted in both categories. 2. Numbers in parentheses indicate the number of persons reporting this ancestry/race alone, not in combination with any other ancestry/race. 3. Refer to the Explanation of Data in the front of the book for more detailed information.

Ancestry/Race	Number	%
French Canadian	15	0.12
German	405	3.33
Hawaii Native/Pacific Islander:	13	0.11
Micronesian:	1	0.01
Guamanian/Chamorro	1	0.01
Polynesian:	1	0.01
Native Hawaiian	1	0.01
Other Pac. Isl., specified	11	0.09
Hispanic or Latino:	120	0.99
Cuban	2	0.02
Mexican	71	0.58
Puerto Rican	4	0.03
South American:	2	0.02
Colombian	1	0.01
Venezuelan	1	0.01
Other Hispanic or Latino	41	0.34
Hungarian	9	0.07
Irish	695	5.72
Italian	94	0.77
Northern European	11	0.09
Norwegian	18	0.15
Polish	23	0.19
Scotch-Irish	222	1.83
Scottish	52	0.43
Swedish	15	0.12
Swiss	5	0.04
United States or American	690	5.68
Welsh	25	0.21
West Indian, excl. Hispanic:	37	0.30
British West Indian	10	0.08
Haitian	27	0.22
White:	5,256	43.28
Not Hispanic (5,165)	5,201	42.82
Hispanic (46)	55	0.45

Yazoo City

Place Type: City
County: Yazoo
Population: 14,550

Ancestry/Race	Number	%
African American/Black:	10,202	70.12
Not Hispanic (10,055)	10,111	69.49
Hispanic (83)	91	0.63
African, sub-Saharan:	147	1.00
African	134	0.92
Nigerian	8	0.05
Sudanese	5	0.03
Am. Ind. or Alaska Nat., not spec.	32	0.22
American Indian tribes, specified:	16	0.11
Blackfeet	4	0.03
Cherokee (8)	8	0.05
Cheyenne (1)	1	0.01
Choctaw	1	0.01
Sioux (1)	1	0.01
All other tribes	1	0.01
American Indian tribes, not spec.	10	0.07
Arab:	14	0.10
Lebanese	14	0.10
Asian:	124	0.85
Chinese, ex. Taiwanese (12)	14	0.10
Filipino (14)	15	0.10
Indian (22)	30	0.21
Japanese	3	0.02
Korean (8)	12	0.08
Laotian (8)	12	0.08
Thai (6)	6	0.04
Vietnamese (5)	8	0.05
Other Asian, specified (1)	2	0.01
Other Asian, not specified (5)	22	0.15
Australian	5	0.03
Austrian	7	0.05
British	5	0.03
Dutch	73	0.50
English	415	2.84
French, except Basque	52	0.36
French Canadian	19	0.13
German	194	1.33
Greek	7	0.05
Hawaii Native/Pacific Islander:	3	0.02
Other Pac. Isl., specified	1	0.01
Other Pac. Isl., not spec.	2	0.01
Hispanic or Latino:	1,087	7.47
Central American:	11	0.08
Costa Rican	1	0.01
Guatemalan	2	0.01
Honduran	3	0.02
Nicaraguan	1	0.01
Salvadoran	4	0.03
Cuban	58	0.40
Dominican Republic	31	0.21
Mexican	735	5.05
Puerto Rican	39	0.27
South American:	85	0.58
Argentinean	3	0.02
Chilean	1	0.01
Colombian	73	0.50
Ecuadorian	2	0.01
Paraguayan	1	0.01
Venezuelan	5	0.03
Other Hispanic or Latino	128	0.88
Irish	409	2.80
Italian	36	0.25
Norwegian	11	0.08
Polish	4	0.03
Russian	14	0.10
Scotch-Irish	240	1.64
Scottish	60	0.41
Swedish	4	0.03
Swiss	4	0.03
United States or American	548	3.75
West Indian, excl. Hispanic:	43	0.29
Haitian	9	0.06
Jamaican	34	0.23
White:	4,214	28.96
Not Hispanic (3,224)	3,257	22.38
Hispanic (956)	957	6.58

Affton

Place Type: Census Designated Place
County: Saint Louis
Population: 20,535

Ancestry/Race	Number	%
African American/Black:	123	0.60
Not Hispanic (93)	121	0.59
Hispanic (1)	2	0.01
African, sub-Saharan:	4	0.02
South African	4	0.02
Alaska Native tribes, specified:	1	0.00
Aleut	1	0.00
Am. Ind. or Alaska Nat., not spec.	11	0.05
Albanian	74	0.35
American Indian tribes, specified:	66	0.32
Apache (2)	2	0.01
Blackfeet	1	0.00
Cherokee (16)	37	0.18
Chickasaw	1	0.00
Chippewa (2)	5	0.02
Choctaw	1	0.00
Iroquois (4)	5	0.02
Latin American Indians (1)	2	0.01
Ottawa	1	0.00
Potawatomi (1)	1	0.00
Pueblo (2)	2	0.01
Sioux	4	0.02
All other tribes (3)	4	0.02
American Indian tribes, not spec.	5	0.02
Arab:	127	0.61
Iraqi	59	0.28
Lebanese	53	0.25
Other Arab	15	0.07
Armenian	5	0.02
Asian:	336	1.64
Bangladeshi (3)	3	0.01
Chinese, ex. Taiwanese (47)	60	0.29
Filipino (42)	56	0.27
Indian (47)	49	0.24
Japanese (5)	11	0.05
Korean (15)	21	0.10
Laotian (4)	8	0.04
Pakistani (3)	6	0.03
Thai	3	0.01
Vietnamese (96)	99	0.48
Other Asian, specified	1	0.00
Other Asian, not specified (1)	19	0.09
Austrian	123	0.59
British	31	0.15
Canadian	28	0.13
Croatian	158	0.76
Czech	342	1.64
Czechoslovakian	101	0.48
Danish	45	0.22
Dutch	300	1.44
English	1,856	8.88
European	96	0.46
French, except Basque	1,257	6.01
French Canadian	66	0.32
German	8,982	42.97
Greek	178	0.85
Hawaii Native/Pacific Islander:	18	0.09
Micronesian: (3)	5	0.02
Guamanian/Chamorro (3)	5	0.02
Polynesian: (1)	4	0.02
Native Hawaiian	3	0.01
Samoan (1)	1	0.00
Other Pac. Isl., specified	1	0.00
Other Pac. Isl., not spec. (2)	8	0.04
Hispanic or Latino:	207	1.01
Central American:	16	0.08
Guatemalan	12	0.06
Honduran	1	0.00
Nicaraguan	2	0.01
Salvadoran	1	0.00
Cuban	11	0.05
Dominican Republic	3	0.01
Mexican	80	0.39
Puerto Rican	27	0.13
South American:	11	0.05
Colombian	4	0.02
Ecuadorian	3	0.01
Peruvian	4	0.02
Other Hispanic or Latino	59	0.29
Hungarian	169	0.81
Irish	4,130	19.76
Italian	1,938	9.27
Lithuanian	115	0.55
Luxemburger	8	0.04
Norwegian	93	0.44
Pennsylvania German	8	0.04
Polish	560	2.68
Portuguese	7	0.03
Romanian	16	0.08
Russian	88	0.42
Scandinavian	17	0.08
Scotch-Irish	369	1.77
Scottish	389	1.86
Serbian	7	0.03
Slavic	30	0.14
Slovak	42	0.20
Slovene	103	0.49
Swedish	173	0.83
Swiss	174	0.83
Ukrainian	56	0.27
United States or American	1,386	6.63
Welsh	67	0.32
White:	20,057	97.67
Not Hispanic (19,686)	19,891	96.86
Hispanic (155)	166	0.81
Yugoslavian	309	1.48

Arnold

Place Type: City
County: Jefferson
Population: 19,965

Ancestry/Race	Number	%

Notes: 1. Figures in the "Number" column do not add up to the total population due to: a) Ancestry/Race overlap — e.g. persons can report being both White and Irish, b) persons of Hispanic origin can report being any race, c) persons reporting two ancestries are counted in both categories. 2. Numbers in parentheses indicate the number of persons reporting this ancestry/race alone, not in combination with any other ancestry/race. 3. Refer to the Explanation of Data in the front of the book for more detailed information.

Ancestry/Race	Number	%
African American/Black:	78	0.39
Not Hispanic (59)	77	0.39
Hispanic	1	0.01
Alaska Native tribes, specified:	2	0.01
Aleut (1)	2	0.01
Am. Ind. or Alaska Nat., not spec.	29	0.15
Alsatian	9	0.04
American Indian tribes, specified:	86	0.43
Apache (1)	1	0.01
Blackfeet (2)	3	0.02
Cherokee (21)	62	0.31
Chickasaw	1	0.01
Choctaw	1	0.01
Comanche	1	0.01
Creek (1)	1	0.01
Iroquois (1)	1	0.01
Latin American Indians	1	0.01
Osage	2	0.01
Shoshone (1)	1	0.01
Sioux (2)	5	0.03
All other tribes (1)	6	0.03
American Indian tribes, not spec.	2	0.01
Arab:	50	0.25
Iraqi	17	0.08
Lebanese	27	0.13
Syrian	6	0.03
Asian:	133	0.67
Chinese, ex. Taiwanese (4)	6	0.03
Filipino (19)	45	0.23
Indian (12)	19	0.10
Japanese (6)	15	0.08
Korean (10)	16	0.08
Laotian (3)	3	0.02
Thai (1)	2	0.01
Vietnamese (16)	17	0.09
Other Asian, not specified (4)	10	0.05
Austrian	5	0.02
Belgian	7	0.03
British	36	0.18
Canadian	5	0.02
Croatian	81	0.40
Czech	201	1.00
Czechoslovakian	13	0.06
Danish	28	0.14
Dutch	432	2.15
English	1,770	8.81
European	98	0.49
Finnish	17	0.08
French, except Basque	1,442	7.18
French Canadian	43	0.21
German	7,308	36.39
Greek	73	0.36
Hawaii Native/Pacific Islander:	6	0.03
Polynesian: (4)	5	0.03
Native Hawaiian (3)	4	0.02
Samoan (1)	1	0.01
Other Pac. Isl., not spec.	1	0.01
Hispanic or Latino:	207	1.04
Central American:	7	0.04
Guatemalan	4	0.02
Honduran	3	0.02
Cuban	2	0.01
Mexican	126	0.63
Puerto Rican	16	0.08
South American:	3	0.02
Peruvian	1	0.01
Other South American	2	0.01
Other Hispanic or Latino	53	0.27
Hungarian	40	0.20
Irish	3,322	16.54
Italian	1,261	6.28
Latvian	18	0.09
Lithuanian	7	0.03
Northern European	8	0.04
Norwegian	101	0.50
Polish	396	1.97
Portuguese	15	0.07
Romanian	7	0.03
Russian	42	0.21
Scotch-Irish	392	1.95
Scottish	298	1.48
Serbian	8	0.04
Slovak	24	0.12
Swedish	56	0.28
Swiss	63	0.31
Ukrainian	32	0.16
United States or American	2,224	11.08
Welsh	78	0.39
White:	19,729	98.82
Not Hispanic (19,408)	19,565	98.00
Hispanic (140)	164	0.82
Yugoslavian	33	0.16

Ballwin

Place Type: City
County: Saint Louis
Population: 31,283

Ancestry/Race	Number	%
African American/Black:	542	1.73
Not Hispanic (461)	523	1.67
Hispanic (7)	19	0.06
African, sub-Saharan:	139	0.45
African	139	0.45
Am. Ind. or Alaska Nat., not spec.	40	0.13
Albanian	51	0.16
American Indian tribes, specified:	122	0.39
Apache	1	0.00
Blackfeet (1)	2	0.01
Cherokee (17)	63	0.20
Cheyenne	2	0.01
Chickasaw (2)	8	0.03
Chippewa	1	0.00
Choctaw (4)	7	0.02
Comanche (1)	1	0.00
Cree	1	0.00
Iroquois (2)	3	0.01
Kiowa	1	0.00
Latin American Indians (7)	15	0.05
Navajo	1	0.00
Osage (3)	3	0.01
Potawatomi (1)	1	0.00
Pueblo (1)	4	0.01
Sioux	2	0.01
All other tribes (4)	6	0.02
American Indian tribes, not spec.	15	0.05
Arab:	121	0.39
Lebanese	89	0.29
Syrian	24	0.08
Other Arab	8	0.03
Armenian	55	0.18
Asian:	1,168	3.73
Bangladeshi (2)	2	0.01
Chinese, ex. Taiwanese (276)	306	0.98
Filipino (136)	170	0.54
Indian (295)	312	1.00
Indonesian (6)	7	0.02
Japanese (28)	55	0.18
Korean (136)	150	0.48
Laotian (1)	1	0.00
Malaysian (2)	2	0.01
Pakistani (37)	39	0.12
Taiwanese (19)	21	0.07
Thai (12)	14	0.04
Vietnamese (43)	50	0.16
Other Asian, specified (2)	4	0.01
Other Asian, not specified (15)	35	0.11
Austrian	119	0.38
Basque	8	0.03
Belgian	8	0.03
Brazilian	16	0.05
British	123	0.39
Canadian	109	0.35
Carpatho Rusyn	17	0.05
Celtic	11	0.04
Croatian	122	0.39
Czech	245	0.78
Czechoslovakian	30	0.10
Danish	113	0.36
Dutch	469	1.50
Eastern European	30	0.10
English	4,076	13.05
European	261	0.84
Finnish	62	0.20
French, except Basque	1,327	4.25
French Canadian	174	0.56
German	12,425	39.79
Greek	208	0.67
Hawaii Native/Pacific Islander:	20	0.06
Micronesian: (2)	3	0.01
Guamanian/Chamorro (2)	3	0.01
Polynesian: (8)	12	0.04
Native Hawaiian (4)	6	0.02
Samoan (4)	4	0.01
Other Polynesian	2	0.01
Other Pac. Isl., specified	1	0.00
Other Pac. Isl., not spec. (3)	4	0.01
Hispanic or Latino:	583	1.86
Central American:	26	0.08
Costa Rican	7	0.02
Guatemalan	7	0.02
Honduran	1	0.00
Nicaraguan	4	0.01
Panamanian	1	0.00
Salvadoran	6	0.02
Cuban	38	0.12
Mexican	284	0.91
Puerto Rican	60	0.19
South American:	45	0.14
Argentinean	8	0.03
Bolivian	1	0.00
Chilean	5	0.02
Colombian	11	0.04
Ecuadorian	5	0.02
Peruvian	13	0.04
Venezuelan	2	0.01
Other Hispanic or Latino	130	0.42
Hungarian	238	0.76
Icelander	28	0.09
Iranian	42	0.13
Irish	6,640	21.27
Israeli	2	0.01
Italian	2,396	7.67
Latvian	17	0.05
Lithuanian	98	0.31
Northern European	8	0.03
Norwegian	391	1.25
Pennsylvania German	8	0.03
Polish	1,362	4.36
Portuguese	22	0.07
Romanian	23	0.07
Russian	478	1.53
Scandinavian	42	0.13
Scotch-Irish	594	1.90
Scottish	718	2.30
Serbian	23	0.07
Slavic	11	0.04
Slovak	103	0.33
Slovene	6	0.02
Swedish	494	1.58
Swiss	196	0.63
Turkish	4	0.01
Ukrainian	174	0.56
United States or American	1,571	5.03
Welsh	360	1.15
White:	29,516	94.35
Not Hispanic (28,844)	29,098	93.02
Hispanic (371)	418	1.34
Yugoslavian	106	0.34

Bellefontaine Neighbors

Place Type: City
County: Saint Louis
Population: 11,271

Ancestry/Race	Number	%
African American/Black:	5,076	45.04
Not Hispanic (4,986)	5,054	44.84

Notes: 1. Figures in the "Number" column do not add up to the total population due to: a) Ancestry/Race overlap — e.g. persons can report being both White and Irish, b) persons of Hispanic origin can report being any race, c) persons reporting two ancestries are counted in both categories. 2. Numbers in parentheses indicate the number of persons reporting this ancestry/race alone, not in combination with any other ancestry/race. 3. Refer to the Explanation of Data in the front of the book for more detailed information.

Ancestry/Race	Number	%
Hispanic (20)	22	0.20
African, sub-Saharan:	127	1.14
African	127	1.14
Alaska Native tribes, specified:	1	0.01
Tlingit-Haida (1)	1	0.01
Am. Ind. or Alaska Nat., not spec.	21	0.19
Albanian	8	0.07
American Indian tribes, specified:	25	0.22
Apache	3	0.03
Blackfeet (1)	2	0.02
Cherokee (1)	5	0.04
Cheyenne	1	0.01
Chippewa (1)	1	0.01
Menominee	3	0.03
Navajo	1	0.01
Seminole	3	0.03
Sioux (1)	5	0.04
All other tribes	1	0.01
American Indian tribes, not spec.	2	0.02
Arab:	5	0.04
Egyptian	5	0.04
Asian:	66	0.59
Chinese, ex. Taiwanese (3)	4	0.04
Filipino (5)	16	0.14
Indian (13)	15	0.13
Japanese (2)	6	0.05
Korean (3)	7	0.06
Taiwanese (1)	1	0.01
Vietnamese (1)	1	0.01
Other Asian, not specified (1)	16	0.14
Austrian	85	0.76
British	9	0.08
Canadian	15	0.13
Czech	52	0.47
Danish	9	0.08
Dutch	77	0.69
English	436	3.92
French, except Basque	198	1.78
French Canadian	24	0.22
German	2,261	20.33
Greek	8	0.07
Hawaii Native/Pacific Islander:	17	0.15
Polynesian: (1)	1	0.01
Native Hawaiian (1)	1	0.01
Other Pac. Isl., not spec. (1)	16	0.14
Hispanic or Latino:	76	0.67
Central American:	2	0.02
Guatemalan	1	0.01
Panamanian	1	0.01
Mexican	35	0.31
Puerto Rican	3	0.03
South American:	3	0.03
Argentinean	1	0.01
Peruvian	1	0.01
Venezuelan	1	0.01
Other Hispanic or Latino	33	0.29
Hungarian	62	0.56
Irish	1,269	11.41
Italian	500	4.49
Norwegian	11	0.10
Polish	395	3.55
Portuguese	18	0.16
Russian	44	0.40
Scandinavian	6	0.05
Scotch-Irish	104	0.93
Scottish	56	0.50
Serbian	10	0.09
Slovak	48	0.43
Swedish	7	0.06
Swiss	28	0.25
Ukrainian	8	0.07
United States or American	366	3.29
Welsh	30	0.27
West Indian, excl. Hispanic:	25	0.22
Haitian	16	0.14
Jamaican	9	0.08
White:	6,143	54.50
Not Hispanic (6,034)	6,115	54.25
Hispanic (22)	28	0.25

Belton

Place Type: City
County: Cass
Population: 21,730

Ancestry/Race	Number	%
Acadian/Cajun	11	0.05
African American/Black:	711	3.27
Not Hispanic (610)	698	3.21
Hispanic (11)	13	0.06
African, sub-Saharan:	15	0.07
African	15	0.07
Am. Ind. or Alaska Nat., not spec.	70	0.32
American Indian tribes, specified:	217	1.00
Apache (1)	5	0.02
Blackfeet (1)	18	0.08
Cherokee (54)	114	0.52
Cheyenne (2)	2	0.01
Chickasaw (1)	1	0.00
Chippewa	1	0.00
Choctaw (8)	11	0.05
Cree	1	0.00
Creek (3)	5	0.02
Crow	2	0.01
Iroquois	3	0.01
Latin American Indians (1)	9	0.04
Navajo (2)	2	0.01
Osage (1)	2	0.01
Potawatomi (4)	5	0.02
Shoshone (5)	5	0.02
Sioux (13)	14	0.06
All other tribes (7)	17	0.08
American Indian tribes, not spec.	6	0.03
Arab:	32	0.15
Arab/Arabic	14	0.06
Syrian	18	0.08
Asian:	228	1.05
Chinese, ex. Taiwanese (21)	38	0.17
Filipino (28)	49	0.23
Indian (14)	17	0.08
Indonesian (1)	1	0.00
Japanese (18)	40	0.18
Korean (23)	39	0.18
Laotian (3)	7	0.03
Taiwanese	1	0.00
Thai (6)	10	0.05
Vietnamese (9)	19	0.09
Other Asian, specified	1	0.00
Other Asian, not specified (5)	6	0.03
Austrian	17	0.08
Belgian	44	0.20
British	76	0.35
Canadian	23	0.11
Croatian	124	0.57
Czech	200	0.92
Czechoslovakian	48	0.22
Danish	93	0.43
Dutch	671	3.09
English	2,364	10.87
European	265	1.22
Finnish	7	0.03
French, except Basque	723	3.32
French Canadian	47	0.22
German	4,884	22.46
Greek	29	0.13
Hawaii Native/Pacific Islander:	41	0.19
Micronesian: (1)	3	0.01
Guamanian/Chamorro (1)	3	0.01
Polynesian: (15)	27	0.12
Native Hawaiian (7)	18	0.08
Samoan (8)	8	0.04
Other Polynesian	1	0.00
Other Pac. Isl., not spec. (1)	11	0.05
Hispanic or Latino:	1,017	4.68
Central American:	19	0.09
Costa Rican	1	0.00
Guatemalan	4	0.02
Honduran	4	0.02
Nicaraguan	3	0.01
Panamanian	3	0.01
Salvadoran	4	0.02
Cuban	5	0.02
Dominican Republic	5	0.02
Mexican	812	3.74
Puerto Rican	43	0.20
South American:	17	0.08
Bolivian	1	0.00
Chilean	4	0.02
Colombian	4	0.02
Ecuadorian	6	0.03
Venezuelan	1	0.00
Other South American	1	0.00
Other Hispanic or Latino	116	0.53
Hungarian	88	0.40
Irish	3,357	15.44
Italian	587	2.70
New Zealander	11	0.05
Norwegian	222	1.02
Polish	310	1.43
Romanian	9	0.04
Russian	81	0.37
Scandinavian	12	0.06
Scotch-Irish	681	3.13
Scottish	426	1.96
Slavic	13	0.06
Slovak	35	0.16
Swedish	391	1.80
Turkish	8	0.04
United States or American	2,677	12.31
Welsh	255	1.17
White:	20,588	94.74
Not Hispanic (19,516)	19,825	91.23
Hispanic (689)	763	3.51

Berkeley

Place Type: City
County: Saint Louis
Population: 10,063

Ancestry/Race	Number	%
African American/Black:	7,841	77.92
Not Hispanic (7,688)	7,809	77.60
Hispanic (29)	32	0.32
African, sub-Saharan:	75	0.75
African	75	0.75
Am. Ind. or Alaska Nat., not spec.	50	0.50
American Indian tribes, specified:	37	0.37
Blackfeet (2)	5	0.05
Cherokee (2)	11	0.11
Chickasaw	3	0.03
Choctaw	8	0.08
Kiowa (4)	4	0.04
Navajo (1)	1	0.01
Osage	1	0.01
Seminole	3	0.03
All other tribes	1	0.01
American Indian tribes, not spec.	1	0.01
Arab:	4	0.04
Arab/Arabic	4	0.04
Asian:	61	0.61
Chinese, ex. Taiwanese (1)	4	0.04
Filipino (24)	30	0.30
Indian (5)	8	0.08
Japanese (1)	1	0.01
Korean (3)	10	0.10
Pakistani	2	0.02
Thai (3)	3	0.03
Other Asian, specified	1	0.01
Other Asian, not specified	2	0.02
British	13	0.13
Canadian	6	0.06
Czech	6	0.06
Danish	8	0.08
Dutch	31	0.31
English	188	1.87
French, except Basque	89	0.89
French Canadian	14	0.14
German	757	7.53

Notes: 1. Figures in the "Number" column do not add up to the total population due to: a) Ancestry/Race overlap — e.g. persons can report being both White and Irish, b) persons of Hispanic origin can report being any race, c) persons reporting two ancestries are counted in both categories. 2. Numbers in parentheses indicate the number of persons reporting this ancestry/race alone, not in combination with any other ancestry/race. 3. Refer to the Explanation of Data in the front of the book for more detailed information.

Greek	9	0.09
Hawaii Native/Pacific Islander:	7	0.07
Polynesian:	2	0.02
Samoan	2	0.02
Other Pac. Isl., specified	1	0.01
Other Pac. Isl., not spec. (2)	4	0.04
Hispanic or Latino:	109	1.08
Central American:	1	0.01
Panamanian	1	0.01
Cuban	5	0.05
Mexican	64	0.64
Puerto Rican	21	0.21
South American:	1	0.01
Peruvian	1	0.01
Other Hispanic or Latino	17	0.17
Hungarian	10	0.10
Irish	499	4.96
Italian	149	1.48
Polish	97	0.96
Russian	6	0.06
Scandinavian	13	0.13
Scotch-Irish	38	0.38
Scottish	5	0.05
Serbian	7	0.07
Slavic	8	0.08
Swedish	11	0.11
Swiss	6	0.06
Ukrainian	27	0.27
United States or American	263	2.62
Welsh	10	0.10
West Indian, excl. Hispanic:	24	0.24
Jamaican	24	0.24
White:	2,179	21.65
Not Hispanic (2,038)	2,132	21.19
Hispanic (39)	47	0.47

Blue Springs

Place Type: City
County: Jackson
Population: 48,080

Ancestry/Race	Number	%
African American/Black:	1,618	3.37
Not Hispanic (1,395)	1,592	3.31
Hispanic (15)	26	0.05
African, sub-Saharan:	157	0.33
African	119	0.25
Ethiopian	10	0.02
Kenyan	10	0.02
Nigerian	8	0.02
Sierra Leonean	10	0.02
Alaska Native tribes, specified:	1	0.00
Tlingit-Haida (1)	1	0.00
Am. Ind. or Alaska Nat., not spec.	100	0.21
American Indian tribes, specified:	391	0.81
Apache (6)	8	0.02
Blackfeet (2)	7	0.01
Cherokee (81)	203	0.42
Cheyenne	3	0.01
Chickasaw (2)	3	0.01
Chippewa (3)	7	0.01
Choctaw (16)	31	0.06
Comanche	7	0.01
Cree	1	0.00
Creek (8)	15	0.03
Crow	1	0.00
Delaware (1)	1	0.00
Iroquois (12)	12	0.02
Latin American Indians (2)	8	0.02
Lumbee (4)	4	0.01
Osage	6	0.01
Ottawa (4)	10	0.02
Paiute (1)	1	0.00
Potawatomi (6)	12	0.02
Pueblo	5	0.01
Seminole (1)	5	0.01
Sioux (6)	15	0.03
Tohono O'Odham (1)	1	0.00
Ute	1	0.00
All other tribes (11)	24	0.05
American Indian tribes, not spec.	11	0.02
Arab:	164	0.34
Arab/Arabic	35	0.07
Jordanian	22	0.05
Lebanese	81	0.17
Syrian	9	0.02
Other Arab	17	0.04
Armenian	9	0.02
Asian:	575	1.20
Bangladeshi (4)	4	0.01
Cambodian (1)	1	0.00
Chinese, ex. Taiwanese (51)	62	0.13
Filipino (144)	176	0.37
Indian (81)	92	0.19
Indonesian (2)	4	0.01
Japanese (19)	37	0.08
Korean (78)	94	0.20
Laotian (7)	4	0.01
Pakistani (22)	22	0.05
Taiwanese (11)	11	0.02
Thai (5)	13	0.03
Vietnamese (26)	28	0.06
Other Asian, specified (1)	2	0.00
Other Asian, not specified (10)	22	0.05
Australian	6	0.01
Austrian	94	0.20
Belgian	56	0.12
Brazilian	34	0.07
British	145	0.30
Canadian	19	0.04
Celtic	10	0.02
Croatian	129	0.27
Czech	124	0.26
Czechoslovakian	43	0.09
Danish	246	0.51
Dutch	729	1.52
English	6,784	14.14
European	789	1.64
Finnish	17	0.04
French, except Basque	1,515	3.16
French Canadian	214	0.45
German	12,189	25.40
Greek	132	0.28
Hawaii Native/Pacific Islander:	122	0.25
Micronesian: (11)	20	0.04
Guamanian/Chamorro (10)	19	0.04
Other Micronesian (1)	1	0.00
Polynesian: (40)	90	0.19
Native Hawaiian (12)	34	0.07
Samoan (26)	47	0.10
Tongan (2)	8	0.02
Other Polynesian	1	0.00
Other Pac. Isl., not spec. (3)	12	0.02
Hispanic or Latino:	1,329	2.76
Central American:	27	0.06
Honduran	4	0.01
Panamanian	18	0.04
Salvadoran	1	0.00
Other Central American	4	0.01
Cuban	16	0.03
Dominican Republic	1	0.00
Mexican	1,019	2.12
Puerto Rican	71	0.15
South American:	29	0.06
Chilean	1	0.00
Colombian	17	0.04
Ecuadorian	1	0.00
Peruvian	3	0.01
Venezuelan	5	0.01
Other South American	2	0.00
Other Hispanic or Latino	166	0.35
Hungarian	28	0.06
Iranian	74	0.15
Irish	7,006	14.60
Italian	1,698	3.54
Latvian	15	0.03
Lithuanian	23	0.05
Luxemburger	7	0.01
Norwegian	784	1.63
Pennsylvania German	10	0.02
Polish	834	1.74
Portuguese	114	0.24
Romanian	8	0.02
Russian	72	0.15
Scandinavian	10	0.02
Scotch-Irish	825	1.72
Scottish	766	1.60
Serbian	18	0.04
Slavic	97	0.20
Slovak	40	0.08
Slovene	29	0.06
Swedish	889	1.85
Swiss	150	0.31
Turkish	15	0.03
Ukrainian	18	0.04
United States or American	4,146	8.64
Welsh	431	0.90
West Indian, excl. Hispanic:	28	0.06
Jamaican	15	0.03
Trinidadian and Tobagonian	13	0.03
White:	45,472	94.58
Not Hispanic (44,045)	44,582	92.72
Hispanic (756)	890	1.85
Yugoslavian	45	0.09

Bridgeton

Place Type: City
County: Saint Louis
Population: 15,550

Ancestry/Race	Number	%
African American/Black:	1,486	9.56
Not Hispanic (1,407)	1,482	9.53
Hispanic (1)	4	0.03
African, sub-Saharan:	145	0.95
African	137	0.90
Kenyan	8	0.05
Am. Ind. or Alaska Nat., not spec.	30	0.19
American Indian tribes, specified:	47	0.30
Blackfeet (3)	5	0.03
Cherokee (8)	18	0.12
Cheyenne (2)	2	0.01
Chickasaw	1	0.01
Chippewa	2	0.01
Choctaw (5)	6	0.04
Cree	1	0.01
Creek	1	0.01
Crow	2	0.01
Iroquois	2	0.01
Kiowa	1	0.01
Pueblo	2	0.01
Sioux (1)	2	0.01
All other tribes	2	0.01
American Indian tribes, not spec.	7	0.05
Arab:	54	0.35
Lebanese	54	0.35
Asian:	417	2.68
Bangladeshi (4)	4	0.03
Chinese, ex. Taiwanese (99)	102	0.66
Filipino (45)	60	0.39
Indian (84)	92	0.59
Japanese (10)	21	0.14
Korean (30)	34	0.22
Laotian (13)	13	0.08
Pakistani (13)	13	0.08
Thai (6)	10	0.06
Vietnamese (44)	46	0.30
Other Asian, not specified (2)	22	0.14
Austrian	45	0.29
Basque	20	0.13
Belgian	6	0.04
British	40	0.26
Canadian	36	0.24
Croatian	28	0.18
Czech	122	0.80
Czechoslovakian	26	0.17
Danish	36	0.24
Dutch	214	1.40

Notes: 1. Figures in the "Number" column do not add up to the total population due to: a) Ancestry/Race overlap — e.g. persons can report being both White and Irish, b) persons of Hispanic origin can report being any race, c) persons reporting two ancestries are counted in both categories. 2. Numbers in parentheses indicate the number of persons reporting this ancestry/race alone, not in combination with any other ancestry/race. 3. Refer to the Explanation of Data in the front of the book for more detailed information.

Ancestry/Race	Number	%
English	1,523	9.98
European	85	0.56
French, except Basque	762	5.00
French Canadian	66	0.43
German	4,837	31.71
Greek	121	0.79
Hawaii Native/Pacific Islander:	4	0.03
Micronesian:	2	0.01
Other Micronesian	2	0.01
Polynesian: (1)	2	0.01
Native Hawaiian (1)	2	0.01
Hispanic or Latino:	345	2.22
Central American:	18	0.12
Costa Rican	2	0.01
Guatemalan	9	0.06
Honduran	2	0.01
Nicaraguan	1	0.01
Panamanian	4	0.03
Cuban	4	0.03
Mexican	246	1.58
Puerto Rican	28	0.18
South American:	20	0.13
Chilean	1	0.01
Colombian	5	0.03
Ecuadorian	2	0.01
Peruvian	7	0.05
Venezuelan	5	0.03
Other Hispanic or Latino	29	0.19
Hungarian	86	0.56
Irish	2,948	19.32
Italian	955	6.26
Lithuanian	6	0.04
Macedonian	8	0.05
Northern European	9	0.06
Norwegian	144	0.94
Polish	416	2.73
Portuguese	18	0.12
Russian	77	0.50
Scotch-Irish	277	1.82
Scottish	319	2.09
Slavic	6	0.04
Slovak	19	0.12
Swedish	107	0.70
Swiss	83	0.54
Ukrainian	17	0.11
United States or American	844	5.53
Welsh	75	0.49
West Indian, excl. Hispanic:	15	0.10
Jamaican	15	0.10
White:	13,623	87.61
Not Hispanic (13,211)	13,375	86.01
Hispanic (235)	248	1.59
Yugoslavian	43	0.28

Cape Girardeau

Place Type: City
County: Cape Girardeau
Population: 35,349

Ancestry/Race	Number	%
African American/Black:	3,504	9.91
Not Hispanic (3,276)	3,473	9.82
Hispanic (12)	31	0.09
African, sub-Saharan:	158	0.45
African	130	0.37
Ethiopian	4	0.01
Nigerian	24	0.07
Alaska Native tribes, specified:	1	0.00
Alaska Athabascan (1)	1	0.00
Am. Ind. or Alaska Nat., not spec.	101	0.29
American Indian tribes, specified:	214	0.61
Apache (1)	5	0.01
Blackfeet (5)	6	0.02
Cherokee (80)	158	0.45
Cheyenne (1)	2	0.01
Chickasaw (3)	5	0.01
Chippewa (1)	2	0.01
Choctaw (1)	2	0.01
Comanche (1)	2	0.01
Creek	2	0.01
Crow	2	0.00
Iroquois	1	0.00
Latin American Indians (1)	2	0.01
Navajo	1	0.00
Osage	1	0.00
Potawatomi (2)	2	0.01
Puget Sound Salish	2	0.01
Seminole	2	0.01
Sioux (1)	4	0.01
All other tribes (5)	14	0.04
American Indian tribes, not spec.	21	0.06
Arab:	5	0.01
Lebanese	5	0.01
Asian:	490	1.39
Bangladeshi (2)	2	0.01
Chinese, ex. Taiwanese (75)	93	0.26
Filipino (34)	54	0.15
Indian (67)	69	0.20
Japanese (94)	111	0.31
Korean (43)	50	0.14
Laotian (1)	1	0.00
Malaysian (9)	11	0.03
Pakistani (16)	16	0.05
Sri Lankan (3)	3	0.01
Taiwanese (12)	13	0.04
Thai (5)	5	0.01
Vietnamese (18)	23	0.07
Other Asian, specified (3)	5	0.01
Other Asian, not specified (16)	34	0.10
Australian	36	0.10
Austrian	64	0.18
Belgian	86	0.24
British	92	0.26
Bulgarian	27	0.08
Canadian	22	0.06
Celtic	11	0.03
Croatian	14	0.04
Czech	104	0.29
Czechoslovakian	41	0.12
Danish	133	0.38
Dutch	792	2.24
Eastern European	13	0.04
English	2,823	7.99
European	343	0.97
Finnish	23	0.07
French, except Basque	1,287	3.64
French Canadian	75	0.21
German	9,926	28.10
Greek	74	0.21
Hawaii Native/Pacific Islander:	28	0.08
Melanesian: (1)	1	0.00
Fijian (1)	1	0.00
Micronesian: (5)	6	0.02
Guamanian/Chamorro (5)	6	0.02
Polynesian: (3)	10	0.03
Native Hawaiian (3)	10	0.03
Other Pac. Isl., specified	1	0.00
Other Pac. Isl., not spec. (4)	10	0.03
Hispanic or Latino:	388	1.10
Central American:	14	0.04
Guatemalan	2	0.01
Nicaraguan	5	0.01
Panamanian	2	0.01
Salvadoran	2	0.01
Other Central American	3	0.01
Cuban	13	0.04
Mexican	234	0.66
Puerto Rican	38	0.11
South American:	15	0.04
Argentinean	1	0.00
Colombian	8	0.02
Peruvian	3	0.01
Venezuelan	3	0.01
Other Hispanic or Latino	74	0.21
Hungarian	73	0.21
Irish	3,767	10.67
Israeli	8	0.02
Italian	722	2.04
Lithuanian	25	0.07
Norwegian	194	0.55
Pennsylvania German	3	0.01
Polish	414	1.17
Portuguese	13	0.04
Russian	65	0.18
Scandinavian	38	0.11
Scotch-Irish	706	2.00
Scottish	569	1.61
Slovak	59	0.17
Swedish	239	0.68
Swiss	117	0.33
Turkish	20	0.06
Ukrainian	24	0.07
United States or American	3,751	10.62
Welsh	242	0.69
West Indian, excl. Hispanic:	7	0.02
British West Indian	4	0.01
Haitian	3	0.01
White:	31,300	88.55
Not Hispanic (30,650)	31,049	87.84
Hispanic (215)	251	0.71
Yugoslavian	10	0.03

Carthage

Place Type: City
County: Jasper
Population: 12,668

Ancestry/Race	Number	%
Acadian/Cajun	5	0.04
African American/Black:	266	2.10
Not Hispanic (191)	253	2.00
Hispanic (4)	13	0.10
Alaska Native tribes, specified:	3	0.02
Aleut	3	0.02
Am. Ind. or Alaska Nat., not spec.	45	0.36
American Indian tribes, specified:	254	2.01
Apache	5	0.04
Blackfeet (1)	5	0.04
Cherokee (58)	122	0.96
Chippewa (1)	1	0.01
Choctaw (5)	11	0.09
Comanche	1	0.01
Creek (4)	5	0.04
Crow	1	0.01
Delaware	3	0.02
Iroquois (4)	7	0.06
Kiowa	1	0.01
Latin American Indians (9)	48	0.38
Navajo (12)	16	0.13
Osage	3	0.02
Potawatomi (1)	3	0.02
Seminole (4)	4	0.03
Sioux (1)	11	0.09
All other tribes (4)	7	0.06
American Indian tribes, not spec.	5	0.04
Asian:	224	1.77
Chinese, ex. Taiwanese (1)	1	0.01
Filipino (13)	25	0.20
Indian (14)	16	0.13
Japanese (6)	7	0.06
Korean (4)	5	0.04
Thai	1	0.01
Vietnamese (155)	160	1.26
Other Asian, not specified (5)	9	0.07
Austrian	15	0.12
Belgian	8	0.06
British	32	0.25
Canadian	6	0.05
Czech	15	0.12
Danish	43	0.34
Dutch	192	1.53
English	1,186	9.44
European	97	0.77
French, except Basque	252	2.01
French Canadian	31	0.25
German	1,960	15.61
Hawaii Native/Pacific Islander:	38	0.30
Micronesian: (20)	27	0.21

Notes: 1. Figures in the "Number" column do not add up to the total population due to: a) Ancestry/Race overlap — e.g. persons can report being both White and Irish, b) persons of Hispanic origin can report being any race, c) persons reporting two ancestries are counted in both categories. 2. Numbers in parentheses indicate the number of persons reporting this ancestry/race alone, not in combination with any other ancestry/race. 3. Refer to the Explanation of Data in the front of the book for more detailed information.

Ancestry/Race	Number	%
Guamanian/Chamorro (20)	25	0.20
Other Micronesian	2	0.02
Polynesian: (5)	8	0.06
Native Hawaiian	3	0.02
Samoan (5)	5	0.04
Other Pac. Isl., not spec. (2)	3	0.02
Hispanic or Latino:	1,589	12.54
Central American:	588	4.64
Guatemalan	514	4.06
Honduran	9	0.07
Panamanian	1	0.01
Salvadoran	64	0.51
Cuban	5	0.04
Mexican	760	6.00
Puerto Rican	23	0.18
South American:	3	0.02
Colombian	1	0.01
Peruvian	2	0.02
Other Hispanic or Latino	210	1.66
Hungarian	7	0.06
Icelander	8	0.06
Irish	1,232	9.81
Italian	183	1.46
Lithuanian	40	0.32
Norwegian	99	0.79
Pennsylvania German	24	0.19
Polish	57	0.45
Portuguese	15	0.12
Romanian	9	0.07
Scandinavian	22	0.18
Scotch-Irish	285	2.27
Scottish	202	1.61
Swedish	47	0.37
Swiss	35	0.28
Ukrainian	5	0.04
United States or American	1,489	11.86
Welsh	69	0.55
West Indian, excl. Hispanic:	7	0.06
Jamaican	7	0.06
White:	11,222	88.59
Not Hispanic (10,351)	10,535	83.16
Hispanic (633)	687	5.42
Yugoslavian	5	0.04

Chesterfield

Place Type: City
County: Saint Louis
Population: 46,802

Ancestry/Race	Number	%
African American/Black:	930	1.99
Not Hispanic (867)	924	1.97
Hispanic (5)	6	0.01
African, sub-Saharan:	94	0.20
African	29	0.06
Nigerian	41	0.09
South African	6	0.01
Sudanese	18	0.04
Alaska Native tribes, specified:	2	0.00
Aleut	2	0.00
Am. Ind. or Alaska Nat., not spec.	37	0.08
Albanian	7	0.01
Alsatian	10	0.02
American Indian tribes, specified:	98	0.21
Apache	1	0.00
Blackfeet	2	0.00
Cherokee (14)	31	0.07
Cheyenne	1	0.00
Chickasaw (4)	7	0.01
Choctaw (1)	4	0.01
Cree (1)	7	0.01
Creek	8	0.02
Iroquois (1)	2	0.00
Latin American Indians (1)	2	0.00
Menominee (1)	1	0.00
Navajo	1	0.00
Osage	4	0.01
Potawatomi (1)	2	0.00
Pueblo (3)	5	0.01
Puget Sound Salish	2	0.00
Yaqui (1)	1	0.00
All other tribes (9)	17	0.04
American Indian tribes, not spec.	10	0.02
Arab:	154	0.33
Arab/Arabic	27	0.06
Egyptian	32	0.07
Lebanese	60	0.13
Syrian	35	0.07
Armenian	28	0.06
Asian:	2,808	6.00
Bangladeshi (5)	5	0.01
Chinese, ex. Taiwanese (934)	977	2.09
Filipino (142)	180	0.38
Indian (671)	719	1.54
Indonesian (1)	3	0.01
Japanese (127)	148	0.32
Korean (346)	380	0.81
Malaysian	1	0.00
Pakistani (92)	103	0.22
Sri Lankan (14)	14	0.03
Taiwanese (149)	152	0.32
Thai (34)	44	0.09
Vietnamese (41)	42	0.09
Other Asian, not specified (21)	40	0.09
Assyrian/Chaldean/Syriac	13	0.03
Australian	25	0.05
Austrian	292	0.62
Basque	8	0.02
Belgian	50	0.11
Brazilian	23	0.05
British	234	0.50
Bulgarian	35	0.07
Canadian	247	0.53
Croatian	122	0.26
Czech	242	0.52
Czechoslovakian	117	0.25
Danish	257	0.55
Dutch	771	1.64
Eastern European	295	0.63
English	6,238	13.28
Estonian	8	0.02
European	818	1.74
Finnish	97	0.21
French, except Basque	1,884	4.01
French Canadian	200	0.43
German	14,551	30.98
Greek	477	1.02
Hawaii Native/Pacific Islander:	22	0.05
Micronesian: (1)	1	0.00
Guamanian/Chamorro (1)	1	0.00
Polynesian: (4)	10	0.02
Native Hawaiian (1)	4	0.01
Samoan (3)	6	0.01
Other Pac. Isl., not spec. (4)	11	0.02
Hispanic or Latino:	726	1.55
Central American:	21	0.04
Costa Rican	3	0.01
Guatemalan	6	0.01
Honduran	2	0.00
Nicaraguan	2	0.00
Panamanian	4	0.01
Salvadoran	3	0.01
Other Central American	1	0.00
Cuban	50	0.11
Dominican Republic	3	0.01
Mexican	329	0.70
Puerto Rican	60	0.13
South American:	98	0.21
Argentinean	20	0.04
Bolivian	9	0.02
Chilean	13	0.03
Colombian	28	0.06
Ecuadorian	2	0.00
Paraguayan	2	0.00
Peruvian	18	0.04
Venezuelan	6	0.01
Other Hispanic or Latino	165	0.35
Hungarian	324	0.69
Iranian	64	0.14
Irish	7,529	16.03
Israeli	34	0.07
Italian	2,734	5.82
Latvian	51	0.11
Lithuanian	182	0.39
Luxemburger	18	0.04
Northern European	35	0.07
Norwegian	478	1.02
Polish	2,188	4.66
Portuguese	80	0.17
Romanian	152	0.32
Russian	2,410	5.13
Scandinavian	52	0.11
Scotch-Irish	1,019	2.17
Scottish	1,077	2.29
Serbian	24	0.05
Slavic	19	0.04
Slovak	148	0.32
Slovene	47	0.10
Swedish	772	1.64
Swiss	330	0.70
Turkish	59	0.13
Ukrainian	450	0.96
United States or American	2,960	6.30
Welsh	366	0.78
West Indian, excl. Hispanic:	16	0.03
Jamaican	8	0.02
U.S. Virgin Islander	8	0.02
White:	43,039	91.96
Not Hispanic (42,190)	42,476	90.76
Hispanic (540)	563	1.20
Yugoslavian	59	0.13

Clayton

Place Type: City
County: Saint Louis
Population: 12,825

Ancestry/Race	Number	%
African American/Black:	1,023	7.98
Not Hispanic (996)	1,022	7.97
Hispanic (1)	1	0.01
African, sub-Saharan:	41	0.32
African	5	0.04
Other sub-Saharan African	36	0.28
Am. Ind. or Alaska Nat., not spec.	18	0.14
Albanian	6	0.05
Alsatian	20	0.16
American Indian tribes, specified:	37	0.29
Apache	1	0.01
Blackfeet	1	0.01
Cherokee (7)	23	0.18
Chickasaw	1	0.01
Choctaw	2	0.02
Creek	2	0.02
Latin American Indians (1)	2	0.02
Sioux (3)	4	0.03
All other tribes	1	0.01
American Indian tribes, not spec.	7	0.05
Arab:	9	0.07
Lebanese	9	0.07
Armenian	15	0.12
Asian:	798	6.22
Chinese, ex. Taiwanese (352)	363	2.83
Filipino (39)	45	0.35
Indian (120)	136	1.06
Indonesian (1)	1	0.01
Japanese (52)	76	0.59
Korean (108)	120	0.94
Malaysian (1)	1	0.01
Pakistani (2)	5	0.04
Sri Lankan (1)	1	0.01
Taiwanese (17)	17	0.13
Thai (3)	7	0.05
Vietnamese (8)	10	0.08
Other Asian, specified (1)	1	0.01
Other Asian, not specified (9)	15	0.12
Australian	46	0.36
Austrian	78	0.61

Notes: 1. Figures in the "Number" column do not add up to the total population due to: a) Ancestry/Race overlap — e.g. persons can report being both White and Irish, b) persons of Hispanic origin can report being any race, c) persons reporting two ancestries are counted in both categories. 2. Numbers in parentheses indicate the number of persons reporting this ancestry/race alone, not in combination with any other ancestry/race. 3. Refer to the Explanation of Data in the front of the book for more detailed information.

Belgian	23	0.18
British	128	1.00
Canadian	88	0.69
Croatian	14	0.11
Czech	36	0.28
Czechoslovakian	23	0.18
Danish	83	0.65
Dutch	128	1.00
Eastern European	150	1.17
English	1,800	14.03
European	253	1.97
Finnish	7	0.05
French, except Basque	421	3.28
French Canadian	32	0.25
German	3,126	24.37
Greek	51	0.40
Guyanese	5	0.04
Hawaii Native/Pacific Islander:	13	0.10
Micronesian: (2)	2	0.02
Guamanian/Chamorro (2)	2	0.02
Polynesian: (1)	2	0.02
Native Hawaiian (1)	2	0.02
Other Pac. Isl., not spec. (1)	9	0.07
Hispanic or Latino:	191	1.49
Central American:	9	0.07
Guatemalan	2	0.02
Honduran	2	0.02
Panamanian	1	0.01
Other Central American	4	0.03
Cuban	8	0.06
Mexican	51	0.40
Puerto Rican	11	0.09
South American:	55	0.43
Argentinean	20	0.16
Chilean	6	0.05
Colombian	10	0.08
Ecuadorian	1	0.01
Paraguayan	1	0.01
Peruvian	14	0.11
Other South American	3	0.02
Other Hispanic or Latino	57	0.44
Hungarian	105	0.82
Iranian	21	0.16
Irish	1,685	13.14
Italian	484	3.77
Latvian	14	0.11
Lithuanian	100	0.78
Norwegian	155	1.21
Polish	522	4.07
Portuguese	5	0.04
Romanian	23	0.18
Russian	970	7.56
Scandinavian	10	0.08
Scotch-Irish	314	2.45
Scottish	245	1.91
Slovak	11	0.09
Slovene	5	0.04
Swedish	209	1.63
Swiss	119	0.93
Ukrainian	50	0.39
United States or American	618	4.82
Welsh	94	0.73
West Indian, excl. Hispanic:	17	0.13
Belizean	10	0.08
Jamaican	7	0.05
White:	11,032	86.02
Not Hispanic (10,740)	10,865	84.72
Hispanic (154)	167	1.30
Yugoslavian	11	0.09

Columbia

Place Type: City
County: Boone
Population: 84,531

Ancestry/Race	Number	%
African American/Black:	9,931	11.75
Not Hispanic (9,106)	9,824	11.62
Hispanic (67)	107	0.13
African, sub-Saharan:	903	1.07
African	543	0.64
Ethiopian	92	0.11
Ghanian	6	0.01
Kenyan	5	0.01
Nigerian	159	0.19
Somalian	9	0.01
South African	14	0.02
Other sub-Saharan African	75	0.09
Alaska Native tribes, specified:	4	0.00
Aleut (1)	2	0.00
Eskimo (1)	2	0.00
Alaska Native tribes, not specified	1	0.00
Am. Ind. or Alaska Nat., not spec.	237	0.28
Albanian	5	0.01
Alsatian	6	0.01
American Indian tribes, specified:	538	0.64
Apache (10)	33	0.04
Blackfeet (2)	22	0.03
Cherokee (96)	292	0.35
Cheyenne (5)	6	0.01
Chickasaw (1)	5	0.01
Chippewa (2)	5	0.01
Choctaw (9)	23	0.03
Comanche (3)	5	0.01
Cree (1)	1	0.00
Creek (7)	12	0.01
Crow	1	0.00
Delaware (5)	6	0.01
Houma (1)	1	0.00
Iroquois (3)	7	0.01
Kiowa (3)	3	0.00
Latin American Indians (14)	23	0.03
Lumbee (3)	3	0.00
Navajo (2)	5	0.01
Osage (2)	4	0.00
Ottawa (1)	4	0.00
Paiute	1	0.00
Potawatomi (3)	7	0.01
Pueblo (2)	3	0.00
Seminole (1)	3	0.00
Shoshone	3	0.00
Sioux (6)	20	0.02
Ute (1)	1	0.00
Yaqui (3)	4	0.00
All other tribes (14)	35	0.04
American Indian tribes, not spec.	42	0.05
Arab:	761	0.90
Arab/Arabic	67	0.08
Egyptian	107	0.13
Iraqi	87	0.10
Jordanian	63	0.07
Lebanese	148	0.17
Moroccan	30	0.04
Palestinian	39	0.05
Syrian	57	0.07
Other Arab	163	0.19
Armenian	31	0.04
Asian:	4,173	4.94
Bangladeshi (14)	15	0.02
Cambodian (207)	228	0.27
Chinese, ex. Taiwanese (1,076)	1,165	1.38
Filipino (186)	259	0.31
Hmong (1)	1	0.00
Indian (801)	881	1.04
Indonesian (32)	40	0.05
Japanese (128)	207	0.24
Korean (526)	602	0.71
Laotian (6)	10	0.01
Malaysian (31)	36	0.04
Pakistani (58)	66	0.08
Sri Lankan (27)	32	0.04
Taiwanese (64)	74	0.09
Thai (119)	141	0.17
Vietnamese (194)	224	0.26
Other Asian, specified (8)	15	0.02
Other Asian, not specified (89)	177	0.21
Australian	22	0.03
Austrian	167	0.20
Basque	21	0.02
Belgian	122	0.14
Brazilian	19	0.02
British	586	0.69
Bulgarian	45	0.05
Canadian	192	0.23
Celtic	11	0.01
Croatian	85	0.10
Czech	401	0.47
Czechoslovakian	149	0.18
Danish	508	0.60
Dutch	1,567	1.85
Eastern European	97	0.11
English	10,904	12.86
Estonian	8	0.01
European	1,230	1.45
Finnish	24	0.03
French, except Basque	2,271	2.68
French Canadian	297	0.35
German	21,702	25.60
German Russian	15	0.02
Greek	196	0.23
Hawaii Native/Pacific Islander:	89	0.11
Melanesian: (5)	5	0.01
Fijian (5)	5	0.01
Micronesian: (5)	10	0.01
Guamanian/Chamorro (5)	9	0.01
Other Micronesian	1	0.00
Polynesian: (15)	30	0.04
Native Hawaiian (10)	23	0.03
Samoan (5)	7	0.01
Other Pac. Isl., specified	2	0.00
Other Pac. Isl., not spec. (5)	42	0.05
Hispanic or Latino:	1,733	2.05
Central American:	95	0.11
Costa Rican	9	0.01
Guatemalan	14	0.02
Honduran	14	0.02
Nicaraguan	14	0.02
Panamanian	21	0.02
Salvadoran	19	0.02
Other Central American	4	0.00
Cuban	73	0.09
Dominican Republic	13	0.02
Mexican	932	1.10
Puerto Rican	133	0.16
South American:	136	0.16
Argentinean	13	0.02
Bolivian	11	0.01
Chilean	7	0.01
Colombian	28	0.03
Ecuadorian	6	0.01
Paraguayan	4	0.00
Peruvian	40	0.05
Uruguayan	5	0.01
Venezuelan	17	0.02
Other South American	5	0.01
Other Hispanic or Latino	351	0.42
Hungarian	280	0.33
Icelander	26	0.03
Iranian	173	0.20
Irish	11,363	13.40
Italian	2,433	2.87
Lithuanian	48	0.06
Macedonian	10	0.01
New Zealander	8	0.01
Northern European	90	0.11
Norwegian	996	1.17
Pennsylvania German	10	0.01
Polish	1,232	1.45
Portuguese	97	0.11
Romanian	109	0.13
Russian	710	0.84
Scandinavian	145	0.17
Scotch-Irish	2,049	2.42
Scottish	2,257	2.66
Serbian	28	0.03
Slavic	15	0.02
Slovak	52	0.06
Slovene	25	0.03
Swedish	1,493	1.76

Notes: 1. Figures in the "Number" column do not add up to the total population due to: a) Ancestry/Race overlap — e.g. persons can report being both White and Irish, b) persons of Hispanic origin can report being any race, c) persons reporting two ancestries are counted in both categories. 2. Numbers in parentheses indicate the number of persons reporting this ancestry/race alone, not in combination with any other ancestry/race. 3. Refer to the Explanation of Data in the front of the book for more detailed information.

Swiss	217	0.26
Turkish	75	0.09
Ukrainian	158	0.19
United States or American	6,096	7.19
Welsh	862	1.02
West Indian, excl. Hispanic:	201	0.24
Haitian	130	0.15
Jamaican	30	0.04
Trinidadian and Tobagonian	23	0.03
West Indian	11	0.01
Other West Indian	7	0.01
White:	70,427	83.31
Not Hispanic (67,984)	69,344	82.03
Hispanic (939)	1,083	1.28
Yugoslavian	105	0.12

Concord

Place Type: Census Designated Place
County: Saint Louis
Population: 16,689

Ancestry/Race	Number	%
African American/Black:	79	0.47
Not Hispanic (52)	76	0.46
Hispanic	3	0.02
African, sub-Saharan:	9	0.05
African	9	0.05
Alaska Native tribes, specified:	1	0.01
Alaska Athabascan	1	0.01
Am. Ind. or Alaska Nat., not spec.	11	0.07
American Indian tribes, specified:	21	0.13
Cherokee (4)	8	0.05
Chippewa (1)	1	0.01
Choctaw	1	0.01
Crow	1	0.01
Delaware (1)	1	0.01
Latin American Indians (2)	4	0.02
Osage (3)	3	0.02
Sioux (1)	2	0.01
American Indian tribes, not spec.	3	0.02
Arab:	110	0.66
Arab/Arabic	17	0.10
Lebanese	82	0.49
Syrian	5	0.03
Other Arab	6	0.04
Armenian	26	0.16
Asian:	168	1.01
Cambodian (1)	1	0.01
Chinese, ex. Taiwanese (30)	31	0.19
Filipino (36)	47	0.28
Indian (39)	41	0.25
Japanese (6)	10	0.06
Korean (10)	10	0.06
Pakistani (1)	1	0.01
Taiwanese (1)	1	0.01
Thai (4)	4	0.02
Vietnamese (6)	10	0.06
Other Asian, not specified (3)	12	0.07
Australian	9	0.05
Austrian	135	0.81
Belgian	5	0.03
British	35	0.21
Bulgarian	8	0.05
Carpatho Rusyn	9	0.05
Croatian	151	0.91
Czech	335	2.01
Czechoslovakian	133	0.80
Danish	71	0.43
Dutch	246	1.48
English	1,507	9.04
European	49	0.29
French, except Basque	985	5.91
French Canadian	13	0.08
German	8,212	49.24
Greek	97	0.58
Hawaii Native/Pacific Islander:	4	0.02
Polynesian: (1)	2	0.01
Native Hawaiian (1)	2	0.01
Other Pac. Isl., not spec.	2	0.01
Hispanic or Latino:	141	0.84
Central American:	12	0.07
Costa Rican	4	0.02
Guatemalan	7	0.04
Honduran	1	0.01
Cuban	5	0.03
Mexican	83	0.50
Puerto Rican	4	0.02
South American:	7	0.04
Bolivian	1	0.01
Colombian	1	0.01
Paraguayan	1	0.01
Peruvian	3	0.02
Venezuelan	1	0.01
Other Hispanic or Latino	30	0.18
Hungarian	120	0.72
Iranian	23	0.14
Irish	3,060	18.35
Italian	971	5.82
Lithuanian	29	0.17
Norwegian	54	0.32
Polish	493	2.96
Portuguese	12	0.07
Romanian	81	0.49
Russian	67	0.40
Scotch-Irish	308	1.85
Scottish	128	0.77
Serbian	22	0.13
Slavic	8	0.05
Slovak	55	0.33
Slovene	6	0.04
Swedish	194	1.16
Swiss	201	1.21
Turkish	6	0.04
Ukrainian	26	0.16
United States or American	1,126	6.75
Welsh	128	0.77
White:	16,437	98.49
Not Hispanic (16,262)	16,338	97.90
Hispanic (85)	99	0.59
Yugoslavian	49	0.29

Crestwood

Place Type: City
County: Saint Louis
Population: 11,863

Ancestry/Race	Number	%
African American/Black:	113	0.95
Not Hispanic (85)	113	0.95
Am. Ind. or Alaska Nat., not spec.	22	0.19
Albanian	19	0.16
American Indian tribes, specified:	44	0.37
Apache	3	0.03
Blackfeet (1)	3	0.03
Cherokee (11)	19	0.16
Chippewa	1	0.01
Choctaw	2	0.02
Creek (1)	1	0.01
Latin American Indians (4)	4	0.03
Osage	1	0.01
Sioux	1	0.01
Yaqui	1	0.01
All other tribes (3)	8	0.07
American Indian tribes, not spec.	2	0.02
Arab:	47	0.40
Lebanese	39	0.33
Syrian	8	0.07
Armenian	36	0.31
Asian:	213	1.80
Cambodian (3)	3	0.03
Chinese, ex. Taiwanese (33)	41	0.35
Filipino (9)	11	0.09
Indian (34)	37	0.31
Indonesian (4)	5	0.04
Japanese (11)	21	0.18
Korean (17)	19	0.16
Laotian (5)	5	0.04
Pakistani (2)	2	0.02
Taiwanese (1)	1	0.01
Thai (2)	2	0.02
Vietnamese (39)	50	0.42
Other Asian, specified	2	0.02
Other Asian, not specified (6)	14	0.12
Australian	19	0.16
Austrian	91	0.78
British	28	0.24
Bulgarian	19	0.16
Canadian	12	0.10
Croatian	51	0.44
Czech	98	0.84
Czechoslovakian	112	0.96
Danish	53	0.45
Dutch	169	1.44
Eastern European	8	0.07
English	1,411	12.04
European	89	0.76
Finnish	1	0.01
French, except Basque	615	5.25
French Canadian	41	0.35
German	5,394	46.02
Greek	200	1.71
Hawaii Native/Pacific Islander:	11	0.09
Polynesian:	3	0.03
Native Hawaiian	3	0.03
Other Pac. Isl., specified	2	0.02
Other Pac. Isl., not spec. (1)	6	0.05
Hispanic or Latino:	119	1.00
Central American:	9	0.08
Guatemalan	3	0.03
Honduran	2	0.02
Nicaraguan	3	0.03
Other Central American	1	0.01
Cuban	9	0.08
Dominican Republic	3	0.03
Mexican	51	0.43
Puerto Rican	2	0.02
South American:	13	0.11
Argentinean	1	0.01
Bolivian	1	0.01
Chilean	1	0.01
Colombian	8	0.07
Ecuadorian	1	0.01
Other South American	1	0.01
Other Hispanic or Latino	32	0.27
Hungarian	41	0.35
Icelander	9	0.08
Irish	2,428	20.72
Italian	937	7.99
Latvian	5	0.04
Lithuanian	50	0.43
Northern European	31	0.26
Norwegian	57	0.49
Polish	271	2.31
Portuguese	9	0.08
Romanian	7	0.06
Russian	35	0.30
Scandinavian	7	0.06
Scotch-Irish	326	2.78
Scottish	218	1.86
Serbian	12	0.10
Slovak	28	0.24
Swedish	127	1.08
Swiss	80	0.68
Ukrainian	8	0.07
United States or American	536	4.57
Welsh	56	0.48
White:	11,540	97.28
Not Hispanic (11,356)	11,451	96.53
Hispanic (81)	89	0.75
Yugoslavian	8	0.07

Creve Coeur

Place Type: City
County: Saint Louis
Population: 16,500

Ancestry/Race	Number	%

Notes: 1. Figures in the "Number" column do not add up to the total population due to: a) Ancestry/Race overlap — e.g. persons can report being both White and Irish, b) persons of Hispanic origin can report being any race, c) persons reporting two ancestries are counted in both categories. 2. Numbers in parentheses indicate the number of persons reporting this ancestry/race alone, not in combination with any other ancestry/race. 3. Refer to the Explanation of Data in the front of the book for more detailed information.

Ancestry/Race	Number	%
African American/Black:	619	3.75
Not Hispanic (566)	607	3.68
Hispanic (3)	12	0.07
African, sub-Saharan:	39	0.24
African	32	0.20
Nigerian	7	0.04
Am. Ind. or Alaska Nat., not spec.	39	0.24
American Indian tribes, specified:	35	0.21
Cherokee (2)	14	0.08
Chippewa (6)	6	0.04
Comanche (3)	3	0.02
Creek	1	0.01
Latin American Indians	1	0.01
Seminole (4)	4	0.02
Sioux (4)	4	0.02
All other tribes	2	0.01
American Indian tribes, not spec.	3	0.02
Arab:	106	0.65
Egyptian	31	0.19
Lebanese	41	0.25
Palestinian	5	0.03
Syrian	29	0.18
Armenian	21	0.13
Asian:	1,076	6.52
Chinese, ex. Taiwanese (200)	232	1.41
Filipino (72)	85	0.52
Indian (323)	342	2.07
Indonesian (4)	4	0.02
Japanese (75)	81	0.49
Korean (193)	199	1.21
Pakistani (18)	23	0.14
Sri Lankan (3)	3	0.02
Taiwanese (35)	36	0.22
Thai (24)	27	0.16
Vietnamese (13)	13	0.08
Other Asian, specified (1)	3	0.02
Other Asian, not specified (13)	28	0.17
Austrian	99	0.61
Belgian	43	0.26
Brazilian	13	0.08
British	82	0.50
Canadian	47	0.29
Croatian	27	0.17
Czech	156	0.96
Czechoslovakian	39	0.24
Danish	94	0.58
Dutch	136	0.83
Eastern European	114	0.70
English	1,517	9.31
European	305	1.87
Finnish	12	0.07
French, except Basque	601	3.69
French Canadian	28	0.17
German	3,738	22.95
Greek	134	0.82
Hawaii Native/Pacific Islander:	4	0.02
Micronesian:	1	0.01
Guamanian/Chamorro	1	0.01
Polynesian:	1	0.01
Native Hawaiian	1	0.01
Other Pac. Isl., specified	1	0.01
Other Pac. Isl., not spec. (1)	1	0.01
Hispanic or Latino:	292	1.77
Central American:	15	0.09
Costa Rican	6	0.04
Guatemalan	5	0.03
Honduran	1	0.01
Nicaraguan	2	0.01
Salvadoran	1	0.01
Cuban	21	0.13
Dominican Republic	2	0.01
Mexican	116	0.70
Puerto Rican	30	0.18
South American:	65	0.39
Argentinean	26	0.16
Bolivian	1	0.01
Chilean	5	0.03
Colombian	9	0.05
Ecuadorian	2	0.01
Peruvian	12	0.07
Venezuelan	2	0.01
Other South American	8	0.05
Other Hispanic or Latino	43	0.26
Hungarian	135	0.83
Iranian	28	0.17
Irish	2,088	12.82
Israeli	54	0.33
Italian	665	4.08
Latvian	22	0.14
Lithuanian	106	0.65
Northern European	32	0.20
Norwegian	112	0.69
Polish	851	5.22
Portuguese	24	0.15
Romanian	58	0.36
Russian	1,500	9.21
Scandinavian	39	0.24
Scotch-Irish	262	1.61
Scottish	254	1.56
Serbian	8	0.05
Slovak	31	0.19
Slovene	30	0.18
Swedish	100	0.61
Swiss	45	0.28
Ukrainian	137	0.84
United States or American	894	5.49
Welsh	62	0.38
West Indian, excl. Hispanic:	20	0.12
Bahamian	5	0.03
Barbadian	6	0.04
Haitian	9	0.06
White:	14,786	89.61
Not Hispanic (14,461)	14,582	88.38
Hispanic (190)	204	1.24
Yugoslavian	26	0.16

Excelsior Springs

Place Type: City
County: Clay
Population: 10,847

Ancestry/Race	Number	%
African American/Black:	444	4.09
Not Hispanic (358)	429	3.96
Hispanic (7)	15	0.14
African, sub-Saharan:	12	0.11
African	5	0.05
Nigerian	7	0.06
Am. Ind. or Alaska Nat., not spec.	39	0.36
American Indian tribes, specified:	108	1.00
Apache	3	0.03
Blackfeet	6	0.06
Cherokee (26)	55	0.51
Cheyenne	1	0.01
Choctaw (2)	2	0.02
Comanche (3)	3	0.03
Crow	6	0.06
Delaware (1)	1	0.01
Iroquois	1	0.01
Kiowa (2)	2	0.02
Latin American Indians (2)	6	0.06
Navajo (1)	2	0.02
Osage	1	0.01
Potawatomi (5)	6	0.06
Sioux	3	0.03
All other tribes (5)	10	0.09
American Indian tribes, not spec.	3	0.03
Arab:	23	0.21
Iraqi	23	0.21
Asian:	58	0.53
Chinese, ex. Taiwanese (8)	10	0.09
Filipino	6	0.06
Indian (2)	4	0.04
Japanese (2)	5	0.05
Korean (14)	15	0.14
Thai (8)	8	0.07
Vietnamese (1)	2	0.02
Other Asian, specified (1)	2	0.02
Other Asian, not specified (1)	6	0.06
Austrian	13	0.12
Belgian	9	0.08
British	32	0.30
Bulgarian	7	0.06
Canadian	11	0.10
Croatian	7	0.06
Czech	98	0.90
Czechoslovakian	33	0.30
Danish	45	0.42
Dutch	181	1.67
English	953	8.79
European	72	0.66
Finnish	9	0.08
French, except Basque	235	2.17
French Canadian	24	0.22
German	1,983	18.30
Greek	9	0.08
Hawaii Native/Pacific Islander:	14	0.13
Micronesian:	3	0.03
Guamanian/Chamorro	2	0.02
Other Micronesian	1	0.01
Polynesian: (1)	7	0.06
Native Hawaiian (1)	5	0.05
Samoan	1	0.01
Other Polynesian	1	0.01
Other Pac. Isl., specified	1	0.01
Other Pac. Isl., not spec. (3)	3	0.03
Hispanic or Latino:	201	1.85
Central American:	3	0.03
Nicaraguan	1	0.01
Panamanian	1	0.01
Salvadoran	1	0.01
Cuban	2	0.02
Dominican Republic	1	0.01
Mexican	156	1.44
Puerto Rican	11	0.10
South American:	1	0.01
Peruvian	1	0.01
Other Hispanic or Latino	27	0.25
Irish	1,191	10.99
Italian	329	3.04
Norwegian	117	1.08
Pennsylvania German	28	0.26
Polish	52	0.48
Russian	47	0.43
Scandinavian	13	0.12
Scotch-Irish	246	2.27
Scottish	281	2.59
Swedish	106	0.98
Swiss	7	0.06
United States or American	1,478	13.64
Welsh	133	1.23
West Indian, excl. Hispanic:	23	0.21
Barbadian	14	0.13
Belizean	9	0.08
White:	10,308	95.03
Not Hispanic (10,030)	10,188	93.92
Hispanic (89)	120	1.11

Farmington

Place Type: City
County: Saint Francois
Population: 13,924

Ancestry/Race	Number	%
African American/Black:	1,099	7.89
Not Hispanic (1,004)	1,074	7.71
Hispanic (21)	25	0.18
African, sub-Saharan:	61	0.44
African	54	0.39
Nigerian	7	0.05
Alaska Native tribes, specified:	1	0.01
Eskimo (1)	1	0.01
Am. Ind. or Alaska Nat., not spec.	54	0.39
American Indian tribes, specified:	119	0.85
Apache (3)	8	0.06
Blackfeet (4)	9	0.06
Cherokee (24)	67	0.48
Cheyenne	1	0.01

Notes: 1. Figures in the "Number" column do not add up to the total population due to: a) Ancestry/Race overlap — e.g. persons can report being both White and Irish, b) persons of Hispanic origin can report being any race, c) persons reporting two ancestries are counted in both categories. 2. Numbers in parentheses indicate the number of persons reporting this ancestry/race alone, not in combination with any other ancestry/race. 3. Refer to the Explanation of Data in the front of the book for more detailed information.

Ancestry/Race	Number	%
Chickasaw (1)	2	0.01
Chippewa (1)	1	0.01
Choctaw	2	0.01
Comanche	1	0.01
Cree	1	0.01
Creek (1)	1	0.01
Iroquois	1	0.01
Latin American Indians (1)	3	0.02
Navajo (1)	1	0.01
Osage	1	0.01
Potawatomi (1)	1	0.01
Sioux (2)	5	0.04
All other tribes (10)	14	0.10
American Indian tribes, not spec.	6	0.04
Arab:	28	0.20
Lebanese	10	0.07
Moroccan	18	0.13
Armenian	6	0.04
Asian:	144	1.03
Chinese, ex. Taiwanese (23)	26	0.19
Filipino (12)	16	0.11
Indian (25)	30	0.22
Japanese (4)	7	0.05
Korean (5)	6	0.04
Pakistani (5)	7	0.05
Sri Lankan (2)	2	0.01
Taiwanese	1	0.01
Thai (2)	2	0.01
Vietnamese (3)	4	0.03
Other Asian, not specified (21)	43	0.31
Assyrian/Chaldean/Syriac	6	0.04
Austrian	5	0.04
Belgian	10	0.07
British	5	0.04
Canadian	41	0.29
Czech	15	0.11
Czechoslovakian	16	0.12
Danish	13	0.09
Dutch	287	2.06
English	1,258	9.05
European	94	0.68
Finnish	13	0.09
French, except Basque	868	6.24
French Canadian	56	0.40
German	2,145	15.43
Greek	63	0.45
Hawaii Native/Pacific Islander:	6	0.04
Micronesian: (1)	2	0.01
Guamanian/Chamorro (1)	2	0.01
Polynesian: (1)	2	0.01
Native Hawaiian	1	0.01
Samoan (1)	1	0.01
Other Pac. Isl., not spec.	2	0.01
Hispanic or Latino:	161	1.16
Central American:	2	0.01
Salvadoran	2	0.01
Cuban	8	0.06
Dominican Republic	4	0.03
Mexican	90	0.65
Puerto Rican	8	0.06
South American:	1	0.01
Chilean	1	0.01
Other Hispanic or Latino	48	0.34
Hungarian	13	0.09
Irish	1,549	11.14
Israeli	14	0.10
Italian	266	1.91
Lithuanian	13	0.09
Northern European	9	0.06
Norwegian	16	0.12
Polish	99	0.71
Scotch-Irish	294	2.12
Scottish	121	0.87
Swedish	92	0.66
Swiss	26	0.19
United States or American	1,821	13.10
Welsh	48	0.35
White:	12,627	90.69
Not Hispanic (12,408)	12,533	90.01
Hispanic (86)	94	0.68
Yugoslavian	7	0.05

Ferguson

Place Type: City
County: Saint Louis
Population: 22,406

Ancestry/Race	Number	%
African American/Black:	11,994	53.53
Not Hispanic (11,718)	11,958	53.37
Hispanic (25)	36	0.16
African, sub-Saharan:	294	1.33
African	266	1.20
Ghanian	8	0.04
Nigerian	8	0.04
Senegalese	12	0.05
Am. Ind. or Alaska Nat., not spec.	86	0.38
American Indian tribes, specified:	71	0.32
Apache (1)	5	0.02
Blackfeet (2)	8	0.04
Cherokee (6)	35	0.16
Chippewa	3	0.01
Choctaw	4	0.02
Comanche	6	0.03
Creek	1	0.00
Crow	1	0.00
Latin American Indians	1	0.00
Navajo	1	0.00
Paiute	1	0.00
Pueblo (1)	1	0.00
Seminole	1	0.00
Sioux	3	0.01
American Indian tribes, not spec.	9	0.04
Arab:	19	0.09
Arab/Arabic	5	0.02
Palestinian	3	0.01
Other Arab	11	0.05
Armenian	15	0.07
Asian:	210	0.94
Chinese, ex. Taiwanese (45)	57	0.25
Filipino (13)	26	0.12
Indian (12)	22	0.10
Japanese (9)	21	0.09
Korean (6)	9	0.04
Laotian (6)	6	0.03
Pakistani	7	0.03
Taiwanese (2)	4	0.02
Thai (2)	3	0.01
Vietnamese (39)	43	0.19
Other Asian, specified	1	0.00
Other Asian, not specified (5)	11	0.05
Austrian	34	0.15
Belgian	7	0.03
British	50	0.23
Bulgarian	4	0.02
Canadian	16	0.07
Croatian	16	0.07
Czech	29	0.13
Czechoslovakian	21	0.10
Danish	44	0.20
Dutch	267	1.21
English	1,309	5.93
European	174	0.79
Finnish	61	0.28
French, except Basque	728	3.30
French Canadian	28	0.13
German	3,527	15.97
Greek	85	0.38
Guyanese	12	0.05
Hawaii Native/Pacific Islander:	10	0.04
Micronesian:	1	0.00
Guamanian/Chamorro	1	0.00
Polynesian: (2)	5	0.02
Native Hawaiian	1	0.00
Samoan (2)	4	0.02
Other Pac. Isl., specified	1	0.00
Other Pac. Isl., not spec. (2)	3	0.01
Hispanic or Latino:	228	1.02
Central American:	17	0.08
Costa Rican	2	0.01
Guatemalan	8	0.04
Honduran	4	0.02
Panamanian	3	0.01
Cuban	9	0.04
Dominican Republic	5	0.02
Mexican	127	0.57
Puerto Rican	23	0.10
South American:	8	0.04
Colombian	1	0.00
Peruvian	3	0.01
Venezuelan	4	0.02
Other Hispanic or Latino	39	0.17
Hungarian	77	0.35
Irish	1,903	8.61
Israeli	8	0.04
Italian	634	2.87
Latvian	6	0.03
Lithuanian	33	0.15
Northern European	7	0.03
Norwegian	51	0.23
Polish	369	1.67
Portuguese	14	0.06
Romanian	17	0.08
Russian	50	0.23
Scandinavian	7	0.03
Scotch-Irish	287	1.30
Scottish	193	0.87
Serbian	2	0.01
Slovak	13	0.06
Swedish	112	0.51
Swiss	66	0.30
Ukrainian	19	0.09
United States or American	700	3.17
Welsh	80	0.36
West Indian, excl. Hispanic:	19	0.09
Jamaican	14	0.06
West Indian	5	0.02
White:	10,304	45.99
Not Hispanic (9,903)	10,167	45.38
Hispanic (123)	137	0.61

Florissant

Place Type: City
County: Saint Louis
Population: 50,497

Ancestry/Race	Number	%
Acadian/Cajun	14	0.03
African American/Black:	6,136	12.15
Not Hispanic (5,775)	6,096	12.07
Hispanic (35)	40	0.08
African, sub-Saharan:	292	0.58
African	292	0.58
Alaska Native tribes, specified:	1	0.00
Aleut	1	0.00
Am. Ind. or Alaska Nat., not spec.	100	0.20
Albanian	7	0.01
Alsatian	8	0.02
American Indian tribes, specified:	222	0.44
Apache (1)	7	0.01
Blackfeet (2)	19	0.04
Cherokee (16)	111	0.22
Chickasaw (1)	1	0.00
Chippewa (3)	4	0.01
Choctaw (1)	4	0.01
Creek (1)	5	0.01
Delaware (2)	2	0.00
Iroquois (5)	8	0.02
Kiowa	1	0.00
Latin American Indians (6)	7	0.01
Menominee	1	0.00
Navajo (4)	9	0.02
Osage	4	0.01
Ottawa	1	0.00
Paiute (1)	1	0.00
Potawatomi	1	0.00
Pueblo (1)	4	0.01
Seminole (1)	3	0.01

Notes: 1. Figures in the "Number" column do not add up to the total population due to: a) Ancestry/Race overlap — e.g. persons can report being both White and Irish, b) persons of Hispanic origin can report being any race, c) persons reporting two ancestries are counted in both categories. 2. Numbers in parentheses indicate the number of persons reporting this ancestry/race alone, not in combination with any other ancestry/race. 3. Refer to the Explanation of Data in the front of the book for more detailed information.

Ancestry/Race	Number	%
Sioux (3)	8	0.02
All other tribes (10)	21	0.04
American Indian tribes, not spec.	6	0.01
Arab:	104	0.21
Arab/Arabic	7	0.01
Jordanian	7	0.01
Lebanese	52	0.10
Moroccan	11	0.02
Palestinian	20	0.04
Syrian	7	0.01
Armenian	24	0.05
Asian:	487	0.96
Chinese, ex. Taiwanese (50)	68	0.13
Filipino (58)	97	0.19
Indian (50)	62	0.12
Indonesian	2	0.00
Japanese (23)	61	0.12
Korean (30)	58	0.11
Malaysian (2)	3	0.01
Pakistani (8)	25	0.05
Taiwanese	1	0.00
Thai (20)	25	0.05
Vietnamese (51)	56	0.11
Other Asian, specified	1	0.00
Other Asian, not specified (8)	28	0.06
Austrian	173	0.34
Belgian	45	0.09
Brazilian	12	0.02
British	101	0.20
Canadian	70	0.14
Croatian	106	0.21
Czech	215	0.43
Czechoslovakian	57	0.11
Danish	117	0.23
Dutch	854	1.70
English	4,538	9.03
European	241	0.48
Finnish	34	0.07
French, except Basque	2,560	5.10
French Canadian	169	0.34
German	17,183	34.21
Greek	211	0.42
Hawaii Native/Pacific Islander:	36	0.07
Micronesian: (7)	7	0.01
Guamanian/Chamorro (5)	5	0.01
Other Micronesian (2)	2	0.00
Polynesian: (6)	18	0.04
Native Hawaiian (1)	11	0.02
Samoan (5)	7	0.01
Other Pac. Isl., specified	1	0.00
Other Pac. Isl., not spec. (2)	10	0.02
Hispanic or Latino:	753	1.49
Central American:	18	0.04
Costa Rican	2	0.00
Guatemalan	5	0.01
Honduran	7	0.01
Panamanian	4	0.01
Cuban	22	0.04
Dominican Republic	17	0.03
Mexican	390	0.77
Puerto Rican	72	0.14
South American:	43	0.09
Bolivian	9	0.02
Chilean	6	0.01
Colombian	12	0.02
Ecuadorian	4	0.01
Peruvian	4	0.01
Uruguayan	1	0.00
Venezuelan	3	0.01
Other South American	4	0.01
Other Hispanic or Latino	191	0.38
Hungarian	323	0.64
Iranian	40	0.08
Irish	10,207	20.32
Italian	3,599	7.17
Lithuanian	77	0.15
Maltese	9	0.02
Northern European	15	0.03
Norwegian	190	0.38
Pennsylvania German	22	0.04
Polish	2,401	4.78
Portuguese	28	0.06
Romanian	31	0.06
Russian	125	0.25
Scandinavian	20	0.04
Scotch-Irish	717	1.43
Scottish	676	1.35
Serbian	29	0.06
Slavic	15	0.03
Slovak	145	0.29
Slovene	6	0.01
Swedish	275	0.55
Swiss	292	0.58
Ukrainian	48	0.10
United States or American	2,847	5.67
Welsh	303	0.60
West Indian, excl. Hispanic:	17	0.03
Haitian	9	0.02
Trinidadian and Tobagonian	8	0.02
White:	43,878	86.89
Not Hispanic (42,807)	43,370	85.89
Hispanic (450)	508	1.01
Yugoslavian	53	0.11

Fort Leonard Wood

Place Type: Census Designated Place
County: Pulaski
Population: 13,666

Ancestry/Race	Number	%
Acadian/Cajun	28	0.20
African American/Black:	3,150	23.05
Not Hispanic (2,907)	3,052	22.33
Hispanic (43)	98	0.72
African, sub-Saharan:	138	1.01
African	110	0.80
Ghanian	11	0.08
Nigerian	17	0.12
Alaska Native tribes, specified:	7	0.05
Aleut (1)	2	0.01
Eskimo (1)	1	0.01
Tlingit-Haida (3)	3	0.02
All other tribes	1	0.01
Am. Ind. or Alaska Nat., not spec.	83	0.61
Albanian	7	0.05
American Indian tribes, specified:	174	1.27
Apache (1)	2	0.01
Blackfeet (6)	11	0.08
Cherokee (29)	64	0.47
Chickasaw	2	0.01
Chippewa (6)	12	0.09
Choctaw (7)	11	0.08
Colville (1)	1	0.01
Cree (1)	1	0.01
Creek (1)	4	0.03
Houma	1	0.01
Iroquois (2)	2	0.01
Latin American Indians (5)	5	0.04
Lumbee (1)	1	0.01
Menominee (2)	2	0.01
Navajo (12)	12	0.09
Osage	1	0.01
Pueblo (9)	10	0.07
Puget Sound Salish	1	0.01
Seminole	2	0.01
Shoshone (1)	1	0.01
Sioux (7)	9	0.07
Tohono O'Odham (2)	2	0.01
Yaqui	1	0.01
Yuman (1)	1	0.01
All other tribes (3)	15	0.11
American Indian tribes, not spec.	18	0.13
Arab:	29	0.21
Arab/Arabic	17	0.12
Lebanese	6	0.04
Other Arab	6	0.04
Asian:	513	3.75
Bangladeshi (1)	1	0.01
Cambodian (3)	3	0.02
Chinese, ex. Taiwanese (11)	41	0.30
Filipino (139)	199	1.46
Hmong (3)	3	0.02
Indian (19)	28	0.20
Indonesian	1	0.01
Japanese (10)	33	0.24
Korean (95)	138	1.01
Laotian (6)	7	0.05
Thai (10)	14	0.10
Vietnamese (9)	15	0.11
Other Asian, specified (3)	3	0.02
Other Asian, not specified (16)	27	0.20
Austrian	10	0.07
Belgian	17	0.12
British	65	0.48
Canadian	12	0.09
Celtic	7	0.05
Croatian	18	0.13
Czech	65	0.48
Czechoslovakian	8	0.06
Danish	23	0.17
Dutch	156	1.14
Eastern European	27	0.20
English	627	4.59
European	148	1.08
Finnish	59	0.43
French, except Basque	279	2.04
French Canadian	111	0.81
German	2,258	16.52
German Russian	12	0.09
Guyanese	12	0.09
Hawaii Native/Pacific Islander:	141	1.03
Micronesian: (26)	41	0.30
Guamanian/Chamorro (25)	40	0.29
Other Micronesian (1)	1	0.01
Polynesian: (32)	76	0.56
Native Hawaiian (14)	49	0.36
Samoan (11)	20	0.15
Tongan (2)	2	0.01
Other Polynesian (5)	5	0.04
Other Pac. Isl., not spec. (3)	24	0.18
Hispanic or Latino:	1,562	11.43
Central American:	105	0.77
Costa Rican	4	0.03
Guatemalan	6	0.04
Honduran	2	0.01
Nicaraguan	7	0.05
Panamanian	72	0.53
Salvadoran	9	0.07
Other Central American	5	0.04
Cuban	13	0.10
Dominican Republic	41	0.30
Mexican	695	5.09
Puerto Rican	414	3.03
South American:	78	0.57
Argentinean	1	0.01
Bolivian	4	0.03
Chilean	3	0.02
Colombian	26	0.19
Ecuadorian	12	0.09
Peruvian	22	0.16
Venezuelan	9	0.07
Other South American	1	0.01
Other Hispanic or Latino	216	1.58
Hungarian	48	0.35
Irish	1,409	10.31
Israeli	6	0.04
Italian	599	4.38
Lithuanian	15	0.11
Norwegian	173	1.27
Polish	248	1.81
Portuguese	117	0.86
Russian	27	0.20
Scotch-Irish	124	0.91
Scottish	266	1.95
Serbian	6	0.04
Slovak	27	0.20
Slovene	6	0.04
Swedish	59	0.43
Swiss	25	0.18

Notes: 1. Figures in the "Number" column do not add up to the total population due to: a) Ancestry/Race overlap — e.g. persons can report being both White and Irish, b) persons of Hispanic origin can report being any race, c) persons reporting two ancestries are counted in both categories. 2. Numbers in parentheses indicate the number of persons reporting this ancestry/race alone, not in combination with any other ancestry/race. 3. Refer to the Explanation of Data in the front of the book for more detailed information.

Turkish	14	0.10
Ukrainian	10	0.07
United States or American	1,037	7.59
Welsh	8	0.06
West Indian, excl. Hispanic:	104	0.76
Belizean	6	0.04
British West Indian	15	0.11
Jamaican	69	0.50
Trinidadian and Tobagonian	14	0.10
White:	9,350	68.42
Not Hispanic (8,204)	8,557	62.62
Hispanic (653)	793	5.80
Yugoslavian	8	0.06

Fulton

Place Type: City
County: Callaway
Population: 12,128

Ancestry/Race	Number	%
African American/Black:	1,949	16.07
Not Hispanic (1,871)	1,944	16.03
Hispanic (1)	5	0.04
African, sub-Saharan:	206	1.70
African	206	1.70
Alaska Native tribes, specified:	1	0.01
Eskimo (1)	1	0.01
Am. Ind. or Alaska Nat., not spec.	43	0.35
Albanian	7	0.06
American Indian tribes, specified:	75	0.62
Apache (2)	2	0.02
Blackfeet (1)	6	0.05
Cherokee (12)	37	0.31
Cheyenne (3)	4	0.03
Chickasaw	1	0.01
Chippewa (1)	2	0.02
Choctaw (1)	3	0.02
Iroquois (2)	2	0.02
Navajo (3)	4	0.03
Potawatomi	1	0.01
Seminole (1)	1	0.01
Sioux (5)	7	0.06
All other tribes (2)	5	0.04
American Indian tribes, not spec.	1	0.01
Asian:	164	1.35
Bangladeshi (4)	4	0.03
Chinese, ex. Taiwanese (37)	44	0.36
Filipino (7)	17	0.14
Indian (14)	17	0.14
Japanese (8)	15	0.12
Korean (7)	10	0.08
Pakistani (5)	5	0.04
Taiwanese (32)	36	0.30
Thai (1)	4	0.03
Vietnamese (2)	6	0.05
Other Asian, specified (3)	3	0.02
Other Asian, not specified (1)	3	0.02
Austrian	14	0.12
British	30	0.25
Canadian	7	0.06
Czech	21	0.17
Czechoslovakian	7	0.06
Danish	80	0.66
Dutch	189	1.56
English	1,180	9.76
European	87	0.72
French, except Basque	509	4.21
French Canadian	6	0.05
German	2,699	22.34
Greek	7	0.06
Hawaii Native/Pacific Islander:	19	0.16
Micronesian:	3	0.02
Guamanian/Chamorro	3	0.02
Polynesian: (3)	14	0.12
Native Hawaiian (3)	13	0.11
Samoan	1	0.01
Other Pac. Isl., not spec.	2	0.02
Hispanic or Latino:	132	1.09
Central American:	3	0.02
Costa Rican	1	0.01
Salvadoran	2	0.02
Cuban	8	0.07
Dominican Republic	1	0.01
Mexican	76	0.63
Puerto Rican	3	0.02
South American:	6	0.05
Argentinean	2	0.02
Peruvian	1	0.01
Venezuelan	2	0.02
Other South American	1	0.01
Other Hispanic or Latino	35	0.29
Irish	1,397	11.56
Italian	279	2.31
Lithuanian	26	0.22
Northern European	10	0.08
Norwegian	63	0.52
Polish	67	0.55
Russian	36	0.30
Scandinavian	18	0.15
Scotch-Irish	262	2.17
Scottish	142	1.18
Slavic	7	0.06
Slovak	19	0.16
Swedish	87	0.72
Swiss	18	0.15
Ukrainian	14	0.12
United States or American	1,097	9.08
Welsh	115	0.95
White:	10,002	82.47
Not Hispanic (9,781)	9,916	81.76
Hispanic (74)	86	0.71

Gladstone

Place Type: City
County: Clay
Population: 26,365

Ancestry/Race	Number	%
African American/Black:	620	2.35
Not Hispanic (533)	603	2.29
Hispanic (7)	17	0.06
African, sub-Saharan:	19	0.07
African	19	0.07
Am. Ind. or Alaska Nat., not spec.	72	0.27
American Indian tribes, specified:	220	0.83
Apache (3)	5	0.02
Blackfeet (1)	4	0.02
Cherokee (42)	106	0.40
Cheyenne	1	0.00
Chickasaw (1)	2	0.01
Chippewa (3)	3	0.01
Choctaw (10)	16	0.06
Comanche (1)	1	0.00
Creek (3)	5	0.02
Crow	1	0.00
Houma (1)	1	0.00
Iroquois (3)	5	0.02
Navajo (2)	2	0.01
Potawatomi (14)	18	0.07
Sioux (5)	12	0.05
All other tribes (18)	38	0.14
American Indian tribes, not spec.	12	0.05
Arab:	58	0.22
Arab/Arabic	13	0.05
Lebanese	22	0.08
Palestinian	14	0.05
Syrian	9	0.03
Armenian	7	0.03
Asian:	408	1.55
Bangladeshi (3)	3	0.01
Chinese, ex. Taiwanese (65)	72	0.27
Filipino (57)	71	0.27
Indian (36)	42	0.16
Indonesian	1	0.00
Japanese (12)	20	0.08
Korean (49)	58	0.22
Laotian	3	0.01
Malaysian (2)	3	0.01
Pakistani (16)	17	0.06
Sri Lankan (2)	2	0.01
Thai (4)	14	0.05
Vietnamese (76)	79	0.30
Other Asian, not specified (7)	23	0.09
Australian	4	0.02
Austrian	107	0.41
Belgian	91	0.35
British	165	0.63
Canadian	34	0.13
Croatian	49	0.19
Czech	127	0.48
Czechoslovakian	20	0.08
Danish	158	0.60
Dutch	730	2.77
English	3,617	13.73
European	264	1.00
French, except Basque	713	2.71
French Canadian	103	0.39
German	6,616	25.12
Greek	97	0.37
Hawaii Native/Pacific Islander:	73	0.28
Micronesian: (27)	43	0.16
Guamanian/Chamorro (2)	2	0.01
Other Micronesian (25)	41	0.16
Polynesian: (7)	16	0.06
Native Hawaiian (5)	10	0.04
Samoan (2)	4	0.02
Other Polynesian	2	0.01
Other Pac. Isl., not spec. (2)	14	0.05
Hispanic or Latino:	938	3.56
Central American:	20	0.08
Costa Rican	2	0.01
Guatemalan	4	0.02
Honduran	7	0.03
Nicaraguan	1	0.00
Panamanian	2	0.01
Salvadoran	4	0.02
Cuban	30	0.11
Dominican Republic	6	0.02
Mexican	642	2.44
Puerto Rican	39	0.15
South American:	21	0.08
Argentinean	9	0.03
Bolivian	2	0.01
Colombian	7	0.03
Ecuadorian	1	0.00
Venezuelan	1	0.00
Other South American	1	0.00
Other Hispanic or Latino	180	0.68
Hungarian	60	0.23
Iranian	25	0.09
Irish	4,498	17.08
Italian	1,847	7.01
Lithuanian	22	0.08
Luxemburger	6	0.02
Northern European	40	0.15
Norwegian	303	1.15
Pennsylvania German	55	0.21
Polish	280	1.06
Portuguese	25	0.09
Romanian	4	0.02
Russian	117	0.44
Scandinavian	36	0.14
Scotch-Irish	650	2.47
Scottish	649	2.46
Slavic	37	0.14
Slovak	39	0.15
Slovene	31	0.12
Swedish	702	2.67
Swiss	73	0.28
Ukrainian	27	0.10
United States or American	2,498	9.48
Welsh	198	0.75
West Indian, excl. Hispanic:	27	0.10
Jamaican	15	0.06
Trinidadian and Tobagonian	12	0.05
White:	24,979	94.74
Not Hispanic (24,018)	24,341	92.32
Hispanic (567)	638	2.42

Notes: 1. Figures in the "Number" column do not add up to the total population due to: a) Ancestry/Race overlap — e.g. persons can report being both White and Irish, b) persons of Hispanic origin can report being any race, c) persons reporting two ancestries are counted in both categories. 2. Numbers in parentheses indicate the number of persons reporting this ancestry/race alone, not in combination with any other ancestry/race. 3. Refer to the Explanation of Data in the front of the book for more detailed information.

Yugoslavian	39	0.15

Grandview

Place Type: City
County: Jackson
Population: 24,881

Ancestry/Race	Number	%
Acadian/Cajun	20	0.08
African American/Black:	8,763	35.22
Not Hispanic (8,295)	8,675	34.87
Hispanic (51)	88	0.35
African, sub-Saharan:	329	1.32
African	224	0.90
Kenyan	13	0.05
Liberian	79	0.32
Nigerian	13	0.05
Am. Ind. or Alaska Nat., not spec.	115	0.46
American Indian tribes, specified:	331	1.33
Apache (1)	7	0.03
Blackfeet (2)	37	0.15
Cherokee (30)	176	0.71
Chickasaw (2)	3	0.01
Chippewa (2)	5	0.02
Choctaw (3)	23	0.09
Comanche (1)	1	0.00
Creek	2	0.01
Iroquois (2)	5	0.02
Latin American Indians (10)	15	0.06
Lumbee (1)	1	0.00
Navajo	3	0.01
Osage	3	0.01
Ottawa (1)	1	0.00
Potawatomi (6)	6	0.02
Pueblo	2	0.01
Seminole (1)	2	0.01
Sioux (13)	18	0.07
Yaqui (1)	1	0.00
All other tribes (11)	20	0.08
American Indian tribes, not spec.	14	0.06
Arab:	53	0.21
Iraqi	21	0.08
Lebanese	19	0.08
Syrian	13	0.05
Asian:	373	1.50
Cambodian (9)	9	0.04
Chinese, ex. Taiwanese (27)	41	0.16
Filipino (72)	106	0.43
Indian (29)	35	0.14
Japanese (24)	42	0.17
Korean (41)	63	0.25
Laotian	1	0.00
Pakistani (14)	15	0.06
Thai (3)	7	0.03
Vietnamese (40)	45	0.18
Other Asian, specified (1)	1	0.00
Other Asian, not specified (1)	8	0.03
Austrian	45	0.18
Belgian	22	0.09
British	98	0.39
Canadian	36	0.14
Croatian	18	0.07
Czech	67	0.27
Czechoslovakian	9	0.04
Danish	113	0.45
Dutch	485	1.94
English	2,171	8.70
European	140	0.56
Finnish	33	0.13
French, except Basque	539	2.16
French Canadian	105	0.42
German	4,288	17.17
German Russian	8	0.03
Greek	55	0.22
Hawaii Native/Pacific Islander:	55	0.22
Micronesian: (3)	14	0.06
Guamanian/Chamorro (3)	14	0.06
Polynesian: (17)	24	0.10
Native Hawaiian (10)	14	0.06
Samoan (7)	9	0.04
Other Polynesian	1	0.00
Other Pac. Isl., not spec. (3)	17	0.07
Hispanic or Latino:	1,077	4.33
Central American:	94	0.38
Costa Rican	1	0.00
Guatemalan	7	0.03
Honduran	19	0.08
Nicaraguan	1	0.00
Panamanian	4	0.02
Salvadoran	56	0.23
Other Central American	6	0.02
Cuban	11	0.04
Dominican Republic	14	0.06
Mexican	714	2.87
Puerto Rican	67	0.27
South American:	10	0.04
Bolivian	1	0.00
Chilean	3	0.01
Colombian	4	0.02
Peruvian	1	0.00
Venezuelan	1	0.00
Other Hispanic or Latino	167	0.67
Hungarian	33	0.13
Irish	2,707	10.84
Italian	526	2.11
Latvian	8	0.03
Norwegian	175	0.70
Pennsylvania German	8	0.03
Polish	203	0.81
Portuguese	19	0.08
Russian	69	0.28
Scandinavian	19	0.08
Scotch-Irish	572	2.29
Scottish	361	1.45
Slavic	5	0.02
Slovak	27	0.11
Swedish	331	1.33
Swiss	81	0.32
United States or American	1,483	5.94
Welsh	138	0.55
West Indian, excl. Hispanic:	104	0.42
Dutch West Indian	16	0.06
Jamaican	59	0.24
West Indian	14	0.06
Other West Indian	15	0.06
White:	15,467	62.16
Not Hispanic (14,435)	14,952	60.09
Hispanic (447)	515	2.07
Yugoslavian	11	0.04

Hannibal

Place Type: City
County: Marion
Population: 17,757

Ancestry/Race	Number	%
Acadian/Cajun	5	0.03
African American/Black:	1,302	7.33
Not Hispanic (1,163)	1,292	7.28
Hispanic (4)	10	0.06
African, sub-Saharan:	48	0.27
African	48	0.27
Am. Ind. or Alaska Nat., not spec.	57	0.32
Albanian	13	0.07
American Indian tribes, specified:	118	0.66
Apache (3)	8	0.05
Blackfeet (4)	17	0.10
Cherokee (14)	72	0.41
Comanche	1	0.01
Creek (1)	2	0.01
Crow (1)	1	0.01
Iroquois	2	0.01
Pueblo	1	0.01
Sioux (1)	2	0.01
All other tribes (10)	13	0.07
American Indian tribes, not spec.	15	0.08
Arab:	6	0.03
Other Arab	6	0.03
Asian:	100	0.56
Chinese, ex. Taiwanese (13)	13	0.07
Filipino (22)	42	0.24
Indian (15)	21	0.12
Japanese (4)	6	0.03
Korean (7)	11	0.06
Vietnamese (2)	2	0.01
Other Asian, specified	2	0.01
Other Asian, not specified	3	0.02
Austrian	14	0.08
British	75	0.42
Canadian	5	0.03
Czech	26	0.15
Czechoslovakian	6	0.03
Danish	7	0.04
Dutch	324	1.81
Eastern European	14	0.08
English	1,912	10.66
European	140	0.78
French, except Basque	268	1.49
French Canadian	100	0.56
German	3,509	19.57
Greek	13	0.07
Hawaii Native/Pacific Islander:	21	0.12
Melanesian: (11)	11	0.06
Fijian (11)	11	0.06
Micronesian:	3	0.02
Guamanian/Chamorro	3	0.02
Polynesian:	1	0.01
Native Hawaiian	1	0.01
Other Pac. Isl., specified	1	0.01
Other Pac. Isl., not spec. (2)	5	0.03
Hispanic or Latino:	200	1.13
Central American:	12	0.07
Costa Rican	4	0.02
Nicaraguan	2	0.01
Panamanian	3	0.02
Salvadoran	2	0.01
Other Central American	1	0.01
Cuban	7	0.04
Dominican Republic	2	0.01
Mexican	109	0.61
Puerto Rican	6	0.03
South American:	2	0.01
Argentinean	1	0.01
Chilean	1	0.01
Other Hispanic or Latino	62	0.35
Hungarian	22	0.12
Irish	2,090	11.66
Italian	208	1.16
Latvian	11	0.06
Norwegian	54	0.30
Polish	85	0.47
Portuguese	19	0.11
Romanian	23	0.13
Russian	70	0.39
Scandinavian	54	0.30
Scotch-Irish	279	1.56
Scottish	185	1.03
Slovak	11	0.06
Swedish	221	1.23
Swiss	17	0.09
United States or American	3,053	17.03
Welsh	62	0.35
White:	16,387	92.28
Not Hispanic (15,978)	16,234	91.42
Hispanic (112)	153	0.86

Hazelwood

Place Type: City
County: Saint Louis
Population: 26,206

Ancestry/Race	Number	%
African American/Black:	4,412	16.84
Not Hispanic (4,188)	4,393	16.76
Hispanic (15)	19	0.07
African, sub-Saharan:	246	0.94
African	187	0.71

Notes: 1. Figures in the "Number" column do not add up to the total population due to: a) Ancestry/Race overlap — e.g. persons can report being both White and Irish, b) persons of Hispanic origin can report being any race, c) persons reporting two ancestries are counted in both categories. 2. Numbers in parentheses indicate the number of persons reporting this ancestry/race alone, not in combination with any other ancestry/race. 3. Refer to the Explanation of Data in the front of the book for more detailed information.

Ethiopian	6	0.02
Kenyan	41	0.16
Other sub-Saharan African	12	0.05
Am. Ind. or Alaska Nat., not spec.	56	0.21
Albanian	34	0.13
American Indian tribes, specified:	118	0.45
Apache	2	0.01
Blackfeet	3	0.01
Cherokee (15)	65	0.25
Chickasaw	1	0.00
Chippewa (1)	6	0.02
Choctaw (2)	3	0.01
Creek	3	0.01
Crow	2	0.01
Iroquois (1)	1	0.00
Latin American Indians (1)	1	0.00
Osage (1)	6	0.02
Ottawa	5	0.02
Pueblo (3)	3	0.01
Sioux	3	0.01
All other tribes (10)	14	0.05
American Indian tribes, not spec.	8	0.03
Arab:	208	0.79
Arab/Arabic	12	0.05
Jordanian	17	0.06
Lebanese	103	0.39
Moroccan	10	0.04
Palestinian	54	0.21
Other Arab	12	0.05
Armenian	32	0.12
Asian:	434	1.66
Bangladeshi (4)	4	0.02
Chinese, ex. Taiwanese (65)	77	0.29
Filipino (65)	95	0.36
Indian (63)	71	0.27
Japanese (17)	26	0.10
Korean (30)	40	0.15
Laotian (2)	2	0.01
Malaysian (2)	3	0.01
Pakistani (7)	12	0.05
Thai (4)	8	0.03
Vietnamese (44)	50	0.19
Other Asian, specified	1	0.00
Other Asian, not specified (7)	45	0.17
Austrian	84	0.32
Belgian	22	0.08
Brazilian	6	0.02
British	72	0.28
Canadian	8	0.03
Celtic	17	0.06
Croatian	63	0.24
Czech	134	0.51
Czechoslovakian	49	0.19
Danish	22	0.08
Dutch	394	1.51
Eastern European	7	0.03
English	2,179	8.33
European	118	0.45
Finnish	21	0.08
French, except Basque	1,209	4.62
French Canadian	83	0.32
German	7,875	30.09
German Russian	10	0.04
Greek	135	0.52
Hawaii Native/Pacific Islander:	27	0.10
Melanesian: (6)	6	0.02
Fijian (6)	6	0.02
Micronesian: (3)	4	0.02
Guamanian/Chamorro (1)	2	0.01
Other Micronesian (2)	2	0.01
Polynesian: (4)	8	0.03
Samoan (3)	6	0.02
Tongan (1)	2	0.01
Other Pac. Isl., not spec. (4)	9	0.03
Hispanic or Latino:	419	1.60
Central American:	17	0.06
Guatemalan	3	0.01
Honduran	10	0.04
Panamanian	3	0.01
Other Central American	1	0.00
Cuban	18	0.07
Dominican Republic	7	0.03
Mexican	270	1.03
Puerto Rican	27	0.10
South American:	7	0.03
Argentinean	1	0.00
Bolivian	1	0.00
Ecuadorian	3	0.01
Peruvian	2	0.01
Other Hispanic or Latino	73	0.28
Hungarian	177	0.68
Irish	4,638	17.72
Italian	1,608	6.14
Lithuanian	28	0.11
Macedonian	10	0.04
Norwegian	51	0.19
Polish	1,129	4.31
Portuguese	18	0.07
Romanian	3	0.01
Russian	146	0.56
Scandinavian	14	0.05
Scotch-Irish	409	1.56
Scottish	218	0.83
Slavic	14	0.05
Slovak	12	0.05
Swedish	125	0.48
Swiss	80	0.31
Ukrainian	6	0.02
United States or American	1,674	6.40
Welsh	62	0.24
West Indian, excl. Hispanic:	8	0.03
Haitian	8	0.03
White:	21,418	81.73
Not Hispanic (20,778)	21,138	80.66
Hispanic (249)	280	1.07

Independence

Place Type: City
County: Jackson
Population: 113,288

Ancestry/Race	Number	%
African American/Black:	3,631	3.21
Not Hispanic (2,874)	3,492	3.08
Hispanic (65)	139	0.12
African, sub-Saharan:	171	0.15
African	161	0.14
Nigerian	4	0.00
South African	6	0.01
Alaska Native tribes, specified:	12	0.01
Alaska Athabascan (1)	4	0.00
Aleut (4)	4	0.00
Eskimo (1)	1	0.00
Tlingit-Haida (2)	3	0.00
Alaska Native tribes, not specified	1	0.00
Am. Ind. or Alaska Nat., not spec.	418	0.37
American Indian tribes, specified:	1,461	1.29
Apache (9)	43	0.04
Blackfeet (8)	80	0.07
Cherokee (224)	696	0.61
Cheyenne (2)	12	0.01
Chickasaw (5)	11	0.01
Chippewa (22)	36	0.03
Choctaw (31)	72	0.06
Comanche	6	0.01
Cree (1)	3	0.00
Creek (13)	36	0.03
Crow (5)	5	0.00
Delaware (10)	20	0.02
Iroquois (4)	15	0.01
Kiowa (1)	3	0.00
Latin American Indians (22)	51	0.05
Lumbee (1)	3	0.00
Menominee (1)	1	0.00
Navajo (10)	24	0.02
Osage (6)	23	0.02
Ottawa (1)	4	0.00
Paiute (1)	4	0.00
Potawatomi (12)	20	0.02
Pueblo (4)	8	0.01
Puget Sound Salish (1)	1	0.00
Seminole (6)	20	0.02
Shoshone	4	0.00
Sioux (59)	106	0.09
Tohono O'Odham (3)	3	0.00
Ute (3)	6	0.01
Yakama	1	0.00
Yaqui	3	0.00
All other tribes (64)	141	0.12
American Indian tribes, not spec.	81	0.07
Arab:	302	0.27
Arab/Arabic	62	0.05
Jordanian	50	0.04
Lebanese	67	0.06
Syrian	70	0.06
Other Arab	53	0.05
Armenian	24	0.02
Asian:	1,138	1.00
Bangladeshi	2	0.00
Cambodian (10)	10	0.01
Chinese, ex. Taiwanese (130)	173	0.15
Filipino (199)	319	0.28
Indian (62)	87	0.08
Indonesian (4)	5	0.00
Japanese (48)	107	0.09
Korean (72)	100	0.09
Laotian (46)	53	0.05
Malaysian (1)	2	0.00
Pakistani (30)	37	0.03
Sri Lankan (6)	6	0.01
Taiwanese (9)	13	0.01
Thai (23)	34	0.03
Vietnamese (105)	120	0.11
Other Asian, specified (1)	6	0.01
Other Asian, not specified (30)	64	0.06
Australian	15	0.01
Austrian	244	0.22
Belgian	205	0.18
Brazilian	49	0.04
British	278	0.25
Bulgarian	24	0.02
Canadian	315	0.28
Celtic	18	0.02
Croatian	200	0.18
Czech	307	0.27
Czechoslovakian	186	0.16
Danish	648	0.57
Dutch	2,636	2.33
English	14,823	13.09
European	859	0.76
Finnish	64	0.06
French, except Basque	3,433	3.03
French Canadian	478	0.42
German	23,598	20.85
German Russian	5	0.00
Greek	247	0.22
Hawaii Native/Pacific Islander:	720	0.64
Melanesian:	1	0.00
Other Melanesian	1	0.00
Micronesian: (9)	19	0.02
Guamanian/Chamorro (5)	9	0.01
Other Micronesian (4)	10	0.01
Polynesian: (477)	665	0.59
Native Hawaiian (38)	86	0.08
Samoan (415)	536	0.47
Tongan (11)	21	0.02
Other Polynesian (13)	22	0.02
Other Pac. Isl., specified	2	0.00
Other Pac. Isl., not spec. (12)	33	0.03
Hispanic or Latino:	4,175	3.69
Central American:	228	0.20
Costa Rican	9	0.01
Guatemalan	38	0.03
Honduran	119	0.11
Nicaraguan	6	0.01
Panamanian	24	0.02
Salvadoran	20	0.02
Other Central American	12	0.01
Cuban	57	0.05

Notes: 1. Figures in the "Number" column do not add up to the total population due to: a) Ancestry/Race overlap — e.g. persons can report being both White and Irish, b) persons of Hispanic origin can report being any race, c) persons reporting two ancestries are counted in both categories. 2. Numbers in parentheses indicate the number of persons reporting this ancestry/race alone, not in combination with any other ancestry/race. 3. Refer to the Explanation of Data in the front of the book for more detailed information.

Dominican Republic	110	0.10
Mexican	2,882	2.54
Puerto Rican	185	0.16
South American:	82	0.07
Argentinean	14	0.01
Bolivian	2	0.00
Chilean	1	0.00
Colombian	27	0.02
Ecuadorian	12	0.01
Peruvian	3	0.00
Uruguayan	2	0.00
Venezuelan	14	0.01
Other South American	7	0.01
Other Hispanic or Latino	631	0.56
Hungarian	247	0.22
Iranian	40	0.04
Irish	15,468	13.66
Israeli	7	0.01
Italian	3,756	3.32
Latvian	9	0.01
Lithuanian	89	0.08
Luxemburger	14	0.01
Northern European	58	0.05
Norwegian	1,186	1.05
Pennsylvania German	28	0.02
Polish	1,355	1.20
Portuguese	29	0.03
Romanian	13	0.01
Russian	306	0.27
Scandinavian	166	0.15
Scotch-Irish	2,742	2.42
Scottish	1,995	1.76
Serbian	5	0.00
Slavic	137	0.12
Slovak	83	0.07
Slovene	21	0.02
Swedish	1,759	1.55
Swiss	289	0.26
Ukrainian	96	0.08
United States or American	11,544	10.20
Welsh	1,181	1.04
West Indian, excl. Hispanic:	27	0.02
Barbadian	9	0.01
Belizean	6	0.01
Dutch West Indian	7	0.01
Jamaican	5	0.00
White:	106,517	94.02
Not Hispanic (102,040)	104,073	91.87
Hispanic (2,041)	2,444	2.16
Yugoslavian	93	0.08

Jackson

Place Type: City
County: Cape Girardeau
Population: 11,947

Ancestry/Race	Number	%
African American/Black:	183	1.53
Not Hispanic (159)	180	1.51
Hispanic (3)	3	0.03
African, sub-Saharan:	7	0.06
African	7	0.06
Am. Ind. or Alaska Nat., not spec.	29	0.24
American Indian tribes, specified:	64	0.54
Apache	3	0.03
Cherokee (11)	50	0.42
Chickasaw (1)	1	0.01
Chippewa	1	0.01
Creek (1)	1	0.01
Iroquois	1	0.01
Latin American Indians (1)	1	0.01
Lumbee	3	0.03
Menominee	1	0.01
Navajo (1)	1	0.01
Sioux (1)	1	0.01
American Indian tribes, not spec.	4	0.03
Arab:	10	0.08
Lebanese	10	0.08
Asian:	100	0.84
Chinese, ex. Taiwanese (10)	11	0.09
Filipino (13)	29	0.24
Indian (17)	22	0.18
Japanese (2)	7	0.06
Korean (9)	15	0.13
Pakistani (3)	3	0.03
Sri Lankan (1)	1	0.01
Taiwanese (1)	1	0.01
Thai (8)	8	0.07
Vietnamese (1)	1	0.01
Other Asian, not specified (2)	2	0.02
Austrian	48	0.41
British	5	0.04
Canadian	15	0.13
Czech	38	0.32
Czechoslovakian	7	0.06
Danish	32	0.27
Dutch	262	2.22
English	866	7.33
European	40	0.34
French, except Basque	449	3.80
French Canadian	26	0.22
German	3,933	33.29
Hawaii Native/Pacific Islander:	13	0.11
Micronesian: (2)	11	0.09
Guamanian/Chamorro (1)	8	0.07
Other Micronesian (1)	3	0.03
Polynesian: (1)	2	0.02
Native Hawaiian (1)	1	0.01
Samoan	1	0.01
Hispanic or Latino:	91	0.76
Central American:	2	0.02
Salvadoran	2	0.02
Mexican	45	0.38
Puerto Rican	4	0.03
South American:	3	0.03
Colombian	2	0.02
Peruvian	1	0.01
Other Hispanic or Latino	37	0.31
Hungarian	39	0.33
Irish	1,039	8.79
Italian	204	1.73
Lithuanian	8	0.07
Northern European	32	0.27
Norwegian	60	0.51
Polish	195	1.65
Scotch-Irish	105	0.89
Scottish	150	1.27
Slovak	6	0.05
Swedish	58	0.49
Turkish	11	0.09
United States or American	1,613	13.65
Welsh	19	0.16
White:	11,645	97.47
Not Hispanic (11,481)	11,583	96.95
Hispanic (56)	62	0.52

Jefferson City

Place Type: City
County: Cole
Population: 39,636

Ancestry/Race	Number	%
African American/Black:	6,093	15.37
Not Hispanic (5,807)	6,060	15.29
Hispanic (21)	33	0.08
African, sub-Saharan:	523	1.32
African	444	1.12
Ethiopian	12	0.03
Nigerian	55	0.14
Sierra Leonean	12	0.03
Alaska Native tribes, not specified	2	0.01
Am. Ind. or Alaska Nat., not spec.	92	0.23
American Indian tribes, specified:	292	0.74
Apache (5)	13	0.03
Blackfeet (3)	23	0.06
Cherokee (56)	159	0.40
Cheyenne (1)	1	0.00
Chickasaw	4	0.01
Chippewa (6)	7	0.02
Choctaw (5)	13	0.03
Comanche (3)	3	0.01
Cree (1)	1	0.00
Creek (1)	7	0.02
Iroquois	1	0.00
Latin American Indians (3)	4	0.01
Lumbee (3)	4	0.01
Navajo	2	0.01
Osage (2)	4	0.01
Paiute (1)	1	0.00
Pueblo (1)	2	0.01
Sioux (6)	15	0.04
All other tribes (12)	28	0.07
American Indian tribes, not spec.	17	0.04
Arab:	93	0.24
Moroccan	93	0.24
Asian:	648	1.63
Bangladeshi (1)	1	0.00
Cambodian (7)	12	0.03
Chinese, ex. Taiwanese (81)	106	0.27
Filipino (47)	70	0.18
Indian (237)	258	0.65
Indonesian (3)	3	0.01
Japanese (23)	39	0.10
Korean (24)	43	0.11
Malaysian (1)	4	0.01
Pakistani (1)	1	0.00
Taiwanese (3)	7	0.02
Thai (2)	5	0.01
Vietnamese (24)	27	0.07
Other Asian, specified (4)	5	0.01
Other Asian, not specified (23)	67	0.17
Austrian	9	0.02
Belgian	23	0.06
British	114	0.29
Canadian	37	0.09
Celtic	12	0.03
Croatian	42	0.11
Czech	66	0.17
Czechoslovakian	41	0.10
Danish	110	0.28
Dutch	543	1.37
Eastern European	7	0.02
English	3,951	10.00
European	362	0.92
Finnish	26	0.07
French, except Basque	1,424	3.60
French Canadian	83	0.21
German	12,397	31.37
Greek	32	0.08
Guyanese	7	0.02
Hawaii Native/Pacific Islander:	45	0.11
Micronesian: (7)	8	0.02
Guamanian/Chamorro (7)	8	0.02
Polynesian: (11)	24	0.06
Native Hawaiian (4)	11	0.03
Samoan (7)	13	0.03
Other Pac. Isl., specified	1	0.00
Other Pac. Isl., not spec. (2)	12	0.03
Hispanic or Latino:	616	1.55
Central American:	35	0.09
Costa Rican	3	0.01
Guatemalan	1	0.00
Honduran	6	0.02
Nicaraguan	14	0.04
Panamanian	3	0.01
Salvadoran	7	0.02
Other Central American	1	0.00
Cuban	33	0.08
Dominican Republic	5	0.01
Mexican	360	0.91
Puerto Rican	23	0.06
South American:	14	0.04
Colombian	7	0.02
Ecuadorian	2	0.01
Peruvian	4	0.01
Venezuelan	1	0.00
Other Hispanic or Latino	146	0.37
Hungarian	60	0.15

Notes: 1. Figures in the "Number" column do not add up to the total population due to: a) Ancestry/Race overlap — e.g. persons can report being both White and Irish, b) persons of Hispanic origin can report being any race, c) persons reporting two ancestries are counted in both categories. 2. Numbers in parentheses indicate the number of persons reporting this ancestry/race alone, not in combination with any other ancestry/race. 3. Refer to the Explanation of Data in the front of the book for more detailed information.

Ancestry/Race	Number	%
Iranian	65	0.16
Irish	3,991	10.10
Italian	742	1.88
Latvian	9	0.02
Lithuanian	31	0.08
Luxemburger	25	0.06
Northern European	10	0.03
Norwegian	392	0.99
Pennsylvania German	6	0.02
Polish	406	1.03
Portuguese	16	0.04
Romanian	16	0.04
Russian	73	0.18
Scandinavian	78	0.20
Scotch-Irish	521	1.32
Scottish	794	2.01
Serbian	10	0.03
Slavic	9	0.02
Slovak	34	0.09
Slovene	6	0.02
Swedish	275	0.70
Swiss	242	0.61
Ukrainian	30	0.08
United States or American	3,714	9.40
Welsh	280	0.71
West Indian, excl. Hispanic:	81	0.20
Bahamian	26	0.07
Jamaican	36	0.09
Trinidadian and Tobagonian	11	0.03
West Indian	8	0.02
White:	32,769	82.67
Not Hispanic (31,997)	32,417	81.79
Hispanic (306)	352	0.89
Yugoslavian	32	0.08

Jennings

Place Type: City
County: Saint Louis
Population: 15,469

Ancestry/Race	Number	%
African American/Black:	12,326	79.68
Not Hispanic (12,099)	12,261	79.26
Hispanic (56)	65	0.42
African, sub-Saharan:	281	1.82
African	279	1.80
Nigerian	2	0.01
Am. Ind. or Alaska Nat., not spec.	42	0.27
American Indian tribes, specified:	42	0.27
Blackfeet	1	0.01
Cherokee (12)	36	0.23
Chippewa	1	0.01
Choctaw	1	0.01
Creek (1)	1	0.01
Pueblo	1	0.01
Sioux	1	0.01
American Indian tribes, not spec.	2	0.01
Arab:	8	0.05
Arab/Arabic	8	0.05
Asian:	95	0.61
Chinese, ex. Taiwanese (15)	20	0.13
Filipino (8)	18	0.12
Indian (2)	14	0.09
Japanese (3)	3	0.02
Thai (4)	4	0.03
Vietnamese (21)	28	0.18
Other Asian, specified	1	0.01
Other Asian, not specified (2)	7	0.05
Canadian	11	0.07
Croatian	14	0.09
Czech	26	0.17
Czechoslovakian	10	0.06
Danish	2	0.01
Dutch	45	0.29
English	242	1.56
European	17	0.11
French, except Basque	83	0.54
French Canadian	14	0.09
German	1,256	8.12
German Russian	57	0.37
Greek	6	0.04
Hawaii Native/Pacific Islander:	6	0.04
Micronesian: (1)	1	0.01
Guamanian/Chamorro (1)	1	0.01
Polynesian:	1	0.01
Native Hawaiian	1	0.01
Other Pac. Isl., specified	1	0.01
Other Pac. Isl., not spec. (3)	3	0.02
Hispanic or Latino:	113	0.73
Central American:	4	0.03
Honduran	4	0.03
Mexican	52	0.34
Puerto Rican	16	0.10
Other Hispanic or Latino	41	0.27
Hungarian	3	0.02
Iranian	6	0.04
Irish	880	5.69
Italian	219	1.42
Latvian	9	0.06
Lithuanian	8	0.05
Norwegian	16	0.10
Polish	85	0.55
Russian	22	0.14
Scotch-Irish	151	0.98
Scottish	88	0.57
Swedish	21	0.14
Swiss	22	0.14
Ukrainian	8	0.05
United States or American	333	2.15
Welsh	4	0.03
West Indian, excl. Hispanic:	6	0.04
West Indian	6	0.04
White:	3,117	20.15
Not Hispanic (2,955)	3,081	19.92
Hispanic (33)	36	0.23
Yugoslavian	7	0.05

Joplin

Place Type: City
County: Jasper
Population: 45,504

Ancestry/Race	Number	%
Acadian/Cajun	7	0.02
African American/Black:	1,516	3.33
Not Hispanic (1,190)	1,476	3.24
Hispanic (27)	40	0.09
African, sub-Saharan:	59	0.13
African	59	0.13
Alaska Native tribes, specified:	5	0.01
Aleut (1)	3	0.01
Tlingit-Haida	2	0.00
Alaska Native tribes, not specified	1	0.00
Am. Ind. or Alaska Nat., not spec.	245	0.54
American Indian tribes, specified:	1,148	2.52
Apache (8)	23	0.05
Blackfeet	25	0.05
Cherokee (294)	624	1.37
Cheyenne (2)	2	0.00
Chickasaw (9)	13	0.03
Chippewa (3)	6	0.01
Choctaw (33)	61	0.13
Comanche (3)	7	0.02
Creek (12)	31	0.07
Crow	1	0.00
Delaware (9)	25	0.05
Iroquois (41)	67	0.15
Kiowa (2)	7	0.02
Latin American Indians (7)	8	0.02
Lumbee (1)	2	0.00
Navajo (7)	12	0.03
Osage (12)	36	0.08
Ottawa (11)	14	0.03
Potawatomi (6)	8	0.02
Pueblo (2)	3	0.01
Seminole (3)	6	0.01
Shoshone (5)	7	0.02
Sioux (7)	24	0.05
All other tribes (90)	136	0.30
American Indian tribes, not spec.	28	0.06
Arab:	147	0.32
Arab/Arabic	8	0.02
Egyptian	4	0.01
Lebanese	71	0.16
Palestinian	21	0.05
Syrian	43	0.09
Asian:	445	0.98
Cambodian (1)	1	0.00
Chinese, ex. Taiwanese (39)	50	0.11
Filipino (58)	93	0.20
Indian (72)	81	0.18
Japanese (19)	36	0.08
Korean (25)	36	0.08
Pakistani (9)	9	0.02
Sri Lankan (1)	2	0.00
Taiwanese	3	0.01
Thai (5)	6	0.01
Vietnamese (100)	105	0.23
Other Asian, specified	1	0.00
Other Asian, not specified (5)	22	0.05
Austrian	49	0.11
Basque	14	0.03
Belgian	16	0.04
British	149	0.33
Bulgarian	6	0.01
Canadian	58	0.13
Celtic	21	0.05
Croatian	59	0.13
Czech	84	0.18
Czechoslovakian	22	0.05
Danish	98	0.22
Dutch	1,091	2.39
English	4,412	9.68
European	306	0.67
Finnish	25	0.05
French, except Basque	1,289	2.83
French Canadian	104	0.23
German	7,802	17.12
Greek	102	0.22
Hawaii Native/Pacific Islander:	51	0.11
Melanesian: (1)	1	0.00
Other Melanesian (1)	1	0.00
Micronesian: (7)	15	0.03
Guamanian/Chamorro (4)	9	0.02
Other Micronesian (3)	6	0.01
Polynesian: (7)	26	0.06
Native Hawaiian (4)	21	0.05
Samoan (2)	3	0.01
Other Polynesian (1)	2	0.00
Other Pac. Isl., not spec. (2)	9	0.02
Hispanic or Latino:	1,144	2.51
Central American:	35	0.08
Guatemalan	16	0.04
Honduran	10	0.02
Panamanian	3	0.01
Salvadoran	6	0.01
Cuban	14	0.03
Mexican	723	1.59
Puerto Rican	146	0.32
South American:	25	0.05
Argentinean	2	0.00
Chilean	2	0.00
Colombian	8	0.02
Ecuadorian	3	0.01
Peruvian	7	0.02
Venezuelan	1	0.00
Other South American	2	0.00
Other Hispanic or Latino	201	0.44
Hungarian	59	0.13
Irish	5,478	12.02
Israeli	8	0.02
Italian	1,039	2.28
Lithuanian	4	0.01
Luxemburger	12	0.03
Macedonian	20	0.04
Northern European	1	0.00
Norwegian	576	1.26
Pennsylvania German	48	0.11

Notes: 1. Figures in the "Number" column do not add up to the total population due to: a) Ancestry/Race overlap — e.g. persons can report being both White and Irish, b) persons of Hispanic origin can report being any race, c) persons reporting two ancestries are counted in both categories. 2. Numbers in parentheses indicate the number of persons reporting this ancestry/race alone, not in combination with any other ancestry/race. 3. Refer to the Explanation of Data in the front of the book for more detailed information.

Polish	458	1.01
Portuguese	59	0.13
Romanian	44	0.10
Russian	208	0.46
Scandinavian	57	0.13
Scotch-Irish	1,208	2.65
Scottish	842	1.85
Serbian	39	0.09
Slavic	5	0.01
Slovak	27	0.06
Slovene	17	0.04
Swedish	549	1.20
Swiss	103	0.23
Ukrainian	62	0.14
United States or American	5,749	12.62
Welsh	311	0.68
West Indian, excl. Hispanic:	42	0.09
Dutch West Indian	33	0.07
Haitian	8	0.02
Jamaican	1	0.00
White:	42,721	93.88
Not Hispanic (41,058)	42,053	92.42
Hispanic (551)	668	1.47
Yugoslavian	2	0.00

Kansas City

Place Type: City
County: Jackson
Population: 441,545

Ancestry/Race	Number	%
Acadian/Cajun	59	0.01
Afghan	35	0.01
African American/Black:	142,621	32.30
Not Hispanic (136,921)	141,182	31.97
Hispanic (958)	1,439	0.33
African, sub-Saharan:	5,177	1.17
African	3,403	0.77
Cape Verdean	29	0.01
Ethiopian	351	0.08
Ghanian	56	0.01
Kenyan	132	0.03
Liberian	65	0.01
Nigerian	358	0.08
Senegalese	53	0.01
Sierra Leonean	29	0.01
Somalian	456	0.10
South African	65	0.01
Sudanese	111	0.03
Ugandan	8	0.00
Other sub-Saharan African	61	0.01
Alaska Native tribes, specified:	22	0.00
Alaska Athabascan (3)	4	0.00
Aleut (6)	7	0.00
Eskimo (4)	6	0.00
Tlingit-Haida (2)	4	0.00
All other tribes	1	0.00
Alaska Native tribes, not specified	1	0.00
Am. Ind. or Alaska Nat., not spec.	1,800	0.41
Albanian	27	0.01
Alsatian	24	0.01
American Indian tribes, specified:	3,506	0.79
Apache (38)	90	0.02
Blackfeet (34)	223	0.05
Cherokee (461)	1,550	0.35
Cheyenne (10)	23	0.01
Chickasaw (21)	67	0.02
Chippewa (22)	57	0.01
Choctaw (78)	200	0.05
Colville (2)	2	0.00
Comanche (8)	21	0.00
Cree (1)	11	0.00
Creek (56)	131	0.03
Crow (4)	12	0.00
Delaware (17)	47	0.01
Iroquois (34)	68	0.02
Kiowa (20)	38	0.01
Latin American Indians (95)	144	0.03
Lumbee (2)	2	0.00
Menominee (4)	6	0.00
Navajo (29)	57	0.01
Osage (20)	52	0.01
Ottawa (3)	5	0.00
Paiute	1	0.00
Pima (1)	1	0.00
Potawatomi (79)	116	0.03
Pueblo (18)	30	0.01
Puget Sound Salish (2)	4	0.00
Seminole (21)	45	0.01
Shoshone (3)	9	0.00
Sioux (81)	187	0.04
Tohono O'Odham (9)	9	0.00
Ute (4)	4	0.00
Yakama (1)	1	0.00
Yaqui (6)	11	0.00
Yuman	1	0.00
All other tribes (147)	281	0.06
American Indian tribes, not spec.	251	0.06
Arab:	1,545	0.35
Arab/Arabic	342	0.08
Egyptian	64	0.01
Iraqi	84	0.02
Jordanian	74	0.02
Lebanese	573	0.13
Moroccan	126	0.03
Palestinian	77	0.02
Syrian	115	0.03
Other Arab	90	0.02
Armenian	106	0.02
Asian:	10,251	2.32
Bangladeshi (9)	14	0.00
Cambodian (238)	318	0.07
Chinese, ex. Taiwanese (962)	1,175	0.27
Filipino (1,006)	1,405	0.32
Hmong (4)	4	0.00
Indian (1,035)	1,271	0.29
Indonesian (29)	44	0.01
Japanese (295)	558	0.13
Korean (569)	760	0.17
Laotian (102)	135	0.03
Malaysian (48)	70	0.02
Pakistani (129)	195	0.04
Sri Lankan (10)	13	0.00
Taiwanese (68)	80	0.02
Thai (142)	192	0.04
Vietnamese (3,192)	3,386	0.77
Other Asian, specified (11)	48	0.01
Other Asian, not specified (177)	583	0.13
Assyrian/Chaldean/Syriac	8	0.00
Australian	124	0.03
Austrian	691	0.16
Belgian	759	0.17
Brazilian	40	0.01
British	1,420	0.32
Bulgarian	67	0.02
Canadian	638	0.14
Celtic	65	0.01
Croatian	827	0.19
Czech	1,553	0.35
Czechoslovakian	445	0.10
Danish	1,794	0.41
Dutch	5,678	1.29
Eastern European	137	0.03
English	35,525	8.05
Estonian	29	0.01
European	2,891	0.66
Finnish	275	0.06
French, except Basque	9,441	2.14
French Canadian	1,174	0.27
German	67,780	15.36
German Russian	74	0.02
Greek	851	0.19
Guyanese	6	0.00
Hawaii Native/Pacific Islander:	942	0.21
Melanesian: (1)	3	0.00
Fijian (1)	1	0.00
Other Melanesian	2	0.00
Micronesian: (171)	199	0.05
Guamanian/Chamorro (53)	69	0.02
Other Micronesian (118)	130	0.03
Polynesian: (251)	490	0.11
Native Hawaiian (75)	197	0.04
Samoan (172)	265	0.06
Tongan (1)	1	0.00
Other Polynesian (3)	27	0.01
Other Pac. Isl., specified	30	0.01
Other Pac. Isl., not spec. (66)	220	0.05
Hispanic or Latino:	30,604	6.93
Central American:	929	0.21
Costa Rican	32	0.01
Guatemalan	187	0.04
Honduran	295	0.07
Nicaraguan	25	0.01
Panamanian	56	0.01
Salvadoran	273	0.06
Other Central American	61	0.01
Cuban	787	0.18
Dominican Republic	97	0.02
Mexican	24,042	5.44
Puerto Rican	740	0.17
South American:	527	0.12
Argentinean	24	0.01
Bolivian	16	0.00
Chilean	51	0.01
Colombian	165	0.04
Ecuadorian	85	0.02
Paraguayan	6	0.00
Peruvian	59	0.01
Uruguayan	4	0.00
Venezuelan	76	0.02
Other South American	41	0.01
Other Hispanic or Latino	3,482	0.79
Hungarian	806	0.18
Icelander	17	0.00
Iranian	425	0.10
Irish	45,655	10.35
Israeli	56	0.01
Italian	15,818	3.58
Latvian	69	0.02
Lithuanian	377	0.09
Luxemburger	35	0.01
Macedonian	9	0.00
Maltese	11	0.00
New Zealander	9	0.00
Northern European	423	0.10
Norwegian	3,462	0.78
Pennsylvania German	167	0.04
Polish	5,995	1.36
Portuguese	264	0.06
Romanian	177	0.04
Russian	1,840	0.42
Scandinavian	329	0.07
Scotch-Irish	6,904	1.56
Scottish	6,667	1.51
Serbian	190	0.04
Slavic	148	0.03
Slovak	187	0.04
Slovene	103	0.02
Soviet Union	10	0.00
Swedish	5,368	1.22
Swiss	1,554	0.35
Turkish	114	0.03
Ukrainian	430	0.10
United States or American	25,807	5.85
Welsh	3,001	0.68
West Indian, excl. Hispanic:	1,189	0.27
Bahamian	9	0.00
Barbadian	34	0.01
Belizean	52	0.01
British West Indian	3	0.00
Dutch West Indian	14	0.00
Haitian	481	0.11
Jamaican	510	0.12
Trinidadian and Tobagonian	5	0.00
U.S. Virgin Islander	18	0.00
West Indian	52	0.01
Other West Indian	11	0.00
White:	276,006	62.51
Not Hispanic (254,471)	260,692	59.04

Notes: 1. Figures in the "Number" column do not add up to the total population due to: a) Ancestry/Race overlap — e.g. persons can report being both White and Irish, b) persons of Hispanic origin can report being any race, c) persons reporting two ancestries are counted in both categories. 2. Numbers in parentheses indicate the number of persons reporting this ancestry/race alone, not in combination with any other ancestry/race. 3. Refer to the Explanation of Data in the front of the book for more detailed information.

Hispanic (13,460)	15,314	3.47
Yugoslavian	297	0.07

Kennett

Place Type: City
County: Dunklin
Population: 11,260

Ancestry/Race	Number	%
African American/Black:	1,544	13.71
Not Hispanic (1,491)	1,541	13.69
Hispanic (3)	3	0.03
African, sub-Saharan:	129	1.14
African	129	1.14
Am. Ind. or Alaska Nat., not spec.	33	0.29
American Indian tribes, specified:	46	0.41
Apache (3)	5	0.04
Blackfeet (1)	1	0.01
Cherokee (8)	29	0.26
Chippewa (1)	1	0.01
Choctaw (3)	6	0.05
Creek	1	0.01
Potawatomi (1)	1	0.01
Sioux (2)	2	0.02
American Indian tribes, not spec.	4	0.04
Asian:	69	0.61
Chinese, ex. Taiwanese	3	0.03
Filipino (24)	25	0.22
Indian (16)	21	0.19
Japanese (2)	4	0.04
Korean (1)	1	0.01
Taiwanese (3)	3	0.03
Thai (8)	8	0.07
Vietnamese (4)	4	0.04
British	5	0.04
Danish	6	0.05
Dutch	147	1.30
English	694	6.16
European	11	0.10
Finnish	17	0.15
French, except Basque	198	1.76
French Canadian	6	0.05
German	793	7.04
Greek	6	0.05
Hawaii Native/Pacific Islander:	1	0.01
Micronesian: (1)	1	0.01
Guamanian/Chamorro (1)	1	0.01
Hispanic or Latino:	202	1.79
Mexican	166	1.47
Puerto Rican	10	0.09
Other Hispanic or Latino	26	0.23
Irish	1,270	11.27
Italian	16	0.14
Norwegian	30	0.27
Polish	47	0.42
Russian	5	0.04
Scotch-Irish	75	0.67
Scottish	90	0.80
Slavic	5	0.04
United States or American	2,578	22.87
Welsh	13	0.12
White:	9,636	85.58
Not Hispanic (9,368)	9,477	84.17
Hispanic (140)	159	1.41

Kirksville

Place Type: City
County: Adair
Population: 16,988

Ancestry/Race	Number	%
African American/Black:	338	1.99
Not Hispanic (286)	328	1.93
Hispanic (8)	10	0.06
African, sub-Saharan:	28	0.17
African	11	0.07
Nigerian	9	0.05
South African	8	0.05
Alaska Native tribes, specified:	1	0.01
Eskimo (1)	1	0.01
Am. Ind. or Alaska Nat., not spec.	16	0.09
American Indian tribes, specified:	86	0.51
Apache (1)	4	0.02
Blackfeet (1)	4	0.02
Cherokee (24)	52	0.31
Cheyenne	1	0.01
Chickasaw	1	0.01
Chippewa (1)	1	0.01
Choctaw (1)	5	0.03
Creek	1	0.01
Latin American Indians (2)	3	0.02
Osage (1)	3	0.02
Paiute (1)	1	0.01
Sioux (1)	6	0.04
All other tribes	4	0.02
American Indian tribes, not spec.	4	0.02
Arab:	22	0.13
Egyptian	11	0.07
Lebanese	11	0.07
Asian:	399	2.35
Bangladeshi (2)	3	0.02
Cambodian (1)	1	0.01
Chinese, ex. Taiwanese (100)	114	0.67
Filipino (29)	40	0.24
Hmong (1)	1	0.01
Indian (77)	89	0.52
Japanese (30)	44	0.26
Korean (36)	40	0.24
Laotian (1)	2	0.01
Pakistani (5)	5	0.03
Sri Lankan (9)	10	0.06
Taiwanese (10)	10	0.06
Thai (1)	1	0.01
Vietnamese (18)	21	0.12
Other Asian, specified (1)	2	0.01
Other Asian, not specified (5)	16	0.09
Australian	9	0.05
Austrian	57	0.34
Belgian	26	0.15
British	68	0.40
Bulgarian	20	0.12
Canadian	24	0.14
Croatian	73	0.43
Czech	69	0.41
Czechoslovakian	43	0.25
Danish	80	0.47
Dutch	350	2.07
Eastern European	8	0.05
English	2,076	12.28
European	148	0.88
Finnish	44	0.26
French, except Basque	527	3.12
French Canadian	54	0.32
German	4,459	26.38
Greek	87	0.51
Hawaii Native/Pacific Islander:	14	0.08
Polynesian: (4)	7	0.04
Native Hawaiian (3)	4	0.02
Samoan	1	0.01
Tongan (1)	2	0.01
Other Pac. Isl., not spec. (3)	7	0.04
Hispanic or Latino:	262	1.54
Central American:	13	0.08
Costa Rican	5	0.03
Guatemalan	2	0.01
Honduran	2	0.01
Nicaraguan	1	0.01
Panamanian	2	0.01
Other Central American	1	0.01
Cuban	9	0.05
Dominican Republic	3	0.02
Mexican	142	0.84
Puerto Rican	21	0.12
South American:	25	0.15
Argentinean	12	0.07
Bolivian	1	0.01
Chilean	2	0.01
Colombian	2	0.01
Ecuadorian	6	0.04
Peruvian	1	0.01
Other South American	1	0.01
Other Hispanic or Latino	49	0.29
Hungarian	71	0.42
Icelander	7	0.04
Iranian	4	0.02
Irish	2,500	14.79
Italian	582	3.44
Lithuanian	7	0.04
Northern European	9	0.05
Norwegian	335	1.98
Polish	274	1.62
Portuguese	7	0.04
Romanian	15	0.09
Russian	59	0.35
Scandinavian	7	0.04
Scotch-Irish	419	2.48
Scottish	586	3.47
Slovak	9	0.05
Slovene	10	0.06
Swedish	331	1.96
Swiss	54	0.32
Turkish	16	0.09
Ukrainian	42	0.25
United States or American	1,668	9.87
Welsh	128	0.76
West Indian, excl. Hispanic:	24	0.14
Barbadian	7	0.04
Haitian	12	0.07
Trinidadian and Tobagonian	5	0.03
White:	16,193	95.32
Not Hispanic (15,887)	16,035	94.39
Hispanic (147)	158	0.93
Yugoslavian	21	0.12

Kirkwood

Place Type: City
County: Saint Louis
Population: 27,324

Ancestry/Race	Number	%
African American/Black:	2,040	7.47
Not Hispanic (1,920)	2,024	7.41
Hispanic (12)	16	0.06
African, sub-Saharan:	43	0.16
African	43	0.16
Alaska Native tribes, specified:	2	0.01
Tlingit-Haida	1	0.00
All other tribes	1	0.00
Am. Ind. or Alaska Nat., not spec.	34	0.12
Albanian	6	0.02
American Indian tribes, specified:	76	0.28
Apache	1	0.00
Blackfeet (1)	6	0.02
Cherokee (5)	42	0.15
Cheyenne (1)	4	0.01
Chickasaw (1)	2	0.01
Chippewa (1)	1	0.00
Choctaw (2)	6	0.02
Comanche	2	0.01
Kiowa	1	0.00
Latin American Indians (2)	2	0.01
Navajo (1)	1	0.00
Osage	1	0.00
Sioux (1)	3	0.01
All other tribes (3)	4	0.01
American Indian tribes, not spec.	4	0.01
Arab:	93	0.34
Arab/Arabic	18	0.07
Lebanese	60	0.22
Syrian	15	0.06
Armenian	26	0.10
Asian:	290	1.06
Chinese, ex. Taiwanese (40)	53	0.19
Filipino (31)	45	0.16
Indian (35)	46	0.17
Indonesian (2)	2	0.01
Japanese (21)	36	0.13

Notes: 1. Figures in the "Number" column do not add up to the total population due to: a) Ancestry/Race overlap — e.g. persons can report being both White and Irish, b) persons of Hispanic origin can report being any race, c) persons reporting two ancestries are counted in both categories. 2. Numbers in parentheses indicate the number of persons reporting this ancestry/race alone, not in combination with any other ancestry/race. 3. Refer to the Explanation of Data in the front of the book for more detailed information.

Ancestry/Race	Number	%
Korean (32)	33	0.12
Laotian (7)	7	0.03
Pakistani (15)	18	0.07
Sri Lankan (4)	4	0.01
Taiwanese (2)	2	0.01
Thai (5)	5	0.02
Vietnamese (22)	24	0.09
Other Asian, specified	4	0.01
Other Asian, not specified (3)	11	0.04
Austrian	192	0.70
Basque	16	0.06
Belgian	56	0.21
British	194	0.71
Canadian	80	0.29
Celtic	9	0.03
Croatian	70	0.26
Czech	132	0.48
Czechoslovakian	59	0.22
Danish	217	0.80
Dutch	560	2.05
Eastern European	24	0.09
English	4,214	15.45
European	332	1.22
Finnish	25	0.09
French, except Basque	1,268	4.65
French Canadian	91	0.33
German	9,853	36.13
Greek	77	0.28
Hawaii Native/Pacific Islander:	24	0.09
Melanesian:	1	0.00
Fijian	1	0.00
Micronesian:	3	0.01
Guamanian/Chamorro	3	0.01
Polynesian: (9)	13	0.05
Native Hawaiian (2)	2	0.01
Samoan (7)	11	0.04
Other Pac. Isl., specified	4	0.01
Other Pac. Isl., not spec. (1)	3	0.01
Hispanic or Latino:	298	1.09
Central American:	15	0.05
Guatemalan	7	0.03
Honduran	3	0.01
Nicaraguan	1	0.00
Salvadoran	1	0.00
Other Central American	3	0.01
Cuban	12	0.04
Dominican Republic	4	0.01
Mexican	135	0.49
Puerto Rican	20	0.07
South American:	44	0.16
Argentinean	13	0.05
Chilean	2	0.01
Colombian	18	0.07
Ecuadorian	3	0.01
Peruvian	7	0.03
Venezuelan	1	0.00
Other Hispanic or Latino	68	0.25
Hungarian	115	0.42
Irish	5,648	20.71
Italian	1,159	4.25
Latvian	17	0.06
Lithuanian	64	0.23
Luxemburger	13	0.05
Macedonian	11	0.04
Maltese	25	0.09
Northern European	73	0.27
Norwegian	342	1.25
Pennsylvania German	16	0.06
Polish	643	2.36
Portuguese	38	0.14
Romanian	2	0.01
Russian	218	0.80
Scandinavian	32	0.12
Scotch-Irish	603	2.21
Scottish	909	3.33
Serbian	5	0.02
Slavic	37	0.14
Slovak	46	0.17
Slovene	16	0.06
Swedish	445	1.63
Swiss	177	0.65
Ukrainian	39	0.14
United States or American	1,184	4.34
Welsh	413	1.51
West Indian, excl. Hispanic:	21	0.08
Belizean	8	0.03
Haitian	2	0.01
Jamaican	11	0.04
White:	25,032	91.61
Not Hispanic (24,603)	24,810	90.80
Hispanic (197)	222	0.81
Yugoslavian	13	0.05

Lake Saint Louis

Place Type: City
County: Saint Charles
Population: 10,169

Ancestry/Race	Number	%
African American/Black:	209	2.06
Not Hispanic (183)	202	1.99
Hispanic (4)	7	0.07
Am. Ind. or Alaska Nat., not spec.	15	0.15
American Indian tribes, specified:	38	0.37
Cherokee (9)	18	0.18
Chippewa (1)	1	0.01
Choctaw	2	0.02
Comanche (1)	1	0.01
Creek (3)	4	0.04
Delaware	1	0.01
Latin American Indians (1)	1	0.01
Ottawa (5)	5	0.05
Sioux	1	0.01
All other tribes (1)	4	0.04
American Indian tribes, not spec.	2	0.02
Arab:	28	0.28
Egyptian	7	0.07
Lebanese	12	0.12
Palestinian	9	0.09
Asian:	134	1.32
Chinese, ex. Taiwanese (13)	19	0.19
Filipino (17)	30	0.30
Indian (25)	26	0.26
Japanese (8)	14	0.14
Korean (20)	24	0.24
Pakistani (7)	7	0.07
Thai (2)	2	0.02
Vietnamese (3)	5	0.05
Other Asian, not specified (3)	7	0.07
Australian	8	0.08
Austrian	31	0.31
Belgian	15	0.15
British	137	1.36
Bulgarian	27	0.27
Canadian	14	0.14
Celtic	10	0.10
Croatian	42	0.42
Czech	60	0.60
Czechoslovakian	32	0.32
Danish	78	0.78
Dutch	194	1.93
Eastern European	11	0.11
English	1,520	15.11
European	55	0.55
Finnish	11	0.11
French, except Basque	469	4.66
French Canadian	32	0.32
German	4,075	40.51
Greek	15	0.15
Hawaii Native/Pacific Islander:	8	0.08
Polynesian: (4)	5	0.05
Native Hawaiian (3)	3	0.03
Samoan (1)	2	0.02
Other Pac. Isl., not spec.	3	0.03
Hispanic or Latino:	137	1.35
Central American:	12	0.12
Costa Rican	2	0.02
Guatemalan	1	0.01
Honduran	3	0.03
Nicaraguan	2	0.02
Panamanian	4	0.04
Mexican	83	0.82
Puerto Rican	3	0.03
South American:	8	0.08
Bolivian	1	0.01
Colombian	5	0.05
Peruvian	1	0.01
Venezuelan	1	0.01
Other Hispanic or Latino	31	0.30
Hungarian	55	0.55
Iranian	42	0.42
Irish	1,863	18.52
Italian	574	5.71
Lithuanian	113	1.12
Norwegian	126	1.25
Polish	316	3.14
Portuguese	27	0.27
Russian	69	0.69
Scandinavian	22	0.22
Scotch-Irish	251	2.50
Scottish	224	2.23
Serbian	11	0.11
Slavic	11	0.11
Slovak	27	0.27
Swedish	175	1.74
Swiss	64	0.64
Turkish	39	0.39
Ukrainian	51	0.51
United States or American	451	4.48
Welsh	79	0.79
White:	9,806	96.43
Not Hispanic (9,641)	9,718	95.56
Hispanic (81)	88	0.87

Lebanon

Place Type: City
County: Laclede
Population: 12,155

Ancestry/Race	Number	%
African American/Black:	141	1.16
Not Hispanic (110)	140	1.15
Hispanic	1	0.01
African, sub-Saharan:	4	0.03
African	4	0.03
Alaska Native tribes, specified:	1	0.01
Tlingit-Haida	1	0.01
Am. Ind. or Alaska Nat., not spec.	53	0.44
American Indian tribes, specified:	119	0.98
Apache (1)	1	0.01
Blackfeet (2)	7	0.06
Cherokee (15)	67	0.55
Cheyenne (1)	3	0.02
Chippewa (1)	1	0.01
Choctaw (1)	4	0.03
Creek	1	0.01
Iroquois (3)	3	0.02
Latin American Indians (3)	4	0.03
Navajo (2)	4	0.03
Osage (4)	5	0.04
Ottawa (1)	3	0.02
Sioux (3)	9	0.07
All other tribes (3)	7	0.06
American Indian tribes, not spec.	11	0.09
Asian:	103	0.85
Chinese, ex. Taiwanese (4)	7	0.06
Filipino (12)	22	0.18
Indian (28)	38	0.31
Japanese (7)	14	0.12
Korean (4)	8	0.07
Taiwanese (2)	3	0.02
Thai	1	0.01
Vietnamese	3	0.02
Other Asian, specified (3)	4	0.03
Other Asian, not specified (1)	3	0.02
British	20	0.16
Canadian	7	0.06
Czech	97	0.79

Notes: 1. Figures in the "Number" column do not add up to the total population due to: a) Ancestry/Race overlap — e.g. persons can report being both White and Irish, b) persons of Hispanic origin can report being any race, c) persons reporting two ancestries are counted in both categories. 2. Numbers in parentheses indicate the number of persons reporting this ancestry/race alone, not in combination with any other ancestry/race. 3. Refer to the Explanation of Data in the front of the book for more detailed information.

Danish	50	0.41
Dutch	262	2.14
English	897	7.31
European	88	0.72
French, except Basque	459	3.74
French Canadian	61	0.50
German	2,099	17.12
Greek	13	0.11
Hawaii Native/Pacific Islander:	11	0.09
Micronesian: (1)	2	0.02
Guamanian/Chamorro (1)	2	0.02
Polynesian: (2)	7	0.06
Native Hawaiian	3	0.02
Samoan (1)	3	0.02
Tongan (1)	1	0.01
Other Pac. Isl., specified	1	0.01
Other Pac. Isl., not spec.	1	0.01
Hispanic or Latino:	201	1.65
Central American:	6	0.05
Costa Rican	4	0.03
Honduran	1	0.01
Salvadoran	1	0.01
Cuban	2	0.02
Mexican	140	1.15
Puerto Rican	7	0.06
South American:	6	0.05
Ecuadorian	6	0.05
Other Hispanic or Latino	40	0.33
Irish	1,586	12.93
Italian	176	1.44
Lithuanian	18	0.15
Norwegian	62	0.51
Pennsylvania German	13	0.11
Polish	159	1.30
Russian	24	0.20
Scandinavian	4	0.03
Scotch-Irish	167	1.36
Scottish	188	1.53
Slovene	9	0.07
Swedish	116	0.95
Swiss	20	0.16
United States or American	2,359	19.24
Welsh	22	0.18
West Indian, excl. Hispanic:	42	0.34
Dutch West Indian	25	0.20
Jamaican	17	0.14
White:	11,857	97.55
Not Hispanic (11,535)	11,708	96.32
Hispanic (132)	149	1.23

Lee's Summit

Place Type: City
County: Jackson
Population: 70,700

Ancestry/Race	Number	%
Acadian/Cajun	15	0.02
African American/Black:	2,773	3.92
Not Hispanic (2,437)	2,738	3.87
Hispanic (17)	35	0.05
African, sub-Saharan:	179	0.25
African	94	0.13
Ethiopian	75	0.11
Ugandan	10	0.01
Alaska Native tribes, specified:	1	0.00
Alaska Athabascan (1)	1	0.00
Alaska Native tribes, not specified	1	0.00
Am. Ind. or Alaska Nat., not spec.	128	0.18
American Indian tribes, specified:	478	0.68
Apache	9	0.01
Blackfeet (3)	34	0.05
Cherokee (89)	239	0.34
Cheyenne	1	0.00
Chickasaw (1)	5	0.01
Chippewa (1)	5	0.01
Choctaw (22)	27	0.04
Comanche	1	0.00
Creek (6)	13	0.02
Crow	1	0.00
Delaware (4)	5	0.01
Iroquois (7)	11	0.02
Latin American Indians (5)	9	0.01
Navajo (11)	14	0.02
Osage (4)	10	0.01
Ottawa	1	0.00
Paiute (2)	3	0.00
Potawatomi (10)	19	0.03
Pueblo (2)	2	0.00
Seminole (4)	5	0.01
Shoshone	1	0.00
Sioux (9)	16	0.02
Ute (1)	2	0.00
Yaqui	1	0.00
All other tribes (26)	44	0.06
American Indian tribes, not spec.	10	0.01
Arab:	315	0.44
Arab/Arabic	59	0.08
Egyptian	17	0.02
Lebanese	158	0.22
Palestinian	6	0.01
Syrian	75	0.11
Armenian	9	0.01
Asian:	923	1.31
Cambodian (14)	18	0.03
Chinese, ex. Taiwanese (148)	172	0.24
Filipino (108)	154	0.22
Hmong (6)	6	0.01
Indian (102)	115	0.16
Indonesian (3)	4	0.01
Japanese (43)	98	0.14
Korean (131)	172	0.24
Laotian (3)	3	0.00
Malaysian (4)	5	0.01
Pakistani (13)	22	0.03
Sri Lankan (2)	2	0.00
Taiwanese (2)	4	0.01
Thai (7)	10	0.01
Vietnamese (84)	93	0.13
Other Asian, specified (3)	7	0.01
Other Asian, not specified (17)	38	0.05
Australian	16	0.02
Austrian	146	0.21
Belgian	161	0.23
British	268	0.38
Canadian	103	0.14
Croatian	243	0.34
Czech	394	0.55
Czechoslovakian	283	0.40
Danish	394	0.55
Dutch	1,740	2.45
Eastern European	32	0.05
English	10,243	14.41
European	809	1.14
Finnish	32	0.05
French, except Basque	2,590	3.64
French Canadian	301	0.42
German	19,795	27.85
German Russian	6	0.01
Greek	177	0.25
Hawaii Native/Pacific Islander:	81	0.11
Micronesian: (9)	12	0.02
Guamanian/Chamorro (5)	8	0.01
Other Micronesian (4)	4	0.01
Polynesian: (28)	51	0.07
Native Hawaiian (8)	26	0.04
Samoan (11)	14	0.02
Tongan (1)	1	0.00
Other Polynesian (8)	10	0.01
Other Pac. Isl., specified	1	0.00
Other Pac. Isl., not spec. (7)	17	0.02
Hispanic or Latino:	1,394	1.97
Central American:	45	0.06
Costa Rican	3	0.00
Guatemalan	7	0.01
Honduran	2	0.00
Nicaraguan	7	0.01
Panamanian	15	0.02
Salvadoran	5	0.01
Other Central American	6	0.01
Cuban	29	0.04
Dominican Republic	2	0.00
Mexican	981	1.39
Puerto Rican	97	0.14
South American:	51	0.07
Argentinean	6	0.01
Bolivian	3	0.00
Chilean	1	0.00
Colombian	10	0.01
Ecuadorian	7	0.01
Paraguayan	1	0.00
Peruvian	5	0.01
Venezuelan	15	0.02
Other South American	3	0.00
Other Hispanic or Latino	189	0.27
Hungarian	155	0.22
Iranian	17	0.02
Irish	10,639	14.97
Italian	3,326	4.68
Latvian	45	0.06
Lithuanian	35	0.05
Luxemburger	13	0.02
Macedonian	8	0.01
Northern European	77	0.11
Norwegian	1,049	1.48
Pennsylvania German	20	0.03
Polish	1,285	1.81
Portuguese	77	0.11
Romanian	9	0.01
Russian	231	0.33
Scandinavian	56	0.08
Scotch-Irish	1,979	2.78
Scottish	1,914	2.69
Serbian	55	0.08
Slavic	17	0.02
Slovak	92	0.13
Slovene	54	0.08
Swedish	1,492	2.10
Swiss	426	0.60
Turkish	35	0.05
Ukrainian	79	0.11
United States or American	6,418	9.03
Welsh	865	1.22
West Indian, excl. Hispanic:	90	0.13
Haitian	5	0.01
Jamaican	77	0.11
West Indian	8	0.01
White:	66,804	94.49
Not Hispanic (64,991)	65,788	93.05
Hispanic (883)	1,016	1.44
Yugoslavian	52	0.07

Lemay

Place Type: Census Designated Place
County: Saint Louis
Population: 17,215

Ancestry/Race	Number	%
African American/Black:	207	1.20
Not Hispanic (175)	205	1.19
Hispanic	2	0.01
African, sub-Saharan:	9	0.05
African	9	0.05
Alaska Native tribes, specified:	4	0.02
Tlingit-Haida (4)	4	0.02
Am. Ind. or Alaska Nat., not spec.	57	0.33
American Indian tribes, specified:	65	0.38
Blackfeet (5)	7	0.04
Cherokee (10)	34	0.20
Cheyenne	1	0.01
Chickasaw	3	0.02
Chippewa (6)	6	0.03
Cree	1	0.01
Delaware (1)	1	0.01
Iroquois (2)	8	0.05
Latin American Indians (1)	1	0.01
Shoshone (1)	1	0.01
Sioux	1	0.01
All other tribes (1)	1	0.01

Notes: 1. Figures in the "Number" column do not add up to the total population due to: a) Ancestry/Race overlap — e.g. persons can report being both White and Irish, b) persons of Hispanic origin can report being any race, c) persons reporting two ancestries are counted in both categories. 2. Numbers in parentheses indicate the number of persons reporting this ancestry/race alone, not in combination with any other ancestry/race. 3. Refer to the Explanation of Data in the front of the book for more detailed information.

Ancestry/Race	Number	%
American Indian tribes, not spec.	2	0.01
Arab:	50	0.29
Lebanese	50	0.29
Asian:	123	0.71
Chinese, ex. Taiwanese (16)	20	0.12
Filipino (17)	30	0.17
Indian (1)	1	0.01
Japanese (7)	14	0.08
Korean (5)	6	0.03
Laotian (7)	7	0.04
Pakistani (1)	1	0.01
Thai (2)	4	0.02
Vietnamese (32)	35	0.20
Other Asian, specified	2	0.01
Other Asian, not specified (1)	3	0.02
Austrian	43	0.25
Belgian	16	0.09
Brazilian	18	0.10
Croatian	74	0.43
Czech	189	1.10
Czechoslovakian	29	0.17
Danish	23	0.13
Dutch	352	2.05
English	1,016	5.93
European	3	0.02
Finnish	16	0.09
French, except Basque	1,198	6.99
French Canadian	41	0.24
German	6,479	37.79
Greek	52	0.30
Hawaii Native/Pacific Islander:	5	0.03
Micronesian: (1)	1	0.01
Guamanian/Chamorro (1)	1	0.01
Polynesian: (1)	1	0.01
Samoan (1)	1	0.01
Other Pac. Isl., not spec.	3	0.02
Hispanic or Latino:	349	2.03
Central American:	7	0.04
Costa Rican	2	0.01
Guatemalan	3	0.02
Honduran	2	0.01
Cuban	5	0.03
Mexican	240	1.39
Puerto Rican	9	0.05
South American:	4	0.02
Bolivian	2	0.01
Peruvian	2	0.01
Other Hispanic or Latino	84	0.49
Hungarian	124	0.72
Iranian	11	0.06
Irish	2,812	16.40
Italian	958	5.59
Lithuanian	49	0.29
Norwegian	10	0.06
Polish	554	3.23
Romanian	14	0.08
Russian	40	0.23
Scandinavian	2	0.01
Scotch-Irish	152	0.89
Scottish	121	0.71
Serbian	7	0.04
Slavic	10	0.06
Slovak	38	0.22
Swedish	173	1.01
Swiss	84	0.49
Ukrainian	53	0.31
United States or American	1,139	6.64
Welsh	86	0.50
White:	16,770	97.42
Not Hispanic (16,415)	16,546	96.11
Hispanic (200)	224	1.30
Yugoslavian	136	0.79

Liberty

Place Type: City
County: Clay
Population: 26,232

Ancestry/Race	Number	%
African American/Black:	791	3.02
Not Hispanic (661)	769	2.93
Hispanic (19)	22	0.08
African, sub-Saharan:	9	0.03
South African	9	0.03
Am. Ind. or Alaska Nat., not spec.	64	0.24
American Indian tribes, specified:	221	0.84
Apache (4)	9	0.03
Blackfeet (2)	11	0.04
Cherokee (28)	103	0.39
Chickasaw	8	0.03
Chippewa (1)	1	0.00
Choctaw (6)	11	0.04
Creek	1	0.00
Crow	1	0.00
Delaware (4)	8	0.03
Iroquois (2)	3	0.01
Kiowa (2)	2	0.01
Latin American Indians (1)	2	0.01
Lumbee (1)	1	0.00
Menominee (1)	2	0.01
Navajo (6)	6	0.02
Osage (6)	7	0.03
Potawatomi (4)	10	0.04
Pueblo (3)	3	0.01
Seminole	4	0.02
Sioux (6)	15	0.06
All other tribes (4)	13	0.05
American Indian tribes, not spec.	8	0.03
Arab:	42	0.16
Arab/Arabic	34	0.13
Lebanese	8	0.03
Armenian	23	0.09
Asian:	237	0.90
Chinese, ex. Taiwanese (35)	43	0.16
Filipino (20)	29	0.11
Indian (31)	35	0.13
Indonesian	3	0.01
Japanese (19)	46	0.18
Korean (26)	37	0.14
Pakistani (3)	6	0.02
Thai (12)	14	0.05
Vietnamese (11)	12	0.05
Other Asian, not specified (2)	12	0.05
Austrian	97	0.37
Belgian	39	0.15
British	85	0.33
Bulgarian	7	0.03
Canadian	25	0.10
Celtic	3	0.01
Croatian	99	0.38
Czech	190	0.73
Czechoslovakian	16	0.06
Danish	207	0.80
Dutch	516	1.98
English	3,567	13.70
Estonian	9	0.03
European	376	1.44
Finnish	45	0.17
French, except Basque	763	2.93
French Canadian	61	0.23
German	6,529	25.08
Greek	70	0.27
Hawaii Native/Pacific Islander:	34	0.13
Micronesian: (7)	14	0.05
Guamanian/Chamorro (5)	12	0.05
Other Micronesian (2)	2	0.01
Polynesian: (8)	14	0.05
Native Hawaiian (1)	3	0.01
Samoan (7)	11	0.04
Other Pac. Isl., not spec.	6	0.02
Hispanic or Latino:	703	2.68
Central American:	17	0.06
Guatemalan	4	0.02
Honduran	7	0.03
Panamanian	5	0.02
Salvadoran	1	0.00
Cuban	19	0.07
Mexican	486	1.85
Puerto Rican	31	0.12
South American:	17	0.06
Argentinean	1	0.00
Chilean	1	0.00
Colombian	2	0.01
Ecuadorian	5	0.02
Paraguayan	1	0.00
Peruvian	6	0.02
Other South American	1	0.00
Other Hispanic or Latino	133	0.51
Hungarian	34	0.13
Irish	3,606	13.85
Italian	940	3.61
Lithuanian	33	0.13
New Zealander	9	0.03
Northern European	8	0.03
Norwegian	402	1.54
Pennsylvania German	10	0.04
Polish	382	1.47
Portuguese	11	0.04
Russian	159	0.61
Scandinavian	36	0.14
Scotch-Irish	729	2.80
Scottish	878	3.37
Serbian	34	0.13
Slovak	74	0.28
Slovene	30	0.12
Swedish	479	1.84
Swiss	143	0.55
Ukrainian	31	0.12
United States or American	2,567	9.86
Welsh	349	1.34
West Indian, excl. Hispanic:	15	0.06
Dutch West Indian	15	0.06
White:	24,993	95.28
Not Hispanic (24,236)	24,558	93.62
Hispanic (356)	435	1.66
Yugoslavian	7	0.03

Manchester

Place Type: City
County: Saint Louis
Population: 19,161

Ancestry/Race	Number	%
African American/Black:	511	2.67
Not Hispanic (462)	510	2.66
Hispanic (1)	1	0.01
African, sub-Saharan:	151	0.79
African	82	0.43
Ethiopian	30	0.16
Nigerian	2	0.01
Sudanese	37	0.19
Alaska Native tribes, specified:	1	0.01
Tlingit-Haida (1)	1	0.01
Am. Ind. or Alaska Nat., not spec.	23	0.12
American Indian tribes, specified:	42	0.22
Blackfeet	2	0.01
Cherokee (4)	14	0.07
Choctaw	10	0.05
Comanche (1)	1	0.01
Latin American Indians (5)	6	0.03
Osage	1	0.01
Potawatomi	1	0.01
Sioux (2)	6	0.03
All other tribes (1)	1	0.01
American Indian tribes, not spec.	3	0.02
Arab:	185	0.97
Arab/Arabic	48	0.25
Jordanian	33	0.17
Lebanese	43	0.23
Other Arab	61	0.32
Asian:	947	4.94
Bangladeshi (12)	12	0.06
Chinese, ex. Taiwanese (216)	229	1.20
Filipino (62)	96	0.50
Indian (271)	295	1.54
Japanese (28)	47	0.25
Korean (55)	62	0.32
Malaysian (3)	6	0.03

Notes: 1. Figures in the "Number" column do not add up to the total population due to: a) Ancestry/Race overlap — e.g. persons can report being both White and Irish, b) persons of Hispanic origin can report being any race, c) persons reporting two ancestries are counted in both categories. 2. Numbers in parentheses indicate the number of persons reporting this ancestry/race alone, not in combination with any other ancestry/race. 3. Refer to the Explanation of Data in the front of the book for more detailed information.

Ancestry/Race	Number	%
Pakistani (105)	122	0.64
Taiwanese (22)	22	0.11
Thai (8)	8	0.04
Vietnamese (34)	35	0.18
Other Asian, not specified (6)	13	0.07
Assyrian/Chaldean/Syriac	34	0.18
Austrian	42	0.22
British	73	0.38
Bulgarian	30	0.16
Canadian	34	0.18
Celtic	8	0.04
Croatian	79	0.41
Czech	137	0.72
Czechoslovakian	27	0.14
Danish	30	0.16
Dutch	341	1.79
Eastern European	7	0.04
English	2,861	14.99
European	239	1.25
Finnish	22	0.12
French, except Basque	905	4.74
French Canadian	138	0.72
German	7,449	39.04
Greek	120	0.63
Hawaii Native/Pacific Islander:	8	0.04
Micronesian: (2)	2	0.01
Guamanian/Chamorro (2)	2	0.01
Polynesian: (3)	4	0.02
Native Hawaiian (1)	2	0.01
Samoan (2)	2	0.01
Other Pac. Isl., not spec. (1)	2	0.01
Hispanic or Latino:	292	1.52
Central American:	5	0.03
Nicaraguan	1	0.01
Panamanian	2	0.01
Salvadoran	2	0.01
Cuban	25	0.13
Dominican Republic	3	0.02
Mexican	105	0.55
Puerto Rican	32	0.17
South American:	55	0.29
Argentinean	5	0.03
Bolivian	3	0.02
Chilean	3	0.02
Colombian	4	0.02
Ecuadorian	3	0.02
Peruvian	29	0.15
Uruguayan	2	0.01
Venezuelan	4	0.02
Other South American	2	0.01
Other Hispanic or Latino	67	0.35
Hungarian	68	0.36
Iranian	70	0.37
Irish	3,258	17.08
Italian	977	5.12
Lithuanian	22	0.12
Northern European	8	0.04
Norwegian	223	1.17
Polish	660	3.46
Portuguese	47	0.25
Romanian	36	0.19
Russian	191	1.00
Scandinavian	57	0.30
Scotch-Irish	385	2.02
Scottish	588	3.08
Serbian	27	0.14
Slavic	22	0.12
Slovak	36	0.19
Slovene	24	0.13
Swedish	291	1.53
Swiss	77	0.40
Ukrainian	51	0.27
United States or American	1,162	6.09
Welsh	131	0.69
White:	17,734	92.55
Not Hispanic (17,355)	17,522	91.45
Hispanic (197)	212	1.11
Yugoslavian	8	0.04

Marshall

Place Type: City
County: Saline
Population: 12,433

Ancestry/Race	Number	%
Afghan	32	0.26
African American/Black:	1,047	8.42
Not Hispanic (909)	1,028	8.27
Hispanic (11)	19	0.15
African, sub-Saharan:	20	0.16
African	12	0.10
Nigerian	8	0.06
Alaska Native tribes, specified:	1	0.01
Alaska Athabascan	1	0.01
Am. Ind. or Alaska Nat., not spec.	42	0.34
Albanian	8	0.06
American Indian tribes, specified:	67	0.54
Apache	1	0.01
Blackfeet (1)	4	0.03
Cherokee (7)	30	0.24
Cheyenne	2	0.02
Chippewa (2)	2	0.02
Choctaw (2)	3	0.02
Creek (1)	3	0.02
Crow	1	0.01
Latin American Indians (11)	12	0.10
Navajo	1	0.01
Pueblo (3)	3	0.02
Seminole	1	0.01
Ute (3)	3	0.02
All other tribes (1)	1	0.01
American Indian tribes, not spec.	3	0.02
Arab:	8	0.06
Lebanese	8	0.06
Asian:	73	0.59
Chinese, ex. Taiwanese (15)	18	0.14
Filipino (15)	21	0.17
Indian (2)	3	0.02
Japanese (8)	12	0.10
Korean (3)	5	0.04
Thai (1)	2	0.02
Vietnamese (4)	7	0.06
Other Asian, not specified	5	0.04
Assyrian/Chaldean/Syriac	5	0.04
Austrian	29	0.23
Belgian	12	0.10
British	31	0.25
Bulgarian	12	0.10
Canadian	30	0.24
Croatian	7	0.06
Czech	5	0.04
Danish	24	0.19
Dutch	207	1.66
English	1,132	9.08
European	177	1.42
French, except Basque	251	2.01
French Canadian	47	0.38
German	2,475	19.85
Hawaii Native/Pacific Islander:	59	0.47
Micronesian: (35)	37	0.30
Other Micronesian (35)	37	0.30
Polynesian: (3)	13	0.10
Native Hawaiian (2)	7	0.06
Samoan (1)	4	0.03
Other Polynesian	2	0.02
Other Pac. Isl., not spec. (4)	9	0.07
Hispanic or Latino:	891	7.17
Central American:	262	2.11
Guatemalan	9	0.07
Honduran	3	0.02
Nicaraguan	12	0.10
Panamanian	1	0.01
Salvadoran	237	1.91
Cuban	3	0.02
Mexican	383	3.08
Puerto Rican	18	0.14
South American:	7	0.06
Chilean	2	0.02
Colombian	2	0.02
Ecuadorian	1	0.01
Peruvian	2	0.02
Other Hispanic or Latino	218	1.75
Hungarian	11	0.09
Iranian	13	0.10
Irish	1,264	10.14
Italian	91	0.73
Latvian	11	0.09
Northern European	6	0.05
Norwegian	100	0.80
Polish	51	0.41
Russian	12	0.10
Scandinavian	11	0.09
Scotch-Irish	246	1.97
Scottish	199	1.60
Slovene	9	0.07
Swedish	107	0.86
Swiss	11	0.09
United States or American	1,530	12.27
Welsh	53	0.42
West Indian, excl. Hispanic:	12	0.10
Belizean	5	0.04
British West Indian	7	0.06
White:	10,918	87.81
Not Hispanic (10,309)	10,488	84.36
Hispanic (390)	430	3.46
Yugoslavian	5	0.04

Maryland Heights

Place Type: City
County: Saint Louis
Population: 25,756

Ancestry/Race	Number	%
African American/Black:	1,527	5.93
Not Hispanic (1,419)	1,509	5.86
Hispanic (17)	18	0.07
African, sub-Saharan:	105	0.40
African	69	0.27
Kenyan	20	0.08
Other sub-Saharan African	16	0.06
Am. Ind. or Alaska Nat., not spec.	39	0.15
Alsatian	8	0.03
American Indian tribes, specified:	83	0.32
Blackfeet (4)	7	0.03
Cherokee (10)	39	0.15
Chippewa (4)	5	0.02
Choctaw (2)	7	0.03
Colville	1	0.00
Comanche	3	0.01
Creek	1	0.00
Kiowa (1)	1	0.00
Latin American Indians (1)	4	0.02
Menominee	1	0.00
Navajo (3)	6	0.02
Osage (1)	1	0.00
Sioux (1)	5	0.02
All other tribes (1)	2	0.01
American Indian tribes, not spec.	2	0.01
Arab:	241	0.93
Arab/Arabic	44	0.17
Egyptian	35	0.13
Iraqi	45	0.17
Lebanese	34	0.13
Syrian	9	0.03
Other Arab	74	0.29
Armenian	13	0.05
Asian:	1,960	7.61
Bangladeshi (1)	1	0.00
Cambodian (4)	5	0.02
Chinese, ex. Taiwanese (402)	435	1.69
Filipino (141)	157	0.61
Indian (873)	896	3.48
Indonesian (4)	5	0.02
Japanese (37)	50	0.19
Korean (183)	197	0.76
Laotian (9)	10	0.04
Malaysian (5)	5	0.02

Notes: 1. Figures in the "Number" column do not add up to the total population due to: a) Ancestry/Race overlap — e.g. persons can report being both White and Irish, b) persons of Hispanic origin can report being any race, c) persons reporting two ancestries are counted in both categories. 2. Numbers in parentheses indicate the number of persons reporting this ancestry/race alone, not in combination with any other ancestry/race. 3. Refer to the Explanation of Data in the front of the book for more detailed information.

Pakistani (38)	38	0.15
Sri Lankan (1)	1	0.00
Taiwanese (23)	26	0.10
Thai (11)	18	0.07
Vietnamese (59)	79	0.31
Other Asian, not specified (19)	37	0.14
Australian	59	0.23
Austrian	100	0.39
Belgian	22	0.08
British	125	0.48
Canadian	45	0.17
Celtic	13	0.05
Croatian	112	0.43
Czech	60	0.23
Czechoslovakian	19	0.07
Danish	103	0.40
Dutch	524	2.02
Eastern European	20	0.08
English	2,745	10.58
European	277	1.07
Finnish	26	0.10
French, except Basque	1,438	5.54
French Canadian	42	0.16
German	8,398	32.38
German Russian	23	0.09
Greek	109	0.42
Hawaii Native/Pacific Islander:	23	0.09
Micronesian: (3)	3	0.01
Guamanian/Chamorro (1)	1	0.00
Other Micronesian (2)	2	0.01
Polynesian: (4)	10	0.04
Native Hawaiian (2)	8	0.03
Samoan (2)	2	0.01
Other Pac. Isl., not spec. (2)	10	0.04
Hispanic or Latino:	599	2.33
Central American:	21	0.08
Costa Rican	5	0.02
Guatemalan	2	0.01
Honduran	2	0.01
Panamanian	4	0.02
Salvadoran	6	0.02
Other Central American	2	0.01
Cuban	22	0.09
Dominican Republic	8	0.03
Mexican	331	1.29
Puerto Rican	64	0.25
South American:	59	0.23
Argentinean	11	0.04
Bolivian	4	0.02
Chilean	6	0.02
Colombian	7	0.03
Ecuadorian	1	0.00
Peruvian	11	0.04
Venezuelan	16	0.06
Other South American	3	0.01
Other Hispanic or Latino	94	0.36
Hungarian	96	0.37
Iranian	42	0.16
Irish	4,369	16.84
Italian	1,361	5.25
Lithuanian	38	0.15
Northern European	50	0.19
Norwegian	68	0.26
Polish	882	3.40
Portuguese	54	0.21
Romanian	6	0.02
Russian	379	1.46
Scandinavian	68	0.26
Scotch-Irish	341	1.31
Scottish	479	1.85
Slavic	10	0.04
Slovak	54	0.21
Slovene	19	0.07
Swedish	235	0.91
Swiss	113	0.44
Turkish	15	0.06
Ukrainian	115	0.44
United States or American	1,276	4.92
Welsh	239	0.92
West Indian, excl. Hispanic:	6	0.02
West Indian	6	0.02
White:	22,196	86.18
Not Hispanic (21,593)	21,790	84.60
Hispanic (390)	406	1.58
Yugoslavian	14	0.05

Maryville

Place Type: City
County: Nodaway
Population: 10,581

Ancestry/Race	Number	%
African American/Black:	180	1.70
Not Hispanic (156)	178	1.68
Hispanic (1)	2	0.02
African, sub-Saharan:	49	0.47
African	39	0.37
Sierra Leonean	10	0.10
Am. Ind. or Alaska Nat., not spec.	27	0.26
American Indian tribes, specified:	28	0.26
Cherokee (1)	13	0.12
Chickasaw	1	0.01
Chippewa	1	0.01
Delaware (1)	1	0.01
Iroquois (1)	1	0.01
Osage (1)	1	0.01
Potawatomi	1	0.01
Sioux (1)	2	0.02
All other tribes (3)	7	0.07
Arab:	7	0.07
Lebanese	7	0.07
Asian:	173	1.64
Bangladeshi (5)	5	0.05
Chinese, ex. Taiwanese (32)	32	0.30
Filipino (12)	16	0.15
Indian (17)	21	0.20
Japanese (61)	64	0.60
Korean (23)	24	0.23
Pakistani (1)	1	0.01
Vietnamese (1)	1	0.01
Other Asian, specified	3	0.03
Other Asian, not specified (1)	6	0.06
Austrian	3	0.03
Belgian	24	0.23
British	90	0.86
Canadian	12	0.11
Croatian	19	0.18
Czech	68	0.65
Czechoslovakian	7	0.07
Danish	70	0.67
Dutch	303	2.88
English	1,418	13.47
European	64	0.61
Finnish	38	0.36
French, except Basque	256	2.43
French Canadian	6	0.06
German	3,049	28.97
Greek	22	0.21
Hawaii Native/Pacific Islander:	6	0.06
Polynesian: (2)	4	0.04
Samoan (2)	4	0.04
Other Pac. Isl., specified	2	0.02
Hispanic or Latino:	104	0.98
Central American:	4	0.04
Guatemalan	2	0.02
Honduran	2	0.02
Cuban	3	0.03
Dominican Republic	1	0.01
Mexican	72	0.68
Puerto Rican	7	0.07
South American:	4	0.04
Colombian	1	0.01
Ecuadorian	2	0.02
Peruvian	1	0.01
Other Hispanic or Latino	13	0.12
Icelander	4	0.04
Irish	1,688	16.04
Italian	165	1.57
Lithuanian	7	0.07
Northern European	15	0.14
Norwegian	106	1.01
Polish	121	1.15
Russian	17	0.16
Scotch-Irish	233	2.21
Scottish	286	2.72
Swedish	185	1.76
Swiss	41	0.39
Turkish	15	0.14
Ukrainian	27	0.26
United States or American	833	7.91
Welsh	64	0.61
White:	10,212	96.51
Not Hispanic (10,071)	10,142	95.85
Hispanic (63)	70	0.66

Mehlville

Place Type: Census Designated Place
County: Saint Louis
Population: 28,822

Ancestry/Race	Number	%
African American/Black:	601	2.09
Not Hispanic (503)	596	2.07
Hispanic (2)	5	0.02
African, sub-Saharan:	76	0.26
African	66	0.23
Nigerian	10	0.03
Am. Ind. or Alaska Nat., not spec.	39	0.14
Albanian	24	0.08
American Indian tribes, specified:	68	0.24
Apache	3	0.01
Blackfeet (1)	2	0.01
Cherokee (12)	40	0.14
Cheyenne	1	0.00
Choctaw (1)	3	0.01
Cree	1	0.00
Delaware	1	0.00
Latin American Indians (3)	3	0.01
Navajo (1)	3	0.01
Potawatomi (1)	1	0.00
Pueblo (2)	2	0.01
Seminole (3)	3	0.01
Sioux (1)	1	0.00
All other tribes	4	0.01
American Indian tribes, not spec.	12	0.04
Arab:	126	0.44
Arab/Arabic	47	0.16
Egyptian	15	0.05
Iraqi	8	0.03
Lebanese	56	0.19
Armenian	18	0.06
Asian:	604	2.10
Bangladeshi (8)	8	0.03
Cambodian (1)	1	0.00
Chinese, ex. Taiwanese (99)	111	0.39
Filipino (92)	112	0.39
Indian (106)	114	0.40
Japanese (13)	22	0.08
Korean (36)	45	0.16
Laotian (21)	21	0.07
Pakistani (8)	8	0.03
Taiwanese (3)	3	0.01
Thai (5)	12	0.04
Vietnamese (103)	118	0.41
Other Asian, specified	2	0.01
Other Asian, not specified (5)	27	0.09
Austrian	158	0.55
Belgian	53	0.18
British	80	0.28
Bulgarian	11	0.04
Canadian	56	0.19
Croatian	314	1.09
Czech	577	2.00
Czechoslovakian	89	0.31
Danish	155	0.54
Dutch	264	0.92
Eastern European	55	0.19
English	2,398	8.33

Notes: 1. Figures in the "Number" column do not add up to the total population due to: a) Ancestry/Race overlap — e.g. persons can report being both White and Irish, b) persons of Hispanic origin can report being any race, c) persons reporting two ancestries are counted in both categories. 2. Numbers in parentheses indicate the number of persons reporting this ancestry/race alone, not in combination with any other ancestry/race. 3. Refer to the Explanation of Data in the front of the book for more detailed information.

European	146	0.51
Finnish	20	0.07
French, except Basque	1,894	6.58
French Canadian	114	0.40
German	12,035	41.82
Greek	63	0.22
Hawaii Native/Pacific Islander:	8	0.03
Micronesian: (2)	4	0.01
Guamanian/Chamorro (1)	2	0.01
Other Micronesian (1)	2	0.01
Polynesian: (3)	3	0.01
Native Hawaiian (2)	2	0.01
Samoan (1)	1	0.00
Other Pac. Isl., specified	1	0.00
Hispanic or Latino:	417	1.45
Central American:	5	0.02
Salvadoran	2	0.01
Other Central American	3	0.01
Cuban	22	0.08
Dominican Republic	1	0.00
Mexican	219	0.76
Puerto Rican	37	0.13
South American:	20	0.07
Argentinean	1	0.00
Bolivian	7	0.02
Colombian	2	0.01
Ecuadorian	4	0.01
Peruvian	1	0.00
Uruguayan	5	0.02
Other Hispanic or Latino	113	0.39
Hungarian	189	0.66
Icelander	15	0.05
Irish	5,506	19.13
Italian	1,721	5.98
Lithuanian	78	0.27
Luxemburger	24	0.08
Norwegian	115	0.40
Pennsylvania German	27	0.09
Polish	1,105	3.84
Romanian	23	0.08
Russian	46	0.16
Scandinavian	68	0.24
Scotch-Irish	289	1.00
Scottish	212	0.74
Serbian	26	0.09
Slavic	7	0.02
Slovak	81	0.28
Slovene	17	0.06
Swedish	138	0.48
Swiss	267	0.93
Ukrainian	102	0.35
United States or American	1,757	6.11
Welsh	152	0.53
White:	27,643	95.91
Not Hispanic (27,056)	27,324	94.80
Hispanic (291)	319	1.11
Yugoslavian	942	3.27

Mexico

Place Type: City
County: Audrain
Population: 11,320

Ancestry/Race	Number	%
African American/Black:	1,091	9.64
Not Hispanic (1,032)	1,076	9.51
Hispanic (8)	15	0.13
African, sub-Saharan:	8	0.07
African	8	0.07
Alaska Native tribes, specified:	1	0.01
Tlingit-Haida	1	0.01
Am. Ind. or Alaska Nat., not spec.	8	0.07
Albanian	8	0.07
American Indian tribes, specified:	55	0.49
Apache (1)	4	0.04
Blackfeet	3	0.03
Cherokee (14)	35	0.31
Chippewa (1)	1	0.01
Creek (3)	3	0.03
Iroquois (1)	3	0.03
Menominee	1	0.01
Shoshone	4	0.04
Sioux (1)	1	0.01
American Indian tribes, not spec.	2	0.02
Arab:	11	0.10
Syrian	11	0.10
Asian:	73	0.64
Cambodian (1)	1	0.01
Chinese, ex. Taiwanese (3)	5	0.04
Filipino (5)	9	0.08
Indian (20)	20	0.18
Japanese (9)	11	0.10
Korean (2)	6	0.05
Pakistani (14)	14	0.12
Vietnamese	2	0.02
Other Asian, not specified (3)	5	0.04
Austrian	10	0.09
Belgian	18	0.16
British	26	0.23
Canadian	44	0.39
Czech	5	0.04
Czechoslovakian	21	0.19
Danish	22	0.19
Dutch	200	1.77
English	1,154	10.19
European	45	0.40
French, except Basque	317	2.80
French Canadian	41	0.36
German	2,305	20.36
Hawaii Native/Pacific Islander:	2	0.02
Other Pac. Isl., not spec. (2)	2	0.02
Hispanic or Latino:	99	0.87
Central American:	2	0.02
Panamanian	2	0.02
Cuban	5	0.04
Mexican	28	0.25
Puerto Rican	14	0.12
South American:	3	0.03
Other South American	3	0.03
Other Hispanic or Latino	47	0.42
Irish	1,065	9.41
Italian	184	1.63
Lithuanian	42	0.37
Luxemburger	9	0.08
Norwegian	13	0.11
Polish	84	0.74
Portuguese	5	0.04
Russian	49	0.43
Scandinavian	4	0.04
Scotch-Irish	231	2.04
Scottish	122	1.08
Swedish	31	0.27
Swiss	37	0.33
Ukrainian	7	0.06
United States or American	1,679	14.83
Welsh	52	0.46
White:	10,151	89.67
Not Hispanic (9,992)	10,087	89.11
Hispanic (59)	64	0.57
Yugoslavian	5	0.04

Moberly

Place Type: City
County: Randolph
Population: 11,945

Ancestry/Race	Number	%
African American/Black:	862	7.22
Not Hispanic (790)	848	7.10
Hispanic (12)	14	0.12
African, sub-Saharan:	51	0.42
African	44	0.37
Nigerian	7	0.06
Alaska Native tribes, specified:	2	0.02
Tlingit-Haida (2)	2	0.02
Am. Ind. or Alaska Nat., not spec.	22	0.18
American Indian tribes, specified:	91	0.76
Blackfeet	5	0.04
Cherokee (13)	50	0.42
Chickasaw (1)	1	0.01
Chippewa (1)	1	0.01
Choctaw	1	0.01
Comanche (1)	1	0.01
Creek	2	0.02
Iroquois	5	0.04
Latin American Indians (1)	2	0.02
Osage	1	0.01
Potawatomi (5)	9	0.08
Sioux (1)	4	0.03
Tohono O'Odham (1)	1	0.01
All other tribes (8)	8	0.07
American Indian tribes, not spec.	2	0.02
Asian:	106	0.89
Chinese, ex. Taiwanese (17)	17	0.14
Filipino (16)	27	0.23
Indian (11)	21	0.18
Indonesian (1)	1	0.01
Japanese (6)	8	0.07
Korean (4)	7	0.06
Pakistani	3	0.03
Thai (1)	1	0.01
Vietnamese (18)	18	0.15
Other Asian, not specified	3	0.03
Austrian	17	0.14
British	180	1.50
Canadian	5	0.04
Croatian	10	0.08
Czech	14	0.12
Czechoslovakian	20	0.17
Danish	44	0.37
Dutch	192	1.60
English	1,115	9.28
European	14	0.12
French, except Basque	230	1.92
French Canadian	31	0.26
German	2,190	18.23
Greek	9	0.07
Hawaii Native/Pacific Islander:	7	0.06
Micronesian:	4	0.03
Guamanian/Chamorro	4	0.03
Polynesian: (1)	2	0.02
Native Hawaiian	1	0.01
Samoan (1)	1	0.01
Other Pac. Isl., not spec. (1)	1	0.01
Hispanic or Latino:	199	1.67
Central American:	9	0.08
Guatemalan	1	0.01
Panamanian	7	0.06
Salvadoran	1	0.01
Cuban	5	0.04
Mexican	119	1.00
Puerto Rican	14	0.12
South American:	2	0.02
Paraguayan	1	0.01
Other South American	1	0.01
Other Hispanic or Latino	50	0.42
Irish	1,107	9.22
Italian	247	2.06
Norwegian	44	0.37
Pennsylvania German	7	0.06
Polish	110	0.92
Portuguese	2	0.02
Russian	8	0.07
Scotch-Irish	245	2.04
Scottish	178	1.48
Slovak	7	0.06
Swedish	100	0.83
Swiss	11	0.09
Ukrainian	7	0.06
United States or American	1,703	14.18
Welsh	96	0.80
White:	10,969	91.83
Not Hispanic (10,695)	10,833	90.69
Hispanic (117)	136	1.14
Yugoslavian	10	0.08

Notes: 1. Figures in the "Number" column do not add up to the total population due to: a) Ancestry/Race overlap — e.g. persons can report being both White and Irish, b) persons of Hispanic origin can report being any race, c) persons reporting two ancestries are counted in both categories. 2. Numbers in parentheses indicate the number of persons reporting this ancestry/race alone, not in combination with any other ancestry/race. 3. Refer to the Explanation of Data in the front of the book for more detailed information.

Neosho

Place Type: City
County: Newton
Population: 10,505

Ancestry/Race	Number	%
African American/Black:	155	1.48
Not Hispanic (105)	149	1.42
Hispanic (4)	6	0.06
African, sub-Saharan:	17	0.16
African	17	0.16
Alaska Native tribes, specified:	1	0.01
Eskimo (1)	1	0.01
Am. Ind. or Alaska Nat., not spec.	63	0.60
American Indian tribes, specified:	236	2.25
Apache (2)	3	0.03
Blackfeet	1	0.01
Cherokee (79)	147	1.40
Chippewa (2)	7	0.07
Choctaw (4)	4	0.04
Creek (3)	3	0.03
Delaware	2	0.02
Iroquois (20)	28	0.27
Kiowa (1)	1	0.01
Latin American Indians	4	0.04
Osage (3)	4	0.04
Ottawa (4)	7	0.07
Pima (2)	2	0.02
Pueblo (1)	1	0.01
Puget Sound Salish	1	0.01
Seminole (1)	1	0.01
Sioux	3	0.03
All other tribes (13)	17	0.16
American Indian tribes, not spec.	14	0.13
Asian:	71	0.68
Chinese, ex. Taiwanese (3)	6	0.06
Filipino (1)	4	0.04
Indian (10)	13	0.12
Japanese (4)	6	0.06
Korean (16)	16	0.15
Taiwanese (1)	1	0.01
Thai (1)	2	0.02
Vietnamese (4)	4	0.04
Other Asian, specified	4	0.04
Other Asian, not specified (1)	15	0.14
Australian	5	0.05
Austrian	15	0.14
British	63	0.60
Canadian	74	0.71
Czech	41	0.39
Czechoslovakian	11	0.10
Danish	16	0.15
Dutch	324	3.09
English	1,014	9.66
European	82	0.78
French, except Basque	120	1.14
French Canadian	18	0.17
German	1,629	15.52
Greek	7	0.07
Hawaii Native/Pacific Islander:	125	1.19
Micronesian: (86)	93	0.89
Guamanian/Chamorro (1)	1	0.01
Other Micronesian (85)	92	0.88
Polynesian:	2	0.02
Native Hawaiian	2	0.02
Other Pac. Isl., specified	3	0.03
Other Pac. Isl., not spec. (19)	27	0.26
Hispanic or Latino:	444	4.23
Central American:	61	0.58
Guatemalan	45	0.43
Honduran	8	0.08
Salvadoran	2	0.02
Other Central American	6	0.06
Cuban	11	0.10
Mexican	290	2.76
Puerto Rican	9	0.09
South American:	4	0.04
Ecuadorian	2	0.02
Peruvian	2	0.02
Other Hispanic or Latino	69	0.66
Irish	1,163	11.08
Italian	141	1.34
Norwegian	166	1.58
Polish	100	0.95
Russian	28	0.27
Scandinavian	20	0.19
Scotch-Irish	293	2.79
Scottish	135	1.29
Swedish	141	1.34
Swiss	12	0.11
United States or American	1,598	15.23
Welsh	55	0.52
West Indian, excl. Hispanic:	4	0.04
Dutch West Indian	4	0.04
White:	9,759	92.90
Not Hispanic (9,436)	9,607	91.45
Hispanic (123)	152	1.45

Nixa

Place Type: City
County: Christian
Population: 12,124

Ancestry/Race	Number	%
Acadian/Cajun	13	0.11
African American/Black:	83	0.68
Not Hispanic (56)	83	0.68
African, sub-Saharan:	8	0.07
African	8	0.07
Am. Ind. or Alaska Nat., not spec.	12	0.10
American Indian tribes, specified:	96	0.79
Apache (1)	6	0.05
Blackfeet	1	0.01
Cherokee (17)	52	0.43
Chickasaw (1)	1	0.01
Chippewa (1)	2	0.02
Choctaw (3)	4	0.03
Creek (4)	4	0.03
Delaware	1	0.01
Iroquois (1)	1	0.01
Osage (1)	5	0.04
Ottawa (3)	3	0.02
Puget Sound Salish	1	0.01
Seminole (2)	2	0.02
Sioux	5	0.04
All other tribes (6)	8	0.07
American Indian tribes, not spec.	2	0.02
Arab:	19	0.16
Lebanese	13	0.11
Syrian	6	0.05
Asian:	82	0.68
Chinese, ex. Taiwanese (4)	8	0.07
Filipino (20)	25	0.21
Indian (2)	4	0.03
Japanese (6)	13	0.11
Korean (19)	24	0.20
Thai	2	0.02
Vietnamese (1)	5	0.04
Other Asian, not specified	1	0.01
Austrian	18	0.15
Belgian	7	0.06
British	15	0.12
Croatian	28	0.23
Czech	61	0.50
Czechoslovakian	17	0.14
Danish	52	0.43
Dutch	124	1.02
Eastern European	8	0.07
English	1,287	10.56
European	108	0.89
French, except Basque	440	3.61
French Canadian	28	0.23
German	2,538	20.82
Greek	69	0.57
Hawaii Native/Pacific Islander:	5	0.04
Polynesian: (2)	5	0.04
Native Hawaiian	1	0.01
Samoan (2)	4	0.03
Hispanic or Latino:	153	1.26
Central American:	2	0.02
Nicaraguan	1	0.01
Salvadoran	1	0.01
Cuban	5	0.04
Dominican Republic	1	0.01
Mexican	76	0.63
Puerto Rican	17	0.14
South American:	5	0.04
Colombian	2	0.02
Peruvian	1	0.01
Other South American	2	0.02
Other Hispanic or Latino	47	0.39
Hungarian	39	0.32
Irish	1,824	14.96
Italian	351	2.88
Norwegian	192	1.57
Polish	195	1.60
Portuguese	25	0.21
Russian	65	0.53
Scotch-Irish	94	0.77
Scottish	246	2.02
Swedish	182	1.49
United States or American	1,980	16.24
Welsh	113	0.93
White:	11,932	98.42
Not Hispanic (11,697)	11,811	97.42
Hispanic (115)	121	1.00

O'Fallon

Place Type: City
County: Saint Charles
Population: 46,169

Ancestry/Race	Number	%
African American/Black:	1,186	2.57
Not Hispanic (1,029)	1,176	2.55
Hispanic (4)	10	0.02
African, sub-Saharan:	94	0.20
African	82	0.18
Ghanian	4	0.01
Sierra Leonean	8	0.02
Alaska Native tribes, specified:	1	0.00
Eskimo (1)	1	0.00
Am. Ind. or Alaska Nat., not spec.	80	0.17
Albanian	28	0.06
American Indian tribes, specified:	181	0.39
Apache (3)	3	0.01
Blackfeet (2)	8	0.02
Cherokee (31)	96	0.21
Chickasaw (3)	4	0.01
Chippewa (3)	3	0.01
Choctaw (4)	9	0.02
Comanche	1	0.00
Creek (1)	2	0.00
Iroquois	2	0.00
Kiowa (1)	1	0.00
Latin American Indians (3)	6	0.01
Lumbee (3)	3	0.01
Navajo (2)	6	0.01
Osage (2)	3	0.01
Potawatomi (3)	4	0.01
Seminole (1)	1	0.00
Sioux (8)	11	0.02
All other tribes (14)	19	0.04
American Indian tribes, not spec.	7	0.02
Arab:	77	0.17
Egyptian	2	0.00
Lebanese	18	0.04
Syrian	48	0.10
Other Arab	9	0.02
Armenian	15	0.03
Asian:	470	1.02
Cambodian (1)	1	0.00
Chinese, ex. Taiwanese (95)	108	0.23
Filipino (67)	115	0.25
Indian (37)	42	0.09
Japanese (15)	32	0.07
Korean (64)	86	0.19

Notes: 1. Figures in the "Number" column do not add up to the total population due to: a) Ancestry/Race overlap — e.g. persons can report being both White and Irish, b) persons of Hispanic origin can report being any race, c) persons reporting two ancestries are counted in both categories. 2. Numbers in parentheses indicate the number of persons reporting this ancestry/race alone, not in combination with any other ancestry/race. 3. Refer to the Explanation of Data in the front of the book for more detailed information.

Ancestry/Race	Number	%
Laotian (1)	1	0.00
Malaysian (4)	6	0.01
Pakistani (3)	4	0.01
Taiwanese (2)	5	0.01
Thai (4)	6	0.01
Vietnamese (32)	44	0.10
Other Asian, not specified (10)	20	0.04
Australian	8	0.02
Austrian	173	0.38
Belgian	52	0.11
British	155	0.34
Bulgarian	8	0.02
Canadian	78	0.17
Celtic	7	0.02
Croatian	36	0.08
Czech	196	0.43
Czechoslovakian	71	0.15
Danish	67	0.15
Dutch	754	1.64
English	4,097	8.93
European	332	0.72
Finnish	42	0.09
French, except Basque	2,638	5.75
French Canadian	245	0.53
German	17,038	37.13
Greek	167	0.36
Guyanese	7	0.02
Hawaii Native/Pacific Islander:	43	0.09
Micronesian: (3)	3	0.01
Guamanian/Chamorro (1)	1	0.00
Other Micronesian (2)	2	0.00
Polynesian: (10)	34	0.07
Native Hawaiian (8)	30	0.06
Samoan (2)	4	0.01
Other Pac. Isl., not spec.	6	0.01
Hispanic or Latino:	671	1.45
Central American:	20	0.04
Costa Rican	3	0.01
Guatemalan	9	0.02
Honduran	4	0.01
Panamanian	2	0.00
Salvadoran	2	0.00
Cuban	27	0.06
Dominican Republic	3	0.01
Mexican	373	0.81
Puerto Rican	45	0.10
South American:	40	0.09
Argentinean	2	0.00
Chilean	4	0.01
Colombian	8	0.02
Ecuadorian	12	0.03
Paraguayan	1	0.00
Peruvian	7	0.02
Venezuelan	6	0.01
Other Hispanic or Latino	163	0.35
Hungarian	227	0.49
Iranian	21	0.05
Irish	8,323	18.14
Italian	2,651	5.78
Lithuanian	67	0.15
New Zealander	3	0.01
Norwegian	643	1.40
Pennsylvania German	16	0.03
Polish	2,014	4.39
Portuguese	16	0.03
Romanian	31	0.07
Russian	218	0.48
Scandinavian	15	0.03
Scotch-Irish	667	1.45
Scottish	682	1.49
Serbian	45	0.10
Slovak	26	0.06
Slovene	15	0.03
Swedish	324	0.71
Swiss	146	0.32
Ukrainian	47	0.10
United States or American	3,699	8.06
Welsh	235	0.51
West Indian, excl. Hispanic:	15	0.03
British West Indian	7	0.02
Jamaican	8	0.02
White:	44,438	96.25
Not Hispanic (43,576)	43,946	95.19
Hispanic (430)	492	1.07
Yugoslavian	109	0.24

Oakville

Place Type: Census Designated Place
County: Saint Louis
Population: 35,309

Ancestry/Race	Number	%
African American/Black:	127	0.36
Not Hispanic (84)	124	0.35
Hispanic (2)	3	0.01
African, sub-Saharan:	44	0.12
African	44	0.12
Am. Ind. or Alaska Nat., not spec.	47	0.13
Albanian	6	0.02
American Indian tribes, specified:	62	0.18
Blackfeet (1)	1	0.00
Cherokee (10)	31	0.09
Chickasaw	3	0.01
Chippewa (1)	2	0.01
Choctaw	2	0.01
Creek	1	0.00
Delaware (1)	1	0.00
Iroquois (1)	1	0.00
Latin American Indians (1)	3	0.01
Lumbee (3)	3	0.01
Osage	1	0.00
Potawatomi (1)	2	0.01
Puget Sound Salish (1)	1	0.00
Sioux (1)	4	0.01
Ute	1	0.00
All other tribes (3)	5	0.01
American Indian tribes, not spec.	7	0.02
Arab:	264	0.75
Egyptian	25	0.07
Lebanese	207	0.58
Syrian	32	0.09
Armenian	22	0.06
Asian:	406	1.15
Chinese, ex. Taiwanese (68)	74	0.21
Filipino (64)	88	0.25
Indian (63)	75	0.21
Japanese (15)	35	0.10
Korean (26)	28	0.08
Laotian (14)	15	0.04
Pakistani (9)	9	0.03
Sri Lankan (1)	5	0.01
Taiwanese (4)	5	0.01
Thai (14)	15	0.04
Vietnamese (35)	41	0.12
Other Asian, specified	1	0.00
Other Asian, not specified (6)	15	0.04
Australian	20	0.06
Austrian	171	0.48
Belgian	30	0.08
British	146	0.41
Bulgarian	58	0.16
Croatian	192	0.54
Czech	532	1.50
Czechoslovakian	149	0.42
Danish	71	0.20
Dutch	464	1.31
English	3,121	8.82
European	305	0.86
Finnish	32	0.09
French, except Basque	2,194	6.20
French Canadian	98	0.28
German	16,930	47.83
German Russian	9	0.03
Greek	144	0.41
Hawaii Native/Pacific Islander:	13	0.04
Micronesian: (1)	1	0.00
Guamanian/Chamorro (1)	1	0.00
Polynesian: (5)	5	0.01
Native Hawaiian (1)	1	0.00
Samoan (4)	4	0.01
Other Pac. Isl., specified	1	0.00
Other Pac. Isl., not spec.	6	0.02
Hispanic or Latino:	365	1.03
Central American:	12	0.03
Guatemalan	7	0.02
Honduran	1	0.00
Panamanian	2	0.01
Salvadoran	2	0.01
Cuban	23	0.07
Mexican	160	0.45
Puerto Rican	41	0.12
South American:	18	0.05
Argentinean	1	0.00
Chilean	4	0.01
Colombian	11	0.03
Ecuadorian	1	0.00
Other South American	1	0.00
Other Hispanic or Latino	111	0.31
Hungarian	208	0.59
Irish	6,604	18.66
Italian	3,483	9.84
Lithuanian	80	0.23
New Zealander	39	0.11
Northern European	61	0.17
Norwegian	302	0.85
Pennsylvania German	4	0.01
Polish	1,641	4.64
Portuguese	17	0.05
Romanian	57	0.16
Russian	144	0.41
Scotch-Irish	480	1.36
Scottish	404	1.14
Serbian	49	0.14
Slavic	38	0.11
Slovak	98	0.28
Swedish	272	0.77
Swiss	345	0.97
Turkish	17	0.05
Ukrainian	64	0.18
United States or American	1,878	5.31
Welsh	118	0.33
White:	34,770	98.47
Not Hispanic (34,290)	34,474	97.64
Hispanic (273)	296	0.84
Yugoslavian	44	0.12

Overland

Place Type: City
County: Saint Louis
Population: 16,838

Ancestry/Race	Number	%
African American/Black:	2,034	12.08
Not Hispanic (1,880)	2,027	12.04
Hispanic (5)	7	0.04
African, sub-Saharan:	25	0.15
African	17	0.10
Nigerian	8	0.05
Am. Ind. or Alaska Nat., not spec.	46	0.27
American Indian tribes, specified:	113	0.67
Apache (1)	2	0.01
Blackfeet	4	0.02
Cherokee (16)	69	0.41
Chickasaw	1	0.01
Chippewa	3	0.02
Choctaw (1)	2	0.01
Comanche	3	0.02
Creek (1)	1	0.01
Delaware	1	0.01
Iroquois	2	0.01
Latin American Indians (2)	2	0.01
Navajo (1)	1	0.01
Osage	1	0.01
Ottawa	3	0.02
Sioux (5)	6	0.04
Ute (1)	2	0.01
All other tribes (6)	10	0.06
American Indian tribes, not spec.	12	0.07

Notes: 1. Figures in the "Number" column do not add up to the total population due to: a) Ancestry/Race overlap — e.g. persons can report being both White and Irish, b) persons of Hispanic origin can report being any race, c) persons reporting two ancestries are counted in both categories. 2. Numbers in parentheses indicate the number of persons reporting this ancestry/race alone, not in combination with any other ancestry/race. 3. Refer to the Explanation of Data in the front of the book for more detailed information.

Arab:	48	0.29
Syrian	48	0.29
Armenian	8	0.05
Asian:	403	2.39
Chinese, ex. Taiwanese (47)	58	0.34
Filipino (60)	76	0.45
Hmong (2)	2	0.01
Indian (61)	62	0.37
Japanese (6)	10	0.06
Korean (26)	39	0.23
Laotian (7)	12	0.07
Thai (11)	13	0.08
Vietnamese (101)	113	0.67
Other Asian, specified	2	0.01
Other Asian, not specified (8)	16	0.10
Austrian	40	0.24
British	14	0.08
Croatian	24	0.14
Czech	92	0.55
Czechoslovakian	7	0.04
Danish	7	0.04
Dutch	321	1.92
English	1,649	9.88
European	134	0.80
Finnish	14	0.08
French, except Basque	764	4.58
French Canadian	20	0.12
German	4,885	29.27
Greek	73	0.44
Hawaii Native/Pacific Islander:	26	0.15
Micronesian:	1	0.01
Guamanian/Chamorro	1	0.01
Polynesian: (2)	10	0.06
Native Hawaiian (1)	5	0.03
Samoan (1)	5	0.03
Other Pac. Isl., specified	2	0.01
Other Pac. Isl., not spec. (3)	13	0.08
Hispanic or Latino:	368	2.19
Central American:	17	0.10
Guatemalan	4	0.02
Honduran	1	0.01
Nicaraguan	1	0.01
Panamanian	8	0.05
Salvadoran	3	0.02
Cuban	4	0.02
Mexican	271	1.61
Puerto Rican	17	0.10
South American:	10	0.06
Colombian	1	0.01
Ecuadorian	1	0.01
Peruvian	5	0.03
Other South American	3	0.02
Other Hispanic or Latino	49	0.29
Hungarian	109	0.65
Irish	2,594	15.54
Italian	819	4.91
Latvian	10	0.06
Lithuanian	14	0.08
Norwegian	32	0.19
Polish	541	3.24
Romanian	44	0.26
Russian	84	0.50
Scandinavian	14	0.08
Scotch-Irish	265	1.59
Scottish	219	1.31
Serbian	28	0.17
Slovene	12	0.07
Swedish	61	0.37
Swiss	43	0.26
Ukrainian	53	0.32
United States or American	1,366	8.19
Welsh	50	0.30
West Indian, excl. Hispanic:	8	0.05
Bahamian	8	0.05
White:	14,370	85.34
Not Hispanic (13,875)	14,141	83.98
Hispanic (194)	229	1.36

Poplar Bluff

Place Type: City
County: Butler
Population: 16,651

Ancestry/Race	Number	%
African American/Black:	1,716	10.31
Not Hispanic (1,605)	1,702	10.22
Hispanic (12)	14	0.08
African, sub-Saharan:	11	0.07
African	11	0.07
Alaska Native tribes, specified:	2	0.01
Aleut	2	0.01
Am. Ind. or Alaska Nat., not spec.	74	0.44
American Indian tribes, specified:	138	0.83
Apache	3	0.02
Blackfeet (3)	5	0.03
Cherokee (48)	104	0.62
Cheyenne (2)	2	0.01
Chickasaw (2)	3	0.02
Chippewa (2)	2	0.01
Choctaw	1	0.01
Comanche (1)	1	0.01
Creek	1	0.01
Crow	1	0.01
Iroquois (1)	1	0.01
Latin American Indians (1)	1	0.01
Menominee	1	0.01
Navajo (2)	2	0.01
Shoshone	1	0.01
Sioux	3	0.02
All other tribes (1)	5	0.03
American Indian tribes, not spec.	12	0.07
Asian:	117	0.70
Cambodian (3)	4	0.02
Chinese, ex. Taiwanese (9)	10	0.06
Filipino (12)	15	0.09
Indian (20)	22	0.13
Japanese (7)	9	0.05
Korean (10)	15	0.09
Pakistani (4)	4	0.02
Taiwanese	1	0.01
Thai (4)	4	0.02
Vietnamese (7)	9	0.05
Other Asian, specified	2	0.01
Other Asian, not specified (9)	22	0.13
Australian	6	0.04
Austrian	9	0.05
British	109	0.66
Canadian	8	0.05
Celtic	5	0.03
Czech	28	0.17
Czechoslovakian	4	0.02
Danish	12	0.07
Dutch	442	2.68
English	1,378	8.34
European	146	0.88
Finnish	7	0.04
French, except Basque	285	1.73
French Canadian	42	0.25
German	1,966	11.90
Greek	30	0.18
Hawaii Native/Pacific Islander:	4	0.02
Polynesian:	1	0.01
Native Hawaiian	1	0.01
Other Pac. Isl., specified	1	0.01
Other Pac. Isl., not spec.	2	0.01
Hispanic or Latino:	224	1.35
Central American:	7	0.04
Guatemalan	4	0.02
Salvadoran	3	0.02
Cuban	5	0.03
Mexican	129	0.77
Puerto Rican	14	0.08
South American:	1	0.01
Colombian	1	0.01
Other Hispanic or Latino	68	0.41
Hungarian	6	0.04
Irish	1,770	10.71
Italian	358	2.17
Norwegian	39	0.24
Pennsylvania German	7	0.04
Polish	65	0.39
Russian	29	0.18
Scotch-Irish	159	0.96
Scottish	119	0.72
Slavic	19	0.12
Slovak	7	0.04
Swedish	67	0.41
Swiss	23	0.14
United States or American	2,551	15.44
Welsh	108	0.65
White:	14,756	88.62
Not Hispanic (14,384)	14,620	87.80
Hispanic (109)	136	0.82

Raymore

Place Type: City
County: Cass
Population: 11,146

Ancestry/Race	Number	%
African American/Black:	239	2.14
Not Hispanic (205)	235	2.11
Hispanic	4	0.04
Am. Ind. or Alaska Nat., not spec.	26	0.23
American Indian tribes, specified:	103	0.92
Apache	1	0.01
Blackfeet	1	0.01
Cherokee (26)	51	0.46
Chickasaw	1	0.01
Chippewa (1)	1	0.01
Choctaw (3)	10	0.09
Creek	6	0.05
Delaware (3)	5	0.04
Latin American Indians (4)	4	0.04
Navajo	1	0.01
Osage	3	0.03
Potawatomi	1	0.01
Sioux (7)	10	0.09
All other tribes (1)	8	0.07
American Indian tribes, not spec.	4	0.04
Asian:	118	1.06
Chinese, ex. Taiwanese (24)	27	0.24
Filipino (12)	25	0.22
Indian (9)	12	0.11
Indonesian	3	0.03
Japanese (6)	10	0.09
Korean (9)	13	0.12
Sri Lankan (1)	1	0.01
Taiwanese (1)	3	0.03
Thai (6)	9	0.08
Vietnamese (5)	8	0.07
Other Asian, specified	1	0.01
Other Asian, not specified (1)	6	0.05
Australian	8	0.07
Austrian	19	0.17
Belgian	7	0.06
British	46	0.42
Croatian	24	0.22
Czech	109	0.99
Danish	86	0.78
Dutch	296	2.70
English	1,664	15.15
European	165	1.50
Finnish	7	0.06
French, except Basque	229	2.09
French Canadian	44	0.40
German	2,826	25.74
Greek	7	0.06
Hawaii Native/Pacific Islander:	16	0.14
Micronesian: (1)	4	0.04
Guamanian/Chamorro (1)	4	0.04
Polynesian: (1)	1	0.01
Tongan (1)	1	0.01
Other Pac. Isl., not spec. (3)	11	0.10
Hispanic or Latino:	226	2.03
Central American:	13	0.12

Notes: 1. Figures in the "Number" column do not add up to the total population due to: a) Ancestry/Race overlap — e.g. persons can report being both White and Irish, b) persons of Hispanic origin can report being any race, c) persons reporting two ancestries are counted in both categories. 2. Numbers in parentheses indicate the number of persons reporting this ancestry/race alone, not in combination with any other ancestry/race. 3. Refer to the Explanation of Data in the front of the book for more detailed information.

Ancestry/Race	Number	%
Guatemalan	1	0.01
Panamanian	11	0.10
Salvadoran	1	0.01
Cuban	5	0.04
Mexican	151	1.35
Puerto Rican	12	0.11
South American:	2	0.02
Ecuadorian	2	0.02
Other Hispanic or Latino	43	0.39
Hungarian	29	0.26
Irish	1,757	16.00
Italian	409	3.72
Lithuanian	8	0.07
Norwegian	201	1.83
Pennsylvania German	8	0.07
Polish	157	1.43
Portuguese	45	0.41
Russian	28	0.25
Scandinavian	14	0.13
Scotch-Irish	181	1.65
Scottish	282	2.57
Serbian	9	0.08
Swedish	367	3.34
Swiss	116	1.06
Ukrainian	11	0.10
United States or American	1,138	10.36
Welsh	32	0.29
White:	10,759	96.53
Not Hispanic (10,453)	10,581	94.93
Hispanic (167)	178	1.60
Yugoslavian	11	0.10

Raytown

Place Type: City
County: Jackson
Population: 30,388

Ancestry/Race	Number	%
African American/Black:	3,773	12.42
Not Hispanic (3,544)	3,736	12.29
Hispanic (23)	37	0.12
African, sub-Saharan:	301	0.99
African	274	0.90
Cape Verdean	21	0.07
Liberian	6	0.02
Alaska Native tribes, specified:	1	0.00
Alaska Athabascan (1)	1	0.00
Am. Ind. or Alaska Nat., not spec.	76	0.25
American Indian tribes, specified:	266	0.88
Apache (3)	7	0.02
Blackfeet (2)	12	0.04
Cherokee (39)	129	0.42
Cheyenne	2	0.01
Chickasaw (1)	3	0.01
Chippewa (9)	12	0.04
Choctaw (4)	16	0.05
Comanche	3	0.01
Cree	1	0.00
Creek (2)	5	0.02
Crow (1)	2	0.01
Iroquois (1)	1	0.00
Kiowa (1)	4	0.01
Latin American Indians	7	0.02
Lumbee (2)	2	0.01
Navajo (1)	4	0.01
Osage	2	0.01
Ottawa (1)	2	0.01
Potawatomi (4)	7	0.02
Seminole (1)	2	0.01
Shoshone (1)	2	0.01
Sioux (5)	13	0.04
Ute (3)	4	0.01
Yakama (2)	2	0.01
Yaqui	1	0.00
All other tribes (12)	21	0.07
American Indian tribes, not spec.	9	0.03
Arab:	15	0.05
Lebanese	6	0.02
Syrian	9	0.03
Asian:	341	1.12
Bangladeshi (2)	2	0.01
Cambodian (12)	20	0.07
Chinese, ex. Taiwanese (24)	29	0.10
Filipino (46)	64	0.21
Indian (39)	53	0.17
Japanese (19)	40	0.13
Korean (12)	20	0.07
Laotian (13)	13	0.04
Malaysian (1)	1	0.00
Pakistani	6	0.02
Thai (2)	5	0.02
Vietnamese (52)	59	0.19
Other Asian, specified	1	0.00
Other Asian, not specified (10)	28	0.09
Austrian	87	0.29
Basque	6	0.02
Belgian	34	0.11
British	152	0.50
Bulgarian	5	0.02
Canadian	14	0.05
Croatian	30	0.10
Czech	68	0.22
Czechoslovakian	33	0.11
Danish	115	0.38
Dutch	601	1.98
English	3,743	12.31
European	257	0.85
Finnish	8	0.03
French, except Basque	800	2.63
French Canadian	215	0.71
German	6,281	20.66
Greek	106	0.35
Hawaii Native/Pacific Islander:	72	0.24
Micronesian: (25)	33	0.11
Guamanian/Chamorro	1	0.00
Other Micronesian (25)	32	0.11
Polynesian: (15)	29	0.10
Native Hawaiian (8)	18	0.06
Samoan (6)	8	0.03
Other Polynesian (1)	3	0.01
Other Pac. Isl., not spec. (6)	10	0.03
Hispanic or Latino:	712	2.34
Central American:	31	0.10
Guatemalan	1	0.00
Honduran	5	0.02
Panamanian	1	0.00
Salvadoran	22	0.07
Other Central American	2	0.01
Cuban	9	0.03
Mexican	510	1.68
Puerto Rican	40	0.13
South American:	14	0.05
Argentinean	1	0.00
Bolivian	2	0.01
Colombian	8	0.03
Peruvian	1	0.00
Other South American	2	0.01
Other Hispanic or Latino	108	0.36
Hungarian	38	0.12
Icelander	8	0.03
Iranian	21	0.07
Irish	4,056	13.34
Italian	1,064	3.50
Lithuanian	19	0.06
Luxemburger	33	0.11
Norwegian	219	0.72
Pennsylvania German	29	0.10
Polish	345	1.13
Portuguese	32	0.11
Romanian	13	0.04
Russian	38	0.12
Scandinavian	42	0.14
Scotch-Irish	894	2.94
Scottish	589	1.94
Slavic	21	0.07
Slovak	15	0.05
Swedish	473	1.56
Swiss	126	0.41
Ukrainian	16	0.05
United States or American	2,997	9.86
Welsh	235	0.77
West Indian, excl. Hispanic:	13	0.04
Jamaican	13	0.04
White:	26,075	85.81
Not Hispanic (25,233)	25,651	84.41
Hispanic (361)	424	1.40

Rolla

Place Type: City
County: Phelps
Population: 16,367

Ancestry/Race	Number	%
Acadian/Cajun	16	0.10
Afghan	7	0.04
African American/Black:	536	3.27
Not Hispanic (470)	523	3.20
Hispanic (8)	13	0.08
African, sub-Saharan:	126	0.76
African	31	0.19
Liberian	7	0.04
Nigerian	63	0.38
Other sub-Saharan African	25	0.15
Alaska Native tribes, not specified	4	0.02
Am. Ind. or Alaska Nat., not spec.	33	0.20
American Indian tribes, specified:	129	0.79
Apache (1)	1	0.01
Blackfeet (1)	5	0.03
Cherokee (28)	78	0.48
Chickasaw (1)	2	0.01
Chippewa (1)	2	0.01
Choctaw (6)	7	0.04
Comanche (1)	1	0.01
Creek (1)	6	0.04
Iroquois (1)	2	0.01
Menominee (1)	1	0.01
Navajo (1)	1	0.01
Osage	1	0.01
Potawatomi (1)	2	0.01
Seminole (1)	1	0.01
Shoshone	1	0.01
Sioux (1)	3	0.02
Tohono O'Odham	1	0.01
All other tribes (7)	14	0.09
American Indian tribes, not spec.	4	0.02
Arab:	176	1.06
Arab/Arabic	84	0.51
Egyptian	28	0.17
Moroccan	6	0.04
Other Arab	58	0.35
Armenian	9	0.05
Asian:	890	5.44
Bangladeshi (1)	1	0.01
Chinese, ex. Taiwanese (307)	331	2.02
Filipino (36)	49	0.30
Indian (248)	255	1.56
Indonesian (4)	4	0.02
Japanese (18)	29	0.18
Korean (63)	71	0.43
Malaysian (6)	7	0.04
Pakistani (11)	12	0.07
Sri Lankan (11)	11	0.07
Taiwanese (12)	17	0.10
Thai (27)	29	0.18
Vietnamese (32)	37	0.23
Other Asian, specified (1)	1	0.01
Other Asian, not specified (8)	36	0.22
Austrian	13	0.08
Belgian	18	0.11
British	58	0.35
Croatian	12	0.07
Czech	60	0.36
Czechoslovakian	7	0.04
Danish	44	0.27
Dutch	238	1.44
English	1,781	10.77
Estonian	4	0.02
European	233	1.41

Notes: 1. Figures in the "Number" column do not add up to the total population due to: a) Ancestry/Race overlap — e.g. persons can report being both White and Irish, b) persons of Hispanic origin can report being any race, c) persons reporting two ancestries are counted in both categories. 2. Numbers in parentheses indicate the number of persons reporting this ancestry/race alone, not in combination with any other ancestry/race. 3. Refer to the Explanation of Data in the front of the book for more detailed information.

French, except Basque	572	3.46
French Canadian	33	0.20
German	3,873	23.42
Greek	60	0.36
Hawaii Native/Pacific Islander:	37	0.23
Micronesian: (10)	10	0.06
Guamanian/Chamorro (10)	10	0.06
Polynesian: (9)	17	0.10
Native Hawaiian (1)	9	0.05
Samoan (7)	7	0.04
Other Polynesian (1)	1	0.01
Other Pac. Isl., not spec. (1)	10	0.06
Hispanic or Latino:	282	1.72
Central American:	12	0.07
Costa Rican	3	0.02
Guatemalan	2	0.01
Honduran	2	0.01
Panamanian	4	0.02
Salvadoran	1	0.01
Cuban	10	0.06
Mexican	151	0.92
Puerto Rican	22	0.13
South American:	30	0.18
Argentinean	1	0.01
Chilean	1	0.01
Peruvian	8	0.05
Venezuelan	15	0.09
Other South American	5	0.03
Other Hispanic or Latino	57	0.35
Hungarian	26	0.16
Iranian	33	0.20
Irish	2,067	12.50
Italian	458	2.77
Lithuanian	31	0.19
Northern European	28	0.17
Norwegian	162	0.98
Polish	322	1.95
Portuguese	33	0.20
Russian	74	0.45
Scandinavian	41	0.25
Scotch-Irish	368	2.22
Scottish	337	2.04
Slavic	15	0.09
Slovak	11	0.07
Swedish	134	0.81
Swiss	55	0.33
Turkish	101	0.61
Ukrainian	21	0.13
United States or American	1,695	10.25
Welsh	148	0.89
West Indian, excl. Hispanic:	10	0.06
Haitian	10	0.06
White:	14,848	90.72
Not Hispanic (14,459)	14,683	89.71
Hispanic (140)	165	1.01
Yugoslavian	22	0.13

Saint Ann

Place Type: City
County: Saint Louis
Population: 13,607

Ancestry/Race	Number	%
African American/Black:	1,662	12.21
Not Hispanic (1,529)	1,627	11.96
Hispanic (28)	35	0.26
African, sub-Saharan:	167	1.24
African	11	0.08
Ethiopian	40	0.30
Sudanese	39	0.29
Other sub-Saharan African	77	0.57
Am. Ind. or Alaska Nat., not spec.	51	0.37
American Indian tribes, specified:	73	0.54
Apache	2	0.01
Blackfeet	6	0.04
Cherokee (9)	43	0.32
Chippewa (2)	3	0.02
Choctaw (5)	11	0.08
Comanche (3)	3	0.02
Navajo (1)	1	0.01
Osage	1	0.01
Pueblo	1	0.01
All other tribes (1)	2	0.01
American Indian tribes, not spec.	4	0.03
Arab:	66	0.49
Arab/Arabic	34	0.25
Lebanese	32	0.24
Asian:	327	2.40
Bangladeshi (4)	4	0.03
Cambodian (1)	3	0.02
Chinese, ex. Taiwanese (53)	64	0.47
Filipino (31)	40	0.29
Indian (68)	76	0.56
Japanese (10)	17	0.12
Korean (19)	28	0.21
Pakistani (2)	4	0.03
Thai (11)	12	0.09
Vietnamese (64)	68	0.50
Other Asian, not specified (3)	11	0.08
Austrian	28	0.21
Belgian	17	0.13
Canadian	2	0.01
Celtic	8	0.06
Croatian	21	0.16
Czech	81	0.60
Danish	27	0.20
Dutch	121	0.90
Eastern European	13	0.10
English	1,249	9.26
European	38	0.28
French, except Basque	841	6.23
French Canadian	61	0.45
German	4,067	30.14
Greek	9	0.07
Hawaii Native/Pacific Islander:	8	0.06
Polynesian: (2)	5	0.04
Native Hawaiian (2)	5	0.04
Other Pac. Isl., not spec.	3	0.02
Hispanic or Latino:	560	4.12
Central American:	17	0.12
Costa Rican	1	0.01
Guatemalan	4	0.03
Honduran	1	0.01
Nicaraguan	2	0.01
Panamanian	5	0.04
Salvadoran	4	0.03
Cuban	4	0.03
Dominican Republic	8	0.06
Mexican	373	2.74
Puerto Rican	49	0.36
South American:	15	0.11
Bolivian	1	0.01
Colombian	10	0.07
Ecuadorian	1	0.01
Peruvian	1	0.01
Venezuelan	2	0.01
Other Hispanic or Latino	94	0.69
Hungarian	43	0.32
Irish	2,112	15.65
Italian	486	3.60
Latvian	10	0.07
Lithuanian	17	0.13
Norwegian	73	0.54
Polish	392	2.90
Portuguese	28	0.21
Romanian	3	0.02
Russian	26	0.19
Scotch-Irish	201	1.49
Scottish	140	1.04
Slovak	9	0.07
Slovene	8	0.06
Swedish	53	0.39
Swiss	93	0.69
United States or American	1,039	7.70
Welsh	49	0.36
West Indian, excl. Hispanic:	2	0.01
Bahamian	2	0.01
White:	11,455	84.18
Not Hispanic (10,974)	11,151	81.95
Hispanic (280)	304	2.23
Yugoslavian	10	0.07

Saint Charles

Place Type: City
County: Saint Charles
Population: 60,321

Ancestry/Race	Number	%
African American/Black:	2,370	3.93
Not Hispanic (2,079)	2,339	3.88
Hispanic (18)	31	0.05
African, sub-Saharan:	83	0.14
African	76	0.13
Kenyan	7	0.01
Am. Ind. or Alaska Nat., not spec.	138	0.23
American Indian tribes, specified:	264	0.44
Apache (2)	13	0.02
Blackfeet (2)	12	0.02
Cherokee (35)	125	0.21
Chickasaw (1)	3	0.00
Chippewa (4)	5	0.01
Choctaw (9)	14	0.02
Cree	1	0.00
Creek	9	0.01
Crow (1)	1	0.00
Delaware	1	0.00
Iroquois (4)	8	0.01
Latin American Indians (11)	19	0.03
Navajo (3)	3	0.00
Osage	1	0.00
Ottawa (2)	2	0.00
Potawatomi (1)	1	0.00
Seminole (1)	4	0.01
Shoshone (1)	1	0.00
Sioux (8)	26	0.04
Ute	1	0.00
Yakama	1	0.00
All other tribes (7)	13	0.02
American Indian tribes, not spec.	23	0.04
Arab:	114	0.19
Egyptian	17	0.03
Lebanese	47	0.08
Moroccan	22	0.04
Syrian	10	0.02
Other Arab	18	0.03
Armenian	39	0.07
Asian:	774	1.28
Cambodian (1)	1	0.00
Chinese, ex. Taiwanese (113)	132	0.22
Filipino (80)	134	0.22
Indian (137)	163	0.27
Indonesian (1)	3	0.00
Japanese (29)	53	0.09
Korean (87)	101	0.17
Laotian (10)	10	0.02
Malaysian (4)	5	0.01
Pakistani (18)	20	0.03
Sri Lankan (1)	1	0.00
Taiwanese (13)	13	0.02
Thai (19)	23	0.04
Vietnamese (73)	78	0.13
Other Asian, specified (1)	1	0.00
Other Asian, not specified (18)	36	0.06
Austrian	187	0.31
Belgian	57	0.10
Brazilian	14	0.02
British	127	0.21
Bulgarian	14	0.02
Canadian	36	0.06
Celtic	6	0.01
Croatian	215	0.36
Czech	272	0.45
Czechoslovakian	109	0.18
Danish	260	0.43
Dutch	1,173	1.96
Eastern European	32	0.05
English	5,877	9.80
European	563	0.94

Notes: 1. Figures in the "Number" column do not add up to the total population due to: a) Ancestry/Race overlap — e.g. persons can report being both White and Irish, b) persons of Hispanic origin can report being any race, c) persons reporting two ancestries are counted in both categories. 2. Numbers in parentheses indicate the number of persons reporting this ancestry/race alone, not in combination with any other ancestry/race. 3. Refer to the Explanation of Data in the front of the book for more detailed information.

Ancestry/Race	Number	%
Finnish	77	0.13
French, except Basque	2,595	4.33
French Canadian	373	0.62
German	22,743	37.91
Greek	312	0.52
Hawaii Native/Pacific Islander:	37	0.06
Micronesian: (5)	6	0.01
Guamanian/Chamorro (1)	2	0.00
Other Micronesian (4)	4	0.01
Polynesian: (4)	11	0.02
Native Hawaiian (4)	10	0.02
Samoan	1	0.00
Other Pac. Isl., not spec. (13)	20	0.03
Hispanic or Latino:	1,187	1.97
Central American:	82	0.14
Costa Rican	1	0.00
Guatemalan	9	0.01
Honduran	16	0.03
Nicaraguan	3	0.00
Panamanian	46	0.08
Salvadoran	6	0.01
Other Central American	1	0.00
Cuban	13	0.02
Mexican	782	1.30
Puerto Rican	88	0.15
South American:	36	0.06
Argentinean	1	0.00
Bolivian	5	0.01
Chilean	4	0.01
Colombian	11	0.02
Ecuadorian	1	0.00
Peruvian	6	0.01
Uruguayan	1	0.00
Venezuelan	5	0.01
Other South American	2	0.00
Other Hispanic or Latino	186	0.31
Hungarian	249	0.42
Icelander	34	0.06
Irish	9,434	15.72
Italian	3,158	5.26
Latvian	8	0.01
Lithuanian	95	0.16
Macedonian	8	0.01
New Zealander	8	0.01
Northern European	44	0.07
Norwegian	384	0.64
Pennsylvania German	14	0.02
Polish	1,359	2.27
Portuguese	44	0.07
Romanian	52	0.09
Russian	277	0.46
Scandinavian	38	0.06
Scotch-Irish	882	1.47
Scottish	985	1.64
Serbian	12	0.02
Slavic	94	0.16
Slovak	49	0.08
Slovene	19	0.03
Swedish	672	1.12
Swiss	353	0.59
Ukrainian	30	0.05
United States or American	4,241	7.07
Welsh	500	0.83
West Indian, excl. Hispanic:	27	0.05
Bahamian	16	0.03
Jamaican	11	0.02
White:	56,933	94.38
Not Hispanic (55,582)	56,156	93.10
Hispanic (688)	777	1.29
Yugoslavian	15	0.03

Saint Joseph

Place Type: City
County: Buchanan
Population: 73,990

Ancestry/Race	Number	%
African American/Black:	4,204	5.68
Not Hispanic (3,685)	4,141	5.60
Hispanic (37)	63	0.09
African, sub-Saharan:	219	0.30
African	214	0.29
Nigerian	5	0.01
Alaska Native tribes, specified:	4	0.01
Eskimo	3	0.00
Tlingit-Haida (1)	1	0.00
Am. Ind. or Alaska Nat., not spec.	252	0.34
American Indian tribes, specified:	426	0.58
Apache (8)	20	0.03
Blackfeet (12)	25	0.03
Cherokee (65)	166	0.22
Cheyenne	1	0.00
Chippewa (6)	10	0.01
Choctaw (4)	10	0.01
Colville (1)	1	0.00
Comanche	4	0.01
Cree	3	0.00
Crow (17)	21	0.03
Delaware (1)	1	0.00
Iroquois (9)	11	0.01
Kiowa	1	0.00
Latin American Indians (1)	6	0.01
Menominee (3)	3	0.00
Navajo (1)	2	0.00
Osage (2)	2	0.00
Ottawa (1)	3	0.00
Paiute (3)	10	0.01
Potawatomi (6)	9	0.01
Pueblo	1	0.00
Seminole (2)	3	0.00
Shoshone (2)	5	0.01
Sioux (21)	40	0.05
Ute	1	0.00
All other tribes (34)	67	0.09
American Indian tribes, not spec.	22	0.03
Arab:	77	0.10
Jordanian	8	0.01
Lebanese	53	0.07
Moroccan	11	0.01
Syrian	5	0.01
Armenian	56	0.08
Asian:	491	0.66
Cambodian (1)	2	0.00
Chinese, ex. Taiwanese (78)	92	0.12
Filipino (64)	106	0.14
Indian (76)	90	0.12
Indonesian (1)	2	0.00
Japanese (39)	66	0.09
Korean (41)	60	0.08
Laotian	1	0.00
Malaysian	1	0.00
Pakistani (1)	1	0.00
Taiwanese (4)	4	0.01
Thai (6)	6	0.01
Vietnamese (31)	37	0.05
Other Asian, specified (1)	5	0.01
Other Asian, not specified (5)	18	0.02
Australian	15	0.02
Austrian	130	0.18
Belgian	25	0.03
British	203	0.27
Canadian	33	0.04
Celtic	8	0.01
Croatian	99	0.13
Czech	147	0.20
Czechoslovakian	97	0.13
Danish	297	0.40
Dutch	1,565	2.12
English	7,399	10.02
European	704	0.95
Finnish	21	0.03
French, except Basque	2,028	2.75
French Canadian	294	0.40
German	15,167	20.54
Greek	99	0.13
Guyanese	11	0.01
Hawaii Native/Pacific Islander:	62	0.08
Micronesian: (4)	9	0.01
Guamanian/Chamorro (4)	8	0.01
Other Micronesian	1	0.00
Polynesian: (12)	37	0.05
Native Hawaiian (7)	29	0.04
Samoan (4)	7	0.01
Other Polynesian (1)	1	0.00
Other Pac. Isl., specified	3	0.00
Other Pac. Isl., not spec. (3)	13	0.02
Hispanic or Latino:	1,929	2.61
Central American:	14	0.02
Costa Rican	1	0.00
Guatemalan	1	0.00
Nicaraguan	3	0.00
Panamanian	7	0.01
Salvadoran	2	0.00
Cuban	37	0.05
Dominican Republic	1	0.00
Mexican	1,452	1.96
Puerto Rican	73	0.10
South American:	35	0.05
Argentinean	8	0.01
Bolivian	6	0.01
Chilean	2	0.00
Colombian	9	0.01
Ecuadorian	4	0.01
Peruvian	3	0.00
Venezuelan	3	0.00
Other Hispanic or Latino	317	0.43
Hungarian	72	0.10
Icelander	7	0.01
Iranian	11	0.01
Irish	9,927	13.45
Italian	959	1.30
Latvian	4	0.01
Lithuanian	30	0.04
Luxemburger	9	0.01
Northern European	58	0.08
Norwegian	703	0.95
Pennsylvania German	17	0.02
Polish	1,683	2.28
Portuguese	36	0.05
Romanian	97	0.13
Russian	191	0.26
Scandinavian	31	0.04
Scotch-Irish	1,362	1.84
Scottish	1,232	1.67
Serbian	6	0.01
Slavic	13	0.02
Slovak	5	0.01
Swedish	783	1.06
Swiss	583	0.79
Turkish	25	0.03
Ukrainian	117	0.16
United States or American	7,852	10.64
Welsh	551	0.75
West Indian, excl. Hispanic:	73	0.10
Haitian	21	0.03
Jamaican	52	0.07
White:	68,975	93.22
Not Hispanic (66,741)	67,593	91.35
Hispanic (1,240)	1,382	1.87
Yugoslavian	18	0.02

Saint Louis

Place Type: Independent City
County: Saint Louis Independent City
Population: 348,189

Ancestry/Race	Number	%
Acadian/Cajun	43	0.01
Afghan	235	0.07
African American/Black:	181,503	52.13
Not Hispanic (177,446)	180,487	51.84
Hispanic (820)	1,016	0.29
African, sub-Saharan:	5,481	1.57
African	4,172	1.20
Ethiopian	405	0.12
Ghanian	14	0.00
Kenyan	8	0.00
Nigerian	295	0.08

Notes: 1. Figures in the "Number" column do not add up to the total population due to: a) Ancestry/Race overlap — e.g. persons can report being both White and Irish, b) persons of Hispanic origin can report being any race, c) persons reporting two ancestries are counted in both categories. 2. Numbers in parentheses indicate the number of persons reporting this ancestry/race alone, not in combination with any other ancestry/race. 3. Refer to the Explanation of Data in the front of the book for more detailed information.

Ancestry/Race	Number	%
Sierra Leonean	51	0.01
Somalian	340	0.10
South African	50	0.01
Other sub-Saharan African	146	0.04
Alaska Native tribes, specified:	18	0.01
Alaska Athabascan (2)	2	0.00
Aleut	1	0.00
Eskimo (2)	3	0.00
Tlingit-Haida (9)	12	0.00
Alaska Native tribes, not specified	3	0.00
Am. Ind. or Alaska Nat., not spec.	1,160	0.33
Albanian	576	0.17
Alsatian	17	0.00
American Indian tribes, specified:	1,621	0.47
Apache (9)	37	0.01
Blackfeet (25)	164	0.05
Cherokee (228)	883	0.25
Cheyenne (2)	10	0.00
Chickasaw (2)	17	0.00
Chippewa (27)	44	0.01
Choctaw (12)	63	0.02
Comanche	4	0.00
Cree (3)	8	0.00
Creek (5)	15	0.00
Crow (1)	4	0.00
Delaware (4)	9	0.00
Houma	3	0.00
Iroquois (19)	25	0.01
Kiowa (2)	5	0.00
Latin American Indians (52)	71	0.02
Lumbee (4)	7	0.00
Menominee	1	0.00
Navajo (15)	29	0.01
Osage (5)	15	0.00
Ottawa	2	0.00
Pima (1)	5	0.00
Potawatomi (2)	6	0.00
Pueblo (3)	11	0.00
Seminole (4)	25	0.01
Shoshone	3	0.00
Sioux (24)	76	0.02
Tohono O'Odham (1)	1	0.00
Ute (1)	1	0.00
Yuman (1)	4	0.00
All other tribes (37)	73	0.02
American Indian tribes, not spec.	134	0.04
Arab:	1,643	0.47
Arab/Arabic	170	0.05
Egyptian	17	0.00
Iraqi	318	0.09
Jordanian	7	0.00
Lebanese	758	0.22
Moroccan	70	0.02
Palestinian	30	0.01
Syrian	88	0.03
Other Arab	185	0.05
Armenian	151	0.04
Asian:	8,242	2.37
Bangladeshi (1)	4	0.00
Cambodian (34)	60	0.02
Chinese, ex. Taiwanese (980)	1,149	0.33
Filipino (454)	639	0.18
Hmong (6)	7	0.00
Indian (845)	1,025	0.29
Indonesian (10)	12	0.00
Japanese (217)	336	0.10
Korean (289)	394	0.11
Laotian (290)	317	0.09
Malaysian (18)	22	0.01
Pakistani (46)	63	0.02
Sri Lankan (11)	13	0.00
Taiwanese (58)	70	0.02
Thai (75)	99	0.03
Vietnamese (3,319)	3,464	0.99
Other Asian, specified (7)	80	0.02
Other Asian, not specified (142)	488	0.14
Assyrian/Chaldean/Syriac	7	0.00
Australian	25	0.01
Austrian	733	0.21
Belgian	215	0.06
Brazilian	42	0.01
British	424	0.12
Bulgarian	31	0.01
Canadian	197	0.06
Carpatho Rusyn	4	0.00
Celtic	25	0.01
Croatian	811	0.23
Cypriot	31	0.01
Czech	1,819	0.52
Czechoslovakian	456	0.13
Danish	328	0.09
Dutch	2,450	0.70
Eastern European	181	0.05
English	13,435	3.86
European	1,304	0.37
Finnish	197	0.06
French, except Basque	8,376	2.41
French Canadian	522	0.15
German	50,575	14.53
German Russian	7	0.00
Greek	994	0.29
Guyanese	12	0.00
Hawaii Native/Pacific Islander:	334	0.10
Melanesian: (3)	5	0.00
Fijian (3)	5	0.00
Micronesian: (29)	63	0.02
Guamanian/Chamorro (23)	53	0.02
Other Micronesian (6)	10	0.00
Polynesian: (48)	110	0.03
Native Hawaiian (16)	56	0.02
Samoan (31)	50	0.01
Other Polynesian (1)	4	0.00
Other Pac. Isl., specified	65	0.02
Other Pac. Isl., not spec. (14)	91	0.03
Hispanic or Latino:	7,022	2.02
Central American:	299	0.09
Costa Rican	13	0.00
Guatemalan	39	0.01
Honduran	82	0.02
Nicaraguan	48	0.01
Panamanian	64	0.02
Salvadoran	42	0.01
Other Central American	11	0.00
Cuban	373	0.11
Dominican Republic	41	0.01
Mexican	4,111	1.18
Puerto Rican	500	0.14
South American:	256	0.07
Argentinean	20	0.01
Bolivian	25	0.01
Chilean	39	0.01
Colombian	65	0.02
Ecuadorian	18	0.01
Paraguayan	1	0.00
Peruvian	40	0.01
Uruguayan	5	0.00
Venezuelan	26	0.01
Other South American	17	0.00
Other Hispanic or Latino	1,442	0.41
Hungarian	1,013	0.29
Icelander	24	0.01
Iranian	94	0.03
Irish	30,092	8.64
Israeli	36	0.01
Italian	12,579	3.61
Latvian	60	0.02
Lithuanian	478	0.14
Luxemburger	40	0.01
Macedonian	96	0.03
New Zealander	6	0.00
Northern European	235	0.07
Norwegian	928	0.27
Pennsylvania German	24	0.01
Polish	5,324	1.53
Portuguese	150	0.04
Romanian	281	0.08
Russian	1,253	0.36
Scandinavian	111	0.03
Scotch-Irish	2,429	0.70
Scottish	2,435	0.70
Serbian	202	0.06
Slavic	212	0.06
Slovak	420	0.12
Slovene	93	0.03
Swedish	1,176	0.34
Swiss	749	0.22
Turkish	47	0.01
Ukrainian	423	0.12
United States or American	10,641	3.06
Welsh	885	0.25
West Indian, excl. Hispanic:	498	0.14
Bahamian	8	0.00
Barbadian	14	0.00
Belizean	10	0.00
Haitian	272	0.08
Jamaican	174	0.05
West Indian	20	0.01
White:	157,460	45.22
Not Hispanic (149,329)	153,721	44.15
Hispanic (3,337)	3,739	1.07
Yugoslavian	5,128	1.47

Saint Peters

Place Type: City
County: Saint Charles
Population: 51,381

Ancestry/Race	Number	%
African American/Black:	1,604	3.12
Not Hispanic (1,424)	1,580	3.08
Hispanic (16)	24	0.05
African, sub-Saharan:	73	0.14
African	48	0.09
Liberian	25	0.05
Alaska Native tribes, specified:	2	0.00
Aleut	2	0.00
Am. Ind. or Alaska Nat., not spec.	67	0.13
American Indian tribes, specified:	178	0.35
Blackfeet (3)	7	0.01
Cherokee (42)	89	0.17
Cheyenne	3	0.01
Chickasaw	4	0.01
Chippewa (1)	4	0.01
Choctaw (5)	11	0.02
Comanche	2	0.00
Cree (1)	4	0.01
Creek	1	0.00
Delaware (1)	2	0.00
Iroquois (5)	6	0.01
Latin American Indians (2)	4	0.01
Navajo (3)	5	0.01
Osage	3	0.01
Ottawa (1)	1	0.00
Pueblo (1)	2	0.00
Seminole (1)	1	0.00
Sioux (7)	11	0.02
All other tribes (13)	18	0.04
American Indian tribes, not spec.	5	0.01
Arab:	133	0.26
Arab/Arabic	7	0.01
Lebanese	85	0.17
Syrian	35	0.07
Other Arab	6	0.01
Armenian	13	0.03
Asian:	806	1.57
Chinese, ex. Taiwanese (98)	122	0.24
Filipino (141)	194	0.38
Indian (128)	142	0.28
Indonesian (1)	1	0.00
Japanese (30)	55	0.11
Korean (91)	114	0.22
Laotian (6)	6	0.01
Malaysian (2)	3	0.01
Pakistani (18)	20	0.04
Sri Lankan (1)	1	0.00
Thai (9)	14	0.03
Vietnamese (71)	89	0.17
Other Asian, specified (4)	4	0.01
Other Asian, not specified (19)	41	0.08

Notes: 1. Figures in the "Number" column do not add up to the total population due to: a) Ancestry/Race overlap — e.g. persons can report being both White and Irish, b) persons of Hispanic origin can report being any race, c) persons reporting two ancestries are counted in both categories. 2. Numbers in parentheses indicate the number of persons reporting this ancestry/race alone, not in combination with any other ancestry/race. 3. Refer to the Explanation of Data in the front of the book for more detailed information.

Australian	8	0.02
Austrian	277	0.54
Belgian	39	0.08
British	78	0.15
Bulgarian	29	0.06
Canadian	93	0.18
Celtic	13	0.03
Croatian	152	0.30
Czech	305	0.59
Czechoslovakian	117	0.23
Danish	150	0.29
Dutch	1,018	1.98
Eastern European	8	0.02
English	6,059	11.80
European	469	0.91
Finnish	38	0.07
French, except Basque	2,546	4.96
French Canadian	290	0.56
German	20,120	39.20
Greek	128	0.25
Hawaii Native/Pacific Islander:	40	0.08
Micronesian:	4	0.01
Guamanian/Chamorro	4	0.01
Polynesian: (3)	32	0.06
Native Hawaiian (1)	24	0.05
Samoan (2)	7	0.01
Tongan	1	0.00
Other Pac. Isl., not spec. (1)	4	0.01
Hispanic or Latino:	768	1.49
Central American:	33	0.06
Costa Rican	2	0.00
Guatemalan	11	0.02
Nicaraguan	4	0.01
Panamanian	13	0.03
Salvadoran	3	0.01
Cuban	24	0.05
Dominican Republic	2	0.00
Mexican	467	0.91
Puerto Rican	94	0.18
South American:	30	0.06
Argentinean	1	0.00
Bolivian	3	0.01
Colombian	13	0.03
Ecuadorian	4	0.01
Peruvian	7	0.01
Venezuelan	2	0.00
Other Hispanic or Latino	118	0.23
Hungarian	134	0.26
Iranian	17	0.03
Irish	9,392	18.30
Italian	3,726	7.26
Lithuanian	86	0.17
Luxemburger	5	0.01
Norwegian	411	0.80
Pennsylvania German	6	0.01
Polish	1,940	3.78
Portuguese	48	0.09
Romanian	29	0.06
Russian	171	0.33
Scandinavian	86	0.17
Scotch-Irish	799	1.56
Scottish	816	1.59
Serbian	17	0.03
Slavic	19	0.04
Slovak	93	0.18
Slovene	49	0.10
Swedish	786	1.53
Swiss	203	0.40
Ukrainian	69	0.13
United States or American	3,424	6.67
Welsh	236	0.46
White:	48,934	95.24
Not Hispanic (47,929)	48,379	94.16
Hispanic (498)	555	1.08
Yugoslavian	53	0.10

Sedalia

Place Type: City
County: Pettis
Population: 20,339

Ancestry/Race	Number	%
African American/Black:	1,136	5.59
Not Hispanic (992)	1,115	5.48
Hispanic (15)	21	0.10
African, sub-Saharan:	50	0.24
African	36	0.18
Somalian	14	0.07
Am. Ind. or Alaska Nat., not spec.	65	0.32
American Indian tribes, specified:	169	0.83
Apache (2)	3	0.01
Blackfeet (2)	6	0.03
Cherokee (20)	87	0.43
Chickasaw	3	0.01
Choctaw (5)	8	0.04
Comanche	1	0.00
Creek	2	0.01
Iroquois	2	0.01
Latin American Indians (2)	3	0.01
Navajo	5	0.02
Osage (1)	11	0.05
Puget Sound Salish (2)	2	0.01
Seminole (1)	1	0.00
Sioux (8)	15	0.07
Tohono O'Odham (1)	1	0.00
Ute (1)	2	0.01
All other tribes (5)	17	0.08
American Indian tribes, not spec.	8	0.04
Arab:	25	0.12
Lebanese	25	0.12
Asian:	134	0.66
Chinese, ex. Taiwanese (14)	14	0.07
Filipino (22)	40	0.20
Indian (7)	15	0.07
Indonesian (1)	1	0.00
Japanese (8)	14	0.07
Korean (4)	11	0.05
Laotian	1	0.00
Thai (6)	8	0.04
Vietnamese (11)	14	0.07
Other Asian, not specified (8)	16	0.08
Austrian	11	0.05
British	36	0.18
Canadian	15	0.07
Czech	46	0.22
Czechoslovakian	47	0.23
Danish	79	0.39
Dutch	414	2.02
English	1,866	9.13
European	80	0.39
Finnish	13	0.06
French, except Basque	565	2.76
French Canadian	25	0.12
German	4,398	21.51
Greek	12	0.06
Hawaii Native/Pacific Islander:	25	0.12
Micronesian: (2)	3	0.01
Guamanian/Chamorro (2)	3	0.01
Polynesian: (2)	8	0.04
Native Hawaiian (1)	7	0.03
Samoan (1)	1	0.00
Other Pac. Isl., not spec.	14	0.07
Hispanic or Latino:	1,129	5.55
Central American:	51	0.25
Guatemalan	13	0.06
Honduran	8	0.04
Panamanian	2	0.01
Salvadoran	28	0.14
Cuban	8	0.04
Mexican	930	4.57
Puerto Rican	21	0.10
South American:	4	0.02
Ecuadorian	4	0.02
Other Hispanic or Latino	115	0.57
Hungarian	13	0.06
Iranian	6	0.03
Irish	2,001	9.79
Italian	298	1.46
Luxemburger	7	0.03
New Zealander	5	0.02
Northern European	24	0.12
Norwegian	111	0.54
Pennsylvania German	6	0.03
Polish	154	0.75
Portuguese	6	0.03
Romanian	4	0.02
Russian	23	0.11
Scandinavian	29	0.14
Scotch-Irish	473	2.31
Scottish	255	1.25
Slovak	3	0.01
Swedish	174	0.85
Swiss	68	0.33
Turkish	2	0.01
Ukrainian	22	0.11
United States or American	2,368	11.58
Welsh	156	0.76
West Indian, excl. Hispanic:	5	0.02
Dutch West Indian	5	0.02
White:	18,375	90.34
Not Hispanic (17,717)	18,030	88.65
Hispanic (308)	345	1.70

Sikeston

Place Type: City
County: Scott
Population: 16,992

Ancestry/Race	Number	%
African American/Black:	3,882	22.85
Not Hispanic (3,772)	3,851	22.66
Hispanic (28)	31	0.18
African, sub-Saharan:	47	0.28
African	47	0.28
Alaska Native tribes, specified:	2	0.01
Eskimo (2)	2	0.01
Am. Ind. or Alaska Nat., not spec.	25	0.15
American Indian tribes, specified:	84	0.49
Apache	5	0.03
Blackfeet	2	0.01
Cherokee (19)	57	0.34
Chickasaw (1)	1	0.01
Chippewa (1)	1	0.01
Choctaw (9)	11	0.06
Iroquois (1)	1	0.01
Latin American Indians (2)	2	0.01
Navajo	1	0.01
Sioux (2)	2	0.01
Yuman	1	0.01
Arab:	6	0.04
Jordanian	4	0.02
Lebanese	2	0.01
Armenian	24	0.14
Asian:	83	0.49
Chinese, ex. Taiwanese (15)	20	0.12
Filipino (5)	7	0.04
Indian (11)	13	0.08
Indonesian	3	0.02
Japanese (2)	3	0.02
Korean (2)	4	0.02
Pakistani (13)	13	0.08
Vietnamese (12)	12	0.07
Other Asian, not specified (1)	8	0.05
Austrian	6	0.04
British	16	0.09
Celtic	15	0.09
Czech	19	0.11
Danish	17	0.10
Dutch	229	1.35
English	1,155	6.79
European	46	0.27
French, except Basque	501	2.94
French Canadian	18	0.11
German	2,011	11.82

Notes: 1. Figures in the "Number" column do not add up to the total population due to: a) Ancestry/Race overlap — e.g. persons can report being both White and Irish, b) persons of Hispanic origin can report being any race, c) persons reporting two ancestries are counted in both categories. 2. Numbers in parentheses indicate the number of persons reporting this ancestry/race alone, not in combination with any other ancestry/race. 3. Refer to the Explanation of Data in the front of the book for more detailed information.

Ancestry/Race	Number	%
Greek	20	0.12
Hispanic or Latino:	204	1.20
Central American:	9	0.05
Costa Rican	2	0.01
Guatemalan	1	0.01
Honduran	5	0.03
Salvadoran	1	0.01
Cuban	4	0.02
Mexican	111	0.65
Puerto Rican	6	0.04
South American:	2	0.01
Venezuelan	2	0.01
Other Hispanic or Latino	72	0.42
Irish	1,935	11.37
Italian	88	0.52
Northern European	5	0.03
Norwegian	20	0.12
Polish	160	0.94
Russian	17	0.10
Scandinavian	5	0.03
Scotch-Irish	248	1.46
Scottish	144	0.85
Swedish	30	0.18
Swiss	31	0.18
United States or American	2,909	17.10
Welsh	75	0.44
West Indian, excl. Hispanic:	26	0.15
Dutch West Indian	3	0.02
Jamaican	23	0.14
White:	12,975	76.36
Not Hispanic (12,752)	12,877	75.78
Hispanic (80)	98	0.58

Spanish Lake

Place Type: Census Designated Place
County: Saint Louis
Population: 21,337

Ancestry/Race	Number	%
African American/Black:	11,948	56.00
Not Hispanic (11,638)	11,866	55.61
Hispanic (53)	82	0.38
African, sub-Saharan:	414	1.93
African	343	1.60
Nigerian	71	0.33
Am. Ind. or Alaska Nat., not spec.	59	0.28
Albanian	6	0.03
American Indian tribes, specified:	95	0.45
Blackfeet	18	0.08
Cherokee (14)	45	0.21
Cheyenne	3	0.01
Chickasaw	4	0.02
Chippewa (3)	3	0.01
Choctaw	13	0.06
Cree	2	0.01
Creek (1)	1	0.00
Iroquois	1	0.00
Osage (1)	1	0.00
All other tribes (2)	4	0.02
American Indian tribes, not spec.	5	0.02
Arab:	17	0.08
Lebanese	8	0.04
Moroccan	9	0.04
Armenian	8	0.04
Asian:	192	0.90
Chinese, ex. Taiwanese (27)	32	0.15
Filipino (40)	51	0.24
Indian (21)	28	0.13
Indonesian	1	0.00
Japanese (5)	8	0.04
Korean (21)	30	0.14
Laotian (1)	1	0.00
Malaysian (1)	1	0.00
Pakistani	2	0.01
Taiwanese	1	0.00
Thai (1)	3	0.01
Vietnamese (11)	15	0.07
Other Asian, specified (3)	3	0.01
Other Asian, not specified (6)	16	0.07
Austrian	65	0.30
Belgian	17	0.08
Canadian	30	0.14
Croatian	44	0.21
Czech	108	0.50
Czechoslovakian	28	0.13
Danish	14	0.07
Dutch	166	0.77
English	655	3.05
European	68	0.32
French, except Basque	475	2.21
French Canadian	18	0.08
German	3,594	16.75
Greek	15	0.07
Hawaii Native/Pacific Islander:	8	0.04
Polynesian: (5)	6	0.03
Native Hawaiian (5)	6	0.03
Other Pac. Isl., not spec. (1)	2	0.01
Hispanic or Latino:	220	1.03
Central American:	7	0.03
Nicaraguan	1	0.00
Panamanian	6	0.03
Cuban	10	0.05
Dominican Republic	3	0.01
Mexican	98	0.46
Puerto Rican	46	0.22
South American:	3	0.01
Argentinean	1	0.00
Colombian	1	0.00
Peruvian	1	0.00
Other Hispanic or Latino	53	0.25
Hungarian	55	0.26
Irish	2,047	9.54
Italian	810	3.78
Lithuanian	6	0.03
Norwegian	36	0.17
Pennsylvania German	25	0.12
Polish	452	2.11
Romanian	8	0.04
Russian	20	0.09
Scotch-Irish	131	0.61
Scottish	26	0.12
Slovak	17	0.08
Swedish	108	0.50
Swiss	46	0.21
Ukrainian	31	0.14
United States or American	731	3.41
Welsh	51	0.24
West Indian, excl. Hispanic:	23	0.11
Jamaican	23	0.11
White:	9,247	43.34
Not Hispanic (8,934)	9,149	42.88
Hispanic (80)	98	0.46
Yugoslavian	33	0.15

Springfield

Place Type: City
County: Greene
Population: 151,580

Ancestry/Race	Number	%
Acadian/Cajun	5	0.00
African American/Black:	5,841	3.85
Not Hispanic (4,863)	5,674	3.74
Hispanic (98)	167	0.11
African, sub-Saharan:	467	0.31
African	330	0.22
Cape Verdean	7	0.00
Ethiopian	20	0.01
Ghanian	13	0.01
Kenyan	24	0.02
Nigerian	36	0.02
South African	6	0.00
Zimbabwean	31	0.02
Alaska Native tribes, specified:	33	0.02
Alaska Athabascan (6)	8	0.01
Aleut (3)	7	0.00
Eskimo (6)	12	0.01
Tlingit-Haida (2)	6	0.00
Alaska Native tribes, not specified	2	0.00
Am. Ind. or Alaska Nat., not spec.	618	0.41
Albanian	4	0.00
Alsatian	34	0.02
American Indian tribes, specified:	1,949	1.29
Apache (27)	66	0.04
Blackfeet (14)	85	0.06
Cherokee (356)	1,045	0.69
Cheyenne (7)	21	0.01
Chickasaw (7)	20	0.01
Chippewa (42)	60	0.04
Choctaw (44)	107	0.07
Colville	1	0.00
Comanche (16)	28	0.02
Cree (3)	3	0.00
Creek (17)	31	0.02
Crow (3)	9	0.01
Delaware (3)	8	0.01
Iroquois (19)	37	0.02
Kiowa (4)	7	0.00
Latin American Indians (8)	27	0.02
Lumbee (1)	2	0.00
Menominee (1)	4	0.00
Navajo (24)	37	0.02
Osage (12)	38	0.03
Ottawa (8)	17	0.01
Pima (1)	2	0.00
Potawatomi (16)	23	0.02
Pueblo (6)	9	0.01
Puget Sound Salish (2)	2	0.00
Seminole (12)	21	0.01
Shoshone (7)	11	0.01
Sioux (47)	104	0.07
Tohono O'Odham (3)	3	0.00
Ute (6)	7	0.00
Yaqui (4)	4	0.00
All other tribes (64)	110	0.07
American Indian tribes, not spec.	98	0.06
Arab:	312	0.21
Arab/Arabic	53	0.03
Egyptian	12	0.01
Lebanese	125	0.08
Moroccan	19	0.01
Palestinian	34	0.02
Syrian	30	0.02
Other Arab	39	0.03
Armenian	8	0.01
Asian:	2,603	1.72
Bangladeshi (9)	12	0.01
Cambodian (21)	34	0.02
Chinese, ex. Taiwanese (369)	415	0.27
Filipino (193)	301	0.20
Indian (208)	259	0.17
Indonesian (25)	35	0.02
Japanese (118)	214	0.14
Korean (360)	441	0.29
Laotian (14)	14	0.01
Malaysian (12)	19	0.01
Pakistani (20)	26	0.02
Sri Lankan (11)	12	0.01
Taiwanese (10)	15	0.01
Thai (49)	60	0.04
Vietnamese (514)	578	0.38
Other Asian, specified (7)	20	0.01
Other Asian, not specified (81)	148	0.10
Australian	40	0.03
Austrian	231	0.15
Basque	38	0.03
Belgian	122	0.08
Brazilian	29	0.02
British	622	0.41
Bulgarian	19	0.01
Canadian	106	0.07
Celtic	63	0.04
Croatian	93	0.06
Czech	340	0.22
Czechoslovakian	188	0.12
Danish	583	0.38
Dutch	3,362	2.21
English	16,555	10.90

Notes: 1. Figures in the "Number" column do not add up to the total population due to: a) Ancestry/Race overlap — e.g. persons can report being both White and Irish, b) persons of Hispanic origin can report being any race, c) persons reporting two ancestries are counted in both categories. 2. Numbers in parentheses indicate the number of persons reporting this ancestry/race alone, not in combination with any other ancestry/race. 3. Refer to the Explanation of Data in the front of the book for more detailed information.

Ancestry/Race	Number	%
Estonian	13	0.01
European	2,187	1.44
Finnish	123	0.08
French, except Basque	4,728	3.11
French Canadian	481	0.32
German	28,331	18.66
German Russian	47	0.03
Greek	285	0.19
Hawaii Native/Pacific Islander:	249	0.16
Melanesian: (1)	3	0.00
Other Melanesian (1)	3	0.00
Micronesian: (54)	71	0.05
Guamanian/Chamorro (19)	28	0.02
Other Micronesian (35)	43	0.03
Polynesian: (63)	120	0.08
Native Hawaiian (28)	63	0.04
Samoan (33)	51	0.03
Tongan (1)	2	0.00
Other Polynesian (1)	4	0.00
Other Pac. Isl., specified	10	0.01
Other Pac. Isl., not spec. (11)	45	0.03
Hispanic or Latino:	3,501	2.31
Central American:	132	0.09
Costa Rican	10	0.01
Guatemalan	10	0.01
Honduran	16	0.01
Nicaraguan	13	0.01
Panamanian	25	0.02
Salvadoran	46	0.03
Other Central American	12	0.01
Cuban	108	0.07
Dominican Republic	16	0.01
Mexican	2,055	1.36
Puerto Rican	303	0.20
South American:	138	0.09
Argentinean	8	0.01
Bolivian	12	0.01
Chilean	13	0.01
Colombian	53	0.03
Ecuadorian	17	0.01
Paraguayan	1	0.00
Peruvian	13	0.01
Uruguayan	4	0.00
Venezuelan	11	0.01
Other South American	6	0.00
Other Hispanic or Latino	749	0.49
Hungarian	346	0.23
Icelander	22	0.01
Irish	19,438	12.80
Italian	3,560	2.34
Latvian	8	0.01
Lithuanian	103	0.07
New Zealander	17	0.01
Northern European	120	0.08
Norwegian	1,753	1.15
Pennsylvania German	96	0.06
Polish	1,963	1.29
Portuguese	89	0.06
Romanian	144	0.09
Russian	455	0.30
Scandinavian	242	0.16
Scotch-Irish	3,485	2.30
Scottish	3,167	2.09
Serbian	7	0.00
Slavic	47	0.03
Slovak	68	0.04
Slovene	32	0.02
Swedish	2,116	1.39
Swiss	447	0.29
Turkish	23	0.02
Ukrainian	84	0.06
United States or American	17,304	11.40
Welsh	1,016	0.67
West Indian, excl. Hispanic:	143	0.09
Belizean	26	0.02
Dutch West Indian	57	0.04
Jamaican	38	0.03
West Indian	22	0.01
White:	141,722	93.50
Not Hispanic (137,140)	139,565	92.07
Hispanic (1,847)	2,157	1.42
Yugoslavian	22	0.01

Town and Country

Place Type: City
County: Saint Louis
Population: 10,894

Ancestry/Race	Number	%
African American/Black:	229	2.10
Not Hispanic (218)	227	2.08
Hispanic (1)	2	0.02
Alaska Native tribes, specified:	2	0.02
Alaska Athabascan (1)	2	0.02
Am. Ind. or Alaska Nat., not spec.	8	0.07
Albanian	32	0.29
Alsatian	5	0.05
American Indian tribes, specified:	10	0.09
Cherokee	5	0.05
Choctaw (1)	1	0.01
Creek (1)	1	0.01
Lumbee	1	0.01
All other tribes	2	0.02
Arab:	138	1.27
Arab/Arabic	8	0.07
Egyptian	39	0.36
Jordanian	46	0.42
Lebanese	41	0.38
Other Arab	4	0.04
Armenian	12	0.11
Asian:	798	7.33
Bangladeshi (1)	1	0.01
Chinese, ex. Taiwanese (90)	112	1.03
Filipino (63)	89	0.82
Indian (300)	326	2.99
Japanese (16)	23	0.21
Korean (58)	58	0.53
Pakistani (57)	76	0.70
Sri Lankan (8)	8	0.07
Taiwanese (47)	52	0.48
Thai (20)	23	0.21
Vietnamese (7)	9	0.08
Other Asian, not specified (9)	21	0.19
Australian	9	0.08
Austrian	58	0.53
Belgian	15	0.14
British	78	0.72
Canadian	20	0.18
Croatian	23	0.21
Czech	96	0.88
Czechoslovakian	10	0.09
Danish	45	0.41
Dutch	193	1.77
English	1,678	15.42
European	78	0.72
French, except Basque	454	4.17
French Canadian	39	0.36
German	3,270	30.06
Greek	183	1.68
Hawaii Native/Pacific Islander:	15	0.14
Polynesian: (1)	1	0.01
Native Hawaiian (1)	1	0.01
Other Pac. Isl., not spec.	14	0.13
Hispanic or Latino:	117	1.07
Central American:	7	0.06
Guatemalan	3	0.03
Honduran	2	0.02
Nicaraguan	1	0.01
Panamanian	1	0.01
Cuban	16	0.15
Mexican	35	0.32
Puerto Rican	23	0.21
South American:	12	0.11
Argentinean	1	0.01
Bolivian	3	0.03
Colombian	1	0.01
Paraguayan	1	0.01
Peruvian	1	0.01
Venezuelan	1	0.01
Other South American	4	0.04
Other Hispanic or Latino	24	0.22
Hungarian	86	0.79
Iranian	98	0.90
Irish	1,824	16.77
Italian	523	4.81
Latvian	6	0.06
Lithuanian	47	0.43
Luxemburger	2	0.02
Macedonian	13	0.12
Northern European	12	0.11
Norwegian	119	1.09
Polish	402	3.70
Romanian	71	0.65
Russian	239	2.20
Scotch-Irish	202	1.86
Scottish	191	1.76
Slavic	2	0.02
Slovak	9	0.08
Swedish	154	1.42
Swiss	92	0.85
Turkish	33	0.30
Ukrainian	23	0.21
United States or American	578	5.31
Welsh	45	0.41
West Indian, excl. Hispanic:	7	0.06
Jamaican	7	0.06
White:	9,941	91.25
Not Hispanic (9,738)	9,850	90.42
Hispanic (84)	91	0.84
Yugoslavian	10	0.09

University City

Place Type: City
County: Saint Louis
Population: 37,428

Ancestry/Race	Number	%
Acadian/Cajun	7	0.02
African American/Black:	17,366	46.40
Not Hispanic (16,895)	17,267	46.13
Hispanic (79)	99	0.26
African, sub-Saharan:	716	1.91
African	500	1.33
Ethiopian	87	0.23
Ghanian	11	0.03
Kenyan	23	0.06
Liberian	25	0.07
Nigerian	12	0.03
South African	48	0.13
Other sub-Saharan African	10	0.03
Am. Ind. or Alaska Nat., not spec.	113	0.30
Albanian	6	0.02
Alsatian	9	0.02
American Indian tribes, specified:	122	0.33
Apache (1)	1	0.00
Blackfeet	5	0.01
Cherokee (6)	40	0.11
Cheyenne	2	0.01
Chickasaw (1)	1	0.00
Chippewa	2	0.01
Choctaw (1)	16	0.04
Creek (1)	2	0.01
Crow	1	0.00
Delaware	1	0.00
Iroquois (1)	6	0.02
Kiowa	1	0.00
Latin American Indians (4)	12	0.03
Lumbee (1)	1	0.00
Navajo	2	0.01
Osage	3	0.01
Potawatomi (1)	1	0.00
Pueblo	1	0.00
Seminole	6	0.02
Sioux (6)	8	0.02
Ute (1)	2	0.01
All other tribes (4)	8	0.02
American Indian tribes, not spec.	5	0.01
Arab:	154	0.41

Notes: 1. Figures in the "Number" column do not add up to the total population due to: a) Ancestry/Race overlap — e.g. persons can report being both White and Irish, b) persons of Hispanic origin can report being any race, c) persons reporting two ancestries are counted in both categories. 2. Numbers in parentheses indicate the number of persons reporting this ancestry/race alone, not in combination with any other ancestry/race. 3. Refer to the Explanation of Data in the front of the book for more detailed information.

Ancestry/Race	Number	%
Arab/Arabic	9	0.02
Egyptian	22	0.06
Iraqi	20	0.05
Lebanese	50	0.13
Moroccan	15	0.04
Syrian	30	0.08
Other Arab	8	0.02
Armenian	61	0.16
Asian:	1,269	3.39
Bangladeshi (4)	4	0.01
Chinese, ex. Taiwanese (415)	462	1.23
Filipino (62)	93	0.25
Indian (247)	279	0.75
Indonesian (4)	4	0.01
Japanese (75)	99	0.26
Korean (90)	115	0.31
Malaysian (8)	13	0.03
Pakistani (23)	26	0.07
Sri Lankan (4)	4	0.01
Taiwanese (24)	33	0.09
Thai (13)	15	0.04
Vietnamese (37)	43	0.11
Other Asian, specified (15)	30	0.08
Other Asian, not specified (26)	49	0.13
Austrian	165	0.44
Belgian	18	0.05
Brazilian	16	0.04
British	136	0.36
Bulgarian	23	0.06
Canadian	78	0.21
Celtic	6	0.02
Croatian	73	0.19
Czech	117	0.31
Czechoslovakian	34	0.09
Danish	125	0.33
Dutch	291	0.78
Eastern European	255	0.68
English	2,353	6.28
European	450	1.20
Finnish	6	0.02
French, except Basque	994	2.65
French Canadian	116	0.31
German	4,929	13.16
Greek	108	0.29
Hawaii Native/Pacific Islander:	33	0.09
Micronesian: (2)	4	0.01
Guamanian/Chamorro (2)	3	0.01
Other Micronesian	1	0.00
Polynesian: (6)	9	0.02
Native Hawaiian (3)	4	0.01
Samoan (1)	2	0.01
Tongan (1)	1	0.00
Other Polynesian (1)	2	0.01
Other Pac. Isl., specified	10	0.03
Other Pac. Isl., not spec. (3)	10	0.03
Hispanic or Latino:	583	1.56
Central American:	38	0.10
Costa Rican	2	0.01
Guatemalan	13	0.03
Honduran	10	0.03
Panamanian	7	0.02
Salvadoran	3	0.01
Other Central American	3	0.01
Cuban	27	0.07
Dominican Republic	5	0.01
Mexican	205	0.55
Puerto Rican	54	0.14
South American:	105	0.28
Argentinean	13	0.03
Bolivian	4	0.01
Chilean	6	0.02
Colombian	24	0.06
Ecuadorian	3	0.01
Paraguayan	3	0.01
Peruvian	30	0.08
Venezuelan	19	0.05
Other South American	3	0.01
Other Hispanic or Latino	149	0.40
Hungarian	203	0.54
Iranian	7	0.02
Irish	3,422	9.13
Israeli	19	0.05
Italian	1,056	2.82
Latvian	41	0.11
Lithuanian	50	0.13
New Zealander	10	0.03
Northern European	18	0.05
Norwegian	171	0.46
Polish	969	2.59
Portuguese	8	0.02
Romanian	59	0.16
Russian	1,431	3.82
Scandinavian	36	0.10
Scotch-Irish	407	1.09
Scottish	510	1.36
Serbian	55	0.15
Slavic	8	0.02
Slovak	35	0.09
Slovene	26	0.07
Swedish	290	0.77
Swiss	77	0.21
Turkish	42	0.11
Ukrainian	222	0.59
United States or American	1,012	2.70
Welsh	170	0.45
West Indian, excl. Hispanic:	111	0.30
Dutch West Indian	12	0.03
Haitian	8	0.02
Jamaican	57	0.15
West Indian	34	0.09
White:	18,943	50.61
Not Hispanic (18,112)	18,584	49.65
Hispanic (325)	359	0.96
Yugoslavian	16	0.04

Warrensburg

Place Type: City
County: Johnson
Population: 16,340

Ancestry/Race	Number	%
African American/Black:	1,176	7.20
Not Hispanic (1,048)	1,160	7.10
Hispanic (7)	16	0.10
African, sub-Saharan:	125	0.76
African	74	0.45
Kenyan	9	0.05
Nigerian	16	0.10
South African	9	0.05
Other sub-Saharan African	17	0.10
Am. Ind. or Alaska Nat., not spec.	49	0.30
Albanian	14	0.09
American Indian tribes, specified:	147	0.90
Apache (2)	3	0.02
Blackfeet (1)	4	0.02
Cherokee (33)	71	0.43
Cheyenne	1	0.01
Chickasaw (2)	4	0.02
Chippewa (11)	11	0.07
Choctaw (13)	14	0.09
Cree	1	0.01
Creek	2	0.01
Delaware (1)	2	0.01
Houma	1	0.01
Iroquois (1)	2	0.01
Latin American Indians	1	0.01
Lumbee (1)	1	0.01
Navajo (1)	1	0.01
Osage	1	0.01
Ottawa (1)	1	0.01
Potawatomi (1)	2	0.01
Pueblo (3)	4	0.02
Seminole (1)	1	0.01
Sioux (4)	10	0.06
All other tribes (4)	9	0.06
American Indian tribes, not spec.	12	0.07
Arab:	37	0.23
Jordanian	37	0.23
Armenian	4	0.02
Asian:	586	3.59
Bangladeshi (3)	10	0.06
Cambodian (1)	1	0.01
Chinese, ex. Taiwanese (128)	139	0.85
Filipino (59)	84	0.51
Hmong	1	0.01
Indian (80)	93	0.57
Indonesian (8)	8	0.05
Japanese (40)	56	0.34
Korean (40)	50	0.31
Laotian	1	0.01
Malaysian (8)	11	0.07
Pakistani (2)	7	0.04
Taiwanese (7)	16	0.10
Thai (15)	23	0.14
Vietnamese (34)	42	0.26
Other Asian, specified (4)	4	0.02
Other Asian, not specified (13)	40	0.24
Australian	6	0.04
Austrian	8	0.05
Basque	7	0.04
Belgian	21	0.13
British	85	0.52
Canadian	34	0.21
Croatian	19	0.12
Czech	29	0.18
Czechoslovakian	6	0.04
Danish	80	0.49
Dutch	221	1.35
Eastern European	5	0.03
English	1,826	11.12
European	232	1.41
Finnish	23	0.14
French, except Basque	582	3.54
French Canadian	99	0.60
German	4,269	25.99
Greek	17	0.10
Hawaii Native/Pacific Islander:	58	0.35
Micronesian: (6)	12	0.07
Guamanian/Chamorro (6)	12	0.07
Polynesian: (13)	25	0.15
Native Hawaiian (1)	7	0.04
Samoan (11)	17	0.10
Other Polynesian (1)	1	0.01
Other Pac. Isl., not spec. (4)	21	0.13
Hispanic or Latino:	398	2.44
Central American:	6	0.04
Costa Rican	2	0.01
Honduran	1	0.01
Panamanian	3	0.02
Cuban	12	0.07
Dominican Republic	2	0.01
Mexican	232	1.42
Puerto Rican	56	0.34
South American:	13	0.08
Argentinean	1	0.01
Colombian	6	0.04
Venezuelan	6	0.04
Other Hispanic or Latino	77	0.47
Hungarian	7	0.04
Iranian	10	0.06
Irish	2,351	14.31
Italian	407	2.48
New Zealander	6	0.04
Northern European	58	0.35
Norwegian	302	1.84
Polish	164	1.00
Portuguese	21	0.13
Russian	69	0.42
Scandinavian	47	0.29
Scotch-Irish	339	2.06
Scottish	355	2.16
Slavic	8	0.05
Swedish	269	1.64
Swiss	39	0.24
Turkish	62	0.38
United States or American	1,437	8.75
Welsh	93	0.57
West Indian, excl. Hispanic:	33	0.20
British West Indian	26	0.16

Notes: 1. Figures in the "Number" column do not add up to the total population due to: a) Ancestry/Race overlap — e.g. persons can report being both White and Irish, b) persons of Hispanic origin can report being any race, c) persons reporting two ancestries are counted in both categories. 2. Numbers in parentheses indicate the number of persons reporting this ancestry/race alone, not in combination with any other ancestry/race. 3. Refer to the Explanation of Data in the front of the book for more detailed information.

Ancestry/Race	Number	%
Haitian	7	0.04
White:	14,506	88.78
Not Hispanic (13,966)	14,223	87.04
Hispanic (234)	283	1.73
Yugoslavian	18	0.11

Washington

Place Type: City
County: Franklin
Population: 13,243

Ancestry/Race	Number	%
African American/Black:	127	0.96
Not Hispanic (112)	127	0.96
Am. Ind. or Alaska Nat., not spec.	12	0.09
American Indian tribes, specified:	42	0.32
Blackfeet	1	0.01
Cherokee (7)	20	0.15
Chickasaw	1	0.01
Chippewa (1)	1	0.01
Choctaw (3)	5	0.04
Iroquois (3)	3	0.02
Latin American Indians	1	0.01
Navajo	1	0.01
Puget Sound Salish (2)	2	0.02
Sioux	2	0.02
All other tribes (1)	5	0.04
Arab:	48	0.37
Arab/Arabic	16	0.12
Lebanese	32	0.24
Armenian	14	0.11
Asian:	83	0.63
Chinese, ex. Taiwanese (4)	4	0.03
Filipino (14)	28	0.21
Indian (15)	16	0.12
Japanese (2)	9	0.07
Korean (12)	16	0.12
Vietnamese (5)	5	0.04
Other Asian, specified (1)	1	0.01
Other Asian, not specified (1)	4	0.03
Austrian	7	0.05
Belgian	7	0.05
British	12	0.09
Croatian	19	0.15
Czech	39	0.30
Czechoslovakian	36	0.27
Dutch	179	1.37
English	1,296	9.90
European	57	0.44
Finnish	7	0.05
French, except Basque	541	4.13
French Canadian	67	0.51
German	6,498	49.63
Greek	15	0.11
Hawaii Native/Pacific Islander:	4	0.03
Polynesian:	3	0.02
Native Hawaiian	2	0.02
Samoan	1	0.01
Other Pac. Isl., not spec.	1	0.01
Hispanic or Latino:	88	0.66
Central American:	1	0.01
Guatemalan	1	0.01
Mexican	56	0.42
Puerto Rican	8	0.06
Other Hispanic or Latino	23	0.17
Hungarian	48	0.37
Irish	1,526	11.66
Italian	219	1.67
Lithuanian	64	0.49
Norwegian	99	0.76
Polish	241	1.84
Portuguese	25	0.19
Romanian	7	0.05
Russian	25	0.19
Scandinavian	11	0.08
Scotch-Irish	203	1.55
Scottish	200	1.53
Serbian	7	0.05
Slovak	11	0.08
Swedish	129	0.99
Swiss	62	0.47
United States or American	852	6.51
Welsh	105	0.80
White:	13,025	98.35
Not Hispanic (12,890)	12,960	97.86
Hispanic (56)	65	0.49

Webster Groves

Place Type: City
County: Saint Louis
Population: 23,230

Ancestry/Race	Number	%
African American/Black:	1,579	6.80
Not Hispanic (1,472)	1,560	6.72
Hispanic (10)	19	0.08
African, sub-Saharan:	83	0.36
African	67	0.29
Ghanian	16	0.07
Am. Ind. or Alaska Nat., not spec.	39	0.17
Albanian	16	0.07
Alsatian	24	0.10
American Indian tribes, specified:	88	0.38
Apache	1	0.00
Blackfeet (1)	1	0.00
Cherokee (13)	50	0.22
Chippewa (1)	2	0.01
Choctaw (3)	4	0.02
Creek (1)	1	0.00
Iroquois (1)	1	0.00
Latin American Indians (2)	4	0.02
Navajo (1)	2	0.01
Osage	1	0.00
Ottawa	1	0.00
Pima	2	0.01
Potawatomi	4	0.02
Seminole (1)	1	0.00
Sioux (1)	6	0.03
All other tribes (2)	7	0.03
American Indian tribes, not spec.	4	0.02
Arab:	72	0.31
Arab/Arabic	11	0.05
Lebanese	56	0.24
Moroccan	5	0.02
Armenian	25	0.11
Asian:	354	1.52
Chinese, ex. Taiwanese (54)	74	0.32
Filipino (23)	34	0.15
Indian (43)	47	0.20
Indonesian (2)	3	0.01
Japanese (65)	84	0.36
Korean (24)	32	0.14
Laotian (1)	2	0.01
Pakistani (1)	1	0.00
Taiwanese (11)	13	0.06
Thai (15)	15	0.06
Vietnamese (28)	37	0.16
Other Asian, specified	6	0.03
Other Asian, not specified (3)	6	0.03
Australian	22	0.10
Austrian	127	0.55
Belgian	57	0.25
British	115	0.50
Canadian	24	0.10
Celtic	8	0.03
Croatian	70	0.30
Czech	268	1.16
Czechoslovakian	24	0.10
Danish	81	0.35
Dutch	373	1.62
English	3,391	14.70
European	244	1.06
Finnish	10	0.04
French, except Basque	1,148	4.98
French Canadian	71	0.31
German	9,012	39.07
Greek	153	0.66
Hawaii Native/Pacific Islander:	14	0.06
Micronesian:	1	0.00
Guamanian/Chamorro	1	0.00
Polynesian: (3)	7	0.03
Native Hawaiian (2)	3	0.01
Tongan (1)	4	0.02
Other Pac. Isl., specified	6	0.03
Hispanic or Latino:	291	1.25
Central American:	26	0.11
Costa Rican	4	0.02
Guatemalan	10	0.04
Panamanian	7	0.03
Salvadoran	2	0.01
Other Central American	3	0.01
Cuban	9	0.04
Dominican Republic	3	0.01
Mexican	117	0.50
Puerto Rican	15	0.06
South American:	46	0.20
Argentinean	1	0.00
Bolivian	1	0.00
Chilean	3	0.01
Colombian	24	0.10
Ecuadorian	4	0.02
Paraguayan	1	0.00
Peruvian	9	0.04
Venezuelan	3	0.01
Other Hispanic or Latino	75	0.32
Hungarian	202	0.88
Icelander	8	0.03
Iranian	54	0.23
Irish	4,879	21.15
Israeli	5	0.02
Italian	1,212	5.25
Latvian	11	0.05
Lithuanian	78	0.34
Luxemburger	16	0.07
Macedonian	4	0.02
Northern European	45	0.20
Norwegian	291	1.26
Polish	513	2.22
Romanian	9	0.04
Russian	244	1.06
Scandinavian	57	0.25
Scotch-Irish	614	2.66
Scottish	681	2.95
Serbian	6	0.03
Slavic	20	0.09
Slovak	70	0.30
Slovene	10	0.04
Swedish	273	1.18
Swiss	143	0.62
Ukrainian	114	0.49
United States or American	946	4.10
Welsh	177	0.77
West Indian, excl. Hispanic:	9	0.04
Bahamian	3	0.01
Haitian	6	0.03
White:	21,327	91.81
Not Hispanic (20,927)	21,127	90.95
Hispanic (181)	200	0.86
Yugoslavian	17	0.07

West Plains

Place Type: City
County: Howell
Population: 10,866

Ancestry/Race	Number	%
African American/Black:	90	0.83
Not Hispanic (79)	89	0.82
Hispanic	1	0.01
African, sub-Saharan:	16	0.15
South African	10	0.09
Other sub-Saharan African	6	0.06
Am. Ind. or Alaska Nat., not spec.	49	0.45
American Indian tribes, specified:	141	1.30
Apache (2)	3	0.03
Blackfeet (1)	5	0.05
Cherokee (51)	99	0.91

Notes: 1. Figures in the "Number" column do not add up to the total population due to: a) Ancestry/Race overlap — e.g. persons can report being both White and Irish, b) persons of Hispanic origin can report being any race, c) persons reporting two ancestries are counted in both categories. 2. Numbers in parentheses indicate the number of persons reporting this ancestry/race alone, not in combination with any other ancestry/race. 3. Refer to the Explanation of Data in the front of the book for more detailed information.

Ancestry/Race	Number	%
Chickasaw	1	0.01
Choctaw (1)	5	0.05
Cree	3	0.03
Iroquois	1	0.01
Latin American Indians (2)	2	0.02
Navajo (1)	1	0.01
Osage (3)	3	0.03
Pima (1)	3	0.03
Potawatomi (1)	1	0.01
Shoshone (1)	2	0.02
Sioux (2)	2	0.02
Yuman (2)	5	0.05
All other tribes (3)	5	0.05
American Indian tribes, not spec.	10	0.09
Arab:	7	0.07
Arab/Arabic	7	0.07
Asian:	111	1.02
Chinese, ex. Taiwanese (10)	10	0.09
Filipino (7)	19	0.17
Indian (26)	31	0.29
Japanese (2)	7	0.06
Korean (6)	13	0.12
Malaysian	1	0.01
Pakistani (13)	13	0.12
Taiwanese (3)	3	0.03
Thai	1	0.01
Vietnamese (4)	6	0.06
Other Asian, not specified (4)	7	0.06
Austrian	22	0.20
Belgian	5	0.05
British	14	0.13
Celtic	9	0.08
Czech	2	0.02
Czechoslovakian	11	0.10
Danish	48	0.45
Dutch	232	2.16
Eastern European	5	0.05
English	899	8.37
European	133	1.24
Finnish	11	0.10
French, except Basque	267	2.49
French Canadian	58	0.54
German	1,500	13.97
Greek	37	0.34
Hawaii Native/Pacific Islander:	18	0.17
Micronesian: (1)	1	0.01
Guamanian/Chamorro (1)	1	0.01
Polynesian: (4)	17	0.16
Native Hawaiian (1)	6	0.06
Samoan (2)	6	0.06
Tongan (1)	2	0.02
Other Polynesian	3	0.03
Hispanic or Latino:	179	1.65
Central American:	3	0.03
Honduran	2	0.02
Other Central American	1	0.01
Cuban	2	0.02
Mexican	116	1.07
Puerto Rican	4	0.04
South American:	1	0.01
Colombian	1	0.01
Other Hispanic or Latino	53	0.49
Hungarian	14	0.13
Irish	1,209	11.26
Italian	111	1.03
Lithuanian	4	0.04
Norwegian	95	0.88
Polish	118	1.10
Portuguese	15	0.14
Russian	52	0.48
Scandinavian	4	0.04
Scotch-Irish	151	1.41
Scottish	159	1.48
Slovak	5	0.05
Swedish	79	0.74
Swiss	10	0.09
Turkish	5	0.05
Ukrainian	8	0.07
United States or American	1,575	14.67
Welsh	59	0.55
West Indian, excl. Hispanic:	8	0.07
Jamaican	8	0.07
White:	10,534	96.94
Not Hispanic (10,304)	10,416	95.86
Hispanic (97)	118	1.09
Yugoslavian	8	0.07

Wildwood

Place Type: City
County: Saint Louis
Population: 32,884

Ancestry/Race	Number	%
African American/Black:	581	1.77
Not Hispanic (524)	569	1.73
Hispanic (10)	12	0.04
African, sub-Saharan:	11	0.03
African	5	0.01
South African	6	0.02
Alaska Native tribes, specified:	1	0.00
Eskimo (1)	1	0.00
Am. Ind. or Alaska Nat., not spec.	19	0.06
American Indian tribes, specified:	103	0.31
Apache (2)	9	0.03
Blackfeet	3	0.01
Cherokee (14)	62	0.19
Chippewa	2	0.01
Choctaw (1)	2	0.01
Creek (2)	2	0.01
Iroquois (1)	1	0.00
Latin American Indians (1)	5	0.02
Paiute	1	0.00
Pueblo (3)	4	0.01
Sioux (1)	8	0.02
All other tribes (2)	4	0.01
American Indian tribes, not spec.	5	0.02
Arab:	200	0.60
Arab/Arabic	32	0.10
Egyptian	13	0.04
Iraqi	22	0.07
Lebanese	118	0.35
Palestinian	15	0.04
Armenian	6	0.02
Asian:	898	2.73
Bangladeshi	4	0.01
Chinese, ex. Taiwanese (244)	269	0.82
Filipino (66)	90	0.27
Indian (262)	279	0.85
Indonesian (6)	6	0.02
Japanese (28)	62	0.19
Korean (87)	89	0.27
Laotian (2)	2	0.01
Malaysian (6)	6	0.02
Pakistani (9)	9	0.03
Sri Lankan (2)	2	0.01
Taiwanese (9)	12	0.04
Thai (6)	7	0.02
Vietnamese (37)	41	0.12
Other Asian, not specified (11)	20	0.06
Australian	16	0.05
Austrian	237	0.71
Belgian	32	0.10
Brazilian	117	0.35
British	89	0.27
Canadian	84	0.25
Croatian	94	0.28
Czech	333	1.00
Czechoslovakian	200	0.60
Danish	159	0.48
Dutch	732	2.19
English	4,568	13.66
European	500	1.49
Finnish	42	0.13
French, except Basque	1,697	5.07
French Canadian	99	0.30
German	12,568	37.58
Greek	176	0.53
Hawaii Native/Pacific Islander:	10	0.03
Micronesian:	2	0.01
Guamanian/Chamorro	2	0.01
Polynesian: (2)	4	0.01
Native Hawaiian	1	0.00
Samoan (2)	3	0.01
Other Pac. Isl., not spec.	4	0.01
Hispanic or Latino:	454	1.38
Central American:	20	0.06
Costa Rican	1	0.00
Guatemalan	10	0.03
Honduran	6	0.02
Nicaraguan	1	0.00
Salvadoran	2	0.01
Cuban	27	0.08
Dominican Republic	2	0.01
Mexican	230	0.70
Puerto Rican	51	0.16
South American:	37	0.11
Argentinean	12	0.04
Bolivian	4	0.01
Chilean	4	0.01
Colombian	8	0.02
Peruvian	5	0.02
Venezuelan	3	0.01
Other South American	1	0.00
Other Hispanic or Latino	87	0.26
Hungarian	219	0.65
Iranian	24	0.07
Irish	6,632	19.83
Italian	2,716	8.12
Lithuanian	173	0.52
Norwegian	604	1.81
Pennsylvania German	9	0.03
Polish	1,339	4.00
Portuguese	70	0.21
Romanian	49	0.15
Russian	398	1.19
Scandinavian	70	0.21
Scotch-Irish	698	2.09
Scottish	818	2.45
Serbian	23	0.07
Slavic	34	0.10
Slovak	139	0.42
Slovene	14	0.04
Swedish	742	2.22
Swiss	241	0.72
Turkish	19	0.06
Ukrainian	69	0.21
United States or American	1,534	4.59
Welsh	354	1.06
West Indian, excl. Hispanic:	56	0.17
British West Indian	26	0.08
Haitian	13	0.04
West Indian	17	0.05
White:	31,406	95.51
Not Hispanic (30,830)	31,038	94.39
Hispanic (325)	368	1.12
Yugoslavian	56	0.17

Billings

Place Type: City
County: Yellowstone
Population: 89,847

Ancestry/Race	Number	%
African American/Black:	849	0.94
Not Hispanic (466)	737	0.82
Hispanic (29)	112	0.12
African, sub-Saharan:	55	0.06
African	32	0.04
Nigerian	15	0.02
South African	8	0.01
Alaska Native tribes, specified:	21	0.02
Alaska Athabascan (5)	5	0.01
Aleut (3)	5	0.01
Eskimo (1)	2	0.00
Tlingit-Haida (8)	8	0.01
All other tribes (1)	1	0.00
Alaska Native tribes, not specified	2	0.00
Am. Ind. or Alaska Nat., not spec.	722	0.80

Notes: 1. Figures in the "Number" column do not add up to the total population due to: a) Ancestry/Race overlap — e.g. persons can report being both White and Irish, b) persons of Hispanic origin can report being any race, c) persons reporting two ancestries are counted in both categories. 2. Numbers in parentheses indicate the number of persons reporting this ancestry/race alone, not in combination with any other ancestry/race. 3. Refer to the Explanation of Data in the front of the book for more detailed information.

Ancestry/Race	Number	%
American Indian tribes, specified:	3,285	3.66
Apache (13)	20	0.02
Blackfeet (109)	150	0.17
Cherokee (21)	96	0.11
Cheyenne (378)	487	0.54
Chickasaw (2)	3	0.00
Chippewa (235)	342	0.38
Choctaw (4)	5	0.01
Colville	4	0.00
Comanche (4)	4	0.00
Cree (15)	25	0.03
Creek (13)	18	0.02
Crow (780)	925	1.03
Delaware (2)	3	0.00
Iroquois (4)	7	0.01
Kiowa (10)	10	0.01
Latin American Indians (14)	24	0.03
Menominee	1	0.00
Navajo (20)	31	0.03
Osage (1)	2	0.00
Ottawa (2)	2	0.00
Paiute (1)	1	0.00
Pima (1)	3	0.00
Potawatomi (2)	4	0.00
Pueblo (3)	8	0.01
Puget Sound Salish (4)	5	0.01
Seminole	9	0.01
Shoshone (15)	19	0.02
Sioux (317)	430	0.48
Ute (3)	10	0.01
Yakama (5)	9	0.01
Yaqui (1)	4	0.00
Yuman (3)	3	0.00
All other tribes (459)	621	0.69
American Indian tribes, not spec.	117	0.13
Arab:	142	0.16
Arab/Arabic	7	0.01
Iraqi	15	0.02
Lebanese	82	0.09
Palestinian	17	0.02
Other Arab	21	0.02
Armenian	91	0.10
Asian:	891	0.99
Bangladeshi	2	0.00
Chinese, ex. Taiwanese (111)	171	0.19
Filipino (54)	147	0.16
Hmong	1	0.00
Indian (39)	62	0.07
Indonesian	2	0.00
Japanese (95)	189	0.21
Korean (135)	174	0.19
Laotian (6)	8	0.01
Malaysian	2	0.00
Pakistani (1)	1	0.00
Sri Lankan (3)	3	0.00
Taiwanese (8)	10	0.01
Thai (15)	21	0.02
Vietnamese (36)	48	0.05
Other Asian, specified	6	0.01
Other Asian, not specified (18)	44	0.05
Australian	31	0.03
Austrian	256	0.29
Basque	36	0.04
Belgian	316	0.35
British	309	0.35
Bulgarian	26	0.03
Canadian	182	0.20
Celtic	56	0.06
Croatian	123	0.14
Czech	642	0.72
Czechoslovakian	260	0.29
Danish	1,524	1.71
Dutch	2,089	2.34
Eastern European	9	0.01
English	11,582	12.96
European	646	0.72
Finnish	596	0.67
French, except Basque	3,858	4.32
French Canadian	935	1.05
German	29,442	32.95
German Russian	6	0.01
Greek	268	0.30
Hawaii Native/Pacific Islander:	136	0.15
Micronesian: (5)	12	0.01
Guamanian/Chamorro (4)	9	0.01
Other Micronesian (1)	3	0.00
Polynesian: (29)	104	0.12
Native Hawaiian (23)	85	0.09
Samoan (4)	13	0.01
Tongan (2)	6	0.01
Other Pac. Isl., specified	1	0.00
Other Pac. Isl., not spec. (3)	19	0.02
Hispanic or Latino:	3,758	4.18
Central American:	42	0.05
Costa Rican	7	0.01
Guatemalan	3	0.00
Honduran	5	0.01
Nicaraguan	9	0.01
Panamanian	9	0.01
Salvadoran	6	0.01
Other Central American	3	0.00
Cuban	30	0.03
Dominican Republic	2	0.00
Mexican	2,706	3.01
Puerto Rican	120	0.13
South American:	17	0.02
Argentinean	6	0.01
Bolivian	1	0.00
Chilean	1	0.00
Colombian	7	0.01
Peruvian	1	0.00
Other South American	1	0.00
Other Hispanic or Latino	841	0.94
Hungarian	366	0.41
Icelander	19	0.02
Iranian	11	0.01
Irish	12,955	14.50
Italian	2,439	2.73
Lithuanian	39	0.04
Luxemburger	26	0.03
Macedonian	3	0.00
Northern European	121	0.14
Norwegian	10,492	11.74
Pennsylvania German	63	0.07
Polish	1,680	1.88
Portuguese	50	0.06
Romanian	80	0.09
Russian	1,451	1.62
Scandinavian	385	0.43
Scotch-Irish	2,310	2.58
Scottish	2,729	3.05
Serbian	67	0.07
Slavic	106	0.12
Slovak	89	0.10
Slovene	85	0.10
Swedish	2,668	2.99
Swiss	411	0.46
Turkish	7	0.01
Ukrainian	299	0.33
United States or American	3,632	4.06
Welsh	990	1.11
West Indian, excl. Hispanic:	51	0.06
Dutch West Indian	26	0.03
Jamaican	8	0.01
Trinidadian and Tobagonian	17	0.02
White:	84,211	93.73
Not Hispanic (80,770)	82,058	91.33
Hispanic (1,769)	2,153	2.40
Yugoslavian	496	0.56

Bozeman

Place Type: City
County: Gallatin
Population: 27,509

Ancestry/Race	Number	%
Acadian/Cajun	9	0.03
African American/Black:	143	0.52
Not Hispanic (88)	132	0.48
Hispanic (4)	11	0.04
African, sub-Saharan:	13	0.05
Zimbabwean	13	0.05
Alaska Native tribes, specified:	9	0.03
Alaska Athabascan (4)	4	0.01
Aleut	1	0.00
Eskimo (1)	1	0.00
All other tribes	3	0.01
Alaska Native tribes, not specified	3	0.01
Am. Ind. or Alaska Nat., not spec.	102	0.37
American Indian tribes, specified:	381	1.39
Apache (1)	5	0.02
Blackfeet (47)	54	0.20
Cherokee (8)	37	0.13
Cheyenne (16)	21	0.08
Chickasaw (1)	1	0.00
Chippewa (37)	51	0.19
Choctaw (1)	4	0.01
Cree (4)	6	0.02
Crow (41)	46	0.17
Iroquois (1)	2	0.01
Latin American Indians (2)	4	0.01
Lumbee (1)	1	0.00
Navajo (2)	5	0.02
Osage (1)	1	0.00
Potawatomi (2)	7	0.03
Pueblo	1	0.00
Puget Sound Salish (2)	2	0.01
Seminole	2	0.01
Shoshone (2)	3	0.01
Sioux (21)	28	0.10
Ute (3)	6	0.02
Yaqui	1	0.00
All other tribes (66)	93	0.34
American Indian tribes, not spec.	22	0.08
Arab:	26	0.09
Lebanese	12	0.04
Syrian	9	0.03
Other Arab	5	0.02
Armenian	7	0.02
Asian:	598	2.17
Bangladeshi (4)	4	0.01
Chinese, ex. Taiwanese (123)	141	0.51
Filipino (27)	65	0.24
Hmong (1)	1	0.00
Indian (44)	51	0.19
Indonesian (6)	9	0.03
Japanese (91)	130	0.47
Korean (94)	105	0.38
Malaysian (4)	21	0.08
Taiwanese (5)	6	0.02
Thai (22)	26	0.09
Vietnamese (7)	10	0.04
Other Asian, specified	5	0.02
Other Asian, not specified (9)	24	0.09
Australian	18	0.06
Austrian	149	0.53
Basque	21	0.07
Belgian	49	0.17
Brazilian	6	0.02
British	255	0.91
Bulgarian	25	0.09
Canadian	39	0.14
Celtic	10	0.04
Croatian	24	0.09
Czech	181	0.65
Czechoslovakian	127	0.45
Danish	526	1.88
Dutch	774	2.76
Eastern European	15	0.05
English	3,183	11.37
Estonian	6	0.02
European	501	1.79
Finnish	79	0.28
French, except Basque	1,040	3.71
French Canadian	230	0.82
German	7,283	26.01
Greek	126	0.45
Hawaii Native/Pacific Islander:	48	0.17
Micronesian: (2)	5	0.02

Notes: 1. Figures in the "Number" column do not add up to the total population due to: a) Ancestry/Race overlap — e.g. persons can report being both White and Irish, b) persons of Hispanic origin can report being any race, c) persons reporting two ancestries are counted in both categories. 2. Numbers in parentheses indicate the number of persons reporting this ancestry/race alone, not in combination with any other ancestry/race. 3. Refer to the Explanation of Data in the front of the book for more detailed information.

Ancestry/Race	Number	%
Guamanian/Chamorro (2)	5	0.02
Polynesian: (14)	34	0.12
Native Hawaiian (11)	27	0.10
Samoan (3)	6	0.02
Other Polynesian	1	0.00
Other Pac. Isl., specified	1	0.00
Other Pac. Isl., not spec. (2)	8	0.03
Hispanic or Latino:	438	1.59
Central American:	4	0.01
Costa Rican	1	0.00
Guatemalan	2	0.01
Panamanian	1	0.00
Cuban	9	0.03
Dominican Republic	6	0.02
Mexican	211	0.77
Puerto Rican	46	0.17
South American:	30	0.11
Argentinean	2	0.01
Bolivian	1	0.00
Chilean	3	0.01
Colombian	5	0.02
Ecuadorian	6	0.02
Peruvian	7	0.03
Uruguayan	1	0.00
Venezuelan	5	0.02
Other Hispanic or Latino	132	0.48
Hungarian	136	0.49
Icelander	21	0.07
Iranian	11	0.04
Irish	4,239	15.14
Italian	1,092	3.90
Latvian	20	0.07
Lithuanian	98	0.35
Luxemburger	8	0.03
Macedonian	13	0.05
New Zealander	9	0.03
Northern European	44	0.16
Norwegian	2,632	9.40
Pennsylvania German	7	0.02
Polish	686	2.45
Portuguese	42	0.15
Romanian	23	0.08
Russian	381	1.36
Scandinavian	246	0.88
Scotch-Irish	628	2.24
Scottish	1,081	3.86
Serbian	6	0.02
Slavic	21	0.07
Slovak	53	0.19
Slovene	5	0.02
Swedish	1,135	4.05
Swiss	219	0.78
Ukrainian	88	0.31
United States or American	1,107	3.95
Welsh	394	1.41
White:	26,424	96.06
Not Hispanic (25,817)	26,138	95.02
Hispanic (241)	286	1.04
Yugoslavian	83	0.30

Butte-Silver Bow

Place Type: Special City
County: Silver Bow
Population: 33,892

Ancestry/Race	Number	%
African American/Black:	87	0.26
Not Hispanic (45)	74	0.22
Hispanic (8)	13	0.04
African, sub-Saharan:	6	0.02
African	6	0.02
Alaska Native tribes, specified:	8	0.02
Aleut (1)	1	0.00
Eskimo (6)	7	0.02
Am. Ind. or Alaska Nat., not spec.	251	0.74
American Indian tribes, specified:	727	2.15
Apache (6)	19	0.06
Blackfeet (53)	74	0.22
Cherokee (26)	51	0.15
Cheyenne (18)	26	0.08
Chippewa (77)	112	0.33
Choctaw	7	0.02
Colville (1)	2	0.01
Cree (17)	24	0.07
Creek (1)	1	0.00
Crow (24)	41	0.12
Delaware (1)	2	0.01
Iroquois (7)	11	0.03
Latin American Indians (2)	5	0.01
Lumbee (2)	3	0.01
Navajo (5)	5	0.01
Paiute	4	0.01
Potawatomi (1)	5	0.01
Pueblo	1	0.00
Seminole	7	0.02
Shoshone (8)	11	0.03
Sioux (34)	49	0.14
Ute (1)	2	0.01
All other tribes (194)	268	0.79
American Indian tribes, not spec.	35	0.10
Arab:	183	0.54
Arab/Arabic	12	0.04
Egyptian	7	0.02
Lebanese	164	0.48
Asian:	230	0.68
Chinese, ex. Taiwanese (28)	35	0.10
Filipino (34)	66	0.19
Indian (36)	44	0.13
Indonesian (3)	3	0.01
Japanese (9)	19	0.06
Korean (21)	32	0.09
Laotian	1	0.00
Pakistani (2)	2	0.01
Sri Lankan (2)	2	0.01
Thai (3)	5	0.01
Vietnamese (7)	9	0.03
Other Asian, not specified (1)	12	0.04
Australian	4	0.01
Austrian	914	2.70
Basque	11	0.03
Belgian	90	0.27
British	54	0.16
Bulgarian	24	0.07
Canadian	90	0.27
Celtic	28	0.08
Croatian	173	0.51
Czech	81	0.24
Czechoslovakian	21	0.06
Danish	430	1.27
Dutch	470	1.39
Eastern European	17	0.05
English	5,174	15.26
Estonian	5	0.01
European	123	0.36
Finnish	950	2.80
French, except Basque	1,734	5.11
French Canadian	442	1.30
German	6,168	18.19
German Russian	10	0.03
Greek	94	0.28
Hawaii Native/Pacific Islander:	35	0.10
Polynesian: (19)	31	0.09
Native Hawaiian (13)	22	0.06
Samoan (6)	9	0.03
Other Pac. Isl., not spec. (2)	4	0.01
Hispanic or Latino:	927	2.74
Central American:	2	0.01
Guatemalan	2	0.01
Cuban	3	0.01
Mexican	622	1.84
Puerto Rican	19	0.06
South American:	12	0.04
Colombian	3	0.01
Ecuadorian	2	0.01
Peruvian	3	0.01
Uruguayan	1	0.00
Other South American	3	0.01
Other Hispanic or Latino	269	0.79
Hungarian	54	0.16
Icelander	2	0.01
Irish	9,245	27.27
Israeli	9	0.03
Italian	2,152	6.35
Latvian	7	0.02
Lithuanian	8	0.02
Luxemburger	17	0.05
New Zealander	12	0.04
Northern European	9	0.03
Norwegian	1,850	5.46
Pennsylvania German	19	0.06
Polish	660	1.95
Portuguese	35	0.10
Russian	163	0.48
Scandinavian	203	0.60
Scotch-Irish	713	2.10
Scottish	659	1.94
Serbian	189	0.56
Slavic	58	0.17
Slovak	37	0.11
Slovene	95	0.28
Swedish	1,179	3.48
Swiss	186	0.55
Ukrainian	9	0.03
United States or American	1,276	3.76
Welsh	419	1.24
West Indian, excl. Hispanic:	23	0.07
Haitian	3	0.01
Jamaican	20	0.06
White:	32,781	96.72
Not Hispanic (31,753)	32,135	94.82
Hispanic (572)	646	1.91
Yugoslavian	414	1.22

Great Falls

Place Type: City
County: Cascade
Population: 56,690

Ancestry/Race	Number	%
African American/Black:	782	1.38
Not Hispanic (503)	721	1.27
Hispanic (37)	61	0.11
African, sub-Saharan:	68	0.12
African	56	0.10
Nigerian	6	0.01
Other sub-Saharan African	6	0.01
Alaska Native tribes, specified:	21	0.04
Alaska Athabascan	1	0.00
Aleut (1)	5	0.01
Eskimo (3)	5	0.01
Tlingit-Haida (6)	9	0.02
All other tribes (1)	1	0.00
Alaska Native tribes, not specified	1	0.00
Am. Ind. or Alaska Nat., not spec.	842	1.49
American Indian tribes, specified:	2,866	5.06
Apache (2)	13	0.02
Blackfeet (582)	699	1.23
Cherokee (26)	94	0.17
Cheyenne (22)	26	0.05
Chickasaw	1	0.00
Chippewa (311)	470	0.83
Choctaw (1)	11	0.02
Colville (5)	6	0.01
Cree (56)	98	0.17
Creek (3)	12	0.02
Crow (17)	22	0.04
Iroquois (6)	8	0.01
Latin American Indians (5)	13	0.02
Lumbee (1)	1	0.00
Menominee	1	0.00
Navajo (15)	24	0.04
Ottawa (1)	1	0.00
Paiute (1)	1	0.00
Pima (1)	2	0.00
Potawatomi (1)	3	0.01
Pueblo (3)	3	0.01
Puget Sound Salish (2)	2	0.00
Seminole (1)	2	0.00

Notes: 1. Figures in the "Number" column do not add up to the total population due to: a) Ancestry/Race overlap — e.g. persons can report being both White and Irish, b) persons of Hispanic origin can report being any race, c) persons reporting two ancestries are counted in both categories. 2. Numbers in parentheses indicate the number of persons reporting this ancestry/race alone, not in combination with any other ancestry/race. 3. Refer to the Explanation of Data in the front of the book for more detailed information.

Ancestry/Race	Number	%
Shoshone	1	0.00
Sioux (102)	141	0.25
Tohono O'Odham	5	0.01
Ute (2)	8	0.01
Yakama (1)	2	0.00
Yaqui (1)	3	0.01
Yuman (1)	2	0.00
All other tribes (902)	1,191	2.10
American Indian tribes, not spec.	117	0.21
Arab:	67	0.12
Egyptian	6	0.01
Lebanese	49	0.09
Syrian	12	0.02
Asian:	801	1.41
Cambodian (1)	1	0.00
Chinese, ex. Taiwanese (56)	94	0.17
Filipino (192)	338	0.60
Hmong	3	0.01
Indian (38)	58	0.10
Indonesian (1)	1	0.00
Japanese (39)	73	0.13
Korean (79)	111	0.20
Laotian (12)	16	0.03
Malaysian	2	0.00
Sri Lankan (1)	1	0.00
Taiwanese (1)	3	0.01
Thai (26)	40	0.07
Vietnamese (14)	21	0.04
Other Asian, specified (2)	3	0.01
Other Asian, not specified (15)	36	0.06
Australian	14	0.02
Austrian	294	0.52
Basque	32	0.06
Belgian	193	0.34
British	251	0.44
Bulgarian	12	0.02
Canadian	69	0.12
Celtic	11	0.02
Croatian	179	0.32
Czech	434	0.77
Czechoslovakian	248	0.44
Danish	836	1.48
Dutch	1,493	2.64
English	6,299	11.12
Estonian	12	0.02
European	507	0.90
Finnish	533	0.94
French, except Basque	2,436	4.30
French Canadian	713	1.26
German	14,350	25.33
German Russian	5	0.01
Greek	231	0.41
Hawaii Native/Pacific Islander:	102	0.18
Micronesian: (24)	37	0.07
Guamanian/Chamorro (19)	31	0.05
Other Micronesian (5)	6	0.01
Polynesian: (23)	50	0.09
Native Hawaiian (18)	44	0.08
Samoan (3)	4	0.01
Other Polynesian (2)	2	0.00
Other Pac. Isl., specified	1	0.00
Other Pac. Isl., not spec. (1)	14	0.02
Hispanic or Latino:	1,354	2.39
Central American:	23	0.04
Costa Rican	3	0.01
Guatemalan	1	0.00
Honduran	3	0.01
Nicaraguan	1	0.00
Panamanian	11	0.02
Salvadoran	3	0.01
Other Central American	1	0.00
Cuban	22	0.04
Dominican Republic	16	0.03
Mexican	784	1.38
Puerto Rican	109	0.19
South American:	13	0.02
Argentinean	2	0.00
Colombian	5	0.01
Ecuadorian	1	0.00
Peruvian	4	0.01
Uruguayan	1	0.00
Other Hispanic or Latino	387	0.68
Hungarian	239	0.42
Icelander	19	0.03
Irish	8,619	15.22
Israeli	10	0.02
Italian	2,005	3.54
Lithuanian	36	0.06
Luxemburger	23	0.04
Northern European	67	0.12
Norwegian	6,488	11.45
Pennsylvania German	49	0.09
Polish	1,518	2.68
Portuguese	126	0.22
Romanian	27	0.05
Russian	377	0.67
Scandinavian	345	0.61
Scotch-Irish	1,352	2.39
Scottish	1,647	2.91
Serbian	28	0.05
Slavic	67	0.12
Slovak	175	0.31
Slovene	70	0.12
Swedish	2,031	3.59
Swiss	291	0.51
Turkish	25	0.04
Ukrainian	111	0.20
United States or American	3,273	5.78
Welsh	517	0.91
West Indian, excl. Hispanic:	24	0.04
Jamaican	14	0.02
Trinidadian and Tobagonian	4	0.01
West Indian	6	0.01
White:	52,266	92.20
Not Hispanic (50,292)	51,428	90.72
Hispanic (704)	838	1.48
Yugoslavian	247	0.44

Helena

Place Type: City
County: Lewis and Clark
Population: 25,780

Ancestry/Race	Number	%
African American/Black:	111	0.43
Not Hispanic (56)	108	0.42
Hispanic (3)	3	0.01
African, sub-Saharan:	11	0.04
African	7	0.03
Ghanian	4	0.02
Alaska Native tribes, specified:	14	0.05
Eskimo (10)	10	0.04
Tlingit-Haida (4)	4	0.02
Alaska Native tribes, not specified	4	0.02
Am. Ind. or Alaska Nat., not spec.	169	0.66
American Indian tribes, specified:	565	2.19
Apache (1)	7	0.03
Blackfeet (70)	88	0.34
Cherokee (22)	48	0.19
Cheyenne (20)	23	0.09
Chickasaw (1)	1	0.00
Chippewa (98)	135	0.52
Choctaw (8)	10	0.04
Cree (7)	14	0.05
Crow (2)	5	0.02
Delaware (1)	1	0.00
Iroquois (1)	1	0.00
Latin American Indians (3)	5	0.02
Navajo (3)	9	0.03
Paiute	2	0.01
Potawatomi (5)	5	0.02
Pueblo (1)	4	0.02
Puget Sound Salish (1)	1	0.00
Seminole (1)	1	0.00
Sioux (23)	36	0.14
All other tribes (124)	169	0.66
American Indian tribes, not spec.	29	0.11
Arab:	17	0.07
Lebanese	9	0.04
Syrian	8	0.03
Armenian	14	0.05
Asian:	307	1.19
Chinese, ex. Taiwanese (40)	61	0.24
Filipino (24)	46	0.18
Hmong (1)	1	0.00
Indian (56)	58	0.22
Indonesian (1)	1	0.00
Japanese (36)	59	0.23
Korean (34)	57	0.22
Pakistani	1	0.00
Taiwanese (1)	2	0.01
Thai (1)	2	0.01
Vietnamese (1)	5	0.02
Other Asian, not specified (5)	14	0.05
Australian	5	0.02
Austrian	212	0.83
Basque	49	0.19
Belgian	34	0.13
Brazilian	5	0.02
British	162	0.63
Canadian	89	0.35
Celtic	29	0.11
Croatian	112	0.44
Cypriot	10	0.04
Czech	162	0.63
Czechoslovakian	76	0.30
Danish	391	1.53
Dutch	404	1.58
Eastern European	42	0.16
English	3,889	15.21
European	210	0.82
Finnish	187	0.73
French, except Basque	1,373	5.37
French Canadian	192	0.75
German	6,794	26.58
Greek	89	0.35
Hawaii Native/Pacific Islander:	41	0.16
Micronesian: (3)	8	0.03
Guamanian/Chamorro (3)	8	0.03
Polynesian: (6)	20	0.08
Native Hawaiian (3)	12	0.05
Samoan (2)	4	0.02
Tongan (1)	4	0.02
Other Pac. Isl., not spec. (8)	13	0.05
Hispanic or Latino:	430	1.67
Central American:	7	0.03
Costa Rican	1	0.00
Guatemalan	4	0.02
Honduran	2	0.01
Cuban	18	0.07
Dominican Republic	1	0.00
Mexican	229	0.89
Puerto Rican	21	0.08
South American:	14	0.05
Argentinean	1	0.00
Bolivian	1	0.00
Chilean	1	0.00
Colombian	1	0.00
Paraguayan	1	0.00
Venezuelan	8	0.03
Other South American	1	0.00
Other Hispanic or Latino	140	0.54
Hungarian	111	0.43
Irish	5,444	21.30
Italian	1,216	4.76
Lithuanian	82	0.32
Luxemburger	32	0.13
Northern European	58	0.23
Norwegian	2,550	9.98
Polish	542	2.12
Portuguese	101	0.40
Romanian	18	0.07
Russian	190	0.74
Scandinavian	190	0.74
Scotch-Irish	945	3.70
Scottish	852	3.33
Serbian	21	0.08
Slavic	16	0.06
Slovak	82	0.32

Notes: 1. Figures in the "Number" column do not add up to the total population due to: a) Ancestry/Race overlap — e.g. persons can report being both White and Irish, b) persons of Hispanic origin can report being any race, c) persons reporting two ancestries are counted in both categories. 2. Numbers in parentheses indicate the number of persons reporting this ancestry/race alone, not in combination with any other ancestry/race. 3. Refer to the Explanation of Data in the front of the book for more detailed information.

Ancestry/Race	Number	%
Slovene	54	0.21
Swedish	793	3.10
Swiss	94	0.37
United States or American	1,154	4.51
Welsh	296	1.16
West Indian, excl. Hispanic:	8	0.03
Dutch West Indian	8	0.03
White:	24,850	96.39
Not Hispanic (24,191)	24,557	95.26
Hispanic (243)	293	1.14
Yugoslavian	127	0.50

Kalispell

Place Type: City
County: Flathead
Population: 14,223

Ancestry/Race	Number	%
African American/Black:	68	0.48
Not Hispanic (39)	63	0.44
Hispanic (1)	5	0.04
Alaska Native tribes, specified:	8	0.06
Aleut (1)	1	0.01
Eskimo (1)	2	0.01
Tlingit-Haida (5)	5	0.04
Alaska Native tribes, not specified	3	0.02
Am. Ind. or Alaska Nat., not spec.	63	0.44
American Indian tribes, specified:	211	1.48
Apache	3	0.02
Blackfeet (35)	49	0.34
Cherokee (4)	14	0.10
Chippewa (17)	32	0.22
Cree (3)	7	0.05
Crow (1)	1	0.01
Iroquois	2	0.01
Latin American Indians	1	0.01
Navajo (1)	1	0.01
Puget Sound Salish (5)	5	0.04
Shoshone	2	0.01
Sioux (11)	16	0.11
Ute (1)	1	0.01
All other tribes (52)	77	0.54
American Indian tribes, not spec.	22	0.15
Arab:	22	0.16
Syrian	22	0.16
Asian:	133	0.94
Chinese, ex. Taiwanese (24)	38	0.27
Filipino (18)	34	0.24
Indian (1)	3	0.02
Japanese (8)	21	0.15
Korean (9)	11	0.08
Thai (6)	8	0.06
Vietnamese (9)	13	0.09
Other Asian, specified (1)	2	0.01
Other Asian, not specified (2)	3	0.02
Austrian	65	0.46
Belgian	45	0.32
British	91	0.64
Canadian	58	0.41
Croatian	17	0.12
Czech	163	1.15
Czechoslovakian	25	0.18
Danish	314	2.22
Dutch	371	2.62
Eastern European	9	0.06
English	1,910	13.49
European	46	0.32
Finnish	124	0.88
French, except Basque	863	6.09
French Canadian	138	0.97
German	3,522	24.87
Greek	17	0.12
Hawaii Native/Pacific Islander:	20	0.14
Micronesian:	1	0.01
Other Micronesian	1	0.01
Polynesian: (6)	17	0.12
Native Hawaiian (2)	10	0.07
Samoan (4)	7	0.05
Other Pac. Isl., specified	1	0.01
Other Pac. Isl., not spec.	1	0.01
Hispanic or Latino:	220	1.55
Central American:	4	0.03
Guatemalan	1	0.01
Honduran	1	0.01
Panamanian	2	0.01
Cuban	3	0.02
Mexican	155	1.09
Puerto Rican	11	0.08
South American:	3	0.02
Argentinean	1	0.01
Chilean	1	0.01
Colombian	1	0.01
Other Hispanic or Latino	44	0.31
Hungarian	46	0.32
Icelander	7	0.05
Irish	2,110	14.90
Italian	480	3.39
Lithuanian	28	0.20
Macedonian	8	0.06
Norwegian	1,667	11.77
Pennsylvania German	6	0.04
Polish	201	1.42
Portuguese	31	0.22
Russian	111	0.78
Scandinavian	100	0.71
Scotch-Irish	406	2.87
Scottish	441	3.11
Serbian	30	0.21
Slavic	15	0.11
Slovak	9	0.06
Swedish	476	3.36
Swiss	82	0.58
Ukrainian	15	0.11
United States or American	715	5.05
Welsh	314	2.22
White:	13,859	97.44
Not Hispanic (13,504)	13,700	96.32
Hispanic (128)	159	1.12
Yugoslavian	32	0.23

Missoula

Place Type: City
County: Missoula
Population: 57,053

Ancestry/Race	Number	%
African American/Black:	370	0.65
Not Hispanic (201)	342	0.60
Hispanic (6)	28	0.05
African, sub-Saharan:	19	0.03
African	17	0.03
Kenyan	2	0.00
Alaska Native tribes, specified:	27	0.05
Alaska Athabascan (5)	8	0.01
Aleut (4)	6	0.01
Eskimo (3)	8	0.01
Tlingit-Haida (4)	4	0.01
All other tribes	1	0.00
Alaska Native tribes, not specified	5	0.01
Am. Ind. or Alaska Nat., not spec.	424	0.74
Albanian	8	0.01
American Indian tribes, specified:	1,492	2.62
Apache (7)	9	0.02
Blackfeet (256)	325	0.57
Cherokee (35)	133	0.23
Cheyenne (46)	62	0.11
Chippewa (70)	120	0.21
Choctaw (10)	21	0.04
Colville (2)	5	0.01
Comanche (1)	2	0.00
Cree (8)	23	0.04
Creek (3)	4	0.01
Crow (36)	54	0.09
Iroquois (5)	15	0.03
Kiowa (1)	1	0.00
Latin American Indians (11)	14	0.02
Menominee (1)	1	0.00
Navajo (20)	29	0.05
Osage (5)	9	0.02
Ottawa (1)	1	0.00
Paiute (1)	4	0.01
Pima (3)	5	0.01
Potawatomi (3)	4	0.01
Pueblo (4)	7	0.01
Puget Sound Salish (6)	6	0.01
Seminole (1)	7	0.01
Shoshone (4)	10	0.02
Sioux (40)	83	0.15
Tohono O'Odham (1)	1	0.00
Ute (1)	2	0.00
Yakama (1)	1	0.00
Yaqui (2)	2	0.00
Yuman (2)	2	0.00
All other tribes (368)	530	0.93
American Indian tribes, not spec.	88	0.15
Arab:	132	0.23
Lebanese	99	0.17
Palestinian	6	0.01
Syrian	19	0.03
Other Arab	8	0.01
Armenian	34	0.06
Asian:	914	1.60
Cambodian (1)	1	0.00
Chinese, ex. Taiwanese (142)	180	0.32
Filipino (36)	71	0.12
Hmong (101)	108	0.19
Indian (34)	46	0.08
Indonesian (6)	14	0.02
Japanese (183)	223	0.39
Korean (60)	89	0.16
Laotian (23)	26	0.05
Malaysian (11)	17	0.03
Pakistani (2)	3	0.01
Sri Lankan	1	0.00
Taiwanese (4)	4	0.01
Thai (5)	11	0.02
Vietnamese (61)	74	0.13
Other Asian, specified	5	0.01
Other Asian, not specified (18)	41	0.07
Australian	14	0.02
Austrian	370	0.65
Basque	42	0.07
Belgian	99	0.17
British	306	0.54
Bulgarian	50	0.09
Canadian	214	0.38
Celtic	46	0.08
Croatian	98	0.17
Czech	329	0.58
Czechoslovakian	140	0.25
Danish	865	1.52
Dutch	1,089	1.91
Eastern European	19	0.03
English	7,301	12.82
Estonian	27	0.05
European	984	1.73
Finnish	575	1.01
French, except Basque	2,823	4.96
French Canadian	711	1.25
German	14,165	24.86
Greek	215	0.38
Hawaii Native/Pacific Islander:	107	0.19
Melanesian: (9)	9	0.02
Fijian (9)	9	0.02
Micronesian: (7)	13	0.02
Guamanian/Chamorro (6)	11	0.02
Other Micronesian (1)	2	0.00
Polynesian: (30)	51	0.09
Native Hawaiian (24)	42	0.07
Samoan (5)	7	0.01
Tongan (1)	1	0.00
Other Polynesian	1	0.00
Other Pac. Isl., specified	3	0.01
Other Pac. Isl., not spec. (11)	31	0.05
Hispanic or Latino:	1,004	1.76
Central American:	20	0.04
Costa Rican	3	0.01
Guatemalan	4	0.01

Notes: 1. Figures in the "Number" column do not add up to the total population due to: a) Ancestry/Race overlap — e.g. persons can report being both White and Irish, b) persons of Hispanic origin can report being any race, c) persons reporting two ancestries are counted in both categories. 2. Numbers in parentheses indicate the number of persons reporting this ancestry/race alone, not in combination with any other ancestry/race. 3. Refer to the Explanation of Data in the front of the book for more detailed information.

Honduran	1	0.00
Nicaraguan	2	0.00
Panamanian	2	0.00
Salvadoran	6	0.01
Other Central American	2	0.00
Cuban	28	0.05
Dominican Republic	2	0.00
Mexican	577	1.01
Puerto Rican	52	0.09
South American:	45	0.08
Argentinean	7	0.01
Chilean	7	0.01
Colombian	13	0.02
Ecuadorian	3	0.01
Peruvian	10	0.02
Venezuelan	1	0.00
Other South American	4	0.01
Other Hispanic or Latino	280	0.49
Hungarian	316	0.55
Iranian	11	0.02
Irish	9,749	17.11
Israeli	5	0.01
Italian	2,565	4.50
Latvian	17	0.03
Lithuanian	97	0.17
Luxemburger	36	0.06
Macedonian	5	0.01
Northern European	62	0.11
Norwegian	5,400	9.48
Pennsylvania German	23	0.04
Polish	1,224	2.15
Portuguese	62	0.11
Romanian	57	0.10
Russian	593	1.04
Scandinavian	451	0.79
Scotch-Irish	1,591	2.79
Scottish	2,104	3.69
Serbian	57	0.10
Slavic	63	0.11
Slovak	64	0.11
Slovene	57	0.10
Swedish	2,177	3.82
Swiss	327	0.57
Turkish	13	0.02
Ukrainian	105	0.18
United States or American	2,094	3.68
Welsh	836	1.47
West Indian, excl. Hispanic:	16	0.03
Jamaican	10	0.02
Trinidadian and Tobagonian	6	0.01
White:	54,389	95.33
Not Hispanic (52,843)	53,714	94.15
Hispanic (544)	675	1.18
Yugoslavian	131	0.23

Beatrice

Place Type: City
County: Gage
Population: 12,496

Ancestry/Race	Number	%
African American/Black:	78	0.62
Not Hispanic (40)	76	0.61
Hispanic (2)	2	0.02
Alaska Native tribes, specified:	1	0.01
Aleut (1)	1	0.01
Am. Ind. or Alaska Nat., not spec.	28	0.22
American Indian tribes, specified:	103	0.82
Apache	4	0.03
Cherokee (3)	27	0.22
Chippewa (2)	6	0.05
Choctaw (1)	2	0.02
Cree (1)	1	0.01
Creek	4	0.03
Latin American Indians (1)	1	0.01
Osage (1)	3	0.02
Potawatomi (8)	12	0.10
Seminole	1	0.01
Shoshone (3)	3	0.02
Sioux (13)	25	0.20
All other tribes (8)	14	0.11
American Indian tribes, not spec.	7	0.06
Arab:	8	0.06
Arab/Arabic	8	0.06
Asian:	53	0.42
Chinese, ex. Taiwanese (7)	15	0.12
Filipino (3)	3	0.02
Hmong (2)	2	0.02
Indian (5)	5	0.04
Japanese (4)	6	0.05
Korean (3)	3	0.02
Laotian (7)	8	0.06
Vietnamese (6)	6	0.05
Other Asian, not specified (4)	5	0.04
Austrian	35	0.28
British	20	0.16
Canadian	6	0.05
Czech	464	3.72
Czechoslovakian	74	0.59
Danish	232	1.86
Dutch	373	2.99
English	1,003	8.04
European	64	0.51
French, except Basque	409	3.28
French Canadian	16	0.13
German	5,929	47.50
Greek	34	0.27
Hawaii Native/Pacific Islander:	24	0.19
Micronesian: (1)	11	0.09
Guamanian/Chamorro (1)	11	0.09
Polynesian: (3)	7	0.06
Native Hawaiian (2)	6	0.05
Samoan (1)	1	0.01
Other Pac. Isl., not spec.	6	0.05
Hispanic or Latino:	120	0.96
Central American:	2	0.02
Nicaraguan	2	0.02
Cuban	2	0.02
Mexican	81	0.65
Puerto Rican	4	0.03
South American:	2	0.02
Chilean	1	0.01
Paraguayan	1	0.01
Other Hispanic or Latino	29	0.23
Hungarian	7	0.06
Iranian	3	0.02
Irish	1,419	11.37
Italian	164	1.31
Luxemburger	6	0.05
Norwegian	151	1.21
Pennsylvania German	38	0.30
Polish	192	1.54
Portuguese	15	0.12
Romanian	8	0.06
Russian	27	0.22
Scandinavian	22	0.18
Scotch-Irish	172	1.38
Scottish	106	0.85
Slovak	7	0.06
Swedish	386	3.09
Swiss	128	1.03
Ukrainian	16	0.13
United States or American	735	5.89
Welsh	172	1.38
West Indian, excl. Hispanic:	7	0.06
Jamaican	7	0.06
White:	12,308	98.50
Not Hispanic (12,118)	12,232	97.89
Hispanic (66)	76	0.61

Bellevue

Place Type: City
County: Sarpy
Population: 44,382

Ancestry/Race	Number	%
Acadian/Cajun	22	0.05
African American/Black:	3,100	6.98
Not Hispanic (2,674)	3,028	6.82
Hispanic (45)	72	0.16
African, sub-Saharan:	260	0.59
African	172	0.39
Ghanian	10	0.02
South African	5	0.01
Sudanese	63	0.14
Ugandan	4	0.01
Other sub-Saharan African	6	0.01
Alaska Native tribes, specified:	6	0.01
Eskimo (3)	3	0.01
Tlingit-Haida (1)	1	0.00
All other tribes	2	0.00
Am. Ind. or Alaska Nat., not spec.	136	0.31
American Indian tribes, specified:	309	0.70
Apache (4)	6	0.01
Blackfeet (7)	21	0.05
Cherokee (17)	83	0.19
Chickasaw (1)	2	0.00
Chippewa (6)	11	0.02
Choctaw (7)	7	0.02
Colville	1	0.00
Comanche (1)	2	0.00
Creek (2)	3	0.01
Crow	1	0.00
Delaware	1	0.00
Iroquois (1)	5	0.01
Latin American Indians (4)	9	0.02
Navajo (4)	4	0.01
Osage (1)	2	0.00
Pima (4)	4	0.01
Potawatomi (7)	7	0.02
Pueblo (3)	3	0.01
Seminole (3)	3	0.01
Sioux (27)	57	0.13
Ute	1	0.00
Yaqui	1	0.00
All other tribes (53)	75	0.17
American Indian tribes, not spec.	35	0.08
Arab:	112	0.25
Iraqi	6	0.01
Lebanese	54	0.12
Syrian	52	0.12
Asian:	1,366	3.08
Bangladeshi (3)	3	0.01
Cambodian (1)	4	0.01
Chinese, ex. Taiwanese (63)	101	0.23
Filipino (282)	436	0.98
Indian (78)	94	0.21
Indonesian (1)	7	0.02
Japanese (103)	177	0.40
Korean (148)	215	0.48
Laotian (8)	11	0.02
Malaysian	1	0.00
Pakistani (3)	4	0.01
Sri Lankan (2)	3	0.01
Thai (84)	119	0.27
Vietnamese (49)	59	0.13
Other Asian, specified (66)	82	0.18
Other Asian, not specified (26)	50	0.11
Assyrian/Chaldean/Syriac	9	0.02
Australian	15	0.03
Austrian	128	0.29
Belgian	124	0.28
British	239	0.54
Canadian	93	0.21
Celtic	23	0.05
Croatian	213	0.48
Czech	2,288	5.16
Czechoslovakian	377	0.85
Danish	780	1.76
Dutch	878	1.98
English	4,781	10.79
European	345	0.78
Finnish	41	0.09
French, except Basque	1,436	3.24
French Canadian	369	0.83
German	12,662	28.57
German Russian	18	0.04
Greek	90	0.20

Notes: 1. Figures in the "Number" column do not add up to the total population due to: a) Ancestry/Race overlap — e.g. persons can report being both White and Irish, b) persons of Hispanic origin can report being any race, c) persons reporting two ancestries are counted in both categories. 2. Numbers in parentheses indicate the number of persons reporting this ancestry/race alone, not in combination with any other ancestry/race. 3. Refer to the Explanation of Data in the front of the book for more detailed information.

Ancestry/Race	Number	%
Guyanese	12	0.03
Hawaii Native/Pacific Islander:	100	0.23
Melanesian:	1	0.00
Other Melanesian	1	0.00
Micronesian: (19)	30	0.07
Guamanian/Chamorro (12)	23	0.05
Other Micronesian (7)	7	0.02
Polynesian: (20)	48	0.11
Native Hawaiian (19)	42	0.09
Samoan (1)	5	0.01
Other Polynesian	1	0.00
Other Pac. Isl., not spec. (10)	21	0.05
Hispanic or Latino:	2,609	5.88
Central American:	136	0.31
Costa Rican	2	0.00
Guatemalan	24	0.05
Honduran	8	0.02
Nicaraguan	9	0.02
Panamanian	32	0.07
Salvadoran	59	0.13
Other Central American	2	0.00
Cuban	29	0.07
Dominican Republic	10	0.02
Mexican	1,883	4.24
Puerto Rican	152	0.34
South American:	39	0.09
Argentinean	6	0.01
Bolivian	1	0.00
Chilean	1	0.00
Colombian	14	0.03
Ecuadorian	2	0.00
Peruvian	8	0.02
Venezuelan	2	0.00
Other South American	5	0.01
Other Hispanic or Latino	360	0.81
Hungarian	224	0.51
Icelander	32	0.07
Iranian	26	0.06
Irish	6,845	15.44
Italian	2,218	5.00
Latvian	18	0.04
Lithuanian	178	0.40
Luxemburger	47	0.11
Northern European	51	0.12
Norwegian	1,094	2.47
Pennsylvania German	29	0.07
Polish	2,602	5.87
Portuguese	173	0.39
Romanian	21	0.05
Russian	211	0.48
Scandinavian	138	0.31
Scotch-Irish	757	1.71
Scottish	736	1.66
Serbian	59	0.13
Slavic	21	0.05
Slovak	35	0.08
Slovene	12	0.03
Swedish	1,580	3.56
Swiss	203	0.46
Turkish	21	0.05
Ukrainian	62	0.14
United States or American	2,322	5.24
Welsh	193	0.44
West Indian, excl. Hispanic:	28	0.06
British West Indian	13	0.03
West Indian	15	0.03
White:	39,046	87.98
Not Hispanic (36,916)	37,725	85.00
Hispanic (1,176)	1,321	2.98
Yugoslavian	12	0.03

Chalco

Place Type: Census Designated Place
County: Sarpy
Population: 10,736

Ancestry/Race	Number	%
Acadian/Cajun	8	0.07
African American/Black:	122	1.14
Not Hispanic (85)	118	1.10
Hispanic (3)	4	0.04
African, sub-Saharan:	34	0.32
African	34	0.32
Am. Ind. or Alaska Nat., not spec.	22	0.20
American Indian tribes, specified:	60	0.56
Blackfeet (3)	3	0.03
Cherokee (6)	17	0.16
Chickasaw	1	0.01
Chippewa (2)	3	0.03
Choctaw	2	0.02
Comanche	2	0.02
Creek	3	0.03
Houma	1	0.01
Navajo	4	0.04
Sioux (8)	14	0.13
All other tribes (4)	10	0.09
American Indian tribes, not spec.	2	0.02
Arab:	43	0.40
Lebanese	43	0.40
Asian:	188	1.75
Cambodian (1)	1	0.01
Chinese, ex. Taiwanese (15)	18	0.17
Filipino (18)	44	0.41
Hmong (13)	13	0.12
Indian (13)	16	0.15
Indonesian (2)	4	0.04
Japanese (11)	27	0.25
Korean (9)	16	0.15
Laotian (4)	5	0.05
Malaysian (1)	1	0.01
Sri Lankan	1	0.01
Thai (1)	2	0.02
Vietnamese (20)	22	0.20
Other Asian, specified (1)	1	0.01
Other Asian, not specified (3)	17	0.16
Austrian	39	0.36
Belgian	8	0.07
British	73	0.68
Canadian	22	0.21
Croatian	44	0.41
Czech	569	5.31
Czechoslovakian	37	0.35
Danish	437	4.08
Dutch	368	3.44
Eastern European	36	0.34
English	1,002	9.35
European	21	0.20
Finnish	20	0.19
French, except Basque	368	3.44
French Canadian	51	0.48
German	4,750	44.34
Greek	8	0.07
Hawaii Native/Pacific Islander:	9	0.08
Micronesian: (1)	1	0.01
Guamanian/Chamorro (1)	1	0.01
Polynesian: (1)	5	0.05
Native Hawaiian (1)	5	0.05
Other Pac. Isl., not spec.	3	0.03
Hispanic or Latino:	302	2.81
Central American:	4	0.04
Guatemalan	1	0.01
Salvadoran	3	0.03
Cuban	1	0.01
Mexican	232	2.16
Puerto Rican	14	0.13
South American:	5	0.05
Argentinean	1	0.01
Colombian	4	0.04
Other Hispanic or Latino	46	0.43
Hungarian	24	0.22
Irish	2,114	19.73
Italian	714	6.66
Lithuanian	25	0.23
Luxemburger	9	0.08
Northern European	7	0.07
Norwegian	295	2.75
Polish	555	5.18
Romanian	32	0.30
Russian	33	0.31
Scandinavian	51	0.48
Scotch-Irish	165	1.54
Scottish	209	1.95
Slovak	7	0.07
Slovene	7	0.07
Swedish	802	7.49
Swiss	62	0.58
Ukrainian	42	0.39
United States or American	201	1.88
Welsh	84	0.78
White:	10,383	96.71
Not Hispanic (10,070)	10,186	94.88
Hispanic (155)	197	1.83
Yugoslavian	9	0.08

Columbus

Place Type: City
County: Platte
Population: 20,971

Ancestry/Race	Number	%
African American/Black:	129	0.62
Not Hispanic (79)	109	0.52
Hispanic (16)	20	0.10
African, sub-Saharan:	18	0.09
African	10	0.05
Nigerian	8	0.04
Am. Ind. or Alaska Nat., not spec.	26	0.12
American Indian tribes, specified:	109	0.52
Apache	6	0.03
Blackfeet (1)	1	0.00
Cherokee (3)	11	0.05
Chickasaw (2)	4	0.02
Chippewa (1)	5	0.02
Choctaw (5)	6	0.03
Comanche (4)	6	0.03
Creek (1)	2	0.01
Crow	1	0.00
Delaware	1	0.00
Latin American Indians (2)	2	0.01
Navajo (1)	4	0.02
Pima (1)	1	0.00
Pueblo (1)	1	0.00
Sioux (21)	35	0.17
All other tribes (15)	23	0.11
American Indian tribes, not spec.	3	0.01
Arab:	71	0.34
Iraqi	31	0.15
Lebanese	7	0.03
Syrian	16	0.08
Other Arab	17	0.08
Asian:	131	0.62
Cambodian (1)	3	0.01
Chinese, ex. Taiwanese (17)	19	0.09
Filipino (10)	14	0.07
Indian (8)	9	0.04
Indonesian	1	0.00
Japanese (5)	20	0.10
Korean (22)	24	0.11
Laotian (1)	1	0.00
Thai (9)	9	0.04
Vietnamese (22)	25	0.12
Other Asian, not specified (5)	6	0.03
Austrian	49	0.23
Belgian	43	0.20
British	8	0.04
Canadian	19	0.09
Croatian	24	0.11
Czech	1,377	6.56
Czechoslovakian	178	0.85
Danish	392	1.87
Dutch	481	2.29
Eastern European	11	0.05
English	1,503	7.16
European	79	0.38
Finnish	7	0.03
French, except Basque	362	1.72
French Canadian	29	0.14
German	9,746	46.43

Notes: 1. Figures in the "Number" column do not add up to the total population due to: a) Ancestry/Race overlap — e.g. persons can report being both White and Irish, b) persons of Hispanic origin can report being any race, c) persons reporting two ancestries are counted in both categories. 2. Numbers in parentheses indicate the number of persons reporting this ancestry/race alone, not in combination with any other ancestry/race. 3. Refer to the Explanation of Data in the front of the book for more detailed information.

Ancestry/Race	Number	%
Hawaii Native/Pacific Islander:	16	0.08
Polynesian: (3)	6	0.03
Native Hawaiian (1)	4	0.02
Samoan (2)	2	0.01
Other Pac. Isl., not spec. (5)	10	0.05
Hispanic or Latino:	1,395	6.65
Central American:	91	0.43
Guatemalan	43	0.21
Honduran	16	0.08
Nicaraguan	6	0.03
Salvadoran	25	0.12
Other Central American	1	0.00
Cuban	7	0.03
Mexican	1,019	4.86
Puerto Rican	19	0.09
South American:	13	0.06
Bolivian	2	0.01
Chilean	7	0.03
Peruvian	4	0.02
Other Hispanic or Latino	246	1.17
Hungarian	43	0.20
Irish	2,321	11.06
Italian	212	1.01
Lithuanian	21	0.10
Luxemburger	31	0.15
Northern European	6	0.03
Norwegian	361	1.72
Pennsylvania German	12	0.06
Polish	2,597	12.37
Romanian	9	0.04
Russian	83	0.40
Scandinavian	105	0.50
Scotch-Irish	199	0.95
Scottish	248	1.18
Swedish	904	4.31
Swiss	344	1.64
Ukrainian	7	0.03
United States or American	438	2.09
Welsh	164	0.78
West Indian, excl. Hispanic:	2	0.01
Jamaican	2	0.01
White:	19,949	95.13
Not Hispanic (19,209)	19,318	92.12
Hispanic (544)	631	3.01

Fremont

Place Type: City
County: Dodge
Population: 25,174

Ancestry/Race	Number	%
African American/Black:	185	0.73
Not Hispanic (133)	171	0.68
Hispanic (11)	14	0.06
African, sub-Saharan:	17	0.07
African	5	0.02
South African	12	0.05
Am. Ind. or Alaska Nat., not spec.	49	0.19
American Indian tribes, specified:	116	0.46
Apache	1	0.00
Cherokee (2)	19	0.08
Cheyenne	3	0.01
Chippewa (1)	4	0.02
Choctaw (1)	1	0.00
Iroquois	2	0.01
Latin American Indians (8)	19	0.08
Navajo (4)	4	0.02
Sioux (20)	33	0.13
All other tribes (26)	30	0.12
American Indian tribes, not spec.	4	0.02
Arab:	63	0.25
Arab/Arabic	5	0.02
Lebanese	24	0.10
Syrian	34	0.14
Armenian	11	0.04
Asian:	219	0.87
Chinese, ex. Taiwanese (16)	19	0.08
Filipino (26)	40	0.16
Indian (6)	9	0.04
Indonesian (1)	1	0.00
Japanese (15)	18	0.07
Korean (21)	29	0.12
Laotian (20)	20	0.08
Pakistani	5	0.02
Thai (1)	5	0.02
Vietnamese (37)	49	0.19
Other Asian, specified	13	0.05
Other Asian, not specified (9)	11	0.04
Belgian	67	0.27
Brazilian	19	0.08
British	13	0.05
Canadian	15	0.06
Croatian	6	0.02
Czech	1,289	5.12
Czechoslovakian	238	0.95
Danish	1,323	5.26
Dutch	594	2.36
English	2,335	9.28
European	49	0.19
Finnish	30	0.12
French, except Basque	718	2.85
French Canadian	39	0.16
German	11,267	44.79
Greek	28	0.11
Hawaii Native/Pacific Islander:	53	0.21
Micronesian: (16)	18	0.07
Guamanian/Chamorro (14)	16	0.06
Other Micronesian (2)	2	0.01
Polynesian: (5)	8	0.03
Native Hawaiian (4)	5	0.02
Samoan (1)	2	0.01
Other Polynesian	1	0.00
Other Pac. Isl., specified	11	0.04
Other Pac. Isl., not spec. (6)	16	0.06
Hispanic or Latino:	1,085	4.31
Central American:	59	0.23
Guatemalan	38	0.15
Honduran	1	0.00
Salvadoran	14	0.06
Other Central American	6	0.02
Cuban	3	0.01
Mexican	813	3.23
Puerto Rican	5	0.02
South American:	10	0.04
Ecuadorian	1	0.00
Peruvian	4	0.02
Other South American	5	0.02
Other Hispanic or Latino	195	0.77
Hungarian	24	0.10
Iranian	12	0.05
Irish	3,465	13.77
Italian	432	1.72
Lithuanian	18	0.07
Luxemburger	14	0.06
Norwegian	637	2.53
Pennsylvania German	41	0.16
Polish	703	2.79
Portuguese	6	0.02
Russian	93	0.37
Scandinavian	29	0.12
Scotch-Irish	344	1.37
Scottish	333	1.32
Slovak	15	0.06
Swedish	1,591	6.32
Swiss	109	0.43
Ukrainian	11	0.04
United States or American	1,102	4.38
Welsh	104	0.41
White:	24,161	95.98
Not Hispanic (23,570)	23,698	94.14
Hispanic (417)	463	1.84
Yugoslavian	7	0.03

Grand Island

Place Type: City
County: Hall
Population: 42,940

Ancestry/Race	Number	%
African American/Black:	264	0.61
Not Hispanic (145)	208	0.48
Hispanic (35)	56	0.13
African, sub-Saharan:	1	0.00
African	1	0.00
Am. Ind. or Alaska Nat., not spec.	88	0.20
American Indian tribes, specified:	179	0.42
Apache	5	0.01
Blackfeet	5	0.01
Cherokee (9)	34	0.08
Cheyenne	1	0.00
Chickasaw (1)	2	0.00
Chippewa (2)	5	0.01
Choctaw (2)	6	0.01
Creek (2)	2	0.00
Crow	1	0.00
Latin American Indians (13)	18	0.04
Navajo (10)	15	0.03
Osage (1)	1	0.00
Pima	1	0.00
Potawatomi (1)	3	0.01
Pueblo (1)	1	0.00
Seminole	1	0.00
Sioux (26)	51	0.12
Yaqui	3	0.01
All other tribes (16)	24	0.06
American Indian tribes, not spec.	18	0.04
Arab:	36	0.08
Iraqi	10	0.02
Lebanese	14	0.03
Syrian	12	0.03
Asian:	662	1.54
Chinese, ex. Taiwanese (24)	27	0.06
Filipino (44)	61	0.14
Indian (37)	45	0.10
Indonesian (1)	1	0.00
Japanese (4)	19	0.04
Korean (23)	35	0.08
Laotian (205)	232	0.54
Thai (7)	7	0.02
Vietnamese (182)	190	0.44
Other Asian, specified (3)	5	0.01
Other Asian, not specified (29)	40	0.09
Australian	2	0.00
Austrian	69	0.16
Belgian	30	0.07
British	119	0.28
Canadian	24	0.06
Czech	1,519	3.55
Czechoslovakian	177	0.41
Danish	1,557	3.64
Dutch	779	1.82
Eastern European	5	0.01
English	3,461	8.08
European	122	0.28
Finnish	7	0.02
French, except Basque	932	2.18
French Canadian	129	0.30
German	15,876	37.08
German Russian	12	0.03
Greek	62	0.14
Hawaii Native/Pacific Islander:	91	0.21
Micronesian: (66)	70	0.16
Guamanian/Chamorro (66)	70	0.16
Polynesian: (5)	13	0.03
Native Hawaiian (4)	10	0.02
Samoan (1)	3	0.01
Other Pac. Isl., specified	2	0.00
Other Pac. Isl., not spec.	6	0.01
Hispanic or Latino:	6,845	15.94
Central American:	954	2.22
Guatemalan	571	1.33
Honduran	90	0.21

Notes: 1. Figures in the "Number" column do not add up to the total population due to: a) Ancestry/Race overlap — e.g. persons can report being both White and Irish, b) persons of Hispanic origin can report being any race, c) persons reporting two ancestries are counted in both categories. 2. Numbers in parentheses indicate the number of persons reporting this ancestry/race alone, not in combination with any other ancestry/race. 3. Refer to the Explanation of Data in the front of the book for more detailed information.

Ancestry/Race	Number	%
Salvadoran	245	0.57
Other Central American	48	0.11
Cuban	19	0.04
Dominican Republic	1	0.00
Mexican	4,846	11.29
Puerto Rican	38	0.09
South American:	39	0.09
Argentinean	3	0.01
Chilean	5	0.01
Colombian	24	0.06
Peruvian	2	0.00
Venezuelan	5	0.01
Other Hispanic or Latino	948	2.21
Hungarian	7	0.02
Irish	4,913	11.47
Italian	335	0.78
Latvian	35	0.08
Luxemburger	24	0.06
Norwegian	600	1.40
Pennsylvania German	47	0.11
Polish	2,257	5.27
Portuguese	17	0.04
Romanian	28	0.07
Russian	216	0.50
Scandinavian	62	0.14
Scotch-Irish	559	1.31
Scottish	450	1.05
Serbian	7	0.02
Swedish	1,797	4.20
Swiss	176	0.41
Turkish	7	0.02
Ukrainian	3	0.01
United States or American	2,081	4.86
Welsh	268	0.63
White:	37,781	87.99
Not Hispanic (34,960)	35,210	82.00
Hispanic (2,277)	2,571	5.99
Yugoslavian	57	0.13

Hastings

Place Type: City
County: Adams
Population: 24,064

Ancestry/Race	Number	%
African American/Black:	230	0.96
Not Hispanic (177)	213	0.89
Hispanic (12)	17	0.07
African, sub-Saharan:	39	0.16
African	5	0.02
Ethiopian	34	0.14
Am. Ind. or Alaska Nat., not spec.	64	0.27
American Indian tribes, specified:	112	0.47
Apache (1)	2	0.01
Cherokee (15)	27	0.11
Chickasaw	1	0.00
Chippewa (2)	5	0.02
Choctaw (2)	2	0.01
Comanche (1)	4	0.02
Cree (1)	1	0.00
Delaware (1)	2	0.01
Iroquois (1)	4	0.02
Latin American Indians (3)	4	0.02
Menominee	1	0.00
Navajo (1)	1	0.00
Potawatomi (1)	1	0.00
Pueblo (3)	5	0.02
Sioux (22)	35	0.15
Yaqui (2)	2	0.01
All other tribes (10)	15	0.06
American Indian tribes, not spec.	9	0.04
Arab:	61	0.25
Arab/Arabic	8	0.03
Lebanese	33	0.14
Syrian	20	0.08
Asian:	533	2.21
Chinese, ex. Taiwanese (29)	37	0.15
Filipino (23)	36	0.15
Indian (10)	15	0.06
Japanese (14)	23	0.10
Korean (23)	27	0.11
Laotian (12)	13	0.05
Sri Lankan (1)	1	0.00
Taiwanese (2)	2	0.01
Thai (2)	4	0.02
Vietnamese (353)	354	1.47
Other Asian, not specified (15)	21	0.09
Austrian	59	0.25
Belgian	35	0.15
British	49	0.20
Canadian	26	0.11
Croatian	22	0.09
Czech	742	3.08
Czechoslovakian	69	0.29
Danish	682	2.83
Dutch	432	1.79
English	2,826	11.74
European	136	0.56
Finnish	19	0.08
French, except Basque	860	3.57
French Canadian	199	0.83
German	10,009	41.58
German Russian	2	0.01
Greek	73	0.30
Hawaii Native/Pacific Islander:	22	0.09
Micronesian: (4)	8	0.03
Guamanian/Chamorro (3)	7	0.03
Other Micronesian (1)	1	0.00
Polynesian: (6)	14	0.06
Native Hawaiian (2)	9	0.04
Samoan (4)	5	0.02
Hispanic or Latino:	1,343	5.58
Central American:	80	0.33
Costa Rican	1	0.00
Guatemalan	21	0.09
Honduran	22	0.09
Nicaraguan	1	0.00
Panamanian	2	0.01
Salvadoran	30	0.12
Other Central American	3	0.01
Cuban	138	0.57
Mexican	875	3.64
Puerto Rican	22	0.09
South American:	3	0.01
Peruvian	1	0.00
Venezuelan	1	0.00
Other South American	1	0.00
Other Hispanic or Latino	225	0.94
Hungarian	21	0.09
Irish	3,117	12.95
Italian	214	0.89
Lithuanian	2	0.01
Luxemburger	19	0.08
Northern European	9	0.04
Norwegian	400	1.66
Pennsylvania German	80	0.33
Polish	659	2.74
Portuguese	7	0.03
Romanian	7	0.03
Russian	227	0.94
Scandinavian	67	0.28
Scotch-Irish	461	1.92
Scottish	385	1.60
Slovak	14	0.06
Swedish	1,185	4.92
Swiss	92	0.38
Turkish	5	0.02
United States or American	1,375	5.71
Welsh	141	0.59
White:	22,684	94.27
Not Hispanic (21,790)	21,932	91.14
Hispanic (684)	752	3.13

Kearney

Place Type: City
County: Buffalo
Population: 27,431

Ancestry/Race	Number	%
Acadian/Cajun	7	0.03
African American/Black:	261	0.95
Not Hispanic (170)	253	0.92
Hispanic (2)	8	0.03
African, sub-Saharan:	19	0.07
African	14	0.05
Kenyan	5	0.02
Alaska Native tribes, not specified	1	0.00
Am. Ind. or Alaska Nat., not spec.	43	0.16
American Indian tribes, specified:	131	0.48
Apache	3	0.01
Blackfeet (1)	5	0.02
Cherokee (5)	25	0.09
Cheyenne	1	0.00
Chippewa (1)	1	0.00
Choctaw	1	0.00
Cree	2	0.01
Creek (1)	4	0.01
Latin American Indians (2)	6	0.02
Navajo (2)	4	0.01
Osage	4	0.01
Pueblo (2)	2	0.01
Sioux (46)	60	0.22
All other tribes (10)	13	0.05
American Indian tribes, not spec.	7	0.03
Arab:	125	0.46
Arab/Arabic	6	0.02
Iraqi	23	0.09
Lebanese	73	0.27
Syrian	15	0.06
Other Arab	8	0.03
Asian:	330	1.20
Cambodian (5)	5	0.02
Chinese, ex. Taiwanese (39)	49	0.18
Filipino (39)	46	0.17
Indian (49)	59	0.22
Japanese (29)	47	0.17
Korean (18)	32	0.12
Laotian (1)	3	0.01
Pakistani (1)	1	0.00
Sri Lankan (5)	6	0.02
Taiwanese (1)	4	0.01
Thai (12)	19	0.07
Vietnamese (10)	11	0.04
Other Asian, specified (31)	33	0.12
Other Asian, not specified (8)	15	0.05
Austrian	39	0.14
Brazilian	16	0.06
British	98	0.36
Canadian	33	0.12
Czech	848	3.14
Czechoslovakian	129	0.48
Danish	1,128	4.17
Dutch	726	2.69
English	2,924	10.82
European	205	0.76
Finnish	19	0.07
French, except Basque	585	2.16
French Canadian	77	0.28
German	11,344	41.96
Greek	92	0.34
Hawaii Native/Pacific Islander:	19	0.07
Polynesian: (8)	10	0.04
Native Hawaiian (3)	5	0.02
Samoan (5)	5	0.02
Other Pac. Isl., not spec. (4)	9	0.03
Hispanic or Latino:	1,118	4.08
Central American:	23	0.08
Costa Rican	2	0.01
Guatemalan	9	0.03
Honduran	3	0.01
Panamanian	4	0.01
Salvadoran	5	0.02

Notes: 1. Figures in the "Number" column do not add up to the total population due to: a) Ancestry/Race overlap — e.g. persons can report being both White and Irish, b) persons of Hispanic origin can report being any race, c) persons reporting two ancestries are counted in both categories. 2. Numbers in parentheses indicate the number of persons reporting this ancestry/race alone, not in combination with any other ancestry/race. 3. Refer to the Explanation of Data in the front of the book for more detailed information.

Cuban	5	0.02
Dominican Republic	3	0.01
Mexican	858	3.13
Puerto Rican	21	0.08
South American:	15	0.05
Chilean	2	0.01
Colombian	6	0.02
Ecuadorian	6	0.02
Uruguayan	1	0.00
Other Hispanic or Latino	193	0.70
Hungarian	11	0.04
Irish	3,372	12.47
Israeli	31	0.11
Italian	445	1.65
Lithuanian	11	0.04
Luxemburger	5	0.02
Norwegian	600	2.22
Pennsylvania German	89	0.33
Polish	917	3.39
Portuguese	20	0.07
Russian	190	0.70
Scandinavian	61	0.23
Scotch-Irish	422	1.56
Scottish	410	1.52
Slavic	9	0.03
Swedish	2,202	8.14
Swiss	183	0.68
Turkish	38	0.14
Ukrainian	4	0.01
United States or American	1,367	5.06
Welsh	201	0.74
West Indian, excl. Hispanic:	50	0.18
Bahamian	43	0.16
Trinidadian and Tobagonian	7	0.03
White:	26,401	96.25
Not Hispanic (25,525)	25,734	93.81
Hispanic (584)	667	2.43

La Vista

Place Type: City
County: Sarpy
Population: 11,699

Ancestry/Race	Number	%
African American/Black:	428	3.66
Not Hispanic (344)	423	3.62
Hispanic	5	0.04
African, sub-Saharan:	34	0.29
African	26	0.22
Cape Verdean	8	0.07
Alaska Native tribes, specified:	4	0.03
Aleut (3)	3	0.03
Eskimo	1	0.01
Am. Ind. or Alaska Nat., not spec.	11	0.09
American Indian tribes, specified:	84	0.72
Apache	2	0.02
Blackfeet	5	0.04
Cherokee (7)	26	0.22
Cheyenne (6)	6	0.05
Chippewa (6)	10	0.09
Choctaw (1)	1	0.01
Creek (2)	4	0.03
Iroquois	1	0.01
Navajo	1	0.01
Osage	2	0.02
Paiute (1)	1	0.01
Potawatomi (2)	4	0.03
Sioux (4)	5	0.04
Ute (1)	1	0.01
All other tribes (8)	15	0.13
American Indian tribes, not spec.	5	0.04
Asian:	358	3.06
Cambodian (2)	3	0.03
Chinese, ex. Taiwanese (19)	24	0.21
Filipino (65)	99	0.85
Indian (12)	15	0.13
Japanese (15)	36	0.31
Korean (34)	49	0.42
Pakistani (1)	1	0.01
Thai (6)	9	0.08
Vietnamese (100)	107	0.91
Other Asian, specified (1)	1	0.01
Other Asian, not specified (12)	14	0.12
Australian	6	0.05
Austrian	27	0.23
Belgian	21	0.18
British	30	0.26
Canadian	30	0.26
Croatian	68	0.58
Czech	791	6.75
Czechoslovakian	71	0.61
Danish	311	2.65
Dutch	294	2.51
English	876	7.48
European	128	1.09
Finnish	16	0.14
French, except Basque	299	2.55
French Canadian	83	0.71
German	4,339	37.03
Greek	6	0.05
Hawaii Native/Pacific Islander:	28	0.24
Micronesian: (4)	11	0.09
Guamanian/Chamorro (4)	11	0.09
Polynesian: (8)	8	0.07
Native Hawaiian (3)	3	0.03
Samoan (3)	3	0.03
Other Polynesian (2)	2	0.02
Other Pac. Isl., not spec.	9	0.08
Hispanic or Latino:	485	4.15
Central American:	13	0.11
Guatemalan	2	0.02
Honduran	2	0.02
Nicaraguan	2	0.02
Panamanian	7	0.06
Cuban	4	0.03
Dominican Republic	2	0.02
Mexican	324	2.77
Puerto Rican	49	0.42
South American:	13	0.11
Chilean	5	0.04
Colombian	6	0.05
Venezuelan	2	0.02
Other Hispanic or Latino	80	0.68
Hungarian	27	0.23
Icelander	6	0.05
Irish	1,926	16.43
Italian	772	6.59
Lithuanian	69	0.59
Luxemburger	14	0.12
Norwegian	341	2.91
Pennsylvania German	43	0.37
Polish	698	5.96
Portuguese	37	0.32
Romanian	5	0.04
Russian	33	0.28
Scotch-Irish	137	1.17
Scottish	184	1.57
Serbian	6	0.05
Slovak	7	0.06
Swedish	499	4.26
Swiss	7	0.06
Ukrainian	6	0.05
United States or American	538	4.59
Welsh	61	0.52
White:	10,808	92.38
Not Hispanic (10,334)	10,518	89.91
Hispanic (248)	290	2.48

Lexington

Place Type: City
County: Dawson
Population: 10,011

Ancestry/Race	Number	%
African American/Black:	64	0.64
Not Hispanic (32)	40	0.40
Hispanic (12)	24	0.24
African, sub-Saharan:	10	0.10
Ghanian	10	0.10
Am. Ind. or Alaska Nat., not spec.	67	0.67
American Indian tribes, specified:	87	0.87
Apache (1)	2	0.02
Cherokee (8)	11	0.11
Cheyenne (1)	5	0.05
Iroquois (1)	3	0.03
Latin American Indians (8)	18	0.18
Navajo (3)	3	0.03
Sioux (17)	25	0.25
All other tribes (16)	20	0.20
American Indian tribes, not spec.	4	0.04
Arab:	20	0.20
Lebanese	20	0.20
Asian:	129	1.29
Chinese, ex. Taiwanese (9)	9	0.09
Filipino (7)	7	0.07
Indian (5)	6	0.06
Japanese (4)	4	0.04
Korean	2	0.02
Laotian (10)	21	0.21
Vietnamese (69)	72	0.72
Other Asian, not specified (6)	8	0.08
Czech	146	1.46
Czechoslovakian	13	0.13
Danish	155	1.55
Dutch	149	1.49
English	547	5.46
European	28	0.28
French, except Basque	89	0.89
French Canadian	7	0.07
German	2,011	20.08
Greek	19	0.19
Hawaii Native/Pacific Islander:	4	0.04
Micronesian: (2)	3	0.03
Guamanian/Chamorro (2)	3	0.03
Other Pac. Isl., not spec.	1	0.01
Hispanic or Latino:	5,121	51.15
Central American:	698	6.97
Guatemalan	490	4.89
Honduran	18	0.18
Nicaraguan	13	0.13
Salvadoran	157	1.57
Other Central American	20	0.20
Cuban	7	0.07
Mexican	3,754	37.50
Puerto Rican	11	0.11
South American:	15	0.15
Bolivian	2	0.02
Chilean	9	0.09
Colombian	1	0.01
Peruvian	3	0.03
Other Hispanic or Latino	636	6.35
Irish	632	6.31
Italian	90	0.90
Luxemburger	5	0.05
Northern European	14	0.14
Norwegian	78	0.78
Polish	100	1.00
Russian	25	0.25
Scotch-Irish	36	0.36
Scottish	91	0.91
Serbian	11	0.11
Swedish	144	1.44
Swiss	8	0.08
United States or American	268	2.68
Welsh	13	0.13
White:	6,619	66.12
Not Hispanic (4,635)	4,660	46.55
Hispanic (1,792)	1,959	19.57
Yugoslavian	12	0.12

Lincoln

Place Type: City
County: Lancaster
Population: 225,581

Ancestry/Race	Number	%
Afghan	107	0.05

Notes: 1. Figures in the "Number" column do not add up to the total population due to: a) Ancestry/Race overlap — e.g. persons can report being both White and Irish, b) persons of Hispanic origin can report being any race, c) persons reporting two ancestries are counted in both categories. 2. Numbers in parentheses indicate the number of persons reporting this ancestry/race alone, not in combination with any other ancestry/race. 3. Refer to the Explanation of Data in the front of the book for more detailed information.

Ancestry/Race	Number	%
African American/Black:	8,607	3.82
Not Hispanic (6,803)	8,315	3.69
Hispanic (157)	292	0.13
African, sub-Saharan:	893	0.40
African	501	0.22
Ethiopian	59	0.03
Ghanian	44	0.02
Kenyan	6	0.00
Liberian	20	0.01
Nigerian	146	0.06
South African	52	0.02
Sudanese	46	0.02
Other sub-Saharan African	19	0.01
Alaska Native tribes, specified:	5	0.00
Aleut (1)	1	0.00
Eskimo (2)	2	0.00
Tlingit-Haida (2)	2	0.00
Alaska Native tribes, not specified	2	0.00
Am. Ind. or Alaska Nat., not spec.	766	0.34
Albanian	57	0.03
American Indian tribes, specified:	1,820	0.81
Apache (8)	29	0.01
Blackfeet (6)	27	0.01
Cherokee (74)	262	0.12
Cheyenne (4)	13	0.01
Chickasaw (7)	10	0.00
Chippewa (34)	58	0.03
Choctaw (14)	43	0.02
Colville (3)	3	0.00
Comanche (2)	3	0.00
Cree (6)	7	0.00
Creek (2)	6	0.00
Crow	3	0.00
Delaware (2)	3	0.00
Houma (1)	1	0.00
Iroquois (10)	21	0.01
Kiowa (3)	7	0.00
Latin American Indians (37)	57	0.03
Menominee (3)	5	0.00
Navajo (37)	51	0.02
Osage (1)	13	0.01
Ottawa (2)	2	0.00
Potawatomi (3)	5	0.00
Pueblo (5)	9	0.00
Seminole (1)	3	0.00
Shoshone (1)	3	0.00
Sioux (331)	541	0.24
Yakama	1	0.00
Yaqui (1)	2	0.00
All other tribes (416)	632	0.28
American Indian tribes, not spec.	146	0.06
Arab:	1,208	0.54
Arab/Arabic	245	0.11
Egyptian	130	0.06
Iraqi	214	0.09
Lebanese	257	0.11
Palestinian	7	0.00
Syrian	46	0.02
Other Arab	309	0.14
Armenian	151	0.07
Asian:	8,155	3.62
Bangladeshi (3)	4	0.00
Cambodian (42)	57	0.03
Chinese, ex. Taiwanese (1,036)	1,181	0.52
Filipino (185)	308	0.14
Hmong (1)	1	0.00
Indian (715)	844	0.37
Indonesian (42)	53	0.02
Japanese (254)	388	0.17
Korean (534)	637	0.28
Laotian (41)	48	0.02
Malaysian (31)	55	0.02
Pakistani (48)	61	0.03
Sri Lankan (12)	16	0.01
Taiwanese (21)	34	0.02
Thai (61)	89	0.04
Vietnamese (3,756)	3,925	1.74
Other Asian, specified (39)	56	0.02
Other Asian, not specified (142)	398	0.18
Australian	78	0.03
Austrian	485	0.22
Basque	33	0.01
Belgian	161	0.07
Brazilian	21	0.01
British	726	0.32
Bulgarian	49	0.02
Canadian	302	0.13
Celtic	71	0.03
Croatian	172	0.08
Czech	11,510	5.11
Czechoslovakian	1,632	0.72
Danish	5,832	2.59
Dutch	5,651	2.51
Eastern European	58	0.03
English	24,766	10.99
Estonian	9	0.00
European	2,335	1.04
Finnish	154	0.07
French, except Basque	6,258	2.78
French Canadian	896	0.40
German	89,621	39.75
German Russian	99	0.04
Greek	452	0.20
Guyanese	4	0.00
Hawaii Native/Pacific Islander:	280	0.12
Melanesian: (4)	4	0.00
Fijian (4)	4	0.00
Micronesian: (41)	72	0.03
Guamanian/Chamorro (17)	37	0.02
Other Micronesian (24)	35	0.02
Polynesian: (54)	104	0.05
Native Hawaiian (35)	78	0.03
Samoan (19)	26	0.01
Other Pac. Isl., specified	8	0.00
Other Pac. Isl., not spec. (38)	92	0.04
Hispanic or Latino:	8,154	3.61
Central American:	404	0.18
Costa Rican	18	0.01
Guatemalan	135	0.06
Honduran	60	0.03
Nicaraguan	13	0.01
Panamanian	29	0.01
Salvadoran	125	0.06
Other Central American	24	0.01
Cuban	140	0.06
Dominican Republic	21	0.01
Mexican	5,309	2.35
Puerto Rican	315	0.14
South American:	302	0.13
Argentinean	41	0.02
Bolivian	8	0.00
Chilean	24	0.01
Colombian	93	0.04
Ecuadorian	17	0.01
Peruvian	66	0.03
Uruguayan	2	0.00
Venezuelan	38	0.02
Other South American	13	0.01
Other Hispanic or Latino	1,663	0.74
Hungarian	312	0.14
Icelander	5	0.00
Iranian	239	0.11
Irish	28,602	12.69
Israeli	9	0.00
Italian	4,032	1.79
Latvian	315	0.14
Lithuanian	212	0.09
Luxemburger	179	0.08
Northern European	169	0.07
Norwegian	5,477	2.43
Pennsylvania German	235	0.10
Polish	5,468	2.43
Portuguese	157	0.07
Romanian	169	0.07
Russian	2,454	1.09
Scandinavian	315	0.14
Scotch-Irish	3,943	1.75
Scottish	3,675	1.63
Serbian	49	0.02
Slavic	115	0.05
Slovak	186	0.08
Slovene	121	0.05
Swedish	11,296	5.01
Swiss	1,319	0.59
Turkish	51	0.02
Ukrainian	796	0.35
United States or American	8,895	3.95
Welsh	1,750	0.78
West Indian, excl. Hispanic:	165	0.07
Bahamian	17	0.01
Barbadian	5	0.00
British West Indian	13	0.01
Haitian	29	0.01
Jamaican	71	0.03
Trinidadian and Tobagonian	9	0.00
West Indian	21	0.01
White:	205,351	91.03
Not Hispanic (198,087)	201,485	89.32
Hispanic (3,235)	3,866	1.71
Yugoslavian	345	0.15

Norfolk

Place Type: City
County: Madison
Population: 23,516

Ancestry/Race	Number	%
African American/Black:	341	1.45
Not Hispanic (271)	333	1.42
Hispanic (1)	8	0.03
African, sub-Saharan:	9	0.04
Other sub-Saharan African	9	0.04
Alaska Native tribes, specified:	1	0.00
Aleut	1	0.00
Am. Ind. or Alaska Nat., not spec.	62	0.26
American Indian tribes, specified:	387	1.65
Apache	2	0.01
Blackfeet (1)	4	0.02
Cherokee (2)	6	0.03
Chickasaw	1	0.00
Chippewa	2	0.01
Choctaw	1	0.00
Iroquois (1)	1	0.00
Kiowa (3)	3	0.01
Latin American Indians (13)	15	0.06
Potawatomi (1)	1	0.00
Sioux (143)	190	0.81
Tohono O'Odham	1	0.00
Yaqui (2)	2	0.01
All other tribes (134)	158	0.67
American Indian tribes, not spec.	8	0.03
Asian:	154	0.65
Bangladeshi (1)	1	0.00
Chinese, ex. Taiwanese (24)	25	0.11
Filipino (15)	31	0.13
Indian (38)	38	0.16
Japanese (6)	9	0.04
Korean (16)	18	0.08
Thai (2)	4	0.02
Vietnamese (10)	13	0.06
Other Asian, not specified (2)	15	0.06
Australian	5	0.02
Austrian	54	0.23
Belgian	6	0.03
British	26	0.11
Croatian	4	0.02
Czech	1,042	4.43
Czechoslovakian	130	0.55
Danish	714	3.03
Dutch	484	2.06
English	1,547	6.57
European	86	0.37
Finnish	13	0.06
French, except Basque	499	2.12
French Canadian	90	0.38
German	11,730	49.83
Greek	31	0.13
Hawaii Native/Pacific Islander:	15	0.06
Micronesian: (4)	6	0.03

Notes: 1. Figures in the "Number" column do not add up to the total population due to: a) Ancestry/Race overlap — e.g. persons can report being both White and Irish, b) persons of Hispanic origin can report being any race, c) persons reporting two ancestries are counted in both categories. 2. Numbers in parentheses indicate the number of persons reporting this ancestry/race alone, not in combination with any other ancestry/race. 3. Refer to the Explanation of Data in the front of the book for more detailed information.

Guamanian/Chamorro (3)	5	0.02
Other Micronesian (1)	1	0.00
Polynesian: (4)	7	0.03
Native Hawaiian	1	0.00
Samoan (4)	6	0.03
Other Pac. Isl., not spec.	2	0.01
Hispanic or Latino:	1,790	7.61
Central American:	15	0.06
Guatemalan	1	0.00
Honduran	1	0.00
Nicaraguan	9	0.04
Salvadoran	2	0.01
Other Central American	2	0.01
Cuban	4	0.02
Mexican	1,546	6.57
Puerto Rican	9	0.04
South American:	18	0.08
Colombian	4	0.02
Ecuadorian	1	0.00
Paraguayan	1	0.00
Venezuelan	11	0.05
Other South American	1	0.00
Other Hispanic or Latino	198	0.84
Hungarian	7	0.03
Icelander	7	0.03
Irish	2,763	11.74
Italian	234	0.99
Lithuanian	42	0.18
Northern European	9	0.04
Norwegian	683	2.90
Pennsylvania German	32	0.14
Polish	424	1.80
Portuguese	6	0.03
Russian	73	0.31
Scandinavian	9	0.04
Scotch-Irish	276	1.17
Scottish	186	0.79
Slovak	2	0.01
Swedish	1,278	5.43
Swiss	90	0.38
Turkish	6	0.03
Ukrainian	10	0.04
United States or American	890	3.78
Welsh	142	0.60
White:	21,750	92.49
Not Hispanic (20,834)	21,005	89.32
Hispanic (663)	745	3.17
Yugoslavian	32	0.14

North Platte

Place Type: City
County: Lincoln
Population: 23,878

Ancestry/Race	Number	%
African American/Black:	242	1.01
Not Hispanic (161)	220	0.92
Hispanic (9)	22	0.09
African, sub-Saharan:	76	0.32
African	37	0.16
Nigerian	25	0.10
Somalian	14	0.06
Alaska Native tribes, specified:	5	0.02
Eskimo (4)	4	0.02
All other tribes (1)	1	0.00
Am. Ind. or Alaska Nat., not spec.	54	0.23
American Indian tribes, specified:	178	0.75
Apache (1)	3	0.01
Blackfeet (2)	7	0.03
Cherokee (24)	37	0.15
Chippewa (2)	6	0.03
Choctaw (2)	2	0.01
Creek (2)	3	0.01
Crow	1	0.00
Latin American Indians (7)	12	0.05
Navajo (14)	27	0.11
Ottawa (3)	3	0.01
Paiute (1)	1	0.00
Sioux (38)	55	0.23
Yaqui	1	0.00
Yuman (1)	2	0.01
All other tribes (12)	18	0.08
American Indian tribes, not spec.	15	0.06
Arab:	22	0.09
Lebanese	16	0.07
Moroccan	6	0.03
Asian:	143	0.60
Cambodian	2	0.01
Chinese, ex. Taiwanese (20)	28	0.12
Filipino (18)	29	0.12
Indian (5)	12	0.05
Indonesian (1)	1	0.00
Japanese (15)	23	0.10
Korean (13)	19	0.08
Thai (4)	4	0.02
Vietnamese (9)	10	0.04
Other Asian, not specified (8)	15	0.06
Australian	9	0.04
Austrian	41	0.17
Belgian	85	0.36
British	37	0.16
Canadian	12	0.05
Celtic	25	0.10
Czech	465	1.95
Czechoslovakian	104	0.44
Danish	529	2.22
Dutch	699	2.93
English	2,835	11.89
European	81	0.34
Finnish	19	0.08
French, except Basque	717	3.01
French Canadian	101	0.42
German	8,036	33.70
Greek	97	0.41
Hawaii Native/Pacific Islander:	13	0.05
Polynesian: (2)	6	0.03
Native Hawaiian (1)	1	0.00
Samoan (1)	4	0.02
Tongan	1	0.00
Other Pac. Isl., not spec. (5)	7	0.03
Hispanic or Latino:	1,596	6.68
Central American:	7	0.03
Costa Rican	2	0.01
Panamanian	3	0.01
Salvadoran	2	0.01
Cuban	3	0.01
Mexican	1,302	5.45
Puerto Rican	4	0.02
South American:	10	0.04
Colombian	7	0.03
Paraguayan	1	0.00
Peruvian	1	0.00
Venezuelan	1	0.00
Other Hispanic or Latino	270	1.13
Hungarian	28	0.12
Irish	3,161	13.26
Italian	339	1.42
Lithuanian	32	0.13
Luxemburger	30	0.13
Macedonian	14	0.06
Norwegian	425	1.78
Pennsylvania German	21	0.09
Polish	666	2.79
Portuguese	37	0.16
Romanian	8	0.03
Russian	117	0.49
Scandinavian	61	0.26
Scotch-Irish	340	1.43
Scottish	486	2.04
Swedish	1,199	5.03
Swiss	61	0.26
Ukrainian	17	0.07
United States or American	1,850	7.76
Welsh	231	0.97
White:	22,629	94.77
Not Hispanic (21,725)	21,890	91.67
Hispanic (594)	739	3.09

Omaha

Place Type: City
County: Douglas
Population: 390,007

Ancestry/Race	Number	%
Acadian/Cajun	28	0.01
Afghan	257	0.07
African American/Black:	55,197	14.15
Not Hispanic (51,427)	54,484	13.97
Hispanic (490)	713	0.18
African, sub-Saharan:	3,252	0.83
African	2,341	0.60
Cape Verdean	7	0.00
Ethiopian	34	0.01
Ghanian	18	0.00
Kenyan	59	0.02
Liberian	15	0.00
Nigerian	141	0.04
Senegalese	35	0.01
Somalian	9	0.00
South African	39	0.01
Sudanese	330	0.08
Ugandan	10	0.00
Zimbabwean	12	0.00
Other sub-Saharan African	202	0.05
Alaska Native tribes, specified:	20	0.01
Alaska Athabascan (4)	4	0.00
Aleut	1	0.00
Eskimo (8)	13	0.00
Tlingit-Haida	2	0.00
Alaska Native tribes, not specified	14	0.00
Am. Ind. or Alaska Nat., not spec.	1,448	0.37
Albanian	9	0.00
American Indian tribes, specified:	3,178	0.81
Apache (36)	71	0.02
Blackfeet (13)	105	0.03
Cherokee (129)	512	0.13
Cheyenne (1)	20	0.01
Chickasaw (15)	29	0.01
Chippewa (55)	104	0.03
Choctaw (19)	51	0.01
Colville (1)	1	0.00
Comanche (9)	11	0.00
Cree (3)	8	0.00
Creek (18)	35	0.01
Crow (2)	3	0.00
Delaware (2)	9	0.00
Iroquois (9)	25	0.01
Kiowa (8)	11	0.00
Latin American Indians (95)	175	0.04
Lumbee (7)	8	0.00
Menominee (4)	5	0.00
Navajo (45)	53	0.01
Osage (1)	7	0.00
Ottawa (2)	2	0.00
Paiute (1)	3	0.00
Potawatomi (14)	29	0.01
Pueblo (14)	20	0.01
Puget Sound Salish (1)	3	0.00
Seminole (9)	17	0.00
Shoshone	4	0.00
Sioux (390)	651	0.17
Tohono O'Odham (1)	1	0.00
Ute (3)	3	0.00
Yaqui (1)	3	0.00
All other tribes (857)	1,199	0.31
American Indian tribes, not spec.	186	0.05
Arab:	1,574	0.40
Arab/Arabic	170	0.04
Egyptian	112	0.03
Jordanian	81	0.02
Lebanese	897	0.23
Moroccan	7	0.00
Palestinian	59	0.02
Syrian	196	0.05
Other Arab	52	0.01
Armenian	44	0.01
Asian:	8,386	2.15

Notes: 1. Figures in the "Number" column do not add up to the total population due to: a) Ancestry/Race overlap — e.g. persons can report being both White and Irish, b) persons of Hispanic origin can report being any race, c) persons reporting two ancestries are counted in both categories. 2. Numbers in parentheses indicate the number of persons reporting this ancestry/race alone, not in combination with any other ancestry/race. 3. Refer to the Explanation of Data in the front of the book for more detailed information.

Ancestry/Race	Number	%
Bangladeshi (10)	11	0.00
Cambodian (40)	50	0.01
Chinese, ex. Taiwanese (1,090)	1,345	0.34
Filipino (672)	979	0.25
Hmong (75)	82	0.02
Indian (1,712)	1,889	0.48
Indonesian (46)	66	0.02
Japanese (610)	907	0.23
Korean (748)	921	0.24
Laotian (100)	120	0.03
Malaysian (8)	9	0.00
Pakistani (79)	111	0.03
Sri Lankan (28)	30	0.01
Taiwanese (65)	80	0.02
Thai (128)	178	0.05
Vietnamese (1,011)	1,095	0.28
Other Asian, specified (99)	136	0.03
Other Asian, not specified (131)	377	0.10
Australian	79	0.02
Austrian	974	0.25
Basque	8	0.00
Belgian	614	0.16
Brazilian	71	0.02
British	1,218	0.31
Bulgarian	66	0.02
Canadian	300	0.08
Carpatho Rusyn	10	0.00
Celtic	106	0.03
Croatian	1,273	0.33
Czech	16,796	4.31
Czechoslovakian	2,106	0.54
Danish	11,367	2.91
Dutch	6,897	1.77
Eastern European	136	0.03
English	33,296	8.53
Estonian	13	0.00
European	2,220	0.57
Finnish	393	0.10
French, except Basque	9,878	2.53
French Canadian	1,514	0.39
German	112,024	28.72
German Russian	40	0.01
Greek	950	0.24
Hawaii Native/Pacific Islander:	513	0.13
Melanesian:	1	0.00
Fijian	1	0.00
Micronesian: (81)	118	0.03
Guamanian/Chamorro (67)	103	0.03
Other Micronesian (14)	15	0.00
Polynesian: (121)	251	0.06
Native Hawaiian (90)	194	0.05
Samoan (30)	49	0.01
Tongan (1)	6	0.00
Other Polynesian	2	0.00
Other Pac. Isl., specified	13	0.00
Other Pac. Isl., not spec. (26)	130	0.03
Hispanic or Latino:	29,397	7.54
Central American:	1,369	0.35
Costa Rican	21	0.01
Guatemalan	383	0.10
Honduran	127	0.03
Nicaraguan	26	0.01
Panamanian	71	0.02
Salvadoran	664	0.17
Other Central American	77	0.02
Cuban	272	0.07
Dominican Republic	65	0.02
Mexican	23,290	5.97
Puerto Rican	591	0.15
South American:	431	0.11
Argentinean	22	0.01
Bolivian	24	0.01
Chilean	38	0.01
Colombian	171	0.04
Ecuadorian	32	0.01
Paraguayan	3	0.00
Peruvian	60	0.02
Uruguayan	3	0.00
Venezuelan	65	0.02
Other South American	13	0.00
Other Hispanic or Latino	3,379	0.87
Hungarian	1,118	0.29
Icelander	60	0.02
Iranian	159	0.04
Irish	62,349	15.98
Israeli	16	0.00
Italian	18,716	4.80
Latvian	191	0.05
Lithuanian	1,761	0.45
Luxemburger	230	0.06
Macedonian	32	0.01
Maltese	17	0.00
New Zealander	6	0.00
Northern European	218	0.06
Norwegian	9,233	2.37
Pennsylvania German	334	0.09
Polish	18,447	4.73
Portuguese	312	0.08
Romanian	337	0.09
Russian	2,487	0.64
Scandinavian	845	0.22
Scotch-Irish	5,565	1.43
Scottish	5,076	1.30
Serbian	407	0.10
Slavic	131	0.03
Slovak	232	0.06
Slovene	137	0.04
Swedish	14,061	3.60
Swiss	1,232	0.32
Turkish	55	0.01
Ukrainian	469	0.12
United States or American	13,521	3.47
Welsh	2,054	0.53
West Indian, excl. Hispanic:	285	0.07
Barbadian	8	0.00
Bermudan	4	0.00
British West Indian	37	0.01
Haitian	63	0.02
Jamaican	82	0.02
Trinidadian and Tobagonian	6	0.00
U.S. Virgin Islander	39	0.01
West Indian	46	0.01
White:	311,843	79.96
Not Hispanic (293,876)	298,507	76.54
Hispanic (11,869)	13,336	3.42
Yugoslavian	417	0.11

Papillion

Place Type: City
County: Sarpy
Population: 16,363

Ancestry/Race	Number	%
African American/Black:	502	3.07
Not Hispanic (394)	472	2.88
Hispanic (8)	30	0.18
African, sub-Saharan:	6	0.04
African	6	0.04
Alaska Native tribes, specified:	4	0.02
Tlingit-Haida (3)	4	0.02
Am. Ind. or Alaska Nat., not spec.	30	0.18
American Indian tribes, specified:	93	0.57
Blackfeet (2)	2	0.01
Cherokee (7)	30	0.18
Chippewa (1)	3	0.02
Choctaw (2)	4	0.02
Cree	4	0.02
Creek	3	0.02
Latin American Indians (6)	10	0.06
Lumbee (5)	5	0.03
Navajo (1)	1	0.01
Potawatomi (4)	4	0.02
Sioux (12)	13	0.08
All other tribes (9)	14	0.09
American Indian tribes, not spec.	7	0.04
Arab:	39	0.24
Arab/Arabic	14	0.09
Lebanese	8	0.05
Syrian	17	0.10
Armenian	16	0.10
Asian:	331	2.02
Chinese, ex. Taiwanese (25)	45	0.28
Filipino (47)	86	0.53
Indian (27)	32	0.20
Japanese (9)	26	0.16
Korean (49)	58	0.35
Laotian (2)	2	0.01
Malaysian	1	0.01
Pakistani (2)	2	0.01
Thai (11)	14	0.09
Vietnamese (37)	45	0.28
Other Asian, specified (2)	6	0.04
Other Asian, not specified (13)	14	0.09
Australian	5	0.03
Austrian	81	0.50
Belgian	36	0.22
British	159	0.98
Bulgarian	4	0.02
Canadian	27	0.17
Celtic	10	0.06
Croatian	35	0.22
Czech	835	5.14
Czechoslovakian	76	0.47
Danish	502	3.09
Dutch	474	2.92
English	2,266	13.94
European	171	1.05
Finnish	38	0.23
French, except Basque	616	3.79
French Canadian	76	0.47
German	6,371	39.20
Greek	93	0.57
Hawaii Native/Pacific Islander:	17	0.10
Micronesian: (2)	5	0.03
Guamanian/Chamorro (2)	5	0.03
Polynesian: (2)	5	0.03
Native Hawaiian (2)	4	0.02
Samoan	1	0.01
Other Pac. Isl., specified	3	0.02
Other Pac. Isl., not spec.	4	0.02
Hispanic or Latino:	478	2.92
Central American:	13	0.08
Costa Rican	1	0.01
Guatemalan	6	0.04
Panamanian	5	0.03
Salvadoran	1	0.01
Cuban	12	0.07
Dominican Republic	2	0.01
Mexican	305	1.86
Puerto Rican	36	0.22
South American:	10	0.06
Chilean	3	0.02
Colombian	5	0.03
Peruvian	1	0.01
Other South American	1	0.01
Other Hispanic or Latino	100	0.61
Hungarian	33	0.20
Icelander	10	0.06
Irish	2,794	17.19
Italian	705	4.34
Lithuanian	6	0.04
Northern European	23	0.14
Norwegian	561	3.45
Pennsylvania German	19	0.12
Polish	810	4.98
Portuguese	13	0.08
Romanian	28	0.17
Russian	78	0.48
Scandinavian	51	0.31
Scotch-Irish	354	2.18
Scottish	394	2.42
Serbian	17	0.10
Slovak	15	0.09
Slovene	7	0.04
Swedish	629	3.87
Swiss	70	0.43
Ukrainian	19	0.12
United States or American	597	3.67
Welsh	148	0.91

Notes: 1. Figures in the "Number" column do not add up to the total population due to: a) Ancestry/Race overlap — e.g. persons can report being both White and Irish, b) persons of Hispanic origin can report being any race, c) persons reporting two ancestries are counted in both categories. 2. Numbers in parentheses indicate the number of persons reporting this ancestry/race alone, not in combination with any other ancestry/race. 3. Refer to the Explanation of Data in the front of the book for more detailed information.

Ancestry/Race	Number	%
White:	15,457	94.46
Not Hispanic (14,976)	15,152	92.60
Hispanic (245)	305	1.86
Yugoslavian	5	0.03

Scottsbluff

Place Type: City
County: Scotts Bluff
Population: 14,732

Ancestry/Race	Number	%
African American/Black:	108	0.73
Not Hispanic (56)	90	0.61
Hispanic (9)	18	0.12
African, sub-Saharan:	5	0.03
African	5	0.03
Alaska Native tribes, specified:	3	0.02
Eskimo (2)	3	0.02
Am. Ind. or Alaska Nat., not spec.	68	0.46
American Indian tribes, specified:	459	3.12
Apache (2)	2	0.01
Cherokee (1)	12	0.08
Cheyenne	8	0.05
Chippewa (1)	1	0.01
Choctaw	1	0.01
Iroquois	1	0.01
Latin American Indians (18)	24	0.16
Navajo (3)	3	0.02
Osage	1	0.01
Sioux (344)	392	2.66
Yuman	1	0.01
All other tribes (4)	13	0.09
American Indian tribes, not spec.	40	0.27
Arab:	30	0.20
Syrian	30	0.20
Asian:	147	1.00
Chinese, ex. Taiwanese (28)	31	0.21
Filipino (14)	29	0.20
Hmong (1)	1	0.01
Indian (3)	3	0.02
Japanese (43)	58	0.39
Korean (4)	5	0.03
Laotian (1)	3	0.02
Vietnamese (9)	9	0.06
Other Asian, not specified (7)	8	0.05
Austrian	30	0.20
Brazilian	6	0.04
British	47	0.32
Czech	175	1.18
Czechoslovakian	45	0.30
Danish	187	1.26
Dutch	290	1.95
English	1,420	9.57
European	11	0.07
Finnish	27	0.18
French, except Basque	352	2.37
French Canadian	25	0.17
German	5,012	33.78
German Russian	9	0.06
Greek	42	0.28
Hawaii Native/Pacific Islander:	12	0.08
Polynesian: (5)	8	0.05
Native Hawaiian (4)	7	0.05
Samoan (1)	1	0.01
Other Pac. Isl., not spec. (1)	4	0.03
Hispanic or Latino:	3,476	23.59
Central American:	9	0.06
Guatemalan	3	0.02
Honduran	3	0.02
Panamanian	1	0.01
Salvadoran	1	0.01
Other Central American	1	0.01
Cuban	4	0.03
Mexican	2,842	19.29
Puerto Rican	17	0.12
South American:	13	0.09
Peruvian	12	0.08
Other South American	1	0.01
Other Hispanic or Latino	591	4.01
Iranian	8	0.05
Irish	1,394	9.40
Italian	223	1.50
Norwegian	336	2.26
Pennsylvania German	33	0.22
Polish	176	1.19
Portuguese	7	0.05
Russian	325	2.19
Scandinavian	32	0.22
Scotch-Irish	192	1.29
Scottish	158	1.06
Serbian	11	0.07
Swedish	366	2.47
Swiss	77	0.52
Turkish	5	0.03
United States or American	538	3.63
Welsh	66	0.44
White:	12,326	83.67
Not Hispanic (10,548)	10,670	72.43
Hispanic (1,514)	1,656	11.24

South Sioux City

Place Type: City
County: Dakota
Population: 11,925

Ancestry/Race	Number	%
African American/Black:	157	1.32
Not Hispanic (96)	142	1.19
Hispanic (6)	15	0.13
African, sub-Saharan:	21	0.18
African	21	0.18
Am. Ind. or Alaska Nat., not spec.	92	0.77
American Indian tribes, specified:	277	2.32
Apache	2	0.02
Cherokee	10	0.08
Chippewa	3	0.03
Choctaw	5	0.04
Latin American Indians (2)	9	0.08
Lumbee (1)	2	0.02
Seminole	1	0.01
Sioux (74)	94	0.79
All other tribes (126)	151	1.27
American Indian tribes, not spec.	14	0.12
Arab:	5	0.04
Syrian	5	0.04
Asian:	443	3.71
Cambodian (1)	1	0.01
Chinese, ex. Taiwanese (15)	24	0.20
Filipino (2)	11	0.09
Indian (35)	37	0.31
Indonesian (5)	5	0.04
Japanese (2)	4	0.03
Korean (10)	13	0.11
Laotian (113)	139	1.17
Pakistani (5)	5	0.04
Thai (3)	7	0.06
Vietnamese (170)	181	1.52
Other Asian, not specified (8)	16	0.13
Austrian	6	0.05
British	6	0.05
Czech	110	0.92
Czechoslovakian	2	0.02
Danish	242	2.02
Dutch	253	2.11
English	796	6.65
European	82	0.69
French, except Basque	380	3.18
French Canadian	116	0.97
German	3,195	26.70
Greek	27	0.23
Hawaii Native/Pacific Islander:	19	0.16
Micronesian: (3)	3	0.03
Guamanian/Chamorro (3)	3	0.03
Other Pac. Isl., not spec. (8)	16	0.13
Hispanic or Latino:	2,958	24.81
Central American:	102	0.86
Guatemalan	68	0.57
Honduran	1	0.01
Nicaraguan	2	0.02
Salvadoran	31	0.26
Cuban	4	0.03
Mexican	2,511	21.06
Puerto Rican	16	0.13
South American:	11	0.09
Chilean	1	0.01
Ecuadorian	1	0.01
Peruvian	9	0.08
Other Hispanic or Latino	314	2.63
Irish	1,602	13.39
Italian	173	1.45
Lithuanian	7	0.06
Luxemburger	12	0.10
Norwegian	510	4.26
Polish	182	1.52
Scotch-Irish	105	0.88
Scottish	138	1.15
Slovak	27	0.23
Swedish	305	2.55
Swiss	71	0.59
Ukrainian	11	0.09
United States or American	373	3.12
Welsh	19	0.16
West Indian, excl. Hispanic:	4	0.03
West Indian	4	0.03
White:	9,354	78.44
Not Hispanic (8,074)	8,202	68.78
Hispanic (975)	1,152	9.66
Yugoslavian	7	0.06

Boulder City

Place Type: City
County: Clark
Population: 14,966

Ancestry/Race	Number	%
African American/Black:	138	0.92
Not Hispanic (102)	131	0.88
Hispanic (5)	7	0.05
African, sub-Saharan:	8	0.05
South African	8	0.05
Alaska Native tribes, specified:	2	0.01
Eskimo (1)	1	0.01
Tlingit-Haida (1)	1	0.01
Alaska Native tribes, not specified	1	0.01
Am. Ind. or Alaska Nat., not spec.	70	0.47
Alsatian	8	0.05
American Indian tribes, specified:	164	1.10
Apache (5)	5	0.03
Blackfeet (1)	4	0.03
Cherokee (10)	50	0.33
Chickasaw (2)	2	0.01
Chippewa (3)	14	0.09
Choctaw (5)	13	0.09
Crow (1)	1	0.01
Delaware (2)	2	0.01
Iroquois (2)	4	0.03
Latin American Indians (1)	5	0.03
Lumbee (1)	1	0.01
Navajo (12)	13	0.09
Osage	3	0.02
Paiute (1)	1	0.01
Potawatomi (1)	3	0.02
Pueblo (4)	5	0.03
Puget Sound Salish	1	0.01
Seminole (5)	6	0.04
Shoshone (6)	9	0.06
Sioux (5)	9	0.06
Tohono O'Odham (2)	2	0.01
Yakama	1	0.01
Yuman	1	0.01
All other tribes (3)	9	0.06
American Indian tribes, not spec.	21	0.14
Asian:	175	1.17
Chinese, ex. Taiwanese (7)	22	0.15
Filipino (30)	50	0.33
Indian (9)	13	0.09
Japanese (23)	38	0.25

Notes: 1. Figures in the "Number" column do not add up to the total population due to: a) Ancestry/Race overlap — e.g. persons can report being both White and Irish, b) persons of Hispanic origin can report being any race, c) persons reporting two ancestries are counted in both categories. 2. Numbers in parentheses indicate the number of persons reporting this ancestry/race alone, not in combination with any other ancestry/race. 3. Refer to the Explanation of Data in the front of the book for more detailed information.

Korean (23)	28	0.19
Pakistani (1)	1	0.01
Thai (3)	4	0.03
Vietnamese (8)	10	0.07
Other Asian, not specified	9	0.06
Australian	7	0.05
Austrian	74	0.49
Basque	28	0.19
Belgian	20	0.13
British	148	0.99
Canadian	36	0.24
Celtic	16	0.11
Croatian	14	0.09
Czech	73	0.49
Czechoslovakian	17	0.11
Danish	261	1.74
Dutch	364	2.43
Eastern European	11	0.07
English	2,622	17.52
European	133	0.89
Finnish	39	0.26
French, except Basque	621	4.15
French Canadian	83	0.55
German	2,780	18.58
Hawaii Native/Pacific Islander:	39	0.26
Micronesian: (1)	2	0.01
Guamanian/Chamorro (1)	2	0.01
Polynesian: (18)	27	0.18
Native Hawaiian (5)	14	0.09
Samoan (5)	5	0.03
Tongan (3)	3	0.02
Other Polynesian (5)	5	0.03
Other Pac. Isl., not spec. (4)	10	0.07
Hispanic or Latino:	650	4.34
Central American:	9	0.06
Costa Rican	5	0.03
Honduran	1	0.01
Panamanian	2	0.01
Other Central American	1	0.01
Cuban	14	0.09
Dominican Republic	4	0.03
Mexican	430	2.87
Puerto Rican	39	0.26
South American:	8	0.05
Argentinean	1	0.01
Bolivian	2	0.01
Colombian	3	0.02
Peruvian	2	0.01
Other Hispanic or Latino	146	0.98
Hungarian	123	0.82
Irish	2,259	15.09
Italian	865	5.78
Lithuanian	28	0.19
Luxemburger	8	0.05
Norwegian	391	2.61
Polish	505	3.37
Portuguese	72	0.48
Romanian	19	0.13
Russian	152	1.02
Scandinavian	119	0.80
Scotch-Irish	362	2.42
Scottish	383	2.56
Slavic	6	0.04
Slovak	33	0.22
Slovene	5	0.03
Swedish	523	3.49
Swiss	65	0.43
Ukrainian	36	0.24
United States or American	750	5.01
Welsh	249	1.66
West Indian, excl. Hispanic:	7	0.05
Dutch West Indian	7	0.05
White:	14,424	96.38
Not Hispanic (13,747)	13,987	93.46
Hispanic (402)	437	2.92
Yugoslavian	16	0.11

Carson City

Place Type: Special City
County: Carson City Independent City
Population: 52,457

Ancestry/Race	Number	%
Afghan	8	0.02
African American/Black:	1,085	2.07
Not Hispanic (909)	1,013	1.93
Hispanic (37)	72	0.14
African, sub-Saharan:	28	0.05
African	8	0.02
Ethiopian	9	0.02
Nigerian	11	0.02
Alaska Native tribes, specified:	22	0.04
Alaska Athabascan (1)	1	0.00
Aleut (5)	5	0.01
Eskimo (4)	4	0.01
Tlingit-Haida (6)	7	0.01
All other tribes	5	0.01
Alaska Native tribes, not specified	1	0.00
Am. Ind. or Alaska Nat., not spec.	308	0.59
American Indian tribes, specified:	1,375	2.62
Apache (12)	23	0.04
Blackfeet (6)	26	0.05
Cherokee (81)	189	0.36
Cheyenne (5)	5	0.01
Chickasaw	7	0.01
Chippewa (12)	24	0.05
Choctaw (10)	42	0.08
Colville	1	0.00
Comanche (1)	3	0.01
Cree (3)	4	0.01
Creek (7)	14	0.03
Crow	2	0.00
Delaware	1	0.00
Iroquois (7)	18	0.03
Kiowa (1)	4	0.01
Latin American Indians (10)	15	0.03
Menominee (3)	3	0.01
Navajo (32)	45	0.09
Osage (2)	4	0.01
Paiute (162)	239	0.46
Pima (7)	7	0.01
Potawatomi (3)	3	0.01
Pueblo (56)	78	0.15
Seminole (1)	6	0.01
Shoshone (32)	42	0.08
Sioux (26)	43	0.08
Ute (2)	2	0.00
Yaqui	9	0.02
Yuman (12)	12	0.02
All other tribes (374)	504	0.96
American Indian tribes, not spec.	122	0.23
Arab:	147	0.28
Egyptian	6	0.01
Jordanian	53	0.10
Lebanese	66	0.13
Syrian	22	0.04
Armenian	106	0.20
Asian:	1,179	2.25
Cambodian (15)	15	0.03
Chinese, ex. Taiwanese (158)	187	0.36
Filipino (254)	357	0.68
Hmong (4)	4	0.01
Indian (171)	185	0.35
Indonesian (3)	5	0.01
Japanese (111)	165	0.31
Korean (72)	86	0.16
Laotian (6)	7	0.01
Malaysian	3	0.01
Pakistani	4	0.01
Taiwanese (5)	5	0.01
Thai (14)	19	0.04
Vietnamese (92)	102	0.19
Other Asian, not specified (18)	35	0.07
Assyrian/Chaldean/Syriac	13	0.02
Austrian	171	0.33
Basque	278	0.53
Belgian	54	0.10
Brazilian	48	0.09
British	213	0.41
Bulgarian	4	0.01
Canadian	163	0.31
Celtic	49	0.09
Croatian	30	0.06
Czech	157	0.30
Czechoslovakian	68	0.13
Danish	798	1.52
Dutch	993	1.89
Eastern European	10	0.02
English	7,059	13.46
European	418	0.80
Finnish	76	0.14
French, except Basque	2,104	4.01
French Canadian	499	0.95
German	8,900	16.97
Greek	205	0.39
Guyanese	8	0.02
Hawaii Native/Pacific Islander:	139	0.26
Micronesian: (21)	29	0.06
Guamanian/Chamorro (19)	27	0.05
Other Micronesian (2)	2	0.00
Polynesian: (39)	79	0.15
Native Hawaiian (27)	59	0.11
Samoan (12)	17	0.03
Tongan	3	0.01
Other Pac. Isl., not spec. (16)	31	0.06
Hispanic or Latino:	7,466	14.23
Central American:	461	0.88
Costa Rican	12	0.02
Guatemalan	36	0.07
Honduran	57	0.11
Nicaraguan	216	0.41
Panamanian	1	0.00
Salvadoran	133	0.25
Other Central American	6	0.01
Cuban	61	0.12
Dominican Republic	5	0.01
Mexican	5,520	10.52
Puerto Rican	89	0.17
South American:	66	0.13
Argentinean	3	0.01
Chilean	14	0.03
Colombian	24	0.05
Ecuadorian	2	0.00
Paraguayan	1	0.00
Peruvian	17	0.03
Venezuelan	1	0.00
Other South American	4	0.01
Other Hispanic or Latino	1,264	2.41
Hungarian	233	0.44
Icelander	86	0.16
Iranian	13	0.02
Irish	6,655	12.69
Italian	3,495	6.66
Lithuanian	50	0.10
Macedonian	7	0.01
Northern European	53	0.10
Norwegian	1,468	2.80
Pennsylvania German	19	0.04
Polish	943	1.80
Portuguese	560	1.07
Romanian	66	0.13
Russian	417	0.79
Scandinavian	190	0.36
Scotch-Irish	1,215	2.32
Scottish	1,226	2.34
Serbian	32	0.06
Slavic	20	0.04
Slovak	50	0.10
Slovene	34	0.06
Swedish	940	1.79
Swiss	294	0.56
Turkish	9	0.02
Ukrainian	65	0.12
United States or American	2,652	5.06
Welsh	612	1.17
West Indian, excl. Hispanic:	21	0.04

Notes: 1. Figures in the "Number" column do not add up to the total population due to: a) Ancestry/Race overlap — e.g. persons can report being both White and Irish, b) persons of Hispanic origin can report being any race, c) persons reporting two ancestries are counted in both categories. 2. Numbers in parentheses indicate the number of persons reporting this ancestry/race alone, not in combination with any other ancestry/race. 3. Refer to the Explanation of Data in the front of the book for more detailed information.

Dutch West Indian	21	0.04
White:	45,760	87.23
Not Hispanic (41,204)	41,872	79.82
Hispanic (3,540)	3,888	7.41
Yugoslavian	64	0.12

Elko

Place Type: City
County: Elko
Population: 16,708

Ancestry/Race	Number	%
African American/Black:	104	0.62
Not Hispanic (58)	92	0.55
Hispanic (4)	12	0.07
African, sub-Saharan:	35	0.21
Ghanian	22	0.13
Nigerian	13	0.08
Alaska Native tribes, specified:	3	0.02
Alaska Athabascan	1	0.01
Tlingit-Haida	2	0.01
Am. Ind. or Alaska Nat., not spec.	81	0.48
American Indian tribes, specified:	509	3.05
Apache (5)	10	0.06
Blackfeet	2	0.01
Cherokee (10)	30	0.18
Cheyenne (3)	6	0.04
Chippewa (5)	12	0.07
Choctaw (1)	3	0.02
Colville (2)	2	0.01
Comanche	1	0.01
Cree	3	0.02
Creek	1	0.01
Crow (3)	3	0.02
Iroquois (1)	5	0.03
Latin American Indians (3)	27	0.16
Menominee (1)	1	0.01
Navajo (33)	36	0.22
Ottawa (2)	2	0.01
Paiute (18)	23	0.14
Pima (1)	1	0.01
Pueblo	1	0.01
Puget Sound Salish (2)	2	0.01
Shoshone (171)	189	1.13
Sioux (4)	8	0.05
Tohono O'Odham	2	0.01
Yaqui (1)	3	0.02
Yuman (4)	4	0.02
All other tribes (98)	132	0.79
American Indian tribes, not spec.	23	0.14
Arab:	6	0.04
Lebanese	6	0.04
Armenian	11	0.07
Asian:	249	1.49
Chinese, ex. Taiwanese (34)	35	0.21
Filipino (54)	78	0.47
Indian (58)	64	0.38
Indonesian (2)	5	0.03
Japanese (12)	27	0.16
Korean (11)	15	0.09
Pakistani (1)	3	0.02
Taiwanese	1	0.01
Thai (1)	1	0.01
Vietnamese (8)	11	0.07
Other Asian, specified	2	0.01
Other Asian, not specified (4)	7	0.04
Australian	7	0.04
Austrian	31	0.19
Basque	642	3.87
Belgian	41	0.25
British	85	0.51
Canadian	65	0.39
Croatian	15	0.09
Czech	85	0.51
Czechoslovakian	12	0.07
Danish	266	1.60
Dutch	252	1.52
English	1,796	10.82
European	59	0.36
Finnish	52	0.31
French, except Basque	595	3.58
French Canadian	170	1.02
German	2,656	16.00
Greek	44	0.27
Hawaii Native/Pacific Islander:	39	0.23
Melanesian: (3)	3	0.02
Fijian (3)	3	0.02
Micronesian: (2)	5	0.03
Guamanian/Chamorro (2)	5	0.03
Polynesian: (6)	15	0.09
Native Hawaiian (5)	7	0.04
Samoan (1)	1	0.01
Tongan	6	0.04
Other Polynesian	1	0.01
Other Pac. Isl., specified	2	0.01
Other Pac. Isl., not spec. (9)	14	0.08
Hispanic or Latino:	3,528	21.12
Central American:	16	0.10
Costa Rican	1	0.01
Guatemalan	7	0.04
Honduran	2	0.01
Salvadoran	5	0.03
Other Central American	1	0.01
Cuban	2	0.01
Mexican	2,878	17.23
Puerto Rican	37	0.22
South American:	14	0.08
Chilean	5	0.03
Ecuadorian	1	0.01
Peruvian	6	0.04
Venezuelan	2	0.01
Other Hispanic or Latino	581	3.48
Hungarian	29	0.17
Icelander	44	0.27
Iranian	8	0.05
Irish	1,866	11.24
Italian	688	4.14
Lithuanian	15	0.09
Northern European	24	0.14
Norwegian	328	1.98
Pennsylvania German	6	0.04
Polish	256	1.54
Portuguese	78	0.47
Romanian	6	0.04
Russian	34	0.20
Scandinavian	46	0.28
Scotch-Irish	283	1.70
Scottish	383	2.31
Slavic	11	0.07
Slovene	14	0.08
Swedish	403	2.43
Swiss	103	0.62
Ukrainian	45	0.27
United States or American	1,021	6.15
Welsh	162	0.98
White:	14,322	85.72
Not Hispanic (12,248)	12,486	74.73
Hispanic (1,646)	1,836	10.99
Yugoslavian	29	0.17

Enterprise

Place Type: Census Designated Place
County: Clark
Population: 14,676

Ancestry/Race	Number	%
African American/Black:	562	3.83
Not Hispanic (442)	522	3.56
Hispanic (22)	40	0.27
African, sub-Saharan:	39	0.27
African	10	0.07
Cape Verdean	9	0.06
Ghanian	20	0.14
Alaska Native tribes, specified:	4	0.03
Alaska Athabascan (1)	1	0.01
All other tribes (3)	3	0.02
Am. Ind. or Alaska Nat., not spec.	58	0.40
American Indian tribes, specified:	140	0.95
Apache (1)	10	0.07
Blackfeet (1)	3	0.02
Cherokee (15)	44	0.30
Cheyenne (1)	2	0.01
Chickasaw (3)	3	0.02
Chippewa (10)	13	0.09
Choctaw (5)	13	0.09
Comanche (2)	3	0.02
Creek (5)	6	0.04
Iroquois (5)	5	0.03
Latin American Indians (5)	6	0.04
Lumbee	1	0.01
Navajo (2)	6	0.04
Paiute (1)	2	0.01
Potawatomi (1)	1	0.01
Pueblo (4)	4	0.03
Seminole (1)	1	0.01
Shoshone	1	0.01
Sioux (1)	6	0.04
Yaqui (1)	2	0.01
All other tribes (4)	8	0.05
American Indian tribes, not spec.	24	0.16
Arab:	145	1.00
Egyptian	8	0.06
Lebanese	72	0.50
Syrian	38	0.26
Other Arab	27	0.19
Armenian	72	0.50
Asian:	1,038	7.07
Cambodian (1)	3	0.02
Chinese, ex. Taiwanese (50)	102	0.70
Filipino (417)	524	3.57
Indian (35)	52	0.35
Indonesian (2)	7	0.05
Japanese (78)	139	0.95
Korean (67)	82	0.56
Laotian (8)	10	0.07
Pakistani	2	0.01
Taiwanese (8)	11	0.07
Thai (13)	18	0.12
Vietnamese (49)	56	0.38
Other Asian, specified (1)	1	0.01
Other Asian, not specified (10)	31	0.21
Basque	70	0.48
Belgian	7	0.05
Brazilian	15	0.10
British	22	0.15
Bulgarian	27	0.19
Canadian	82	0.57
Croatian	13	0.09
Czech	33	0.23
Czechoslovakian	22	0.15
Danish	39	0.27
Dutch	197	1.36
English	1,642	11.37
European	52	0.36
Finnish	28	0.19
French, except Basque	397	2.75
French Canadian	132	0.91
German	1,871	12.96
Greek	104	0.72
Hawaii Native/Pacific Islander:	159	1.08
Melanesian:	2	0.01
Fijian	2	0.01
Micronesian: (25)	41	0.28
Guamanian/Chamorro (18)	32	0.22
Other Micronesian (7)	9	0.06
Polynesian: (41)	89	0.61
Native Hawaiian (30)	68	0.46
Samoan (4)	13	0.09
Tongan (5)	5	0.03
Other Polynesian (2)	3	0.02
Other Pac. Isl., not spec. (14)	27	0.18
Hispanic or Latino:	1,766	12.03
Central American:	97	0.66
Costa Rican	7	0.05
Guatemalan	32	0.22
Honduran	9	0.06
Nicaraguan	14	0.10
Panamanian	8	0.05

Notes: 1. Figures in the "Number" column do not add up to the total population due to: a) Ancestry/Race overlap — e.g. persons can report being both White and Irish, b) persons of Hispanic origin can report being any race, c) persons reporting two ancestries are counted in both categories. 2. Numbers in parentheses indicate the number of persons reporting this ancestry/race alone, not in combination with any other ancestry/race. 3. Refer to the Explanation of Data in the front of the book for more detailed information.

Ancestry/Race	Number	%
Salvadoran	27	0.18
Cuban	92	0.63
Dominican Republic	4	0.03
Mexican	1,133	7.72
Puerto Rican	78	0.53
South American:	47	0.32
Argentinean	11	0.07
Bolivian	2	0.01
Chilean	6	0.04
Colombian	16	0.11
Ecuadorian	2	0.01
Peruvian	4	0.03
Uruguayan	1	0.01
Venezuelan	2	0.01
Other South American	3	0.02
Other Hispanic or Latino	315	2.15
Hungarian	41	0.28
Iranian	10	0.07
Irish	1,796	12.44
Italian	1,018	7.05
Latvian	14	0.10
Lithuanian	31	0.21
Norwegian	277	1.92
Pennsylvania German	7	0.05
Polish	519	3.59
Portuguese	134	0.93
Romanian	28	0.19
Russian	164	1.14
Scandinavian	57	0.39
Scotch-Irish	246	1.70
Scottish	329	2.28
Slovak	45	0.31
Slovene	8	0.06
Swedish	118	0.82
Swiss	8	0.06
Ukrainian	35	0.24
United States or American	933	6.46
Welsh	119	0.82
White:	12,551	85.52
Not Hispanic (11,086)	11,450	78.02
Hispanic (992)	1,101	7.50
Yugoslavian	81	0.56

Gardnerville Ranchos

Place Type: Census Designated Place
County: Douglas
Population: 11,054

Ancestry/Race	Number	%
African American/Black:	53	0.48
Not Hispanic (28)	43	0.39
Hispanic (2)	10	0.09
Alaska Native tribes, specified:	3	0.03
Aleut (2)	2	0.02
All other tribes (1)	1	0.01
Am. Ind. or Alaska Nat., not spec.	53	0.48
American Indian tribes, specified:	294	2.66
Apache (3)	3	0.03
Blackfeet (4)	8	0.07
Cherokee (5)	30	0.27
Chickasaw (3)	4	0.04
Chippewa (2)	3	0.03
Choctaw (1)	6	0.05
Iroquois	3	0.03
Kiowa	1	0.01
Latin American Indians (1)	7	0.06
Navajo (1)	5	0.05
Paiute (14)	29	0.26
Potawatomi (1)	2	0.02
Pueblo (3)	4	0.04
Shoshone (2)	7	0.06
Sioux (2)	7	0.06
Yakama (1)	1	0.01
Yaqui (1)	1	0.01
All other tribes (118)	173	1.57
American Indian tribes, not spec.	31	0.28
Arab:	9	0.08
Syrian	9	0.08
Armenian	60	0.54
Asian:	205	1.85
Chinese, ex. Taiwanese (15)	34	0.31
Filipino (55)	95	0.86
Indian (3)	5	0.05
Indonesian (2)	3	0.03
Japanese (22)	42	0.38
Korean (7)	12	0.11
Malaysian (1)	1	0.01
Thai (2)	2	0.02
Other Asian, not specified (3)	11	0.10
Australian	41	0.37
Austrian	34	0.31
Basque	30	0.27
Belgian	24	0.22
British	44	0.39
Canadian	68	0.61
Czech	35	0.31
Czechoslovakian	12	0.11
Danish	181	1.62
Dutch	173	1.55
English	1,657	14.87
European	141	1.27
Finnish	14	0.13
French, except Basque	429	3.85
French Canadian	144	1.29
German	2,348	21.07
Greek	19	0.17
Hawaii Native/Pacific Islander:	35	0.32
Micronesian: (5)	6	0.05
Guamanian/Chamorro (5)	6	0.05
Polynesian: (7)	24	0.22
Native Hawaiian (3)	16	0.14
Samoan (4)	8	0.07
Other Pac. Isl., not spec. (1)	5	0.05
Hispanic or Latino:	830	7.51
Central American:	15	0.14
Costa Rican	4	0.04
Guatemalan	2	0.02
Nicaraguan	2	0.02
Panamanian	2	0.02
Salvadoran	5	0.05
Cuban	16	0.14
Dominican Republic	1	0.01
Mexican	544	4.92
Puerto Rican	32	0.29
South American:	26	0.24
Argentinean	1	0.01
Chilean	1	0.01
Colombian	18	0.16
Ecuadorian	1	0.01
Peruvian	5	0.05
Other Hispanic or Latino	196	1.77
Hungarian	56	0.50
Iranian	7	0.06
Irish	1,534	13.77
Italian	707	6.35
Latvian	10	0.09
Lithuanian	18	0.16
Maltese	16	0.14
New Zealander	13	0.12
Northern European	40	0.36
Norwegian	392	3.52
Pennsylvania German	14	0.13
Polish	126	1.13
Portuguese	129	1.16
Romanian	8	0.07
Russian	177	1.59
Scandinavian	60	0.54
Scotch-Irish	344	3.09
Scottish	359	3.22
Slavic	47	0.42
Swedish	363	3.26
Swiss	151	1.36
Ukrainian	55	0.49
United States or American	445	3.99
Welsh	115	1.03
West Indian, excl. Hispanic:	6	0.05
Haitian	6	0.05
White:	10,409	94.17
Not Hispanic (9,653)	9,853	89.14
Hispanic (488)	556	5.03
Yugoslavian	42	0.38

Henderson

Place Type: City
County: Clark
Population: 175,381

Ancestry/Race	Number	%
Acadian/Cajun	43	0.02
Afghan	48	0.03
African American/Black:	7,728	4.41
Not Hispanic (6,376)	7,352	4.19
Hispanic (214)	376	0.21
African, sub-Saharan:	601	0.34
African	388	0.22
Cape Verdean	45	0.03
Ethiopian	61	0.03
South African	90	0.05
Other sub-Saharan African	17	0.01
Alaska Native tribes, specified:	41	0.02
Alaska Athabascan (5)	5	0.00
Aleut (5)	6	0.00
Eskimo (12)	22	0.01
Tlingit-Haida (1)	6	0.00
All other tribes (2)	2	0.00
Alaska Native tribes, not specified	5	0.00
Am. Ind. or Alaska Nat., not spec.	655	0.37
Albanian	77	0.04
American Indian tribes, specified:	1,764	1.01
Apache (44)	106	0.06
Blackfeet (25)	81	0.05
Cherokee (189)	494	0.28
Cheyenne (1)	6	0.00
Chickasaw (11)	30	0.02
Chippewa (43)	64	0.04
Choctaw (50)	133	0.08
Colville (1)	2	0.00
Comanche (2)	10	0.01
Cree (3)	8	0.00
Creek (22)	30	0.02
Crow	4	0.00
Delaware	2	0.00
Iroquois (18)	40	0.02
Kiowa	1	0.00
Latin American Indians (55)	95	0.05
Lumbee (4)	4	0.00
Menominee (1)	3	0.00
Navajo (141)	178	0.10
Osage (3)	14	0.01
Ottawa (4)	5	0.00
Paiute (16)	38	0.02
Pima (1)	3	0.00
Potawatomi (16)	24	0.01
Pueblo (21)	44	0.03
Puget Sound Salish (3)	6	0.00
Seminole (1)	13	0.01
Shoshone (18)	27	0.02
Sioux (36)	70	0.04
Tohono O'Odham (3)	7	0.00
Ute (2)	2	0.00
Yakama (3)	3	0.00
Yaqui (3)	9	0.01
Yuman (6)	7	0.00
All other tribes (109)	201	0.11
American Indian tribes, not spec.	104	0.06
Arab:	1,210	0.69
Arab/Arabic	105	0.06
Egyptian	242	0.14
Iraqi	83	0.05
Lebanese	447	0.25
Moroccan	22	0.01
Palestinian	99	0.06
Syrian	136	0.08
Other Arab	76	0.04
Armenian	440	0.25
Asian:	9,768	5.57
Bangladeshi (4)	7	0.00
Cambodian (12)	22	0.01

Notes: 1. Figures in the "Number" column do not add up to the total population due to: a) Ancestry/Race overlap — e.g. persons can report being both White and Irish, b) persons of Hispanic origin can report being any race, c) persons reporting two ancestries are counted in both categories. 2. Numbers in parentheses indicate the number of persons reporting this ancestry/race alone, not in combination with any other ancestry/race. 3. Refer to the Explanation of Data in the front of the book for more detailed information.

Chinese, ex. Taiwanese (871)	1,377	0.79
Filipino (2,916)	4,040	2.30
Hmong (7)	7	0.00
Indian (590)	682	0.39
Indonesian (47)	85	0.05
Japanese (883)	1,506	0.86
Korean (709)	944	0.54
Laotian (48)	57	0.03
Malaysian (4)	7	0.00
Pakistani (30)	55	0.03
Sri Lankan (19)	23	0.01
Taiwanese (24)	39	0.02
Thai (225)	297	0.17
Vietnamese (291)	377	0.21
Other Asian, specified (15)	30	0.02
Other Asian, not specified (75)	213	0.12
Assyrian/Chaldean/Syriac	17	0.01
Australian	33	0.02
Austrian	644	0.37
Basque	134	0.08
Belgian	111	0.06
Brazilian	47	0.03
British	902	0.51
Bulgarian	55	0.03
Canadian	627	0.36
Celtic	7	0.00
Croatian	304	0.17
Czech	939	0.53
Czechoslovakian	332	0.19
Danish	1,932	1.10
Dutch	3,576	2.03
Eastern European	102	0.06
English	20,088	11.41
Estonian	7	0.00
European	1,584	0.90
Finnish	414	0.24
French, except Basque	6,032	3.43
French Canadian	1,332	0.76
German	30,027	17.06
German Russian	13	0.01
Greek	1,048	0.60
Hawaii Native/Pacific Islander:	1,687	0.96
Melanesian: (11)	18	0.01
Fijian (11)	18	0.01
Micronesian: (97)	167	0.10
Guamanian/Chamorro (90)	155	0.09
Other Micronesian (7)	12	0.01
Polynesian: (509)	1,216	0.69
Native Hawaiian (382)	957	0.55
Samoan (83)	179	0.10
Tongan (35)	57	0.03
Other Polynesian (9)	23	0.01
Other Pac. Isl., specified	6	0.00
Other Pac. Isl., not spec. (90)	280	0.16
Hispanic or Latino:	18,785	10.71
Central American:	558	0.32
Costa Rican	43	0.02
Guatemalan	128	0.07
Honduran	19	0.01
Nicaraguan	65	0.04
Panamanian	48	0.03
Salvadoran	210	0.12
Other Central American	45	0.03
Cuban	787	0.45
Dominican Republic	64	0.04
Mexican	11,000	6.27
Puerto Rican	1,100	0.63
South American:	719	0.41
Argentinean	185	0.11
Bolivian	8	0.00
Chilean	57	0.03
Colombian	220	0.13
Ecuadorian	57	0.03
Paraguayan	2	0.00
Peruvian	124	0.07
Uruguayan	3	0.00
Venezuelan	39	0.02
Other South American	24	0.01
Other Hispanic or Latino	4,557	2.60
Hungarian	1,177	0.67
Icelander	78	0.04
Iranian	245	0.14
Irish	23,090	13.12
Israeli	139	0.08
Italian	15,863	9.01
Latvian	58	0.03
Lithuanian	552	0.31
Luxemburger	11	0.01
Macedonian	14	0.01
Maltese	87	0.05
New Zealander	9	0.01
Northern European	169	0.10
Norwegian	3,400	1.93
Polish	6,144	3.49
Portuguese	851	0.48
Romanian	280	0.16
Russian	2,478	1.41
Scandinavian	459	0.26
Scotch-Irish	2,815	1.60
Scottish	3,810	2.16
Serbian	161	0.09
Slavic	127	0.07
Slovak	326	0.19
Slovene	56	0.03
Swedish	4,016	2.28
Swiss	790	0.45
Turkish	110	0.06
Ukrainian	578	0.33
United States or American	9,306	5.29
Welsh	1,648	0.94
West Indian, excl. Hispanic:	221	0.13
Bahamian	8	0.00
Barbadian	8	0.00
British West Indian	10	0.01
Dutch West Indian	14	0.01
Haitian	13	0.01
Jamaican	72	0.04
Trinidadian and Tobagonian	55	0.03
West Indian	41	0.02
White:	153,372	87.45
Not Hispanic (137,174)	140,808	80.29
Hispanic (11,007)	12,564	7.16
Yugoslavian	342	0.19

Las Vegas

Place Type: City
County: Clark
Population: 478,434

Ancestry/Race	Number	%
Acadian/Cajun	29	0.01
Afghan	91	0.02
African American/Black:	53,923	11.27
Not Hispanic (48,380)	51,888	10.85
Hispanic (1,190)	2,035	0.43
African, sub-Saharan:	3,034	0.63
African	2,465	0.51
Cape Verdean	10	0.00
Ethiopian	286	0.06
Ghanian	7	0.00
Kenyan	6	0.00
Nigerian	124	0.03
Somalian	22	0.00
South African	87	0.02
Sudanese	11	0.00
Other sub-Saharan African	16	0.00
Alaska Native tribes, specified:	83	0.02
Alaska Athabascan (13)	15	0.00
Aleut (5)	16	0.00
Eskimo (13)	23	0.00
Tlingit-Haida (17)	26	0.01
All other tribes (3)	3	0.00
Alaska Native tribes, not specified	11	0.00
Am. Ind. or Alaska Nat., not spec.	2,316	0.48
Albanian	40	0.01
Alsatian	20	0.00
American Indian tribes, specified:	4,364	0.91
Apache (133)	278	0.06
Blackfeet (48)	170	0.04
Cherokee (298)	1,075	0.22
Cheyenne (8)	16	0.00
Chickasaw (26)	60	0.01
Chippewa (75)	138	0.03
Choctaw (64)	195	0.04
Colville (2)	2	0.00
Comanche (17)	34	0.01
Cree (9)	24	0.01
Creek (12)	51	0.01
Crow (3)	11	0.00
Delaware (7)	24	0.01
Houma	2	0.00
Iroquois (45)	118	0.02
Kiowa (6)	8	0.00
Latin American Indians (265)	495	0.10
Lumbee (8)	11	0.00
Menominee (5)	10	0.00
Navajo (282)	366	0.08
Osage (12)	30	0.01
Ottawa (8)	11	0.00
Paiute (118)	153	0.03
Pima (18)	21	0.00
Potawatomi (21)	48	0.01
Pueblo (65)	94	0.02
Puget Sound Salish (14)	23	0.00
Seminole (13)	44	0.01
Shoshone (31)	43	0.01
Sioux (116)	258	0.05
Tohono O'Odham (9)	16	0.00
Ute (16)	20	0.00
Yakama (5)	8	0.00
Yaqui (14)	35	0.01
Yuman (14)	15	0.00
All other tribes (290)	457	0.10
American Indian tribes, not spec.	404	0.08
Arab:	1,844	0.39
Arab/Arabic	279	0.06
Egyptian	174	0.04
Iraqi	29	0.01
Jordanian	35	0.01
Lebanese	882	0.18
Moroccan	64	0.01
Palestinian	30	0.01
Syrian	297	0.06
Other Arab	54	0.01
Armenian	661	0.14
Asian:	29,987	6.27
Bangladeshi (1)	5	0.00
Cambodian (160)	214	0.04
Chinese, ex. Taiwanese (2,663)	3,929	0.82
Filipino (11,182)	14,139	2.96
Hmong (32)	33	0.01
Indian (1,229)	1,517	0.32
Indonesian (45)	99	0.02
Japanese (2,422)	3,751	0.78
Korean (1,571)	2,080	0.43
Laotian (379)	478	0.10
Malaysian (17)	26	0.01
Pakistani (101)	154	0.03
Sri Lankan (56)	66	0.01
Taiwanese (121)	165	0.03
Thai (895)	1,226	0.26
Vietnamese (946)	1,139	0.24
Other Asian, specified (41)	104	0.02
Other Asian, not specified (357)	862	0.18
Australian	177	0.04
Austrian	1,187	0.25
Basque	248	0.05
Belgian	387	0.08
Brazilian	343	0.07
British	1,846	0.39
Bulgarian	297	0.06
Canadian	1,969	0.41
Celtic	118	0.02
Croatian	829	0.17
Czech	1,574	0.33
Czechoslovakian	633	0.13
Danish	3,763	0.79
Dutch	6,663	1.39
Eastern European	147	0.03

Notes: 1. Figures in the "Number" column do not add up to the total population due to: a) Ancestry/Race overlap — e.g. persons can report being both White and Irish, b) persons of Hispanic origin can report being any race, c) persons reporting two ancestries are counted in both categories. 2. Numbers in parentheses indicate the number of persons reporting this ancestry/race alone, not in combination with any other ancestry/race. 3. Refer to the Explanation of Data in the front of the book for more detailed information.

English	40,378	8.43
Estonian	5	0.00
European	2,634	0.55
Finnish	796	0.17
French, except Basque	13,241	2.77
French Canadian	3,158	0.66
German	58,288	12.17
German Russian	53	0.01
Greek	2,380	0.50
Guyanese	60	0.01
Hawaii Native/Pacific Islander:	4,440	0.93
Melanesian: (6)	11	0.00
Fijian (6)	11	0.00
Micronesian: (412)	586	0.12
Guamanian/Chamorro (379)	531	0.11
Other Micronesian (33)	55	0.01
Polynesian: (1,454)	3,170	0.66
Native Hawaiian (956)	2,396	0.50
Samoan (403)	610	0.13
Tongan (77)	100	0.02
Other Polynesian (18)	64	0.01
Other Pac. Isl., specified	23	0.00
Other Pac. Isl., not spec. (220)	650	0.14
Hispanic or Latino:	112,962	23.61
Central American:	5,669	1.18
Costa Rican	158	0.03
Guatemalan	1,263	0.26
Honduran	424	0.09
Nicaraguan	493	0.10
Panamanian	194	0.04
Salvadoran	2,832	0.59
Other Central American	305	0.06
Cuban	3,393	0.71
Dominican Republic	293	0.06
Mexican	83,490	17.45
Puerto Rican	2,866	0.60
South American:	1,850	0.39
Argentinean	378	0.08
Bolivian	40	0.01
Chilean	193	0.04
Colombian	489	0.10
Ecuadorian	196	0.04
Paraguayan	19	0.00
Peruvian	334	0.07
Uruguayan	27	0.01
Venezuelan	59	0.01
Other South American	115	0.02
Other Hispanic or Latino	15,401	3.22
Hungarian	2,985	0.62
Icelander	60	0.01
Iranian	453	0.09
Irish	46,617	9.73
Israeli	238	0.05
Italian	32,124	6.71
Latvian	158	0.03
Lithuanian	743	0.16
Luxemburger	31	0.01
Macedonian	17	0.00
Maltese	14	0.00
New Zealander	71	0.01
Northern European	83	0.02
Norwegian	7,125	1.49
Pennsylvania German	108	0.02
Polish	12,188	2.55
Portuguese	1,411	0.29
Romanian	933	0.19
Russian	6,593	1.38
Scandinavian	925	0.19
Scotch-Irish	5,616	1.17
Scottish	7,916	1.65
Serbian	350	0.07
Slavic	188	0.04
Slovak	771	0.16
Slovene	193	0.04
Swedish	6,808	1.42
Swiss	1,237	0.26
Turkish	303	0.06
Ukrainian	1,210	0.25
United States or American	21,393	4.47
Welsh	2,832	0.59
West Indian, excl. Hispanic:	1,058	0.22
Bahamian	13	0.00
Barbadian	62	0.01
Belizean	69	0.01
Bermudan	15	0.00
British West Indian	21	0.00
Haitian	273	0.06
Jamaican	354	0.07
Trinidadian and Tobagonian	61	0.01
U.S. Virgin Islander	15	0.00
West Indian	175	0.04
White:	350,136	73.18
Not Hispanic (277,704)	287,272	60.04
Hispanic (56,526)	62,864	13.14
Yugoslavian	804	0.17

North Las Vegas

Place Type: City
County: Clark
Population: 115,488

Ancestry/Race	Number	%
Acadian/Cajun	14	0.01
African American/Black:	23,335	20.21
Not Hispanic (21,528)	22,627	19.59
Hispanic (442)	708	0.61
African, sub-Saharan:	1,176	1.02
African	1,122	0.97
Ghanian	8	0.01
South African	37	0.03
Other sub-Saharan African	9	0.01
Alaska Native tribes, specified:	20	0.02
Alaska Athabascan (1)	1	0.00
Aleut (5)	6	0.01
Eskimo (5)	9	0.01
Tlingit-Haida (2)	4	0.00
Alaska Native tribes, not specified	4	0.00
Am. Ind. or Alaska Nat., not spec.	629	0.54
American Indian tribes, specified:	1,004	0.87
Apache (13)	31	0.03
Blackfeet (14)	60	0.05
Cherokee (77)	223	0.19
Cheyenne (4)	5	0.00
Chickasaw (2)	3	0.00
Chippewa (20)	29	0.03
Choctaw (20)	55	0.05
Colville (1)	1	0.00
Comanche (1)	4	0.00
Cree (2)	3	0.00
Creek (5)	28	0.02
Crow (3)	8	0.01
Delaware (6)	8	0.01
Houma	1	0.00
Iroquois (13)	18	0.02
Latin American Indians (126)	191	0.17
Menominee (1)	2	0.00
Navajo (41)	66	0.06
Osage (7)	8	0.01
Ottawa (2)	3	0.00
Paiute (35)	49	0.04
Pima (2)	3	0.00
Potawatomi (4)	5	0.00
Pueblo (12)	17	0.01
Puget Sound Salish (4)	10	0.01
Seminole (2)	7	0.01
Shoshone (5)	7	0.01
Sioux (15)	36	0.03
Tohono O'Odham (2)	2	0.00
Ute (2)	2	0.00
Yaqui (1)	3	0.00
Yuman (4)	5	0.00
All other tribes (67)	111	0.10
American Indian tribes, not spec.	83	0.07
Arab:	241	0.21
Arab/Arabic	52	0.05
Egyptian	14	0.01
Iraqi	31	0.03
Lebanese	47	0.04
Palestinian	28	0.02
Syrian	41	0.04
Other Arab	28	0.02
Armenian	101	0.09
Asian:	5,386	4.66
Bangladeshi (1)	1	0.00
Cambodian (10)	13	0.01
Chinese, ex. Taiwanese (169)	413	0.36
Filipino (2,188)	2,916	2.52
Hmong (2)	10	0.01
Indian (169)	206	0.18
Indonesian (10)	19	0.02
Japanese (276)	562	0.49
Korean (223)	351	0.30
Laotian (100)	135	0.12
Malaysian	1	0.00
Pakistani (4)	7	0.01
Sri Lankan (5)	5	0.00
Taiwanese (14)	28	0.02
Thai (264)	351	0.30
Vietnamese (109)	153	0.13
Other Asian, specified (2)	14	0.01
Other Asian, not specified (95)	201	0.17
Australian	62	0.05
Austrian	206	0.18
Belgian	47	0.04
Brazilian	6	0.01
British	341	0.30
Canadian	243	0.21
Croatian	99	0.09
Czech	234	0.20
Czechoslovakian	66	0.06
Danish	356	0.31
Dutch	872	0.76
English	5,854	5.07
European	403	0.35
Finnish	111	0.10
French, except Basque	2,101	1.82
French Canadian	434	0.38
German	9,586	8.30
German Russian	6	0.01
Greek	196	0.17
Hawaii Native/Pacific Islander:	1,175	1.02
Melanesian: (8)	8	0.01
Fijian (8)	8	0.01
Micronesian: (132)	204	0.18
Guamanian/Chamorro (132)	203	0.18
Other Micronesian	1	0.00
Polynesian: (396)	740	0.64
Native Hawaiian (249)	530	0.46
Samoan (136)	185	0.16
Tongan (8)	18	0.02
Other Polynesian (3)	7	0.01
Other Pac. Isl., specified	4	0.00
Other Pac. Isl., not spec. (55)	219	0.19
Hispanic or Latino:	43,435	37.61
Central American:	1,629	1.41
Costa Rican	28	0.02
Guatemalan	333	0.29
Honduran	112	0.10
Nicaraguan	109	0.09
Panamanian	97	0.08
Salvadoran	876	0.76
Other Central American	74	0.06
Cuban	476	0.41
Dominican Republic	45	0.04
Mexican	34,848	30.17
Puerto Rican	745	0.65
South American:	305	0.26
Argentinean	54	0.05
Bolivian	3	0.00
Chilean	19	0.02
Colombian	111	0.10
Ecuadorian	34	0.03
Paraguayan	3	0.00
Peruvian	45	0.04
Uruguayan	9	0.01
Venezuelan	18	0.02
Other South American	9	0.01
Other Hispanic or Latino	5,387	4.66
Hungarian	248	0.21

Notes: 1. Figures in the "Number" column do not add up to the total population due to: a) Ancestry/Race overlap — e.g. persons can report being both White and Irish, b) persons of Hispanic origin can report being any race, c) persons reporting two ancestries are counted in both categories. 2. Numbers in parentheses indicate the number of persons reporting this ancestry/race alone, not in combination with any other ancestry/race. 3. Refer to the Explanation of Data in the front of the book for more detailed information.

Icelander	46	0.04
Iranian	101	0.09
Irish	7,354	6.37
Israeli	7	0.01
Italian	4,827	4.18
Lithuanian	135	0.12
Macedonian	9	0.01
Northern European	45	0.04
Norwegian	1,123	0.97
Pennsylvania German	12	0.01
Polish	1,795	1.55
Portuguese	348	0.30
Romanian	57	0.05
Russian	390	0.34
Scandinavian	147	0.13
Scotch-Irish	707	0.61
Scottish	1,312	1.14
Serbian	10	0.01
Slavic	7	0.01
Slovak	65	0.06
Slovene	22	0.02
Swedish	1,096	0.95
Swiss	256	0.22
Turkish	16	0.01
Ukrainian	168	0.15
United States or American	3,937	3.41
Welsh	421	0.36
West Indian, excl. Hispanic:	157	0.14
Barbadian	7	0.01
British West Indian	44	0.04
Dutch West Indian	9	0.01
Jamaican	84	0.07
West Indian	13	0.01
White:	69,012	59.76
Not Hispanic (42,880)	44,989	38.96
Hispanic (21,711)	24,023	20.80
Yugoslavian	84	0.07

Pahrump

Place Type: Census Designated Place
County: Nye
Population: 24,631

Ancestry/Race	Number	%
Acadian/Cajun	28	0.11
African American/Black:	412	1.67
Not Hispanic (314)	392	1.59
Hispanic (7)	20	0.08
African, sub-Saharan:	57	0.23
African	57	0.23
Alaska Native tribes, specified:	8	0.03
Eskimo (1)	1	0.00
Tlingit-Haida (6)	7	0.03
Am. Ind. or Alaska Nat., not spec.	168	0.68
American Indian tribes, specified:	428	1.74
Apache (4)	14	0.06
Blackfeet (9)	21	0.09
Cherokee (57)	169	0.69
Cheyenne (2)	7	0.03
Chickasaw (4)	5	0.02
Chippewa (8)	12	0.05
Choctaw (11)	25	0.10
Comanche (2)	4	0.02
Cree (1)	3	0.01
Creek (3)	4	0.02
Crow (1)	5	0.02
Delaware (1)	1	0.00
Iroquois (1)	8	0.03
Kiowa (1)	1	0.00
Latin American Indians (3)	7	0.03
Navajo (19)	21	0.09
Osage (1)	3	0.01
Paiute (11)	17	0.07
Pima (1)	1	0.00
Potawatomi	1	0.00
Pueblo	1	0.00
Seminole	2	0.01
Shoshone (12)	13	0.05
Sioux (17)	37	0.15
Tohono O'Odham	1	0.00
All other tribes (28)	45	0.18
American Indian tribes, not spec.	36	0.15
Armenian	11	0.04
Asian:	322	1.31
Chinese, ex. Taiwanese (9)	35	0.14
Filipino (81)	118	0.48
Indian (20)	30	0.12
Indonesian	4	0.02
Japanese (59)	77	0.31
Korean (15)	25	0.10
Laotian (1)	1	0.00
Taiwanese (2)	2	0.01
Thai (9)	16	0.06
Vietnamese (1)	1	0.00
Other Asian, specified (1)	1	0.00
Other Asian, not specified (8)	12	0.05
Assyrian/Chaldean/Syriac	11	0.04
Australian	47	0.19
Austrian	28	0.11
Belgian	76	0.31
British	134	0.54
Canadian	29	0.12
Croatian	18	0.07
Czech	73	0.30
Czechoslovakian	46	0.19
Danish	191	0.77
Dutch	689	2.79
English	3,699	14.97
European	217	0.88
Finnish	53	0.21
French, except Basque	1,290	5.22
French Canadian	117	0.47
German	5,706	23.09
Greek	166	0.67
Hawaii Native/Pacific Islander:	140	0.57
Micronesian: (26)	30	0.12
Guamanian/Chamorro (26)	27	0.11
Other Micronesian	3	0.01
Polynesian: (56)	97	0.39
Native Hawaiian (47)	77	0.31
Samoan (7)	15	0.06
Other Polynesian (2)	5	0.02
Other Pac. Isl., not spec. (9)	13	0.05
Hispanic or Latino:	1,879	7.63
Central American:	28	0.11
Costa Rican	2	0.01
Guatemalan	13	0.05
Honduran	2	0.01
Panamanian	3	0.01
Salvadoran	7	0.03
Other Central American	1	0.00
Cuban	24	0.10
Dominican Republic	1	0.00
Mexican	1,413	5.74
Puerto Rican	70	0.28
South American:	16	0.06
Argentinean	11	0.04
Chilean	1	0.00
Colombian	2	0.01
Ecuadorian	1	0.00
Peruvian	1	0.00
Other Hispanic or Latino	327	1.33
Hungarian	134	0.54
Irish	4,565	18.48
Italian	1,498	6.06
Latvian	8	0.03
Lithuanian	48	0.19
Maltese	12	0.05
Norwegian	449	1.82
Pennsylvania German	69	0.28
Polish	490	1.98
Portuguese	193	0.78
Romanian	23	0.09
Russian	146	0.59
Scandinavian	138	0.56
Scotch-Irish	554	2.24
Scottish	686	2.78
Slavic	11	0.04
Slovak	40	0.16
Slovene	16	0.06
Swedish	558	2.26
Swiss	80	0.32
Ukrainian	24	0.10
United States or American	1,917	7.76
Welsh	305	1.23
West Indian, excl. Hispanic:	10	0.04
Jamaican	10	0.04
White:	23,073	93.67
Not Hispanic (21,183)	21,774	88.40
Hispanic (1,236)	1,299	5.27
Yugoslavian	18	0.07

Paradise

Place Type: Census Designated Place
County: Clark
Population: 186,070

Ancestry/Race	Number	%
Acadian/Cajun	15	0.01
Afghan	26	0.01
African American/Black:	13,930	7.49
Not Hispanic (11,734)	13,125	7.05
Hispanic (526)	805	0.43
African, sub-Saharan:	2,435	1.31
African	1,202	0.65
Cape Verdean	74	0.04
Ethiopian	864	0.46
Ghanian	117	0.06
Kenyan	7	0.00
Nigerian	7	0.00
Sierra Leonean	10	0.01
Somalian	26	0.01
South African	67	0.04
Ugandan	34	0.02
Other sub-Saharan African	27	0.01
Alaska Native tribes, specified:	32	0.02
Alaska Athabascan (6)	9	0.00
Aleut (2)	2	0.00
Eskimo (2)	3	0.00
Tlingit-Haida (9)	18	0.01
Alaska Native tribes, not specified	5	0.00
Am. Ind. or Alaska Nat., not spec.	850	0.46
Albanian	25	0.01
Alsatian	17	0.01
American Indian tribes, specified:	1,746	0.94
Apache (54)	101	0.05
Blackfeet (36)	99	0.05
Cherokee (171)	474	0.25
Cheyenne (3)	9	0.00
Chickasaw (4)	18	0.01
Chippewa (37)	67	0.04
Choctaw (30)	87	0.05
Colville (4)	4	0.00
Comanche (3)	11	0.01
Cree (1)	12	0.01
Creek (7)	24	0.01
Crow	6	0.00
Delaware (10)	10	0.01
Houma (1)	1	0.00
Iroquois (20)	43	0.02
Kiowa (8)	8	0.00
Latin American Indians (89)	151	0.08
Lumbee (2)	3	0.00
Menominee (2)	2	0.00
Navajo (135)	164	0.09
Osage (6)	10	0.01
Ottawa (1)	3	0.00
Paiute (18)	25	0.01
Pima (7)	10	0.01
Potawatomi (13)	15	0.01
Pueblo (21)	32	0.02
Puget Sound Salish (1)	2	0.00
Seminole (1)	20	0.01
Shoshone (11)	15	0.01
Sioux (44)	74	0.04
Tohono O'Odham (4)	4	0.00
Ute (5)	6	0.00
Yakama (1)	3	0.00

Notes: 1. Figures in the "Number" column do not add up to the total population due to: a) Ancestry/Race overlap — e.g. persons can report being both White and Irish, b) persons of Hispanic origin can report being any race, c) persons reporting two ancestries are counted in both categories. 2. Numbers in parentheses indicate the number of persons reporting this ancestry/race alone, not in combination with any other ancestry/race. 3. Refer to the Explanation of Data in the front of the book for more detailed information.

Yaqui (13)	28	0.02
Yuman (5)	10	0.01
All other tribes (114)	195	0.10
American Indian tribes, not spec.	141	0.08
Arab:	1,168	0.63
Arab/Arabic	242	0.13
Egyptian	94	0.05
Iraqi	42	0.02
Jordanian	28	0.02
Lebanese	417	0.22
Moroccan	91	0.05
Palestinian	25	0.01
Syrian	117	0.06
Other Arab	112	0.06
Armenian	314	0.17
Asian:	15,488	8.32
Bangladeshi (9)	15	0.01
Cambodian (51)	66	0.04
Chinese, ex. Taiwanese (1,644)	2,308	1.24
Filipino (5,418)	6,743	3.62
Hmong (28)	28	0.02
Indian (678)	853	0.46
Indonesian (48)	81	0.04
Japanese (1,293)	1,907	1.02
Korean (1,202)	1,423	0.76
Laotian (113)	132	0.07
Malaysian (11)	27	0.01
Pakistani (40)	84	0.05
Sri Lankan (48)	58	0.03
Taiwanese (93)	119	0.06
Thai (329)	472	0.25
Vietnamese (626)	701	0.38
Other Asian, specified (24)	54	0.03
Other Asian, not specified (150)	417	0.22
Assyrian/Chaldean/Syriac	22	0.01
Australian	84	0.05
Austrian	540	0.29
Basque	123	0.07
Belgian	191	0.10
Brazilian	120	0.06
British	707	0.38
Bulgarian	256	0.14
Canadian	561	0.30
Celtic	83	0.04
Croatian	424	0.23
Cypriot	16	0.01
Czech	532	0.29
Czechoslovakian	365	0.20
Danish	1,495	0.80
Dutch	1,917	1.03
Eastern European	124	0.07
English	15,008	8.08
Estonian	33	0.02
European	1,169	0.63
Finnish	383	0.21
French, except Basque	5,555	2.99
French Canadian	995	0.54
German	22,417	12.06
German Russian	24	0.01
Greek	989	0.53
Guyanese	21	0.01
Hawaii Native/Pacific Islander:	2,201	1.18
Melanesian: (16)	25	0.01
Fijian (16)	25	0.01
Micronesian: (164)	262	0.14
Guamanian/Chamorro (150)	238	0.13
Other Micronesian (14)	24	0.01
Polynesian: (817)	1,660	0.89
Native Hawaiian (619)	1,332	0.72
Samoan (169)	256	0.14
Tongan (11)	24	0.01
Other Polynesian (18)	48	0.03
Other Pac. Isl., specified	4	0.00
Other Pac. Isl., not spec. (73)	250	0.13
Hispanic or Latino:	43,663	23.47
Central American:	2,657	1.43
Costa Rican	94	0.05
Guatemalan	609	0.33
Honduran	214	0.12
Nicaraguan	190	0.10
Panamanian	83	0.04
Salvadoran	1,315	0.71
Other Central American	152	0.08
Cuban	2,684	1.44
Dominican Republic	146	0.08
Mexican	28,936	15.55
Puerto Rican	1,406	0.76
South American:	1,245	0.67
Argentinean	270	0.15
Bolivian	16	0.01
Chilean	121	0.07
Colombian	301	0.16
Ecuadorian	97	0.05
Paraguayan	7	0.00
Peruvian	290	0.16
Uruguayan	18	0.01
Venezuelan	43	0.02
Other South American	82	0.04
Other Hispanic or Latino	6,589	3.54
Hungarian	1,137	0.61
Icelander	36	0.02
Iranian	505	0.27
Irish	18,033	9.70
Israeli	239	0.13
Italian	13,395	7.21
Latvian	35	0.02
Lithuanian	424	0.23
Luxemburger	32	0.02
Macedonian	8	0.00
Maltese	9	0.00
New Zealander	17	0.01
Northern European	47	0.03
Norwegian	2,541	1.37
Pennsylvania German	63	0.03
Polish	5,096	2.74
Portuguese	710	0.38
Romanian	308	0.17
Russian	2,083	1.12
Scandinavian	366	0.20
Scotch-Irish	2,153	1.16
Scottish	2,880	1.55
Serbian	201	0.11
Slavic	122	0.07
Slovak	267	0.14
Slovene	36	0.02
Swedish	2,695	1.45
Swiss	591	0.32
Turkish	37	0.02
Ukrainian	363	0.20
United States or American	7,854	4.23
Welsh	1,140	0.61
West Indian, excl. Hispanic:	459	0.25
Barbadian	21	0.01
Belizean	32	0.02
Bermudan	8	0.00
British West Indian	3	0.00
Dutch West Indian	46	0.02
Haitian	135	0.07
Jamaican	136	0.07
Trinidadian and Tobagonian	21	0.01
West Indian	57	0.03
White:	142,055	76.34
Not Hispanic (111,017)	115,248	61.94
Hispanic (23,910)	26,807	14.41
Yugoslavian	512	0.28

Reno

Place Type: City
County: Washoe
Population: 180,480

Ancestry/Race	Number	%
Acadian/Cajun	25	0.01
African American/Black:	5,751	3.19
Not Hispanic (4,414)	5,342	2.96
Hispanic (237)	409	0.23
African, sub-Saharan:	434	0.24
African	273	0.15
Cape Verdean	16	0.01
Ethiopian	11	0.01
Ghanian	10	0.01
Kenyan	18	0.01
Nigerian	56	0.03
South African	39	0.02
Other sub-Saharan African	11	0.01
Alaska Native tribes, specified:	73	0.04
Alaska Athabascan (20)	24	0.01
Aleut (3)	11	0.01
Eskimo (14)	20	0.01
Tlingit-Haida (7)	18	0.01
Alaska Native tribes, not specified	3	0.00
Am. Ind. or Alaska Nat., not spec.	1,016	0.56
Albanian	22	0.01
American Indian tribes, specified:	2,652	1.47
Apache (41)	102	0.06
Blackfeet (28)	93	0.05
Cherokee (176)	489	0.27
Cheyenne (8)	13	0.01
Chickasaw (17)	23	0.01
Chippewa (37)	70	0.04
Choctaw (32)	75	0.04
Colville (1)	2	0.00
Comanche (8)	21	0.01
Cree (5)	13	0.01
Creek (13)	27	0.01
Crow (9)	15	0.01
Delaware (3)	5	0.00
Iroquois (14)	46	0.03
Kiowa (4)	5	0.00
Latin American Indians (145)	205	0.11
Lumbee (2)	4	0.00
Navajo (68)	110	0.06
Osage (2)	8	0.00
Ottawa (3)	8	0.00
Paiute (314)	423	0.23
Pima (14)	17	0.01
Potawatomi (19)	33	0.02
Pueblo (23)	41	0.02
Puget Sound Salish (5)	7	0.00
Seminole (2)	8	0.00
Shoshone (124)	162	0.09
Sioux (62)	100	0.06
Tohono O'Odham (3)	5	0.00
Ute (3)	9	0.00
Yakama	1	0.00
Yaqui (3)	4	0.00
Yuman (4)	6	0.00
All other tribes (327)	502	0.28
American Indian tribes, not spec.	227	0.13
Arab:	446	0.25
Arab/Arabic	14	0.01
Egyptian	63	0.03
Jordanian	38	0.02
Lebanese	202	0.11
Moroccan	42	0.02
Syrian	79	0.04
Other Arab	8	0.00
Armenian	248	0.14
Asian:	11,722	6.49
Bangladeshi (128)	170	0.09
Cambodian (12)	22	0.01
Chinese, ex. Taiwanese (1,791)	2,151	1.19
Filipino (4,066)	4,889	2.71
Hmong (9)	12	0.01
Indian (1,036)	1,190	0.66
Indonesian (17)	43	0.02
Japanese (799)	1,171	0.65
Korean (541)	674	0.37
Laotian (31)	34	0.02
Malaysian (8)	21	0.01
Pakistani (61)	102	0.06
Sri Lankan (11)	11	0.01
Taiwanese (44)	56	0.03
Thai (202)	244	0.14
Vietnamese (452)	557	0.31
Other Asian, specified (10)	41	0.02
Other Asian, not specified (135)	334	0.19
Assyrian/Chaldean/Syriac	45	0.02
Australian	144	0.08

Notes: 1. Figures in the "Number" column do not add up to the total population due to: a) Ancestry/Race overlap — e.g. persons can report being both White and Irish, b) persons of Hispanic origin can report being any race, c) persons reporting two ancestries are counted in both categories. 2. Numbers in parentheses indicate the number of persons reporting this ancestry/race alone, not in combination with any other ancestry/race. 3. Refer to the Explanation of Data in the front of the book for more detailed information.

Austrian	544	0.30
Basque	1,226	0.68
Belgian	141	0.08
Brazilian	60	0.03
British	973	0.54
Bulgarian	54	0.03
Canadian	580	0.32
Carpatho Rusyn	12	0.01
Celtic	85	0.05
Croatian	228	0.13
Czech	508	0.28
Czechoslovakian	271	0.15
Danish	2,089	1.16
Dutch	3,274	1.81
Eastern European	23	0.01
English	20,590	11.40
Estonian	19	0.01
European	1,366	0.76
Finnish	485	0.27
French, except Basque	6,302	3.49
French Canadian	1,454	0.80
German	28,740	15.91
German Russian	7	0.00
Greek	1,006	0.56
Hawaii Native/Pacific Islander:	1,600	0.89
Melanesian: (14)	17	0.01
Fijian (14)	17	0.01
Micronesian: (137)	218	0.12
Guamanian/Chamorro (60)	124	0.07
Other Micronesian (77)	94	0.05
Polynesian: (764)	1,110	0.62
Native Hawaiian (161)	411	0.23
Samoan (191)	230	0.13
Tongan (385)	427	0.24
Other Polynesian (27)	42	0.02
Other Pac. Isl., specified	18	0.01
Other Pac. Isl., not spec. (68)	237	0.13
Hispanic or Latino:	34,616	19.18
Central American:	2,509	1.39
Costa Rican	100	0.06
Guatemalan	744	0.41
Honduran	76	0.04
Nicaraguan	73	0.04
Panamanian	26	0.01
Salvadoran	1,351	0.75
Other Central American	139	0.08
Cuban	203	0.11
Dominican Republic	23	0.01
Mexican	25,601	14.18
Puerto Rican	643	0.36
South American:	402	0.22
Argentinean	35	0.02
Bolivian	13	0.01
Chilean	50	0.03
Colombian	107	0.06
Ecuadorian	34	0.02
Paraguayan	4	0.00
Peruvian	109	0.06
Uruguayan	6	0.00
Venezuelan	9	0.00
Other South American	35	0.02
Other Hispanic or Latino	5,235	2.90
Hungarian	822	0.46
Icelander	156	0.09
Iranian	285	0.16
Irish	22,897	12.67
Israeli	17	0.01
Italian	11,948	6.61
Latvian	100	0.06
Lithuanian	302	0.17
Luxemburger	4	0.00
Macedonian	28	0.02
Maltese	7	0.00
New Zealander	19	0.01
Northern European	296	0.16
Norwegian	4,775	2.64
Pennsylvania German	40	0.02
Polish	3,102	1.72
Portuguese	1,850	1.02
Romanian	214	0.12
Russian	1,894	1.05
Scandinavian	501	0.28
Scotch-Irish	3,375	1.87
Scottish	4,697	2.60
Serbian	135	0.07
Slavic	51	0.03
Slovak	193	0.11
Slovene	52	0.03
Swedish	3,808	2.11
Swiss	759	0.42
Turkish	37	0.02
Ukrainian	281	0.16
United States or American	8,167	4.52
Welsh	1,456	0.81
West Indian, excl. Hispanic:	92	0.05
Belizean	17	0.01
Dutch West Indian	6	0.00
Haitian	12	0.01
Jamaican	47	0.03
Trinidadian and Tobagonian	5	0.00
West Indian	5	0.00
White:	145,315	80.52
Not Hispanic (124,870)	128,351	71.12
Hispanic (14,923)	16,964	9.40
Yugoslavian	523	0.29

Sparks

Place Type: City
County: Washoe
Population: 66,346

Ancestry/Race	Number	%
African American/Black:	1,931	2.91
Not Hispanic (1,507)	1,788	2.69
Hispanic (84)	143	0.22
African, sub-Saharan:	199	0.30
African	131	0.20
Nigerian	10	0.02
South African	49	0.07
Other sub-Saharan African	9	0.01
Alaska Native tribes, specified:	15	0.02
Alaska Athabascan	2	0.00
Aleut (10)	10	0.02
Eskimo	2	0.00
Tlingit-Haida (1)	1	0.00
Alaska Native tribes, not specified	1	0.00
Am. Ind. or Alaska Nat., not spec.	311	0.47
Albanian	19	0.03
American Indian tribes, specified:	916	1.38
Apache (13)	33	0.05
Blackfeet (7)	28	0.04
Cherokee (53)	167	0.25
Cheyenne (2)	4	0.01
Chickasaw (2)	5	0.01
Chippewa (11)	32	0.05
Choctaw (13)	31	0.05
Colville (1)	2	0.00
Comanche (5)	10	0.02
Cree	6	0.01
Creek (8)	12	0.02
Crow	1	0.00
Delaware (1)	1	0.00
Iroquois (10)	17	0.03
Kiowa (2)	3	0.00
Latin American Indians (45)	73	0.11
Lumbee (1)	1	0.00
Menominee (2)	2	0.00
Navajo (25)	43	0.06
Osage (3)	6	0.01
Ottawa	1	0.00
Paiute (135)	168	0.25
Pima (2)	2	0.00
Potawatomi	2	0.00
Pueblo (14)	23	0.03
Puget Sound Salish (4)	5	0.01
Seminole	1	0.00
Shoshone (17)	21	0.03
Sioux (16)	27	0.04
Ute (1)	7	0.01
Yaqui	2	0.00
Yuman (1)	2	0.00
All other tribes (125)	178	0.27
American Indian tribes, not spec.	58	0.09
Arab:	66	0.10
Egyptian	33	0.05
Lebanese	8	0.01
Syrian	6	0.01
Other Arab	19	0.03
Armenian	20	0.03
Asian:	4,093	6.17
Bangladeshi (13)	18	0.03
Cambodian (9)	9	0.01
Chinese, ex. Taiwanese (559)	691	1.04
Filipino (1,453)	1,754	2.64
Indian (349)	408	0.61
Indonesian (2)	11	0.02
Japanese (168)	276	0.42
Korean (311)	378	0.57
Laotian (4)	4	0.01
Malaysian (1)	3	0.00
Pakistani (20)	35	0.05
Sri Lankan (5)	8	0.01
Taiwanese (11)	12	0.02
Thai (48)	68	0.10
Vietnamese (254)	322	0.49
Other Asian, specified (2)	11	0.02
Other Asian, not specified (40)	85	0.13
Austrian	145	0.22
Basque	440	0.66
Belgian	58	0.09
Brazilian	65	0.10
British	237	0.36
Canadian	165	0.25
Celtic	33	0.05
Croatian	64	0.10
Czech	196	0.29
Czechoslovakian	92	0.14
Danish	570	0.86
Dutch	1,282	1.93
Eastern European	9	0.01
English	8,396	12.62
European	805	1.21
Finnish	127	0.19
French, except Basque	2,645	3.98
French Canadian	257	0.39
German	11,004	16.54
Greek	342	0.51
Hawaii Native/Pacific Islander:	562	0.85
Melanesian: (5)	6	0.01
Fijian (5)	6	0.01
Micronesian: (42)	56	0.08
Guamanian/Chamorro (19)	33	0.05
Other Micronesian (23)	23	0.03
Polynesian: (233)	403	0.61
Native Hawaiian (58)	164	0.25
Samoan (57)	79	0.12
Tongan (114)	134	0.20
Other Polynesian (4)	26	0.04
Other Pac. Isl., specified	1	0.00
Other Pac. Isl., not spec. (34)	96	0.14
Hispanic or Latino:	13,068	19.70
Central American:	751	1.13
Costa Rican	42	0.06
Guatemalan	144	0.22
Honduran	28	0.04
Nicaraguan	22	0.03
Panamanian	23	0.03
Salvadoran	466	0.70
Other Central American	26	0.04
Cuban	59	0.09
Dominican Republic	12	0.02
Mexican	10,018	15.10
Puerto Rican	188	0.28
South American:	141	0.21
Argentinean	14	0.02
Bolivian	1	0.00
Chilean	16	0.02
Colombian	40	0.06
Ecuadorian	7	0.01

Notes: 1. Figures in the "Number" column do not add up to the total population due to: a) Ancestry/Race overlap — e.g. persons can report being both White and Irish, b) persons of Hispanic origin can report being any race, c) persons reporting two ancestries are counted in both categories. 2. Numbers in parentheses indicate the number of persons reporting this ancestry/race alone, not in combination with any other ancestry/race. 3. Refer to the Explanation of Data in the front of the book for more detailed information.

Peruvian	56	0.08
Venezuelan	5	0.01
Other South American	2	0.00
Other Hispanic or Latino	1,899	2.86
Hungarian	340	0.51
Icelander	18	0.03
Iranian	75	0.11
Irish	9,122	13.71
Italian	4,845	7.28
Lithuanian	88	0.13
Luxemburger	16	0.02
New Zealander	19	0.03
Northern European	106	0.16
Norwegian	1,645	2.47
Pennsylvania German	64	0.10
Polish	1,258	1.89
Portuguese	872	1.31
Romanian	42	0.06
Russian	219	0.33
Scandinavian	200	0.30
Scotch-Irish	1,124	1.69
Scottish	1,398	2.10
Serbian	48	0.07
Slavic	48	0.07
Slovak	134	0.20
Slovene	27	0.04
Swedish	1,464	2.20
Swiss	203	0.31
Turkish	20	0.03
Ukrainian	53	0.08
United States or American	2,462	3.70
Welsh	547	0.82
West Indian, excl. Hispanic:	22	0.03
West Indian	22	0.03
White:	53,989	81.37
Not Hispanic (46,122)	47,282	71.27
Hispanic (5,879)	6,707	10.11
Yugoslavian	156	0.23

Spring Creek

Place Type: Census Designated Place
County: Elko
Population: 10,548

Ancestry/Race	Number	%
Acadian/Cajun	7	0.06
African American/Black:	51	0.48
Not Hispanic (20)	47	0.45
Hispanic (2)	4	0.04
Alaska Native tribes, specified:	6	0.06
Eskimo	1	0.01
Tlingit-Haida (5)	5	0.05
Am. Ind. or Alaska Nat., not spec.	57	0.54
American Indian tribes, specified:	197	1.87
Apache (2)	2	0.02
Blackfeet (2)	5	0.05
Cherokee (3)	14	0.13
Cheyenne (3)	3	0.03
Chickasaw	2	0.02
Chippewa (4)	4	0.04
Choctaw (4)	10	0.09
Comanche	2	0.02
Cree (1)	1	0.01
Creek (1)	1	0.01
Latin American Indians (3)	4	0.04
Lumbee	2	0.02
Navajo (9)	24	0.23
Ottawa (2)	2	0.02
Paiute (6)	9	0.09
Pueblo (2)	3	0.03
Puget Sound Salish	3	0.03
Shoshone (12)	15	0.14
Sioux (6)	11	0.10
Tohono O'Odham (4)	4	0.04
Ute	1	0.01
All other tribes (60)	75	0.71
American Indian tribes, not spec.	17	0.16
Arab:	12	0.11
Lebanese	12	0.11
Armenian	8	0.07
Asian:	76	0.72
Chinese, ex. Taiwanese (4)	7	0.07
Filipino (15)	27	0.26
Indian (4)	4	0.04
Indonesian (2)	2	0.02
Japanese (4)	21	0.20
Korean (1)	8	0.08
Vietnamese (3)	3	0.03
Other Asian, specified	4	0.04
Australian	11	0.10
Austrian	40	0.36
Basque	115	1.05
Belgian	5	0.05
British	66	0.60
Canadian	32	0.29
Celtic	9	0.08
Croatian	6	0.05
Czech	30	0.27
Czechoslovakian	15	0.14
Danish	278	2.53
Dutch	287	2.61
English	1,714	15.61
European	130	1.18
Finnish	54	0.49
French, except Basque	331	3.02
French Canadian	107	0.97
German	2,258	20.57
Greek	37	0.34
Hawaii Native/Pacific Islander:	37	0.35
Micronesian: (3)	6	0.06
Guamanian/Chamorro (1)	1	0.01
Other Micronesian (2)	5	0.05
Polynesian: (13)	24	0.23
Native Hawaiian (12)	19	0.18
Samoan (1)	5	0.05
Other Pac. Isl., specified	4	0.04
Other Pac. Isl., not spec. (2)	3	0.03
Hispanic or Latino:	690	6.54
Central American:	8	0.08
Costa Rican	5	0.05
Honduran	3	0.03
Cuban	2	0.02
Mexican	431	4.09
Puerto Rican	16	0.15
Other Hispanic or Latino	233	2.21
Hungarian	21	0.19
Irish	1,481	13.49
Italian	580	5.28
Northern European	17	0.15
Norwegian	342	3.12
Pennsylvania German	6	0.05
Polish	152	1.38
Portuguese	44	0.40
Russian	81	0.74
Scandinavian	22	0.20
Scotch-Irish	129	1.18
Scottish	291	2.65
Slavic	11	0.10
Slovene	10	0.09
Swedish	411	3.74
Swiss	46	0.42
Ukrainian	24	0.22
United States or American	749	6.82
Welsh	150	1.37
West Indian, excl. Hispanic:	5	0.05
Haitian	5	0.05
White:	10,060	95.37
Not Hispanic (9,477)	9,640	91.39
Hispanic (339)	420	3.98
Yugoslavian	96	0.87

Spring Valley

Place Type: Census Designated Place
County: Clark
Population: 117,390

Ancestry/Race	Number	%
Afghan	87	0.07
African American/Black:	7,244	6.17
Not Hispanic (6,011)	6,893	5.87
Hispanic (203)	351	0.30
African, sub-Saharan:	965	0.82
African	549	0.47
Ethiopian	346	0.29
Ghanian	28	0.02
South African	33	0.03
Other sub-Saharan African	9	0.01
Alaska Native tribes, specified:	15	0.01
Alaska Athabascan (6)	6	0.01
Aleut (1)	4	0.00
Eskimo (3)	4	0.00
Tlingit-Haida	1	0.00
Alaska Native tribes, not specified	4	0.00
Am. Ind. or Alaska Nat., not spec.	437	0.37
Albanian	31	0.03
American Indian tribes, specified:	969	0.83
Apache (21)	49	0.04
Blackfeet (10)	34	0.03
Cherokee (87)	293	0.25
Cheyenne	1	0.00
Chickasaw (3)	10	0.01
Chippewa (16)	34	0.03
Choctaw (21)	61	0.05
Colville (1)	1	0.00
Comanche (4)	10	0.01
Cree (1)	5	0.00
Creek (16)	27	0.02
Crow	5	0.00
Delaware (1)	4	0.00
Iroquois (3)	27	0.02
Kiowa (6)	11	0.01
Latin American Indians (21)	52	0.04
Lumbee (4)	5	0.00
Navajo (57)	79	0.07
Osage (2)	7	0.01
Ottawa (2)	2	0.00
Paiute (15)	21	0.02
Potawatomi (5)	6	0.01
Pueblo (17)	34	0.03
Puget Sound Salish (3)	4	0.00
Seminole (1)	6	0.01
Shoshone (12)	20	0.02
Sioux (19)	40	0.03
Tohono O'Odham	1	0.00
Ute (5)	9	0.01
Yakama	1	0.00
Yaqui (5)	5	0.00
All other tribes (61)	105	0.09
American Indian tribes, not spec.	74	0.06
Arab:	882	0.75
Arab/Arabic	268	0.23
Egyptian	33	0.03
Iraqi	5	0.00
Jordanian	37	0.03
Lebanese	356	0.30
Moroccan	21	0.02
Palestinian	46	0.04
Syrian	39	0.03
Other Arab	77	0.07
Armenian	440	0.37
Asian:	15,596	13.29
Bangladeshi (13)	19	0.02
Cambodian (48)	55	0.05
Chinese, ex. Taiwanese (4,042)	4,571	3.89
Filipino (4,020)	4,813	4.10
Hmong (4)	8	0.01
Indian (393)	492	0.42
Indonesian (24)	48	0.04
Japanese (845)	1,236	1.05
Korean (1,546)	1,768	1.51
Laotian (76)	94	0.08
Malaysian (9)	22	0.02
Pakistani (62)	106	0.09
Sri Lankan (33)	44	0.04
Taiwanese (129)	173	0.15
Thai (405)	519	0.44
Vietnamese (963)	1,155	0.98
Other Asian, specified (21)	30	0.03

Notes: 1. Figures in the "Number" column do not add up to the total population due to: a) Ancestry/Race overlap — e.g. persons can report being both White and Irish, b) persons of Hispanic origin can report being any race, c) persons reporting two ancestries are counted in both categories. 2. Numbers in parentheses indicate the number of persons reporting this ancestry/race alone, not in combination with any other ancestry/race. 3. Refer to the Explanation of Data in the front of the book for more detailed information.

Other Asian, not specified (205)	443	0.38
Assyrian/Chaldean/Syriac	72	0.06
Australian	79	0.07
Austrian	437	0.37
Basque	84	0.07
Belgian	105	0.09
Brazilian	24	0.02
British	524	0.45
Bulgarian	128	0.11
Canadian	493	0.42
Croatian	196	0.17
Czech	362	0.31
Czechoslovakian	188	0.16
Danish	743	0.63
Dutch	1,786	1.52
Eastern European	84	0.07
English	9,101	7.74
Estonian	20	0.02
European	922	0.78
Finnish	189	0.16
French, except Basque	3,432	2.92
French Canadian	907	0.77
German	15,597	13.26
German Russian	4	0.00
Greek	965	0.82
Guyanese	22	0.02
Hawaii Native/Pacific Islander:	1,148	0.98
Melanesian: (5)	5	0.00
Fijian (5)	5	0.00
Micronesian: (96)	138	0.12
Guamanian/Chamorro (85)	126	0.11
Other Micronesian (11)	12	0.01
Polynesian: (421)	809	0.69
Native Hawaiian (318)	648	0.55
Samoan (91)	123	0.10
Tongan (4)	13	0.01
Other Polynesian (8)	25	0.02
Other Pac. Isl., specified	5	0.00
Other Pac. Isl., not spec. (32)	191	0.16
Hispanic or Latino:	16,165	13.77
Central American:	843	0.72
Costa Rican	43	0.04
Guatemalan	171	0.15
Honduran	59	0.05
Nicaraguan	82	0.07
Panamanian	38	0.03
Salvadoran	382	0.33
Other Central American	68	0.06
Cuban	892	0.76
Dominican Republic	119	0.10
Mexican	9,704	8.27
Puerto Rican	772	0.66
South American:	742	0.63
Argentinean	185	0.16
Bolivian	8	0.01
Chilean	88	0.07
Colombian	193	0.16
Ecuadorian	57	0.05
Paraguayan	6	0.01
Peruvian	117	0.10
Uruguayan	20	0.02
Venezuelan	17	0.01
Other South American	51	0.04
Other Hispanic or Latino	3,093	2.63
Hungarian	859	0.73
Icelander	57	0.05
Iranian	536	0.46
Irish	12,815	10.89
Israeli	241	0.20
Italian	11,377	9.67
Latvian	16	0.01
Lithuanian	239	0.20
Luxemburger	17	0.01
Macedonian	15	0.01
Maltese	42	0.04
New Zealander	16	0.01
Northern European	21	0.02
Norwegian	1,936	1.65
Pennsylvania German	25	0.02
Polish	3,731	3.17
Portuguese	502	0.43
Romanian	295	0.25
Russian	1,905	1.62
Scandinavian	168	0.14
Scotch-Irish	1,263	1.07
Scottish	1,425	1.21
Serbian	277	0.24
Slavic	29	0.02
Slovak	174	0.15
Slovene	44	0.04
Swedish	1,837	1.56
Swiss	358	0.30
Turkish	105	0.09
Ukrainian	352	0.30
United States or American	4,836	4.11
Welsh	696	0.59
West Indian, excl. Hispanic:	92	0.08
Barbadian	6	0.01
Dutch West Indian	8	0.01
Haitian	8	0.01
Jamaican	47	0.04
Trinidadian and Tobagonian	23	0.02
White:	89,696	76.41
Not Hispanic (76,766)	80,065	68.20
Hispanic (8,458)	9,631	8.20
Yugoslavian	235	0.20

Sun Valley

Place Type: Census Designated Place
County: Washoe
Population: 19,461

Ancestry/Race	Number	%
Acadian/Cajun	8	0.04
African American/Black:	532	2.73
Not Hispanic (411)	495	2.54
Hispanic (18)	37	0.19
African, sub-Saharan:	29	0.15
African	29	0.15
Alaska Native tribes, specified:	19	0.10
Alaska Athabascan (5)	5	0.03
Aleut (3)	4	0.02
Eskimo	7	0.04
Tlingit-Haida (3)	3	0.02
Am. Ind. or Alaska Nat., not spec.	132	0.68
American Indian tribes, specified:	450	2.31
Apache (3)	4	0.02
Blackfeet (4)	8	0.04
Cherokee (44)	109	0.56
Cheyenne	2	0.01
Chippewa (5)	10	0.05
Choctaw (5)	22	0.11
Colville	1	0.01
Comanche	1	0.01
Cree	1	0.01
Crow (2)	2	0.01
Delaware	2	0.01
Iroquois	4	0.02
Latin American Indians (12)	21	0.11
Navajo (12)	18	0.09
Osage	1	0.01
Paiute (68)	85	0.44
Pima (1)	3	0.02
Potawatomi (11)	14	0.07
Pueblo (2)	5	0.03
Shoshone (26)	35	0.18
Sioux (13)	18	0.09
Ute	1	0.01
Yakama	3	0.02
Yaqui	4	0.02
Yuman (1)	1	0.01
All other tribes (47)	75	0.39
American Indian tribes, not spec.	24	0.12
Arab:	62	0.32
Egyptian	13	0.07
Syrian	38	0.20
Other Arab	11	0.06
Asian:	591	3.04
Cambodian (1)	2	0.01
Chinese, ex. Taiwanese (32)	47	0.24
Filipino (221)	302	1.55
Indian (66)	69	0.35
Indonesian (1)	1	0.01
Japanese (34)	57	0.29
Korean (18)	35	0.18
Pakistani (10)	18	0.09
Thai (6)	10	0.05
Vietnamese (25)	36	0.18
Other Asian, specified	2	0.01
Other Asian, not specified (4)	12	0.06
Australian	6	0.03
Austrian	6	0.03
Basque	14	0.07
British	18	0.09
Canadian	43	0.22
Czech	65	0.33
Danish	46	0.24
Dutch	414	2.13
English	1,930	9.92
European	244	1.25
Finnish	6	0.03
French, except Basque	863	4.43
French Canadian	203	1.04
German	3,569	18.34
Greek	71	0.36
Hawaii Native/Pacific Islander:	182	0.94
Micronesian: (15)	19	0.10
Guamanian/Chamorro (4)	5	0.03
Other Micronesian (11)	14	0.07
Polynesian: (88)	136	0.70
Native Hawaiian (14)	37	0.19
Samoan (22)	25	0.13
Tongan (50)	64	0.33
Other Polynesian (2)	10	0.05
Other Pac. Isl., specified	2	0.01
Other Pac. Isl., not spec. (8)	25	0.13
Hispanic or Latino:	4,113	21.13
Central American:	197	1.01
Guatemalan	51	0.26
Honduran	8	0.04
Nicaraguan	18	0.09
Panamanian	2	0.01
Salvadoran	103	0.53
Other Central American	15	0.08
Cuban	22	0.11
Dominican Republic	2	0.01
Mexican	3,242	16.66
Puerto Rican	64	0.33
South American:	24	0.12
Argentinean	5	0.03
Bolivian	2	0.01
Chilean	2	0.01
Colombian	3	0.02
Ecuadorian	2	0.01
Peruvian	6	0.03
Venezuelan	1	0.01
Other South American	3	0.02
Other Hispanic or Latino	562	2.89
Hungarian	34	0.17
Icelander	16	0.08
Irish	3,175	16.32
Italian	1,016	5.22
Lithuanian	12	0.06
Northern European	7	0.04
Norwegian	515	2.65
Polish	303	1.56
Portuguese	229	1.18
Romanian	18	0.09
Russian	120	0.62
Scandinavian	30	0.15
Scotch-Irish	329	1.69
Scottish	333	1.71
Serbian	52	0.27
Slavic	11	0.06
Slovak	8	0.04
Swedish	322	1.65
Swiss	46	0.24
Ukrainian	6	0.03
United States or American	1,077	5.53

Notes: 1. Figures in the "Number" column do not add up to the total population due to: a) Ancestry/Race overlap — e.g. persons can report being both White and Irish, b) persons of Hispanic origin can report being any race, c) persons reporting two ancestries are counted in both categories. 2. Numbers in parentheses indicate the number of persons reporting this ancestry/race alone, not in combination with any other ancestry/race. 3. Refer to the Explanation of Data in the front of the book for more detailed information.

Welsh	160	0.82
White:	16,180	83.14
Not Hispanic (13,675)	14,075	72.32
Hispanic (1,851)	2,105	10.82
Yugoslavian	29	0.15

Sunrise Manor

Place Type: Census Designated Place
County: Clark
Population: 156,120

Ancestry/Race	Number	%
Acadian/Cajun	10	0.01
Afghan	125	0.08
African American/Black:	22,112	14.16
Not Hispanic (19,533)	21,210	13.59
Hispanic (584)	902	0.58
African, sub-Saharan:	1,375	0.88
African	1,237	0.79
Ethiopian	115	0.07
Ghanian	14	0.01
Nigerian	9	0.01
Alaska Native tribes, specified:	22	0.01
Alaska Athabascan (4)	4	0.00
Aleut (2)	3	0.00
Eskimo (5)	7	0.00
Tlingit-Haida (4)	7	0.00
All other tribes	1	0.00
Alaska Native tribes, not specified	6	0.00
Am. Ind. or Alaska Nat., not spec.	911	0.58
Albanian	16	0.01
American Indian tribes, specified:	1,786	1.14
Apache (47)	113	0.07
Blackfeet (18)	74	0.05
Cherokee (144)	438	0.28
Cheyenne (9)	9	0.01
Chickasaw (6)	11	0.01
Chippewa (23)	32	0.02
Choctaw (33)	78	0.05
Colville (4)	4	0.00
Comanche (4)	11	0.01
Cree (3)	5	0.00
Creek (9)	32	0.02
Crow	2	0.00
Delaware (6)	13	0.01
Iroquois (20)	46	0.03
Kiowa (11)	11	0.01
Latin American Indians (79)	135	0.09
Lumbee (3)	3	0.00
Menominee (4)	6	0.00
Navajo (205)	252	0.16
Osage (1)	1	0.00
Ottawa (3)	5	0.00
Paiute (53)	69	0.04
Pima (2)	3	0.00
Potawatomi (11)	17	0.01
Pueblo (22)	47	0.03
Puget Sound Salish (3)	3	0.00
Seminole (5)	17	0.01
Shoshone (11)	17	0.01
Sioux (55)	92	0.06
Tohono O'Odham (5)	6	0.00
Ute (5)	8	0.01
Yakama (9)	10	0.01
Yaqui (9)	22	0.01
Yuman (14)	22	0.01
All other tribes (90)	172	0.11
American Indian tribes, not spec.	176	0.11
Arab:	374	0.24
Arab/Arabic	110	0.07
Egyptian	37	0.02
Iraqi	20	0.01
Lebanese	95	0.06
Moroccan	9	0.01
Palestinian	8	0.01
Syrian	47	0.03
Other Arab	48	0.03
Armenian	148	0.10
Asian:	11,140	7.14
Bangladeshi	3	0.00
Cambodian (92)	121	0.08
Chinese, ex. Taiwanese (558)	938	0.60
Filipino (4,830)	5,971	3.82
Hmong (6)	9	0.01
Indian (277)	399	0.26
Indonesian (29)	38	0.02
Japanese (465)	819	0.52
Korean (642)	882	0.56
Laotian (338)	415	0.27
Malaysian (3)	7	0.00
Pakistani (41)	79	0.05
Sri Lankan (4)	12	0.01
Taiwanese (30)	44	0.03
Thai (439)	628	0.40
Vietnamese (309)	421	0.27
Other Asian, specified (2)	17	0.01
Other Asian, not specified (164)	337	0.22
Assyrian/Chaldean/Syriac	52	0.03
Australian	71	0.05
Austrian	272	0.17
Basque	17	0.01
Belgian	120	0.08
Brazilian	13	0.01
British	848	0.54
Bulgarian	35	0.02
Canadian	414	0.27
Celtic	39	0.03
Croatian	139	0.09
Czech	410	0.26
Czechoslovakian	202	0.13
Danish	843	0.54
Dutch	1,789	1.15
Eastern European	29	0.02
English	12,110	7.78
European	1,086	0.70
Finnish	312	0.20
French, except Basque	4,121	2.65
French Canadian	1,051	0.68
German	17,353	11.15
German Russian	22	0.01
Greek	555	0.36
Hawaii Native/Pacific Islander:	1,532	0.98
Melanesian: (4)	5	0.00
Fijian (4)	5	0.00
Micronesian: (243)	347	0.22
Guamanian/Chamorro (229)	327	0.21
Other Micronesian (14)	20	0.01
Polynesian: (398)	952	0.61
Native Hawaiian (250)	693	0.44
Samoan (115)	193	0.12
Tongan (12)	22	0.01
Other Polynesian (21)	44	0.03
Other Pac. Isl., specified	7	0.00
Other Pac. Isl., not spec. (57)	221	0.14
Hispanic or Latino:	40,619	26.02
Central American:	1,730	1.11
Costa Rican	36	0.02
Guatemalan	328	0.21
Honduran	180	0.12
Nicaraguan	135	0.09
Panamanian	57	0.04
Salvadoran	919	0.59
Other Central American	75	0.05
Cuban	1,342	0.86
Dominican Republic	66	0.04
Mexican	29,891	19.15
Puerto Rican	1,182	0.76
South American:	536	0.34
Argentinean	103	0.07
Bolivian	2	0.00
Chilean	60	0.04
Colombian	141	0.09
Ecuadorian	77	0.05
Paraguayan	7	0.00
Peruvian	96	0.06
Uruguayan	4	0.00
Venezuelan	28	0.02
Other South American	18	0.01
Other Hispanic or Latino	5,872	3.76
Hungarian	568	0.36
Icelander	13	0.01
Iranian	199	0.13
Irish	12,792	8.22
Israeli	36	0.02
Italian	7,422	4.77
Latvian	5	0.00
Lithuanian	215	0.14
Luxemburger	7	0.00
Macedonian	17	0.01
Maltese	17	0.01
Northern European	159	0.10
Norwegian	2,162	1.39
Pennsylvania German	15	0.01
Polish	3,340	2.15
Portuguese	562	0.36
Romanian	115	0.07
Russian	882	0.57
Scandinavian	128	0.08
Scotch-Irish	1,544	0.99
Scottish	2,057	1.32
Serbian	48	0.03
Slavic	77	0.05
Slovak	113	0.07
Slovene	52	0.03
Swedish	1,959	1.26
Swiss	574	0.37
Turkish	43	0.03
Ukrainian	197	0.13
United States or American	7,516	4.83
Welsh	836	0.54
West Indian, excl. Hispanic:	225	0.14
Bahamian	7	0.00
Barbadian	7	0.00
Belizean	62	0.04
Bermudan	3	0.00
Haitian	35	0.02
Jamaican	70	0.04
Trinidadian and Tobagonian	36	0.02
West Indian	5	0.00
White:	108,082	69.23
Not Hispanic (81,044)	84,656	54.22
Hispanic (21,168)	23,426	15.01
Yugoslavian	102	0.07

Whitney

Place Type: Census Designated Place
County: Clark
Population: 18,273

Ancestry/Race	Number	%
African American/Black:	1,455	7.96
Not Hispanic (1,168)	1,318	7.21
Hispanic (79)	137	0.75
African, sub-Saharan:	144	0.81
African	130	0.73
Cape Verdean	7	0.04
Nigerian	7	0.04
Alaska Native tribes, specified:	7	0.04
Aleut (3)	3	0.02
Eskimo	3	0.02
Tlingit-Haida (1)	1	0.01
Am. Ind. or Alaska Nat., not spec.	114	0.62
American Indian tribes, specified:	242	1.32
Apache (15)	16	0.09
Blackfeet (1)	7	0.04
Cherokee (19)	71	0.39
Cheyenne	2	0.01
Chippewa (3)	3	0.02
Choctaw (1)	9	0.05
Cree (1)	2	0.01
Creek (3)	4	0.02
Crow	1	0.01
Delaware (1)	1	0.01
Iroquois	3	0.02
Kiowa (2)	3	0.02
Latin American Indians (16)	21	0.11
Navajo (13)	22	0.12
Osage	1	0.01

Notes: 1. Figures in the "Number" column do not add up to the total population due to: a) Ancestry/Race overlap — e.g. persons can report being both White and Irish, b) persons of Hispanic origin can report being any race, c) persons reporting two ancestries are counted in both categories. 2. Numbers in parentheses indicate the number of persons reporting this ancestry/race alone, not in combination with any other ancestry/race. 3. Refer to the Explanation of Data in the front of the book for more detailed information.

Ancestry/Race	Number	%
Paiute (1)	4	0.02
Potawatomi (2)	2	0.01
Pueblo (1)	10	0.05
Seminole (3)	7	0.04
Shoshone	6	0.03
Sioux (13)	16	0.09
Yakama (1)	1	0.01
All other tribes (16)	30	0.16
American Indian tribes, not spec.	36	0.20
Arab:	76	0.43
Arab/Arabic	12	0.07
Lebanese	53	0.30
Syrian	11	0.06
Armenian	27	0.15
Asian:	947	5.18
Cambodian	1	0.01
Chinese, ex. Taiwanese (43)	83	0.45
Filipino (416)	543	2.97
Hmong (1)	1	0.01
Indian (33)	51	0.28
Indonesian (3)	3	0.02
Japanese (60)	94	0.51
Korean (44)	61	0.33
Laotian (13)	17	0.09
Malaysian (1)	11	0.06
Pakistani (1)	1	0.01
Sri Lankan (1)	1	0.01
Taiwanese (1)	1	0.01
Thai (27)	39	0.21
Vietnamese (24)	28	0.15
Other Asian, not specified (5)	12	0.07
Austrian	18	0.10
Belgian	9	0.05
Brazilian	72	0.41
British	7	0.04
Bulgarian	18	0.10
Canadian	48	0.27
Croatian	9	0.05
Czech	56	0.32
Czechoslovakian	38	0.21
Danish	68	0.38
Dutch	225	1.27
English	1,346	7.59
European	81	0.46
Finnish	22	0.12
French, except Basque	503	2.84
French Canadian	120	0.68
German	2,035	11.48
German Russian	14	0.08
Greek	32	0.18
Hawaii Native/Pacific Islander:	182	1.00
Micronesian: (18)	24	0.13
Guamanian/Chamorro (16)	19	0.10
Other Micronesian (2)	5	0.03
Polynesian: (59)	123	0.67
Native Hawaiian (40)	102	0.56
Samoan (19)	20	0.11
Other Polynesian	1	0.01
Other Pac. Isl., not spec. (5)	35	0.19
Hispanic or Latino:	4,622	25.29
Central American:	240	1.31
Costa Rican	3	0.02
Guatemalan	33	0.18
Honduran	21	0.11
Nicaraguan	29	0.16
Panamanian	22	0.12
Salvadoran	120	0.66
Other Central American	12	0.07
Cuban	255	1.40
Dominican Republic	11	0.06
Mexican	3,113	17.04
Puerto Rican	139	0.76
South American:	79	0.43
Argentinean	9	0.05
Bolivian	1	0.01
Chilean	2	0.01
Colombian	18	0.10
Ecuadorian	18	0.10
Paraguayan	1	0.01
Peruvian	22	0.12
Venezuelan	6	0.03
Other South American	2	0.01
Other Hispanic or Latino	785	4.30
Hungarian	83	0.47
Iranian	20	0.11
Irish	1,523	8.59
Italian	1,083	6.11
Lithuanian	19	0.11
Northern European	20	0.11
Norwegian	216	1.22
Pennsylvania German	9	0.05
Polish	550	3.10
Romanian	11	0.06
Russian	55	0.31
Scandinavian	11	0.06
Scotch-Irish	132	0.74
Scottish	176	0.99
Serbian	10	0.06
Slavic	11	0.06
Slovak	19	0.11
Slovene	10	0.06
Swedish	257	1.45
Swiss	24	0.14
Turkish	9	0.05
Ukrainian	20	0.11
United States or American	1,099	6.20
Welsh	86	0.49
West Indian, excl. Hispanic:	51	0.29
Belizean	22	0.12
Jamaican	16	0.09
West Indian	13	0.07
White:	13,863	75.87
Not Hispanic (11,019)	11,457	62.70
Hispanic (2,181)	2,406	13.17

Winchester

Place Type: Census Designated Place
County: Clark
Population: 26,958

Ancestry/Race	Number	%
African American/Black:	2,166	8.03
Not Hispanic (1,811)	2,024	7.51
Hispanic (84)	142	0.53
African, sub-Saharan:	273	1.02
African	186	0.69
Ethiopian	49	0.18
Kenyan	31	0.12
Senegalese	7	0.03
Alaska Native tribes, specified:	4	0.01
Eskimo (2)	2	0.01
Tlingit-Haida (2)	2	0.01
Am. Ind. or Alaska Nat., not spec.	114	0.42
American Indian tribes, specified:	295	1.09
Apache (4)	9	0.03
Blackfeet (7)	8	0.03
Cherokee (26)	75	0.28
Cheyenne (2)	2	0.01
Chickasaw (1)	6	0.02
Chippewa (2)	3	0.01
Choctaw	4	0.01
Comanche (3)	9	0.03
Cree (3)	3	0.01
Creek	3	0.01
Crow	1	0.00
Delaware	3	0.01
Iroquois (2)	6	0.02
Kiowa (1)	1	0.00
Latin American Indians (17)	31	0.11
Navajo (32)	39	0.14
Osage (1)	1	0.00
Ottawa (3)	3	0.01
Paiute (6)	6	0.02
Pima	7	0.03
Potawatomi	1	0.00
Pueblo (5)	7	0.03
Seminole	1	0.00
Shoshone	1	0.00
Sioux (12)	24	0.09
Yakama (1)	6	0.02
Yuman (6)	6	0.02
All other tribes (19)	29	0.11
American Indian tribes, not spec.	30	0.11
Arab:	119	0.44
Egyptian	34	0.13
Jordanian	30	0.11
Lebanese	38	0.14
Moroccan	8	0.03
Syrian	9	0.03
Armenian	37	0.14
Asian:	1,849	6.86
Bangladeshi (8)	8	0.03
Cambodian (12)	19	0.07
Chinese, ex. Taiwanese (240)	318	1.18
Filipino (629)	779	2.89
Indian (73)	104	0.39
Indonesian (4)	5	0.02
Japanese (94)	160	0.59
Korean (102)	128	0.47
Laotian (7)	20	0.07
Malaysian (9)	11	0.04
Pakistani (2)	14	0.05
Sri Lankan (7)	9	0.03
Taiwanese (2)	9	0.03
Thai (77)	102	0.38
Vietnamese (74)	88	0.33
Other Asian, specified (12)	17	0.06
Other Asian, not specified (23)	58	0.22
Australian	21	0.08
Austrian	89	0.33
British	74	0.28
Bulgarian	32	0.12
Canadian	143	0.53
Celtic	9	0.03
Croatian	56	0.21
Czech	61	0.23
Czechoslovakian	21	0.08
Danish	236	0.88
Dutch	277	1.03
English	2,063	7.70
European	181	0.68
Finnish	38	0.14
French, except Basque	952	3.55
French Canadian	92	0.34
German	2,479	9.25
Greek	101	0.38
Hawaii Native/Pacific Islander:	201	0.75
Melanesian: (2)	2	0.01
Fijian (2)	2	0.01
Micronesian: (12)	24	0.09
Guamanian/Chamorro (12)	24	0.09
Polynesian: (90)	150	0.56
Native Hawaiian (71)	113	0.42
Samoan (17)	31	0.11
Tongan (1)	2	0.01
Other Polynesian (1)	4	0.01
Other Pac. Isl., not spec. (14)	25	0.09
Hispanic or Latino:	7,820	29.01
Central American:	471	1.75
Costa Rican	16	0.06
Guatemalan	67	0.25
Honduran	33	0.12
Nicaraguan	26	0.10
Panamanian	6	0.02
Salvadoran	282	1.05
Other Central American	41	0.15
Cuban	737	2.73
Dominican Republic	23	0.09
Mexican	5,205	19.31
Puerto Rican	208	0.77
South American:	131	0.49
Argentinean	28	0.10
Bolivian	2	0.01
Chilean	8	0.03
Colombian	29	0.11
Ecuadorian	17	0.06
Peruvian	34	0.13
Venezuelan	5	0.02
Other South American	8	0.03

Notes: 1. Figures in the "Number" column do not add up to the total population due to: a) Ancestry/Race overlap — e.g. persons can report being both White and Irish, b) persons of Hispanic origin can report being any race, c) persons reporting two ancestries are counted in both categories. 2. Numbers in parentheses indicate the number of persons reporting this ancestry/race alone, not in combination with any other ancestry/race. 3. Refer to the Explanation of Data in the front of the book for more detailed information.

Ancestry/Race	Number	%
Other Hispanic or Latino	1,045	3.88
Hungarian	117	0.44
Iranian	29	0.11
Irish	2,343	8.74
Israeli	13	0.05
Italian	1,513	5.65
Latvian	10	0.04
Lithuanian	119	0.44
Macedonian	10	0.04
Northern European	7	0.03
Norwegian	364	1.36
Polish	651	2.43
Portuguese	72	0.27
Romanian	142	0.53
Russian	341	1.27
Scandinavian	37	0.14
Scotch-Irish	288	1.07
Scottish	296	1.10
Serbian	51	0.19
Slovak	23	0.09
Swedish	359	1.34
Swiss	64	0.24
Turkish	7	0.03
Ukrainian	74	0.28
United States or American	1,449	5.41
Welsh	129	0.48
West Indian, excl. Hispanic:	35	0.13
Bahamian	9	0.03
British West Indian	13	0.05
Haitian	13	0.05
White:	20,410	75.71
Not Hispanic (14,790)	15,388	57.08
Hispanic (4,574)	5,022	18.63
Yugoslavian	15	0.06

Amherst

Place Type: Town
County: Hillsborough
Population: 10,769

Ancestry/Race	Number	%
African American/Black:	63	0.59
Not Hispanic (38)	54	0.50
Hispanic (8)	9	0.08
African, sub-Saharan:	47	0.44
Cape Verdean	21	0.20
Ghanian	6	0.06
South African	20	0.19
Alaska Native tribes, not specified	1	0.01
Am. Ind. or Alaska Nat., not spec.	10	0.09
American Indian tribes, specified:	29	0.27
Blackfeet	2	0.02
Cherokee (2)	5	0.05
Delaware (1)	1	0.01
Iroquois (1)	1	0.01
Latin American Indians (1)	2	0.02
Sioux (1)	1	0.01
All other tribes (6)	17	0.16
American Indian tribes, not spec.	1	0.01
Arab:	31	0.29
Lebanese	27	0.25
Syrian	4	0.04
Armenian	9	0.08
Asian:	189	1.76
Chinese, ex. Taiwanese (73)	84	0.78
Filipino (11)	13	0.12
Indian (12)	13	0.12
Indonesian	2	0.02
Japanese (7)	22	0.20
Korean (25)	25	0.23
Malaysian (1)	1	0.01
Sri Lankan (1)	1	0.01
Thai (3)	10	0.09
Vietnamese (5)	9	0.08
Other Asian, not specified (6)	9	0.08
Austrian	38	0.35
British	213	1.98
Canadian	88	0.82
Carpatho Rusyn	6	0.06
Czech	30	0.28
Czechoslovakian	12	0.11
Danish	39	0.36
Dutch	146	1.36
Eastern European	26	0.24
English	2,318	21.52
European	107	0.99
Finnish	95	0.88
French, except Basque	972	9.03
French Canadian	702	6.52
German	1,659	15.41
Greek	81	0.75
Hawaii Native/Pacific Islander:	2	0.02
Polynesian: (2)	2	0.02
Native Hawaiian (2)	2	0.02
Hispanic or Latino:	109	1.01
Central American:	6	0.06
Guatemalan	6	0.06
Cuban	14	0.13
Dominican Republic	4	0.04
Mexican	28	0.26
Puerto Rican	16	0.15
South American:	6	0.06
Colombian	2	0.02
Ecuadorian	1	0.01
Other South American	3	0.03
Other Hispanic or Latino	35	0.33
Hungarian	84	0.78
Icelander	9	0.08
Iranian	22	0.20
Irish	2,411	22.39
Israeli	10	0.09
Italian	1,128	10.47
Latvian	19	0.18
Lithuanian	49	0.46
Norwegian	101	0.94
Pennsylvania German	13	0.12
Polish	510	4.74
Portuguese	112	1.04
Romanian	7	0.07
Russian	179	1.66
Scandinavian	42	0.39
Scotch-Irish	213	1.98
Scottish	622	5.78
Slavic	12	0.11
Slovak	17	0.16
Swedish	299	2.78
Swiss	123	1.14
Turkish	7	0.07
Ukrainian	48	0.45
United States or American	349	3.24
Welsh	115	1.07
West Indian, excl. Hispanic:	18	0.17
Haitian	18	0.17
White:	10,536	97.84
Not Hispanic (10,365)	10,449	97.03
Hispanic (81)	87	0.81

Bedford

Place Type: Town
County: Hillsborough
Population: 18,274

Ancestry/Race	Number	%
African American/Black:	90	0.49
Not Hispanic (56)	87	0.48
Hispanic (3)	3	0.02
African, sub-Saharan:	30	0.16
Cape Verdean	18	0.10
Other sub-Saharan African	12	0.07
Alaska Native tribes, specified:	6	0.03
Alaska Athabascan	4	0.02
Tlingit-Haida	2	0.01
Am. Ind. or Alaska Nat., not spec.	25	0.14
Albanian	13	0.07
American Indian tribes, specified:	21	0.11
Cherokee (1)	3	0.02
Chippewa (1)	2	0.01
Choctaw	3	0.02
Comanche	1	0.01
Delaware	1	0.01
Iroquois (1)	2	0.01
Pueblo (1)	1	0.01
All other tribes (3)	8	0.04
American Indian tribes, not spec.	6	0.03
Arab:	88	0.48
Arab/Arabic	16	0.09
Lebanese	44	0.24
Syrian	28	0.15
Armenian	39	0.21
Asian:	318	1.74
Cambodian (1)	1	0.01
Chinese, ex. Taiwanese (69)	90	0.49
Filipino (19)	32	0.18
Indian (74)	78	0.43
Japanese (16)	36	0.20
Korean (37)	50	0.27
Pakistani	1	0.01
Taiwanese (2)	2	0.01
Vietnamese (4)	6	0.03
Other Asian, specified	10	0.05
Other Asian, not specified (6)	12	0.07
Australian	25	0.14
Austrian	42	0.23
Basque	9	0.05
Belgian	24	0.13
British	136	0.74
Canadian	344	1.88
Croatian	41	0.22
Czech	28	0.15
Danish	27	0.15
Dutch	151	0.83
English	2,709	14.82
European	102	0.56
Finnish	69	0.38
French, except Basque	1,936	10.59
French Canadian	2,222	12.16
German	2,074	11.35
Greek	399	2.18
Hawaii Native/Pacific Islander:	15	0.08
Polynesian: (4)	4	0.02
Native Hawaiian (3)	3	0.02
Samoan (1)	1	0.01
Other Pac. Isl., specified	10	0.05
Other Pac. Isl., not spec.	1	0.01
Hispanic or Latino:	165	0.90
Central American:	6	0.03
Costa Rican	1	0.01
Guatemalan	2	0.01
Panamanian	1	0.01
Salvadoran	2	0.01
Cuban	8	0.04
Dominican Republic	9	0.05
Mexican	42	0.23
Puerto Rican	30	0.16
South American:	23	0.13
Bolivian	3	0.02
Chilean	2	0.01
Colombian	7	0.04
Ecuadorian	4	0.02
Peruvian	2	0.01
Venezuelan	5	0.03
Other Hispanic or Latino	47	0.26
Hungarian	66	0.36
Iranian	15	0.08
Irish	4,077	22.31
Israeli	8	0.04
Italian	1,670	9.14
Latvian	9	0.05
Lithuanian	112	0.61
New Zealander	9	0.05
Norwegian	138	0.76
Pennsylvania German	9	0.05
Polish	1,419	7.77
Portuguese	194	1.06
Russian	403	2.21
Scandinavian	109	0.60
Scotch-Irish	299	1.64
Scottish	615	3.37

Notes: 1. Figures in the "Number" column do not add up to the total population due to: a) Ancestry/Race overlap — e.g. persons can report being both White and Irish, b) persons of Hispanic origin can report being any race, c) persons reporting two ancestries are counted in both categories. 2. Numbers in parentheses indicate the number of persons reporting this ancestry/race alone, not in combination with any other ancestry/race. 3. Refer to the Explanation of Data in the front of the book for more detailed information.

Slovak	51	0.28
Slovene	9	0.05
Swedish	516	2.82
Swiss	10	0.05
Turkish	33	0.18
Ukrainian	104	0.57
United States or American	969	5.30
Welsh	113	0.62
West Indian, excl. Hispanic:	11	0.06
Haitian	11	0.06
White:	17,942	98.18
Not Hispanic (17,669)	17,802	97.42
Hispanic (132)	140	0.77

Berlin

Place Type: City
County: Coos
Population: 10,331

Ancestry/Race	Number	%
African American/Black:	37	0.36
Not Hispanic (19)	36	0.35
Hispanic	1	0.01
African, sub-Saharan:	7	0.07
Cape Verdean	7	0.07
Alaska Native tribes, specified:	3	0.03
Eskimo (1)	3	0.03
Alaska Native tribes, not specified	1	0.01
Am. Ind. or Alaska Nat., not spec.	27	0.26
American Indian tribes, specified:	41	0.40
Blackfeet (1)	2	0.02
Cherokee (2)	9	0.09
Choctaw (1)	1	0.01
Crow	1	0.01
Iroquois (1)	3	0.03
Latin American Indians (1)	1	0.01
All other tribes (10)	24	0.23
Arab:	20	0.19
Egyptian	20	0.19
Asian:	55	0.53
Cambodian	1	0.01
Chinese, ex. Taiwanese (10)	13	0.13
Filipino (13)	18	0.17
Indian (6)	6	0.06
Japanese (1)	4	0.04
Korean (1)	5	0.05
Taiwanese (1)	1	0.01
Vietnamese (3)	3	0.03
Other Asian, specified	1	0.01
Other Asian, not specified (2)	3	0.03
Belgian	17	0.16
British	13	0.13
Canadian	180	1.74
Danish	5	0.05
Dutch	44	0.43
English	833	8.06
European	51	0.49
French, except Basque	2,071	20.05
French Canadian	4,022	38.93
German	269	2.60
Greek	5	0.05
Hawaii Native/Pacific Islander:	3	0.03
Micronesian:	1	0.01
Guamanian/Chamorro	1	0.01
Other Pac. Isl., specified	1	0.01
Other Pac. Isl., not spec. (1)	1	0.01
Hispanic or Latino:	68	0.66
Central American:	4	0.04
Guatemalan	2	0.02
Other Central American	2	0.02
Cuban	2	0.02
Mexican	19	0.18
Puerto Rican	21	0.20
South American:	4	0.04
Uruguayan	4	0.04
Other Hispanic or Latino	18	0.17
Hungarian	5	0.05
Irish	1,037	10.04
Italian	367	3.55
Latvian	7	0.07
Lithuanian	14	0.14
Norwegian	229	2.22
Pennsylvania German	6	0.06
Polish	78	0.76
Portuguese	25	0.24
Russian	58	0.56
Scandinavian	4	0.04
Scotch-Irish	141	1.36
Scottish	212	2.05
Swedish	26	0.25
Ukrainian	25	0.24
United States or American	652	6.31
Welsh	19	0.18
White:	10,229	99.01
Not Hispanic (10,105)	10,178	98.52
Hispanic (45)	51	0.49

Claremont

Place Type: City
County: Sullivan
Population: 13,151

Ancestry/Race	Number	%
African American/Black:	68	0.52
Not Hispanic (41)	64	0.49
Hispanic	4	0.03
Am. Ind. or Alaska Nat., not spec.	43	0.33
American Indian tribes, specified:	66	0.50
Apache	1	0.01
Blackfeet	5	0.04
Cherokee (3)	8	0.06
Chippewa (1)	1	0.01
Cree	1	0.01
Iroquois (1)	6	0.05
Seminole	1	0.01
Shoshone	1	0.01
Sioux (2)	3	0.02
Ute	1	0.01
All other tribes (23)	38	0.29
American Indian tribes, not spec.	2	0.02
Arab:	10	0.08
Lebanese	10	0.08
Asian:	99	0.75
Cambodian (8)	8	0.06
Chinese, ex. Taiwanese (23)	26	0.20
Filipino (13)	17	0.13
Indian (6)	6	0.05
Japanese (6)	7	0.05
Korean (8)	12	0.09
Laotian (7)	7	0.05
Thai (2)	2	0.02
Vietnamese (8)	12	0.09
Other Asian, specified	1	0.01
Other Asian, not specified	1	0.01
Belgian	8	0.06
Brazilian	14	0.11
British	42	0.32
Canadian	78	0.59
Czech	7	0.05
Danish	6	0.05
Dutch	164	1.25
Eastern European	10	0.08
English	1,935	14.71
European	12	0.09
Finnish	80	0.61
French, except Basque	2,567	19.52
French Canadian	1,504	11.44
German	796	6.05
Greek	80	0.61
Hawaii Native/Pacific Islander:	5	0.04
Polynesian: (4)	4	0.03
Native Hawaiian (4)	4	0.03
Other Pac. Isl., specified	1	0.01
Hispanic or Latino:	66	0.50
Central American:	4	0.03
Costa Rican	1	0.01
Guatemalan	2	0.02
Salvadoran	1	0.01
Cuban	1	0.01
Mexican	17	0.13
Puerto Rican	23	0.17
South American:	3	0.02
Argentinean	2	0.02
Colombian	1	0.01
Other Hispanic or Latino	18	0.14
Hungarian	8	0.06
Irish	1,680	12.77
Italian	745	5.66
Lithuanian	59	0.45
Norwegian	104	0.79
Polish	736	5.60
Portuguese	71	0.54
Russian	197	1.50
Scotch-Irish	317	2.41
Scottish	480	3.65
Slavic	7	0.05
Slovak	14	0.11
Swedish	103	0.78
Swiss	37	0.28
Ukrainian	6	0.05
United States or American	1,264	9.61
Welsh	25	0.19
White:	12,961	98.56
Not Hispanic (12,798)	12,907	98.14
Hispanic (47)	54	0.41
Yugoslavian	12	0.09

Concord

Place Type: City
County: Merrimack
Population: 40,687

Ancestry/Race	Number	%
African American/Black:	576	1.42
Not Hispanic (398)	537	1.32
Hispanic (23)	39	0.10
African, sub-Saharan:	98	0.24
African	24	0.06
Ghanian	5	0.01
Nigerian	14	0.03
Sudanese	5	0.01
Ugandan	14	0.03
Other sub-Saharan African	36	0.09
Alaska Native tribes, specified:	1	0.00
Tlingit-Haida (1)	1	0.00
Am. Ind. or Alaska Nat., not spec.	84	0.21
Albanian	177	0.44
American Indian tribes, specified:	217	0.53
Apache (2)	8	0.02
Blackfeet	14	0.03
Cherokee (15)	40	0.10
Cheyenne (1)	4	0.01
Chickasaw (1)	1	0.00
Chippewa	2	0.00
Choctaw (6)	7	0.02
Comanche (3)	3	0.01
Cree	3	0.01
Creek (2)	3	0.01
Crow	4	0.01
Delaware	1	0.00
Iroquois (12)	18	0.04
Latin American Indians (2)	7	0.02
Menominee (2)	2	0.00
Navajo (1)	1	0.00
Osage	1	0.00
Pima	3	0.01
Pueblo	1	0.00
Seminole	1	0.00
Sioux (9)	13	0.03
All other tribes (24)	80	0.20
American Indian tribes, not spec.	23	0.06
Arab:	148	0.36
Arab/Arabic	6	0.01
Egyptian	5	0.01
Lebanese	65	0.16
Syrian	59	0.15
Other Arab	13	0.03

Notes: 1. Figures in the "Number" column do not add up to the total population due to: a) Ancestry/Race overlap — e.g. persons can report being both White and Irish, b) persons of Hispanic origin can report being any race, c) persons reporting two ancestries are counted in both categories. 2. Numbers in parentheses indicate the number of persons reporting this ancestry/race alone, not in combination with any other ancestry/race. 3. Refer to the Explanation of Data in the front of the book for more detailed information.

Ancestry/Race	Number	%
Armenian	82	0.20
Asian:	737	1.81
Cambodian (2)	3	0.01
Chinese, ex. Taiwanese (104)	128	0.31
Filipino (74)	110	0.27
Hmong (1)	3	0.01
Indian (147)	161	0.40
Indonesian (1)	1	0.00
Japanese (45)	59	0.15
Korean (115)	139	0.34
Laotian (5)	5	0.01
Malaysian (1)	1	0.00
Pakistani (5)	7	0.02
Taiwanese (1)	2	0.00
Thai (6)	8	0.02
Vietnamese (35)	42	0.10
Other Asian, specified (31)	34	0.08
Other Asian, not specified (14)	34	0.08
Australian	10	0.02
Austrian	136	0.33
Belgian	30	0.07
Brazilian	56	0.14
British	203	0.50
Canadian	236	0.58
Czech	46	0.11
Czechoslovakian	61	0.15
Danish	99	0.24
Dutch	450	1.11
Eastern European	91	0.22
English	7,982	19.62
European	208	0.51
Finnish	233	0.57
French, except Basque	5,797	14.25
French Canadian	4,150	10.20
German	3,302	8.12
German Russian	7	0.02
Greek	591	1.45
Hawaii Native/Pacific Islander:	26	0.06
Polynesian: (9)	15	0.04
Native Hawaiian (9)	14	0.03
Samoan	1	0.00
Other Pac. Isl., specified	1	0.00
Other Pac. Isl., not spec. (4)	10	0.02
Hispanic or Latino:	591	1.45
Central American:	33	0.08
Costa Rican	7	0.02
Guatemalan	6	0.01
Honduran	7	0.02
Panamanian	6	0.01
Salvadoran	1	0.00
Other Central American	6	0.01
Cuban	28	0.07
Dominican Republic	14	0.03
Mexican	104	0.26
Puerto Rican	208	0.51
South American:	42	0.10
Argentinean	5	0.01
Chilean	5	0.01
Colombian	13	0.03
Ecuadorian	6	0.01
Peruvian	3	0.01
Uruguayan	8	0.02
Venezuelan	2	0.00
Other Hispanic or Latino	162	0.40
Hungarian	93	0.23
Iranian	10	0.02
Irish	7,491	18.41
Israeli	9	0.02
Italian	3,064	7.53
Latvian	18	0.04
Lithuanian	156	0.38
Northern European	19	0.05
Norwegian	284	0.70
Pennsylvania German	20	0.05
Polish	1,201	2.95
Portuguese	280	0.69
Romanian	15	0.04
Russian	360	0.88
Scandinavian	83	0.20
Scotch-Irish	1,163	2.86
Scottish	2,094	5.15
Serbian	10	0.02
Slovak	8	0.02
Swedish	935	2.30
Swiss	112	0.28
Ukrainian	95	0.23
United States or American	2,405	5.91
Welsh	412	1.01
West Indian, excl. Hispanic:	49	0.12
Haitian	20	0.05
Jamaican	16	0.04
Trinidadian and Tobagonian	5	0.01
West Indian	8	0.02
White:	39,342	96.69
Not Hispanic (38,484)	38,896	95.60
Hispanic (379)	446	1.10

Derry

Place Type: Town
County: Rockingham
Population: 34,021

Ancestry/Race	Number	%
African American/Black:	399	1.17
Not Hispanic (287)	375	1.10
Hispanic (18)	24	0.07
African, sub-Saharan:	104	0.31
African	81	0.24
South African	23	0.07
Am. Ind. or Alaska Nat., not spec.	57	0.17
Albanian	8	0.02
Alsatian	9	0.03
American Indian tribes, specified:	121	0.36
Blackfeet (1)	9	0.03
Cherokee (6)	18	0.05
Chickasaw	1	0.00
Chippewa (1)	1	0.00
Choctaw	1	0.00
Cree	1	0.00
Delaware	1	0.00
Iroquois (1)	4	0.01
Kiowa	1	0.00
Latin American Indians (5)	12	0.04
Lumbee (4)	4	0.01
Navajo (1)	2	0.01
Sioux (5)	11	0.03
All other tribes (26)	55	0.16
American Indian tribes, not spec.	12	0.04
Arab:	399	1.17
Arab/Arabic	20	0.06
Lebanese	361	1.06
Syrian	18	0.05
Armenian	71	0.21
Asian:	471	1.38
Cambodian (2)	2	0.01
Chinese, ex. Taiwanese (71)	92	0.27
Filipino (31)	54	0.16
Indian (114)	125	0.37
Indonesian	6	0.02
Japanese (22)	35	0.10
Korean (68)	84	0.25
Laotian	1	0.00
Pakistani (4)	5	0.01
Sri Lankan (1)	2	0.01
Taiwanese (2)	2	0.01
Thai (10)	14	0.04
Vietnamese (26)	35	0.10
Other Asian, specified (1)	1	0.00
Other Asian, not specified (2)	13	0.04
Australian	11	0.03
Austrian	60	0.18
Belgian	42	0.12
Brazilian	7	0.02
British	159	0.47
Canadian	421	1.24
Celtic	8	0.02
Croatian	19	0.06
Czech	57	0.17
Czechoslovakian	7	0.02
Danish	45	0.13
Dutch	102	0.30
Eastern European	33	0.10
English	5,227	15.36
European	68	0.20
Finnish	128	0.38
French, except Basque	5,029	14.78
French Canadian	2,790	8.20
German	3,296	9.69
Greek	435	1.28
Hawaii Native/Pacific Islander:	19	0.06
Micronesian: (1)	1	0.00
Guamanian/Chamorro (1)	1	0.00
Polynesian: (10)	12	0.04
Native Hawaiian (10)	10	0.03
Samoan	2	0.01
Other Pac. Isl., not spec. (5)	6	0.02
Hispanic or Latino:	643	1.89
Central American:	39	0.11
Costa Rican	1	0.00
Guatemalan	17	0.05
Honduran	5	0.01
Nicaraguan	12	0.04
Salvadoran	4	0.01
Cuban	29	0.09
Dominican Republic	51	0.15
Mexican	94	0.28
Puerto Rican	223	0.66
South American:	77	0.23
Argentinean	2	0.01
Chilean	4	0.01
Colombian	30	0.09
Ecuadorian	14	0.04
Peruvian	15	0.04
Uruguayan	1	0.00
Venezuelan	7	0.02
Other South American	4	0.01
Other Hispanic or Latino	130	0.38
Hungarian	95	0.28
Iranian	69	0.20
Irish	8,685	25.53
Italian	5,014	14.74
Latvian	9	0.03
Lithuanian	248	0.73
Norwegian	215	0.63
Pennsylvania German	31	0.09
Polish	1,503	4.42
Portuguese	631	1.85
Romanian	8	0.02
Russian	211	0.62
Scandinavian	9	0.03
Scotch-Irish	892	2.62
Scottish	1,314	3.86
Slavic	20	0.06
Slovak	16	0.05
Swedish	630	1.85
Swiss	36	0.11
Turkish	7	0.02
Ukrainian	143	0.42
United States or American	1,185	3.48
Welsh	85	0.25
West Indian, excl. Hispanic:	40	0.12
Haitian	6	0.02
Jamaican	8	0.02
Trinidadian and Tobagonian	8	0.02
West Indian	18	0.05
White:	33,032	97.09
Not Hispanic (32,292)	32,603	95.83
Hispanic (384)	429	1.26
Yugoslavian	20	0.06

Dover

Place Type: City
County: Strafford
Population: 26,884

Ancestry/Race	Number	%
African American/Black:	414	1.54
Not Hispanic (289)	392	1.46

Notes: 1. Figures in the "Number" column do not add up to the total population due to: a) Ancestry/Race overlap — e.g. persons can report being both White and Irish, b) persons of Hispanic origin can report being any race, c) persons reporting two ancestries are counted in both categories. 2. Numbers in parentheses indicate the number of persons reporting this ancestry/race alone, not in combination with any other ancestry/race. 3. Refer to the Explanation of Data in the front of the book for more detailed information.

Hispanic (12)	22	0.08
African, sub-Saharan:	53	0.20
African	53	0.20
Alaska Native tribes, specified:	12	0.04
Alaska Athabascan (6)	10	0.04
Aleut	1	0.00
Eskimo	1	0.00
Am. Ind. or Alaska Nat., not spec.	71	0.26
Albanian	33	0.12
American Indian tribes, specified:	106	0.39
Apache (2)	5	0.02
Blackfeet (3)	12	0.04
Cherokee (5)	27	0.10
Chippewa (1)	2	0.01
Cree	3	0.01
Iroquois (1)	11	0.04
Latin American Indians	3	0.01
Navajo	2	0.01
Ottawa	1	0.00
Seminole	2	0.01
Sioux	1	0.00
All other tribes (16)	37	0.14
American Indian tribes, not spec.	3	0.01
Arab:	393	1.46
Arab/Arabic	12	0.04
Egyptian	22	0.08
Lebanese	327	1.22
Other Arab	32	0.12
Armenian	49	0.18
Asian:	754	2.80
Cambodian (31)	38	0.14
Chinese, ex. Taiwanese (107)	132	0.49
Filipino (46)	69	0.26
Indian (101)	116	0.43
Indonesian (118)	125	0.46
Japanese (18)	32	0.12
Korean (17)	24	0.09
Laotian (55)	61	0.23
Malaysian (10)	10	0.04
Pakistani	1	0.00
Taiwanese (4)	4	0.01
Thai (24)	32	0.12
Vietnamese (77)	86	0.32
Other Asian, specified (3)	4	0.01
Other Asian, not specified (13)	20	0.07
Australian	6	0.02
Austrian	36	0.13
Belgian	33	0.12
Brazilian	15	0.06
British	208	0.77
Bulgarian	8	0.03
Canadian	253	0.94
Celtic	49	0.18
Croatian	8	0.03
Czech	62	0.23
Czechoslovakian	35	0.13
Danish	58	0.22
Dutch	346	1.29
Eastern European	33	0.12
English	5,041	18.75
European	160	0.60
Finnish	79	0.29
French, except Basque	4,031	14.99
French Canadian	2,270	8.44
German	2,346	8.73
Greek	528	1.96
Hawaii Native/Pacific Islander:	29	0.11
Micronesian: (7)	8	0.03
Guamanian/Chamorro (7)	8	0.03
Polynesian: (6)	8	0.03
Native Hawaiian (4)	5	0.02
Samoan (2)	3	0.01
Other Pac. Isl., specified	1	0.00
Other Pac. Isl., not spec. (2)	12	0.04
Hispanic or Latino:	306	1.14
Central American:	5	0.02
Guatemalan	2	0.00
Honduran	2	0.01
Panamanian	1	0.00
Other Central American	1	0.00
Cuban	20	0.07
Dominican Republic	28	0.10
Mexican	51	0.19
Puerto Rican	86	0.32
South American:	32	0.12
Argentinean	5	0.02
Chilean	1	0.00
Colombian	15	0.06
Ecuadorian	5	0.02
Peruvian	2	0.01
Venezuelan	4	0.01
Other Hispanic or Latino	84	0.31
Hungarian	30	0.11
Icelander	8	0.03
Irish	5,724	21.29
Italian	1,980	7.36
Lithuanian	76	0.28
Northern European	11	0.04
Norwegian	256	0.95
Pennsylvania German	6	0.02
Polish	1,012	3.76
Portuguese	199	0.74
Russian	249	0.93
Scandinavian	43	0.16
Scotch-Irish	716	2.66
Scottish	1,225	4.56
Slavic	7	0.03
Slovak	17	0.06
Swedish	575	2.14
Swiss	22	0.08
Ukrainian	61	0.23
United States or American	1,432	5.33
Welsh	151	0.56
West Indian, excl. Hispanic:	38	0.14
Bahamian	5	0.02
British West Indian	8	0.03
Jamaican	25	0.09
White:	25,756	95.80
Not Hispanic (25,217)	25,554	95.05
Hispanic (179)	202	0.75
Yugoslavian	16	0.06

Durham

Place Type: Town
County: Strafford
Population: 12,664

Ancestry/Race	Number	%
African American/Black:	133	1.05
Not Hispanic (84)	117	0.92
Hispanic (14)	16	0.13
African, sub-Saharan:	10	0.08
Kenyan	10	0.08
Alaska Native tribes, specified:	2	0.02
Eskimo	1	0.01
Tlingit-Haida (1)	1	0.01
Am. Ind. or Alaska Nat., not spec.	26	0.21
Albanian	14	0.11
American Indian tribes, specified:	25	0.20
Blackfeet	2	0.02
Cherokee (1)	4	0.03
Chippewa (2)	2	0.02
Choctaw	1	0.01
Cree	1	0.01
Delaware	1	0.01
Iroquois (1)	3	0.02
Latin American Indians (3)	3	0.02
Seminole (1)	1	0.01
Shoshone (1)	1	0.01
All other tribes (1)	6	0.05
American Indian tribes, not spec.	8	0.06
Arab:	78	0.62
Lebanese	65	0.51
Other Arab	13	0.10
Armenian	64	0.51
Asian:	448	3.54
Bangladeshi (5)	5	0.04
Cambodian (2)	4	0.03
Chinese, ex. Taiwanese (193)	199	1.57
Filipino (10)	15	0.12
Indian (73)	76	0.60
Japanese (15)	24	0.19
Korean (43)	55	0.43
Laotian (9)	9	0.07
Malaysian (9)	9	0.07
Sri Lankan (3)	3	0.02
Taiwanese (2)	3	0.02
Thai (3)	6	0.05
Vietnamese (6)	10	0.08
Other Asian, specified (6)	6	0.05
Other Asian, not specified (11)	24	0.19
Australian	8	0.06
Austrian	64	0.51
British	219	1.73
Canadian	125	0.99
Croatian	7	0.06
Czech	49	0.39
Czechoslovakian	13	0.10
Danish	45	0.36
Dutch	213	1.68
English	2,511	19.83
European	78	0.62
Finnish	85	0.67
French, except Basque	865	6.83
French Canadian	897	7.08
German	1,672	13.20
Greek	104	0.82
Hawaii Native/Pacific Islander:	17	0.13
Micronesian: (8)	8	0.06
Guamanian/Chamorro (8)	8	0.06
Polynesian: (4)	5	0.04
Native Hawaiian (4)	5	0.04
Other Pac. Isl., not spec. (4)	4	0.03
Hispanic or Latino:	157	1.24
Central American:	17	0.13
Costa Rican	4	0.03
Guatemalan	6	0.05
Honduran	2	0.02
Panamanian	4	0.03
Salvadoran	1	0.01
Cuban	10	0.08
Dominican Republic	4	0.03
Mexican	24	0.19
Puerto Rican	24	0.19
South American:	26	0.21
Argentinean	3	0.02
Chilean	2	0.02
Colombian	6	0.05
Ecuadorian	1	0.01
Paraguayan	2	0.02
Peruvian	5	0.04
Uruguayan	2	0.02
Other South American	5	0.04
Other Hispanic or Latino	52	0.41
Hungarian	83	0.66
Irish	2,544	20.09
Israeli	15	0.12
Italian	1,405	11.09
Latvian	18	0.14
Lithuanian	117	0.92
Luxemburger	8	0.06
Norwegian	166	1.31
Polish	658	5.20
Portuguese	154	1.22
Romanian	5	0.04
Russian	173	1.37
Scandinavian	17	0.13
Scotch-Irish	390	3.08
Scottish	519	4.10
Swedish	459	3.62
Swiss	58	0.46
Ukrainian	32	0.25
United States or American	307	2.42
Welsh	133	1.05
West Indian, excl. Hispanic:	30	0.24
Haitian	22	0.17
Trinidadian and Tobagonian	8	0.06
White:	12,094	95.50
Not Hispanic (11,868)	11,986	94.65

Notes: 1. Figures in the "Number" column do not add up to the total population due to: a) Ancestry/Race overlap — e.g. persons can report being both White and Irish, b) persons of Hispanic origin can report being any race, c) persons reporting two ancestries are counted in both categories. 2. Numbers in parentheses indicate the number of persons reporting this ancestry/race alone, not in combination with any other ancestry/race. 3. Refer to the Explanation of Data in the front of the book for more detailed information.

Hispanic (106)	108	0.85

Exeter

Place Type: Town
County: Rockingham
Population: 14,058

Ancestry/Race	Number	%
African American/Black:	101	0.72
Not Hispanic (53)	93	0.66
Hispanic (6)	8	0.06
African, sub-Saharan:	6	0.04
African	6	0.04
Am. Ind. or Alaska Nat., not spec.	17	0.12
American Indian tribes, specified:	43	0.31
Apache	1	0.01
Blackfeet	1	0.01
Cherokee (1)	6	0.04
Chippewa (2)	2	0.01
Creek	3	0.02
Delaware (1)	1	0.01
Iroquois (1)	1	0.01
Navajo (1)	2	0.01
Sioux	6	0.04
All other tribes (9)	20	0.14
American Indian tribes, not spec.	4	0.03
Arab:	59	0.42
Arab/Arabic	25	0.18
Lebanese	29	0.21
Syrian	5	0.04
Armenian	6	0.04
Asian:	187	1.33
Chinese, ex. Taiwanese (35)	43	0.31
Filipino (17)	25	0.18
Indian (19)	19	0.14
Japanese (9)	23	0.16
Korean (31)	40	0.28
Laotian (8)	11	0.08
Taiwanese	1	0.01
Thai (3)	8	0.06
Vietnamese (9)	9	0.06
Other Asian, specified	4	0.03
Other Asian, not specified	4	0.03
Australian	19	0.14
Austrian	128	0.91
Basque	10	0.07
British	122	0.87
Canadian	150	1.07
Celtic	62	0.44
Croatian	9	0.06
Czech	82	0.58
Czechoslovakian	31	0.22
Danish	137	0.97
Dutch	252	1.79
Eastern European	37	0.26
English	3,370	23.97
European	54	0.38
Finnish	53	0.38
French, except Basque	1,762	12.53
French Canadian	1,168	8.31
German	1,409	10.02
Greek	129	0.92
Hawaii Native/Pacific Islander:	12	0.09
Other Pac. Isl., specified	4	0.03
Other Pac. Isl., not spec.	8	0.06
Hispanic or Latino:	122	0.87
Central American:	13	0.09
Guatemalan	7	0.05
Honduran	4	0.03
Nicaraguan	1	0.01
Other Central American	1	0.01
Cuban	4	0.03
Dominican Republic	6	0.04
Mexican	24	0.17
Puerto Rican	36	0.26
South American:	9	0.06
Chilean	2	0.01
Colombian	2	0.01
Ecuadorian	2	0.01
Peruvian	2	0.01
Other South American	1	0.01
Other Hispanic or Latino	30	0.21
Hungarian	22	0.16
Irish	2,684	19.09
Italian	1,266	9.01
Lithuanian	27	0.19
Northern European	13	0.09
Norwegian	153	1.09
Polish	650	4.62
Portuguese	78	0.55
Romanian	9	0.06
Russian	99	0.70
Scandinavian	57	0.41
Scotch-Irish	248	1.76
Scottish	589	4.19
Serbian	9	0.06
Slovak	26	0.18
Swedish	337	2.40
Swiss	22	0.16
Ukrainian	20	0.14
United States or American	524	3.73
Welsh	113	0.80
West Indian, excl. Hispanic:	17	0.12
Jamaican	5	0.04
West Indian	12	0.09
White:	13,786	98.07
Not Hispanic (13,583)	13,702	97.47
Hispanic (79)	84	0.60

Goffstown

Place Type: Town
County: Hillsborough
Population: 16,929

Ancestry/Race	Number	%
African American/Black:	67	0.40
Not Hispanic (43)	62	0.37
Hispanic	5	0.03
Alaska Native tribes, specified:	2	0.01
Eskimo (2)	2	0.01
Am. Ind. or Alaska Nat., not spec.	29	0.17
Albanian	20	0.12
American Indian tribes, specified:	60	0.35
Blackfeet (3)	7	0.04
Cherokee (7)	15	0.09
Chippewa	2	0.01
Iroquois (3)	3	0.02
Latin American Indians	3	0.02
Sioux (1)	1	0.01
All other tribes (15)	29	0.17
Arab:	59	0.35
Lebanese	10	0.06
Moroccan	7	0.04
Syrian	42	0.25
Armenian	20	0.12
Asian:	84	0.50
Cambodian (3)	3	0.02
Chinese, ex. Taiwanese (17)	26	0.15
Filipino (9)	19	0.11
Indian (3)	6	0.04
Japanese (3)	5	0.03
Korean (9)	11	0.06
Vietnamese (6)	9	0.05
Other Asian, not specified (1)	5	0.03
Australian	8	0.05
Austrian	20	0.12
Belgian	69	0.41
British	57	0.34
Canadian	322	1.90
Celtic	8	0.05
Czech	81	0.48
Czechoslovakian	9	0.05
Danish	29	0.17
Dutch	144	0.85
English	2,608	15.41
European	83	0.49
Finnish	26	0.15
French, except Basque	2,696	15.93
French Canadian	3,300	19.49
German	1,542	9.11
Greek	155	0.92
Hawaii Native/Pacific Islander:	10	0.06
Polynesian: (2)	8	0.05
Native Hawaiian (2)	8	0.05
Other Pac. Isl., not spec.	2	0.01
Hispanic or Latino:	141	0.83
Central American:	7	0.04
Guatemalan	2	0.01
Nicaraguan	4	0.02
Salvadoran	1	0.01
Cuban	7	0.04
Dominican Republic	12	0.07
Mexican	20	0.12
Puerto Rican	33	0.19
South American:	27	0.16
Argentinean	4	0.02
Bolivian	1	0.01
Colombian	7	0.04
Ecuadorian	1	0.01
Peruvian	6	0.04
Uruguayan	5	0.03
Venezuelan	2	0.01
Other South American	1	0.01
Other Hispanic or Latino	35	0.21
Hungarian	8	0.05
Iranian	9	0.05
Irish	3,480	20.56
Italian	1,288	7.61
Latvian	8	0.05
Lithuanian	120	0.71
Maltese	16	0.09
Norwegian	209	1.23
Polish	757	4.47
Portuguese	195	1.15
Russian	87	0.51
Scandinavian	6	0.04
Scotch-Irish	279	1.65
Scottish	654	3.86
Slavic	6	0.04
Slovak	15	0.09
Swedish	288	1.70
Swiss	13	0.08
Ukrainian	20	0.12
United States or American	858	5.07
Welsh	90	0.53
West Indian, excl. Hispanic:	6	0.04
Bahamian	6	0.04
White:	16,728	98.81
Not Hispanic (16,534)	16,631	98.24
Hispanic (91)	97	0.57

Hampton

Place Type: Town
County: Rockingham
Population: 14,937

Ancestry/Race	Number	%
African American/Black:	84	0.56
Not Hispanic (53)	72	0.48
Hispanic (6)	12	0.08
African, sub-Saharan:	54	0.36
Cape Verdean	34	0.23
South African	20	0.13
Am. Ind. or Alaska Nat., not spec.	10	0.07
Albanian	4	0.03
Alsatian	9	0.06
American Indian tribes, specified:	50	0.33
Apache	1	0.01
Cherokee (7)	12	0.08
Chippewa (1)	3	0.02
Choctaw	1	0.01
Comanche (1)	1	0.01
Cree	4	0.03
Iroquois (4)	8	0.05
Seminole (1)	1	0.01
Sioux (1)	1	0.01
All other tribes (4)	18	0.12

Notes: 1. Figures in the "Number" column do not add up to the total population due to: a) Ancestry/Race overlap — e.g. persons can report being both White and Irish, b) persons of Hispanic origin can report being any race, c) persons reporting two ancestries are counted in both categories. 2. Numbers in parentheses indicate the number of persons reporting this ancestry/race alone, not in combination with any other ancestry/race. 3. Refer to the Explanation of Data in the front of the book for more detailed information.

Ancestry/Race	Number	%
American Indian tribes, not spec.	4	0.03
Arab:	215	1.44
Egyptian	15	0.10
Lebanese	189	1.27
Palestinian	11	0.07
Armenian	120	0.80
Asian:	155	1.04
Chinese, ex. Taiwanese (44)	47	0.31
Filipino (14)	18	0.12
Indian (13)	13	0.09
Indonesian (1)	1	0.01
Japanese (6)	11	0.07
Korean (26)	30	0.20
Laotian (1)	3	0.02
Malaysian (3)	3	0.02
Pakistani (4)	4	0.03
Taiwanese (1)	2	0.01
Thai (1)	1	0.01
Vietnamese (10)	10	0.07
Other Asian, specified	1	0.01
Other Asian, not specified (4)	11	0.07
Austrian	19	0.13
British	56	0.37
Canadian	123	0.82
Celtic	9	0.06
Czech	7	0.05
Czechoslovakian	20	0.13
Danish	21	0.14
Dutch	137	0.92
English	3,059	20.48
European	26	0.17
Finnish	83	0.56
French, except Basque	1,689	11.31
French Canadian	1,251	8.38
German	1,328	8.89
Greek	228	1.53
Hawaii Native/Pacific Islander:	19	0.13
Micronesian: (3)	3	0.02
Guamanian/Chamorro (3)	3	0.02
Polynesian: (7)	12	0.08
Native Hawaiian (4)	9	0.06
Samoan (3)	3	0.02
Other Pac. Isl., specified	1	0.01
Other Pac. Isl., not spec.	3	0.02
Hispanic or Latino:	135	0.90
Central American:	22	0.15
Guatemalan	3	0.02
Honduran	4	0.03
Nicaraguan	4	0.03
Panamanian	3	0.02
Salvadoran	8	0.05
Cuban	3	0.02
Dominican Republic	9	0.06
Mexican	35	0.23
Puerto Rican	43	0.29
South American:	8	0.05
Colombian	6	0.04
Ecuadorian	2	0.01
Other Hispanic or Latino	15	0.10
Hungarian	53	0.35
Irish	4,142	27.73
Israeli	8	0.05
Italian	1,723	11.54
Latvian	9	0.06
Lithuanian	106	0.71
Norwegian	101	0.68
Polish	670	4.49
Portuguese	176	1.18
Romanian	35	0.23
Russian	96	0.64
Scandinavian	29	0.19
Scotch-Irish	360	2.41
Scottish	729	4.88
Slovak	41	0.27
Swedish	408	2.73
Swiss	68	0.46
Ukrainian	45	0.30
United States or American	569	3.81
Welsh	73	0.49
West Indian, excl. Hispanic:	18	0.12
British West Indian	9	0.06
Jamaican	9	0.06
White:	14,670	98.21
Not Hispanic (14,490)	14,575	97.58
Hispanic (84)	95	0.64

Hanover

Place Type: Town
County: Grafton
Population: 10,850

Ancestry/Race	Number	%
African American/Black:	258	2.38
Not Hispanic (186)	245	2.26
Hispanic (3)	13	0.12
African, sub-Saharan:	47	0.43
African	19	0.18
Cape Verdean	8	0.07
Nigerian	13	0.12
Other sub-Saharan African	7	0.06
Alaska Native tribes, specified:	4	0.04
Aleut	1	0.01
Eskimo (1)	2	0.02
Tlingit-Haida	1	0.01
Am. Ind. or Alaska Nat., not spec.	25	0.23
American Indian tribes, specified:	84	0.77
Apache (1)	2	0.02
Blackfeet (1)	6	0.06
Cherokee (2)	8	0.07
Chickasaw	1	0.01
Chippewa (2)	4	0.04
Choctaw (1)	4	0.04
Comanche	2	0.02
Cree	1	0.01
Creek	1	0.01
Crow (2)	5	0.05
Delaware	1	0.01
Iroquois (1)	8	0.07
Kiowa	1	0.01
Latin American Indians (3)	6	0.06
Lumbee (2)	2	0.02
Navajo (5)	10	0.09
Pueblo (4)	5	0.05
Seminole	1	0.01
Sioux	1	0.01
Yakama (1)	1	0.01
All other tribes (8)	14	0.13
American Indian tribes, not spec.	6	0.06
Arab:	75	0.69
Arab/Arabic	9	0.08
Lebanese	59	0.54
Syrian	7	0.06
Armenian	81	0.75
Asian:	860	7.93
Chinese, ex. Taiwanese (278)	323	2.98
Filipino (5)	18	0.17
Indian (152)	172	1.59
Japanese (56)	80	0.74
Korean (108)	118	1.09
Pakistani (11)	15	0.14
Sri Lankan (2)	2	0.02
Taiwanese (25)	27	0.25
Thai (5)	5	0.05
Vietnamese (8)	9	0.08
Other Asian, specified (6)	7	0.06
Other Asian, not specified (67)	84	0.77
Australian	9	0.08
Austrian	141	1.30
Basque	10	0.09
Belgian	9	0.08
Brazilian	12	0.11
British	203	1.87
Bulgarian	8	0.07
Canadian	95	0.88
Croatian	15	0.14
Czech	65	0.60
Czechoslovakian	26	0.24
Danish	32	0.29
Dutch	272	2.51
Eastern European	77	0.71
English	2,293	21.13
European	199	1.83
Finnish	30	0.28
French, except Basque	306	2.82
French Canadian	187	1.72
German	1,779	16.40
Greek	184	1.70
Guyanese	12	0.11
Hawaii Native/Pacific Islander:	14	0.13
Polynesian: (5)	10	0.09
Native Hawaiian (4)	9	0.08
Samoan (1)	1	0.01
Other Pac. Isl., not spec. (2)	4	0.04
Hispanic or Latino:	276	2.54
Central American:	12	0.11
Costa Rican	3	0.03
Guatemalan	2	0.02
Honduran	1	0.01
Nicaraguan	3	0.03
Salvadoran	1	0.01
Other Central American	2	0.02
Cuban	18	0.17
Dominican Republic	6	0.06
Mexican	56	0.52
Puerto Rican	35	0.32
South American:	62	0.57
Argentinean	15	0.14
Bolivian	1	0.01
Chilean	6	0.06
Colombian	14	0.13
Ecuadorian	5	0.05
Peruvian	14	0.13
Venezuelan	5	0.05
Other South American	2	0.02
Other Hispanic or Latino	87	0.80
Hungarian	92	0.85
Iranian	14	0.13
Irish	1,560	14.38
Israeli	12	0.11
Italian	649	5.98
Latvian	29	0.27
Lithuanian	69	0.64
Northern European	19	0.18
Norwegian	158	1.46
Polish	510	4.70
Portuguese	29	0.27
Romanian	46	0.42
Russian	440	4.06
Scandinavian	20	0.18
Scotch-Irish	190	1.75
Scottish	624	5.75
Serbian	8	0.07
Slovak	12	0.11
Swedish	278	2.56
Swiss	74	0.68
Ukrainian	71	0.65
United States or American	379	3.49
Welsh	130	1.20
West Indian, excl. Hispanic:	31	0.29
Barbadian	6	0.06
Trinidadian and Tobagonian	8	0.07
West Indian	17	0.16
White:	9,739	89.76
Not Hispanic (9,397)	9,563	88.14
Hispanic (149)	176	1.62
Yugoslavian	6	0.06

Hooksett

Place Type: Town
County: Merrimack
Population: 11,721

Ancestry/Race	Number	%
African American/Black:	110	0.94
Not Hispanic (77)	98	0.84
Hispanic (3)	12	0.10
African, sub-Saharan:	73	0.62
African	29	0.25

Notes: 1. Figures in the "Number" column do not add up to the total population due to: a) Ancestry/Race overlap — e.g. persons can report being both White and Irish, b) persons of Hispanic origin can report being any race, c) persons reporting two ancestries are counted in both categories. 2. Numbers in parentheses indicate the number of persons reporting this ancestry/race alone, not in combination with any other ancestry/race. 3. Refer to the Explanation of Data in the front of the book for more detailed information.

Ancestry/Race	Number	%
Nigerian	14	0.12
Other sub-Saharan African	30	0.26
Am. Ind. or Alaska Nat., not spec.	23	0.20
Albanian	11	0.09
American Indian tribes, specified:	24	0.20
Blackfeet (2)	3	0.03
Cherokee (2)	2	0.02
Delaware	1	0.01
Iroquois (2)	2	0.02
Pueblo	1	0.01
Yakama	1	0.01
All other tribes (7)	14	0.12
American Indian tribes, not spec.	4	0.03
Arab:	136	1.16
Egyptian	72	0.61
Lebanese	50	0.43
Syrian	14	0.12
Armenian	32	0.27
Asian:	219	1.87
Chinese, ex. Taiwanese (51)	56	0.48
Filipino (9)	11	0.09
Indian (47)	48	0.41
Indonesian (4)	4	0.03
Japanese (16)	20	0.17
Korean (36)	36	0.31
Malaysian (1)	2	0.02
Pakistani (3)	7	0.06
Thai (12)	15	0.13
Vietnamese (1)	1	0.01
Other Asian, not specified (12)	19	0.16
Austrian	29	0.25
Belgian	23	0.20
British	104	0.89
Canadian	169	1.44
Croatian	23	0.20
Czech	29	0.25
Danish	32	0.27
Dutch	186	1.59
English	1,529	13.04
European	31	0.26
Finnish	22	0.19
French, except Basque	1,826	15.58
French Canadian	1,961	16.73
German	859	7.33
Greek	214	1.83
Hawaii Native/Pacific Islander:	6	0.05
Micronesian: (1)	1	0.01
Other Micronesian (1)	1	0.01
Polynesian:	2	0.02
Native Hawaiian	2	0.02
Other Pac. Isl., not spec. (2)	3	0.03
Hispanic or Latino:	170	1.45
Central American:	4	0.03
Nicaraguan	4	0.03
Cuban	11	0.09
Dominican Republic	6	0.05
Mexican	19	0.16
Puerto Rican	46	0.39
South American:	28	0.24
Chilean	5	0.04
Colombian	11	0.09
Ecuadorian	1	0.01
Peruvian	1	0.01
Uruguayan	8	0.07
Venezuelan	2	0.02
Other Hispanic or Latino	56	0.48
Hungarian	48	0.41
Irish	2,076	17.71
Italian	969	8.27
Latvian	7	0.06
Lithuanian	103	0.88
Northern European	10	0.09
Norwegian	10	0.09
Polish	491	4.19
Portuguese	166	1.42
Romanian	12	0.10
Russian	41	0.35
Scandinavian	22	0.19
Scotch-Irish	272	2.32
Scottish	252	2.15
Swedish	251	2.14
Turkish	40	0.34
Ukrainian	34	0.29
United States or American	764	6.52
Welsh	10	0.09
White:	11,384	97.12
Not Hispanic (11,188)	11,250	95.98
Hispanic (117)	134	1.14
Yugoslavian	33	0.28

Hudson

Place Type: Town
County: Hillsborough
Population: 22,928

Ancestry/Race	Number	%
African American/Black:	266	1.16
Not Hispanic (189)	250	1.09
Hispanic (4)	16	0.07
African, sub-Saharan:	63	0.27
African	32	0.14
Cape Verdean	31	0.14
Am. Ind. or Alaska Nat., not spec.	32	0.14
Albanian	43	0.19
American Indian tribes, specified:	73	0.32
Apache (1)	1	0.00
Blackfeet	6	0.03
Cherokee (2)	12	0.05
Cheyenne	1	0.00
Choctaw	1	0.00
Comanche	2	0.01
Creek (1)	4	0.02
Iroquois (2)	14	0.06
Latin American Indians (3)	3	0.01
Menominee (2)	2	0.01
Ottawa (1)	1	0.00
Sioux	3	0.01
All other tribes (9)	23	0.10
American Indian tribes, not spec.	3	0.01
Arab:	98	0.43
Arab/Arabic	12	0.05
Lebanese	77	0.34
Syrian	9	0.04
Armenian	80	0.35
Asian:	307	1.34
Bangladeshi (1)	1	0.00
Chinese, ex. Taiwanese (58)	71	0.31
Filipino (35)	44	0.19
Indian (59)	62	0.27
Indonesian	2	0.01
Japanese (13)	22	0.10
Korean (27)	32	0.14
Laotian (9)	9	0.04
Taiwanese (1)	1	0.00
Thai (2)	3	0.01
Vietnamese (37)	41	0.18
Other Asian, specified (4)	5	0.02
Other Asian, not specified (6)	14	0.06
Australian	14	0.06
Austrian	78	0.34
Basque	41	0.18
Belgian	11	0.05
Brazilian	13	0.06
British	130	0.57
Canadian	293	1.28
Croatian	9	0.04
Czech	36	0.16
Czechoslovakian	88	0.38
Danish	95	0.41
Dutch	192	0.84
English	3,421	14.92
European	57	0.25
Finnish	97	0.42
French, except Basque	3,688	16.09
French Canadian	3,113	13.58
German	1,692	7.38
Greek	309	1.35
Hawaii Native/Pacific Islander:	36	0.16
Melanesian: (1)	1	0.00
Fijian (1)	1	0.00
Micronesian: (5)	12	0.05
Guamanian/Chamorro (2)	3	0.01
Other Micronesian (3)	9	0.04
Polynesian:	5	0.02
Native Hawaiian	3	0.01
Samoan	2	0.01
Other Pac. Isl., not spec. (7)	18	0.08
Hispanic or Latino:	356	1.55
Central American:	20	0.09
Costa Rican	1	0.00
Guatemalan	3	0.01
Honduran	3	0.01
Nicaraguan	1	0.00
Panamanian	7	0.03
Salvadoran	1	0.00
Other Central American	4	0.02
Cuban	7	0.03
Dominican Republic	18	0.08
Mexican	66	0.29
Puerto Rican	132	0.58
South American:	56	0.24
Argentinean	1	0.00
Colombian	36	0.16
Ecuadorian	9	0.04
Peruvian	2	0.01
Venezuelan	3	0.01
Other South American	5	0.02
Other Hispanic or Latino	57	0.25
Hungarian	121	0.53
Iranian	19	0.08
Irish	5,386	23.49
Italian	2,134	9.31
Latvian	14	0.06
Lithuanian	338	1.47
New Zealander	15	0.07
Northern European	7	0.03
Norwegian	207	0.90
Polish	1,147	5.00
Portuguese	427	1.86
Romanian	17	0.07
Russian	104	0.45
Scandinavian	8	0.03
Scotch-Irish	435	1.90
Scottish	738	3.22
Serbian	8	0.03
Slovak	91	0.40
Slovene	10	0.04
Swedish	283	1.23
Swiss	18	0.08
Ukrainian	63	0.27
United States or American	1,386	6.05
Welsh	82	0.36
West Indian, excl. Hispanic:	34	0.15
Haitian	10	0.04
Jamaican	24	0.10
White:	22,291	97.22
Not Hispanic (21,871)	22,037	96.11
Hispanic (220)	254	1.11

Keene

Place Type: City
County: Cheshire
Population: 22,563

Ancestry/Race	Number	%
African American/Black:	133	0.59
Not Hispanic (81)	119	0.53
Hispanic (8)	14	0.06
African, sub-Saharan:	34	0.15
African	11	0.05
Sudanese	23	0.10
Am. Ind. or Alaska Nat., not spec.	51	0.23
Alsatian	7	0.03
American Indian tribes, specified:	78	0.35
Apache	1	0.00
Blackfeet (2)	15	0.07
Cherokee (7)	15	0.07
Comanche (1)	1	0.00

Notes: 1. Figures in the "Number" column do not add up to the total population due to: a) Ancestry/Race overlap — e.g. persons can report being both White and Irish, b) persons of Hispanic origin can report being any race, c) persons reporting two ancestries are counted in both categories. 2. Numbers in parentheses indicate the number of persons reporting this ancestry/race alone, not in combination with any other ancestry/race. 3. Refer to the Explanation of Data in the front of the book for more detailed information.

Ancestry/Race	Number	%
Cree	2	0.01
Iroquois (3)	7	0.03
Latin American Indians (1)	1	0.00
Navajo (3)	4	0.02
Seminole	2	0.01
Shoshone	2	0.01
Sioux (3)	5	0.02
Ute (1)	1	0.00
All other tribes (7)	22	0.10
American Indian tribes, not spec.	6	0.03
Arab:	95	0.42
Lebanese	56	0.25
Syrian	13	0.06
Other Arab	26	0.12
Armenian	32	0.14
Asian:	212	0.94
Cambodian (13)	13	0.06
Chinese, ex. Taiwanese (45)	54	0.24
Filipino (13)	18	0.08
Indian (24)	32	0.14
Japanese (20)	28	0.12
Korean (15)	24	0.11
Malaysian	4	0.02
Pakistani (5)	5	0.02
Thai (5)	5	0.02
Vietnamese (11)	15	0.07
Other Asian, specified (1)	1	0.00
Other Asian, not specified (1)	13	0.06
Australian	5	0.02
Austrian	48	0.21
British	81	0.36
Canadian	135	0.60
Croatian	22	0.10
Czech	38	0.17
Czechoslovakian	7	0.03
Danish	105	0.47
Dutch	209	0.93
English	3,794	16.82
Estonian	8	0.04
European	155	0.69
Finnish	339	1.50
French, except Basque	2,984	13.23
French Canadian	1,839	8.15
German	2,157	9.56
Greek	292	1.29
Hawaii Native/Pacific Islander:	16	0.07
Polynesian: (4)	4	0.02
Native Hawaiian (4)	4	0.02
Other Pac. Isl., not spec. (3)	12	0.05
Hispanic or Latino:	172	0.76
Central American:	9	0.04
Costa Rican	2	0.01
Guatemalan	1	0.00
Nicaraguan	1	0.00
Panamanian	2	0.01
Salvadoran	3	0.01
Cuban	5	0.02
Dominican Republic	1	0.00
Mexican	41	0.18
Puerto Rican	38	0.17
South American:	16	0.07
Argentinean	2	0.01
Bolivian	1	0.00
Chilean	1	0.00
Colombian	8	0.04
Peruvian	3	0.01
Other South American	1	0.00
Other Hispanic or Latino	62	0.27
Hungarian	103	0.46
Irish	3,749	16.62
Italian	1,938	8.59
Lithuanian	131	0.58
Northern European	19	0.08
Norwegian	120	0.53
Pennsylvania German	21	0.09
Polish	675	2.99
Portuguese	135	0.60
Romanian	38	0.17
Russian	147	0.65
Scandinavian	26	0.12
Scotch-Irish	380	1.68
Scottish	860	3.81
Slavic	11	0.05
Slovak	8	0.04
Slovene	6	0.03
Swedish	538	2.38
Swiss	54	0.24
Ukrainian	67	0.30
United States or American	1,524	6.75
Welsh	266	1.18
White:	22,197	98.38
Not Hispanic (21,916)	22,072	97.82
Hispanic (118)	125	0.55
Yugoslavian	9	0.04

Laconia

Place Type: City
County: Belknap
Population: 16,411

Ancestry/Race	Number	%
African American/Black:	128	0.78
Not Hispanic (82)	119	0.73
Hispanic (8)	9	0.05
Alaska Native tribes, specified:	3	0.02
Alaska Athabascan (2)	2	0.01
Eskimo (1)	1	0.01
Am. Ind. or Alaska Nat., not spec.	60	0.37
American Indian tribes, specified:	100	0.61
Blackfeet (1)	14	0.09
Cherokee (8)	18	0.11
Chippewa	1	0.01
Choctaw (4)	5	0.03
Cree	5	0.03
Iroquois (4)	4	0.02
Latin American Indians (2)	2	0.01
Navajo	1	0.01
Ottawa (1)	1	0.01
Sioux	1	0.01
All other tribes (21)	48	0.29
Arab:	45	0.27
Arab/Arabic	13	0.08
Lebanese	24	0.15
Syrian	8	0.05
Armenian	29	0.18
Asian:	177	1.08
Cambodian (2)	8	0.05
Chinese, ex. Taiwanese (34)	44	0.27
Filipino (12)	20	0.12
Indian (17)	26	0.16
Japanese (5)	11	0.07
Korean (10)	19	0.12
Laotian (18)	23	0.14
Taiwanese	1	0.01
Thai (4)	5	0.03
Vietnamese (14)	14	0.09
Other Asian, not specified	6	0.04
Austrian	17	0.10
Belgian	30	0.18
Brazilian	4	0.02
British	87	0.53
Canadian	173	1.05
Croatian	19	0.12
Czech	47	0.29
Czechoslovakian	19	0.12
Danish	13	0.08
Dutch	87	0.53
English	2,750	16.76
European	81	0.49
Finnish	68	0.41
French, except Basque	2,643	16.11
French Canadian	2,484	15.14
German	1,026	6.25
Greek	273	1.66
Hawaii Native/Pacific Islander:	8	0.05
Micronesian: (3)	4	0.02
Guamanian/Chamorro (2)	3	0.02
Other Micronesian (1)	1	0.01
Polynesian: (1)	3	0.02
Native Hawaiian	1	0.01
Samoan (1)	1	0.01
Other Polynesian	1	0.01
Other Pac. Isl., not spec.	1	0.01
Hispanic or Latino:	162	0.99
Central American:	6	0.04
Guatemalan	1	0.01
Panamanian	4	0.02
Salvadoran	1	0.01
Cuban	4	0.02
Dominican Republic	5	0.03
Mexican	44	0.27
Puerto Rican	67	0.41
South American:	2	0.01
Other South American	2	0.01
Other Hispanic or Latino	34	0.21
Hungarian	12	0.07
Icelander	6	0.04
Irish	2,749	16.75
Italian	955	5.82
Latvian	12	0.07
Lithuanian	83	0.51
New Zealander	25	0.15
Northern European	30	0.18
Norwegian	161	0.98
Polish	376	2.29
Portuguese	190	1.16
Romanian	11	0.07
Russian	65	0.40
Scandinavian	53	0.32
Scotch-Irish	376	2.29
Scottish	631	3.84
Serbian	8	0.05
Swedish	326	1.99
Ukrainian	12	0.07
United States or American	1,190	7.25
Welsh	50	0.30
White:	16,063	97.88
Not Hispanic (15,777)	15,951	97.20
Hispanic (108)	112	0.68
Yugoslavian	77	0.47

Lebanon

Place Type: City
County: Grafton
Population: 12,568

Ancestry/Race	Number	%
African American/Black:	147	1.17
Not Hispanic (99)	134	1.07
Hispanic (5)	13	0.10
African, sub-Saharan:	15	0.12
Nigerian	7	0.06
Other sub-Saharan African	8	0.06
Am. Ind. or Alaska Nat., not spec.	29	0.23
American Indian tribes, specified:	78	0.62
Apache (1)	1	0.01
Blackfeet (2)	2	0.02
Cherokee (1)	11	0.09
Cheyenne (1)	1	0.01
Cree	3	0.02
Delaware	1	0.01
Houma (2)	2	0.02
Iroquois (5)	9	0.07
Kiowa (1)	1	0.01
Latin American Indians (2)	7	0.06
Lumbee (6)	6	0.05
Navajo (2)	2	0.02
Sioux (3)	4	0.03
Ute (2)	2	0.02
Yakama (1)	1	0.01
All other tribes (13)	25	0.20
American Indian tribes, not spec.	7	0.06
Arab:	36	0.29
Iraqi	15	0.12
Lebanese	21	0.17
Armenian	12	0.10
Asian:	393	3.13
Bangladeshi (1)	1	0.01

Notes: 1. Figures in the "Number" column do not add up to the total population due to: a) Ancestry/Race overlap — e.g. persons can report being both White and Irish, b) persons of Hispanic origin can report being any race, c) persons reporting two ancestries are counted in both categories. 2. Numbers in parentheses indicate the number of persons reporting this ancestry/race alone, not in combination with any other ancestry/race. 3. Refer to the Explanation of Data in the front of the book for more detailed information.

Ancestry/Race	Number	%
Cambodian (5)	8	0.06
Chinese, ex. Taiwanese (137)	154	1.23
Filipino (10)	15	0.12
Indian (86)	92	0.73
Japanese (29)	38	0.30
Korean (31)	38	0.30
Laotian (9)	13	0.10
Malaysian	1	0.01
Pakistani (8)	9	0.07
Thai (3)	5	0.04
Vietnamese (11)	12	0.10
Other Asian, not specified (1)	7	0.06
Australian	36	0.29
Austrian	35	0.28
British	77	0.61
Canadian	159	1.27
Czech	21	0.17
Czechoslovakian	7	0.06
Danish	93	0.74
Dutch	104	0.83
English	2,274	18.09
European	210	1.67
Finnish	44	0.35
French, except Basque	1,487	11.83
French Canadian	1,104	8.78
German	1,055	8.39
Greek	97	0.77
Hawaii Native/Pacific Islander:	8	0.06
Micronesian: (1)	3	0.02
Guamanian/Chamorro (1)	3	0.02
Polynesian:	1	0.01
Native Hawaiian	1	0.01
Other Pac. Isl., not spec. (3)	4	0.03
Hispanic or Latino:	206	1.64
Central American:	3	0.02
Costa Rican	1	0.01
Guatemalan	2	0.02
Cuban	7	0.06
Mexican	66	0.53
Puerto Rican	47	0.37
South American:	27	0.21
Argentinean	4	0.03
Colombian	6	0.05
Ecuadorian	5	0.04
Paraguayan	1	0.01
Peruvian	8	0.06
Uruguayan	1	0.01
Other South American	2	0.02
Other Hispanic or Latino	56	0.45
Hungarian	64	0.51
Icelander	18	0.14
Irish	1,858	14.78
Italian	501	3.99
Lithuanian	52	0.41
New Zealander	11	0.09
Norwegian	112	0.89
Polish	295	2.35
Portuguese	98	0.78
Russian	89	0.71
Scandinavian	5	0.04
Scotch-Irish	250	1.99
Scottish	537	4.27
Serbian	19	0.15
Slovak	23	0.18
Swedish	219	1.74
Swiss	69	0.55
Ukrainian	41	0.33
United States or American	706	5.62
Welsh	128	1.02
West Indian, excl. Hispanic:	20	0.16
Haitian	20	0.16
White:	12,003	95.50
Not Hispanic (11,738)	11,855	94.33
Hispanic (124)	148	1.18

Londonderry

Place Type: Town
County: Rockingham
Population: 23,236

Ancestry/Race	Number	%
African American/Black:	184	0.79
Not Hispanic (125)	170	0.73
Hispanic (4)	14	0.06
Alaska Native tribes, specified:	5	0.02
Eskimo (5)	5	0.02
Am. Ind. or Alaska Nat., not spec.	27	0.12
American Indian tribes, specified:	67	0.29
Apache	5	0.02
Blackfeet	5	0.02
Cherokee	7	0.03
Chippewa (1)	1	0.00
Choctaw	1	0.00
Colville (3)	3	0.01
Comanche (1)	1	0.00
Cree	2	0.01
Delaware	7	0.03
Iroquois (3)	7	0.03
Latin American Indians	1	0.00
Navajo	5	0.02
Sioux (3)	9	0.04
Yaqui	1	0.00
All other tribes (5)	12	0.05
American Indian tribes, not spec.	8	0.03
Arab:	143	0.62
Arab/Arabic	6	0.03
Egyptian	35	0.15
Lebanese	59	0.25
Moroccan	6	0.03
Palestinian	3	0.01
Syrian	34	0.15
Armenian	39	0.17
Asian:	339	1.46
Cambodian (3)	3	0.01
Chinese, ex. Taiwanese (85)	101	0.43
Filipino (20)	35	0.15
Hmong (1)	1	0.00
Indian (78)	94	0.40
Indonesian (1)	6	0.03
Japanese (9)	14	0.06
Korean (51)	57	0.25
Pakistani (7)	7	0.03
Taiwanese (4)	4	0.02
Thai (1)	3	0.01
Vietnamese (6)	9	0.04
Other Asian, not specified	5	0.02
Australian	8	0.03
Austrian	119	0.51
Belgian	105	0.45
Brazilian	19	0.08
British	149	0.64
Canadian	243	1.05
Czech	65	0.28
Czechoslovakian	11	0.05
Danish	35	0.15
Dutch	215	0.93
English	4,018	17.29
European	94	0.40
Finnish	85	0.37
French, except Basque	2,882	12.40
French Canadian	1,717	7.39
German	2,201	9.47
Greek	263	1.13
Hawaii Native/Pacific Islander:	10	0.04
Melanesian: (1)	1	0.00
Other Melanesian (1)	1	0.00
Other Pac. Isl., not spec. (5)	9	0.04
Hispanic or Latino:	356	1.53
Central American:	20	0.09
Costa Rican	5	0.02
Guatemalan	5	0.02
Honduran	5	0.02
Nicaraguan	1	0.00
Panamanian	2	0.01
Salvadoran	2	0.01
Cuban	17	0.07
Dominican Republic	16	0.07
Mexican	83	0.36
Puerto Rican	133	0.57
South American:	30	0.13
Chilean	3	0.01
Colombian	11	0.05
Peruvian	2	0.01
Venezuelan	9	0.04
Other South American	5	0.02
Other Hispanic or Latino	57	0.25
Hungarian	115	0.49
Irish	6,025	25.93
Italian	3,976	17.11
Latvian	18	0.08
Lithuanian	197	0.85
Luxemburger	9	0.04
Norwegian	226	0.97
Polish	1,195	5.14
Portuguese	256	1.10
Romanian	6	0.03
Russian	220	0.95
Scotch-Irish	698	3.00
Scottish	726	3.12
Serbian	9	0.04
Slavic	7	0.03
Slovak	26	0.11
Slovene	6	0.03
Swedish	515	2.22
Swiss	43	0.19
Ukrainian	91	0.39
United States or American	928	3.99
Welsh	155	0.67
West Indian, excl. Hispanic:	76	0.33
Haitian	47	0.20
Jamaican	29	0.12
White:	22,706	97.72
Not Hispanic (22,268)	22,428	96.52
Hispanic (253)	278	1.20

Manchester

Place Type: City
County: Hillsborough
Population: 107,006

Ancestry/Race	Number	%
Afghan	9	0.01
African American/Black:	2,820	2.64
Not Hispanic (2,045)	2,542	2.38
Hispanic (201)	278	0.26
African, sub-Saharan:	544	0.51
African	193	0.18
Cape Verdean	32	0.03
Kenyan	19	0.02
Nigerian	55	0.05
South African	14	0.01
Sudanese	118	0.11
Other sub-Saharan African	113	0.11
Alaska Native tribes, specified:	9	0.01
Alaska Athabascan (1)	1	0.00
Aleut (3)	3	0.00
Eskimo (1)	3	0.00
Tlingit-Haida (2)	2	0.00
Am. Ind. or Alaska Nat., not spec.	300	0.28
Albanian	436	0.41
Alsatian	10	0.01
American Indian tribes, specified:	457	0.43
Apache (8)	18	0.02
Blackfeet (19)	56	0.05
Cherokee (21)	89	0.08
Cheyenne	2	0.00
Chickasaw (2)	2	0.00
Chippewa (11)	13	0.01
Choctaw (5)	11	0.01
Comanche	2	0.00
Cree	4	0.00
Creek	1	0.00
Delaware	1	0.00

Notes: 1. Figures in the "Number" column do not add up to the total population due to: a) Ancestry/Race overlap — e.g. persons can report being both White and Irish, b) persons of Hispanic origin can report being any race, c) persons reporting two ancestries are counted in both categories. 2. Numbers in parentheses indicate the number of persons reporting this ancestry/race alone, not in combination with any other ancestry/race. 3. Refer to the Explanation of Data in the front of the book for more detailed information.

Ancestry/Race	Number	%
Iroquois (5)	14	0.01
Latin American Indians (17)	17	0.02
Lumbee (1)	2	0.00
Navajo (1)	2	0.00
Ottawa (1)	3	0.00
Pima (2)	2	0.00
Potawatomi	2	0.00
Pueblo (1)	5	0.00
Puget Sound Salish	2	0.00
Seminole (1)	2	0.00
Sioux (9)	23	0.02
All other tribes (83)	184	0.17
American Indian tribes, not spec.	46	0.04
Arab:	862	0.81
Arab/Arabic	32	0.03
Egyptian	10	0.01
Iraqi	61	0.06
Lebanese	424	0.40
Moroccan	18	0.02
Palestinian	54	0.05
Syrian	117	0.11
Other Arab	146	0.14
Armenian	185	0.17
Asian:	2,924	2.73
Bangladeshi (9)	13	0.01
Cambodian (53)	64	0.06
Chinese, ex. Taiwanese (522)	604	0.56
Filipino (131)	191	0.18
Indian (376)	437	0.41
Indonesian (26)	32	0.03
Japanese (67)	106	0.10
Korean (269)	304	0.28
Laotian (16)	19	0.02
Malaysian (2)	7	0.01
Pakistani (54)	61	0.06
Sri Lankan (1)	1	0.00
Taiwanese (17)	20	0.02
Thai (16)	27	0.03
Vietnamese (804)	873	0.82
Other Asian, specified (19)	26	0.02
Other Asian, not specified (48)	139	0.13
Assyrian/Chaldean/Syriac	13	0.01
Australian	20	0.02
Austrian	143	0.13
Belgian	190	0.18
Brazilian	99	0.09
British	360	0.34
Bulgarian	37	0.03
Canadian	1,570	1.47
Celtic	33	0.03
Croatian	18	0.02
Czech	147	0.14
Czechoslovakian	106	0.10
Danish	169	0.16
Dutch	735	0.69
Eastern European	46	0.04
English	10,675	9.98
Estonian	27	0.03
European	158	0.15
Finnish	252	0.24
French, except Basque	19,235	17.98
French Canadian	17,681	16.52
German	6,764	6.32
Greek	3,066	2.87
Hawaii Native/Pacific Islander:	102	0.10
Micronesian: (12)	23	0.02
Guamanian/Chamorro (11)	22	0.02
Other Micronesian (1)	1	0.00
Polynesian: (21)	47	0.04
Native Hawaiian (10)	33	0.03
Samoan (9)	12	0.01
Other Polynesian (2)	2	0.00
Other Pac. Isl., specified	6	0.01
Other Pac. Isl., not spec. (5)	26	0.02
Hispanic or Latino:	4,944	4.62
Central American:	195	0.18
Costa Rican	11	0.01
Guatemalan	11	0.01
Honduran	42	0.04
Nicaraguan	7	0.01
Panamanian	19	0.02
Salvadoran	83	0.08
Other Central American	22	0.02
Cuban	78	0.07
Dominican Republic	367	0.34
Mexican	1,220	1.14
Puerto Rican	1,811	1.69
South American:	392	0.37
Argentinean	12	0.01
Chilean	5	0.00
Colombian	172	0.16
Ecuadorian	17	0.02
Peruvian	27	0.03
Uruguayan	121	0.11
Venezuelan	13	0.01
Other South American	25	0.02
Other Hispanic or Latino	881	0.82
Hungarian	276	0.26
Icelander	10	0.01
Iranian	8	0.01
Irish	19,368	18.10
Israeli	8	0.01
Italian	6,596	6.16
Latvian	8	0.01
Lithuanian	579	0.54
Luxemburger	8	0.01
Macedonian	10	0.01
New Zealander	23	0.02
Northern European	13	0.01
Norwegian	515	0.48
Pennsylvania German	29	0.03
Polish	5,172	4.83
Portuguese	1,180	1.10
Romanian	312	0.29
Russian	910	0.85
Scandinavian	108	0.10
Scotch-Irish	1,833	1.71
Scottish	3,088	2.89
Serbian	8	0.01
Slavic	22	0.02
Slovak	84	0.08
Slovene	12	0.01
Swedish	1,619	1.51
Swiss	130	0.12
Turkish	87	0.08
Ukrainian	578	0.54
United States or American	5,104	4.77
Welsh	357	0.33
West Indian, excl. Hispanic:	583	0.54
British West Indian	15	0.01
Haitian	399	0.37
Jamaican	139	0.13
West Indian	30	0.03
White:	99,784	93.25
Not Hispanic (95,581)	96,903	90.56
Hispanic (2,597)	2,881	2.69
Yugoslavian	818	0.76

Merrimack

Place Type: Town
County: Hillsborough
Population: 25,119

Ancestry/Race	Number	%
African American/Black:	235	0.94
Not Hispanic (181)	226	0.90
Hispanic (3)	9	0.04
African, sub-Saharan:	49	0.20
African	16	0.06
Nigerian	33	0.13
Am. Ind. or Alaska Nat., not spec.	19	0.08
Albanian	22	0.09
American Indian tribes, specified:	70	0.28
Apache	2	0.01
Blackfeet	1	0.00
Cherokee (7)	15	0.06
Chippewa (2)	3	0.01
Choctaw (1)	3	0.01
Crow	1	0.00
Iroquois (4)	4	0.02
Kiowa (2)	2	0.01
Latin American Indians (2)	2	0.01
Navajo (5)	5	0.02
Pueblo (1)	1	0.00
Puget Sound Salish	1	0.00
Sioux (3)	7	0.03
All other tribes (7)	23	0.09
American Indian tribes, not spec.	1	0.00
Arab:	75	0.30
Arab/Arabic	7	0.03
Lebanese	36	0.14
Moroccan	25	0.10
Syrian	7	0.03
Armenian	117	0.47
Asian:	464	1.85
Chinese, ex. Taiwanese (99)	125	0.50
Filipino (28)	44	0.18
Hmong (11)	11	0.04
Indian (111)	121	0.48
Indonesian (1)	1	0.00
Japanese (32)	47	0.19
Korean (39)	54	0.21
Malaysian	1	0.00
Pakistani	1	0.00
Sri Lankan (8)	8	0.03
Taiwanese (8)	9	0.04
Thai (6)	7	0.03
Vietnamese (16)	16	0.06
Other Asian, specified	3	0.01
Other Asian, not specified (13)	16	0.06
Austrian	72	0.29
Belgian	20	0.08
Brazilian	33	0.13
British	7	0.03
Canadian	442	1.76
Czech	71	0.28
Czechoslovakian	70	0.28
Danish	37	0.15
Dutch	342	1.36
Eastern European	16	0.06
English	4,083	16.25
European	138	0.55
Finnish	74	0.29
French, except Basque	3,481	13.86
French Canadian	2,982	11.87
German	2,894	11.52
Greek	408	1.62
Hawaii Native/Pacific Islander:	15	0.06
Polynesian: (9)	11	0.04
Native Hawaiian (8)	10	0.04
Samoan (1)	1	0.00
Other Pac. Isl., not spec. (1)	4	0.02
Hispanic or Latino:	272	1.08
Central American:	9	0.04
Guatemalan	3	0.01
Honduran	4	0.02
Panamanian	1	0.00
Other Central American	1	0.00
Cuban	20	0.08
Dominican Republic	17	0.07
Mexican	68	0.27
Puerto Rican	66	0.26
South American:	31	0.12
Argentinean	7	0.03
Colombian	19	0.08
Ecuadorian	1	0.00
Peruvian	2	0.01
Uruguayan	1	0.00
Venezuelan	1	0.00
Other Hispanic or Latino	61	0.24
Hungarian	133	0.53
Irish	4,974	19.80
Israeli	9	0.04
Italian	2,874	11.44
Latvian	5	0.02
Lithuanian	298	1.19
Norwegian	193	0.77
Polish	1,328	5.29
Portuguese	419	1.67

Notes: 1. Figures in the "Number" column do not add up to the total population due to: a) Ancestry/Race overlap — e.g. persons can report being both White and Irish, b) persons of Hispanic origin can report being any race, c) persons reporting two ancestries are counted in both categories. 2. Numbers in parentheses indicate the number of persons reporting this ancestry/race alone, not in combination with any other ancestry/race. 3. Refer to the Explanation of Data in the front of the book for more detailed information.

Ancestry/Race	Number	%
Romanian	9	0.04
Russian	173	0.69
Scandinavian	54	0.21
Scotch-Irish	805	3.20
Scottish	1,184	4.71
Slavic	23	0.09
Slovak	18	0.07
Swedish	455	1.81
Swiss	30	0.12
Ukrainian	63	0.25
United States or American	1,051	4.18
Welsh	162	0.64
West Indian, excl. Hispanic:	31	0.12
Haitian	11	0.04
Jamaican	20	0.08
White:	24,434	97.27
Not Hispanic (24,035)	24,194	96.32
Hispanic (225)	240	0.96

Milford

Place Type: Town
County: Hillsborough
Population: 13,535

Ancestry/Race	Number	%
African American/Black:	166	1.23
Not Hispanic (115)	159	1.17
Hispanic (7)	7	0.05
African, sub-Saharan:	43	0.32
African	43	0.32
Am. Ind. or Alaska Nat., not spec.	17	0.13
Albanian	9	0.07
American Indian tribes, specified:	39	0.29
Apache (1)	2	0.01
Cherokee (1)	1	0.01
Chippewa (1)	1	0.01
Cree	3	0.02
Creek	1	0.01
Iroquois (2)	8	0.06
Latin American Indians (1)	1	0.01
Seminole	4	0.03
Sioux (2)	4	0.03
All other tribes (8)	14	0.10
American Indian tribes, not spec.	10	0.07
Arab:	34	0.25
Egyptian	25	0.18
Lebanese	9	0.07
Armenian	8	0.06
Asian:	159	1.17
Bangladeshi (1)	1	0.01
Cambodian (12)	12	0.09
Chinese, ex. Taiwanese (22)	31	0.23
Filipino (15)	22	0.16
Indian (21)	22	0.16
Indonesian (1)	2	0.01
Japanese (23)	30	0.22
Korean (10)	14	0.10
Laotian (1)	1	0.01
Pakistani (6)	8	0.06
Taiwanese	1	0.01
Thai (4)	4	0.03
Vietnamese (3)	5	0.04
Other Asian, specified (1)	1	0.01
Other Asian, not specified (4)	5	0.04
Austrian	44	0.33
Basque	23	0.17
Belgian	8	0.06
Brazilian	36	0.27
British	61	0.45
Canadian	104	0.77
Celtic	11	0.08
Danish	72	0.53
Dutch	124	0.92
Eastern European	22	0.16
English	2,359	17.43
Estonian	21	0.16
Finnish	169	1.25
French, except Basque	2,009	14.84
French Canadian	1,165	8.61
German	1,466	10.83
Greek	55	0.41
Hawaii Native/Pacific Islander:	14	0.10
Micronesian:	2	0.01
Guamanian/Chamorro	2	0.01
Polynesian: (1)	5	0.04
Native Hawaiian (1)	5	0.04
Other Pac. Isl., not spec.	7	0.05
Hispanic or Latino:	158	1.17
Central American:	15	0.11
Costa Rican	1	0.01
Guatemalan	2	0.01
Honduran	6	0.04
Panamanian	2	0.01
Salvadoran	4	0.03
Cuban	11	0.08
Dominican Republic	4	0.03
Mexican	26	0.19
Puerto Rican	56	0.41
South American:	16	0.12
Argentinean	4	0.03
Chilean	1	0.01
Colombian	5	0.04
Ecuadorian	3	0.02
Peruvian	2	0.01
Venezuelan	1	0.01
Other Hispanic or Latino	30	0.22
Hungarian	18	0.13
Icelander	6	0.04
Irish	2,501	18.48
Italian	1,305	9.64
Lithuanian	62	0.46
Norwegian	233	1.72
Polish	353	2.61
Portuguese	143	1.06
Romanian	22	0.16
Russian	45	0.33
Scandinavian	47	0.35
Scotch-Irish	296	2.19
Scottish	609	4.50
Slovak	28	0.21
Swedish	332	2.45
Swiss	9	0.07
Ukrainian	85	0.63
United States or American	797	5.89
Welsh	84	0.62
West Indian, excl. Hispanic:	78	0.58
Dutch West Indian	5	0.04
Jamaican	48	0.35
West Indian	25	0.18
White:	13,234	97.78
Not Hispanic (12,986)	13,112	96.87
Hispanic (110)	122	0.90
Yugoslavian	51	0.38

Nashua

Place Type: City
County: Hillsborough
Population: 86,605

Ancestry/Race	Number	%
Acadian/Cajun	11	0.01
African American/Black:	2,131	2.46
Not Hispanic (1,571)	1,872	2.16
Hispanic (169)	259	0.30
African, sub-Saharan:	380	0.44
African	231	0.27
Cape Verdean	59	0.07
Ghanian	8	0.01
Kenyan	48	0.06
Nigerian	10	0.01
Sierra Leonean	13	0.02
South African	11	0.01
Alaska Native tribes, specified:	10	0.01
Aleut	1	0.00
Eskimo (5)	9	0.01
Alaska Native tribes, not specified	4	0.00
Am. Ind. or Alaska Nat., not spec.	179	0.21
Albanian	25	0.03
Alsatian	7	0.01
American Indian tribes, specified:	324	0.37
Apache (3)	5	0.01
Blackfeet (16)	31	0.04
Cherokee (24)	64	0.07
Cheyenne (1)	1	0.00
Chickasaw (1)	1	0.00
Chippewa (6)	7	0.01
Choctaw (2)	6	0.01
Colville (1)	1	0.00
Comanche	1	0.00
Cree (2)	8	0.01
Creek (1)	3	0.00
Crow (2)	6	0.01
Iroquois (11)	22	0.03
Latin American Indians (3)	10	0.01
Lumbee (3)	5	0.01
Menominee	1	0.00
Navajo (2)	2	0.00
Osage (1)	1	0.00
Potawatomi (1)	1	0.00
Pueblo (9)	11	0.01
Seminole	6	0.01
Sioux (17)	22	0.03
Yaqui (2)	3	0.00
All other tribes (62)	106	0.12
American Indian tribes, not spec.	27	0.03
Arab:	501	0.58
Arab/Arabic	5	0.01
Egyptian	69	0.08
Lebanese	295	0.34
Moroccan	19	0.02
Syrian	61	0.07
Other Arab	52	0.06
Armenian	350	0.40
Asian:	3,733	4.31
Bangladeshi (8)	8	0.01
Cambodian (22)	24	0.03
Chinese, ex. Taiwanese (838)	906	1.05
Filipino (171)	234	0.27
Indian (1,506)	1,558	1.80
Indonesian (11)	16	0.02
Japanese (78)	112	0.13
Korean (197)	228	0.26
Laotian (10)	23	0.03
Malaysian (5)	8	0.01
Pakistani (60)	75	0.09
Sri Lankan (2)	4	0.00
Taiwanese (36)	43	0.05
Thai (46)	62	0.07
Vietnamese (287)	309	0.36
Other Asian, specified (15)	20	0.02
Other Asian, not specified (45)	103	0.12
Assyrian/Chaldean/Syriac	7	0.01
Australian	9	0.01
Austrian	268	0.31
Belgian	144	0.17
Brazilian	315	0.36
British	540	0.62
Bulgarian	12	0.01
Canadian	980	1.13
Celtic	63	0.07
Croatian	75	0.09
Cypriot	25	0.03
Czech	148	0.17
Czechoslovakian	98	0.11
Danish	229	0.26
Dutch	774	0.89
Eastern European	37	0.04
English	10,836	12.51
Estonian	7	0.01
European	290	0.33
Finnish	213	0.25
French, except Basque	11,651	13.45
French Canadian	11,038	12.75
German	6,845	7.90
Greek	1,422	1.64
Guyanese	34	0.04
Hawaii Native/Pacific Islander:	77	0.09
Micronesian: (5)	14	0.02

Notes: 1. Figures in the "Number" column do not add up to the total population due to: a) Ancestry/Race overlap — e.g. persons can report being both White and Irish, b) persons of Hispanic origin can report being any race, c) persons reporting two ancestries are counted in both categories. 2. Numbers in parentheses indicate the number of persons reporting this ancestry/race alone, not in combination with any other ancestry/race. 3. Refer to the Explanation of Data in the front of the book for more detailed information.

Ancestry/Race	Number	%
Guamanian/Chamorro (5)	12	0.01
Other Micronesian	2	0.00
Polynesian: (11)	21	0.02
Native Hawaiian (9)	18	0.02
Samoan (2)	3	0.00
Other Pac. Isl., specified	3	0.00
Other Pac. Isl., not spec. (13)	39	0.05
Hispanic or Latino:	5,388	6.22
Central American:	170	0.20
Costa Rican	5	0.01
Guatemalan	21	0.02
Honduran	38	0.04
Panamanian	24	0.03
Salvadoran	80	0.09
Other Central American	2	0.00
Cuban	98	0.11
Dominican Republic	624	0.72
Mexican	1,306	1.51
Puerto Rican	1,468	1.70
South American:	591	0.68
Argentinean	6	0.01
Bolivian	15	0.02
Chilean	6	0.01
Colombian	396	0.46
Ecuadorian	76	0.09
Peruvian	31	0.04
Uruguayan	3	0.00
Venezuelan	35	0.04
Other South American	23	0.03
Other Hispanic or Latino	1,131	1.31
Hungarian	256	0.30
Icelander	6	0.01
Iranian	70	0.08
Irish	17,958	20.74
Israeli	41	0.05
Italian	7,796	9.00
Latvian	23	0.03
Lithuanian	812	0.94
Maltese	14	0.02
New Zealander	6	0.01
Northern European	29	0.03
Norwegian	549	0.63
Pennsylvania German	19	0.02
Polish	3,978	4.59
Portuguese	1,365	1.58
Romanian	140	0.16
Russian	950	1.10
Scandinavian	72	0.08
Scotch-Irish	1,539	1.78
Scottish	2,298	2.65
Serbian	13	0.02
Slavic	20	0.02
Slovak	95	0.11
Slovene	7	0.01
Swedish	1,123	1.30
Swiss	264	0.30
Turkish	39	0.05
Ukrainian	206	0.24
United States or American	4,120	4.76
Welsh	476	0.55
West Indian, excl. Hispanic:	224	0.26
Barbadian	31	0.04
Haitian	72	0.08
Jamaican	98	0.11
West Indian	23	0.03
White:	78,393	90.52
Not Hispanic (74,907)	75,716	87.43
Hispanic (2,384)	2,677	3.09
Yugoslavian	44	0.05

Pelham

Place Type: Town
County: Hillsborough
Population: 10,914

Ancestry/Race	Number	%
African American/Black:	62	0.57
Not Hispanic (48)	62	0.57
Am. Ind. or Alaska Nat., not spec.	23	0.21
American Indian tribes, specified:	27	0.25
Blackfeet (4)	4	0.04
Cherokee (2)	4	0.04
Choctaw	1	0.01
Latin American Indians (2)	8	0.07
Yaqui (1)	1	0.01
All other tribes (7)	9	0.08
American Indian tribes, not spec.	9	0.08
Arab:	67	0.61
Arab/Arabic	6	0.05
Lebanese	61	0.56
Armenian	54	0.49
Asian:	151	1.38
Cambodian	6	0.05
Chinese, ex. Taiwanese (6)	20	0.18
Filipino (17)	29	0.27
Indian (49)	51	0.47
Japanese (5)	10	0.09
Korean (4)	5	0.05
Thai (2)	3	0.03
Vietnamese (23)	23	0.21
Other Asian, not specified (1)	4	0.04
Belgian	22	0.20
Brazilian	46	0.42
Canadian	109	1.00
Croatian	28	0.26
Czechoslovakian	15	0.14
Danish	8	0.07
Dutch	57	0.52
English	1,520	13.93
European	32	0.29
Finnish	44	0.40
French, except Basque	2,271	20.81
French Canadian	1,374	12.59
German	750	6.87
Greek	203	1.86
Hispanic or Latino:	105	0.96
Central American:	3	0.03
Guatemalan	1	0.01
Salvadoran	2	0.02
Cuban	6	0.05
Dominican Republic	4	0.04
Mexican	17	0.16
Puerto Rican	41	0.38
South American:	8	0.07
Colombian	6	0.05
Ecuadorian	1	0.01
Paraguayan	1	0.01
Other Hispanic or Latino	26	0.24
Hungarian	57	0.52
Iranian	7	0.06
Irish	2,955	27.08
Italian	1,445	13.24
Lithuanian	144	1.32
Northern European	13	0.12
Norwegian	38	0.35
Polish	662	6.07
Portuguese	309	2.83
Romanian	17	0.16
Russian	94	0.86
Scotch-Irish	212	1.94
Scottish	387	3.55
Slavic	15	0.14
Slovak	21	0.19
Swedish	105	0.96
Swiss	4	0.04
Ukrainian	21	0.19
United States or American	380	3.48
Welsh	23	0.21
West Indian, excl. Hispanic:	7	0.06
Haitian	7	0.06
White:	10,689	97.94
Not Hispanic (10,544)	10,605	97.17
Hispanic (80)	84	0.77

Portsmouth

Place Type: City
County: Rockingham
Population: 20,784

Ancestry/Race	Number	%
Acadian/Cajun	12	0.06
African American/Black:	554	2.67
Not Hispanic (416)	520	2.50
Hispanic (26)	34	0.16
African, sub-Saharan:	67	0.32
African	49	0.24
Cape Verdean	12	0.06
South African	6	0.03
Alaska Native tribes, specified:	1	0.00
Eskimo	1	0.00
Am. Ind. or Alaska Nat., not spec.	35	0.17
Albanian	17	0.08
American Indian tribes, specified:	82	0.39
Apache (1)	2	0.01
Blackfeet (2)	8	0.04
Cherokee (9)	19	0.09
Cheyenne	1	0.00
Chippewa	2	0.01
Choctaw (2)	2	0.01
Comanche	1	0.00
Delaware (1)	2	0.01
Iroquois (3)	9	0.04
Latin American Indians (3)	5	0.02
Navajo (2)	2	0.01
Pueblo	1	0.00
Sioux	1	0.00
All other tribes (7)	27	0.13
American Indian tribes, not spec.	9	0.04
Arab:	160	0.77
Arab/Arabic	14	0.07
Egyptian	35	0.17
Lebanese	88	0.42
Syrian	23	0.11
Armenian	24	0.12
Asian:	617	2.97
Cambodian (3)	4	0.02
Chinese, ex. Taiwanese (112)	135	0.65
Filipino (24)	45	0.22
Indian (141)	150	0.72
Indonesian (35)	41	0.20
Japanese (22)	35	0.17
Korean (42)	59	0.28
Laotian (20)	22	0.11
Taiwanese (1)	1	0.00
Thai (19)	22	0.11
Vietnamese (63)	75	0.36
Other Asian, specified (1)	7	0.03
Other Asian, not specified (15)	21	0.10
Assyrian/Chaldean/Syriac	5	0.02
Austrian	49	0.24
Belgian	35	0.17
Brazilian	7	0.03
British	203	0.98
Canadian	236	1.14
Celtic	36	0.17
Croatian	22	0.11
Czech	29	0.14
Czechoslovakian	48	0.23
Danish	53	0.25
Dutch	260	1.25
Eastern European	14	0.07
English	4,018	19.33
Estonian	11	0.05
European	91	0.44
Finnish	107	0.51
French, except Basque	1,763	8.48
French Canadian	1,220	5.87
German	2,076	9.99
Greek	371	1.78
Hawaii Native/Pacific Islander:	19	0.09
Micronesian:	1	0.00
Other Micronesian	1	0.00
Polynesian: (4)	6	0.03

Notes: 1. Figures in the "Number" column do not add up to the total population due to: a) Ancestry/Race overlap — e.g. persons can report being both White and Irish, b) persons of Hispanic origin can report being any race, c) persons reporting two ancestries are counted in both categories. 2. Numbers in parentheses indicate the number of persons reporting this ancestry/race alone, not in combination with any other ancestry/race. 3. Refer to the Explanation of Data in the front of the book for more detailed information.

Native Hawaiian	1	0.00
Samoan (4)	4	0.02
Other Polynesian	1	0.00
Other Pac. Isl., specified	1	0.00
Other Pac. Isl., not spec. (1)	11	0.05
Hispanic or Latino:	280	1.35
Central American:	13	0.06
Honduran	7	0.03
Nicaraguan	4	0.02
Other Central American	2	0.01
Cuban	22	0.11
Dominican Republic	13	0.06
Mexican	48	0.23
Puerto Rican	88	0.42
South American:	30	0.14
Argentinean	4	0.02
Bolivian	1	0.00
Chilean	6	0.03
Colombian	8	0.04
Ecuadorian	3	0.01
Peruvian	3	0.01
Venezuelan	2	0.01
Other South American	3	0.01
Other Hispanic or Latino	66	0.32
Hungarian	114	0.55
Irish	4,479	21.55
Italian	1,941	9.34
Latvian	7	0.03
Lithuanian	178	0.86
Northern European	27	0.13
Norwegian	158	0.76
Pennsylvania German	16	0.08
Polish	788	3.79
Portuguese	207	1.00
Romanian	19	0.09
Russian	289	1.39
Scandinavian	51	0.25
Scotch-Irish	465	2.24
Scottish	1,040	5.00
Slovak	6	0.03
Slovene	8	0.04
Swedish	394	1.90
Swiss	112	0.54
Turkish	8	0.04
Ukrainian	60	0.29
United States or American	995	4.79
Welsh	194	0.93
West Indian, excl. Hispanic:	22	0.11
Haitian	11	0.05
Jamaican	6	0.03
Trinidadian and Tobagonian	5	0.02
White:	19,683	94.70
Not Hispanic (19,263)	19,488	93.76
Hispanic (180)	195	0.94
Yugoslavian	18	0.09

Rochester

Place Type: City
County: Strafford
Population: 28,461

Ancestry/Race	Number	%
Acadian/Cajun	6	0.02
African American/Black:	215	0.76
Not Hispanic (140)	202	0.71
Hispanic (9)	13	0.05
African, sub-Saharan:	10	0.04
African	10	0.04
Am. Ind. or Alaska Nat., not spec.	75	0.26
American Indian tribes, specified:	93	0.33
Apache	1	0.00
Blackfeet (1)	4	0.01
Cherokee (2)	23	0.08
Cheyenne (1)	1	0.00
Chippewa	1	0.00
Choctaw (1)	2	0.01
Cree	2	0.01
Creek (1)	1	0.00
Iroquois (6)	9	0.03
Latin American Indians (3)	5	0.02
Navajo	1	0.00
Osage	1	0.00
All other tribes (22)	42	0.15
American Indian tribes, not spec.	5	0.02
Arab:	102	0.36
Arab/Arabic	8	0.03
Egyptian	4	0.01
Lebanese	85	0.30
Syrian	5	0.02
Armenian	14	0.05
Asian:	335	1.18
Cambodian (12)	12	0.04
Chinese, ex. Taiwanese (46)	61	0.21
Filipino (22)	38	0.13
Indian (35)	42	0.15
Indonesian (50)	57	0.20
Japanese (11)	28	0.10
Korean (22)	31	0.11
Laotian	5	0.02
Malaysian (2)	2	0.01
Thai (11)	12	0.04
Vietnamese (13)	18	0.06
Other Asian, specified (3)	6	0.02
Other Asian, not specified (19)	23	0.08
Australian	13	0.05
Austrian	29	0.10
Belgian	21	0.07
Brazilian	15	0.05
British	120	0.42
Canadian	255	0.90
Croatian	5	0.02
Czech	38	0.13
Czechoslovakian	5	0.02
Danish	91	0.32
Dutch	285	1.00
Eastern European	12	0.04
English	5,635	19.80
European	64	0.22
Finnish	52	0.18
French, except Basque	5,586	19.63
French Canadian	3,366	11.83
German	1,996	7.01
Greek	355	1.25
Hawaii Native/Pacific Islander:	21	0.07
Micronesian: (2)	2	0.01
Guamanian/Chamorro (2)	2	0.01
Polynesian: (7)	17	0.06
Native Hawaiian (2)	7	0.02
Samoan (5)	10	0.04
Other Pac. Isl., specified	1	0.00
Other Pac. Isl., not spec.	1	0.00
Hispanic or Latino:	255	0.90
Central American:	6	0.02
Costa Rican	6	0.02
Cuban	13	0.05
Dominican Republic	11	0.04
Mexican	73	0.26
Puerto Rican	62	0.22
South American:	10	0.04
Colombian	4	0.01
Peruvian	4	0.01
Venezuelan	1	0.00
Other South American	1	0.00
Other Hispanic or Latino	80	0.28
Hungarian	58	0.20
Irish	5,412	19.02
Italian	1,813	6.37
Lithuanian	32	0.11
Northern European	10	0.04
Norwegian	202	0.71
Polish	812	2.85
Portuguese	228	0.80
Russian	114	0.40
Scandinavian	12	0.04
Scotch-Irish	603	2.12
Scottish	1,044	3.67
Slovak	12	0.04
Swedish	293	1.03
Swiss	29	0.10
Ukrainian	17	0.06
United States or American	1,866	6.56
Welsh	185	0.65
West Indian, excl. Hispanic:	42	0.15
Jamaican	42	0.15
White:	27,899	98.03
Not Hispanic (27,501)	27,728	97.42
Hispanic (139)	171	0.60
Yugoslavian	5	0.02

Salem

Place Type: Town
County: Rockingham
Population: 28,112

Ancestry/Race	Number	%
Acadian/Cajun	11	0.04
African American/Black:	202	0.72
Not Hispanic (143)	179	0.64
Hispanic (13)	23	0.08
African, sub-Saharan:	8	0.03
African	8	0.03
Am. Ind. or Alaska Nat., not spec.	36	0.13
Alsatian	4	0.01
American Indian tribes, specified:	86	0.31
Apache	2	0.01
Blackfeet	2	0.01
Cherokee (7)	25	0.09
Chickasaw	1	0.00
Chippewa (3)	3	0.01
Choctaw	1	0.00
Creek	1	0.00
Iroquois (5)	5	0.02
Latin American Indians (6)	7	0.02
Sioux (1)	6	0.02
All other tribes (14)	33	0.12
American Indian tribes, not spec.	7	0.02
Arab:	600	2.13
Lebanese	594	2.11
Syrian	6	0.02
Armenian	310	1.10
Asian:	724	2.58
Cambodian (5)	6	0.02
Chinese, ex. Taiwanese (142)	157	0.56
Filipino (86)	99	0.35
Indian (148)	151	0.54
Indonesian (1)	1	0.00
Japanese (23)	32	0.11
Korean (101)	119	0.42
Laotian (2)	4	0.01
Pakistani (20)	22	0.08
Taiwanese (10)	20	0.07
Thai (10)	11	0.04
Vietnamese (71)	76	0.27
Other Asian, specified (1)	1	0.00
Other Asian, not specified (6)	25	0.09
Australian	22	0.08
Austrian	78	0.28
Belgian	85	0.30
Brazilian	23	0.08
British	51	0.18
Canadian	446	1.59
Celtic	8	0.03
Czech	31	0.11
Czechoslovakian	11	0.04
Danish	89	0.32
Dutch	120	0.43
English	4,538	16.14
Estonian	23	0.08
European	38	0.14
Finnish	19	0.07
French, except Basque	4,220	15.01
French Canadian	2,323	8.26
German	2,082	7.41
Greek	261	0.93
Hawaii Native/Pacific Islander:	24	0.09
Micronesian: (1)	1	0.00
Guamanian/Chamorro (1)	1	0.00
Polynesian: (8)	9	0.03

Notes: 1. Figures in the "Number" column do not add up to the total population due to: a) Ancestry/Race overlap — e.g. persons can report being both White and Irish, b) persons of Hispanic origin can report being any race, c) persons reporting two ancestries are counted in both categories. 2. Numbers in parentheses indicate the number of persons reporting this ancestry/race alone, not in combination with any other ancestry/race. 3. Refer to the Explanation of Data in the front of the book for more detailed information.

Ancestry/Race	Number	%
Native Hawaiian (3)	4	0.01
Samoan (5)	5	0.02
Other Pac. Isl., not spec. (9)	14	0.05
Hispanic or Latino:	552	1.96
Central American:	48	0.17
Costa Rican	13	0.05
Guatemalan	19	0.07
Honduran	1	0.00
Panamanian	7	0.02
Salvadoran	1	0.00
Other Central American	7	0.02
Cuban	33	0.12
Dominican Republic	97	0.35
Mexican	45	0.16
Puerto Rican	154	0.55
South American:	43	0.15
Argentinean	4	0.01
Colombian	16	0.06
Ecuadorian	5	0.02
Peruvian	8	0.03
Uruguayan	5	0.02
Venezuelan	5	0.02
Other Hispanic or Latino	132	0.47
Hungarian	49	0.17
Icelander	30	0.11
Iranian	66	0.23
Irish	6,728	23.93
Italian	5,656	20.12
Latvian	9	0.03
Lithuanian	235	0.84
Norwegian	51	0.18
Polish	1,655	5.89
Portuguese	539	1.92
Romanian	39	0.14
Russian	307	1.09
Scotch-Irish	414	1.47
Scottish	916	3.26
Slovak	16	0.06
Swedish	494	1.76
Swiss	16	0.06
Turkish	12	0.04
Ukrainian	36	0.13
United States or American	1,340	4.77
Welsh	141	0.50
West Indian, excl. Hispanic:	13	0.05
West Indian	13	0.05
White:	26,981	95.98
Not Hispanic (26,446)	26,674	94.88
Hispanic (262)	307	1.09
Yugoslavian	9	0.03

Somersworth

Place Type: City
County: Strafford
Population: 11,477

Ancestry/Race	Number	%
African American/Black:	127	1.11
Not Hispanic (63)	122	1.06
Hispanic (3)	5	0.04
Alaska Native tribes, specified:	2	0.02
Aleut (2)	2	0.02
Am. Ind. or Alaska Nat., not spec.	44	0.38
American Indian tribes, specified:	33	0.29
Blackfeet (1)	1	0.01
Cherokee (1)	5	0.04
Chippewa	1	0.01
Iroquois	3	0.03
Latin American Indians	2	0.02
Navajo (1)	3	0.03
Sioux	1	0.01
Ute (2)	2	0.02
All other tribes (1)	15	0.13
American Indian tribes, not spec.	1	0.01
Arab:	108	0.94
Lebanese	108	0.94
Armenian	13	0.11
Asian:	155	1.35
Cambodian (13)	18	0.16
Chinese, ex. Taiwanese (13)	16	0.14
Filipino (9)	17	0.15
Indian (25)	28	0.24
Indonesian (5)	6	0.05
Japanese (7)	19	0.17
Korean (4)	5	0.04
Laotian (5)	6	0.05
Thai (10)	15	0.13
Vietnamese (11)	13	0.11
Other Asian, not specified (6)	12	0.10
Austrian	6	0.05
British	38	0.33
Canadian	182	1.59
Croatian	33	0.29
Czech	8	0.07
Czechoslovakian	9	0.08
Danish	69	0.60
Dutch	83	0.72
English	1,737	15.13
Finnish	35	0.30
French, except Basque	2,311	20.14
French Canadian	1,761	15.34
German	821	7.15
Greek	171	1.49
Hawaii Native/Pacific Islander:	3	0.03
Micronesian:	1	0.01
Guamanian/Chamorro	1	0.01
Polynesian: (1)	1	0.01
Native Hawaiian (1)	1	0.01
Other Pac. Isl., not spec.	1	0.01
Hispanic or Latino:	185	1.61
Central American:	8	0.07
Costa Rican	2	0.02
Guatemalan	2	0.02
Nicaraguan	4	0.03
Cuban	4	0.03
Dominican Republic	10	0.09
Mexican	47	0.41
Puerto Rican	42	0.37
South American:	16	0.14
Chilean	4	0.03
Colombian	4	0.03
Ecuadorian	7	0.06
Venezuelan	1	0.01
Other Hispanic or Latino	58	0.51
Hungarian	10	0.09
Irish	2,243	19.54
Italian	596	5.19
Lithuanian	27	0.24
Norwegian	121	1.05
Polish	449	3.91
Portuguese	67	0.58
Russian	36	0.31
Scandinavian	7	0.06
Scotch-Irish	213	1.86
Scottish	456	3.97
Slovak	11	0.10
Swedish	123	1.07
Swiss	32	0.28
Ukrainian	82	0.71
United States or American	809	7.05
Welsh	81	0.71
West Indian, excl. Hispanic:	10	0.09
Haitian	10	0.09
White:	11,187	97.47
Not Hispanic (10,929)	11,060	96.37
Hispanic (108)	127	1.11
Yugoslavian	9	0.08

Windham

Place Type: Town
County: Rockingham
Population: 10,709

Ancestry/Race	Number	%
African American/Black:	44	0.41
Not Hispanic (33)	43	0.40
Hispanic (1)	1	0.01
Am. Ind. or Alaska Nat., not spec.	7	0.07
Albanian	19	0.18
American Indian tribes, specified:	6	0.06
Cherokee (2)	2	0.02
Chippewa (1)	1	0.01
Sioux	1	0.01
All other tribes (1)	2	0.02
Arab:	80	0.75
Lebanese	80	0.75
Armenian	124	1.16
Asian:	216	2.02
Chinese, ex. Taiwanese (52)	59	0.55
Filipino (8)	11	0.10
Indian (38)	54	0.50
Japanese (14)	22	0.21
Korean (15)	23	0.21
Pakistani (10)	14	0.13
Taiwanese (5)	5	0.05
Thai (2)	3	0.03
Vietnamese (9)	9	0.08
Other Asian, not specified (10)	16	0.15
Austrian	36	0.34
Belgian	68	0.63
Canadian	166	1.55
Danish	38	0.35
Dutch	90	0.84
Eastern European	6	0.06
English	1,713	16.00
European	52	0.49
Finnish	44	0.41
French, except Basque	1,152	10.76
French Canadian	851	7.95
German	868	8.11
Greek	252	2.35
Hawaii Native/Pacific Islander:	13	0.12
Micronesian: (11)	11	0.10
Guamanian/Chamorro (11)	11	0.10
Polynesian: (2)	2	0.02
Native Hawaiian (2)	2	0.02
Hispanic or Latino:	106	0.99
Central American:	6	0.06
Guatemalan	4	0.04
Honduran	1	0.01
Panamanian	1	0.01
Cuban	11	0.10
Dominican Republic	14	0.13
Mexican	14	0.13
Puerto Rican	22	0.21
South American:	8	0.07
Argentinean	1	0.01
Colombian	1	0.01
Ecuadorian	3	0.03
Peruvian	1	0.01
Venezuelan	2	0.02
Other Hispanic or Latino	31	0.29
Hungarian	85	0.79
Iranian	59	0.55
Irish	2,895	27.03
Italian	1,857	17.34
Lithuanian	68	0.63
New Zealander	12	0.11
Northern European	8	0.07
Norwegian	91	0.85
Polish	752	7.02
Portuguese	169	1.58
Russian	143	1.34
Scandinavian	10	0.09
Scotch-Irish	254	2.37
Scottish	448	4.18
Slovak	7	0.07
Swedish	278	2.60
Swiss	53	0.49
Ukrainian	31	0.29
United States or American	373	3.48
Welsh	87	0.81
White:	10,447	97.55
Not Hispanic (10,295)	10,363	96.77
Hispanic (81)	84	0.78

Notes: 1. Figures in the "Number" column do not add up to the total population due to: a) Ancestry/Race overlap — e.g. persons can report being both White and Irish, b) persons of Hispanic origin can report being any race, c) persons reporting two ancestries are counted in both categories. 2. Numbers in parentheses indicate the number of persons reporting this ancestry/race alone, not in combination with any other ancestry/race. 3. Refer to the Explanation of Data in the front of the book for more detailed information.

Aberdeen

Place Type: Township
County: Monmouth
Population: 17,454

Ancestry/Race	Number	%
African American/Black:	2,211	12.67
Not Hispanic (2,040)	2,128	12.19
Hispanic (58)	83	0.48
African, sub-Saharan:	65	0.37
African	65	0.37
Am. Ind. or Alaska Nat., not spec.	32	0.18
American Indian tribes, specified:	45	0.26
Blackfeet	3	0.02
Cherokee	13	0.07
Creek (2)	4	0.02
Delaware (1)	4	0.02
Iroquois (10)	12	0.07
Latin American Indians (4)	5	0.03
Sioux	2	0.01
All other tribes	2	0.01
American Indian tribes, not spec.	2	0.01
Arab:	80	0.46
Egyptian	59	0.34
Lebanese	16	0.09
Syrian	5	0.03
Armenian	11	0.06
Asian:	1,082	6.20
Bangladeshi (7)	8	0.05
Cambodian (3)	3	0.02
Chinese, ex. Taiwanese (255)	286	1.64
Filipino (138)	149	0.85
Indian (416)	438	2.51
Indonesian (1)	1	0.01
Japanese (9)	17	0.10
Korean (74)	83	0.48
Malaysian (1)	1	0.01
Pakistani (14)	18	0.10
Sri Lankan (4)	4	0.02
Taiwanese (4)	14	0.08
Thai (2)	4	0.02
Vietnamese (14)	15	0.09
Other Asian, specified (1)	4	0.02
Other Asian, not specified (11)	37	0.21
Australian	10	0.06
Austrian	109	0.63
Brazilian	64	0.37
British	26	0.15
Bulgarian	6	0.03
Canadian	63	0.36
Croatian	57	0.33
Czech	98	0.56
Czechoslovakian	54	0.31
Danish	76	0.44
Dutch	182	1.05
Eastern European	49	0.28
English	881	5.07
European	79	0.45
French, except Basque	372	2.14
French Canadian	79	0.45
German	2,279	13.11
Greek	215	1.24
Hawaii Native/Pacific Islander:	20	0.11
Polynesian:	3	0.02
Native Hawaiian	3	0.02
Other Pac. Isl., specified	3	0.02
Other Pac. Isl., not spec. (1)	14	0.08
Hispanic or Latino:	1,225	7.02
Central American:	51	0.29
Costa Rican	22	0.13
Guatemalan	1	0.01
Honduran	9	0.05
Nicaraguan	4	0.02
Panamanian	4	0.02
Salvadoran	11	0.06
Cuban	96	0.55
Dominican Republic	43	0.25
Mexican	90	0.52
Puerto Rican	648	3.71
South American:	120	0.69
Argentinean	12	0.07
Bolivian	2	0.01
Chilean	6	0.03
Colombian	46	0.26
Ecuadorian	18	0.10
Paraguayan	1	0.01
Peruvian	23	0.13
Uruguayan	6	0.03
Venezuelan	2	0.01
Other South American	4	0.02
Other Hispanic or Latino	177	1.01
Hungarian	374	2.15
Iranian	68	0.39
Irish	3,986	22.93
Israeli	43	0.25
Italian	3,997	22.99
Lithuanian	69	0.40
Northern European	5	0.03
Norwegian	132	0.76
Polish	1,324	7.61
Portuguese	167	0.96
Romanian	71	0.41
Russian	613	3.53
Scandinavian	11	0.06
Scotch-Irish	212	1.22
Scottish	226	1.30
Serbian	12	0.07
Slavic	14	0.08
Slovak	114	0.66
Slovene	14	0.08
Swedish	128	0.74
Swiss	10	0.06
Turkish	39	0.22
Ukrainian	118	0.68
United States or American	466	2.68
Welsh	94	0.54
West Indian, excl. Hispanic:	329	1.89
Barbadian	19	0.11
Bermudan	7	0.04
British West Indian	5	0.03
Haitian	80	0.46
Jamaican	67	0.39
Trinidadian and Tobagonian	56	0.32
West Indian	95	0.55
White:	13,981	80.10
Not Hispanic (12,943)	13,119	75.16
Hispanic (815)	862	4.94

Asbury Park

Place Type: City
County: Monmouth
Population: 16,930

Ancestry/Race	Number	%
African American/Black:	11,240	66.39
Not Hispanic (10,236)	10,864	64.17
Hispanic (279)	376	2.22
African, sub-Saharan:	276	1.63
African	276	1.63
Alaska Native tribes, specified:	4	0.02
Eskimo	2	0.01
Tlingit-Haida	2	0.01
Alaska Native tribes, not specified	2	0.01
Am. Ind. or Alaska Nat., not spec.	113	0.67
American Indian tribes, specified:	85	0.50
Apache (1)	2	0.01
Blackfeet (1)	10	0.06
Cherokee (11)	50	0.30
Chickasaw	2	0.01
Chippewa (2)	2	0.01
Choctaw	4	0.02
Delaware (1)	3	0.02
Iroquois	1	0.01
Latin American Indians (1)	1	0.01
Seminole	4	0.02
Sioux	1	0.01
Tohono O'Odham	4	0.02
All other tribes (1)	1	0.01
American Indian tribes, not spec.	6	0.04
Arab:	74	0.44
Egyptian	20	0.12
Lebanese	24	0.14
Palestinian	7	0.04
Syrian	23	0.14
Armenian	32	0.19
Asian:	180	1.06
Chinese, ex. Taiwanese (29)	36	0.21
Filipino (13)	17	0.10
Indian (36)	54	0.32
Indonesian (2)	2	0.01
Japanese (3)	5	0.03
Korean (9)	16	0.09
Pakistani (14)	17	0.10
Taiwanese	1	0.01
Vietnamese (5)	7	0.04
Other Asian, specified	6	0.04
Other Asian, not specified (5)	19	0.11
Brazilian	5	0.03
Canadian	17	0.10
Czech	19	0.11
Danish	5	0.03
Dutch	64	0.38
English	266	1.57
Estonian	6	0.04
European	6	0.04
Finnish	4	0.02
French, except Basque	44	0.26
French Canadian	16	0.09
German	454	2.68
German Russian	17	0.10
Greek	105	0.62
Hawaii Native/Pacific Islander:	65	0.38
Micronesian: (4)	8	0.05
Guamanian/Chamorro (4)	8	0.05
Polynesian: (4)	10	0.06
Native Hawaiian (2)	7	0.04
Samoan (2)	3	0.02
Other Pac. Isl., specified	6	0.04
Other Pac. Isl., not spec. (4)	41	0.24
Hispanic or Latino:	2,637	15.58
Central American:	194	1.15
Costa Rican	8	0.05
Guatemalan	44	0.26
Honduran	13	0.08
Nicaraguan	64	0.38
Panamanian	13	0.08
Salvadoran	44	0.26
Other Central American	8	0.05
Cuban	35	0.21
Dominican Republic	43	0.25
Mexican	956	5.65
Puerto Rican	1,021	6.03
South American:	98	0.58
Argentinean	2	0.01
Bolivian	14	0.08
Chilean	5	0.03
Colombian	31	0.18
Ecuadorian	27	0.16
Paraguayan	1	0.01
Peruvian	11	0.06
Other South American	7	0.04
Other Hispanic or Latino	290	1.71
Hungarian	34	0.20
Irish	833	4.92
Italian	753	4.45
Latvian	6	0.04
Lithuanian	71	0.42
Norwegian	16	0.09
Pennsylvania German	8	0.05
Polish	201	1.19
Portuguese	6	0.04
Russian	29	0.17
Scotch-Irish	31	0.18
Scottish	69	0.41
Slovak	8	0.05
Swedish	32	0.19
Swiss	5	0.03
Turkish	10	0.06

Notes: 1. Figures in the "Number" column do not add up to the total population due to: a) Ancestry/Race overlap — e.g. persons can report being both White and Irish, b) persons of Hispanic origin can report being any race, c) persons reporting two ancestries are counted in both categories. 2. Numbers in parentheses indicate the number of persons reporting this ancestry/race alone, not in combination with any other ancestry/race. 3. Refer to the Explanation of Data in the front of the book for more detailed information.

Ancestry/Race	Number	%
Ukrainian	22	0.13
United States or American	305	1.80
Welsh	59	0.35
West Indian, excl. Hispanic:	1,629	9.62
Bahamian	13	0.08
Barbadian	45	0.27
Belizean	48	0.28
British West Indian	14	0.08
Haitian	974	5.75
Jamaican	449	2.65
Trinidadian and Tobagonian	27	0.16
West Indian	59	0.35
White:	4,519	26.69
Not Hispanic (3,147)	3,332	19.68
Hispanic (1,047)	1,187	7.01
Yugoslavian	14	0.08

Atlantic City

Place Type: City
County: Atlantic
Population: 40,517

Ancestry/Race	Number	%
African American/Black:	18,587	45.87
Not Hispanic (17,168)	17,621	43.49
Hispanic (724)	966	2.38
African, sub-Saharan:	662	1.63
African	476	1.17
Cape Verdean	6	0.01
Ethiopian	18	0.04
Liberian	106	0.26
Nigerian	36	0.09
Senegalese	4	0.01
Sudanese	7	0.02
Other sub-Saharan African	9	0.02
Alaska Native tribes, specified:	1	0.00
Eskimo	1	0.00
Am. Ind. or Alaska Nat., not spec.	234	0.58
Albanian	36	0.09
American Indian tribes, specified:	259	0.64
Apache	2	0.00
Blackfeet (3)	26	0.06
Cherokee (15)	81	0.20
Cheyenne (1)	1	0.00
Chippewa (1)	2	0.00
Creek (3)	5	0.01
Delaware (1)	4	0.01
Iroquois (1)	7	0.02
Latin American Indians (24)	74	0.18
Lumbee (1)	1	0.00
Navajo (3)	4	0.01
Osage	1	0.00
Pueblo (8)	15	0.04
Seminole	5	0.01
Sioux (1)	4	0.01
Ute	1	0.00
All other tribes (9)	26	0.06
American Indian tribes, not spec.	10	0.02
Arab:	134	0.33
Arab/Arabic	5	0.01
Egyptian	27	0.07
Jordanian	14	0.03
Lebanese	30	0.07
Moroccan	33	0.08
Syrian	11	0.03
Other Arab	14	0.03
Armenian	7	0.02
Asian:	4,812	11.88
Bangladeshi (193)	303	0.75
Cambodian (11)	13	0.03
Chinese, ex. Taiwanese (927)	1,031	2.54
Filipino (467)	531	1.31
Indian (803)	968	2.39
Indonesian	2	0.00
Japanese (14)	33	0.08
Korean (58)	64	0.16
Laotian (14)	26	0.06
Malaysian (10)	11	0.03
Pakistani (219)	309	0.76
Taiwanese (2)	11	0.03
Thai (10)	18	0.04
Vietnamese (1,257)	1,352	3.34
Other Asian, specified (5)	8	0.02
Other Asian, not specified (76)	132	0.33
Austrian	64	0.16
Brazilian	7	0.02
British	33	0.08
Bulgarian	8	0.02
Canadian	17	0.04
Cypriot	10	0.02
Czech	13	0.03
Danish	11	0.03
Dutch	97	0.24
English	604	1.49
European	29	0.07
French, except Basque	201	0.50
French Canadian	13	0.03
German	825	2.04
Greek	190	0.47
Hawaii Native/Pacific Islander:	89	0.22
Micronesian: (6)	7	0.02
Guamanian/Chamorro (5)	6	0.01
Other Micronesian (1)	1	0.00
Polynesian: (10)	20	0.05
Native Hawaiian (5)	10	0.02
Samoan (5)	10	0.02
Other Pac. Isl., specified	1	0.00
Other Pac. Isl., not spec. (8)	61	0.15
Hispanic or Latino:	10,107	24.95
Central American:	818	2.02
Costa Rican	9	0.02
Guatemalan	26	0.06
Honduran	450	1.11
Nicaraguan	52	0.13
Panamanian	23	0.06
Salvadoran	221	0.55
Other Central American	37	0.09
Cuban	238	0.59
Dominican Republic	840	2.07
Mexican	2,199	5.43
Puerto Rican	3,635	8.97
South American:	672	1.66
Argentinean	12	0.03
Chilean	9	0.02
Colombian	444	1.10
Ecuadorian	61	0.15
Peruvian	108	0.27
Venezuelan	7	0.02
Other South American	31	0.08
Other Hispanic or Latino	1,705	4.21
Hungarian	104	0.26
Iranian	31	0.08
Irish	1,653	4.08
Italian	1,990	4.91
Latvian	12	0.03
Lithuanian	61	0.15
Norwegian	33	0.08
Pennsylvania German	14	0.03
Polish	425	1.05
Portuguese	30	0.07
Romanian	31	0.08
Russian	444	1.10
Scandinavian	7	0.02
Scotch-Irish	124	0.31
Scottish	101	0.25
Serbian	7	0.02
Slavic	11	0.03
Slovak	15	0.04
Swedish	41	0.10
Swiss	7	0.02
Turkish	9	0.02
Ukrainian	52	0.13
United States or American	953	2.35
Welsh	75	0.19
West Indian, excl. Hispanic:	390	0.96
Bahamian	4	0.01
Barbadian	51	0.13
Haitian	74	0.18
Jamaican	136	0.34
Trinidadian and Tobagonian	40	0.10
West Indian	85	0.21
White:	11,846	29.24
Not Hispanic (7,878)	8,382	20.69
Hispanic (2,931)	3,464	8.55
Yugoslavian	13	0.03

Avenel

Place Type: Census Designated Place
County: Middlesex
Population: 17,552

Ancestry/Race	Number	%
Afghan	37	0.21
African American/Black:	3,637	20.72
Not Hispanic (3,296)	3,424	19.51
Hispanic (155)	213	1.21
African, sub-Saharan:	602	3.43
African	386	2.20
Liberian	18	0.10
Nigerian	116	0.66
Sudanese	25	0.14
Ugandan	20	0.11
Other sub-Saharan African	37	0.21
Am. Ind. or Alaska Nat., not spec.	114	0.65
American Indian tribes, specified:	65	0.37
Apache (2)	8	0.05
Blackfeet (1)	4	0.02
Cherokee (3)	20	0.11
Choctaw (1)	1	0.01
Comanche	1	0.01
Delaware (2)	4	0.02
Iroquois (1)	3	0.02
Latin American Indians (7)	11	0.06
Seminole (1)	1	0.01
Sioux	5	0.03
All other tribes (1)	7	0.04
American Indian tribes, not spec.	13	0.07
Arab:	363	2.07
Arab/Arabic	63	0.36
Egyptian	259	1.48
Jordanian	5	0.03
Moroccan	7	0.04
Other Arab	29	0.17
Armenian	6	0.03
Asian:	3,640	20.74
Bangladeshi (20)	22	0.13
Chinese, ex. Taiwanese (150)	164	0.93
Filipino (257)	274	1.56
Indian (2,282)	2,395	13.65
Indonesian (86)	108	0.62
Japanese (5)	7	0.04
Korean (149)	154	0.88
Laotian (1)	1	0.01
Pakistani (259)	330	1.88
Sri Lankan (5)	5	0.03
Taiwanese (8)	8	0.05
Vietnamese (58)	60	0.34
Other Asian, specified	6	0.03
Other Asian, not specified (20)	106	0.60
Austrian	52	0.30
Brazilian	16	0.09
British	5	0.03
Canadian	9	0.05
Czech	21	0.12
Czechoslovakian	13	0.07
Danish	54	0.31
Dutch	103	0.59
Eastern European	9	0.05
English	659	3.75
European	19	0.11
Finnish	13	0.07
French, except Basque	175	1.00
French Canadian	44	0.25
German	1,352	7.70
Greek	37	0.21
Guyanese	16	0.09
Hawaii Native/Pacific Islander:	16	0.09
Polynesian: (2)	4	0.02

Notes: 1. Figures in the "Number" column do not add up to the total population due to: a) Ancestry/Race overlap — e.g. persons can report being both White and Irish, b) persons of Hispanic origin can report being any race, c) persons reporting two ancestries are counted in both categories. 2. Numbers in parentheses indicate the number of persons reporting this ancestry/race alone, not in combination with any other ancestry/race. 3. Refer to the Explanation of Data in the front of the book for more detailed information.

Ancestry/Race	Number	%
Native Hawaiian (2)	3	0.02
Samoan	1	0.01
Other Pac. Isl., specified	6	0.03
Other Pac. Isl., not spec. (3)	6	0.03
Hispanic or Latino:	1,729	9.85
Central American:	64	0.36
Costa Rican	8	0.05
Guatemalan	15	0.09
Honduran	11	0.06
Nicaraguan	1	0.01
Panamanian	6	0.03
Salvadoran	22	0.13
Other Central American	1	0.01
Cuban	110	0.63
Dominican Republic	83	0.47
Mexican	71	0.40
Puerto Rican	725	4.13
South American:	325	1.85
Argentinean	11	0.06
Chilean	1	0.01
Colombian	104	0.59
Ecuadorian	28	0.16
Paraguayan	4	0.02
Peruvian	147	0.84
Uruguayan	16	0.09
Venezuelan	1	0.01
Other South American	13	0.07
Other Hispanic or Latino	351	2.00
Hungarian	551	3.14
Iranian	7	0.04
Irish	2,164	12.33
Israeli	8	0.05
Italian	2,250	12.82
Lithuanian	122	0.70
Maltese	8	0.05
Norwegian	38	0.22
Polish	1,183	6.74
Portuguese	127	0.72
Romanian	10	0.06
Russian	285	1.62
Scandinavian	20	0.11
Scotch-Irish	94	0.54
Scottish	110	0.63
Slavic	57	0.32
Slovak	157	0.89
Slovene	5	0.03
Swedish	50	0.28
Swiss	13	0.07
Turkish	34	0.19
Ukrainian	204	1.16
United States or American	428	2.44
Welsh	35	0.20
West Indian, excl. Hispanic:	237	1.35
British West Indian	15	0.09
Haitian	67	0.38
Jamaican	49	0.28
Trinidadian and Tobagonian	57	0.32
U.S. Virgin Islander	11	0.06
West Indian	38	0.22
White:	9,797	55.82
Not Hispanic (8,596)	8,877	50.58
Hispanic (797)	920	5.24

Barclay-Kingston

Place Type: Census Designated Place
County: Camden
Population: 10,728

Ancestry/Race	Number	%
African American/Black:	437	4.07
Not Hispanic (375)	424	3.95
Hispanic (11)	13	0.12
African, sub-Saharan:	14	0.13
African	14	0.13
Am. Ind. or Alaska Nat., not spec.	14	0.13
American Indian tribes, specified:	28	0.26
Blackfeet	5	0.05
Cherokee (6)	10	0.09
Creek (1)	1	0.01
Iroquois (3)	3	0.03
Latin American Indians	5	0.05
Lumbee (1)	1	0.01
All other tribes (1)	3	0.03
American Indian tribes, not spec.	1	0.01
Arab:	125	1.16
Egyptian	9	0.08
Iraqi	6	0.06
Jordanian	53	0.49
Lebanese	46	0.43
Moroccan	11	0.10
Armenian	22	0.20
Asian:	809	7.54
Cambodian (17)	21	0.20
Chinese, ex. Taiwanese (116)	132	1.23
Filipino (288)	304	2.83
Indian (109)	130	1.21
Indonesian (2)	2	0.02
Japanese (5)	8	0.07
Korean (101)	106	0.99
Pakistani (16)	16	0.15
Taiwanese (5)	6	0.06
Thai (7)	8	0.07
Vietnamese (44)	52	0.48
Other Asian, not specified (10)	24	0.22
Austrian	76	0.71
Belgian	4	0.04
British	31	0.29
Canadian	28	0.26
Czech	45	0.42
Czechoslovakian	19	0.18
Danish	6	0.06
Dutch	73	0.68
Eastern European	49	0.45
English	1,275	11.83
European	22	0.20
Finnish	43	0.40
French, except Basque	318	2.95
French Canadian	85	0.79
German	2,077	19.27
Greek	94	0.87
Hawaii Native/Pacific Islander:	6	0.06
Polynesian: (1)	5	0.05
Native Hawaiian (1)	4	0.04
Samoan	1	0.01
Other Pac. Isl., not spec.	1	0.01
Hispanic or Latino:	244	2.27
Central American:	2	0.02
Guatemalan	1	0.01
Salvadoran	1	0.01
Cuban	19	0.18
Dominican Republic	3	0.03
Mexican	35	0.33
Puerto Rican	97	0.90
South American:	44	0.41
Argentinean	5	0.05
Bolivian	1	0.01
Chilean	4	0.04
Colombian	20	0.19
Ecuadorian	7	0.07
Paraguayan	1	0.01
Venezuelan	4	0.04
Other South American	2	0.02
Other Hispanic or Latino	44	0.41
Hungarian	114	1.06
Irish	2,420	22.45
Italian	1,895	17.58
Lithuanian	78	0.72
Maltese	17	0.16
Norwegian	68	0.63
Pennsylvania German	6	0.06
Polish	623	5.78
Romanian	12	0.11
Russian	413	3.83
Scandinavian	40	0.37
Scotch-Irish	233	2.16
Scottish	324	3.01
Slavic	14	0.13
Slovak	47	0.44
Swedish	52	0.48
Swiss	26	0.24
Ukrainian	136	1.26
United States or American	462	4.29
Welsh	178	1.65
West Indian, excl. Hispanic:	25	0.23
British West Indian	4	0.04
Trinidadian and Tobagonian	10	0.09
West Indian	11	0.10
White:	9,489	88.45
Not Hispanic (9,219)	9,323	86.90
Hispanic (152)	166	1.55

Barnegat

Place Type: Township
County: Ocean
Population: 15,270

Ancestry/Race	Number	%
African American/Black:	389	2.55
Not Hispanic (320)	358	2.34
Hispanic (18)	31	0.20
Am. Ind. or Alaska Nat., not spec.	19	0.12
Albanian	5	0.03
Alsatian	10	0.07
American Indian tribes, specified:	40	0.26
Apache (1)	1	0.01
Blackfeet	2	0.01
Cherokee (4)	20	0.13
Crow	2	0.01
Delaware (3)	5	0.03
Iroquois	3	0.02
Latin American Indians	3	0.02
Potawatomi	1	0.01
All other tribes (2)	3	0.02
American Indian tribes, not spec.	1	0.01
Arab:	24	0.16
Egyptian	15	0.10
Syrian	9	0.06
Asian:	203	1.33
Chinese, ex. Taiwanese (18)	27	0.18
Filipino (73)	93	0.61
Indian (32)	33	0.22
Japanese (5)	14	0.09
Korean (12)	18	0.12
Thai (4)	5	0.03
Vietnamese (7)	9	0.06
Other Asian, not specified	4	0.03
Austrian	95	0.62
British	106	0.69
Canadian	10	0.07
Czech	8	0.05
Czechoslovakian	47	0.31
Danish	93	0.61
Dutch	521	3.41
English	1,432	9.37
European	36	0.24
Finnish	28	0.18
French, except Basque	361	2.36
French Canadian	178	1.16
German	3,407	22.29
Greek	119	0.78
Hawaii Native/Pacific Islander:	2	0.01
Other Pac. Isl., not spec.	2	0.01
Hispanic or Latino:	590	3.86
Central American:	23	0.15
Costa Rican	5	0.03
Guatemalan	7	0.05
Honduran	7	0.05
Salvadoran	4	0.03
Cuban	68	0.45
Dominican Republic	6	0.04
Mexican	39	0.26
Puerto Rican	281	1.84
South American:	52	0.34
Argentinean	7	0.05
Chilean	4	0.03
Colombian	20	0.13
Ecuadorian	6	0.04
Peruvian	5	0.03

Notes: 1. Figures in the "Number" column do not add up to the total population due to: a) Ancestry/Race overlap — e.g. persons can report being both White and Irish, b) persons of Hispanic origin can report being any race, c) persons reporting two ancestries are counted in both categories. 2. Numbers in parentheses indicate the number of persons reporting this ancestry/race alone, not in combination with any other ancestry/race. 3. Refer to the Explanation of Data in the front of the book for more detailed information.

Ancestry/Race	Number	%
Uruguayan	4	0.03
Other South American	6	0.04
Other Hispanic or Latino	121	0.79
Hungarian	463	3.03
Irish	4,059	26.56
Italian	4,250	27.81
Latvian	8	0.05
Lithuanian	84	0.55
Northern European	9	0.06
Norwegian	76	0.50
Polish	1,305	8.54
Portuguese	137	0.90
Romanian	33	0.22
Russian	131	0.86
Scotch-Irish	253	1.66
Scottish	336	2.20
Slovak	106	0.69
Swedish	231	1.51
Swiss	17	0.11
Turkish	26	0.17
Ukrainian	160	1.05
United States or American	396	2.59
Welsh	79	0.52
West Indian, excl. Hispanic:	71	0.46
Jamaican	71	0.46
White:	14,647	95.92
Not Hispanic (14,050)	14,187	92.91
Hispanic (418)	460	3.01

Bayonne

Place Type: City
County: Hudson
Population: 61,842

Ancestry/Race	Number	%
Afghan	59	0.10
African American/Black:	3,909	6.32
Not Hispanic (3,098)	3,405	5.51
Hispanic (318)	504	0.81
African, sub-Saharan:	261	0.42
African	254	0.41
Ghanian	7	0.01
Alaska Native tribes, specified:	1	0.00
Eskimo	1	0.00
Am. Ind. or Alaska Nat., not spec.	146	0.24
Albanian	28	0.05
American Indian tribes, specified:	121	0.20
Apache	2	0.00
Blackfeet	5	0.01
Cherokee (6)	40	0.06
Cree	6	0.01
Delaware (1)	4	0.01
Iroquois (1)	1	0.00
Latin American Indians (26)	36	0.06
Navajo (1)	2	0.00
Pueblo	3	0.00
Seminole	3	0.00
Shoshone	1	0.00
Sioux (4)	4	0.01
All other tribes (4)	14	0.02
American Indian tribes, not spec.	14	0.02
Arab:	2,345	3.79
Arab/Arabic	155	0.25
Egyptian	1,958	3.17
Jordanian	93	0.15
Lebanese	32	0.05
Moroccan	15	0.02
Palestinian	30	0.05
Syrian	4	0.01
Other Arab	58	0.09
Armenian	17	0.03
Asian:	3,031	4.90
Bangladeshi (5)	9	0.01
Chinese, ex. Taiwanese (205)	236	0.38
Filipino (1,176)	1,284	2.08
Indian (535)	616	1.00
Indonesian (2)	7	0.01
Japanese (21)	31	0.05
Korean (330)	345	0.56
Laotian (1)	1	0.00
Pakistani (145)	242	0.39
Sri Lankan (12)	12	0.02
Taiwanese (6)	6	0.01
Thai (10)	16	0.03
Vietnamese (51)	56	0.09
Other Asian, specified (1)	13	0.02
Other Asian, not specified (24)	157	0.25
Austrian	125	0.20
Belgian	16	0.03
Brazilian	7	0.01
British	17	0.03
Bulgarian	27	0.04
Canadian	36	0.06
Celtic	7	0.01
Croatian	21	0.03
Cypriot	6	0.01
Czech	161	0.26
Czechoslovakian	231	0.37
Danish	72	0.12
Dutch	313	0.51
Eastern European	52	0.08
English	1,263	2.04
Estonian	8	0.01
European	64	0.10
Finnish	57	0.09
French, except Basque	442	0.71
French Canadian	131	0.21
German	3,775	6.10
Greek	266	0.43
Guyanese	116	0.19
Hawaii Native/Pacific Islander:	97	0.16
Micronesian: (2)	5	0.01
Guamanian/Chamorro (2)	5	0.01
Polynesian: (9)	10	0.02
Native Hawaiian (8)	9	0.01
Samoan (1)	1	0.00
Other Pac. Isl., specified	9	0.01
Other Pac. Isl., not spec. (19)	73	0.12
Hispanic or Latino:	11,015	17.81
Central American:	998	1.61
Costa Rican	16	0.03
Guatemalan	297	0.48
Honduran	207	0.33
Nicaraguan	47	0.08
Panamanian	97	0.16
Salvadoran	243	0.39
Other Central American	91	0.15
Cuban	454	0.73
Dominican Republic	1,072	1.73
Mexican	631	1.02
Puerto Rican	4,244	6.86
South American:	1,136	1.84
Argentinean	77	0.12
Bolivian	21	0.03
Chilean	128	0.21
Colombian	359	0.58
Ecuadorian	294	0.48
Peruvian	157	0.25
Uruguayan	12	0.02
Venezuelan	36	0.06
Other South American	52	0.08
Other Hispanic or Latino	2,480	4.01
Hungarian	371	0.60
Iranian	62	0.10
Irish	11,606	18.77
Italian	12,416	20.08
Latvian	15	0.02
Lithuanian	408	0.66
Maltese	55	0.09
Northern European	7	0.01
Norwegian	95	0.15
Pennsylvania German	20	0.03
Polish	11,095	17.94
Portuguese	147	0.24
Romanian	25	0.04
Russian	890	1.44
Scandinavian	7	0.01
Scotch-Irish	344	0.56
Scottish	325	0.53
Slavic	383	0.62
Slovak	857	1.39
Slovene	9	0.01
Swedish	245	0.40
Swiss	24	0.04
Turkish	7	0.01
Ukrainian	772	1.25
United States or American	1,546	2.50
Welsh	89	0.14
West Indian, excl. Hispanic:	226	0.37
Bahamian	8	0.01
Belizean	7	0.01
British West Indian	9	0.01
Dutch West Indian	8	0.01
Haitian	92	0.15
Jamaican	24	0.04
Trinidadian and Tobagonian	34	0.05
West Indian	44	0.07
White:	50,684	81.96
Not Hispanic (43,217)	44,710	72.30
Hispanic (5,414)	5,974	9.66
Yugoslavian	16	0.03

Beachwood

Place Type: Borough
County: Ocean
Population: 10,375

Ancestry/Race	Number	%
African American/Black:	137	1.32
Not Hispanic (95)	125	1.20
Hispanic (6)	12	0.12
Am. Ind. or Alaska Nat., not spec.	6	0.06
American Indian tribes, specified:	15	0.14
Blackfeet	4	0.04
Cherokee (4)	6	0.06
Delaware	1	0.01
Iroquois (3)	3	0.03
Navajo	1	0.01
American Indian tribes, not spec.	4	0.04
Arab:	30	0.29
Arab/Arabic	2	0.02
Egyptian	18	0.17
Syrian	10	0.10
Armenian	29	0.28
Asian:	138	1.33
Chinese, ex. Taiwanese (18)	23	0.22
Filipino (46)	52	0.50
Indian (13)	15	0.14
Japanese (6)	11	0.11
Korean (26)	26	0.25
Thai	1	0.01
Vietnamese (1)	1	0.01
Other Asian, not specified (7)	9	0.09
Austrian	30	0.29
Canadian	34	0.33
Czech	9	0.09
Czechoslovakian	22	0.21
Danish	32	0.31
Dutch	282	2.73
English	660	6.40
Estonian	9	0.09
European	79	0.77
Finnish	16	0.16
French, except Basque	287	2.78
French Canadian	89	0.86
German	2,238	21.69
Greek	113	1.10
Hawaii Native/Pacific Islander:	9	0.09
Micronesian: (2)	2	0.02
Guamanian/Chamorro (2)	2	0.02
Polynesian: (4)	6	0.06
Native Hawaiian	1	0.01
Samoan (4)	5	0.05
Other Pac. Isl., not spec.	1	0.01
Hispanic or Latino:	438	4.22
Central American:	6	0.06
Costa Rican	3	0.03
Guatemalan	2	0.02

Notes: 1. Figures in the "Number" column do not add up to the total population due to: a) Ancestry/Race overlap — e.g. persons can report being both White and Irish, b) persons of Hispanic origin can report being any race, c) persons reporting two ancestries are counted in both categories. 2. Numbers in parentheses indicate the number of persons reporting this ancestry/race alone, not in combination with any other ancestry/race. 3. Refer to the Explanation of Data in the front of the book for more detailed information.

Honduran	1	0.01
Cuban	53	0.51
Dominican Republic	1	0.01
Mexican	106	1.02
Puerto Rican	196	1.89
South American:	27	0.26
Argentinean	5	0.05
Colombian	11	0.11
Ecuadorian	7	0.07
Peruvian	3	0.03
Other South American	1	0.01
Other Hispanic or Latino	49	0.47
Hungarian	191	1.85
Irish	2,626	25.46
Italian	2,917	28.28
Latvian	9	0.09
Lithuanian	24	0.23
Norwegian	153	1.48
Polish	999	9.68
Portuguese	22	0.21
Romanian	8	0.08
Russian	135	1.31
Scotch-Irish	92	0.89
Scottish	224	2.17
Slavic	29	0.28
Slovak	42	0.41
Swedish	154	1.49
Ukrainian	87	0.84
United States or American	465	4.51
Welsh	23	0.22
White:	10,020	96.58
Not Hispanic (9,635)	9,707	93.56
Hispanic (290)	313	3.02
Yugoslavian	47	0.46

Belleville

Place Type: Census Designated Place
County: Essex
Population: 35,928

Ancestry/Race	Number	%
African American/Black:	2,114	5.88
Not Hispanic (1,708)	1,848	5.14
Hispanic (218)	266	0.74
African, sub-Saharan:	199	0.55
African	126	0.35
Kenyan	12	0.03
Nigerian	61	0.17
Alaska Native tribes, specified:	3	0.01
Alaska Athabascan	1	0.00
Tlingit-Haida (1)	2	0.01
Am. Ind. or Alaska Nat., not spec.	97	0.27
Albanian	84	0.23
American Indian tribes, specified:	55	0.15
Blackfeet	2	0.01
Cherokee (4)	19	0.05
Creek	5	0.01
Delaware	2	0.01
Iroquois	2	0.01
Latin American Indians (6)	14	0.04
Potawatomi (1)	1	0.00
Pueblo (3)	7	0.02
Seminole	1	0.00
Sioux (1)	1	0.00
All other tribes	1	0.00
American Indian tribes, not spec.	11	0.03
Arab:	392	1.09
Arab/Arabic	92	0.26
Egyptian	172	0.48
Lebanese	52	0.14
Moroccan	4	0.01
Palestinian	67	0.19
Syrian	5	0.01
Armenian	61	0.17
Asian:	4,391	12.22
Bangladeshi (1)	1	0.00
Chinese, ex. Taiwanese (242)	293	0.82
Filipino (2,116)	2,224	6.19
Indian (1,038)	1,114	3.10
Indonesian (14)	15	0.04
Japanese (35)	50	0.14
Korean (87)	96	0.27
Malaysian (1)	3	0.01
Pakistani (66)	83	0.23
Sri Lankan (4)	8	0.02
Taiwanese (9)	12	0.03
Thai (33)	41	0.11
Vietnamese (317)	349	0.97
Other Asian, specified (6)	12	0.03
Other Asian, not specified (34)	90	0.25
Austrian	78	0.22
Belgian	36	0.10
Brazilian	236	0.66
British	36	0.10
Canadian	47	0.13
Croatian	59	0.16
Czech	35	0.10
Czechoslovakian	104	0.29
Danish	14	0.04
Dutch	182	0.51
Eastern European	31	0.09
English	784	2.18
European	62	0.17
Finnish	14	0.04
French, except Basque	294	0.82
French Canadian	103	0.29
German	2,463	6.86
Greek	164	0.46
Guyanese	42	0.12
Hawaii Native/Pacific Islander:	73	0.20
Micronesian: (3)	10	0.03
Guamanian/Chamorro (3)	10	0.03
Polynesian: (11)	26	0.07
Native Hawaiian (4)	14	0.04
Samoan (7)	12	0.03
Other Pac. Isl., specified	6	0.02
Other Pac. Isl., not spec. (11)	31	0.09
Hispanic or Latino:	8,507	23.68
Central American:	350	0.97
Costa Rican	38	0.11
Guatemalan	125	0.35
Honduran	68	0.19
Nicaraguan	18	0.05
Panamanian	18	0.05
Salvadoran	53	0.15
Other Central American	30	0.08
Cuban	454	1.26
Dominican Republic	409	1.14
Mexican	158	0.44
Puerto Rican	3,430	9.55
South American:	1,939	5.40
Argentinean	66	0.18
Bolivian	4	0.01
Chilean	18	0.05
Colombian	232	0.65
Ecuadorian	1,098	3.06
Peruvian	382	1.06
Uruguayan	50	0.14
Venezuelan	27	0.08
Other South American	62	0.17
Other Hispanic or Latino	1,767	4.92
Hungarian	229	0.64
Icelander	7	0.02
Iranian	51	0.14
Irish	3,371	9.38
Italian	11,115	30.94
Latvian	9	0.03
Lithuanian	118	0.33
Norwegian	41	0.11
Polish	1,611	4.48
Portuguese	610	1.70
Romanian	52	0.14
Russian	253	0.70
Scotch-Irish	151	0.42
Scottish	228	0.63
Serbian	23	0.06
Slavic	22	0.06
Slovak	47	0.13
Swedish	37	0.10
Swiss	31	0.09
Turkish	183	0.51
Ukrainian	122	0.34
United States or American	918	2.56
Welsh	96	0.27
West Indian, excl. Hispanic:	385	1.07
British West Indian	8	0.02
Haitian	194	0.54
Jamaican	54	0.15
Trinidadian and Tobagonian	37	0.10
West Indian	92	0.26
White:	26,086	72.61
Not Hispanic (20,669)	21,336	59.39
Hispanic (4,281)	4,750	13.22
Yugoslavian	172	0.48

Bellmawr

Place Type: Borough
County: Camden
Population: 11,262

Ancestry/Race	Number	%
African American/Black:	163	1.45
Not Hispanic (130)	156	1.39
Hispanic (3)	7	0.06
Am. Ind. or Alaska Nat., not spec.	16	0.14
Albanian	9	0.08
Alsatian	6	0.05
American Indian tribes, specified:	29	0.26
Blackfeet (1)	8	0.07
Cherokee	7	0.06
Chickasaw	1	0.01
Chippewa	6	0.05
Delaware (1)	1	0.01
Iroquois	3	0.03
Latin American Indians (1)	2	0.02
All other tribes	1	0.01
American Indian tribes, not spec.	3	0.03
Arab:	13	0.12
Syrian	13	0.12
Armenian	5	0.04
Asian:	412	3.66
Bangladeshi (8)	11	0.10
Chinese, ex. Taiwanese (64)	66	0.59
Filipino (11)	27	0.24
Indian (156)	170	1.51
Indonesian (3)	3	0.03
Japanese (4)	4	0.04
Korean (5)	7	0.06
Laotian (5)	6	0.05
Pakistani (71)	100	0.89
Taiwanese	2	0.02
Vietnamese (4)	5	0.04
Other Asian, specified (2)	2	0.02
Other Asian, not specified (7)	9	0.08
Austrian	25	0.22
Brazilian	11	0.10
British	6	0.05
Canadian	5	0.04
Celtic	23	0.20
Croatian	11	0.10
Czechoslovakian	11	0.10
Dutch	107	0.95
English	983	8.73
French, except Basque	193	1.71
French Canadian	17	0.15
German	2,422	21.51
Greek	49	0.44
Hawaii Native/Pacific Islander:	3	0.03
Melanesian: (1)	1	0.01
Fijian (1)	1	0.01
Micronesian: (1)	1	0.01
Guamanian/Chamorro (1)	1	0.01
Polynesian:	1	0.01
Native Hawaiian	1	0.01
Hispanic or Latino:	394	3.50
Central American:	6	0.05
Guatemalan	4	0.04
Honduran	1	0.01

Notes: 1. Figures in the "Number" column do not add up to the total population due to: a) Ancestry/Race overlap — e.g. persons can report being both White and Irish, b) persons of Hispanic origin can report being any race, c) persons reporting two ancestries are counted in both categories. 2. Numbers in parentheses indicate the number of persons reporting this ancestry/race alone, not in combination with any other ancestry/race. 3. Refer to the Explanation of Data in the front of the book for more detailed information.

Panamanian	1	0.01
Cuban	1	0.01
Dominican Republic	2	0.02
Mexican	115	1.02
Puerto Rican	202	1.79
South American:	14	0.12
Argentinean	3	0.03
Colombian	5	0.04
Peruvian	1	0.01
Uruguayan	2	0.02
Other South American	3	0.03
Other Hispanic or Latino	54	0.48
Hungarian	59	0.52
Irish	3,515	31.21
Italian	3,501	31.09
Lithuanian	94	0.83
Norwegian	61	0.54
Pennsylvania German	16	0.14
Polish	1,355	12.03
Portuguese	5	0.04
Russian	55	0.49
Scotch-Irish	79	0.70
Scottish	103	0.91
Slovak	42	0.37
Swedish	32	0.28
Ukrainian	35	0.31
United States or American	324	2.88
Welsh	103	0.91
West Indian, excl. Hispanic:	11	0.10
Jamaican	11	0.10
White:	10,565	93.81
Not Hispanic (10,238)	10,333	91.75
Hispanic (212)	232	2.06
Yugoslavian	13	0.12

Bergenfield

Place Type: Borough
County: Bergen
Population: 26,247

Ancestry/Race	Number	%
African American/Black:	2,050	7.81
Not Hispanic (1,665)	1,850	7.05
Hispanic (147)	200	0.76
African, sub-Saharan:	313	1.19
African	150	0.57
Ghanian	15	0.06
Nigerian	138	0.53
Other sub-Saharan African	10	0.04
Alaska Native tribes, specified:	2	0.01
Tlingit-Haida	2	0.01
Am. Ind. or Alaska Nat., not spec.	102	0.39
Albanian	36	0.14
American Indian tribes, specified:	53	0.20
Apache	1	0.00
Blackfeet	7	0.03
Cherokee (2)	13	0.05
Chickasaw	1	0.00
Delaware	4	0.02
Iroquois	5	0.02
Latin American Indians (5)	14	0.05
Seminole	2	0.01
Sioux (1)	3	0.01
All other tribes	3	0.01
American Indian tribes, not spec.	21	0.08
Arab:	154	0.59
Arab/Arabic	26	0.10
Egyptian	47	0.18
Iraqi	10	0.04
Lebanese	29	0.11
Syrian	22	0.08
Other Arab	20	0.08
Armenian	221	0.84
Asian:	5,678	21.63
Chinese, ex. Taiwanese (220)	254	0.97
Filipino (3,133)	3,254	12.40
Indian (1,504)	1,602	6.10
Indonesian (1)	1	0.00
Japanese (65)	79	0.30
Korean (203)	212	0.81
Malaysian (2)	3	0.01
Pakistani (56)	103	0.39
Sri Lankan (20)	23	0.09
Taiwanese (12)	13	0.05
Thai (10)	11	0.04
Vietnamese (24)	24	0.09
Other Asian, specified (17)	19	0.07
Other Asian, not specified (47)	80	0.30
Australian	5	0.02
Austrian	138	0.53
Belgian	30	0.11
Brazilian	12	0.05
British	123	0.47
Canadian	25	0.10
Croatian	43	0.16
Czech	57	0.22
Czechoslovakian	100	0.38
Danish	21	0.08
Dutch	287	1.09
Eastern European	62	0.24
English	951	3.62
Estonian	24	0.09
European	180	0.69
Finnish	29	0.11
French, except Basque	328	1.25
French Canadian	37	0.14
German	2,807	10.69
Greek	409	1.56
Guyanese	78	0.30
Hawaii Native/Pacific Islander:	27	0.10
Micronesian:	8	0.03
Guamanian/Chamorro	8	0.03
Polynesian: (2)	3	0.01
Native Hawaiian (1)	2	0.01
Tongan (1)	1	0.00
Other Pac. Isl., not spec. (2)	16	0.06
Hispanic or Latino:	4,474	17.05
Central American:	272	1.04
Costa Rican	33	0.13
Guatemalan	49	0.19
Honduran	42	0.16
Nicaraguan	18	0.07
Panamanian	6	0.02
Salvadoran	109	0.42
Other Central American	15	0.06
Cuban	247	0.94
Dominican Republic	638	2.43
Mexican	220	0.84
Puerto Rican	926	3.53
South American:	1,121	4.27
Argentinean	17	0.06
Bolivian	4	0.02
Chilean	45	0.17
Colombian	850	3.24
Ecuadorian	120	0.46
Paraguayan	2	0.01
Peruvian	43	0.16
Uruguayan	1	0.00
Venezuelan	18	0.07
Other South American	21	0.08
Other Hispanic or Latino	1,050	4.00
Hungarian	137	0.52
Icelander	6	0.02
Iranian	21	0.08
Irish	4,242	16.16
Israeli	41	0.16
Italian	4,419	16.84
Lithuanian	35	0.13
Macedonian	16	0.06
Maltese	4	0.02
Norwegian	119	0.45
Polish	809	3.08
Portuguese	45	0.17
Romanian	30	0.11
Russian	350	1.33
Scandinavian	42	0.16
Scotch-Irish	199	0.76
Scottish	208	0.79
Serbian	21	0.08
Slavic	20	0.08
Slovak	67	0.26
Swedish	173	0.66
Swiss	131	0.50
Ukrainian	99	0.38
United States or American	699	2.66
Welsh	48	0.18
West Indian, excl. Hispanic:	590	2.25
British West Indian	39	0.15
Haitian	12	0.05
Jamaican	318	1.21
Trinidadian and Tobagonian	169	0.64
West Indian	52	0.20
White:	17,040	64.92
Not Hispanic (14,165)	14,404	54.88
Hispanic (2,345)	2,636	10.04
Yugoslavian	129	0.49

Berkeley Heights

Place Type: Census Designated Place
County: Union
Population: 13,407

Ancestry/Race	Number	%
African American/Black:	164	1.22
Not Hispanic (143)	158	1.18
Hispanic (6)	6	0.04
African, sub-Saharan:	23	0.17
African	23	0.17
Am. Ind. or Alaska Nat., not spec.	6	0.04
Albanian	41	0.31
American Indian tribes, specified:	17	0.13
Cherokee (2)	5	0.04
Cree	1	0.01
Delaware (1)	1	0.01
Iroquois (1)	2	0.01
Latin American Indians (2)	2	0.01
Potawatomi	4	0.03
Pueblo	1	0.01
All other tribes	1	0.01
American Indian tribes, not spec.	3	0.02
Arab:	95	0.71
Arab/Arabic	8	0.06
Lebanese	46	0.34
Syrian	41	0.31
Armenian	48	0.36
Asian:	1,110	8.28
Chinese, ex. Taiwanese (504)	535	3.99
Filipino (45)	55	0.41
Indian (278)	286	2.13
Indonesian (5)	5	0.04
Japanese (23)	25	0.19
Korean (101)	104	0.78
Malaysian (2)	2	0.01
Pakistani (12)	14	0.10
Taiwanese (42)	45	0.34
Thai (2)	2	0.01
Vietnamese (15)	17	0.13
Other Asian, specified (2)	2	0.01
Other Asian, not specified (16)	18	0.13
Assyrian/Chaldean/Syriac	6	0.04
Austrian	110	0.82
Belgian	15	0.11
Brazilian	32	0.24
British	262	1.95
Canadian	62	0.46
Celtic	5	0.04
Croatian	9	0.07
Czech	115	0.86
Czechoslovakian	44	0.33
Danish	111	0.83
Dutch	189	1.41
Eastern European	158	1.18
English	1,206	9.00
Estonian	7	0.05
European	81	0.60
French, except Basque	276	2.06
French Canadian	41	0.31
German	2,319	17.30

Notes: 1. Figures in the "Number" column do not add up to the total population due to: a) Ancestry/Race overlap — e.g. persons can report being both White and Irish, b) persons of Hispanic origin can report being any race, c) persons reporting two ancestries are counted in both categories. 2. Numbers in parentheses indicate the number of persons reporting this ancestry/race alone, not in combination with any other ancestry/race. 3. Refer to the Explanation of Data in the front of the book for more detailed information.

Greek	149	1.11
Hispanic or Latino:	494	3.68
Central American:	115	0.86
Costa Rican	98	0.73
Guatemalan	2	0.01
Honduran	3	0.02
Nicaraguan	4	0.03
Salvadoran	7	0.05
Other Central American	1	0.01
Cuban	45	0.34
Dominican Republic	5	0.04
Mexican	37	0.28
Puerto Rican	93	0.69
South American:	82	0.61
Argentinean	7	0.05
Chilean	5	0.04
Colombian	25	0.19
Ecuadorian	14	0.10
Paraguayan	6	0.04
Peruvian	9	0.07
Uruguayan	5	0.04
Venezuelan	10	0.07
Other South American	1	0.01
Other Hispanic or Latino	117	0.87
Hungarian	295	2.20
Iranian	26	0.19
Irish	3,011	22.46
Italian	3,407	25.41
Latvian	17	0.13
Lithuanian	123	0.92
Luxemburger	9	0.07
New Zealander	7	0.05
Norwegian	110	0.82
Pennsylvania German	27	0.20
Polish	758	5.65
Portuguese	142	1.06
Romanian	6	0.04
Russian	627	4.68
Scandinavian	7	0.05
Scotch-Irish	151	1.13
Scottish	346	2.58
Slovak	124	0.92
Slovene	11	0.08
Swedish	99	0.74
Swiss	71	0.53
Ukrainian	94	0.70
United States or American	307	2.29
Welsh	33	0.25
West Indian, excl. Hispanic:	34	0.25
Jamaican	34	0.25
White:	12,106	90.30
Not Hispanic (11,611)	11,683	87.14
Hispanic (408)	423	3.16
Yugoslavian	11	0.08

Berkeley

Place Type: Township
County: Ocean
Population: 39,991

Ancestry/Race	Number	%
African American/Black:	583	1.46
Not Hispanic (482)	542	1.36
Hispanic (37)	41	0.10
African, sub-Saharan:	7	0.02
Cape Verdean	7	0.02
Alaska Native tribes, specified:	2	0.01
Eskimo	2	0.01
Am. Ind. or Alaska Nat., not spec.	33	0.08
Albanian	7	0.02
American Indian tribes, specified:	72	0.18
Apache (1)	1	0.00
Blackfeet	3	0.01
Cherokee (5)	28	0.07
Choctaw	3	0.01
Comanche	5	0.01
Delaware (2)	6	0.02
Iroquois (1)	8	0.02
Kiowa	5	0.01
Latin American Indians (1)	2	0.01
Navajo	2	0.01
Ottawa	1	0.00
Seminole	1	0.00
Sioux (2)	4	0.01
All other tribes	3	0.01
American Indian tribes, not spec.	3	0.01
Arab:	62	0.16
Lebanese	17	0.04
Syrian	45	0.11
Armenian	101	0.25
Asian:	237	0.59
Cambodian (1)	1	0.00
Chinese, ex. Taiwanese (42)	49	0.12
Filipino (60)	77	0.19
Indian (17)	25	0.06
Japanese (18)	23	0.06
Korean (27)	33	0.08
Thai	1	0.00
Vietnamese (12)	14	0.04
Other Asian, specified (1)	1	0.00
Other Asian, not specified (2)	13	0.03
Austrian	261	0.65
Belgian	94	0.24
British	94	0.24
Bulgarian	8	0.02
Canadian	68	0.17
Croatian	44	0.11
Czech	183	0.46
Czechoslovakian	228	0.57
Danish	155	0.39
Dutch	709	1.77
English	2,734	6.84
Estonian	13	0.03
European	105	0.26
Finnish	36	0.09
French, except Basque	786	1.97
French Canadian	140	0.35
German	6,929	17.33
Greek	130	0.33
Hawaii Native/Pacific Islander:	9	0.02
Micronesian: (1)	1	0.00
Guamanian/Chamorro (1)	1	0.00
Polynesian: (2)	6	0.02
Native Hawaiian (2)	5	0.01
Samoan	1	0.00
Other Pac. Isl., not spec. (1)	2	0.01
Hispanic or Latino:	932	2.33
Central American:	18	0.05
Costa Rican	8	0.02
Guatemalan	4	0.01
Honduran	2	0.01
Nicaraguan	1	0.00
Salvadoran	3	0.01
Cuban	78	0.20
Dominican Republic	4	0.01
Mexican	228	0.57
Puerto Rican	354	0.89
South American:	63	0.16
Argentinean	9	0.02
Chilean	6	0.02
Colombian	19	0.05
Ecuadorian	4	0.01
Peruvian	6	0.02
Uruguayan	8	0.02
Venezuelan	4	0.01
Other South American	7	0.02
Other Hispanic or Latino	187	0.47
Hungarian	658	1.65
Icelander	8	0.02
Irish	8,541	21.36
Italian	11,757	29.40
Latvian	30	0.08
Lithuanian	287	0.72
Maltese	16	0.04
Northern European	22	0.06
Norwegian	395	0.99
Pennsylvania German	35	0.09
Polish	3,686	9.22
Portuguese	163	0.41
Romanian	59	0.15
Russian	713	1.78
Scandinavian	18	0.05
Scotch-Irish	421	1.05
Scottish	792	1.98
Slavic	67	0.17
Slovak	419	1.05
Slovene	19	0.05
Swedish	293	0.73
Swiss	74	0.19
Turkish	59	0.15
Ukrainian	554	1.39
United States or American	1,322	3.31
Welsh	291	0.73
West Indian, excl. Hispanic:	30	0.08
Barbadian	12	0.03
Jamaican	18	0.05
White:	39,071	97.70
Not Hispanic (38,153)	38,347	95.89
Hispanic (680)	724	1.81
Yugoslavian	83	0.21

Bernards

Place Type: Township
County: Somerset
Population: 24,575

Ancestry/Race	Number	%
African American/Black:	392	1.60
Not Hispanic (341)	373	1.52
Hispanic (13)	19	0.08
African, sub-Saharan:	55	0.22
African	19	0.08
Ghanian	5	0.02
Kenyan	14	0.06
South African	12	0.05
Zimbabwean	5	0.02
Alaska Native tribes, specified:	1	0.00
Alaska Athabascan	1	0.00
Am. Ind. or Alaska Nat., not spec.	17	0.07
Albanian	9	0.04
American Indian tribes, specified:	30	0.12
Apache (4)	4	0.02
Blackfeet	1	0.00
Cherokee (1)	9	0.04
Creek (1)	1	0.00
Crow	1	0.00
Delaware (1)	5	0.02
Iroquois (1)	2	0.01
Menominee	2	0.01
Osage	1	0.00
Sioux	2	0.01
All other tribes (1)	2	0.01
American Indian tribes, not spec.	2	0.01
Arab:	194	0.79
Egyptian	42	0.17
Lebanese	53	0.22
Syrian	99	0.40
Armenian	69	0.28
Asian:	2,122	8.63
Chinese, ex. Taiwanese (758)	814	3.31
Filipino (90)	116	0.47
Indian (701)	729	2.97
Indonesian (1)	3	0.01
Japanese (57)	94	0.38
Korean (171)	192	0.78
Malaysian	3	0.01
Pakistani (39)	48	0.20
Taiwanese (49)	56	0.23
Thai (6)	8	0.03
Vietnamese (12)	14	0.06
Other Asian, specified (5)	8	0.03
Other Asian, not specified (8)	37	0.15
Australian	18	0.07
Austrian	188	0.77
Basque	9	0.04
Belgian	64	0.26
Brazilian	56	0.23
British	234	0.95

Notes: 1. Figures in the "Number" column do not add up to the total population due to: a) Ancestry/Race overlap — e.g. persons can report being both White and Irish, b) persons of Hispanic origin can report being any race, c) persons reporting two ancestries are counted in both categories. 2. Numbers in parentheses indicate the number of persons reporting this ancestry/race alone, not in combination with any other ancestry/race. 3. Refer to the Explanation of Data in the front of the book for more detailed information.

Ancestry/Race	Number	%
Bulgarian	5	0.02
Canadian	115	0.47
Carpatho Rusyn	10	0.04
Celtic	24	0.10
Croatian	40	0.16
Czech	206	0.84
Czechoslovakian	156	0.63
Danish	170	0.69
Dutch	298	1.21
Eastern European	121	0.49
English	2,699	10.98
Estonian	41	0.17
European	119	0.48
Finnish	30	0.12
French, except Basque	478	1.95
French Canadian	94	0.38
German	4,607	18.75
Greek	168	0.68
Guyanese	21	0.09
Hawaii Native/Pacific Islander:	10	0.04
Micronesian: (2)	5	0.02
Guamanian/Chamorro (1)	1	0.00
Other Micronesian (1)	4	0.02
Polynesian:	3	0.01
Native Hawaiian	3	0.01
Other Pac. Isl., not spec. (1)	2	0.01
Hispanic or Latino:	646	2.63
Central American:	35	0.14
Costa Rican	19	0.08
Guatemalan	3	0.01
Honduran	3	0.01
Nicaraguan	3	0.01
Panamanian	4	0.02
Salvadoran	3	0.01
Cuban	82	0.33
Dominican Republic	14	0.06
Mexican	60	0.24
Puerto Rican	105	0.43
South American:	154	0.63
Argentinean	32	0.13
Bolivian	7	0.03
Chilean	22	0.09
Colombian	37	0.15
Ecuadorian	10	0.04
Paraguayan	16	0.07
Peruvian	11	0.04
Uruguayan	1	0.00
Venezuelan	11	0.04
Other South American	7	0.03
Other Hispanic or Latino	196	0.80
Hungarian	402	1.64
Iranian	234	0.95
Irish	5,765	23.46
Israeli	7	0.03
Italian	4,689	19.08
Latvian	5	0.02
Lithuanian	129	0.52
Maltese	5	0.02
Northern European	6	0.02
Norwegian	177	0.72
Pennsylvania German	8	0.03
Polish	1,740	7.08
Portuguese	269	1.09
Romanian	13	0.05
Russian	714	2.91
Scandinavian	46	0.19
Scotch-Irish	349	1.42
Scottish	787	3.20
Slavic	10	0.04
Slovak	212	0.86
Slovene	5	0.02
Swedish	457	1.86
Swiss	115	0.47
Turkish	8	0.03
Ukrainian	166	0.68
United States or American	819	3.33
Welsh	217	0.88
West Indian, excl. Hispanic:	48	0.20
British West Indian	8	0.03
Jamaican	33	0.13
Trinidadian and Tobagonian	7	0.03
White:	22,145	90.11
Not Hispanic (21,398)	21,593	87.87
Hispanic (523)	552	2.25
Yugoslavian	73	0.30

Bloomfield

Place Type: Census Designated Place
County: Essex
Population: 47,683

Ancestry/Race	Number	%
African American/Black:	6,074	12.74
Not Hispanic (5,332)	5,716	11.99
Hispanic (241)	358	0.75
African, sub-Saharan:	496	1.04
African	332	0.70
Ghanian	25	0.05
Kenyan	25	0.05
Nigerian	94	0.20
South African	8	0.02
Other sub-Saharan African	12	0.03
Am. Ind. or Alaska Nat., not spec.	137	0.29
Albanian	109	0.23
Alsatian	4	0.01
American Indian tribes, specified:	116	0.24
Apache (1)	2	0.00
Blackfeet (1)	6	0.01
Cherokee (4)	36	0.08
Choctaw	2	0.00
Cree	1	0.00
Creek	1	0.00
Delaware (1)	4	0.01
Iroquois	2	0.00
Latin American Indians (21)	45	0.09
Navajo (1)	1	0.00
Osage	1	0.00
Potawatomi	1	0.00
Puget Sound Salish	1	0.00
Sioux (1)	2	0.00
All other tribes (1)	11	0.02
American Indian tribes, not spec.	28	0.06
Arab:	620	1.30
Arab/Arabic	35	0.07
Egyptian	300	0.63
Jordanian	9	0.02
Lebanese	156	0.33
Moroccan	36	0.08
Syrian	75	0.16
Other Arab	9	0.02
Armenian	116	0.24
Asian:	4,364	9.15
Bangladeshi (11)	13	0.03
Cambodian (1)	1	0.00
Chinese, ex. Taiwanese (535)	599	1.26
Filipino (1,586)	1,714	3.59
Indian (1,301)	1,409	2.95
Indonesian (10)	15	0.03
Japanese (56)	73	0.15
Korean (158)	172	0.36
Malaysian (3)	4	0.01
Pakistani (72)	79	0.17
Sri Lankan (10)	14	0.03
Taiwanese (7)	8	0.02
Thai (60)	62	0.13
Vietnamese (86)	98	0.21
Other Asian, specified (9)	10	0.02
Other Asian, not specified (54)	93	0.20
Assyrian/Chaldean/Syriac	9	0.02
Austrian	202	0.42
Basque	12	0.03
Belgian	45	0.09
Brazilian	128	0.27
British	106	0.22
Bulgarian	31	0.07
Canadian	29	0.06
Celtic	9	0.02
Croatian	10	0.02
Czech	119	0.25
Czechoslovakian	65	0.14
Danish	120	0.25
Dutch	306	0.64
Eastern European	83	0.17
English	1,982	4.16
European	104	0.22
Finnish	53	0.11
French, except Basque	659	1.38
French Canadian	112	0.23
German	4,865	10.20
Greek	380	0.80
Guyanese	394	0.83
Hawaii Native/Pacific Islander:	95	0.20
Melanesian: (1)	1	0.00
Fijian (1)	1	0.00
Micronesian: (11)	15	0.03
Guamanian/Chamorro (11)	15	0.03
Polynesian: (3)	10	0.02
Native Hawaiian (1)	6	0.01
Samoan (2)	4	0.01
Other Pac. Isl., specified	1	0.00
Other Pac. Isl., not spec. (16)	68	0.14
Hispanic or Latino:	6,901	14.47
Central American:	544	1.14
Costa Rican	197	0.41
Guatemalan	137	0.29
Honduran	53	0.11
Nicaraguan	39	0.08
Panamanian	8	0.02
Salvadoran	93	0.20
Other Central American	17	0.04
Cuban	377	0.79
Dominican Republic	399	0.84
Mexican	160	0.34
Puerto Rican	2,724	5.71
South American:	1,291	2.71
Argentinean	71	0.15
Bolivian	3	0.01
Chilean	55	0.12
Colombian	234	0.49
Ecuadorian	514	1.08
Peruvian	297	0.62
Uruguayan	27	0.06
Venezuelan	43	0.09
Other South American	47	0.10
Other Hispanic or Latino	1,406	2.95
Hungarian	401	0.84
Icelander	6	0.01
Iranian	55	0.12
Irish	6,607	13.86
Israeli	13	0.03
Italian	12,590	26.40
Latvian	35	0.07
Lithuanian	280	0.59
Macedonian	7	0.01
Northern European	17	0.04
Norwegian	77	0.16
Pennsylvania German	11	0.02
Polish	3,315	6.95
Portuguese	368	0.77
Romanian	66	0.14
Russian	939	1.97
Scandinavian	69	0.14
Scotch-Irish	467	0.98
Scottish	745	1.56
Serbian	12	0.03
Slavic	33	0.07
Slovak	166	0.35
Swedish	198	0.42
Swiss	123	0.26
Turkish	40	0.08
Ukrainian	225	0.47
United States or American	790	1.66
Welsh	160	0.34
West Indian, excl. Hispanic:	1,069	2.24
Bahamian	9	0.02
British West Indian	43	0.09
Haitian	339	0.71
Jamaican	464	0.97
Trinidadian and Tobagonian	123	0.26

Notes: 1. Figures in the "Number" column do not add up to the total population due to: a) Ancestry/Race overlap — e.g. persons can report being both White and Irish, b) persons of Hispanic origin can report being any race, c) persons reporting two ancestries are counted in both categories. 2. Numbers in parentheses indicate the number of persons reporting this ancestry/race alone, not in combination with any other ancestry/race. 3. Refer to the Explanation of Data in the front of the book for more detailed information.

West Indian	91	0.19
White:	34,463	72.28
Not Hispanic (30,036)	30,715	64.41
Hispanic (3,385)	3,748	7.86
Yugoslavian	55	0.12

Bound Brook

Place Type: Borough
County: Somerset
Population: 10,155

Ancestry/Race	Number	%
Acadian/Cajun	6	0.06
African American/Black:	300	2.95
Not Hispanic (222)	251	2.47
Hispanic (34)	49	0.48
African, sub-Saharan:	39	0.38
Ghanian	24	0.24
South African	15	0.15
Am. Ind. or Alaska Nat., not spec.	23	0.23
American Indian tribes, specified:	23	0.23
Blackfeet	1	0.01
Cherokee (1)	2	0.02
Iroquois	2	0.02
Latin American Indians (1)	11	0.11
Lumbee (5)	5	0.05
Seminole	1	0.01
All other tribes (1)	1	0.01
American Indian tribes, not spec.	13	0.13
Arab:	128	1.26
Arab/Arabic	6	0.06
Egyptian	69	0.68
Jordanian	18	0.18
Palestinian	28	0.27
Other Arab	7	0.07
Armenian	6	0.06
Asian:	343	3.38
Chinese, ex. Taiwanese (51)	65	0.64
Filipino (20)	35	0.34
Indian (129)	140	1.38
Indonesian (3)	7	0.07
Japanese (6)	11	0.11
Korean (12)	12	0.12
Laotian (3)	7	0.07
Pakistani (11)	12	0.12
Taiwanese (9)	9	0.09
Vietnamese (36)	36	0.35
Other Asian, not specified (5)	9	0.09
Austrian	24	0.24
Belgian	8	0.08
Brazilian	17	0.17
British	11	0.11
Canadian	10	0.10
Czech	33	0.32
Czechoslovakian	19	0.19
Dutch	95	0.93
Eastern European	21	0.21
English	397	3.90
European	47	0.46
French, except Basque	124	1.22
French Canadian	24	0.24
German	1,013	9.94
Greek	69	0.68
Guyanese	14	0.14
Hawaii Native/Pacific Islander:	11	0.11
Micronesian: (6)	6	0.06
Guamanian/Chamorro (6)	6	0.06
Polynesian: (1)	2	0.02
Samoan	1	0.01
Other Polynesian (1)	1	0.01
Other Pac. Isl., not spec.	3	0.03
Hispanic or Latino:	3,541	34.87
Central American:	1,202	11.84
Costa Rican	941	9.27
Guatemalan	64	0.63
Honduran	20	0.20
Nicaraguan	17	0.17
Panamanian	4	0.04
Salvadoran	131	1.29
Other Central American	25	0.25
Cuban	43	0.42
Dominican Republic	27	0.27
Mexican	706	6.95
Puerto Rican	246	2.42
South American:	532	5.24
Argentinean	9	0.09
Chilean	6	0.06
Colombian	270	2.66
Ecuadorian	95	0.94
Paraguayan	8	0.08
Peruvian	120	1.18
Uruguayan	2	0.02
Venezuelan	14	0.14
Other South American	8	0.08
Other Hispanic or Latino	785	7.73
Hungarian	138	1.35
Irish	1,212	11.89
Italian	1,902	18.66
Lithuanian	31	0.30
Macedonian	34	0.33
Norwegian	27	0.26
Pennsylvania German	5	0.05
Polish	842	8.26
Portuguese	62	0.61
Russian	137	1.34
Scotch-Irish	67	0.66
Scottish	116	1.14
Serbian	12	0.12
Slavic	8	0.08
Slovak	53	0.52
Slovene	6	0.06
Swedish	35	0.34
Swiss	49	0.48
Ukrainian	73	0.72
United States or American	264	2.59
Welsh	82	0.80
West Indian, excl. Hispanic:	25	0.25
British West Indian	25	0.25
White:	8,642	85.10
Not Hispanic (5,964)	6,039	59.47
Hispanic (2,421)	2,603	25.63
Yugoslavian	29	0.28

Branchburg

Place Type: Township
County: Somerset
Population: 14,566

Ancestry/Race	Number	%
African American/Black:	308	2.11
Not Hispanic (273)	295	2.03
Hispanic (11)	13	0.09
African, sub-Saharan:	11	0.08
African	11	0.08
Am. Ind. or Alaska Nat., not spec.	5	0.03
American Indian tribes, specified:	47	0.32
Apache	4	0.03
Blackfeet	2	0.01
Cherokee	9	0.06
Chickasaw (1)	1	0.01
Chippewa (1)	1	0.01
Choctaw (1)	1	0.01
Delaware (2)	2	0.01
Iroquois	3	0.02
Latin American Indians (4)	4	0.03
Lumbee (3)	3	0.02
Osage	1	0.01
Seminole	5	0.03
Sioux (1)	1	0.01
All other tribes (1)	10	0.07
Arab:	132	0.91
Arab/Arabic	41	0.28
Egyptian	11	0.08
Iraqi	10	0.07
Lebanese	64	0.44
Other Arab	6	0.04
Armenian	22	0.15
Asian:	977	6.71
Cambodian (3)	3	0.02
Chinese, ex. Taiwanese (274)	302	2.07
Filipino (81)	98	0.67
Indian (407)	413	2.84
Japanese (20)	36	0.25
Korean (51)	60	0.41
Pakistani (1)	1	0.01
Sri Lankan (1)	1	0.01
Taiwanese (29)	32	0.22
Thai (4)	4	0.03
Vietnamese (17)	20	0.14
Other Asian, specified (1)	1	0.01
Other Asian, not specified (1)	6	0.04
Austrian	99	0.68
Belgian	49	0.34
Brazilian	21	0.14
British	62	0.43
Canadian	18	0.12
Croatian	11	0.08
Czech	59	0.41
Czechoslovakian	63	0.43
Danish	120	0.82
Dutch	336	2.31
Eastern European	52	0.36
English	1,486	10.20
Estonian	9	0.06
European	79	0.54
French, except Basque	435	2.99
French Canadian	178	1.22
German	2,728	18.73
Greek	179	1.23
Hawaii Native/Pacific Islander:	7	0.05
Polynesian: (4)	6	0.04
Native Hawaiian (3)	5	0.03
Samoan (1)	1	0.01
Other Pac. Isl., not spec.	1	0.01
Hispanic or Latino:	392	2.69
Central American:	11	0.08
Costa Rican	5	0.03
Honduran	1	0.01
Nicaraguan	1	0.01
Salvadoran	4	0.03
Cuban	51	0.35
Dominican Republic	3	0.02
Mexican	20	0.14
Puerto Rican	137	0.94
South American:	80	0.55
Argentinean	12	0.08
Chilean	6	0.04
Colombian	36	0.25
Ecuadorian	5	0.03
Paraguayan	3	0.02
Peruvian	9	0.06
Venezuelan	6	0.04
Other South American	3	0.02
Other Hispanic or Latino	90	0.62
Hungarian	463	3.18
Irish	2,655	18.23
Israeli	8	0.05
Italian	3,102	21.30
Latvian	10	0.07
Lithuanian	115	0.79
Northern European	8	0.05
Norwegian	170	1.17
Pennsylvania German	17	0.12
Polish	1,327	9.11
Portuguese	151	1.04
Romanian	93	0.64
Russian	325	2.23
Scotch-Irish	100	0.69
Scottish	245	1.68
Serbian	19	0.13
Slavic	52	0.36
Slovak	191	1.31
Slovene	18	0.12
Swedish	175	1.20
Swiss	72	0.49
Turkish	36	0.25
Ukrainian	336	2.31
United States or American	448	3.08

Notes: 1. Figures in the "Number" column do not add up to the total population due to: a) Ancestry/Race overlap — e.g. persons can report being both White and Irish, b) persons of Hispanic origin can report being any race, c) persons reporting two ancestries are counted in both categories. 2. Numbers in parentheses indicate the number of persons reporting this ancestry/race alone, not in combination with any other ancestry/race. 3. Refer to the Explanation of Data in the front of the book for more detailed information.

Ancestry/Race	Number	%
Welsh	64	0.44
West Indian, excl. Hispanic:	38	0.26
Barbadian	9	0.06
Jamaican	24	0.16
West Indian	5	0.03
White:	13,292	91.25
Not Hispanic (12,856)	12,965	89.01
Hispanic (318)	327	2.24
Yugoslavian	18	0.12

Brick

Place Type: Township
County: Ocean
Population: 76,119

Ancestry/Race	Number	%
African American/Black:	948	1.25
Not Hispanic (705)	864	1.14
Hispanic (46)	84	0.11
African, sub-Saharan:	141	0.19
African	103	0.14
Ghanian	28	0.04
Nigerian	10	0.01
Am. Ind. or Alaska Nat., not spec.	101	0.13
Albanian	13	0.02
Alsatian	14	0.02
American Indian tribes, specified:	165	0.22
Apache	6	0.01
Blackfeet (1)	14	0.02
Cherokee (15)	58	0.08
Cheyenne (1)	1	0.00
Chippewa (3)	4	0.01
Comanche	4	0.01
Delaware	12	0.02
Iroquois (3)	22	0.03
Latin American Indians (8)	10	0.01
Lumbee (1)	2	0.00
Paiute (1)	1	0.00
Potawatomi (1)	1	0.00
Pueblo	3	0.00
Seminole	3	0.00
Sioux	5	0.01
All other tribes (3)	19	0.02
American Indian tribes, not spec.	28	0.04
Arab:	386	0.51
Arab/Arabic	7	0.01
Egyptian	131	0.17
Lebanese	169	0.22
Syrian	79	0.10
Armenian	99	0.13
Asian:	1,106	1.45
Bangladeshi	5	0.01
Chinese, ex. Taiwanese (183)	221	0.29
Filipino (254)	293	0.38
Indian (217)	255	0.34
Indonesian (2)	6	0.01
Japanese (21)	40	0.05
Korean (122)	147	0.19
Laotian (1)	1	0.00
Pakistani (2)	4	0.01
Taiwanese (5)	11	0.01
Thai (11)	13	0.02
Vietnamese (45)	55	0.07
Other Asian, not specified (24)	55	0.07
Australian	14	0.02
Austrian	439	0.58
Belgian	26	0.03
British	217	0.29
Canadian	77	0.10
Celtic	18	0.02
Croatian	203	0.27
Czech	274	0.36
Czechoslovakian	304	0.40
Danish	369	0.48
Dutch	1,831	2.41
Eastern European	87	0.11
English	6,484	8.52
Estonian	27	0.04
European	131	0.17
Finnish	39	0.05
French, except Basque	1,760	2.31
French Canadian	393	0.52
German	15,859	20.83
Greek	708	0.93
Guyanese	15	0.02
Hawaii Native/Pacific Islander:	33	0.04
Micronesian: (1)	2	0.00
Guamanian/Chamorro (1)	2	0.00
Polynesian: (2)	10	0.01
Native Hawaiian (1)	9	0.01
Samoan (1)	1	0.00
Other Pac. Isl., not spec. (9)	21	0.03
Hispanic or Latino:	2,930	3.85
Central American:	81	0.11
Costa Rican	33	0.04
Guatemalan	20	0.03
Honduran	11	0.01
Nicaraguan	1	0.00
Panamanian	4	0.01
Salvadoran	9	0.01
Other Central American	3	0.00
Cuban	200	0.26
Dominican Republic	49	0.06
Mexican	491	0.65
Puerto Rican	1,229	1.61
South American:	313	0.41
Argentinean	41	0.05
Bolivian	1	0.00
Chilean	21	0.03
Colombian	133	0.17
Ecuadorian	24	0.03
Paraguayan	1	0.00
Peruvian	64	0.08
Uruguayan	7	0.01
Venezuelan	6	0.01
Other South American	15	0.02
Other Hispanic or Latino	567	0.74
Hungarian	1,463	1.92
Icelander	34	0.04
Irish	22,022	28.93
Italian	23,161	30.43
Latvian	123	0.16
Lithuanian	575	0.76
Luxemburger	6	0.01
Maltese	8	0.01
Northern European	28	0.04
Norwegian	763	1.00
Pennsylvania German	9	0.01
Polish	6,973	9.16
Portuguese	544	0.71
Romanian	129	0.17
Russian	1,226	1.61
Scandinavian	95	0.12
Scotch-Irish	1,266	1.66
Scottish	1,517	1.99
Slavic	68	0.09
Slovak	552	0.73
Slovene	20	0.03
Swedish	677	0.89
Swiss	305	0.40
Turkish	35	0.05
Ukrainian	616	0.81
United States or American	2,058	2.70
Welsh	415	0.55
West Indian, excl. Hispanic:	124	0.16
British West Indian	8	0.01
Dutch West Indian	33	0.04
Haitian	26	0.03
Jamaican	10	0.01
Trinidadian and Tobagonian	32	0.04
West Indian	15	0.02
White:	73,643	96.75
Not Hispanic (70,860)	71,379	93.77
Hispanic (2,072)	2,264	2.97
Yugoslavian	89	0.12

Bridgeton

Place Type: City
County: Cumberland
Population: 22,771

Ancestry/Race	Number	%
African American/Black:	9,966	43.77
Not Hispanic (9,303)	9,623	42.26
Hispanic (225)	343	1.51
African, sub-Saharan:	350	1.54
African	330	1.45
Nigerian	11	0.05
South African	9	0.04
Am. Ind. or Alaska Nat., not spec.	207	0.91
Albanian	9	0.04
American Indian tribes, specified:	280	1.23
Apache (2)	4	0.02
Blackfeet	8	0.04
Cherokee (13)	41	0.18
Cheyenne	1	0.00
Crow	2	0.01
Delaware (45)	76	0.33
Iroquois	3	0.01
Latin American Indians (31)	55	0.24
Lumbee (1)	1	0.00
Navajo	1	0.00
Pueblo (7)	7	0.03
Sioux (2)	2	0.01
Yuman	1	0.00
All other tribes (55)	78	0.34
American Indian tribes, not spec.	30	0.13
Arab:	12	0.05
Lebanese	12	0.05
Asian:	266	1.17
Chinese, ex. Taiwanese (15)	20	0.09
Filipino (44)	53	0.23
Indian (37)	57	0.25
Japanese (39)	60	0.26
Korean (6)	6	0.03
Sri Lankan	2	0.01
Vietnamese (6)	8	0.04
Other Asian, specified	6	0.03
Other Asian, not specified (9)	54	0.24
Austrian	22	0.10
Canadian	4	0.02
Czech	29	0.13
Czechoslovakian	7	0.03
Danish	35	0.15
Dutch	172	0.76
English	999	4.39
Estonian	17	0.07
European	22	0.10
Finnish	16	0.07
French, except Basque	133	0.58
French Canadian	22	0.10
German	1,333	5.85
Greek	35	0.15
Hawaii Native/Pacific Islander:	59	0.26
Micronesian: (16)	17	0.07
Guamanian/Chamorro (16)	17	0.07
Polynesian: (2)	5	0.02
Native Hawaiian (1)	3	0.01
Samoan (1)	2	0.01
Other Pac. Isl., specified	6	0.03
Other Pac. Isl., not spec. (2)	31	0.14
Hispanic or Latino:	5,576	24.49
Central American:	71	0.31
Guatemalan	49	0.22
Honduran	3	0.01
Nicaraguan	1	0.00
Panamanian	8	0.04
Salvadoran	10	0.04
Cuban	62	0.27
Dominican Republic	40	0.18
Mexican	3,264	14.33
Puerto Rican	1,558	6.84
South American:	70	0.31
Chilean	1	0.00
Colombian	27	0.12

Notes: 1. Figures in the "Number" column do not add up to the total population due to: a) Ancestry/Race overlap — e.g. persons can report being both White and Irish, b) persons of Hispanic origin can report being any race, c) persons reporting two ancestries are counted in both categories. 2. Numbers in parentheses indicate the number of persons reporting this ancestry/race alone, not in combination with any other ancestry/race. 3. Refer to the Explanation of Data in the front of the book for more detailed information.

Ecuadorian	11	0.05
Peruvian	29	0.13
Venezuelan	1	0.00
Other South American	1	0.00
Other Hispanic or Latino	511	2.24
Hungarian	33	0.14
Irish	1,329	5.84
Italian	1,292	5.67
Latvian	13	0.06
Lithuanian	43	0.19
Norwegian	11	0.05
Pennsylvania German	4	0.02
Polish	256	1.12
Portuguese	17	0.07
Russian	89	0.39
Scotch-Irish	83	0.36
Scottish	76	0.33
Serbian	7	0.03
Slavic	7	0.03
Slovak	17	0.07
Swedish	110	0.48
Swiss	6	0.03
Ukrainian	58	0.25
United States or American	643	2.82
Welsh	80	0.35
West Indian, excl. Hispanic:	159	0.70
Bahamian	12	0.05
Barbadian	16	0.07
Belizean	9	0.04
Jamaican	104	0.46
West Indian	18	0.08
White:	9,336	41.00
Not Hispanic (7,109)	7,341	32.24
Hispanic (1,745)	1,995	8.76
Yugoslavian	8	0.04

Bridgewater

Place Type: Township
County: Somerset
Population: 42,940

Ancestry/Race	Number	%
African American/Black:	1,022	2.38
Not Hispanic (899)	967	2.25
Hispanic (32)	55	0.13
African, sub-Saharan:	97	0.23
African	64	0.15
Nigerian	20	0.05
South African	13	0.03
Am. Ind. or Alaska Nat., not spec.	36	0.08
Albanian	85	0.20
American Indian tribes, specified:	75	0.17
Blackfeet (1)	7	0.02
Cherokee (3)	19	0.04
Chippewa	5	0.01
Choctaw (1)	3	0.01
Comanche (2)	2	0.00
Delaware	2	0.00
Iroquois (1)	2	0.00
Latin American Indians (6)	18	0.04
Osage	3	0.01
Seminole (1)	2	0.00
Sioux	3	0.01
All other tribes (2)	9	0.02
American Indian tribes, not spec.	2	0.00
Arab:	221	0.52
Arab/Arabic	28	0.07
Egyptian	50	0.12
Jordanian	49	0.11
Lebanese	39	0.09
Palestinian	6	0.01
Syrian	49	0.11
Armenian	61	0.14
Asian:	4,831	11.25
Bangladeshi (4)	4	0.01
Cambodian (3)	5	0.01
Chinese, ex. Taiwanese (1,611)	1,717	4.00
Filipino (370)	426	0.99
Indian (1,819)	1,885	4.39
Indonesian (2)	2	0.00
Japanese (53)	74	0.17
Korean (193)	227	0.53
Laotian (7)	9	0.02
Pakistani (123)	133	0.31
Sri Lankan (9)	10	0.02
Taiwanese (152)	167	0.39
Thai (11)	13	0.03
Vietnamese (110)	121	0.28
Other Asian, specified (3)	5	0.01
Other Asian, not specified (11)	33	0.08
Austrian	381	0.89
Belgian	26	0.06
Brazilian	16	0.04
British	110	0.26
Canadian	165	0.38
Croatian	34	0.08
Czech	346	0.81
Czechoslovakian	162	0.38
Danish	265	0.62
Dutch	746	1.74
Eastern European	235	0.55
English	3,158	7.36
Estonian	18	0.04
European	402	0.94
Finnish	48	0.11
French, except Basque	887	2.07
French Canadian	211	0.49
German	7,142	16.66
German Russian	15	0.03
Greek	406	0.95
Hawaii Native/Pacific Islander:	17	0.04
Micronesian: (1)	1	0.00
Guamanian/Chamorro (1)	1	0.00
Polynesian: (4)	7	0.02
Native Hawaiian (4)	6	0.01
Other Polynesian	1	0.00
Other Pac. Isl., specified	1	0.00
Other Pac. Isl., not spec.	8	0.02
Hispanic or Latino:	2,056	4.79
Central American:	428	1.00
Costa Rican	316	0.74
Guatemalan	36	0.08
Honduran	7	0.02
Panamanian	11	0.03
Salvadoran	36	0.08
Other Central American	22	0.05
Cuban	143	0.33
Dominican Republic	17	0.04
Mexican	194	0.45
Puerto Rican	352	0.82
South American:	363	0.85
Argentinean	34	0.08
Chilean	24	0.06
Colombian	140	0.33
Ecuadorian	45	0.10
Paraguayan	23	0.05
Peruvian	74	0.17
Uruguayan	7	0.02
Venezuelan	3	0.01
Other South American	13	0.03
Other Hispanic or Latino	559	1.30
Hungarian	889	2.07
Icelander	7	0.02
Iranian	25	0.06
Irish	7,328	17.09
Israeli	44	0.10
Italian	9,143	21.32
Latvian	15	0.03
Lithuanian	450	1.05
Luxemburger	9	0.02
Macedonian	5	0.01
Maltese	79	0.18
Northern European	23	0.05
Norwegian	370	0.86
Pennsylvania German	21	0.05
Polish	5,047	11.77
Portuguese	329	0.77
Romanian	79	0.18
Russian	1,725	4.02
Scandinavian	52	0.12
Scotch-Irish	458	1.07
Scottish	846	1.97
Serbian	15	0.03
Slavic	112	0.26
Slovak	513	1.20
Slovene	16	0.04
Swedish	424	0.99
Swiss	211	0.49
Ukrainian	696	1.62
United States or American	1,201	2.80
Welsh	204	0.48
West Indian, excl. Hispanic:	165	0.38
British West Indian	5	0.01
Haitian	31	0.07
Jamaican	96	0.22
West Indian	33	0.08
White:	36,988	86.14
Not Hispanic (34,995)	35,343	82.31
Hispanic (1,532)	1,645	3.83
Yugoslavian	36	0.08

Brigantine

Place Type: City
County: Atlantic
Population: 12,594

Ancestry/Race	Number	%
African American/Black:	582	4.62
Not Hispanic (432)	488	3.87
Hispanic (64)	94	0.75
African, sub-Saharan:	147	1.17
African	47	0.37
Liberian	34	0.27
Sudanese	66	0.52
Alaska Native tribes, not specified	2	0.02
Am. Ind. or Alaska Nat., not spec.	39	0.31
Albanian	34	0.27
American Indian tribes, specified:	35	0.28
Apache	2	0.02
Blackfeet	2	0.02
Cherokee (5)	14	0.11
Choctaw (1)	1	0.01
Delaware (1)	3	0.02
Iroquois (2)	2	0.02
Latin American Indians (6)	6	0.05
Seminole	4	0.03
All other tribes	1	0.01
American Indian tribes, not spec.	13	0.10
Arab:	18	0.14
Lebanese	7	0.06
Palestinian	6	0.05
Syrian	5	0.04
Armenian	72	0.57
Asian:	838	6.65
Bangladeshi (14)	30	0.24
Chinese, ex. Taiwanese (80)	92	0.73
Filipino (70)	79	0.63
Indian (328)	372	2.95
Japanese (4)	8	0.06
Korean (12)	13	0.10
Laotian (2)	2	0.02
Malaysian	1	0.01
Pakistani (97)	111	0.88
Taiwanese (1)	1	0.01
Thai (6)	6	0.05
Vietnamese (91)	113	0.90
Other Asian, specified (1)	1	0.01
Other Asian, not specified (3)	9	0.07
Australian	5	0.04
Austrian	53	0.42
Belgian	12	0.10
British	19	0.15
Bulgarian	83	0.66
Canadian	26	0.21
Czech	8	0.06
Danish	16	0.13
Dutch	181	1.44
English	1,259	10.00

Notes: 1. Figures in the "Number" column do not add up to the total population due to: a) Ancestry/Race overlap — e.g. persons can report being both White and Irish, b) persons of Hispanic origin can report being any race, c) persons reporting two ancestries are counted in both categories. 2. Numbers in parentheses indicate the number of persons reporting this ancestry/race alone, not in combination with any other ancestry/race. 3. Refer to the Explanation of Data in the front of the book for more detailed information.

European	26	0.21
French, except Basque	307	2.44
French Canadian	17	0.13
German	2,047	16.25
Greek	126	1.00
Hawaii Native/Pacific Islander:	13	0.10
Polynesian: (6)	10	0.08
Native Hawaiian (4)	8	0.06
Samoan (2)	2	0.02
Other Pac. Isl., not spec.	3	0.02
Hispanic or Latino:	1,185	9.41
Central American:	124	0.98
Costa Rican	1	0.01
Guatemalan	9	0.07
Honduran	50	0.40
Nicaraguan	8	0.06
Panamanian	5	0.04
Salvadoran	42	0.33
Other Central American	9	0.07
Cuban	29	0.23
Dominican Republic	43	0.34
Mexican	171	1.36
Puerto Rican	526	4.18
South American:	91	0.72
Argentinean	1	0.01
Chilean	1	0.01
Colombian	44	0.35
Ecuadorian	13	0.10
Peruvian	24	0.19
Venezuelan	8	0.06
Other Hispanic or Latino	201	1.60
Hungarian	105	0.83
Irish	3,080	24.46
Italian	2,796	22.20
Lithuanian	105	0.83
Macedonian	40	0.32
New Zealander	4	0.03
Norwegian	57	0.45
Pennsylvania German	11	0.09
Polish	797	6.33
Portuguese	22	0.17
Romanian	10	0.08
Russian	194	1.54
Scotch-Irish	198	1.57
Scottish	149	1.18
Serbian	7	0.06
Slovak	38	0.30
Swedish	68	0.54
Swiss	17	0.13
Ukrainian	154	1.22
United States or American	304	2.41
Welsh	107	0.85
West Indian, excl. Hispanic:	23	0.18
West Indian	23	0.18
White:	10,658	84.63
Not Hispanic (10,014)	10,132	80.45
Hispanic (458)	526	4.18
Yugoslavian	7	0.06

Browns Mills

Place Type: Census Designated Place
County: Burlington
Population: 11,257

Ancestry/Race	Number	%
African American/Black:	2,885	25.63
Not Hispanic (2,496)	2,756	24.48
Hispanic (72)	129	1.15
African, sub-Saharan:	111	0.98
African	105	0.92
Nigerian	6	0.05
Alaska Native tribes, not specified	1	0.01
Am. Ind. or Alaska Nat., not spec.	53	0.47
American Indian tribes, specified:	120	1.07
Blackfeet	11	0.10
Cherokee (9)	56	0.50
Chickasaw	1	0.01
Choctaw	1	0.01
Delaware (3)	3	0.03
Iroquois (13)	16	0.14
Latin American Indians (2)	6	0.05
Navajo	2	0.02
Osage (1)	1	0.01
Shoshone (1)	1	0.01
Sioux (1)	11	0.10
All other tribes (6)	11	0.10
American Indian tribes, not spec.	7	0.06
Arab:	11	0.10
Moroccan	11	0.10
Asian:	619	5.50
Bangladeshi (4)	4	0.04
Chinese, ex. Taiwanese (22)	32	0.28
Filipino (78)	119	1.06
Indian (17)	25	0.22
Japanese (43)	107	0.95
Korean (195)	239	2.12
Pakistani (2)	5	0.04
Taiwanese	1	0.01
Thai (33)	49	0.44
Vietnamese (9)	18	0.16
Other Asian, specified (1)	2	0.02
Other Asian, not specified (11)	18	0.16
Austrian	26	0.23
British	47	0.41
Canadian	9	0.08
Czech	35	0.31
Danish	28	0.25
Dutch	136	1.20
English	716	6.31
European	62	0.55
Finnish	24	0.21
French, except Basque	255	2.25
French Canadian	33	0.29
German	1,827	16.09
Greek	6	0.05
Guyanese	40	0.35
Hawaii Native/Pacific Islander:	22	0.20
Polynesian: (3)	10	0.09
Native Hawaiian (3)	8	0.07
Samoan	2	0.02
Other Pac. Isl., specified	1	0.01
Other Pac. Isl., not spec. (5)	11	0.10
Hispanic or Latino:	1,052	9.35
Central American:	52	0.46
Guatemalan	1	0.01
Honduran	1	0.01
Panamanian	45	0.40
Salvadoran	5	0.04
Cuban	20	0.18
Dominican Republic	7	0.06
Mexican	91	0.81
Puerto Rican	701	6.23
South American:	34	0.30
Argentinean	4	0.04
Colombian	5	0.04
Ecuadorian	10	0.09
Peruvian	7	0.06
Uruguayan	1	0.01
Venezuelan	6	0.05
Other South American	1	0.01
Other Hispanic or Latino	147	1.31
Hungarian	98	0.86
Irish	1,807	15.92
Italian	1,101	9.70
Lithuanian	22	0.19
Northern European	9	0.08
Norwegian	8	0.07
Pennsylvania German	31	0.27
Polish	574	5.06
Portuguese	10	0.09
Russian	68	0.60
Scandinavian	8	0.07
Scotch-Irish	143	1.26
Scottish	151	1.33
Slovak	12	0.11
Swedish	44	0.39
Swiss	8	0.07
Turkish	10	0.09
Ukrainian	48	0.42
United States or American	741	6.53
Welsh	50	0.44
West Indian, excl. Hispanic:	52	0.46
Barbadian	4	0.04
Belizean	29	0.26
British West Indian	9	0.08
Jamaican	10	0.09
White:	7,698	68.38
Not Hispanic (6,752)	7,098	63.05
Hispanic (509)	600	5.33

Burlington

Place Type: Township
County: Burlington
Population: 20,294

Ancestry/Race	Number	%
Acadian/Cajun	18	0.09
African American/Black:	5,271	25.97
Not Hispanic (4,839)	5,090	25.08
Hispanic (132)	181	0.89
African, sub-Saharan:	383	1.89
African	153	0.75
Ghanian	21	0.10
Kenyan	6	0.03
Liberian	49	0.24
Nigerian	65	0.32
Sierra Leonean	25	0.12
Zairian	13	0.06
Other sub-Saharan African	51	0.25
Alaska Native tribes, specified:	1	0.00
Tlingit-Haida	1	0.00
Am. Ind. or Alaska Nat., not spec.	43	0.21
American Indian tribes, specified:	85	0.42
Blackfeet (4)	15	0.07
Cherokee (6)	34	0.17
Chippewa	2	0.01
Choctaw (4)	6	0.03
Delaware	4	0.02
Iroquois	2	0.01
Latin American Indians (3)	9	0.04
Pima (1)	1	0.00
Puget Sound Salish (1)	1	0.00
All other tribes (4)	11	0.05
American Indian tribes, not spec.	11	0.05
Arab:	36	0.18
Egyptian	19	0.09
Syrian	4	0.02
Other Arab	13	0.06
Armenian	22	0.11
Asian:	902	4.44
Cambodian (1)	2	0.01
Chinese, ex. Taiwanese (106)	119	0.59
Filipino (109)	123	0.61
Indian (333)	361	1.78
Indonesian (1)	1	0.00
Japanese (19)	52	0.26
Korean (112)	144	0.71
Laotian (2)	2	0.01
Pakistani (11)	32	0.16
Sri Lankan (3)	4	0.02
Taiwanese (1)	3	0.01
Thai (4)	7	0.03
Vietnamese (30)	30	0.15
Other Asian, specified	1	0.00
Other Asian, not specified (12)	21	0.10
Australian	4	0.02
Austrian	81	0.40
Belgian	7	0.03
Brazilian	4	0.02
British	60	0.30
Canadian	34	0.17
Croatian	34	0.17
Czech	72	0.35
Czechoslovakian	35	0.17
Danish	67	0.33
Dutch	253	1.25
Eastern European	14	0.07
English	1,756	8.65

Notes: 1. Figures in the "Number" column do not add up to the total population due to: a) Ancestry/Race overlap — e.g. persons can report being both White and Irish, b) persons of Hispanic origin can report being any race, c) persons reporting two ancestries are counted in both categories. 2. Numbers in parentheses indicate the number of persons reporting this ancestry/race alone, not in combination with any other ancestry/race. 3. Refer to the Explanation of Data in the front of the book for more detailed information.

Estonian	6	0.03
European	84	0.41
Finnish	8	0.04
French, except Basque	315	1.55
French Canadian	109	0.54
German	3,552	17.50
Greek	90	0.44
Guyanese	45	0.22
Hawaii Native/Pacific Islander:	10	0.05
Micronesian: (4)	4	0.02
Guamanian/Chamorro (4)	4	0.02
Polynesian: (1)	2	0.01
Native Hawaiian	1	0.00
Samoan (1)	1	0.00
Other Pac. Isl., specified	1	0.00
Other Pac. Isl., not spec. (1)	3	0.01
Hispanic or Latino:	814	4.01
Central American:	78	0.38
Costa Rican	1	0.00
Guatemalan	13	0.06
Honduran	14	0.07
Nicaraguan	4	0.02
Panamanian	40	0.20
Salvadoran	5	0.02
Other Central American	1	0.00
Cuban	28	0.14
Dominican Republic	33	0.16
Mexican	84	0.41
Puerto Rican	401	1.98
South American:	61	0.30
Argentinean	1	0.00
Colombian	31	0.15
Ecuadorian	6	0.03
Paraguayan	1	0.00
Peruvian	19	0.09
Venezuelan	1	0.00
Other South American	2	0.01
Other Hispanic or Latino	129	0.64
Hungarian	227	1.12
Iranian	5	0.02
Irish	3,462	17.06
Italian	3,001	14.79
Latvian	7	0.03
Lithuanian	147	0.72
Norwegian	153	0.75
Pennsylvania German	12	0.06
Polish	1,621	7.99
Portuguese	38	0.19
Romanian	44	0.22
Russian	239	1.18
Scandinavian	16	0.08
Scotch-Irish	258	1.27
Scottish	200	0.99
Serbian	10	0.05
Slavic	17	0.08
Slovak	111	0.55
Slovene	27	0.13
Swedish	110	0.54
Swiss	12	0.06
Turkish	54	0.27
Ukrainian	119	0.59
United States or American	437	2.15
Welsh	89	0.44
West Indian, excl. Hispanic:	268	1.32
Bahamian	17	0.08
Barbadian	16	0.08
Bermudan	11	0.05
British West Indian	23	0.11
Jamaican	159	0.78
Trinidadian and Tobagonian	15	0.07
West Indian	27	0.13
White:	14,078	69.37
Not Hispanic (13,406)	13,698	67.50
Hispanic (336)	380	1.87
Yugoslavian	29	0.14

Camden

Place Type: City
County: Camden
Population: 79,904

Ancestry/Race	Number	%
African American/Black:	44,224	55.35
Not Hispanic (39,753)	40,651	50.87
Hispanic (2,875)	3,573	4.47
African, sub-Saharan:	1,098	1.37
African	1,006	1.26
Ethiopian	32	0.04
Nigerian	22	0.03
Sierra Leonean	7	0.01
Other sub-Saharan African	31	0.04
Alaska Native tribes, specified:	1	0.00
Alaska Athabascan	1	0.00
Am. Ind. or Alaska Nat., not spec.	588	0.74
American Indian tribes, specified:	367	0.46
Apache (1)	2	0.00
Blackfeet (5)	24	0.03
Cherokee (22)	131	0.16
Chippewa	2	0.00
Comanche (1)	3	0.00
Creek	3	0.00
Crow	2	0.00
Delaware (1)	16	0.02
Iroquois (4)	12	0.02
Latin American Indians (37)	88	0.11
Navajo	8	0.01
Ottawa (1)	1	0.00
Pueblo (9)	15	0.02
Seminole	2	0.00
Shoshone	2	0.00
Sioux (4)	14	0.02
All other tribes (17)	42	0.05
American Indian tribes, not spec.	56	0.07
Arab:	27	0.03
Lebanese	20	0.03
Syrian	7	0.01
Asian:	2,453	3.07
Bangladeshi	1	0.00
Cambodian (195)	267	0.33
Chinese, ex. Taiwanese (141)	199	0.25
Filipino (50)	71	0.09
Indian (113)	196	0.25
Indonesian	1	0.00
Japanese (20)	48	0.06
Korean (64)	81	0.10
Laotian (6)	7	0.01
Pakistani (13)	22	0.03
Taiwanese (3)	4	0.01
Thai	3	0.00
Vietnamese (1,246)	1,344	1.68
Other Asian, specified	10	0.01
Other Asian, not specified (43)	199	0.25
Basque	11	0.01
Canadian	25	0.03
Croatian	8	0.01
Czech	18	0.02
Czechoslovakian	6	0.01
Danish	17	0.02
Dutch	150	0.19
English	724	0.91
European	36	0.05
French, except Basque	182	0.23
French Canadian	40	0.05
German	1,254	1.57
Greek	93	0.12
Guyanese	15	0.02
Hawaii Native/Pacific Islander:	246	0.31
Melanesian:	5	0.01
Fijian	5	0.01
Micronesian: (12)	19	0.02
Guamanian/Chamorro (12)	19	0.02
Polynesian: (30)	46	0.06
Native Hawaiian (23)	34	0.04
Samoan (7)	12	0.02
Other Pac. Isl., specified	9	0.01
Other Pac. Isl., not spec. (17)	167	0.21
Hispanic or Latino:	31,019	38.82
Central American:	920	1.15
Costa Rican	21	0.03
Guatemalan	111	0.14
Honduran	49	0.06
Nicaraguan	607	0.76
Panamanian	37	0.05
Salvadoran	58	0.07
Other Central American	37	0.05
Cuban	206	0.26
Dominican Republic	1,874	2.35
Mexican	1,908	2.39
Puerto Rican	23,051	28.85
South American:	173	0.22
Argentinean	3	0.00
Bolivian	5	0.01
Chilean	6	0.01
Colombian	32	0.04
Ecuadorian	72	0.09
Peruvian	39	0.05
Venezuelan	14	0.02
Other South American	2	0.00
Other Hispanic or Latino	2,887	3.61
Hungarian	44	0.06
Irish	1,562	1.95
Israeli	8	0.01
Italian	1,237	1.55
Latvian	8	0.01
Lithuanian	6	0.01
Northern European	13	0.02
Norwegian	30	0.04
Pennsylvania German	47	0.06
Polish	677	0.85
Portuguese	41	0.05
Russian	94	0.12
Scotch-Irish	86	0.11
Scottish	105	0.13
Slavic	8	0.01
Swedish	68	0.09
Swiss	9	0.01
Ukrainian	24	0.03
United States or American	946	1.18
Welsh	54	0.07
West Indian, excl. Hispanic:	718	0.90
Bahamian	7	0.01
Belizean	10	0.01
Bermudan	9	0.01
British West Indian	17	0.02
Dutch West Indian	45	0.06
Haitian	21	0.03
Jamaican	506	0.63
Trinidadian and Tobagonian	27	0.03
West Indian	76	0.10
White:	15,151	18.96
Not Hispanic (5,671)	6,254	7.83
Hispanic (7,783)	8,897	11.13
Yugoslavian	13	0.02

Carteret

Place Type: Borough
County: Middlesex
Population: 20,709

Ancestry/Race	Number	%
Afghan	24	0.12
African American/Black:	2,169	10.47
Not Hispanic (1,856)	1,984	9.58
Hispanic (119)	185	0.89
African, sub-Saharan:	107	0.52
African	77	0.37
Ghanian	16	0.08
Nigerian	14	0.07
Am. Ind. or Alaska Nat., not spec.	61	0.29
Albanian	18	0.09
American Indian tribes, specified:	44	0.21
Cherokee (2)	11	0.05
Iroquois	7	0.03
Latin American Indians (5)	14	0.07

Notes: 1. Figures in the "Number" column do not add up to the total population due to: a) Ancestry/Race overlap — e.g. persons can report being both White and Irish, b) persons of Hispanic origin can report being any race, c) persons reporting two ancestries are counted in both categories. 2. Numbers in parentheses indicate the number of persons reporting this ancestry/race alone, not in combination with any other ancestry/race. 3. Refer to the Explanation of Data in the front of the book for more detailed information.

Paiute (1)	4	0.02
Sioux (3)	3	0.01
All other tribes (2)	5	0.02
American Indian tribes, not spec.	12	0.06
Arab:	120	0.58
Arab/Arabic	13	0.06
Egyptian	104	0.50
Syrian	3	0.01
Asian:	1,890	9.13
Chinese, ex. Taiwanese (64)	91	0.44
Filipino (260)	280	1.35
Indian (1,219)	1,311	6.33
Indonesian (1)	1	0.00
Japanese (7)	8	0.04
Korean (55)	58	0.28
Malaysian (1)	1	0.00
Pakistani (45)	63	0.30
Sri Lankan (6)	6	0.03
Thai (3)	5	0.02
Vietnamese (20)	25	0.12
Other Asian, specified	2	0.01
Other Asian, not specified (24)	39	0.19
Austrian	70	0.34
Brazilian	36	0.17
British	14	0.07
Canadian	5	0.02
Croatian	6	0.03
Czech	98	0.47
Czechoslovakian	50	0.24
Danish	48	0.23
Dutch	84	0.41
English	365	1.76
European	17	0.08
French, except Basque	185	0.89
French Canadian	31	0.15
German	1,482	7.16
Greek	66	0.32
Guyanese	48	0.23
Hawaii Native/Pacific Islander:	37	0.18
Micronesian: (2)	2	0.01
Guamanian/Chamorro (2)	2	0.01
Polynesian: (2)	5	0.02
Native Hawaiian (2)	5	0.02
Other Pac. Isl., specified	2	0.01
Other Pac. Isl., not spec. (3)	28	0.14
Hispanic or Latino:	4,839	23.37
Central American:	133	0.64
Costa Rican	29	0.14
Guatemalan	4	0.02
Honduran	38	0.18
Nicaraguan	11	0.05
Panamanian	3	0.01
Salvadoran	41	0.20
Other Central American	7	0.03
Cuban	244	1.18
Dominican Republic	291	1.41
Mexican	184	0.89
Puerto Rican	2,216	10.70
South American:	756	3.65
Argentinean	35	0.17
Bolivian	19	0.09
Chilean	32	0.15
Colombian	105	0.51
Ecuadorian	75	0.36
Peruvian	417	2.01
Uruguayan	37	0.18
Venezuelan	7	0.03
Other South American	29	0.14
Other Hispanic or Latino	1,015	4.90
Hungarian	958	4.63
Irish	2,665	12.87
Italian	2,955	14.27
Lithuanian	78	0.38
Norwegian	36	0.17
Polish	2,546	12.29
Portuguese	270	1.30
Romanian	23	0.11
Russian	318	1.54
Scotch-Irish	143	0.69
Scottish	61	0.29
Slavic	34	0.16
Slovak	635	3.07
Slovene	20	0.10
Swedish	47	0.23
Turkish	7	0.03
Ukrainian	764	3.69
United States or American	496	2.40
Welsh	36	0.17
West Indian, excl. Hispanic:	311	1.50
Bahamian	5	0.02
Barbadian	5	0.02
British West Indian	12	0.06
Haitian	32	0.15
Jamaican	85	0.41
Trinidadian and Tobagonian	75	0.36
U.S. Virgin Islander	5	0.02
West Indian	87	0.42
Other West Indian	5	0.02
White:	14,848	71.70
Not Hispanic (11,855)	12,079	58.33
Hispanic (2,384)	2,769	13.37

Cedar Grove

Place Type: Census Designated Place
County: Essex
Population: 12,300

Ancestry/Race	Number	%
African American/Black:	386	3.14
Not Hispanic (364)	381	3.10
Hispanic (4)	5	0.04
African, sub-Saharan:	43	0.35
African	26	0.21
Kenyan	17	0.14
Am. Ind. or Alaska Nat., not spec.	5	0.04
Albanian	15	0.12
American Indian tribes, specified:	10	0.08
Blackfeet	1	0.01
Cherokee (1)	1	0.01
Choctaw	2	0.02
Delaware (1)	1	0.01
Iroquois	2	0.02
Latin American Indians (2)	2	0.02
Pueblo (1)	1	0.01
Arab:	63	0.51
Arab/Arabic	14	0.11
Egyptian	15	0.12
Lebanese	11	0.09
Syrian	19	0.15
Other Arab	4	0.03
Armenian	28	0.23
Asian:	721	5.86
Chinese, ex. Taiwanese (164)	171	1.39
Filipino (148)	162	1.32
Indian (210)	213	1.73
Indonesian (8)	12	0.10
Japanese (20)	23	0.19
Korean (44)	52	0.42
Malaysian	1	0.01
Pakistani (6)	7	0.06
Sri Lankan (3)	3	0.02
Taiwanese (41)	44	0.36
Thai (1)	1	0.01
Vietnamese (10)	21	0.17
Other Asian, not specified (3)	11	0.09
Austrian	65	0.53
British	86	0.70
Canadian	43	0.35
Croatian	25	0.20
Czech	25	0.20
Czechoslovakian	9	0.07
Danish	14	0.11
Dutch	174	1.41
Eastern European	26	0.21
English	752	6.11
European	20	0.16
Finnish	28	0.23
French, except Basque	133	1.08
French Canadian	11	0.09
German	1,488	12.10
Greek	40	0.33
Guyanese	30	0.24
Hawaii Native/Pacific Islander:	6	0.05
Micronesian: (1)	1	0.01
Guamanian/Chamorro (1)	1	0.01
Polynesian: (2)	2	0.02
Samoan (2)	2	0.02
Other Pac. Isl., not spec.	3	0.02
Hispanic or Latino:	393	3.20
Central American:	11	0.09
Costa Rican	2	0.02
Guatemalan	2	0.02
Nicaraguan	4	0.03
Salvadoran	1	0.01
Other Central American	2	0.02
Cuban	55	0.45
Dominican Republic	17	0.14
Mexican	23	0.19
Puerto Rican	112	0.91
South American:	68	0.55
Argentinean	12	0.10
Bolivian	1	0.01
Chilean	1	0.01
Colombian	21	0.17
Ecuadorian	6	0.05
Paraguayan	1	0.01
Peruvian	15	0.12
Uruguayan	2	0.02
Venezuelan	5	0.04
Other South American	4	0.03
Other Hispanic or Latino	107	0.87
Hungarian	246	2.00
Icelander	9	0.07
Iranian	54	0.44
Irish	2,671	21.72
Israeli	30	0.24
Italian	4,278	34.78
Lithuanian	89	0.72
Norwegian	33	0.27
Pennsylvania German	9	0.07
Polish	826	6.72
Portuguese	52	0.42
Romanian	35	0.28
Russian	350	2.85
Scandinavian	12	0.10
Scotch-Irish	161	1.31
Scottish	122	0.99
Slovak	32	0.26
Swedish	151	1.23
Swiss	29	0.24
Turkish	18	0.15
Ukrainian	115	0.93
United States or American	392	3.19
Welsh	16	0.13
West Indian, excl. Hispanic:	53	0.43
Haitian	6	0.05
Jamaican	36	0.29
West Indian	11	0.09
White:	11,190	90.98
Not Hispanic (10,777)	10,855	88.25
Hispanic (299)	335	2.72

Chatham

Place Type: Township
County: Morris
Population: 10,086

Ancestry/Race	Number	%
Acadian/Cajun	17	0.17
Afghan	8	0.08
African American/Black:	49	0.49
Not Hispanic (41)	45	0.45
Hispanic (4)	4	0.04
Am. Ind. or Alaska Nat., not spec.	3	0.03
Albanian	6	0.06
American Indian tribes, specified:	13	0.13
Blackfeet (1)	1	0.01
Cherokee	4	0.04

Notes: 1. Figures in the "Number" column do not add up to the total population due to: a) Ancestry/Race overlap — e.g. persons can report being both White and Irish, b) persons of Hispanic origin can report being any race, c) persons reporting two ancestries are counted in both categories. 2. Numbers in parentheses indicate the number of persons reporting this ancestry/race alone, not in combination with any other ancestry/race. 3. Refer to the Explanation of Data in the front of the book for more detailed information.

Ancestry/Race	Number	%
Creek	4	0.04
Iroquois	2	0.02
Latin American Indians (1)	2	0.02
American Indian tribes, not spec.	4	0.04
Arab:	96	0.95
Arab/Arabic	11	0.11
Iraqi	8	0.08
Lebanese	39	0.39
Syrian	38	0.38
Armenian	17	0.17
Asian:	546	5.41
Chinese, ex. Taiwanese (195)	215	2.13
Filipino (20)	29	0.29
Indian (131)	145	1.44
Japanese (38)	45	0.45
Korean (66)	74	0.73
Pakistani (5)	7	0.07
Sri Lankan (1)	1	0.01
Taiwanese (14)	16	0.16
Thai (5)	6	0.06
Vietnamese (4)	4	0.04
Other Asian, not specified (3)	4	0.04
Austrian	77	0.76
Belgian	22	0.22
British	184	1.82
Canadian	84	0.83
Celtic	20	0.20
Croatian	7	0.07
Czech	63	0.62
Czechoslovakian	23	0.23
Danish	42	0.42
Dutch	187	1.85
Eastern European	29	0.29
English	1,485	14.72
European	96	0.95
Finnish	18	0.18
French, except Basque	278	2.76
French Canadian	51	0.51
German	1,986	19.69
Greek	104	1.03
Hawaii Native/Pacific Islander:	4	0.04
Polynesian: (1)	1	0.01
Native Hawaiian (1)	1	0.01
Other Pac. Isl., not spec.	3	0.03
Hispanic or Latino:	197	1.95
Central American:	22	0.22
Costa Rican	19	0.19
Guatemalan	2	0.02
Nicaraguan	1	0.01
Cuban	22	0.22
Mexican	27	0.27
Puerto Rican	26	0.26
South American:	44	0.44
Argentinean	1	0.01
Bolivian	1	0.01
Chilean	3	0.03
Colombian	21	0.21
Ecuadorian	5	0.05
Peruvian	6	0.06
Venezuelan	4	0.04
Other South American	3	0.03
Other Hispanic or Latino	56	0.56
Hungarian	77	0.76
Iranian	7	0.07
Irish	2,436	24.15
Italian	1,944	19.27
Latvian	15	0.15
Lithuanian	56	0.56
Luxemburger	5	0.05
Northern European	5	0.05
Norwegian	151	1.50
Polish	593	5.88
Portuguese	72	0.71
Romanian	7	0.07
Russian	288	2.86
Scandinavian	4	0.04
Scotch-Irish	110	1.09
Scottish	333	3.30
Slavic	13	0.13
Slovak	66	0.65
Swedish	167	1.66
Swiss	140	1.39
Turkish	69	0.68
Ukrainian	101	1.00
United States or American	477	4.73
Welsh	87	0.86
White:	9,524	94.43
Not Hispanic (9,282)	9,345	92.65
Hispanic (170)	179	1.77
Yugoslavian	7	0.07

Cherry Hill Mall

Place Type: Census Designated Place
County: Camden
Population: 13,238

Ancestry/Race	Number	%
African American/Black:	716	5.41
Not Hispanic (655)	698	5.27
Hispanic (13)	18	0.14
African, sub-Saharan:	29	0.22
African	29	0.22
Am. Ind. or Alaska Nat., not spec.	7	0.05
Albanian	10	0.07
Alsatian	11	0.08
American Indian tribes, specified:	16	0.12
Blackfeet (1)	1	0.01
Cherokee	8	0.06
Choctaw (1)	1	0.01
Navajo	1	0.01
Sioux (2)	2	0.02
All other tribes (1)	3	0.02
Arab:	70	0.52
Arab/Arabic	4	0.03
Egyptian	18	0.13
Iraqi	8	0.06
Moroccan	31	0.23
Other Arab	9	0.07
Armenian	7	0.05
Asian:	1,300	9.82
Cambodian (8)	10	0.08
Chinese, ex. Taiwanese (211)	228	1.72
Filipino (233)	244	1.84
Indian (161)	167	1.26
Japanese (19)	21	0.16
Korean (376)	395	2.98
Pakistani (25)	33	0.25
Taiwanese (18)	23	0.17
Vietnamese (119)	122	0.92
Other Asian, not specified (12)	57	0.43
Austrian	158	1.17
Brazilian	7	0.05
British	7	0.05
Carpatho Rusyn	14	0.10
Cypriot	18	0.13
Czech	46	0.34
Czechoslovakian	14	0.10
Danish	48	0.36
Dutch	120	0.89
Eastern European	106	0.79
English	873	6.48
European	88	0.65
Finnish	7	0.05
French, except Basque	240	1.78
French Canadian	31	0.23
German	1,899	14.10
Greek	154	1.14
Hawaii Native/Pacific Islander:	16	0.12
Micronesian: (2)	4	0.03
Guamanian/Chamorro (2)	4	0.03
Polynesian: (9)	11	0.08
Native Hawaiian	2	0.02
Samoan (9)	9	0.07
Other Pac. Isl., not spec.	1	0.01
Hispanic or Latino:	399	3.01
Central American:	17	0.13
Costa Rican	4	0.03
Guatemalan	5	0.04
Nicaraguan	7	0.05
Panamanian	1	0.01
Cuban	19	0.14
Dominican Republic	18	0.14
Mexican	41	0.31
Puerto Rican	230	1.74
South American:	21	0.16
Argentinean	2	0.02
Chilean	2	0.02
Colombian	10	0.08
Ecuadorian	2	0.02
Venezuelan	1	0.01
Other South American	4	0.03
Other Hispanic or Latino	53	0.40
Hungarian	124	0.92
Iranian	22	0.16
Irish	2,386	17.71
Israeli	29	0.22
Italian	2,547	18.91
Latvian	34	0.25
Lithuanian	94	0.70
Norwegian	116	0.86
Pennsylvania German	28	0.21
Polish	893	6.63
Romanian	66	0.49
Russian	924	6.86
Scotch-Irish	174	1.29
Scottish	118	0.88
Slavic	19	0.14
Slovak	87	0.65
Swedish	49	0.36
Swiss	65	0.48
Turkish	15	0.11
Ukrainian	283	2.10
United States or American	320	2.38
Welsh	126	0.94
West Indian, excl. Hispanic:	45	0.33
Jamaican	37	0.27
Trinidadian and Tobagonian	8	0.06
White:	11,169	84.37
Not Hispanic (10,789)	10,925	82.53
Hispanic (219)	244	1.84

Cherry Hill

Place Type: Township
County: Camden
Population: 69,965

Ancestry/Race	Number	%
African American/Black:	3,368	4.81
Not Hispanic (3,020)	3,242	4.63
Hispanic (101)	126	0.18
African, sub-Saharan:	219	0.31
African	126	0.18
Nigerian	37	0.05
South African	56	0.08
Alaska Native tribes, not specified	1	0.00
Am. Ind. or Alaska Nat., not spec.	79	0.11
Albanian	10	0.01
Alsatian	22	0.03
American Indian tribes, specified:	119	0.17
Blackfeet (3)	9	0.01
Cherokee (13)	46	0.07
Choctaw (1)	1	0.00
Creek (1)	3	0.00
Delaware (4)	5	0.01
Iroquois (4)	8	0.01
Latin American Indians (2)	13	0.02
Lumbee (1)	1	0.00
Navajo	1	0.00
Osage	1	0.00
Pima (1)	1	0.00
Pueblo (1)	2	0.00
Sioux (3)	5	0.01
All other tribes (9)	23	0.03
American Indian tribes, not spec.	12	0.02
Arab:	322	0.46
Arab/Arabic	19	0.03
Egyptian	32	0.05
Iraqi	14	0.02

Notes: 1. Figures in the "Number" column do not add up to the total population due to: a) Ancestry/Race overlap — e.g. persons can report being both White and Irish, b) persons of Hispanic origin can report being any race, c) persons reporting two ancestries are counted in both categories. 2. Numbers in parentheses indicate the number of persons reporting this ancestry/race alone, not in combination with any other ancestry/race. 3. Refer to the Explanation of Data in the front of the book for more detailed information.

Ancestry/Race	Number	%
Jordanian	53	0.08
Lebanese	106	0.15
Moroccan	78	0.11
Other Arab	20	0.03
Armenian	114	0.16
Asian:	6,630	9.48
Bangladeshi (13)	17	0.02
Cambodian (52)	65	0.09
Chinese, ex. Taiwanese (1,457)	1,524	2.18
Filipino (1,253)	1,333	1.91
Indian (1,285)	1,361	1.95
Indonesian (3)	3	0.00
Japanese (90)	118	0.17
Korean (1,363)	1,409	2.01
Laotian	3	0.00
Malaysian	4	0.01
Pakistani (60)	81	0.12
Sri Lankan (7)	7	0.01
Taiwanese (137)	156	0.22
Thai (19)	22	0.03
Vietnamese (339)	366	0.52
Other Asian, specified	3	0.00
Other Asian, not specified (56)	158	0.23
Austrian	648	0.93
Basque	14	0.02
Belgian	19	0.03
Brazilian	42	0.06
British	177	0.25
Bulgarian	6	0.01
Canadian	105	0.15
Carpatho Rusyn	14	0.02
Croatian	43	0.06
Cypriot	18	0.03
Czech	248	0.35
Czechoslovakian	67	0.10
Danish	158	0.23
Dutch	517	0.74
Eastern European	876	1.25
English	5,494	7.85
Estonian	5	0.01
European	305	0.44
Finnish	69	0.10
French, except Basque	1,096	1.57
French Canadian	210	0.30
German	9,617	13.75
Greek	959	1.37
Hawaii Native/Pacific Islander:	48	0.07
Micronesian: (9)	13	0.02
Guamanian/Chamorro (9)	13	0.02
Polynesian: (13)	22	0.03
Native Hawaiian (2)	10	0.01
Samoan (11)	12	0.02
Other Pac. Isl., specified	3	0.00
Other Pac. Isl., not spec. (2)	10	0.01
Hispanic or Latino:	1,778	2.54
Central American:	90	0.13
Costa Rican	11	0.02
Guatemalan	22	0.03
Honduran	4	0.01
Nicaraguan	30	0.04
Panamanian	12	0.02
Salvadoran	10	0.01
Other Central American	1	0.00
Cuban	96	0.14
Dominican Republic	49	0.07
Mexican	252	0.36
Puerto Rican	823	1.18
South American:	166	0.24
Argentinean	22	0.03
Bolivian	2	0.00
Chilean	20	0.03
Colombian	68	0.10
Ecuadorian	15	0.02
Paraguayan	1	0.00
Peruvian	3	0.00
Uruguayan	3	0.00
Venezuelan	17	0.02
Other South American	15	0.02
Other Hispanic or Latino	302	0.43
Hungarian	733	1.05
Icelander	7	0.01
Iranian	91	0.13
Irish	11,910	17.02
Israeli	225	0.32
Italian	11,780	16.84
Latvian	92	0.13
Lithuanian	656	0.94
Luxemburger	18	0.03
Maltese	27	0.04
New Zealander	9	0.01
Northern European	8	0.01
Norwegian	338	0.48
Pennsylvania German	80	0.11
Polish	4,954	7.08
Portuguese	52	0.07
Romanian	429	0.61
Russian	5,620	8.03
Scandinavian	50	0.07
Scotch-Irish	777	1.11
Scottish	914	1.31
Serbian	27	0.04
Slavic	69	0.10
Slovak	231	0.33
Slovene	6	0.01
Swedish	516	0.74
Swiss	191	0.27
Turkish	29	0.04
Ukrainian	976	1.39
United States or American	2,777	3.97
Welsh	621	0.89
West Indian, excl. Hispanic:	210	0.30
Bahamian	6	0.01
Barbadian	21	0.03
British West Indian	5	0.01
Haitian	39	0.06
Jamaican	110	0.16
Trinidadian and Tobagonian	18	0.03
West Indian	11	0.02
White:	59,874	85.58
Not Hispanic (58,165)	58,695	83.89
Hispanic (1,075)	1,179	1.69
Yugoslavian	44	0.06

Cinnaminson

Place Type: Township
County: Burlington
Population: 14,595

Ancestry/Race	Number	%
African American/Black:	797	5.46
Not Hispanic (737)	785	5.38
Hispanic (5)	12	0.08
African, sub-Saharan:	9	0.06
African	9	0.06
Alaska Native tribes, specified:	1	0.01
Tlingit-Haida	1	0.01
Am. Ind. or Alaska Nat., not spec.	28	0.19
Albanian	5	0.03
Alsatian	6	0.04
American Indian tribes, specified:	35	0.24
Blackfeet	1	0.01
Cherokee	16	0.11
Delaware	1	0.01
Seminole (1)	1	0.01
Sioux	1	0.01
All other tribes (9)	15	0.10
American Indian tribes, not spec.	1	0.01
Arab:	62	0.42
Egyptian	20	0.14
Lebanese	30	0.21
Syrian	12	0.08
Armenian	23	0.16
Asian:	304	2.08
Cambodian (6)	6	0.04
Chinese, ex. Taiwanese (60)	67	0.46
Filipino (28)	34	0.23
Indian (92)	93	0.64
Japanese (6)	10	0.07
Korean (43)	47	0.32
Sri Lankan (2)	3	0.02
Taiwanese (11)	11	0.08
Thai (2)	4	0.03
Vietnamese (13)	13	0.09
Other Asian, specified (2)	3	0.02
Other Asian, not specified (7)	13	0.09
Austrian	70	0.48
Belgian	15	0.10
Brazilian	23	0.16
British	32	0.22
Canadian	58	0.40
Celtic	23	0.16
Croatian	46	0.32
Cypriot	13	0.09
Czech	35	0.24
Czechoslovakian	21	0.14
Danish	6	0.04
Dutch	99	0.68
Eastern European	29	0.20
English	1,710	11.72
European	151	1.03
Finnish	6	0.04
French, except Basque	231	1.58
French Canadian	45	0.31
German	3,718	25.47
Greek	41	0.28
Hawaii Native/Pacific Islander:	9	0.06
Polynesian: (1)	3	0.02
Native Hawaiian (1)	3	0.02
Other Pac. Isl., specified	1	0.01
Other Pac. Isl., not spec.	5	0.03
Hispanic or Latino:	224	1.53
Central American:	11	0.08
Guatemalan	4	0.03
Panamanian	4	0.03
Salvadoran	3	0.02
Cuban	19	0.13
Dominican Republic	6	0.04
Mexican	24	0.16
Puerto Rican	126	0.86
South American:	13	0.09
Argentinean	1	0.01
Colombian	11	0.08
Ecuadorian	1	0.01
Other Hispanic or Latino	25	0.17
Hungarian	145	0.99
Irish	4,513	30.92
Israeli	7	0.05
Italian	3,083	21.12
Lithuanian	143	0.98
Northern European	11	0.08
Norwegian	44	0.30
Pennsylvania German	39	0.27
Polish	1,243	8.52
Portuguese	5	0.03
Romanian	23	0.16
Russian	180	1.23
Scotch-Irish	272	1.86
Scottish	339	2.32
Serbian	4	0.03
Slavic	10	0.07
Slovak	163	1.12
Swedish	181	1.24
Swiss	59	0.40
Ukrainian	180	1.23
United States or American	465	3.19
Welsh	51	0.35
West Indian, excl. Hispanic:	14	0.10
Jamaican	14	0.10
White:	13,465	92.26
Not Hispanic (13,204)	13,311	91.20
Hispanic (130)	154	1.06
Yugoslavian	9	0.06

Notes: 1. Figures in the "Number" column do not add up to the total population due to: a) Ancestry/Race overlap — e.g. persons can report being both White and Irish, b) persons of Hispanic origin can report being any race, c) persons reporting two ancestries are counted in both categories. 2. Numbers in parentheses indicate the number of persons reporting this ancestry/race alone, not in combination with any other ancestry/race. 3. Refer to the Explanation of Data in the front of the book for more detailed information.

Clark

Place Type: Census Designated Place
County: Union
Population: 14,597

Ancestry/Race	Number	%
African American/Black:	55	0.38
Not Hispanic (35)	45	0.31
Hispanic (9)	10	0.07
African, sub-Saharan:	3	0.02
African	3	0.02
Am. Ind. or Alaska Nat., not spec.	14	0.10
Albanian	26	0.18
American Indian tribes, specified:	12	0.08
Apache	1	0.01
Blackfeet	2	0.01
Cherokee	1	0.01
Chippewa (1)	1	0.01
Delaware (1)	2	0.01
Iroquois	4	0.03
Latin American Indians	1	0.01
American Indian tribes, not spec.	9	0.06
Arab:	154	1.06
Egyptian	94	0.64
Lebanese	60	0.41
Armenian	6	0.04
Asian:	434	2.97
Chinese, ex. Taiwanese (94)	103	0.71
Filipino (115)	123	0.84
Indian (85)	91	0.62
Japanese (7)	10	0.07
Korean (76)	77	0.53
Laotian (1)	1	0.01
Malaysian	4	0.03
Pakistani (10)	10	0.07
Taiwanese	1	0.01
Vietnamese (9)	12	0.08
Other Asian, not specified	2	0.01
Australian	25	0.17
Austrian	98	0.67
Brazilian	61	0.42
British	48	0.33
Canadian	20	0.14
Carpatho Rusyn	9	0.06
Croatian	11	0.08
Czech	45	0.31
Czechoslovakian	68	0.47
Danish	44	0.30
Dutch	187	1.28
Eastern European	35	0.24
English	676	4.63
European	67	0.46
Finnish	23	0.16
French, except Basque	108	0.74
French Canadian	121	0.83
German	2,360	16.17
Greek	64	0.44
Hispanic or Latino:	535	3.67
Central American:	19	0.13
Costa Rican	1	0.01
Guatemalan	2	0.01
Honduran	4	0.03
Nicaraguan	1	0.01
Salvadoran	11	0.08
Cuban	97	0.66
Dominican Republic	9	0.06
Mexican	21	0.14
Puerto Rican	99	0.68
South American:	118	0.81
Argentinean	13	0.09
Bolivian	2	0.01
Chilean	4	0.03
Colombian	46	0.32
Ecuadorian	26	0.18
Peruvian	6	0.04
Uruguayan	11	0.08
Venezuelan	4	0.03
Other South American	6	0.04
Other Hispanic or Latino	172	1.18
Hungarian	291	1.99
Irish	2,737	18.75
Italian	4,599	31.51
Latvian	17	0.12
Lithuanian	150	1.03
Luxemburger	9	0.06
Norwegian	146	1.00
Polish	2,588	17.73
Portuguese	500	3.43
Romanian	21	0.14
Russian	401	2.75
Scotch-Irish	120	0.82
Scottish	190	1.30
Serbian	11	0.08
Slavic	16	0.11
Slovak	356	2.44
Swedish	69	0.47
Swiss	41	0.28
Ukrainian	376	2.58
United States or American	350	2.40
Welsh	21	0.14
West Indian, excl. Hispanic:	11	0.08
Jamaican	8	0.05
West Indian	3	0.02
White:	14,055	96.29
Not Hispanic (13,534)	13,606	93.21
Hispanic (422)	449	3.08
Yugoslavian	5	0.03

Cliffside Park

Place Type: Borough
County: Bergen
Population: 23,007

Ancestry/Race	Number	%
African American/Black:	507	2.20
Not Hispanic (356)	403	1.75
Hispanic (66)	104	0.45
African, sub-Saharan:	57	0.25
African	9	0.04
Nigerian	48	0.21
Am. Ind. or Alaska Nat., not spec.	57	0.25
Albanian	172	0.75
Alsatian	9	0.04
American Indian tribes, specified:	60	0.26
Apache	2	0.01
Blackfeet	4	0.02
Cherokee	4	0.02
Choctaw	1	0.00
Comanche	1	0.00
Iroquois (17)	17	0.07
Latin American Indians (5)	22	0.10
Lumbee (1)	1	0.00
All other tribes (6)	8	0.03
American Indian tribes, not spec.	3	0.01
Arab:	483	2.10
Arab/Arabic	27	0.12
Egyptian	24	0.10
Iraqi	43	0.19
Jordanian	25	0.11
Lebanese	119	0.52
Moroccan	57	0.25
Palestinian	58	0.25
Syrian	52	0.23
Other Arab	78	0.34
Armenian	879	3.82
Asian:	2,954	12.84
Bangladeshi (17)	21	0.09
Cambodian (4)	4	0.02
Chinese, ex. Taiwanese (358)	384	1.67
Filipino (135)	152	0.66
Indian (198)	222	0.96
Indonesian (3)	3	0.01
Japanese (408)	424	1.84
Korean (1,588)	1,620	7.04
Laotian	1	0.00
Malaysian (2)	2	0.01
Pakistani (3)	4	0.02
Taiwanese (11)	16	0.07
Thai (2)	6	0.03
Vietnamese (3)	4	0.02
Other Asian, specified (3)	3	0.01
Other Asian, not specified (19)	88	0.38
Austrian	233	1.01
Brazilian	503	2.19
British	125	0.54
Bulgarian	8	0.03
Canadian	10	0.04
Croatian	661	2.87
Czech	21	0.09
Czechoslovakian	60	0.26
Danish	25	0.11
Dutch	159	0.69
Eastern European	24	0.10
English	423	1.84
European	70	0.30
Finnish	49	0.21
French, except Basque	147	0.64
French Canadian	23	0.10
German	1,200	5.22
Greek	489	2.13
Guyanese	23	0.10
Hawaii Native/Pacific Islander:	24	0.10
Melanesian:	1	0.00
Other Melanesian	1	0.00
Micronesian: (1)	1	0.00
Other Micronesian (1)	1	0.00
Polynesian: (2)	4	0.02
Native Hawaiian (1)	2	0.01
Samoan	1	0.00
Other Polynesian (1)	1	0.00
Other Pac. Isl., not spec. (2)	18	0.08
Hispanic or Latino:	4,177	18.16
Central American:	798	3.47
Costa Rican	9	0.04
Guatemalan	256	1.11
Honduran	22	0.10
Nicaraguan	9	0.04
Panamanian	8	0.03
Salvadoran	467	2.03
Other Central American	27	0.12
Cuban	565	2.46
Dominican Republic	323	1.40
Mexican	89	0.39
Puerto Rican	578	2.51
South American:	769	3.34
Argentinean	77	0.33
Bolivian	5	0.02
Chilean	39	0.17
Colombian	350	1.52
Ecuadorian	133	0.58
Paraguayan	5	0.02
Peruvian	99	0.43
Uruguayan	7	0.03
Venezuelan	33	0.14
Other South American	21	0.09
Other Hispanic or Latino	1,055	4.59
Hungarian	287	1.25
Iranian	182	0.79
Irish	1,620	7.04
Israeli	143	0.62
Italian	5,032	21.87
Latvian	16	0.07
Lithuanian	69	0.30
Northern European	9	0.04
Norwegian	83	0.36
Polish	817	3.55
Portuguese	45	0.20
Romanian	130	0.57
Russian	779	3.39
Scandinavian	20	0.09
Scotch-Irish	30	0.13
Scottish	45	0.20
Slavic	28	0.12
Slovak	27	0.12
Swedish	71	0.31
Swiss	44	0.19
Turkish	306	1.33
Ukrainian	351	1.53

Notes: 1. Figures in the "Number" column do not add up to the total population due to: a) Ancestry/Race overlap — e.g. persons can report being both White and Irish, b) persons of Hispanic origin can report being any race, c) persons reporting two ancestries are counted in both categories. 2. Numbers in parentheses indicate the number of persons reporting this ancestry/race alone, not in combination with any other ancestry/race. 3. Refer to the Explanation of Data in the front of the book for more detailed information.

Ancestry/Race	Number	%
United States or American	664	2.89
West Indian, excl. Hispanic:	44	0.19
Barbadian	20	0.09
British West Indian	4	0.02
Trinidadian and Tobagonian	10	0.04
West Indian	10	0.04
White:	18,494	80.38
Not Hispanic (15,262)	15,569	67.67
Hispanic (2,649)	2,925	12.71
Yugoslavian	189	0.82

Clifton

Place Type: City
County: Passaic
Population: 78,672

Ancestry/Race	Number	%
Afghan	40	0.05
African American/Black:	2,588	3.29
Not Hispanic (2,002)	2,196	2.79
Hispanic (275)	392	0.50
African, sub-Saharan:	112	0.14
African	72	0.09
Nigerian	29	0.04
South African	11	0.01
Alaska Native tribes, specified:	1	0.00
Tlingit-Haida	1	0.00
Am. Ind. or Alaska Nat., not spec.	183	0.23
Albanian	170	0.22
American Indian tribes, specified:	169	0.21
Apache (4)	4	0.01
Blackfeet (1)	9	0.01
Cherokee (5)	28	0.04
Chippewa (1)	1	0.00
Delaware	3	0.00
Iroquois (3)	9	0.01
Kiowa	2	0.00
Latin American Indians (57)	99	0.13
Pueblo (1)	2	0.00
Puget Sound Salish (1)	1	0.00
Sioux	3	0.00
All other tribes (3)	8	0.01
American Indian tribes, not spec.	30	0.04
Arab:	2,641	3.36
Arab/Arabic	729	0.93
Egyptian	228	0.29
Jordanian	143	0.18
Lebanese	163	0.21
Moroccan	11	0.01
Palestinian	298	0.38
Syrian	1,010	1.28
Other Arab	59	0.07
Armenian	227	0.29
Asian:	5,705	7.25
Bangladeshi (14)	23	0.03
Chinese, ex. Taiwanese (421)	516	0.66
Filipino (1,526)	1,670	2.12
Indian (2,397)	2,503	3.18
Indonesian (10)	12	0.02
Japanese (68)	116	0.15
Korean (315)	329	0.42
Laotian (2)	8	0.01
Malaysian	6	0.01
Pakistani (93)	118	0.15
Sri Lankan (9)	11	0.01
Taiwanese (16)	21	0.03
Thai (54)	58	0.07
Vietnamese (38)	57	0.07
Other Asian, specified (2)	4	0.01
Other Asian, not specified (45)	253	0.32
Assyrian/Chaldean/Syriac	5	0.01
Australian	15	0.02
Austrian	799	1.02
Basque	27	0.03
Belgian	41	0.05
Brazilian	107	0.14
British	202	0.26
Bulgarian	18	0.02
Canadian	72	0.09
Carpatho Rusyn	7	0.01
Celtic	10	0.01
Croatian	197	0.25
Cypriot	11	0.01
Czech	400	0.51
Czechoslovakian	257	0.33
Danish	70	0.09
Dutch	2,091	2.66
Eastern European	64	0.08
English	2,299	2.92
Estonian	14	0.02
European	139	0.18
Finnish	51	0.06
French, except Basque	805	1.02
French Canadian	241	0.31
German	6,834	8.69
Greek	746	0.95
Guyanese	48	0.06
Hawaii Native/Pacific Islander:	91	0.12
Melanesian: (1)	1	0.00
Fijian (1)	1	0.00
Micronesian: (6)	11	0.01
Guamanian/Chamorro (6)	11	0.01
Polynesian: (6)	20	0.03
Native Hawaiian (5)	11	0.01
Samoan (1)	6	0.01
Other Polynesian	3	0.00
Other Pac. Isl., specified	2	0.00
Other Pac. Isl., not spec. (14)	57	0.07
Hispanic or Latino:	15,608	19.84
Central American:	459	0.58
Costa Rican	87	0.11
Guatemalan	77	0.10
Honduran	131	0.17
Nicaraguan	23	0.03
Panamanian	13	0.02
Salvadoran	98	0.12
Other Central American	30	0.04
Cuban	510	0.65
Dominican Republic	1,853	2.36
Mexican	1,591	2.02
Puerto Rican	3,923	4.99
South American:	4,305	5.47
Argentinean	160	0.20
Bolivian	118	0.15
Chilean	84	0.11
Colombian	1,581	2.01
Ecuadorian	406	0.52
Paraguayan	8	0.01
Peruvian	1,788	2.27
Uruguayan	23	0.03
Venezuelan	50	0.06
Other South American	87	0.11
Other Hispanic or Latino	2,967	3.77
Hungarian	1,688	2.15
Icelander	10	0.01
Iranian	57	0.07
Irish	7,709	9.80
Israeli	40	0.05
Italian	15,108	19.20
Latvian	6	0.01
Lithuanian	276	0.35
Macedonian	298	0.38
Maltese	13	0.02
Norwegian	115	0.15
Pennsylvania German	12	0.02
Polish	11,451	14.56
Portuguese	258	0.33
Romanian	159	0.20
Russian	2,135	2.71
Scandinavian	23	0.03
Scotch-Irish	444	0.56
Scottish	786	1.00
Serbian	144	0.18
Slavic	134	0.17
Slovak	1,163	1.48
Swedish	417	0.53
Swiss	124	0.16
Turkish	839	1.07
Ukrainian	1,795	2.28
United States or American	1,947	2.47
Welsh	201	0.26
West Indian, excl. Hispanic:	623	0.79
Bahamian	7	0.01
Barbadian	17	0.02
Belizean	11	0.01
Bermudan	13	0.02
British West Indian	15	0.02
Haitian	79	0.10
Jamaican	358	0.46
Trinidadian and Tobagonian	59	0.07
U.S. Virgin Islander	4	0.01
West Indian	56	0.07
Other West Indian	4	0.01
White:	63,141	80.26
Not Hispanic (53,206)	55,485	70.53
Hispanic (6,754)	7,656	9.73
Yugoslavian	278	0.35

Clinton

Place Type: Township
County: Hunterdon
Population: 12,957

Ancestry/Race	Number	%
African American/Black:	961	7.42
Not Hispanic (858)	897	6.92
Hispanic (44)	64	0.49
African, sub-Saharan:	58	0.45
African	58	0.45
Am. Ind. or Alaska Nat., not spec.	28	0.22
American Indian tribes, specified:	30	0.23
Blackfeet (1)	1	0.01
Cherokee (6)	14	0.11
Delaware	1	0.01
Iroquois (1)	2	0.02
Latin American Indians (3)	6	0.05
Navajo (1)	2	0.02
Sioux (1)	2	0.02
All other tribes (1)	2	0.02
American Indian tribes, not spec.	3	0.02
Armenian	8	0.06
Asian:	362	2.79
Chinese, ex. Taiwanese (121)	138	1.07
Filipino (12)	25	0.19
Indian (100)	114	0.88
Indonesian	1	0.01
Japanese (12)	16	0.12
Korean (39)	44	0.34
Pakistani (1)	1	0.01
Sri Lankan	4	0.03
Taiwanese (6)	6	0.05
Thai (3)	3	0.02
Vietnamese (2)	3	0.02
Other Asian, not specified	7	0.05
Australian	7	0.05
Austrian	193	1.49
Belgian	56	0.43
British	31	0.24
Canadian	19	0.15
Croatian	22	0.17
Czech	60	0.46
Czechoslovakian	40	0.31
Danish	56	0.43
Dutch	351	2.71
Eastern European	23	0.18
English	1,360	10.50
European	52	0.40
Finnish	22	0.17
French, except Basque	294	2.27
French Canadian	41	0.32
German	3,185	24.58
Greek	88	0.68
Hawaii Native/Pacific Islander:	17	0.13
Micronesian: (1)	1	0.01
Other Micronesian (1)	1	0.01
Polynesian: (4)	6	0.05
Native Hawaiian (4)	5	0.04
Samoan	1	0.01

Notes: 1. Figures in the "Number" column do not add up to the total population due to: a) Ancestry/Race overlap — e.g. persons can report being both White and Irish, b) persons of Hispanic origin can report being any race, c) persons reporting two ancestries are counted in both categories. 2. Numbers in parentheses indicate the number of persons reporting this ancestry/race alone, not in combination with any other ancestry/race. 3. Refer to the Explanation of Data in the front of the book for more detailed information.

Other Pac. Isl., not spec. (4)	10	0.08
Hispanic or Latino:	507	3.91
Central American:	18	0.14
Costa Rican	5	0.04
Guatemalan	5	0.04
Honduran	1	0.01
Nicaraguan	1	0.01
Panamanian	2	0.02
Salvadoran	4	0.03
Cuban	46	0.36
Dominican Republic	25	0.19
Mexican	36	0.28
Puerto Rican	253	1.95
South American:	50	0.39
Argentinean	3	0.02
Chilean	4	0.03
Colombian	19	0.15
Ecuadorian	9	0.07
Paraguayan	1	0.01
Peruvian	5	0.04
Venezuelan	6	0.05
Other South American	3	0.02
Other Hispanic or Latino	79	0.61
Hungarian	211	1.63
Irish	2,421	18.68
Italian	2,958	22.83
Latvian	14	0.11
Lithuanian	130	1.00
Luxemburger	23	0.18
Norwegian	150	1.16
Pennsylvania German	21	0.16
Polish	1,232	9.51
Portuguese	128	0.99
Romanian	10	0.08
Russian	182	1.40
Scandinavian	7	0.05
Scotch-Irish	214	1.65
Scottish	213	1.64
Slavic	8	0.06
Slovak	177	1.37
Slovene	8	0.06
Swedish	228	1.76
Swiss	78	0.60
Ukrainian	203	1.57
United States or American	901	6.95
Welsh	89	0.69
West Indian, excl. Hispanic:	61	0.47
Jamaican	17	0.13
West Indian	44	0.34
White:	11,459	88.44
Not Hispanic (11,140)	11,215	86.56
Hispanic (225)	244	1.88
Yugoslavian	52	0.40

Collingswood

Place Type: Borough
County: Camden
Population: 14,326

Ancestry/Race	Number	%
African American/Black:	1,046	7.30
Not Hispanic (901)	982	6.85
Hispanic (54)	64	0.45
African, sub-Saharan:	42	0.29
African	4	0.03
Sierra Leonean	38	0.27
Am. Ind. or Alaska Nat., not spec.	44	0.31
American Indian tribes, specified:	57	0.40
Blackfeet	4	0.03
Cherokee (5)	11	0.08
Chippewa	1	0.01
Creek (1)	4	0.03
Delaware	5	0.03
Iroquois (3)	8	0.06
Kiowa	1	0.01
Latin American Indians (6)	6	0.04
Navajo	2	0.01
Seminole	1	0.01
Sioux (6)	6	0.04
All other tribes (3)	8	0.06
American Indian tribes, not spec.	13	0.09
Arab:	23	0.16
Egyptian	13	0.09
Lebanese	10	0.07
Armenian	93	0.65
Asian:	429	2.99
Cambodian (1)	1	0.01
Chinese, ex. Taiwanese (172)	180	1.26
Filipino (45)	53	0.37
Indian (75)	81	0.57
Indonesian (1)	1	0.01
Japanese (11)	14	0.10
Korean (30)	37	0.26
Taiwanese (1)	1	0.01
Vietnamese (53)	54	0.38
Other Asian, specified	1	0.01
Other Asian, not specified (5)	6	0.04
Austrian	42	0.29
Brazilian	6	0.04
British	48	0.33
Canadian	7	0.05
Celtic	8	0.06
Croatian	19	0.13
Czech	9	0.06
Czechoslovakian	15	0.10
Danish	27	0.19
Dutch	298	2.08
Eastern European	21	0.15
English	1,920	13.39
Estonian	4	0.03
European	102	0.71
Finnish	24	0.17
French, except Basque	304	2.12
French Canadian	82	0.57
German	2,910	20.30
Greek	48	0.33
Guyanese	7	0.05
Hawaii Native/Pacific Islander:	10	0.07
Micronesian: (2)	3	0.02
Guamanian/Chamorro (2)	3	0.02
Polynesian: (1)	2	0.01
Native Hawaiian (1)	2	0.01
Other Pac. Isl., not spec.	5	0.03
Hispanic or Latino:	812	5.67
Central American:	46	0.32
Costa Rican	7	0.05
Honduran	9	0.06
Nicaraguan	24	0.17
Panamanian	1	0.01
Salvadoran	5	0.03
Cuban	9	0.06
Dominican Republic	35	0.24
Mexican	112	0.78
Puerto Rican	450	3.14
South American:	33	0.23
Argentinean	2	0.01
Bolivian	1	0.01
Colombian	12	0.08
Ecuadorian	3	0.02
Peruvian	8	0.06
Venezuelan	2	0.01
Other South American	5	0.03
Other Hispanic or Latino	127	0.89
Hungarian	60	0.42
Irish	3,663	25.55
Italian	2,683	18.71
Latvian	7	0.05
Lithuanian	128	0.89
Maltese	12	0.08
Northern European	16	0.11
Norwegian	120	0.84
Pennsylvania German	47	0.33
Polish	1,087	7.58
Portuguese	51	0.36
Romanian	14	0.10
Russian	209	1.46
Scandinavian	6	0.04
Scotch-Irish	314	2.19
Scottish	289	2.02
Slavic	22	0.15
Slovak	42	0.29
Swedish	27	0.19
Swiss	27	0.19
Turkish	9	0.06
Ukrainian	178	1.24
United States or American	661	4.61
Welsh	219	1.53
West Indian, excl. Hispanic:	44	0.31
Haitian	9	0.06
West Indian	35	0.24
White:	12,540	87.53
Not Hispanic (12,024)	12,144	84.77
Hispanic (364)	396	2.76
Yugoslavian	31	0.22

Colonia

Place Type: Census Designated Place
County: Middlesex
Population: 17,811

Ancestry/Race	Number	%
African American/Black:	910	5.11
Not Hispanic (828)	873	4.90
Hispanic (19)	37	0.21
African, sub-Saharan:	34	0.19
African	29	0.16
Other sub-Saharan African	5	0.03
Alaska Native tribes, specified:	1	0.01
Eskimo	1	0.01
Am. Ind. or Alaska Nat., not spec.	22	0.12
Albanian	16	0.09
Alsatian	8	0.05
American Indian tribes, specified:	29	0.16
Blackfeet	2	0.01
Cherokee (4)	13	0.07
Cheyenne (1)	1	0.01
Choctaw	2	0.01
Delaware	1	0.01
Iroquois (1)	4	0.02
Latin American Indians	2	0.01
Pueblo	1	0.01
All other tribes (1)	3	0.02
Arab:	155	0.87
Arab/Arabic	40	0.23
Egyptian	22	0.12
Jordanian	21	0.12
Lebanese	58	0.33
Syrian	14	0.08
Asian:	1,219	6.84
Chinese, ex. Taiwanese (161)	181	1.02
Filipino (338)	372	2.09
Indian (455)	473	2.66
Japanese (3)	6	0.03
Korean (73)	77	0.43
Malaysian (1)	2	0.01
Pakistani (24)	35	0.20
Sri Lankan (6)	7	0.04
Taiwanese (6)	10	0.06
Thai (1)	1	0.01
Vietnamese (33)	33	0.19
Other Asian, specified (1)	1	0.01
Other Asian, not specified (8)	21	0.12
Assyrian/Chaldean/Syriac	5	0.03
Austrian	115	0.65
Belgian	5	0.03
Canadian	67	0.38
Carpatho Rusyn	33	0.19
Croatian	12	0.07
Czech	113	0.64
Czechoslovakian	40	0.23
Danish	77	0.43
Dutch	92	0.52
Eastern European	28	0.16
English	697	3.93
European	35	0.20
French, except Basque	179	1.01
French Canadian	51	0.29
German	2,556	14.40

Notes: 1. Figures in the "Number" column do not add up to the total population due to: a) Ancestry/Race overlap — e.g. persons can report being both White and Irish, b) persons of Hispanic origin can report being any race, c) persons reporting two ancestries are counted in both categories. 2. Numbers in parentheses indicate the number of persons reporting this ancestry/race alone, not in combination with any other ancestry/race. 3. Refer to the Explanation of Data in the front of the book for more detailed information.

Greek	102	0.57
Guyanese	31	0.17
Hawaii Native/Pacific Islander:	35	0.20
Micronesian: (1)	7	0.04
Guamanian/Chamorro (1)	2	0.01
Other Micronesian	5	0.03
Polynesian: (6)	14	0.08
Native Hawaiian	4	0.02
Samoan (6)	9	0.05
Tongan	1	0.01
Other Pac. Isl., not spec. (3)	14	0.08
Hispanic or Latino:	886	4.97
Central American:	44	0.25
Costa Rican	18	0.10
Guatemalan	4	0.02
Honduran	4	0.02
Nicaraguan	4	0.02
Panamanian	8	0.04
Salvadoran	5	0.03
Other Central American	1	0.01
Cuban	123	0.69
Dominican Republic	29	0.16
Mexican	15	0.08
Puerto Rican	363	2.04
South American:	115	0.65
Argentinean	11	0.06
Bolivian	1	0.01
Chilean	4	0.02
Colombian	57	0.32
Ecuadorian	8	0.04
Peruvian	22	0.12
Uruguayan	4	0.02
Venezuelan	1	0.01
Other South American	7	0.04
Other Hispanic or Latino	197	1.11
Hungarian	471	2.65
Iranian	26	0.15
Irish	3,560	20.05
Israeli	33	0.19
Italian	4,376	24.65
Latvian	14	0.08
Lithuanian	157	0.88
Norwegian	198	1.12
Polish	2,612	14.71
Portuguese	689	3.88
Romanian	33	0.19
Russian	544	3.06
Scandinavian	42	0.24
Scotch-Irish	175	0.99
Scottish	212	1.19
Slavic	48	0.27
Slovak	284	1.60
Slovene	4	0.02
Swedish	110	0.62
Swiss	35	0.20
Turkish	22	0.12
Ukrainian	425	2.39
United States or American	443	2.49
Welsh	78	0.44
West Indian, excl. Hispanic:	92	0.52
Haitian	38	0.21
Jamaican	46	0.26
Trinidadian and Tobagonian	8	0.05
White:	15,533	87.21
Not Hispanic (14,713)	14,877	83.53
Hispanic (604)	656	3.68
Yugoslavian	22	0.12

Colts Neck

Place Type: Township
County: Monmouth
Population: 12,331

Ancestry/Race	Number	%
African American/Black:	1,021	8.28
Not Hispanic (916)	949	7.70
Hispanic (57)	72	0.58
African, sub-Saharan:	15	0.12
African	15	0.12
Alaska Native tribes, specified:	1	0.01
Tlingit-Haida (1)	1	0.01
Am. Ind. or Alaska Nat., not spec.	21	0.17
American Indian tribes, specified:	46	0.37
Apache	1	0.01
Blackfeet	4	0.03
Cherokee (4)	18	0.15
Choctaw (1)	1	0.01
Comanche	1	0.01
Creek	1	0.01
Crow (1)	1	0.01
Iroquois (1)	4	0.03
Latin American Indians (2)	4	0.03
Lumbee (2)	3	0.02
Navajo (4)	4	0.03
Ottawa (1)	1	0.01
Sioux (1)	1	0.01
All other tribes (1)	2	0.02
American Indian tribes, not spec.	5	0.04
Arab:	228	1.85
Egyptian	71	0.58
Lebanese	27	0.22
Syrian	130	1.05
Armenian	19	0.15
Asian:	507	4.11
Bangladeshi (5)	5	0.04
Cambodian (1)	1	0.01
Chinese, ex. Taiwanese (127)	136	1.10
Filipino (113)	129	1.05
Hmong (2)	2	0.02
Indian (84)	91	0.74
Indonesian (1)	2	0.02
Japanese (11)	18	0.15
Korean (29)	36	0.29
Laotian (2)	2	0.02
Malaysian (1)	2	0.02
Pakistani (12)	12	0.10
Taiwanese (23)	24	0.19
Thai (1)	1	0.01
Vietnamese (27)	30	0.24
Other Asian, not specified (8)	16	0.13
Austrian	76	0.62
Belgian	15	0.12
Brazilian	5	0.04
British	52	0.42
Croatian	6	0.05
Czech	34	0.28
Czechoslovakian	13	0.11
Danish	20	0.16
Dutch	133	1.08
Eastern European	42	0.34
English	867	7.03
European	57	0.46
Finnish	16	0.13
French, except Basque	183	1.48
French Canadian	51	0.41
German	2,076	16.84
Greek	123	1.00
Hawaii Native/Pacific Islander:	6	0.05
Polynesian: (1)	4	0.03
Native Hawaiian	2	0.02
Samoan (1)	2	0.02
Other Pac. Isl., not spec.	2	0.02
Hispanic or Latino:	520	4.22
Central American:	35	0.28
Costa Rican	9	0.07
Guatemalan	2	0.02
Honduran	13	0.11
Nicaraguan	3	0.02
Panamanian	6	0.05
Salvadoran	2	0.02
Cuban	15	0.12
Dominican Republic	30	0.24
Mexican	113	0.92
Puerto Rican	186	1.51
South American:	44	0.36
Argentinean	12	0.10
Chilean	8	0.06
Colombian	8	0.06
Ecuadorian	11	0.09
Peruvian	3	0.02
Venezuelan	1	0.01
Other South American	1	0.01
Other Hispanic or Latino	97	0.79
Hungarian	130	1.05
Irish	2,813	22.81
Italian	3,039	24.65
Latvian	16	0.13
Lithuanian	69	0.56
Norwegian	186	1.51
Polish	920	7.46
Portuguese	149	1.21
Romanian	22	0.18
Russian	352	2.85
Scotch-Irish	200	1.62
Scottish	243	1.97
Slovak	51	0.41
Swedish	92	0.75
Swiss	50	0.41
Turkish	39	0.32
Ukrainian	89	0.72
United States or American	512	4.15
Welsh	40	0.32
West Indian, excl. Hispanic:	82	0.66
British West Indian	7	0.06
Haitian	15	0.12
Jamaican	27	0.22
Trinidadian and Tobagonian	7	0.06
West Indian	26	0.21
White:	10,673	86.55
Not Hispanic (10,289)	10,397	84.32
Hispanic (255)	276	2.24
Yugoslavian	6	0.05

Cranford

Place Type: Census Designated Place
County: Union
Population: 22,578

Ancestry/Race	Number	%
African American/Black:	628	2.78
Not Hispanic (579)	617	2.73
Hispanic (4)	11	0.05
African, sub-Saharan:	30	0.13
African	24	0.11
South African	6	0.03
Alaska Native tribes, specified:	1	0.00
Aleut	1	0.00
Am. Ind. or Alaska Nat., not spec.	16	0.07
Albanian	27	0.12
American Indian tribes, specified:	17	0.08
Apache	2	0.01
Cherokee (2)	5	0.02
Delaware	2	0.01
Latin American Indians (3)	4	0.02
Shoshone	2	0.01
All other tribes	2	0.01
American Indian tribes, not spec.	3	0.01
Arab:	186	0.82
Egyptian	38	0.17
Lebanese	108	0.48
Palestinian	8	0.04
Syrian	32	0.14
Armenian	10	0.04
Asian:	574	2.54
Bangladeshi	2	0.01
Chinese, ex. Taiwanese (168)	191	0.85
Filipino (112)	156	0.69
Indian (113)	117	0.52
Indonesian (1)	1	0.00
Japanese (20)	25	0.11
Korean (29)	31	0.14
Pakistani (9)	10	0.04
Sri Lankan (4)	4	0.02
Taiwanese (4)	4	0.02
Thai (3)	7	0.03
Vietnamese (10)	11	0.05
Other Asian, specified (1)	1	0.00
Other Asian, not specified (4)	14	0.06

Notes: 1. Figures in the "Number" column do not add up to the total population due to: a) Ancestry/Race overlap — e.g. persons can report being both White and Irish, b) persons of Hispanic origin can report being any race, c) persons reporting two ancestries are counted in both categories. 2. Numbers in parentheses indicate the number of persons reporting this ancestry/race alone, not in combination with any other ancestry/race. 3. Refer to the Explanation of Data in the front of the book for more detailed information.

Australian	12	0.05
Austrian	171	0.76
Brazilian	21	0.09
British	72	0.32
Canadian	38	0.17
Carpatho Rusyn	12	0.05
Croatian	9	0.04
Czech	105	0.47
Czechoslovakian	127	0.56
Danish	229	1.01
Dutch	254	1.12
Eastern European	115	0.51
English	1,616	7.16
Estonian	7	0.03
European	19	0.08
Finnish	13	0.06
French, except Basque	318	1.41
French Canadian	145	0.64
German	4,097	18.15
Greek	162	0.72
Guyanese	7	0.03
Hawaii Native/Pacific Islander:	13	0.06
Micronesian: (1)	4	0.02
Guamanian/Chamorro (1)	4	0.02
Polynesian: (3)	6	0.03
Native Hawaiian (2)	4	0.02
Samoan (1)	2	0.01
Other Pac. Isl., not spec. (1)	3	0.01
Hispanic or Latino:	879	3.89
Central American:	33	0.15
Costa Rican	5	0.02
Guatemalan	8	0.04
Honduran	8	0.04
Nicaraguan	1	0.00
Salvadoran	10	0.04
Other Central American	1	0.00
Cuban	198	0.88
Dominican Republic	12	0.05
Mexican	47	0.21
Puerto Rican	241	1.07
South American:	136	0.60
Argentinean	17	0.08
Bolivian	3	0.01
Chilean	5	0.02
Colombian	50	0.22
Ecuadorian	25	0.11
Paraguayan	1	0.00
Peruvian	13	0.06
Uruguayan	4	0.02
Venezuelan	13	0.06
Other South American	5	0.02
Other Hispanic or Latino	212	0.94
Hungarian	468	2.07
Irish	5,549	24.58
Israeli	30	0.13
Italian	5,742	25.43
Lithuanian	406	1.80
Luxemburger	11	0.05
Northern European	9	0.04
Norwegian	110	0.49
Pennsylvania German	17	0.08
Polish	2,705	11.98
Portuguese	326	1.44
Romanian	39	0.17
Russian	750	3.32
Scandinavian	25	0.11
Scotch-Irish	269	1.19
Scottish	545	2.41
Serbian	6	0.03
Slavic	52	0.23
Slovak	223	0.99
Slovene	19	0.08
Swedish	260	1.15
Swiss	84	0.37
Ukrainian	412	1.82
United States or American	662	2.93
Welsh	183	0.81
West Indian, excl. Hispanic:	42	0.19
British West Indian	5	0.02
Haitian	14	0.06
West Indian	23	0.10
White:	21,317	94.41
Not Hispanic (20,464)	20,578	91.14
Hispanic (692)	739	3.27
Yugoslavian	38	0.17

Delran

Place Type: Township
County: Burlington
Population: 15,536

Ancestry/Race	Number	%
African American/Black:	1,561	10.05
Not Hispanic (1,425)	1,507	9.70
Hispanic (39)	54	0.35
African, sub-Saharan:	185	1.19
African	77	0.50
Cape Verdean	4	0.03
Ghanian	80	0.51
Nigerian	17	0.11
Ugandan	7	0.05
Am. Ind. or Alaska Nat., not spec.	34	0.22
Albanian	13	0.08
American Indian tribes, specified:	36	0.23
Blackfeet	3	0.02
Cherokee (3)	11	0.07
Comanche	3	0.02
Delaware	3	0.02
Iroquois (2)	2	0.01
Latin American Indians (4)	4	0.03
Shoshone	3	0.02
All other tribes (6)	7	0.05
American Indian tribes, not spec.	2	0.01
Arab:	20	0.13
Lebanese	20	0.13
Asian:	523	3.37
Cambodian (1)	2	0.01
Chinese, ex. Taiwanese (36)	45	0.29
Filipino (36)	45	0.29
Indian (176)	185	1.19
Japanese (20)	38	0.24
Korean (119)	135	0.87
Pakistani (2)	10	0.06
Sri Lankan (4)	4	0.03
Taiwanese (12)	12	0.08
Vietnamese (13)	15	0.10
Other Asian, specified (1)	1	0.01
Other Asian, not specified (13)	31	0.20
Austrian	87	0.56
Brazilian	217	1.40
British	49	0.32
Canadian	5	0.03
Croatian	12	0.08
Czech	16	0.10
Czechoslovakian	37	0.24
Danish	43	0.28
Dutch	217	1.40
Eastern European	5	0.03
English	1,626	10.47
European	82	0.53
Finnish	26	0.17
French, except Basque	424	2.73
French Canadian	52	0.33
German	3,465	22.30
Greek	44	0.28
Hawaii Native/Pacific Islander:	37	0.24
Micronesian: (6)	6	0.04
Guamanian/Chamorro (4)	4	0.03
Other Micronesian (2)	2	0.01
Polynesian: (17)	22	0.14
Native Hawaiian (3)	7	0.05
Samoan (14)	14	0.09
Other Polynesian	1	0.01
Other Pac. Isl., not spec. (2)	9	0.06
Hispanic or Latino:	505	3.25
Central American:	22	0.14
Guatemalan	1	0.01
Honduran	16	0.10
Panamanian	2	0.01
Salvadoran	3	0.02
Cuban	7	0.05
Dominican Republic	7	0.05
Mexican	51	0.33
Puerto Rican	253	1.63
South American:	46	0.30
Argentinean	4	0.03
Chilean	4	0.03
Colombian	18	0.12
Ecuadorian	5	0.03
Paraguayan	2	0.01
Peruvian	8	0.05
Venezuelan	2	0.01
Other South American	3	0.02
Other Hispanic or Latino	119	0.77
Hungarian	252	1.62
Iranian	17	0.11
Irish	4,240	27.29
Italian	3,113	20.04
Lithuanian	90	0.58
Luxemburger	5	0.03
New Zealander	7	0.05
Norwegian	60	0.39
Pennsylvania German	16	0.10
Polish	1,184	7.62
Portuguese	113	0.73
Romanian	36	0.23
Russian	199	1.28
Scotch-Irish	126	0.81
Scottish	186	1.20
Slovak	38	0.24
Swedish	159	1.02
Turkish	226	1.45
Ukrainian	99	0.64
United States or American	525	3.38
Welsh	82	0.53
West Indian, excl. Hispanic:	35	0.23
Jamaican	35	0.23
White:	13,276	85.45
Not Hispanic (12,641)	13,019	83.80
Hispanic (234)	257	1.65
Yugoslavian	87	0.56

Denville

Place Type: Township
County: Morris
Population: 15,824

Ancestry/Race	Number	%
African American/Black:	205	1.30
Not Hispanic (169)	192	1.21
Hispanic (12)	13	0.08
African, sub-Saharan:	23	0.15
African	19	0.12
Ghanian	4	0.03
Am. Ind. or Alaska Nat., not spec.	15	0.09
American Indian tribes, specified:	49	0.31
Apache (1)	1	0.01
Blackfeet	2	0.01
Cherokee (2)	16	0.10
Creek	1	0.01
Crow	1	0.01
Delaware	3	0.02
Iroquois (4)	9	0.06
Latin American Indians (2)	4	0.03
Osage (1)	2	0.01
All other tribes	10	0.06
Arab:	72	0.46
Egyptian	39	0.25
Lebanese	33	0.21
Armenian	76	0.48
Asian:	808	5.11
Chinese, ex. Taiwanese (212)	228	1.44
Filipino (90)	110	0.70
Indian (255)	264	1.67
Indonesian (1)	1	0.01
Japanese (20)	31	0.20
Korean (70)	75	0.47
Pakistani (8)	10	0.06

Notes: 1. Figures in the "Number" column do not add up to the total population due to: a) Ancestry/Race overlap — e.g. persons can report being both White and Irish, b) persons of Hispanic origin can report being any race, c) persons reporting two ancestries are counted in both categories. 2. Numbers in parentheses indicate the number of persons reporting this ancestry/race alone, not in combination with any other ancestry/race. 3. Refer to the Explanation of Data in the front of the book for more detailed information.

Ancestry/Race	Number	%
Sri Lankan (2)	2	0.01
Taiwanese (16)	16	0.10
Thai (6)	9	0.06
Vietnamese (39)	39	0.25
Other Asian, not specified (11)	23	0.15
Australian	12	0.08
Austrian	92	0.58
Belgian	10	0.06
Brazilian	54	0.34
British	41	0.26
Canadian	30	0.19
Czech	127	0.80
Czechoslovakian	37	0.23
Danish	79	0.50
Dutch	328	2.07
Eastern European	36	0.23
English	1,351	8.54
Estonian	33	0.21
European	177	1.12
Finnish	38	0.24
French, except Basque	384	2.43
French Canadian	138	0.87
German	3,106	19.63
Greek	223	1.41
Guyanese	2	0.01
Hawaii Native/Pacific Islander:	9	0.06
Micronesian: (1)	1	0.01
Other Micronesian (1)	1	0.01
Polynesian: (3)	6	0.04
Native Hawaiian (3)	6	0.04
Other Pac. Isl., not spec. (1)	2	0.01
Hispanic or Latino:	418	2.64
Central American:	17	0.11
Costa Rican	1	0.01
Honduran	5	0.03
Nicaraguan	4	0.03
Salvadoran	6	0.04
Other Central American	1	0.01
Cuban	55	0.35
Dominican Republic	8	0.05
Mexican	30	0.19
Puerto Rican	115	0.73
South American:	102	0.64
Argentinean	8	0.05
Bolivian	1	0.01
Chilean	10	0.06
Colombian	51	0.32
Ecuadorian	9	0.06
Paraguayan	3	0.02
Peruvian	19	0.12
Venezuelan	1	0.01
Other Hispanic or Latino	91	0.58
Hungarian	386	2.44
Iranian	19	0.12
Irish	3,977	25.13
Italian	4,134	26.12
Lithuanian	54	0.34
Northern European	9	0.06
Norwegian	89	0.56
Polish	1,216	7.68
Portuguese	90	0.57
Romanian	38	0.24
Russian	392	2.48
Scotch-Irish	158	1.00
Scottish	349	2.21
Slavic	31	0.20
Slovak	168	1.06
Swedish	254	1.61
Swiss	109	0.69
Ukrainian	242	1.53
United States or American	616	3.89
Welsh	74	0.47
West Indian, excl. Hispanic:	16	0.10
Haitian	8	0.05
Trinidadian and Tobagonian	8	0.05
White:	14,807	93.57
Not Hispanic (14,327)	14,455	91.35
Hispanic (332)	352	2.22
Yugoslavian	11	0.07

Deptford

Place Type: Township
County: Gloucester
Population: 26,763

Ancestry/Race	Number	%
African American/Black:	3,505	13.10
Not Hispanic (3,252)	3,418	12.77
Hispanic (62)	87	0.33
African, sub-Saharan:	136	0.51
African	64	0.24
Nigerian	16	0.06
South African	56	0.21
Am. Ind. or Alaska Nat., not spec.	48	0.18
American Indian tribes, specified:	89	0.33
Blackfeet (1)	3	0.01
Cherokee (8)	26	0.10
Chippewa	5	0.02
Comanche	1	0.00
Delaware (5)	9	0.03
Iroquois (10)	10	0.04
Latin American Indians (2)	6	0.02
Lumbee (1)	1	0.00
Ottawa (2)	2	0.01
Pueblo	3	0.01
Sioux	1	0.00
All other tribes (11)	22	0.08
American Indian tribes, not spec.	1	0.00
Arab:	38	0.14
Lebanese	24	0.09
Moroccan	9	0.03
Syrian	5	0.02
Armenian	6	0.02
Asian:	507	1.89
Bangladeshi (16)	16	0.06
Chinese, ex. Taiwanese (85)	89	0.33
Filipino (121)	141	0.53
Indian (114)	132	0.49
Japanese (11)	21	0.08
Korean (43)	56	0.21
Pakistani	5	0.02
Taiwanese (1)	2	0.01
Thai (3)	5	0.02
Vietnamese (11)	13	0.05
Other Asian, specified	1	0.00
Other Asian, not specified (4)	26	0.10
Austrian	102	0.38
Belgian	3	0.01
British	18	0.07
Canadian	18	0.07
Croatian	61	0.23
Czech	38	0.14
Czechoslovakian	16	0.06
Danish	35	0.13
Dutch	368	1.38
English	2,620	9.79
Estonian	6	0.02
European	69	0.26
Finnish	11	0.04
French, except Basque	539	2.01
French Canadian	65	0.24
German	5,652	21.12
Greek	179	0.67
Hawaii Native/Pacific Islander:	16	0.06
Micronesian: (1)	1	0.00
Guamanian/Chamorro (1)	1	0.00
Polynesian: (6)	10	0.04
Native Hawaiian (5)	8	0.03
Samoan (1)	2	0.01
Other Pac. Isl., specified	1	0.00
Other Pac. Isl., not spec. (2)	4	0.01
Hispanic or Latino:	766	2.86
Central American:	32	0.12
Costa Rican	1	0.00
Guatemalan	16	0.06
Honduran	5	0.02
Panamanian	7	0.03
Salvadoran	2	0.01
Other Central American	1	0.00
Cuban	25	0.09
Dominican Republic	13	0.05
Mexican	114	0.43
Puerto Rican	421	1.57
South American:	51	0.19
Argentinean	7	0.03
Bolivian	1	0.00
Chilean	5	0.02
Colombian	15	0.06
Ecuadorian	6	0.02
Peruvian	9	0.03
Venezuelan	4	0.01
Other South American	4	0.01
Other Hispanic or Latino	110	0.41
Hungarian	156	0.58
Iranian	9	0.03
Irish	7,514	28.08
Italian	6,128	22.90
Latvian	34	0.13
Lithuanian	113	0.42
Norwegian	148	0.55
Pennsylvania German	125	0.47
Polish	1,776	6.64
Portuguese	46	0.17
Romanian	40	0.15
Russian	274	1.02
Scotch-Irish	272	1.02
Scottish	245	0.92
Serbian	5	0.02
Slavic	20	0.07
Slovak	48	0.18
Swedish	205	0.77
Swiss	16	0.06
Ukrainian	195	0.73
United States or American	687	2.57
Welsh	205	0.77
West Indian, excl. Hispanic:	103	0.38
Bermudan	8	0.03
Haitian	17	0.06
Jamaican	78	0.29
White:	22,635	84.58
Not Hispanic (21,933)	22,191	82.92
Hispanic (397)	444	1.66
Yugoslavian	9	0.03

Dover

Place Type: Town
County: Morris
Population: 18,188

Ancestry/Race	Number	%
African American/Black:	1,379	7.58
Not Hispanic (1,035)	1,108	6.09
Hispanic (207)	271	1.49
African, sub-Saharan:	47	0.26
African	27	0.15
Ethiopian	16	0.09
Kenyan	4	0.02
Alaska Native tribes, specified:	1	0.01
Alaska Athabascan (1)	1	0.01
Am. Ind. or Alaska Nat., not spec.	45	0.25
Alsatian	8	0.04
American Indian tribes, specified:	87	0.48
Apache	5	0.03
Cherokee	5	0.03
Chickasaw	3	0.02
Chippewa	3	0.02
Delaware (2)	4	0.02
Iroquois	1	0.01
Latin American Indians (18)	45	0.25
Navajo (1)	1	0.01
Pueblo	7	0.04
Seminole	1	0.01
Shoshone (1)	1	0.01
Sioux	6	0.03
Tohono O'Odham	2	0.01
Yakama	1	0.01
All other tribes	2	0.01
American Indian tribes, not spec.	17	0.09

Notes: 1. Figures in the "Number" column do not add up to the total population due to: a) Ancestry/Race overlap — e.g. persons can report being both White and Irish, b) persons of Hispanic origin can report being any race, c) persons reporting two ancestries are counted in both categories. 2. Numbers in parentheses indicate the number of persons reporting this ancestry/race alone, not in combination with any other ancestry/race. 3. Refer to the Explanation of Data in the front of the book for more detailed information.

Ancestry/Race	Number	%
Arab:	11	0.06
Lebanese	5	0.03
Syrian	6	0.03
Armenian	6	0.03
Asian:	512	2.82
Bangladeshi (3)	3	0.02
Chinese, ex. Taiwanese (74)	77	0.42
Filipino (116)	130	0.71
Hmong (1)	1	0.01
Indian (116)	132	0.73
Indonesian (3)	3	0.02
Japanese (3)	3	0.02
Korean (24)	26	0.14
Laotian (3)	3	0.02
Pakistani (5)	12	0.07
Taiwanese (4)	4	0.02
Vietnamese (90)	90	0.49
Other Asian, specified (1)	1	0.01
Other Asian, not specified (4)	27	0.15
Austrian	40	0.22
Brazilian	19	0.10
British	16	0.09
Czech	60	0.33
Czechoslovakian	11	0.06
Danish	14	0.08
Dutch	61	0.34
English	805	4.43
European	37	0.20
Finnish	6	0.03
French, except Basque	89	0.49
French Canadian	12	0.07
German	985	5.42
Greek	288	1.58
Hawaii Native/Pacific Islander:	12	0.07
Micronesian: (2)	2	0.01
Guamanian/Chamorro (2)	2	0.01
Polynesian:	1	0.01
Samoan	1	0.01
Other Pac. Isl., not spec. (3)	9	0.05
Hispanic or Latino:	10,539	57.94
Central American:	618	3.40
Costa Rican	239	1.31
Guatemalan	85	0.47
Honduran	176	0.97
Nicaraguan	2	0.01
Panamanian	3	0.02
Salvadoran	71	0.39
Other Central American	42	0.23
Cuban	98	0.54
Dominican Republic	279	1.53
Mexican	1,557	8.56
Puerto Rican	2,413	13.27
South American:	3,440	18.91
Argentinean	48	0.26
Bolivian	7	0.04
Chilean	275	1.51
Colombian	2,050	11.27
Ecuadorian	613	3.37
Peruvian	212	1.17
Uruguayan	157	0.86
Venezuelan	20	0.11
Other South American	58	0.32
Other Hispanic or Latino	2,134	11.73
Hungarian	157	0.86
Irish	1,181	6.49
Italian	1,320	7.26
Lithuanian	49	0.27
Macedonian	7	0.04
Norwegian	69	0.38
Polish	446	2.45
Portuguese	125	0.69
Romanian	7	0.04
Russian	51	0.28
Scandinavian	7	0.04
Scotch-Irish	109	0.60
Scottish	60	0.33
Slavic	9	0.05
Slovak	39	0.21
Swedish	92	0.51
Swiss	7	0.04
United States or American	698	3.84
Welsh	37	0.20
West Indian, excl. Hispanic:	166	0.91
Haitian	8	0.04
Jamaican	141	0.78
Trinidadian and Tobagonian	3	0.02
West Indian	14	0.08
White:	13,406	73.71
Not Hispanic (5,937)	6,096	33.52
Hispanic (6,694)	7,310	40.19
Yugoslavian	9	0.05

Dover

Place Type: Township
County: Ocean
Population: 89,706

Ancestry/Race	Number	%
African American/Black:	1,841	2.05
Not Hispanic (1,490)	1,695	1.89
Hispanic (78)	146	0.16
African, sub-Saharan:	132	0.15
African	83	0.09
Kenyan	16	0.02
South African	33	0.04
Alaska Native tribes, specified:	8	0.01
Aleut (3)	4	0.00
Tlingit-Haida (4)	4	0.00
Alaska Native tribes, not specified	4	0.00
Am. Ind. or Alaska Nat., not spec.	121	0.13
Albanian	67	0.07
American Indian tribes, specified:	205	0.23
Apache	3	0.00
Blackfeet (6)	20	0.02
Cherokee (10)	49	0.05
Chickasaw (1)	1	0.00
Chippewa	5	0.01
Choctaw	1	0.00
Comanche	2	0.00
Creek (2)	10	0.01
Crow	1	0.00
Delaware (3)	34	0.04
Iroquois (7)	17	0.02
Latin American Indians (14)	23	0.03
Navajo (2)	3	0.00
Paiute (1)	1	0.00
Sioux (4)	5	0.01
Ute (1)	1	0.00
Yaqui	1	0.00
All other tribes (10)	28	0.03
American Indian tribes, not spec.	21	0.02
Arab:	338	0.38
Arab/Arabic	14	0.02
Egyptian	16	0.02
Iraqi	16	0.02
Lebanese	121	0.13
Syrian	161	0.18
Other Arab	10	0.01
Armenian	66	0.07
Asian:	2,561	2.85
Cambodian	1	0.00
Chinese, ex. Taiwanese (295)	336	0.37
Filipino (983)	1,145	1.28
Indian (529)	589	0.66
Indonesian (4)	7	0.01
Japanese (46)	57	0.06
Korean (162)	195	0.22
Malaysian (5)	10	0.01
Pakistani (48)	57	0.06
Sri Lankan (19)	19	0.02
Taiwanese (5)	6	0.01
Thai (11)	21	0.02
Vietnamese (26)	35	0.04
Other Asian, specified (6)	15	0.02
Other Asian, not specified (24)	68	0.08
Australian	23	0.03
Austrian	361	0.40
Basque	9	0.01
Belgian	106	0.12
Brazilian	55	0.06
British	222	0.25
Bulgarian	35	0.04
Canadian	141	0.16
Carpatho Rusyn	4	0.00
Celtic	3	0.00
Croatian	85	0.09
Cypriot	9	0.01
Czech	465	0.52
Czechoslovakian	280	0.31
Danish	384	0.43
Dutch	1,730	1.93
Eastern European	52	0.06
English	7,646	8.52
Estonian	12	0.01
European	381	0.42
Finnish	72	0.08
French, except Basque	1,758	1.96
French Canadian	472	0.53
German	16,833	18.75
Greek	840	0.94
Hawaii Native/Pacific Islander:	50	0.06
Micronesian: (1)	1	0.00
Guamanian/Chamorro (1)	1	0.00
Polynesian: (6)	14	0.02
Native Hawaiian (4)	10	0.01
Samoan (2)	4	0.00
Other Pac. Isl., specified	7	0.01
Other Pac. Isl., not spec. (14)	28	0.03
Hispanic or Latino:	4,070	4.54
Central American:	115	0.13
Costa Rican	46	0.05
Guatemalan	20	0.02
Honduran	9	0.01
Nicaraguan	5	0.01
Panamanian	6	0.01
Salvadoran	27	0.03
Other Central American	2	0.00
Cuban	326	0.36
Dominican Republic	54	0.06
Mexican	720	0.80
Puerto Rican	1,764	1.97
South American:	496	0.55
Argentinean	37	0.04
Bolivian	3	0.00
Chilean	14	0.02
Colombian	164	0.18
Ecuadorian	48	0.05
Paraguayan	6	0.01
Peruvian	158	0.18
Uruguayan	9	0.01
Venezuelan	32	0.04
Other South American	25	0.03
Other Hispanic or Latino	595	0.66
Hungarian	1,808	2.01
Iranian	59	0.07
Irish	21,766	24.25
Italian	28,261	31.48
Latvian	62	0.07
Lithuanian	517	0.58
Luxemburger	7	0.01
Norwegian	723	0.81
Pennsylvania German	25	0.03
Polish	8,088	9.01
Portuguese	571	0.64
Romanian	92	0.10
Russian	1,416	1.58
Scandinavian	60	0.07
Scotch-Irish	1,444	1.61
Scottish	1,757	1.96
Serbian	85	0.09
Slavic	107	0.12
Slovak	505	0.56
Slovene	27	0.03
Swedish	994	1.11
Swiss	196	0.22
Turkish	75	0.08
Ukrainian	1,139	1.27
United States or American	2,586	2.88
Welsh	434	0.48

Notes: 1. Figures in the "Number" column do not add up to the total population due to: a) Ancestry/Race overlap — e.g. persons can report being both White and Irish, b) persons of Hispanic origin can report being any race, c) persons reporting two ancestries are counted in both categories. 2. Numbers in parentheses indicate the number of persons reporting this ancestry/race alone, not in combination with any other ancestry/race. 3. Refer to the Explanation of Data in the front of the book for more detailed information.

Ancestry/Race	Number	%
West Indian, excl. Hispanic:	121	0.13
Haitian	14	0.02
Jamaican	94	0.10
Trinidadian and Tobagonian	8	0.01
West Indian	5	0.01
White:	84,835	94.57
Not Hispanic (81,093)	81,737	91.12
Hispanic (2,846)	3,098	3.45
Yugoslavian	85	0.09

Dumont

Place Type: Borough
County: Bergen
Population: 17,503

Ancestry/Race	Number	%
African American/Black:	316	1.81
Not Hispanic (222)	255	1.46
Hispanic (39)	61	0.35
African, sub-Saharan:	23	0.13
Other sub-Saharan African	23	0.13
Am. Ind. or Alaska Nat., not spec.	25	0.14
Albanian	62	0.35
American Indian tribes, specified:	20	0.11
Blackfeet (1)	1	0.01
Cherokee (4)	9	0.05
Delaware	3	0.02
Latin American Indians (1)	6	0.03
Sioux (1)	1	0.01
American Indian tribes, not spec.	2	0.01
Arab:	172	0.98
Arab/Arabic	15	0.09
Jordanian	18	0.10
Lebanese	46	0.26
Syrian	79	0.45
Other Arab	14	0.08
Armenian	142	0.81
Asian:	2,066	11.80
Bangladeshi (4)	4	0.02
Chinese, ex. Taiwanese (193)	215	1.23
Filipino (836)	884	5.05
Indian (478)	501	2.86
Indonesian (1)	1	0.01
Japanese (89)	112	0.64
Korean (242)	258	1.47
Malaysian (2)	2	0.01
Pakistani (8)	13	0.07
Sri Lankan (7)	7	0.04
Taiwanese (3)	3	0.02
Thai (11)	13	0.07
Vietnamese (6)	8	0.05
Other Asian, specified (5)	5	0.03
Other Asian, not specified (13)	40	0.23
Assyrian/Chaldean/Syriac	5	0.03
Austrian	122	0.70
Belgian	13	0.07
Brazilian	17	0.10
British	19	0.11
Canadian	37	0.21
Croatian	84	0.48
Cypriot	22	0.13
Czech	53	0.30
Czechoslovakian	62	0.35
Danish	30	0.17
Dutch	285	1.63
English	863	4.93
European	114	0.65
Finnish	20	0.11
French, except Basque	220	1.26
French Canadian	59	0.34
German	2,822	16.12
Greek	344	1.97
Hawaii Native/Pacific Islander:	20	0.11
Micronesian:	1	0.01
Guamanian/Chamorro	1	0.01
Polynesian:	2	0.01
Native Hawaiian	1	0.01
Samoan	1	0.01
Other Pac. Isl., not spec. (1)	17	0.10
Hispanic or Latino:	1,463	8.36
Central American:	63	0.36
Costa Rican	7	0.04
Guatemalan	11	0.06
Honduran	12	0.07
Nicaraguan	1	0.01
Panamanian	3	0.02
Salvadoran	23	0.13
Other Central American	6	0.03
Cuban	160	0.91
Dominican Republic	161	0.92
Mexican	59	0.34
Puerto Rican	419	2.39
South American:	249	1.42
Argentinean	13	0.07
Bolivian	7	0.04
Chilean	1	0.01
Colombian	160	0.91
Ecuadorian	39	0.22
Peruvian	19	0.11
Venezuelan	1	0.01
Other South American	9	0.05
Other Hispanic or Latino	352	2.01
Hungarian	157	0.90
Iranian	7	0.04
Irish	4,688	26.78
Israeli	8	0.05
Italian	4,583	26.18
Lithuanian	47	0.27
Northern European	55	0.31
Norwegian	183	1.05
Polish	644	3.68
Portuguese	55	0.31
Romanian	18	0.10
Russian	257	1.47
Scotch-Irish	164	0.94
Scottish	256	1.46
Serbian	6	0.03
Slavic	13	0.07
Slovak	80	0.46
Slovene	9	0.05
Swedish	118	0.67
Swiss	85	0.49
Turkish	27	0.15
Ukrainian	220	1.26
United States or American	495	2.83
Welsh	69	0.39
West Indian, excl. Hispanic:	113	0.65
Jamaican	18	0.10
Trinidadian and Tobagonian	83	0.47
West Indian	12	0.07
White:	14,892	85.08
Not Hispanic (13,692)	13,827	79.00
Hispanic (971)	1,065	6.08
Yugoslavian	81	0.46

East Brunswick

Place Type: Census Designated Place
County: Middlesex
Population: 46,756

Ancestry/Race	Number	%
African American/Black:	1,492	3.19
Not Hispanic (1,282)	1,428	3.05
Hispanic (39)	64	0.14
African, sub-Saharan:	220	0.47
African	88	0.19
Ethiopian	37	0.08
Liberian	7	0.01
Nigerian	37	0.08
Sierra Leonean	31	0.07
South African	20	0.04
Am. Ind. or Alaska Nat., not spec.	53	0.11
American Indian tribes, specified:	79	0.17
Apache (1)	1	0.00
Blackfeet	2	0.00
Cherokee (7)	21	0.04
Cree	1	0.00
Delaware (1)	8	0.02
Iroquois (9)	11	0.02
Latin American Indians (4)	17	0.04
Potawatomi (1)	1	0.00
Pueblo (1)	1	0.00
Seminole	1	0.00
Sioux (3)	4	0.01
All other tribes (7)	11	0.02
American Indian tribes, not spec.	4	0.01
Arab:	1,307	2.80
Egyptian	1,128	2.41
Iraqi	16	0.03
Lebanese	115	0.25
Moroccan	8	0.02
Syrian	40	0.09
Armenian	87	0.19
Asian:	8,027	17.17
Bangladeshi (7)	8	0.02
Chinese, ex. Taiwanese (3,088)	3,245	6.94
Filipino (597)	663	1.42
Indian (2,587)	2,662	5.69
Indonesian (6)	10	0.02
Japanese (47)	60	0.13
Korean (617)	632	1.35
Malaysian (1)	17	0.04
Pakistani (153)	179	0.38
Sri Lankan (23)	28	0.06
Taiwanese (232)	285	0.61
Thai (11)	14	0.03
Vietnamese (66)	71	0.15
Other Asian, specified (31)	40	0.09
Other Asian, not specified (39)	113	0.24
Australian	13	0.03
Austrian	546	1.17
Belgian	24	0.05
Brazilian	102	0.22
British	136	0.29
Canadian	125	0.27
Celtic	10	0.02
Croatian	28	0.06
Cypriot	52	0.11
Czech	239	0.51
Czechoslovakian	162	0.35
Danish	197	0.42
Dutch	380	0.81
Eastern European	387	0.83
English	1,676	3.58
Estonian	14	0.03
European	231	0.49
Finnish	47	0.10
French, except Basque	713	1.52
French Canadian	122	0.26
German	4,973	10.64
German Russian	7	0.01
Greek	407	0.87
Guyanese	91	0.19
Hawaii Native/Pacific Islander:	33	0.07
Micronesian: (3)	5	0.01
Guamanian/Chamorro (1)	2	0.00
Other Micronesian (2)	3	0.01
Polynesian:	2	0.00
Native Hawaiian	2	0.00
Other Pac. Isl., specified	3	0.01
Other Pac. Isl., not spec. (2)	23	0.05
Hispanic or Latino:	1,957	4.19
Central American:	83	0.18
Costa Rican	11	0.02
Guatemalan	16	0.03
Honduran	10	0.02
Nicaraguan	12	0.03
Panamanian	9	0.02
Salvadoran	15	0.03
Other Central American	10	0.02
Cuban	189	0.40
Dominican Republic	84	0.18
Mexican	160	0.34
Puerto Rican	718	1.54
South American:	335	0.72
Argentinean	41	0.09
Bolivian	1	0.00
Chilean	15	0.03

Notes: 1. Figures in the "Number" column do not add up to the total population due to: a) Ancestry/Race overlap— e.g. persons can report being both White and Irish, b) persons of Hispanic origin can report being any race, c) persons reporting two ancestries are counted in both categories. 2. Numbers in parentheses indicate the number of persons reporting this ancestry/race alone, not in combination with any other ancestry/race. 3. Refer to the Explanation of Data in the front of the book for more detailed information.

Ancestry/Race	Number	%
Colombian	92	0.20
Ecuadorian	54	0.12
Paraguayan	4	0.01
Peruvian	101	0.22
Uruguayan	8	0.02
Venezuelan	11	0.02
Other South American	8	0.02
Other Hispanic or Latino	388	0.83
Hungarian	1,779	3.80
Icelander	6	0.01
Iranian	127	0.27
Irish	6,424	13.74
Israeli	178	0.38
Italian	7,020	15.01
Latvian	155	0.33
Lithuanian	194	0.41
Macedonian	28	0.06
Maltese	61	0.13
Northern European	26	0.06
Norwegian	286	0.61
Pennsylvania German	7	0.01
Polish	5,369	11.48
Portuguese	212	0.45
Romanian	331	0.71
Russian	3,627	7.76
Scandinavian	15	0.03
Scotch-Irish	311	0.67
Scottish	512	1.10
Serbian	16	0.03
Slavic	36	0.08
Slovak	333	0.71
Slovene	8	0.02
Swedish	219	0.47
Swiss	128	0.27
Turkish	70	0.15
Ukrainian	706	1.51
United States or American	1,960	4.19
Welsh	83	0.18
West Indian, excl. Hispanic:	220	0.47
Barbadian	12	0.03
British West Indian	49	0.10
Dutch West Indian	7	0.01
Haitian	17	0.04
Jamaican	76	0.16
Trinidadian and Tobagonian	12	0.03
West Indian	47	0.10
White:	37,111	79.37
Not Hispanic (35,004)	35,718	76.39
Hispanic (1,261)	1,393	2.98
Yugoslavian	77	0.16

East Hanover

Place Type: Township
County: Morris
Population: 11,393

Ancestry/Race	Number	%
African American/Black:	72	0.63
Not Hispanic (64)	68	0.60
Hispanic (2)	4	0.04
Am. Ind. or Alaska Nat., not spec.	8	0.07
American Indian tribes, specified:	10	0.09
Blackfeet	2	0.02
Cherokee	3	0.03
Latin American Indians	4	0.04
Lumbee (1)	1	0.01
Arab:	205	1.80
Egyptian	43	0.38
Lebanese	98	0.86
Syrian	64	0.56
Armenian	31	0.27
Asian:	1,336	11.73
Bangladeshi	4	0.04
Chinese, ex. Taiwanese (499)	524	4.60
Filipino (129)	141	1.24
Indian (280)	287	2.52
Japanese (11)	16	0.14
Korean (141)	142	1.25
Laotian (1)	1	0.01
Malaysian (1)	1	0.01
Pakistani (25)	30	0.26
Taiwanese (121)	133	1.17
Thai (1)	1	0.01
Vietnamese (34)	36	0.32
Other Asian, not specified (14)	20	0.18
Austrian	44	0.39
British	12	0.11
Canadian	21	0.18
Carpatho Rusyn	9	0.08
Czech	56	0.49
Czechoslovakian	13	0.11
Danish	40	0.35
Dutch	134	1.18
Eastern European	6	0.05
English	434	3.81
European	31	0.27
French, except Basque	119	1.04
French Canadian	26	0.23
German	1,407	12.35
Greek	171	1.50
Guyanese	17	0.15
Hawaii Native/Pacific Islander:	6	0.05
Polynesian:	1	0.01
Samoan	1	0.01
Other Pac. Isl., not spec.	5	0.04
Hispanic or Latino:	312	2.74
Central American:	4	0.04
Guatemalan	1	0.01
Salvadoran	2	0.02
Other Central American	1	0.01
Cuban	53	0.47
Dominican Republic	3	0.03
Mexican	22	0.19
Puerto Rican	71	0.62
South American:	78	0.68
Argentinean	4	0.04
Chilean	2	0.02
Colombian	24	0.21
Ecuadorian	28	0.25
Paraguayan	1	0.01
Peruvian	11	0.10
Uruguayan	3	0.03
Venezuelan	2	0.02
Other South American	3	0.03
Other Hispanic or Latino	81	0.71
Hungarian	142	1.25
Iranian	20	0.18
Irish	1,468	12.89
Israeli	45	0.39
Italian	4,759	41.77
Lithuanian	45	0.39
Norwegian	50	0.44
Polish	792	6.95
Portuguese	158	1.39
Romanian	47	0.41
Russian	203	1.78
Scotch-Irish	101	0.89
Scottish	135	1.18
Slovak	90	0.79
Swedish	34	0.30
Swiss	41	0.36
Ukrainian	141	1.24
United States or American	387	3.40
Welsh	38	0.33
West Indian, excl. Hispanic:	43	0.38
Barbadian	12	0.11
Jamaican	31	0.27
White:	10,002	87.79
Not Hispanic (9,668)	9,732	85.42
Hispanic (253)	270	2.37
Yugoslavian	8	0.07

East Orange

Place Type: City
County: Essex
Population: 69,824

Ancestry/Race	Number	%
African American/Black:	64,797	92.80
Not Hispanic (61,604)	63,742	91.29
Hispanic (858)	1,055	1.51
African, sub-Saharan:	2,774	3.97
African	1,598	2.29
Cape Verdean	6	0.01
Ethiopian	149	0.21
Ghanian	217	0.31
Liberian	162	0.23
Nigerian	495	0.71
Sudanese	7	0.01
Ugandan	10	0.01
Other sub-Saharan African	130	0.19
Alaska Native tribes, specified:	2	0.00
Eskimo	1	0.00
Tlingit-Haida	1	0.00
Alaska Native tribes, not specified	1	0.00
Am. Ind. or Alaska Nat., not spec.	339	0.49
American Indian tribes, specified:	243	0.35
Apache (3)	5	0.01
Blackfeet (7)	42	0.06
Cherokee (10)	96	0.14
Cheyenne	2	0.00
Chippewa (1)	4	0.01
Cree (1)	6	0.01
Creek	1	0.00
Crow	1	0.00
Delaware	2	0.00
Iroquois (4)	19	0.03
Latin American Indians (15)	35	0.05
Navajo (1)	3	0.00
Pueblo	1	0.00
Seminole	7	0.01
Sioux	6	0.01
All other tribes	13	0.02
American Indian tribes, not spec.	57	0.08
Arab:	100	0.14
Arab/Arabic	33	0.05
Egyptian	52	0.07
Jordanian	10	0.01
Moroccan	5	0.01
Asian:	493	0.71
Bangladeshi (1)	1	0.00
Chinese, ex. Taiwanese (34)	62	0.09
Filipino (89)	112	0.16
Indian (137)	227	0.33
Japanese (4)	11	0.02
Korean (2)	4	0.01
Pakistani (2)	5	0.01
Taiwanese	1	0.00
Thai (4)	9	0.01
Vietnamese (14)	15	0.02
Other Asian, specified	10	0.01
Other Asian, not specified (9)	36	0.05
Austrian	15	0.02
Belgian	6	0.01
Brazilian	47	0.07
British	51	0.07
Canadian	16	0.02
Danish	6	0.01
Dutch	76	0.11
English	180	0.26
European	18	0.03
Finnish	5	0.01
French, except Basque	87	0.12
French Canadian	21	0.03
German	246	0.35
Guyanese	1,460	2.09
Hawaii Native/Pacific Islander:	212	0.30
Melanesian:	1	0.00
Other Melanesian	1	0.00
Micronesian: (4)	10	0.01
Guamanian/Chamorro (4)	10	0.01
Polynesian: (24)	52	0.07
Native Hawaiian (10)	12	0.02
Samoan (14)	26	0.04
Other Polynesian	14	0.02
Other Pac. Isl., specified	10	0.01
Other Pac. Isl., not spec. (23)	139	0.20
Hispanic or Latino:	3,284	4.70

Notes: 1. Figures in the "Number" column do not add up to the total population due to: a) Ancestry/Race overlap — e.g. persons can report being both White and Irish, b) persons of Hispanic origin can report being any race, c) persons reporting two ancestries are counted in both categories. 2. Numbers in parentheses indicate the number of persons reporting this ancestry/race alone, not in combination with any other ancestry/race. 3. Refer to the Explanation of Data in the front of the book for more detailed information.

Ancestry/Race	Number	%
Central American:	190	0.27
Costa Rican	9	0.01
Guatemalan	85	0.12
Honduran	10	0.01
Nicaraguan	9	0.01
Panamanian	27	0.04
Salvadoran	33	0.05
Other Central American	17	0.02
Cuban	138	0.20
Dominican Republic	582	0.83
Mexican	196	0.28
Puerto Rican	1,248	1.79
South American:	209	0.30
Argentinean	8	0.01
Colombian	68	0.10
Ecuadorian	36	0.05
Paraguayan	1	0.00
Peruvian	53	0.08
Uruguayan	8	0.01
Venezuelan	4	0.01
Other South American	31	0.04
Other Hispanic or Latino	721	1.03
Hungarian	21	0.03
Irish	538	0.77
Israeli	13	0.02
Italian	581	0.83
Lithuanian	12	0.02
Northern European	6	0.01
Polish	60	0.09
Portuguese	79	0.11
Russian	25	0.04
Scotch-Irish	40	0.06
Scottish	31	0.04
Serbian	23	0.03
Ukrainian	30	0.04
United States or American	1,147	1.64
Welsh	18	0.03
West Indian, excl. Hispanic:	7,743	11.08
Bahamian	18	0.03
Barbadian	193	0.28
Belizean	59	0.08
Bermudan	37	0.05
British West Indian	260	0.37
Haitian	2,852	4.08
Jamaican	3,368	4.82
Trinidadian and Tobagonian	518	0.74
U.S. Virgin Islander	23	0.03
West Indian	406	0.58
Other West Indian	9	0.01
White:	3,163	4.53
Not Hispanic (1,874)	2,212	3.17
Hispanic (809)	951	1.36

East Windsor

Place Type: Township
County: Mercer
Population: 24,919

Ancestry/Race	Number	%
African American/Black:	2,385	9.57
Not Hispanic (2,122)	2,259	9.07
Hispanic (95)	126	0.51
African, sub-Saharan:	422	1.69
African	160	0.64
Ghanian	97	0.39
Liberian	58	0.23
Nigerian	107	0.43
Am. Ind. or Alaska Nat., not spec.	70	0.28
Albanian	7	0.03
American Indian tribes, specified:	63	0.25
Apache	1	0.00
Blackfeet (1)	7	0.03
Cherokee	19	0.08
Choctaw	3	0.01
Creek	1	0.00
Crow	1	0.00
Delaware	2	0.01
Iroquois (1)	2	0.01
Latin American Indians (9)	15	0.06
Osage	3	0.01
Pueblo	2	0.01
Seminole (1)	1	0.00
Sioux	1	0.00
Yaqui	1	0.00
All other tribes	4	0.02
American Indian tribes, not spec.	1	0.00
Arab:	321	1.29
Egyptian	163	0.65
Jordanian	33	0.13
Lebanese	32	0.13
Palestinian	18	0.07
Syrian	34	0.14
Other Arab	41	0.16
Armenian	14	0.06
Asian:	2,544	10.21
Bangladeshi (15)	16	0.06
Cambodian	1	0.00
Chinese, ex. Taiwanese (395)	410	1.65
Filipino (146)	168	0.67
Indian (1,465)	1,520	6.10
Indonesian	2	0.01
Japanese (27)	48	0.19
Korean (82)	90	0.36
Laotian (2)	2	0.01
Malaysian (5)	8	0.03
Pakistani (118)	140	0.56
Taiwanese (18)	19	0.08
Thai (6)	9	0.04
Vietnamese (48)	55	0.22
Other Asian, specified (6)	6	0.02
Other Asian, not specified (25)	50	0.20
Assyrian/Chaldean/Syriac	6	0.02
Australian	31	0.12
Austrian	174	0.70
Brazilian	9	0.04
British	123	0.49
Canadian	98	0.39
Croatian	21	0.08
Czech	101	0.41
Czechoslovakian	77	0.31
Danish	106	0.43
Dutch	137	0.55
Eastern European	177	0.71
English	1,627	6.53
European	150	0.60
Finnish	33	0.13
French, except Basque	417	1.67
French Canadian	95	0.38
German	2,854	11.45
Greek	82	0.33
Guyanese	74	0.30
Hawaii Native/Pacific Islander:	50	0.20
Micronesian: (12)	18	0.07
Guamanian/Chamorro (12)	18	0.07
Polynesian: (6)	8	0.03
Native Hawaiian (3)	5	0.02
Samoan (3)	3	0.01
Other Pac. Isl., not spec. (13)	24	0.10
Hispanic or Latino:	3,559	14.28
Central American:	520	2.09
Costa Rican	33	0.13
Guatemalan	383	1.54
Honduran	33	0.13
Nicaraguan	22	0.09
Panamanian	14	0.06
Salvadoran	17	0.07
Other Central American	18	0.07
Cuban	96	0.39
Dominican Republic	110	0.44
Mexican	282	1.13
Puerto Rican	515	2.07
South American:	1,197	4.80
Argentinean	9	0.04
Bolivian	3	0.01
Chilean	7	0.03
Colombian	215	0.86
Ecuadorian	846	3.39
Peruvian	67	0.27
Uruguayan	6	0.02
Venezuelan	16	0.06
Other South American	28	0.11
Other Hispanic or Latino	839	3.37
Hungarian	598	2.40
Irish	3,141	12.60
Israeli	38	0.15
Italian	2,937	11.79
Lithuanian	202	0.81
Luxemburger	7	0.03
Norwegian	131	0.53
Pennsylvania German	9	0.04
Polish	2,368	9.50
Portuguese	31	0.12
Romanian	136	0.55
Russian	1,353	5.43
Scandinavian	5	0.02
Scotch-Irish	262	1.05
Scottish	229	0.92
Serbian	7	0.03
Slavic	18	0.07
Slovak	157	0.63
Swedish	190	0.76
Swiss	92	0.37
Turkish	113	0.45
Ukrainian	208	0.83
United States or American	875	3.51
Welsh	219	0.88
West Indian, excl. Hispanic:	347	1.39
British West Indian	33	0.13
Haitian	135	0.54
Jamaican	93	0.37
West Indian	86	0.35
White:	18,956	76.07
Not Hispanic (16,433)	16,660	66.86
Hispanic (2,112)	2,296	9.21
Yugoslavian	17	0.07

Eatontown

Place Type: Borough
County: Monmouth
Population: 14,008

Ancestry/Race	Number	%
African American/Black:	1,808	12.91
Not Hispanic (1,572)	1,724	12.31
Hispanic (54)	84	0.60
African, sub-Saharan:	92	0.66
African	85	0.61
Ethiopian	7	0.05
Am. Ind. or Alaska Nat., not spec.	38	0.27
American Indian tribes, specified:	104	0.74
Apache (1)	3	0.02
Blackfeet	6	0.04
Cherokee (10)	39	0.28
Comanche	1	0.01
Cree	2	0.01
Creek	2	0.01
Delaware (1)	7	0.05
Iroquois	1	0.01
Latin American Indians (14)	28	0.20
Ottawa	2	0.01
Seminole	2	0.01
Sioux	4	0.03
All other tribes (2)	7	0.05
American Indian tribes, not spec.	5	0.04
Arab:	65	0.46
Lebanese	6	0.04
Other Arab	59	0.42
Asian:	1,466	10.47
Bangladeshi (3)	3	0.02
Cambodian (3)	3	0.02
Chinese, ex. Taiwanese (368)	419	2.99
Filipino (160)	191	1.36
Indian (429)	440	3.14
Indonesian (2)	5	0.04
Japanese (27)	42	0.30
Korean (155)	181	1.29
Laotian (1)	1	0.01
Pakistani (9)	9	0.06

Notes: 1. Figures in the "Number" column do not add up to the total population due to: a) Ancestry/Race overlap — e.g. persons can report being both White and Irish, b) persons of Hispanic origin can report being any race, c) persons reporting two ancestries are counted in both categories. 2. Numbers in parentheses indicate the number of persons reporting this ancestry/race alone, not in combination with any other ancestry/race. 3. Refer to the Explanation of Data in the front of the book for more detailed information.

Ancestry/Race	Number	%
Sri Lankan (2)	2	0.01
Taiwanese (16)	26	0.19
Thai (2)	7	0.05
Vietnamese (94)	103	0.74
Other Asian, specified (4)	5	0.04
Other Asian, not specified (11)	29	0.21
Austrian	50	0.36
Belgian	5	0.04
Brazilian	29	0.21
British	91	0.65
Canadian	32	0.23
Celtic	4	0.03
Croatian	40	0.29
Czech	9	0.06
Czechoslovakian	24	0.17
Danish	27	0.19
Dutch	170	1.21
Eastern European	10	0.07
English	1,129	8.07
European	101	0.72
Finnish	16	0.11
French, except Basque	302	2.16
French Canadian	86	0.61
German	1,975	14.11
Greek	95	0.68
Hawaii Native/Pacific Islander:	17	0.12
Micronesian:	1	0.01
Guamanian/Chamorro	1	0.01
Polynesian: (4)	11	0.08
Native Hawaiian (1)	7	0.05
Samoan (3)	4	0.03
Other Pac. Isl., not spec. (1)	5	0.04
Hispanic or Latino:	928	6.62
Central American:	73	0.52
Costa Rican	14	0.10
Guatemalan	3	0.02
Honduran	5	0.04
Nicaraguan	4	0.03
Panamanian	30	0.21
Salvadoran	10	0.07
Other Central American	7	0.05
Cuban	35	0.25
Dominican Republic	39	0.28
Mexican	158	1.13
Puerto Rican	378	2.70
South American:	85	0.61
Argentinean	6	0.04
Bolivian	1	0.01
Chilean	15	0.11
Colombian	14	0.10
Ecuadorian	20	0.14
Peruvian	18	0.13
Venezuelan	8	0.06
Other South American	3	0.02
Other Hispanic or Latino	160	1.14
Hungarian	66	0.47
Iranian	5	0.04
Irish	2,688	19.20
Israeli	59	0.42
Italian	2,992	21.37
Lithuanian	69	0.49
Maltese	16	0.11
Norwegian	101	0.72
Pennsylvania German	23	0.16
Polish	762	5.44
Portuguese	96	0.69
Romanian	14	0.10
Russian	229	1.64
Scandinavian	20	0.14
Scotch-Irish	130	0.93
Scottish	287	2.05
Serbian	8	0.06
Slovak	51	0.36
Swedish	136	0.97
Swiss	50	0.36
Turkish	88	0.63
Ukrainian	131	0.94
United States or American	467	3.34
Welsh	99	0.71
West Indian, excl. Hispanic:	204	1.46
Barbadian	6	0.04
Belizean	26	0.19
British West Indian	6	0.04
Haitian	76	0.54
Jamaican	51	0.36
Trinidadian and Tobagonian	23	0.16
West Indian	16	0.11
White:	10,613	75.76
Not Hispanic (9,806)	10,060	71.82
Hispanic (461)	553	3.95

Echelon

Place Type: Census Designated Place
County: Camden
Population: 10,440

Ancestry/Race	Number	%
Acadian/Cajun	6	0.06
African American/Black:	1,138	10.90
Not Hispanic (1,048)	1,115	10.68
Hispanic (9)	23	0.22
African, sub-Saharan:	55	0.53
African	45	0.43
Other sub-Saharan African	10	0.10
Alaska Native tribes, specified:	1	0.01
Alaska Athabascan (1)	1	0.01
Am. Ind. or Alaska Nat., not spec.	29	0.28
American Indian tribes, specified:	26	0.25
Blackfeet	1	0.01
Cherokee (2)	12	0.11
Chippewa (1)	1	0.01
Choctaw	3	0.03
Creek	1	0.01
Delaware (1)	2	0.02
Latin American Indians	1	0.01
Sioux	2	0.02
All other tribes (2)	3	0.03
American Indian tribes, not spec.	4	0.04
Arab:	130	1.25
Jordanian	40	0.39
Lebanese	56	0.54
Syrian	34	0.33
Asian:	1,478	14.16
Bangladeshi (19)	21	0.20
Chinese, ex. Taiwanese (241)	260	2.49
Filipino (179)	194	1.86
Indian (660)	695	6.66
Japanese (20)	32	0.31
Korean (161)	171	1.64
Laotian (1)	1	0.01
Pakistani (18)	21	0.20
Taiwanese (9)	10	0.10
Thai (8)	9	0.09
Vietnamese (40)	41	0.39
Other Asian, specified	1	0.01
Other Asian, not specified (14)	22	0.21
Austrian	25	0.24
Brazilian	30	0.29
British	17	0.16
Canadian	25	0.24
Croatian	10	0.10
Czech	33	0.32
Czechoslovakian	8	0.08
Danish	9	0.09
Dutch	147	1.41
English	947	9.12
Estonian	29	0.28
European	87	0.84
Finnish	6	0.06
French, except Basque	285	2.74
French Canadian	75	0.72
German	1,478	14.23
Greek	65	0.63
Hawaii Native/Pacific Islander:	5	0.05
Polynesian: (1)	3	0.03
Native Hawaiian	2	0.02
Samoan (1)	1	0.01
Other Pac. Isl., not spec. (1)	2	0.02
Hispanic or Latino:	317	3.04
Central American:	12	0.11
Costa Rican	5	0.05
Guatemalan	1	0.01
Honduran	1	0.01
Panamanian	1	0.01
Salvadoran	4	0.04
Cuban	16	0.15
Dominican Republic	4	0.04
Mexican	63	0.60
Puerto Rican	145	1.39
South American:	39	0.37
Argentinean	6	0.06
Chilean	4	0.04
Colombian	13	0.12
Ecuadorian	1	0.01
Peruvian	7	0.07
Venezuelan	6	0.06
Other South American	2	0.02
Other Hispanic or Latino	38	0.36
Hungarian	114	1.10
Irish	1,797	17.30
Israeli	106	1.02
Italian	1,955	18.82
Latvian	6	0.06
Lithuanian	55	0.53
Norwegian	79	0.76
Pennsylvania German	7	0.07
Polish	573	5.52
Portuguese	21	0.20
Romanian	40	0.39
Russian	301	2.90
Scotch-Irish	71	0.68
Scottish	111	1.07
Slovak	55	0.53
Swedish	69	0.66
Ukrainian	106	1.02
United States or American	335	3.22
Welsh	91	0.88
West Indian, excl. Hispanic:	40	0.39
Jamaican	19	0.18
West Indian	21	0.20
White:	7,839	75.09
Not Hispanic (7,484)	7,615	72.94
Hispanic (194)	224	2.15
Yugoslavian	15	0.14

Edison

Place Type: Census Designated Place
County: Middlesex
Population: 97,687

Ancestry/Race	Number	%
African American/Black:	7,190	7.36
Not Hispanic (6,458)	6,830	6.99
Hispanic (270)	360	0.37
African, sub-Saharan:	1,309	1.34
African	699	0.72
Ethiopian	13	0.01
Ghanian	119	0.12
Kenyan	132	0.14
Liberian	25	0.03
Nigerian	158	0.16
Senegalese	9	0.01
Sierra Leonean	81	0.08
Sudanese	10	0.01
Other sub-Saharan African	63	0.06
Alaska Native tribes, specified:	4	0.00
Eskimo (2)	4	0.00
Am. Ind. or Alaska Nat., not spec.	283	0.29
Albanian	68	0.07
American Indian tribes, specified:	162	0.17
Apache	3	0.00
Blackfeet (2)	12	0.01
Cherokee (10)	73	0.07
Chickasaw	2	0.00
Chippewa (1)	1	0.00
Choctaw	3	0.00
Cree (1)	1	0.00
Creek	2	0.00

Notes: 1. Figures in the "Number" column do not add up to the total population due to: a) Ancestry/Race overlap — e.g. persons can report being both White and Irish, b) persons of Hispanic origin can report being any race, c) persons reporting two ancestries are counted in both categories. 2. Numbers in parentheses indicate the number of persons reporting this ancestry/race alone, not in combination with any other ancestry/race. 3. Refer to the Explanation of Data in the front of the book for more detailed information.

Ancestry/Race	Number	%
Iroquois (1)	8	0.01
Latin American Indians (10)	25	0.03
Lumbee (1)	2	0.00
Navajo (1)	2	0.00
Pueblo (2)	3	0.00
Seminole	2	0.00
Sioux (3)	9	0.01
All other tribes (8)	15	0.02
American Indian tribes, not spec.	37	0.04
Arab:	1,003	1.03
Arab/Arabic	22	0.02
Egyptian	562	0.58
Jordanian	5	0.01
Lebanese	185	0.19
Moroccan	7	0.01
Palestinian	86	0.09
Syrian	35	0.04
Other Arab	101	0.10
Armenian	24	0.02
Asian:	29,669	30.37
Bangladeshi (63)	87	0.09
Cambodian (4)	4	0.00
Chinese, ex. Taiwanese (5,589)	5,824	5.96
Filipino (2,354)	2,516	2.58
Indian (16,898)	17,343	17.75
Indonesian (158)	182	0.19
Japanese (148)	176	0.18
Korean (1,597)	1,647	1.69
Laotian (1)	8	0.01
Malaysian (5)	10	0.01
Pakistani (671)	737	0.75
Sri Lankan (53)	54	0.06
Taiwanese (399)	465	0.48
Thai (42)	56	0.06
Vietnamese (330)	345	0.35
Other Asian, specified (21)	31	0.03
Other Asian, not specified (92)	184	0.19
Assyrian/Chaldean/Syriac	6	0.01
Australian	6	0.01
Austrian	503	0.51
Basque	5	0.01
Belgian	27	0.03
Brazilian	77	0.08
British	187	0.19
Canadian	59	0.06
Celtic	12	0.01
Croatian	36	0.04
Cypriot	21	0.02
Czech	233	0.24
Czechoslovakian	364	0.37
Danish	565	0.58
Dutch	712	0.73
Eastern European	395	0.40
English	3,438	3.52
Estonian	53	0.05
European	351	0.36
Finnish	68	0.07
French, except Basque	886	0.91
French Canadian	345	0.35
German	8,467	8.67
Greek	990	1.01
Guyanese	160	0.16
Hawaii Native/Pacific Islander:	117	0.12
Melanesian: (1)	1	0.00
Fijian (1)	1	0.00
Micronesian: (9)	10	0.01
Guamanian/Chamorro (8)	9	0.01
Other Micronesian (1)	1	0.00
Polynesian: (5)	9	0.01
Native Hawaiian (4)	8	0.01
Samoan (1)	1	0.00
Other Pac. Isl., specified	3	0.00
Other Pac. Isl., not spec. (22)	94	0.10
Hispanic or Latino:	6,226	6.37
Central American:	277	0.28
Costa Rican	49	0.05
Guatemalan	58	0.06
Honduran	50	0.05
Nicaraguan	26	0.03
Panamanian	20	0.02
Salvadoran	63	0.06
Other Central American	11	0.01
Cuban	590	0.60
Dominican Republic	366	0.37
Mexican	546	0.56
Puerto Rican	2,095	2.14
South American:	1,032	1.06
Argentinean	59	0.06
Bolivian	4	0.00
Chilean	33	0.03
Colombian	486	0.50
Ecuadorian	132	0.14
Paraguayan	6	0.01
Peruvian	201	0.21
Uruguayan	25	0.03
Venezuelan	46	0.05
Other South American	40	0.04
Other Hispanic or Latino	1,320	1.35
Hungarian	3,121	3.19
Iranian	125	0.13
Irish	10,793	11.05
Israeli	107	0.11
Italian	14,431	14.77
Latvian	89	0.09
Lithuanian	327	0.33
Luxemburger	6	0.01
Macedonian	6	0.01
Maltese	19	0.02
Northern European	4	0.00
Norwegian	376	0.38
Pennsylvania German	19	0.02
Polish	7,251	7.42
Portuguese	721	0.74
Romanian	404	0.41
Russian	3,097	3.17
Scandinavian	39	0.04
Scotch-Irish	523	0.54
Scottish	769	0.79
Serbian	78	0.08
Slavic	174	0.18
Slovak	1,097	1.12
Slovene	51	0.05
Swedish	427	0.44
Swiss	191	0.20
Turkish	199	0.20
Ukrainian	1,048	1.07
United States or American	2,356	2.41
Welsh	207	0.21
West Indian, excl. Hispanic:	1,075	1.10
Bahamian	3	0.00
Barbadian	21	0.02
Bermudan	6	0.01
British West Indian	37	0.04
Haitian	218	0.22
Jamaican	408	0.42
Trinidadian and Tobagonian	294	0.30
U.S. Virgin Islander	17	0.02
West Indian	71	0.07
White:	59,524	60.93
Not Hispanic (54,461)	55,459	56.77
Hispanic (3,655)	4,065	4.16
Yugoslavian	120	0.12

Egg Harbor

Place Type: Township
County: Atlantic
Population: 30,726

Ancestry/Race	Number	%
Acadian/Cajun	5	0.02
African American/Black:	3,419	11.13
Not Hispanic (3,100)	3,278	10.67
Hispanic (85)	141	0.46
African, sub-Saharan:	271	0.89
African	216	0.71
Ethiopian	9	0.03
Ghanian	10	0.03
Liberian	15	0.05
Nigerian	16	0.05
Sudanese	5	0.02
Alaska Native tribes, specified:	1	0.00
Eskimo (1)	1	0.00
Am. Ind. or Alaska Nat., not spec.	72	0.23
Albanian	47	0.15
Alsatian	9	0.03
American Indian tribes, specified:	98	0.32
Apache (1)	3	0.01
Blackfeet (2)	15	0.05
Cherokee (3)	26	0.08
Cheyenne	1	0.00
Chickasaw	1	0.00
Chippewa (2)	2	0.01
Choctaw (1)	1	0.00
Comanche (2)	2	0.01
Delaware	4	0.01
Houma (2)	2	0.01
Iroquois (1)	5	0.02
Potawatomi (4)	4	0.01
Seminole	4	0.01
Shoshone (1)	1	0.00
Sioux	5	0.02
All other tribes (12)	22	0.07
American Indian tribes, not spec.	14	0.05
Arab:	131	0.43
Egyptian	47	0.15
Jordanian	20	0.07
Lebanese	51	0.17
Moroccan	4	0.01
Syrian	9	0.03
Armenian	91	0.30
Asian:	1,747	5.69
Bangladeshi (16)	26	0.08
Cambodian (2)	2	0.01
Chinese, ex. Taiwanese (394)	439	1.43
Filipino (286)	335	1.09
Indian (253)	268	0.87
Indonesian	1	0.00
Japanese (24)	44	0.14
Korean (191)	209	0.68
Laotian (64)	72	0.23
Malaysian (2)	4	0.01
Pakistani (31)	32	0.10
Sri Lankan (4)	4	0.01
Taiwanese (12)	16	0.05
Thai (13)	18	0.06
Vietnamese (203)	218	0.71
Other Asian, specified (3)	7	0.02
Other Asian, not specified (25)	54	0.18
Austrian	85	0.28
Belgian	22	0.07
British	113	0.37
Canadian	53	0.17
Celtic	7	0.02
Czech	26	0.08
Czechoslovakian	21	0.07
Danish	21	0.07
Dutch	417	1.36
Eastern European	30	0.10
English	3,187	10.41
European	251	0.82
Finnish	58	0.19
French, except Basque	645	2.11
French Canadian	169	0.55
German	5,564	18.17
German Russian	10	0.03
Greek	231	0.75
Guyanese	23	0.08
Hawaii Native/Pacific Islander:	35	0.11
Micronesian: (3)	10	0.03
Guamanian/Chamorro (3)	10	0.03
Polynesian: (8)	12	0.04
Native Hawaiian (8)	11	0.04
Samoan	1	0.00
Other Pac. Isl., specified	2	0.01
Other Pac. Isl., not spec. (4)	11	0.04
Hispanic or Latino:	2,076	6.76
Central American:	101	0.33
Costa Rican	5	0.02
Guatemalan	11	0.04

Notes: 1. Figures in the "Number" column do not add up to the total population due to: a) Ancestry/Race overlap — e.g. persons can report being both White and Irish, b) persons of Hispanic origin can report being any race, c) persons reporting two ancestries are counted in both categories. 2. Numbers in parentheses indicate the number of persons reporting this ancestry/race alone, not in combination with any other ancestry/race. 3. Refer to the Explanation of Data in the front of the book for more detailed information.

Honduran	45	0.15
Nicaraguan	4	0.01
Panamanian	11	0.04
Salvadoran	22	0.07
Other Central American	3	0.01
Cuban	44	0.14
Dominican Republic	113	0.37
Mexican	213	0.69
Puerto Rican	1,098	3.57
South American:	158	0.51
Argentinean	15	0.05
Colombian	55	0.18
Ecuadorian	15	0.05
Peruvian	51	0.17
Uruguayan	5	0.02
Venezuelan	2	0.01
Other South American	15	0.05
Other Hispanic or Latino	349	1.14
Hungarian	169	0.55
Iranian	33	0.11
Irish	7,078	23.12
Italian	5,334	17.42
Lithuanian	95	0.31
Northern European	16	0.05
Norwegian	191	0.62
Pennsylvania German	64	0.21
Polish	1,387	4.53
Portuguese	45	0.15
Romanian	16	0.05
Russian	466	1.52
Scandinavian	46	0.15
Scotch-Irish	416	1.36
Scottish	429	1.40
Slavic	43	0.14
Slovak	84	0.27
Swedish	264	0.86
Swiss	45	0.15
Ukrainian	138	0.45
United States or American	1,301	4.25
Welsh	239	0.78
West Indian, excl. Hispanic:	140	0.46
Haitian	30	0.10
Jamaican	91	0.30
Trinidadian and Tobagonian	8	0.03
U.S. Virgin Islander	5	0.02
West Indian	6	0.02
White:	24,900	81.04
Not Hispanic (23,512)	23,831	77.56
Hispanic (892)	1,069	3.48
Yugoslavian	33	0.11

Elizabeth

Place Type: City
County: Union
Population: 120,568

Ancestry/Race	Number	%
African American/Black:	26,038	21.60
Not Hispanic (22,329)	23,586	19.56
Hispanic (1,761)	2,452	2.03
African, sub-Saharan:	1,550	1.29
African	1,118	0.93
Cape Verdean	6	0.00
Ghanian	96	0.08
Kenyan	32	0.03
Liberian	97	0.08
Nigerian	105	0.09
South African	37	0.03
Sudanese	10	0.01
Other sub-Saharan African	49	0.04
Alaska Native tribes, specified:	12	0.01
Aleut	1	0.00
Tlingit-Haida (1)	11	0.01
Am. Ind. or Alaska Nat., not spec.	548	0.45
Albanian	81	0.07
American Indian tribes, specified:	307	0.25
Apache (2)	4	0.00
Blackfeet (2)	13	0.01
Cherokee (4)	25	0.02
Cheyenne	1	0.00
Choctaw	1	0.00
Creek (2)	4	0.00
Delaware (3)	3	0.00
Iroquois (2)	10	0.01
Latin American Indians (114)	193	0.16
Lumbee	1	0.00
Pueblo (6)	17	0.01
Seminole (1)	2	0.00
Sioux (5)	8	0.01
All other tribes (2)	25	0.02
American Indian tribes, not spec.	116	0.10
Arab:	567	0.47
Arab/Arabic	158	0.13
Egyptian	170	0.14
Jordanian	11	0.01
Lebanese	67	0.06
Moroccan	19	0.02
Palestinian	74	0.06
Syrian	58	0.05
Other Arab	10	0.01
Armenian	7	0.01
Asian:	3,387	2.81
Bangladeshi (34)	72	0.06
Cambodian (5)	5	0.00
Chinese, ex. Taiwanese (324)	411	0.34
Filipino (856)	969	0.80
Hmong	1	0.00
Indian (1,196)	1,336	1.11
Indonesian (1)	1	0.00
Japanese (25)	54	0.04
Korean (83)	94	0.08
Malaysian (1)	1	0.00
Pakistani (90)	145	0.12
Sri Lankan (54)	55	0.05
Taiwanese (8)	8	0.01
Thai (1)	2	0.00
Vietnamese (44)	56	0.05
Other Asian, specified	4	0.00
Other Asian, not specified (55)	173	0.14
Assyrian/Chaldean/Syriac	54	0.04
Australian	6	0.00
Austrian	140	0.12
Brazilian	1,349	1.12
British	72	0.06
Canadian	82	0.07
Celtic	8	0.01
Croatian	105	0.09
Czech	89	0.07
Czechoslovakian	137	0.11
Danish	38	0.03
Dutch	154	0.13
Eastern European	61	0.05
English	636	0.53
European	265	0.22
Finnish	8	0.01
French, except Basque	309	0.26
French Canadian	31	0.03
German	2,264	1.88
Greek	499	0.41
Guyanese	77	0.06
Hawaii Native/Pacific Islander:	229	0.19
Melanesian: (1)	2	0.00
Fijian	1	0.00
Other Melanesian (1)	1	0.00
Micronesian: (6)	11	0.01
Guamanian/Chamorro (6)	10	0.01
Other Micronesian	1	0.00
Polynesian: (15)	28	0.02
Native Hawaiian (6)	14	0.01
Samoan (8)	13	0.01
Other Polynesian (1)	1	0.00
Other Pac. Isl., specified	4	0.00
Other Pac. Isl., not spec. (33)	184	0.15
Hispanic or Latino:	59,627	49.46
Central American:	6,126	5.08
Costa Rican	323	0.27
Guatemalan	537	0.45
Honduran	1,094	0.91
Nicaraguan	277	0.23
Panamanian	57	0.05
Salvadoran	3,518	2.92
Other Central American	320	0.27
Cuban	7,069	5.86
Dominican Republic	3,629	3.01
Mexican	1,612	1.34
Puerto Rican	12,989	10.77
South American:	14,831	12.30
Argentinean	312	0.26
Bolivian	121	0.10
Chilean	209	0.17
Colombian	7,793	6.46
Ecuadorian	2,135	1.77
Paraguayan	7	0.01
Peruvian	2,830	2.35
Uruguayan	772	0.64
Venezuelan	296	0.25
Other South American	356	0.30
Other Hispanic or Latino	13,371	11.09
Hungarian	239	0.20
Icelander	26	0.02
Iranian	32	0.03
Irish	3,932	3.26
Israeli	82	0.07
Italian	6,017	4.99
Latvian	64	0.05
Lithuanian	398	0.33
Norwegian	46	0.04
Pennsylvania German	23	0.02
Polish	4,269	3.54
Portuguese	6,639	5.51
Romanian	105	0.09
Russian	899	0.75
Scandinavian	15	0.01
Scotch-Irish	91	0.08
Scottish	169	0.14
Slavic	52	0.04
Slovak	265	0.22
Swedish	152	0.13
Swiss	46	0.04
Turkish	25	0.02
Ukrainian	607	0.50
United States or American	3,703	3.07
Welsh	86	0.07
West Indian, excl. Hispanic:	4,021	3.34
Bahamian	18	0.01
Barbadian	36	0.03
Belizean	22	0.02
Bermudan	8	0.01
British West Indian	47	0.04
Haitian	3,016	2.50
Jamaican	433	0.36
Trinidadian and Tobagonian	252	0.21
U.S. Virgin Islander	40	0.03
West Indian	126	0.10
Other West Indian	23	0.02
White:	72,547	60.17
Not Hispanic (32,338)	34,023	28.22
Hispanic (34,912)	38,524	31.95
Yugoslavian	112	0.09

Elmwood Park

Place Type: Borough
County: Bergen
Population: 18,925

Ancestry/Race	Number	%
Afghan	29	0.15
African American/Black:	461	2.44
Not Hispanic (379)	412	2.18
Hispanic (30)	49	0.26
African, sub-Saharan:	49	0.26
African	31	0.16
Sudanese	18	0.10
Am. Ind. or Alaska Nat., not spec.	29	0.15
American Indian tribes, specified:	20	0.11
Cherokee (1)	5	0.03
Delaware	1	0.01
Iroquois	1	0.01

Notes: 1. Figures in the "Number" column do not add up to the total population due to: a) Ancestry/Race overlap — e.g. persons can report being both White and Irish, b) persons of Hispanic origin can report being any race, c) persons reporting two ancestries are counted in both categories. 2. Numbers in parentheses indicate the number of persons reporting this ancestry/race alone, not in combination with any other ancestry/race. 3. Refer to the Explanation of Data in the front of the book for more detailed information.

Latin American Indians (2)	9	0.05
Pueblo (1)	2	0.01
Sioux	1	0.01
All other tribes (1)	1	0.01
American Indian tribes, not spec.	4	0.02
Arab:	297	1.57
Arab/Arabic	86	0.45
Egyptian	39	0.21
Lebanese	45	0.24
Palestinian	67	0.35
Syrian	53	0.28
Other Arab	7	0.04
Armenian	27	0.14
Asian:	1,655	8.75
Bangladeshi (31)	39	0.21
Chinese, ex. Taiwanese (140)	150	0.79
Filipino (216)	248	1.31
Indian (860)	903	4.77
Japanese (22)	28	0.15
Korean (83)	86	0.45
Malaysian (1)	1	0.01
Pakistani (94)	140	0.74
Thai (9)	9	0.05
Vietnamese (2)	4	0.02
Other Asian, specified (5)	5	0.03
Other Asian, not specified	42	0.22
Australian	18	0.10
Austrian	104	0.55
Belgian	16	0.08
Brazilian	9	0.05
British	25	0.13
Bulgarian	24	0.13
Canadian	64	0.34
Croatian	15	0.08
Czech	67	0.35
Czechoslovakian	75	0.40
Danish	29	0.15
Dutch	492	2.60
English	480	2.54
Estonian	10	0.05
European	39	0.21
Finnish	29	0.15
French, except Basque	193	1.02
French Canadian	33	0.17
German	1,673	8.84
Greek	232	1.23
Guyanese	107	0.57
Hawaii Native/Pacific Islander:	4	0.02
Micronesian: (1)	2	0.01
Guamanian/Chamorro (1)	1	0.01
Other Micronesian	1	0.01
Polynesian:	1	0.01
Native Hawaiian	1	0.01
Other Pac. Isl., not spec.	1	0.01
Hispanic or Latino:	2,535	13.39
Central American:	93	0.49
Costa Rican	34	0.18
Guatemalan	11	0.06
Honduran	2	0.01
Nicaraguan	7	0.04
Panamanian	2	0.01
Salvadoran	24	0.13
Other Central American	13	0.07
Cuban	237	1.25
Dominican Republic	189	1.00
Mexican	43	0.23
Puerto Rican	535	2.83
South American:	845	4.46
Argentinean	31	0.16
Bolivian	18	0.10
Chilean	43	0.23
Colombian	353	1.87
Ecuadorian	79	0.42
Peruvian	273	1.44
Uruguayan	21	0.11
Venezuelan	13	0.07
Other South American	14	0.07
Other Hispanic or Latino	593	3.13
Hungarian	376	1.99
Irish	1,716	9.07
Israeli	12	0.06
Italian	4,775	25.23
Latvian	8	0.04
Lithuanian	46	0.24
Macedonian	306	1.62
Norwegian	27	0.14
Polish	2,386	12.61
Portuguese	74	0.39
Romanian	57	0.30
Russian	685	3.62
Scotch-Irish	143	0.76
Scottish	104	0.55
Slavic	11	0.06
Slovak	290	1.53
Slovene	10	0.05
Swedish	68	0.36
Swiss	11	0.06
Turkish	45	0.24
Ukrainian	323	1.71
United States or American	673	3.56
Welsh	6	0.03
West Indian, excl. Hispanic:	50	0.26
Jamaican	7	0.04
Trinidadian and Tobagonian	20	0.11
West Indian	16	0.08
Other West Indian	7	0.04
White:	16,067	84.90
Not Hispanic (14,138)	14,409	76.14
Hispanic (1,481)	1,658	8.76
Yugoslavian	61	0.32

Englewood

Place Type: City
County: Bergen
Population: 26,203

Ancestry/Race	Number	%
African American/Black:	10,863	41.46
Not Hispanic (9,887)	10,428	39.80
Hispanic (328)	435	1.66
African, sub-Saharan:	436	1.66
African	354	1.35
Nigerian	49	0.19
South African	33	0.13
Am. Ind. or Alaska Nat., not spec.	132	0.50
Albanian	7	0.03
American Indian tribes, specified:	123	0.47
Blackfeet	8	0.03
Cherokee (6)	37	0.14
Choctaw	2	0.01
Crow (1)	2	0.01
Delaware (8)	8	0.03
Iroquois (4)	5	0.02
Latin American Indians (19)	46	0.18
Ottawa	1	0.00
Pueblo	1	0.00
Seminole	6	0.02
Sioux (2)	2	0.01
All other tribes	5	0.02
American Indian tribes, not spec.	19	0.07
Arab:	305	1.16
Arab/Arabic	53	0.20
Egyptian	79	0.30
Iraqi	8	0.03
Lebanese	115	0.44
Moroccan	7	0.03
Palestinian	7	0.03
Syrian	27	0.10
Other Arab	9	0.03
Armenian	73	0.28
Asian:	1,563	5.96
Chinese, ex. Taiwanese (90)	117	0.45
Filipino (470)	506	1.93
Indian (372)	436	1.66
Indonesian (3)	5	0.02
Japanese (98)	109	0.42
Korean (235)	246	0.94
Laotian	1	0.00
Pakistani (35)	50	0.19
Sri Lankan (13)	14	0.05
Taiwanese (4)	4	0.02
Thai (2)	8	0.03
Vietnamese (7)	9	0.03
Other Asian, specified	7	0.03
Other Asian, not specified (24)	51	0.19
Austrian	127	0.48
Belgian	26	0.10
Brazilian	14	0.05
British	125	0.48
Canadian	14	0.05
Croatian	8	0.03
Cypriot	14	0.05
Czech	40	0.15
Czechoslovakian	14	0.05
Danish	28	0.11
Dutch	64	0.24
Eastern European	298	1.14
English	554	2.11
European	129	0.49
Finnish	10	0.04
French, except Basque	238	0.91
French Canadian	22	0.08
German	933	3.56
Greek	180	0.69
Guyanese	306	1.17
Hawaii Native/Pacific Islander:	43	0.16
Micronesian:	1	0.00
Guamanian/Chamorro	1	0.00
Polynesian: (3)	10	0.04
Native Hawaiian (2)	3	0.01
Samoan	6	0.02
Tongan (1)	1	0.00
Other Pac. Isl., specified	6	0.02
Other Pac. Isl., not spec. (9)	26	0.10
Hispanic or Latino:	5,703	21.76
Central American:	418	1.60
Costa Rican	31	0.12
Guatemalan	59	0.23
Honduran	86	0.33
Nicaraguan	16	0.06
Panamanian	23	0.09
Salvadoran	189	0.72
Other Central American	14	0.05
Cuban	257	0.98
Dominican Republic	617	2.35
Mexican	251	0.96
Puerto Rican	666	2.54
South American:	2,130	8.13
Argentinean	31	0.12
Bolivian	18	0.07
Chilean	18	0.07
Colombian	1,878	7.17
Ecuadorian	58	0.22
Paraguayan	3	0.01
Peruvian	69	0.26
Uruguayan	4	0.02
Venezuelan	13	0.05
Other South American	38	0.15
Other Hispanic or Latino	1,364	5.21
Hungarian	213	0.81
Iranian	50	0.19
Irish	937	3.58
Israeli	181	0.69
Italian	1,176	4.49
Latvian	22	0.08
Lithuanian	60	0.23
Northern European	7	0.03
Norwegian	21	0.08
Polish	711	2.71
Portuguese	35	0.13
Romanian	48	0.18
Russian	636	2.43
Scandinavian	4	0.02
Scotch-Irish	93	0.35
Scottish	127	0.48
Slovak	18	0.07
Swedish	88	0.34
Swiss	51	0.19
Turkish	46	0.18

Notes: 1. Figures in the "Number" column do not add up to the total population due to: a) Ancestry/Race overlap — e.g. persons can report being both White and Irish, b) persons of Hispanic origin can report being any race, c) persons reporting two ancestries are counted in both categories. 2. Numbers in parentheses indicate the number of persons reporting this ancestry/race alone, not in combination with any other ancestry/race. 3. Refer to the Explanation of Data in the front of the book for more detailed information.

Ancestry/Race	Number	%
Ukrainian	88	0.34
United States or American	941	3.59
Welsh	39	0.15
West Indian, excl. Hispanic:	2,034	7.76
Bahamian	15	0.06
Barbadian	6	0.02
Bermudan	9	0.03
British West Indian	106	0.40
Haitian	274	1.05
Jamaican	1,307	4.99
Trinidadian and Tobagonian	152	0.58
U.S. Virgin Islander	20	0.08
West Indian	145	0.55
White:	11,746	44.83
Not Hispanic (8,389)	8,653	33.02
Hispanic (2,745)	3,093	11.80
Yugoslavian	7	0.03

Evesham

Place Type: Township
County: Burlington
Population: 42,275

Ancestry/Race	Number	%
African American/Black:	1,438	3.40
Not Hispanic (1,272)	1,373	3.25
Hispanic (41)	65	0.15
African, sub-Saharan:	76	0.18
African	53	0.12
Ghanian	16	0.04
Liberian	7	0.02
Alaska Native tribes, specified:	1	0.00
Alaska Athabascan (1)	1	0.00
Am. Ind. or Alaska Nat., not spec.	36	0.09
Albanian	55	0.13
Alsatian	10	0.02
American Indian tribes, specified:	80	0.19
Apache (4)	5	0.01
Blackfeet	2	0.00
Cherokee (3)	24	0.06
Chickasaw (1)	1	0.00
Chippewa (1)	1	0.00
Choctaw (2)	2	0.00
Creek	2	0.00
Delaware (3)	3	0.01
Iroquois (1)	7	0.02
Latin American Indians (2)	8	0.02
Lumbee	1	0.00
Navajo	1	0.00
Potawatomi (1)	2	0.00
Pueblo	3	0.01
Sioux (4)	11	0.03
All other tribes	7	0.02
American Indian tribes, not spec.	2	0.00
Arab:	193	0.45
Arab/Arabic	29	0.07
Egyptian	60	0.14
Lebanese	84	0.20
Palestinian	20	0.05
Armenian	79	0.19
Asian:	1,935	4.58
Bangladeshi (1)	1	0.00
Cambodian (13)	13	0.03
Chinese, ex. Taiwanese (381)	428	1.01
Filipino (255)	309	0.73
Indian (540)	574	1.36
Indonesian	2	0.00
Japanese (73)	97	0.23
Korean (277)	300	0.71
Pakistani (9)	10	0.02
Sri Lankan (14)	15	0.04
Taiwanese (41)	51	0.12
Thai (15)	15	0.04
Vietnamese (49)	60	0.14
Other Asian, not specified (36)	60	0.14
Australian	6	0.01
Austrian	302	0.71
Belgian	58	0.14
Brazilian	13	0.03
British	119	0.28
Bulgarian	17	0.04
Canadian	90	0.21
Croatian	45	0.11
Cypriot	13	0.03
Czech	145	0.34
Czechoslovakian	84	0.20
Danish	69	0.16
Dutch	560	1.32
Eastern European	148	0.35
English	4,204	9.91
European	146	0.34
Finnish	48	0.11
French, except Basque	909	2.14
French Canadian	275	0.65
German	8,671	20.44
Greek	338	0.80
Guyanese	12	0.03
Hawaii Native/Pacific Islander:	17	0.04
Micronesian: (1)	3	0.01
Guamanian/Chamorro (1)	1	0.00
Other Micronesian	2	0.00
Polynesian: (2)	7	0.02
Native Hawaiian (2)	7	0.02
Other Pac. Isl., not spec. (5)	7	0.02
Hispanic or Latino:	829	1.96
Central American:	29	0.07
Costa Rican	2	0.00
Guatemalan	4	0.01
Honduran	2	0.00
Nicaraguan	2	0.00
Panamanian	12	0.03
Salvadoran	5	0.01
Other Central American	2	0.00
Cuban	81	0.19
Dominican Republic	24	0.06
Mexican	136	0.32
Puerto Rican	330	0.78
South American:	76	0.18
Argentinean	6	0.01
Chilean	2	0.00
Colombian	25	0.06
Ecuadorian	9	0.02
Paraguayan	1	0.00
Peruvian	9	0.02
Uruguayan	3	0.01
Venezuelan	9	0.02
Other South American	12	0.03
Other Hispanic or Latino	153	0.36
Hungarian	403	0.95
Iranian	58	0.14
Irish	11,802	27.82
Israeli	35	0.08
Italian	11,269	26.56
Latvian	10	0.02
Lithuanian	361	0.85
Luxemburger	6	0.01
Northern European	10	0.02
Norwegian	244	0.58
Pennsylvania German	75	0.18
Polish	3,912	9.22
Portuguese	108	0.25
Romanian	150	0.35
Russian	1,475	3.48
Scandinavian	96	0.23
Scotch-Irish	568	1.34
Scottish	746	1.76
Serbian	38	0.09
Slavic	87	0.21
Slovak	210	0.49
Swedish	354	0.83
Swiss	90	0.21
Ukrainian	347	0.82
United States or American	1,300	3.06
Welsh	338	0.80
West Indian, excl. Hispanic:	129	0.30
Belizean	10	0.02
Haitian	20	0.05
Jamaican	71	0.17
West Indian	28	0.07
White:	38,940	92.11
Not Hispanic (38,026)	38,341	90.69
Hispanic (553)	599	1.42
Yugoslavian	34	0.08

Ewing

Place Type: Census Designated Place
County: Mercer
Population: 35,707

Ancestry/Race	Number	%
African American/Black:	9,204	25.78
Not Hispanic (8,707)	8,992	25.18
Hispanic (156)	212	0.59
African, sub-Saharan:	364	1.02
African	160	0.45
Kenyan	12	0.03
Liberian	49	0.14
Nigerian	76	0.21
Sierra Leonean	67	0.19
Alaska Native tribes, specified:	2	0.01
Tlingit-Haida (1)	2	0.01
Am. Ind. or Alaska Nat., not spec.	93	0.26
Albanian	16	0.04
Alsatian	6	0.02
American Indian tribes, specified:	141	0.39
Apache	2	0.01
Blackfeet (1)	10	0.03
Cherokee (13)	57	0.16
Chippewa	6	0.02
Choctaw (1)	1	0.00
Creek	1	0.00
Delaware (6)	25	0.07
Iroquois (1)	5	0.01
Latin American Indians (2)	8	0.02
Navajo (1)	1	0.00
Osage (2)	2	0.01
Seminole	2	0.01
Sioux (2)	3	0.01
All other tribes (1)	18	0.05
American Indian tribes, not spec.	14	0.04
Arab:	147	0.41
Arab/Arabic	48	0.13
Egyptian	71	0.20
Jordanian	4	0.01
Lebanese	4	0.01
Palestinian	8	0.02
Syrian	12	0.03
Armenian	55	0.15
Asian:	964	2.70
Cambodian (10)	10	0.03
Chinese, ex. Taiwanese (96)	126	0.35
Filipino (152)	175	0.49
Indian (304)	326	0.91
Indonesian	9	0.03
Japanese (17)	23	0.06
Korean (104)	120	0.34
Laotian	2	0.01
Malaysian (2)	2	0.01
Pakistani (54)	68	0.19
Taiwanese (5)	5	0.01
Thai (12)	15	0.04
Vietnamese (13)	15	0.04
Other Asian, not specified (28)	68	0.19
Austrian	125	0.35
British	92	0.26
Canadian	28	0.08
Croatian	10	0.03
Czech	199	0.56
Czechoslovakian	116	0.32
Danish	61	0.17
Dutch	653	1.83
Eastern European	3	0.01
English	3,600	10.08
European	162	0.45
Finnish	8	0.02
French, except Basque	517	1.45
French Canadian	92	0.26
German	5,016	14.05

Notes: 1. Figures in the "Number" column do not add up to the total population due to: a) Ancestry/Race overlap — e.g. persons can report being both White and Irish, b) persons of Hispanic origin can report being any race, c) persons reporting two ancestries are counted in both categories. 2. Numbers in parentheses indicate the number of persons reporting this ancestry/race alone, not in combination with any other ancestry/race. 3. Refer to the Explanation of Data in the front of the book for more detailed information.

Ancestry/Race	Number	%
Greek	168	0.47
Guyanese	5	0.01
Hawaii Native/Pacific Islander:	36	0.10
Polynesian: (5)	7	0.02
Native Hawaiian (4)	5	0.01
Samoan	1	0.00
Other Polynesian (1)	1	0.00
Other Pac. Isl., not spec. (17)	29	0.08
Hispanic or Latino:	1,586	4.44
Central American:	129	0.36
Costa Rican	29	0.08
Guatemalan	54	0.15
Honduran	11	0.03
Panamanian	19	0.05
Salvadoran	13	0.04
Other Central American	3	0.01
Cuban	72	0.20
Dominican Republic	59	0.17
Mexican	97	0.27
Puerto Rican	900	2.52
South American:	130	0.36
Argentinean	15	0.04
Bolivian	2	0.01
Chilean	9	0.03
Colombian	50	0.14
Ecuadorian	22	0.06
Peruvian	26	0.07
Uruguayan	2	0.01
Venezuelan	4	0.01
Other Hispanic or Latino	199	0.56
Hungarian	763	2.14
Irish	5,501	15.41
Italian	5,955	16.68
Latvian	12	0.03
Lithuanian	194	0.54
Macedonian	6	0.02
Maltese	21	0.06
Northern European	6	0.02
Norwegian	174	0.49
Pennsylvania German	13	0.04
Polish	3,091	8.66
Portuguese	30	0.08
Romanian	18	0.05
Russian	692	1.94
Scandinavian	14	0.04
Scotch-Irish	531	1.49
Scottish	670	1.88
Slavic	62	0.17
Slovak	397	1.11
Slovene	31	0.09
Swedish	147	0.41
Swiss	34	0.10
Ukrainian	260	0.73
United States or American	1,060	2.97
Welsh	209	0.59
West Indian, excl. Hispanic:	524	1.47
Bahamian	15	0.04
Barbadian	8	0.02
British West Indian	28	0.08
Haitian	156	0.44
Jamaican	272	0.76
Trinidadian and Tobagonian	27	0.08
West Indian	18	0.05
White:	25,072	70.22
Not Hispanic (23,968)	24,322	68.12
Hispanic (677)	750	2.10
Yugoslavian	38	0.11

Fair Lawn

Place Type: Borough
County: Bergen
Population: 31,637

Ancestry/Race	Number	%
Afghan	7	0.02
African American/Black:	308	0.97
Not Hispanic (208)	271	0.86
Hispanic (26)	37	0.12
African, sub-Saharan:	31	0.10
African	17	0.05
South African	14	0.04
Am. Ind. or Alaska Nat., not spec.	38	0.12
Albanian	89	0.28
American Indian tribes, specified:	29	0.09
Apache	1	0.00
Blackfeet	1	0.00
Cherokee (1)	7	0.02
Delaware	1	0.00
Iroquois (1)	1	0.00
Latin American Indians (4)	10	0.03
Paiute (2)	2	0.01
Sioux	1	0.00
All other tribes (1)	5	0.02
American Indian tribes, not spec.	4	0.01
Arab:	272	0.86
Arab/Arabic	21	0.07
Egyptian	7	0.02
Iraqi	14	0.04
Lebanese	70	0.22
Moroccan	34	0.11
Syrian	126	0.40
Armenian	182	0.58
Asian:	1,720	5.44
Bangladeshi (5)	5	0.02
Chinese, ex. Taiwanese (330)	353	1.12
Filipino (335)	364	1.15
Indian (498)	532	1.68
Indonesian (1)	1	0.00
Japanese (43)	49	0.15
Korean (231)	238	0.75
Malaysian (1)	1	0.00
Pakistani (40)	41	0.13
Sri Lankan (1)	2	0.01
Taiwanese (20)	30	0.09
Thai (3)	3	0.01
Vietnamese (26)	33	0.10
Other Asian, specified (3)	7	0.02
Other Asian, not specified (13)	61	0.19
Austrian	339	1.07
Basque	8	0.03
Belgian	38	0.12
British	41	0.13
Canadian	40	0.13
Carpatho Rusyn	9	0.03
Celtic	32	0.10
Croatian	29	0.09
Czech	110	0.35
Czechoslovakian	55	0.17
Danish	13	0.04
Dutch	763	2.41
Eastern European	267	0.84
English	1,269	4.01
Estonian	24	0.08
European	135	0.43
Finnish	15	0.05
French, except Basque	475	1.50
French Canadian	78	0.25
German	3,158	9.98
Greek	380	1.20
Guyanese	8	0.03
Hawaii Native/Pacific Islander:	20	0.06
Polynesian: (1)	3	0.01
Native Hawaiian (1)	3	0.01
Other Pac. Isl., specified	3	0.01
Other Pac. Isl., not spec.	14	0.04
Hispanic or Latino:	1,744	5.51
Central American:	74	0.23
Costa Rican	9	0.03
Guatemalan	13	0.04
Honduran	9	0.03
Nicaraguan	1	0.00
Panamanian	3	0.01
Salvadoran	38	0.12
Other Central American	1	0.00
Cuban	171	0.54
Dominican Republic	170	0.54
Mexican	55	0.17
Puerto Rican	456	1.44
South American:	433	1.37
Argentinean	40	0.13
Bolivian	11	0.03
Chilean	32	0.10
Colombian	147	0.46
Ecuadorian	72	0.23
Peruvian	99	0.31
Uruguayan	5	0.02
Venezuelan	12	0.04
Other South American	15	0.05
Other Hispanic or Latino	385	1.22
Hungarian	681	2.15
Iranian	58	0.18
Irish	3,133	9.90
Israeli	926	2.93
Italian	6,228	19.69
Latvian	107	0.34
Lithuanian	277	0.88
Macedonian	9	0.03
Maltese	30	0.09
New Zealander	48	0.15
Northern European	8	0.03
Norwegian	97	0.31
Pennsylvania German	6	0.02
Polish	3,125	9.88
Portuguese	113	0.36
Romanian	207	0.65
Russian	3,699	11.69
Scandinavian	5	0.02
Scotch-Irish	172	0.54
Scottish	288	0.91
Slavic	53	0.17
Slovak	52	0.16
Slovene	14	0.04
Soviet Union	7	0.02
Swedish	226	0.71
Swiss	109	0.34
Turkish	79	0.25
Ukrainian	898	2.84
United States or American	1,647	5.21
Welsh	23	0.07
West Indian, excl. Hispanic:	55	0.17
British West Indian	7	0.02
Haitian	11	0.03
Jamaican	15	0.05
Trinidadian and Tobagonian	11	0.03
West Indian	11	0.03
White:	29,332	92.71
Not Hispanic (27,737)	28,032	88.61
Hispanic (1,223)	1,300	4.11
Yugoslavian	16	0.05

Fairview

Place Type: Borough
County: Bergen
Population: 13,255

Ancestry/Race	Number	%
African American/Black:	311	2.35
Not Hispanic (161)	188	1.42
Hispanic (65)	123	0.93
African, sub-Saharan:	22	0.17
African	22	0.17
Am. Ind. or Alaska Nat., not spec.	52	0.39
Albanian	52	0.39
American Indian tribes, specified:	32	0.24
Cherokee (5)	6	0.05
Choctaw	1	0.01
Creek	1	0.01
Latin American Indians (19)	23	0.17
Sioux (1)	1	0.01
American Indian tribes, not spec.	2	0.02
Arab:	565	4.26
Arab/Arabic	169	1.27
Egyptian	141	1.06
Jordanian	19	0.14
Lebanese	69	0.52
Palestinian	120	0.91
Syrian	33	0.25
Other Arab	14	0.11

Notes: 1. Figures in the "Number" column do not add up to the total population due to: a) Ancestry/Race overlap — e.g. persons can report being both White and Irish, b) persons of Hispanic origin can report being any race, c) persons reporting two ancestries are counted in both categories. 2. Numbers in parentheses indicate the number of persons reporting this ancestry/race alone, not in combination with any other ancestry/race. 3. Refer to the Explanation of Data in the front of the book for more detailed information.

Armenian	320	2.41
Asian:	783	5.91
Cambodian (1)	1	0.01
Chinese, ex. Taiwanese (63)	79	0.60
Filipino (52)	58	0.44
Indian (126)	151	1.14
Indonesian	1	0.01
Japanese (34)	51	0.38
Korean (332)	355	2.68
Pakistani (22)	24	0.18
Sri Lankan (7)	9	0.07
Vietnamese (9)	9	0.07
Other Asian, not specified (7)	45	0.34
Austrian	29	0.22
Brazilian	261	1.97
British	19	0.14
Canadian	6	0.05
Croatian	607	4.58
Czech	40	0.30
Czechoslovakian	13	0.10
Danish	15	0.11
Dutch	42	0.32
English	78	0.59
European	10	0.08
Finnish	12	0.09
French, except Basque	37	0.28
French Canadian	21	0.16
German	634	4.78
Greek	185	1.40
Guyanese	17	0.13
Hawaii Native/Pacific Islander:	26	0.20
Micronesian:	5	0.04
Guamanian/Chamorro	3	0.02
Other Micronesian	2	0.02
Other Pac. Isl., not spec. (4)	21	0.16
Hispanic or Latino:	4,911	37.05
Central American:	1,283	9.68
Costa Rican	6	0.05
Guatemalan	722	5.45
Honduran	40	0.30
Nicaraguan	14	0.11
Panamanian	7	0.05
Salvadoran	456	3.44
Other Central American	38	0.29
Cuban	562	4.24
Dominican Republic	405	3.06
Mexican	149	1.12
Puerto Rican	452	3.41
South American:	876	6.61
Argentinean	40	0.30
Bolivian	7	0.05
Chilean	27	0.20
Colombian	463	3.49
Ecuadorian	201	1.52
Peruvian	85	0.64
Uruguayan	9	0.07
Venezuelan	27	0.20
Other South American	17	0.13
Other Hispanic or Latino	1,184	8.93
Hungarian	23	0.17
Iranian	69	0.52
Irish	770	5.81
Italian	2,896	21.85
Lithuanian	12	0.09
Maltese	9	0.07
Norwegian	20	0.15
Pennsylvania German	5	0.04
Polish	256	1.93
Portuguese	17	0.13
Romanian	13	0.10
Russian	98	0.74
Slavic	7	0.05
Slovak	46	0.35
Soviet Union	11	0.08
Swiss	25	0.19
Turkish	230	1.74
Ukrainian	6	0.05
United States or American	358	2.70
Welsh	25	0.19
West Indian, excl. Hispanic:	61	0.46
Haitian	19	0.14
Jamaican	6	0.05
Trinidadian and Tobagonian	36	0.27
White:	10,522	79.38
Not Hispanic (6,872)	7,346	55.42
Hispanic (2,733)	3,176	23.96
Yugoslavian	76	0.57

Florence

Place Type: Township
County: Burlington
Population: 10,746

Ancestry/Race	Number	%
Acadian/Cajun	8	0.07
African American/Black:	1,138	10.59
Not Hispanic (1,042)	1,124	10.46
Hispanic (5)	14	0.13
African, sub-Saharan:	28	0.26
African	28	0.26
Am. Ind. or Alaska Nat., not spec.	25	0.23
American Indian tribes, specified:	22	0.20
Blackfeet	4	0.04
Cherokee (3)	7	0.07
Delaware	1	0.01
Latin American Indians (7)	7	0.07
Sioux	1	0.01
All other tribes (1)	2	0.02
American Indian tribes, not spec.	3	0.03
Arab:	6	0.06
Syrian	6	0.06
Armenian	7	0.07
Asian:	313	2.91
Chinese, ex. Taiwanese (27)	32	0.30
Filipino (7)	14	0.13
Indian (173)	185	1.72
Japanese (2)	9	0.08
Korean (22)	32	0.30
Pakistani	11	0.10
Sri Lankan (1)	1	0.01
Taiwanese (5)	5	0.05
Thai (2)	3	0.03
Vietnamese (5)	13	0.12
Other Asian, not specified (5)	8	0.07
Austrian	15	0.14
Belgian	4	0.04
British	13	0.12
Canadian	14	0.13
Carpatho Rusyn	7	0.07
Croatian	30	0.28
Czech	44	0.41
Czechoslovakian	41	0.38
Danish	77	0.72
Dutch	83	0.77
Eastern European	7	0.07
English	1,303	12.13
French, except Basque	367	3.42
French Canadian	134	1.25
German	2,228	20.73
Greek	35	0.33
Hawaii Native/Pacific Islander:	10	0.09
Micronesian: (1)	2	0.02
Guamanian/Chamorro (1)	2	0.02
Polynesian:	8	0.07
Native Hawaiian	6	0.06
Samoan	2	0.02
Hispanic or Latino:	253	2.35
Central American:	10	0.09
Guatemalan	8	0.07
Panamanian	2	0.02
Cuban	11	0.10
Dominican Republic	13	0.12
Mexican	23	0.21
Puerto Rican	126	1.17
South American:	17	0.16
Argentinean	2	0.02
Chilean	1	0.01
Colombian	4	0.04
Ecuadorian	1	0.01
Peruvian	7	0.07
Venezuelan	2	0.02
Other Hispanic or Latino	53	0.49
Hungarian	802	7.46
Irish	2,597	24.17
Italian	2,001	18.62
Lithuanian	67	0.62
Luxemburger	10	0.09
Norwegian	16	0.15
Pennsylvania German	8	0.07
Polish	898	8.36
Portuguese	19	0.18
Romanian	188	1.75
Russian	85	0.79
Scandinavian	7	0.07
Scotch-Irish	117	1.09
Scottish	113	1.05
Slavic	79	0.74
Slovak	234	2.18
Slovene	34	0.32
Swedish	129	1.20
Swiss	6	0.06
Turkish	75	0.70
Ukrainian	91	0.85
United States or American	351	3.27
Welsh	121	1.13
West Indian, excl. Hispanic:	19	0.18
Barbadian	15	0.14
Jamaican	4	0.04
White:	9,318	86.71
Not Hispanic (9,023)	9,142	85.07
Hispanic (167)	176	1.64
Yugoslavian	7	0.07

Fords

Place Type: Census Designated Place
County: Middlesex
Population: 15,032

Ancestry/Race	Number	%
Afghan	27	0.18
African American/Black:	957	6.37
Not Hispanic (877)	928	6.17
Hispanic (14)	29	0.19
African, sub-Saharan:	205	1.35
African	53	0.35
Ghanian	116	0.77
Nigerian	36	0.24
Am. Ind. or Alaska Nat., not spec.	37	0.25
Albanian	13	0.09
American Indian tribes, specified:	33	0.22
Blackfeet	3	0.02
Cherokee	10	0.07
Iroquois (1)	2	0.01
Latin American Indians (4)	7	0.05
Pueblo	1	0.01
Seminole	1	0.01
Sioux	2	0.01
All other tribes (4)	7	0.05
American Indian tribes, not spec.	1	0.01
Arab:	161	1.06
Arab/Arabic	32	0.21
Egyptian	62	0.41
Jordanian	7	0.05
Lebanese	9	0.06
Palestinian	38	0.25
Syrian	13	0.09
Armenian	6	0.04
Asian:	2,563	17.05
Bangladeshi (4)	4	0.03
Chinese, ex. Taiwanese (292)	315	2.10
Filipino (643)	677	4.50
Indian (1,247)	1,290	8.58
Indonesian (6)	7	0.05
Japanese (6)	8	0.05
Korean (58)	61	0.41
Pakistani (61)	67	0.45
Sri Lankan (7)	9	0.06
Taiwanese (6)	10	0.07

Notes: 1. Figures in the "Number" column do not add up to the total population due to: a) Ancestry/Race overlap — e.g. persons can report being both White and Irish, b) persons of Hispanic origin can report being any race, c) persons reporting two ancestries are counted in both categories. 2. Numbers in parentheses indicate the number of persons reporting this ancestry/race alone, not in combination with any other ancestry/race. 3. Refer to the Explanation of Data in the front of the book for more detailed information.

Ancestry/Race	Number	%
Thai (1)	2	0.01
Vietnamese (75)	76	0.51
Other Asian, not specified (11)	37	0.25
Austrian	16	0.11
Belgian	20	0.13
Brazilian	5	0.03
British	45	0.30
Canadian	5	0.03
Croatian	11	0.07
Czech	68	0.45
Czechoslovakian	91	0.60
Danish	152	1.00
Dutch	174	1.15
English	585	3.86
Finnish	6	0.04
French, except Basque	160	1.06
French Canadian	30	0.20
German	1,773	11.71
Greek	122	0.81
Guyanese	8	0.05
Hawaii Native/Pacific Islander:	13	0.09
Other Pac. Isl., not spec.	13	0.09
Hispanic or Latino:	1,388	9.23
Central American:	60	0.40
Costa Rican	25	0.17
Guatemalan	13	0.09
Honduran	7	0.05
Salvadoran	13	0.09
Other Central American	2	0.01
Cuban	114	0.76
Dominican Republic	44	0.29
Mexican	18	0.12
Puerto Rican	654	4.35
South American:	253	1.68
Argentinean	27	0.18
Chilean	7	0.05
Colombian	70	0.47
Ecuadorian	52	0.35
Peruvian	70	0.47
Uruguayan	13	0.09
Venezuelan	4	0.03
Other South American	10	0.07
Other Hispanic or Latino	245	1.63
Hungarian	934	6.17
Irish	2,739	18.10
Israeli	15	0.10
Italian	2,705	17.87
Lithuanian	104	0.69
Maltese	12	0.08
Norwegian	34	0.22
Pennsylvania German	12	0.08
Polish	1,863	12.31
Portuguese	147	0.97
Romanian	32	0.21
Russian	342	2.26
Scandinavian	14	0.09
Scotch-Irish	185	1.22
Scottish	99	0.65
Slavic	38	0.25
Slovak	318	2.10
Slovene	5	0.03
Swedish	101	0.67
Swiss	22	0.15
Turkish	25	0.17
Ukrainian	221	1.46
United States or American	323	2.13
Welsh	57	0.38
West Indian, excl. Hispanic:	142	0.94
Haitian	15	0.10
Jamaican	37	0.24
Trinidadian and Tobagonian	37	0.24
West Indian	53	0.35
White:	11,202	74.52
Not Hispanic (10,070)	10,248	68.17
Hispanic (882)	954	6.35
Yugoslavian	37	0.24

Fort Lee

Place Type: Borough
County: Bergen
Population: 35,461

Ancestry/Race	Number	%
Afghan	42	0.12
African American/Black:	756	2.13
Not Hispanic (555)	630	1.78
Hispanic (60)	126	0.36
African, sub-Saharan:	95	0.27
African	27	0.08
South African	48	0.14
Zimbabwean	7	0.02
Other sub-Saharan African	13	0.04
Alaska Native tribes, specified:	1	0.00
Eskimo	1	0.00
Am. Ind. or Alaska Nat., not spec.	50	0.14
Albanian	25	0.07
American Indian tribes, specified:	31	0.09
Blackfeet (1)	4	0.01
Cherokee	2	0.01
Choctaw (1)	2	0.01
Latin American Indians (5)	16	0.05
Navajo	1	0.00
Yaqui	1	0.00
All other tribes (1)	5	0.01
American Indian tribes, not spec.	4	0.01
Arab:	545	1.54
Arab/Arabic	128	0.36
Egyptian	83	0.23
Iraqi	8	0.02
Jordanian	8	0.02
Lebanese	138	0.39
Moroccan	22	0.06
Palestinian	19	0.05
Syrian	48	0.14
Other Arab	91	0.26
Armenian	582	1.64
Asian:	11,548	32.57
Bangladeshi (3)	4	0.01
Chinese, ex. Taiwanese (1,880)	1,971	5.56
Filipino (309)	325	0.92
Indian (509)	553	1.56
Indonesian (12)	14	0.04
Japanese (2,091)	2,161	6.09
Korean (5,978)	6,091	17.18
Malaysian (12)	16	0.05
Pakistani (42)	51	0.14
Taiwanese (108)	132	0.37
Thai (13)	14	0.04
Vietnamese (29)	34	0.10
Other Asian, specified (27)	28	0.08
Other Asian, not specified (49)	154	0.43
Assyrian/Chaldean/Syriac	17	0.05
Australian	18	0.05
Austrian	400	1.13
Belgian	77	0.22
Brazilian	73	0.21
British	70	0.20
Bulgarian	20	0.06
Canadian	32	0.09
Croatian	395	1.11
Czech	49	0.14
Czechoslovakian	42	0.12
Danish	43	0.12
Dutch	113	0.32
Eastern European	233	0.66
English	520	1.47
Estonian	7	0.02
European	112	0.32
Finnish	7	0.02
French, except Basque	232	0.65
French Canadian	65	0.18
German	1,461	4.12
Greek	1,346	3.80
Guyanese	6	0.02
Hawaii Native/Pacific Islander:	38	0.11
Micronesian: (6)	8	0.02
Guamanian/Chamorro (6)	8	0.02
Polynesian: (4)	5	0.01
Native Hawaiian (2)	3	0.01
Samoan (2)	2	0.01
Other Pac. Isl., not spec. (10)	25	0.07
Hispanic or Latino:	2,791	7.87
Central American:	285	0.80
Costa Rican	23	0.06
Guatemalan	38	0.11
Honduran	9	0.03
Nicaraguan	17	0.05
Panamanian	9	0.03
Salvadoran	179	0.50
Other Central American	10	0.03
Cuban	425	1.20
Dominican Republic	338	0.95
Mexican	78	0.22
Puerto Rican	562	1.58
South American:	467	1.32
Argentinean	64	0.18
Bolivian	13	0.04
Chilean	23	0.06
Colombian	206	0.58
Ecuadorian	90	0.25
Peruvian	29	0.08
Uruguayan	5	0.01
Venezuelan	12	0.03
Other South American	25	0.07
Other Hispanic or Latino	636	1.79
Hungarian	551	1.55
Iranian	244	0.69
Irish	1,734	4.89
Israeli	122	0.34
Italian	4,148	11.70
Latvian	72	0.20
Lithuanian	132	0.37
Luxemburger	10	0.03
New Zealander	21	0.06
Norwegian	49	0.14
Pennsylvania German	12	0.03
Polish	1,370	3.86
Portuguese	38	0.11
Romanian	219	0.62
Russian	2,858	8.06
Scotch-Irish	44	0.12
Scottish	135	0.38
Serbian	10	0.03
Slavic	27	0.08
Slovak	45	0.13
Slovene	8	0.02
Swedish	87	0.25
Swiss	44	0.12
Turkish	172	0.49
Ukrainian	246	0.69
United States or American	1,325	3.74
Welsh	24	0.07
West Indian, excl. Hispanic:	121	0.34
Barbadian	15	0.04
British West Indian	5	0.01
Jamaican	35	0.10
Trinidadian and Tobagonian	20	0.06
U.S. Virgin Islander	7	0.02
West Indian	39	0.11
White:	22,918	64.63
Not Hispanic (20,350)	20,806	58.67
Hispanic (1,903)	2,112	5.96
Yugoslavian	160	0.45

Franklin Lakes

Place Type: Borough
County: Bergen
Population: 10,422

Ancestry/Race	Number	%
African American/Black:	115	1.10
Not Hispanic (96)	113	1.08
Hispanic	2	0.02
African, sub-Saharan:	28	0.27
African	6	0.06

Notes: 1. Figures in the "Number" column do not add up to the total population due to: a) Ancestry/Race overlap — e.g. persons can report being both White and Irish, b) persons of Hispanic origin can report being any race, c) persons reporting two ancestries are counted in both categories. 2. Numbers in parentheses indicate the number of persons reporting this ancestry/race alone, not in combination with any other ancestry/race. 3. Refer to the Explanation of Data in the front of the book for more detailed information.

Ancestry/Race	Number	%
South African	22	0.21
Am. Ind. or Alaska Nat., not spec.	7	0.07
American Indian tribes, specified:	11	0.11
Cherokee	1	0.01
Iroquois (5)	5	0.05
Latin American Indians (1)	1	0.01
All other tribes (3)	4	0.04
Arab:	109	1.05
Egyptian	7	0.07
Iraqi	8	0.08
Jordanian	3	0.03
Lebanese	23	0.22
Syrian	68	0.65
Armenian	72	0.69
Asian:	707	6.78
Chinese, ex. Taiwanese (149)	158	1.52
Filipino (46)	49	0.47
Indian (151)	165	1.58
Japanese (37)	48	0.46
Korean (221)	226	2.17
Laotian	1	0.01
Pakistani (2)	2	0.02
Sri Lankan (7)	7	0.07
Taiwanese (27)	33	0.32
Thai (9)	11	0.11
Vietnamese (3)	3	0.03
Other Asian, not specified (1)	4	0.04
Assyrian/Chaldean/Syriac	7	0.07
Austrian	33	0.32
Belgian	7	0.07
Brazilian	19	0.18
British	40	0.38
Canadian	35	0.34
Croatian	6	0.06
Czech	63	0.60
Czechoslovakian	51	0.49
Danish	49	0.47
Dutch	509	4.88
Eastern European	37	0.36
English	803	7.70
European	45	0.43
Finnish	3	0.03
French, except Basque	152	1.46
French Canadian	59	0.57
German	1,583	15.19
Greek	61	0.59
Hawaii Native/Pacific Islander:	2	0.02
Micronesian: (1)	1	0.01
Guamanian/Chamorro (1)	1	0.01
Other Pac. Isl., not spec.	1	0.01
Hispanic or Latino:	286	2.74
Central American:	20	0.19
Costa Rican	3	0.03
Guatemalan	1	0.01
Honduran	3	0.03
Nicaraguan	4	0.04
Salvadoran	8	0.08
Other Central American	1	0.01
Cuban	60	0.58
Dominican Republic	23	0.22
Mexican	11	0.11
Puerto Rican	62	0.59
South American:	41	0.39
Argentinean	3	0.03
Colombian	11	0.11
Ecuadorian	8	0.08
Paraguayan	1	0.01
Peruvian	11	0.11
Other South American	7	0.07
Other Hispanic or Latino	69	0.66
Hungarian	100	0.96
Iranian	109	1.05
Irish	2,060	19.77
Israeli	50	0.48
Italian	3,110	29.84
Latvian	7	0.07
Lithuanian	50	0.48
Norwegian	66	0.63
Polish	874	8.39
Portuguese	34	0.33
Romanian	39	0.37
Russian	634	6.08
Scotch-Irish	132	1.27
Scottish	131	1.26
Slavic	7	0.07
Slovak	52	0.50
Swedish	158	1.52
Swiss	75	0.72
Ukrainian	92	0.88
United States or American	325	3.12
Welsh	27	0.26
West Indian, excl. Hispanic:	72	0.69
British West Indian	6	0.06
Haitian	25	0.24
Jamaican	14	0.13
Trinidadian and Tobagonian	16	0.15
U.S. Virgin Islander	11	0.11
White:	9,586	91.98
Not Hispanic (9,285)	9,341	89.63
Hispanic (236)	245	2.35
Yugoslavian	5	0.05

Franklin

Place Type: Township
County: Gloucester
Population: 15,466

Ancestry/Race	Number	%
African American/Black:	1,112	7.19
Not Hispanic (1,000)	1,075	6.95
Hispanic (30)	37	0.24
African, sub-Saharan:	163	1.05
African	135	0.87
Other sub-Saharan African	28	0.18
Alaska Native tribes, specified:	1	0.01
Aleut (1)	1	0.01
Am. Ind. or Alaska Nat., not spec.	55	0.36
Albanian	26	0.17
American Indian tribes, specified:	58	0.38
Apache (3)	3	0.02
Blackfeet (1)	5	0.03
Cherokee (3)	14	0.09
Chickasaw	5	0.03
Crow	1	0.01
Delaware (4)	6	0.04
Iroquois	2	0.01
Latin American Indians (8)	8	0.05
Lumbee	1	0.01
All other tribes (7)	13	0.08
American Indian tribes, not spec.	2	0.01
Arab:	8	0.05
Lebanese	8	0.05
Asian:	84	0.54
Chinese, ex. Taiwanese (5)	9	0.06
Filipino (8)	15	0.10
Indian (7)	7	0.05
Japanese (1)	8	0.05
Korean (23)	25	0.16
Thai (1)	1	0.01
Vietnamese (10)	10	0.06
Other Asian, not specified (8)	9	0.06
Australian	8	0.05
Austrian	97	0.63
Belgian	51	0.33
Brazilian	6	0.04
British	36	0.23
Canadian	20	0.13
Czech	83	0.54
Czechoslovakian	34	0.22
Danish	56	0.36
Dutch	173	1.12
English	1,819	11.76
Estonian	6	0.04
European	11	0.07
French, except Basque	396	2.56
French Canadian	125	0.81
German	3,684	23.82
Greek	25	0.16
Hawaii Native/Pacific Islander:	3	0.02
Polynesian: (2)	3	0.02
Native Hawaiian	1	0.01
Samoan (2)	2	0.01
Hispanic or Latino:	543	3.51
Central American:	7	0.05
Nicaraguan	2	0.01
Panamanian	3	0.02
Salvadoran	2	0.01
Cuban	13	0.08
Dominican Republic	6	0.04
Mexican	86	0.56
Puerto Rican	365	2.36
South American:	11	0.07
Argentinean	2	0.01
Chilean	4	0.03
Colombian	1	0.01
Ecuadorian	1	0.01
Uruguayan	2	0.01
Venezuelan	1	0.01
Other Hispanic or Latino	55	0.36
Hungarian	138	0.89
Irish	3,730	24.12
Israeli	15	0.10
Italian	3,653	23.62
Latvian	5	0.03
Lithuanian	67	0.43
Norwegian	55	0.36
Pennsylvania German	24	0.16
Polish	1,123	7.26
Portuguese	53	0.34
Romanian	9	0.06
Russian	128	0.83
Scotch-Irish	136	0.88
Scottish	248	1.60
Slavic	24	0.16
Slovak	6	0.04
Swedish	188	1.22
Swiss	117	0.76
Ukrainian	154	1.00
United States or American	358	2.31
Welsh	125	0.81
West Indian, excl. Hispanic:	5	0.03
Jamaican	5	0.03
White:	14,114	91.26
Not Hispanic (13,658)	13,796	89.20
Hispanic (296)	318	2.06
Yugoslavian	23	0.15

Franklin

Place Type: Township
County: Somerset
Population: 50,903

Ancestry/Race	Number	%
Afghan	28	0.06
African American/Black:	13,790	27.09
Not Hispanic (12,888)	13,321	26.17
Hispanic (335)	469	0.92
African, sub-Saharan:	1,987	3.90
African	1,273	2.50
Cape Verdean	14	0.03
Ghanian	259	0.51
Kenyan	27	0.05
Liberian	31	0.06
Nigerian	277	0.54
Sierra Leonean	106	0.21
Alaska Native tribes, specified:	1	0.00
Tlingit-Haida	1	0.00
Am. Ind. or Alaska Nat., not spec.	137	0.27
American Indian tribes, specified:	145	0.28
Blackfeet (3)	8	0.02
Cherokee (7)	41	0.08
Chickasaw (2)	5	0.01
Choctaw (1)	5	0.01
Comanche	2	0.00
Cree	1	0.00
Creek (2)	2	0.00
Delaware (1)	8	0.02
Iroquois (1)	4	0.01

Notes: 1. Figures in the "Number" column do not add up to the total population due to: a) Ancestry/Race overlap — e.g. persons can report being both White and Irish, b) persons of Hispanic origin can report being any race, c) persons reporting two ancestries are counted in both categories. 2. Numbers in parentheses indicate the number of persons reporting this ancestry/race alone, not in combination with any other ancestry/race. 3. Refer to the Explanation of Data in the front of the book for more detailed information.

Ancestry/Race	Number	%
Latin American Indians (17)	32	0.06
Lumbee (1)	2	0.00
Navajo (1)	3	0.01
Paiute	1	0.00
Pueblo	4	0.01
Seminole (1)	6	0.01
Sioux	2	0.00
All other tribes (8)	19	0.04
American Indian tribes, not spec.	9	0.02
Arab:	772	1.52
Egyptian	285	0.56
Jordanian	10	0.02
Lebanese	394	0.77
Moroccan	58	0.11
Palestinian	10	0.02
Syrian	5	0.01
Other Arab	10	0.02
Armenian	76	0.15
Asian:	6,875	13.51
Bangladeshi (15)	16	0.03
Cambodian (3)	3	0.01
Chinese, ex. Taiwanese (1,229)	1,308	2.57
Filipino (888)	969	1.90
Hmong (7)	8	0.02
Indian (3,472)	3,574	7.02
Indonesian (3)	4	0.01
Japanese (88)	108	0.21
Korean (288)	311	0.61
Laotian (2)	5	0.01
Malaysian (4)	4	0.01
Pakistani (222)	247	0.49
Sri Lankan (14)	15	0.03
Taiwanese (62)	83	0.16
Thai (24)	31	0.06
Vietnamese (84)	91	0.18
Other Asian, specified (1)	2	0.00
Other Asian, not specified (33)	96	0.19
Australian	14	0.03
Austrian	246	0.48
Basque	11	0.02
Belgian	10	0.02
Brazilian	52	0.10
British	215	0.42
Bulgarian	16	0.03
Canadian	87	0.17
Carpatho Rusyn	16	0.03
Croatian	63	0.12
Czech	102	0.20
Czechoslovakian	100	0.20
Danish	90	0.18
Dutch	609	1.20
Eastern European	96	0.19
English	1,839	3.61
Estonian	8	0.02
European	204	0.40
Finnish	41	0.08
French, except Basque	477	0.94
French Canadian	315	0.62
German	4,346	8.54
Greek	244	0.48
Guyanese	131	0.26
Hawaii Native/Pacific Islander:	65	0.13
Micronesian: (9)	10	0.02
Guamanian/Chamorro (9)	10	0.02
Polynesian: (2)	11	0.02
Native Hawaiian (1)	9	0.02
Samoan (1)	2	0.00
Other Pac. Isl., not spec. (10)	44	0.09
Hispanic or Latino:	4,127	8.11
Central American:	312	0.61
Costa Rican	32	0.06
Guatemalan	42	0.08
Honduran	137	0.27
Nicaraguan	43	0.08
Panamanian	27	0.05
Salvadoran	23	0.05
Other Central American	8	0.02
Cuban	206	0.40
Dominican Republic	567	1.11
Mexican	522	1.03
Puerto Rican	1,372	2.70
South American:	396	0.78
Argentinean	35	0.07
Bolivian	3	0.01
Chilean	10	0.02
Colombian	141	0.28
Ecuadorian	88	0.17
Paraguayan	3	0.01
Peruvian	69	0.14
Uruguayan	6	0.01
Venezuelan	20	0.04
Other South American	21	0.04
Other Hispanic or Latino	752	1.48
Hungarian	1,717	3.37
Icelander	7	0.01
Iranian	202	0.40
Irish	5,111	10.04
Israeli	16	0.03
Italian	6,131	12.04
Latvian	54	0.11
Lithuanian	260	0.51
Luxemburger	4	0.01
Macedonian	40	0.08
Maltese	36	0.07
Northern European	20	0.04
Norwegian	530	1.04
Pennsylvania German	9	0.02
Polish	3,528	6.93
Portuguese	127	0.25
Romanian	111	0.22
Russian	1,230	2.42
Scandinavian	90	0.18
Scotch-Irish	198	0.39
Scottish	504	0.99
Slavic	111	0.22
Slovak	245	0.48
Slovene	15	0.03
Swedish	310	0.61
Swiss	157	0.31
Turkish	62	0.12
Ukrainian	606	1.19
United States or American	1,177	2.31
Welsh	182	0.36
West Indian, excl. Hispanic:	1,925	3.78
Bahamian	5	0.01
Barbadian	92	0.18
Belizean	7	0.01
British West Indian	92	0.18
Haitian	108	0.21
Jamaican	1,295	2.54
Trinidadian and Tobagonian	95	0.19
U.S. Virgin Islander	6	0.01
West Indian	214	0.42
Other West Indian	11	0.02
White:	28,832	56.64
Not Hispanic (26,226)	26,782	52.61
Hispanic (1,826)	2,050	4.03
Yugoslavian	71	0.14

Freehold

Place Type: Borough
County: Monmouth
Population: 10,976

Ancestry/Race	Number	%
African American/Black:	1,819	16.57
Not Hispanic (1,635)	1,685	15.35
Hispanic (103)	134	1.22
African, sub-Saharan:	45	0.41
African	38	0.35
Cape Verdean	4	0.04
Nigerian	3	0.03
Am. Ind. or Alaska Nat., not spec.	62	0.56
Albanian	30	0.27
American Indian tribes, specified:	61	0.56
Cherokee (4)	15	0.14
Delaware	3	0.03
Latin American Indians (29)	36	0.33
Pueblo	1	0.01
Seminole	1	0.01
Sioux (1)	1	0.01
All other tribes (2)	4	0.04
American Indian tribes, not spec.	11	0.10
Arab:	53	0.48
Arab/Arabic	27	0.25
Moroccan	12	0.11
Palestinian	14	0.13
Armenian	28	0.26
Asian:	325	2.96
Chinese, ex. Taiwanese (79)	90	0.82
Filipino (39)	43	0.39
Indian (73)	77	0.70
Japanese (4)	7	0.06
Korean (6)	11	0.10
Laotian	1	0.01
Malaysian	3	0.03
Pakistani (1)	10	0.09
Taiwanese (4)	4	0.04
Thai (2)	2	0.02
Vietnamese (38)	44	0.40
Other Asian, specified (7)	7	0.06
Other Asian, not specified (8)	26	0.24
Austrian	32	0.29
Belgian	7	0.06
Brazilian	26	0.24
British	59	0.54
Canadian	29	0.26
Czech	17	0.15
Czechoslovakian	16	0.15
Danish	23	0.21
Dutch	130	1.18
English	710	6.47
European	24	0.22
French, except Basque	176	1.60
French Canadian	81	0.74
German	961	8.76
Greek	90	0.82
Hawaii Native/Pacific Islander:	10	0.09
Micronesian: (2)	3	0.03
Guamanian/Chamorro (2)	3	0.03
Polynesian:	1	0.01
Native Hawaiian	1	0.01
Other Pac. Isl., not spec.	6	0.05
Hispanic or Latino:	3,081	28.07
Central American:	149	1.36
Costa Rican	12	0.11
Guatemalan	50	0.46
Honduran	43	0.39
Nicaraguan	5	0.05
Panamanian	10	0.09
Salvadoran	20	0.18
Other Central American	9	0.08
Cuban	31	0.28
Dominican Republic	23	0.21
Mexican	1,903	17.34
Puerto Rican	627	5.71
South American:	156	1.42
Argentinean	2	0.02
Bolivian	1	0.01
Colombian	36	0.33
Ecuadorian	12	0.11
Peruvian	91	0.83
Uruguayan	1	0.01
Venezuelan	2	0.02
Other South American	11	0.10
Other Hispanic or Latino	192	1.75
Hungarian	154	1.40
Iranian	6	0.05
Irish	1,883	17.16
Israeli	30	0.27
Italian	1,173	10.69
Latvian	32	0.29
Lithuanian	105	0.96
Norwegian	30	0.27
Pennsylvania German	14	0.13
Polish	634	5.78
Russian	340	3.10
Scandinavian	18	0.16
Scotch-Irish	91	0.83

Notes: 1. Figures in the "Number" column do not add up to the total population due to: a) Ancestry/Race overlap — e.g. persons can report being both White and Irish, b) persons of Hispanic origin can report being any race, c) persons reporting two ancestries are counted in both categories. 2. Numbers in parentheses indicate the number of persons reporting this ancestry/race alone, not in combination with any other ancestry/race. 3. Refer to the Explanation of Data in the front of the book for more detailed information.

Scottish	161	1.47
Slavic	5	0.05
Slovak	56	0.51
Swedish	94	0.86
Swiss	14	0.13
Ukrainian	76	0.69
United States or American	311	2.83
Welsh	61	0.56
West Indian, excl. Hispanic:	112	1.02
Barbadian	15	0.14
Belizean	34	0.31
British West Indian	6	0.05
Haitian	11	0.10
Jamaican	6	0.05
West Indian	32	0.29
Other West Indian	8	0.07
White:	8,107	73.86
Not Hispanic (5,853)	5,941	54.13
Hispanic (1,942)	2,166	19.73

Freehold

Place Type: Township
County: Monmouth
Population: 31,537

Ancestry/Race	Number	%
African American/Black:	1,727	5.48
Not Hispanic (1,550)	1,644	5.21
Hispanic (66)	83	0.26
African, sub-Saharan:	38	0.12
African	32	0.10
South African	6	0.02
Am. Ind. or Alaska Nat., not spec.	47	0.15
Albanian	51	0.16
American Indian tribes, specified:	65	0.21
Apache (1)	1	0.00
Blackfeet	6	0.02
Cherokee (4)	24	0.08
Chippewa	3	0.01
Crow	1	0.00
Iroquois (2)	8	0.03
Latin American Indians (5)	8	0.03
Lumbee	1	0.00
Navajo	1	0.00
Pueblo (5)	6	0.02
Sioux	4	0.01
All other tribes	3	0.01
American Indian tribes, not spec.	11	0.03
Arab:	321	1.02
Arab/Arabic	16	0.05
Egyptian	54	0.17
Lebanese	101	0.32
Syrian	150	0.48
Armenian	22	0.07
Asian:	1,789	5.67
Bangladeshi (2)	2	0.01
Cambodian (1)	1	0.00
Chinese, ex. Taiwanese (527)	567	1.80
Filipino (377)	423	1.34
Indian (497)	540	1.71
Indonesian (3)	3	0.01
Japanese (17)	36	0.11
Korean (105)	117	0.37
Pakistani (5)	5	0.02
Sri Lankan (3)	3	0.01
Taiwanese (13)	13	0.04
Thai (4)	4	0.01
Vietnamese (37)	42	0.13
Other Asian, not specified (21)	33	0.10
Austrian	393	1.25
Belgian	26	0.08
Brazilian	67	0.21
British	101	0.32
Canadian	55	0.17
Croatian	37	0.12
Cypriot	13	0.04
Czech	143	0.45
Czechoslovakian	95	0.30
Danish	150	0.48
Dutch	330	1.05
Eastern European	156	0.49
English	2,044	6.48
European	75	0.24
Finnish	15	0.05
French, except Basque	622	1.97
French Canadian	103	0.33
German	4,063	12.88
Greek	445	1.41
Guyanese	24	0.08
Hawaii Native/Pacific Islander:	13	0.04
Melanesian:	1	0.00
Other Melanesian	1	0.00
Micronesian: (1)	1	0.00
Guamanian/Chamorro (1)	1	0.00
Polynesian: (4)	9	0.03
Native Hawaiian (4)	8	0.03
Samoan	1	0.00
Other Pac. Isl., not spec.	2	0.01
Hispanic or Latino:	1,637	5.19
Central American:	60	0.19
Costa Rican	8	0.03
Guatemalan	12	0.04
Honduran	18	0.06
Nicaraguan	1	0.00
Panamanian	12	0.04
Salvadoran	8	0.03
Other Central American	1	0.00
Cuban	133	0.42
Dominican Republic	48	0.15
Mexican	328	1.04
Puerto Rican	607	1.92
South American:	187	0.59
Argentinean	13	0.04
Bolivian	2	0.01
Chilean	5	0.02
Colombian	80	0.25
Ecuadorian	37	0.12
Paraguayan	1	0.00
Peruvian	27	0.09
Uruguayan	5	0.02
Venezuelan	8	0.03
Other South American	9	0.03
Other Hispanic or Latino	274	0.87
Hungarian	454	1.44
Irish	5,734	18.18
Israeli	46	0.15
Italian	8,218	26.06
Latvian	14	0.04
Lithuanian	128	0.41
Maltese	32	0.10
Norwegian	185	0.59
Pennsylvania German	22	0.07
Polish	3,202	10.15
Portuguese	162	0.51
Romanian	116	0.37
Russian	1,373	4.35
Scandinavian	107	0.34
Scotch-Irish	264	0.84
Scottish	311	0.99
Serbian	19	0.06
Slavic	58	0.18
Slovak	57	0.18
Swedish	184	0.58
Swiss	61	0.19
Turkish	111	0.35
Ukrainian	340	1.08
United States or American	778	2.47
Welsh	55	0.17
West Indian, excl. Hispanic:	182	0.58
Barbadian	18	0.06
British West Indian	25	0.08
Haitian	18	0.06
Jamaican	87	0.28
Trinidadian and Tobagonian	15	0.05
West Indian	19	0.06
White:	27,801	88.15
Not Hispanic (26,371)	26,602	84.35
Hispanic (1,095)	1,199	3.80
Yugoslavian	82	0.26

Galloway

Place Type: Township
County: Atlantic
Population: 31,209

Ancestry/Race	Number	%
African American/Black:	3,279	10.51
Not Hispanic (2,959)	3,140	10.06
Hispanic (99)	139	0.45
African, sub-Saharan:	149	0.48
African	54	0.17
Ethiopian	10	0.03
Nigerian	80	0.26
Sierra Leonean	5	0.02
Am. Ind. or Alaska Nat., not spec.	75	0.24
Albanian	14	0.04
American Indian tribes, specified:	107	0.34
Blackfeet (2)	11	0.04
Cherokee (7)	43	0.14
Chippewa (1)	2	0.01
Cree	2	0.01
Delaware (3)	12	0.04
Iroquois (1)	4	0.01
Latin American Indians (5)	11	0.04
Navajo	1	0.00
Osage (1)	1	0.00
Seminole	2	0.01
Shoshone (1)	1	0.00
Sioux (1)	1	0.00
All other tribes (4)	16	0.05
American Indian tribes, not spec.	21	0.07
Arab:	125	0.40
Egyptian	90	0.29
Lebanese	7	0.02
Syrian	28	0.09
Armenian	65	0.21
Asian:	2,772	8.88
Bangladeshi (5)	10	0.03
Cambodian (2)	2	0.01
Chinese, ex. Taiwanese (571)	638	2.04
Filipino (270)	328	1.05
Hmong	1	0.00
Indian (923)	971	3.11
Japanese (16)	38	0.12
Korean (206)	223	0.71
Laotian (16)	19	0.06
Malaysian (1)	1	0.00
Pakistani (110)	138	0.44
Taiwanese (2)	4	0.01
Thai (22)	29	0.09
Vietnamese (233)	261	0.84
Other Asian, specified (1)	1	0.00
Other Asian, not specified (84)	108	0.35
Assyrian/Chaldean/Syriac	8	0.03
Australian	21	0.07
Austrian	199	0.64
Belgian	34	0.11
British	53	0.17
Canadian	39	0.13
Celtic	10	0.03
Croatian	29	0.09
Cypriot	5	0.02
Czech	52	0.17
Czechoslovakian	65	0.21
Danish	67	0.22
Dutch	427	1.37
Eastern European	41	0.13
English	2,560	8.22
European	88	0.28
Finnish	19	0.06
French, except Basque	687	2.20
French Canadian	165	0.53
German	5,963	19.14
Greek	181	0.58
Guyanese	25	0.08
Hawaii Native/Pacific Islander:	39	0.12
Micronesian: (3)	5	0.02
Guamanian/Chamorro (3)	5	0.02
Polynesian: (10)	21	0.07

Notes: 1. Figures in the "Number" column do not add up to the total population due to: a) Ancestry/Race overlap — e.g. persons can report being both White and Irish, b) persons of Hispanic origin can report being any race, c) persons reporting two ancestries are counted in both categories. 2. Numbers in parentheses indicate the number of persons reporting this ancestry/race alone, not in combination with any other ancestry/race. 3. Refer to the Explanation of Data in the front of the book for more detailed information.

Native Hawaiian (9)	18	0.06
Samoan (1)	2	0.01
Tongan	1	0.00
Other Pac. Isl., not spec. (1)	13	0.04
Hispanic or Latino:	1,924	6.16
Central American:	51	0.16
Costa Rican	6	0.02
Guatemalan	4	0.01
Honduran	13	0.04
Nicaraguan	4	0.01
Panamanian	1	0.00
Salvadoran	19	0.06
Other Central American	4	0.01
Cuban	69	0.22
Dominican Republic	97	0.31
Mexican	126	0.40
Puerto Rican	1,048	3.36
South American:	192	0.62
Argentinean	8	0.03
Bolivian	2	0.01
Chilean	3	0.01
Colombian	58	0.19
Ecuadorian	15	0.05
Peruvian	88	0.28
Venezuelan	8	0.03
Other South American	10	0.03
Other Hispanic or Latino	341	1.09
Hungarian	421	1.35
Irish	6,444	20.68
Italian	6,082	19.52
Lithuanian	198	0.64
Luxemburger	9	0.03
Norwegian	172	0.55
Pennsylvania German	20	0.06
Polish	1,443	4.63
Portuguese	21	0.07
Romanian	100	0.32
Russian	489	1.57
Scandinavian	15	0.05
Scotch-Irish	318	1.02
Scottish	410	1.32
Slavic	45	0.14
Slovak	36	0.12
Swedish	203	0.65
Swiss	65	0.21
Turkish	18	0.06
Ukrainian	191	0.61
United States or American	1,536	4.93
Welsh	212	0.68
West Indian, excl. Hispanic:	237	0.76
Bahamian	59	0.19
Barbadian	10	0.03
Bermudan	14	0.04
Haitian	49	0.16
Jamaican	87	0.28
West Indian	18	0.06
White:	24,604	78.84
Not Hispanic (23,188)	23,608	75.64
Hispanic (893)	996	3.19
Yugoslavian	12	0.04

Garfield

Place Type: City
County: Bergen
Population: 29,786

Ancestry/Race	Number	%
African American/Black:	1,184	3.98
Not Hispanic (778)	900	3.02
Hispanic (109)	284	0.95
African, sub-Saharan:	50	0.17
African	50	0.17
Am. Ind. or Alaska Nat., not spec.	104	0.35
Albanian	370	1.24
American Indian tribes, specified:	70	0.24
Blackfeet	1	0.00
Cherokee (8)	16	0.05
Choctaw	2	0.01
Delaware	2	0.01
Iroquois (1)	5	0.02
Latin American Indians (14)	43	0.14
All other tribes	1	0.00
American Indian tribes, not spec.	15	0.05
Arab:	676	2.27
Arab/Arabic	171	0.57
Egyptian	163	0.55
Jordanian	82	0.28
Lebanese	60	0.20
Palestinian	121	0.41
Syrian	79	0.27
Armenian	39	0.13
Asian:	935	3.14
Bangladeshi	2	0.01
Chinese, ex. Taiwanese (113)	130	0.44
Filipino (232)	248	0.83
Indian (223)	250	0.84
Japanese (36)	47	0.16
Korean (66)	68	0.23
Laotian (6)	6	0.02
Pakistani (78)	87	0.29
Taiwanese (1)	4	0.01
Thai (10)	12	0.04
Vietnamese (22)	24	0.08
Other Asian, not specified (8)	57	0.19
Australian	7	0.02
Austrian	80	0.27
Belgian	8	0.03
Brazilian	39	0.13
British	15	0.05
Bulgarian	29	0.10
Canadian	4	0.01
Carpatho Rusyn	19	0.06
Croatian	113	0.38
Czech	117	0.39
Czechoslovakian	147	0.49
Danish	27	0.09
Dutch	457	1.53
English	490	1.65
French, except Basque	267	0.90
French Canadian	47	0.16
German	1,624	5.45
Greek	276	0.93
Guyanese	11	0.04
Hawaii Native/Pacific Islander:	24	0.08
Polynesian: (2)	7	0.02
Native Hawaiian (1)	6	0.02
Samoan (1)	1	0.00
Other Pac. Isl., not spec.	17	0.06
Hispanic or Latino:	5,989	20.11
Central American:	157	0.53
Costa Rican	31	0.10
Guatemalan	26	0.09
Honduran	30	0.10
Nicaraguan	20	0.07
Panamanian	9	0.03
Salvadoran	35	0.12
Other Central American	6	0.02
Cuban	130	0.44
Dominican Republic	623	2.09
Mexican	469	1.57
Puerto Rican	1,348	4.53
South American:	1,868	6.27
Argentinean	128	0.43
Bolivian	53	0.18
Chilean	34	0.11
Colombian	542	1.82
Ecuadorian	260	0.87
Paraguayan	3	0.01
Peruvian	761	2.55
Uruguayan	25	0.08
Venezuelan	16	0.05
Other South American	46	0.15
Other Hispanic or Latino	1,394	4.68
Hungarian	432	1.45
Iranian	13	0.04
Irish	2,002	6.72
Italian	5,794	19.45
Latvian	6	0.02
Lithuanian	38	0.13
Macedonian	834	2.80
Norwegian	17	0.06
Polish	7,431	24.95
Portuguese	315	1.06
Romanian	28	0.09
Russian	630	2.12
Scotch-Irish	44	0.15
Scottish	156	0.52
Serbian	39	0.13
Slavic	99	0.33
Slovak	523	1.76
Swedish	24	0.08
Swiss	92	0.31
Turkish	90	0.30
Ukrainian	410	1.38
United States or American	785	2.64
Welsh	20	0.07
West Indian, excl. Hispanic:	197	0.66
Bahamian	14	0.05
Jamaican	74	0.25
Trinidadian and Tobagonian	50	0.17
West Indian	59	0.20
White:	25,451	85.45
Not Hispanic (21,560)	22,096	74.18
Hispanic (2,896)	3,355	11.26
Yugoslavian	277	0.93

Glassboro

Place Type: Borough
County: Gloucester
Population: 19,068

Ancestry/Race	Number	%
African American/Black:	3,936	20.64
Not Hispanic (3,617)	3,818	20.02
Hispanic (95)	118	0.62
African, sub-Saharan:	135	0.71
African	110	0.58
Ghanian	12	0.06
Somalian	13	0.07
Am. Ind. or Alaska Nat., not spec.	35	0.18
Albanian	5	0.03
American Indian tribes, specified:	91	0.48
Apache	1	0.01
Blackfeet (4)	7	0.04
Cherokee (11)	30	0.16
Choctaw	1	0.01
Cree	1	0.01
Crow	2	0.01
Delaware (2)	13	0.07
Iroquois	8	0.04
Latin American Indians (2)	8	0.04
Lumbee	2	0.01
Pueblo (1)	3	0.02
Seminole	1	0.01
Sioux (1)	4	0.02
All other tribes (6)	10	0.05
American Indian tribes, not spec.	1	0.01
Arab:	11	0.06
Egyptian	11	0.06
Armenian	22	0.12
Asian:	534	2.80
Bangladeshi (5)	5	0.03
Chinese, ex. Taiwanese (86)	107	0.56
Filipino (69)	110	0.58
Indian (92)	108	0.57
Indonesian	1	0.01
Japanese (13)	19	0.10
Korean (42)	49	0.26
Laotian (10)	10	0.05
Pakistani (19)	19	0.10
Sri Lankan (9)	9	0.05
Taiwanese (7)	7	0.04
Thai (6)	6	0.03
Vietnamese (36)	36	0.19
Other Asian, not specified (36)	48	0.25
Austrian	53	0.28
Brazilian	16	0.08
British	16	0.08

Notes: 1. Figures in the "Number" column do not add up to the total population due to: a) Ancestry/Race overlap — e.g. persons can report being both White and Irish, b) persons of Hispanic origin can report being any race, c) persons reporting two ancestries are counted in both categories. 2. Numbers in parentheses indicate the number of persons reporting this ancestry/race alone, not in combination with any other ancestry/race. 3. Refer to the Explanation of Data in the front of the book for more detailed information.

Ancestry/Race	Number	%
Canadian	16	0.08
Czech	22	0.12
Czechoslovakian	30	0.16
Danish	15	0.08
Dutch	207	1.09
Eastern European	8	0.04
English	1,549	8.12
European	123	0.65
Finnish	4	0.02
French, except Basque	319	1.67
French Canadian	18	0.09
German	3,245	17.02
Greek	104	0.55
Guyanese	18	0.09
Hawaii Native/Pacific Islander:	36	0.19
Micronesian:	1	0.01
Guamanian/Chamorro	1	0.01
Polynesian: (13)	17	0.09
Native Hawaiian (4)	7	0.04
Samoan	1	0.01
Other Polynesian (9)	9	0.05
Other Pac. Isl., not spec. (4)	18	0.09
Hispanic or Latino:	728	3.82
Central American:	16	0.08
Guatemalan	10	0.05
Panamanian	6	0.03
Cuban	28	0.15
Dominican Republic	12	0.06
Mexican	62	0.33
Puerto Rican	468	2.45
South American:	26	0.14
Argentinean	1	0.01
Colombian	11	0.06
Ecuadorian	3	0.02
Peruvian	6	0.03
Uruguayan	2	0.01
Other South American	3	0.02
Other Hispanic or Latino	116	0.61
Hungarian	133	0.70
Irish	3,861	20.25
Italian	4,106	21.53
Lithuanian	53	0.28
Norwegian	91	0.48
Polish	963	5.05
Portuguese	84	0.44
Romanian	23	0.12
Russian	270	1.42
Scandinavian	15	0.08
Scotch-Irish	179	0.94
Scottish	163	0.85
Serbian	8	0.04
Slovak	13	0.07
Swedish	161	0.84
Swiss	24	0.13
Turkish	9	0.05
Ukrainian	74	0.39
United States or American	391	2.05
Welsh	88	0.46
West Indian, excl. Hispanic:	30	0.16
Bahamian	7	0.04
Haitian	6	0.03
Jamaican	4	0.02
Trinidadian and Tobagonian	13	0.07
White:	14,485	75.96
Not Hispanic (13,904)	14,147	74.19
Hispanic (308)	338	1.77

Glen Rock

Place Type: Borough
County: Bergen
Population: 11,546

Ancestry/Race	Number	%
African American/Black:	232	2.01
Not Hispanic (206)	226	1.96
Hispanic (3)	6	0.05
African, sub-Saharan:	9	0.08
African	9	0.08
Am. Ind. or Alaska Nat., not spec.	8	0.07
Albanian	16	0.14
American Indian tribes, specified:	17	0.15
Blackfeet (1)	1	0.01
Cherokee (1)	2	0.02
Iroquois	3	0.03
Latin American Indians (1)	1	0.01
Yaqui	1	0.01
All other tribes (9)	9	0.08
Arab:	41	0.36
Arab/Arabic	8	0.07
Iraqi	15	0.13
Syrian	18	0.16
Armenian	51	0.44
Asian:	807	6.99
Chinese, ex. Taiwanese (118)	140	1.21
Filipino (73)	79	0.68
Indian (115)	122	1.06
Indonesian	3	0.03
Japanese (143)	149	1.29
Korean (244)	253	2.19
Taiwanese (20)	21	0.18
Thai (12)	16	0.14
Other Asian, not specified (15)	24	0.21
Austrian	241	2.09
Belgian	18	0.16
British	100	0.87
Canadian	25	0.22
Celtic	6	0.05
Croatian	17	0.15
Czech	30	0.26
Czechoslovakian	38	0.33
Danish	26	0.23
Dutch	318	2.75
Eastern European	66	0.57
English	1,077	9.33
Estonian	6	0.05
European	149	1.29
Finnish	10	0.09
French, except Basque	105	0.91
French Canadian	61	0.53
German	1,975	17.11
Greek	53	0.46
Hawaii Native/Pacific Islander:	2	0.02
Polynesian: (2)	2	0.02
Native Hawaiian (2)	2	0.02
Hispanic or Latino:	314	2.72
Central American:	25	0.22
Costa Rican	2	0.02
Guatemalan	1	0.01
Honduran	5	0.04
Salvadoran	17	0.15
Cuban	57	0.49
Dominican Republic	9	0.08
Mexican	37	0.32
Puerto Rican	99	0.86
South American:	40	0.35
Argentinean	5	0.04
Chilean	5	0.04
Colombian	16	0.14
Ecuadorian	6	0.05
Paraguayan	2	0.02
Peruvian	2	0.02
Other South American	4	0.03
Other Hispanic or Latino	47	0.41
Hungarian	110	0.95
Irish	2,865	24.81
Israeli	30	0.26
Italian	2,783	24.10
Lithuanian	23	0.20
Maltese	10	0.09
Norwegian	78	0.68
Pennsylvania German	7	0.06
Polish	859	7.44
Portuguese	21	0.18
Romanian	23	0.20
Russian	577	5.00
Scotch-Irish	84	0.73
Scottish	195	1.69
Slavic	6	0.05
Slovak	55	0.48
Swedish	125	1.08
Swiss	110	0.95
Ukrainian	107	0.93
United States or American	664	5.75
Welsh	92	0.80
West Indian, excl. Hispanic:	59	0.51
Bahamian	12	0.10
Barbadian	20	0.17
British West Indian	8	0.07
Haitian	7	0.06
West Indian	12	0.10
White:	10,493	90.88
Not Hispanic (10,163)	10,242	88.71
Hispanic (236)	251	2.17

Gloucester City

Place Type: City
County: Camden
Population: 11,484

Ancestry/Race	Number	%
African American/Black:	90	0.78
Not Hispanic (76)	86	0.75
Hispanic (3)	4	0.03
African, sub-Saharan:	5	0.04
African	5	0.04
Am. Ind. or Alaska Nat., not spec.	20	0.17
American Indian tribes, specified:	31	0.27
Blackfeet	1	0.01
Cherokee (4)	14	0.12
Chippewa	3	0.03
Choctaw	1	0.01
Delaware	3	0.03
Iroquois (2)	3	0.03
Latin American Indians (4)	4	0.03
Seminole	1	0.01
Sioux (1)	1	0.01
American Indian tribes, not spec.	8	0.07
Asian:	92	0.80
Bangladeshi	3	0.03
Chinese, ex. Taiwanese (44)	46	0.40
Filipino (7)	10	0.09
Indian (14)	14	0.12
Japanese (3)	5	0.04
Korean (2)	3	0.03
Pakistani (1)	2	0.02
Vietnamese (6)	7	0.06
Other Asian, not specified (1)	2	0.02
Austrian	18	0.16
British	30	0.26
Celtic	4	0.03
Czech	4	0.03
Czechoslovakian	6	0.05
Danish	5	0.04
Dutch	153	1.33
English	1,150	10.02
European	50	0.44
French, except Basque	292	2.54
French Canadian	18	0.16
German	2,543	22.16
Greek	16	0.14
Hawaii Native/Pacific Islander:	4	0.03
Micronesian: (4)	4	0.03
Guamanian/Chamorro (4)	4	0.03
Hispanic or Latino:	216	1.88
Central American:	1	0.01
Costa Rican	1	0.01
Cuban	10	0.09
Dominican Republic	8	0.07
Mexican	15	0.13
Puerto Rican	142	1.24
South American:	13	0.11
Colombian	9	0.08
Peruvian	3	0.03
Uruguayan	1	0.01
Other Hispanic or Latino	27	0.24
Hungarian	47	0.41
Irish	4,859	42.34
Italian	2,173	18.94

Notes: 1. Figures in the "Number" column do not add up to the total population due to: a) Ancestry/Race overlap — e.g. persons can report being both White and Irish, b) persons of Hispanic origin can report being any race, c) persons reporting two ancestries are counted in both categories. 2. Numbers in parentheses indicate the number of persons reporting this ancestry/race alone, not in combination with any other ancestry/race. 3. Refer to the Explanation of Data in the front of the book for more detailed information.

Ancestry/Race	Number	%
Lithuanian	46	0.40
Northern European	7	0.06
Norwegian	62	0.54
Pennsylvania German	19	0.17
Polish	798	6.95
Russian	81	0.71
Scotch-Irish	215	1.87
Scottish	151	1.32
Slovak	23	0.20
Swedish	130	1.13
Ukrainian	28	0.24
United States or American	588	5.12
Welsh	148	1.29
West Indian, excl. Hispanic:	7	0.06
Jamaican	7	0.06
White:	11,221	97.71
Not Hispanic (11,026)	11,081	96.49
Hispanic (129)	140	1.22
Yugoslavian	11	0.10

Gloucester

Place Type: Township
County: Camden
Population: 64,350

Ancestry/Race	Number	%
African American/Black:	7,853	12.20
Not Hispanic (7,268)	7,606	11.82
Hispanic (164)	247	0.38
African, sub-Saharan:	448	0.70
African	308	0.48
Ethiopian	42	0.07
Ghanian	23	0.04
Nigerian	44	0.07
Sierra Leonean	7	0.01
Other sub-Saharan African	24	0.04
Am. Ind. or Alaska Nat., not spec.	112	0.17
Albanian	25	0.04
Alsatian	9	0.01
American Indian tribes, specified:	160	0.25
Apache (4)	8	0.01
Blackfeet (1)	14	0.02
Cherokee (12)	65	0.10
Cheyenne	3	0.00
Choctaw (3)	3	0.00
Creek (1)	2	0.00
Delaware (8)	18	0.03
Iroquois (5)	11	0.02
Latin American Indians (2)	3	0.00
Lumbee (1)	1	0.00
Seminole	1	0.00
Sioux (1)	7	0.01
Ute	1	0.00
All other tribes (18)	23	0.04
American Indian tribes, not spec.	26	0.04
Arab:	225	0.35
Egyptian	148	0.23
Lebanese	48	0.07
Moroccan	6	0.01
Palestinian	11	0.02
Syrian	12	0.02
Armenian	70	0.11
Asian:	1,966	3.06
Bangladeshi (17)	21	0.03
Cambodian (3)	3	0.00
Chinese, ex. Taiwanese (220)	254	0.39
Filipino (642)	739	1.15
Hmong (5)	5	0.01
Indian (456)	484	0.75
Indonesian	1	0.00
Japanese (26)	62	0.10
Korean (88)	115	0.18
Laotian (3)	6	0.01
Malaysian	3	0.00
Pakistani (24)	32	0.05
Taiwanese (5)	5	0.01
Thai (5)	11	0.02
Vietnamese (124)	145	0.23
Other Asian, specified (1)	1	0.00
Other Asian, not specified (32)	79	0.12
Australian	14	0.02
Austrian	140	0.22
Belgian	7	0.01
Brazilian	20	0.03
British	157	0.24
Canadian	94	0.15
Croatian	41	0.06
Czech	147	0.23
Czechoslovakian	114	0.18
Danish	65	0.10
Dutch	542	0.84
Eastern European	12	0.02
English	5,249	8.16
Estonian	10	0.02
European	196	0.30
Finnish	60	0.09
French, except Basque	1,215	1.89
French Canadian	226	0.35
German	12,253	19.05
Greek	323	0.50
Hawaii Native/Pacific Islander:	33	0.05
Polynesian: (9)	16	0.02
Native Hawaiian (5)	11	0.02
Samoan (4)	5	0.01
Other Pac. Isl., not spec. (7)	17	0.03
Hispanic or Latino:	1,962	3.05
Central American:	78	0.12
Costa Rican	11	0.02
Guatemalan	25	0.04
Honduran	2	0.00
Nicaraguan	12	0.02
Panamanian	21	0.03
Salvadoran	7	0.01
Cuban	81	0.13
Dominican Republic	16	0.02
Mexican	248	0.39
Puerto Rican	1,160	1.80
South American:	124	0.19
Argentinean	23	0.04
Chilean	5	0.01
Colombian	28	0.04
Ecuadorian	11	0.02
Paraguayan	2	0.00
Peruvian	15	0.02
Venezuelan	25	0.04
Other South American	15	0.02
Other Hispanic or Latino	255	0.40
Hungarian	405	0.63
Iranian	14	0.02
Irish	16,582	25.78
Italian	18,860	29.32
Latvian	41	0.06
Lithuanian	303	0.47
Maltese	6	0.01
Norwegian	331	0.51
Pennsylvania German	214	0.33
Polish	4,952	7.70
Portuguese	135	0.21
Romanian	92	0.14
Russian	827	1.29
Scandinavian	7	0.01
Scotch-Irish	719	1.12
Scottish	712	1.11
Serbian	8	0.01
Slavic	57	0.09
Slovak	150	0.23
Slovene	7	0.01
Swedish	301	0.47
Swiss	104	0.16
Turkish	55	0.09
Ukrainian	290	0.45
United States or American	1,877	2.92
Welsh	563	0.88
West Indian, excl. Hispanic:	207	0.32
Jamaican	137	0.21
Trinidadian and Tobagonian	44	0.07
West Indian	26	0.04
White:	54,200	84.23
Not Hispanic (52,555)	53,162	82.61
Hispanic (929)	1,038	1.61
Yugoslavian	34	0.05

Greentree

Place Type: Census Designated Place
County: Camden
Population: 11,536

Ancestry/Race	Number	%
African American/Black:	739	6.41
Not Hispanic (675)	714	6.19
Hispanic (23)	25	0.22
African, sub-Saharan:	64	0.56
Nigerian	37	0.32
South African	27	0.23
Am. Ind. or Alaska Nat., not spec.	17	0.15
American Indian tribes, specified:	8	0.07
Blackfeet	1	0.01
Cherokee	2	0.02
Latin American Indians (2)	2	0.02
Pima (1)	1	0.01
All other tribes	2	0.02
American Indian tribes, not spec.	5	0.04
Arab:	42	0.37
Lebanese	18	0.16
Moroccan	24	0.21
Armenian	31	0.27
Asian:	1,776	15.40
Bangladeshi (4)	4	0.03
Cambodian (6)	6	0.05
Chinese, ex. Taiwanese (472)	482	4.18
Filipino (231)	247	2.14
Indian (484)	498	4.32
Indonesian (1)	1	0.01
Japanese (16)	19	0.16
Korean (369)	374	3.24
Laotian	3	0.03
Pakistani (4)	4	0.03
Sri Lankan (4)	4	0.03
Taiwanese (62)	69	0.60
Thai (4)	4	0.03
Vietnamese (41)	44	0.38
Other Asian, not specified (5)	17	0.15
Austrian	67	0.58
Basque	5	0.04
British	8	0.07
Canadian	9	0.08
Croatian	24	0.21
Czech	10	0.09
Czechoslovakian	9	0.08
Danish	10	0.09
Dutch	45	0.39
Eastern European	152	1.32
English	716	6.23
Estonian	5	0.04
European	102	0.89
Finnish	12	0.10
French, except Basque	112	0.97
German	1,297	11.28
Greek	179	1.56
Hawaii Native/Pacific Islander:	4	0.03
Micronesian: (1)	1	0.01
Guamanian/Chamorro (1)	1	0.01
Polynesian: (1)	1	0.01
Native Hawaiian (1)	1	0.01
Other Pac. Isl., not spec.	2	0.02
Hispanic or Latino:	236	2.05
Central American:	13	0.11
Costa Rican	5	0.04
Guatemalan	3	0.03
Honduran	2	0.02
Salvadoran	3	0.03
Cuban	17	0.15
Dominican Republic	6	0.05
Mexican	28	0.24
Puerto Rican	97	0.84
South American:	19	0.16
Colombian	7	0.06
Ecuadorian	1	0.01

Notes: 1. Figures in the "Number" column do not add up to the total population due to: a) Ancestry/Race overlap — e.g. persons can report being both White and Irish, b) persons of Hispanic origin can report being any race, c) persons reporting two ancestries are counted in both categories. 2. Numbers in parentheses indicate the number of persons reporting this ancestry/race alone, not in combination with any other ancestry/race. 3. Refer to the Explanation of Data in the front of the book for more detailed information.

Uruguayan	3	0.03
Venezuelan	3	0.03
Other South American	5	0.04
Other Hispanic or Latino	56	0.49
Hungarian	104	0.90
Irish	1,690	14.70
Israeli	14	0.12
Italian	1,643	14.29
Lithuanian	213	1.85
Maltese	10	0.09
New Zealander	9	0.08
Northern European	8	0.07
Norwegian	70	0.61
Polish	828	7.20
Portuguese	6	0.05
Romanian	111	0.97
Russian	1,149	9.99
Scotch-Irish	110	0.96
Scottish	82	0.71
Slovak	17	0.15
Swedish	167	1.45
Swiss	52	0.45
Turkish	8	0.07
Ukrainian	201	1.75
United States or American	531	4.62
Welsh	92	0.80
West Indian, excl. Hispanic:	17	0.15
Jamaican	17	0.15
White:	9,020	78.19
Not Hispanic (8,806)	8,873	76.92
Hispanic (136)	147	1.27

Guttenberg

Place Type: Town
County: Hudson
Population: 10,807

Ancestry/Race	Number	%
African American/Black:	513	4.75
Not Hispanic (307)	349	3.23
Hispanic (105)	164	1.52
African, sub-Saharan:	36	0.34
African	9	0.08
Nigerian	27	0.25
Am. Ind. or Alaska Nat., not spec.	51	0.47
Albanian	18	0.17
American Indian tribes, specified:	24	0.22
Cherokee	4	0.04
Creek (3)	3	0.03
Latin American Indians (7)	13	0.12
Pueblo (1)	2	0.02
All other tribes (2)	2	0.02
American Indian tribes, not spec.	8	0.07
Arab:	182	1.70
Arab/Arabic	69	0.65
Egyptian	18	0.17
Jordanian	19	0.18
Lebanese	25	0.23
Moroccan	51	0.48
Armenian	29	0.27
Asian:	890	8.24
Chinese, ex. Taiwanese (157)	172	1.59
Filipino (41)	47	0.43
Indian (386)	430	3.98
Indonesian (1)	1	0.01
Japanese (60)	65	0.60
Korean (133)	141	1.30
Pakistani (3)	10	0.09
Taiwanese	2	0.02
Thai	2	0.02
Vietnamese (2)	2	0.02
Other Asian, specified (1)	1	0.01
Other Asian, not specified	17	0.16
Basque	7	0.07
Brazilian	86	0.80
British	12	0.11
Canadian	20	0.19
Croatian	49	0.46
Czech	41	0.38
Czechoslovakian	25	0.23
Danish	19	0.18
Dutch	77	0.72
Eastern European	8	0.07
English	168	1.57
European	35	0.33
French, except Basque	155	1.45
French Canadian	17	0.16
German	434	4.06
Greek	63	0.59
Hawaii Native/Pacific Islander:	15	0.14
Micronesian:	1	0.01
Guamanian/Chamorro	1	0.01
Polynesian: (1)	1	0.01
Native Hawaiian (1)	1	0.01
Other Pac. Isl., not spec.	13	0.12
Hispanic or Latino:	5,871	54.33
Central American:	582	5.39
Costa Rican	7	0.06
Guatemalan	62	0.57
Honduran	109	1.01
Nicaraguan	35	0.32
Panamanian	11	0.10
Salvadoran	318	2.94
Other Central American	40	0.37
Cuban	1,203	11.13
Dominican Republic	550	5.09
Mexican	233	2.16
Puerto Rican	608	5.63
South American:	1,410	13.05
Argentinean	76	0.70
Bolivian	8	0.07
Chilean	71	0.66
Colombian	571	5.28
Ecuadorian	419	3.88
Paraguayan	1	0.01
Peruvian	144	1.33
Uruguayan	22	0.20
Venezuelan	47	0.43
Other South American	51	0.47
Other Hispanic or Latino	1,285	11.89
Hungarian	17	0.16
Iranian	10	0.09
Irish	698	6.53
Israeli	11	0.10
Italian	983	9.19
New Zealander	17	0.16
Norwegian	41	0.38
Polish	170	1.59
Portuguese	73	0.68
Romanian	11	0.10
Russian	278	2.60
Scotch-Irish	78	0.73
Scottish	66	0.62
Slovak	20	0.19
Swedish	57	0.53
Swiss	21	0.20
Turkish	10	0.09
Ukrainian	56	0.52
United States or American	284	2.66
West Indian, excl. Hispanic:	113	1.06
British West Indian	23	0.22
Haitian	12	0.11
Jamaican	34	0.32
Trinidadian and Tobagonian	44	0.41
White:	7,669	70.96
Not Hispanic (3,485)	3,739	34.60
Hispanic (3,537)	3,930	36.37
Yugoslavian	69	0.65

Hackensack

Place Type: City
County: Bergen
Population: 42,677

Ancestry/Race	Number	%
Afghan	20	0.05
African American/Black:	11,307	26.49
Not Hispanic (10,092)	10,658	24.97
Hispanic (426)	649	1.52
African, sub-Saharan:	759	1.78
African	461	1.08
Ethiopian	4	0.01
Ghanian	86	0.20
Kenyan	15	0.04
Liberian	8	0.02
Nigerian	119	0.28
Sierra Leonean	29	0.07
Somalian	6	0.01
South African	10	0.02
Sudanese	12	0.03
Other sub-Saharan African	9	0.02
Alaska Native tribes, specified:	1	0.00
Alaska Athabascan (1)	1	0.00
Am. Ind. or Alaska Nat., not spec.	265	0.62
Albanian	33	0.08
Alsatian	7	0.02
American Indian tribes, specified:	186	0.44
Apache	1	0.00
Blackfeet (4)	23	0.05
Cherokee (14)	85	0.20
Chippewa (1)	1	0.00
Creek	1	0.00
Crow (1)	3	0.01
Delaware	5	0.01
Iroquois	7	0.02
Latin American Indians (15)	34	0.08
Lumbee	1	0.00
Navajo (1)	5	0.01
Pueblo (2)	2	0.00
Sioux (5)	9	0.02
All other tribes (1)	9	0.02
American Indian tribes, not spec.	29	0.07
Arab:	528	1.24
Arab/Arabic	59	0.14
Egyptian	223	0.52
Jordanian	13	0.03
Lebanese	67	0.16
Moroccan	14	0.03
Palestinian	23	0.05
Syrian	67	0.16
Other Arab	62	0.15
Armenian	134	0.31
Asian:	3,510	8.22
Bangladeshi (35)	47	0.11
Cambodian (1)	1	0.00
Chinese, ex. Taiwanese (313)	352	0.82
Filipino (809)	902	2.11
Indian (1,089)	1,167	2.73
Indonesian (16)	19	0.04
Japanese (132)	150	0.35
Korean (550)	576	1.35
Laotian (1)	3	0.01
Malaysian (1)	2	0.00
Pakistani (62)	76	0.18
Sri Lankan (6)	7	0.02
Taiwanese (28)	36	0.08
Thai (30)	32	0.07
Vietnamese (56)	59	0.14
Other Asian, specified	1	0.00
Other Asian, not specified (19)	80	0.19
Austrian	289	0.68
Belgian	9	0.02
Brazilian	79	0.19
British	121	0.28
Bulgarian	9	0.02
Canadian	23	0.05
Celtic	13	0.03
Croatian	32	0.07
Czech	112	0.26
Czechoslovakian	129	0.30
Danish	50	0.12
Dutch	211	0.49
Eastern European	82	0.19
English	895	2.10
Estonian	41	0.10
European	72	0.17
Finnish	64	0.15
French, except Basque	402	0.94

Notes: 1. Figures in the "Number" column do not add up to the total population due to: a) Ancestry/Race overlap — e.g. persons can report being both White and Irish, b) persons of Hispanic origin can report being any race, c) persons reporting two ancestries are counted in both categories. 2. Numbers in parentheses indicate the number of persons reporting this ancestry/race alone, not in combination with any other ancestry/race. 3. Refer to the Explanation of Data in the front of the book for more detailed information.

French Canadian	30	0.07
German	2,426	5.68
Greek	331	0.78
Guyanese	73	0.17
Hawaii Native/Pacific Islander:	62	0.15
Micronesian: (1)	2	0.00
Guamanian/Chamorro (1)	2	0.00
Polynesian: (5)	11	0.03
Native Hawaiian	6	0.01
Samoan (5)	5	0.01
Other Pac. Isl., not spec. (17)	49	0.11
Hispanic or Latino:	11,061	25.92
Central American:	554	1.30
Costa Rican	82	0.19
Guatemalan	77	0.18
Honduran	39	0.09
Nicaraguan	43	0.10
Panamanian	39	0.09
Salvadoran	254	0.60
Other Central American	20	0.05
Cuban	298	0.70
Dominican Republic	1,573	3.69
Mexican	340	0.80
Puerto Rican	1,371	3.21
South American:	4,266	10.00
Argentinean	74	0.17
Bolivian	49	0.11
Chilean	41	0.10
Colombian	1,634	3.83
Ecuadorian	2,040	4.78
Paraguayan	4	0.01
Peruvian	296	0.69
Uruguayan	30	0.07
Venezuelan	36	0.08
Other South American	62	0.15
Other Hispanic or Latino	2,659	6.23
Hungarian	328	0.77
Iranian	113	0.26
Irish	3,157	7.40
Israeli	92	0.22
Italian	5,831	13.66
Latvian	25	0.06
Lithuanian	117	0.27
Macedonian	106	0.25
Norwegian	115	0.27
Polish	1,416	3.32
Portuguese	112	0.26
Romanian	152	0.36
Russian	1,068	2.50
Scandinavian	6	0.01
Scotch-Irish	136	0.32
Scottish	206	0.48
Slavic	51	0.12
Slovak	30	0.07
Slovene	22	0.05
Swedish	52	0.12
Swiss	45	0.11
Turkish	64	0.15
Ukrainian	175	0.41
United States or American	1,225	2.87
Welsh	60	0.14
West Indian, excl. Hispanic:	1,816	4.26
Bahamian	30	0.07
Barbadian	14	0.03
Belizean	17	0.04
Bermudan	9	0.02
British West Indian	146	0.34
Haitian	106	0.25
Jamaican	1,226	2.87
Trinidadian and Tobagonian	197	0.46
West Indian	71	0.17
White:	24,007	56.25
Not Hispanic (17,013)	17,698	41.47
Hispanic (5,438)	6,309	14.78
Yugoslavian	59	0.14

Hackettstown

Place Type: Town
County: Warren
Population: 10,403

Ancestry/Race	Number	%
African American/Black:	283	2.72
Not Hispanic (221)	265	2.55
Hispanic (6)	18	0.17
African, sub-Saharan:	49	0.47
African	43	0.41
Other sub-Saharan African	6	0.06
Alaska Native tribes, specified:	1	0.01
Tlingit-Haida	1	0.01
Am. Ind. or Alaska Nat., not spec.	22	0.21
Albanian	10	0.10
American Indian tribes, specified:	27	0.26
Cherokee (1)	8	0.08
Chippewa	1	0.01
Comanche	1	0.01
Delaware	6	0.06
Iroquois	3	0.03
Lumbee (3)	3	0.03
Osage	1	0.01
Seminole	1	0.01
Sioux	1	0.01
Yaqui	1	0.01
All other tribes (1)	1	0.01
American Indian tribes, not spec.	1	0.01
Arab:	42	0.40
Egyptian	20	0.19
Lebanese	6	0.06
Moroccan	16	0.15
Asian:	369	3.55
Chinese, ex. Taiwanese (84)	95	0.91
Filipino (23)	34	0.33
Indian (80)	93	0.89
Indonesian	1	0.01
Japanese (20)	26	0.25
Korean (41)	46	0.44
Pakistani (8)	9	0.09
Taiwanese (1)	2	0.02
Thai (1)	1	0.01
Vietnamese (34)	36	0.35
Other Asian, specified (1)	1	0.01
Other Asian, not specified (7)	25	0.24
Austrian	69	0.66
Belgian	6	0.06
British	76	0.73
Canadian	5	0.05
Celtic	16	0.15
Croatian	12	0.12
Czech	18	0.17
Danish	41	0.39
Dutch	389	3.74
English	877	8.43
French, except Basque	197	1.89
French Canadian	83	0.80
German	2,087	20.06
Greek	60	0.58
Guyanese	31	0.30
Hawaii Native/Pacific Islander:	12	0.12
Micronesian: (4)	4	0.04
Guamanian/Chamorro (2)	2	0.02
Other Micronesian (2)	2	0.02
Other Pac. Isl., not spec. (2)	8	0.08
Hispanic or Latino:	833	8.01
Central American:	130	1.25
Costa Rican	69	0.66
Guatemalan	34	0.33
Honduran	13	0.12
Nicaraguan	3	0.03
Salvadoran	4	0.04
Other Central American	7	0.07
Cuban	48	0.46
Dominican Republic	13	0.12
Mexican	79	0.76
Puerto Rican	188	1.81
South American:	250	2.40
Argentinean	11	0.11
Chilean	24	0.23
Colombian	97	0.93
Ecuadorian	66	0.63
Paraguayan	1	0.01
Peruvian	43	0.41
Venezuelan	1	0.01
Other South American	7	0.07
Other Hispanic or Latino	125	1.20
Hungarian	189	1.82
Irish	1,982	19.05
Israeli	28	0.27
Italian	1,914	18.40
Latvian	20	0.19
Lithuanian	61	0.59
Northern European	9	0.09
Norwegian	95	0.91
Pennsylvania German	7	0.07
Polish	876	8.42
Romanian	6	0.06
Russian	84	0.81
Scandinavian	7	0.07
Scotch-Irish	203	1.95
Scottish	201	1.93
Slavic	14	0.13
Slovak	30	0.29
Swedish	92	0.88
Swiss	44	0.42
Ukrainian	155	1.49
United States or American	353	3.39
Welsh	96	0.92
West Indian, excl. Hispanic:	70	0.67
Barbadian	42	0.40
British West Indian	8	0.08
Jamaican	20	0.19
White:	9,597	92.25
Not Hispanic (8,814)	8,964	86.17
Hispanic (575)	633	6.08
Yugoslavian	118	1.13

Haddon

Place Type: Township
County: Camden
Population: 14,651

Ancestry/Race	Number	%
African American/Black:	199	1.36
Not Hispanic (162)	184	1.26
Hispanic (11)	15	0.10
Am. Ind. or Alaska Nat., not spec.	6	0.04
American Indian tribes, specified:	19	0.13
Apache	1	0.01
Cherokee (2)	3	0.02
Chippewa (1)	1	0.01
Creek	1	0.01
Delaware	1	0.01
Iroquois (1)	4	0.03
Navajo (1)	1	0.01
Ottawa	4	0.03
All other tribes (1)	3	0.02
Arab:	15	0.10
Arab/Arabic	15	0.10
Armenian	17	0.12
Asian:	341	2.33
Chinese, ex. Taiwanese (130)	139	0.95
Filipino (25)	39	0.27
Indian (36)	46	0.31
Japanese (12)	19	0.13
Korean (43)	47	0.32
Vietnamese (44)	44	0.30
Other Asian, not specified (4)	7	0.05
Austrian	107	0.73
Belgian	10	0.07
British	45	0.31
Canadian	4	0.03
Croatian	30	0.20
Czechoslovakian	23	0.16
Danish	16	0.11
Dutch	181	1.23

Notes: 1. Figures in the "Number" column do not add up to the total population due to: a) Ancestry/Race overlap — e.g. persons can report being both White and Irish, b) persons of Hispanic origin can report being any race, c) persons reporting two ancestries are counted in both categories. 2. Numbers in parentheses indicate the number of persons reporting this ancestry/race alone, not in combination with any other ancestry/race. 3. Refer to the Explanation of Data in the front of the book for more detailed information.

Eastern European	42	0.29
English	2,208	15.06
European	100	0.68
French, except Basque	261	1.78
French Canadian	30	0.20
German	3,695	25.20
Greek	133	0.91
Hawaii Native/Pacific Islander:	18	0.12
Micronesian: (5)	6	0.04
Guamanian/Chamorro (5)	6	0.04
Polynesian:	10	0.07
Native Hawaiian	8	0.05
Samoan	2	0.01
Other Pac. Isl., not spec. (1)	2	0.01
Hispanic or Latino:	226	1.54
Central American:	10	0.07
Costa Rican	1	0.01
Guatemalan	5	0.03
Honduran	1	0.01
Salvadoran	3	0.02
Cuban	19	0.13
Dominican Republic	8	0.05
Mexican	39	0.27
Puerto Rican	114	0.78
South American:	2	0.01
Peruvian	1	0.01
Venezuelan	1	0.01
Other Hispanic or Latino	34	0.23
Hungarian	150	1.02
Irish	4,394	29.97
Italian	3,653	24.92
Lithuanian	51	0.35
Maltese	12	0.08
Norwegian	134	0.91
Pennsylvania German	62	0.42
Polish	1,198	8.17
Portuguese	14	0.10
Romanian	14	0.10
Russian	178	1.21
Scandinavian	9	0.06
Scotch-Irish	255	1.74
Scottish	307	2.09
Serbian	11	0.08
Slovak	125	0.85
Swedish	160	1.09
Swiss	39	0.27
Ukrainian	82	0.56
United States or American	378	2.58
Welsh	177	1.21
White:	14,074	96.06
Not Hispanic (13,864)	13,942	95.16
Hispanic (116)	132	0.90
Yugoslavian	25	0.17

Haddonfield

Place Type: Borough
County: Camden
Population: 11,659

Ancestry/Race	Number	%
African American/Black:	179	1.54
Not Hispanic (146)	168	1.44
Hispanic (2)	11	0.09
African, sub-Saharan:	16	0.14
African	16	0.14
Am. Ind. or Alaska Nat., not spec.	12	0.10
American Indian tribes, specified:	15	0.13
Blackfeet	1	0.01
Cherokee (4)	8	0.07
Delaware (1)	2	0.02
Latin American Indians	3	0.03
All other tribes	1	0.01
American Indian tribes, not spec.	9	0.08
Arab:	49	0.42
Lebanese	31	0.27
Palestinian	6	0.05
Syrian	12	0.10
Armenian	57	0.49
Asian:	165	1.42
Chinese, ex. Taiwanese (39)	46	0.39
Filipino (19)	22	0.19
Indian (14)	17	0.15
Japanese (17)	26	0.22
Korean (27)	32	0.27
Pakistani (4)	4	0.03
Taiwanese (4)	4	0.03
Thai (1)	1	0.01
Other Asian, specified	2	0.02
Other Asian, not specified (5)	11	0.09
Australian	14	0.12
Austrian	117	1.00
Belgian	8	0.07
British	140	1.20
Canadian	53	0.45
Celtic	19	0.16
Croatian	12	0.10
Czech	66	0.57
Czechoslovakian	28	0.24
Danish	14	0.12
Dutch	142	1.22
Eastern European	86	0.74
English	2,251	19.31
European	84	0.72
Finnish	33	0.28
French, except Basque	309	2.65
French Canadian	56	0.48
German	2,433	20.87
Greek	116	0.99
Hawaii Native/Pacific Islander:	5	0.04
Micronesian: (2)	2	0.02
Guamanian/Chamorro (2)	2	0.02
Other Pac. Isl., specified	2	0.02
Other Pac. Isl., not spec. (1)	1	0.01
Hispanic or Latino:	170	1.46
Central American:	5	0.04
Honduran	3	0.03
Nicaraguan	2	0.02
Cuban	24	0.21
Dominican Republic	2	0.02
Mexican	22	0.19
Puerto Rican	54	0.46
South American:	36	0.31
Argentinean	6	0.05
Bolivian	1	0.01
Chilean	1	0.01
Colombian	7	0.06
Ecuadorian	12	0.10
Peruvian	8	0.07
Other South American	1	0.01
Other Hispanic or Latino	27	0.23
Hungarian	108	0.93
Iranian	7	0.06
Irish	3,523	30.21
Italian	2,221	19.05
Latvian	34	0.29
Lithuanian	91	0.78
Macedonian	5	0.04
Northern European	7	0.06
Norwegian	123	1.05
Pennsylvania German	31	0.27
Polish	901	7.73
Portuguese	8	0.07
Romanian	13	0.11
Russian	392	3.36
Scandinavian	7	0.06
Scotch-Irish	268	2.30
Scottish	388	3.33
Serbian	14	0.12
Slavic	8	0.07
Slovak	94	0.81
Swedish	155	1.33
Swiss	60	0.51
Turkish	7	0.06
Ukrainian	93	0.80
United States or American	247	2.12
Welsh	182	1.56
West Indian, excl. Hispanic:	17	0.15
Jamaican	7	0.06
West Indian	10	0.09
White:	11,319	97.08
Not Hispanic (11,121)	11,183	95.92
Hispanic (126)	136	1.17
Yugoslavian	5	0.04

Hamilton

Place Type: Township
County: Atlantic
Population: 20,499

Ancestry/Race	Number	%
African American/Black:	4,163	20.31
Not Hispanic (3,837)	4,010	19.56
Hispanic (112)	153	0.75
African, sub-Saharan:	207	1.01
African	207	1.01
Alaska Native tribes, specified:	1	0.00
Tlingit-Haida (1)	1	0.00
Am. Ind. or Alaska Nat., not spec.	66	0.32
American Indian tribes, specified:	97	0.47
Blackfeet (1)	6	0.03
Cherokee (7)	21	0.10
Chippewa (9)	16	0.08
Choctaw (1)	1	0.00
Creek (1)	6	0.03
Delaware (3)	13	0.06
Latin American Indians (6)	9	0.04
Potawatomi	5	0.02
Seminole	2	0.01
Shoshone (4)	6	0.03
Sioux (1)	2	0.01
All other tribes (3)	10	0.05
American Indian tribes, not spec.	7	0.03
Arab:	70	0.34
Egyptian	10	0.05
Lebanese	26	0.13
Syrian	34	0.17
Armenian	28	0.14
Asian:	764	3.73
Bangladeshi (5)	5	0.02
Chinese, ex. Taiwanese (216)	237	1.16
Filipino (122)	158	0.77
Indian (105)	106	0.52
Japanese (7)	21	0.10
Korean (57)	61	0.30
Laotian (35)	36	0.18
Pakistani (1)	1	0.00
Sri Lankan (10)	10	0.05
Taiwanese (11)	14	0.07
Thai (11)	15	0.07
Vietnamese (64)	70	0.34
Other Asian, specified (1)	1	0.00
Other Asian, not specified (21)	29	0.14
Austrian	86	0.42
Basque	8	0.04
Belgian	22	0.11
British	26	0.13
Canadian	61	0.30
Croatian	30	0.15
Czech	41	0.20
Czechoslovakian	11	0.05
Danish	42	0.20
Dutch	347	1.69
English	1,794	8.75
Estonian	9	0.04
European	93	0.45
Finnish	47	0.23
French, except Basque	430	2.10
French Canadian	106	0.52
German	4,030	19.66
Greek	62	0.30
Guyanese	19	0.09
Hawaii Native/Pacific Islander:	34	0.17
Melanesian: (1)	1	0.00
Fijian (1)	1	0.00
Micronesian:	9	0.04
Guamanian/Chamorro	7	0.03
Other Micronesian	2	0.01
Polynesian: (9)	12	0.06

Notes: 1. Figures in the "Number" column do not add up to the total population due to: a) Ancestry/Race overlap — e.g. persons can report being both White and Irish, b) persons of Hispanic origin can report being any race, c) persons reporting two ancestries are counted in both categories. 2. Numbers in parentheses indicate the number of persons reporting this ancestry/race alone, not in combination with any other ancestry/race. 3. Refer to the Explanation of Data in the front of the book for more detailed information.

Ancestry/Race	Number	%
Native Hawaiian (4)	7	0.03
Samoan (4)	4	0.02
Tongan (1)	1	0.00
Other Pac. Isl., not spec.	12	0.06
Hispanic or Latino:	1,621	7.91
Central American:	33	0.16
Costa Rican	1	0.00
Guatemalan	8	0.04
Honduran	10	0.05
Nicaraguan	7	0.03
Panamanian	2	0.01
Salvadoran	4	0.02
Other Central American	1	0.00
Cuban	34	0.17
Dominican Republic	73	0.36
Mexican	91	0.44
Puerto Rican	960	4.68
South American:	94	0.46
Argentinean	6	0.03
Chilean	3	0.01
Colombian	55	0.27
Ecuadorian	20	0.10
Peruvian	3	0.01
Venezuelan	3	0.01
Other South American	4	0.02
Other Hispanic or Latino	336	1.64
Hungarian	161	0.79
Iranian	10	0.05
Irish	3,780	18.44
Israeli	6	0.03
Italian	3,520	17.17
Latvian	23	0.11
Lithuanian	60	0.29
Norwegian	208	1.01
Pennsylvania German	6	0.03
Polish	1,035	5.05
Portuguese	6	0.03
Romanian	39	0.19
Russian	181	0.88
Scandinavian	28	0.14
Scotch-Irish	187	0.91
Scottish	283	1.38
Slavic	9	0.04
Slovak	56	0.27
Swedish	119	0.58
Swiss	36	0.18
Ukrainian	217	1.06
United States or American	504	2.46
Welsh	84	0.41
West Indian, excl. Hispanic:	133	0.65
Barbadian	9	0.04
Haitian	11	0.05
Jamaican	65	0.32
West Indian	48	0.23
White:	15,021	73.28
Not Hispanic (13,952)	14,238	69.46
Hispanic (694)	783	3.82
Yugoslavian	35	0.17

Hamilton

Place Type: Township
County: Mercer
Population: 87,109

Ancestry/Race	Number	%
Afghan	29	0.03
African American/Black:	7,774	8.92
Not Hispanic (6,907)	7,489	8.60
Hispanic (205)	285	0.33
African, sub-Saharan:	435	0.50
African	229	0.26
Liberian	187	0.21
Nigerian	8	0.01
South African	11	0.01
Alaska Native tribes, specified:	2	0.00
Alaska Athabascan (1)	2	0.00
Am. Ind. or Alaska Nat., not spec.	155	0.18
Alsatian	40	0.05
American Indian tribes, specified:	184	0.21
Apache (1)	4	0.00
Blackfeet	12	0.01
Cherokee (17)	70	0.08
Chippewa	2	0.00
Choctaw	2	0.00
Cree (1)	1	0.00
Crow	1	0.00
Delaware (4)	16	0.02
Houma (4)	4	0.00
Iroquois (7)	14	0.02
Kiowa (1)	1	0.00
Latin American Indians (11)	16	0.02
Lumbee (3)	4	0.00
Navajo (3)	6	0.01
Seminole (1)	5	0.01
Sioux (2)	9	0.01
All other tribes (11)	17	0.02
American Indian tribes, not spec.	16	0.02
Arab:	537	0.62
Arab/Arabic	38	0.04
Egyptian	301	0.34
Jordanian	26	0.03
Lebanese	99	0.11
Syrian	57	0.07
Other Arab	16	0.02
Armenian	40	0.05
Asian:	2,576	2.96
Bangladeshi	6	0.01
Cambodian (21)	23	0.03
Chinese, ex. Taiwanese (374)	430	0.49
Filipino (276)	315	0.36
Indian (831)	901	1.03
Japanese (36)	75	0.09
Korean (334)	353	0.41
Malaysian (2)	7	0.01
Pakistani (234)	270	0.31
Sri Lankan (11)	11	0.01
Taiwanese (5)	17	0.02
Thai (3)	3	0.00
Vietnamese (37)	39	0.04
Other Asian, specified (6)	13	0.01
Other Asian, not specified (44)	113	0.13
Austrian	334	0.38
Belgian	80	0.09
Brazilian	55	0.06
British	424	0.49
Bulgarian	10	0.01
Canadian	86	0.10
Carpatho Rusyn	7	0.01
Celtic	39	0.04
Croatian	67	0.08
Cypriot	19	0.02
Czech	404	0.46
Czechoslovakian	465	0.53
Danish	222	0.25
Dutch	1,019	1.17
Eastern European	73	0.08
English	8,574	9.83
Estonian	11	0.01
European	155	0.18
Finnish	31	0.04
French, except Basque	1,395	1.60
French Canadian	460	0.53
German	14,425	16.53
Greek	604	0.69
Guyanese	65	0.07
Hawaii Native/Pacific Islander:	77	0.09
Melanesian:	1	0.00
Other Melanesian	1	0.00
Micronesian: (20)	24	0.03
Guamanian/Chamorro (20)	24	0.03
Polynesian: (5)	10	0.01
Native Hawaiian (2)	6	0.01
Samoan (3)	4	0.00
Other Pac. Isl., specified	7	0.01
Other Pac. Isl., not spec. (6)	35	0.04
Hispanic or Latino:	4,471	5.13
Central American:	534	0.61
Costa Rican	111	0.13
Guatemalan	317	0.36
Honduran	18	0.02
Nicaraguan	11	0.01
Panamanian	18	0.02
Salvadoran	19	0.02
Other Central American	40	0.05
Cuban	113	0.13
Dominican Republic	154	0.18
Mexican	221	0.25
Puerto Rican	2,409	2.77
South American:	267	0.31
Argentinean	33	0.04
Bolivian	1	0.00
Chilean	12	0.01
Colombian	91	0.10
Ecuadorian	69	0.08
Peruvian	10	0.01
Uruguayan	3	0.00
Venezuelan	35	0.04
Other South American	13	0.01
Other Hispanic or Latino	773	0.89
Hungarian	3,648	4.18
Iranian	50	0.06
Irish	15,948	18.28
Israeli	53	0.06
Italian	22,684	26.00
Lithuanian	340	0.39
Luxemburger	18	0.02
Macedonian	8	0.01
Northern European	42	0.05
Norwegian	485	0.56
Pennsylvania German	140	0.16
Polish	10,751	12.32
Portuguese	183	0.21
Romanian	282	0.32
Russian	969	1.11
Scandinavian	25	0.03
Scotch-Irish	964	1.10
Scottish	1,401	1.61
Serbian	12	0.01
Slavic	339	0.39
Slovak	1,785	2.05
Slovene	36	0.04
Swedish	486	0.56
Swiss	88	0.10
Turkish	100	0.11
Ukrainian	1,208	1.38
United States or American	2,537	2.91
Welsh	451	0.52
West Indian, excl. Hispanic:	1,351	1.55
British West Indian	25	0.03
Haitian	914	1.05
Jamaican	342	0.39
Trinidadian and Tobagonian	64	0.07
West Indian	6	0.01
White:	75,198	86.33
Not Hispanic (72,118)	72,843	83.62
Hispanic (2,055)	2,355	2.70
Yugoslavian	79	0.09

Hammonton

Place Type: Town
County: Atlantic
Population: 12,604

Ancestry/Race	Number	%
African American/Black:	256	2.03
Not Hispanic (187)	208	1.65
Hispanic (32)	48	0.38
Am. Ind. or Alaska Nat., not spec.	22	0.17
American Indian tribes, specified:	27	0.21
Blackfeet	1	0.01
Cherokee	5	0.04
Chippewa (1)	1	0.01
Delaware	2	0.02
Iroquois	3	0.02
Lumbee	1	0.01
Seminole (2)	7	0.06
Sioux	4	0.03
All other tribes (1)	3	0.02

Notes: 1. Figures in the "Number" column do not add up to the total population due to: a) Ancestry/Race overlap — e.g. persons can report being both White and Irish, b) persons of Hispanic origin can report being any race, c) persons reporting two ancestries are counted in both categories. 2. Numbers in parentheses indicate the number of persons reporting this ancestry/race alone, not in combination with any other ancestry/race. 3. Refer to the Explanation of Data in the front of the book for more detailed information.

Ancestry/Race	Number	%
American Indian tribes, not spec.	4	0.03
Arab:	19	0.15
Lebanese	19	0.15
Armenian	6	0.05
Asian:	163	1.29
Cambodian (1)	2	0.02
Chinese, ex. Taiwanese (42)	43	0.34
Filipino (48)	53	0.42
Indian (24)	25	0.20
Japanese (4)	8	0.06
Korean (15)	21	0.17
Vietnamese (3)	3	0.02
Other Asian, not specified (7)	8	0.06
Belgian	6	0.05
British	8	0.06
Czechoslovakian	25	0.20
Danish	25	0.20
Dutch	76	0.60
English	730	5.79
European	20	0.16
Finnish	7	0.06
French, except Basque	209	1.66
French Canadian	43	0.34
German	1,519	12.05
Greek	40	0.32
Hawaii Native/Pacific Islander:	7	0.06
Micronesian: (1)	1	0.01
Guamanian/Chamorro (1)	1	0.01
Polynesian: (2)	2	0.02
Native Hawaiian (2)	2	0.02
Other Pac. Isl., not spec.	4	0.03
Hispanic or Latino:	1,876	14.88
Central American:	46	0.36
Guatemalan	5	0.04
Honduran	34	0.27
Nicaraguan	1	0.01
Salvadoran	6	0.05
Cuban	11	0.09
Dominican Republic	12	0.10
Mexican	685	5.43
Puerto Rican	994	7.89
South American:	28	0.22
Argentinean	6	0.05
Colombian	14	0.11
Ecuadorian	2	0.02
Peruvian	6	0.05
Other Hispanic or Latino	100	0.79
Hungarian	69	0.55
Irish	1,856	14.73
Italian	6,841	54.28
Lithuanian	56	0.44
Norwegian	43	0.34
Polish	515	4.09
Russian	53	0.42
Scotch-Irish	63	0.50
Scottish	88	0.70
Serbian	9	0.07
Slavic	7	0.06
Slovak	31	0.25
Swedish	73	0.58
Swiss	28	0.22
Ukrainian	123	0.98
United States or American	173	1.37
Welsh	47	0.37
White:	11,210	88.94
Not Hispanic (10,292)	10,373	82.30
Hispanic (781)	837	6.64

Hanover

Place Type: Township
County: Morris
Population: 12,898

Ancestry/Race	Number	%
African American/Black:	142	1.10
Not Hispanic (127)	128	0.99
Hispanic (13)	14	0.11
African, sub-Saharan:	6	0.05
African	6	0.05
Am. Ind. or Alaska Nat., not spec.	10	0.08
American Indian tribes, specified:	7	0.05
Blackfeet (1)	1	0.01
Cherokee	3	0.02
Delaware	1	0.01
Latin American Indians (1)	1	0.01
Sioux (1)	1	0.01
Arab:	38	0.29
Arab/Arabic	7	0.05
Syrian	31	0.24
Armenian	32	0.25
Asian:	1,189	9.22
Chinese, ex. Taiwanese (551)	571	4.43
Filipino (77)	96	0.74
Indian (231)	243	1.88
Indonesian (2)	3	0.02
Japanese (36)	37	0.29
Korean (73)	75	0.58
Pakistani (11)	15	0.12
Taiwanese (87)	102	0.79
Thai (1)	3	0.02
Vietnamese (29)	33	0.26
Other Asian, specified (9)	11	0.09
Assyrian/Chaldean/Syriac	14	0.11
Austrian	63	0.49
Belgian	6	0.05
Brazilian	7	0.05
British	10	0.08
Canadian	58	0.45
Carpatho Rusyn	19	0.15
Czech	23	0.18
Czechoslovakian	44	0.34
Danish	14	0.11
Dutch	154	1.19
Eastern European	22	0.17
English	1,169	9.06
European	74	0.57
Finnish	37	0.29
French, except Basque	236	1.83
French Canadian	82	0.64
German	2,000	15.51
Greek	151	1.17
Guyanese	7	0.05
Hawaii Native/Pacific Islander:	5	0.04
Polynesian: (1)	1	0.01
Samoan (1)	1	0.01
Other Pac. Isl., not spec.	4	0.03
Hispanic or Latino:	452	3.50
Central American:	55	0.43
Costa Rican	5	0.04
Guatemalan	18	0.14
Honduran	9	0.07
Nicaraguan	2	0.02
Panamanian	1	0.01
Salvadoran	12	0.09
Other Central American	8	0.06
Cuban	56	0.43
Dominican Republic	19	0.15
Mexican	44	0.34
Puerto Rican	63	0.49
South American:	108	0.84
Argentinean	9	0.07
Bolivian	3	0.02
Chilean	6	0.05
Colombian	37	0.29
Ecuadorian	28	0.22
Paraguayan	3	0.02
Peruvian	11	0.09
Uruguayan	1	0.01
Venezuelan	6	0.05
Other South American	4	0.03
Other Hispanic or Latino	107	0.83
Hungarian	135	1.05
Icelander	10	0.08
Irish	2,716	21.06
Israeli	6	0.05
Italian	3,917	30.37
Latvian	7	0.05
Lithuanian	60	0.47
Norwegian	80	0.62
Pennsylvania German	16	0.12
Polish	1,255	9.73
Portuguese	35	0.27
Romanian	19	0.15
Russian	208	1.61
Scandinavian	37	0.29
Scotch-Irish	152	1.18
Scottish	265	2.05
Serbian	5	0.04
Slavic	21	0.16
Slovak	116	0.90
Slovene	7	0.05
Swedish	107	0.83
Swiss	51	0.40
Turkish	9	0.07
Ukrainian	454	3.52
United States or American	488	3.78
Welsh	35	0.27
West Indian, excl. Hispanic:	5	0.04
Bermudan	5	0.04
White:	11,529	89.39
Not Hispanic (11,113)	11,164	86.56
Hispanic (339)	365	2.83
Yugoslavian	13	0.10

Harrison

Place Type: Town
County: Hudson
Population: 14,424

Ancestry/Race	Number	%
African American/Black:	185	1.28
Not Hispanic (87)	104	0.72
Hispanic (55)	81	0.56
African, sub-Saharan:	87	0.60
African	39	0.27
Cape Verdean	28	0.19
South African	8	0.06
Other sub-Saharan African	12	0.08
Am. Ind. or Alaska Nat., not spec.	51	0.35
American Indian tribes, specified:	45	0.31
Cherokee (1)	4	0.03
Iroquois	1	0.01
Latin American Indians (20)	34	0.24
Navajo	1	0.01
Pima	1	0.01
Pueblo (4)	4	0.03
American Indian tribes, not spec.	7	0.05
Arab:	61	0.42
Arab/Arabic	14	0.10
Egyptian	28	0.19
Jordanian	7	0.05
Moroccan	12	0.08
Asian:	1,822	12.63
Bangladeshi (11)	11	0.08
Chinese, ex. Taiwanese (1,007)	1,042	7.22
Filipino (77)	87	0.60
Indian (350)	381	2.64
Japanese (11)	17	0.12
Korean (13)	13	0.09
Pakistani (138)	168	1.16
Sri Lankan (2)	2	0.01
Taiwanese (34)	42	0.29
Thai (9)	12	0.08
Vietnamese (1)	2	0.01
Other Asian, specified (8)	8	0.06
Other Asian, not specified (21)	37	0.26
Brazilian	726	5.03
British	20	0.14
Bulgarian	15	0.10
Canadian	13	0.09
Czech	20	0.14
Czechoslovakian	10	0.07
Dutch	31	0.21
English	137	0.95
European	54	0.37
French, except Basque	69	0.48
German	389	2.70
Greek	64	0.44

Notes: 1. Figures in the "Number" column do not add up to the total population due to: a) Ancestry/Race overlap — e.g. persons can report being both White and Irish, b) persons of Hispanic origin can report being any race, c) persons reporting two ancestries are counted in both categories. 2. Numbers in parentheses indicate the number of persons reporting this ancestry/race alone, not in combination with any other ancestry/race. 3. Refer to the Explanation of Data in the front of the book for more detailed information.

Ancestry/Race	Number	%
Guyanese	70	0.49
Hawaii Native/Pacific Islander:	25	0.17
Polynesian:	3	0.02
Native Hawaiian	2	0.01
Other Polynesian	1	0.01
Other Pac. Isl., not spec. (4)	22	0.15
Hispanic or Latino:	5,333	36.97
Central American:	226	1.57
Costa Rican	25	0.17
Guatemalan	61	0.42
Honduran	34	0.24
Nicaraguan	35	0.24
Panamanian	3	0.02
Salvadoran	56	0.39
Other Central American	12	0.08
Cuban	438	3.04
Dominican Republic	225	1.56
Mexican	139	0.96
Puerto Rican	605	4.19
South American:	2,034	14.10
Argentinean	46	0.32
Chilean	30	0.21
Colombian	172	1.19
Ecuadorian	562	3.90
Peruvian	1,011	7.01
Uruguayan	66	0.46
Venezuelan	41	0.28
Other South American	106	0.73
Other Hispanic or Latino	1,666	11.55
Hungarian	35	0.24
Irish	1,117	7.74
Italian	1,095	7.59
Lithuanian	120	0.83
Polish	1,161	8.05
Portuguese	1,961	13.60
Romanian	15	0.10
Russian	54	0.37
Scotch-Irish	153	1.06
Scottish	67	0.46
Slavic	9	0.06
Slovak	17	0.12
Swedish	6	0.04
Turkish	6	0.04
Ukrainian	53	0.37
United States or American	360	2.50
Welsh	7	0.05
White:	10,148	70.35
Not Hispanic (6,756)	7,046	48.85
Hispanic (2,778)	3,102	21.51

Hasbrouck Heights

Place Type: Borough
County: Bergen
Population: 11,662

Ancestry/Race	Number	%
African American/Black:	249	2.14
Not Hispanic (188)	209	1.79
Hispanic (12)	40	0.34
African, sub-Saharan:	58	0.50
African	42	0.36
South African	16	0.14
Am. Ind. or Alaska Nat., not spec.	14	0.12
American Indian tribes, specified:	7	0.06
Apache	1	0.01
Blackfeet	2	0.02
Delaware	2	0.02
Latin American Indians	1	0.01
Seminole (1)	1	0.01
Arab:	146	1.25
Jordanian	37	0.32
Lebanese	31	0.27
Palestinian	23	0.20
Syrian	55	0.47
Armenian	109	0.93
Asian:	850	7.29
Bangladeshi (5)	5	0.04
Chinese, ex. Taiwanese (71)	85	0.73
Filipino (132)	150	1.29
Indian (280)	299	2.56
Indonesian (4)	4	0.03
Japanese (18)	22	0.19
Korean (185)	188	1.61
Laotian	5	0.04
Pakistani (25)	29	0.25
Taiwanese (11)	12	0.10
Thai (15)	17	0.15
Other Asian, not specified (14)	34	0.29
Australian	9	0.08
Austrian	30	0.26
Belgian	67	0.57
Brazilian	30	0.26
British	43	0.37
Canadian	70	0.60
Croatian	56	0.48
Czech	9	0.08
Czechoslovakian	73	0.63
Danish	34	0.29
Dutch	291	2.50
Eastern European	11	0.09
English	481	4.12
French, except Basque	202	1.73
French Canadian	28	0.24
German	1,784	15.30
Greek	32	0.27
Hawaii Native/Pacific Islander:	3	0.03
Polynesian: (1)	1	0.01
Native Hawaiian (1)	1	0.01
Other Pac. Isl., not spec.	2	0.02
Hispanic or Latino:	964	8.27
Central American:	35	0.30
Costa Rican	3	0.03
Guatemalan	4	0.03
Honduran	3	0.03
Nicaraguan	3	0.03
Salvadoran	16	0.14
Other Central American	6	0.05
Cuban	184	1.58
Dominican Republic	67	0.57
Mexican	28	0.24
Puerto Rican	241	2.07
South American:	220	1.89
Argentinean	21	0.18
Bolivian	4	0.03
Chilean	7	0.06
Colombian	90	0.77
Ecuadorian	59	0.51
Peruvian	32	0.27
Uruguayan	1	0.01
Venezuelan	4	0.03
Other South American	2	0.02
Other Hispanic or Latino	189	1.62
Hungarian	76	0.65
Iranian	27	0.23
Irish	1,997	17.12
Italian	4,486	38.47
Lithuanian	13	0.11
Macedonian	47	0.40
Norwegian	36	0.31
Polish	1,177	10.09
Portuguese	53	0.45
Romanian	32	0.27
Russian	218	1.87
Scandinavian	14	0.12
Scotch-Irish	70	0.60
Scottish	107	0.92
Serbian	8	0.07
Slavic	29	0.25
Slovak	68	0.58
Swedish	54	0.46
Swiss	32	0.27
Ukrainian	186	1.59
United States or American	192	1.65
Welsh	17	0.15
West Indian, excl. Hispanic:	37	0.32
Bahamian	24	0.21
British West Indian	6	0.05
West Indian	7	0.06
White:	10,403	89.20
Not Hispanic (9,611)	9,705	83.22
Hispanic (636)	698	5.99
Yugoslavian	8	0.07

Hawthorne

Place Type: Borough
County: Passaic
Population: 18,218

Ancestry/Race	Number	%
African American/Black:	189	1.04
Not Hispanic (130)	155	0.85
Hispanic (7)	34	0.19
Alaska Native tribes, not specified	1	0.01
Am. Ind. or Alaska Nat., not spec.	14	0.08
Albanian	39	0.21
Alsatian	8	0.04
American Indian tribes, specified:	43	0.24
Blackfeet	1	0.01
Cherokee (1)	7	0.04
Choctaw (1)	1	0.01
Delaware	1	0.01
Iroquois (4)	4	0.02
Latin American Indians (11)	15	0.08
Navajo	9	0.05
Pueblo (3)	3	0.02
All other tribes	2	0.01
American Indian tribes, not spec.	7	0.04
Arab:	521	2.86
Arab/Arabic	65	0.36
Egyptian	29	0.16
Iraqi	18	0.10
Jordanian	79	0.43
Lebanese	37	0.20
Palestinian	10	0.05
Syrian	266	1.46
Other Arab	17	0.09
Armenian	29	0.16
Asian:	427	2.34
Bangladeshi (2)	2	0.01
Chinese, ex. Taiwanese (54)	59	0.32
Filipino (51)	74	0.41
Indian (159)	170	0.93
Indonesian (3)	4	0.02
Japanese (16)	19	0.10
Korean (28)	46	0.25
Pakistani (10)	16	0.09
Taiwanese (2)	2	0.01
Vietnamese (4)	4	0.02
Other Asian, specified	1	0.01
Other Asian, not specified (15)	30	0.16
Assyrian/Chaldean/Syriac	12	0.07
Australian	9	0.05
Austrian	112	0.61
Belgian	55	0.30
Brazilian	8	0.04
British	43	0.24
Canadian	34	0.19
Croatian	44	0.24
Czech	24	0.13
Czechoslovakian	17	0.09
Danish	51	0.28
Dutch	2,014	11.06
Eastern European	24	0.13
English	1,171	6.43
European	14	0.08
Finnish	9	0.05
French, except Basque	463	2.54
French Canadian	104	0.57
German	2,671	14.66
Greek	125	0.69
Hawaii Native/Pacific Islander:	29	0.16
Polynesian:	2	0.01
Native Hawaiian	1	0.01
Samoan	1	0.01
Other Pac. Isl., specified	1	0.01
Other Pac. Isl., not spec. (3)	26	0.14
Hispanic or Latino:	1,354	7.43
Central American:	122	0.67

Notes: 1. Figures in the "Number" column do not add up to the total population due to: a) Ancestry/Race overlap — e.g. persons can report being both White and Irish, b) persons of Hispanic origin can report being any race, c) persons reporting two ancestries are counted in both categories. 2. Numbers in parentheses indicate the number of persons reporting this ancestry/race alone, not in combination with any other ancestry/race. 3. Refer to the Explanation of Data in the front of the book for more detailed information.

Ancestry/Race	Number	%
Costa Rican	63	0.35
Guatemalan	13	0.07
Honduran	1	0.01
Nicaraguan	8	0.04
Salvadoran	27	0.15
Other Central American	10	0.05
Cuban	99	0.54
Dominican Republic	77	0.42
Mexican	55	0.30
Puerto Rican	345	1.89
South American:	336	1.84
Argentinean	6	0.03
Bolivian	4	0.02
Chilean	11	0.06
Colombian	96	0.53
Ecuadorian	55	0.30
Peruvian	147	0.81
Uruguayan	4	0.02
Venezuelan	7	0.04
Other South American	6	0.03
Other Hispanic or Latino	320	1.76
Hungarian	303	1.66
Icelander	12	0.07
Iranian	33	0.18
Irish	3,267	17.93
Italian	6,096	33.46
Lithuanian	41	0.23
Northern European	17	0.09
Norwegian	69	0.38
Polish	1,182	6.49
Portuguese	63	0.35
Romanian	13	0.07
Russian	249	1.37
Scotch-Irish	148	0.81
Scottish	349	1.92
Serbian	39	0.21
Slavic	38	0.21
Slovak	59	0.32
Swedish	73	0.40
Swiss	162	0.89
Turkish	70	0.38
Ukrainian	148	0.81
United States or American	453	2.49
Welsh	73	0.40
West Indian, excl. Hispanic:	17	0.09
Jamaican	17	0.09
White:	17,368	95.33
Not Hispanic (16,141)	16,341	89.70
Hispanic (939)	1,027	5.64
Yugoslavian	34	0.19

Hazlet

Place Type: Township
County: Monmouth
Population: 21,378

Ancestry/Race	Number	%
African American/Black:	290	1.36
Not Hispanic (210)	251	1.17
Hispanic (25)	39	0.18
African, sub-Saharan:	4	0.02
African	4	0.02
Alaska Native tribes, not specified	4	0.02
Am. Ind. or Alaska Nat., not spec.	15	0.07
Albanian	6	0.03
American Indian tribes, specified:	36	0.17
Apache	1	0.00
Blackfeet	5	0.02
Cherokee (1)	9	0.04
Cheyenne (1)	2	0.01
Delaware	3	0.01
Iroquois (1)	7	0.03
Latin American Indians	5	0.02
Pueblo	1	0.00
All other tribes (2)	3	0.01
Arab:	140	0.65
Egyptian	93	0.44
Jordanian	22	0.10
Lebanese	25	0.12
Armenian	16	0.07
Asian:	798	3.73
Chinese, ex. Taiwanese (256)	268	1.25
Filipino (222)	264	1.23
Indian (170)	177	0.83
Indonesian (1)	1	0.00
Japanese (11)	13	0.06
Korean (30)	39	0.18
Pakistani (10)	11	0.05
Thai (4)	5	0.02
Other Asian, not specified (10)	20	0.09
Austrian	192	0.90
Brazilian	24	0.11
British	57	0.27
Canadian	40	0.19
Croatian	23	0.11
Czech	110	0.51
Czechoslovakian	32	0.15
Danish	119	0.56
Dutch	215	1.01
Eastern European	39	0.18
English	1,422	6.65
European	43	0.20
Finnish	20	0.09
French, except Basque	360	1.68
French Canadian	152	0.71
German	3,144	14.71
Greek	303	1.42
Guyanese	65	0.30
Hawaii Native/Pacific Islander:	9	0.04
Micronesian:	1	0.00
Guamanian/Chamorro	1	0.00
Polynesian: (1)	2	0.01
Native Hawaiian	1	0.00
Samoan (1)	1	0.00
Other Pac. Isl., not spec.	6	0.03
Hispanic or Latino:	1,254	5.87
Central American:	42	0.20
Costa Rican	4	0.02
Guatemalan	10	0.05
Honduran	5	0.02
Panamanian	12	0.06
Salvadoran	8	0.04
Other Central American	3	0.01
Cuban	107	0.50
Dominican Republic	18	0.08
Mexican	137	0.64
Puerto Rican	564	2.64
South American:	152	0.71
Argentinean	14	0.07
Colombian	54	0.25
Ecuadorian	27	0.13
Paraguayan	2	0.01
Peruvian	36	0.17
Uruguayan	7	0.03
Venezuelan	6	0.03
Other South American	6	0.03
Other Hispanic or Latino	234	1.09
Hungarian	345	1.61
Irish	7,033	32.90
Italian	7,032	32.89
Lithuanian	49	0.23
Maltese	53	0.25
Norwegian	242	1.13
Pennsylvania German	8	0.04
Polish	1,647	7.70
Portuguese	169	0.79
Romanian	57	0.27
Russian	295	1.38
Scandinavian	7	0.03
Scotch-Irish	249	1.16
Scottish	330	1.54
Slavic	16	0.07
Slovak	143	0.67
Swedish	287	1.34
Swiss	22	0.10
Ukrainian	132	0.62
United States or American	539	2.52
Welsh	29	0.14
West Indian, excl. Hispanic:	58	0.27
Barbadian	29	0.14
Haitian	12	0.06
Jamaican	11	0.05
West Indian	6	0.03
White:	20,135	94.19
Not Hispanic (18,989)	19,138	89.52
Hispanic (929)	997	4.66
Yugoslavian	42	0.20

Highland Park

Place Type: Borough
County: Middlesex
Population: 13,999

Ancestry/Race	Number	%
African American/Black:	1,244	8.89
Not Hispanic (1,067)	1,156	8.26
Hispanic (44)	88	0.63
African, sub-Saharan:	186	1.33
African	28	0.20
Ethiopian	22	0.16
Nigerian	10	0.07
Sierra Leonean	110	0.79
South African	16	0.11
Am. Ind. or Alaska Nat., not spec.	42	0.30
Albanian	26	0.19
American Indian tribes, specified:	35	0.25
Cherokee (1)	14	0.10
Chippewa	3	0.02
Creek	1	0.01
Iroquois	1	0.01
Latin American Indians (2)	10	0.07
Shoshone	1	0.01
Sioux	1	0.01
Yaqui	1	0.01
All other tribes	3	0.02
American Indian tribes, not spec.	1	0.01
Arab:	123	0.88
Arab/Arabic	11	0.08
Egyptian	28	0.20
Lebanese	42	0.30
Moroccan	10	0.07
Other Arab	32	0.23
Armenian	23	0.16
Asian:	2,043	14.59
Bangladeshi (17)	18	0.13
Cambodian (1)	1	0.01
Chinese, ex. Taiwanese (699)	731	5.22
Filipino (83)	91	0.65
Indian (663)	694	4.96
Indonesian (6)	6	0.04
Japanese (64)	79	0.56
Korean (233)	241	1.72
Laotian (1)	2	0.01
Malaysian	1	0.01
Pakistani (41)	46	0.33
Sri Lankan (3)	7	0.05
Taiwanese (31)	39	0.28
Thai (9)	11	0.08
Vietnamese (21)	26	0.19
Other Asian, specified (1)	2	0.01
Other Asian, not specified (25)	48	0.34
Assyrian/Chaldean/Syriac	7	0.05
Austrian	95	0.68
Belgian	33	0.24
Brazilian	58	0.41
British	79	0.56
Canadian	17	0.12
Croatian	13	0.09
Czech	65	0.46
Czechoslovakian	55	0.39
Danish	10	0.07
Dutch	70	0.50
Eastern European	315	2.25
English	704	5.03
European	155	1.11
Finnish	10	0.07
French, except Basque	168	1.20
French Canadian	55	0.39

Notes: 1. Figures in the "Number" column do not add up to the total population due to: a) Ancestry/Race overlap — e.g. persons can report being both White and Irish, b) persons of Hispanic origin can report being any race, c) persons reporting two ancestries are counted in both categories. 2. Numbers in parentheses indicate the number of persons reporting this ancestry/race alone, not in combination with any other ancestry/race. 3. Refer to the Explanation of Data in the front of the book for more detailed information.

Ancestry/Race	Number	%
German	1,129	8.06
Greek	221	1.58
Guyanese	32	0.23
Hawaii Native/Pacific Islander:	21	0.15
Micronesian: (2)	2	0.01
Guamanian/Chamorro (2)	2	0.01
Polynesian: (1)	1	0.01
Samoan (1)	1	0.01
Other Pac. Isl., not spec. (9)	18	0.13
Hispanic or Latino:	1,145	8.18
Central American:	91	0.65
Costa Rican	4	0.03
Guatemalan	10	0.07
Honduran	30	0.21
Nicaraguan	7	0.05
Panamanian	13	0.09
Salvadoran	12	0.09
Other Central American	15	0.11
Cuban	46	0.33
Dominican Republic	27	0.19
Mexican	247	1.76
Puerto Rican	287	2.05
South American:	217	1.55
Argentinean	23	0.16
Bolivian	12	0.09
Chilean	9	0.06
Colombian	49	0.35
Ecuadorian	49	0.35
Peruvian	58	0.41
Uruguayan	4	0.03
Venezuelan	3	0.02
Other South American	10	0.07
Other Hispanic or Latino	230	1.64
Hungarian	655	4.68
Iranian	4	0.03
Irish	1,272	9.09
Israeli	114	0.81
Italian	1,373	9.81
Latvian	62	0.44
Lithuanian	59	0.42
Northern European	11	0.08
Norwegian	88	0.63
Polish	1,052	7.51
Portuguese	6	0.04
Romanian	132	0.94
Russian	1,091	7.79
Scandinavian	28	0.20
Scotch-Irish	75	0.54
Scottish	213	1.52
Serbian	11	0.08
Slavic	25	0.18
Slovak	53	0.38
Slovene	23	0.16
Swedish	104	0.74
Swiss	30	0.21
Turkish	59	0.42
Ukrainian	203	1.45
United States or American	438	3.13
Welsh	61	0.44
West Indian, excl. Hispanic:	186	1.33
Barbadian	9	0.06
Jamaican	73	0.52
Trinidadian and Tobagonian	72	0.51
U.S. Virgin Islander	13	0.09
West Indian	19	0.14
White:	10,341	73.87
Not Hispanic (9,517)	9,716	69.40
Hispanic (570)	625	4.46

Hillsborough

Place Type: Township
County: Somerset
Population: 36,634

Ancestry/Race	Number	%
Acadian/Cajun	9	0.02
African American/Black:	1,520	4.15
Not Hispanic (1,325)	1,458	3.98
Hispanic (54)	62	0.17
African, sub-Saharan:	216	0.59
African	96	0.26
Ethiopian	8	0.02
Ghanian	112	0.31
Alaska Native tribes, specified:	1	0.00
Eskimo	1	0.00
Am. Ind. or Alaska Nat., not spec.	39	0.11
Albanian	7	0.02
American Indian tribes, specified:	67	0.18
Apache	2	0.01
Blackfeet	2	0.01
Cherokee (10)	26	0.07
Chickasaw	5	0.01
Chippewa (1)	3	0.01
Choctaw (1)	1	0.00
Delaware	2	0.01
Iroquois	1	0.00
Latin American Indians (5)	13	0.04
Osage	1	0.00
Potawatomi	1	0.00
Sioux	2	0.01
All other tribes (7)	8	0.02
American Indian tribes, not spec.	8	0.02
Arab:	189	0.52
Arab/Arabic	15	0.04
Egyptian	12	0.03
Lebanese	74	0.20
Palestinian	24	0.07
Syrian	64	0.17
Armenian	24	0.07
Asian:	2,951	8.06
Bangladeshi (4)	4	0.01
Cambodian (1)	1	0.00
Chinese, ex. Taiwanese (857)	932	2.54
Filipino (303)	354	0.97
Indian (1,038)	1,090	2.98
Indonesian (6)	8	0.02
Japanese (52)	69	0.19
Korean (131)	149	0.41
Pakistani (128)	155	0.42
Sri Lankan	1	0.00
Taiwanese (65)	70	0.19
Thai (2)	3	0.01
Vietnamese (44)	49	0.13
Other Asian, specified (1)	1	0.00
Other Asian, not specified (29)	65	0.18
Austrian	292	0.80
Belgian	7	0.02
Brazilian	15	0.04
British	118	0.32
Canadian	85	0.23
Croatian	64	0.17
Cypriot	9	0.02
Czech	224	0.61
Czechoslovakian	158	0.43
Danish	198	0.54
Dutch	776	2.12
Eastern European	79	0.22
English	2,692	7.34
Estonian	20	0.05
European	260	0.71
Finnish	71	0.19
French, except Basque	678	1.85
French Canadian	245	0.67
German	6,071	16.56
Greek	269	0.73
Guyanese	50	0.14
Hawaii Native/Pacific Islander:	43	0.12
Micronesian: (17)	17	0.05
Guamanian/Chamorro (2)	2	0.01
Other Micronesian (15)	15	0.04
Polynesian: (4)	10	0.03
Native Hawaiian (1)	7	0.02
Samoan (3)	3	0.01
Other Pac. Isl., not spec. (2)	16	0.04
Hispanic or Latino:	1,740	4.75
Central American:	261	0.71
Costa Rican	210	0.57
Guatemalan	19	0.05
Nicaraguan	2	0.01
Panamanian	7	0.02
Salvadoran	22	0.06
Other Central American	1	0.00
Cuban	133	0.36
Dominican Republic	27	0.07
Mexican	203	0.55
Puerto Rican	436	1.19
South American:	301	0.82
Argentinean	34	0.09
Bolivian	1	0.00
Chilean	15	0.04
Colombian	135	0.37
Ecuadorian	34	0.09
Paraguayan	4	0.01
Peruvian	44	0.12
Uruguayan	11	0.03
Venezuelan	9	0.02
Other South American	14	0.04
Other Hispanic or Latino	379	1.03
Hungarian	845	2.31
Iranian	21	0.06
Irish	6,642	18.12
Italian	8,310	22.67
Lithuanian	237	0.65
Maltese	26	0.07
Northern European	32	0.09
Norwegian	420	1.15
Pennsylvania German	8	0.02
Polish	4,790	13.07
Portuguese	220	0.60
Romanian	91	0.25
Russian	1,473	4.02
Scandinavian	25	0.07
Scotch-Irish	385	1.05
Scottish	678	1.85
Slavic	53	0.14
Slovak	392	1.07
Swedish	245	0.67
Swiss	172	0.47
Turkish	23	0.06
Ukrainian	668	1.82
United States or American	1,487	4.06
Welsh	275	0.75
West Indian, excl. Hispanic:	156	0.43
Bermudan	25	0.07
Jamaican	114	0.31
Trinidadian and Tobagonian	11	0.03
West Indian	6	0.02
White:	31,902	87.08
Not Hispanic (30,362)	30,662	83.70
Hispanic (1,129)	1,240	3.38
Yugoslavian	16	0.04

Hillsdale

Place Type: Borough
County: Bergen
Population: 10,087

Ancestry/Race	Number	%
African American/Black:	109	1.08
Not Hispanic (86)	107	1.06
Hispanic	2	0.02
African, sub-Saharan:	63	0.62
African	6	0.06
Nigerian	22	0.22
South African	19	0.19
Other sub-Saharan African	16	0.16
Am. Ind. or Alaska Nat., not spec.	14	0.14
Albanian	7	0.07
American Indian tribes, specified:	8	0.08
Blackfeet	1	0.01
Cherokee (1)	4	0.04
Cheyenne	1	0.01
Iroquois	1	0.01
Sioux	1	0.01
American Indian tribes, not spec.	2	0.02
Arab:	149	1.48
Lebanese	94	0.93
Palestinian	33	0.33

Notes: 1. Figures in the "Number" column do not add up to the total population due to: a) Ancestry/Race overlap — e.g. persons can report being both White and Irish, b) persons of Hispanic origin can report being any race, c) persons reporting two ancestries are counted in both categories. 2. Numbers in parentheses indicate the number of persons reporting this ancestry/race alone, not in combination with any other ancestry/race. 3. Refer to the Explanation of Data in the front of the book for more detailed information.

Ancestry/Race	Number	%
Syrian	7	0.07
Other Arab	15	0.15
Armenian	120	1.19
Asian:	557	5.52
Chinese, ex. Taiwanese (143)	153	1.52
Filipino (55)	62	0.61
Indian (111)	116	1.15
Japanese (75)	86	0.85
Korean (108)	115	1.14
Pakistani	1	0.01
Thai (2)	2	0.02
Vietnamese (14)	14	0.14
Other Asian, not specified	8	0.08
Assyrian/Chaldean/Syriac	7	0.07
Australian	6	0.06
Austrian	51	0.51
Belgian	6	0.06
Brazilian	12	0.12
British	26	0.26
Canadian	54	0.54
Croatian	25	0.25
Czech	51	0.51
Czechoslovakian	63	0.62
Danish	68	0.67
Dutch	270	2.68
Eastern European	30	0.30
English	593	5.88
Estonian	7	0.07
European	79	0.78
Finnish	39	0.39
French, except Basque	167	1.66
French Canadian	76	0.75
German	1,831	18.15
Greek	158	1.57
Hawaii Native/Pacific Islander:	5	0.05
Micronesian: (3)	3	0.03
Guamanian/Chamorro (3)	3	0.03
Other Pac. Isl., not spec. (1)	2	0.02
Hispanic or Latino:	429	4.25
Central American:	37	0.37
Costa Rican	27	0.27
Guatemalan	1	0.01
Honduran	5	0.05
Panamanian	2	0.02
Other Central American	2	0.02
Cuban	55	0.55
Dominican Republic	29	0.29
Mexican	76	0.75
Puerto Rican	70	0.69
South American:	70	0.69
Argentinean	8	0.08
Chilean	1	0.01
Colombian	12	0.12
Ecuadorian	43	0.43
Peruvian	2	0.02
Uruguayan	2	0.02
Other South American	2	0.02
Other Hispanic or Latino	92	0.91
Hungarian	140	1.39
Iranian	5	0.05
Irish	2,476	24.55
Italian	2,491	24.70
Lithuanian	55	0.55
Northern European	81	0.80
Norwegian	127	1.26
Polish	577	5.72
Portuguese	42	0.42
Romanian	77	0.76
Russian	446	4.42
Scotch-Irish	94	0.93
Scottish	132	1.31
Serbian	7	0.07
Slavic	4	0.04
Slovak	44	0.44
Swedish	83	0.82
Swiss	5	0.05
Turkish	37	0.37
Ukrainian	44	0.44
United States or American	349	3.46
Welsh	48	0.48
West Indian, excl. Hispanic:	6	0.06
Jamaican	6	0.06
White:	9,382	93.01
Not Hispanic (8,983)	9,035	89.57
Hispanic (338)	347	3.44
Yugoslavian	5	0.05

Hillside

Place Type: Census Designated Place
County: Union
Population: 21,747

Ancestry/Race	Number	%
African American/Black:	10,500	48.28
Not Hispanic (9,961)	10,285	47.29
Hispanic (161)	215	0.99
African, sub-Saharan:	615	2.83
African	253	1.16
Ghanian	109	0.50
Kenyan	48	0.22
Nigerian	205	0.94
Am. Ind. or Alaska Nat., not spec.	78	0.36
Albanian	41	0.19
American Indian tribes, specified:	65	0.30
Apache	1	0.00
Blackfeet	5	0.02
Cherokee	18	0.08
Chippewa (5)	5	0.02
Choctaw	1	0.00
Iroquois (3)	4	0.02
Latin American Indians (13)	23	0.11
All other tribes (5)	8	0.04
American Indian tribes, not spec.	12	0.06
Arab:	151	0.69
Arab/Arabic	59	0.27
Egyptian	71	0.33
Lebanese	21	0.10
Asian:	889	4.09
Chinese, ex. Taiwanese (83)	109	0.50
Filipino (422)	479	2.20
Indian (158)	190	0.87
Indonesian (4)	7	0.03
Japanese (6)	11	0.05
Korean (9)	9	0.04
Pakistani (36)	38	0.17
Thai (3)	4	0.02
Vietnamese (5)	5	0.02
Other Asian, not specified (11)	37	0.17
Austrian	33	0.15
Basque	17	0.08
Brazilian	469	2.16
British	14	0.06
Canadian	16	0.07
Carpatho Rusyn	6	0.03
Croatian	14	0.06
Czech	28	0.13
Czechoslovakian	34	0.16
Dutch	35	0.16
Eastern European	44	0.20
English	205	0.94
European	27	0.12
French, except Basque	64	0.29
German	462	2.12
Greek	64	0.29
Guyanese	123	0.57
Hawaii Native/Pacific Islander:	40	0.18
Polynesian: (4)	6	0.03
Native Hawaiian (3)	5	0.02
Samoan (1)	1	0.00
Other Pac. Isl., not spec. (13)	34	0.16
Hispanic or Latino:	3,153	14.50
Central American:	281	1.29
Costa Rican	46	0.21
Guatemalan	59	0.27
Honduran	38	0.17
Nicaraguan	8	0.04
Panamanian	22	0.10
Salvadoran	103	0.47
Other Central American	5	0.02
Cuban	402	1.85
Dominican Republic	146	0.67
Mexican	56	0.26
Puerto Rican	832	3.83
South American:	646	2.97
Argentinean	20	0.09
Bolivian	2	0.01
Chilean	37	0.17
Colombian	212	0.97
Ecuadorian	156	0.72
Paraguayan	6	0.03
Peruvian	102	0.47
Uruguayan	59	0.27
Venezuelan	12	0.06
Other South American	40	0.18
Other Hispanic or Latino	790	3.63
Hungarian	101	0.46
Iranian	12	0.06
Irish	707	3.25
Israeli	11	0.05
Italian	896	4.12
Lithuanian	27	0.12
Maltese	35	0.16
Norwegian	34	0.16
Polish	1,095	5.04
Portuguese	2,391	10.99
Romanian	18	0.08
Russian	229	1.05
Scotch-Irish	68	0.31
Scottish	6	0.03
Slavic	31	0.14
Slovak	99	0.46
Swedish	3	0.01
Swiss	28	0.13
Turkish	45	0.21
Ukrainian	136	0.63
United States or American	503	2.31
Welsh	46	0.21
West Indian, excl. Hispanic:	928	4.27
Barbadian	46	0.21
Bermudan	20	0.09
British West Indian	6	0.03
Haitian	540	2.48
Jamaican	201	0.92
Trinidadian and Tobagonian	91	0.42
West Indian	24	0.11
White:	9,337	42.93
Not Hispanic (6,991)	7,392	33.99
Hispanic (1,714)	1,945	8.94
Yugoslavian	5	0.02

Hoboken

Place Type: City
County: Hudson
Population: 38,577

Ancestry/Race	Number	%
African American/Black:	1,951	5.06
Not Hispanic (1,299)	1,442	3.74
Hispanic (345)	509	1.32
African, sub-Saharan:	180	0.47
African	116	0.30
Nigerian	22	0.06
Senegalese	10	0.03
South African	21	0.05
Zimbabwean	11	0.03
Alaska Native tribes, specified:	1	0.00
Eskimo	1	0.00
Am. Ind. or Alaska Nat., not spec.	77	0.20
Albanian	31	0.08
Alsatian	18	0.05
American Indian tribes, specified:	86	0.22
Blackfeet	1	0.00
Cherokee (2)	25	0.06
Creek	1	0.00
Delaware	2	0.01
Iroquois (1)	2	0.01
Latin American Indians (14)	40	0.10
Pueblo (1)	1	0.00

Notes: 1. Figures in the "Number" column do not add up to the total population due to: a) Ancestry/Race overlap — e.g. persons can report being both White and Irish, b) persons of Hispanic origin can report being any race, c) persons reporting two ancestries are counted in both categories. 2. Numbers in parentheses indicate the number of persons reporting this ancestry/race alone, not in combination with any other ancestry/race. 3. Refer to the Explanation of Data in the front of the book for more detailed information.

Ancestry/Race	Number	%
Sioux (1)	3	0.01
All other tribes (2)	11	0.03
American Indian tribes, not spec.	10	0.03
Arab:	191	0.49
Arab/Arabic	29	0.07
Egyptian	73	0.19
Lebanese	52	0.13
Moroccan	8	0.02
Syrian	29	0.07
Armenian	69	0.18
Asian:	1,935	5.02
Bangladeshi (1)	2	0.01
Chinese, ex. Taiwanese (450)	519	1.35
Filipino (136)	192	0.50
Indian (625)	670	1.74
Indonesian (6)	7	0.02
Japanese (126)	161	0.42
Korean (182)	202	0.52
Malaysian (3)	5	0.01
Pakistani (9)	14	0.04
Sri Lankan (4)	5	0.01
Taiwanese (15)	21	0.05
Thai (32)	36	0.09
Vietnamese (27)	34	0.09
Other Asian, specified (1)	1	0.00
Other Asian, not specified (22)	66	0.17
Assyrian/Chaldean/Syriac	8	0.02
Australian	28	0.07
Austrian	240	0.62
Basque	17	0.04
Belgian	48	0.12
Brazilian	90	0.23
British	326	0.84
Bulgarian	20	0.05
Canadian	90	0.23
Croatian	172	0.44
Czech	155	0.40
Czechoslovakian	176	0.46
Danish	133	0.34
Dutch	351	0.91
Eastern European	249	0.64
English	2,126	5.50
Estonian	17	0.04
European	286	0.74
Finnish	27	0.07
French, except Basque	613	1.59
French Canadian	203	0.52
German	4,127	10.67
Greek	270	0.70
Guyanese	9	0.02
Hawaii Native/Pacific Islander:	49	0.13
Micronesian: (10)	11	0.03
Guamanian/Chamorro (10)	11	0.03
Polynesian: (4)	12	0.03
Native Hawaiian (2)	8	0.02
Samoan (2)	4	0.01
Other Pac. Isl., not spec. (7)	26	0.07
Hispanic or Latino:	7,783	20.18
Central American:	149	0.39
Costa Rican	13	0.03
Guatemalan	22	0.06
Honduran	43	0.11
Nicaraguan	6	0.02
Panamanian	8	0.02
Salvadoran	39	0.10
Other Central American	18	0.05
Cuban	560	1.45
Dominican Republic	536	1.39
Mexican	359	0.93
Puerto Rican	4,660	12.08
South American:	605	1.57
Argentinean	53	0.14
Bolivian	12	0.03
Chilean	25	0.06
Colombian	124	0.32
Ecuadorian	309	0.80
Paraguayan	1	0.00
Peruvian	42	0.11
Uruguayan	7	0.02
Venezuelan	18	0.05
Other South American	14	0.04
Other Hispanic or Latino	914	2.37
Hungarian	453	1.17
Iranian	64	0.17
Irish	7,408	19.16
Israeli	49	0.13
Italian	8,052	20.82
Latvian	22	0.06
Lithuanian	189	0.49
Maltese	17	0.04
New Zealander	19	0.05
Northern European	5	0.01
Norwegian	321	0.83
Pennsylvania German	8	0.02
Polish	1,954	5.05
Portuguese	84	0.22
Romanian	141	0.36
Russian	1,187	3.07
Scandinavian	29	0.07
Scotch-Irish	313	0.81
Scottish	650	1.68
Serbian	12	0.03
Slavic	10	0.03
Slovak	152	0.39
Slovene	15	0.04
Swedish	311	0.80
Swiss	101	0.26
Turkish	66	0.17
Ukrainian	292	0.76
United States or American	1,125	2.91
Welsh	179	0.46
West Indian, excl. Hispanic:	187	0.48
Barbadian	21	0.05
Haitian	16	0.04
Jamaican	56	0.14
Trinidadian and Tobagonian	30	0.08
West Indian	56	0.14
Other West Indian	8	0.02
White:	32,045	83.07
Not Hispanic (27,196)	27,651	71.68
Hispanic (3,982)	4,394	11.39
Yugoslavian	55	0.14

Holiday City-Berkeley

Place Type: Census Designated Place
County: Ocean
Population: 13,884

Ancestry/Race	Number	%
African American/Black:	59	0.42
Not Hispanic (53)	59	0.42
Am. Ind. or Alaska Nat., not spec.	11	0.08
Albanian	7	0.05
American Indian tribes, specified:	4	0.03
Cherokee	1	0.01
Iroquois	1	0.01
All other tribes	2	0.01
American Indian tribes, not spec.	1	0.01
Arab:	29	0.21
Syrian	29	0.21
Armenian	8	0.06
Asian:	39	0.28
Chinese, ex. Taiwanese (6)	8	0.06
Filipino (9)	11	0.08
Indian (2)	2	0.01
Japanese (7)	7	0.05
Korean (5)	7	0.05
Other Asian, not specified (2)	4	0.03
Austrian	60	0.43
Belgian	35	0.25
British	18	0.13
Canadian	50	0.36
Croatian	9	0.06
Czech	87	0.63
Czechoslovakian	67	0.48
Danish	31	0.22
Dutch	214	1.54
English	995	7.15
European	44	0.32
Finnish	17	0.12
French, except Basque	244	1.75
French Canadian	76	0.55
German	2,167	15.58
Greek	56	0.40
Hawaii Native/Pacific Islander:	4	0.03
Polynesian: (1)	3	0.02
Native Hawaiian (1)	2	0.01
Samoan	1	0.01
Other Pac. Isl., not spec. (1)	1	0.01
Hispanic or Latino:	151	1.09
Central American:	2	0.01
Costa Rican	1	0.01
Salvadoran	1	0.01
Cuban	19	0.14
Dominican Republic	1	0.01
Mexican	9	0.06
Puerto Rican	65	0.47
South American:	13	0.09
Argentinean	3	0.02
Chilean	2	0.01
Colombian	3	0.02
Peruvian	1	0.01
Venezuelan	3	0.02
Other South American	1	0.01
Other Hispanic or Latino	42	0.30
Hungarian	178	1.28
Icelander	8	0.06
Irish	2,495	17.94
Italian	4,195	30.16
Latvian	10	0.07
Lithuanian	93	0.67
Maltese	16	0.12
Norwegian	106	0.76
Pennsylvania German	27	0.19
Polish	1,249	8.98
Portuguese	17	0.12
Romanian	24	0.17
Russian	222	1.60
Scotch-Irish	119	0.86
Scottish	217	1.56
Slavic	39	0.28
Slovak	234	1.68
Swedish	90	0.65
Swiss	33	0.24
Ukrainian	246	1.77
United States or American	358	2.57
Welsh	78	0.56
West Indian, excl. Hispanic:	11	0.08
Jamaican	11	0.08
White:	13,787	99.30
Not Hispanic (13,608)	13,646	98.29
Hispanic (133)	141	1.02
Yugoslavian	10	0.07

Holmdel

Place Type: Township
County: Monmouth
Population: 15,781

Ancestry/Race	Number	%
African American/Black:	127	0.80
Not Hispanic (101)	126	0.80
Hispanic (1)	1	0.01
African, sub-Saharan:	61	0.39
African	8	0.05
Kenyan	13	0.08
Nigerian	40	0.25
Am. Ind. or Alaska Nat., not spec.	18	0.11
Alsatian	34	0.22
American Indian tribes, specified:	8	0.05
Apache	1	0.01
Blackfeet	1	0.01
Creek (1)	1	0.01
Delaware	3	0.02
Latin American Indians	1	0.01
All other tribes (1)	1	0.01
American Indian tribes, not spec.	3	0.02
Arab:	147	0.93

Notes: 1. Figures in the "Number" column do not add up to the total population due to: a) Ancestry/Race overlap — e.g. persons can report being both White and Irish, b) persons of Hispanic origin can report being any race, c) persons reporting two ancestries are counted in both categories. 2. Numbers in parentheses indicate the number of persons reporting this ancestry/race alone, not in combination with any other ancestry/race. 3. Refer to the Explanation of Data in the front of the book for more detailed information.

Ancestry/Race	Number	%
Egyptian	103	0.65
Lebanese	32	0.20
Syrian	12	0.08
Armenian	64	0.41
Asian:	2,909	18.43
Chinese, ex. Taiwanese (1,514)	1,574	9.97
Filipino (133)	152	0.96
Indian (560)	591	3.75
Indonesian (1)	1	0.01
Japanese (22)	33	0.21
Korean (256)	267	1.69
Pakistani (11)	22	0.14
Taiwanese (186)	216	1.37
Thai (2)	2	0.01
Vietnamese (9)	10	0.06
Other Asian, specified (2)	2	0.01
Other Asian, not specified (17)	39	0.25
Australian	34	0.22
Austrian	95	0.60
Belgian	39	0.25
Brazilian	44	0.28
British	61	0.39
Czech	86	0.54
Danish	14	0.09
Dutch	168	1.06
Eastern European	32	0.20
English	886	5.61
European	93	0.59
Finnish	55	0.35
French, except Basque	230	1.46
French Canadian	99	0.63
German	1,895	12.01
Greek	270	1.71
Hawaii Native/Pacific Islander:	16	0.10
Polynesian: (1)	2	0.01
Native Hawaiian (1)	2	0.01
Other Pac. Isl., not spec.	14	0.09
Hispanic or Latino:	387	2.45
Central American:	14	0.09
Costa Rican	2	0.01
Guatemalan	3	0.02
Honduran	1	0.01
Nicaraguan	1	0.01
Panamanian	1	0.01
Salvadoran	6	0.04
Cuban	78	0.49
Dominican Republic	20	0.13
Mexican	30	0.19
Puerto Rican	105	0.67
South American:	62	0.39
Argentinean	2	0.01
Bolivian	4	0.03
Chilean	3	0.02
Colombian	22	0.14
Ecuadorian	10	0.06
Peruvian	10	0.06
Uruguayan	1	0.01
Venezuelan	5	0.03
Other South American	5	0.03
Other Hispanic or Latino	78	0.49
Hungarian	208	1.32
Iranian	129	0.82
Irish	2,630	16.67
Italian	4,426	28.05
Latvian	8	0.05
Lithuanian	95	0.60
Norwegian	121	0.77
Pennsylvania German	6	0.04
Polish	889	5.63
Portuguese	96	0.61
Romanian	59	0.37
Russian	376	2.38
Scotch-Irish	111	0.70
Scottish	247	1.57
Slavic	22	0.14
Slovak	71	0.45
Swedish	135	0.86
Swiss	14	0.09
Turkish	146	0.93
Ukrainian	38	0.24
United States or American	361	2.29
Welsh	40	0.25
West Indian, excl. Hispanic:	52	0.33
Belizean	8	0.05
Jamaican	44	0.28
White:	12,796	81.08
Not Hispanic (12,342)	12,470	79.02
Hispanic (315)	326	2.07

Hopatcong

Place Type: Borough
County: Sussex
Population: 15,888

Ancestry/Race	Number	%
African American/Black:	372	2.34
Not Hispanic (296)	343	2.16
Hispanic (14)	29	0.18
African, sub-Saharan:	28	0.18
African	21	0.13
South African	7	0.04
Am. Ind. or Alaska Nat., not spec.	29	0.18
American Indian tribes, specified:	38	0.24
Apache	1	0.01
Blackfeet	7	0.04
Cherokee	7	0.04
Chippewa (2)	4	0.03
Cree (1)	1	0.01
Delaware	1	0.01
Iroquois (3)	10	0.06
Pueblo (1)	1	0.01
Seminole	1	0.01
All other tribes (1)	5	0.03
American Indian tribes, not spec.	1	0.01
Arab:	61	0.38
Egyptian	35	0.22
Lebanese	26	0.16
Armenian	16	0.10
Asian:	337	2.12
Cambodian (7)	8	0.05
Chinese, ex. Taiwanese (33)	48	0.30
Filipino (55)	62	0.39
Indian (99)	101	0.64
Japanese (10)	20	0.13
Korean (23)	25	0.16
Pakistani (14)	15	0.09
Sri Lankan (2)	2	0.01
Taiwanese	1	0.01
Thai (5)	5	0.03
Vietnamese (24)	29	0.18
Other Asian, specified (1)	1	0.01
Other Asian, not specified (2)	20	0.13
Austrian	77	0.48
Belgian	12	0.08
Brazilian	35	0.22
British	69	0.43
Canadian	23	0.14
Czech	91	0.57
Czechoslovakian	41	0.26
Danish	68	0.43
Dutch	423	2.65
Eastern European	20	0.13
English	1,237	7.75
European	51	0.32
Finnish	29	0.18
French, except Basque	332	2.08
French Canadian	86	0.54
German	3,307	20.73
Greek	107	0.67
Hawaii Native/Pacific Islander:	2	0.01
Other Pac. Isl., not spec.	2	0.01
Hispanic or Latino:	952	5.99
Central American:	43	0.27
Costa Rican	10	0.06
Guatemalan	5	0.03
Honduran	15	0.09
Panamanian	4	0.03
Salvadoran	8	0.05
Other Central American	1	0.01
Cuban	72	0.45
Dominican Republic	37	0.23
Mexican	45	0.28
Puerto Rican	352	2.22
South American:	174	1.10
Argentinean	11	0.07
Bolivian	2	0.01
Chilean	21	0.13
Colombian	76	0.48
Ecuadorian	31	0.20
Peruvian	18	0.11
Uruguayan	11	0.07
Venezuelan	2	0.01
Other South American	2	0.01
Other Hispanic or Latino	229	1.44
Hungarian	250	1.57
Irish	3,869	24.26
Israeli	7	0.04
Italian	4,119	25.82
Lithuanian	75	0.47
Maltese	19	0.12
Norwegian	163	1.02
Pennsylvania German	15	0.09
Polish	1,213	7.60
Portuguese	92	0.58
Romanian	23	0.14
Russian	312	1.96
Scandinavian	18	0.11
Scotch-Irish	167	1.05
Scottish	396	2.48
Serbian	13	0.08
Slavic	24	0.15
Slovak	116	0.73
Swedish	195	1.22
Swiss	54	0.34
Turkish	21	0.13
Ukrainian	126	0.79
United States or American	743	4.66
Welsh	149	0.93
West Indian, excl. Hispanic:	51	0.32
Jamaican	29	0.18
Trinidadian and Tobagonian	22	0.14
White:	15,026	94.57
Not Hispanic (14,144)	14,304	90.03
Hispanic (648)	722	4.54
Yugoslavian	13	0.08

Hopewell

Place Type: Township
County: Mercer
Population: 16,105

Ancestry/Race	Number	%
African American/Black:	987	6.13
Not Hispanic (905)	941	5.84
Hispanic (34)	46	0.29
African, sub-Saharan:	94	0.58
African	70	0.43
South African	24	0.15
Am. Ind. or Alaska Nat., not spec.	21	0.13
Albanian	10	0.06
American Indian tribes, specified:	39	0.24
Blackfeet (2)	3	0.02
Cherokee (2)	11	0.07
Cheyenne	3	0.02
Choctaw (1)	1	0.01
Cree	3	0.02
Delaware	8	0.05
Latin American Indians (3)	5	0.03
Navajo	1	0.01
Sioux (2)	2	0.01
All other tribes	2	0.01
American Indian tribes, not spec.	2	0.01
Armenian	31	0.19
Asian:	716	4.45
Chinese, ex. Taiwanese (221)	238	1.48
Filipino (39)	50	0.31
Indian (228)	251	1.56
Japanese (22)	30	0.19

Notes: 1. Figures in the "Number" column do not add up to the total population due to: a) Ancestry/Race overlap — e.g. persons can report being both White and Irish, b) persons of Hispanic origin can report being any race, c) persons reporting two ancestries are counted in both categories. 2. Numbers in parentheses indicate the number of persons reporting this ancestry/race alone, not in combination with any other ancestry/race. 3. Refer to the Explanation of Data in the front of the book for more detailed information.

Ancestry/Race	Number	%
Korean (86)	93	0.58
Pakistani (16)	17	0.11
Taiwanese (5)	8	0.05
Thai (4)	4	0.02
Vietnamese (7)	7	0.04
Other Asian, specified	2	0.01
Other Asian, not specified (8)	16	0.10
Austrian	74	0.46
Belgian	49	0.30
British	86	0.53
Canadian	37	0.23
Czech	87	0.54
Czechoslovakian	63	0.39
Danish	66	0.41
Dutch	456	2.83
Eastern European	67	0.42
English	2,441	15.16
European	272	1.69
Finnish	10	0.06
French, except Basque	331	2.06
French Canadian	155	0.96
German	2,859	17.75
Greek	51	0.32
Hawaii Native/Pacific Islander:	9	0.06
Polynesian: (3)	3	0.02
Native Hawaiian (2)	2	0.01
Samoan (1)	1	0.01
Other Pac. Isl., not spec. (1)	6	0.04
Hispanic or Latino:	395	2.45
Central American:	31	0.19
Costa Rican	5	0.03
Guatemalan	17	0.11
Honduran	2	0.01
Nicaraguan	3	0.02
Panamanian	3	0.02
Salvadoran	1	0.01
Cuban	50	0.31
Dominican Republic	1	0.01
Mexican	36	0.22
Puerto Rican	152	0.94
South American:	57	0.35
Argentinean	7	0.04
Chilean	12	0.07
Colombian	17	0.11
Ecuadorian	8	0.05
Paraguayan	3	0.02
Peruvian	5	0.03
Uruguayan	1	0.01
Venezuelan	1	0.01
Other South American	3	0.02
Other Hispanic or Latino	68	0.42
Hungarian	386	2.40
Irish	3,040	18.88
Italian	2,576	16.00
Latvian	24	0.15
Lithuanian	37	0.23
Luxemburger	7	0.04
Norwegian	131	0.81
Pennsylvania German	75	0.47
Polish	1,090	6.77
Portuguese	26	0.16
Romanian	46	0.29
Russian	404	2.51
Scandinavian	9	0.06
Scotch-Irish	280	1.74
Scottish	504	3.13
Slavic	17	0.11
Slovak	180	1.12
Swedish	315	1.96
Swiss	60	0.37
Turkish	71	0.44
Ukrainian	247	1.53
United States or American	870	5.40
Welsh	140	0.87
White:	14,374	89.25
Not Hispanic (13,978)	14,103	87.57
Hispanic (242)	271	1.68
Yugoslavian	25	0.16

Howell

Place Type: Township
County: Monmouth
Population: 48,903

Ancestry/Race	Number	%
Acadian/Cajun	23	0.05
African American/Black:	1,947	3.98
Not Hispanic (1,669)	1,811	3.70
Hispanic (70)	136	0.28
African, sub-Saharan:	120	0.25
African	93	0.19
Nigerian	27	0.06
Am. Ind. or Alaska Nat., not spec.	69	0.14
Albanian	47	0.10
American Indian tribes, specified:	112	0.23
Apache	9	0.02
Blackfeet (4)	14	0.03
Cherokee (4)	42	0.09
Chippewa	3	0.01
Choctaw	6	0.01
Creek (1)	1	0.00
Crow	1	0.00
Delaware	4	0.01
Iroquois (4)	12	0.02
Latin American Indians (3)	8	0.02
Paiute (1)	1	0.00
Seminole	1	0.00
Sioux	5	0.01
All other tribes (2)	5	0.01
American Indian tribes, not spec.	16	0.03
Arab:	430	0.88
Arab/Arabic	14	0.03
Egyptian	126	0.26
Jordanian	22	0.04
Lebanese	64	0.13
Palestinian	86	0.18
Syrian	90	0.18
Other Arab	28	0.06
Armenian	79	0.16
Asian:	2,040	4.17
Bangladeshi (11)	12	0.02
Chinese, ex. Taiwanese (378)	437	0.89
Filipino (407)	484	0.99
Indian (535)	582	1.19
Indonesian	4	0.01
Japanese (19)	39	0.08
Korean (139)	157	0.32
Pakistani (13)	24	0.05
Sri Lankan (12)	18	0.04
Taiwanese (6)	13	0.03
Thai (7)	13	0.03
Vietnamese (87)	97	0.20
Other Asian, specified	2	0.00
Other Asian, not specified (114)	158	0.32
Assyrian/Chaldean/Syriac	24	0.05
Austrian	227	0.46
Belgian	49	0.10
Brazilian	126	0.26
British	92	0.19
Bulgarian	16	0.03
Canadian	94	0.19
Celtic	11	0.02
Croatian	64	0.13
Cypriot	24	0.05
Czech	162	0.33
Czechoslovakian	208	0.43
Danish	125	0.26
Dutch	561	1.15
Eastern European	51	0.10
English	3,080	6.30
Estonian	30	0.06
European	196	0.40
Finnish	21	0.04
French, except Basque	947	1.94
French Canadian	352	0.72
German	8,051	16.46
Greek	444	0.91
Guyanese	42	0.09
Hawaii Native/Pacific Islander:	34	0.07
Micronesian: (1)	3	0.01
Guamanian/Chamorro (1)	3	0.01
Polynesian: (4)	8	0.02
Native Hawaiian (2)	6	0.01
Samoan (2)	2	0.00
Other Pac. Isl., specified	2	0.00
Other Pac. Isl., not spec.	21	0.04
Hispanic or Latino:	2,610	5.34
Central American:	114	0.23
Costa Rican	29	0.06
Guatemalan	38	0.08
Honduran	21	0.04
Nicaraguan	2	0.00
Panamanian	10	0.02
Salvadoran	12	0.02
Other Central American	2	0.00
Cuban	202	0.41
Dominican Republic	61	0.12
Mexican	229	0.47
Puerto Rican	1,252	2.56
South American:	291	0.60
Argentinean	22	0.04
Chilean	18	0.04
Colombian	103	0.21
Ecuadorian	62	0.13
Peruvian	60	0.12
Uruguayan	10	0.02
Venezuelan	5	0.01
Other South American	11	0.02
Other Hispanic or Latino	461	0.94
Hungarian	631	1.29
Iranian	33	0.07
Irish	11,826	24.18
Israeli	31	0.06
Italian	15,020	30.71
Latvian	18	0.04
Lithuanian	174	0.36
Maltese	49	0.10
Northern European	11	0.02
Norwegian	423	0.86
Pennsylvania German	18	0.04
Polish	4,833	9.88
Portuguese	383	0.78
Romanian	87	0.18
Russian	1,879	3.84
Scandinavian	38	0.08
Scotch-Irish	573	1.17
Scottish	658	1.35
Serbian	59	0.12
Slavic	25	0.05
Slovak	361	0.74
Swedish	274	0.56
Swiss	62	0.13
Turkish	29	0.06
Ukrainian	488	1.00
United States or American	1,859	3.80
Welsh	158	0.32
West Indian, excl. Hispanic:	132	0.27
British West Indian	28	0.06
Haitian	34	0.07
Jamaican	26	0.05
Trinidadian and Tobagonian	18	0.04
West Indian	26	0.05
White:	44,600	91.20
Not Hispanic (42,263)	42,685	87.29
Hispanic (1,745)	1,915	3.92
Yugoslavian	200	0.41

Irvington

Place Type: Census Designated Place
County: Essex
Population: 60,695

Ancestry/Race	Number	%
African American/Black:	51,726	85.22
Not Hispanic (48,852)	50,878	83.83
Hispanic (714)	848	1.40
African, sub-Saharan:	2,422	4.00

Notes: 1. Figures in the "Number" column do not add up to the total population due to: a) Ancestry/Race overlap — e.g. persons can report being both White and Irish, b) persons of Hispanic origin can report being any race, c) persons reporting two ancestries are counted in both categories. 2. Numbers in parentheses indicate the number of persons reporting this ancestry/race alone, not in combination with any other ancestry/race. 3. Refer to the Explanation of Data in the front of the book for more detailed information.

African	1,377	2.27
Ghanian	308	0.51
Kenyan	14	0.02
Liberian	59	0.10
Nigerian	598	0.99
Sierra Leonean	19	0.03
Sudanese	22	0.04
Other sub-Saharan African	25	0.04
Alaska Native tribes, specified:	3	0.00
Alaska Athabascan	1	0.00
Tlingit-Haida	2	0.00
Am. Ind. or Alaska Nat., not spec.	215	0.35
American Indian tribes, specified:	146	0.24
Apache	5	0.01
Blackfeet (3)	16	0.03
Cherokee (9)	66	0.11
Cheyenne	1	0.00
Chickasaw	1	0.00
Chippewa	3	0.00
Creek	1	0.00
Delaware (1)	2	0.00
Iroquois (3)	11	0.02
Latin American Indians (16)	27	0.04
Lumbee (1)	1	0.00
Navajo (1)	1	0.00
Pueblo	5	0.01
Seminole	1	0.00
Sioux	2	0.00
All other tribes (1)	3	0.00
American Indian tribes, not spec.	16	0.03
Arab:	13	0.02
Lebanese	13	0.02
Armenian	10	0.02
Asian:	836	1.38
Bangladeshi (5)	5	0.01
Cambodian (1)	1	0.00
Chinese, ex. Taiwanese (63)	67	0.11
Filipino (299)	320	0.53
Indian (166)	229	0.38
Japanese (6)	11	0.02
Korean (37)	43	0.07
Laotian (6)	6	0.01
Pakistani (12)	26	0.04
Sri Lankan (2)	7	0.01
Taiwanese (3)	3	0.00
Thai (2)	2	0.00
Vietnamese (44)	47	0.08
Other Asian, specified	3	0.00
Other Asian, not specified (18)	66	0.11
Australian	16	0.03
Austrian	32	0.05
Brazilian	9	0.01
British	7	0.01
Canadian	6	0.01
Czech	8	0.01
Dutch	22	0.04
English	206	0.34
Estonian	10	0.02
European	15	0.02
French, except Basque	69	0.11
French Canadian	25	0.04
German	447	0.74
Greek	132	0.22
Guyanese	920	1.52
Hawaii Native/Pacific Islander:	198	0.33
Micronesian: (13)	15	0.02
Guamanian/Chamorro (13)	15	0.02
Polynesian: (15)	21	0.03
Native Hawaiian (6)	11	0.02
Samoan (9)	10	0.02
Other Pac. Isl., specified	3	0.00
Other Pac. Isl., not spec. (31)	159	0.26
Hispanic or Latino:	5,086	8.38
Central American:	494	0.81
Costa Rican	89	0.15
Guatemalan	118	0.19
Honduran	18	0.03
Nicaraguan	12	0.02
Panamanian	35	0.06
Salvadoran	202	0.33
Other Central American	20	0.03
Cuban	105	0.17
Dominican Republic	396	0.65
Mexican	357	0.59
Puerto Rican	2,083	3.43
South American:	617	1.02
Argentinean	13	0.02
Chilean	5	0.01
Colombian	82	0.14
Ecuadorian	438	0.72
Paraguayan	2	0.00
Peruvian	36	0.06
Uruguayan	8	0.01
Venezuelan	10	0.02
Other South American	23	0.04
Other Hispanic or Latino	1,034	1.70
Hungarian	54	0.09
Irish	477	0.79
Italian	705	1.16
Lithuanian	92	0.15
Norwegian	14	0.02
Pennsylvania German	9	0.01
Polish	669	1.10
Portuguese	131	0.22
Romanian	18	0.03
Russian	86	0.14
Scotch-Irish	15	0.02
Scottish	41	0.07
Serbian	6	0.01
Slovak	75	0.12
Turkish	66	0.11
Ukrainian	123	0.20
United States or American	1,149	1.90
West Indian, excl. Hispanic:	9,590	15.82
Bahamian	28	0.05
Barbadian	113	0.19
Belizean	24	0.04
Bermudan	33	0.05
British West Indian	153	0.25
Haitian	5,812	9.59
Jamaican	2,585	4.26
Trinidadian and Tobagonian	491	0.81
U.S. Virgin Islander	25	0.04
West Indian	326	0.54
White:	5,937	9.78
Not Hispanic (3,465)	3,769	6.21
Hispanic (1,981)	2,168	3.57

Iselin

Place Type: Census Designated Place
County: Middlesex
Population: 16,698

Ancestry/Race	Number	%
African American/Black:	1,072	6.42
Not Hispanic (974)	1,022	6.12
Hispanic (32)	50	0.30
African, sub-Saharan:	114	0.69
African	44	0.27
Ethiopian	23	0.14
Kenyan	6	0.04
Nigerian	41	0.25
Alaska Native tribes, specified:	2	0.01
Aleut (2)	2	0.01
Am. Ind. or Alaska Nat., not spec.	50	0.30
American Indian tribes, specified:	16	0.10
Cherokee	7	0.04
Iroquois (1)	1	0.01
Latin American Indians (1)	3	0.02
Pueblo (1)	1	0.01
Seminole	1	0.01
All other tribes (3)	3	0.02
American Indian tribes, not spec.	7	0.04
Arab:	95	0.57
Arab/Arabic	36	0.22
Egyptian	48	0.29
Jordanian	11	0.07
Asian:	4,409	26.40
Bangladeshi (10)	15	0.09
Chinese, ex. Taiwanese (452)	486	2.91
Filipino (423)	455	2.72
Indian (2,843)	2,912	17.44
Indonesian (21)	35	0.21
Japanese (11)	17	0.10
Korean (173)	179	1.07
Laotian	1	0.01
Pakistani (143)	164	0.98
Sri Lankan (23)	23	0.14
Taiwanese (2)	6	0.04
Thai (3)	7	0.04
Vietnamese (41)	52	0.31
Other Asian, specified (2)	6	0.04
Other Asian, not specified (22)	51	0.31
Australian	16	0.10
Austrian	17	0.10
British	41	0.25
Canadian	5	0.03
Croatian	46	0.28
Czech	96	0.58
Czechoslovakian	86	0.52
Danish	37	0.22
Dutch	55	0.33
Eastern European	15	0.09
English	570	3.43
European	22	0.13
Finnish	22	0.13
French, except Basque	100	0.60
French Canadian	13	0.08
German	1,934	11.65
Greek	105	0.63
Guyanese	62	0.37
Hawaii Native/Pacific Islander:	24	0.14
Polynesian: (2)	9	0.05
Native Hawaiian (1)	7	0.04
Samoan (1)	2	0.01
Other Pac. Isl., specified	4	0.02
Other Pac. Isl., not spec.	11	0.07
Hispanic or Latino:	914	5.47
Central American:	46	0.28
Costa Rican	12	0.07
Guatemalan	13	0.08
Honduran	5	0.03
Nicaraguan	2	0.01
Panamanian	1	0.01
Salvadoran	12	0.07
Other Central American	1	0.01
Cuban	94	0.56
Dominican Republic	46	0.28
Mexican	46	0.28
Puerto Rican	358	2.14
South American:	132	0.79
Argentinean	19	0.11
Chilean	2	0.01
Colombian	41	0.25
Ecuadorian	11	0.07
Paraguayan	4	0.02
Peruvian	33	0.20
Uruguayan	6	0.04
Venezuelan	6	0.04
Other South American	10	0.06
Other Hispanic or Latino	192	1.15
Hungarian	511	3.08
Irish	3,034	18.28
Italian	3,010	18.14
Lithuanian	115	0.69
Northern European	5	0.03
Norwegian	131	0.79
Pennsylvania German	7	0.04
Polish	1,596	9.62
Portuguese	199	1.20
Romanian	43	0.26
Russian	331	1.99
Scotch-Irish	230	1.39
Scottish	271	1.63
Slavic	14	0.08
Slovak	246	1.48
Slovene	9	0.05
Swedish	76	0.46
Ukrainian	292	1.76

Notes: 1. Figures in the "Number" column do not add up to the total population due to: a) Ancestry/Race overlap — e.g. persons can report being both White and Irish, b) persons of Hispanic origin can report being any race, c) persons reporting two ancestries are counted in both categories. 2. Numbers in parentheses indicate the number of persons reporting this ancestry/race alone, not in combination with any other ancestry/race. 3. Refer to the Explanation of Data in the front of the book for more detailed information.

Ancestry/Race	Number	%
United States or American	315	1.90
Welsh	103	0.62
West Indian, excl. Hispanic:	193	1.16
Barbadian	12	0.07
Belizean	22	0.13
British West Indian	14	0.08
Haitian	59	0.36
Jamaican	59	0.36
Trinidadian and Tobagonian	12	0.07
West Indian	15	0.09
White:	11,048	66.16
Not Hispanic (10,252)	10,435	62.49
Hispanic (544)	613	3.67
Yugoslavian	25	0.15

Jackson

Place Type: Township
County: Ocean
Population: 42,816

Ancestry/Race	Number	%
African American/Black:	1,854	4.33
Not Hispanic (1,569)	1,699	3.97
Hispanic (101)	155	0.36
African, sub-Saharan:	167	0.39
African	108	0.25
Nigerian	59	0.14
Am. Ind. or Alaska Nat., not spec.	76	0.18
Albanian	23	0.05
American Indian tribes, specified:	137	0.32
Blackfeet	17	0.04
Cherokee (3)	43	0.10
Chippewa	1	0.00
Choctaw	3	0.01
Cree (1)	1	0.00
Creek	2	0.00
Delaware (2)	14	0.03
Iroquois (1)	7	0.02
Latin American Indians (8)	12	0.03
Navajo	2	0.00
Pueblo (3)	3	0.01
Seminole (3)	6	0.01
Sioux	1	0.00
Yaqui	3	0.01
Yuman (3)	3	0.01
All other tribes (9)	19	0.04
American Indian tribes, not spec.	19	0.04
Arab:	231	0.54
Egyptian	143	0.33
Lebanese	44	0.10
Palestinian	8	0.02
Syrian	36	0.08
Armenian	72	0.17
Asian:	1,071	2.50
Chinese, ex. Taiwanese (154)	185	0.43
Filipino (227)	283	0.66
Indian (253)	285	0.67
Indonesian	7	0.02
Japanese (36)	51	0.12
Korean (65)	87	0.20
Malaysian (2)	2	0.00
Pakistani (20)	30	0.07
Sri Lankan (3)	3	0.01
Taiwanese (1)	3	0.01
Thai (8)	9	0.02
Vietnamese (48)	55	0.13
Other Asian, specified (5)	10	0.02
Other Asian, not specified (39)	61	0.14
Assyrian/Chaldean/Syriac	13	0.03
Australian	10	0.02
Austrian	178	0.42
Belgian	20	0.05
Brazilian	35	0.08
British	95	0.22
Canadian	115	0.27
Celtic	7	0.02
Croatian	42	0.10
Czech	121	0.28
Czechoslovakian	130	0.30
Danish	208	0.49
Dutch	505	1.18
Eastern European	37	0.09
English	3,249	7.59
Estonian	126	0.29
European	137	0.32
French, except Basque	1,086	2.54
French Canadian	263	0.61
German	7,588	17.72
Greek	459	1.07
Hawaii Native/Pacific Islander:	26	0.06
Micronesian: (1)	2	0.00
Guamanian/Chamorro (1)	2	0.00
Polynesian: (1)	14	0.03
Native Hawaiian	11	0.03
Samoan (1)	2	0.00
Other Polynesian	1	0.00
Other Pac. Isl., specified	3	0.01
Other Pac. Isl., not spec. (1)	7	0.02
Hispanic or Latino:	2,474	5.78
Central American:	69	0.16
Costa Rican	9	0.02
Guatemalan	8	0.02
Honduran	7	0.02
Nicaraguan	18	0.04
Panamanian	6	0.01
Salvadoran	13	0.03
Other Central American	8	0.02
Cuban	161	0.38
Dominican Republic	40	0.09
Mexican	201	0.47
Puerto Rican	1,316	3.07
South American:	239	0.56
Argentinean	20	0.05
Chilean	10	0.02
Colombian	126	0.29
Ecuadorian	36	0.08
Peruvian	23	0.05
Uruguayan	6	0.01
Venezuelan	5	0.01
Other South American	13	0.03
Other Hispanic or Latino	448	1.05
Hungarian	1,042	2.43
Iranian	42	0.10
Irish	10,048	23.47
Israeli	21	0.05
Italian	11,311	26.42
Latvian	9	0.02
Lithuanian	311	0.73
Macedonian	22	0.05
Maltese	14	0.03
Northern European	9	0.02
Norwegian	420	0.98
Pennsylvania German	9	0.02
Polish	4,810	11.24
Portuguese	159	0.37
Romanian	67	0.16
Russian	1,183	2.76
Scandinavian	20	0.05
Scotch-Irish	519	1.21
Scottish	508	1.19
Slavic	16	0.04
Slovak	266	0.62
Swedish	386	0.90
Swiss	118	0.28
Turkish	58	0.14
Ukrainian	468	1.09
United States or American	1,109	2.59
Welsh	258	0.60
West Indian, excl. Hispanic:	119	0.28
Haitian	8	0.02
Jamaican	67	0.16
Trinidadian and Tobagonian	19	0.04
West Indian	25	0.06
White:	39,694	92.71
Not Hispanic (37,348)	37,776	88.23
Hispanic (1,725)	1,918	4.48
Yugoslavian	62	0.14

Jefferson

Place Type: Township
County: Morris
Population: 19,717

Ancestry/Race	Number	%
African American/Black:	213	1.08
Not Hispanic (153)	198	1.00
Hispanic (10)	15	0.08
African, sub-Saharan:	36	0.18
South African	36	0.18
Am. Ind. or Alaska Nat., not spec.	39	0.20
Albanian	50	0.25
American Indian tribes, specified:	50	0.25
Apache (1)	1	0.01
Blackfeet	1	0.01
Cherokee	9	0.05
Comanche (3)	3	0.02
Delaware (4)	7	0.04
Iroquois (2)	8	0.04
Latin American Indians (2)	3	0.02
Navajo (1)	1	0.01
Ottawa (2)	3	0.02
Pueblo (1)	1	0.01
Sioux	9	0.05
All other tribes (1)	4	0.02
American Indian tribes, not spec.	8	0.04
Arab:	110	0.56
Arab/Arabic	14	0.07
Lebanese	34	0.17
Syrian	62	0.31
Asian:	275	1.39
Cambodian (1)	1	0.01
Chinese, ex. Taiwanese (54)	59	0.30
Filipino (34)	53	0.27
Hmong (2)	2	0.01
Indian (47)	49	0.25
Japanese (13)	24	0.12
Korean (40)	48	0.24
Pakistani (4)	5	0.03
Taiwanese (1)	2	0.01
Vietnamese (10)	12	0.06
Other Asian, specified (3)	4	0.02
Other Asian, not specified	16	0.08
Austrian	201	1.02
British	91	0.46
Canadian	106	0.54
Carpatho Rusyn	27	0.14
Croatian	75	0.38
Czech	57	0.29
Czechoslovakian	111	0.56
Danish	46	0.23
Dutch	975	4.94
Eastern European	7	0.04
English	2,286	11.59
European	66	0.33
Finnish	16	0.08
French, except Basque	599	3.04
French Canadian	173	0.88
German	4,274	21.68
Greek	324	1.64
Guyanese	12	0.06
Hawaii Native/Pacific Islander:	14	0.07
Micronesian: (2)	2	0.01
Guamanian/Chamorro (2)	2	0.01
Polynesian: (8)	10	0.05
Native Hawaiian (1)	2	0.01
Samoan (7)	8	0.04
Other Pac. Isl., not spec.	2	0.01
Hispanic or Latino:	672	3.41
Central American:	28	0.14
Costa Rican	4	0.02
Guatemalan	10	0.05
Honduran	3	0.02
Nicaraguan	2	0.01
Panamanian	1	0.01
Salvadoran	1	0.01
Other Central American	7	0.04
Cuban	53	0.27

Notes: 1. Figures in the "Number" column do not add up to the total population due to: a) Ancestry/Race overlap — e.g. persons can report being both White and Irish, b) persons of Hispanic origin can report being any race, c) persons reporting two ancestries are counted in both categories. 2. Numbers in parentheses indicate the number of persons reporting this ancestry/race alone, not in combination with any other ancestry/race. 3. Refer to the Explanation of Data in the front of the book for more detailed information.

Dominican Republic	6	0.03
Mexican	50	0.25
Puerto Rican	244	1.24
South American:	157	0.80
Argentinean	9	0.05
Chilean	12	0.06
Colombian	68	0.34
Ecuadorian	24	0.12
Peruvian	23	0.12
Uruguayan	10	0.05
Venezuelan	3	0.02
Other South American	8	0.04
Other Hispanic or Latino	134	0.68
Hungarian	334	1.69
Irish	4,508	22.86
Italian	5,060	25.66
Lithuanian	151	0.77
Northern European	8	0.04
Norwegian	289	1.47
Pennsylvania German	16	0.08
Polish	1,967	9.98
Portuguese	69	0.35
Romanian	15	0.08
Russian	437	2.22
Scandinavian	24	0.12
Scotch-Irish	255	1.29
Scottish	703	3.57
Serbian	5	0.03
Slavic	40	0.20
Slovak	199	1.01
Slovene	9	0.05
Swedish	199	1.01
Swiss	69	0.35
Ukrainian	239	1.21
United States or American	628	3.19
Welsh	142	0.72
West Indian, excl. Hispanic:	57	0.29
Barbadian	23	0.12
Haitian	13	0.07
Jamaican	8	0.04
Trinidadian and Tobagonian	13	0.07
White:	19,158	97.16
Not Hispanic (18,444)	18,613	94.40
Hispanic (511)	545	2.76
Yugoslavian	85	0.43

Jersey City

Place Type: City
County: Hudson
Population: 240,055

Ancestry/Race	Number	%
Afghan	82	0.03
African American/Black:	72,080	30.03
Not Hispanic (64,389)	67,172	27.98
Hispanic (3,605)	4,908	2.04
African, sub-Saharan:	5,342	2.23
African	3,546	1.48
Cape Verdean	124	0.05
Ethiopian	221	0.09
Ghanian	114	0.05
Kenyan	209	0.09
Liberian	50	0.02
Nigerian	449	0.19
Senegalese	110	0.05
Sierra Leonean	44	0.02
Somalian	49	0.02
South African	59	0.02
Sudanese	146	0.06
Ugandan	10	0.00
Other sub-Saharan African	211	0.09
Alaska Native tribes, specified:	5	0.00
Alaska Athabascan (1)	2	0.00
Eskimo (1)	2	0.00
Tlingit-Haida	1	0.00
Alaska Native tribes, not specified	1	0.00
Am. Ind. or Alaska Nat., not spec.	1,368	0.57
Albanian	21	0.01
Alsatian	26	0.01
American Indian tribes, specified:	828	0.34
Apache	8	0.00
Blackfeet (2)	44	0.02
Cherokee (56)	224	0.09
Cheyenne (2)	2	0.00
Chickasaw (1)	4	0.00
Chippewa (1)	7	0.00
Choctaw (2)	10	0.00
Comanche (2)	2	0.00
Cree (1)	2	0.00
Creek	4	0.00
Crow	6	0.00
Delaware (6)	9	0.00
Iroquois (3)	16	0.01
Latin American Indians (171)	367	0.15
Lumbee (1)	1	0.00
Menominee	2	0.00
Navajo (3)	11	0.00
Paiute	1	0.00
Pueblo (22)	31	0.01
Puget Sound Salish	1	0.00
Seminole (1)	10	0.00
Shoshone (1)	1	0.00
Sioux (3)	20	0.01
Yuman (1)	1	0.00
All other tribes (17)	44	0.02
American Indian tribes, not spec.	188	0.08
Arab:	6,764	2.82
Arab/Arabic	770	0.32
Egyptian	4,820	2.01
Iraqi	11	0.00
Jordanian	143	0.06
Lebanese	387	0.16
Moroccan	223	0.09
Palestinian	37	0.02
Syrian	181	0.08
Other Arab	192	0.08
Armenian	102	0.04
Asian:	42,849	17.85
Bangladeshi (135)	182	0.08
Cambodian (11)	12	0.00
Chinese, ex. Taiwanese (3,490)	3,811	1.59
Filipino (15,860)	16,777	6.99
Indian (12,973)	14,206	5.92
Indonesian (26)	45	0.02
Japanese (404)	486	0.20
Korean (1,428)	1,507	0.63
Laotian (15)	18	0.01
Malaysian (29)	56	0.02
Pakistani (1,877)	2,617	1.09
Sri Lankan (23)	33	0.01
Taiwanese (110)	140	0.06
Thai (125)	171	0.07
Vietnamese (1,602)	1,701	0.71
Other Asian, specified (16)	62	0.03
Other Asian, not specified (326)	1,025	0.43
Assyrian/Chaldean/Syriac	6	0.00
Australian	75	0.03
Austrian	231	0.10
Basque	17	0.01
Belgian	53	0.02
Brazilian	256	0.11
British	277	0.12
Bulgarian	42	0.02
Canadian	212	0.09
Celtic	43	0.02
Croatian	147	0.06
Cypriot	6	0.00
Czech	127	0.05
Czechoslovakian	124	0.05
Danish	234	0.10
Dutch	616	0.26
Eastern European	202	0.08
English	2,605	1.09
European	388	0.16
Finnish	156	0.06
French, except Basque	1,055	0.44
French Canadian	234	0.10
German	6,476	2.70
German Russian	6	0.00
Greek	1,011	0.42
Guyanese	1,986	0.83
Hawaii Native/Pacific Islander:	617	0.26
Melanesian: (2)	3	0.00
Fijian (2)	3	0.00
Micronesian: (33)	47	0.02
Guamanian/Chamorro (33)	47	0.02
Polynesian: (57)	104	0.04
Native Hawaiian (29)	57	0.02
Samoan (28)	45	0.02
Other Polynesian	2	0.00
Other Pac. Isl., specified	37	0.02
Other Pac. Isl., not spec. (88)	426	0.18
Hispanic or Latino:	67,952	28.31
Central American:	4,752	1.98
Costa Rican	188	0.08
Guatemalan	520	0.22
Honduran	2,192	0.91
Nicaraguan	351	0.15
Panamanian	236	0.10
Salvadoran	932	0.39
Other Central American	333	0.14
Cuban	1,860	0.77
Dominican Republic	9,186	3.83
Mexican	2,495	1.04
Puerto Rican	29,777	12.40
South American:	7,807	3.25
Argentinean	300	0.12
Bolivian	244	0.10
Chilean	269	0.11
Colombian	1,683	0.70
Ecuadorian	3,920	1.63
Paraguayan	23	0.01
Peruvian	786	0.33
Uruguayan	44	0.02
Venezuelan	165	0.07
Other South American	373	0.16
Other Hispanic or Latino	12,075	5.03
Hungarian	638	0.27
Icelander	10	0.00
Iranian	170	0.07
Irish	13,500	5.62
Israeli	197	0.08
Italian	15,731	6.55
Latvian	39	0.02
Lithuanian	142	0.06
Macedonian	7	0.00
Northern European	54	0.02
Norwegian	408	0.17
Pennsylvania German	42	0.02
Polish	7,215	3.01
Portuguese	375	0.16
Romanian	167	0.07
Russian	1,653	0.69
Scandinavian	72	0.03
Scotch-Irish	523	0.22
Scottish	800	0.33
Serbian	32	0.01
Slavic	107	0.04
Slovak	365	0.15
Slovene	28	0.01
Soviet Union	5	0.00
Swedish	409	0.17
Swiss	150	0.06
Turkish	158	0.07
Ukrainian	682	0.28
United States or American	4,513	1.88
Welsh	220	0.09
West Indian, excl. Hispanic:	5,769	2.40
Bahamian	43	0.02
Barbadian	82	0.03
Belizean	153	0.06
British West Indian	377	0.16
Dutch West Indian	7	0.00
Haitian	1,931	0.80
Jamaican	1,154	0.48
Trinidadian and Tobagonian	1,031	0.43
U.S. Virgin Islander	29	0.01
West Indian	923	0.38
Other West Indian	39	0.02

Notes: 1. Figures in the "Number" column do not add up to the total population due to: a) Ancestry/Race overlap — e.g. persons can report being both White and Irish, b) persons of Hispanic origin can report being any race, c) persons reporting two ancestries are counted in both categories. 2. Numbers in parentheses indicate the number of persons reporting this ancestry/race alone, not in combination with any other ancestry/race. 3. Refer to the Explanation of Data in the front of the book for more detailed information.

White:	90,383	37.65
Not Hispanic (56,736)	62,186	25.90
Hispanic (24,901)	28,197	11.75
Yugoslavian	59	0.02

Keansburg

Place Type: Borough
County: Monmouth
Population: 10,732

Ancestry/Race	Number	%
African American/Black:	281	2.62
Not Hispanic (207)	250	2.33
Hispanic (22)	31	0.29
African, sub-Saharan:	7	0.07
African	7	0.07
Am. Ind. or Alaska Nat., not spec.	16	0.15
American Indian tribes, specified:	27	0.25
Cherokee (5)	12	0.11
Chickasaw (1)	1	0.01
Comanche	2	0.02
Delaware (1)	8	0.07
Latin American Indians (2)	3	0.03
Navajo	1	0.01
American Indian tribes, not spec.	3	0.03
Arab:	92	0.86
Jordanian	43	0.40
Lebanese	39	0.36
Other Arab	10	0.09
Asian:	170	1.58
Chinese, ex. Taiwanese (34)	37	0.34
Filipino (51)	69	0.64
Indian (9)	16	0.15
Indonesian (1)	1	0.01
Japanese (4)	8	0.07
Korean (6)	6	0.06
Pakistani (13)	16	0.15
Taiwanese (2)	2	0.02
Vietnamese (4)	4	0.04
Other Asian, not specified (7)	11	0.10
Austrian	8	0.07
Brazilian	5	0.05
British	7	0.07
Canadian	14	0.13
Celtic	6	0.06
Czech	18	0.17
Czechoslovakian	20	0.19
Danish	50	0.47
Dutch	181	1.69
English	506	4.71
European	22	0.20
French, except Basque	226	2.11
French Canadian	98	0.91
German	1,846	17.20
Greek	135	1.26
Hawaii Native/Pacific Islander:	14	0.13
Micronesian: (3)	3	0.03
Guamanian/Chamorro (3)	3	0.03
Polynesian: (2)	2	0.02
Native Hawaiian (1)	1	0.01
Samoan (1)	1	0.01
Other Pac. Isl., not spec. (2)	9	0.08
Hispanic or Latino:	853	7.95
Central American:	13	0.12
Costa Rican	1	0.01
Guatemalan	1	0.01
Nicaraguan	1	0.01
Panamanian	4	0.04
Salvadoran	6	0.06
Cuban	70	0.65
Dominican Republic	28	0.26
Mexican	61	0.57
Puerto Rican	473	4.41
South American:	59	0.55
Argentinean	3	0.03
Colombian	38	0.35
Ecuadorian	11	0.10
Peruvian	7	0.07
Other Hispanic or Latino	149	1.39
Hungarian	107	1.00
Irish	3,710	34.57
Italian	2,521	23.49
Lithuanian	53	0.49
Norwegian	108	1.01
Polish	686	6.39
Portuguese	86	0.80
Romanian	6	0.06
Russian	121	1.13
Scotch-Irish	132	1.23
Scottish	239	2.23
Slavic	7	0.07
Slovak	48	0.45
Swedish	146	1.36
Swiss	11	0.10
Ukrainian	165	1.54
United States or American	253	2.36
Welsh	14	0.13
West Indian, excl. Hispanic:	42	0.39
Haitian	13	0.12
Jamaican	29	0.27
White:	10,141	94.49
Not Hispanic (9,403)	9,494	88.46
Hispanic (611)	647	6.03

Kearny

Place Type: Town
County: Hudson
Population: 40,513

Ancestry/Race	Number	%
African American/Black:	1,867	4.61
Not Hispanic (1,442)	1,592	3.93
Hispanic (167)	275	0.68
African, sub-Saharan:	321	0.79
African	245	0.60
Ghanian	9	0.02
Kenyan	19	0.05
Liberian	8	0.02
South African	9	0.02
Other sub-Saharan African	31	0.08
Am. Ind. or Alaska Nat., not spec.	124	0.31
American Indian tribes, specified:	109	0.27
Apache (1)	2	0.00
Blackfeet (1)	4	0.01
Cherokee (5)	9	0.02
Iroquois (8)	9	0.02
Latin American Indians (40)	64	0.16
Osage	1	0.00
Pueblo (3)	5	0.01
Sioux (1)	1	0.00
All other tribes (7)	14	0.03
American Indian tribes, not spec.	10	0.02
Arab:	337	0.83
Arab/Arabic	51	0.13
Egyptian	202	0.50
Lebanese	30	0.07
Moroccan	36	0.09
Syrian	12	0.03
Other Arab	6	0.01
Armenian	69	0.17
Asian:	2,451	6.05
Bangladeshi (11)	13	0.03
Chinese, ex. Taiwanese (840)	864	2.13
Filipino (293)	324	0.80
Indian (831)	912	2.25
Indonesian (3)	3	0.01
Japanese (22)	31	0.08
Korean (72)	85	0.21
Malaysian (2)	2	0.00
Pakistani (56)	80	0.20
Sri Lankan (14)	14	0.03
Taiwanese (15)	16	0.04
Thai (24)	32	0.08
Vietnamese (8)	12	0.03
Other Asian, specified	1	0.00
Other Asian, not specified (10)	62	0.15
Austrian	121	0.30
Basque	55	0.14
Belgian	6	0.01
Brazilian	1,629	4.02
British	72	0.18
Bulgarian	8	0.02
Canadian	35	0.09
Celtic	7	0.02
Croatian	33	0.08
Czech	63	0.16
Czechoslovakian	41	0.10
Danish	24	0.06
Dutch	143	0.35
Eastern European	5	0.01
English	983	2.43
European	64	0.16
French, except Basque	407	1.00
French Canadian	71	0.18
German	2,492	6.15
Greek	336	0.83
Guyanese	47	0.12
Hawaii Native/Pacific Islander:	72	0.18
Micronesian: (2)	6	0.01
Guamanian/Chamorro (2)	6	0.01
Polynesian: (9)	17	0.04
Native Hawaiian (2)	4	0.01
Samoan (7)	13	0.03
Other Pac. Isl., specified	1	0.00
Other Pac. Isl., not spec. (16)	48	0.12
Hispanic or Latino:	11,075	27.34
Central American:	510	1.26
Costa Rican	28	0.07
Guatemalan	164	0.40
Honduran	64	0.16
Nicaraguan	26	0.06
Panamanian	6	0.01
Salvadoran	204	0.50
Other Central American	18	0.04
Cuban	847	2.09
Dominican Republic	469	1.16
Mexican	375	0.93
Puerto Rican	2,237	5.52
South American:	3,235	7.99
Argentinean	105	0.26
Bolivian	2	0.00
Chilean	64	0.16
Colombian	382	0.94
Ecuadorian	856	2.11
Paraguayan	6	0.01
Peruvian	1,549	3.82
Uruguayan	98	0.24
Venezuelan	59	0.15
Other South American	114	0.28
Other Hispanic or Latino	3,402	8.40
Hungarian	152	0.38
Iranian	8	0.02
Irish	5,413	13.36
Italian	4,889	12.07
Latvian	13	0.03
Lithuanian	442	1.09
Macedonian	52	0.13
Maltese	4	0.01
Norwegian	48	0.12
Polish	3,156	7.79
Portuguese	4,773	11.78
Romanian	23	0.06
Russian	204	0.50
Scotch-Irish	646	1.59
Scottish	1,023	2.53
Slavic	19	0.05
Slovak	121	0.30
Swedish	131	0.32
Swiss	25	0.06
Turkish	36	0.09
Ukrainian	234	0.58
United States or American	1,129	2.79
Welsh	99	0.24
West Indian, excl. Hispanic:	134	0.33
Bermudan	6	0.01
British West Indian	14	0.03
Haitian	28	0.07
Jamaican	29	0.07

Notes: 1. Figures in the "Number" column do not add up to the total population due to: a) Ancestry/Race overlap — e.g. persons can report being both White and Irish, b) persons of Hispanic origin can report being any race, c) persons reporting two ancestries are counted in both categories. 2. Numbers in parentheses indicate the number of persons reporting this ancestry/race alone, not in combination with any other ancestry/race. 3. Refer to the Explanation of Data in the front of the book for more detailed information.

Ancestry/Race	Number	%
Trinidadian and Tobagonian	47	0.12
West Indian	10	0.02
White:	32,219	79.53
Not Hispanic (24,425)	25,233	62.28
Hispanic (6,262)	6,986	17.24
Yugoslavian	11	0.03

Lacey

Place Type: Township
County: Ocean
Population: 25,346

Ancestry/Race	Number	%
African American/Black:	127	0.50
Not Hispanic (89)	120	0.47
Hispanic (2)	7	0.03
Am. Ind. or Alaska Nat., not spec.	32	0.13
Alsatian	13	0.05
American Indian tribes, specified:	63	0.25
Apache	3	0.01
Blackfeet	6	0.02
Cherokee (12)	15	0.06
Chickasaw (1)	2	0.01
Choctaw	5	0.02
Creek	2	0.01
Delaware	6	0.02
Iroquois (3)	3	0.01
Latin American Indians (8)	9	0.04
Seminole (1)	1	0.00
Sioux	5	0.02
All other tribes (2)	6	0.02
American Indian tribes, not spec.	5	0.02
Arab:	68	0.27
Egyptian	20	0.08
Lebanese	9	0.04
Palestinian	39	0.15
Armenian	9	0.04
Asian:	193	0.76
Chinese, ex. Taiwanese (41)	44	0.17
Filipino (39)	61	0.24
Indian (14)	21	0.08
Indonesian (1)	1	0.00
Japanese (7)	17	0.07
Korean (25)	28	0.11
Pakistani (1)	2	0.01
Taiwanese	2	0.01
Thai (1)	1	0.00
Vietnamese (8)	11	0.04
Other Asian, specified	2	0.01
Other Asian, not specified (2)	3	0.01
Austrian	133	0.52
Belgian	41	0.16
British	24	0.09
Canadian	42	0.17
Celtic	30	0.12
Croatian	40	0.16
Czech	139	0.55
Czechoslovakian	43	0.17
Danish	83	0.33
Dutch	430	1.70
Eastern European	12	0.05
English	2,372	9.36
European	141	0.56
French, except Basque	636	2.51
French Canadian	114	0.45
German	5,278	20.82
Greek	303	1.20
Hawaii Native/Pacific Islander:	5	0.02
Micronesian: (1)	1	0.00
Guamanian/Chamorro (1)	1	0.00
Polynesian: (1)	1	0.00
Native Hawaiian (1)	1	0.00
Other Pac. Isl., specified	2	0.01
Other Pac. Isl., not spec.	1	0.00
Hispanic or Latino:	545	2.15
Central American:	23	0.09
Costa Rican	6	0.02
Guatemalan	11	0.04
Honduran	1	0.00
Salvadoran	4	0.02
Other Central American	1	0.00
Cuban	49	0.19
Dominican Republic	11	0.04
Mexican	78	0.31
Puerto Rican	216	0.85
South American:	28	0.11
Argentinean	5	0.02
Chilean	2	0.01
Colombian	13	0.05
Ecuadorian	4	0.02
Peruvian	1	0.00
Uruguayan	2	0.01
Other South American	1	0.00
Other Hispanic or Latino	140	0.55
Hungarian	504	1.99
Iranian	9	0.04
Irish	6,640	26.20
Italian	7,872	31.06
Latvian	10	0.04
Lithuanian	273	1.08
Maltese	7	0.03
Norwegian	319	1.26
Pennsylvania German	16	0.06
Polish	2,461	9.71
Portuguese	199	0.79
Romanian	9	0.04
Russian	393	1.55
Scandinavian	7	0.03
Scotch-Irish	484	1.91
Scottish	699	2.76
Slavic	18	0.07
Slovak	129	0.51
Swedish	300	1.18
Swiss	81	0.32
Turkish	10	0.04
Ukrainian	321	1.27
United States or American	881	3.48
Welsh	134	0.53
West Indian, excl. Hispanic:	19	0.07
Jamaican	19	0.07
White:	24,960	98.48
Not Hispanic (24,393)	24,530	96.78
Hispanic (407)	430	1.70
Yugoslavian	27	0.11

Lakewood

Place Type: Township
County: Ocean
Population: 60,352

Ancestry/Race	Number	%
African American/Black:	7,778	12.89
Not Hispanic (6,878)	7,216	11.96
Hispanic (392)	562	0.93
African, sub-Saharan:	439	0.73
African	400	0.66
Nigerian	18	0.03
South African	21	0.03
Am. Ind. or Alaska Nat., not spec.	101	0.17
Albanian	8	0.01
American Indian tribes, specified:	204	0.34
Apache (5)	5	0.01
Blackfeet (2)	13	0.02
Cherokee (4)	51	0.08
Chippewa	1	0.00
Delaware (1)	5	0.01
Iroquois (2)	3	0.00
Latin American Indians (38)	97	0.16
Lumbee	1	0.00
Navajo (1)	3	0.00
Potawatomi (3)	3	0.00
Pueblo	7	0.01
Seminole	2	0.00
Sioux (1)	3	0.00
All other tribes (4)	10	0.02
American Indian tribes, not spec.	29	0.05
Arab:	294	0.49
Egyptian	44	0.07
Iraqi	5	0.01
Lebanese	56	0.09
Moroccan	88	0.15
Syrian	83	0.14
Other Arab	18	0.03
Armenian	18	0.03
Asian:	1,016	1.68
Bangladeshi (2)	4	0.01
Cambodian (1)	1	0.00
Chinese, ex. Taiwanese (108)	128	0.21
Filipino (322)	370	0.61
Indian (236)	280	0.46
Indonesian (3)	5	0.01
Japanese (14)	29	0.05
Korean (51)	60	0.10
Pakistani (17)	19	0.03
Sri Lankan (1)	1	0.00
Taiwanese	1	0.00
Thai (10)	12	0.02
Vietnamese (27)	34	0.06
Other Asian, specified	1	0.00
Other Asian, not specified (37)	71	0.12
Assyrian/Chaldean/Syriac	7	0.01
Australian	20	0.03
Austrian	476	0.79
Belgian	24	0.04
Brazilian	23	0.04
British	156	0.26
Canadian	159	0.26
Croatian	19	0.03
Czech	104	0.17
Czechoslovakian	133	0.22
Danish	140	0.23
Dutch	596	0.99
Eastern European	493	0.82
English	2,149	3.56
Estonian	160	0.27
European	643	1.07
Finnish	46	0.08
French, except Basque	534	0.88
French Canadian	175	0.29
German	4,610	7.64
Greek	217	0.36
Guyanese	13	0.02
Hawaii Native/Pacific Islander:	45	0.07
Micronesian: (2)	2	0.00
Guamanian/Chamorro (2)	2	0.00
Polynesian: (11)	23	0.04
Native Hawaiian (8)	13	0.02
Samoan (2)	9	0.01
Tongan (1)	1	0.00
Other Pac. Isl., specified	1	0.00
Other Pac. Isl., not spec. (6)	19	0.03
Hispanic or Latino:	8,935	14.80
Central American:	485	0.80
Costa Rican	150	0.25
Guatemalan	58	0.10
Honduran	15	0.02
Nicaraguan	51	0.08
Panamanian	15	0.02
Salvadoran	171	0.28
Other Central American	25	0.04
Cuban	214	0.35
Dominican Republic	235	0.39
Mexican	2,825	4.68
Puerto Rican	3,730	6.18
South American:	507	0.84
Argentinean	16	0.03
Bolivian	1	0.00
Chilean	5	0.01
Colombian	216	0.36
Ecuadorian	120	0.20
Peruvian	115	0.19
Uruguayan	4	0.01
Venezuelan	12	0.02
Other South American	18	0.03
Other Hispanic or Latino	939	1.56
Hungarian	1,354	2.24
Iranian	20	0.03
Irish	5,532	9.17

Notes: 1. Figures in the "Number" column do not add up to the total population due to: a) Ancestry/Race overlap — e.g. persons can report being both White and Irish, b) persons of Hispanic origin can report being any race, c) persons reporting two ancestries are counted in both categories. 2. Numbers in parentheses indicate the number of persons reporting this ancestry/race alone, not in combination with any other ancestry/race. 3. Refer to the Explanation of Data in the front of the book for more detailed information.

Israeli	191	0.32
Italian	5,946	9.85
Latvian	18	0.03
Lithuanian	508	0.84
Luxemburger	8	0.01
Northern European	5	0.01
Norwegian	216	0.36
Pennsylvania German	9	0.01
Polish	3,686	6.11
Portuguese	74	0.12
Romanian	138	0.23
Russian	1,592	2.64
Scandinavian	23	0.04
Scotch-Irish	161	0.27
Scottish	539	0.89
Slavic	27	0.04
Slovak	211	0.35
Swedish	261	0.43
Swiss	121	0.20
Turkish	30	0.05
Ukrainian	394	0.65
United States or American	3,043	5.04
Welsh	99	0.16
West Indian, excl. Hispanic:	695	1.15
Barbadian	6	0.01
Bermudan	11	0.02
British West Indian	20	0.03
Haitian	7	0.01
Jamaican	471	0.78
Trinidadian and Tobagonian	91	0.15
West Indian	89	0.15
White:	49,013	81.21
Not Hispanic (42,816)	43,428	71.96
Hispanic (4,726)	5,585	9.25
Yugoslavian	8	0.01

Lawrence

Place Type: Township
County: Mercer
Population: 29,159

Ancestry/Race	Number	%
Afghan	48	0.16
African American/Black:	2,867	9.83
Not Hispanic (2,669)	2,793	9.58
Hispanic (38)	74	0.25
African, sub-Saharan:	294	1.01
African	124	0.43
Kenyan	17	0.06
Nigerian	46	0.16
Sierra Leonean	107	0.37
Alaska Native tribes, specified:	1	0.00
Tlingit-Haida (1)	1	0.00
Am. Ind. or Alaska Nat., not spec.	53	0.18
American Indian tribes, specified:	53	0.18
Blackfeet	3	0.01
Cherokee (1)	13	0.04
Choctaw	1	0.00
Cree	2	0.01
Creek (1)	1	0.00
Delaware (2)	5	0.02
Iroquois (3)	6	0.02
Latin American Indians (1)	7	0.02
Lumbee	4	0.01
Navajo	2	0.01
Seminole (1)	1	0.00
Sioux	1	0.00
All other tribes	7	0.02
Arab:	232	0.80
Arab/Arabic	9	0.03
Egyptian	70	0.24
Jordanian	16	0.05
Lebanese	77	0.26
Syrian	30	0.10
Other Arab	30	0.10
Armenian	9	0.03
Asian:	2,493	8.55
Bangladeshi (16)	16	0.05
Chinese, ex. Taiwanese (547)	592	2.03
Filipino (156)	174	0.60
Indian (1,073)	1,119	3.84
Indonesian (2)	2	0.01
Japanese (77)	107	0.37
Korean (211)	224	0.77
Laotian	1	0.00
Pakistani (70)	85	0.29
Sri Lankan (28)	31	0.11
Taiwanese (43)	44	0.15
Thai (8)	9	0.03
Vietnamese (30)	31	0.11
Other Asian, specified (1)	2	0.01
Other Asian, not specified (20)	56	0.19
Austrian	146	0.50
Belgian	18	0.06
British	281	0.96
Bulgarian	19	0.07
Canadian	103	0.35
Celtic	9	0.03
Croatian	41	0.14
Czech	105	0.36
Czechoslovakian	73	0.25
Danish	64	0.22
Dutch	539	1.85
Eastern European	167	0.57
English	2,504	8.59
Estonian	17	0.06
European	124	0.43
French, except Basque	447	1.53
French Canadian	45	0.15
German	3,652	12.52
Greek	167	0.57
Hawaii Native/Pacific Islander:	53	0.18
Micronesian: (5)	5	0.02
Guamanian/Chamorro (5)	5	0.02
Polynesian: (4)	17	0.06
Native Hawaiian (1)	7	0.02
Samoan (3)	10	0.03
Other Pac. Isl., not spec. (22)	31	0.11
Hispanic or Latino:	1,344	4.61
Central American:	155	0.53
Costa Rican	10	0.03
Guatemalan	120	0.41
Honduran	5	0.02
Nicaraguan	1	0.00
Panamanian	6	0.02
Other Central American	13	0.04
Cuban	42	0.14
Dominican Republic	22	0.08
Mexican	180	0.62
Puerto Rican	365	1.25
South American:	190	0.65
Argentinean	26	0.09
Chilean	5	0.02
Colombian	94	0.32
Ecuadorian	14	0.05
Paraguayan	1	0.00
Peruvian	21	0.07
Uruguayan	4	0.01
Venezuelan	18	0.06
Other South American	7	0.02
Other Hispanic or Latino	390	1.34
Hungarian	564	1.93
Iranian	37	0.13
Irish	4,243	14.55
Israeli	20	0.07
Italian	4,980	17.08
Latvian	36	0.12
Lithuanian	75	0.26
Northern European	22	0.08
Norwegian	170	0.58
Pennsylvania German	37	0.13
Polish	3,420	11.73
Portuguese	48	0.16
Romanian	75	0.26
Russian	811	2.78
Scandinavian	18	0.06
Scotch-Irish	388	1.33
Scottish	541	1.86
Slavic	65	0.22
Slovak	293	1.00
Slovene	8	0.03
Swedish	272	0.93
Swiss	112	0.38
Turkish	38	0.13
Ukrainian	285	0.98
United States or American	600	2.06
Welsh	135	0.46
West Indian, excl. Hispanic:	388	1.33
Bahamian	22	0.08
Haitian	66	0.23
Jamaican	143	0.49
U.S. Virgin Islander	12	0.04
West Indian	145	0.50
White:	23,461	80.46
Not Hispanic (22,325)	22,623	77.58
Hispanic (776)	838	2.87
Yugoslavian	15	0.05

Leisure Village West-Pine Lake Park

Place Type: Census Designated Place
County: Ocean
Population: 11,085

Ancestry/Race	Number	%
African American/Black:	373	3.36
Not Hispanic (305)	353	3.18
Hispanic (12)	20	0.18
African, sub-Saharan:	19	0.17
African	19	0.17
Alaska Native tribes, specified:	1	0.01
Alaska Athabascan (1)	1	0.01
Alaska Native tribes, not specified	1	0.01
Am. Ind. or Alaska Nat., not spec.	25	0.23
Albanian	9	0.08
American Indian tribes, specified:	31	0.28
Blackfeet (4)	4	0.04
Cherokee (7)	22	0.20
Delaware (3)	3	0.03
Iroquois (1)	1	0.01
Sioux	1	0.01
American Indian tribes, not spec.	2	0.02
Arab:	11	0.10
Egyptian	11	0.10
Armenian	62	0.56
Asian:	152	1.37
Chinese, ex. Taiwanese (7)	8	0.07
Filipino (95)	101	0.91
Indian	1	0.01
Japanese (5)	9	0.08
Korean (6)	9	0.08
Laotian (6)	11	0.10
Pakistani (3)	5	0.05
Thai (3)	3	0.03
Vietnamese	1	0.01
Other Asian, specified	1	0.01
Other Asian, not specified	3	0.03
Assyrian/Chaldean/Syriac	7	0.06
Austrian	125	1.13
Belgian	7	0.06
British	33	0.30
Czech	56	0.51
Czechoslovakian	22	0.20
Danish	52	0.47
Dutch	155	1.40
English	738	6.68
Estonian	8	0.07
European	48	0.43
Finnish	29	0.26
French, except Basque	188	1.70
French Canadian	87	0.79
German	2,150	19.46
Greek	99	0.90
Hawaii Native/Pacific Islander:	7	0.06
Polynesian: (5)	6	0.05
Native Hawaiian	1	0.01
Samoan (5)	5	0.05
Other Pac. Isl., specified	1	0.01

Notes: 1. Figures in the "Number" column do not add up to the total population due to: a) Ancestry/Race overlap — e.g. persons can report being both White and Irish, b) persons of Hispanic origin can report being any race, c) persons reporting two ancestries are counted in both categories. 2. Numbers in parentheses indicate the number of persons reporting this ancestry/race alone, not in combination with any other ancestry/race. 3. Refer to the Explanation of Data in the front of the book for more detailed information.

Hispanic or Latino:	437	3.94
Central American:	9	0.08
Costa Rican	2	0.02
Guatemalan	1	0.01
Honduran	1	0.01
Nicaraguan	1	0.01
Panamanian	1	0.01
Salvadoran	1	0.01
Other Central American	2	0.02
Cuban	12	0.11
Dominican Republic	20	0.18
Mexican	16	0.14
Puerto Rican	269	2.43
South American:	31	0.28
Argentinean	1	0.01
Colombian	16	0.14
Ecuadorian	5	0.05
Peruvian	8	0.07
Other South American	1	0.01
Other Hispanic or Latino	80	0.72
Hungarian	145	1.31
Irish	2,301	20.82
Italian	2,467	22.32
Latvian	44	0.40
Lithuanian	65	0.59
Norwegian	106	0.96
Polish	1,000	9.05
Portuguese	77	0.70
Romanian	58	0.52
Russian	384	3.47
Scandinavian	16	0.14
Scotch-Irish	154	1.39
Scottish	239	2.16
Slavic	8	0.07
Slovak	111	1.00
Swedish	92	0.83
Swiss	57	0.52
Ukrainian	165	1.49
United States or American	654	5.92
Welsh	61	0.55
West Indian, excl. Hispanic:	30	0.27
Jamaican	24	0.22
West Indian	6	0.05
White:	10,478	94.52
Not Hispanic (10,078)	10,186	91.89
Hispanic (268)	292	2.63
Yugoslavian	17	0.15

Lincoln Park

Place Type: Borough
County: Morris
Population: 10,930

Ancestry/Race	Number	%
African American/Black:	212	1.94
Not Hispanic (177)	198	1.81
Hispanic (14)	14	0.13
African, sub-Saharan:	16	0.15
Ghanian	16	0.15
Alaska Native tribes, specified:	1	0.01
Tlingit-Haida	1	0.01
Am. Ind. or Alaska Nat., not spec.	11	0.10
Albanian	200	1.83
American Indian tribes, specified:	18	0.16
Cherokee	7	0.06
Delaware (1)	1	0.01
Latin American Indians (5)	10	0.09
American Indian tribes, not spec.	1	0.01
Arab:	97	0.89
Egyptian	31	0.28
Lebanese	17	0.16
Moroccan	10	0.09
Palestinian	8	0.07
Syrian	31	0.28
Armenian	7	0.06
Asian:	661	6.05
Chinese, ex. Taiwanese (86)	104	0.95
Filipino (166)	188	1.72
Indian (181)	190	1.74
Japanese (47)	54	0.49
Korean (63)	70	0.64
Malaysian (1)	1	0.01
Pakistani (2)	2	0.02
Taiwanese	4	0.04
Thai (4)	4	0.04
Vietnamese (2)	9	0.08
Other Asian, not specified (14)	35	0.32
Australian	7	0.06
Austrian	13	0.12
Belgian	20	0.18
Brazilian	14	0.13
British	22	0.20
Canadian	7	0.06
Croatian	29	0.27
Czech	26	0.24
Czechoslovakian	16	0.15
Danish	39	0.36
Dutch	357	3.27
Eastern European	38	0.35
English	761	6.96
European	14	0.13
Finnish	16	0.15
French, except Basque	155	1.42
French Canadian	53	0.48
German	1,814	16.60
Greek	57	0.52
Hawaii Native/Pacific Islander:	2	0.02
Other Pac. Isl., not spec. (1)	2	0.02
Hispanic or Latino:	633	5.79
Central American:	21	0.19
Costa Rican	3	0.03
Guatemalan	13	0.12
Salvadoran	5	0.05
Cuban	75	0.69
Dominican Republic	18	0.16
Mexican	41	0.38
Puerto Rican	214	1.96
South American:	159	1.45
Argentinean	14	0.13
Chilean	6	0.05
Colombian	46	0.42
Ecuadorian	32	0.29
Peruvian	47	0.43
Venezuelan	10	0.09
Other South American	4	0.04
Other Hispanic or Latino	105	0.96
Hungarian	158	1.45
Iranian	13	0.12
Irish	2,103	19.24
Italian	2,919	26.71
Lithuanian	51	0.47
Macedonian	140	1.28
Maltese	8	0.07
Norwegian	76	0.70
Pennsylvania German	22	0.20
Polish	1,078	9.86
Portuguese	71	0.65
Russian	166	1.52
Scotch-Irish	46	0.42
Scottish	216	1.98
Serbian	18	0.16
Slavic	7	0.06
Slovak	95	0.87
Slovene	6	0.05
Swedish	96	0.88
Swiss	28	0.26
Turkish	14	0.13
Ukrainian	145	1.33
United States or American	390	3.57
Welsh	29	0.27
West Indian, excl. Hispanic:	23	0.21
Jamaican	23	0.21
White:	9,994	91.44
Not Hispanic (9,398)	9,516	87.06
Hispanic (447)	478	4.37
Yugoslavian	32	0.29

Linden

Place Type: City
County: Union
Population: 39,394

Ancestry/Race	Number	%
African American/Black:	9,612	24.40
Not Hispanic (8,782)	9,274	23.54
Hispanic (199)	338	0.86
African, sub-Saharan:	497	1.26
African	411	1.04
Liberian	23	0.06
Nigerian	37	0.09
South African	7	0.02
Other sub-Saharan African	19	0.05
Alaska Native tribes, specified:	1	0.00
Tlingit-Haida	1	0.00
Am. Ind. or Alaska Nat., not spec.	91	0.23
Albanian	18	0.05
Alsatian	20	0.05
American Indian tribes, specified:	107	0.27
Blackfeet	12	0.03
Cherokee (3)	33	0.08
Cheyenne	4	0.01
Chickasaw	1	0.00
Chippewa (1)	4	0.01
Delaware (2)	18	0.05
Iroquois	1	0.00
Latin American Indians (5)	10	0.03
Lumbee (1)	1	0.00
Navajo	2	0.01
Potawatomi (2)	2	0.01
Seminole	8	0.02
Sioux	6	0.02
All other tribes (2)	5	0.01
American Indian tribes, not spec.	11	0.03
Arab:	211	0.54
Arab/Arabic	57	0.14
Egyptian	85	0.22
Moroccan	24	0.06
Syrian	7	0.02
Other Arab	38	0.10
Armenian	16	0.04
Asian:	1,088	2.76
Bangladeshi (5)	6	0.02
Chinese, ex. Taiwanese (134)	172	0.44
Filipino (266)	306	0.78
Indian (359)	398	1.01
Japanese (11)	23	0.06
Korean (44)	45	0.11
Laotian	1	0.00
Malaysian	9	0.02
Pakistani (49)	51	0.13
Taiwanese (3)	6	0.02
Thai (2)	2	0.01
Vietnamese (29)	38	0.10
Other Asian, specified (1)	1	0.00
Other Asian, not specified (7)	30	0.08
Austrian	103	0.26
Belgian	5	0.01
Brazilian	162	0.41
British	47	0.12
Bulgarian	30	0.08
Canadian	18	0.05
Carpatho Rusyn	19	0.05
Croatian	17	0.04
Czech	138	0.35
Czechoslovakian	273	0.69
Danish	66	0.17
Dutch	151	0.38
Eastern European	9	0.02
English	1,068	2.71
European	114	0.29
Finnish	12	0.03
French, except Basque	374	0.95
French Canadian	71	0.18
German	2,692	6.83
Greek	271	0.69
Guyanese	121	0.31

Notes: 1. Figures in the "Number" column do not add up to the total population due to: a) Ancestry/Race overlap — e.g. persons can report being both White and Irish, b) persons of Hispanic origin can report being any race, c) persons reporting two ancestries are counted in both categories. 2. Numbers in parentheses indicate the number of persons reporting this ancestry/race alone, not in combination with any other ancestry/race. 3. Refer to the Explanation of Data in the front of the book for more detailed information.

Hawaii Native/Pacific Islander:	44	0.11
Micronesian: (4)	5	0.01
Guamanian/Chamorro (4)	5	0.01
Polynesian: (1)	3	0.01
Native Hawaiian (1)	3	0.01
Other Pac. Isl., not spec. (10)	36	0.09
Hispanic or Latino:	5,674	14.40
Central American:	335	0.85
Costa Rican	73	0.19
Guatemalan	25	0.06
Honduran	64	0.16
Nicaraguan	23	0.06
Panamanian	13	0.03
Salvadoran	118	0.30
Other Central American	19	0.05
Cuban	593	1.51
Dominican Republic	275	0.70
Mexican	153	0.39
Puerto Rican	1,512	3.84
South American:	1,479	3.75
Argentinean	98	0.25
Bolivian	6	0.02
Chilean	19	0.05
Colombian	852	2.16
Ecuadorian	111	0.28
Peruvian	263	0.67
Uruguayan	46	0.12
Venezuelan	27	0.07
Other South American	57	0.14
Other Hispanic or Latino	1,327	3.37
Hungarian	366	0.93
Irish	3,541	8.99
Italian	4,039	10.25
Lithuanian	438	1.11
Luxemburger	4	0.01
Norwegian	52	0.13
Pennsylvania German	5	0.01
Polish	7,098	18.02
Portuguese	1,216	3.09
Romanian	38	0.10
Russian	508	1.29
Scandinavian	13	0.03
Scotch-Irish	102	0.26
Scottish	142	0.36
Slavic	112	0.28
Slovak	927	2.35
Slovene	5	0.01
Swedish	115	0.29
Swiss	7	0.02
Turkish	36	0.09
Ukrainian	697	1.77
United States or American	957	2.43
Welsh	52	0.13
West Indian, excl. Hispanic:	1,723	4.37
Barbadian	49	0.12
Bermudan	7	0.02
British West Indian	53	0.13
Haitian	1,360	3.45
Jamaican	157	0.40
Trinidadian and Tobagonian	64	0.16
West Indian	33	0.08
White:	26,993	68.52
Not Hispanic (22,827)	23,430	59.48
Hispanic (3,204)	3,563	9.04
Yugoslavian	48	0.12

Lindenwold

Place Type: Borough
County: Camden
Population: 17,414

Ancestry/Race	Number	%
African American/Black:	5,232	30.04
Not Hispanic (4,776)	5,025	28.86
Hispanic (139)	207	1.19
African, sub-Saharan:	220	1.26
African	169	0.97
Ethiopian	16	0.09
Ghanian	17	0.10
Nigerian	7	0.04
Sierra Leonean	11	0.06
Alaska Native tribes, specified:	1	0.01
Eskimo (1)	1	0.01
Am. Ind. or Alaska Nat., not spec.	105	0.60
Albanian	13	0.07
American Indian tribes, specified:	111	0.64
Apache	1	0.01
Blackfeet	9	0.05
Cherokee (11)	37	0.21
Chippewa	1	0.01
Choctaw (2)	2	0.01
Creek	2	0.01
Delaware (4)	11	0.06
Iroquois (1)	6	0.03
Latin American Indians (3)	8	0.05
Menominee (1)	1	0.01
Navajo (1)	3	0.02
Potawatomi	1	0.01
Pueblo (1)	2	0.01
Seminole	1	0.01
Sioux (2)	4	0.02
All other tribes (9)	22	0.13
American Indian tribes, not spec.	15	0.09
Arab:	8	0.05
Egyptian	8	0.05
Armenian	26	0.15
Asian:	748	4.30
Bangladeshi (36)	44	0.25
Cambodian (9)	11	0.06
Chinese, ex. Taiwanese (65)	86	0.49
Filipino (115)	152	0.87
Indian (220)	241	1.38
Indonesian	1	0.01
Japanese (11)	28	0.16
Korean (43)	50	0.29
Laotian (4)	5	0.03
Malaysian	2	0.01
Pakistani (15)	24	0.14
Taiwanese (3)	3	0.02
Thai (1)	1	0.01
Vietnamese (45)	54	0.31
Other Asian, specified (1)	7	0.04
Other Asian, not specified (24)	39	0.22
Austrian	66	0.38
Belgian	8	0.05
British	15	0.09
Canadian	19	0.11
Czechoslovakian	28	0.16
Danish	45	0.26
Dutch	140	0.80
Eastern European	37	0.21
English	1,171	6.72
European	41	0.24
Finnish	20	0.11
French, except Basque	419	2.41
French Canadian	120	0.69
German	2,612	15.00
German Russian	18	0.10
Greek	60	0.34
Hawaii Native/Pacific Islander:	39	0.22
Micronesian:	2	0.01
Guamanian/Chamorro	2	0.01
Polynesian: (8)	12	0.07
Native Hawaiian (8)	12	0.07
Other Pac. Isl., specified	6	0.03
Other Pac. Isl., not spec. (2)	19	0.11
Hispanic or Latino:	1,316	7.56
Central American:	262	1.50
Costa Rican	5	0.03
Guatemalan	7	0.04
Honduran	67	0.38
Nicaraguan	1	0.01
Panamanian	11	0.06
Salvadoran	169	0.97
Other Central American	2	0.01
Cuban	30	0.17
Dominican Republic	29	0.17
Mexican	203	1.17
Puerto Rican	587	3.37
South American:	26	0.15
Argentinean	8	0.05
Chilean	2	0.01
Colombian	8	0.05
Ecuadorian	1	0.01
Venezuelan	6	0.03
Other South American	1	0.01
Other Hispanic or Latino	179	1.03
Hungarian	39	0.22
Iranian	3	0.02
Irish	3,232	18.56
Italian	2,726	15.65
Lithuanian	72	0.41
Norwegian	102	0.59
Pennsylvania German	26	0.15
Polish	850	4.88
Portuguese	19	0.11
Romanian	62	0.36
Russian	116	0.67
Scotch-Irish	237	1.36
Scottish	229	1.32
Slovak	47	0.27
Swedish	146	0.84
Swiss	12	0.07
Ukrainian	129	0.74
United States or American	438	2.52
Welsh	186	1.07
West Indian, excl. Hispanic:	92	0.53
Jamaican	66	0.38
Trinidadian and Tobagonian	16	0.09
West Indian	10	0.06
White:	11,043	63.41
Not Hispanic (10,214)	10,486	60.22
Hispanic (481)	557	3.20

Little Egg Harbor

Place Type: Township
County: Ocean
Population: 15,945

Ancestry/Race	Number	%
Afghan	8	0.05
African American/Black:	157	0.98
Not Hispanic (117)	146	0.92
Hispanic (9)	11	0.07
African, sub-Saharan:	21	0.13
African	21	0.13
Alaska Native tribes, not specified	1	0.01
Am. Ind. or Alaska Nat., not spec.	30	0.19
American Indian tribes, specified:	76	0.48
Apache (1)	4	0.03
Blackfeet (2)	4	0.03
Cherokee (11)	23	0.14
Cree	1	0.01
Delaware (5)	8	0.05
Iroquois (1)	12	0.08
Latin American Indians (1)	6	0.04
Pueblo	5	0.03
Seminole (1)	1	0.01
Sioux	1	0.01
All other tribes (4)	11	0.07
American Indian tribes, not spec.	10	0.06
Arab:	68	0.42
Arab/Arabic	14	0.09
Egyptian	17	0.11
Syrian	37	0.23
Armenian	8	0.05
Asian:	145	0.91
Bangladeshi (2)	2	0.01
Chinese, ex. Taiwanese (17)	21	0.13
Filipino (33)	48	0.30
Indian (5)	10	0.06
Indonesian	2	0.01
Japanese (4)	11	0.07
Korean (18)	29	0.18
Laotian	1	0.01
Pakistani (1)	1	0.01
Thai (4)	5	0.03
Vietnamese (5)	7	0.04

Notes: 1. Figures in the "Number" column do not add up to the total population due to: a) Ancestry/Race overlap — e.g. persons can report being both White and Irish, b) persons of Hispanic origin can report being any race, c) persons reporting two ancestries are counted in both categories. 2. Numbers in parentheses indicate the number of persons reporting this ancestry/race alone, not in combination with any other ancestry/race. 3. Refer to the Explanation of Data in the front of the book for more detailed information.

Ancestry/Race	Number	%
Other Asian, specified	1	0.01
Other Asian, not specified (2)	7	0.04
Austrian	147	0.92
Belgian	8	0.05
Brazilian	6	0.04
British	124	0.77
Canadian	49	0.31
Croatian	8	0.05
Czech	57	0.36
Czechoslovakian	88	0.55
Danish	99	0.62
Dutch	365	2.28
English	1,778	11.10
European	47	0.29
Finnish	88	0.55
French, except Basque	417	2.60
French Canadian	141	0.88
German	3,850	24.03
Greek	25	0.16
Hawaii Native/Pacific Islander:	5	0.03
Polynesian: (1)	1	0.01
Native Hawaiian (1)	1	0.01
Other Pac. Isl., specified	1	0.01
Other Pac. Isl., not spec.	3	0.02
Hispanic or Latino:	520	3.26
Central American:	19	0.12
Guatemalan	5	0.03
Honduran	2	0.01
Nicaraguan	1	0.01
Salvadoran	2	0.01
Other Central American	9	0.06
Cuban	19	0.12
Dominican Republic	11	0.07
Mexican	79	0.50
Puerto Rican	253	1.59
South American:	41	0.26
Argentinean	7	0.04
Colombian	16	0.10
Ecuadorian	5	0.03
Peruvian	7	0.04
Venezuelan	6	0.04
Other Hispanic or Latino	98	0.61
Hungarian	357	2.23
Irish	3,779	23.59
Italian	3,993	24.93
Lithuanian	106	0.66
Maltese	7	0.04
Norwegian	256	1.60
Polish	1,483	9.26
Portuguese	62	0.39
Romanian	28	0.17
Russian	207	1.29
Scandinavian	16	0.10
Scotch-Irish	261	1.63
Scottish	326	2.04
Slavic	8	0.05
Slovak	112	0.70
Slovene	20	0.12
Swedish	241	1.50
Swiss	108	0.67
Ukrainian	164	1.02
United States or American	568	3.55
Welsh	182	1.14
West Indian, excl. Hispanic:	11	0.07
Jamaican	11	0.07
White:	15,504	97.23
Not Hispanic (15,030)	15,155	95.05
Hispanic (312)	349	2.19
Yugoslavian	17	0.11

Little Falls

Place Type: Census Designated Place
County: Passaic
Population: 10,855

Ancestry/Race	Number	%
African American/Black:	81	0.75
Not Hispanic (71)	80	0.74
Hispanic	1	0.01
African, sub-Saharan:	21	0.19
South African	21	0.19
Alaska Native tribes, specified:	1	0.01
Aleut (1)	1	0.01
Am. Ind. or Alaska Nat., not spec.	11	0.10
American Indian tribes, specified:	9	0.08
Cherokee	4	0.04
Chickasaw	3	0.03
Latin American Indians (1)	1	0.01
All other tribes (1)	1	0.01
Arab:	319	2.94
Egyptian	9	0.08
Jordanian	24	0.22
Lebanese	113	1.04
Syrian	173	1.59
Armenian	29	0.27
Asian:	525	4.84
Bangladeshi	4	0.04
Chinese, ex. Taiwanese (66)	80	0.74
Filipino (63)	72	0.66
Indian (193)	205	1.89
Indonesian (4)	4	0.04
Japanese (14)	19	0.18
Korean (56)	59	0.54
Laotian (1)	1	0.01
Pakistani (15)	15	0.14
Taiwanese (4)	9	0.08
Thai (5)	5	0.05
Vietnamese (21)	22	0.20
Other Asian, specified	1	0.01
Other Asian, not specified (1)	29	0.27
Assyrian/Chaldean/Syriac	18	0.17
Austrian	174	1.60
Basque	33	0.30
Belgian	31	0.29
Brazilian	17	0.16
British	15	0.14
Canadian	16	0.15
Croatian	13	0.12
Czech	62	0.57
Czechoslovakian	14	0.13
Danish	27	0.25
Dutch	413	3.80
Eastern European	16	0.15
English	567	5.22
European	18	0.17
Finnish	17	0.16
French, except Basque	203	1.87
French Canadian	5	0.05
German	1,337	12.32
Greek	130	1.20
Hawaii Native/Pacific Islander:	5	0.05
Polynesian: (2)	3	0.03
Native Hawaiian (1)	2	0.02
Samoan (1)	1	0.01
Other Pac. Isl., specified	1	0.01
Other Pac. Isl., not spec.	1	0.01
Hispanic or Latino:	579	5.33
Central American:	31	0.29
Costa Rican	11	0.10
Guatemalan	2	0.02
Nicaraguan	3	0.03
Panamanian	1	0.01
Salvadoran	14	0.13
Cuban	66	0.61
Dominican Republic	20	0.18
Mexican	56	0.52
Puerto Rican	166	1.53
South American:	160	1.47
Argentinean	14	0.13
Chilean	11	0.10
Colombian	73	0.67
Ecuadorian	14	0.13
Peruvian	34	0.31
Uruguayan	1	0.01
Venezuelan	6	0.06
Other South American	7	0.06
Other Hispanic or Latino	80	0.74
Hungarian	78	0.72
Icelander	7	0.06
Irish	2,172	20.01
Italian	3,755	34.59
Lithuanian	72	0.66
Maltese	7	0.06
Norwegian	33	0.30
Polish	792	7.30
Portuguese	30	0.28
Romanian	20	0.18
Russian	400	3.68
Scandinavian	12	0.11
Scotch-Irish	67	0.62
Scottish	123	1.13
Serbian	7	0.06
Slavic	43	0.40
Slovak	69	0.64
Swedish	83	0.76
Swiss	68	0.63
Turkish	47	0.43
Ukrainian	242	2.23
United States or American	181	1.67
Welsh	23	0.21
West Indian, excl. Hispanic:	30	0.28
British West Indian	7	0.06
Jamaican	23	0.21
White:	10,168	93.67
Not Hispanic (9,593)	9,732	89.65
Hispanic (408)	436	4.02

Little Ferry

Place Type: Borough
County: Bergen
Population: 10,800

Ancestry/Race	Number	%
African American/Black:	564	5.22
Not Hispanic (487)	517	4.79
Hispanic (22)	47	0.44
African, sub-Saharan:	192	1.78
African	79	0.73
Ghanian	91	0.84
Other sub-Saharan African	22	0.20
Alaska Native tribes, specified:	1	0.01
Alaska Athabascan (1)	1	0.01
Am. Ind. or Alaska Nat., not spec.	31	0.29
Albanian	27	0.25
American Indian tribes, specified:	15	0.14
Blackfeet	1	0.01
Cherokee (1)	7	0.06
Iroquois	1	0.01
Latin American Indians (4)	5	0.05
All other tribes (1)	1	0.01
American Indian tribes, not spec.	2	0.02
Arab:	98	0.91
Egyptian	46	0.43
Moroccan	30	0.28
Palestinian	22	0.20
Armenian	31	0.29
Asian:	2,015	18.66
Chinese, ex. Taiwanese (92)	94	0.87
Filipino (343)	363	3.36
Indian (384)	438	4.06
Japanese (82)	88	0.81
Korean (851)	865	8.01
Pakistani (45)	61	0.56
Taiwanese (1)	1	0.01
Vietnamese (5)	5	0.05
Other Asian, specified (9)	9	0.08
Other Asian, not specified (17)	91	0.84
Austrian	16	0.15
British	43	0.40
Croatian	143	1.32
Czech	148	1.37
Czechoslovakian	43	0.40
Danish	10	0.09
Dutch	188	1.74
Eastern European	9	0.08
English	204	1.89
Finnish	8	0.07
French, except Basque	120	1.11

Notes: 1. Figures in the "Number" column do not add up to the total population due to: a) Ancestry/Race overlap — e.g. persons can report being both White and Irish, b) persons of Hispanic origin can report being any race, c) persons reporting two ancestries are counted in both categories. 2. Numbers in parentheses indicate the number of persons reporting this ancestry/race alone, not in combination with any other ancestry/race. 3. Refer to the Explanation of Data in the front of the book for more detailed information.

French Canadian	14	0.13
German	1,340	12.41
Greek	65	0.60
Guyanese	40	0.37
Hawaii Native/Pacific Islander:	11	0.10
Micronesian: (2)	3	0.03
Guamanian/Chamorro (2)	2	0.02
Other Micronesian	1	0.01
Polynesian: (4)	5	0.05
Native Hawaiian (4)	5	0.05
Other Pac. Isl., not spec.	3	0.03
Hispanic or Latino:	1,641	15.19
Central American:	98	0.91
Costa Rican	19	0.18
Guatemalan	7	0.06
Honduran	12	0.11
Nicaraguan	6	0.06
Panamanian	9	0.08
Salvadoran	41	0.38
Other Central American	4	0.04
Cuban	199	1.84
Dominican Republic	223	2.06
Mexican	43	0.40
Puerto Rican	344	3.19
South American:	379	3.51
Argentinean	13	0.12
Chilean	6	0.06
Colombian	190	1.76
Ecuadorian	132	1.22
Peruvian	22	0.20
Uruguayan	2	0.02
Other South American	14	0.13
Other Hispanic or Latino	355	3.29
Hungarian	55	0.51
Iranian	59	0.55
Irish	1,519	14.06
Italian	2,844	26.33
Lithuanian	14	0.13
Norwegian	18	0.17
Pennsylvania German	30	0.28
Polish	583	5.40
Portuguese	39	0.36
Romanian	16	0.15
Russian	109	1.01
Scotch-Irish	19	0.18
Scottish	56	0.52
Slovak	8	0.07
Swedish	36	0.33
Swiss	47	0.44
Turkish	17	0.16
Ukrainian	37	0.34
United States or American	308	2.85
Welsh	5	0.05
West Indian, excl. Hispanic:	69	0.64
Barbadian	11	0.10
British West Indian	3	0.03
Jamaican	38	0.35
Trinidadian and Tobagonian	8	0.07
West Indian	9	0.08
White:	7,714	71.43
Not Hispanic (6,504)	6,734	62.35
Hispanic (922)	980	9.07
Yugoslavian	19	0.18

Livingston

Place Type: Census Designated Place
County: Essex
Population: 27,391

Ancestry/Race	Number	%
African American/Black:	374	1.37
Not Hispanic (325)	368	1.34
Hispanic (3)	6	0.02
African, sub-Saharan:	29	0.11
Ethiopian	13	0.05
Nigerian	16	0.06
Alaska Native tribes, specified:	1	0.00
Tlingit-Haida	1	0.00
Am. Ind. or Alaska Nat., not spec.	19	0.07
Alsatian	7	0.03
American Indian tribes, specified:	18	0.07
Cherokee (2)	6	0.02
Creek	2	0.01
Iroquois	3	0.01
Latin American Indians (3)	4	0.01
Osage	1	0.00
All other tribes	2	0.01
American Indian tribes, not spec.	10	0.04
Arab:	274	1.00
Egyptian	91	0.33
Iraqi	20	0.07
Lebanese	92	0.34
Syrian	63	0.23
Other Arab	8	0.03
Armenian	32	0.12
Asian:	4,163	15.20
Chinese, ex. Taiwanese (1,655)	1,723	6.29
Filipino (482)	528	1.93
Indian (734)	771	2.81
Japanese (26)	30	0.11
Korean (685)	696	2.54
Malaysian (5)	6	0.02
Pakistani (32)	34	0.12
Sri Lankan (10)	10	0.04
Taiwanese (230)	269	0.98
Thai (8)	9	0.03
Vietnamese (51)	52	0.19
Other Asian, not specified (10)	35	0.13
Austrian	500	1.83
Belgian	18	0.07
British	66	0.24
Canadian	50	0.18
Carpatho Rusyn	6	0.02
Czech	79	0.29
Czechoslovakian	63	0.23
Danish	111	0.41
Dutch	70	0.26
Eastern European	743	2.71
English	1,132	4.13
Estonian	16	0.06
European	326	1.19
Finnish	12	0.04
French, except Basque	143	0.52
French Canadian	79	0.29
German	2,022	7.38
Greek	243	0.89
Guyanese	36	0.13
Hawaii Native/Pacific Islander:	20	0.07
Micronesian: (1)	1	0.00
Guamanian/Chamorro (1)	1	0.00
Polynesian: (2)	4	0.01
Native Hawaiian (2)	3	0.01
Samoan	1	0.00
Other Pac. Isl., not spec.	15	0.05
Hispanic or Latino:	695	2.54
Central American:	38	0.14
Costa Rican	18	0.07
Guatemalan	2	0.01
Honduran	1	0.00
Nicaraguan	1	0.00
Salvadoran	12	0.04
Other Central American	4	0.01
Cuban	88	0.32
Dominican Republic	31	0.11
Mexican	39	0.14
Puerto Rican	128	0.47
South American:	192	0.70
Argentinean	19	0.07
Chilean	5	0.02
Colombian	29	0.11
Ecuadorian	17	0.06
Peruvian	83	0.30
Uruguayan	22	0.08
Venezuelan	2	0.01
Other South American	15	0.05
Other Hispanic or Latino	179	0.65
Hungarian	286	1.04
Iranian	185	0.68
Irish	2,833	10.34
Israeli	176	0.64
Italian	4,846	17.69
Latvian	25	0.09
Lithuanian	116	0.42
Northern European	3	0.01
Norwegian	101	0.37
Pennsylvania German	7	0.03
Polish	1,799	6.57
Portuguese	83	0.30
Romanian	213	0.78
Russian	2,693	9.83
Scandinavian	10	0.04
Scotch-Irish	185	0.68
Scottish	220	0.80
Serbian	9	0.03
Slavic	5	0.02
Slovak	80	0.29
Slovene	22	0.08
Swedish	113	0.41
Swiss	24	0.09
Turkish	46	0.17
Ukrainian	363	1.33
United States or American	1,927	7.04
Welsh	81	0.30
West Indian, excl. Hispanic:	40	0.15
Jamaican	9	0.03
Trinidadian and Tobagonian	31	0.11
White:	22,829	83.34
Not Hispanic (22,150)	22,319	81.48
Hispanic (487)	510	1.86
Yugoslavian	10	0.04

Lodi

Place Type: Borough
County: Bergen
Population: 23,971

Ancestry/Race	Number	%
African American/Black:	1,005	4.19
Not Hispanic (769)	873	3.64
Hispanic (83)	132	0.55
African, sub-Saharan:	83	0.35
African	69	0.29
Liberian	14	0.06
Alaska Native tribes, specified:	1	0.00
Aleut (1)	1	0.00
Am. Ind. or Alaska Nat., not spec.	56	0.23
Albanian	245	1.02
American Indian tribes, specified:	39	0.16
Cherokee (4)	21	0.09
Cheyenne (1)	1	0.00
Choctaw	2	0.01
Iroquois (1)	1	0.00
Latin American Indians (4)	6	0.03
Seminole (1)	1	0.00
Sioux	1	0.00
All other tribes (3)	6	0.03
American Indian tribes, not spec.	11	0.05
Arab:	466	1.94
Arab/Arabic	112	0.47
Egyptian	4	0.02
Iraqi	7	0.03
Lebanese	15	0.06
Syrian	215	0.90
Other Arab	113	0.47
Armenian	104	0.43
Asian:	2,303	9.61
Bangladeshi (10)	10	0.04
Chinese, ex. Taiwanese (106)	122	0.51
Filipino (467)	500	2.09
Indian (1,248)	1,317	5.49
Indonesian (3)	3	0.01
Japanese (22)	28	0.12
Korean (121)	126	0.53
Laotian (22)	23	0.10
Pakistani (59)	73	0.30
Sri Lankan (2)	2	0.01
Taiwanese (4)	8	0.03
Thai (6)	6	0.03

Notes: 1. Figures in the "Number" column do not add up to the total population due to: a) Ancestry/Race overlap — e.g. persons can report being both White and Irish, b) persons of Hispanic origin can report being any race, c) persons reporting two ancestries are counted in both categories. 2. Numbers in parentheses indicate the number of persons reporting this ancestry/race alone, not in combination with any other ancestry/race. 3. Refer to the Explanation of Data in the front of the book for more detailed information.

Vietnamese (23)	26	0.11
Other Asian, specified (1)	1	0.00
Other Asian, not specified (9)	58	0.24
Australian	7	0.03
Austrian	54	0.23
Belgian	18	0.08
Brazilian	121	0.50
British	70	0.29
Bulgarian	39	0.16
Canadian	47	0.20
Croatian	41	0.17
Czech	56	0.23
Czechoslovakian	57	0.24
Danish	66	0.28
Dutch	301	1.26
Eastern European	10	0.04
English	530	2.21
European	48	0.20
French, except Basque	321	1.34
French Canadian	67	0.28
German	2,038	8.50
Greek	179	0.75
Guyanese	60	0.25
Hawaii Native/Pacific Islander:	24	0.10
Micronesian: (2)	2	0.01
Guamanian/Chamorro (2)	2	0.01
Polynesian:	1	0.00
Native Hawaiian	1	0.00
Other Pac. Isl., not spec. (6)	21	0.09
Hispanic or Latino:	4,309	17.98
Central American:	157	0.65
Costa Rican	29	0.12
Guatemalan	21	0.09
Honduran	22	0.09
Nicaraguan	14	0.06
Panamanian	5	0.02
Salvadoran	50	0.21
Other Central American	16	0.07
Cuban	178	0.74
Dominican Republic	365	1.52
Mexican	212	0.88
Puerto Rican	912	3.80
South American:	1,524	6.36
Argentinean	97	0.40
Bolivian	33	0.14
Chilean	14	0.06
Colombian	704	2.94
Ecuadorian	238	0.99
Peruvian	365	1.52
Uruguayan	4	0.02
Venezuelan	33	0.14
Other South American	36	0.15
Other Hispanic or Latino	961	4.01
Hungarian	197	0.82
Irish	2,475	10.32
Israeli	23	0.10
Italian	7,986	33.32
Macedonian	62	0.26
Norwegian	105	0.44
Polish	1,900	7.93
Portuguese	649	2.71
Romanian	54	0.23
Russian	175	0.73
Scotch-Irish	67	0.28
Scottish	72	0.30
Serbian	40	0.17
Slavic	71	0.30
Slovak	151	0.63
Swedish	32	0.13
Swiss	44	0.18
Turkish	61	0.25
Ukrainian	136	0.57
United States or American	416	1.74
West Indian, excl. Hispanic:	216	0.90
Barbadian	19	0.08
British West Indian	8	0.03
Haitian	36	0.15
Jamaican	115	0.48
West Indian	38	0.16
White:	19,304	80.53
Not Hispanic (16,277)	16,575	69.15
Hispanic (2,459)	2,729	11.38
Yugoslavian	86	0.36

Long Branch

Place Type: City
County: Monmouth
Population: 31,340

Ancestry/Race	Number	%
African American/Black:	6,253	19.95
Not Hispanic (5,471)	5,782	18.45
Hispanic (376)	471	1.50
African, sub-Saharan:	202	0.64
African	191	0.61
South African	11	0.04
Alaska Native tribes, specified:	1	0.00
Tlingit-Haida	1	0.00
Am. Ind. or Alaska Nat., not spec.	122	0.39
American Indian tribes, specified:	107	0.34
Apache	5	0.02
Blackfeet	10	0.03
Cherokee (4)	27	0.09
Cheyenne (1)	1	0.00
Chippewa (3)	3	0.01
Creek	1	0.00
Crow	1	0.00
Delaware (2)	4	0.01
Iroquois (1)	2	0.01
Latin American Indians (23)	27	0.09
Lumbee (1)	1	0.00
Navajo (1)	4	0.01
Ottawa (3)	3	0.01
Potawatomi (1)	1	0.00
Pueblo	1	0.00
Seminole	1	0.00
Shoshone (1)	1	0.00
Sioux	1	0.00
All other tribes (5)	13	0.04
American Indian tribes, not spec.	18	0.06
Arab:	312	1.00
Egyptian	104	0.33
Iraqi	7	0.02
Lebanese	19	0.06
Moroccan	9	0.03
Syrian	173	0.55
Armenian	24	0.08
Asian:	657	2.10
Bangladeshi (3)	3	0.01
Cambodian (5)	8	0.03
Chinese, ex. Taiwanese (111)	115	0.37
Filipino (133)	160	0.51
Indian (141)	171	0.55
Indonesian (1)	1	0.00
Japanese (9)	30	0.10
Korean (52)	56	0.18
Pakistani (6)	18	0.06
Taiwanese (1)	2	0.01
Thai (4)	5	0.02
Vietnamese (23)	43	0.14
Other Asian, specified (1)	1	0.00
Other Asian, not specified (14)	44	0.14
Austrian	117	0.37
Basque	6	0.02
Belgian	7	0.02
Brazilian	890	2.84
British	49	0.16
Bulgarian	9	0.03
Canadian	43	0.14
Croatian	28	0.09
Czech	68	0.22
Czechoslovakian	27	0.09
Danish	77	0.25
Dutch	241	0.77
Eastern European	17	0.05
English	1,276	4.07
Estonian	7	0.02
European	13	0.04
Finnish	19	0.06
French, except Basque	397	1.27
French Canadian	82	0.26
German	2,080	6.64
Greek	179	0.57
Guyanese	31	0.10
Hawaii Native/Pacific Islander:	55	0.18
Micronesian: (3)	5	0.02
Guamanian/Chamorro (3)	5	0.02
Polynesian: (7)	18	0.06
Native Hawaiian (3)	11	0.04
Samoan (4)	7	0.02
Other Pac. Isl., not spec. (5)	32	0.10
Hispanic or Latino:	6,477	20.67
Central American:	548	1.75
Costa Rican	41	0.13
Guatemalan	166	0.53
Honduran	41	0.13
Nicaraguan	29	0.09
Panamanian	16	0.05
Salvadoran	233	0.74
Other Central American	22	0.07
Cuban	84	0.27
Dominican Republic	109	0.35
Mexican	1,448	4.62
Puerto Rican	2,778	8.86
South American:	411	1.31
Argentinean	18	0.06
Bolivian	1	0.00
Chilean	55	0.18
Colombian	188	0.60
Ecuadorian	89	0.28
Paraguayan	1	0.00
Peruvian	39	0.12
Uruguayan	1	0.00
Venezuelan	8	0.03
Other South American	11	0.04
Other Hispanic or Latino	1,099	3.51
Hungarian	210	0.67
Iranian	32	0.10
Irish	3,500	11.17
Israeli	28	0.09
Italian	5,489	17.51
Latvian	30	0.10
Lithuanian	53	0.17
Maltese	5	0.02
Norwegian	148	0.47
Polish	771	2.46
Portuguese	1,067	3.40
Romanian	54	0.17
Russian	495	1.58
Scandinavian	32	0.10
Scotch-Irish	205	0.65
Scottish	305	0.97
Slavic	36	0.11
Slovak	53	0.17
Slovene	7	0.02
Swedish	232	0.74
Swiss	9	0.03
Turkish	19	0.06
Ukrainian	135	0.43
United States or American	1,011	3.23
Welsh	111	0.35
West Indian, excl. Hispanic:	447	1.43
Barbadian	14	0.04
Belizean	52	0.17
Haitian	122	0.39
Jamaican	155	0.49
Trinidadian and Tobagonian	18	0.06
West Indian	86	0.27
White:	22,409	71.50
Not Hispanic (17,831)	18,457	58.89
Hispanic (3,489)	3,952	12.61
Yugoslavian	87	0.28

Notes: 1. Figures in the "Number" column do not add up to the total population due to: a) Ancestry/Race overlap — e.g. persons can report being both White and Irish, b) persons of Hispanic origin can report being any race, c) persons reporting two ancestries are counted in both categories. 2. Numbers in parentheses indicate the number of persons reporting this ancestry/race alone, not in combination with any other ancestry/race. 3. Refer to the Explanation of Data in the front of the book for more detailed information.

Lower

Place Type: Township
County: Cape May
Population: 22,945

Ancestry/Race	Number	%
African American/Black:	405	1.77
Not Hispanic (288)	369	1.61
Hispanic (31)	36	0.16
African, sub-Saharan:	48	0.21
African	48	0.21
Alaska Native tribes, specified:	1	0.00
Tlingit-Haida (1)	1	0.00
Am. Ind. or Alaska Nat., not spec.	27	0.12
Albanian	40	0.17
American Indian tribes, specified:	77	0.34
Blackfeet (7)	10	0.04
Cherokee (4)	19	0.08
Chippewa (3)	6	0.03
Choctaw (1)	1	0.00
Cree	1	0.00
Creek	1	0.00
Delaware (2)	6	0.03
Iroquois (2)	8	0.03
Latin American Indians (1)	1	0.00
Navajo (1)	4	0.02
Sioux (1)	4	0.02
All other tribes (11)	16	0.07
American Indian tribes, not spec.	8	0.03
Armenian	6	0.03
Asian:	171	0.75
Chinese, ex. Taiwanese (20)	23	0.10
Filipino (50)	73	0.32
Indian (13)	13	0.06
Japanese (3)	7	0.03
Korean (9)	16	0.07
Malaysian (4)	4	0.02
Pakistani (2)	2	0.01
Taiwanese (3)	5	0.02
Thai (4)	9	0.04
Vietnamese (9)	12	0.05
Other Asian, specified	3	0.01
Other Asian, not specified (3)	4	0.02
Austrian	59	0.26
Belgian	10	0.04
British	108	0.47
Bulgarian	6	0.03
Canadian	28	0.12
Croatian	8	0.03
Czech	35	0.15
Czechoslovakian	26	0.11
Danish	62	0.27
Dutch	274	1.19
English	3,003	13.09
European	20	0.09
Finnish	37	0.16
French, except Basque	667	2.91
French Canadian	117	0.51
German	5,690	24.80
Greek	218	0.95
Hawaii Native/Pacific Islander:	18	0.08
Micronesian: (1)	2	0.01
Guamanian/Chamorro (1)	2	0.01
Polynesian: (2)	9	0.04
Native Hawaiian	1	0.00
Samoan (2)	5	0.02
Other Polynesian	3	0.01
Other Pac. Isl., specified	2	0.01
Other Pac. Isl., not spec. (1)	5	0.02
Hispanic or Latino:	432	1.88
Central American:	9	0.04
Costa Rican	1	0.00
Nicaraguan	1	0.00
Panamanian	1	0.00
Salvadoran	6	0.03
Cuban	30	0.13
Mexican	74	0.32
Puerto Rican	250	1.09
South American:	19	0.08
Argentinean	1	0.00
Colombian	14	0.06
Ecuadorian	1	0.00
Paraguayan	1	0.00
Peruvian	2	0.01
Other Hispanic or Latino	50	0.22
Hungarian	147	0.64
Irish	7,350	32.03
Italian	3,802	16.57
Latvian	10	0.04
Lithuanian	150	0.65
Maltese	6	0.03
Norwegian	317	1.38
Pennsylvania German	31	0.14
Polish	1,320	5.75
Portuguese	80	0.35
Romanian	15	0.07
Russian	156	0.68
Scandinavian	5	0.02
Scotch-Irish	477	2.08
Scottish	315	1.37
Serbian	11	0.05
Slavic	8	0.03
Slovak	65	0.28
Swedish	317	1.38
Swiss	42	0.18
Ukrainian	243	1.06
United States or American	925	4.03
Welsh	411	1.79
West Indian, excl. Hispanic:	46	0.20
Jamaican	39	0.17
Trinidadian and Tobagonian	7	0.03
White:	22,275	97.08
Not Hispanic (21,869)	22,025	95.99
Hispanic (219)	250	1.09

Lumberton

Place Type: Township
County: Burlington
Population: 10,461

Ancestry/Race	Number	%
Acadian/Cajun	11	0.11
African American/Black:	1,554	14.86
Not Hispanic (1,400)	1,513	14.46
Hispanic (38)	41	0.39
African, sub-Saharan:	67	0.65
African	67	0.65
Alaska Native tribes, specified:	1	0.01
Alaska Athabascan (1)	1	0.01
Am. Ind. or Alaska Nat., not spec.	15	0.14
American Indian tribes, specified:	59	0.56
Apache	3	0.03
Blackfeet	4	0.04
Cherokee (5)	21	0.20
Chippewa (2)	2	0.02
Cree	1	0.01
Crow (1)	3	0.03
Delaware (1)	2	0.02
Iroquois	3	0.03
Latin American Indians (1)	2	0.02
Lumbee (1)	1	0.01
Potawatomi (2)	2	0.02
Seminole	3	0.03
All other tribes (6)	12	0.11
American Indian tribes, not spec.	5	0.05
Arab:	48	0.46
Egyptian	21	0.20
Lebanese	27	0.26
Armenian	12	0.12
Asian:	442	4.23
Bangladeshi (11)	11	0.11
Chinese, ex. Taiwanese (41)	47	0.45
Filipino (59)	79	0.76
Indian (115)	126	1.20
Japanese (19)	37	0.35
Korean (67)	81	0.77
Pakistani (6)	6	0.06
Thai (7)	9	0.09
Vietnamese (15)	18	0.17
Other Asian, not specified (12)	28	0.27
Austrian	57	0.55
British	14	0.14
Canadian	17	0.16
Croatian	11	0.11
Czechoslovakian	10	0.10
Danish	66	0.64
Dutch	100	0.97
Eastern European	6	0.06
English	1,241	12.00
European	47	0.45
Finnish	22	0.21
French, except Basque	154	1.49
French Canadian	61	0.59
German	2,186	21.14
Greek	18	0.17
Hawaii Native/Pacific Islander:	11	0.11
Micronesian:	1	0.01
Guamanian/Chamorro	1	0.01
Polynesian:	1	0.01
Native Hawaiian	1	0.01
Other Pac. Isl., not spec. (2)	9	0.09
Hispanic or Latino:	539	5.15
Central American:	30	0.29
Guatemalan	2	0.02
Honduran	2	0.02
Nicaraguan	2	0.02
Panamanian	21	0.20
Salvadoran	3	0.03
Cuban	17	0.16
Dominican Republic	3	0.03
Mexican	46	0.44
Puerto Rican	337	3.22
South American:	30	0.29
Argentinean	2	0.02
Chilean	1	0.01
Colombian	4	0.04
Ecuadorian	15	0.14
Paraguayan	4	0.04
Peruvian	3	0.03
Other South American	1	0.01
Other Hispanic or Latino	76	0.73
Hungarian	114	1.10
Irish	2,257	21.83
Israeli	11	0.11
Italian	1,519	14.69
Lithuanian	23	0.22
Maltese	7	0.07
Norwegian	31	0.30
Pennsylvania German	8	0.08
Polish	563	5.44
Portuguese	6	0.06
Russian	54	0.52
Scotch-Irish	107	1.03
Scottish	219	2.12
Slovak	62	0.60
Swedish	39	0.38
Swiss	8	0.08
Ukrainian	66	0.64
United States or American	343	3.32
Welsh	102	0.99
West Indian, excl. Hispanic:	60	0.58
Jamaican	60	0.58
White:	8,405	80.35
Not Hispanic (7,916)	8,097	77.40
Hispanic (276)	308	2.94

Lyndhurst

Place Type: Census Designated Place
County: Bergen
Population: 19,383

Ancestry/Race	Number	%
Afghan	24	0.12
African American/Black:	176	0.91
Not Hispanic (98)	138	0.71
Hispanic (21)	38	0.20
Am. Ind. or Alaska Nat., not spec.	27	0.14

Notes: 1. Figures in the "Number" column do not add up to the total population due to: a) Ancestry/Race overlap — e.g. persons can report being both White and Irish, b) persons of Hispanic origin can report being any race, c) persons reporting two ancestries are counted in both categories. 2. Numbers in parentheses indicate the number of persons reporting this ancestry/race alone, not in combination with any other ancestry/race. 3. Refer to the Explanation of Data in the front of the book for more detailed information.

American Indian tribes, specified:	16	0.08
Blackfeet	1	0.01
Cherokee	7	0.04
Iroquois	3	0.02
Latin American Indians (1)	2	0.01
All other tribes (1)	3	0.02
Arab:	176	0.91
Arab/Arabic	24	0.12
Egyptian	57	0.29
Lebanese	43	0.22
Moroccan	6	0.03
Syrian	39	0.20
Other Arab	7	0.04
Asian:	1,145	5.91
Bangladeshi (4)	4	0.02
Chinese, ex. Taiwanese (164)	171	0.88
Filipino (190)	209	1.08
Indian (166)	187	0.96
Indonesian (1)	4	0.02
Japanese (10)	15	0.08
Korean (412)	433	2.23
Laotian (10)	19	0.10
Malaysian (1)	1	0.01
Pakistani (11)	13	0.07
Sri Lankan (2)	2	0.01
Taiwanese (9)	9	0.05
Thai (32)	35	0.18
Vietnamese (9)	14	0.07
Other Asian, specified (2)	2	0.01
Other Asian, not specified (10)	27	0.14
Assyrian/Chaldean/Syriac	10	0.05
Austrian	63	0.33
Belgian	20	0.10
Brazilian	17	0.09
British	23	0.12
Canadian	38	0.20
Croatian	48	0.25
Cypriot	13	0.07
Czech	81	0.42
Czechoslovakian	29	0.15
Danish	24	0.12
Dutch	257	1.33
English	513	2.65
French, except Basque	216	1.11
French Canadian	27	0.14
German	1,813	9.35
Greek	176	0.91
Guyanese	14	0.07
Hawaii Native/Pacific Islander:	4	0.02
Polynesian:	2	0.01
Native Hawaiian	2	0.01
Other Pac. Isl., not spec. (1)	2	0.01
Hispanic or Latino:	1,744	9.00
Central American:	36	0.19
Costa Rican	6	0.03
Guatemalan	8	0.04
Honduran	5	0.03
Nicaraguan	2	0.01
Panamanian	4	0.02
Salvadoran	2	0.01
Other Central American	9	0.05
Cuban	273	1.41
Dominican Republic	39	0.20
Mexican	97	0.50
Puerto Rican	465	2.40
South American:	375	1.93
Argentinean	29	0.15
Bolivian	1	0.01
Chilean	17	0.09
Colombian	117	0.60
Ecuadorian	79	0.41
Peruvian	94	0.48
Uruguayan	8	0.04
Venezuelan	7	0.04
Other South American	23	0.12
Other Hispanic or Latino	459	2.37
Hungarian	178	0.92
Iranian	7	0.04
Irish	3,538	18.25
Italian	7,914	40.83
Lithuanian	97	0.50
Macedonian	6	0.03
Maltese	19	0.10
New Zealander	18	0.09
Norwegian	61	0.31
Pennsylvania German	5	0.03
Polish	2,394	12.35
Portuguese	543	2.80
Romanian	28	0.14
Russian	152	0.78
Scotch-Irish	222	1.15
Scottish	268	1.38
Slavic	7	0.04
Slovak	56	0.29
Swedish	113	0.58
Swiss	43	0.22
Turkish	166	0.86
Ukrainian	160	0.83
United States or American	414	2.14
Welsh	46	0.24
West Indian, excl. Hispanic:	22	0.11
Haitian	6	0.03
Trinidadian and Tobagonian	5	0.03
West Indian	11	0.06
White:	17,758	91.62
Not Hispanic (16,166)	16,404	84.63
Hispanic (1,267)	1,354	6.99
Yugoslavian	30	0.15

Madison

Place Type: Borough
County: Morris
Population: 16,530

Ancestry/Race	Number	%
African American/Black:	563	3.41
Not Hispanic (481)	539	3.26
Hispanic (15)	24	0.15
African, sub-Saharan:	21	0.13
African	21	0.13
Alaska Native tribes, specified:	4	0.02
Aleut (1)	1	0.01
Eskimo (3)	3	0.02
Alaska Native tribes, not specified	2	0.01
Am. Ind. or Alaska Nat., not spec.	27	0.16
Alsatian	4	0.02
American Indian tribes, specified:	26	0.16
Apache	1	0.01
Blackfeet (2)	2	0.01
Cherokee (2)	8	0.05
Chippewa	1	0.01
Choctaw	1	0.01
Delaware	2	0.01
Latin American Indians (4)	8	0.05
Sioux	1	0.01
All other tribes	2	0.01
American Indian tribes, not spec.	4	0.02
Arab:	63	0.38
Arab/Arabic	9	0.05
Egyptian	13	0.08
Lebanese	24	0.15
Syrian	17	0.10
Armenian	19	0.11
Asian:	739	4.47
Cambodian (1)	3	0.02
Chinese, ex. Taiwanese (191)	207	1.25
Filipino (45)	62	0.38
Indian (130)	142	0.86
Indonesian (4)	6	0.04
Japanese (56)	65	0.39
Korean (136)	145	0.88
Laotian (8)	8	0.05
Pakistani (6)	6	0.04
Sri Lankan (2)	2	0.01
Taiwanese (13)	13	0.08
Thai (8)	8	0.05
Vietnamese (8)	10	0.06
Other Asian, specified (4)	5	0.03
Other Asian, not specified (4)	57	0.34
Australian	5	0.03
Austrian	88	0.53
Basque	7	0.04
Belgian	6	0.04
Brazilian	5	0.03
British	247	1.49
Bulgarian	7	0.04
Canadian	84	0.51
Celtic	7	0.04
Croatian	40	0.24
Czech	87	0.53
Czechoslovakian	49	0.30
Danish	68	0.41
Dutch	330	2.00
Eastern European	23	0.14
English	1,824	11.03
European	85	0.51
Finnish	35	0.21
French, except Basque	420	2.54
French Canadian	86	0.52
German	2,137	12.93
Greek	124	0.75
Hawaii Native/Pacific Islander:	91	0.55
Melanesian: (1)	1	0.01
Fijian (1)	1	0.01
Polynesian: (2)	3	0.02
Native Hawaiian (1)	2	0.01
Samoan (1)	1	0.01
Other Pac. Isl., not spec. (35)	87	0.53
Hispanic or Latino:	987	5.97
Central American:	63	0.38
Costa Rican	33	0.20
Guatemalan	3	0.02
Honduran	3	0.02
Nicaraguan	1	0.01
Panamanian	11	0.07
Salvadoran	5	0.03
Other Central American	7	0.04
Cuban	30	0.18
Dominican Republic	31	0.19
Mexican	43	0.26
Puerto Rican	70	0.42
South American:	431	2.61
Argentinean	10	0.06
Bolivian	4	0.02
Chilean	7	0.04
Colombian	362	2.19
Ecuadorian	7	0.04
Paraguayan	10	0.06
Peruvian	12	0.07
Uruguayan	6	0.04
Venezuelan	7	0.04
Other South American	6	0.04
Other Hispanic or Latino	319	1.93
Hungarian	219	1.32
Iranian	38	0.23
Irish	3,255	19.69
Italian	3,907	23.64
Latvian	30	0.18
Lithuanian	79	0.48
Luxemburger	22	0.13
Northern European	70	0.42
Norwegian	240	1.45
Pennsylvania German	8	0.05
Polish	933	5.64
Portuguese	105	0.64
Romanian	12	0.07
Russian	377	2.28
Scandinavian	23	0.14
Scotch-Irish	376	2.27
Scottish	504	3.05
Slavic	14	0.08
Slovak	19	0.11
Slovene	11	0.07
Swedish	272	1.65
Swiss	118	0.71
Turkish	51	0.31
Ukrainian	122	0.74
United States or American	457	2.76
Welsh	258	1.56

Notes: 1. Figures in the "Number" column do not add up to the total population due to: a) Ancestry/Race overlap — e.g. persons can report being both White and Irish, b) persons of Hispanic origin can report being any race, c) persons reporting two ancestries are counted in both categories. 2. Numbers in parentheses indicate the number of persons reporting this ancestry/race alone, not in combination with any other ancestry/race. 3. Refer to the Explanation of Data in the front of the book for more detailed information.

West Indian, excl. Hispanic:	98	0.59
Barbadian	18	0.11
Haitian	27	0.16
Jamaican	48	0.29
West Indian	5	0.03
White:	15,020	90.87
Not Hispanic (14,172)	14,293	86.47
Hispanic (654)	727	4.40
Yugoslavian	54	0.33

Mahwah

Place Type: Township
County: Bergen
Population: 24,062

Ancestry/Race	Number	%
Acadian/Cajun	14	0.06
African American/Black:	578	2.40
Not Hispanic (510)	562	2.34
Hispanic (9)	16	0.07
African, sub-Saharan:	103	0.43
African	38	0.16
Nigerian	20	0.08
South African	45	0.19
Am. Ind. or Alaska Nat., not spec.	70	0.29
Albanian	25	0.10
Alsatian	23	0.10
American Indian tribes, specified:	162	0.67
Cherokee (4)	13	0.05
Creek (1)	1	0.00
Delaware (117)	131	0.54
Iroquois (6)	9	0.04
Latin American Indians (1)	2	0.01
Seminole	1	0.00
Sioux (1)	3	0.01
All other tribes (1)	2	0.01
American Indian tribes, not spec.	11	0.05
Arab:	201	0.84
Arab/Arabic	28	0.12
Egyptian	58	0.24
Lebanese	42	0.17
Moroccan	7	0.03
Syrian	50	0.21
Other Arab	16	0.07
Armenian	161	0.67
Asian:	1,658	6.89
Bangladeshi (3)	3	0.01
Cambodian (1)	2	0.01
Chinese, ex. Taiwanese (368)	389	1.62
Filipino (110)	125	0.52
Indian (529)	571	2.37
Indonesian (1)	5	0.02
Japanese (197)	208	0.86
Korean (224)	243	1.01
Malaysian (1)	1	0.00
Pakistani (34)	38	0.16
Sri Lankan (2)	4	0.02
Taiwanese (2)	2	0.01
Thai (12)	12	0.05
Vietnamese (15)	15	0.06
Other Asian, specified (3)	4	0.02
Other Asian, not specified (6)	36	0.15
Assyrian/Chaldean/Syriac	6	0.02
Australian	7	0.03
Austrian	271	1.13
Belgian	89	0.37
British	74	0.31
Bulgarian	9	0.04
Canadian	33	0.14
Croatian	128	0.53
Czech	169	0.70
Czechoslovakian	47	0.20
Danish	83	0.34
Dutch	782	3.25
Eastern European	82	0.34
English	1,343	5.58
Estonian	7	0.03
European	115	0.48
Finnish	18	0.07
French, except Basque	525	2.18
French Canadian	65	0.27
German	3,798	15.78
Greek	418	1.74
Guyanese	12	0.05
Hawaii Native/Pacific Islander:	23	0.10
Melanesian: (1)	1	0.00
Fijian (1)	1	0.00
Polynesian: (6)	9	0.04
Native Hawaiian	3	0.01
Samoan (6)	6	0.02
Other Pac. Isl., specified	1	0.00
Other Pac. Isl., not spec.	12	0.05
Hispanic or Latino:	1,028	4.27
Central American:	59	0.25
Costa Rican	3	0.01
Guatemalan	1	0.00
Honduran	20	0.08
Nicaraguan	3	0.01
Salvadoran	28	0.12
Other Central American	4	0.02
Cuban	89	0.37
Dominican Republic	79	0.33
Mexican	136	0.57
Puerto Rican	264	1.10
South American:	185	0.77
Argentinean	7	0.03
Bolivian	4	0.02
Chilean	11	0.05
Colombian	58	0.24
Ecuadorian	34	0.14
Peruvian	60	0.25
Uruguayan	2	0.01
Venezuelan	7	0.03
Other South American	2	0.01
Other Hispanic or Latino	216	0.90
Hungarian	484	2.01
Iranian	17	0.07
Irish	4,739	19.69
Israeli	12	0.05
Italian	6,128	25.47
Latvian	10	0.04
Lithuanian	182	0.76
Macedonian	47	0.20
Maltese	7	0.03
Norwegian	361	1.50
Pennsylvania German	39	0.16
Polish	1,961	8.15
Portuguese	88	0.37
Romanian	145	0.60
Russian	876	3.64
Scotch-Irish	323	1.34
Scottish	373	1.55
Serbian	15	0.06
Slavic	24	0.10
Slovak	151	0.63
Swedish	259	1.08
Swiss	226	0.94
Ukrainian	205	0.85
United States or American	658	2.73
Welsh	107	0.44
West Indian, excl. Hispanic:	96	0.40
Haitian	10	0.04
Jamaican	46	0.19
Trinidadian and Tobagonian	22	0.09
West Indian	18	0.07
White:	21,414	89.00
Not Hispanic (20,555)	20,764	86.29
Hispanic (602)	650	2.70
Yugoslavian	96	0.40

Manalapan

Place Type: Township
County: Monmouth
Population: 33,423

Ancestry/Race	Number	%
African American/Black:	766	2.29
Not Hispanic (641)	714	2.14
Hispanic (23)	52	0.16
African, sub-Saharan:	72	0.22
African	53	0.16
Ethiopian	19	0.06
Am. Ind. or Alaska Nat., not spec.	34	0.10
Albanian	29	0.09
American Indian tribes, specified:	34	0.10
Apache	1	0.00
Cherokee (4)	14	0.04
Chippewa	1	0.00
Cree (1)	1	0.00
Delaware	8	0.02
Latin American Indians (2)	6	0.02
Sioux	2	0.01
All other tribes	1	0.00
American Indian tribes, not spec.	1	0.00
Arab:	273	0.82
Egyptian	135	0.40
Lebanese	70	0.21
Moroccan	5	0.01
Syrian	63	0.19
Armenian	80	0.24
Asian:	1,665	4.98
Bangladeshi	5	0.01
Chinese, ex. Taiwanese (670)	726	2.17
Filipino (171)	207	0.62
Indian (462)	484	1.45
Indonesian (2)	2	0.01
Japanese (14)	27	0.08
Korean (101)	118	0.35
Malaysian (1)	1	0.00
Pakistani (18)	19	0.06
Sri Lankan (2)	2	0.01
Taiwanese (21)	23	0.07
Thai (4)	5	0.01
Vietnamese (19)	20	0.06
Other Asian, specified (3)	7	0.02
Other Asian, not specified (4)	19	0.06
Australian	5	0.01
Austrian	753	2.25
Belgian	25	0.07
Brazilian	9	0.03
British	39	0.12
Canadian	167	0.50
Croatian	63	0.19
Czech	158	0.47
Czechoslovakian	105	0.31
Danish	42	0.13
Dutch	161	0.48
Eastern European	214	0.64
English	1,132	3.39
European	164	0.49
Finnish	29	0.09
French, except Basque	340	1.02
French Canadian	129	0.39
German	2,814	8.42
Greek	338	1.01
Guyanese	12	0.04
Hawaii Native/Pacific Islander:	17	0.05
Micronesian: (2)	5	0.01
Guamanian/Chamorro (2)	5	0.01
Polynesian: (3)	6	0.02
Native Hawaiian (2)	4	0.01
Samoan (1)	2	0.01
Other Pac. Isl., not spec.	6	0.02
Hispanic or Latino:	1,183	3.54
Central American:	36	0.11
Costa Rican	6	0.02
Guatemalan	9	0.03
Honduran	3	0.01
Nicaraguan	9	0.03
Panamanian	6	0.02
Salvadoran	2	0.01
Other Central American	1	0.00
Cuban	143	0.43
Dominican Republic	34	0.10
Mexican	86	0.26
Puerto Rican	579	1.73
South American:	152	0.45
Argentinean	31	0.09

Notes: 1. Figures in the "Number" column do not add up to the total population due to: a) Ancestry/Race overlap — e.g. persons can report being both White and Irish, b) persons of Hispanic origin can report being any race, c) persons reporting two ancestries are counted in both categories. 2. Numbers in parentheses indicate the number of persons reporting this ancestry/race alone, not in combination with any other ancestry/race. 3. Refer to the Explanation of Data in the front of the book for more detailed information.

Ancestry/Race	Number	%
Bolivian	6	0.02
Chilean	2	0.01
Colombian	76	0.23
Ecuadorian	20	0.06
Paraguayan	1	0.00
Peruvian	10	0.03
Uruguayan	2	0.01
Venezuelan	2	0.01
Other South American	2	0.01
Other Hispanic or Latino	153	0.46
Hungarian	560	1.68
Icelander	9	0.03
Iranian	35	0.10
Irish	4,391	13.14
Israeli	141	0.42
Italian	9,335	27.93
Latvian	63	0.19
Lithuanian	139	0.42
Norwegian	185	0.55
Pennsylvania German	11	0.03
Polish	3,919	11.73
Portuguese	423	1.27
Romanian	195	0.58
Russian	3,333	9.97
Scotch-Irish	205	0.61
Scottish	257	0.77
Slavic	26	0.08
Slovak	164	0.49
Swedish	158	0.47
Swiss	49	0.15
Turkish	84	0.25
Ukrainian	410	1.23
United States or American	1,781	5.33
Welsh	64	0.19
West Indian, excl. Hispanic:	171	0.51
Barbadian	36	0.11
Belizean	6	0.02
Haitian	60	0.18
Jamaican	60	0.18
Trinidadian and Tobagonian	9	0.03
White:	31,002	92.76
Not Hispanic (29,763)	29,990	89.73
Hispanic (924)	1,012	3.03
Yugoslavian	57	0.17

Manchester

Place Type: Township
County: Ocean
Population: 38,928

Ancestry/Race	Number	%
African American/Black:	1,322	3.40
Not Hispanic (1,153)	1,262	3.24
Hispanic (37)	60	0.15
African, sub-Saharan:	33	0.08
African	33	0.08
Alaska Native tribes, specified:	1	0.00
Alaska Athabascan (1)	1	0.00
Alaska Native tribes, not specified	1	0.00
Am. Ind. or Alaska Nat., not spec.	60	0.15
Albanian	16	0.04
American Indian tribes, specified:	84	0.22
Apache (1)	1	0.00
Blackfeet (5)	13	0.03
Cherokee (12)	32	0.08
Comanche (1)	2	0.01
Creek (1)	1	0.00
Delaware (4)	13	0.03
Iroquois (1)	8	0.02
Latin American Indians (1)	5	0.01
Osage (1)	1	0.00
Seminole	1	0.00
Sioux	3	0.01
All other tribes (3)	4	0.01
American Indian tribes, not spec.	13	0.03
Arab:	50	0.13
Egyptian	20	0.05
Syrian	30	0.08
Armenian	99	0.25
Asian:	409	1.05
Chinese, ex. Taiwanese (45)	57	0.15
Filipino (190)	218	0.56
Indian (26)	31	0.08
Japanese (11)	19	0.05
Korean (38)	45	0.12
Laotian (9)	14	0.04
Pakistani (3)	5	0.01
Thai (5)	6	0.02
Vietnamese	1	0.00
Other Asian, specified (1)	4	0.01
Other Asian, not specified (1)	9	0.02
Assyrian/Chaldean/Syriac	7	0.02
Australian	8	0.02
Austrian	341	0.88
Belgian	56	0.14
British	138	0.35
Canadian	66	0.17
Croatian	15	0.04
Czech	166	0.43
Czechoslovakian	130	0.33
Danish	219	0.56
Dutch	962	2.47
Eastern European	19	0.05
English	3,802	9.76
Estonian	15	0.04
European	95	0.24
Finnish	87	0.22
French, except Basque	779	2.00
French Canadian	256	0.66
German	7,793	20.00
Greek	231	0.59
Hawaii Native/Pacific Islander:	24	0.06
Micronesian:	4	0.01
Guamanian/Chamorro	4	0.01
Polynesian: (8)	12	0.03
Native Hawaiian (2)	4	0.01
Samoan (6)	7	0.02
Other Polynesian	1	0.00
Other Pac. Isl., specified	3	0.01
Other Pac. Isl., not spec. (2)	5	0.01
Hispanic or Latino:	1,024	2.63
Central American:	27	0.07
Costa Rican	6	0.02
Guatemalan	4	0.01
Honduran	2	0.01
Nicaraguan	9	0.02
Panamanian	2	0.01
Salvadoran	2	0.01
Other Central American	2	0.01
Cuban	48	0.12
Dominican Republic	46	0.12
Mexican	62	0.16
Puerto Rican	590	1.52
South American:	79	0.20
Argentinean	8	0.02
Colombian	29	0.07
Ecuadorian	13	0.03
Peruvian	16	0.04
Uruguayan	5	0.01
Venezuelan	5	0.01
Other South American	3	0.01
Other Hispanic or Latino	172	0.44
Hungarian	644	1.65
Irish	8,341	21.41
Italian	8,032	20.62
Latvian	109	0.28
Lithuanian	257	0.66
Maltese	7	0.02
Norwegian	472	1.21
Pennsylvania German	36	0.09
Polish	3,003	7.71
Portuguese	193	0.50
Romanian	112	0.29
Russian	760	1.95
Scandinavian	24	0.06
Scotch-Irish	502	1.29
Scottish	958	2.46
Slavic	15	0.04
Slovak	339	0.87
Swedish	524	1.34
Swiss	154	0.40
Ukrainian	368	0.94
United States or American	1,545	3.97
Welsh	291	0.75
West Indian, excl. Hispanic:	74	0.19
Bermudan	19	0.05
Haitian	4	0.01
Jamaican	45	0.12
West Indian	6	0.02
White:	37,045	95.16
Not Hispanic (36,071)	36,334	93.34
Hispanic (653)	711	1.83
Yugoslavian	42	0.11

Mantua

Place Type: Township
County: Gloucester
Population: 14,217

Ancestry/Race	Number	%
African American/Black:	321	2.26
Not Hispanic (292)	318	2.24
Hispanic (2)	3	0.02
African, sub-Saharan:	24	0.17
African	24	0.17
Am. Ind. or Alaska Nat., not spec.	21	0.15
American Indian tribes, specified:	44	0.31
Blackfeet	3	0.02
Cherokee (7)	11	0.08
Chippewa (2)	2	0.01
Comanche (1)	1	0.01
Delaware (4)	6	0.04
Iroquois (1)	9	0.06
Latin American Indians	2	0.01
Lumbee (1)	1	0.01
Navajo (1)	1	0.01
Seminole	4	0.03
All other tribes (2)	4	0.03
American Indian tribes, not spec.	3	0.02
Arab:	47	0.33
Moroccan	8	0.06
Palestinian	39	0.27
Asian:	150	1.06
Chinese, ex. Taiwanese (30)	33	0.23
Filipino (9)	17	0.12
Indian (42)	45	0.32
Indonesian (1)	2	0.01
Japanese (8)	15	0.11
Korean (22)	25	0.18
Pakistani (1)	1	0.01
Vietnamese (3)	7	0.05
Other Asian, not specified (5)	5	0.04
Australian	24	0.17
Austrian	57	0.40
Belgian	7	0.05
Brazilian	13	0.09
British	23	0.16
Czech	34	0.24
Czechoslovakian	25	0.18
Danish	33	0.23
Dutch	186	1.31
Eastern European	10	0.07
English	2,100	14.77
European	26	0.18
French, except Basque	412	2.90
French Canadian	19	0.13
German	4,000	28.14
Greek	218	1.53
Hawaii Native/Pacific Islander:	3	0.02
Polynesian:	2	0.01
Native Hawaiian	2	0.01
Other Pac. Isl., not spec.	1	0.01
Hispanic or Latino:	179	1.26
Central American:	8	0.06
Honduran	3	0.02
Nicaraguan	4	0.03
Panamanian	1	0.01
Cuban	12	0.08

Notes: 1. Figures in the "Number" column do not add up to the total population due to: a) Ancestry/Race overlap — e.g. persons can report being both White and Irish, b) persons of Hispanic origin can report being any race, c) persons reporting two ancestries are counted in both categories. 2. Numbers in parentheses indicate the number of persons reporting this ancestry/race alone, not in combination with any other ancestry/race. 3. Refer to the Explanation of Data in the front of the book for more detailed information.

Dominican Republic	1	0.01
Mexican	19	0.13
Puerto Rican	81	0.57
South American:	16	0.11
Argentinean	2	0.01
Chilean	1	0.01
Colombian	6	0.04
Paraguayan	3	0.02
Other South American	4	0.03
Other Hispanic or Latino	42	0.30
Hungarian	88	0.62
Irish	3,904	27.46
Italian	3,286	23.11
Lithuanian	147	1.03
Norwegian	134	0.94
Pennsylvania German	104	0.73
Polish	921	6.48
Portuguese	33	0.23
Romanian	7	0.05
Russian	100	0.70
Scotch-Irish	333	2.34
Scottish	203	1.43
Slovak	142	1.00
Swedish	76	0.53
Swiss	53	0.37
Ukrainian	65	0.46
United States or American	451	3.17
Welsh	174	1.22
West Indian, excl. Hispanic:	25	0.18
Haitian	25	0.18
White:	13,731	96.58
Not Hispanic (13,488)	13,586	95.56
Hispanic (134)	145	1.02

Manville

Place Type: Borough
County: Somerset
Population: 10,343

Ancestry/Race	Number	%
African American/Black:	64	0.62
Not Hispanic (45)	52	0.50
Hispanic (2)	12	0.12
Am. Ind. or Alaska Nat., not spec.	8	0.08
American Indian tribes, specified:	21	0.20
Apache (1)	1	0.01
Cherokee (1)	12	0.12
Iroquois	4	0.04
Latin American Indians (1)	1	0.01
Sioux	1	0.01
All other tribes (2)	2	0.02
American Indian tribes, not spec.	1	0.01
Arab:	15	0.15
Lebanese	15	0.15
Asian:	159	1.54
Cambodian	1	0.01
Chinese, ex. Taiwanese (22)	29	0.28
Filipino (57)	63	0.61
Indian (25)	26	0.25
Japanese (2)	8	0.08
Korean (6)	7	0.07
Pakistani (3)	3	0.03
Vietnamese (14)	16	0.15
Other Asian, specified (1)	1	0.01
Other Asian, not specified (4)	5	0.05
Australian	9	0.09
Austrian	69	0.67
Belgian	25	0.24
Brazilian	33	0.32
British	16	0.16
Bulgarian	20	0.19
Canadian	5	0.05
Celtic	17	0.16
Czech	73	0.71
Czechoslovakian	119	1.15
Danish	11	0.11
Dutch	271	2.63
English	631	6.12
European	20	0.19
French, except Basque	135	1.31
French Canadian	49	0.48
German	1,579	15.32
Greek	56	0.54
Hawaii Native/Pacific Islander:	7	0.07
Polynesian: (3)	5	0.05
Native Hawaiian (3)	4	0.04
Samoan	1	0.01
Other Pac. Isl., not spec.	2	0.02
Hispanic or Latino:	559	5.40
Central American:	168	1.62
Costa Rican	128	1.24
Guatemalan	24	0.23
Honduran	1	0.01
Nicaraguan	3	0.03
Panamanian	1	0.01
Salvadoran	7	0.07
Other Central American	4	0.04
Cuban	7	0.07
Dominican Republic	1	0.01
Mexican	46	0.44
Puerto Rican	121	1.17
South American:	83	0.80
Colombian	40	0.39
Ecuadorian	4	0.04
Paraguayan	12	0.12
Peruvian	21	0.20
Venezuelan	3	0.03
Other South American	3	0.03
Other Hispanic or Latino	133	1.29
Hungarian	568	5.51
Irish	1,274	12.36
Italian	2,117	20.54
Lithuanian	96	0.93
Northern European	29	0.28
Norwegian	87	0.84
Pennsylvania German	6	0.06
Polish	2,999	29.10
Portuguese	76	0.74
Romanian	40	0.39
Russian	432	4.19
Scotch-Irish	61	0.59
Scottish	47	0.46
Serbian	48	0.47
Slavic	74	0.72
Slovak	388	3.76
Swedish	46	0.45
Swiss	3	0.03
Ukrainian	318	3.09
United States or American	226	2.19
Welsh	82	0.80
West Indian, excl. Hispanic:	6	0.06
Jamaican	6	0.06
White:	10,025	96.93
Not Hispanic (9,524)	9,589	92.71
Hispanic (404)	436	4.22
Yugoslavian	18	0.17

Maple Shade

Place Type: Township
County: Burlington
Population: 19,079

Ancestry/Race	Number	%
African American/Black:	1,485	7.78
Not Hispanic (1,327)	1,402	7.35
Hispanic (49)	83	0.44
African, sub-Saharan:	119	0.62
African	94	0.49
South African	25	0.13
Am. Ind. or Alaska Nat., not spec.	42	0.22
Albanian	5	0.03
American Indian tribes, specified:	55	0.29
Apache	3	0.02
Blackfeet	5	0.03
Cherokee (3)	16	0.08
Chippewa	1	0.01
Choctaw	1	0.01
Delaware	1	0.01
Iroquois (1)	3	0.02
Latin American Indians (4)	14	0.07
Navajo (1)	1	0.01
Seminole	2	0.01
Sioux (2)	4	0.02
All other tribes (2)	4	0.02
American Indian tribes, not spec.	3	0.02
Arab:	23	0.12
Egyptian	17	0.09
Lebanese	6	0.03
Armenian	78	0.41
Asian:	1,267	6.64
Bangladeshi (7)	9	0.05
Chinese, ex. Taiwanese (149)	160	0.84
Filipino (148)	180	0.94
Indian (557)	570	2.99
Indonesian (2)	4	0.02
Japanese (19)	30	0.16
Korean (197)	207	1.08
Pakistani (17)	17	0.09
Sri Lankan (1)	1	0.01
Taiwanese (1)	1	0.01
Thai (3)	9	0.05
Vietnamese (45)	52	0.27
Other Asian, specified (1)	7	0.04
Other Asian, not specified (9)	20	0.10
Australian	15	0.08
Austrian	54	0.28
British	95	0.50
Canadian	9	0.05
Celtic	5	0.03
Croatian	35	0.18
Czech	63	0.33
Czechoslovakian	40	0.21
Danish	45	0.24
Dutch	175	0.92
Eastern European	9	0.05
English	1,890	9.91
European	26	0.14
Finnish	40	0.21
French, except Basque	247	1.29
French Canadian	61	0.32
German	3,891	20.39
Greek	97	0.51
Hawaii Native/Pacific Islander:	16	0.08
Polynesian: (6)	8	0.04
Native Hawaiian (5)	7	0.04
Samoan (1)	1	0.01
Other Pac. Isl., specified	3	0.02
Other Pac. Isl., not spec. (2)	5	0.03
Hispanic or Latino:	850	4.46
Central American:	37	0.19
Costa Rican	4	0.02
Honduran	2	0.01
Nicaraguan	11	0.06
Panamanian	10	0.05
Salvadoran	8	0.04
Other Central American	2	0.01
Cuban	19	0.10
Dominican Republic	33	0.17
Mexican	154	0.81
Puerto Rican	446	2.34
South American:	71	0.37
Argentinean	3	0.02
Bolivian	1	0.01
Chilean	8	0.04
Colombian	19	0.10
Ecuadorian	20	0.10
Peruvian	7	0.04
Venezuelan	8	0.04
Other South American	5	0.03
Other Hispanic or Latino	90	0.47
Hungarian	187	0.98
Iranian	9	0.05
Irish	4,752	24.91
Italian	3,831	20.08
Latvian	11	0.06
Lithuanian	98	0.51
Luxemburger	12	0.06
Norwegian	112	0.59

Notes: 1. Figures in the "Number" column do not add up to the total population due to: a) Ancestry/Race overlap — e.g. persons can report being both White and Irish, b) persons of Hispanic origin can report being any race, c) persons reporting two ancestries are counted in both categories. 2. Numbers in parentheses indicate the number of persons reporting this ancestry/race alone, not in combination with any other ancestry/race. 3. Refer to the Explanation of Data in the front of the book for more detailed information.

Ancestry/Race	Number	%
Pennsylvania German	29	0.15
Polish	1,555	8.15
Portuguese	16	0.08
Romanian	15	0.08
Russian	280	1.47
Scandinavian	17	0.09
Scotch-Irish	255	1.34
Scottish	307	1.61
Slavic	17	0.09
Slovak	50	0.26
Swedish	103	0.54
Swiss	12	0.06
Turkish	36	0.19
Ukrainian	156	0.82
United States or American	593	3.11
Welsh	135	0.71
West Indian, excl. Hispanic:	79	0.41
Jamaican	43	0.23
West Indian	36	0.19
White:	16,121	84.50
Not Hispanic (15,455)	15,656	82.06
Hispanic (413)	465	2.44
Yugoslavian	18	0.09

Maplewood

Place Type: Census Designated Place
County: Essex
Population: 23,868

Ancestry/Race	Number	%
Afghan	6	0.03
African American/Black:	8,416	35.26
Not Hispanic (7,644)	8,206	34.38
Hispanic (144)	210	0.88
African, sub-Saharan:	611	2.56
African	281	1.18
Ghanian	67	0.28
Kenyan	35	0.15
Nigerian	212	0.89
Sierra Leonean	16	0.07
Am. Ind. or Alaska Nat., not spec.	44	0.18
Albanian	6	0.03
American Indian tribes, specified:	101	0.42
Blackfeet (1)	2	0.01
Cherokee (5)	39	0.16
Cheyenne	1	0.00
Chippewa (2)	2	0.01
Choctaw	2	0.01
Cree	1	0.00
Creek (2)	2	0.01
Delaware	2	0.01
Iroquois	8	0.03
Latin American Indians (4)	13	0.05
Seminole	7	0.03
Sioux	5	0.02
All other tribes (6)	17	0.07
American Indian tribes, not spec.	7	0.03
Arab:	5	0.02
Lebanese	5	0.02
Armenian	12	0.05
Asian:	885	3.71
Chinese, ex. Taiwanese (173)	235	0.98
Filipino (144)	195	0.82
Indian (198)	229	0.96
Indonesian (1)	2	0.01
Japanese (47)	70	0.29
Korean (58)	61	0.26
Pakistani (3)	10	0.04
Sri Lankan (2)	5	0.02
Taiwanese (5)	5	0.02
Thai	1	0.00
Vietnamese (27)	31	0.13
Other Asian, specified	3	0.01
Other Asian, not specified (12)	38	0.16
Austrian	233	0.98
Belgian	4	0.02
Brazilian	129	0.54
British	216	0.90
Bulgarian	22	0.09
Canadian	23	0.10
Celtic	13	0.05
Croatian	9	0.04
Cypriot	12	0.05
Czech	85	0.36
Czechoslovakian	43	0.18
Danish	44	0.18
Dutch	214	0.90
Eastern European	237	0.99
English	1,434	6.01
European	228	0.96
Finnish	13	0.05
French, except Basque	266	1.11
French Canadian	106	0.44
German	2,267	9.50
Greek	154	0.65
Guyanese	216	0.90
Hawaii Native/Pacific Islander:	28	0.12
Micronesian: (1)	1	0.00
Guamanian/Chamorro (1)	1	0.00
Polynesian: (4)	5	0.02
Native Hawaiian (1)	2	0.01
Samoan (3)	3	0.01
Other Pac. Isl., specified	3	0.01
Other Pac. Isl., not spec. (2)	19	0.08
Hispanic or Latino:	1,248	5.23
Central American:	116	0.49
Costa Rican	44	0.18
Guatemalan	19	0.08
Honduran	9	0.04
Nicaraguan	5	0.02
Panamanian	10	0.04
Salvadoran	15	0.06
Other Central American	14	0.06
Cuban	97	0.41
Dominican Republic	43	0.18
Mexican	69	0.29
Puerto Rican	438	1.84
South American:	234	0.98
Argentinean	23	0.10
Bolivian	15	0.06
Chilean	28	0.12
Colombian	86	0.36
Ecuadorian	17	0.07
Paraguayan	4	0.02
Peruvian	22	0.09
Uruguayan	27	0.11
Venezuelan	4	0.02
Other South American	8	0.03
Other Hispanic or Latino	251	1.05
Hungarian	227	0.95
Iranian	34	0.14
Irish	2,815	11.79
Israeli	33	0.14
Italian	2,392	10.02
Latvian	21	0.09
Lithuanian	142	0.59
Norwegian	217	0.91
Polish	1,423	5.96
Portuguese	52	0.22
Romanian	54	0.23
Russian	1,194	5.00
Scandinavian	21	0.09
Scotch-Irish	229	0.96
Scottish	321	1.34
Slavic	15	0.06
Slovak	92	0.39
Slovene	6	0.03
Swedish	91	0.38
Swiss	39	0.16
Turkish	24	0.10
Ukrainian	278	1.16
United States or American	712	2.98
Welsh	131	0.55
West Indian, excl. Hispanic:	2,423	10.15
Barbadian	67	0.28
Belizean	13	0.05
British West Indian	62	0.26
Haitian	1,181	4.95
Jamaican	735	3.08
Trinidadian and Tobagonian	234	0.98
U.S. Virgin Islander	6	0.03
West Indian	125	0.52
White:	14,496	60.73
Not Hispanic (13,382)	13,750	57.61
Hispanic (648)	746	3.13
Yugoslavian	19	0.08

Marlboro

Place Type: Township
County: Monmouth
Population: 36,398

Ancestry/Race	Number	%
Afghan	55	0.15
African American/Black:	814	2.24
Not Hispanic (721)	774	2.13
Hispanic (31)	40	0.11
African, sub-Saharan:	86	0.24
African	24	0.07
Kenyan	36	0.10
South African	26	0.07
Am. Ind. or Alaska Nat., not spec.	38	0.10
American Indian tribes, specified:	25	0.07
Cherokee	3	0.01
Chippewa	1	0.00
Creek (1)	1	0.00
Delaware	4	0.01
Iroquois	1	0.00
Latin American Indians (1)	2	0.01
Potawatomi	4	0.01
Sioux (1)	2	0.01
All other tribes	7	0.02
American Indian tribes, not spec.	7	0.02
Arab:	268	0.74
Egyptian	92	0.25
Iraqi	10	0.03
Lebanese	61	0.17
Moroccan	8	0.02
Palestinian	34	0.09
Syrian	63	0.17
Armenian	78	0.21
Asian:	4,857	13.34
Bangladeshi (17)	18	0.05
Chinese, ex. Taiwanese (2,112)	2,206	6.06
Filipino (326)	350	0.96
Indian (1,578)	1,634	4.49
Indonesian (9)	11	0.03
Japanese (18)	29	0.08
Korean (248)	260	0.71
Pakistani (42)	51	0.14
Taiwanese (118)	138	0.38
Thai (18)	19	0.05
Vietnamese (64)	78	0.21
Other Asian, not specified (18)	63	0.17
Austrian	682	1.87
Basque	8	0.02
Brazilian	29	0.08
British	57	0.16
Canadian	29	0.08
Croatian	37	0.10
Czech	27	0.07
Czechoslovakian	70	0.19
Danish	27	0.07
Dutch	383	1.05
Eastern European	525	1.44
English	1,042	2.86
European	474	1.30
Finnish	15	0.04
French, except Basque	271	0.74
French Canadian	81	0.22
German	2,435	6.69
Greek	408	1.12
Hawaii Native/Pacific Islander:	27	0.07
Micronesian: (1)	1	0.00
Guamanian/Chamorro (1)	1	0.00
Polynesian: (4)	6	0.02
Native Hawaiian (4)	6	0.02
Other Pac. Isl., not spec.	20	0.05

Notes: 1. Figures in the "Number" column do not add up to the total population due to: a) Ancestry/Race overlap — e.g. persons can report being both White and Irish, b) persons of Hispanic origin can report being any race, c) persons reporting two ancestries are counted in both categories. 2. Numbers in parentheses indicate the number of persons reporting this ancestry/race alone, not in combination with any other ancestry/race. 3. Refer to the Explanation of Data in the front of the book for more detailed information.

…		
Hispanic or Latino:	1,051	2.89
Central American:	23	0.06
Costa Rican	5	0.01
Guatemalan	9	0.02
Honduran	3	0.01
Nicaraguan	2	0.01
Panamanian	2	0.01
Salvadoran	2	0.01
Cuban	107	0.29
Dominican Republic	33	0.09
Mexican	123	0.34
Puerto Rican	350	0.96
South American:	173	0.48
Argentinean	30	0.08
Bolivian	1	0.00
Chilean	10	0.03
Colombian	78	0.21
Ecuadorian	17	0.05
Peruvian	17	0.05
Uruguayan	3	0.01
Venezuelan	6	0.02
Other South American	11	0.03
Other Hispanic or Latino	242	0.66
Hungarian	599	1.65
Iranian	14	0.04
Irish	3,872	10.64
Israeli	92	0.25
Italian	7,332	20.14
Latvian	21	0.06
Lithuanian	178	0.49
Maltese	18	0.05
Northern European	8	0.02
Norwegian	182	0.50
Polish	3,844	10.56
Portuguese	104	0.29
Romanian	373	1.02
Russian	3,914	10.75
Scotch-Irish	324	0.89
Scottish	224	0.62
Serbian	37	0.10
Slavic	20	0.05
Slovak	103	0.28
Slovene	9	0.02
Swedish	161	0.44
Swiss	35	0.10
Turkish	59	0.16
Ukrainian	442	1.21
United States or American	2,341	6.43
Welsh	43	0.12
West Indian, excl. Hispanic:	45	0.12
Jamaican	14	0.04
West Indian	31	0.09
White:	30,775	84.55
Not Hispanic (29,671)	29,914	82.19
Hispanic (816)	861	2.37
Yugoslavian	43	0.12

Marlton

Place Type: Census Designated Place
County: Burlington
Population: 10,260

Ancestry/Race	Number	%
African American/Black:	319	3.11
Not Hispanic (286)	306	2.98
Hispanic (9)	13	0.13
African, sub-Saharan:	5	0.05
African	5	0.05
Am. Ind. or Alaska Nat., not spec.	12	0.12
Albanian	41	0.40
American Indian tribes, specified:	29	0.28
Apache (4)	4	0.04
Blackfeet	1	0.01
Cherokee (2)	11	0.11
Chippewa (1)	1	0.01
Choctaw (2)	2	0.02
Creek	2	0.02
Pueblo	3	0.03
Sioux	3	0.03
All other tribes	2	0.02
American Indian tribes, not spec.	1	0.01
Arab:	6	0.06
Egyptian	6	0.06
Armenian	14	0.14
Asian:	473	4.61
Cambodian (4)	4	0.04
Chinese, ex. Taiwanese (104)	110	1.07
Filipino (48)	62	0.60
Indian (176)	186	1.81
Japanese (5)	9	0.09
Korean (63)	70	0.68
Sri Lankan	1	0.01
Taiwanese (10)	12	0.12
Thai (4)	4	0.04
Vietnamese (8)	8	0.08
Other Asian, not specified (5)	7	0.07
Australian	6	0.06
Austrian	55	0.54
Brazilian	5	0.05
British	25	0.24
Bulgarian	17	0.17
Canadian	16	0.16
Croatian	17	0.17
Cypriot	13	0.13
Czech	28	0.27
Czechoslovakian	31	0.30
Danish	18	0.18
Dutch	162	1.58
Eastern European	45	0.44
English	862	8.41
European	27	0.26
Finnish	27	0.26
French, except Basque	165	1.61
French Canadian	34	0.33
German	2,221	21.67
Greek	70	0.68
Hawaii Native/Pacific Islander:	4	0.04
Polynesian: (1)	3	0.03
Native Hawaiian (1)	3	0.03
Other Pac. Isl., not spec.	1	0.01
Hispanic or Latino:	240	2.34
Central American:	7	0.07
Guatemalan	2	0.02
Panamanian	4	0.04
Salvadoran	1	0.01
Cuban	14	0.14
Dominican Republic	6	0.06
Mexican	54	0.53
Puerto Rican	108	1.05
South American:	22	0.21
Argentinean	2	0.02
Chilean	1	0.01
Colombian	8	0.08
Ecuadorian	3	0.03
Peruvian	3	0.03
Venezuelan	4	0.04
Other South American	1	0.01
Other Hispanic or Latino	29	0.28
Hungarian	67	0.65
Iranian	21	0.20
Irish	2,951	28.79
Italian	2,674	26.09
Latvian	10	0.10
Lithuanian	124	1.21
Norwegian	20	0.20
Pennsylvania German	14	0.14
Polish	889	8.67
Portuguese	42	0.41
Romanian	14	0.14
Russian	282	2.75
Scandinavian	10	0.10
Scotch-Irish	209	2.04
Scottish	184	1.80
Serbian	28	0.27
Slavic	25	0.24
Slovak	30	0.29
Swedish	55	0.54
Swiss	17	0.17
Ukrainian	98	0.96
United States or American	358	3.49
Welsh	109	1.06
West Indian, excl. Hispanic:	55	0.54
Jamaican	55	0.54
White:	9,448	92.09
Not Hispanic (9,203)	9,275	90.40
Hispanic (166)	173	1.69

Medford

Place Type: Township
County: Burlington
Population: 22,253

Ancestry/Race	Number	%
African American/Black:	204	0.92
Not Hispanic (165)	196	0.88
Hispanic (5)	8	0.04
African, sub-Saharan:	22	0.10
Liberian	7	0.03
South African	15	0.07
Am. Ind. or Alaska Nat., not spec.	15	0.07
Albanian	6	0.03
American Indian tribes, specified:	47	0.21
Apache (2)	2	0.01
Blackfeet (1)	2	0.01
Cherokee (2)	9	0.04
Chippewa (1)	1	0.00
Choctaw	1	0.00
Cree	1	0.00
Creek (1)	1	0.00
Delaware	7	0.03
Iroquois (2)	2	0.01
Latin American Indians (1)	4	0.02
Puget Sound Salish (4)	4	0.02
All other tribes (6)	13	0.06
Arab:	56	0.25
Lebanese	8	0.04
Moroccan	5	0.02
Palestinian	10	0.04
Other Arab	33	0.15
Armenian	68	0.31
Asian:	389	1.75
Bangladeshi (5)	5	0.02
Chinese, ex. Taiwanese (80)	90	0.40
Filipino (34)	51	0.23
Indian (104)	106	0.48
Japanese (25)	33	0.15
Korean (43)	53	0.24
Taiwanese (9)	12	0.05
Vietnamese (5)	5	0.02
Other Asian, specified	1	0.00
Other Asian, not specified (21)	33	0.15
Austrian	172	0.77
Belgian	69	0.31
Brazilian	6	0.03
British	99	0.44
Canadian	125	0.56
Celtic	11	0.05
Czech	112	0.50
Czechoslovakian	27	0.12
Danish	123	0.55
Dutch	354	1.59
Eastern European	34	0.15
English	2,876	12.92
Estonian	8	0.04
European	204	0.92
Finnish	32	0.14
French, except Basque	609	2.74
French Canadian	153	0.69
German	5,195	23.35
Greek	177	0.80
Hawaii Native/Pacific Islander:	19	0.09
Micronesian: (4)	8	0.04
Guamanian/Chamorro (4)	8	0.04
Polynesian: (5)	6	0.03
Native Hawaiian (2)	3	0.01
Samoan (3)	3	0.01
Other Pac. Isl., specified	1	0.00
Other Pac. Isl., not spec.	4	0.02

Notes: 1. Figures in the "Number" column do not add up to the total population due to: a) Ancestry/Race overlap — e.g. persons can report being both White and Irish, b) persons of Hispanic origin can report being any race, c) persons reporting two ancestries are counted in both categories. 2. Numbers in parentheses indicate the number of persons reporting this ancestry/race alone, not in combination with any other ancestry/race. 3. Refer to the Explanation of Data in the front of the book for more detailed information.

Hispanic or Latino:	252	1.13
Central American:	18	0.08
Costa Rican	2	0.01
Guatemalan	5	0.02
Panamanian	1	0.00
Salvadoran	4	0.02
Other Central American	6	0.03
Cuban	18	0.08
Dominican Republic	5	0.02
Mexican	37	0.17
Puerto Rican	99	0.44
South American:	30	0.13
Argentinean	5	0.02
Colombian	12	0.05
Ecuadorian	6	0.03
Paraguayan	2	0.01
Peruvian	5	0.02
Other Hispanic or Latino	45	0.20
Hungarian	378	1.70
Irish	5,832	26.21
Israeli	4	0.02
Italian	4,704	21.14
Lithuanian	141	0.63
Macedonian	8	0.04
Maltese	7	0.03
Northern European	8	0.04
Norwegian	388	1.74
Pennsylvania German	24	0.11
Polish	1,846	8.30
Portuguese	71	0.32
Romanian	76	0.34
Russian	427	1.92
Scandinavian	10	0.04
Scotch-Irish	513	2.31
Scottish	617	2.77
Slavic	48	0.22
Slovak	75	0.34
Slovene	10	0.04
Swedish	490	2.20
Swiss	130	0.58
Turkish	11	0.05
Ukrainian	193	0.87
United States or American	890	4.00
Welsh	273	1.23
West Indian, excl. Hispanic:	20	0.09
Jamaican	16	0.07
West Indian	4	0.02
White:	21,646	97.27
Not Hispanic (21,353)	21,462	96.45
Hispanic (174)	184	0.83
Yugoslavian	38	0.17

Mercerville-Hamilton Square

Place Type: Census Designated Place
County: Mercer
Population: 26,419

Ancestry/Race	Number	%
African American/Black:	453	1.71
Not Hispanic (367)	423	1.60
Hispanic (17)	30	0.11
Alaska Native tribes, specified:	1	0.00
Alaska Athabascan (1)	1	0.00
Am. Ind. or Alaska Nat., not spec.	38	0.14
American Indian tribes, specified:	51	0.19
Apache	1	0.00
Blackfeet	4	0.02
Cherokee (3)	19	0.07
Chippewa	1	0.00
Choctaw	1	0.00
Delaware (1)	1	0.00
Iroquois (6)	7	0.03
Lumbee (3)	4	0.02
Navajo (3)	6	0.02
Seminole	1	0.00
Sioux (1)	2	0.01
All other tribes (2)	4	0.02
Arab:	200	0.76
Egyptian	137	0.52
Lebanese	18	0.07
Syrian	40	0.15
Other Arab	5	0.02
Armenian	19	0.07
Asian:	739	2.80
Chinese, ex. Taiwanese (134)	149	0.56
Filipino (83)	97	0.37
Indian (233)	251	0.95
Japanese (6)	13	0.05
Korean (115)	119	0.45
Pakistani (56)	58	0.22
Taiwanese (1)	4	0.02
Thai (1)	1	0.00
Vietnamese (24)	24	0.09
Other Asian, not specified (12)	23	0.09
Austrian	125	0.47
Belgian	53	0.20
Brazilian	32	0.12
British	193	0.73
Canadian	17	0.06
Celtic	11	0.04
Croatian	12	0.05
Cypriot	19	0.07
Czech	117	0.44
Czechoslovakian	142	0.54
Danish	88	0.33
Dutch	376	1.42
Eastern European	29	0.11
English	3,396	12.82
European	52	0.20
Finnish	19	0.07
French, except Basque	536	2.02
French Canadian	204	0.77
German	4,870	18.39
Greek	262	0.99
Guyanese	42	0.16
Hawaii Native/Pacific Islander:	3	0.01
Polynesian: (2)	3	0.01
Native Hawaiian (1)	1	0.00
Samoan (1)	2	0.01
Hispanic or Latino:	671	2.54
Central American:	73	0.28
Costa Rican	16	0.06
Guatemalan	49	0.19
Honduran	3	0.01
Panamanian	4	0.02
Other Central American	1	0.00
Cuban	23	0.09
Dominican Republic	4	0.02
Mexican	69	0.26
Puerto Rican	282	1.07
South American:	75	0.28
Argentinean	12	0.05
Chilean	5	0.02
Colombian	22	0.08
Ecuadorian	24	0.09
Peruvian	3	0.01
Venezuelan	5	0.02
Other South American	4	0.02
Other Hispanic or Latino	145	0.55
Hungarian	1,117	4.22
Iranian	30	0.11
Irish	5,779	21.82
Israeli	53	0.20
Italian	7,710	29.11
Lithuanian	102	0.39
Luxemburger	9	0.03
Macedonian	8	0.03
Northern European	21	0.08
Norwegian	266	1.00
Pennsylvania German	52	0.20
Polish	3,678	13.89
Portuguese	89	0.34
Romanian	39	0.15
Russian	295	1.11
Scandinavian	7	0.03
Scotch-Irish	371	1.40
Scottish	592	2.24
Serbian	12	0.05
Slavic	103	0.39
Slovak	641	2.42
Swedish	183	0.69
Swiss	48	0.18
Ukrainian	233	0.88
United States or American	701	2.65
Welsh	195	0.74
West Indian, excl. Hispanic:	52	0.20
Haitian	35	0.13
Jamaican	17	0.06
White:	25,089	94.97
Not Hispanic (24,471)	24,631	93.23
Hispanic (401)	458	1.73

Metuchen

Place Type: Borough
County: Middlesex
Population: 12,840

Ancestry/Race	Number	%
African American/Black:	769	5.99
Not Hispanic (668)	745	5.80
Hispanic (13)	24	0.19
African, sub-Saharan:	85	0.66
African	85	0.66
Am. Ind. or Alaska Nat., not spec.	13	0.10
Albanian	7	0.05
American Indian tribes, specified:	27	0.21
Cherokee (5)	7	0.05
Chippewa (1)	1	0.01
Comanche	3	0.02
Cree (1)	1	0.01
Creek	1	0.01
Delaware	1	0.01
Iroquois	2	0.02
Latin American Indians	2	0.02
Navajo	1	0.01
Seminole	2	0.02
Sioux	4	0.03
All other tribes (1)	2	0.02
American Indian tribes, not spec.	4	0.03
Arab:	57	0.44
Arab/Arabic	33	0.26
Lebanese	16	0.12
Other Arab	8	0.06
Armenian	39	0.30
Asian:	1,033	8.05
Chinese, ex. Taiwanese (209)	227	1.77
Filipino (146)	160	1.25
Indian (327)	341	2.66
Indonesian (24)	30	0.23
Japanese (17)	31	0.24
Korean (72)	86	0.67
Malaysian	1	0.01
Pakistani (32)	54	0.42
Sri Lankan (5)	5	0.04
Taiwanese (4)	8	0.06
Thai (2)	2	0.02
Vietnamese (74)	75	0.58
Other Asian, not specified (6)	13	0.10
Australian	10	0.08
Austrian	148	1.15
Belgian	15	0.12
Brazilian	62	0.48
British	46	0.36
Canadian	37	0.29
Celtic	8	0.06
Croatian	7	0.05
Czech	35	0.27
Czechoslovakian	87	0.68
Danish	179	1.39
Dutch	138	1.07
Eastern European	45	0.35
English	984	7.66
Estonian	12	0.09
European	48	0.37
Finnish	13	0.10
French, except Basque	252	1.96
French Canadian	184	1.43

Notes: 1. Figures in the "Number" column do not add up to the total population due to: a) Ancestry/Race overlap — e.g. persons can report being both White and Irish, b) persons of Hispanic origin can report being any race, c) persons reporting two ancestries are counted in both categories. 2. Numbers in parentheses indicate the number of persons reporting this ancestry/race alone, not in combination with any other ancestry/race. 3. Refer to the Explanation of Data in the front of the book for more detailed information.

Ancestry/Race	Number	%
German	1,863	14.51
Greek	57	0.44
Guyanese	12	0.09
Hawaii Native/Pacific Islander:	7	0.05
Polynesian:	1	0.01
Native Hawaiian	1	0.01
Other Pac. Isl., not spec.	6	0.05
Hispanic or Latino:	508	3.96
Central American:	26	0.20
Costa Rican	3	0.02
Guatemalan	4	0.03
Honduran	9	0.07
Nicaraguan	1	0.01
Panamanian	5	0.04
Salvadoran	4	0.03
Cuban	51	0.40
Dominican Republic	11	0.09
Mexican	50	0.39
Puerto Rican	188	1.46
South American:	76	0.59
Argentinean	15	0.12
Chilean	4	0.03
Colombian	21	0.16
Ecuadorian	17	0.13
Peruvian	10	0.08
Uruguayan	3	0.02
Venezuelan	2	0.02
Other South American	4	0.03
Other Hispanic or Latino	106	0.83
Hungarian	694	5.40
Icelander	21	0.16
Iranian	49	0.38
Irish	2,863	22.30
Israeli	17	0.13
Italian	2,210	17.21
Latvian	7	0.05
Lithuanian	120	0.93
Norwegian	104	0.81
Polish	1,115	8.68
Portuguese	47	0.37
Romanian	74	0.58
Russian	743	5.79
Scandinavian	8	0.06
Scotch-Irish	140	1.09
Scottish	145	1.13
Slavic	5	0.04
Slovak	175	1.36
Slovene	5	0.04
Soviet Union	7	0.05
Swedish	199	1.55
Swiss	38	0.30
Ukrainian	148	1.15
United States or American	327	2.55
Welsh	48	0.37
West Indian, excl. Hispanic:	104	0.81
Haitian	37	0.29
Jamaican	23	0.18
Trinidadian and Tobagonian	17	0.13
West Indian	27	0.21
White:	11,016	85.79
Not Hispanic (10,483)	10,638	82.85
Hispanic (352)	378	2.94
Yugoslavian	10	0.08

Middle

Place Type: Township
County: Cape May
Population: 16,405

Ancestry/Race	Number	%
African American/Black:	1,943	11.84
Not Hispanic (1,745)	1,883	11.48
Hispanic (36)	60	0.37
African, sub-Saharan:	68	0.41
African	68	0.41
Alaska Native tribes, not specified	2	0.01
Am. Ind. or Alaska Nat., not spec.	40	0.24
American Indian tribes, specified:	74	0.45
Apache (1)	1	0.01
Blackfeet	11	0.07
Cherokee (10)	32	0.20
Cheyenne (2)	2	0.01
Choctaw (1)	1	0.01
Creek	2	0.01
Delaware (1)	4	0.02
Iroquois (4)	9	0.05
Latin American Indians (3)	3	0.02
Potawatomi	1	0.01
Yakama	4	0.02
All other tribes (1)	3	0.02
American Indian tribes, not spec.	12	0.07
Arab:	19	0.12
Lebanese	13	0.08
Syrian	6	0.04
Asian:	282	1.72
Chinese, ex. Taiwanese (33)	41	0.25
Filipino (105)	115	0.70
Indian (44)	52	0.32
Indonesian (1)	1	0.01
Japanese (1)	6	0.04
Korean (16)	23	0.14
Malaysian	2	0.01
Pakistani (3)	3	0.02
Taiwanese (5)	5	0.03
Thai (4)	5	0.03
Vietnamese (18)	23	0.14
Other Asian, not specified (1)	6	0.04
Austrian	75	0.46
British	81	0.49
Canadian	6	0.04
Croatian	9	0.05
Czech	5	0.03
Czechoslovakian	69	0.42
Danish	48	0.29
Dutch	245	1.49
English	2,062	12.57
European	10	0.06
Finnish	29	0.18
French, except Basque	347	2.12
French Canadian	47	0.29
German	3,054	18.62
Greek	97	0.59
Hawaii Native/Pacific Islander:	14	0.09
Polynesian: (3)	12	0.07
Native Hawaiian	6	0.04
Other Polynesian (3)	6	0.04
Other Pac. Isl., not spec. (1)	2	0.01
Hispanic or Latino:	347	2.12
Central American:	31	0.19
Costa Rican	2	0.01
Nicaraguan	1	0.01
Panamanian	27	0.16
Other Central American	1	0.01
Cuban	15	0.09
Dominican Republic	15	0.09
Mexican	27	0.16
Puerto Rican	173	1.05
South American:	19	0.12
Argentinean	4	0.02
Chilean	2	0.01
Colombian	11	0.07
Venezuelan	2	0.01
Other Hispanic or Latino	67	0.41
Hungarian	78	0.48
Irish	3,655	22.28
Italian	2,244	13.68
Latvian	8	0.05
Lithuanian	60	0.37
Northern European	59	0.36
Norwegian	102	0.62
Pennsylvania German	29	0.18
Polish	829	5.05
Portuguese	33	0.20
Russian	110	0.67
Scandinavian	4	0.02
Scotch-Irish	213	1.30
Scottish	266	1.62
Slavic	6	0.04
Slovak	49	0.30
Swedish	306	1.87
Swiss	22	0.13
Turkish	5	0.03
Ukrainian	94	0.57
United States or American	1,599	9.75
Welsh	162	0.99
West Indian, excl. Hispanic:	64	0.39
Bahamian	7	0.04
Jamaican	26	0.16
West Indian	31	0.19
White:	14,180	86.44
Not Hispanic (13,823)	14,004	85.36
Hispanic (156)	176	1.07

Middlesex

Place Type: Borough
County: Middlesex
Population: 13,717

Ancestry/Race	Number	%
African American/Black:	500	3.65
Not Hispanic (440)	467	3.40
Hispanic (21)	33	0.24
African, sub-Saharan:	66	0.48
African	13	0.09
Ghanian	30	0.22
Liberian	7	0.05
Sierra Leonean	16	0.12
Am. Ind. or Alaska Nat., not spec.	19	0.14
Albanian	20	0.15
American Indian tribes, specified:	22	0.16
Cherokee (1)	11	0.08
Delaware (2)	2	0.01
Iroquois	2	0.01
Latin American Indians (4)	4	0.03
Lumbee (1)	1	0.01
Sioux (1)	1	0.01
All other tribes	1	0.01
American Indian tribes, not spec.	7	0.05
Arab:	99	0.72
Arab/Arabic	45	0.33
Egyptian	27	0.20
Lebanese	27	0.20
Armenian	6	0.04
Asian:	633	4.61
Chinese, ex. Taiwanese (90)	94	0.69
Filipino (104)	111	0.81
Indian (175)	180	1.31
Indonesian (6)	19	0.14
Japanese (5)	14	0.10
Korean (29)	42	0.31
Laotian (4)	4	0.03
Pakistani (7)	14	0.10
Taiwanese (12)	12	0.09
Thai (3)	4	0.03
Vietnamese (129)	131	0.96
Other Asian, specified (2)	2	0.01
Other Asian, not specified (1)	6	0.04
Austrian	103	0.75
Belgian	20	0.15
Brazilian	21	0.15
British	63	0.46
Bulgarian	10	0.07
Canadian	22	0.16
Croatian	7	0.05
Czech	30	0.22
Czechoslovakian	47	0.34
Danish	43	0.31
Dutch	288	2.10
Eastern European	21	0.15
English	829	6.04
European	59	0.43
Finnish	33	0.24
French, except Basque	129	0.94
French Canadian	121	0.88
German	2,657	19.37
Greek	123	0.90
Guyanese	8	0.06
Hawaii Native/Pacific Islander:	21	0.15

Notes: 1. Figures in the "Number" column do not add up to the total population due to: a) Ancestry/Race overlap — e.g. persons can report being both White and Irish, b) persons of Hispanic origin can report being any race, c) persons reporting two ancestries are counted in both categories. 2. Numbers in parentheses indicate the number of persons reporting this ancestry/race alone, not in combination with any other ancestry/race. 3. Refer to the Explanation of Data in the front of the book for more detailed information.

Micronesian: (2)	5	0.04
Guamanian/Chamorro (2)	2	0.01
Other Micronesian	3	0.02
Polynesian: (1)	1	0.01
Samoan (1)	1	0.01
Other Pac. Isl., not spec.	15	0.11
Hispanic or Latino:	1,235	9.00
Central American:	160	1.17
Costa Rican	49	0.36
Guatemalan	43	0.31
Honduran	7	0.05
Nicaraguan	1	0.01
Panamanian	4	0.03
Salvadoran	29	0.21
Other Central American	27	0.20
Cuban	27	0.20
Dominican Republic	39	0.28
Mexican	48	0.35
Puerto Rican	244	1.78
South American:	345	2.52
Argentinean	12	0.09
Bolivian	1	0.01
Chilean	4	0.03
Colombian	132	0.96
Ecuadorian	55	0.40
Paraguayan	1	0.01
Peruvian	105	0.77
Uruguayan	3	0.02
Venezuelan	5	0.04
Other South American	27	0.20
Other Hispanic or Latino	372	2.71
Hungarian	322	2.35
Iranian	31	0.23
Irish	2,781	20.27
Israeli	16	0.12
Italian	3,561	25.96
Latvian	13	0.09
Lithuanian	99	0.72
Macedonian	6	0.04
Norwegian	215	1.57
Pennsylvania German	39	0.28
Polish	1,983	14.46
Portuguese	71	0.52
Russian	300	2.19
Scandinavian	17	0.12
Scotch-Irish	153	1.12
Scottish	261	1.90
Slavic	24	0.17
Slovak	242	1.76
Swedish	77	0.56
Swiss	26	0.19
Ukrainian	216	1.57
United States or American	178	1.30
Welsh	147	1.07
West Indian, excl. Hispanic:	76	0.55
Haitian	10	0.07
Jamaican	66	0.48
White:	12,187	88.85
Not Hispanic (11,299)	11,420	83.25
Hispanic (671)	767	5.59
Yugoslavian	8	0.06

Middletown

Place Type: Township
County: Monmouth
Population: 66,327

Ancestry/Race	Number	%
African American/Black:	936	1.41
Not Hispanic (769)	882	1.33
Hispanic (34)	54	0.08
African, sub-Saharan:	75	0.11
African	14	0.02
Nigerian	54	0.08
Other sub-Saharan African	7	0.01
Am. Ind. or Alaska Nat., not spec.	51	0.08
Albanian	15	0.02
Alsatian	27	0.04
American Indian tribes, specified:	91	0.14
Apache	7	0.01
Blackfeet (1)	4	0.01
Cherokee (8)	27	0.04
Chickasaw	2	0.00
Chippewa (2)	4	0.01
Choctaw (3)	3	0.00
Comanche (1)	2	0.00
Delaware (8)	12	0.02
Iroquois (2)	11	0.02
Latin American Indians (2)	4	0.01
Pueblo (3)	3	0.00
Puget Sound Salish	1	0.00
Seminole	4	0.01
Sioux (3)	5	0.01
All other tribes	2	0.00
American Indian tribes, not spec.	17	0.03
Arab:	508	0.77
Arab/Arabic	13	0.02
Egyptian	110	0.17
Lebanese	169	0.25
Palestinian	7	0.01
Syrian	176	0.27
Other Arab	33	0.05
Armenian	66	0.10
Asian:	1,956	2.95
Bangladeshi (4)	4	0.01
Cambodian (1)	1	0.00
Chinese, ex. Taiwanese (644)	706	1.06
Filipino (228)	287	0.43
Indian (445)	476	0.72
Indonesian (1)	1	0.00
Japanese (40)	81	0.12
Korean (142)	154	0.23
Pakistani (39)	51	0.08
Taiwanese (80)	94	0.14
Thai (2)	4	0.01
Vietnamese (44)	55	0.08
Other Asian, specified (1)	3	0.00
Other Asian, not specified (19)	39	0.06
Australian	23	0.03
Austrian	520	0.78
Belgian	22	0.03
Brazilian	49	0.07
British	142	0.21
Bulgarian	22	0.03
Canadian	156	0.24
Celtic	36	0.05
Croatian	61	0.09
Czech	264	0.40
Czechoslovakian	212	0.32
Danish	438	0.66
Dutch	891	1.34
Eastern European	81	0.12
English	5,816	8.77
Estonian	19	0.03
European	141	0.21
Finnish	75	0.11
French, except Basque	1,511	2.28
French Canadian	303	0.46
German	11,573	17.45
Greek	451	0.68
Guyanese	55	0.08
Hawaii Native/Pacific Islander:	36	0.05
Micronesian: (6)	6	0.01
Guamanian/Chamorro (3)	3	0.00
Other Micronesian (3)	3	0.00
Polynesian: (8)	12	0.02
Native Hawaiian (2)	4	0.01
Samoan (6)	7	0.01
Other Polynesian	1	0.00
Other Pac. Isl., specified	1	0.00
Other Pac. Isl., not spec. (3)	17	0.03
Hispanic or Latino:	2,265	3.41
Central American:	74	0.11
Costa Rican	7	0.01
Guatemalan	22	0.03
Honduran	13	0.02
Nicaraguan	6	0.01
Panamanian	12	0.02
Salvadoran	13	0.02
Other Central American	1	0.00
Cuban	188	0.28
Dominican Republic	73	0.11
Mexican	116	0.17
Puerto Rican	1,087	1.64
South American:	313	0.47
Argentinean	25	0.04
Bolivian	5	0.01
Chilean	20	0.03
Colombian	100	0.15
Ecuadorian	69	0.10
Paraguayan	11	0.02
Peruvian	38	0.06
Uruguayan	5	0.01
Venezuelan	17	0.03
Other South American	23	0.03
Other Hispanic or Latino	414	0.62
Hungarian	994	1.50
Icelander	18	0.03
Iranian	41	0.06
Irish	21,756	32.80
Israeli	16	0.02
Italian	19,142	28.86
Latvian	6	0.01
Lithuanian	403	0.61
Maltese	46	0.07
Norwegian	850	1.28
Pennsylvania German	16	0.02
Polish	5,797	8.74
Portuguese	249	0.38
Romanian	127	0.19
Russian	1,170	1.76
Scandinavian	113	0.17
Scotch-Irish	1,234	1.86
Scottish	1,195	1.80
Serbian	25	0.04
Slavic	97	0.15
Slovak	533	0.80
Slovene	53	0.08
Swedish	902	1.36
Swiss	101	0.15
Turkish	89	0.13
Ukrainian	728	1.10
United States or American	1,848	2.79
Welsh	393	0.59
West Indian, excl. Hispanic:	86	0.13
Belizean	9	0.01
British West Indian	6	0.01
Haitian	22	0.03
Jamaican	15	0.02
Trinidadian and Tobagonian	29	0.04
Other West Indian	5	0.01
White:	63,324	95.47
Not Hispanic (61,067)	61,440	92.63
Hispanic (1,752)	1,884	2.84
Yugoslavian	46	0.07

Millburn

Place Type: Census Designated Place
County: Essex
Population: 19,765

Ancestry/Race	Number	%
African American/Black:	238	1.20
Not Hispanic (212)	225	1.14
Hispanic (5)	13	0.07
African, sub-Saharan:	33	0.17
African	5	0.03
Cape Verdean	6	0.03
South African	22	0.11
Am. Ind. or Alaska Nat., not spec.	11	0.06
Albanian	25	0.13
Alsatian	6	0.03
American Indian tribes, specified:	11	0.06
Cherokee	3	0.02
Creek	1	0.01
Latin American Indians (2)	4	0.02
Navajo (1)	1	0.01
Sioux (1)	1	0.01

Notes: 1. Figures in the "Number" column do not add up to the total population due to: a) Ancestry/Race overlap — e.g. persons can report being both White and Irish, b) persons of Hispanic origin can report being any race, c) persons reporting two ancestries are counted in both categories. 2. Numbers in parentheses indicate the number of persons reporting this ancestry/race alone, not in combination with any other ancestry/race. 3. Refer to the Explanation of Data in the front of the book for more detailed information.

Ancestry/Race	Number	%
All other tribes	1	0.01
American Indian tribes, not spec.	1	0.01
Arab:	127	0.64
Arab/Arabic	12	0.06
Egyptian	22	0.11
Lebanese	18	0.09
Moroccan	42	0.21
Syrian	23	0.12
Other Arab	10	0.05
Armenian	70	0.35
Asian:	1,829	9.25
Bangladeshi (1)	1	0.01
Cambodian (1)	1	0.01
Chinese, ex. Taiwanese (702)	764	3.87
Filipino (130)	147	0.74
Indian (343)	374	1.89
Indonesian (1)	1	0.01
Japanese (91)	110	0.56
Korean (217)	235	1.19
Laotian (1)	3	0.02
Malaysian (4)	6	0.03
Pakistani (42)	47	0.24
Sri Lankan (8)	8	0.04
Taiwanese (72)	84	0.42
Thai (5)	5	0.03
Vietnamese (5)	9	0.05
Other Asian, specified (3)	5	0.03
Other Asian, not specified (8)	29	0.15
Austrian	482	2.44
Brazilian	9	0.05
British	204	1.03
Bulgarian	23	0.12
Canadian	24	0.12
Celtic	5	0.03
Croatian	14	0.07
Czech	53	0.27
Czechoslovakian	14	0.07
Danish	55	0.28
Dutch	171	0.87
Eastern European	495	2.50
English	1,345	6.80
Estonian	7	0.04
European	324	1.64
Finnish	14	0.07
French, except Basque	337	1.71
French Canadian	26	0.13
German	2,277	11.52
Greek	208	1.05
Guyanese	3	0.02
Hawaii Native/Pacific Islander:	13	0.07
Micronesian: (1)	1	0.01
Guamanian/Chamorro (1)	1	0.01
Polynesian: (5)	8	0.04
Native Hawaiian (3)	6	0.03
Samoan (2)	2	0.01
Other Pac. Isl., specified	1	0.01
Other Pac. Isl., not spec.	3	0.02
Hispanic or Latino:	404	2.04
Central American:	44	0.22
Costa Rican	27	0.14
Guatemalan	6	0.03
Honduran	6	0.03
Panamanian	1	0.01
Salvadoran	2	0.01
Other Central American	2	0.01
Cuban	35	0.18
Dominican Republic	13	0.07
Mexican	48	0.24
Puerto Rican	64	0.32
South American:	95	0.48
Argentinean	21	0.11
Bolivian	3	0.02
Chilean	15	0.08
Colombian	28	0.14
Ecuadorian	4	0.02
Paraguayan	1	0.01
Peruvian	15	0.08
Venezuelan	2	0.01
Other South American	6	0.03
Other Hispanic or Latino	105	0.53
Hungarian	465	2.35
Iranian	84	0.42
Irish	2,398	12.13
Israeli	199	1.01
Italian	2,668	13.50
Latvian	48	0.24
Lithuanian	137	0.69
Northern European	26	0.13
Norwegian	168	0.85
Polish	1,265	6.40
Portuguese	89	0.45
Romanian	201	1.02
Russian	2,309	11.68
Scandinavian	23	0.12
Scotch-Irish	270	1.37
Scottish	319	1.61
Serbian	7	0.04
Slavic	6	0.03
Slovak	74	0.37
Swedish	300	1.52
Swiss	111	0.56
Turkish	24	0.12
Ukrainian	170	0.86
United States or American	1,306	6.61
Welsh	161	0.81
West Indian, excl. Hispanic:	44	0.22
Jamaican	16	0.08
Trinidadian and Tobagonian	14	0.07
West Indian	14	0.07
White:	17,763	89.87
Not Hispanic (17,262)	17,430	88.19
Hispanic (311)	333	1.68
Yugoslavian	31	0.16

Millville

Place Type: City
County: Cumberland
Population: 26,847

Ancestry/Race	Number	%
African American/Black:	4,356	16.23
Not Hispanic (3,851)	4,093	15.25
Hispanic (174)	263	0.98
African, sub-Saharan:	218	0.81
African	218	0.81
Alaska Native tribes, specified:	2	0.01
Tlingit-Haida	2	0.01
Am. Ind. or Alaska Nat., not spec.	141	0.53
American Indian tribes, specified:	183	0.68
Blackfeet (6)	16	0.06
Cherokee (8)	44	0.16
Choctaw	1	0.00
Delaware (16)	48	0.18
Iroquois	1	0.00
Latin American Indians (5)	6	0.02
Seminole (2)	2	0.01
Sioux (1)	2	0.01
All other tribes (28)	63	0.23
American Indian tribes, not spec.	13	0.05
Asian:	287	1.07
Chinese, ex. Taiwanese (33)	46	0.17
Filipino (57)	72	0.27
Indian (22)	32	0.12
Japanese (14)	29	0.11
Korean (54)	62	0.23
Malaysian	1	0.00
Pakistani (7)	10	0.04
Sri Lankan (1)	2	0.01
Thai (4)	5	0.02
Vietnamese (12)	13	0.05
Other Asian, not specified (6)	15	0.06
Austrian	68	0.25
British	114	0.42
Canadian	31	0.12
Croatian	7	0.03
Czech	82	0.31
Czechoslovakian	40	0.15
Dutch	419	1.56
English	3,500	13.04
European	42	0.16
Finnish	5	0.02
French, except Basque	603	2.25
French Canadian	91	0.34
German	4,669	17.39
German Russian	8	0.03
Greek	130	0.48
Hawaii Native/Pacific Islander:	20	0.07
Micronesian: (6)	9	0.03
Guamanian/Chamorro (2)	3	0.01
Other Micronesian (4)	6	0.02
Polynesian: (1)	4	0.01
Native Hawaiian (1)	4	0.01
Other Pac. Isl., not spec. (1)	7	0.03
Hispanic or Latino:	2,998	11.17
Central American:	22	0.08
Costa Rican	8	0.03
Guatemalan	4	0.01
Honduran	4	0.01
Nicaraguan	1	0.00
Panamanian	1	0.00
Salvadoran	3	0.01
Other Central American	1	0.00
Cuban	14	0.05
Dominican Republic	29	0.11
Mexican	168	0.63
Puerto Rican	2,392	8.91
South American:	38	0.14
Argentinean	1	0.00
Chilean	2	0.01
Colombian	14	0.05
Ecuadorian	10	0.04
Peruvian	8	0.03
Venezuelan	3	0.01
Other Hispanic or Latino	335	1.25
Hungarian	82	0.31
Irish	4,214	15.70
Italian	3,652	13.60
Latvian	26	0.10
Lithuanian	30	0.11
Norwegian	121	0.45
Pennsylvania German	26	0.10
Polish	922	3.43
Portuguese	20	0.07
Russian	382	1.42
Scandinavian	28	0.10
Scotch-Irish	289	1.08
Scottish	347	1.29
Serbian	18	0.07
Slavic	8	0.03
Slovak	32	0.12
Slovene	7	0.03
Swedish	236	0.88
Swiss	92	0.34
Ukrainian	397	1.48
United States or American	1,308	4.87
Welsh	244	0.91
West Indian, excl. Hispanic:	103	0.38
Barbadian	9	0.03
Haitian	9	0.03
Jamaican	40	0.15
Trinidadian and Tobagonian	37	0.14
West Indian	8	0.03
White:	20,912	77.89
Not Hispanic (19,215)	19,565	72.88
Hispanic (1,223)	1,347	5.02
Yugoslavian	10	0.04

Monroe

Place Type: Township
County: Gloucester
Population: 28,967

Ancestry/Race	Number	%
African American/Black:	3,422	11.81
Not Hispanic (3,177)	3,345	11.55
Hispanic (54)	77	0.27
African, sub-Saharan:	138	0.48
African	81	0.28

Notes: 1. Figures in the "Number" column do not add up to the total population due to: a) Ancestry/Race overlap — e.g. persons can report being both White and Irish, b) persons of Hispanic origin can report being any race, c) persons reporting two ancestries are counted in both categories. 2. Numbers in parentheses indicate the number of persons reporting this ancestry/race alone, not in combination with any other ancestry/race. 3. Refer to the Explanation of Data in the front of the book for more detailed information.

Ancestry/Race	Number	%
Ghanian	7	0.02
Liberian	50	0.17
Alaska Native tribes, specified:	1	0.00
Tlingit-Haida (1)	1	0.00
Am. Ind. or Alaska Nat., not spec.	76	0.26
American Indian tribes, specified:	86	0.30
Apache (1)	3	0.01
Blackfeet (1)	3	0.01
Cherokee (8)	23	0.08
Choctaw (1)	1	0.00
Creek (1)	1	0.00
Crow (1)	1	0.00
Delaware (2)	5	0.02
Iroquois	4	0.01
Latin American Indians	1	0.00
Lumbee (5)	5	0.02
Navajo	1	0.00
Pueblo	1	0.00
Seminole	6	0.02
Sioux	11	0.04
All other tribes (14)	20	0.07
American Indian tribes, not spec.	15	0.05
Arab:	95	0.33
Arab/Arabic	13	0.04
Egyptian	34	0.12
Lebanese	33	0.11
Syrian	15	0.05
Armenian	63	0.22
Asian:	458	1.58
Cambodian (4)	4	0.01
Chinese, ex. Taiwanese (53)	68	0.23
Filipino (148)	189	0.65
Indian (70)	87	0.30
Japanese (16)	28	0.10
Korean (39)	45	0.16
Pakistani	1	0.00
Thai (1)	3	0.01
Vietnamese (14)	15	0.05
Other Asian, specified (1)	1	0.00
Other Asian, not specified (10)	17	0.06
Austrian	56	0.19
Belgian	6	0.02
Brazilian	6	0.02
British	21	0.07
Canadian	15	0.05
Croatian	3	0.01
Czech	16	0.06
Czechoslovakian	37	0.13
Danish	40	0.14
Dutch	275	0.95
Eastern European	40	0.14
English	2,795	9.65
European	64	0.22
French, except Basque	556	1.92
French Canadian	116	0.40
German	6,674	23.04
Greek	105	0.36
Hawaii Native/Pacific Islander:	15	0.05
Micronesian: (1)	2	0.01
Guamanian/Chamorro (1)	2	0.01
Polynesian: (6)	6	0.02
Native Hawaiian (1)	1	0.00
Samoan (5)	5	0.02
Other Pac. Isl., not spec. (2)	7	0.02
Hispanic or Latino:	785	2.71
Central American:	10	0.03
Costa Rican	1	0.00
Guatemalan	1	0.00
Honduran	2	0.01
Panamanian	2	0.01
Salvadoran	4	0.01
Cuban	24	0.08
Dominican Republic	2	0.01
Mexican	96	0.33
Puerto Rican	486	1.68
South American:	33	0.11
Argentinean	1	0.00
Chilean	1	0.00
Colombian	16	0.06
Ecuadorian	8	0.03
Peruvian	2	0.01
Other South American	5	0.02
Other Hispanic or Latino	134	0.46
Hungarian	107	0.37
Irish	7,433	25.66
Italian	6,977	24.09
Latvian	12	0.04
Lithuanian	133	0.46
Macedonian	15	0.05
Norwegian	126	0.43
Pennsylvania German	122	0.42
Polish	2,216	7.65
Portuguese	17	0.06
Romanian	35	0.12
Russian	183	0.63
Scandinavian	10	0.03
Scotch-Irish	294	1.01
Scottish	287	0.99
Serbian	19	0.07
Slavic	8	0.03
Slovak	102	0.35
Swedish	229	0.79
Swiss	7	0.02
Ukrainian	238	0.82
United States or American	1,032	3.56
Welsh	199	0.69
West Indian, excl. Hispanic:	102	0.35
Dutch West Indian	10	0.03
Haitian	7	0.02
Jamaican	32	0.11
Trinidadian and Tobagonian	39	0.13
West Indian	14	0.05
White:	24,932	86.07
Not Hispanic (24,178)	24,489	84.54
Hispanic (395)	443	1.53
Yugoslavian	28	0.10

Monroe

Place Type: Township
County: Middlesex
Population: 27,999

Ancestry/Race	Number	%
African American/Black:	865	3.09
Not Hispanic (792)	825	2.95
Hispanic (28)	40	0.14
African, sub-Saharan:	57	0.20
African	57	0.20
Am. Ind. or Alaska Nat., not spec.	23	0.08
American Indian tribes, specified:	26	0.09
Cherokee (1)	6	0.02
Chickasaw	1	0.00
Choctaw	1	0.00
Creek (3)	3	0.01
Iroquois (5)	6	0.02
Latin American Indians	4	0.01
All other tribes (4)	5	0.02
American Indian tribes, not spec.	5	0.02
Arab:	92	0.33
Arab/Arabic	9	0.03
Egyptian	68	0.24
Lebanese	15	0.05
Armenian	13	0.05
Asian:	742	2.65
Cambodian	1	0.00
Chinese, ex. Taiwanese (206)	233	0.83
Filipino (92)	108	0.39
Indian (256)	290	1.04
Japanese (9)	11	0.04
Korean (50)	51	0.18
Pakistani (10)	10	0.04
Taiwanese (1)	3	0.01
Thai (1)	1	0.00
Vietnamese (8)	13	0.05
Other Asian, not specified	21	0.08
Austrian	656	2.34
Belgian	6	0.02
Brazilian	61	0.22
British	90	0.32
Bulgarian	21	0.08
Canadian	30	0.11
Croatian	19	0.07
Czech	103	0.37
Czechoslovakian	61	0.22
Danish	118	0.42
Dutch	285	1.02
Eastern European	122	0.44
English	1,868	6.67
European	97	0.35
Finnish	7	0.03
French, except Basque	474	1.69
French Canadian	89	0.32
German	3,417	12.20
Greek	245	0.88
Hawaii Native/Pacific Islander:	27	0.10
Micronesian: (1)	1	0.00
Guamanian/Chamorro (1)	1	0.00
Polynesian: (2)	2	0.01
Native Hawaiian (1)	1	0.00
Samoan (1)	1	0.00
Other Pac. Isl., not spec. (21)	24	0.09
Hispanic or Latino:	666	2.38
Central American:	20	0.07
Costa Rican	5	0.02
Guatemalan	2	0.01
Honduran	5	0.02
Nicaraguan	2	0.01
Panamanian	1	0.00
Salvadoran	3	0.01
Other Central American	2	0.01
Cuban	57	0.20
Dominican Republic	11	0.04
Mexican	63	0.23
Puerto Rican	295	1.05
South American:	63	0.23
Argentinean	7	0.03
Colombian	19	0.07
Ecuadorian	11	0.04
Peruvian	13	0.05
Uruguayan	5	0.02
Venezuelan	1	0.00
Other South American	7	0.03
Other Hispanic or Latino	157	0.56
Hungarian	1,043	3.73
Iranian	20	0.07
Irish	4,024	14.37
Israeli	6	0.02
Italian	5,795	20.70
Latvian	49	0.18
Lithuanian	156	0.56
Maltese	11	0.04
Norwegian	140	0.50
Pennsylvania German	9	0.03
Polish	3,569	12.75
Portuguese	126	0.45
Romanian	285	1.02
Russian	2,597	9.28
Scandinavian	18	0.06
Scotch-Irish	284	1.01
Scottish	294	1.05
Serbian	47	0.17
Slavic	71	0.25
Slovak	178	0.64
Slovene	6	0.02
Swedish	130	0.46
Swiss	59	0.21
Turkish	47	0.17
Ukrainian	364	1.30
United States or American	1,313	4.69
Welsh	107	0.38
West Indian, excl. Hispanic:	79	0.28
Jamaican	71	0.25
West Indian	8	0.03
White:	26,272	93.83
Not Hispanic (25,693)	25,809	92.18
Hispanic (434)	463	1.65
Yugoslavian	43	0.15

Notes: 1. Figures in the "Number" column do not add up to the total population due to: a) Ancestry/Race overlap — e.g. persons can report being both White and Irish, b) persons of Hispanic origin can report being any race, c) persons reporting two ancestries are counted in both categories. 2. Numbers in parentheses indicate the number of persons reporting this ancestry/race alone, not in combination with any other ancestry/race. 3. Refer to the Explanation of Data in the front of the book for more detailed information.

Montclair

Place Type: Census Designated Place
County: Essex
Population: 38,977

Ancestry/Race	Number	%
African American/Black:	13,298	34.12
Not Hispanic (12,194)	12,899	33.09
Hispanic (303)	399	1.02
African, sub-Saharan:	899	2.30
African	390	1.00
Cape Verdean	71	0.18
Ethiopian	18	0.05
Ghanian	56	0.14
Kenyan	48	0.12
Nigerian	193	0.49
Senegalese	24	0.06
Sierra Leonean	19	0.05
South African	63	0.16
Sudanese	6	0.02
Other sub-Saharan African	11	0.03
Am. Ind. or Alaska Nat., not spec.	158	0.41
Albanian	14	0.04
Alsatian	15	0.04
American Indian tribes, specified:	193	0.50
Apache (1)	2	0.01
Blackfeet	14	0.04
Cherokee (5)	95	0.24
Chippewa	2	0.01
Choctaw (1)	4	0.01
Creek	2	0.01
Delaware (4)	12	0.03
Houma	1	0.00
Iroquois (2)	8	0.02
Latin American Indians (8)	20	0.05
Menominee	1	0.00
Navajo (2)	3	0.01
Pueblo (1)	1	0.00
Seminole	6	0.02
Sioux (4)	5	0.01
All other tribes (3)	17	0.04
American Indian tribes, not spec.	23	0.06
Arab:	283	0.72
Arab/Arabic	24	0.06
Egyptian	34	0.09
Jordanian	6	0.02
Lebanese	112	0.29
Moroccan	27	0.07
Palestinian	43	0.11
Syrian	37	0.09
Armenian	76	0.19
Asian:	1,529	3.92
Bangladeshi (37)	47	0.12
Chinese, ex. Taiwanese (302)	378	0.97
Filipino (136)	168	0.43
Indian (478)	560	1.44
Indonesian	4	0.01
Japanese (72)	114	0.29
Korean (135)	158	0.41
Laotian	4	0.01
Malaysian (3)	3	0.01
Pakistani (1)	8	0.02
Sri Lankan (3)	6	0.02
Taiwanese (5)	8	0.02
Thai (4)	4	0.01
Vietnamese (11)	13	0.03
Other Asian, specified (3)	4	0.01
Other Asian, not specified (15)	50	0.13
Assyrian/Chaldean/Syriac	6	0.02
Australian	19	0.05
Austrian	256	0.66
Belgian	66	0.17
Brazilian	57	0.15
British	244	0.62
Bulgarian	4	0.01
Canadian	166	0.42
Croatian	45	0.12
Czech	97	0.25
Czechoslovakian	42	0.11
Danish	88	0.23
Dutch	413	1.06
Eastern European	340	0.87
English	2,975	7.61
Estonian	29	0.07
European	303	0.78
Finnish	26	0.07
French, except Basque	893	2.29
French Canadian	165	0.42
German	3,604	9.22
Greek	137	0.35
Guyanese	221	0.57
Hawaii Native/Pacific Islander:	36	0.09
Micronesian:	2	0.01
Guamanian/Chamorro	2	0.01
Polynesian: (11)	14	0.04
Native Hawaiian (3)	5	0.01
Samoan (8)	9	0.02
Other Pac. Isl., not spec. (3)	20	0.05
Hispanic or Latino:	1,995	5.12
Central American:	141	0.36
Costa Rican	30	0.08
Guatemalan	28	0.07
Honduran	21	0.05
Nicaraguan	6	0.02
Panamanian	28	0.07
Salvadoran	19	0.05
Other Central American	9	0.02
Cuban	171	0.44
Dominican Republic	109	0.28
Mexican	183	0.47
Puerto Rican	584	1.50
South American:	376	0.96
Argentinean	42	0.11
Bolivian	4	0.01
Chilean	12	0.03
Colombian	150	0.38
Ecuadorian	40	0.10
Paraguayan	6	0.02
Peruvian	73	0.19
Uruguayan	11	0.03
Venezuelan	26	0.07
Other South American	12	0.03
Other Hispanic or Latino	431	1.11
Hungarian	275	0.70
Iranian	83	0.21
Irish	5,339	13.67
Israeli	51	0.13
Italian	3,948	10.11
Latvian	74	0.19
Lithuanian	237	0.61
Luxemburger	4	0.01
Macedonian	10	0.03
New Zealander	7	0.02
Northern European	20	0.05
Norwegian	343	0.88
Polish	1,900	4.86
Portuguese	52	0.13
Romanian	58	0.15
Russian	1,604	4.11
Scandinavian	48	0.12
Scotch-Irish	504	1.29
Scottish	937	2.40
Serbian	3	0.01
Slavic	27	0.07
Slovak	93	0.24
Slovene	22	0.06
Soviet Union	6	0.02
Swedish	271	0.69
Swiss	206	0.53
Turkish	23	0.06
Ukrainian	278	0.71
United States or American	967	2.48
Welsh	180	0.46
West Indian, excl. Hispanic:	2,015	5.16
Barbadian	74	0.19
Bermudan	48	0.12
British West Indian	44	0.11
Dutch West Indian	8	0.02
Haitian	468	1.20
Jamaican	978	2.50
Trinidadian and Tobagonian	134	0.34
West Indian	261	0.67
White:	24,082	61.79
Not Hispanic (22,268)	22,950	58.88
Hispanic (1,029)	1,132	2.90
Yugoslavian	41	0.10

Montgomery

Place Type: Township
County: Somerset
Population: 17,481

Ancestry/Race	Number	%
African American/Black:	416	2.38
Not Hispanic (350)	393	2.25
Hispanic (11)	23	0.13
African, sub-Saharan:	141	0.81
African	10	0.06
Nigerian	112	0.64
Other sub-Saharan African	19	0.11
Am. Ind. or Alaska Nat., not spec.	23	0.13
Alsatian	54	0.31
American Indian tribes, specified:	21	0.12
Blackfeet	1	0.01
Cherokee (2)	3	0.02
Cree (1)	1	0.01
Delaware (3)	4	0.02
Iroquois	1	0.01
Latin American Indians	6	0.03
All other tribes (5)	5	0.03
American Indian tribes, not spec.	2	0.01
Arab:	141	0.81
Egyptian	91	0.52
Iraqi	7	0.04
Lebanese	28	0.16
Palestinian	7	0.04
Syrian	8	0.05
Armenian	37	0.21
Asian:	2,171	12.42
Bangladeshi	1	0.01
Cambodian (4)	4	0.02
Chinese, ex. Taiwanese (976)	1,023	5.85
Filipino (86)	98	0.56
Indian (556)	585	3.35
Indonesian (5)	6	0.03
Japanese (68)	94	0.54
Korean (121)	136	0.78
Laotian (1)	1	0.01
Pakistani (16)	16	0.09
Sri Lankan (19)	19	0.11
Taiwanese (119)	134	0.77
Thai (1)	1	0.01
Vietnamese (11)	16	0.09
Other Asian, specified (1)	5	0.03
Other Asian, not specified (7)	32	0.18
Austrian	264	1.51
Belgian	21	0.12
Brazilian	8	0.05
British	125	0.72
Canadian	42	0.24
Celtic	6	0.03
Croatian	25	0.14
Czech	184	1.05
Czechoslovakian	63	0.36
Danish	29	0.17
Dutch	265	1.52
Eastern European	90	0.52
English	1,668	9.55
European	152	0.87
Finnish	7	0.04
French, except Basque	346	1.98
French Canadian	110	0.63
German	2,680	15.34
Greek	275	1.57
Hawaii Native/Pacific Islander:	10	0.06
Micronesian: (1)	1	0.01
Guamanian/Chamorro (1)	1	0.01
Polynesian: (1)	1	0.01

Notes: 1. Figures in the "Number" column do not add up to the total population due to: a) Ancestry/Race overlap — e.g. persons can report being both White and Irish, b) persons of Hispanic origin can report being any race, c) persons reporting two ancestries are counted in both categories. 2. Numbers in parentheses indicate the number of persons reporting this ancestry/race alone, not in combination with any other ancestry/race. 3. Refer to the Explanation of Data in the front of the book for more detailed information.

Native Hawaiian (1)	1	0.01
Other Pac. Isl., not spec.	8	0.05
Hispanic or Latino:	387	2.21
Central American:	20	0.11
Costa Rican	9	0.05
Guatemalan	4	0.02
Panamanian	2	0.01
Salvadoran	3	0.02
Other Central American	2	0.01
Cuban	47	0.27
Dominican Republic	5	0.03
Mexican	76	0.43
Puerto Rican	96	0.55
South American:	54	0.31
Argentinean	4	0.02
Bolivian	2	0.01
Chilean	2	0.01
Colombian	17	0.10
Ecuadorian	12	0.07
Paraguayan	4	0.02
Peruvian	4	0.02
Uruguayan	1	0.01
Venezuelan	1	0.01
Other South American	7	0.04
Other Hispanic or Latino	89	0.51
Hungarian	269	1.54
Iranian	18	0.10
Irish	3,188	18.25
Israeli	19	0.11
Italian	3,052	17.47
Latvian	8	0.05
Lithuanian	146	0.84
Northern European	118	0.68
Norwegian	294	1.68
Polish	1,770	10.13
Portuguese	22	0.13
Romanian	99	0.57
Russian	653	3.74
Scandinavian	48	0.27
Scotch-Irish	284	1.63
Scottish	475	2.72
Serbian	7	0.04
Slavic	7	0.04
Slovak	148	0.85
Swedish	410	2.35
Swiss	41	0.23
Turkish	48	0.27
Ukrainian	343	1.96
United States or American	645	3.69
Welsh	97	0.56
West Indian, excl. Hispanic:	32	0.18
British West Indian	7	0.04
Jamaican	10	0.06
West Indian	15	0.09
White:	14,968	85.62
Not Hispanic (14,507)	14,677	83.96
Hispanic (274)	291	1.66
Yugoslavian	22	0.13

Montville

Place Type: Township
County: Morris
Population: 20,839

Ancestry/Race	Number	%
Afghan	65	0.31
African American/Black:	232	1.11
Not Hispanic (188)	223	1.07
Hispanic (5)	9	0.04
African, sub-Saharan:	17	0.08
African	17	0.08
Am. Ind. or Alaska Nat., not spec.	16	0.08
Albanian	117	0.56
American Indian tribes, specified:	22	0.11
Apache	1	0.00
Cherokee (1)	8	0.04
Chickasaw	1	0.00
Chippewa	3	0.01
Iroquois	2	0.01
Potawatomi	1	0.00
Pueblo	1	0.00
Shoshone (3)	3	0.01
Sioux (1)	1	0.00
All other tribes	1	0.00
American Indian tribes, not spec.	3	0.01
Arab:	55	0.26
Lebanese	15	0.07
Syrian	29	0.14
Other Arab	11	0.05
Armenian	79	0.38
Asian:	2,779	13.34
Chinese, ex. Taiwanese (1,054)	1,098	5.27
Filipino (99)	128	0.61
Indian (810)	843	4.05
Indonesian	2	0.01
Japanese (47)	52	0.25
Korean (349)	358	1.72
Laotian (3)	3	0.01
Pakistani (32)	44	0.21
Sri Lankan (2)	2	0.01
Taiwanese (168)	187	0.90
Thai (1)	1	0.00
Vietnamese (15)	15	0.07
Other Asian, specified (1)	2	0.01
Other Asian, not specified (10)	44	0.21
Austrian	264	1.27
Brazilian	7	0.03
British	179	0.86
Canadian	8	0.04
Croatian	10	0.05
Cypriot	8	0.04
Czech	73	0.35
Czechoslovakian	152	0.73
Danish	91	0.44
Dutch	583	2.80
Eastern European	111	0.53
English	1,274	6.11
European	152	0.73
Finnish	38	0.18
French, except Basque	262	1.26
French Canadian	67	0.32
German	2,847	13.66
Greek	263	1.26
Hawaii Native/Pacific Islander:	22	0.11
Micronesian: (3)	3	0.01
Guamanian/Chamorro (3)	3	0.01
Polynesian:	4	0.02
Native Hawaiian	1	0.00
Samoan	3	0.01
Other Pac. Isl., not spec. (1)	15	0.07
Hispanic or Latino:	531	2.55
Central American:	36	0.17
Costa Rican	2	0.01
Guatemalan	4	0.02
Honduran	18	0.09
Nicaraguan	2	0.01
Salvadoran	8	0.04
Other Central American	2	0.01
Cuban	75	0.36
Dominican Republic	6	0.03
Mexican	69	0.33
Puerto Rican	158	0.76
South American:	71	0.34
Argentinean	8	0.04
Bolivian	1	0.00
Chilean	3	0.01
Colombian	34	0.16
Ecuadorian	6	0.03
Peruvian	10	0.05
Uruguayan	5	0.02
Venezuelan	2	0.01
Other South American	2	0.01
Other Hispanic or Latino	116	0.56
Hungarian	335	1.61
Icelander	10	0.05
Iranian	28	0.13
Irish	2,976	14.28
Israeli	20	0.10
Italian	5,594	26.84
Latvian	56	0.27
Lithuanian	64	0.31
Macedonian	35	0.17
Maltese	27	0.13
Norwegian	171	0.82
Pennsylvania German	7	0.03
Polish	1,928	9.25
Portuguese	76	0.36
Romanian	123	0.59
Russian	1,262	6.06
Scandinavian	15	0.07
Scotch-Irish	103	0.49
Scottish	275	1.32
Slavic	24	0.12
Slovak	165	0.79
Slovene	8	0.04
Swedish	159	0.76
Swiss	238	1.14
Turkish	35	0.17
Ukrainian	283	1.36
United States or American	681	3.27
Welsh	98	0.47
West Indian, excl. Hispanic:	52	0.25
British West Indian	10	0.05
Jamaican	37	0.18
Trinidadian and Tobagonian	5	0.02
White:	17,901	85.90
Not Hispanic (17,274)	17,439	83.68
Hispanic (429)	462	2.22
Yugoslavian	50	0.24

Moorestown

Place Type: Township
County: Burlington
Population: 19,017

Ancestry/Race	Number	%
African American/Black:	1,176	6.18
Not Hispanic (1,056)	1,148	6.04
Hispanic (26)	28	0.15
African, sub-Saharan:	49	0.26
African	29	0.15
Nigerian	13	0.07
South African	7	0.04
Am. Ind. or Alaska Nat., not spec.	38	0.20
Albanian	4	0.02
American Indian tribes, specified:	59	0.31
Blackfeet	1	0.01
Cherokee (2)	20	0.11
Cheyenne	2	0.01
Chippewa (3)	3	0.02
Choctaw (2)	2	0.01
Delaware	1	0.01
Lumbee (1)	1	0.01
Navajo	2	0.01
Seminole	1	0.01
Sioux	4	0.02
All other tribes (10)	22	0.12
American Indian tribes, not spec.	3	0.02
Arab:	37	0.19
Egyptian	7	0.04
Lebanese	8	0.04
Other Arab	22	0.12
Armenian	80	0.42
Asian:	743	3.91
Chinese, ex. Taiwanese (124)	155	0.82
Filipino (51)	74	0.39
Indian (245)	259	1.36
Indonesian (1)	2	0.01
Japanese (26)	57	0.30
Korean (69)	83	0.44
Laotian (6)	7	0.04
Pakistani (23)	24	0.13
Sri Lankan (9)	9	0.05
Taiwanese (14)	14	0.07
Thai	1	0.01
Vietnamese (27)	31	0.16
Other Asian, specified	4	0.02
Other Asian, not specified (14)	23	0.12

Notes: 1. Figures in the "Number" column do not add up to the total population due to: a) Ancestry/Race overlap — e.g. persons can report being both White and Irish, b) persons of Hispanic origin can report being any race, c) persons reporting two ancestries are counted in both categories. 2. Numbers in parentheses indicate the number of persons reporting this ancestry/race alone, not in combination with any other ancestry/race. 3. Refer to the Explanation of Data in the front of the book for more detailed information.

Australian	42	0.22
Austrian	135	0.71
British	194	1.02
Canadian	24	0.13
Croatian	64	0.34
Czech	97	0.51
Czechoslovakian	33	0.17
Danish	112	0.59
Dutch	143	0.75
Eastern European	93	0.49
English	2,808	14.77
Estonian	17	0.09
European	222	1.17
Finnish	51	0.27
French, except Basque	509	2.68
French Canadian	134	0.70
German	3,742	19.68
Greek	168	0.88
Hawaii Native/Pacific Islander:	5	0.03
Other Pac. Isl., specified	4	0.02
Other Pac. Isl., not spec. (1)	1	0.01
Hispanic or Latino:	332	1.75
Central American:	14	0.07
Costa Rican	1	0.01
Guatemalan	1	0.01
Honduran	1	0.01
Nicaraguan	2	0.01
Panamanian	6	0.03
Salvadoran	3	0.02
Cuban	26	0.14
Dominican Republic	17	0.09
Mexican	49	0.26
Puerto Rican	140	0.74
South American:	35	0.18
Argentinean	10	0.05
Chilean	12	0.06
Colombian	7	0.04
Paraguayan	1	0.01
Peruvian	3	0.02
Venezuelan	1	0.01
Other South American	1	0.01
Other Hispanic or Latino	51	0.27
Hungarian	150	0.79
Irish	4,796	25.22
Italian	2,977	15.65
Latvian	19	0.10
Lithuanian	93	0.49
Northern European	34	0.18
Norwegian	216	1.14
Pennsylvania German	45	0.24
Polish	1,192	6.27
Portuguese	68	0.36
Romanian	101	0.53
Russian	616	3.24
Scandinavian	9	0.05
Scotch-Irish	548	2.88
Scottish	430	2.26
Serbian	7	0.04
Slavic	35	0.18
Slovak	55	0.29
Slovene	17	0.09
Swedish	337	1.77
Swiss	87	0.46
Turkish	29	0.15
Ukrainian	101	0.53
United States or American	877	4.61
Welsh	255	1.34
West Indian, excl. Hispanic:	33	0.17
Jamaican	33	0.17
White:	17,162	90.25
Not Hispanic (16,742)	16,927	89.01
Hispanic (220)	235	1.24
Yugoslavian	17	0.09

Moorestown-Lenola

Place Type: Census Designated Place
County: Burlington
Population: 13,860

Ancestry/Race	Number	%
African American/Black:	1,048	7.56
Not Hispanic (939)	1,021	7.37
Hispanic (25)	27	0.19
African, sub-Saharan:	36	0.26
African	29	0.21
South African	7	0.05
Am. Ind. or Alaska Nat., not spec.	33	0.24
American Indian tribes, specified:	55	0.40
Blackfeet	1	0.01
Cherokee (1)	18	0.13
Cheyenne	2	0.01
Chippewa (1)	1	0.01
Choctaw (2)	2	0.01
Delaware	1	0.01
Lumbee (1)	1	0.01
Navajo	2	0.01
Seminole	1	0.01
Sioux	4	0.03
All other tribes (10)	22	0.16
American Indian tribes, not spec.	3	0.02
Arab:	7	0.05
Egyptian	7	0.05
Armenian	41	0.30
Asian:	386	2.78
Chinese, ex. Taiwanese (56)	80	0.58
Filipino (25)	43	0.31
Indian (93)	101	0.73
Japanese (18)	41	0.30
Korean (36)	46	0.33
Laotian (6)	7	0.05
Pakistani (10)	10	0.07
Taiwanese (7)	7	0.05
Vietnamese (24)	28	0.20
Other Asian, not specified (14)	23	0.17
Austrian	81	0.59
British	137	0.99
Croatian	45	0.33
Czech	45	0.33
Czechoslovakian	15	0.11
Danish	81	0.59
Dutch	124	0.90
Eastern European	54	0.39
English	2,062	14.94
Estonian	17	0.12
European	188	1.36
Finnish	51	0.37
French, except Basque	393	2.85
French Canadian	79	0.57
German	2,684	19.44
Greek	119	0.86
Hawaii Native/Pacific Islander:	1	0.01
Other Pac. Isl., not spec. (1)	1	0.01
Hispanic or Latino:	274	1.98
Central American:	14	0.10
Costa Rican	1	0.01
Guatemalan	1	0.01
Honduran	1	0.01
Nicaraguan	2	0.01
Panamanian	6	0.04
Salvadoran	3	0.02
Cuban	21	0.15
Dominican Republic	17	0.12
Mexican	30	0.22
Puerto Rican	126	0.91
South American:	18	0.13
Argentinean	2	0.01
Chilean	6	0.04
Colombian	4	0.03
Paraguayan	1	0.01
Peruvian	3	0.02
Venezuelan	1	0.01
Other South American	1	0.01
Other Hispanic or Latino	48	0.35
Hungarian	93	0.67
Irish	3,419	24.77
Italian	1,932	14.00
Latvian	19	0.14
Lithuanian	33	0.24
Northern European	6	0.04
Norwegian	146	1.06
Pennsylvania German	45	0.33
Polish	964	6.98
Portuguese	68	0.49
Romanian	50	0.36
Russian	435	3.15
Scandinavian	9	0.07
Scotch-Irish	385	2.79
Scottish	374	2.71
Serbian	7	0.05
Slavic	27	0.20
Slovak	48	0.35
Swedish	230	1.67
Swiss	87	0.63
Turkish	29	0.21
Ukrainian	75	0.54
United States or American	662	4.80
Welsh	189	1.37
West Indian, excl. Hispanic:	15	0.11
Jamaican	15	0.11
White:	12,462	89.91
Not Hispanic (12,122)	12,278	88.59
Hispanic (169)	184	1.33
Yugoslavian	17	0.12

Morganville

Place Type: Census Designated Place
County: Monmouth
Population: 11,255

Ancestry/Race	Number	%
African American/Black:	216	1.92
Not Hispanic (183)	201	1.79
Hispanic (10)	15	0.13
African, sub-Saharan:	15	0.13
African	15	0.13
Am. Ind. or Alaska Nat., not spec.	5	0.04
American Indian tribes, specified:	3	0.03
All other tribes	3	0.03
Arab:	124	1.11
Egyptian	54	0.48
Iraqi	10	0.09
Lebanese	8	0.07
Syrian	52	0.47
Armenian	38	0.34
Asian:	1,151	10.23
Bangladeshi (10)	11	0.10
Chinese, ex. Taiwanese (537)	565	5.02
Filipino (92)	95	0.84
Indian (299)	301	2.67
Indonesian (1)	3	0.03
Japanese (3)	6	0.05
Korean (83)	89	0.79
Pakistani (11)	13	0.12
Taiwanese (24)	30	0.27
Thai (6)	7	0.06
Vietnamese (13)	19	0.17
Other Asian, not specified (5)	12	0.11
Austrian	299	2.69
Brazilian	22	0.20
British	28	0.25
Canadian	22	0.20
Czechoslovakian	28	0.25
Danish	7	0.06
Dutch	156	1.40
Eastern European	172	1.54
English	297	2.67
European	127	1.14
Finnish	15	0.13
French, except Basque	32	0.29
French Canadian	28	0.25
German	660	5.93
Greek	126	1.13

Notes: 1. Figures in the "Number" column do not add up to the total population due to: a) Ancestry/Race overlap — e.g. persons can report being both White and Irish, b) persons of Hispanic origin can report being any race, c) persons reporting two ancestries are counted in both categories. 2. Numbers in parentheses indicate the number of persons reporting this ancestry/race alone, not in combination with any other ancestry/race. 3. Refer to the Explanation of Data in the front of the book for more detailed information.

Ancestry/Race	Number	%
Hawaii Native/Pacific Islander:	15	0.13
Micronesian: (1)	1	0.01
Guamanian/Chamorro (1)	1	0.01
Polynesian: (4)	4	0.04
Native Hawaiian (4)	4	0.04
Other Pac. Isl., not spec.	10	0.09
Hispanic or Latino:	331	2.94
Central American:	11	0.10
Costa Rican	1	0.01
Guatemalan	5	0.04
Honduran	2	0.02
Nicaraguan	1	0.01
Salvadoran	2	0.02
Cuban	35	0.31
Dominican Republic	14	0.12
Mexican	18	0.16
Puerto Rican	122	1.08
South American:	49	0.44
Argentinean	6	0.05
Chilean	2	0.02
Colombian	27	0.24
Ecuadorian	2	0.02
Peruvian	3	0.03
Uruguayan	2	0.02
Venezuelan	4	0.04
Other South American	3	0.03
Other Hispanic or Latino	82	0.73
Hungarian	122	1.10
Irish	1,247	11.20
Israeli	10	0.09
Italian	1,747	15.69
Lithuanian	22	0.20
Northern European	8	0.07
Norwegian	69	0.62
Polish	1,334	11.98
Portuguese	28	0.25
Romanian	111	1.00
Russian	1,440	12.93
Scotch-Irish	68	0.61
Scottish	29	0.26
Slovak	33	0.30
Slovene	9	0.08
Swedish	31	0.28
Swiss	7	0.06
Turkish	9	0.08
Ukrainian	127	1.14
United States or American	850	7.63
Welsh	10	0.09
West Indian, excl. Hispanic:	29	0.26
Jamaican	5	0.04
West Indian	24	0.22
White:	9,885	87.83
Not Hispanic (9,565)	9,616	85.44
Hispanic (257)	269	2.39

Morris

Place Type: Township
County: Morris
Population: 21,796

Ancestry/Race	Number	%
African American/Black:	1,266	5.81
Not Hispanic (1,154)	1,223	5.61
Hispanic (35)	43	0.20
African, sub-Saharan:	63	0.29
African	51	0.23
Ghanian	5	0.02
South African	7	0.03
Alaska Native tribes, specified:	1	0.00
Aleut (1)	1	0.00
Alaska Native tribes, not specified	1	0.00
Am. Ind. or Alaska Nat., not spec.	24	0.11
Alsatian	21	0.10
American Indian tribes, specified:	40	0.18
Blackfeet	3	0.01
Cherokee (5)	13	0.06
Chippewa (1)	1	0.00
Choctaw	1	0.00
Cree	1	0.00
Crow	2	0.01
Delaware	2	0.01
Houma (2)	2	0.01
Iroquois (1)	4	0.02
Latin American Indians	1	0.00
Pueblo (1)	1	0.00
Seminole	1	0.00
Sioux	1	0.00
All other tribes (3)	7	0.03
American Indian tribes, not spec.	7	0.03
Arab:	137	0.63
Arab/Arabic	15	0.07
Egyptian	43	0.20
Lebanese	41	0.19
Syrian	30	0.14
Other Arab	8	0.04
Armenian	20	0.09
Asian:	949	4.35
Bangladeshi (1)	1	0.00
Chinese, ex. Taiwanese (310)	340	1.56
Filipino (70)	93	0.43
Indian (255)	269	1.23
Japanese (61)	71	0.33
Korean (69)	75	0.34
Malaysian (1)	1	0.00
Pakistani (7)	7	0.03
Sri Lankan (2)	2	0.01
Taiwanese (29)	31	0.14
Thai (1)	1	0.00
Vietnamese (22)	23	0.11
Other Asian, specified	1	0.00
Other Asian, not specified (13)	34	0.16
Australian	54	0.25
Austrian	186	0.85
Basque	9	0.04
Belgian	9	0.04
Brazilian	26	0.12
British	134	0.61
Canadian	152	0.70
Celtic	12	0.06
Croatian	30	0.14
Czech	130	0.60
Czechoslovakian	42	0.19
Danish	74	0.34
Dutch	300	1.38
Eastern European	213	0.98
English	2,279	10.46
Estonian	15	0.07
European	208	0.95
Finnish	25	0.11
French, except Basque	483	2.22
French Canadian	34	0.16
German	3,152	14.46
Greek	166	0.76
Hawaii Native/Pacific Islander:	18	0.08
Micronesian:	3	0.01
Guamanian/Chamorro	3	0.01
Polynesian: (1)	2	0.01
Native Hawaiian (1)	2	0.01
Other Pac. Isl., not spec. (2)	13	0.06
Hispanic or Latino:	830	3.81
Central American:	82	0.38
Costa Rican	2	0.01
Guatemalan	15	0.07
Honduran	23	0.11
Nicaraguan	2	0.01
Panamanian	11	0.05
Salvadoran	28	0.13
Other Central American	1	0.00
Cuban	56	0.26
Dominican Republic	15	0.07
Mexican	62	0.28
Puerto Rican	157	0.72
South American:	231	1.06
Argentinean	23	0.11
Chilean	4	0.02
Colombian	118	0.54
Ecuadorian	33	0.15
Paraguayan	4	0.02
Peruvian	24	0.11
Uruguayan	12	0.06
Venezuelan	10	0.05
Other South American	3	0.01
Other Hispanic or Latino	227	1.04
Hungarian	309	1.42
Icelander	17	0.08
Iranian	182	0.84
Irish	4,677	21.46
Israeli	33	0.15
Italian	3,958	18.16
Latvian	64	0.29
Lithuanian	104	0.48
Maltese	31	0.14
Northern European	43	0.20
Norwegian	183	0.84
Polish	1,154	5.29
Portuguese	29	0.13
Romanian	57	0.26
Russian	823	3.78
Scandinavian	50	0.23
Scotch-Irish	432	1.98
Scottish	504	2.31
Serbian	7	0.03
Slavic	19	0.09
Slovak	88	0.40
Slovene	16	0.07
Swedish	176	0.81
Swiss	85	0.39
Turkish	7	0.03
Ukrainian	201	0.92
United States or American	1,010	4.63
Welsh	178	0.82
West Indian, excl. Hispanic:	207	0.95
Barbadian	13	0.06
Bermudan	6	0.03
Haitian	82	0.38
Jamaican	87	0.40
West Indian	19	0.09
White:	19,483	89.39
Not Hispanic (18,742)	18,887	86.65
Hispanic (575)	596	2.73
Yugoslavian	22	0.10

Morristown

Place Type: Town
County: Morris
Population: 18,544

Ancestry/Race	Number	%
African American/Black:	3,318	17.89
Not Hispanic (3,066)	3,213	17.33
Hispanic (78)	105	0.57
African, sub-Saharan:	255	1.38
African	249	1.34
Other sub-Saharan African	6	0.03
Alaska Native tribes, specified:	1	0.01
Eskimo (1)	1	0.01
Am. Ind. or Alaska Nat., not spec.	64	0.35
Albanian	35	0.19
Alsatian	7	0.04
American Indian tribes, specified:	60	0.32
Blackfeet	1	0.01
Cherokee (4)	19	0.10
Choctaw	5	0.03
Cree	1	0.01
Delaware (3)	5	0.03
Iroquois (1)	3	0.02
Latin American Indians (6)	18	0.10
Menominee	1	0.01
Navajo	2	0.01
All other tribes (3)	5	0.03
American Indian tribes, not spec.	6	0.03
Arab:	78	0.42
Egyptian	43	0.23
Lebanese	15	0.08
Other Arab	20	0.11
Armenian	53	0.29
Asian:	808	4.36
Bangladeshi (3)	3	0.02

Notes: 1. Figures in the "Number" column do not add up to the total population due to: a) Ancestry/Race overlap — e.g. persons can report being both White and Irish, b) persons of Hispanic origin can report being any race, c) persons reporting two ancestries are counted in both categories. 2. Numbers in parentheses indicate the number of persons reporting this ancestry/race alone, not in combination with any other ancestry/race. 3. Refer to the Explanation of Data in the front of the book for more detailed information.

Ancestry/Race	Number	%
Chinese, ex. Taiwanese (187)	207	1.12
Filipino (141)	157	0.85
Indian (226)	263	1.42
Indonesian	1	0.01
Japanese (28)	31	0.17
Korean (52)	60	0.32
Pakistani (5)	6	0.03
Sri Lankan (2)	2	0.01
Taiwanese (12)	19	0.10
Thai (5)	8	0.04
Vietnamese (21)	22	0.12
Other Asian, not specified (9)	29	0.16
Austrian	100	0.54
Belgian	31	0.17
Brazilian	6	0.03
British	152	0.82
Bulgarian	20	0.11
Canadian	69	0.37
Czech	24	0.13
Czechoslovakian	73	0.39
Danish	31	0.17
Dutch	160	0.86
Eastern European	34	0.18
English	1,125	6.07
European	97	0.52
Finnish	10	0.05
French, except Basque	219	1.18
French Canadian	116	0.63
German	1,386	7.47
Greek	109	0.59
Guyanese	30	0.16
Hawaii Native/Pacific Islander:	20	0.11
Micronesian: (3)	3	0.02
Guamanian/Chamorro (3)	3	0.02
Polynesian: (7)	8	0.04
Native Hawaiian (6)	6	0.03
Samoan (1)	1	0.01
Other Polynesian	1	0.01
Other Pac. Isl., not spec. (2)	9	0.05
Hispanic or Latino:	5,034	27.15
Central American:	1,139	6.14
Costa Rican	17	0.09
Guatemalan	259	1.40
Honduran	638	3.44
Nicaraguan	1	0.01
Salvadoran	154	0.83
Other Central American	70	0.38
Cuban	50	0.27
Dominican Republic	42	0.23
Mexican	139	0.75
Puerto Rican	286	1.54
South American:	1,814	9.78
Argentinean	15	0.08
Chilean	15	0.08
Colombian	1,479	7.98
Ecuadorian	165	0.89
Peruvian	72	0.39
Uruguayan	10	0.05
Venezuelan	15	0.08
Other South American	43	0.23
Other Hispanic or Latino	1,564	8.43
Hungarian	122	0.66
Iranian	4	0.02
Irish	2,676	14.43
Israeli	16	0.09
Italian	1,998	10.77
Lithuanian	28	0.15
Luxemburger	7	0.04
Maltese	5	0.03
Northern European	28	0.15
Norwegian	122	0.66
Polish	646	3.48
Portuguese	42	0.23
Romanian	18	0.10
Russian	394	2.12
Scandinavian	12	0.06
Scotch-Irish	141	0.76
Scottish	204	1.10
Serbian	16	0.09
Slavic	14	0.08
Slovak	70	0.38
Swedish	141	0.76
Swiss	29	0.16
Turkish	28	0.15
Ukrainian	107	0.58
United States or American	494	2.66
Welsh	52	0.28
West Indian, excl. Hispanic:	392	2.11
British West Indian	21	0.11
Haitian	71	0.38
Jamaican	283	1.53
Trinidadian and Tobagonian	10	0.05
West Indian	7	0.04
White:	12,937	69.76
Not Hispanic (9,402)	9,573	51.62
Hispanic (3,050)	3,364	18.14
Yugoslavian	7	0.04

Mount Holly

Place Type: Township
County: Burlington
Population: 10,728

Ancestry/Race	Number	%
African American/Black:	2,494	23.25
Not Hispanic (2,231)	2,387	22.25
Hispanic (83)	107	1.00
African, sub-Saharan:	114	1.06
African	114	1.06
Am. Ind. or Alaska Nat., not spec.	29	0.27
American Indian tribes, specified:	53	0.49
Apache (1)	2	0.02
Blackfeet (1)	1	0.01
Cherokee (5)	16	0.15
Chippewa	2	0.02
Cree	1	0.01
Creek (1)	1	0.01
Delaware (10)	10	0.09
Iroquois (1)	2	0.02
Latin American Indians (1)	3	0.03
Navajo	3	0.03
Pueblo	2	0.02
Sioux (1)	3	0.03
Yakama (1)	1	0.01
Yuman (1)	1	0.01
All other tribes (5)	5	0.05
American Indian tribes, not spec.	6	0.06
Arab:	28	0.26
Egyptian	28	0.26
Asian:	225	2.10
Bangladeshi (4)	6	0.06
Chinese, ex. Taiwanese (11)	22	0.21
Filipino (32)	54	0.50
Indian (13)	14	0.13
Japanese (20)	38	0.35
Korean (55)	68	0.63
Thai	4	0.04
Vietnamese (8)	10	0.09
Other Asian, not specified (1)	9	0.08
Austrian	7	0.07
Belgian	13	0.12
British	67	0.62
Canadian	14	0.13
Czech	45	0.42
Czechoslovakian	4	0.04
Danish	7	0.07
Dutch	227	2.11
English	1,296	12.06
European	88	0.82
Finnish	5	0.05
French, except Basque	270	2.51
French Canadian	151	1.41
German	1,806	16.81
Greek	62	0.58
Hawaii Native/Pacific Islander:	14	0.13
Micronesian:	4	0.04
Guamanian/Chamorro	4	0.04
Polynesian: (1)	4	0.04
Native Hawaiian	3	0.03
Samoan (1)	1	0.01
Other Pac. Isl., not spec. (5)	6	0.06
Hispanic or Latino:	942	8.78
Central American:	49	0.46
Guatemalan	1	0.01
Honduran	15	0.14
Nicaraguan	2	0.02
Panamanian	24	0.22
Salvadoran	7	0.07
Cuban	15	0.14
Dominican Republic	24	0.22
Mexican	71	0.66
Puerto Rican	638	5.95
South American:	35	0.33
Bolivian	2	0.02
Chilean	1	0.01
Colombian	19	0.18
Ecuadorian	5	0.05
Peruvian	7	0.07
Venezuelan	1	0.01
Other Hispanic or Latino	110	1.03
Hungarian	128	1.19
Iranian	5	0.05
Irish	1,601	14.90
Italian	1,267	11.79
Lithuanian	34	0.32
Northern European	25	0.23
Norwegian	82	0.76
Pennsylvania German	20	0.19
Polish	562	5.23
Portuguese	54	0.50
Romanian	8	0.07
Russian	35	0.33
Scandinavian	31	0.29
Scotch-Irish	153	1.42
Scottish	115	1.07
Slovak	11	0.10
Swedish	59	0.55
Swiss	24	0.22
Turkish	7	0.07
Ukrainian	51	0.47
United States or American	497	4.63
Welsh	143	1.33
West Indian, excl. Hispanic:	91	0.85
Jamaican	66	0.61
Trinidadian and Tobagonian	20	0.19
West Indian	5	0.05
White:	7,640	71.22
Not Hispanic (7,101)	7,308	68.12
Hispanic (267)	332	3.09

Mount Laurel

Place Type: Township
County: Burlington
Population: 40,221

Ancestry/Race	Number	%
African American/Black:	3,049	7.58
Not Hispanic (2,752)	2,975	7.40
Hispanic (33)	74	0.18
African, sub-Saharan:	70	0.17
African	33	0.08
Cape Verdean	23	0.06
Ethiopian	7	0.02
Zairian	7	0.02
Alaska Native tribes, specified:	4	0.01
Tlingit-Haida	4	0.01
Am. Ind. or Alaska Nat., not spec.	66	0.16
Albanian	25	0.06
American Indian tribes, specified:	112	0.28
Apache (1)	6	0.01
Blackfeet (2)	14	0.03
Cherokee (6)	27	0.07
Chippewa (1)	5	0.01
Choctaw	1	0.00
Comanche	1	0.00
Cree	1	0.00
Delaware	6	0.01
Iroquois (1)	14	0.03

Notes: 1. Figures in the "Number" column do not add up to the total population due to: a) Ancestry/Race overlap — e.g. persons can report being both White and Irish, b) persons of Hispanic origin can report being any race, c) persons reporting two ancestries are counted in both categories. 2. Numbers in parentheses indicate the number of persons reporting this ancestry/race alone, not in combination with any other ancestry/race. 3. Refer to the Explanation of Data in the front of the book for more detailed information.

Ancestry/Race	Number	%
Latin American Indians (6)	7	0.02
Lumbee (1)	4	0.01
Potawatomi	1	0.00
Sioux	4	0.01
All other tribes (9)	21	0.05
American Indian tribes, not spec.	8	0.02
Arab:	261	0.65
Arab/Arabic	56	0.14
Egyptian	61	0.15
Jordanian	21	0.05
Lebanese	47	0.12
Moroccan	32	0.08
Syrian	44	0.11
Armenian	113	0.28
Asian:	1,737	4.32
Bangladeshi (4)	4	0.01
Cambodian (3)	6	0.01
Chinese, ex. Taiwanese (431)	479	1.19
Filipino (204)	251	0.62
Indian (497)	516	1.28
Indonesian	1	0.00
Japanese (51)	99	0.25
Korean (202)	221	0.55
Laotian (1)	1	0.00
Malaysian (1)	1	0.00
Pakistani (17)	20	0.05
Sri Lankan (2)	2	0.00
Taiwanese (27)	37	0.09
Thai (17)	20	0.05
Vietnamese (39)	43	0.11
Other Asian, specified	1	0.00
Other Asian, not specified (14)	35	0.09
Australian	10	0.02
Austrian	233	0.58
Belgian	17	0.04
Brazilian	42	0.10
British	203	0.50
Canadian	127	0.32
Celtic	6	0.01
Croatian	36	0.09
Cypriot	11	0.03
Czech	189	0.47
Czechoslovakian	95	0.24
Danish	63	0.16
Dutch	360	0.90
Eastern European	73	0.18
English	4,810	11.96
Estonian	5	0.01
European	220	0.55
Finnish	131	0.33
French, except Basque	850	2.11
French Canadian	152	0.38
German	7,638	18.99
Greek	252	0.63
Guyanese	22	0.05
Hawaii Native/Pacific Islander:	44	0.11
Micronesian: (8)	10	0.02
Guamanian/Chamorro (8)	10	0.02
Polynesian: (2)	23	0.06
Native Hawaiian (1)	18	0.04
Tongan (1)	5	0.01
Other Pac. Isl., not spec. (2)	11	0.03
Hispanic or Latino:	901	2.24
Central American:	38	0.09
Costa Rican	6	0.01
Guatemalan	6	0.01
Nicaraguan	7	0.02
Panamanian	8	0.02
Salvadoran	7	0.02
Other Central American	4	0.01
Cuban	60	0.15
Dominican Republic	22	0.05
Mexican	110	0.27
Puerto Rican	407	1.01
South American:	105	0.26
Argentinean	16	0.04
Bolivian	4	0.01
Chilean	15	0.04
Colombian	26	0.06
Ecuadorian	10	0.02
Peruvian	22	0.05
Venezuelan	8	0.02
Other South American	4	0.01
Other Hispanic or Latino	159	0.40
Hungarian	501	1.25
Iranian	24	0.06
Irish	8,497	21.13
Israeli	64	0.16
Italian	7,930	19.72
Latvian	23	0.06
Lithuanian	321	0.80
Northern European	10	0.02
Norwegian	394	0.98
Pennsylvania German	91	0.23
Polish	3,083	7.67
Portuguese	72	0.18
Romanian	137	0.34
Russian	1,552	3.86
Scandinavian	46	0.11
Scotch-Irish	530	1.32
Scottish	649	1.61
Serbian	28	0.07
Slavic	45	0.11
Slovak	340	0.85
Slovene	5	0.01
Swedish	416	1.03
Swiss	152	0.38
Turkish	55	0.14
Ukrainian	462	1.15
United States or American	1,134	2.82
Welsh	288	0.72
West Indian, excl. Hispanic:	157	0.39
Barbadian	9	0.02
Bermudan	10	0.02
Haitian	5	0.01
Jamaican	71	0.18
Trinidadian and Tobagonian	40	0.10
West Indian	22	0.05
White:	35,493	88.24
Not Hispanic (34,482)	34,858	86.67
Hispanic (552)	635	1.58
Yugoslavian	10	0.02

Mount Olive

Place Type: Township
County: Morris
Population: 24,193

Ancestry/Race	Number	%
African American/Black:	1,011	4.18
Not Hispanic (895)	974	4.03
Hispanic (23)	37	0.15
African, sub-Saharan:	152	0.63
African	63	0.26
Ethiopian	11	0.05
Nigerian	78	0.32
Am. Ind. or Alaska Nat., not spec.	37	0.15
American Indian tribes, specified:	69	0.29
Apache	1	0.00
Blackfeet	3	0.01
Cherokee (9)	28	0.12
Chickasaw (1)	1	0.00
Chippewa	1	0.00
Delaware	2	0.01
Iroquois (3)	4	0.02
Latin American Indians (3)	4	0.02
Potawatomi	2	0.01
Pueblo (1)	1	0.00
Seminole	1	0.00
Sioux (11)	13	0.05
All other tribes (1)	8	0.03
American Indian tribes, not spec.	10	0.04
Arab:	144	0.60
Arab/Arabic	13	0.05
Egyptian	55	0.23
Lebanese	59	0.24
Syrian	17	0.07
Armenian	12	0.05
Asian:	1,601	6.62
Bangladeshi (12)	12	0.05
Cambodian (5)	5	0.02
Chinese, ex. Taiwanese (253)	279	1.15
Filipino (152)	168	0.69
Indian (732)	772	3.19
Indonesian (14)	17	0.07
Japanese (16)	30	0.12
Korean (127)	129	0.53
Malaysian	3	0.01
Pakistani (54)	76	0.31
Sri Lankan (5)	8	0.03
Taiwanese (7)	7	0.03
Thai (7)	9	0.04
Vietnamese (33)	35	0.14
Other Asian, specified (1)	1	0.00
Other Asian, not specified (16)	50	0.21
Australian	7	0.03
Austrian	153	0.63
Belgian	14	0.06
Brazilian	35	0.14
British	42	0.17
Canadian	35	0.14
Celtic	51	0.21
Croatian	26	0.11
Czech	158	0.65
Czechoslovakian	137	0.57
Danish	83	0.34
Dutch	392	1.62
Eastern European	16	0.07
English	2,092	8.65
European	80	0.33
French, except Basque	637	2.63
French Canadian	218	0.90
German	4,744	19.61
Greek	105	0.43
Guyanese	78	0.32
Hawaii Native/Pacific Islander:	13	0.05
Polynesian: (1)	3	0.01
Native Hawaiian	2	0.01
Samoan (1)	1	0.00
Other Pac. Isl., not spec. (1)	10	0.04
Hispanic or Latino:	1,445	5.97
Central American:	110	0.45
Costa Rican	31	0.13
Guatemalan	20	0.08
Honduran	11	0.05
Nicaraguan	4	0.02
Panamanian	1	0.00
Salvadoran	32	0.13
Other Central American	11	0.05
Cuban	86	0.36
Dominican Republic	38	0.16
Mexican	102	0.42
Puerto Rican	466	1.93
South American:	343	1.42
Argentinean	20	0.08
Bolivian	1	0.00
Chilean	41	0.17
Colombian	131	0.54
Ecuadorian	54	0.22
Paraguayan	1	0.00
Peruvian	39	0.16
Uruguayan	28	0.12
Venezuelan	10	0.04
Other South American	18	0.07
Other Hispanic or Latino	300	1.24
Hungarian	460	1.90
Iranian	20	0.08
Irish	5,485	22.67
Israeli	17	0.07
Italian	5,481	22.66
Lithuanian	196	0.81
Macedonian	28	0.12
Norwegian	227	0.94
Polish	2,117	8.75
Portuguese	121	0.50
Romanian	20	0.08
Russian	573	2.37
Scandinavian	18	0.07
Scotch-Irish	333	1.38

Notes: 1. Figures in the "Number" column do not add up to the total population due to: a) Ancestry/Race overlap — e.g. persons can report being both White and Irish, b) persons of Hispanic origin can report being any race, c) persons reporting two ancestries are counted in both categories. 2. Numbers in parentheses indicate the number of persons reporting this ancestry/race alone, not in combination with any other ancestry/race. 3. Refer to the Explanation of Data in the front of the book for more detailed information.

Ancestry/Race	Number	%
Scottish	402	1.66
Serbian	11	0.05
Slavic	27	0.11
Slovak	111	0.46
Slovene	24	0.10
Swedish	282	1.17
Swiss	47	0.19
Turkish	88	0.36
Ukrainian	303	1.25
United States or American	763	3.15
Welsh	242	1.00
West Indian, excl. Hispanic:	76	0.31
Barbadian	8	0.03
British West Indian	6	0.02
Jamaican	35	0.14
Trinidadian and Tobagonian	6	0.02
West Indian	21	0.09
White:	21,344	88.22
Not Hispanic (19,989)	20,261	83.75
Hispanic (985)	1,083	4.48
Yugoslavian	138	0.57

Neptune

Place Type: Township
County: Monmouth
Population: 27,690

Ancestry/Race	Number	%
African American/Black:	11,053	39.92
Not Hispanic (10,310)	10,715	38.70
Hispanic (257)	338	1.22
African, sub-Saharan:	307	1.11
African	241	0.87
Ethiopian	4	0.01
Ghanian	17	0.06
Nigerian	18	0.07
Other sub-Saharan African	27	0.10
Am. Ind. or Alaska Nat., not spec.	115	0.42
Alsatian	7	0.03
American Indian tribes, specified:	141	0.51
Blackfeet (1)	15	0.05
Cherokee (8)	69	0.25
Cheyenne (1)	2	0.01
Chickasaw	1	0.00
Choctaw (3)	3	0.01
Comanche	1	0.00
Creek	2	0.01
Delaware (5)	17	0.06
Iroquois	5	0.02
Latin American Indians (4)	8	0.03
Navajo	4	0.01
Seminole (1)	2	0.01
Sioux (1)	7	0.03
All other tribes (1)	5	0.02
American Indian tribes, not spec.	16	0.06
Arab:	85	0.31
Egyptian	51	0.18
Syrian	34	0.12
Armenian	69	0.25
Asian:	433	1.56
Chinese, ex. Taiwanese (49)	68	0.25
Filipino (133)	161	0.58
Indian (50)	53	0.19
Japanese (20)	38	0.14
Korean (45)	69	0.25
Pakistani (6)	6	0.02
Sri Lankan (2)	2	0.01
Taiwanese (1)	2	0.01
Vietnamese (11)	11	0.04
Other Asian, specified	11	0.04
Other Asian, not specified (6)	12	0.04
Assyrian/Chaldean/Syriac	6	0.02
Austrian	146	0.53
Belgian	4	0.01
British	116	0.42
Canadian	18	0.07
Czech	65	0.23
Czechoslovakian	86	0.31
Danish	91	0.33
Dutch	344	1.24
English	2,068	7.47
Estonian	5	0.02
European	72	0.26
Finnish	13	0.05
French, except Basque	490	1.77
French Canadian	88	0.32
German	3,230	11.66
Greek	130	0.47
Guyanese	26	0.09
Hawaii Native/Pacific Islander:	46	0.17
Micronesian: (4)	10	0.04
Guamanian/Chamorro (4)	10	0.04
Polynesian: (8)	16	0.06
Native Hawaiian (2)	9	0.03
Samoan (6)	7	0.03
Other Pac. Isl., specified	10	0.04
Other Pac. Isl., not spec.	10	0.04
Hispanic or Latino:	1,537	5.55
Central American:	71	0.26
Costa Rican	10	0.04
Guatemalan	3	0.01
Honduran	2	0.01
Nicaraguan	12	0.04
Panamanian	22	0.08
Salvadoran	10	0.04
Other Central American	12	0.04
Cuban	46	0.17
Dominican Republic	25	0.09
Mexican	296	1.07
Puerto Rican	791	2.86
South American:	76	0.27
Argentinean	5	0.02
Bolivian	1	0.00
Chilean	6	0.02
Colombian	32	0.12
Ecuadorian	13	0.05
Paraguayan	1	0.00
Peruvian	9	0.03
Uruguayan	2	0.01
Venezuelan	3	0.01
Other South American	4	0.01
Other Hispanic or Latino	232	0.84
Hungarian	167	0.60
Irish	4,021	14.52
Italian	3,405	12.30
Latvian	13	0.05
Lithuanian	65	0.23
Norwegian	239	0.86
Pennsylvania German	6	0.02
Polish	879	3.17
Portuguese	73	0.26
Romanian	5	0.02
Russian	194	0.70
Scotch-Irish	218	0.79
Scottish	570	2.06
Slavic	19	0.07
Slovak	36	0.13
Swedish	235	0.85
Swiss	63	0.23
Turkish	16	0.06
Ukrainian	64	0.23
United States or American	1,061	3.83
Welsh	140	0.51
West Indian, excl. Hispanic:	1,043	3.77
Bahamian	12	0.04
Barbadian	39	0.14
Bermudan	10	0.04
British West Indian	20	0.07
Haitian	409	1.48
Jamaican	497	1.79
Trinidadian and Tobagonian	32	0.12
West Indian	24	0.09
White:	15,876	57.33
Not Hispanic (14,859)	15,164	54.76
Hispanic (626)	712	2.57
Yugoslavian	28	0.10

New Brunswick

Place Type: City
County: Middlesex
Population: 48,573

Ancestry/Race	Number	%
African American/Black:	11,895	24.49
Not Hispanic (10,043)	10,408	21.43
Hispanic (1,142)	1,487	3.06
African, sub-Saharan:	1,043	2.15
African	793	1.63
Ethiopian	7	0.01
Ghanian	14	0.03
Kenyan	12	0.02
Nigerian	169	0.35
Somalian	7	0.01
South African	16	0.03
Ugandan	11	0.02
Other sub-Saharan African	14	0.03
Alaska Native tribes, specified:	4	0.01
Alaska Athabascan (1)	1	0.00
Aleut (1)	1	0.00
Eskimo (1)	2	0.00
Am. Ind. or Alaska Nat., not spec.	286	0.59
Albanian	3	0.01
American Indian tribes, specified:	261	0.54
Blackfeet	4	0.01
Cherokee (12)	58	0.12
Chippewa (1)	2	0.00
Choctaw	1	0.00
Cree	1	0.00
Creek	3	0.01
Delaware (3)	10	0.02
Iroquois (1)	3	0.01
Latin American Indians (48)	145	0.30
Navajo (2)	3	0.01
Ottawa	1	0.00
Pueblo (3)	15	0.03
Seminole	1	0.00
Shoshone	1	0.00
Sioux (1)	2	0.00
Yaqui (1)	1	0.00
All other tribes (3)	10	0.02
American Indian tribes, not spec.	30	0.06
Arab:	572	1.18
Arab/Arabic	42	0.09
Egyptian	154	0.32
Lebanese	223	0.46
Moroccan	38	0.08
Syrian	104	0.21
Other Arab	11	0.02
Armenian	48	0.10
Asian:	2,902	5.97
Bangladeshi (19)	22	0.05
Cambodian	2	0.00
Chinese, ex. Taiwanese (534)	585	1.20
Filipino (314)	364	0.75
Indian (1,014)	1,119	2.30
Indonesian (8)	10	0.02
Japanese (57)	75	0.15
Korean (418)	446	0.92
Laotian (3)	5	0.01
Malaysian (1)	2	0.00
Pakistani (53)	67	0.14
Sri Lankan (12)	13	0.03
Taiwanese (22)	25	0.05
Thai (18)	21	0.04
Vietnamese (43)	55	0.11
Other Asian, specified (6)	8	0.02
Other Asian, not specified (28)	83	0.17
Australian	7	0.01
Austrian	154	0.32
Basque	9	0.02
Belgian	34	0.07
Brazilian	33	0.07
British	89	0.18
Bulgarian	37	0.08
Canadian	52	0.11
Croatian	9	0.02

Notes: 1. Figures in the "Number" column do not add up to the total population due to: a) Ancestry/Race overlap — e.g. persons can report being both White and Irish, b) persons of Hispanic origin can report being any race, c) persons reporting two ancestries are counted in both categories. 2. Numbers in parentheses indicate the number of persons reporting this ancestry/race alone, not in combination with any other ancestry/race. 3. Refer to the Explanation of Data in the front of the book for more detailed information.

Ancestry/Race	Number	%
Czech	48	0.10
Czechoslovakian	82	0.17
Danish	69	0.14
Dutch	195	0.40
Eastern European	147	0.30
English	943	1.94
European	118	0.24
Finnish	15	0.03
French, except Basque	273	0.56
French Canadian	82	0.17
German	2,562	5.27
Greek	242	0.50
Guyanese	201	0.41
Hawaii Native/Pacific Islander:	113	0.23
Micronesian: (17)	18	0.04
Guamanian/Chamorro (17)	18	0.04
Polynesian: (11)	28	0.06
Native Hawaiian (9)	19	0.04
Samoan (2)	8	0.02
Other Polynesian	1	0.00
Other Pac. Isl., specified	1	0.00
Other Pac. Isl., not spec. (11)	66	0.14
Hispanic or Latino:	18,947	39.01
Central American:	2,198	4.53
Costa Rican	40	0.08
Guatemalan	163	0.34
Honduran	1,451	2.99
Nicaraguan	258	0.53
Panamanian	39	0.08
Salvadoran	100	0.21
Other Central American	147	0.30
Cuban	254	0.52
Dominican Republic	2,855	5.88
Mexican	7,364	15.16
Puerto Rican	3,178	6.54
South American:	709	1.46
Argentinean	36	0.07
Bolivian	8	0.02
Chilean	41	0.08
Colombian	210	0.43
Ecuadorian	192	0.40
Peruvian	146	0.30
Uruguayan	4	0.01
Venezuelan	30	0.06
Other South American	42	0.09
Other Hispanic or Latino	2,389	4.92
Hungarian	959	1.97
Icelander	8	0.02
Iranian	28	0.06
Irish	3,383	6.96
Israeli	86	0.18
Italian	3,544	7.30
Latvian	34	0.07
Lithuanian	117	0.24
Macedonian	32	0.07
Norwegian	138	0.28
Pennsylvania German	16	0.03
Polish	1,718	3.54
Portuguese	150	0.31
Romanian	46	0.09
Russian	827	1.70
Scandinavian	6	0.01
Scotch-Irish	160	0.33
Scottish	186	0.38
Slavic	9	0.02
Slovak	133	0.27
Swedish	199	0.41
Swiss	16	0.03
Turkish	78	0.16
Ukrainian	246	0.51
United States or American	651	1.34
Welsh	92	0.19
West Indian, excl. Hispanic:	668	1.38
Barbadian	14	0.03
British West Indian	24	0.05
Haitian	83	0.17
Jamaican	404	0.83
Trinidadian and Tobagonian	70	0.14
West Indian	73	0.15
White:	25,113	51.70
Not Hispanic (15,964)	16,467	33.90
Hispanic (7,737)	8,646	17.80
Yugoslavian	56	0.12

New Milford

Place Type: Borough
County: Bergen
Population: 16,400

Ancestry/Race	Number	%
Afghan	36	0.22
African American/Black:	486	2.96
Not Hispanic (396)	435	2.65
Hispanic (33)	51	0.31
African, sub-Saharan:	32	0.20
African	24	0.15
Nigerian	8	0.05
Am. Ind. or Alaska Nat., not spec.	20	0.12
Albanian	7	0.04
Alsatian	6	0.04
American Indian tribes, specified:	24	0.15
Cherokee (1)	8	0.05
Chippewa (1)	1	0.01
Delaware (2)	3	0.02
Latin American Indians (7)	11	0.07
All other tribes	1	0.01
American Indian tribes, not spec.	3	0.02
Arab:	362	2.21
Arab/Arabic	26	0.16
Egyptian	46	0.28
Jordanian	42	0.26
Lebanese	58	0.35
Syrian	167	1.02
Other Arab	23	0.14
Armenian	367	2.24
Asian:	2,607	15.90
Chinese, ex. Taiwanese (311)	360	2.20
Filipino (1,046)	1,119	6.82
Indian (631)	651	3.97
Indonesian (6)	7	0.04
Japanese (65)	79	0.48
Korean (223)	230	1.40
Malaysian (1)	1	0.01
Pakistani (29)	29	0.18
Sri Lankan (4)	4	0.02
Taiwanese (17)	28	0.17
Thai (19)	24	0.15
Vietnamese (11)	15	0.09
Other Asian, specified (5)	5	0.03
Other Asian, not specified (16)	56	0.34
Assyrian/Chaldean/Syriac	88	0.54
Austrian	126	0.77
Belgian	18	0.11
Brazilian	6	0.04
British	34	0.21
Bulgarian	25	0.15
Canadian	11	0.07
Carpatho Rusyn	6	0.04
Celtic	15	0.09
Croatian	13	0.08
Czech	28	0.17
Czechoslovakian	72	0.44
Danish	45	0.27
Dutch	207	1.26
Eastern European	30	0.18
English	592	3.61
Estonian	21	0.13
European	45	0.27
Finnish	29	0.18
French, except Basque	288	1.76
French Canadian	23	0.14
German	2,325	14.18
German Russian	8	0.05
Greek	373	2.27
Guyanese	22	0.13
Hawaii Native/Pacific Islander:	25	0.15
Melanesian: (1)	1	0.01
Fijian (1)	1	0.01
Micronesian:	1	0.01
Other Micronesian	1	0.01
Polynesian: (1)	1	0.01
Samoan (1)	1	0.01
Other Pac. Isl., not spec. (2)	22	0.13
Hispanic or Latino:	1,326	8.09
Central American:	45	0.27
Costa Rican	12	0.07
Guatemalan	6	0.04
Honduran	10	0.06
Nicaraguan	3	0.02
Panamanian	2	0.01
Salvadoran	11	0.07
Other Central American	1	0.01
Cuban	190	1.16
Dominican Republic	166	1.01
Mexican	47	0.29
Puerto Rican	328	2.00
South American:	297	1.81
Argentinean	11	0.07
Bolivian	3	0.02
Chilean	8	0.05
Colombian	173	1.05
Ecuadorian	51	0.31
Paraguayan	2	0.01
Peruvian	19	0.12
Uruguayan	23	0.14
Venezuelan	2	0.01
Other South American	5	0.03
Other Hispanic or Latino	253	1.54
Hungarian	154	0.94
Irish	3,219	19.63
Israeli	17	0.10
Italian	3,847	23.46
Latvian	6	0.04
Lithuanian	20	0.12
Norwegian	140	0.85
Polish	777	4.74
Portuguese	25	0.15
Romanian	43	0.26
Russian	440	2.68
Scandinavian	5	0.03
Scotch-Irish	118	0.72
Scottish	146	0.89
Slavic	13	0.08
Slovak	30	0.18
Soviet Union	21	0.13
Swedish	78	0.48
Swiss	68	0.41
Turkish	60	0.37
Ukrainian	67	0.41
United States or American	413	2.52
Welsh	43	0.26
West Indian, excl. Hispanic:	68	0.41
British West Indian	8	0.05
Jamaican	34	0.21
Trinidadian and Tobagonian	8	0.05
U.S. Virgin Islander	9	0.05
West Indian	9	0.05
White:	13,149	80.18
Not Hispanic (12,008)	12,188	74.32
Hispanic (880)	961	5.86
Yugoslavian	47	0.29

New Providence

Place Type: Borough
County: Union
Population: 11,907

Ancestry/Race	Number	%
African American/Black:	120	1.01
Not Hispanic (104)	116	0.97
Hispanic (1)	4	0.03
Am. Ind. or Alaska Nat., not spec.	9	0.08
Albanian	9	0.08
American Indian tribes, specified:	15	0.13
Blackfeet	1	0.01
Chickasaw (3)	3	0.03
Latin American Indians (1)	2	0.02
Sioux	1	0.01

Notes: 1. Figures in the "Number" column do not add up to the total population due to: a) Ancestry/Race overlap — e.g. persons can report being both White and Irish, b) persons of Hispanic origin can report being any race, c) persons reporting two ancestries are counted in both categories. 2. Numbers in parentheses indicate the number of persons reporting this ancestry/race alone, not in combination with any other ancestry/race. 3. Refer to the Explanation of Data in the front of the book for more detailed information.

All other tribes	8	0.07
American Indian tribes, not spec.	3	0.03
Arab:	75	0.63
Egyptian	42	0.35
Lebanese	15	0.13
Syrian	18	0.15
Armenian	8	0.07
Asian:	983	8.26
Chinese, ex. Taiwanese (347)	372	3.12
Filipino (63)	84	0.71
Indian (309)	317	2.66
Japanese (64)	72	0.60
Korean (66)	69	0.58
Sri Lankan (5)	5	0.04
Taiwanese (23)	26	0.22
Thai (3)	6	0.05
Vietnamese (7)	7	0.06
Other Asian, not specified (14)	25	0.21
Australian	8	0.07
Austrian	110	0.92
Belgian	8	0.07
Brazilian	59	0.50
British	168	1.41
Canadian	50	0.42
Croatian	6	0.05
Czech	120	1.01
Czechoslovakian	30	0.25
Danish	54	0.45
Dutch	184	1.55
Eastern European	54	0.45
English	1,031	8.66
Estonian	9	0.08
European	111	0.93
French, except Basque	205	1.72
French Canadian	94	0.79
German	1,896	15.92
Greek	159	1.34
Hawaii Native/Pacific Islander:	10	0.08
Micronesian: (1)	1	0.01
Guamanian/Chamorro (1)	1	0.01
Polynesian: (1)	1	0.01
Native Hawaiian (1)	1	0.01
Other Pac. Isl., not spec. (1)	8	0.07
Hispanic or Latino:	417	3.50
Central American:	81	0.68
Costa Rican	54	0.45
Guatemalan	3	0.03
Honduran	11	0.09
Panamanian	2	0.02
Salvadoran	3	0.03
Other Central American	8	0.07
Cuban	44	0.37
Mexican	37	0.31
Puerto Rican	57	0.48
South American:	104	0.87
Argentinean	12	0.10
Chilean	9	0.08
Colombian	49	0.41
Ecuadorian	14	0.12
Peruvian	12	0.10
Uruguayan	2	0.02
Venezuelan	5	0.04
Other South American	1	0.01
Other Hispanic or Latino	94	0.79
Hungarian	294	2.47
Irish	2,611	21.93
Italian	3,085	25.91
Latvian	9	0.08
Lithuanian	152	1.28
New Zealander	30	0.25
Norwegian	112	0.94
Pennsylvania German	16	0.13
Polish	757	6.36
Portuguese	91	0.76
Romanian	47	0.39
Russian	328	2.75
Scandinavian	32	0.27
Scotch-Irish	112	0.94
Scottish	248	2.08
Slavic	13	0.11
Slovak	104	0.87
Swedish	137	1.15
Swiss	70	0.59
Turkish	48	0.40
Ukrainian	209	1.76
United States or American	386	3.24
Welsh	82	0.69
West Indian, excl. Hispanic:	46	0.39
Bahamian	8	0.07
Haitian	11	0.09
Jamaican	12	0.10
West Indian	15	0.13
White:	10,788	90.60
Not Hispanic (10,359)	10,448	87.75
Hispanic (330)	340	2.86
Yugoslavian	7	0.06

Newark

Place Type: City
County: Essex
Population: 273,546

Ancestry/Race	Number	%
Afghan	162	0.06
African American/Black:	150,384	54.98
Not Hispanic (142,083)	144,900	52.97
Hispanic (4,167)	5,484	2.00
African, sub-Saharan:	7,114	2.60
African	3,920	1.43
Cape Verdean	96	0.04
Ethiopian	9	0.00
Ghanian	868	0.32
Kenyan	85	0.03
Liberian	427	0.16
Nigerian	1,325	0.48
Senegalese	15	0.01
South African	24	0.01
Zairian	8	0.00
Other sub-Saharan African	337	0.12
Alaska Native tribes, specified:	6	0.00
Alaska Athabascan	1	0.00
Aleut (1)	1	0.00
Tlingit-Haida (2)	4	0.00
Am. Ind. or Alaska Nat., not spec.	1,285	0.47
Albanian	85	0.03
American Indian tribes, specified:	774	0.28
Apache (2)	13	0.00
Blackfeet (21)	96	0.04
Cherokee (52)	237	0.09
Cheyenne	1	0.00
Chickasaw	1	0.00
Chippewa (2)	4	0.00
Choctaw	2	0.00
Comanche (1)	1	0.00
Creek (1)	2	0.00
Crow	1	0.00
Delaware (5)	12	0.00
Iroquois (7)	48	0.02
Latin American Indians (109)	217	0.08
Navajo (5)	11	0.00
Pueblo (9)	17	0.01
Seminole (10)	29	0.01
Shoshone	1	0.00
Sioux (3)	14	0.01
Tohono O'Odham (1)	1	0.00
All other tribes (23)	65	0.02
American Indian tribes, not spec.	180	0.07
Arab:	426	0.16
Arab/Arabic	162	0.06
Egyptian	82	0.03
Lebanese	60	0.02
Moroccan	22	0.01
Palestinian	57	0.02
Syrian	9	0.00
Other Arab	34	0.01
Armenian	128	0.05
Asian:	4,378	1.60
Bangladeshi (58)	67	0.02
Cambodian (13)	15	0.01
Chinese, ex. Taiwanese (478)	568	0.21
Filipino (586)	693	0.25
Hmong	1	0.00
Indian (1,428)	1,746	0.64
Indonesian (2)	2	0.00
Japanese (99)	155	0.06
Korean (133)	162	0.06
Laotian (5)	5	0.00
Malaysian (3)	6	0.00
Pakistani (170)	242	0.09
Sri Lankan (26)	40	0.01
Taiwanese (11)	15	0.01
Thai (18)	22	0.01
Vietnamese (127)	154	0.06
Other Asian, specified	35	0.01
Other Asian, not specified (80)	450	0.16
Austrian	66	0.02
Basque	27	0.01
Belgian	8	0.00
Brazilian	5,805	2.12
British	143	0.05
Bulgarian	13	0.00
Canadian	102	0.04
Celtic	16	0.01
Czech	23	0.01
Czechoslovakian	39	0.01
Dutch	265	0.10
English	696	0.25
European	365	0.13
Finnish	8	0.00
French, except Basque	396	0.14
French Canadian	75	0.03
German	1,671	0.61
German Russian	13	0.00
Greek	192	0.07
Guyanese	1,313	0.48
Hawaii Native/Pacific Islander:	634	0.23
Micronesian: (32)	54	0.02
Guamanian/Chamorro (32)	54	0.02
Polynesian: (57)	126	0.05
Native Hawaiian (24)	80	0.03
Samoan (33)	46	0.02
Other Pac. Isl., specified	34	0.01
Other Pac. Isl., not spec. (46)	420	0.15
Hispanic or Latino:	80,622	29.47
Central American:	3,785	1.38
Costa Rican	282	0.10
Guatemalan	776	0.28
Honduran	657	0.24
Nicaraguan	174	0.06
Panamanian	152	0.06
Salvadoran	1,565	0.57
Other Central American	179	0.07
Cuban	2,962	1.08
Dominican Republic	6,266	2.29
Mexican	2,295	0.84
Puerto Rican	39,650	14.49
South American:	11,134	4.07
Argentinean	213	0.08
Bolivian	29	0.01
Chilean	74	0.03
Colombian	1,071	0.39
Ecuadorian	7,611	2.78
Paraguayan	6	0.00
Peruvian	1,405	0.51
Uruguayan	239	0.09
Venezuelan	246	0.09
Other South American	240	0.09
Other Hispanic or Latino	14,530	5.31
Hungarian	223	0.08
Iranian	34	0.01
Irish	2,478	0.91
Israeli	10	0.00
Italian	7,223	2.64
Lithuanian	110	0.04
Luxemburger	7	0.00
Macedonian	9	0.00
New Zealander	21	0.01
Norwegian	77	0.03
Polish	2,134	0.78

Notes: 1. Figures in the "Number" column do not add up to the total population due to: a) Ancestry/Race overlap — e.g. persons can report being both White and Irish, b) persons of Hispanic origin can report being any race, c) persons reporting two ancestries are counted in both categories. 2. Numbers in parentheses indicate the number of persons reporting this ancestry/race alone, not in combination with any other ancestry/race. 3. Refer to the Explanation of Data in the front of the book for more detailed information.

Portuguese	15,801	5.78
Romanian	19	0.01
Russian	440	0.16
Scandinavian	14	0.01
Scotch-Irish	181	0.07
Scottish	190	0.07
Slavic	13	0.00
Slovak	60	0.02
Slovene	15	0.01
Soviet Union	10	0.00
Swedish	86	0.03
Swiss	27	0.01
Turkish	53	0.02
Ukrainian	534	0.20
United States or American	4,976	1.82
Welsh	30	0.01
West Indian, excl. Hispanic:	6,424	2.35
Bahamian	21	0.01
Barbadian	53	0.02
Belizean	14	0.01
Bermudan	13	0.00
British West Indian	248	0.09
Haitian	2,634	0.96
Jamaican	2,008	0.73
Trinidadian and Tobagonian	585	0.21
U.S. Virgin Islander	36	0.01
West Indian	812	0.30
White:	80,495	29.43
Not Hispanic (38,950)	42,428	15.51
Hispanic (33,587)	38,067	13.92
Yugoslavian	25	0.01

North Arlington

Place Type: Borough
County: Bergen
Population: 15,181

Ancestry/Race	Number	%
Afghan	23	0.15
African American/Black:	91	0.60
Not Hispanic (58)	77	0.51
Hispanic (12)	14	0.09
African, sub-Saharan:	55	0.36
African	55	0.36
Am. Ind. or Alaska Nat., not spec.	22	0.14
Albanian	12	0.08
American Indian tribes, specified:	18	0.12
Apache (1)	1	0.01
Blackfeet	2	0.01
Cherokee (2)	7	0.05
Iroquois	1	0.01
Latin American Indians (1)	1	0.01
Sioux (1)	1	0.01
All other tribes (2)	5	0.03
American Indian tribes, not spec.	5	0.03
Arab:	262	1.73
Arab/Arabic	72	0.47
Egyptian	92	0.61
Jordanian	90	0.59
Lebanese	8	0.05
Armenian	25	0.16
Asian:	938	6.18
Chinese, ex. Taiwanese (165)	174	1.15
Filipino (190)	198	1.30
Indian (233)	241	1.59
Indonesian (1)	2	0.01
Japanese (13)	22	0.14
Korean (204)	224	1.48
Pakistani (7)	14	0.09
Sri Lankan (2)	2	0.01
Taiwanese (2)	2	0.01
Thai (15)	15	0.10
Vietnamese (7)	8	0.05
Other Asian, not specified (6)	36	0.24
Austrian	30	0.20
Belgian	27	0.18
Brazilian	110	0.72
British	40	0.26
Bulgarian	9	0.06
Canadian	7	0.05
Celtic	9	0.06
Croatian	10	0.07
Czech	39	0.26
Czechoslovakian	69	0.45
Dutch	95	0.63
English	485	3.19
European	60	0.40
French, except Basque	160	1.05
French Canadian	33	0.22
German	1,278	8.42
Greek	287	1.89
Guyanese	6	0.04
Hawaii Native/Pacific Islander:	9	0.06
Micronesian:	1	0.01
Guamanian/Chamorro	1	0.01
Polynesian: (1)	3	0.02
Native Hawaiian (1)	1	0.01
Other Polynesian	2	0.01
Other Pac. Isl., not spec. (1)	5	0.03
Hispanic or Latino:	1,605	10.57
Central American:	33	0.22
Costa Rican	4	0.03
Guatemalan	3	0.02
Honduran	12	0.08
Nicaraguan	4	0.03
Salvadoran	10	0.07
Cuban	241	1.59
Dominican Republic	42	0.28
Mexican	56	0.37
Puerto Rican	390	2.57
South American:	325	2.14
Argentinean	20	0.13
Bolivian	2	0.01
Chilean	15	0.10
Colombian	71	0.47
Ecuadorian	103	0.68
Paraguayan	4	0.03
Peruvian	86	0.57
Uruguayan	8	0.05
Venezuelan	6	0.04
Other South American	10	0.07
Other Hispanic or Latino	518	3.41
Hungarian	140	0.92
Irish	3,597	23.69
Italian	4,164	27.43
Latvian	4	0.03
Lithuanian	102	0.67
Norwegian	33	0.22
Polish	1,753	11.55
Portuguese	731	4.82
Russian	133	0.88
Scandinavian	8	0.05
Scotch-Irish	331	2.18
Scottish	278	1.83
Slavic	20	0.13
Slovak	65	0.43
Slovene	7	0.05
Swedish	86	0.57
Swiss	18	0.12
Turkish	91	0.60
Ukrainian	202	1.33
United States or American	299	1.97
Welsh	49	0.32
West Indian, excl. Hispanic:	55	0.36
Haitian	25	0.16
Jamaican	30	0.20
White:	13,856	91.27
Not Hispanic (12,438)	12,615	83.10
Hispanic (1,165)	1,241	8.17

North Bergen

Place Type: Township
County: Hudson
Population: 58,092

Ancestry/Race	Number	%
Acadian/Cajun	6	0.01
African American/Black:	2,097	3.61
Not Hispanic (900)	1,056	1.82
Hispanic (681)	1,041	1.79
African, sub-Saharan:	127	0.22
African	49	0.08
Cape Verdean	42	0.07
Liberian	20	0.03
Senegalese	7	0.01
South African	9	0.02
Alaska Native tribes, specified:	1	0.00
Tlingit-Haida	1	0.00
Am. Ind. or Alaska Nat., not spec.	295	0.51
Albanian	61	0.10
American Indian tribes, specified:	148	0.25
Apache	1	0.00
Blackfeet	3	0.01
Cherokee (1)	22	0.04
Chippewa (1)	2	0.00
Creek	2	0.00
Delaware	3	0.01
Iroquois (1)	1	0.00
Latin American Indians (59)	92	0.16
Navajo (2)	8	0.01
Pima	1	0.00
Pueblo	1	0.00
Sioux	1	0.00
All other tribes (3)	11	0.02
American Indian tribes, not spec.	31	0.05
Arab:	1,830	3.14
Arab/Arabic	416	0.71
Egyptian	485	0.83
Jordanian	120	0.21
Lebanese	320	0.55
Moroccan	50	0.09
Palestinian	354	0.61
Syrian	77	0.13
Other Arab	8	0.01
Armenian	269	0.46
Asian:	4,275	7.36
Bangladeshi (9)	9	0.02
Cambodian (5)	6	0.01
Chinese, ex. Taiwanese (367)	430	0.74
Filipino (278)	327	0.56
Indian (2,637)	2,796	4.81
Indonesian (7)	8	0.01
Japanese (64)	83	0.14
Korean (257)	284	0.49
Malaysian (4)	4	0.01
Pakistani (20)	30	0.05
Sri Lankan (7)	7	0.01
Taiwanese (4)	6	0.01
Thai (13)	18	0.03
Vietnamese (24)	29	0.05
Other Asian, specified (5)	6	0.01
Other Asian, not specified (24)	232	0.40
Assyrian/Chaldean/Syriac	7	0.01
Austrian	154	0.26
Belgian	8	0.01
Brazilian	384	0.66
British	41	0.07
Bulgarian	8	0.01
Croatian	325	0.56
Czech	121	0.21
Czechoslovakian	100	0.17
Danish	26	0.04
Dutch	150	0.26
Eastern European	10	0.02
English	417	0.72
Estonian	10	0.02
European	66	0.11
Finnish	18	0.03
French, except Basque	294	0.51
French Canadian	41	0.07
German	2,599	4.47
Greek	489	0.84
Guyanese	62	0.11
Hawaii Native/Pacific Islander:	61	0.11
Micronesian: (4)	5	0.01
Guamanian/Chamorro (4)	5	0.01
Polynesian: (9)	14	0.02
Native Hawaiian (4)	9	0.02

Notes: 1. Figures in the "Number" column do not add up to the total population due to: a) Ancestry/Race overlap — e.g. persons can report being both White and Irish, b) persons of Hispanic origin can report being any race, c) persons reporting two ancestries are counted in both categories. 2. Numbers in parentheses indicate the number of persons reporting this ancestry/race alone, not in combination with any other ancestry/race. 3. Refer to the Explanation of Data in the front of the book for more detailed information.

Ancestry/Race	Number	%
Samoan (4)	4	0.01
Tongan (1)	1	0.00
Other Pac. Isl., not spec. (15)	42	0.07
Hispanic or Latino:	33,260	57.25
Central American:	2,739	4.71
Costa Rican	116	0.20
Guatemalan	467	0.80
Honduran	509	0.88
Nicaraguan	150	0.26
Panamanian	55	0.09
Salvadoran	1,273	2.19
Other Central American	169	0.29
Cuban	7,635	13.14
Dominican Republic	3,228	5.56
Mexican	553	0.95
Puerto Rican	4,535	7.81
South American:	7,781	13.39
Argentinean	414	0.71
Bolivian	37	0.06
Chilean	315	0.54
Colombian	3,351	5.77
Ecuadorian	2,334	4.02
Paraguayan	16	0.03
Peruvian	848	1.46
Uruguayan	104	0.18
Venezuelan	150	0.26
Other South American	212	0.36
Other Hispanic or Latino	6,789	11.69
Hungarian	254	0.44
Iranian	23	0.04
Irish	3,344	5.75
Israeli	62	0.11
Italian	6,127	10.53
Latvian	9	0.02
Lithuanian	50	0.09
Maltese	9	0.02
Norwegian	133	0.23
Polish	894	1.54
Portuguese	110	0.19
Romanian	105	0.18
Russian	519	0.89
Scotch-Irish	133	0.23
Scottish	128	0.22
Slovak	30	0.05
Swedish	39	0.07
Swiss	37	0.06
Turkish	101	0.17
Ukrainian	56	0.10
United States or American	1,509	2.59
Welsh	68	0.12
West Indian, excl. Hispanic:	374	0.64
Barbadian	13	0.02
British West Indian	27	0.05
Dutch West Indian	8	0.01
Haitian	34	0.06
Jamaican	143	0.25
Trinidadian and Tobagonian	98	0.17
West Indian	41	0.07
Other West Indian	10	0.02
White:	43,006	74.03
Not Hispanic (18,427)	19,687	33.89
Hispanic (20,704)	23,319	40.14
Yugoslavian	44	0.08

North Brunswick Township

Place Type: Census Designated Place
County: Middlesex
Population: 36,287

Ancestry/Race	Number	%
African American/Black:	5,932	16.35
Not Hispanic (5,370)	5,660	15.60
Hispanic (172)	272	0.75
African, sub-Saharan:	715	1.97
African	362	1.00
Ghanian	217	0.60
Kenyan	25	0.07
Nigerian	22	0.06
Sierra Leonean	89	0.25
Am. Ind. or Alaska Nat., not spec.	119	0.33
Albanian	38	0.10
Alsatian	10	0.03
American Indian tribes, specified:	99	0.27
Blackfeet	9	0.02
Cherokee (11)	38	0.10
Comanche (1)	3	0.01
Delaware	2	0.01
Iroquois (4)	15	0.04
Latin American Indians (10)	16	0.04
Pueblo (1)	1	0.00
Puget Sound Salish	1	0.00
Sioux	3	0.01
All other tribes	11	0.03
American Indian tribes, not spec.	24	0.07
Arab:	809	2.23
Arab/Arabic	59	0.16
Egyptian	292	0.80
Lebanese	381	1.05
Palestinian	53	0.15
Syrian	15	0.04
Other Arab	9	0.02
Armenian	12	0.03
Asian:	5,530	15.24
Bangladeshi (19)	24	0.07
Cambodian (1)	1	0.00
Chinese, ex. Taiwanese (798)	862	2.38
Filipino (383)	433	1.19
Indian (3,012)	3,158	8.70
Indonesian (5)	5	0.01
Japanese (42)	58	0.16
Korean (449)	472	1.30
Laotian (1)	1	0.00
Malaysian (4)	4	0.01
Pakistani (221)	245	0.68
Sri Lankan (31)	38	0.10
Taiwanese (74)	77	0.21
Thai (13)	14	0.04
Vietnamese (28)	31	0.09
Other Asian, specified	3	0.01
Other Asian, not specified (29)	104	0.29
Australian	6	0.02
Austrian	134	0.37
Basque	20	0.06
Belgian	35	0.10
Brazilian	11	0.03
British	40	0.11
Canadian	69	0.19
Croatian	27	0.07
Cypriot	34	0.09
Czech	58	0.16
Czechoslovakian	30	0.08
Danish	151	0.42
Dutch	354	0.98
Eastern European	33	0.09
English	1,432	3.95
European	211	0.58
French, except Basque	497	1.37
French Canadian	91	0.25
German	3,164	8.72
Greek	279	0.77
Guyanese	40	0.11
Hawaii Native/Pacific Islander:	38	0.10
Micronesian: (1)	1	0.00
Guamanian/Chamorro (1)	1	0.00
Polynesian: (9)	16	0.04
Native Hawaiian (1)	8	0.02
Samoan (8)	8	0.02
Other Pac. Isl., specified	3	0.01
Other Pac. Isl., not spec.	18	0.05
Hispanic or Latino:	3,775	10.40
Central American:	208	0.57
Costa Rican	9	0.02
Guatemalan	41	0.11
Honduran	88	0.24
Nicaraguan	36	0.10
Panamanian	16	0.04
Salvadoran	12	0.03
Other Central American	6	0.02
Cuban	161	0.44
Dominican Republic	392	1.08
Mexican	522	1.44
Puerto Rican	1,316	3.63
South American:	501	1.38
Argentinean	27	0.07
Bolivian	2	0.01
Chilean	7	0.02
Colombian	172	0.47
Ecuadorian	163	0.45
Paraguayan	1	0.00
Peruvian	79	0.22
Uruguayan	1	0.00
Venezuelan	22	0.06
Other South American	27	0.07
Other Hispanic or Latino	675	1.86
Hungarian	1,581	4.36
Icelander	12	0.03
Iranian	51	0.14
Irish	4,507	12.42
Israeli	46	0.13
Italian	6,139	16.92
Latvian	46	0.13
Lithuanian	143	0.39
Northern European	70	0.19
Norwegian	131	0.36
Pennsylvania German	7	0.02
Polish	2,453	6.76
Portuguese	187	0.52
Romanian	41	0.11
Russian	1,126	3.10
Scandinavian	10	0.03
Scotch-Irish	226	0.62
Scottish	244	0.67
Serbian	14	0.04
Slavic	39	0.11
Slovak	229	0.63
Slovene	5	0.01
Swedish	118	0.33
Swiss	8	0.02
Turkish	40	0.11
Ukrainian	337	0.93
United States or American	1,027	2.83
Welsh	64	0.18
West Indian, excl. Hispanic:	651	1.79
Barbadian	24	0.07
Belizean	13	0.04
British West Indian	19	0.05
Haitian	68	0.19
Jamaican	316	0.87
Trinidadian and Tobagonian	58	0.16
U.S. Virgin Islander	27	0.07
West Indian	119	0.33
Other West Indian	7	0.02
White:	23,478	64.70
Not Hispanic (21,056)	21,582	59.48
Hispanic (1,707)	1,896	5.23
Yugoslavian	10	0.03

North Plainfield

Place Type: Borough
County: Somerset
Population: 21,103

Ancestry/Race	Number	%
African American/Black:	3,004	14.23
Not Hispanic (2,580)	2,723	12.90
Hispanic (244)	281	1.33
African, sub-Saharan:	245	1.16
African	73	0.35
Ghanian	27	0.13
Kenyan	28	0.13
Liberian	8	0.04
Nigerian	100	0.47
Other sub-Saharan African	9	0.04
Am. Ind. or Alaska Nat., not spec.	70	0.33
American Indian tribes, specified:	62	0.29
Apache	2	0.01
Blackfeet (2)	4	0.02

Notes: 1. Figures in the "Number" column do not add up to the total population due to: a) Ancestry/Race overlap — e.g. persons can report being both White and Irish, b) persons of Hispanic origin can report being any race, c) persons reporting two ancestries are counted in both categories. 2. Numbers in parentheses indicate the number of persons reporting this ancestry/race alone, not in combination with any other ancestry/race. 3. Refer to the Explanation of Data in the front of the book for more detailed information.

Cherokee (7)	26	0.12
Cheyenne (1)	1	0.00
Chickasaw (1)	1	0.00
Choctaw (1)	5	0.02
Delaware	2	0.01
Iroquois	2	0.01
Latin American Indians (1)	7	0.03
Pueblo	1	0.00
Sioux (2)	4	0.02
Tohono O'Odham (2)	2	0.01
All other tribes	5	0.02
American Indian tribes, not spec.	13	0.06
Arab:	303	1.44
Arab/Arabic	44	0.21
Egyptian	145	0.69
Jordanian	44	0.21
Lebanese	6	0.03
Moroccan	25	0.12
Palestinian	17	0.08
Syrian	22	0.10
Armenian	19	0.09
Asian:	1,270	6.02
Bangladeshi	2	0.01
Chinese, ex. Taiwanese (231)	254	1.20
Filipino (128)	147	0.70
Indian (320)	379	1.80
Indonesian (2)	2	0.01
Japanese (11)	16	0.08
Korean (54)	64	0.30
Laotian (14)	14	0.07
Malaysian	2	0.01
Pakistani (107)	170	0.81
Sri Lankan (13)	13	0.06
Taiwanese (14)	14	0.07
Thai	3	0.01
Vietnamese (133)	149	0.71
Other Asian, specified (2)	2	0.01
Other Asian, not specified (13)	39	0.18
Assyrian/Chaldean/Syriac	11	0.05
Austrian	90	0.43
British	83	0.39
Canadian	43	0.20
Croatian	23	0.11
Czech	38	0.18
Czechoslovakian	21	0.10
Danish	46	0.22
Dutch	115	0.54
English	1,040	4.93
European	87	0.41
Finnish	55	0.26
French, except Basque	243	1.15
French Canadian	75	0.36
German	2,123	10.06
Greek	137	0.65
Guyanese	121	0.57
Hawaii Native/Pacific Islander:	29	0.14
Micronesian: (1)	2	0.01
Guamanian/Chamorro (1)	2	0.01
Polynesian: (6)	12	0.06
Native Hawaiian (4)	9	0.04
Samoan (2)	3	0.01
Other Pac. Isl., not spec. (9)	15	0.07
Hispanic or Latino:	6,916	32.77
Central American:	1,311	6.21
Costa Rican	39	0.18
Guatemalan	431	2.04
Honduran	237	1.12
Nicaraguan	40	0.19
Panamanian	11	0.05
Salvadoran	488	2.31
Other Central American	65	0.31
Cuban	93	0.44
Dominican Republic	178	0.84
Mexican	332	1.57
Puerto Rican	787	3.73
South American:	2,249	10.66
Argentinean	33	0.16
Chilean	30	0.14
Colombian	704	3.34
Ecuadorian	1,138	5.39
Paraguayan	2	0.01
Peruvian	266	1.26
Uruguayan	5	0.02
Venezuelan	18	0.09
Other South American	53	0.25
Other Hispanic or Latino	1,966	9.32
Hungarian	130	0.62
Irish	2,161	10.24
Israeli	18	0.09
Italian	2,927	13.87
Lithuanian	57	0.27
Maltese	6	0.03
Northern European	16	0.08
Norwegian	93	0.44
Pennsylvania German	6	0.03
Polish	975	4.62
Portuguese	126	0.60
Romanian	27	0.13
Russian	172	0.82
Scandinavian	6	0.03
Scotch-Irish	104	0.49
Scottish	295	1.40
Serbian	4	0.02
Slavic	16	0.08
Slovak	139	0.66
Swedish	49	0.23
Swiss	63	0.30
Turkish	53	0.25
Ukrainian	117	0.55
United States or American	708	3.35
Welsh	81	0.38
West Indian, excl. Hispanic:	400	1.90
Barbadian	17	0.08
British West Indian	7	0.03
Haitian	75	0.36
Jamaican	203	0.96
Trinidadian and Tobagonian	51	0.24
West Indian	47	0.22
White:	14,033	66.50
Not Hispanic (10,023)	10,297	48.79
Hispanic (3,284)	3,736	17.70
Yugoslavian	39	0.18

Nutley

Place Type: Census Designated Place
County: Essex
Population: 27,362

Ancestry/Race	Number	%
Afghan	55	0.20
African American/Black:	559	2.04
Not Hispanic (484)	520	1.90
Hispanic (27)	39	0.14
African, sub-Saharan:	37	0.14
African	13	0.05
Other sub-Saharan African	24	0.09
Am. Ind. or Alaska Nat., not spec.	25	0.09
Albanian	15	0.05
American Indian tribes, specified:	31	0.11
Apache	1	0.00
Cherokee	9	0.03
Cheyenne	1	0.00
Chippewa (1)	1	0.00
Delaware	4	0.01
Iroquois (1)	1	0.00
Latin American Indians (5)	6	0.02
Navajo	3	0.01
Seminole	1	0.00
Sioux	2	0.01
All other tribes (1)	2	0.01
American Indian tribes, not spec.	8	0.03
Arab:	175	0.64
Arab/Arabic	28	0.10
Egyptian	118	0.43
Lebanese	10	0.04
Moroccan	7	0.03
Syrian	12	0.04
Armenian	67	0.24
Asian:	2,113	7.72
Bangladeshi (1)	1	0.00
Cambodian (1)	6	0.02
Chinese, ex. Taiwanese (347)	386	1.41
Filipino (448)	494	1.81
Indian (600)	630	2.30
Indonesian (2)	4	0.01
Japanese (75)	99	0.36
Korean (201)	214	0.78
Malaysian	1	0.00
Pakistani (71)	73	0.27
Sri Lankan (6)	7	0.03
Taiwanese (23)	31	0.11
Thai (35)	38	0.14
Vietnamese (73)	87	0.32
Other Asian, not specified (22)	42	0.15
Australian	6	0.02
Austrian	155	0.57
Brazilian	46	0.17
British	22	0.08
Canadian	21	0.08
Celtic	14	0.05
Croatian	8	0.03
Czech	85	0.31
Czechoslovakian	116	0.42
Danish	51	0.19
Dutch	261	0.95
Eastern European	11	0.04
English	1,152	4.21
European	119	0.43
Finnish	9	0.03
French, except Basque	364	1.33
French Canadian	96	0.35
German	3,166	11.57
Greek	247	0.90
Hawaii Native/Pacific Islander:	21	0.08
Micronesian:	2	0.01
Guamanian/Chamorro	2	0.01
Polynesian: (7)	15	0.05
Native Hawaiian (3)	5	0.02
Samoan (4)	10	0.04
Other Pac. Isl., not spec. (2)	4	0.01
Hispanic or Latino:	1,830	6.69
Central American:	89	0.33
Costa Rican	26	0.10
Guatemalan	12	0.04
Honduran	10	0.04
Nicaraguan	4	0.01
Panamanian	5	0.02
Salvadoran	28	0.10
Other Central American	4	0.01
Cuban	178	0.65
Dominican Republic	91	0.33
Mexican	72	0.26
Puerto Rican	585	2.14
South American:	451	1.65
Argentinean	32	0.12
Bolivian	6	0.02
Chilean	37	0.14
Colombian	80	0.29
Ecuadorian	155	0.57
Paraguayan	1	0.00
Peruvian	98	0.36
Uruguayan	7	0.03
Venezuelan	14	0.05
Other South American	21	0.08
Other Hispanic or Latino	364	1.33
Hungarian	358	1.31
Iranian	95	0.35
Irish	4,985	18.22
Israeli	12	0.04
Italian	12,183	44.53
Latvian	35	0.13
Lithuanian	140	0.51
Macedonian	19	0.07
Norwegian	112	0.41
Polish	1,912	6.99
Portuguese	493	1.80
Romanian	41	0.15
Russian	531	1.94
Scandinavian	7	0.03

Notes: 1. Figures in the "Number" column do not add up to the total population due to: a) Ancestry/Race overlap — e.g. persons can report being both White and Irish, b) persons of Hispanic origin can report being any race, c) persons reporting two ancestries are counted in both categories. 2. Numbers in parentheses indicate the number of persons reporting this ancestry/race alone, not in combination with any other ancestry/race. 3. Refer to the Explanation of Data in the front of the book for more detailed information.

Ancestry/Race	Number	%
Scotch-Irish	227	0.83
Scottish	498	1.82
Serbian	16	0.06
Slavic	12	0.04
Slovak	95	0.35
Slovene	9	0.03
Swedish	102	0.37
Swiss	88	0.32
Turkish	38	0.14
Ukrainian	292	1.07
United States or American	563	2.06
Welsh	151	0.55
West Indian, excl. Hispanic:	109	0.40
Bahamian	14	0.05
Barbadian	5	0.02
British West Indian	8	0.03
Haitian	12	0.04
Jamaican	22	0.08
Trinidadian and Tobagonian	32	0.12
West Indian	16	0.06
White:	24,350	88.99
Not Hispanic (22,795)	23,003	84.07
Hispanic (1,269)	1,347	4.92
Yugoslavian	13	0.05

Oakland

Place Type: Borough
County: Bergen
Population: 12,466

Ancestry/Race	Number	%
Afghan	8	0.06
African American/Black:	130	1.04
Not Hispanic (94)	118	0.95
Hispanic (3)	12	0.10
Am. Ind. or Alaska Nat., not spec.	6	0.05
Albanian	11	0.09
Alsatian	6	0.05
American Indian tribes, specified:	14	0.11
Cherokee	2	0.02
Chippewa (1)	1	0.01
Cree	1	0.01
Delaware (4)	5	0.04
Iroquois	1	0.01
Latin American Indians (1)	1	0.01
Seminole	1	0.01
All other tribes	2	0.02
Arab:	145	1.16
Arab/Arabic	13	0.10
Egyptian	38	0.30
Lebanese	49	0.39
Syrian	42	0.34
Other Arab	3	0.02
Armenian	17	0.14
Asian:	407	3.26
Chinese, ex. Taiwanese (69)	84	0.67
Filipino (48)	63	0.51
Indian (97)	110	0.88
Japanese (29)	39	0.31
Korean (65)	69	0.55
Pakistani (7)	7	0.06
Taiwanese (4)	4	0.03
Thai (1)	1	0.01
Vietnamese (7)	7	0.06
Other Asian, not specified (6)	23	0.18
Assyrian/Chaldean/Syriac	9	0.07
Austrian	195	1.56
Basque	12	0.10
Belgian	34	0.27
British	72	0.58
Canadian	18	0.14
Croatian	40	0.32
Czech	107	0.86
Czechoslovakian	46	0.37
Danish	29	0.23
Dutch	676	5.42
Eastern European	48	0.39
English	1,063	8.53
Estonian	29	0.23
European	23	0.18
Finnish	13	0.10
French, except Basque	371	2.98
French Canadian	68	0.55
German	2,258	18.11
Greek	107	0.86
Hawaii Native/Pacific Islander:	3	0.02
Polynesian: (1)	3	0.02
Native Hawaiian (1)	3	0.02
Hispanic or Latino:	483	3.87
Central American:	19	0.15
Costa Rican	6	0.05
Guatemalan	2	0.02
Honduran	1	0.01
Nicaraguan	3	0.02
Panamanian	2	0.02
Salvadoran	5	0.04
Cuban	62	0.50
Dominican Republic	12	0.10
Mexican	49	0.39
Puerto Rican	146	1.17
South American:	92	0.74
Argentinean	14	0.11
Bolivian	1	0.01
Chilean	7	0.06
Colombian	29	0.23
Ecuadorian	8	0.06
Peruvian	17	0.14
Uruguayan	6	0.05
Venezuelan	3	0.02
Other South American	7	0.06
Other Hispanic or Latino	103	0.83
Hungarian	251	2.01
Iranian	7	0.06
Irish	2,639	21.17
Italian	3,334	26.74
Lithuanian	21	0.17
Luxemburger	14	0.11
Maltese	7	0.06
Northern European	12	0.10
Norwegian	172	1.38
Polish	1,158	9.29
Portuguese	41	0.33
Romanian	38	0.30
Russian	392	3.14
Scandinavian	22	0.18
Scotch-Irish	100	0.80
Scottish	247	1.98
Slavic	17	0.14
Slovak	85	0.68
Swedish	169	1.36
Swiss	111	0.89
Ukrainian	156	1.25
United States or American	543	4.36
Welsh	80	0.64
West Indian, excl. Hispanic:	58	0.47
Jamaican	43	0.34
Trinidadian and Tobagonian	5	0.04
West Indian	10	0.08
White:	11,913	95.56
Not Hispanic (11,441)	11,519	92.40
Hispanic (372)	394	3.16
Yugoslavian	91	0.73

Ocean Acres

Place Type: Census Designated Place
County: Ocean
Population: 13,155

Ancestry/Race	Number	%
African American/Black:	166	1.26
Not Hispanic (123)	154	1.17
Hispanic (9)	12	0.09
African, sub-Saharan:	28	0.21
Cape Verdean	28	0.21
Am. Ind. or Alaska Nat., not spec.	10	0.08
Albanian	15	0.11
American Indian tribes, specified:	42	0.32
Blackfeet	5	0.04
Cherokee (4)	19	0.14
Chickasaw (2)	2	0.02
Chippewa (1)	1	0.01
Delaware	2	0.02
Iroquois (6)	6	0.05
Sioux	4	0.03
All other tribes (1)	3	0.02
Arab:	28	0.21
Lebanese	8	0.06
Syrian	20	0.15
Armenian	15	0.11
Asian:	165	1.25
Chinese, ex. Taiwanese (11)	11	0.08
Filipino (56)	83	0.63
Indian (27)	31	0.24
Indonesian (2)	2	0.02
Japanese	4	0.03
Korean (19)	22	0.17
Vietnamese (3)	3	0.02
Other Asian, not specified (4)	9	0.07
Austrian	70	0.53
Belgian	27	0.20
Brazilian	24	0.18
British	68	0.51
Croatian	35	0.26
Czech	81	0.61
Czechoslovakian	73	0.55
Danish	24	0.18
Dutch	222	1.68
English	1,371	10.38
Estonian	10	0.08
European	121	0.92
French, except Basque	421	3.19
French Canadian	78	0.59
German	3,025	22.90
Greek	134	1.01
Hawaii Native/Pacific Islander:	8	0.06
Micronesian:	1	0.01
Guamanian/Chamorro	1	0.01
Polynesian: (2)	5	0.04
Native Hawaiian	2	0.02
Samoan (2)	3	0.02
Other Pac. Isl., not spec. (1)	2	0.02
Hispanic or Latino:	365	2.77
Central American:	11	0.08
Costa Rican	3	0.02
Guatemalan	4	0.03
Panamanian	4	0.03
Cuban	33	0.25
Dominican Republic	16	0.12
Mexican	52	0.40
Puerto Rican	160	1.22
South American:	38	0.29
Argentinean	4	0.03
Chilean	3	0.02
Colombian	15	0.11
Ecuadorian	7	0.05
Peruvian	3	0.02
Uruguayan	3	0.02
Venezuelan	2	0.02
Other South American	1	0.01
Other Hispanic or Latino	55	0.42
Hungarian	181	1.37
Irish	3,740	28.32
Italian	3,674	27.82
Lithuanian	116	0.88
Luxemburger	28	0.21
Northern European	20	0.15
Norwegian	180	1.36
Pennsylvania German	24	0.18
Polish	1,260	9.54
Portuguese	71	0.54
Romanian	40	0.30
Russian	67	0.51
Scandinavian	10	0.08
Scotch-Irish	201	1.52
Scottish	244	1.85
Slavic	8	0.06
Slovak	46	0.35
Swedish	123	0.93

Notes: 1. Figures in the "Number" column do not add up to the total population due to: a) Ancestry/Race overlap — e.g. persons can report being both White and Irish, b) persons of Hispanic origin can report being any race, c) persons reporting two ancestries are counted in both categories. 2. Numbers in parentheses indicate the number of persons reporting this ancestry/race alone, not in combination with any other ancestry/race. 3. Refer to the Explanation of Data in the front of the book for more detailed information.

Swiss	25	0.19
Ukrainian	157	1.19
United States or American	472	3.57
Welsh	85	0.64
West Indian, excl. Hispanic:	14	0.11
Jamaican	14	0.11
White:	12,802	97.32
Not Hispanic (12,406)	12,511	95.10
Hispanic (267)	291	2.21
Yugoslavian	7	0.05

Ocean City

Place Type: City
County: Cape May
Population: 15,378

Ancestry/Race	Number	%
African American/Black:	720	4.68
Not Hispanic (632)	679	4.42
Hispanic (31)	41	0.27
African, sub-Saharan:	26	0.17
African	7	0.05
Ethiopian	19	0.12
Alaska Native tribes, specified:	1	0.01
Alaska Athabascan	1	0.01
Am. Ind. or Alaska Nat., not spec.	20	0.13
Albanian	16	0.10
American Indian tribes, specified:	32	0.21
Blackfeet	1	0.01
Cherokee (2)	13	0.08
Crow (1)	1	0.01
Delaware	5	0.03
Iroquois (1)	3	0.02
Latin American Indians (1)	1	0.01
Navajo (1)	1	0.01
Puget Sound Salish	1	0.01
Sioux (3)	3	0.02
All other tribes (2)	3	0.02
American Indian tribes, not spec.	4	0.03
Arab:	52	0.34
Egyptian	52	0.34
Armenian	20	0.13
Asian:	116	0.75
Chinese, ex. Taiwanese (31)	39	0.25
Filipino (12)	16	0.10
Indian (19)	23	0.15
Indonesian (1)	5	0.03
Japanese (6)	10	0.07
Korean (11)	11	0.07
Laotian (1)	1	0.01
Pakistani (1)	1	0.01
Taiwanese	1	0.01
Thai (1)	2	0.01
Vietnamese (2)	2	0.01
Other Asian, not specified	5	0.03
Australian	7	0.05
Austrian	82	0.53
Belgian	9	0.06
Brazilian	9	0.06
British	173	1.12
Canadian	19	0.12
Celtic	7	0.05
Croatian	39	0.25
Czech	29	0.19
Czechoslovakian	16	0.10
Danish	74	0.48
Dutch	193	1.26
Eastern European	9	0.06
English	2,292	14.90
European	62	0.40
Finnish	17	0.11
French, except Basque	376	2.45
French Canadian	26	0.17
German	3,453	22.45
Greek	156	1.01
Hawaii Native/Pacific Islander:	17	0.11
Micronesian: (3)	4	0.03
Guamanian/Chamorro (3)	4	0.03
Polynesian: (7)	8	0.05
Native Hawaiian (1)	2	0.01
Samoan (6)	6	0.04
Other Pac. Isl., not spec.	5	0.03
Hispanic or Latino:	306	1.99
Central American:	7	0.05
Costa Rican	3	0.02
Honduran	2	0.01
Panamanian	2	0.01
Cuban	15	0.10
Dominican Republic	18	0.12
Mexican	60	0.39
Puerto Rican	140	0.91
South American:	13	0.08
Argentinean	2	0.01
Chilean	2	0.01
Colombian	3	0.02
Ecuadorian	1	0.01
Peruvian	2	0.01
Uruguayan	3	0.02
Other Hispanic or Latino	53	0.34
Hungarian	79	0.51
Irish	4,259	27.70
Italian	2,961	19.25
Latvian	11	0.07
Lithuanian	97	0.63
Northern European	9	0.06
Norwegian	84	0.55
Pennsylvania German	25	0.16
Polish	492	3.20
Portuguese	16	0.10
Romanian	8	0.05
Russian	140	0.91
Scandinavian	9	0.06
Scotch-Irish	451	2.93
Scottish	444	2.89
Serbian	70	0.46
Slavic	38	0.25
Slovak	51	0.33
Swedish	149	0.97
Swiss	44	0.29
Ukrainian	109	0.71
United States or American	540	3.51
Welsh	261	1.70
White:	14,503	94.31
Not Hispanic (14,211)	14,311	93.06
Hispanic (178)	192	1.25
Yugoslavian	8	0.05

Ocean

Place Type: Township
County: Monmouth
Population: 26,959

Ancestry/Race	Number	%
Afghan	90	0.33
African American/Black:	1,731	6.42
Not Hispanic (1,466)	1,654	6.14
Hispanic (63)	77	0.29
African, sub-Saharan:	102	0.38
African	84	0.31
Nigerian	9	0.03
Other sub-Saharan African	9	0.03
Am. Ind. or Alaska Nat., not spec.	50	0.19
American Indian tribes, specified:	45	0.17
Blackfeet (1)	3	0.01
Cherokee (1)	10	0.04
Cheyenne (1)	1	0.00
Cree	1	0.00
Delaware	2	0.01
Latin American Indians (6)	7	0.03
Paiute (5)	9	0.03
Seminole (1)	1	0.00
Shoshone	1	0.00
Sioux (2)	2	0.01
Yaqui (1)	1	0.00
All other tribes	7	0.03
American Indian tribes, not spec.	5	0.02
Arab:	687	2.55
Arab/Arabic	34	0.13
Egyptian	47	0.17
Iraqi	7	0.03
Jordanian	7	0.03
Lebanese	126	0.47
Syrian	337	1.25
Other Arab	129	0.48
Armenian	27	0.10
Asian:	1,872	6.94
Bangladeshi (22)	27	0.10
Cambodian (5)	5	0.02
Chinese, ex. Taiwanese (326)	351	1.30
Filipino (255)	285	1.06
Indian (622)	665	2.47
Indonesian (1)	1	0.00
Japanese (17)	40	0.15
Korean (277)	300	1.11
Malaysian (2)	3	0.01
Pakistani (46)	57	0.21
Sri Lankan	1	0.00
Taiwanese (10)	18	0.07
Thai (6)	12	0.04
Vietnamese (47)	59	0.22
Other Asian, specified (3)	3	0.01
Other Asian, not specified (15)	45	0.17
Assyrian/Chaldean/Syriac	24	0.09
Austrian	341	1.26
Belgian	50	0.19
Brazilian	76	0.28
British	70	0.26
Canadian	50	0.19
Celtic	21	0.08
Croatian	43	0.16
Czech	28	0.10
Czechoslovakian	81	0.30
Danish	43	0.16
Dutch	361	1.34
Eastern European	191	0.71
English	1,934	7.17
Estonian	11	0.04
European	179	0.66
Finnish	11	0.04
French, except Basque	456	1.69
French Canadian	82	0.30
German	3,478	12.90
Greek	482	1.79
Hawaii Native/Pacific Islander:	60	0.22
Micronesian: (7)	7	0.03
Guamanian/Chamorro (7)	7	0.03
Polynesian: (6)	13	0.05
Native Hawaiian (5)	12	0.04
Samoan (1)	1	0.00
Other Pac. Isl., not spec. (7)	40	0.15
Hispanic or Latino:	1,215	4.51
Central American:	91	0.34
Costa Rican	12	0.04
Guatemalan	12	0.04
Honduran	15	0.06
Nicaraguan	4	0.01
Panamanian	8	0.03
Salvadoran	35	0.13
Other Central American	5	0.02
Cuban	63	0.23
Dominican Republic	56	0.21
Mexican	148	0.55
Puerto Rican	335	1.24
South American:	265	0.98
Argentinean	5	0.02
Bolivian	3	0.01
Chilean	36	0.13
Colombian	105	0.39
Ecuadorian	21	0.08
Paraguayan	1	0.00
Peruvian	38	0.14
Uruguayan	1	0.00
Venezuelan	50	0.19
Other South American	5	0.02
Other Hispanic or Latino	257	0.95
Hungarian	334	1.24
Iranian	74	0.27
Irish	4,912	18.22

Notes: 1. Figures in the "Number" column do not add up to the total population due to: a) Ancestry/Race overlap — e.g. persons can report being both White and Irish, b) persons of Hispanic origin can report being any race, c) persons reporting two ancestries are counted in both categories. 2. Numbers in parentheses indicate the number of persons reporting this ancestry/race alone, not in combination with any other ancestry/race. 3. Refer to the Explanation of Data in the front of the book for more detailed information.

Ancestry/Race	Number	%
Israeli	108	0.40
Italian	5,657	20.98
Latvian	57	0.21
Lithuanian	96	0.36
Northern European	4	0.01
Norwegian	133	0.49
Polish	1,688	6.26
Portuguese	83	0.31
Romanian	157	0.58
Russian	1,272	4.72
Scandinavian	19	0.07
Scotch-Irish	276	1.02
Scottish	361	1.34
Serbian	11	0.04
Slavic	18	0.07
Slovak	70	0.26
Swedish	172	0.64
Swiss	70	0.26
Turkish	48	0.18
Ukrainian	202	0.75
United States or American	1,287	4.77
Welsh	108	0.40
West Indian, excl. Hispanic:	568	2.11
Barbadian	13	0.05
Belizean	13	0.05
Bermudan	4	0.01
Haitian	406	1.51
Jamaican	110	0.41
West Indian	22	0.08
White:	23,077	85.60
Not Hispanic (22,052)	22,319	82.79
Hispanic (686)	758	2.81
Yugoslavian	37	0.14

Old Bridge

Place Type: Township
County: Middlesex
Population: 60,456

Ancestry/Race	Number	%
Afghan	45	0.07
African American/Black:	3,524	5.83
Not Hispanic (3,052)	3,279	5.42
Hispanic (155)	245	0.41
African, sub-Saharan:	573	0.95
African	240	0.40
Ethiopian	48	0.08
Ghanian	102	0.17
Liberian	17	0.03
Nigerian	122	0.20
Sierra Leonean	23	0.04
Other sub-Saharan African	21	0.03
Alaska Native tribes, specified:	1	0.00
Alaska Athabascan (1)	1	0.00
Am. Ind. or Alaska Nat., not spec.	147	0.24
Albanian	41	0.07
American Indian tribes, specified:	132	0.22
Apache (3)	5	0.01
Blackfeet (1)	5	0.01
Cherokee (5)	45	0.07
Cheyenne	1	0.00
Chippewa	1	0.00
Choctaw	1	0.00
Comanche	1	0.00
Delaware (4)	10	0.02
Iroquois (8)	16	0.03
Latin American Indians (5)	20	0.03
Paiute (1)	1	0.00
Pueblo	4	0.01
Seminole	1	0.00
Shoshone (4)	4	0.01
Sioux	2	0.00
All other tribes (3)	15	0.02
American Indian tribes, not spec.	25	0.04
Arab:	1,140	1.89
Arab/Arabic	147	0.24
Egyptian	900	1.49
Jordanian	8	0.01
Moroccan	16	0.03
Syrian	69	0.11
Armenian	43	0.07
Asian:	7,203	11.91
Bangladeshi (28)	32	0.05
Cambodian (5)	5	0.01
Chinese, ex. Taiwanese (1,332)	1,417	2.34
Filipino (1,221)	1,350	2.23
Indian (3,019)	3,219	5.32
Indonesian (5)	6	0.01
Japanese (38)	70	0.12
Korean (230)	253	0.42
Malaysian (2)	4	0.01
Pakistani (399)	526	0.87
Sri Lankan (22)	31	0.05
Taiwanese (9)	16	0.03
Thai (28)	29	0.05
Vietnamese (65)	68	0.11
Other Asian, specified (6)	16	0.03
Other Asian, not specified (44)	161	0.27
Australian	10	0.02
Austrian	388	0.64
Belgian	64	0.11
Brazilian	45	0.07
British	92	0.15
Bulgarian	31	0.05
Canadian	113	0.19
Carpatho Rusyn	6	0.01
Croatian	132	0.22
Cypriot	13	0.02
Czech	210	0.35
Czechoslovakian	156	0.26
Danish	213	0.35
Dutch	461	0.76
Eastern European	198	0.33
English	2,406	3.98
Estonian	74	0.12
European	113	0.19
Finnish	26	0.04
French, except Basque	749	1.24
French Canadian	203	0.34
German	6,902	11.42
Greek	482	0.80
Guyanese	80	0.13
Hawaii Native/Pacific Islander:	59	0.10
Micronesian: (9)	9	0.01
Guamanian/Chamorro (9)	9	0.01
Polynesian: (12)	19	0.03
Native Hawaiian (4)	7	0.01
Samoan (8)	11	0.02
Other Polynesian	1	0.00
Other Pac. Isl., specified	2	0.00
Other Pac. Isl., not spec. (6)	29	0.05
Hispanic or Latino:	4,578	7.57
Central American:	175	0.29
Costa Rican	12	0.02
Guatemalan	36	0.06
Honduran	15	0.02
Nicaraguan	9	0.01
Panamanian	12	0.02
Salvadoran	75	0.12
Other Central American	16	0.03
Cuban	377	0.62
Dominican Republic	188	0.31
Mexican	439	0.73
Puerto Rican	2,002	3.31
South American:	602	1.00
Argentinean	72	0.12
Bolivian	4	0.01
Chilean	25	0.04
Colombian	244	0.40
Ecuadorian	108	0.18
Peruvian	60	0.10
Uruguayan	44	0.07
Venezuelan	13	0.02
Other South American	32	0.05
Other Hispanic or Latino	795	1.32
Hungarian	1,071	1.77
Icelander	5	0.01
Irish	12,378	20.47
Israeli	48	0.08
Italian	14,722	24.35
Latvian	16	0.03
Lithuanian	236	0.39
Macedonian	13	0.02
Maltese	64	0.11
Northern European	25	0.04
Norwegian	585	0.97
Pennsylvania German	11	0.02
Polish	5,830	9.64
Portuguese	508	0.84
Romanian	114	0.19
Russian	2,187	3.62
Scandinavian	15	0.02
Scotch-Irish	395	0.65
Scottish	527	0.87
Slavic	79	0.13
Slovak	491	0.81
Slovene	24	0.04
Swedish	477	0.79
Swiss	68	0.11
Turkish	73	0.12
Ukrainian	643	1.06
United States or American	1,707	2.82
Welsh	179	0.30
West Indian, excl. Hispanic:	638	1.06
Barbadian	71	0.12
Bermudan	8	0.01
British West Indian	40	0.07
Haitian	150	0.25
Jamaican	187	0.31
Trinidadian and Tobagonian	108	0.18
West Indian	63	0.10
Other West Indian	11	0.02
White:	49,059	81.15
Not Hispanic (45,028)	45,787	75.74
Hispanic (3,021)	3,272	5.41
Yugoslavian	32	0.05

Orange

Place Type: Census Designated Place
County: Essex
Population: 32,868

Ancestry/Race	Number	%
African American/Black:	25,879	78.74
Not Hispanic (24,318)	25,425	77.35
Hispanic (367)	454	1.38
African, sub-Saharan:	1,492	4.54
African	801	2.44
Ethiopian	13	0.04
Ghanian	196	0.60
Liberian	36	0.11
Nigerian	417	1.27
Other sub-Saharan African	29	0.09
Alaska Native tribes, not specified	2	0.01
Am. Ind. or Alaska Nat., not spec.	126	0.38
American Indian tribes, specified:	145	0.44
Blackfeet (2)	9	0.03
Cherokee (14)	53	0.16
Choctaw	1	0.00
Delaware (1)	2	0.01
Iroquois (2)	4	0.01
Latin American Indians (16)	47	0.14
Lumbee (2)	8	0.02
Seminole (5)	7	0.02
Sioux (3)	4	0.01
All other tribes (1)	10	0.03
American Indian tribes, not spec.	24	0.07
Arab:	26	0.08
Arab/Arabic	12	0.04
Egyptian	14	0.04
Armenian	6	0.02
Asian:	545	1.66
Chinese, ex. Taiwanese (43)	63	0.19
Filipino (99)	107	0.33
Indian (211)	278	0.85
Japanese (5)	6	0.02
Korean (31)	32	0.10
Malaysian (1)	1	0.00

Notes: 1. Figures in the "Number" column do not add up to the total population due to: a) Ancestry/Race overlap — e.g. persons can report being both White and Irish, b) persons of Hispanic origin can report being any race, c) persons reporting two ancestries are counted in both categories. 2. Numbers in parentheses indicate the number of persons reporting this ancestry/race alone, not in combination with any other ancestry/race. 3. Refer to the Explanation of Data in the front of the book for more detailed information.

Ancestry/Race	Number	%
Pakistani (6)	7	0.02
Vietnamese (13)	13	0.04
Other Asian, specified (2)	4	0.01
Other Asian, not specified (4)	34	0.10
Austrian	13	0.04
Basque	9	0.03
Belgian	13	0.04
Brazilian	10	0.03
British	42	0.13
Canadian	43	0.13
Czech	16	0.05
Danish	5	0.02
Dutch	14	0.04
English	92	0.28
Estonian	14	0.04
European	50	0.15
French, except Basque	78	0.24
German	340	1.03
Greek	36	0.11
Guyanese	821	2.50
Hawaii Native/Pacific Islander:	111	0.34
Micronesian: (10)	12	0.04
Guamanian/Chamorro (10)	12	0.04
Polynesian: (6)	6	0.02
Samoan (6)	6	0.02
Other Pac. Isl., specified	1	0.00
Other Pac. Isl., not spec. (17)	92	0.28
Hispanic or Latino:	4,097	12.47
Central American:	581	1.77
Costa Rican	48	0.15
Guatemalan	102	0.31
Honduran	41	0.12
Nicaraguan	4	0.01
Panamanian	12	0.04
Salvadoran	350	1.06
Other Central American	24	0.07
Cuban	38	0.12
Dominican Republic	326	0.99
Mexican	387	1.18
Puerto Rican	538	1.64
South American:	1,134	3.45
Argentinean	58	0.18
Bolivian	52	0.16
Chilean	5	0.02
Colombian	88	0.27
Ecuadorian	290	0.88
Peruvian	391	1.19
Uruguayan	190	0.58
Venezuelan	12	0.04
Other South American	48	0.15
Other Hispanic or Latino	1,093	3.33
Hungarian	23	0.07
Irish	508	1.55
Italian	1,061	3.23
Polish	140	0.43
Portuguese	6	0.02
Romanian	6	0.02
Russian	82	0.25
Scotch-Irish	13	0.04
Scottish	46	0.14
Slovak	19	0.06
Swedish	18	0.05
Ukrainian	32	0.10
United States or American	1,051	3.20
Welsh	11	0.03
West Indian, excl. Hispanic:	5,505	16.75
Barbadian	61	0.19
British West Indian	66	0.20
Dutch West Indian	27	0.08
Haitian	3,250	9.89
Jamaican	1,238	3.77
Trinidadian and Tobagonian	630	1.92
U.S. Virgin Islander	19	0.06
West Indian	191	0.58
Other West Indian	23	0.07
White:	4,791	14.58
Not Hispanic (2,502)	2,736	8.32
Hispanic (1,835)	2,055	6.25

Palisades Park

Place Type: Borough
County: Bergen
Population: 17,073

Ancestry/Race	Number	%
African American/Black:	286	1.68
Not Hispanic (176)	208	1.22
Hispanic (59)	78	0.46
Am. Ind. or Alaska Nat., not spec.	46	0.27
Albanian	67	0.39
American Indian tribes, specified:	29	0.17
Apache	1	0.01
Choctaw	1	0.01
Creek	1	0.01
Latin American Indians (13)	20	0.12
Tohono O'Odham (2)	2	0.01
All other tribes (4)	4	0.02
American Indian tribes, not spec.	5	0.03
Arab:	190	1.11
Arab/Arabic	83	0.49
Egyptian	41	0.24
Lebanese	20	0.12
Moroccan	9	0.05
Palestinian	21	0.12
Syrian	16	0.09
Armenian	320	1.87
Asian:	7,259	42.52
Bangladeshi (1)	1	0.01
Chinese, ex. Taiwanese (388)	403	2.36
Filipino (111)	121	0.71
Indian (172)	197	1.15
Indonesian (4)	4	0.02
Japanese (189)	203	1.19
Korean (6,065)	6,211	36.38
Malaysian (2)	2	0.01
Pakistani (13)	19	0.11
Taiwanese (21)	25	0.15
Thai (6)	6	0.04
Vietnamese (4)	8	0.05
Other Asian, not specified (12)	59	0.35
Assyrian/Chaldean/Syriac	7	0.04
Austrian	19	0.11
Brazilian	150	0.88
Croatian	541	3.17
Cypriot	5	0.03
Czechoslovakian	6	0.04
Danish	17	0.10
Dutch	39	0.23
Eastern European	12	0.07
English	187	1.10
Estonian	20	0.12
Finnish	13	0.08
French, except Basque	89	0.52
French Canadian	52	0.30
German	632	3.70
Greek	610	3.57
Hawaii Native/Pacific Islander:	10	0.06
Polynesian: (3)	5	0.03
Native Hawaiian	2	0.01
Samoan (3)	3	0.02
Other Pac. Isl., not spec. (2)	5	0.03
Hispanic or Latino:	2,813	16.48
Central American:	549	3.22
Costa Rican	8	0.05
Guatemalan	451	2.64
Honduran	7	0.04
Nicaraguan	6	0.04
Panamanian	1	0.01
Salvadoran	65	0.38
Other Central American	11	0.06
Cuban	279	1.63
Dominican Republic	283	1.66
Mexican	86	0.50
Puerto Rican	293	1.72
South American:	604	3.54
Argentinean	25	0.15
Chilean	10	0.06
Colombian	406	2.38
Ecuadorian	85	0.50
Peruvian	35	0.21
Uruguayan	8	0.05
Venezuelan	7	0.04
Other South American	28	0.16
Other Hispanic or Latino	719	4.21
Hungarian	47	0.28
Irish	670	3.92
Israeli	17	0.10
Italian	2,524	14.78
Latvian	12	0.07
Lithuanian	32	0.19
Norwegian	49	0.29
Polish	267	1.56
Russian	170	1.00
Scandinavian	12	0.07
Scotch-Irish	55	0.32
Scottish	51	0.30
Swedish	29	0.17
Swiss	31	0.18
Turkish	139	0.81
Ukrainian	41	0.24
United States or American	294	1.72
West Indian, excl. Hispanic:	56	0.33
Belizean	17	0.10
Haitian	12	0.07
Trinidadian and Tobagonian	7	0.04
West Indian	20	0.12
White:	8,671	50.79
Not Hispanic (6,668)	6,910	40.47
Hispanic (1,573)	1,761	10.31
Yugoslavian	36	0.21

Paramus

Place Type: Borough
County: Bergen
Population: 25,737

Ancestry/Race	Number	%
African American/Black:	340	1.32
Not Hispanic (278)	314	1.22
Hispanic (13)	26	0.10
African, sub-Saharan:	64	0.25
African	25	0.10
Ghanian	9	0.03
Nigerian	30	0.12
Am. Ind. or Alaska Nat., not spec.	22	0.09
Albanian	51	0.20
Alsatian	7	0.03
American Indian tribes, specified:	20	0.08
Apache	1	0.00
Blackfeet	1	0.00
Cherokee (1)	8	0.03
Delaware (1)	1	0.00
Latin American Indians	3	0.01
Seminole	1	0.00
Ute	1	0.00
All other tribes	4	0.02
American Indian tribes, not spec.	4	0.02
Arab:	542	2.11
Arab/Arabic	5	0.02
Egyptian	76	0.30
Iraqi	40	0.16
Lebanese	122	0.47
Moroccan	13	0.05
Palestinian	59	0.23
Syrian	155	0.60
Other Arab	72	0.28
Armenian	445	1.73
Asian:	4,681	18.19
Bangladeshi (3)	3	0.01
Chinese, ex. Taiwanese (885)	929	3.61
Filipino (566)	608	2.36
Indian (1,155)	1,199	4.66
Indonesian (1)	5	0.02
Japanese (308)	326	1.27
Korean (1,238)	1,253	4.87
Malaysian (10)	10	0.04
Pakistani (46)	60	0.23

Notes: 1. Figures in the "Number" column do not add up to the total population due to: a) Ancestry/Race overlap — e.g. persons can report being both White and Irish, b) persons of Hispanic origin can report being any race, c) persons reporting two ancestries are counted in both categories. 2. Numbers in parentheses indicate the number of persons reporting this ancestry/race alone, not in combination with any other ancestry/race. 3. Refer to the Explanation of Data in the front of the book for more detailed information.

Ancestry/Race	Number	%
Taiwanese (123)	132	0.51
Thai (9)	15	0.06
Vietnamese (23)	24	0.09
Other Asian, specified	3	0.01
Other Asian, not specified (38)	114	0.44
Assyrian/Chaldean/Syriac	24	0.09
Austrian	321	1.25
Brazilian	43	0.17
British	33	0.13
Bulgarian	16	0.06
Canadian	13	0.05
Croatian	59	0.23
Cypriot	96	0.37
Czech	94	0.37
Czechoslovakian	32	0.12
Danish	50	0.19
Dutch	319	1.24
Eastern European	101	0.39
English	1,014	3.94
European	62	0.24
Finnish	42	0.16
French, except Basque	313	1.22
French Canadian	86	0.33
German	3,254	12.64
Greek	307	1.19
Hawaii Native/Pacific Islander:	11	0.04
Polynesian:	1	0.00
Native Hawaiian	1	0.00
Other Pac. Isl., not spec. (3)	10	0.04
Hispanic or Latino:	1,253	4.87
Central American:	33	0.13
Costa Rican	8	0.03
Guatemalan	4	0.02
Honduran	6	0.02
Nicaraguan	1	0.00
Panamanian	9	0.03
Salvadoran	3	0.01
Other Central American	2	0.01
Cuban	285	1.11
Dominican Republic	143	0.56
Mexican	60	0.23
Puerto Rican	211	0.82
South American:	256	0.99
Argentinean	20	0.08
Bolivian	6	0.02
Chilean	9	0.03
Colombian	137	0.53
Ecuadorian	37	0.14
Peruvian	24	0.09
Uruguayan	1	0.00
Venezuelan	12	0.05
Other South American	10	0.04
Other Hispanic or Latino	265	1.03
Hungarian	358	1.39
Iranian	425	1.65
Irish	3,710	14.42
Israeli	153	0.59
Italian	6,122	23.79
Latvian	42	0.16
Lithuanian	62	0.24
Macedonian	11	0.04
Norwegian	170	0.66
Polish	1,742	6.77
Portuguese	11	0.04
Romanian	72	0.28
Russian	1,074	4.17
Scandinavian	12	0.05
Scotch-Irish	83	0.32
Scottish	153	0.59
Serbian	30	0.12
Slavic	21	0.08
Slovak	77	0.30
Swedish	157	0.61
Swiss	81	0.31
Turkish	70	0.27
Ukrainian	136	0.53
United States or American	1,072	4.17
Welsh	73	0.28
West Indian, excl. Hispanic:	34	0.13
Barbadian	3	0.01
Jamaican	31	0.12
White:	20,703	80.44
Not Hispanic (19,433)	19,713	76.59
Hispanic (947)	990	3.85
Yugoslavian	45	0.17

Parsippany-Troy Hills

Place Type: Township
County: Morris
Population: 50,649

Ancestry/Race	Number	%
Afghan	361	0.71
African American/Black:	1,817	3.59
Not Hispanic (1,510)	1,726	3.41
Hispanic (64)	91	0.18
African, sub-Saharan:	204	0.40
African	124	0.24
Cape Verdean	6	0.01
Nigerian	22	0.04
South African	44	0.09
Other sub-Saharan African	8	0.02
Am. Ind. or Alaska Nat., not spec.	110	0.22
Albanian	22	0.04
American Indian tribes, specified:	76	0.15
Blackfeet	1	0.00
Cherokee (4)	20	0.04
Chippewa (1)	1	0.00
Colville (1)	1	0.00
Cree	1	0.00
Crow (1)	1	0.00
Delaware	12	0.02
Iroquois (2)	3	0.01
Latin American Indians (4)	17	0.03
Menominee	1	0.00
Navajo	1	0.00
Pueblo (5)	8	0.02
Sioux (1)	3	0.01
Yaqui	3	0.01
All other tribes	3	0.01
American Indian tribes, not spec.	22	0.04
Arab:	623	1.23
Arab/Arabic	50	0.10
Egyptian	244	0.48
Lebanese	131	0.26
Moroccan	8	0.02
Syrian	170	0.34
Other Arab	20	0.04
Armenian	55	0.11
Asian:	9,870	19.49
Bangladeshi (15)	22	0.04
Cambodian (6)	10	0.02
Chinese, ex. Taiwanese (2,714)	2,870	5.67
Filipino (782)	826	1.63
Indian (4,099)	4,251	8.39
Indonesian (10)	10	0.02
Japanese (75)	90	0.18
Korean (469)	497	0.98
Laotian (7)	10	0.02
Malaysian (5)	15	0.03
Pakistani (186)	212	0.42
Sri Lankan (9)	11	0.02
Taiwanese (330)	400	0.79
Thai (14)	20	0.04
Vietnamese (236)	248	0.49
Other Asian, specified (24)	29	0.06
Other Asian, not specified (53)	349	0.69
Australian	6	0.01
Austrian	343	0.68
Belgian	13	0.03
Brazilian	76	0.15
British	197	0.39
Bulgarian	21	0.04
Canadian	114	0.23
Carpatho Rusyn	5	0.01
Celtic	5	0.01
Croatian	40	0.08
Cypriot	8	0.02
Czech	145	0.29
Czechoslovakian	140	0.28
Danish	167	0.33
Dutch	613	1.21
Eastern European	142	0.28
English	2,707	5.34
Estonian	31	0.06
European	235	0.46
Finnish	42	0.08
French, except Basque	781	1.54
French Canadian	218	0.43
German	6,512	12.86
Greek	596	1.18
Guyanese	15	0.03
Hawaii Native/Pacific Islander:	75	0.15
Micronesian: (1)	6	0.01
Guamanian/Chamorro (1)	6	0.01
Polynesian: (3)	8	0.02
Native Hawaiian	2	0.00
Samoan (3)	5	0.01
Other Polynesian	1	0.00
Other Pac. Isl., specified	1	0.00
Other Pac. Isl., not spec. (24)	60	0.12
Hispanic or Latino:	3,535	6.98
Central American:	296	0.58
Costa Rican	48	0.09
Guatemalan	63	0.12
Honduran	110	0.22
Nicaraguan	8	0.02
Panamanian	1	0.00
Salvadoran	50	0.10
Other Central American	16	0.03
Cuban	228	0.45
Dominican Republic	99	0.20
Mexican	221	0.44
Puerto Rican	709	1.40
South American:	1,151	2.27
Argentinean	42	0.08
Bolivian	5	0.01
Chilean	63	0.12
Colombian	739	1.46
Ecuadorian	77	0.15
Paraguayan	5	0.01
Peruvian	132	0.26
Uruguayan	45	0.09
Venezuelan	16	0.03
Other South American	27	0.05
Other Hispanic or Latino	831	1.64
Hungarian	706	1.39
Iranian	38	0.08
Irish	7,700	15.20
Israeli	33	0.07
Italian	10,590	20.91
Latvian	20	0.04
Lithuanian	264	0.52
Luxemburger	7	0.01
Macedonian	193	0.38
Maltese	19	0.04
Northern European	15	0.03
Norwegian	387	0.76
Pennsylvania German	28	0.06
Polish	3,553	7.01
Portuguese	344	0.68
Romanian	206	0.41
Russian	1,781	3.52
Scandinavian	39	0.08
Scotch-Irish	358	0.71
Scottish	647	1.28
Slavic	41	0.08
Slovak	362	0.71
Soviet Union	9	0.02
Swedish	352	0.69
Swiss	156	0.31
Turkish	196	0.39
Ukrainian	468	0.92
United States or American	1,391	2.75
Welsh	265	0.52
West Indian, excl. Hispanic:	413	0.82
Haitian	46	0.09
Jamaican	325	0.64
Trinidadian and Tobagonian	10	0.02

Notes: 1. Figures in the "Number" column do not add up to the total population due to: a) Ancestry/Race overlap — e.g. persons can report being both White and Irish, b) persons of Hispanic origin can report being any race, c) persons reporting two ancestries are counted in both categories. 2. Numbers in parentheses indicate the number of persons reporting this ancestry/race alone, not in combination with any other ancestry/race. 3. Refer to the Explanation of Data in the front of the book for more detailed information.

West Indian	32	0.06
White:	38,553	76.12
Not Hispanic (35,283)	36,029	71.13
Hispanic (2,337)	2,524	4.98
Yugoslavian	44	0.09

Passaic

Place Type: City
County: Passaic
Population: 67,861

Ancestry/Race	Number	%
African American/Black:	10,300	15.18
Not Hispanic (8,042)	8,342	12.29
Hispanic (1,343)	1,958	2.89
African, sub-Saharan:	480	0.71
African	394	0.58
Kenyan	12	0.02
Liberian	23	0.03
Nigerian	36	0.05
Sudanese	5	0.01
Other sub-Saharan African	10	0.01
Am. Ind. or Alaska Nat., not spec.	533	0.79
American Indian tribes, specified:	258	0.38
Apache (1)	1	0.00
Cherokee (1)	14	0.02
Cheyenne (1)	1	0.00
Chickasaw	1	0.00
Delaware (2)	15	0.02
Iroquois (4)	4	0.01
Kiowa	2	0.00
Latin American Indians (148)	195	0.29
Navajo (1)	1	0.00
Pueblo	8	0.01
Seminole (1)	1	0.00
Sioux (1)	1	0.00
All other tribes (2)	14	0.02
American Indian tribes, not spec.	44	0.06
Arab:	531	0.78
Arab/Arabic	51	0.08
Egyptian	107	0.16
Iraqi	55	0.08
Jordanian	6	0.01
Lebanese	45	0.07
Palestinian	207	0.31
Syrian	60	0.09
Asian:	4,181	6.16
Bangladeshi (12)	12	0.02
Chinese, ex. Taiwanese (166)	186	0.27
Filipino (832)	888	1.31
Hmong (4)	4	0.01
Indian (2,493)	2,692	3.97
Indonesian (11)	14	0.02
Japanese (44)	69	0.10
Korean (52)	60	0.09
Pakistani (57)	79	0.12
Taiwanese (6)	7	0.01
Thai (10)	13	0.02
Vietnamese (2)	10	0.01
Other Asian, not specified (36)	147	0.22
Austrian	113	0.17
Basque	23	0.03
Belgian	35	0.05
Brazilian	14	0.02
British	24	0.04
Bulgarian	13	0.02
Canadian	53	0.08
Celtic	22	0.03
Czech	89	0.13
Czechoslovakian	33	0.05
Danish	8	0.01
Dutch	282	0.42
Eastern European	168	0.25
English	432	0.64
European	238	0.35
Finnish	9	0.01
French, except Basque	91	0.13
French Canadian	37	0.05
German	634	0.93
Greek	124	0.18
Guyanese	112	0.17
Hawaii Native/Pacific Islander:	110	0.16
Polynesian: (5)	19	0.03
Native Hawaiian (5)	17	0.03
Samoan	2	0.00
Other Pac. Isl., not spec. (24)	91	0.13
Hispanic or Latino:	42,387	62.46
Central American:	809	1.19
Costa Rican	49	0.07
Guatemalan	163	0.24
Honduran	301	0.44
Nicaraguan	34	0.05
Panamanian	17	0.03
Salvadoran	218	0.32
Other Central American	27	0.04
Cuban	654	0.96
Dominican Republic	8,865	13.06
Mexican	13,346	19.67
Puerto Rican	9,122	13.44
South American:	3,796	5.59
Argentinean	56	0.08
Bolivian	103	0.15
Chilean	42	0.06
Colombian	1,260	1.86
Ecuadorian	512	0.75
Paraguayan	1	0.00
Peruvian	1,643	2.42
Uruguayan	27	0.04
Venezuelan	44	0.06
Other South American	108	0.16
Other Hispanic or Latino	5,795	8.54
Hungarian	620	0.91
Icelander	9	0.01
Iranian	56	0.08
Irish	714	1.05
Israeli	53	0.08
Italian	1,785	2.63
Lithuanian	36	0.05
Macedonian	8	0.01
Polish	2,350	3.46
Portuguese	21	0.03
Romanian	20	0.03
Russian	524	0.77
Scotch-Irish	104	0.15
Scottish	99	0.15
Serbian	42	0.06
Slavic	17	0.03
Slovak	188	0.28
Slovene	6	0.01
Soviet Union	8	0.01
Swedish	52	0.08
Swiss	13	0.02
Turkish	36	0.05
Ukrainian	454	0.67
United States or American	1,574	2.32
Welsh	36	0.05
West Indian, excl. Hispanic:	589	0.87
Belizean	40	0.06
Bermudan	10	0.01
British West Indian	13	0.02
Jamaican	412	0.61
Trinidadian and Tobagonian	45	0.07
West Indian	69	0.10
White:	26,477	39.02
Not Hispanic (12,405)	13,149	19.38
Hispanic (11,639)	13,328	19.64
Yugoslavian	74	0.11

Paterson

Place Type: City
County: Passaic
Population: 149,222

Ancestry/Race	Number	%
Acadian/Cajun	8	0.01
African American/Black:	51,663	34.62
Not Hispanic (46,882)	48,404	32.44
Hispanic (2,213)	3,259	2.18
African, sub-Saharan:	1,930	1.29
African	1,733	1.16
Ethiopian	18	0.01
Ghanian	47	0.03
Kenyan	23	0.02
Liberian	56	0.04
Nigerian	53	0.04
Alaska Native tribes, specified:	4	0.00
Alaska Athabascan (1)	1	0.00
Aleut	1	0.00
Tlingit-Haida (1)	2	0.00
Am. Ind. or Alaska Nat., not spec.	918	0.62
Albanian	255	0.17
American Indian tribes, specified:	532	0.36
Apache (3)	3	0.00
Blackfeet (11)	41	0.03
Cherokee (12)	76	0.05
Chickasaw (6)	7	0.00
Chippewa (1)	1	0.00
Creek	1	0.00
Crow	4	0.00
Delaware (12)	26	0.02
Iroquois (1)	9	0.01
Latin American Indians (187)	280	0.19
Lumbee (1)	2	0.00
Navajo (2)	2	0.00
Pueblo (19)	45	0.03
Seminole	4	0.00
Sioux	2	0.00
Yaqui	1	0.00
All other tribes (11)	29	0.02
American Indian tribes, not spec.	91	0.06
Arab:	2,634	1.77
Arab/Arabic	1,171	0.78
Egyptian	54	0.04
Jordanian	165	0.11
Lebanese	181	0.12
Moroccan	115	0.08
Palestinian	556	0.37
Syrian	329	0.22
Other Arab	63	0.04
Armenian	78	0.05
Asian:	3,832	2.57
Bangladeshi (396)	729	0.49
Chinese, ex. Taiwanese (182)	210	0.14
Filipino (387)	433	0.29
Indian (1,422)	1,775	1.19
Japanese (36)	66	0.04
Korean (49)	57	0.04
Laotian	7	0.00
Malaysian	6	0.00
Pakistani (57)	94	0.06
Sri Lankan (2)	2	0.00
Taiwanese (6)	6	0.00
Thai (18)	19	0.01
Vietnamese (38)	47	0.03
Other Asian, specified	14	0.01
Other Asian, not specified (99)	367	0.25
Assyrian/Chaldean/Syriac	6	0.00
Australian	13	0.01
Austrian	63	0.04
Belgian	76	0.05
Brazilian	83	0.06
British	46	0.03
Canadian	55	0.04
Croatian	17	0.01
Czech	20	0.01
Czechoslovakian	54	0.04
Danish	38	0.03
Dutch	675	0.45
Eastern European	10	0.01
English	1,106	0.74
European	92	0.06
French, except Basque	277	0.19
French Canadian	40	0.03
German	1,718	1.15
Greek	148	0.10
Guyanese	193	0.13
Hawaii Native/Pacific Islander:	504	0.34
Melanesian:	4	0.00

Notes: 1. Figures in the "Number" column do not add up to the total population due to: a) Ancestry/Race overlap — e.g. persons can report being both White and Irish, b) persons of Hispanic origin can report being any race, c) persons reporting two ancestries are counted in both categories. 2. Numbers in parentheses indicate the number of persons reporting this ancestry/race alone, not in combination with any other ancestry/race. 3. Refer to the Explanation of Data in the front of the book for more detailed information.

Ancestry/Race	Number	%
Fijian	4	0.00
Micronesian: (10)	21	0.01
Guamanian/Chamorro (10)	20	0.01
Other Micronesian	1	0.00
Polynesian: (28)	58	0.04
Native Hawaiian (10)	24	0.02
Samoan (18)	34	0.02
Other Pac. Isl., specified	14	0.01
Other Pac. Isl., not spec. (42)	407	0.27
Hispanic or Latino:	74,774	50.11
Central American:	2,284	1.53
Costa Rican	789	0.53
Guatemalan	464	0.31
Honduran	177	0.12
Nicaraguan	177	0.12
Panamanian	47	0.03
Salvadoran	514	0.34
Other Central American	116	0.08
Cuban	858	0.57
Dominican Republic	15,331	10.27
Mexican	5,004	3.35
Puerto Rican	24,013	16.09
South American:	13,852	9.28
Argentinean	213	0.14
Bolivian	63	0.04
Chilean	95	0.06
Colombian	5,110	3.42
Ecuadorian	778	0.52
Paraguayan	6	0.00
Peruvian	7,038	4.72
Uruguayan	71	0.05
Venezuelan	248	0.17
Other South American	230	0.15
Other Hispanic or Latino	13,432	9.00
Hungarian	224	0.15
Irish	2,422	1.62
Israeli	23	0.02
Italian	6,955	4.66
Lithuanian	102	0.07
Macedonian	281	0.19
Norwegian	88	0.06
Pennsylvania German	11	0.01
Polish	943	0.63
Portuguese	82	0.05
Romanian	124	0.08
Russian	344	0.23
Scandinavian	9	0.01
Scotch-Irish	136	0.09
Scottish	236	0.16
Serbian	82	0.05
Slavic	14	0.01
Slovak	41	0.03
Swedish	84	0.06
Swiss	89	0.06
Turkish	842	0.56
Ukrainian	226	0.15
United States or American	4,732	3.17
Welsh	20	0.01
West Indian, excl. Hispanic:	5,479	3.67
Bahamian	25	0.02
Barbadian	55	0.04
Belizean	7	0.00
Bermudan	11	0.01
British West Indian	113	0.08
Dutch West Indian	7	0.00
Haitian	266	0.18
Jamaican	4,776	3.20
Trinidadian and Tobagonian	76	0.05
U.S. Virgin Islander	27	0.02
West Indian	116	0.08
White:	52,281	35.04
Not Hispanic (19,765)	22,421	15.03
Hispanic (26,148)	29,860	20.01
Yugoslavian	273	0.18

Pemberton

Place Type: Township
County: Burlington
Population: 28,691

Ancestry/Race	Number	%
African American/Black:	7,247	25.26
Not Hispanic (6,410)	6,909	24.08
Hispanic (222)	338	1.18
African, sub-Saharan:	236	0.82
African	212	0.74
Ghanian	6	0.02
Liberian	5	0.02
Nigerian	13	0.05
Alaska Native tribes, specified:	1	0.00
Eskimo (1)	1	0.00
Alaska Native tribes, not specified	1	0.00
Am. Ind. or Alaska Nat., not spec.	135	0.47
American Indian tribes, specified:	237	0.83
Apache	7	0.02
Blackfeet (1)	18	0.06
Cherokee (27)	111	0.39
Cheyenne (1)	1	0.00
Chickasaw	1	0.00
Chippewa	2	0.01
Choctaw (1)	5	0.02
Comanche (1)	1	0.00
Delaware (10)	12	0.04
Iroquois (13)	17	0.06
Latin American Indians (6)	10	0.03
Navajo	2	0.01
Osage (1)	1	0.00
Seminole	4	0.01
Shoshone (1)	1	0.00
Sioux (3)	14	0.05
All other tribes (23)	30	0.10
American Indian tribes, not spec.	12	0.04
Arab:	16	0.06
Arab/Arabic	5	0.02
Moroccan	11	0.04
Armenian	12	0.04
Asian:	1,351	4.71
Bangladeshi (4)	4	0.01
Chinese, ex. Taiwanese (36)	61	0.21
Filipino (188)	290	1.01
Indian (73)	87	0.30
Indonesian (1)	1	0.00
Japanese (138)	270	0.94
Korean (348)	432	1.51
Laotian (2)	2	0.01
Malaysian (1)	3	0.01
Pakistani (3)	7	0.02
Taiwanese	3	0.01
Thai (54)	82	0.29
Vietnamese (29)	48	0.17
Other Asian, specified (4)	7	0.02
Other Asian, not specified (22)	54	0.19
Austrian	64	0.22
Belgian	9	0.03
British	85	0.30
Canadian	21	0.07
Croatian	14	0.05
Czech	52	0.18
Czechoslovakian	22	0.08
Danish	103	0.36
Dutch	462	1.61
English	2,113	7.38
European	115	0.40
Finnish	33	0.12
French, except Basque	672	2.35
French Canadian	142	0.50
German	4,616	16.11
German Russian	21	0.07
Greek	50	0.17
Guyanese	46	0.16
Hawaii Native/Pacific Islander:	64	0.22
Micronesian: (4)	6	0.02
Guamanian/Chamorro (4)	6	0.02
Polynesian: (14)	38	0.13
Native Hawaiian (10)	30	0.10
Samoan (3)	6	0.02
Other Polynesian (1)	2	0.01
Other Pac. Isl., specified	1	0.00
Other Pac. Isl., not spec. (5)	19	0.07
Hispanic or Latino:	2,477	8.63
Central American:	131	0.46
Costa Rican	2	0.01
Guatemalan	5	0.02
Honduran	3	0.01
Nicaraguan	1	0.00
Panamanian	107	0.37
Salvadoran	13	0.05
Cuban	44	0.15
Dominican Republic	61	0.21
Mexican	225	0.78
Puerto Rican	1,560	5.44
South American:	75	0.26
Argentinean	5	0.02
Chilean	3	0.01
Colombian	23	0.08
Ecuadorian	23	0.08
Peruvian	9	0.03
Uruguayan	3	0.01
Venezuelan	7	0.02
Other South American	2	0.01
Other Hispanic or Latino	381	1.33
Hungarian	289	1.01
Irish	4,440	15.50
Italian	2,532	8.84
Lithuanian	100	0.35
Northern European	9	0.03
Norwegian	99	0.35
Pennsylvania German	72	0.25
Polish	1,369	4.78
Portuguese	52	0.18
Romanian	62	0.22
Russian	119	0.42
Scandinavian	8	0.03
Scotch-Irish	264	0.92
Scottish	450	1.57
Slavic	8	0.03
Slovak	61	0.21
Swedish	73	0.25
Swiss	33	0.12
Turkish	44	0.15
Ukrainian	115	0.40
United States or American	1,947	6.80
Welsh	151	0.53
West Indian, excl. Hispanic:	101	0.35
Barbadian	4	0.01
Belizean	29	0.10
British West Indian	9	0.03
Dutch West Indian	6	0.02
Jamaican	22	0.08
Trinidadian and Tobagonian	28	0.10
West Indian	3	0.01
White:	19,860	69.22
Not Hispanic (17,701)	18,427	64.23
Hispanic (1,245)	1,433	4.99
Yugoslavian	12	0.04

Pennsauken

Place Type: Census Designated Place
County: Camden
Population: 35,737

Ancestry/Race	Number	%
Afghan	36	0.10
African American/Black:	9,048	25.32
Not Hispanic (8,396)	8,684	24.30
Hispanic (245)	364	1.02
African, sub-Saharan:	400	1.12
African	279	0.78
Ghanian	10	0.03
Nigerian	13	0.04
Sierra Leonean	90	0.25
Other sub-Saharan African	8	0.02
Am. Ind. or Alaska Nat., not spec.	111	0.31

Notes: 1. Figures in the "Number" column do not add up to the total population due to: a) Ancestry/Race overlap — e.g. persons can report being both White and Irish, b) persons of Hispanic origin can report being any race, c) persons reporting two ancestries are counted in both categories. 2. Numbers in parentheses indicate the number of persons reporting this ancestry/race alone, not in combination with any other ancestry/race. 3. Refer to the Explanation of Data in the front of the book for more detailed information.

Albanian	13	0.04
American Indian tribes, specified:	148	0.41
Apache (1)	5	0.01
Blackfeet	11	0.03
Cherokee (5)	33	0.09
Choctaw	7	0.02
Delaware	5	0.01
Iroquois (3)	9	0.03
Latin American Indians (4)	8	0.02
Navajo (1)	1	0.00
Pueblo	1	0.00
Seminole	3	0.01
Shoshone	2	0.01
Sioux (2)	6	0.02
All other tribes (45)	57	0.16
American Indian tribes, not spec.	15	0.04
Arab:	49	0.14
Lebanese	9	0.03
Moroccan	36	0.10
Palestinian	4	0.01
Armenian	20	0.06
Asian:	1,900	5.32
Bangladeshi	5	0.01
Cambodian (76)	122	0.34
Chinese, ex. Taiwanese (218)	250	0.70
Filipino (212)	262	0.73
Indian (99)	136	0.38
Japanese (14)	23	0.06
Korean (76)	89	0.25
Laotian (10)	10	0.03
Pakistani (23)	35	0.10
Sri Lankan (1)	1	0.00
Taiwanese (4)	6	0.02
Thai (4)	5	0.01
Vietnamese (825)	883	2.47
Other Asian, specified (1)	2	0.01
Other Asian, not specified (42)	71	0.20
Austrian	97	0.27
Belgian	14	0.04
British	33	0.09
Canadian	25	0.07
Croatian	7	0.02
Czech	70	0.20
Czechoslovakian	19	0.05
Danish	81	0.23
Dutch	230	0.64
Eastern European	25	0.07
English	2,425	6.79
Estonian	7	0.02
European	81	0.23
Finnish	41	0.11
French, except Basque	388	1.09
French Canadian	44	0.12
German	5,098	14.28
Greek	230	0.64
Hawaii Native/Pacific Islander:	35	0.10
Micronesian: (1)	1	0.00
Guamanian/Chamorro (1)	1	0.00
Polynesian: (1)	8	0.02
Native Hawaiian (1)	7	0.02
Samoan	1	0.00
Other Pac. Isl., specified	1	0.00
Other Pac. Isl., not spec. (5)	25	0.07
Hispanic or Latino:	5,126	14.34
Central American:	273	0.76
Costa Rican	5	0.01
Guatemalan	18	0.05
Honduran	10	0.03
Nicaraguan	177	0.50
Panamanian	20	0.06
Salvadoran	26	0.07
Other Central American	17	0.05
Cuban	32	0.09
Dominican Republic	252	0.71
Mexican	218	0.61
Puerto Rican	3,629	10.15
South American:	91	0.25
Bolivian	1	0.00
Chilean	4	0.01
Colombian	40	0.11
Ecuadorian	14	0.04
Peruvian	11	0.03
Uruguayan	1	0.00
Venezuelan	15	0.04
Other South American	5	0.01
Other Hispanic or Latino	631	1.77
Hungarian	202	0.57
Iranian	14	0.04
Irish	6,567	18.39
Israeli	6	0.02
Italian	5,118	14.33
Latvian	21	0.06
Lithuanian	168	0.47
Norwegian	129	0.36
Pennsylvania German	38	0.11
Polish	2,007	5.62
Portuguese	12	0.03
Romanian	5	0.01
Russian	288	0.81
Scotch-Irish	357	1.00
Scottish	332	0.93
Slavic	34	0.10
Slovak	25	0.07
Swedish	187	0.52
Swiss	109	0.31
Ukrainian	179	0.50
United States or American	934	2.62
Welsh	189	0.53
West Indian, excl. Hispanic:	192	0.54
Bermudan	10	0.03
Haitian	16	0.04
Jamaican	131	0.37
U.S. Virgin Islander	14	0.04
West Indian	21	0.06
White:	22,070	61.76
Not Hispanic (19,845)	20,202	56.53
Hispanic (1,634)	1,868	5.23
Yugoslavian	13	0.04

Pennsville

Place Type: Township
County: Salem
Population: 13,194

Ancestry/Race	Number	%
Afghan	9	0.07
African American/Black:	150	1.14
Not Hispanic (110)	125	0.95
Hispanic (17)	25	0.19
African, sub-Saharan:	29	0.22
African	29	0.22
Am. Ind. or Alaska Nat., not spec.	13	0.10
Albanian	10	0.08
American Indian tribes, specified:	52	0.39
Blackfeet (1)	3	0.02
Cherokee (4)	32	0.24
Chippewa	1	0.01
Comanche	1	0.01
Delaware (2)	6	0.05
Latin American Indians (1)	1	0.01
Navajo (1)	1	0.01
Pueblo (2)	2	0.02
Sioux	2	0.02
All other tribes (2)	3	0.02
American Indian tribes, not spec.	6	0.05
Arab:	12	0.09
Lebanese	6	0.05
Palestinian	6	0.05
Armenian	22	0.17
Asian:	156	1.18
Bangladeshi (1)	1	0.01
Cambodian (1)	1	0.01
Chinese, ex. Taiwanese (23)	31	0.23
Filipino (18)	27	0.20
Indian (34)	34	0.26
Japanese (10)	16	0.12
Korean (22)	25	0.19
Pakistani (11)	11	0.08
Thai (2)	4	0.03
Vietnamese (2)	2	0.02
Other Asian, not specified (2)	4	0.03
Austrian	22	0.17
British	48	0.36
Canadian	15	0.11
Celtic	5	0.04
Czech	21	0.16
Czechoslovakian	34	0.26
Danish	22	0.17
Dutch	334	2.52
Eastern European	7	0.05
English	2,261	17.07
European	57	0.43
French, except Basque	346	2.61
French Canadian	123	0.93
German	2,928	22.11
Greek	154	1.16
Hawaii Native/Pacific Islander:	3	0.02
Polynesian: (2)	3	0.02
Native Hawaiian (1)	1	0.01
Samoan (1)	2	0.02
Hispanic or Latino:	211	1.60
Central American:	5	0.04
Guatemalan	4	0.03
Panamanian	1	0.01
Cuban	6	0.05
Mexican	45	0.34
Puerto Rican	102	0.77
South American:	14	0.11
Argentinean	1	0.01
Colombian	8	0.06
Ecuadorian	1	0.01
Uruguayan	1	0.01
Venezuelan	2	0.02
Other South American	1	0.01
Other Hispanic or Latino	39	0.30
Hungarian	90	0.68
Irish	2,911	21.98
Italian	1,805	13.63
Latvian	18	0.14
Lithuanian	30	0.23
Norwegian	75	0.57
Pennsylvania German	62	0.47
Polish	638	4.82
Portuguese	57	0.43
Romanian	26	0.20
Russian	45	0.34
Scotch-Irish	178	1.34
Scottish	293	2.21
Slavic	12	0.09
Slovak	13	0.10
Swedish	169	1.28
Swiss	13	0.10
Turkish	25	0.19
Ukrainian	80	0.60
United States or American	959	7.24
Welsh	189	1.43
White:	12,860	97.47
Not Hispanic (12,625)	12,715	96.37
Hispanic (131)	145	1.10

Pequannock

Place Type: Township
County: Morris
Population: 13,888

Ancestry/Race	Number	%
African American/Black:	62	0.45
Not Hispanic (39)	57	0.41
Hispanic (2)	5	0.04
Am. Ind. or Alaska Nat., not spec.	12	0.09
American Indian tribes, specified:	19	0.14
Cherokee (1)	7	0.05
Chippewa (1)	2	0.01
Delaware (1)	1	0.01
Latin American Indians (5)	5	0.04
Navajo (1)	1	0.01
Sioux	1	0.01
All other tribes (2)	2	0.01

Notes: 1. Figures in the "Number" column do not add up to the total population due to: a) Ancestry/Race overlap — e.g. persons can report being both White and Irish, b) persons of Hispanic origin can report being any race, c) persons reporting two ancestries are counted in both categories. 2. Numbers in parentheses indicate the number of persons reporting this ancestry/race alone, not in combination with any other ancestry/race. 3. Refer to the Explanation of Data in the front of the book for more detailed information.

Ancestry/Race	Number	%
Arab:	182	1.31
Arab/Arabic	39	0.28
Egyptian	8	0.06
Lebanese	52	0.37
Syrian	83	0.60
Armenian	90	0.65
Asian:	299	2.15
Chinese, ex. Taiwanese (45)	54	0.39
Filipino (88)	96	0.69
Indian (59)	69	0.50
Japanese (3)	7	0.05
Korean (40)	41	0.30
Pakistani (4)	4	0.03
Taiwanese	2	0.01
Thai (3)	3	0.02
Vietnamese (12)	12	0.09
Other Asian, not specified (7)	11	0.08
Australian	15	0.11
Austrian	125	0.90
Belgian	21	0.15
Brazilian	46	0.33
British	85	0.61
Canadian	18	0.13
Croatian	15	0.11
Czech	139	1.00
Czechoslovakian	47	0.34
Danish	66	0.48
Dutch	1,141	8.22
Eastern European	16	0.12
English	1,250	9.00
European	16	0.12
French, except Basque	392	2.82
French Canadian	62	0.45
German	2,464	17.74
Greek	130	0.94
Hispanic or Latino:	408	2.94
Central American:	38	0.27
Costa Rican	26	0.19
Guatemalan	5	0.04
Honduran	2	0.01
Other Central American	5	0.04
Cuban	42	0.30
Dominican Republic	18	0.13
Mexican	29	0.21
Puerto Rican	144	1.04
South American:	55	0.40
Argentinean	9	0.06
Colombian	19	0.14
Ecuadorian	8	0.06
Peruvian	13	0.09
Uruguayan	3	0.02
Venezuelan	1	0.01
Other South American	2	0.01
Other Hispanic or Latino	82	0.59
Hungarian	231	1.66
Irish	3,677	26.48
Italian	4,049	29.15
Lithuanian	35	0.25
Macedonian	82	0.59
Northern European	9	0.06
Norwegian	238	1.71
Pennsylvania German	8	0.06
Polish	959	6.91
Portuguese	42	0.30
Romanian	10	0.07
Russian	131	0.94
Scandinavian	36	0.26
Scotch-Irish	231	1.66
Scottish	250	1.80
Serbian	10	0.07
Slavic	10	0.07
Slovak	70	0.50
Swedish	82	0.59
Swiss	138	0.99
Turkish	29	0.21
Ukrainian	42	0.30
United States or American	453	3.26
Welsh	57	0.41
White:	13,487	97.11
Not Hispanic (13,099)	13,154	94.71
Hispanic (317)	333	2.40
Yugoslavian	20	0.14

Perth Amboy

Place Type: City
County: Middlesex
Population: 47,303

Ancestry/Race	Number	%
African American/Black:	5,400	11.42
Not Hispanic (3,790)	3,980	8.41
Hispanic (959)	1,420	3.00
African, sub-Saharan:	268	0.57
African	189	0.40
Cape Verdean	4	0.01
Ghanian	62	0.13
Nigerian	5	0.01
Other sub-Saharan African	8	0.02
Alaska Native tribes, specified:	1	0.00
Alaska Athabascan (1)	1	0.00
Am. Ind. or Alaska Nat., not spec.	267	0.56
American Indian tribes, specified:	238	0.50
Apache (1)	1	0.00
Blackfeet	5	0.01
Cherokee	12	0.03
Choctaw	1	0.00
Creek	7	0.01
Iroquois (1)	1	0.00
Latin American Indians (83)	152	0.32
Navajo (1)	1	0.00
Pueblo (10)	36	0.08
Sioux	3	0.01
All other tribes (11)	19	0.04
American Indian tribes, not spec.	32	0.07
Arab:	7	0.01
Egyptian	7	0.01
Asian:	847	1.79
Bangladeshi (4)	4	0.01
Chinese, ex. Taiwanese (136)	146	0.31
Filipino (197)	212	0.45
Indian (232)	278	0.59
Indonesian (5)	6	0.01
Japanese (8)	13	0.03
Korean (33)	41	0.09
Laotian (2)	2	0.00
Malaysian (10)	10	0.02
Pakistani (12)	13	0.03
Thai (5)	5	0.01
Vietnamese (60)	66	0.14
Other Asian, not specified (19)	51	0.11
Australian	4	0.01
Austrian	33	0.07
Basque	3	0.01
Belgian	7	0.01
Brazilian	147	0.31
British	14	0.03
Carpatho Rusyn	12	0.03
Czech	13	0.03
Czechoslovakian	76	0.16
Danish	86	0.18
Dutch	51	0.11
Eastern European	18	0.04
English	353	0.75
European	26	0.05
French, except Basque	130	0.27
French Canadian	19	0.04
German	637	1.35
Greek	143	0.30
Guyanese	12	0.03
Hawaii Native/Pacific Islander:	117	0.25
Micronesian: (7)	9	0.02
Guamanian/Chamorro (7)	9	0.02
Polynesian: (17)	27	0.06
Native Hawaiian (5)	12	0.03
Samoan (11)	14	0.03
Other Polynesian (1)	1	0.00
Other Pac. Isl., not spec. (36)	81	0.17
Hispanic or Latino:	33,033	69.83
Central American:	768	1.62
Costa Rican	81	0.17
Guatemalan	81	0.17
Honduran	227	0.48
Nicaraguan	14	0.03
Panamanian	16	0.03
Salvadoran	317	0.67
Other Central American	32	0.07
Cuban	918	1.94
Dominican Republic	8,897	18.81
Mexican	3,056	6.46
Puerto Rican	13,145	27.79
South American:	1,955	4.13
Argentinean	166	0.35
Bolivian	16	0.03
Chilean	39	0.08
Colombian	382	0.81
Ecuadorian	166	0.35
Paraguayan	1	0.00
Peruvian	1,041	2.20
Uruguayan	31	0.07
Venezuelan	53	0.11
Other South American	60	0.13
Other Hispanic or Latino	4,294	9.08
Hungarian	899	1.90
Iranian	43	0.09
Irish	924	1.95
Israeli	6	0.01
Italian	1,393	2.94
Lithuanian	98	0.21
Norwegian	76	0.16
Polish	2,435	5.15
Portuguese	811	1.71
Romanian	7	0.01
Russian	98	0.21
Scandinavian	22	0.05
Scotch-Irish	58	0.12
Scottish	29	0.06
Slavic	79	0.17
Slovak	626	1.32
Swedish	40	0.08
Turkish	56	0.12
Ukrainian	350	0.74
United States or American	809	1.71
Welsh	63	0.13
West Indian, excl. Hispanic:	645	1.36
Barbadian	20	0.04
Belizean	15	0.03
British West Indian	21	0.04
Haitian	84	0.18
Jamaican	294	0.62
Trinidadian and Tobagonian	97	0.21
U.S. Virgin Islander	15	0.03
West Indian	89	0.19
Other West Indian	10	0.02
White:	24,089	50.92
Not Hispanic (8,919)	9,428	19.93
Hispanic (13,032)	14,661	30.99

Phillipsburg

Place Type: Town
County: Warren
Population: 15,166

Ancestry/Race	Number	%
African American/Black:	642	4.23
Not Hispanic (502)	601	3.96
Hispanic (25)	41	0.27
African, sub-Saharan:	64	0.42
African	37	0.24
Ethiopian	27	0.18
Alaska Native tribes, specified:	2	0.01
Eskimo	2	0.01
Am. Ind. or Alaska Nat., not spec.	42	0.28
American Indian tribes, specified:	28	0.18
Cherokee (1)	10	0.07
Creek	6	0.04
Delaware (2)	6	0.04
Iroquois	4	0.03
Tohono O'Odham (1)	1	0.01

Notes: 1. Figures in the "Number" column do not add up to the total population due to: a) Ancestry/Race overlap — e.g. persons can report being both White and Irish, b) persons of Hispanic origin can report being any race, c) persons reporting two ancestries are counted in both categories. 2. Numbers in parentheses indicate the number of persons reporting this ancestry/race alone, not in combination with any other ancestry/race. 3. Refer to the Explanation of Data in the front of the book for more detailed information.

Ancestry/Race	Number	%
All other tribes (1)	1	0.01
American Indian tribes, not spec.	3	0.02
Arab:	39	0.26
Lebanese	26	0.17
Syrian	13	0.09
Armenian	6	0.04
Asian:	162	1.07
Chinese, ex. Taiwanese (10)	11	0.07
Filipino (23)	30	0.20
Indian (51)	60	0.40
Japanese (2)	9	0.06
Korean (9)	9	0.06
Laotian (3)	3	0.02
Pakistani (1)	1	0.01
Sri Lankan (5)	5	0.03
Thai (2)	5	0.03
Vietnamese (18)	20	0.13
Other Asian, not specified (1)	9	0.06
Austrian	11	0.07
British	27	0.18
Canadian	29	0.19
Czech	59	0.39
Czechoslovakian	43	0.28
Danish	41	0.27
Dutch	938	6.18
English	1,273	8.39
Finnish	12	0.08
French, except Basque	311	2.05
French Canadian	77	0.51
German	3,607	23.78
Greek	21	0.14
Hawaii Native/Pacific Islander:	5	0.03
Polynesian: (2)	2	0.01
Samoan (2)	2	0.01
Other Pac. Isl., not spec.	3	0.02
Hispanic or Latino:	816	5.38
Central American:	63	0.42
Costa Rican	23	0.15
Guatemalan	12	0.08
Honduran	3	0.02
Nicaraguan	2	0.01
Panamanian	3	0.02
Salvadoran	6	0.04
Other Central American	14	0.09
Cuban	30	0.20
Dominican Republic	10	0.07
Mexican	120	0.79
Puerto Rican	374	2.47
South American:	79	0.52
Chilean	5	0.03
Colombian	27	0.18
Ecuadorian	11	0.07
Peruvian	28	0.18
Uruguayan	5	0.03
Venezuelan	3	0.02
Other Hispanic or Latino	140	0.92
Hungarian	671	4.42
Irish	2,775	18.30
Italian	2,617	17.26
Lithuanian	123	0.81
Norwegian	31	0.20
Pennsylvania German	251	1.66
Polish	1,000	6.59
Portuguese	69	0.45
Russian	134	0.88
Scandinavian	10	0.07
Scotch-Irish	201	1.33
Scottish	151	1.00
Slavic	19	0.13
Slovak	96	0.63
Soviet Union	9	0.06
Swedish	94	0.62
Swiss	41	0.27
Ukrainian	97	0.64
United States or American	600	3.96
Welsh	220	1.45
West Indian, excl. Hispanic:	61	0.40
Haitian	23	0.15
Jamaican	38	0.25
White:	14,148	93.29
Not Hispanic (13,495)	13,661	90.08
Hispanic (433)	487	3.21

Pine Hill

Place Type: Borough
County: Camden
Population: 10,880

Ancestry/Race	Number	%
African American/Black:	2,108	19.38
Not Hispanic (1,948)	2,045	18.80
Hispanic (48)	63	0.58
African, sub-Saharan:	115	1.05
African	103	0.94
Sierra Leonean	12	0.11
Alaska Native tribes, specified:	1	0.01
Alaska Athabascan (1)	1	0.01
Am. Ind. or Alaska Nat., not spec.	37	0.34
American Indian tribes, specified:	43	0.40
Blackfeet (4)	8	0.07
Cherokee (2)	8	0.07
Chippewa	2	0.02
Delaware (3)	4	0.04
Iroquois (1)	2	0.02
Navajo	1	0.01
Seminole	4	0.04
Sioux	4	0.04
All other tribes (5)	10	0.09
American Indian tribes, not spec.	4	0.04
Armenian	12	0.11
Asian:	189	1.74
Chinese, ex. Taiwanese (48)	53	0.49
Filipino (53)	68	0.63
Indian (16)	22	0.20
Japanese (1)	4	0.04
Korean (12)	15	0.14
Pakistani (6)	6	0.06
Sri Lankan (3)	3	0.03
Vietnamese (11)	13	0.12
Other Asian, not specified (3)	5	0.05
Austrian	4	0.04
Canadian	12	0.11
Croatian	36	0.33
Czech	36	0.33
Czechoslovakian	9	0.08
Danish	22	0.20
Dutch	153	1.40
English	959	8.78
French, except Basque	223	2.04
French Canadian	18	0.16
German	2,161	19.79
Greek	82	0.75
Hawaii Native/Pacific Islander:	7	0.06
Polynesian: (1)	5	0.05
Native Hawaiian (1)	4	0.04
Samoan	1	0.01
Other Pac. Isl., not spec. (1)	2	0.02
Hispanic or Latino:	396	3.64
Central American:	14	0.13
Costa Rican	1	0.01
Honduran	2	0.02
Panamanian	5	0.05
Salvadoran	6	0.06
Cuban	16	0.15
Dominican Republic	5	0.05
Mexican	47	0.43
Puerto Rican	252	2.32
South American:	17	0.16
Argentinean	4	0.04
Chilean	10	0.09
Colombian	2	0.02
Other South American	1	0.01
Other Hispanic or Latino	45	0.41
Hungarian	44	0.40
Irish	2,868	26.27
Italian	2,408	22.05
Lithuanian	33	0.30
Norwegian	8	0.07
Pennsylvania German	20	0.18
Polish	706	6.47
Portuguese	11	0.10
Russian	76	0.70
Scotch-Irish	106	0.97
Scottish	79	0.72
Slovak	30	0.27
Swedish	71	0.65
Ukrainian	80	0.73
United States or American	332	3.04
Welsh	33	0.30
West Indian, excl. Hispanic:	56	0.51
Trinidadian and Tobagonian	56	0.51
White:	8,522	78.33
Not Hispanic (8,165)	8,301	76.30
Hispanic (190)	221	2.03
Yugoslavian	40	0.37

Piscataway

Place Type: Township
County: Middlesex
Population: 50,482

Ancestry/Race	Number	%
African American/Black:	10,776	21.35
Not Hispanic (9,985)	10,419	20.64
Hispanic (269)	357	0.71
African, sub-Saharan:	996	1.97
African	517	1.02
Cape Verdean	14	0.03
Ghanian	43	0.09
Liberian	23	0.05
Nigerian	229	0.45
Sierra Leonean	74	0.15
South African	44	0.09
Other sub-Saharan African	52	0.10
Alaska Native tribes, specified:	1	0.00
Eskimo (1)	1	0.00
Am. Ind. or Alaska Nat., not spec.	176	0.35
Albanian	39	0.08
American Indian tribes, specified:	152	0.30
Apache	1	0.00
Blackfeet	16	0.03
Cherokee (2)	49	0.10
Chickasaw	1	0.00
Chippewa	3	0.01
Choctaw	3	0.01
Cree (1)	2	0.00
Creek (1)	1	0.00
Delaware (1)	11	0.02
Iroquois (2)	9	0.02
Latin American Indians (10)	16	0.03
Lumbee	3	0.01
Menominee	1	0.00
Navajo	3	0.01
Paiute	1	0.00
Seminole	2	0.00
Sioux (1)	5	0.01
Ute	1	0.00
All other tribes (14)	24	0.05
American Indian tribes, not spec.	22	0.04
Arab:	324	0.64
Egyptian	153	0.30
Jordanian	49	0.10
Lebanese	80	0.16
Palestinian	6	0.01
Syrian	27	0.05
Other Arab	9	0.02
Armenian	6	0.01
Asian:	13,167	26.08
Bangladeshi (28)	28	0.06
Cambodian (3)	4	0.01
Chinese, ex. Taiwanese (2,357)	2,478	4.91
Filipino (2,100)	2,235	4.43
Indian (6,067)	6,307	12.49
Indonesian (19)	30	0.06
Japanese (43)	69	0.14
Korean (638)	675	1.34
Laotian (3)	3	0.01
Malaysian (9)	11	0.02

Notes: 1. Figures in the "Number" column do not add up to the total population due to: a) Ancestry/Race overlap — e.g. persons can report being both White and Irish, b) persons of Hispanic origin can report being any race, c) persons reporting two ancestries are counted in both categories. 2. Numbers in parentheses indicate the number of persons reporting this ancestry/race alone, not in combination with any other ancestry/race. 3. Refer to the Explanation of Data in the front of the book for more detailed information.

Ancestry/Race	Number	%
Pakistani (318)	355	0.70
Sri Lankan (32)	36	0.07
Taiwanese (158)	178	0.35
Thai (20)	29	0.06
Vietnamese (526)	550	1.09
Other Asian, specified (29)	31	0.06
Other Asian, not specified (79)	148	0.29
Australian	8	0.02
Austrian	179	0.35
Belgian	20	0.04
Brazilian	55	0.11
British	129	0.26
Canadian	56	0.11
Carpatho Rusyn	13	0.03
Croatian	28	0.06
Czech	157	0.31
Czechoslovakian	161	0.32
Danish	211	0.42
Dutch	441	0.87
Eastern European	36	0.07
English	1,951	3.86
Estonian	5	0.01
European	91	0.18
Finnish	19	0.04
French, except Basque	521	1.03
French Canadian	148	0.29
German	4,386	8.69
Greek	283	0.56
Guyanese	269	0.53
Hawaii Native/Pacific Islander:	68	0.13
Melanesian: (2)	2	0.00
Fijian (2)	2	0.00
Micronesian: (4)	4	0.01
Guamanian/Chamorro (1)	1	0.00
Other Micronesian (3)	3	0.01
Polynesian: (3)	6	0.01
Native Hawaiian (3)	4	0.01
Samoan	2	0.00
Other Pac. Isl., not spec. (4)	56	0.11
Hispanic or Latino:	4,002	7.93
Central American:	386	0.76
Costa Rican	59	0.12
Guatemalan	78	0.15
Honduran	31	0.06
Nicaraguan	22	0.04
Panamanian	41	0.08
Salvadoran	136	0.27
Other Central American	19	0.04
Cuban	202	0.40
Dominican Republic	188	0.37
Mexican	185	0.37
Puerto Rican	1,060	2.10
South American:	1,193	2.36
Argentinean	51	0.10
Bolivian	1	0.00
Chilean	31	0.06
Colombian	693	1.37
Ecuadorian	116	0.23
Paraguayan	2	0.00
Peruvian	237	0.47
Uruguayan	10	0.02
Venezuelan	22	0.04
Other South American	30	0.06
Other Hispanic or Latino	788	1.56
Hungarian	994	1.97
Icelander	5	0.01
Iranian	33	0.07
Irish	4,764	9.44
Israeli	60	0.12
Italian	6,185	12.25
Latvian	20	0.04
Lithuanian	201	0.40
Northern European	28	0.06
Norwegian	108	0.21
Pennsylvania German	18	0.04
Polish	3,373	6.68
Portuguese	178	0.35
Romanian	49	0.10
Russian	808	1.60
Scandinavian	43	0.09
Scotch-Irish	178	0.35
Scottish	405	0.80
Serbian	56	0.11
Slavic	61	0.12
Slovak	309	0.61
Swedish	274	0.54
Swiss	47	0.09
Turkish	61	0.12
Ukrainian	728	1.44
United States or American	1,164	2.31
Welsh	207	0.41
West Indian, excl. Hispanic:	1,156	2.29
Bahamian	14	0.03
Barbadian	50	0.10
Bermudan	10	0.02
British West Indian	57	0.11
Dutch West Indian	22	0.04
Haitian	221	0.44
Jamaican	577	1.14
Trinidadian and Tobagonian	109	0.22
West Indian	90	0.18
Other West Indian	6	0.01
White:	25,577	50.67
Not Hispanic (22,682)	23,343	46.24
Hispanic (1,960)	2,234	4.43
Yugoslavian	17	0.03

Plainfield

Place Type: City
County: Union
Population: 47,829

Ancestry/Race	Number	%
African American/Black:	30,557	63.89
Not Hispanic (28,698)	29,406	61.48
Hispanic (852)	1,151	2.41
African, sub-Saharan:	756	1.58
African	499	1.04
Cape Verdean	5	0.01
Ghanian	29	0.06
Liberian	7	0.01
Nigerian	145	0.30
Sierra Leonean	54	0.11
Somalian	6	0.01
Other sub-Saharan African	11	0.02
Alaska Native tribes, specified:	1	0.00
Eskimo	1	0.00
Am. Ind. or Alaska Nat., not spec.	261	0.55
Alsatian	7	0.01
American Indian tribes, specified:	245	0.51
Apache (3)	7	0.01
Blackfeet (5)	17	0.04
Cherokee (9)	60	0.13
Choctaw	4	0.01
Creek	3	0.01
Delaware	4	0.01
Houma	1	0.00
Iroquois (3)	12	0.03
Latin American Indians (29)	104	0.22
Lumbee (1)	1	0.00
Navajo	1	0.00
Pueblo (2)	6	0.01
Seminole	4	0.01
Sioux	7	0.01
All other tribes (7)	14	0.03
American Indian tribes, not spec.	28	0.06
Arab:	99	0.21
Egyptian	49	0.10
Jordanian	35	0.07
Lebanese	11	0.02
Syrian	4	0.01
Asian:	582	1.22
Bangladeshi (1)	1	0.00
Cambodian (1)	1	0.00
Chinese, ex. Taiwanese (47)	68	0.14
Filipino (68)	94	0.20
Hmong (1)	1	0.00
Indian (161)	218	0.46
Japanese (5)	12	0.03
Korean (11)	12	0.03
Laotian (9)	9	0.02
Malaysian (1)	1	0.00
Pakistani (17)	26	0.05
Taiwanese (2)	4	0.01
Vietnamese (109)	111	0.23
Other Asian, specified (1)	4	0.01
Other Asian, not specified (4)	20	0.04
Assyrian/Chaldean/Syriac	5	0.01
Austrian	28	0.06
Belgian	6	0.01
Brazilian	20	0.04
British	76	0.16
Canadian	34	0.07
Celtic	4	0.01
Croatian	10	0.02
Czech	60	0.13
Czechoslovakian	34	0.07
Danish	10	0.02
Dutch	79	0.17
Eastern European	9	0.02
English	859	1.80
European	50	0.10
Finnish	15	0.03
French, except Basque	156	0.33
French Canadian	7	0.01
German	1,054	2.20
Greek	20	0.04
Guyanese	149	0.31
Hawaii Native/Pacific Islander:	133	0.28
Micronesian: (34)	54	0.11
Guamanian/Chamorro (34)	54	0.11
Polynesian: (6)	13	0.03
Native Hawaiian (2)	5	0.01
Samoan (4)	7	0.01
Other Polynesian	1	0.00
Other Pac. Isl., specified	3	0.01
Other Pac. Isl., not spec. (6)	63	0.13
Hispanic or Latino:	12,033	25.16
Central American:	3,846	8.04
Costa Rican	69	0.14
Guatemalan	1,443	3.02
Honduran	779	1.63
Nicaraguan	56	0.12
Panamanian	56	0.12
Salvadoran	1,260	2.63
Other Central American	183	0.38
Cuban	145	0.30
Dominican Republic	702	1.47
Mexican	807	1.69
Puerto Rican	1,782	3.73
South American:	1,826	3.82
Argentinean	18	0.04
Bolivian	13	0.03
Chilean	15	0.03
Colombian	616	1.29
Ecuadorian	863	1.80
Paraguayan	1	0.00
Peruvian	233	0.49
Uruguayan	4	0.01
Venezuelan	23	0.05
Other South American	40	0.08
Other Hispanic or Latino	2,925	6.12
Hungarian	138	0.29
Irish	1,074	2.25
Italian	1,176	2.46
Latvian	10	0.02
Lithuanian	56	0.12
Northern European	14	0.03
Norwegian	36	0.08
Pennsylvania German	15	0.03
Polish	659	1.38
Portuguese	54	0.11
Romanian	19	0.04
Russian	168	0.35
Scandinavian	21	0.04
Scotch-Irish	167	0.35
Scottish	180	0.38
Slavic	5	0.01
Slovak	51	0.11

Notes: 1. Figures in the "Number" column do not add up to the total population due to: a) Ancestry/Race overlap — e.g. persons can report being both White and Irish, b) persons of Hispanic origin can report being any race, c) persons reporting two ancestries are counted in both categories. 2. Numbers in parentheses indicate the number of persons reporting this ancestry/race alone, not in combination with any other ancestry/race. 3. Refer to the Explanation of Data in the front of the book for more detailed information.

Swedish	76	0.16
Swiss	10	0.02
Turkish	10	0.02
Ukrainian	152	0.32
United States or American	987	2.06
Welsh	41	0.09
West Indian, excl. Hispanic:	2,465	5.15
Barbadian	270	0.56
Bermudan	35	0.07
British West Indian	41	0.09
Haitian	192	0.40
Jamaican	1,450	3.03
Trinidadian and Tobagonian	221	0.46
U.S. Virgin Islander	29	0.06
West Indian	227	0.47
White:	11,675	24.41
Not Hispanic (5,508)	5,937	12.41
Hispanic (4,750)	5,738	12.00

Plainsboro

Place Type: Township
County: Middlesex
Population: 20,215

Ancestry/Race	Number	%
African American/Black:	1,683	8.33
Not Hispanic (1,490)	1,617	8.00
Hispanic (43)	66	0.33
African, sub-Saharan:	209	1.03
African	87	0.43
Ethiopian	15	0.07
Ghanian	44	0.22
Liberian	6	0.03
Nigerian	13	0.06
Somalian	6	0.03
South African	16	0.08
Sudanese	22	0.11
Alaska Native tribes, specified:	1	0.00
Eskimo (1)	1	0.00
Am. Ind. or Alaska Nat., not spec.	31	0.15
American Indian tribes, specified:	45	0.22
Blackfeet (1)	1	0.00
Cherokee (3)	21	0.10
Chippewa	1	0.00
Choctaw (1)	1	0.00
Iroquois	1	0.00
Latin American Indians (2)	11	0.05
Ottawa	2	0.01
Shoshone	3	0.01
All other tribes	4	0.02
American Indian tribes, not spec.	5	0.02
Arab:	241	1.19
Arab/Arabic	9	0.04
Egyptian	97	0.48
Lebanese	110	0.54
Syrian	25	0.12
Armenian	49	0.24
Asian:	6,432	31.82
Bangladeshi (14)	18	0.09
Cambodian (3)	3	0.01
Chinese, ex. Taiwanese (1,680)	1,729	8.55
Filipino (325)	367	1.82
Indian (3,357)	3,431	16.97
Indonesian (9)	14	0.07
Japanese (129)	164	0.81
Korean (343)	364	1.80
Malaysian	2	0.01
Pakistani (94)	101	0.50
Sri Lankan (17)	18	0.09
Taiwanese (74)	99	0.49
Thai (15)	17	0.08
Vietnamese (36)	38	0.19
Other Asian, specified (9)	10	0.05
Other Asian, not specified (34)	57	0.28
Australian	22	0.11
Austrian	254	1.26
Belgian	68	0.34
Brazilian	46	0.23
British	139	0.69
Bulgarian	17	0.08
Canadian	47	0.23
Croatian	41	0.20
Czech	86	0.43
Czechoslovakian	23	0.11
Danish	63	0.31
Dutch	185	0.92
Eastern European	133	0.66
English	1,170	5.79
European	70	0.35
Finnish	7	0.03
French, except Basque	419	2.07
French Canadian	36	0.18
German	2,300	11.38
Greek	148	0.73
Guyanese	30	0.15
Hawaii Native/Pacific Islander:	38	0.19
Micronesian:	4	0.02
Guamanian/Chamorro	4	0.02
Polynesian:	4	0.02
Native Hawaiian	4	0.02
Other Pac. Isl., not spec. (2)	30	0.15
Hispanic or Latino:	937	4.64
Central American:	108	0.53
Costa Rican	6	0.03
Guatemalan	72	0.36
Honduran	6	0.03
Nicaraguan	7	0.03
Panamanian	9	0.04
Salvadoran	6	0.03
Other Central American	2	0.01
Cuban	77	0.38
Dominican Republic	26	0.13
Mexican	79	0.39
Puerto Rican	284	1.40
South American:	153	0.76
Argentinean	17	0.08
Chilean	13	0.06
Colombian	57	0.28
Ecuadorian	15	0.07
Paraguayan	1	0.00
Peruvian	12	0.06
Uruguayan	7	0.03
Venezuelan	16	0.08
Other South American	15	0.07
Other Hispanic or Latino	210	1.04
Hungarian	243	1.20
Iranian	42	0.21
Irish	2,308	11.42
Israeli	73	0.36
Italian	2,027	10.03
Latvian	21	0.10
Lithuanian	74	0.37
Luxemburger	6	0.03
Northern European	6	0.03
Norwegian	109	0.54
Polish	1,286	6.36
Portuguese	21	0.10
Romanian	104	0.51
Russian	861	4.26
Scandinavian	18	0.09
Scotch-Irish	203	1.00
Scottish	266	1.32
Serbian	70	0.35
Slavic	17	0.08
Slovak	79	0.39
Swedish	226	1.12
Swiss	37	0.18
Turkish	49	0.24
Ukrainian	144	0.71
United States or American	515	2.55
Welsh	122	0.60
West Indian, excl. Hispanic:	242	1.20
Bahamian	28	0.14
Barbadian	15	0.07
Haitian	28	0.14
Jamaican	123	0.61
Trinidadian and Tobagonian	24	0.12
U.S. Virgin Islander	8	0.04
West Indian	16	0.08
White:	12,055	59.63
Not Hispanic (11,212)	11,428	56.53
Hispanic (553)	627	3.10
Yugoslavian	5	0.02

Pleasantville

Place Type: City
County: Atlantic
Population: 19,012

Ancestry/Race	Number	%
African American/Black:	11,429	60.11
Not Hispanic (10,572)	10,927	57.47
Hispanic (397)	502	2.64
African, sub-Saharan:	424	2.22
African	383	2.01
Nigerian	33	0.17
Senegalese	8	0.04
Alaska Native tribes, specified:	1	0.01
Eskimo (1)	1	0.01
Am. Ind. or Alaska Nat., not spec.	94	0.49
American Indian tribes, specified:	100	0.53
Apache	2	0.01
Blackfeet (3)	15	0.08
Cherokee (6)	33	0.17
Cheyenne	2	0.01
Chippewa	4	0.02
Delaware	3	0.02
Iroquois	1	0.01
Latin American Indians (12)	17	0.09
Osage	3	0.02
Potawatomi (1)	1	0.01
Pueblo (6)	7	0.04
Seminole	1	0.01
All other tribes (1)	11	0.06
American Indian tribes, not spec.	13	0.07
Arab:	116	0.61
Arab/Arabic	40	0.21
Egyptian	39	0.20
Moroccan	37	0.19
Asian:	439	2.31
Bangladeshi	4	0.02
Chinese, ex. Taiwanese (43)	49	0.26
Filipino (64)	74	0.39
Indian (109)	120	0.63
Japanese (5)	8	0.04
Korean (22)	23	0.12
Laotian (48)	58	0.31
Pakistani (7)	18	0.09
Taiwanese	1	0.01
Thai (4)	7	0.04
Vietnamese (41)	43	0.23
Other Asian, specified (1)	2	0.01
Other Asian, not specified (23)	32	0.17
Austrian	9	0.05
Brazilian	14	0.07
British	14	0.07
Canadian	6	0.03
Czechoslovakian	31	0.16
Danish	6	0.03
Dutch	40	0.21
English	547	2.86
European	27	0.14
French, except Basque	103	0.54
French Canadian	5	0.03
German	914	4.79
Greek	31	0.16
Guyanese	23	0.12
Hawaii Native/Pacific Islander:	30	0.16
Micronesian:	1	0.01
Guamanian/Chamorro	1	0.01
Polynesian: (3)	7	0.04
Native Hawaiian (1)	4	0.02
Samoan (1)	2	0.01
Other Polynesian (1)	1	0.01
Other Pac. Isl., specified	1	0.01
Other Pac. Isl., not spec. (2)	21	0.11
Hispanic or Latino:	4,158	21.87
Central American:	183	0.96

Notes: 1. Figures in the "Number" column do not add up to the total population due to: a) Ancestry/Race overlap — e.g. persons can report being both White and Irish, b) persons of Hispanic origin can report being any race, c) persons reporting two ancestries are counted in both categories. 2. Numbers in parentheses indicate the number of persons reporting this ancestry/race alone, not in combination with any other ancestry/race. 3. Refer to the Explanation of Data in the front of the book for more detailed information.

Ancestry/Race	Number	%
Costa Rican	10	0.05
Guatemalan	15	0.08
Honduran	46	0.24
Nicaraguan	18	0.09
Panamanian	14	0.07
Salvadoran	70	0.37
Other Central American	10	0.05
Cuban	61	0.32
Dominican Republic	548	2.88
Mexican	451	2.37
Puerto Rican	2,085	10.97
South American:	208	1.09
Argentinean	4	0.02
Chilean	3	0.02
Colombian	99	0.52
Ecuadorian	22	0.12
Peruvian	80	0.42
Other Hispanic or Latino	622	3.27
Hungarian	46	0.24
Irish	936	4.90
Italian	631	3.30
Lithuanian	14	0.07
Norwegian	8	0.04
Polish	238	1.25
Portuguese	22	0.12
Romanian	14	0.07
Russian	28	0.15
Scotch-Irish	21	0.11
Scottish	45	0.24
Slavic	9	0.05
Slovak	15	0.08
Swedish	45	0.24
Ukrainian	26	0.14
United States or American	446	2.34
Welsh	37	0.19
West Indian, excl. Hispanic:	1,001	5.24
Bahamian	13	0.07
Barbadian	18	0.09
British West Indian	22	0.12
Haitian	575	3.01
Jamaican	352	1.84
Trinidadian and Tobagonian	6	0.03
West Indian	15	0.08
White:	5,200	27.35
Not Hispanic (3,402)	3,606	18.97
Hispanic (1,353)	1,594	8.38

Point Pleasant

Place Type: Borough
County: Ocean
Population: 19,306

Ancestry/Race	Number	%
African American/Black:	69	0.36
Not Hispanic (47)	59	0.31
Hispanic (9)	10	0.05
Am. Ind. or Alaska Nat., not spec.	19	0.10
Albanian	9	0.05
American Indian tribes, specified:	48	0.25
Apache	1	0.01
Cherokee (7)	20	0.10
Cheyenne (4)	4	0.02
Chippewa	1	0.01
Choctaw (1)	1	0.01
Delaware	1	0.01
Iroquois (3)	3	0.02
Latin American Indians (2)	5	0.03
Navajo (1)	1	0.01
Seminole	3	0.02
Ute	1	0.01
All other tribes (4)	7	0.04
American Indian tribes, not spec.	8	0.04
Arab:	55	0.28
Lebanese	28	0.15
Moroccan	9	0.05
Syrian	18	0.09
Armenian	33	0.17
Asian:	151	0.78
Chinese, ex. Taiwanese (49)	54	0.28
Filipino (18)	32	0.17
Indian (10)	11	0.06
Indonesian (1)	3	0.02
Japanese (5)	20	0.10
Korean (11)	12	0.06
Thai (1)	2	0.01
Vietnamese (7)	7	0.04
Other Asian, not specified (2)	10	0.05
Australian	13	0.07
Austrian	178	0.92
Belgian	21	0.11
Brazilian	17	0.09
British	88	0.46
Canadian	36	0.19
Croatian	35	0.18
Czech	124	0.64
Czechoslovakian	100	0.52
Danish	96	0.50
Dutch	491	2.54
English	1,933	10.01
Estonian	19	0.10
European	17	0.09
Finnish	15	0.08
French, except Basque	536	2.78
French Canadian	50	0.26
German	4,153	21.51
Greek	86	0.45
Hawaii Native/Pacific Islander:	5	0.03
Polynesian: (2)	5	0.03
Native Hawaiian (1)	2	0.01
Samoan (1)	3	0.02
Hispanic or Latino:	465	2.41
Central American:	20	0.10
Costa Rican	2	0.01
Guatemalan	5	0.03
Honduran	1	0.01
Nicaraguan	2	0.01
Salvadoran	10	0.05
Cuban	35	0.18
Dominican Republic	1	0.01
Mexican	171	0.89
Puerto Rican	117	0.61
South American:	48	0.25
Argentinean	7	0.04
Chilean	1	0.01
Colombian	18	0.09
Ecuadorian	14	0.07
Peruvian	2	0.01
Venezuelan	2	0.01
Other South American	4	0.02
Other Hispanic or Latino	73	0.38
Hungarian	212	1.10
Irish	6,317	32.72
Israeli	30	0.16
Italian	4,864	25.19
Lithuanian	150	0.78
Norwegian	354	1.83
Pennsylvania German	15	0.08
Polish	1,936	10.03
Portuguese	49	0.25
Romanian	29	0.15
Russian	288	1.49
Scandinavian	30	0.16
Scotch-Irish	378	1.96
Scottish	551	2.85
Slavic	15	0.08
Slovak	151	0.78
Slovene	23	0.12
Swedish	262	1.36
Swiss	22	0.11
Turkish	18	0.09
Ukrainian	222	1.15
United States or American	542	2.81
Welsh	86	0.45
West Indian, excl. Hispanic:	12	0.06
U.S. Virgin Islander	12	0.06
White:	19,015	98.49
Not Hispanic (18,556)	18,655	96.63
Hispanic (331)	360	1.86
Yugoslavian	52	0.27

Pompton Lakes

Place Type: Borough
County: Passaic
Population: 10,640

Ancestry/Race	Number	%
African American/Black:	146	1.37
Not Hispanic (127)	144	1.35
Hispanic (2)	2	0.02
Am. Ind. or Alaska Nat., not spec.	5	0.05
Albanian	173	1.63
American Indian tribes, specified:	21	0.20
Cherokee (2)	3	0.03
Delaware (2)	2	0.02
Iroquois	2	0.02
Latin American Indians (13)	13	0.12
Seminole (1)	1	0.01
American Indian tribes, not spec.	2	0.02
Arab:	138	1.30
Egyptian	8	0.08
Jordanian	31	0.29
Lebanese	79	0.74
Syrian	20	0.19
Armenian	67	0.63
Asian:	360	3.38
Bangladeshi (1)	1	0.01
Chinese, ex. Taiwanese (50)	58	0.55
Filipino (143)	156	1.47
Indian (61)	68	0.64
Indonesian (3)	3	0.03
Japanese (7)	10	0.09
Korean (25)	26	0.24
Pakistani (3)	7	0.07
Vietnamese (22)	25	0.23
Other Asian, not specified (3)	6	0.06
Austrian	114	1.07
Belgian	7	0.07
British	21	0.20
Canadian	28	0.26
Carpatho Rusyn	6	0.06
Celtic	6	0.06
Croatian	36	0.34
Czech	62	0.58
Czechoslovakian	56	0.53
Danish	46	0.43
Dutch	792	7.44
English	901	8.47
European	51	0.48
Finnish	7	0.07
French, except Basque	246	2.31
French Canadian	40	0.38
German	2,189	20.57
Greek	92	0.86
Hawaii Native/Pacific Islander:	2	0.02
Micronesian: (1)	1	0.01
Guamanian/Chamorro (1)	1	0.01
Other Pac. Isl., not spec.	1	0.01
Hispanic or Latino:	611	5.74
Central American:	14	0.13
Costa Rican	2	0.02
Guatemalan	2	0.02
Honduran	3	0.03
Nicaraguan	1	0.01
Panamanian	1	0.01
Salvadoran	5	0.05
Cuban	62	0.58
Dominican Republic	5	0.05
Mexican	180	1.69
Puerto Rican	148	1.39
South American:	103	0.97
Argentinean	12	0.11
Chilean	2	0.02
Colombian	35	0.33
Ecuadorian	10	0.09
Peruvian	44	0.41
Other Hispanic or Latino	99	0.93
Hungarian	208	1.95
Irish	2,469	23.20
Italian	2,821	26.51

Notes: 1. Figures in the "Number" column do not add up to the total population due to: a) Ancestry/Race overlap — e.g. persons can report being both White and Irish, b) persons of Hispanic origin can report being any race, c) persons reporting two ancestries are counted in both categories. 2. Numbers in parentheses indicate the number of persons reporting this ancestry/race alone, not in combination with any other ancestry/race. 3. Refer to the Explanation of Data in the front of the book for more detailed information.

Latvian	6	0.06
Lithuanian	38	0.36
New Zealander	9	0.08
Norwegian	54	0.51
Polish	853	8.02
Portuguese	52	0.49
Russian	327	3.07
Scotch-Irish	98	0.92
Scottish	168	1.58
Slavic	7	0.07
Slovak	50	0.47
Swedish	86	0.81
Swiss	102	0.96
Ukrainian	58	0.55
United States or American	306	2.88
Welsh	24	0.23
West Indian, excl. Hispanic:	6	0.06
Jamaican	6	0.06
White:	9,994	93.93
Not Hispanic (9,477)	9,553	89.78
Hispanic (419)	441	4.14
Yugoslavian	14	0.13

Princeton Meadows

Place Type: Census Designated Place
County: Middlesex
Population: 13,436

Ancestry/Race	Number	%
African American/Black:	1,410	10.49
Not Hispanic (1,257)	1,355	10.08
Hispanic (38)	55	0.41
African, sub-Saharan:	190	1.43
African	87	0.66
Ethiopian	8	0.06
Ghanian	44	0.33
Nigerian	13	0.10
South African	16	0.12
Sudanese	22	0.17
Alaska Native tribes, specified:	1	0.01
Eskimo (1)	1	0.01
Am. Ind. or Alaska Nat., not spec.	23	0.17
American Indian tribes, specified:	32	0.24
Blackfeet (1)	1	0.01
Cherokee (2)	11	0.08
Chippewa	1	0.01
Choctaw (1)	1	0.01
Iroquois	1	0.01
Latin American Indians (2)	10	0.07
Shoshone	3	0.02
All other tribes	4	0.03
American Indian tribes, not spec.	5	0.04
Arab:	93	0.70
Arab/Arabic	9	0.07
Lebanese	84	0.63
Armenian	43	0.32
Asian:	4,211	31.34
Bangladeshi (9)	13	0.10
Cambodian (3)	3	0.02
Chinese, ex. Taiwanese (1,007)	1,037	7.72
Filipino (240)	272	2.02
Indian (2,257)	2,305	17.16
Indonesian (1)	4	0.03
Japanese (75)	98	0.73
Korean (227)	243	1.81
Malaysian	1	0.01
Pakistani (70)	77	0.57
Sri Lankan (13)	14	0.10
Taiwanese (36)	49	0.36
Thai (13)	13	0.10
Vietnamese (29)	31	0.23
Other Asian, specified (8)	8	0.06
Other Asian, not specified (26)	43	0.32
Australian	7	0.05
Austrian	168	1.27
Belgian	28	0.21
Brazilian	46	0.35
British	67	0.51
Canadian	39	0.29
Croatian	12	0.09
Czech	43	0.32
Czechoslovakian	18	0.14
Danish	41	0.31
Dutch	66	0.50
Eastern European	81	0.61
English	795	6.00
European	35	0.26
French, except Basque	312	2.36
French Canadian	36	0.27
German	1,397	10.55
Greek	93	0.70
Guyanese	30	0.23
Hawaii Native/Pacific Islander:	24	0.18
Micronesian:	3	0.02
Guamanian/Chamorro	3	0.02
Polynesian:	4	0.03
Native Hawaiian	4	0.03
Other Pac. Isl., not spec.	17	0.13
Hispanic or Latino:	708	5.27
Central American:	88	0.65
Costa Rican	2	0.01
Guatemalan	59	0.44
Honduran	6	0.04
Nicaraguan	6	0.04
Panamanian	9	0.07
Salvadoran	4	0.03
Other Central American	2	0.01
Cuban	55	0.41
Dominican Republic	25	0.19
Mexican	60	0.45
Puerto Rican	199	1.48
South American:	117	0.87
Argentinean	14	0.10
Chilean	13	0.10
Colombian	37	0.28
Ecuadorian	14	0.10
Paraguayan	1	0.01
Peruvian	7	0.05
Uruguayan	6	0.04
Venezuelan	14	0.10
Other South American	11	0.08
Other Hispanic or Latino	164	1.22
Hungarian	143	1.08
Iranian	42	0.32
Irish	1,365	10.31
Israeli	38	0.29
Italian	1,423	10.74
Lithuanian	19	0.14
Northern European	6	0.05
Norwegian	79	0.60
Polish	986	7.44
Portuguese	21	0.16
Romanian	85	0.64
Russian	528	3.99
Scandinavian	11	0.08
Scotch-Irish	111	0.84
Scottish	152	1.15
Serbian	51	0.39
Slavic	9	0.07
Slovak	61	0.46
Swedish	95	0.72
Swiss	8	0.06
Turkish	34	0.26
Ukrainian	77	0.58
United States or American	324	2.45
Welsh	53	0.40
West Indian, excl. Hispanic:	182	1.37
Bahamian	28	0.21
Barbadian	15	0.11
Haitian	28	0.21
Jamaican	63	0.48
Trinidadian and Tobagonian	24	0.18
U.S. Virgin Islander	8	0.06
West Indian	16	0.12
White:	7,739	57.60
Not Hispanic (7,155)	7,288	54.24
Hispanic (391)	451	3.36
Yugoslavian	5	0.04

Princeton

Place Type: Borough
County: Mercer
Population: 14,203

Ancestry/Race	Number	%
African American/Black:	970	6.83
Not Hispanic (882)	929	6.54
Hispanic (26)	41	0.29
African, sub-Saharan:	89	0.63
African	44	0.31
Ghanian	12	0.08
South African	33	0.23
Am. Ind. or Alaska Nat., not spec.	28	0.20
Alsatian	31	0.22
American Indian tribes, specified:	56	0.39
Cherokee (1)	11	0.08
Chippewa (1)	1	0.01
Delaware (2)	2	0.01
Latin American Indians (17)	36	0.25
Navajo (1)	1	0.01
All other tribes	5	0.04
American Indian tribes, not spec.	3	0.02
Arab:	98	0.69
Arab/Arabic	9	0.06
Egyptian	11	0.08
Lebanese	46	0.32
Syrian	23	0.16
Other Arab	9	0.06
Armenian	9	0.06
Asian:	1,297	9.13
Cambodian (1)	3	0.02
Chinese, ex. Taiwanese (491)	588	4.14
Filipino (59)	74	0.52
Indian (202)	265	1.87
Indonesian (1)	1	0.01
Japanese (98)	127	0.89
Korean (135)	149	1.05
Pakistani (1)	1	0.01
Sri Lankan (5)	8	0.06
Taiwanese (4)	4	0.03
Thai (3)	3	0.02
Vietnamese (34)	39	0.27
Other Asian, specified (2)	2	0.01
Other Asian, not specified (17)	33	0.23
Australian	42	0.30
Austrian	71	0.50
Belgian	18	0.13
Brazilian	5	0.04
British	190	1.34
Bulgarian	22	0.15
Canadian	160	1.13
Croatian	8	0.06
Czech	42	0.30
Czechoslovakian	39	0.27
Danish	42	0.30
Dutch	151	1.06
Eastern European	65	0.46
English	945	6.65
European	56	0.39
French, except Basque	306	2.15
French Canadian	39	0.27
German	927	6.53
Greek	81	0.57
Hawaii Native/Pacific Islander:	30	0.21
Micronesian: (15)	20	0.14
Guamanian/Chamorro (15)	20	0.14
Polynesian: (5)	8	0.06
Native Hawaiian (3)	6	0.04
Samoan (2)	2	0.01
Other Pac. Isl., not spec.	2	0.01
Hispanic or Latino:	1,009	7.10
Central American:	291	2.05
Costa Rican	1	0.01
Guatemalan	264	1.86
Honduran	6	0.04
Nicaraguan	1	0.01
Panamanian	3	0.02
Salvadoran	1	0.01

Notes: 1. Figures in the "Number" column do not add up to the total population due to: a) Ancestry/Race overlap — e.g. persons can report being both White and Irish, b) persons of Hispanic origin can report being any race, c) persons reporting two ancestries are counted in both categories. 2. Numbers in parentheses indicate the number of persons reporting this ancestry/race alone, not in combination with any other ancestry/race. 3. Refer to the Explanation of Data in the front of the book for more detailed information.

Other Central American	15	0.11
Cuban	30	0.21
Dominican Republic	12	0.08
Mexican	340	2.39
Puerto Rican	113	0.80
South American:	43	0.30
Argentinean	12	0.08
Chilean	2	0.01
Colombian	20	0.14
Peruvian	3	0.02
Uruguayan	3	0.02
Other South American	3	0.02
Other Hispanic or Latino	180	1.27
Hungarian	103	0.73
Irish	1,043	7.34
Israeli	21	0.15
Italian	556	3.91
Lithuanian	84	0.59
Northern European	27	0.19
Norwegian	45	0.32
Polish	462	3.25
Portuguese	1	0.01
Romanian	15	0.11
Russian	259	1.82
Scandinavian	10	0.07
Scotch-Irish	94	0.66
Scottish	127	0.89
Slovak	22	0.15
Swedish	90	0.63
Swiss	96	0.68
Ukrainian	95	0.67
United States or American	190	1.34
Welsh	93	0.65
West Indian, excl. Hispanic:	50	0.35
Barbadian	5	0.04
British West Indian	9	0.06
Haitian	13	0.09
Jamaican	23	0.16
White:	11,764	82.83
Not Hispanic (10,859)	11,136	78.41
Hispanic (540)	628	4.42
Yugoslavian	8	0.06

Princeton

Place Type: Township
County: Mercer
Population: 16,027

Ancestry/Race	Number	%
African American/Black:	986	6.15
Not Hispanic (837)	947	5.91
Hispanic (15)	39	0.24
African, sub-Saharan:	27	0.17
African	12	0.07
Kenyan	7	0.04
Nigerian	1	0.01
South African	7	0.04
Am. Ind. or Alaska Nat., not spec.	19	0.12
Albanian	62	0.39
Alsatian	11	0.07
American Indian tribes, specified:	40	0.25
Cherokee (2)	13	0.08
Chippewa (1)	1	0.01
Choctaw	2	0.01
Delaware (3)	3	0.02
Iroquois	1	0.01
Latin American Indians (11)	13	0.08
Tohono O'Odham	1	0.01
All other tribes (1)	6	0.04
American Indian tribes, not spec.	1	0.01
Arab:	178	1.11
Egyptian	35	0.22
Iraqi	57	0.36
Lebanese	54	0.34
Syrian	20	0.12
Other Arab	12	0.07
Armenian	8	0.05
Asian:	1,775	11.08
Cambodian (1)	1	0.01
Chinese, ex. Taiwanese (668)	731	4.56
Filipino (63)	76	0.47
Indian (390)	418	2.61
Japanese (117)	146	0.91
Korean (220)	232	1.45
Laotian (2)	4	0.02
Malaysian (1)	4	0.02
Pakistani (21)	32	0.20
Sri Lankan (6)	6	0.04
Taiwanese (51)	69	0.43
Thai (5)	8	0.05
Vietnamese (8)	9	0.06
Other Asian, specified (7)	7	0.04
Other Asian, not specified (13)	32	0.20
Austrian	190	1.19
Belgian	44	0.27
Brazilian	43	0.27
British	245	1.53
Bulgarian	19	0.12
Canadian	58	0.36
Celtic	11	0.07
Croatian	29	0.18
Czech	56	0.35
Czechoslovakian	16	0.10
Danish	47	0.29
Dutch	285	1.78
Eastern European	110	0.69
English	2,140	13.35
European	210	1.31
Finnish	52	0.32
French, except Basque	488	3.04
French Canadian	65	0.41
German	1,855	11.57
Greek	146	0.91
Hawaii Native/Pacific Islander:	24	0.15
Micronesian: (1)	1	0.01
Guamanian/Chamorro (1)	1	0.01
Polynesian: (5)	8	0.05
Native Hawaiian (1)	2	0.01
Samoan (3)	3	0.02
Tongan (1)	2	0.01
Other Polynesian	1	0.01
Other Pac. Isl., not spec. (2)	15	0.09
Hispanic or Latino:	847	5.28
Central American:	123	0.77
Costa Rican	1	0.01
Guatemalan	102	0.64
Honduran	3	0.02
Nicaraguan	5	0.03
Panamanian	3	0.02
Salvadoran	4	0.02
Other Central American	5	0.03
Cuban	23	0.14
Dominican Republic	10	0.06
Mexican	309	1.93
Puerto Rican	70	0.44
South American:	154	0.96
Argentinean	33	0.21
Bolivian	8	0.05
Chilean	10	0.06
Colombian	52	0.32
Ecuadorian	9	0.06
Paraguayan	5	0.03
Peruvian	19	0.12
Venezuelan	14	0.09
Other South American	4	0.02
Other Hispanic or Latino	158	0.99
Hungarian	209	1.30
Icelander	11	0.07
Irish	1,724	10.76
Israeli	157	0.98
Italian	1,280	7.99
Latvian	16	0.10
Lithuanian	102	0.64
Luxemburger	8	0.05
Macedonian	8	0.05
New Zealander	14	0.09
Northern European	12	0.07
Norwegian	226	1.41
Polish	727	4.54
Portuguese	47	0.29
Romanian	40	0.25
Russian	1,046	6.53
Scandinavian	9	0.06
Scotch-Irish	351	2.19
Scottish	485	3.03
Slavic	35	0.22
Slovak	111	0.69
Swedish	171	1.07
Swiss	112	0.70
Ukrainian	107	0.67
United States or American	614	3.83
Welsh	155	0.97
West Indian, excl. Hispanic:	222	1.39
Haitian	107	0.67
Jamaican	40	0.25
Trinidadian and Tobagonian	7	0.04
West Indian	68	0.42
White:	13,137	81.97
Not Hispanic (12,377)	12,645	78.90
Hispanic (430)	492	3.07

Rahway

Place Type: City
County: Union
Population: 26,500

Ancestry/Race	Number	%
African American/Black:	7,593	28.65
Not Hispanic (7,058)	7,406	27.95
Hispanic (115)	187	0.71
African, sub-Saharan:	406	1.53
African	226	0.85
Ghanian	40	0.15
Nigerian	140	0.53
Am. Ind. or Alaska Nat., not spec.	78	0.29
Albanian	23	0.09
American Indian tribes, specified:	113	0.43
Blackfeet (3)	12	0.05
Cherokee (4)	51	0.19
Chickasaw	7	0.03
Delaware (1)	4	0.02
Iroquois (1)	3	0.01
Latin American Indians (6)	12	0.05
Lumbee (4)	4	0.02
Navajo	4	0.02
Seminole	2	0.01
Sioux (1)	2	0.01
All other tribes (5)	12	0.05
American Indian tribes, not spec.	15	0.06
Arab:	130	0.49
Arab/Arabic	5	0.02
Egyptian	39	0.15
Iraqi	19	0.07
Lebanese	38	0.14
Moroccan	8	0.03
Syrian	21	0.08
Asian:	1,082	4.08
Bangladeshi (1)	1	0.00
Chinese, ex. Taiwanese (151)	174	0.66
Filipino (418)	471	1.78
Indian (250)	278	1.05
Indonesian (4)	5	0.02
Japanese (18)	25	0.09
Korean (44)	47	0.18
Pakistani (12)	12	0.05
Sri Lankan (4)	4	0.02
Taiwanese (3)	3	0.01
Thai (5)	9	0.03
Vietnamese (16)	16	0.06
Other Asian, specified (1)	10	0.04
Other Asian, not specified (9)	27	0.10
Assyrian/Chaldean/Syriac	12	0.05
Austrian	114	0.43
Belgian	10	0.04
Brazilian	9	0.03
British	28	0.11
Bulgarian	8	0.03
Canadian	19	0.07

Notes: 1. Figures in the "Number" column do not add up to the total population due to: a) Ancestry/Race overlap — e.g. persons can report being both White and Irish, b) persons of Hispanic origin can report being any race, c) persons reporting two ancestries are counted in both categories. 2. Numbers in parentheses indicate the number of persons reporting this ancestry/race alone, not in combination with any other ancestry/race. 3. Refer to the Explanation of Data in the front of the book for more detailed information.

Ancestry/Race	Number	%
Croatian	20	0.08
Czech	75	0.28
Czechoslovakian	60	0.23
Danish	108	0.41
Dutch	253	0.95
Eastern European	15	0.06
English	1,006	3.80
Estonian	6	0.02
European	103	0.39
Finnish	10	0.04
French, except Basque	176	0.66
French Canadian	80	0.30
German	2,663	10.05
Greek	216	0.82
Guyanese	48	0.18
Hawaii Native/Pacific Islander:	38	0.14
Micronesian: (2)	2	0.01
Guamanian/Chamorro (2)	2	0.01
Polynesian: (4)	9	0.03
Native Hawaiian (2)	7	0.03
Samoan (2)	2	0.01
Other Pac. Isl., specified	1	0.00
Other Pac. Isl., not spec. (8)	26	0.10
Hispanic or Latino:	3,675	13.87
Central American:	419	1.58
Costa Rican	33	0.12
Guatemalan	51	0.19
Honduran	48	0.18
Nicaraguan	4	0.02
Panamanian	17	0.06
Salvadoran	251	0.95
Other Central American	15	0.06
Cuban	216	0.82
Dominican Republic	155	0.58
Mexican	424	1.60
Puerto Rican	887	3.35
South American:	780	2.94
Argentinean	39	0.15
Bolivian	1	0.00
Chilean	18	0.07
Colombian	266	1.00
Ecuadorian	97	0.37
Paraguayan	3	0.01
Peruvian	290	1.09
Uruguayan	27	0.10
Venezuelan	21	0.08
Other South American	18	0.07
Other Hispanic or Latino	794	3.00
Hungarian	449	1.69
Iranian	16	0.06
Irish	3,028	11.43
Italian	3,187	12.03
Lithuanian	151	0.57
Northern European	8	0.03
Norwegian	98	0.37
Polish	2,507	9.46
Portuguese	499	1.88
Romanian	24	0.09
Russian	445	1.68
Scotch-Irish	195	0.74
Scottish	312	1.18
Slavic	54	0.20
Slovak	349	1.32
Slovene	8	0.03
Swedish	138	0.52
Swiss	15	0.06
Turkish	15	0.06
Ukrainian	324	1.22
United States or American	781	2.95
Welsh	67	0.25
West Indian, excl. Hispanic:	741	2.80
Bahamian	22	0.08
Bermudan	7	0.03
British West Indian	8	0.03
Haitian	492	1.86
Jamaican	104	0.39
Trinidadian and Tobagonian	44	0.17
U.S. Virgin Islander	8	0.03
West Indian	56	0.21
White:	16,508	62.29
Not Hispanic (14,099)	14,427	54.44
Hispanic (1,851)	2,081	7.85
Yugoslavian	15	0.06

Ramsey

Place Type: Borough
County: Bergen
Population: 14,351

Ancestry/Race	Number	%
African American/Black:	153	1.07
Not Hispanic (110)	144	1.00
Hispanic (2)	9	0.06
African, sub-Saharan:	9	0.06
African	9	0.06
Am. Ind. or Alaska Nat., not spec.	24	0.17
Albanian	22	0.15
American Indian tribes, specified:	28	0.20
Apache (1)	2	0.01
Cherokee	13	0.09
Choctaw (1)	1	0.01
Delaware (4)	4	0.03
Latin American Indians	1	0.01
All other tribes	7	0.05
American Indian tribes, not spec.	1	0.01
Arab:	62	0.43
Egyptian	16	0.11
Lebanese	46	0.32
Armenian	84	0.59
Asian:	924	6.44
Chinese, ex. Taiwanese (243)	276	1.92
Filipino (56)	67	0.47
Indian (156)	167	1.16
Indonesian (6)	6	0.04
Japanese (140)	154	1.07
Korean (189)	194	1.35
Pakistani (23)	25	0.17
Sri Lankan (8)	8	0.06
Taiwanese (1)	5	0.03
Thai (2)	6	0.04
Vietnamese (3)	8	0.06
Other Asian, not specified	8	0.06
Australian	8	0.06
Austrian	162	1.13
British	94	0.66
Canadian	29	0.20
Czech	75	0.52
Czechoslovakian	89	0.62
Danish	59	0.41
Dutch	434	3.02
Eastern European	56	0.39
English	1,449	10.10
European	93	0.65
Finnish	12	0.08
French, except Basque	275	1.92
French Canadian	109	0.76
German	2,393	16.67
Greek	141	0.98
Hawaii Native/Pacific Islander:	5	0.03
Polynesian: (1)	2	0.01
Native Hawaiian (1)	2	0.01
Other Pac. Isl., not spec.	3	0.02
Hispanic or Latino:	420	2.93
Central American:	31	0.22
Costa Rican	3	0.02
Guatemalan	2	0.01
Salvadoran	26	0.18
Cuban	36	0.25
Dominican Republic	11	0.08
Mexican	82	0.57
Puerto Rican	81	0.56
South American:	92	0.64
Argentinean	5	0.03
Bolivian	6	0.04
Chilean	2	0.01
Colombian	36	0.25
Ecuadorian	20	0.14
Peruvian	12	0.08
Venezuelan	9	0.06
Other South American	2	0.01
Other Hispanic or Latino	87	0.61
Hungarian	197	1.37
Irish	3,444	24.00
Israeli	10	0.07
Italian	3,997	27.85
Latvian	26	0.18
Lithuanian	79	0.55
New Zealander	19	0.13
Norwegian	82	0.57
Polish	864	6.02
Portuguese	32	0.22
Romanian	49	0.34
Russian	386	2.69
Scandinavian	5	0.03
Scotch-Irish	123	0.86
Scottish	321	2.24
Serbian	17	0.12
Slovak	105	0.73
Swedish	131	0.91
Swiss	100	0.70
Turkish	12	0.08
Ukrainian	81	0.56
United States or American	502	3.50
Welsh	128	0.89
West Indian, excl. Hispanic:	77	0.54
Dutch West Indian	4	0.03
Haitian	32	0.22
Jamaican	31	0.22
Trinidadian and Tobagonian	10	0.07
White:	13,275	92.50
Not Hispanic (12,846)	12,942	90.18
Hispanic (302)	333	2.32
Yugoslavian	37	0.26

Randolph

Place Type: Township
County: Morris
Population: 24,847

Ancestry/Race	Number	%
African American/Black:	657	2.64
Not Hispanic (555)	629	2.53
Hispanic (17)	28	0.11
African, sub-Saharan:	95	0.38
African	50	0.20
South African	19	0.08
Other sub-Saharan African	26	0.10
Am. Ind. or Alaska Nat., not spec.	29	0.12
American Indian tribes, specified:	26	0.10
Cherokee (2)	7	0.03
Delaware (1)	3	0.01
Iroquois (1)	5	0.02
Latin American Indians	7	0.03
Pueblo (2)	2	0.01
Sioux (1)	1	0.00
All other tribes	1	0.00
American Indian tribes, not spec.	4	0.02
Arab:	208	0.84
Arab/Arabic	33	0.13
Egyptian	27	0.11
Lebanese	29	0.12
Syrian	108	0.43
Other Arab	11	0.04
Armenian	20	0.08
Asian:	2,486	10.01
Bangladeshi (9)	9	0.04
Chinese, ex. Taiwanese (546)	608	2.45
Filipino (130)	173	0.70
Indian (1,237)	1,271	5.12
Indonesian (1)	4	0.02
Japanese (36)	67	0.27
Korean (145)	169	0.68
Pakistani (40)	48	0.19
Sri Lankan (15)	15	0.06
Taiwanese (45)	56	0.23
Thai (2)	2	0.01
Vietnamese (33)	36	0.14
Other Asian, not specified (6)	28	0.11

Notes: 1. Figures in the "Number" column do not add up to the total population due to: a) Ancestry/Race overlap — e.g. persons can report being both White and Irish, b) persons of Hispanic origin can report being any race, c) persons reporting two ancestries are counted in both categories. 2. Numbers in parentheses indicate the number of persons reporting this ancestry/race alone, not in combination with any other ancestry/race. 3. Refer to the Explanation of Data in the front of the book for more detailed information.

Assyrian/Chaldean/Syriac	20	0.08
Australian	28	0.11
Austrian	358	1.44
Belgian	32	0.13
Brazilian	8	0.03
British	155	0.62
Bulgarian	44	0.18
Canadian	182	0.73
Carpatho Rusyn	13	0.05
Celtic	17	0.07
Croatian	69	0.28
Czech	95	0.38
Czechoslovakian	92	0.37
Danish	133	0.54
Dutch	441	1.77
Eastern European	352	1.42
English	1,668	6.71
European	228	0.92
Finnish	48	0.19
French, except Basque	418	1.68
French Canadian	183	0.74
German	4,030	16.22
Greek	287	1.16
Hawaii Native/Pacific Islander:	24	0.10
Melanesian: (1)	1	0.00
Fijian (1)	1	0.00
Polynesian:	6	0.02
Native Hawaiian	6	0.02
Other Pac. Isl., not spec. (4)	17	0.07
Hispanic or Latino:	1,208	4.86
Central American:	59	0.24
Costa Rican	12	0.05
Guatemalan	9	0.04
Honduran	18	0.07
Nicaraguan	2	0.01
Panamanian	2	0.01
Salvadoran	16	0.06
Cuban	81	0.33
Dominican Republic	40	0.16
Mexican	130	0.52
Puerto Rican	257	1.03
South American:	332	1.34
Argentinean	10	0.04
Bolivian	1	0.00
Chilean	15	0.06
Colombian	166	0.67
Ecuadorian	69	0.28
Paraguayan	5	0.02
Peruvian	20	0.08
Uruguayan	11	0.04
Venezuelan	15	0.06
Other South American	20	0.08
Other Hispanic or Latino	309	1.24
Hungarian	308	1.24
Icelander	22	0.09
Iranian	24	0.10
Irish	4,234	17.04
Italian	4,801	19.32
Latvian	60	0.24
Lithuanian	99	0.40
Maltese	32	0.13
Northern European	23	0.09
Norwegian	320	1.29
Pennsylvania German	9	0.04
Polish	1,796	7.23
Portuguese	114	0.46
Romanian	80	0.32
Russian	1,275	5.13
Scandinavian	74	0.30
Scotch-Irish	172	0.69
Scottish	631	2.54
Serbian	13	0.05
Slavic	54	0.22
Slovak	127	0.51
Slovene	16	0.06
Swedish	286	1.15
Swiss	101	0.41
Turkish	76	0.31
Ukrainian	330	1.33
United States or American	912	3.67
Welsh	353	1.42
West Indian, excl. Hispanic:	36	0.14
Jamaican	23	0.09
Trinidadian and Tobagonian	13	0.05
White:	21,594	86.91
Not Hispanic (20,457)	20,686	83.25
Hispanic (836)	908	3.65
Yugoslavian	19	0.08

Raritan

Place Type: Township
County: Hunterdon
Population: 19,809

Ancestry/Race	Number	%
African American/Black:	285	1.44
Not Hispanic (237)	277	1.40
Hispanic (7)	8	0.04
African, sub-Saharan:	8	0.04
African	3	0.02
Nigerian	5	0.03
Am. Ind. or Alaska Nat., not spec.	14	0.07
Albanian	34	0.17
Alsatian	8	0.04
American Indian tribes, specified:	38	0.19
Apache	1	0.01
Cherokee (2)	11	0.06
Chickasaw (1)	1	0.01
Chippewa (2)	5	0.03
Choctaw	1	0.01
Iroquois (1)	4	0.02
Latin American Indians (4)	5	0.03
Seminole	2	0.01
All other tribes (5)	8	0.04
Arab:	206	1.04
Egyptian	65	0.33
Lebanese	105	0.53
Moroccan	11	0.06
Palestinian	17	0.09
Syrian	8	0.04
Armenian	20	0.10
Asian:	797	4.02
Bangladeshi (5)	5	0.03
Chinese, ex. Taiwanese (222)	258	1.30
Filipino (64)	76	0.38
Indian (284)	306	1.54
Indonesian	3	0.02
Japanese (10)	22	0.11
Korean (61)	65	0.33
Pakistani (5)	7	0.04
Taiwanese (8)	8	0.04
Thai	1	0.01
Vietnamese (25)	29	0.15
Other Asian, specified (1)	7	0.04
Other Asian, not specified (1)	10	0.05
Austrian	144	0.73
Belgian	52	0.26
Brazilian	16	0.08
British	57	0.29
Canadian	37	0.19
Celtic	33	0.17
Croatian	27	0.14
Cypriot	42	0.21
Czech	169	0.85
Czechoslovakian	127	0.64
Danish	100	0.50
Dutch	679	3.43
Eastern European	23	0.12
English	2,469	12.46
Estonian	7	0.04
European	119	0.60
Finnish	53	0.27
French, except Basque	348	1.76
French Canadian	159	0.80
German	4,585	23.15
Greek	253	1.28
Hawaii Native/Pacific Islander:	15	0.08
Polynesian: (1)	4	0.02
Native Hawaiian	2	0.01
Samoan (1)	2	0.01
Other Pac. Isl., specified	6	0.03
Other Pac. Isl., not spec. (1)	5	0.03
Hispanic or Latino:	552	2.79
Central American:	27	0.14
Costa Rican	11	0.06
Honduran	8	0.04
Nicaraguan	1	0.01
Salvadoran	7	0.04
Cuban	80	0.40
Dominican Republic	3	0.02
Mexican	86	0.43
Puerto Rican	173	0.87
South American:	75	0.38
Argentinean	6	0.03
Chilean	5	0.03
Colombian	31	0.16
Ecuadorian	16	0.08
Paraguayan	3	0.02
Peruvian	2	0.01
Uruguayan	1	0.01
Venezuelan	8	0.04
Other South American	3	0.02
Other Hispanic or Latino	108	0.55
Hungarian	427	2.16
Iranian	6	0.03
Irish	3,756	18.96
Italian	4,653	23.49
Latvian	19	0.10
Lithuanian	195	0.98
Maltese	17	0.09
Norwegian	93	0.47
Pennsylvania German	1	0.01
Polish	1,971	9.95
Portuguese	15	0.08
Romanian	59	0.30
Russian	526	2.66
Scandinavian	24	0.12
Scotch-Irish	385	1.94
Scottish	447	2.26
Slavic	54	0.27
Slovak	258	1.30
Slovene	8	0.04
Swedish	243	1.23
Swiss	62	0.31
Ukrainian	334	1.69
United States or American	685	3.46
Welsh	251	1.27
White:	18,696	94.38
Not Hispanic (18,085)	18,280	92.28
Hispanic (381)	416	2.10

Readington

Place Type: Township
County: Hunterdon
Population: 15,803

Ancestry/Race	Number	%
African American/Black:	139	0.88
Not Hispanic (118)	137	0.87
Hispanic (2)	2	0.01
African, sub-Saharan:	12	0.08
South African	12	0.08
Am. Ind. or Alaska Nat., not spec.	14	0.09
Albanian	16	0.10
American Indian tribes, specified:	25	0.16
Blackfeet (1)	1	0.01
Cherokee (3)	13	0.08
Chickasaw	1	0.01
Chippewa	1	0.01
Choctaw	1	0.01
Cree	1	0.01
Iroquois	4	0.03
Sioux	2	0.01
All other tribes (1)	1	0.01
Arab:	75	0.47
Egyptian	11	0.07
Lebanese	14	0.09
Palestinian	29	0.18

Notes: 1. Figures in the "Number" column do not add up to the total population due to: a) Ancestry/Race overlap — e.g. persons can report being both White and Irish, b) persons of Hispanic origin can report being any race, c) persons reporting two ancestries are counted in both categories. 2. Numbers in parentheses indicate the number of persons reporting this ancestry/race alone, not in combination with any other ancestry/race. 3. Refer to the Explanation of Data in the front of the book for more detailed information.

Syrian	21	0.13
Asian:	480	3.04
Cambodian (5)	5	0.03
Chinese, ex. Taiwanese (121)	146	0.92
Filipino (28)	42	0.27
Indian (173)	188	1.19
Japanese (15)	21	0.13
Korean (37)	46	0.29
Pakistani (6)	6	0.04
Taiwanese (12)	13	0.08
Thai (6)	7	0.04
Vietnamese (1)	1	0.01
Other Asian, not specified	5	0.03
Austrian	169	1.07
Basque	7	0.04
Belgian	6	0.04
Brazilian	15	0.09
British	60	0.38
Canadian	17	0.11
Carpatho Rusyn	10	0.06
Croatian	18	0.11
Czech	161	1.02
Czechoslovakian	76	0.48
Danish	151	0.96
Dutch	317	2.01
English	1,842	11.66
Estonian	9	0.06
European	94	0.59
Finnish	7	0.04
French, except Basque	478	3.02
French Canadian	102	0.65
German	3,516	22.25
Greek	110	0.70
Hawaii Native/Pacific Islander:	6	0.04
Micronesian:	4	0.03
Guamanian/Chamorro	4	0.03
Polynesian:	1	0.01
Native Hawaiian	1	0.01
Other Pac. Isl., not spec.	1	0.01
Hispanic or Latino:	324	2.05
Central American:	28	0.18
Costa Rican	5	0.03
Guatemalan	2	0.01
Honduran	10	0.06
Salvadoran	11	0.07
Cuban	35	0.22
Dominican Republic	4	0.03
Mexican	34	0.22
Puerto Rican	103	0.65
South American:	79	0.50
Argentinean	13	0.08
Bolivian	4	0.03
Chilean	8	0.05
Colombian	19	0.12
Ecuadorian	11	0.07
Peruvian	6	0.04
Uruguayan	4	0.03
Venezuelan	7	0.04
Other South American	7	0.04
Other Hispanic or Latino	41	0.26
Hungarian	428	2.71
Irish	3,575	22.62
Italian	3,284	20.78
Lithuanian	88	0.56
Norwegian	334	2.11
Pennsylvania German	21	0.13
Polish	2,047	12.95
Portuguese	109	0.69
Romanian	9	0.06
Russian	392	2.48
Scotch-Irish	311	1.97
Scottish	320	2.02
Slavic	25	0.16
Slovak	401	2.54
Slovene	15	0.09
Swedish	275	1.74
Swiss	64	0.40
Ukrainian	250	1.58
United States or American	706	4.47
Welsh	191	1.21
West Indian, excl. Hispanic:	26	0.16
Bermudan	10	0.06
Jamaican	16	0.10
White:	15,173	96.01
Not Hispanic (14,807)	14,923	94.43
Hispanic (228)	250	1.58
Yugoslavian	20	0.13

Red Bank

Place Type: Borough
County: Monmouth
Population: 11,844

Ancestry/Race	Number	%
African American/Black:	2,509	21.18
Not Hispanic (2,287)	2,397	20.24
Hispanic (88)	112	0.95
African, sub-Saharan:	107	0.90
African	95	0.80
Nigerian	12	0.10
Am. Ind. or Alaska Nat., not spec.	54	0.46
American Indian tribes, specified:	59	0.50
Apache (1)	1	0.01
Blackfeet (2)	12	0.10
Cherokee (3)	10	0.08
Delaware	6	0.05
Iroquois	2	0.02
Latin American Indians (8)	14	0.12
Pueblo	8	0.07
Seminole (1)	1	0.01
Sioux	2	0.02
All other tribes	3	0.03
American Indian tribes, not spec.	1	0.01
Arab:	20	0.17
Arab/Arabic	13	0.11
Lebanese	7	0.06
Armenian	14	0.12
Asian:	313	2.64
Chinese, ex. Taiwanese (72)	81	0.68
Filipino (103)	115	0.97
Indian (30)	42	0.35
Indonesian (2)	4	0.03
Japanese (11)	21	0.18
Korean (13)	16	0.14
Taiwanese	2	0.02
Thai (2)	3	0.03
Vietnamese (12)	13	0.11
Other Asian, specified (6)	8	0.07
Other Asian, not specified (4)	8	0.07
Austrian	81	0.68
Belgian	25	0.21
Brazilian	10	0.08
British	20	0.17
Bulgarian	8	0.07
Canadian	34	0.29
Czech	26	0.22
Czechoslovakian	16	0.14
Danish	61	0.52
Dutch	123	1.04
Eastern European	28	0.24
English	773	6.53
European	32	0.27
French, except Basque	164	1.38
French Canadian	44	0.37
German	1,341	11.32
Greek	41	0.35
Guyanese	8	0.07
Hawaii Native/Pacific Islander:	20	0.17
Micronesian: (1)	1	0.01
Guamanian/Chamorro (1)	1	0.01
Polynesian: (6)	9	0.08
Native Hawaiian (4)	7	0.06
Samoan (1)	1	0.01
Other Polynesian (1)	1	0.01
Other Pac. Isl., specified	2	0.02
Other Pac. Isl., not spec. (3)	8	0.07
Hispanic or Latino:	2,027	17.11
Central American:	178	1.50
Costa Rican	23	0.19
Guatemalan	4	0.03
Honduran	8	0.07
Nicaraguan	6	0.05
Panamanian	3	0.03
Salvadoran	120	1.01
Other Central American	14	0.12
Cuban	24	0.20
Dominican Republic	12	0.10
Mexican	1,171	9.89
Puerto Rican	296	2.50
South American:	83	0.70
Argentinean	7	0.06
Bolivian	3	0.03
Chilean	6	0.05
Colombian	31	0.26
Ecuadorian	18	0.15
Peruvian	4	0.03
Venezuelan	9	0.08
Other South American	5	0.04
Other Hispanic or Latino	263	2.22
Hungarian	62	0.52
Irish	2,326	19.64
Italian	1,657	13.99
Latvian	9	0.08
Lithuanian	45	0.38
Norwegian	110	0.93
Polish	494	4.17
Portuguese	6	0.05
Romanian	50	0.42
Russian	279	2.36
Scandinavian	8	0.07
Scotch-Irish	137	1.16
Scottish	165	1.39
Slavic	6	0.05
Slovak	34	0.29
Swedish	115	0.97
Swiss	14	0.12
Ukrainian	46	0.39
United States or American	384	3.24
Welsh	25	0.21
West Indian, excl. Hispanic:	112	0.95
Belizean	11	0.09
Jamaican	68	0.57
Trinidadian and Tobagonian	23	0.19
U.S. Virgin Islander	10	0.08
White:	8,282	69.93
Not Hispanic (7,063)	7,188	60.69
Hispanic (1,014)	1,094	9.24
Yugoslavian	6	0.05

Ridgefield Park

Place Type: Village
County: Bergen
Population: 12,873

Ancestry/Race	Number	%
African American/Black:	600	4.66
Not Hispanic (446)	494	3.84
Hispanic (82)	106	0.82
African, sub-Saharan:	26	0.20
African	26	0.20
Alaska Native tribes, specified:	8	0.06
Eskimo	8	0.06
Am. Ind. or Alaska Nat., not spec.	30	0.23
Albanian	10	0.08
Alsatian	8	0.06
American Indian tribes, specified:	22	0.17
Blackfeet (1)	1	0.01
Cherokee (2)	5	0.04
Colville (1)	1	0.01
Creek	1	0.01
Delaware	1	0.01
Iroquois	1	0.01
Latin American Indians (6)	11	0.09
All other tribes (1)	1	0.01
American Indian tribes, not spec.	15	0.12
Arab:	270	2.10
Arab/Arabic	35	0.27
Egyptian	161	1.25

Notes: 1. Figures in the "Number" column do not add up to the total population due to: a) Ancestry/Race overlap — e.g. persons can report being both White and Irish, b) persons of Hispanic origin can report being any race, c) persons reporting two ancestries are counted in both categories. 2. Numbers in parentheses indicate the number of persons reporting this ancestry/race alone, not in combination with any other ancestry/race. 3. Refer to the Explanation of Data in the front of the book for more detailed information.

Lebanese	62	0.48
Syrian	12	0.09
Armenian	84	0.65
Asian:	1,097	8.52
Bangladeshi (3)	5	0.04
Chinese, ex. Taiwanese (74)	85	0.66
Filipino (243)	260	2.02
Indian (177)	217	1.69
Indonesian (1)	1	0.01
Japanese (41)	46	0.36
Korean (407)	407	3.16
Pakistani (24)	37	0.29
Taiwanese (1)	1	0.01
Thai (3)	3	0.02
Vietnamese (2)	4	0.03
Other Asian, specified (2)	2	0.02
Other Asian, not specified (16)	29	0.23
Australian	20	0.16
Austrian	75	0.58
Belgian	10	0.08
Brazilian	9	0.07
British	38	0.30
Canadian	27	0.21
Croatian	30	0.23
Czech	39	0.30
Czechoslovakian	25	0.19
Danish	34	0.26
Dutch	86	0.67
Eastern European	14	0.11
English	693	5.38
Estonian	7	0.05
European	23	0.18
French, except Basque	231	1.79
French Canadian	113	0.88
German	1,748	13.58
Greek	198	1.54
Guyanese	11	0.09
Hawaii Native/Pacific Islander:	16	0.12
Micronesian: (1)	1	0.01
Guamanian/Chamorro (1)	1	0.01
Polynesian: (3)	5	0.04
Samoan (3)	5	0.04
Other Pac. Isl., not spec.	10	0.08
Hispanic or Latino:	2,863	22.24
Central American:	150	1.17
Costa Rican	35	0.27
Guatemalan	16	0.12
Honduran	17	0.13
Nicaraguan	14	0.11
Panamanian	18	0.14
Salvadoran	46	0.36
Other Central American	4	0.03
Cuban	513	3.99
Dominican Republic	404	3.14
Mexican	64	0.50
Puerto Rican	491	3.81
South American:	636	4.94
Argentinean	23	0.18
Bolivian	6	0.05
Chilean	25	0.19
Colombian	347	2.70
Ecuadorian	185	1.44
Peruvian	25	0.19
Uruguayan	4	0.03
Venezuelan	6	0.05
Other South American	15	0.12
Other Hispanic or Latino	605	4.70
Hungarian	60	0.47
Irish	2,712	21.07
Italian	2,796	21.72
Latvian	8	0.06
Lithuanian	28	0.22
Norwegian	75	0.58
Polish	429	3.33
Portuguese	24	0.19
Russian	121	0.94
Scandinavian	5	0.04
Scotch-Irish	91	0.71
Scottish	145	1.13
Slovak	5	0.04
Swedish	101	0.78
Swiss	25	0.19
Turkish	13	0.10
Ukrainian	68	0.53
United States or American	301	2.34
Welsh	6	0.05
West Indian, excl. Hispanic:	127	0.99
British West Indian	4	0.03
Jamaican	76	0.59
Trinidadian and Tobagonian	16	0.12
West Indian	31	0.24
White:	10,392	80.73
Not Hispanic (8,338)	8,475	65.84
Hispanic (1,729)	1,917	14.89
Yugoslavian	56	0.44

Ridgefield

Place Type: Borough
County: Bergen
Population: 10,830

Ancestry/Race	Number	%
African American/Black:	122	1.13
Not Hispanic (71)	96	0.89
Hispanic (12)	26	0.24
African, sub-Saharan:	8	0.07
South African	8	0.07
Am. Ind. or Alaska Nat., not spec.	16	0.15
Albanian	8	0.07
American Indian tribes, specified:	19	0.18
Apache	1	0.01
Blackfeet (1)	2	0.02
Cherokee (1)	4	0.04
Creek (1)	1	0.01
Delaware	1	0.01
Latin American Indians (3)	7	0.06
Shoshone	2	0.02
Sioux (1)	1	0.01
American Indian tribes, not spec.	1	0.01
Arab:	206	1.90
Arab/Arabic	7	0.06
Egyptian	4	0.04
Lebanese	68	0.63
Palestinian	53	0.49
Syrian	74	0.68
Armenian	294	2.71
Asian:	1,962	18.12
Bangladeshi	1	0.01
Cambodian (1)	1	0.01
Chinese, ex. Taiwanese (129)	133	1.23
Filipino (60)	62	0.57
Indian (120)	133	1.23
Japanese (36)	39	0.36
Korean (1,519)	1,550	14.31
Pakistani (4)	4	0.04
Taiwanese (5)	5	0.05
Vietnamese (5)	5	0.05
Other Asian, not specified (3)	29	0.27
Assyrian/Chaldean/Syriac	25	0.23
Austrian	15	0.14
Belgian	13	0.12
Brazilian	44	0.41
British	8	0.07
Canadian	5	0.05
Croatian	366	3.38
Czech	50	0.46
Czechoslovakian	17	0.16
Danish	22	0.20
Dutch	99	0.91
English	269	2.48
Estonian	10	0.09
European	25	0.23
Finnish	5	0.05
French, except Basque	188	1.74
German	1,081	9.98
Greek	252	2.33
Hawaii Native/Pacific Islander:	19	0.18
Micronesian:	1	0.01
Guamanian/Chamorro	1	0.01
Other Pac. Isl., not spec. (4)	18	0.17
Hispanic or Latino:	1,494	13.80
Central American:	85	0.78
Costa Rican	9	0.08
Guatemalan	38	0.35
Honduran	2	0.02
Nicaraguan	3	0.03
Salvadoran	27	0.25
Other Central American	6	0.06
Cuban	361	3.33
Dominican Republic	121	1.12
Mexican	30	0.28
Puerto Rican	244	2.25
South American:	332	3.07
Argentinean	26	0.24
Chilean	15	0.14
Colombian	148	1.37
Ecuadorian	91	0.84
Paraguayan	1	0.01
Peruvian	30	0.28
Uruguayan	5	0.05
Venezuelan	9	0.08
Other South American	7	0.06
Other Hispanic or Latino	321	2.96
Hungarian	137	1.27
Iranian	26	0.24
Irish	1,392	12.85
Italian	2,623	24.22
Latvian	9	0.08
Lithuanian	17	0.16
Norwegian	29	0.27
Polish	264	2.44
Romanian	22	0.20
Russian	110	1.02
Scandinavian	5	0.05
Scotch-Irish	73	0.67
Scottish	65	0.60
Slovak	19	0.18
Slovene	6	0.06
Swedish	19	0.18
Swiss	56	0.52
Turkish	152	1.40
Ukrainian	102	0.94
United States or American	350	3.23
Welsh	16	0.15
West Indian, excl. Hispanic:	83	0.77
Barbadian	7	0.06
British West Indian	60	0.55
Jamaican	8	0.07
Other West Indian	8	0.07
White:	8,427	77.81
Not Hispanic (7,189)	7,319	67.58
Hispanic (1,028)	1,108	10.23
Yugoslavian	18	0.17

Ridgewood

Place Type: Village
County: Bergen
Population: 24,936

Ancestry/Race	Number	%
African American/Black:	492	1.97
Not Hispanic (395)	473	1.90
Hispanic (14)	19	0.08
African, sub-Saharan:	33	0.13
African	33	0.13
Alaska Native tribes, specified:	2	0.01
Alaska Athabascan	1	0.00
Eskimo (1)	1	0.00
Am. Ind. or Alaska Nat., not spec.	21	0.08
Albanian	32	0.13
American Indian tribes, specified:	16	0.06
Cherokee (2)	8	0.03
Chippewa	1	0.00
Latin American Indians (1)	1	0.00
Seminole	2	0.01
All other tribes	4	0.02
Arab:	278	1.11
Arab/Arabic	39	0.16

Notes: 1. Figures in the "Number" column do not add up to the total population due to: a) Ancestry/Race overlap — e.g. persons can report being both White and Irish, b) persons of Hispanic origin can report being any race, c) persons reporting two ancestries are counted in both categories. 2. Numbers in parentheses indicate the number of persons reporting this ancestry/race alone, not in combination with any other ancestry/race. 3. Refer to the Explanation of Data in the front of the book for more detailed information.

Ancestry/Race	Number	%
Egyptian	33	0.13
Iraqi	33	0.13
Lebanese	109	0.44
Palestinian	13	0.05
Syrian	41	0.16
Other Arab	10	0.04
Armenian	131	0.53
Asian:	2,325	9.32
Chinese, ex. Taiwanese (442)	485	1.94
Filipino (240)	276	1.11
Indian (327)	344	1.38
Indonesian (1)	1	0.00
Japanese (379)	423	1.70
Korean (664)	681	2.73
Malaysian (1)	3	0.01
Pakistani (14)	16	0.06
Sri Lankan (6)	6	0.02
Taiwanese (30)	35	0.14
Thai (13)	13	0.05
Vietnamese (15)	18	0.07
Other Asian, not specified (11)	24	0.10
Australian	74	0.30
Austrian	309	1.24
Belgian	82	0.33
Brazilian	12	0.05
British	138	0.55
Canadian	93	0.37
Celtic	7	0.03
Croatian	86	0.34
Cypriot	22	0.09
Czech	121	0.49
Czechoslovakian	124	0.50
Danish	114	0.46
Dutch	697	2.80
Eastern European	188	0.75
English	2,667	10.70
European	175	0.70
Finnish	55	0.22
French, except Basque	616	2.47
French Canadian	59	0.24
German	3,625	14.54
Greek	314	1.26
Hawaii Native/Pacific Islander:	11	0.04
Polynesian:	7	0.03
Native Hawaiian	6	0.02
Samoan	1	0.00
Other Pac. Isl., not spec.	4	0.02
Hispanic or Latino:	942	3.78
Central American:	134	0.54
Costa Rican	72	0.29
Guatemalan	4	0.02
Nicaraguan	4	0.02
Panamanian	1	0.00
Salvadoran	51	0.20
Other Central American	2	0.01
Cuban	134	0.54
Dominican Republic	48	0.19
Mexican	110	0.44
Puerto Rican	173	0.69
South American:	157	0.63
Argentinean	33	0.13
Bolivian	1	0.01
Chilean	4	0.02
Colombian	38	0.15
Ecuadorian	10	0.04
Peruvian	42	0.17
Uruguayan	7	0.03
Venezuelan	13	0.05
Other South American	8	0.03
Other Hispanic or Latino	186	0.75
Hungarian	191	0.77
Icelander	14	0.06
Iranian	85	0.34
Irish	5,605	22.48
Israeli	54	0.22
Italian	4,482	17.97
Latvian	42	0.17
Lithuanian	133	0.53
Macedonian	53	0.21
Northern European	5	0.02
Norwegian	209	0.84
Pennsylvania German	6	0.02
Polish	1,418	5.69
Portuguese	35	0.14
Romanian	87	0.35
Russian	1,067	4.28
Scandinavian	23	0.09
Scotch-Irish	405	1.62
Scottish	681	2.73
Serbian	49	0.20
Slavic	18	0.07
Slovak	144	0.58
Soviet Union	10	0.04
Swedish	286	1.15
Swiss	146	0.59
Turkish	138	0.55
Ukrainian	137	0.55
United States or American	1,109	4.45
Welsh	203	0.81
West Indian, excl. Hispanic:	94	0.38
Bahamian	15	0.06
Barbadian	13	0.05
Jamaican	48	0.19
Trinidadian and Tobagonian	7	0.03
West Indian	11	0.04
White:	22,152	88.84
Not Hispanic (21,164)	21,356	85.64
Hispanic (735)	796	3.19
Yugoslavian	11	0.04

Ringwood

Place Type: Borough
County: Passaic
Population: 12,396

Ancestry/Race	Number	%
African American/Black:	269	2.17
Not Hispanic (183)	232	1.87
Hispanic (16)	37	0.30
African, sub-Saharan:	17	0.14
South African	17	0.14
Am. Ind. or Alaska Nat., not spec.	42	0.34
American Indian tribes, specified:	182	1.47
Cherokee (3)	14	0.11
Chippewa (8)	8	0.06
Delaware (132)	145	1.17
Iroquois (7)	8	0.06
Latin American Indians (1)	1	0.01
Seminole (1)	1	0.01
Sioux (1)	1	0.01
All other tribes (4)	4	0.03
American Indian tribes, not spec.	10	0.08
Arab:	74	0.60
Lebanese	25	0.20
Syrian	49	0.40
Armenian	15	0.12
Asian:	190	1.53
Chinese, ex. Taiwanese (28)	37	0.30
Filipino (15)	19	0.15
Indian (63)	71	0.57
Japanese (9)	23	0.19
Korean (22)	27	0.22
Pakistani (3)	3	0.02
Taiwanese (4)	4	0.03
Thai	1	0.01
Vietnamese (1)	2	0.02
Other Asian, not specified (2)	3	0.02
Austrian	139	1.12
Belgian	33	0.27
Brazilian	10	0.08
British	52	0.42
Bulgarian	12	0.10
Canadian	7	0.06
Croatian	9	0.07
Czech	37	0.30
Czechoslovakian	88	0.71
Danish	30	0.24
Dutch	529	4.27
Eastern European	43	0.35
English	1,033	8.33
Estonian	9	0.07
European	65	0.52
Finnish	44	0.35
French, except Basque	310	2.50
French Canadian	58	0.47
German	2,915	23.52
Greek	71	0.57
Hawaii Native/Pacific Islander:	3	0.02
Other Pac. Isl., not spec. (1)	3	0.02
Hispanic or Latino:	527	4.25
Central American:	17	0.14
Costa Rican	3	0.02
Guatemalan	5	0.04
Honduran	1	0.01
Salvadoran	6	0.05
Other Central American	2	0.02
Cuban	61	0.49
Dominican Republic	17	0.14
Mexican	40	0.32
Puerto Rican	195	1.57
South American:	73	0.59
Argentinean	8	0.06
Bolivian	1	0.01
Chilean	2	0.02
Colombian	35	0.28
Ecuadorian	10	0.08
Paraguayan	1	0.01
Peruvian	11	0.09
Uruguayan	1	0.01
Venezuelan	2	0.02
Other South American	2	0.02
Other Hispanic or Latino	124	1.00
Hungarian	218	1.76
Iranian	32	0.26
Irish	3,117	25.15
Italian	3,309	26.69
Lithuanian	93	0.75
Macedonian	38	0.31
Maltese	8	0.06
Northern European	33	0.27
Norwegian	50	0.40
Polish	1,008	8.13
Portuguese	44	0.35
Romanian	28	0.23
Russian	426	3.44
Scandinavian	44	0.35
Scotch-Irish	121	0.98
Scottish	246	1.98
Serbian	10	0.08
Slovak	47	0.38
Slovene	8	0.06
Swedish	154	1.24
Swiss	116	0.94
Ukrainian	137	1.11
United States or American	193	1.56
Welsh	17	0.14
White:	11,747	94.76
Not Hispanic (11,256)	11,329	91.39
Hispanic (380)	418	3.37
Yugoslavian	112	0.90

River Edge

Place Type: Borough
County: Bergen
Population: 10,946

Ancestry/Race	Number	%
African American/Black:	140	1.28
Not Hispanic (108)	124	1.13
Hispanic (8)	16	0.15
African, sub-Saharan:	33	0.30
African	28	0.26
Ethiopian	5	0.05
Alaska Native tribes, specified:	1	0.01
Tlingit-Haida (1)	1	0.01
Am. Ind. or Alaska Nat., not spec.	8	0.07
American Indian tribes, specified:	12	0.11
Blackfeet	1	0.01

Notes: 1. Figures in the "Number" column do not add up to the total population due to: a) Ancestry/Race overlap — e.g. persons can report being both White and Irish, b) persons of Hispanic origin can report being any race, c) persons reporting two ancestries are counted in both categories. 2. Numbers in parentheses indicate the number of persons reporting this ancestry/race alone, not in combination with any other ancestry/race. 3. Refer to the Explanation of Data in the front of the book for more detailed information.

Ancestry/Race	Number	%
Cherokee (1)	6	0.05
Iroquois	1	0.01
Latin American Indians (1)	4	0.04
American Indian tribes, not spec.	4	0.04
Arab:	98	0.90
Jordanian	17	0.16
Lebanese	49	0.45
Syrian	25	0.23
Other Arab	7	0.06
Armenian	147	1.34
Asian:	1,455	13.29
Bangladeshi (5)	6	0.05
Chinese, ex. Taiwanese (299)	328	3.00
Filipino (154)	165	1.51
Indian (160)	172	1.57
Indonesian (3)	3	0.03
Japanese (142)	154	1.41
Korean (542)	553	5.05
Malaysian (8)	8	0.07
Pakistani (7)	7	0.06
Sri Lankan (3)	3	0.03
Taiwanese (2)	4	0.04
Thai (28)	28	0.26
Vietnamese (7)	10	0.09
Other Asian, specified (1)	2	0.02
Other Asian, not specified (7)	12	0.11
Austrian	98	0.90
Belgian	37	0.34
Brazilian	16	0.15
British	21	0.19
Croatian	20	0.18
Czech	47	0.43
Czechoslovakian	30	0.27
Danish	37	0.34
Dutch	52	0.48
Eastern European	47	0.43
English	551	5.03
European	39	0.36
French, except Basque	132	1.21
French Canadian	55	0.50
German	1,653	15.10
Greek	375	3.43
Guyanese	16	0.15
Hawaii Native/Pacific Islander:	2	0.02
Micronesian: (1)	1	0.01
Guamanian/Chamorro (1)	1	0.01
Other Pac. Isl., specified	1	0.01
Hispanic or Latino:	581	5.31
Central American:	29	0.26
Costa Rican	18	0.16
Guatemalan	4	0.04
Honduran	1	0.01
Nicaraguan	1	0.01
Panamanian	4	0.04
Salvadoran	1	0.01
Cuban	113	1.03
Dominican Republic	31	0.28
Mexican	32	0.29
Puerto Rican	141	1.29
South American:	126	1.15
Argentinean	12	0.11
Chilean	8	0.07
Colombian	53	0.48
Ecuadorian	25	0.23
Peruvian	12	0.11
Venezuelan	11	0.10
Other South American	5	0.05
Other Hispanic or Latino	109	1.00
Hungarian	71	0.65
Iranian	13	0.12
Irish	2,798	25.56
Israeli	17	0.16
Italian	2,253	20.58
Latvian	8	0.07
Lithuanian	27	0.25
Norwegian	69	0.63
Polish	696	6.36
Portuguese	5	0.05
Romanian	69	0.63
Russian	698	6.38
Scandinavian	47	0.43
Scotch-Irish	80	0.73
Scottish	154	1.41
Slovak	25	0.23
Swedish	64	0.58
Swiss	17	0.16
Turkish	7	0.06
Ukrainian	132	1.21
United States or American	292	2.67
Welsh	29	0.26
West Indian, excl. Hispanic:	51	0.47
Trinidadian and Tobagonian	12	0.11
West Indian	39	0.36
White:	9,331	85.25
Not Hispanic (8,758)	8,846	80.81
Hispanic (450)	485	4.43

Rockaway

Place Type: Township
County: Morris
Population: 22,930

Ancestry/Race	Number	%
African American/Black:	659	2.87
Not Hispanic (538)	615	2.68
Hispanic (27)	44	0.19
African, sub-Saharan:	157	0.68
African	32	0.14
Nigerian	109	0.48
South African	9	0.04
Sudanese	7	0.03
Am. Ind. or Alaska Nat., not spec.	48	0.21
American Indian tribes, specified:	28	0.12
Blackfeet	1	0.00
Cherokee	6	0.03
Chippewa	1	0.00
Choctaw (1)	1	0.00
Delaware (5)	5	0.02
Iroquois (1)	3	0.01
Latin American Indians (2)	2	0.01
Pueblo	1	0.00
All other tribes (4)	8	0.03
American Indian tribes, not spec.	3	0.01
Arab:	118	0.51
Arab/Arabic	14	0.06
Egyptian	10	0.04
Lebanese	38	0.17
Palestinian	32	0.14
Syrian	24	0.10
Armenian	65	0.28
Asian:	1,433	6.25
Bangladeshi (2)	2	0.01
Chinese, ex. Taiwanese (259)	281	1.23
Filipino (211)	241	1.05
Indian (553)	588	2.56
Japanese (38)	49	0.21
Korean (115)	125	0.55
Laotian (1)	1	0.00
Malaysian (2)	2	0.01
Pakistani (9)	10	0.04
Sri Lankan (4)	4	0.02
Taiwanese (6)	10	0.04
Thai (13)	14	0.06
Vietnamese (53)	54	0.24
Other Asian, specified	8	0.03
Other Asian, not specified (11)	44	0.19
Assyrian/Chaldean/Syriac	8	0.03
Austrian	195	0.85
Basque	13	0.06
Belgian	27	0.12
Brazilian	8	0.03
British	35	0.15
Canadian	19	0.08
Croatian	44	0.19
Czech	100	0.44
Czechoslovakian	87	0.38
Danish	119	0.52
Dutch	539	2.35
Eastern European	108	0.47
English	1,812	7.90
European	97	0.42
Finnish	12	0.05
French, except Basque	397	1.73
French Canadian	141	0.61
German	3,495	15.24
Greek	123	0.54
Guyanese	10	0.04
Hawaii Native/Pacific Islander:	14	0.06
Micronesian: (1)	1	0.00
Guamanian/Chamorro (1)	1	0.00
Polynesian: (3)	3	0.01
Native Hawaiian (3)	3	0.01
Other Pac. Isl., specified	7	0.03
Other Pac. Isl., not spec.	3	0.01
Hispanic or Latino:	1,440	6.28
Central American:	73	0.32
Costa Rican	19	0.08
Guatemalan	19	0.08
Honduran	14	0.06
Panamanian	7	0.03
Salvadoran	5	0.02
Other Central American	9	0.04
Cuban	109	0.48
Dominican Republic	29	0.13
Mexican	127	0.55
Puerto Rican	455	1.98
South American:	356	1.55
Argentinean	12	0.05
Chilean	21	0.09
Colombian	187	0.82
Ecuadorian	54	0.24
Paraguayan	3	0.01
Peruvian	46	0.20
Uruguayan	8	0.03
Venezuelan	6	0.03
Other South American	19	0.08
Other Hispanic or Latino	291	1.27
Hungarian	412	1.80
Iranian	36	0.16
Irish	4,429	19.32
Israeli	16	0.07
Italian	5,373	23.43
Latvian	15	0.07
Lithuanian	215	0.94
Macedonian	13	0.06
Norwegian	394	1.72
Polish	2,300	10.03
Portuguese	93	0.41
Romanian	161	0.70
Russian	1,034	4.51
Scandinavian	5	0.02
Scotch-Irish	349	1.52
Scottish	368	1.60
Serbian	33	0.14
Slavic	48	0.21
Slovak	183	0.80
Swedish	353	1.54
Swiss	90	0.39
Turkish	68	0.30
Ukrainian	244	1.06
United States or American	889	3.88
Welsh	171	0.75
West Indian, excl. Hispanic:	122	0.53
Haitian	61	0.27
Jamaican	46	0.20
Trinidadian and Tobagonian	4	0.02
West Indian	11	0.05
White:	20,616	89.91
Not Hispanic (19,393)	19,569	85.34
Hispanic (982)	1,047	4.57
Yugoslavian	40	0.17

Roselle Park

Place Type: Borough
County: Union
Population: 13,281

Ancestry/Race	Number	%

Notes: 1. Figures in the "Number" column do not add up to the total population due to: a) Ancestry/Race overlap — e.g. persons can report being both White and Irish, b) persons of Hispanic origin can report being any race, c) persons reporting two ancestries are counted in both categories. 2. Numbers in parentheses indicate the number of persons reporting this ancestry/race alone, not in combination with any other ancestry/race. 3. Refer to the Explanation of Data in the front of the book for more detailed information.

Ancestry/Race	Number	%
African American/Black:	378	2.85
Not Hispanic (298)	335	2.52
Hispanic (24)	43	0.32
African, sub-Saharan:	28	0.21
African	9	0.07
Ghanian	19	0.14
Am. Ind. or Alaska Nat., not spec.	34	0.26
Albanian	72	0.54
American Indian tribes, specified:	16	0.12
Cherokee (1)	2	0.02
Cheyenne	1	0.01
Latin American Indians	7	0.05
Lumbee (1)	1	0.01
Sioux (1)	4	0.03
All other tribes	1	0.01
American Indian tribes, not spec.	3	0.02
Arab:	89	0.67
Arab/Arabic	11	0.08
Egyptian	64	0.48
Jordanian	7	0.05
Lebanese	7	0.05
Armenian	23	0.17
Asian:	1,300	9.79
Bangladeshi (2)	2	0.02
Cambodian (1)	2	0.02
Chinese, ex. Taiwanese (78)	89	0.67
Filipino (207)	237	1.78
Indian (859)	896	6.75
Indonesian (2)	2	0.02
Japanese (9)	13	0.10
Korean (14)	15	0.11
Pakistani (14)	14	0.11
Thai (3)	4	0.03
Vietnamese (10)	10	0.08
Other Asian, specified	1	0.01
Other Asian, not specified (9)	15	0.11
Austrian	75	0.56
Basque	6	0.05
Belgian	8	0.06
British	43	0.32
Canadian	28	0.21
Croatian	16	0.12
Czechoslovakian	31	0.23
Danish	21	0.16
Dutch	145	1.09
English	534	4.02
European	26	0.20
Finnish	14	0.11
French, except Basque	187	1.41
French Canadian	52	0.39
German	1,650	12.42
Greek	146	1.10
Guyanese	10	0.08
Hawaii Native/Pacific Islander:	5	0.04
Other Pac. Isl., not spec. (2)	5	0.04
Hispanic or Latino:	2,170	16.34
Central American:	116	0.87
Costa Rican	19	0.14
Guatemalan	19	0.14
Honduran	23	0.17
Nicaraguan	7	0.05
Panamanian	14	0.11
Salvadoran	26	0.20
Other Central American	8	0.06
Cuban	275	2.07
Dominican Republic	53	0.40
Mexican	242	1.82
Puerto Rican	423	3.19
South American:	558	4.20
Argentinean	27	0.20
Bolivian	1	0.01
Chilean	27	0.20
Colombian	259	1.95
Ecuadorian	75	0.56
Peruvian	99	0.75
Uruguayan	39	0.29
Venezuelan	8	0.06
Other South American	23	0.17
Other Hispanic or Latino	503	3.79
Hungarian	133	1.00
Irish	2,651	19.96
Italian	3,350	25.22
Lithuanian	95	0.72
Norwegian	48	0.36
Polish	1,042	7.85
Portuguese	211	1.59
Romanian	66	0.50
Russian	215	1.62
Scotch-Irish	177	1.33
Scottish	164	1.23
Serbian	4	0.03
Slovak	157	1.18
Slovene	7	0.05
Swedish	61	0.46
Swiss	12	0.09
Ukrainian	278	2.09
United States or American	343	2.58
Welsh	43	0.32
West Indian, excl. Hispanic:	123	0.93
Barbadian	9	0.07
Haitian	114	0.86
White:	10,999	82.82
Not Hispanic (9,397)	9,536	71.80
Hispanic (1,343)	1,463	11.02
Yugoslavian	50	0.38

Roselle

Place Type: Borough
County: Union
Population: 21,274

Ancestry/Race	Number	%
African American/Black:	11,395	53.56
Not Hispanic (10,669)	11,069	52.03
Hispanic (248)	326	1.53
African, sub-Saharan:	525	2.47
African	246	1.16
Ghanian	86	0.40
Liberian	8	0.04
Nigerian	103	0.48
Sierra Leonean	25	0.12
Other sub-Saharan African	57	0.27
Am. Ind. or Alaska Nat., not spec.	81	0.38
Albanian	18	0.08
American Indian tribes, specified:	82	0.39
Blackfeet	4	0.02
Cherokee (2)	30	0.14
Chippewa	3	0.01
Choctaw	2	0.01
Crow	1	0.00
Delaware (1)	1	0.00
Iroquois (1)	3	0.01
Latin American Indians (7)	23	0.11
Lumbee (1)	1	0.00
Navajo	3	0.01
Seminole	4	0.02
Sioux	1	0.00
All other tribes (1)	6	0.03
American Indian tribes, not spec.	11	0.05
Arab:	169	0.79
Arab/Arabic	7	0.03
Egyptian	91	0.43
Lebanese	4	0.02
Moroccan	43	0.20
Syrian	24	0.11
Asian:	671	3.15
Chinese, ex. Taiwanese (46)	59	0.28
Filipino (209)	233	1.10
Indian (226)	261	1.23
Japanese (5)	10	0.05
Korean (29)	30	0.14
Pakistani (24)	29	0.14
Sri Lankan (1)	1	0.00
Taiwanese (3)	4	0.02
Thai (1)	1	0.00
Vietnamese (17)	18	0.08
Other Asian, not specified (10)	25	0.12
Austrian	70	0.33
Brazilian	33	0.16
British	27	0.13
Croatian	11	0.05
Czech	59	0.28
Czechoslovakian	18	0.08
Danish	27	0.13
Dutch	80	0.38
English	455	2.14
Finnish	15	0.07
French, except Basque	142	0.67
French Canadian	65	0.31
German	1,210	5.69
Greek	19	0.09
Guyanese	202	0.95
Hawaii Native/Pacific Islander:	41	0.19
Micronesian: (10)	11	0.05
Guamanian/Chamorro (9)	10	0.05
Other Micronesian (1)	1	0.00
Polynesian: (5)	13	0.06
Native Hawaiian (4)	11	0.05
Samoan (1)	2	0.01
Other Pac. Isl., not spec.	17	0.08
Hispanic or Latino:	3,641	17.11
Central American:	266	1.25
Costa Rican	16	0.08
Guatemalan	34	0.16
Honduran	47	0.22
Nicaraguan	15	0.07
Panamanian	16	0.08
Salvadoran	107	0.50
Other Central American	31	0.15
Cuban	230	1.08
Dominican Republic	177	0.83
Mexican	597	2.81
Puerto Rican	876	4.12
South American:	809	3.80
Argentinean	35	0.16
Bolivian	8	0.04
Chilean	13	0.06
Colombian	428	2.01
Ecuadorian	77	0.36
Peruvian	155	0.73
Uruguayan	44	0.21
Venezuelan	10	0.05
Other South American	39	0.18
Other Hispanic or Latino	686	3.22
Hungarian	126	0.59
Irish	1,633	7.68
Italian	1,378	6.48
Latvian	4	0.02
Lithuanian	101	0.47
Norwegian	21	0.10
Polish	1,065	5.01
Portuguese	204	0.96
Russian	124	0.58
Scotch-Irish	43	0.20
Scottish	91	0.43
Slavic	14	0.07
Slovak	104	0.49
Swedish	50	0.24
Turkish	34	0.16
Ukrainian	112	0.53
United States or American	283	1.33
Welsh	104	0.49
West Indian, excl. Hispanic:	2,331	10.96
British West Indian	45	0.21
Dutch West Indian	5	0.02
Haitian	1,709	8.03
Jamaican	386	1.81
Trinidadian and Tobagonian	141	0.66
West Indian	45	0.21
White:	8,016	37.68
Not Hispanic (5,674)	5,907	27.77
Hispanic (1,896)	2,109	9.91

Notes: 1. Figures in the "Number" column do not add up to the total population due to: a) Ancestry/Race overlap — e.g. persons can report being both White and Irish, b) persons of Hispanic origin can report being any race, c) persons reporting two ancestries are counted in both categories. 2. Numbers in parentheses indicate the number of persons reporting this ancestry/race alone, not in combination with any other ancestry/race. 3. Refer to the Explanation of Data in the front of the book for more detailed information.

Roxbury

Place Type: Township
County: Morris
Population: 23,883

Ancestry/Race	Number	%
African American/Black:	528	2.21
Not Hispanic (432)	498	2.09
Hispanic (24)	30	0.13
African, sub-Saharan:	60	0.25
African	60	0.25
Am. Ind. or Alaska Nat., not spec.	32	0.13
Albanian	8	0.03
Alsatian	8	0.03
American Indian tribes, specified:	37	0.15
Blackfeet	5	0.02
Cherokee (2)	11	0.05
Choctaw	1	0.00
Cree	1	0.00
Creek	1	0.00
Delaware (4)	4	0.02
Latin American Indians (4)	4	0.02
Ottawa (1)	1	0.00
Pueblo (1)	2	0.01
Seminole (3)	3	0.01
Sioux	1	0.00
All other tribes (1)	3	0.01
American Indian tribes, not spec.	9	0.04
Arab:	74	0.31
Arab/Arabic	12	0.05
Egyptian	30	0.13
Jordanian	14	0.06
Syrian	18	0.08
Armenian	13	0.05
Asian:	970	4.06
Bangladeshi (3)	3	0.01
Chinese, ex. Taiwanese (203)	240	1.00
Filipino (126)	149	0.62
Indian (344)	359	1.50
Indonesian (1)	1	0.00
Japanese (17)	27	0.11
Korean (92)	106	0.44
Sri Lankan (1)	1	0.00
Taiwanese (4)	7	0.03
Thai (4)	6	0.03
Vietnamese (30)	44	0.18
Other Asian, specified (1)	5	0.02
Other Asian, not specified (7)	22	0.09
Australian	22	0.09
Austrian	209	0.88
Basque	16	0.07
Belgian	11	0.05
Brazilian	14	0.06
British	82	0.34
Canadian	48	0.20
Croatian	9	0.04
Czech	138	0.58
Czechoslovakian	88	0.37
Danish	164	0.69
Dutch	473	1.98
Eastern European	57	0.24
English	2,180	9.13
European	186	0.78
Finnish	29	0.12
French, except Basque	465	1.95
French Canadian	90	0.38
German	4,583	19.19
Greek	183	0.77
Hawaii Native/Pacific Islander:	20	0.08
Micronesian: (3)	4	0.02
Guamanian/Chamorro (3)	4	0.02
Polynesian:	1	0.00
Native Hawaiian	1	0.00
Other Pac. Isl., not spec. (14)	15	0.06
Hispanic or Latino:	1,154	4.83
Central American:	61	0.26
Costa Rican	17	0.07
Guatemalan	9	0.04
Honduran	18	0.08
Panamanian	1	0.00
Salvadoran	12	0.05
Other Central American	4	0.02
Cuban	103	0.43
Dominican Republic	18	0.08
Mexican	77	0.32
Puerto Rican	393	1.65
South American:	227	0.95
Argentinean	12	0.05
Bolivian	1	0.00
Chilean	22	0.09
Colombian	112	0.47
Ecuadorian	42	0.18
Peruvian	7	0.03
Uruguayan	19	0.08
Venezuelan	4	0.02
Other South American	8	0.03
Other Hispanic or Latino	275	1.15
Hungarian	398	1.67
Iranian	16	0.07
Irish	5,008	20.97
Italian	6,634	27.78
Latvian	88	0.37
Lithuanian	115	0.48
Macedonian	44	0.18
Norwegian	544	2.28
Pennsylvania German	19	0.08
Polish	2,459	10.30
Portuguese	79	0.33
Romanian	107	0.45
Russian	778	3.26
Scandinavian	12	0.05
Scotch-Irish	341	1.43
Scottish	524	2.19
Serbian	13	0.05
Slavic	32	0.13
Slovak	292	1.22
Slovene	14	0.06
Swedish	264	1.11
Swiss	138	0.58
Turkish	16	0.07
Ukrainian	226	0.95
United States or American	944	3.95
Welsh	205	0.86
West Indian, excl. Hispanic:	78	0.33
Bermudan	9	0.04
British West Indian	6	0.03
Jamaican	10	0.04
Trinidadian and Tobagonian	53	0.22
White:	22,332	93.51
Not Hispanic (21,211)	21,370	89.48
Hispanic (899)	962	4.03
Yugoslavian	12	0.05

Rutherford

Place Type: Borough
County: Bergen
Population: 18,110

Ancestry/Race	Number	%
African American/Black:	579	3.20
Not Hispanic (475)	550	3.04
Hispanic (14)	29	0.16
African, sub-Saharan:	31	0.17
African	3	0.02
Ethiopian	8	0.04
Other sub-Saharan African	20	0.11
Alaska Native tribes, specified:	3	0.02
Eskimo	3	0.02
Am. Ind. or Alaska Nat., not spec.	38	0.21
Albanian	5	0.03
Alsatian	5	0.03
American Indian tribes, specified:	28	0.15
Apache	4	0.02
Blackfeet	2	0.01
Cherokee	10	0.06
Delaware (1)	1	0.01
Iroquois (1)	8	0.04
Latin American Indians	1	0.01
All other tribes	2	0.01
American Indian tribes, not spec.	4	0.02
Arab:	278	1.54
Arab/Arabic	10	0.06
Egyptian	174	0.96
Jordanian	24	0.13
Lebanese	17	0.09
Moroccan	11	0.06
Palestinian	5	0.03
Syrian	23	0.13
Other Arab	14	0.08
Armenian	41	0.23
Asian:	2,195	12.12
Bangladeshi (7)	7	0.04
Chinese, ex. Taiwanese (253)	267	1.47
Filipino (186)	208	1.15
Indian (520)	553	3.05
Indonesian (3)	3	0.02
Japanese (25)	37	0.20
Korean (965)	995	5.49
Pakistani (4)	6	0.03
Sri Lankan (6)	6	0.03
Taiwanese (3)	3	0.02
Thai (40)	40	0.22
Vietnamese (21)	27	0.15
Other Asian, not specified (11)	43	0.24
Austrian	103	0.57
Belgian	46	0.25
Brazilian	34	0.19
British	34	0.19
Canadian	11	0.06
Celtic	18	0.10
Croatian	40	0.22
Czech	77	0.43
Czechoslovakian	47	0.26
Danish	58	0.32
Dutch	210	1.16
Eastern European	15	0.08
English	1,142	6.31
Estonian	7	0.04
European	17	0.09
Finnish	13	0.07
French, except Basque	273	1.51
French Canadian	80	0.44
German	2,153	11.89
Greek	220	1.21
Guyanese	25	0.14
Hawaii Native/Pacific Islander:	9	0.05
Polynesian: (2)	2	0.01
Native Hawaiian (1)	1	0.01
Samoan (1)	1	0.01
Other Pac. Isl., not spec. (3)	7	0.04
Hispanic or Latino:	1,555	8.59
Central American:	75	0.41
Costa Rican	22	0.12
Guatemalan	1	0.01
Honduran	21	0.12
Nicaraguan	6	0.03
Panamanian	5	0.03
Salvadoran	16	0.09
Other Central American	4	0.02
Cuban	280	1.55
Dominican Republic	102	0.56
Mexican	88	0.49
Puerto Rican	348	1.92
South American:	333	1.84
Argentinean	52	0.29
Bolivian	9	0.05
Chilean	16	0.09
Colombian	86	0.47
Ecuadorian	90	0.50
Peruvian	52	0.29
Uruguayan	13	0.07
Venezuelan	5	0.03
Other South American	10	0.06
Other Hispanic or Latino	329	1.82
Hungarian	169	0.93
Iranian	88	0.49
Irish	4,215	23.27
Israeli	16	0.09

Notes: 1. Figures in the "Number" column do not add up to the total population due to: a) Ancestry/Race overlap — e.g. persons can report being both White and Irish, b) persons of Hispanic origin can report being any race, c) persons reporting two ancestries are counted in both categories. 2. Numbers in parentheses indicate the number of persons reporting this ancestry/race alone, not in combination with any other ancestry/race. 3. Refer to the Explanation of Data in the front of the book for more detailed information.

Italian	4,687	25.88
Latvian	11	0.06
Lithuanian	127	0.70
Norwegian	80	0.44
Polish	1,529	8.44
Portuguese	118	0.65
Romanian	19	0.10
Russian	219	1.21
Scandinavian	15	0.08
Scotch-Irish	268	1.48
Scottish	279	1.54
Slavic	32	0.18
Slovak	53	0.29
Soviet Union	5	0.03
Swedish	67	0.37
Swiss	89	0.49
Turkish	33	0.18
Ukrainian	171	0.94
United States or American	390	2.15
Welsh	64	0.35
West Indian, excl. Hispanic:	65	0.36
Barbadian	4	0.02
Belizean	14	0.08
Jamaican	36	0.20
Trinidadian and Tobagonian	11	0.06
White:	15,151	83.66
Not Hispanic (13,696)	13,920	76.86
Hispanic (1,153)	1,231	6.80
Yugoslavian	29	0.16

Saddle Brook

Place Type: Census Designated Place
County: Bergen
Population: 13,155

Ancestry/Race	Number	%
African American/Black:	205	1.56
Not Hispanic (162)	182	1.38
Hispanic (21)	23	0.17
African, sub-Saharan:	11	0.08
Kenyan	11	0.08
Am. Ind. or Alaska Nat., not spec.	7	0.05
Albanian	17	0.13
American Indian tribes, specified:	11	0.08
Blackfeet	2	0.02
Cherokee	1	0.01
Cree	1	0.01
Delaware (1)	3	0.02
Latin American Indians (1)	2	0.02
Pima (1)	1	0.01
All other tribes	1	0.01
Arab:	342	2.60
Arab/Arabic	36	0.27
Lebanese	66	0.50
Palestinian	143	1.09
Syrian	97	0.74
Armenian	61	0.46
Asian:	689	5.24
Bangladeshi (3)	3	0.02
Chinese, ex. Taiwanese (100)	112	0.85
Filipino (183)	206	1.57
Indian (240)	254	1.93
Indonesian (1)	1	0.01
Japanese (14)	17	0.13
Korean (49)	54	0.41
Pakistani (4)	8	0.06
Sri Lankan (8)	8	0.06
Taiwanese (5)	5	0.04
Thai (1)	1	0.01
Vietnamese (7)	8	0.06
Other Asian, not specified (4)	12	0.09
Austrian	94	0.71
Belgian	20	0.15
British	10	0.08
Canadian	6	0.05
Croatian	26	0.20
Czech	76	0.58
Czechoslovakian	75	0.57
Danish	9	0.07
Dutch	319	2.42
Eastern European	7	0.05
English	394	3.00
European	22	0.17
Finnish	13	0.10
French, except Basque	179	1.36
French Canadian	71	0.54
German	1,446	10.99
Greek	129	0.98
Hawaii Native/Pacific Islander:	1	0.01
Other Pac. Isl., not spec.	1	0.01
Hispanic or Latino:	825	6.27
Central American:	25	0.19
Costa Rican	8	0.06
Guatemalan	5	0.04
Honduran	1	0.01
Nicaraguan	2	0.02
Panamanian	6	0.05
Salvadoran	3	0.02
Cuban	87	0.66
Dominican Republic	58	0.44
Mexican	19	0.14
Puerto Rican	198	1.51
South American:	261	1.98
Argentinean	37	0.28
Bolivian	2	0.02
Chilean	15	0.11
Colombian	92	0.70
Ecuadorian	55	0.42
Peruvian	44	0.33
Uruguayan	2	0.02
Other South American	14	0.11
Other Hispanic or Latino	177	1.35
Hungarian	261	1.98
Irish	2,066	15.71
Israeli	10	0.08
Italian	4,700	35.73
Lithuanian	99	0.75
Macedonian	44	0.33
Maltese	24	0.18
Norwegian	42	0.32
Pennsylvania German	8	0.06
Polish	1,725	13.11
Portuguese	7	0.05
Romanian	56	0.43
Russian	272	2.07
Scandinavian	18	0.14
Scotch-Irish	59	0.45
Scottish	92	0.70
Serbian	22	0.17
Slavic	35	0.27
Slovak	222	1.69
Swedish	86	0.65
Swiss	21	0.16
Turkish	61	0.46
Ukrainian	200	1.52
United States or American	509	3.87
Welsh	7	0.05
West Indian, excl. Hispanic:	32	0.24
Belizean	20	0.15
West Indian	12	0.09
White:	12,097	91.96
Not Hispanic (11,400)	11,511	87.50
Hispanic (536)	586	4.45
Yugoslavian	44	0.33

Sayreville

Place Type: Borough
County: Middlesex
Population: 40,377

Ancestry/Race	Number	%
African American/Black:	3,657	9.06
Not Hispanic (3,334)	3,479	8.62
Hispanic (147)	178	0.44
African, sub-Saharan:	927	2.30
African	314	0.78
Cape Verdean	11	0.03
Ethiopian	9	0.02
Ghanian	289	0.72
Kenyan	14	0.03
Liberian	26	0.06
Nigerian	209	0.52
Sierra Leonean	33	0.08
South African	10	0.02
Ugandan	12	0.03
Am. Ind. or Alaska Nat., not spec.	83	0.21
Albanian	19	0.05
American Indian tribes, specified:	59	0.15
Cherokee (2)	21	0.05
Chippewa	5	0.01
Choctaw	1	0.00
Comanche (1)	1	0.00
Cree (2)	3	0.01
Delaware (2)	2	0.00
Iroquois	4	0.01
Latin American Indians (11)	17	0.04
Seminole	3	0.01
All other tribes (1)	2	0.00
American Indian tribes, not spec.	16	0.04
Arab:	629	1.56
Arab/Arabic	135	0.33
Egyptian	355	0.88
Jordanian	46	0.11
Lebanese	22	0.05
Syrian	13	0.03
Other Arab	58	0.14
Asian:	4,625	11.45
Bangladeshi (22)	25	0.06
Chinese, ex. Taiwanese (554)	599	1.48
Filipino (672)	751	1.86
Indian (2,530)	2,657	6.58
Indonesian (3)	8	0.02
Japanese (21)	26	0.06
Korean (98)	110	0.27
Malaysian (2)	3	0.01
Pakistani (239)	297	0.74
Sri Lankan (12)	12	0.03
Taiwanese (5)	5	0.01
Thai (2)	2	0.00
Vietnamese (27)	28	0.07
Other Asian, specified (4)	4	0.01
Other Asian, not specified (32)	98	0.24
Austrian	135	0.33
Belgian	7	0.02
Brazilian	124	0.31
British	96	0.24
Canadian	55	0.14
Celtic	4	0.01
Croatian	47	0.12
Cypriot	8	0.02
Czech	69	0.17
Czechoslovakian	93	0.23
Danish	314	0.78
Dutch	310	0.77
Eastern European	73	0.18
English	1,271	3.15
Estonian	28	0.07
European	95	0.24
Finnish	23	0.06
French, except Basque	490	1.21
French Canadian	132	0.33
German	4,316	10.69
Greek	336	0.83
Guyanese	66	0.16
Hawaii Native/Pacific Islander:	40	0.10
Micronesian: (5)	8	0.02
Guamanian/Chamorro (4)	6	0.01
Other Micronesian (1)	2	0.00
Polynesian: (2)	8	0.02
Native Hawaiian	6	0.01
Samoan (2)	2	0.00
Other Pac. Isl., not spec. (1)	24	0.06
Hispanic or Latino:	2,942	7.29
Central American:	143	0.35
Costa Rican	10	0.02
Guatemalan	17	0.04
Honduran	21	0.05
Nicaraguan	16	0.04

Notes: 1. Figures in the "Number" column do not add up to the total population due to: a) Ancestry/Race overlap — e.g. persons can report being both White and Irish, b) persons of Hispanic origin can report being any race, c) persons reporting two ancestries are counted in both categories. 2. Numbers in parentheses indicate the number of persons reporting this ancestry/race alone, not in combination with any other ancestry/race. 3. Refer to the Explanation of Data in the front of the book for more detailed information.

Ancestry/Race	Number	%
Panamanian	36	0.09
Salvadoran	28	0.07
Other Central American	15	0.04
Cuban	194	0.48
Dominican Republic	138	0.34
Mexican	105	0.26
Puerto Rican	1,365	3.38
South American:	400	0.99
Argentinean	64	0.16
Bolivian	5	0.01
Chilean	13	0.03
Colombian	133	0.33
Ecuadorian	72	0.18
Paraguayan	2	0.00
Peruvian	59	0.15
Uruguayan	21	0.05
Venezuelan	7	0.02
Other South American	24	0.06
Other Hispanic or Latino	597	1.48
Hungarian	1,162	2.88
Icelander	6	0.01
Iranian	39	0.10
Irish	7,458	18.47
Israeli	14	0.03
Italian	7,512	18.60
Lithuanian	168	0.42
Macedonian	6	0.01
Norwegian	287	0.71
Polish	8,133	20.14
Portuguese	565	1.40
Romanian	34	0.08
Russian	854	2.12
Scotch-Irish	253	0.63
Scottish	303	0.75
Slavic	110	0.27
Slovak	510	1.26
Slovene	6	0.01
Swedish	207	0.51
Swiss	40	0.10
Turkish	88	0.22
Ukrainian	486	1.20
United States or American	888	2.20
Welsh	89	0.22
West Indian, excl. Hispanic:	386	0.96
British West Indian	33	0.08
Haitian	91	0.23
Jamaican	148	0.37
Trinidadian and Tobagonian	38	0.09
West Indian	76	0.19
White:	31,513	78.05
Not Hispanic (29,068)	29,563	73.22
Hispanic (1,807)	1,950	4.83
Yugoslavian	23	0.06

Scotch Plains

Place Type: Census Designated Place
County: Union
Population: 22,732

Ancestry/Race	Number	%
African American/Black:	2,678	11.78
Not Hispanic (2,532)	2,624	11.54
Hispanic (36)	54	0.24
African, sub-Saharan:	237	1.04
African	174	0.77
Ghanian	31	0.14
Kenyan	32	0.14
Am. Ind. or Alaska Nat., not spec.	21	0.09
Albanian	7	0.03
Alsatian	22	0.10
American Indian tribes, specified:	43	0.19
Blackfeet (1)	3	0.01
Cherokee (5)	18	0.08
Cheyenne	3	0.01
Chippewa (1)	2	0.01
Choctaw	2	0.01
Creek (5)	5	0.02
Delaware	1	0.00
Latin American Indians (3)	6	0.03
Potawatomi	1	0.00
All other tribes (1)	2	0.01
American Indian tribes, not spec.	3	0.01
Arab:	308	1.35
Arab/Arabic	66	0.29
Egyptian	170	0.75
Lebanese	51	0.22
Palestinian	5	0.02
Syrian	16	0.07
Armenian	45	0.20
Asian:	1,778	7.82
Chinese, ex. Taiwanese (450)	486	2.14
Filipino (245)	299	1.32
Indian (676)	701	3.08
Indonesian (1)	5	0.02
Japanese (26)	29	0.13
Korean (153)	159	0.70
Malaysian (1)	1	0.00
Pakistani (13)	13	0.06
Taiwanese (17)	18	0.08
Thai (5)	5	0.02
Vietnamese (29)	29	0.13
Other Asian, specified	2	0.01
Other Asian, not specified (12)	31	0.14
Australian	8	0.04
Austrian	281	1.24
Basque	6	0.03
Belgian	22	0.10
Brazilian	113	0.50
British	155	0.68
Canadian	74	0.33
Croatian	19	0.08
Czech	62	0.27
Czechoslovakian	48	0.21
Danish	118	0.52
Dutch	309	1.36
Eastern European	149	0.66
English	1,426	6.27
Estonian	13	0.06
European	59	0.26
Finnish	25	0.11
French, except Basque	336	1.48
French Canadian	38	0.17
German	3,057	13.45
Greek	124	0.55
Hawaii Native/Pacific Islander:	8	0.04
Polynesian:	1	0.00
Samoan	1	0.00
Other Pac. Isl., specified	2	0.01
Other Pac. Isl., not spec. (3)	5	0.02
Hispanic or Latino:	895	3.94
Central American:	87	0.38
Costa Rican	34	0.15
Guatemalan	17	0.07
Honduran	3	0.01
Panamanian	9	0.04
Salvadoran	24	0.11
Cuban	106	0.47
Dominican Republic	28	0.12
Mexican	53	0.23
Puerto Rican	229	1.01
South American:	185	0.81
Argentinean	14	0.06
Chilean	6	0.03
Colombian	84	0.37
Ecuadorian	19	0.08
Paraguayan	8	0.04
Peruvian	22	0.10
Uruguayan	10	0.04
Venezuelan	7	0.03
Other South American	15	0.07
Other Hispanic or Latino	207	0.91
Hungarian	329	1.45
Iranian	53	0.23
Irish	4,153	18.27
Israeli	59	0.26
Italian	5,124	22.54
Latvian	20	0.09
Lithuanian	134	0.59
Northern European	6	0.03
Norwegian	194	0.85
Pennsylvania German	25	0.11
Polish	2,286	10.06
Portuguese	189	0.83
Romanian	49	0.22
Russian	1,211	5.33
Scandinavian	25	0.11
Scotch-Irish	250	1.10
Scottish	268	1.18
Slavic	20	0.09
Slovak	219	0.96
Slovene	19	0.08
Swedish	238	1.05
Swiss	31	0.14
Ukrainian	221	0.97
United States or American	671	2.95
Welsh	151	0.66
West Indian, excl. Hispanic:	430	1.89
Bahamian	6	0.03
Barbadian	5	0.02
British West Indian	38	0.17
Haitian	8	0.04
Jamaican	100	0.44
Trinidadian and Tobagonian	231	1.02
West Indian	42	0.18
White:	18,242	80.25
Not Hispanic (17,335)	17,590	77.38
Hispanic (596)	652	2.87
Yugoslavian	17	0.07

Secaucus

Place Type: Town
County: Hudson
Population: 15,931

Ancestry/Race	Number	%
Afghan	34	0.21
African American/Black:	749	4.70
Not Hispanic (651)	684	4.29
Hispanic (58)	65	0.41
African, sub-Saharan:	124	0.78
African	57	0.36
Ethiopian	48	0.30
Ghanian	9	0.06
South African	10	0.06
Am. Ind. or Alaska Nat., not spec.	27	0.17
Albanian	56	0.35
American Indian tribes, specified:	7	0.04
Blackfeet	2	0.01
Cherokee	2	0.01
Creek	1	0.01
Latin American Indians (1)	2	0.01
American Indian tribes, not spec.	1	0.01
Arab:	336	2.12
Arab/Arabic	148	0.93
Egyptian	159	1.00
Jordanian	8	0.05
Lebanese	21	0.13
Armenian	49	0.31
Asian:	2,037	12.79
Chinese, ex. Taiwanese (314)	333	2.09
Filipino (500)	549	3.45
Indian (525)	559	3.51
Indonesian (44)	44	0.28
Japanese (38)	41	0.26
Korean (251)	266	1.67
Malaysian	5	0.03
Pakistani (41)	64	0.40
Sri Lankan (1)	1	0.01
Taiwanese (3)	3	0.02
Thai (3)	3	0.02
Vietnamese (102)	103	0.65
Other Asian, specified (1)	5	0.03
Other Asian, not specified (10)	61	0.38
Assyrian/Chaldean/Syriac	7	0.04
Austrian	41	0.26
Belgian	15	0.09
Brazilian	20	0.13
British	59	0.37

Notes: 1. Figures in the "Number" column do not add up to the total population due to: a) Ancestry/Race overlap — e.g. persons can report being both White and Irish, b) persons of Hispanic origin can report being any race, c) persons reporting two ancestries are counted in both categories. 2. Numbers in parentheses indicate the number of persons reporting this ancestry/race alone, not in combination with any other ancestry/race. 3. Refer to the Explanation of Data in the front of the book for more detailed information.

Bulgarian	11	0.07
Croatian	7	0.04
Czech	23	0.15
Czechoslovakian	28	0.18
Danish	46	0.29
Dutch	163	1.03
Eastern European	21	0.13
English	394	2.49
European	25	0.16
French, except Basque	107	0.68
French Canadian	26	0.16
German	2,349	14.83
Greek	178	1.12
Guyanese	19	0.12
Hawaii Native/Pacific Islander:	8	0.05
Micronesian: (4)	4	0.03
Guamanian/Chamorro (4)	4	0.03
Polynesian: (2)	3	0.02
Native Hawaiian	1	0.01
Samoan (2)	2	0.01
Other Pac. Isl., not spec.	1	0.01
Hispanic or Latino:	1,953	12.26
Central American:	85	0.53
Costa Rican	9	0.06
Guatemalan	6	0.04
Honduran	19	0.12
Nicaraguan	4	0.03
Panamanian	3	0.02
Salvadoran	25	0.16
Other Central American	19	0.12
Cuban	376	2.36
Dominican Republic	92	0.58
Mexican	47	0.30
Puerto Rican	521	3.27
South American:	406	2.55
Argentinean	50	0.31
Chilean	19	0.12
Colombian	148	0.93
Ecuadorian	114	0.72
Peruvian	44	0.28
Uruguayan	6	0.04
Venezuelan	13	0.08
Other South American	12	0.08
Other Hispanic or Latino	426	2.67
Hungarian	89	0.56
Iranian	33	0.21
Irish	2,810	17.74
Israeli	11	0.07
Italian	4,358	27.51
Latvian	8	0.05
Macedonian	74	0.47
Maltese	46	0.29
Norwegian	25	0.16
Polish	1,114	7.03
Portuguese	33	0.21
Romanian	63	0.40
Russian	158	1.00
Scotch-Irish	68	0.43
Scottish	86	0.54
Slavic	6	0.04
Swedish	59	0.37
Swiss	87	0.55
Turkish	35	0.22
Ukrainian	145	0.92
United States or American	197	1.24
Welsh	23	0.15
West Indian, excl. Hispanic:	60	0.38
Haitian	7	0.04
West Indian	53	0.33
White:	12,828	80.52
Not Hispanic (11,172)	11,378	71.42
Hispanic (1,340)	1,450	9.10
Yugoslavian	22	0.14

Somers Point

Place Type: City
County: Atlantic
Population: 11,614

Ancestry/Race	Number	%
African American/Black:	897	7.72
Not Hispanic (778)	855	7.36
Hispanic (36)	42	0.36
African, sub-Saharan:	30	0.26
African	23	0.20
Ghanian	7	0.06
Am. Ind. or Alaska Nat., not spec.	36	0.31
Albanian	7	0.06
American Indian tribes, specified:	50	0.43
Apache	1	0.01
Blackfeet	3	0.03
Cherokee (6)	23	0.20
Chippewa (2)	2	0.02
Choctaw	1	0.01
Comanche (3)	3	0.03
Delaware (1)	1	0.01
Iroquois (1)	3	0.03
Navajo	3	0.03
Osage (1)	1	0.01
Seminole	1	0.01
All other tribes (4)	8	0.07
American Indian tribes, not spec.	3	0.03
Arab:	47	0.40
Egyptian	31	0.27
Lebanese	16	0.14
Armenian	10	0.09
Asian:	410	3.53
Bangladeshi (3)	3	0.03
Chinese, ex. Taiwanese (50)	56	0.48
Filipino (123)	131	1.13
Indian (112)	122	1.05
Indonesian (1)	1	0.01
Japanese (5)	13	0.11
Korean (11)	13	0.11
Laotian (7)	7	0.06
Malaysian (1)	1	0.01
Pakistani (8)	13	0.11
Thai (4)	8	0.07
Vietnamese (26)	28	0.24
Other Asian, specified (5)	5	0.04
Other Asian, not specified (6)	9	0.08
Austrian	18	0.15
British	40	0.34
Canadian	13	0.11
Celtic	8	0.07
Croatian	29	0.25
Czech	11	0.09
Czechoslovakian	12	0.10
Danish	46	0.40
Dutch	205	1.77
Eastern European	8	0.07
English	1,342	11.56
Estonian	8	0.07
European	41	0.35
Finnish	16	0.14
French, except Basque	350	3.01
French Canadian	39	0.34
German	1,974	17.00
Greek	103	0.89
Hawaii Native/Pacific Islander:	8	0.07
Micronesian: (1)	2	0.02
Guamanian/Chamorro (1)	2	0.02
Polynesian: (1)	1	0.01
Samoan (1)	1	0.01
Other Pac. Isl., not spec. (2)	5	0.04
Hispanic or Latino:	696	5.99
Central American:	11	0.09
Guatemalan	3	0.03
Honduran	4	0.03
Other Central American	4	0.03
Cuban	10	0.09
Dominican Republic	33	0.28
Mexican	132	1.14
Puerto Rican	332	2.86
South American:	72	0.62
Argentinean	1	0.01
Chilean	1	0.01
Colombian	7	0.06
Ecuadorian	9	0.08
Peruvian	39	0.34
Venezuelan	2	0.02
Other South American	13	0.11
Other Hispanic or Latino	106	0.91
Hungarian	96	0.83
Icelander	7	0.06
Iranian	63	0.54
Irish	3,373	29.04
Israeli	19	0.16
Italian	2,356	20.29
Latvian	5	0.04
Lithuanian	83	0.71
Macedonian	28	0.24
Norwegian	99	0.85
Pennsylvania German	10	0.09
Polish	615	5.30
Portuguese	5	0.04
Russian	202	1.74
Scandinavian	21	0.18
Scotch-Irish	314	2.70
Scottish	125	1.08
Slavic	6	0.05
Slovak	63	0.54
Slovene	6	0.05
Swedish	77	0.66
Swiss	26	0.22
Ukrainian	74	0.64
United States or American	221	1.90
Welsh	108	0.93
West Indian, excl. Hispanic:	96	0.83
British West Indian	5	0.04
Haitian	38	0.33
Jamaican	40	0.34
Trinidadian and Tobagonian	13	0.11
White:	10,101	86.97
Not Hispanic (9,587)	9,710	83.61
Hispanic (361)	391	3.37
Yugoslavian	8	0.07

Somerset

Place Type: Census Designated Place
County: Somerset
Population: 23,040

Ancestry/Race	Number	%
African American/Black:	9,239	40.10
Not Hispanic (8,666)	8,937	38.79
Hispanic (215)	302	1.31
African, sub-Saharan:	1,426	6.19
African	964	4.18
Ghanian	164	0.71
Kenyan	5	0.02
Liberian	7	0.03
Nigerian	180	0.78
Sierra Leonean	106	0.46
Alaska Native tribes, specified:	1	0.00
Tlingit-Haida	1	0.00
Am. Ind. or Alaska Nat., not spec.	83	0.36
American Indian tribes, specified:	84	0.36
Blackfeet	3	0.01
Cherokee (4)	27	0.12
Chickasaw	3	0.01
Choctaw	2	0.01
Comanche	2	0.01
Creek (1)	1	0.00
Delaware	5	0.02
Iroquois (1)	4	0.02
Latin American Indians (15)	23	0.10
Lumbee (1)	1	0.00
Seminole (1)	1	0.00
Sioux	1	0.00
All other tribes (5)	11	0.05
American Indian tribes, not spec.	6	0.03

Notes: 1. Figures in the "Number" column do not add up to the total population due to: a) Ancestry/Race overlap — e.g. persons can report being both White and Irish, b) persons of Hispanic origin can report being any race, c) persons reporting two ancestries are counted in both categories. 2. Numbers in parentheses indicate the number of persons reporting this ancestry/race alone, not in combination with any other ancestry/race. 3. Refer to the Explanation of Data in the front of the book for more detailed information.

Arab:	210	0.91
Egyptian	152	0.66
Jordanian	10	0.04
Lebanese	40	0.17
Moroccan	7	0.03
Palestinian	1	0.00
Armenian	24	0.10
Asian:	2,057	8.93
Bangladeshi (3)	3	0.01
Cambodian (1)	1	0.00
Chinese, ex. Taiwanese (375)	416	1.81
Filipino (425)	467	2.03
Hmong (3)	3	0.01
Indian (861)	898	3.90
Japanese (14)	20	0.09
Korean (102)	119	0.52
Malaysian (2)	2	0.01
Pakistani (32)	32	0.14
Sri Lankan (4)	4	0.02
Taiwanese (11)	14	0.06
Thai (11)	17	0.07
Vietnamese (23)	23	0.10
Other Asian, not specified (13)	38	0.16
Australian	6	0.03
Austrian	86	0.37
Belgian	10	0.04
British	89	0.39
Canadian	30	0.13
Carpatho Rusyn	6	0.03
Croatian	37	0.16
Czech	39	0.17
Czechoslovakian	33	0.14
Danish	52	0.23
Dutch	319	1.38
Eastern European	27	0.12
English	672	2.92
Estonian	8	0.03
European	36	0.16
Finnish	10	0.04
French, except Basque	204	0.88
French Canadian	116	0.50
German	1,425	6.18
Greek	87	0.38
Guyanese	61	0.26
Hawaii Native/Pacific Islander:	45	0.20
Micronesian: (1)	1	0.00
Guamanian/Chamorro (1)	1	0.00
Polynesian: (1)	9	0.04
Native Hawaiian	7	0.03
Samoan (1)	2	0.01
Other Pac. Isl., not spec. (9)	35	0.15
Hispanic or Latino:	2,764	12.00
Central American:	223	0.97
Costa Rican	15	0.07
Guatemalan	25	0.11
Honduran	114	0.49
Nicaraguan	39	0.17
Panamanian	10	0.04
Salvadoran	16	0.07
Other Central American	4	0.02
Cuban	97	0.42
Dominican Republic	508	2.20
Mexican	409	1.78
Puerto Rican	871	3.78
South American:	204	0.89
Argentinean	12	0.05
Bolivian	2	0.01
Chilean	3	0.01
Colombian	75	0.33
Ecuadorian	54	0.23
Peruvian	43	0.19
Uruguayan	2	0.01
Venezuelan	3	0.01
Other South American	10	0.04
Other Hispanic or Latino	452	1.96
Hungarian	619	2.69
Iranian	50	0.22
Irish	1,780	7.72
Israeli	11	0.05
Italian	1,972	8.55
Latvian	23	0.10
Lithuanian	40	0.17
Maltese	13	0.06
Northern European	6	0.03
Norwegian	41	0.18
Polish	1,285	5.57
Portuguese	47	0.20
Romanian	34	0.15
Russian	370	1.60
Scandinavian	6	0.03
Scotch-Irish	56	0.24
Scottish	236	1.02
Slovak	81	0.35
Slovene	15	0.07
Swedish	135	0.59
Swiss	41	0.18
Ukrainian	147	0.64
United States or American	396	1.72
Welsh	101	0.44
West Indian, excl. Hispanic:	1,149	4.98
Bahamian	5	0.02
Barbadian	45	0.20
British West Indian	14	0.06
Haitian	55	0.24
Jamaican	910	3.95
Trinidadian and Tobagonian	22	0.10
U.S. Virgin Islander	6	0.03
West Indian	92	0.40
White:	10,562	45.84
Not Hispanic (9,067)	9,352	40.59
Hispanic (1,057)	1,210	5.25

Somerville

Place Type: Borough
County: Somerset
Population: 12,423

Ancestry/Race	Number	%
Afghan	46	0.37
African American/Black:	1,751	14.09
Not Hispanic (1,548)	1,685	13.56
Hispanic (58)	66	0.53
African, sub-Saharan:	136	1.09
African	89	0.71
Ghanian	38	0.30
South African	9	0.07
Am. Ind. or Alaska Nat., not spec.	23	0.19
Albanian	29	0.23
American Indian tribes, specified:	51	0.41
Apache	4	0.03
Blackfeet	1	0.01
Cherokee (1)	21	0.17
Chickasaw	1	0.01
Choctaw (1)	3	0.02
Creek	1	0.01
Delaware	2	0.02
Latin American Indians (8)	8	0.06
Navajo	3	0.02
Seminole	1	0.01
Sioux	4	0.03
All other tribes (1)	2	0.02
American Indian tribes, not spec.	6	0.05
Arab:	118	0.95
Arab/Arabic	40	0.32
Egyptian	48	0.38
Lebanese	4	0.03
Syrian	9	0.07
Other Arab	17	0.14
Asian:	1,026	8.26
Bangladeshi (9)	9	0.07
Cambodian (1)	1	0.01
Chinese, ex. Taiwanese (193)	205	1.65
Filipino (258)	294	2.37
Indian (289)	316	2.54
Indonesian (2)	3	0.02
Japanese (18)	24	0.19
Korean (31)	40	0.32
Malaysian (2)	3	0.02
Pakistani (50)	53	0.43
Sri Lankan (3)	6	0.05
Taiwanese (8)	9	0.07
Thai (5)	7	0.06
Vietnamese (25)	31	0.25
Other Asian, specified (3)	4	0.03
Other Asian, not specified (6)	21	0.17
Austrian	49	0.39
Belgian	9	0.07
British	42	0.34
Canadian	36	0.29
Croatian	28	0.22
Czech	47	0.38
Czechoslovakian	35	0.28
Danish	34	0.27
Dutch	194	1.55
Eastern European	5	0.04
English	781	6.26
European	36	0.29
French, except Basque	248	1.99
French Canadian	30	0.24
German	1,609	12.89
Greek	48	0.38
Guyanese	21	0.17
Hawaii Native/Pacific Islander:	10	0.08
Polynesian: (2)	4	0.03
Samoan (2)	4	0.03
Other Pac. Isl., not spec. (1)	6	0.05
Hispanic or Latino:	2,112	17.00
Central American:	578	4.65
Costa Rican	464	3.74
Guatemalan	45	0.36
Honduran	16	0.13
Nicaraguan	3	0.02
Panamanian	1	0.01
Salvadoran	26	0.21
Other Central American	23	0.19
Cuban	46	0.37
Dominican Republic	40	0.32
Mexican	278	2.24
Puerto Rican	402	3.24
South American:	321	2.58
Argentinean	6	0.05
Bolivian	2	0.02
Chilean	4	0.03
Colombian	120	0.97
Ecuadorian	41	0.33
Paraguayan	49	0.39
Peruvian	71	0.57
Uruguayan	2	0.02
Venezuelan	7	0.06
Other South American	19	0.15
Other Hispanic or Latino	447	3.60
Hungarian	100	0.80
Irish	1,670	13.38
Italian	1,888	15.13
Latvian	11	0.09
Lithuanian	41	0.33
Maltese	21	0.17
Norwegian	78	0.62
Pennsylvania German	12	0.10
Polish	845	6.77
Portuguese	47	0.38
Russian	207	1.66
Scandinavian	13	0.10
Scotch-Irish	36	0.29
Scottish	163	1.31
Slavic	17	0.14
Slovak	202	1.62
Swedish	60	0.48
Swiss	21	0.17
Turkish	13	0.10
Ukrainian	167	1.34
United States or American	320	2.56
Welsh	87	0.70
West Indian, excl. Hispanic:	158	1.27
Bahamian	12	0.10
Barbadian	6	0.05
Haitian	96	0.77
Jamaican	29	0.23
West Indian	8	0.06

Notes: 1. Figures in the "Number" column do not add up to the total population due to: a) Ancestry/Race overlap — e.g. persons can report being both White and Irish, b) persons of Hispanic origin can report being any race, c) persons reporting two ancestries are counted in both categories. 2. Numbers in parentheses indicate the number of persons reporting this ancestry/race alone, not in combination with any other ancestry/race. 3. Refer to the Explanation of Data in the front of the book for more detailed information.

Other West Indian	7	0.06
White:	9,169	73.81
Not Hispanic (7,532)	7,739	62.30
Hispanic (1,315)	1,430	11.51
Yugoslavian	6	0.05

South Brunswick

Place Type: Township
County: Middlesex
Population: 37,734

Ancestry/Race	Number	%
Afghan	8	0.02
African American/Black:	3,235	8.57
Not Hispanic (2,886)	3,098	8.21
Hispanic (89)	137	0.36
African, sub-Saharan:	519	1.38
African	353	0.94
Ethiopian	30	0.08
Ghanian	69	0.18
Liberian	32	0.08
Sierra Leonean	23	0.06
Other sub-Saharan African	12	0.03
Alaska Native tribes, specified:	2	0.01
Eskimo (2)	2	0.01
Am. Ind. or Alaska Nat., not spec.	87	0.23
Albanian	4	0.01
American Indian tribes, specified:	104	0.28
Blackfeet	4	0.01
Cherokee (13)	45	0.12
Chickasaw	2	0.01
Choctaw	4	0.01
Delaware	7	0.02
Iroquois	7	0.02
Latin American Indians (7)	17	0.05
Menominee	1	0.00
Navajo (1)	1	0.00
Seminole	6	0.02
Sioux (1)	1	0.00
All other tribes	7	0.02
American Indian tribes, not spec.	6	0.02
Arab:	650	1.72
Arab/Arabic	61	0.16
Egyptian	363	0.96
Jordanian	27	0.07
Lebanese	87	0.23
Moroccan	28	0.07
Palestinian	51	0.14
Syrian	33	0.09
Armenian	30	0.08
Asian:	7,160	18.97
Bangladeshi (15)	17	0.05
Chinese, ex. Taiwanese (1,494)	1,583	4.20
Filipino (556)	611	1.62
Indian (3,845)	3,954	10.48
Indonesian (7)	12	0.03
Japanese (75)	90	0.24
Korean (319)	338	0.90
Laotian (2)	2	0.01
Malaysian (3)	9	0.02
Pakistani (184)	204	0.54
Sri Lankan (63)	68	0.18
Taiwanese (81)	98	0.26
Thai (22)	29	0.08
Vietnamese (53)	53	0.14
Other Asian, specified (8)	10	0.03
Other Asian, not specified (32)	82	0.22
Australian	5	0.01
Austrian	303	0.80
Belgian	22	0.06
Brazilian	8	0.02
British	67	0.18
Bulgarian	31	0.08
Canadian	135	0.36
Carpatho Rusyn	11	0.03
Celtic	6	0.02
Croatian	43	0.11
Cypriot	73	0.19
Czech	217	0.58
Czechoslovakian	119	0.32
Danish	138	0.37
Dutch	567	1.50
Eastern European	151	0.40
English	2,193	5.81
Estonian	21	0.06
European	144	0.38
Finnish	74	0.20
French, except Basque	584	1.55
French Canadian	140	0.37
German	5,056	13.40
Greek	200	0.53
Guyanese	87	0.23
Hawaii Native/Pacific Islander:	48	0.13
Micronesian: (1)	1	0.00
Guamanian/Chamorro (1)	1	0.00
Polynesian: (8)	17	0.05
Native Hawaiian (6)	11	0.03
Samoan (2)	6	0.02
Other Pac. Isl., specified	1	0.00
Other Pac. Isl., not spec. (5)	29	0.08
Hispanic or Latino:	1,918	5.08
Central American:	137	0.36
Costa Rican	17	0.05
Guatemalan	58	0.15
Honduran	18	0.05
Nicaraguan	10	0.03
Panamanian	15	0.04
Salvadoran	16	0.04
Other Central American	3	0.01
Cuban	141	0.37
Dominican Republic	72	0.19
Mexican	190	0.50
Puerto Rican	700	1.86
South American:	259	0.69
Argentinean	28	0.07
Bolivian	6	0.02
Chilean	19	0.05
Colombian	112	0.30
Ecuadorian	30	0.08
Paraguayan	5	0.01
Peruvian	30	0.08
Uruguayan	7	0.02
Venezuelan	19	0.05
Other South American	3	0.01
Other Hispanic or Latino	419	1.11
Hungarian	1,186	3.14
Iranian	19	0.05
Irish	5,296	14.04
Israeli	52	0.14
Italian	7,231	19.16
Latvian	13	0.03
Lithuanian	142	0.38
Luxemburger	10	0.03
New Zealander	6	0.02
Northern European	6	0.02
Norwegian	434	1.15
Polish	3,074	8.15
Portuguese	63	0.17
Romanian	92	0.24
Russian	1,615	4.28
Scotch-Irish	238	0.63
Scottish	759	2.01
Serbian	6	0.02
Slavic	6	0.02
Slovak	162	0.43
Slovene	7	0.02
Swedish	319	0.85
Swiss	40	0.11
Turkish	68	0.18
Ukrainian	284	0.75
United States or American	971	2.57
Welsh	224	0.59
West Indian, excl. Hispanic:	415	1.10
Barbadian	10	0.03
British West Indian	37	0.10
Haitian	45	0.12
Jamaican	125	0.33
Trinidadian and Tobagonian	81	0.21
U.S. Virgin Islander	9	0.02
West Indian	92	0.24
Other West Indian	16	0.04
White:	27,185	72.04
Not Hispanic (25,392)	25,862	68.54
Hispanic (1,208)	1,323	3.51
Yugoslavian	54	0.14

South Orange

Place Type: Census Designated Place
County: Essex
Population: 16,964

Ancestry/Race	Number	%
African American/Black:	5,620	33.13
Not Hispanic (5,150)	5,409	31.89
Hispanic (159)	211	1.24
African, sub-Saharan:	560	3.30
African	184	1.08
Ethiopian	16	0.09
Ghanian	19	0.11
Liberian	8	0.05
Nigerian	231	1.36
Somalian	17	0.10
South African	7	0.04
Sudanese	8	0.05
Zimbabwean	17	0.10
Other sub-Saharan African	53	0.31
Am. Ind. or Alaska Nat., not spec.	36	0.21
Albanian	6	0.04
American Indian tribes, specified:	81	0.48
Apache	9	0.05
Blackfeet	3	0.02
Cherokee (7)	40	0.24
Chippewa	5	0.03
Iroquois (1)	4	0.02
Latin American Indians (2)	6	0.04
Pueblo (1)	1	0.01
Sioux	4	0.02
All other tribes (2)	9	0.05
American Indian tribes, not spec.	2	0.01
Arab:	145	0.85
Egyptian	76	0.45
Lebanese	66	0.39
Other Arab	3	0.02
Asian:	786	4.63
Chinese, ex. Taiwanese (217)	239	1.41
Filipino (111)	135	0.80
Indian (177)	205	1.21
Indonesian	3	0.02
Japanese (32)	43	0.25
Korean (51)	63	0.37
Malaysian	1	0.01
Pakistani (11)	15	0.09
Sri Lankan (10)	10	0.06
Taiwanese (15)	15	0.09
Thai (3)	3	0.02
Vietnamese (15)	15	0.09
Other Asian, specified (3)	3	0.02
Other Asian, not specified (12)	36	0.21
Australian	32	0.19
Austrian	176	1.04
Belgian	10	0.06
Brazilian	36	0.21
British	107	0.63
Canadian	74	0.44
Croatian	15	0.09
Czech	52	0.31
Czechoslovakian	48	0.28
Danish	53	0.31
Dutch	140	0.83
Eastern European	153	0.90
English	736	4.34
European	166	0.98
Finnish	7	0.04
French, except Basque	285	1.68
French Canadian	19	0.11
German	1,580	9.31
Greek	81	0.48
Guyanese	116	0.68

Notes: 1. Figures in the "Number" column do not add up to the total population due to: a) Ancestry/Race overlap — e.g. persons can report being both White and Irish, b) persons of Hispanic origin can report being any race, c) persons reporting two ancestries are counted in both categories. 2. Numbers in parentheses indicate the number of persons reporting this ancestry/race alone, not in combination with any other ancestry/race. 3. Refer to the Explanation of Data in the front of the book for more detailed information.

Ancestry/Race	Number	%
Hawaii Native/Pacific Islander:	33	0.19
Micronesian:	2	0.01
Guamanian/Chamorro	1	0.01
Other Micronesian	1	0.01
Polynesian: (4)	15	0.09
Native Hawaiian (4)	8	0.05
Samoan	5	0.03
Other Polynesian	2	0.01
Other Pac. Isl., not spec. (1)	16	0.09
Hispanic or Latino:	837	4.93
Central American:	58	0.34
Costa Rican	7	0.04
Guatemalan	14	0.08
Honduran	4	0.02
Nicaraguan	7	0.04
Panamanian	11	0.06
Salvadoran	15	0.09
Cuban	60	0.35
Dominican Republic	58	0.34
Mexican	92	0.54
Puerto Rican	266	1.57
South American:	133	0.78
Argentinean	9	0.05
Bolivian	4	0.02
Chilean	4	0.02
Colombian	43	0.25
Ecuadorian	22	0.13
Paraguayan	1	0.01
Peruvian	33	0.19
Uruguayan	8	0.05
Venezuelan	1	0.01
Other South American	8	0.05
Other Hispanic or Latino	170	1.00
Hungarian	235	1.39
Icelander	6	0.04
Iranian	23	0.14
Irish	2,003	11.81
Israeli	6	0.04
Italian	1,887	11.12
Lithuanian	27	0.16
Maltese	6	0.04
New Zealander	5	0.03
Northern European	6	0.04
Norwegian	67	0.39
Polish	921	5.43
Portuguese	110	0.65
Romanian	180	1.06
Russian	819	4.83
Scotch-Irish	154	0.91
Scottish	132	0.78
Slavic	42	0.25
Slovak	58	0.34
Swedish	92	0.54
Swiss	21	0.12
Turkish	14	0.08
Ukrainian	120	0.71
United States or American	442	2.61
Welsh	63	0.37
West Indian, excl. Hispanic:	1,177	6.94
Barbadian	23	0.14
Belizean	7	0.04
British West Indian	79	0.47
Haitian	488	2.88
Jamaican	383	2.26
Trinidadian and Tobagonian	90	0.53
West Indian	107	0.63
White:	10,518	62.00
Not Hispanic (9,871)	10,082	59.43
Hispanic (377)	436	2.57
Yugoslavian	34	0.20

South Plainfield

Place Type: Borough
County: Middlesex
Population: 21,810

Ancestry/Race	Number	%
Afghan	53	0.24
African American/Black:	2,024	9.28
Not Hispanic (1,798)	1,917	8.79
Hispanic (68)	107	0.49
African, sub-Saharan:	71	0.33
African	52	0.24
Nigerian	19	0.09
Am. Ind. or Alaska Nat., not spec.	49	0.22
American Indian tribes, specified:	84	0.39
Blackfeet	3	0.01
Cherokee (1)	37	0.17
Choctaw (2)	3	0.01
Delaware (7)	12	0.06
Iroquois (1)	1	0.00
Latin American Indians (6)	16	0.07
Seminole	1	0.00
Sioux (2)	2	0.01
All other tribes (9)	9	0.04
American Indian tribes, not spec.	12	0.06
Arab:	303	1.39
Arab/Arabic	87	0.40
Egyptian	56	0.26
Lebanese	76	0.35
Moroccan	20	0.09
Palestinian	33	0.15
Syrian	31	0.14
Asian:	1,825	8.37
Bangladeshi (1)	4	0.02
Chinese, ex. Taiwanese (149)	159	0.73
Filipino (445)	484	2.22
Indian (589)	633	2.90
Indonesian (24)	28	0.13
Japanese (8)	13	0.06
Korean (50)	65	0.30
Pakistani (10)	23	0.11
Sri Lankan (2)	2	0.01
Taiwanese (4)	14	0.06
Thai (1)	3	0.01
Vietnamese (329)	339	1.55
Other Asian, not specified (20)	58	0.27
Austrian	105	0.48
Belgian	14	0.06
British	26	0.12
Bulgarian	15	0.07
Canadian	21	0.10
Czech	150	0.69
Czechoslovakian	59	0.27
Danish	145	0.66
Dutch	272	1.25
Eastern European	13	0.06
English	1,228	5.63
European	8	0.04
Finnish	58	0.27
French, except Basque	305	1.40
French Canadian	135	0.62
German	3,434	15.75
Greek	95	0.44
Guyanese	342	1.57
Hawaii Native/Pacific Islander:	14	0.06
Polynesian: (1)	1	0.00
Native Hawaiian (1)	1	0.00
Other Pac. Isl., not spec.	13	0.06
Hispanic or Latino:	1,888	8.66
Central American:	226	1.04
Costa Rican	7	0.03
Guatemalan	71	0.33
Honduran	13	0.06
Nicaraguan	14	0.06
Panamanian	20	0.09
Salvadoran	87	0.40
Other Central American	14	0.06
Cuban	99	0.45
Dominican Republic	59	0.27
Mexican	131	0.60
Puerto Rican	517	2.37
South American:	467	2.14
Argentinean	30	0.14
Chilean	4	0.02
Colombian	239	1.10
Ecuadorian	97	0.44
Paraguayan	1	0.00
Peruvian	75	0.34
Uruguayan	7	0.03
Venezuelan	2	0.01
Other South American	12	0.06
Other Hispanic or Latino	389	1.78
Hungarian	615	2.82
Icelander	16	0.07
Irish	3,600	16.51
Italian	5,452	25.00
Latvian	5	0.02
Lithuanian	98	0.45
Norwegian	113	0.52
Pennsylvania German	25	0.11
Polish	2,487	11.40
Portuguese	88	0.40
Romanian	49	0.22
Russian	493	2.26
Scandinavian	6	0.03
Scotch-Irish	158	0.72
Scottish	339	1.55
Slavic	42	0.19
Slovak	357	1.64
Slovene	12	0.06
Swedish	85	0.39
Swiss	26	0.12
Turkish	17	0.08
Ukrainian	427	1.96
United States or American	570	2.61
Welsh	78	0.36
West Indian, excl. Hispanic:	375	1.72
Barbadian	64	0.29
British West Indian	7	0.03
Haitian	22	0.10
Jamaican	206	0.94
Trinidadian and Tobagonian	31	0.14
West Indian	45	0.21
White:	17,334	79.48
Not Hispanic (15,902)	16,165	74.12
Hispanic (1,054)	1,169	5.36
Yugoslavian	6	0.03

South River

Place Type: Borough
County: Middlesex
Population: 15,322

Ancestry/Race	Number	%
African American/Black:	1,025	6.69
Not Hispanic (892)	965	6.30
Hispanic (37)	60	0.39
African, sub-Saharan:	81	0.53
African	42	0.27
Ghanian	8	0.05
Nigerian	31	0.20
Am. Ind. or Alaska Nat., not spec.	31	0.20
American Indian tribes, specified:	37	0.24
Blackfeet (1)	1	0.01
Cherokee (2)	14	0.09
Crow	1	0.01
Iroquois (1)	6	0.04
Latin American Indians (5)	10	0.07
Sioux	1	0.01
All other tribes	4	0.03
American Indian tribes, not spec.	1	0.01
Arab:	177	1.16
Egyptian	74	0.48
Jordanian	8	0.05
Lebanese	27	0.18
Palestinian	18	0.12
Syrian	11	0.07
Other Arab	39	0.25
Asian:	634	4.14
Bangladeshi (1)	1	0.01
Chinese, ex. Taiwanese (140)	157	1.02
Filipino (165)	196	1.28
Indian (171)	190	1.24
Japanese (3)	11	0.07
Korean (16)	21	0.14
Pakistani (13)	16	0.10
Taiwanese (2)	2	0.01

Notes: 1. Figures in the "Number" column do not add up to the total population due to: a) Ancestry/Race overlap — e.g. persons can report being both White and Irish, b) persons of Hispanic origin can report being any race, c) persons reporting two ancestries are counted in both categories. 2. Numbers in parentheses indicate the number of persons reporting this ancestry/race alone, not in combination with any other ancestry/race. 3. Refer to the Explanation of Data in the front of the book for more detailed information.

Ancestry/Race	Number	%
Thai (2)	2	0.01
Vietnamese (14)	14	0.09
Other Asian, specified (3)	3	0.02
Other Asian, not specified (5)	21	0.14
Australian	21	0.14
Austrian	49	0.32
Belgian	10	0.07
Brazilian	376	2.45
British	23	0.15
Czech	31	0.20
Czechoslovakian	56	0.37
Danish	46	0.30
Dutch	92	0.60
English	578	3.77
European	34	0.22
Finnish	11	0.07
French, except Basque	189	1.23
French Canadian	71	0.46
German	1,916	12.50
Greek	230	1.50
Guyanese	21	0.14
Hawaii Native/Pacific Islander:	10	0.07
Polynesian: (7)	7	0.05
Native Hawaiian (6)	6	0.04
Samoan (1)	1	0.01
Other Pac. Isl., not spec. (1)	3	0.02
Hispanic or Latino:	1,480	9.66
Central American:	92	0.60
Costa Rican	2	0.01
Guatemalan	4	0.03
Honduran	31	0.20
Nicaraguan	32	0.21
Panamanian	4	0.03
Salvadoran	16	0.10
Other Central American	3	0.02
Cuban	53	0.35
Dominican Republic	53	0.35
Mexican	248	1.62
Puerto Rican	435	2.84
South American:	305	1.99
Argentinean	54	0.35
Bolivian	12	0.08
Chilean	3	0.02
Colombian	62	0.40
Ecuadorian	64	0.42
Paraguayan	5	0.03
Peruvian	34	0.22
Uruguayan	8	0.05
Venezuelan	50	0.33
Other South American	13	0.08
Other Hispanic or Latino	294	1.92
Hungarian	638	4.16
Irish	1,985	12.96
Italian	2,237	14.60
Lithuanian	41	0.27
Norwegian	60	0.39
Polish	2,894	18.89
Portuguese	1,432	9.35
Romanian	9	0.06
Russian	695	4.54
Scotch-Irish	74	0.48
Scottish	96	0.63
Serbian	23	0.15
Slavic	6	0.04
Slovak	72	0.47
Swedish	44	0.29
Swiss	14	0.09
Ukrainian	290	1.89
United States or American	375	2.45
Welsh	22	0.14
West Indian, excl. Hispanic:	111	0.72
British West Indian	5	0.03
Haitian	57	0.37
Jamaican	27	0.18
Trinidadian and Tobagonian	9	0.06
West Indian	13	0.08
White:	13,180	86.02
Not Hispanic (11,995)	12,282	80.16
Hispanic (806)	898	5.86

Southampton

Place Type: Township
County: Burlington
Population: 10,388

Ancestry/Race	Number	%
African American/Black:	149	1.43
Not Hispanic (125)	148	1.42
Hispanic	1	0.01
Am. Ind. or Alaska Nat., not spec.	23	0.22
American Indian tribes, specified:	26	0.25
Blackfeet	1	0.01
Cherokee (5)	7	0.07
Chickasaw	2	0.02
Choctaw	1	0.01
Delaware	1	0.01
Iroquois (1)	3	0.03
Lumbee (1)	1	0.01
Navajo	1	0.01
Sioux	3	0.03
All other tribes (4)	6	0.06
Arab:	8	0.08
Lebanese	8	0.08
Asian:	80	0.77
Chinese, ex. Taiwanese (9)	9	0.09
Filipino (5)	8	0.08
Indian (11)	12	0.12
Japanese (9)	18	0.17
Korean (24)	25	0.24
Thai (2)	2	0.02
Vietnamese (3)	3	0.03
Other Asian, not specified (2)	3	0.03
Australian	6	0.06
Austrian	57	0.55
Belgian	6	0.06
British	20	0.19
Canadian	22	0.21
Croatian	24	0.23
Czech	38	0.37
Czechoslovakian	24	0.23
Danish	41	0.40
Dutch	182	1.76
English	1,696	16.41
European	37	0.36
Finnish	16	0.15
French, except Basque	249	2.41
French Canadian	41	0.40
German	2,715	26.28
Greek	80	0.77
Hawaii Native/Pacific Islander:	1	0.01
Polynesian:	1	0.01
Native Hawaiian	1	0.01
Hispanic or Latino:	134	1.29
Central American:	7	0.07
Costa Rican	1	0.01
Honduran	1	0.01
Panamanian	5	0.05
Cuban	5	0.05
Mexican	34	0.33
Puerto Rican	63	0.61
Other Hispanic or Latino	25	0.24
Hungarian	142	1.37
Irish	2,386	23.09
Italian	1,243	12.03
Lithuanian	83	0.80
Norwegian	93	0.90
Pennsylvania German	111	1.07
Polish	833	8.06
Portuguese	6	0.06
Romanian	23	0.22
Russian	70	0.68
Scotch-Irish	207	2.00
Scottish	191	1.85
Slavic	8	0.08
Slovak	35	0.34
Swedish	75	0.73
Swiss	22	0.21
Ukrainian	43	0.42
United States or American	766	7.41
Welsh	207	2.00
White:	10,134	97.55
Not Hispanic (9,983)	10,030	96.55
Hispanic (103)	104	1.00

Sparta

Place Type: Township
County: Sussex
Population: 18,080

Ancestry/Race	Number	%
African American/Black:	84	0.46
Not Hispanic (50)	72	0.40
Hispanic (2)	12	0.07
African, sub-Saharan:	14	0.08
African	14	0.08
Am. Ind. or Alaska Nat., not spec.	27	0.15
Albanian	18	0.10
American Indian tribes, specified:	36	0.20
Apache	3	0.02
Blackfeet	3	0.02
Cherokee (3)	11	0.06
Chippewa	1	0.01
Choctaw	1	0.01
Houma	1	0.01
Iroquois (1)	7	0.04
Latin American Indians	2	0.01
Pima (1)	1	0.01
Shoshone	1	0.01
Sioux (1)	2	0.01
Tohono O'Odham (1)	1	0.01
All other tribes	2	0.01
American Indian tribes, not spec.	5	0.03
Arab:	147	0.81
Egyptian	51	0.28
Lebanese	35	0.19
Syrian	61	0.34
Armenian	48	0.27
Asian:	326	1.80
Cambodian (1)	1	0.01
Chinese, ex. Taiwanese (65)	82	0.45
Filipino (39)	52	0.29
Indian (67)	79	0.44
Indonesian (1)	1	0.01
Japanese (6)	10	0.06
Korean (22)	37	0.20
Pakistani (12)	12	0.07
Taiwanese (3)	3	0.02
Vietnamese (33)	36	0.20
Other Asian, not specified (1)	13	0.07
Australian	9	0.05
Austrian	169	0.93
Belgian	19	0.10
Brazilian	23	0.13
British	111	0.61
Canadian	50	0.28
Croatian	36	0.20
Czech	177	0.98
Czechoslovakian	63	0.35
Danish	141	0.78
Dutch	508	2.81
Eastern European	13	0.07
English	2,031	11.22
European	108	0.60
Finnish	45	0.25
French, except Basque	400	2.21
French Canadian	96	0.53
German	4,217	23.29
Greek	194	1.07
Hawaii Native/Pacific Islander:	22	0.12
Micronesian: (4)	5	0.03
Guamanian/Chamorro (4)	5	0.03
Polynesian: (1)	8	0.04
Native Hawaiian (1)	6	0.03
Samoan	1	0.01
Other Polynesian	1	0.01
Other Pac. Isl., not spec.	9	0.05
Hispanic or Latino:	459	2.54
Central American:	28	0.15

Notes: 1. Figures in the "Number" column do not add up to the total population due to: a) Ancestry/Race overlap — e.g. persons can report being both White and Irish, b) persons of Hispanic origin can report being any race, c) persons reporting two ancestries are counted in both categories. 2. Numbers in parentheses indicate the number of persons reporting this ancestry/race alone, not in combination with any other ancestry/race. 3. Refer to the Explanation of Data in the front of the book for more detailed information.

Costa Rican	10	0.06
Guatemalan	4	0.02
Honduran	1	0.01
Nicaraguan	7	0.04
Salvadoran	6	0.03
Cuban	55	0.30
Dominican Republic	16	0.09
Mexican	81	0.45
Puerto Rican	106	0.59
South American:	64	0.35
Argentinean	14	0.08
Bolivian	1	0.01
Chilean	2	0.01
Colombian	24	0.13
Ecuadorian	14	0.08
Paraguayan	2	0.01
Peruvian	4	0.02
Uruguayan	2	0.01
Venezuelan	1	0.01
Other Hispanic or Latino	109	0.60
Hungarian	156	0.86
Iranian	27	0.15
Irish	4,999	27.61
Italian	4,089	22.58
Latvian	20	0.11
Lithuanian	75	0.41
Northern European	21	0.12
Norwegian	225	1.24
Pennsylvania German	8	0.04
Polish	1,461	8.07
Portuguese	42	0.23
Romanian	66	0.36
Russian	475	2.62
Scandinavian	18	0.10
Scotch-Irish	623	3.44
Scottish	527	2.91
Slavic	37	0.20
Slovak	151	0.83
Swedish	308	1.70
Swiss	104	0.57
Turkish	26	0.14
Ukrainian	232	1.28
United States or American	701	3.87
Welsh	188	1.04
White:	17,664	97.70
Not Hispanic (17,135)	17,280	95.58
Hispanic (346)	384	2.12
Yugoslavian	68	0.38

Springdale

Place Type: Census Designated Place
County: Camden
Population: 14,409

Ancestry/Race	Number	%
African American/Black:	384	2.67
Not Hispanic (345)	377	2.62
Hispanic (1)	7	0.05
African, sub-Saharan:	45	0.31
African	30	0.21
South African	15	0.10
Am. Ind. or Alaska Nat., not spec.	6	0.04
American Indian tribes, specified:	24	0.17
Cherokee (5)	12	0.08
Delaware (1)	1	0.01
Iroquois	1	0.01
Latin American Indians	4	0.03
Pueblo	1	0.01
All other tribes	5	0.03
American Indian tribes, not spec.	2	0.01
Arab:	38	0.26
Arab/Arabic	15	0.10
Egyptian	5	0.03
Lebanese	13	0.09
Other Arab	5	0.03
Armenian	43	0.30
Asian:	1,359	9.43
Bangladeshi (3)	4	0.03
Cambodian (6)	6	0.04
Chinese, ex. Taiwanese (379)	390	2.71
Filipino (136)	154	1.07
Indian (295)	310	2.15
Japanese (25)	32	0.22
Korean (383)	389	2.70
Malaysian	4	0.03
Pakistani (6)	6	0.04
Taiwanese (39)	42	0.29
Thai	2	0.01
Vietnamese (7)	9	0.06
Other Asian, not specified (8)	11	0.08
Austrian	226	1.57
Basque	9	0.06
Belgian	10	0.07
Brazilian	26	0.18
British	56	0.39
Canadian	23	0.16
Croatian	5	0.03
Czech	112	0.78
Czechoslovakian	8	0.06
Danish	19	0.13
Dutch	115	0.80
Eastern European	434	3.01
English	927	6.43
European	41	0.28
French, except Basque	184	1.28
German	1,223	8.49
Greek	245	1.70
Hawaii Native/Pacific Islander:	3	0.02
Polynesian: (1)	1	0.01
Samoan (1)	1	0.01
Other Pac. Isl., not spec.	2	0.01
Hispanic or Latino:	176	1.22
Central American:	11	0.08
Guatemalan	1	0.01
Honduran	1	0.01
Nicaraguan	4	0.03
Panamanian	3	0.02
Salvadoran	2	0.01
Cuban	19	0.13
Dominican Republic	4	0.03
Mexican	35	0.24
Puerto Rican	46	0.32
South American:	24	0.17
Argentinean	7	0.05
Bolivian	1	0.01
Chilean	3	0.02
Colombian	8	0.06
Venezuelan	3	0.02
Other South American	2	0.01
Other Hispanic or Latino	37	0.26
Hungarian	167	1.16
Iranian	61	0.42
Irish	1,753	12.16
Israeli	58	0.40
Italian	1,817	12.61
Latvian	33	0.23
Lithuanian	112	0.78
Luxemburger	18	0.12
Norwegian	30	0.21
Pennsylvania German	7	0.05
Polish	1,149	7.97
Portuguese	30	0.21
Romanian	132	0.92
Russian	2,014	13.97
Scotch-Irish	40	0.28
Scottish	135	0.94
Serbian	27	0.19
Slovak	67	0.46
Swedish	117	0.81
Swiss	13	0.09
Ukrainian	208	1.44
United States or American	679	4.71
Welsh	86	0.60
West Indian, excl. Hispanic:	68	0.47
Barbadian	21	0.15
Haitian	21	0.15
Jamaican	26	0.18
White:	12,713	88.23
Not Hispanic (12,492)	12,558	87.15
Hispanic (147)	155	1.08

Springfield

Place Type: Census Designated Place
County: Union
Population: 14,429

Ancestry/Race	Number	%
Afghan	10	0.07
African American/Black:	561	3.89
Not Hispanic (536)	556	3.85
Hispanic (1)	5	0.03
African, sub-Saharan:	96	0.67
South African	87	0.60
Zimbabwean	9	0.06
Am. Ind. or Alaska Nat., not spec.	17	0.12
American Indian tribes, specified:	6	0.04
Apache	1	0.01
Cherokee	1	0.01
Chippewa	1	0.01
Delaware (1)	1	0.01
Iroquois (1)	2	0.01
American Indian tribes, not spec.	3	0.02
Arab:	22	0.15
Egyptian	8	0.06
Lebanese	8	0.06
Moroccan	6	0.04
Armenian	40	0.28
Asian:	744	5.16
Chinese, ex. Taiwanese (228)	242	1.68
Filipino (120)	134	0.93
Indian (220)	240	1.66
Indonesian (1)	1	0.01
Japanese (14)	20	0.14
Korean (57)	60	0.42
Pakistani (6)	7	0.05
Sri Lankan (2)	2	0.01
Taiwanese (1)	2	0.01
Thai (1)	1	0.01
Vietnamese (13)	13	0.09
Other Asian, not specified (9)	22	0.15
Assyrian/Chaldean/Syriac	70	0.49
Austrian	200	1.39
British	10	0.07
Canadian	28	0.19
Carpatho Rusyn	6	0.04
Czech	63	0.44
Czechoslovakian	15	0.10
Danish	43	0.30
Dutch	154	1.07
Eastern European	124	0.86
English	419	2.90
European	100	0.69
French, except Basque	89	0.62
French Canadian	55	0.38
German	1,538	10.66
Greek	250	1.73
Guyanese	47	0.33
Hawaii Native/Pacific Islander:	6	0.04
Polynesian:	4	0.03
Native Hawaiian	3	0.02
Samoan	1	0.01
Other Pac. Isl., not spec.	2	0.01
Hispanic or Latino:	597	4.14
Central American:	131	0.91
Costa Rican	108	0.75
Guatemalan	7	0.05
Honduran	2	0.01
Panamanian	5	0.03
Salvadoran	9	0.06
Cuban	48	0.33
Dominican Republic	7	0.05
Mexican	20	0.14
Puerto Rican	78	0.54
South American:	169	1.17
Argentinean	10	0.07
Bolivian	2	0.01
Chilean	5	0.03
Colombian	55	0.38

Notes: 1. Figures in the "Number" column do not add up to the total population due to: a) Ancestry/Race overlap — e.g. persons can report being both White and Irish, b) persons of Hispanic origin can report being any race, c) persons reporting two ancestries are counted in both categories. 2. Numbers in parentheses indicate the number of persons reporting this ancestry/race alone, not in combination with any other ancestry/race. 3. Refer to the Explanation of Data in the front of the book for more detailed information.

Ecuadorian	33	0.23
Peruvian	26	0.18
Uruguayan	12	0.08
Venezuelan	13	0.09
Other South American	13	0.09
Other Hispanic or Latino	144	1.00
Hungarian	216	1.50
Iranian	26	0.18
Irish	1,471	10.19
Israeli	74	0.51
Italian	3,036	21.04
Latvian	31	0.21
Lithuanian	37	0.26
Macedonian	29	0.20
Norwegian	38	0.26
Polish	1,328	9.20
Portuguese	165	1.14
Romanian	103	0.71
Russian	1,493	10.35
Scotch-Irish	81	0.56
Scottish	114	0.79
Slavic	18	0.12
Slovak	100	0.69
Slovene	20	0.14
Swedish	41	0.28
Swiss	23	0.16
Turkish	65	0.45
Ukrainian	348	2.41
United States or American	689	4.78
Welsh	26	0.18
West Indian, excl. Hispanic:	116	0.80
Barbadian	7	0.05
British West Indian	21	0.15
Haitian	26	0.18
Jamaican	45	0.31
Trinidadian and Tobagonian	7	0.05
West Indian	10	0.07
White:	13,052	90.46
Not Hispanic (12,491)	12,580	87.19
Hispanic (455)	472	3.27

Stafford

Place Type: Township
County: Ocean
Population: 22,532

Ancestry/Race	Number	%
African American/Black:	220	0.98
Not Hispanic (157)	206	0.91
Hispanic (9)	14	0.06
African, sub-Saharan:	33	0.15
African	5	0.02
Cape Verdean	28	0.12
Alaska Native tribes, specified:	1	0.00
Tlingit-Haida (1)	1	0.00
Am. Ind. or Alaska Nat., not spec.	19	0.08
Albanian	15	0.07
American Indian tribes, specified:	56	0.25
Blackfeet	6	0.03
Cherokee (5)	28	0.12
Chickasaw (2)	2	0.01
Chippewa (1)	1	0.00
Comanche	1	0.00
Delaware	3	0.01
Iroquois (7)	7	0.03
Sioux	4	0.02
All other tribes (1)	4	0.02
American Indian tribes, not spec.	1	0.00
Arab:	58	0.26
Egyptian	6	0.03
Lebanese	15	0.07
Syrian	37	0.16
Armenian	24	0.11
Asian:	268	1.19
Chinese, ex. Taiwanese (32)	33	0.15
Filipino (68)	100	0.44
Indian (62)	66	0.29
Indonesian (2)	2	0.01
Japanese (3)	9	0.04
Korean (34)	37	0.16
Vietnamese (11)	11	0.05
Other Asian, not specified (5)	10	0.04
Australian	8	0.04
Austrian	107	0.48
Belgian	48	0.21
Brazilian	24	0.11
British	90	0.40
Canadian	14	0.06
Croatian	49	0.22
Czech	101	0.45
Czechoslovakian	138	0.61
Danish	24	0.11
Dutch	333	1.48
Eastern European	8	0.04
English	2,526	11.22
Estonian	10	0.04
European	154	0.68
Finnish	26	0.12
French, except Basque	671	2.98
French Canadian	166	0.74
German	5,169	22.96
Greek	141	0.63
Hawaii Native/Pacific Islander:	19	0.08
Micronesian:	1	0.00
Guamanian/Chamorro	1	0.00
Polynesian: (6)	10	0.04
Native Hawaiian (4)	7	0.03
Samoan (2)	3	0.01
Other Pac. Isl., not spec. (1)	8	0.04
Hispanic or Latino:	542	2.41
Central American:	13	0.06
Costa Rican	3	0.01
Guatemalan	5	0.02
Panamanian	4	0.02
Salvadoran	1	0.00
Cuban	55	0.24
Dominican Republic	20	0.09
Mexican	88	0.39
Puerto Rican	202	0.90
South American:	69	0.31
Argentinean	5	0.02
Chilean	4	0.02
Colombian	26	0.12
Ecuadorian	15	0.07
Peruvian	6	0.03
Uruguayan	10	0.04
Venezuelan	2	0.01
Other South American	1	0.00
Other Hispanic or Latino	95	0.42
Hungarian	308	1.37
Irish	6,627	29.43
Italian	5,553	24.66
Lithuanian	225	1.00
Luxemburger	28	0.12
Northern European	20	0.09
Norwegian	326	1.45
Pennsylvania German	56	0.25
Polish	2,042	9.07
Portuguese	88	0.39
Romanian	40	0.18
Russian	184	0.82
Scandinavian	10	0.04
Scotch-Irish	368	1.63
Scottish	481	2.14
Slavic	41	0.18
Slovak	131	0.58
Swedish	302	1.34
Swiss	66	0.29
Ukrainian	174	0.77
United States or American	809	3.59
Welsh	181	0.80
West Indian, excl. Hispanic:	14	0.06
Jamaican	14	0.06
White:	21,995	97.62
Not Hispanic (21,411)	21,568	95.72
Hispanic (397)	427	1.90
Yugoslavian	12	0.05

Succasunna-Kenvil

Place Type: Census Designated Place
County: Morris
Population: 12,569

Ancestry/Race	Number	%
African American/Black:	199	1.58
Not Hispanic (164)	189	1.50
Hispanic (4)	10	0.08
African, sub-Saharan:	10	0.08
African	10	0.08
Am. Ind. or Alaska Nat., not spec.	13	0.10
Alsatian	8	0.06
American Indian tribes, specified:	10	0.08
Cherokee (2)	7	0.06
Delaware (1)	1	0.01
Latin American Indians (1)	1	0.01
Seminole (1)	1	0.01
American Indian tribes, not spec.	6	0.05
Arab:	8	0.06
Syrian	8	0.06
Armenian	13	0.10
Asian:	572	4.55
Bangladeshi (3)	3	0.02
Chinese, ex. Taiwanese (129)	148	1.18
Filipino (50)	60	0.48
Indian (222)	233	1.85
Japanese (15)	16	0.13
Korean (69)	75	0.60
Sri Lankan (1)	1	0.01
Taiwanese (4)	7	0.06
Thai (3)	4	0.03
Vietnamese (10)	12	0.10
Other Asian, not specified (5)	13	0.10
Australian	22	0.18
Austrian	136	1.09
Belgian	11	0.09
Brazilian	14	0.11
British	65	0.52
Canadian	48	0.38
Czech	67	0.53
Czechoslovakian	21	0.17
Danish	86	0.69
Dutch	270	2.15
Eastern European	52	0.42
English	951	7.59
European	92	0.73
Finnish	29	0.23
French, except Basque	289	2.31
French Canadian	34	0.27
German	2,453	19.58
Greek	128	1.02
Hawaii Native/Pacific Islander:	1	0.01
Polynesian:	1	0.01
Native Hawaiian	1	0.01
Hispanic or Latino:	487	3.87
Central American:	32	0.25
Costa Rican	11	0.09
Guatemalan	5	0.04
Honduran	6	0.05
Panamanian	1	0.01
Salvadoran	5	0.04
Other Central American	4	0.03
Cuban	58	0.46
Dominican Republic	5	0.04
Mexican	22	0.18
Puerto Rican	162	1.29
South American:	84	0.67
Argentinean	7	0.06
Bolivian	1	0.01
Chilean	5	0.04
Colombian	30	0.24
Ecuadorian	28	0.22
Peruvian	1	0.01
Uruguayan	6	0.05
Venezuelan	4	0.03
Other South American	2	0.02
Other Hispanic or Latino	124	0.99
Hungarian	216	1.72

Notes: 1. Figures in the "Number" column do not add up to the total population due to: a) Ancestry/Race overlap — e.g. persons can report being both White and Irish, b) persons of Hispanic origin can report being any race, c) persons reporting two ancestries are counted in both categories. 2. Numbers in parentheses indicate the number of persons reporting this ancestry/race alone, not in combination with any other ancestry/race. 3. Refer to the Explanation of Data in the front of the book for more detailed information.

Iranian	8	0.06
Irish	2,448	19.54
Italian	3,553	28.36
Latvian	9	0.07
Lithuanian	40	0.32
Macedonian	8	0.06
Norwegian	376	3.00
Pennsylvania German	13	0.10
Polish	1,290	10.30
Portuguese	70	0.56
Romanian	49	0.39
Russian	468	3.74
Scandinavian	6	0.05
Scotch-Irish	187	1.49
Scottish	356	2.84
Slavic	7	0.06
Slovak	180	1.44
Slovene	14	0.11
Swedish	89	0.71
Swiss	98	0.78
Turkish	16	0.13
Ukrainian	118	0.94
United States or American	500	3.99
Welsh	104	0.83
West Indian, excl. Hispanic:	10	0.08
Jamaican	10	0.08
White:	11,776	93.69
Not Hispanic (11,307)	11,374	90.49
Hispanic (380)	402	3.20

Summit

Place Type: City
County: Union
Population: 21,131

Ancestry/Race	Number	%
African American/Black:	988	4.68
Not Hispanic (877)	939	4.44
Hispanic (37)	49	0.23
African, sub-Saharan:	58	0.27
African	9	0.04
South African	49	0.23
Am. Ind. or Alaska Nat., not spec.	35	0.17
Albanian	13	0.06
American Indian tribes, specified:	35	0.17
Blackfeet	4	0.02
Cherokee (2)	7	0.03
Chickasaw (3)	3	0.01
Choctaw (1)	1	0.00
Cree (1)	1	0.00
Iroquois	1	0.00
Latin American Indians (3)	16	0.08
Sioux	1	0.00
All other tribes	1	0.00
American Indian tribes, not spec.	9	0.04
Arab:	69	0.33
Egyptian	20	0.09
Lebanese	23	0.11
Moroccan	8	0.04
Syrian	8	0.04
Other Arab	10	0.05
Armenian	61	0.29
Asian:	1,077	5.10
Bangladeshi (2)	2	0.01
Chinese, ex. Taiwanese (253)	300	1.42
Filipino (119)	134	0.63
Indian (307)	336	1.59
Indonesian (3)	3	0.01
Japanese (52)	72	0.34
Korean (78)	91	0.43
Laotian (2)	2	0.01
Malaysian (4)	4	0.02
Pakistani (53)	54	0.26
Sri Lankan (5)	5	0.02
Taiwanese (11)	11	0.05
Thai (4)	5	0.02
Vietnamese (19)	21	0.10
Other Asian, specified (7)	8	0.04
Other Asian, not specified (11)	29	0.14
Australian	14	0.07
Austrian	181	0.86
Belgian	39	0.18
Brazilian	83	0.39
British	245	1.16
Bulgarian	21	0.10
Canadian	82	0.39
Celtic	7	0.03
Croatian	57	0.27
Czech	38	0.18
Czechoslovakian	57	0.27
Danish	79	0.37
Dutch	341	1.61
Eastern European	133	0.63
English	2,737	12.95
Estonian	43	0.20
European	150	0.71
Finnish	53	0.25
French, except Basque	513	2.43
French Canadian	93	0.44
German	3,151	14.91
Greek	170	0.80
Guyanese	26	0.12
Hawaii Native/Pacific Islander:	6	0.03
Micronesian: (1)	1	0.00
Guamanian/Chamorro (1)	1	0.00
Polynesian: (2)	3	0.01
Native Hawaiian (1)	1	0.00
Other Polynesian (1)	2	0.01
Other Pac. Isl., not spec.	2	0.01
Hispanic or Latino:	2,150	10.17
Central American:	742	3.51
Costa Rican	640	3.03
Guatemalan	34	0.16
Honduran	31	0.15
Nicaraguan	5	0.02
Panamanian	5	0.02
Salvadoran	7	0.03
Other Central American	20	0.09
Cuban	159	0.75
Dominican Republic	28	0.13
Mexican	162	0.77
Puerto Rican	207	0.98
South American:	320	1.51
Argentinean	27	0.13
Bolivian	1	0.00
Chilean	36	0.17
Colombian	143	0.68
Ecuadorian	46	0.22
Paraguayan	1	0.00
Peruvian	51	0.24
Uruguayan	4	0.02
Venezuelan	6	0.03
Other South American	5	0.02
Other Hispanic or Latino	532	2.52
Hungarian	248	1.17
Iranian	19	0.09
Irish	4,351	20.59
Italian	3,228	15.28
Lithuanian	101	0.48
Northern European	7	0.03
Norwegian	213	1.01
Pennsylvania German	22	0.10
Polish	1,016	4.81
Portuguese	36	0.17
Romanian	57	0.27
Russian	651	3.08
Scandinavian	8	0.04
Scotch-Irish	434	2.05
Scottish	678	3.21
Serbian	22	0.10
Slavic	14	0.07
Slovak	76	0.36
Slovene	15	0.07
Swedish	256	1.21
Swiss	135	0.64
Turkish	37	0.18
Ukrainian	160	0.76
United States or American	527	2.49
Welsh	171	0.81
West Indian, excl. Hispanic:	205	0.97
Barbadian	59	0.28
Jamaican	136	0.64
Other West Indian	10	0.05
White:	18,843	89.17
Not Hispanic (16,926)	17,094	80.90
Hispanic (1,620)	1,749	8.28
Yugoslavian	5	0.02

Teaneck

Place Type: Census Designated Place
County: Bergen
Population: 39,260

Ancestry/Race	Number	%
Afghan	35	0.09
African American/Black:	11,973	30.50
Not Hispanic (10,905)	11,460	29.19
Hispanic (393)	513	1.31
African, sub-Saharan:	775	1.97
African	511	1.30
Cape Verdean	16	0.04
Ethiopian	30	0.08
Ghanian	9	0.02
Kenyan	25	0.06
Nigerian	71	0.18
Sierra Leonean	22	0.06
South African	24	0.06
Zairian	17	0.04
Other sub-Saharan African	50	0.13
Alaska Native tribes, specified:	2	0.01
Aleut	1	0.00
Tlingit-Haida	1	0.00
Am. Ind. or Alaska Nat., not spec.	114	0.29
American Indian tribes, specified:	220	0.56
Apache (1)	2	0.01
Blackfeet (1)	10	0.03
Cherokee (4)	80	0.20
Cheyenne	2	0.01
Chickasaw	3	0.01
Chippewa (2)	3	0.01
Choctaw	2	0.01
Cree	2	0.01
Delaware	3	0.01
Iroquois (3)	13	0.03
Latin American Indians (11)	61	0.16
Lumbee (1)	2	0.01
Navajo	13	0.03
Seminole	9	0.02
Sioux	2	0.01
All other tribes (3)	13	0.03
American Indian tribes, not spec.	20	0.05
Arab:	446	1.14
Arab/Arabic	71	0.18
Egyptian	143	0.36
Lebanese	65	0.17
Moroccan	49	0.12
Palestinian	20	0.05
Syrian	72	0.18
Other Arab	26	0.07
Armenian	57	0.15
Asian:	3,192	8.13
Bangladeshi (14)	15	0.04
Cambodian (2)	2	0.01
Chinese, ex. Taiwanese (360)	432	1.10
Filipino (853)	918	2.34
Indian (981)	1,131	2.88
Japanese (108)	131	0.33
Korean (151)	167	0.43
Laotian (1)	1	0.00
Malaysian (12)	13	0.03
Pakistani (151)	186	0.47
Sri Lankan (11)	11	0.03
Taiwanese (23)	33	0.08
Thai (14)	16	0.04
Vietnamese (34)	35	0.09
Other Asian, specified (3)	11	0.03
Other Asian, not specified (25)	90	0.23
Austrian	346	0.88

Notes: 1. Figures in the "Number" column do not add up to the total population due to: a) Ancestry/Race overlap — e.g. persons can report being both White and Irish, b) persons of Hispanic origin can report being any race, c) persons reporting two ancestries are counted in both categories. 2. Numbers in parentheses indicate the number of persons reporting this ancestry/race alone, not in combination with any other ancestry/race. 3. Refer to the Explanation of Data in the front of the book for more detailed information.

Ancestry/Race	Number	%
Belgian	36	0.09
Brazilian	8	0.02
British	115	0.29
Bulgarian	22	0.06
Canadian	163	0.42
Croatian	34	0.09
Czech	160	0.41
Czechoslovakian	80	0.20
Danish	29	0.07
Dutch	185	0.47
Eastern European	734	1.87
English	902	2.30
European	571	1.45
Finnish	21	0.05
French, except Basque	387	0.99
French Canadian	67	0.17
German	2,342	5.97
German Russian	53	0.13
Greek	351	0.89
Guyanese	205	0.52
Hawaii Native/Pacific Islander:	39	0.10
Polynesian: (5)	5	0.01
Native Hawaiian (1)	1	0.00
Samoan (4)	4	0.01
Other Pac. Isl., specified	8	0.02
Other Pac. Isl., not spec. (6)	26	0.07
Hispanic or Latino:	4,103	10.45
Central American:	184	0.47
Costa Rican	16	0.04
Guatemalan	8	0.02
Honduran	29	0.07
Nicaraguan	6	0.02
Panamanian	41	0.10
Salvadoran	67	0.17
Other Central American	17	0.04
Cuban	329	0.84
Dominican Republic	780	1.99
Mexican	151	0.38
Puerto Rican	1,132	2.88
South American:	681	1.73
Argentinean	40	0.10
Bolivian	11	0.03
Chilean	24	0.06
Colombian	382	0.97
Ecuadorian	112	0.29
Paraguayan	2	0.01
Peruvian	76	0.19
Uruguayan	8	0.02
Venezuelan	8	0.02
Other South American	18	0.05
Other Hispanic or Latino	846	2.15
Hungarian	569	1.45
Iranian	103	0.26
Irish	2,017	5.14
Israeli	291	0.74
Italian	2,447	6.23
Latvian	38	0.10
Lithuanian	99	0.25
Norwegian	139	0.35
Pennsylvania German	8	0.02
Polish	1,632	4.16
Portuguese	53	0.13
Romanian	181	0.46
Russian	2,093	5.33
Scandinavian	10	0.03
Scotch-Irish	129	0.33
Scottish	242	0.62
Serbian	26	0.07
Slavic	44	0.11
Slovak	20	0.05
Swedish	167	0.43
Swiss	42	0.11
Turkish	135	0.34
Ukrainian	150	0.38
United States or American	1,679	4.28
Welsh	57	0.15
West Indian, excl. Hispanic:	2,469	6.29
Barbadian	19	0.05
Belizean	61	0.16
British West Indian	196	0.50
Dutch West Indian	7	0.02
Haitian	251	0.64
Jamaican	1,351	3.44
Trinidadian and Tobagonian	186	0.47
U.S. Virgin Islander	18	0.05
West Indian	363	0.92
Other West Indian	17	0.04
White:	22,968	58.50
Not Hispanic (20,237)	20,866	53.15
Hispanic (1,845)	2,102	5.35
Yugoslavian	36	0.09

Tenafly

Place Type: Borough
County: Bergen
Population: 13,806

Ancestry/Race	Number	%
African American/Black:	167	1.21
Not Hispanic (122)	148	1.07
Hispanic (10)	19	0.14
African, sub-Saharan:	10	0.07
African	10	0.07
Am. Ind. or Alaska Nat., not spec.	20	0.14
Alsatian	9	0.07
American Indian tribes, specified:	6	0.04
Apache (1)	1	0.01
Cherokee (3)	4	0.03
Latin American Indians (1)	1	0.01
American Indian tribes, not spec.	3	0.02
Arab:	93	0.67
Egyptian	56	0.41
Iraqi	12	0.09
Lebanese	17	0.12
Syrian	8	0.06
Armenian	229	1.66
Asian:	2,791	20.22
Chinese, ex. Taiwanese (644)	698	5.06
Filipino (149)	165	1.20
Indian (177)	185	1.34
Indonesian (6)	11	0.08
Japanese (251)	282	2.04
Korean (1,294)	1,332	9.65
Malaysian (1)	1	0.01
Pakistani (17)	20	0.14
Sri Lankan (1)	1	0.01
Taiwanese (41)	47	0.34
Thai (4)	6	0.04
Vietnamese (13)	13	0.09
Other Asian, not specified (8)	30	0.22
Australian	8	0.06
Austrian	170	1.23
Basque	26	0.19
Brazilian	6	0.04
British	33	0.24
Canadian	32	0.23
Carpatho Rusyn	20	0.14
Croatian	16	0.12
Czech	63	0.46
Czechoslovakian	44	0.32
Danish	47	0.34
Dutch	118	0.85
Eastern European	234	1.69
English	395	2.86
European	321	2.33
French, except Basque	180	1.30
French Canadian	60	0.43
German	1,074	7.78
Greek	247	1.79
Hawaii Native/Pacific Islander:	3	0.02
Micronesian: (2)	2	0.01
Guamanian/Chamorro (2)	2	0.01
Polynesian: (1)	1	0.01
Samoan (1)	1	0.01
Hispanic or Latino:	642	4.65
Central American:	63	0.46
Costa Rican	9	0.07
Guatemalan	17	0.12
Honduran	2	0.01
Nicaraguan	1	0.01
Panamanian	4	0.03
Salvadoran	28	0.20
Other Central American	2	0.01
Cuban	98	0.71
Dominican Republic	45	0.33
Mexican	42	0.30
Puerto Rican	99	0.72
South American:	117	0.85
Argentinean	17	0.12
Chilean	9	0.07
Colombian	65	0.47
Ecuadorian	7	0.05
Peruvian	10	0.07
Venezuelan	6	0.04
Other South American	3	0.02
Other Hispanic or Latino	178	1.29
Hungarian	215	1.56
Iranian	21	0.15
Irish	1,533	11.10
Israeli	200	1.45
Italian	1,192	8.63
Latvian	22	0.16
Lithuanian	108	0.78
Norwegian	47	0.34
Polish	862	6.24
Portuguese	26	0.19
Romanian	109	0.79
Russian	1,208	8.75
Scandinavian	8	0.06
Scotch-Irish	44	0.32
Scottish	84	0.61
Serbian	8	0.06
Slavic	34	0.25
Slovak	8	0.06
Soviet Union	21	0.15
Swedish	114	0.83
Swiss	76	0.55
Turkish	102	0.74
Ukrainian	144	1.04
United States or American	1,092	7.91
Welsh	18	0.13
West Indian, excl. Hispanic:	71	0.51
Haitian	45	0.33
Jamaican	8	0.06
Trinidadian and Tobagonian	9	0.07
West Indian	9	0.07
White:	10,776	78.05
Not Hispanic (10,176)	10,324	74.78
Hispanic (425)	452	3.27

Tinton Falls

Place Type: Borough
County: Monmouth
Population: 15,053

Ancestry/Race	Number	%
African American/Black:	2,106	13.99
Not Hispanic (1,916)	2,049	13.61
Hispanic (47)	57	0.38
African, sub-Saharan:	72	0.48
African	52	0.35
Cape Verdean	10	0.07
South African	10	0.07
Am. Ind. or Alaska Nat., not spec.	34	0.23
Albanian	6	0.04
American Indian tribes, specified:	59	0.39
Apache	2	0.01
Blackfeet (2)	15	0.10
Cherokee (4)	8	0.05
Chippewa	3	0.02
Creek (1)	1	0.01
Delaware (3)	5	0.03
Iroquois (1)	5	0.03
Latin American Indians (12)	12	0.08
Osage (1)	1	0.01
Sioux	3	0.02
All other tribes	4	0.03
American Indian tribes, not spec.	1	0.01

Notes: 1. Figures in the "Number" column do not add up to the total population due to: a) Ancestry/Race overlap — e.g. persons can report being both White and Irish, b) persons of Hispanic origin can report being any race, c) persons reporting two ancestries are counted in both categories. 2. Numbers in parentheses indicate the number of persons reporting this ancestry/race alone, not in combination with any other ancestry/race. 3. Refer to the Explanation of Data in the front of the book for more detailed information.

Arab:	186	1.24
Arab/Arabic	19	0.13
Egyptian	20	0.13
Lebanese	49	0.33
Syrian	98	0.65
Armenian	24	0.16
Asian:	861	5.72
Chinese, ex. Taiwanese (201)	222	1.47
Filipino (113)	139	0.92
Indian (174)	192	1.28
Indonesian	1	0.01
Japanese (14)	23	0.15
Korean (150)	177	1.18
Laotian (1)	3	0.02
Malaysian (2)	2	0.01
Pakistani (28)	29	0.19
Sri Lankan (1)	1	0.01
Taiwanese (9)	11	0.07
Thai (1)	1	0.01
Vietnamese (39)	40	0.27
Other Asian, specified	3	0.02
Other Asian, not specified (6)	17	0.11
Austrian	231	1.53
Belgian	6	0.04
Brazilian	6	0.04
British	67	0.45
Canadian	9	0.06
Czech	11	0.07
Czechoslovakian	30	0.20
Danish	33	0.22
Dutch	141	0.94
Eastern European	23	0.15
English	1,116	7.41
Estonian	7	0.05
European	36	0.24
Finnish	5	0.03
French, except Basque	344	2.28
French Canadian	112	0.74
German	2,149	14.27
Greek	190	1.26
Guyanese	10	0.07
Hawaii Native/Pacific Islander:	5	0.03
Polynesian: (2)	5	0.03
Native Hawaiian (2)	5	0.03
Hispanic or Latino:	707	4.70
Central American:	18	0.12
Costa Rican	5	0.03
Guatemalan	3	0.02
Honduran	1	0.01
Nicaraguan	4	0.03
Panamanian	4	0.03
Salvadoran	1	0.01
Cuban	49	0.33
Dominican Republic	14	0.09
Mexican	122	0.81
Puerto Rican	305	2.03
South American:	74	0.49
Argentinean	6	0.04
Bolivian	2	0.01
Chilean	5	0.03
Colombian	14	0.09
Ecuadorian	6	0.04
Paraguayan	2	0.01
Peruvian	23	0.15
Uruguayan	1	0.01
Venezuelan	10	0.07
Other South American	5	0.03
Other Hispanic or Latino	125	0.83
Hungarian	190	1.26
Iranian	19	0.13
Irish	3,193	21.21
Israeli	8	0.05
Italian	3,406	22.62
Latvian	15	0.10
Lithuanian	47	0.31
Luxemburger	13	0.09
Northern European	31	0.21
Norwegian	140	0.93
Polish	1,076	7.15
Portuguese	92	0.61
Romanian	9	0.06
Russian	377	2.50
Scandinavian	12	0.08
Scotch-Irish	123	0.82
Scottish	336	2.23
Slavic	19	0.13
Slovak	75	0.50
Slovene	7	0.05
Swedish	239	1.59
Swiss	22	0.15
Ukrainian	158	1.05
United States or American	400	2.66
Welsh	122	0.81
West Indian, excl. Hispanic:	130	0.86
Haitian	51	0.34
Jamaican	59	0.39
Trinidadian and Tobagonian	20	0.13
White:	12,069	80.18
Not Hispanic (11,396)	11,571	76.87
Hispanic (466)	498	3.31

Toms River

Place Type: Census Designated Place
County: Ocean
Population: 86,327

Ancestry/Race	Number	%
African American/Black:	1,831	2.12
Not Hispanic (1,487)	1,685	1.95
Hispanic (78)	146	0.17
African, sub-Saharan:	132	0.15
African	83	0.10
Kenyan	16	0.02
South African	33	0.04
Alaska Native tribes, specified:	8	0.01
Aleut (3)	4	0.00
Tlingit-Haida (4)	4	0.00
Alaska Native tribes, not specified	4	0.00
Am. Ind. or Alaska Nat., not spec.	119	0.14
Albanian	67	0.08
American Indian tribes, specified:	197	0.23
Apache	3	0.00
Blackfeet (2)	16	0.02
Cherokee (10)	47	0.05
Chippewa	5	0.01
Choctaw	1	0.00
Comanche	2	0.00
Creek (2)	10	0.01
Crow	1	0.00
Delaware (3)	34	0.04
Iroquois (7)	17	0.02
Latin American Indians (14)	23	0.03
Navajo (2)	3	0.00
Paiute (1)	1	0.00
Sioux (4)	5	0.01
Ute (1)	1	0.00
Yaqui	1	0.00
All other tribes (10)	27	0.03
American Indian tribes, not spec.	19	0.02
Arab:	338	0.39
Arab/Arabic	14	0.02
Egyptian	16	0.02
Iraqi	16	0.02
Lebanese	121	0.14
Syrian	161	0.19
Other Arab	10	0.01
Armenian	66	0.08
Asian:	2,547	2.95
Cambodian	1	0.00
Chinese, ex. Taiwanese (292)	333	0.39
Filipino (978)	1,140	1.32
Indian (529)	589	0.68
Indonesian (4)	7	0.01
Japanese (44)	54	0.06
Korean (160)	192	0.22
Malaysian (5)	10	0.01
Pakistani (48)	57	0.07
Sri Lankan (19)	19	0.02
Taiwanese (5)	6	0.01
Thai (11)	21	0.02
Vietnamese (26)	35	0.04
Other Asian, specified (6)	15	0.02
Other Asian, not specified (24)	68	0.08
Australian	23	0.03
Austrian	341	0.39
Basque	9	0.01
Belgian	106	0.12
Brazilian	55	0.06
British	205	0.24
Bulgarian	35	0.04
Canadian	128	0.15
Carpatho Rusyn	4	0.00
Celtic	3	0.00
Croatian	85	0.10
Cypriot	9	0.01
Czech	440	0.51
Czechoslovakian	266	0.31
Danish	369	0.43
Dutch	1,670	1.93
Eastern European	52	0.06
English	7,326	8.47
Estonian	12	0.01
European	368	0.43
Finnish	72	0.08
French, except Basque	1,652	1.91
French Canadian	465	0.54
German	16,217	18.76
Greek	832	0.96
Hawaii Native/Pacific Islander:	50	0.06
Micronesian: (1)	1	0.00
Guamanian/Chamorro (1)	1	0.00
Polynesian: (6)	14	0.02
Native Hawaiian (4)	10	0.01
Samoan (2)	4	0.00
Other Pac. Isl., specified	7	0.01
Other Pac. Isl., not spec. (14)	28	0.03
Hispanic or Latino:	4,010	4.65
Central American:	115	0.13
Costa Rican	46	0.05
Guatemalan	20	0.02
Honduran	9	0.01
Nicaraguan	5	0.01
Panamanian	6	0.01
Salvadoran	27	0.03
Other Central American	2	0.00
Cuban	320	0.37
Dominican Republic	54	0.06
Mexican	714	0.83
Puerto Rican	1,744	2.02
South American:	484	0.56
Argentinean	36	0.04
Bolivian	3	0.00
Chilean	14	0.02
Colombian	164	0.19
Ecuadorian	45	0.05
Paraguayan	6	0.01
Peruvian	158	0.18
Uruguayan	9	0.01
Venezuelan	32	0.04
Other South American	17	0.02
Other Hispanic or Latino	579	0.67
Hungarian	1,755	2.03
Iranian	59	0.07
Irish	20,815	24.08
Italian	27,250	31.52
Latvian	62	0.07
Lithuanian	510	0.59
Norwegian	692	0.80
Pennsylvania German	25	0.03
Polish	7,691	8.90
Portuguese	549	0.64
Romanian	86	0.10
Russian	1,380	1.60
Scandinavian	60	0.07
Scotch-Irish	1,357	1.57
Scottish	1,681	1.94
Serbian	85	0.10
Slavic	80	0.09
Slovak	471	0.54

Notes: 1. Figures in the "Number" column do not add up to the total population due to: a) Ancestry/Race overlap — e.g. persons can report being both White and Irish, b) persons of Hispanic origin can report being any race, c) persons reporting two ancestries are counted in both categories. 2. Numbers in parentheses indicate the number of persons reporting this ancestry/race alone, not in combination with any other ancestry/race. 3. Refer to the Explanation of Data in the front of the book for more detailed information.

Ancestry/Race	Number	%
Slovene	27	0.03
Swedish	981	1.13
Swiss	196	0.23
Turkish	75	0.09
Ukrainian	1,052	1.22
United States or American	2,521	2.92
Welsh	388	0.45
West Indian, excl. Hispanic:	115	0.13
Haitian	14	0.02
Jamaican	88	0.10
Trinidadian and Tobagonian	8	0.01
West Indian	5	0.01
White:	81,480	94.39
Not Hispanic (77,807)	78,438	90.86
Hispanic (2,791)	3,042	3.52
Yugoslavian	85	0.10

Trenton

Place Type: City
County: Mercer
Population: 85,403

Ancestry/Race	Number	%
African American/Black:	45,762	53.58
Not Hispanic (43,497)	44,481	52.08
Hispanic (968)	1,281	1.50
African, sub-Saharan:	2,555	3.00
African	1,603	1.88
Ghanian	27	0.03
Liberian	739	0.87
Nigerian	97	0.11
Sierra Leonean	9	0.01
Sudanese	6	0.01
Other sub-Saharan African	74	0.09
Am. Ind. or Alaska Nat., not spec.	381	0.45
Albanian	8	0.01
American Indian tribes, specified:	276	0.32
Apache (2)	5	0.01
Blackfeet (2)	14	0.02
Cherokee (25)	107	0.13
Chickasaw	1	0.00
Chippewa	1	0.00
Choctaw	5	0.01
Cree	1	0.00
Delaware (6)	13	0.02
Iroquois	9	0.01
Latin American Indians (44)	79	0.09
Lumbee	1	0.00
Navajo (3)	7	0.01
Pueblo	1	0.00
Seminole (1)	8	0.01
Sioux (2)	9	0.01
All other tribes (2)	15	0.02
American Indian tribes, not spec.	41	0.05
Arab:	71	0.08
Egyptian	63	0.07
Lebanese	8	0.01
Armenian	14	0.02
Asian:	1,051	1.23
Bangladeshi (17)	17	0.02
Cambodian (6)	24	0.03
Chinese, ex. Taiwanese (75)	96	0.11
Filipino (80)	121	0.14
Indian (228)	303	0.35
Indonesian (18)	22	0.03
Japanese (25)	47	0.06
Korean (49)	59	0.07
Laotian (1)	1	0.00
Malaysian	2	0.00
Pakistani (79)	103	0.12
Sri Lankan (1)	1	0.00
Thai (1)	3	0.00
Vietnamese (78)	92	0.11
Other Asian, specified	7	0.01
Other Asian, not specified (42)	153	0.18
Assyrian/Chaldean/Syriac	8	0.01
Australian	3	0.00
Austrian	108	0.13
Brazilian	26	0.03
British	20	0.02
Bulgarian	6	0.01
Canadian	18	0.02
Carpatho Rusyn	15	0.02
Celtic	13	0.02
Czech	80	0.09
Czechoslovakian	44	0.05
Danish	56	0.07
Dutch	300	0.35
English	1,720	2.02
European	95	0.11
Finnish	6	0.01
French, except Basque	290	0.34
French Canadian	69	0.08
German	3,181	3.73
Greek	177	0.21
Guyanese	67	0.08
Hawaii Native/Pacific Islander:	369	0.43
Micronesian: (135)	158	0.19
Guamanian/Chamorro (135)	158	0.19
Polynesian: (16)	26	0.03
Native Hawaiian (8)	11	0.01
Samoan (8)	13	0.02
Tongan	2	0.00
Other Pac. Isl., specified	4	0.00
Other Pac. Isl., not spec. (48)	181	0.21
Hispanic or Latino:	18,391	21.53
Central American:	3,902	4.57
Costa Rican	795	0.93
Guatemalan	2,644	3.10
Honduran	151	0.18
Nicaraguan	18	0.02
Panamanian	29	0.03
Salvadoran	80	0.09
Other Central American	185	0.22
Cuban	200	0.23
Dominican Republic	458	0.54
Mexican	925	1.08
Puerto Rican	8,952	10.48
South American:	606	0.71
Argentinean	24	0.03
Chilean	21	0.02
Colombian	163	0.19
Ecuadorian	309	0.36
Paraguayan	1	0.00
Peruvian	36	0.04
Uruguayan	12	0.01
Venezuelan	18	0.02
Other South American	22	0.03
Other Hispanic or Latino	3,348	3.92
Hungarian	925	1.08
Irish	3,823	4.48
Italian	6,230	7.31
Latvian	14	0.02
Lithuanian	99	0.12
Northern European	8	0.01
Norwegian	71	0.08
Pennsylvania German	63	0.07
Polish	3,272	3.84
Portuguese	31	0.04
Romanian	53	0.06
Russian	449	0.53
Scotch-Irish	168	0.20
Scottish	302	0.35
Serbian	6	0.01
Slavic	159	0.19
Slovak	529	0.62
Slovene	8	0.01
Swedish	82	0.10
Swiss	60	0.07
Turkish	44	0.05
Ukrainian	340	0.40
United States or American	2,082	2.44
Welsh	123	0.14
West Indian, excl. Hispanic:	2,019	2.37
British West Indian	7	0.01
Haitian	737	0.86
Jamaican	1,134	1.33
Trinidadian and Tobagonian	55	0.06
West Indian	86	0.10
White:	29,439	34.47
Not Hispanic (21,022)	21,741	25.46
Hispanic (6,780)	7,698	9.01
Yugoslavian	6	0.01

Union

Place Type: Census Designated Place
County: Union
Population: 54,405

Ancestry/Race	Number	%
Afghan	41	0.08
African American/Black:	11,211	20.61
Not Hispanic (10,563)	10,966	20.16
Hispanic (189)	245	0.45
African, sub-Saharan:	1,265	2.33
African	549	1.01
Cape Verdean	18	0.03
Ghanian	143	0.26
Kenyan	19	0.03
Liberian	7	0.01
Nigerian	518	0.95
South African	11	0.02
Am. Ind. or Alaska Nat., not spec.	113	0.21
Albanian	78	0.14
Alsatian	17	0.03
American Indian tribes, specified:	89	0.16
Blackfeet	4	0.01
Cherokee (10)	33	0.06
Chippewa	1	0.00
Creek	1	0.00
Delaware (3)	3	0.01
Iroquois (2)	7	0.01
Latin American Indians (16)	22	0.04
Lumbee (3)	5	0.01
Seminole (2)	3	0.01
Sioux (3)	4	0.01
All other tribes (3)	6	0.01
American Indian tribes, not spec.	13	0.02
Arab:	241	0.44
Arab/Arabic	72	0.13
Egyptian	74	0.14
Lebanese	19	0.03
Palestinian	34	0.06
Syrian	42	0.08
Asian:	4,545	8.35
Cambodian (13)	13	0.02
Chinese, ex. Taiwanese (404)	456	0.84
Filipino (2,080)	2,184	4.01
Indian (1,240)	1,341	2.46
Indonesian (1)	2	0.00
Japanese (38)	53	0.10
Korean (109)	127	0.23
Malaysian (1)	8	0.01
Pakistani (101)	121	0.22
Sri Lankan (6)	8	0.01
Taiwanese (11)	11	0.02
Thai (5)	9	0.02
Vietnamese (87)	101	0.19
Other Asian, specified	5	0.01
Other Asian, not specified (40)	106	0.19
Assyrian/Chaldean/Syriac	13	0.02
Australian	7	0.01
Austrian	242	0.44
Basque	5	0.01
Belgian	23	0.04
Brazilian	331	0.61
British	99	0.18
Canadian	41	0.08
Croatian	71	0.13
Czech	161	0.30
Czechoslovakian	173	0.32
Danish	50	0.09
Dutch	192	0.35
Eastern European	46	0.08
English	1,416	2.60
European	62	0.11
French, except Basque	305	0.56
French Canadian	59	0.11

Notes: 1. Figures in the "Number" column do not add up to the total population due to: a) Ancestry/Race overlap — e.g. persons can report being both White and Irish, b) persons of Hispanic origin can report being any race, c) persons reporting two ancestries are counted in both categories. 2. Numbers in parentheses indicate the number of persons reporting this ancestry/race alone, not in combination with any other ancestry/race. 3. Refer to the Explanation of Data in the front of the book for more detailed information.

Ancestry/Race	Number	%
German	5,538	10.18
Greek	523	0.96
Guyanese	314	0.58
Hawaii Native/Pacific Islander:	48	0.09
Micronesian: (1)	1	0.00
Guamanian/Chamorro (1)	1	0.00
Polynesian: (7)	12	0.02
Native Hawaiian (2)	7	0.01
Samoan (5)	5	0.01
Other Pac. Isl., specified	5	0.01
Other Pac. Isl., not spec. (5)	30	0.06
Hispanic or Latino:	4,861	8.93
Central American:	301	0.55
Costa Rican	150	0.28
Guatemalan	29	0.05
Honduran	16	0.03
Nicaraguan	10	0.02
Panamanian	15	0.03
Salvadoran	56	0.10
Other Central American	25	0.05
Cuban	666	1.22
Dominican Republic	169	0.31
Mexican	113	0.21
Puerto Rican	1,398	2.57
South American:	980	1.80
Argentinean	59	0.11
Bolivian	14	0.03
Chilean	24	0.04
Colombian	385	0.71
Ecuadorian	230	0.42
Paraguayan	6	0.01
Peruvian	149	0.27
Uruguayan	52	0.10
Venezuelan	28	0.05
Other South American	33	0.06
Other Hispanic or Latino	1,234	2.27
Hungarian	604	1.11
Iranian	10	0.02
Irish	5,395	9.92
Israeli	42	0.08
Italian	9,378	17.24
Latvian	6	0.01
Lithuanian	185	0.34
Northern European	5	0.01
Norwegian	133	0.24
Polish	4,896	9.00
Portuguese	3,725	6.85
Romanian	262	0.48
Russian	893	1.64
Scotch-Irish	241	0.44
Scottish	303	0.56
Slavic	55	0.10
Slovak	443	0.81
Slovene	6	0.01
Swedish	155	0.28
Swiss	99	0.18
Turkish	21	0.04
Ukrainian	1,045	1.92
United States or American	1,590	2.92
Welsh	65	0.12
West Indian, excl. Hispanic:	1,977	3.63
Barbadian	26	0.05
Bermudan	10	0.02
British West Indian	27	0.05
Haitian	1,156	2.12
Jamaican	427	0.78
Trinidadian and Tobagonian	250	0.46
U.S. Virgin Islander	11	0.02
West Indian	70	0.13
White:	37,649	69.20
Not Hispanic (33,661)	34,269	62.99
Hispanic (3,148)	3,380	6.21
Yugoslavian	62	0.11

Union City

Place Type: City
County: Hudson
Population: 67,088

Ancestry/Race	Number	%
African American/Black:	3,544	5.28
Not Hispanic (875)	985	1.47
Hispanic (1,567)	2,559	3.81
African, sub-Saharan:	206	0.31
African	130	0.19
Cape Verdean	10	0.01
Ghanian	16	0.02
Nigerian	21	0.03
Senegalese	20	0.03
Other sub-Saharan African	9	0.01
Alaska Native tribes, specified:	1	0.00
Alaska Athabascan (1)	1	0.00
Am. Ind. or Alaska Nat., not spec.	468	0.70
Albanian	13	0.02
American Indian tribes, specified:	275	0.41
Blackfeet	1	0.00
Cherokee (2)	8	0.01
Delaware	1	0.00
Iroquois	1	0.00
Latin American Indians (128)	226	0.34
Navajo (1)	1	0.00
Pueblo	14	0.02
Seminole	1	0.00
Sioux	3	0.00
Ute	3	0.00
All other tribes (8)	16	0.02
American Indian tribes, not spec.	67	0.10
Arab:	379	0.56
Arab/Arabic	78	0.12
Egyptian	97	0.14
Jordanian	12	0.02
Lebanese	80	0.12
Moroccan	15	0.02
Palestinian	88	0.13
Other Arab	9	0.01
Armenian	57	0.08
Asian:	1,761	2.62
Bangladeshi (8)	17	0.03
Cambodian (5)	5	0.01
Chinese, ex. Taiwanese (176)	219	0.33
Filipino (180)	220	0.33
Indian (825)	904	1.35
Indonesian (12)	16	0.02
Japanese (26)	49	0.07
Korean (93)	100	0.15
Malaysian	2	0.00
Pakistani (31)	46	0.07
Sri Lankan (15)	15	0.02
Taiwanese (3)	6	0.01
Thai (9)	10	0.01
Vietnamese (17)	21	0.03
Other Asian, specified	15	0.02
Other Asian, not specified (23)	116	0.17
Australian	7	0.01
Austrian	21	0.03
Basque	6	0.01
Belgian	60	0.09
Brazilian	138	0.21
British	44	0.07
Canadian	5	0.01
Croatian	17	0.03
Cypriot	28	0.04
Czechoslovakian	34	0.05
Danish	78	0.12
Dutch	82	0.12
English	251	0.37
European	60	0.09
French, except Basque	248	0.37
French Canadian	82	0.12
German	1,081	1.61
Greek	165	0.25
Guyanese	49	0.07
Hawaii Native/Pacific Islander:	141	0.21
Micronesian: (5)	6	0.01
Guamanian/Chamorro (5)	6	0.01
Polynesian: (12)	20	0.03
Native Hawaiian (11)	16	0.02
Samoan (1)	4	0.01
Other Pac. Isl., specified	15	0.02
Other Pac. Isl., not spec. (37)	100	0.15
Hispanic or Latino:	55,226	82.32
Central American:	5,750	8.57
Costa Rican	89	0.13
Guatemalan	525	0.78
Honduran	1,541	2.30
Nicaraguan	196	0.29
Panamanian	58	0.09
Salvadoran	3,099	4.62
Other Central American	242	0.36
Cuban	10,296	15.35
Dominican Republic	7,688	11.46
Mexican	2,752	4.10
Puerto Rican	7,388	11.01
South American:	10,080	15.03
Argentinean	404	0.60
Bolivian	71	0.11
Chilean	352	0.52
Colombian	3,039	4.53
Ecuadorian	3,984	5.94
Paraguayan	5	0.01
Peruvian	1,694	2.53
Uruguayan	100	0.15
Venezuelan	218	0.32
Other South American	213	0.32
Other Hispanic or Latino	11,272	16.80
Hungarian	71	0.11
Irish	1,351	2.01
Israeli	42	0.06
Italian	2,988	4.45
Lithuanian	25	0.04
Luxemburger	7	0.01
Northern European	8	0.01
Norwegian	62	0.09
Polish	177	0.26
Portuguese	112	0.17
Romanian	47	0.07
Russian	60	0.09
Scotch-Irish	89	0.13
Scottish	149	0.22
Slavic	28	0.04
Slovak	30	0.04
Swedish	45	0.07
Swiss	77	0.11
Turkish	25	0.04
Ukrainian	17	0.03
United States or American	1,647	2.45
Welsh	40	0.06
West Indian, excl. Hispanic:	218	0.32
Belizean	7	0.01
Dutch West Indian	6	0.01
Haitian	55	0.08
Jamaican	51	0.08
Trinidadian and Tobagonian	39	0.06
U.S. Virgin Islander	13	0.02
West Indian	40	0.06
Other West Indian	7	0.01
White:	43,044	64.16
Not Hispanic (8,890)	9,303	13.87
Hispanic (30,277)	33,741	50.29
Yugoslavian	37	0.06

Upper

Place Type: Township
County: Cape May
Population: 12,115

Ancestry/Race	Number	%
African American/Black:	121	1.00
Not Hispanic (79)	114	0.94
Hispanic (4)	7	0.06
Am. Ind. or Alaska Nat., not spec.	6	0.05
Albanian	36	0.30

Notes: 1. Figures in the "Number" column do not add up to the total population due to: a) Ancestry/Race overlap — e.g. persons can report being both White and Irish, b) persons of Hispanic origin can report being any race, c) persons reporting two ancestries are counted in both categories. 2. Numbers in parentheses indicate the number of persons reporting this ancestry/race alone, not in combination with any other ancestry/race. 3. Refer to the Explanation of Data in the front of the book for more detailed information.

American Indian tribes, specified:	34	0.28
Apache	2	0.02
Blackfeet	1	0.01
Cherokee (1)	11	0.09
Cree	1	0.01
Creek	3	0.02
Delaware (1)	5	0.04
All other tribes (8)	11	0.09
American Indian tribes, not spec.	4	0.03
Arab:	19	0.16
Syrian	19	0.16
Asian:	95	0.78
Chinese, ex. Taiwanese (3)	7	0.06
Filipino (27)	28	0.23
Indian (12)	15	0.12
Japanese (6)	10	0.08
Korean (15)	17	0.14
Pakistani (1)	1	0.01
Thai (3)	6	0.05
Vietnamese (6)	6	0.05
Other Asian, not specified	5	0.04
Austrian	40	0.33
Belgian	75	0.62
Brazilian	5	0.04
British	48	0.40
Canadian	16	0.13
Croatian	28	0.23
Czech	17	0.14
Danish	58	0.48
Dutch	210	1.73
Eastern European	13	0.11
English	2,011	16.60
European	150	1.24
Finnish	25	0.21
French, except Basque	445	3.67
French Canadian	62	0.51
German	3,117	25.73
Greek	79	0.65
Hawaii Native/Pacific Islander:	10	0.08
Micronesian: (1)	1	0.01
Guamanian/Chamorro (1)	1	0.01
Polynesian: (4)	7	0.06
Native Hawaiian (4)	7	0.06
Other Pac. Isl., not spec. (2)	2	0.02
Hispanic or Latino:	155	1.28
Central American:	11	0.09
Costa Rican	4	0.03
Guatemalan	2	0.02
Honduran	1	0.01
Salvadoran	2	0.02
Other Central American	2	0.02
Cuban	2	0.02
Dominican Republic	1	0.01
Mexican	40	0.33
Puerto Rican	66	0.54
South American:	10	0.08
Argentinean	1	0.01
Chilean	2	0.02
Colombian	1	0.01
Ecuadorian	2	0.02
Peruvian	2	0.02
Venezuelan	2	0.02
Other Hispanic or Latino	25	0.21
Hungarian	96	0.79
Irish	3,933	32.46
Italian	2,357	19.46
Latvian	4	0.03
Lithuanian	68	0.56
New Zealander	21	0.17
Norwegian	129	1.06
Pennsylvania German	29	0.24
Polish	557	4.60
Russian	316	2.61
Scandinavian	7	0.06
Scotch-Irish	270	2.23
Scottish	283	2.34
Serbian	18	0.15
Slovak	20	0.17
Swedish	194	1.60
Swiss	41	0.34
Ukrainian	50	0.41
United States or American	413	3.41
Welsh	130	1.07
West Indian, excl. Hispanic:	15	0.12
Jamaican	15	0.12
White:	11,908	98.29
Not Hispanic (11,706)	11,784	97.27
Hispanic (117)	124	1.02

Ventnor City

Place Type: City
County: Atlantic
Population: 12,910

Ancestry/Race	Number	%
African American/Black:	452	3.50
Not Hispanic (319)	369	2.86
Hispanic (60)	83	0.64
Alaska Native tribes, specified:	1	0.01
Aleut (1)	1	0.01
Am. Ind. or Alaska Nat., not spec.	26	0.20
Albanian	115	0.89
American Indian tribes, specified:	42	0.33
Blackfeet (1)	2	0.02
Cherokee (1)	2	0.02
Chippewa (1)	1	0.01
Cree	1	0.01
Delaware (1)	2	0.02
Iroquois	1	0.01
Latin American Indians (7)	13	0.10
Pueblo (5)	12	0.09
All other tribes (1)	8	0.06
American Indian tribes, not spec.	1	0.01
Arab:	130	1.01
Egyptian	94	0.73
Moroccan	28	0.22
Syrian	8	0.06
Armenian	13	0.10
Asian:	1,055	8.17
Bangladeshi (47)	64	0.50
Cambodian	4	0.03
Chinese, ex. Taiwanese (141)	151	1.17
Filipino (47)	55	0.43
Indian (340)	364	2.82
Japanese (5)	5	0.04
Korean (16)	20	0.15
Malaysian	1	0.01
Pakistani (76)	84	0.65
Sri Lankan (3)	3	0.02
Thai (1)	1	0.01
Vietnamese (226)	245	1.90
Other Asian, specified (9)	14	0.11
Other Asian, not specified (39)	44	0.34
Austrian	56	0.43
British	9	0.07
Bulgarian	33	0.26
Canadian	7	0.05
Danish	30	0.23
Dutch	168	1.30
Eastern European	14	0.11
English	795	6.16
European	7	0.05
Finnish	18	0.14
French, except Basque	320	2.48
French Canadian	22	0.17
German	1,125	8.71
Greek	255	1.98
Hawaii Native/Pacific Islander:	12	0.09
Micronesian: (2)	2	0.02
Guamanian/Chamorro (2)	2	0.02
Polynesian: (1)	5	0.04
Native Hawaiian (1)	4	0.03
Samoan	1	0.01
Other Pac. Isl., specified	1	0.01
Other Pac. Isl., not spec. (1)	4	0.03
Hispanic or Latino:	2,213	17.14
Central American:	234	1.81
Costa Rican	3	0.02
Guatemalan	4	0.03
Honduran	112	0.87
Nicaraguan	30	0.23
Panamanian	5	0.04
Salvadoran	70	0.54
Other Central American	10	0.08
Cuban	44	0.34
Dominican Republic	180	1.39
Mexican	365	2.83
Puerto Rican	629	4.87
South American:	356	2.76
Argentinean	6	0.05
Chilean	4	0.03
Colombian	235	1.82
Ecuadorian	17	0.13
Peruvian	83	0.64
Venezuelan	11	0.09
Other Hispanic or Latino	405	3.14
Hungarian	30	0.23
Iranian	9	0.07
Irish	1,995	15.45
Israeli	22	0.17
Italian	2,940	22.77
Latvian	17	0.13
Lithuanian	42	0.33
Norwegian	32	0.25
Pennsylvania German	19	0.15
Polish	470	3.64
Romanian	31	0.24
Russian	536	4.15
Scotch-Irish	70	0.54
Scottish	153	1.19
Slovak	8	0.06
Swedish	40	0.31
Swiss	10	0.08
Ukrainian	87	0.67
United States or American	350	2.71
Welsh	76	0.59
West Indian, excl. Hispanic:	104	0.81
British West Indian	21	0.16
Haitian	39	0.30
Jamaican	34	0.26
Trinidadian and Tobagonian	10	0.08
White:	10,241	79.33
Not Hispanic (9,145)	9,318	72.18
Hispanic (808)	923	7.15
Yugoslavian	8	0.06

Vernon

Place Type: Township
County: Sussex
Population: 24,686

Ancestry/Race	Number	%
African American/Black:	253	1.02
Not Hispanic (178)	225	0.91
Hispanic (10)	28	0.11
African, sub-Saharan:	34	0.14
South African	34	0.14
Am. Ind. or Alaska Nat., not spec.	32	0.13
Albanian	21	0.09
American Indian tribes, specified:	57	0.23
Apache	2	0.01
Blackfeet	6	0.02
Cherokee (2)	11	0.04
Chippewa (1)	1	0.00
Crow	5	0.02
Delaware (6)	15	0.06
Houma	1	0.00
Iroquois	4	0.02
Latin American Indians (3)	3	0.01
Navajo (1)	1	0.00
Osage	1	0.00
Seminole	3	0.01
Sioux	1	0.00
All other tribes (1)	3	0.01
American Indian tribes, not spec.	2	0.01
Arab:	38	0.15
Egyptian	21	0.09
Syrian	7	0.03

Notes: 1. Figures in the "Number" column do not add up to the total population due to: a) Ancestry/Race overlap — e.g. persons can report being both White and Irish, b) persons of Hispanic origin can report being any race, c) persons reporting two ancestries are counted in both categories. 2. Numbers in parentheses indicate the number of persons reporting this ancestry/race alone, not in combination with any other ancestry/race. 3. Refer to the Explanation of Data in the front of the book for more detailed information.

Ancestry/Race	Number	%
Other Arab	10	0.04
Armenian	35	0.14
Asian:	233	0.94
Chinese, ex. Taiwanese (34)	50	0.20
Filipino (40)	57	0.23
Indian (38)	41	0.17
Japanese (12)	17	0.07
Korean (30)	36	0.15
Pakistani	1	0.00
Thai (4)	5	0.02
Vietnamese (5)	7	0.03
Other Asian, specified (1)	1	0.00
Other Asian, not specified (3)	18	0.07
Austrian	104	0.42
Belgian	25	0.10
Brazilian	7	0.03
British	62	0.25
Canadian	52	0.21
Czech	164	0.66
Czechoslovakian	46	0.19
Danish	78	0.32
Dutch	1,593	6.45
Eastern European	6	0.02
English	1,997	8.09
Estonian	9	0.04
European	19	0.08
Finnish	43	0.17
French, except Basque	827	3.35
French Canadian	135	0.55
German	6,294	25.50
Greek	147	0.60
Hawaii Native/Pacific Islander:	11	0.04
Micronesian:	2	0.01
Guamanian/Chamorro	2	0.01
Polynesian: (3)	3	0.01
Native Hawaiian (3)	3	0.01
Other Pac. Isl., not spec. (4)	6	0.02
Hispanic or Latino:	889	3.60
Central American:	48	0.19
Costa Rican	17	0.07
Guatemalan	7	0.03
Honduran	1	0.00
Nicaraguan	1	0.00
Panamanian	4	0.02
Salvadoran	18	0.07
Cuban	85	0.34
Dominican Republic	42	0.17
Mexican	62	0.25
Puerto Rican	352	1.43
South American:	144	0.58
Argentinean	10	0.04
Chilean	12	0.05
Colombian	41	0.17
Ecuadorian	40	0.16
Peruvian	27	0.11
Uruguayan	7	0.03
Venezuelan	6	0.02
Other South American	1	0.00
Other Hispanic or Latino	156	0.63
Hungarian	365	1.48
Icelander	5	0.02
Iranian	7	0.03
Irish	7,005	28.38
Israeli	38	0.15
Italian	6,588	26.69
Lithuanian	76	0.31
Norwegian	338	1.37
Pennsylvania German	3	0.01
Polish	2,351	9.52
Portuguese	114	0.46
Romanian	53	0.21
Russian	408	1.65
Scandinavian	56	0.23
Scotch-Irish	453	1.84
Scottish	395	1.60
Slavic	42	0.17
Slovak	122	0.49
Swedish	284	1.15
Swiss	176	0.71
Turkish	41	0.17
Ukrainian	272	1.10
United States or American	869	3.52
Welsh	145	0.59
West Indian, excl. Hispanic:	22	0.09
Barbadian	7	0.03
Haitian	9	0.04
West Indian	6	0.02
White:	24,084	97.56
Not Hispanic (23,214)	23,386	94.73
Hispanic (623)	698	2.83
Yugoslavian	53	0.21

Verona

Place Type: Census Designated Place
County: Essex
Population: 13,533

Ancestry/Race	Number	%
African American/Black:	235	1.74
Not Hispanic (197)	218	1.61
Hispanic (10)	17	0.13
Am. Ind. or Alaska Nat., not spec.	9	0.07
Albanian	6	0.04
American Indian tribes, specified:	15	0.11
Blackfeet	2	0.01
Choctaw	3	0.02
Delaware (1)	1	0.01
Iroquois (1)	4	0.03
Latin American Indians (1)	2	0.01
Seminole	2	0.01
Sioux	1	0.01
American Indian tribes, not spec.	4	0.03
Arab:	27	0.20
Jordanian	6	0.04
Syrian	21	0.16
Armenian	18	0.13
Asian:	561	4.15
Chinese, ex. Taiwanese (147)	174	1.29
Filipino (57)	76	0.56
Indian (161)	177	1.31
Japanese (26)	43	0.32
Korean (37)	46	0.34
Pakistani (4)	5	0.04
Sri Lankan (4)	4	0.03
Taiwanese (8)	8	0.06
Thai (2)	2	0.01
Vietnamese (4)	5	0.04
Other Asian, not specified (3)	21	0.16
Austrian	147	1.09
British	137	1.01
Bulgarian	18	0.13
Canadian	32	0.24
Czech	83	0.61
Czechoslovakian	40	0.30
Danish	37	0.27
Dutch	172	1.27
Eastern European	35	0.26
English	977	7.22
Estonian	8	0.06
European	28	0.21
French, except Basque	251	1.85
French Canadian	59	0.44
German	1,847	13.65
Greek	105	0.78
Guyanese	12	0.09
Hawaii Native/Pacific Islander:	14	0.10
Micronesian: (5)	6	0.04
Guamanian/Chamorro (5)	6	0.04
Polynesian: (3)	6	0.04
Native Hawaiian (2)	5	0.04
Other Polynesian (1)	1	0.01
Other Pac. Isl., not spec.	2	0.01
Hispanic or Latino:	467	3.45
Central American:	13	0.10
Costa Rican	6	0.04
Guatemalan	2	0.01
Nicaraguan	1	0.01
Panamanian	2	0.01
Salvadoran	2	0.01
Cuban	72	0.53
Dominican Republic	12	0.09
Mexican	38	0.28
Puerto Rican	127	0.94
South American:	90	0.67
Argentinean	12	0.09
Bolivian	2	0.01
Chilean	2	0.01
Colombian	25	0.18
Ecuadorian	20	0.15
Paraguayan	1	0.01
Peruvian	19	0.14
Uruguayan	4	0.03
Venezuelan	4	0.03
Other South American	1	0.01
Other Hispanic or Latino	115	0.85
Hungarian	207	1.53
Iranian	28	0.21
Irish	3,060	22.61
Israeli	6	0.04
Italian	4,638	34.27
Lithuanian	108	0.80
Norwegian	104	0.77
Polish	1,059	7.83
Portuguese	132	0.98
Romanian	66	0.49
Russian	733	5.42
Scandinavian	9	0.07
Scotch-Irish	114	0.84
Scottish	361	2.67
Slavic	8	0.06
Slovak	54	0.40
Slovene	7	0.05
Swedish	237	1.75
Swiss	41	0.30
Turkish	5	0.04
Ukrainian	194	1.43
United States or American	312	2.31
Welsh	92	0.68
West Indian, excl. Hispanic:	62	0.46
Haitian	40	0.30
Jamaican	17	0.13
Trinidadian and Tobagonian	5	0.04
White:	12,713	93.94
Not Hispanic (12,260)	12,362	91.35
Hispanic (325)	351	2.59
Yugoslavian	7	0.05

Vineland

Place Type: City
County: Cumberland
Population: 56,271

Ancestry/Race	Number	%
African American/Black:	8,327	14.80
Not Hispanic (6,885)	7,258	12.90
Hispanic (779)	1,069	1.90
African, sub-Saharan:	247	0.44
African	247	0.44
Alaska Native tribes, specified:	1	0.00
Aleut (1)	1	0.00
Am. Ind. or Alaska Nat., not spec.	288	0.51
American Indian tribes, specified:	271	0.48
Apache	1	0.00
Blackfeet (1)	20	0.04
Cherokee (7)	52	0.09
Cheyenne	1	0.00
Chippewa (1)	1	0.00
Choctaw	3	0.01
Creek	2	0.00
Delaware (23)	47	0.08
Iroquois (4)	5	0.01
Kiowa	1	0.00
Latin American Indians (30)	55	0.10
Menominee (1)	1	0.00
Ottawa (1)	1	0.00
Pueblo (4)	6	0.01
Seminole (1)	2	0.00
Sioux (2)	6	0.01

Notes: 1. Figures in the "Number" column do not add up to the total population due to: a) Ancestry/Race overlap — e.g. persons can report being both White and Irish, b) persons of Hispanic origin can report being any race, c) persons reporting two ancestries are counted in both categories. 2. Numbers in parentheses indicate the number of persons reporting this ancestry/race alone, not in combination with any other ancestry/race. 3. Refer to the Explanation of Data in the front of the book for more detailed information.

Ute	1	0.00
All other tribes (52)	66	0.12
American Indian tribes, not spec.	36	0.06
Arab:	31	0.06
Arab/Arabic	13	0.02
Lebanese	5	0.01
Moroccan	9	0.02
Syrian	4	0.01
Armenian	33	0.06
Asian:	821	1.46
Bangladeshi	2	0.00
Chinese, ex. Taiwanese (87)	99	0.18
Filipino (106)	140	0.25
Indian (308)	352	0.63
Indonesian	3	0.01
Japanese (32)	54	0.10
Korean (50)	63	0.11
Pakistani (40)	43	0.08
Taiwanese (1)	2	0.00
Thai	7	0.01
Vietnamese (11)	15	0.03
Other Asian, specified (3)	3	0.01
Other Asian, not specified (8)	38	0.07
Australian	9	0.02
Austrian	168	0.30
Belgian	8	0.01
Brazilian	7	0.01
British	86	0.15
Canadian	103	0.18
Carpatho Rusyn	11	0.02
Croatian	17	0.03
Czech	66	0.12
Czechoslovakian	80	0.14
Danish	54	0.10
Dutch	454	0.81
English	3,297	5.86
Estonian	44	0.08
European	382	0.68
Finnish	55	0.10
French, except Basque	723	1.28
French Canadian	194	0.34
German	5,408	9.61
Greek	171	0.30
Hawaii Native/Pacific Islander:	102	0.18
Micronesian: (7)	8	0.01
Guamanian/Chamorro (7)	8	0.01
Polynesian: (20)	45	0.08
Native Hawaiian (9)	21	0.04
Samoan (11)	16	0.03
Other Polynesian	8	0.01
Other Pac. Isl., not spec. (16)	49	0.09
Hispanic or Latino:	16,880	30.00
Central American:	151	0.27
Costa Rican	21	0.04
Guatemalan	46	0.08
Honduran	40	0.07
Nicaraguan	1	0.00
Panamanian	8	0.01
Salvadoran	27	0.05
Other Central American	8	0.01
Cuban	232	0.41
Dominican Republic	283	0.50
Mexican	1,365	2.43
Puerto Rican	13,284	23.61
South American:	182	0.32
Argentinean	20	0.04
Bolivian	3	0.01
Chilean	4	0.01
Colombian	108	0.19
Ecuadorian	19	0.03
Paraguayan	1	0.00
Peruvian	16	0.03
Uruguayan	3	0.01
Venezuelan	5	0.01
Other South American	3	0.01
Other Hispanic or Latino	1,383	2.46
Hungarian	405	0.72
Iranian	7	0.01
Irish	4,732	8.41
Israeli	7	0.01
Italian	12,847	22.83
Latvian	68	0.12
Lithuanian	106	0.19
Maltese	33	0.06
Norwegian	127	0.23
Pennsylvania German	67	0.12
Polish	1,699	3.02
Portuguese	14	0.02
Romanian	37	0.07
Russian	589	1.05
Scandinavian	44	0.08
Scotch-Irish	300	0.53
Scottish	407	0.72
Serbian	9	0.02
Slavic	15	0.03
Slovak	62	0.11
Swedish	374	0.66
Swiss	81	0.14
Turkish	25	0.04
Ukrainian	547	0.97
United States or American	1,334	2.37
Welsh	138	0.25
West Indian, excl. Hispanic:	593	1.05
Dutch West Indian	21	0.04
Haitian	101	0.18
Jamaican	409	0.73
Trinidadian and Tobagonian	8	0.01
U.S. Virgin Islander	8	0.01
West Indian	46	0.08
White:	39,267	69.78
Not Hispanic (30,842)	31,416	55.83
Hispanic (7,122)	7,851	13.95

Voorhees

Place Type: Township
County: Camden
Population: 28,126

Ancestry/Race	Number	%
Acadian/Cajun	6	0.02
African American/Black:	2,395	8.52
Not Hispanic (2,225)	2,346	8.34
Hispanic (24)	49	0.17
African, sub-Saharan:	195	0.69
African	132	0.47
Ghanian	16	0.06
South African	37	0.13
Other sub-Saharan African	10	0.04
Alaska Native tribes, specified:	1	0.00
Alaska Athabascan (1)	1	0.00
Am. Ind. or Alaska Nat., not spec.	53	0.19
American Indian tribes, specified:	53	0.19
Blackfeet	1	0.00
Cherokee (5)	20	0.07
Chippewa (1)	1	0.00
Choctaw	4	0.01
Creek	1	0.00
Delaware (2)	3	0.01
Latin American Indians (1)	2	0.01
Sioux	2	0.01
All other tribes (11)	19	0.07
American Indian tribes, not spec.	8	0.03
Arab:	237	0.84
Egyptian	46	0.16
Jordanian	40	0.14
Lebanese	86	0.31
Syrian	43	0.15
Other Arab	22	0.08
Armenian	61	0.22
Asian:	3,453	12.28
Bangladeshi (22)	24	0.09
Chinese, ex. Taiwanese (515)	573	2.04
Filipino (476)	511	1.82
Indian (1,455)	1,532	5.45
Indonesian	1	0.00
Japanese (35)	57	0.20
Korean (463)	485	1.72
Laotian (1)	1	0.00
Malaysian (1)	1	0.00
Pakistani (44)	62	0.22
Sri Lankan	2	0.01
Taiwanese (60)	70	0.25
Thai (10)	12	0.04
Vietnamese (62)	63	0.22
Other Asian, specified (2)	5	0.02
Other Asian, not specified (28)	54	0.19
Australian	23	0.08
Austrian	105	0.37
Belgian	10	0.04
Brazilian	30	0.11
British	64	0.23
Bulgarian	7	0.02
Canadian	53	0.19
Croatian	37	0.13
Czech	58	0.21
Czechoslovakian	50	0.18
Danish	81	0.29
Dutch	269	0.96
Eastern European	259	0.92
English	2,333	8.29
Estonian	29	0.10
European	167	0.59
Finnish	6	0.02
French, except Basque	672	2.39
French Canadian	171	0.61
German	4,027	14.32
Greek	238	0.85
Hawaii Native/Pacific Islander:	19	0.07
Micronesian: (3)	3	0.01
Guamanian/Chamorro (3)	3	0.01
Polynesian: (2)	6	0.02
Native Hawaiian (1)	3	0.01
Samoan (1)	1	0.00
Other Polynesian	2	0.01
Other Pac. Isl., not spec. (3)	10	0.04
Hispanic or Latino:	694	2.47
Central American:	24	0.09
Costa Rican	5	0.02
Guatemalan	7	0.02
Honduran	1	0.00
Nicaraguan	1	0.00
Panamanian	4	0.01
Salvadoran	5	0.02
Other Central American	1	0.00
Cuban	52	0.18
Dominican Republic	15	0.05
Mexican	102	0.36
Puerto Rican	301	1.07
South American:	82	0.29
Argentinean	8	0.03
Bolivian	1	0.00
Chilean	8	0.03
Colombian	30	0.11
Ecuadorian	7	0.02
Paraguayan	2	0.01
Peruvian	7	0.02
Uruguayan	1	0.00
Venezuelan	9	0.03
Other South American	9	0.03
Other Hispanic or Latino	118	0.42
Hungarian	226	0.80
Iranian	72	0.26
Irish	5,098	18.13
Israeli	177	0.63
Italian	5,487	19.51
Latvian	39	0.14
Lithuanian	194	0.69
Macedonian	8	0.03
Norwegian	170	0.60
Pennsylvania German	31	0.11
Polish	1,669	5.93
Portuguese	30	0.11
Romanian	153	0.54
Russian	1,155	4.11
Scandinavian	21	0.07
Scotch-Irish	198	0.70
Scottish	328	1.17
Slavic	10	0.04
Slovak	74	0.26

Notes: 1. Figures in the "Number" column do not add up to the total population due to: a) Ancestry/Race overlap — e.g. persons can report being both White and Irish, b) persons of Hispanic origin can report being any race, c) persons reporting two ancestries are counted in both categories. 2. Numbers in parentheses indicate the number of persons reporting this ancestry/race alone, not in combination with any other ancestry/race. 3. Refer to the Explanation of Data in the front of the book for more detailed information.

Slovene	10	0.04
Swedish	245	0.87
Swiss	58	0.21
Ukrainian	253	0.90
United States or American	1,003	3.57
Welsh	126	0.45
West Indian, excl. Hispanic:	102	0.36
Jamaican	47	0.17
Trinidadian and Tobagonian	34	0.12
West Indian	21	0.07
White:	22,354	79.48
Not Hispanic (21,551)	21,838	77.64
Hispanic (460)	516	1.83
Yugoslavian	47	0.17

Wall

Place Type: Township
County: Monmouth
Population: 25,261

Ancestry/Race	Number	%
African American/Black:	191	0.76
Not Hispanic (149)	184	0.73
Hispanic (6)	7	0.03
African, sub-Saharan:	6	0.02
African	6	0.02
Alaska Native tribes, specified:	1	0.00
Aleut (1)	1	0.00
Am. Ind. or Alaska Nat., not spec.	20	0.08
Alsatian	8	0.03
American Indian tribes, specified:	51	0.20
Apache	1	0.00
Cherokee (1)	12	0.05
Delaware (4)	10	0.04
Iroquois (1)	6	0.02
Latin American Indians (1)	1	0.00
Navajo (1)	3	0.01
Osage	2	0.01
Paiute (1)	1	0.00
Pueblo (1)	1	0.00
Ute	4	0.02
All other tribes (7)	10	0.04
American Indian tribes, not spec.	1	0.00
Arab:	116	0.46
Arab/Arabic	5	0.02
Egyptian	11	0.04
Lebanese	55	0.22
Palestinian	21	0.08
Syrian	24	0.10
Armenian	123	0.49
Asian:	367	1.45
Chinese, ex. Taiwanese (62)	73	0.29
Filipino (68)	85	0.34
Indian (109)	113	0.45
Japanese (6)	15	0.06
Korean (47)	49	0.19
Malaysian (1)	1	0.00
Pakistani (5)	5	0.02
Taiwanese (13)	13	0.05
Vietnamese (3)	4	0.02
Other Asian, not specified (4)	9	0.04
Assyrian/Chaldean/Syriac	22	0.09
Austrian	156	0.62
British	62	0.25
Canadian	25	0.10
Croatian	29	0.11
Czech	134	0.53
Czechoslovakian	83	0.33
Danish	88	0.35
Dutch	443	1.75
Eastern European	15	0.06
English	2,897	11.47
Estonian	6	0.02
European	79	0.31
Finnish	21	0.08
French, except Basque	626	2.48
French Canadian	141	0.56
German	5,273	20.87
Greek	484	1.92
Hawaii Native/Pacific Islander:	10	0.04
Polynesian: (7)	8	0.03
Native Hawaiian (5)	6	0.02
Samoan (2)	2	0.01
Other Pac. Isl., not spec. (2)	2	0.01
Hispanic or Latino:	391	1.55
Central American:	24	0.10
Costa Rican	6	0.02
Guatemalan	7	0.03
Honduran	6	0.02
Salvadoran	5	0.02
Cuban	43	0.17
Dominican Republic	6	0.02
Mexican	60	0.24
Puerto Rican	128	0.51
South American:	54	0.21
Argentinean	6	0.02
Chilean	14	0.06
Colombian	19	0.08
Ecuadorian	2	0.01
Peruvian	10	0.04
Venezuelan	3	0.01
Other Hispanic or Latino	76	0.30
Hungarian	321	1.27
Irish	8,809	34.87
Italian	6,503	25.74
Latvian	25	0.10
Lithuanian	98	0.39
Northern European	7	0.03
Norwegian	290	1.15
Pennsylvania German	8	0.03
Polish	2,071	8.20
Portuguese	144	0.57
Romanian	17	0.07
Russian	423	1.67
Scandinavian	41	0.16
Scotch-Irish	351	1.39
Scottish	704	2.79
Slavic	15	0.06
Slovak	167	0.66
Slovene	22	0.09
Swedish	268	1.06
Swiss	29	0.11
Ukrainian	143	0.57
United States or American	686	2.72
Welsh	159	0.63
White:	24,663	97.63
Not Hispanic (24,226)	24,349	96.39
Hispanic (300)	314	1.24
Yugoslavian	32	0.13

Wallington

Place Type: Borough
County: Bergen
Population: 11,583

Ancestry/Race	Number	%
African American/Black:	354	3.06
Not Hispanic (284)	318	2.75
Hispanic (25)	36	0.31
African, sub-Saharan:	92	0.79
African	16	0.14
Ghanian	63	0.54
Nigerian	13	0.11
Am. Ind. or Alaska Nat., not spec.	18	0.16
American Indian tribes, specified:	11	0.09
Cherokee (2)	5	0.04
Chippewa (1)	1	0.01
Creek	1	0.01
Iroquois	1	0.01
Latin American Indians (1)	1	0.01
Navajo (1)	1	0.01
Sioux (1)	1	0.01
American Indian tribes, not spec.	9	0.08
Arab:	181	1.56
Arab/Arabic	56	0.48
Egyptian	54	0.47
Jordanian	45	0.39
Lebanese	5	0.04
Palestinian	7	0.06
Other Arab	14	0.12
Armenian	20	0.17
Asian:	630	5.44
Chinese, ex. Taiwanese (36)	40	0.35
Filipino (56)	62	0.54
Indian (364)	390	3.37
Indonesian (3)	4	0.03
Japanese (4)	5	0.04
Korean (82)	84	0.73
Pakistani (3)	3	0.03
Sri Lankan (7)	7	0.06
Taiwanese (2)	4	0.03
Thai (6)	10	0.09
Vietnamese (4)	4	0.03
Other Asian, not specified (6)	17	0.15
Austrian	26	0.22
Brazilian	25	0.22
British	6	0.05
Canadian	7	0.06
Croatian	44	0.38
Czech	49	0.42
Czechoslovakian	26	0.22
Dutch	229	1.98
English	206	1.78
European	9	0.08
French, except Basque	120	1.04
French Canadian	14	0.12
German	583	5.03
Greek	64	0.55
Hawaii Native/Pacific Islander:	6	0.05
Micronesian: (1)	2	0.02
Guamanian/Chamorro (1)	2	0.02
Polynesian: (1)	2	0.02
Native Hawaiian (1)	2	0.02
Other Pac. Isl., not spec.	2	0.02
Hispanic or Latino:	776	6.70
Central American:	16	0.14
Costa Rican	4	0.03
Guatemalan	1	0.01
Honduran	6	0.05
Panamanian	3	0.03
Salvadoran	1	0.01
Other Central American	1	0.01
Cuban	66	0.57
Dominican Republic	82	0.71
Mexican	37	0.32
Puerto Rican	252	2.18
South American:	181	1.56
Argentinean	6	0.05
Bolivian	4	0.03
Chilean	1	0.01
Colombian	63	0.54
Ecuadorian	27	0.23
Peruvian	53	0.46
Uruguayan	2	0.02
Venezuelan	9	0.08
Other South American	16	0.14
Other Hispanic or Latino	142	1.23
Hungarian	206	1.78
Irish	828	7.15
Israeli	23	0.20
Italian	1,741	15.03
Lithuanian	18	0.16
Norwegian	15	0.13
Polish	5,967	51.52
Portuguese	40	0.35
Romanian	9	0.08
Russian	190	1.64
Scandinavian	6	0.05
Scotch-Irish	6	0.05
Scottish	45	0.39
Slavic	32	0.28
Slovak	178	1.54
Swedish	13	0.11
Ukrainian	180	1.55
United States or American	209	1.80
Welsh	35	0.30
West Indian, excl. Hispanic:	91	0.79
British West Indian	10	0.09

Notes: 1. Figures in the "Number" column do not add up to the total population due to: a) Ancestry/Race overlap — e.g. persons can report being both White and Irish, b) persons of Hispanic origin can report being any race, c) persons reporting two ancestries are counted in both categories. 2. Numbers in parentheses indicate the number of persons reporting this ancestry/race alone, not in combination with any other ancestry/race. 3. Refer to the Explanation of Data in the front of the book for more detailed information.

Ancestry/Race	Number	%
Haitian	6	0.05
Jamaican	45	0.39
West Indian	30	0.26
White:	10,364	89.48
Not Hispanic (9,733)	9,899	85.46
Hispanic (414)	465	4.01
Yugoslavian	8	0.07

Wanaque

Place Type: Borough
County: Passaic
Population: 10,266

Ancestry/Race	Number	%
African American/Black:	218	2.12
Not Hispanic (147)	197	1.92
Hispanic (8)	21	0.20
African, sub-Saharan:	10	0.10
Other sub-Saharan African	10	0.10
Am. Ind. or Alaska Nat., not spec.	17	0.17
Albanian	11	0.11
American Indian tribes, specified:	67	0.65
Apache	4	0.04
Blackfeet (1)	1	0.01
Cherokee (4)	12	0.12
Chippewa (1)	1	0.01
Choctaw	4	0.04
Delaware (9)	27	0.26
Iroquois	6	0.06
Latin American Indians (2)	2	0.02
Navajo	3	0.03
Sioux (5)	6	0.06
All other tribes	1	0.01
American Indian tribes, not spec.	3	0.03
Arab:	264	2.57
Arab/Arabic	42	0.41
Egyptian	79	0.77
Lebanese	82	0.80
Moroccan	7	0.07
Palestinian	18	0.18
Syrian	36	0.35
Armenian	12	0.12
Asian:	431	4.20
Bangladeshi (5)	5	0.05
Chinese, ex. Taiwanese (40)	48	0.47
Filipino (227)	258	2.51
Indian (69)	78	0.76
Indonesian (1)	1	0.01
Japanese (7)	8	0.08
Korean (12)	16	0.16
Taiwanese (1)	1	0.01
Thai (4)	4	0.04
Vietnamese (2)	3	0.03
Other Asian, not specified (2)	9	0.09
Austrian	66	0.64
Belgian	14	0.14
Brazilian	25	0.24
British	61	0.59
Canadian	12	0.12
Croatian	10	0.10
Czech	60	0.58
Czechoslovakian	28	0.27
Danish	29	0.28
Dutch	621	6.05
Eastern European	11	0.11
English	587	5.72
European	96	0.94
Finnish	8	0.08
French, except Basque	310	3.02
French Canadian	61	0.59
German	1,943	18.93
Greek	52	0.51
Hawaii Native/Pacific Islander:	3	0.03
Micronesian: (1)	1	0.01
Guamanian/Chamorro (1)	1	0.01
Polynesian: (1)	1	0.01
Other Polynesian (1)	1	0.01
Other Pac. Isl., not spec. (1)	1	0.01
Hispanic or Latino:	554	5.40
Central American:	29	0.28
Costa Rican	10	0.10
Guatemalan	9	0.09
Honduran	2	0.02
Panamanian	3	0.03
Salvadoran	1	0.01
Other Central American	4	0.04
Cuban	44	0.43
Dominican Republic	10	0.10
Mexican	69	0.67
Puerto Rican	179	1.74
South American:	114	1.11
Argentinean	8	0.08
Chilean	2	0.02
Colombian	34	0.33
Ecuadorian	21	0.20
Peruvian	44	0.43
Uruguayan	2	0.02
Venezuelan	1	0.01
Other South American	2	0.02
Other Hispanic or Latino	109	1.06
Hungarian	242	2.36
Iranian	86	0.84
Irish	2,053	20.00
Israeli	10	0.10
Italian	2,642	25.74
Lithuanian	30	0.29
Maltese	12	0.12
Norwegian	35	0.34
Polish	936	9.12
Portuguese	6	0.06
Russian	193	1.88
Scotch-Irish	103	1.00
Scottish	133	1.30
Serbian	9	0.09
Slavic	9	0.09
Slovak	20	0.19
Swedish	66	0.64
Swiss	64	0.62
Turkish	53	0.52
Ukrainian	53	0.52
United States or American	365	3.56
Welsh	42	0.41
West Indian, excl. Hispanic:	4	0.04
Jamaican	4	0.04
White:	9,447	92.02
Not Hispanic (8,997)	9,117	88.81
Hispanic (311)	330	3.21
Yugoslavian	42	0.41

Wantage

Place Type: Township
County: Sussex
Population: 10,387

Ancestry/Race	Number	%
African American/Black:	83	0.80
Not Hispanic (66)	80	0.77
Hispanic (1)	3	0.03
Am. Ind. or Alaska Nat., not spec.	13	0.13
Albanian	7	0.07
American Indian tribes, specified:	31	0.30
Blackfeet (1)	5	0.05
Cherokee (2)	13	0.13
Chippewa	1	0.01
Comanche (1)	1	0.01
Iroquois	8	0.08
Latin American Indians	1	0.01
Seminole	1	0.01
Sioux	1	0.01
American Indian tribes, not spec.	2	0.02
Arab:	116	1.12
Arab/Arabic	6	0.06
Egyptian	41	0.39
Lebanese	14	0.13
Moroccan	43	0.41
Syrian	12	0.12
Armenian	25	0.24
Asian:	87	0.84
Chinese, ex. Taiwanese (14)	15	0.14
Filipino (13)	22	0.21
Indian (23)	23	0.22
Japanese (1)	1	0.01
Korean (14)	18	0.17
Sri Lankan (2)	2	0.02
Vietnamese (1)	1	0.01
Other Asian, not specified (2)	5	0.05
Austrian	99	0.95
Basque	6	0.06
Belgian	4	0.04
Brazilian	16	0.15
British	38	0.37
Canadian	57	0.55
Czech	81	0.78
Danish	76	0.73
Dutch	946	9.11
English	1,566	15.08
French, except Basque	240	2.31
French Canadian	32	0.31
German	2,562	24.67
Greek	65	0.63
Hawaii Native/Pacific Islander:	3	0.03
Micronesian: (1)	1	0.01
Guamanian/Chamorro (1)	1	0.01
Other Pac. Isl., not spec.	2	0.02
Hispanic or Latino:	300	2.89
Central American:	12	0.12
Costa Rican	5	0.05
Guatemalan	1	0.01
Honduran	2	0.02
Nicaraguan	1	0.01
Salvadoran	3	0.03
Cuban	34	0.33
Dominican Republic	12	0.12
Mexican	23	0.22
Puerto Rican	130	1.25
South American:	35	0.34
Argentinean	1	0.01
Bolivian	1	0.01
Chilean	2	0.02
Colombian	12	0.12
Ecuadorian	6	0.06
Peruvian	6	0.06
Venezuelan	3	0.03
Other South American	4	0.04
Other Hispanic or Latino	54	0.52
Hungarian	123	1.18
Icelander	9	0.09
Iranian	8	0.08
Irish	2,132	20.53
Israeli	42	0.40
Italian	1,757	16.92
Lithuanian	54	0.52
Macedonian	35	0.34
Norwegian	105	1.01
Pennsylvania German	10	0.10
Polish	827	7.96
Portuguese	97	0.93
Russian	173	1.67
Scotch-Irish	67	0.65
Scottish	187	1.80
Slavic	6	0.06
Slovak	75	0.72
Swedish	110	1.06
Swiss	35	0.34
Turkish	7	0.07
Ukrainian	75	0.72
United States or American	621	5.98
Welsh	69	0.66
West Indian, excl. Hispanic:	17	0.16
Bahamian	11	0.11
West Indian	6	0.06
White:	10,196	98.16
Not Hispanic (9,857)	9,942	95.72
Hispanic (229)	254	2.45
Yugoslavian	12	0.12

Notes: 1. Figures in the "Number" column do not add up to the total population due to: a) Ancestry/Race overlap — e.g. persons can report being both White and Irish, b) persons of Hispanic origin can report being any race, c) persons reporting two ancestries are counted in both categories. 2. Numbers in parentheses indicate the number of persons reporting this ancestry/race alone, not in combination with any other ancestry/race. 3. Refer to the Explanation of Data in the front of the book for more detailed information.

Warren

Place Type: Township
County: Somerset
Population: 14,259

Ancestry/Race	Number	%
African American/Black:	206	1.44
Not Hispanic (169)	193	1.35
Hispanic (11)	13	0.09
African, sub-Saharan:	14	0.10
African	7	0.05
Cape Verdean	7	0.05
Am. Ind. or Alaska Nat., not spec.	9	0.06
American Indian tribes, specified:	8	0.06
Blackfeet	2	0.01
Cherokee	3	0.02
Iroquois	1	0.01
Latin American Indians (1)	1	0.01
All other tribes	1	0.01
American Indian tribes, not spec.	1	0.01
Arab:	134	0.94
Arab/Arabic	7	0.05
Egyptian	8	0.06
Lebanese	35	0.25
Palestinian	22	0.15
Syrian	62	0.43
Armenian	29	0.20
Asian:	1,632	11.45
Chinese, ex. Taiwanese (633)	677	4.75
Filipino (135)	151	1.06
Indian (443)	466	3.27
Indonesian (1)	1	0.01
Japanese (23)	28	0.20
Korean (154)	163	1.14
Pakistani (23)	26	0.18
Sri Lankan (4)	5	0.04
Taiwanese (67)	76	0.53
Thai (4)	7	0.05
Vietnamese (14)	15	0.11
Other Asian, not specified (3)	17	0.12
Australian	10	0.07
Austrian	247	1.73
Brazilian	9	0.06
British	26	0.18
Canadian	9	0.06
Celtic	7	0.05
Cypriot	18	0.13
Czech	63	0.44
Czechoslovakian	78	0.55
Danish	35	0.25
Dutch	178	1.25
Eastern European	207	1.45
English	784	5.50
European	199	1.40
Finnish	38	0.27
French, except Basque	265	1.86
French Canadian	49	0.34
German	1,972	13.83
Greek	159	1.12
Hawaii Native/Pacific Islander:	11	0.08
Micronesian: (2)	2	0.01
Guamanian/Chamorro (2)	2	0.01
Polynesian: (5)	5	0.04
Native Hawaiian (3)	3	0.02
Samoan (2)	2	0.01
Other Pac. Isl., not spec. (1)	4	0.03
Hispanic or Latino:	455	3.19
Central American:	23	0.16
Costa Rican	12	0.08
Guatemalan	2	0.01
Honduran	1	0.01
Nicaraguan	2	0.01
Salvadoran	6	0.04
Cuban	76	0.53
Dominican Republic	2	0.01
Mexican	33	0.23
Puerto Rican	66	0.46
South American:	119	0.83
Argentinean	8	0.06
Bolivian	5	0.04
Chilean	9	0.06
Colombian	25	0.18
Ecuadorian	20	0.14
Paraguayan	31	0.22
Peruvian	11	0.08
Uruguayan	2	0.01
Other South American	8	0.06
Other Hispanic or Latino	136	0.95
Hungarian	358	2.51
Iranian	73	0.51
Irish	1,909	13.39
Italian	3,346	23.47
Latvian	23	0.16
Lithuanian	52	0.36
Norwegian	130	0.91
Pennsylvania German	8	0.06
Polish	1,136	7.97
Portuguese	315	2.21
Romanian	29	0.20
Russian	812	5.69
Scandinavian	7	0.05
Scotch-Irish	125	0.88
Scottish	204	1.43
Slavic	39	0.27
Slovak	77	0.54
Swedish	105	0.74
Swiss	61	0.43
Turkish	9	0.06
Ukrainian	176	1.23
United States or American	515	3.61
Welsh	25	0.18
West Indian, excl. Hispanic:	13	0.09
Haitian	8	0.06
Jamaican	5	0.04
White:	12,454	87.34
Not Hispanic (11,918)	12,056	84.55
Hispanic (385)	398	2.79
Yugoslavian	8	0.06

Washington

Place Type: Township
County: Gloucester
Population: 47,114

Ancestry/Race	Number	%
African American/Black:	2,457	5.22
Not Hispanic (2,246)	2,395	5.08
Hispanic (40)	62	0.13
African, sub-Saharan:	94	0.20
African	91	0.19
Cape Verdean	3	0.01
Am. Ind. or Alaska Nat., not spec.	49	0.10
Albanian	31	0.07
Alsatian	5	0.01
American Indian tribes, specified:	69	0.15
Apache	3	0.01
Blackfeet (1)	3	0.01
Cherokee (7)	28	0.06
Chickasaw (1)	1	0.00
Chippewa	1	0.00
Choctaw	1	0.00
Delaware (2)	9	0.02
Iroquois (4)	8	0.02
Latin American Indians (1)	3	0.01
Seminole	3	0.01
All other tribes (6)	9	0.02
American Indian tribes, not spec.	6	0.01
Arab:	140	0.30
Egyptian	28	0.06
Iraqi	6	0.01
Lebanese	28	0.06
Palestinian	6	0.01
Syrian	36	0.08
Other Arab	36	0.08
Armenian	45	0.10
Asian:	1,747	3.71
Cambodian (8)	8	0.02
Chinese, ex. Taiwanese (252)	289	0.61
Filipino (650)	711	1.51
Indian (369)	404	0.86
Indonesian	2	0.00
Japanese (29)	52	0.11
Korean (133)	143	0.30
Laotian (5)	5	0.01
Pakistani (10)	16	0.03
Sri Lankan (5)	5	0.01
Taiwanese (2)	2	0.00
Thai (18)	19	0.04
Vietnamese (47)	57	0.12
Other Asian, not specified (13)	34	0.07
Austrian	174	0.37
Belgian	7	0.01
British	37	0.08
Canadian	24	0.05
Celtic	7	0.01
Croatian	25	0.05
Czech	99	0.21
Czechoslovakian	81	0.17
Danish	57	0.12
Dutch	614	1.30
Eastern European	9	0.02
English	4,618	9.80
Estonian	35	0.07
European	133	0.28
Finnish	66	0.14
French, except Basque	920	1.95
French Canadian	223	0.47
German	9,433	20.02
Greek	335	0.71
Guyanese	21	0.04
Hawaii Native/Pacific Islander:	30	0.06
Melanesian:	7	0.01
Fijian	7	0.01
Micronesian: (1)	5	0.01
Guamanian/Chamorro (1)	5	0.01
Polynesian: (3)	9	0.02
Native Hawaiian (2)	7	0.01
Samoan (1)	2	0.00
Other Pac. Isl., not spec. (2)	9	0.02
Hispanic or Latino:	955	2.03
Central American:	27	0.06
Guatemalan	5	0.01
Honduran	4	0.01
Nicaraguan	9	0.02
Panamanian	1	0.00
Salvadoran	5	0.01
Other Central American	3	0.01
Cuban	53	0.11
Dominican Republic	24	0.05
Mexican	138	0.29
Puerto Rican	464	0.98
South American:	84	0.18
Argentinean	26	0.06
Bolivian	1	0.00
Chilean	2	0.00
Colombian	17	0.04
Ecuadorian	15	0.03
Peruvian	8	0.02
Uruguayan	11	0.02
Venezuelan	2	0.00
Other South American	2	0.00
Other Hispanic or Latino	165	0.35
Hungarian	354	0.75
Iranian	46	0.10
Irish	13,639	28.95
Italian	15,966	33.89
Latvian	11	0.02
Lithuanian	352	0.75
Luxemburger	7	0.01
Macedonian	5	0.01
Northern European	9	0.02
Norwegian	141	0.30
Pennsylvania German	58	0.12
Polish	3,615	7.67
Portuguese	55	0.12
Romanian	113	0.24
Russian	830	1.76
Scandinavian	16	0.03

Notes: 1. Figures in the "Number" column do not add up to the total population due to: a) Ancestry/Race overlap — e.g. persons can report being both White and Irish, b) persons of Hispanic origin can report being any race, c) persons reporting two ancestries are counted in both categories. 2. Numbers in parentheses indicate the number of persons reporting this ancestry/race alone, not in combination with any other ancestry/race. 3. Refer to the Explanation of Data in the front of the book for more detailed information.

Ancestry/Race	Number	%
Scotch-Irish	611	1.30
Scottish	594	1.26
Serbian	5	0.01
Slavic	14	0.03
Slovak	171	0.36
Swedish	302	0.64
Swiss	98	0.21
Turkish	12	0.03
Ukrainian	424	0.90
United States or American	1,049	2.23
Welsh	358	0.76
West Indian, excl. Hispanic:	72	0.15
British West Indian	6	0.01
Dutch West Indian	19	0.04
Haitian	41	0.09
Jamaican	6	0.01
White:	42,877	91.01
Not Hispanic (41,909)	42,227	89.63
Hispanic (588)	650	1.38
Yugoslavian	68	0.14

Washington

Place Type: Township
County: Mercer
Population: 10,275

Ancestry/Race	Number	%
African American/Black:	323	3.14
Not Hispanic (293)	311	3.03
Hispanic (4)	12	0.12
African, sub-Saharan:	9	0.09
African	9	0.09
Am. Ind. or Alaska Nat., not spec.	10	0.10
Albanian	29	0.28
American Indian tribes, specified:	21	0.20
Blackfeet	3	0.03
Cherokee (1)	3	0.03
Comanche	2	0.02
Delaware	2	0.02
Iroquois	2	0.02
Navajo (2)	4	0.04
All other tribes (4)	5	0.05
American Indian tribes, not spec.	8	0.08
Arab:	169	1.64
Egyptian	72	0.70
Iraqi	21	0.20
Lebanese	52	0.51
Palestinian	24	0.23
Armenian	10	0.10
Asian:	502	4.89
Chinese, ex. Taiwanese (100)	110	1.07
Filipino (68)	82	0.80
Indian (189)	207	2.01
Indonesian (1)	8	0.08
Japanese (6)	13	0.13
Korean (52)	58	0.56
Pakistani (12)	16	0.16
Taiwanese (1)	1	0.01
Thai (1)	1	0.01
Vietnamese (1)	4	0.04
Other Asian, specified (1)	1	0.01
Other Asian, not specified (1)	1	0.01
Austrian	46	0.45
Belgian	15	0.15
British	41	0.40
Bulgarian	32	0.31
Croatian	7	0.07
Cypriot	10	0.10
Czech	37	0.36
Czechoslovakian	29	0.28
Danish	42	0.41
Dutch	118	1.15
English	1,072	10.43
Estonian	26	0.25
European	6	0.06
French, except Basque	124	1.21
French Canadian	54	0.53
German	2,021	19.67
Greek	121	1.18
Hawaii Native/Pacific Islander:	7	0.07
Other Pac. Isl., not spec.	7	0.07
Hispanic or Latino:	279	2.72
Central American:	10	0.10
Costa Rican	1	0.01
Guatemalan	3	0.03
Nicaraguan	1	0.01
Panamanian	1	0.01
Salvadoran	4	0.04
Cuban	34	0.33
Dominican Republic	10	0.10
Mexican	29	0.28
Puerto Rican	95	0.92
South American:	40	0.39
Argentinean	3	0.03
Colombian	25	0.24
Ecuadorian	7	0.07
Peruvian	2	0.02
Uruguayan	2	0.02
Other South American	1	0.01
Other Hispanic or Latino	61	0.59
Hungarian	261	2.54
Icelander	21	0.20
Iranian	7	0.07
Irish	2,454	23.88
Italian	2,641	25.70
Lithuanian	42	0.41
Norwegian	53	0.52
Pennsylvania German	27	0.26
Polish	1,156	11.25
Portuguese	7	0.07
Romanian	28	0.27
Russian	188	1.83
Scotch-Irish	152	1.48
Scottish	166	1.62
Slavic	15	0.15
Slovak	124	1.21
Swedish	82	0.80
Swiss	15	0.15
Ukrainian	192	1.87
United States or American	268	2.61
Welsh	82	0.80
West Indian, excl. Hispanic:	39	0.38
Barbadian	8	0.08
Haitian	22	0.21
West Indian	9	0.09
White:	9,438	91.85
Not Hispanic (9,137)	9,212	89.65
Hispanic (213)	226	2.20

Washington

Place Type: Township
County: Morris
Population: 17,592

Ancestry/Race	Number	%
African American/Black:	183	1.04
Not Hispanic (143)	178	1.01
Hispanic (3)	5	0.03
African, sub-Saharan:	19	0.11
South African	19	0.11
Am. Ind. or Alaska Nat., not spec.	21	0.12
Alsatian	12	0.07
American Indian tribes, specified:	26	0.15
Cherokee	10	0.06
Choctaw (1)	1	0.01
Creek (3)	3	0.02
Delaware	4	0.02
Iroquois (1)	2	0.01
Latin American Indians (2)	2	0.01
Pima (1)	1	0.01
Seminole (1)	1	0.01
Sioux (1)	1	0.01
All other tribes	1	0.01
American Indian tribes, not spec.	2	0.01
Arab:	185	1.05
Arab/Arabic	6	0.03
Egyptian	109	0.62
Lebanese	15	0.09
Moroccan	26	0.15
Palestinian	5	0.03
Syrian	24	0.14
Armenian	18	0.10
Asian:	370	2.10
Chinese, ex. Taiwanese (107)	117	0.67
Filipino (45)	54	0.31
Indian (110)	119	0.68
Japanese (9)	11	0.06
Korean (36)	39	0.22
Malaysian (1)	1	0.01
Pakistani (4)	8	0.05
Sri Lankan (1)	1	0.01
Taiwanese (5)	5	0.03
Vietnamese (8)	10	0.06
Other Asian, not specified (1)	5	0.03
Austrian	116	0.66
Brazilian	8	0.05
British	58	0.33
Canadian	103	0.59
Celtic	4	0.02
Czech	89	0.51
Czechoslovakian	39	0.22
Danish	91	0.52
Dutch	572	3.25
Eastern European	42	0.24
English	2,083	11.84
Estonian	18	0.10
European	107	0.61
Finnish	75	0.43
French, except Basque	362	2.06
French Canadian	85	0.48
German	3,862	21.95
Greek	128	0.73
Hawaii Native/Pacific Islander:	9	0.05
Micronesian: (3)	3	0.02
Guamanian/Chamorro (3)	3	0.02
Polynesian: (6)	6	0.03
Samoan (6)	6	0.03
Hispanic or Latino:	389	2.21
Central American:	19	0.11
Costa Rican	5	0.03
Guatemalan	3	0.02
Honduran	4	0.02
Nicaraguan	3	0.02
Panamanian	1	0.01
Salvadoran	3	0.02
Cuban	62	0.35
Dominican Republic	11	0.06
Mexican	47	0.27
Puerto Rican	127	0.72
South American:	68	0.39
Argentinean	9	0.05
Chilean	9	0.05
Colombian	18	0.10
Ecuadorian	13	0.07
Paraguayan	3	0.02
Peruvian	9	0.05
Venezuelan	6	0.03
Other South American	1	0.01
Other Hispanic or Latino	55	0.31
Hungarian	308	1.75
Irish	4,489	25.52
Italian	4,143	23.55
Latvian	26	0.15
Lithuanian	185	1.05
Maltese	48	0.27
Northern European	12	0.07
Norwegian	208	1.18
Polish	1,445	8.21
Portuguese	133	0.76
Romanian	29	0.16
Russian	379	2.15
Scandinavian	62	0.35
Scotch-Irish	435	2.47
Scottish	613	3.48
Slavic	24	0.14
Slovak	149	0.85
Slovene	10	0.06
Swedish	254	1.44

Notes: 1. Figures in the "Number" column do not add up to the total population due to: a) Ancestry/Race overlap — e.g. persons can report being both White and Irish, b) persons of Hispanic origin can report being any race, c) persons reporting two ancestries are counted in both categories. 2. Numbers in parentheses indicate the number of persons reporting this ancestry/race alone, not in combination with any other ancestry/race. 3. Refer to the Explanation of Data in the front of the book for more detailed information.

Ancestry/Race	Number	%
Swiss	47	0.27
Ukrainian	276	1.57
United States or American	767	4.36
Welsh	126	0.72
West Indian, excl. Hispanic:	18	0.10
British West Indian	6	0.03
Trinidadian and Tobagonian	12	0.07
White:	17,007	96.67
Not Hispanic (16,610)	16,688	94.86
Hispanic (307)	319	1.81
Yugoslavian	28	0.16

Waterford

Place Type: Township
County: Camden
Population: 10,494

Ancestry/Race	Number	%
African American/Black:	491	4.68
Not Hispanic (428)	479	4.56
Hispanic (11)	12	0.11
African, sub-Saharan:	32	0.31
African	32	0.31
Am. Ind. or Alaska Nat., not spec.	38	0.36
Albanian	10	0.10
American Indian tribes, specified:	26	0.25
Cherokee	10	0.10
Delaware	1	0.01
Iroquois (1)	3	0.03
Latin American Indians	3	0.03
Navajo (1)	1	0.01
Seminole	2	0.02
Sioux (1)	6	0.06
American Indian tribes, not spec.	1	0.01
Asian:	122	1.16
Chinese, ex. Taiwanese (7)	11	0.10
Filipino (8)	15	0.14
Indian (45)	47	0.45
Indonesian	2	0.02
Japanese (4)	11	0.10
Korean (19)	22	0.21
Sri Lankan (4)	4	0.04
Taiwanese (5)	5	0.05
Vietnamese	2	0.02
Other Asian, not specified (1)	3	0.03
Austrian	6	0.06
British	25	0.24
Canadian	3	0.03
Czech	50	0.48
Czechoslovakian	8	0.08
Danish	11	0.10
Dutch	78	0.74
English	1,126	10.74
European	35	0.33
Finnish	11	0.10
French, except Basque	321	3.06
French Canadian	11	0.10
German	2,665	25.42
Greek	86	0.82
Hawaii Native/Pacific Islander:	8	0.08
Micronesian: (1)	1	0.01
Guamanian/Chamorro (1)	1	0.01
Polynesian:	3	0.03
Native Hawaiian	3	0.03
Other Pac. Isl., not spec.	4	0.04
Hispanic or Latino:	217	2.07
Central American:	14	0.13
Guatemalan	6	0.06
Honduran	1	0.01
Nicaraguan	4	0.04
Other Central American	3	0.03
Cuban	6	0.06
Dominican Republic	1	0.01
Mexican	24	0.23
Puerto Rican	127	1.21
South American:	11	0.10
Argentinean	2	0.02
Colombian	6	0.06
Peruvian	3	0.03
Other Hispanic or Latino	34	0.32
Hungarian	57	0.54
Irish	2,989	28.51
Italian	2,598	24.78
Lithuanian	174	1.66
Norwegian	41	0.39
Pennsylvania German	24	0.23
Polish	622	5.93
Portuguese	5	0.05
Romanian	36	0.34
Russian	150	1.43
Scandinavian	61	0.58
Scotch-Irish	149	1.42
Scottish	129	1.23
Serbian	32	0.31
Slovak	21	0.20
Swedish	59	0.56
Swiss	42	0.40
Ukrainian	59	0.56
United States or American	404	3.85
Welsh	71	0.68
West Indian, excl. Hispanic:	28	0.27
Haitian	15	0.14
Jamaican	13	0.12
White:	9,854	93.90
Not Hispanic (9,602)	9,716	92.59
Hispanic (131)	138	1.32
Yugoslavian	33	0.31

Wayne

Place Type: Census Designated Place
County: Passaic
Population: 54,069

Ancestry/Race	Number	%
Afghan	17	0.03
African American/Black:	1,030	1.90
Not Hispanic (843)	940	1.74
Hispanic (52)	90	0.17
African, sub-Saharan:	77	0.14
African	16	0.03
Ethiopian	12	0.02
Nigerian	29	0.05
Sierra Leonean	9	0.02
South African	11	0.02
Am. Ind. or Alaska Nat., not spec.	62	0.11
Albanian	466	0.86
Alsatian	7	0.01
American Indian tribes, specified:	97	0.18
Blackfeet (1)	3	0.01
Cherokee (2)	21	0.04
Cheyenne	1	0.00
Chickasaw	1	0.00
Chippewa (3)	3	0.01
Choctaw	6	0.01
Delaware (2)	14	0.03
Iroquois (1)	4	0.01
Latin American Indians (1)	23	0.04
Navajo (2)	2	0.00
Ottawa	1	0.00
Seminole	1	0.00
Shoshone	2	0.00
Sioux (1)	1	0.00
All other tribes (4)	14	0.03
American Indian tribes, not spec.	12	0.02
Arab:	1,448	2.68
Arab/Arabic	132	0.24
Egyptian	189	0.35
Iraqi	12	0.02
Jordanian	25	0.05
Lebanese	196	0.36
Syrian	853	1.58
Other Arab	41	0.08
Armenian	309	0.57
Asian:	3,342	6.18
Bangladeshi (20)	25	0.05
Chinese, ex. Taiwanese (602)	662	1.22
Filipino (456)	503	0.93
Indian (986)	1,005	1.86
Indonesian (1)	6	0.01
Japanese (84)	102	0.19
Korean (712)	738	1.36
Malaysian (1)	5	0.01
Pakistani (49)	49	0.09
Sri Lankan (12)	16	0.03
Taiwanese (52)	63	0.12
Thai (11)	13	0.02
Vietnamese (43)	46	0.09
Other Asian, specified	3	0.01
Other Asian, not specified (11)	106	0.20
Assyrian/Chaldean/Syriac	77	0.14
Australian	9	0.02
Austrian	578	1.07
Belgian	141	0.26
Brazilian	48	0.09
British	196	0.36
Bulgarian	4	0.01
Canadian	89	0.16
Carpatho Rusyn	9	0.02
Celtic	7	0.01
Croatian	77	0.14
Czech	301	0.56
Czechoslovakian	134	0.25
Danish	159	0.29
Dutch	2,035	3.76
Eastern European	285	0.53
English	3,177	5.87
Estonian	11	0.02
European	145	0.27
Finnish	26	0.05
French, except Basque	812	1.50
French Canadian	183	0.34
German	6,964	12.87
Greek	652	1.20
Hawaii Native/Pacific Islander:	21	0.04
Micronesian: (2)	3	0.01
Guamanian/Chamorro (2)	3	0.01
Polynesian: (3)	4	0.01
Native Hawaiian (2)	3	0.01
Samoan (1)	1	0.00
Other Pac. Isl., specified	3	0.01
Other Pac. Isl., not spec. (6)	11	0.02
Hispanic or Latino:	2,754	5.09
Central American:	145	0.27
Costa Rican	66	0.12
Guatemalan	23	0.04
Honduran	16	0.03
Nicaraguan	10	0.02
Panamanian	12	0.02
Salvadoran	16	0.03
Other Central American	2	0.00
Cuban	320	0.59
Dominican Republic	149	0.28
Mexican	164	0.30
Puerto Rican	726	1.34
South American:	577	1.07
Argentinean	71	0.13
Bolivian	4	0.01
Chilean	16	0.03
Colombian	219	0.41
Ecuadorian	82	0.15
Paraguayan	1	0.00
Peruvian	146	0.27
Uruguayan	8	0.01
Venezuelan	16	0.03
Other South American	14	0.03
Other Hispanic or Latino	673	1.24
Hungarian	932	1.72
Iranian	124	0.23
Irish	8,625	15.94
Israeli	121	0.22
Italian	16,166	29.87
Latvian	23	0.04
Lithuanian	302	0.56
Macedonian	66	0.12
Northern European	8	0.01
Norwegian	389	0.72
Polish	4,930	9.11
Portuguese	136	0.25

Notes: 1. Figures in the "Number" column do not add up to the total population due to: a) Ancestry/Race overlap — e.g. persons can report being both White and Irish, b) persons of Hispanic origin can report being any race, c) persons reporting two ancestries are counted in both categories. 2. Numbers in parentheses indicate the number of persons reporting this ancestry/race alone, not in combination with any other ancestry/race. 3. Refer to the Explanation of Data in the front of the book for more detailed information.

Romanian	368	0.68
Russian	2,185	4.04
Scandinavian	10	0.02
Scotch-Irish	499	0.92
Scottish	845	1.56
Serbian	25	0.05
Slavic	61	0.11
Slovak	274	0.51
Slovene	7	0.01
Swedish	405	0.75
Swiss	206	0.38
Turkish	250	0.46
Ukrainian	620	1.15
United States or American	1,588	2.93
Welsh	179	0.33
West Indian, excl. Hispanic:	122	0.23
Haitian	19	0.04
Jamaican	71	0.13
West Indian	32	0.06
White:	49,314	91.21
Not Hispanic (46,766)	47,249	87.39
Hispanic (1,921)	2,065	3.82
Yugoslavian	215	0.40

Weehawken

Place Type: Township
County: Hudson
Population: 13,501

Ancestry/Race	Number	%
African American/Black:	628	4.65
Not Hispanic (312)	368	2.73
Hispanic (171)	260	1.93
African, sub-Saharan:	39	0.29
African	32	0.24
Other sub-Saharan African	7	0.05
Am. Ind. or Alaska Nat., not spec.	33	0.24
Albanian	7	0.05
American Indian tribes, specified:	38	0.28
Apache	1	0.01
Cherokee (1)	6	0.04
Choctaw	1	0.01
Delaware	2	0.01
Iroquois	2	0.01
Latin American Indians (7)	19	0.14
Lumbee (2)	2	0.01
Seminole	1	0.01
Sioux	1	0.01
Yakama (2)	2	0.01
All other tribes	1	0.01
American Indian tribes, not spec.	6	0.04
Arab:	197	1.46
Arab/Arabic	22	0.16
Iraqi	15	0.11
Lebanese	62	0.46
Palestinian	30	0.22
Syrian	31	0.23
Other Arab	37	0.27
Armenian	95	0.70
Asian:	723	5.36
Chinese, ex. Taiwanese (121)	136	1.01
Filipino (102)	111	0.82
Indian (201)	218	1.61
Indonesian	1	0.01
Japanese (65)	85	0.63
Korean (61)	71	0.53
Laotian (1)	1	0.01
Malaysian	1	0.01
Pakistani (26)	28	0.21
Sri Lankan (3)	3	0.02
Taiwanese (6)	13	0.10
Thai (6)	6	0.04
Vietnamese (8)	13	0.10
Other Asian, specified	1	0.01
Other Asian, not specified (14)	35	0.26
Austrian	63	0.47
Basque	26	0.19
Belgian	5	0.04
Brazilian	41	0.30
British	46	0.34
Canadian	25	0.19
Carpatho Rusyn	30	0.22
Celtic	7	0.05
Croatian	44	0.33
Czech	28	0.21
Czechoslovakian	22	0.16
Danish	34	0.25
Dutch	120	0.89
Eastern European	39	0.29
English	459	3.40
Estonian	12	0.09
European	38	0.28
Finnish	10	0.07
French, except Basque	176	1.30
French Canadian	40	0.30
German	1,081	8.01
Greek	63	0.47
Guyanese	29	0.21
Hawaii Native/Pacific Islander:	20	0.15
Micronesian: (1)	1	0.01
Guamanian/Chamorro (1)	1	0.01
Polynesian: (1)	4	0.03
Native Hawaiian (1)	3	0.02
Other Polynesian	1	0.01
Other Pac. Isl., not spec. (12)	15	0.11
Hispanic or Latino:	5,487	40.64
Central American:	340	2.52
Costa Rican	12	0.09
Guatemalan	30	0.22
Honduran	83	0.61
Nicaraguan	15	0.11
Panamanian	7	0.05
Salvadoran	176	1.30
Other Central American	17	0.13
Cuban	1,182	8.75
Dominican Republic	775	5.74
Mexican	177	1.31
Puerto Rican	822	6.09
South American:	1,074	7.95
Argentinean	59	0.44
Bolivian	7	0.05
Chilean	57	0.42
Colombian	330	2.44
Ecuadorian	382	2.83
Peruvian	154	1.14
Uruguayan	27	0.20
Venezuelan	23	0.17
Other South American	35	0.26
Other Hispanic or Latino	1,117	8.27
Hungarian	87	0.64
Irish	1,618	11.98
Israeli	19	0.14
Italian	2,156	15.97
Latvian	9	0.07
Lithuanian	6	0.04
Norwegian	49	0.36
Polish	386	2.86
Portuguese	63	0.47
Romanian	17	0.13
Russian	269	1.99
Scandinavian	17	0.13
Scotch-Irish	48	0.36
Scottish	131	0.97
Serbian	8	0.06
Slovak	47	0.35
Swedish	98	0.73
Swiss	30	0.22
Turkish	121	0.90
Ukrainian	50	0.37
United States or American	379	2.81
Welsh	50	0.37
West Indian, excl. Hispanic:	71	0.53
Jamaican	7	0.05
Trinidadian and Tobagonian	34	0.25
West Indian	30	0.22
White:	10,383	76.91
Not Hispanic (6,766)	6,979	51.69
Hispanic (3,096)	3,404	25.21
Yugoslavian	43	0.32

West Caldwell

Place Type: Census Designated Place
County: Essex
Population: 11,233

Ancestry/Race	Number	%
African American/Black:	116	1.03
Not Hispanic (100)	116	1.03
African, sub-Saharan:	3	0.03
African	3	0.03
Am. Ind. or Alaska Nat., not spec.	2	0.02
American Indian tribes, specified:	6	0.05
Iroquois (1)	1	0.01
Latin American Indians (2)	2	0.02
All other tribes	3	0.03
American Indian tribes, not spec.	6	0.05
Arab:	50	0.45
Arab/Arabic	17	0.15
Lebanese	33	0.29
Armenian	17	0.15
Asian:	479	4.26
Chinese, ex. Taiwanese (106)	113	1.01
Filipino (77)	91	0.81
Indian (126)	142	1.26
Japanese (11)	13	0.12
Korean (70)	74	0.66
Pakistani (3)	3	0.03
Taiwanese (3)	8	0.07
Thai (3)	3	0.03
Vietnamese (24)	24	0.21
Other Asian, not specified (2)	8	0.07
Austrian	86	0.77
Belgian	14	0.12
Brazilian	56	0.50
British	26	0.23
Canadian	14	0.12
Croatian	8	0.07
Czech	26	0.23
Czechoslovakian	33	0.29
Danish	11	0.10
Dutch	201	1.79
Eastern European	146	1.30
English	754	6.71
Estonian	21	0.19
European	138	1.23
Finnish	6	0.05
French, except Basque	231	2.06
French Canadian	18	0.16
German	1,618	14.40
Greek	111	0.99
Guyanese	5	0.04
Hawaii Native/Pacific Islander:	7	0.06
Other Pac. Isl., not spec. (4)	7	0.06
Hispanic or Latino:	314	2.80
Central American:	15	0.13
Costa Rican	2	0.02
Guatemalan	5	0.04
Honduran	1	0.01
Nicaraguan	2	0.02
Salvadoran	4	0.04
Other Central American	1	0.01
Cuban	68	0.61
Dominican Republic	18	0.16
Mexican	23	0.20
Puerto Rican	85	0.76
South American:	45	0.40
Argentinean	3	0.03
Chilean	7	0.06
Colombian	7	0.06
Ecuadorian	6	0.05
Paraguayan	2	0.02
Peruvian	15	0.13
Uruguayan	3	0.03
Venezuelan	2	0.02
Other Hispanic or Latino	60	0.53
Hungarian	137	1.22
Irish	2,438	21.70
Italian	3,958	35.24
Latvian	13	0.12

Notes: 1. Figures in the "Number" column do not add up to the total population due to: a) Ancestry/Race overlap — e.g. persons can report being both White and Irish, b) persons of Hispanic origin can report being any race, c) persons reporting two ancestries are counted in both categories. 2. Numbers in parentheses indicate the number of persons reporting this ancestry/race alone, not in combination with any other ancestry/race. 3. Refer to the Explanation of Data in the front of the book for more detailed information.

Ancestry/Race	Number	%
Lithuanian	19	0.17
Norwegian	163	1.45
Polish	616	5.48
Portuguese	95	0.85
Romanian	57	0.51
Russian	257	2.29
Scotch-Irish	90	0.80
Scottish	205	1.82
Slovak	86	0.77
Swedish	133	1.18
Swiss	65	0.58
Turkish	34	0.30
Ukrainian	45	0.40
United States or American	467	4.16
Welsh	30	0.27
West Indian, excl. Hispanic:	55	0.49
Jamaican	6	0.05
Trinidadian and Tobagonian	49	0.44
White:	10,609	94.44
Not Hispanic (10,300)	10,356	92.19
Hispanic (241)	253	2.25
Yugoslavian	27	0.24

West Deptford

Place Type: Township
County: Gloucester
Population: 19,368

Ancestry/Race	Number	%
African American/Black:	1,047	5.41
Not Hispanic (964)	1,025	5.29
Hispanic (20)	22	0.11
African, sub-Saharan:	92	0.48
African	71	0.37
Cape Verdean	7	0.04
Ethiopian	14	0.07
Am. Ind. or Alaska Nat., not spec.	35	0.18
Alsatian	11	0.06
American Indian tribes, specified:	47	0.24
Blackfeet (1)	3	0.02
Cherokee (6)	20	0.10
Cheyenne (1)	1	0.01
Delaware (3)	7	0.04
Lumbee	1	0.01
Navajo (3)	3	0.02
Sioux (1)	1	0.01
All other tribes (9)	11	0.06
American Indian tribes, not spec.	4	0.02
Arab:	52	0.27
Lebanese	45	0.23
Syrian	7	0.04
Armenian	6	0.03
Asian:	253	1.31
Cambodian (5)	5	0.03
Chinese, ex. Taiwanese (35)	37	0.19
Filipino (37)	50	0.26
Indian (64)	68	0.35
Japanese (1)	4	0.02
Korean (39)	45	0.23
Laotian	1	0.01
Pakistani (3)	3	0.02
Taiwanese	1	0.01
Thai (6)	9	0.05
Vietnamese (20)	22	0.11
Other Asian, not specified (6)	8	0.04
Australian	5	0.03
Austrian	35	0.18
Brazilian	21	0.11
British	7	0.04
Canadian	5	0.03
Croatian	55	0.28
Czech	35	0.18
Czechoslovakian	15	0.08
Danish	17	0.09
Dutch	310	1.60
English	2,814	14.53
Estonian	19	0.10
European	24	0.12
Finnish	8	0.04
French, except Basque	502	2.59
French Canadian	55	0.28
German	5,435	28.06
Greek	107	0.55
Hawaii Native/Pacific Islander:	15	0.08
Polynesian: (4)	11	0.06
Native Hawaiian (4)	11	0.06
Other Pac. Isl., not spec.	4	0.02
Hispanic or Latino:	341	1.76
Central American:	6	0.03
Guatemalan	2	0.01
Panamanian	1	0.01
Salvadoran	2	0.01
Other Central American	1	0.01
Cuban	9	0.05
Dominican Republic	2	0.01
Mexican	29	0.15
Puerto Rican	172	0.89
South American:	50	0.26
Argentinean	12	0.06
Colombian	7	0.04
Ecuadorian	23	0.12
Peruvian	1	0.01
Venezuelan	6	0.03
Other South American	1	0.01
Other Hispanic or Latino	73	0.38
Hungarian	102	0.53
Irish	6,423	33.16
Italian	4,519	23.33
Latvian	27	0.14
Lithuanian	136	0.70
Norwegian	65	0.34
Pennsylvania German	41	0.21
Polish	1,520	7.85
Portuguese	27	0.14
Romanian	24	0.12
Russian	165	0.85
Scotch-Irish	278	1.44
Scottish	352	1.82
Slovak	44	0.23
Swedish	185	0.96
Swiss	35	0.18
Ukrainian	69	0.36
United States or American	532	2.75
Welsh	245	1.26
West Indian, excl. Hispanic:	12	0.06
Bahamian	5	0.03
Jamaican	7	0.04
White:	18,021	93.05
Not Hispanic (17,651)	17,782	91.81
Hispanic (224)	239	1.23
Yugoslavian	22	0.11

West Freehold

Place Type: Census Designated Place
County: Monmouth
Population: 12,498

Ancestry/Race	Number	%
African American/Black:	339	2.71
Not Hispanic (301)	326	2.61
Hispanic (7)	13	0.10
Am. Ind. or Alaska Nat., not spec.	18	0.14
Albanian	33	0.26
American Indian tribes, specified:	29	0.23
Apache (1)	1	0.01
Blackfeet	1	0.01
Cherokee (1)	10	0.08
Crow	1	0.01
Iroquois (1)	5	0.04
Latin American Indians (3)	3	0.02
Navajo	1	0.01
Pueblo (5)	5	0.04
Sioux	1	0.01
All other tribes	1	0.01
American Indian tribes, not spec.	7	0.06
Arab:	134	1.07
Egyptian	15	0.12
Lebanese	22	0.18
Syrian	97	0.77
Asian:	605	4.84
Cambodian (1)	1	0.01
Chinese, ex. Taiwanese (188)	208	1.66
Filipino (112)	127	1.02
Indian (145)	167	1.34
Japanese (2)	8	0.06
Korean (43)	50	0.40
Pakistani (4)	4	0.03
Sri Lankan (3)	3	0.02
Taiwanese (9)	9	0.07
Thai (4)	4	0.03
Vietnamese (18)	21	0.17
Other Asian, not specified (1)	3	0.02
Austrian	267	2.13
Belgian	26	0.21
Brazilian	30	0.24
British	22	0.18
Canadian	42	0.34
Croatian	24	0.19
Cypriot	5	0.04
Czech	60	0.48
Czechoslovakian	70	0.56
Danish	122	0.97
Dutch	126	1.01
Eastern European	100	0.80
English	721	5.75
European	45	0.36
Finnish	6	0.05
French, except Basque	281	2.24
French Canadian	43	0.34
German	1,747	13.94
Greek	107	0.85
Hawaii Native/Pacific Islander:	5	0.04
Polynesian: (3)	3	0.02
Native Hawaiian (3)	3	0.02
Other Pac. Isl., not spec.	2	0.02
Hispanic or Latino:	673	5.38
Central American:	33	0.26
Costa Rican	4	0.03
Guatemalan	10	0.08
Honduran	9	0.07
Nicaraguan	1	0.01
Panamanian	4	0.03
Salvadoran	5	0.04
Cuban	52	0.42
Dominican Republic	21	0.17
Mexican	185	1.48
Puerto Rican	231	1.85
South American:	72	0.58
Argentinean	5	0.04
Bolivian	1	0.01
Chilean	3	0.02
Colombian	35	0.28
Ecuadorian	14	0.11
Peruvian	7	0.06
Uruguayan	2	0.02
Venezuelan	3	0.02
Other South American	2	0.02
Other Hispanic or Latino	79	0.63
Hungarian	211	1.68
Irish	2,329	18.58
Israeli	14	0.11
Italian	3,123	24.92
Lithuanian	89	0.71
Maltese	32	0.26
Norwegian	53	0.42
Pennsylvania German	15	0.12
Polish	1,523	12.15
Portuguese	54	0.43
Romanian	67	0.53
Russian	632	5.04
Scandinavian	60	0.48
Scotch-Irish	59	0.47
Scottish	167	1.33
Serbian	19	0.15
Slavic	20	0.16
Slovak	35	0.28
Swedish	115	0.92
Swiss	42	0.34

Notes: 1. Figures in the "Number" column do not add up to the total population due to: a) Ancestry/Race overlap — e.g. persons can report being both White and Irish, b) persons of Hispanic origin can report being any race, c) persons reporting two ancestries are counted in both categories. 2. Numbers in parentheses indicate the number of persons reporting this ancestry/race alone, not in combination with any other ancestry/race. 3. Refer to the Explanation of Data in the front of the book for more detailed information.

Ancestry/Race	Number	%
Turkish	86	0.69
Ukrainian	175	1.40
United States or American	262	2.09
Welsh	43	0.34
West Indian, excl. Hispanic:	47	0.37
Jamaican	32	0.26
Trinidadian and Tobagonian	15	0.12
White:	11,468	91.76
Not Hispanic (10,842)	10,931	87.46
Hispanic (491)	537	4.30
Yugoslavian	31	0.25

West Milford

Place Type: Census Designated Place
County: Passaic
Population: 26,410

Ancestry/Race	Number	%
African American/Black:	453	1.72
Not Hispanic (314)	422	1.60
Hispanic (12)	31	0.12
African, sub-Saharan:	20	0.08
African	13	0.05
South African	7	0.03
Alaska Native tribes, not specified	1	0.00
Am. Ind. or Alaska Nat., not spec.	125	0.47
Albanian	18	0.07
American Indian tribes, specified:	193	0.73
Blackfeet	4	0.02
Cherokee (11)	49	0.19
Cheyenne (2)	2	0.01
Chippewa (1)	4	0.02
Choctaw	1	0.00
Comanche	3	0.01
Cree	2	0.01
Creek	3	0.01
Delaware (58)	88	0.33
Iroquois (2)	8	0.03
Latin American Indians (3)	4	0.02
Navajo (1)	6	0.02
Sioux (1)	3	0.01
All other tribes (4)	16	0.06
American Indian tribes, not spec.	11	0.04
Arab:	120	0.45
Arab/Arabic	6	0.02
Egyptian	14	0.05
Jordanian	22	0.08
Lebanese	9	0.03
Palestinian	39	0.15
Syrian	30	0.11
Armenian	72	0.27
Asian:	357	1.35
Chinese, ex. Taiwanese (38)	55	0.21
Filipino (52)	80	0.30
Indian (81)	93	0.35
Japanese (10)	20	0.08
Korean (65)	77	0.29
Laotian	8	0.03
Taiwanese (3)	3	0.01
Thai (6)	7	0.03
Vietnamese (4)	5	0.02
Other Asian, specified (1)	3	0.01
Other Asian, not specified (5)	6	0.02
Australian	8	0.03
Austrian	277	1.05
Basque	9	0.03
Belgian	88	0.33
Brazilian	27	0.10
British	111	0.42
Bulgarian	16	0.06
Canadian	117	0.44
Celtic	8	0.03
Croatian	31	0.12
Czech	125	0.47
Czechoslovakian	156	0.59
Danish	65	0.25
Dutch	1,668	6.32
Eastern European	26	0.10
English	2,779	10.52
Estonian	7	0.03
European	156	0.59
Finnish	74	0.28
French, except Basque	707	2.68
French Canadian	175	0.66
German	6,514	24.66
Greek	229	0.87
Hawaii Native/Pacific Islander:	7	0.03
Micronesian: (1)	1	0.00
Guamanian/Chamorro (1)	1	0.00
Polynesian: (3)	3	0.01
Native Hawaiian (1)	1	0.00
Samoan (2)	2	0.01
Other Pac. Isl., specified	2	0.01
Other Pac. Isl., not spec.	1	0.00
Hispanic or Latino:	893	3.38
Central American:	40	0.15
Costa Rican	14	0.05
Guatemalan	13	0.05
Honduran	6	0.02
Nicaraguan	5	0.02
Panamanian	1	0.00
Salvadoran	1	0.00
Cuban	97	0.37
Dominican Republic	28	0.11
Mexican	97	0.37
Puerto Rican	305	1.15
South American:	151	0.57
Argentinean	11	0.04
Bolivian	2	0.01
Chilean	13	0.05
Colombian	37	0.14
Ecuadorian	19	0.07
Peruvian	45	0.17
Uruguayan	1	0.00
Venezuelan	4	0.02
Other South American	19	0.07
Other Hispanic or Latino	175	0.66
Hungarian	443	1.68
Iranian	12	0.05
Irish	6,709	25.40
Israeli	4	0.02
Italian	6,950	26.32
Latvian	19	0.07
Lithuanian	148	0.56
Macedonian	38	0.14
Maltese	16	0.06
Northern European	14	0.05
Norwegian	251	0.95
Pennsylvania German	9	0.03
Polish	2,555	9.67
Portuguese	70	0.27
Romanian	38	0.14
Russian	609	2.31
Scandinavian	11	0.04
Scotch-Irish	417	1.58
Scottish	471	1.78
Slavic	37	0.14
Slovak	140	0.53
Slovene	22	0.08
Swedish	396	1.50
Swiss	168	0.64
Turkish	23	0.09
Ukrainian	304	1.15
United States or American	690	2.61
Welsh	141	0.53
West Indian, excl. Hispanic:	6	0.02
Barbadian	6	0.02
White:	25,411	96.22
Not Hispanic (24,474)	24,728	93.63
Hispanic (636)	683	2.59
Yugoslavian	35	0.13

West New York

Place Type: Town
County: Hudson
Population: 45,768

Ancestry/Race	Number	%
African American/Black:	2,188	4.78
Not Hispanic (658)	754	1.65
Hispanic (968)	1,434	3.13
African, sub-Saharan:	209	0.46
African	86	0.19
Ethiopian	16	0.03
Senegalese	30	0.07
South African	37	0.08
Ugandan	40	0.09
Am. Ind. or Alaska Nat., not spec.	256	0.56
Albanian	50	0.11
American Indian tribes, specified:	181	0.40
Apache (5)	5	0.01
Blackfeet	1	0.00
Cherokee	6	0.01
Chippewa (4)	4	0.01
Latin American Indians (82)	133	0.29
Pueblo (1)	5	0.01
Seminole (1)	1	0.00
All other tribes (8)	26	0.06
American Indian tribes, not spec.	51	0.11
Arab:	520	1.14
Arab/Arabic	203	0.44
Egyptian	150	0.33
Iraqi	7	0.02
Lebanese	71	0.16
Moroccan	14	0.03
Palestinian	52	0.11
Syrian	18	0.04
Other Arab	5	0.01
Armenian	83	0.18
Asian:	1,548	3.38
Chinese, ex. Taiwanese (168)	213	0.47
Filipino (132)	146	0.32
Indian (589)	668	1.46
Indonesian (2)	2	0.00
Japanese (68)	75	0.16
Korean (286)	294	0.64
Malaysian (2)	2	0.00
Pakistani (32)	38	0.08
Sri Lankan (1)	1	0.00
Taiwanese (1)	5	0.01
Thai (25)	30	0.07
Vietnamese (12)	17	0.04
Other Asian, specified (1)	4	0.01
Other Asian, not specified (9)	53	0.12
Australian	22	0.05
Austrian	35	0.08
Basque	9	0.02
Belgian	16	0.03
Brazilian	71	0.16
British	42	0.09
Canadian	21	0.05
Carpatho Rusyn	7	0.02
Celtic	6	0.01
Croatian	73	0.16
Czechoslovakian	28	0.06
Danish	23	0.05
Dutch	49	0.11
Eastern European	26	0.06
English	246	0.54
European	126	0.28
French, except Basque	222	0.49
French Canadian	34	0.07
German	781	1.71
Greek	124	0.27
Guyanese	40	0.09
Hawaii Native/Pacific Islander:	67	0.15
Polynesian:	9	0.02
Native Hawaiian	8	0.02
Samoan	1	0.00
Other Pac. Isl., not spec. (15)	58	0.13
Hispanic or Latino:	36,038	78.74
Central American:	3,978	8.69
Costa Rican	82	0.18
Guatemalan	364	0.80
Honduran	542	1.18
Nicaraguan	113	0.25
Panamanian	35	0.08
Salvadoran	2,491	5.44

Notes: 1. Figures in the "Number" column do not add up to the total population due to: a) Ancestry/Race overlap — e.g. persons can report being both White and Irish, b) persons of Hispanic origin can report being any race, c) persons reporting two ancestries are counted in both categories. 2. Numbers in parentheses indicate the number of persons reporting this ancestry/race alone, not in combination with any other ancestry/race. 3. Refer to the Explanation of Data in the front of the book for more detailed information.

Ancestry/Race	Number	%
Other Central American	351	0.77
Cuban	8,991	19.64
Dominican Republic	3,847	8.41
Mexican	2,982	6.52
Puerto Rican	2,791	6.10
South American:	6,237	13.63
Argentinean	179	0.39
Bolivian	48	0.10
Chilean	196	0.43
Colombian	2,664	5.82
Ecuadorian	2,035	4.45
Peruvian	771	1.68
Uruguayan	42	0.09
Venezuelan	148	0.32
Other South American	154	0.34
Other Hispanic or Latino	7,212	15.76
Hungarian	120	0.26
Iranian	22	0.05
Irish	769	1.68
Israeli	18	0.04
Italian	1,769	3.87
Latvian	9	0.02
Lithuanian	27	0.06
Macedonian	5	0.01
Maltese	6	0.01
Norwegian	28	0.06
Polish	214	0.47
Portuguese	76	0.17
Romanian	27	0.06
Russian	148	0.32
Scotch-Irish	25	0.05
Scottish	62	0.14
Slavic	11	0.02
Slovak	14	0.03
Swedish	72	0.16
Swiss	42	0.09
Turkish	156	0.34
Ukrainian	26	0.06
United States or American	1,207	2.64
Welsh	10	0.02
West Indian, excl. Hispanic:	289	0.63
Bahamian	10	0.02
British West Indian	35	0.08
Dutch West Indian	17	0.04
Haitian	64	0.14
Jamaican	111	0.24
Trinidadian and Tobagonian	29	0.06
West Indian	13	0.03
Other West Indian	10	0.02
White:	30,516	66.68
Not Hispanic (7,088)	7,526	16.44
Hispanic (20,415)	22,990	50.23
Yugoslavian	42	0.09

West Orange

Place Type: Census Designated Place
County: Essex
Population: 44,943

Ancestry/Race	Number	%
African American/Black:	8,504	18.92
Not Hispanic (7,672)	8,270	18.40
Hispanic (176)	234	0.52
African, sub-Saharan:	893	1.99
African	494	1.10
Ethiopian	104	0.23
Ghanian	88	0.20
Liberian	24	0.05
Nigerian	154	0.34
South African	29	0.06
Am. Ind. or Alaska Nat., not spec.	102	0.23
Albanian	23	0.05
American Indian tribes, specified:	98	0.22
Apache	1	0.00
Blackfeet (1)	2	0.00
Cherokee	27	0.06
Cree	1	0.00
Creek	2	0.00
Delaware	6	0.01
Iroquois (2)	4	0.01
Latin American Indians (13)	33	0.07
Navajo (1)	3	0.01
Pueblo (2)	2	0.00
Seminole	2	0.00
Sioux	1	0.00
Tohono O'Odham (1)	1	0.00
All other tribes (5)	13	0.03
American Indian tribes, not spec.	18	0.04
Arab:	500	1.11
Arab/Arabic	66	0.15
Egyptian	181	0.40
Lebanese	35	0.08
Moroccan	98	0.22
Palestinian	5	0.01
Syrian	90	0.20
Other Arab	24	0.05
Armenian	87	0.19
Asian:	4,013	8.93
Chinese, ex. Taiwanese (720)	794	1.77
Filipino (932)	1,003	2.23
Indian (1,306)	1,437	3.20
Indonesian (2)	2	0.00
Japanese (32)	51	0.11
Korean (312)	336	0.75
Pakistani (57)	73	0.16
Sri Lankan (19)	19	0.04
Taiwanese (50)	65	0.14
Thai (10)	13	0.03
Vietnamese (107)	122	0.27
Other Asian, specified (3)	4	0.01
Other Asian, not specified (30)	94	0.21
Austrian	382	0.85
Brazilian	31	0.07
British	86	0.19
Canadian	43	0.10
Celtic	15	0.03
Croatian	17	0.04
Cypriot	38	0.08
Czech	119	0.27
Czechoslovakian	123	0.27
Danish	162	0.36
Dutch	159	0.35
Eastern European	489	1.09
English	1,338	2.98
Estonian	78	0.17
European	253	0.56
Finnish	27	0.06
French, except Basque	406	0.91
French Canadian	48	0.11
German	3,063	6.83
Greek	529	1.18
Guyanese	199	0.44
Hawaii Native/Pacific Islander:	48	0.11
Micronesian: (4)	6	0.01
Guamanian/Chamorro (3)	4	0.01
Other Micronesian (1)	2	0.00
Polynesian: (9)	9	0.02
Native Hawaiian (5)	5	0.01
Samoan (4)	4	0.01
Other Pac. Isl., specified	1	0.00
Other Pac. Isl., not spec. (4)	32	0.07
Hispanic or Latino:	4,514	10.04
Central American:	383	0.85
Costa Rican	89	0.20
Guatemalan	43	0.10
Honduran	48	0.11
Nicaraguan	8	0.02
Panamanian	20	0.04
Salvadoran	155	0.34
Other Central American	20	0.04
Cuban	214	0.48
Dominican Republic	174	0.39
Mexican	277	0.62
Puerto Rican	672	1.50
South American:	1,585	3.53
Argentinean	51	0.11
Bolivian	16	0.04
Chilean	11	0.02
Colombian	299	0.67
Ecuadorian	160	0.36
Paraguayan	6	0.01
Peruvian	577	1.28
Uruguayan	384	0.85
Venezuelan	14	0.03
Other South American	67	0.15
Other Hispanic or Latino	1,209	2.69
Hungarian	432	0.96
Iranian	146	0.33
Irish	4,874	10.87
Israeli	23	0.05
Italian	7,474	16.66
Latvian	56	0.12
Lithuanian	113	0.25
Norwegian	210	0.47
Pennsylvania German	8	0.02
Polish	2,394	5.34
Portuguese	152	0.34
Romanian	185	0.41
Russian	2,620	5.84
Scandinavian	6	0.01
Scotch-Irish	203	0.45
Scottish	468	1.04
Slavic	25	0.06
Slovak	70	0.16
Slovene	7	0.02
Swedish	277	0.62
Swiss	72	0.16
Turkish	34	0.08
Ukrainian	467	1.04
United States or American	1,944	4.33
Welsh	86	0.19
West Indian, excl. Hispanic:	2,674	5.96
Barbadian	53	0.12
British West Indian	48	0.11
Haitian	1,618	3.61
Jamaican	646	1.44
Trinidadian and Tobagonian	143	0.32
U.S. Virgin Islander	19	0.04
West Indian	139	0.31
Other West Indian	8	0.02
White:	31,220	69.47
Not Hispanic (27,907)	28,450	63.30
Hispanic (2,452)	2,770	6.16
Yugoslavian	16	0.04

West Paterson

Place Type: Borough
County: Passaic
Population: 10,987

Ancestry/Race	Number	%
African American/Black:	377	3.43
Not Hispanic (327)	351	3.19
Hispanic (20)	26	0.24
African, sub-Saharan:	58	0.53
African	44	0.40
Nigerian	14	0.13
Am. Ind. or Alaska Nat., not spec.	14	0.13
American Indian tribes, specified:	12	0.11
Cherokee (2)	5	0.05
Comanche (1)	1	0.01
Delaware	1	0.01
Iroquois	2	0.02
Pueblo (2)	2	0.02
All other tribes	1	0.01
American Indian tribes, not spec.	5	0.05
Arab:	298	2.71
Arab/Arabic	82	0.75
Egyptian	40	0.36
Iraqi	32	0.29
Lebanese	32	0.29
Syrian	71	0.65
Other Arab	41	0.37
Armenian	16	0.15
Asian:	572	5.21
Bangladeshi (3)	6	0.05
Chinese, ex. Taiwanese (58)	63	0.57
Filipino (56)	62	0.56

Notes: 1. Figures in the "Number" column do not add up to the total population due to: a) Ancestry/Race overlap — e.g. persons can report being both White and Irish, b) persons of Hispanic origin can report being any race, c) persons reporting two ancestries are counted in both categories. 2. Numbers in parentheses indicate the number of persons reporting this ancestry/race alone, not in combination with any other ancestry/race. 3. Refer to the Explanation of Data in the front of the book for more detailed information.

Ancestry/Race	Number	%
Indian (180)	211	1.92
Japanese (4)	6	0.05
Korean (73)	83	0.76
Pakistani (24)	34	0.31
Sri Lankan	3	0.03
Thai (6)	6	0.05
Vietnamese (1)	2	0.02
Other Asian, specified	2	0.02
Other Asian, not specified	94	0.86
Assyrian/Chaldean/Syriac	41	0.37
Austrian	36	0.33
Basque	30	0.27
Belgian	13	0.12
Brazilian	35	0.32
British	8	0.07
Canadian	13	0.12
Croatian	15	0.14
Czech	63	0.57
Czechoslovakian	17	0.15
Dutch	292	2.66
English	279	2.54
European	8	0.07
French, except Basque	139	1.27
French Canadian	47	0.43
German	1,183	10.77
Greek	153	1.39
Guyanese	12	0.11
Hawaii Native/Pacific Islander:	6	0.05
Polynesian: (4)	4	0.04
Samoan (4)	4	0.04
Other Pac. Isl., not spec.	2	0.02
Hispanic or Latino:	1,105	10.06
Central American:	35	0.32
Costa Rican	17	0.15
Guatemalan	1	0.01
Honduran	5	0.05
Salvadoran	10	0.09
Other Central American	2	0.02
Cuban	60	0.55
Dominican Republic	76	0.69
Mexican	38	0.35
Puerto Rican	355	3.23
South American:	316	2.88
Argentinean	32	0.29
Bolivian	3	0.03
Chilean	9	0.08
Colombian	146	1.33
Ecuadorian	6	0.05
Peruvian	93	0.85
Uruguayan	10	0.09
Venezuelan	7	0.06
Other South American	10	0.09
Other Hispanic or Latino	225	2.05
Hungarian	144	1.31
Iranian	11	0.10
Irish	1,695	15.43
Italian	4,452	40.52
Lithuanian	70	0.64
Macedonian	12	0.11
Northern European	12	0.11
Polish	767	6.98
Portuguese	69	0.63
Romanian	8	0.07
Russian	185	1.68
Scandinavian	10	0.09
Scotch-Irish	54	0.49
Scottish	105	0.96
Serbian	14	0.13
Slavic	11	0.10
Slovak	106	0.96
Swedish	46	0.42
Swiss	42	0.38
Turkish	76	0.69
Ukrainian	58	0.53
United States or American	167	1.52
Welsh	61	0.56
West Indian, excl. Hispanic:	54	0.49
Jamaican	42	0.38
Trinidadian and Tobagonian	12	0.11
White:	9,829	89.46
Not Hispanic (8,814)	9,088	82.72
Hispanic (693)	741	6.74
Yugoslavian	19	0.17

West Windsor

Place Type: Township
County: Mercer
Population: 21,907

Ancestry/Race	Number	%
Afghan	13	0.06
African American/Black:	706	3.22
Not Hispanic (587)	667	3.04
Hispanic (18)	39	0.18
African, sub-Saharan:	75	0.34
African	18	0.08
Cape Verdean	8	0.04
Nigerian	19	0.09
South African	25	0.11
Ugandan	5	0.02
Am. Ind. or Alaska Nat., not spec.	32	0.15
American Indian tribes, specified:	25	0.11
Blackfeet	2	0.01
Cherokee (1)	7	0.03
Creek (1)	1	0.00
Iroquois (1)	1	0.00
Latin American Indians (2)	7	0.03
Shoshone	1	0.00
All other tribes (3)	6	0.03
American Indian tribes, not spec.	5	0.02
Arab:	308	1.41
Egyptian	167	0.76
Iraqi	6	0.03
Lebanese	97	0.44
Moroccan	4	0.02
Syrian	16	0.07
Other Arab	18	0.08
Asian:	5,268	24.05
Bangladeshi (20)	22	0.10
Chinese, ex. Taiwanese (1,732)	1,820	8.31
Filipino (156)	206	0.94
Indian (1,927)	1,973	9.01
Indonesian (2)	2	0.01
Japanese (181)	232	1.06
Korean (495)	514	2.35
Malaysian (3)	5	0.02
Pakistani (102)	111	0.51
Sri Lankan (16)	19	0.09
Taiwanese (215)	253	1.15
Thai (11)	12	0.05
Vietnamese (12)	17	0.08
Other Asian, specified (1)	1	0.00
Other Asian, not specified (57)	81	0.37
Australian	18	0.08
Austrian	155	0.71
Belgian	7	0.03
Brazilian	50	0.23
British	153	0.70
Bulgarian	31	0.14
Canadian	56	0.26
Celtic	5	0.02
Croatian	8	0.04
Czech	113	0.52
Czechoslovakian	79	0.36
Danish	92	0.42
Dutch	437	1.99
Eastern European	386	1.76
English	2,185	9.97
European	206	0.94
Finnish	28	0.13
French, except Basque	454	2.07
French Canadian	143	0.65
German	2,811	12.83
Greek	113	0.52
Hawaii Native/Pacific Islander:	19	0.09
Micronesian:	1	0.00
Guamanian/Chamorro	1	0.00
Polynesian: (2)	2	0.01
Native Hawaiian (2)	2	0.01
Other Pac. Isl., not spec.	16	0.07
Hispanic or Latino:	892	4.07
Central American:	119	0.54
Costa Rican	6	0.03
Guatemalan	71	0.32
Honduran	1	0.00
Nicaraguan	6	0.03
Panamanian	8	0.04
Salvadoran	8	0.04
Other Central American	19	0.09
Cuban	63	0.29
Dominican Republic	11	0.05
Mexican	177	0.81
Puerto Rican	152	0.69
South American:	149	0.68
Argentinean	22	0.10
Bolivian	7	0.03
Chilean	14	0.06
Colombian	64	0.29
Ecuadorian	6	0.03
Paraguayan	2	0.01
Peruvian	4	0.02
Uruguayan	3	0.01
Venezuelan	13	0.06
Other South American	14	0.06
Other Hispanic or Latino	221	1.01
Hungarian	314	1.43
Iranian	86	0.39
Irish	3,352	15.30
Italian	3,178	14.51
Latvian	10	0.05
Lithuanian	78	0.36
Luxemburger	11	0.05
Macedonian	8	0.04
Northern European	49	0.22
Norwegian	167	0.76
Pennsylvania German	10	0.05
Polish	1,211	5.53
Portuguese	54	0.25
Romanian	113	0.52
Russian	1,181	5.39
Scandinavian	7	0.03
Scotch-Irish	311	1.42
Scottish	378	1.73
Slavic	37	0.17
Slovak	88	0.40
Slovene	7	0.03
Swedish	132	0.60
Swiss	136	0.62
Ukrainian	116	0.53
United States or American	526	2.40
Welsh	111	0.51
West Indian, excl. Hispanic:	85	0.39
Haitian	32	0.15
Jamaican	23	0.10
Trinidadian and Tobagonian	30	0.14
White:	15,982	72.95
Not Hispanic (15,084)	15,326	69.96
Hispanic (586)	656	2.99
Yugoslavian	19	0.09

Westfield

Place Type: Town
County: Union
Population: 29,644

Ancestry/Race	Number	%
Acadian/Cajun	6	0.02
Afghan	14	0.05
African American/Black:	1,269	4.28
Not Hispanic (1,137)	1,238	4.18
Hispanic (14)	31	0.10
African, sub-Saharan:	36	0.12
African	23	0.08
Nigerian	8	0.03
Sudanese	5	0.02
Am. Ind. or Alaska Nat., not spec.	33	0.11
American Indian tribes, specified:	50	0.17
Apache	1	0.00

Notes: 1. Figures in the "Number" column do not add up to the total population due to: a) Ancestry/Race overlap — e.g. persons can report being both White and Irish, b) persons of Hispanic origin can report being any race, c) persons reporting two ancestries are counted in both categories. 2. Numbers in parentheses indicate the number of persons reporting this ancestry/race alone, not in combination with any other ancestry/race. 3. Refer to the Explanation of Data in the front of the book for more detailed information.

Ancestry/Race	Number	%
Blackfeet	1	0.00
Cherokee (4)	24	0.08
Delaware	2	0.01
Iroquois (3)	3	0.01
Latin American Indians (3)	5	0.02
Lumbee	1	0.00
Potawatomi (1)	1	0.00
Sioux (2)	2	0.01
All other tribes (4)	10	0.03
American Indian tribes, not spec.	2	0.01
Arab:	116	0.39
Arab/Arabic	4	0.01
Egyptian	13	0.04
Iraqi	26	0.09
Lebanese	52	0.18
Syrian	7	0.02
Other Arab	14	0.05
Armenian	45	0.15
Asian:	1,430	4.82
Bangladeshi (2)	2	0.01
Cambodian (1)	1	0.00
Chinese, ex. Taiwanese (463)	538	1.81
Filipino (109)	140	0.47
Indian (244)	288	0.97
Indonesian (2)	3	0.01
Japanese (50)	81	0.27
Korean (231)	252	0.85
Malaysian (6)	6	0.02
Pakistani (9)	24	0.08
Sri Lankan (5)	5	0.02
Taiwanese (20)	29	0.10
Thai (5)	5	0.02
Vietnamese (31)	36	0.12
Other Asian, not specified (12)	20	0.07
Australian	19	0.06
Austrian	272	0.92
Belgian	63	0.21
Brazilian	51	0.17
British	284	0.96
Canadian	87	0.29
Czech	201	0.68
Czechoslovakian	102	0.34
Danish	66	0.22
Dutch	359	1.21
Eastern European	398	1.34
English	3,334	11.25
European	215	0.73
Finnish	38	0.13
French, except Basque	569	1.92
French Canadian	132	0.45
German	5,063	17.08
Greek	308	1.04
Hawaii Native/Pacific Islander:	17	0.06
Polynesian: (2)	3	0.01
Native Hawaiian (1)	2	0.01
Samoan (1)	1	0.00
Other Pac. Isl., not spec. (1)	14	0.05
Hispanic or Latino:	836	2.82
Central American:	57	0.19
Costa Rican	31	0.10
Guatemalan	10	0.03
Honduran	1	0.00
Nicaraguan	1	0.00
Panamanian	3	0.01
Salvadoran	7	0.02
Other Central American	4	0.01
Cuban	103	0.35
Dominican Republic	28	0.09
Mexican	104	0.35
Puerto Rican	176	0.59
South American:	169	0.57
Argentinean	31	0.10
Bolivian	3	0.01
Chilean	11	0.04
Colombian	49	0.17
Ecuadorian	27	0.09
Paraguayan	1	0.00
Peruvian	36	0.12
Uruguayan	5	0.02
Venezuelan	4	0.01
Other South American	2	0.01
Other Hispanic or Latino	199	0.67
Hungarian	559	1.89
Iranian	79	0.27
Irish	6,796	22.93
Israeli	28	0.09
Italian	5,963	20.12
Latvian	37	0.12
Lithuanian	277	0.93
Northern European	34	0.11
Norwegian	331	1.12
Pennsylvania German	32	0.11
Polish	2,509	8.46
Portuguese	50	0.17
Romanian	111	0.37
Russian	1,422	4.80
Scandinavian	5	0.02
Scotch-Irish	396	1.34
Scottish	717	2.42
Serbian	10	0.03
Slavic	34	0.11
Slovak	200	0.67
Slovene	11	0.04
Swedish	223	0.75
Swiss	83	0.28
Turkish	18	0.06
Ukrainian	281	0.95
United States or American	1,065	3.59
Welsh	226	0.76
West Indian, excl. Hispanic:	136	0.46
Barbadian	26	0.09
Bermudan	7	0.02
Jamaican	77	0.26
Trinidadian and Tobagonian	26	0.09
White:	27,013	91.12
Not Hispanic (26,047)	26,332	88.83
Hispanic (628)	681	2.30

Westwood

Place Type: Borough
County: Bergen
Population: 10,999

Ancestry/Race	Number	%
African American/Black:	672	6.11
Not Hispanic (624)	651	5.92
Hispanic (5)	21	0.19
African, sub-Saharan:	8	0.07
Nigerian	8	0.07
Am. Ind. or Alaska Nat., not spec.	20	0.18
Albanian	19	0.17
Alsatian	10	0.09
American Indian tribes, specified:	35	0.32
Blackfeet	3	0.03
Cherokee (1)	3	0.03
Delaware (6)	14	0.13
Iroquois	1	0.01
Latin American Indians (5)	10	0.09
All other tribes	4	0.04
American Indian tribes, not spec.	2	0.02
Arab:	92	0.84
Lebanese	16	0.15
Syrian	54	0.49
Other Arab	22	0.20
Armenian	142	1.29
Asian:	530	4.82
Chinese, ex. Taiwanese (95)	104	0.95
Filipino (36)	43	0.39
Indian (163)	179	1.63
Indonesian (1)	2	0.02
Japanese (41)	42	0.38
Korean (127)	132	1.20
Pakistani (3)	3	0.03
Taiwanese (5)	8	0.07
Thai (3)	3	0.03
Vietnamese (7)	8	0.07
Other Asian, not specified	6	0.05
Austrian	234	2.13
Belgian	16	0.15
Canadian	36	0.33
Croatian	41	0.37
Czech	108	0.98
Czechoslovakian	24	0.22
Danish	83	0.75
Dutch	78	0.71
Eastern European	29	0.26
English	780	7.09
Estonian	35	0.32
European	78	0.71
Finnish	5	0.05
French, except Basque	211	1.92
French Canadian	82	0.75
German	1,937	17.61
Greek	120	1.09
Hawaii Native/Pacific Islander:	5	0.05
Polynesian: (1)	4	0.04
Native Hawaiian (1)	4	0.04
Other Pac. Isl., not spec.	1	0.01
Hispanic or Latino:	660	6.00
Central American:	55	0.50
Costa Rican	32	0.29
Guatemalan	2	0.02
Honduran	6	0.05
Nicaraguan	3	0.03
Panamanian	3	0.03
Salvadoran	8	0.07
Other Central American	1	0.01
Cuban	60	0.55
Dominican Republic	43	0.39
Mexican	135	1.23
Puerto Rican	113	1.03
South American:	128	1.16
Argentinean	8	0.07
Chilean	5	0.05
Colombian	66	0.60
Ecuadorian	27	0.25
Peruvian	14	0.13
Uruguayan	5	0.05
Venezuelan	2	0.02
Other South American	1	0.01
Other Hispanic or Latino	126	1.15
Hungarian	159	1.45
Iranian	42	0.38
Irish	2,268	20.62
Italian	2,708	24.62
Lithuanian	109	0.99
Northern European	8	0.07
Norwegian	111	1.01
Polish	571	5.19
Portuguese	83	0.75
Romanian	38	0.35
Russian	285	2.59
Scotch-Irish	71	0.65
Scottish	154	1.40
Serbian	12	0.11
Slavic	8	0.07
Slovak	55	0.50
Swedish	115	1.05
Swiss	31	0.28
Turkish	34	0.31
Ukrainian	20	0.18
United States or American	464	4.22
Welsh	78	0.71
West Indian, excl. Hispanic:	98	0.89
Bermudan	8	0.07
Jamaican	29	0.26
Trinidadian and Tobagonian	37	0.34
West Indian	24	0.22
White:	9,648	87.72
Not Hispanic (9,111)	9,176	83.43
Hispanic (414)	472	4.29

Williamstown

Place Type: Census Designated Place
County: Gloucester
Population: 11,812

Ancestry/Race	Number	%

Notes: 1. Figures in the "Number" column do not add up to the total population due to: a) Ancestry/Race overlap — e.g. persons can report being both White and Irish, b) persons of Hispanic origin can report being any race, c) persons reporting two ancestries are counted in both categories. 2. Numbers in parentheses indicate the number of persons reporting this ancestry/race alone, not in combination with any other ancestry/race. 3. Refer to the Explanation of Data in the front of the book for more detailed information.

African American/Black:	1,321	11.18
Not Hispanic (1,193)	1,285	10.88
Hispanic (30)	36	0.30
African, sub-Saharan:	25	0.21
African	25	0.21
Alaska Native tribes, specified:	1	0.01
Tlingit-Haida (1)	1	0.01
Am. Ind. or Alaska Nat., not spec.	20	0.17
American Indian tribes, specified:	47	0.40
Apache (1)	1	0.01
Blackfeet (1)	2	0.02
Cherokee (5)	12	0.10
Creek (1)	1	0.01
Crow (1)	1	0.01
Delaware (2)	2	0.02
Lumbee (5)	5	0.04
Navajo	1	0.01
Pueblo	1	0.01
Seminole	4	0.03
Sioux	11	0.09
All other tribes (6)	6	0.05
American Indian tribes, not spec.	11	0.09
Arab:	74	0.63
Arab/Arabic	13	0.11
Egyptian	34	0.29
Lebanese	27	0.23
Armenian	6	0.05
Asian:	158	1.34
Cambodian (4)	4	0.03
Chinese, ex. Taiwanese (21)	29	0.25
Filipino (27)	47	0.40
Indian (25)	29	0.25
Japanese (11)	15	0.13
Korean (13)	16	0.14
Pakistani	1	0.01
Thai (1)	3	0.03
Vietnamese (2)	2	0.02
Other Asian, specified (1)	1	0.01
Other Asian, not specified (8)	11	0.09
Austrian	21	0.18
British	15	0.13
Danish	9	0.08
Dutch	79	0.67
Eastern European	14	0.12
English	1,209	10.24
European	8	0.07
French, except Basque	237	2.01
French Canadian	27	0.23
German	2,923	24.75
Greek	16	0.14
Hawaii Native/Pacific Islander:	8	0.07
Polynesian: (5)	5	0.04
Samoan (5)	5	0.04
Other Pac. Isl., not spec. (2)	3	0.03
Hispanic or Latino:	339	2.87
Central American:	2	0.02
Guatemalan	1	0.01
Panamanian	1	0.01
Cuban	10	0.08
Dominican Republic	2	0.02
Mexican	37	0.31
Puerto Rican	202	1.71
South American:	25	0.21
Colombian	11	0.09
Ecuadorian	8	0.07
Peruvian	1	0.01
Other South American	5	0.04
Other Hispanic or Latino	61	0.52
Hungarian	15	0.13
Irish	2,836	24.01
Italian	2,966	25.11
Lithuanian	65	0.55
Norwegian	103	0.87
Pennsylvania German	36	0.30
Polish	1,046	8.86
Russian	43	0.36
Scandinavian	10	0.08
Scotch-Irish	122	1.03
Scottish	147	1.24
Serbian	12	0.10
Slavic	8	0.07
Slovak	30	0.25
Swedish	87	0.74
Ukrainian	29	0.25
United States or American	458	3.88
Welsh	67	0.57
West Indian, excl. Hispanic:	32	0.27
Jamaican	32	0.27
White:	10,290	87.11
Not Hispanic (9,954)	10,100	85.51
Hispanic (166)	190	1.61
Yugoslavian	17	0.14

Willingboro

Place Type: Township
County: Burlington
Population: 33,008

Ancestry/Race	Number	%
African American/Black:	23,069	69.89
Not Hispanic (21,616)	22,507	68.19
Hispanic (405)	562	1.70
African, sub-Saharan:	604	1.83
African	417	1.26
Cape Verdean	9	0.03
Ghanian	44	0.13
Kenyan	21	0.06
Liberian	48	0.15
Nigerian	60	0.18
Sierra Leonean	5	0.02
Am. Ind. or Alaska Nat., not spec.	156	0.47
American Indian tribes, specified:	274	0.83
Apache (4)	6	0.02
Blackfeet (5)	41	0.12
Cherokee (21)	122	0.37
Chippewa (8)	8	0.02
Choctaw (1)	4	0.01
Creek	7	0.02
Delaware (1)	2	0.01
Iroquois (3)	20	0.06
Kiowa	2	0.01
Latin American Indians (2)	9	0.03
Osage	3	0.01
Potawatomi	5	0.02
Seminole (1)	5	0.02
Shoshone	2	0.01
Sioux (4)	7	0.02
All other tribes (14)	31	0.09
American Indian tribes, not spec.	14	0.04
Arab:	36	0.11
Egyptian	36	0.11
Armenian	26	0.08
Asian:	803	2.43
Bangladeshi (1)	1	0.00
Cambodian (6)	6	0.02
Chinese, ex. Taiwanese (34)	57	0.17
Filipino (76)	126	0.38
Indian (146)	188	0.57
Indonesian (1)	6	0.02
Japanese (59)	96	0.29
Korean (51)	74	0.22
Pakistani (53)	79	0.24
Thai (10)	14	0.04
Vietnamese (93)	104	0.32
Other Asian, specified (12)	17	0.05
Other Asian, not specified (15)	35	0.11
Australian	15	0.05
Austrian	52	0.16
Belgian	3	0.01
British	71	0.22
Canadian	23	0.07
Celtic	17	0.05
Croatian	9	0.03
Czech	30	0.09
Czechoslovakian	29	0.09
Danish	6	0.02
Dutch	161	0.49
English	1,279	3.87
Estonian	8	0.02
European	50	0.15
Finnish	8	0.02
French, except Basque	394	1.19
French Canadian	63	0.19
German	2,286	6.93
German Russian	25	0.08
Greek	25	0.08
Guyanese	89	0.27
Hawaii Native/Pacific Islander:	65	0.20
Micronesian: (2)	3	0.01
Guamanian/Chamorro (2)	3	0.01
Polynesian: (5)	11	0.03
Native Hawaiian (4)	10	0.03
Samoan (1)	1	0.00
Other Pac. Isl., not spec. (5)	51	0.15
Hispanic or Latino:	1,998	6.05
Central American:	128	0.39
Costa Rican	3	0.01
Guatemalan	2	0.01
Honduran	28	0.08
Nicaraguan	8	0.02
Panamanian	76	0.23
Salvadoran	5	0.02
Other Central American	6	0.02
Cuban	46	0.14
Dominican Republic	60	0.18
Mexican	103	0.31
Puerto Rican	1,273	3.86
South American:	70	0.21
Argentinean	1	0.00
Chilean	3	0.01
Colombian	31	0.09
Ecuadorian	3	0.01
Peruvian	24	0.07
Venezuelan	1	0.00
Other South American	7	0.02
Other Hispanic or Latino	318	0.96
Hungarian	127	0.38
Irish	1,972	5.97
Italian	1,154	3.50
Latvian	14	0.04
Lithuanian	52	0.16
Northern European	17	0.05
Norwegian	46	0.14
Pennsylvania German	17	0.05
Polish	624	1.89
Portuguese	28	0.08
Romanian	19	0.06
Russian	251	0.76
Scotch-Irish	216	0.65
Scottish	200	0.61
Slavic	12	0.04
Slovak	92	0.28
Slovene	6	0.02
Swedish	68	0.21
Swiss	14	0.04
Ukrainian	78	0.24
United States or American	603	1.83
Welsh	170	0.52
West Indian, excl. Hispanic:	1,357	4.11
Barbadian	65	0.20
Bermudan	22	0.07
British West Indian	20	0.06
Haitian	288	0.87
Jamaican	611	1.85
Trinidadian and Tobagonian	123	0.37
West Indian	228	0.69
White:	8,886	26.92
Not Hispanic (7,560)	8,169	24.75
Hispanic (584)	717	2.17

Winslow

Place Type: Township
County: Camden
Population: 34,611

Ancestry/Race	Number	%
African American/Black:	10,522	30.40
Not Hispanic (9,968)	10,274	29.68

Notes: 1. Figures in the "Number" column do not add up to the total population due to: a) Ancestry/Race overlap — e.g. persons can report being both White and Irish, b) persons of Hispanic origin can report being any race, c) persons reporting two ancestries are counted in both categories. 2. Numbers in parentheses indicate the number of persons reporting this ancestry/race alone, not in combination with any other ancestry/race. 3. Refer to the Explanation of Data in the front of the book for more detailed information.

Hispanic (186)	248	0.72
African, sub-Saharan:	602	1.74
African	477	1.38
Ethiopian	40	0.12
Nigerian	67	0.19
Other sub-Saharan African	18	0.05
Alaska Native tribes, not specified	1	0.00
Am. Ind. or Alaska Nat., not spec.	110	0.32
Albanian	30	0.09
American Indian tribes, specified:	168	0.49
Apache	3	0.01
Blackfeet (10)	31	0.09
Cherokee (11)	45	0.13
Chippewa (2)	5	0.01
Comanche	2	0.01
Creek (2)	6	0.02
Crow (2)	2	0.01
Delaware (3)	7	0.02
Iroquois	11	0.03
Latin American Indians (4)	10	0.03
Lumbee (3)	3	0.01
Navajo	2	0.01
Ottawa	2	0.01
Paiute	1	0.00
Seminole (2)	3	0.01
Sioux	3	0.01
All other tribes (9)	32	0.09
American Indian tribes, not spec.	15	0.04
Arab:	185	0.53
Arab/Arabic	28	0.08
Egyptian	40	0.12
Lebanese	85	0.25
Moroccan	32	0.09
Armenian	67	0.19
Asian:	566	1.64
Chinese, ex. Taiwanese (81)	94	0.27
Filipino (167)	209	0.60
Indian (85)	104	0.30
Japanese (12)	24	0.07
Korean (59)	71	0.21
Laotian	1	0.00
Pakistani (6)	8	0.02
Taiwanese (5)	5	0.01
Thai	2	0.01
Vietnamese (19)	21	0.06
Other Asian, specified (6)	14	0.04
Other Asian, not specified (5)	13	0.04
Austrian	81	0.23
Belgian	32	0.09
British	33	0.10
Canadian	86	0.25
Croatian	12	0.03
Czech	68	0.20
Czechoslovakian	52	0.15
Danish	82	0.24
Dutch	383	1.11
English	2,305	6.65
European	104	0.30
Finnish	6	0.02
French, except Basque	883	2.55
French Canadian	163	0.47
German	5,985	17.27
German Russian	6	0.02
Greek	100	0.29
Hawaii Native/Pacific Islander:	29	0.08
Micronesian: (4)	8	0.02
Guamanian/Chamorro (4)	8	0.02
Polynesian: (4)	12	0.03
Native Hawaiian (1)	4	0.01
Samoan (3)	8	0.02
Other Pac. Isl., not spec. (2)	9	0.03
Hispanic or Latino:	1,492	4.31
Central American:	50	0.14
Costa Rican	7	0.02
Guatemalan	3	0.01
Honduran	5	0.01
Nicaraguan	8	0.02
Panamanian	17	0.05
Salvadoran	6	0.02
Other Central American	4	0.01
Cuban	38	0.11
Dominican Republic	14	0.04
Mexican	217	0.63
Puerto Rican	958	2.77
South American:	36	0.10
Argentinean	4	0.01
Chilean	5	0.01
Colombian	12	0.03
Ecuadorian	2	0.01
Peruvian	5	0.01
Venezuelan	7	0.02
Other South American	1	0.00
Other Hispanic or Latino	179	0.52
Hungarian	116	0.33
Irish	6,790	19.59
Italian	6,960	20.08
Lithuanian	106	0.31
Norwegian	151	0.44
Pennsylvania German	69	0.20
Polish	2,029	5.85
Portuguese	41	0.12
Romanian	55	0.16
Russian	195	0.56
Scotch-Irish	302	0.87
Scottish	322	0.93
Slavic	11	0.03
Slovak	37	0.11
Swedish	213	0.61
Swiss	75	0.22
Ukrainian	272	0.78
United States or American	780	2.25
Welsh	196	0.57
West Indian, excl. Hispanic:	165	0.48
Haitian	43	0.12
Jamaican	122	0.35
White:	23,173	66.95
Not Hispanic (22,044)	22,451	64.87
Hispanic (626)	722	2.09
Yugoslavian	22	0.06

Woodbridge

Place Type: Township
County: Middlesex
Population: 97,203

Ancestry/Race	Number	%
Afghan	64	0.07
African American/Black:	9,070	9.33
Not Hispanic (8,154)	8,555	8.80
Hispanic (353)	515	0.53
African, sub-Saharan:	1,183	1.22
African	597	0.61
Ethiopian	23	0.02
Ghanian	134	0.14
Kenyan	6	0.01
Liberian	30	0.03
Nigerian	292	0.30
Sudanese	39	0.04
Ugandan	20	0.02
Other sub-Saharan African	42	0.04
Alaska Native tribes, specified:	3	0.00
Aleut (2)	2	0.00
Eskimo	1	0.00
Am. Ind. or Alaska Nat., not spec.	282	0.29
Albanian	36	0.04
Alsatian	8	0.01
American Indian tribes, specified:	191	0.20
Apache (3)	9	0.01
Blackfeet (1)	9	0.01
Cherokee (8)	64	0.07
Cheyenne (1)	1	0.00
Choctaw (2)	5	0.01
Comanche	1	0.00
Crow	1	0.00
Delaware (3)	6	0.01
Iroquois (4)	14	0.01
Latin American Indians (24)	43	0.04
Pueblo (1)	3	0.00
Seminole (1)	3	0.00
Sioux (1)	8	0.01
All other tribes (12)	24	0.02
American Indian tribes, not spec.	38	0.04
Arab:	1,027	1.06
Arab/Arabic	185	0.19
Egyptian	562	0.58
Jordanian	44	0.05
Lebanese	97	0.10
Moroccan	16	0.02
Palestinian	51	0.05
Syrian	37	0.04
Other Arab	35	0.04
Armenian	40	0.04
Asian:	15,042	15.47
Bangladeshi (40)	50	0.05
Cambodian (2)	2	0.00
Chinese, ex. Taiwanese (1,327)	1,442	1.48
Filipino (2,126)	2,284	2.35
Indian (8,592)	8,937	9.19
Indonesian (117)	154	0.16
Japanese (39)	58	0.06
Korean (670)	702	0.72
Laotian (1)	2	0.00
Malaysian (4)	5	0.01
Pakistani (619)	755	0.78
Sri Lankan (47)	55	0.06
Taiwanese (28)	40	0.04
Thai (9)	15	0.02
Vietnamese (248)	263	0.27
Other Asian, specified (3)	13	0.01
Other Asian, not specified (70)	265	0.27
Assyrian/Chaldean/Syriac	5	0.01
Australian	16	0.02
Austrian	280	0.29
Belgian	61	0.06
Brazilian	67	0.07
British	146	0.15
Bulgarian	28	0.03
Canadian	142	0.15
Carpatho Rusyn	33	0.03
Celtic	13	0.01
Croatian	69	0.07
Czech	465	0.48
Czechoslovakian	399	0.41
Danish	560	0.58
Dutch	652	0.67
Eastern European	52	0.05
English	3,410	3.51
European	108	0.11
Finnish	60	0.06
French, except Basque	978	1.01
French Canadian	197	0.20
German	10,547	10.85
Greek	536	0.55
Guyanese	206	0.21
Hawaii Native/Pacific Islander:	112	0.12
Micronesian: (4)	12	0.01
Guamanian/Chamorro (4)	7	0.01
Other Micronesian	5	0.01
Polynesian: (11)	29	0.03
Native Hawaiian (4)	15	0.02
Samoan (7)	13	0.01
Tongan	1	0.00
Other Pac. Isl., specified	10	0.01
Other Pac. Isl., not spec. (8)	61	0.06
Hispanic or Latino:	8,956	9.21
Central American:	355	0.37
Costa Rican	97	0.10
Guatemalan	73	0.08
Honduran	61	0.06
Nicaraguan	9	0.01
Panamanian	36	0.04
Salvadoran	72	0.07
Other Central American	7	0.01
Cuban	680	0.70
Dominican Republic	679	0.70
Mexican	390	0.40
Puerto Rican	3,838	3.95
South American:	1,390	1.43
Argentinean	105	0.11

Notes: 1. Figures in the "Number" column do not add up to the total population due to: a) Ancestry/Race overlap — e.g. persons can report being both White and Irish, b) persons of Hispanic origin can report being any race, c) persons reporting two ancestries are counted in both categories. 2. Numbers in parentheses indicate the number of persons reporting this ancestry/race alone, not in combination with any other ancestry/race. 3. Refer to the Explanation of Data in the front of the book for more detailed information.

Ancestry/Race	Number	%
Bolivian	1	0.00
Chilean	36	0.04
Colombian	434	0.45
Ecuadorian	158	0.16
Paraguayan	8	0.01
Peruvian	508	0.52
Uruguayan	60	0.06
Venezuelan	27	0.03
Other South American	53	0.05
Other Hispanic or Latino	1,624	1.67
Hungarian	5,000	5.14
Iranian	33	0.03
Irish	16,323	16.79
Israeli	101	0.10
Italian	17,734	18.24
Latvian	25	0.03
Lithuanian	738	0.76
Maltese	20	0.02
Northern European	5	0.01
Norwegian	618	0.64
Pennsylvania German	32	0.03
Polish	10,694	11.00
Portuguese	1,369	1.41
Romanian	189	0.19
Russian	2,101	2.16
Scandinavian	81	0.08
Scotch-Irish	884	0.91
Scottish	883	0.91
Slavic	234	0.24
Slovak	1,833	1.89
Slovene	38	0.04
Swedish	479	0.49
Swiss	112	0.12
Turkish	91	0.09
Ukrainian	1,848	1.90
United States or American	2,172	2.23
Welsh	378	0.39
West Indian, excl. Hispanic:	1,177	1.21
Bahamian	19	0.02
Barbadian	35	0.04
Belizean	22	0.02
Bermudan	6	0.01
British West Indian	51	0.05
Haitian	196	0.20
Jamaican	455	0.47
Trinidadian and Tobagonian	252	0.26
U.S. Virgin Islander	11	0.01
West Indian	130	0.13
White:	70,514	72.54
Not Hispanic (63,999)	65,106	66.98
Hispanic (4,849)	5,408	5.56
Yugoslavian	131	0.13

Woodbury

Place Type: City
County: Gloucester
Population: 10,307

Ancestry/Race	Number	%
African American/Black:	2,510	24.35
Not Hispanic (2,283)	2,429	23.57
Hispanic (70)	81	0.79
African, sub-Saharan:	87	0.84
African	62	0.60
Nigerian	5	0.05
Sierra Leonean	20	0.19
Am. Ind. or Alaska Nat., not spec.	34	0.33
Alsatian	6	0.06
American Indian tribes, specified:	26	0.25
Apache (1)	1	0.01
Blackfeet	4	0.04
Cherokee (2)	8	0.08
Choctaw	2	0.02
Latin American Indians	1	0.01
Navajo (1)	1	0.01
Pueblo (1)	2	0.02
Sioux	2	0.02
All other tribes (5)	5	0.05
American Indian tribes, not spec.	3	0.03
Arab:	9	0.09
Syrian	9	0.09
Armenian	9	0.09
Asian:	126	1.22
Chinese, ex. Taiwanese (43)	44	0.43
Filipino (22)	30	0.29
Indian (18)	18	0.17
Japanese (7)	16	0.16
Korean (7)	8	0.08
Vietnamese (4)	8	0.08
Other Asian, not specified	2	0.02
Austrian	29	0.28
Belgian	13	0.13
British	25	0.24
Canadian	12	0.12
Czech	16	0.16
Czechoslovakian	6	0.06
Danish	23	0.22
Dutch	81	0.79
Eastern European	11	0.11
English	1,197	11.61
European	4	0.04
Finnish	11	0.11
French, except Basque	270	2.62
French Canadian	18	0.17
German	2,074	20.12
Greek	53	0.51
Hawaii Native/Pacific Islander:	22	0.21
Micronesian: (5)	8	0.08
Guamanian/Chamorro (5)	8	0.08
Polynesian: (6)	11	0.11
Native Hawaiian (3)	7	0.07
Samoan (3)	4	0.04
Other Pac. Isl., not spec. (3)	3	0.03
Hispanic or Latino:	406	3.94
Central American:	45	0.44
Guatemalan	39	0.38
Honduran	1	0.01
Nicaraguan	1	0.01
Panamanian	2	0.02
Salvadoran	1	0.01
Other Central American	1	0.01
Cuban	17	0.16
Dominican Republic	1	0.01
Mexican	28	0.27
Puerto Rican	235	2.28
South American:	15	0.15
Argentinean	5	0.05
Chilean	4	0.04
Colombian	4	0.04
Ecuadorian	1	0.01
Venezuelan	1	0.01
Other Hispanic or Latino	65	0.63
Hungarian	60	0.58
Irish	2,143	20.79
Italian	1,421	13.79
Lithuanian	71	0.69
Macedonian	21	0.20
Norwegian	18	0.17
Pennsylvania German	7	0.07
Polish	442	4.29
Romanian	6	0.06
Russian	96	0.93
Scotch-Irish	234	2.27
Scottish	199	1.93
Slavic	19	0.18
Slovak	23	0.22
Swedish	143	1.39
Swiss	13	0.13
Ukrainian	27	0.26
United States or American	478	4.64
Welsh	167	1.62
West Indian, excl. Hispanic:	28	0.27
Jamaican	28	0.27
White:	7,644	74.16
Not Hispanic (7,290)	7,448	72.26
Hispanic (177)	196	1.90
Yugoslavian	15	0.15

Wyckoff

Place Type: Census Designated Place
County: Bergen
Population: 16,508

Ancestry/Race	Number	%
Afghan	11	0.07
African American/Black:	94	0.57
Not Hispanic (73)	89	0.54
Hispanic (4)	5	0.03
Alaska Native tribes, specified:	6	0.04
Alaska Athabascan (5)	5	0.03
Eskimo (1)	1	0.01
Am. Ind. or Alaska Nat., not spec.	11	0.07
Albanian	60	0.36
Alsatian	37	0.22
American Indian tribes, specified:	14	0.08
Cherokee	1	0.01
Choctaw (2)	2	0.01
Latin American Indians (2)	6	0.04
Paiute	1	0.01
All other tribes (4)	4	0.02
American Indian tribes, not spec.	7	0.04
Arab:	177	1.07
Arab/Arabic	13	0.08
Egyptian	50	0.30
Lebanese	32	0.19
Syrian	82	0.50
Armenian	196	1.19
Asian:	676	4.09
Chinese, ex. Taiwanese (125)	152	0.92
Filipino (36)	48	0.29
Indian (63)	70	0.42
Indonesian (1)	3	0.02
Japanese (99)	113	0.68
Korean (261)	269	1.63
Taiwanese (2)	7	0.04
Thai (4)	4	0.02
Vietnamese (2)	2	0.01
Other Asian, not specified (6)	8	0.05
Assyrian/Chaldean/Syriac	37	0.22
Austrian	200	1.21
Belgian	12	0.07
British	80	0.48
Canadian	32	0.19
Celtic	4	0.02
Croatian	120	0.73
Czech	61	0.37
Czechoslovakian	50	0.30
Danish	41	0.25
Dutch	1,374	8.32
Eastern European	123	0.75
English	1,709	10.35
Estonian	26	0.16
European	129	0.78
Finnish	22	0.13
French, except Basque	201	1.22
French Canadian	23	0.14
German	2,273	13.77
Greek	165	1.00
Hawaii Native/Pacific Islander:	6	0.04
Micronesian: (1)	1	0.01
Guamanian/Chamorro (1)	1	0.01
Other Pac. Isl., not spec. (1)	5	0.03
Hispanic or Latino:	376	2.28
Central American:	4	0.02
Guatemalan	1	0.01
Honduran	2	0.01
Salvadoran	1	0.01
Cuban	62	0.38
Dominican Republic	20	0.12
Mexican	19	0.12
Puerto Rican	94	0.57
South American:	72	0.44
Argentinean	2	0.01
Bolivian	1	0.01
Chilean	3	0.02
Colombian	38	0.23
Ecuadorian	8	0.05

Notes: 1. Figures in the "Number" column do not add up to the total population due to: a) Ancestry/Race overlap — e.g. persons can report being both White and Irish, b) persons of Hispanic origin can report being any race, c) persons reporting two ancestries are counted in both categories. 2. Numbers in parentheses indicate the number of persons reporting this ancestry/race alone, not in combination with any other ancestry/race. 3. Refer to the Explanation of Data in the front of the book for more detailed information.

Paraguayan	1	0.01
Peruvian	15	0.09
Venezuelan	1	0.01
Other South American	3	0.02
Other Hispanic or Latino	105	0.64
Hungarian	243	1.47
Irish	3,985	24.14
Israeli	13	0.08
Italian	3,782	22.91
Latvian	18	0.11
Lithuanian	85	0.51
New Zealander	7	0.04
Norwegian	237	1.44
Polish	1,118	6.77
Portuguese	35	0.21
Romanian	72	0.44
Russian	577	3.50
Scandinavian	29	0.18
Scotch-Irish	241	1.46
Scottish	229	1.39
Serbian	6	0.04
Slavic	13	0.08
Slovak	77	0.47
Swedish	182	1.10
Swiss	145	0.88
Turkish	51	0.31
Ukrainian	245	1.48
United States or American	659	3.99
Welsh	87	0.53
West Indian, excl. Hispanic:	4	0.02
Jamaican	4	0.02
White:	15,712	95.18
Not Hispanic (15,312)	15,409	93.34
Hispanic (295)	303	1.84

Alamogordo

Place Type: City
County: Otero
Population: 35,582

Ancestry/Race	Number	%
Acadian/Cajun	17	0.05
African American/Black:	2,291	6.44
Not Hispanic (1,882)	2,116	5.95
Hispanic (103)	175	0.49
African, sub-Saharan:	86	0.24
African	86	0.24
Alaska Native tribes, specified:	12	0.03
Aleut (1)	6	0.02
Eskimo (5)	5	0.01
Tlingit-Haida	1	0.00
Alaska Native tribes, not specified	3	0.01
Am. Ind. or Alaska Nat., not spec.	149	0.42
American Indian tribes, specified:	459	1.29
Apache (65)	86	0.24
Blackfeet (2)	8	0.02
Cherokee (39)	116	0.33
Cheyenne (1)	2	0.01
Chickasaw (3)	11	0.03
Chippewa (5)	6	0.02
Choctaw (11)	24	0.07
Comanche (1)	6	0.02
Creek	1	0.00
Iroquois (6)	8	0.02
Kiowa	3	0.01
Latin American Indians (13)	24	0.07
Menominee (1)	1	0.00
Navajo (35)	48	0.13
Ottawa (2)	2	0.01
Pima (2)	3	0.01
Potawatomi (3)	5	0.01
Pueblo (31)	39	0.11
Puget Sound Salish	1	0.00
Seminole (1)	2	0.01
Shoshone (2)	2	0.01
Sioux (14)	20	0.06
Yaqui (2)	3	0.01
All other tribes (21)	38	0.11
American Indian tribes, not spec.	32	0.09
Arab:	16	0.05
Lebanese	16	0.05
Armenian	8	0.02
Asian:	859	2.41
Cambodian (1)	1	0.00
Chinese, ex. Taiwanese (42)	62	0.17
Filipino (207)	331	0.93
Indian (36)	41	0.12
Indonesian (1)	2	0.01
Japanese (74)	130	0.37
Korean (81)	130	0.37
Laotian (1)	1	0.00
Taiwanese (11)	13	0.04
Thai (46)	73	0.21
Vietnamese (16)	20	0.06
Other Asian, specified	3	0.01
Other Asian, not specified (24)	52	0.15
Austrian	102	0.29
Belgian	35	0.10
British	216	0.61
Bulgarian	14	0.04
Canadian	154	0.44
Croatian	7	0.02
Czech	55	0.16
Czechoslovakian	78	0.22
Danish	227	0.64
Dutch	420	1.19
English	2,835	8.01
European	235	0.66
Finnish	43	0.12
French, except Basque	814	2.30
French Canadian	309	0.87
German	5,705	16.12
Greek	60	0.17
Hawaii Native/Pacific Islander:	118	0.33
Micronesian: (23)	29	0.08
Guamanian/Chamorro (23)	28	0.08
Other Micronesian	1	0.00
Polynesian: (31)	65	0.18
Native Hawaiian (20)	39	0.11
Samoan (9)	18	0.05
Tongan	1	0.00
Other Polynesian (2)	7	0.02
Other Pac. Isl., specified	2	0.01
Other Pac. Isl., not spec. (5)	22	0.06
Hispanic or Latino:	11,383	31.99
Central American:	48	0.13
Costa Rican	4	0.01
Guatemalan	3	0.01
Honduran	11	0.03
Nicaraguan	1	0.00
Panamanian	24	0.07
Salvadoran	4	0.01
Other Central American	1	0.00
Cuban	25	0.07
Dominican Republic	4	0.01
Mexican	7,908	22.22
Puerto Rican	261	0.73
South American:	41	0.12
Chilean	5	0.01
Colombian	21	0.06
Ecuadorian	4	0.01
Peruvian	9	0.03
Other South American	2	0.01
Other Hispanic or Latino	3,096	8.70
Hungarian	84	0.24
Irish	3,154	8.91
Italian	985	2.78
Lithuanian	54	0.15
Maltese	10	0.03
Northern European	23	0.06
Norwegian	326	0.92
Polish	455	1.29
Portuguese	27	0.08
Russian	66	0.19
Scandinavian	48	0.14
Scotch-Irish	543	1.53
Scottish	501	1.42
Slavic	11	0.03
Slovak	54	0.15
Slovene	18	0.05
Swedish	423	1.20
Swiss	66	0.19
Turkish	20	0.06
Ukrainian	97	0.27
United States or American	2,549	7.20
Welsh	93	0.26
West Indian, excl. Hispanic:	46	0.13
Dutch West Indian	4	0.01
Haitian	8	0.02
Jamaican	34	0.10
White:	28,162	79.15
Not Hispanic (20,570)	21,343	59.98
Hispanic (6,242)	6,819	19.16
Yugoslavian	36	0.10

Albuquerque

Place Type: City
County: Bernalillo
Population: 448,607

Ancestry/Race	Number	%
Acadian/Cajun	60	0.01
Afghan	82	0.02
African American/Black:	16,938	3.78
Not Hispanic (12,376)	14,343	3.20
Hispanic (1,478)	2,595	0.58
African, sub-Saharan:	1,188	0.26
African	1,003	0.22
Cape Verdean	11	0.00
Ethiopian	12	0.00
Ghanian	6	0.00
Kenyan	6	0.00
Nigerian	31	0.01
South African	36	0.01
Sudanese	5	0.00
Zimbabwean	10	0.00
Other sub-Saharan African	68	0.02
Alaska Native tribes, specified:	114	0.03
Alaska Athabascan (17)	38	0.01
Aleut (15)	18	0.00
Eskimo (17)	36	0.01
Tlingit-Haida (13)	17	0.00
All other tribes (2)	5	0.00
Alaska Native tribes, not specified	35	0.01
Am. Ind. or Alaska Nat., not spec.	3,056	0.68
Albanian	6	0.00
Alsatian	37	0.01
American Indian tribes, specified:	18,309	4.08
Apache (501)	810	0.18
Blackfeet (55)	114	0.03
Cherokee (352)	1,105	0.25
Cheyenne (46)	77	0.02
Chickasaw (41)	102	0.02
Chippewa (136)	222	0.05
Choctaw (138)	323	0.07
Colville (11)	13	0.00
Comanche (97)	146	0.03
Cree (9)	21	0.00
Creek (65)	128	0.03
Crow (27)	45	0.01
Delaware (32)	52	0.01
Iroquois (87)	170	0.04
Kiowa (64)	85	0.02
Latin American Indians (291)	477	0.11
Lumbee (14)	23	0.01
Menominee (7)	9	0.00
Navajo (6,958)	7,889	1.76
Osage (26)	50	0.01
Ottawa (13)	18	0.00
Paiute (10)	18	0.00
Pima (23)	45	0.01
Potawatomi (24)	49	0.01
Pueblo (3,855)	4,695	1.05
Puget Sound Salish (6)	9	0.00
Seminole (27)	73	0.02
Shoshone (32)	59	0.01
Sioux (389)	577	0.13
Tohono O'Odham (15)	17	0.00

Notes: 1. Figures in the "Number" column do not add up to the total population due to: a) Ancestry/Race overlap — e.g. persons can report being both White and Irish, b) persons of Hispanic origin can report being any race, c) persons reporting two ancestries are counted in both categories. 2. Numbers in parentheses indicate the number of persons reporting this ancestry/race alone, not in combination with any other ancestry/race. 3. Refer to the Explanation of Data in the front of the book for more detailed information.

Ute (75)	87	0.02
Yakama (4)	4	0.00
Yaqui (19)	40	0.01
Yuman (40)	47	0.01
All other tribes (456)	710	0.16
American Indian tribes, not spec.	1,151	0.26
Arab:	1,838	0.41
Arab/Arabic	394	0.09
Egyptian	137	0.03
Iraqi	59	0.01
Jordanian	71	0.02
Lebanese	893	0.20
Moroccan	56	0.01
Palestinian	75	0.02
Syrian	70	0.02
Other Arab	83	0.02
Armenian	198	0.04
Asian:	13,290	2.96
Bangladeshi (26)	34	0.01
Cambodian (28)	39	0.01
Chinese, ex. Taiwanese (1,868)	2,414	0.54
Filipino (1,050)	1,730	0.39
Hmong (9)	12	0.00
Indian (1,421)	1,679	0.37
Indonesian (19)	38	0.01
Japanese (835)	1,593	0.36
Korean (825)	1,125	0.25
Laotian (275)	344	0.08
Malaysian (4)	10	0.00
Pakistani (111)	167	0.04
Sri Lankan (32)	35	0.01
Taiwanese (78)	111	0.02
Thai (155)	248	0.06
Vietnamese (2,829)	3,058	0.68
Other Asian, specified (28)	70	0.02
Other Asian, not specified (220)	583	0.13
Assyrian/Chaldean/Syriac	10	0.00
Australian	152	0.03
Austrian	953	0.21
Basque	205	0.05
Belgian	337	0.08
Brazilian	89	0.02
British	2,265	0.50
Bulgarian	103	0.02
Canadian	1,086	0.24
Carpatho Rusyn	26	0.01
Celtic	337	0.08
Croatian	412	0.09
Czech	1,801	0.40
Czechoslovakian	733	0.16
Danish	2,399	0.53
Dutch	5,833	1.30
Eastern European	470	0.10
English	40,280	8.98
Estonian	49	0.01
European	3,535	0.79
Finnish	740	0.16
French, except Basque	11,529	2.57
French Canadian	2,425	0.54
German	56,320	12.55
German Russian	16	0.00
Greek	1,679	0.37
Guyanese	47	0.01
Hawaii Native/Pacific Islander:	982	0.22
Micronesian: (137)	195	0.04
Guamanian/Chamorro (122)	177	0.04
Other Micronesian (15)	18	0.00
Polynesian: (238)	572	0.13
Native Hawaiian (160)	431	0.10
Samoan (63)	118	0.03
Tongan (8)	11	0.00
Other Polynesian (7)	12	0.00
Other Pac. Isl., specified	21	0.00
Other Pac. Isl., not spec. (73)	194	0.04
Hispanic or Latino:	179,075	39.92
Central American:	826	0.18
Costa Rican	54	0.01
Guatemalan	197	0.04
Honduran	76	0.02
Nicaraguan	86	0.02
Panamanian	141	0.03
Salvadoran	223	0.05
Other Central American	49	0.01
Cuban	1,694	0.38
Dominican Republic	50	0.01
Mexican	68,537	15.28
Puerto Rican	1,716	0.38
South American:	871	0.19
Argentinean	80	0.02
Bolivian	50	0.01
Chilean	133	0.03
Colombian	239	0.05
Ecuadorian	103	0.02
Paraguayan	6	0.00
Peruvian	141	0.03
Uruguayan	6	0.00
Venezuelan	52	0.01
Other South American	61	0.01
Other Hispanic or Latino	105,381	23.49
Hungarian	1,686	0.38
Icelander	91	0.02
Iranian	617	0.14
Irish	41,090	9.16
Israeli	153	0.03
Italian	16,721	3.73
Latvian	88	0.02
Lithuanian	663	0.15
Luxemburger	65	0.01
Macedonian	12	0.00
Maltese	50	0.01
New Zealander	18	0.00
Northern European	364	0.08
Norwegian	6,528	1.46
Pennsylvania German	94	0.02
Polish	7,468	1.66
Portuguese	624	0.14
Romanian	384	0.09
Russian	3,024	0.67
Scandinavian	873	0.19
Scotch-Irish	7,923	1.77
Scottish	9,761	2.18
Serbian	159	0.04
Slavic	230	0.05
Slovak	579	0.13
Slovene	198	0.04
Swedish	5,708	1.27
Swiss	1,320	0.29
Turkish	88	0.02
Ukrainian	714	0.16
United States or American	18,480	4.12
Welsh	3,728	0.83
West Indian, excl. Hispanic:	380	0.08
Barbadian	18	0.00
Belizean	9	0.00
Bermudan	6	0.00
Dutch West Indian	7	0.00
Haitian	39	0.01
Jamaican	202	0.05
Trinidadian and Tobagonian	33	0.01
West Indian	66	0.01
White:	337,780	75.30
Not Hispanic (223,895)	230,367	51.35
Hispanic (97,284)	107,413	23.94
Yugoslavian	413	0.09

Artesia

Place Type: City
County: Eddy
Population: 10,692

Ancestry/Race	Number	%
African American/Black:	192	1.80
Not Hispanic (129)	149	1.39
Hispanic (25)	43	0.40
Alaska Native tribes, specified:	3	0.03
Tlingit-Haida (3)	3	0.03
Am. Ind. or Alaska Nat., not spec.	62	0.58
American Indian tribes, specified:	149	1.39
Apache (2)	11	0.10
Blackfeet	3	0.03
Cherokee (16)	27	0.25
Chickasaw (1)	1	0.01
Chippewa (3)	3	0.03
Choctaw (5)	14	0.13
Comanche (3)	3	0.03
Creek (1)	1	0.01
Delaware (1)	1	0.01
Latin American Indians (5)	10	0.09
Navajo (27)	35	0.33
Osage	1	0.01
Pima (3)	3	0.03
Potawatomi	1	0.01
Pueblo (9)	10	0.09
Seminole (2)	2	0.02
Shoshone (1)	1	0.01
Sioux (1)	1	0.01
Tohono O'Odham (3)	3	0.03
Ute (3)	3	0.03
All other tribes (13)	15	0.14
American Indian tribes, not spec.	17	0.16
Arab:	26	0.24
Egyptian	11	0.10
Lebanese	15	0.14
Asian:	47	0.44
Chinese, ex. Taiwanese (3)	8	0.07
Filipino (6)	15	0.14
Indian (5)	7	0.07
Japanese (2)	6	0.06
Korean (1)	1	0.01
Pakistani (1)	2	0.02
Thai (1)	1	0.01
Vietnamese	1	0.01
Other Asian, not specified (2)	6	0.06
Austrian	6	0.05
Basque	9	0.08
British	16	0.15
Canadian	10	0.09
Danish	6	0.05
Dutch	190	1.74
English	861	7.88
European	36	0.33
Finnish	9	0.08
French, except Basque	54	0.49
French Canadian	52	0.48
German	602	5.51
Hawaii Native/Pacific Islander:	20	0.19
Polynesian: (11)	14	0.13
Native Hawaiian (2)	5	0.05
Samoan (9)	9	0.08
Other Pac. Isl., not spec. (5)	6	0.06
Hispanic or Latino:	4,809	44.98
Mexican	3,106	29.05
Puerto Rican	19	0.18
South American:	6	0.06
Colombian	6	0.06
Other Hispanic or Latino	1,678	15.69
Hungarian	12	0.11
Irish	671	6.14
Italian	59	0.54
Norwegian	35	0.32
Polish	9	0.08
Russian	16	0.15
Scandinavian	24	0.22
Scotch-Irish	111	1.02
Scottish	175	1.60
Swedish	54	0.49
Ukrainian	9	0.08
United States or American	797	7.29
Welsh	30	0.27
West Indian, excl. Hispanic:	8	0.07
Dutch West Indian	8	0.07
White:	7,984	74.67
Not Hispanic (5,533)	5,622	52.58
Hispanic (2,192)	2,362	22.09
Yugoslavian	6	0.05

Notes: 1. Figures in the "Number" column do not add up to the total population due to: a) Ancestry/Race overlap — e.g. persons can report being both White and Irish, b) persons of Hispanic origin can report being any race, c) persons reporting two ancestries are counted in both categories. 2. Numbers in parentheses indicate the number of persons reporting this ancestry/race alone, not in combination with any other ancestry/race. 3. Refer to the Explanation of Data in the front of the book for more detailed information.

Carlsbad

Place Type: City
County: Eddy
Population: 25,625

Ancestry/Race	Number	%
African American/Black:	657	2.56
Not Hispanic (488)	547	2.13
Hispanic (75)	110	0.43
African, sub-Saharan:	15	0.06
African	8	0.03
South African	7	0.03
Alaska Native tribes, specified:	2	0.01
Aleut	1	0.00
Eskimo	1	0.00
Am. Ind. or Alaska Nat., not spec.	171	0.67
American Indian tribes, specified:	274	1.07
Apache (29)	38	0.15
Blackfeet (1)	2	0.01
Cherokee (38)	74	0.29
Cheyenne (1)	1	0.00
Chickasaw (2)	7	0.03
Chippewa (3)	3	0.01
Choctaw (19)	30	0.12
Comanche	1	0.00
Creek (7)	9	0.04
Delaware	1	0.00
Iroquois (1)	1	0.00
Kiowa (1)	1	0.00
Latin American Indians (13)	15	0.06
Navajo (13)	21	0.08
Osage (3)	5	0.02
Ottawa (1)	2	0.01
Potawatomi (8)	8	0.03
Pueblo (23)	30	0.12
Shoshone (4)	4	0.02
Sioux (5)	5	0.02
Ute (1)	1	0.00
All other tribes (7)	15	0.06
American Indian tribes, not spec.	45	0.18
Arab:	15	0.06
Egyptian	7	0.03
Iraqi	8	0.03
Asian:	224	0.87
Chinese, ex. Taiwanese (30)	40	0.16
Filipino (22)	26	0.10
Indian (79)	82	0.32
Japanese (21)	34	0.13
Korean (9)	16	0.06
Malaysian (1)	3	0.01
Taiwanese (3)	3	0.01
Vietnamese (11)	12	0.05
Other Asian, specified (4)	5	0.02
Other Asian, not specified	3	0.01
Austrian	6	0.02
Basque	8	0.03
Belgian	34	0.13
British	107	0.41
Canadian	59	0.23
Croatian	6	0.02
Czech	29	0.11
Czechoslovakian	25	0.10
Danish	37	0.14
Dutch	451	1.74
English	2,504	9.65
European	206	0.79
Finnish	44	0.17
French, except Basque	590	2.27
French Canadian	75	0.29
German	2,705	10.43
Greek	37	0.14
Hawaii Native/Pacific Islander:	30	0.12
Micronesian: (7)	8	0.03
Guamanian/Chamorro (7)	8	0.03
Polynesian: (11)	16	0.06
Native Hawaiian (10)	14	0.05
Samoan	1	0.00
Tongan (1)	1	0.00
Other Pac. Isl., specified	1	0.00
Other Pac. Isl., not spec. (2)	5	0.02
Hispanic or Latino:	9,417	36.75
Central American:	13	0.05
Costa Rican	6	0.02
Guatemalan	3	0.01
Honduran	1	0.00
Salvadoran	3	0.01
Cuban	14	0.05
Mexican	5,057	19.73
Puerto Rican	46	0.18
South American:	14	0.05
Argentinean	2	0.01
Chilean	2	0.01
Colombian	1	0.00
Peruvian	7	0.03
Venezuelan	2	0.01
Other Hispanic or Latino	4,273	16.68
Hungarian	19	0.07
Irish	2,090	8.05
Italian	276	1.06
Lithuanian	30	0.12
New Zealander	8	0.03
Northern European	15	0.06
Norwegian	119	0.46
Pennsylvania German	14	0.05
Polish	143	0.55
Portuguese	26	0.10
Russian	23	0.09
Scandinavian	25	0.10
Scotch-Irish	517	1.99
Scottish	354	1.36
Slovak	4	0.02
Swedish	158	0.61
Swiss	64	0.25
Ukrainian	8	0.03
United States or American	2,228	8.59
Welsh	81	0.31
West Indian, excl. Hispanic:	24	0.09
Dutch West Indian	17	0.07
West Indian	7	0.03
White:	20,422	79.70
Not Hispanic (15,070)	15,318	59.78
Hispanic (4,764)	5,104	19.92
Yugoslavian	20	0.08

Clovis

Place Type: City
County: Curry
Population: 32,667

Ancestry/Race	Number	%
African American/Black:	2,708	8.29
Not Hispanic (2,270)	2,470	7.56
Hispanic (122)	238	0.73
African, sub-Saharan:	130	0.40
African	123	0.38
Nigerian	7	0.02
Alaska Native tribes, specified:	6	0.02
Alaska Athabascan	2	0.01
Aleut (1)	1	0.00
Tlingit-Haida (2)	2	0.01
Am. Ind. or Alaska Nat., not spec.	198	0.61
American Indian tribes, specified:	356	1.09
Apache (19)	24	0.07
Blackfeet (2)	7	0.02
Cherokee (28)	105	0.32
Chickasaw	2	0.01
Chippewa (1)	2	0.01
Choctaw (23)	41	0.13
Comanche (1)	2	0.01
Creek (6)	8	0.02
Crow	2	0.01
Delaware (1)	1	0.00
Houma (1)	1	0.00
Iroquois	2	0.01
Kiowa	1	0.00
Latin American Indians (13)	33	0.10
Navajo (30)	59	0.18
Osage (2)	3	0.01
Potawatomi (2)	3	0.01
Pueblo (6)	17	0.05
Seminole (4)	12	0.04
Sioux (4)	4	0.01
Ute (1)	1	0.00
Yaqui (1)	1	0.00
Yuman	1	0.00
All other tribes (16)	23	0.07
American Indian tribes, not spec.	49	0.15
Asian:	759	2.32
Chinese, ex. Taiwanese (143)	175	0.54
Filipino (110)	161	0.49
Indian (44)	62	0.19
Japanese (43)	88	0.27
Korean (37)	66	0.20
Laotian (52)	61	0.19
Pakistani (13)	14	0.04
Taiwanese (1)	4	0.01
Thai (27)	46	0.14
Vietnamese (21)	25	0.08
Other Asian, specified (7)	15	0.05
Other Asian, not specified (13)	42	0.13
Australian	15	0.05
British	105	0.32
Canadian	19	0.06
Celtic	6	0.02
Croatian	13	0.04
Czech	140	0.43
Czechoslovakian	14	0.04
Danish	59	0.18
Dutch	410	1.26
English	2,794	8.59
European	280	0.86
Finnish	5	0.02
French, except Basque	761	2.34
French Canadian	81	0.25
German	3,407	10.47
Greek	44	0.14
Hawaii Native/Pacific Islander:	79	0.24
Micronesian: (16)	24	0.07
Guamanian/Chamorro (16)	24	0.07
Polynesian: (18)	38	0.12
Native Hawaiian (14)	33	0.10
Samoan (4)	5	0.02
Other Pac. Isl., not spec. (6)	17	0.05
Hispanic or Latino:	10,924	33.44
Central American:	13	0.04
Honduran	3	0.01
Panamanian	7	0.02
Salvadoran	3	0.01
Cuban	13	0.04
Dominican Republic	1	0.00
Mexican	5,131	15.71
Puerto Rican	113	0.35
South American:	26	0.08
Argentinean	7	0.02
Chilean	3	0.01
Colombian	5	0.02
Ecuadorian	1	0.00
Peruvian	8	0.02
Venezuelan	1	0.00
Other South American	1	0.00
Other Hispanic or Latino	5,627	17.23
Hungarian	83	0.26
Irish	2,445	7.51
Italian	612	1.88
Lithuanian	10	0.03
Norwegian	348	1.07
Polish	239	0.73
Portuguese	26	0.08
Russian	59	0.18
Scandinavian	8	0.02
Scotch-Irish	420	1.29
Scottish	394	1.21
Serbian	6	0.02
Slavic	5	0.02
Slovak	6	0.02
Slovene	16	0.05
Swedish	261	0.80
Swiss	25	0.08

Notes: 1. Figures in the "Number" column do not add up to the total population due to: a) Ancestry/Race overlap — e.g. persons can report being both White and Irish, b) persons of Hispanic origin can report being any race, c) persons reporting two ancestries are counted in both categories. 2. Numbers in parentheses indicate the number of persons reporting this ancestry/race alone, not in combination with any other ancestry/race. 3. Refer to the Explanation of Data in the front of the book for more detailed information.

Ukrainian	19	0.06
United States or American	2,573	7.91
Welsh	206	0.63
West Indian, excl. Hispanic:	37	0.11
Dutch West Indian	33	0.10
West Indian	4	0.01
White:	24,261	74.27
Not Hispanic (18,176)	18,632	57.04
Hispanic (5,117)	5,629	17.23
Yugoslavian	38	0.12

Deming

Place Type: City
County: Luna
Population: 14,116

Ancestry/Race	Number	%
African American/Black:	205	1.45
Not Hispanic (148)	161	1.14
Hispanic (25)	44	0.31
Am. Ind. or Alaska Nat., not spec.	112	0.79
American Indian tribes, specified:	134	0.95
Apache (7)	11	0.08
Blackfeet (1)	1	0.01
Cherokee (7)	22	0.16
Chickasaw (3)	3	0.02
Choctaw (9)	10	0.07
Iroquois (2)	2	0.01
Latin American Indians (25)	32	0.23
Navajo (15)	26	0.18
Potawatomi	1	0.01
Pueblo (13)	18	0.13
Seminole	2	0.01
Tohono O'Odham (1)	1	0.01
Yaqui (1)	1	0.01
All other tribes (3)	4	0.03
American Indian tribes, not spec.	46	0.33
Arab:	8	0.06
Syrian	8	0.06
Asian:	94	0.67
Chinese, ex. Taiwanese (14)	18	0.13
Filipino (19)	22	0.16
Indian (22)	31	0.22
Japanese (3)	8	0.06
Korean (3)	3	0.02
Pakistani (4)	4	0.03
Thai (1)	1	0.01
Other Asian, not specified (2)	7	0.05
Australian	9	0.06
Austrian	24	0.17
Basque	7	0.05
Belgian	8	0.06
British	18	0.13
Croatian	6	0.04
Czechoslovakian	22	0.15
Danish	59	0.41
Dutch	159	1.12
English	629	4.42
European	14	0.10
Finnish	21	0.15
French, except Basque	211	1.48
French Canadian	69	0.48
German	1,043	7.33
Greek	6	0.04
Hawaii Native/Pacific Islander:	4	0.03
Polynesian: (1)	3	0.02
Native Hawaiian	1	0.01
Samoan (1)	2	0.01
Other Pac. Isl., not spec.	1	0.01
Hispanic or Latino:	9,116	64.58
Central American:	4	0.03
Costa Rican	1	0.01
Guatemalan	1	0.01
Panamanian	1	0.01
Salvadoran	1	0.01
Cuban	6	0.04
Mexican	6,659	47.17
Puerto Rican	16	0.11
South American:	11	0.08
Colombian	6	0.04
Ecuadorian	3	0.02
Peruvian	1	0.01
Venezuelan	1	0.01
Other Hispanic or Latino	2,420	17.14
Hungarian	26	0.18
Irish	866	6.08
Italian	164	1.15
Latvian	7	0.05
Norwegian	97	0.68
Pennsylvania German	7	0.05
Polish	123	0.86
Russian	17	0.12
Scotch-Irish	140	0.98
Scottish	112	0.79
Slovak	19	0.13
Swedish	15	0.11
Swiss	9	0.06
Ukrainian	8	0.06
United States or American	912	6.41
Welsh	22	0.15
West Indian, excl. Hispanic:	4	0.03
Jamaican	4	0.03
White:	10,222	72.41
Not Hispanic (4,578)	4,672	33.10
Hispanic (5,255)	5,550	39.32

Farmington

Place Type: City
County: San Juan
Population: 37,844

Ancestry/Race	Number	%
African American/Black:	484	1.28
Not Hispanic (287)	407	1.08
Hispanic (29)	77	0.20
African, sub-Saharan:	44	0.12
African	44	0.12
Alaska Native tribes, specified:	25	0.07
Alaska Athabascan (5)	9	0.02
Aleut (1)	1	0.00
Eskimo (12)	14	0.04
Tlingit-Haida (1)	1	0.00
Alaska Native tribes, not specified	4	0.01
Am. Ind. or Alaska Nat., not spec.	408	1.08
American Indian tribes, specified:	6,381	16.86
Apache (53)	65	0.17
Blackfeet (2)	6	0.02
Cherokee (47)	114	0.30
Cheyenne (3)	4	0.01
Chickasaw (3)	7	0.02
Chippewa (15)	22	0.06
Choctaw (14)	22	0.06
Colville	3	0.01
Comanche	18	0.05
Cree (1)	1	0.00
Creek (11)	18	0.05
Delaware (2)	2	0.01
Iroquois (4)	8	0.02
Kiowa (2)	11	0.03
Latin American Indians (3)	6	0.02
Lumbee (2)	2	0.01
Menominee	1	0.00
Navajo (5,399)	5,793	15.31
Osage (4)	5	0.01
Paiute (1)	3	0.01
Pima (3)	7	0.02
Pueblo (51)	97	0.26
Seminole	1	0.00
Shoshone (1)	2	0.01
Sioux (25)	62	0.16
Tohono O'Odham	1	0.00
Ute (26)	41	0.11
Yuman (2)	2	0.01
All other tribes (24)	57	0.15
American Indian tribes, not spec.	276	0.73
Arab:	128	0.34
Lebanese	128	0.34
Armenian	15	0.04
Asian:	329	0.87
Chinese, ex. Taiwanese (29)	52	0.14
Filipino (44)	74	0.20
Indian (43)	56	0.15
Indonesian (6)	6	0.02
Japanese (24)	61	0.16
Korean (25)	37	0.10
Malaysian (1)	2	0.01
Sri Lankan (1)	1	0.00
Taiwanese (4)	4	0.01
Thai (1)	1	0.00
Vietnamese (8)	12	0.03
Other Asian, specified	1	0.00
Other Asian, not specified (7)	22	0.06
Austrian	60	0.16
Basque	9	0.02
Belgian	29	0.08
British	270	0.72
Canadian	8	0.02
Celtic	15	0.04
Czech	128	0.34
Czechoslovakian	50	0.13
Danish	331	0.88
Dutch	599	1.59
English	4,098	10.90
European	274	0.73
Finnish	23	0.06
French, except Basque	805	2.14
French Canadian	162	0.43
German	4,733	12.58
Greek	32	0.09
Hawaii Native/Pacific Islander:	48	0.13
Micronesian: (4)	6	0.02
Guamanian/Chamorro (1)	3	0.01
Other Micronesian (3)	3	0.01
Polynesian: (15)	31	0.08
Native Hawaiian (8)	20	0.05
Samoan (6)	6	0.02
Tongan (1)	1	0.00
Other Polynesian	4	0.01
Other Pac. Isl., specified	1	0.00
Other Pac. Isl., not spec. (5)	10	0.03
Hispanic or Latino:	6,684	17.66
Central American:	8	0.02
Costa Rican	1	0.00
Guatemalan	5	0.01
Honduran	2	0.01
Cuban	22	0.06
Dominican Republic	1	0.00
Mexican	2,680	7.08
Puerto Rican	46	0.12
South American:	19	0.05
Bolivian	1	0.00
Chilean	3	0.01
Colombian	7	0.02
Ecuadorian	1	0.00
Peruvian	1	0.00
Venezuelan	4	0.01
Other South American	2	0.01
Other Hispanic or Latino	3,908	10.33
Hungarian	56	0.15
Iranian	53	0.14
Irish	3,513	9.34
Italian	778	2.07
Lithuanian	29	0.08
Northern European	48	0.13
Norwegian	505	1.34
Pennsylvania German	27	0.07
Polish	356	0.95
Portuguese	28	0.07
Romanian	22	0.06
Russian	39	0.10
Scandinavian	41	0.11
Scotch-Irish	614	1.63
Scottish	811	2.16
Slavic	16	0.04
Slovak	13	0.03
Slovene	14	0.04
Swedish	387	1.03
Swiss	82	0.22

Notes: 1. Figures in the "Number" column do not add up to the total population due to: a) Ancestry/Race overlap — e.g. persons can report being both White and Irish, b) persons of Hispanic origin can report being any race, c) persons reporting two ancestries are counted in both categories. 2. Numbers in parentheses indicate the number of persons reporting this ancestry/race alone, not in combination with any other ancestry/race. 3. Refer to the Explanation of Data in the front of the book for more detailed information.

Ancestry/Race	Number	%
Ukrainian	43	0.11
United States or American	2,584	6.87
Welsh	174	0.46
West Indian, excl. Hispanic:	25	0.07
Belizean	5	0.01
Dutch West Indian	9	0.02
Jamaican	11	0.03
White:	27,785	73.42
Not Hispanic (23,780)	24,331	64.29
Hispanic (2,991)	3,454	9.13
Yugoslavian	31	0.08

Gallup

Place Type: City
County: McKinley
Population: 20,209

Ancestry/Race	Number	%
African American/Black:	352	1.74
Not Hispanic (210)	321	1.59
Hispanic (9)	31	0.15
African, sub-Saharan:	10	0.05
African	10	0.05
Alaska Native tribes, specified:	11	0.05
Alaska Athabascan	5	0.02
Eskimo	2	0.01
All other tribes	4	0.02
Alaska Native tribes, not specified	16	0.08
Am. Ind. or Alaska Nat., not spec.	454	2.25
American Indian tribes, specified:	7,324	36.24
Apache (30)	50	0.25
Blackfeet (4)	10	0.05
Cherokee (23)	52	0.26
Cheyenne (9)	27	0.13
Chickasaw (5)	6	0.03
Chippewa (6)	11	0.05
Choctaw (22)	27	0.13
Comanche (4)	6	0.03
Cree (5)	5	0.02
Creek (1)	7	0.03
Crow (2)	2	0.01
Houma	1	0.00
Iroquois (5)	9	0.04
Kiowa (6)	16	0.08
Latin American Indians (13)	23	0.11
Lumbee (1)	1	0.00
Menominee (1)	4	0.02
Navajo (5,730)	6,279	31.07
Osage (6)	7	0.03
Paiute (10)	11	0.05
Pima (4)	4	0.02
Potawatomi	2	0.01
Pueblo (451)	624	3.09
Seminole (1)	2	0.01
Shoshone (1)	2	0.01
Sioux (19)	39	0.19
Tohono O'Odham (6)	8	0.04
Ute (7)	12	0.06
Yaqui (2)	2	0.01
Yuman (6)	7	0.03
All other tribes (54)	68	0.34
American Indian tribes, not spec.	454	2.25
Arab:	89	0.44
Arab/Arabic	49	0.24
Jordanian	7	0.03
Palestinian	33	0.16
Asian:	406	2.01
Chinese, ex. Taiwanese (46)	54	0.27
Filipino (62)	88	0.44
Indian (101)	116	0.57
Japanese (28)	73	0.36
Korean (12)	14	0.07
Pakistani (5)	9	0.04
Taiwanese (1)	2	0.01
Thai (2)	3	0.01
Vietnamese (4)	4	0.02
Other Asian, specified (19)	19	0.09
Other Asian, not specified (7)	24	0.12
Austrian	33	0.16
Belgian	9	0.04
British	37	0.18
Canadian	45	0.22
Celtic	17	0.08
Croatian	56	0.28
Czechoslovakian	12	0.06
Danish	59	0.29
Dutch	148	0.73
Eastern European	8	0.04
English	917	4.52
European	121	0.60
Finnish	8	0.04
French, except Basque	165	0.81
French Canadian	16	0.08
German	1,391	6.86
Greek	45	0.22
Hawaii Native/Pacific Islander:	42	0.21
Micronesian: (3)	6	0.03
Guamanian/Chamorro (3)	6	0.03
Polynesian: (12)	33	0.16
Native Hawaiian (4)	14	0.07
Samoan (5)	12	0.06
Other Polynesian (3)	7	0.03
Other Pac. Isl., not spec.	3	0.01
Hispanic or Latino:	6,699	33.15
Central American:	6	0.03
Costa Rican	1	0.00
Honduran	2	0.01
Nicaraguan	1	0.00
Panamanian	1	0.00
Other Central American	1	0.00
Cuban	8	0.04
Dominican Republic	5	0.02
Mexican	3,420	16.92
Puerto Rican	22	0.11
South American:	11	0.05
Chilean	2	0.01
Colombian	4	0.02
Ecuadorian	5	0.02
Other Hispanic or Latino	3,227	15.97
Hungarian	51	0.25
Iranian	2	0.01
Irish	1,252	6.18
Italian	528	2.60
Lithuanian	7	0.03
Luxemburger	5	0.02
Northern European	32	0.16
Norwegian	138	0.68
Polish	243	1.20
Russian	39	0.19
Scandinavian	20	0.10
Scotch-Irish	182	0.90
Scottish	164	0.81
Slavic	74	0.36
Slovak	17	0.08
Slovene	7	0.03
Swedish	31	0.15
Swiss	37	0.18
Ukrainian	38	0.19
United States or American	554	2.73
Welsh	65	0.32
White:	8,952	44.30
Not Hispanic (5,436)	5,946	29.42
Hispanic (2,670)	3,006	14.87
Yugoslavian	69	0.34

Hobbs

Place Type: City
County: Lea
Population: 28,657

Ancestry/Race	Number	%
Acadian/Cajun	5	0.02
African American/Black:	2,109	7.36
Not Hispanic (1,885)	1,994	6.96
Hispanic (60)	115	0.40
African, sub-Saharan:	103	0.36
African	92	0.32
Ethiopian	11	0.04
Alaska Native tribes, specified:	6	0.02
Alaska Athabascan (4)	4	0.01
Eskimo	1	0.00
Tlingit-Haida	1	0.00
Alaska Native tribes, not specified	1	0.00
Am. Ind. or Alaska Nat., not spec.	194	0.68
American Indian tribes, specified:	291	1.02
Apache (10)	19	0.07
Blackfeet (2)	3	0.01
Cherokee (34)	90	0.31
Cheyenne	7	0.02
Chickasaw (7)	14	0.05
Chippewa (3)	3	0.01
Choctaw (13)	36	0.13
Comanche (3)	6	0.02
Cree	2	0.01
Creek (6)	12	0.04
Delaware (1)	1	0.00
Iroquois	1	0.00
Latin American Indians (23)	29	0.10
Navajo (11)	15	0.05
Osage (2)	2	0.01
Potawatomi (5)	8	0.03
Pueblo (5)	15	0.05
Seminole (1)	3	0.01
Shoshone	2	0.01
Sioux (2)	11	0.04
Ute	3	0.01
Yaqui (1)	3	0.01
All other tribes (3)	6	0.02
American Indian tribes, not spec.	33	0.12
Arab:	26	0.09
Arab/Arabic	26	0.09
Asian:	156	0.54
Chinese, ex. Taiwanese (13)	14	0.05
Filipino (24)	34	0.12
Indian (54)	58	0.20
Japanese (7)	14	0.05
Korean (16)	20	0.07
Malaysian (1)	1	0.00
Thai (2)	2	0.01
Vietnamese (1)	1	0.00
Other Asian, not specified (5)	12	0.04
Belgian	33	0.12
Brazilian	9	0.03
British	94	0.33
Canadian	16	0.06
Celtic	8	0.03
Czech	31	0.11
Czechoslovakian	24	0.08
Danish	82	0.29
Dutch	467	1.64
English	1,593	5.59
European	114	0.40
Finnish	7	0.02
French, except Basque	440	1.55
French Canadian	16	0.06
German	2,065	7.25
Greek	34	0.12
Hawaii Native/Pacific Islander:	28	0.10
Micronesian: (6)	9	0.03
Guamanian/Chamorro (6)	9	0.03
Polynesian: (3)	10	0.03
Native Hawaiian (1)	4	0.01
Samoan (2)	3	0.01
Other Polynesian	3	0.01
Other Pac. Isl., not spec. (3)	9	0.03
Hispanic or Latino:	12,088	42.18
Central American:	7	0.02
Guatemalan	3	0.01
Salvadoran	3	0.01
Other Central American	1	0.00
Cuban	8	0.03
Mexican	7,995	27.90
Puerto Rican	28	0.10
South American:	5	0.02
Chilean	1	0.00
Colombian	2	0.01
Venezuelan	2	0.01
Other Hispanic or Latino	4,045	14.12

Notes: 1. Figures in the "Number" column do not add up to the total population due to: a) Ancestry/Race overlap — e.g. persons can report being both White and Irish, b) persons of Hispanic origin can report being any race, c) persons reporting two ancestries are counted in both categories. 2. Numbers in parentheses indicate the number of persons reporting this ancestry/race alone, not in combination with any other ancestry/race. 3. Refer to the Explanation of Data in the front of the book for more detailed information.

Hungarian	10	0.04
Icelander	8	0.03
Iranian	5	0.02
Irish	1,835	6.44
Italian	359	1.26
Lithuanian	5	0.02
Norwegian	186	0.65
Polish	133	0.47
Portuguese	16	0.06
Russian	36	0.13
Scandinavian	20	0.07
Scotch-Irish	364	1.28
Scottish	288	1.01
Serbian	8	0.03
Slovene	6	0.02
Swedish	227	0.80
Swiss	31	0.11
Turkish	5	0.02
United States or American	1,777	6.24
Welsh	38	0.13
West Indian, excl. Hispanic:	91	0.32
Dutch West Indian	91	0.32
White:	19,163	66.87
Not Hispanic (14,027)	14,316	49.96
Hispanic (4,176)	4,847	16.91
Yugoslavian	42	0.15

Las Cruces

Place Type: City
County: Dona Ana
Population: 74,267

Ancestry/Race	Number	%
Acadian/Cajun	7	0.01
African American/Black:	2,154	2.90
Not Hispanic (1,486)	1,724	2.32
Hispanic (252)	430	0.58
African, sub-Saharan:	203	0.27
African	164	0.22
Cape Verdean	5	0.01
Ethiopian	8	0.01
South African	6	0.01
Other sub-Saharan African	20	0.03
Alaska Native tribes, specified:	12	0.02
Alaska Athabascan (1)	4	0.01
Eskimo (4)	5	0.01
Tlingit-Haida (2)	3	0.00
Alaska Native tribes, not specified	4	0.01
Am. Ind. or Alaska Nat., not spec.	568	0.76
American Indian tribes, specified:	1,293	1.74
Apache (140)	176	0.24
Blackfeet (3)	11	0.01
Cherokee (66)	191	0.26
Cheyenne (3)	5	0.01
Chickasaw (5)	12	0.02
Chippewa (2)	9	0.01
Choctaw (8)	31	0.04
Comanche (3)	10	0.01
Creek (2)	7	0.01
Crow	1	0.00
Delaware (3)	3	0.00
Iroquois (5)	10	0.01
Kiowa (4)	5	0.01
Latin American Indians (75)	116	0.16
Lumbee (3)	3	0.00
Navajo (192)	233	0.31
Osage	4	0.01
Ottawa (1)	4	0.01
Paiute (2)	2	0.00
Pima (9)	15	0.02
Potawatomi (3)	8	0.01
Pueblo (270)	332	0.45
Puget Sound Salish (1)	1	0.00
Seminole	3	0.00
Shoshone (1)	3	0.00
Sioux (6)	24	0.03
Tohono O'Odham (2)	4	0.01
Ute (5)	8	0.01
Yakama	6	0.01
Yaqui (9)	12	0.02
All other tribes (26)	44	0.06
American Indian tribes, not spec.	152	0.20
Arab:	266	0.36
Arab/Arabic	64	0.09
Jordanian	17	0.02
Lebanese	125	0.17
Palestinian	14	0.02
Syrian	12	0.02
Other Arab	34	0.05
Armenian	9	0.01
Asian:	1,314	1.77
Bangladeshi (2)	2	0.00
Cambodian (2)	7	0.01
Chinese, ex. Taiwanese (206)	289	0.39
Filipino (104)	189	0.25
Indian (191)	221	0.30
Indonesian (13)	22	0.03
Japanese (116)	211	0.28
Korean (76)	119	0.16
Pakistani (27)	27	0.04
Sri Lankan (10)	10	0.01
Taiwanese (4)	6	0.01
Thai (27)	36	0.05
Vietnamese (37)	50	0.07
Other Asian, specified (11)	18	0.02
Other Asian, not specified (31)	107	0.14
Australian	39	0.05
Austrian	131	0.18
Basque	15	0.02
Belgian	89	0.12
Brazilian	26	0.03
British	355	0.48
Canadian	73	0.10
Celtic	21	0.03
Croatian	41	0.06
Czech	216	0.29
Czechoslovakian	50	0.07
Danish	326	0.44
Dutch	756	1.01
Eastern European	20	0.03
English	5,586	7.50
European	812	1.09
Finnish	138	0.19
French, except Basque	1,427	1.92
French Canadian	339	0.46
German	7,620	10.23
Greek	100	0.13
Hawaii Native/Pacific Islander:	160	0.22
Melanesian: (1)	1	0.00
Other Melanesian (1)	1	0.00
Micronesian: (15)	21	0.03
Guamanian/Chamorro (14)	19	0.03
Other Micronesian (1)	2	0.00
Polynesian: (32)	99	0.13
Native Hawaiian (18)	76	0.10
Samoan (10)	17	0.02
Tongan (3)	3	0.00
Other Polynesian (1)	3	0.00
Other Pac. Isl., specified	5	0.01
Other Pac. Isl., not spec. (7)	34	0.05
Hispanic or Latino:	38,421	51.73
Central American:	75	0.10
Costa Rican	2	0.00
Guatemalan	15	0.02
Honduran	4	0.01
Nicaraguan	15	0.02
Panamanian	22	0.03
Salvadoran	11	0.01
Other Central American	6	0.01
Cuban	57	0.08
Dominican Republic	5	0.01
Mexican	24,155	32.52
Puerto Rican	285	0.38
South American:	108	0.15
Argentinean	5	0.01
Bolivian	10	0.01
Chilean	10	0.01
Colombian	30	0.04
Ecuadorian	11	0.01
Peruvian	13	0.02
Venezuelan	17	0.02
Other South American	12	0.02
Other Hispanic or Latino	13,736	18.50
Hungarian	222	0.30
Icelander	30	0.04
Iranian	18	0.02
Irish	5,145	6.91
Italian	1,355	1.82
Latvian	16	0.02
Lithuanian	58	0.08
Northern European	102	0.14
Norwegian	788	1.06
Pennsylvania German	21	0.03
Polish	852	1.14
Portuguese	119	0.16
Romanian	51	0.07
Russian	503	0.68
Scandinavian	117	0.16
Scotch-Irish	1,133	1.52
Scottish	1,003	1.35
Serbian	21	0.03
Slavic	13	0.02
Slovak	29	0.04
Slovene	13	0.02
Swedish	814	1.09
Swiss	197	0.26
Turkish	12	0.02
Ukrainian	38	0.05
United States or American	3,069	4.12
Welsh	528	0.71
West Indian, excl. Hispanic:	51	0.07
Dutch West Indian	21	0.03
Jamaican	16	0.02
West Indian	14	0.02
White:	53,919	72.60
Not Hispanic (31,208)	32,198	43.35
Hispanic (20,040)	21,721	29.25
Yugoslavian	34	0.05

Las Vegas

Place Type: City
County: San Miguel
Population: 14,565

Ancestry/Race	Number	%
African American/Black:	194	1.33
Not Hispanic (108)	130	0.89
Hispanic (36)	64	0.44
Alaska Native tribes, specified:	2	0.01
Alaska Athabascan (2)	2	0.01
Am. Ind. or Alaska Nat., not spec.	112	0.77
American Indian tribes, specified:	272	1.87
Apache (25)	38	0.26
Blackfeet (2)	3	0.02
Cherokee	11	0.08
Chickasaw	3	0.02
Chippewa (1)	3	0.02
Choctaw (3)	5	0.03
Comanche (3)	4	0.03
Creek (1)	1	0.01
Iroquois	1	0.01
Latin American Indians (8)	15	0.10
Navajo (103)	129	0.89
Osage	3	0.02
Pima (2)	2	0.01
Potawatomi (2)	2	0.01
Pueblo (27)	32	0.22
Seminole	1	0.01
Sioux (2)	10	0.07
Ute (1)	3	0.02
All other tribes (1)	6	0.04
American Indian tribes, not spec.	53	0.36
Arab:	8	0.05
Lebanese	8	0.05
Asian:	139	0.95
Bangladeshi (1)	1	0.01
Chinese, ex. Taiwanese (29)	38	0.26
Filipino (6)	9	0.06

Notes: 1. Figures in the "Number" column do not add up to the total population due to: a) Ancestry/Race overlap — e.g. persons can report being both White and Irish, b) persons of Hispanic origin can report being any race, c) persons reporting two ancestries are counted in both categories. 2. Numbers in parentheses indicate the number of persons reporting this ancestry/race alone, not in combination with any other ancestry/race. 3. Refer to the Explanation of Data in the front of the book for more detailed information.

Ancestry/Race	Number	%
Indian (31)	42	0.29
Indonesian (1)	3	0.02
Japanese (2)	15	0.10
Korean (10)	11	0.08
Laotian (1)	1	0.01
Malaysian (1)	3	0.02
Vietnamese (2)	4	0.03
Other Asian, specified (3)	3	0.02
Other Asian, not specified (1)	9	0.06
Basque	9	0.06
Belgian	7	0.05
Canadian	11	0.08
Czech	43	0.29
Czechoslovakian	14	0.10
Danish	32	0.22
Dutch	11	0.08
Eastern European	13	0.09
English	279	1.91
European	29	0.20
Finnish	5	0.03
French, except Basque	110	0.75
French Canadian	47	0.32
German	453	3.10
Greek	12	0.08
Hawaii Native/Pacific Islander:	41	0.28
Micronesian:	4	0.03
Guamanian/Chamorro	4	0.03
Polynesian: (3)	25	0.17
Native Hawaiian	13	0.09
Samoan (3)	7	0.05
Tongan	1	0.01
Other Polynesian	4	0.03
Other Pac. Isl., not spec. (8)	12	0.08
Hispanic or Latino:	12,080	82.94
Central American:	10	0.07
Honduran	1	0.01
Panamanian	6	0.04
Salvadoran	2	0.01
Other Central American	1	0.01
Cuban	4	0.03
Mexican	1,930	13.25
Puerto Rican	28	0.19
South American:	2	0.01
Colombian	1	0.01
Peruvian	1	0.01
Other Hispanic or Latino	10,106	69.39
Hungarian	13	0.09
Irish	361	2.47
Italian	172	1.18
Lithuanian	16	0.11
Norwegian	28	0.19
Polish	73	0.50
Russian	18	0.12
Scotch-Irish	171	1.17
Scottish	90	0.62
Swedish	81	0.55
Swiss	17	0.12
United States or American	475	3.25
White:	8,527	58.54
Not Hispanic (1,962)	2,064	14.17
Hispanic (5,933)	6,463	44.37

Los Alamos

Place Type: Census Designated Place
County: Los Alamos
Population: 11,909

Ancestry/Race	Number	%
African American/Black:	75	0.63
Not Hispanic (48)	71	0.60
Hispanic (4)	4	0.03
African, sub-Saharan:	20	0.17
South African	20	0.17
Alaska Native tribes, specified:	1	0.01
Eskimo (1)	1	0.01
Am. Ind. or Alaska Nat., not spec.	27	0.23
Alsatian	9	0.08
American Indian tribes, specified:	105	0.88
Apache (1)	4	0.03
Cherokee (6)	25	0.21
Chickasaw (1)	2	0.02
Chippewa (3)	5	0.04
Choctaw (1)	3	0.03
Houma (2)	2	0.02
Iroquois (2)	3	0.03
Kiowa (1)	1	0.01
Latin American Indians (2)	3	0.03
Navajo (8)	12	0.10
Osage	2	0.02
Potawatomi (7)	7	0.06
Pueblo (14)	22	0.18
Sioux (1)	1	0.01
All other tribes (2)	13	0.11
American Indian tribes, not spec.	5	0.04
Arab:	43	0.36
Lebanese	30	0.25
Syrian	13	0.11
Asian:	636	5.34
Cambodian (1)	3	0.03
Chinese, ex. Taiwanese (264)	297	2.49
Filipino (16)	30	0.25
Indian (69)	82	0.69
Indonesian (4)	6	0.05
Japanese (37)	61	0.51
Korean (86)	98	0.82
Laotian	1	0.01
Malaysian	1	0.01
Pakistani (1)	1	0.01
Taiwanese (5)	7	0.06
Thai (1)	3	0.03
Vietnamese (32)	34	0.29
Other Asian, not specified (5)	12	0.10
Australian	5	0.04
Austrian	35	0.29
Basque	6	0.05
Belgian	85	0.71
British	141	1.18
Canadian	35	0.29
Celtic	10	0.08
Croatian	15	0.13
Czech	100	0.84
Czechoslovakian	43	0.36
Danish	96	0.81
Dutch	228	1.92
Eastern European	7	0.06
English	1,866	15.68
European	244	2.05
Finnish	58	0.49
French, except Basque	382	3.21
French Canadian	73	0.61
German	2,298	19.31
Greek	50	0.42
Hawaii Native/Pacific Islander:	9	0.08
Polynesian:	2	0.02
Native Hawaiian	2	0.02
Other Pac. Isl., not spec. (5)	7	0.06
Hispanic or Latino:	1,454	12.21
Central American:	11	0.09
Costa Rican	3	0.03
Guatemalan	1	0.01
Honduran	1	0.01
Nicaraguan	3	0.03
Panamanian	3	0.03
Cuban	16	0.13
Mexican	363	3.05
Puerto Rican	14	0.12
South American:	10	0.08
Argentinean	5	0.04
Colombian	1	0.01
Venezuelan	2	0.02
Other South American	2	0.02
Other Hispanic or Latino	1,040	8.73
Hungarian	90	0.76
Irish	1,489	12.51
Italian	436	3.66
Latvian	4	0.03
Lithuanian	50	0.42
Norwegian	234	1.97
Pennsylvania German	6	0.05
Polish	395	3.32
Portuguese	51	0.43
Romanian	11	0.09
Russian	175	1.47
Scandinavian	25	0.21
Scotch-Irish	310	2.60
Scottish	337	2.83
Slovak	32	0.27
Swedish	283	2.38
Swiss	103	0.87
Ukrainian	10	0.08
United States or American	607	5.10
Welsh	140	1.18
White:	10,883	91.38
Not Hispanic (9,619)	9,786	82.17
Hispanic (995)	1,097	9.21
Yugoslavian	52	0.44

Los Lunas

Place Type: Village
County: Valencia
Population: 10,034

Ancestry/Race	Number	%
African American/Black:	153	1.52
Not Hispanic (89)	111	1.11
Hispanic (27)	42	0.42
Am. Ind. or Alaska Nat., not spec.	66	0.66
American Indian tribes, specified:	275	2.74
Apache (15)	24	0.24
Cherokee (4)	16	0.16
Chickasaw (2)	2	0.02
Choctaw (3)	4	0.04
Creek (1)	3	0.03
Iroquois (1)	1	0.01
Kiowa	1	0.01
Latin American Indians (5)	7	0.07
Navajo (57)	77	0.77
Potawatomi (1)	1	0.01
Pueblo (79)	111	1.11
Seminole	2	0.02
Sioux (4)	8	0.08
Yaqui (1)	6	0.06
Yuman (1)	2	0.02
All other tribes (9)	10	0.10
American Indian tribes, not spec.	35	0.35
Asian:	73	0.73
Chinese, ex. Taiwanese (5)	10	0.10
Filipino (29)	38	0.38
Indian	3	0.03
Japanese (3)	7	0.07
Korean (5)	5	0.05
Pakistani (1)	1	0.01
Thai (1)	1	0.01
Vietnamese (4)	4	0.04
Other Asian, not specified (2)	4	0.04
Basque	9	0.09
British	52	0.51
Canadian	16	0.16
Croatian	6	0.06
Czech	8	0.08
Czechoslovakian	7	0.07
Danish	19	0.19
Dutch	98	0.97
English	668	6.61
European	79	0.78
Finnish	12	0.12
French, except Basque	224	2.22
French Canadian	107	1.06
German	797	7.88
Greek	8	0.08
Hawaii Native/Pacific Islander:	12	0.12
Polynesian: (5)	9	0.09
Native Hawaiian (1)	3	0.03
Samoan (4)	6	0.06
Other Pac. Isl., not spec. (1)	3	0.03
Hispanic or Latino:	5,894	58.74
Central American:	3	0.03
Nicaraguan	1	0.01

Notes: 1. Figures in the "Number" column do not add up to the total population due to: a) Ancestry/Race overlap — e.g. persons can report being both White and Irish, b) persons of Hispanic origin can report being any race, c) persons reporting two ancestries are counted in both categories. 2. Numbers in parentheses indicate the number of persons reporting this ancestry/race alone, not in combination with any other ancestry/race. 3. Refer to the Explanation of Data in the front of the book for more detailed information.

Panamanian	1	0.01
Salvadoran	1	0.01
Cuban	16	0.16
Mexican	1,479	14.74
Puerto Rican	10	0.10
South American:	9	0.09
Bolivian	1	0.01
Chilean	1	0.01
Colombian	6	0.06
Ecuadorian	1	0.01
Other Hispanic or Latino	4,377	43.62
Hungarian	32	0.32
Irish	599	5.93
Italian	144	1.42
Norwegian	11	0.11
Polish	142	1.40
Portuguese	18	0.18
Romanian	12	0.12
Russian	23	0.23
Scandinavian	9	0.09
Scotch-Irish	145	1.43
Scottish	213	2.11
Serbian	9	0.09
Slovak	9	0.09
Swedish	98	0.97
Swiss	18	0.18
United States or American	378	3.74
Welsh	44	0.44
West Indian, excl. Hispanic:	9	0.09
Dutch West Indian	9	0.09
White:	6,768	67.45
Not Hispanic (3,715)	3,818	38.05
Hispanic (2,721)	2,950	29.40
Yugoslavian	7	0.07

North Valley

Place Type: Census Designated Place
County: Bernalillo
Population: 11,923

Ancestry/Race	Number	%
African American/Black:	164	1.38
Not Hispanic (94)	119	1.00
Hispanic (30)	45	0.38
African, sub-Saharan:	9	0.07
African	9	0.07
Alaska Native tribes, specified:	3	0.03
Alaska Athabascan (1)	1	0.01
Eskimo (1)	1	0.01
Tlingit-Haida	1	0.01
Alaska Native tribes, not specified	1	0.01
Am. Ind. or Alaska Nat., not spec.	102	0.86
American Indian tribes, specified:	339	2.84
Apache (13)	18	0.15
Blackfeet	5	0.04
Cherokee (4)	22	0.18
Cheyenne	2	0.02
Chickasaw (4)	4	0.03
Chippewa (4)	8	0.07
Choctaw (2)	4	0.03
Comanche	1	0.01
Creek (3)	3	0.03
Iroquois (4)	5	0.04
Kiowa (1)	1	0.01
Latin American Indians (13)	15	0.13
Lumbee	1	0.01
Navajo (123)	146	1.22
Pueblo (48)	61	0.51
Seminole	1	0.01
Shoshone (1)	1	0.01
Sioux (10)	22	0.18
Ute (2)	4	0.03
All other tribes (8)	15	0.13
American Indian tribes, not spec.	33	0.28
Arab:	78	0.64
Arab/Arabic	60	0.49
Lebanese	18	0.15
Asian:	84	0.70
Chinese, ex. Taiwanese (9)	13	0.11
Filipino (11)	24	0.20
Indian (6)	7	0.06
Indonesian (1)	1	0.01
Japanese (14)	21	0.18
Korean (5)	13	0.11
Malaysian (1)	3	0.03
Other Asian, specified	1	0.01
Other Asian, not specified (1)	1	0.01
Austrian	26	0.21
Belgian	27	0.22
British	64	0.53
Croatian	38	0.31
Czech	9	0.07
Czechoslovakian	21	0.17
Danish	23	0.19
Dutch	176	1.45
Eastern European	10	0.08
English	870	7.14
European	87	0.71
French, except Basque	156	1.28
French Canadian	40	0.33
German	1,059	8.70
Greek	52	0.43
Hawaii Native/Pacific Islander:	7	0.06
Micronesian: (4)	4	0.03
Guamanian/Chamorro (4)	4	0.03
Polynesian: (3)	3	0.03
Native Hawaiian (2)	2	0.02
Other Polynesian (1)	1	0.01
Hispanic or Latino:	6,773	56.81
Central American:	34	0.29
Guatemalan	12	0.10
Honduran	5	0.04
Panamanian	12	0.10
Salvadoran	4	0.03
Other Central American	1	0.01
Cuban	23	0.19
Mexican	1,890	15.85
Puerto Rican	29	0.24
South American:	4	0.03
Chilean	1	0.01
Colombian	2	0.02
Ecuadorian	1	0.01
Other Hispanic or Latino	4,793	40.20
Irish	735	6.04
Italian	460	3.78
Norwegian	108	0.89
Polish	96	0.79
Russian	44	0.36
Scandinavian	59	0.48
Scotch-Irish	140	1.15
Scottish	134	1.10
Slovak	35	0.29
Slovene	10	0.08
Swedish	140	1.15
Swiss	6	0.05
Turkish	10	0.08
United States or American	534	4.38
Welsh	76	0.62
West Indian, excl. Hispanic:	6	0.05
Dutch West Indian	6	0.05
White:	9,194	77.11
Not Hispanic (4,615)	4,739	39.75
Hispanic (4,163)	4,455	37.36

Portales

Place Type: City
County: Roosevelt
Population: 11,131

Ancestry/Race	Number	%
African American/Black:	305	2.74
Not Hispanic (246)	279	2.51
Hispanic (8)	26	0.23
African, sub-Saharan:	78	0.72
African	70	0.65
Liberian	8	0.07
Am. Ind. or Alaska Nat., not spec.	43	0.39
American Indian tribes, specified:	138	1.24
Apache (7)	10	0.09
Blackfeet	1	0.01
Cherokee (11)	26	0.23
Cheyenne	2	0.02
Chickasaw	1	0.01
Chippewa (1)	1	0.01
Choctaw (9)	16	0.14
Creek	1	0.01
Iroquois	1	0.01
Kiowa (1)	1	0.01
Latin American Indians (2)	10	0.09
Lumbee	1	0.01
Navajo (26)	34	0.31
Pueblo (10)	17	0.15
Shoshone (1)	1	0.01
Sioux (4)	7	0.06
All other tribes (4)	8	0.07
American Indian tribes, not spec.	33	0.30
Asian:	149	1.34
Chinese, ex. Taiwanese (34)	41	0.37
Filipino (16)	28	0.25
Indian (10)	15	0.13
Japanese (12)	16	0.14
Korean (17)	20	0.18
Pakistani (3)	6	0.05
Thai (4)	6	0.05
Vietnamese	2	0.02
Other Asian, specified (2)	6	0.05
Other Asian, not specified (6)	9	0.08
Austrian	6	0.06
Belgian	41	0.38
British	22	0.20
Canadian	30	0.28
Czech	27	0.25
Czechoslovakian	16	0.15
Danish	58	0.53
Dutch	92	0.85
English	644	5.94
European	42	0.39
Finnish	9	0.08
French, except Basque	149	1.37
French Canadian	48	0.44
German	867	7.99
Greek	9	0.08
Hawaii Native/Pacific Islander:	17	0.15
Micronesian: (1)	2	0.02
Guamanian/Chamorro (1)	2	0.02
Polynesian: (5)	10	0.09
Native Hawaiian (3)	4	0.04
Samoan (2)	6	0.05
Other Pac. Isl., specified	2	0.02
Other Pac. Isl., not spec. (3)	3	0.03
Hispanic or Latino:	4,244	38.13
Central American:	10	0.09
Guatemalan	2	0.02
Honduran	2	0.02
Nicaraguan	1	0.01
Panamanian	3	0.03
Salvadoran	1	0.01
Other Central American	1	0.01
Cuban	19	0.17
Mexican	2,068	18.58
Puerto Rican	13	0.12
South American:	3	0.03
Colombian	3	0.03
Other Hispanic or Latino	2,131	19.14
Hungarian	8	0.07
Irish	979	9.02
Italian	163	1.50
Latvian	15	0.14
Norwegian	77	0.71
Pennsylvania German	6	0.06
Polish	42	0.39
Russian	28	0.26
Scotch-Irish	189	1.74
Scottish	150	1.38
Slavic	9	0.08
Swedish	80	0.74
United States or American	989	9.12
Welsh	50	0.46

Notes: 1. Figures in the "Number" column do not add up to the total population due to: a) Ancestry/Race overlap — e.g. persons can report being both White and Irish, b) persons of Hispanic origin can report being any race, c) persons reporting two ancestries are counted in both categories. 2. Numbers in parentheses indicate the number of persons reporting this ancestry/race alone, not in combination with any other ancestry/race. 3. Refer to the Explanation of Data in the front of the book for more detailed information.

West Indian, excl. Hispanic:	7	0.06
Dutch West Indian	7	0.06
White:	7,988	71.76
Not Hispanic (6,303)	6,413	57.61
Hispanic (1,355)	1,575	14.15

Rio Rancho

Place Type: City
County: Sandoval
Population: 51,765

Ancestry/Race	Number	%
Afghan	6	0.01
African American/Black:	1,776	3.43
Not Hispanic (1,286)	1,564	3.02
Hispanic (90)	212	0.41
African, sub-Saharan:	83	0.16
African	74	0.14
Nigerian	9	0.02
Alaska Native tribes, specified:	20	0.04
Alaska Athabascan (3)	9	0.02
Aleut (2)	4	0.01
Eskimo (5)	5	0.01
Tlingit-Haida (2)	2	0.00
Alaska Native tribes, not specified	2	0.00
Am. Ind. or Alaska Nat., not spec.	229	0.44
Albanian	10	0.02
American Indian tribes, specified:	1,482	2.86
Apache (48)	83	0.16
Blackfeet (6)	27	0.05
Cherokee (41)	144	0.28
Cheyenne (6)	7	0.01
Chickasaw (9)	18	0.03
Chippewa (18)	33	0.06
Choctaw (14)	31	0.06
Colville	1	0.00
Comanche (6)	15	0.03
Creek (4)	9	0.02
Crow (5)	5	0.01
Delaware (6)	9	0.02
Iroquois (5)	12	0.02
Kiowa (7)	8	0.02
Latin American Indians (13)	38	0.07
Navajo (386)	453	0.88
Osage (5)	5	0.01
Ottawa	2	0.00
Paiute (1)	1	0.00
Pima (3)	3	0.01
Potawatomi (10)	12	0.02
Pueblo (299)	375	0.72
Puget Sound Salish (1)	2	0.00
Seminole (4)	7	0.01
Sioux (31)	52	0.10
Tohono O'Odham (3)	3	0.01
Ute (10)	18	0.03
Yakama (4)	4	0.01
Yaqui (4)	11	0.02
Yuman (3)	3	0.01
All other tribes (51)	91	0.18
American Indian tribes, not spec.	104	0.20
Arab:	216	0.42
Arab/Arabic	8	0.02
Jordanian	18	0.03
Lebanese	153	0.30
Palestinian	12	0.02
Syrian	15	0.03
Other Arab	10	0.02
Armenian	73	0.14
Asian:	1,139	2.20
Cambodian (1)	1	0.00
Chinese, ex. Taiwanese (99)	157	0.30
Filipino (250)	385	0.74
Indian (77)	99	0.19
Indonesian (1)	2	0.00
Japanese (85)	177	0.34
Korean (82)	108	0.21
Laotian (20)	23	0.04
Malaysian (1)	1	0.00
Pakistani (9)	11	0.02
Sri Lankan (3)	3	0.01
Taiwanese (8)	12	0.02
Thai (21)	36	0.07
Vietnamese (60)	68	0.13
Other Asian, specified	4	0.01
Other Asian, not specified (26)	52	0.10
Australian	76	0.15
Austrian	154	0.30
Basque	13	0.03
Belgian	78	0.15
Brazilian	89	0.17
British	327	0.63
Canadian	94	0.18
Celtic	51	0.10
Croatian	44	0.09
Czech	184	0.36
Czechoslovakian	89	0.17
Danish	466	0.90
Dutch	938	1.81
Eastern European	19	0.04
English	5,418	10.48
Estonian	5	0.01
European	638	1.23
Finnish	111	0.21
French, except Basque	1,803	3.49
French Canadian	391	0.76
German	8,462	16.36
Greek	145	0.28
Hawaii Native/Pacific Islander:	175	0.34
Micronesian: (32)	35	0.07
Guamanian/Chamorro (28)	31	0.06
Other Micronesian (4)	4	0.01
Polynesian: (53)	113	0.22
Native Hawaiian (39)	85	0.16
Samoan (14)	24	0.05
Other Polynesian	4	0.01
Other Pac. Isl., specified	3	0.01
Other Pac. Isl., not spec. (2)	24	0.05
Hispanic or Latino:	14,329	27.68
Central American:	109	0.21
Costa Rican	7	0.01
Guatemalan	19	0.04
Honduran	14	0.03
Nicaraguan	11	0.02
Panamanian	16	0.03
Salvadoran	27	0.05
Other Central American	15	0.03
Cuban	51	0.10
Dominican Republic	19	0.04
Mexican	4,266	8.24
Puerto Rican	317	0.61
South American:	90	0.17
Argentinean	12	0.02
Bolivian	1	0.00
Chilean	15	0.03
Colombian	32	0.06
Ecuadorian	12	0.02
Peruvian	9	0.02
Uruguayan	1	0.00
Venezuelan	1	0.00
Other South American	7	0.01
Other Hispanic or Latino	9,477	18.31
Hungarian	308	0.60
Iranian	88	0.17
Irish	5,732	11.08
Israeli	36	0.07
Italian	3,435	6.64
Latvian	15	0.03
Lithuanian	43	0.08
Luxemburger	8	0.02
Macedonian	23	0.04
Maltese	17	0.03
Northern European	24	0.05
Norwegian	842	1.63
Pennsylvania German	23	0.04
Polish	1,402	2.71
Portuguese	121	0.23
Romanian	50	0.10
Russian	383	0.74
Scandinavian	122	0.24
Scotch-Irish	1,148	2.22
Scottish	1,196	2.31
Serbian	43	0.08
Slavic	19	0.04
Slovak	89	0.17
Slovene	40	0.08
Swedish	862	1.67
Swiss	176	0.34
Turkish	19	0.04
Ukrainian	91	0.18
United States or American	2,933	5.67
Welsh	319	0.62
West Indian, excl. Hispanic:	95	0.18
Dutch West Indian	11	0.02
Haitian	7	0.01
Jamaican	46	0.09
West Indian	31	0.06
White:	42,424	81.95
Not Hispanic (33,176)	34,085	65.85
Hispanic (7,387)	8,339	16.11
Yugoslavian	51	0.10

Roswell

Place Type: City
County: Chaves
Population: 45,293

Ancestry/Race	Number	%
Acadian/Cajun	10	0.02
African American/Black:	1,298	2.87
Not Hispanic (1,020)	1,130	2.49
Hispanic (97)	168	0.37
African, sub-Saharan:	33	0.07
African	25	0.06
Other sub-Saharan African	8	0.02
Alaska Native tribes, specified:	3	0.01
Alaska Athabascan (1)	1	0.00
Aleut (1)	1	0.00
Eskimo	1	0.00
Alaska Native tribes, not specified	10	0.02
Am. Ind. or Alaska Nat., not spec.	333	0.74
American Indian tribes, specified:	539	1.19
Apache (42)	78	0.17
Blackfeet (6)	15	0.03
Cherokee (49)	146	0.32
Cheyenne	2	0.00
Chickasaw (5)	11	0.02
Chippewa	1	0.00
Choctaw (15)	49	0.11
Comanche (4)	12	0.03
Creek (1)	6	0.01
Crow	1	0.00
Delaware	4	0.01
Iroquois (4)	7	0.02
Kiowa (2)	3	0.01
Latin American Indians (39)	46	0.10
Lumbee	1	0.00
Navajo (31)	49	0.11
Osage (1)	2	0.00
Potawatomi (1)	3	0.01
Pueblo (34)	40	0.09
Seminole (4)	5	0.01
Sioux (13)	19	0.04
Ute (3)	4	0.01
Yaqui (3)	5	0.01
All other tribes (22)	30	0.07
American Indian tribes, not spec.	76	0.17
Arab:	5	0.01
Lebanese	5	0.01
Asian:	448	0.99
Chinese, ex. Taiwanese (44)	58	0.13
Filipino (61)	96	0.21
Indian (45)	78	0.17
Indonesian (1)	1	0.00
Japanese (37)	69	0.15
Korean (13)	20	0.04
Laotian (1)	1	0.00
Pakistani (10)	13	0.03
Sri Lankan (1)	1	0.00

Notes: 1. Figures in the "Number" column do not add up to the total population due to: a) Ancestry/Race overlap — e.g. persons can report being both White and Irish, b) persons of Hispanic origin can report being any race, c) persons reporting two ancestries are counted in both categories. 2. Numbers in parentheses indicate the number of persons reporting this ancestry/race alone, not in combination with any other ancestry/race. 3. Refer to the Explanation of Data in the front of the book for more detailed information.

Ancestry/Race	Number	%
Taiwanese (4)	5	0.01
Thai (13)	16	0.04
Vietnamese (49)	53	0.12
Other Asian, specified	8	0.02
Other Asian, not specified (9)	29	0.06
Austrian	50	0.11
Belgian	8	0.02
Brazilian	8	0.02
British	100	0.22
Canadian	48	0.11
Celtic	11	0.02
Croatian	22	0.05
Czech	133	0.29
Czechoslovakian	13	0.03
Danish	116	0.26
Dutch	464	1.02
English	3,937	8.66
Estonian	23	0.05
European	234	0.51
Finnish	49	0.11
French, except Basque	859	1.89
French Canadian	227	0.50
German	4,196	9.23
Greek	17	0.04
Hawaii Native/Pacific Islander:	58	0.13
Melanesian:	1	0.00
Other Melanesian	1	0.00
Micronesian: (6)	9	0.02
Guamanian/Chamorro (6)	9	0.02
Polynesian: (11)	28	0.06
Native Hawaiian (7)	15	0.03
Samoan (4)	13	0.03
Other Pac. Isl., specified	8	0.02
Other Pac. Isl., not spec. (6)	12	0.03
Hispanic or Latino:	20,084	44.34
Central American:	41	0.09
Costa Rican	3	0.01
Guatemalan	9	0.02
Honduran	3	0.01
Nicaraguan	5	0.01
Panamanian	16	0.04
Salvadoran	4	0.01
Other Central American	1	0.00
Cuban	13	0.03
Mexican	12,284	27.12
Puerto Rican	88	0.19
South American:	12	0.03
Chilean	2	0.00
Colombian	4	0.01
Ecuadorian	1	0.00
Peruvian	1	0.00
Venezuelan	2	0.00
Other South American	2	0.00
Other Hispanic or Latino	7,646	16.88
Hungarian	61	0.13
Iranian	12	0.03
Irish	3,351	7.37
Italian	834	1.83
Lithuanian	22	0.05
Northern European	15	0.03
Norwegian	440	0.97
Pennsylvania German	22	0.05
Polish	417	0.92
Portuguese	53	0.12
Romanian	8	0.02
Russian	91	0.20
Scandinavian	24	0.05
Scotch-Irish	739	1.63
Scottish	592	1.30
Serbian	6	0.01
Slavic	17	0.04
Slovak	21	0.05
Slovene	14	0.03
Swedish	268	0.59
Swiss	71	0.16
United States or American	2,870	6.31
Welsh	165	0.36
West Indian, excl. Hispanic:	25	0.06
Dutch West Indian	25	0.06
White:	33,478	73.91
Not Hispanic (23,063)	23,517	51.92
Hispanic (9,078)	9,961	21.99
Yugoslavian	27	0.06

Santa Fe

Place Type: City
County: Santa Fe
Population: 62,203

Ancestry/Race	Number	%
Acadian/Cajun	7	0.01
Afghan	24	0.04
African American/Black:	621	1.00
Not Hispanic (341)	491	0.79
Hispanic (68)	130	0.21
African, sub-Saharan:	120	0.19
African	80	0.13
Cape Verdean	7	0.01
South African	33	0.05
Alaska Native tribes, specified:	28	0.05
Alaska Athabascan (2)	2	0.00
Aleut	2	0.00
Eskimo (7)	12	0.02
Tlingit-Haida (7)	12	0.02
Alaska Native tribes, not specified	4	0.01
Am. Ind. or Alaska Nat., not spec.	386	0.62
Alsatian	7	0.01
American Indian tribes, specified:	1,493	2.40
Apache (44)	92	0.15
Blackfeet (9)	21	0.03
Cherokee (36)	126	0.20
Cheyenne (7)	7	0.01
Chickasaw (2)	4	0.01
Chippewa (33)	44	0.07
Choctaw (14)	33	0.05
Colville (2)	2	0.00
Comanche (9)	11	0.02
Cree	3	0.00
Creek (4)	15	0.02
Crow (6)	7	0.01
Delaware (1)	2	0.00
Iroquois (21)	30	0.05
Kiowa (10)	16	0.03
Latin American Indians (57)	107	0.17
Lumbee	1	0.00
Menominee (2)	2	0.00
Navajo (247)	305	0.49
Osage (8)	13	0.02
Paiute (3)	3	0.00
Pima (6)	6	0.01
Potawatomi (3)	7	0.01
Pueblo (335)	409	0.66
Puget Sound Salish (1)	1	0.00
Seminole (5)	8	0.01
Shoshone (10)	18	0.03
Sioux (40)	51	0.08
Tohono O'Odham (9)	9	0.01
Ute (5)	7	0.01
Yakama (1)	2	0.00
Yaqui (1)	4	0.01
All other tribes (75)	127	0.20
American Indian tribes, not spec.	169	0.27
Arab:	228	0.37
Arab/Arabic	33	0.05
Iraqi	6	0.01
Lebanese	130	0.21
Moroccan	4	0.01
Palestinian	15	0.02
Syrian	12	0.02
Other Arab	28	0.05
Armenian	71	0.11
Asian:	1,063	1.71
Bangladeshi (1)	1	0.00
Cambodian (3)	3	0.00
Chinese, ex. Taiwanese (220)	279	0.45
Filipino (49)	95	0.15
Hmong	1	0.00
Indian (248)	293	0.47
Indonesian (2)	4	0.01
Japanese (83)	141	0.23
Korean (71)	96	0.15
Laotian (2)	2	0.00
Malaysian (1)	2	0.00
Pakistani (5)	7	0.01
Taiwanese (5)	5	0.01
Thai (6)	7	0.01
Vietnamese (42)	43	0.07
Other Asian, specified (4)	11	0.02
Other Asian, not specified (36)	73	0.12
Australian	19	0.03
Austrian	283	0.46
Basque	31	0.05
Belgian	57	0.09
British	521	0.84
Bulgarian	20	0.03
Canadian	173	0.28
Celtic	63	0.10
Croatian	61	0.10
Czech	223	0.36
Czechoslovakian	59	0.10
Danish	250	0.40
Dutch	808	1.31
Eastern European	102	0.17
English	6,323	10.23
Estonian	14	0.02
European	609	0.99
Finnish	115	0.19
French, except Basque	1,655	2.68
French Canadian	175	0.28
German	6,640	10.74
Greek	297	0.48
Guyanese	7	0.01
Hawaii Native/Pacific Islander:	108	0.17
Melanesian:	1	0.00
Fijian	1	0.00
Micronesian: (22)	32	0.05
Guamanian/Chamorro (15)	25	0.04
Other Micronesian (7)	7	0.01
Polynesian: (21)	56	0.09
Native Hawaiian (17)	44	0.07
Samoan (4)	7	0.01
Tongan	1	0.00
Other Polynesian	4	0.01
Other Pac. Isl., specified	5	0.01
Other Pac. Isl., not spec. (6)	14	0.02
Hispanic or Latino:	29,744	47.82
Central American:	333	0.54
Costa Rican	11	0.02
Guatemalan	173	0.28
Honduran	26	0.04
Nicaraguan	9	0.01
Panamanian	11	0.02
Salvadoran	79	0.13
Other Central American	24	0.04
Cuban	66	0.11
Dominican Republic	9	0.01
Mexican	8,325	13.38
Puerto Rican	128	0.21
South American:	156	0.25
Argentinean	15	0.02
Bolivian	6	0.01
Chilean	22	0.04
Colombian	24	0.04
Ecuadorian	11	0.02
Paraguayan	2	0.00
Peruvian	39	0.06
Uruguayan	5	0.01
Venezuelan	14	0.02
Other South American	18	0.03
Other Hispanic or Latino	20,727	33.32
Hungarian	250	0.40
Icelander	7	0.01
Iranian	62	0.10
Irish	5,352	8.66
Israeli	33	0.05
Italian	1,742	2.82
Latvian	32	0.05
Lithuanian	215	0.35
New Zealander	8	0.01

Notes: 1. Figures in the "Number" column do not add up to the total population due to: a) Ancestry/Race overlap — e.g. persons can report being both White and Irish, b) persons of Hispanic origin can report being any race, c) persons reporting two ancestries are counted in both categories. 2. Numbers in parentheses indicate the number of persons reporting this ancestry/race alone, not in combination with any other ancestry/race. 3. Refer to the Explanation of Data in the front of the book for more detailed information.

Ancestry/Race	Number	%
Northern European	184	0.30
Norwegian	862	1.39
Pennsylvania German	33	0.05
Polish	1,169	1.89
Portuguese	182	0.29
Romanian	96	0.16
Russian	981	1.59
Scandinavian	114	0.18
Scotch-Irish	1,398	2.26
Scottish	1,555	2.52
Serbian	11	0.02
Slavic	34	0.06
Slovak	39	0.06
Soviet Union	5	0.01
Swedish	735	1.19
Swiss	224	0.36
Ukrainian	157	0.25
United States or American	2,446	3.96
Welsh	616	1.00
West Indian, excl. Hispanic:	55	0.09
Bahamian	5	0.01
Belizean	13	0.02
British West Indian	5	0.01
Jamaican	18	0.03
Trinidadian and Tobagonian	8	0.01
U.S. Virgin Islander	6	0.01
White:	49,794	80.05
Not Hispanic (29,300)	30,102	48.39
Hispanic (18,159)	19,692	31.66
Yugoslavian	9	0.01

Silver City

Place Type: Town
County: Grant
Population: 10,545

Ancestry/Race	Number	%
Acadian/Cajun	5	0.05
African American/Black:	135	1.28
Not Hispanic (67)	86	0.82
Hispanic (24)	49	0.46
African, sub-Saharan:	16	0.15
African	16	0.15
Alaska Native tribes, specified:	4	0.04
Aleut (1)	1	0.01
Eskimo (2)	2	0.02
Tlingit-Haida (1)	1	0.01
Am. Ind. or Alaska Nat., not spec.	48	0.46
American Indian tribes, specified:	160	1.52
Apache (23)	32	0.30
Blackfeet	1	0.01
Cherokee (4)	34	0.32
Chickasaw (1)	2	0.02
Chippewa (3)	3	0.03
Choctaw (3)	4	0.04
Comanche (1)	1	0.01
Cree	1	0.01
Creek (1)	1	0.01
Delaware	1	0.01
Iroquois (1)	3	0.03
Kiowa	1	0.01
Latin American Indians (9)	12	0.11
Navajo (15)	16	0.15
Osage	5	0.05
Pima (5)	5	0.05
Potawatomi (1)	1	0.01
Pueblo (3)	11	0.10
Shoshone (1)	5	0.05
Sioux (2)	5	0.05
Tohono O'Odham (4)	8	0.08
Yaqui (3)	3	0.03
All other tribes (1)	5	0.05
American Indian tribes, not spec.	11	0.10
Arab:	11	0.10
Lebanese	6	0.06
Other Arab	5	0.05
Armenian	6	0.06
Asian:	71	0.67
Chinese, ex. Taiwanese (10)	13	0.12
Filipino (11)	12	0.11
Indian (3)	6	0.06
Japanese (13)	26	0.25
Korean (5)	5	0.05
Thai (1)	1	0.01
Vietnamese (3)	5	0.05
Other Asian, not specified	3	0.03
Assyrian/Chaldean/Syriac	6	0.06
Australian	8	0.08
Austrian	36	0.34
Belgian	7	0.07
British	30	0.28
Canadian	11	0.10
Celtic	15	0.14
Croatian	8	0.08
Czechoslovakian	71	0.67
Danish	44	0.42
Dutch	76	0.72
English	1,106	10.43
European	80	0.75
Finnish	36	0.34
French, except Basque	236	2.23
French Canadian	89	0.84
German	1,119	10.56
Greek	37	0.35
Hawaii Native/Pacific Islander:	13	0.12
Micronesian: (2)	2	0.02
Guamanian/Chamorro (1)	1	0.01
Other Micronesian (1)	1	0.01
Polynesian: (1)	4	0.04
Native Hawaiian	3	0.03
Samoan (1)	1	0.01
Other Pac. Isl., not spec. (2)	7	0.07
Hispanic or Latino:	5,529	52.43
Central American:	6	0.06
Costa Rican	3	0.03
Panamanian	2	0.02
Salvadoran	1	0.01
Cuban	14	0.13
Dominican Republic	1	0.01
Mexican	3,071	29.12
Puerto Rican	13	0.12
South American:	20	0.19
Argentinean	4	0.04
Bolivian	1	0.01
Colombian	2	0.02
Paraguayan	2	0.02
Peruvian	6	0.06
Venezuelan	5	0.05
Other Hispanic or Latino	2,404	22.80
Irish	712	6.72
Italian	293	2.76
Lithuanian	7	0.07
Norwegian	107	1.01
Pennsylvania German	6	0.06
Polish	74	0.70
Russian	59	0.56
Scotch-Irish	139	1.31
Scottish	182	1.72
Slavic	9	0.08
Swedish	121	1.14
Swiss	33	0.31
Turkish	10	0.09
Ukrainian	31	0.29
United States or American	653	6.16
Welsh	23	0.22
White:	7,880	74.73
Not Hispanic (4,693)	4,809	45.60
Hispanic (2,870)	3,071	29.12
Yugoslavian	5	0.05

South Valley

Place Type: Census Designated Place
County: Bernalillo
Population: 39,060

Ancestry/Race	Number	%
Afghan	40	0.10
African American/Black:	564	1.44
Not Hispanic (355)	409	1.05
Hispanic (92)	155	0.40
African, sub-Saharan:	8	0.02
Other sub-Saharan African	8	0.02
Alaska Native tribes, specified:	12	0.03
Alaska Athabascan (4)	8	0.02
Eskimo (3)	3	0.01
Tlingit-Haida	1	0.00
Am. Ind. or Alaska Nat., not spec.	261	0.67
Alsatian	9	0.02
American Indian tribes, specified:	729	1.87
Apache (22)	41	0.10
Blackfeet	7	0.02
Cherokee (29)	68	0.17
Cheyenne (1)	3	0.01
Chickasaw (1)	1	0.00
Chippewa	2	0.01
Choctaw (3)	15	0.04
Comanche (3)	5	0.01
Creek	3	0.01
Crow (9)	10	0.03
Delaware	1	0.00
Iroquois (4)	9	0.02
Kiowa (1)	1	0.00
Latin American Indians (33)	54	0.14
Lumbee	2	0.01
Navajo (187)	224	0.57
Osage	2	0.01
Ottawa (1)	1	0.00
Potawatomi (2)	5	0.01
Pueblo (152)	207	0.53
Seminole	1	0.00
Sioux (14)	21	0.05
Tohono O'Odham (3)	3	0.01
Ute	2	0.01
Yaqui	2	0.01
Yuman (2)	2	0.01
All other tribes (22)	37	0.09
American Indian tribes, not spec.	85	0.22
Arab:	43	0.11
Lebanese	43	0.11
Armenian	11	0.03
Asian:	233	0.60
Chinese, ex. Taiwanese (21)	33	0.08
Filipino (24)	42	0.11
Indian (14)	22	0.06
Japanese (13)	42	0.11
Korean (23)	33	0.08
Laotian (3)	3	0.01
Pakistani (2)	3	0.01
Vietnamese (15)	21	0.05
Other Asian, not specified (8)	34	0.09
Austrian	36	0.09
Belgian	48	0.12
Brazilian	9	0.02
British	48	0.12
Canadian	32	0.08
Croatian	6	0.02
Czech	45	0.11
Czechoslovakian	18	0.05
Danish	47	0.12
Dutch	78	0.20
English	1,263	3.22
European	158	0.40
Finnish	22	0.06
French, except Basque	451	1.15
French Canadian	64	0.16
German	1,665	4.24
Greek	38	0.10
Hawaii Native/Pacific Islander:	75	0.19
Melanesian: (3)	3	0.01
Fijian (3)	3	0.01
Micronesian: (7)	8	0.02
Guamanian/Chamorro (7)	8	0.02
Polynesian: (29)	42	0.11
Native Hawaiian (11)	22	0.06
Samoan (18)	20	0.05
Other Pac. Isl., not spec. (9)	22	0.06
Hispanic or Latino:	30,307	77.59
Central American:	45	0.12

Notes: 1. Figures in the "Number" column do not add up to the total population due to: a) Ancestry/Race overlap — e.g. persons can report being both White and Irish, b) persons of Hispanic origin can report being any race, c) persons reporting two ancestries are counted in both categories. 2. Numbers in parentheses indicate the number of persons reporting this ancestry/race alone, not in combination with any other ancestry/race. 3. Refer to the Explanation of Data in the front of the book for more detailed information.

Ancestry/Race	Number	%
Costa Rican	3	0.01
Guatemalan	16	0.04
Honduran	1	0.00
Nicaraguan	13	0.03
Panamanian	1	0.00
Salvadoran	5	0.01
Other Central American	6	0.02
Cuban	67	0.17
Dominican Republic	3	0.01
Mexican	12,280	31.44
Puerto Rican	63	0.16
South American:	22	0.06
Argentinean	1	0.00
Bolivian	3	0.01
Colombian	7	0.02
Ecuadorian	3	0.01
Paraguayan	1	0.00
Peruvian	5	0.01
Other South American	2	0.01
Other Hispanic or Latino	17,827	45.64
Hungarian	94	0.24
Iranian	6	0.02
Irish	1,183	3.01
Italian	573	1.46
Latvian	9	0.02
Lithuanian	14	0.04
Northern European	78	0.20
Norwegian	164	0.42
Pennsylvania German	6	0.02
Polish	188	0.48
Portuguese	41	0.10
Romanian	18	0.05
Russian	64	0.16
Scandinavian	11	0.03
Scotch-Irish	260	0.66
Scottish	157	0.40
Slavic	15	0.04
Slovak	11	0.03
Slovene	5	0.01
Swedish	124	0.32
Swiss	3	0.01
Ukrainian	19	0.05
United States or American	1,637	4.17
Welsh	153	0.39
West Indian, excl. Hispanic:	12	0.03
Dutch West Indian	12	0.03
White:	23,835	61.02
Not Hispanic (7,480)	7,740	19.82
Hispanic (14,857)	16,095	41.21
Yugoslavian	10	0.03

Sunland Park

Place Type: City
County: Dona Ana
Population: 13,309

Ancestry/Race	Number	%
African American/Black:	95	0.71
Not Hispanic (21)	27	0.20
Hispanic (50)	68	0.51
African, sub-Saharan:	13	0.10
African	13	0.10
Am. Ind. or Alaska Nat., not spec.	72	0.54
American Indian tribes, specified:	44	0.33
Apache (8)	10	0.08
Cherokee (2)	4	0.03
Latin American Indians (14)	14	0.11
Navajo (7)	7	0.05
Pueblo (7)	7	0.05
All other tribes (1)	2	0.02
American Indian tribes, not spec.	10	0.08
Asian:	21	0.16
Chinese, ex. Taiwanese (1)	2	0.02
Filipino (1)	4	0.03
Indian (3)	7	0.05
Japanese (4)	6	0.05
Other Asian, specified	2	0.02
Bulgarian	6	0.05
Canadian	14	0.11
Dutch	10	0.08
English	63	0.47
French, except Basque	34	0.26
French Canadian	14	0.11
German	47	0.35
Hawaii Native/Pacific Islander:	7	0.05
Polynesian: (1)	3	0.02
Native Hawaiian	1	0.01
Samoan (1)	2	0.02
Other Pac. Isl., specified	2	0.02
Other Pac. Isl., not spec.	2	0.02
Hispanic or Latino:	12,835	96.44
Central American:	14	0.11
Costa Rican	2	0.02
Guatemalan	4	0.03
Honduran	2	0.02
Panamanian	1	0.01
Salvadoran	4	0.03
Other Central American	1	0.01
Cuban	1	0.01
Mexican	11,009	82.72
Puerto Rican	11	0.08
South American:	3	0.02
Chilean	1	0.01
Peruvian	2	0.02
Other Hispanic or Latino	1,797	13.50
Irish	38	0.29
Italian	9	0.07
Pennsylvania German	11	0.08
Polish	5	0.04
Scotch-Irish	9	0.07
Scottish	4	0.03
United States or American	273	2.05
White:	9,638	72.42
Not Hispanic (381)	395	2.97
Hispanic (8,909)	9,243	69.45

Albany

Place Type: City
County: Albany
Population: 95,658

Ancestry/Race	Number	%
Afghan	50	0.05
African American/Black:	28,638	29.94
Not Hispanic (26,042)	27,401	28.64
Hispanic (873)	1,237	1.29
African, sub-Saharan:	1,810	1.89
African	1,188	1.24
Ethiopian	28	0.03
Ghanian	210	0.22
Kenyan	25	0.03
Liberian	28	0.03
Nigerian	103	0.11
South African	14	0.01
Sudanese	105	0.11
Ugandan	13	0.01
Zimbabwean	18	0.02
Other sub-Saharan African	78	0.08
Alaska Native tribes, specified:	2	0.00
Eskimo (1)	2	0.00
Am. Ind. or Alaska Nat., not spec.	470	0.49
Albanian	111	0.12
Alsatian	16	0.02
American Indian tribes, specified:	448	0.47
Apache (1)	14	0.01
Blackfeet (6)	41	0.04
Cherokee (30)	134	0.14
Cheyenne	4	0.00
Chippewa (3)	5	0.01
Choctaw (1)	7	0.01
Cree	2	0.00
Creek	1	0.00
Delaware (2)	2	0.00
Iroquois (35)	100	0.10
Latin American Indians (14)	34	0.04
Navajo (4)	7	0.01
Potawatomi (1)	3	0.00
Seminole (3)	11	0.01
Shoshone (1)	1	0.00
Sioux (6)	16	0.02
All other tribes (31)	66	0.07
American Indian tribes, not spec.	52	0.05
Arab:	400	0.42
Arab/Arabic	152	0.16
Egyptian	75	0.08
Iraqi	7	0.01
Lebanese	88	0.09
Moroccan	11	0.01
Palestinian	15	0.02
Syrian	44	0.05
Other Arab	8	0.01
Armenian	139	0.15
Asian:	3,779	3.95
Bangladeshi (14)	26	0.03
Cambodian (9)	10	0.01
Chinese, ex. Taiwanese (941)	1,049	1.10
Filipino (159)	216	0.23
Hmong (1)	1	0.00
Indian (785)	925	0.97
Indonesian (14)	20	0.02
Japanese (133)	183	0.19
Korean (336)	379	0.40
Laotian (2)	2	0.00
Malaysian (2)	9	0.01
Pakistani (155)	236	0.25
Sri Lankan (3)	3	0.00
Taiwanese (48)	60	0.06
Thai (18)	24	0.03
Vietnamese (328)	353	0.37
Other Asian, specified (14)	19	0.02
Other Asian, not specified (88)	264	0.28
Assyrian/Chaldean/Syriac	23	0.02
Australian	24	0.03
Austrian	410	0.43
Basque	22	0.02
Belgian	21	0.02
Brazilian	19	0.02
British	317	0.33
Bulgarian	55	0.06
Canadian	197	0.21
Celtic	68	0.07
Croatian	71	0.07
Czech	160	0.17
Czechoslovakian	169	0.18
Danish	195	0.20
Dutch	1,814	1.90
Eastern European	161	0.17
English	5,013	5.24
European	523	0.55
Finnish	117	0.12
French, except Basque	2,904	3.04
French Canadian	950	0.99
German	9,927	10.38
German Russian	12	0.01
Greek	521	0.54
Guyanese	235	0.25
Hawaii Native/Pacific Islander:	111	0.12
Micronesian: (5)	11	0.01
Guamanian/Chamorro (5)	11	0.01
Polynesian: (15)	36	0.04
Native Hawaiian (6)	24	0.03
Samoan (9)	12	0.01
Other Pac. Isl., specified	5	0.01
Other Pac. Isl., not spec. (13)	59	0.06
Hispanic or Latino:	5,349	5.59
Central American:	144	0.15
Costa Rican	17	0.02
Guatemalan	15	0.02
Honduran	26	0.03
Nicaraguan	6	0.01
Panamanian	51	0.05
Salvadoran	20	0.02
Other Central American	9	0.01
Cuban	169	0.18
Dominican Republic	337	0.35
Mexican	359	0.38
Puerto Rican	3,094	3.23
South American:	279	0.29

Notes: 1. Figures in the "Number" column do not add up to the total population due to: a) Ancestry/Race overlap — e.g. persons can report being both White and Irish, b) persons of Hispanic origin can report being any race, c) persons reporting two ancestries are counted in both categories. 2. Numbers in parentheses indicate the number of persons reporting this ancestry/race alone, not in combination with any other ancestry/race. 3. Refer to the Explanation of Data in the front of the book for more detailed information.

	Number	%
Argentinean	19	0.02
Bolivian	2	0.00
Chilean	13	0.01
Colombian	116	0.12
Ecuadorian	47	0.05
Paraguayan	1	0.00
Peruvian	39	0.04
Uruguayan	4	0.00
Venezuelan	22	0.02
Other South American	16	0.02
Other Hispanic or Latino	967	1.01
Hungarian	445	0.47
Iranian	56	0.06
Irish	17,209	17.99
Israeli	102	0.11
Italian	11,816	12.35
Latvian	34	0.04
Lithuanian	314	0.33
Luxemburger	16	0.02
Macedonian	8	0.01
Maltese	53	0.06
Northern European	37	0.04
Norwegian	271	0.28
Polish	4,108	4.29
Portuguese	174	0.18
Romanian	108	0.11
Russian	2,065	2.16
Scandinavian	25	0.03
Scotch-Irish	684	0.72
Scottish	994	1.04
Serbian	11	0.01
Slavic	57	0.06
Slovak	149	0.16
Slovene	6	0.01
Swedish	496	0.52
Swiss	144	0.15
Turkish	37	0.04
Ukrainian	662	0.69
United States or American	2,356	2.46
Welsh	492	0.51
West Indian, excl. Hispanic:	1,672	1.75
Barbadian	76	0.08
British West Indian	84	0.09
Haitian	172	0.18
Jamaican	1,064	1.11
Trinidadian and Tobagonian	58	0.06
U.S. Virgin Islander	17	0.02
West Indian	197	0.21
Other West Indian	4	0.00
White:	62,320	65.15
Not Hispanic (58,459)	60,000	62.72
Hispanic (1,924)	2,320	2.43
Yugoslavian	93	0.10

Alden

Place Type: Town
County: Erie
Population: 10,470

Ancestry/Race	Number	%
African American/Black:	724	6.91
Not Hispanic (691)	706	6.74
Hispanic (18)	18	0.17
African, sub-Saharan:	16	0.15
African	16	0.15
Am. Ind. or Alaska Nat., not spec.	18	0.17
American Indian tribes, specified:	21	0.20
Cherokee (1)	6	0.06
Iroquois (14)	14	0.13
Sioux	1	0.01
American Indian tribes, not spec.	1	0.01
Arab:	48	0.46
Jordanian	11	0.11
Lebanese	37	0.35
Asian:	30	0.29
Chinese, ex. Taiwanese (9)	9	0.09
Filipino (4)	5	0.05
Indian (2)	4	0.04
Japanese (5)	5	0.05
Korean (3)	4	0.04
Vietnamese	1	0.01
Other Asian, not specified (1)	2	0.02
Austrian	49	0.47
Belgian	14	0.13
British	7	0.07
Bulgarian	18	0.17
Canadian	39	0.37
Czech	82	0.78
Danish	8	0.08
Dutch	199	1.90
English	756	7.22
European	8	0.08
French, except Basque	208	1.99
French Canadian	153	1.46
German	3,964	37.86
German Russian	1	0.01
Greek	46	0.44
Hawaii Native/Pacific Islander:	7	0.07
Polynesian: (4)	4	0.04
Native Hawaiian (2)	2	0.02
Samoan (2)	2	0.02
Other Pac. Isl., not spec. (2)	3	0.03
Hispanic or Latino:	285	2.72
Central American:	4	0.04
Guatemalan	2	0.02
Honduran	1	0.01
Nicaraguan	1	0.01
Cuban	12	0.11
Dominican Republic	28	0.27
Mexican	14	0.13
Puerto Rican	174	1.66
South American:	14	0.13
Chilean	5	0.05
Colombian	4	0.04
Ecuadorian	4	0.04
Peruvian	1	0.01
Other Hispanic or Latino	39	0.37
Hungarian	55	0.53
Irish	1,452	13.87
Italian	1,083	10.34
Lithuanian	5	0.05
Macedonian	8	0.08
Norwegian	16	0.15
Pennsylvania German	7	0.07
Polish	2,572	24.57
Portuguese	7	0.07
Russian	67	0.64
Scandinavian	7	0.07
Scotch-Irish	72	0.69
Scottish	164	1.57
Serbian	16	0.15
Swedish	64	0.61
Swiss	21	0.20
Ukrainian	42	0.40
United States or American	389	3.72
Welsh	19	0.18
White:	9,550	91.21
Not Hispanic (9,409)	9,434	90.11
Hispanic (114)	116	1.11
Yugoslavian	15	0.14

Amherst

Place Type: Town
County: Erie
Population: 116,510

Ancestry/Race	Number	%
African American/Black:	5,004	4.29
Not Hispanic (4,478)	4,882	4.19
Hispanic (66)	122	0.10
African, sub-Saharan:	275	0.24
African	91	0.08
Ethiopian	18	0.02
Ghanian	48	0.04
Kenyan	11	0.01
Nigerian	71	0.06
South African	36	0.03
Alaska Native tribes, specified:	2	0.00
Alaska Athabascan (2)	2	0.00
Am. Ind. or Alaska Nat., not spec.	113	0.10
Albanian	52	0.04
Alsatian	19	0.02
American Indian tribes, specified:	234	0.20
Apache	1	0.00
Blackfeet (1)	12	0.01
Cherokee (13)	36	0.03
Cheyenne	7	0.01
Chippewa (6)	7	0.01
Choctaw (1)	1	0.00
Comanche (1)	1	0.00
Cree	3	0.00
Creek (2)	2	0.00
Delaware (6)	6	0.01
Iroquois (74)	131	0.11
Latin American Indians	4	0.00
Navajo (1)	2	0.00
Osage	1	0.00
Ottawa (1)	1	0.00
Potawatomi	2	0.00
Seminole (1)	3	0.00
Sioux	1	0.00
All other tribes (3)	13	0.01
American Indian tribes, not spec.	8	0.01
Arab:	959	0.82
Arab/Arabic	65	0.06
Egyptian	101	0.09
Iraqi	28	0.02
Jordanian	9	0.01
Lebanese	664	0.57
Palestinian	15	0.01
Syrian	50	0.04
Other Arab	27	0.02
Armenian	130	0.11
Asian:	6,611	5.67
Bangladeshi (14)	14	0.01
Cambodian (5)	6	0.01
Chinese, ex. Taiwanese (1,814)	1,940	1.67
Filipino (181)	240	0.21
Indian (1,949)	2,055	1.76
Indonesian (35)	37	0.03
Japanese (312)	372	0.32
Korean (1,104)	1,145	0.98
Malaysian (6)	15	0.01
Pakistani (173)	185	0.16
Sri Lankan (52)	54	0.05
Taiwanese (105)	125	0.11
Thai (40)	47	0.04
Vietnamese (149)	157	0.13
Other Asian, specified (12)	17	0.01
Other Asian, not specified (66)	202	0.17
Assyrian/Chaldean/Syriac	9	0.01
Australian	20	0.02
Austrian	748	0.64
Basque	30	0.03
Belgian	81	0.07
Brazilian	62	0.05
British	611	0.52
Canadian	985	0.85
Carpatho Rusyn	6	0.01
Croatian	191	0.16
Czech	352	0.30
Czechoslovakian	194	0.17
Danish	343	0.29
Dutch	1,366	1.17
Eastern European	314	0.27
English	11,843	10.16
Estonian	57	0.05
European	745	0.64
Finnish	36	0.03
French, except Basque	3,805	3.27
French Canadian	662	0.57
German	29,827	25.60
Greek	904	0.78
Guyanese	47	0.04
Hawaii Native/Pacific Islander:	66	0.06
Micronesian: (1)	3	0.00
Guamanian/Chamorro (1)	1	0.00
Other Micronesian	2	0.00

Notes: 1. Figures in the "Number" column do not add up to the total population due to: a) Ancestry/Race overlap — e.g. persons can report being both White and Irish, b) persons of Hispanic origin can report being any race, c) persons reporting two ancestries are counted in both categories. 2. Numbers in parentheses indicate the number of persons reporting this ancestry/race alone, not in combination with any other ancestry/race. 3. Refer to the Explanation of Data in the front of the book for more detailed information.

Ancestry/Race	Number	%
Polynesian: (5)	21	0.02
Native Hawaiian (2)	15	0.01
Samoan (3)	6	0.01
Other Pac. Isl., not spec. (23)	42	0.04
Hispanic or Latino:	1,579	1.36
Central American:	57	0.05
Costa Rican	9	0.01
Guatemalan	10	0.01
Honduran	8	0.01
Nicaraguan	3	0.00
Panamanian	19	0.02
Salvadoran	8	0.01
Cuban	96	0.08
Dominican Republic	52	0.04
Mexican	257	0.22
Puerto Rican	590	0.51
South American:	210	0.18
Argentinean	39	0.03
Bolivian	5	0.00
Chilean	15	0.01
Colombian	79	0.07
Ecuadorian	28	0.02
Paraguayan	2	0.00
Peruvian	22	0.02
Venezuelan	9	0.01
Other South American	11	0.01
Other Hispanic or Latino	317	0.27
Hungarian	1,316	1.13
Icelander	8	0.01
Iranian	147	0.13
Irish	19,215	16.49
Israeli	42	0.04
Italian	20,696	17.76
Latvian	91	0.08
Lithuanian	373	0.32
Luxemburger	28	0.02
Macedonian	36	0.03
Maltese	35	0.03
Northern European	43	0.04
Norwegian	509	0.44
Pennsylvania German	48	0.04
Polish	15,136	12.99
Romanian	315	0.27
Russian	2,937	2.52
Scandinavian	134	0.12
Scotch-Irish	1,500	1.29
Scottish	2,546	2.19
Serbian	58	0.05
Slavic	70	0.06
Slovak	270	0.23
Slovene	34	0.03
Soviet Union	6	0.01
Swedish	1,399	1.20
Swiss	459	0.39
Turkish	167	0.14
Ukrainian	1,158	0.99
United States or American	2,585	2.22
Welsh	899	0.77
West Indian, excl. Hispanic:	398	0.34
Bahamian	7	0.01
British West Indian	10	0.01
Haitian	50	0.04
Jamaican	277	0.24
Trinidadian and Tobagonian	9	0.01
West Indian	45	0.04
White:	105,096	90.20
Not Hispanic (102,941)	103,945	89.22
Hispanic (1,077)	1,151	0.99
Yugoslavian	45	0.04

Amsterdam

Place Type: City
County: Montgomery
Population: 18,355

Ancestry/Race	Number	%
Afghan	25	0.14
African American/Black:	532	2.90
Not Hispanic (294)	369	2.01
Hispanic (105)	163	0.89
African, sub-Saharan:	18	0.10
African	18	0.10
Am. Ind. or Alaska Nat., not spec.	71	0.39
American Indian tribes, specified:	35	0.19
Cherokee (2)	4	0.02
Chippewa	1	0.01
Cree (1)	1	0.01
Iroquois (5)	15	0.08
Latin American Indians (2)	3	0.02
Sioux (1)	3	0.02
All other tribes (1)	8	0.04
American Indian tribes, not spec.	3	0.02
Arab:	13	0.07
Arab/Arabic	5	0.03
Lebanese	8	0.04
Armenian	6	0.03
Asian:	163	0.89
Bangladeshi (1)	1	0.01
Chinese, ex. Taiwanese (25)	29	0.16
Filipino (19)	22	0.12
Indian (45)	61	0.33
Japanese (6)	7	0.04
Korean (11)	13	0.07
Laotian (2)	2	0.01
Pakistani (7)	9	0.05
Thai (1)	3	0.02
Vietnamese (8)	11	0.06
Other Asian, not specified	5	0.03
Austrian	41	0.22
Belgian	13	0.07
British	18	0.10
Canadian	24	0.13
Czech	19	0.10
Czechoslovakian	16	0.09
Dutch	482	2.63
Eastern European	23	0.13
English	1,105	6.02
European	7	0.04
Finnish	9	0.05
French, except Basque	723	3.94
French Canadian	227	1.24
German	2,204	12.01
Greek	65	0.35
Guyanese	8	0.04
Hawaii Native/Pacific Islander:	9	0.05
Polynesian: (4)	7	0.04
Native Hawaiian (4)	7	0.04
Other Pac. Isl., not spec.	2	0.01
Hispanic or Latino:	2,941	16.02
Central American:	160	0.87
Costa Rican	128	0.70
Guatemalan	8	0.04
Honduran	2	0.01
Panamanian	10	0.05
Salvadoran	7	0.04
Other Central American	5	0.03
Cuban	57	0.31
Dominican Republic	93	0.51
Mexican	61	0.33
Puerto Rican	2,124	11.57
South American:	39	0.21
Argentinean	5	0.03
Colombian	21	0.11
Ecuadorian	5	0.03
Peruvian	3	0.02
Venezuelan	5	0.03
Other Hispanic or Latino	407	2.22
Hungarian	51	0.28
Irish	2,542	13.85
Italian	4,546	24.77
Lithuanian	530	2.89
Norwegian	29	0.16
Polish	3,670	19.99
Portuguese	42	0.23
Russian	51	0.28
Scotch-Irish	91	0.50
Scottish	143	0.78
Slovak	14	0.08
Swedish	49	0.27
Swiss	18	0.10
Turkish	8	0.04
Ukrainian	193	1.05
United States or American	808	4.40
Welsh	80	0.44
West Indian, excl. Hispanic:	30	0.16
Barbadian	5	0.03
British West Indian	6	0.03
Jamaican	8	0.04
West Indian	11	0.06
White:	16,839	91.74
Not Hispanic (14,797)	14,925	81.31
Hispanic (1,725)	1,914	10.43
Yugoslavian	19	0.10

Arcadia

Place Type: Town
County: Wayne
Population: 14,889

Ancestry/Race	Number	%
African American/Black:	722	4.85
Not Hispanic (527)	651	4.37
Hispanic (45)	71	0.48
African, sub-Saharan:	21	0.14
African	21	0.14
Am. Ind. or Alaska Nat., not spec.	45	0.30
American Indian tribes, specified:	65	0.44
Blackfeet	9	0.06
Cherokee (5)	17	0.11
Chippewa (1)	1	0.01
Delaware (1)	1	0.01
Iroquois (17)	34	0.23
All other tribes (1)	3	0.02
American Indian tribes, not spec.	2	0.01
Arab:	82	0.55
Lebanese	41	0.27
Syrian	41	0.27
Asian:	79	0.53
Bangladeshi (2)	2	0.01
Cambodian (5)	5	0.03
Chinese, ex. Taiwanese (7)	7	0.05
Filipino (8)	9	0.06
Indian (8)	8	0.05
Japanese (7)	10	0.07
Korean (21)	23	0.15
Laotian (4)	4	0.03
Thai (1)	3	0.02
Vietnamese (2)	2	0.01
Other Asian, not specified (1)	6	0.04
Austrian	16	0.11
Belgian	41	0.27
British	31	0.21
Canadian	72	0.48
Croatian	7	0.05
Czech	18	0.12
Czechoslovakian	21	0.14
Danish	37	0.25
Dutch	2,672	17.80
English	2,654	17.68
European	63	0.42
Finnish	8	0.05
French, except Basque	699	4.66
French Canadian	178	1.19
German	2,994	19.95
Greek	30	0.20
Hawaii Native/Pacific Islander:	5	0.03
Micronesian: (5)	5	0.03
Guamanian/Chamorro (1)	1	0.01
Other Micronesian (4)	4	0.03
Hispanic or Latino:	823	5.53
Central American:	51	0.34
Honduran	42	0.28
Panamanian	8	0.05
Salvadoran	1	0.01
Cuban	7	0.05
Dominican Republic	9	0.06
Mexican	41	0.28
Puerto Rican	617	4.14

Notes: 1. Figures in the "Number" column do not add up to the total population due to: a) Ancestry/Race overlap — e.g. persons can report being both White and Irish, b) persons of Hispanic origin can report being any race, c) persons reporting two ancestries are counted in both categories. 2. Numbers in parentheses indicate the number of persons reporting this ancestry/race alone, not in combination with any other ancestry/race. 3. Refer to the Explanation of Data in the front of the book for more detailed information.

South American:	8	0.05
Colombian	2	0.01
Ecuadorian	1	0.01
Peruvian	2	0.01
Uruguayan	1	0.01
Venezuelan	2	0.01
Other Hispanic or Latino	90	0.60
Hungarian	43	0.29
Irish	1,983	13.21
Italian	1,912	12.74
Lithuanian	25	0.17
Norwegian	10	0.07
Pennsylvania German	24	0.16
Polish	383	2.55
Portuguese	5	0.03
Russian	24	0.16
Scandinavian	22	0.15
Scotch-Irish	151	1.01
Scottish	331	2.21
Slovak	33	0.22
Swedish	26	0.17
Swiss	9	0.06
Ukrainian	24	0.16
United States or American	853	5.68
Welsh	143	0.95
West Indian, excl. Hispanic:	24	0.16
Jamaican	24	0.16
White:	13,864	93.12
Not Hispanic (13,245)	13,419	90.13
Hispanic (369)	445	2.99
Yugoslavian	19	0.13

Arlington

Place Type: Census Designated Place
County: Dutchess
Population: 12,481

Ancestry/Race	Number	%
African American/Black:	1,648	13.20
Not Hispanic (1,483)	1,584	12.69
Hispanic (49)	64	0.51
African, sub-Saharan:	159	1.28
African	27	0.22
Cape Verdean	25	0.20
Ghanian	22	0.18
Kenyan	41	0.33
Nigerian	20	0.16
Somalian	24	0.19
Am. Ind. or Alaska Nat., not spec.	28	0.22
American Indian tribes, specified:	47	0.38
Apache	1	0.01
Blackfeet	5	0.04
Cherokee (9)	25	0.20
Chickasaw (1)	1	0.01
Choctaw	1	0.01
Creek	2	0.02
Iroquois (1)	2	0.02
Latin American Indians (4)	5	0.04
Sioux (1)	2	0.02
All other tribes	3	0.02
American Indian tribes, not spec.	2	0.02
Arab:	149	1.20
Arab/Arabic	99	0.80
Jordanian	14	0.11
Lebanese	29	0.23
Palestinian	7	0.06
Armenian	18	0.14
Asian:	891	7.14
Bangladeshi (7)	7	0.06
Cambodian (1)	1	0.01
Chinese, ex. Taiwanese (162)	196	1.57
Filipino (44)	62	0.50
Indian (369)	389	3.12
Indonesian (1)	1	0.01
Japanese (19)	42	0.34
Korean (76)	84	0.67
Laotian (4)	4	0.03
Malaysian	1	0.01
Pakistani (25)	28	0.22
Sri Lankan (1)	1	0.01
Taiwanese (5)	7	0.06
Thai (8)	11	0.09
Vietnamese (17)	20	0.16
Other Asian, specified (2)	4	0.03
Other Asian, not specified (10)	33	0.26
Austrian	57	0.46
Basque	9	0.07
Brazilian	29	0.23
British	191	1.54
Canadian	9	0.07
Celtic	10	0.08
Czech	23	0.18
Czechoslovakian	16	0.13
Danish	26	0.21
Dutch	244	1.96
Eastern European	6	0.05
English	1,281	10.30
European	58	0.47
Finnish	56	0.45
French, except Basque	375	3.01
French Canadian	234	1.88
German	1,639	13.18
Greek	145	1.17
Hawaii Native/Pacific Islander:	24	0.19
Micronesian:	2	0.02
Guamanian/Chamorro	2	0.02
Polynesian: (5)	16	0.13
Native Hawaiian (5)	14	0.11
Samoan	2	0.02
Other Pac. Isl., not spec.	6	0.05
Hispanic or Latino:	672	5.38
Central American:	36	0.29
Costa Rican	1	0.01
Guatemalan	5	0.04
Honduran	5	0.04
Nicaraguan	2	0.02
Panamanian	19	0.15
Salvadoran	4	0.03
Cuban	27	0.22
Dominican Republic	24	0.19
Mexican	117	0.94
Puerto Rican	289	2.32
South American:	67	0.54
Argentinean	8	0.06
Chilean	6	0.05
Colombian	22	0.18
Ecuadorian	7	0.06
Peruvian	21	0.17
Venezuelan	2	0.02
Other South American	1	0.01
Other Hispanic or Latino	112	0.90
Hungarian	223	1.79
Iranian	56	0.45
Irish	1,991	16.01
Israeli	19	0.15
Italian	2,184	17.56
Latvian	9	0.07
Lithuanian	25	0.20
Norwegian	111	0.89
Polish	706	5.68
Portuguese	62	0.50
Romanian	84	0.68
Russian	411	3.30
Scandinavian	49	0.39
Scotch-Irish	63	0.51
Scottish	239	1.92
Serbian	19	0.15
Slavic	17	0.14
Slovak	45	0.36
Swedish	233	1.87
Swiss	38	0.31
Turkish	9	0.07
Ukrainian	92	0.74
United States or American	402	3.23
Welsh	91	0.73
West Indian, excl. Hispanic:	462	3.71
Bahamian	25	0.20
Barbadian	10	0.08
Jamaican	391	3.14
Trinidadian and Tobagonian	36	0.29
White:	9,864	79.03
Not Hispanic (9,256)	9,479	75.95
Hispanic (355)	385	3.08
Yugoslavian	36	0.29

Auburn

Place Type: City
County: Cayuga
Population: 28,574

Ancestry/Race	Number	%
African American/Black:	2,451	8.58
Not Hispanic (2,113)	2,367	8.28
Hispanic (57)	84	0.29
African, sub-Saharan:	39	0.14
African	39	0.14
Am. Ind. or Alaska Nat., not spec.	77	0.27
American Indian tribes, specified:	135	0.47
Blackfeet (1)	5	0.02
Cherokee (7)	22	0.08
Chippewa (1)	13	0.05
Choctaw (2)	8	0.03
Cree	1	0.00
Creek	4	0.01
Iroquois (29)	58	0.20
Latin American Indians (1)	2	0.01
Seminole	4	0.01
Sioux (3)	3	0.01
All other tribes (1)	15	0.05
American Indian tribes, not spec.	7	0.02
Arab:	103	0.36
Arab/Arabic	11	0.04
Egyptian	18	0.06
Lebanese	20	0.07
Syrian	35	0.12
Other Arab	19	0.07
Armenian	8	0.03
Asian:	193	0.68
Chinese, ex. Taiwanese (30)	36	0.13
Filipino (16)	19	0.07
Indian (41)	43	0.15
Indonesian	1	0.00
Japanese (7)	7	0.02
Korean (20)	24	0.08
Laotian (11)	12	0.04
Pakistani (6)	7	0.02
Taiwanese (1)	1	0.00
Thai (2)	6	0.02
Vietnamese (16)	21	0.07
Other Asian, not specified (9)	16	0.06
Australian	8	0.03
Austrian	76	0.27
Brazilian	10	0.03
British	28	0.10
Canadian	89	0.31
Czech	36	0.13
Czechoslovakian	95	0.33
Danish	111	0.39
Dutch	777	2.72
Eastern European	10	0.03
English	4,180	14.63
European	28	0.10
French, except Basque	1,012	3.54
French Canadian	505	1.77
German	3,539	12.39
Greek	60	0.21
Hawaii Native/Pacific Islander:	15	0.05
Micronesian: (1)	3	0.01
Guamanian/Chamorro (1)	3	0.01
Polynesian: (5)	9	0.03
Native Hawaiian (2)	4	0.01
Samoan (3)	4	0.01
Other Polynesian	1	0.00
Other Pac. Isl., not spec.	3	0.01
Hispanic or Latino:	806	2.82
Central American:	23	0.08
Costa Rican	1	0.00
Guatemalan	5	0.02

Notes: 1. Figures in the "Number" column do not add up to the total population due to: a) Ancestry/Race overlap — e.g. persons can report being both White and Irish, b) persons of Hispanic origin can report being any race, c) persons reporting two ancestries are counted in both categories. 2. Numbers in parentheses indicate the number of persons reporting this ancestry/race alone, not in combination with any other ancestry/race. 3. Refer to the Explanation of Data in the front of the book for more detailed information.

Ancestry/Race	Number	%
Honduran	2	0.01
Nicaraguan	2	0.01
Panamanian	3	0.01
Salvadoran	10	0.03
Cuban	30	0.10
Dominican Republic	69	0.24
Mexican	81	0.28
Puerto Rican	446	1.56
South American:	23	0.08
Argentinean	1	0.00
Colombian	12	0.04
Ecuadorian	6	0.02
Peruvian	3	0.01
Other South American	1	0.00
Other Hispanic or Latino	134	0.47
Hungarian	105	0.37
Irish	5,781	20.23
Italian	6,310	22.08
Lithuanian	24	0.08
Macedonian	15	0.05
Norwegian	80	0.28
Pennsylvania German	14	0.05
Polish	2,575	9.01
Portuguese	8	0.03
Romanian	7	0.02
Russian	225	0.79
Scandinavian	10	0.03
Scotch-Irish	293	1.03
Scottish	348	1.22
Serbian	32	0.11
Slavic	30	0.10
Slovak	14	0.05
Swedish	69	0.24
Swiss	76	0.27
Ukrainian	1,352	4.73
United States or American	1,282	4.49
Welsh	129	0.45
West Indian, excl. Hispanic:	40	0.14
Jamaican	40	0.14
White:	25,694	89.92
Not Hispanic (24,971)	25,321	88.62
Hispanic (336)	373	1.31

Aurora

Place Type: Town
County: Erie
Population: 13,996

Ancestry/Race	Number	%
African American/Black:	51	0.36
Not Hispanic (25)	49	0.35
Hispanic	2	0.01
Am. Ind. or Alaska Nat., not spec.	17	0.12
American Indian tribes, specified:	11	0.08
Cherokee	3	0.02
Iroquois (3)	6	0.04
Latin American Indians (2)	2	0.01
Arab:	88	0.63
Lebanese	88	0.63
Asian:	60	0.43
Chinese, ex. Taiwanese (6)	6	0.04
Filipino (8)	9	0.06
Indian (8)	11	0.08
Japanese (5)	6	0.04
Korean (12)	13	0.09
Laotian (1)	1	0.01
Thai (6)	8	0.06
Vietnamese (1)	1	0.01
Other Asian, not specified (3)	5	0.04
Austrian	73	0.52
Belgian	12	0.09
British	90	0.64
Bulgarian	22	0.16
Canadian	67	0.48
Celtic	11	0.08
Croatian	7	0.05
Czech	74	0.53
Czechoslovakian	20	0.14
Danish	64	0.46
Dutch	191	1.36
English	2,530	18.08
European	87	0.62
Finnish	5	0.04
French, except Basque	594	4.24
French Canadian	263	1.88
German	5,502	39.31
Greek	27	0.19
Hawaii Native/Pacific Islander:	3	0.02
Polynesian: (1)	2	0.01
Native Hawaiian	1	0.01
Samoan (1)	1	0.01
Other Pac. Isl., not spec. (1)	1	0.01
Hispanic or Latino:	82	0.59
Central American:	5	0.04
Costa Rican	1	0.01
Guatemalan	1	0.01
Panamanian	3	0.02
Cuban	8	0.06
Dominican Republic	2	0.01
Mexican	18	0.13
Puerto Rican	16	0.11
South American:	18	0.13
Chilean	2	0.01
Colombian	12	0.09
Peruvian	3	0.02
Venezuelan	1	0.01
Other Hispanic or Latino	15	0.11
Hungarian	96	0.69
Iranian	8	0.06
Irish	2,962	21.16
Italian	1,592	11.37
Latvian	34	0.24
Lithuanian	71	0.51
Norwegian	111	0.79
Pennsylvania German	7	0.05
Polish	2,109	15.07
Portuguese	5	0.04
Romanian	8	0.06
Russian	109	0.78
Scotch-Irish	182	1.30
Scottish	327	2.34
Slavic	5	0.04
Slovak	21	0.15
Swedish	240	1.71
Swiss	57	0.41
Ukrainian	170	1.21
United States or American	502	3.59
Welsh	155	1.11
West Indian, excl. Hispanic:	11	0.08
Haitian	6	0.04
West Indian	5	0.04
White:	13,895	99.28
Not Hispanic (13,768)	13,826	98.79
Hispanic (64)	69	0.49
Yugoslavian	7	0.05

Babylon

Place Type: Town
County: Suffolk
Population: 211,792

Ancestry/Race	Number	%
Acadian/Cajun	6	0.00
Afghan	98	0.05
African American/Black:	35,262	16.65
Not Hispanic (31,945)	33,704	15.91
Hispanic (1,192)	1,558	0.74
African, sub-Saharan:	1,409	0.67
African	1,140	0.54
Ethiopian	126	0.06
Ghanian	45	0.02
Nigerian	89	0.04
South African	4	0.00
Other sub-Saharan African	5	0.00
Alaska Native tribes, specified:	2	0.00
Tlingit-Haida	2	0.00
Alaska Native tribes, not specified	2	0.00
Am. Ind. or Alaska Nat., not spec.	632	0.30
Albanian	146	0.07
American Indian tribes, specified:	836	0.39
Apache (1)	7	0.00
Blackfeet (7)	48	0.02
Cherokee (45)	261	0.12
Cheyenne	1	0.00
Chickasaw (2)	2	0.00
Chippewa (2)	4	0.00
Choctaw (4)	12	0.01
Cree	1	0.00
Creek (1)	5	0.00
Houma	1	0.00
Iroquois (26)	70	0.03
Latin American Indians (37)	84	0.04
Lumbee (1)	2	0.00
Navajo (1)	4	0.00
Pima (2)	4	0.00
Pueblo (1)	5	0.00
Seminole (2)	12	0.01
Sioux (9)	20	0.01
Yuman (1)	1	0.00
All other tribes (154)	292	0.14
American Indian tribes, not spec.	107	0.05
Arab:	557	0.26
Arab/Arabic	96	0.05
Egyptian	128	0.06
Iraqi	7	0.00
Lebanese	166	0.08
Moroccan	62	0.03
Palestinian	10	0.00
Syrian	88	0.04
Armenian	162	0.08
Asian:	4,982	2.35
Bangladeshi (45)	76	0.04
Chinese, ex. Taiwanese (868)	1,041	0.49
Filipino (468)	620	0.29
Indian (1,508)	1,779	0.84
Indonesian (6)	6	0.00
Japanese (72)	121	0.06
Korean (347)	385	0.18
Laotian (2)	2	0.00
Malaysian	1	0.00
Pakistani (265)	387	0.18
Sri Lankan (7)	9	0.00
Taiwanese (12)	12	0.01
Thai (52)	67	0.03
Vietnamese (191)	216	0.10
Other Asian, specified	2	0.00
Other Asian, not specified (77)	258	0.12
Australian	24	0.01
Austrian	1,006	0.48
Basque	22	0.01
Belgian	57	0.03
Brazilian	163	0.08
British	264	0.12
Canadian	242	0.11
Celtic	6	0.00
Croatian	272	0.13
Cypriot	23	0.01
Czech	609	0.29
Czechoslovakian	474	0.22
Danish	545	0.26
Dutch	1,310	0.62
Eastern European	180	0.08
English	8,227	3.88
Estonian	45	0.02
European	289	0.14
Finnish	162	0.08
French, except Basque	2,434	1.15
French Canadian	772	0.36
German	31,723	14.98
Greek	2,273	1.07
Guyanese	502	0.24
Hawaii Native/Pacific Islander:	211	0.10
Melanesian: (1)	1	0.00
Fijian (1)	1	0.00
Micronesian: (19)	29	0.01
Guamanian/Chamorro (19)	26	0.01
Other Micronesian	3	0.00
Polynesian: (29)	62	0.03

Notes: 1. Figures in the "Number" column do not add up to the total population due to: a) Ancestry/Race overlap — e.g. persons can report being both White and Irish, b) persons of Hispanic origin can report being any race, c) persons reporting two ancestries are counted in both categories. 2. Numbers in parentheses indicate the number of persons reporting this ancestry/race alone, not in combination with any other ancestry/race. 3. Refer to the Explanation of Data in the front of the book for more detailed information.

Ancestry/Race	Number	%
Native Hawaiian (21)	49	0.02
Samoan (7)	11	0.01
Tongan	1	0.00
Other Polynesian (1)	1	0.00
Other Pac. Isl., not spec. (14)	119	0.06
Hispanic or Latino:	21,275	10.05
Central American:	3,552	1.68
Costa Rican	85	0.04
Guatemalan	234	0.11
Honduran	377	0.18
Nicaraguan	35	0.02
Panamanian	173	0.08
Salvadoran	2,549	1.20
Other Central American	99	0.05
Cuban	487	0.23
Dominican Republic	3,188	1.51
Mexican	756	0.36
Puerto Rican	6,170	2.91
South American:	2,514	1.19
Argentinean	149	0.07
Bolivian	29	0.01
Chilean	105	0.05
Colombian	1,071	0.51
Ecuadorian	540	0.25
Paraguayan	9	0.00
Peruvian	402	0.19
Uruguayan	50	0.02
Venezuelan	59	0.03
Other South American	100	0.05
Other Hispanic or Latino	4,608	2.18
Hungarian	1,402	0.66
Icelander	76	0.04
Iranian	52	0.02
Irish	43,411	20.50
Israeli	48	0.02
Italian	63,967	30.20
Latvian	170	0.08
Lithuanian	505	0.24
Maltese	218	0.10
New Zealander	6	0.00
Northern European	4	0.00
Norwegian	1,678	0.79
Pennsylvania German	32	0.02
Polish	11,519	5.44
Portuguese	572	0.27
Romanian	249	0.12
Russian	2,973	1.40
Scandinavian	136	0.06
Scotch-Irish	1,575	0.74
Scottish	1,540	0.73
Serbian	15	0.01
Slavic	105	0.05
Slovak	139	0.07
Slovene	76	0.04
Swedish	1,434	0.68
Swiss	246	0.12
Turkish	544	0.26
Ukrainian	1,323	0.62
United States or American	5,586	2.64
Welsh	368	0.17
West Indian, excl. Hispanic:	6,081	2.87
Bahamian	28	0.01
Barbadian	105	0.05
Belizean	38	0.02
Bermudan	34	0.02
British West Indian	168	0.08
Dutch West Indian	45	0.02
Haitian	1,819	0.86
Jamaican	2,491	1.18
Trinidadian and Tobagonian	595	0.28
U.S. Virgin Islander	17	0.01
West Indian	741	0.35
White:	165,170	77.99
Not Hispanic (150,180)	152,316	71.92
Hispanic (11,495)	12,854	6.07
Yugoslavian	293	0.14

Babylon

Place Type: Village
County: Suffolk
Population: 12,615

Ancestry/Race	Number	%
African American/Black:	404	3.20
Not Hispanic (315)	374	2.96
Hispanic (24)	30	0.24
African, sub-Saharan:	49	0.39
African	49	0.39
Am. Ind. or Alaska Nat., not spec.	20	0.16
Albanian	26	0.21
American Indian tribes, specified:	24	0.19
Blackfeet	3	0.02
Cherokee (1)	14	0.11
Iroquois (1)	2	0.02
Sioux (1)	2	0.02
All other tribes	3	0.02
American Indian tribes, not spec.	4	0.03
Arab:	20	0.16
Arab/Arabic	6	0.05
Egyptian	9	0.07
Lebanese	5	0.04
Armenian	33	0.26
Asian:	225	1.78
Chinese, ex. Taiwanese (40)	50	0.40
Filipino (18)	27	0.21
Indian (57)	62	0.49
Japanese (7)	17	0.13
Korean (37)	43	0.34
Pakistani (17)	17	0.13
Thai	1	0.01
Vietnamese (6)	7	0.06
Other Asian, not specified (1)	1	0.01
Austrian	55	0.44
Basque	22	0.17
Belgian	6	0.05
Brazilian	7	0.06
British	12	0.10
Canadian	3	0.02
Croatian	6	0.05
Czech	70	0.55
Czechoslovakian	35	0.28
Danish	32	0.25
Dutch	128	1.01
Eastern European	27	0.21
English	968	7.67
Estonian	4	0.03
European	13	0.10
Finnish	9	0.07
French, except Basque	123	0.98
French Canadian	79	0.63
German	2,877	22.81
Greek	125	0.99
Hawaii Native/Pacific Islander:	12	0.10
Micronesian:	4	0.03
Guamanian/Chamorro	1	0.01
Other Micronesian	3	0.02
Polynesian: (1)	1	0.01
Samoan (1)	1	0.01
Other Pac. Isl., not spec.	7	0.06
Hispanic or Latino:	644	5.11
Central American:	46	0.36
Costa Rican	2	0.02
Guatemalan	1	0.01
Honduran	6	0.05
Nicaraguan	5	0.04
Panamanian	2	0.02
Salvadoran	25	0.20
Other Central American	5	0.04
Cuban	26	0.21
Dominican Republic	117	0.93
Mexican	36	0.29
Puerto Rican	199	1.58
South American:	103	0.82
Argentinean	4	0.03
Bolivian	2	0.02
Chilean	11	0.09
Colombian	33	0.26
Ecuadorian	35	0.28
Paraguayan	2	0.02
Peruvian	12	0.10
Uruguayan	4	0.03
Other Hispanic or Latino	117	0.93
Hungarian	131	1.04
Iranian	6	0.05
Irish	3,877	30.73
Italian	3,803	30.15
Latvian	23	0.18
Lithuanian	51	0.40
Maltese	16	0.13
Norwegian	127	1.01
Polish	596	4.72
Portuguese	6	0.05
Romanian	28	0.22
Russian	236	1.87
Scandinavian	12	0.10
Scotch-Irish	290	2.30
Scottish	245	1.94
Slavic	9	0.07
Slovak	13	0.10
Slovene	6	0.05
Swedish	124	0.98
Swiss	27	0.21
Turkish	7	0.06
Ukrainian	81	0.64
United States or American	356	2.82
Welsh	28	0.22
West Indian, excl. Hispanic:	54	0.43
Haitian	22	0.17
Jamaican	9	0.07
Trinidadian and Tobagonian	6	0.05
West Indian	17	0.13
White:	11,866	94.06
Not Hispanic (11,244)	11,419	90.52
Hispanic (420)	447	3.54
Yugoslavian	5	0.04

Baldwin

Place Type: Census Designated Place
County: Nassau
Population: 23,455

Ancestry/Race	Number	%
Afghan	15	0.06
African American/Black:	5,776	24.63
Not Hispanic (5,226)	5,541	23.62
Hispanic (142)	235	1.00
African, sub-Saharan:	261	1.11
African	76	0.32
Ghanian	35	0.15
Nigerian	126	0.54
Sierra Leonean	18	0.08
South African	6	0.03
Am. Ind. or Alaska Nat., not spec.	90	0.38
Albanian	37	0.16
American Indian tribes, specified:	96	0.41
Apache	3	0.01
Blackfeet	2	0.01
Cherokee (6)	28	0.12
Chickasaw	4	0.02
Chippewa (1)	1	0.00
Choctaw	1	0.00
Iroquois (1)	6	0.03
Latin American Indians (10)	24	0.10
Paiute	1	0.00
Potawatomi	1	0.00
Pueblo	1	0.00
Seminole	6	0.03
Sioux (1)	1	0.00
All other tribes (9)	17	0.07
American Indian tribes, not spec.	15	0.06
Arab:	84	0.36
Arab/Arabic	7	0.03
Egyptian	48	0.20
Jordanian	7	0.03
Lebanese	7	0.03

Notes: 1. Figures in the "Number" column do not add up to the total population due to: a) Ancestry/Race overlap — e.g. persons can report being both White and Irish, b) persons of Hispanic origin can report being any race, c) persons reporting two ancestries are counted in both categories. 2. Numbers in parentheses indicate the number of persons reporting this ancestry/race alone, not in combination with any other ancestry/race. 3. Refer to the Explanation of Data in the front of the book for more detailed information.

Ancestry/Race	Number	%
Other Arab	15	0.06
Asian:	906	3.86
Chinese, ex. Taiwanese (189)	214	0.91
Filipino (161)	176	0.75
Indian (313)	353	1.51
Indonesian (2)	2	0.01
Japanese (11)	18	0.08
Korean (72)	75	0.32
Pakistani (16)	24	0.10
Thai (4)	5	0.02
Vietnamese (3)	4	0.02
Other Asian, specified	4	0.02
Other Asian, not specified (2)	31	0.13
Austrian	195	0.83
Brazilian	45	0.19
British	27	0.12
Canadian	14	0.06
Croatian	16	0.07
Czech	26	0.11
Czechoslovakian	30	0.13
Danish	7	0.03
Dutch	126	0.54
Eastern European	40	0.17
English	1,032	4.40
European	97	0.41
Finnish	5	0.02
French, except Basque	306	1.30
French Canadian	22	0.09
German	2,738	11.67
Greek	159	0.68
Guyanese	102	0.43
Hawaii Native/Pacific Islander:	24	0.10
Micronesian: (2)	2	0.01
Guamanian/Chamorro (2)	2	0.01
Polynesian:	4	0.02
Native Hawaiian	1	0.00
Samoan	3	0.01
Other Pac. Isl., specified	4	0.02
Other Pac. Isl., not spec. (4)	14	0.06
Hispanic or Latino:	2,721	11.60
Central American:	411	1.75
Costa Rican	18	0.08
Guatemalan	67	0.29
Honduran	35	0.15
Nicaraguan	8	0.03
Panamanian	33	0.14
Salvadoran	220	0.94
Other Central American	30	0.13
Cuban	130	0.55
Dominican Republic	453	1.93
Mexican	54	0.23
Puerto Rican	721	3.07
South American:	340	1.45
Argentinean	28	0.12
Bolivian	3	0.01
Chilean	15	0.06
Colombian	106	0.45
Ecuadorian	82	0.35
Paraguayan	1	0.00
Peruvian	63	0.27
Uruguayan	5	0.02
Venezuelan	16	0.07
Other South American	21	0.09
Other Hispanic or Latino	612	2.61
Hungarian	147	0.63
Iranian	73	0.31
Irish	4,684	19.97
Italian	4,844	20.65
Latvian	7	0.03
Lithuanian	22	0.09
Maltese	6	0.03
New Zealander	6	0.03
Norwegian	161	0.69
Polish	888	3.79
Portuguese	64	0.27
Romanian	154	0.66
Russian	470	2.00
Scandinavian	27	0.12
Scotch-Irish	184	0.78
Scottish	218	0.93
Slavic	8	0.03
Slovak	36	0.15
Slovene	8	0.03
Swedish	152	0.65
Swiss	48	0.20
Turkish	19	0.08
Ukrainian	123	0.52
United States or American	879	3.75
Welsh	28	0.12
West Indian, excl. Hispanic:	2,578	10.99
Barbadian	30	0.13
Belizean	26	0.11
British West Indian	68	0.29
Haitian	1,104	4.71
Jamaican	1,005	4.28
Trinidadian and Tobagonian	113	0.48
West Indian	232	0.99
White:	15,853	67.59
Not Hispanic (14,143)	14,380	61.31
Hispanic (1,299)	1,473	6.28
Yugoslavian	22	0.09

Batavia

Place Type: City
County: Genesee
Population: 16,256

Ancestry/Race	Number	%
Afghan	12	0.07
African American/Black:	1,055	6.49
Not Hispanic (827)	973	5.99
Hispanic (56)	82	0.50
African, sub-Saharan:	51	0.31
African	51	0.31
Am. Ind. or Alaska Nat., not spec.	76	0.47
American Indian tribes, specified:	105	0.65
Apache	2	0.01
Blackfeet	2	0.01
Cherokee	12	0.07
Cheyenne	2	0.01
Chippewa (2)	2	0.01
Iroquois (45)	74	0.46
Latin American Indians (1)	3	0.02
Navajo	2	0.01
Paiute	1	0.01
Potawatomi	2	0.01
Pueblo	1	0.01
Sioux (1)	1	0.01
All other tribes (1)	1	0.01
American Indian tribes, not spec.	3	0.02
Arab:	62	0.38
Arab/Arabic	9	0.06
Egyptian	13	0.08
Lebanese	40	0.25
Asian:	191	1.17
Cambodian (2)	2	0.01
Chinese, ex. Taiwanese (19)	23	0.14
Filipino (30)	42	0.26
Indian (42)	44	0.27
Japanese (7)	13	0.08
Korean (20)	24	0.15
Laotian (3)	3	0.02
Malaysian (1)	1	0.01
Pakistani (6)	6	0.04
Sri Lankan	2	0.01
Vietnamese (10)	12	0.07
Other Asian, not specified (2)	19	0.12
Austrian	46	0.28
Belgian	7	0.04
Brazilian	22	0.14
British	54	0.33
Canadian	110	0.68
Czech	12	0.07
Czechoslovakian	15	0.09
Danish	36	0.22
Dutch	336	2.07
English	2,483	15.27
Estonian	7	0.04
European	51	0.31
French, except Basque	562	3.46
French Canadian	214	1.32
German	3,814	23.46
Greek	35	0.22
Guyanese	18	0.11
Hawaii Native/Pacific Islander:	8	0.05
Micronesian:	2	0.01
Guamanian/Chamorro	2	0.01
Polynesian: (4)	6	0.04
Native Hawaiian (4)	5	0.03
Samoan	1	0.01
Hispanic or Latino:	399	2.45
Central American:	25	0.15
Guatemalan	5	0.03
Honduran	4	0.02
Nicaraguan	1	0.01
Panamanian	7	0.04
Salvadoran	8	0.05
Cuban	21	0.13
Dominican Republic	73	0.45
Mexican	63	0.39
Puerto Rican	138	0.85
South American:	16	0.10
Bolivian	3	0.02
Colombian	6	0.04
Ecuadorian	2	0.01
Venezuelan	1	0.01
Other South American	4	0.02
Other Hispanic or Latino	63	0.39
Hungarian	65	0.40
Irish	2,782	17.11
Italian	3,489	21.46
Lithuanian	27	0.17
Northern European	15	0.09
Norwegian	22	0.14
Pennsylvania German	7	0.04
Polish	1,817	11.18
Portuguese	7	0.04
Russian	66	0.41
Scandinavian	18	0.11
Scotch-Irish	194	1.19
Scottish	315	1.94
Serbian	8	0.05
Slavic	12	0.07
Slovak	18	0.11
Swedish	163	1.00
Swiss	43	0.26
Ukrainian	65	0.40
United States or American	724	4.45
Welsh	132	0.81
West Indian, excl. Hispanic:	50	0.31
Bahamian	11	0.07
Dutch West Indian	9	0.06
Jamaican	9	0.06
Trinidadian and Tobagonian	9	0.06
West Indian	12	0.07
White:	14,915	91.75
Not Hispanic (14,517)	14,731	90.62
Hispanic (150)	184	1.13

Bath

Place Type: Town
County: Steuben
Population: 12,097

Ancestry/Race	Number	%
African American/Black:	267	2.21
Not Hispanic (213)	262	2.17
Hispanic (4)	5	0.04
African, sub-Saharan:	14	0.12
African	14	0.12
Am. Ind. or Alaska Nat., not spec.	34	0.28
Alsatian	6	0.05
American Indian tribes, specified:	71	0.59
Apache	2	0.02
Blackfeet (3)	7	0.06
Cherokee (6)	19	0.16
Cheyenne	3	0.02
Colville	1	0.01

Notes: 1. Figures in the "Number" column do not add up to the total population due to: a) Ancestry/Race overlap — e.g. persons can report being both White and Irish, b) persons of Hispanic origin can report being any race, c) persons reporting two ancestries are counted in both categories. 2. Numbers in parentheses indicate the number of persons reporting this ancestry/race alone, not in combination with any other ancestry/race. 3. Refer to the Explanation of Data in the front of the book for more detailed information.

Ancestry/Race	Number	%
Crow (1)	1	0.01
Iroquois (10)	29	0.24
Latin American Indians	1	0.01
Navajo (1)	1	0.01
All other tribes (5)	7	0.06
American Indian tribes, not spec.	7	0.06
Arab:	38	0.31
Egyptian	10	0.08
Syrian	28	0.23
Asian:	98	0.81
Chinese, ex. Taiwanese (22)	22	0.18
Filipino (14)	17	0.14
Indian (32)	34	0.28
Japanese (5)	8	0.07
Korean (8)	10	0.08
Pakistani	2	0.02
Taiwanese (2)	2	0.02
Other Asian, not specified (1)	3	0.02
Austrian	16	0.13
Belgian	6	0.05
British	21	0.17
Canadian	9	0.07
Czech	39	0.32
Czechoslovakian	27	0.22
Danish	27	0.22
Dutch	490	4.05
English	2,100	17.36
European	61	0.50
Finnish	1	0.01
French, except Basque	345	2.85
French Canadian	125	1.03
German	1,775	14.67
Greek	53	0.44
Hawaii Native/Pacific Islander:	7	0.06
Micronesian: (1)	1	0.01
Guamanian/Chamorro (1)	1	0.01
Polynesian: (3)	5	0.04
Native Hawaiian (2)	4	0.03
Samoan (1)	1	0.01
Other Pac. Isl., not spec.	1	0.01
Hispanic or Latino:	85	0.70
Central American:	4	0.03
Salvadoran	4	0.03
Cuban	2	0.02
Mexican	24	0.20
Puerto Rican	32	0.26
South American:	4	0.03
Colombian	2	0.02
Paraguayan	1	0.01
Other South American	1	0.01
Other Hispanic or Latino	19	0.16
Hungarian	52	0.43
Irish	1,912	15.81
Italian	768	6.35
Lithuanian	9	0.07
Luxemburger	3	0.02
Norwegian	19	0.16
Pennsylvania German	19	0.16
Polish	752	6.22
Portuguese	7	0.06
Romanian	2	0.02
Russian	46	0.38
Scandinavian	20	0.17
Scotch-Irish	208	1.72
Scottish	234	1.93
Slavic	6	0.05
Slovak	27	0.22
Slovene	6	0.05
Swedish	101	0.83
Swiss	22	0.18
Ukrainian	71	0.59
United States or American	1,493	12.34
Welsh	169	1.40
West Indian, excl. Hispanic:	4	0.03
West Indian	4	0.03
White:	11,728	96.95
Not Hispanic (11,576)	11,672	96.49
Hispanic (42)	56	0.46
Yugoslavian	18	0.15

Bay Shore

Place Type: Census Designated Place
County: Suffolk
Population: 23,852

Ancestry/Race	Number	%
Afghan	13	0.05
African American/Black:	4,481	18.79
Not Hispanic (3,857)	4,148	17.39
Hispanic (234)	333	1.40
African, sub-Saharan:	277	1.16
African	147	0.62
Cape Verdean	15	0.06
Ethiopian	37	0.16
Ghanian	78	0.33
Am. Ind. or Alaska Nat., not spec.	124	0.52
American Indian tribes, specified:	163	0.68
Apache	1	0.00
Blackfeet (3)	10	0.04
Cherokee (10)	56	0.23
Cheyenne	2	0.01
Chickasaw	1	0.00
Choctaw	4	0.02
Creek	2	0.01
Iroquois (2)	9	0.04
Latin American Indians (8)	14	0.06
Lumbee	1	0.00
Navajo	1	0.00
Seminole	1	0.00
Sioux	2	0.01
All other tribes (11)	59	0.25
American Indian tribes, not spec.	33	0.14
Arab:	109	0.46
Arab/Arabic	9	0.04
Egyptian	47	0.20
Lebanese	30	0.13
Other Arab	23	0.10
Asian:	754	3.16
Bangladeshi (9)	10	0.04
Chinese, ex. Taiwanese (88)	127	0.53
Filipino (56)	76	0.32
Indian (247)	300	1.26
Indonesian (3)	6	0.03
Japanese (20)	28	0.12
Korean (34)	37	0.16
Malaysian (2)	2	0.01
Pakistani (42)	67	0.28
Taiwanese (1)	2	0.01
Thai (1)	3	0.01
Vietnamese (24)	25	0.10
Other Asian, not specified (21)	71	0.30
Austrian	35	0.15
Belgian	8	0.03
British	87	0.36
Bulgarian	12	0.05
Canadian	32	0.13
Croatian	31	0.13
Czech	134	0.56
Czechoslovakian	63	0.26
Danish	52	0.22
Dutch	130	0.55
Eastern European	68	0.29
English	1,029	4.31
Estonian	32	0.13
European	6	0.03
Finnish	15	0.06
French, except Basque	498	2.09
French Canadian	146	0.61
German	3,057	12.82
Greek	194	0.81
Guyanese	78	0.33
Hawaii Native/Pacific Islander:	39	0.16
Polynesian: (2)	6	0.03
Native Hawaiian (1)	4	0.02
Samoan (1)	1	0.00
Other Polynesian	1	0.00
Other Pac. Isl., not spec. (5)	33	0.14
Hispanic or Latino:	4,738	19.86
Central American:	618	2.59
Costa Rican	9	0.04
Guatemalan	86	0.36
Honduran	65	0.27
Nicaraguan	4	0.02
Panamanian	4	0.02
Salvadoran	420	1.76
Other Central American	30	0.13
Cuban	72	0.30
Dominican Republic	301	1.26
Mexican	111	0.47
Puerto Rican	1,855	7.78
South American:	795	3.33
Argentinean	19	0.08
Bolivian	3	0.01
Chilean	8	0.03
Colombian	282	1.18
Ecuadorian	369	1.55
Paraguayan	5	0.02
Peruvian	73	0.31
Uruguayan	7	0.03
Venezuelan	6	0.03
Other South American	23	0.10
Other Hispanic or Latino	986	4.13
Hungarian	135	0.57
Irish	4,638	19.44
Israeli	28	0.12
Italian	4,951	20.76
Latvian	6	0.03
Lithuanian	28	0.12
Maltese	34	0.14
Norwegian	116	0.49
Polish	794	3.33
Portuguese	250	1.05
Romanian	9	0.04
Russian	310	1.30
Scandinavian	27	0.11
Scotch-Irish	257	1.08
Scottish	131	0.55
Slovak	16	0.07
Swedish	150	0.63
Swiss	11	0.05
Turkish	50	0.21
Ukrainian	60	0.25
United States or American	630	2.64
Welsh	64	0.27
West Indian, excl. Hispanic:	562	2.36
Barbadian	22	0.09
British West Indian	7	0.03
Haitian	39	0.16
Jamaican	335	1.40
Trinidadian and Tobagonian	33	0.14
West Indian	126	0.53
White:	17,052	71.49
Not Hispanic (14,018)	14,336	60.10
Hispanic (2,401)	2,716	11.39
Yugoslavian	22	0.09

Beacon

Place Type: City
County: Dutchess
Population: 13,808

Ancestry/Race	Number	%
African American/Black:	2,951	21.37
Not Hispanic (2,556)	2,729	19.76
Hispanic (157)	222	1.61
African, sub-Saharan:	87	0.63
African	82	0.59
Nigerian	5	0.04
Alaska Native tribes, specified:	5	0.04
Tlingit-Haida (5)	5	0.04
Am. Ind. or Alaska Nat., not spec.	66	0.48
Albanian	32	0.23
American Indian tribes, specified:	75	0.54
Blackfeet (2)	4	0.03
Cherokee (5)	33	0.24
Cheyenne (1)	1	0.01
Chippewa (1)	5	0.04
Creek	1	0.01

Notes: 1. Figures in the "Number" column do not add up to the total population due to: a) Ancestry/Race overlap — e.g. persons can report being both White and Irish, b) persons of Hispanic origin can report being any race, c) persons reporting two ancestries are counted in both categories. 2. Numbers in parentheses indicate the number of persons reporting this ancestry/race alone, not in combination with any other ancestry/race. 3. Refer to the Explanation of Data in the front of the book for more detailed information.

Delaware	3	0.02
Iroquois	1	0.01
Latin American Indians (5)	12	0.09
Pueblo (1)	1	0.01
Seminole (2)	3	0.02
Sioux	7	0.05
All other tribes (1)	4	0.03
American Indian tribes, not spec.	6	0.04
Arab:	91	0.66
Arab/Arabic	10	0.07
Lebanese	67	0.48
Syrian	14	0.10
Armenian	7	0.05
Asian:	246	1.78
Cambodian (1)	1	0.01
Chinese, ex. Taiwanese (32)	48	0.35
Filipino (17)	24	0.17
Indian (83)	92	0.67
Japanese (6)	13	0.09
Korean (9)	14	0.10
Laotian (1)	1	0.01
Malaysian	1	0.01
Pakistani (4)	9	0.07
Sri Lankan (4)	9	0.07
Thai (3)	3	0.02
Vietnamese (4)	6	0.04
Other Asian, specified	5	0.04
Other Asian, not specified (14)	20	0.14
Austrian	7	0.05
British	28	0.20
Canadian	51	0.37
Celtic	5	0.04
Czech	19	0.14
Czechoslovakian	47	0.34
Danish	25	0.18
Dutch	263	1.90
Eastern European	5	0.04
English	908	6.56
European	39	0.28
Finnish	6	0.04
French, except Basque	294	2.12
French Canadian	170	1.23
German	1,826	13.19
German Russian	9	0.07
Greek	83	0.60
Hawaii Native/Pacific Islander:	9	0.07
Polynesian:	2	0.01
Native Hawaiian	2	0.01
Other Pac. Isl., specified	4	0.03
Other Pac. Isl., not spec.	3	0.02
Hispanic or Latino:	2,334	16.90
Central American:	58	0.42
Costa Rican	6	0.04
Guatemalan	9	0.07
Honduran	9	0.07
Nicaraguan	2	0.01
Panamanian	12	0.09
Salvadoran	20	0.14
Cuban	12	0.09
Dominican Republic	108	0.78
Mexican	185	1.34
Puerto Rican	1,436	10.40
South American:	197	1.43
Argentinean	8	0.06
Bolivian	4	0.03
Chilean	14	0.10
Colombian	101	0.73
Ecuadorian	45	0.33
Peruvian	19	0.14
Venezuelan	3	0.02
Other South American	3	0.02
Other Hispanic or Latino	338	2.45
Hungarian	109	0.79
Irish	2,230	16.11
Italian	2,416	17.46
Lithuanian	6	0.04
Maltese	39	0.28
Northern European	23	0.17
Norwegian	66	0.48
Pennsylvania German	9	0.07
Polish	582	4.21
Portuguese	64	0.46
Russian	183	1.32
Scandinavian	12	0.09
Scotch-Irish	147	1.06
Scottish	188	1.36
Slavic	23	0.17
Slovak	65	0.47
Swedish	123	0.89
Swiss	14	0.10
Ukrainian	34	0.25
United States or American	342	2.47
Welsh	40	0.29
West Indian, excl. Hispanic:	51	0.37
Barbadian	6	0.04
Jamaican	28	0.20
West Indian	17	0.12
White:	9,817	71.10
Not Hispanic (8,377)	8,634	62.53
Hispanic (1,063)	1,183	8.57
Yugoslavian	9	0.07

Bedford

Place Type: Town
County: Westchester
Population: 18,133

Ancestry/Race	Number	%
African American/Black:	1,331	7.34
Not Hispanic (1,167)	1,202	6.63
Hispanic (124)	129	0.71
African, sub-Saharan:	8	0.04
African	8	0.04
Am. Ind. or Alaska Nat., not spec.	16	0.09
Albanian	23	0.13
Alsatian	8	0.04
American Indian tribes, specified:	32	0.18
Apache	3	0.02
Cherokee (4)	12	0.07
Chippewa	1	0.01
Delaware	1	0.01
Iroquois	1	0.01
Latin American Indians (1)	9	0.05
Lumbee (4)	4	0.02
All other tribes	1	0.01
Arab:	63	0.35
Lebanese	16	0.09
Moroccan	7	0.04
Syrian	33	0.18
Other Arab	7	0.04
Armenian	34	0.19
Asian:	444	2.45
Chinese, ex. Taiwanese (82)	112	0.62
Filipino (98)	107	0.59
Indian (91)	99	0.55
Japanese (24)	43	0.24
Korean (42)	52	0.29
Laotian (2)	2	0.01
Pakistani (4)	6	0.03
Sri Lankan (7)	7	0.04
Vietnamese (3)	4	0.02
Other Asian, specified	3	0.02
Other Asian, not specified (1)	9	0.05
Australian	5	0.03
Austrian	225	1.24
Belgian	16	0.09
Brazilian	33	0.18
British	154	0.85
Bulgarian	10	0.06
Canadian	63	0.35
Croatian	33	0.18
Cypriot	18	0.10
Czech	51	0.28
Czechoslovakian	43	0.24
Danish	126	0.69
Dutch	208	1.15
Eastern European	210	1.16
English	2,056	11.34
Estonian	9	0.05
European	98	0.54
Finnish	92	0.51
French, except Basque	403	2.22
French Canadian	152	0.84
German	2,084	11.49
Greek	105	0.58
Guyanese	21	0.12
Hawaii Native/Pacific Islander:	23	0.13
Micronesian: (5)	5	0.03
Guamanian/Chamorro (5)	5	0.03
Polynesian: (1)	1	0.01
Native Hawaiian (1)	1	0.01
Other Pac. Isl., specified	3	0.02
Other Pac. Isl., not spec. (8)	14	0.08
Hispanic or Latino:	1,372	7.57
Central American:	204	1.13
Costa Rican	1	0.01
Guatemalan	152	0.84
Honduran	11	0.06
Nicaraguan	1	0.01
Panamanian	6	0.03
Salvadoran	25	0.14
Other Central American	8	0.04
Cuban	31	0.17
Dominican Republic	37	0.20
Mexican	143	0.79
Puerto Rican	341	1.88
South American:	286	1.58
Argentinean	10	0.06
Bolivian	1	0.01
Chilean	7	0.04
Colombian	104	0.57
Ecuadorian	95	0.52
Paraguayan	15	0.08
Peruvian	42	0.23
Uruguayan	3	0.02
Venezuelan	4	0.02
Other South American	5	0.03
Other Hispanic or Latino	330	1.82
Hungarian	170	0.94
Iranian	18	0.10
Irish	3,025	16.68
Israeli	33	0.18
Italian	3,464	19.10
Latvian	36	0.20
Lithuanian	38	0.21
Luxemburger	7	0.04
Macedonian	6	0.03
New Zealander	17	0.09
Northern European	25	0.14
Norwegian	139	0.77
Pennsylvania German	6	0.03
Polish	811	4.47
Portuguese	62	0.34
Romanian	40	0.22
Russian	1,008	5.56
Scandinavian	21	0.12
Scotch-Irish	216	1.19
Scottish	342	1.89
Slavic	14	0.08
Slovak	63	0.35
Slovene	13	0.07
Swedish	205	1.13
Swiss	31	0.17
Ukrainian	62	0.34
United States or American	851	4.69
Welsh	124	0.68
West Indian, excl. Hispanic:	62	0.34
Barbadian	6	0.03
Jamaican	43	0.24
West Indian	13	0.07
White:	16,089	88.73
Not Hispanic (15,058)	15,181	83.72
Hispanic (809)	908	5.01
Yugoslavian	5	0.03

Notes: 1. Figures in the "Number" column do not add up to the total population due to: a) Ancestry/Race overlap — e.g. persons can report being both White and Irish, b) persons of Hispanic origin can report being any race, c) persons reporting two ancestries are counted in both categories. 2. Numbers in parentheses indicate the number of persons reporting this ancestry/race alone, not in combination with any other ancestry/race. 3. Refer to the Explanation of Data in the front of the book for more detailed information.

Beekman

Place Type: Town
County: Dutchess
Population: 11,452

Ancestry/Race	Number	%
Acadian/Cajun	13	0.11
African American/Black:	330	2.88
Not Hispanic (264)	309	2.70
Hispanic (13)	21	0.18
African, sub-Saharan:	4	0.03
African	4	0.03
Am. Ind. or Alaska Nat., not spec.	33	0.29
Albanian	114	1.00
American Indian tribes, specified:	40	0.35
Blackfeet	5	0.04
Cherokee (1)	13	0.11
Chippewa	1	0.01
Delaware	1	0.01
Iroquois (1)	9	0.08
Latin American Indians	5	0.04
Navajo (1)	1	0.01
Potawatomi (3)	3	0.03
Sioux (1)	1	0.01
All other tribes	1	0.01
American Indian tribes, not spec.	8	0.07
Arab:	38	0.33
Arab/Arabic	8	0.07
Egyptian	20	0.17
Syrian	10	0.09
Asian:	250	2.18
Chinese, ex. Taiwanese (74)	94	0.82
Filipino (11)	21	0.18
Indian (68)	76	0.66
Indonesian	1	0.01
Japanese (9)	12	0.10
Korean (8)	12	0.10
Malaysian	2	0.02
Pakistani (2)	3	0.03
Thai (3)	3	0.03
Vietnamese (5)	7	0.06
Other Asian, specified	4	0.03
Other Asian, not specified (14)	15	0.13
Austrian	63	0.55
British	38	0.33
Canadian	18	0.16
Czech	15	0.13
Czechoslovakian	25	0.22
Danish	15	0.13
Dutch	186	1.63
Eastern European	7	0.06
English	978	8.55
European	11	0.10
Finnish	19	0.17
French, except Basque	288	2.52
French Canadian	221	1.93
German	1,594	13.94
Greek	69	0.60
Hawaii Native/Pacific Islander:	14	0.12
Micronesian: (2)	4	0.03
Guamanian/Chamorro (2)	4	0.03
Polynesian: (1)	4	0.03
Native Hawaiian	3	0.03
Samoan (1)	1	0.01
Other Pac. Isl., specified	4	0.03
Other Pac. Isl., not spec.	2	0.02
Hispanic or Latino:	616	5.38
Central American:	17	0.15
Costa Rican	2	0.02
Guatemalan	8	0.07
Honduran	1	0.01
Nicaraguan	1	0.01
Salvadoran	4	0.03
Other Central American	1	0.01
Cuban	33	0.29
Dominican Republic	19	0.17
Mexican	101	0.88
Puerto Rican	296	2.58
South American:	52	0.45
Argentinean	1	0.01
Bolivian	6	0.05
Chilean	2	0.02
Colombian	33	0.29
Ecuadorian	3	0.03
Paraguayan	1	0.01
Peruvian	4	0.03
Other South American	2	0.02
Other Hispanic or Latino	98	0.86
Hungarian	67	0.59
Icelander	11	0.10
Irish	2,957	25.86
Italian	3,764	32.92
Latvian	11	0.10
Lithuanian	82	0.72
Maltese	11	0.10
Norwegian	136	1.19
Polish	485	4.24
Portuguese	54	0.47
Romanian	4	0.03
Russian	166	1.45
Scandinavian	8	0.07
Scotch-Irish	151	1.32
Scottish	147	1.29
Slavic	8	0.07
Slovak	64	0.56
Swedish	211	1.85
Swiss	30	0.26
Ukrainian	69	0.60
United States or American	606	5.30
Welsh	37	0.32
West Indian, excl. Hispanic:	61	0.53
Haitian	45	0.39
Jamaican	13	0.11
West Indian	3	0.03
White:	10,806	94.36
Not Hispanic (10,211)	10,315	90.07
Hispanic (467)	491	4.29
Yugoslavian	13	0.11

Bellmore

Place Type: Census Designated Place
County: Nassau
Population: 16,441

Ancestry/Race	Number	%
African American/Black:	111	0.68
Not Hispanic (69)	96	0.58
Hispanic (8)	15	0.09
African, sub-Saharan:	37	0.23
Liberian	37	0.23
Am. Ind. or Alaska Nat., not spec.	14	0.09
American Indian tribes, specified:	16	0.10
Cherokee (3)	7	0.04
Cheyenne	1	0.01
Cree	1	0.01
Delaware (1)	1	0.01
Latin American Indians (4)	4	0.02
All other tribes (2)	2	0.01
American Indian tribes, not spec.	3	0.02
Arab:	125	0.76
Egyptian	5	0.03
Jordanian	30	0.18
Lebanese	5	0.03
Moroccan	15	0.09
Syrian	43	0.26
Other Arab	27	0.16
Asian:	387	2.35
Chinese, ex. Taiwanese (135)	153	0.93
Filipino (26)	38	0.23
Indian (103)	122	0.74
Japanese (12)	17	0.10
Korean (33)	33	0.20
Pakistani (8)	12	0.07
Vietnamese (3)	5	0.03
Other Asian, specified (2)	2	0.01
Other Asian, not specified	5	0.03
Australian	5	0.03
Austrian	263	1.60
Belgian	13	0.08
Brazilian	17	0.10
British	43	0.26
Canadian	52	0.32
Croatian	10	0.06
Czech	119	0.72
Czechoslovakian	77	0.47
Danish	18	0.11
Dutch	76	0.46
Eastern European	212	1.29
English	558	3.39
European	101	0.61
French, except Basque	200	1.22
French Canadian	18	0.11
German	2,860	17.40
Greek	309	1.88
Hawaii Native/Pacific Islander:	7	0.04
Micronesian: (1)	1	0.01
Guamanian/Chamorro (1)	1	0.01
Polynesian: (3)	4	0.02
Native Hawaiian (3)	4	0.02
Other Pac. Isl., not spec.	2	0.01
Hispanic or Latino:	515	3.13
Central American:	66	0.40
Costa Rican	3	0.02
Guatemalan	4	0.02
Honduran	7	0.04
Nicaraguan	5	0.03
Panamanian	2	0.01
Salvadoran	45	0.27
Cuban	40	0.24
Dominican Republic	18	0.11
Mexican	19	0.12
Puerto Rican	151	0.92
South American:	83	0.50
Argentinean	11	0.07
Chilean	10	0.06
Colombian	35	0.21
Ecuadorian	15	0.09
Paraguayan	1	0.01
Peruvian	3	0.02
Uruguayan	1	0.01
Other South American	7	0.04
Other Hispanic or Latino	138	0.84
Hungarian	209	1.27
Iranian	5	0.03
Irish	3,629	22.07
Israeli	78	0.47
Italian	4,307	26.20
Lithuanian	108	0.66
Maltese	22	0.13
Norwegian	190	1.16
Polish	1,145	6.96
Portuguese	38	0.23
Romanian	76	0.46
Russian	1,062	6.46
Scandinavian	19	0.12
Scotch-Irish	63	0.38
Scottish	178	1.08
Slovak	5	0.03
Swedish	158	0.96
Swiss	9	0.05
Turkish	53	0.32
Ukrainian	141	0.86
United States or American	1,058	6.44
West Indian, excl. Hispanic:	14	0.09
Jamaican	14	0.09
White:	15,905	96.74
Not Hispanic (15,389)	15,483	94.17
Hispanic (395)	422	2.57
Yugoslavian	28	0.17

Bethlehem

Place Type: Town
County: Albany
Population: 31,304

Ancestry/Race	Number	%
African American/Black:	793	2.53

Notes: 1. Figures in the "Number" column do not add up to the total population due to: a) Ancestry/Race overlap — e.g. persons can report being both White and Irish, b) persons of Hispanic origin can report being any race, c) persons reporting two ancestries are counted in both categories. 2. Numbers in parentheses indicate the number of persons reporting this ancestry/race alone, not in combination with any other ancestry/race. 3. Refer to the Explanation of Data in the front of the book for more detailed information.

Not Hispanic (685)	764	2.44
Hispanic (21)	29	0.09
African, sub-Saharan:	16	0.05
African	16	0.05
Alaska Native tribes, specified:	1	0.00
Eskimo (1)	1	0.00
Am. Ind. or Alaska Nat., not spec.	42	0.13
American Indian tribes, specified:	52	0.17
Blackfeet	1	0.00
Cherokee (6)	9	0.03
Chickasaw (2)	2	0.01
Delaware	2	0.01
Iroquois (6)	18	0.06
Latin American Indians (6)	10	0.03
Navajo (1)	1	0.00
Sioux	1	0.00
All other tribes (3)	8	0.03
American Indian tribes, not spec.	4	0.01
Arab:	207	0.66
Arab/Arabic	19	0.06
Egyptian	28	0.09
Jordanian	22	0.07
Lebanese	106	0.34
Syrian	32	0.10
Armenian	118	0.38
Asian:	638	2.04
Cambodian (1)	1	0.00
Chinese, ex. Taiwanese (192)	219	0.70
Filipino (28)	40	0.13
Indian (141)	170	0.54
Indonesian (1)	3	0.01
Japanese (25)	44	0.14
Korean (73)	81	0.26
Malaysian (1)	1	0.00
Pakistani (26)	33	0.11
Taiwanese (8)	10	0.03
Thai (1)	4	0.01
Vietnamese (5)	9	0.03
Other Asian, not specified (17)	23	0.07
Austrian	261	0.83
Belgian	5	0.02
British	136	0.43
Canadian	94	0.30
Celtic	38	0.12
Croatian	13	0.04
Czech	126	0.40
Czechoslovakian	48	0.15
Danish	107	0.34
Dutch	1,407	4.49
Eastern European	142	0.45
English	4,284	13.69
Estonian	8	0.03
European	216	0.69
Finnish	43	0.14
French, except Basque	1,577	5.04
French Canadian	530	1.69
German	6,718	21.46
Greek	387	1.24
Guyanese	33	0.11
Hawaii Native/Pacific Islander:	28	0.09
Micronesian:	3	0.01
Guamanian/Chamorro	3	0.01
Polynesian: (10)	15	0.05
Native Hawaiian (6)	11	0.04
Samoan (4)	4	0.01
Other Pac. Isl., not spec. (3)	10	0.03
Hispanic or Latino:	544	1.74
Central American:	27	0.09
Costa Rican	2	0.01
Guatemalan	11	0.04
Honduran	1	0.00
Panamanian	3	0.01
Salvadoran	10	0.03
Cuban	21	0.07
Dominican Republic	27	0.09
Mexican	95	0.30
Puerto Rican	170	0.54
South American:	56	0.18
Argentinean	6	0.02
Bolivian	1	0.00
Chilean	3	0.01
Colombian	21	0.07
Ecuadorian	1	0.00
Peruvian	9	0.03
Uruguayan	3	0.01
Venezuelan	3	0.01
Other South American	9	0.03
Other Hispanic or Latino	148	0.47
Hungarian	229	0.73
Iranian	35	0.11
Irish	7,565	24.17
Italian	5,005	15.99
Latvian	23	0.07
Lithuanian	183	0.58
Luxemburger	26	0.08
Maltese	9	0.03
Northern European	8	0.03
Norwegian	256	0.82
Polish	1,935	6.18
Portuguese	59	0.19
Romanian	153	0.49
Russian	1,056	3.37
Scandinavian	23	0.07
Scotch-Irish	413	1.32
Scottish	739	2.36
Slavic	15	0.05
Slovak	105	0.34
Slovene	14	0.04
Swedish	417	1.33
Swiss	97	0.31
Ukrainian	171	0.55
United States or American	1,295	4.14
Welsh	415	1.33
West Indian, excl. Hispanic:	48	0.15
Belizean	8	0.03
Haitian	11	0.04
Jamaican	21	0.07
Trinidadian and Tobagonian	8	0.03
White:	29,884	95.46
Not Hispanic (29,256)	29,456	94.10
Hispanic (400)	428	1.37
Yugoslavian	56	0.18

Bethpage

Place Type: Census Designated Place
County: Nassau
Population: 16,543

Ancestry/Race	Number	%
African American/Black:	72	0.44
Not Hispanic (36)	54	0.33
Hispanic (12)	18	0.11
African, sub-Saharan:	5	0.03
Ghanian	5	0.03
Am. Ind. or Alaska Nat., not spec.	14	0.08
American Indian tribes, specified:	13	0.08
Cherokee (1)	3	0.02
Cree	1	0.01
Creek	1	0.01
Iroquois	2	0.01
Latin American Indians (1)	2	0.01
Sioux	2	0.01
All other tribes (1)	2	0.01
American Indian tribes, not spec.	7	0.04
Arab:	21	0.13
Egyptian	21	0.13
Armenian	55	0.33
Asian:	564	3.41
Cambodian (1)	1	0.01
Chinese, ex. Taiwanese (135)	159	0.96
Filipino (78)	96	0.58
Indian (141)	152	0.92
Japanese (27)	33	0.20
Korean (84)	89	0.54
Pakistani (6)	11	0.07
Taiwanese (8)	8	0.05
Thai (3)	3	0.02
Other Asian, specified	1	0.01
Other Asian, not specified (3)	11	0.07
Austrian	115	0.70
Belgian	14	0.08
Brazilian	70	0.42
British	28	0.17
Canadian	21	0.13
Croatian	89	0.54
Czech	103	0.62
Czechoslovakian	60	0.36
Danish	101	0.61
Dutch	48	0.29
Eastern European	7	0.04
English	582	3.52
European	28	0.17
Finnish	12	0.07
French, except Basque	267	1.61
French Canadian	58	0.35
German	2,807	16.97
Greek	573	3.46
Hawaii Native/Pacific Islander:	21	0.13
Polynesian:	4	0.02
Native Hawaiian	4	0.02
Other Pac. Isl., specified	1	0.01
Other Pac. Isl., not spec.	16	0.10
Hispanic or Latino:	785	4.75
Central American:	75	0.45
Costa Rican	2	0.01
Guatemalan	6	0.04
Honduran	10	0.06
Panamanian	1	0.01
Salvadoran	55	0.33
Other Central American	1	0.01
Cuban	41	0.25
Dominican Republic	26	0.16
Mexican	54	0.33
Puerto Rican	225	1.36
South American:	180	1.09
Argentinean	15	0.09
Bolivian	12	0.07
Chilean	2	0.01
Colombian	81	0.49
Ecuadorian	38	0.23
Peruvian	20	0.12
Venezuelan	1	0.01
Other South American	11	0.07
Other Hispanic or Latino	184	1.11
Hungarian	224	1.35
Irish	4,349	26.29
Israeli	53	0.32
Italian	6,507	39.33
Latvian	5	0.03
Lithuanian	43	0.26
Norwegian	165	1.00
Polish	1,087	6.57
Portuguese	67	0.41
Romanian	50	0.30
Russian	382	2.31
Scandinavian	17	0.10
Scotch-Irish	98	0.59
Scottish	158	0.96
Slovak	8	0.05
Swedish	232	1.40
Swiss	35	0.21
Turkish	12	0.07
Ukrainian	63	0.38
United States or American	365	2.21
Welsh	51	0.31
White:	15,800	95.51
Not Hispanic (15,066)	15,193	91.84
Hispanic (512)	607	3.67

Binghamton

Place Type: City
County: Broome
Population: 47,380

Ancestry/Race	Number	%
African American/Black:	4,737	10.00
Not Hispanic (3,765)	4,425	9.34
Hispanic (222)	312	0.66

Notes: 1. Figures in the "Number" column do not add up to the total population due to: a) Ancestry/Race overlap — e.g. persons can report being both White and Irish, b) persons of Hispanic origin can report being any race, c) persons reporting two ancestries are counted in both categories. 2. Numbers in parentheses indicate the number of persons reporting this ancestry/race alone, not in combination with any other ancestry/race. 3. Refer to the Explanation of Data in the front of the book for more detailed information.

African, sub-Saharan:	496	1.05
African	334	0.70
Ethiopian	8	0.02
Ghanian	29	0.06
Liberian	30	0.06
Somalian	22	0.05
South African	7	0.01
Sudanese	55	0.12
Other sub-Saharan African	11	0.02
Am. Ind. or Alaska Nat., not spec.	134	0.28
American Indian tribes, specified:	255	0.54
Apache (2)	4	0.01
Blackfeet (9)	37	0.08
Cherokee (20)	74	0.16
Cheyenne (2)	2	0.00
Chippewa (3)	3	0.01
Choctaw (2)	5	0.01
Comanche (2)	2	0.00
Cree	1	0.00
Delaware (2)	9	0.02
Iroquois (13)	59	0.12
Latin American Indians (1)	7	0.01
Lumbee (1)	2	0.00
Navajo	3	0.01
Seminole (1)	6	0.01
Sioux (6)	7	0.01
Tohono O'Odham (1)	1	0.00
Yaqui (1)	1	0.00
All other tribes (9)	32	0.07
American Indian tribes, not spec.	15	0.03
Arab:	407	0.86
Arab/Arabic	21	0.04
Egyptian	19	0.04
Iraqi	32	0.07
Lebanese	158	0.33
Moroccan	12	0.03
Palestinian	12	0.03
Syrian	19	0.04
Other Arab	134	0.28
Armenian	242	0.51
Asian:	1,885	3.98
Cambodian (3)	3	0.01
Chinese, ex. Taiwanese (394)	437	0.92
Filipino (89)	117	0.25
Indian (216)	250	0.53
Indonesian (8)	8	0.02
Japanese (54)	66	0.14
Korean (134)	149	0.31
Laotian (160)	200	0.42
Pakistani (43)	46	0.10
Sri Lankan (1)	2	0.00
Taiwanese (26)	31	0.07
Thai (15)	20	0.04
Vietnamese (359)	395	0.83
Other Asian, specified (2)	3	0.01
Other Asian, not specified (38)	158	0.33
Australian	21	0.04
Austrian	300	0.63
Basque	12	0.03
Belgian	26	0.05
Brazilian	32	0.07
British	184	0.39
Canadian	56	0.12
Carpatho Rusyn	52	0.11
Celtic	28	0.06
Croatian	6	0.01
Czech	306	0.65
Czechoslovakian	314	0.66
Danish	85	0.18
Dutch	1,161	2.45
Eastern European	35	0.07
English	5,264	11.11
European	268	0.57
Finnish	46	0.10
French, except Basque	1,057	2.23
French Canadian	286	0.60
German	5,702	12.03
Greek	479	1.01
Guyanese	24	0.05
Hawaii Native/Pacific Islander:	44	0.09
Micronesian: (8)	16	0.03
Guamanian/Chamorro (2)	4	0.01
Other Micronesian (6)	12	0.03
Polynesian: (4)	7	0.01
Native Hawaiian (3)	5	0.01
Samoan (1)	2	0.00
Other Pac. Isl., not spec. (6)	21	0.04
Hispanic or Latino:	1,849	3.90
Central American:	50	0.11
Guatemalan	16	0.03
Honduran	8	0.02
Nicaraguan	3	0.01
Panamanian	12	0.03
Salvadoran	9	0.02
Other Central American	2	0.00
Cuban	111	0.23
Dominican Republic	95	0.20
Mexican	152	0.32
Puerto Rican	1,021	2.15
South American:	106	0.22
Argentinean	24	0.05
Bolivian	1	0.00
Chilean	6	0.01
Colombian	30	0.06
Ecuadorian	15	0.03
Peruvian	20	0.04
Uruguayan	2	0.00
Venezuelan	5	0.01
Other South American	3	0.01
Other Hispanic or Latino	314	0.66
Hungarian	335	0.71
Iranian	53	0.11
Irish	9,318	19.67
Israeli	5	0.01
Italian	6,057	12.78
Lithuanian	314	0.66
Norwegian	168	0.35
Pennsylvania German	223	0.47
Polish	2,850	6.02
Portuguese	35	0.07
Romanian	33	0.07
Russian	1,271	2.68
Scandinavian	22	0.05
Scotch-Irish	609	1.29
Scottish	819	1.73
Slavic	70	0.15
Slovak	1,704	3.60
Slovene	13	0.03
Swedish	347	0.73
Swiss	150	0.32
Turkish	53	0.11
Ukrainian	787	1.66
United States or American	2,291	4.84
Welsh	852	1.80
West Indian, excl. Hispanic:	402	0.85
Barbadian	8	0.02
British West Indian	54	0.11
Haitian	133	0.28
Jamaican	167	0.35
Trinidadian and Tobagonian	20	0.04
West Indian	20	0.04
White:	40,607	85.70
Not Hispanic (38,717)	39,773	83.94
Hispanic (695)	834	1.76
Yugoslavian	249	0.53

Blooming Grove

Place Type: Town
County: Orange
Population: 17,351

Ancestry/Race	Number	%
African American/Black:	765	4.41
Not Hispanic (599)	692	3.99
Hispanic (60)	73	0.42
African, sub-Saharan:	51	0.29
African	51	0.29
Am. Ind. or Alaska Nat., not spec.	69	0.40
Albanian	15	0.09
American Indian tribes, specified:	109	0.63
Apache	1	0.01
Blackfeet (1)	6	0.03
Cherokee (3)	12	0.07
Chippewa (1)	4	0.02
Choctaw	1	0.01
Delaware (22)	33	0.19
Iroquois (4)	16	0.09
Latin American Indians (6)	17	0.10
Pueblo	1	0.01
Seminole (1)	1	0.01
Sioux (6)	10	0.06
All other tribes (5)	7	0.04
American Indian tribes, not spec.	16	0.09
Arab:	69	0.40
Arab/Arabic	19	0.11
Jordanian	6	0.03
Lebanese	22	0.13
Syrian	17	0.10
Other Arab	5	0.03
Asian:	311	1.79
Chinese, ex. Taiwanese (61)	84	0.48
Filipino (33)	41	0.24
Indian (54)	64	0.37
Indonesian (1)	3	0.02
Japanese (29)	40	0.23
Korean (32)	35	0.20
Thai (7)	7	0.04
Vietnamese (20)	23	0.13
Other Asian, not specified (5)	14	0.08
Australian	12	0.07
Austrian	201	1.16
British	31	0.18
Bulgarian	20	0.12
Canadian	27	0.16
Czech	77	0.44
Czechoslovakian	81	0.47
Danish	18	0.10
Dutch	488	2.81
Eastern European	7	0.04
English	1,174	6.77
Estonian	8	0.05
European	70	0.40
Finnish	32	0.18
French, except Basque	363	2.09
French Canadian	79	0.46
German	3,008	17.34
Greek	87	0.50
Hawaii Native/Pacific Islander:	6	0.03
Micronesian:	1	0.01
Guamanian/Chamorro	1	0.01
Polynesian: (2)	2	0.01
Samoan (2)	2	0.01
Other Pac. Isl., not spec. (1)	3	0.02
Hispanic or Latino:	1,556	8.97
Central American:	45	0.26
Costa Rican	7	0.04
Guatemalan	5	0.03
Honduran	6	0.03
Nicaraguan	11	0.06
Panamanian	8	0.05
Salvadoran	8	0.05
Cuban	58	0.33
Dominican Republic	52	0.30
Mexican	79	0.46
Puerto Rican	1,013	5.84
South American:	96	0.55
Argentinean	4	0.02
Bolivian	1	0.01
Chilean	4	0.02
Colombian	31	0.18
Ecuadorian	34	0.20
Peruvian	14	0.08
Venezuelan	1	0.01
Other South American	7	0.04
Other Hispanic or Latino	213	1.23
Hungarian	206	1.19
Iranian	22	0.13
Irish	5,166	29.77
Israeli	8	0.05

Notes: 1. Figures in the "Number" column do not add up to the total population due to: a) Ancestry/Race overlap — e.g. persons can report being both White and Irish, b) persons of Hispanic origin can report being any race, c) persons reporting two ancestries are counted in both categories. 2. Numbers in parentheses indicate the number of persons reporting this ancestry/race alone, not in combination with any other ancestry/race. 3. Refer to the Explanation of Data in the front of the book for more detailed information.

Italian	4,485	25.85
Latvian	9	0.05
Lithuanian	10	0.06
Luxemburger	9	0.05
Maltese	58	0.33
Northern European	39	0.22
Norwegian	256	1.48
Polish	1,177	6.78
Portuguese	69	0.40
Romanian	7	0.04
Russian	285	1.64
Scandinavian	10	0.06
Scotch-Irish	299	1.72
Scottish	237	1.37
Slavic	15	0.09
Slovak	75	0.43
Swedish	233	1.34
Swiss	47	0.27
Ukrainian	100	0.58
United States or American	479	2.76
Welsh	38	0.22
West Indian, excl. Hispanic:	120	0.69
Haitian	39	0.22
Jamaican	27	0.16
Trinidadian and Tobagonian	28	0.16
West Indian	26	0.15
White:	15,899	91.63
Not Hispanic (14,646)	14,822	85.42
Hispanic (1,012)	1,077	6.21
Yugoslavian	19	0.11

Brentwood

Place Type: Census Designated Place
County: Suffolk
Population: 53,917

Ancestry/Race	Number	%
Afghan	60	0.11
African American/Black:	10,926	20.26
Not Hispanic (8,654)	9,413	17.46
Hispanic (1,081)	1,513	2.81
African, sub-Saharan:	366	0.68
African	333	0.62
Cape Verdean	17	0.03
Nigerian	16	0.03
Alaska Native tribes, specified:	1	0.00
Tlingit-Haida	1	0.00
Am. Ind. or Alaska Nat., not spec.	291	0.54
American Indian tribes, specified:	434	0.80
Apache	1	0.00
Blackfeet (6)	23	0.04
Cherokee	82	0.15
Comanche	2	0.00
Creek	1	0.00
Iroquois (4)	15	0.03
Latin American Indians (72)	213	0.40
Lumbee (2)	2	0.00
Navajo	3	0.01
Osage (1)	2	0.00
Paiute	1	0.00
Pueblo (9)	26	0.05
Seminole	3	0.01
Shoshone	3	0.01
Sioux (3)	6	0.01
All other tribes (23)	51	0.09
American Indian tribes, not spec.	61	0.11
Arab:	178	0.33
Arab/Arabic	75	0.14
Egyptian	17	0.03
Jordanian	12	0.02
Lebanese	13	0.02
Moroccan	5	0.01
Palestinian	50	0.09
Syrian	6	0.01
Armenian	26	0.05
Asian:	1,424	2.64
Bangladeshi (9)	10	0.02
Chinese, ex. Taiwanese (113)	141	0.26
Filipino (131)	159	0.29
Hmong	1	0.00
Indian (509)	648	1.20
Indonesian (3)	7	0.01
Japanese (9)	18	0.03
Korean (13)	21	0.04
Laotian (6)	6	0.01
Malaysian	4	0.01
Pakistani (132)	193	0.36
Sri Lankan (4)	4	0.01
Taiwanese (3)	3	0.01
Thai (48)	50	0.09
Vietnamese (71)	77	0.14
Other Asian, specified	9	0.02
Other Asian, not specified (12)	73	0.14
Australian	7	0.01
Austrian	101	0.19
Brazilian	64	0.12
British	20	0.04
Canadian	53	0.10
Cypriot	7	0.01
Czech	45	0.08
Czechoslovakian	26	0.05
Danish	14	0.03
Dutch	133	0.25
Eastern European	25	0.05
English	863	1.60
European	83	0.15
Finnish	14	0.03
French, except Basque	344	0.64
French Canadian	122	0.23
German	2,353	4.37
Greek	333	0.62
Guyanese	77	0.14
Hawaii Native/Pacific Islander:	135	0.25
Micronesian: (28)	31	0.06
Guamanian/Chamorro (28)	31	0.06
Polynesian: (13)	16	0.03
Native Hawaiian (7)	9	0.02
Samoan (6)	7	0.01
Other Pac. Isl., specified	5	0.01
Other Pac. Isl., not spec. (20)	83	0.15
Hispanic or Latino:	29,251	54.25
Central American:	8,221	15.25
Costa Rican	72	0.13
Guatemalan	710	1.32
Honduran	546	1.01
Nicaraguan	32	0.06
Panamanian	137	0.25
Salvadoran	6,387	11.85
Other Central American	337	0.63
Cuban	205	0.38
Dominican Republic	2,744	5.09
Mexican	469	0.87
Puerto Rican	8,254	15.31
South American:	3,139	5.82
Argentinean	81	0.15
Bolivian	51	0.09
Chilean	95	0.18
Colombian	1,357	2.52
Ecuadorian	798	1.48
Paraguayan	10	0.02
Peruvian	544	1.01
Uruguayan	36	0.07
Venezuelan	65	0.12
Other South American	102	0.19
Other Hispanic or Latino	6,219	11.53
Hungarian	132	0.24
Iranian	27	0.05
Irish	3,650	6.77
Italian	4,273	7.93
Latvian	30	0.06
Lithuanian	88	0.16
Maltese	34	0.06
Norwegian	187	0.35
Polish	791	1.47
Portuguese	456	0.85
Romanian	7	0.01
Russian	254	0.47
Scotch-Irish	147	0.27
Scottish	143	0.27
Slavic	6	0.01
Slovak	34	0.06
Swedish	167	0.31
Swiss	6	0.01
Turkish	58	0.11
Ukrainian	45	0.08
United States or American	1,373	2.55
Welsh	8	0.01
West Indian, excl. Hispanic:	2,493	4.63
Barbadian	98	0.18
British West Indian	61	0.11
Haitian	1,431	2.66
Jamaican	510	0.95
Trinidadian and Tobagonian	235	0.44
West Indian	158	0.29
White:	27,830	51.62
Not Hispanic (13,439)	13,916	25.81
Hispanic (12,297)	13,914	25.81

Brighton

Place Type: Town
County: Monroe
Population: 35,588

Ancestry/Race	Number	%
African American/Black:	1,460	4.10
Not Hispanic (1,303)	1,427	4.01
Hispanic (12)	33	0.09
African, sub-Saharan:	251	0.71
African	150	0.42
Ethiopian	3	0.01
Ghanian	3	0.01
Somalian	15	0.04
South African	10	0.03
Zimbabwean	49	0.14
Other sub-Saharan African	21	0.06
Alaska Native tribes, specified:	2	0.01
Eskimo	1	0.00
Tlingit-Haida	1	0.00
Alaska Native tribes, not specified	1	0.00
Am. Ind. or Alaska Nat., not spec.	50	0.14
American Indian tribes, specified:	60	0.17
Blackfeet	1	0.00
Cherokee	3	0.01
Chippewa (4)	7	0.02
Choctaw	1	0.00
Comanche (1)	1	0.00
Cree (1)	1	0.00
Iroquois (12)	23	0.06
Latin American Indians (2)	16	0.04
Lumbee	1	0.00
Sioux (1)	2	0.01
All other tribes (1)	4	0.01
American Indian tribes, not spec.	5	0.01
Arab:	208	0.58
Arab/Arabic	29	0.08
Egyptian	53	0.15
Iraqi	18	0.05
Lebanese	30	0.08
Syrian	78	0.22
Armenian	14	0.04
Asian:	3,147	8.84
Bangladeshi (13)	15	0.04
Cambodian (1)	5	0.01
Chinese, ex. Taiwanese (830)	883	2.48
Filipino (97)	128	0.36
Hmong (1)	1	0.00
Indian (987)	1,041	2.93
Indonesian (15)	19	0.05
Japanese (152)	170	0.48
Korean (429)	449	1.26
Laotian (24)	28	0.08
Malaysian (6)	6	0.02
Pakistani (81)	94	0.26
Sri Lankan (9)	12	0.03
Taiwanese (55)	62	0.17
Thai (28)	31	0.09
Vietnamese (85)	89	0.25
Other Asian, specified (22)	28	0.08

Notes: 1. Figures in the "Number" column do not add up to the total population due to: a) Ancestry/Race overlap — e.g. persons can report being both White and Irish, b) persons of Hispanic origin can report being any race, c) persons reporting two ancestries are counted in both categories. 2. Numbers in parentheses indicate the number of persons reporting this ancestry/race alone, not in combination with any other ancestry/race. 3. Refer to the Explanation of Data in the front of the book for more detailed information.

Other Asian, not specified (38)	86	0.24
Assyrian/Chaldean/Syriac	19	0.05
Australian	18	0.05
Austrian	256	0.72
Belgian	83	0.23
Brazilian	10	0.03
British	230	0.65
Bulgarian	29	0.08
Canadian	264	0.74
Croatian	12	0.03
Czech	68	0.19
Czechoslovakian	32	0.09
Danish	100	0.28
Dutch	743	2.09
Eastern European	260	0.73
English	4,735	13.31
European	312	0.88
Finnish	41	0.12
French, except Basque	820	2.30
French Canadian	376	1.06
German	6,460	18.15
Greek	298	0.84
Hawaii Native/Pacific Islander:	27	0.08
Melanesian:	1	0.00
Other Melanesian	1	0.00
Micronesian: (3)	4	0.01
Guamanian/Chamorro (3)	4	0.01
Polynesian: (6)	12	0.03
Native Hawaiian (1)	7	0.02
Samoan (4)	4	0.01
Other Polynesian (1)	1	0.00
Other Pac. Isl., specified	5	0.01
Other Pac. Isl., not spec. (1)	5	0.01
Hispanic or Latino:	831	2.34
Central American:	42	0.12
Costa Rican	7	0.02
Guatemalan	6	0.02
Honduran	3	0.01
Nicaraguan	17	0.05
Salvadoran	5	0.01
Other Central American	4	0.01
Cuban	63	0.18
Dominican Republic	18	0.05
Mexican	140	0.39
Puerto Rican	266	0.75
South American:	148	0.42
Argentinean	25	0.07
Bolivian	6	0.02
Chilean	12	0.03
Colombian	44	0.12
Ecuadorian	6	0.02
Paraguayan	4	0.01
Peruvian	22	0.06
Uruguayan	6	0.02
Venezuelan	14	0.04
Other South American	9	0.03
Other Hispanic or Latino	154	0.43
Hungarian	357	1.00
Irish	6,005	16.87
Israeli	34	0.10
Italian	4,167	11.71
Latvian	74	0.21
Lithuanian	178	0.50
Northern European	59	0.17
Norwegian	259	0.73
Pennsylvania German	29	0.08
Polish	2,307	6.48
Portuguese	74	0.21
Romanian	107	0.30
Russian	1,979	5.56
Scandinavian	13	0.04
Scotch-Irish	560	1.57
Scottish	851	2.39
Serbian	27	0.08
Slavic	16	0.04
Slovak	62	0.17
Slovene	14	0.04
Swedish	297	0.83
Swiss	149	0.42
Turkish	104	0.29
Ukrainian	496	1.39
United States or American	1,583	4.45
Welsh	252	0.71
West Indian, excl. Hispanic:	64	0.18
Dutch West Indian	9	0.03
Haitian	8	0.02
Jamaican	36	0.10
Trinidadian and Tobagonian	7	0.02
U.S. Virgin Islander	4	0.01
White:	31,024	87.18
Not Hispanic (30,089)	30,410	85.45
Hispanic (550)	614	1.73
Yugoslavian	81	0.23

Brookhaven

Place Type: Town
County: Suffolk
Population: 448,248

Ancestry/Race	Number	%
Afghan	101	0.02
African American/Black:	22,437	5.01
Not Hispanic (18,196)	20,580	4.59
Hispanic (1,215)	1,857	0.41
African, sub-Saharan:	1,302	0.29
African	975	0.22
Ethiopian	7	0.00
Ghanian	29	0.01
Kenyan	7	0.00
Liberian	6	0.00
Nigerian	206	0.05
Sierra Leonean	13	0.00
South African	10	0.00
Zimbabwean	33	0.01
Other sub-Saharan African	16	0.00
Alaska Native tribes, specified:	2	0.00
Alaska Athabascan (1)	1	0.00
Eskimo (1)	1	0.00
Alaska Native tribes, not specified	4	0.00
Am. Ind. or Alaska Nat., not spec.	1,137	0.25
Albanian	158	0.04
Alsatian	35	0.01
American Indian tribes, specified:	1,622	0.36
Apache (8)	37	0.01
Blackfeet (26)	118	0.03
Cherokee (118)	506	0.11
Cheyenne (2)	5	0.00
Chickasaw (8)	8	0.00
Chippewa (5)	12	0.00
Choctaw (8)	17	0.00
Comanche	6	0.00
Cree (2)	6	0.00
Creek (1)	7	0.00
Crow (1)	6	0.00
Delaware	7	0.00
Iroquois (49)	131	0.03
Latin American Indians (64)	207	0.05
Lumbee (3)	5	0.00
Navajo (4)	16	0.00
Osage (1)	4	0.00
Paiute (1)	2	0.00
Potawatomi	1	0.00
Pueblo (10)	13	0.00
Puget Sound Salish	1	0.00
Seminole (8)	32	0.01
Sioux (11)	40	0.01
Ute (1)	4	0.00
Yakama	1	0.00
All other tribes (172)	430	0.10
American Indian tribes, not spec.	169	0.04
Arab:	1,513	0.34
Arab/Arabic	116	0.03
Egyptian	552	0.12
Iraqi	36	0.01
Jordanian	69	0.02
Lebanese	385	0.09
Moroccan	8	0.00
Palestinian	50	0.01
Syrian	208	0.05
Other Arab	89	0.02
Armenian	694	0.15
Asian:	15,288	3.41
Bangladeshi (99)	120	0.03
Cambodian (11)	24	0.01
Chinese, ex. Taiwanese (4,721)	5,140	1.15
Filipino (1,338)	1,723	0.38
Indian (3,293)	3,738	0.83
Indonesian (18)	36	0.01
Japanese (333)	513	0.11
Korean (1,489)	1,689	0.38
Laotian (27)	37	0.01
Malaysian (9)	13	0.00
Pakistani (626)	869	0.19
Sri Lankan (34)	38	0.01
Taiwanese (155)	191	0.04
Thai (109)	143	0.03
Vietnamese (338)	379	0.08
Other Asian, specified (30)	65	0.01
Other Asian, not specified (172)	570	0.13
Australian	250	0.06
Austrian	3,427	0.76
Basque	22	0.00
Belgian	415	0.09
Brazilian	195	0.04
British	1,167	0.26
Bulgarian	130	0.03
Canadian	1,179	0.26
Celtic	98	0.02
Croatian	533	0.12
Cypriot	137	0.03
Czech	2,115	0.47
Czechoslovakian	1,281	0.29
Danish	1,660	0.37
Dutch	4,271	0.95
Eastern European	836	0.19
English	26,741	5.97
Estonian	161	0.04
European	1,270	0.28
Finnish	872	0.19
French, except Basque	9,044	2.02
French Canadian	2,741	0.61
German	87,375	19.49
German Russian	9	0.00
Greek	6,580	1.47
Guyanese	423	0.09
Hawaii Native/Pacific Islander:	332	0.07
Melanesian: (5)	5	0.00
Fijian (1)	1	0.00
Other Melanesian (4)	4	0.00
Micronesian: (15)	27	0.01
Guamanian/Chamorro (15)	25	0.01
Other Micronesian	2	0.00
Polynesian: (63)	104	0.02
Native Hawaiian (33)	63	0.01
Samoan (29)	38	0.01
Other Polynesian (1)	3	0.00
Other Pac. Isl., specified	18	0.00
Other Pac. Isl., not spec. (30)	178	0.04
Hispanic or Latino:	36,041	8.04
Central American:	2,604	0.58
Costa Rican	82	0.02
Guatemalan	457	0.10
Honduran	164	0.04
Nicaraguan	55	0.01
Panamanian	134	0.03
Salvadoran	1,581	0.35
Other Central American	131	0.03
Cuban	1,032	0.23
Dominican Republic	2,132	0.48
Mexican	2,018	0.45
Puerto Rican	16,438	3.67
South American:	4,746	1.06
Argentinean	265	0.06
Bolivian	67	0.01
Chilean	168	0.04
Colombian	1,400	0.31
Ecuadorian	2,055	0.46
Paraguayan	20	0.00
Peruvian	415	0.09

Notes: 1. Figures in the "Number" column do not add up to the total population due to: a) Ancestry/Race overlap — e.g. persons can report being both White and Irish, b) persons of Hispanic origin can report being any race, c) persons reporting two ancestries are counted in both categories. 2. Numbers in parentheses indicate the number of persons reporting this ancestry/race alone, not in combination with any other ancestry/race. 3. Refer to the Explanation of Data in the front of the book for more detailed information.

Ancestry/Race	Number	%
Uruguayan	33	0.01
Venezuelan	103	0.02
Other South American	220	0.05
Other Hispanic or Latino	7,071	1.58
Hungarian	4,122	0.92
Icelander	63	0.01
Iranian	325	0.07
Irish	112,354	25.06
Israeli	360	0.08
Italian	147,077	32.81
Latvian	261	0.06
Lithuanian	1,800	0.40
Luxemburger	10	0.00
Macedonian	9	0.00
Maltese	587	0.13
New Zealander	17	0.00
Northern European	86	0.02
Norwegian	5,636	1.26
Pennsylvania German	38	0.01
Polish	26,848	5.99
Portuguese	2,972	0.66
Romanian	919	0.21
Russian	10,157	2.27
Scandinavian	505	0.11
Scotch-Irish	4,402	0.98
Scottish	4,974	1.11
Serbian	61	0.01
Slavic	103	0.02
Slovak	687	0.15
Slovene	26	0.01
Swedish	5,546	1.24
Swiss	901	0.20
Turkish	1,182	0.26
Ukrainian	2,385	0.53
United States or American	12,588	2.81
Welsh	1,023	0.23
West Indian, excl. Hispanic:	4,646	1.04
Bahamian	17	0.00
Barbadian	116	0.03
Belizean	31	0.01
Bermudan	56	0.01
British West Indian	195	0.04
Dutch West Indian	20	0.00
Haitian	1,089	0.24
Jamaican	1,649	0.37
Trinidadian and Tobagonian	746	0.17
U.S. Virgin Islander	29	0.01
West Indian	635	0.14
Other West Indian	63	0.01
White:	402,768	89.85
Not Hispanic (373,872)	378,052	84.34
Hispanic (22,509)	24,716	5.51
Yugoslavian	470	0.10

Brunswick

Place Type: Town
County: Rensselaer
Population: 11,664

Ancestry/Race	Number	%
African American/Black:	119	1.02
Not Hispanic (104)	112	0.96
Hispanic (1)	7	0.06
Alaska Native tribes, specified:	5	0.04
Eskimo (1)	5	0.04
Am. Ind. or Alaska Nat., not spec.	4	0.03
American Indian tribes, specified:	28	0.24
Apache (1)	1	0.01
Cherokee (2)	3	0.03
Choctaw	3	0.03
Cree	1	0.01
Iroquois (1)	18	0.15
Ute	1	0.01
All other tribes (1)	1	0.01
American Indian tribes, not spec.	1	0.01
Arab:	23	0.20
Lebanese	23	0.20
Armenian	132	1.13
Asian:	203	1.74
Chinese, ex. Taiwanese (35)	37	0.32
Filipino (9)	11	0.09
Indian (41)	44	0.38
Japanese (24)	26	0.22
Korean (67)	73	0.63
Taiwanese (1)	1	0.01
Thai (4)	4	0.03
Vietnamese (4)	5	0.04
Other Asian, not specified (1)	2	0.02
Austrian	45	0.38
British	67	0.57
Canadian	52	0.44
Czech	36	0.31
Danish	216	1.84
Dutch	526	4.49
Eastern European	29	0.25
English	1,347	11.49
Estonian	36	0.31
European	99	0.84
French, except Basque	1,248	10.65
French Canadian	238	2.03
German	2,239	19.11
Greek	42	0.36
Hawaii Native/Pacific Islander:	2	0.02
Micronesian: (1)	1	0.01
Guamanian/Chamorro (1)	1	0.01
Polynesian: (1)	1	0.01
Native Hawaiian (1)	1	0.01
Hispanic or Latino:	93	0.80
Central American:	4	0.03
Guatemalan	4	0.03
Cuban	2	0.02
Dominican Republic	2	0.02
Mexican	17	0.15
Puerto Rican	35	0.30
South American:	9	0.08
Chilean	1	0.01
Colombian	4	0.03
Ecuadorian	2	0.02
Peruvian	1	0.01
Uruguayan	1	0.01
Other Hispanic or Latino	24	0.21
Hungarian	27	0.23
Icelander	30	0.26
Irish	3,757	32.06
Italian	1,722	14.69
Latvian	8	0.07
Lithuanian	16	0.14
Northern European	8	0.07
Norwegian	84	0.72
Pennsylvania German	5	0.04
Polish	713	6.08
Portuguese	8	0.07
Romanian	18	0.15
Russian	169	1.44
Scandinavian	11	0.09
Scotch-Irish	208	1.77
Scottish	258	2.20
Serbian	11	0.09
Slovak	15	0.13
Swedish	77	0.66
Swiss	21	0.18
Turkish	21	0.18
Ukrainian	242	2.07
United States or American	524	4.47
Welsh	114	0.97
White:	11,322	97.07
Not Hispanic (11,177)	11,252	96.47
Hispanic (65)	70	0.60

Buffalo

Place Type: City
County: Erie
Population: 292,648

Ancestry/Race	Number	%
African American/Black:	112,880	38.57
Not Hispanic (107,066)	110,334	37.70
Hispanic (1,885)	2,546	0.87
African, sub-Saharan:	3,810	1.30
African	2,870	0.98
Cape Verdean	12	0.00
Ethiopian	31	0.01
Kenyan	14	0.00
Liberian	12	0.00
Nigerian	129	0.04
Somalian	457	0.16
South African	6	0.00
Sudanese	161	0.06
Ugandan	5	0.00
Other sub-Saharan African	113	0.04
Alaska Native tribes, specified:	7	0.00
Alaska Athabascan	1	0.00
Aleut	1	0.00
Eskimo (1)	1	0.00
Tlingit-Haida (1)	4	0.00
Alaska Native tribes, not specified	1	0.00
Am. Ind. or Alaska Nat., not spec.	1,386	0.47
Albanian	50	0.02
Alsatian	23	0.01
American Indian tribes, specified:	2,474	0.85
Apache (12)	29	0.01
Blackfeet (20)	106	0.04
Cherokee (56)	363	0.12
Cheyenne (2)	2	0.00
Chickasaw	1	0.00
Chippewa (35)	61	0.02
Choctaw (2)	22	0.01
Comanche (1)	4	0.00
Cree (1)	11	0.00
Creek (3)	9	0.00
Crow	5	0.00
Delaware (7)	9	0.00
Iroquois (1,234)	1,604	0.55
Kiowa (1)	1	0.00
Latin American Indians (24)	68	0.02
Lumbee (1)	6	0.00
Menominee (1)	1	0.00
Navajo (4)	8	0.00
Osage	1	0.00
Potawatomi (2)	3	0.00
Pueblo	1	0.00
Seminole (6)	22	0.01
Shoshone (1)	1	0.00
Sioux (21)	46	0.02
Tohono O'Odham (1)	2	0.00
Yaqui (3)	3	0.00
All other tribes (34)	85	0.03
American Indian tribes, not spec.	249	0.09
Arab:	1,737	0.59
Arab/Arabic	522	0.18
Egyptian	38	0.01
Iraqi	11	0.00
Jordanian	37	0.01
Lebanese	801	0.27
Moroccan	15	0.01
Palestinian	82	0.03
Syrian	53	0.02
Other Arab	178	0.06
Armenian	111	0.04
Asian:	4,979	1.70
Bangladeshi (14)	18	0.01
Cambodian (53)	60	0.02
Chinese, ex. Taiwanese (651)	736	0.25
Filipino (189)	292	0.10
Indian (730)	900	0.31
Indonesian (34)	44	0.02
Japanese (145)	243	0.08
Korean (245)	309	0.11
Laotian (298)	332	0.11
Malaysian (8)	9	0.00
Pakistani (47)	54	0.02
Sri Lankan (34)	36	0.01
Taiwanese (11)	15	0.01
Thai (35)	49	0.02
Vietnamese (1,325)	1,402	0.48
Other Asian, specified (35)	59	0.02
Other Asian, not specified (179)	421	0.14
Assyrian/Chaldean/Syriac	9	0.00

Notes: 1. Figures in the "Number" column do not add up to the total population due to: a) Ancestry/Race overlap — e.g. persons can report being both White and Irish, b) persons of Hispanic origin can report being any race, c) persons reporting two ancestries are counted in both categories. 2. Numbers in parentheses indicate the number of persons reporting this ancestry/race alone, not in combination with any other ancestry/race. 3. Refer to the Explanation of Data in the front of the book for more detailed information.

Australian	46	0.02
Austrian	545	0.19
Basque	28	0.01
Belgian	116	0.04
Brazilian	51	0.02
British	492	0.17
Bulgarian	29	0.01
Canadian	753	0.26
Celtic	65	0.02
Croatian	363	0.12
Czech	328	0.11
Czechoslovakian	297	0.10
Danish	300	0.10
Dutch	1,739	0.59
Eastern European	141	0.05
English	11,765	4.02
Estonian	19	0.01
European	451	0.15
Finnish	111	0.04
French, except Basque	5,292	1.81
French Canadian	1,340	0.46
German	39,692	13.56
Greek	937	0.32
Guyanese	79	0.03
Hawaii Native/Pacific Islander:	289	0.10
Micronesian: (24)	36	0.01
Guamanian/Chamorro (23)	35	0.01
Other Micronesian (1)	1	0.00
Polynesian: (30)	75	0.03
Native Hawaiian (18)	41	0.01
Samoan (11)	25	0.01
Tongan	4	0.00
Other Polynesian (1)	5	0.00
Other Pac. Isl., specified	17	0.01
Other Pac. Isl., not spec. (66)	161	0.06
Hispanic or Latino:	22,076	7.54
Central American:	233	0.08
Costa Rican	25	0.01
Guatemalan	45	0.02
Honduran	29	0.01
Nicaraguan	20	0.01
Panamanian	60	0.02
Salvadoran	35	0.01
Other Central American	19	0.01
Cuban	353	0.12
Dominican Republic	445	0.15
Mexican	1,030	0.35
Puerto Rican	17,250	5.89
South American:	333	0.11
Argentinean	39	0.01
Bolivian	8	0.00
Chilean	35	0.01
Colombian	107	0.04
Ecuadorian	40	0.01
Paraguayan	1	0.00
Peruvian	50	0.02
Uruguayan	4	0.00
Venezuelan	35	0.01
Other South American	14	0.00
Other Hispanic or Latino	2,432	0.83
Hungarian	2,190	0.75
Iranian	95	0.03
Irish	35,608	12.17
Israeli	89	0.03
Italian	34,379	11.75
Latvian	144	0.05
Lithuanian	366	0.13
Luxemburger	28	0.01
Macedonian	40	0.01
Northern European	15	0.01
Norwegian	627	0.21
Pennsylvania German	125	0.04
Polish	34,254	11.70
Portuguese	307	0.10
Romanian	337	0.12
Russian	1,668	0.57
Scandinavian	31	0.01
Scotch-Irish	1,671	0.57
Scottish	2,657	0.91
Serbian	278	0.09
Slavic	165	0.06
Slovak	385	0.13
Slovene	13	0.00
Swedish	1,323	0.45
Swiss	245	0.08
Turkish	61	0.02
Ukrainian	1,439	0.49
United States or American	4,765	1.63
Welsh	878	0.30
West Indian, excl. Hispanic:	1,344	0.46
Barbadian	38	0.01
Bermudan	7	0.00
British West Indian	37	0.01
Dutch West Indian	6	0.00
Haitian	195	0.07
Jamaican	710	0.24
Trinidadian and Tobagonian	93	0.03
West Indian	258	0.09
White:	164,588	56.24
Not Hispanic (151,450)	155,570	53.16
Hispanic (7,850)	9,018	3.08
Yugoslavian	254	0.09

Camillus

Place Type: Town
County: Onondaga
Population: 23,152

Ancestry/Race	Number	%
African American/Black:	278	1.20
Not Hispanic (208)	263	1.14
Hispanic (11)	15	0.06
African, sub-Saharan:	36	0.16
African	36	0.16
Am. Ind. or Alaska Nat., not spec.	35	0.15
Albanian	9	0.04
American Indian tribes, specified:	106	0.46
Blackfeet	1	0.00
Cherokee	6	0.03
Chippewa	1	0.00
Choctaw	1	0.00
Creek	1	0.00
Iroquois (62)	80	0.35
Kiowa (2)	2	0.01
Latin American Indians	2	0.01
Lumbee	1	0.00
Pueblo	1	0.00
Sioux (2)	2	0.01
All other tribes (4)	8	0.03
American Indian tribes, not spec.	7	0.03
Arab:	302	1.30
Arab/Arabic	78	0.34
Lebanese	99	0.43
Palestinian	101	0.44
Syrian	24	0.10
Armenian	34	0.15
Asian:	297	1.28
Cambodian (1)	1	0.00
Chinese, ex. Taiwanese (47)	62	0.27
Filipino (21)	33	0.14
Indian (89)	98	0.42
Japanese (2)	2	0.01
Korean (50)	52	0.22
Laotian (1)	1	0.00
Pakistani (8)	11	0.05
Sri Lankan (2)	2	0.01
Taiwanese (9)	9	0.04
Thai (2)	3	0.01
Vietnamese (11)	20	0.09
Other Asian, not specified (1)	3	0.01
Austrian	158	0.68
Belgian	6	0.03
British	34	0.15
Canadian	41	0.18
Celtic	10	0.04
Croatian	20	0.09
Czech	51	0.22
Czechoslovakian	20	0.09
Danish	75	0.32
Dutch	500	2.16
Eastern European	15	0.06
English	3,753	16.21
European	22	0.10
Finnish	13	0.06
French, except Basque	979	4.23
French Canadian	506	2.19
German	4,425	19.11
Greek	182	0.79
Hawaii Native/Pacific Islander:	7	0.03
Micronesian: (2)	2	0.01
Guamanian/Chamorro (1)	1	0.00
Other Micronesian (1)	1	0.00
Polynesian: (2)	5	0.02
Native Hawaiian (2)	5	0.02
Hispanic or Latino:	213	0.92
Central American:	10	0.04
Guatemalan	2	0.01
Honduran	4	0.02
Nicaraguan	1	0.00
Panamanian	2	0.01
Salvadoran	1	0.00
Cuban	9	0.04
Dominican Republic	4	0.02
Mexican	42	0.18
Puerto Rican	68	0.29
South American:	20	0.09
Chilean	3	0.01
Colombian	15	0.06
Peruvian	2	0.01
Other Hispanic or Latino	60	0.26
Hungarian	192	0.83
Icelander	8	0.03
Irish	6,372	27.52
Italian	4,601	19.87
Latvian	11	0.05
Lithuanian	85	0.37
Macedonian	42	0.18
Northern European	3	0.01
Norwegian	177	0.76
Pennsylvania German	2	0.01
Polish	2,606	11.26
Portuguese	76	0.33
Romanian	4	0.02
Russian	174	0.75
Scandinavian	10	0.04
Scotch-Irish	284	1.23
Scottish	508	2.19
Slavic	13	0.06
Slovak	96	0.41
Swedish	160	0.69
Swiss	103	0.44
Ukrainian	809	3.49
United States or American	536	2.32
Welsh	215	0.93
West Indian, excl. Hispanic:	28	0.12
Jamaican	11	0.05
Trinidadian and Tobagonian	17	0.07
White:	22,516	97.25
Not Hispanic (22,188)	22,358	96.57
Hispanic (143)	158	0.68
Yugoslavian	11	0.05

Canandaigua

Place Type: City
County: Ontario
Population: 11,264

Ancestry/Race	Number	%
African American/Black:	225	2.00
Not Hispanic (170)	218	1.94
Hispanic (2)	7	0.06
African, sub-Saharan:	12	0.11
African	12	0.11
Am. Ind. or Alaska Nat., not spec.	34	0.30
American Indian tribes, specified:	42	0.37
Apache	1	0.01
Blackfeet	2	0.02
Cherokee (2)	7	0.06

Notes: 1. Figures in the "Number" column do not add up to the total population due to: a) Ancestry/Race overlap — e.g. persons can report being both White and Irish, b) persons of Hispanic origin can report being any race, c) persons reporting two ancestries are counted in both categories. 2. Numbers in parentheses indicate the number of persons reporting this ancestry/race alone, not in combination with any other ancestry/race. 3. Refer to the Explanation of Data in the front of the book for more detailed information.

Ancestry/Race	Number	%
Cheyenne (1)	1	0.01
Chippewa	1	0.01
Choctaw	4	0.04
Cree (1)	1	0.01
Iroquois (6)	18	0.16
Ottawa (1)	1	0.01
Pueblo	1	0.01
All other tribes (4)	5	0.04
American Indian tribes, not spec.	5	0.04
Arab:	46	0.41
Arab/Arabic	18	0.16
Egyptian	5	0.04
Lebanese	6	0.05
Syrian	17	0.15
Armenian	10	0.09
Asian:	98	0.87
Bangladeshi (2)	3	0.03
Chinese, ex. Taiwanese (26)	30	0.27
Filipino (14)	17	0.15
Indian (3)	4	0.04
Indonesian	1	0.01
Japanese (2)	7	0.06
Korean (10)	16	0.14
Laotian (6)	7	0.06
Pakistani (1)	1	0.01
Sri Lankan (1)	1	0.01
Thai (1)	2	0.02
Vietnamese (1)	1	0.01
Other Asian, specified (6)	6	0.05
Other Asian, not specified	2	0.02
Austrian	12	0.11
Belgian	6	0.05
British	62	0.55
Canadian	55	0.49
Czech	32	0.28
Czechoslovakian	15	0.13
Danish	95	0.84
Dutch	717	6.37
English	2,131	18.92
European	94	0.83
Finnish	22	0.20
French, except Basque	533	4.73
French Canadian	174	1.54
German	2,301	20.43
Greek	16	0.14
Hawaii Native/Pacific Islander:	9	0.08
Micronesian: (6)	6	0.05
Guamanian/Chamorro (6)	6	0.05
Polynesian: (1)	3	0.03
Native Hawaiian	1	0.01
Samoan (1)	2	0.02
Hispanic or Latino:	115	1.02
Central American:	5	0.04
Honduran	1	0.01
Other Central American	4	0.04
Cuban	7	0.06
Mexican	18	0.16
Puerto Rican	48	0.43
South American:	12	0.11
Colombian	8	0.07
Peruvian	4	0.04
Other Hispanic or Latino	25	0.22
Hungarian	36	0.32
Irish	2,463	21.87
Italian	1,325	11.76
Lithuanian	11	0.10
Northern European	5	0.04
Norwegian	37	0.33
Pennsylvania German	25	0.22
Polish	519	4.61
Portuguese	22	0.20
Russian	64	0.57
Scotch-Irish	199	1.77
Scottish	395	3.51
Slavic	10	0.09
Slovak	17	0.15
Swedish	232	2.06
Swiss	20	0.18
Turkish	7	0.06
Ukrainian	46	0.41
United States or American	729	6.47
Welsh	133	1.18
West Indian, excl. Hispanic:	11	0.10
Jamaican	11	0.10
White:	10,947	97.19
Not Hispanic (10,745)	10,857	96.39
Hispanic (73)	90	0.80
Yugoslavian	21	0.19

Canton

Place Type: Town
County: Saint Lawrence
Population: 10,334

Ancestry/Race	Number	%
African American/Black:	310	3.00
Not Hispanic (261)	288	2.79
Hispanic (14)	22	0.21
African, sub-Saharan:	17	0.16
African	9	0.09
South African	8	0.08
Am. Ind. or Alaska Nat., not spec.	34	0.33
American Indian tribes, specified:	41	0.40
Blackfeet	1	0.01
Cherokee (2)	4	0.04
Crow (1)	1	0.01
Iroquois (16)	25	0.24
Latin American Indians (1)	1	0.01
Lumbee (3)	3	0.03
Navajo (1)	1	0.01
Sioux (2)	2	0.02
Yaqui (1)	1	0.01
All other tribes (2)	2	0.02
American Indian tribes, not spec.	10	0.10
Arab:	19	0.18
Lebanese	8	0.08
Syrian	7	0.07
Other Arab	4	0.04
Armenian	6	0.06
Asian:	94	0.91
Chinese, ex. Taiwanese (13)	19	0.18
Filipino (10)	15	0.15
Indian (15)	17	0.16
Indonesian	2	0.02
Japanese (14)	19	0.18
Korean (7)	8	0.08
Sri Lankan	1	0.01
Thai (1)	2	0.02
Vietnamese (6)	6	0.06
Other Asian, not specified (3)	5	0.05
Australian	11	0.11
Austrian	34	0.33
Basque	7	0.07
Belgian	14	0.14
British	82	0.79
Bulgarian	9	0.09
Canadian	127	1.23
Czech	17	0.16
Czechoslovakian	14	0.14
Danish	28	0.27
Dutch	279	2.70
Eastern European	15	0.15
English	1,795	17.36
European	50	0.48
Finnish	17	0.16
French, except Basque	1,209	11.69
French Canadian	472	4.56
German	1,130	10.93
Greek	27	0.26
Hawaii Native/Pacific Islander:	4	0.04
Polynesian:	1	0.01
Samoan	1	0.01
Other Pac. Isl., not spec.	3	0.03
Hispanic or Latino:	144	1.39
Central American:	6	0.06
Costa Rican	1	0.01
Guatemalan	1	0.01
Honduran	4	0.04
Cuban	4	0.04
Dominican Republic	15	0.15
Mexican	18	0.17
Puerto Rican	43	0.42
South American:	16	0.15
Argentinean	3	0.03
Chilean	2	0.02
Colombian	6	0.06
Ecuadorian	3	0.03
Venezuelan	1	0.01
Other South American	1	0.01
Other Hispanic or Latino	42	0.41
Hungarian	90	0.87
Iranian	9	0.09
Irish	1,886	18.24
Italian	683	6.61
Lithuanian	31	0.30
Norwegian	89	0.86
Polish	253	2.45
Russian	82	0.79
Scandinavian	12	0.12
Scotch-Irish	176	1.70
Scottish	401	3.88
Slavic	22	0.21
Slovak	4	0.04
Swedish	145	1.40
Swiss	13	0.13
Ukrainian	20	0.19
United States or American	947	9.16
Welsh	104	1.01
West Indian, excl. Hispanic:	77	0.74
British West Indian	12	0.12
Haitian	10	0.10
Jamaican	40	0.39
Trinidadian and Tobagonian	7	0.07
U.S. Virgin Islander	8	0.08
White:	9,865	95.46
Not Hispanic (9,718)	9,795	94.78
Hispanic (58)	70	0.68

Carmel

Place Type: Town
County: Putnam
Population: 33,006

Ancestry/Race	Number	%
African American/Black:	471	1.43
Not Hispanic (325)	393	1.19
Hispanic (37)	78	0.24
African, sub-Saharan:	11	0.03
African	4	0.01
South African	7	0.02
Alaska Native tribes, specified:	1	0.00
Aleut	1	0.00
Alaska Native tribes, not specified	4	0.01
Am. Ind. or Alaska Nat., not spec.	64	0.19
Albanian	57	0.17
Alsatian	6	0.02
American Indian tribes, specified:	52	0.16
Blackfeet (1)	1	0.00
Cherokee	20	0.06
Choctaw (2)	2	0.01
Iroquois (1)	7	0.02
Latin American Indians (9)	12	0.04
Menominee (1)	1	0.00
Osage (2)	2	0.01
Sioux	1	0.00
All other tribes (1)	6	0.02
American Indian tribes, not spec.	4	0.01
Arab:	98	0.30
Arab/Arabic	20	0.06
Egyptian	11	0.03
Jordanian	44	0.13
Lebanese	11	0.03
Moroccan	6	0.02
Syrian	6	0.02
Armenian	118	0.36
Asian:	473	1.43
Cambodian (1)	1	0.00
Chinese, ex. Taiwanese (106)	131	0.40

Notes: 1. Figures in the "Number" column do not add up to the total population due to: a) Ancestry/Race overlap — e.g. persons can report being both White and Irish, b) persons of Hispanic origin can report being any race, c) persons reporting two ancestries are counted in both categories. 2. Numbers in parentheses indicate the number of persons reporting this ancestry/race alone, not in combination with any other ancestry/race. 3. Refer to the Explanation of Data in the front of the book for more detailed information.

Ancestry/Race	Number	%
Filipino (48)	59	0.18
Indian (126)	133	0.40
Japanese (9)	18	0.05
Korean (47)	48	0.15
Malaysian (3)	6	0.02
Pakistani (24)	29	0.09
Sri Lankan	1	0.00
Taiwanese	3	0.01
Thai (10)	11	0.03
Vietnamese (9)	9	0.03
Other Asian, specified (1)	5	0.02
Other Asian, not specified (4)	19	0.06
Austrian	424	1.28
Belgian	20	0.06
Brazilian	29	0.09
British	21	0.06
Bulgarian	6	0.02
Canadian	100	0.30
Celtic	13	0.04
Croatian	30	0.09
Czech	192	0.58
Czechoslovakian	105	0.32
Danish	63	0.19
Dutch	325	0.98
Eastern European	61	0.18
English	1,652	5.01
European	67	0.20
Finnish	12	0.04
French, except Basque	535	1.62
French Canadian	188	0.57
German	5,112	15.49
Greek	379	1.15
Guyanese	56	0.17
Hawaii Native/Pacific Islander:	17	0.05
Micronesian: (1)	1	0.00
Guamanian/Chamorro (1)	1	0.00
Polynesian: (2)	14	0.04
Native Hawaiian (2)	14	0.04
Other Pac. Isl., not spec.	2	0.01
Hispanic or Latino:	1,955	5.92
Central American:	145	0.44
Costa Rican	15	0.05
Guatemalan	44	0.13
Honduran	9	0.03
Nicaraguan	4	0.01
Panamanian	5	0.02
Salvadoran	56	0.17
Other Central American	12	0.04
Cuban	94	0.28
Dominican Republic	63	0.19
Mexican	247	0.75
Puerto Rican	807	2.45
South American:	264	0.80
Argentinean	34	0.10
Bolivian	14	0.04
Chilean	7	0.02
Colombian	81	0.25
Ecuadorian	65	0.20
Paraguayan	6	0.02
Peruvian	25	0.08
Venezuelan	18	0.05
Other South American	14	0.04
Other Hispanic or Latino	335	1.01
Hungarian	394	1.19
Icelander	20	0.06
Iranian	13	0.04
Irish	8,253	25.00
Israeli	22	0.07
Italian	11,655	35.31
Latvian	12	0.04
Lithuanian	83	0.25
Maltese	8	0.02
Northern European	17	0.05
Norwegian	201	0.61
Polish	1,812	5.49
Portuguese	377	1.14
Romanian	91	0.28
Russian	861	2.61
Scandinavian	10	0.03
Scotch-Irish	354	1.07
Scottish	403	1.22
Serbian	13	0.04
Slavic	36	0.11
Slovak	256	0.78
Slovene	6	0.02
Swedish	477	1.45
Swiss	115	0.35
Turkish	8	0.02
Ukrainian	135	0.41
United States or American	1,226	3.71
Welsh	66	0.20
West Indian, excl. Hispanic:	72	0.22
British West Indian	25	0.08
Jamaican	6	0.02
Trinidadian and Tobagonian	5	0.02
West Indian	36	0.11
White:	31,688	96.01
Not Hispanic (29,938)	30,253	91.66
Hispanic (1,285)	1,435	4.35
Yugoslavian	123	0.37

Catskill

Place Type: Town
County: Greene
Population: 11,849

Ancestry/Race	Number	%
African American/Black:	841	7.10
Not Hispanic (683)	787	6.64
Hispanic (32)	54	0.46
African, sub-Saharan:	17	0.14
African	8	0.07
Kenyan	9	0.08
Am. Ind. or Alaska Nat., not spec.	54	0.46
Albanian	56	0.47
American Indian tribes, specified:	71	0.60
Apache (1)	1	0.01
Blackfeet (3)	13	0.11
Cherokee (2)	13	0.11
Cheyenne	1	0.01
Chippewa (1)	1	0.01
Choctaw (2)	4	0.03
Cree (1)	4	0.03
Creek (1)	2	0.02
Delaware	1	0.01
Iroquois (5)	18	0.15
Latin American Indians (1)	2	0.02
Seminole (1)	2	0.02
Tohono O'Odham (4)	4	0.03
All other tribes	5	0.04
American Indian tribes, not spec.	1	0.01
Arab:	9	0.08
Lebanese	9	0.08
Armenian	8	0.07
Asian:	115	0.97
Chinese, ex. Taiwanese (24)	25	0.21
Filipino (9)	13	0.11
Indian (20)	29	0.24
Japanese (2)	3	0.03
Korean (8)	11	0.09
Pakistani (4)	4	0.03
Thai (2)	3	0.03
Vietnamese (1)	1	0.01
Other Asian, specified	2	0.02
Other Asian, not specified (1)	24	0.20
Assyrian/Chaldean/Syriac	15	0.13
Austrian	99	0.84
Brazilian	6	0.05
British	51	0.43
Celtic	5	0.04
Croatian	36	0.30
Czech	45	0.38
Czechoslovakian	44	0.37
Danish	29	0.24
Dutch	659	5.56
English	894	7.54
Estonian	15	0.13
European	48	0.41
French, except Basque	491	4.14
French Canadian	49	0.41
German	2,436	20.56
Greek	38	0.32
Hawaii Native/Pacific Islander:	11	0.09
Micronesian: (1)	1	0.01
Guamanian/Chamorro (1)	1	0.01
Polynesian: (1)	5	0.04
Native Hawaiian (1)	5	0.04
Other Pac. Isl., not spec.	5	0.04
Hispanic or Latino:	477	4.03
Central American:	22	0.19
Honduran	5	0.04
Nicaraguan	1	0.01
Salvadoran	15	0.13
Other Central American	1	0.01
Cuban	10	0.08
Dominican Republic	8	0.07
Mexican	63	0.53
Puerto Rican	286	2.41
South American:	18	0.15
Argentinean	8	0.07
Chilean	1	0.01
Colombian	8	0.07
Venezuelan	1	0.01
Other Hispanic or Latino	70	0.59
Hungarian	12	0.10
Irish	2,631	22.20
Italian	2,159	18.22
Lithuanian	58	0.49
Norwegian	56	0.47
Pennsylvania German	7	0.06
Polish	551	4.65
Portuguese	7	0.06
Romanian	31	0.26
Russian	88	0.74
Scotch-Irish	101	0.85
Scottish	159	1.34
Slavic	31	0.26
Swedish	58	0.49
Swiss	44	0.37
Ukrainian	23	0.19
United States or American	815	6.88
Welsh	21	0.18
West Indian, excl. Hispanic:	88	0.74
Jamaican	66	0.56
Trinidadian and Tobagonian	22	0.19
White:	10,884	91.86
Not Hispanic (10,348)	10,558	89.10
Hispanic (297)	326	2.75
Yugoslavian	98	0.83

Centereach

Place Type: Census Designated Place
County: Suffolk
Population: 27,285

Ancestry/Race	Number	%
African American/Black:	643	2.36
Not Hispanic (501)	583	2.14
Hispanic (38)	60	0.22
African, sub-Saharan:	45	0.17
African	45	0.17
Alaska Native tribes, not specified	1	0.00
Am. Ind. or Alaska Nat., not spec.	60	0.22
American Indian tribes, specified:	69	0.25
Apache (1)	1	0.00
Blackfeet (5)	15	0.05
Cherokee (4)	14	0.05
Choctaw (2)	2	0.01
Cree (1)	1	0.00
Creek	1	0.00
Iroquois (4)	9	0.03
Latin American Indians (3)	3	0.01
Lumbee	1	0.00
Seminole (1)	1	0.00
Sioux	1	0.00
All other tribes (3)	20	0.07
American Indian tribes, not spec.	6	0.02
Arab:	210	0.77

Notes: 1. Figures in the "Number" column do not add up to the total population due to: a) Ancestry/Race overlap — e.g. persons can report being both White and Irish, b) persons of Hispanic origin can report being any race, c) persons reporting two ancestries are counted in both categories. 2. Numbers in parentheses indicate the number of persons reporting this ancestry/race alone, not in combination with any other ancestry/race. 3. Refer to the Explanation of Data in the front of the book for more detailed information.

Arab/Arabic	17	0.06
Egyptian	84	0.31
Iraqi	13	0.05
Lebanese	69	0.25
Syrian	19	0.07
Other Arab	8	0.03
Armenian	58	0.21
Asian:	969	3.55
Bangladeshi (6)	6	0.02
Chinese, ex. Taiwanese (263)	286	1.05
Filipino (151)	169	0.62
Indian (234)	240	0.88
Indonesian (2)	2	0.01
Japanese (22)	31	0.11
Korean (68)	90	0.33
Pakistani (38)	44	0.16
Sri Lankan (3)	3	0.01
Taiwanese (10)	12	0.04
Thai (6)	12	0.04
Vietnamese (26)	29	0.11
Other Asian, specified (3)	9	0.03
Other Asian, not specified (30)	36	0.13
Austrian	253	0.93
Belgian	26	0.10
Brazilian	11	0.04
British	102	0.38
Canadian	76	0.28
Croatian	8	0.03
Czech	64	0.24
Czechoslovakian	99	0.36
Danish	122	0.45
Dutch	258	0.95
Eastern European	12	0.04
English	1,190	4.38
Estonian	5	0.02
European	59	0.22
Finnish	8	0.03
French, except Basque	416	1.53
French Canadian	145	0.53
German	5,184	19.07
Greek	369	1.36
Guyanese	9	0.03
Hawaii Native/Pacific Islander:	17	0.06
Micronesian: (1)	1	0.00
Guamanian/Chamorro (1)	1	0.00
Polynesian: (1)	1	0.00
Samoan (1)	1	0.00
Other Pac. Isl., not spec.	15	0.05
Hispanic or Latino:	1,932	7.08
Central American:	86	0.32
Costa Rican	11	0.04
Guatemalan	15	0.05
Honduran	9	0.03
Panamanian	1	0.00
Salvadoran	43	0.16
Other Central American	7	0.03
Cuban	84	0.31
Dominican Republic	60	0.22
Mexican	96	0.35
Puerto Rican	911	3.34
South American:	214	0.78
Argentinean	21	0.08
Bolivian	10	0.04
Chilean	8	0.03
Colombian	94	0.34
Ecuadorian	51	0.19
Peruvian	14	0.05
Uruguayan	3	0.01
Venezuelan	9	0.03
Other South American	4	0.01
Other Hispanic or Latino	481	1.76
Hungarian	214	0.79
Iranian	4	0.01
Irish	6,746	24.82
Israeli	23	0.08
Italian	9,983	36.73
Latvian	9	0.03
Lithuanian	148	0.54
Macedonian	9	0.03
Maltese	11	0.04
Northern European	8	0.03
Norwegian	315	1.16
Polish	1,781	6.55
Portuguese	212	0.78
Romanian	52	0.19
Russian	673	2.48
Scandinavian	48	0.18
Scotch-Irish	205	0.75
Scottish	282	1.04
Slovak	41	0.15
Swedish	509	1.87
Swiss	20	0.07
Turkish	27	0.10
Ukrainian	92	0.34
United States or American	826	3.04
Welsh	17	0.06
West Indian, excl. Hispanic:	145	0.53
Bermudan	9	0.03
British West Indian	6	0.02
Haitian	65	0.24
Jamaican	24	0.09
Trinidadian and Tobagonian	3	0.01
Other West Indian	38	0.14
White:	25,402	93.10
Not Hispanic (23,658)	23,877	87.51
Hispanic (1,414)	1,525	5.59
Yugoslavian	30	0.11

Central Islip

Place Type: Census Designated Place
County: Suffolk
Population: 31,950

Ancestry/Race	Number	%
Afghan	17	0.05
African American/Black:	9,506	29.75
Not Hispanic (8,244)	8,791	27.51
Hispanic (525)	715	2.24
African, sub-Saharan:	332	1.04
African	271	0.85
Liberian	4	0.01
Nigerian	44	0.14
Sierra Leonean	6	0.02
Other sub-Saharan African	7	0.02
Am. Ind. or Alaska Nat., not spec.	173	0.54
American Indian tribes, specified:	214	0.67
Apache (1)	4	0.01
Blackfeet (1)	10	0.03
Cherokee (10)	52	0.16
Cheyenne (3)	3	0.01
Choctaw (1)	1	0.00
Cree	1	0.00
Iroquois	2	0.01
Latin American Indians (23)	52	0.16
Lumbee (1)	1	0.00
Navajo	2	0.01
Pueblo (4)	8	0.03
Seminole (1)	2	0.01
Sioux	8	0.03
Ute	3	0.01
All other tribes (47)	65	0.20
American Indian tribes, not spec.	23	0.07
Arab:	92	0.29
Arab/Arabic	21	0.07
Egyptian	16	0.05
Moroccan	9	0.03
Palestinian	34	0.11
Other Arab	12	0.04
Armenian	34	0.11
Asian:	1,244	3.89
Cambodian (1)	1	0.00
Chinese, ex. Taiwanese (107)	149	0.47
Filipino (100)	117	0.37
Indian (513)	611	1.91
Indonesian	2	0.01
Japanese (13)	28	0.09
Korean (37)	47	0.15
Laotian (7)	7	0.02
Malaysian (2)	2	0.01
Pakistani (80)	115	0.36
Sri Lankan (3)	7	0.02
Thai (6)	8	0.03
Vietnamese (83)	93	0.29
Other Asian, specified (2)	5	0.02
Other Asian, not specified (24)	52	0.16
Austrian	88	0.28
Basque	6	0.02
Belgian	17	0.05
Brazilian	9	0.03
British	37	0.12
Canadian	40	0.13
Czech	108	0.34
Czechoslovakian	96	0.30
Danish	21	0.07
Dutch	82	0.26
English	699	2.19
European	100	0.31
French, except Basque	303	0.95
French Canadian	82	0.26
German	2,065	6.48
Greek	195	0.61
Guyanese	244	0.77
Hawaii Native/Pacific Islander:	65	0.20
Micronesian: (25)	30	0.09
Guamanian/Chamorro (25)	30	0.09
Polynesian: (8)	14	0.04
Native Hawaiian (3)	9	0.03
Samoan (5)	5	0.02
Other Pac. Isl., specified	2	0.01
Other Pac. Isl., not spec. (4)	19	0.06
Hispanic or Latino:	11,452	35.84
Central American:	2,821	8.83
Costa Rican	24	0.08
Guatemalan	236	0.74
Honduran	300	0.94
Nicaraguan	33	0.10
Panamanian	85	0.27
Salvadoran	1,967	6.16
Other Central American	176	0.55
Cuban	129	0.40
Dominican Republic	711	2.23
Mexican	284	0.89
Puerto Rican	4,050	12.68
South American:	1,156	3.62
Argentinean	62	0.19
Bolivian	27	0.08
Chilean	27	0.08
Colombian	406	1.27
Ecuadorian	324	1.01
Paraguayan	3	0.01
Peruvian	238	0.74
Uruguayan	3	0.01
Venezuelan	26	0.08
Other South American	40	0.13
Other Hispanic or Latino	2,301	7.20
Hungarian	136	0.43
Irish	3,130	9.82
Israeli	24	0.08
Italian	3,182	9.98
Lithuanian	98	0.31
Maltese	29	0.09
Norwegian	60	0.19
Polish	540	1.69
Portuguese	147	0.46
Romanian	7	0.02
Russian	147	0.46
Scandinavian	29	0.09
Scotch-Irish	136	0.43
Scottish	150	0.47
Slavic	6	0.02
Slovak	21	0.07
Swedish	128	0.40
Swiss	108	0.34
Turkish	12	0.04
Ukrainian	32	0.10
United States or American	695	2.18
Welsh	13	0.04
West Indian, excl. Hispanic:	2,040	6.40
Barbadian	95	0.30

Notes: 1. Figures in the "Number" column do not add up to the total population due to: a) Ancestry/Race overlap — e.g. persons can report being both White and Irish, b) persons of Hispanic origin can report being any race, c) persons reporting two ancestries are counted in both categories. 2. Numbers in parentheses indicate the number of persons reporting this ancestry/race alone, not in combination with any other ancestry/race. 3. Refer to the Explanation of Data in the front of the book for more detailed information.

Ancestry/Race	Number	%
Belizean	84	0.26
Bermudan	10	0.03
British West Indian	20	0.06
Dutch West Indian	5	0.02
Haitian	470	1.47
Jamaican	874	2.74
Trinidadian and Tobagonian	326	1.02
U.S. Virgin Islander	10	0.03
West Indian	146	0.46
White:	16,244	50.84
Not Hispanic (10,162)	10,524	32.94
Hispanic (5,107)	5,720	17.90
Yugoslavian	10	0.03

Cheektowaga

Place Type: Town
County: Erie
Population: 94,019

Ancestry/Race	Number	%
African American/Black:	3,060	3.25
Not Hispanic (2,706)	2,990	3.18
Hispanic (48)	70	0.07
African, sub-Saharan:	84	0.09
African	78	0.08
Other sub-Saharan African	6	0.01
Alaska Native tribes, specified:	5	0.01
Alaska Athabascan	1	0.00
Aleut	1	0.00
Eskimo (2)	3	0.00
Am. Ind. or Alaska Nat., not spec.	103	0.11
Albanian	12	0.01
Alsatian	38	0.04
American Indian tribes, specified:	239	0.25
Apache (5)	8	0.01
Blackfeet	14	0.01
Cherokee (2)	23	0.02
Chippewa (4)	8	0.01
Choctaw	1	0.00
Cree (3)	3	0.00
Creek (1)	1	0.00
Iroquois (89)	147	0.16
Latin American Indians	4	0.00
Lumbee	1	0.00
Navajo (1)	2	0.00
Ottawa (1)	1	0.00
Pueblo (1)	1	0.00
Seminole	1	0.00
Sioux	1	0.00
Yaqui (1)	1	0.00
All other tribes (8)	22	0.02
American Indian tribes, not spec.	10	0.01
Arab:	257	0.27
Arab/Arabic	46	0.05
Jordanian	18	0.02
Lebanese	150	0.16
Palestinian	21	0.02
Syrian	15	0.02
Other Arab	7	0.01
Armenian	13	0.01
Asian:	1,066	1.13
Bangladeshi	3	0.00
Cambodian (2)	3	0.00
Chinese, ex. Taiwanese (193)	208	0.22
Filipino (56)	92	0.10
Indian (284)	309	0.33
Indonesian	1	0.00
Japanese (26)	64	0.07
Korean (101)	126	0.13
Laotian (47)	51	0.05
Malaysian (8)	9	0.01
Pakistani (13)	15	0.02
Sri Lankan	3	0.00
Taiwanese (1)	3	0.00
Thai (3)	5	0.01
Vietnamese (127)	135	0.14
Other Asian, specified	3	0.00
Other Asian, not specified (9)	36	0.04
Austrian	318	0.34
Belgian	76	0.08
Brazilian	21	0.02
British	227	0.24
Bulgarian	10	0.01
Canadian	286	0.30
Croatian	172	0.18
Czech	218	0.23
Czechoslovakian	128	0.14
Danish	74	0.08
Dutch	685	0.73
Eastern European	16	0.02
English	5,441	5.79
Estonian	7	0.01
European	54	0.06
Finnish	76	0.08
French, except Basque	2,535	2.70
French Canadian	681	0.72
German	28,147	29.94
Greek	331	0.35
Hawaii Native/Pacific Islander:	29	0.03
Polynesian: (6)	14	0.01
Native Hawaiian (4)	9	0.01
Samoan (1)	4	0.00
Other Polynesian (1)	1	0.00
Other Pac. Isl., not spec. (1)	15	0.02
Hispanic or Latino:	908	0.97
Central American:	12	0.01
Costa Rican	2	0.00
Guatemalan	2	0.00
Honduran	1	0.00
Panamanian	1	0.00
Salvadoran	6	0.01
Cuban	25	0.03
Dominican Republic	2	0.00
Mexican	135	0.14
Puerto Rican	503	0.53
South American:	51	0.05
Argentinean	6	0.01
Bolivian	1	0.00
Chilean	1	0.00
Colombian	21	0.02
Ecuadorian	6	0.01
Paraguayan	4	0.00
Peruvian	2	0.00
Uruguayan	1	0.00
Venezuelan	6	0.01
Other South American	3	0.00
Other Hispanic or Latino	180	0.19
Hungarian	698	0.74
Irish	13,260	14.10
Israeli	14	0.01
Italian	15,047	16.00
Latvian	23	0.02
Lithuanian	124	0.13
Macedonian	23	0.02
Norwegian	224	0.24
Pennsylvania German	88	0.09
Polish	37,560	39.95
Portuguese	36	0.04
Russian	415	0.44
Scandinavian	13	0.01
Scotch-Irish	475	0.51
Scottish	1,141	1.21
Serbian	34	0.04
Slavic	39	0.04
Slovak	153	0.16
Slovene	8	0.01
Swedish	738	0.78
Swiss	141	0.15
Ukrainian	830	0.88
United States or American	2,021	2.15
Welsh	330	0.35
West Indian, excl. Hispanic:	166	0.18
British West Indian	20	0.02
Haitian	24	0.03
Jamaican	91	0.10
Trinidadian and Tobagonian	10	0.01
West Indian	21	0.02
White:	89,883	95.60
Not Hispanic (88,674)	89,234	94.91
Hispanic (592)	649	0.69
Yugoslavian	169	0.18

Chenango

Place Type: Town
County: Broome
Population: 11,454

Ancestry/Race	Number	%
Acadian/Cajun	6	0.05
African American/Black:	109	0.95
Not Hispanic (67)	106	0.93
Hispanic	3	0.03
African, sub-Saharan:	8	0.07
African	8	0.07
Am. Ind. or Alaska Nat., not spec.	17	0.15
American Indian tribes, specified:	36	0.31
Blackfeet	4	0.03
Cherokee	5	0.04
Cree (1)	2	0.02
Delaware	2	0.02
Iroquois (2)	13	0.11
Kiowa	1	0.01
Latin American Indians (2)	2	0.02
Potawatomi (1)	1	0.01
Sioux (3)	4	0.03
All other tribes	2	0.02
American Indian tribes, not spec.	1	0.01
Arab:	53	0.46
Arab/Arabic	7	0.06
Iraqi	10	0.09
Lebanese	28	0.24
Syrian	8	0.07
Armenian	31	0.27
Asian:	82	0.72
Chinese, ex. Taiwanese (33)	38	0.33
Filipino (2)	2	0.02
Indian (8)	8	0.07
Japanese (1)	6	0.05
Korean (6)	6	0.05
Laotian (1)	1	0.01
Thai (3)	4	0.03
Vietnamese (4)	11	0.10
Other Asian, specified	2	0.02
Other Asian, not specified (3)	4	0.03
Austrian	51	0.45
Belgian	7	0.06
British	44	0.38
Canadian	10	0.09
Carpatho Rusyn	20	0.17
Croatian	10	0.09
Czech	136	1.19
Czechoslovakian	121	1.06
Danish	37	0.32
Dutch	436	3.81
English	1,955	17.07
European	64	0.56
Finnish	12	0.10
French, except Basque	272	2.37
French Canadian	136	1.19
German	2,267	19.79
Greek	45	0.39
Hawaii Native/Pacific Islander:	6	0.05
Micronesian: (1)	1	0.01
Guamanian/Chamorro (1)	1	0.01
Polynesian: (1)	2	0.02
Native Hawaiian (1)	2	0.02
Other Pac. Isl., specified	2	0.02
Other Pac. Isl., not spec.	1	0.01
Hispanic or Latino:	107	0.93
Central American:	10	0.09
Guatemalan	3	0.03
Honduran	5	0.04
Nicaraguan	2	0.02
Cuban	10	0.09
Dominican Republic	5	0.04
Mexican	17	0.15
Puerto Rican	28	0.24
South American:	22	0.19

Notes: 1. Figures in the "Number" column do not add up to the total population due to: a) Ancestry/Race overlap — e.g. persons can report being both White and Irish, b) persons of Hispanic origin can report being any race, c) persons reporting two ancestries are counted in both categories. 2. Numbers in parentheses indicate the number of persons reporting this ancestry/race alone, not in combination with any other ancestry/race. 3. Refer to the Explanation of Data in the front of the book for more detailed information.

Colombian	6	0.05
Ecuadorian	11	0.10
Peruvian	4	0.03
Other South American	1	0.01
Other Hispanic or Latino	15	0.13
Hungarian	90	0.79
Icelander	7	0.06
Irish	2,662	23.24
Italian	1,223	10.68
Lithuanian	93	0.81
Norwegian	58	0.51
Pennsylvania German	5	0.04
Polish	757	6.61
Portuguese	6	0.05
Romanian	5	0.04
Russian	230	2.01
Scandinavian	10	0.09
Scotch-Irish	130	1.13
Scottish	288	2.51
Slavic	57	0.50
Slovak	517	4.51
Slovene	5	0.04
Swedish	84	0.73
Swiss	36	0.31
Ukrainian	116	1.01
United States or American	730	6.37
Welsh	388	3.39
White:	11,261	98.31
Not Hispanic (11,101)	11,192	97.71
Hispanic (60)	69	0.60

Chester

Place Type: Town
County: Orange
Population: 12,140

Ancestry/Race	Number	%
African American/Black:	871	7.17
Not Hispanic (768)	820	6.75
Hispanic (36)	51	0.42
African, sub-Saharan:	43	0.35
African	20	0.16
Ethiopian	23	0.19
Am. Ind. or Alaska Nat., not spec.	25	0.21
Albanian	7	0.06
American Indian tribes, specified:	44	0.36
Blackfeet (1)	1	0.01
Cherokee (4)	12	0.10
Chippewa (1)	2	0.02
Crow	1	0.01
Delaware (5)	13	0.11
Iroquois (1)	1	0.01
Latin American Indians	3	0.02
Navajo (1)	1	0.01
Ottawa	1	0.01
Seminole	1	0.01
Sioux	3	0.02
All other tribes	5	0.04
American Indian tribes, not spec.	12	0.10
Arab:	25	0.21
Egyptian	8	0.07
Lebanese	8	0.07
Moroccan	9	0.07
Asian:	352	2.90
Chinese, ex. Taiwanese (117)	130	1.07
Filipino (16)	19	0.16
Indian (135)	138	1.14
Japanese (3)	3	0.02
Korean (32)	37	0.30
Pakistani (2)	2	0.02
Thai (3)	3	0.02
Vietnamese (7)	8	0.07
Other Asian, not specified (8)	12	0.10
Austrian	59	0.49
Belgian	8	0.07
British	18	0.15
Canadian	26	0.21
Carpatho Rusyn	14	0.12
Czech	28	0.23
Czechoslovakian	47	0.39
Danish	24	0.20
Dutch	310	2.55
Eastern European	24	0.20
English	534	4.40
Estonian	5	0.04
European	15	0.12
Finnish	25	0.21
French, except Basque	204	1.68
French Canadian	162	1.33
German	1,844	15.19
German Russian	10	0.08
Greek	128	1.05
Hawaii Native/Pacific Islander:	6	0.05
Polynesian: (6)	6	0.05
Native Hawaiian (5)	5	0.04
Samoan (1)	1	0.01
Hispanic or Latino:	1,231	10.14
Central American:	19	0.16
Guatemalan	1	0.01
Nicaraguan	8	0.07
Panamanian	10	0.08
Cuban	67	0.55
Dominican Republic	25	0.21
Mexican	92	0.76
Puerto Rican	779	6.42
South American:	67	0.55
Argentinean	4	0.03
Chilean	2	0.02
Colombian	26	0.21
Ecuadorian	16	0.13
Paraguayan	1	0.01
Peruvian	11	0.09
Venezuelan	3	0.02
Other South American	4	0.03
Other Hispanic or Latino	182	1.50
Hungarian	151	1.24
Iranian	18	0.15
Irish	2,918	24.04
Israeli	11	0.09
Italian	2,733	22.51
Lithuanian	16	0.13
Maltese	17	0.14
Norwegian	59	0.49
Polish	1,055	8.69
Romanian	60	0.49
Russian	304	2.50
Scandinavian	12	0.10
Scotch-Irish	175	1.44
Scottish	145	1.19
Serbian	19	0.16
Slavic	19	0.16
Slovak	32	0.26
Slovene	5	0.04
Soviet Union	9	0.07
Swedish	146	1.20
Swiss	32	0.26
Ukrainian	62	0.51
United States or American	368	3.03
Welsh	24	0.20
West Indian, excl. Hispanic:	53	0.44
Haitian	4	0.03
Jamaican	19	0.16
Trinidadian and Tobagonian	30	0.25
White:	10,705	88.18
Not Hispanic (9,669)	9,744	80.26
Hispanic (915)	961	7.92
Yugoslavian	40	0.33

Chili

Place Type: Town
County: Monroe
Population: 27,638

Ancestry/Race	Number	%
African American/Black:	1,713	6.20
Not Hispanic (1,546)	1,679	6.07
Hispanic (33)	34	0.12
African, sub-Saharan:	153	0.55
African	114	0.41
Nigerian	19	0.07
Sudanese	20	0.07
Am. Ind. or Alaska Nat., not spec.	31	0.11
Albanian	38	0.14
American Indian tribes, specified:	92	0.33
Blackfeet	2	0.01
Cherokee	3	0.01
Chippewa (4)	4	0.01
Cree (1)	1	0.00
Creek (1)	1	0.00
Iroquois (41)	68	0.25
Potawatomi (2)	2	0.01
Shoshone (1)	1	0.00
Sioux (1)	1	0.00
All other tribes (1)	9	0.03
American Indian tribes, not spec.	9	0.03
Arab:	122	0.44
Egyptian	10	0.04
Lebanese	67	0.24
Palestinian	32	0.12
Syrian	13	0.05
Armenian	23	0.08
Asian:	399	1.44
Cambodian (5)	5	0.02
Chinese, ex. Taiwanese (25)	31	0.11
Filipino (6)	17	0.06
Indian (72)	96	0.35
Japanese (23)	35	0.13
Korean (67)	72	0.26
Laotian (32)	34	0.12
Pakistani (1)	1	0.00
Sri Lankan	4	0.01
Thai (2)	4	0.01
Vietnamese (64)	69	0.25
Other Asian, specified	4	0.01
Other Asian, not specified (11)	27	0.10
Austrian	112	0.41
Belgian	13	0.05
British	175	0.63
Canadian	95	0.34
Celtic	34	0.12
Croatian	11	0.04
Czech	29	0.10
Czechoslovakian	27	0.10
Danish	138	0.50
Dutch	887	3.21
English	4,007	14.50
European	177	0.64
Finnish	9	0.03
French, except Basque	1,113	4.03
French Canadian	416	1.51
German	7,522	27.22
Greek	318	1.15
Guyanese	24	0.09
Hawaii Native/Pacific Islander:	22	0.08
Micronesian: (4)	4	0.01
Guamanian/Chamorro (3)	3	0.01
Other Micronesian (1)	1	0.00
Polynesian: (1)	5	0.02
Native Hawaiian	3	0.01
Samoan (1)	1	0.00
Tongan	1	0.00
Other Pac. Isl., specified	1	0.00
Other Pac. Isl., not spec. (1)	12	0.04
Hispanic or Latino:	456	1.65
Central American:	28	0.10
Costa Rican	3	0.01
Guatemalan	13	0.05
Honduran	2	0.01
Nicaraguan	1	0.00
Panamanian	1	0.00
Salvadoran	8	0.03
Cuban	39	0.14
Dominican Republic	15	0.05
Mexican	44	0.16
Puerto Rican	226	0.82
South American:	20	0.07
Chilean	3	0.01
Colombian	10	0.04

Notes: 1. Figures in the "Number" column do not add up to the total population due to: a) Ancestry/Race overlap — e.g. persons can report being both White and Irish, b) persons of Hispanic origin can report being any race, c) persons reporting two ancestries are counted in both categories. 2. Numbers in parentheses indicate the number of persons reporting this ancestry/race alone, not in combination with any other ancestry/race. 3. Refer to the Explanation of Data in the front of the book for more detailed information.

Ancestry/Race	Number	%
Paraguayan	1	0.00
Peruvian	5	0.02
Other South American	1	0.00
Other Hispanic or Latino	84	0.30
Hungarian	179	0.65
Irish	5,189	18.78
Italian	5,271	19.08
Latvian	16	0.06
Lithuanian	116	0.42
Macedonian	220	0.80
Maltese	9	0.03
Northern European	33	0.12
Norwegian	92	0.33
Polish	1,537	5.56
Portuguese	92	0.33
Romanian	37	0.13
Russian	152	0.55
Scandinavian	22	0.08
Scotch-Irish	401	1.45
Scottish	958	3.47
Slavic	7	0.03
Slovak	78	0.28
Swedish	327	1.18
Swiss	77	0.28
Turkish	114	0.41
Ukrainian	413	1.49
United States or American	1,151	4.17
Welsh	186	0.67
West Indian, excl. Hispanic:	188	0.68
Haitian	34	0.12
Jamaican	137	0.50
Trinidadian and Tobagonian	7	0.03
West Indian	10	0.04
White:	25,486	92.21
Not Hispanic (24,926)	25,201	91.18
Hispanic (262)	285	1.03
Yugoslavian	22	0.08

Cicero

Place Type: Town
County: Onondaga
Population: 27,982

Ancestry/Race	Number	%
African American/Black:	449	1.60
Not Hispanic (330)	433	1.55
Hispanic (3)	16	0.06
African, sub-Saharan:	15	0.05
African	15	0.05
Alaska Native tribes, specified:	8	0.03
Alaska Athabascan	1	0.00
Aleut	4	0.01
Eskimo (2)	2	0.01
Tlingit-Haida (1)	1	0.00
Am. Ind. or Alaska Nat., not spec.	56	0.20
American Indian tribes, specified:	164	0.59
Apache (2)	2	0.01
Blackfeet	1	0.00
Cherokee (2)	14	0.05
Choctaw (1)	1	0.00
Delaware	1	0.00
Houma (1)	1	0.00
Iroquois (70)	123	0.44
Latin American Indians (1)	1	0.00
Navajo	3	0.01
Potawatomi	1	0.00
All other tribes (8)	16	0.06
American Indian tribes, not spec.	4	0.01
Arab:	143	0.51
Arab/Arabic	25	0.09
Jordanian	14	0.05
Lebanese	59	0.21
Palestinian	15	0.05
Syrian	30	0.11
Armenian	17	0.06
Asian:	288	1.03
Cambodian (4)	4	0.01
Chinese, ex. Taiwanese (15)	23	0.08
Filipino (23)	44	0.16
Hmong (14)	14	0.05
Indian (41)	48	0.17
Japanese (11)	21	0.08
Korean (42)	54	0.19
Malaysian (1)	2	0.01
Pakistani (8)	18	0.06
Thai (1)	2	0.01
Vietnamese (32)	36	0.13
Other Asian, not specified (6)	22	0.08
Australian	8	0.03
Austrian	108	0.39
Belgian	7	0.03
British	85	0.30
Bulgarian	6	0.02
Canadian	111	0.40
Celtic	10	0.04
Croatian	6	0.02
Czech	57	0.20
Czechoslovakian	17	0.06
Danish	35	0.13
Dutch	816	2.92
Eastern European	16	0.06
English	3,882	13.87
European	248	0.89
Finnish	13	0.05
French, except Basque	2,009	7.18
French Canadian	903	3.23
German	6,626	23.68
Greek	140	0.50
Hawaii Native/Pacific Islander:	9	0.03
Polynesian: (4)	7	0.03
Native Hawaiian (3)	5	0.02
Samoan (1)	1	0.00
Other Polynesian	1	0.00
Other Pac. Isl., not spec. (1)	2	0.01
Hispanic or Latino:	245	0.88
Central American:	15	0.05
Costa Rican	1	0.00
Guatemalan	4	0.01
Panamanian	10	0.04
Cuban	12	0.04
Dominican Republic	2	0.01
Mexican	52	0.19
Puerto Rican	88	0.31
South American:	12	0.04
Argentinean	1	0.00
Chilean	1	0.00
Colombian	2	0.01
Ecuadorian	3	0.01
Peruvian	2	0.01
Venezuelan	1	0.00
Other South American	2	0.01
Other Hispanic or Latino	64	0.23
Hungarian	157	0.56
Icelander	7	0.03
Irish	6,653	23.78
Israeli	7	0.03
Italian	6,351	22.70
Latvian	7	0.03
Lithuanian	107	0.38
Northern European	5	0.02
Norwegian	89	0.32
Pennsylvania German	25	0.09
Polish	2,677	9.57
Portuguese	50	0.18
Romanian	30	0.11
Russian	143	0.51
Scandinavian	16	0.06
Scotch-Irish	528	1.89
Scottish	470	1.68
Slavic	13	0.05
Slovak	48	0.17
Slovene	16	0.06
Swedish	198	0.71
Swiss	97	0.35
Ukrainian	249	0.89
United States or American	1,062	3.80
Welsh	293	1.05
West Indian, excl. Hispanic:	8	0.03
Jamaican	8	0.03
White:	27,252	97.39
Not Hispanic (26,801)	27,076	96.76
Hispanic (149)	176	0.63
Yugoslavian	15	0.05

Clarence

Place Type: Town
County: Erie
Population: 26,123

Ancestry/Race	Number	%
African American/Black:	203	0.78
Not Hispanic (166)	199	0.76
Hispanic (3)	4	0.02
African, sub-Saharan:	16	0.06
South African	16	0.06
Am. Ind. or Alaska Nat., not spec.	22	0.08
Alsatian	39	0.15
American Indian tribes, specified:	50	0.19
Apache	2	0.01
Blackfeet	1	0.00
Cherokee	2	0.01
Chippewa (6)	6	0.02
Iroquois (14)	26	0.10
Latin American Indians (8)	8	0.03
All other tribes	5	0.02
American Indian tribes, not spec.	9	0.03
Arab:	100	0.38
Lebanese	91	0.35
Moroccan	9	0.03
Armenian	38	0.15
Asian:	412	1.58
Cambodian (1)	1	0.00
Chinese, ex. Taiwanese (60)	75	0.29
Filipino (28)	35	0.13
Indian (162)	174	0.67
Indonesian	1	0.00
Japanese (8)	10	0.04
Korean (63)	68	0.26
Pakistani (12)	12	0.05
Taiwanese (6)	8	0.03
Vietnamese (16)	18	0.07
Other Asian, not specified (5)	10	0.04
Austrian	197	0.75
Belgian	41	0.16
British	49	0.19
Bulgarian	26	0.10
Canadian	138	0.53
Celtic	8	0.03
Croatian	52	0.20
Czech	92	0.35
Czechoslovakian	40	0.15
Danish	38	0.15
Dutch	303	1.16
Eastern European	34	0.13
English	3,179	12.17
Estonian	62	0.24
European	78	0.30
Finnish	9	0.03
French, except Basque	936	3.58
French Canadian	202	0.77
German	9,289	35.56
Greek	149	0.57
Hawaii Native/Pacific Islander:	18	0.07
Micronesian: (1)	2	0.01
Guamanian/Chamorro (1)	2	0.01
Polynesian: (9)	13	0.05
Native Hawaiian (4)	8	0.03
Samoan (5)	5	0.02
Other Pac. Isl., not spec.	3	0.01
Hispanic or Latino:	208	0.80
Central American:	12	0.05
Costa Rican	5	0.02
Guatemalan	7	0.03
Cuban	14	0.05
Mexican	59	0.23
Puerto Rican	60	0.23
South American:	23	0.09
Chilean	3	0.01

Notes: 1. Figures in the "Number" column do not add up to the total population due to: a) Ancestry/Race overlap — e.g. persons can report being both White and Irish, b) persons of Hispanic origin can report being any race, c) persons reporting two ancestries are counted in both categories. 2. Numbers in parentheses indicate the number of persons reporting this ancestry/race alone, not in combination with any other ancestry/race. 3. Refer to the Explanation of Data in the front of the book for more detailed information.

Ancestry/Race	Number	%
Colombian	15	0.06
Ecuadorian	1	0.00
Venezuelan	4	0.02
Other Hispanic or Latino	40	0.15
Hungarian	406	1.55
Iranian	44	0.17
Irish	5,049	19.33
Italian	5,781	22.13
Lithuanian	103	0.39
Macedonian	7	0.03
Northern European	7	0.03
Norwegian	92	0.35
Pennsylvania German	8	0.03
Polish	3,910	14.97
Portuguese	34	0.13
Romanian	18	0.07
Russian	296	1.13
Scotch-Irish	377	1.44
Scottish	583	2.23
Serbian	20	0.08
Slavic	28	0.11
Slovak	5	0.02
Slovene	20	0.08
Swedish	276	1.06
Swiss	56	0.21
Turkish	8	0.03
Ukrainian	229	0.88
United States or American	742	2.84
Welsh	190	0.73
West Indian, excl. Hispanic:	19	0.07
Trinidadian and Tobagonian	19	0.07
White:	25,480	97.54
Not Hispanic (25,189)	25,310	96.89
Hispanic (154)	170	0.65
Yugoslavian	22	0.08

Clarkstown

Place Type: Town
County: Rockland
Population: 82,082

Ancestry/Race	Number	%
Acadian/Cajun	11	0.01
Afghan	19	0.02
African American/Black:	7,227	8.80
Not Hispanic (6,178)	6,826	8.32
Hispanic (281)	401	0.49
African, sub-Saharan:	377	0.46
African	330	0.40
Cape Verdean	6	0.01
Kenyan	7	0.01
Nigerian	8	0.01
South African	26	0.03
Am. Ind. or Alaska Nat., not spec.	187	0.23
Albanian	257	0.31
American Indian tribes, specified:	135	0.16
Blackfeet (1)	5	0.01
Cherokee (6)	32	0.04
Chickasaw	1	0.00
Chippewa (1)	4	0.00
Choctaw (1)	1	0.00
Creek	4	0.00
Delaware (8)	16	0.02
Iroquois (2)	12	0.01
Latin American Indians (16)	34	0.04
Potawatomi	2	0.00
Seminole	1	0.00
Shoshone	2	0.00
Sioux (2)	3	0.00
Tohono O'Odham (1)	1	0.00
All other tribes (3)	17	0.02
American Indian tribes, not spec.	37	0.05
Arab:	380	0.46
Arab/Arabic	26	0.03
Egyptian	158	0.19
Lebanese	61	0.07
Moroccan	5	0.01
Syrian	113	0.14
Other Arab	17	0.02
Armenian	186	0.23
Asian:	6,999	8.53
Bangladeshi (16)	20	0.02
Cambodian (6)	11	0.01
Chinese, ex. Taiwanese (948)	1,081	1.32
Filipino (1,729)	1,856	2.26
Indian (2,454)	2,596	3.16
Indonesian (4)	6	0.01
Japanese (77)	102	0.12
Korean (784)	805	0.98
Laotian (5)	6	0.01
Malaysian (2)	10	0.01
Pakistani (133)	143	0.17
Sri Lankan (12)	20	0.02
Taiwanese (25)	31	0.04
Thai (65)	75	0.09
Vietnamese (115)	125	0.15
Other Asian, specified (2)	12	0.01
Other Asian, not specified (38)	100	0.12
Assyrian/Chaldean/Syriac	13	0.02
Australian	22	0.03
Austrian	927	1.13
Belgian	37	0.05
Brazilian	19	0.02
British	136	0.17
Canadian	193	0.24
Carpatho Rusyn	18	0.02
Celtic	8	0.01
Croatian	175	0.21
Cypriot	19	0.02
Czech	287	0.35
Czechoslovakian	218	0.27
Danish	88	0.11
Dutch	732	0.89
Eastern European	818	1.00
English	3,343	4.07
Estonian	46	0.06
European	682	0.83
Finnish	66	0.08
French, except Basque	923	1.12
French Canadian	302	0.37
German	8,094	9.86
Greek	954	1.16
Guyanese	13	0.02
Hawaii Native/Pacific Islander:	150	0.18
Micronesian: (52)	61	0.07
Guamanian/Chamorro (52)	61	0.07
Polynesian: (16)	24	0.03
Native Hawaiian (11)	14	0.02
Samoan (5)	10	0.01
Other Pac. Isl., specified	9	0.01
Other Pac. Isl., not spec. (13)	56	0.07
Hispanic or Latino:	5,683	6.92
Central American:	444	0.54
Costa Rican	26	0.03
Guatemalan	187	0.23
Honduran	27	0.03
Nicaraguan	10	0.01
Panamanian	18	0.02
Salvadoran	166	0.20
Other Central American	10	0.01
Cuban	336	0.41
Dominican Republic	327	0.40
Mexican	511	0.62
Puerto Rican	2,609	3.18
South American:	462	0.56
Argentinean	33	0.04
Bolivian	5	0.01
Chilean	24	0.03
Colombian	104	0.13
Ecuadorian	199	0.24
Paraguayan	2	0.00
Peruvian	48	0.06
Uruguayan	1	0.00
Venezuelan	10	0.01
Other South American	36	0.04
Other Hispanic or Latino	994	1.21
Hungarian	987	1.20
Icelander	7	0.01
Iranian	99	0.12
Irish	14,853	18.10
Israeli	160	0.19
Italian	18,611	22.67
Latvian	6	0.01
Lithuanian	143	0.17
Maltese	50	0.06
Northern European	30	0.04
Norwegian	418	0.51
Pennsylvania German	21	0.03
Polish	4,270	5.20
Portuguese	179	0.22
Romanian	545	0.66
Russian	5,482	6.68
Scandinavian	52	0.06
Scotch-Irish	600	0.73
Scottish	678	0.83
Serbian	16	0.02
Slavic	26	0.03
Slovak	116	0.14
Slovene	13	0.02
Soviet Union	45	0.05
Swedish	376	0.46
Swiss	137	0.17
Turkish	67	0.08
Ukrainian	505	0.62
United States or American	3,786	4.61
Welsh	115	0.14
West Indian, excl. Hispanic:	2,505	3.05
British West Indian	3	0.00
Haitian	1,586	1.93
Jamaican	737	0.90
Trinidadian and Tobagonian	5	0.01
U.S. Virgin Islander	11	0.01
West Indian	163	0.20
White:	66,715	81.28
Not Hispanic (62,351)	63,033	76.79
Hispanic (3,292)	3,682	4.49
Yugoslavian	90	0.11

Clay

Place Type: Town
County: Onondaga
Population: 58,805

Ancestry/Race	Number	%
African American/Black:	2,446	4.16
Not Hispanic (2,019)	2,373	4.04
Hispanic (41)	73	0.12
African, sub-Saharan:	155	0.26
African	76	0.13
Liberian	69	0.12
Nigerian	10	0.02
Alaska Native tribes, specified:	1	0.00
Alaska Athabascan (1)	1	0.00
Am. Ind. or Alaska Nat., not spec.	146	0.25
Albanian	19	0.03
Alsatian	18	0.03
American Indian tribes, specified:	398	0.68
Apache (3)	4	0.01
Blackfeet (2)	11	0.02
Cherokee (7)	41	0.07
Chippewa (4)	9	0.02
Choctaw (2)	2	0.00
Comanche	1	0.00
Cree	2	0.00
Creek	1	0.00
Iroquois (174)	280	0.48
Latin American Indians (1)	6	0.01
Lumbee (1)	1	0.00
Navajo (2)	3	0.01
Potawatomi	1	0.00
Sioux (1)	7	0.01
Yaqui	5	0.01
All other tribes (13)	24	0.04
American Indian tribes, not spec.	6	0.01
Arab:	593	1.01
Arab/Arabic	185	0.31
Egyptian	20	0.03
Jordanian	48	0.08

Notes: 1. Figures in the "Number" column do not add up to the total population due to: a) Ancestry/Race overlap — e.g. persons can report being both White and Irish, b) persons of Hispanic origin can report being any race, c) persons reporting two ancestries are counted in both categories. 2. Numbers in parentheses indicate the number of persons reporting this ancestry/race alone, not in combination with any other ancestry/race. 3. Refer to the Explanation of Data in the front of the book for more detailed information.

Ancestry/Race	Number	%
Lebanese	136	0.23
Syrian	98	0.17
Other Arab	106	0.18
Armenian	23	0.04
Asian:	1,399	2.38
Bangladeshi (8)	10	0.02
Cambodian (17)	23	0.04
Chinese, ex. Taiwanese (242)	272	0.46
Filipino (112)	151	0.26
Hmong (22)	27	0.05
Indian (382)	423	0.72
Indonesian (1)	5	0.01
Japanese (30)	57	0.10
Korean (130)	152	0.26
Laotian (14)	15	0.03
Pakistani (21)	23	0.04
Taiwanese (5)	6	0.01
Thai (12)	17	0.03
Vietnamese (158)	177	0.30
Other Asian, not specified (10)	41	0.07
Austrian	216	0.37
Belgian	31	0.05
Brazilian	29	0.05
British	153	0.26
Canadian	304	0.52
Celtic	8	0.01
Croatian	6	0.01
Czech	149	0.25
Czechoslovakian	110	0.19
Danish	117	0.20
Dutch	1,364	2.32
Eastern European	37	0.06
English	7,941	13.50
European	282	0.48
Finnish	45	0.08
French, except Basque	4,167	7.09
French Canadian	1,468	2.50
German	12,722	21.63
Greek	350	0.60
Hawaii Native/Pacific Islander:	34	0.06
Micronesian: (3)	6	0.01
Guamanian/Chamorro (1)	4	0.01
Other Micronesian (2)	2	0.00
Polynesian: (11)	23	0.04
Native Hawaiian (2)	14	0.02
Samoan (7)	7	0.01
Other Polynesian (2)	2	0.00
Other Pac. Isl., not spec.	5	0.01
Hispanic or Latino:	816	1.39
Central American:	35	0.06
Costa Rican	1	0.00
Guatemalan	8	0.01
Honduran	8	0.01
Panamanian	12	0.02
Salvadoran	6	0.01
Cuban	56	0.10
Dominican Republic	17	0.03
Mexican	154	0.26
Puerto Rican	337	0.57
South American:	68	0.12
Argentinean	4	0.01
Bolivian	1	0.00
Chilean	2	0.00
Colombian	25	0.04
Ecuadorian	7	0.01
Paraguayan	2	0.00
Peruvian	19	0.03
Venezuelan	2	0.00
Other South American	6	0.01
Other Hispanic or Latino	149	0.25
Hungarian	290	0.49
Irish	13,410	22.80
Italian	13,040	22.17
Latvian	63	0.11
Lithuanian	117	0.20
Macedonian	215	0.37
Northern European	53	0.09
Norwegian	163	0.28
Pennsylvania German	28	0.05
Polish	4,721	8.03
Portuguese	77	0.13
Romanian	13	0.02
Russian	497	0.85
Scandinavian	13	0.02
Scotch-Irish	711	1.21
Scottish	1,339	2.28
Slavic	78	0.13
Slovak	266	0.45
Slovene	6	0.01
Swedish	463	0.79
Swiss	141	0.24
Ukrainian	766	1.30
United States or American	1,782	3.03
Welsh	594	1.01
West Indian, excl. Hispanic:	95	0.16
Barbadian	6	0.01
British West Indian	14	0.02
Haitian	16	0.03
Jamaican	9	0.02
West Indian	50	0.09
White:	54,964	93.47
Not Hispanic (53,677)	54,397	92.50
Hispanic (500)	567	0.96
Yugoslavian	112	0.19

Clifton Park

Place Type: Town
County: Saratoga
Population: 32,995

Ancestry/Race	Number	%
Afghan	24	0.07
African American/Black:	470	1.42
Not Hispanic (393)	452	1.37
Hispanic (10)	18	0.05
African, sub-Saharan:	20	0.06
African	20	0.06
Alaska Native tribes, specified:	1	0.00
Eskimo (1)	1	0.00
Am. Ind. or Alaska Nat., not spec.	29	0.09
Albanian	27	0.08
American Indian tribes, specified:	73	0.22
Blackfeet	3	0.01
Cherokee (1)	18	0.05
Chickasaw (1)	1	0.00
Chippewa (1)	1	0.00
Choctaw	2	0.01
Creek	1	0.00
Delaware	3	0.01
Iroquois (8)	18	0.05
Latin American Indians (1)	7	0.02
Potawatomi	1	0.00
Seminole	1	0.00
All other tribes (12)	17	0.05
American Indian tribes, not spec.	14	0.04
Arab:	263	0.80
Arab/Arabic	32	0.10
Egyptian	49	0.15
Jordanian	29	0.09
Lebanese	83	0.25
Syrian	62	0.19
Other Arab	8	0.02
Armenian	148	0.45
Asian:	949	2.88
Chinese, ex. Taiwanese (257)	282	0.85
Filipino (46)	59	0.18
Indian (341)	363	1.10
Japanese (21)	33	0.10
Korean (93)	105	0.32
Malaysian (3)	3	0.01
Pakistani (16)	27	0.08
Sri Lankan (8)	8	0.02
Taiwanese (4)	5	0.02
Thai (3)	3	0.01
Vietnamese (13)	19	0.06
Other Asian, specified (7)	8	0.02
Other Asian, not specified (5)	34	0.10
Australian	28	0.08
Austrian	176	0.53
Basque	10	0.03
Belgian	13	0.04
Brazilian	7	0.02
British	187	0.57
Bulgarian	32	0.10
Canadian	205	0.62
Croatian	66	0.20
Czech	135	0.41
Czechoslovakian	67	0.20
Danish	164	0.50
Dutch	1,007	3.05
Eastern European	124	0.38
English	4,567	13.84
European	215	0.65
Finnish	10	0.03
French, except Basque	2,526	7.66
French Canadian	881	2.67
German	6,247	18.93
Greek	284	0.86
Hawaii Native/Pacific Islander:	7	0.02
Micronesian: (1)	2	0.01
Guamanian/Chamorro (1)	2	0.01
Polynesian: (2)	3	0.01
Native Hawaiian (1)	2	0.01
Samoan (1)	1	0.00
Other Pac. Isl., specified	1	0.00
Other Pac. Isl., not spec.	1	0.00
Hispanic or Latino:	473	1.43
Central American:	19	0.06
Costa Rican	2	0.01
Guatemalan	2	0.01
Honduran	2	0.01
Nicaraguan	3	0.01
Panamanian	5	0.02
Salvadoran	2	0.01
Other Central American	3	0.01
Cuban	45	0.14
Dominican Republic	15	0.05
Mexican	89	0.27
Puerto Rican	156	0.47
South American:	42	0.13
Argentinean	3	0.01
Chilean	3	0.01
Colombian	21	0.06
Ecuadorian	10	0.03
Peruvian	3	0.01
Uruguayan	1	0.00
Other South American	1	0.00
Other Hispanic or Latino	107	0.32
Hungarian	198	0.60
Iranian	45	0.14
Irish	9,197	27.87
Israeli	8	0.02
Italian	6,419	19.45
Latvian	47	0.14
Lithuanian	200	0.61
Maltese	16	0.05
New Zealander	5	0.02
Northern European	40	0.12
Norwegian	337	1.02
Polish	2,908	8.81
Portuguese	30	0.09
Romanian	50	0.15
Russian	679	2.06
Scandinavian	54	0.16
Scotch-Irish	559	1.69
Scottish	807	2.45
Slavic	13	0.04
Slovak	74	0.22
Slovene	27	0.08
Swedish	308	0.93
Swiss	153	0.46
Turkish	22	0.07
Ukrainian	492	1.49
United States or American	757	2.29
Welsh	190	0.58
West Indian, excl. Hispanic:	39	0.12
Jamaican	39	0.12
White:	31,559	95.65
Not Hispanic (30,977)	31,202	94.57

Notes: 1. Figures in the "Number" column do not add up to the total population due to: a) Ancestry/Race overlap — e.g. persons can report being both White and Irish, b) persons of Hispanic origin can report being any race, c) persons reporting two ancestries are counted in both categories. 2. Numbers in parentheses indicate the number of persons reporting this ancestry/race alone, not in combination with any other ancestry/race. 3. Refer to the Explanation of Data in the front of the book for more detailed information.

Ancestry/Race	Number	%
Hispanic (332)	357	1.08
Yugoslavian	68	0.21

Cohoes

Place Type: City
County: Albany
Population: 15,521

Ancestry/Race	Number	%
African American/Black:	429	2.76
Not Hispanic (313)	393	2.53
Hispanic (22)	36	0.23
African, sub-Saharan:	27	0.17
African	27	0.17
Am. Ind. or Alaska Nat., not spec.	26	0.17
American Indian tribes, specified:	45	0.29
Blackfeet (1)	9	0.06
Cherokee (1)	6	0.04
Choctaw	4	0.03
Cree	1	0.01
Crow	1	0.01
Iroquois (4)	11	0.07
Pueblo	1	0.01
Sioux	3	0.02
All other tribes (8)	9	0.06
American Indian tribes, not spec.	2	0.01
Arab:	32	0.21
Arab/Arabic	5	0.03
Lebanese	8	0.05
Syrian	19	0.12
Armenian	44	0.28
Asian:	146	0.94
Cambodian (1)	1	0.01
Chinese, ex. Taiwanese (18)	21	0.14
Filipino (19)	30	0.19
Indian (24)	29	0.19
Indonesian (2)	2	0.01
Japanese (4)	8	0.05
Korean (25)	31	0.20
Thai (1)	1	0.01
Vietnamese (10)	14	0.09
Other Asian, specified	1	0.01
Other Asian, not specified (1)	8	0.05
Australian	13	0.08
Austrian	35	0.23
British	13	0.08
Canadian	116	0.75
Czech	32	0.21
Danish	37	0.24
Dutch	368	2.37
English	1,183	7.62
European	8	0.05
French, except Basque	2,984	19.23
French Canadian	1,177	7.58
German	1,733	11.17
Greek	19	0.12
Guyanese	9	0.06
Hawaii Native/Pacific Islander:	11	0.07
Polynesian: (3)	6	0.04
Native Hawaiian	3	0.02
Samoan (3)	3	0.02
Other Pac. Isl., not spec. (3)	5	0.03
Hispanic or Latino:	315	2.03
Central American:	17	0.11
Guatemalan	1	0.01
Panamanian	5	0.03
Salvadoran	9	0.06
Other Central American	2	0.01
Cuban	13	0.08
Dominican Republic	9	0.06
Mexican	30	0.19
Puerto Rican	163	1.05
South American:	4	0.03
Argentinean	1	0.01
Colombian	1	0.01
Ecuadorian	1	0.01
Peruvian	1	0.01
Other Hispanic or Latino	79	0.51
Hungarian	23	0.15
Irish	3,963	25.53
Italian	2,150	13.85
Lithuanian	49	0.32
Norwegian	47	0.30
Pennsylvania German	9	0.06
Polish	1,606	10.35
Portuguese	19	0.12
Romanian	51	0.33
Russian	311	2.00
Scandinavian	5	0.03
Scotch-Irish	124	0.80
Scottish	194	1.25
Slavic	6	0.04
Slovak	52	0.34
Swedish	58	0.37
Turkish	20	0.13
Ukrainian	522	3.36
United States or American	471	3.03
Welsh	59	0.38
West Indian, excl. Hispanic:	4	0.03
Jamaican	4	0.03
White:	14,942	96.27
Not Hispanic (14,582)	14,734	94.93
Hispanic (185)	208	1.34

Colonie

Place Type: Town
County: Albany
Population: 79,258

Ancestry/Race	Number	%
Afghan	148	0.19
African American/Black:	3,443	4.34
Not Hispanic (3,026)	3,273	4.13
Hispanic (111)	170	0.21
African, sub-Saharan:	238	0.30
African	128	0.16
Cape Verdean	11	0.01
Nigerian	29	0.04
Sudanese	9	0.01
Ugandan	14	0.02
Other sub-Saharan African	47	0.06
Am. Ind. or Alaska Nat., not spec.	111	0.14
Albanian	30	0.04
Alsatian	8	0.01
American Indian tribes, specified:	219	0.28
Apache (7)	9	0.01
Blackfeet (1)	12	0.02
Cherokee (6)	42	0.05
Chippewa	1	0.00
Choctaw (1)	7	0.01
Comanche (2)	2	0.00
Cree	5	0.01
Creek	1	0.00
Iroquois (25)	63	0.08
Latin American Indians (4)	16	0.02
Navajo (2)	3	0.00
Osage	1	0.00
Pima (7)	7	0.01
Seminole	8	0.01
Shoshone	1	0.00
Sioux (4)	6	0.01
Tohono O'Odham (1)	1	0.00
All other tribes (12)	34	0.04
American Indian tribes, not spec.	19	0.02
Arab:	540	0.68
Arab/Arabic	99	0.12
Egyptian	52	0.07
Iraqi	9	0.01
Lebanese	227	0.29
Syrian	131	0.17
Other Arab	22	0.03
Armenian	398	0.50
Asian:	3,220	4.06
Bangladeshi (4)	10	0.01
Cambodian (6)	7	0.01
Chinese, ex. Taiwanese (663)	745	0.94
Filipino (193)	241	0.30
Indian (1,026)	1,105	1.39
Indonesian (12)	12	0.02
Japanese (55)	74	0.09
Korean (317)	348	0.44
Laotian	1	0.00
Malaysian	6	0.01
Pakistani (256)	309	0.39
Taiwanese (32)	45	0.06
Thai (13)	18	0.02
Vietnamese (134)	158	0.20
Other Asian, specified	5	0.01
Other Asian, not specified (53)	136	0.17
Australian	7	0.01
Austrian	297	0.37
Belgian	49	0.06
Brazilian	2	0.00
British	188	0.24
Canadian	173	0.22
Carpatho Rusyn	3	0.00
Croatian	39	0.05
Czech	201	0.25
Czechoslovakian	179	0.23
Danish	225	0.28
Dutch	2,859	3.61
Eastern European	134	0.17
English	7,706	9.72
Estonian	6	0.01
European	263	0.33
Finnish	29	0.04
French, except Basque	5,256	6.63
French Canadian	2,452	3.09
German	13,968	17.62
German Russian	6	0.01
Greek	592	0.75
Guyanese	36	0.05
Hawaii Native/Pacific Islander:	31	0.04
Micronesian: (2)	2	0.00
Guamanian/Chamorro (2)	2	0.00
Polynesian: (5)	9	0.01
Native Hawaiian (4)	6	0.01
Samoan (1)	2	0.00
Other Polynesian	1	0.00
Other Pac. Isl., not spec. (6)	20	0.03
Hispanic or Latino:	1,476	1.86
Central American:	55	0.07
Costa Rican	15	0.02
Guatemalan	7	0.01
Honduran	17	0.02
Nicaraguan	1	0.00
Panamanian	3	0.00
Salvadoran	9	0.01
Other Central American	3	0.00
Cuban	52	0.07
Dominican Republic	74	0.09
Mexican	219	0.28
Puerto Rican	641	0.81
South American:	141	0.18
Argentinean	22	0.03
Bolivian	5	0.01
Chilean	8	0.01
Colombian	42	0.05
Ecuadorian	17	0.02
Paraguayan	3	0.00
Peruvian	27	0.03
Uruguayan	4	0.01
Venezuelan	10	0.01
Other South American	3	0.00
Other Hispanic or Latino	294	0.37
Hungarian	356	0.45
Iranian	25	0.03
Irish	22,194	28.00
Israeli	15	0.02
Italian	16,064	20.27
Latvian	27	0.03
Lithuanian	280	0.35
Northern European	21	0.03
Norwegian	344	0.43
Pennsylvania German	44	0.06
Polish	6,515	8.22
Portuguese	202	0.25
Romanian	89	0.11

Notes: 1. Figures in the "Number" column do not add up to the total population due to: a) Ancestry/Race overlap — e.g. persons can report being both White and Irish, b) persons of Hispanic origin can report being any race, c) persons reporting two ancestries are counted in both categories. 2. Numbers in parentheses indicate the number of persons reporting this ancestry/race alone, not in combination with any other ancestry/race. 3. Refer to the Explanation of Data in the front of the book for more detailed information.

Ancestry/Race	Number	%
Russian	1,176	1.48
Scandinavian	29	0.04
Scotch-Irish	958	1.21
Scottish	1,519	1.92
Serbian	19	0.02
Slovak	164	0.21
Slovene	10	0.01
Swedish	609	0.77
Swiss	116	0.15
Turkish	40	0.05
Ukrainian	943	1.19
United States or American	2,951	3.72
Welsh	624	0.79
West Indian, excl. Hispanic:	237	0.30
Barbadian	17	0.02
British West Indian	43	0.05
Haitian	18	0.02
Jamaican	129	0.16
Trinidadian and Tobagonian	16	0.02
U.S. Virgin Islander	8	0.01
West Indian	6	0.01
White:	72,476	91.44
Not Hispanic (70,974)	71,585	90.32
Hispanic (797)	891	1.12
Yugoslavian	141	0.18

Commack

Place Type: Census Designated Place
County: Suffolk
Population: 36,367

Ancestry/Race	Number	%
Afghan	26	0.07
African American/Black:	257	0.71
Not Hispanic (214)	239	0.66
Hispanic (17)	18	0.05
African, sub-Saharan:	59	0.16
African	59	0.16
Am. Ind. or Alaska Nat., not spec.	14	0.04
Albanian	7	0.02
Alsatian	6	0.02
American Indian tribes, specified:	14	0.04
Cherokee (1)	4	0.01
Iroquois (1)	1	0.00
Latin American Indians (1)	1	0.00
Navajo	1	0.00
All other tribes (2)	7	0.02
American Indian tribes, not spec.	4	0.01
Arab:	214	0.59
Arab/Arabic	39	0.11
Egyptian	61	0.17
Lebanese	50	0.14
Moroccan	6	0.02
Syrian	58	0.16
Armenian	90	0.25
Asian:	1,479	4.07
Chinese, ex. Taiwanese (354)	389	1.07
Filipino (93)	116	0.32
Indian (403)	421	1.16
Japanese (46)	59	0.16
Korean (373)	385	1.06
Pakistani (41)	50	0.14
Sri Lankan (2)	4	0.01
Taiwanese (16)	17	0.05
Thai (8)	8	0.02
Vietnamese (5)	5	0.01
Other Asian, specified (4)	4	0.01
Other Asian, not specified (12)	21	0.06
Austrian	360	0.99
Belgian	31	0.09
Brazilian	8	0.02
British	104	0.29
Canadian	89	0.24
Croatian	107	0.29
Cypriot	19	0.05
Czech	63	0.17
Czechoslovakian	59	0.16
Danish	82	0.23
Dutch	245	0.67
Eastern European	216	0.59
English	1,461	4.02
Estonian	8	0.02
European	144	0.40
Finnish	22	0.06
French, except Basque	410	1.13
French Canadian	119	0.33
German	5,124	14.10
Greek	1,083	2.98
Guyanese	26	0.07
Hawaii Native/Pacific Islander:	7	0.02
Polynesian:	5	0.01
Native Hawaiian	5	0.01
Other Pac. Isl., not spec.	2	0.01
Hispanic or Latino:	1,055	2.90
Central American:	67	0.18
Costa Rican	1	0.00
Guatemalan	5	0.01
Honduran	15	0.04
Nicaraguan	5	0.01
Panamanian	1	0.00
Salvadoran	29	0.08
Other Central American	11	0.03
Cuban	110	0.30
Dominican Republic	29	0.08
Mexican	48	0.13
Puerto Rican	359	0.99
South American:	181	0.50
Argentinean	11	0.03
Bolivian	8	0.02
Chilean	20	0.05
Colombian	69	0.19
Ecuadorian	37	0.10
Paraguayan	2	0.01
Peruvian	18	0.05
Uruguayan	4	0.01
Venezuelan	5	0.01
Other South American	7	0.02
Other Hispanic or Latino	261	0.72
Hungarian	496	1.37
Iranian	154	0.42
Irish	7,061	19.44
Israeli	91	0.25
Italian	12,124	33.37
Latvian	18	0.05
Lithuanian	195	0.54
Maltese	24	0.07
New Zealander	6	0.02
Northern European	36	0.10
Norwegian	315	0.87
Pennsylvania German	20	0.06
Polish	2,786	7.67
Portuguese	51	0.14
Romanian	164	0.45
Russian	2,112	5.81
Scandinavian	19	0.05
Scotch-Irish	180	0.50
Scottish	201	0.55
Slavic	18	0.05
Slovak	34	0.09
Slovene	30	0.08
Swedish	190	0.52
Swiss	78	0.21
Turkish	229	0.63
Ukrainian	248	0.68
United States or American	1,492	4.11
Welsh	37	0.10
West Indian, excl. Hispanic:	101	0.28
Belizean	12	0.03
British West Indian	11	0.03
Haitian	9	0.02
Jamaican	36	0.10
Trinidadian and Tobagonian	33	0.09
White:	34,557	95.02
Not Hispanic (33,490)	33,653	92.54
Hispanic (853)	904	2.49
Yugoslavian	17	0.05

Copiague

Place Type: Census Designated Place
County: Suffolk
Population: 21,922

Ancestry/Race	Number	%
African American/Black:	1,096	5.00
Not Hispanic (843)	917	4.18
Hispanic (117)	179	0.82
African, sub-Saharan:	87	0.40
African	81	0.37
Ethiopian	6	0.03
Am. Ind. or Alaska Nat., not spec.	27	0.12
Albanian	10	0.05
American Indian tribes, specified:	56	0.26
Blackfeet	1	0.00
Cherokee (1)	7	0.03
Choctaw (1)	1	0.00
Houma	1	0.00
Iroquois (1)	2	0.01
Latin American Indians (8)	13	0.06
Pueblo	1	0.00
Seminole	1	0.00
Sioux (2)	2	0.01
All other tribes (18)	27	0.12
American Indian tribes, not spec.	8	0.04
Arab:	8	0.04
Egyptian	8	0.04
Armenian	7	0.03
Asian:	495	2.26
Bangladeshi (11)	26	0.12
Chinese, ex. Taiwanese (105)	124	0.57
Filipino (46)	58	0.26
Indian (144)	187	0.85
Japanese (2)	10	0.05
Korean (21)	30	0.14
Pakistani (14)	27	0.12
Sri Lankan	1	0.00
Taiwanese (4)	4	0.02
Thai (4)	4	0.02
Vietnamese (12)	12	0.05
Other Asian, not specified (1)	12	0.05
Australian	11	0.05
Austrian	103	0.47
Belgian	11	0.05
Brazilian	37	0.17
British	31	0.14
Canadian	42	0.19
Croatian	42	0.19
Czech	66	0.30
Czechoslovakian	27	0.12
Danish	24	0.11
Dutch	160	0.73
Eastern European	9	0.04
English	845	3.85
European	47	0.21
Finnish	12	0.05
French, except Basque	380	1.73
French Canadian	49	0.22
German	3,162	14.42
Greek	161	0.73
Guyanese	18	0.08
Hawaii Native/Pacific Islander:	27	0.12
Micronesian: (4)	5	0.02
Guamanian/Chamorro (4)	5	0.02
Polynesian: (9)	11	0.05
Native Hawaiian (9)	11	0.05
Other Pac. Isl., not spec. (3)	11	0.05
Hispanic or Latino:	4,489	20.48
Central American:	760	3.47
Costa Rican	15	0.07
Guatemalan	50	0.23
Honduran	77	0.35
Nicaraguan	7	0.03
Panamanian	13	0.06
Salvadoran	581	2.65
Other Central American	17	0.08
Cuban	84	0.38
Dominican Republic	1,440	6.57

Notes: 1. Figures in the "Number" column do not add up to the total population due to: a) Ancestry/Race overlap — e.g. persons can report being both White and Irish, b) persons of Hispanic origin can report being any race, c) persons reporting two ancestries are counted in both categories. 2. Numbers in parentheses indicate the number of persons reporting this ancestry/race alone, not in combination with any other ancestry/race. 3. Refer to the Explanation of Data in the front of the book for more detailed information.

Ancestry/Race	Number	%
Mexican	113	0.52
Puerto Rican	737	3.36
South American:	404	1.84
Argentinean	13	0.06
Bolivian	1	0.00
Chilean	17	0.08
Colombian	200	0.91
Ecuadorian	76	0.35
Paraguayan	1	0.00
Peruvian	63	0.29
Uruguayan	5	0.02
Venezuelan	9	0.04
Other South American	19	0.09
Other Hispanic or Latino	951	4.34
Hungarian	97	0.44
Icelander	9	0.04
Irish	4,262	19.44
Italian	6,765	30.86
Lithuanian	26	0.12
Maltese	13	0.06
Norwegian	132	0.60
Polish	1,412	6.44
Portuguese	49	0.22
Romanian	26	0.12
Russian	357	1.63
Scandinavian	41	0.19
Scotch-Irish	102	0.47
Scottish	133	0.61
Slavic	18	0.08
Slovak	13	0.06
Swedish	173	0.79
Swiss	30	0.14
Turkish	68	0.31
Ukrainian	250	1.14
United States or American	667	3.04
Welsh	55	0.25
West Indian, excl. Hispanic:	232	1.06
Belizean	7	0.03
Haitian	34	0.16
Jamaican	102	0.47
Trinidadian and Tobagonian	41	0.19
West Indian	48	0.22
White:	18,544	84.59
Not Hispanic (15,849)	16,058	73.25
Hispanic (2,127)	2,486	11.34
Yugoslavian	30	0.14

Coram

Place Type: Census Designated Place
County: Suffolk
Population: 34,923

Ancestry/Race	Number	%
Afghan	49	0.14
African American/Black:	3,410	9.76
Not Hispanic (2,869)	3,173	9.09
Hispanic (155)	237	0.68
African, sub-Saharan:	250	0.71
African	169	0.48
Nigerian	48	0.14
Zimbabwean	33	0.09
Am. Ind. or Alaska Nat., not spec.	113	0.32
Albanian	19	0.05
Alsatian	27	0.08
American Indian tribes, specified:	139	0.40
Apache (1)	7	0.02
Blackfeet	8	0.02
Cherokee (12)	64	0.18
Choctaw (1)	1	0.00
Creek (1)	1	0.00
Crow (1)	2	0.01
Iroquois	5	0.01
Latin American Indians (7)	12	0.03
Navajo (1)	1	0.00
Potawatomi	1	0.00
Pueblo	1	0.00
Seminole (1)	2	0.01
Sioux (4)	4	0.01
All other tribes (16)	30	0.09
American Indian tribes, not spec.	7	0.02
Arab:	149	0.43
Egyptian	76	0.22
Lebanese	27	0.08
Syrian	46	0.13
Armenian	38	0.11
Asian:	1,375	3.94
Bangladeshi (9)	9	0.03
Cambodian (1)	7	0.02
Chinese, ex. Taiwanese (315)	350	1.00
Filipino (168)	202	0.58
Indian (346)	422	1.21
Indonesian (1)	2	0.01
Japanese (10)	16	0.05
Korean (129)	140	0.40
Laotian (1)	1	0.00
Malaysian (1)	1	0.00
Pakistani (113)	136	0.39
Sri Lankan (6)	6	0.02
Taiwanese (7)	7	0.02
Thai (13)	14	0.04
Vietnamese (10)	10	0.03
Other Asian, specified (2)	2	0.01
Other Asian, not specified (13)	50	0.14
Australian	23	0.07
Austrian	355	1.01
Belgian	76	0.22
Brazilian	14	0.04
British	50	0.14
Bulgarian	16	0.05
Canadian	148	0.42
Celtic	12	0.03
Croatian	8	0.02
Czech	109	0.31
Czechoslovakian	68	0.19
Danish	58	0.17
Dutch	274	0.78
Eastern European	104	0.30
English	1,389	3.97
European	106	0.30
Finnish	94	0.27
French, except Basque	618	1.77
French Canadian	135	0.39
German	5,420	15.50
Greek	400	1.14
Guyanese	74	0.21
Hawaii Native/Pacific Islander:	22	0.06
Melanesian: (1)	1	0.00
Fijian (1)	1	0.00
Micronesian:	1	0.00
Guamanian/Chamorro	1	0.00
Polynesian: (2)	4	0.01
Native Hawaiian (2)	4	0.01
Other Pac. Isl., not spec. (4)	16	0.05
Hispanic or Latino:	3,314	9.49
Central American:	118	0.34
Costa Rican	5	0.01
Guatemalan	15	0.04
Honduran	11	0.03
Nicaraguan	5	0.01
Panamanian	24	0.07
Salvadoran	40	0.11
Other Central American	18	0.05
Cuban	96	0.27
Dominican Republic	360	1.03
Mexican	142	0.41
Puerto Rican	1,420	4.07
South American:	503	1.44
Argentinean	43	0.12
Bolivian	7	0.02
Chilean	27	0.08
Colombian	217	0.62
Ecuadorian	111	0.32
Paraguayan	7	0.02
Peruvian	45	0.13
Uruguayan	1	0.00
Venezuelan	16	0.05
Other South American	29	0.08
Other Hispanic or Latino	675	1.93
Hungarian	534	1.53
Icelander	27	0.08
Iranian	28	0.08
Irish	7,118	20.35
Israeli	35	0.10
Italian	11,086	31.69
Lithuanian	98	0.28
Maltese	7	0.02
Norwegian	217	0.62
Polish	2,355	6.73
Portuguese	140	0.40
Romanian	150	0.43
Russian	1,022	2.92
Scandinavian	17	0.05
Scotch-Irish	280	0.80
Scottish	247	0.71
Slovak	49	0.14
Swedish	286	0.82
Swiss	72	0.21
Turkish	181	0.52
Ukrainian	270	0.77
United States or American	948	2.71
Welsh	98	0.28
West Indian, excl. Hispanic:	798	2.28
Barbadian	28	0.08
Bermudan	7	0.02
British West Indian	12	0.03
Haitian	124	0.35
Jamaican	466	1.33
Trinidadian and Tobagonian	84	0.24
West Indian	60	0.17
Other West Indian	17	0.05
White:	29,291	83.87
Not Hispanic (26,897)	27,246	78.02
Hispanic (1,860)	2,045	5.86
Yugoslavian	7	0.02

Corning

Place Type: City
County: Steuben
Population: 10,842

Ancestry/Race	Number	%
African American/Black:	367	3.38
Not Hispanic (305)	364	3.36
Hispanic (3)	3	0.03
African, sub-Saharan:	10	0.09
Nigerian	5	0.05
South African	5	0.05
Alaska Native tribes, specified:	1	0.01
Aleut	1	0.01
Am. Ind. or Alaska Nat., not spec.	22	0.20
Alsatian	5	0.05
American Indian tribes, specified:	52	0.48
Apache (2)	2	0.02
Blackfeet	5	0.05
Cherokee	8	0.07
Iroquois (23)	30	0.28
Navajo (4)	4	0.04
Seminole	1	0.01
Sioux	1	0.01
All other tribes	1	0.01
American Indian tribes, not spec.	5	0.05
Arab:	53	0.49
Egyptian	9	0.08
Lebanese	44	0.41
Asian:	191	1.76
Bangladeshi (1)	1	0.01
Chinese, ex. Taiwanese (44)	50	0.46
Filipino (10)	16	0.15
Indian (55)	66	0.61
Japanese (9)	9	0.08
Korean (15)	16	0.15
Laotian (6)	6	0.06
Malaysian	3	0.03
Pakistani (5)	5	0.05
Taiwanese (1)	1	0.01
Thai (2)	2	0.02
Vietnamese (2)	2	0.02
Other Asian, specified (1)	4	0.04

Notes: 1. Figures in the "Number" column do not add up to the total population due to: a) Ancestry/Race overlap — e.g. persons can report being both White and Irish, b) persons of Hispanic origin can report being any race, c) persons reporting two ancestries are counted in both categories. 2. Numbers in parentheses indicate the number of persons reporting this ancestry/race alone, not in combination with any other ancestry/race. 3. Refer to the Explanation of Data in the front of the book for more detailed information.

Other Asian, not specified (5)	10	0.09
Austrian	34	0.31
Basque	5	0.05
Belgian	6	0.06
British	66	0.61
Canadian	21	0.19
Celtic	18	0.17
Croatian	6	0.06
Czech	45	0.42
Czechoslovakian	71	0.65
Danish	9	0.08
Dutch	367	3.38
Eastern European	5	0.05
English	1,517	13.99
Estonian	6	0.06
European	94	0.87
Finnish	19	0.18
French, except Basque	401	3.70
French Canadian	133	1.23
German	1,910	17.62
Greek	57	0.53
Hawaii Native/Pacific Islander:	2	0.02
Polynesian: (1)	1	0.01
Native Hawaiian (1)	1	0.01
Other Pac. Isl., not spec.	1	0.01
Hispanic or Latino:	86	0.79
Central American:	4	0.04
Costa Rican	3	0.03
Salvadoran	1	0.01
Cuban	3	0.03
Dominican Republic	4	0.04
Mexican	16	0.15
Puerto Rican	23	0.21
South American:	5	0.05
Colombian	4	0.04
Other South American	1	0.01
Other Hispanic or Latino	31	0.29
Hungarian	16	0.15
Irish	1,769	16.32
Italian	1,280	11.81
Lithuanian	49	0.45
Northern European	20	0.18
Norwegian	66	0.61
Pennsylvania German	50	0.46
Polish	483	4.45
Portuguese	37	0.34
Romanian	13	0.12
Russian	60	0.55
Scandinavian	8	0.07
Scotch-Irish	166	1.53
Scottish	240	2.21
Slavic	29	0.27
Slovak	52	0.48
Slovene	6	0.06
Swedish	240	2.21
Swiss	38	0.35
Ukrainian	133	1.23
United States or American	888	8.19
Welsh	135	1.25
West Indian, excl. Hispanic:	14	0.13
British West Indian	4	0.04
Jamaican	10	0.09
White:	10,290	94.91
Not Hispanic (10,124)	10,225	94.31
Hispanic (61)	65	0.60

Cornwall

Place Type: Town
County: Orange
Population: 12,307

Ancestry/Race	Number	%
African American/Black:	210	1.71
Not Hispanic (144)	184	1.50
Hispanic (18)	26	0.21
African, sub-Saharan:	7	0.06
African	7	0.06
Alaska Native tribes, specified:	1	0.01
Aleut (1)	1	0.01
Am. Ind. or Alaska Nat., not spec.	19	0.15
American Indian tribes, specified:	34	0.28
Apache	1	0.01
Blackfeet	2	0.02
Cherokee (7)	12	0.10
Choctaw	3	0.02
Creek	1	0.01
Delaware (3)	3	0.02
Iroquois	1	0.01
Latin American Indians (1)	1	0.01
Lumbee (3)	3	0.02
Seminole	1	0.01
All other tribes (4)	6	0.05
American Indian tribes, not spec.	1	0.01
Arab:	29	0.24
Lebanese	14	0.11
Syrian	15	0.12
Armenian	8	0.06
Asian:	218	1.77
Chinese, ex. Taiwanese (29)	35	0.28
Filipino (19)	42	0.34
Indian (32)	43	0.35
Japanese (11)	20	0.16
Korean (52)	58	0.47
Malaysian (1)	1	0.01
Pakistani (1)	6	0.05
Thai (1)	1	0.01
Vietnamese (8)	8	0.07
Other Asian, not specified (1)	4	0.03
Assyrian/Chaldean/Syriac	3	0.02
Australian	9	0.07
Austrian	156	1.27
Belgian	9	0.07
British	44	0.36
Canadian	36	0.29
Carpatho Rusyn	4	0.03
Croatian	3	0.02
Czech	56	0.45
Czechoslovakian	24	0.19
Danish	95	0.77
Dutch	254	2.06
Eastern European	30	0.24
English	1,284	10.42
Estonian	4	0.03
European	70	0.57
Finnish	21	0.17
French, except Basque	274	2.22
French Canadian	103	0.84
German	2,198	17.83
Greek	134	1.09
Hawaii Native/Pacific Islander:	11	0.09
Micronesian: (1)	1	0.01
Other Micronesian (1)	1	0.01
Polynesian: (4)	7	0.06
Native Hawaiian	3	0.02
Samoan (4)	4	0.03
Other Pac. Isl., not spec. (1)	3	0.02
Hispanic or Latino:	629	5.11
Central American:	10	0.08
Costa Rican	1	0.01
Guatemalan	3	0.02
Honduran	1	0.01
Panamanian	4	0.03
Salvadoran	1	0.01
Cuban	21	0.17
Dominican Republic	18	0.15
Mexican	49	0.40
Puerto Rican	357	2.90
South American:	61	0.50
Argentinean	5	0.04
Bolivian	1	0.01
Chilean	11	0.09
Colombian	23	0.19
Ecuadorian	5	0.04
Peruvian	12	0.10
Venezuelan	1	0.01
Other South American	3	0.02
Other Hispanic or Latino	113	0.92
Hungarian	185	1.50
Icelander	2	0.02
Iranian	33	0.27
Irish	3,351	27.19
Israeli	13	0.11
Italian	2,879	23.36
Lithuanian	37	0.30
Luxemburger	2	0.02
Maltese	3	0.02
Northern European	18	0.15
Norwegian	165	1.34
Polish	631	5.12
Portuguese	54	0.44
Romanian	29	0.24
Russian	209	1.70
Scandinavian	13	0.11
Scotch-Irish	176	1.43
Scottish	361	2.93
Slavic	5	0.04
Slovak	56	0.45
Swedish	237	1.92
Swiss	65	0.53
Turkish	11	0.09
Ukrainian	71	0.58
United States or American	511	4.15
Welsh	100	0.81
West Indian, excl. Hispanic:	24	0.19
Jamaican	22	0.18
West Indian	2	0.02
White:	11,807	95.94
Not Hispanic (11,226)	11,348	92.21
Hispanic (426)	459	3.73
Yugoslavian	4	0.03

Cortland

Place Type: City
County: Cortland
Population: 18,740

Ancestry/Race	Number	%
African American/Black:	407	2.17
Not Hispanic (278)	387	2.07
Hispanic (14)	20	0.11
African, sub-Saharan:	35	0.19
African	18	0.10
Ethiopian	12	0.06
Nigerian	5	0.03
Am. Ind. or Alaska Nat., not spec.	53	0.28
American Indian tribes, specified:	75	0.40
Blackfeet (1)	5	0.03
Cherokee (3)	17	0.09
Chippewa	1	0.01
Cree	1	0.01
Delaware	1	0.01
Iroquois (17)	37	0.20
Latin American Indians (1)	3	0.02
Lumbee	2	0.01
Navajo	1	0.01
All other tribes (4)	7	0.04
American Indian tribes, not spec.	6	0.03
Arab:	74	0.39
Arab/Arabic	19	0.10
Lebanese	37	0.20
Syrian	18	0.10
Armenian	30	0.16
Asian:	140	0.75
Bangladeshi (1)	1	0.01
Chinese, ex. Taiwanese (26)	36	0.19
Filipino (10)	12	0.06
Indian (31)	41	0.22
Japanese (7)	7	0.04
Korean (16)	17	0.09
Laotian (6)	6	0.03
Taiwanese (2)	7	0.04
Vietnamese (2)	3	0.02
Other Asian, specified (4)	5	0.03
Other Asian, not specified (1)	5	0.03
Austrian	32	0.17
Brazilian	5	0.03
British	81	0.43
Canadian	46	0.25

Notes: 1. Figures in the "Number" column do not add up to the total population due to: a) Ancestry/Race overlap — e.g. persons can report being both White and Irish, b) persons of Hispanic origin can report being any race, c) persons reporting two ancestries are counted in both categories. 2. Numbers in parentheses indicate the number of persons reporting this ancestry/race alone, not in combination with any other ancestry/race. 3. Refer to the Explanation of Data in the front of the book for more detailed information.

Ancestry/Race	Number	%
Celtic	30	0.16
Czech	74	0.39
Czechoslovakian	40	0.21
Danish	18	0.10
Dutch	792	4.23
English	3,092	16.50
European	107	0.57
Finnish	18	0.10
French, except Basque	695	3.71
French Canadian	260	1.39
German	3,179	16.96
Greek	56	0.30
Guyanese	12	0.06
Hawaii Native/Pacific Islander:	14	0.07
Polynesian: (2)	4	0.02
Native Hawaiian (2)	4	0.02
Other Pac. Isl., specified	1	0.01
Other Pac. Isl., not spec. (1)	9	0.05
Hispanic or Latino:	322	1.72
Central American:	6	0.03
Guatemalan	3	0.02
Honduran	1	0.01
Panamanian	2	0.01
Cuban	13	0.07
Dominican Republic	17	0.09
Mexican	32	0.17
Puerto Rican	167	0.89
South American:	27	0.14
Argentinean	3	0.02
Bolivian	4	0.02
Chilean	1	0.01
Colombian	10	0.05
Ecuadorian	3	0.02
Peruvian	5	0.03
Uruguayan	1	0.01
Other Hispanic or Latino	60	0.32
Hungarian	48	0.26
Iranian	5	0.03
Irish	3,973	21.20
Italian	3,453	18.43
Lithuanian	35	0.19
Maltese	7	0.04
Northern European	4	0.02
Norwegian	129	0.69
Pennsylvania German	12	0.06
Polish	759	4.05
Portuguese	54	0.29
Romanian	12	0.06
Russian	146	0.78
Scandinavian	17	0.09
Scotch-Irish	239	1.28
Scottish	302	1.61
Serbian	6	0.03
Slavic	7	0.04
Slovak	38	0.20
Swedish	163	0.87
Swiss	31	0.17
Ukrainian	209	1.12
United States or American	1,176	6.28
Welsh	252	1.34
West Indian, excl. Hispanic:	4	0.02
Jamaican	4	0.02
White:	18,175	96.99
Not Hispanic (17,737)	17,952	95.80
Hispanic (200)	223	1.19
Yugoslavian	16	0.09

Cortlandt

Place Type: Town
County: Westchester
Population: 38,467

Ancestry/Race	Number	%
Acadian/Cajun	9	0.02
African American/Black:	2,006	5.21
Not Hispanic (1,672)	1,864	4.85
Hispanic (93)	142	0.37
African, sub-Saharan:	129	0.34
African	101	0.26
South African	28	0.07
Am. Ind. or Alaska Nat., not spec.	96	0.25
Albanian	78	0.20
Alsatian	11	0.03
American Indian tribes, specified:	104	0.27
Apache (1)	1	0.00
Blackfeet (2)	5	0.01
Cherokee (4)	25	0.06
Cheyenne	1	0.00
Creek	3	0.01
Crow	3	0.01
Delaware (4)	4	0.01
Iroquois (10)	24	0.06
Latin American Indians (8)	16	0.04
Navajo	3	0.01
Potawatomi (3)	3	0.01
Pueblo (1)	1	0.00
Sioux (1)	3	0.01
All other tribes (3)	12	0.03
American Indian tribes, not spec.	3	0.01
Arab:	47	0.12
Arab/Arabic	6	0.02
Egyptian	9	0.02
Lebanese	32	0.08
Armenian	68	0.18
Asian:	1,174	3.05
Cambodian (11)	11	0.03
Chinese, ex. Taiwanese (310)	355	0.92
Filipino (91)	115	0.30
Indian (332)	386	1.00
Indonesian (2)	3	0.01
Japanese (59)	75	0.19
Korean (79)	99	0.26
Malaysian (1)	1	0.00
Pakistani (41)	50	0.13
Sri Lankan (4)	5	0.01
Taiwanese (12)	13	0.03
Thai (9)	9	0.02
Vietnamese (11)	11	0.03
Other Asian, specified (7)	10	0.03
Other Asian, not specified (10)	31	0.08
Assyrian/Chaldean/Syriac	47	0.12
Australian	69	0.18
Austrian	426	1.11
Belgian	19	0.05
Brazilian	20	0.05
British	138	0.36
Bulgarian	19	0.05
Canadian	89	0.23
Celtic	20	0.05
Croatian	29	0.08
Czech	230	0.60
Czechoslovakian	104	0.27
Danish	104	0.27
Dutch	668	1.74
Eastern European	295	0.77
English	2,340	6.08
Estonian	7	0.02
European	214	0.56
Finnish	72	0.19
French, except Basque	712	1.85
French Canadian	229	0.60
German	4,829	12.55
German Russian	10	0.03
Greek	371	0.96
Guyanese	52	0.14
Hawaii Native/Pacific Islander:	16	0.04
Micronesian: (4)	4	0.01
Guamanian/Chamorro (4)	4	0.01
Polynesian: (1)	2	0.01
Native Hawaiian (1)	2	0.01
Other Pac. Isl., specified	1	0.00
Other Pac. Isl., not spec.	9	0.02
Hispanic or Latino:	2,766	7.19
Central American:	123	0.32
Costa Rican	8	0.02
Guatemalan	31	0.08
Honduran	19	0.05
Nicaraguan	3	0.01
Panamanian	10	0.03
Salvadoran	43	0.11
Other Central American	9	0.02
Cuban	104	0.27
Dominican Republic	118	0.31
Mexican	139	0.36
Puerto Rican	1,185	3.08
South American:	539	1.40
Argentinean	22	0.06
Bolivian	6	0.02
Chilean	20	0.05
Colombian	132	0.34
Ecuadorian	213	0.55
Paraguayan	9	0.02
Peruvian	73	0.19
Uruguayan	35	0.09
Venezuelan	7	0.02
Other South American	22	0.06
Other Hispanic or Latino	558	1.45
Hungarian	517	1.34
Icelander	18	0.05
Iranian	71	0.18
Irish	9,064	23.56
Israeli	54	0.14
Italian	10,177	26.46
Latvian	53	0.14
Lithuanian	121	0.31
Luxemburger	25	0.06
Macedonian	6	0.02
Maltese	23	0.06
Northern European	45	0.12
Norwegian	334	0.87
Pennsylvania German	9	0.02
Polish	1,996	5.19
Portuguese	338	0.88
Romanian	157	0.41
Russian	1,562	4.06
Scandinavian	49	0.13
Scotch-Irish	483	1.26
Scottish	422	1.10
Serbian	13	0.03
Slavic	17	0.04
Slovak	202	0.53
Slovene	20	0.05
Soviet Union	8	0.02
Swedish	413	1.07
Swiss	183	0.48
Turkish	21	0.05
Ukrainian	404	1.05
United States or American	1,859	4.83
Welsh	166	0.43
West Indian, excl. Hispanic:	532	1.38
Barbadian	59	0.15
Belizean	34	0.09
Bermudan	15	0.04
British West Indian	6	0.02
Haitian	62	0.16
Jamaican	254	0.66
West Indian	102	0.27
White:	34,615	89.99
Not Hispanic (32,470)	32,844	85.38
Hispanic (1,612)	1,771	4.60
Yugoslavian	6	0.02

De Witt

Place Type: Town
County: Onondaga
Population: 24,071

Ancestry/Race	Number	%
African American/Black:	1,326	5.51
Not Hispanic (1,149)	1,287	5.35
Hispanic (28)	39	0.16
African, sub-Saharan:	102	0.42
African	74	0.31
Ethiopian	21	0.09
Liberian	7	0.03
Am. Ind. or Alaska Nat., not spec.	83	0.34
Albanian	8	0.03
American Indian tribes, specified:	167	0.69

Notes: 1. Figures in the "Number" column do not add up to the total population due to: a) Ancestry/Race overlap — e.g. persons can report being both White and Irish, b) persons of Hispanic origin can report being any race, c) persons reporting two ancestries are counted in both categories. 2. Numbers in parentheses indicate the number of persons reporting this ancestry/race alone, not in combination with any other ancestry/race. 3. Refer to the Explanation of Data in the front of the book for more detailed information.

Apache (1)	2	0.01
Blackfeet (5)	6	0.02
Cherokee (8)	22	0.09
Chippewa (2)	4	0.02
Choctaw	1	0.00
Crow	2	0.01
Iroquois (77)	122	0.51
Pima (1)	1	0.00
Seminole	1	0.00
Sioux	1	0.00
All other tribes (2)	5	0.02
American Indian tribes, not spec.	8	0.03
Arab:	307	1.28
Arab/Arabic	92	0.38
Egyptian	54	0.22
Jordanian	16	0.07
Lebanese	76	0.32
Palestinian	30	0.12
Syrian	39	0.16
Armenian	89	0.37
Asian:	819	3.40
Bangladeshi (4)	4	0.02
Cambodian (5)	5	0.02
Chinese, ex. Taiwanese (235)	249	1.03
Filipino (25)	33	0.14
Indian (236)	258	1.07
Japanese (24)	32	0.13
Korean (78)	83	0.34
Malaysian (3)	5	0.02
Pakistani (8)	18	0.07
Taiwanese (27)	33	0.14
Thai (10)	12	0.05
Vietnamese (47)	50	0.21
Other Asian, specified (7)	9	0.04
Other Asian, not specified (1)	28	0.12
Australian	13	0.05
Austrian	148	0.61
Belgian	10	0.04
British	172	0.71
Bulgarian	15	0.06
Canadian	70	0.29
Croatian	6	0.02
Czech	62	0.26
Czechoslovakian	17	0.07
Danish	80	0.33
Dutch	489	2.03
Eastern European	73	0.30
English	3,151	13.09
Estonian	31	0.13
European	196	0.81
Finnish	7	0.03
French, except Basque	1,220	5.07
French Canadian	522	2.17
German	4,660	19.36
Greek	192	0.80
Hawaii Native/Pacific Islander:	16	0.07
Micronesian: (1)	1	0.00
Other Micronesian (1)	1	0.00
Polynesian: (4)	8	0.03
Native Hawaiian (4)	8	0.03
Other Pac. Isl., not spec. (1)	7	0.03
Hispanic or Latino:	324	1.35
Central American:	5	0.02
Guatemalan	3	0.01
Honduran	1	0.00
Panamanian	1	0.00
Cuban	19	0.08
Dominican Republic	14	0.06
Mexican	58	0.24
Puerto Rican	118	0.49
South American:	28	0.12
Argentinean	1	0.00
Chilean	11	0.05
Colombian	10	0.04
Ecuadorian	2	0.01
Paraguayan	2	0.01
Peruvian	1	0.00
Venezuelan	1	0.00
Other Hispanic or Latino	82	0.34
Hungarian	149	0.62
Iranian	42	0.17
Irish	4,973	20.66
Israeli	138	0.57
Italian	3,709	15.41
Latvian	135	0.56
Lithuanian	106	0.44
Macedonian	51	0.21
Northern European	10	0.04
Norwegian	60	0.25
Pennsylvania German	9	0.04
Polish	1,852	7.69
Portuguese	30	0.12
Romanian	89	0.37
Russian	607	2.52
Scandinavian	14	0.06
Scotch-Irish	296	1.23
Scottish	644	2.68
Slavic	9	0.04
Slovak	44	0.18
Slovene	6	0.02
Swedish	175	0.73
Swiss	181	0.75
Turkish	15	0.06
Ukrainian	326	1.35
United States or American	984	4.09
Welsh	176	0.73
West Indian, excl. Hispanic:	57	0.24
British West Indian	10	0.04
Jamaican	41	0.17
Trinidadian and Tobagonian	6	0.02
White:	21,917	91.05
Not Hispanic (21,390)	21,684	90.08
Hispanic (202)	233	0.97
Yugoslavian	17	0.07

Deer Park

Place Type: Census Designated Place
County: Suffolk
Population: 28,316

Ancestry/Race	Number	%
African American/Black:	2,832	10.00
Not Hispanic (2,500)	2,715	9.59
Hispanic (77)	117	0.41
African, sub-Saharan:	97	0.34
African	97	0.34
Am. Ind. or Alaska Nat., not spec.	77	0.27
American Indian tribes, specified:	61	0.22
Apache	1	0.00
Blackfeet	2	0.01
Cherokee (8)	37	0.13
Choctaw	1	0.00
Iroquois (1)	1	0.00
Latin American Indians (3)	5	0.02
Navajo	1	0.00
Pima (1)	1	0.00
Sioux	1	0.00
All other tribes (7)	11	0.04
American Indian tribes, not spec.	5	0.02
Arab:	66	0.23
Arab/Arabic	10	0.04
Lebanese	26	0.09
Moroccan	30	0.11
Armenian	39	0.14
Asian:	998	3.52
Bangladeshi (13)	27	0.10
Chinese, ex. Taiwanese (167)	190	0.67
Filipino (84)	109	0.38
Indian (342)	404	1.43
Japanese (14)	17	0.06
Korean (98)	104	0.37
Pakistani (46)	81	0.29
Taiwanese (2)	2	0.01
Thai (12)	19	0.07
Vietnamese (7)	7	0.02
Other Asian, specified	1	0.00
Other Asian, not specified (11)	37	0.13
Austrian	126	0.45
Belgian	5	0.02
Brazilian	42	0.15
British	10	0.04
Canadian	11	0.04
Celtic	6	0.02
Croatian	14	0.05
Czech	59	0.21
Czechoslovakian	66	0.23
Danish	29	0.10
Dutch	117	0.41
English	955	3.38
Estonian	33	0.12
European	34	0.12
French, except Basque	242	0.86
French Canadian	120	0.42
German	3,452	12.21
Greek	398	1.41
Guyanese	137	0.48
Hawaii Native/Pacific Islander:	15	0.05
Micronesian: (2)	2	0.01
Guamanian/Chamorro (2)	2	0.01
Polynesian:	1	0.00
Samoan	1	0.00
Other Pac. Isl., not spec. (1)	12	0.04
Hispanic or Latino:	2,139	7.55
Central American:	219	0.77
Costa Rican	8	0.03
Guatemalan	13	0.05
Honduran	46	0.16
Nicaraguan	9	0.03
Panamanian	14	0.05
Salvadoran	121	0.43
Other Central American	8	0.03
Cuban	72	0.25
Dominican Republic	112	0.40
Mexican	62	0.22
Puerto Rican	817	2.89
South American:	410	1.45
Argentinean	34	0.12
Bolivian	1	0.00
Chilean	31	0.11
Colombian	173	0.61
Ecuadorian	95	0.34
Paraguayan	2	0.01
Peruvian	36	0.13
Uruguayan	14	0.05
Venezuelan	6	0.02
Other South American	18	0.06
Other Hispanic or Latino	447	1.58
Hungarian	277	0.98
Iranian	22	0.08
Irish	5,890	20.84
Israeli	11	0.04
Italian	11,899	42.10
Latvian	60	0.21
Lithuanian	89	0.31
Maltese	16	0.06
Norwegian	305	1.08
Polish	1,357	4.80
Portuguese	115	0.41
Romanian	65	0.23
Russian	558	1.97
Scotch-Irish	245	0.87
Scottish	211	0.75
Serbian	15	0.05
Slavic	15	0.05
Slovak	6	0.02
Swedish	157	0.56
Swiss	5	0.02
Turkish	70	0.25
Ukrainian	236	0.84
United States or American	698	2.47
Welsh	58	0.21
West Indian, excl. Hispanic:	820	2.90
Barbadian	5	0.02
British West Indian	30	0.11
Haitian	216	0.76
Jamaican	421	1.49
Trinidadian and Tobagonian	90	0.32
West Indian	58	0.21
White:	24,030	84.86

Notes: 1. Figures in the "Number" column do not add up to the total population due to: a) Ancestry/Race overlap — e.g. persons can report being both White and Irish, b) persons of Hispanic origin can report being any race, c) persons reporting two ancestries are counted in both categories. 2. Numbers in parentheses indicate the number of persons reporting this ancestry/race alone, not in combination with any other ancestry/race. 3. Refer to the Explanation of Data in the front of the book for more detailed information.

	Number	%
Not Hispanic (22,299)	22,545	79.62
Hispanic (1,319)	1,485	5.24
Yugoslavian	97	0.34

Depew

Place Type: Village
County: Erie
Population: 16,629

Ancestry/Race	Number	%
African American/Black:	141	0.85
Not Hispanic (102)	133	0.80
Hispanic (3)	8	0.05
Alaska Native tribes, specified:	4	0.02
Aleut	1	0.01
Eskimo (2)	3	0.02
Am. Ind. or Alaska Nat., not spec.	9	0.05
Alsatian	8	0.05
American Indian tribes, specified:	40	0.24
Blackfeet (1)	4	0.02
Cherokee (1)	2	0.01
Chippewa (1)	1	0.01
Iroquois (20)	31	0.19
All other tribes (2)	2	0.01
American Indian tribes, not spec.	3	0.02
Arab:	74	0.45
Lebanese	74	0.45
Asian:	104	0.63
Chinese, ex. Taiwanese (12)	16	0.10
Filipino (11)	19	0.11
Indian (26)	26	0.16
Indonesian	3	0.02
Japanese (1)	3	0.02
Korean (10)	17	0.10
Laotian (5)	7	0.04
Vietnamese (2)	4	0.02
Other Asian, not specified	9	0.05
Austrian	25	0.15
British	14	0.08
Canadian	40	0.24
Czech	36	0.22
Czechoslovakian	39	0.23
Dutch	125	0.75
English	1,125	6.77
Finnish	5	0.03
French, except Basque	395	2.38
French Canadian	72	0.43
German	5,565	33.49
Greek	40	0.24
Hawaii Native/Pacific Islander:	8	0.05
Micronesian: (1)	1	0.01
Guamanian/Chamorro (1)	1	0.01
Polynesian: (1)	4	0.02
Native Hawaiian (1)	4	0.02
Other Pac. Isl., not spec.	3	0.02
Hispanic or Latino:	122	0.73
Central American:	9	0.05
Costa Rican	4	0.02
Panamanian	1	0.01
Salvadoran	4	0.02
Cuban	1	0.01
Mexican	23	0.14
Puerto Rican	66	0.40
South American:	4	0.02
Chilean	1	0.01
Colombian	2	0.01
Ecuadorian	1	0.01
Other Hispanic or Latino	19	0.11
Hungarian	62	0.37
Icelander	20	0.12
Irish	2,515	15.14
Italian	2,881	17.34
Latvian	8	0.05
Lithuanian	31	0.19
Norwegian	12	0.07
Polish	6,687	40.24
Portuguese	5	0.03
Romanian	11	0.07
Russian	51	0.31
Scotch-Irish	88	0.53
Scottish	239	1.44
Slovak	11	0.07
Swedish	87	0.52
Ukrainian	164	0.99
United States or American	409	2.46
Welsh	80	0.48
White:	16,377	98.48
Not Hispanic (16,213)	16,292	97.97
Hispanic (73)	85	0.51

Dix Hills

Place Type: Census Designated Place
County: Suffolk
Population: 26,024

Ancestry/Race	Number	%
African American/Black:	957	3.68
Not Hispanic (819)	926	3.56
Hispanic (27)	31	0.12
African, sub-Saharan:	43	0.16
African	7	0.03
Ghanian	8	0.03
Kenyan	14	0.05
Other sub-Saharan African	14	0.05
Am. Ind. or Alaska Nat., not spec.	19	0.07
Albanian	39	0.15
Alsatian	8	0.03
American Indian tribes, specified:	37	0.14
Blackfeet	2	0.01
Cherokee (2)	19	0.07
Choctaw	1	0.00
Creek (1)	1	0.00
Iroquois (1)	2	0.01
Latin American Indians (2)	7	0.03
Ottawa	1	0.00
Seminole	1	0.00
All other tribes (2)	3	0.01
American Indian tribes, not spec.	5	0.02
Arab:	100	0.38
Egyptian	66	0.25
Lebanese	20	0.08
Syrian	8	0.03
Other Arab	6	0.02
Armenian	121	0.46
Asian:	2,160	8.30
Bangladeshi (21)	22	0.08
Chinese, ex. Taiwanese (495)	547	2.10
Filipino (164)	185	0.71
Indian (665)	718	2.76
Japanese (28)	47	0.18
Korean (297)	315	1.21
Malaysian (2)	2	0.01
Pakistani (92)	132	0.51
Taiwanese (46)	53	0.20
Thai (5)	6	0.02
Vietnamese (13)	13	0.05
Other Asian, specified (8)	9	0.03
Other Asian, not specified (42)	111	0.43
Assyrian/Chaldean/Syriac	7	0.03
Austrian	336	1.29
Belgian	8	0.03
British	64	0.25
Canadian	44	0.17
Croatian	10	0.04
Cypriot	33	0.13
Czech	76	0.29
Czechoslovakian	107	0.41
Danish	17	0.07
Dutch	212	0.81
Eastern European	267	1.02
English	912	3.49
Estonian	14	0.05
European	319	1.22
Finnish	28	0.11
French, except Basque	284	1.09
French Canadian	36	0.14
German	2,887	11.06
Greek	553	2.12
Guyanese	34	0.13
Hawaii Native/Pacific Islander:	20	0.08
Micronesian: (2)	2	0.01
Guamanian/Chamorro (2)	2	0.01
Polynesian: (1)	1	0.00
Samoan (1)	1	0.00
Other Pac. Isl., specified	1	0.00
Other Pac. Isl., not spec. (1)	16	0.06
Hispanic or Latino:	995	3.82
Central American:	44	0.17
Costa Rican	4	0.02
Guatemalan	15	0.06
Honduran	4	0.02
Panamanian	2	0.01
Salvadoran	18	0.07
Other Central American	1	0.00
Cuban	65	0.25
Dominican Republic	50	0.19
Mexican	52	0.20
Puerto Rican	315	1.21
South American:	200	0.77
Argentinean	15	0.06
Bolivian	5	0.02
Chilean	10	0.04
Colombian	82	0.32
Ecuadorian	38	0.15
Paraguayan	4	0.02
Peruvian	27	0.10
Uruguayan	5	0.02
Venezuelan	4	0.02
Other South American	10	0.04
Other Hispanic or Latino	269	1.03
Hungarian	385	1.48
Iranian	110	0.42
Irish	3,570	13.68
Israeli	76	0.29
Italian	7,359	28.20
Latvian	24	0.09
Lithuanian	144	0.55
Northern European	6	0.02
Norwegian	91	0.35
Polish	1,591	6.10
Portuguese	78	0.30
Romanian	262	1.00
Russian	2,164	8.29
Scandinavian	10	0.04
Scotch-Irish	63	0.24
Scottish	208	0.80
Slavic	39	0.15
Slovak	66	0.25
Slovene	8	0.03
Swedish	194	0.74
Swiss	28	0.11
Turkish	72	0.28
Ukrainian	120	0.46
United States or American	1,070	4.10
Welsh	67	0.26
West Indian, excl. Hispanic:	392	1.50
Barbadian	19	0.07
Belizean	12	0.05
Bermudan	5	0.02
British West Indian	6	0.02
Haitian	236	0.90
Jamaican	85	0.33
Trinidadian and Tobagonian	29	0.11
White:	22,910	88.03
Not Hispanic (21,833)	22,129	85.03
Hispanic (733)	781	3.00
Yugoslavian	54	0.21

Dobbs Ferry

Place Type: Village
County: Westchester
Population: 10,622

Ancestry/Race	Number	%
African American/Black:	862	8.12
Not Hispanic (745)	803	7.56
Hispanic (39)	59	0.56

Notes: 1. Figures in the "Number" column do not add up to the total population due to: a) Ancestry/Race overlap — e.g. persons can report being both White and Irish, b) persons of Hispanic origin can report being any race, c) persons reporting two ancestries are counted in both categories. 2. Numbers in parentheses indicate the number of persons reporting this ancestry/race alone, not in combination with any other ancestry/race. 3. Refer to the Explanation of Data in the front of the book for more detailed information.

Ancestry/Race	Number	%
African, sub-Saharan:	58	0.55
African	58	0.55
Am. Ind. or Alaska Nat., not spec.	33	0.31
American Indian tribes, specified:	16	0.15
Cherokee	2	0.02
Creek (1)	2	0.02
Iroquois (2)	3	0.03
Latin American Indians (3)	9	0.08
American Indian tribes, not spec.	1	0.01
Arab:	29	0.27
Arab/Arabic	5	0.05
Other Arab	24	0.23
Armenian	10	0.09
Asian:	903	8.50
Cambodian (1)	2	0.02
Chinese, ex. Taiwanese (127)	139	1.31
Filipino (57)	74	0.70
Indian (217)	241	2.27
Japanese (156)	172	1.62
Korean (161)	168	1.58
Malaysian	1	0.01
Pakistani (45)	58	0.55
Taiwanese	4	0.04
Thai (4)	4	0.04
Vietnamese	1	0.01
Other Asian, specified (9)	10	0.09
Other Asian, not specified (21)	29	0.27
Australian	12	0.11
Austrian	224	2.11
Belgian	30	0.28
Brazilian	44	0.41
British	41	0.39
Bulgarian	10	0.09
Canadian	55	0.52
Croatian	48	0.45
Czech	31	0.29
Danish	32	0.30
Dutch	107	1.01
Eastern European	114	1.07
English	596	5.61
European	111	1.05
French, except Basque	109	1.03
French Canadian	74	0.70
German	885	8.33
Greek	133	1.25
Guyanese	36	0.34
Hawaii Native/Pacific Islander:	23	0.22
Micronesian: (8)	9	0.08
Guamanian/Chamorro (8)	9	0.08
Polynesian: (1)	3	0.03
Samoan (1)	3	0.03
Other Pac. Isl., specified	1	0.01
Other Pac. Isl., not spec. (1)	10	0.09
Hispanic or Latino:	744	7.00
Central American:	84	0.79
Guatemalan	54	0.51
Honduran	5	0.05
Nicaraguan	2	0.02
Panamanian	3	0.03
Salvadoran	20	0.19
Cuban	47	0.44
Dominican Republic	38	0.36
Mexican	75	0.71
Puerto Rican	226	2.13
South American:	65	0.61
Argentinean	11	0.10
Chilean	4	0.04
Colombian	17	0.16
Ecuadorian	18	0.17
Paraguayan	2	0.02
Peruvian	11	0.10
Uruguayan	1	0.01
Other South American	1	0.01
Other Hispanic or Latino	209	1.97
Hungarian	297	2.80
Iranian	21	0.20
Irish	1,756	16.53
Israeli	40	0.38
Italian	2,277	21.44
Latvian	10	0.09
Lithuanian	61	0.57
Maltese	12	0.11
Norwegian	56	0.53
Polish	514	4.84
Portuguese	125	1.18
Romanian	31	0.29
Russian	667	6.28
Scandinavian	27	0.25
Scotch-Irish	130	1.22
Scottish	198	1.86
Slovak	56	0.53
Swedish	52	0.49
Swiss	53	0.50
Turkish	46	0.43
Ukrainian	99	0.93
United States or American	156	1.47
Welsh	10	0.09
West Indian, excl. Hispanic:	136	1.28
British West Indian	23	0.22
Haitian	31	0.29
Jamaican	39	0.37
Trinidadian and Tobagonian	35	0.33
West Indian	8	0.08
White:	8,751	82.39
Not Hispanic (8,134)	8,261	77.77
Hispanic (438)	490	4.61
Yugoslavian	6	0.06

Dryden

Place Type: Town
County: Tompkins
Population: 13,532

Ancestry/Race	Number	%
African American/Black:	271	2.00
Not Hispanic (188)	251	1.85
Hispanic (13)	20	0.15
African, sub-Saharan:	25	0.18
African	6	0.04
Ethiopian	4	0.03
Kenyan	6	0.04
Nigerian	2	0.01
South African	7	0.05
Am. Ind. or Alaska Nat., not spec.	32	0.24
American Indian tribes, specified:	88	0.65
Apache (6)	10	0.07
Blackfeet	4	0.03
Cherokee (9)	25	0.18
Chippewa	1	0.01
Choctaw (1)	1	0.01
Delaware (2)	10	0.07
Iroquois (14)	20	0.15
Latin American Indians (3)	6	0.04
Lumbee (1)	1	0.01
Navajo	1	0.01
Shoshone	1	0.01
Sioux (1)	4	0.03
All other tribes (2)	4	0.03
American Indian tribes, not spec.	2	0.01
Arab:	64	0.47
Arab/Arabic	18	0.13
Lebanese	25	0.18
Syrian	21	0.15
Armenian	11	0.08
Asian:	236	1.74
Cambodian	2	0.01
Chinese, ex. Taiwanese (101)	112	0.83
Filipino (10)	14	0.10
Indian (21)	23	0.17
Indonesian (2)	4	0.03
Japanese (16)	19	0.14
Korean (32)	35	0.26
Malaysian (1)	1	0.01
Pakistani (1)	3	0.02
Taiwanese (6)	6	0.04
Thai (4)	7	0.05
Vietnamese (2)	2	0.01
Other Asian, specified (2)	2	0.01
Other Asian, not specified (2)	6	0.04
Australian	19	0.14
Austrian	88	0.64
British	144	1.05
Bulgarian	6	0.04
Canadian	61	0.45
Croatian	36	0.26
Czech	42	0.31
Czechoslovakian	19	0.14
Danish	117	0.85
Dutch	661	4.82
Eastern European	90	0.66
English	2,752	20.09
Estonian	12	0.09
European	229	1.67
Finnish	114	0.83
French, except Basque	647	4.72
French Canadian	179	1.31
German	2,523	18.42
Greek	29	0.21
Hawaii Native/Pacific Islander:	18	0.13
Polynesian: (4)	14	0.10
Native Hawaiian (2)	7	0.05
Samoan (2)	5	0.04
Other Polynesian	2	0.01
Other Pac. Isl., not spec.	4	0.03
Hispanic or Latino:	223	1.65
Central American:	22	0.16
Guatemalan	6	0.04
Honduran	2	0.01
Nicaraguan	2	0.01
Panamanian	8	0.06
Salvadoran	1	0.01
Other Central American	3	0.02
Cuban	6	0.04
Mexican	41	0.30
Puerto Rican	66	0.49
South American:	36	0.27
Argentinean	1	0.01
Bolivian	1	0.01
Chilean	4	0.03
Colombian	9	0.07
Ecuadorian	4	0.03
Paraguayan	1	0.01
Peruvian	7	0.05
Venezuelan	7	0.05
Other South American	2	0.01
Other Hispanic or Latino	52	0.38
Hungarian	110	0.80
Iranian	4	0.03
Irish	2,199	16.05
Italian	1,226	8.95
Latvian	13	0.09
Lithuanian	92	0.67
Northern European	9	0.07
Norwegian	109	0.80
Pennsylvania German	47	0.34
Polish	566	4.13
Portuguese	34	0.25
Romanian	34	0.25
Russian	227	1.66
Scandinavian	10	0.07
Scotch-Irish	258	1.88
Scottish	395	2.88
Slovak	28	0.20
Slovene	4	0.03
Swedish	141	1.03
Swiss	46	0.34
Turkish	2	0.01
Ukrainian	97	0.71
United States or American	893	6.52
Welsh	194	1.42
West Indian, excl. Hispanic:	59	0.43
Barbadian	5	0.04
Belizean	30	0.22
Jamaican	5	0.04
Trinidadian and Tobagonian	1	0.01
West Indian	18	0.13
White:	12,985	95.96
Not Hispanic (12,678)	12,836	94.86
Hispanic (138)	149	1.10

Notes: 1. Figures in the "Number" column do not add up to the total population due to: a) Ancestry/Race overlap — e.g. persons can report being both White and Irish, b) persons of Hispanic origin can report being any race, c) persons reporting two ancestries are counted in both categories. 2. Numbers in parentheses indicate the number of persons reporting this ancestry/race alone, not in combination with any other ancestry/race. 3. Refer to the Explanation of Data in the front of the book for more detailed information.

Yugoslavian	14	0.10

Dunkirk

Place Type: City
County: Chautauqua
Population: 13,131

Ancestry/Race	Number	%
African American/Black:	764	5.82
Not Hispanic (586)	659	5.02
Hispanic (79)	105	0.80
African, sub-Saharan:	48	0.37
African	48	0.37
Am. Ind. or Alaska Nat., not spec.	33	0.25
Albanian	6	0.05
American Indian tribes, specified:	99	0.75
Blackfeet (1)	2	0.02
Cherokee	3	0.02
Iroquois (36)	59	0.45
Latin American Indians (9)	27	0.21
Ottawa	3	0.02
Sioux	2	0.02
All other tribes	3	0.02
American Indian tribes, not spec.	3	0.02
Arab:	62	0.47
Egyptian	5	0.04
Lebanese	20	0.15
Syrian	37	0.28
Asian:	43	0.33
Chinese, ex. Taiwanese (6)	6	0.05
Filipino (7)	9	0.07
Indian (5)	7	0.05
Japanese (6)	6	0.05
Korean (4)	5	0.04
Laotian (2)	3	0.02
Pakistani	1	0.01
Thai	1	0.01
Other Asian, not specified	5	0.04
Australian	9	0.07
Austrian	56	0.43
Belgian	5	0.04
British	27	0.21
Canadian	5	0.04
Czech	6	0.05
Danish	24	0.18
Dutch	170	1.29
English	861	6.56
European	7	0.05
French, except Basque	225	1.71
French Canadian	14	0.11
German	2,542	19.36
Greek	13	0.10
Hawaii Native/Pacific Islander:	7	0.05
Micronesian: (2)	3	0.02
Guamanian/Chamorro (2)	3	0.02
Polynesian: (3)	3	0.02
Native Hawaiian (2)	2	0.02
Samoan (1)	1	0.01
Other Pac. Isl., not spec.	1	0.01
Hispanic or Latino:	2,608	19.86
Central American:	4	0.03
Guatemalan	3	0.02
Honduran	1	0.01
Cuban	10	0.08
Dominican Republic	3	0.02
Mexican	183	1.39
Puerto Rican	2,238	17.04
South American:	12	0.09
Colombian	4	0.03
Ecuadorian	7	0.05
Peruvian	1	0.01
Other Hispanic or Latino	158	1.20
Hungarian	43	0.33
Irish	1,428	10.88
Italian	1,980	15.08
Lithuanian	5	0.04
Luxemburger	8	0.06
Norwegian	5	0.04
Polish	3,641	27.73
Portuguese	6	0.05
Russian	69	0.53
Scotch-Irish	70	0.53
Scottish	201	1.53
Slavic	6	0.05
Slovak	14	0.11
Slovene	11	0.08
Swedish	249	1.90
Swiss	13	0.10
Ukrainian	58	0.44
United States or American	317	2.41
Welsh	18	0.14
West Indian, excl. Hispanic:	12	0.09
West Indian	12	0.09
White:	11,117	84.66
Not Hispanic (9,710)	9,833	74.88
Hispanic (1,147)	1,284	9.78

East Fishkill

Place Type: Town
County: Dutchess
Population: 25,589

Ancestry/Race	Number	%
African American/Black:	679	2.65
Not Hispanic (563)	636	2.49
Hispanic (22)	43	0.17
African, sub-Saharan:	97	0.38
Kenyan	63	0.25
Liberian	15	0.06
Nigerian	19	0.07
Am. Ind. or Alaska Nat., not spec.	43	0.17
Albanian	64	0.25
American Indian tribes, specified:	72	0.28
Apache (1)	1	0.00
Blackfeet (1)	2	0.01
Cherokee (3)	14	0.05
Chippewa (1)	1	0.00
Creek	5	0.02
Crow	1	0.00
Delaware	1	0.00
Iroquois (3)	15	0.06
Latin American Indians (3)	9	0.04
Lumbee (2)	2	0.01
Seminole	2	0.01
Sioux	1	0.00
All other tribes (8)	18	0.07
American Indian tribes, not spec.	14	0.05
Arab:	163	0.64
Arab/Arabic	6	0.02
Egyptian	12	0.05
Jordanian	65	0.25
Lebanese	77	0.30
Palestinian	3	0.01
Armenian	70	0.27
Asian:	822	3.21
Bangladeshi (8)	8	0.03
Chinese, ex. Taiwanese (187)	209	0.82
Filipino (28)	38	0.15
Indian (314)	354	1.38
Japanese (22)	27	0.11
Korean (88)	97	0.38
Malaysian (3)	3	0.01
Pakistani (14)	21	0.08
Sri Lankan	1	0.00
Taiwanese (5)	11	0.04
Thai (5)	7	0.03
Vietnamese (19)	20	0.08
Other Asian, specified (1)	1	0.00
Other Asian, not specified (10)	25	0.10
Australian	14	0.05
Austrian	199	0.78
Belgian	17	0.07
British	55	0.21
Canadian	123	0.48
Croatian	15	0.06
Czech	148	0.58
Czechoslovakian	57	0.22
Danish	88	0.34
Dutch	486	1.89
Eastern European	46	0.18
English	2,466	9.62
Estonian	8	0.03
European	161	0.63
Finnish	101	0.39
French, except Basque	615	2.40
French Canadian	290	1.13
German	4,971	19.38
Greek	159	0.62
Hawaii Native/Pacific Islander:	15	0.06
Micronesian: (3)	7	0.03
Other Micronesian (3)	7	0.03
Polynesian: (3)	7	0.03
Native Hawaiian	3	0.01
Samoan (3)	3	0.01
Other Polynesian	1	0.00
Other Pac. Isl., not spec.	1	0.00
Hispanic or Latino:	1,035	4.04
Central American:	42	0.16
Costa Rican	5	0.02
Guatemalan	6	0.02
Honduran	5	0.02
Panamanian	3	0.01
Salvadoran	16	0.06
Other Central American	7	0.03
Cuban	60	0.23
Dominican Republic	26	0.10
Mexican	54	0.21
Puerto Rican	524	2.05
South American:	90	0.35
Argentinean	6	0.02
Chilean	3	0.01
Colombian	47	0.18
Ecuadorian	18	0.07
Peruvian	15	0.06
Venezuelan	1	0.00
Other Hispanic or Latino	239	0.93
Hungarian	346	1.35
Iranian	27	0.11
Irish	6,640	25.89
Israeli	13	0.05
Italian	7,705	30.04
Latvian	17	0.07
Lithuanian	84	0.33
New Zealander	5	0.02
Northern European	4	0.02
Norwegian	133	0.52
Pennsylvania German	15	0.06
Polish	1,397	5.45
Portuguese	89	0.35
Romanian	30	0.12
Russian	412	1.61
Scotch-Irish	434	1.69
Scottish	457	1.78
Serbian	13	0.05
Slovak	109	0.43
Swedish	354	1.38
Swiss	61	0.24
Ukrainian	187	0.73
United States or American	953	3.72
Welsh	115	0.45
West Indian, excl. Hispanic:	159	0.62
British West Indian	36	0.14
Dutch West Indian	13	0.05
Haitian	7	0.03
Jamaican	103	0.40
White:	23,988	93.74
Not Hispanic (22,945)	23,193	90.64
Hispanic (734)	795	3.11
Yugoslavian	10	0.04

East Greenbush

Place Type: Town
County: Rensselaer
Population: 15,560

Ancestry/Race	Number	%
African American/Black:	493	3.17

Notes: 1. Figures in the "Number" column do not add up to the total population due to: a) Ancestry/Race overlap — e.g. persons can report being both White and Irish, b) persons of Hispanic origin can report being any race, c) persons reporting two ancestries are counted in both categories. 2. Numbers in parentheses indicate the number of persons reporting this ancestry/race alone, not in combination with any other ancestry/race. 3. Refer to the Explanation of Data in the front of the book for more detailed information.

Ancestry/Race	Number	%
Not Hispanic (436)	483	3.10
Hispanic (7)	10	0.06
African, sub-Saharan:	93	0.60
African	22	0.14
Ethiopian	23	0.15
Liberian	48	0.31
Am. Ind. or Alaska Nat., not spec.	26	0.17
American Indian tribes, specified:	39	0.25
Cherokee (2)	11	0.07
Creek	3	0.02
Iroquois (2)	5	0.03
Latin American Indians (1)	3	0.02
Ottawa (1)	1	0.01
Sioux (1)	1	0.01
All other tribes (9)	15	0.10
American Indian tribes, not spec.	3	0.02
Arab:	78	0.50
Egyptian	27	0.17
Lebanese	35	0.22
Palestinian	9	0.06
Syrian	7	0.04
Armenian	76	0.49
Asian:	335	2.15
Cambodian (1)	1	0.01
Chinese, ex. Taiwanese (72)	82	0.53
Filipino (30)	37	0.24
Indian (107)	109	0.70
Japanese (10)	16	0.10
Korean (29)	33	0.21
Pakistani (29)	33	0.21
Sri Lankan (2)	2	0.01
Thai (3)	3	0.02
Vietnamese (1)	2	0.01
Other Asian, specified (3)	3	0.02
Other Asian, not specified (12)	14	0.09
Australian	17	0.11
Austrian	15	0.10
Basque	20	0.13
British	51	0.33
Canadian	73	0.47
Croatian	7	0.04
Czech	64	0.41
Czechoslovakian	57	0.37
Danish	19	0.12
Dutch	827	5.30
Eastern European	7	0.04
English	2,133	13.66
European	61	0.39
Finnish	32	0.20
French, except Basque	1,207	7.73
French Canadian	299	1.92
German	3,567	22.85
Greek	117	0.75
Hawaii Native/Pacific Islander:	4	0.03
Polynesian:	1	0.01
Native Hawaiian	1	0.01
Other Pac. Isl., not spec. (3)	3	0.02
Hispanic or Latino:	207	1.33
Cuban	7	0.04
Dominican Republic	4	0.03
Mexican	25	0.16
Puerto Rican	110	0.71
South American:	19	0.12
Argentinean	1	0.01
Chilean	4	0.03
Colombian	3	0.02
Ecuadorian	1	0.01
Peruvian	4	0.03
Venezuelan	3	0.02
Other South American	3	0.02
Other Hispanic or Latino	42	0.27
Hungarian	80	0.51
Iranian	19	0.12
Irish	4,601	29.47
Israeli	6	0.04
Italian	3,536	22.65
Lithuanian	152	0.97
Macedonian	8	0.05
Northern European	32	0.20
Norwegian	192	1.23
Polish	1,154	7.39
Portuguese	22	0.14
Romanian	14	0.09
Russian	238	1.52
Scandinavian	8	0.05
Scotch-Irish	293	1.88
Scottish	285	1.83
Slavic	18	0.12
Slovak	28	0.18
Slovene	9	0.06
Swedish	124	0.79
Swiss	16	0.10
Ukrainian	206	1.32
United States or American	395	2.53
Welsh	114	0.73
West Indian, excl. Hispanic:	74	0.47
Haitian	5	0.03
Jamaican	57	0.37
Trinidadian and Tobagonian	12	0.08
White:	14,729	94.66
Not Hispanic (14,476)	14,567	93.62
Hispanic (152)	162	1.04
Yugoslavian	20	0.13

East Hampton

Place Type: Town
County: Suffolk
Population: 19,719

Ancestry/Race	Number	%
African American/Black:	848	4.30
Not Hispanic (681)	792	4.02
Hispanic (25)	56	0.28
African, sub-Saharan:	57	0.29
African	51	0.26
South African	6	0.03
Am. Ind. or Alaska Nat., not spec.	52	0.26
Albanian	5	0.03
Alsatian	4	0.02
American Indian tribes, specified:	86	0.44
Blackfeet (1)	7	0.04
Cherokee (5)	24	0.12
Chickasaw (2)	2	0.01
Chippewa	1	0.01
Choctaw	2	0.01
Delaware	1	0.01
Iroquois (3)	7	0.04
Latin American Indians (5)	27	0.14
Seminole	1	0.01
Shoshone	1	0.01
All other tribes (6)	13	0.07
American Indian tribes, not spec.	20	0.10
Arab:	69	0.35
Arab/Arabic	7	0.04
Egyptian	7	0.04
Lebanese	32	0.16
Moroccan	11	0.06
Palestinian	2	0.01
Other Arab	10	0.05
Armenian	51	0.26
Asian:	330	1.67
Bangladeshi	3	0.02
Chinese, ex. Taiwanese (47)	68	0.34
Filipino (19)	25	0.13
Indian (29)	39	0.20
Japanese (22)	38	0.19
Korean (25)	41	0.21
Laotian (2)	6	0.03
Sri Lankan	2	0.01
Taiwanese	3	0.02
Thai (2)	3	0.02
Vietnamese (83)	88	0.45
Other Asian, not specified (3)	14	0.07
Australian	6	0.03
Austrian	158	0.80
Belgian	9	0.05
Brazilian	6	0.03
British	54	0.27
Bulgarian	3	0.02
Canadian	45	0.23
Celtic	22	0.11
Croatian	37	0.19
Czech	106	0.54
Czechoslovakian	57	0.29
Danish	72	0.37
Dutch	258	1.31
Eastern European	60	0.30
English	2,911	14.76
Estonian	30	0.15
European	304	1.54
Finnish	32	0.16
French, except Basque	708	3.59
French Canadian	188	0.95
German	3,271	16.59
Greek	170	0.86
Hawaii Native/Pacific Islander:	12	0.06
Micronesian: (2)	3	0.02
Guamanian/Chamorro (2)	3	0.02
Polynesian: (3)	5	0.03
Native Hawaiian (3)	4	0.02
Samoan	1	0.01
Other Pac. Isl., not spec.	4	0.02
Hispanic or Latino:	2,914	14.78
Central American:	310	1.57
Costa Rican	178	0.90
Guatemalan	57	0.29
Honduran	8	0.04
Nicaraguan	5	0.03
Panamanian	5	0.03
Salvadoran	50	0.25
Other Central American	7	0.04
Cuban	30	0.15
Dominican Republic	119	0.60
Mexican	280	1.42
Puerto Rican	175	0.89
South American:	1,757	8.91
Argentinean	27	0.14
Bolivian	1	0.01
Chilean	56	0.28
Colombian	850	4.31
Ecuadorian	752	3.81
Peruvian	22	0.11
Uruguayan	14	0.07
Venezuelan	30	0.15
Other South American	5	0.03
Other Hispanic or Latino	243	1.23
Hungarian	131	0.66
Iranian	8	0.04
Irish	4,374	22.18
Israeli	5	0.03
Italian	2,417	12.26
Latvian	28	0.14
Lithuanian	189	0.96
Macedonian	7	0.04
Northern European	12	0.06
Norwegian	312	1.58
Polish	1,098	5.57
Portuguese	74	0.38
Romanian	53	0.27
Russian	723	3.67
Scandinavian	77	0.39
Scotch-Irish	397	2.01
Scottish	385	1.95
Slovak	12	0.06
Slovene	3	0.02
Swedish	270	1.37
Swiss	39	0.20
Turkish	20	0.10
Ukrainian	55	0.28
United States or American	1,070	5.43
Welsh	124	0.63
West Indian, excl. Hispanic:	139	0.70
British West Indian	12	0.06
Jamaican	22	0.11
West Indian	105	0.53
White:	17,682	89.67
Not Hispanic (15,447)	15,700	79.62
Hispanic (1,875)	1,982	10.05
Yugoslavian	19	0.10

Notes: 1. Figures in the "Number" column do not add up to the total population due to: a) Ancestry/Race overlap — e.g. persons can report being both White and Irish, b) persons of Hispanic origin can report being any race, c) persons reporting two ancestries are counted in both categories. 2. Numbers in parentheses indicate the number of persons reporting this ancestry/race alone, not in combination with any other ancestry/race. 3. Refer to the Explanation of Data in the front of the book for more detailed information.

East Islip

Place Type: Census Designated Place
County: Suffolk
Population: 14,078

Ancestry/Race	Number	%
African American/Black:	101	0.72
Not Hispanic (71)	88	0.63
Hispanic (9)	13	0.09
Am. Ind. or Alaska Nat., not spec.	11	0.08
Albanian	33	0.23
American Indian tribes, specified:	18	0.13
Cherokee	5	0.04
Iroquois (2)	5	0.04
Latin American Indians	4	0.03
Lumbee (1)	1	0.01
Sioux (2)	2	0.01
All other tribes	1	0.01
Arab:	83	0.59
Egyptian	33	0.23
Iraqi	22	0.16
Lebanese	7	0.05
Syrian	21	0.15
Armenian	18	0.13
Asian:	234	1.66
Chinese, ex. Taiwanese (57)	65	0.46
Filipino (17)	20	0.14
Indian (62)	67	0.48
Japanese (1)	2	0.01
Korean (34)	34	0.24
Pakistani (11)	14	0.10
Taiwanese (3)	3	0.02
Thai (3)	11	0.08
Vietnamese (2)	6	0.04
Other Asian, not specified (5)	12	0.09
Austrian	92	0.65
Belgian	17	0.12
British	10	0.07
Canadian	12	0.09
Croatian	7	0.05
Czech	191	1.36
Czechoslovakian	60	0.43
Danish	45	0.32
Dutch	182	1.29
Eastern European	12	0.09
English	863	6.13
European	81	0.58
Finnish	12	0.09
French, except Basque	269	1.91
French Canadian	16	0.11
German	3,027	21.49
Greek	108	0.77
Guyanese	11	0.08
Hawaii Native/Pacific Islander:	3	0.02
Polynesian: (1)	1	0.01
Samoan (1)	1	0.01
Other Pac. Isl., not spec. (2)	2	0.01
Hispanic or Latino:	547	3.89
Central American:	31	0.22
Costa Rican	1	0.01
Guatemalan	2	0.01
Honduran	4	0.03
Panamanian	1	0.01
Salvadoran	23	0.16
Cuban	15	0.11
Dominican Republic	21	0.15
Mexican	22	0.16
Puerto Rican	277	1.97
South American:	66	0.47
Argentinean	2	0.01
Bolivian	1	0.01
Chilean	1	0.01
Colombian	47	0.33
Ecuadorian	4	0.03
Paraguayan	1	0.01
Peruvian	6	0.04
Uruguayan	2	0.01
Other South American	2	0.01
Other Hispanic or Latino	115	0.82
Hungarian	128	0.91
Icelander	6	0.04
Irish	4,404	31.27
Italian	4,942	35.09
Latvian	12	0.09
Lithuanian	74	0.53
Maltese	14	0.10
Norwegian	230	1.63
Polish	854	6.06
Portuguese	54	0.38
Romanian	7	0.05
Russian	381	2.71
Scandinavian	4	0.03
Scotch-Irish	104	0.74
Scottish	147	1.04
Slovak	6	0.04
Swedish	208	1.48
Swiss	33	0.23
Ukrainian	65	0.46
United States or American	502	3.56
Welsh	41	0.29
West Indian, excl. Hispanic:	52	0.37
Barbadian	10	0.07
Haitian	25	0.18
Jamaican	7	0.05
West Indian	10	0.07
White:	13,640	96.89
Not Hispanic (13,142)	13,218	93.89
Hispanic (401)	422	3.00
Yugoslavian	20	0.14

East Massapequa

Place Type: Census Designated Place
County: Nassau
Population: 19,565

Ancestry/Race	Number	%
African American/Black:	2,604	13.31
Not Hispanic (2,328)	2,490	12.73
Hispanic (87)	114	0.58
African, sub-Saharan:	12	0.06
African	12	0.06
Am. Ind. or Alaska Nat., not spec.	55	0.28
Albanian	8	0.04
American Indian tribes, specified:	32	0.16
Blackfeet	1	0.01
Cherokee (1)	10	0.05
Chippewa	3	0.02
Choctaw	1	0.01
Iroquois (5)	5	0.03
Latin American Indians (6)	8	0.04
All other tribes (3)	4	0.02
American Indian tribes, not spec.	2	0.01
Arab:	109	0.56
Egyptian	61	0.31
Lebanese	24	0.12
Palestinian	18	0.09
Other Arab	6	0.03
Armenian	12	0.06
Asian:	540	2.76
Cambodian (5)	5	0.03
Chinese, ex. Taiwanese (154)	179	0.91
Filipino (62)	82	0.42
Indian (135)	159	0.81
Japanese (5)	13	0.07
Korean (29)	39	0.20
Laotian (4)	4	0.02
Pakistani (15)	17	0.09
Taiwanese (1)	2	0.01
Vietnamese (15)	20	0.10
Other Asian, not specified (5)	20	0.10
Austrian	131	0.67
Belgian	12	0.06
Brazilian	6	0.03
British	45	0.23
Canadian	63	0.32
Czech	83	0.42
Czechoslovakian	57	0.29
Danish	16	0.08
Dutch	113	0.58
Eastern European	18	0.09
English	719	3.67
European	6	0.03
Finnish	17	0.09
French, except Basque	365	1.87
French Canadian	136	0.70
German	3,183	16.27
Greek	250	1.28
Guyanese	49	0.25
Hawaii Native/Pacific Islander:	11	0.06
Micronesian: (4)	4	0.02
Guamanian/Chamorro (4)	4	0.02
Polynesian: (1)	1	0.01
Samoan (1)	1	0.01
Other Pac. Isl., not spec.	6	0.03
Hispanic or Latino:	1,466	7.49
Central American:	243	1.24
Costa Rican	4	0.02
Guatemalan	17	0.09
Honduran	28	0.14
Nicaraguan	6	0.03
Panamanian	25	0.13
Salvadoran	161	0.82
Other Central American	2	0.01
Cuban	62	0.32
Dominican Republic	54	0.28
Mexican	49	0.25
Puerto Rican	453	2.32
South American:	257	1.31
Argentinean	13	0.07
Chilean	9	0.05
Colombian	118	0.60
Ecuadorian	57	0.29
Paraguayan	7	0.04
Peruvian	32	0.16
Uruguayan	1	0.01
Venezuelan	5	0.03
Other South American	15	0.08
Other Hispanic or Latino	348	1.78
Hungarian	121	0.62
Iranian	30	0.15
Irish	4,587	23.44
Israeli	4	0.02
Italian	5,785	29.57
Latvian	15	0.08
Lithuanian	67	0.34
Maltese	12	0.06
Norwegian	223	1.14
Polish	977	4.99
Portuguese	7	0.04
Romanian	19	0.10
Russian	607	3.10
Scandinavian	5	0.03
Scotch-Irish	125	0.64
Scottish	129	0.66
Slovak	50	0.26
Swedish	116	0.59
Swiss	31	0.16
Turkish	99	0.51
Ukrainian	108	0.55
United States or American	551	2.82
Welsh	62	0.32
West Indian, excl. Hispanic:	1,119	5.72
Bahamian	15	0.08
Barbadian	19	0.10
Bermudan	8	0.04
British West Indian	49	0.25
Haitian	497	2.54
Jamaican	403	2.06
Trinidadian and Tobagonian	38	0.19
West Indian	90	0.46
White:	16,043	82.00
Not Hispanic (15,013)	15,158	77.48
Hispanic (799)	885	4.52
Yugoslavian	41	0.21

Notes: 1. Figures in the "Number" column do not add up to the total population due to: a) Ancestry/Race overlap — e.g. persons can report being both White and Irish, b) persons of Hispanic origin can report being any race, c) persons reporting two ancestries are counted in both categories. 2. Numbers in parentheses indicate the number of persons reporting this ancestry/race alone, not in combination with any other ancestry/race. 3. Refer to the Explanation of Data in the front of the book for more detailed information.

East Meadow

Place Type: Census Designated Place
County: Nassau
Population: 37,461

Ancestry/Race	Number	%
African American/Black:	1,756	4.69
Not Hispanic (1,513)	1,619	4.32
Hispanic (104)	137	0.37
African, sub-Saharan:	140	0.37
African	79	0.21
Nigerian	61	0.16
Am. Ind. or Alaska Nat., not spec.	43	0.11
American Indian tribes, specified:	61	0.16
Apache	1	0.00
Blackfeet	1	0.00
Cherokee (7)	27	0.07
Chippewa	1	0.00
Choctaw	2	0.01
Latin American Indians (8)	8	0.02
Menominee (2)	2	0.01
Navajo (3)	3	0.01
Pueblo (1)	1	0.00
Seminole	1	0.00
Sioux	3	0.01
All other tribes (8)	11	0.03
American Indian tribes, not spec.	13	0.03
Arab:	290	0.77
Arab/Arabic	59	0.16
Egyptian	51	0.14
Iraqi	8	0.02
Jordanian	30	0.08
Lebanese	49	0.13
Moroccan	51	0.14
Syrian	42	0.11
Armenian	159	0.42
Asian:	2,812	7.51
Bangladeshi	4	0.01
Cambodian (2)	4	0.01
Chinese, ex. Taiwanese (431)	493	1.32
Filipino (438)	492	1.31
Indian (1,099)	1,165	3.11
Indonesian	1	0.00
Japanese (17)	23	0.06
Korean (128)	135	0.36
Pakistani (238)	302	0.81
Sri Lankan (5)	9	0.02
Taiwanese (3)	5	0.01
Thai (3)	6	0.02
Vietnamese (40)	53	0.14
Other Asian, specified (10)	12	0.03
Other Asian, not specified (41)	108	0.29
Australian	8	0.02
Austrian	202	0.54
Brazilian	37	0.10
British	41	0.11
Bulgarian	8	0.02
Canadian	35	0.09
Croatian	117	0.31
Czech	125	0.33
Czechoslovakian	53	0.14
Danish	156	0.42
Dutch	196	0.52
Eastern European	283	0.75
English	861	2.30
Estonian	12	0.03
European	146	0.39
Finnish	36	0.10
French, except Basque	475	1.27
French Canadian	98	0.26
German	4,433	11.82
Greek	564	1.50
Guyanese	140	0.37
Hawaii Native/Pacific Islander:	36	0.10
Micronesian: (10)	11	0.03
Guamanian/Chamorro (10)	11	0.03
Polynesian: (3)	11	0.03
Native Hawaiian (3)	7	0.02
Samoan	4	0.01
Other Pac. Isl., specified	2	0.01
Other Pac. Isl., not spec. (1)	12	0.03
Hispanic or Latino:	2,626	7.01
Central American:	327	0.87
Costa Rican	19	0.05
Guatemalan	20	0.05
Honduran	31	0.08
Nicaraguan	3	0.01
Panamanian	12	0.03
Salvadoran	227	0.61
Other Central American	15	0.04
Cuban	122	0.33
Dominican Republic	102	0.27
Mexican	91	0.24
Puerto Rican	717	1.91
South American:	511	1.36
Argentinean	46	0.12
Bolivian	2	0.01
Chilean	24	0.06
Colombian	230	0.61
Ecuadorian	124	0.33
Paraguayan	8	0.02
Peruvian	41	0.11
Uruguayan	8	0.02
Venezuelan	11	0.03
Other South American	17	0.05
Other Hispanic or Latino	756	2.02
Hungarian	465	1.24
Iranian	47	0.13
Irish	6,539	17.44
Israeli	50	0.13
Italian	10,662	28.43
Latvian	47	0.13
Lithuanian	94	0.25
Maltese	40	0.11
Northern European	8	0.02
Norwegian	237	0.63
Pennsylvania German	9	0.02
Polish	3,288	8.77
Portuguese	447	1.19
Romanian	301	0.80
Russian	2,155	5.75
Scandinavian	8	0.02
Scotch-Irish	176	0.47
Scottish	170	0.45
Serbian	10	0.03
Slavic	9	0.02
Swedish	361	0.96
Swiss	132	0.35
Turkish	127	0.34
Ukrainian	217	0.58
United States or American	1,886	5.03
Welsh	49	0.13
West Indian, excl. Hispanic:	207	0.55
Barbadian	27	0.07
Belizean	2	0.01
Haitian	100	0.27
Jamaican	60	0.16
Trinidadian and Tobagonian	8	0.02
West Indian	10	0.03
White:	32,376	86.43
Not Hispanic (30,355)	30,630	81.77
Hispanic (1,594)	1,746	4.66
Yugoslavian	39	0.10

East Northport

Place Type: Census Designated Place
County: Suffolk
Population: 20,845

Ancestry/Race	Number	%
African American/Black:	241	1.16
Not Hispanic (181)	225	1.08
Hispanic (8)	16	0.08
African, sub-Saharan:	12	0.06
African	12	0.06
Am. Ind. or Alaska Nat., not spec.	19	0.09
Albanian	19	0.09
American Indian tribes, specified:	46	0.22
Cherokee (1)	13	0.06
Chippewa (1)	1	0.00
Choctaw (4)	6	0.03
Iroquois	3	0.01
Latin American Indians (5)	15	0.07
Lumbee (1)	1	0.00
Sioux	4	0.02
All other tribes (3)	3	0.01
American Indian tribes, not spec.	8	0.04
Arab:	67	0.32
Arab/Arabic	14	0.07
Egyptian	17	0.08
Lebanese	6	0.03
Syrian	8	0.04
Other Arab	22	0.11
Armenian	90	0.43
Asian:	613	2.94
Chinese, ex. Taiwanese (113)	156	0.75
Filipino (33)	55	0.26
Indian (64)	94	0.45
Japanese (21)	34	0.16
Korean (155)	161	0.77
Laotian (4)	4	0.02
Malaysian	2	0.01
Pakistani (34)	34	0.16
Taiwanese (6)	6	0.03
Thai (10)	10	0.05
Vietnamese (11)	15	0.07
Other Asian, specified (10)	10	0.05
Other Asian, not specified (8)	32	0.15
Australian	15	0.07
Austrian	178	0.86
Belgian	14	0.07
British	69	0.33
Canadian	27	0.13
Croatian	122	0.59
Cypriot	22	0.11
Czech	122	0.59
Czechoslovakian	67	0.32
Danish	73	0.35
Dutch	269	1.29
Eastern European	46	0.22
English	1,584	7.61
European	26	0.12
Finnish	46	0.22
French, except Basque	435	2.09
French Canadian	144	0.69
German	4,398	21.13
Greek	408	1.96
Hawaii Native/Pacific Islander:	14	0.07
Micronesian:	2	0.01
Guamanian/Chamorro	2	0.01
Polynesian: (1)	2	0.01
Native Hawaiian (1)	2	0.01
Other Pac. Isl., not spec. (5)	10	0.05
Hispanic or Latino:	814	3.91
Central American:	147	0.71
Costa Rican	3	0.01
Guatemalan	6	0.03
Honduran	41	0.20
Nicaraguan	3	0.01
Panamanian	4	0.02
Salvadoran	81	0.39
Other Central American	9	0.04
Cuban	40	0.19
Dominican Republic	31	0.15
Mexican	50	0.24
Puerto Rican	288	1.38
South American:	128	0.61
Argentinean	16	0.08
Bolivian	12	0.06
Chilean	5	0.02
Colombian	54	0.26
Ecuadorian	16	0.08
Paraguayan	2	0.01
Peruvian	13	0.06
Uruguayan	3	0.01
Venezuelan	2	0.01
Other South American	5	0.02
Other Hispanic or Latino	130	0.62

Notes: 1. Figures in the "Number" column do not add up to the total population due to: a) Ancestry/Race overlap — e.g. persons can report being both White and Irish, b) persons of Hispanic origin can report being any race, c) persons reporting two ancestries are counted in both categories. 2. Numbers in parentheses indicate the number of persons reporting this ancestry/race alone, not in combination with any other ancestry/race. 3. Refer to the Explanation of Data in the front of the book for more detailed information.

Hungarian	202	0.97
Iranian	34	0.16
Irish	6,098	29.30
Israeli	20	0.10
Italian	5,759	27.67
Latvian	19	0.09
Lithuanian	64	0.31
Macedonian	4	0.02
Maltese	20	0.10
New Zealander	7	0.03
Northern European	10	0.05
Norwegian	294	1.41
Pennsylvania German	5	0.02
Polish	1,296	6.23
Portuguese	29	0.14
Romanian	52	0.25
Russian	737	3.54
Scandinavian	14	0.07
Scotch-Irish	269	1.29
Scottish	169	0.81
Slavic	6	0.03
Slovak	28	0.13
Swedish	384	1.85
Swiss	67	0.32
Turkish	41	0.20
Ukrainian	177	0.85
United States or American	732	3.52
Welsh	37	0.18
West Indian, excl. Hispanic:	22	0.11
Trinidadian and Tobagonian	7	0.03
West Indian	15	0.07
White:	19,962	95.76
Not Hispanic (19,134)	19,310	92.64
Hispanic (611)	652	3.13
Yugoslavian	13	0.06

East Patchogue

Place Type: Census Designated Place
County: Suffolk
Population: 20,824

Ancestry/Race	Number	%
Afghan	24	0.12
African American/Black:	793	3.81
Not Hispanic (625)	729	3.50
Hispanic (40)	64	0.31
African, sub-Saharan:	67	0.32
African	12	0.06
Liberian	6	0.03
Nigerian	39	0.19
South African	10	0.05
Am. Ind. or Alaska Nat., not spec.	41	0.20
Albanian	22	0.11
Alsatian	8	0.04
American Indian tribes, specified:	53	0.25
Apache (1)	1	0.00
Blackfeet	2	0.01
Cherokee	11	0.05
Cheyenne	1	0.00
Iroquois (5)	5	0.02
Latin American Indians (1)	11	0.05
Navajo	1	0.00
All other tribes (9)	21	0.10
American Indian tribes, not spec.	9	0.04
Arab:	78	0.37
Egyptian	66	0.32
Lebanese	12	0.06
Armenian	11	0.05
Asian:	519	2.49
Chinese, ex. Taiwanese (97)	106	0.51
Filipino (24)	45	0.22
Indian (160)	192	0.92
Japanese (9)	20	0.10
Korean (26)	32	0.15
Pakistani (43)	51	0.24
Sri Lankan (3)	3	0.01
Taiwanese (5)	8	0.04
Thai (7)	11	0.05
Vietnamese (11)	12	0.06
Other Asian, specified	7	0.03
Other Asian, not specified (7)	32	0.15
Austrian	206	0.99
Belgian	23	0.11
Brazilian	8	0.04
British	52	0.25
Canadian	57	0.27
Czech	148	0.71
Czechoslovakian	36	0.17
Danish	71	0.34
Dutch	146	0.70
Eastern European	7	0.03
English	1,520	7.28
Estonian	16	0.08
European	56	0.27
Finnish	5	0.02
French, except Basque	519	2.49
French Canadian	99	0.47
German	4,117	19.73
Greek	198	0.95
Guyanese	11	0.05
Hawaii Native/Pacific Islander:	13	0.06
Polynesian: (2)	4	0.02
Native Hawaiian	2	0.01
Samoan (2)	2	0.01
Other Pac. Isl., specified	1	0.00
Other Pac. Isl., not spec. (1)	8	0.04
Hispanic or Latino:	1,895	9.10
Central American:	219	1.05
Costa Rican	2	0.01
Guatemalan	38	0.18
Honduran	3	0.01
Nicaraguan	1	0.00
Salvadoran	165	0.79
Other Central American	10	0.05
Cuban	29	0.14
Dominican Republic	36	0.17
Mexican	65	0.31
Puerto Rican	888	4.26
South American:	323	1.55
Argentinean	20	0.10
Bolivian	5	0.02
Chilean	6	0.03
Colombian	57	0.27
Ecuadorian	194	0.93
Peruvian	19	0.09
Venezuelan	14	0.07
Other South American	8	0.04
Other Hispanic or Latino	335	1.61
Hungarian	166	0.80
Iranian	43	0.21
Irish	4,968	23.81
Italian	6,867	32.91
Latvian	11	0.05
Lithuanian	74	0.35
Maltese	21	0.10
Norwegian	208	1.00
Polish	1,084	5.20
Portuguese	76	0.36
Romanian	25	0.12
Russian	384	1.84
Scandinavian	11	0.05
Scotch-Irish	133	0.64
Scottish	230	1.10
Slovak	5	0.02
Swedish	214	1.03
Swiss	53	0.25
Turkish	51	0.24
Ukrainian	99	0.47
United States or American	542	2.60
Welsh	84	0.40
West Indian, excl. Hispanic:	166	0.80
Bahamian	17	0.08
British West Indian	9	0.04
Haitian	36	0.17
Jamaican	79	0.38
Trinidadian and Tobagonian	19	0.09
West Indian	6	0.03
White:	18,962	91.06
Not Hispanic (17,560)	17,767	85.32
Hispanic (1,073)	1,195	5.74
Yugoslavian	7	0.03

East Rockaway

Place Type: Village
County: Nassau
Population: 10,414

Ancestry/Race	Number	%
African American/Black:	78	0.75
Not Hispanic (56)	64	0.61
Hispanic (8)	14	0.13
African, sub-Saharan:	20	0.19
African	20	0.19
Am. Ind. or Alaska Nat., not spec.	10	0.10
Albanian	31	0.30
American Indian tribes, specified:	6	0.06
Blackfeet	1	0.01
Cherokee	1	0.01
Iroquois (1)	1	0.01
Latin American Indians (1)	1	0.01
Seminole	2	0.02
Arab:	18	0.17
Egyptian	9	0.09
Lebanese	9	0.09
Armenian	9	0.09
Asian:	217	2.08
Chinese, ex. Taiwanese (58)	69	0.66
Filipino (20)	28	0.27
Indian (56)	61	0.59
Japanese (3)	7	0.07
Korean (27)	27	0.26
Pakistani (9)	11	0.11
Vietnamese (2)	4	0.04
Other Asian, specified	5	0.05
Other Asian, not specified	5	0.05
Austrian	68	0.65
Brazilian	41	0.39
British	49	0.47
Canadian	19	0.18
Croatian	8	0.08
Cypriot	22	0.21
Czech	59	0.56
Czechoslovakian	9	0.09
Danish	37	0.35
Dutch	76	0.73
Eastern European	74	0.71
English	369	3.53
European	93	0.89
Finnish	51	0.49
French, except Basque	77	0.74
French Canadian	38	0.36
German	1,321	12.63
Greek	113	1.08
Guyanese	13	0.12
Hawaii Native/Pacific Islander:	6	0.06
Polynesian: (1)	1	0.01
Native Hawaiian (1)	1	0.01
Other Pac. Isl., specified	5	0.05
Hispanic or Latino:	603	5.79
Central American:	93	0.89
Guatemalan	16	0.15
Honduran	15	0.14
Nicaraguan	7	0.07
Salvadoran	52	0.50
Other Central American	3	0.03
Cuban	40	0.38
Dominican Republic	27	0.26
Mexican	7	0.07
Puerto Rican	165	1.58
South American:	148	1.42
Argentinean	12	0.12
Bolivian	20	0.19
Chilean	7	0.07
Colombian	45	0.43
Ecuadorian	12	0.12
Paraguayan	1	0.01
Peruvian	31	0.30
Uruguayan	2	0.02

Notes: 1. Figures in the "Number" column do not add up to the total population due to: a) Ancestry/Race overlap — e.g. persons can report being both White and Irish, b) persons of Hispanic origin can report being any race, c) persons reporting two ancestries are counted in both categories. 2. Numbers in parentheses indicate the number of persons reporting this ancestry/race alone, not in combination with any other ancestry/race. 3. Refer to the Explanation of Data in the front of the book for more detailed information.

Ancestry/Race	Number	%
Venezuelan	10	0.10
Other South American	8	0.08
Other Hispanic or Latino	123	1.18
Hungarian	190	1.82
Iranian	39	0.37
Irish	2,678	25.59
Israeli	15	0.14
Italian	2,872	27.45
Lithuanian	30	0.29
Northern European	33	0.32
Norwegian	103	0.98
Pennsylvania German	8	0.08
Polish	616	5.89
Portuguese	25	0.24
Romanian	26	0.25
Russian	649	6.20
Scotch-Irish	51	0.49
Scottish	98	0.94
Serbian	4	0.04
Slavic	8	0.08
Slovak	13	0.12
Swedish	143	1.37
Swiss	11	0.11
Turkish	88	0.84
Ukrainian	121	1.16
United States or American	539	5.15
Welsh	15	0.14
West Indian, excl. Hispanic:	79	0.76
Jamaican	27	0.26
Trinidadian and Tobagonian	52	0.50
White:	10,050	96.50
Not Hispanic (9,518)	9,568	91.88
Hispanic (442)	482	4.63

Eastchester

Place Type: Town
County: Westchester
Population: 31,318

Ancestry/Race	Number	%
African American/Black:	958	3.06
Not Hispanic (825)	879	2.81
Hispanic (53)	79	0.25
African, sub-Saharan:	70	0.22
African	43	0.14
Ethiopian	27	0.09
Am. Ind. or Alaska Nat., not spec.	27	0.09
Albanian	68	0.22
American Indian tribes, specified:	36	0.11
Blackfeet	2	0.01
Cherokee	12	0.04
Chippewa	3	0.01
Choctaw	1	0.00
Iroquois (1)	9	0.03
Latin American Indians (3)	7	0.02
All other tribes (1)	2	0.01
American Indian tribes, not spec.	7	0.02
Arab:	144	0.46
Arab/Arabic	9	0.03
Egyptian	19	0.06
Lebanese	75	0.24
Palestinian	22	0.07
Syrian	6	0.02
Other Arab	13	0.04
Armenian	85	0.27
Asian:	2,322	7.41
Bangladeshi (4)	4	0.01
Cambodian (1)	1	0.00
Chinese, ex. Taiwanese (241)	285	0.91
Filipino (95)	129	0.41
Indian (281)	303	0.97
Indonesian (1)	2	0.01
Japanese (1,058)	1,110	3.54
Korean (338)	364	1.16
Malaysian	3	0.01
Pakistani (22)	23	0.07
Sri Lankan (4)	4	0.01
Taiwanese (17)	18	0.06
Thai (35)	42	0.13
Vietnamese (6)	7	0.02
Other Asian, specified (9)	10	0.03
Other Asian, not specified (6)	17	0.05
Australian	17	0.05
Austrian	269	0.86
Basque	10	0.03
Belgian	29	0.09
Brazilian	15	0.05
British	161	0.51
Canadian	53	0.17
Carpatho Rusyn	8	0.03
Celtic	6	0.02
Croatian	47	0.15
Czech	178	0.57
Czechoslovakian	78	0.25
Danish	104	0.33
Dutch	300	0.96
Eastern European	143	0.46
English	1,803	5.76
Estonian	16	0.05
European	378	1.21
Finnish	38	0.12
French, except Basque	493	1.57
French Canadian	117	0.37
German	2,865	9.15
Greek	231	0.74
Guyanese	10	0.03
Hawaii Native/Pacific Islander:	18	0.06
Micronesian: (3)	4	0.01
Guamanian/Chamorro	1	0.00
Other Micronesian (3)	3	0.01
Polynesian: (2)	6	0.02
Native Hawaiian (1)	5	0.02
Samoan (1)	1	0.00
Other Pac. Isl., not spec. (4)	8	0.03
Hispanic or Latino:	1,402	4.48
Central American:	76	0.24
Costa Rican	4	0.01
Guatemalan	31	0.10
Honduran	7	0.02
Panamanian	9	0.03
Salvadoran	24	0.08
Other Central American	1	0.00
Cuban	82	0.26
Dominican Republic	77	0.25
Mexican	136	0.43
Puerto Rican	495	1.58
South American:	210	0.67
Argentinean	34	0.11
Bolivian	3	0.01
Chilean	8	0.03
Colombian	31	0.10
Ecuadorian	42	0.13
Paraguayan	4	0.01
Peruvian	45	0.14
Uruguayan	4	0.01
Venezuelan	22	0.07
Other South American	17	0.05
Other Hispanic or Latino	326	1.04
Hungarian	422	1.35
Iranian	32	0.10
Irish	6,189	19.76
Israeli	8	0.03
Italian	10,844	34.63
Latvian	7	0.02
Lithuanian	60	0.19
Maltese	8	0.03
New Zealander	6	0.02
Northern European	30	0.10
Norwegian	138	0.44
Polish	1,348	4.30
Portuguese	61	0.19
Romanian	100	0.32
Russian	1,302	4.16
Scandinavian	29	0.09
Scotch-Irish	301	0.96
Scottish	458	1.46
Slavic	6	0.02
Slovak	170	0.54
Slovene	6	0.02
Swedish	317	1.01
Swiss	131	0.42
Turkish	49	0.16
Ukrainian	116	0.37
United States or American	969	3.09
Welsh	141	0.45
West Indian, excl. Hispanic:	173	0.55
Barbadian	38	0.12
British West Indian	32	0.10
Haitian	11	0.04
Jamaican	39	0.12
Trinidadian and Tobagonian	24	0.08
West Indian	29	0.09
White:	27,781	88.71
Not Hispanic (26,501)	26,855	85.75
Hispanic (854)	926	2.96
Yugoslavian	10	0.03

Elma

Place Type: Town
County: Erie
Population: 11,304

Ancestry/Race	Number	%
African American/Black:	22	0.19
Not Hispanic (4)	16	0.14
Hispanic (2)	6	0.05
Alaska Native tribes, specified:	1	0.01
Aleut	1	0.01
Am. Ind. or Alaska Nat., not spec.	13	0.12
American Indian tribes, specified:	15	0.13
Cherokee	2	0.02
Iroquois (3)	10	0.09
Latin American Indians	1	0.01
All other tribes (2)	2	0.02
American Indian tribes, not spec.	2	0.02
Arab:	50	0.44
Lebanese	50	0.44
Asian:	39	0.35
Chinese, ex. Taiwanese (1)	2	0.02
Filipino (2)	2	0.02
Indian (3)	5	0.04
Japanese (8)	10	0.09
Korean (10)	12	0.11
Taiwanese (6)	6	0.05
Other Asian, not specified	2	0.02
Austrian	80	0.71
Belgian	23	0.20
British	42	0.37
Bulgarian	10	0.09
Canadian	23	0.20
Croatian	41	0.36
Czech	40	0.35
Danish	61	0.54
Dutch	147	1.30
Eastern European	22	0.19
English	1,037	9.17
European	37	0.33
French, except Basque	295	2.61
French Canadian	141	1.25
German	3,892	34.43
Greek	44	0.39
Hawaii Native/Pacific Islander:	1	0.01
Polynesian: (1)	1	0.01
Samoan (1)	1	0.01
Hispanic or Latino:	68	0.60
Central American:	1	0.01
Salvadoran	1	0.01
Cuban	10	0.09
Mexican	22	0.19
Puerto Rican	10	0.09
South American:	10	0.09
Colombian	5	0.04
Ecuadorian	1	0.01
Peruvian	4	0.04
Other Hispanic or Latino	15	0.13
Hungarian	234	2.07
Irish	1,602	14.17
Italian	1,624	14.37

Notes: 1. Figures in the "Number" column do not add up to the total population due to: a) Ancestry/Race overlap — e.g. persons can report being both White and Irish, b) persons of Hispanic origin can report being any race, c) persons reporting two ancestries are counted in both categories. 2. Numbers in parentheses indicate the number of persons reporting this ancestry/race alone, not in combination with any other ancestry/race. 3. Refer to the Explanation of Data in the front of the book for more detailed information.

Latvian	32	0.28
Lithuanian	8	0.07
Macedonian	27	0.24
Maltese	8	0.07
Norwegian	30	0.27
Polish	3,284	29.05
Romanian	9	0.08
Russian	123	1.09
Scotch-Irish	116	1.03
Scottish	285	2.52
Serbian	11	0.10
Slavic	12	0.11
Slovak	67	0.59
Swedish	112	0.99
Swiss	34	0.30
Ukrainian	132	1.17
United States or American	267	2.36
Welsh	99	0.88
White:	11,253	99.55
Not Hispanic (11,149)	11,196	99.04
Hispanic (52)	57	0.50
Yugoslavian	66	0.58

Elmira

Place Type: City
County: Chemung
Population: 30,940

Ancestry/Race	Number	%
African American/Black:	4,609	14.90
Not Hispanic (3,935)	4,461	14.42
Hispanic (104)	148	0.48
African, sub-Saharan:	48	0.16
African	41	0.13
Zimbabwean	7	0.02
Alaska Native tribes, not specified	1	0.00
Am. Ind. or Alaska Nat., not spec.	100	0.32
American Indian tribes, specified:	156	0.50
Apache	1	0.00
Blackfeet (1)	6	0.02
Cherokee (21)	57	0.18
Cheyenne	5	0.02
Chippewa	1	0.00
Choctaw	3	0.01
Cree (1)	1	0.00
Crow	5	0.02
Delaware	3	0.01
Iroquois (15)	39	0.13
Latin American Indians (1)	3	0.01
Navajo (2)	2	0.01
Pueblo (1)	1	0.00
Puget Sound Salish	1	0.00
Seminole	1	0.00
Sioux (3)	7	0.02
All other tribes (14)	20	0.06
American Indian tribes, not spec.	18	0.06
Arab:	187	0.60
Lebanese	163	0.53
Syrian	24	0.08
Asian:	223	0.72
Chinese, ex. Taiwanese (31)	37	0.12
Filipino (15)	26	0.08
Indian (18)	30	0.10
Japanese (31)	47	0.15
Korean (20)	27	0.09
Laotian (16)	18	0.06
Malaysian (1)	1	0.00
Pakistani	1	0.00
Taiwanese (2)	2	0.01
Thai (1)	1	0.00
Vietnamese (2)	6	0.02
Other Asian, not specified (13)	27	0.09
Austrian	67	0.22
Belgian	9	0.03
British	89	0.29
Canadian	32	0.10
Croatian	13	0.04
Czech	47	0.15
Czechoslovakian	58	0.19
Danish	49	0.16
Dutch	777	2.51
English	2,955	9.55
European	121	0.39
Finnish	41	0.13
French, except Basque	813	2.63
French Canadian	250	0.81
German	5,105	16.50
Greek	96	0.31
Hawaii Native/Pacific Islander:	18	0.06
Micronesian: (2)	2	0.01
Guamanian/Chamorro (2)	2	0.01
Polynesian: (6)	11	0.04
Native Hawaiian (3)	5	0.02
Samoan (3)	6	0.02
Other Pac. Isl., not spec. (1)	5	0.02
Hispanic or Latino:	970	3.14
Central American:	17	0.05
Costa Rican	2	0.01
Guatemalan	4	0.01
Honduran	5	0.02
Nicaraguan	3	0.01
Panamanian	2	0.01
Salvadoran	1	0.00
Cuban	20	0.06
Dominican Republic	48	0.16
Mexican	98	0.32
Puerto Rican	550	1.78
South American:	22	0.07
Colombian	13	0.04
Ecuadorian	6	0.02
Peruvian	3	0.01
Other Hispanic or Latino	215	0.69
Hungarian	56	0.18
Irish	5,387	17.41
Israeli	7	0.02
Italian	3,412	11.03
Latvian	5	0.02
Lithuanian	50	0.16
Northern European	9	0.03
Norwegian	83	0.27
Pennsylvania German	203	0.66
Polish	2,068	6.68
Portuguese	75	0.24
Russian	165	0.53
Scandinavian	16	0.05
Scotch-Irish	308	1.00
Scottish	477	1.54
Slavic	20	0.06
Slovak	75	0.24
Slovene	4	0.01
Swedish	229	0.74
Swiss	39	0.13
Ukrainian	490	1.58
United States or American	1,424	4.60
Welsh	382	1.23
West Indian, excl. Hispanic:	72	0.23
Bahamian	7	0.02
British West Indian	22	0.07
Haitian	8	0.03
Jamaican	23	0.07
Trinidadian and Tobagonian	6	0.02
U.S. Virgin Islander	6	0.02
White:	26,109	84.39
Not Hispanic (25,002)	25,642	82.88
Hispanic (377)	467	1.51
Yugoslavian	18	0.06

Elmont

Place Type: Census Designated Place
County: Nassau
Population: 32,657

Ancestry/Race	Number	%
Afghan	26	0.08
African American/Black:	12,044	36.88
Not Hispanic (10,902)	11,533	35.32
Hispanic (427)	511	1.56
African, sub-Saharan:	868	2.66
African	390	1.19
Cape Verdean	15	0.05
Ghanian	61	0.19
Nigerian	383	1.17
South African	11	0.03
Other sub-Saharan African	8	0.02
Am. Ind. or Alaska Nat., not spec.	137	0.42
American Indian tribes, specified:	128	0.39
Blackfeet	3	0.01
Cherokee (17)	32	0.10
Choctaw	3	0.01
Creek	4	0.01
Iroquois (1)	4	0.01
Latin American Indians (27)	51	0.16
Pueblo	1	0.00
Seminole	6	0.02
Shoshone	4	0.01
Sioux (1)	2	0.01
All other tribes (9)	18	0.06
American Indian tribes, not spec.	21	0.06
Arab:	142	0.43
Arab/Arabic	5	0.02
Egyptian	84	0.26
Jordanian	46	0.14
Palestinian	7	0.02
Armenian	20	0.06
Asian:	3,435	10.52
Bangladeshi (14)	18	0.06
Chinese, ex. Taiwanese (194)	277	0.85
Filipino (432)	491	1.50
Indian (1,919)	2,113	6.47
Indonesian (1)	1	0.00
Japanese (14)	29	0.09
Korean (53)	54	0.17
Pakistani (200)	243	0.74
Sri Lankan (3)	6	0.02
Thai (40)	52	0.16
Vietnamese (23)	35	0.11
Other Asian, specified (4)	7	0.02
Other Asian, not specified (22)	109	0.33
Australian	8	0.02
Austrian	71	0.22
Belgian	8	0.02
British	195	0.60
Canadian	31	0.09
Croatian	24	0.07
Czech	20	0.06
Czechoslovakian	16	0.05
Danish	4	0.01
Dutch	114	0.35
Eastern European	28	0.09
English	329	1.01
Estonian	21	0.06
European	16	0.05
Finnish	44	0.13
French, except Basque	329	1.01
French Canadian	50	0.15
German	2,050	6.28
Greek	234	0.72
Guyanese	603	1.85
Hawaii Native/Pacific Islander:	90	0.28
Melanesian: (1)	1	0.00
Fijian (1)	1	0.00
Micronesian: (6)	7	0.02
Guamanian/Chamorro (6)	7	0.02
Polynesian:	1	0.00
Native Hawaiian	1	0.00
Other Pac. Isl., not spec. (20)	81	0.25
Hispanic or Latino:	4,672	14.31
Central American:	719	2.20
Costa Rican	23	0.07
Guatemalan	90	0.28
Honduran	85	0.26
Nicaraguan	5	0.02
Panamanian	87	0.27
Salvadoran	371	1.14
Other Central American	58	0.18
Cuban	118	0.36
Dominican Republic	402	1.23
Mexican	446	1.37

Notes: 1. Figures in the "Number" column do not add up to the total population due to: a) Ancestry/Race overlap — e.g. persons can report being both White and Irish, b) persons of Hispanic origin can report being any race, c) persons reporting two ancestries are counted in both categories. 2. Numbers in parentheses indicate the number of persons reporting this ancestry/race alone, not in combination with any other ancestry/race. 3. Refer to the Explanation of Data in the front of the book for more detailed information.

Ancestry/Race	Number	%
Puerto Rican	971	2.97
South American:	966	2.96
Argentinean	86	0.26
Bolivian	13	0.04
Chilean	107	0.33
Colombian	427	1.31
Ecuadorian	126	0.39
Paraguayan	1	0.00
Peruvian	158	0.48
Uruguayan	6	0.02
Venezuelan	19	0.06
Other South American	23	0.07
Other Hispanic or Latino	1,050	3.22
Hungarian	128	0.39
Irish	1,861	5.70
Italian	5,997	18.36
Latvian	6	0.02
Lithuanian	23	0.07
Maltese	53	0.16
Norwegian	63	0.19
Pennsylvania German	10	0.03
Polish	948	2.90
Portuguese	137	0.42
Romanian	27	0.08
Russian	265	0.81
Scotch-Irish	59	0.18
Scottish	71	0.22
Serbian	25	0.08
Slavic	6	0.02
Swedish	96	0.29
Swiss	25	0.08
Turkish	68	0.21
Ukrainian	49	0.15
United States or American	859	2.63
Welsh	32	0.10
West Indian, excl. Hispanic:	6,585	20.16
Barbadian	315	0.96
Belizean	93	0.28
British West Indian	145	0.44
Haitian	3,572	10.94
Jamaican	1,962	6.01
Trinidadian and Tobagonian	329	1.01
U.S. Virgin Islander	6	0.02
West Indian	163	0.50
White:	15,516	47.51
Not Hispanic (12,631)	12,960	39.69
Hispanic (2,247)	2,556	7.83
Yugoslavian	51	0.16

Elwood

Place Type: Census Designated Place
County: Suffolk
Population: 10,916

Ancestry/Race	Number	%
African American/Black:	678	6.21
Not Hispanic (586)	641	5.87
Hispanic (26)	37	0.34
African, sub-Saharan:	21	0.19
African	21	0.19
Alaska Native tribes, specified:	1	0.01
Tlingit-Haida (1)	1	0.01
Am. Ind. or Alaska Nat., not spec.	18	0.16
Alsatian	6	0.06
American Indian tribes, specified:	30	0.27
Cherokee	7	0.06
Comanche	1	0.01
Creek	2	0.02
Iroquois (5)	5	0.05
Kiowa	1	0.01
Latin American Indians (4)	4	0.04
Lumbee (3)	3	0.03
All other tribes (3)	7	0.06
American Indian tribes, not spec.	1	0.01
Arab:	24	0.22
Lebanese	5	0.05
Syrian	19	0.18
Armenian	7	0.06
Asian:	656	6.01
Bangladeshi (1)	2	0.02
Chinese, ex. Taiwanese (132)	139	1.27
Filipino (40)	46	0.42
Indian (161)	171	1.57
Japanese (14)	18	0.16
Korean (198)	207	1.90
Malaysian (2)	4	0.04
Pakistani (34)	43	0.39
Taiwanese (6)	6	0.05
Thai (3)	3	0.03
Other Asian, not specified (14)	17	0.16
Assyrian/Chaldean/Syriac	12	0.11
Austrian	98	0.90
Belgian	5	0.05
British	6	0.06
Canadian	16	0.15
Croatian	37	0.34
Czech	101	0.93
Czechoslovakian	32	0.30
Danish	38	0.35
Dutch	58	0.53
Eastern European	53	0.49
English	416	3.84
European	28	0.26
Finnish	15	0.14
French, except Basque	138	1.27
French Canadian	125	1.15
German	1,740	16.04
Greek	113	1.04
Hawaii Native/Pacific Islander:	3	0.03
Other Pac. Isl., not spec. (3)	3	0.03
Hispanic or Latino:	550	5.04
Central American:	59	0.54
Costa Rican	2	0.02
Guatemalan	10	0.09
Honduran	10	0.09
Panamanian	1	0.01
Salvadoran	35	0.32
Other Central American	1	0.01
Cuban	11	0.10
Dominican Republic	15	0.14
Mexican	18	0.16
Puerto Rican	206	1.89
South American:	94	0.86
Argentinean	10	0.09
Chilean	6	0.05
Colombian	24	0.22
Ecuadorian	20	0.18
Paraguayan	11	0.10
Peruvian	12	0.11
Uruguayan	5	0.05
Venezuelan	2	0.02
Other South American	4	0.04
Other Hispanic or Latino	147	1.35
Hungarian	91	0.84
Iranian	5	0.05
Irish	2,136	19.70
Italian	3,179	29.31
Lithuanian	5	0.05
Maltese	6	0.06
Norwegian	77	0.71
Polish	934	8.61
Portuguese	13	0.12
Romanian	46	0.42
Russian	495	4.56
Scotch-Irish	73	0.67
Scottish	115	1.06
Slavic	7	0.06
Slovak	29	0.27
Swedish	96	0.89
Swiss	25	0.23
Turkish	6	0.06
Ukrainian	15	0.14
United States or American	564	5.20
Welsh	13	0.12
West Indian, excl. Hispanic:	241	2.22
Haitian	145	1.34
Jamaican	29	0.27
West Indian	67	0.62
White:	9,477	86.82
Not Hispanic (9,023)	9,081	83.19
Hispanic (367)	396	3.63

Endicott

Place Type: Village
County: Broome
Population: 13,038

Ancestry/Race	Number	%
Acadian/Cajun	10	0.08
African American/Black:	583	4.47
Not Hispanic (475)	563	4.32
Hispanic (14)	20	0.15
African, sub-Saharan:	37	0.28
African	9	0.07
Nigerian	20	0.15
Other sub-Saharan African	8	0.06
Am. Ind. or Alaska Nat., not spec.	32	0.25
American Indian tribes, specified:	66	0.51
Apache (1)	1	0.01
Blackfeet (3)	7	0.05
Cherokee (7)	16	0.12
Chippewa (2)	2	0.02
Comanche	2	0.02
Delaware	5	0.04
Iroquois (4)	24	0.18
Kiowa	2	0.02
Ottawa	1	0.01
Potawatomi (1)	1	0.01
Seminole (1)	1	0.01
Sioux (1)	1	0.01
All other tribes (2)	3	0.02
American Indian tribes, not spec.	8	0.06
Arab:	52	0.40
Arab/Arabic	11	0.08
Egyptian	9	0.07
Lebanese	32	0.25
Asian:	295	2.26
Bangladeshi (1)	1	0.01
Chinese, ex. Taiwanese (41)	45	0.35
Filipino (19)	27	0.21
Indian (38)	42	0.32
Indonesian (3)	3	0.02
Japanese (9)	11	0.08
Korean (13)	15	0.12
Laotian (27)	33	0.25
Pakistani	2	0.02
Thai	1	0.01
Vietnamese (99)	109	0.84
Other Asian, not specified (2)	6	0.05
Australian	24	0.18
Austrian	45	0.35
British	31	0.24
Canadian	53	0.41
Carpatho Rusyn	12	0.09
Celtic	29	0.22
Croatian	24	0.18
Czech	76	0.58
Czechoslovakian	109	0.84
Danish	15	0.12
Dutch	491	3.77
English	1,629	12.49
European	11	0.08
Finnish	7	0.05
French, except Basque	315	2.42
French Canadian	164	1.26
German	1,737	13.32
Greek	115	0.88
Hawaii Native/Pacific Islander:	12	0.09
Micronesian: (3)	3	0.02
Guamanian/Chamorro (3)	3	0.02
Polynesian: (6)	6	0.05
Native Hawaiian (6)	6	0.05
Other Pac. Isl., not spec.	3	0.02
Hispanic or Latino:	218	1.67
Central American:	2	0.02
Guatemalan	1	0.01
Panamanian	1	0.01
Cuban	4	0.03

Notes: 1. Figures in the "Number" column do not add up to the total population due to: a) Ancestry/Race overlap — e.g. persons can report being both White and Irish, b) persons of Hispanic origin can report being any race, c) persons reporting two ancestries are counted in both categories. 2. Numbers in parentheses indicate the number of persons reporting this ancestry/race alone, not in combination with any other ancestry/race. 3. Refer to the Explanation of Data in the front of the book for more detailed information.

Ancestry/Race	Number	%
Dominican Republic	6	0.05
Mexican	33	0.25
Puerto Rican	117	0.90
South American:	6	0.05
Argentinean	1	0.01
Bolivian	1	0.01
Colombian	1	0.01
Peruvian	3	0.02
Other Hispanic or Latino	50	0.38
Hungarian	53	0.41
Irish	2,496	19.14
Italian	2,721	20.87
Lithuanian	83	0.64
Norwegian	57	0.44
Pennsylvania German	35	0.27
Polish	1,009	7.74
Portuguese	6	0.05
Romanian	4	0.03
Russian	217	1.66
Scandinavian	17	0.13
Scotch-Irish	148	1.14
Scottish	271	2.08
Serbian	6	0.05
Slavic	37	0.28
Slovak	457	3.51
Slovene	5	0.04
Swedish	150	1.15
Swiss	33	0.25
Turkish	13	0.10
Ukrainian	158	1.21
United States or American	614	4.71
Welsh	193	1.48
West Indian, excl. Hispanic:	63	0.48
British West Indian	6	0.05
Jamaican	40	0.31
Trinidadian and Tobagonian	10	0.08
West Indian	7	0.05
White:	12,152	93.20
Not Hispanic (11,853)	12,029	92.26
Hispanic (96)	123	0.94
Yugoslavian	5	0.04

Endwell

Place Type: Census Designated Place
County: Broome
Population: 11,706

Ancestry/Race	Number	%
African American/Black:	209	1.79
Not Hispanic (153)	206	1.76
Hispanic (2)	3	0.03
African, sub-Saharan:	29	0.25
African	29	0.25
Am. Ind. or Alaska Nat., not spec.	21	0.18
American Indian tribes, specified:	15	0.13
Cherokee (1)	7	0.06
Iroquois (2)	3	0.03
All other tribes (4)	5	0.04
Arab:	28	0.24
Egyptian	6	0.05
Lebanese	22	0.19
Armenian	13	0.11
Asian:	228	1.95
Bangladeshi (3)	3	0.03
Chinese, ex. Taiwanese (60)	60	0.51
Filipino (16)	26	0.22
Indian (49)	51	0.44
Indonesian	1	0.01
Japanese (3)	3	0.03
Korean (16)	17	0.15
Laotian (9)	10	0.09
Malaysian (1)	1	0.01
Pakistani (10)	10	0.09
Taiwanese (11)	11	0.09
Thai (2)	2	0.02
Vietnamese (18)	26	0.22
Other Asian, not specified (3)	7	0.06
Austrian	125	1.07
Belgian	5	0.04
Brazilian	7	0.06
British	56	0.48
Canadian	26	0.22
Carpatho Rusyn	20	0.17
Czech	88	0.75
Czechoslovakian	157	1.34
Danish	55	0.47
Dutch	334	2.85
Eastern European	36	0.31
English	1,560	13.32
European	5	0.04
French, except Basque	468	4.00
French Canadian	74	0.63
German	1,774	15.15
Greek	115	0.98
Hawaii Native/Pacific Islander:	1	0.01
Polynesian: (1)	1	0.01
Native Hawaiian (1)	1	0.01
Hispanic or Latino:	149	1.27
Central American:	5	0.04
Costa Rican	3	0.03
Guatemalan	1	0.01
Panamanian	1	0.01
Cuban	5	0.04
Dominican Republic	1	0.01
Mexican	15	0.13
Puerto Rican	76	0.65
South American:	7	0.06
Argentinean	2	0.02
Bolivian	1	0.01
Chilean	1	0.01
Colombian	2	0.02
Other South American	1	0.01
Other Hispanic or Latino	40	0.34
Hungarian	83	0.71
Irish	2,208	18.86
Italian	2,356	20.12
Lithuanian	24	0.20
Northern European	7	0.06
Norwegian	40	0.34
Pennsylvania German	62	0.53
Polish	986	8.42
Portuguese	7	0.06
Russian	314	2.68
Scotch-Irish	136	1.16
Scottish	130	1.11
Slavic	24	0.20
Slovak	634	5.41
Slovene	7	0.06
Swedish	151	1.29
Swiss	40	0.34
Ukrainian	205	1.75
United States or American	442	3.77
Welsh	283	2.42
West Indian, excl. Hispanic:	14	0.12
Jamaican	7	0.06
West Indian	7	0.06
White:	11,276	96.33
Not Hispanic (11,087)	11,180	95.51
Hispanic (90)	96	0.82
Yugoslavian	5	0.04

Evans

Place Type: Town
County: Erie
Population: 17,594

Ancestry/Race	Number	%
African American/Black:	94	0.53
Not Hispanic (60)	87	0.49
Hispanic (6)	7	0.04
Am. Ind. or Alaska Nat., not spec.	40	0.23
American Indian tribes, specified:	135	0.77
Blackfeet	3	0.02
Cherokee	8	0.05
Cheyenne	1	0.01
Chippewa (4)	4	0.02
Iroquois (82)	109	0.62
Kiowa	1	0.01
Latin American Indians	1	0.01
Navajo	2	0.01
Osage (1)	1	0.01
All other tribes (5)	5	0.03
American Indian tribes, not spec.	16	0.09
Arab:	36	0.20
Lebanese	36	0.20
Asian:	64	0.36
Chinese, ex. Taiwanese (10)	13	0.07
Filipino (6)	12	0.07
Indian	3	0.02
Japanese (4)	12	0.07
Korean (6)	10	0.06
Laotian	1	0.01
Thai (6)	10	0.06
Vietnamese (3)	3	0.02
Austrian	108	0.61
Belgian	29	0.16
British	57	0.32
Canadian	48	0.27
Croatian	59	0.34
Czech	45	0.26
Czechoslovakian	10	0.06
Danish	14	0.08
Dutch	389	2.21
English	1,461	8.30
European	75	0.43
Finnish	32	0.18
French, except Basque	659	3.75
French Canadian	263	1.49
German	6,173	35.09
Greek	53	0.30
Hawaii Native/Pacific Islander:	5	0.03
Polynesian: (3)	5	0.03
Native Hawaiian	2	0.01
Samoan (3)	3	0.02
Hispanic or Latino:	212	1.20
Cuban	2	0.01
Mexican	38	0.22
Puerto Rican	116	0.66
South American:	12	0.07
Argentinean	2	0.01
Chilean	2	0.01
Colombian	2	0.01
Peruvian	6	0.03
Other Hispanic or Latino	44	0.25
Hungarian	165	0.94
Irish	3,830	21.77
Italian	3,038	17.27
Lithuanian	13	0.07
Macedonian	13	0.07
Northern European	8	0.05
Norwegian	151	0.86
Pennsylvania German	3	0.02
Polish	3,608	20.51
Portuguese	64	0.36
Romanian	6	0.03
Russian	185	1.05
Scandinavian	8	0.05
Scotch-Irish	257	1.46
Scottish	267	1.52
Slavic	11	0.06
Slovak	24	0.14
Swedish	158	0.90
Swiss	34	0.19
Turkish	23	0.13
Ukrainian	199	1.13
United States or American	633	3.60
Welsh	103	0.59
White:	17,342	98.57
Not Hispanic (17,045)	17,164	97.56
Hispanic (164)	178	1.01
Yugoslavian	13	0.07

Notes: 1. Figures in the "Number" column do not add up to the total population due to: a) Ancestry/Race overlap — e.g. persons can report being both White and Irish, b) persons of Hispanic origin can report being any race, c) persons reporting two ancestries are counted in both categories. 2. Numbers in parentheses indicate the number of persons reporting this ancestry/race alone, not in combination with any other ancestry/race. 3. Refer to the Explanation of Data in the front of the book for more detailed information.

Fairmount

Place Type: Census Designated Place
County: Onondaga
Population: 10,795

Ancestry/Race	Number	%
African American/Black:	169	1.57
Not Hispanic (129)	155	1.44
Hispanic (10)	14	0.13
African, sub-Saharan:	36	0.33
African	36	0.33
Am. Ind. or Alaska Nat., not spec.	14	0.13
Albanian	9	0.08
American Indian tribes, specified:	50	0.46
Blackfeet	1	0.01
Cherokee	6	0.06
Chippewa	1	0.01
Iroquois (29)	36	0.33
Latin American Indians	1	0.01
Lumbee	1	0.01
Pueblo	1	0.01
All other tribes (1)	3	0.03
Arab:	174	1.61
Arab/Arabic	59	0.55
Lebanese	50	0.46
Palestinian	58	0.54
Syrian	7	0.06
Armenian	20	0.18
Asian:	168	1.56
Chinese, ex. Taiwanese (28)	36	0.33
Filipino (12)	21	0.19
Indian (50)	53	0.49
Japanese (2)	2	0.02
Korean (27)	28	0.26
Pakistani (3)	4	0.04
Sri Lankan (2)	2	0.02
Taiwanese (4)	4	0.04
Thai (2)	3	0.03
Vietnamese (8)	13	0.12
Other Asian, not specified (1)	2	0.02
Austrian	78	0.72
Belgian	6	0.06
British	5	0.05
Canadian	12	0.11
Croatian	18	0.17
Czech	49	0.45
Czechoslovakian	18	0.17
Dutch	173	1.60
English	1,632	15.09
European	20	0.18
Finnish	13	0.12
French, except Basque	338	3.13
French Canadian	219	2.03
German	2,082	19.26
Greek	65	0.60
Hawaii Native/Pacific Islander:	6	0.06
Micronesian: (2)	3	0.03
Guamanian/Chamorro (1)	2	0.02
Other Micronesian (1)	1	0.01
Polynesian: (1)	3	0.03
Native Hawaiian (1)	3	0.03
Hispanic or Latino:	115	1.07
Central American:	4	0.04
Guatemalan	1	0.01
Honduran	1	0.01
Panamanian	2	0.02
Cuban	3	0.03
Dominican Republic	1	0.01
Mexican	21	0.19
Puerto Rican	43	0.40
South American:	2	0.02
Chilean	1	0.01
Colombian	1	0.01
Other Hispanic or Latino	41	0.38
Hungarian	101	0.93
Irish	2,832	26.19
Italian	2,113	19.54
Lithuanian	37	0.34
Macedonian	42	0.39
Norwegian	76	0.70
Polish	1,245	11.51
Russian	67	0.62
Scandinavian	10	0.09
Scotch-Irish	125	1.16
Scottish	190	1.76
Slavic	9	0.08
Slovak	57	0.53
Swedish	39	0.36
Swiss	46	0.43
Ukrainian	456	4.22
United States or American	255	2.36
Welsh	104	0.96
West Indian, excl. Hispanic:	17	0.16
Trinidadian and Tobagonian	17	0.16
White:	10,440	96.71
Not Hispanic (10,259)	10,354	95.91
Hispanic (77)	86	0.80
Yugoslavian	9	0.08

Fallsburg

Place Type: Town
County: Sullivan
Population: 12,234

Ancestry/Race	Number	%
African American/Black:	2,050	16.76
Not Hispanic (1,780)	1,858	15.19
Hispanic (124)	192	1.57
African, sub-Saharan:	46	0.38
African	46	0.38
Am. Ind. or Alaska Nat., not spec.	49	0.40
Albanian	4	0.03
American Indian tribes, specified:	52	0.43
Apache	1	0.01
Blackfeet (3)	5	0.04
Cherokee (7)	15	0.12
Cheyenne	2	0.02
Chippewa	1	0.01
Cree	1	0.01
Creek (1)	1	0.01
Crow	1	0.01
Delaware (2)	2	0.02
Iroquois (5)	12	0.10
Latin American Indians	3	0.02
Navajo (2)	2	0.02
Potawatomi (1)	1	0.01
Sioux	1	0.01
All other tribes (2)	4	0.03
American Indian tribes, not spec.	9	0.07
Arab:	54	0.44
Egyptian	15	0.12
Lebanese	25	0.20
Syrian	14	0.11
Asian:	199	1.63
Chinese, ex. Taiwanese (50)	60	0.49
Filipino (11)	26	0.21
Indian (47)	60	0.49
Japanese (5)	8	0.07
Korean (13)	16	0.13
Malaysian (1)	1	0.01
Pakistani (5)	12	0.10
Taiwanese (1)	1	0.01
Thai (1)	2	0.02
Vietnamese (6)	6	0.05
Other Asian, specified (1)	2	0.02
Other Asian, not specified (2)	5	0.04
Australian	12	0.10
Austrian	43	0.35
Brazilian	35	0.29
British	39	0.32
Canadian	48	0.39
Czech	87	0.71
Czechoslovakian	17	0.14
Danish	35	0.29
Dutch	347	2.83
Eastern European	44	0.36
English	640	5.22
European	56	0.46
Finnish	22	0.18
French, except Basque	170	1.39
French Canadian	34	0.28
German	1,268	10.34
Greek	83	0.68
Hawaii Native/Pacific Islander:	10	0.08
Polynesian: (4)	4	0.03
Native Hawaiian (4)	4	0.03
Other Pac. Isl., specified	1	0.01
Other Pac. Isl., not spec.	5	0.04
Hispanic or Latino:	1,777	14.53
Central American:	187	1.53
Costa Rican	4	0.03
Guatemalan	29	0.24
Honduran	42	0.34
Nicaraguan	4	0.03
Panamanian	15	0.12
Salvadoran	83	0.68
Other Central American	10	0.08
Cuban	69	0.56
Dominican Republic	119	0.97
Mexican	81	0.66
Puerto Rican	916	7.49
South American:	108	0.88
Argentinean	7	0.06
Chilean	7	0.06
Colombian	66	0.54
Ecuadorian	14	0.11
Peruvian	9	0.07
Venezuelan	4	0.03
Other South American	1	0.01
Other Hispanic or Latino	297	2.43
Hungarian	114	0.93
Irish	1,417	11.55
Italian	1,202	9.80
Latvian	15	0.12
Lithuanian	16	0.13
Luxemburger	11	0.09
Norwegian	62	0.51
Pennsylvania German	13	0.11
Polish	610	4.97
Portuguese	23	0.19
Romanian	20	0.16
Russian	386	3.15
Scandinavian	24	0.20
Scotch-Irish	64	0.52
Scottish	169	1.38
Slovak	20	0.16
Swedish	61	0.50
Swiss	10	0.08
Ukrainian	93	0.76
United States or American	750	6.12
Welsh	29	0.24
West Indian, excl. Hispanic:	68	0.55
British West Indian	5	0.04
Jamaican	47	0.38
West Indian	16	0.13
White:	9,429	77.07
Not Hispanic (8,300)	8,406	68.71
Hispanic (899)	1,023	8.36
Yugoslavian	15	0.12

Farmington

Place Type: Town
County: Ontario
Population: 10,585

Ancestry/Race	Number	%
African American/Black:	145	1.37
Not Hispanic (102)	134	1.27
Hispanic (6)	11	0.10
African, sub-Saharan:	6	0.06
Cape Verdean	6	0.06
Alaska Native tribes, specified:	3	0.03
Tlingit-Haida (2)	3	0.03
Am. Ind. or Alaska Nat., not spec.	16	0.15
American Indian tribes, specified:	40	0.38
Blackfeet	1	0.01
Cherokee	4	0.04

Notes: 1. Figures in the "Number" column do not add up to the total population due to: a) Ancestry/Race overlap — e.g. persons can report being both White and Irish, b) persons of Hispanic origin can report being any race, c) persons reporting two ancestries are counted in both categories. 2. Numbers in parentheses indicate the number of persons reporting this ancestry/race alone, not in combination with any other ancestry/race. 3. Refer to the Explanation of Data in the front of the book for more detailed information.

Ancestry/Race	Number	%
Comanche	1	0.01
Iroquois (17)	22	0.21
Kiowa	1	0.01
Latin American Indians (1)	2	0.02
Sioux	2	0.02
Ute (1)	3	0.03
All other tribes	4	0.04
American Indian tribes, not spec.	2	0.02
Arab:	40	0.38
Lebanese	40	0.38
Asian:	128	1.21
Cambodian (1)	1	0.01
Chinese, ex. Taiwanese (16)	21	0.20
Filipino (4)	8	0.08
Indian (17)	17	0.16
Indonesian	3	0.03
Japanese (1)	3	0.03
Korean (29)	36	0.34
Laotian (6)	9	0.09
Sri Lankan (1)	1	0.01
Taiwanese (2)	2	0.02
Thai (6)	6	0.06
Vietnamese (11)	14	0.13
Other Asian, not specified (5)	7	0.07
Austrian	25	0.24
Belgian	7	0.07
British	22	0.21
Canadian	50	0.47
Celtic	8	0.08
Croatian	30	0.28
Czech	16	0.15
Czechoslovakian	7	0.07
Danish	68	0.64
Dutch	623	5.89
Eastern European	7	0.07
English	2,020	19.08
European	86	0.81
Finnish	6	0.06
French, except Basque	510	4.82
French Canadian	147	1.39
German	3,141	29.67
Greek	46	0.43
Hawaii Native/Pacific Islander:	10	0.09
Polynesian: (1)	4	0.04
Native Hawaiian (1)	3	0.03
Other Polynesian	1	0.01
Other Pac. Isl., not spec.	6	0.06
Hispanic or Latino:	128	1.21
Central American:	7	0.07
Guatemalan	2	0.02
Panamanian	2	0.02
Other Central American	3	0.03
Cuban	2	0.02
Dominican Republic	2	0.02
Mexican	19	0.18
Puerto Rican	66	0.62
South American:	7	0.07
Argentinean	2	0.02
Colombian	1	0.01
Ecuadorian	1	0.01
Peruvian	1	0.01
Uruguayan	1	0.01
Venezuelan	1	0.01
Other Hispanic or Latino	25	0.24
Hungarian	58	0.55
Icelander	7	0.07
Irish	2,077	19.62
Italian	1,662	15.70
Lithuanian	45	0.43
Macedonian	14	0.13
Norwegian	92	0.87
Pennsylvania German	10	0.09
Polish	657	6.21
Portuguese	19	0.18
Russian	40	0.38
Scotch-Irish	125	1.18
Scottish	357	3.37
Serbian	35	0.33
Slovak	30	0.28
Swedish	126	1.19
Swiss	20	0.19
Turkish	15	0.14
Ukrainian	124	1.17
United States or American	565	5.34
Welsh	74	0.70
White:	10,313	97.43
Not Hispanic (10,134)	10,215	96.50
Hispanic (84)	98	0.93

Farmingville

Place Type: Census Designated Place
County: Suffolk
Population: 16,458

Ancestry/Race	Number	%
African American/Black:	284	1.73
Not Hispanic (187)	255	1.55
Hispanic (17)	29	0.18
Am. Ind. or Alaska Nat., not spec.	36	0.22
American Indian tribes, specified:	47	0.29
Blackfeet	1	0.01
Cherokee (2)	9	0.05
Creek	1	0.01
Delaware	3	0.02
Iroquois (2)	3	0.02
Latin American Indians (5)	17	0.10
Lumbee (3)	3	0.02
Navajo (1)	2	0.01
Sioux (3)	3	0.02
All other tribes	5	0.03
Arab:	75	0.45
Egyptian	21	0.13
Lebanese	35	0.21
Syrian	19	0.12
Armenian	52	0.32
Asian:	366	2.22
Chinese, ex. Taiwanese (70)	85	0.52
Filipino (21)	29	0.18
Indian (96)	107	0.65
Indonesian (1)	2	0.01
Japanese (4)	8	0.05
Korean (12)	15	0.09
Laotian	2	0.01
Malaysian (1)	1	0.01
Pakistani (42)	49	0.30
Sri Lankan (3)	3	0.02
Thai (1)	1	0.01
Vietnamese (29)	31	0.19
Other Asian, specified	4	0.02
Other Asian, not specified (7)	29	0.18
Austrian	198	1.20
Belgian	24	0.15
Brazilian	16	0.10
Canadian	49	0.30
Cypriot	9	0.05
Czech	84	0.51
Czechoslovakian	33	0.20
Danish	15	0.09
Dutch	128	0.78
Eastern European	46	0.28
English	670	4.06
European	61	0.37
Finnish	32	0.19
French, except Basque	284	1.72
French Canadian	96	0.58
German	3,252	19.72
Greek	312	1.89
Hawaii Native/Pacific Islander:	7	0.04
Other Pac. Isl., specified	4	0.02
Other Pac. Isl., not spec.	3	0.02
Hispanic or Latino:	1,336	8.12
Central American:	92	0.56
Costa Rican	7	0.04
Guatemalan	32	0.19
Panamanian	4	0.02
Salvadoran	49	0.30
Cuban	32	0.19
Dominican Republic	20	0.12
Mexican	233	1.42
Puerto Rican	531	3.23
South American:	147	0.89
Argentinean	8	0.05
Bolivian	4	0.02
Chilean	1	0.01
Colombian	61	0.37
Ecuadorian	32	0.19
Paraguayan	2	0.01
Peruvian	25	0.15
Venezuelan	1	0.01
Other South American	13	0.08
Other Hispanic or Latino	281	1.71
Hungarian	109	0.66
Icelander	8	0.05
Irish	4,537	27.52
Israeli	7	0.04
Italian	6,530	39.60
Latvian	22	0.13
Lithuanian	94	0.57
Maltese	25	0.15
Norwegian	331	2.01
Polish	1,182	7.17
Portuguese	313	1.90
Romanian	8	0.05
Russian	375	2.27
Scandinavian	16	0.10
Scotch-Irish	173	1.05
Scottish	95	0.58
Slovak	23	0.14
Slovene	10	0.06
Swedish	105	0.64
Swiss	19	0.12
Ukrainian	156	0.95
United States or American	262	1.59
Welsh	18	0.11
West Indian, excl. Hispanic:	90	0.55
British West Indian	14	0.08
Trinidadian and Tobagonian	58	0.35
West Indian	18	0.11
White:	15,645	95.06
Not Hispanic (14,451)	14,589	88.64
Hispanic (945)	1,056	6.42

Fishkill

Place Type: Town
County: Dutchess
Population: 20,258

Ancestry/Race	Number	%
African American/Black:	2,936	14.49
Not Hispanic (2,734)	2,784	13.74
Hispanic (129)	152	0.75
African, sub-Saharan:	39	0.19
African	17	0.08
Nigerian	22	0.11
Am. Ind. or Alaska Nat., not spec.	22	0.11
Albanian	46	0.23
American Indian tribes, specified:	40	0.20
Blackfeet	1	0.00
Cherokee (3)	8	0.04
Iroquois (5)	11	0.05
Latin American Indians (4)	6	0.03
Lumbee	1	0.00
Sioux	6	0.03
All other tribes (5)	7	0.03
American Indian tribes, not spec.	10	0.05
Arab:	111	0.55
Arab/Arabic	9	0.04
Jordanian	16	0.08
Lebanese	39	0.19
Palestinian	21	0.10
Syrian	26	0.13
Armenian	17	0.08
Asian:	681	3.36
Bangladeshi (2)	2	0.01
Chinese, ex. Taiwanese (194)	219	1.08
Filipino (40)	61	0.30
Indian (213)	226	1.12
Indonesian (5)	5	0.02

Notes: 1. Figures in the "Number" column do not add up to the total population due to: a) Ancestry/Race overlap — e.g. persons can report being both White and Irish, b) persons of Hispanic origin can report being any race, c) persons reporting two ancestries are counted in both categories. 2. Numbers in parentheses indicate the number of persons reporting this ancestry/race alone, not in combination with any other ancestry/race. 3. Refer to the Explanation of Data in the front of the book for more detailed information.

Ancestry/Race	Number	%
Japanese (33)	34	0.17
Korean (54)	56	0.28
Pakistani (9)	9	0.04
Taiwanese (11)	20	0.10
Thai (3)	6	0.03
Vietnamese (21)	21	0.10
Other Asian, not specified (12)	22	0.11
Australian	16	0.08
Austrian	119	0.59
Belgian	26	0.13
Brazilian	11	0.05
British	40	0.20
Canadian	30	0.15
Croatian	14	0.07
Czech	79	0.39
Czechoslovakian	55	0.27
Danish	19	0.09
Dutch	355	1.76
English	1,386	6.87
Estonian	6	0.03
European	105	0.52
Finnish	57	0.28
French, except Basque	351	1.74
French Canadian	219	1.09
German	2,712	13.44
Greek	113	0.56
Guyanese	20	0.10
Hawaii Native/Pacific Islander:	8	0.04
Polynesian: (1)	2	0.01
Native Hawaiian (1)	2	0.01
Other Pac. Isl., not spec. (4)	6	0.03
Hispanic or Latino:	2,121	10.47
Central American:	62	0.31
Costa Rican	2	0.01
Guatemalan	6	0.03
Honduran	16	0.08
Nicaraguan	3	0.01
Panamanian	14	0.07
Salvadoran	20	0.10
Other Central American	1	0.00
Cuban	104	0.51
Dominican Republic	204	1.01
Mexican	95	0.47
Puerto Rican	1,214	5.99
South American:	141	0.70
Argentinean	9	0.04
Chilean	1	0.00
Colombian	54	0.27
Ecuadorian	43	0.21
Peruvian	16	0.08
Uruguayan	2	0.01
Venezuelan	7	0.03
Other South American	9	0.04
Other Hispanic or Latino	301	1.49
Hungarian	158	0.78
Irish	3,495	17.32
Italian	4,668	23.13
Lithuanian	82	0.41
Maltese	16	0.08
Norwegian	145	0.72
Polish	994	4.93
Portuguese	93	0.46
Romanian	24	0.12
Russian	266	1.32
Scotch-Irish	179	0.89
Scottish	390	1.93
Slavic	22	0.11
Slovak	154	0.76
Swedish	284	1.41
Swiss	32	0.16
Turkish	29	0.14
Ukrainian	110	0.55
United States or American	468	2.32
Welsh	82	0.41
West Indian, excl. Hispanic:	75	0.37
Haitian	14	0.07
Jamaican	40	0.20
Trinidadian and Tobagonian	10	0.05
West Indian	11	0.05
White:	15,802	78.00
Not Hispanic (14,596)	14,711	72.62
Hispanic (1,042)	1,091	5.39
Yugoslavian	45	0.22

Floral Park

Place Type: Village
County: Nassau
Population: 15,967

Ancestry/Race	Number	%
African American/Black:	103	0.65
Not Hispanic (59)	80	0.50
Hispanic (15)	23	0.14
African, sub-Saharan:	26	0.16
African	26	0.16
Am. Ind. or Alaska Nat., not spec.	8	0.05
Albanian	5	0.03
American Indian tribes, specified:	12	0.08
Cherokee	2	0.01
Iroquois (1)	6	0.04
Latin American Indians (4)	4	0.03
American Indian tribes, not spec.	4	0.03
Arab:	67	0.42
Arab/Arabic	10	0.06
Egyptian	11	0.07
Lebanese	6	0.04
Moroccan	12	0.08
Palestinian	6	0.04
Syrian	22	0.14
Armenian	38	0.24
Asian:	668	4.18
Bangladeshi (5)	5	0.03
Chinese, ex. Taiwanese (120)	143	0.90
Filipino (54)	60	0.38
Indian (335)	349	2.19
Indonesian (3)	3	0.02
Japanese (9)	12	0.08
Korean (29)	29	0.18
Pakistani (55)	55	0.34
Taiwanese (1)	1	0.01
Thai (3)	3	0.02
Other Asian, specified (1)	1	0.01
Other Asian, not specified (5)	7	0.04
Australian	11	0.07
Austrian	164	1.03
Belgian	5	0.03
Bulgarian	13	0.08
Canadian	56	0.35
Croatian	123	0.77
Czech	46	0.29
Czechoslovakian	17	0.11
Danish	51	0.32
Dutch	85	0.53
Eastern European	17	0.11
English	777	4.86
European	23	0.14
Finnish	7	0.04
French, except Basque	247	1.55
French Canadian	47	0.29
German	2,938	18.38
Greek	247	1.55
Hawaii Native/Pacific Islander:	5	0.03
Polynesian: (1)	1	0.01
Samoan (1)	1	0.01
Other Pac. Isl., not spec. (4)	4	0.03
Hispanic or Latino:	859	5.38
Central American:	67	0.42
Costa Rican	4	0.03
Guatemalan	7	0.04
Honduran	5	0.03
Nicaraguan	4	0.03
Panamanian	12	0.08
Salvadoran	31	0.19
Other Central American	4	0.03
Cuban	69	0.43
Dominican Republic	52	0.33
Mexican	20	0.13
Puerto Rican	231	1.45
South American:	206	1.29
Argentinean	10	0.06
Chilean	15	0.09
Colombian	88	0.55
Ecuadorian	44	0.28
Paraguayan	1	0.01
Peruvian	31	0.19
Uruguayan	4	0.03
Venezuelan	7	0.04
Other South American	6	0.04
Other Hispanic or Latino	214	1.34
Hungarian	96	0.60
Icelander	6	0.04
Iranian	12	0.08
Irish	5,771	36.10
Israeli	12	0.08
Italian	4,887	30.57
Latvian	6	0.04
Lithuanian	87	0.54
Maltese	5	0.03
Norwegian	121	0.76
Polish	985	6.16
Portuguese	63	0.39
Romanian	10	0.06
Russian	152	0.95
Scotch-Irish	178	1.11
Scottish	246	1.54
Slavic	6	0.04
Slovak	46	0.29
Slovene	29	0.18
Swedish	181	1.13
Swiss	29	0.18
Turkish	10	0.06
Ukrainian	57	0.36
United States or American	432	2.70
Welsh	23	0.14
West Indian, excl. Hispanic:	65	0.41
Haitian	36	0.23
Jamaican	29	0.18
White:	15,069	94.38
Not Hispanic (14,290)	14,368	89.99
Hispanic (648)	701	4.39
Yugoslavian	43	0.27

Fort Drum

Place Type: Census Designated Place
County: Jefferson
Population: 12,123

Ancestry/Race	Number	%
Acadian/Cajun	8	0.07
African American/Black:	2,627	21.67
Not Hispanic (2,335)	2,501	20.63
Hispanic (63)	126	1.04
African, sub-Saharan:	154	1.27
African	83	0.68
Ethiopian	18	0.15
Liberian	7	0.06
Sierra Leonean	29	0.24
South African	17	0.14
Alaska Native tribes, specified:	7	0.06
Eskimo (2)	4	0.03
Tlingit-Haida (1)	3	0.02
Alaska Native tribes, not specified	3	0.02
Am. Ind. or Alaska Nat., not spec.	52	0.43
American Indian tribes, specified:	165	1.36
Apache (2)	10	0.08
Blackfeet (1)	7	0.06
Cherokee (15)	47	0.39
Cheyenne (1)	2	0.02
Chippewa (3)	4	0.03
Choctaw (6)	7	0.06
Comanche (7)	7	0.06
Creek (7)	7	0.06
Crow (1)	2	0.02
Iroquois (2)	6	0.05
Latin American Indians (5)	5	0.04
Lumbee (3)	3	0.02
Menominee	3	0.02
Navajo (13)	14	0.12

Notes: 1. Figures in the "Number" column do not add up to the total population due to: a) Ancestry/Race overlap — e.g. persons can report being both White and Irish, b) persons of Hispanic origin can report being any race, c) persons reporting two ancestries are counted in both categories. 2. Numbers in parentheses indicate the number of persons reporting this ancestry/race alone, not in combination with any other ancestry/race. 3. Refer to the Explanation of Data in the front of the book for more detailed information.

Ancestry/Race	Number	%
Ottawa (1)	5	0.04
Pueblo (1)	1	0.01
Seminole (2)	2	0.02
Sioux (4)	13	0.11
Ute	2	0.02
All other tribes (10)	18	0.15
American Indian tribes, not spec.	4	0.03
Arab:	74	0.61
Arab/Arabic	8	0.07
Egyptian	11	0.09
Lebanese	22	0.18
Other Arab	33	0.27
Armenian	6	0.05
Asian:	453	3.74
Cambodian (3)	3	0.02
Chinese, ex. Taiwanese (8)	29	0.24
Filipino (122)	182	1.50
Indian (6)	12	0.10
Indonesian (1)	1	0.01
Japanese (11)	28	0.23
Korean (99)	142	1.17
Laotian (3)	3	0.02
Pakistani (2)	2	0.02
Sri Lankan (1)	1	0.01
Taiwanese (2)	2	0.02
Thai (2)	5	0.04
Vietnamese (13)	17	0.14
Other Asian, not specified (6)	26	0.21
Austrian	16	0.13
Belgian	8	0.07
British	74	0.61
Canadian	14	0.12
Croatian	11	0.09
Czech	8	0.07
Czechoslovakian	31	0.26
Danish	46	0.38
Dutch	165	1.36
English	646	5.33
European	66	0.54
French, except Basque	437	3.60
French Canadian	200	1.65
German	1,867	15.40
Greek	31	0.26
Guyanese	14	0.12
Hawaii Native/Pacific Islander:	143	1.18
Micronesian: (34)	41	0.34
Guamanian/Chamorro (19)	25	0.21
Other Micronesian (15)	16	0.13
Polynesian: (40)	77	0.64
Native Hawaiian (15)	45	0.37
Samoan (24)	30	0.25
Tongan (1)	2	0.02
Other Pac. Isl., not spec. (10)	25	0.21
Hispanic or Latino:	1,609	13.27
Central American:	107	0.88
Costa Rican	4	0.03
Guatemalan	11	0.09
Honduran	7	0.06
Nicaraguan	8	0.07
Panamanian	57	0.47
Salvadoran	20	0.16
Cuban	17	0.14
Dominican Republic	59	0.49
Mexican	563	4.64
Puerto Rican	592	4.88
South American:	73	0.60
Argentinean	7	0.06
Bolivian	4	0.03
Chilean	1	0.01
Colombian	23	0.19
Ecuadorian	10	0.08
Paraguayan	1	0.01
Peruvian	21	0.17
Venezuelan	3	0.02
Other South American	3	0.02
Other Hispanic or Latino	198	1.63
Iranian	16	0.13
Irish	1,349	11.13
Israeli	19	0.16
Italian	869	7.17
Latvian	20	0.16
Lithuanian	11	0.09
Northern European	36	0.30
Norwegian	150	1.24
Polish	297	2.45
Portuguese	40	0.33
Romanian	9	0.07
Russian	73	0.60
Scotch-Irish	140	1.15
Scottish	174	1.44
Slovak	24	0.20
Slovene	8	0.07
Swedish	108	0.89
Swiss	5	0.04
Turkish	5	0.04
Ukrainian	17	0.14
United States or American	542	4.47
Welsh	66	0.54
West Indian, excl. Hispanic:	277	2.28
Barbadian	13	0.11
Belizean	8	0.07
British West Indian	15	0.12
Haitian	14	0.12
Jamaican	154	1.27
Trinidadian and Tobagonian	46	0.38
U.S. Virgin Islander	8	0.07
West Indian	19	0.16
White:	8,187	67.53
Not Hispanic (7,328)	7,623	62.88
Hispanic (451)	564	4.65

Franklin Square

Place Type: Census Designated Place
County: Nassau
Population: 29,342

Ancestry/Race	Number	%
Afghan	59	0.20
African American/Black:	349	1.19
Not Hispanic (277)	314	1.07
Hispanic (13)	35	0.12
Am. Ind. or Alaska Nat., not spec.	20	0.07
Albanian	9	0.03
American Indian tribes, specified:	31	0.11
Blackfeet	1	0.00
Cherokee (1)	3	0.01
Choctaw	1	0.00
Creek (1)	2	0.01
Iroquois (1)	1	0.00
Latin American Indians (12)	15	0.05
Seminole (1)	1	0.00
Sioux	4	0.01
All other tribes (2)	3	0.01
American Indian tribes, not spec.	19	0.06
Arab:	79	0.27
Arab/Arabic	58	0.20
Moroccan	21	0.07
Armenian	61	0.21
Asian:	1,246	4.25
Chinese, ex. Taiwanese (298)	323	1.10
Filipino (195)	222	0.76
Indian (393)	423	1.44
Japanese (24)	30	0.10
Korean (74)	77	0.26
Pakistani (49)	70	0.24
Sri Lankan (1)	1	0.00
Taiwanese (1)	5	0.02
Thai (15)	15	0.05
Vietnamese (28)	29	0.10
Other Asian, not specified (17)	51	0.17
Australian	6	0.02
Austrian	230	0.78
Belgian	14	0.05
Brazilian	32	0.11
British	60	0.20
Canadian	58	0.20
Croatian	18	0.06
Cypriot	6	0.02
Czech	37	0.13
Czechoslovakian	125	0.43
Danish	38	0.13
Dutch	203	0.69
Eastern European	31	0.11
English	641	2.18
Estonian	25	0.09
European	7	0.02
Finnish	31	0.11
French, except Basque	335	1.14
French Canadian	62	0.21
German	4,009	13.66
Greek	639	2.18
Guyanese	87	0.30
Hawaii Native/Pacific Islander:	12	0.04
Micronesian:	2	0.01
Guamanian/Chamorro	2	0.01
Polynesian: (1)	3	0.01
Native Hawaiian (1)	3	0.01
Other Pac. Isl., not spec. (2)	7	0.02
Hispanic or Latino:	2,023	6.89
Central American:	198	0.67
Costa Rican	5	0.02
Guatemalan	35	0.12
Honduran	33	0.11
Nicaraguan	5	0.02
Panamanian	6	0.02
Salvadoran	98	0.33
Other Central American	16	0.05
Cuban	104	0.35
Dominican Republic	89	0.30
Mexican	89	0.30
Puerto Rican	602	2.05
South American:	471	1.61
Argentinean	42	0.14
Bolivian	5	0.02
Chilean	15	0.05
Colombian	136	0.46
Ecuadorian	121	0.41
Paraguayan	1	0.00
Peruvian	95	0.32
Uruguayan	9	0.03
Venezuelan	14	0.05
Other South American	33	0.11
Other Hispanic or Latino	470	1.60
Hungarian	234	0.80
Iranian	95	0.32
Irish	5,613	19.13
Italian	13,970	47.61
Latvian	11	0.04
Lithuanian	78	0.27
Maltese	123	0.42
Norwegian	211	0.72
Polish	1,128	3.84
Portuguese	192	0.65
Romanian	31	0.11
Russian	575	1.96
Scandinavian	10	0.03
Scotch-Irish	134	0.46
Scottish	124	0.42
Slavic	58	0.20
Slovak	28	0.10
Slovene	17	0.06
Swedish	193	0.66
Swiss	51	0.17
Turkish	24	0.08
Ukrainian	135	0.46
United States or American	669	2.28
Welsh	73	0.25
West Indian, excl. Hispanic:	66	0.22
Haitian	46	0.16
Jamaican	20	0.07
White:	27,328	93.14
Not Hispanic (25,557)	25,799	87.93
Hispanic (1,430)	1,529	5.21
Yugoslavian	73	0.25

Notes: 1. Figures in the "Number" column do not add up to the total population due to: a) Ancestry/Race overlap — e.g. persons can report being both White and Irish, b) persons of Hispanic origin can report being any race, c) persons reporting two ancestries are counted in both categories. 2. Numbers in parentheses indicate the number of persons reporting this ancestry/race alone, not in combination with any other ancestry/race. 3. Refer to the Explanation of Data in the front of the book for more detailed information.

Fredonia

Place Type: Village
County: Chautauqua
Population: 10,706

Ancestry/Race	Number	%
African American/Black:	130	1.21
Not Hispanic (107)	125	1.17
Hispanic (2)	5	0.05
African, sub-Saharan:	18	0.17
African	18	0.17
Alaska Native tribes, specified:	1	0.01
Eskimo (1)	1	0.01
Am. Ind. or Alaska Nat., not spec.	14	0.13
Albanian	39	0.36
American Indian tribes, specified:	46	0.43
Blackfeet (1)	6	0.06
Cherokee	7	0.07
Chippewa (1)	1	0.01
Choctaw	1	0.01
Iroquois (22)	27	0.25
Latin American Indians	1	0.01
Sioux	1	0.01
All other tribes (1)	2	0.02
American Indian tribes, not spec.	1	0.01
Arab:	84	0.78
Arab/Arabic	12	0.11
Egyptian	4	0.04
Lebanese	59	0.55
Syrian	9	0.08
Asian:	137	1.28
Chinese, ex. Taiwanese (31)	37	0.35
Filipino (6)	8	0.07
Indian (30)	32	0.30
Indonesian (1)	1	0.01
Japanese (11)	12	0.11
Korean (14)	14	0.13
Laotian (1)	1	0.01
Pakistani (7)	14	0.13
Sri Lankan (3)	3	0.03
Thai (5)	6	0.06
Other Asian, not specified (4)	9	0.08
Austrian	29	0.27
British	41	0.38
Canadian	72	0.67
Croatian	8	0.07
Czech	34	0.32
Czechoslovakian	28	0.26
Danish	35	0.32
Dutch	185	1.72
English	1,463	13.57
European	86	0.80
French, except Basque	275	2.55
French Canadian	104	0.96
German	2,780	25.79
Greek	38	0.35
Hawaii Native/Pacific Islander:	5	0.05
Micronesian: (1)	1	0.01
Guamanian/Chamorro (1)	1	0.01
Polynesian: (1)	4	0.04
Native Hawaiian	1	0.01
Samoan (1)	3	0.03
Hispanic or Latino:	181	1.69
Central American:	2	0.02
Nicaraguan	1	0.01
Salvadoran	1	0.01
Cuban	8	0.07
Dominican Republic	8	0.07
Mexican	21	0.20
Puerto Rican	107	1.00
South American:	7	0.07
Argentinean	1	0.01
Chilean	1	0.01
Colombian	4	0.04
Peruvian	1	0.01
Other Hispanic or Latino	28	0.26
Hungarian	76	0.70
Irish	1,817	16.85
Italian	2,424	22.48
Latvian	7	0.06
Lithuanian	37	0.34
Luxemburger	4	0.04
Northern European	11	0.10
Norwegian	44	0.41
Pennsylvania German	6	0.06
Polish	1,889	17.52
Portuguese	25	0.23
Romanian	10	0.09
Russian	74	0.69
Scandinavian	17	0.16
Scotch-Irish	195	1.81
Scottish	234	2.17
Serbian	7	0.06
Slavic	15	0.14
Slovak	24	0.22
Slovene	5	0.05
Swedish	429	3.98
Swiss	30	0.28
Ukrainian	87	0.81
United States or American	398	3.69
Welsh	83	0.77
West Indian, excl. Hispanic:	36	0.33
Jamaican	18	0.17
Trinidadian and Tobagonian	11	0.10
West Indian	7	0.06
White:	10,379	96.95
Not Hispanic (10,194)	10,244	95.68
Hispanic (122)	135	1.26
Yugoslavian	30	0.28

Freeport

Place Type: Village
County: Nassau
Population: 43,783

Ancestry/Race	Number	%
Afghan	53	0.12
African American/Black:	15,177	34.66
Not Hispanic (13,610)	14,243	32.53
Hispanic (648)	934	2.13
African, sub-Saharan:	371	0.85
African	248	0.57
Cape Verdean	39	0.09
Ghanian	34	0.08
Liberian	8	0.02
Nigerian	6	0.01
Zimbabwean	19	0.04
Other sub-Saharan African	17	0.04
Alaska Native tribes, specified:	2	0.00
Tlingit-Haida	1	0.00
All other tribes (1)	1	0.00
Am. Ind. or Alaska Nat., not spec.	209	0.48
Albanian	7	0.02
American Indian tribes, specified:	279	0.64
Blackfeet	19	0.04
Cherokee (10)	86	0.20
Cheyenne	2	0.00
Chippewa	4	0.01
Choctaw (1)	4	0.01
Cree (1)	2	0.00
Crow (1)	6	0.01
Delaware (1)	1	0.00
Iroquois (1)	8	0.02
Latin American Indians (34)	59	0.13
Navajo	6	0.01
Osage (2)	4	0.01
Pueblo (1)	5	0.01
Seminole	1	0.00
Sioux (1)	9	0.02
All other tribes (22)	63	0.14
American Indian tribes, not spec.	48	0.11
Arab:	57	0.13
Arab/Arabic	13	0.03
Egyptian	12	0.03
Lebanese	18	0.04
Moroccan	14	0.03
Armenian	19	0.04
Asian:	819	1.87
Bangladeshi (3)	7	0.02
Chinese, ex. Taiwanese (139)	198	0.45
Filipino (78)	97	0.22
Indian (269)	346	0.79
Japanese (14)	24	0.05
Korean (45)	50	0.11
Laotian (1)	1	0.00
Pakistani (25)	49	0.11
Sri Lankan (1)	1	0.00
Thai (7)	7	0.02
Vietnamese (7)	16	0.04
Other Asian, specified	1	0.00
Other Asian, not specified (8)	22	0.05
Australian	13	0.03
Austrian	174	0.40
Belgian	8	0.02
Brazilian	22	0.05
British	86	0.20
Canadian	21	0.05
Czech	52	0.12
Czechoslovakian	42	0.10
Danish	46	0.11
Dutch	201	0.46
Eastern European	75	0.17
English	993	2.27
Estonian	6	0.01
European	116	0.26
Finnish	36	0.08
French, except Basque	462	1.06
French Canadian	28	0.06
German	3,295	7.53
Greek	218	0.50
Guyanese	326	0.74
Hawaii Native/Pacific Islander:	78	0.18
Micronesian: (5)	6	0.01
Guamanian/Chamorro (5)	6	0.01
Polynesian: (5)	14	0.03
Native Hawaiian (1)	7	0.02
Samoan (4)	6	0.01
Other Polynesian	1	0.00
Other Pac. Isl., not spec. (14)	58	0.13
Hispanic or Latino:	14,648	33.46
Central American:	4,249	9.70
Costa Rican	71	0.16
Guatemalan	535	1.22
Honduran	254	0.58
Nicaraguan	26	0.06
Panamanian	89	0.20
Salvadoran	3,094	7.07
Other Central American	180	0.41
Cuban	429	0.98
Dominican Republic	3,226	7.37
Mexican	301	0.69
Puerto Rican	1,554	3.55
South American:	1,074	2.45
Argentinean	51	0.12
Bolivian	6	0.01
Chilean	19	0.04
Colombian	562	1.28
Ecuadorian	230	0.53
Paraguayan	6	0.01
Peruvian	143	0.33
Uruguayan	8	0.02
Venezuelan	28	0.06
Other South American	21	0.05
Other Hispanic or Latino	3,815	8.71
Hungarian	215	0.49
Irish	3,837	8.76
Israeli	39	0.09
Italian	3,981	9.09
Latvian	13	0.03
Lithuanian	105	0.24
Maltese	14	0.03
Norwegian	222	0.51
Polish	889	2.03
Portuguese	117	0.27
Romanian	43	0.10
Russian	670	1.53
Scotch-Irish	220	0.50
Scottish	160	0.37

Notes: 1. Figures in the "Number" column do not add up to the total population due to: a) Ancestry/Race overlap — e.g. persons can report being both White and Irish, b) persons of Hispanic origin can report being any race, c) persons reporting two ancestries are counted in both categories. 2. Numbers in parentheses indicate the number of persons reporting this ancestry/race alone, not in combination with any other ancestry/race. 3. Refer to the Explanation of Data in the front of the book for more detailed information.

Slavic	7	0.02
Slovak	33	0.08
Slovene	7	0.02
Swedish	140	0.32
Swiss	106	0.24
Turkish	56	0.13
Ukrainian	48	0.11
United States or American	1,365	3.12
Welsh	34	0.08
West Indian, excl. Hispanic:	3,076	7.03
Barbadian	186	0.42
Belizean	49	0.11
British West Indian	139	0.32
Dutch West Indian	26	0.06
Haitian	568	1.30
Jamaican	1,327	3.03
Trinidadian and Tobagonian	380	0.87
U.S. Virgin Islander	25	0.06
West Indian	376	0.86
White:	20,499	46.82
Not Hispanic (13,835)	14,252	32.55
Hispanic (4,956)	6,247	14.27
Yugoslavian	8	0.02

Fulton

Place Type: City
County: Oswego
Population: 11,855

Ancestry/Race	Number	%
African American/Black:	115	0.97
Not Hispanic (78)	104	0.88
Hispanic (10)	11	0.09
African, sub-Saharan:	5	0.04
Nigerian	5	0.04
Am. Ind. or Alaska Nat., not spec.	15	0.13
American Indian tribes, specified:	75	0.63
Blackfeet (2)	2	0.02
Cherokee (1)	12	0.10
Chippewa	1	0.01
Choctaw	1	0.01
Delaware (1)	1	0.01
Iroquois (26)	42	0.35
Latin American Indians (2)	3	0.03
Lumbee (2)	6	0.05
Navajo	1	0.01
All other tribes (3)	6	0.05
Arab:	43	0.36
Lebanese	40	0.34
Syrian	3	0.03
Asian:	57	0.48
Chinese, ex. Taiwanese (4)	4	0.03
Filipino (3)	6	0.05
Indian (21)	21	0.18
Japanese (2)	10	0.08
Korean (8)	11	0.09
Pakistani	1	0.01
Thai	1	0.01
Vietnamese (1)	2	0.02
Other Asian, not specified	1	0.01
British	21	0.18
Canadian	24	0.20
Danish	41	0.35
Dutch	318	2.68
English	1,652	13.94
European	193	1.63
Finnish	18	0.15
French, except Basque	1,173	9.89
French Canadian	430	3.63
German	1,813	15.29
Greek	35	0.30
Hawaii Native/Pacific Islander:	9	0.08
Micronesian: (2)	2	0.02
Guamanian/Chamorro (2)	2	0.02
Polynesian: (1)	1	0.01
Native Hawaiian (1)	1	0.01
Other Pac. Isl., not spec.	6	0.05
Hispanic or Latino:	228	1.92
Central American:	34	0.29
Guatemalan	33	0.28
Other Central American	1	0.01
Cuban	2	0.02
Dominican Republic	1	0.01
Mexican	37	0.31
Puerto Rican	101	0.85
Other Hispanic or Latino	53	0.45
Hungarian	29	0.24
Irish	2,112	17.82
Italian	2,059	17.37
Lithuanian	34	0.29
Norwegian	14	0.12
Polish	673	5.68
Portuguese	17	0.14
Russian	57	0.48
Scotch-Irish	150	1.27
Scottish	200	1.69
Slovak	12	0.10
Swedish	48	0.40
Swiss	29	0.24
Turkish	14	0.12
Ukrainian	140	1.18
United States or American	984	8.30
Welsh	91	0.77
West Indian, excl. Hispanic:	18	0.15
Haitian	9	0.08
West Indian	9	0.08
White:	11,568	97.58
Not Hispanic (11,370)	11,449	96.58
Hispanic (106)	119	1.00

Garden City

Place Type: Village
County: Nassau
Population: 21,672

Ancestry/Race	Number	%
African American/Black:	300	1.38
Not Hispanic (254)	282	1.30
Hispanic (12)	18	0.08
African, sub-Saharan:	46	0.21
African	17	0.08
Nigerian	29	0.13
Am. Ind. or Alaska Nat., not spec.	8	0.04
Albanian	51	0.24
American Indian tribes, specified:	24	0.11
Blackfeet	3	0.01
Cherokee	8	0.04
Latin American Indians (4)	8	0.04
All other tribes (1)	5	0.02
American Indian tribes, not spec.	7	0.03
Arab:	62	0.29
Egyptian	15	0.07
Lebanese	32	0.15
Syrian	15	0.07
Armenian	186	0.86
Asian:	811	3.74
Bangladeshi (1)	1	0.00
Cambodian (2)	2	0.01
Chinese, ex. Taiwanese (273)	316	1.46
Filipino (58)	77	0.36
Indian (135)	147	0.68
Indonesian (2)	4	0.02
Japanese (91)	98	0.45
Korean (92)	99	0.46
Malaysian	1	0.00
Pakistani (9)	9	0.04
Sri Lankan (2)	2	0.01
Taiwanese (7)	14	0.06
Thai (4)	4	0.02
Vietnamese (12)	17	0.08
Other Asian, not specified (5)	20	0.09
Austrian	163	0.75
Basque	21	0.10
Brazilian	21	0.10
British	130	0.60
Canadian	87	0.40
Celtic	20	0.09
Croatian	55	0.25
Czech	75	0.35
Czechoslovakian	148	0.68
Danish	49	0.23
Dutch	286	1.32
Eastern European	30	0.14
English	1,520	7.02
European	218	1.01
French, except Basque	373	1.72
French Canadian	127	0.59
German	4,094	18.90
Greek	691	3.19
Guyanese	63	0.29
Hawaii Native/Pacific Islander:	10	0.05
Micronesian: (5)	5	0.02
Guamanian/Chamorro (5)	5	0.02
Polynesian:	1	0.00
Native Hawaiian	1	0.00
Other Pac. Isl., not spec. (2)	4	0.02
Hispanic or Latino:	600	2.77
Central American:	42	0.19
Costa Rican	1	0.00
Guatemalan	6	0.03
Honduran	4	0.02
Panamanian	3	0.01
Salvadoran	27	0.12
Other Central American	1	0.00
Cuban	93	0.43
Dominican Republic	16	0.07
Mexican	55	0.25
Puerto Rican	123	0.57
South American:	93	0.43
Argentinean	16	0.07
Bolivian	1	0.00
Chilean	7	0.03
Colombian	36	0.17
Ecuadorian	14	0.06
Peruvian	5	0.02
Uruguayan	5	0.02
Venezuelan	1	0.00
Other South American	8	0.04
Other Hispanic or Latino	178	0.82
Hungarian	113	0.52
Icelander	32	0.15
Irish	7,627	35.21
Israeli	8	0.04
Italian	6,552	30.25
Latvian	28	0.13
Lithuanian	94	0.43
Maltese	33	0.15
Northern European	25	0.12
Norwegian	156	0.72
Pennsylvania German	11	0.05
Polish	1,046	4.83
Portuguese	59	0.27
Romanian	52	0.24
Russian	330	1.52
Scandinavian	5	0.02
Scotch-Irish	260	1.20
Scottish	217	1.00
Slavic	13	0.06
Slovak	44	0.20
Slovene	6	0.03
Swedish	128	0.59
Swiss	112	0.52
Turkish	19	0.09
Ukrainian	86	0.40
United States or American	582	2.69
Welsh	54	0.25
West Indian, excl. Hispanic:	110	0.51
Barbadian	12	0.06
British West Indian	20	0.09
Haitian	54	0.25
Jamaican	24	0.11
White:	20,573	94.93
Not Hispanic (19,938)	20,059	92.56
Hispanic (480)	514	2.37
Yugoslavian	18	0.08

Notes: 1. Figures in the "Number" column do not add up to the total population due to: a) Ancestry/Race overlap — e.g. persons can report being both White and Irish, b) persons of Hispanic origin can report being any race, c) persons reporting two ancestries are counted in both categories. 2. Numbers in parentheses indicate the number of persons reporting this ancestry/race alone, not in combination with any other ancestry/race. 3. Refer to the Explanation of Data in the front of the book for more detailed information.

Gates

Place Type: Town
County: Monroe
Population: 29,275

Ancestry/Race	Number	%
African American/Black:	1,987	6.79
Not Hispanic (1,823)	1,925	6.58
Hispanic (45)	62	0.21
African, sub-Saharan:	112	0.38
African	93	0.32
Ethiopian	9	0.03
Nigerian	10	0.03
Alaska Native tribes, specified:	1	0.00
Alaska Athabascan (1)	1	0.00
Am. Ind. or Alaska Nat., not spec.	46	0.16
Albanian	9	0.03
American Indian tribes, specified:	66	0.23
Apache	2	0.01
Cherokee (3)	12	0.04
Delaware	1	0.00
Iroquois (24)	40	0.14
Latin American Indians (2)	7	0.02
Sioux (1)	1	0.00
All other tribes	3	0.01
American Indian tribes, not spec.	3	0.01
Arab:	102	0.35
Arab/Arabic	61	0.21
Lebanese	24	0.08
Syrian	17	0.06
Asian:	814	2.78
Cambodian (13)	13	0.04
Chinese, ex. Taiwanese (126)	157	0.54
Filipino (24)	38	0.13
Indian (70)	91	0.31
Indonesian (8)	8	0.03
Japanese (12)	21	0.07
Korean (102)	114	0.39
Laotian (55)	70	0.24
Pakistani (13)	14	0.05
Sri Lankan	5	0.02
Taiwanese (6)	6	0.02
Thai (13)	16	0.05
Vietnamese (215)	237	0.81
Other Asian, specified (3)	7	0.02
Other Asian, not specified (9)	17	0.06
Austrian	50	0.17
Belgian	74	0.25
British	50	0.17
Canadian	141	0.48
Celtic	16	0.05
Croatian	28	0.10
Czech	34	0.12
Czechoslovakian	75	0.26
Danish	17	0.06
Dutch	776	2.65
Eastern European	21	0.07
English	2,822	9.63
European	40	0.14
Finnish	21	0.07
French, except Basque	905	3.09
French Canadian	299	1.02
German	5,883	20.08
Greek	330	1.13
Hawaii Native/Pacific Islander:	29	0.10
Micronesian: (2)	2	0.01
Guamanian/Chamorro (2)	2	0.01
Polynesian: (5)	14	0.05
Native Hawaiian (4)	11	0.04
Samoan (1)	3	0.01
Other Pac. Isl., specified	3	0.01
Other Pac. Isl., not spec. (5)	10	0.03
Hispanic or Latino:	855	2.92
Central American:	21	0.07
Guatemalan	4	0.01
Honduran	2	0.01
Panamanian	4	0.01
Salvadoran	11	0.04
Cuban	101	0.35
Dominican Republic	18	0.06
Mexican	68	0.23
Puerto Rican	499	1.70
South American:	59	0.20
Argentinean	3	0.01
Chilean	18	0.06
Colombian	15	0.05
Ecuadorian	6	0.02
Peruvian	6	0.02
Venezuelan	11	0.04
Other Hispanic or Latino	89	0.30
Hungarian	72	0.25
Iranian	5	0.02
Irish	4,309	14.71
Italian	9,541	32.57
Latvian	34	0.12
Lithuanian	176	0.60
Macedonian	71	0.24
Norwegian	40	0.14
Polish	1,423	4.86
Portuguese	152	0.52
Romanian	23	0.08
Russian	24	0.08
Scotch-Irish	210	0.72
Scottish	357	1.22
Slavic	4	0.01
Slovak	16	0.05
Swedish	162	0.55
Swiss	42	0.14
Turkish	44	0.15
Ukrainian	258	0.88
United States or American	1,101	3.76
Welsh	171	0.58
West Indian, excl. Hispanic:	184	0.63
Barbadian	61	0.21
Jamaican	123	0.42
White:	26,290	89.80
Not Hispanic (25,507)	25,802	88.14
Hispanic (436)	488	1.67
Yugoslavian	64	0.22

Gates-North Gates

Place Type: Census Designated Place
County: Monroe
Population: 15,138

Ancestry/Race	Number	%
African American/Black:	1,002	6.62
Not Hispanic (913)	974	6.43
Hispanic (16)	28	0.18
African, sub-Saharan:	66	0.44
African	56	0.37
Nigerian	10	0.07
Alaska Native tribes, specified:	1	0.01
Alaska Athabascan (1)	1	0.01
Am. Ind. or Alaska Nat., not spec.	35	0.23
American Indian tribes, specified:	33	0.22
Cherokee (2)	7	0.05
Iroquois (11)	20	0.13
Latin American Indians	5	0.03
Sioux (1)	1	0.01
American Indian tribes, not spec.	3	0.02
Arab:	43	0.28
Arab/Arabic	10	0.07
Lebanese	16	0.11
Syrian	17	0.11
Asian:	497	3.28
Cambodian (9)	9	0.06
Chinese, ex. Taiwanese (93)	108	0.71
Filipino (17)	23	0.15
Indian (30)	44	0.29
Indonesian (7)	7	0.05
Japanese (4)	10	0.07
Korean (57)	62	0.41
Laotian (44)	56	0.37
Pakistani (9)	9	0.06
Sri Lankan	5	0.03
Taiwanese (1)	1	0.01
Thai (6)	7	0.05
Vietnamese (129)	144	0.95
Other Asian, specified (3)	4	0.03
Other Asian, not specified (6)	8	0.05
Austrian	41	0.27
Belgian	38	0.25
British	22	0.15
Canadian	55	0.36
Celtic	16	0.11
Czech	18	0.12
Czechoslovakian	42	0.28
Danish	11	0.07
Dutch	395	2.61
Eastern European	9	0.06
English	1,107	7.31
European	5	0.03
Finnish	18	0.12
French, except Basque	478	3.16
French Canadian	172	1.14
German	2,573	17.00
Greek	172	1.14
Hawaii Native/Pacific Islander:	15	0.10
Polynesian: (4)	11	0.07
Native Hawaiian (4)	11	0.07
Other Pac. Isl., not spec. (1)	4	0.03
Hispanic or Latino:	497	3.28
Central American:	16	0.11
Guatemalan	3	0.02
Honduran	2	0.01
Panamanian	3	0.02
Salvadoran	8	0.05
Cuban	55	0.36
Dominican Republic	5	0.03
Mexican	34	0.22
Puerto Rican	299	1.98
South American:	37	0.24
Argentinean	1	0.01
Chilean	13	0.09
Colombian	11	0.07
Ecuadorian	6	0.04
Peruvian	1	0.01
Venezuelan	5	0.03
Other Hispanic or Latino	51	0.34
Hungarian	34	0.22
Irish	1,898	12.54
Italian	5,454	36.03
Latvian	34	0.22
Lithuanian	113	0.75
Macedonian	7	0.05
Norwegian	14	0.09
Polish	687	4.54
Portuguese	76	0.50
Romanian	17	0.11
Russian	24	0.16
Scotch-Irish	111	0.73
Scottish	134	0.89
Slovak	12	0.08
Swedish	63	0.42
Swiss	11	0.07
Turkish	6	0.04
Ukrainian	115	0.76
United States or American	507	3.35
Welsh	40	0.26
West Indian, excl. Hispanic:	115	0.76
Barbadian	45	0.30
Jamaican	70	0.46
White:	13,501	89.19
Not Hispanic (13,071)	13,233	87.42
Hispanic (229)	268	1.77
Yugoslavian	58	0.38

Geddes

Place Type: Town
County: Onondaga
Population: 17,740

Ancestry/Race	Number	%
Acadian/Cajun	5	0.03
African American/Black:	134	0.76
Not Hispanic (83)	131	0.74

Notes: 1. Figures in the "Number" column do not add up to the total population due to: a) Ancestry/Race overlap — e.g. persons can report being both White and Irish, b) persons of Hispanic origin can report being any race, c) persons reporting two ancestries are counted in both categories. 2. Numbers in parentheses indicate the number of persons reporting this ancestry/race alone, not in combination with any other ancestry/race. 3. Refer to the Explanation of Data in the front of the book for more detailed information.

Hispanic (3)	3	0.02
African, sub-Saharan:	21	0.12
African	6	0.03
Ghanian	15	0.08
Alaska Native tribes, specified:	1	0.01
Eskimo	1	0.01
Am. Ind. or Alaska Nat., not spec.	54	0.30
Albanian	12	0.07
American Indian tribes, specified:	153	0.86
Blackfeet (1)	2	0.01
Cherokee	2	0.01
Choctaw	1	0.01
Crow	1	0.01
Iroquois (66)	115	0.65
Latin American Indians (4)	7	0.04
Navajo	1	0.01
Seminole	1	0.01
Sioux	3	0.02
All other tribes (7)	20	0.11
American Indian tribes, not spec.	6	0.03
Arab:	147	0.83
Arab/Arabic	67	0.38
Egyptian	22	0.12
Jordanian	23	0.13
Lebanese	29	0.16
Syrian	6	0.03
Armenian	18	0.10
Asian:	118	0.67
Cambodian (1)	1	0.01
Chinese, ex. Taiwanese (15)	16	0.09
Filipino (27)	33	0.19
Indian (18)	19	0.11
Japanese (1)	1	0.01
Korean (19)	20	0.11
Malaysian	1	0.01
Vietnamese (14)	19	0.11
Other Asian, not specified (2)	8	0.05
Austrian	196	1.11
Brazilian	10	0.06
British	31	0.17
Canadian	61	0.34
Czech	48	0.27
Czechoslovakian	37	0.21
Danish	10	0.06
Dutch	319	1.80
English	1,853	10.46
European	74	0.42
French, except Basque	834	4.71
French Canadian	284	1.60
German	2,512	14.17
Greek	112	0.63
Hawaii Native/Pacific Islander:	10	0.06
Micronesian: (3)	5	0.03
Guamanian/Chamorro (3)	4	0.02
Other Micronesian	1	0.01
Polynesian: (2)	2	0.01
Samoan (2)	2	0.01
Other Pac. Isl., not spec. (1)	3	0.02
Hispanic or Latino:	268	1.51
Central American:	3	0.02
Nicaraguan	2	0.01
Other Central American	1	0.01
Cuban	11	0.06
Dominican Republic	2	0.01
Mexican	58	0.33
Puerto Rican	99	0.56
South American:	20	0.11
Colombian	11	0.06
Peruvian	2	0.01
Venezuelan	7	0.04
Other Hispanic or Latino	75	0.42
Hungarian	56	0.32
Irish	4,625	26.10
Italian	4,986	28.13
Latvian	7	0.04
Lithuanian	10	0.06
Norwegian	15	0.08
Pennsylvania German	36	0.20
Polish	2,501	14.11
Portuguese	38	0.21
Romanian	4	0.02
Russian	242	1.37
Scotch-Irish	156	0.88
Scottish	208	1.17
Slavic	21	0.12
Slovak	72	0.41
Swedish	70	0.39
Swiss	27	0.15
Ukrainian	735	4.15
United States or American	341	1.92
Welsh	172	0.97
West Indian, excl. Hispanic:	5	0.03
Jamaican	5	0.03
White:	17,410	98.14
Not Hispanic (17,021)	17,188	96.89
Hispanic (197)	222	1.25
Yugoslavian	14	0.08

Geneva

Place Type: City
County: Ontario
Population: 13,617

Ancestry/Race	Number	%
African American/Black:	1,675	12.30
Not Hispanic (1,261)	1,490	10.94
Hispanic (130)	185	1.36
African, sub-Saharan:	107	0.78
African	107	0.78
Am. Ind. or Alaska Nat., not spec.	35	0.26
Albanian	6	0.04
Alsatian	8	0.06
American Indian tribes, specified:	65	0.48
Apache (1)	1	0.01
Cherokee (1)	10	0.07
Chippewa (1)	1	0.01
Choctaw (1)	2	0.01
Comanche (1)	1	0.01
Creek	1	0.01
Delaware	2	0.01
Iroquois (7)	17	0.12
Latin American Indians (1)	7	0.05
Navajo (1)	1	0.01
Pueblo (3)	3	0.02
Puget Sound Salish (3)	3	0.02
Seminole	5	0.04
Sioux (5)	10	0.07
All other tribes (1)	1	0.01
American Indian tribes, not spec.	7	0.05
Arab:	93	0.68
Arab/Arabic	7	0.05
Lebanese	19	0.14
Syrian	67	0.49
Asian:	210	1.54
Chinese, ex. Taiwanese (64)	69	0.51
Filipino (3)	6	0.04
Indian (19)	28	0.21
Indonesian (1)	1	0.01
Japanese (20)	24	0.18
Korean (29)	44	0.32
Laotian (9)	9	0.07
Pakistani (4)	4	0.03
Taiwanese (4)	4	0.03
Thai (3)	3	0.02
Vietnamese (4)	4	0.03
Other Asian, specified (4)	6	0.04
Other Asian, not specified (1)	8	0.06
Austrian	20	0.15
Belgian	13	0.10
Brazilian	5	0.04
British	71	0.52
Bulgarian	15	0.11
Canadian	25	0.18
Czech	26	0.19
Czechoslovakian	5	0.04
Danish	112	0.82
Dutch	419	3.07
Eastern European	13	0.10
English	1,600	11.72
European	67	0.49
Finnish	13	0.10
French, except Basque	376	2.75
French Canadian	155	1.14
German	1,843	13.50
Greek	26	0.19
Hawaii Native/Pacific Islander:	19	0.14
Micronesian: (1)	5	0.04
Guamanian/Chamorro (1)	4	0.03
Other Micronesian	1	0.01
Polynesian: (2)	2	0.01
Native Hawaiian (2)	2	0.01
Other Pac. Isl., specified	1	0.01
Other Pac. Isl., not spec. (4)	11	0.08
Hispanic or Latino:	1,157	8.50
Central American:	33	0.24
Costa Rican	5	0.04
Guatemalan	10	0.07
Honduran	9	0.07
Nicaraguan	3	0.02
Panamanian	3	0.02
Salvadoran	3	0.02
Cuban	25	0.18
Dominican Republic	38	0.28
Mexican	133	0.98
Puerto Rican	801	5.88
South American:	25	0.18
Argentinean	3	0.02
Bolivian	2	0.01
Chilean	2	0.01
Colombian	8	0.06
Ecuadorian	3	0.02
Peruvian	5	0.04
Venezuelan	1	0.01
Other South American	1	0.01
Other Hispanic or Latino	102	0.75
Hungarian	23	0.17
Irish	2,834	20.76
Italian	3,122	22.87
Lithuanian	14	0.10
Maltese	7	0.05
Northern European	9	0.07
Norwegian	92	0.67
Pennsylvania German	20	0.15
Polish	360	2.64
Portuguese	36	0.26
Russian	84	0.62
Scandinavian	5	0.04
Scotch-Irish	219	1.60
Scottish	313	2.29
Slavic	6	0.04
Slovak	19	0.14
Swedish	167	1.22
Swiss	27	0.20
Ukrainian	11	0.08
United States or American	494	3.62
Welsh	91	0.67
West Indian, excl. Hispanic:	71	0.52
Haitian	6	0.04
Jamaican	65	0.48
White:	11,482	84.32
Not Hispanic (10,662)	10,946	80.38
Hispanic (439)	536	3.94
Yugoslavian	18	0.13

German Flatts

Place Type: Town
County: Herkimer
Population: 13,629

Ancestry/Race	Number	%
African American/Black:	138	1.01
Not Hispanic (74)	119	0.87
Hispanic (6)	19	0.14
African, sub-Saharan:	2	0.01
African	2	0.01
Am. Ind. or Alaska Nat., not spec.	28	0.21
American Indian tribes, specified:	65	0.48
Cherokee (2)	12	0.09

Notes: 1. Figures in the "Number" column do not add up to the total population due to: a) Ancestry/Race overlap — e.g. persons can report being both White and Irish, b) persons of Hispanic origin can report being any race, c) persons reporting two ancestries are counted in both categories. 2. Numbers in parentheses indicate the number of persons reporting this ancestry/race alone, not in combination with any other ancestry/race. 3. Refer to the Explanation of Data in the front of the book for more detailed information.

Ancestry/Race	Number	%
Chickasaw	1	0.01
Chippewa	3	0.02
Delaware	4	0.03
Iroquois (7)	34	0.25
Latin American Indians (1)	1	0.01
Sioux	7	0.05
Tohono O'Odham (1)	1	0.01
All other tribes	2	0.01
American Indian tribes, not spec.	1	0.01
Arab:	30	0.22
Lebanese	30	0.22
Asian:	38	0.28
Chinese, ex. Taiwanese (1)	1	0.01
Filipino (6)	11	0.08
Indian (4)	6	0.04
Japanese (3)	5	0.04
Korean (5)	7	0.05
Laotian (1)	1	0.01
Thai	1	0.01
Vietnamese (2)	3	0.02
Other Asian, not specified (1)	3	0.02
Austrian	55	0.40
British	32	0.23
Canadian	26	0.19
Czech	19	0.14
Czechoslovakian	51	0.37
Danish	70	0.51
Dutch	682	4.99
English	1,799	13.17
European	22	0.16
French, except Basque	1,159	8.49
French Canadian	391	2.86
German	3,113	22.79
Greek	29	0.21
Hawaii Native/Pacific Islander:	3	0.02
Polynesian: (1)	2	0.01
Native Hawaiian (1)	2	0.01
Other Pac. Isl., not spec. (1)	1	0.01
Hispanic or Latino:	196	1.44
Central American:	1	0.01
Panamanian	1	0.01
Cuban	1	0.01
Dominican Republic	9	0.07
Mexican	45	0.33
Puerto Rican	98	0.72
South American:	7	0.05
Colombian	4	0.03
Peruvian	1	0.01
Other South American	2	0.01
Other Hispanic or Latino	35	0.26
Hungarian	35	0.26
Irish	2,676	19.59
Italian	2,240	16.40
Lithuanian	48	0.35
Northern European	2	0.01
Norwegian	28	0.21
Pennsylvania German	4	0.03
Polish	1,058	7.75
Portuguese	58	0.42
Russian	90	0.66
Scotch-Irish	79	0.58
Scottish	349	2.56
Slavic	20	0.15
Slovak	62	0.45
Swedish	66	0.48
Swiss	45	0.33
Ukrainian	145	1.06
United States or American	774	5.67
Welsh	472	3.46
West Indian, excl. Hispanic:	11	0.08
Haitian	5	0.04
Jamaican	6	0.04
White:	13,459	98.75
Not Hispanic (13,209)	13,297	97.56
Hispanic (130)	162	1.19
Yugoslavian	28	0.21

Glen Cove

Place Type: City
County: Nassau
Population: 26,622

Ancestry/Race	Number	%
Afghan	33	0.12
African American/Black:	1,871	7.03
Not Hispanic (1,614)	1,722	6.47
Hispanic (89)	149	0.56
African, sub-Saharan:	110	0.41
African	110	0.41
Am. Ind. or Alaska Nat., not spec.	63	0.24
Albanian	8	0.03
American Indian tribes, specified:	102	0.38
Apache (1)	1	0.00
Blackfeet	9	0.03
Cherokee (1)	18	0.07
Chickasaw	1	0.00
Chippewa (1)	4	0.02
Comanche (1)	1	0.00
Cree (1)	1	0.00
Delaware	1	0.00
Iroquois (1)	3	0.01
Latin American Indians (26)	49	0.18
Lumbee	1	0.00
Pueblo (1)	2	0.01
Sioux (1)	2	0.01
All other tribes (5)	9	0.03
American Indian tribes, not spec.	8	0.03
Arab:	69	0.26
Egyptian	44	0.17
Iraqi	12	0.05
Lebanese	9	0.03
Syrian	4	0.02
Armenian	11	0.04
Asian:	1,282	4.82
Bangladeshi (2)	2	0.01
Chinese, ex. Taiwanese (250)	281	1.06
Filipino (146)	178	0.67
Indian (327)	366	1.37
Japanese (92)	116	0.44
Korean (214)	229	0.86
Malaysian (4)	4	0.02
Pakistani (6)	11	0.04
Taiwanese (21)	32	0.12
Thai (9)	12	0.05
Vietnamese (9)	10	0.04
Other Asian, specified	1	0.00
Other Asian, not specified (4)	40	0.15
Australian	7	0.03
Austrian	197	0.74
Belgian	13	0.05
Brazilian	81	0.30
British	63	0.24
Bulgarian	7	0.03
Canadian	20	0.08
Celtic	4	0.02
Croatian	74	0.28
Cypriot	37	0.14
Czech	76	0.29
Czechoslovakian	74	0.28
Danish	21	0.08
Dutch	147	0.55
Eastern European	40	0.15
English	988	3.71
Estonian	14	0.05
European	54	0.20
Finnish	15	0.06
French, except Basque	288	1.08
French Canadian	79	0.30
German	1,961	7.37
Greek	358	1.34
Guyanese	12	0.05
Hawaii Native/Pacific Islander:	46	0.17
Micronesian: (1)	1	0.00
Guamanian/Chamorro (1)	1	0.00
Polynesian: (4)	9	0.03
Native Hawaiian (3)	6	0.02
Samoan	1	0.00
Tongan (1)	2	0.01
Other Pac. Isl., specified	1	0.00
Other Pac. Isl., not spec. (9)	35	0.13
Hispanic or Latino:	5,336	20.04
Central American:	1,434	5.39
Costa Rican	42	0.16
Guatemalan	73	0.27
Honduran	140	0.53
Nicaraguan	5	0.02
Panamanian	6	0.02
Salvadoran	1,131	4.25
Other Central American	37	0.14
Cuban	82	0.31
Dominican Republic	148	0.56
Mexican	224	0.84
Puerto Rican	975	3.66
South American:	1,208	4.54
Argentinean	42	0.16
Bolivian	9	0.03
Chilean	132	0.50
Colombian	221	0.83
Ecuadorian	63	0.24
Paraguayan	6	0.02
Peruvian	659	2.48
Uruguayan	8	0.03
Venezuelan	34	0.13
Other South American	34	0.13
Other Hispanic or Latino	1,265	4.75
Hungarian	232	0.87
Iranian	179	0.67
Irish	3,420	12.85
Israeli	76	0.29
Italian	7,103	26.68
Latvian	26	0.10
Lithuanian	67	0.25
Norwegian	167	0.63
Polish	1,661	6.24
Portuguese	36	0.14
Romanian	132	0.50
Russian	738	2.77
Scandinavian	7	0.03
Scotch-Irish	170	0.64
Scottish	347	1.30
Slavic	17	0.06
Slovak	24	0.09
Swedish	141	0.53
Swiss	22	0.08
Turkish	45	0.17
Ukrainian	53	0.20
United States or American	821	3.08
Welsh	36	0.14
West Indian, excl. Hispanic:	158	0.59
British West Indian	13	0.05
Haitian	58	0.22
Jamaican	78	0.29
Trinidadian and Tobagonian	9	0.03
White:	22,068	82.89
Not Hispanic (18,144)	18,442	69.27
Hispanic (3,229)	3,626	13.62
Yugoslavian	31	0.12

Glens Falls

Place Type: City
County: Warren
Population: 14,354

Ancestry/Race	Number	%
African American/Black:	265	1.85
Not Hispanic (174)	239	1.67
Hispanic (12)	26	0.18
Am. Ind. or Alaska Nat., not spec.	36	0.25
American Indian tribes, specified:	42	0.29
Apache (1)	1	0.01
Blackfeet (2)	8	0.06
Cherokee	2	0.01
Chippewa (1)	2	0.01
Iroquois (8)	15	0.10
Latin American Indians	1	0.01

Notes: 1. Figures in the "Number" column do not add up to the total population due to: a) Ancestry/Race overlap — e.g. persons can report being both White and Irish, b) persons of Hispanic origin can report being any race, c) persons reporting two ancestries are counted in both categories. 2. Numbers in parentheses indicate the number of persons reporting this ancestry/race alone, not in combination with any other ancestry/race. 3. Refer to the Explanation of Data in the front of the book for more detailed information.

Ancestry/Race	Number	%
Seminole (1)	1	0.01
Sioux (2)	3	0.02
All other tribes	9	0.06
American Indian tribes, not spec.	5	0.03
Arab:	147	1.02
Egyptian	4	0.03
Lebanese	12	0.08
Syrian	131	0.91
Armenian	27	0.19
Asian:	103	0.72
Chinese, ex. Taiwanese (14)	17	0.12
Filipino (6)	18	0.13
Indian (11)	14	0.10
Indonesian	1	0.01
Japanese (3)	10	0.07
Korean (10)	19	0.13
Pakistani (6)	6	0.04
Thai	1	0.01
Vietnamese (8)	8	0.06
Other Asian, specified	1	0.01
Other Asian, not specified (3)	8	0.06
Austrian	38	0.26
Brazilian	8	0.06
British	16	0.11
Canadian	36	0.25
Czechoslovakian	33	0.23
Danish	27	0.19
Dutch	402	2.78
English	1,936	13.40
European	22	0.15
Finnish	30	0.21
French, except Basque	2,450	16.96
French Canadian	678	4.69
German	1,717	11.89
Greek	85	0.59
Hawaii Native/Pacific Islander:	8	0.06
Micronesian: (1)	1	0.01
Guamanian/Chamorro (1)	1	0.01
Polynesian: (1)	1	0.01
Native Hawaiian (1)	1	0.01
Other Pac. Isl., specified	1	0.01
Other Pac. Isl., not spec.	5	0.03
Hispanic or Latino:	199	1.39
Central American:	14	0.10
Costa Rican	3	0.02
Honduran	2	0.01
Panamanian	4	0.03
Salvadoran	5	0.03
Cuban	6	0.04
Dominican Republic	5	0.03
Mexican	18	0.13
Puerto Rican	114	0.79
South American:	7	0.05
Bolivian	1	0.01
Colombian	2	0.01
Paraguayan	4	0.03
Other Hispanic or Latino	35	0.24
Hungarian	57	0.39
Iranian	4	0.03
Irish	3,178	22.00
Italian	1,755	12.15
Lithuanian	40	0.28
Northern European	9	0.06
Norwegian	68	0.47
Polish	414	2.87
Portuguese	22	0.15
Russian	47	0.33
Scotch-Irish	219	1.52
Scottish	371	2.57
Slovak	13	0.09
Swedish	118	0.82
Swiss	28	0.19
Ukrainian	69	0.48
United States or American	1,096	7.59
Welsh	192	1.33
West Indian, excl. Hispanic:	4	0.03
Jamaican	4	0.03
White:	14,026	97.71
Not Hispanic (13,736)	13,882	96.71
Hispanic (121)	144	1.00

Glenville

Place Type: Town
County: Schenectady
Population: 28,183

Ancestry/Race	Number	%
Afghan	14	0.05
African American/Black:	278	0.99
Not Hispanic (195)	254	0.90
Hispanic (9)	24	0.09
African, sub-Saharan:	24	0.09
African	24	0.09
Am. Ind. or Alaska Nat., not spec.	45	0.16
Albanian	52	0.19
American Indian tribes, specified:	61	0.22
Blackfeet	1	0.00
Cherokee	10	0.04
Cheyenne	2	0.01
Choctaw	1	0.00
Comanche	1	0.00
Creek (4)	4	0.01
Delaware	1	0.00
Iroquois (3)	23	0.08
Menominee (1)	1	0.00
Potawatomi (2)	2	0.01
Sioux (2)	2	0.01
All other tribes (5)	13	0.05
American Indian tribes, not spec.	5	0.02
Arab:	42	0.15
Syrian	33	0.12
Other Arab	9	0.03
Armenian	30	0.11
Asian:	300	1.06
Cambodian (1)	1	0.00
Chinese, ex. Taiwanese (58)	63	0.22
Filipino (32)	37	0.13
Indian (60)	65	0.23
Indonesian (1)	1	0.00
Japanese (17)	22	0.08
Korean (56)	73	0.26
Pakistani (2)	2	0.01
Thai (2)	2	0.01
Vietnamese (12)	19	0.07
Other Asian, not specified (11)	15	0.05
Australian	18	0.06
Austrian	90	0.32
Belgian	29	0.10
Brazilian	21	0.07
British	82	0.29
Canadian	85	0.30
Czech	316	1.13
Czechoslovakian	197	0.70
Danish	247	0.88
Dutch	1,412	5.03
Eastern European	41	0.15
English	4,127	14.71
European	237	0.84
Finnish	73	0.26
French, except Basque	2,277	8.11
French Canadian	671	2.39
German	5,752	20.50
Greek	153	0.55
Hawaii Native/Pacific Islander:	15	0.05
Micronesian: (3)	3	0.01
Guamanian/Chamorro (3)	3	0.01
Polynesian: (1)	2	0.01
Native Hawaiian (1)	2	0.01
Other Pac. Isl., not spec. (2)	10	0.04
Hispanic or Latino:	337	1.20
Central American:	16	0.06
Costa Rican	2	0.01
Guatemalan	2	0.01
Honduran	2	0.01
Panamanian	4	0.01
Salvadoran	6	0.02
Cuban	18	0.06
Dominican Republic	10	0.04
Mexican	36	0.13
Puerto Rican	112	0.40
South American:	48	0.17
Argentinean	5	0.02
Bolivian	1	0.00
Chilean	4	0.01
Colombian	25	0.09
Ecuadorian	6	0.02
Peruvian	2	0.01
Venezuelan	3	0.01
Other South American	2	0.01
Other Hispanic or Latino	97	0.34
Hungarian	234	0.83
Irish	5,877	20.94
Italian	5,286	18.84
Latvian	17	0.06
Lithuanian	265	0.94
Northern European	17	0.06
Norwegian	246	0.88
Pennsylvania German	20	0.07
Polish	2,860	10.19
Portuguese	56	0.20
Russian	237	0.84
Scandinavian	29	0.10
Scotch-Irish	707	2.52
Scottish	1,050	3.74
Slavic	17	0.06
Slovak	143	0.51
Swedish	420	1.50
Swiss	129	0.46
Ukrainian	151	0.54
United States or American	988	3.52
Welsh	285	1.02
West Indian, excl. Hispanic:	16	0.06
Haitian	16	0.06
White:	27,630	98.04
Not Hispanic (27,197)	27,357	97.07
Hispanic (240)	273	0.97
Yugoslavian	46	0.16

Gloversville

Place Type: City
County: Fulton
Population: 15,413

Ancestry/Race	Number	%
African American/Black:	386	2.50
Not Hispanic (275)	365	2.37
Hispanic (11)	21	0.14
African, sub-Saharan:	8	0.05
African	8	0.05
Am. Ind. or Alaska Nat., not spec.	45	0.29
American Indian tribes, specified:	49	0.32
Apache (1)	1	0.01
Blackfeet (1)	2	0.01
Cherokee (5)	12	0.08
Chippewa (1)	1	0.01
Cree	2	0.01
Iroquois (7)	24	0.16
Navajo (1)	1	0.01
Sioux (1)	2	0.01
All other tribes (1)	4	0.03
Arab:	35	0.23
Lebanese	13	0.08
Syrian	22	0.14
Asian:	126	0.82
Chinese, ex. Taiwanese (19)	27	0.18
Filipino (19)	28	0.18
Indian (8)	9	0.06
Japanese (27)	29	0.19
Korean (14)	18	0.12
Taiwanese (1)	1	0.01
Thai (1)	1	0.01
Vietnamese (2)	5	0.03
Other Asian, specified	1	0.01
Other Asian, not specified	7	0.05
Austrian	42	0.27
British	5	0.03
Bulgarian	3	0.02
Canadian	42	0.27
Croatian	13	0.08

Notes: 1. Figures in the "Number" column do not add up to the total population due to: a) Ancestry/Race overlap — e.g. persons can report being both White and Irish, b) persons of Hispanic origin can report being any race, c) persons reporting two ancestries are counted in both categories. 2. Numbers in parentheses indicate the number of persons reporting this ancestry/race alone, not in combination with any other ancestry/race. 3. Refer to the Explanation of Data in the front of the book for more detailed information.

Ancestry/Race	Number	%
Czech	131	0.85
Czechoslovakian	91	0.59
Danish	35	0.23
Dutch	930	6.03
English	1,889	12.26
European	46	0.30
French, except Basque	1,013	6.57
French Canadian	246	1.60
German	2,452	15.91
Greek	70	0.45
Hawaii Native/Pacific Islander:	19	0.12
Polynesian: (3)	13	0.08
Native Hawaiian (1)	11	0.07
Samoan (1)	1	0.01
Other Polynesian (1)	1	0.01
Other Pac. Isl., not spec. (1)	6	0.04
Hispanic or Latino:	258	1.67
Central American:	5	0.03
Costa Rican	4	0.03
Guatemalan	1	0.01
Cuban	10	0.06
Dominican Republic	10	0.06
Mexican	17	0.11
Puerto Rican	150	0.97
South American:	8	0.05
Colombian	6	0.04
Ecuadorian	2	0.01
Other Hispanic or Latino	58	0.38
Hungarian	13	0.08
Irish	2,500	16.22
Italian	3,354	21.76
Lithuanian	79	0.51
Norwegian	42	0.27
Polish	766	4.97
Portuguese	29	0.19
Romanian	51	0.33
Russian	50	0.32
Scotch-Irish	145	0.94
Scottish	193	1.25
Slavic	19	0.12
Slovak	242	1.57
Swedish	67	0.43
Swiss	22	0.14
Ukrainian	48	0.31
United States or American	966	6.27
Welsh	53	0.34
West Indian, excl. Hispanic:	8	0.05
Jamaican	8	0.05
White:	14,901	96.68
Not Hispanic (14,557)	14,735	95.60
Hispanic (142)	166	1.08
Yugoslavian	90	0.58

Goshen

Place Type: Town
County: Orange
Population: 12,913

Ancestry/Race	Number	%
African American/Black:	916	7.09
Not Hispanic (801)	837	6.48
Hispanic (67)	79	0.61
African, sub-Saharan:	33	0.26
African	4	0.03
South African	24	0.19
Sudanese	5	0.04
Am. Ind. or Alaska Nat., not spec.	15	0.12
Alsatian	5	0.04
American Indian tribes, specified:	33	0.26
Blackfeet (2)	4	0.03
Cherokee (3)	8	0.06
Choctaw (1)	1	0.01
Delaware (7)	7	0.05
Latin American Indians	4	0.03
Navajo (1)	2	0.02
All other tribes (2)	7	0.05
American Indian tribes, not spec.	4	0.03
Arab:	44	0.34
Lebanese	6	0.05
Moroccan	10	0.08
Syrian	28	0.22
Armenian	12	0.09
Asian:	247	1.91
Chinese, ex. Taiwanese (47)	53	0.41
Filipino (30)	33	0.26
Indian (77)	84	0.65
Indonesian (1)	1	0.01
Japanese (15)	17	0.13
Korean (37)	41	0.32
Pakistani (4)	5	0.04
Vietnamese (7)	7	0.05
Other Asian, not specified (2)	6	0.05
Assyrian/Chaldean/Syriac	12	0.09
Austrian	45	0.35
British	47	0.36
Canadian	71	0.55
Croatian	21	0.16
Czech	98	0.76
Czechoslovakian	34	0.26
Danish	28	0.22
Dutch	361	2.80
Eastern European	36	0.28
English	1,054	8.16
Estonian	6	0.05
European	70	0.54
Finnish	14	0.11
French, except Basque	177	1.37
French Canadian	123	0.95
German	1,894	14.67
Greek	103	0.80
Hawaii Native/Pacific Islander:	9	0.07
Melanesian: (1)	1	0.01
Fijian (1)	1	0.01
Micronesian: (2)	2	0.02
Other Micronesian (2)	2	0.02
Polynesian: (2)	3	0.02
Native Hawaiian (2)	3	0.02
Other Pac. Isl., not spec.	3	0.02
Hispanic or Latino:	950	7.36
Central American:	27	0.21
Costa Rican	7	0.05
Guatemalan	12	0.09
Honduran	4	0.03
Nicaraguan	2	0.02
Salvadoran	2	0.02
Cuban	11	0.09
Dominican Republic	28	0.22
Mexican	309	2.39
Puerto Rican	395	3.06
South American:	43	0.33
Argentinean	6	0.05
Bolivian	2	0.02
Chilean	12	0.09
Colombian	5	0.04
Ecuadorian	6	0.05
Peruvian	2	0.02
Other South American	10	0.08
Other Hispanic or Latino	137	1.06
Hungarian	75	0.58
Iranian	43	0.33
Irish	2,788	21.59
Israeli	3	0.02
Italian	1,948	15.09
Lithuanian	26	0.20
Norwegian	182	1.41
Pennsylvania German	6	0.05
Polish	1,307	10.12
Portuguese	20	0.15
Romanian	13	0.10
Russian	269	2.08
Scotch-Irish	129	1.00
Scottish	173	1.34
Slovak	24	0.19
Swedish	125	0.97
Swiss	23	0.18
Turkish	17	0.13
Ukrainian	67	0.52
United States or American	386	2.99
Welsh	68	0.53
West Indian, excl. Hispanic:	94	0.73
Haitian	44	0.34
Jamaican	9	0.07
Trinidadian and Tobagonian	9	0.07
West Indian	32	0.25
White:	11,541	89.38
Not Hispanic (10,838)	10,898	84.40
Hispanic (614)	643	4.98
Yugoslavian	12	0.09

Grand Island

Place Type: Town
County: Erie
Population: 18,621

Ancestry/Race	Number	%
African American/Black:	355	1.91
Not Hispanic (307)	353	1.90
Hispanic (1)	2	0.01
African, sub-Saharan:	19	0.10
African	19	0.10
Am. Ind. or Alaska Nat., not spec.	22	0.12
Alsatian	8	0.04
American Indian tribes, specified:	62	0.33
Blackfeet	1	0.01
Cherokee (3)	3	0.02
Chippewa (1)	1	0.01
Choctaw (2)	2	0.01
Iroquois (26)	44	0.24
Latin American Indians	3	0.02
Navajo (1)	1	0.01
All other tribes (5)	7	0.04
American Indian tribes, not spec.	2	0.01
Arab:	285	1.53
Arab/Arabic	22	0.12
Jordanian	11	0.06
Lebanese	185	0.99
Moroccan	9	0.05
Palestinian	58	0.31
Armenian	33	0.18
Asian:	271	1.46
Bangladeshi (1)	1	0.01
Chinese, ex. Taiwanese (31)	33	0.18
Filipino (24)	34	0.18
Indian (101)	118	0.63
Japanese (8)	15	0.08
Korean (29)	34	0.18
Malaysian	3	0.02
Pakistani (9)	9	0.05
Sri Lankan (4)	4	0.02
Taiwanese (3)	4	0.02
Thai (3)	3	0.02
Vietnamese	1	0.01
Other Asian, specified	2	0.01
Other Asian, not specified (3)	10	0.05
Austrian	76	0.41
Brazilian	21	0.11
British	114	0.61
Canadian	272	1.46
Croatian	19	0.10
Czech	59	0.32
Czechoslovakian	66	0.35
Danish	32	0.17
Dutch	201	1.08
Eastern European	36	0.19
English	2,492	13.38
European	156	0.84
Finnish	20	0.11
French, except Basque	915	4.91
French Canadian	316	1.70
German	5,650	30.34
Greek	78	0.42
Hawaii Native/Pacific Islander:	8	0.04
Polynesian: (2)	2	0.01
Samoan (2)	2	0.01
Other Pac. Isl., specified	2	0.01
Other Pac. Isl., not spec.	4	0.02
Hispanic or Latino:	203	1.09
Central American:	8	0.04

Notes: 1. Figures in the "Number" column do not add up to the total population due to: a) Ancestry/Race overlap — e.g. persons can report being both White and Irish, b) persons of Hispanic origin can report being any race, c) persons reporting two ancestries are counted in both categories. 2. Numbers in parentheses indicate the number of persons reporting this ancestry/race alone, not in combination with any other ancestry/race. 3. Refer to the Explanation of Data in the front of the book for more detailed information.

Ancestry/Race	Number	%
Nicaraguan	4	0.02
Panamanian	2	0.01
Salvadoran	1	0.01
Other Central American	1	0.01
Cuban	5	0.03
Dominican Republic	1	0.01
Mexican	34	0.18
Puerto Rican	86	0.46
South American:	16	0.09
Argentinean	3	0.02
Chilean	1	0.01
Colombian	7	0.04
Paraguayan	2	0.01
Peruvian	1	0.01
Venezuelan	1	0.01
Other South American	1	0.01
Other Hispanic or Latino	53	0.28
Hungarian	660	3.54
Icelander	9	0.05
Irish	3,981	21.38
Italian	3,734	20.05
Lithuanian	97	0.52
Maltese	22	0.12
Norwegian	90	0.48
Pennsylvania German	59	0.32
Polish	2,804	15.06
Romanian	8	0.04
Russian	180	0.97
Scotch-Irish	335	1.80
Scottish	637	3.42
Serbian	84	0.45
Slavic	39	0.21
Slovak	118	0.63
Swedish	209	1.12
Swiss	13	0.07
Ukrainian	142	0.76
United States or American	630	3.38
Welsh	228	1.22
White:	17,985	96.58
Not Hispanic (17,693)	17,827	95.74
Hispanic (145)	158	0.85
Yugoslavian	66	0.35

Greece

Place Type: Town
County: Monroe
Population: 94,141

Ancestry/Race	Number	%
African American/Black:	3,132	3.33
Not Hispanic (2,626)	2,992	3.18
Hispanic (86)	140	0.15
African, sub-Saharan:	297	0.32
African	252	0.27
Ethiopian	28	0.03
Other sub-Saharan African	17	0.02
Alaska Native tribes, specified:	3	0.00
Eskimo (1)	3	0.00
Alaska Native tribes, not specified	1	0.00
Am. Ind. or Alaska Nat., not spec.	141	0.15
Albanian	50	0.05
American Indian tribes, specified:	298	0.32
Apache (2)	5	0.01
Blackfeet (1)	5	0.01
Cherokee (6)	42	0.04
Chickasaw (1)	1	0.00
Chippewa (5)	7	0.01
Choctaw (1)	1	0.00
Creek	1	0.00
Iroquois (134)	186	0.20
Lumbee (3)	3	0.00
Navajo (1)	3	0.00
Osage	3	0.00
Pueblo	3	0.00
Seminole (1)	8	0.01
Sioux (6)	12	0.01
Ute (1)	1	0.00
Yuman (1)	1	0.00
All other tribes (8)	16	0.02
American Indian tribes, not spec.	15	0.02
Arab:	401	0.43
Arab/Arabic	28	0.03
Egyptian	33	0.04
Lebanese	224	0.24
Palestinian	28	0.03
Syrian	68	0.07
Other Arab	20	0.02
Armenian	70	0.07
Asian:	1,641	1.74
Cambodian (14)	23	0.02
Chinese, ex. Taiwanese (267)	315	0.33
Filipino (95)	133	0.14
Hmong (1)	1	0.00
Indian (256)	279	0.30
Indonesian (7)	10	0.01
Japanese (17)	47	0.05
Korean (321)	361	0.38
Laotian (75)	89	0.09
Pakistani (4)	4	0.00
Sri Lankan (2)	2	0.00
Taiwanese (6)	8	0.01
Thai (11)	13	0.01
Vietnamese (291)	311	0.33
Other Asian, not specified (15)	45	0.05
Australian	24	0.03
Austrian	197	0.21
Basque	7	0.01
Belgian	273	0.29
Brazilian	34	0.04
British	334	0.35
Bulgarian	6	0.01
Canadian	516	0.55
Celtic	7	0.01
Croatian	116	0.12
Cypriot	7	0.01
Czech	81	0.09
Czechoslovakian	78	0.08
Danish	273	0.29
Dutch	2,776	2.95
Eastern European	17	0.02
English	11,642	12.37
Estonian	4	0.00
European	731	0.78
Finnish	31	0.03
French, except Basque	3,630	3.86
French Canadian	1,640	1.74
German	24,689	26.23
Greek	356	0.38
Guyanese	17	0.02
Hawaii Native/Pacific Islander:	60	0.06
Micronesian: (11)	11	0.01
Guamanian/Chamorro (11)	11	0.01
Polynesian: (9)	26	0.03
Native Hawaiian (8)	25	0.03
Samoan (1)	1	0.00
Other Pac. Isl., not spec. (4)	23	0.02
Hispanic or Latino:	2,404	2.55
Central American:	82	0.09
Costa Rican	12	0.01
Guatemalan	9	0.01
Honduran	5	0.01
Nicaraguan	8	0.01
Panamanian	14	0.01
Salvadoran	33	0.04
Other Central American	1	0.00
Cuban	153	0.16
Dominican Republic	65	0.07
Mexican	191	0.20
Puerto Rican	1,484	1.58
South American:	138	0.15
Argentinean	6	0.01
Bolivian	2	0.00
Chilean	39	0.04
Colombian	34	0.04
Ecuadorian	4	0.00
Paraguayan	2	0.00
Peruvian	26	0.03
Uruguayan	1	0.00
Venezuelan	12	0.01
Other South American	12	0.01
Other Hispanic or Latino	291	0.31
Hungarian	423	0.45
Iranian	25	0.03
Irish	17,425	18.51
Italian	26,253	27.89
Latvian	37	0.04
Lithuanian	397	0.42
Macedonian	68	0.07
Northern European	7	0.01
Norwegian	260	0.28
Pennsylvania German	59	0.06
Polish	6,174	6.56
Portuguese	421	0.45
Romanian	171	0.18
Russian	468	0.50
Scandinavian	40	0.04
Scotch-Irish	912	0.97
Scottish	1,892	2.01
Slavic	58	0.06
Slovak	54	0.06
Slovene	38	0.04
Swedish	701	0.74
Swiss	189	0.20
Turkish	227	0.24
Ukrainian	1,726	1.83
United States or American	2,911	3.09
Welsh	560	0.59
West Indian, excl. Hispanic:	430	0.46
Bahamian	18	0.02
Barbadian	28	0.03
British West Indian	39	0.04
Haitian	11	0.01
Jamaican	287	0.30
Trinidadian and Tobagonian	6	0.01
West Indian	41	0.04
White:	88,790	94.32
Not Hispanic (86,578)	87,282	92.71
Hispanic (1,325)	1,508	1.60
Yugoslavian	354	0.38

Greenburgh

Place Type: Town
County: Westchester
Population: 86,764

Ancestry/Race	Number	%
African American/Black:	12,163	14.02
Not Hispanic (10,993)	11,662	13.44
Hispanic (351)	501	0.58
African, sub-Saharan:	788	0.91
African	351	0.40
Cape Verdean	7	0.01
Ethiopian	19	0.02
Ghanian	35	0.04
Nigerian	220	0.25
Senegalese	7	0.01
Sierra Leonean	29	0.03
South African	107	0.12
Other sub-Saharan African	13	0.01
Alaska Native tribes, specified:	1	0.00
Eskimo (1)	1	0.00
Am. Ind. or Alaska Nat., not spec.	230	0.27
Albanian	109	0.13
American Indian tribes, specified:	221	0.25
Apache (1)	4	0.00
Blackfeet (2)	9	0.01
Cherokee (13)	74	0.09
Cheyenne	1	0.00
Chickasaw	3	0.00
Choctaw	6	0.01
Comanche	2	0.00
Cree	2	0.00
Creek (1)	3	0.00
Delaware (1)	1	0.00
Houma (1)	3	0.00
Iroquois (6)	17	0.02
Latin American Indians (41)	75	0.09
Navajo	2	0.00

Notes: 1. Figures in the "Number" column do not add up to the total population due to: a) Ancestry/Race overlap — e.g. persons can report being both White and Irish, b) persons of Hispanic origin can report being any race, c) persons reporting two ancestries are counted in both categories. 2. Numbers in parentheses indicate the number of persons reporting this ancestry/race alone, not in combination with any other ancestry/race. 3. Refer to the Explanation of Data in the front of the book for more detailed information.

Ancestry/Race	Number	%
Potawatomi (1)	1	0.00
Pueblo	1	0.00
Seminole	1	0.00
Sioux (1)	2	0.00
All other tribes (2)	14	0.02
American Indian tribes, not spec.	53	0.06
Arab:	459	0.53
Arab/Arabic	63	0.07
Egyptian	39	0.04
Iraqi	62	0.07
Jordanian	44	0.05
Lebanese	66	0.08
Moroccan	14	0.02
Palestinian	78	0.09
Syrian	41	0.05
Other Arab	52	0.06
Armenian	143	0.16
Asian:	8,392	9.67
Bangladeshi (18)	19	0.02
Cambodian (4)	5	0.01
Chinese, ex. Taiwanese (1,310)	1,496	1.72
Filipino (628)	742	0.86
Indian (2,333)	2,481	2.86
Indonesian (15)	16	0.02
Japanese (1,741)	1,894	2.18
Korean (1,100)	1,196	1.38
Laotian (1)	4	0.00
Malaysian	11	0.01
Pakistani (133)	164	0.19
Sri Lankan (11)	15	0.02
Taiwanese (57)	71	0.08
Thai (34)	46	0.05
Vietnamese (32)	37	0.04
Other Asian, specified (20)	25	0.03
Other Asian, not specified (83)	170	0.20
Assyrian/Chaldean/Syriac	47	0.05
Australian	32	0.04
Austrian	1,111	1.28
Basque	19	0.02
Belgian	188	0.22
Brazilian	210	0.24
British	369	0.43
Bulgarian	147	0.17
Canadian	225	0.26
Celtic	28	0.03
Croatian	141	0.16
Cypriot	47	0.05
Czech	327	0.38
Czechoslovakian	181	0.21
Danish	293	0.34
Dutch	548	0.63
Eastern European	1,338	1.54
English	3,987	4.60
Estonian	8	0.01
European	756	0.87
Finnish	92	0.11
French, except Basque	987	1.14
French Canadian	521	0.60
German	6,720	7.75
German Russian	3	0.00
Greek	927	1.07
Guyanese	127	0.15
Hawaii Native/Pacific Islander:	84	0.10
Micronesian: (21)	22	0.03
Guamanian/Chamorro (12)	13	0.01
Other Micronesian (9)	9	0.01
Polynesian: (7)	12	0.01
Native Hawaiian (5)	7	0.01
Samoan (2)	5	0.01
Other Pac. Isl., specified	3	0.00
Other Pac. Isl., not spec. (13)	47	0.05
Hispanic or Latino:	7,825	9.02
Central American:	390	0.45
Costa Rican	9	0.01
Guatemalan	181	0.21
Honduran	40	0.05
Nicaraguan	11	0.01
Panamanian	36	0.04
Salvadoran	101	0.12
Other Central American	12	0.01
Cuban	501	0.58
Dominican Republic	579	0.67
Mexican	925	1.07
Puerto Rican	1,818	2.10
South American:	1,787	2.06
Argentinean	100	0.12
Bolivian	15	0.02
Chilean	140	0.16
Colombian	419	0.48
Ecuadorian	566	0.65
Paraguayan	37	0.04
Peruvian	388	0.45
Uruguayan	24	0.03
Venezuelan	37	0.04
Other South American	61	0.07
Other Hispanic or Latino	1,825	2.10
Hungarian	1,356	1.56
Icelander	8	0.01
Iranian	193	0.22
Irish	11,757	13.55
Israeli	279	0.32
Italian	15,494	17.86
Latvian	101	0.12
Lithuanian	323	0.37
Maltese	33	0.04
New Zealander	9	0.01
Northern European	34	0.04
Norwegian	275	0.32
Pennsylvania German	6	0.01
Polish	4,690	5.41
Portuguese	506	0.58
Romanian	341	0.39
Russian	4,988	5.75
Scandinavian	75	0.09
Scotch-Irish	606	0.70
Scottish	938	1.08
Serbian	20	0.02
Slavic	62	0.07
Slovak	340	0.39
Slovene	31	0.04
Swedish	541	0.62
Swiss	302	0.35
Turkish	194	0.22
Ukrainian	600	0.69
United States or American	2,906	3.35
Welsh	236	0.27
West Indian, excl. Hispanic:	2,582	2.98
Bahamian	25	0.03
Barbadian	114	0.13
Belizean	24	0.03
British West Indian	157	0.18
Dutch West Indian	43	0.05
Haitian	405	0.47
Jamaican	1,434	1.65
Trinidadian and Tobagonian	153	0.18
West Indian	227	0.26
White:	64,484	74.32
Not Hispanic (58,450)	59,538	68.62
Hispanic (4,375)	4,946	5.70
Yugoslavian	62	0.07

Greenlawn

Place Type: Census Designated Place
County: Suffolk
Population: 13,286

Ancestry/Race	Number	%
African American/Black:	2,178	16.39
Not Hispanic (1,967)	2,109	15.87
Hispanic (60)	69	0.52
African, sub-Saharan:	183	1.38
African	148	1.11
Kenyan	12	0.09
Liberian	17	0.13
Other sub-Saharan African	6	0.05
Am. Ind. or Alaska Nat., not spec.	28	0.21
Albanian	20	0.15
American Indian tribes, specified:	42	0.32
Blackfeet	4	0.03
Cherokee (1)	11	0.08
Iroquois	1	0.01
Latin American Indians (4)	6	0.05
Lumbee (1)	1	0.01
Navajo (2)	4	0.03
All other tribes (9)	15	0.11
American Indian tribes, not spec.	5	0.04
Arab:	21	0.16
Lebanese	5	0.04
Palestinian	6	0.05
Syrian	10	0.08
Armenian	56	0.42
Asian:	429	3.23
Bangladeshi (1)	1	0.01
Cambodian (1)	1	0.01
Chinese, ex. Taiwanese (98)	110	0.83
Filipino (26)	34	0.26
Indian (118)	119	0.90
Indonesian (1)	1	0.01
Japanese (12)	16	0.12
Korean (51)	55	0.41
Pakistani (41)	54	0.41
Taiwanese (9)	9	0.07
Thai (4)	4	0.03
Other Asian, specified	3	0.02
Other Asian, not specified (7)	22	0.17
Austrian	90	0.68
Belgian	18	0.14
Brazilian	5	0.04
British	20	0.15
Canadian	39	0.29
Croatian	41	0.31
Czech	56	0.42
Czechoslovakian	24	0.18
Danish	25	0.19
Dutch	176	1.32
Eastern European	17	0.13
English	701	5.28
Estonian	10	0.08
European	34	0.26
Finnish	50	0.38
French, except Basque	177	1.33
French Canadian	25	0.19
German	2,190	16.48
Greek	216	1.63
Hawaii Native/Pacific Islander:	11	0.08
Micronesian:	1	0.01
Guamanian/Chamorro	1	0.01
Polynesian: (1)	2	0.02
Native Hawaiian (1)	1	0.01
Samoan	1	0.01
Other Pac. Isl., not spec. (3)	8	0.06
Hispanic or Latino:	905	6.81
Central American:	186	1.40
Costa Rican	2	0.02
Guatemalan	61	0.46
Honduran	12	0.09
Panamanian	4	0.03
Salvadoran	101	0.76
Other Central American	6	0.05
Cuban	33	0.25
Dominican Republic	34	0.26
Mexican	30	0.23
Puerto Rican	277	2.08
South American:	161	1.21
Argentinean	20	0.15
Chilean	18	0.14
Colombian	39	0.29
Ecuadorian	40	0.30
Paraguayan	12	0.09
Peruvian	17	0.13
Uruguayan	3	0.02
Venezuelan	2	0.02
Other South American	10	0.08
Other Hispanic or Latino	184	1.38
Hungarian	103	0.78
Irish	2,944	22.16
Israeli	3	0.02
Italian	3,092	23.27
Latvian	10	0.08

Notes: 1. Figures in the "Number" column do not add up to the total population due to: a) Ancestry/Race overlap — e.g. persons can report being both White and Irish, b) persons of Hispanic origin can report being any race, c) persons reporting two ancestries are counted in both categories. 2. Numbers in parentheses indicate the number of persons reporting this ancestry/race alone, not in combination with any other ancestry/race. 3. Refer to the Explanation of Data in the front of the book for more detailed information.

Lithuanian	72	0.54
Maltese	14	0.11
Norwegian	146	1.10
Polish	727	5.47
Portuguese	46	0.35
Romanian	23	0.17
Russian	415	3.12
Scandinavian	60	0.45
Scotch-Irish	212	1.60
Scottish	250	1.88
Slavic	12	0.09
Slovak	63	0.47
Slovene	10	0.08
Swedish	192	1.45
Swiss	44	0.33
Turkish	47	0.35
Ukrainian	122	0.92
United States or American	429	3.23
Welsh	93	0.70
West Indian, excl. Hispanic:	513	3.86
British West Indian	15	0.11
Haitian	282	2.12
Jamaican	161	1.21
Trinidadian and Tobagonian	55	0.41
White:	10,431	78.51
Not Hispanic (9,792)	9,891	74.45
Hispanic (477)	540	4.06
Yugoslavian	52	0.39

Guilderland

Place Type: Town
County: Albany
Population: 32,688

Ancestry/Race	Number	%
African American/Black:	923	2.82
Not Hispanic (788)	870	2.66
Hispanic (32)	53	0.16
African, sub-Saharan:	9	0.03
African	9	0.03
Am. Ind. or Alaska Nat., not spec.	38	0.12
Albanian	20	0.06
American Indian tribes, specified:	95	0.29
Apache	1	0.00
Blackfeet (1)	4	0.01
Cherokee (3)	17	0.05
Chippewa (2)	3	0.01
Choctaw (1)	1	0.00
Cree	4	0.01
Delaware (3)	4	0.01
Iroquois (8)	26	0.08
Latin American Indians (4)	10	0.03
Lumbee (1)	1	0.00
Pueblo (1)	2	0.01
Seminole (1)	1	0.00
Shoshone	4	0.01
Sioux (6)	8	0.02
All other tribes (1)	9	0.03
American Indian tribes, not spec.	15	0.05
Arab:	180	0.55
Arab/Arabic	21	0.06
Egyptian	25	0.08
Jordanian	13	0.04
Lebanese	31	0.09
Palestinian	16	0.05
Syrian	66	0.20
Other Arab	8	0.02
Armenian	91	0.28
Asian:	1,386	4.24
Bangladeshi (6)	6	0.02
Cambodian (1)	1	0.00
Chinese, ex. Taiwanese (303)	333	1.02
Filipino (42)	66	0.20
Indian (494)	518	1.58
Indonesian (2)	3	0.01
Japanese (27)	37	0.11
Korean (265)	274	0.84
Laotian (1)	2	0.01
Malaysian (1)	2	0.01
Pakistani (21)	34	0.10
Sri Lankan (1)	1	0.00
Taiwanese (23)	27	0.08
Thai (4)	4	0.01
Vietnamese (27)	34	0.10
Other Asian, specified (1)	2	0.01
Other Asian, not specified (11)	42	0.13
Australian	38	0.12
Austrian	170	0.52
Brazilian	6	0.02
British	119	0.36
Bulgarian	10	0.03
Canadian	83	0.25
Croatian	25	0.08
Czech	90	0.28
Czechoslovakian	36	0.11
Danish	107	0.33
Dutch	1,455	4.45
Eastern European	112	0.34
English	3,840	11.75
Estonian	2	0.01
European	197	0.60
Finnish	32	0.10
French, except Basque	1,608	4.92
French Canadian	758	2.32
German	6,659	20.37
Greek	254	0.78
Hawaii Native/Pacific Islander:	14	0.04
Polynesian: (3)	8	0.02
Native Hawaiian (2)	6	0.02
Samoan (1)	1	0.00
Other Polynesian	1	0.00
Other Pac. Isl., specified	1	0.00
Other Pac. Isl., not spec. (1)	5	0.02
Hispanic or Latino:	585	1.79
Central American:	29	0.09
Costa Rican	7	0.02
Guatemalan	4	0.01
Nicaraguan	6	0.02
Panamanian	7	0.02
Salvadoran	4	0.01
Other Central American	1	0.00
Cuban	25	0.08
Dominican Republic	10	0.03
Mexican	94	0.29
Puerto Rican	243	0.74
South American:	57	0.17
Argentinean	12	0.04
Chilean	6	0.02
Colombian	13	0.04
Ecuadorian	4	0.01
Paraguayan	1	0.00
Peruvian	10	0.03
Uruguayan	1	0.00
Venezuelan	7	0.02
Other South American	3	0.01
Other Hispanic or Latino	127	0.39
Hungarian	249	0.76
Iranian	20	0.06
Irish	7,880	24.11
Israeli	25	0.08
Italian	6,689	20.46
Latvian	21	0.06
Lithuanian	198	0.61
Luxemburger	8	0.02
Macedonian	14	0.04
New Zealander	2	0.01
Northern European	16	0.05
Norwegian	150	0.46
Pennsylvania German	13	0.04
Polish	2,460	7.53
Portuguese	71	0.22
Romanian	19	0.06
Russian	755	2.31
Scandinavian	22	0.07
Scotch-Irish	507	1.55
Scottish	618	1.89
Serbian	7	0.02
Slavic	7	0.02
Slovak	116	0.35
Slovene	45	0.14
Swedish	252	0.77
Swiss	98	0.30
Turkish	38	0.12
Ukrainian	335	1.02
United States or American	1,123	3.44
Welsh	226	0.69
West Indian, excl. Hispanic:	88	0.27
British West Indian	14	0.04
Haitian	12	0.04
Jamaican	42	0.13
Trinidadian and Tobagonian	10	0.03
West Indian	10	0.03
White:	30,381	92.94
Not Hispanic (29,715)	29,952	91.63
Hispanic (382)	429	1.31
Yugoslavian	22	0.07

Halfmoon

Place Type: Town
County: Saratoga
Population: 18,474

Ancestry/Race	Number	%
Afghan	10	0.05
African American/Black:	295	1.60
Not Hispanic (223)	270	1.46
Hispanic (11)	25	0.14
Am. Ind. or Alaska Nat., not spec.	44	0.24
Alsatian	9	0.05
American Indian tribes, specified:	89	0.48
Blackfeet (1)	15	0.08
Cherokee (6)	21	0.11
Cheyenne	4	0.02
Chippewa	1	0.01
Iroquois (6)	20	0.11
Latin American Indians (4)	4	0.02
Potawatomi	1	0.01
Sioux (2)	6	0.03
All other tribes (4)	17	0.09
American Indian tribes, not spec.	1	0.01
Arab:	104	0.56
Jordanian	44	0.24
Lebanese	51	0.28
Syrian	9	0.05
Armenian	61	0.33
Asian:	427	2.31
Bangladeshi (2)	2	0.01
Cambodian (5)	5	0.03
Chinese, ex. Taiwanese (96)	101	0.55
Filipino (19)	37	0.20
Indian (135)	148	0.80
Indonesian (8)	10	0.05
Japanese (11)	24	0.13
Korean (31)	43	0.23
Laotian (2)	2	0.01
Malaysian	1	0.01
Pakistani (20)	25	0.14
Taiwanese (3)	3	0.02
Thai	3	0.02
Vietnamese (11)	14	0.08
Other Asian, not specified (5)	9	0.05
Australian	9	0.05
Austrian	101	0.55
Belgian	41	0.22
British	51	0.28
Canadian	55	0.30
Celtic	8	0.04
Czech	110	0.60
Czechoslovakian	7	0.04
Danish	135	0.73
Dutch	676	3.66
Eastern European	27	0.15
English	2,285	12.37
Estonian	14	0.08
European	46	0.25
Finnish	33	0.18
French, except Basque	2,157	11.68
French Canadian	909	4.92

Notes: 1. Figures in the "Number" column do not add up to the total population due to: a) Ancestry/Race overlap — e.g. persons can report being both White and Irish, b) persons of Hispanic origin can report being any race, c) persons reporting two ancestries are counted in both categories. 2. Numbers in parentheses indicate the number of persons reporting this ancestry/race alone, not in combination with any other ancestry/race. 3. Refer to the Explanation of Data in the front of the book for more detailed information.

Ancestry/Race	Number	%
German	3,019	16.34
Greek	53	0.29
Hawaii Native/Pacific Islander:	5	0.03
Polynesian: (3)	3	0.02
Samoan (3)	3	0.02
Other Pac. Isl., not spec.	2	0.01
Hispanic or Latino:	304	1.65
Central American:	11	0.06
Costa Rican	1	0.01
Guatemalan	1	0.01
Nicaraguan	1	0.01
Panamanian	4	0.02
Salvadoran	3	0.02
Other Central American	1	0.01
Cuban	22	0.12
Dominican Republic	13	0.07
Mexican	82	0.44
Puerto Rican	96	0.52
South American:	21	0.11
Argentinean	3	0.02
Chilean	4	0.02
Colombian	3	0.02
Ecuadorian	2	0.01
Peruvian	1	0.01
Venezuelan	3	0.02
Other South American	5	0.03
Other Hispanic or Latino	59	0.32
Hungarian	87	0.47
Iranian	19	0.10
Irish	4,606	24.93
Italian	3,203	17.34
Lithuanian	102	0.55
Norwegian	205	1.11
Polish	1,806	9.78
Portuguese	11	0.06
Romanian	3	0.02
Russian	213	1.15
Scandinavian	6	0.03
Scotch-Irish	168	0.91
Scottish	313	1.69
Serbian	15	0.08
Slovak	130	0.70
Swedish	130	0.70
Swiss	46	0.25
Ukrainian	293	1.59
United States or American	603	3.26
Welsh	186	1.01
West Indian, excl. Hispanic:	27	0.15
Haitian	8	0.04
Jamaican	19	0.10
White:	17,757	96.12
Not Hispanic (17,344)	17,539	94.94
Hispanic (195)	218	1.18
Yugoslavian	42	0.23

Hamburg

Place Type: Town
County: Erie
Population: 56,259

Ancestry/Race	Number	%
African American/Black:	380	0.68
Not Hispanic (258)	358	0.64
Hispanic (19)	22	0.04
African, sub-Saharan:	31	0.06
African	4	0.01
Ethiopian	27	0.05
Alaska Native tribes, specified:	1	0.00
Tlingit-Haida	1	0.00
Am. Ind. or Alaska Nat., not spec.	70	0.12
Albanian	25	0.04
American Indian tribes, specified:	154	0.27
Apache	1	0.00
Blackfeet	2	0.00
Cherokee (3)	18	0.03
Chippewa (2)	2	0.00
Cree (1)	4	0.01
Delaware (1)	1	0.00
Iroquois (62)	105	0.19
Latin American Indians (5)	8	0.01
Navajo (2)	4	0.01
Pueblo (1)	1	0.00
Yuman	1	0.00
All other tribes (5)	7	0.01
American Indian tribes, not spec.	7	0.01
Arab:	133	0.24
Lebanese	108	0.19
Moroccan	11	0.02
Syrian	14	0.02
Asian:	292	0.52
Cambodian (1)	1	0.00
Chinese, ex. Taiwanese (55)	66	0.12
Filipino (29)	49	0.09
Indian (41)	51	0.09
Indonesian (1)	1	0.00
Japanese (7)	16	0.03
Korean (54)	60	0.11
Laotian (1)	3	0.01
Malaysian	1	0.00
Pakistani (1)	1	0.00
Taiwanese (4)	4	0.01
Thai (8)	13	0.02
Vietnamese (7)	9	0.02
Other Asian, not specified (3)	17	0.03
Austrian	221	0.39
Basque	6	0.01
Belgian	15	0.03
Brazilian	22	0.04
British	133	0.24
Bulgarian	14	0.02
Canadian	268	0.48
Croatian	458	0.82
Czech	123	0.22
Czechoslovakian	110	0.20
Danish	232	0.41
Dutch	566	1.01
Eastern European	19	0.03
English	5,738	10.21
Estonian	20	0.04
European	77	0.14
Finnish	60	0.11
French, except Basque	1,928	3.43
French Canadian	564	1.00
German	19,071	33.94
Greek	105	0.19
Hawaii Native/Pacific Islander:	23	0.04
Micronesian: (3)	7	0.01
Guamanian/Chamorro (3)	7	0.01
Polynesian: (2)	11	0.02
Native Hawaiian (1)	10	0.02
Samoan (1)	1	0.00
Other Pac. Isl., not spec.	5	0.01
Hispanic or Latino:	876	1.56
Central American:	8	0.01
Costa Rican	1	0.00
Guatemalan	2	0.00
Panamanian	3	0.01
Other Central American	2	0.00
Cuban	9	0.02
Dominican Republic	6	0.01
Mexican	259	0.46
Puerto Rican	355	0.63
South American:	22	0.04
Argentinean	1	0.00
Chilean	2	0.00
Colombian	12	0.02
Paraguayan	2	0.00
Peruvian	2	0.00
Venezuelan	1	0.00
Other South American	2	0.00
Other Hispanic or Latino	217	0.39
Hungarian	658	1.17
Iranian	31	0.06
Irish	13,597	24.20
Italian	10,049	17.88
Lithuanian	82	0.15
Luxemburger	10	0.02
Macedonian	198	0.35
Norwegian	265	0.47
Pennsylvania German	30	0.05
Polish	12,779	22.74
Portuguese	22	0.04
Romanian	19	0.03
Russian	352	0.63
Scandinavian	17	0.03
Scotch-Irish	675	1.20
Scottish	1,163	2.07
Serbian	42	0.07
Slavic	66	0.12
Slovak	175	0.31
Slovene	20	0.04
Swedish	691	1.23
Swiss	120	0.21
Ukrainian	652	1.16
United States or American	1,273	2.27
Welsh	410	0.73
West Indian, excl. Hispanic:	11	0.02
Jamaican	11	0.02
White:	55,402	98.48
Not Hispanic (54,490)	54,751	97.32
Hispanic (606)	651	1.16
Yugoslavian	188	0.33

Hamburg

Place Type: Village
County: Erie
Population: 10,116

Ancestry/Race	Number	%
African American/Black:	35	0.35
Not Hispanic (20)	35	0.35
Am. Ind. or Alaska Nat., not spec.	6	0.06
Albanian	25	0.25
American Indian tribes, specified:	23	0.23
Blackfeet	2	0.02
Cherokee (1)	3	0.03
Iroquois (9)	15	0.15
Latin American Indians (1)	1	0.01
Navajo (2)	2	0.02
American Indian tribes, not spec.	1	0.01
Arab:	35	0.35
Lebanese	21	0.21
Syrian	14	0.14
Asian:	56	0.55
Chinese, ex. Taiwanese (12)	14	0.14
Filipino (4)	7	0.07
Indian (3)	3	0.03
Indonesian (1)	1	0.01
Japanese	1	0.01
Korean (15)	15	0.15
Laotian	1	0.01
Thai (3)	3	0.03
Vietnamese	1	0.01
Other Asian, not specified (1)	10	0.10
Austrian	37	0.37
British	41	0.41
Canadian	79	0.78
Croatian	75	0.74
Czech	9	0.09
Czechoslovakian	21	0.21
Danish	121	1.20
Dutch	88	0.87
English	1,558	15.42
Estonian	12	0.12
European	10	0.10
Finnish	19	0.19
French, except Basque	324	3.21
French Canadian	163	1.61
German	3,649	36.10
Hawaii Native/Pacific Islander:	1	0.01
Micronesian:	1	0.01
Guamanian/Chamorro	1	0.01
Hispanic or Latino:	76	0.75
Mexican	26	0.26
Puerto Rican	21	0.21
South American:	9	0.09
Argentinean	1	0.01
Chilean	2	0.02

Notes: 1. Figures in the "Number" column do not add up to the total population due to: a) Ancestry/Race overlap — e.g. persons can report being both White and Irish, b) persons of Hispanic origin can report being any race, c) persons reporting two ancestries are counted in both categories. 2. Numbers in parentheses indicate the number of persons reporting this ancestry/race alone, not in combination with any other ancestry/race. 3. Refer to the Explanation of Data in the front of the book for more detailed information.

Ancestry/Race	Number	%
Colombian	4	0.04
Other South American	2	0.02
Other Hispanic or Latino	20	0.20
Hungarian	105	1.04
Iranian	18	0.18
Irish	2,732	27.03
Italian	1,885	18.65
Lithuanian	7	0.07
Macedonian	8	0.08
Norwegian	45	0.45
Polish	1,416	14.01
Portuguese	6	0.06
Romanian	8	0.08
Russian	43	0.43
Scotch-Irish	160	1.58
Scottish	271	2.68
Serbian	21	0.21
Slavic	6	0.06
Slovak	32	0.32
Swedish	173	1.71
Swiss	35	0.35
Ukrainian	113	1.12
United States or American	328	3.25
Welsh	71	0.70
White:	10,022	99.07
Not Hispanic (9,918)	9,960	98.46
Hispanic (60)	62	0.61
Yugoslavian	21	0.21

Hampton Bays

Place Type: Census Designated Place
County: Suffolk
Population: 12,236

Ancestry/Race	Number	%
African American/Black:	142	1.16
Not Hispanic (92)	126	1.03
Hispanic (15)	16	0.13
Alaska Native tribes, specified:	1	0.01
Eskimo (1)	1	0.01
Am. Ind. or Alaska Nat., not spec.	22	0.18
Albanian	22	0.18
American Indian tribes, specified:	28	0.23
Blackfeet	2	0.02
Cherokee	8	0.07
Choctaw (1)	1	0.01
Iroquois (1)	4	0.03
Latin American Indians (2)	2	0.02
Osage	1	0.01
Shoshone	4	0.03
All other tribes (2)	6	0.05
Arab:	26	0.21
Arab/Arabic	9	0.07
Lebanese	8	0.07
Syrian	9	0.07
Armenian	6	0.05
Asian:	116	0.95
Chinese, ex. Taiwanese (20)	20	0.16
Filipino (16)	26	0.21
Indian (9)	11	0.09
Japanese (8)	14	0.11
Korean (9)	14	0.11
Laotian (1)	5	0.04
Malaysian (1)	8	0.07
Pakistani (4)	4	0.03
Thai (1)	1	0.01
Vietnamese (6)	6	0.05
Other Asian, specified	1	0.01
Other Asian, not specified (4)	6	0.05
Austrian	111	0.91
Belgian	8	0.07
Brazilian	50	0.41
British	36	0.29
Canadian	17	0.14
Celtic	9	0.07
Czech	150	1.23
Czechoslovakian	48	0.39
Danish	42	0.34
Dutch	176	1.44
Eastern European	34	0.28
English	1,411	11.56
European	55	0.45
Finnish	12	0.10
French, except Basque	376	3.08
French Canadian	105	0.86
German	2,114	17.31
Greek	186	1.52
Hawaii Native/Pacific Islander:	18	0.15
Micronesian: (6)	6	0.05
Guamanian/Chamorro (6)	6	0.05
Polynesian: (3)	3	0.02
Native Hawaiian (2)	2	0.02
Samoan (1)	1	0.01
Other Pac. Isl., specified	1	0.01
Other Pac. Isl., not spec. (3)	8	0.07
Hispanic or Latino:	1,529	12.50
Central American:	345	2.82
Costa Rican	193	1.58
Guatemalan	81	0.66
Honduran	21	0.17
Nicaraguan	3	0.02
Panamanian	2	0.02
Salvadoran	41	0.34
Other Central American	4	0.03
Cuban	18	0.15
Dominican Republic	17	0.14
Mexican	299	2.44
Puerto Rican	140	1.14
South American:	345	2.82
Argentinean	9	0.07
Chilean	3	0.02
Colombian	235	1.92
Ecuadorian	53	0.43
Paraguayan	1	0.01
Peruvian	21	0.17
Venezuelan	8	0.07
Other South American	15	0.12
Other Hispanic or Latino	365	2.98
Hungarian	71	0.58
Irish	3,124	25.58
Israeli	6	0.05
Italian	2,643	21.64
Latvian	39	0.32
Lithuanian	109	0.89
Maltese	14	0.11
Northern European	16	0.13
Norwegian	172	1.41
Polish	1,005	8.23
Portuguese	66	0.54
Romanian	30	0.25
Russian	169	1.38
Scotch-Irish	227	1.86
Scottish	205	1.68
Slovak	17	0.14
Swedish	138	1.13
Swiss	41	0.34
Turkish	7	0.06
Ukrainian	76	0.62
United States or American	386	3.16
Welsh	106	0.87
West Indian, excl. Hispanic:	41	0.34
Jamaican	41	0.34
White:	11,546	94.36
Not Hispanic (10,402)	10,480	85.65
Hispanic (971)	1,066	8.71
Yugoslavian	23	0.19

Harrison

Place Type: Village
County: Westchester
Population: 24,154

Ancestry/Race	Number	%
African American/Black:	402	1.66
Not Hispanic (308)	349	1.44
Hispanic (37)	53	0.22
African, sub-Saharan:	69	0.29
African	16	0.07
Cape Verdean	9	0.04
Nigerian	9	0.04
South African	20	0.08
Ugandan	7	0.03
Zimbabwean	8	0.03
Am. Ind. or Alaska Nat., not spec.	24	0.10
Albanian	77	0.32
American Indian tribes, specified:	35	0.14
Apache	1	0.00
Blackfeet	2	0.01
Cherokee (5)	10	0.04
Comanche	1	0.00
Iroquois (4)	9	0.04
Latin American Indians (6)	8	0.03
Osage (1)	1	0.00
Seminole	1	0.00
All other tribes (1)	2	0.01
American Indian tribes, not spec.	2	0.01
Arab:	134	0.56
Arab/Arabic	19	0.08
Egyptian	19	0.08
Iraqi	60	0.25
Lebanese	29	0.12
Moroccan	7	0.03
Armenian	104	0.43
Asian:	1,429	5.92
Cambodian (3)	3	0.01
Chinese, ex. Taiwanese (199)	228	0.94
Filipino (81)	96	0.40
Indian (145)	160	0.66
Indonesian	4	0.02
Japanese (661)	694	2.87
Korean (144)	151	0.63
Laotian (2)	3	0.01
Pakistani (27)	32	0.13
Taiwanese (2)	3	0.01
Thai (10)	12	0.05
Vietnamese (3)	5	0.02
Other Asian, specified (4)	4	0.02
Other Asian, not specified (23)	34	0.14
Australian	6	0.02
Austrian	147	0.61
Basque	10	0.04
Belgian	36	0.15
Brazilian	62	0.26
British	121	0.50
Bulgarian	39	0.16
Canadian	77	0.32
Croatian	16	0.07
Czech	82	0.34
Czechoslovakian	49	0.20
Danish	64	0.27
Dutch	170	0.70
Eastern European	143	0.59
English	1,012	4.19
Estonian	5	0.02
European	159	0.66
Finnish	10	0.04
French, except Basque	512	2.12
French Canadian	51	0.21
German	1,836	7.60
Greek	380	1.57
Guyanese	8	0.03
Hawaii Native/Pacific Islander:	15	0.06
Micronesian: (2)	3	0.01
Guamanian/Chamorro (2)	3	0.01
Polynesian:	5	0.02
Native Hawaiian	4	0.02
Samoan	1	0.00
Other Pac. Isl., not spec.	7	0.03
Hispanic or Latino:	1,618	6.70
Central American:	54	0.22
Costa Rican	4	0.02
Guatemalan	18	0.07
Honduran	1	0.00
Nicaraguan	2	0.01
Panamanian	8	0.03
Salvadoran	19	0.08
Other Central American	2	0.01
Cuban	48	0.20

Notes: 1. Figures in the "Number" column do not add up to the total population due to: a) Ancestry/Race overlap — e.g. persons can report being both White and Irish, b) persons of Hispanic origin can report being any race, c) persons reporting two ancestries are counted in both categories. 2. Numbers in parentheses indicate the number of persons reporting this ancestry/race alone, not in combination with any other ancestry/race. 3. Refer to the Explanation of Data in the front of the book for more detailed information.

Ancestry/Race	Number	%
Dominican Republic	85	0.35
Mexican	182	0.75
Puerto Rican	269	1.11
South American:	603	2.50
Argentinean	42	0.17
Bolivian	18	0.07
Chilean	29	0.12
Colombian	199	0.82
Ecuadorian	37	0.15
Paraguayan	94	0.39
Peruvian	124	0.51
Uruguayan	27	0.11
Venezuelan	17	0.07
Other South American	16	0.07
Other Hispanic or Latino	377	1.56
Hungarian	267	1.11
Irish	3,835	15.88
Israeli	52	0.22
Italian	9,185	38.04
Latvian	20	0.08
Lithuanian	38	0.16
Luxemburger	7	0.03
Macedonian	10	0.04
Maltese	6	0.02
Northern European	20	0.08
Norwegian	147	0.61
Polish	822	3.40
Portuguese	137	0.57
Romanian	127	0.53
Russian	991	4.10
Scandinavian	21	0.09
Scotch-Irish	147	0.61
Scottish	293	1.21
Slovak	50	0.21
Swedish	151	0.63
Swiss	129	0.53
Turkish	7	0.03
Ukrainian	106	0.44
United States or American	835	3.46
Welsh	65	0.27
West Indian, excl. Hispanic:	66	0.27
Haitian	46	0.19
Jamaican	17	0.07
Trinidadian and Tobagonian	3	0.01
White:	22,028	91.20
Not Hispanic (20,584)	20,833	86.25
Hispanic (1,102)	1,195	4.95
Yugoslavian	9	0.04

Hauppauge

Place Type: Census Designated Place
County: Suffolk
Population: 20,100

Ancestry/Race	Number	%
African American/Black:	292	1.45
Not Hispanic (216)	267	1.33
Hispanic (14)	25	0.12
African, sub-Saharan:	9	0.04
Ghanian	5	0.02
South African	4	0.02
Am. Ind. or Alaska Nat., not spec.	26	0.13
Albanian	37	0.18
Alsatian	20	0.10
American Indian tribes, specified:	25	0.12
Blackfeet	1	0.00
Cherokee	4	0.02
Cree (1)	1	0.00
Iroquois	12	0.06
Latin American Indians (1)	1	0.00
All other tribes (1)	6	0.03
Arab:	73	0.36
Arab/Arabic	19	0.09
Jordanian	9	0.04
Lebanese	22	0.11
Palestinian	17	0.08
Other Arab	6	0.03
Armenian	47	0.23
Asian:	832	4.14
Chinese, ex. Taiwanese (186)	204	1.01
Filipino (69)	90	0.45
Indian (288)	321	1.60
Japanese (11)	16	0.08
Korean (111)	119	0.59
Laotian	1	0.00
Pakistani (32)	38	0.19
Taiwanese (7)	8	0.04
Thai (6)	6	0.03
Vietnamese (2)	2	0.01
Other Asian, not specified (5)	27	0.13
Austrian	130	0.65
Belgian	13	0.06
British	28	0.14
Bulgarian	37	0.18
Canadian	38	0.19
Celtic	37	0.18
Croatian	17	0.08
Czech	78	0.39
Czechoslovakian	68	0.34
Danish	53	0.26
Dutch	182	0.90
Eastern European	87	0.43
English	1,050	5.22
European	60	0.30
Finnish	51	0.25
French, except Basque	398	1.98
French Canadian	100	0.50
German	3,749	18.63
Greek	275	1.37
Hawaii Native/Pacific Islander:	11	0.05
Micronesian: (1)	3	0.01
Guamanian/Chamorro (1)	3	0.01
Polynesian: (5)	5	0.02
Native Hawaiian (4)	4	0.02
Samoan (1)	1	0.00
Other Pac. Isl., not spec.	3	0.01
Hispanic or Latino:	887	4.41
Central American:	75	0.37
Costa Rican	24	0.12
Guatemalan	12	0.06
Honduran	3	0.01
Nicaraguan	4	0.02
Panamanian	3	0.01
Salvadoran	28	0.14
Other Central American	1	0.00
Cuban	51	0.25
Dominican Republic	21	0.10
Mexican	41	0.20
Puerto Rican	397	1.98
South American:	132	0.66
Argentinean	22	0.11
Chilean	18	0.09
Colombian	39	0.19
Ecuadorian	18	0.09
Paraguayan	1	0.00
Peruvian	27	0.13
Uruguayan	2	0.01
Venezuelan	2	0.01
Other South American	3	0.01
Other Hispanic or Latino	170	0.85
Hungarian	230	1.14
Icelander	26	0.13
Iranian	42	0.21
Irish	4,864	24.17
Israeli	24	0.12
Italian	7,556	37.54
Latvian	5	0.02
Lithuanian	78	0.39
Macedonian	6	0.03
Maltese	24	0.12
Norwegian	113	0.56
Polish	1,334	6.63
Portuguese	58	0.29
Romanian	49	0.24
Russian	663	3.29
Scandinavian	11	0.05
Scotch-Irish	206	1.02
Scottish	244	1.21
Slovak	7	0.03
Swedish	114	0.57
Swiss	36	0.18
Turkish	45	0.22
Ukrainian	149	0.74
United States or American	588	2.92
Welsh	50	0.25
West Indian, excl. Hispanic:	154	0.77
Belizean	16	0.08
Haitian	86	0.43
Jamaican	45	0.22
West Indian	7	0.03
White:	18,919	94.12
Not Hispanic (18,052)	18,189	90.49
Hispanic (691)	730	3.63

Haverstraw

Place Type: Town
County: Rockland
Population: 33,811

Ancestry/Race	Number	%
Afghan	67	0.20
African American/Black:	3,951	11.69
Not Hispanic (3,146)	3,453	10.21
Hispanic (325)	498	1.47
African, sub-Saharan:	186	0.55
African	169	0.50
Liberian	8	0.02
Nigerian	9	0.03
Am. Ind. or Alaska Nat., not spec.	157	0.46
Albanian	26	0.08
American Indian tribes, specified:	157	0.46
Blackfeet	6	0.02
Cherokee (9)	36	0.11
Chickasaw	1	0.00
Comanche (1)	1	0.00
Delaware (11)	29	0.09
Iroquois (1)	12	0.04
Latin American Indians (13)	48	0.14
Lumbee (1)	1	0.00
Navajo	2	0.01
Pueblo	2	0.01
Shoshone	1	0.00
Sioux	5	0.01
Tohono O'Odham (1)	1	0.00
All other tribes (10)	12	0.04
American Indian tribes, not spec.	26	0.08
Arab:	117	0.35
Egyptian	34	0.10
Iraqi	4	0.01
Lebanese	50	0.15
Syrian	29	0.09
Armenian	6	0.02
Asian:	1,314	3.89
Bangladeshi (16)	24	0.07
Cambodian (34)	41	0.12
Chinese, ex. Taiwanese (145)	184	0.54
Filipino (214)	253	0.75
Indian (466)	542	1.60
Indonesian (2)	7	0.02
Japanese (15)	24	0.07
Korean (77)	81	0.24
Laotian (1)	1	0.00
Pakistani (34)	62	0.18
Taiwanese (6)	6	0.02
Thai (8)	12	0.04
Vietnamese (29)	34	0.10
Other Asian, specified (5)	5	0.01
Other Asian, not specified (20)	38	0.11
Australian	9	0.03
Austrian	268	0.79
Brazilian	80	0.24
British	6	0.02
Bulgarian	9	0.03
Canadian	22	0.07
Celtic	10	0.03
Croatian	36	0.11
Czech	126	0.37
Czechoslovakian	41	0.12

Notes: 1. Figures in the "Number" column do not add up to the total population due to: a) Ancestry/Race overlap — e.g. persons can report being both White and Irish, b) persons of Hispanic origin can report being any race, c) persons reporting two ancestries are counted in both categories. 2. Numbers in parentheses indicate the number of persons reporting this ancestry/race alone, not in combination with any other ancestry/race. 3. Refer to the Explanation of Data in the front of the book for more detailed information.

Danish	28	0.08
Dutch	296	0.88
Eastern European	71	0.21
English	1,144	3.39
European	45	0.13
Finnish	14	0.04
French, except Basque	527	1.56
French Canadian	125	0.37
German	2,657	7.88
German Russian	11	0.03
Greek	252	0.75
Guyanese	26	0.08
Hawaii Native/Pacific Islander:	51	0.15
Micronesian: (5)	5	0.01
Guamanian/Chamorro (5)	5	0.01
Polynesian: (10)	12	0.04
Native Hawaiian (6)	8	0.02
Samoan (4)	4	0.01
Other Pac. Isl., not spec. (18)	34	0.10
Hispanic or Latino:	10,729	31.73
Central American:	280	0.83
Costa Rican	22	0.07
Guatemalan	99	0.29
Honduran	9	0.03
Nicaraguan	17	0.05
Panamanian	22	0.07
Salvadoran	89	0.26
Other Central American	22	0.07
Cuban	115	0.34
Dominican Republic	3,764	11.13
Mexican	587	1.74
Puerto Rican	3,812	11.27
South American:	420	1.24
Argentinean	26	0.08
Bolivian	4	0.01
Chilean	11	0.03
Colombian	93	0.28
Ecuadorian	192	0.57
Paraguayan	1	0.00
Peruvian	62	0.18
Uruguayan	1	0.00
Venezuelan	15	0.04
Other South American	15	0.04
Other Hispanic or Latino	1,751	5.18
Hungarian	325	0.96
Icelander	28	0.08
Iranian	45	0.13
Irish	5,218	15.47
Israeli	68	0.20
Italian	6,280	18.62
Lithuanian	72	0.21
Norwegian	129	0.38
Polish	1,472	4.37
Portuguese	34	0.10
Romanian	74	0.22
Russian	870	2.58
Scandinavian	37	0.11
Scotch-Irish	113	0.34
Scottish	191	0.57
Slavic	25	0.07
Slovak	85	0.25
Swedish	146	0.43
Swiss	48	0.14
Turkish	21	0.06
Ukrainian	100	0.30
United States or American	1,368	4.06
Welsh	24	0.07
West Indian, excl. Hispanic:	1,338	3.97
British West Indian	10	0.03
Haitian	793	2.35
Jamaican	349	1.03
Trinidadian and Tobagonian	72	0.21
West Indian	114	0.34
White:	23,370	69.12
Not Hispanic (18,133)	18,466	54.62
Hispanic (4,265)	4,904	14.50
Yugoslavian	6	0.02

Haverstraw

Place Type: Village
County: Rockland
Population: 10,117

Ancestry/Race	Number	%
Afghan	5	0.05
African American/Black:	1,401	13.85
Not Hispanic (1,061)	1,152	11.39
Hispanic (160)	249	2.46
African, sub-Saharan:	65	0.65
African	65	0.65
Am. Ind. or Alaska Nat., not spec.	63	0.62
American Indian tribes, specified:	57	0.56
Blackfeet	2	0.02
Cherokee	11	0.11
Delaware	8	0.08
Iroquois	2	0.02
Latin American Indians (6)	29	0.29
Lumbee (1)	1	0.01
Pueblo	2	0.02
Tohono O'Odham (1)	1	0.01
All other tribes	1	0.01
American Indian tribes, not spec.	6	0.06
Asian:	127	1.26
Cambodian (4)	5	0.05
Chinese, ex. Taiwanese (8)	11	0.11
Filipino (34)	41	0.41
Indian (45)	48	0.47
Japanese (3)	3	0.03
Korean (6)	6	0.06
Laotian (1)	1	0.01
Pakistani (1)	1	0.01
Thai (3)	4	0.04
Vietnamese (4)	4	0.04
Other Asian, not specified	3	0.03
Austrian	14	0.14
Brazilian	5	0.05
Czech	33	0.33
Czechoslovakian	4	0.04
Danish	7	0.07
Dutch	23	0.23
Eastern European	8	0.08
English	254	2.53
European	6	0.06
French, except Basque	110	1.10
French Canadian	10	0.10
German	443	4.42
Greek	18	0.18
Hawaii Native/Pacific Islander:	25	0.25
Polynesian: (1)	3	0.03
Native Hawaiian (1)	3	0.03
Other Pac. Isl., not spec. (12)	22	0.22
Hispanic or Latino:	5,998	59.29
Central American:	105	1.04
Costa Rican	12	0.12
Guatemalan	32	0.32
Honduran	7	0.07
Nicaraguan	5	0.05
Panamanian	8	0.08
Salvadoran	39	0.39
Other Central American	2	0.02
Cuban	24	0.24
Dominican Republic	2,727	26.95
Mexican	419	4.14
Puerto Rican	1,494	14.77
South American:	192	1.90
Argentinean	4	0.04
Bolivian	4	0.04
Chilean	4	0.04
Colombian	35	0.35
Ecuadorian	116	1.15
Peruvian	19	0.19
Venezuelan	2	0.02
Other South American	8	0.08
Other Hispanic or Latino	1,037	10.25
Hungarian	21	0.21
Iranian	11	0.11
Irish	921	9.19
Israeli	21	0.21
Italian	780	7.78
Norwegian	26	0.26
Polish	175	1.75
Portuguese	11	0.11
Russian	75	0.75
Scotch-Irish	14	0.14
Scottish	16	0.16
Slovak	53	0.53
Swedish	21	0.21
Ukrainian	7	0.07
United States or American	374	3.73
West Indian, excl. Hispanic:	194	1.93
British West Indian	5	0.05
Haitian	70	0.70
Jamaican	98	0.98
West Indian	21	0.21
White:	5,080	50.21
Not Hispanic (2,775)	2,866	28.33
Hispanic (1,881)	2,214	21.88

Hempstead

Place Type: Town
County: Nassau
Population: 755,924

Ancestry/Race	Number	%
Acadian/Cajun	36	0.00
Afghan	223	0.03
African American/Black:	118,490	15.67
Not Hispanic (107,929)	113,317	14.99
Hispanic (3,794)	5,173	0.68
African, sub-Saharan:	5,025	0.66
African	3,042	0.40
Cape Verdean	90	0.01
Ethiopian	28	0.00
Ghanian	193	0.03
Liberian	218	0.03
Nigerian	1,196	0.16
Sierra Leonean	39	0.01
South African	67	0.01
Sudanese	14	0.00
Zimbabwean	27	0.00
Other sub-Saharan African	111	0.01
Alaska Native tribes, specified:	17	0.00
Alaska Athabascan	3	0.00
Eskimo	1	0.00
Tlingit-Haida (1)	12	0.00
All other tribes (1)	1	0.00
Am. Ind. or Alaska Nat., not spec.	1,681	0.22
Albanian	488	0.06
Alsatian	87	0.01
American Indian tribes, specified:	1,917	0.25
Apache (10)	38	0.01
Blackfeet (7)	112	0.01
Cherokee (125)	627	0.08
Cheyenne	8	0.00
Chickasaw	4	0.00
Chippewa (4)	21	0.00
Choctaw (2)	29	0.00
Comanche	5	0.00
Cree (1)	3	0.00
Creek (8)	21	0.00
Crow (1)	7	0.00
Delaware (3)	10	0.00
Iroquois (27)	105	0.01
Latin American Indians (227)	449	0.06
Lumbee (16)	19	0.00
Menominee (2)	3	0.00
Navajo (3)	27	0.00
Osage (2)	4	0.00
Ottawa (1)	1	0.00
Paiute (1)	2	0.00
Pima	1	0.00
Potawatomi	3	0.00
Pueblo (8)	23	0.00
Seminole (1)	37	0.00
Shoshone	5	0.00
Sioux (14)	61	0.01

Notes: 1. Figures in the "Number" column do not add up to the total population due to: a) Ancestry/Race overlap — e.g. persons can report being both White and Irish, b) persons of Hispanic origin can report being any race, c) persons reporting two ancestries are counted in both categories. 2. Numbers in parentheses indicate the number of persons reporting this ancestry/race alone, not in combination with any other ancestry/race. 3. Refer to the Explanation of Data in the front of the book for more detailed information.

Ute (1)	1	0.00
Yaqui (1)	1	0.00
All other tribes (99)	290	0.04
American Indian tribes, not spec.	360	0.05
Arab:	3,264	0.43
Arab/Arabic	460	0.06
Egyptian	965	0.13
Iraqi	127	0.02
Jordanian	191	0.03
Lebanese	498	0.07
Moroccan	258	0.03
Palestinian	133	0.02
Syrian	424	0.06
Other Arab	208	0.03
Armenian	1,270	0.17
Asian:	31,057	4.11
Bangladeshi (120)	150	0.02
Cambodian (30)	35	0.00
Chinese, ex. Taiwanese (5,636)	6,607	0.87
Filipino (4,168)	4,712	0.62
Indian (10,698)	11,966	1.58
Indonesian (33)	60	0.01
Japanese (453)	647	0.09
Korean (2,372)	2,559	0.34
Laotian (8)	9	0.00
Malaysian (5)	14	0.00
Pakistani (1,561)	2,039	0.27
Sri Lankan (50)	64	0.01
Taiwanese (193)	248	0.03
Thai (207)	255	0.03
Vietnamese (411)	499	0.07
Other Asian, specified (50)	102	0.01
Other Asian, not specified (310)	1,091	0.14
Assyrian/Chaldean/Syriac	17	0.00
Australian	85	0.01
Austrian	6,437	0.85
Basque	91	0.01
Belgian	321	0.04
Brazilian	581	0.08
British	1,552	0.21
Bulgarian	102	0.01
Canadian	1,319	0.17
Celtic	78	0.01
Croatian	1,092	0.14
Cypriot	203	0.03
Czech	1,842	0.24
Czechoslovakian	1,549	0.20
Danish	1,279	0.17
Dutch	3,964	0.52
Eastern European	3,765	0.50
English	23,832	3.15
Estonian	203	0.03
European	3,388	0.45
Finnish	574	0.08
French, except Basque	8,604	1.14
French Canadian	1,971	0.26
German	87,201	11.54
German Russian	18	0.00
Greek	10,576	1.40
Guyanese	3,420	0.45
Hawaii Native/Pacific Islander:	792	0.10
Melanesian: (4)	5	0.00
Fijian (1)	2	0.00
Other Melanesian (3)	3	0.00
Micronesian: (66)	82	0.01
Guamanian/Chamorro (64)	76	0.01
Other Micronesian (2)	6	0.00
Polynesian: (59)	163	0.02
Native Hawaiian (31)	93	0.01
Samoan (25)	53	0.01
Other Polynesian (3)	17	0.00
Other Pac. Isl., specified	33	0.00
Other Pac. Isl., not spec. (111)	509	0.07
Hispanic or Latino:	86,657	11.46
Central American:	22,455	2.97
Costa Rican	445	0.06
Guatemalan	2,094	0.28
Honduran	2,452	0.32
Nicaraguan	187	0.02
Panamanian	597	0.08
Salvadoran	15,659	2.07
Other Central American	1,021	0.14
Cuban	2,934	0.39
Dominican Republic	8,433	1.12
Mexican	2,971	0.39
Puerto Rican	15,779	2.09
South American:	11,430	1.51
Argentinean	859	0.11
Bolivian	228	0.03
Chilean	893	0.12
Colombian	4,403	0.58
Ecuadorian	2,343	0.31
Paraguayan	62	0.01
Peruvian	1,724	0.23
Uruguayan	185	0.02
Venezuelan	235	0.03
Other South American	498	0.07
Other Hispanic or Latino	22,655	3.00
Hungarian	7,004	0.93
Icelander	97	0.01
Iranian	954	0.13
Irish	133,307	17.63
Israeli	1,877	0.25
Italian	179,140	23.70
Latvian	490	0.06
Lithuanian	2,517	0.33
Luxemburger	9	0.00
Macedonian	6	0.00
Maltese	730	0.10
New Zealander	86	0.01
Northern European	156	0.02
Norwegian	4,339	0.57
Pennsylvania German	90	0.01
Polish	38,256	5.06
Portuguese	2,111	0.28
Romanian	3,220	0.43
Russian	30,246	4.00
Scandinavian	317	0.04
Scotch-Irish	4,687	0.62
Scottish	5,207	0.69
Serbian	114	0.02
Slavic	263	0.03
Slovak	908	0.12
Slovene	176	0.02
Soviet Union	51	0.01
Swedish	4,688	0.62
Swiss	1,191	0.16
Turkish	1,424	0.19
Ukrainian	4,023	0.53
United States or American	31,416	4.16
Welsh	1,013	0.13
West Indian, excl. Hispanic:	36,824	4.87
Bahamian	54	0.01
Barbadian	1,180	0.16
Belizean	209	0.03
Bermudan	26	0.00
British West Indian	1,135	0.15
Dutch West Indian	53	0.01
Haitian	13,599	1.80
Jamaican	15,339	2.03
Trinidadian and Tobagonian	2,770	0.37
U.S. Virgin Islander	83	0.01
West Indian	2,280	0.30
Other West Indian	96	0.01
White:	575,620	76.15
Not Hispanic (521,352)	526,808	69.69
Hispanic (42,908)	48,812	6.46
Yugoslavian	765	0.10

Hempstead

Place Type: Village
County: Nassau
Population: 56,554

Ancestry/Race	Number	%
Acadian/Cajun	30	0.05
African American/Black:	30,923	54.68
Not Hispanic (28,729)	29,729	52.57
Hispanic (949)	1,194	2.11
African, sub-Saharan:	1,300	2.30
African	1,011	1.79
Ethiopian	19	0.03
Ghanian	11	0.02
Liberian	2	0.00
Nigerian	219	0.39
Other sub-Saharan African	38	0.07
Am. Ind. or Alaska Nat., not spec.	355	0.63
Albanian	56	0.10
American Indian tribes, specified:	340	0.60
Apache (1)	9	0.02
Blackfeet	19	0.03
Cherokee (21)	131	0.23
Cheyenne	1	0.00
Chippewa (1)	5	0.01
Choctaw (1)	6	0.01
Creek (2)	6	0.01
Delaware	1	0.00
Iroquois (1)	8	0.01
Latin American Indians (35)	68	0.12
Lumbee (12)	13	0.02
Navajo	1	0.00
Ottawa (1)	1	0.00
Pima	1	0.00
Pueblo	1	0.00
Seminole	5	0.01
Sioux (3)	9	0.02
All other tribes (16)	55	0.10
American Indian tribes, not spec.	99	0.18
Arab:	175	0.31
Lebanese	88	0.16
Moroccan	37	0.07
Palestinian	25	0.04
Other Arab	25	0.04
Armenian	62	0.11
Asian:	1,052	1.86
Bangladeshi (3)	3	0.01
Cambodian (11)	12	0.02
Chinese, ex. Taiwanese (101)	171	0.30
Filipino (104)	131	0.23
Indian (304)	415	0.73
Indonesian	3	0.01
Japanese (28)	38	0.07
Korean (107)	108	0.19
Malaysian	1	0.00
Pakistani (32)	56	0.10
Sri Lankan (6)	8	0.01
Taiwanese (5)	9	0.02
Thai (4)	5	0.01
Vietnamese (24)	27	0.05
Other Asian, specified	10	0.02
Other Asian, not specified (6)	55	0.10
Austrian	64	0.11
Belgian	4	0.01
Brazilian	16	0.03
British	90	0.16
Canadian	44	0.08
Croatian	14	0.02
Czech	41	0.07
Czechoslovakian	14	0.02
Danish	31	0.05
Dutch	113	0.20
English	565	1.00
Estonian	5	0.01
European	122	0.22
Finnish	12	0.02
French, except Basque	195	0.34
French Canadian	22	0.04
German	1,230	2.18
German Russian	18	0.03
Greek	92	0.16
Guyanese	503	0.89
Hawaii Native/Pacific Islander:	126	0.22
Micronesian: (1)	5	0.01
Guamanian/Chamorro (1)	1	0.00
Other Micronesian	4	0.01
Polynesian: (10)	24	0.04
Native Hawaiian (3)	8	0.01
Samoan (7)	16	0.03
Other Pac. Isl., specified	10	0.02

Notes: 1. Figures in the "Number" column do not add up to the total population due to: a) Ancestry/Race overlap — e.g. persons can report being both White and Irish, b) persons of Hispanic origin can report being any race, c) persons reporting two ancestries are counted in both categories. 2. Numbers in parentheses indicate the number of persons reporting this ancestry/race alone, not in combination with any other ancestry/race. 3. Refer to the Explanation of Data in the front of the book for more detailed information.

Other Pac. Isl., not spec. (22)	87	0.15
Hispanic or Latino:	17,991	31.81
Central American:	8,382	14.82
Costa Rican	35	0.06
Guatemalan	482	0.85
Honduran	1,450	2.56
Nicaraguan	23	0.04
Panamanian	119	0.21
Salvadoran	5,949	10.52
Other Central American	324	0.57
Cuban	216	0.38
Dominican Republic	887	1.57
Mexican	505	0.89
Puerto Rican	1,381	2.44
South American:	1,070	1.89
Argentinean	29	0.05
Bolivian	3	0.01
Chilean	13	0.02
Colombian	388	0.69
Ecuadorian	395	0.70
Paraguayan	6	0.01
Peruvian	173	0.31
Uruguayan	3	0.01
Venezuelan	24	0.04
Other South American	36	0.06
Other Hispanic or Latino	5,550	9.81
Hungarian	48	0.08
Icelander	28	0.05
Iranian	28	0.05
Irish	1,336	2.36
Israeli	37	0.07
Italian	1,548	2.74
Latvian	37	0.07
Lithuanian	42	0.07
Maltese	6	0.01
Northern European	25	0.04
Norwegian	34	0.06
Polish	732	1.29
Portuguese	124	0.22
Romanian	23	0.04
Russian	323	0.57
Scandinavian	4	0.01
Scotch-Irish	97	0.17
Scottish	49	0.09
Slovak	6	0.01
Swedish	87	0.15
Swiss	8	0.01
Turkish	24	0.04
Ukrainian	154	0.27
United States or American	1,283	2.27
Welsh	7	0.01
West Indian, excl. Hispanic:	6,264	11.08
Bahamian	13	0.02
Barbadian	239	0.42
Belizean	7	0.01
Bermudan	8	0.01
British West Indian	247	0.44
Haitian	1,601	2.83
Jamaican	3,064	5.42
Trinidadian and Tobagonian	583	1.03
U.S. Virgin Islander	19	0.03
West Indian	448	0.79
Other West Indian	35	0.06
White:	16,127	28.52
Not Hispanic (7,460)	7,917	14.00
Hispanic (7,055)	8,210	14.52

Henrietta

Place Type: Town
County: Monroe
Population: 39,028

Ancestry/Race	Number	%
Acadian/Cajun	7	0.02
African American/Black:	3,010	7.71
Not Hispanic (2,642)	2,922	7.49
Hispanic (66)	88	0.23
African, sub-Saharan:	199	0.51
African	143	0.37
Ethiopian	18	0.05
Nigerian	25	0.06
South African	7	0.02
Other sub-Saharan African	6	0.02
Alaska Native tribes, specified:	3	0.01
Alaska Athabascan (1)	1	0.00
Eskimo (1)	1	0.00
Tlingit-Haida (1)	1	0.00
Alaska Native tribes, not specified	1	0.00
Am. Ind. or Alaska Nat., not spec.	110	0.28
Albanian	8	0.02
Alsatian	10	0.03
American Indian tribes, specified:	218	0.56
Apache	2	0.01
Blackfeet	13	0.03
Cherokee (6)	43	0.11
Cheyenne (1)	2	0.01
Chippewa (1)	4	0.01
Choctaw (4)	7	0.02
Cree	1	0.00
Creek	1	0.00
Delaware	2	0.01
Iroquois (58)	92	0.24
Kiowa	2	0.01
Latin American Indians (1)	14	0.04
Menominee	1	0.00
Navajo (2)	4	0.01
Osage	2	0.01
Potawatomi	2	0.01
Pueblo (3)	4	0.01
Seminole	5	0.01
Sioux (1)	2	0.01
All other tribes (5)	15	0.04
American Indian tribes, not spec.	3	0.01
Arab:	123	0.32
Arab/Arabic	5	0.01
Lebanese	92	0.24
Moroccan	16	0.04
Syrian	10	0.03
Armenian	13	0.03
Asian:	2,469	6.33
Bangladeshi (2)	2	0.01
Cambodian (13)	20	0.05
Chinese, ex. Taiwanese (569)	639	1.64
Filipino (41)	67	0.17
Indian (703)	756	1.94
Indonesian (7)	14	0.04
Japanese (71)	111	0.28
Korean (188)	215	0.55
Laotian (103)	115	0.29
Malaysian (1)	1	0.00
Pakistani (66)	93	0.24
Sri Lankan (8)	9	0.02
Taiwanese (35)	47	0.12
Thai (35)	40	0.10
Vietnamese (188)	217	0.56
Other Asian, specified (7)	9	0.02
Other Asian, not specified (48)	114	0.29
Australian	13	0.03
Austrian	135	0.35
Belgian	57	0.15
British	151	0.39
Bulgarian	17	0.04
Canadian	155	0.40
Celtic	9	0.02
Croatian	8	0.02
Cypriot	6	0.02
Czech	161	0.41
Czechoslovakian	45	0.12
Danish	203	0.52
Dutch	1,180	3.02
Eastern European	55	0.14
English	5,071	12.99
Estonian	17	0.04
European	228	0.58
Finnish	46	0.12
French, except Basque	1,546	3.96
French Canadian	677	1.73
German	9,157	23.46
Greek	253	0.65
Guyanese	12	0.03
Hawaii Native/Pacific Islander:	51	0.13
Micronesian: (3)	5	0.01
Guamanian/Chamorro (3)	5	0.01
Polynesian: (6)	15	0.04
Native Hawaiian (6)	13	0.03
Samoan	2	0.01
Other Pac. Isl., specified	2	0.01
Other Pac. Isl., not spec. (2)	29	0.07
Hispanic or Latino:	1,181	3.03
Central American:	34	0.09
Costa Rican	5	0.01
Guatemalan	3	0.01
Honduran	5	0.01
Nicaraguan	2	0.01
Panamanian	11	0.03
Salvadoran	7	0.02
Other Central American	1	0.00
Cuban	60	0.15
Dominican Republic	72	0.18
Mexican	123	0.32
Puerto Rican	569	1.46
South American:	101	0.26
Argentinean	3	0.01
Bolivian	3	0.01
Chilean	21	0.05
Colombian	38	0.10
Ecuadorian	10	0.03
Peruvian	11	0.03
Venezuelan	8	0.02
Other South American	7	0.02
Other Hispanic or Latino	222	0.57
Hungarian	342	0.88
Iranian	5	0.01
Irish	6,616	16.95
Israeli	26	0.07
Italian	6,320	16.19
Latvian	62	0.16
Lithuanian	142	0.36
Macedonian	74	0.19
New Zealander	7	0.02
Northern European	5	0.01
Norwegian	166	0.43
Pennsylvania German	25	0.06
Polish	2,574	6.60
Portuguese	32	0.08
Romanian	67	0.17
Russian	491	1.26
Scotch-Irish	431	1.10
Scottish	834	2.14
Serbian	8	0.02
Slavic	14	0.04
Slovak	41	0.11
Slovene	15	0.04
Swedish	405	1.04
Swiss	115	0.29
Turkish	63	0.16
Ukrainian	441	1.13
United States or American	1,737	4.45
Welsh	281	0.72
West Indian, excl. Hispanic:	316	0.81
Barbadian	25	0.06
Bermudan	9	0.02
British West Indian	10	0.03
Haitian	24	0.06
Jamaican	228	0.58
Trinidadian and Tobagonian	7	0.02
West Indian	13	0.03
White:	33,527	85.90
Not Hispanic (32,238)	32,786	84.01
Hispanic (652)	741	1.90
Yugoslavian	61	0.16

Hicksville

Place Type: Census Designated Place
County: Nassau
Population: 41,260

Ancestry/Race	Number	%

Notes: 1. Figures in the "Number" column do not add up to the total population due to: a) Ancestry/Race overlap — e.g. persons can report being both White and Irish, b) persons of Hispanic origin can report being any race, c) persons reporting two ancestries are counted in both categories. 2. Numbers in parentheses indicate the number of persons reporting this ancestry/race alone, not in combination with any other ancestry/race. 3. Refer to the Explanation of Data in the front of the book for more detailed information.

Afghan	213	0.52
African American/Black:	643	1.56
Not Hispanic (538)	606	1.47
Hispanic (24)	37	0.09
African, sub-Saharan:	12	0.03
African	12	0.03
Am. Ind. or Alaska Nat., not spec.	54	0.13
Alsatian	7	0.02
American Indian tribes, specified:	52	0.13
Blackfeet	3	0.01
Cherokee (5)	16	0.04
Chickasaw	1	0.00
Chippewa	1	0.00
Delaware (1)	1	0.00
Iroquois	3	0.01
Latin American Indians (3)	6	0.01
Potawatomi	2	0.00
Sioux (3)	4	0.01
All other tribes (12)	15	0.04
American Indian tribes, not spec.	16	0.04
Arab:	200	0.48
Arab/Arabic	58	0.14
Egyptian	70	0.17
Jordanian	31	0.08
Lebanese	8	0.02
Syrian	33	0.08
Armenian	69	0.17
Asian:	4,025	9.76
Bangladeshi (31)	40	0.10
Cambodian (18)	24	0.06
Chinese, ex. Taiwanese (812)	865	2.10
Filipino (410)	451	1.09
Indian (1,772)	1,876	4.55
Indonesian (10)	10	0.02
Japanese (24)	31	0.08
Korean (293)	300	0.73
Laotian (6)	6	0.01
Malaysian	1	0.00
Pakistani (163)	193	0.47
Sri Lankan (1)	1	0.00
Taiwanese (18)	23	0.06
Thai (20)	20	0.05
Vietnamese (90)	93	0.23
Other Asian, specified (8)	8	0.02
Other Asian, not specified (25)	83	0.20
Austrian	391	0.95
Belgian	32	0.08
Brazilian	15	0.04
British	97	0.24
Canadian	88	0.21
Carpatho Rusyn	7	0.02
Celtic	25	0.06
Croatian	43	0.10
Cypriot	72	0.17
Czech	188	0.46
Czechoslovakian	128	0.31
Danish	62	0.15
Dutch	180	0.44
Eastern European	117	0.28
English	1,729	4.19
Estonian	15	0.04
European	151	0.37
Finnish	35	0.08
French, except Basque	357	0.87
French Canadian	123	0.30
German	6,852	16.61
Greek	1,103	2.67
Hawaii Native/Pacific Islander:	34	0.08
Melanesian: (2)	2	0.00
Fijian (2)	2	0.00
Polynesian: (8)	8	0.02
Native Hawaiian (2)	2	0.00
Samoan (6)	6	0.01
Other Pac. Isl., not spec. (4)	24	0.06
Hispanic or Latino:	3,819	9.26
Central American:	917	2.22
Costa Rican	17	0.04
Guatemalan	17	0.04
Honduran	71	0.17
Nicaraguan	10	0.02
Panamanian	1	0.00
Salvadoran	756	1.83
Other Central American	45	0.11
Cuban	172	0.42
Dominican Republic	152	0.37
Mexican	204	0.49
Puerto Rican	615	1.49
South American:	699	1.69
Argentinean	40	0.10
Bolivian	5	0.01
Chilean	50	0.12
Colombian	286	0.69
Ecuadorian	108	0.26
Paraguayan	2	0.00
Peruvian	157	0.38
Uruguayan	9	0.02
Venezuelan	18	0.04
Other South American	24	0.06
Other Hispanic or Latino	1,060	2.57
Hungarian	457	1.11
Iranian	109	0.26
Irish	9,644	23.37
Israeli	8	0.02
Italian	11,616	28.15
Latvian	34	0.08
Lithuanian	148	0.36
Maltese	28	0.07
Northern European	5	0.01
Norwegian	279	0.68
Polish	2,576	6.24
Portuguese	91	0.22
Romanian	96	0.23
Russian	920	2.23
Scotch-Irish	222	0.54
Scottish	273	0.66
Serbian	11	0.03
Slavic	5	0.01
Slovak	96	0.23
Slovene	25	0.06
Swedish	257	0.62
Swiss	53	0.13
Turkish	43	0.10
Ukrainian	229	0.56
United States or American	1,547	3.75
Welsh	60	0.15
West Indian, excl. Hispanic:	288	0.70
Bahamian	7	0.02
Barbadian	17	0.04
Haitian	42	0.10
Jamaican	181	0.44
West Indian	41	0.10
White:	35,485	86.00
Not Hispanic (32,645)	32,942	79.84
Hispanic (2,246)	2,543	6.16
Yugoslavian	57	0.14

Highlands

Place Type: Town
County: Orange
Population: 12,484

Ancestry/Race	Number	%
Acadian/Cajun	8	0.06
African American/Black:	1,286	10.30
Not Hispanic (1,064)	1,165	9.33
Hispanic (79)	121	0.97
African, sub-Saharan:	85	0.68
African	49	0.39
Kenyan	36	0.29
Alaska Native tribes, specified:	1	0.01
Alaska Athabascan (1)	1	0.01
Am. Ind. or Alaska Nat., not spec.	35	0.28
Albanian	7	0.06
American Indian tribes, specified:	90	0.72
Apache (4)	4	0.03
Blackfeet (1)	6	0.05
Cherokee (12)	27	0.22
Chickasaw (2)	4	0.03
Chippewa (1)	1	0.01
Choctaw (2)	3	0.02
Creek	2	0.02
Delaware (2)	3	0.02
Iroquois (4)	12	0.10
Latin American Indians	6	0.05
Lumbee (3)	3	0.02
Navajo (5)	5	0.04
Pima	2	0.02
Seminole	1	0.01
All other tribes (3)	11	0.09
American Indian tribes, not spec.	9	0.07
Arab:	41	0.33
Lebanese	35	0.28
Syrian	6	0.05
Armenian	72	0.58
Asian:	480	3.84
Chinese, ex. Taiwanese (45)	67	0.54
Filipino (82)	108	0.87
Indian (27)	30	0.24
Japanese (21)	59	0.47
Korean (137)	178	1.43
Pakistani	2	0.02
Sri Lankan (1)	2	0.02
Taiwanese (2)	5	0.04
Thai (2)	2	0.02
Vietnamese (8)	11	0.09
Other Asian, specified (1)	3	0.02
Other Asian, not specified (3)	13	0.10
Australian	7	0.06
Austrian	53	0.43
Belgian	26	0.21
British	90	0.72
Bulgarian	6	0.05
Croatian	34	0.27
Czech	71	0.57
Czechoslovakian	38	0.30
Danish	45	0.36
Dutch	195	1.56
Eastern European	6	0.05
English	1,286	10.31
European	63	0.51
Finnish	27	0.22
French, except Basque	426	3.42
French Canadian	176	1.41
German	2,638	21.16
Greek	75	0.60
Guyanese	5	0.04
Hawaii Native/Pacific Islander:	31	0.25
Micronesian: (8)	9	0.07
Guamanian/Chamorro (4)	4	0.03
Other Micronesian (4)	5	0.04
Polynesian: (8)	13	0.10
Native Hawaiian (3)	8	0.06
Samoan (5)	5	0.04
Other Pac. Isl., not spec. (4)	9	0.07
Hispanic or Latino:	962	7.71
Central American:	84	0.67
Costa Rican	7	0.06
Guatemalan	28	0.22
Honduran	12	0.10
Nicaraguan	3	0.02
Panamanian	29	0.23
Salvadoran	3	0.02
Other Central American	2	0.02
Cuban	26	0.21
Dominican Republic	68	0.54
Mexican	199	1.59
Puerto Rican	311	2.49
South American:	106	0.85
Argentinean	7	0.06
Chilean	2	0.02
Colombian	27	0.22
Ecuadorian	8	0.06
Peruvian	49	0.39
Venezuelan	12	0.10
Other South American	1	0.01
Other Hispanic or Latino	168	1.35
Hungarian	63	0.51
Irish	2,657	21.31
Italian	1,534	12.30

Notes: 1. Figures in the "Number" column do not add up to the total population due to: a) Ancestry/Race overlap — e.g. persons can report being both White and Irish, b) persons of Hispanic origin can report being any race, c) persons reporting two ancestries are counted in both categories. 2. Numbers in parentheses indicate the number of persons reporting this ancestry/race alone, not in combination with any other ancestry/race. 3. Refer to the Explanation of Data in the front of the book for more detailed information.

Latvian	20	0.16
Lithuanian	53	0.43
Luxemburger	6	0.05
Maltese	5	0.04
Norwegian	252	2.02
Pennsylvania German	9	0.07
Polish	545	4.37
Portuguese	52	0.42
Romanian	21	0.17
Russian	155	1.24
Scandinavian	25	0.20
Scotch-Irish	226	1.81
Scottish	560	4.49
Slavic	17	0.14
Slovak	61	0.49
Slovene	13	0.10
Swedish	205	1.64
Swiss	13	0.10
Turkish	5	0.04
Ukrainian	31	0.25
United States or American	723	5.80
Welsh	130	1.04
West Indian, excl. Hispanic:	190	1.52
Haitian	100	0.80
Jamaican	76	0.61
Trinidadian and Tobagonian	5	0.04
West Indian	9	0.07
White:	10,579	84.74
Not Hispanic (9,761)	9,996	80.07
Hispanic (498)	583	4.67
Yugoslavian	7	0.06

Holbrook

Place Type: Census Designated Place
County: Suffolk
Population: 27,512

Ancestry/Race	Number	%
African American/Black:	433	1.57
Not Hispanic (341)	402	1.46
Hispanic (22)	31	0.11
African, sub-Saharan:	53	0.19
African	53	0.19
Alaska Native tribes, specified:	1	0.00
Alaska Athabascan (1)	1	0.00
Am. Ind. or Alaska Nat., not spec.	17	0.06
American Indian tribes, specified:	45	0.16
Blackfeet (3)	6	0.02
Cherokee (2)	13	0.05
Chickasaw (1)	1	0.00
Chippewa (2)	2	0.01
Choctaw	2	0.01
Cree	2	0.01
Iroquois	5	0.02
Latin American Indians (1)	1	0.00
All other tribes (8)	13	0.05
Arab:	63	0.23
Egyptian	45	0.16
Lebanese	7	0.03
Syrian	5	0.02
Other Arab	6	0.02
Armenian	82	0.30
Asian:	921	3.35
Cambodian (10)	10	0.04
Chinese, ex. Taiwanese (145)	163	0.59
Filipino (264)	300	1.09
Indian (236)	259	0.94
Indonesian	5	0.02
Japanese (14)	16	0.06
Korean (54)	58	0.21
Laotian (1)	1	0.00
Pakistani (30)	55	0.20
Taiwanese (5)	5	0.02
Thai (1)	1	0.00
Vietnamese (12)	16	0.06
Other Asian, specified	1	0.00
Other Asian, not specified (9)	31	0.11
Australian	10	0.04
Austrian	191	0.69
Basque	5	0.02
Brazilian	6	0.02
British	33	0.12
Canadian	33	0.12
Celtic	14	0.05
Czech	122	0.44
Czechoslovakian	51	0.19
Danish	21	0.08
Dutch	247	0.90
Eastern European	121	0.44
English	1,340	4.87
Estonian	9	0.03
European	106	0.39
Finnish	57	0.21
French, except Basque	454	1.65
French Canadian	170	0.62
German	5,188	18.85
Greek	406	1.47
Guyanese	5	0.02
Hawaii Native/Pacific Islander:	20	0.07
Micronesian: (4)	4	0.01
Guamanian/Chamorro (4)	4	0.01
Polynesian: (4)	6	0.02
Native Hawaiian (1)	3	0.01
Samoan (3)	3	0.01
Other Pac. Isl., not spec. (4)	10	0.04
Hispanic or Latino:	1,616	5.87
Central American:	58	0.21
Costa Rican	4	0.01
Honduran	4	0.01
Nicaraguan	4	0.01
Panamanian	6	0.02
Salvadoran	38	0.14
Other Central American	2	0.01
Cuban	87	0.32
Dominican Republic	44	0.16
Mexican	62	0.23
Puerto Rican	877	3.19
South American:	179	0.65
Argentinean	17	0.06
Bolivian	1	0.00
Chilean	7	0.03
Colombian	74	0.27
Ecuadorian	43	0.16
Paraguayan	1	0.00
Peruvian	15	0.05
Uruguayan	4	0.01
Venezuelan	4	0.01
Other South American	13	0.05
Other Hispanic or Latino	309	1.12
Hungarian	275	1.00
Irish	7,559	27.46
Israeli	39	0.14
Italian	10,982	39.89
Lithuanian	76	0.28
Maltese	40	0.15
Norwegian	233	0.85
Pennsylvania German	5	0.02
Polish	1,638	5.95
Portuguese	161	0.58
Romanian	65	0.24
Russian	866	3.15
Scandinavian	23	0.08
Scotch-Irish	269	0.98
Scottish	440	1.60
Slavic	14	0.05
Slovak	34	0.12
Swedish	234	0.85
Swiss	26	0.09
Turkish	77	0.28
Ukrainian	89	0.32
United States or American	728	2.64
Welsh	124	0.45
West Indian, excl. Hispanic:	152	0.55
Barbadian	32	0.12
British West Indian	10	0.04
Jamaican	45	0.16
Trinidadian and Tobagonian	37	0.13
West Indian	28	0.10
White:	26,073	94.77
Not Hispanic (24,511)	24,677	89.70
Hispanic (1,336)	1,396	5.07
Yugoslavian	13	0.05

Holtsville

Place Type: Census Designated Place
County: Suffolk
Population: 17,006

Ancestry/Race	Number	%
Afghan	35	0.21
African American/Black:	244	1.43
Not Hispanic (174)	216	1.27
Hispanic (15)	28	0.16
African, sub-Saharan:	8	0.05
African	8	0.05
Am. Ind. or Alaska Nat., not spec.	23	0.14
American Indian tribes, specified:	44	0.26
Blackfeet (2)	5	0.03
Cherokee (8)	10	0.06
Choctaw	1	0.01
Delaware	1	0.01
Iroquois (2)	5	0.03
Latin American Indians	10	0.06
Navajo	3	0.02
Sioux	7	0.04
All other tribes (2)	2	0.01
American Indian tribes, not spec.	11	0.06
Arab:	12	0.07
Arab/Arabic	4	0.02
Lebanese	8	0.05
Armenian	39	0.23
Asian:	343	2.02
Chinese, ex. Taiwanese (71)	79	0.46
Filipino (49)	65	0.38
Indian (98)	106	0.62
Japanese (10)	18	0.11
Korean (36)	39	0.23
Laotian (1)	1	0.01
Pakistani (9)	10	0.06
Taiwanese (1)	2	0.01
Thai (4)	5	0.03
Vietnamese (9)	9	0.05
Other Asian, not specified (7)	9	0.05
Austrian	42	0.25
Basque	6	0.04
Brazilian	9	0.05
British	26	0.15
Canadian	78	0.46
Cypriot	30	0.18
Czech	116	0.68
Czechoslovakian	35	0.21
Danish	31	0.18
Dutch	119	0.70
Eastern European	27	0.16
English	747	4.40
Estonian	6	0.04
European	46	0.27
Finnish	54	0.32
French, except Basque	248	1.46
French Canadian	77	0.45
German	3,453	20.34
Greek	336	1.98
Guyanese	5	0.03
Hawaii Native/Pacific Islander:	2	0.01
Other Pac. Isl., not spec. (1)	2	0.01
Hispanic or Latino:	1,200	7.06
Central American:	38	0.22
Costa Rican	1	0.01
Guatemalan	7	0.04
Honduran	5	0.03
Nicaraguan	1	0.01
Panamanian	2	0.01
Salvadoran	17	0.10
Other Central American	5	0.03
Cuban	54	0.32
Dominican Republic	31	0.18
Mexican	124	0.73
Puerto Rican	626	3.68

Notes: 1. Figures in the "Number" column do not add up to the total population due to: a) Ancestry/Race overlap — e.g. persons can report being both White and Irish, b) persons of Hispanic origin can report being any race, c) persons reporting two ancestries are counted in both categories. 2. Numbers in parentheses indicate the number of persons reporting this ancestry/race alone, not in combination with any other ancestry/race. 3. Refer to the Explanation of Data in the front of the book for more detailed information.

South American:	124	0.73
Argentinean	12	0.07
Chilean	4	0.02
Colombian	42	0.25
Ecuadorian	41	0.24
Peruvian	18	0.11
Venezuelan	1	0.01
Other South American	6	0.04
Other Hispanic or Latino	203	1.19
Hungarian	195	1.15
Icelander	5	0.03
Irish	4,929	29.04
Italian	6,821	40.18
Lithuanian	70	0.41
Maltese	44	0.26
Norwegian	165	0.97
Polish	955	5.63
Portuguese	173	1.02
Romanian	34	0.20
Russian	366	2.16
Scandinavian	22	0.13
Scotch-Irish	231	1.36
Scottish	65	0.38
Serbian	26	0.15
Slovak	15	0.09
Swedish	166	0.98
Swiss	7	0.04
Turkish	21	0.12
Ukrainian	190	1.12
United States or American	539	3.18
Welsh	43	0.25
West Indian, excl. Hispanic:	130	0.77
Barbadian	6	0.04
Jamaican	28	0.16
Trinidadian and Tobagonian	69	0.41
West Indian	27	0.16
White:	16,256	95.59
Not Hispanic (15,141)	15,289	89.90
Hispanic (908)	967	5.69
Yugoslavian	24	0.14

Horseheads

Place Type: Town
County: Chemung
Population: 19,561

Ancestry/Race	Number	%
African American/Black:	323	1.65
Not Hispanic (249)	313	1.60
Hispanic (4)	10	0.05
Am. Ind. or Alaska Nat., not spec.	33	0.17
American Indian tribes, specified:	48	0.25
Apache (1)	1	0.01
Cherokee (2)	12	0.06
Choctaw (1)	1	0.01
Delaware	1	0.01
Iroquois (5)	19	0.10
Shoshone	1	0.01
Sioux (3)	5	0.03
All other tribes	8	0.04
American Indian tribes, not spec.	7	0.04
Arab:	49	0.25
Lebanese	27	0.14
Syrian	22	0.11
Asian:	355	1.81
Chinese, ex. Taiwanese (93)	102	0.52
Filipino (25)	42	0.21
Indian (87)	93	0.48
Japanese (18)	28	0.14
Korean (24)	24	0.12
Laotian (3)	5	0.03
Pakistani (27)	30	0.15
Taiwanese (5)	6	0.03
Thai (1)	3	0.02
Vietnamese (9)	9	0.05
Other Asian, not specified (5)	13	0.07
Austrian	131	0.67
Belgian	6	0.03
British	120	0.62
Canadian	77	0.39
Celtic	60	0.31
Croatian	6	0.03
Czech	184	0.94
Czechoslovakian	64	0.33
Danish	26	0.13
Dutch	589	3.02
English	3,246	16.65
European	55	0.28
Finnish	55	0.28
French, except Basque	613	3.14
French Canadian	167	0.86
German	3,885	19.93
German Russian	25	0.13
Greek	87	0.45
Hawaii Native/Pacific Islander:	4	0.02
Micronesian: (1)	2	0.01
Guamanian/Chamorro (1)	2	0.01
Polynesian:	1	0.01
Native Hawaiian	1	0.01
Other Pac. Isl., not spec. (1)	1	0.01
Hispanic or Latino:	145	0.74
Central American:	5	0.03
Guatemalan	4	0.02
Honduran	1	0.01
Cuban	7	0.04
Dominican Republic	1	0.01
Mexican	23	0.12
Puerto Rican	50	0.26
South American:	20	0.10
Bolivian	3	0.02
Colombian	2	0.01
Ecuadorian	8	0.04
Peruvian	5	0.03
Other South American	2	0.01
Other Hispanic or Latino	39	0.20
Hungarian	100	0.51
Irish	3,462	17.76
Italian	2,316	11.88
Lithuanian	42	0.22
Northern European	22	0.11
Norwegian	62	0.32
Pennsylvania German	102	0.52
Polish	1,435	7.36
Portuguese	5	0.03
Romanian	7	0.04
Russian	83	0.43
Scotch-Irish	304	1.56
Scottish	423	2.17
Slavic	5	0.03
Slovak	37	0.19
Swedish	239	1.23
Swiss	81	0.42
Ukrainian	330	1.69
United States or American	1,232	6.32
Welsh	407	2.09
White:	18,936	96.80
Not Hispanic (18,668)	18,832	96.27
Hispanic (89)	104	0.53
Yugoslavian	17	0.09

Huntington Station

Place Type: Census Designated Place
County: Suffolk
Population: 29,910

Ancestry/Race	Number	%
Afghan	181	0.60
African American/Black:	3,818	12.76
Not Hispanic (3,296)	3,584	11.98
Hispanic (163)	234	0.78
African, sub-Saharan:	111	0.37
African	84	0.28
Nigerian	27	0.09
Alaska Native tribes, specified:	1	0.00
Tlingit-Haida (1)	1	0.00
Am. Ind. or Alaska Nat., not spec.	113	0.38
Alsatian	4	0.01
American Indian tribes, specified:	111	0.37
Apache (3)	4	0.01
Blackfeet	5	0.02
Cherokee (10)	25	0.08
Choctaw	1	0.00
Cree	1	0.00
Iroquois	2	0.01
Latin American Indians (4)	15	0.05
Seminole	3	0.01
Sioux	4	0.01
All other tribes (29)	51	0.17
American Indian tribes, not spec.	17	0.06
Arab:	130	0.43
Egyptian	73	0.24
Lebanese	27	0.09
Moroccan	24	0.08
Syrian	6	0.02
Armenian	69	0.23
Asian:	1,084	3.62
Bangladeshi (1)	1	0.00
Cambodian (4)	4	0.01
Chinese, ex. Taiwanese (227)	256	0.86
Filipino (94)	115	0.38
Indian (271)	304	1.02
Indonesian (2)	2	0.01
Japanese (68)	78	0.26
Korean (68)	85	0.28
Malaysian	1	0.00
Pakistani (112)	153	0.51
Sri Lankan	3	0.01
Taiwanese (5)	5	0.02
Thai (16)	18	0.06
Vietnamese (12)	14	0.05
Other Asian, specified (2)	2	0.01
Other Asian, not specified (24)	43	0.14
Austrian	155	0.52
Brazilian	2	0.01
British	7	0.02
Canadian	45	0.15
Croatian	38	0.13
Czech	133	0.44
Czechoslovakian	18	0.06
Danish	69	0.23
Dutch	232	0.77
Eastern European	117	0.39
English	1,363	4.55
European	172	0.57
Finnish	77	0.26
French, except Basque	472	1.58
French Canadian	60	0.20
German	4,186	13.97
Greek	390	1.30
Guyanese	44	0.15
Hawaii Native/Pacific Islander:	25	0.08
Micronesian: (2)	4	0.01
Guamanian/Chamorro (2)	4	0.01
Polynesian: (1)	5	0.02
Native Hawaiian (1)	5	0.02
Other Pac. Isl., not spec. (1)	16	0.05
Hispanic or Latino:	6,802	22.74
Central American:	2,851	9.53
Costa Rican	22	0.07
Guatemalan	169	0.57
Honduran	252	0.84
Nicaraguan	15	0.05
Panamanian	2	0.01
Salvadoran	2,304	7.70
Other Central American	87	0.29
Cuban	57	0.19
Dominican Republic	263	0.88
Mexican	357	1.19
Puerto Rican	1,427	4.77
South American:	524	1.75
Argentinean	34	0.11
Chilean	40	0.13
Colombian	165	0.55
Ecuadorian	141	0.47
Paraguayan	1	0.00
Peruvian	117	0.39
Uruguayan	8	0.03
Venezuelan	11	0.04

Notes: 1. Figures in the "Number" column do not add up to the total population due to: a) Ancestry/Race overlap — e.g. persons can report being both White and Irish, b) persons of Hispanic origin can report being any race, c) persons reporting two ancestries are counted in both categories. 2. Numbers in parentheses indicate the number of persons reporting this ancestry/race alone, not in combination with any other ancestry/race. 3. Refer to the Explanation of Data in the front of the book for more detailed information.

Ancestry/Race	Number	%
Other South American	7	0.02
Other Hispanic or Latino	1,323	4.42
Hungarian	134	0.45
Iranian	154	0.51
Irish	5,178	17.28
Israeli	14	0.05
Italian	6,080	20.29
Latvian	11	0.04
Lithuanian	93	0.31
Maltese	22	0.07
Northern European	12	0.04
Norwegian	269	0.90
Pennsylvania German	18	0.06
Polish	1,371	4.57
Portuguese	67	0.22
Romanian	38	0.13
Russian	670	2.24
Scandinavian	43	0.14
Scotch-Irish	228	0.76
Scottish	313	1.04
Serbian	8	0.03
Slavic	22	0.07
Slovak	42	0.14
Swedish	289	0.96
Swiss	48	0.16
Turkish	42	0.14
Ukrainian	108	0.36
United States or American	980	3.27
Welsh	77	0.26
West Indian, excl. Hispanic:	723	2.41
British West Indian	7	0.02
Haitian	384	1.28
Jamaican	240	0.80
Trinidadian and Tobagonian	21	0.07
West Indian	71	0.24
White:	22,132	74.00
Not Hispanic (18,187)	18,561	62.06
Hispanic (3,214)	3,571	11.94
Yugoslavian	22	0.07

Huntington

Place Type: Town
County: Suffolk
Population: 195,289

Ancestry/Race	Number	%
Afghan	285	0.15
African American/Black:	9,162	4.69
Not Hispanic (7,934)	8,722	4.47
Hispanic (307)	440	0.23
African, sub-Saharan:	548	0.28
African	351	0.18
Ghanian	8	0.00
Kenyan	26	0.01
Liberian	17	0.01
Nigerian	27	0.01
South African	67	0.03
Other sub-Saharan African	52	0.03
Alaska Native tribes, specified:	6	0.00
Alaska Athabascan (1)	1	0.00
Aleut	2	0.00
Eskimo	1	0.00
Tlingit-Haida (2)	2	0.00
Am. Ind. or Alaska Nat., not spec.	278	0.14
Albanian	91	0.05
Alsatian	55	0.03
American Indian tribes, specified:	382	0.20
Apache (3)	5	0.00
Blackfeet (1)	15	0.01
Cherokee (17)	109	0.06
Chickasaw	1	0.00
Chippewa (2)	2	0.00
Choctaw (6)	11	0.01
Comanche	4	0.00
Cree	1	0.00
Creek (1)	7	0.00
Crow	2	0.00
Iroquois (6)	18	0.01
Kiowa	1	0.00
Latin American Indians (24)	59	0.03
Lumbee (5)	6	0.00
Navajo (2)	5	0.00
Ottawa	1	0.00
Pima	1	0.00
Pueblo (1)	4	0.00
Seminole (3)	7	0.00
Sioux	8	0.00
Tohono O'Odham (5)	5	0.00
Yaqui	2	0.00
All other tribes (59)	108	0.06
American Indian tribes, not spec.	40	0.02
Arab:	908	0.46
Arab/Arabic	14	0.01
Egyptian	303	0.16
Iraqi	15	0.01
Jordanian	6	0.00
Lebanese	226	0.12
Moroccan	99	0.05
Palestinian	6	0.00
Syrian	149	0.08
Other Arab	90	0.05
Armenian	621	0.32
Asian:	7,887	4.04
Bangladeshi (38)	40	0.02
Cambodian (5)	5	0.00
Chinese, ex. Taiwanese (1,788)	2,027	1.04
Filipino (547)	696	0.36
Indian (1,951)	2,156	1.10
Indonesian (5)	6	0.00
Japanese (305)	394	0.20
Korean (1,260)	1,352	0.69
Laotian (5)	5	0.00
Malaysian (5)	11	0.01
Pakistani (480)	600	0.31
Sri Lankan (5)	8	0.00
Taiwanese (106)	116	0.06
Thai (51)	59	0.03
Vietnamese (55)	64	0.03
Other Asian, specified (24)	34	0.02
Other Asian, not specified (111)	314	0.16
Assyrian/Chaldean/Syriac	19	0.01
Australian	22	0.01
Austrian	2,004	1.03
Basque	9	0.00
Belgian	197	0.10
Brazilian	45	0.02
British	736	0.38
Canadian	362	0.19
Carpatho Rusyn	4	0.00
Celtic	6	0.00
Croatian	398	0.20
Cypriot	120	0.06
Czech	1,006	0.52
Czechoslovakian	631	0.32
Danish	587	0.30
Dutch	1,975	1.01
Eastern European	1,175	0.60
English	12,454	6.38
Estonian	45	0.02
European	1,178	0.60
Finnish	341	0.17
French, except Basque	3,567	1.83
French Canadian	877	0.45
German	31,620	16.19
Greek	3,492	1.79
Guyanese	123	0.06
Hawaii Native/Pacific Islander:	113	0.06
Micronesian: (12)	23	0.01
Guamanian/Chamorro (12)	20	0.01
Other Micronesian	3	0.00
Polynesian: (9)	26	0.01
Native Hawaiian (8)	22	0.01
Samoan (1)	4	0.00
Other Pac. Isl., specified	2	0.00
Other Pac. Isl., not spec. (15)	62	0.03
Hispanic or Latino:	12,844	6.58
Central American:	3,623	1.86
Costa Rican	47	0.02
Guatemalan	298	0.15
Honduran	354	0.18
Nicaraguan	20	0.01
Panamanian	23	0.01
Salvadoran	2,747	1.41
Other Central American	134	0.07
Cuban	366	0.19
Dominican Republic	489	0.25
Mexican	721	0.37
Puerto Rican	3,465	1.77
South American:	1,535	0.79
Argentinean	160	0.08
Bolivian	32	0.02
Chilean	115	0.06
Colombian	489	0.25
Ecuadorian	334	0.17
Paraguayan	40	0.02
Peruvian	239	0.12
Uruguayan	38	0.02
Venezuelan	37	0.02
Other South American	51	0.03
Other Hispanic or Latino	2,645	1.35
Hungarian	1,955	1.00
Icelander	7	0.00
Iranian	464	0.24
Irish	41,599	21.30
Israeli	260	0.13
Italian	51,869	26.56
Latvian	167	0.09
Lithuanian	962	0.49
Luxemburger	3	0.00
Macedonian	4	0.00
Maltese	140	0.07
New Zealander	7	0.00
Northern European	82	0.04
Norwegian	1,904	0.97
Pennsylvania German	45	0.02
Polish	11,435	5.86
Portuguese	434	0.22
Romanian	951	0.49
Russian	8,974	4.60
Scandinavian	181	0.09
Scotch-Irish	1,808	0.93
Scottish	2,489	1.27
Serbian	52	0.03
Slavic	161	0.08
Slovak	429	0.22
Slovene	66	0.03
Swedish	2,447	1.25
Swiss	622	0.32
Turkish	432	0.22
Ukrainian	1,234	0.63
United States or American	7,252	3.71
Welsh	749	0.38
West Indian, excl. Hispanic:	2,103	1.08
Barbadian	26	0.01
Belizean	12	0.01
Bermudan	7	0.00
British West Indian	28	0.01
Haitian	1,220	0.62
Jamaican	521	0.27
Trinidadian and Tobagonian	116	0.06
West Indian	173	0.09
White:	174,756	89.49
Not Hispanic (165,027)	166,630	85.32
Hispanic (7,432)	8,126	4.16
Yugoslavian	290	0.15

Hyde Park

Place Type: Town
County: Dutchess
Population: 20,851

Ancestry/Race	Number	%
African American/Black:	1,055	5.06
Not Hispanic (846)	983	4.71
Hispanic (41)	72	0.35
African, sub-Saharan:	67	0.32
African	53	0.25
Ghanian	14	0.07

Notes: 1. Figures in the "Number" column do not add up to the total population due to: a) Ancestry/Race overlap — e.g. persons can report being both White and Irish, b) persons of Hispanic origin can report being any race, c) persons reporting two ancestries are counted in both categories. 2. Numbers in parentheses indicate the number of persons reporting this ancestry/race alone, not in combination with any other ancestry/race. 3. Refer to the Explanation of Data in the front of the book for more detailed information.

Am. Ind. or Alaska Nat., not spec.	70	0.34
American Indian tribes, specified:	89	0.43
Apache	1	0.00
Blackfeet (1)	8	0.04
Cherokee (1)	6	0.03
Chippewa	2	0.01
Choctaw	1	0.00
Delaware	1	0.00
Iroquois (3)	31	0.15
Latin American Indians (6)	10	0.05
Lumbee (1)	3	0.01
Pueblo (2)	3	0.01
Sioux	2	0.01
All other tribes (8)	21	0.10
Amcrican Indian tribes, not spec.	1	0.00
Arab:	202	0.97
Arab/Arabic	32	0.15
Egyptian	53	0.25
Jordanian	103	0.49
Lebanese	14	0.07
Armenian	18	0.09
Asian:	341	1.64
Cambodian (1)	1	0.00
Chinese, ex. Taiwanese (52)	61	0.29
Filipino (71)	88	0.42
Indian (76)	82	0.39
Japanese (9)	12	0.06
Korean (50)	62	0.30
Pakistani (3)	3	0.01
Sri Lankan (1)	2	0.01
Thai (1)	3	0.01
Vietnamese (21)	23	0.11
Other Asian, specified (1)	1	0.00
Other Asian, not specified (1)	3	0.01
Australian	5	0.02
Austrian	85	0.41
Belgian	63	0.30
Brazilian	8	0.04
British	148	0.71
Canadian	27	0.13
Czech	112	0.54
Czechoslovakian	116	0.56
Danish	59	0.28
Dutch	928	4.45
Eastern European	15	0.07
English	2,342	11.23
European	167	0.80
Finnish	36	0.17
French, except Basque	705	3.38
French Canadian	241	1.16
German	3,819	18.32
Greek	162	0.78
Guyanese	6	0.03
Hawaii Native/Pacific Islander:	24	0.12
Micronesian: (3)	3	0.01
Guamanian/Chamorro (3)	3	0.01
Polynesian: (12)	14	0.07
Native Hawaiian (1)	1	0.00
Samoan (5)	7	0.03
Tongan (6)	6	0.03
Other Pac. Isl., not spec. (2)	7	0.03
Hispanic or Latino:	674	3.23
Central American:	23	0.11
Costa Rican	1	0.00
Guatemalan	5	0.02
Honduran	11	0.05
Panamanian	2	0.01
Salvadoran	2	0.01
Other Central American	2	0.01
Cuban	29	0.14
Dominican Republic	10	0.05
Mexican	158	0.76
Puerto Rican	294	1.41
South American:	46	0.22
Argentinean	1	0.00
Bolivian	1	0.00
Chilean	3	0.01
Colombian	27	0.13
Ecuadorian	4	0.02
Peruvian	2	0.01
Uruguayan	1	0.00
Venezuelan	4	0.02
Other South American	3	0.01
Other Hispanic or Latino	114	0.55
Hungarian	313	1.50
Irish	4,572	21.93
Israeli	9	0.04
Italian	4,091	19.62
Latvian	25	0.12
Lithuanian	83	0.40
Maltese	8	0.04
Norwegian	227	1.09
Pennsylvania German	5	0.02
Polish	896	4.30
Portuguese	44	0.21
Romanian	11	0.05
Russian	220	1.06
Scandinavian	35	0.17
Scotch-Irish	292	1.40
Scottish	275	1.32
Slavic	40	0.19
Slovak	104	0.50
Slovene	6	0.03
Swedish	260	1.25
Swiss	99	0.47
Ukrainian	96	0.46
United States or American	798	3.83
Welsh	151	0.72
West Indian, excl. Hispanic:	217	1.04
British West Indian	27	0.13
Haitian	40	0.19
Jamaican	48	0.23
Trinidadian and Tobagonian	22	0.11
West Indian	80	0.38
White:	19,307	92.60
Not Hispanic (18,628)	18,907	90.68
Hispanic (350)	400	1.92
Yugoslavian	37	0.18

Irondequoit

Place Type: Census Designated Place
County: Monroe
Population: 52,354

Ancestry/Race	Number	%
Acadian/Cajun	6	0.01
African American/Black:	2,062	3.94
Not Hispanic (1,765)	1,922	3.67
Hispanic (92)	140	0.27
African, sub-Saharan:	121	0.23
African	71	0.14
Cape Verdean	10	0.02
Kenyan	6	0.01
Nigerian	28	0.05
South African	6	0.01
Alaska Native tribes, specified:	1	0.00
Alaska Athabascan	1	0.00
Am. Ind. or Alaska Nat., not spec.	97	0.19
Albanian	8	0.02
American Indian tribes, specified:	110	0.21
Blackfeet	5	0.01
Cherokee (1)	17	0.03
Chickasaw (1)	1	0.00
Chippewa (4)	10	0.02
Creek	1	0.00
Iroquois (35)	59	0.11
Latin American Indians	1	0.00
Pueblo (1)	1	0.00
Seminole	3	0.01
Sioux (1)	2	0.00
All other tribes (5)	10	0.02
American Indian tribes, not spec.	13	0.02
Arab:	296	0.57
Arab/Arabic	12	0.02
Egyptian	55	0.11
Jordanian	8	0.02
Lebanese	189	0.36
Syrian	32	0.06
Armenian	94	0.18
Asian:	698	1.33
Cambodian (21)	23	0.04
Chinese, ex. Taiwanese (83)	107	0.20
Filipino (47)	64	0.12
Indian (90)	110	0.21
Japanese (17)	42	0.08
Korean (68)	81	0.15
Laotian (45)	58	0.11
Pakistani (11)	12	0.02
Sri Lankan (4)	4	0.01
Taiwanese (2)	3	0.01
Thai (9)	15	0.03
Vietnamese (82)	99	0.19
Other Asian, specified (1)	1	0.00
Other Asian, not specified (17)	79	0.15
Australian	4	0.01
Austrian	112	0.21
Belgian	306	0.58
Brazilian	41	0.08
British	285	0.54
Bulgarian	28	0.05
Canadian	358	0.68
Celtic	20	0.04
Croatian	33	0.06
Czech	117	0.22
Czechoslovakian	59	0.11
Danish	152	0.29
Dutch	1,688	3.22
Eastern European	67	0.13
English	6,005	11.47
Estonian	4	0.01
European	222	0.42
Finnish	119	0.23
French, except Basque	1,728	3.30
French Canadian	499	0.95
German	11,896	22.73
Greek	236	0.45
Hawaii Native/Pacific Islander:	23	0.04
Micronesian: (2)	5	0.01
Guamanian/Chamorro (2)	4	0.01
Other Micronesian	1	0.00
Polynesian: (6)	11	0.02
Native Hawaiian (5)	9	0.02
Other Polynesian (1)	2	0.00
Other Pac. Isl., not spec. (2)	7	0.01
Hispanic or Latino:	1,602	3.06
Central American:	18	0.03
Costa Rican	3	0.01
Guatemalan	8	0.02
Nicaraguan	2	0.00
Panamanian	3	0.01
Salvadoran	2	0.00
Cuban	72	0.14
Dominican Republic	37	0.07
Mexican	103	0.20
Puerto Rican	1,123	2.15
South American:	48	0.09
Argentinean	6	0.01
Chilean	10	0.02
Colombian	8	0.02
Ecuadorian	5	0.01
Paraguayan	4	0.01
Peruvian	7	0.01
Venezuelan	5	0.01
Other South American	3	0.01
Other Hispanic or Latino	201	0.38
Hungarian	263	0.50
Irish	9,861	18.84
Israeli	5	0.01
Italian	14,968	28.59
Latvian	30	0.06
Lithuanian	377	0.72
Macedonian	319	0.61
New Zealander	7	0.01
Northern European	26	0.05
Norwegian	123	0.23
Pennsylvania German	34	0.06
Polish	3,341	6.38
Portuguese	29	0.06
Romanian	61	0.12

Notes: 1. Figures in the "Number" column do not add up to the total population due to: a) Ancestry/Race overlap — e.g. persons can report being both White and Irish, b) persons of Hispanic origin can report being any race, c) persons reporting two ancestries are counted in both categories. 2. Numbers in parentheses indicate the number of persons reporting this ancestry/race alone, not in combination with any other ancestry/race. 3. Refer to the Explanation of Data in the front of the book for more detailed information.

Russian	463	0.88
Scandinavian	16	0.03
Scotch-Irish	532	1.02
Scottish	975	1.86
Slavic	19	0.04
Slovak	38	0.07
Slovene	10	0.02
Swedish	412	0.79
Swiss	140	0.27
Turkish	459	0.88
Ukrainian	1,643	3.14
United States or American	1,589	3.04
Welsh	464	0.89
West Indian, excl. Hispanic:	237	0.45
Bermudan	11	0.02
British West Indian	27	0.05
Haitian	34	0.06
Jamaican	143	0.27
Trinidadian and Tobagonian	22	0.04
White:	49,281	94.13
Not Hispanic (47,845)	48,322	92.30
Hispanic (862)	959	1.83
Yugoslavian	48	0.09

Islip

Place Type: Town
County: Suffolk
Population: 322,612

Ancestry/Race	Number	%
Acadian/Cajun	15	0.00
Afghan	125	0.04
African American/Black:	32,429	10.05
Not Hispanic (26,827)	29,186	9.05
Hispanic (2,283)	3,243	1.01
African, sub-Saharan:	1,421	0.44
African	1,088	0.34
Cape Verdean	32	0.01
Ethiopian	37	0.01
Ghanian	106	0.03
Liberian	18	0.01
Nigerian	105	0.03
Sierra Leonean	6	0.00
South African	10	0.00
Sudanese	12	0.00
Other sub-Saharan African	7	0.00
Alaska Native tribes, specified:	7	0.00
Alaska Athabascan (1)	1	0.00
Aleut	1	0.00
Eskimo (3)	3	0.00
Tlingit-Haida	2	0.00
Am. Ind. or Alaska Nat., not spec.	923	0.29
Albanian	138	0.04
Alsatian	50	0.02
American Indian tribes, specified:	1,206	0.37
Apache (6)	22	0.01
Blackfeet (23)	83	0.03
Cherokee (38)	295	0.09
Cheyenne (3)	6	0.00
Chickasaw (2)	3	0.00
Chippewa (9)	12	0.00
Choctaw (3)	16	0.00
Comanche	3	0.00
Cree (1)	7	0.00
Creek (1)	8	0.00
Iroquois (20)	76	0.02
Latin American Indians (126)	336	0.10
Lumbee (4)	6	0.00
Navajo	9	0.00
Osage (1)	2	0.00
Paiute	1	0.00
Pueblo (13)	34	0.01
Puget Sound Salish	2	0.00
Seminole (1)	11	0.00
Shoshone	3	0.00
Sioux (9)	29	0.01
Ute (1)	4	0.00
All other tribes (99)	238	0.07
American Indian tribes, not spec.	169	0.05
Arab:	1,027	0.32
Arab/Arabic	198	0.06
Egyptian	318	0.10
Iraqi	22	0.01
Jordanian	25	0.01
Lebanese	153	0.05
Moroccan	19	0.01
Palestinian	174	0.05
Syrian	55	0.02
Other Arab	63	0.02
Armenian	329	0.10
Asian:	8,817	2.73
Bangladeshi (62)	78	0.02
Cambodian (11)	11	0.00
Chinese, ex. Taiwanese (1,269)	1,548	0.48
Filipino (905)	1,155	0.36
Hmong	1	0.00
Indian (2,827)	3,360	1.04
Indonesian (18)	32	0.01
Japanese (119)	214	0.07
Korean (517)	584	0.18
Laotian (17)	19	0.01
Malaysian (5)	10	0.00
Pakistani (522)	755	0.23
Sri Lankan (10)	14	0.00
Taiwanese (36)	42	0.01
Thai (91)	110	0.03
Vietnamese (365)	424	0.13
Other Asian, specified (3)	34	0.01
Other Asian, not specified (131)	426	0.13
Assyrian/Chaldean/Syriac	10	0.00
Australian	12	0.00
Austrian	1,537	0.48
Basque	12	0.00
Belgian	191	0.06
Brazilian	171	0.05
British	568	0.18
Bulgarian	73	0.02
Canadian	583	0.18
Celtic	60	0.02
Croatian	204	0.06
Cypriot	14	0.00
Czech	1,662	0.52
Czechoslovakian	922	0.29
Danish	623	0.19
Dutch	2,588	0.80
Eastern European	363	0.11
English	14,592	4.52
Estonian	48	0.01
European	755	0.23
Finnish	379	0.12
French, except Basque	4,982	1.54
French Canadian	1,534	0.48
German	47,823	14.82
Greek	2,970	0.92
Guyanese	553	0.17
Hawaii Native/Pacific Islander:	383	0.12
Micronesian: (75)	87	0.03
Guamanian/Chamorro (75)	86	0.03
Other Micronesian	1	0.00
Polynesian: (50)	85	0.03
Native Hawaiian (32)	59	0.02
Samoan (17)	23	0.01
Tongan	1	0.00
Other Polynesian (1)	2	0.00
Other Pac. Isl., specified	18	0.01
Other Pac. Isl., not spec. (36)	193	0.06
Hispanic or Latino:	65,031	20.16
Central American:	14,851	4.60
Costa Rican	187	0.06
Guatemalan	1,347	0.42
Honduran	1,211	0.38
Nicaraguan	105	0.03
Panamanian	298	0.09
Salvadoran	11,046	3.42
Other Central American	657	0.20
Cuban	929	0.29
Dominican Republic	4,792	1.49
Mexican	1,410	0.44
Puerto Rican	22,298	6.91
South American:	7,398	2.29
Argentinean	300	0.09
Bolivian	107	0.03
Chilean	249	0.08
Colombian	2,951	0.91
Ecuadorian	2,052	0.64
Paraguayan	27	0.01
Peruvian	1,244	0.39
Uruguayan	88	0.03
Venezuelan	139	0.04
Other South American	241	0.07
Other Hispanic or Latino	13,353	4.14
Hungarian	1,931	0.60
Icelander	37	0.01
Iranian	229	0.07
Irish	69,514	21.55
Israeli	187	0.06
Italian	83,408	25.85
Latvian	135	0.04
Lithuanian	967	0.30
Maltese	388	0.12
New Zealander	9	0.00
Northern European	30	0.01
Norwegian	2,627	0.81
Pennsylvania German	21	0.01
Polish	14,034	4.35
Portuguese	1,771	0.55
Romanian	369	0.11
Russian	5,270	1.63
Scandinavian	152	0.05
Scotch-Irish	2,406	0.75
Scottish	2,878	0.89
Serbian	42	0.01
Slavic	120	0.04
Slovak	268	0.08
Slovene	12	0.00
Soviet Union	8	0.00
Swedish	2,577	0.80
Swiss	550	0.17
Turkish	585	0.18
Ukrainian	1,168	0.36
United States or American	8,893	2.76
Welsh	566	0.18
West Indian, excl. Hispanic:	6,903	2.14
Barbadian	270	0.08
Belizean	107	0.03
Bermudan	10	0.00
British West Indian	190	0.06
Dutch West Indian	12	0.00
Haitian	2,487	0.77
Jamaican	2,379	0.74
Trinidadian and Tobagonian	733	0.23
U.S. Virgin Islander	10	0.00
West Indian	694	0.22
Other West Indian	11	0.00
White:	255,698	79.26
Not Hispanic (217,803)	220,676	68.40
Hispanic (31,407)	35,022	10.86
Yugoslavian	173	0.05

Ithaca

Place Type: City
County: Tompkins
Population: 29,287

Ancestry/Race	Number	%
Acadian/Cajun	5	0.02
African American/Black:	2,282	7.79
Not Hispanic (1,854)	2,106	7.19
Hispanic (111)	176	0.60
African, sub-Saharan:	168	0.58
African	64	0.22
Ethiopian	6	0.02
Ghanian	16	0.06
Nigerian	50	0.17
Sierra Leonean	16	0.06
Ugandan	16	0.06
Alaska Native tribes, specified:	1	0.00
All other tribes	1	0.00

Notes: 1. Figures in the "Number" column do not add up to the total population due to: a) Ancestry/Race overlap — e.g. persons can report being both White and Irish, b) persons of Hispanic origin can report being any race, c) persons reporting two ancestries are counted in both categories. 2. Numbers in parentheses indicate the number of persons reporting this ancestry/race alone, not in combination with any other ancestry/race. 3. Refer to the Explanation of Data in the front of the book for more detailed information.

Am. Ind. or Alaska Nat., not spec.	121	0.41
Alsatian	11	0.04
American Indian tribes, specified:	153	0.52
Apache (4)	4	0.01
Blackfeet	4	0.01
Cherokee (10)	42	0.14
Cheyenne	1	0.00
Chickasaw	1	0.00
Chippewa (1)	4	0.01
Choctaw	1	0.00
Crow	2	0.01
Delaware (1)	2	0.01
Iroquois (16)	38	0.13
Latin American Indians (5)	14	0.05
Navajo (6)	6	0.02
Osage (1)	1	0.00
Potawatomi	1	0.00
Pueblo (2)	2	0.01
Seminole	4	0.01
Sioux (1)	6	0.02
Ute (1)	1	0.00
Yaqui (1)	2	0.01
All other tribes (9)	17	0.06
American Indian tribes, not spec.	17	0.06
Arab:	189	0.65
Arab/Arabic	13	0.04
Egyptian	43	0.15
Lebanese	56	0.19
Moroccan	14	0.05
Syrian	48	0.17
Other Arab	15	0.05
Armenian	83	0.29
Asian:	4,528	15.46
Bangladeshi (13)	15	0.05
Cambodian (61)	65	0.22
Chinese, ex. Taiwanese (1,568)	1,700	5.80
Filipino (93)	140	0.48
Hmong (1)	2	0.01
Indian (570)	625	2.13
Indonesian (30)	39	0.13
Japanese (207)	286	0.98
Korean (469)	507	1.73
Laotian (46)	52	0.18
Malaysian (17)	25	0.09
Pakistani (13)	30	0.10
Sri Lankan (13)	17	0.06
Taiwanese (91)	101	0.34
Thai (90)	109	0.37
Vietnamese (125)	143	0.49
Other Asian, specified (39)	52	0.18
Other Asian, not specified (466)	620	2.12
Australian	23	0.08
Austrian	284	0.98
Basque	4	0.01
Belgian	39	0.13
Brazilian	19	0.07
British	425	1.47
Bulgarian	11	0.04
Canadian	134	0.46
Celtic	8	0.03
Czech	196	0.68
Czechoslovakian	23	0.08
Danish	109	0.38
Dutch	534	1.84
Eastern European	225	0.78
English	2,700	9.31
Estonian	13	0.04
European	630	2.17
Finnish	136	0.47
French, except Basque	615	2.12
French Canadian	257	0.89
German	3,982	13.73
Greek	307	1.06
Guyanese	62	0.21
Hawaii Native/Pacific Islander:	135	0.46
Melanesian:	1	0.00
Fijian	1	0.00
Micronesian: (2)	8	0.03
Guamanian/Chamorro (2)	8	0.03
Polynesian: (9)	23	0.08
Native Hawaiian (5)	13	0.04
Samoan (4)	7	0.02
Tongan	2	0.01
Other Polynesian	1	0.00
Other Pac. Isl., not spec. (4)	103	0.35
Hispanic or Latino:	1,555	5.31
Central American:	91	0.31
Costa Rican	10	0.03
Guatemalan	16	0.05
Honduran	10	0.03
Nicaraguan	13	0.04
Panamanian	11	0.04
Salvadoran	28	0.10
Other Central American	3	0.01
Cuban	80	0.27
Dominican Republic	84	0.29
Mexican	236	0.81
Puerto Rican	406	1.39
South American:	262	0.89
Argentinean	14	0.05
Bolivian	14	0.05
Chilean	33	0.11
Colombian	78	0.27
Ecuadorian	38	0.13
Paraguayan	2	0.01
Peruvian	44	0.15
Uruguayan	2	0.01
Venezuelan	24	0.08
Other South American	13	0.04
Other Hispanic or Latino	396	1.35
Hungarian	259	0.89
Iranian	79	0.27
Irish	3,628	12.51
Israeli	67	0.23
Italian	2,853	9.84
Latvian	13	0.04
Lithuanian	143	0.49
New Zealander	7	0.02
Northern European	27	0.09
Norwegian	480	1.65
Pennsylvania German	38	0.13
Polish	1,823	6.28
Portuguese	94	0.32
Romanian	171	0.59
Russian	1,518	5.23
Scandinavian	45	0.16
Scotch-Irish	416	1.43
Scottish	524	1.81
Serbian	22	0.08
Slovak	85	0.29
Swedish	416	1.43
Swiss	143	0.49
Turkish	50	0.17
Ukrainian	175	0.60
United States or American	743	2.56
Welsh	459	1.58
West Indian, excl. Hispanic:	254	0.88
British West Indian	27	0.09
Haitian	34	0.12
Jamaican	155	0.53
Trinidadian and Tobagonian	16	0.06
West Indian	9	0.03
Other West Indian	13	0.04
White:	22,376	76.40
Not Hispanic (20,893)	21,469	73.31
Hispanic (770)	907	3.10
Yugoslavian	95	0.33

Ithaca

Place Type: Town
County: Tompkins
Population: 18,198

Ancestry/Race	Number	%
Acadian/Cajun	8	0.04
African American/Black:	630	3.46
Not Hispanic (512)	604	3.32
Hispanic (21)	26	0.14
African, sub-Saharan:	193	1.05
African	36	0.20
Cape Verdean	8	0.04
Ghanian	31	0.17
Kenyan	33	0.18
Senegalese	10	0.05
Sudanese	16	0.09
Other sub-Saharan African	59	0.32
Alaska Native tribes, specified:	1	0.01
Eskimo (1)	1	0.01
Am. Ind. or Alaska Nat., not spec.	36	0.20
American Indian tribes, specified:	51	0.28
Apache	1	0.01
Blackfeet	3	0.02
Cherokee (1)	17	0.09
Chippewa (3)	4	0.02
Creek	3	0.02
Iroquois (3)	6	0.03
Latin American Indians (2)	8	0.04
Lumbee (2)	2	0.01
Potawatomi (3)	3	0.02
Sioux	1	0.01
All other tribes (1)	3	0.02
American Indian tribes, not spec.	4	0.02
Arab:	152	0.82
Egyptian	20	0.11
Lebanese	87	0.47
Syrian	24	0.13
Other Arab	21	0.11
Armenian	19	0.10
Asian:	1,909	10.49
Bangladeshi (4)	7	0.04
Cambodian (17)	22	0.12
Chinese, ex. Taiwanese (591)	647	3.56
Filipino (49)	73	0.40
Indian (327)	357	1.96
Indonesian (26)	28	0.15
Japanese (132)	160	0.88
Korean (294)	318	1.75
Malaysian (4)	4	0.02
Pakistani (16)	16	0.09
Sri Lankan (2)	4	0.02
Taiwanese (78)	97	0.53
Thai (43)	46	0.25
Vietnamese (27)	30	0.16
Other Asian, specified (16)	20	0.11
Other Asian, not specified (22)	80	0.44
Australian	7	0.04
Austrian	179	0.97
Belgian	31	0.17
Brazilian	81	0.44
British	319	1.73
Bulgarian	18	0.10
Canadian	116	0.63
Celtic	4	0.02
Croatian	26	0.14
Czech	148	0.80
Czechoslovakian	48	0.26
Danish	61	0.33
Dutch	430	2.33
Eastern European	116	0.63
English	2,692	14.58
European	216	1.17
Finnish	175	0.95
French, except Basque	480	2.60
French Canadian	254	1.38
German	3,002	16.26
Greek	179	0.97
Guyanese	8	0.04
Hawaii Native/Pacific Islander:	77	0.42
Melanesian: (1)	2	0.01
Other Melanesian (1)	2	0.01
Micronesian: (2)	3	0.02
Guamanian/Chamorro (2)	3	0.02
Polynesian: (3)	10	0.05
Native Hawaiian (1)	8	0.04
Samoan (2)	2	0.01
Other Pac. Isl., not spec. (2)	62	0.34
Hispanic or Latino:	611	3.36
Central American:	25	0.14
Costa Rican	3	0.02

Notes: 1. Figures in the "Number" column do not add up to the total population due to: a) Ancestry/Race overlap — e.g. persons can report being both White and Irish, b) persons of Hispanic origin can report being any race, c) persons reporting two ancestries are counted in both categories. 2. Numbers in parentheses indicate the number of persons reporting this ancestry/race alone, not in combination with any other ancestry/race. 3. Refer to the Explanation of Data in the front of the book for more detailed information.

Ancestry/Race	Number	%
Guatemalan	6	0.03
Honduran	2	0.01
Nicaraguan	4	0.02
Panamanian	4	0.02
Salvadoran	5	0.03
Other Central American	1	0.01
Cuban	37	0.20
Dominican Republic	14	0.08
Mexican	123	0.68
Puerto Rican	104	0.57
South American:	135	0.74
Argentinean	31	0.17
Bolivian	1	0.01
Chilean	11	0.06
Colombian	28	0.15
Ecuadorian	13	0.07
Paraguayan	3	0.02
Peruvian	15	0.08
Uruguayan	2	0.01
Venezuelan	19	0.10
Other South American	12	0.07
Other Hispanic or Latino	173	0.95
Hungarian	155	0.84
Icelander	10	0.05
Iranian	14	0.08
Irish	2,710	14.68
Israeli	11	0.06
Italian	2,049	11.10
Latvian	30	0.16
Lithuanian	67	0.36
Luxemburger	7	0.04
New Zealander	22	0.12
Northern European	33	0.18
Norwegian	144	0.78
Pennsylvania German	15	0.08
Polish	1,034	5.60
Portuguese	36	0.20
Romanian	41	0.22
Russian	754	4.08
Scandinavian	16	0.09
Scotch-Irish	454	2.46
Scottish	746	4.04
Serbian	28	0.15
Slavic	39	0.21
Slovak	68	0.37
Slovene	29	0.16
Swedish	410	2.22
Swiss	136	0.74
Turkish	75	0.41
Ukrainian	112	0.61
United States or American	614	3.33
Welsh	288	1.56
West Indian, excl. Hispanic:	58	0.31
Jamaican	40	0.22
Trinidadian and Tobagonian	5	0.03
West Indian	13	0.07
White:	15,614	85.80
Not Hispanic (14,965)	15,237	83.73
Hispanic (347)	377	2.07
Yugoslavian	13	0.07

Jamestown

Place Type: City
County: Chautauqua
Population: 31,730

Ancestry/Race	Number	%
African American/Black:	1,428	4.50
Not Hispanic (989)	1,299	4.09
Hispanic (86)	129	0.41
African, sub-Saharan:	7	0.02
African	7	0.02
Alaska Native tribes, specified:	1	0.00
Alaska Athabascan	1	0.00
Am. Ind. or Alaska Nat., not spec.	125	0.39
Albanian	123	0.39
American Indian tribes, specified:	238	0.75
Apache (1)	2	0.01
Blackfeet (3)	12	0.04
Cherokee (8)	27	0.09
Cheyenne (1)	1	0.00
Chippewa (1)	1	0.00
Creek (4)	6	0.02
Crow	1	0.00
Iroquois (104)	160	0.50
Latin American Indians (1)	6	0.02
Navajo (2)	3	0.01
Sioux (1)	7	0.02
All other tribes (5)	12	0.04
American Indian tribes, not spec.	14	0.04
Arab:	9	0.03
Lebanese	9	0.03
Armenian	6	0.02
Asian:	195	0.61
Cambodian (4)	4	0.01
Chinese, ex. Taiwanese (18)	19	0.06
Filipino (24)	35	0.11
Indian (29)	38	0.12
Japanese (5)	12	0.04
Korean (26)	36	0.11
Laotian (3)	9	0.03
Pakistani (14)	15	0.05
Taiwanese (1)	1	0.00
Thai (1)	1	0.00
Vietnamese (13)	16	0.05
Other Asian, not specified (3)	9	0.03
Australian	6	0.02
Austrian	25	0.08
Belgian	34	0.11
British	128	0.40
Canadian	20	0.06
Croatian	35	0.11
Cypriot	30	0.09
Czech	64	0.20
Czechoslovakian	36	0.11
Danish	132	0.42
Dutch	816	2.57
English	4,163	13.12
European	41	0.13
Finnish	14	0.04
French, except Basque	808	2.55
French Canadian	183	0.58
German	5,520	17.40
Greek	154	0.49
Hawaii Native/Pacific Islander:	30	0.09
Melanesian: (1)	1	0.00
Fijian (1)	1	0.00
Micronesian: (2)	6	0.02
Guamanian/Chamorro (2)	6	0.02
Polynesian: (7)	11	0.03
Native Hawaiian (1)	3	0.01
Samoan (6)	8	0.03
Other Pac. Isl., not spec. (6)	12	0.04
Hispanic or Latino:	1,567	4.94
Central American:	5	0.02
Costa Rican	1	0.00
Guatemalan	3	0.01
Other Central American	1	0.00
Cuban	9	0.03
Dominican Republic	29	0.09
Mexican	60	0.19
Puerto Rican	1,287	4.06
South American:	7	0.02
Argentinean	1	0.00
Ecuadorian	4	0.01
Peruvian	1	0.00
Other South American	1	0.00
Other Hispanic or Latino	170	0.54
Hungarian	126	0.40
Irish	4,479	14.12
Italian	5,853	18.45
Latvian	21	0.07
Lithuanian	18	0.06
Luxemburger	8	0.03
Northern European	16	0.05
Norwegian	345	1.09
Pennsylvania German	63	0.20
Polish	1,628	5.13
Portuguese	41	0.13
Romanian	13	0.04
Russian	111	0.35
Scandinavian	52	0.16
Scotch-Irish	442	1.39
Scottish	439	1.38
Serbian	8	0.03
Slavic	4	0.01
Slovak	71	0.22
Slovene	23	0.07
Swedish	6,062	19.10
Swiss	104	0.33
Ukrainian	101	0.32
United States or American	1,454	4.58
Welsh	262	0.83
White:	29,661	93.48
Not Hispanic (28,235)	28,743	90.59
Hispanic (805)	918	2.89
Yugoslavian	13	0.04

Jefferson Valley-Yorktown

Place Type: Census Designated Place
County: Westchester
Population: 14,891

Ancestry/Race	Number	%
African American/Black:	379	2.55
Not Hispanic (327)	350	2.35
Hispanic (20)	29	0.19
Alaska Native tribes, specified:	1	0.01
Tlingit-Haida	1	0.01
Am. Ind. or Alaska Nat., not spec.	22	0.15
Albanian	72	0.48
American Indian tribes, specified:	22	0.15
Blackfeet (1)	3	0.02
Cherokee (3)	4	0.03
Chippewa	5	0.03
Iroquois	2	0.01
Latin American Indians (1)	3	0.02
Sioux (5)	5	0.03
American Indian tribes, not spec.	2	0.01
Arab:	41	0.28
Egyptian	41	0.28
Armenian	22	0.15
Asian:	546	3.67
Chinese, ex. Taiwanese (156)	179	1.20
Filipino (43)	56	0.38
Indian (173)	196	1.32
Japanese (15)	20	0.13
Korean (35)	37	0.25
Pakistani (15)	15	0.10
Sri Lankan	4	0.03
Taiwanese (2)	8	0.05
Thai (10)	10	0.07
Vietnamese (8)	11	0.07
Other Asian, not specified (6)	10	0.07
Austrian	255	1.71
British	24	0.16
Canadian	9	0.06
Croatian	16	0.11
Czech	47	0.32
Czechoslovakian	68	0.46
Danish	9	0.06
Dutch	227	1.52
Eastern European	110	0.74
English	920	6.18
Estonian	25	0.17
European	42	0.28
Finnish	14	0.09
French, except Basque	268	1.80
French Canadian	130	0.87
German	1,932	12.97
Greek	90	0.60
Hawaii Native/Pacific Islander:	6	0.04
Micronesian: (1)	1	0.01
Guamanian/Chamorro (1)	1	0.01
Other Pac. Isl., not spec.	5	0.03
Hispanic or Latino:	699	4.69
Central American:	8	0.05

Notes: 1. Figures in the "Number" column do not add up to the total population due to: a) Ancestry/Race overlap — e.g. persons can report being both White and Irish, b) persons of Hispanic origin can report being any race, c) persons reporting two ancestries are counted in both categories. 2. Numbers in parentheses indicate the number of persons reporting this ancestry/race alone, not in combination with any other ancestry/race. 3. Refer to the Explanation of Data in the front of the book for more detailed information.

Ancestry/Race	Number	%
Guatemalan	2	0.01
Honduran	4	0.03
Nicaraguan	1	0.01
Other Central American	1	0.01
Cuban	26	0.17
Dominican Republic	36	0.24
Mexican	15	0.10
Puerto Rican	393	2.64
South American:	87	0.58
Argentinean	1	0.01
Bolivian	2	0.01
Chilean	3	0.02
Colombian	16	0.11
Ecuadorian	30	0.20
Peruvian	17	0.11
Uruguayan	5	0.03
Venezuelan	4	0.03
Other South American	9	0.06
Other Hispanic or Latino	134	0.90
Hungarian	155	1.04
Iranian	8	0.05
Irish	3,533	23.73
Italian	5,485	36.83
Lithuanian	97	0.65
Northern European	10	0.07
Norwegian	67	0.45
Polish	691	4.64
Portuguese	36	0.24
Romanian	101	0.68
Russian	724	4.86
Scandinavian	9	0.06
Scotch-Irish	95	0.64
Scottish	194	1.30
Slavic	17	0.11
Slovak	42	0.28
Swedish	102	0.68
Swiss	108	0.73
Turkish	30	0.20
Ukrainian	78	0.52
United States or American	617	4.14
Welsh	57	0.38
West Indian, excl. Hispanic:	15	0.10
Jamaican	15	0.10
White:	13,867	93.12
Not Hispanic (13,265)	13,353	89.67
Hispanic (481)	514	3.45
Yugoslavian	14	0.09

Jericho

Place Type: Census Designated Place
County: Nassau
Population: 13,045

Ancestry/Race	Number	%
African American/Black:	213	1.63
Not Hispanic (179)	203	1.56
Hispanic (6)	10	0.08
African, sub-Saharan:	20	0.15
South African	20	0.15
Am. Ind. or Alaska Nat., not spec.	13	0.10
Albanian	7	0.05
American Indian tribes, specified:	7	0.05
Cherokee	5	0.04
Creek (1)	1	0.01
All other tribes (1)	1	0.01
American Indian tribes, not spec.	6	0.05
Arab:	31	0.24
Egyptian	4	0.03
Iraqi	15	0.12
Lebanese	12	0.09
Armenian	11	0.08
Asian:	1,465	11.23
Bangladeshi (3)	3	0.02
Chinese, ex. Taiwanese (375)	391	3.00
Filipino (50)	57	0.44
Indian (337)	365	2.80
Indonesian	2	0.02
Japanese (21)	24	0.18
Korean (525)	535	4.10
Laotian (4)	4	0.03
Malaysian (1)	3	0.02
Pakistani (25)	25	0.19
Sri Lankan (6)	6	0.05
Taiwanese (20)	23	0.18
Thai (1)	1	0.01
Vietnamese (11)	11	0.08
Other Asian, not specified (4)	15	0.11
Austrian	407	3.13
Brazilian	36	0.28
British	26	0.20
Celtic	7	0.05
Croatian	43	0.33
Czech	15	0.12
Czechoslovakian	51	0.39
Danish	7	0.05
Dutch	41	0.32
Eastern European	377	2.90
English	286	2.20
European	154	1.19
French, except Basque	106	0.82
French Canadian	19	0.15
German	745	5.74
Greek	78	0.60
Hawaii Native/Pacific Islander:	5	0.04
Micronesian:	1	0.01
Guamanian/Chamorro	1	0.01
Polynesian: (1)	1	0.01
Native Hawaiian (1)	1	0.01
Other Pac. Isl., not spec.	3	0.02
Hispanic or Latino:	318	2.44
Central American:	31	0.24
Costa Rican	2	0.02
Honduran	4	0.03
Panamanian	2	0.02
Salvadoran	23	0.18
Cuban	23	0.18
Dominican Republic	19	0.15
Mexican	15	0.11
Puerto Rican	75	0.57
South American:	72	0.55
Argentinean	6	0.05
Bolivian	2	0.02
Chilean	8	0.06
Colombian	25	0.19
Ecuadorian	23	0.18
Peruvian	6	0.05
Venezuelan	1	0.01
Other South American	1	0.01
Other Hispanic or Latino	83	0.64
Hungarian	243	1.87
Iranian	20	0.15
Irish	912	7.02
Israeli	74	0.57
Italian	1,514	11.66
Latvian	23	0.18
Lithuanian	109	0.84
Maltese	34	0.26
Norwegian	36	0.28
Polish	1,368	10.54
Portuguese	20	0.15
Romanian	171	1.32
Russian	2,096	16.14
Scotch-Irish	12	0.09
Scottish	55	0.42
Slovak	46	0.35
Swedish	34	0.26
Swiss	12	0.09
Turkish	33	0.25
Ukrainian	83	0.64
United States or American	924	7.12
Welsh	13	0.10
West Indian, excl. Hispanic:	70	0.54
Haitian	47	0.36
Trinidadian and Tobagonian	18	0.14
West Indian	5	0.04
White:	11,365	87.12
Not Hispanic (11,034)	11,121	85.25
Hispanic (232)	244	1.87
Yugoslavian	35	0.27

Johnson City

Place Type: Village
County: Broome
Population: 15,535

Ancestry/Race	Number	%
African American/Black:	634	4.08
Not Hispanic (473)	595	3.83
Hispanic (7)	39	0.25
African, sub-Saharan:	39	0.25
African	15	0.10
Ethiopian	9	0.06
Nigerian	9	0.06
South African	6	0.04
Am. Ind. or Alaska Nat., not spec.	57	0.37
Albanian	25	0.16
American Indian tribes, specified:	55	0.35
Apache (1)	3	0.02
Blackfeet (2)	6	0.04
Cherokee (1)	17	0.11
Chippewa	1	0.01
Choctaw (2)	2	0.01
Iroquois (3)	17	0.11
Latin American Indians (1)	1	0.01
Navajo (1)	2	0.01
Seminole (1)	1	0.01
Sioux	2	0.01
All other tribes (1)	3	0.02
American Indian tribes, not spec.	6	0.04
Arab:	17	0.11
Jordanian	5	0.03
Moroccan	6	0.04
Syrian	6	0.04
Armenian	40	0.26
Asian:	852	5.48
Chinese, ex. Taiwanese (160)	172	1.11
Filipino (20)	33	0.21
Indian (133)	145	0.93
Indonesian	2	0.01
Japanese (7)	16	0.10
Korean (96)	103	0.66
Laotian (201)	220	1.42
Pakistani (30)	30	0.19
Taiwanese (13)	15	0.10
Thai	3	0.02
Vietnamese (54)	59	0.38
Other Asian, specified (3)	4	0.03
Other Asian, not specified (39)	50	0.32
Austrian	79	0.51
British	54	0.35
Canadian	12	0.08
Carpatho Rusyn	30	0.19
Celtic	13	0.08
Croatian	13	0.08
Czech	150	0.97
Czechoslovakian	182	1.17
Danish	26	0.17
Dutch	451	2.90
Eastern European	27	0.17
English	2,255	14.51
European	78	0.50
Finnish	6	0.04
French, except Basque	353	2.27
French Canadian	145	0.93
German	2,225	14.32
Greek	68	0.44
Guyanese	11	0.07
Hawaii Native/Pacific Islander:	23	0.15
Micronesian: (1)	2	0.01
Guamanian/Chamorro (1)	2	0.01
Polynesian: (1)	6	0.04
Native Hawaiian	3	0.02
Samoan (1)	3	0.02
Other Pac. Isl., not spec. (5)	15	0.10
Hispanic or Latino:	347	2.23
Central American:	6	0.04
Guatemalan	5	0.03
Nicaraguan	1	0.01
Cuban	23	0.15

Notes: 1. Figures in the "Number" column do not add up to the total population due to: a) Ancestry/Race overlap — e.g. persons can report being both White and Irish, b) persons of Hispanic origin can report being any race, c) persons reporting two ancestries are counted in both categories. 2. Numbers in parentheses indicate the number of persons reporting this ancestry/race alone, not in combination with any other ancestry/race. 3. Refer to the Explanation of Data in the front of the book for more detailed information.

Ancestry/Race	Number	%
Dominican Republic	12	0.08
Mexican	32	0.21
Puerto Rican	198	1.27
South American:	13	0.08
Argentinean	1	0.01
Chilean	5	0.03
Colombian	3	0.02
Ecuadorian	1	0.01
Peruvian	1	0.01
Uruguayan	1	0.01
Venezuelan	1	0.01
Other Hispanic or Latino	63	0.41
Hungarian	55	0.35
Iranian	15	0.10
Irish	2,679	17.24
Israeli	9	0.06
Italian	1,421	9.14
Latvian	13	0.08
Lithuanian	160	1.03
Northern European	6	0.04
Norwegian	54	0.35
Pennsylvania German	60	0.39
Polish	1,381	8.89
Portuguese	22	0.14
Romanian	62	0.40
Russian	491	3.16
Scandinavian	9	0.06
Scotch-Irish	160	1.03
Scottish	313	2.01
Slavic	49	0.32
Slovak	1,044	6.72
Slovene	24	0.15
Swedish	147	0.95
Swiss	68	0.44
Ukrainian	492	3.17
United States or American	784	5.04
Welsh	309	1.99
West Indian, excl. Hispanic:	42	0.27
Barbadian	8	0.05
British West Indian	15	0.10
Jamaican	11	0.07
West Indian	8	0.05
White:	14,059	90.50
Not Hispanic (13,647)	13,865	89.25
Hispanic (158)	194	1.25
Yugoslavian	39	0.25

Kenmore

Place Type: Village
County: Erie
Population: 16,426

Ancestry/Race	Number	%
African American/Black:	205	1.25
Not Hispanic (159)	200	1.22
Hispanic (4)	5	0.03
Am. Ind. or Alaska Nat., not spec.	33	0.20
American Indian tribes, specified:	72	0.44
Blackfeet	2	0.01
Cherokee	1	0.01
Chickasaw	1	0.01
Chippewa (1)	1	0.01
Delaware	4	0.02
Iroquois (35)	56	0.34
Lumbee	2	0.01
Sioux (1)	1	0.01
All other tribes (4)	4	0.02
American Indian tribes, not spec.	7	0.04
Arab:	150	0.91
Lebanese	121	0.74
Syrian	29	0.18
Armenian	16	0.10
Asian:	135	0.82
Chinese, ex. Taiwanese (13)	17	0.10
Filipino (7)	12	0.07
Indian (25)	30	0.18
Japanese (1)	10	0.06
Korean (25)	33	0.20
Laotian (3)	4	0.02
Sri Lankan (1)	1	0.01
Taiwanese (1)	1	0.01
Thai (2)	4	0.02
Vietnamese (11)	11	0.07
Other Asian, specified	1	0.01
Other Asian, not specified (4)	11	0.07
Australian	4	0.02
Austrian	50	0.30
Belgian	3	0.02
British	111	0.68
Bulgarian	35	0.21
Canadian	95	0.58
Croatian	50	0.30
Czech	71	0.43
Czechoslovakian	64	0.39
Dutch	170	1.03
Eastern European	7	0.04
English	1,671	10.17
Estonian	5	0.03
European	98	0.60
French, except Basque	595	3.62
French Canadian	179	1.09
German	5,053	30.76
Greek	74	0.45
Hawaii Native/Pacific Islander:	11	0.07
Micronesian: (2)	2	0.01
Guamanian/Chamorro (2)	2	0.01
Polynesian: (5)	7	0.04
Native Hawaiian (4)	6	0.04
Samoan (1)	1	0.01
Other Pac. Isl., specified	1	0.01
Other Pac. Isl., not spec.	1	0.01
Hispanic or Latino:	213	1.30
Central American:	5	0.03
Nicaraguan	1	0.01
Panamanian	4	0.02
Cuban	7	0.04
Dominican Republic	1	0.01
Mexican	33	0.20
Puerto Rican	121	0.74
South American:	9	0.05
Argentinean	1	0.01
Bolivian	2	0.01
Colombian	3	0.02
Ecuadorian	3	0.02
Other Hispanic or Latino	37	0.23
Hungarian	263	1.60
Irish	3,693	22.48
Italian	4,401	26.79
Lithuanian	43	0.26
Maltese	13	0.08
Norwegian	84	0.51
Pennsylvania German	8	0.05
Polish	1,958	11.92
Portuguese	14	0.09
Romanian	10	0.06
Russian	144	0.88
Scandinavian	7	0.04
Scotch-Irish	194	1.18
Scottish	476	2.90
Slavic	9	0.05
Slovak	10	0.06
Swedish	118	0.72
Swiss	22	0.13
Turkish	20	0.12
Ukrainian	131	0.80
United States or American	362	2.20
Welsh	151	0.92
West Indian, excl. Hispanic:	20	0.12
Bahamian	5	0.03
Belizean	10	0.06
Jamaican	5	0.03
White:	16,039	97.64
Not Hispanic (15,769)	15,885	96.71
Hispanic (140)	154	0.94
Yugoslavian	6	0.04

Kent

Place Type: Town
County: Putnam
Population: 14,009

Ancestry/Race	Number	%
African American/Black:	253	1.81
Not Hispanic (193)	234	1.67
Hispanic (5)	19	0.14
African, sub-Saharan:	10	0.07
African	10	0.07
Am. Ind. or Alaska Nat., not spec.	35	0.25
Alsatian	9	0.06
American Indian tribes, specified:	51	0.36
Cherokee (3)	22	0.16
Cheyenne	2	0.01
Chippewa (2)	2	0.01
Crow	1	0.01
Delaware	1	0.01
Iroquois (1)	3	0.02
Latin American Indians (3)	6	0.04
Seminole	1	0.01
Sioux (5)	8	0.06
All other tribes	5	0.04
American Indian tribes, not spec.	7	0.05
Arab:	55	0.39
Arab/Arabic	23	0.16
Jordanian	32	0.23
Armenian	29	0.21
Asian:	208	1.48
Chinese, ex. Taiwanese (78)	93	0.66
Filipino (33)	41	0.29
Indian (35)	41	0.29
Indonesian (1)	2	0.01
Japanese (4)	7	0.05
Korean (9)	10	0.07
Malaysian (1)	1	0.01
Thai (4)	4	0.03
Vietnamese (4)	4	0.03
Other Asian, specified (1)	1	0.01
Other Asian, not specified (2)	4	0.03
Austrian	114	0.81
Belgian	27	0.19
British	42	0.30
Canadian	41	0.29
Croatian	11	0.08
Czech	55	0.39
Czechoslovakian	56	0.40
Danish	55	0.39
Dutch	138	0.99
Eastern European	16	0.11
English	987	7.05
Estonian	11	0.08
European	69	0.49
Finnish	40	0.29
French, except Basque	300	2.14
French Canadian	135	0.96
German	2,131	15.21
Greek	77	0.55
Hawaii Native/Pacific Islander:	7	0.05
Polynesian: (1)	3	0.02
Samoan (1)	3	0.02
Other Pac. Isl., not spec. (1)	4	0.03
Hispanic or Latino:	808	5.77
Central American:	43	0.31
Costa Rican	2	0.01
Guatemalan	21	0.15
Honduran	4	0.03
Nicaraguan	8	0.06
Panamanian	1	0.01
Salvadoran	7	0.05
Cuban	27	0.19
Dominican Republic	47	0.34
Mexican	43	0.31
Puerto Rican	397	2.83
South American:	87	0.62
Argentinean	4	0.03
Bolivian	5	0.04
Chilean	1	0.01

Notes: 1. Figures in the "Number" column do not add up to the total population due to: a) Ancestry/Race overlap — e.g. persons can report being both White and Irish, b) persons of Hispanic origin can report being any race, c) persons reporting two ancestries are counted in both categories. 2. Numbers in parentheses indicate the number of persons reporting this ancestry/race alone, not in combination with any other ancestry/race. 3. Refer to the Explanation of Data in the front of the book for more detailed information.

Ancestry/Race	Number	%
Colombian	17	0.12
Ecuadorian	26	0.19
Paraguayan	3	0.02
Peruvian	21	0.15
Uruguayan	2	0.01
Other South American	8	0.06
Other Hispanic or Latino	164	1.17
Hungarian	109	0.78
Irish	4,733	33.79
Italian	4,386	31.31
Latvian	14	0.10
Lithuanian	25	0.18
Norwegian	188	1.34
Polish	594	4.24
Portuguese	84	0.60
Romanian	15	0.11
Russian	314	2.24
Scandinavian	5	0.04
Scotch-Irish	99	0.71
Scottish	270	1.93
Slavic	18	0.13
Slovak	102	0.73
Swedish	220	1.57
Swiss	32	0.23
Ukrainian	35	0.25
United States or American	547	3.90
Welsh	106	0.76
West Indian, excl. Hispanic:	65	0.46
Jamaican	65	0.46
White:	13,343	95.25
Not Hispanic (12,643)	12,789	91.29
Hispanic (499)	554	3.95

Kings Park

Place Type: Census Designated Place
County: Suffolk
Population: 16,146

Ancestry/Race	Number	%
Afghan	86	0.53
African American/Black:	170	1.05
Not Hispanic (131)	161	1.00
Hispanic (5)	9	0.06
African, sub-Saharan:	5	0.03
African	5	0.03
Alaska Native tribes, specified:	1	0.01
Eskimo (1)	1	0.01
Am. Ind. or Alaska Nat., not spec.	24	0.15
Alsatian	6	0.04
American Indian tribes, specified:	30	0.19
Blackfeet (1)	2	0.01
Cherokee (2)	9	0.06
Choctaw (1)	1	0.01
Iroquois	6	0.04
Latin American Indians (2)	2	0.01
Navajo	1	0.01
Pueblo	1	0.01
Sioux	1	0.01
Ute (1)	1	0.01
All other tribes	6	0.04
American Indian tribes, not spec.	2	0.01
Arab:	62	0.38
Egyptian	62	0.38
Armenian	33	0.20
Asian:	393	2.43
Chinese, ex. Taiwanese (86)	96	0.59
Filipino (45)	58	0.36
Indian (80)	86	0.53
Japanese (16)	20	0.12
Korean (47)	55	0.34
Pakistani (21)	25	0.15
Thai (3)	3	0.02
Other Asian, specified	7	0.04
Other Asian, not specified (2)	43	0.27
Austrian	141	0.87
Brazilian	22	0.14
British	18	0.11
Canadian	33	0.20
Carpatho Rusyn	6	0.04
Croatian	10	0.06
Czech	59	0.37
Czechoslovakian	23	0.14
Danish	27	0.17
Dutch	143	0.89
Eastern European	40	0.25
English	717	4.44
European	107	0.66
Finnish	31	0.19
French, except Basque	278	1.72
French Canadian	46	0.29
German	3,243	20.10
Greek	279	1.73
Guyanese	28	0.17
Hawaii Native/Pacific Islander:	14	0.09
Micronesian: (1)	1	0.01
Guamanian/Chamorro (1)	1	0.01
Polynesian: (4)	4	0.02
Native Hawaiian (3)	3	0.02
Samoan (1)	1	0.01
Other Pac. Isl., specified	4	0.02
Other Pac. Isl., not spec.	5	0.03
Hispanic or Latino:	538	3.33
Central American:	46	0.28
Guatemalan	8	0.05
Honduran	6	0.04
Salvadoran	30	0.19
Other Central American	2	0.01
Cuban	32	0.20
Dominican Republic	13	0.08
Mexican	54	0.33
Puerto Rican	181	1.12
South American:	116	0.72
Argentinean	8	0.05
Bolivian	2	0.01
Chilean	7	0.04
Colombian	32	0.20
Ecuadorian	20	0.12
Peruvian	16	0.10
Uruguayan	4	0.02
Venezuelan	1	0.01
Other South American	26	0.16
Other Hispanic or Latino	96	0.59
Hungarian	141	0.87
Iranian	9	0.06
Irish	4,944	30.64
Italian	5,910	36.63
Lithuanian	125	0.77
Luxemburger	6	0.04
Maltese	44	0.27
Norwegian	167	1.03
Pennsylvania German	7	0.04
Polish	1,138	7.05
Portuguese	74	0.46
Romanian	34	0.21
Russian	409	2.53
Scotch-Irish	113	0.70
Scottish	111	0.69
Slavic	12	0.07
Slovak	33	0.20
Swedish	141	0.87
Swiss	17	0.11
Turkish	21	0.13
Ukrainian	104	0.64
United States or American	503	3.12
Welsh	70	0.43
West Indian, excl. Hispanic:	30	0.19
Haitian	17	0.11
Jamaican	13	0.08
White:	15,549	96.30
Not Hispanic (15,000)	15,112	93.60
Hispanic (411)	437	2.71
Yugoslavian	49	0.30

Kingsbury

Place Type: Town
County: Washington
Population: 11,171

Ancestry/Race	Number	%
African American/Black:	62	0.56
Not Hispanic (40)	59	0.53
Hispanic (1)	3	0.03
Am. Ind. or Alaska Nat., not spec.	24	0.21
American Indian tribes, specified:	44	0.39
Apache (2)	3	0.03
Blackfeet	1	0.01
Cherokee	9	0.08
Chippewa	2	0.02
Delaware (1)	1	0.01
Iroquois (9)	11	0.10
Sioux	2	0.02
All other tribes (1)	15	0.13
Arab:	45	0.40
Arab/Arabic	11	0.10
Lebanese	13	0.12
Syrian	21	0.19
Asian:	44	0.39
Chinese, ex. Taiwanese (8)	8	0.07
Filipino (4)	10	0.09
Indian (5)	5	0.04
Japanese (1)	3	0.03
Korean (4)	16	0.14
Thai (1)	1	0.01
Other Asian, not specified	1	0.01
Australian	16	0.14
Austrian	39	0.35
Belgian	8	0.07
British	12	0.11
Canadian	44	0.39
Czech	10	0.09
Czechoslovakian	16	0.14
Dutch	268	2.40
English	1,262	11.30
French, except Basque	2,289	20.49
French Canadian	641	5.74
German	657	5.88
Greek	6	0.05
Hawaii Native/Pacific Islander:	4	0.04
Other Pac. Isl., not spec. (1)	4	0.04
Hispanic or Latino:	67	0.60
Central American:	2	0.02
Salvadoran	2	0.02
Cuban	1	0.01
Dominican Republic	1	0.01
Mexican	9	0.08
Puerto Rican	34	0.30
South American:	3	0.03
Chilean	1	0.01
Colombian	2	0.02
Other Hispanic or Latino	17	0.15
Hungarian	72	0.64
Irish	2,098	18.78
Italian	1,066	9.54
Lithuanian	29	0.26
Norwegian	24	0.21
Polish	315	2.82
Russian	29	0.26
Scotch-Irish	238	2.13
Scottish	326	2.92
Slovak	17	0.15
Swedish	103	0.92
Swiss	18	0.16
Ukrainian	5	0.04
United States or American	925	8.28
Welsh	239	2.14
White:	11,061	99.02
Not Hispanic (10,929)	11,011	98.57
Hispanic (38)	50	0.45

Notes: 1. Figures in the "Number" column do not add up to the total population due to: a) Ancestry/Race overlap — e.g. persons can report being both White and Irish, b) persons of Hispanic origin can report being any race, c) persons reporting two ancestries are counted in both categories. 2. Numbers in parentheses indicate the number of persons reporting this ancestry/race alone, not in combination with any other ancestry/race. 3. Refer to the Explanation of Data in the front of the book for more detailed information.

Kingston

Place Type: City
County: Ulster
Population: 23,456

Ancestry/Race	Number	%
African American/Black:	3,487	14.87
Not Hispanic (2,820)	3,234	13.79
Hispanic (175)	253	1.08
African, sub-Saharan:	120	0.51
African	111	0.47
Kenyan	9	0.04
Alaska Native tribes, specified:	1	0.00
Eskimo (1)	1	0.00
Am. Ind. or Alaska Nat., not spec.	123	0.52
Albanian	5	0.02
American Indian tribes, specified:	106	0.45
Blackfeet	14	0.06
Cherokee (8)	41	0.17
Chippewa	2	0.01
Choctaw	2	0.01
Creek	1	0.00
Delaware	1	0.00
Iroquois (2)	24	0.10
Latin American Indians (10)	11	0.05
Lumbee (1)	1	0.00
Navajo (1)	1	0.00
Pueblo	1	0.00
Sioux (1)	1	0.00
All other tribes (1)	6	0.03
American Indian tribes, not spec.	5	0.02
Arab:	20	0.09
Lebanese	11	0.05
Syrian	9	0.04
Armenian	47	0.20
Asian:	455	1.94
Cambodian (3)	3	0.01
Chinese, ex. Taiwanese (121)	135	0.58
Filipino (38)	54	0.23
Indian (95)	111	0.47
Indonesian (1)	1	0.00
Japanese (12)	22	0.09
Korean (33)	35	0.15
Laotian	2	0.01
Malaysian	3	0.01
Pakistani (27)	47	0.20
Taiwanese (4)	5	0.02
Thai	1	0.00
Vietnamese (18)	19	0.08
Other Asian, specified	2	0.01
Other Asian, not specified (5)	15	0.06
Australian	5	0.02
Austrian	178	0.76
Belgian	17	0.07
Brazilian	6	0.03
British	77	0.33
Canadian	21	0.09
Croatian	19	0.08
Cypriot	6	0.03
Czech	28	0.12
Czechoslovakian	54	0.23
Danish	23	0.10
Dutch	1,127	4.82
Eastern European	35	0.15
English	1,427	6.10
Estonian	5	0.02
European	77	0.33
Finnish	54	0.23
French, except Basque	642	2.75
French Canadian	187	0.80
German	4,392	18.78
Greek	179	0.77
Guyanese	7	0.03
Hawaii Native/Pacific Islander:	15	0.06
Polynesian: (1)	5	0.02
Native Hawaiian	3	0.01
Samoan (1)	2	0.01
Other Pac. Isl., specified	2	0.01
Other Pac. Isl., not spec.	8	0.03
Hispanic or Latino:	1,516	6.46
Central American:	105	0.45
Costa Rican	3	0.01
Guatemalan	15	0.06
Honduran	16	0.07
Panamanian	9	0.04
Salvadoran	49	0.21
Other Central American	13	0.06
Cuban	37	0.16
Dominican Republic	33	0.14
Mexican	441	1.88
Puerto Rican	608	2.59
South American:	50	0.21
Argentinean	1	0.00
Chilean	3	0.01
Colombian	17	0.07
Ecuadorian	3	0.01
Peruvian	13	0.06
Venezuelan	13	0.06
Other Hispanic or Latino	242	1.03
Hungarian	159	0.68
Icelander	14	0.06
Iranian	26	0.11
Irish	5,117	21.88
Israeli	9	0.04
Italian	3,762	16.09
Latvian	11	0.05
Lithuanian	55	0.24
Norwegian	96	0.41
Polish	1,363	5.83
Portuguese	20	0.09
Romanian	20	0.09
Russian	354	1.51
Scandinavian	10	0.04
Scotch-Irish	229	0.98
Scottish	256	1.09
Slavic	5	0.02
Slovak	23	0.10
Swedish	85	0.36
Swiss	60	0.26
Ukrainian	79	0.34
United States or American	713	3.05
Welsh	69	0.30
West Indian, excl. Hispanic:	254	1.09
Haitian	74	0.32
Jamaican	152	0.65
West Indian	28	0.12
White:	19,442	82.89
Not Hispanic (18,076)	18,547	79.07
Hispanic (777)	895	3.82
Yugoslavian	15	0.06

Kirkland

Place Type: Town
County: Oneida
Population: 10,138

Ancestry/Race	Number	%
African American/Black:	145	1.43
Not Hispanic (118)	137	1.35
Hispanic (4)	8	0.08
Am. Ind. or Alaska Nat., not spec.	10	0.10
Albanian	8	0.08
American Indian tribes, specified:	25	0.25
Cherokee (2)	8	0.08
Choctaw	1	0.01
Iroquois (2)	6	0.06
Latin American Indians	2	0.02
Puget Sound Salish	1	0.01
Seminole	1	0.01
Sioux	1	0.01
All other tribes (2)	5	0.05
American Indian tribes, not spec.	2	0.02
Arab:	149	1.47
Arab/Arabic	6	0.06
Iraqi	2	0.02
Lebanese	111	1.09
Syrian	15	0.15
Other Arab	15	0.15
Armenian	8	0.08
Asian:	160	1.58
Bangladeshi (1)	1	0.01
Chinese, ex. Taiwanese (55)	69	0.68
Filipino (4)	5	0.05
Indian (14)	15	0.15
Indonesian	1	0.01
Japanese (10)	15	0.15
Korean (27)	34	0.34
Laotian (1)	1	0.01
Pakistani (2)	3	0.03
Taiwanese (2)	2	0.02
Thai	1	0.01
Vietnamese (4)	4	0.04
Other Asian, not specified (2)	9	0.09
Assyrian/Chaldean/Syriac	23	0.23
Austrian	66	0.65
Belgian	6	0.06
British	103	1.02
Canadian	50	0.49
Croatian	7	0.07
Czech	35	0.35
Czechoslovakian	17	0.17
Danish	42	0.41
Dutch	130	1.28
Eastern European	40	0.39
English	1,833	18.08
Estonian	5	0.05
European	104	1.03
Finnish	10	0.10
French, except Basque	515	5.08
French Canadian	246	2.43
German	2,068	20.40
Greek	42	0.41
Guyanese	5	0.05
Hawaii Native/Pacific Islander:	4	0.04
Polynesian: (3)	3	0.03
Native Hawaiian (2)	2	0.02
Samoan (1)	1	0.01
Other Pac. Isl., not spec.	1	0.01
Hispanic or Latino:	134	1.32
Central American:	5	0.05
Costa Rican	2	0.02
Salvadoran	3	0.03
Cuban	15	0.15
Dominican Republic	11	0.11
Mexican	26	0.26
Puerto Rican	28	0.28
South American:	24	0.24
Argentinean	7	0.07
Chilean	1	0.01
Colombian	5	0.05
Ecuadorian	5	0.05
Peruvian	2	0.02
Venezuelan	2	0.02
Other South American	2	0.02
Other Hispanic or Latino	25	0.25
Hungarian	58	0.57
Irish	2,401	23.68
Italian	1,430	14.11
Latvian	6	0.06
Lithuanian	27	0.27
New Zealander	7	0.07
Northern European	15	0.15
Norwegian	130	1.28
Polish	1,081	10.66
Portuguese	11	0.11
Romanian	8	0.08
Russian	118	1.16
Scandinavian	21	0.21
Scotch-Irish	123	1.21
Scottish	319	3.15
Slavic	2	0.02
Slovak	12	0.12
Slovene	2	0.02
Swedish	133	1.31
Swiss	57	0.56
Turkish	13	0.13
Ukrainian	122	1.20
United States or American	406	4.00

Notes: 1. Figures in the "Number" column do not add up to the total population due to: a) Ancestry/Race overlap — e.g. persons can report being both White and Irish, b) persons of Hispanic origin can report being any race, c) persons reporting two ancestries are counted in both categories. 2. Numbers in parentheses indicate the number of persons reporting this ancestry/race alone, not in combination with any other ancestry/race. 3. Refer to the Explanation of Data in the front of the book for more detailed information.

Ancestry/Race	Number	%
Welsh	431	4.25
West Indian, excl. Hispanic:	27	0.27
British West Indian	5	0.05
Haitian	7	0.07
Jamaican	8	0.08
Trinidadian and Tobagonian	7	0.07
White:	9,853	97.19
Not Hispanic (9,668)	9,747	96.14
Hispanic (97)	106	1.05

Kiryas Joel

Place Type: Village
County: Orange
Population: 13,138

Ancestry/Race	Number	%
African American/Black:	39	0.30
Not Hispanic (26)	36	0.27
Hispanic (1)	3	0.02
Am. Ind. or Alaska Nat., not spec.	9	0.07
Asian:	28	0.21
Filipino (2)	6	0.05
Indian	8	0.06
Japanese (1)	1	0.01
Other Asian, not specified	13	0.10
British	19	0.14
Canadian	20	0.15
Cypriot	4	0.03
Czech	30	0.23
Czechoslovakian	13	0.10
Dutch	6	0.05
Eastern European	7	0.05
European	60	0.45
German	25	0.19
Hawaii Native/Pacific Islander:	2	0.02
Other Pac. Isl., not spec.	2	0.02
Hispanic or Latino:	122	0.93
Central American:	1	0.01
Panamanian	1	0.01
Mexican	45	0.34
Puerto Rican	15	0.11
South American:	28	0.21
Argentinean	27	0.21
Uruguayan	1	0.01
Other Hispanic or Latino	33	0.25
Hungarian	2,010	15.21
Iranian	8	0.06
Irish	10	0.08
Israeli	274	2.07
Italian	18	0.14
Polish	93	0.70
Romanian	234	1.77
Russian	42	0.32
Swiss	6	0.05
Ukrainian	15	0.11
United States or American	1,052	7.96
White:	13,076	99.53
Not Hispanic (12,921)	12,976	98.77
Hispanic (88)	100	0.76

La Grange

Place Type: Town
County: Dutchess
Population: 14,928

Ancestry/Race	Number	%
African American/Black:	428	2.87
Not Hispanic (340)	399	2.67
Hispanic (20)	29	0.19
Am. Ind. or Alaska Nat., not spec.	23	0.15
Albanian	111	0.74
American Indian tribes, specified:	35	0.23
Blackfeet	2	0.01
Cherokee (3)	20	0.13
Iroquois (1)	7	0.05
Kiowa (2)	2	0.01
Latin American Indians	1	0.01
Shoshone	1	0.01
Sioux (2)	2	0.01
Arab:	35	0.23
Arab/Arabic	8	0.05
Egyptian	5	0.03
Lebanese	16	0.11
Syrian	6	0.04
Armenian	19	0.13
Asian:	524	3.51
Chinese, ex. Taiwanese (136)	142	0.95
Filipino (20)	30	0.20
Indian (156)	179	1.20
Indonesian	4	0.03
Japanese (7)	13	0.09
Korean (79)	79	0.53
Pakistani (5)	29	0.19
Sri Lankan	3	0.02
Taiwanese (4)	6	0.04
Thai (2)	4	0.03
Vietnamese (15)	17	0.11
Other Asian, specified (1)	1	0.01
Other Asian, not specified (10)	17	0.11
Austrian	147	0.99
Belgian	31	0.21
Brazilian	46	0.31
British	65	0.44
Canadian	19	0.13
Carpatho Rusyn	5	0.03
Czech	107	0.72
Czechoslovakian	44	0.30
Danish	16	0.11
Dutch	431	2.89
Eastern European	45	0.30
English	1,790	12.01
European	64	0.43
Finnish	55	0.37
French, except Basque	495	3.32
French Canadian	266	1.78
German	3,059	20.52
Greek	167	1.12
Hawaii Native/Pacific Islander:	1	0.01
Other Pac. Isl., not spec.	1	0.01
Hispanic or Latino:	636	4.26
Central American:	17	0.11
Costa Rican	2	0.01
Guatemalan	8	0.05
Honduran	1	0.01
Salvadoran	4	0.03
Other Central American	2	0.01
Cuban	42	0.28
Dominican Republic	36	0.24
Mexican	51	0.34
Puerto Rican	325	2.18
South American:	51	0.34
Argentinean	4	0.03
Bolivian	1	0.01
Chilean	2	0.01
Colombian	11	0.07
Ecuadorian	18	0.12
Peruvian	2	0.01
Venezuelan	5	0.03
Other South American	8	0.05
Other Hispanic or Latino	114	0.76
Hungarian	159	1.07
Iranian	16	0.11
Irish	4,366	29.29
Italian	3,609	24.21
Latvian	78	0.52
Lithuanian	54	0.36
Northern European	38	0.25
Norwegian	116	0.78
Polish	875	5.87
Portuguese	62	0.42
Romanian	52	0.35
Russian	195	1.31
Scandinavian	10	0.07
Scotch-Irish	154	1.03
Scottish	373	2.50
Slavic	26	0.17
Slovak	102	0.68
Slovene	17	0.11
Swedish	234	1.57
Swiss	50	0.34
Turkish	4	0.03
Ukrainian	178	1.19
United States or American	280	1.88
Welsh	75	0.50
West Indian, excl. Hispanic:	88	0.59
Barbadian	13	0.09
Haitian	35	0.23
Jamaican	26	0.17
West Indian	14	0.09
White:	13,897	93.09
Not Hispanic (13,300)	13,432	89.98
Hispanic (431)	465	3.11
Yugoslavian	29	0.19

Lackawanna

Place Type: City
County: Erie
Population: 19,064

Ancestry/Race	Number	%
Acadian/Cajun	37	0.19
African American/Black:	1,932	10.13
Not Hispanic (1,743)	1,856	9.74
Hispanic (69)	76	0.40
African, sub-Saharan:	95	0.50
African	95	0.50
Am. Ind. or Alaska Nat., not spec.	37	0.19
American Indian tribes, specified:	73	0.38
Apache (6)	6	0.03
Cherokee (3)	11	0.06
Chippewa (1)	2	0.01
Cree	1	0.01
Delaware	1	0.01
Iroquois (32)	41	0.22
Tohono O'Odham	1	0.01
Yaqui	1	0.01
All other tribes (6)	9	0.05
American Indian tribes, not spec.	10	0.05
Arab:	1,111	5.83
Arab/Arabic	617	3.24
Lebanese	16	0.08
Other Arab	478	2.51
Asian:	94	0.49
Chinese, ex. Taiwanese (10)	16	0.08
Filipino (6)	8	0.04
Indian (8)	8	0.04
Indonesian (1)	1	0.01
Japanese (2)	3	0.02
Korean (15)	17	0.09
Pakistani (1)	1	0.01
Thai (1)	1	0.01
Vietnamese (5)	10	0.05
Other Asian, specified	1	0.01
Other Asian, not specified (10)	28	0.15
Australian	9	0.05
Austrian	48	0.25
Belgian	6	0.03
British	13	0.07
Canadian	23	0.12
Croatian	273	1.43
Czech	7	0.04
Czechoslovakian	26	0.14
Danish	22	0.12
Dutch	186	0.98
English	566	2.97
Finnish	6	0.03
French, except Basque	315	1.65
French Canadian	137	0.72
German	3,044	15.98
Greek	38	0.20
Hawaii Native/Pacific Islander:	6	0.03
Polynesian: (1)	4	0.02
Native Hawaiian	2	0.01
Samoan (1)	1	0.01
Other Polynesian	1	0.01
Other Pac. Isl., specified	1	0.01
Other Pac. Isl., not spec.	1	0.01

Notes: 1. Figures in the "Number" column do not add up to the total population due to: a) Ancestry/Race overlap — e.g. persons can report being both White and Irish, b) persons of Hispanic origin can report being any race, c) persons reporting two ancestries are counted in both categories. 2. Numbers in parentheses indicate the number of persons reporting this ancestry/race alone, not in combination with any other ancestry/race. 3. Refer to the Explanation of Data in the front of the book for more detailed information.

Ancestry/Race	Number	%
Hispanic or Latino:	969	5.08
Central American:	4	0.02
Guatemalan	1	0.01
Salvadoran	3	0.02
Cuban	5	0.03
Dominican Republic	1	0.01
Mexican	111	0.58
Puerto Rican	676	3.55
South American:	11	0.06
Chilean	2	0.01
Colombian	3	0.02
Peruvian	2	0.01
Venezuelan	4	0.02
Other Hispanic or Latino	161	0.84
Hungarian	310	1.63
Irish	2,766	14.52
Italian	3,231	16.97
Lithuanian	26	0.14
Macedonian	113	0.59
Northern European	17	0.09
Norwegian	34	0.18
Pennsylvania German	22	0.12
Polish	5,656	29.70
Portuguese	20	0.11
Romanian	6	0.03
Russian	173	0.91
Scotch-Irish	41	0.22
Scottish	105	0.55
Serbian	151	0.79
Slavic	22	0.12
Slovak	41	0.22
Slovene	6	0.03
Swedish	143	0.75
Swiss	4	0.02
Ukrainian	178	0.93
United States or American	287	1.51
Welsh	102	0.54
West Indian, excl. Hispanic:	26	0.14
Jamaican	17	0.09
West Indian	9	0.05
White:	16,667	87.43
Not Hispanic (15,546)	16,163	84.78
Hispanic (465)	504	2.64
Yugoslavian	193	1.01

Lake Grove

Place Type: Village
County: Suffolk
Population: 10,250

Ancestry/Race	Number	%
African American/Black:	182	1.78
Not Hispanic (141)	170	1.66
Hispanic (7)	12	0.12
African, sub-Saharan:	14	0.13
African	14	0.13
Am. Ind. or Alaska Nat., not spec.	11	0.11
Albanian	15	0.14
American Indian tribes, specified:	13	0.13
Blackfeet	1	0.01
Cherokee (1)	3	0.03
Chippewa (1)	3	0.03
Choctaw	1	0.01
Cree	1	0.01
Iroquois (1)	1	0.01
Navajo	1	0.01
Pueblo	1	0.01
All other tribes	1	0.01
American Indian tribes, not spec.	13	0.13
Arab:	44	0.42
Lebanese	17	0.16
Palestinian	21	0.20
Syrian	6	0.06
Armenian	13	0.13
Asian:	561	5.47
Bangladeshi (3)	7	0.07
Chinese, ex. Taiwanese (202)	216	2.11
Filipino (44)	52	0.51
Indian (151)	162	1.58
Indonesian (1)	2	0.02
Japanese (2)	2	0.02
Korean (42)	44	0.43
Pakistani (23)	35	0.34
Taiwanese (5)	5	0.05
Vietnamese (1)	5	0.05
Other Asian, specified (6)	6	0.06
Other Asian, not specified (16)	25	0.24
Austrian	75	0.72
Brazilian	4	0.04
Canadian	14	0.13
Croatian	10	0.10
Cypriot	22	0.21
Czech	42	0.40
Czechoslovakian	35	0.34
Danish	98	0.94
Dutch	130	1.25
Eastern European	24	0.23
English	515	4.95
European	46	0.44
Finnish	8	0.08
French, except Basque	249	2.39
French Canadian	62	0.60
German	2,110	20.29
Greek	144	1.39
Hawaii Native/Pacific Islander:	1	0.01
Other Pac. Isl., not spec.	1	0.01
Hispanic or Latino:	496	4.84
Central American:	27	0.26
Costa Rican	2	0.02
Guatemalan	2	0.02
Honduran	2	0.02
Panamanian	3	0.03
Salvadoran	16	0.16
Other Central American	2	0.02
Cuban	15	0.15
Dominican Republic	16	0.16
Mexican	6	0.06
Puerto Rican	249	2.43
South American:	54	0.53
Argentinean	3	0.03
Chilean	4	0.04
Colombian	18	0.18
Ecuadorian	22	0.21
Peruvian	2	0.02
Other South American	5	0.05
Other Hispanic or Latino	129	1.26
Hungarian	64	0.62
Irish	2,555	24.57
Israeli	32	0.31
Italian	4,236	40.74
Latvian	18	0.17
Lithuanian	42	0.40
Maltese	42	0.40
Norwegian	122	1.17
Polish	528	5.08
Portuguese	53	0.51
Romanian	14	0.13
Russian	159	1.53
Scandinavian	11	0.11
Scotch-Irish	68	0.65
Scottish	137	1.32
Slovak	14	0.13
Swedish	132	1.27
Ukrainian	34	0.33
United States or American	276	2.65
Welsh	14	0.13
West Indian, excl. Hispanic:	56	0.54
Haitian	22	0.21
Jamaican	20	0.19
West Indian	14	0.13
White:	9,444	92.14
Not Hispanic (8,990)	9,044	88.23
Hispanic (369)	400	3.90
Yugoslavian	18	0.17

Lake Ronkonkoma

Place Type: Census Designated Place
County: Suffolk
Population: 19,701

Ancestry/Race	Number	%
Afghan	8	0.04
African American/Black:	315	1.60
Not Hispanic (237)	279	1.42
Hispanic (30)	36	0.18
African, sub-Saharan:	14	0.07
Ghanian	9	0.05
Nigerian	5	0.03
Am. Ind. or Alaska Nat., not spec.	28	0.14
Albanian	6	0.03
American Indian tribes, specified:	36	0.18
Blackfeet (1)	5	0.03
Cherokee (2)	14	0.07
Crow	1	0.01
Iroquois (4)	4	0.02
Latin American Indians (2)	3	0.02
Pueblo (1)	1	0.01
Seminole	1	0.01
Sioux	3	0.02
All other tribes (3)	4	0.02
American Indian tribes, not spec.	5	0.03
Arab:	76	0.39
Arab/Arabic	7	0.04
Jordanian	7	0.04
Lebanese	62	0.32
Armenian	6	0.03
Asian:	574	2.91
Bangladeshi (3)	5	0.03
Chinese, ex. Taiwanese (113)	143	0.73
Filipino (101)	123	0.62
Indian (175)	188	0.95
Indonesian (1)	1	0.01
Japanese (6)	13	0.07
Korean (33)	40	0.20
Pakistani (11)	17	0.09
Taiwanese (2)	2	0.01
Thai	1	0.01
Vietnamese (19)	21	0.11
Other Asian, specified (1)	1	0.01
Other Asian, not specified (1)	19	0.10
Australian	15	0.08
Austrian	181	0.92
Belgian	14	0.07
British	26	0.13
Canadian	14	0.07
Croatian	20	0.10
Czech	85	0.43
Czechoslovakian	49	0.25
Danish	96	0.49
Dutch	123	0.63
Eastern European	20	0.10
English	1,221	6.21
European	15	0.08
Finnish	61	0.31
French, except Basque	432	2.20
French Canadian	49	0.25
German	4,026	20.46
Greek	287	1.46
Hawaii Native/Pacific Islander:	15	0.08
Micronesian:	1	0.01
Guamanian/Chamorro	1	0.01
Polynesian: (5)	6	0.03
Native Hawaiian (4)	4	0.02
Samoan (1)	2	0.01
Other Pac. Isl., not spec.	8	0.04
Hispanic or Latino:	1,153	5.85
Central American:	68	0.35
Costa Rican	3	0.02
Guatemalan	9	0.05
Honduran	3	0.02
Nicaraguan	2	0.01
Panamanian	6	0.03
Salvadoran	45	0.23
Cuban	45	0.23

Notes: 1. Figures in the "Number" column do not add up to the total population due to: a) Ancestry/Race overlap — e.g. persons can report being both White and Irish, b) persons of Hispanic origin can report being any race, c) persons reporting two ancestries are counted in both categories. 2. Numbers in parentheses indicate the number of persons reporting this ancestry/race alone, not in combination with any other ancestry/race. 3. Refer to the Explanation of Data in the front of the book for more detailed information.

Ancestry/Race	Number	%
Dominican Republic	46	0.23
Mexican	65	0.33
Puerto Rican	517	2.62
South American:	157	0.80
Argentinean	19	0.10
Bolivian	8	0.04
Chilean	4	0.02
Colombian	51	0.26
Ecuadorian	30	0.15
Paraguayan	1	0.01
Peruvian	31	0.16
Uruguayan	5	0.03
Venezuelan	3	0.02
Other South American	5	0.03
Other Hispanic or Latino	255	1.29
Hungarian	272	1.38
Iranian	36	0.18
Irish	5,753	29.24
Israeli	37	0.19
Italian	7,061	35.89
Latvian	6	0.03
Lithuanian	64	0.33
Norwegian	273	1.39
Pennsylvania German	4	0.02
Polish	1,125	5.72
Portuguese	132	0.67
Romanian	42	0.21
Russian	325	1.65
Scandinavian	5	0.03
Scotch-Irish	269	1.37
Scottish	287	1.46
Slovak	87	0.44
Swedish	390	1.98
Swiss	50	0.25
Turkish	78	0.40
Ukrainian	106	0.54
United States or American	582	2.96
Welsh	32	0.16
West Indian, excl. Hispanic:	196	1.00
Haitian	71	0.36
Jamaican	78	0.40
Trinidadian and Tobagonian	47	0.24
White:	18,627	94.55
Not Hispanic (17,618)	17,756	90.13
Hispanic (809)	871	4.42
Yugoslavian	6	0.03

Lancaster

Place Type: Town
County: Erie
Population: 39,019

Ancestry/Race	Number	%
African American/Black:	357	0.91
Not Hispanic (310)	350	0.90
Hispanic (5)	7	0.02
Alaska Native tribes, specified:	1	0.00
Eskimo (1)	1	0.00
Am. Ind. or Alaska Nat., not spec.	31	0.08
Alsatian	13	0.03
American Indian tribes, specified:	89	0.23
Blackfeet (1)	6	0.02
Cherokee (3)	7	0.02
Chippewa (4)	4	0.01
Iroquois (36)	66	0.17
Kiowa (1)	1	0.00
Latin American Indians (2)	2	0.01
Lumbee (1)	1	0.00
Menominee (1)	1	0.00
All other tribes (1)	1	0.00
American Indian tribes, not spec.	14	0.04
Arab:	123	0.32
Lebanese	104	0.27
Syrian	19	0.05
Asian:	205	0.53
Chinese, ex. Taiwanese (26)	31	0.08
Filipino (20)	30	0.08
Indian (25)	35	0.09
Indonesian	3	0.01
Japanese (2)	3	0.01
Korean (45)	58	0.15
Laotian (4)	5	0.01
Thai (10)	11	0.03
Vietnamese (18)	19	0.05
Other Asian, not specified (1)	10	0.03
Austrian	81	0.21
British	40	0.10
Canadian	108	0.28
Croatian	54	0.14
Czech	84	0.22
Czechoslovakian	79	0.20
Danish	100	0.26
Dutch	429	1.10
English	2,765	7.09
Estonian	8	0.02
Finnish	34	0.09
French, except Basque	1,115	2.86
French Canadian	258	0.66
German	13,820	35.42
Greek	278	0.71
Hawaii Native/Pacific Islander:	16	0.04
Micronesian: (1)	5	0.01
Guamanian/Chamorro (1)	5	0.01
Polynesian:	6	0.02
Native Hawaiian	5	0.01
Samoan	1	0.00
Other Pac. Isl., not spec.	5	0.01
Hispanic or Latino:	262	0.67
Central American:	9	0.02
Costa Rican	5	0.01
Guatemalan	4	0.01
Cuban	5	0.01
Dominican Republic	1	0.00
Mexican	57	0.15
Puerto Rican	114	0.29
South American:	32	0.08
Argentinean	3	0.01
Bolivian	2	0.01
Chilean	2	0.01
Colombian	16	0.04
Ecuadorian	7	0.02
Paraguayan	1	0.00
Venezuelan	1	0.00
Other Hispanic or Latino	44	0.11
Hungarian	244	0.63
Icelander	20	0.05
Irish	5,429	13.91
Italian	7,006	17.96
Latvian	7	0.02
Lithuanian	54	0.14
New Zealander	7	0.02
Norwegian	108	0.28
Pennsylvania German	10	0.03
Polish	13,903	35.63
Portuguese	17	0.04
Romanian	17	0.04
Russian	264	0.68
Scandinavian	7	0.02
Scotch-Irish	280	0.72
Scottish	536	1.37
Serbian	9	0.02
Slovak	67	0.17
Swedish	475	1.22
Swiss	152	0.39
Ukrainian	342	0.88
United States or American	863	2.21
Welsh	168	0.43
West Indian, excl. Hispanic:	8	0.02
Jamaican	8	0.02
White:	38,425	98.48
Not Hispanic (38,042)	38,206	97.92
Hispanic (197)	219	0.56
Yugoslavian	18	0.05

Lancaster

Place Type: Village
County: Erie
Population: 11,188

Ancestry/Race	Number	%
African American/Black:	47	0.42
Not Hispanic (34)	45	0.40
Hispanic (2)	2	0.02
Am. Ind. or Alaska Nat., not spec.	14	0.13
American Indian tribes, specified:	30	0.27
Blackfeet	2	0.02
Cherokee (3)	4	0.04
Chippewa (2)	2	0.02
Iroquois (10)	20	0.18
Latin American Indians (1)	1	0.01
Menominee (1)	1	0.01
American Indian tribes, not spec.	7	0.06
Arab:	25	0.22
Lebanese	6	0.05
Syrian	19	0.17
Asian:	23	0.21
Chinese, ex. Taiwanese (5)	5	0.04
Filipino (2)	5	0.04
Indian	1	0.01
Korean (5)	7	0.06
Thai (3)	3	0.03
Other Asian, not specified	2	0.02
Austrian	58	0.52
British	16	0.14
Canadian	36	0.32
Croatian	38	0.34
Czechoslovakian	12	0.11
Danish	18	0.16
Dutch	169	1.51
English	857	7.66
French, except Basque	427	3.82
French Canadian	116	1.04
German	4,285	38.30
Greek	41	0.37
Hawaii Native/Pacific Islander:	8	0.07
Micronesian:	4	0.04
Guamanian/Chamorro	4	0.04
Polynesian:	2	0.02
Native Hawaiian	1	0.01
Samoan	1	0.01
Other Pac. Isl., not spec.	2	0.02
Hispanic or Latino:	91	0.81
Central American:	1	0.01
Costa Rican	1	0.01
Cuban	1	0.01
Mexican	23	0.21
Puerto Rican	43	0.38
South American:	6	0.05
Bolivian	1	0.01
Colombian	4	0.04
Ecuadorian	1	0.01
Other Hispanic or Latino	17	0.15
Hungarian	69	0.62
Irish	1,664	14.87
Italian	1,671	14.94
Latvian	7	0.06
Lithuanian	9	0.08
New Zealander	7	0.06
Norwegian	22	0.20
Polish	3,317	29.65
Russian	67	0.60
Scandinavian	7	0.06
Scotch-Irish	50	0.45
Scottish	134	1.20
Slovak	42	0.38
Swedish	125	1.12
Swiss	8	0.07
Ukrainian	144	1.29
United States or American	435	3.89
Welsh	25	0.22
White:	11,084	99.07
Not Hispanic (10,970)	11,012	98.43
Hispanic (64)	72	0.64

Notes: 1. Figures in the "Number" column do not add up to the total population due to: a) Ancestry/Race overlap — e.g. persons can report being both White and Irish, b) persons of Hispanic origin can report being any race, c) persons reporting two ancestries are counted in both categories. 2. Numbers in parentheses indicate the number of persons reporting this ancestry/race alone, not in combination with any other ancestry/race. 3. Refer to the Explanation of Data in the front of the book for more detailed information.

Yugoslavian	10	0.09

Lansing

Place Type: Town
County: Tompkins
Population: 10,521

Ancestry/Race	Number	%
African American/Black:	508	4.83
Not Hispanic (396)	470	4.47
Hispanic (34)	38	0.36
African, sub-Saharan:	116	1.13
African	7	0.07
Nigerian	95	0.92
South African	14	0.14
Alaska Native tribes, specified:	1	0.01
Alaska Athabascan (1)	1	0.01
Am. Ind. or Alaska Nat., not spec.	33	0.31
American Indian tribes, specified:	33	0.31
Apache (1)	1	0.01
Blackfeet (1)	1	0.01
Cherokee (1)	6	0.06
Chippewa (2)	2	0.02
Creek	1	0.01
Delaware (1)	2	0.02
Iroquois (4)	12	0.11
Latin American Indians (1)	3	0.03
Lumbee	1	0.01
Sioux (2)	2	0.02
All other tribes (1)	2	0.02
American Indian tribes, not spec.	2	0.02
Arab:	81	0.79
Egyptian	16	0.16
Lebanese	19	0.18
Syrian	39	0.38
Other Arab	7	0.07
Armenian	50	0.49
Asian:	1,013	9.63
Bangladeshi (1)	1	0.01
Cambodian (25)	27	0.26
Chinese, ex. Taiwanese (371)	394	3.74
Filipino (6)	11	0.10
Indian (128)	138	1.31
Indonesian (7)	9	0.09
Japanese (60)	71	0.67
Korean (253)	265	2.52
Malaysian (1)	1	0.01
Pakistani (10)	14	0.13
Sri Lankan (9)	9	0.09
Taiwanese (23)	29	0.28
Thai (1)	2	0.02
Vietnamese (18)	25	0.24
Other Asian, not specified (6)	17	0.16
Australian	14	0.14
Austrian	67	0.65
Belgian	22	0.21
Brazilian	49	0.48
British	110	1.07
Canadian	91	0.88
Celtic	5	0.05
Czech	27	0.26
Czechoslovakian	43	0.42
Danish	6	0.06
Dutch	271	2.63
Eastern European	33	0.32
English	1,836	17.83
European	191	1.85
Finnish	71	0.69
French, except Basque	256	2.49
French Canadian	122	1.18
German	1,689	16.40
Greek	67	0.65
Hawaii Native/Pacific Islander:	11	0.10
Melanesian:	2	0.02
Other Melanesian	2	0.02
Micronesian: (2)	3	0.03
Guamanian/Chamorro (2)	3	0.03
Polynesian: (2)	5	0.05
Native Hawaiian	3	0.03
Samoan (1)	1	0.01
Tongan (1)	1	0.01
Other Pac. Isl., not spec.	1	0.01
Hispanic or Latino:	247	2.35
Central American:	11	0.10
Costa Rican	3	0.03
Guatemalan	1	0.01
Honduran	4	0.04
Panamanian	3	0.03
Cuban	7	0.07
Dominican Republic	1	0.01
Mexican	30	0.29
Puerto Rican	47	0.45
South American:	48	0.46
Argentinean	7	0.07
Bolivian	1	0.01
Chilean	2	0.02
Colombian	10	0.10
Ecuadorian	11	0.10
Peruvian	6	0.06
Venezuelan	6	0.06
Other South American	5	0.05
Other Hispanic or Latino	103	0.98
Hungarian	129	1.25
Irish	1,319	12.81
Italian	772	7.50
Latvian	9	0.09
Lithuanian	24	0.23
Northern European	6	0.06
Norwegian	182	1.77
Pennsylvania German	10	0.10
Polish	380	3.69
Portuguese	8	0.08
Romanian	27	0.26
Russian	122	1.18
Scandinavian	8	0.08
Scotch-Irish	177	1.72
Scottish	432	4.19
Slavic	34	0.33
Slovak	49	0.48
Soviet Union	5	0.05
Swedish	180	1.75
Swiss	35	0.34
Turkish	5	0.05
Ukrainian	38	0.37
United States or American	455	4.42
Welsh	243	2.36
White:	9,033	85.86
Not Hispanic (8,710)	8,882	84.42
Hispanic (137)	151	1.44
Yugoslavian	21	0.20

Le Ray

Place Type: Town
County: Jefferson
Population: 19,836

Ancestry/Race	Number	%
Acadian/Cajun	11	0.06
African American/Black:	3,586	18.08
Not Hispanic (3,145)	3,405	17.17
Hispanic (100)	181	0.91
African, sub-Saharan:	235	1.19
African	164	0.83
Ethiopian	18	0.09
Liberian	8	0.04
Sierra Leonean	29	0.15
South African	17	0.09
Alaska Native tribes, specified:	8	0.04
Aleut (1)	1	0.01
Eskimo (2)	4	0.02
Tlingit-Haida (1)	3	0.02
Alaska Native tribes, not specified	3	0.02
Am. Ind. or Alaska Nat., not spec.	79	0.40
American Indian tribes, specified:	218	1.10
Apache (2)	13	0.07
Blackfeet (6)	12	0.06
Cherokee (16)	56	0.28
Cheyenne (2)	3	0.02
Chippewa (3)	4	0.02
Choctaw (7)	8	0.04
Comanche (7)	7	0.04
Creek (7)	7	0.04
Crow (1)	2	0.01
Iroquois (9)	16	0.08
Latin American Indians (10)	12	0.06
Lumbee (3)	5	0.03
Menominee	3	0.02
Navajo (21)	22	0.11
Ottawa (1)	5	0.03
Pueblo (1)	1	0.01
Seminole (2)	2	0.01
Sioux (8)	17	0.09
Ute	2	0.01
All other tribes (12)	21	0.11
American Indian tribes, not spec.	12	0.06
Arab:	82	0.41
Arab/Arabic	13	0.07
Egyptian	11	0.06
Lebanese	25	0.13
Other Arab	33	0.17
Armenian	27	0.14
Asian:	606	3.06
Cambodian (3)	4	0.02
Chinese, ex. Taiwanese (17)	43	0.22
Filipino (156)	228	1.15
Indian (11)	18	0.09
Indonesian (1)	1	0.01
Japanese (18)	37	0.19
Korean (143)	197	0.99
Laotian (3)	3	0.02
Pakistani (9)	9	0.05
Sri Lankan (1)	1	0.01
Taiwanese (2)	2	0.01
Thai (8)	13	0.07
Vietnamese (13)	18	0.09
Other Asian, not specified (11)	32	0.16
Austrian	45	0.23
Belgian	8	0.04
British	89	0.45
Canadian	66	0.33
Celtic	2	0.01
Croatian	20	0.10
Czech	8	0.04
Czechoslovakian	40	0.20
Danish	61	0.31
Dutch	375	1.89
English	1,492	7.54
European	127	0.64
Finnish	37	0.19
French, except Basque	1,131	5.71
French Canadian	529	2.67
German	2,903	14.67
Greek	57	0.29
Guyanese	30	0.15
Hawaii Native/Pacific Islander:	162	0.82
Micronesian: (37)	44	0.22
Guamanian/Chamorro (22)	28	0.14
Other Micronesian (15)	16	0.08
Polynesian: (50)	88	0.44
Native Hawaiian (25)	56	0.28
Samoan (24)	30	0.15
Tongan (1)	2	0.01
Other Pac. Isl., not spec. (10)	30	0.15
Hispanic or Latino:	2,170	10.94
Central American:	133	0.67
Costa Rican	4	0.02
Guatemalan	14	0.07
Honduran	11	0.06
Nicaraguan	8	0.04
Panamanian	73	0.37
Salvadoran	23	0.12
Cuban	21	0.11
Dominican Republic	73	0.37
Mexican	726	3.66
Puerto Rican	862	4.35
South American:	99	0.50
Argentinean	7	0.04
Bolivian	4	0.02

Notes: 1. Figures in the "Number" column do not add up to the total population due to: a) Ancestry/Race overlap — e.g. persons can report being both White and Irish, b) persons of Hispanic origin can report being any race, c) persons reporting two ancestries are counted in both categories. 2. Numbers in parentheses indicate the number of persons reporting this ancestry/race alone, not in combination with any other ancestry/race. 3. Refer to the Explanation of Data in the front of the book for more detailed information.

Ancestry/Race	Number	%
Chilean	1	0.01
Colombian	33	0.17
Ecuadorian	23	0.12
Paraguayan	1	0.01
Peruvian	21	0.11
Venezuelan	5	0.03
Other South American	4	0.02
Other Hispanic or Latino	256	1.29
Hungarian	39	0.20
Iranian	16	0.08
Irish	2,646	13.37
Israeli	19	0.10
Italian	1,342	6.78
Latvian	20	0.10
Lithuanian	19	0.10
Luxemburger	12	0.06
Northern European	36	0.18
Norwegian	184	0.93
Polish	520	2.63
Portuguese	68	0.34
Romanian	16	0.08
Russian	142	0.72
Scandinavian	22	0.11
Scotch-Irish	200	1.01
Scottish	270	1.36
Slavic	5	0.03
Slovak	33	0.17
Slovene	8	0.04
Swedish	156	0.79
Swiss	38	0.19
Turkish	5	0.03
Ukrainian	21	0.11
United States or American	1,081	5.46
Welsh	131	0.66
West Indian, excl. Hispanic:	351	1.77
Barbadian	13	0.07
Belizean	8	0.04
British West Indian	15	0.08
Haitian	31	0.16
Jamaican	167	0.84
Trinidadian and Tobagonian	46	0.23
U.S. Virgin Islander	8	0.04
West Indian	63	0.32
White:	14,548	73.34
Not Hispanic (13,329)	13,758	69.36
Hispanic (651)	790	3.98

Levittown

Place Type: Census Designated Place
County: Nassau
Population: 53,067

Ancestry/Race	Number	%
African American/Black:	387	0.73
Not Hispanic (247)	333	0.63
Hispanic (19)	54	0.10
African, sub-Saharan:	20	0.04
African	8	0.02
Ghanian	8	0.02
South African	4	0.01
Am. Ind. or Alaska Nat., not spec.	46	0.09
Alsatian	21	0.04
American Indian tribes, specified:	61	0.11
Apache	1	0.00
Blackfeet (1)	3	0.01
Cherokee (6)	19	0.04
Cheyenne	2	0.00
Chippewa	1	0.00
Comanche	4	0.01
Iroquois (1)	9	0.02
Latin American Indians (3)	14	0.03
Lumbee (3)	3	0.01
Sioux (1)	1	0.00
All other tribes (1)	4	0.01
American Indian tribes, not spec.	9	0.02
Arab:	329	0.62
Arab/Arabic	117	0.22
Egyptian	117	0.22
Lebanese	50	0.09
Syrian	45	0.08
Armenian	74	0.14
Asian:	1,742	3.28
Bangladeshi (21)	21	0.04
Cambodian (2)	2	0.00
Chinese, ex. Taiwanese (358)	428	0.81
Filipino (273)	303	0.57
Indian (438)	480	0.90
Indonesian (6)	8	0.02
Japanese (32)	50	0.09
Korean (107)	117	0.22
Malaysian	1	0.00
Pakistani (93)	120	0.23
Sri Lankan (3)	6	0.01
Taiwanese (12)	16	0.03
Thai (25)	29	0.05
Vietnamese (101)	101	0.19
Other Asian, specified (2)	8	0.02
Other Asian, not specified (21)	52	0.10
Assyrian/Chaldean/Syriac	17	0.03
Austrian	404	0.76
Basque	19	0.04
Belgian	29	0.05
Brazilian	125	0.24
British	67	0.13
Bulgarian	45	0.08
Canadian	157	0.30
Croatian	26	0.05
Cypriot	27	0.05
Czech	209	0.39
Czechoslovakian	112	0.21
Danish	90	0.17
Dutch	395	0.74
Eastern European	119	0.22
English	2,270	4.28
Estonian	23	0.04
European	119	0.22
Finnish	59	0.11
French, except Basque	842	1.59
French Canadian	186	0.35
German	9,816	18.50
Greek	1,259	2.37
Guyanese	19	0.04
Hawaii Native/Pacific Islander:	24	0.05
Micronesian: (2)	2	0.00
Guamanian/Chamorro (2)	2	0.00
Polynesian: (5)	10	0.02
Native Hawaiian (2)	4	0.01
Samoan (3)	6	0.01
Other Pac. Isl., not spec. (3)	12	0.02
Hispanic or Latino:	3,601	6.79
Central American:	449	0.85
Costa Rican	23	0.04
Guatemalan	47	0.09
Honduran	22	0.04
Nicaraguan	6	0.01
Panamanian	5	0.01
Salvadoran	322	0.61
Other Central American	24	0.05
Cuban	164	0.31
Dominican Republic	68	0.13
Mexican	104	0.20
Puerto Rican	1,360	2.56
South American:	671	1.26
Argentinean	56	0.11
Bolivian	19	0.04
Chilean	57	0.11
Colombian	302	0.57
Ecuadorian	115	0.22
Paraguayan	4	0.01
Peruvian	76	0.14
Uruguayan	14	0.03
Venezuelan	5	0.01
Other South American	23	0.04
Other Hispanic or Latino	785	1.48
Hungarian	551	1.04
Icelander	25	0.05
Iranian	21	0.04
Irish	16,106	30.35
Israeli	31	0.06
Italian	18,020	33.96
Latvian	17	0.03
Lithuanian	282	0.53
Maltese	47	0.09
New Zealander	56	0.11
Northern European	24	0.05
Norwegian	490	0.92
Polish	2,898	5.46
Portuguese	238	0.45
Romanian	127	0.24
Russian	1,796	3.38
Scandinavian	70	0.13
Scotch-Irish	540	1.02
Scottish	695	1.31
Serbian	4	0.01
Slavic	22	0.04
Slovak	109	0.21
Swedish	322	0.61
Swiss	74	0.14
Turkish	90	0.17
Ukrainian	383	0.72
United States or American	1,276	2.40
Welsh	116	0.22
West Indian, excl. Hispanic:	288	0.54
Bahamian	10	0.02
Belizean	10	0.02
British West Indian	33	0.06
Dutch West Indian	5	0.01
Haitian	98	0.18
Jamaican	107	0.20
Trinidadian and Tobagonian	4	0.01
West Indian	7	0.01
Other West Indian	14	0.03
White:	50,452	95.07
Not Hispanic (47,251)	47,549	89.60
Hispanic (2,711)	2,903	5.47
Yugoslavian	100	0.19

Lewisboro

Place Type: Town
County: Westchester
Population: 12,324

Ancestry/Race	Number	%
African American/Black:	188	1.53
Not Hispanic (144)	178	1.44
Hispanic (3)	10	0.08
Am. Ind. or Alaska Nat., not spec.	16	0.13
Albanian	45	0.37
American Indian tribes, specified:	17	0.14
Blackfeet (1)	6	0.05
Cherokee	4	0.03
Iroquois	1	0.01
Latin American Indians (1)	4	0.03
Ottawa (1)	1	0.01
Potawatomi	1	0.01
American Indian tribes, not spec.	2	0.02
Arab:	113	0.92
Arab/Arabic	21	0.17
Egyptian	37	0.30
Lebanese	40	0.32
Other Arab	15	0.12
Asian:	306	2.48
Chinese, ex. Taiwanese (88)	100	0.81
Filipino (17)	24	0.19
Indian (58)	65	0.53
Indonesian (1)	1	0.01
Japanese (18)	24	0.19
Korean (60)	68	0.55
Pakistani (4)	4	0.03
Thai (1)	1	0.01
Vietnamese (1)	5	0.04
Other Asian, specified (5)	5	0.04
Other Asian, not specified (4)	9	0.07
Australian	7	0.06
Austrian	171	1.39
Belgian	7	0.06
British	95	0.77
Canadian	18	0.15

Notes: 1. Figures in the "Number" column do not add up to the total population due to: a) Ancestry/Race overlap — e.g. persons can report being both White and Irish, b) persons of Hispanic origin can report being any race, c) persons reporting two ancestries are counted in both categories. 2. Numbers in parentheses indicate the number of persons reporting this ancestry/race alone, not in combination with any other ancestry/race. 3. Refer to the Explanation of Data in the front of the book for more detailed information.

Croatian	6	0.05
Cypriot	4	0.03
Czech	104	0.84
Czechoslovakian	70	0.57
Danish	88	0.71
Dutch	99	0.80
Eastern European	226	1.83
English	1,396	11.33
Estonian	14	0.11
European	113	0.92
Finnish	54	0.44
French, except Basque	327	2.65
French Canadian	75	0.61
German	1,609	13.06
Greek	153	1.24
Hispanic or Latino:	306	2.48
Central American:	15	0.12
Guatemalan	12	0.10
Salvadoran	3	0.02
Cuban	23	0.19
Dominican Republic	8	0.06
Mexican	44	0.36
Puerto Rican	96	0.78
South American:	50	0.41
Argentinean	12	0.10
Bolivian	2	0.02
Chilean	2	0.02
Colombian	17	0.14
Ecuadorian	4	0.03
Paraguayan	1	0.01
Peruvian	6	0.05
Uruguayan	4	0.03
Venezuelan	1	0.01
Other South American	1	0.01
Other Hispanic or Latino	70	0.57
Hungarian	277	2.25
Irish	2,464	19.99
Israeli	29	0.24
Italian	2,623	21.28
Latvian	8	0.06
Lithuanian	90	0.73
Luxemburger	7	0.06
Norwegian	118	0.96
Pennsylvania German	7	0.06
Polish	775	6.29
Portuguese	40	0.32
Romanian	85	0.69
Russian	1,059	8.59
Scandinavian	9	0.07
Scotch-Irish	132	1.07
Scottish	271	2.20
Slavic	6	0.05
Slovak	16	0.13
Soviet Union	2	0.02
Swedish	181	1.47
Swiss	22	0.18
Turkish	44	0.36
Ukrainian	113	0.92
United States or American	558	4.53
Welsh	46	0.37
West Indian, excl. Hispanic:	26	0.21
British West Indian	5	0.04
Jamaican	21	0.17
White:	11,839	96.06
Not Hispanic (11,481)	11,573	93.91
Hispanic (249)	266	2.16
Yugoslavian	27	0.22

Lewiston

Place Type: Town
County: Niagara
Population: 16,257

Ancestry/Race	Number	%
African American/Black:	164	1.01
Not Hispanic (147)	161	0.99
Hispanic (2)	3	0.02
African, sub-Saharan:	39	0.24
African	14	0.09
Ethiopian	25	0.15
Am. Ind. or Alaska Nat., not spec.	27	0.17
Albanian	75	0.46
American Indian tribes, specified:	111	0.68
Blackfeet (1)	1	0.01
Cherokee (1)	6	0.04
Chippewa	1	0.01
Comanche	3	0.02
Delaware (1)	1	0.01
Iroquois (86)	95	0.58
Potawatomi	1	0.01
All other tribes (2)	3	0.02
American Indian tribes, not spec.	2	0.01
Arab:	132	0.81
Egyptian	7	0.04
Lebanese	112	0.69
Syrian	13	0.08
Armenian	38	0.23
Asian:	120	0.74
Chinese, ex. Taiwanese (20)	24	0.15
Filipino (5)	12	0.07
Indian (45)	49	0.30
Indonesian	1	0.01
Japanese (5)	9	0.06
Korean (14)	15	0.09
Thai (1)	2	0.01
Other Asian, not specified (3)	8	0.05
Austrian	84	0.52
Belgian	7	0.04
Brazilian	22	0.14
British	74	0.46
Canadian	291	1.79
Croatian	48	0.30
Czech	50	0.31
Czechoslovakian	19	0.12
Danish	25	0.15
Dutch	272	1.67
English	2,310	14.21
European	40	0.25
Finnish	28	0.17
French, except Basque	539	3.32
French Canadian	174	1.07
German	3,933	24.19
Greek	50	0.31
Hawaii Native/Pacific Islander:	4	0.02
Micronesian: (1)	1	0.01
Other Micronesian (1)	1	0.01
Polynesian: (1)	3	0.02
Native Hawaiian (1)	2	0.01
Samoan	1	0.01
Hispanic or Latino:	148	0.91
Central American:	8	0.05
Guatemalan	1	0.01
Honduran	2	0.01
Nicaraguan	4	0.02
Panamanian	1	0.01
Dominican Republic	5	0.03
Mexican	32	0.20
Puerto Rican	39	0.24
South American:	1	0.01
Ecuadorian	1	0.01
Other Hispanic or Latino	63	0.39
Hungarian	174	1.07
Iranian	15	0.09
Irish	3,015	18.55
Italian	4,379	26.94
Lithuanian	29	0.18
Macedonian	7	0.04
New Zealander	14	0.09
Norwegian	114	0.70
Pennsylvania German	27	0.17
Polish	2,185	13.44
Portuguese	23	0.14
Russian	66	0.41
Scandinavian	19	0.12
Scotch-Irish	441	2.71
Scottish	454	2.79
Slovak	69	0.42
Swedish	187	1.15
Swiss	46	0.28
Turkish	17	0.10
Ukrainian	180	1.11
United States or American	416	2.56
Welsh	140	0.86
West Indian, excl. Hispanic:	30	0.18
Jamaican	30	0.18
White:	15,840	97.43
Not Hispanic (15,669)	15,741	96.83
Hispanic (97)	99	0.61
Yugoslavian	42	0.26

Lindenhurst

Place Type: Village
County: Suffolk
Population: 27,819

Ancestry/Race	Number	%
Afghan	41	0.15
African American/Black:	297	1.07
Not Hispanic (220)	272	0.98
Hispanic (13)	25	0.09
African, sub-Saharan:	5	0.02
Other sub-Saharan African	5	0.02
Am. Ind. or Alaska Nat., not spec.	39	0.14
Albanian	87	0.31
American Indian tribes, specified:	64	0.23
Apache	1	0.00
Blackfeet (2)	3	0.01
Cherokee (3)	24	0.09
Cheyenne	1	0.00
Chickasaw (2)	2	0.01
Chippewa (1)	1	0.00
Choctaw (1)	1	0.00
Iroquois (4)	15	0.05
Latin American Indians (1)	5	0.02
Lumbee (1)	1	0.00
Sioux (3)	3	0.01
All other tribes (2)	7	0.03
American Indian tribes, not spec.	12	0.04
Arab:	135	0.48
Arab/Arabic	21	0.08
Lebanese	36	0.13
Palestinian	4	0.01
Syrian	74	0.26
Armenian	37	0.13
Asian:	493	1.77
Bangladeshi (4)	4	0.01
Chinese, ex. Taiwanese (82)	107	0.38
Filipino (39)	69	0.25
Indian (154)	174	0.63
Indonesian (1)	1	0.00
Japanese (6)	9	0.03
Korean (31)	32	0.12
Pakistani (17)	22	0.08
Taiwanese (3)	3	0.01
Thai (10)	10	0.04
Vietnamese (17)	19	0.07
Other Asian, not specified (13)	43	0.15
Austrian	209	0.75
British	19	0.07
Canadian	106	0.38
Croatian	18	0.06
Czech	86	0.31
Czechoslovakian	63	0.23
Danish	97	0.35
Dutch	193	0.69
Eastern European	16	0.06
English	1,062	3.80
European	60	0.21
Finnish	11	0.04
French, except Basque	442	1.58
French Canadian	144	0.52
German	5,642	20.20
Greek	277	0.99
Hawaii Native/Pacific Islander:	15	0.05
Polynesian: (2)	6	0.02
Native Hawaiian (1)	5	0.02
Samoan (1)	1	0.00
Other Pac. Isl., not spec. (1)	9	0.03

Notes: 1. Figures in the "Number" column do not add up to the total population due to: a) Ancestry/Race overlap — e.g. persons can report being both White and Irish, b) persons of Hispanic origin can report being any race, c) persons reporting two ancestries are counted in both categories. 2. Numbers in parentheses indicate the number of persons reporting this ancestry/race alone, not in combination with any other ancestry/race. 3. Refer to the Explanation of Data in the front of the book for more detailed information.

Ancestry/Race	Number	%
Hispanic or Latino:	1,813	6.52
Central American:	210	0.75
Costa Rican	3	0.01
Guatemalan	12	0.04
Honduran	16	0.06
Panamanian	5	0.02
Salvadoran	174	0.63
Cuban	73	0.26
Dominican Republic	231	0.83
Mexican	102	0.37
Puerto Rican	519	1.87
South American:	263	0.95
Argentinean	33	0.12
Bolivian	8	0.03
Chilean	7	0.03
Colombian	119	0.43
Ecuadorian	51	0.18
Peruvian	35	0.13
Uruguayan	1	0.00
Other South American	9	0.03
Other Hispanic or Latino	415	1.49
Hungarian	208	0.74
Irish	7,496	26.84
Israeli	11	0.04
Italian	10,831	38.77
Latvian	11	0.04
Lithuanian	109	0.39
Maltese	40	0.14
Northern European	4	0.01
Norwegian	295	1.06
Polish	2,353	8.42
Portuguese	105	0.38
Romanian	19	0.07
Russian	312	1.12
Scandinavian	20	0.07
Scotch-Irish	245	0.88
Scottish	248	0.89
Slavic	8	0.03
Slovak	51	0.18
Slovene	6	0.02
Swedish	243	0.87
Swiss	48	0.17
Turkish	53	0.19
Ukrainian	168	0.60
United States or American	581	2.08
Welsh	57	0.20
West Indian, excl. Hispanic:	136	0.49
Haitian	68	0.24
Jamaican	6	0.02
Trinidadian and Tobagonian	5	0.02
West Indian	57	0.20
White:	26,654	95.81
Not Hispanic (24,976)	25,313	90.99
Hispanic (1,237)	1,341	4.82
Yugoslavian	19	0.07

Lockport

Place Type: City
County: Niagara
Population: 22,279

Ancestry/Race	Number	%
African American/Black:	1,528	6.86
Not Hispanic (1,265)	1,475	6.62
Hispanic (22)	53	0.24
African, sub-Saharan:	32	0.14
African	26	0.12
Nigerian	6	0.03
Am. Ind. or Alaska Nat., not spec.	72	0.32
Alsatian	11	0.05
American Indian tribes, specified:	131	0.59
Apache	1	0.00
Blackfeet (3)	15	0.07
Cherokee	16	0.07
Chippewa (2)	2	0.01
Choctaw	1	0.00
Iroquois (56)	80	0.36
Latin American Indians (1)	2	0.01
Ottawa	1	0.00
Seminole (2)	2	0.01
Sioux (1)	1	0.00
Yaqui (1)	1	0.00
All other tribes (8)	9	0.04
American Indian tribes, not spec.	3	0.01
Arab:	14	0.06
Lebanese	14	0.06
Armenian	11	0.05
Asian:	171	0.77
Chinese, ex. Taiwanese (33)	49	0.22
Filipino (14)	31	0.14
Indian (14)	22	0.10
Indonesian (1)	3	0.01
Japanese (9)	20	0.09
Korean (26)	33	0.15
Thai (2)	2	0.01
Vietnamese (7)	9	0.04
Other Asian, not specified (2)	2	0.01
Austrian	27	0.12
Belgian	26	0.12
British	42	0.19
Canadian	88	0.39
Croatian	9	0.04
Czech	48	0.22
Czechoslovakian	11	0.05
Danish	31	0.14
Dutch	368	1.65
Eastern European	18	0.08
English	3,216	14.44
Estonian	16	0.07
European	67	0.30
Finnish	10	0.04
French, except Basque	987	4.43
French Canadian	220	0.99
German	7,079	31.77
Greek	47	0.21
Hawaii Native/Pacific Islander:	12	0.05
Polynesian: (1)	4	0.02
Native Hawaiian (1)	3	0.01
Samoan	1	0.00
Other Pac. Isl., not spec. (1)	8	0.04
Hispanic or Latino:	460	2.06
Central American:	10	0.04
Guatemalan	1	0.00
Honduran	2	0.01
Panamanian	2	0.01
Salvadoran	5	0.02
Cuban	6	0.03
Dominican Republic	7	0.03
Mexican	92	0.41
Puerto Rican	246	1.10
South American:	18	0.08
Argentinean	6	0.03
Colombian	3	0.01
Peruvian	7	0.03
Venezuelan	2	0.01
Other Hispanic or Latino	81	0.36
Hungarian	88	0.39
Irish	5,115	22.96
Italian	3,495	15.69
Lithuanian	18	0.08
Northern European	8	0.04
Norwegian	84	0.38
Pennsylvania German	18	0.08
Polish	1,962	8.81
Portuguese	6	0.03
Romanian	10	0.04
Russian	82	0.37
Scandinavian	7	0.03
Scotch-Irish	285	1.28
Scottish	398	1.79
Serbian	14	0.06
Slovak	36	0.16
Swedish	113	0.51
Swiss	6	0.03
Ukrainian	229	1.03
United States or American	1,135	5.09
Welsh	161	0.72
West Indian, excl. Hispanic:	142	0.64
Bahamian	19	0.09
British West Indian	7	0.03
Haitian	27	0.12
Jamaican	61	0.27
Trinidadian and Tobagonian	17	0.08
West Indian	11	0.05
White:	20,615	92.53
Not Hispanic (20,018)	20,294	91.09
Hispanic (264)	321	1.44
Yugoslavian	6	0.03

Lockport

Place Type: Town
County: Niagara
Population: 19,653

Ancestry/Race	Number	%
African American/Black:	926	4.71
Not Hispanic (790)	904	4.60
Hispanic (12)	22	0.11
African, sub-Saharan:	14	0.07
African	14	0.07
Alaska Native tribes, specified:	2	0.01
Eskimo	2	0.01
Am. Ind. or Alaska Nat., not spec.	59	0.30
Alsatian	12	0.06
American Indian tribes, specified:	93	0.47
Apache (1)	1	0.01
Blackfeet	4	0.02
Cherokee (2)	9	0.05
Chippewa (1)	1	0.01
Iroquois (51)	68	0.35
Lumbee	3	0.02
Navajo (1)	1	0.01
Pueblo	1	0.01
Sioux	1	0.01
All other tribes (3)	4	0.02
American Indian tribes, not spec.	8	0.04
Arab:	32	0.16
Lebanese	19	0.10
Syrian	13	0.07
Asian:	252	1.28
Bangladeshi	3	0.02
Chinese, ex. Taiwanese (41)	47	0.24
Filipino (14)	28	0.14
Indian (80)	92	0.47
Indonesian (6)	6	0.03
Japanese (8)	11	0.06
Korean (30)	36	0.18
Taiwanese (3)	3	0.02
Thai (4)	4	0.02
Vietnamese (11)	13	0.07
Other Asian, not specified (2)	9	0.05
Austrian	31	0.16
British	102	0.52
Canadian	128	0.65
Czech	12	0.06
Czechoslovakian	11	0.06
Danish	69	0.35
Dutch	369	1.88
English	2,701	13.74
Estonian	6	0.03
European	35	0.18
French, except Basque	791	4.02
French Canadian	202	1.03
German	6,628	33.73
Greek	39	0.20
Hawaii Native/Pacific Islander:	5	0.03
Polynesian: (1)	3	0.02
Native Hawaiian (1)	3	0.02
Other Pac. Isl., not spec. (1)	2	0.01
Hispanic or Latino:	235	1.20
Cuban	12	0.06
Dominican Republic	5	0.03
Mexican	32	0.16
Puerto Rican	140	0.71
South American:	9	0.05
Colombian	8	0.04
Venezuelan	1	0.01
Other Hispanic or Latino	37	0.19

Notes: 1. Figures in the "Number" column do not add up to the total population due to: a) Ancestry/Race overlap — e.g. persons can report being both White and Irish, b) persons of Hispanic origin can report being any race, c) persons reporting two ancestries are counted in both categories. 2. Numbers in parentheses indicate the number of persons reporting this ancestry/race alone, not in combination with any other ancestry/race. 3. Refer to the Explanation of Data in the front of the book for more detailed information.

Ancestry/Race	Number	%
Hungarian	175	0.89
Irish	3,372	17.16
Italian	2,754	14.01
Lithuanian	20	0.10
Luxemburger	9	0.05
Norwegian	45	0.23
Pennsylvania German	8	0.04
Polish	2,544	12.94
Portuguese	48	0.24
Russian	164	0.83
Scandinavian	12	0.06
Scotch-Irish	267	1.36
Scottish	580	2.95
Slavic	15	0.08
Slovak	41	0.21
Swedish	217	1.10
Swiss	44	0.22
Ukrainian	109	0.55
United States or American	798	4.06
Welsh	122	0.62
West Indian, excl. Hispanic:	43	0.22
British West Indian	7	0.04
Jamaican	36	0.18
White:	18,451	93.88
Not Hispanic (18,118)	18,297	93.10
Hispanic (132)	154	0.78
Yugoslavian	9	0.05

Long Beach

Place Type: City
County: Nassau
Population: 35,462

Ancestry/Race	Number	%
African American/Black:	2,406	6.78
Not Hispanic (2,071)	2,225	6.27
Hispanic (119)	181	0.51
African, sub-Saharan:	88	0.25
African	83	0.23
Ethiopian	5	0.01
Am. Ind. or Alaska Nat., not spec.	71	0.20
Albanian	31	0.09
American Indian tribes, specified:	89	0.25
Apache (3)	4	0.01
Blackfeet	3	0.01
Cherokee (5)	23	0.06
Cheyenne (1)	1	0.00
Chippewa	1	0.00
Comanche	1	0.00
Cree (1)	2	0.01
Creek	3	0.01
Iroquois (2)	4	0.01
Latin American Indians (19)	38	0.11
Pueblo (1)	1	0.00
Sioux (3)	5	0.01
All other tribes	3	0.01
American Indian tribes, not spec.	20	0.06
Arab:	79	0.22
Egyptian	44	0.12
Iraqi	8	0.02
Lebanese	21	0.06
Other Arab	6	0.02
Armenian	58	0.16
Asian:	1,029	2.90
Bangladeshi (2)	7	0.02
Cambodian (1)	1	0.00
Chinese, ex. Taiwanese (128)	153	0.43
Filipino (321)	354	1.00
Indian (258)	334	0.94
Indonesian (2)	2	0.01
Japanese (21)	38	0.11
Korean (41)	51	0.14
Malaysian	2	0.01
Pakistani (11)	19	0.05
Sri Lankan (2)	2	0.01
Thai (9)	13	0.04
Vietnamese (5)	12	0.03
Other Asian, specified	6	0.02
Other Asian, not specified (8)	35	0.10
Austrian	404	1.14
Basque	7	0.02
Belgian	39	0.11
Brazilian	49	0.14
British	67	0.19
Canadian	44	0.12
Celtic	11	0.03
Croatian	8	0.02
Czech	102	0.29
Czechoslovakian	139	0.39
Danish	37	0.10
Dutch	120	0.34
Eastern European	283	0.80
English	1,032	2.91
Estonian	14	0.04
European	393	1.11
Finnish	56	0.16
French, except Basque	353	1.00
French Canadian	60	0.17
German	3,315	9.35
Greek	469	1.32
Guyanese	202	0.57
Hawaii Native/Pacific Islander:	67	0.19
Melanesian: (1)	1	0.00
Fijian (1)	1	0.00
Micronesian: (8)	11	0.03
Guamanian/Chamorro (7)	10	0.03
Other Micronesian (1)	1	0.00
Polynesian: (15)	20	0.06
Native Hawaiian (7)	10	0.03
Samoan (8)	9	0.03
Other Polynesian	1	0.00
Other Pac. Isl., specified	4	0.01
Other Pac. Isl., not spec. (5)	31	0.09
Hispanic or Latino:	4,540	12.80
Central American:	758	2.14
Costa Rican	29	0.08
Guatemalan	142	0.40
Honduran	183	0.52
Nicaraguan	25	0.07
Panamanian	9	0.03
Salvadoran	306	0.86
Other Central American	64	0.18
Cuban	169	0.48
Dominican Republic	195	0.55
Mexican	128	0.36
Puerto Rican	1,071	3.02
South American:	945	2.66
Argentinean	67	0.19
Bolivian	29	0.08
Chilean	31	0.09
Colombian	321	0.91
Ecuadorian	128	0.36
Paraguayan	1	0.00
Peruvian	270	0.76
Uruguayan	27	0.08
Venezuelan	24	0.07
Other South American	47	0.13
Other Hispanic or Latino	1,274	3.59
Hungarian	608	1.71
Icelander	19	0.05
Iranian	26	0.07
Irish	7,409	20.89
Israeli	111	0.31
Italian	5,764	16.25
Latvian	76	0.21
Lithuanian	127	0.36
Maltese	19	0.05
Northern European	11	0.03
Norwegian	191	0.54
Polish	1,983	5.59
Portuguese	101	0.28
Romanian	151	0.43
Russian	2,379	6.71
Scotch-Irish	350	0.99
Scottish	299	0.84
Slavic	9	0.03
Slovak	50	0.14
Slovene	7	0.02
Swedish	193	0.54
Swiss	61	0.17
Turkish	203	0.57
Ukrainian	275	0.78
United States or American	1,887	5.32
Welsh	24	0.07
West Indian, excl. Hispanic:	209	0.59
Haitian	49	0.14
Jamaican	101	0.28
Trinidadian and Tobagonian	24	0.07
West Indian	35	0.10
White:	30,461	85.90
Not Hispanic (27,328)	27,636	77.93
Hispanic (2,532)	2,825	7.97
Yugoslavian	76	0.21

Lynbrook

Place Type: Village
County: Nassau
Population: 19,911

Ancestry/Race	Number	%
African American/Black:	253	1.27
Not Hispanic (174)	218	1.09
Hispanic (9)	35	0.18
African, sub-Saharan:	16	0.08
African	7	0.04
South African	9	0.05
Am. Ind. or Alaska Nat., not spec.	10	0.05
American Indian tribes, specified:	29	0.15
Apache	6	0.03
Blackfeet	4	0.02
Cherokee (1)	7	0.04
Iroquois (1)	2	0.01
Latin American Indians (6)	7	0.04
Seminole	1	0.01
Shoshone	1	0.01
Ute (1)	1	0.01
American Indian tribes, not spec.	4	0.02
Arab:	107	0.54
Egyptian	57	0.29
Iraqi	19	0.10
Lebanese	16	0.08
Syrian	15	0.08
Armenian	91	0.46
Asian:	690	3.47
Cambodian (1)	1	0.01
Chinese, ex. Taiwanese (208)	245	1.23
Filipino (80)	85	0.43
Indian (158)	185	0.93
Indonesian (1)	1	0.01
Japanese (1)	3	0.02
Korean (75)	78	0.39
Pakistani (28)	32	0.16
Sri Lankan (1)	1	0.01
Taiwanese (5)	7	0.04
Thai (8)	8	0.04
Vietnamese (11)	12	0.06
Other Asian, specified (1)	1	0.01
Other Asian, not specified (13)	31	0.16
Austrian	197	0.99
Belgian	33	0.17
Brazilian	6	0.03
British	66	0.33
Canadian	18	0.09
Celtic	20	0.10
Croatian	30	0.15
Cypriot	7	0.04
Czech	31	0.16
Czechoslovakian	33	0.17
Danish	25	0.13
Dutch	88	0.44
Eastern European	117	0.59
English	839	4.22
Estonian	30	0.15
European	69	0.35
Finnish	7	0.04
French, except Basque	183	0.92
French Canadian	70	0.35
German	3,325	16.72

Notes: 1. Figures in the "Number" column do not add up to the total population due to: a) Ancestry/Race overlap — e.g. persons can report being both White and Irish, b) persons of Hispanic origin can report being any race, c) persons reporting two ancestries are counted in both categories. 2. Numbers in parentheses indicate the number of persons reporting this ancestry/race alone, not in combination with any other ancestry/race. 3. Refer to the Explanation of Data in the front of the book for more detailed information.

Ancestry/Race	Number	%
Greek	414	2.08
Guyanese	35	0.18
Hawaii Native/Pacific Islander:	7	0.04
Polynesian:	3	0.02
Native Hawaiian	3	0.02
Other Pac. Isl., not spec.	4	0.02
Hispanic or Latino:	1,648	8.28
Central American:	178	0.89
Costa Rican	14	0.07
Guatemalan	38	0.19
Honduran	4	0.02
Nicaraguan	4	0.02
Panamanian	1	0.01
Salvadoran	111	0.56
Other Central American	6	0.03
Cuban	60	0.30
Dominican Republic	159	0.80
Mexican	44	0.22
Puerto Rican	393	1.97
South American:	404	2.03
Argentinean	34	0.17
Bolivian	19	0.10
Chilean	38	0.19
Colombian	139	0.70
Ecuadorian	79	0.40
Peruvian	62	0.31
Uruguayan	12	0.06
Venezuelan	3	0.02
Other South American	18	0.09
Other Hispanic or Latino	410	2.06
Hungarian	332	1.67
Iranian	45	0.23
Irish	5,018	25.24
Israeli	15	0.08
Italian	7,140	35.91
Latvian	25	0.13
Lithuanian	112	0.56
Luxemburger	3	0.02
Macedonian	6	0.03
Maltese	37	0.19
Norwegian	104	0.52
Polish	939	4.72
Portuguese	9	0.05
Romanian	48	0.24
Russian	821	4.13
Scotch-Irish	270	1.36
Scottish	128	0.64
Slovak	65	0.33
Slovene	11	0.06
Swedish	104	0.52
Swiss	84	0.42
Turkish	105	0.53
Ukrainian	201	1.01
United States or American	662	3.33
Welsh	36	0.18
West Indian, excl. Hispanic:	118	0.59
Barbadian	20	0.10
Haitian	31	0.16
Jamaican	52	0.26
Trinidadian and Tobagonian	15	0.08
White:	18,545	93.14
Not Hispanic (17,285)	17,408	87.43
Hispanic (1,049)	1,137	5.71
Yugoslavian	44	0.22

Lysander

Place Type: Town
County: Onondaga
Population: 19,285

Ancestry/Race	Number	%
African American/Black:	185	0.96
Not Hispanic (136)	175	0.91
Hispanic (5)	10	0.05
African, sub-Saharan:	7	0.04
African	7	0.04
Alaska Native tribes, specified:	1	0.01
Eskimo (1)	1	0.01
Am. Ind. or Alaska Nat., not spec.	30	0.16
Albanian	14	0.07
American Indian tribes, specified:	74	0.38
Cherokee (2)	5	0.03
Chippewa	2	0.01
Choctaw	1	0.01
Iroquois (40)	56	0.29
Latin American Indians	1	0.01
Shoshone	2	0.01
Sioux (2)	2	0.01
All other tribes (2)	6	0.03
American Indian tribes, not spec.	2	0.01
Arab:	14	0.07
Lebanese	14	0.07
Armenian	45	0.23
Asian:	237	1.23
Cambodian (1)	1	0.01
Chinese, ex. Taiwanese (34)	42	0.22
Filipino (28)	36	0.19
Indian (67)	70	0.36
Japanese (9)	25	0.13
Korean (34)	38	0.20
Laotian (1)	2	0.01
Pakistani (11)	11	0.06
Taiwanese (3)	5	0.03
Other Asian, not specified (3)	7	0.04
Austrian	49	0.25
Belgian	48	0.25
British	37	0.19
Canadian	108	0.56
Czech	45	0.23
Czechoslovakian	56	0.29
Danish	8	0.04
Dutch	754	3.91
Eastern European	8	0.04
English	3,756	19.48
Estonian	6	0.03
European	55	0.29
Finnish	34	0.18
French, except Basque	1,121	5.81
French Canadian	388	2.01
German	4,460	23.13
Greek	42	0.22
Hawaii Native/Pacific Islander:	8	0.04
Micronesian: (1)	1	0.01
Guamanian/Chamorro (1)	1	0.01
Polynesian: (1)	4	0.02
Native Hawaiian (1)	4	0.02
Other Pac. Isl., not spec. (1)	3	0.02
Hispanic or Latino:	150	0.78
Central American:	8	0.04
Guatemalan	3	0.02
Panamanian	5	0.03
Cuban	9	0.05
Dominican Republic	3	0.02
Mexican	39	0.20
Puerto Rican	40	0.21
South American:	15	0.08
Chilean	2	0.01
Colombian	1	0.01
Ecuadorian	5	0.03
Paraguayan	2	0.01
Peruvian	5	0.03
Other Hispanic or Latino	36	0.19
Hungarian	70	0.36
Iranian	39	0.20
Irish	4,553	23.61
Italian	3,108	16.12
Lithuanian	24	0.12
Macedonian	18	0.09
Northern European	13	0.07
Norwegian	91	0.47
Pennsylvania German	6	0.03
Polish	1,396	7.24
Portuguese	86	0.45
Romanian	9	0.05
Russian	227	1.18
Scandinavian	43	0.22
Scotch-Irish	279	1.45
Scottish	399	2.07
Serbian	11	0.06
Slavic	7	0.04
Slovak	18	0.09
Slovene	6	0.03
Swedish	240	1.24
Swiss	95	0.49
Ukrainian	204	1.06
United States or American	795	4.12
Welsh	208	1.08
White:	18,836	97.67
Not Hispanic (18,596)	18,724	97.09
Hispanic (90)	112	0.58
Yugoslavian	9	0.05

Malone

Place Type: Town
County: Franklin
Population: 14,981

Ancestry/Race	Number	%
African American/Black:	2,794	18.65
Not Hispanic (2,590)	2,598	17.34
Hispanic (191)	196	1.31
African, sub-Saharan:	11	0.07
African	11	0.07
Am. Ind. or Alaska Nat., not spec.	34	0.23
American Indian tribes, specified:	64	0.43
Apache	1	0.01
Blackfeet	4	0.03
Cherokee (1)	4	0.03
Delaware	1	0.01
Iroquois (37)	44	0.29
Latin American Indians (1)	3	0.02
Sioux	1	0.01
All other tribes (4)	6	0.04
American Indian tribes, not spec.	4	0.03
Arab:	28	0.19
Lebanese	17	0.11
Syrian	11	0.07
Asian:	114	0.76
Bangladeshi (7)	8	0.05
Chinese, ex. Taiwanese (34)	36	0.24
Filipino (6)	12	0.08
Indian (11)	14	0.09
Indonesian (3)	5	0.03
Japanese (1)	1	0.01
Korean (9)	10	0.07
Malaysian (1)	1	0.01
Pakistani (10)	12	0.08
Taiwanese (1)	1	0.01
Thai (1)	1	0.01
Vietnamese (5)	5	0.03
Other Asian, specified (1)	1	0.01
Other Asian, not specified (1)	7	0.05
Austrian	13	0.09
British	50	0.33
Canadian	129	0.86
Celtic	7	0.05
Danish	27	0.18
Dutch	141	0.94
English	846	5.65
European	15	0.10
French, except Basque	2,620	17.49
French Canadian	1,292	8.62
German	498	3.32
Greek	40	0.27
Hawaii Native/Pacific Islander:	7	0.05
Micronesian:	1	0.01
Guamanian/Chamorro	1	0.01
Other Pac. Isl., not spec.	6	0.04
Hispanic or Latino:	1,677	11.19
Central American:	62	0.41
Costa Rican	2	0.01
Guatemalan	4	0.03
Honduran	16	0.11
Nicaraguan	2	0.01
Panamanian	24	0.16
Salvadoran	14	0.09
Cuban	59	0.39
Dominican Republic	256	1.71

Notes: 1. Figures in the "Number" column do not add up to the total population due to: a) Ancestry/Race overlap — e.g. persons can report being both White and Irish, b) persons of Hispanic origin can report being any race, c) persons reporting two ancestries are counted in both categories. 2. Numbers in parentheses indicate the number of persons reporting this ancestry/race alone, not in combination with any other ancestry/race. 3. Refer to the Explanation of Data in the front of the book for more detailed information.

Ancestry/Race	Number	%
Mexican	88	0.59
Puerto Rican	954	6.37
South American:	54	0.36
Argentinean	3	0.02
Colombian	31	0.21
Ecuadorian	14	0.09
Paraguayan	1	0.01
Peruvian	3	0.02
Venezuelan	2	0.01
Other Hispanic or Latino	204	1.36
Hungarian	72	0.48
Irish	1,626	10.85
Italian	478	3.19
Norwegian	20	0.13
Polish	152	1.01
Russian	46	0.31
Scandinavian	6	0.04
Scotch-Irish	96	0.64
Scottish	281	1.88
Slovak	5	0.03
Swedish	37	0.25
Swiss	31	0.21
Ukrainian	13	0.09
United States or American	1,191	7.95
Welsh	26	0.17
White:	11,082	73.97
Not Hispanic (10,491)	10,541	70.36
Hispanic (537)	541	3.61
Yugoslavian	13	0.09

Malta

Place Type: Town
County: Saratoga
Population: 13,005

Ancestry/Race	Number	%
African American/Black:	181	1.39
Not Hispanic (139)	175	1.35
Hispanic (2)	6	0.05
Am. Ind. or Alaska Nat., not spec.	30	0.23
Albanian	7	0.05
American Indian tribes, specified:	33	0.25
Apache	2	0.02
Blackfeet (4)	8	0.06
Cherokee (1)	4	0.03
Iroquois (2)	6	0.05
Latin American Indians (3)	3	0.02
Sioux (1)	1	0.01
All other tribes (4)	9	0.07
Arab:	62	0.48
Egyptian	40	0.31
Lebanese	22	0.17
Armenian	7	0.05
Asian:	164	1.26
Bangladeshi (4)	4	0.03
Chinese, ex. Taiwanese (39)	45	0.35
Filipino (14)	19	0.15
Indian (35)	41	0.32
Indonesian	2	0.02
Japanese (6)	8	0.06
Korean (23)	25	0.19
Pakistani (6)	6	0.05
Taiwanese (1)	1	0.01
Thai (3)	3	0.02
Vietnamese (3)	3	0.02
Other Asian, specified	2	0.02
Other Asian, not specified (3)	5	0.04
Austrian	38	0.29
Belgian	9	0.07
British	33	0.25
Canadian	57	0.44
Croatian	4	0.03
Czech	110	0.85
Czechoslovakian	55	0.42
Danish	51	0.39
Dutch	524	4.03
Eastern European	7	0.05
English	1,965	15.11
Estonian	2	0.02
European	112	0.86
Finnish	24	0.18
French, except Basque	1,200	9.23
French Canadian	481	3.70
German	2,322	17.85
Greek	152	1.17
Hawaii Native/Pacific Islander:	8	0.06
Micronesian: (2)	3	0.02
Guamanian/Chamorro (1)	1	0.01
Other Micronesian (1)	2	0.02
Polynesian:	5	0.04
Native Hawaiian	1	0.01
Samoan	4	0.03
Hispanic or Latino:	188	1.45
Central American:	5	0.04
Nicaraguan	2	0.02
Salvadoran	3	0.02
Cuban	10	0.08
Dominican Republic	6	0.05
Mexican	38	0.29
Puerto Rican	78	0.60
South American:	6	0.05
Argentinean	3	0.02
Bolivian	1	0.01
Ecuadorian	1	0.01
Venezuelan	1	0.01
Other Hispanic or Latino	45	0.35
Hungarian	74	0.57
Iranian	8	0.06
Irish	3,426	26.34
Italian	2,267	17.43
Lithuanian	52	0.40
Northern European	3	0.02
Norwegian	129	0.99
Pennsylvania German	3	0.02
Polish	1,205	9.27
Portuguese	68	0.52
Russian	144	1.11
Scandinavian	8	0.06
Scotch-Irish	266	2.05
Scottish	359	2.76
Slavic	32	0.25
Slovak	85	0.65
Swedish	104	0.80
Swiss	53	0.41
Ukrainian	109	0.84
United States or American	439	3.38
Welsh	78	0.60
West Indian, excl. Hispanic:	15	0.12
Jamaican	8	0.06
Trinidadian and Tobagonian	7	0.05
White:	12,615	97.00
Not Hispanic (12,406)	12,496	96.09
Hispanic (110)	119	0.92
Yugoslavian	15	0.12

Mamakating

Place Type: Town
County: Sullivan
Population: 11,002

Ancestry/Race	Number	%
African American/Black:	282	2.56
Not Hispanic (215)	256	2.33
Hispanic (20)	26	0.24
African, sub-Saharan:	3	0.03
African	3	0.03
Am. Ind. or Alaska Nat., not spec.	49	0.45
Albanian	110	1.00
American Indian tribes, specified:	60	0.55
Apache	1	0.01
Blackfeet	2	0.02
Cherokee (3)	16	0.15
Chickasaw (1)	1	0.01
Delaware (13)	20	0.18
Iroquois (2)	9	0.08
Latin American Indians	1	0.01
Seminole	1	0.01
All other tribes	9	0.08
American Indian tribes, not spec.	10	0.09
Armenian	16	0.15
Asian:	151	1.37
Chinese, ex. Taiwanese (24)	29	0.26
Filipino (7)	16	0.15
Indian (36)	44	0.40
Japanese (5)	7	0.06
Korean (13)	13	0.12
Laotian (2)	5	0.05
Pakistani (9)	10	0.09
Thai (6)	10	0.09
Vietnamese (1)	6	0.05
Other Asian, specified (1)	4	0.04
Other Asian, not specified (5)	7	0.06
Austrian	75	0.68
Belgian	4	0.04
Brazilian	35	0.32
British	63	0.57
Canadian	5	0.05
Celtic	10	0.09
Czech	44	0.40
Czechoslovakian	43	0.39
Danish	70	0.64
Dutch	430	3.91
English	1,319	11.99
Estonian	10	0.09
European	20	0.18
Finnish	18	0.16
French, except Basque	313	2.84
French Canadian	84	0.76
German	2,351	21.37
Greek	53	0.48
Guyanese	25	0.23
Hawaii Native/Pacific Islander:	5	0.05
Polynesian:	1	0.01
Native Hawaiian	1	0.01
Other Pac. Isl., not spec.	4	0.04
Hispanic or Latino:	525	4.77
Central American:	15	0.14
Costa Rican	8	0.07
Guatemalan	1	0.01
Honduran	5	0.05
Panamanian	1	0.01
Cuban	15	0.14
Dominican Republic	4	0.04
Mexican	36	0.33
Puerto Rican	327	2.97
South American:	31	0.28
Argentinean	2	0.02
Chilean	1	0.01
Colombian	21	0.19
Ecuadorian	5	0.05
Peruvian	1	0.01
Venezuelan	1	0.01
Other Hispanic or Latino	97	0.88
Hungarian	152	1.38
Irish	2,430	22.09
Italian	2,175	19.77
Lithuanian	17	0.15
Norwegian	95	0.86
Pennsylvania German	12	0.11
Polish	758	6.89
Portuguese	11	0.10
Romanian	1	0.01
Russian	178	1.62
Scotch-Irish	134	1.22
Scottish	226	2.05
Slovak	45	0.41
Swedish	137	1.25
Swiss	28	0.25
Turkish	15	0.14
Ukrainian	111	1.01
United States or American	485	4.41
Welsh	41	0.37
West Indian, excl. Hispanic:	48	0.44
Jamaican	33	0.30
Trinidadian and Tobagonian	12	0.11
Other West Indian	3	0.03
White:	10,504	95.47
Not Hispanic (9,955)	10,082	91.64

Notes: 1. Figures in the "Number" column do not add up to the total population due to: a) Ancestry/Race overlap — e.g. persons can report being both White and Irish, b) persons of Hispanic origin can report being any race, c) persons reporting two ancestries are counted in both categories. 2. Numbers in parentheses indicate the number of persons reporting this ancestry/race alone, not in combination with any other ancestry/race. 3. Refer to the Explanation of Data in the front of the book for more detailed information.

Hispanic (382)	422	3.84
Yugoslavian	37	0.34

Mamaroneck

Place Type: Town
County: Westchester
Population: 28,967

Ancestry/Race	Number	%
African American/Black:	958	3.31
Not Hispanic (751)	855	2.95
Hispanic (61)	103	0.36
African, sub-Saharan:	133	0.46
Ghanian	28	0.10
South African	100	0.35
Other sub-Saharan African	5	0.02
Alaska Native tribes, specified:	3	0.01
Alaska Athabascan	1	0.00
Aleut	1	0.00
Eskimo	1	0.00
Am. Ind. or Alaska Nat., not spec.	41	0.14
Albanian	10	0.03
Alsatian	8	0.03
American Indian tribes, specified:	38	0.13
Blackfeet	3	0.01
Cherokee	6	0.02
Chickasaw (1)	1	0.00
Crow	5	0.02
Iroquois	6	0.02
Latin American Indians (10)	12	0.04
All other tribes (1)	5	0.02
American Indian tribes, not spec.	2	0.01
Arab:	204	0.70
Arab/Arabic	18	0.06
Egyptian	8	0.03
Iraqi	10	0.03
Jordanian	39	0.13
Lebanese	95	0.33
Moroccan	15	0.05
Syrian	10	0.03
Other Arab	9	0.03
Armenian	79	0.27
Asian:	1,016	3.51
Chinese, ex. Taiwanese (201)	232	0.80
Filipino (85)	96	0.33
Hmong (1)	1	0.00
Indian (170)	186	0.64
Indonesian (6)	6	0.02
Japanese (284)	314	1.08
Korean (109)	119	0.41
Laotian	3	0.01
Malaysian	1	0.00
Pakistani (7)	7	0.02
Sri Lankan	1	0.00
Taiwanese (4)	4	0.01
Thai (6)	6	0.02
Vietnamese (11)	12	0.04
Other Asian, specified (4)	4	0.01
Other Asian, not specified (10)	24	0.08
Australian	88	0.30
Austrian	508	1.75
Belgian	105	0.36
Brazilian	257	0.89
British	237	0.82
Bulgarian	44	0.15
Canadian	111	0.38
Croatian	7	0.02
Cypriot	6	0.02
Czech	163	0.56
Czechoslovakian	80	0.28
Danish	55	0.19
Dutch	261	0.90
Eastern European	527	1.82
English	1,907	6.58
Estonian	21	0.07
European	462	1.59
Finnish	70	0.24
French, except Basque	1,310	4.52
French Canadian	89	0.31
German	2,794	9.65
Greek	218	0.75
Guyanese	10	0.03
Hawaii Native/Pacific Islander:	34	0.12
Melanesian: (1)	3	0.01
Fijian (1)	3	0.01
Micronesian: (8)	16	0.06
Guamanian/Chamorro (5)	11	0.04
Other Micronesian (3)	5	0.02
Polynesian: (5)	9	0.03
Native Hawaiian (3)	6	0.02
Samoan (1)	1	0.00
Other Polynesian (1)	2	0.01
Other Pac. Isl., not spec.	6	0.02
Hispanic or Latino:	3,164	10.92
Central American:	660	2.28
Costa Rican	16	0.06
Guatemalan	471	1.63
Honduran	26	0.09
Nicaraguan	7	0.02
Panamanian	9	0.03
Salvadoran	119	0.41
Other Central American	12	0.04
Cuban	82	0.28
Dominican Republic	69	0.24
Mexican	577	1.99
Puerto Rican	362	1.25
South American:	701	2.42
Argentinean	71	0.25
Bolivian	23	0.08
Chilean	41	0.14
Colombian	184	0.64
Ecuadorian	82	0.28
Paraguayan	12	0.04
Peruvian	226	0.78
Uruguayan	15	0.05
Venezuelan	32	0.11
Other South American	15	0.05
Other Hispanic or Latino	713	2.46
Hungarian	437	1.51
Iranian	4	0.01
Irish	4,216	14.55
Israeli	25	0.09
Italian	5,691	19.65
Latvian	80	0.28
Lithuanian	192	0.66
Luxemburger	43	0.15
Northern European	19	0.07
Norwegian	217	0.75
Polish	1,503	5.19
Portuguese	214	0.74
Romanian	184	0.64
Russian	2,080	7.18
Scandinavian	13	0.04
Scotch-Irish	177	0.61
Scottish	425	1.47
Serbian	10	0.03
Slavic	7	0.02
Slovak	38	0.13
Swedish	182	0.63
Swiss	86	0.30
Turkish	37	0.13
Ukrainian	184	0.64
United States or American	1,146	3.96
Welsh	78	0.27
West Indian, excl. Hispanic:	169	0.58
Haitian	8	0.03
Jamaican	134	0.46
West Indian	27	0.09
White:	26,290	90.76
Not Hispanic (23,744)	24,045	83.01
Hispanic (2,015)	2,245	7.75
Yugoslavian	7	0.02

Mamaroneck

Place Type: Village
County: Westchester
Population: 18,752

Ancestry/Race	Number	%
African American/Black:	895	4.77
Not Hispanic (715)	795	4.24
Hispanic (63)	100	0.53
African, sub-Saharan:	58	0.31
Ghanian	28	0.15
South African	25	0.13
Other sub-Saharan African	5	0.03
Alaska Native tribes, specified:	1	0.01
Alaska Athabascan	1	0.01
Am. Ind. or Alaska Nat., not spec.	46	0.25
Albanian	8	0.04
American Indian tribes, specified:	32	0.17
Cherokee (8)	14	0.07
Iroquois	6	0.03
Latin American Indians (8)	10	0.05
All other tribes (1)	2	0.01
American Indian tribes, not spec.	8	0.04
Arab:	93	0.50
Arab/Arabic	54	0.29
Egyptian	17	0.09
Lebanese	5	0.03
Syrian	10	0.05
Other Arab	7	0.04
Armenian	37	0.20
Asian:	759	4.05
Chinese, ex. Taiwanese (113)	147	0.78
Filipino (75)	85	0.45
Indian (112)	120	0.64
Japanese (264)	285	1.52
Korean (75)	83	0.44
Laotian	3	0.02
Malaysian (2)	4	0.02
Taiwanese (3)	4	0.02
Thai (4)	5	0.03
Vietnamese	1	0.01
Other Asian, not specified (8)	22	0.12
Australian	13	0.07
Austrian	233	1.24
Belgian	34	0.18
Brazilian	107	0.57
British	71	0.38
Bulgarian	44	0.23
Canadian	86	0.46
Cypriot	6	0.03
Czech	73	0.39
Czechoslovakian	25	0.13
Danish	44	0.23
Dutch	164	0.87
Eastern European	162	0.86
English	813	4.33
Estonian	21	0.11
European	100	0.53
Finnish	21	0.11
French, except Basque	477	2.54
French Canadian	67	0.36
German	1,298	6.92
Greek	87	0.46
Hawaii Native/Pacific Islander:	29	0.15
Melanesian:	2	0.01
Fijian	2	0.01
Micronesian: (5)	11	0.06
Guamanian/Chamorro (5)	11	0.06
Polynesian: (6)	7	0.04
Native Hawaiian (2)	3	0.02
Samoan (4)	4	0.02
Other Pac. Isl., not spec. (1)	9	0.05
Hispanic or Latino:	3,284	17.51
Central American:	783	4.18
Costa Rican	18	0.10
Guatemalan	544	2.90
Honduran	25	0.13
Nicaraguan	6	0.03
Panamanian	11	0.06

Notes: 1. Figures in the "Number" column do not add up to the total population due to: a) Ancestry/Race overlap — e.g. persons can report being both White and Irish, b) persons of Hispanic origin can report being any race, c) persons reporting two ancestries are counted in both categories. 2. Numbers in parentheses indicate the number of persons reporting this ancestry/race alone, not in combination with any other ancestry/race. 3. Refer to the Explanation of Data in the front of the book for more detailed information.

Ancestry/Race	Number	%
Salvadoran	164	0.87
Other Central American	15	0.08
Cuban	58	0.31
Dominican Republic	66	0.35
Mexican	575	3.07
Puerto Rican	342	1.82
South American:	699	3.73
Argentinean	47	0.25
Bolivian	20	0.11
Chilean	41	0.22
Colombian	150	0.80
Ecuadorian	71	0.38
Paraguayan	39	0.21
Peruvian	260	1.39
Uruguayan	31	0.17
Venezuelan	25	0.13
Other South American	15	0.08
Other Hispanic or Latino	761	4.06
Hungarian	158	0.84
Irish	2,346	12.50
Israeli	7	0.04
Italian	5,354	28.53
Latvian	20	0.11
Lithuanian	112	0.60
Maltese	7	0.04
Norwegian	70	0.37
Polish	687	3.66
Portuguese	303	1.61
Romanian	48	0.26
Russian	741	3.95
Scandinavian	6	0.03
Scotch-Irish	233	1.24
Scottish	101	0.54
Serbian	4	0.02
Slovak	24	0.13
Slovene	16	0.09
Swedish	130	0.69
Swiss	58	0.31
Turkish	16	0.09
Ukrainian	23	0.12
United States or American	833	4.44
Welsh	21	0.11
West Indian, excl. Hispanic:	187	1.00
Haitian	32	0.17
Jamaican	124	0.66
West Indian	31	0.17
White:	16,299	86.92
Not Hispanic (13,809)	14,037	74.86
Hispanic (2,050)	2,262	12.06

Manlius

Place Type: Town
County: Onondaga
Population: 31,872

Ancestry/Race	Number	%
African American/Black:	343	1.08
Not Hispanic (264)	324	1.02
Hispanic (13)	19	0.06
African, sub-Saharan:	48	0.15
African	6	0.02
Nigerian	8	0.03
South African	34	0.11
Am. Ind. or Alaska Nat., not spec.	36	0.11
Albanian	20	0.06
American Indian tribes, specified:	138	0.43
Cherokee (3)	26	0.08
Chickasaw	1	0.00
Cree (1)	1	0.00
Creek	1	0.00
Crow	3	0.01
Delaware	4	0.01
Houma	2	0.01
Iroquois (48)	80	0.25
Latin American Indians (1)	1	0.00
Navajo (2)	2	0.01
Paiute	1	0.00
Sioux (2)	2	0.01
Yakama	1	0.00
All other tribes (10)	13	0.04
American Indian tribes, not spec.	8	0.03
Arab:	326	1.02
Arab/Arabic	23	0.07
Egyptian	19	0.06
Jordanian	22	0.07
Lebanese	104	0.33
Palestinian	117	0.37
Syrian	33	0.10
Other Arab	8	0.03
Armenian	44	0.14
Asian:	1,064	3.34
Cambodian (11)	11	0.03
Chinese, ex. Taiwanese (228)	268	0.84
Filipino (72)	81	0.25
Hmong (6)	6	0.02
Indian (272)	292	0.92
Indonesian	6	0.02
Japanese (28)	41	0.13
Korean (197)	206	0.65
Laotian (4)	6	0.02
Malaysian (1)	1	0.00
Pakistani (32)	37	0.12
Sri Lankan (1)	1	0.00
Taiwanese (21)	24	0.08
Thai (5)	10	0.03
Vietnamese (23)	31	0.10
Other Asian, specified (1)	1	0.00
Other Asian, not specified (19)	42	0.13
Australian	22	0.07
Austrian	183	0.57
Belgian	27	0.08
British	272	0.85
Canadian	144	0.45
Croatian	52	0.16
Czech	108	0.34
Czechoslovakian	85	0.27
Danish	79	0.25
Dutch	714	2.24
Eastern European	120	0.38
English	5,508	17.28
Estonian	13	0.04
European	234	0.73
Finnish	38	0.12
French, except Basque	1,773	5.56
French Canadian	548	1.72
German	6,967	21.86
Greek	231	0.72
Hawaii Native/Pacific Islander:	27	0.08
Micronesian: (3)	6	0.02
Guamanian/Chamorro (2)	4	0.01
Other Micronesian (1)	2	0.01
Polynesian: (1)	16	0.05
Native Hawaiian (1)	12	0.04
Other Polynesian	4	0.01
Other Pac. Isl., not spec.	5	0.02
Hispanic or Latino:	310	0.97
Central American:	16	0.05
Costa Rican	4	0.01
Guatemalan	3	0.01
Honduran	1	0.00
Panamanian	6	0.02
Salvadoran	1	0.00
Other Central American	1	0.00
Cuban	21	0.07
Dominican Republic	7	0.02
Mexican	78	0.24
Puerto Rican	77	0.24
South American:	45	0.14
Argentinean	7	0.02
Chilean	5	0.02
Colombian	12	0.04
Ecuadorian	2	0.01
Paraguayan	6	0.02
Venezuelan	12	0.04
Other South American	1	0.00
Other Hispanic or Latino	66	0.21
Hungarian	111	0.35
Irish	7,519	23.59
Israeli	25	0.08
Italian	5,017	15.74
Latvian	11	0.03
Lithuanian	151	0.47
Macedonian	55	0.17
Maltese	5	0.02
Northern European	61	0.19
Norwegian	247	0.77
Pennsylvania German	30	0.09
Polish	2,603	8.17
Portuguese	5	0.02
Romanian	47	0.15
Russian	709	2.22
Scandinavian	34	0.11
Scotch-Irish	607	1.90
Scottish	783	2.46
Slavic	37	0.12
Slovak	138	0.43
Slovene	62	0.19
Swedish	392	1.23
Swiss	150	0.47
Turkish	8	0.03
Ukrainian	378	1.19
United States or American	1,497	4.70
Welsh	468	1.47
West Indian, excl. Hispanic:	28	0.09
Jamaican	28	0.09
White:	30,505	95.71
Not Hispanic (29,964)	30,254	94.92
Hispanic (218)	251	0.79
Yugoslavian	15	0.05

Manorville

Place Type: Census Designated Place
County: Suffolk
Population: 11,131

Ancestry/Race	Number	%
African American/Black:	163	1.46
Not Hispanic (120)	148	1.33
Hispanic (11)	15	0.13
African, sub-Saharan:	20	0.18
African	20	0.18
Am. Ind. or Alaska Nat., not spec.	12	0.11
American Indian tribes, specified:	21	0.19
Blackfeet	2	0.02
Cherokee (2)	9	0.08
Chippewa (1)	1	0.01
Iroquois (3)	4	0.04
Seminole (1)	2	0.02
All other tribes (1)	3	0.03
American Indian tribes, not spec.	3	0.03
Arab:	10	0.09
Jordanian	10	0.09
Asian:	105	0.94
Chinese, ex. Taiwanese (18)	20	0.18
Filipino (3)	16	0.14
Indian (13)	15	0.13
Indonesian	1	0.01
Japanese (3)	3	0.03
Korean (24)	24	0.22
Pakistani (3)	8	0.07
Vietnamese (8)	8	0.07
Other Asian, specified	5	0.04
Other Asian, not specified (1)	5	0.04
Australian	7	0.06
Austrian	69	0.62
British	23	0.21
Canadian	15	0.13
Czech	67	0.60
Czechoslovakian	30	0.27
Danish	44	0.39
Dutch	115	1.03
Eastern European	21	0.19
English	643	5.76
European	18	0.16
Finnish	31	0.28
French, except Basque	245	2.19
French Canadian	82	0.73
German	3,042	27.24

Notes: 1. Figures in the "Number" column do not add up to the total population due to: a) Ancestry/Race overlap — e.g. persons can report being both White and Irish, b) persons of Hispanic origin can report being any race, c) persons reporting two ancestries are counted in both categories. 2. Numbers in parentheses indicate the number of persons reporting this ancestry/race alone, not in combination with any other ancestry/race. 3. Refer to the Explanation of Data in the front of the book for more detailed information.

Greek	109	0.98
Guyanese	28	0.25
Hawaii Native/Pacific Islander:	12	0.11
Micronesian: (2)	3	0.03
Guamanian/Chamorro (2)	2	0.02
Other Micronesian	1	0.01
Polynesian: (2)	4	0.04
Native Hawaiian (1)	3	0.03
Samoan (1)	1	0.01
Other Pac. Isl., specified	5	0.04
Hispanic or Latino:	461	4.14
Central American:	22	0.20
Costa Rican	2	0.02
Guatemalan	4	0.04
Honduran	7	0.06
Salvadoran	7	0.06
Other Central American	2	0.02
Cuban	17	0.15
Dominican Republic	13	0.12
Mexican	11	0.10
Puerto Rican	284	2.55
South American:	56	0.50
Argentinean	6	0.05
Chilean	2	0.02
Colombian	29	0.26
Ecuadorian	12	0.11
Uruguayan	2	0.02
Other South American	5	0.04
Other Hispanic or Latino	58	0.52
Hungarian	31	0.28
Iranian	5	0.04
Irish	3,515	31.48
Israeli	7	0.06
Italian	4,374	39.17
Lithuanian	16	0.14
Maltese	34	0.30
Norwegian	162	1.45
Polish	870	7.79
Romanian	23	0.21
Russian	107	0.96
Scandinavian	15	0.13
Scotch-Irish	80	0.72
Scottish	172	1.54
Slovak	47	0.42
Swedish	87	0.78
Swiss	27	0.24
Turkish	20	0.18
Ukrainian	66	0.59
United States or American	461	4.13
Welsh	59	0.53
West Indian, excl. Hispanic:	5	0.04
Barbadian	5	0.04
White:	10,814	97.15
Not Hispanic (10,374)	10,435	93.75
Hispanic (354)	379	3.40
Yugoslavian	17	0.15

Massapequa

Place Type: Census Designated Place
County: Nassau
Population: 22,652

Ancestry/Race	Number	%
African American/Black:	56	0.25
Not Hispanic (35)	51	0.23
Hispanic (3)	5	0.02
African, sub-Saharan:	7	0.03
South African	7	0.03
Alaska Native tribes, specified:	1	0.00
Tlingit-Haida (1)	1	0.00
Am. Ind. or Alaska Nat., not spec.	12	0.05
American Indian tribes, specified:	22	0.10
Apache	2	0.01
Cherokee	2	0.01
Cheyenne (1)	1	0.00
Comanche	2	0.01
Iroquois	8	0.04
Kiowa	2	0.01
Latin American Indians (1)	1	0.00
Sioux (1)	1	0.00
All other tribes	3	0.01
Arab:	96	0.42
Arab/Arabic	21	0.09
Lebanese	72	0.32
Other Arab	3	0.01
Armenian	64	0.28
Asian:	342	1.51
Bangladeshi (4)	5	0.02
Chinese, ex. Taiwanese (130)	138	0.61
Filipino (8)	17	0.08
Indian (60)	79	0.35
Japanese (14)	22	0.10
Korean (26)	32	0.14
Pakistani (13)	14	0.06
Taiwanese (17)	17	0.08
Thai (4)	4	0.02
Vietnamese (1)	1	0.00
Other Asian, specified (3)	4	0.02
Other Asian, not specified (5)	9	0.04
Australian	20	0.09
Austrian	201	0.89
Basque	7	0.03
Belgian	12	0.05
British	29	0.13
Bulgarian	44	0.19
Canadian	16	0.07
Croatian	18	0.08
Czech	44	0.19
Czechoslovakian	42	0.19
Danish	21	0.09
Dutch	122	0.54
Eastern European	126	0.56
English	1,455	6.42
Estonian	13	0.06
European	93	0.41
Finnish	13	0.06
French, except Basque	272	1.20
French Canadian	64	0.28
German	4,623	20.41
Greek	495	2.19
Guyanese	17	0.08
Hawaii Native/Pacific Islander:	11	0.05
Polynesian: (3)	6	0.03
Native Hawaiian (3)	6	0.03
Other Pac. Isl., specified	1	0.00
Other Pac. Isl., not spec. (3)	4	0.02
Hispanic or Latino:	587	2.59
Central American:	28	0.12
Costa Rican	1	0.00
Guatemalan	4	0.02
Honduran	3	0.01
Nicaraguan	4	0.02
Salvadoran	14	0.06
Other Central American	2	0.01
Cuban	40	0.18
Dominican Republic	15	0.07
Mexican	27	0.12
Puerto Rican	217	0.96
South American:	99	0.44
Argentinean	14	0.06
Chilean	12	0.05
Colombian	28	0.12
Ecuadorian	14	0.06
Paraguayan	1	0.00
Peruvian	15	0.07
Uruguayan	8	0.04
Other South American	7	0.03
Other Hispanic or Latino	161	0.71
Hungarian	201	0.89
Iranian	41	0.18
Irish	6,520	28.78
Israeli	78	0.34
Italian	8,969	39.59
Latvian	6	0.03
Lithuanian	161	0.71
Maltese	56	0.25
New Zealander	5	0.02
Norwegian	278	1.23
Polish	1,066	4.71
Portuguese	42	0.19
Romanian	75	0.33
Russian	505	2.23
Scotch-Irish	313	1.38
Scottish	220	0.97
Slavic	13	0.06
Slovak	24	0.11
Swedish	238	1.05
Swiss	64	0.28
Turkish	63	0.28
Ukrainian	221	0.98
United States or American	1,073	4.74
Welsh	84	0.37
West Indian, excl. Hispanic:	19	0.08
Jamaican	7	0.03
Trinidadian and Tobagonian	12	0.05
White:	22,222	98.10
Not Hispanic (21,606)	21,720	95.89
Hispanic (461)	502	2.22
Yugoslavian	49	0.22

Massapequa Park

Place Type: Village
County: Nassau
Population: 17,499

Ancestry/Race	Number	%
African American/Black:	43	0.25
Not Hispanic (37)	42	0.24
Hispanic (1)	1	0.01
Am. Ind. or Alaska Nat., not spec.	11	0.06
Albanian	7	0.04
American Indian tribes, specified:	15	0.09
Blackfeet (1)	1	0.01
Cherokee	7	0.04
Iroquois (2)	3	0.02
Latin American Indians	3	0.02
Seminole	1	0.01
American Indian tribes, not spec.	1	0.01
Arab:	80	0.46
Egyptian	23	0.13
Lebanese	38	0.22
Syrian	19	0.11
Armenian	101	0.58
Asian:	287	1.64
Chinese, ex. Taiwanese (116)	133	0.76
Filipino (24)	32	0.18
Indian (55)	61	0.35
Japanese (5)	11	0.06
Korean (23)	26	0.15
Taiwanese	4	0.02
Thai (7)	7	0.04
Vietnamese (2)	2	0.01
Other Asian, specified (1)	1	0.01
Other Asian, not specified (9)	10	0.06
Austrian	153	0.87
Brazilian	42	0.24
British	53	0.30
Bulgarian	14	0.08
Canadian	38	0.22
Croatian	48	0.27
Cypriot	15	0.09
Czech	62	0.35
Czechoslovakian	71	0.41
Danish	23	0.13
Dutch	116	0.66
Eastern European	40	0.23
English	761	4.35
European	37	0.21
Finnish	26	0.15
French, except Basque	305	1.74
French Canadian	43	0.25
German	2,939	16.80
Greek	308	1.76
Hawaii Native/Pacific Islander:	4	0.02
Micronesian: (2)	2	0.01
Guamanian/Chamorro (2)	2	0.01
Polynesian: (2)	2	0.01
Samoan (2)	2	0.01

Notes: 1. Figures in the "Number" column do not add up to the total population due to: a) Ancestry/Race overlap — e.g. persons can report being both White and Irish, b) persons of Hispanic origin can report being any race, c) persons reporting two ancestries are counted in both categories. 2. Numbers in parentheses indicate the number of persons reporting this ancestry/race alone, not in combination with any other ancestry/race. 3. Refer to the Explanation of Data in the front of the book for more detailed information.

Ancestry/Race	Number	%
Hispanic or Latino:	525	3.00
Central American:	25	0.14
Costa Rican	1	0.01
Guatemalan	15	0.09
Salvadoran	9	0.05
Cuban	39	0.22
Dominican Republic	22	0.13
Mexican	31	0.18
Puerto Rican	197	1.13
South American:	113	0.65
Argentinean	23	0.13
Chilean	12	0.07
Colombian	32	0.18
Ecuadorian	16	0.09
Paraguayan	3	0.02
Peruvian	15	0.09
Uruguayan	6	0.03
Other South American	6	0.03
Other Hispanic or Latino	98	0.56
Hungarian	196	1.12
Irish	5,463	31.22
Israeli	14	0.08
Italian	7,169	40.97
Lithuanian	70	0.40
Maltese	23	0.13
Norwegian	247	1.41
Polish	694	3.97
Portuguese	66	0.38
Romanian	34	0.19
Russian	553	3.16
Scandinavian	40	0.23
Scotch-Irish	133	0.76
Scottish	161	0.92
Slovak	36	0.21
Swedish	275	1.57
Swiss	51	0.29
Turkish	19	0.11
Ukrainian	83	0.47
United States or American	486	2.78
Welsh	74	0.42
West Indian, excl. Hispanic:	18	0.10
Barbadian	5	0.03
Haitian	7	0.04
Trinidadian and Tobagonian	6	0.03
White:	17,131	97.90
Not Hispanic (16,614)	16,682	95.33
Hispanic (425)	449	2.57
Yugoslavian	17	0.10

Massena

Place Type: Town
County: Saint Lawrence
Population: 13,121

Ancestry/Race	Number	%
African American/Black:	55	0.42
Not Hispanic (39)	53	0.40
Hispanic (1)	2	0.02
African, sub-Saharan:	8	0.06
African	8	0.06
Alaska Native tribes, not specified	2	0.02
Am. Ind. or Alaska Nat., not spec.	81	0.62
American Indian tribes, specified:	421	3.21
Apache	3	0.02
Cherokee (6)	12	0.09
Chippewa	1	0.01
Colville (1)	1	0.01
Delaware	1	0.01
Iroquois (345)	397	3.03
Latin American Indians (1)	1	0.01
All other tribes (1)	5	0.04
American Indian tribes, not spec.	8	0.06
Arab:	81	0.62
Lebanese	72	0.55
Syrian	4	0.03
Other Arab	5	0.04
Armenian	37	0.28
Asian:	76	0.58
Cambodian (2)	3	0.02
Chinese, ex. Taiwanese (9)	15	0.11
Filipino (7)	17	0.13
Indian (16)	17	0.13
Japanese (3)	3	0.02
Korean (6)	7	0.05
Taiwanese (2)	2	0.02
Vietnamese (8)	9	0.07
Other Asian, not specified	3	0.02
British	57	0.43
Canadian	182	1.39
Croatian	6	0.05
Czech	11	0.08
Czechoslovakian	12	0.09
Danish	4	0.03
Dutch	278	2.12
English	1,331	10.14
European	17	0.13
French, except Basque	3,373	25.71
French Canadian	1,265	9.64
German	793	6.04
Greek	12	0.09
Hawaii Native/Pacific Islander:	6	0.05
Polynesian: (3)	3	0.02
Native Hawaiian (1)	1	0.01
Samoan (2)	2	0.02
Other Pac. Isl., not spec. (1)	3	0.02
Hispanic or Latino:	141	1.07
Central American:	1	0.01
Honduran	1	0.01
Cuban	2	0.02
Dominican Republic	4	0.03
Mexican	31	0.24
Puerto Rican	48	0.37
South American:	4	0.03
Colombian	2	0.02
Ecuadorian	2	0.02
Other Hispanic or Latino	51	0.39
Hungarian	235	1.79
Irish	2,423	18.47
Italian	998	7.61
Lithuanian	52	0.40
Norwegian	15	0.11
Polish	374	2.85
Portuguese	33	0.25
Romanian	6	0.05
Russian	51	0.39
Scandinavian	8	0.06
Scotch-Irish	225	1.71
Scottish	499	3.80
Slavic	8	0.06
Swedish	53	0.40
Swiss	4	0.03
Ukrainian	45	0.34
United States or American	1,049	7.99
Welsh	61	0.46
West Indian, excl. Hispanic:	7	0.05
Haitian	7	0.05
White:	12,558	95.71
Not Hispanic (12,355)	12,460	94.96
Hispanic (84)	98	0.75
Yugoslavian	17	0.13

Massena

Place Type: Village
County: Saint Lawrence
Population: 11,209

Ancestry/Race	Number	%
African American/Black:	55	0.49
Not Hispanic (35)	49	0.44
Hispanic (5)	6	0.05
African, sub-Saharan:	8	0.07
African	8	0.07
Am. Ind. or Alaska Nat., not spec.	52	0.46
American Indian tribes, specified:	244	2.18
Apache	1	0.01
Cherokee (6)	12	0.11
Chippewa	1	0.01
Colville (1)	1	0.01
Iroquois (182)	223	1.99
Latin American Indians (1)	1	0.01
All other tribes (1)	5	0.04
American Indian tribes, not spec.	7	0.06
Arab:	85	0.76
Lebanese	50	0.45
Syrian	30	0.27
Other Arab	5	0.04
Armenian	57	0.51
Asian:	103	0.92
Cambodian (1)	2	0.02
Chinese, ex. Taiwanese (14)	21	0.19
Filipino (7)	17	0.15
Indian (32)	33	0.29
Japanese (2)	2	0.02
Korean (9)	10	0.09
Malaysian	1	0.01
Pakistani (6)	6	0.05
Taiwanese (2)	2	0.02
Vietnamese (7)	7	0.06
Other Asian, not specified	2	0.02
British	49	0.44
Canadian	146	1.30
Croatian	6	0.05
Czech	32	0.29
Czechoslovakian	5	0.04
Danish	4	0.04
Dutch	204	1.82
English	1,150	10.25
European	17	0.15
French, except Basque	2,901	25.85
French Canadian	1,154	10.28
German	627	5.59
Greek	12	0.11
Hawaii Native/Pacific Islander:	6	0.05
Polynesian: (3)	3	0.03
Native Hawaiian (1)	1	0.01
Samoan (2)	2	0.02
Other Pac. Isl., not spec. (1)	3	0.03
Hispanic or Latino:	133	1.19
Cuban	2	0.02
Dominican Republic	4	0.04
Mexican	27	0.24
Puerto Rican	47	0.42
South American:	3	0.03
Colombian	1	0.01
Ecuadorian	2	0.02
Other Hispanic or Latino	50	0.45
Hungarian	194	1.73
Irish	2,085	18.58
Italian	910	8.11
Lithuanian	27	0.24
Norwegian	8	0.07
Polish	263	2.34
Portuguese	33	0.29
Romanian	6	0.05
Russian	35	0.31
Scotch-Irish	180	1.60
Scottish	525	4.68
Slavic	8	0.07
Swedish	46	0.41
Swiss	4	0.04
Ukrainian	38	0.34
United States or American	891	7.94
Welsh	76	0.68
White:	10,809	96.43
Not Hispanic (10,625)	10,715	95.59
Hispanic (78)	94	0.84
Yugoslavian	17	0.15

Mastic Beach

Place Type: Census Designated Place
County: Suffolk
Population: 11,543

Ancestry/Race	Number	%
African American/Black:	721	6.25
Not Hispanic (544)	664	5.75
Hispanic (36)	57	0.49

Notes: 1. Figures in the "Number" column do not add up to the total population due to: a) Ancestry/Race overlap — e.g. persons can report being both White and Irish, b) persons of Hispanic origin can report being any race, c) persons reporting two ancestries are counted in both categories. 2. Numbers in parentheses indicate the number of persons reporting this ancestry/race alone, not in combination with any other ancestry/race. 3. Refer to the Explanation of Data in the front of the book for more detailed information.

Alaska Native tribes, not specified	1	0.01
Am. Ind. or Alaska Nat., not spec.	39	0.34
Albanian	15	0.13
American Indian tribes, specified:	84	0.73
Apache (2)	10	0.09
Blackfeet (5)	10	0.09
Cherokee (8)	37	0.32
Choctaw (5)	5	0.04
Cree	2	0.02
Iroquois (3)	3	0.03
Latin American Indians (6)	6	0.05
Seminole	3	0.03
All other tribes (1)	8	0.07
American Indian tribes, not spec.	10	0.09
Arab:	29	0.25
Arab/Arabic	29	0.25
Armenian	10	0.09
Asian:	156	1.35
Chinese, ex. Taiwanese (32)	39	0.34
Filipino (15)	24	0.21
Indian (36)	48	0.42
Japanese	3	0.03
Korean (7)	11	0.10
Pakistani (8)	15	0.13
Vietnamese (6)	6	0.05
Other Asian, not specified (1)	10	0.09
Australian	74	0.64
Austrian	17	0.15
Brazilian	7	0.06
British	43	0.37
Canadian	17	0.15
Croatian	8	0.07
Czech	33	0.29
Czechoslovakian	26	0.23
Danish	64	0.55
Dutch	178	1.54
Eastern European	12	0.10
English	710	6.15
French, except Basque	273	2.37
French Canadian	90	0.78
German	2,555	22.13
German Russian	9	0.08
Greek	112	0.97
Hawaii Native/Pacific Islander:	4	0.03
Polynesian: (1)	1	0.01
Native Hawaiian (1)	1	0.01
Other Pac. Isl., not spec.	3	0.03
Hispanic or Latino:	1,222	10.59
Central American:	57	0.49
Costa Rican	7	0.06
Guatemalan	3	0.03
Honduran	6	0.05
Nicaraguan	11	0.10
Panamanian	1	0.01
Salvadoran	23	0.20
Other Central American	6	0.05
Cuban	38	0.33
Dominican Republic	37	0.32
Mexican	38	0.33
Puerto Rican	779	6.75
South American:	102	0.88
Argentinean	2	0.02
Bolivian	8	0.07
Chilean	11	0.10
Colombian	22	0.19
Ecuadorian	36	0.31
Peruvian	15	0.13
Venezuelan	1	0.01
Other South American	7	0.06
Other Hispanic or Latino	171	1.48
Hungarian	13	0.11
Irish	3,227	27.96
Italian	3,877	33.59
Lithuanian	38	0.33
Maltese	88	0.76
Norwegian	177	1.53
Polish	709	6.14
Portuguese	41	0.36
Romanian	15	0.13
Russian	133	1.15
Scotch-Irish	44	0.38
Scottish	92	0.80
Slovak	25	0.22
Swedish	82	0.71
Swiss	30	0.26
Turkish	10	0.09
Ukrainian	23	0.20
United States or American	377	3.27
Welsh	33	0.29
West Indian, excl. Hispanic:	99	0.86
Haitian	22	0.19
Jamaican	24	0.21
Trinidadian and Tobagonian	21	0.18
West Indian	32	0.28
White:	10,434	90.39
Not Hispanic (9,388)	9,570	82.91
Hispanic (788)	864	7.49
Yugoslavian	20	0.17

Mastic

Place Type: Census Designated Place
County: Suffolk
Population: 15,436

Ancestry/Race	Number	%
African American/Black:	1,096	7.10
Not Hispanic (856)	998	6.47
Hispanic (78)	98	0.63
African, sub-Saharan:	56	0.36
African	56	0.36
Am. Ind. or Alaska Nat., not spec.	88	0.57
American Indian tribes, specified:	259	1.68
Apache	6	0.04
Blackfeet	2	0.01
Cherokee (21)	41	0.27
Cheyenne	1	0.01
Crow	1	0.01
Iroquois (4)	13	0.08
Latin American Indians (2)	2	0.01
Osage	1	0.01
Pueblo	1	0.01
Seminole	8	0.05
Ute	3	0.02
All other tribes (155)	180	1.17
American Indian tribes, not spec.	52	0.34
Arab:	42	0.27
Egyptian	3	0.02
Lebanese	39	0.25
Armenian	28	0.18
Asian:	232	1.50
Chinese, ex. Taiwanese (35)	41	0.27
Filipino (27)	30	0.19
Indian (40)	54	0.35
Japanese (8)	15	0.10
Korean (17)	20	0.13
Pakistani (9)	13	0.08
Sri Lankan (4)	4	0.03
Taiwanese (3)	5	0.03
Thai (2)	2	0.01
Vietnamese (21)	24	0.16
Other Asian, specified	1	0.01
Other Asian, not specified (6)	23	0.15
Austrian	59	0.38
British	17	0.11
Canadian	20	0.13
Czech	107	0.69
Czechoslovakian	60	0.39
Danish	46	0.30
Dutch	82	0.53
English	957	6.16
European	33	0.21
Finnish	36	0.23
French, except Basque	291	1.87
French Canadian	76	0.49
German	3,134	20.19
Greek	172	1.11
Hawaii Native/Pacific Islander:	12	0.08
Polynesian: (1)	5	0.03
Native Hawaiian (1)	5	0.03
Other Pac. Isl., specified	1	0.01
Other Pac. Isl., not spec.	6	0.04
Hispanic or Latino:	1,875	12.15
Central American:	109	0.71
Costa Rican	1	0.01
Guatemalan	33	0.21
Honduran	4	0.03
Nicaraguan	1	0.01
Panamanian	6	0.04
Salvadoran	63	0.41
Other Central American	1	0.01
Cuban	53	0.34
Dominican Republic	43	0.28
Mexican	88	0.57
Puerto Rican	1,166	7.55
South American:	129	0.84
Argentinean	3	0.02
Bolivian	5	0.03
Chilean	4	0.03
Colombian	38	0.25
Ecuadorian	42	0.27
Paraguayan	1	0.01
Peruvian	20	0.13
Uruguayan	6	0.04
Venezuelan	7	0.05
Other South American	3	0.02
Other Hispanic or Latino	287	1.86
Hungarian	52	0.33
Irish	4,849	31.23
Italian	5,435	35.01
Latvian	10	0.06
Lithuanian	74	0.48
Maltese	43	0.28
Norwegian	129	0.83
Polish	832	5.36
Portuguese	148	0.95
Romanian	10	0.06
Russian	177	1.14
Scandinavian	27	0.17
Scotch-Irish	210	1.35
Scottish	84	0.54
Slavic	37	0.24
Slovak	9	0.06
Swedish	97	0.62
Swiss	11	0.07
Turkish	44	0.28
Ukrainian	35	0.23
United States or American	336	2.16
Welsh	14	0.09
West Indian, excl. Hispanic:	173	1.11
British West Indian	11	0.07
Haitian	35	0.23
Jamaican	64	0.41
Trinidadian and Tobagonian	49	0.32
West Indian	14	0.09
White:	13,415	86.91
Not Hispanic (11,999)	12,183	78.93
Hispanic (1,162)	1,232	7.98

Medford

Place Type: Census Designated Place
County: Suffolk
Population: 21,985

Ancestry/Race	Number	%
African American/Black:	1,021	4.64
Not Hispanic (812)	912	4.15
Hispanic (63)	109	0.50
African, sub-Saharan:	58	0.26
African	4	0.02
Nigerian	54	0.25
Alaska Native tribes, specified:	2	0.01
Alaska Athabascan (1)	1	0.00
Eskimo (1)	1	0.00
Am. Ind. or Alaska Nat., not spec.	66	0.30
American Indian tribes, specified:	70	0.32
Blackfeet (1)	10	0.05
Cherokee	11	0.05
Chickasaw (3)	3	0.01

Notes: 1. Figures in the "Number" column do not add up to the total population due to: a) Ancestry/Race overlap — e.g. persons can report being both White and Irish, b) persons of Hispanic origin can report being any race, c) persons reporting two ancestries are counted in both categories. 2. Numbers in parentheses indicate the number of persons reporting this ancestry/race alone, not in combination with any other ancestry/race. 3. Refer to the Explanation of Data in the front of the book for more detailed information.

Chippewa (2)	2	0.01
Choctaw	1	0.00
Iroquois (2)	11	0.05
Latin American Indians (3)	24	0.11
Seminole	1	0.00
Sioux (2)	2	0.01
All other tribes (2)	5	0.02
American Indian tribes, not spec.	1	0.00
Arab:	62	0.28
Egyptian	28	0.13
Syrian	34	0.15
Armenian	23	0.10
Asian:	427	1.94
Bangladeshi (8)	8	0.04
Cambodian (2)	3	0.01
Chinese, ex. Taiwanese (75)	98	0.45
Filipino (30)	48	0.22
Indian (90)	117	0.53
Indonesian (2)	3	0.01
Japanese (13)	24	0.11
Korean (32)	44	0.20
Laotian (5)	5	0.02
Pakistani (8)	26	0.12
Sri Lankan (2)	2	0.01
Taiwanese (8)	8	0.04
Thai (2)	5	0.02
Vietnamese (11)	14	0.06
Other Asian, not specified (7)	22	0.10
Australian	18	0.08
Austrian	192	0.87
Belgian	20	0.09
Brazilian	4	0.02
British	47	0.21
Canadian	76	0.35
Croatian	10	0.05
Czech	152	0.69
Czechoslovakian	40	0.18
Danish	36	0.16
Dutch	141	0.64
Eastern European	11	0.05
English	1,410	6.41
Estonian	6	0.03
European	62	0.28
Finnish	27	0.12
French, except Basque	421	1.91
French Canadian	148	0.67
German	4,463	20.30
Greek	230	1.05
Guyanese	38	0.17
Hawaii Native/Pacific Islander:	14	0.06
Micronesian:	1	0.00
Guamanian/Chamorro	1	0.00
Polynesian: (5)	11	0.05
Native Hawaiian (2)	5	0.02
Samoan (3)	6	0.03
Other Pac. Isl., not spec.	2	0.01
Hispanic or Latino:	2,373	10.79
Central American:	138	0.63
Costa Rican	2	0.01
Guatemalan	49	0.22
Honduran	1	0.00
Nicaraguan	1	0.00
Panamanian	5	0.02
Salvadoran	78	0.35
Other Central American	2	0.01
Cuban	55	0.25
Dominican Republic	70	0.32
Mexican	238	1.08
Puerto Rican	1,141	5.19
South American:	269	1.22
Argentinean	15	0.07
Chilean	9	0.04
Colombian	55	0.25
Ecuadorian	142	0.65
Paraguayan	1	0.00
Peruvian	28	0.13
Uruguayan	3	0.01
Venezuelan	3	0.01
Other South American	13	0.06
Other Hispanic or Latino	462	2.10
Hungarian	151	0.69
Irish	5,261	23.93
Israeli	11	0.05
Italian	7,186	32.69
Lithuanian	58	0.26
Maltese	18	0.08
Northern European	8	0.04
Norwegian	252	1.15
Polish	1,153	5.24
Portuguese	221	1.01
Romanian	65	0.30
Russian	498	2.27
Scandinavian	5	0.02
Scotch-Irish	215	0.98
Scottish	305	1.39
Slovak	16	0.07
Swedish	250	1.14
Turkish	138	0.63
Ukrainian	115	0.52
United States or American	580	2.64
Welsh	36	0.16
West Indian, excl. Hispanic:	196	0.89
Belizean	9	0.04
Haitian	115	0.52
Jamaican	27	0.12
Trinidadian and Tobagonian	5	0.02
West Indian	40	0.18
White:	19,946	90.73
Not Hispanic (18,144)	18,347	83.45
Hispanic (1,463)	1,599	7.27
Yugoslavian	17	0.08

Melville

Place Type: Census Designated Place
County: Suffolk
Population: 14,533

Ancestry/Race	Number	%
Afghan	70	0.48
African American/Black:	344	2.37
Not Hispanic (294)	325	2.24
Hispanic (6)	19	0.13
African, sub-Saharan:	48	0.33
African	42	0.29
South African	6	0.04
Am. Ind. or Alaska Nat., not spec.	11	0.08
Alsatian	10	0.07
American Indian tribes, specified:	9	0.06
Apache	1	0.01
Blackfeet	1	0.01
Cherokee (1)	2	0.01
Latin American Indians	3	0.02
All other tribes	2	0.01
Arab:	131	0.90
Egyptian	125	0.86
Jordanian	6	0.04
Armenian	69	0.47
Asian:	877	6.03
Chinese, ex. Taiwanese (209)	219	1.51
Filipino (51)	64	0.44
Indian (304)	330	2.27
Indonesian (1)	1	0.01
Japanese (26)	31	0.21
Korean (98)	105	0.72
Pakistani (66)	69	0.47
Sri Lankan (5)	5	0.03
Taiwanese (11)	11	0.08
Thai (2)	5	0.03
Vietnamese	1	0.01
Other Asian, not specified (7)	36	0.25
Australian	5	0.03
Austrian	184	1.27
Belgian	4	0.03
British	37	0.25
Canadian	26	0.18
Croatian	15	0.10
Czech	49	0.34
Czechoslovakian	71	0.49
Danish	17	0.12
Dutch	49	0.34
Eastern European	244	1.68
English	525	3.61
European	124	0.85
Finnish	30	0.21
French, except Basque	196	1.35
French Canadian	24	0.17
German	1,558	10.72
Greek	243	1.67
Guyanese	10	0.07
Hawaii Native/Pacific Islander:	11	0.08
Micronesian: (8)	8	0.06
Guamanian/Chamorro (8)	8	0.06
Polynesian: (1)	1	0.01
Native Hawaiian (1)	1	0.01
Other Pac. Isl., not spec. (1)	2	0.01
Hispanic or Latino:	540	3.72
Central American:	36	0.25
Guatemalan	2	0.01
Honduran	1	0.01
Panamanian	7	0.05
Salvadoran	25	0.17
Other Central American	1	0.01
Cuban	16	0.11
Dominican Republic	25	0.17
Mexican	37	0.25
Puerto Rican	227	1.56
South American:	66	0.45
Argentinean	12	0.08
Bolivian	1	0.01
Chilean	1	0.01
Colombian	19	0.13
Ecuadorian	14	0.10
Paraguayan	3	0.02
Peruvian	9	0.06
Venezuelan	5	0.03
Other South American	2	0.01
Other Hispanic or Latino	133	0.92
Hungarian	227	1.56
Iranian	20	0.14
Irish	1,571	10.81
Israeli	90	0.62
Italian	3,862	26.56
Latvian	5	0.03
Lithuanian	74	0.51
Maltese	30	0.21
Norwegian	69	0.47
Polish	957	6.58
Portuguese	59	0.41
Romanian	136	0.94
Russian	1,195	8.22
Scotch-Irish	59	0.41
Scottish	107	0.74
Slavic	53	0.36
Slovak	12	0.08
Swedish	151	1.04
Turkish	53	0.36
Ukrainian	128	0.88
United States or American	802	5.52
West Indian, excl. Hispanic:	102	0.70
Haitian	87	0.60
Jamaican	6	0.04
West Indian	9	0.06
White:	13,233	91.05
Not Hispanic (12,711)	12,844	88.38
Hispanic (359)	389	2.68
Yugoslavian	27	0.19

Merrick

Place Type: Census Designated Place
County: Nassau
Population: 22,764

Ancestry/Race	Number	%
Acadian/Cajun	6	0.03
African American/Black:	166	0.73
Not Hispanic (109)	136	0.60
Hispanic (18)	30	0.13
African, sub-Saharan:	9	0.04

Notes: 1. Figures in the "Number" column do not add up to the total population due to: a) Ancestry/Race overlap — e.g. persons can report being both White and Irish, b) persons of Hispanic origin can report being any race, c) persons reporting two ancestries are counted in both categories. 2. Numbers in parentheses indicate the number of persons reporting this ancestry/race alone, not in combination with any other ancestry/race. 3. Refer to the Explanation of Data in the front of the book for more detailed information.

Ancestry/Race	Number	%
African	9	0.04
Am. Ind. or Alaska Nat., not spec.	16	0.07
Alsatian	5	0.02
American Indian tribes, specified:	38	0.17
Blackfeet	3	0.01
Cherokee (4)	13	0.06
Choctaw	1	0.00
Iroquois (8)	11	0.05
Latin American Indians (3)	7	0.03
Pueblo	2	0.01
All other tribes (1)	1	0.00
American Indian tribes, not spec.	3	0.01
Arab:	75	0.33
Egyptian	31	0.14
Lebanese	4	0.02
Moroccan	9	0.04
Palestinian	7	0.03
Syrian	24	0.11
Armenian	6	0.03
Asian:	597	2.62
Bangladeshi (15)	15	0.07
Chinese, ex. Taiwanese (196)	218	0.96
Filipino (33)	48	0.21
Indian (160)	177	0.78
Japanese (4)	13	0.06
Korean (66)	72	0.32
Malaysian	1	0.00
Pakistani (19)	22	0.10
Thai (1)	1	0.00
Vietnamese (6)	10	0.04
Other Asian, not specified (6)	20	0.09
Australian	6	0.03
Austrian	461	2.03
Belgian	18	0.08
Brazilian	21	0.09
British	50	0.22
Canadian	76	0.33
Czech	85	0.37
Czechoslovakian	36	0.16
Danish	24	0.11
Dutch	175	0.77
Eastern European	339	1.49
English	776	3.41
Estonian	13	0.06
European	61	0.27
Finnish	55	0.24
French, except Basque	192	0.84
German	2,638	11.59
Greek	446	1.96
Hawaii Native/Pacific Islander:	4	0.02
Polynesian: (1)	1	0.00
Samoan (1)	1	0.00
Other Pac. Isl., not spec. (1)	3	0.01
Hispanic or Latino:	842	3.70
Central American:	83	0.36
Costa Rican	6	0.03
Guatemalan	21	0.09
Honduran	1	0.00
Panamanian	3	0.01
Salvadoran	48	0.21
Other Central American	4	0.02
Cuban	65	0.29
Dominican Republic	85	0.37
Mexican	40	0.18
Puerto Rican	236	1.04
South American:	145	0.64
Argentinean	16	0.07
Bolivian	4	0.02
Chilean	7	0.03
Colombian	46	0.20
Ecuadorian	40	0.18
Paraguayan	6	0.03
Peruvian	12	0.05
Uruguayan	1	0.00
Venezuelan	3	0.01
Other South American	10	0.04
Other Hispanic or Latino	188	0.83
Hungarian	284	1.25
Iranian	35	0.15
Irish	3,790	16.65
Israeli	125	0.55
Italian	4,998	21.96
Latvian	17	0.07
Lithuanian	106	0.47
Maltese	20	0.09
Norwegian	142	0.62
Polish	2,101	9.23
Portuguese	43	0.19
Romanian	157	0.69
Russian	2,502	10.99
Scandinavian	38	0.17
Scotch-Irish	75	0.33
Scottish	212	0.93
Serbian	11	0.05
Slavic	5	0.02
Slovak	42	0.18
Slovene	18	0.08
Swedish	174	0.76
Swiss	44	0.19
Turkish	59	0.26
Ukrainian	221	0.97
United States or American	1,879	8.25
Welsh	24	0.11
West Indian, excl. Hispanic:	37	0.16
British West Indian	9	0.04
Haitian	4	0.02
Jamaican	8	0.04
West Indian	16	0.07
White:	21,873	96.09
Not Hispanic (21,097)	21,257	93.38
Hispanic (569)	616	2.71
Yugoslavian	59	0.26

Middletown

Place Type: City
County: Orange
Population: 25,388

Ancestry/Race	Number	%
African American/Black:	4,423	17.42
Not Hispanic (3,350)	3,776	14.87
Hispanic (490)	647	2.55
African, sub-Saharan:	131	0.52
African	113	0.45
South African	18	0.07
Alaska Native tribes, specified:	1	0.00
Tlingit-Haida (1)	1	0.00
Am. Ind. or Alaska Nat., not spec.	218	0.86
American Indian tribes, specified:	143	0.56
Apache	2	0.01
Blackfeet (1)	11	0.04
Cherokee (4)	38	0.15
Chippewa	1	0.00
Choctaw	1	0.00
Creek	1	0.00
Delaware (8)	13	0.05
Iroquois (11)	23	0.09
Latin American Indians (20)	31	0.12
Navajo (3)	3	0.01
Osage	1	0.00
Paiute	2	0.01
Pueblo	1	0.00
Sioux	5	0.02
Ute	1	0.00
Yakama	1	0.00
All other tribes (3)	8	0.03
American Indian tribes, not spec.	27	0.11
Arab:	53	0.21
Lebanese	28	0.11
Syrian	25	0.10
Armenian	13	0.05
Asian:	555	2.19
Bangladeshi (1)	1	0.00
Cambodian (10)	18	0.07
Chinese, ex. Taiwanese (61)	86	0.34
Filipino (54)	70	0.28
Indian (201)	225	0.89
Indonesian	1	0.00
Japanese (8)	23	0.09
Korean (21)	25	0.10
Laotian (3)	3	0.01
Pakistani (13)	27	0.11
Sri Lankan (2)	2	0.01
Taiwanese (3)	5	0.02
Thai (5)	8	0.03
Vietnamese (23)	26	0.10
Other Asian, specified (10)	11	0.04
Other Asian, not specified (3)	24	0.09
Austrian	70	0.28
Brazilian	25	0.10
British	54	0.21
Bulgarian	7	0.03
Canadian	43	0.17
Carpatho Rusyn	12	0.05
Czech	29	0.11
Czechoslovakian	49	0.19
Danish	128	0.51
Dutch	618	2.44
Eastern European	38	0.15
English	1,577	6.23
European	39	0.15
Finnish	34	0.13
French, except Basque	435	1.72
French Canadian	93	0.37
German	2,803	11.07
Greek	252	0.99
Guyanese	45	0.18
Hawaii Native/Pacific Islander:	40	0.16
Micronesian:	4	0.02
Guamanian/Chamorro	4	0.02
Polynesian: (1)	19	0.07
Native Hawaiian	18	0.07
Samoan (1)	1	0.00
Other Pac. Isl., not spec. (6)	17	0.07
Hispanic or Latino:	6,375	25.11
Central American:	260	1.02
Costa Rican	15	0.06
Guatemalan	15	0.06
Honduran	124	0.49
Nicaraguan	11	0.04
Panamanian	60	0.24
Salvadoran	33	0.13
Other Central American	2	0.01
Cuban	51	0.20
Dominican Republic	124	0.49
Mexican	2,038	8.03
Puerto Rican	3,066	12.08
South American:	206	0.81
Argentinean	6	0.02
Bolivian	4	0.02
Chilean	3	0.01
Colombian	109	0.43
Ecuadorian	15	0.06
Paraguayan	2	0.01
Peruvian	51	0.20
Uruguayan	1	0.00
Venezuelan	1	0.00
Other South American	14	0.06
Other Hispanic or Latino	630	2.48
Hungarian	164	0.65
Irish	4,276	16.88
Israeli	7	0.03
Italian	3,761	14.85
Latvian	26	0.10
Lithuanian	20	0.08
Macedonian	42	0.17
Northern European	10	0.04
Norwegian	106	0.42
Pennsylvania German	8	0.03
Polish	1,414	5.58
Portuguese	16	0.06
Romanian	21	0.08
Russian	291	1.15
Scandinavian	17	0.07
Scotch-Irish	190	0.75
Scottish	196	0.77
Slovak	35	0.14
Slovene	10	0.04
Swedish	113	0.45

Notes: 1. Figures in the "Number" column do not add up to the total population due to: a) Ancestry/Race overlap — e.g. persons can report being both White and Irish, b) persons of Hispanic origin can report being any race, c) persons reporting two ancestries are counted in both categories. 2. Numbers in parentheses indicate the number of persons reporting this ancestry/race alone, not in combination with any other ancestry/race. 3. Refer to the Explanation of Data in the front of the book for more detailed information.

Swiss	78	0.31
Ukrainian	84	0.33
United States or American	993	3.92
Welsh	103	0.41
West Indian, excl. Hispanic:	503	1.99
Bermudan	5	0.02
British West Indian	27	0.11
Haitian	19	0.08
Jamaican	346	1.37
Trinidadian and Tobagonian	50	0.20
U.S. Virgin Islander	10	0.04
West Indian	46	0.18
White:	18,294	72.06
Not Hispanic (14,423)	14,882	58.62
Hispanic (3,014)	3,412	13.44

Miller Place

Place Type: Census Designated Place
County: Suffolk
Population: 10,580

Ancestry/Race	Number	%
African American/Black:	66	0.62
Not Hispanic (38)	53	0.50
Hispanic (7)	13	0.12
African, sub-Saharan:	11	0.10
African	11	0.10
Am. Ind. or Alaska Nat., not spec.	9	0.09
American Indian tribes, specified:	16	0.15
Blackfeet	2	0.02
Cherokee	2	0.02
Iroquois (2)	4	0.04
Latin American Indians (1)	2	0.02
Pueblo (3)	3	0.03
All other tribes (2)	3	0.03
American Indian tribes, not spec.	11	0.10
Arab:	19	0.18
Syrian	19	0.18
Armenian	68	0.64
Asian:	168	1.59
Chinese, ex. Taiwanese (42)	51	0.48
Filipino (39)	47	0.44
Indian (22)	23	0.22
Japanese (3)	6	0.06
Korean (17)	21	0.20
Laotian	1	0.01
Pakistani (12)	13	0.12
Thai (1)	2	0.02
Vietnamese (2)	3	0.03
Other Asian, not specified	1	0.01
Australian	10	0.09
Austrian	83	0.78
Belgian	10	0.09
Brazilian	15	0.14
British	32	0.30
Canadian	21	0.20
Croatian	5	0.05
Czech	125	1.17
Czechoslovakian	19	0.18
Danish	56	0.52
Dutch	92	0.86
Eastern European	21	0.20
English	755	7.08
European	26	0.24
Finnish	37	0.35
French, except Basque	199	1.87
French Canadian	82	0.77
German	2,368	22.20
Greek	281	2.63
Guyanese	14	0.13
Hispanic or Latino:	339	3.20
Central American:	11	0.10
Costa Rican	3	0.03
Guatemalan	1	0.01
Nicaraguan	1	0.01
Salvadoran	6	0.06
Cuban	15	0.14
Dominican Republic	15	0.14
Mexican	16	0.15
Puerto Rican	160	1.51
South American:	50	0.47
Argentinean	8	0.08
Bolivian	1	0.01
Chilean	3	0.03
Colombian	11	0.10
Ecuadorian	5	0.05
Peruvian	13	0.12
Venezuelan	4	0.04
Other South American	5	0.05
Other Hispanic or Latino	72	0.68
Hungarian	126	1.18
Irish	3,459	32.43
Italian	3,452	32.36
Lithuanian	51	0.48
Norwegian	203	1.90
Polish	655	6.14
Portuguese	79	0.74
Romanian	36	0.34
Russian	320	3.00
Scotch-Irish	161	1.51
Scottish	160	1.50
Swedish	201	1.88
Turkish	31	0.29
Ukrainian	42	0.39
United States or American	469	4.40
Welsh	16	0.15
West Indian, excl. Hispanic:	64	0.60
Jamaican	52	0.49
Trinidadian and Tobagonian	12	0.11
White:	10,318	97.52
Not Hispanic (9,963)	10,029	94.79
Hispanic (274)	289	2.73

Milton

Place Type: Town
County: Saratoga
Population: 17,103

Ancestry/Race	Number	%
African American/Black:	233	1.36
Not Hispanic (169)	223	1.30
Hispanic (6)	10	0.06
African, sub-Saharan:	5	0.03
Cape Verdean	5	0.03
Am. Ind. or Alaska Nat., not spec.	44	0.26
Albanian	7	0.04
American Indian tribes, specified:	87	0.51
Apache (1)	1	0.01
Blackfeet (2)	9	0.05
Cherokee (7)	17	0.10
Cheyenne	1	0.01
Comanche	2	0.01
Iroquois (11)	29	0.17
Latin American Indians	3	0.02
Lumbee (1)	4	0.02
Navajo (4)	4	0.02
Seminole	2	0.01
Sioux (1)	5	0.03
All other tribes (1)	10	0.06
American Indian tribes, not spec.	4	0.02
Arab:	86	0.50
Lebanese	48	0.28
Syrian	38	0.22
Armenian	17	0.10
Asian:	135	0.79
Cambodian (6)	6	0.04
Chinese, ex. Taiwanese (14)	20	0.12
Filipino (25)	37	0.22
Indian (6)	9	0.05
Indonesian	2	0.01
Japanese (11)	22	0.13
Korean (12)	25	0.15
Sri Lankan (2)	2	0.01
Taiwanese (1)	3	0.02
Thai (3)	5	0.03
Vietnamese (1)	3	0.02
Other Asian, not specified	1	0.01
Australian	30	0.18
Austrian	60	0.35
Belgian	17	0.10
British	100	0.58
Canadian	60	0.35
Croatian	8	0.05
Czech	121	0.71
Czechoslovakian	130	0.76
Danish	51	0.30
Dutch	543	3.17
Eastern European	7	0.04
English	2,671	15.61
European	32	0.19
Finnish	18	0.11
French, except Basque	1,803	10.53
French Canadian	646	3.77
German	3,435	20.07
Greek	100	0.58
Hawaii Native/Pacific Islander:	15	0.09
Micronesian: (2)	2	0.01
Guamanian/Chamorro (1)	1	0.01
Other Micronesian (1)	1	0.01
Polynesian: (1)	7	0.04
Native Hawaiian	5	0.03
Samoan (1)	2	0.01
Other Pac. Isl., not spec.	6	0.04
Hispanic or Latino:	299	1.75
Central American:	10	0.06
Honduran	2	0.01
Salvadoran	6	0.04
Other Central American	2	0.01
Cuban	12	0.07
Dominican Republic	4	0.02
Mexican	53	0.31
Puerto Rican	116	0.68
South American:	20	0.12
Chilean	3	0.02
Colombian	3	0.02
Peruvian	12	0.07
Venezuelan	1	0.01
Other South American	1	0.01
Other Hispanic or Latino	84	0.49
Hungarian	131	0.77
Irish	4,394	25.67
Italian	2,808	16.41
Lithuanian	84	0.49
Northern European	21	0.12
Norwegian	185	1.08
Polish	1,165	6.81
Portuguese	41	0.24
Romanian	27	0.16
Russian	112	0.65
Scandinavian	15	0.09
Scotch-Irish	265	1.55
Scottish	379	2.21
Slavic	27	0.16
Slovak	78	0.46
Slovene	44	0.26
Swedish	135	0.79
Swiss	97	0.57
Turkish	9	0.05
Ukrainian	50	0.29
United States or American	691	4.04
Welsh	221	1.29
West Indian, excl. Hispanic:	24	0.14
Jamaican	24	0.14
White:	16,720	97.76
Not Hispanic (16,301)	16,493	96.43
Hispanic (192)	227	1.33
Yugoslavian	35	0.20

Mineola

Place Type: Village
County: Nassau
Population: 19,234

Ancestry/Race	Number	%
African American/Black:	261	1.36
Not Hispanic (179)	221	1.15
Hispanic (20)	40	0.21

Notes: 1. Figures in the "Number" column do not add up to the total population due to: a) Ancestry/Race overlap — e.g. persons can report being both White and Irish, b) persons of Hispanic origin can report being any race, c) persons reporting two ancestries are counted in both categories. 2. Numbers in parentheses indicate the number of persons reporting this ancestry/race alone, not in combination with any other ancestry/race. 3. Refer to the Explanation of Data in the front of the book for more detailed information.

Ancestry/Race	Number	%
African, sub-Saharan:	32	0.17
Cape Verdean	7	0.04
South African	16	0.08
Other sub-Saharan African	9	0.05
Alaska Native tribes, specified:	1	0.01
Alaska Athabascan	1	0.01
Am. Ind. or Alaska Nat., not spec.	54	0.28
Albanian	37	0.19
American Indian tribes, specified:	53	0.28
Apache (2)	2	0.01
Cherokee (1)	4	0.02
Cheyenne (2)	2	0.01
Crow	1	0.01
Iroquois	1	0.01
Latin American Indians (21)	32	0.17
Sioux (1)	1	0.01
All other tribes (5)	10	0.05
American Indian tribes, not spec.	8	0.04
Arab:	92	0.48
Arab/Arabic	7	0.04
Iraqi	37	0.19
Moroccan	35	0.18
Other Arab	13	0.07
Armenian	69	0.36
Asian:	1,000	5.20
Bangladeshi (4)	4	0.02
Chinese, ex. Taiwanese (216)	230	1.20
Filipino (102)	130	0.68
Indian (326)	359	1.87
Indonesian (4)	4	0.02
Japanese (19)	29	0.15
Korean (136)	146	0.76
Malaysian	2	0.01
Pakistani (12)	15	0.08
Sri Lankan (1)	1	0.01
Taiwanese (8)	10	0.05
Thai (2)	5	0.03
Vietnamese (23)	25	0.13
Other Asian, specified (1)	3	0.02
Other Asian, not specified (3)	37	0.19
Austrian	104	0.54
Basque	25	0.13
Belgian	11	0.06
Brazilian	45	0.23
British	50	0.26
Canadian	14	0.07
Croatian	23	0.12
Czech	50	0.26
Czechoslovakian	139	0.72
Danish	28	0.15
Dutch	57	0.30
Eastern European	18	0.09
English	594	3.09
Estonian	19	0.10
European	68	0.35
Finnish	18	0.09
French, except Basque	245	1.27
German	2,741	14.25
Greek	219	1.14
Hawaii Native/Pacific Islander:	27	0.14
Micronesian: (1)	4	0.02
Guamanian/Chamorro (1)	4	0.02
Polynesian:	6	0.03
Samoan	6	0.03
Other Pac. Isl., not spec. (7)	17	0.09
Hispanic or Latino:	2,507	13.03
Central American:	688	3.58
Costa Rican	12	0.06
Guatemalan	54	0.28
Honduran	50	0.26
Panamanian	1	0.01
Salvadoran	532	2.77
Other Central American	39	0.20
Cuban	43	0.22
Dominican Republic	63	0.33
Mexican	90	0.47
Puerto Rican	245	1.27
South American:	527	2.74
Argentinean	32	0.17
Bolivian	1	0.01
Chilean	34	0.18
Colombian	232	1.21
Ecuadorian	95	0.49
Paraguayan	26	0.14
Peruvian	39	0.20
Uruguayan	9	0.05
Venezuelan	13	0.07
Other South American	46	0.24
Other Hispanic or Latino	851	4.42
Hungarian	156	0.81
Iranian	179	0.93
Irish	3,754	19.51
Italian	4,616	23.99
Latvian	14	0.07
Lithuanian	98	0.51
Maltese	8	0.04
Northern European	5	0.03
Norwegian	169	0.88
Pennsylvania German	7	0.04
Polish	906	4.71
Portuguese	2,076	10.79
Romanian	50	0.26
Russian	334	1.74
Scandinavian	52	0.27
Scotch-Irish	61	0.32
Scottish	148	0.77
Slavic	5	0.03
Slovak	23	0.12
Swedish	175	0.91
Swiss	37	0.19
Turkish	25	0.13
Ukrainian	137	0.71
United States or American	447	2.32
Welsh	58	0.30
West Indian, excl. Hispanic:	75	0.39
Haitian	32	0.17
Jamaican	29	0.15
Trinidadian and Tobagonian	5	0.03
West Indian	9	0.05
White:	17,278	89.83
Not Hispanic (15,227)	15,563	80.91
Hispanic (1,390)	1,715	8.92
Yugoslavian	23	0.12

Monroe

Place Type: Town
County: Orange
Population: 31,407

Ancestry/Race	Number	%
Afghan	6	0.02
African American/Black:	477	1.52
Not Hispanic (369)	435	1.39
Hispanic (13)	42	0.13
African, sub-Saharan:	24	0.08
African	7	0.02
Ethiopian	17	0.05
Am. Ind. or Alaska Nat., not spec.	66	0.21
Albanian	47	0.15
American Indian tribes, specified:	80	0.25
Blackfeet	5	0.02
Cherokee (2)	16	0.05
Cheyenne	2	0.01
Chippewa	1	0.00
Choctaw	3	0.01
Delaware (21)	21	0.07
Iroquois (5)	10	0.03
Latin American Indians (9)	21	0.07
All other tribes	1	0.00
American Indian tribes, not spec.	1	0.00
Arab:	107	0.34
Arab/Arabic	7	0.02
Egyptian	36	0.11
Lebanese	12	0.04
Syrian	52	0.17
Armenian	34	0.11
Asian:	532	1.69
Cambodian (1)	1	0.00
Chinese, ex. Taiwanese (130)	141	0.45
Filipino (96)	115	0.37
Indian (118)	137	0.44
Indonesian (2)	4	0.01
Japanese (28)	38	0.12
Korean (31)	39	0.12
Laotian (1)	2	0.01
Sri Lankan (3)	3	0.01
Taiwanese (2)	2	0.01
Thai (3)	3	0.01
Vietnamese (6)	9	0.03
Other Asian, not specified (5)	38	0.12
Austrian	112	0.36
Basque	8	0.03
Belgian	44	0.14
Brazilian	4	0.01
British	130	0.41
Bulgarian	14	0.04
Canadian	76	0.24
Carpatho Rusyn	8	0.03
Croatian	13	0.04
Cypriot	11	0.03
Czech	101	0.32
Czechoslovakian	104	0.33
Danish	10	0.03
Dutch	189	0.60
Eastern European	31	0.10
English	983	3.12
Estonian	5	0.02
European	137	0.43
Finnish	20	0.06
French, except Basque	259	0.82
French Canadian	55	0.17
German	2,829	8.98
Greek	66	0.21
Hawaii Native/Pacific Islander:	9	0.03
Polynesian: (1)	2	0.01
Samoan (1)	2	0.01
Other Pac. Isl., not spec.	7	0.02
Hispanic or Latino:	1,543	4.91
Central American:	20	0.06
Guatemalan	1	0.00
Honduran	11	0.04
Nicaraguan	1	0.00
Panamanian	3	0.01
Salvadoran	3	0.01
Other Central American	1	0.00
Cuban	56	0.18
Dominican Republic	63	0.20
Mexican	282	0.90
Puerto Rican	712	2.27
South American:	172	0.55
Argentinean	56	0.18
Bolivian	3	0.01
Chilean	15	0.05
Colombian	29	0.09
Ecuadorian	43	0.14
Paraguayan	1	0.00
Peruvian	15	0.05
Uruguayan	3	0.01
Venezuelan	2	0.01
Other South American	5	0.02
Other Hispanic or Latino	238	0.76
Hungarian	2,620	8.32
Iranian	19	0.06
Irish	4,599	14.60
Israeli	305	0.97
Italian	4,090	12.99
Latvian	68	0.22
Lithuanian	37	0.12
Maltese	44	0.14
Norwegian	152	0.48
Pennsylvania German	17	0.05
Polish	1,467	4.66
Portuguese	100	0.32
Romanian	311	0.99
Russian	695	2.21
Scotch-Irish	211	0.67
Scottish	250	0.79
Slavic	14	0.04
Slovak	67	0.21

Notes: 1. Figures in the "Number" column do not add up to the total population due to: a) Ancestry/Race overlap — e.g. persons can report being both White and Irish, b) persons of Hispanic origin can report being any race, c) persons reporting two ancestries are counted in both categories. 2. Numbers in parentheses indicate the number of persons reporting this ancestry/race alone, not in combination with any other ancestry/race. 3. Refer to the Explanation of Data in the front of the book for more detailed information.

Swedish	118	0.37
Swiss	43	0.14
Turkish	16	0.05
Ukrainian	475	1.51
United States or American	1,588	5.04
Welsh	28	0.09
West Indian, excl. Hispanic:	147	0.47
British West Indian	4	0.01
Jamaican	52	0.17
Trinidadian and Tobagonian	69	0.22
West Indian	22	0.07
White:	30,089	95.80
Not Hispanic (28,748)	28,943	92.15
Hispanic (1,061)	1,146	3.65
Yugoslavian	80	0.25

Monsey

Place Type: Census Designated Place
County: Rockland
Population: 14,504

Ancestry/Race	Number	%
African American/Black:	677	4.67
Not Hispanic (606)	650	4.48
Hispanic (20)	27	0.19
African, sub-Saharan:	66	0.45
African	62	0.42
Other sub-Saharan African	4	0.03
Am. Ind. or Alaska Nat., not spec.	12	0.08
American Indian tribes, specified:	6	0.04
Cherokee (5)	5	0.03
Delaware	1	0.01
Arab:	90	0.61
Palestinian	58	0.39
Syrian	9	0.06
Other Arab	23	0.16
Asian:	178	1.23
Bangladeshi (3)	3	0.02
Cambodian (2)	2	0.01
Chinese, ex. Taiwanese (18)	30	0.21
Filipino (23)	34	0.23
Indian (47)	55	0.38
Indonesian (1)	1	0.01
Japanese (5)	5	0.03
Korean (21)	21	0.14
Pakistani (2)	4	0.03
Sri Lankan (8)	8	0.06
Thai (4)	4	0.03
Vietnamese (1)	3	0.02
Other Asian, not specified (7)	8	0.06
Australian	23	0.16
Austrian	84	0.57
Belgian	8	0.05
Brazilian	10	0.07
British	14	0.10
Canadian	4	0.03
Czech	20	0.14
Czechoslovakian	49	0.33
Danish	15	0.10
Dutch	49	0.33
Eastern European	251	1.71
English	95	0.65
European	662	4.51
French Canadian	32	0.22
German	325	2.21
Greek	7	0.05
Hawaii Native/Pacific Islander:	4	0.03
Melanesian: (1)	1	0.01
Fijian (1)	1	0.01
Polynesian: (1)	3	0.02
Native Hawaiian (1)	3	0.02
Hispanic or Latino:	415	2.86
Central American:	129	0.89
Costa Rican	1	0.01
Guatemalan	95	0.65
Honduran	14	0.10
Nicaraguan	1	0.01
Panamanian	1	0.01
Salvadoran	17	0.12
Cuban	12	0.08
Dominican Republic	9	0.06
Mexican	35	0.24
Puerto Rican	79	0.54
South American:	65	0.45
Argentinean	7	0.05
Colombian	6	0.04
Ecuadorian	39	0.27
Peruvian	1	0.01
Venezuelan	11	0.08
Other South American	1	0.01
Other Hispanic or Latino	86	0.59
Hungarian	752	5.12
Iranian	6	0.04
Irish	101	0.69
Israeli	330	2.25
Italian	214	1.46
Lithuanian	51	0.35
Norwegian	27	0.18
Polish	789	5.37
Portuguese	35	0.24
Romanian	242	1.65
Russian	426	2.90
Scotch-Irish	26	0.18
Scottish	23	0.16
Swedish	21	0.14
Swiss	23	0.16
Ukrainian	19	0.13
United States or American	1,223	8.32
West Indian, excl. Hispanic:	372	2.53
Haitian	317	2.16
Jamaican	55	0.37
White:	13,577	93.61
Not Hispanic (13,170)	13,263	91.44
Hispanic (292)	314	2.16
Yugoslavian	6	0.04

Montgomery

Place Type: Town
County: Orange
Population: 20,891

Ancestry/Race	Number	%
African American/Black:	904	4.33
Not Hispanic (694)	788	3.77
Hispanic (77)	116	0.56
African, sub-Saharan:	32	0.15
African	26	0.12
South African	6	0.03
Am. Ind. or Alaska Nat., not spec.	73	0.35
American Indian tribes, specified:	76	0.36
Apache (1)	1	0.00
Blackfeet (1)	1	0.00
Cherokee (7)	21	0.10
Cheyenne	2	0.01
Chippewa (5)	6	0.03
Choctaw	1	0.00
Comanche (1)	1	0.00
Delaware (4)	7	0.03
Iroquois (6)	11	0.05
Latin American Indians (5)	11	0.05
Pueblo	1	0.00
Shoshone (1)	1	0.00
All other tribes (2)	12	0.06
American Indian tribes, not spec.	4	0.02
Arab:	10	0.05
Syrian	10	0.05
Armenian	18	0.09
Asian:	213	1.02
Bangladeshi (4)	5	0.02
Chinese, ex. Taiwanese (31)	43	0.21
Filipino (23)	36	0.17
Indian (20)	35	0.17
Japanese (4)	17	0.08
Korean (38)	53	0.25
Pakistani (4)	4	0.02
Taiwanese (2)	2	0.01
Thai (3)	3	0.01
Vietnamese (3)	3	0.01
Other Asian, specified	1	0.00
Other Asian, not specified (6)	11	0.05
Australian	6	0.03
Austrian	113	0.54
Belgian	20	0.10
Brazilian	37	0.18
British	10	0.05
Canadian	41	0.20
Celtic	48	0.23
Czech	134	0.64
Czechoslovakian	71	0.34
Danish	64	0.31
Dutch	908	4.35
Eastern European	12	0.06
English	2,368	11.34
Estonian	10	0.05
European	60	0.29
Finnish	27	0.13
French, except Basque	658	3.15
French Canadian	230	1.10
German	3,729	17.85
Greek	132	0.63
Hawaii Native/Pacific Islander:	21	0.10
Micronesian: (1)	5	0.02
Guamanian/Chamorro (1)	5	0.02
Polynesian: (1)	6	0.03
Native Hawaiian (1)	6	0.03
Other Pac. Isl., specified	1	0.00
Other Pac. Isl., not spec.	9	0.04
Hispanic or Latino:	1,620	7.75
Central American:	31	0.15
Costa Rican	1	0.00
Guatemalan	9	0.04
Honduran	10	0.05
Nicaraguan	1	0.00
Panamanian	2	0.01
Salvadoran	6	0.03
Other Central American	2	0.01
Cuban	33	0.16
Dominican Republic	70	0.34
Mexican	135	0.65
Puerto Rican	1,026	4.91
South American:	48	0.23
Argentinean	9	0.04
Chilean	1	0.00
Colombian	11	0.05
Ecuadorian	7	0.03
Peruvian	8	0.04
Uruguayan	6	0.03
Venezuelan	2	0.01
Other South American	4	0.02
Other Hispanic or Latino	277	1.33
Hungarian	215	1.03
Irish	5,213	24.95
Israeli	5	0.02
Italian	4,810	23.02
Lithuanian	51	0.24
Macedonian	12	0.06
Maltese	5	0.02
Northern European	10	0.05
Norwegian	321	1.54
Polish	1,221	5.84
Portuguese	95	0.45
Romanian	4	0.02
Russian	127	0.61
Scandinavian	79	0.38
Scotch-Irish	332	1.59
Scottish	356	1.70
Slavic	106	0.51
Slovak	42	0.20
Slovene	16	0.08
Swedish	249	1.19
Swiss	56	0.27
Turkish	5	0.02
Ukrainian	87	0.42
United States or American	757	3.62
Welsh	73	0.35
West Indian, excl. Hispanic:	76	0.36
British West Indian	9	0.04
Haitian	16	0.08

Notes: 1. Figures in the "Number" column do not add up to the total population due to: a) Ancestry/Race overlap — e.g. persons can report being both White and Irish, b) persons of Hispanic origin can report being any race, c) persons reporting two ancestries are counted in both categories. 2. Numbers in parentheses indicate the number of persons reporting this ancestry/race alone, not in combination with any other ancestry/race. 3. Refer to the Explanation of Data in the front of the book for more detailed information.

Jamaican	35	0.17
Trinidadian and Tobagonian	16	0.08
White:	19,380	92.77
Not Hispanic (18,138)	18,344	87.81
Hispanic (931)	1,036	4.96
Yugoslavian	67	0.32

Moreau

Place Type: Town
County: Saratoga
Population: 13,826

Ancestry/Race	Number	%
African American/Black:	520	3.76
Not Hispanic (479)	502	3.63
Hispanic (16)	18	0.13
African, sub-Saharan:	6	0.04
African	6	0.04
Am. Ind. or Alaska Nat., not spec.	16	0.12
American Indian tribes, specified:	56	0.41
Cherokee (3)	9	0.07
Comanche (1)	1	0.01
Iroquois (7)	18	0.13
Latin American Indians (1)	4	0.03
Lumbee	1	0.01
Navajo	1	0.01
Pueblo (3)	3	0.02
Sioux	4	0.03
All other tribes (3)	15	0.11
American Indian tribes, not spec.	4	0.03
Arab:	35	0.25
Arab/Arabic	6	0.04
Lebanese	7	0.05
Syrian	22	0.16
Asian:	76	0.55
Chinese, ex. Taiwanese (11)	13	0.09
Filipino (15)	21	0.15
Indian (3)	4	0.03
Japanese (2)	12	0.09
Korean (21)	24	0.17
Vietnamese	1	0.01
Other Asian, not specified	1	0.01
Austrian	5	0.04
Belgian	6	0.04
British	39	0.28
Canadian	77	0.56
Czech	21	0.15
Czechoslovakian	21	0.15
Dutch	650	4.70
English	2,054	14.86
European	39	0.28
Finnish	6	0.04
French, except Basque	2,248	16.26
French Canadian	684	4.95
German	1,517	10.97
Greek	6	0.04
Hawaii Native/Pacific Islander:	15	0.11
Micronesian: (2)	3	0.02
Guamanian/Chamorro (2)	3	0.02
Polynesian: (1)	4	0.03
Native Hawaiian (1)	2	0.01
Samoan	2	0.01
Other Pac. Isl., not spec.	8	0.06
Hispanic or Latino:	289	2.09
Central American:	7	0.05
Panamanian	2	0.01
Salvadoran	4	0.03
Other Central American	1	0.01
Cuban	6	0.04
Dominican Republic	23	0.17
Mexican	22	0.16
Puerto Rican	192	1.39
South American:	8	0.06
Colombian	5	0.04
Ecuadorian	2	0.01
Uruguayan	1	0.01
Other Hispanic or Latino	31	0.22
Hungarian	49	0.35
Irish	3,067	22.18
Italian	1,598	11.56
Latvian	12	0.09
Lithuanian	43	0.31
Maltese	8	0.06
Northern European	6	0.04
Norwegian	111	0.80
Pennsylvania German	10	0.07
Polish	461	3.33
Portuguese	6	0.04
Russian	40	0.29
Scandinavian	34	0.25
Scotch-Irish	255	1.84
Scottish	370	2.68
Slavic	6	0.04
Slovak	15	0.11
Slovene	8	0.06
Swedish	188	1.36
Swiss	40	0.29
Ukrainian	15	0.11
United States or American	839	6.07
Welsh	139	1.01
White:	13,089	94.67
Not Hispanic (12,890)	12,966	93.78
Hispanic (116)	123	0.89

Mount Pleasant

Place Type: Town
County: Westchester
Population: 43,221

Ancestry/Race	Number	%
Afghan	3	0.01
African American/Black:	2,360	5.46
Not Hispanic (1,962)	2,041	4.72
Hispanic (229)	319	0.74
African, sub-Saharan:	105	0.24
African	52	0.12
Ethiopian	7	0.02
Nigerian	11	0.03
South African	35	0.08
Am. Ind. or Alaska Nat., not spec.	104	0.24
Albanian	95	0.22
Alsatian	6	0.01
American Indian tribes, specified:	101	0.23
Blackfeet (1)	3	0.01
Cherokee (5)	27	0.06
Cheyenne (1)	1	0.00
Chippewa (1)	1	0.00
Choctaw (2)	2	0.00
Delaware	1	0.00
Iroquois	5	0.01
Latin American Indians (25)	52	0.12
Navajo	1	0.00
Ottawa (1)	1	0.00
Sioux	2	0.00
All other tribes (2)	5	0.01
American Indian tribes, not spec.	16	0.04
Arab:	370	0.86
Arab/Arabic	19	0.04
Egyptian	106	0.25
Jordanian	33	0.08
Lebanese	185	0.43
Moroccan	5	0.01
Syrian	22	0.05
Armenian	94	0.22
Asian:	1,662	3.85
Bangladeshi (5)	5	0.01
Chinese, ex. Taiwanese (395)	464	1.07
Filipino (105)	133	0.31
Indian (404)	468	1.08
Indonesian (2)	8	0.02
Japanese (136)	170	0.39
Korean (207)	222	0.51
Malaysian	1	0.00
Pakistani (23)	43	0.10
Sri Lankan (1)	1	0.00
Taiwanese (28)	36	0.08
Thai (15)	23	0.05
Vietnamese (29)	37	0.09
Other Asian, specified (20)	31	0.07
Other Asian, not specified (10)	20	0.05
Assyrian/Chaldean/Syriac	35	0.08
Australian	16	0.04
Austrian	255	0.59
Belgian	50	0.12
Brazilian	78	0.18
British	196	0.45
Bulgarian	56	0.13
Canadian	95	0.22
Celtic	14	0.03
Croatian	74	0.17
Czech	125	0.29
Czechoslovakian	130	0.30
Danish	68	0.16
Dutch	450	1.04
Eastern European	268	0.62
English	2,339	5.41
Estonian	10	0.02
European	242	0.56
Finnish	34	0.08
French, except Basque	889	2.06
French Canadian	221	0.51
German	4,388	10.15
Greek	338	0.78
Guyanese	21	0.05
Hawaii Native/Pacific Islander:	62	0.14
Micronesian: (10)	11	0.03
Guamanian/Chamorro (10)	10	0.02
Other Micronesian	1	0.00
Polynesian: (7)	10	0.02
Native Hawaiian (6)	9	0.02
Samoan (1)	1	0.00
Other Pac. Isl., specified	6	0.01
Other Pac. Isl., not spec. (1)	35	0.08
Hispanic or Latino:	6,057	14.01
Central American:	177	0.41
Costa Rican	4	0.01
Guatemalan	120	0.28
Honduran	10	0.02
Nicaraguan	5	0.01
Salvadoran	25	0.06
Other Central American	13	0.03
Cuban	257	0.59
Dominican Republic	1,241	2.87
Mexican	256	0.59
Puerto Rican	850	1.97
South American:	1,667	3.86
Argentinean	25	0.06
Bolivian	3	0.01
Chilean	193	0.45
Colombian	167	0.39
Ecuadorian	1,119	2.59
Paraguayan	21	0.05
Peruvian	78	0.18
Uruguayan	16	0.04
Venezuelan	4	0.01
Other South American	41	0.09
Other Hispanic or Latino	1,609	3.72
Hungarian	432	1.00
Irish	8,010	18.53
Israeli	109	0.25
Italian	12,467	28.84
Latvian	9	0.02
Lithuanian	114	0.26
Macedonian	3	0.01
Maltese	29	0.07
Northern European	21	0.05
Norwegian	267	0.62
Pennsylvania German	7	0.02
Polish	1,422	3.29
Portuguese	479	1.11
Romanian	106	0.25
Russian	1,090	2.52
Scandinavian	22	0.05
Scotch-Irish	399	0.92
Scottish	601	1.39
Slavic	26	0.06
Slovak	225	0.52
Slovene	49	0.11

Notes: 1. Figures in the "Number" column do not add up to the total population due to: a) Ancestry/Race overlap — e.g. persons can report being both White and Irish, b) persons of Hispanic origin can report being any race, c) persons reporting two ancestries are counted in both categories. 2. Numbers in parentheses indicate the number of persons reporting this ancestry/race alone, not in combination with any other ancestry/race. 3. Refer to the Explanation of Data in the front of the book for more detailed information.

Swedish	352	0.81
Swiss	157	0.36
Turkish	75	0.17
Ukrainian	202	0.47
United States or American	1,149	2.66
Welsh	140	0.32
West Indian, excl. Hispanic:	230	0.53
Bahamian	11	0.03
Barbadian	10	0.02
British West Indian	11	0.03
Haitian	49	0.11
Jamaican	112	0.26
Trinidadian and Tobagonian	19	0.04
West Indian	18	0.04
White:	37,183	86.03
Not Hispanic (33,380)	33,675	77.91
Hispanic (3,035)	3,508	8.12
Yugoslavian	71	0.16

Mount Vernon

Place Type: City
County: Westchester
Population: 68,381

Ancestry/Race	Number	%
African American/Black:	42,516	62.18
Not Hispanic (39,889)	41,372	60.50
Hispanic (854)	1,144	1.67
African, sub-Saharan:	1,004	1.47
African	639	0.93
Cape Verdean	10	0.01
Ethiopian	25	0.04
Ghanian	6	0.01
Kenyan	7	0.01
Liberian	22	0.03
Nigerian	165	0.24
Senegalese	9	0.01
Sudanese	9	0.01
Ugandan	3	0.00
Other sub-Saharan African	109	0.16
Alaska Native tribes, specified:	2	0.00
Alaska Athabascan	1	0.00
Eskimo (1)	1	0.00
Am. Ind. or Alaska Nat., not spec.	300	0.44
Albanian	13	0.02
American Indian tribes, specified:	289	0.42
Apache (1)	3	0.00
Blackfeet (2)	27	0.04
Cherokee (25)	126	0.18
Chickasaw	2	0.00
Choctaw	6	0.01
Creek	3	0.00
Crow	2	0.00
Delaware	2	0.00
Iroquois (7)	15	0.02
Latin American Indians (33)	59	0.09
Navajo	1	0.00
Osage (2)	2	0.00
Potawatomi	2	0.00
Pueblo	2	0.00
Seminole	15	0.02
Sioux (1)	3	0.00
Yakama (1)	1	0.00
All other tribes (6)	18	0.03
American Indian tribes, not spec.	49	0.07
Arab:	90	0.13
Arab/Arabic	40	0.06
Jordanian	25	0.04
Lebanese	15	0.02
Moroccan	10	0.01
Armenian	36	0.05
Asian:	1,887	2.76
Cambodian (4)	4	0.01
Chinese, ex. Taiwanese (168)	242	0.35
Filipino (178)	211	0.31
Indian (830)	1,046	1.53
Indonesian (1)	3	0.00
Japanese (61)	77	0.11
Korean (58)	67	0.10
Laotian (1)	1	0.00
Malaysian (1)	2	0.00
Pakistani (30)	53	0.08
Sri Lankan (4)	4	0.01
Taiwanese (14)	15	0.02
Thai (57)	73	0.11
Vietnamese (5)	10	0.01
Other Asian, specified (1)	7	0.01
Other Asian, not specified (24)	72	0.11
Australian	9	0.01
Austrian	174	0.25
Belgian	14	0.02
Brazilian	991	1.45
British	120	0.18
Canadian	25	0.04
Carpatho Rusyn	10	0.01
Croatian	8	0.01
Czech	77	0.11
Czechoslovakian	41	0.06
Danish	36	0.05
Dutch	105	0.15
Eastern European	56	0.08
English	759	1.11
Estonian	14	0.02
European	40	0.06
Finnish	20	0.03
French, except Basque	323	0.47
French Canadian	49	0.07
German	1,648	2.41
Greek	355	0.52
Guyanese	568	0.83
Hawaii Native/Pacific Islander:	185	0.27
Micronesian: (6)	7	0.01
Guamanian/Chamorro (6)	7	0.01
Polynesian: (10)	29	0.04
Native Hawaiian (8)	17	0.02
Samoan (2)	12	0.02
Other Pac. Isl., specified	5	0.01
Other Pac. Isl., not spec. (27)	144	0.21
Hispanic or Latino:	7,083	10.36
Central American:	383	0.56
Costa Rican	28	0.04
Guatemalan	61	0.09
Honduran	124	0.18
Nicaraguan	9	0.01
Panamanian	63	0.09
Salvadoran	67	0.10
Other Central American	31	0.05
Cuban	192	0.28
Dominican Republic	792	1.16
Mexican	1,361	1.99
Puerto Rican	2,212	3.23
South American:	808	1.18
Argentinean	32	0.05
Bolivian	13	0.02
Chilean	38	0.06
Colombian	359	0.52
Ecuadorian	122	0.18
Paraguayan	61	0.09
Peruvian	122	0.18
Uruguayan	11	0.02
Venezuelan	18	0.03
Other South American	32	0.05
Other Hispanic or Latino	1,335	1.95
Hungarian	160	0.23
Iranian	52	0.08
Irish	2,768	4.05
Italian	7,076	10.35
Latvian	31	0.05
Lithuanian	54	0.08
Maltese	50	0.07
Norwegian	78	0.11
Polish	929	1.36
Portuguese	1,498	2.19
Romanian	27	0.04
Russian	468	0.68
Scotch-Irish	111	0.16
Scottish	219	0.32
Slavic	11	0.02
Slovak	54	0.08
Swedish	62	0.09
Swiss	56	0.08
Turkish	8	0.01
Ukrainian	89	0.13
United States or American	1,852	2.71
Welsh	13	0.02
West Indian, excl. Hispanic:	11,360	16.61
Bahamian	23	0.03
Barbadian	457	0.67
Belizean	27	0.04
British West Indian	365	0.53
Dutch West Indian	18	0.03
Haitian	825	1.21
Jamaican	8,419	12.31
Trinidadian and Tobagonian	266	0.39
U.S. Virgin Islander	22	0.03
West Indian	895	1.31
Other West Indian	43	0.06
White:	21,129	30.90
Not Hispanic (16,677)	17,802	26.03
Hispanic (2,900)	3,327	4.87

Nanuet

Place Type: Census Designated Place
County: Rockland
Population: 16,707

Ancestry/Race	Number	%
African American/Black:	2,470	14.78
Not Hispanic (2,147)	2,360	14.13
Hispanic (81)	110	0.66
African, sub-Saharan:	94	0.56
African	88	0.53
Cape Verdean	6	0.04
Am. Ind. or Alaska Nat., not spec.	65	0.39
American Indian tribes, specified:	32	0.19
Blackfeet	1	0.01
Cherokee (4)	9	0.05
Delaware (4)	9	0.05
Iroquois (1)	3	0.02
Latin American Indians	4	0.02
Sioux	1	0.01
All other tribes (1)	5	0.03
American Indian tribes, not spec.	7	0.04
Arab:	70	0.42
Arab/Arabic	26	0.16
Egyptian	34	0.20
Syrian	10	0.06
Armenian	74	0.44
Asian:	1,745	10.44
Bangladeshi (9)	13	0.08
Cambodian	1	0.01
Chinese, ex. Taiwanese (274)	297	1.78
Filipino (399)	424	2.54
Indian (583)	639	3.82
Japanese (18)	18	0.11
Korean (189)	198	1.19
Malaysian (2)	7	0.04
Pakistani (47)	53	0.32
Sri Lankan (1)	2	0.01
Taiwanese (9)	9	0.05
Thai (21)	24	0.14
Vietnamese (33)	33	0.20
Other Asian, specified	2	0.01
Other Asian, not specified (10)	25	0.15
Austrian	115	0.69
Belgian	10	0.06
British	10	0.06
Canadian	35	0.21
Croatian	41	0.25
Cypriot	13	0.08
Czech	45	0.27
Czechoslovakian	8	0.05
Danish	17	0.10
Dutch	136	0.81
Eastern European	33	0.20
English	587	3.51
Estonian	15	0.09
European	103	0.62

Notes: 1. Figures in the "Number" column do not add up to the total population due to: a) Ancestry/Race overlap — e.g. persons can report being both White and Irish, b) persons of Hispanic origin can report being any race, c) persons reporting two ancestries are counted in both categories. 2. Numbers in parentheses indicate the number of persons reporting this ancestry/race alone, not in combination with any other ancestry/race. 3. Refer to the Explanation of Data in the front of the book for more detailed information.

Ancestry/Race	Number	%
Finnish	21	0.13
French, except Basque	116	0.69
French Canadian	120	0.72
German	1,333	7.98
Greek	268	1.60
Guyanese	13	0.08
Hawaii Native/Pacific Islander:	45	0.27
Micronesian: (6)	6	0.04
Guamanian/Chamorro (6)	6	0.04
Polynesian:	2	0.01
Samoan	2	0.01
Other Pac. Isl., specified	2	0.01
Other Pac. Isl., not spec. (8)	35	0.21
Hispanic or Latino:	1,364	8.16
Central American:	102	0.61
Costa Rican	6	0.04
Guatemalan	28	0.17
Honduran	15	0.09
Nicaraguan	3	0.02
Panamanian	5	0.03
Salvadoran	36	0.22
Other Central American	9	0.05
Cuban	52	0.31
Dominican Republic	64	0.38
Mexican	96	0.57
Puerto Rican	670	4.01
South American:	129	0.77
Argentinean	7	0.04
Chilean	8	0.05
Colombian	17	0.10
Ecuadorian	69	0.41
Peruvian	15	0.09
Uruguayan	1	0.01
Venezuelan	8	0.05
Other South American	4	0.02
Other Hispanic or Latino	251	1.50
Hungarian	180	1.08
Iranian	7	0.04
Irish	2,801	16.76
Italian	3,813	22.82
Maltese	6	0.04
Norwegian	71	0.42
Polish	654	3.91
Portuguese	91	0.54
Romanian	119	0.71
Russian	661	3.96
Scandinavian	11	0.07
Scotch-Irish	108	0.65
Scottish	123	0.74
Slavic	8	0.05
Slovak	19	0.11
Slovene	13	0.08
Swedish	40	0.24
Swiss	7	0.04
Turkish	8	0.05
Ukrainian	74	0.44
United States or American	694	4.15
Welsh	11	0.07
West Indian, excl. Hispanic:	1,013	6.06
Haitian	632	3.78
Jamaican	357	2.14
Trinidadian and Tobagonian	5	0.03
U.S. Virgin Islander	11	0.07
West Indian	8	0.05
White:	12,216	73.12
Not Hispanic (11,207)	11,355	67.97
Hispanic (786)	861	5.15
Yugoslavian	20	0.12

Nesconset

Place Type: Census Designated Place
County: Suffolk
Population: 11,992

Ancestry/Race	Number	%
African American/Black:	134	1.12
Not Hispanic (111)	126	1.05
Hispanic (4)	8	0.07
African, sub-Saharan:	11	0.09
African	11	0.09
Alaska Native tribes, specified:	1	0.01
Eskimo (1)	1	0.01
Am. Ind. or Alaska Nat., not spec.	9	0.08
Albanian	12	0.10
American Indian tribes, specified:	20	0.17
Apache (1)	1	0.01
Blackfeet	1	0.01
Cherokee	1	0.01
Cheyenne (1)	1	0.01
Chickasaw (1)	1	0.01
Creek	3	0.03
Iroquois (1)	1	0.01
Latin American Indians (5)	5	0.04
All other tribes (2)	6	0.05
Arab:	45	0.38
Egyptian	18	0.15
Syrian	8	0.07
Other Arab	19	0.16
Armenian	58	0.48
Asian:	440	3.67
Chinese, ex. Taiwanese (114)	124	1.03
Filipino (44)	57	0.48
Indian (84)	104	0.87
Indonesian (1)	3	0.03
Japanese (11)	15	0.13
Korean (33)	37	0.31
Laotian (3)	3	0.03
Pakistani (63)	85	0.71
Taiwanese (2)	2	0.02
Vietnamese	1	0.01
Other Asian, not specified	9	0.08
Austrian	78	0.65
Basque	12	0.10
Belgian	9	0.08
British	27	0.23
Canadian	20	0.17
Croatian	26	0.22
Czech	75	0.63
Czechoslovakian	45	0.38
Danish	86	0.72
Dutch	57	0.48
Eastern European	50	0.42
English	464	3.87
European	26	0.22
French, except Basque	192	1.60
French Canadian	21	0.18
German	2,071	17.27
Greek	137	1.14
Guyanese	19	0.16
Hawaii Native/Pacific Islander:	8	0.07
Polynesian: (6)	6	0.05
Native Hawaiian (3)	3	0.03
Samoan (3)	3	0.03
Other Pac. Isl., not spec. (2)	2	0.02
Hispanic or Latino:	403	3.36
Central American:	19	0.16
Guatemalan	6	0.05
Honduran	2	0.02
Nicaraguan	1	0.01
Salvadoran	10	0.08
Cuban	17	0.14
Dominican Republic	10	0.08
Mexican	33	0.28
Puerto Rican	172	1.43
South American:	65	0.54
Argentinean	11	0.09
Chilean	1	0.01
Colombian	19	0.16
Ecuadorian	11	0.09
Peruvian	17	0.14
Uruguayan	1	0.01
Venezuelan	1	0.01
Other South American	4	0.03
Other Hispanic or Latino	87	0.73
Hungarian	216	1.80
Iranian	8	0.07
Irish	3,234	26.97
Israeli	29	0.24
Italian	4,599	38.35
Lithuanian	38	0.32
Norwegian	200	1.67
Pennsylvania German	10	0.08
Polish	816	6.80
Portuguese	36	0.30
Romanian	6	0.05
Russian	647	5.40
Scotch-Irish	85	0.71
Scottish	236	1.97
Slavic	9	0.08
Slovak	18	0.15
Swedish	161	1.34
Swiss	33	0.28
Ukrainian	138	1.15
United States or American	218	1.82
West Indian, excl. Hispanic:	132	1.10
Haitian	79	0.66
Jamaican	35	0.29
Trinidadian and Tobagonian	18	0.15
White:	11,393	95.01
Not Hispanic (11,006)	11,061	92.24
Hispanic (311)	332	2.77
Yugoslavian	29	0.24

New Cassel

Place Type: Census Designated Place
County: Nassau
Population: 13,298

Ancestry/Race	Number	%
African American/Black:	6,670	50.16
Not Hispanic (6,082)	6,359	47.82
Hispanic (210)	311	2.34
African, sub-Saharan:	427	3.21
African	366	2.75
Ghanian	7	0.05
Liberian	30	0.23
Nigerian	24	0.18
Alaska Native tribes, specified:	1	0.01
Tlingit-Haida	1	0.01
Am. Ind. or Alaska Nat., not spec.	73	0.55
American Indian tribes, specified:	52	0.39
Apache	3	0.02
Blackfeet	3	0.02
Cherokee	10	0.08
Cheyenne (1)	1	0.01
Choctaw	1	0.01
Iroquois	1	0.01
Latin American Indians (8)	12	0.09
Navajo	3	0.02
All other tribes (2)	18	0.14
American Indian tribes, not spec.	15	0.11
Arab:	15	0.11
Egyptian	15	0.11
Asian:	264	1.99
Chinese, ex. Taiwanese (34)	42	0.32
Filipino (32)	41	0.31
Indian (73)	104	0.78
Indonesian (2)	2	0.02
Japanese	3	0.02
Korean (16)	16	0.12
Pakistani (15)	25	0.19
Sri Lankan (6)	6	0.05
Taiwanese	3	0.02
Thai (3)	3	0.02
Vietnamese	2	0.02
Other Asian, specified	1	0.01
Other Asian, not specified (2)	16	0.12
Austrian	27	0.20
Belgian	5	0.04
Brazilian	56	0.42
British	10	0.08
Canadian	6	0.05
English	62	0.47
French, except Basque	30	0.23
German	200	1.50
Guyanese	10	0.08
Hawaii Native/Pacific Islander:	33	0.25
Polynesian:	1	0.01

Notes: 1. Figures in the "Number" column do not add up to the total population due to: a) Ancestry/Race overlap — e.g. persons can report being both White and Irish, b) persons of Hispanic origin can report being any race, c) persons reporting two ancestries are counted in both categories. 2. Numbers in parentheses indicate the number of persons reporting this ancestry/race alone, not in combination with any other ancestry/race. 3. Refer to the Explanation of Data in the front of the book for more detailed information.

Ancestry/Race	Number	%
Samoan	1	0.01
Other Pac. Isl., specified	1	0.01
Other Pac. Isl., not spec. (6)	31	0.23
Hispanic or Latino:	5,467	41.11
Central American:	2,688	20.21
Costa Rican	9	0.07
Guatemalan	18	0.14
Honduran	280	2.11
Nicaraguan	14	0.11
Panamanian	2	0.02
Salvadoran	2,322	17.46
Other Central American	43	0.32
Cuban	27	0.20
Dominican Republic	96	0.72
Mexican	1,166	8.77
Puerto Rican	198	1.49
South American:	216	1.62
Argentinean	1	0.01
Bolivian	3	0.02
Chilean	24	0.18
Colombian	86	0.65
Ecuadorian	54	0.41
Peruvian	24	0.18
Uruguayan	4	0.03
Venezuelan	6	0.05
Other South American	14	0.11
Other Hispanic or Latino	1,076	8.09
Iranian	13	0.10
Irish	251	1.89
Italian	414	3.11
Latvian	4	0.03
Lithuanian	10	0.08
Norwegian	16	0.12
Polish	49	0.37
Portuguese	36	0.27
Russian	47	0.35
Scotch-Irish	19	0.14
Scottish	32	0.24
Swedish	6	0.05
Turkish	10	0.08
Ukrainian	42	0.32
United States or American	295	2.22
Welsh	3	0.02
West Indian, excl. Hispanic:	2,029	15.26
Barbadian	7	0.05
British West Indian	27	0.20
Haitian	1,257	9.45
Jamaican	589	4.43
Trinidadian and Tobagonian	82	0.62
West Indian	67	0.50
White:	4,784	35.98
Not Hispanic (1,194)	1,264	9.51
Hispanic (3,013)	3,520	26.47
Yugoslavian	11	0.08

New Castle

Place Type: Town
County: Westchester
Population: 17,491

Ancestry/Race	Number	%
Acadian/Cajun	15	0.09
African American/Black:	284	1.62
Not Hispanic (231)	264	1.51
Hispanic (9)	20	0.11
African, sub-Saharan:	12	0.07
South African	12	0.07
Am. Ind. or Alaska Nat., not spec.	13	0.07
Albanian	19	0.11
Alsatian	20	0.11
American Indian tribes, specified:	18	0.10
Cherokee (4)	8	0.05
Chippewa	1	0.01
Choctaw	2	0.01
Creek	1	0.01
Iroquois	1	0.01
Latin American Indians	1	0.01
Navajo (1)	1	0.01
All other tribes (2)	3	0.02
Arab:	120	0.69
Arab/Arabic	7	0.04
Egyptian	26	0.15
Iraqi	8	0.05
Lebanese	13	0.07
Syrian	66	0.38
Asian:	1,070	6.12
Bangladeshi (3)	3	0.02
Cambodian (2)	9	0.05
Chinese, ex. Taiwanese (314)	355	2.03
Filipino (62)	72	0.41
Indian (238)	248	1.42
Indonesian (1)	1	0.01
Japanese (135)	165	0.94
Korean (154)	156	0.89
Malaysian	2	0.01
Pakistani (16)	16	0.09
Taiwanese (10)	11	0.06
Thai (8)	8	0.05
Vietnamese (4)	5	0.03
Other Asian, specified (3)	3	0.02
Other Asian, not specified (7)	16	0.09
Assyrian/Chaldean/Syriac	7	0.04
Australian	14	0.08
Austrian	257	1.47
Belgian	33	0.19
British	135	0.77
Canadian	26	0.15
Czech	93	0.53
Czechoslovakian	43	0.25
Danish	58	0.33
Dutch	123	0.70
Eastern European	689	3.94
English	1,317	7.53
European	404	2.31
Finnish	38	0.22
French, except Basque	271	1.55
French Canadian	43	0.25
German	1,524	8.71
Greek	228	1.30
Guyanese	6	0.03
Hawaii Native/Pacific Islander:	10	0.06
Micronesian: (1)	1	0.01
Guamanian/Chamorro (1)	1	0.01
Polynesian: (1)	3	0.02
Native Hawaiian (1)	3	0.02
Other Pac. Isl., not spec. (1)	6	0.03
Hispanic or Latino:	487	2.78
Central American:	31	0.18
Costa Rican	1	0.01
Guatemalan	8	0.05
Nicaraguan	2	0.01
Panamanian	16	0.09
Other Central American	4	0.02
Cuban	39	0.22
Dominican Republic	14	0.08
Mexican	31	0.18
Puerto Rican	106	0.61
South American:	154	0.88
Argentinean	12	0.07
Chilean	3	0.02
Colombian	26	0.15
Ecuadorian	44	0.25
Paraguayan	14	0.08
Peruvian	26	0.15
Uruguayan	17	0.10
Venezuelan	10	0.06
Other South American	2	0.01
Other Hispanic or Latino	112	0.64
Hungarian	274	1.57
Iranian	6	0.03
Irish	2,217	12.68
Israeli	54	0.31
Italian	2,525	14.44
Latvian	14	0.08
Lithuanian	59	0.34
New Zealander	19	0.11
Northern European	5	0.03
Norwegian	169	0.97
Pennsylvania German	8	0.05
Polish	1,105	6.32
Portuguese	140	0.80
Romanian	174	0.99
Russian	1,939	11.09
Scandinavian	6	0.03
Scotch-Irish	183	1.05
Scottish	267	1.53
Serbian	28	0.16
Slovak	22	0.13
Slovene	6	0.03
Swedish	153	0.87
Swiss	67	0.38
Turkish	51	0.29
Ukrainian	209	1.19
United States or American	1,000	5.72
Welsh	96	0.55
West Indian, excl. Hispanic:	71	0.41
British West Indian	11	0.06
Haitian	13	0.07
Jamaican	19	0.11
Trinidadian and Tobagonian	28	0.16
White:	16,156	92.37
Not Hispanic (15,625)	15,767	90.14
Hispanic (379)	389	2.22

New City

Place Type: Census Designated Place
County: Rockland
Population: 34,038

Ancestry/Race	Number	%
Acadian/Cajun	11	0.03
African American/Black:	1,767	5.19
Not Hispanic (1,513)	1,648	4.84
Hispanic (78)	119	0.35
African, sub-Saharan:	149	0.44
African	115	0.34
Nigerian	8	0.02
South African	26	0.08
Am. Ind. or Alaska Nat., not spec.	53	0.16
Albanian	171	0.50
American Indian tribes, specified:	17	0.05
Cherokee (1)	5	0.01
Chippewa	1	0.00
Latin American Indians (2)	4	0.01
Seminole	1	0.00
Tohono O'Odham (1)	1	0.00
All other tribes (2)	5	0.01
American Indian tribes, not spec.	20	0.06
Arab:	255	0.75
Egyptian	106	0.31
Lebanese	48	0.14
Moroccan	5	0.01
Syrian	96	0.28
Armenian	36	0.11
Asian:	2,557	7.51
Bangladeshi (3)	3	0.01
Cambodian (4)	8	0.02
Chinese, ex. Taiwanese (397)	447	1.31
Filipino (531)	577	1.70
Indian (830)	876	2.57
Indonesian (4)	6	0.02
Japanese (33)	42	0.12
Korean (383)	389	1.14
Laotian (5)	6	0.02
Pakistani (73)	73	0.21
Sri Lankan (6)	10	0.03
Taiwanese (10)	15	0.04
Thai (15)	16	0.05
Vietnamese (44)	50	0.15
Other Asian, specified	6	0.02
Other Asian, not specified (14)	33	0.10
Assyrian/Chaldean/Syriac	13	0.04
Australian	7	0.02
Austrian	440	1.29
Belgian	7	0.02
British	80	0.23
Canadian	89	0.26
Croatian	79	0.23

Notes: 1. Figures in the "Number" column do not add up to the total population due to: a) Ancestry/Race overlap — e.g. persons can report being both White and Irish, b) persons of Hispanic origin can report being any race, c) persons reporting two ancestries are counted in both categories. 2. Numbers in parentheses indicate the number of persons reporting this ancestry/race alone, not in combination with any other ancestry/race. 3. Refer to the Explanation of Data in the front of the book for more detailed information.

Czech	120	0.35
Czechoslovakian	103	0.30
Danish	32	0.09
Dutch	243	0.71
Eastern European	594	1.74
English	1,199	3.51
Estonian	20	0.06
European	344	1.01
Finnish	21	0.06
French, except Basque	326	0.95
French Canadian	39	0.11
German	3,392	9.94
Greek	249	0.73
Hawaii Native/Pacific Islander:	24	0.07
Polynesian: (6)	7	0.02
Native Hawaiian (2)	3	0.01
Samoan (4)	4	0.01
Other Pac. Isl., specified	6	0.02
Other Pac. Isl., not spec. (1)	11	0.03
Hispanic or Latino:	1,999	5.87
Central American:	67	0.20
Costa Rican	1	0.00
Guatemalan	18	0.05
Honduran	5	0.01
Nicaraguan	4	0.01
Panamanian	11	0.03
Salvadoran	27	0.08
Other Central American	1	0.00
Cuban	142	0.42
Dominican Republic	135	0.40
Mexican	233	0.68
Puerto Rican	877	2.58
South American:	165	0.48
Argentinean	8	0.02
Chilean	5	0.01
Colombian	62	0.18
Ecuadorian	63	0.19
Paraguayan	2	0.01
Peruvian	10	0.03
Venezuelan	1	0.00
Other South American	14	0.04
Other Hispanic or Latino	380	1.12
Hungarian	484	1.42
Iranian	72	0.21
Irish	5,748	16.84
Israeli	107	0.31
Italian	7,376	21.61
Lithuanian	77	0.23
Maltese	35	0.10
Norwegian	216	0.63
Pennsylvania German	21	0.06
Polish	2,165	6.34
Portuguese	71	0.21
Romanian	291	0.85
Russian	3,352	9.82
Scandinavian	25	0.07
Scotch-Irish	243	0.71
Scottish	279	0.82
Serbian	16	0.05
Slavic	7	0.02
Slovak	26	0.08
Swedish	126	0.37
Swiss	59	0.17
Turkish	25	0.07
Ukrainian	239	0.70
United States or American	1,794	5.26
Welsh	57	0.17
West Indian, excl. Hispanic:	555	1.63
Haitian	252	0.74
Jamaican	203	0.59
West Indian	100	0.29
White:	29,282	86.03
Not Hispanic (27,786)	27,986	82.22
Hispanic (1,177)	1,296	3.81
Yugoslavian	15	0.04

New Hartford

Place Type: Town
County: Oneida
Population: 21,172

Ancestry/Race	Number	%
African American/Black:	203	0.96
Not Hispanic (165)	199	0.94
Hispanic (4)	4	0.02
African, sub-Saharan:	61	0.29
African	13	0.06
Other sub-Saharan African	48	0.23
Am. Ind. or Alaska Nat., not spec.	12	0.06
American Indian tribes, specified:	32	0.15
Cherokee (2)	5	0.02
Iroquois (7)	14	0.07
Latin American Indians (1)	1	0.00
Potawatomi (1)	1	0.00
Yaqui (1)	1	0.00
All other tribes (6)	10	0.05
American Indian tribes, not spec.	3	0.01
Arab:	688	3.25
Arab/Arabic	20	0.09
Lebanese	554	2.62
Syrian	114	0.54
Armenian	34	0.16
Asian:	527	2.49
Bangladeshi (3)	3	0.01
Cambodian (5)	5	0.02
Chinese, ex. Taiwanese (63)	70	0.33
Filipino (9)	13	0.06
Indian (297)	308	1.45
Japanese (8)	9	0.04
Korean (34)	39	0.18
Malaysian (1)	1	0.00
Pakistani (33)	34	0.16
Sri Lankan (8)	8	0.04
Taiwanese (5)	5	0.02
Vietnamese (16)	16	0.08
Other Asian, specified (2)	2	0.01
Other Asian, not specified (10)	14	0.07
Austrian	74	0.35
Belgian	26	0.12
British	74	0.35
Canadian	127	0.60
Celtic	23	0.11
Czech	14	0.07
Czechoslovakian	9	0.04
Danish	48	0.23
Dutch	416	1.97
Eastern European	4	0.02
English	2,539	11.99
European	78	0.37
Finnish	16	0.08
French, except Basque	1,048	4.95
French Canadian	387	1.83
German	3,473	16.41
Greek	37	0.17
Hawaii Native/Pacific Islander:	3	0.01
Polynesian: (3)	3	0.01
Native Hawaiian (3)	3	0.01
Hispanic or Latino:	154	0.73
Central American:	4	0.02
Salvadoran	4	0.02
Cuban	4	0.02
Dominican Republic	6	0.03
Mexican	14	0.07
Puerto Rican	71	0.34
South American:	21	0.10
Argentinean	5	0.02
Chilean	3	0.01
Colombian	6	0.03
Ecuadorian	6	0.03
Peruvian	1	0.00
Other Hispanic or Latino	34	0.16
Hungarian	67	0.32
Iranian	7	0.03
Irish	4,347	20.53
Israeli	15	0.07
Italian	5,718	27.01
Lithuanian	81	0.38
Luxemburger	10	0.05
Norwegian	52	0.25
Polish	2,991	14.13
Romanian	14	0.07
Russian	265	1.25
Scotch-Irish	193	0.91
Scottish	350	1.65
Slovak	62	0.29
Slovene	17	0.08
Swedish	193	0.91
Swiss	106	0.50
Ukrainian	231	1.09
United States or American	441	2.08
Welsh	1,029	4.86
White:	20,425	96.47
Not Hispanic (20,222)	20,306	95.91
Hispanic (110)	119	0.56
Yugoslavian	3	0.01

New Paltz

Place Type: Town
County: Ulster
Population: 12,830

Ancestry/Race	Number	%
Acadian/Cajun	3	0.02
African American/Black:	900	7.01
Not Hispanic (709)	809	6.31
Hispanic (59)	91	0.71
African, sub-Saharan:	86	0.67
African	31	0.24
Ethiopian	13	0.10
Kenyan	14	0.11
Nigerian	6	0.05
South African	22	0.17
Alaska Native tribes, specified:	2	0.02
Eskimo	2	0.02
Am. Ind. or Alaska Nat., not spec.	43	0.34
Albanian	24	0.19
American Indian tribes, specified:	63	0.49
Blackfeet (2)	3	0.02
Cherokee (1)	26	0.20
Chippewa	2	0.02
Choctaw	1	0.01
Cree	1	0.01
Delaware (1)	2	0.02
Iroquois (3)	15	0.12
Latin American Indians (2)	4	0.03
Menominee	1	0.01
Osage (1)	1	0.01
Puget Sound Salish	1	0.01
Seminole	1	0.01
Sioux	1	0.01
All other tribes (2)	4	0.03
American Indian tribes, not spec.	9	0.07
Arab:	65	0.51
Egyptian	10	0.08
Lebanese	36	0.28
Moroccan	13	0.10
Syrian	6	0.05
Armenian	9	0.07
Asian:	600	4.68
Bangladeshi (2)	3	0.02
Cambodian (1)	1	0.01
Chinese, ex. Taiwanese (180)	200	1.56
Filipino (23)	30	0.23
Indian (72)	77	0.60
Indonesian (2)	5	0.04
Japanese (94)	105	0.82
Korean (71)	73	0.57
Laotian (1)	4	0.03
Malaysian	3	0.02
Pakistani (22)	36	0.28
Sri Lankan	1	0.01
Taiwanese (7)	10	0.08
Thai (1)	4	0.03
Vietnamese (14)	15	0.12

Notes: 1. Figures in the "Number" column do not add up to the total population due to: a) Ancestry/Race overlap — e.g. persons can report being both White and Irish, b) persons of Hispanic origin can report being any race, c) persons reporting two ancestries are counted in both categories. 2. Numbers in parentheses indicate the number of persons reporting this ancestry/race alone, not in combination with any other ancestry/race. 3. Refer to the Explanation of Data in the front of the book for more detailed information.

Other Asian, specified (6)	9	0.07
Other Asian, not specified (16)	24	0.19
Australian	10	0.08
Austrian	137	1.07
Basque	5	0.04
Belgian	4	0.03
Brazilian	10	0.08
British	77	0.60
Canadian	25	0.19
Celtic	7	0.05
Croatian	14	0.11
Czech	85	0.66
Czechoslovakian	7	0.05
Danish	58	0.45
Dutch	273	2.13
Eastern European	31	0.24
English	1,014	7.90
European	208	1.62
Finnish	6	0.05
French, except Basque	478	3.73
French Canadian	66	0.51
German	2,142	16.70
Greek	71	0.55
Hawaii Native/Pacific Islander:	12	0.09
Polynesian: (6)	8	0.06
Native Hawaiian (1)	3	0.02
Samoan (5)	5	0.04
Other Pac. Isl., specified	1	0.01
Other Pac. Isl., not spec.	3	0.02
Hispanic or Latino:	1,054	8.22
Central American:	51	0.40
Costa Rican	7	0.05
Guatemalan	7	0.05
Honduran	10	0.08
Nicaraguan	2	0.02
Panamanian	6	0.05
Salvadoran	19	0.15
Cuban	30	0.23
Dominican Republic	166	1.29
Mexican	105	0.82
Puerto Rican	435	3.39
South American:	94	0.73
Argentinean	6	0.05
Chilean	13	0.10
Colombian	33	0.26
Ecuadorian	24	0.19
Peruvian	12	0.09
Uruguayan	1	0.01
Venezuelan	3	0.02
Other South American	2	0.02
Other Hispanic or Latino	173	1.35
Hungarian	140	1.09
Icelander	9	0.07
Iranian	16	0.12
Irish	2,907	22.66
Israeli	21	0.16
Italian	2,467	19.23
Latvian	20	0.16
Lithuanian	24	0.19
New Zealander	11	0.09
Northern European	18	0.14
Norwegian	94	0.73
Pennsylvania German	5	0.04
Polish	688	5.36
Portuguese	16	0.12
Romanian	42	0.33
Russian	481	3.75
Scandinavian	8	0.06
Scotch-Irish	240	1.87
Scottish	223	1.74
Slavic	24	0.19
Slovak	53	0.41
Slovene	6	0.05
Swedish	162	1.26
Swiss	78	0.61
Turkish	12	0.09
Ukrainian	128	1.00
United States or American	246	1.92
Welsh	151	1.18
West Indian, excl. Hispanic:	252	1.96
Dutch West Indian	6	0.05
Haitian	22	0.17
Jamaican	161	1.25
Trinidadian and Tobagonian	36	0.28
West Indian	27	0.21
White:	10,787	84.08
Not Hispanic (10,146)	10,348	80.65
Hispanic (395)	439	3.42
Yugoslavian	3	0.02

New Rochelle

Place Type: City
County: Westchester
Population: 72,182

Ancestry/Race	Number	%
Acadian/Cajun	7	0.01
African American/Black:	14,651	20.30
Not Hispanic (13,389)	14,057	19.47
Hispanic (459)	594	0.82
African, sub-Saharan:	1,140	1.58
African	518	0.72
Cape Verdean	58	0.08
Ethiopian	82	0.11
Ghanian	23	0.03
Nigerian	310	0.43
Sierra Leonean	9	0.01
South African	37	0.05
Sudanese	17	0.02
Other sub-Saharan African	86	0.12
Alaska Native tribes, specified:	6	0.01
Eskimo	5	0.01
All other tribes	1	0.00
Alaska Native tribes, not specified	0	0.00
Am. Ind. or Alaska Nat., not spec.	218	0.30
Albanian	83	0.11
Alsatian	7	0.01
American Indian tribes, specified:	197	0.27
Blackfeet (1)	9	0.01
Cherokee (7)	57	0.08
Cheyenne	2	0.00
Chickasaw	1	0.00
Chippewa	2	0.00
Choctaw	7	0.01
Creek	2	0.00
Iroquois (3)	13	0.02
Latin American Indians (40)	66	0.09
Navajo	5	0.01
Osage (3)	3	0.00
Sioux (1)	2	0.00
All other tribes (6)	28	0.04
American Indian tribes, not spec.	24	0.03
Arab:	190	0.26
Arab/Arabic	31	0.04
Jordanian	10	0.01
Lebanese	38	0.05
Moroccan	63	0.09
Palestinian	4	0.01
Syrian	21	0.03
Other Arab	23	0.03
Armenian	140	0.19
Asian:	2,773	3.84
Bangladeshi (12)	15	0.02
Cambodian (7)	8	0.01
Chinese, ex. Taiwanese (428)	515	0.71
Filipino (373)	412	0.57
Indian (1,073)	1,202	1.67
Indonesian (1)	4	0.01
Japanese (95)	131	0.18
Korean (138)	163	0.23
Laotian (1)	2	0.00
Malaysian (5)	5	0.01
Pakistani (62)	101	0.14
Sri Lankan (38)	43	0.06
Taiwanese (7)	8	0.01
Thai (19)	23	0.03
Vietnamese (11)	13	0.02
Other Asian, specified (5)	20	0.03
Other Asian, not specified (37)	108	0.15
Assyrian/Chaldean/Syriac	8	0.01
Australian	12	0.02
Austrian	556	0.77
Belgian	53	0.07
Brazilian	384	0.53
British	293	0.41
Bulgarian	13	0.02
Canadian	168	0.23
Carpatho Rusyn	11	0.02
Celtic	34	0.05
Croatian	82	0.11
Cypriot	5	0.01
Czech	132	0.18
Czechoslovakian	90	0.12
Danish	80	0.11
Dutch	312	0.43
Eastern European	703	0.97
English	1,841	2.55
Estonian	15	0.02
European	349	0.48
Finnish	56	0.08
French, except Basque	1,039	1.44
French Canadian	295	0.41
German	3,806	5.27
Greek	445	0.62
Guyanese	99	0.14
Hawaii Native/Pacific Islander:	93	0.13
Micronesian: (13)	15	0.02
Guamanian/Chamorro (13)	14	0.02
Other Micronesian	1	0.00
Polynesian: (16)	20	0.03
Native Hawaiian (11)	13	0.02
Samoan (5)	7	0.01
Other Pac. Isl., specified	13	0.02
Other Pac. Isl., not spec. (6)	45	0.06
Hispanic or Latino:	14,492	20.08
Central American:	741	1.03
Costa Rican	47	0.07
Guatemalan	330	0.46
Honduran	92	0.13
Nicaraguan	45	0.06
Panamanian	33	0.05
Salvadoran	145	0.20
Other Central American	49	0.07
Cuban	237	0.33
Dominican Republic	381	0.53
Mexican	6,899	9.56
Puerto Rican	1,918	2.66
South American:	2,435	3.37
Argentinean	80	0.11
Bolivian	10	0.01
Chilean	62	0.09
Colombian	1,071	1.48
Ecuadorian	165	0.23
Paraguayan	29	0.04
Peruvian	791	1.10
Uruguayan	72	0.10
Venezuelan	70	0.10
Other South American	85	0.12
Other Hispanic or Latino	1,881	2.61
Hungarian	839	1.16
Iranian	42	0.06
Irish	6,413	8.88
Israeli	75	0.10
Italian	14,404	19.96
Latvian	44	0.06
Lithuanian	118	0.16
Maltese	64	0.09
Northern European	56	0.08
Norwegian	163	0.23
Polish	2,345	3.25
Portuguese	722	1.00
Romanian	195	0.27
Russian	2,472	3.42
Scandinavian	66	0.09
Scotch-Irish	308	0.43
Scottish	549	0.76
Serbian	6	0.01
Slavic	14	0.02
Slovak	105	0.15

Notes: 1. Figures in the "Number" column do not add up to the total population due to: a) Ancestry/Race overlap — e.g. persons can report being both White and Irish, b) persons of Hispanic origin can report being any race, c) persons reporting two ancestries are counted in both categories. 2. Numbers in parentheses indicate the number of persons reporting this ancestry/race alone, not in combination with any other ancestry/race. 3. Refer to the Explanation of Data in the front of the book for more detailed information.

Ancestry/Race	Number	%
Swedish	400	0.55
Swiss	123	0.17
Turkish	123	0.17
Ukrainian	217	0.30
United States or American	3,191	4.42
Welsh	161	0.22
West Indian, excl. Hispanic:	3,552	4.92
Bahamian	34	0.05
Barbadian	296	0.41
Belizean	7	0.01
British West Indian	110	0.15
Haitian	933	1.29
Jamaican	1,657	2.30
Trinidadian and Tobagonian	128	0.18
U.S. Virgin Islander	23	0.03
West Indian	364	0.50
White:	50,655	70.18
Not Hispanic (40,272)	41,109	56.95
Hispanic (8,729)	9,546	13.22
Yugoslavian	17	0.02

New Windsor

Place Type: Town
County: Orange
Population: 22,866

Ancestry/Race	Number	%
African American/Black:	1,751	7.66
Not Hispanic (1,446)	1,619	7.08
Hispanic (99)	132	0.58
African, sub-Saharan:	107	0.47
African	97	0.42
Nigerian	10	0.04
Am. Ind. or Alaska Nat., not spec.	73	0.32
Albanian	61	0.27
Alsatian	5	0.02
American Indian tribes, specified:	84	0.37
Apache	1	0.00
Blackfeet (1)	7	0.03
Cherokee (4)	21	0.09
Chippewa (2)	2	0.01
Creek	1	0.00
Delaware (8)	15	0.07
Iroquois (5)	9	0.04
Latin American Indians (1)	11	0.05
Lumbee	1	0.00
Menominee (1)	2	0.01
Navajo (2)	2	0.01
Sioux	1	0.00
All other tribes (2)	11	0.05
American Indian tribes, not spec.	8	0.03
Arab:	27	0.12
Jordanian	7	0.03
Lebanese	20	0.09
Asian:	478	2.09
Chinese, ex. Taiwanese (74)	88	0.38
Filipino (56)	60	0.26
Indian (120)	135	0.59
Indonesian (6)	8	0.03
Japanese (20)	35	0.15
Korean (62)	87	0.38
Laotian (1)	1	0.00
Malaysian (1)	1	0.00
Pakistani (15)	15	0.07
Taiwanese	4	0.02
Thai (6)	6	0.03
Vietnamese (19)	20	0.09
Other Asian, not specified (11)	18	0.08
Assyrian/Chaldean/Syriac	8	0.03
Australian	54	0.24
Austrian	61	0.27
Belgian	17	0.07
British	36	0.16
Canadian	41	0.18
Croatian	19	0.08
Czech	65	0.28
Czechoslovakian	70	0.31
Danish	47	0.21
Dutch	447	1.95
English	1,894	8.28
European	24	0.10
Finnish	7	0.03
French, except Basque	580	2.53
French Canadian	200	0.87
German	3,013	13.17
Greek	340	1.49
Hawaii Native/Pacific Islander:	26	0.11
Micronesian: (5)	9	0.04
Guamanian/Chamorro (2)	6	0.03
Other Micronesian (3)	3	0.01
Polynesian: (3)	12	0.05
Native Hawaiian	4	0.02
Samoan (3)	8	0.03
Other Pac. Isl., not spec. (3)	5	0.02
Hispanic or Latino:	2,538	11.10
Central American:	131	0.57
Costa Rican	6	0.03
Guatemalan	25	0.11
Honduran	70	0.31
Nicaraguan	4	0.02
Panamanian	10	0.04
Salvadoran	12	0.05
Other Central American	4	0.02
Cuban	80	0.35
Dominican Republic	90	0.39
Mexican	229	1.00
Puerto Rican	1,382	6.04
South American:	224	0.98
Argentinean	31	0.14
Bolivian	5	0.02
Chilean	13	0.06
Colombian	49	0.21
Ecuadorian	26	0.11
Peruvian	71	0.31
Uruguayan	4	0.02
Venezuelan	10	0.04
Other South American	15	0.07
Other Hispanic or Latino	402	1.76
Hungarian	228	1.00
Iranian	12	0.05
Irish	5,984	26.15
Israeli	9	0.04
Italian	5,393	23.56
Lithuanian	61	0.27
Maltese	65	0.28
Norwegian	100	0.44
Pennsylvania German	22	0.10
Polish	1,373	6.00
Portuguese	56	0.24
Romanian	35	0.15
Russian	231	1.01
Scandinavian	29	0.13
Scotch-Irish	263	1.15
Scottish	388	1.70
Slavic	26	0.11
Slovak	96	0.42
Slovene	8	0.03
Swedish	301	1.32
Swiss	33	0.14
Turkish	7	0.03
Ukrainian	112	0.49
United States or American	738	3.22
Welsh	29	0.13
West Indian, excl. Hispanic:	203	0.89
Haitian	90	0.39
Jamaican	67	0.29
Trinidadian and Tobagonian	14	0.06
West Indian	32	0.14
White:	19,805	86.61
Not Hispanic (18,047)	18,334	80.18
Hispanic (1,325)	1,471	6.43
Yugoslavian	7	0.03

New York

Place Type: City
County: Bronx; Kings; New York; Queens; Richmond
Population: 8,008,278

Ancestry/Race	Number	%
Acadian/Cajun	382	0.00
Afghan	5,446	0.07
African American/Black:	2,274,049	28.40
Not Hispanic (1,962,154)	2,050,764	25.61
Hispanic (167,608)	223,285	2.79
African, sub-Saharan:	122,425	1.53
African	76,791	0.96
Cape Verdean	848	0.01
Ethiopian	1,921	0.02
Ghanian	9,921	0.12
Kenyan	146	0.00
Liberian	2,561	0.03
Nigerian	17,928	0.22
Senegalese	2,136	0.03
Sierra Leonean	798	0.01
Somalian	247	0.00
South African	1,399	0.02
Sudanese	859	0.01
Ugandan	104	0.00
Zairian	14	0.00
Zimbabwean	95	0.00
Other sub-Saharan African	6,657	0.08
Alaska Native tribes, specified:	237	0.00
Alaska Athabascan (19)	49	0.00
Aleut (4)	20	0.00
Eskimo (32)	65	0.00
Tlingit-Haida (13)	77	0.00
All other tribes (6)	26	0.00
Alaska Native tribes, not specified	35	0.00
Am. Ind. or Alaska Nat., not spec.	43,524	0.54
Albanian	24,577	0.31
Alsatian	388	0.00
American Indian tribes, specified:	37,382	0.47
Apache (122)	342	0.00
Blackfeet (258)	1,454	0.02
Cherokee (1,524)	6,631	0.08
Cheyenne (24)	80	0.00
Chickasaw (30)	85	0.00
Chippewa (72)	194	0.00
Choctaw (61)	255	0.00
Colville (2)	3	0.00
Comanche (21)	65	0.00
Cree (21)	94	0.00
Creek (41)	229	0.00
Crow (12)	44	0.00
Delaware (39)	150	0.00
Houma (2)	10	0.00
Iroquois (348)	1,069	0.01
Kiowa (5)	13	0.00
Latin American Indians (9,176)	22,003	0.27
Lumbee (51)	87	0.00
Menominee (1)	6	0.00
Navajo (89)	187	0.00
Osage (19)	40	0.00
Ottawa (9)	13	0.00
Paiute (6)	11	0.00
Pima (2)	5	0.00
Potawatomi (11)	27	0.00
Pueblo (375)	1,162	0.01
Puget Sound Salish (1)	7	0.00
Seminole (69)	374	0.00
Shoshone (9)	24	0.00
Sioux (128)	437	0.01
Tohono O'Odham (28)	43	0.00
Ute (2)	8	0.00
Yakama (1)	3	0.00
Yaqui (9)	29	0.00
Yuman (9)	16	0.00
All other tribes (797)	2,182	0.03
American Indian tribes, not spec.	7,090	0.09
Arab:	70,965	0.89
Arab/Arabic	14,572	0.18

Notes: 1. Figures in the "Number" column do not add up to the total population due to: a) Ancestry/Race overlap — e.g. persons can report being both White and Irish, b) persons of Hispanic origin can report being any race, c) persons reporting two ancestries are counted in both categories. 2. Numbers in parentheses indicate the number of persons reporting this ancestry/race alone, not in combination with any other ancestry/race. 3. Refer to the Explanation of Data in the front of the book for more detailed information.

Egyptian	17,223	0.22
Iraqi	957	0.01
Jordanian	897	0.01
Lebanese	11,419	0.14
Moroccan	5,116	0.06
Palestinian	3,184	0.04
Syrian	10,985	0.14
Other Arab	6,612	0.08
Armenian	10,360	0.13
Asian:	889,642	11.11
Bangladeshi (19,148)	28,269	0.35
Cambodian (1,771)	2,296	0.03
Chinese, ex. Taiwanese (357,243)	374,321	4.67
Filipino (54,993)	62,058	0.77
Hmong (8)	26	0.00
Indian (170,899)	206,228	2.58
Indonesian (2,263)	3,017	0.04
Japanese (22,636)	26,419	0.33
Korean (86,473)	90,208	1.13
Laotian (234)	316	0.00
Malaysian (1,368)	2,287	0.03
Pakistani (24,099)	34,310	0.43
Sri Lankan (2,033)	2,640	0.03
Taiwanese (4,288)	5,488	0.07
Thai (4,169)	5,002	0.06
Vietnamese (11,334)	13,010	0.16
Other Asian, specified (2,546)	3,921	0.05
Other Asian, not specified (8,658)	29,826	0.37
Assyrian/Chaldean/Syriac	300	0.00
Australian	3,155	0.04
Austrian	33,605	0.42
Basque	596	0.01
Belgian	3,426	0.04
Brazilian	12,176	0.15
British	17,030	0.21
Bulgarian	3,826	0.05
Canadian	9,744	0.12
Carpatho Rusyn	138	0.00
Celtic	836	0.01
Croatian	11,948	0.15
Cypriot	1,397	0.02
Czech	10,659	0.13
Czechoslovakian	8,154	0.10
Danish	7,460	0.09
Dutch	19,402	0.24
Eastern European	30,570	0.38
English	124,821	1.56
Estonian	883	0.01
European	32,892	0.41
Finnish	3,466	0.04
French, except Basque	52,907	0.66
French Canadian	10,645	0.13
German	255,536	3.19
German Russian	110	0.00
Greek	80,145	1.00
Guyanese	99,537	1.24
Hawaii Native/Pacific Islander:	19,313	0.24
Melanesian: (56)	339	0.00
Fijian (52)	302	0.00
Other Melanesian (4)	37	0.00
Micronesian: (1,094)	1,552	0.02
Guamanian/Chamorro (1,066)	1,486	0.02
Other Micronesian (28)	66	0.00
Polynesian: (1,785)	3,253	0.04
Native Hawaiian (882)	1,864	0.02
Samoan (879)	1,279	0.02
Tongan (9)	26	0.00
Other Polynesian (15)	84	0.00
Other Pac. Isl., specified	639	0.01
Other Pac. Isl., not spec. (2,484)	13,530	0.17
Hispanic or Latino:	2,160,554	26.98
Central American:	99,099	1.24
Costa Rican	4,939	0.06
Guatemalan	15,212	0.19
Honduran	25,600	0.32
Nicaraguan	6,451	0.08
Panamanian	16,847	0.21
Salvadoran	24,516	0.31
Other Central American	5,534	0.07
Cuban	41,123	0.51
Dominican Republic	406,806	5.08
Mexican	186,872	2.33
Puerto Rican	789,172	9.85
South American:	236,374	2.95
Argentinean	9,578	0.12
Bolivian	2,942	0.04
Chilean	5,014	0.06
Colombian	77,154	0.96
Ecuadorian	101,005	1.26
Paraguayan	1,658	0.02
Peruvian	23,567	0.29
Uruguayan	1,907	0.02
Venezuelan	6,713	0.08
Other South American	6,836	0.09
Other Hispanic or Latino	401,108	5.01
Hungarian	48,879	0.61
Icelander	541	0.01
Iranian	8,506	0.11
Irish	420,810	5.25
Israeli	20,946	0.26
Italian	692,739	8.65
Latvian	3,777	0.05
Lithuanian	13,847	0.17
Luxemburger	233	0.00
Macedonian	1,736	0.02
Maltese	3,082	0.04
New Zealander	559	0.01
Northern European	1,917	0.02
Norwegian	23,849	0.30
Pennsylvania German	350	0.00
Polish	213,447	2.67
Portuguese	11,307	0.14
Romanian	30,360	0.38
Russian	243,015	3.03
Scandinavian	2,129	0.03
Scotch-Irish	21,951	0.27
Scottish	32,024	0.40
Serbian	2,652	0.03
Slavic	2,025	0.03
Slovak	6,459	0.08
Slovene	1,162	0.01
Soviet Union	550	0.01
Swedish	20,644	0.26
Swiss	8,108	0.10
Turkish	12,221	0.15
Ukrainian	62,695	0.78
United States or American	238,385	2.98
Welsh	8,830	0.11
West Indian, excl. Hispanic:	549,664	6.86
Bahamian	1,658	0.02
Barbadian	26,816	0.33
Belizean	6,487	0.08
Bermudan	608	0.01
British West Indian	47,084	0.59
Dutch West Indian	994	0.01
Haitian	118,769	1.48
Jamaican	212,972	2.66
Trinidadian and Tobagonian	75,584	0.94
U.S. Virgin Islander	2,790	0.03
West Indian	54,585	0.68
Other West Indian	1,317	0.02
White:	3,806,508	47.53
Not Hispanic (2,801,267)	2,912,995	36.37
Hispanic (775,118)	893,513	11.16
Yugoslavian	15,273	0.19

Newburgh

Place Type: City
County: Orange
Population: 28,259

Ancestry/Race	Number	%
African American/Black:	10,046	35.55
Not Hispanic (8,961)	9,506	33.64
Hispanic (353)	540	1.91
African, sub-Saharan:	341	1.21
African	341	1.21
Alaska Native tribes, specified:	1	0.00
Aleut (1)	1	0.00
Am. Ind. or Alaska Nat., not spec.	180	0.64
American Indian tribes, specified:	227	0.80
Apache	2	0.01
Blackfeet (4)	37	0.13
Cherokee (11)	47	0.17
Delaware (1)	10	0.04
Iroquois	3	0.01
Latin American Indians (61)	99	0.35
Lumbee	4	0.01
Sioux (4)	18	0.06
All other tribes (3)	7	0.02
American Indian tribes, not spec.	28	0.10
Arab:	48	0.17
Egyptian	24	0.09
Lebanese	8	0.03
Palestinian	5	0.02
Other Arab	11	0.04
Armenian	5	0.02
Asian:	324	1.15
Bangladeshi (4)	6	0.02
Chinese, ex. Taiwanese (63)	82	0.29
Filipino (34)	46	0.16
Indian (46)	67	0.24
Indonesian (2)	2	0.01
Japanese (2)	15	0.05
Korean (21)	30	0.11
Pakistani (10)	12	0.04
Thai (2)	7	0.02
Vietnamese (20)	26	0.09
Other Asian, specified (1)	4	0.01
Other Asian, not specified (1)	27	0.10
Austrian	35	0.12
Belgian	15	0.05
British	6	0.02
Canadian	10	0.04
Celtic	38	0.13
Czech	39	0.14
Czechoslovakian	25	0.09
Danish	6	0.02
Dutch	357	1.26
Eastern European	38	0.13
English	835	2.96
European	71	0.25
Finnish	7	0.02
French, except Basque	364	1.29
French Canadian	143	0.51
German	1,504	5.33
Greek	36	0.13
Guyanese	16	0.06
Hawaii Native/Pacific Islander:	53	0.19
Micronesian: (11)	15	0.05
Guamanian/Chamorro (11)	15	0.05
Polynesian: (1)	5	0.02
Native Hawaiian (1)	4	0.01
Samoan	1	0.00
Other Pac. Isl., not spec. (4)	33	0.12
Hispanic or Latino:	10,257	36.30
Central American:	1,085	3.84
Costa Rican	2	0.01
Guatemalan	78	0.28
Honduran	750	2.65
Nicaraguan	9	0.03
Panamanian	10	0.04
Salvadoran	191	0.68
Other Central American	45	0.16
Cuban	90	0.32
Dominican Republic	109	0.39
Mexican	4,111	14.55
Puerto Rican	3,069	10.86
South American:	584	2.07
Argentinean	57	0.20
Bolivian	4	0.01
Chilean	34	0.12
Colombian	86	0.30
Ecuadorian	46	0.16
Peruvian	330	1.17
Uruguayan	9	0.03
Venezuelan	8	0.03
Other South American	10	0.04

Notes: 1. Figures in the "Number" column do not add up to the total population due to: a) Ancestry/Race overlap — e.g. persons can report being both White and Irish, b) persons of Hispanic origin can report being any race, c) persons reporting two ancestries are counted in both categories. 2. Numbers in parentheses indicate the number of persons reporting this ancestry/race alone, not in combination with any other ancestry/race. 3. Refer to the Explanation of Data in the front of the book for more detailed information.

Ancestry/Race	Number	%
Other Hispanic or Latino	1,209	4.28
Hungarian	142	0.50
Irish	2,322	8.22
Italian	2,599	9.21
Latvian	13	0.05
Lithuanian	5	0.02
Norwegian	34	0.12
Polish	316	1.12
Portuguese	37	0.13
Romanian	20	0.07
Russian	132	0.47
Scandinavian	20	0.07
Scotch-Irish	148	0.52
Scottish	141	0.50
Slovak	17	0.06
Swedish	88	0.31
Swiss	16	0.06
Turkish	11	0.04
Ukrainian	33	0.12
United States or American	454	1.61
Welsh	47	0.17
West Indian, excl. Hispanic:	818	2.90
British West Indian	32	0.11
Haitian	157	0.56
Jamaican	486	1.72
West Indian	143	0.51
White:	12,960	45.86
Not Hispanic (7,969)	8,430	29.83
Hispanic (3,993)	4,530	16.03

Newburgh

Place Type: Town
County: Orange
Population: 27,568

Ancestry/Race	Number	%
African American/Black:	2,318	8.41
Not Hispanic (1,873)	2,034	7.38
Hispanic (210)	284	1.03
African, sub-Saharan:	31	0.11
African	24	0.09
Nigerian	7	0.03
Alaska Native tribes, specified:	2	0.01
Aleut	2	0.01
Am. Ind. or Alaska Nat., not spec.	90	0.33
American Indian tribes, specified:	85	0.31
Apache (1)	6	0.02
Blackfeet (2)	5	0.02
Cherokee	27	0.10
Choctaw	5	0.02
Delaware (2)	6	0.02
Iroquois (2)	12	0.04
Latin American Indians (2)	8	0.03
Lumbee (1)	1	0.00
Sioux	7	0.03
Ute	1	0.00
All other tribes (7)	7	0.03
American Indian tribes, not spec.	11	0.04
Arab:	67	0.24
Lebanese	14	0.05
Palestinian	20	0.07
Other Arab	33	0.12
Armenian	28	0.10
Asian:	679	2.46
Bangladeshi (10)	10	0.04
Chinese, ex. Taiwanese (98)	113	0.41
Filipino (109)	138	0.50
Indian (165)	184	0.67
Japanese (20)	32	0.12
Korean (68)	82	0.30
Pakistani (45)	50	0.18
Sri Lankan (6)	13	0.05
Thai (6)	9	0.03
Vietnamese (17)	19	0.07
Other Asian, not specified (15)	29	0.11
Australian	19	0.07
Austrian	118	0.43
Basque	12	0.04
Brazilian	12	0.04
British	73	0.26
Canadian	57	0.21
Croatian	25	0.09
Czech	100	0.36
Czechoslovakian	76	0.28
Danish	66	0.24
Dutch	975	3.53
Eastern European	83	0.30
English	2,167	7.85
European	261	0.95
Finnish	61	0.22
French, except Basque	857	3.11
French Canadian	323	1.17
German	3,963	14.36
Greek	226	0.82
Hawaii Native/Pacific Islander:	30	0.11
Micronesian: (3)	3	0.01
Guamanian/Chamorro (3)	3	0.01
Polynesian: (4)	6	0.02
Native Hawaiian	2	0.01
Samoan (4)	4	0.01
Other Pac. Isl., not spec.	21	0.08
Hispanic or Latino:	2,644	9.59
Central American:	140	0.51
Costa Rican	6	0.02
Guatemalan	4	0.01
Honduran	64	0.23
Nicaraguan	3	0.01
Panamanian	20	0.07
Salvadoran	30	0.11
Other Central American	13	0.05
Cuban	66	0.24
Dominican Republic	61	0.22
Mexican	177	0.64
Puerto Rican	1,631	5.92
South American:	179	0.65
Argentinean	31	0.11
Chilean	13	0.05
Colombian	34	0.12
Ecuadorian	31	0.11
Peruvian	53	0.19
Uruguayan	5	0.02
Venezuelan	8	0.03
Other South American	4	0.01
Other Hispanic or Latino	390	1.41
Hungarian	474	1.72
Iranian	5	0.02
Irish	6,155	22.31
Italian	7,200	26.09
Lithuanian	153	0.55
Maltese	18	0.07
Northern European	12	0.04
Norwegian	255	0.92
Pennsylvania German	7	0.03
Polish	1,586	5.75
Portuguese	139	0.50
Romanian	65	0.24
Russian	510	1.85
Scandinavian	26	0.09
Scotch-Irish	509	1.84
Scottish	364	1.32
Slavic	23	0.08
Slovak	123	0.45
Swedish	271	0.98
Swiss	115	0.42
Turkish	46	0.17
Ukrainian	262	0.95
United States or American	721	2.61
Welsh	96	0.35
West Indian, excl. Hispanic:	169	0.61
British West Indian	9	0.03
Haitian	4	0.01
Jamaican	130	0.47
West Indian	26	0.09
White:	23,910	86.73
Not Hispanic (22,045)	22,342	81.04
Hispanic (1,410)	1,568	5.69
Yugoslavian	4	0.01

Niagara Falls

Place Type: City
County: Niagara
Population: 55,593

Ancestry/Race	Number	%
African American/Black:	11,015	19.81
Not Hispanic (10,291)	10,844	19.51
Hispanic (118)	171	0.31
African, sub-Saharan:	253	0.45
African	236	0.42
Senegalese	6	0.01
Ugandan	11	0.02
Alaska Native tribes, specified:	1	0.00
Eskimo (1)	1	0.00
Alaska Native tribes, not specified	1	0.00
Am. Ind. or Alaska Nat., not spec.	375	0.67
Albanian	17	0.03
Alsatian	10	0.02
American Indian tribes, specified:	903	1.62
Apache (1)	3	0.01
Blackfeet (3)	10	0.02
Cherokee (12)	33	0.06
Chickasaw (1)	1	0.00
Chippewa (15)	33	0.06
Choctaw	2	0.00
Comanche (1)	1	0.00
Cree	2	0.00
Delaware (1)	5	0.01
Iroquois (601)	767	1.38
Latin American Indians (1)	1	0.00
Menominee	1	0.00
Navajo (3)	4	0.01
Pima	3	0.01
Potawatomi (1)	2	0.00
Pueblo	1	0.00
Seminole	1	0.00
Sioux (1)	2	0.00
All other tribes (20)	31	0.06
American Indian tribes, not spec.	44	0.08
Arab:	453	0.81
Arab/Arabic	17	0.03
Egyptian	26	0.05
Lebanese	388	0.70
Syrian	22	0.04
Armenian	287	0.52
Asian:	516	0.93
Bangladeshi (5)	5	0.01
Chinese, ex. Taiwanese (50)	71	0.13
Filipino (50)	66	0.12
Indian (163)	210	0.38
Japanese (13)	23	0.04
Korean (24)	30	0.05
Laotian (3)	3	0.01
Pakistani (34)	39	0.07
Taiwanese (2)	2	0.00
Thai (2)	2	0.00
Vietnamese (25)	32	0.06
Other Asian, specified	1	0.00
Other Asian, not specified (13)	32	0.06
Australian	4	0.01
Austrian	115	0.21
Belgian	11	0.02
British	132	0.24
Canadian	393	0.71
Celtic	17	0.03
Croatian	68	0.12
Czech	170	0.31
Czechoslovakian	105	0.19
Danish	95	0.17
Dutch	584	1.05
Eastern European	9	0.02
English	4,643	8.34
European	155	0.28
Finnish	26	0.05
French, except Basque	1,758	3.16
French Canadian	785	1.41
German	9,318	16.74
Greek	152	0.27

Notes: 1. Figures in the "Number" column do not add up to the total population due to: a) Ancestry/Race overlap — e.g. persons can report being both White and Irish, b) persons of Hispanic origin can report being any race, c) persons reporting two ancestries are counted in both categories. 2. Numbers in parentheses indicate the number of persons reporting this ancestry/race alone, not in combination with any other ancestry/race. 3. Refer to the Explanation of Data in the front of the book for more detailed information.

Ancestry/Race	Number	%
Guyanese	6	0.01
Hawaii Native/Pacific Islander:	45	0.08
Micronesian: (5)	6	0.01
Guamanian/Chamorro (5)	6	0.01
Polynesian: (18)	26	0.05
Native Hawaiian (16)	20	0.04
Samoan (2)	6	0.01
Other Pac. Isl., specified	1	0.00
Other Pac. Isl., not spec. (3)	12	0.02
Hispanic or Latino:	1,114	2.00
Central American:	21	0.04
Guatemalan	8	0.01
Honduran	2	0.00
Panamanian	10	0.02
Salvadoran	1	0.00
Cuban	62	0.11
Dominican Republic	16	0.03
Mexican	153	0.28
Puerto Rican	558	1.00
South American:	21	0.04
Chilean	2	0.00
Colombian	11	0.02
Ecuadorian	4	0.01
Peruvian	1	0.00
Venezuelan	3	0.01
Other Hispanic or Latino	283	0.51
Hungarian	255	0.46
Irish	7,627	13.70
Italian	12,879	23.13
Latvian	5	0.01
Lithuanian	167	0.30
Luxemburger	7	0.01
Norwegian	111	0.20
Pennsylvania German	91	0.16
Polish	6,100	10.96
Portuguese	56	0.10
Romanian	30	0.05
Russian	239	0.43
Scotch-Irish	591	1.06
Scottish	969	1.74
Serbian	38	0.07
Slavic	26	0.05
Slovak	127	0.23
Slovene	5	0.01
Swedish	318	0.57
Swiss	84	0.15
Ukrainian	276	0.50
United States or American	1,734	3.11
Welsh	388	0.70
West Indian, excl. Hispanic:	179	0.32
Bahamian	9	0.02
Barbadian	5	0.01
Jamaican	152	0.27
Trinidadian and Tobagonian	7	0.01
West Indian	6	0.01
White:	43,315	77.91
Not Hispanic (41,843)	42,721	76.85
Hispanic (527)	594	1.07
Yugoslavian	101	0.18

Niskayuna

Place Type: Town
County: Schenectady
Population: 20,295

Ancestry/Race	Number	%
Afghan	8	0.04
African American/Black:	371	1.83
Not Hispanic (313)	366	1.80
Hispanic (5)	5	0.02
African, sub-Saharan:	7	0.03
African	7	0.03
Am. Ind. or Alaska Nat., not spec.	20	0.10
American Indian tribes, specified:	35	0.17
Blackfeet (1)	2	0.01
Cherokee (1)	7	0.03
Chippewa (1)	1	0.00
Crow	2	0.01
Iroquois (1)	4	0.02
Latin American Indians (2)	7	0.03
Osage	1	0.00
Sioux	3	0.01
All other tribes (4)	8	0.04
American Indian tribes, not spec.	5	0.02
Arab:	172	0.85
Arab/Arabic	21	0.10
Egyptian	41	0.20
Iraqi	27	0.13
Jordanian	12	0.06
Lebanese	25	0.12
Palestinian	46	0.23
Armenian	28	0.14
Asian:	1,333	6.57
Chinese, ex. Taiwanese (347)	376	1.85
Filipino (30)	44	0.22
Indian (626)	656	3.23
Indonesian (8)	13	0.06
Japanese (39)	50	0.25
Korean (87)	94	0.46
Malaysian (1)	1	0.00
Pakistani (28)	34	0.17
Sri Lankan (13)	13	0.06
Taiwanese (7)	7	0.03
Thai (2)	3	0.01
Vietnamese (10)	13	0.06
Other Asian, not specified (10)	29	0.14
Australian	9	0.04
Austrian	97	0.48
Belgian	8	0.04
British	149	0.74
Canadian	57	0.28
Celtic	8	0.04
Croatian	31	0.15
Czech	83	0.41
Czechoslovakian	14	0.07
Danish	78	0.39
Dutch	513	2.53
Eastern European	65	0.32
English	2,493	12.31
European	111	0.55
Finnish	41	0.20
French, except Basque	854	4.22
French Canadian	417	2.06
German	3,075	15.18
Greek	118	0.58
Hawaii Native/Pacific Islander:	6	0.03
Polynesian: (5)	5	0.02
Native Hawaiian (3)	3	0.01
Tongan (2)	2	0.01
Other Pac. Isl., not spec.	1	0.00
Hispanic or Latino:	333	1.64
Central American:	11	0.05
Costa Rican	2	0.01
Guatemalan	3	0.01
Honduran	1	0.00
Panamanian	1	0.00
Salvadoran	3	0.01
Other Central American	1	0.00
Cuban	13	0.06
Dominican Republic	14	0.07
Mexican	52	0.26
Puerto Rican	113	0.56
South American:	52	0.26
Argentinean	11	0.05
Bolivian	5	0.02
Chilean	6	0.03
Colombian	18	0.09
Ecuadorian	4	0.02
Paraguayan	1	0.00
Peruvian	6	0.03
Venezuelan	1	0.00
Other Hispanic or Latino	78	0.38
Hungarian	325	1.60
Iranian	21	0.10
Irish	4,261	21.03
Israeli	40	0.20
Italian	3,985	19.67
Lithuanian	114	0.56
Maltese	9	0.04
Northern European	27	0.13
Norwegian	165	0.81
Pennsylvania German	18	0.09
Polish	1,873	9.25
Portuguese	12	0.06
Romanian	47	0.23
Russian	669	3.30
Scandinavian	37	0.18
Scotch-Irish	244	1.20
Scottish	557	2.75
Serbian	35	0.17
Slavic	31	0.15
Slovak	42	0.21
Slovene	8	0.04
Swedish	332	1.64
Swiss	101	0.50
Turkish	53	0.26
Ukrainian	159	0.78
United States or American	767	3.79
Welsh	119	0.59
West Indian, excl. Hispanic:	11	0.05
Jamaican	11	0.05
White:	18,608	91.69
Not Hispanic (18,186)	18,355	90.44
Hispanic (231)	253	1.25
Yugoslavian	7	0.03

North Amityville

Place Type: Census Designated Place
County: Suffolk
Population: 16,572

Ancestry/Race	Number	%
African American/Black:	11,991	72.36
Not Hispanic (11,071)	11,591	69.94
Hispanic (315)	400	2.41
African, sub-Saharan:	450	2.72
African	422	2.56
Nigerian	28	0.17
Am. Ind. or Alaska Nat., not spec.	146	0.88
American Indian tribes, specified:	244	1.47
Blackfeet (5)	9	0.05
Cherokee (13)	65	0.39
Chippewa	1	0.01
Choctaw	1	0.01
Creek (1)	1	0.01
Iroquois (1)	10	0.06
Latin American Indians	17	0.10
Pima	2	0.01
Seminole (2)	5	0.03
All other tribes (94)	133	0.80
American Indian tribes, not spec.	24	0.14
Arab:	49	0.30
Egyptian	49	0.30
Asian:	232	1.40
Bangladeshi (2)	3	0.02
Chinese, ex. Taiwanese (16)	24	0.14
Filipino (34)	38	0.23
Indian (84)	116	0.70
Japanese (1)	4	0.02
Korean (4)	5	0.03
Pakistani (8)	14	0.08
Sri Lankan (1)	1	0.01
Thai (2)	2	0.01
Vietnamese (11)	11	0.07
Other Asian, not specified (7)	14	0.08
Austrian	4	0.02
Czech	24	0.15
Czechoslovakian	7	0.04
Danish	16	0.10
Dutch	58	0.35
English	184	1.11
European	10	0.06
Finnish	10	0.06
French, except Basque	74	0.45
French Canadian	21	0.13
German	427	2.59
Guyanese	119	0.72
Hawaii Native/Pacific Islander:	45	0.27

Notes: 1. Figures in the "Number" column do not add up to the total population due to: a) Ancestry/Race overlap — e.g. persons can report being both White and Irish, b) persons of Hispanic origin can report being any race, c) persons reporting two ancestries are counted in both categories. 2. Numbers in parentheses indicate the number of persons reporting this ancestry/race alone, not in combination with any other ancestry/race. 3. Refer to the Explanation of Data in the front of the book for more detailed information.

Melanesian: (1)	1	0.01
Fijian (1)	1	0.01
Micronesian: (7)	7	0.04
Guamanian/Chamorro (7)	7	0.04
Polynesian:	4	0.02
Native Hawaiian	4	0.02
Other Pac. Isl., not spec. (4)	33	0.20
Hispanic or Latino:	2,242	13.53
Central American:	685	4.13
Costa Rican	14	0.08
Guatemalan	36	0.22
Honduran	51	0.31
Nicaraguan	1	0.01
Panamanian	58	0.35
Salvadoran	515	3.11
Other Central American	10	0.06
Cuban	36	0.22
Dominican Republic	314	1.89
Mexican	52	0.31
Puerto Rican	477	2.88
South American:	160	0.97
Bolivian	1	0.01
Chilean	4	0.02
Colombian	90	0.54
Ecuadorian	30	0.18
Peruvian	18	0.11
Venezuelan	11	0.07
Other South American	6	0.04
Other Hispanic or Latino	518	3.13
Hungarian	15	0.09
Irish	633	3.83
Italian	654	3.96
New Zealander	6	0.04
Norwegian	24	0.15
Polish	243	1.47
Portuguese	14	0.08
Romanian	8	0.05
Russian	66	0.40
Scotch-Irish	31	0.19
Scottish	44	0.27
Swedish	19	0.12
Turkish	12	0.07
Ukrainian	25	0.15
United States or American	500	3.03
West Indian, excl. Hispanic:	1,901	11.51
Bahamian	28	0.17
Barbadian	62	0.38
Bermudan	18	0.11
British West Indian	65	0.39
Haitian	303	1.83
Jamaican	971	5.88
Trinidadian and Tobagonian	207	1.25
West Indian	247	1.50
White:	3,384	20.42
Not Hispanic (2,279)	2,464	14.87
Hispanic (812)	920	5.55

North Babylon

Place Type: Census Designated Place
County: Suffolk
Population: 17,877

Ancestry/Race	Number	%
Afghan	44	0.25
African American/Black:	425	2.38
Not Hispanic (352)	400	2.24
Hispanic (19)	25	0.14
African, sub-Saharan:	24	0.14
African	24	0.14
Alaska Native tribes, not specified	1	0.01
Am. Ind. or Alaska Nat., not spec.	12	0.07
Albanian	7	0.04
American Indian tribes, specified:	46	0.26
Blackfeet	1	0.01
Cherokee (2)	11	0.06
Choctaw (1)	1	0.01
Creek	1	0.01
Iroquois (8)	9	0.05
Latin American Indians (9)	14	0.08
Pueblo (1)	1	0.01
Sioux (1)	1	0.01
All other tribes (4)	7	0.04
American Indian tribes, not spec.	5	0.03
Arab:	61	0.34
Arab/Arabic	6	0.03
Egyptian	11	0.06
Lebanese	29	0.16
Moroccan	9	0.05
Palestinian	6	0.03
Asian:	446	2.49
Bangladeshi (3)	3	0.02
Chinese, ex. Taiwanese (93)	113	0.63
Filipino (60)	70	0.39
Indian (117)	127	0.71
Japanese (10)	17	0.10
Korean (42)	45	0.25
Pakistani (22)	27	0.15
Sri Lankan (1)	2	0.01
Thai (5)	5	0.03
Vietnamese (16)	20	0.11
Other Asian, not specified (1)	17	0.10
Austrian	116	0.65
British	60	0.34
Canadian	13	0.07
Croatian	43	0.24
Czech	70	0.39
Czechoslovakian	64	0.36
Danish	100	0.56
Dutch	65	0.37
Eastern European	8	0.05
English	957	5.39
Estonian	8	0.05
European	16	0.09
Finnish	24	0.14
French, except Basque	272	1.53
French Canadian	64	0.36
German	3,356	18.89
Greek	328	1.85
Guyanese	60	0.34
Hawaii Native/Pacific Islander:	18	0.10
Polynesian: (5)	14	0.08
Native Hawaiian (1)	10	0.06
Samoan (4)	4	0.02
Other Pac. Isl., not spec. (1)	4	0.02
Hispanic or Latino:	1,313	7.34
Central American:	89	0.50
Costa Rican	5	0.03
Guatemalan	9	0.05
Honduran	7	0.04
Nicaraguan	9	0.05
Salvadoran	55	0.31
Other Central American	4	0.02
Cuban	35	0.20
Dominican Republic	71	0.40
Mexican	41	0.23
Puerto Rican	643	3.60
South American:	194	1.09
Argentinean	17	0.10
Bolivian	5	0.03
Chilean	5	0.03
Colombian	69	0.39
Ecuadorian	50	0.28
Paraguayan	1	0.01
Peruvian	26	0.15
Venezuelan	10	0.06
Other South American	11	0.06
Other Hispanic or Latino	240	1.34
Hungarian	154	0.87
Icelander	12	0.07
Iranian	6	0.03
Irish	4,822	27.14
Israeli	12	0.07
Italian	6,572	36.99
Latvian	26	0.15
Lithuanian	60	0.34
Maltese	15	0.08
Norwegian	186	1.05
Polish	1,222	6.88
Portuguese	36	0.20
Romanian	7	0.04
Russian	407	2.29
Scandinavian	7	0.04
Scotch-Irish	88	0.50
Scottish	120	0.68
Slovak	2	0.01
Swedish	240	1.35
Swiss	30	0.17
Turkish	68	0.38
Ukrainian	174	0.98
United States or American	552	3.11
Welsh	35	0.20
West Indian, excl. Hispanic:	114	0.64
British West Indian	5	0.03
Haitian	41	0.23
Jamaican	39	0.22
West Indian	29	0.16
White:	16,704	93.44
Not Hispanic (15,592)	15,753	88.12
Hispanic (864)	951	5.32
Yugoslavian	36	0.20

North Bay Shore

Place Type: Census Designated Place
County: Suffolk
Population: 14,992

Ancestry/Race	Number	%
African American/Black:	3,198	21.33
Not Hispanic (2,632)	2,885	19.24
Hispanic (189)	313	2.09
African, sub-Saharan:	213	1.42
African	158	1.05
Ghanian	23	0.15
Nigerian	32	0.21
Am. Ind. or Alaska Nat., not spec.	126	0.84
American Indian tribes, specified:	89	0.59
Apache (4)	9	0.06
Blackfeet (6)	14	0.09
Cherokee (1)	16	0.11
Cree	3	0.02
Iroquois (2)	13	0.09
Latin American Indians (8)	13	0.09
Navajo	3	0.02
Puget Sound Salish	2	0.01
All other tribes (2)	16	0.11
American Indian tribes, not spec.	5	0.03
Arab:	85	0.57
Lebanese	8	0.05
Palestinian	77	0.51
Armenian	19	0.13
Asian:	458	3.05
Bangladeshi (3)	10	0.07
Chinese, ex. Taiwanese (30)	48	0.32
Filipino (25)	45	0.30
Indian (124)	179	1.19
Indonesian (1)	1	0.01
Japanese (7)	9	0.06
Korean (1)	2	0.01
Laotian (1)	2	0.01
Pakistani (36)	71	0.47
Taiwanese (1)	1	0.01
Thai (3)	5	0.03
Vietnamese (52)	56	0.37
Other Asian, not specified (14)	29	0.19
Austrian	12	0.08
British	22	0.15
Canadian	58	0.39
Czech	11	0.07
Czechoslovakian	28	0.19
Dutch	50	0.33
Eastern European	9	0.06
English	332	2.21
European	8	0.05
Finnish	9	0.06
French, except Basque	202	1.35
French Canadian	51	0.34
German	1,039	6.92
Greek	62	0.41

Notes: 1. Figures in the "Number" column do not add up to the total population due to: a) Ancestry/Race overlap — e.g. persons can report being both White and Irish, b) persons of Hispanic origin can report being any race, c) persons reporting two ancestries are counted in both categories. 2. Numbers in parentheses indicate the number of persons reporting this ancestry/race alone, not in combination with any other ancestry/race. 3. Refer to the Explanation of Data in the front of the book for more detailed information.

Guyanese	55	0.37
Hawaii Native/Pacific Islander:	29	0.19
Micronesian: (3)	5	0.03
Guamanian/Chamorro (3)	5	0.03
Polynesian: (9)	15	0.10
Native Hawaiian (9)	14	0.09
Samoan	1	0.01
Other Pac. Isl., not spec.	9	0.06
Hispanic or Latino:	7,608	50.75
Central American:	2,152	14.35
Costa Rican	27	0.18
Guatemalan	174	1.16
Honduran	194	1.29
Nicaraguan	7	0.05
Panamanian	36	0.24
Salvadoran	1,630	10.87
Other Central American	84	0.56
Cuban	38	0.25
Dominican Republic	505	3.37
Mexican	122	0.81
Puerto Rican	2,578	17.20
South American:	737	4.92
Argentinean	26	0.17
Chilean	38	0.25
Colombian	269	1.79
Ecuadorian	186	1.24
Paraguayan	5	0.03
Peruvian	166	1.11
Uruguayan	14	0.09
Venezuelan	8	0.05
Other South American	25	0.17
Other Hispanic or Latino	1,476	9.85
Hungarian	66	0.44
Irish	1,398	9.31
Italian	1,516	10.09
Latvian	16	0.11
Lithuanian	17	0.11
Norwegian	7	0.05
Polish	231	1.54
Portuguese	103	0.69
Russian	50	0.33
Scotch-Irish	71	0.47
Scottish	15	0.10
Swedish	13	0.09
Turkish	12	0.08
Ukrainian	12	0.08
United States or American	402	2.68
West Indian, excl. Hispanic:	617	4.11
Barbadian	9	0.06
British West Indian	45	0.30
Haitian	232	1.54
Jamaican	190	1.27
Trinidadian and Tobagonian	56	0.37
West Indian	85	0.57
White:	7,912	52.77
Not Hispanic (3,902)	4,121	27.49
Hispanic (3,367)	3,791	25.29

North Bellmore

Place Type: Census Designated Place
County: Nassau
Population: 20,079

Ancestry/Race	Number	%
Afghan	18	0.09
African American/Black:	491	2.45
Not Hispanic (418)	472	2.35
Hispanic (12)	19	0.09
African, sub-Saharan:	5	0.02
African	5	0.02
Am. Ind. or Alaska Nat., not spec.	23	0.11
Albanian	24	0.12
American Indian tribes, specified:	23	0.11
Cherokee (1)	5	0.02
Iroquois (2)	3	0.01
Latin American Indians	4	0.02
Navajo	1	0.00
All other tribes	10	0.05
Arab:	49	0.24
Egyptian	22	0.11
Palestinian	27	0.13
Armenian	32	0.16
Asian:	747	3.72
Bangladeshi (10)	12	0.06
Chinese, ex. Taiwanese (120)	151	0.75
Filipino (52)	64	0.32
Indian (227)	255	1.27
Japanese (6)	10	0.05
Korean (40)	42	0.21
Pakistani (136)	164	0.82
Taiwanese (3)	3	0.01
Thai (3)	4	0.02
Vietnamese (9)	10	0.05
Other Asian, specified (5)	5	0.02
Other Asian, not specified (8)	27	0.13
Austrian	212	1.06
Brazilian	10	0.05
British	41	0.20
Canadian	18	0.09
Czech	81	0.40
Czechoslovakian	33	0.16
Danish	88	0.44
Dutch	126	0.63
Eastern European	182	0.91
English	1,021	5.08
European	13	0.06
Finnish	9	0.04
French, except Basque	382	1.90
French Canadian	85	0.42
German	3,156	15.72
Greek	533	2.65
Guyanese	48	0.24
Hawaii Native/Pacific Islander:	20	0.10
Micronesian: (1)	1	0.00
Guamanian/Chamorro (1)	1	0.00
Polynesian: (3)	3	0.01
Native Hawaiian (3)	3	0.01
Other Pac. Isl., not spec. (1)	16	0.08
Hispanic or Latino:	913	4.55
Central American:	98	0.49
Costa Rican	2	0.01
Guatemalan	7	0.03
Nicaraguan	2	0.01
Panamanian	1	0.00
Salvadoran	80	0.40
Other Central American	6	0.03
Cuban	53	0.26
Dominican Republic	35	0.17
Mexican	53	0.26
Puerto Rican	294	1.46
South American:	173	0.86
Argentinean	16	0.08
Bolivian	1	0.00
Chilean	16	0.08
Colombian	85	0.42
Ecuadorian	29	0.14
Paraguayan	1	0.00
Peruvian	15	0.07
Uruguayan	2	0.01
Venezuelan	6	0.03
Other South American	2	0.01
Other Hispanic or Latino	207	1.03
Hungarian	243	1.21
Iranian	28	0.14
Irish	4,760	23.71
Israeli	82	0.41
Italian	6,429	32.02
Lithuanian	135	0.67
Maltese	62	0.31
Norwegian	164	0.82
Pennsylvania German	30	0.15
Polish	1,282	6.38
Portuguese	11	0.05
Romanian	93	0.46
Russian	1,188	5.92
Scotch-Irish	137	0.68
Scottish	163	0.81
Slavic	7	0.03
Slovak	83	0.41
Swedish	148	0.74
Swiss	76	0.38
Turkish	86	0.43
Ukrainian	107	0.53
United States or American	888	4.42
Welsh	42	0.21
West Indian, excl. Hispanic:	206	1.03
Haitian	127	0.63
Trinidadian and Tobagonian	35	0.17
West Indian	44	0.22
White:	18,713	93.20
Not Hispanic (17,888)	18,016	89.73
Hispanic (642)	697	3.47

North Castle

Place Type: Town
County: Westchester
Population: 10,849

Ancestry/Race	Number	%
African American/Black:	208	1.92
Not Hispanic (182)	188	1.73
Hispanic (9)	20	0.18
African, sub-Saharan:	41	0.38
African	41	0.38
Am. Ind. or Alaska Nat., not spec.	11	0.10
Albanian	25	0.23
Alsatian	11	0.10
American Indian tribes, specified:	10	0.09
Blackfeet (1)	2	0.02
Cherokee	3	0.03
Choctaw	1	0.01
Iroquois	1	0.01
Latin American Indians	2	0.02
Pueblo (1)	1	0.01
American Indian tribes, not spec.	3	0.03
Arab:	27	0.25
Iraqi	7	0.06
Lebanese	12	0.11
Other Arab	8	0.07
Armenian	7	0.06
Asian:	493	4.54
Chinese, ex. Taiwanese (167)	187	1.72
Filipino (14)	20	0.18
Indian (113)	127	1.17
Indonesian (1)	1	0.01
Japanese (45)	52	0.48
Korean (67)	72	0.66
Taiwanese (11)	11	0.10
Vietnamese (1)	4	0.04
Other Asian, not specified (4)	19	0.18
Austrian	155	1.43
Belgian	14	0.13
British	67	0.62
Bulgarian	37	0.34
Canadian	88	0.81
Celtic	6	0.06
Croatian	20	0.18
Czech	11	0.10
Czechoslovakian	14	0.13
Danish	42	0.39
Dutch	132	1.22
Eastern European	247	2.28
English	871	8.03
European	114	1.05
Finnish	24	0.22
French, except Basque	132	1.22
French Canadian	71	0.65
German	1,109	10.22
Greek	112	1.03
Hawaii Native/Pacific Islander:	6	0.06
Micronesian: (5)	5	0.05
Guamanian/Chamorro (5)	5	0.05
Other Pac. Isl., not spec.	1	0.01
Hispanic or Latino:	449	4.14
Central American:	45	0.41
Guatemalan	15	0.14
Honduran	8	0.07
Nicaraguan	4	0.04

Notes: 1. Figures in the "Number" column do not add up to the total population due to: a) Ancestry/Race overlap — e.g. persons can report being both White and Irish, b) persons of Hispanic origin can report being any race, c) persons reporting two ancestries are counted in both categories. 2. Numbers in parentheses indicate the number of persons reporting this ancestry/race alone, not in combination with any other ancestry/race. 3. Refer to the Explanation of Data in the front of the book for more detailed information.

Panamanian	2	0.02
Salvadoran	4	0.04
Other Central American	12	0.11
Cuban	39	0.36
Dominican Republic	10	0.09
Mexican	54	0.50
Puerto Rican	101	0.93
South American:	117	1.08
Argentinean	9	0.08
Bolivian	2	0.02
Chilean	2	0.02
Colombian	58	0.53
Ecuadorian	13	0.12
Paraguayan	5	0.05
Peruvian	17	0.16
Uruguayan	8	0.07
Other South American	3	0.03
Other Hispanic or Latino	83	0.77
Hungarian	131	1.21
Iranian	38	0.35
Irish	1,656	15.26
Israeli	34	0.31
Italian	2,915	26.87
Latvian	10	0.09
Norwegian	81	0.75
Polish	544	5.01
Portuguese	7	0.06
Romanian	25	0.23
Russian	695	6.41
Scandinavian	5	0.05
Scotch-Irish	97	0.89
Scottish	247	2.28
Serbian	6	0.06
Slavic	8	0.07
Slovak	20	0.18
Swedish	146	1.35
Swiss	144	1.33
Turkish	6	0.06
Ukrainian	56	0.52
United States or American	731	6.74
Welsh	32	0.29
West Indian, excl. Hispanic:	46	0.42
Barbadian	7	0.06
Haitian	32	0.29
Trinidadian and Tobagonian	7	0.06
White:	10,142	93.48
Not Hispanic (9,682)	9,768	90.04
Hispanic (340)	374	3.45
Yugoslavian	17	0.16

North Greenbush

Place Type: Town
County: Rensselaer
Population: 10,805

Ancestry/Race	Number	%
Afghan	24	0.22
African American/Black:	150	1.39
Not Hispanic (106)	144	1.33
Hispanic (3)	6	0.06
Am. Ind. or Alaska Nat., not spec.	9	0.08
American Indian tribes, specified:	26	0.24
Apache	3	0.03
Blackfeet	2	0.02
Cherokee	4	0.04
Chippewa (4)	4	0.04
Cree	1	0.01
Iroquois (1)	4	0.04
Latin American Indians	2	0.02
Sioux	1	0.01
All other tribes (2)	5	0.05
American Indian tribes, not spec.	7	0.06
Arab:	102	0.95
Lebanese	100	0.93
Palestinian	2	0.02
Armenian	78	0.73
Asian:	104	0.96
Bangladeshi	1	0.01
Chinese, ex. Taiwanese (24)	27	0.25
Filipino (4)	10	0.09
Indian (18)	18	0.17
Japanese (6)	6	0.06
Korean (16)	19	0.18
Pakistani (4)	4	0.04
Thai (1)	1	0.01
Other Asian, not specified (9)	18	0.17
Austrian	46	0.43
Belgian	14	0.13
British	70	0.65
Canadian	25	0.23
Celtic	31	0.29
Czech	29	0.27
Czechoslovakian	18	0.17
Danish	50	0.46
Dutch	478	4.44
Eastern European	6	0.06
English	1,068	9.93
European	95	0.88
French, except Basque	926	8.61
French Canadian	303	2.82
German	2,062	19.17
Greek	95	0.88
Guyanese	30	0.28
Hawaii Native/Pacific Islander:	9	0.08
Polynesian:	1	0.01
Samoan	1	0.01
Other Pac. Isl., not spec. (1)	8	0.07
Hispanic or Latino:	92	0.85
Central American:	3	0.03
Costa Rican	2	0.02
Guatemalan	1	0.01
Mexican	8	0.07
Puerto Rican	39	0.36
South American:	10	0.09
Argentinean	2	0.02
Colombian	6	0.06
Venezuelan	2	0.02
Other Hispanic or Latino	32	0.30
Hungarian	32	0.30
Irish	2,877	26.75
Italian	2,035	18.92
Latvian	9	0.08
Lithuanian	42	0.39
Norwegian	60	0.56
Polish	719	6.69
Portuguese	16	0.15
Russian	200	1.86
Scandinavian	8	0.07
Scotch-Irish	175	1.63
Scottish	269	2.50
Slavic	20	0.19
Slovak	2	0.02
Swedish	45	0.42
Swiss	10	0.09
Ukrainian	196	1.82
United States or American	339	3.15
Welsh	86	0.80
White:	10,565	97.78
Not Hispanic (10,405)	10,497	97.15
Hispanic (55)	68	0.63
Yugoslavian	3	0.03

North Hempstead

Place Type: Town
County: Nassau
Population: 222,611

Ancestry/Race	Number	%
Acadian/Cajun	2	0.00
Afghan	69	0.03
African American/Black:	15,454	6.94
Not Hispanic (13,651)	14,582	6.55
Hispanic (587)	872	0.39
African, sub-Saharan:	1,005	0.45
African	598	0.27
Cape Verdean	58	0.03
Ghanian	30	0.01
Liberian	30	0.01
Nigerian	127	0.06
South African	145	0.07
Other sub-Saharan African	17	0.01
Alaska Native tribes, specified:	3	0.00
Alaska Athabascan	1	0.00
Tlingit-Haida	2	0.00
Am. Ind. or Alaska Nat., not spec.	391	0.18
Albanian	247	0.11
Alsatian	22	0.01
American Indian tribes, specified:	373	0.17
Apache (4)	10	0.00
Blackfeet (1)	6	0.00
Cherokee (9)	73	0.03
Cheyenne (3)	3	0.00
Chippewa (1)	5	0.00
Choctaw	9	0.00
Creek	4	0.00
Crow	1	0.00
Delaware	1	0.00
Iroquois (6)	24	0.01
Kiowa	1	0.00
Latin American Indians (66)	128	0.06
Navajo (3)	6	0.00
Potawatomi (1)	1	0.00
Pueblo	2	0.00
Seminole	5	0.00
Sioux (7)	11	0.00
Yaqui (1)	1	0.00
Yuman	1	0.00
All other tribes (24)	81	0.04
American Indian tribes, not spec.	62	0.03
Arab:	1,768	0.79
Arab/Arabic	140	0.06
Egyptian	431	0.19
Iraqi	334	0.15
Jordanian	24	0.01
Lebanese	226	0.10
Moroccan	183	0.08
Palestinian	24	0.01
Syrian	105	0.05
Other Arab	301	0.14
Armenian	717	0.32
Asian:	22,196	9.97
Bangladeshi (130)	159	0.07
Cambodian (1)	1	0.00
Chinese, ex. Taiwanese (5,618)	6,003	2.70
Filipino (1,286)	1,479	0.66
Indian (7,463)	7,951	3.57
Indonesian (22)	25	0.01
Japanese (1,035)	1,130	0.51
Korean (3,315)	3,425	1.54
Malaysian (8)	20	0.01
Pakistani (396)	462	0.21
Sri Lankan (11)	11	0.00
Taiwanese (349)	418	0.19
Thai (78)	93	0.04
Vietnamese (120)	140	0.06
Other Asian, specified (33)	42	0.02
Other Asian, not specified (181)	837	0.38
Australian	61	0.03
Austrian	2,795	1.26
Basque	34	0.02
Belgian	132	0.06
Brazilian	316	0.14
British	542	0.24
Bulgarian	29	0.01
Canadian	280	0.13
Carpatho Rusyn	8	0.00
Celtic	11	0.00
Croatian	667	0.30
Cypriot	76	0.03
Czech	679	0.31
Czechoslovakian	517	0.23
Danish	423	0.19
Dutch	803	0.36
Eastern European	2,251	1.01
English	6,629	2.98
Estonian	49	0.02
European	1,399	0.63
Finnish	117	0.05

Notes: 1. Figures in the "Number" column do not add up to the total population due to: a) Ancestry/Race overlap — e.g. persons can report being both White and Irish, b) persons of Hispanic origin can report being any race, c) persons reporting two ancestries are counted in both categories. 2. Numbers in parentheses indicate the number of persons reporting this ancestry/race alone, not in combination with any other ancestry/race. 3. Refer to the Explanation of Data in the front of the book for more detailed information.

French, except Basque	2,285	1.03
French Canadian	465	0.21
German	19,739	8.87
Greek	3,529	1.59
Guyanese	346	0.16
Hawaii Native/Pacific Islander:	216	0.10
Melanesian: (1)	5	0.00
Fijian (1)	5	0.00
Micronesian: (5)	11	0.00
Guamanian/Chamorro (5)	11	0.00
Polynesian: (28)	48	0.02
Native Hawaiian (11)	20	0.01
Samoan (16)	26	0.01
Other Polynesian (1)	2	0.00
Other Pac. Isl., specified	3	0.00
Other Pac. Isl., not spec. (31)	149	0.07
Hispanic or Latino:	21,872	9.83
Central American:	6,571	2.95
Costa Rican	99	0.04
Guatemalan	550	0.25
Honduran	594	0.27
Nicaraguan	32	0.01
Panamanian	51	0.02
Salvadoran	4,993	2.24
Other Central American	252	0.11
Cuban	526	0.24
Dominican Republic	864	0.39
Mexican	2,403	1.08
Puerto Rican	2,209	0.99
South American:	3,707	1.67
Argentinean	297	0.13
Bolivian	36	0.02
Chilean	521	0.23
Colombian	1,219	0.55
Ecuadorian	815	0.37
Paraguayan	48	0.02
Peruvian	457	0.21
Uruguayan	47	0.02
Venezuelan	81	0.04
Other South American	186	0.08
Other Hispanic or Latino	5,592	2.51
Hungarian	2,470	1.11
Icelander	2	0.00
Iranian	7,622	3.42
Irish	28,740	12.91
Israeli	1,348	0.61
Italian	39,788	17.87
Latvian	234	0.11
Lithuanian	1,128	0.51
Luxemburger	4	0.00
Maltese	158	0.07
New Zealander	19	0.01
Northern European	40	0.02
Norwegian	787	0.35
Pennsylvania German	13	0.01
Polish	13,130	5.90
Portuguese	3,259	1.46
Romanian	1,317	0.59
Russian	12,446	5.59
Scandinavian	142	0.06
Scotch-Irish	1,098	0.49
Scottish	1,513	0.68
Serbian	22	0.01
Slavic	47	0.02
Slovak	345	0.15
Slovene	24	0.01
Soviet Union	5	0.00
Swedish	1,038	0.47
Swiss	439	0.20
Turkish	612	0.27
Ukrainian	1,196	0.54
United States or American	11,272	5.06
Welsh	420	0.19
West Indian, excl. Hispanic:	4,524	2.03
Barbadian	103	0.05
Belizean	69	0.03
Bermudan	12	0.01
British West Indian	170	0.08
Dutch West Indian	5	0.00
Haitian	2,007	0.90
Jamaican	1,534	0.69
Trinidadian and Tobagonian	367	0.16
U.S. Virgin Islander	7	0.00
West Indian	250	0.11
White:	180,100	80.90
Not Hispanic (162,762)	165,291	74.25
Hispanic (13,047)	14,809	6.65
Yugoslavian	248	0.11

North Lindenhurst

Place Type: Census Designated Place
County: Suffolk
Population: 11,767

Ancestry/Race	Number	%
African American/Black:	503	4.27
Not Hispanic (416)	444	3.77
Hispanic (43)	59	0.50
Am. Ind. or Alaska Nat., not spec.	23	0.20
American Indian tribes, specified:	35	0.30
Blackfeet	6	0.05
Cherokee (1)	5	0.04
Chippewa (1)	1	0.01
Iroquois	2	0.02
Latin American Indians (1)	1	0.01
All other tribes (6)	20	0.17
Arab:	38	0.32
Arab/Arabic	38	0.32
Armenian	16	0.14
Asian:	315	2.68
Bangladeshi (1)	2	0.02
Chinese, ex. Taiwanese (50)	54	0.46
Filipino (13)	23	0.20
Indian (90)	109	0.93
Japanese (5)	6	0.05
Korean (23)	24	0.20
Pakistani (46)	53	0.45
Vietnamese (17)	19	0.16
Other Asian, not specified (4)	25	0.21
Australian	7	0.06
Austrian	27	0.23
Brazilian	7	0.06
British	10	0.08
Croatian	59	0.50
Cypriot	6	0.05
Czech	29	0.25
Czechoslovakian	64	0.54
Danish	7	0.06
Dutch	62	0.53
Eastern European	27	0.23
English	387	3.29
Finnish	6	0.05
French, except Basque	138	1.17
French Canadian	19	0.16
German	2,236	19.00
Greek	130	1.10
Guyanese	22	0.19
Hawaii Native/Pacific Islander:	13	0.11
Micronesian: (5)	7	0.06
Guamanian/Chamorro (5)	7	0.06
Polynesian: (1)	5	0.04
Native Hawaiian (1)	5	0.04
Other Pac. Isl., not spec.	1	0.01
Hispanic or Latino:	1,372	11.66
Central American:	202	1.72
Costa Rican	4	0.03
Guatemalan	14	0.12
Honduran	16	0.14
Panamanian	17	0.14
Salvadoran	148	1.26
Other Central American	3	0.03
Cuban	10	0.08
Dominican Republic	196	1.67
Mexican	55	0.47
Puerto Rican	381	3.24
South American:	205	1.74
Argentinean	12	0.10
Chilean	2	0.02
Colombian	108	0.92
Ecuadorian	36	0.31
Paraguayan	1	0.01
Peruvian	25	0.21
Uruguayan	7	0.06
Venezuelan	4	0.03
Other South American	10	0.08
Other Hispanic or Latino	323	2.74
Hungarian	80	0.68
Iranian	5	0.04
Irish	2,611	22.19
Italian	3,652	31.04
Lithuanian	31	0.26
Maltese	22	0.19
Norwegian	38	0.32
Polish	928	7.89
Portuguese	25	0.21
Romanian	12	0.10
Russian	172	1.46
Scandinavian	39	0.33
Scotch-Irish	103	0.88
Scottish	78	0.66
Slavic	6	0.05
Slovak	18	0.15
Slovene	36	0.31
Swedish	54	0.46
Swiss	17	0.14
Turkish	94	0.80
United States or American	432	3.67
Welsh	4	0.03
West Indian, excl. Hispanic:	20	0.17
Jamaican	20	0.17
White:	10,576	89.88
Not Hispanic (9,565)	9,672	82.20
Hispanic (822)	904	7.68
Yugoslavian	66	0.56

North Massapequa

Place Type: Census Designated Place
County: Nassau
Population: 19,152

Ancestry/Race	Number	%
African American/Black:	66	0.34
Not Hispanic (34)	52	0.27
Hispanic (8)	14	0.07
African, sub-Saharan:	34	0.18
Ethiopian	24	0.13
Ghanian	10	0.05
Am. Ind. or Alaska Nat., not spec.	4	0.02
Albanian	47	0.25
American Indian tribes, specified:	15	0.08
Cherokee	1	0.01
Iroquois	3	0.02
Latin American Indians	1	0.01
Navajo	5	0.03
All other tribes (3)	5	0.03
Arab:	118	0.62
Egyptian	47	0.25
Jordanian	15	0.08
Lebanese	17	0.09
Palestinian	5	0.03
Syrian	20	0.10
Other Arab	14	0.07
Armenian	30	0.16
Asian:	271	1.41
Chinese, ex. Taiwanese (90)	102	0.53
Filipino (20)	30	0.16
Indian (47)	60	0.31
Japanese (10)	12	0.06
Korean (31)	38	0.20
Pakistani (12)	13	0.07
Taiwanese (5)	5	0.03
Other Asian, not specified (3)	11	0.06
Austrian	127	0.66
Belgian	5	0.03
Brazilian	22	0.11
British	80	0.42
Canadian	45	0.23
Croatian	36	0.19

Notes: 1. Figures in the "Number" column do not add up to the total population due to: a) Ancestry/Race overlap — e.g. persons can report being both White and Irish, b) persons of Hispanic origin can report being any race, c) persons reporting two ancestries are counted in both categories. 2. Numbers in parentheses indicate the number of persons reporting this ancestry/race alone, not in combination with any other ancestry/race. 3. Refer to the Explanation of Data in the front of the book for more detailed information.

Ancestry/Race	Number	%
Czech	81	0.42
Czechoslovakian	111	0.58
Danish	69	0.36
Dutch	71	0.37
Eastern European	55	0.29
English	638	3.33
European	112	0.58
Finnish	70	0.37
French, except Basque	153	0.80
French Canadian	53	0.28
German	2,922	15.26
Greek	287	1.50
Hawaii Native/Pacific Islander:	1	0.01
Polynesian:	1	0.01
Native Hawaiian	1	0.01
Hispanic or Latino:	619	3.23
Central American:	26	0.14
Costa Rican	2	0.01
Guatemalan	8	0.04
Honduran	1	0.01
Panamanian	1	0.01
Salvadoran	13	0.07
Other Central American	1	0.01
Cuban	55	0.29
Dominican Republic	9	0.05
Mexican	24	0.13
Puerto Rican	278	1.45
South American:	127	0.66
Argentinean	4	0.02
Chilean	11	0.06
Colombian	47	0.25
Ecuadorian	22	0.11
Paraguayan	1	0.01
Peruvian	27	0.14
Uruguayan	4	0.02
Venezuelan	1	0.01
Other South American	10	0.05
Other Hispanic or Latino	100	0.52
Hungarian	249	1.30
Icelander	13	0.07
Iranian	12	0.06
Irish	4,497	23.48
Israeli	6	0.03
Italian	9,368	48.91
Lithuanian	84	0.44
Maltese	6	0.03
Norwegian	118	0.62
Polish	1,257	6.56
Portuguese	38	0.20
Romanian	28	0.15
Russian	605	3.16
Scandinavian	7	0.04
Scotch-Irish	153	0.80
Scottish	126	0.66
Slavic	15	0.08
Slovak	26	0.14
Slovene	7	0.04
Swedish	164	0.86
Swiss	36	0.19
Turkish	7	0.04
Ukrainian	93	0.49
United States or American	580	3.03
West Indian, excl. Hispanic:	27	0.14
Jamaican	13	0.07
West Indian	14	0.07
White:	18,768	97.99
Not Hispanic (18,155)	18,249	95.29
Hispanic (484)	519	2.71
Yugoslavian	15	0.08

North Merrick

Place Type: Census Designated Place
County: Nassau
Population: 11,844

Ancestry/Race	Number	%
African American/Black:	168	1.42
Not Hispanic (119)	156	1.32
Hispanic (8)	12	0.10
Alaska Native tribes, specified:	1	0.01
Eskimo	1	0.01
Am. Ind. or Alaska Nat., not spec.	21	0.18
American Indian tribes, specified:	31	0.26
Apache	4	0.03
Cherokee	8	0.07
Cheyenne	2	0.02
Iroquois (1)	2	0.02
Latin American Indians (3)	3	0.03
Navajo	1	0.01
Pueblo	2	0.02
All other tribes	9	0.08
American Indian tribes, not spec.	1	0.01
Arab:	35	0.30
Egyptian	19	0.16
Lebanese	6	0.05
Syrian	10	0.08
Armenian	16	0.14
Asian:	441	3.72
Bangladeshi (3)	3	0.03
Cambodian (1)	2	0.02
Chinese, ex. Taiwanese (123)	135	1.14
Filipino (35)	42	0.35
Indian (141)	154	1.30
Indonesian	6	0.05
Japanese (8)	11	0.09
Korean (24)	26	0.22
Pakistani (35)	50	0.42
Taiwanese	1	0.01
Thai (2)	2	0.02
Vietnamese (1)	1	0.01
Other Asian, not specified (1)	8	0.07
Australian	7	0.06
Austrian	148	1.25
British	18	0.15
Bulgarian	5	0.04
Canadian	21	0.18
Croatian	13	0.11
Czech	50	0.42
Czechoslovakian	26	0.22
Danish	68	0.57
Dutch	161	1.36
Eastern European	59	0.50
English	540	4.56
European	112	0.95
Finnish	12	0.10
French, except Basque	181	1.53
French Canadian	53	0.45
German	2,226	18.79
Greek	191	1.61
Guyanese	12	0.10
Hawaii Native/Pacific Islander:	11	0.09
Polynesian: (5)	6	0.05
Native Hawaiian (1)	2	0.02
Samoan (4)	4	0.03
Other Pac. Isl., not spec. (1)	5	0.04
Hispanic or Latino:	436	3.68
Central American:	28	0.24
Costa Rican	7	0.06
Guatemalan	3	0.03
Honduran	1	0.01
Nicaraguan	3	0.03
Panamanian	1	0.01
Salvadoran	13	0.11
Cuban	35	0.30
Dominican Republic	6	0.05
Mexican	23	0.19
Puerto Rican	130	1.10
South American:	99	0.84
Argentinean	11	0.09
Bolivian	3	0.03
Chilean	1	0.01
Colombian	53	0.45
Ecuadorian	15	0.13
Peruvian	6	0.05
Venezuelan	2	0.02
Other South American	8	0.07
Other Hispanic or Latino	115	0.97
Hungarian	97	0.82
Irish	2,987	25.22
Israeli	20	0.17
Italian	4,092	34.55
Latvian	13	0.11
Lithuanian	77	0.65
Maltese	19	0.16
Northern European	13	0.11
Norwegian	124	1.05
Polish	875	7.39
Portuguese	18	0.15
Romanian	51	0.43
Russian	591	4.99
Scandinavian	9	0.08
Scotch-Irish	74	0.62
Scottish	117	0.99
Serbian	6	0.05
Slavic	7	0.06
Slovak	14	0.12
Swedish	149	1.26
Swiss	6	0.05
Turkish	10	0.08
Ukrainian	95	0.80
United States or American	323	2.73
Welsh	36	0.30
West Indian, excl. Hispanic:	108	0.91
Haitian	48	0.41
Jamaican	53	0.45
Other West Indian	7	0.06
White:	11,188	94.46
Not Hispanic (10,752)	10,836	91.49
Hispanic (331)	352	2.97

North New Hyde Park

Place Type: Census Designated Place
County: Nassau
Population: 14,542

Ancestry/Race	Number	%
African American/Black:	72	0.50
Not Hispanic (43)	63	0.43
Hispanic (5)	9	0.06
Am. Ind. or Alaska Nat., not spec.	21	0.14
Albanian	109	0.75
American Indian tribes, specified:	7	0.05
Iroquois	3	0.02
Sioux (4)	4	0.03
American Indian tribes, not spec.	8	0.06
Arab:	76	0.52
Arab/Arabic	7	0.05
Moroccan	54	0.37
Other Arab	15	0.10
Armenian	77	0.53
Asian:	2,244	15.43
Bangladeshi (10)	11	0.08
Chinese, ex. Taiwanese (644)	669	4.60
Filipino (161)	173	1.19
Indian (1,094)	1,122	7.72
Indonesian (2)	2	0.01
Japanese (37)	43	0.30
Korean (133)	138	0.95
Malaysian	2	0.01
Pakistani (24)	25	0.17
Taiwanese (23)	23	0.16
Thai (3)	5	0.03
Vietnamese (2)	7	0.05
Other Asian, specified (6)	8	0.06
Other Asian, not specified (10)	16	0.11
Austrian	187	1.29
British	28	0.19
Canadian	23	0.16
Croatian	99	0.68
Czech	38	0.26
Czechoslovakian	24	0.17
Danish	20	0.14
Dutch	30	0.21
Eastern European	26	0.18
English	396	2.72
European	55	0.38
French, except Basque	141	0.97
French Canadian	46	0.32

Notes: 1. Figures in the "Number" column do not add up to the total population due to: a) Ancestry/Race overlap — e.g. persons can report being both White and Irish, b) persons of Hispanic origin can report being any race, c) persons reporting two ancestries are counted in both categories. 2. Numbers in parentheses indicate the number of persons reporting this ancestry/race alone, not in combination with any other ancestry/race. 3. Refer to the Explanation of Data in the front of the book for more detailed information.

Ancestry/Race	Number	%
German	1,787	12.29
Greek	216	1.49
Guyanese	33	0.23
Hawaii Native/Pacific Islander:	4	0.03
Other Pac. Isl., not spec. (3)	4	0.03
Hispanic or Latino:	707	4.86
Central American:	18	0.12
Costa Rican	4	0.03
Guatemalan	3	0.02
Honduran	1	0.01
Panamanian	1	0.01
Salvadoran	8	0.06
Other Central American	1	0.01
Cuban	53	0.36
Dominican Republic	53	0.36
Mexican	17	0.12
Puerto Rican	162	1.11
South American:	218	1.50
Argentinean	17	0.12
Bolivian	2	0.01
Chilean	20	0.14
Colombian	73	0.50
Ecuadorian	73	0.50
Paraguayan	1	0.01
Peruvian	22	0.15
Uruguayan	8	0.06
Venezuelan	2	0.01
Other Hispanic or Latino	186	1.28
Hungarian	80	0.55
Iranian	170	1.17
Irish	3,008	20.68
Israeli	53	0.36
Italian	4,076	28.03
Latvian	9	0.06
Lithuanian	56	0.39
Maltese	24	0.17
Norwegian	45	0.31
Polish	763	5.25
Portuguese	45	0.31
Romanian	24	0.17
Russian	356	2.45
Scandinavian	24	0.17
Scotch-Irish	62	0.43
Scottish	105	0.72
Slovak	17	0.12
Swedish	37	0.25
Swiss	30	0.21
Ukrainian	142	0.98
United States or American	564	3.88
Welsh	17	0.12
West Indian, excl. Hispanic:	99	0.68
Haitian	57	0.39
Jamaican	42	0.29
White:	12,099	83.20
Not Hispanic (11,475)	11,557	79.47
Hispanic (505)	542	3.73
Yugoslavian	52	0.36

North Tonawanda

Place Type: City
County: Niagara
Population: 33,262

Ancestry/Race	Number	%
African American/Black:	152	0.46
Not Hispanic (96)	145	0.44
Hispanic (2)	7	0.02
African, sub-Saharan:	13	0.04
African	13	0.04
Am. Ind. or Alaska Nat., not spec.	66	0.20
Alsatian	8	0.02
American Indian tribes, specified:	143	0.43
Apache (1)	2	0.01
Blackfeet (2)	5	0.02
Cherokee (5)	15	0.05
Chippewa (4)	5	0.02
Choctaw	1	0.00
Iroquois (76)	108	0.32
Lumbee (3)	3	0.01
Sioux (1)	4	0.01
American Indian tribes, not spec.	2	0.01
Arab:	197	0.59
Arab/Arabic	26	0.08
Lebanese	133	0.40
Palestinian	6	0.02
Syrian	32	0.10
Asian:	224	0.67
Chinese, ex. Taiwanese (61)	63	0.19
Filipino (9)	13	0.04
Indian (11)	16	0.05
Indonesian (1)	4	0.01
Japanese (12)	18	0.05
Korean (59)	64	0.19
Laotian (5)	5	0.02
Pakistani (1)	1	0.00
Taiwanese (3)	5	0.02
Thai (2)	3	0.01
Vietnamese (9)	12	0.04
Other Asian, not specified (4)	20	0.06
Austrian	172	0.52
British	77	0.23
Bulgarian	27	0.08
Canadian	208	0.63
Croatian	37	0.11
Czech	98	0.29
Czechoslovakian	69	0.21
Danish	94	0.28
Dutch	498	1.50
English	3,382	10.17
European	64	0.19
Finnish	16	0.05
French, except Basque	1,401	4.21
French Canadian	528	1.59
German	11,748	35.32
Greek	87	0.26
Hawaii Native/Pacific Islander:	7	0.02
Micronesian:	2	0.01
Guamanian/Chamorro	2	0.01
Polynesian: (1)	3	0.01
Native Hawaiian (1)	3	0.01
Other Pac. Isl., not spec. (1)	2	0.01
Hispanic or Latino:	362	1.09
Central American:	17	0.05
Honduran	1	0.00
Panamanian	13	0.04
Salvadoran	3	0.01
Cuban	9	0.03
Mexican	57	0.17
Puerto Rican	198	0.60
South American:	12	0.04
Argentinean	1	0.00
Bolivian	2	0.01
Colombian	1	0.00
Ecuadorian	3	0.01
Peruvian	2	0.01
Venezuelan	1	0.00
Other South American	2	0.01
Other Hispanic or Latino	69	0.21
Hungarian	674	2.03
Icelander	10	0.03
Iranian	8	0.02
Irish	5,654	17.00
Italian	5,665	17.03
Lithuanian	45	0.14
Macedonian	4	0.01
Norwegian	83	0.25
Pennsylvania German	38	0.11
Polish	6,949	20.89
Portuguese	20	0.06
Romanian	62	0.19
Russian	209	0.63
Scandinavian	12	0.04
Scotch-Irish	371	1.12
Scottish	846	2.54
Serbian	11	0.03
Slavic	39	0.12
Slovak	92	0.28
Slovene	15	0.05
Swedish	374	1.12
Swiss	122	0.37
Ukrainian	415	1.25
United States or American	1,074	3.23
Welsh	228	0.69
West Indian, excl. Hispanic:	9	0.03
West Indian	9	0.03
White:	32,762	98.50
Not Hispanic (32,294)	32,482	97.65
Hispanic (255)	280	0.84
Yugoslavian	19	0.06

North Valley Stream

Place Type: Census Designated Place
County: Nassau
Population: 15,789

Ancestry/Race	Number	%
African American/Black:	6,248	39.57
Not Hispanic (5,695)	6,045	38.29
Hispanic (159)	203	1.29
African, sub-Saharan:	394	2.50
African	156	0.99
Cape Verdean	25	0.16
Liberian	42	0.27
Nigerian	146	0.92
Sierra Leonean	11	0.07
Sudanese	14	0.09
Alaska Native tribes, specified:	6	0.04
Alaska Athabascan	3	0.02
Tlingit-Haida	3	0.02
Am. Ind. or Alaska Nat., not spec.	68	0.43
American Indian tribes, specified:	43	0.27
Apache (1)	2	0.01
Blackfeet	5	0.03
Cherokee (2)	8	0.05
Choctaw	1	0.01
Iroquois	2	0.01
Latin American Indians (4)	13	0.08
Navajo	9	0.06
All other tribes (4)	4	0.03
American Indian tribes, not spec.	8	0.05
Arab:	65	0.41
Arab/Arabic	22	0.14
Egyptian	36	0.23
Moroccan	7	0.04
Armenian	7	0.04
Asian:	1,691	10.71
Bangladeshi (6)	10	0.06
Chinese, ex. Taiwanese (228)	268	1.70
Filipino (231)	269	1.70
Indian (657)	752	4.76
Indonesian (1)	2	0.01
Japanese (7)	11	0.07
Korean (75)	89	0.56
Malaysian (3)	6	0.04
Pakistani (134)	151	0.96
Taiwanese (12)	20	0.13
Thai (13)	18	0.11
Vietnamese (2)	3	0.02
Other Asian, not specified (29)	92	0.58
Austrian	102	0.65
British	73	0.46
Canadian	12	0.08
Croatian	57	0.36
Czech	16	0.10
Czechoslovakian	20	0.13
Danish	7	0.04
Dutch	71	0.45
Eastern European	23	0.15
English	346	2.19
European	57	0.36
French, except Basque	98	0.62
French Canadian	6	0.04
German	944	5.98
Greek	102	0.65
Guyanese	236	1.49
Hawaii Native/Pacific Islander:	24	0.15
Melanesian: (3)	4	0.03
Fijian	1	0.01

Notes: 1. Figures in the "Number" column do not add up to the total population due to: a) Ancestry/Race overlap — e.g. persons can report being both White and Irish, b) persons of Hispanic origin can report being any race, c) persons reporting two ancestries are counted in both categories. 2. Numbers in parentheses indicate the number of persons reporting this ancestry/race alone, not in combination with any other ancestry/race. 3. Refer to the Explanation of Data in the front of the book for more detailed information.

Other Melanesian (3)	3	0.02
Polynesian: (1)	3	0.02
Native Hawaiian (1)	3	0.02
Other Pac. Isl., not spec. (6)	17	0.11
Hispanic or Latino:	1,709	10.82
Central American:	166	1.05
Costa Rican	1	0.01
Guatemalan	26	0.16
Honduran	16	0.10
Nicaraguan	11	0.07
Panamanian	29	0.18
Salvadoran	73	0.46
Other Central American	10	0.06
Cuban	62	0.39
Dominican Republic	209	1.32
Mexican	23	0.15
Puerto Rican	497	3.15
South American:	325	2.06
Argentinean	17	0.11
Chilean	8	0.05
Colombian	177	1.12
Ecuadorian	71	0.45
Peruvian	19	0.12
Uruguayan	12	0.08
Venezuelan	4	0.03
Other South American	17	0.11
Other Hispanic or Latino	427	2.70
Hungarian	76	0.48
Iranian	131	0.83
Irish	1,351	8.56
Israeli	31	0.20
Italian	2,669	16.90
Lithuanian	78	0.49
Maltese	17	0.11
Norwegian	20	0.13
Polish	362	2.29
Portuguese	63	0.40
Romanian	35	0.22
Russian	271	1.72
Scotch-Irish	29	0.18
Scottish	74	0.47
Slovak	6	0.04
Swedish	42	0.27
Swiss	3	0.02
Ukrainian	19	0.12
United States or American	549	3.48
Welsh	35	0.22
West Indian, excl. Hispanic:	3,709	23.49
Bahamian	25	0.16
Barbadian	100	0.63
British West Indian	84	0.53
Haitian	1,792	11.35
Jamaican	1,319	8.35
Trinidadian and Tobagonian	188	1.19
U.S. Virgin Islander	22	0.14
West Indian	167	1.06
Other West Indian	12	0.08
White:	7,265	46.01
Not Hispanic (6,278)	6,402	40.55
Hispanic (784)	863	5.47

North Wantagh

Place Type: Census Designated Place
County: Nassau
Population: 12,156

Ancestry/Race	Number	%
African American/Black:	89	0.73
Not Hispanic (45)	76	0.63
Hispanic (10)	13	0.11
Am. Ind. or Alaska Nat., not spec.	7	0.06
American Indian tribes, specified:	9	0.07
Cherokee	2	0.02
Iroquois	4	0.03
All other tribes	3	0.02
American Indian tribes, not spec.	1	0.01
Arab:	11	0.09
Arab/Arabic	5	0.04
Other Arab	6	0.05
Armenian	10	0.08
Asian:	258	2.12
Chinese, ex. Taiwanese (90)	99	0.81
Filipino (32)	39	0.32
Indian (40)	43	0.35
Indonesian (5)	5	0.04
Japanese (2)	2	0.02
Korean (12)	19	0.16
Pakistani (16)	16	0.13
Sri Lankan (1)	1	0.01
Taiwanese (11)	13	0.11
Vietnamese (4)	4	0.03
Other Asian, specified (1)	7	0.06
Other Asian, not specified (7)	10	0.08
Austrian	184	1.51
Belgian	6	0.05
Brazilian	23	0.19
British	18	0.15
Canadian	32	0.26
Croatian	35	0.29
Czech	72	0.59
Czechoslovakian	10	0.08
Danish	26	0.21
Dutch	84	0.69
Eastern European	57	0.47
English	576	4.74
Estonian	5	0.04
European	50	0.41
Finnish	20	0.16
French, except Basque	207	1.70
French Canadian	76	0.63
German	2,257	18.57
Greek	181	1.49
Guyanese	12	0.10
Hawaii Native/Pacific Islander:	10	0.08
Micronesian: (1)	1	0.01
Other Micronesian (1)	1	0.01
Polynesian:	3	0.02
Other Polynesian	3	0.02
Other Pac. Isl., specified	4	0.03
Other Pac. Isl., not spec.	2	0.02
Hispanic or Latino:	556	4.57
Central American:	30	0.25
Costa Rican	3	0.02
Guatemalan	7	0.06
Honduran	4	0.03
Nicaraguan	1	0.01
Salvadoran	14	0.12
Other Central American	1	0.01
Cuban	40	0.33
Dominican Republic	26	0.21
Mexican	14	0.12
Puerto Rican	219	1.80
South American:	98	0.81
Argentinean	9	0.07
Bolivian	12	0.10
Chilean	11	0.09
Colombian	33	0.27
Ecuadorian	21	0.17
Peruvian	8	0.07
Other South American	4	0.03
Other Hispanic or Latino	129	1.06
Hungarian	131	1.08
Icelander	6	0.05
Irish	3,389	27.88
Italian	4,200	34.55
Latvian	12	0.10
Lithuanian	62	0.51
Maltese	25	0.21
Norwegian	121	1.00
Polish	654	5.38
Portuguese	19	0.16
Romanian	50	0.41
Russian	816	6.71
Scandinavian	22	0.18
Scotch-Irish	159	1.31
Scottish	103	0.85
Slavic	4	0.03
Slovak	24	0.20
Slovene	21	0.17
Swedish	123	1.01
Swiss	21	0.17
Turkish	15	0.12
Ukrainian	83	0.68
United States or American	272	2.24
West Indian, excl. Hispanic:	14	0.12
Haitian	6	0.05
Jamaican	8	0.07
White:	11,759	96.73
Not Hispanic (11,248)	11,312	93.06
Hispanic (422)	447	3.68
Yugoslavian	33	0.27

Oceanside

Place Type: Census Designated Place
County: Nassau
Population: 32,733

Ancestry/Race	Number	%
African American/Black:	248	0.76
Not Hispanic (173)	220	0.67
Hispanic (11)	28	0.09
African, sub-Saharan:	4	0.01
South African	4	0.01
Am. Ind. or Alaska Nat., not spec.	26	0.08
Albanian	42	0.13
American Indian tribes, specified:	23	0.07
Apache (1)	1	0.00
Blackfeet	1	0.00
Cherokee (1)	6	0.02
Iroquois (2)	6	0.02
Latin American Indians (2)	6	0.02
All other tribes (1)	3	0.01
American Indian tribes, not spec.	7	0.02
Arab:	146	0.45
Egyptian	16	0.05
Jordanian	9	0.03
Lebanese	44	0.13
Moroccan	24	0.07
Palestinian	7	0.02
Syrian	46	0.14
Armenian	41	0.13
Asian:	687	2.10
Bangladeshi (1)	1	0.00
Chinese, ex. Taiwanese (162)	180	0.55
Filipino (120)	131	0.40
Indian (188)	196	0.60
Indonesian (5)	5	0.02
Japanese (17)	25	0.08
Korean (55)	61	0.19
Laotian (3)	4	0.01
Pakistani (16)	24	0.07
Sri Lankan (6)	7	0.02
Taiwanese (7)	7	0.02
Vietnamese (3)	4	0.01
Other Asian, not specified (7)	42	0.13
Austrian	397	1.21
Belgian	17	0.05
British	88	0.27
Canadian	58	0.18
Celtic	4	0.01
Croatian	49	0.15
Czech	82	0.25
Czechoslovakian	100	0.31
Danish	25	0.08
Dutch	133	0.41
Eastern European	307	0.94
English	1,340	4.09
Estonian	37	0.11
European	324	0.99
Finnish	13	0.04
French, except Basque	407	1.24
French Canadian	146	0.45
German	4,329	13.23
Greek	404	1.23
Guyanese	9	0.03
Hawaii Native/Pacific Islander:	5	0.02
Micronesian: (1)	1	0.00
Guamanian/Chamorro (1)	1	0.00

Notes: 1. Figures in the "Number" column do not add up to the total population due to: a) Ancestry/Race overlap — e.g. persons can report being both White and Irish, b) persons of Hispanic origin can report being any race, c) persons reporting two ancestries are counted in both categories. 2. Numbers in parentheses indicate the number of persons reporting this ancestry/race alone, not in combination with any other ancestry/race. 3. Refer to the Explanation of Data in the front of the book for more detailed information.

Ancestry/Race	Number	%
Other Pac. Isl., not spec. (2)	4	0.01
Hispanic or Latino:	1,931	5.90
Central American:	141	0.43
Costa Rican	16	0.05
Guatemalan	23	0.07
Honduran	5	0.02
Nicaraguan	7	0.02
Panamanian	8	0.02
Salvadoran	79	0.24
Other Central American	3	0.01
Cuban	167	0.51
Dominican Republic	332	1.01
Mexican	84	0.26
Puerto Rican	398	1.22
South American:	390	1.19
Argentinean	36	0.11
Bolivian	4	0.01
Chilean	59	0.18
Colombian	153	0.47
Ecuadorian	44	0.13
Peruvian	58	0.18
Uruguayan	14	0.04
Venezuelan	10	0.03
Other South American	12	0.04
Other Hispanic or Latino	419	1.28
Hungarian	523	1.60
Iranian	57	0.17
Irish	5,868	17.93
Israeli	190	0.58
Italian	9,488	28.99
Latvian	22	0.07
Lithuanian	108	0.33
Luxemburger	6	0.02
Maltese	39	0.12
Northern European	6	0.02
Norwegian	192	0.59
Polish	2,415	7.38
Portuguese	31	0.09
Romanian	259	0.79
Russian	2,418	7.39
Scotch-Irish	269	0.82
Scottish	214	0.65
Serbian	7	0.02
Slavic	34	0.10
Slovak	41	0.13
Slovene	7	0.02
Soviet Union	32	0.10
Swedish	159	0.49
Swiss	26	0.08
Turkish	65	0.20
Ukrainian	301	0.92
United States or American	2,130	6.51
Welsh	14	0.04
West Indian, excl. Hispanic:	58	0.18
Haitian	7	0.02
Jamaican	51	0.16
White:	31,352	95.78
Not Hispanic (29,784)	29,915	91.39
Hispanic (1,295)	1,437	4.39
Yugoslavian	72	0.22

Ogden

Place Type: Town
County: Monroe
Population: 18,492

Ancestry/Race	Number	%
African American/Black:	293	1.58
Not Hispanic (247)	286	1.55
Hispanic (3)	7	0.04
African, sub-Saharan:	40	0.22
African	6	0.03
Ethiopian	34	0.18
Alaska Native tribes, specified:	1	0.01
Tlingit-Haida (1)	1	0.01
Am. Ind. or Alaska Nat., not spec.	31	0.17
Albanian	9	0.05
American Indian tribes, specified:	47	0.25
Chippewa (2)	2	0.01
Iroquois (20)	35	0.19
Latin American Indians (1)	1	0.01
Ottawa (1)	1	0.01
Seminole	1	0.01
Sioux (1)	5	0.03
All other tribes	2	0.01
American Indian tribes, not spec.	3	0.02
Arab:	81	0.44
Egyptian	10	0.05
Lebanese	64	0.35
Syrian	7	0.04
Armenian	12	0.06
Asian:	182	0.98
Cambodian (1)	1	0.01
Chinese, ex. Taiwanese (14)	20	0.11
Filipino (8)	16	0.09
Indian (35)	39	0.21
Japanese (4)	8	0.04
Korean (51)	57	0.31
Laotian (4)	4	0.02
Pakistani (1)	6	0.03
Taiwanese (1)	1	0.01
Vietnamese (14)	26	0.14
Other Asian, not specified (3)	4	0.02
Austrian	73	0.40
Belgian	73	0.40
Brazilian	5	0.03
British	194	1.05
Canadian	183	0.99
Croatian	16	0.09
Czech	21	0.11
Czechoslovakian	33	0.18
Danish	66	0.36
Dutch	684	3.70
Eastern European	7	0.04
English	3,010	16.29
European	125	0.68
Finnish	22	0.12
French, except Basque	592	3.20
French Canadian	234	1.27
German	5,652	30.59
Greek	29	0.16
Hawaii Native/Pacific Islander:	10	0.05
Melanesian:	3	0.02
Fijian	3	0.02
Polynesian: (2)	7	0.04
Native Hawaiian	1	0.01
Samoan (2)	3	0.02
Other Polynesian	3	0.02
Hispanic or Latino:	253	1.37
Central American:	3	0.02
Costa Rican	1	0.01
Panamanian	1	0.01
Salvadoran	1	0.01
Cuban	29	0.16
Dominican Republic	3	0.02
Mexican	34	0.18
Puerto Rican	116	0.63
South American:	19	0.10
Colombian	10	0.05
Ecuadorian	1	0.01
Paraguayan	1	0.01
Peruvian	4	0.02
Venezuelan	2	0.01
Other South American	1	0.01
Other Hispanic or Latino	49	0.26
Hungarian	130	0.70
Irish	3,502	18.95
Israeli	7	0.04
Italian	4,509	24.40
Lithuanian	74	0.40
Luxemburger	6	0.03
Northern European	19	0.10
Norwegian	48	0.26
Pennsylvania German	9	0.05
Polish	1,312	7.10
Portuguese	27	0.15
Romanian	38	0.21
Russian	53	0.29
Scandinavian	7	0.04
Scotch-Irish	217	1.17
Scottish	354	1.92
Serbian	22	0.12
Slovak	8	0.04
Slovene	25	0.14
Swedish	199	1.08
Swiss	42	0.23
Turkish	12	0.06
Ukrainian	281	1.52
United States or American	768	4.16
Welsh	144	0.78
West Indian, excl. Hispanic:	5	0.03
Jamaican	5	0.03
White:	18,003	97.36
Not Hispanic (17,663)	17,802	96.27
Hispanic (187)	201	1.09
Yugoslavian	30	0.16

Ogdensburg

Place Type: City
County: Saint Lawrence
Population: 12,364

Ancestry/Race	Number	%
African American/Black:	1,251	10.12
Not Hispanic (1,161)	1,185	9.58
Hispanic (66)	66	0.53
Alaska Native tribes, specified:	1	0.01
Tlingit-Haida	1	0.01
Am. Ind. or Alaska Nat., not spec.	26	0.21
American Indian tribes, specified:	102	0.82
Blackfeet (1)	1	0.01
Cherokee (3)	4	0.03
Choctaw	2	0.02
Delaware	1	0.01
Iroquois (68)	89	0.72
All other tribes (4)	5	0.04
American Indian tribes, not spec.	10	0.08
Arab:	19	0.15
Syrian	19	0.15
Asian:	95	0.77
Chinese, ex. Taiwanese (21)	21	0.17
Filipino (15)	16	0.13
Indian (31)	34	0.27
Japanese (1)	2	0.02
Korean (8)	11	0.09
Malaysian (1)	1	0.01
Vietnamese (2)	2	0.02
Other Asian, specified	1	0.01
Other Asian, not specified (5)	7	0.06
Brazilian	5	0.04
British	26	0.21
Canadian	178	1.44
Czech	18	0.15
Dutch	214	1.73
English	1,215	9.83
European	5	0.04
French, except Basque	2,571	20.80
French Canadian	996	8.06
German	670	5.42
Hawaii Native/Pacific Islander:	13	0.11
Polynesian:	2	0.02
Native Hawaiian	1	0.01
Samoan	1	0.01
Other Pac. Isl., specified	1	0.01
Other Pac. Isl., not spec. (7)	10	0.08
Hispanic or Latino:	769	6.22
Central American:	31	0.25
Costa Rican	3	0.02
Guatemalan	3	0.02
Honduran	4	0.03
Nicaraguan	1	0.01
Panamanian	8	0.06
Salvadoran	12	0.10
Cuban	26	0.21
Dominican Republic	131	1.06
Mexican	49	0.40
Puerto Rican	411	3.32
South American:	35	0.28

Notes: 1. Figures in the "Number" column do not add up to the total population due to: a) Ancestry/Race overlap — e.g. persons can report being both White and Irish, b) persons of Hispanic origin can report being any race, c) persons reporting two ancestries are counted in both categories. 2. Numbers in parentheses indicate the number of persons reporting this ancestry/race alone, not in combination with any other ancestry/race. 3. Refer to the Explanation of Data in the front of the book for more detailed information.

Argentinean	1	0.01
Colombian	23	0.19
Ecuadorian	6	0.05
Peruvian	2	0.02
Venezuelan	2	0.02
Other South American	1	0.01
Other Hispanic or Latino	86	0.70
Hungarian	12	0.10
Irish	1,778	14.39
Italian	459	3.71
Lithuanian	8	0.06
Norwegian	12	0.10
Pennsylvania German	5	0.04
Polish	242	1.96
Portuguese	3	0.02
Scotch-Irish	120	0.97
Scottish	390	3.16
Swedish	23	0.19
Swiss	7	0.06
Ukrainian	4	0.03
United States or American	1,083	8.76
Welsh	81	0.66
White:	10,595	85.69
Not Hispanic (10,168)	10,239	82.81
Hispanic (347)	356	2.88

Olean

Place Type: City
County: Cattaraugus
Population: 15,347

Ancestry/Race	Number	%
African American/Black:	663	4.32
Not Hispanic (501)	630	4.11
Hispanic (31)	33	0.22
African, sub-Saharan:	47	0.31
African	47	0.31
Alaska Native tribes, specified:	2	0.01
Aleut (1)	1	0.01
Tlingit-Haida (1)	1	0.01
Am. Ind. or Alaska Nat., not spec.	39	0.25
American Indian tribes, specified:	63	0.41
Blackfeet	1	0.01
Cherokee (1)	5	0.03
Chippewa	1	0.01
Iroquois (33)	41	0.27
Latin American Indians (1)	1	0.01
Sioux (1)	6	0.04
All other tribes (8)	8	0.05
American Indian tribes, not spec.	8	0.05
Arab:	408	2.66
Arab/Arabic	5	0.03
Egyptian	7	0.05
Iraqi	72	0.47
Lebanese	310	2.02
Syrian	9	0.06
Other Arab	5	0.03
Armenian	39	0.25
Asian:	171	1.11
Chinese, ex. Taiwanese (21)	23	0.15
Filipino (17)	22	0.14
Indian (51)	61	0.40
Japanese (7)	15	0.10
Korean (8)	9	0.06
Pakistani (14)	17	0.11
Thai (2)	2	0.01
Vietnamese (7)	9	0.06
Other Asian, not specified (5)	13	0.08
Austrian	126	0.82
Basque	5	0.03
Belgian	7	0.05
British	41	0.27
Canadian	33	0.22
Czech	129	0.84
Czechoslovakian	13	0.08
Danish	4	0.03
Dutch	430	2.80
English	1,843	12.01
European	66	0.43
Finnish	10	0.07
French, except Basque	474	3.09
French Canadian	164	1.07
German	4,238	27.61
Greek	40	0.26
Hawaii Native/Pacific Islander:	7	0.05
Polynesian: (4)	4	0.03
Native Hawaiian (1)	1	0.01
Samoan (3)	3	0.02
Other Pac. Isl., not spec.	3	0.02
Hispanic or Latino:	190	1.24
Central American:	3	0.02
Nicaraguan	1	0.01
Panamanian	2	0.01
Cuban	3	0.02
Dominican Republic	9	0.06
Mexican	26	0.17
Puerto Rican	98	0.64
South American:	10	0.07
Chilean	4	0.03
Peruvian	3	0.02
Venezuelan	2	0.01
Other South American	1	0.01
Other Hispanic or Latino	41	0.27
Hungarian	42	0.27
Irish	3,256	21.22
Italian	1,939	12.63
Lithuanian	6	0.04
Macedonian	6	0.04
Northern European	25	0.16
Norwegian	69	0.45
Pennsylvania German	20	0.13
Polish	1,673	10.90
Russian	38	0.25
Scotch-Irish	187	1.22
Scottish	211	1.37
Slovak	63	0.41
Slovene	7	0.05
Swedish	525	3.42
Swiss	34	0.22
Ukrainian	79	0.51
United States or American	733	4.78
Welsh	92	0.60
West Indian, excl. Hispanic:	59	0.38
Bahamian	34	0.22
Jamaican	8	0.05
West Indian	17	0.11
White:	14,527	94.66
Not Hispanic (14,211)	14,407	93.88
Hispanic (110)	120	0.78
Yugoslavian	53	0.35

Oneida

Place Type: City
County: Madison
Population: 10,987

Ancestry/Race	Number	%
African American/Black:	110	1.00
Not Hispanic (85)	107	0.97
Hispanic (3)	3	0.03
African, sub-Saharan:	8	0.07
African	8	0.07
Alaska Native tribes, specified:	1	0.01
Alaska Athabascan (1)	1	0.01
Am. Ind. or Alaska Nat., not spec.	41	0.37
Albanian	15	0.14
American Indian tribes, specified:	100	0.91
Cherokee (2)	4	0.04
Crow (2)	2	0.02
Iroquois (71)	86	0.78
Latin American Indians (1)	1	0.01
Navajo	1	0.01
Pueblo	1	0.01
Sioux	1	0.01
All other tribes (4)	4	0.04
American Indian tribes, not spec.	49	0.45
Arab:	183	1.67
Arab/Arabic	67	0.61
Jordanian	88	0.80
Lebanese	28	0.25
Asian:	64	0.58
Chinese, ex. Taiwanese (10)	11	0.10
Filipino (3)	5	0.05
Indian (20)	21	0.19
Japanese (2)	5	0.05
Korean (4)	4	0.04
Sri Lankan (6)	8	0.07
Vietnamese (3)	4	0.04
Other Asian, not specified (2)	6	0.05
Austrian	27	0.25
Belgian	8	0.07
Brazilian	7	0.06
British	14	0.13
Canadian	40	0.36
Czechoslovakian	5	0.05
Danish	18	0.16
Dutch	371	3.38
English	1,637	14.90
European	69	0.63
French, except Basque	544	4.95
French Canadian	230	2.09
German	2,241	20.40
Greek	41	0.37
Hawaii Native/Pacific Islander:	3	0.03
Micronesian: (2)	3	0.03
Guamanian/Chamorro (2)	3	0.03
Hispanic or Latino:	92	0.84
Cuban	6	0.05
Mexican	17	0.15
Puerto Rican	46	0.42
South American:	2	0.02
Argentinean	1	0.01
Ecuadorian	1	0.01
Other Hispanic or Latino	21	0.19
Hungarian	28	0.25
Irish	2,381	21.67
Italian	1,345	12.24
Norwegian	104	0.95
Polish	548	4.99
Portuguese	9	0.08
Romanian	9	0.08
Russian	62	0.56
Scotch-Irish	100	0.91
Scottish	198	1.80
Slavic	12	0.11
Slovak	21	0.19
Swedish	40	0.36
Swiss	57	0.52
Ukrainian	94	0.86
United States or American	637	5.80
Welsh	341	3.10
White:	10,670	97.11
Not Hispanic (10,510)	10,601	96.49
Hispanic (69)	69	0.63
Yugoslavian	7	0.06

Oneonta

Place Type: City
County: Otsego
Population: 13,292

Ancestry/Race	Number	%
African American/Black:	589	4.43
Not Hispanic (492)	554	4.17
Hispanic (23)	35	0.26
African, sub-Saharan:	66	0.50
African	24	0.18
Nigerian	31	0.23
Other sub-Saharan African	11	0.08
Alaska Native tribes, specified:	1	0.01
Aleut	1	0.01
Am. Ind. or Alaska Nat., not spec.	38	0.29
American Indian tribes, specified:	39	0.29
Blackfeet	2	0.02
Cherokee (2)	9	0.07
Choctaw	2	0.02
Creek	1	0.01

Notes: 1. Figures in the "Number" column do not add up to the total population due to: a) Ancestry/Race overlap — e.g. persons can report being both White and Irish, b) persons of Hispanic origin can report being any race, c) persons reporting two ancestries are counted in both categories. 2. Numbers in parentheses indicate the number of persons reporting this ancestry/race alone, not in combination with any other ancestry/race. 3. Refer to the Explanation of Data in the front of the book for more detailed information.

Iroquois (2)	9	0.07
Latin American Indians (2)	9	0.07
Navajo	1	0.01
Ottawa	1	0.01
Sioux (1)	3	0.02
All other tribes (1)	2	0.02
American Indian tribes, not spec.	5	0.04
Arab:	77	0.58
Arab/Arabic	16	0.12
Lebanese	44	0.33
Moroccan	7	0.05
Syrian	10	0.08
Armenian	17	0.13
Asian:	235	1.77
Chinese, ex. Taiwanese (65)	71	0.53
Filipino (5)	18	0.14
Indian (37)	47	0.35
Indonesian	3	0.02
Japanese (34)	37	0.28
Korean (22)	25	0.19
Pakistani (1)	1	0.01
Sri Lankan (1)	1	0.01
Taiwanese (1)	7	0.05
Thai (2)	3	0.02
Vietnamese (7)	8	0.06
Other Asian, specified	1	0.01
Other Asian, not specified (8)	13	0.10
Australian	4	0.03
Austrian	68	0.51
Belgian	16	0.12
British	38	0.29
Croatian	30	0.23
Czech	51	0.38
Czechoslovakian	23	0.17
Danish	73	0.55
Dutch	431	3.24
Eastern European	13	0.10
English	1,411	10.62
Estonian	15	0.11
European	116	0.87
Finnish	36	0.27
French, except Basque	450	3.39
French Canadian	170	1.28
German	1,860	13.99
Greek	108	0.81
Hawaii Native/Pacific Islander:	22	0.17
Micronesian:	2	0.02
Guamanian/Chamorro	2	0.02
Polynesian: (11)	15	0.11
Native Hawaiian (2)	4	0.03
Samoan (9)	11	0.08
Other Pac. Isl., specified	1	0.01
Other Pac. Isl., not spec. (1)	4	0.03
Hispanic or Latino:	475	3.57
Central American:	20	0.15
Costa Rican	3	0.02
Guatemalan	1	0.01
Honduran	3	0.02
Salvadoran	13	0.10
Cuban	22	0.17
Dominican Republic	37	0.28
Mexican	40	0.30
Puerto Rican	195	1.47
South American:	35	0.26
Argentinean	1	0.01
Bolivian	1	0.01
Chilean	3	0.02
Colombian	5	0.04
Ecuadorian	11	0.08
Peruvian	9	0.07
Uruguayan	2	0.02
Venezuelan	2	0.02
Other South American	1	0.01
Other Hispanic or Latino	126	0.95
Hungarian	50	0.38
Iranian	5	0.04
Irish	2,587	19.46
Israeli	5	0.04
Italian	1,931	14.53
Latvian	9	0.07
Lithuanian	81	0.61
Northern European	28	0.21
Norwegian	149	1.12
Polish	577	4.34
Portuguese	6	0.05
Romanian	12	0.09
Russian	344	2.59
Scandinavian	14	0.11
Scotch-Irish	235	1.77
Scottish	334	2.51
Slavic	7	0.05
Slovak	32	0.24
Swedish	154	1.16
Swiss	41	0.31
Turkish	4	0.03
Ukrainian	69	0.52
United States or American	582	4.38
Welsh	50	0.38
West Indian, excl. Hispanic:	52	0.39
Jamaican	19	0.14
Trinidadian and Tobagonian	11	0.08
West Indian	22	0.17
White:	12,391	93.22
Not Hispanic (11,904)	12,069	90.80
Hispanic (300)	322	2.42
Yugoslavian	8	0.06

Onondaga

Place Type: Town
County: Onondaga
Population: 21,063

Ancestry/Race	Number	%
African American/Black:	479	2.27
Not Hispanic (398)	456	2.16
Hispanic (15)	23	0.11
African, sub-Saharan:	14	0.07
African	14	0.07
Am. Ind. or Alaska Nat., not spec.	66	0.31
Albanian	6	0.03
American Indian tribes, specified:	272	1.29
Apache (2)	2	0.01
Blackfeet	1	0.00
Cherokee	1	0.00
Chippewa (1)	1	0.00
Comanche (3)	4	0.02
Creek (1)	2	0.01
Iroquois (168)	247	1.17
Latin American Indians (5)	5	0.02
Sioux	1	0.00
All other tribes (4)	8	0.04
American Indian tribes, not spec.	5	0.02
Arab:	158	0.75
Jordanian	11	0.05
Lebanese	78	0.37
Palestinian	29	0.14
Syrian	18	0.09
Other Arab	22	0.10
Armenian	29	0.14
Asian:	281	1.33
Cambodian	1	0.00
Chinese, ex. Taiwanese (53)	56	0.27
Filipino (26)	35	0.17
Indian (65)	69	0.33
Japanese (5)	9	0.04
Korean (69)	83	0.39
Pakistani (9)	9	0.04
Taiwanese (1)	1	0.00
Thai (2)	2	0.01
Vietnamese (3)	3	0.01
Other Asian, specified (4)	4	0.02
Other Asian, not specified (7)	9	0.04
Austrian	68	0.32
Belgian	85	0.40
British	103	0.49
Canadian	91	0.43
Celtic	15	0.07
Croatian	8	0.04
Czech	75	0.36
Czechoslovakian	35	0.17
Danish	39	0.19
Dutch	470	2.24
English	3,641	17.33
Estonian	7	0.03
European	94	0.45
French, except Basque	916	4.36
French Canadian	401	1.91
German	3,986	18.97
Greek	90	0.43
Hawaii Native/Pacific Islander:	19	0.09
Micronesian: (2)	2	0.01
Guamanian/Chamorro (2)	2	0.01
Polynesian: (6)	10	0.05
Native Hawaiian (3)	7	0.03
Samoan (3)	3	0.01
Other Pac. Isl., not spec.	7	0.03
Hispanic or Latino:	221	1.05
Central American:	11	0.05
Costa Rican	1	0.00
Guatemalan	5	0.02
Honduran	4	0.02
Panamanian	1	0.00
Cuban	6	0.03
Dominican Republic	3	0.01
Mexican	36	0.17
Puerto Rican	103	0.49
South American:	11	0.05
Chilean	1	0.00
Colombian	3	0.01
Ecuadorian	6	0.03
Venezuelan	1	0.00
Other Hispanic or Latino	51	0.24
Hungarian	189	0.90
Iranian	6	0.03
Irish	6,008	28.59
Italian	3,418	16.27
Latvian	35	0.17
Lithuanian	8	0.04
Macedonian	65	0.31
Northern European	43	0.20
Norwegian	109	0.52
Pennsylvania German	16	0.08
Polish	1,418	6.75
Portuguese	46	0.22
Romanian	16	0.08
Russian	191	0.91
Scandinavian	28	0.13
Scotch-Irish	373	1.78
Scottish	473	2.25
Slavic	21	0.10
Slovak	48	0.23
Swedish	186	0.89
Swiss	92	0.44
Turkish	25	0.12
Ukrainian	293	1.39
United States or American	927	4.41
Welsh	252	1.20
West Indian, excl. Hispanic:	4	0.02
British West Indian	4	0.02
White:	20,126	95.55
Not Hispanic (19,719)	19,959	94.76
Hispanic (142)	167	0.79
Yugoslavian	63	0.30

Orangetown

Place Type: Town
County: Rockland
Population: 47,711

Ancestry/Race	Number	%
African American/Black:	3,255	6.82
Not Hispanic (2,687)	3,084	6.46
Hispanic (119)	171	0.36
African, sub-Saharan:	232	0.49
African	167	0.35
Cape Verdean	7	0.01
Ethiopian	8	0.02
Kenyan	7	0.01

Notes: 1. Figures in the "Number" column do not add up to the total population due to: a) Ancestry/Race overlap — e.g. persons can report being both White and Irish, b) persons of Hispanic origin can report being any race, c) persons reporting two ancestries are counted in both categories. 2. Numbers in parentheses indicate the number of persons reporting this ancestry/race alone, not in combination with any other ancestry/race. 3. Refer to the Explanation of Data in the front of the book for more detailed information.

Nigerian	9	0.02
Other sub-Saharan African	34	0.07
Alaska Native tribes, specified:	4	0.01
Aleut (2)	2	0.00
Eskimo (1)	1	0.00
Tlingit-Haida (1)	1	0.00
Am. Ind. or Alaska Nat., not spec.	77	0.16
Albanian	97	0.20
Alsatian	11	0.02
American Indian tribes, specified:	88	0.18
Blackfeet (1)	7	0.01
Cherokee (2)	16	0.03
Chickasaw	1	0.00
Chippewa (1)	1	0.00
Choctaw	4	0.01
Comanche (4)	4	0.01
Cree	2	0.00
Delaware (2)	4	0.01
Iroquois (5)	12	0.03
Latin American Indians (4)	15	0.03
Lumbee (1)	1	0.00
Potawatomi	1	0.00
Pueblo	3	0.01
Seminole (1)	2	0.00
Sioux	2	0.00
Yaqui (1)	1	0.00
All other tribes (1)	12	0.03
American Indian tribes, not spec.	16	0.03
Arab:	177	0.37
Arab/Arabic	15	0.03
Egyptian	45	0.09
Iraqi	11	0.02
Lebanese	45	0.09
Palestinian	6	0.01
Syrian	47	0.10
Other Arab	8	0.02
Armenian	166	0.35
Asian:	3,391	7.11
Bangladeshi (13)	13	0.03
Cambodian (3)	4	0.01
Chinese, ex. Taiwanese (626)	708	1.48
Filipino (630)	708	1.48
Hmong (1)	1	0.00
Indian (820)	883	1.85
Indonesian (3)	4	0.01
Japanese (75)	102	0.21
Korean (695)	750	1.57
Malaysian (1)	7	0.01
Pakistani (14)	15	0.03
Sri Lankan (10)	10	0.02
Taiwanese (11)	12	0.03
Thai (42)	46	0.10
Vietnamese (27)	45	0.09
Other Asian, not specified (41)	83	0.17
Australian	18	0.04
Austrian	502	1.05
Belgian	17	0.04
Brazilian	84	0.18
British	236	0.49
Bulgarian	11	0.02
Canadian	100	0.21
Celtic	54	0.11
Croatian	107	0.22
Czech	143	0.30
Czechoslovakian	151	0.32
Danish	71	0.15
Dutch	675	1.41
Eastern European	144	0.30
English	2,692	5.63
Estonian	36	0.08
European	210	0.44
Finnish	58	0.12
French, except Basque	656	1.37
French Canadian	191	0.40
German	5,709	11.94
Greek	678	1.42
Guyanese	34	0.07
Hawaii Native/Pacific Islander:	31	0.06
Micronesian: (1)	1	0.00
Guamanian/Chamorro (1)	1	0.00
Polynesian: (3)	6	0.01
Native Hawaiian (1)	2	0.00
Samoan (1)	3	0.01
Tongan (1)	1	0.00
Other Pac. Isl., not spec. (7)	24	0.05
Hispanic or Latino:	2,873	6.02
Central American:	497	1.04
Costa Rican	10	0.02
Guatemalan	35	0.07
Honduran	15	0.03
Nicaraguan	3	0.01
Panamanian	3	0.01
Salvadoran	392	0.82
Other Central American	39	0.08
Cuban	150	0.31
Dominican Republic	194	0.41
Mexican	233	0.49
Puerto Rican	1,067	2.24
South American:	266	0.56
Argentinean	28	0.06
Bolivian	6	0.01
Chilean	3	0.01
Colombian	78	0.16
Ecuadorian	84	0.18
Paraguayan	3	0.01
Peruvian	26	0.05
Uruguayan	3	0.01
Venezuelan	9	0.02
Other South American	26	0.05
Other Hispanic or Latino	466	0.98
Hungarian	414	0.87
Iranian	68	0.14
Irish	14,379	30.08
Israeli	35	0.07
Italian	9,549	19.98
Latvian	23	0.05
Lithuanian	185	0.39
Maltese	11	0.02
Northern European	44	0.09
Norwegian	435	0.91
Pennsylvania German	11	0.02
Polish	1,743	3.65
Portuguese	161	0.34
Romanian	94	0.20
Russian	1,596	3.34
Scandinavian	48	0.10
Scotch-Irish	510	1.07
Scottish	582	1.22
Slavic	15	0.03
Slovak	114	0.24
Slovene	10	0.02
Swedish	415	0.87
Swiss	180	0.38
Turkish	57	0.12
Ukrainian	290	0.61
United States or American	1,911	4.00
Welsh	247	0.52
West Indian, excl. Hispanic:	1,344	2.81
Barbadian	12	0.03
British West Indian	23	0.05
Haitian	1,026	2.15
Jamaican	242	0.51
Trinidadian and Tobagonian	8	0.02
U.S. Virgin Islander	4	0.01
West Indian	29	0.06
White:	40,606	85.11
Not Hispanic (38,214)	38,629	80.96
Hispanic (1,850)	1,977	4.14
Yugoslavian	24	0.05

Orchard Park

Place Type: Town
County: Erie
Population: 27,637

Ancestry/Race	Number	%
African American/Black:	163	0.59
Not Hispanic (130)	160	0.58
Hispanic (3)	3	0.01
African, sub-Saharan:	7	0.03
African	7	0.03
Am. Ind. or Alaska Nat., not spec.	31	0.11
Alsatian	22	0.08
American Indian tribes, specified:	60	0.22
Blackfeet	2	0.01
Cherokee	2	0.01
Chippewa	5	0.02
Cree	1	0.00
Delaware	5	0.02
Iroquois (25)	38	0.14
Latin American Indians	1	0.00
Potawatomi	1	0.00
Sioux (1)	1	0.00
All other tribes (1)	4	0.01
American Indian tribes, not spec.	4	0.01
Arab:	141	0.51
Lebanese	66	0.24
Syrian	75	0.27
Armenian	16	0.06
Asian:	335	1.21
Cambodian (1)	1	0.00
Chinese, ex. Taiwanese (42)	49	0.18
Filipino (28)	42	0.15
Indian (124)	131	0.47
Indonesian (1)	1	0.00
Japanese (19)	26	0.09
Korean (38)	43	0.16
Laotian (3)	3	0.01
Pakistani (3)	3	0.01
Sri Lankan (3)	3	0.01
Thai (6)	6	0.02
Vietnamese (17)	20	0.07
Other Asian, not specified (5)	7	0.03
Australian	11	0.04
Austrian	130	0.47
Belgian	15	0.05
Brazilian	5	0.02
British	157	0.57
Bulgarian	21	0.08
Canadian	93	0.34
Croatian	205	0.74
Czech	39	0.14
Czechoslovakian	73	0.26
Danish	74	0.27
Dutch	415	1.50
Eastern European	10	0.04
English	3,020	10.93
Estonian	11	0.04
European	83	0.30
Finnish	78	0.28
French, except Basque	884	3.20
French Canadian	222	0.80
German	8,845	32.00
Greek	81	0.29
Hawaii Native/Pacific Islander:	11	0.04
Micronesian:	4	0.01
Guamanian/Chamorro	4	0.01
Polynesian: (3)	3	0.01
Native Hawaiian (2)	2	0.01
Samoan (1)	1	0.00
Other Pac. Isl., not spec. (3)	4	0.01
Hispanic or Latino:	265	0.96
Central American:	16	0.06
Guatemalan	4	0.01
Honduran	2	0.01
Nicaraguan	3	0.01
Panamanian	1	0.00
Salvadoran	6	0.02
Cuban	14	0.05
Dominican Republic	1	0.00
Mexican	69	0.25
Puerto Rican	57	0.21
South American:	36	0.13
Argentinean	1	0.00
Chilean	2	0.01
Colombian	24	0.09
Ecuadorian	1	0.00
Paraguayan	1	0.00
Peruvian	2	0.01

Notes: 1. Figures in the "Number" column do not add up to the total population due to: a) Ancestry/Race overlap — e.g. persons can report being both White and Irish, b) persons of Hispanic origin can report being any race, c) persons reporting two ancestries are counted in both categories. 2. Numbers in parentheses indicate the number of persons reporting this ancestry/race alone, not in combination with any other ancestry/race. 3. Refer to the Explanation of Data in the front of the book for more detailed information.

Venezuelan	2	0.01
Other South American	3	0.01
Other Hispanic or Latino	72	0.26
Hungarian	400	1.45
Icelander	9	0.03
Irish	6,982	25.26
Italian	4,816	17.43
Latvian	50	0.18
Lithuanian	43	0.16
Luxemburger	7	0.03
Macedonian	7	0.03
Northern European	7	0.03
Norwegian	213	0.77
Polish	5,165	18.69
Romanian	17	0.06
Russian	228	0.82
Scandinavian	34	0.12
Scotch-Irish	389	1.41
Scottish	645	2.33
Serbian	76	0.27
Slavic	25	0.09
Slovak	88	0.32
Swedish	366	1.32
Swiss	128	0.46
Ukrainian	450	1.63
United States or American	706	2.55
Welsh	209	0.76
West Indian, excl. Hispanic:	7	0.03
Jamaican	7	0.03
White:	27,111	98.10
Not Hispanic (26,763)	26,895	97.32
Hispanic (202)	216	0.78
Yugoslavian	16	0.06

Ossining

Place Type: Town
County: Westchester
Population: 36,534

Ancestry/Race	Number	%
Acadian/Cajun	5	0.01
Afghan	15	0.04
African American/Black:	5,501	15.06
Not Hispanic (4,969)	5,145	14.08
Hispanic (248)	356	0.97
African, sub-Saharan:	255	0.70
African	185	0.51
Ghanian	10	0.03
Other sub-Saharan African	60	0.16
Am. Ind. or Alaska Nat., not spec.	91	0.25
Albanian	159	0.44
Alsatian	14	0.04
American Indian tribes, specified:	144	0.39
Apache (1)	1	0.00
Blackfeet	1	0.00
Cherokee (5)	18	0.05
Creek	1	0.00
Iroquois (2)	8	0.02
Latin American Indians (52)	104	0.28
Sioux (1)	6	0.02
All other tribes (2)	5	0.01
American Indian tribes, not spec.	29	0.08
Arab:	94	0.26
Arab/Arabic	23	0.06
Egyptian	37	0.10
Iraqi	9	0.02
Lebanese	17	0.05
Syrian	8	0.02
Armenian	57	0.16
Asian:	1,893	5.18
Bangladeshi	1	0.00
Cambodian (5)	5	0.01
Chinese, ex. Taiwanese (419)	460	1.26
Filipino (194)	217	0.59
Indian (612)	678	1.86
Indonesian (7)	8	0.02
Japanese (124)	165	0.45
Korean (122)	128	0.35
Laotian (1)	2	0.01
Malaysian (7)	8	0.02
Pakistani (70)	78	0.21
Sri Lankan (8)	12	0.03
Taiwanese (6)	6	0.02
Thai (4)	4	0.01
Vietnamese (46)	48	0.13
Other Asian, specified (2)	5	0.01
Other Asian, not specified (14)	68	0.19
Assyrian/Chaldean/Syriac	78	0.21
Australian	14	0.04
Austrian	306	0.84
Belgian	5	0.01
Brazilian	20	0.05
British	251	0.69
Canadian	60	0.16
Celtic	8	0.02
Croatian	28	0.08
Czech	108	0.30
Czechoslovakian	55	0.15
Danish	49	0.13
Dutch	384	1.05
Eastern European	211	0.58
English	1,786	4.89
Estonian	9	0.02
European	219	0.60
Finnish	69	0.19
French, except Basque	476	1.30
French Canadian	179	0.49
German	2,944	8.06
Greek	183	0.50
Guyanese	14	0.04
Hawaii Native/Pacific Islander:	46	0.13
Micronesian: (3)	6	0.02
Guamanian/Chamorro (3)	6	0.02
Polynesian: (2)	6	0.02
Native Hawaiian (2)	6	0.02
Other Pac. Isl., specified	3	0.01
Other Pac. Isl., not spec. (2)	31	0.08
Hispanic or Latino:	7,282	19.93
Central American:	310	0.85
Costa Rican	32	0.09
Guatemalan	125	0.34
Honduran	59	0.16
Nicaraguan	16	0.04
Panamanian	22	0.06
Salvadoran	44	0.12
Other Central American	12	0.03
Cuban	184	0.50
Dominican Republic	451	1.23
Mexican	210	0.57
Puerto Rican	1,393	3.81
South American:	2,942	8.05
Argentinean	40	0.11
Bolivian	13	0.04
Chilean	159	0.44
Colombian	486	1.33
Ecuadorian	1,818	4.98
Paraguayan	12	0.03
Peruvian	113	0.31
Uruguayan	205	0.56
Venezuelan	22	0.06
Other South American	74	0.20
Other Hispanic or Latino	1,792	4.91
Hungarian	373	1.02
Iranian	41	0.11
Irish	4,364	11.95
Israeli	71	0.19
Italian	5,903	16.16
Latvian	28	0.08
Lithuanian	56	0.15
Macedonian	34	0.09
Maltese	17	0.05
Northern European	10	0.03
Norwegian	196	0.54
Polish	1,202	3.29
Portuguese	615	1.68
Romanian	161	0.44
Russian	1,505	4.12
Scandinavian	32	0.09
Scotch-Irish	210	0.57
Scottish	547	1.50
Slavic	18	0.05
Slovak	76	0.21
Slovene	15	0.04
Swedish	387	1.06
Swiss	72	0.20
Turkish	46	0.13
Ukrainian	231	0.63
United States or American	1,073	2.94
Welsh	46	0.13
West Indian, excl. Hispanic:	713	1.95
Barbadian	61	0.17
Belizean	10	0.03
Bermudan	8	0.02
British West Indian	22	0.06
Haitian	19	0.05
Jamaican	443	1.21
Trinidadian and Tobagonian	78	0.21
West Indian	72	0.20
White:	26,614	72.85
Not Hispanic (22,032)	22,429	61.39
Hispanic (3,635)	4,185	11.46
Yugoslavian	26	0.07

Ossining

Place Type: Village
County: Westchester
Population: 24,010

Ancestry/Race	Number	%
Acadian/Cajun	5	0.02
Afghan	15	0.06
African American/Black:	5,112	21.29
Not Hispanic (4,624)	4,779	19.90
Hispanic (234)	333	1.39
African, sub-Saharan:	248	1.03
African	178	0.74
Ghanian	10	0.04
Other sub-Saharan African	60	0.25
Am. Ind. or Alaska Nat., not spec.	84	0.35
Albanian	94	0.39
American Indian tribes, specified:	127	0.53
Blackfeet	1	0.00
Cherokee (3)	11	0.05
Iroquois (1)	6	0.02
Latin American Indians (49)	100	0.42
Sioux	5	0.02
All other tribes (2)	4	0.02
American Indian tribes, not spec.	28	0.12
Arab:	46	0.19
Arab/Arabic	23	0.10
Egyptian	14	0.06
Lebanese	9	0.04
Armenian	18	0.07
Asian:	1,182	4.92
Bangladeshi	1	0.00
Cambodian (5)	5	0.02
Chinese, ex. Taiwanese (248)	268	1.12
Filipino (140)	158	0.66
Indian (396)	452	1.88
Indonesian (7)	7	0.03
Japanese (60)	89	0.37
Korean (49)	54	0.22
Laotian (1)	2	0.01
Malaysian (1)	1	0.00
Pakistani (25)	30	0.12
Sri Lankan (7)	11	0.05
Taiwanese (1)	1	0.00
Thai (4)	4	0.02
Vietnamese (35)	37	0.15
Other Asian, specified (2)	5	0.02
Other Asian, not specified (12)	57	0.24
Australian	9	0.04
Austrian	150	0.62
British	113	0.47
Canadian	37	0.15
Celtic	8	0.03
Croatian	28	0.12
Czech	57	0.24

Notes: 1. Figures in the "Number" column do not add up to the total population due to: a) Ancestry/Race overlap — e.g. persons can report being both White and Irish, b) persons of Hispanic origin can report being any race, c) persons reporting two ancestries are counted in both categories. 2. Numbers in parentheses indicate the number of persons reporting this ancestry/race alone, not in combination with any other ancestry/race. 3. Refer to the Explanation of Data in the front of the book for more detailed information.

Czechoslovakian	41	0.17
Danish	17	0.07
Dutch	258	1.07
English	1,041	4.34
Estonian	9	0.04
European	54	0.22
Finnish	9	0.04
French, except Basque	255	1.06
French Canadian	97	0.40
German	1,554	6.47
Greek	94	0.39
Guyanese	14	0.06
Hawaii Native/Pacific Islander:	35	0.15
Micronesian: (2)	5	0.02
Guamanian/Chamorro (2)	5	0.02
Other Pac. Isl., specified	3	0.01
Other Pac. Isl., not spec. (1)	27	0.11
Hispanic or Latino:	6,654	27.71
Central American:	280	1.17
Costa Rican	31	0.13
Guatemalan	111	0.46
Honduran	53	0.22
Nicaraguan	11	0.05
Panamanian	22	0.09
Salvadoran	44	0.18
Other Central American	8	0.03
Cuban	132	0.55
Dominican Republic	423	1.76
Mexican	168	0.70
Puerto Rican	1,194	4.97
South American:	2,819	11.74
Argentinean	31	0.13
Bolivian	11	0.05
Chilean	152	0.63
Colombian	456	1.90
Ecuadorian	1,796	7.48
Paraguayan	12	0.05
Peruvian	99	0.41
Uruguayan	179	0.75
Venezuelan	16	0.07
Other South American	67	0.28
Other Hispanic or Latino	1,638	6.82
Hungarian	119	0.50
Iranian	7	0.03
Irish	2,387	9.94
Israeli	16	0.07
Italian	3,464	14.43
Latvian	13	0.05
Lithuanian	23	0.10
Macedonian	34	0.14
Norwegian	117	0.49
Polish	505	2.10
Portuguese	528	2.20
Romanian	75	0.31
Russian	611	2.54
Scandinavian	14	0.06
Scotch-Irish	144	0.60
Scottish	321	1.34
Slavic	4	0.02
Slovak	59	0.25
Swedish	249	1.04
Swiss	27	0.11
Turkish	28	0.12
Ukrainian	92	0.38
United States or American	475	1.98
Welsh	25	0.10
West Indian, excl. Hispanic:	559	2.33
Barbadian	12	0.05
Bermudan	8	0.03
British West Indian	15	0.06
Haitian	19	0.08
Jamaican	412	1.72
Trinidadian and Tobagonian	29	0.12
West Indian	64	0.27
White:	15,320	63.81
Not Hispanic (11,294)	11,581	48.23
Hispanic (3,226)	3,739	15.57
Yugoslavian	22	0.09

Oswego

Place Type: City
County: Oswego
Population: 17,954

Ancestry/Race	Number	%
African American/Black:	253	1.41
Not Hispanic (167)	215	1.20
Hispanic (19)	38	0.21
African, sub-Saharan:	31	0.17
African	31	0.17
Am. Ind. or Alaska Nat., not spec.	40	0.22
American Indian tribes, specified:	97	0.54
Blackfeet (1)	6	0.03
Cherokee (4)	11	0.06
Chickasaw (1)	1	0.01
Chippewa (4)	6	0.03
Choctaw	1	0.01
Cree	2	0.01
Creek	1	0.01
Delaware	3	0.02
Iroquois (23)	45	0.25
Latin American Indians (3)	8	0.04
Ottawa (2)	2	0.01
Seminole	1	0.01
Sioux (2)	2	0.01
Yakama	1	0.01
All other tribes	7	0.04
American Indian tribes, not spec.	3	0.02
Arab:	74	0.41
Egyptian	23	0.13
Jordanian	7	0.04
Lebanese	44	0.25
Armenian	8	0.04
Asian:	199	1.11
Chinese, ex. Taiwanese (27)	31	0.17
Filipino (35)	51	0.28
Indian (50)	54	0.30
Japanese (7)	12	0.07
Korean (12)	17	0.09
Laotian (1)	1	0.01
Malaysian (1)	2	0.01
Pakistani	1	0.01
Taiwanese (1)	1	0.01
Thai (1)	2	0.01
Vietnamese (11)	12	0.07
Other Asian, not specified	15	0.08
Austrian	6	0.03
Belgian	24	0.13
British	46	0.26
Bulgarian	8	0.04
Canadian	25	0.14
Croatian	7	0.04
Czech	6	0.03
Danish	35	0.19
Dutch	328	1.83
Eastern European	28	0.16
English	2,176	12.12
European	53	0.30
French, except Basque	1,570	8.74
French Canadian	496	2.76
German	2,828	15.75
Greek	45	0.25
Hawaii Native/Pacific Islander:	11	0.06
Melanesian:	1	0.01
Other Melanesian	1	0.01
Polynesian:	4	0.02
Native Hawaiian	4	0.02
Other Pac. Isl., not spec.	6	0.03
Hispanic or Latino:	503	2.80
Central American:	14	0.08
Costa Rican	1	0.01
Guatemalan	9	0.05
Nicaraguan	1	0.01
Panamanian	2	0.01
Salvadoran	1	0.01
Cuban	7	0.04
Dominican Republic	20	0.11
Mexican	109	0.61
Puerto Rican	260	1.45
South American:	15	0.08
Argentinean	4	0.02
Colombian	2	0.01
Ecuadorian	6	0.03
Paraguayan	1	0.01
Other South American	2	0.01
Other Hispanic or Latino	78	0.43
Hungarian	76	0.42
Iranian	7	0.04
Irish	4,693	26.14
Israeli	13	0.07
Italian	3,311	18.44
Latvian	23	0.13
Lithuanian	49	0.27
New Zealander	5	0.03
Northern European	6	0.03
Norwegian	55	0.31
Polish	1,152	6.42
Portuguese	4	0.02
Russian	130	0.72
Scotch-Irish	227	1.26
Scottish	310	1.73
Serbian	7	0.04
Swedish	104	0.58
Swiss	36	0.20
Ukrainian	99	0.55
United States or American	880	4.90
Welsh	192	1.07
West Indian, excl. Hispanic:	5	0.03
Jamaican	5	0.03
White:	17,354	96.66
Not Hispanic (16,888)	17,072	95.09
Hispanic (226)	282	1.57

Owego

Place Type: Town
County: Tioga
Population: 20,365

Ancestry/Race	Number	%
African American/Black:	196	0.96
Not Hispanic (139)	186	0.91
Hispanic (4)	10	0.05
African, sub-Saharan:	24	0.12
African	16	0.08
South African	8	0.04
Alaska Native tribes, specified:	1	0.00
Aleut (1)	1	0.00
Am. Ind. or Alaska Nat., not spec.	45	0.22
American Indian tribes, specified:	100	0.49
Apache	5	0.02
Blackfeet (7)	19	0.09
Cherokee (8)	33	0.16
Cheyenne	4	0.02
Comanche	1	0.00
Crow	1	0.00
Delaware	3	0.01
Iroquois (5)	14	0.07
Latin American Indians (2)	4	0.02
Osage	1	0.00
Sioux (5)	11	0.05
All other tribes (1)	4	0.02
American Indian tribes, not spec.	3	0.01
Arab:	70	0.34
Lebanese	70	0.34
Armenian	12	0.06
Asian:	270	1.33
Chinese, ex. Taiwanese (45)	60	0.29
Filipino (17)	22	0.11
Indian (53)	70	0.34
Japanese (8)	13	0.06
Korean (27)	37	0.18
Laotian	1	0.00
Pakistani (10)	15	0.07
Taiwanese (4)	7	0.03
Thai (3)	5	0.02
Vietnamese (29)	32	0.16
Other Asian, not specified	8	0.04

Notes: 1. Figures in the "Number" column do not add up to the total population due to: a) Ancestry/Race overlap — e.g. persons can report being both White and Irish, b) persons of Hispanic origin can report being any race, c) persons reporting two ancestries are counted in both categories. 2. Numbers in parentheses indicate the number of persons reporting this ancestry/race alone, not in combination with any other ancestry/race. 3. Refer to the Explanation of Data in the front of the book for more detailed information.

Austrian	78	0.38
Belgian	13	0.06
British	78	0.38
Bulgarian	11	0.05
Canadian	18	0.09
Carpatho Rusyn	38	0.19
Celtic	13	0.06
Croatian	7	0.03
Czech	141	0.69
Czechoslovakian	152	0.75
Danish	34	0.17
Dutch	816	4.01
Eastern European	8	0.04
English	3,658	17.96
European	130	0.64
Finnish	49	0.24
French, except Basque	700	3.44
French Canadian	226	1.11
German	4,005	19.67
Greek	78	0.38
Guyanese	5	0.02
Hawaii Native/Pacific Islander:	12	0.06
Polynesian: (1)	5	0.02
Native Hawaiian	4	0.02
Samoan (1)	1	0.00
Other Pac. Isl., not spec. (3)	7	0.03
Hispanic or Latino:	226	1.11
Central American:	15	0.07
Guatemalan	1	0.00
Honduran	1	0.00
Nicaraguan	2	0.01
Panamanian	6	0.03
Salvadoran	4	0.02
Other Central American	1	0.00
Cuban	12	0.06
Dominican Republic	7	0.03
Mexican	46	0.23
Puerto Rican	67	0.33
South American:	18	0.09
Chilean	5	0.02
Colombian	2	0.01
Ecuadorian	8	0.04
Peruvian	2	0.01
Other South American	1	0.00
Other Hispanic or Latino	61	0.30
Hungarian	131	0.64
Iranian	6	0.03
Irish	3,662	17.98
Italian	2,159	10.60
Latvian	17	0.08
Lithuanian	87	0.43
Luxemburger	9	0.04
Northern European	29	0.14
Norwegian	277	1.36
Pennsylvania German	46	0.23
Polish	1,321	6.49
Russian	384	1.89
Scandinavian	24	0.12
Scotch-Irish	262	1.29
Scottish	369	1.81
Serbian	13	0.06
Slavic	30	0.15
Slovak	516	2.53
Slovene	15	0.07
Swedish	236	1.16
Swiss	46	0.23
Ukrainian	259	1.27
United States or American	1,591	7.81
Welsh	635	3.12
West Indian, excl. Hispanic:	12	0.06
Haitian	7	0.03
West Indian	5	0.02
White:	19,891	97.67
Not Hispanic (19,574)	19,718	96.82
Hispanic (135)	173	0.85
Yugoslavian	25	0.12

Oyster Bay

Place Type: Town
County: Nassau
Population: 293,925

Ancestry/Race	Number	%
Afghan	374	0.13
African American/Black:	5,490	1.87
Not Hispanic (4,595)	5,141	1.75
Hispanic (224)	349	0.12
African, sub-Saharan:	257	0.09
African	93	0.03
Ethiopian	24	0.01
Ghanian	29	0.01
Nigerian	11	0.00
Sierra Leonean	3	0.00
South African	38	0.01
Other sub-Saharan African	59	0.02
Alaska Native tribes, specified:	6	0.00
Alaska Athabascan (2)	2	0.00
Aleut (1)	1	0.00
Tlingit-Haida (1)	3	0.00
Am. Ind. or Alaska Nat., not spec.	299	0.10
Albanian	111	0.04
Alsatian	16	0.01
American Indian tribes, specified:	331	0.11
Apache	5	0.00
Blackfeet (1)	8	0.00
Cherokee (11)	82	0.03
Cheyenne (1)	1	0.00
Chickasaw (1)	2	0.00
Chippewa (1)	5	0.00
Choctaw (1)	2	0.00
Comanche	2	0.00
Cree	1	0.00
Creek (1)	2	0.00
Delaware (1)	7	0.00
Iroquois (9)	42	0.01
Kiowa	2	0.00
Latin American Indians (41)	75	0.03
Navajo (2)	7	0.00
Osage (1)	1	0.00
Potawatomi (1)	4	0.00
Pueblo	2	0.00
Seminole	1	0.00
Sioux (6)	19	0.01
Yaqui	1	0.00
All other tribes (32)	60	0.02
American Indian tribes, not spec.	54	0.02
Arab:	1,217	0.41
Arab/Arabic	88	0.03
Egyptian	373	0.13
Iraqi	56	0.02
Jordanian	51	0.02
Lebanese	306	0.10
Moroccan	68	0.02
Palestinian	45	0.02
Syrian	163	0.06
Other Arab	67	0.02
Armenian	877	0.30
Asian:	15,630	5.32
Bangladeshi (70)	82	0.03
Cambodian (24)	30	0.01
Chinese, ex. Taiwanese (3,985)	4,286	1.46
Filipino (1,164)	1,372	0.47
Indian (5,047)	5,415	1.84
Indonesian (31)	49	0.02
Japanese (377)	447	0.15
Korean (2,397)	2,505	0.85
Laotian (14)	14	0.00
Malaysian (1)	6	0.00
Pakistani (459)	578	0.20
Sri Lankan (14)	19	0.01
Taiwanese (140)	161	0.05
Thai (54)	59	0.02
Vietnamese (173)	188	0.06
Other Asian, specified (24)	30	0.01
Other Asian, not specified (147)	389	0.13
Assyrian/Chaldean/Syriac	5	0.00
Australian	115	0.04
Austrian	3,802	1.29
Basque	13	0.00
Belgian	259	0.09
Brazilian	253	0.09
British	817	0.28
Bulgarian	81	0.03
Canadian	583	0.20
Carpatho Rusyn	7	0.00
Celtic	57	0.02
Croatian	1,051	0.36
Cypriot	165	0.06
Czech	1,287	0.44
Czechoslovakian	823	0.28
Danish	782	0.27
Dutch	1,739	0.59
Eastern European	2,156	0.73
English	13,218	4.50
Estonian	56	0.02
European	1,925	0.65
Finnish	312	0.11
French, except Basque	3,741	1.27
French Canadian	978	0.33
German	42,703	14.53
Greek	5,932	2.02
Guyanese	238	0.08
Hawaii Native/Pacific Islander:	148	0.05
Melanesian: (2)	2	0.00
Fijian (2)	2	0.00
Micronesian: (12)	15	0.01
Guamanian/Chamorro (12)	15	0.01
Polynesian: (27)	40	0.01
Native Hawaiian (11)	22	0.01
Samoan (15)	17	0.01
Other Polynesian (1)	1	0.00
Other Pac. Isl., specified	4	0.00
Other Pac. Isl., not spec. (11)	87	0.03
Hispanic or Latino:	14,877	5.06
Central American:	2,608	0.89
Costa Rican	60	0.02
Guatemalan	132	0.04
Honduran	318	0.11
Nicaraguan	35	0.01
Panamanian	46	0.02
Salvadoran	1,898	0.65
Other Central American	119	0.04
Cuban	747	0.25
Dominican Republic	492	0.17
Mexican	843	0.29
Puerto Rican	3,506	1.19
South American:	3,052	1.04
Argentinean	242	0.08
Bolivian	59	0.02
Chilean	409	0.14
Colombian	1,066	0.36
Ecuadorian	441	0.15
Paraguayan	42	0.01
Peruvian	538	0.18
Uruguayan	42	0.01
Venezuelan	54	0.02
Other South American	159	0.05
Other Hispanic or Latino	3,629	1.23
Hungarian	3,453	1.17
Icelander	56	0.02
Iranian	751	0.26
Irish	60,453	20.57
Israeli	821	0.28
Italian	87,807	29.87
Latvian	275	0.09
Lithuanian	1,389	0.47
Luxemburger	6	0.00
Macedonian	22	0.01
Maltese	390	0.13
New Zealander	5	0.00
Northern European	16	0.01
Norwegian	2,311	0.79
Pennsylvania German	13	0.00
Polish	19,752	6.72
Portuguese	710	0.24
Romanian	1,381	0.47

Notes: 1. Figures in the "Number" column do not add up to the total population due to: a) Ancestry/Race overlap — e.g. persons can report being both White and Irish, b) persons of Hispanic origin can report being any race, c) persons reporting two ancestries are counted in both categories. 2. Numbers in parentheses indicate the number of persons reporting this ancestry/race alone, not in combination with any other ancestry/race. 3. Refer to the Explanation of Data in the front of the book for more detailed information.

Russian	14,698	5.00
Scandinavian	176	0.06
Scotch-Irish	1,919	0.65
Scottish	2,610	0.89
Serbian	35	0.01
Slavic	139	0.05
Slovak	481	0.16
Slovene	48	0.02
Soviet Union	6	0.00
Swedish	2,515	0.86
Swiss	630	0.21
Turkish	638	0.22
Ukrainian	1,917	0.65
United States or American	13,610	4.63
Welsh	672	0.23
West Indian, excl. Hispanic:	2,024	0.69
Bahamian	22	0.01
Barbadian	61	0.02
Belizean	15	0.01
Bermudan	31	0.01
British West Indian	69	0.02
Haitian	721	0.25
Jamaican	731	0.25
Trinidadian and Tobagonian	136	0.05
West Indian	225	0.08
Other West Indian	13	0.00
White:	269,904	91.83
Not Hispanic (257,361)	259,218	88.19
Hispanic (9,622)	10,686	3.64
Yugoslavian	518	0.18

Parma

Place Type: Town
County: Monroe
Population: 14,822

Ancestry/Race	Number	%
African American/Black:	222	1.50
Not Hispanic (182)	213	1.44
Hispanic (9)	9	0.06
African, sub-Saharan:	29	0.20
African	29	0.20
Am. Ind. or Alaska Nat., not spec.	13	0.09
American Indian tribes, specified:	37	0.25
Blackfeet (1)	2	0.01
Cherokee (4)	4	0.03
Chippewa (1)	3	0.02
Iroquois (10)	17	0.11
Navajo	1	0.01
Pima (2)	2	0.01
Sioux	4	0.03
All other tribes (3)	4	0.03
American Indian tribes, not spec.	12	0.08
Arab:	57	0.38
Arab/Arabic	7	0.05
Lebanese	31	0.21
Syrian	19	0.13
Armenian	53	0.36
Asian:	97	0.65
Cambodian (2)	3	0.02
Chinese, ex. Taiwanese (14)	16	0.11
Filipino (7)	12	0.08
Indian (10)	11	0.07
Indonesian	1	0.01
Japanese (4)	7	0.05
Korean (21)	25	0.17
Thai (1)	2	0.01
Vietnamese (16)	16	0.11
Other Asian, not specified (1)	4	0.03
Austrian	33	0.22
Belgian	56	0.38
British	34	0.23
Canadian	87	0.59
Croatian	5	0.03
Czech	16	0.11
Czechoslovakian	38	0.26
Danish	43	0.29
Dutch	496	3.34
English	3,027	20.40
European	94	0.63
Finnish	7	0.05
French, except Basque	661	4.46
French Canadian	254	1.71
German	5,025	33.87
Greek	78	0.53
Hawaii Native/Pacific Islander:	8	0.05
Polynesian: (3)	3	0.02
Native Hawaiian (2)	2	0.01
Samoan (1)	1	0.01
Other Pac. Isl., not spec. (1)	5	0.03
Hispanic or Latino:	166	1.12
Central American:	6	0.04
Guatemalan	1	0.01
Salvadoran	5	0.03
Cuban	4	0.03
Mexican	30	0.20
Puerto Rican	86	0.58
South American:	12	0.08
Argentinean	2	0.01
Bolivian	2	0.01
Chilean	2	0.01
Colombian	5	0.03
Paraguayan	1	0.01
Other Hispanic or Latino	28	0.19
Irish	3,114	20.99
Italian	2,950	19.88
Lithuanian	31	0.21
Norwegian	56	0.38
Polish	915	6.17
Portuguese	35	0.24
Russian	56	0.38
Scotch-Irish	186	1.25
Scottish	351	2.37
Slovak	3	0.02
Slovene	12	0.08
Swedish	150	1.01
Swiss	11	0.07
Turkish	27	0.18
Ukrainian	241	1.62
United States or American	589	3.97
Welsh	41	0.28
West Indian, excl. Hispanic:	21	0.14
Jamaican	21	0.14
White:	14,484	97.72
Not Hispanic (14,272)	14,361	96.89
Hispanic (117)	123	0.83

Patchogue

Place Type: Village
County: Suffolk
Population: 11,919

Ancestry/Race	Number	%
African American/Black:	606	5.08
Not Hispanic (408)	510	4.28
Hispanic (56)	96	0.81
African, sub-Saharan:	61	0.51
African	61	0.51
Am. Ind. or Alaska Nat., not spec.	57	0.48
American Indian tribes, specified:	58	0.49
Blackfeet	7	0.06
Cherokee (3)	12	0.10
Delaware	1	0.01
Iroquois (1)	3	0.03
Latin American Indians (4)	7	0.06
Seminole	1	0.01
Sioux (1)	4	0.03
All other tribes (8)	23	0.19
American Indian tribes, not spec.	10	0.08
Arab:	48	0.40
Arab/Arabic	10	0.08
Egyptian	23	0.19
Other Arab	15	0.13
Armenian	8	0.07
Asian:	224	1.88
Chinese, ex. Taiwanese (43)	49	0.41
Filipino (14)	27	0.23
Indian (64)	82	0.69
Indonesian	1	0.01
Japanese (6)	9	0.08
Korean (10)	13	0.11
Malaysian	1	0.01
Pakistani (9)	18	0.15
Sri Lankan (3)	3	0.03
Thai (6)	6	0.05
Vietnamese (1)	3	0.03
Other Asian, specified (1)	1	0.01
Other Asian, not specified	11	0.09
Austrian	31	0.26
Belgian	19	0.16
British	50	0.42
Canadian	5	0.04
Croatian	37	0.31
Czech	54	0.45
Czechoslovakian	39	0.33
Danish	5	0.04
Dutch	143	1.20
Eastern European	41	0.34
English	877	7.36
Estonian	7	0.06
European	50	0.42
Finnish	38	0.32
French, except Basque	261	2.19
French Canadian	171	1.43
German	1,776	14.90
Greek	182	1.53
Guyanese	13	0.11
Hawaii Native/Pacific Islander:	14	0.12
Micronesian:	1	0.01
Guamanian/Chamorro	1	0.01
Polynesian: (1)	4	0.03
Native Hawaiian (1)	2	0.02
Samoan	2	0.02
Other Pac. Isl., not spec. (1)	9	0.08
Hispanic or Latino:	2,842	23.84
Central American:	358	3.00
Guatemalan	23	0.19
Honduran	26	0.22
Panamanian	6	0.05
Salvadoran	285	2.39
Other Central American	18	0.15
Cuban	28	0.23
Dominican Republic	74	0.62
Mexican	76	0.64
Puerto Rican	748	6.28
South American:	968	8.12
Argentinean	7	0.06
Colombian	55	0.46
Ecuadorian	845	7.09
Peruvian	8	0.07
Uruguayan	1	0.01
Venezuelan	8	0.07
Other South American	44	0.37
Other Hispanic or Latino	590	4.95
Hungarian	47	0.39
Icelander	13	0.11
Iranian	11	0.09
Irish	2,489	20.89
Italian	2,692	22.59
Lithuanian	14	0.12
Northern European	20	0.17
Norwegian	74	0.62
Polish	561	4.71
Portuguese	22	0.18
Romanian	21	0.18
Russian	177	1.49
Scotch-Irish	151	1.27
Scottish	85	0.71
Slovak	11	0.09
Slovene	8	0.07
Swedish	94	0.79
Swiss	11	0.09
Turkish	47	0.39
Ukrainian	64	0.54
United States or American	329	2.76
Welsh	21	0.18
West Indian, excl. Hispanic:	127	1.07
Haitian	11	0.09

Notes: 1. Figures in the "Number" column do not add up to the total population due to: a) Ancestry/Race overlap — e.g. persons can report being both White and Irish, b) persons of Hispanic origin can report being any race, c) persons reporting two ancestries are counted in both categories. 2. Numbers in parentheses indicate the number of persons reporting this ancestry/race alone, not in combination with any other ancestry/race. 3. Refer to the Explanation of Data in the front of the book for more detailed information.

Jamaican	71	0.60
Trinidadian and Tobagonian	32	0.27
West Indian	13	0.11
White:	10,050	84.32
Not Hispanic (8,231)	8,368	70.21
Hispanic (1,456)	1,682	14.11
Yugoslavian	7	0.06

Patterson

Place Type: Town
County: Putnam
Population: 11,306

Ancestry/Race	Number	%
African American/Black:	468	4.14
Not Hispanic (380)	433	3.83
Hispanic (22)	35	0.31
African, sub-Saharan:	8	0.07
Sierra Leonean	8	0.07
Alaska Native tribes, specified:	1	0.01
Alaska Athabascan	1	0.01
Am. Ind. or Alaska Nat., not spec.	24	0.21
American Indian tribes, specified:	49	0.43
Apache	1	0.01
Blackfeet (1)	9	0.08
Cherokee (1)	8	0.07
Chippewa (1)	7	0.06
Comanche	1	0.01
Iroquois	6	0.05
Latin American Indians (2)	5	0.04
Lumbee (1)	1	0.01
All other tribes (7)	11	0.10
American Indian tribes, not spec.	3	0.03
Arab:	22	0.19
Lebanese	12	0.11
Syrian	10	0.09
Asian:	200	1.77
Bangladeshi (4)	4	0.04
Chinese, ex. Taiwanese (38)	52	0.46
Filipino (17)	27	0.24
Indian (30)	40	0.35
Indonesian (2)	3	0.03
Japanese (17)	31	0.27
Korean (18)	19	0.17
Pakistani (2)	3	0.03
Sri Lankan (1)	2	0.02
Taiwanese (2)	2	0.02
Thai (1)	1	0.01
Vietnamese (8)	9	0.08
Other Asian, not specified (2)	7	0.06
Austrian	89	0.79
Belgian	11	0.10
British	32	0.28
Canadian	73	0.65
Croatian	21	0.19
Czech	105	0.93
Danish	49	0.43
Dutch	233	2.06
Eastern European	17	0.15
English	773	6.84
Estonian	7	0.06
European	37	0.33
Finnish	27	0.24
French, except Basque	345	3.05
French Canadian	132	1.17
German	1,575	13.93
Greek	96	0.85
Guyanese	17	0.15
Hawaii Native/Pacific Islander:	8	0.07
Micronesian: (1)	2	0.02
Guamanian/Chamorro (1)	2	0.02
Polynesian: (2)	3	0.03
Native Hawaiian (1)	2	0.02
Samoan (1)	1	0.01
Other Pac. Isl., not spec.	3	0.03
Hispanic or Latino:	792	7.01
Central American:	54	0.48
Costa Rican	9	0.08
Guatemalan	20	0.18
Honduran	8	0.07
Nicaraguan	4	0.04
Panamanian	5	0.04
Salvadoran	4	0.04
Other Central American	4	0.04
Cuban	37	0.33
Dominican Republic	34	0.30
Mexican	112	0.99
Puerto Rican	317	2.80
South American:	90	0.80
Argentinean	2	0.02
Bolivian	5	0.04
Colombian	30	0.27
Ecuadorian	33	0.29
Paraguayan	1	0.01
Peruvian	12	0.11
Uruguayan	3	0.03
Venezuelan	1	0.01
Other South American	3	0.03
Other Hispanic or Latino	148	1.31
Hungarian	111	0.98
Iranian	4	0.04
Irish	2,784	24.62
Italian	3,248	28.73
Latvian	16	0.14
Lithuanian	26	0.23
Maltese	17	0.15
Norwegian	104	0.92
Polish	614	5.43
Portuguese	70	0.62
Romanian	16	0.14
Russian	175	1.55
Scotch-Irish	141	1.25
Scottish	171	1.51
Slavic	16	0.14
Slovak	51	0.45
Slovene	32	0.28
Swedish	245	2.17
Swiss	57	0.50
Ukrainian	64	0.57
United States or American	494	4.37
Welsh	42	0.37
West Indian, excl. Hispanic:	87	0.77
Haitian	27	0.24
Jamaican	60	0.53
White:	10,481	92.70
Not Hispanic (9,806)	9,934	87.86
Hispanic (514)	547	4.84

Pearl River

Place Type: Census Designated Place
County: Rockland
Population: 15,553

Ancestry/Race	Number	%
African American/Black:	86	0.55
Not Hispanic (59)	84	0.54
Hispanic (2)	2	0.01
African, sub-Saharan:	14	0.09
Cape Verdean	7	0.04
Kenyan	7	0.04
Alaska Native tribes, specified:	1	0.01
Eskimo (1)	1	0.01
Am. Ind. or Alaska Nat., not spec.	13	0.08
Albanian	14	0.09
Alsatian	11	0.07
American Indian tribes, specified:	8	0.05
Blackfeet	2	0.01
Cherokee	3	0.02
Latin American Indians	1	0.01
Sioux	1	0.01
All other tribes	1	0.01
American Indian tribes, not spec.	3	0.02
Arab:	23	0.15
Lebanese	23	0.15
Armenian	61	0.39
Asian:	549	3.53
Bangladeshi (12)	12	0.08
Chinese, ex. Taiwanese (173)	186	1.20
Filipino (50)	56	0.36
Indian (131)	141	0.91
Indonesian (2)	2	0.01
Japanese (11)	26	0.17
Korean (86)	96	0.62
Malaysian	1	0.01
Pakistani (3)	3	0.02
Sri Lankan (1)	1	0.01
Thai (12)	12	0.08
Vietnamese (3)	4	0.03
Other Asian, not specified (5)	9	0.06
Austrian	208	1.34
Belgian	12	0.08
British	35	0.22
Canadian	35	0.22
Celtic	6	0.04
Croatian	15	0.10
Czech	92	0.59
Czechoslovakian	34	0.22
Danish	14	0.09
Dutch	212	1.36
Eastern European	34	0.22
English	766	4.92
European	32	0.21
Finnish	26	0.17
French, except Basque	187	1.20
French Canadian	81	0.52
German	2,124	13.64
Greek	214	1.37
Hawaii Native/Pacific Islander:	5	0.03
Polynesian: (2)	4	0.03
Samoan (1)	3	0.02
Tongan (1)	1	0.01
Other Pac. Isl., not spec. (1)	1	0.01
Hispanic or Latino:	535	3.44
Central American:	45	0.29
Costa Rican	3	0.02
Guatemalan	1	0.01
Honduran	1	0.01
Salvadoran	39	0.25
Other Central American	1	0.01
Cuban	25	0.16
Dominican Republic	11	0.07
Mexican	69	0.44
Puerto Rican	216	1.39
South American:	88	0.57
Argentinean	2	0.01
Bolivian	5	0.03
Chilean	2	0.01
Colombian	25	0.16
Ecuadorian	40	0.26
Peruvian	1	0.01
Venezuelan	2	0.01
Other South American	11	0.07
Other Hispanic or Latino	81	0.52
Hungarian	97	0.62
Iranian	8	0.05
Irish	7,256	46.60
Italian	3,498	22.46
Lithuanian	64	0.41
Norwegian	208	1.34
Pennsylvania German	11	0.07
Polish	467	3.00
Portuguese	31	0.20
Romanian	16	0.10
Russian	388	2.49
Scotch-Irish	238	1.53
Scottish	126	0.81
Slavic	8	0.05
Slovak	18	0.12
Swedish	183	1.18
Swiss	45	0.29
Turkish	6	0.04
Ukrainian	126	0.81
United States or American	596	3.83
Welsh	91	0.58
West Indian, excl. Hispanic:	35	0.22
Barbadian	12	0.08
Jamaican	23	0.15
White:	14,888	95.72

Notes: 1. Figures in the "Number" column do not add up to the total population due to: a) Ancestry/Race overlap — e.g. persons can report being both White and Irish, b) persons of Hispanic origin can report being any race, c) persons reporting two ancestries are counted in both categories. 2. Numbers in parentheses indicate the number of persons reporting this ancestry/race alone, not in combination with any other ancestry/race. 3. Refer to the Explanation of Data in the front of the book for more detailed information.

Not Hispanic (14,366)	14,442	92.86
Hispanic (430)	446	2.87
Yugoslavian	17	0.11

Peekskill

Place Type: City
County: Westchester
Population: 22,441

Ancestry/Race	Number	%
African American/Black:	6,295	28.05
Not Hispanic (5,483)	5,894	26.26
Hispanic (249)	401	1.79
African, sub-Saharan:	142	0.63
African	127	0.57
Ghanian	8	0.04
Other sub-Saharan African	7	0.03
Alaska Native tribes, specified:	1	0.00
Eskimo	1	0.00
Am. Ind. or Alaska Nat., not spec.	141	0.63
Albanian	20	0.09
American Indian tribes, specified:	123	0.55
Apache	3	0.01
Blackfeet	5	0.02
Cherokee (13)	52	0.23
Chippewa (1)	2	0.01
Crow	5	0.02
Delaware	1	0.00
Iroquois (5)	11	0.05
Latin American Indians (16)	32	0.14
Pueblo (1)	1	0.00
Seminole	4	0.02
Sioux (1)	2	0.01
All other tribes (2)	5	0.02
American Indian tribes, not spec.	10	0.04
Arab:	74	0.33
Arab/Arabic	31	0.14
Jordanian	23	0.10
Lebanese	8	0.04
Moroccan	6	0.03
Other Arab	6	0.03
Armenian	17	0.08
Asian:	655	2.92
Bangladeshi (1)	1	0.00
Cambodian (2)	2	0.01
Chinese, ex. Taiwanese (124)	146	0.65
Filipino (94)	115	0.51
Indian (212)	258	1.15
Japanese (5)	8	0.04
Korean (29)	30	0.13
Laotian (9)	10	0.04
Malaysian (1)	2	0.01
Pakistani (3)	6	0.03
Sri Lankan (1)	1	0.00
Taiwanese (1)	1	0.00
Thai (3)	4	0.02
Vietnamese (29)	35	0.16
Other Asian, specified (12)	12	0.05
Other Asian, not specified (5)	24	0.11
Austrian	157	0.70
Basque	10	0.04
Brazilian	36	0.16
British	41	0.18
Bulgarian	5	0.02
Canadian	52	0.23
Celtic	7	0.03
Croatian	39	0.17
Czech	94	0.42
Czechoslovakian	35	0.16
Danish	35	0.16
Dutch	254	1.13
Eastern European	36	0.16
English	729	3.25
European	114	0.51
Finnish	6	0.03
French, except Basque	281	1.25
French Canadian	72	0.32
German	1,601	7.13
Greek	62	0.28
Hawaii Native/Pacific Islander:	25	0.11
Micronesian: (10)	14	0.06
Guamanian/Chamorro (10)	14	0.06
Polynesian: (1)	3	0.01
Native Hawaiian	1	0.00
Samoan (1)	2	0.01
Other Pac. Isl., not spec. (2)	8	0.04
Hispanic or Latino:	4,920	21.92
Central American:	435	1.94
Costa Rican	13	0.06
Guatemalan	261	1.16
Honduran	49	0.22
Nicaraguan	6	0.03
Panamanian	14	0.06
Salvadoran	81	0.36
Other Central American	11	0.05
Cuban	52	0.23
Dominican Republic	144	0.64
Mexican	184	0.82
Puerto Rican	1,454	6.48
South American:	1,314	5.86
Argentinean	20	0.09
Chilean	7	0.03
Colombian	128	0.57
Ecuadorian	970	4.32
Peruvian	102	0.45
Uruguayan	49	0.22
Venezuelan	19	0.08
Other South American	19	0.08
Other Hispanic or Latino	1,337	5.96
Hungarian	154	0.69
Irish	3,008	13.40
Israeli	27	0.12
Italian	3,650	16.26
Latvian	5	0.02
Lithuanian	26	0.12
Maltese	7	0.03
Northern European	4	0.02
Norwegian	59	0.26
Polish	503	2.24
Portuguese	127	0.57
Romanian	36	0.16
Russian	164	0.73
Scotch-Irish	55	0.25
Scottish	146	0.65
Serbian	11	0.05
Slovak	100	0.45
Soviet Union	6	0.03
Swedish	184	0.82
Swiss	32	0.14
Ukrainian	134	0.60
United States or American	929	4.14
Welsh	32	0.14
West Indian, excl. Hispanic:	859	3.83
Barbadian	25	0.11
British West Indian	56	0.25
Dutch West Indian	9	0.04
Haitian	43	0.19
Jamaican	614	2.74
Trinidadian and Tobagonian	68	0.30
West Indian	44	0.20
White:	13,579	60.51
Not Hispanic (10,776)	11,192	49.87
Hispanic (2,043)	2,387	10.64
Yugoslavian	55	0.25

Pelham

Place Type: Town
County: Westchester
Population: 11,866

Ancestry/Race	Number	%
African American/Black:	605	5.10
Not Hispanic (519)	558	4.70
Hispanic (23)	47	0.40
African, sub-Saharan:	49	0.41
African	42	0.35
South African	7	0.06
Am. Ind. or Alaska Nat., not spec.	21	0.18
Albanian	17	0.14
American Indian tribes, specified:	25	0.21
Blackfeet (1)	2	0.02
Cherokee (2)	5	0.04
Iroquois	7	0.06
Latin American Indians (4)	5	0.04
All other tribes	6	0.05
Arab:	87	0.73
Lebanese	12	0.10
Moroccan	48	0.40
Other Arab	27	0.23
Armenian	12	0.10
Asian:	570	4.80
Bangladeshi (5)	5	0.04
Chinese, ex. Taiwanese (89)	116	0.98
Filipino (47)	51	0.43
Indian (225)	249	2.10
Indonesian	1	0.01
Japanese (20)	38	0.32
Korean (41)	44	0.37
Pakistani (4)	5	0.04
Sri Lankan (1)	1	0.01
Thai (20)	25	0.21
Vietnamese	1	0.01
Other Asian, specified (1)	6	0.05
Other Asian, not specified (15)	28	0.24
Australian	25	0.21
Austrian	137	1.15
Belgian	59	0.50
Brazilian	37	0.31
British	87	0.73
Canadian	113	0.95
Croatian	71	0.60
Cypriot	8	0.07
Czech	26	0.22
Czechoslovakian	23	0.19
Danish	64	0.54
Dutch	146	1.23
Eastern European	52	0.44
English	1,182	9.96
Estonian	5	0.04
European	151	1.27
Finnish	12	0.10
French, except Basque	283	2.38
French Canadian	74	0.62
German	1,368	11.53
Greek	97	0.82
Guyanese	33	0.28
Hawaii Native/Pacific Islander:	2	0.02
Other Pac. Isl., not spec.	2	0.02
Hispanic or Latino:	714	6.02
Central American:	30	0.25
Costa Rican	2	0.02
Guatemalan	9	0.08
Honduran	10	0.08
Nicaraguan	1	0.01
Panamanian	3	0.03
Salvadoran	2	0.02
Other Central American	3	0.03
Cuban	49	0.41
Dominican Republic	34	0.29
Mexican	49	0.41
Puerto Rican	319	2.69
South American:	74	0.62
Argentinean	10	0.08
Bolivian	9	0.08
Chilean	2	0.02
Colombian	21	0.18
Ecuadorian	4	0.03
Paraguayan	1	0.01
Peruvian	23	0.19
Venezuelan	4	0.03
Other Hispanic or Latino	159	1.34
Hungarian	52	0.44
Iranian	6	0.05
Irish	2,576	21.71
Israeli	6	0.05
Italian	3,537	29.81
Latvian	7	0.06
Lithuanian	18	0.15

Notes: 1. Figures in the "Number" column do not add up to the total population due to: a) Ancestry/Race overlap — e.g. persons can report being both White and Irish, b) persons of Hispanic origin can report being any race, c) persons reporting two ancestries are counted in both categories. 2. Numbers in parentheses indicate the number of persons reporting this ancestry/race alone, not in combination with any other ancestry/race. 3. Refer to the Explanation of Data in the front of the book for more detailed information.

Luxemburger	7	0.06
New Zealander	7	0.06
Norwegian	79	0.67
Polish	364	3.07
Portuguese	22	0.19
Romanian	18	0.15
Russian	285	2.40
Scotch-Irish	140	1.18
Scottish	269	2.27
Slavic	6	0.05
Slovak	38	0.32
Slovene	9	0.08
Swedish	82	0.69
Swiss	27	0.23
Turkish	28	0.24
Ukrainian	98	0.83
United States or American	298	2.51
Welsh	39	0.33
West Indian, excl. Hispanic:	156	1.31
Barbadian	7	0.06
Haitian	6	0.05
Jamaican	123	1.04
Trinidadian and Tobagonian	20	0.17
White:	10,577	89.14
Not Hispanic (9,912)	10,078	84.93
Hispanic (451)	499	4.21

Penfield

Place Type: Town
County: Monroe
Population: 34,645

Ancestry/Race	Number	%
Afghan	14	0.04
African American/Black:	814	2.35
Not Hispanic (720)	796	2.30
Hispanic (12)	18	0.05
African, sub-Saharan:	25	0.07
African	21	0.06
Nigerian	4	0.01
Am. Ind. or Alaska Nat., not spec.	41	0.12
Albanian	21	0.06
American Indian tribes, specified:	72	0.21
Blackfeet	1	0.00
Cherokee (3)	11	0.03
Chickasaw	5	0.01
Chippewa	4	0.01
Cree	2	0.01
Creek (1)	1	0.00
Delaware (1)	2	0.01
Iroquois (10)	33	0.10
Latin American Indians (4)	4	0.01
Pueblo (3)	4	0.01
Sioux (2)	3	0.01
All other tribes	2	0.01
American Indian tribes, not spec.	7	0.02
Arab:	182	0.53
Egyptian	41	0.12
Lebanese	135	0.39
Syrian	6	0.02
Armenian	39	0.11
Asian:	1,199	3.46
Bangladeshi (1)	3	0.01
Cambodian (1)	3	0.01
Chinese, ex. Taiwanese (352)	383	1.11
Filipino (34)	48	0.14
Indian (321)	354	1.02
Indonesian (3)	8	0.02
Japanese (28)	41	0.12
Korean (106)	121	0.35
Laotian (42)	51	0.15
Malaysian (2)	2	0.01
Pakistani (23)	23	0.07
Sri Lankan (14)	22	0.06
Taiwanese (43)	54	0.16
Thai (3)	8	0.02
Vietnamese (55)	57	0.16
Other Asian, specified	2	0.01
Other Asian, not specified (9)	19	0.05
Assyrian/Chaldean/Syriac	5	0.01
Australian	20	0.06
Austrian	86	0.25
Belgian	146	0.42
Brazilian	46	0.13
British	207	0.60
Canadian	146	0.42
Celtic	9	0.03
Czech	82	0.24
Czechoslovakian	46	0.13
Danish	101	0.29
Dutch	1,235	3.56
Eastern European	50	0.14
English	5,623	16.23
European	158	0.46
Finnish	41	0.12
French, except Basque	1,208	3.49
French Canadian	299	0.86
German	8,410	24.27
Greek	492	1.42
Hawaii Native/Pacific Islander:	20	0.06
Polynesian: (1)	2	0.01
Native Hawaiian (1)	1	0.00
Other Polynesian	1	0.00
Other Pac. Isl., not spec. (6)	18	0.05
Hispanic or Latino:	495	1.43
Central American:	17	0.05
Costa Rican	4	0.01
Guatemalan	6	0.02
Honduran	1	0.00
Nicaraguan	4	0.01
Panamanian	1	0.00
Salvadoran	1	0.00
Cuban	26	0.08
Dominican Republic	17	0.05
Mexican	74	0.21
Puerto Rican	212	0.61
South American:	54	0.16
Argentinean	10	0.03
Bolivian	3	0.01
Chilean	7	0.02
Colombian	15	0.04
Ecuadorian	2	0.01
Paraguayan	3	0.01
Peruvian	8	0.02
Venezuelan	3	0.01
Other South American	3	0.01
Other Hispanic or Latino	95	0.27
Hungarian	130	0.38
Icelander	7	0.02
Irish	6,323	18.25
Italian	8,149	23.52
Latvian	23	0.07
Lithuanian	93	0.27
Macedonian	23	0.07
Northern European	21	0.06
Norwegian	155	0.45
Pennsylvania German	7	0.02
Polish	2,249	6.49
Portuguese	73	0.21
Romanian	68	0.20
Russian	477	1.38
Scandinavian	11	0.03
Scotch-Irish	350	1.01
Scottish	836	2.41
Slavic	23	0.07
Slovak	73	0.21
Slovene	8	0.02
Swedish	369	1.07
Swiss	180	0.52
Turkish	16	0.05
Ukrainian	567	1.64
United States or American	1,427	4.12
Welsh	277	0.80
West Indian, excl. Hispanic:	73	0.21
Barbadian	7	0.02
British West Indian	7	0.02
Jamaican	43	0.12
West Indian	16	0.05
White:	32,672	94.31
Not Hispanic (32,031)	32,283	93.18
Hispanic (355)	389	1.12
Yugoslavian	147	0.42

Perinton

Place Type: Town
County: Monroe
Population: 46,090

Ancestry/Race	Number	%
African American/Black:	941	2.04
Not Hispanic (780)	917	1.99
Hispanic (15)	24	0.05
African, sub-Saharan:	50	0.11
African	19	0.04
Ethiopian	24	0.05
Liberian	7	0.02
Am. Ind. or Alaska Nat., not spec.	38	0.08
Albanian	70	0.15
Alsatian	21	0.05
American Indian tribes, specified:	105	0.23
Apache	1	0.00
Blackfeet	6	0.01
Cherokee (6)	23	0.05
Chippewa	3	0.01
Choctaw	1	0.00
Delaware (2)	2	0.00
Iroquois (17)	40	0.09
Latin American Indians (4)	4	0.01
Navajo	1	0.00
Potawatomi (3)	6	0.01
Sioux	7	0.02
All other tribes (4)	11	0.02
American Indian tribes, not spec.	6	0.01
Arab:	178	0.39
Arab/Arabic	8	0.02
Lebanese	126	0.27
Syrian	44	0.10
Armenian	116	0.25
Asian:	1,495	3.24
Bangladeshi (9)	9	0.02
Cambodian (2)	2	0.00
Chinese, ex. Taiwanese (366)	414	0.90
Filipino (24)	44	0.10
Indian (356)	375	0.81
Indonesian	1	0.00
Japanese (51)	80	0.17
Korean (196)	221	0.48
Laotian (103)	118	0.26
Malaysian (3)	5	0.01
Pakistani (30)	38	0.08
Sri Lankan (10)	11	0.02
Taiwanese (22)	22	0.05
Thai (6)	17	0.04
Vietnamese (99)	103	0.22
Other Asian, specified (2)	6	0.01
Other Asian, not specified (18)	29	0.06
Australian	12	0.03
Austrian	232	0.50
Belgian	153	0.33
Brazilian	28	0.06
British	432	0.94
Canadian	399	0.87
Celtic	50	0.11
Croatian	76	0.16
Czech	169	0.37
Czechoslovakian	70	0.15
Danish	377	0.82
Dutch	1,612	3.50
Eastern European	105	0.23
English	7,417	16.09
Estonian	60	0.13
European	423	0.92
Finnish	45	0.10
French, except Basque	1,641	3.56
French Canadian	838	1.82
German	11,338	24.60
Greek	216	0.47
Hawaii Native/Pacific Islander:	14	0.03

Notes: 1. Figures in the "Number" column do not add up to the total population due to: a) Ancestry/Race overlap — e.g. persons can report being both White and Irish, b) persons of Hispanic origin can report being any race, c) persons reporting two ancestries are counted in both categories. 2. Numbers in parentheses indicate the number of persons reporting this ancestry/race alone, not in combination with any other ancestry/race. 3. Refer to the Explanation of Data in the front of the book for more detailed information.

Ancestry/Race	Number	%
Micronesian: (1)	2	0.00
Guamanian/Chamorro (1)	2	0.00
Polynesian:	4	0.01
Native Hawaiian	3	0.01
Samoan	1	0.00
Other Pac. Isl., specified	4	0.01
Other Pac. Isl., not spec. (2)	4	0.01
Hispanic or Latino:	660	1.43
Central American:	27	0.06
Costa Rican	1	0.00
Guatemalan	8	0.02
Honduran	7	0.02
Nicaraguan	4	0.01
Panamanian	6	0.01
Salvadoran	1	0.00
Cuban	48	0.10
Dominican Republic	17	0.04
Mexican	116	0.25
Puerto Rican	221	0.48
South American:	76	0.16
Argentinean	2	0.00
Bolivian	6	0.01
Chilean	7	0.02
Colombian	33	0.07
Ecuadorian	5	0.01
Paraguayan	4	0.01
Peruvian	7	0.02
Venezuelan	6	0.01
Other South American	6	0.01
Other Hispanic or Latino	155	0.34
Hungarian	323	0.70
Iranian	34	0.07
Irish	9,486	20.58
Israeli	26	0.06
Italian	9,046	19.63
Latvian	55	0.12
Lithuanian	228	0.49
Luxemburger	7	0.02
Macedonian	75	0.16
Maltese	19	0.04
Northern European	50	0.11
Norwegian	253	0.55
Pennsylvania German	39	0.08
Polish	2,924	6.34
Portuguese	102	0.22
Romanian	49	0.11
Russian	703	1.53
Scandinavian	38	0.08
Scotch-Irish	762	1.65
Scottish	1,543	3.35
Serbian	8	0.02
Slavic	20	0.04
Slovak	247	0.54
Slovene	41	0.09
Swedish	740	1.61
Swiss	185	0.40
Turkish	79	0.17
Ukrainian	709	1.54
United States or American	1,754	3.81
Welsh	446	0.97
West Indian, excl. Hispanic:	72	0.16
Barbadian	8	0.02
Haitian	34	0.07
Jamaican	30	0.07
White:	43,674	94.76
Not Hispanic (42,857)	43,210	93.75
Hispanic (421)	464	1.01
Yugoslavian	72	0.16

Pittsford

Place Type: Town
County: Monroe
Population: 27,219

Ancestry/Race	Number	%
African American/Black:	501	1.84
Not Hispanic (426)	478	1.76
Hispanic (10)	23	0.08
African, sub-Saharan:	66	0.24
African	20	0.07
Ethiopian	10	0.04
South African	22	0.08
Ugandan	14	0.05
Am. Ind. or Alaska Nat., not spec.	22	0.08
Albanian	13	0.05
Alsatian	26	0.10
American Indian tribes, specified:	42	0.15
Blackfeet	1	0.00
Cherokee (3)	10	0.04
Choctaw (1)	3	0.01
Iroquois (4)	8	0.03
Latin American Indians (2)	9	0.03
Sioux (2)	7	0.03
All other tribes (2)	4	0.01
American Indian tribes, not spec.	5	0.02
Arab:	218	0.80
Egyptian	45	0.17
Lebanese	114	0.42
Syrian	45	0.17
Other Arab	14	0.05
Armenian	22	0.08
Asian:	1,383	5.08
Bangladeshi (1)	1	0.00
Cambodian (1)	1	0.00
Chinese, ex. Taiwanese (255)	295	1.08
Filipino (24)	37	0.14
Indian (565)	604	2.22
Indonesian	5	0.02
Japanese (51)	63	0.23
Korean (127)	137	0.50
Malaysian	1	0.00
Pakistani (93)	121	0.44
Sri Lankan (2)	4	0.01
Taiwanese (52)	62	0.23
Thai (1)	1	0.00
Vietnamese (26)	28	0.10
Other Asian, specified (3)	4	0.01
Other Asian, not specified (7)	19	0.07
Australian	29	0.11
Austrian	117	0.43
Belgian	63	0.23
Brazilian	9	0.03
British	228	0.84
Bulgarian	8	0.03
Canadian	90	0.33
Croatian	35	0.13
Czech	111	0.41
Czechoslovakian	46	0.17
Danish	136	0.50
Dutch	809	2.97
Eastern European	157	0.58
English	4,672	17.16
Estonian	4	0.01
European	427	1.57
Finnish	47	0.17
French, except Basque	965	3.54
French Canadian	386	1.42
German	6,445	23.68
German Russian	4	0.01
Greek	228	0.84
Hawaii Native/Pacific Islander:	9	0.03
Micronesian: (2)	2	0.01
Guamanian/Chamorro (2)	2	0.01
Polynesian: (3)	5	0.02
Native Hawaiian (1)	3	0.01
Samoan (2)	2	0.01
Other Pac. Isl., not spec.	2	0.01
Hispanic or Latino:	353	1.30
Central American:	21	0.08
Guatemalan	6	0.02
Honduran	3	0.01
Nicaraguan	1	0.00
Panamanian	5	0.02
Salvadoran	2	0.01
Other Central American	4	0.01
Cuban	43	0.16
Dominican Republic	11	0.04
Mexican	76	0.28
Puerto Rican	70	0.26
South American:	67	0.25
Argentinean	5	0.02
Bolivian	1	0.00
Chilean	5	0.02
Colombian	17	0.06
Ecuadorian	4	0.01
Paraguayan	4	0.01
Peruvian	16	0.06
Uruguayan	5	0.02
Venezuelan	7	0.03
Other South American	3	0.01
Other Hispanic or Latino	65	0.24
Hungarian	185	0.68
Icelander	1	0.00
Iranian	20	0.07
Irish	5,688	20.89
Israeli	11	0.04
Italian	4,205	15.45
Latvian	49	0.18
Lithuanian	284	1.04
Macedonian	43	0.16
Northern European	14	0.05
Norwegian	229	0.84
Pennsylvania German	13	0.05
Polish	1,652	6.07
Portuguese	64	0.24
Romanian	98	0.36
Russian	742	2.73
Scandinavian	12	0.04
Scotch-Irish	402	1.48
Scottish	896	3.29
Serbian	15	0.06
Slavic	18	0.07
Slovak	94	0.35
Slovene	14	0.05
Swedish	533	1.96
Swiss	165	0.61
Turkish	45	0.17
Ukrainian	336	1.23
United States or American	989	3.63
Welsh	287	1.05
West Indian, excl. Hispanic:	46	0.17
Haitian	7	0.03
Jamaican	31	0.11
West Indian	8	0.03
White:	25,383	93.25
Not Hispanic (24,974)	25,124	92.30
Hispanic (234)	259	0.95
Yugoslavian	31	0.11

Plainview

Place Type: Census Designated Place
County: Nassau
Population: 25,637

Ancestry/Race	Number	%
Afghan	54	0.21
African American/Black:	133	0.52
Not Hispanic (93)	126	0.49
Hispanic (5)	7	0.03
African, sub-Saharan:	6	0.02
African	6	0.02
Am. Ind. or Alaska Nat., not spec.	6	0.02
American Indian tribes, specified:	6	0.02
Cherokee	2	0.01
Chippewa (1)	1	0.00
Iroquois (1)	2	0.01
Navajo (1)	1	0.00
American Indian tribes, not spec.	2	0.01
Arab:	116	0.45
Arab/Arabic	6	0.02
Egyptian	29	0.11
Iraqi	14	0.05
Moroccan	26	0.10
Palestinian	8	0.03
Syrian	21	0.08
Other Arab	12	0.05
Armenian	55	0.21
Asian:	1,352	5.27

Notes: 1. Figures in the "Number" column do not add up to the total population due to: a) Ancestry/Race overlap — e.g. persons can report being both White and Irish, b) persons of Hispanic origin can report being any race, c) persons reporting two ancestries are counted in both categories. 2. Numbers in parentheses indicate the number of persons reporting this ancestry/race alone, not in combination with any other ancestry/race. 3. Refer to the Explanation of Data in the front of the book for more detailed information.

Ancestry/Race	Number	%
Bangladeshi (11)	11	0.04
Chinese, ex. Taiwanese (326)	355	1.38
Filipino (69)	85	0.33
Indian (418)	435	1.70
Japanese (40)	47	0.18
Korean (299)	313	1.22
Pakistani (29)	45	0.18
Taiwanese (7)	7	0.03
Thai (6)	7	0.03
Vietnamese (7)	7	0.03
Other Asian, not specified (5)	40	0.16
Australian	6	0.02
Austrian	621	2.42
Belgian	6	0.02
Brazilian	4	0.02
British	33	0.13
Canadian	17	0.07
Croatian	176	0.69
Cypriot	27	0.11
Czech	81	0.32
Czechoslovakian	39	0.15
Danish	31	0.12
Dutch	61	0.24
Eastern European	652	2.54
English	615	2.40
Estonian	6	0.02
European	432	1.69
Finnish	13	0.05
French, except Basque	223	0.87
French Canadian	26	0.10
German	1,818	7.09
Greek	586	2.29
Guyanese	25	0.10
Hawaii Native/Pacific Islander:	4	0.02
Polynesian: (1)	1	0.00
Native Hawaiian (1)	1	0.00
Other Pac. Isl., not spec.	3	0.01
Hispanic or Latino:	658	2.57
Central American:	55	0.21
Costa Rican	1	0.00
Guatemalan	9	0.04
Honduran	6	0.02
Panamanian	3	0.01
Salvadoran	32	0.12
Other Central American	4	0.02
Cuban	61	0.24
Dominican Republic	14	0.05
Mexican	27	0.11
Puerto Rican	166	0.65
South American:	144	0.56
Argentinean	27	0.11
Bolivian	3	0.01
Chilean	14	0.05
Colombian	40	0.16
Ecuadorian	31	0.12
Peruvian	10	0.04
Uruguayan	3	0.01
Venezuelan	6	0.02
Other South American	10	0.04
Other Hispanic or Latino	191	0.75
Hungarian	439	1.71
Iranian	86	0.34
Irish	2,549	9.94
Israeli	381	1.49
Italian	4,922	19.20
Latvian	21	0.08
Lithuanian	180	0.70
Luxemburger	6	0.02
Maltese	39	0.15
Norwegian	50	0.20
Pennsylvania German	6	0.02
Polish	2,377	9.27
Portuguese	51	0.20
Romanian	317	1.24
Russian	2,802	10.93
Scotch-Irish	43	0.17
Scottish	86	0.34
Slovak	13	0.05
Soviet Union	6	0.02
Swedish	44	0.17
Swiss	40	0.16
Turkish	105	0.41
Ukrainian	209	0.82
United States or American	1,983	7.73
Welsh	25	0.10
West Indian, excl. Hispanic:	68	0.27
Belizean	6	0.02
British West Indian	6	0.02
Haitian	36	0.14
Jamaican	11	0.04
Other West Indian	9	0.04
White:	24,162	94.25
Not Hispanic (23,477)	23,606	92.08
Hispanic (507)	556	2.17
Yugoslavian	45	0.18

Plattsburgh

Place Type: City
County: Clinton
Population: 18,816

Ancestry/Race	Number	%
African American/Black:	572	3.04
Not Hispanic (437)	530	2.82
Hispanic (26)	42	0.22
African, sub-Saharan:	28	0.15
African	18	0.10
South African	10	0.05
Alaska Native tribes, specified:	3	0.02
Alaska Athabascan (1)	1	0.01
Eskimo (2)	2	0.01
Am. Ind. or Alaska Nat., not spec.	59	0.31
American Indian tribes, specified:	110	0.58
Blackfeet (2)	4	0.02
Cherokee (3)	8	0.04
Cheyenne (3)	3	0.02
Chickasaw (1)	1	0.01
Chippewa (2)	3	0.02
Choctaw	1	0.01
Cree (1)	4	0.02
Creek	1	0.01
Crow	1	0.01
Delaware	3	0.02
Iroquois (47)	55	0.29
Latin American Indians (3)	9	0.05
Pueblo (1)	1	0.01
Sioux (3)	3	0.02
All other tribes (4)	13	0.07
American Indian tribes, not spec.	6	0.03
Arab:	113	0.60
Arab/Arabic	39	0.21
Jordanian	11	0.06
Lebanese	53	0.28
Syrian	10	0.05
Armenian	45	0.24
Asian:	354	1.88
Bangladeshi (3)	3	0.02
Chinese, ex. Taiwanese (79)	92	0.49
Filipino (17)	33	0.18
Indian (55)	66	0.35
Indonesian (4)	5	0.03
Japanese (32)	40	0.21
Korean (25)	29	0.15
Laotian (1)	1	0.01
Pakistani (15)	16	0.09
Sri Lankan (4)	4	0.02
Taiwanese (1)	1	0.01
Thai (5)	7	0.04
Vietnamese (12)	14	0.07
Other Asian, specified (1)	6	0.03
Other Asian, not specified (26)	37	0.20
Austrian	39	0.21
Basque	8	0.04
Belgian	10	0.05
Brazilian	9	0.05
British	130	0.69
Canadian	155	0.83
Celtic	8	0.04
Czech	38	0.20
Czechoslovakian	19	0.10
Danish	46	0.25
Dutch	267	1.42
Eastern European	40	0.21
English	1,898	10.12
Estonian	6	0.03
European	70	0.37
French, except Basque	3,840	20.48
French Canadian	1,622	8.65
German	1,628	8.68
Greek	116	0.62
Hawaii Native/Pacific Islander:	19	0.10
Melanesian: (1)	1	0.01
Fijian (1)	1	0.01
Micronesian: (2)	2	0.01
Guamanian/Chamorro (2)	2	0.01
Polynesian: (6)	10	0.05
Native Hawaiian (3)	7	0.04
Samoan (3)	3	0.02
Other Pac. Isl., specified	4	0.02
Other Pac. Isl., not spec. (1)	2	0.01
Hispanic or Latino:	399	2.12
Central American:	14	0.07
Costa Rican	1	0.01
Guatemalan	1	0.01
Honduran	4	0.02
Nicaraguan	4	0.02
Salvadoran	3	0.02
Other Central American	1	0.01
Cuban	19	0.10
Dominican Republic	23	0.12
Mexican	53	0.28
Puerto Rican	136	0.72
South American:	27	0.14
Argentinean	1	0.01
Chilean	6	0.03
Colombian	8	0.04
Ecuadorian	5	0.03
Paraguayan	2	0.01
Peruvian	2	0.01
Venezuelan	1	0.01
Other South American	2	0.01
Other Hispanic or Latino	127	0.67
Hungarian	88	0.47
Iranian	20	0.11
Irish	3,098	16.52
Italian	1,347	7.18
Lithuanian	27	0.14
New Zealander	5	0.03
Norwegian	56	0.30
Pennsylvania German	7	0.04
Polish	569	3.03
Portuguese	35	0.19
Romanian	43	0.23
Russian	73	0.39
Scandinavian	39	0.21
Scotch-Irish	294	1.57
Scottish	345	1.84
Slovak	33	0.18
Slovene	8	0.04
Swedish	79	0.42
Ukrainian	76	0.41
United States or American	780	4.16
Welsh	172	0.92
West Indian, excl. Hispanic:	88	0.47
Barbadian	9	0.05
Belizean	12	0.06
Haitian	19	0.10
Jamaican	29	0.15
West Indian	19	0.10
White:	17,800	94.60
Not Hispanic (17,334)	17,539	93.21
Hispanic (242)	261	1.39

Notes: 1. Figures in the "Number" column do not add up to the total population due to: a) Ancestry/Race overlap — e.g. persons can report being both White and Irish, b) persons of Hispanic origin can report being any race, c) persons reporting two ancestries are counted in both categories. 2. Numbers in parentheses indicate the number of persons reporting this ancestry/race alone, not in combination with any other ancestry/race. 3. Refer to the Explanation of Data in the front of the book for more detailed information.

Plattsburgh

Place Type: Town
County: Clinton
Population: 11,190

Ancestry/Race	Number	%
African American/Black:	156	1.39
Not Hispanic (119)	154	1.38
Hispanic (1)	2	0.02
Alaska Native tribes, specified:	2	0.02
Alaska Athabascan (1)	1	0.01
Aleut (1)	1	0.01
Alaska Native tribes, not specified	1	0.01
Am. Ind. or Alaska Nat., not spec.	19	0.17
American Indian tribes, specified:	40	0.36
Cherokee (2)	3	0.03
Chippewa (2)	3	0.03
Delaware	2	0.02
Iroquois (11)	14	0.13
Latin American Indians (1)	1	0.01
Menominee (1)	1	0.01
Pueblo (2)	2	0.02
Seminole	1	0.01
All other tribes (11)	13	0.12
American Indian tribes, not spec.	2	0.02
Arab:	71	0.64
Egyptian	16	0.14
Lebanese	27	0.24
Syrian	28	0.25
Armenian	5	0.04
Asian:	86	0.77
Chinese, ex. Taiwanese (15)	19	0.17
Filipino (15)	29	0.26
Indian (6)	8	0.07
Japanese (9)	12	0.11
Korean (5)	5	0.04
Thai (1)	2	0.02
Vietnamese (8)	8	0.07
Other Asian, not specified (2)	3	0.03
Australian	7	0.06
Austrian	43	0.39
British	49	0.44
Canadian	132	1.19
Celtic	10	0.09
Czech	8	0.07
Czechoslovakian	13	0.12
Danish	9	0.08
Dutch	167	1.50
English	1,181	10.62
European	44	0.40
Finnish	25	0.22
French, except Basque	2,705	24.31
French Canadian	1,554	13.97
German	885	7.96
Greek	35	0.31
Hawaii Native/Pacific Islander:	5	0.04
Micronesian:	2	0.02
Guamanian/Chamorro	2	0.02
Polynesian: (1)	2	0.02
Native Hawaiian (1)	2	0.02
Other Pac. Isl., not spec.	1	0.01
Hispanic or Latino:	116	1.04
Central American:	6	0.05
Honduran	1	0.01
Nicaraguan	1	0.01
Panamanian	4	0.04
Cuban	3	0.03
Mexican	30	0.27
Puerto Rican	38	0.34
South American:	4	0.04
Chilean	1	0.01
Venezuelan	3	0.03
Other Hispanic or Latino	35	0.31
Hungarian	62	0.56
Iranian	22	0.20
Irish	1,984	17.83
Italian	490	4.40
Lithuanian	9	0.08
Norwegian	64	0.58
Polish	394	3.54
Portuguese	30	0.27
Russian	43	0.39
Scandinavian	23	0.21
Scotch-Irish	155	1.39
Scottish	239	2.15
Slovene	10	0.09
Swedish	43	0.39
Swiss	6	0.05
Ukrainian	25	0.22
United States or American	1,018	9.15
Welsh	37	0.33
West Indian, excl. Hispanic:	10	0.09
Haitian	10	0.09
White:	10,911	97.51
Not Hispanic (10,760)	10,839	96.86
Hispanic (58)	72	0.64

Pomfret

Place Type: Town
County: Chautauqua
Population: 14,703

Ancestry/Race	Number	%
African American/Black:	338	2.30
Not Hispanic (299)	328	2.23
Hispanic (6)	10	0.07
African, sub-Saharan:	18	0.12
African	18	0.12
Alaska Native tribes, specified:	1	0.01
Eskimo (1)	1	0.01
Am. Ind. or Alaska Nat., not spec.	22	0.15
Albanian	44	0.30
American Indian tribes, specified:	62	0.42
Blackfeet (1)	6	0.04
Cherokee	8	0.05
Chippewa (1)	1	0.01
Choctaw	1	0.01
Iroquois (34)	42	0.29
Latin American Indians	1	0.01
Sioux	1	0.01
All other tribes (1)	2	0.01
American Indian tribes, not spec.	2	0.01
Arab:	113	0.77
Arab/Arabic	24	0.16
Egyptian	4	0.03
Lebanese	59	0.40
Syrian	26	0.18
Asian:	151	1.03
Chinese, ex. Taiwanese (31)	37	0.25
Filipino (7)	9	0.06
Indian (39)	41	0.28
Indonesian (1)	1	0.01
Japanese (12)	13	0.09
Korean (16)	16	0.11
Laotian (1)	1	0.01
Pakistani (7)	14	0.10
Sri Lankan (3)	3	0.02
Thai (5)	6	0.04
Other Asian, not specified (5)	10	0.07
Austrian	39	0.27
Brazilian	6	0.04
British	72	0.49
Canadian	72	0.49
Croatian	8	0.05
Czech	34	0.23
Czechoslovakian	33	0.22
Danish	40	0.27
Dutch	261	1.78
English	2,070	14.10
European	133	0.91
Finnish	5	0.03
French, except Basque	436	2.97
French Canadian	109	0.74
German	3,823	26.04
Greek	38	0.26
Hawaii Native/Pacific Islander:	7	0.05
Micronesian: (1)	1	0.01
Guamanian/Chamorro (1)	1	0.01
Polynesian: (2)	6	0.04
Native Hawaiian (1)	3	0.02
Samoan (1)	3	0.02
Hispanic or Latino:	342	2.33
Central American:	2	0.01
Nicaraguan	1	0.01
Salvadoran	1	0.01
Cuban	10	0.07
Dominican Republic	9	0.06
Mexican	25	0.17
Puerto Rican	220	1.50
South American:	7	0.05
Argentinean	1	0.01
Chilean	1	0.01
Colombian	4	0.03
Peruvian	1	0.01
Other Hispanic or Latino	69	0.47
Hungarian	105	0.72
Irish	2,296	15.64
Italian	2,861	19.48
Latvian	7	0.05
Lithuanian	37	0.25
Luxemburger	4	0.03
Northern European	11	0.07
Norwegian	49	0.33
Pennsylvania German	34	0.23
Polish	2,819	19.20
Portuguese	32	0.22
Romanian	10	0.07
Russian	74	0.50
Scandinavian	17	0.12
Scotch-Irish	250	1.70
Scottish	289	1.97
Serbian	7	0.05
Slavic	15	0.10
Slovak	24	0.16
Slovene	5	0.03
Swedish	665	4.53
Swiss	45	0.31
Ukrainian	114	0.78
United States or American	521	3.55
Welsh	105	0.72
West Indian, excl. Hispanic:	40	0.27
Jamaican	22	0.15
Trinidadian and Tobagonian	11	0.07
West Indian	7	0.05
White:	14,109	95.96
Not Hispanic (13,776)	13,859	94.26
Hispanic (233)	250	1.70
Yugoslavian	37	0.25

Port Chester

Place Type: Village
County: Westchester
Population: 27,867

Ancestry/Race	Number	%
African American/Black:	2,113	7.58
Not Hispanic (1,795)	1,884	6.76
Hispanic (154)	229	0.82
African, sub-Saharan:	75	0.27
African	13	0.05
Ethiopian	7	0.03
Other sub-Saharan African	55	0.20
Am. Ind. or Alaska Nat., not spec.	87	0.31
American Indian tribes, specified:	66	0.24
Blackfeet	2	0.01
Cherokee (3)	7	0.03
Cree	1	0.00
Latin American Indians (31)	50	0.18
Pueblo	1	0.00
Sioux	2	0.01
Ute (3)	3	0.01
American Indian tribes, not spec.	35	0.13
Arab:	53	0.19
Arab/Arabic	38	0.14
Lebanese	5	0.02
Syrian	10	0.04
Armenian	21	0.08

Notes: 1. Figures in the "Number" column do not add up to the total population due to: a) Ancestry/Race overlap — e.g. persons can report being both White and Irish, b) persons of Hispanic origin can report being any race, c) persons reporting two ancestries are counted in both categories. 2. Numbers in parentheses indicate the number of persons reporting this ancestry/race alone, not in combination with any other ancestry/race. 3. Refer to the Explanation of Data in the front of the book for more detailed information.

Ancestry/Race	Number	%
Asian:	654	2.35
Chinese, ex. Taiwanese (96)	107	0.38
Filipino (125)	137	0.49
Indian (238)	251	0.90
Japanese (31)	38	0.14
Korean (24)	29	0.10
Laotian (11)	11	0.04
Malaysian (1)	2	0.01
Pakistani (20)	23	0.08
Taiwanese (1)	1	0.00
Thai (10)	11	0.04
Vietnamese (5)	6	0.02
Other Asian, specified (5)	13	0.05
Other Asian, not specified (5)	25	0.09
Assyrian/Chaldean/Syriac	8	0.03
Australian	8	0.03
Austrian	46	0.17
Belgian	28	0.10
Brazilian	342	1.23
British	57	0.20
Canadian	30	0.11
Celtic	9	0.03
Croatian	31	0.11
Cypriot	12	0.04
Czech	49	0.18
Czechoslovakian	42	0.15
Danish	45	0.16
Dutch	50	0.18
Eastern European	20	0.07
English	523	1.88
Estonian	3	0.01
European	83	0.30
Finnish	9	0.03
French, except Basque	206	0.74
French Canadian	67	0.24
German	1,161	4.17
Greek	113	0.41
Hawaii Native/Pacific Islander:	47	0.17
Micronesian: (5)	13	0.05
Guamanian/Chamorro (5)	13	0.05
Polynesian: (3)	4	0.02
Native Hawaiian (2)	3	0.01
Samoan (1)	2	0.01
Other Pac. Isl., specified	8	0.03
Other Pac. Isl., not spec. (3)	21	0.08
Hispanic or Latino:	12,884	46.23
Central American:	1,819	6.53
Costa Rican	22	0.08
Guatemalan	1,037	3.72
Honduran	97	0.35
Nicaraguan	14	0.05
Panamanian	9	0.03
Salvadoran	558	2.00
Other Central American	82	0.29
Cuban	465	1.67
Dominican Republic	273	0.98
Mexican	3,108	11.15
Puerto Rican	842	3.02
South American:	3,516	12.62
Argentinean	45	0.16
Bolivian	163	0.58
Chilean	111	0.40
Colombian	696	2.50
Ecuadorian	1,366	4.90
Paraguayan	17	0.06
Peruvian	919	3.30
Uruguayan	95	0.34
Venezuelan	9	0.03
Other South American	95	0.34
Other Hispanic or Latino	2,861	10.27
Hungarian	75	0.27
Irish	2,078	7.46
Italian	5,773	20.72
Latvian	7	0.03
Lithuanian	28	0.10
Norwegian	69	0.25
Polish	757	2.72
Portuguese	259	0.93
Romanian	31	0.11
Russian	210	0.75
Scandinavian	6	0.02
Scotch-Irish	117	0.42
Scottish	74	0.27
Serbian	38	0.14
Slavic	7	0.03
Slovak	37	0.13
Swedish	108	0.39
Swiss	64	0.23
Turkish	30	0.11
Ukrainian	19	0.07
United States or American	801	2.87
Welsh	72	0.26
West Indian, excl. Hispanic:	160	0.57
Barbadian	46	0.17
Haitian	28	0.10
Jamaican	48	0.17
Trinidadian and Tobagonian	12	0.04
West Indian	26	0.09
White:	18,669	66.99
Not Hispanic (11,934)	12,376	44.41
Hispanic (4,980)	6,293	22.58
Yugoslavian	60	0.22

Port Washington

Place Type: Census Designated Place
County: Nassau
Population: 15,215

Ancestry/Race	Number	%
African American/Black:	477	3.14
Not Hispanic (394)	432	2.84
Hispanic (33)	45	0.30
African, sub-Saharan:	16	0.11
African	4	0.03
South African	12	0.08
Am. Ind. or Alaska Nat., not spec.	15	0.10
Albanian	20	0.13
American Indian tribes, specified:	25	0.16
Cherokee (1)	8	0.05
Iroquois (3)	4	0.03
Latin American Indians	3	0.02
Yaqui (1)	1	0.01
Yuman	1	0.01
All other tribes (1)	8	0.05
American Indian tribes, not spec.	1	0.01
Arab:	37	0.24
Arab/Arabic	18	0.12
Egyptian	4	0.03
Lebanese	15	0.10
Armenian	46	0.30
Asian:	1,021	6.71
Bangladeshi (4)	5	0.03
Chinese, ex. Taiwanese (225)	255	1.68
Filipino (28)	39	0.26
Indian (141)	166	1.09
Indonesian (1)	1	0.01
Japanese (258)	276	1.81
Korean (216)	226	1.49
Pakistani (1)	3	0.02
Taiwanese (16)	18	0.12
Thai (3)	4	0.03
Vietnamese (13)	13	0.09
Other Asian, not specified (8)	15	0.10
Australian	14	0.09
Austrian	160	1.05
Belgian	6	0.04
Brazilian	21	0.14
British	104	0.68
Bulgarian	12	0.08
Canadian	10	0.07
Carpatho Rusyn	4	0.03
Croatian	93	0.61
Czech	54	0.36
Czechoslovakian	20	0.13
Danish	61	0.40
Dutch	104	0.68
Eastern European	243	1.60
English	993	6.54
Estonian	7	0.05
European	80	0.53
Finnish	27	0.18
French, except Basque	252	1.66
French Canadian	68	0.45
German	1,625	10.70
Greek	197	1.30
Hawaii Native/Pacific Islander:	10	0.07
Melanesian: (1)	5	0.03
Fijian (1)	5	0.03
Micronesian: (1)	1	0.01
Guamanian/Chamorro (1)	1	0.01
Polynesian: (1)	2	0.01
Native Hawaiian (1)	2	0.01
Other Pac. Isl., not spec.	2	0.01
Hispanic or Latino:	1,704	11.20
Central American:	528	3.47
Costa Rican	1	0.01
Guatemalan	140	0.92
Honduran	31	0.20
Nicaraguan	1	0.01
Panamanian	4	0.03
Salvadoran	310	2.04
Other Central American	41	0.27
Cuban	20	0.13
Dominican Republic	40	0.26
Mexican	57	0.37
Puerto Rican	130	0.85
South American:	428	2.81
Argentinean	20	0.13
Bolivian	1	0.01
Chilean	106	0.70
Colombian	87	0.57
Ecuadorian	154	1.01
Paraguayan	5	0.03
Peruvian	34	0.22
Uruguayan	2	0.01
Venezuelan	4	0.03
Other South American	15	0.10
Other Hispanic or Latino	501	3.29
Hungarian	209	1.38
Iranian	25	0.16
Irish	2,576	16.95
Israeli	42	0.28
Italian	3,009	19.80
Latvian	55	0.36
Lithuanian	76	0.50
Maltese	16	0.11
New Zealander	10	0.07
Northern European	2	0.01
Norwegian	108	0.71
Polish	1,132	7.45
Portuguese	83	0.55
Romanian	112	0.74
Russian	1,057	6.96
Scandinavian	30	0.20
Scotch-Irish	186	1.22
Scottish	223	1.47
Serbian	6	0.04
Slovak	15	0.10
Slovene	6	0.04
Swedish	138	0.91
Swiss	41	0.27
Turkish	79	0.52
Ukrainian	64	0.42
United States or American	644	4.24
Welsh	18	0.12
West Indian, excl. Hispanic:	36	0.24
Dutch West Indian	5	0.03
Jamaican	8	0.05
Trinidadian and Tobagonian	9	0.06
West Indian	14	0.09
White:	13,343	87.70
Not Hispanic (11,980)	12,133	79.74
Hispanic (1,101)	1,210	7.95
Yugoslavian	6	0.04

Notes: 1. Figures in the "Number" column do not add up to the total population due to: a) Ancestry/Race overlap — e.g. persons can report being both White and Irish, b) persons of Hispanic origin can report being any race, c) persons reporting two ancestries are counted in both categories. 2. Numbers in parentheses indicate the number of persons reporting this ancestry/race alone, not in combination with any other ancestry/race. 3. Refer to the Explanation of Data in the front of the book for more detailed information.

Potsdam

Place Type: Town
County: Saint Lawrence
Population: 15,957

Ancestry/Race	Number	%
African American/Black:	294	1.84
Not Hispanic (246)	282	1.77
Hispanic (8)	12	0.08
African, sub-Saharan:	67	0.42
African	44	0.28
Ghanian	7	0.04
South African	16	0.10
Alaska Native tribes, specified:	1	0.01
Eskimo (1)	1	0.01
Am. Ind. or Alaska Nat., not spec.	19	0.12
American Indian tribes, specified:	77	0.48
Apache (1)	1	0.01
Cherokee (2)	4	0.03
Chippewa (3)	3	0.02
Delaware	2	0.01
Iroquois (41)	51	0.32
Latin American Indians (2)	4	0.03
Navajo (1)	1	0.01
Sioux	1	0.01
All other tribes (5)	10	0.06
American Indian tribes, not spec.	3	0.02
Arab:	155	0.97
Arab/Arabic	14	0.09
Egyptian	77	0.48
Iraqi	17	0.11
Lebanese	36	0.23
Moroccan	5	0.03
Other Arab	6	0.04
Armenian	7	0.04
Asian:	462	2.90
Bangladeshi (1)	1	0.01
Cambodian (2)	2	0.01
Chinese, ex. Taiwanese (156)	171	1.07
Filipino (6)	6	0.04
Indian (128)	142	0.89
Indonesian (4)	5	0.03
Japanese (17)	20	0.13
Korean (38)	44	0.28
Laotian (1)	1	0.01
Malaysian (2)	3	0.02
Pakistani (2)	2	0.01
Sri Lankan (3)	3	0.02
Taiwanese (8)	10	0.06
Thai (5)	7	0.04
Vietnamese (11)	18	0.11
Other Asian, specified (3)	3	0.02
Other Asian, not specified (9)	24	0.15
Australian	49	0.31
Austrian	48	0.30
Belgian	5	0.03
Brazilian	12	0.08
British	102	0.64
Bulgarian	8	0.05
Canadian	135	0.85
Croatian	8	0.05
Czech	25	0.16
Czechoslovakian	18	0.11
Danish	47	0.29
Dutch	431	2.70
Eastern European	5	0.03
English	1,867	11.70
European	149	0.93
Finnish	37	0.23
French, except Basque	2,006	12.57
French Canadian	920	5.77
German	1,814	11.37
Greek	63	0.39
Hawaii Native/Pacific Islander:	9	0.06
Micronesian: (1)	1	0.01
Guamanian/Chamorro (1)	1	0.01
Polynesian: (1)	2	0.01
Native Hawaiian (1)	1	0.01
Samoan	1	0.01
Other Pac. Isl., not spec.	6	0.04
Hispanic or Latino:	200	1.25
Central American:	11	0.07
Costa Rican	3	0.02
Guatemalan	2	0.01
Honduran	3	0.02
Nicaraguan	1	0.01
Salvadoran	2	0.01
Cuban	16	0.10
Dominican Republic	14	0.09
Mexican	27	0.17
Puerto Rican	66	0.41
South American:	19	0.12
Argentinean	4	0.03
Chilean	4	0.03
Colombian	6	0.04
Ecuadorian	1	0.01
Paraguayan	2	0.01
Peruvian	2	0.01
Other Hispanic or Latino	47	0.29
Hungarian	164	1.03
Iranian	11	0.07
Irish	2,696	16.90
Italian	1,197	7.50
Latvian	2	0.01
Lithuanian	20	0.13
Luxemburger	8	0.05
Norwegian	134	0.84
Pennsylvania German	9	0.06
Polish	560	3.51
Portuguese	18	0.11
Romanian	36	0.23
Russian	105	0.66
Scandinavian	19	0.12
Scotch-Irish	340	2.13
Scottish	442	2.77
Slovak	81	0.51
Slovene	5	0.03
Swedish	134	0.84
Swiss	49	0.31
Turkish	15	0.09
Ukrainian	64	0.40
United States or American	897	5.62
Welsh	135	0.85
West Indian, excl. Hispanic:	73	0.46
Bermudan	7	0.04
British West Indian	15	0.09
Haitian	6	0.04
Jamaican	27	0.17
Trinidadian and Tobagonian	18	0.11
White:	15,153	94.96
Not Hispanic (14,916)	15,023	94.15
Hispanic (117)	130	0.81

Poughkeepsie

Place Type: City
County: Dutchess
Population: 29,871

Ancestry/Race	Number	%
Acadian/Cajun	6	0.02
African American/Black:	11,507	38.52
Not Hispanic (10,354)	11,080	37.09
Hispanic (312)	427	1.43
African, sub-Saharan:	418	1.40
African	345	1.15
Kenyan	6	0.02
Liberian	22	0.07
Nigerian	15	0.05
Ugandan	22	0.07
Other sub-Saharan African	8	0.03
Am. Ind. or Alaska Nat., not spec.	190	0.64
Alsatian	5	0.02
American Indian tribes, specified:	155	0.52
Apache	6	0.02
Blackfeet (1)	7	0.02
Cherokee (4)	53	0.18
Cheyenne	3	0.01
Chickasaw	1	0.00
Choctaw	4	0.01
Colville (1)	1	0.00
Creek	3	0.01
Delaware	3	0.01
Iroquois (6)	20	0.07
Latin American Indians (17)	26	0.09
Lumbee	1	0.00
Osage (1)	1	0.00
Seminole	3	0.01
Sioux (6)	6	0.02
All other tribes (2)	17	0.06
American Indian tribes, not spec.	18	0.06
Arab:	143	0.48
Arab/Arabic	18	0.06
Jordanian	17	0.06
Lebanese	48	0.16
Syrian	43	0.14
Other Arab	17	0.06
Armenian	20	0.07
Asian:	591	1.98
Bangladeshi (2)	2	0.01
Cambodian	1	0.00
Chinese, ex. Taiwanese (80)	101	0.34
Filipino (36)	53	0.18
Indian (167)	197	0.66
Indonesian (2)	4	0.01
Japanese (9)	12	0.04
Korean (48)	54	0.18
Laotian (11)	12	0.04
Pakistani (9)	13	0.04
Sri Lankan (4)	4	0.01
Thai (1)	2	0.01
Vietnamese (99)	107	0.36
Other Asian, specified (4)	4	0.01
Other Asian, not specified (6)	25	0.08
Austrian	73	0.24
Belgian	15	0.05
British	66	0.22
Bulgarian	5	0.02
Canadian	18	0.06
Celtic	18	0.06
Croatian	7	0.02
Czech	39	0.13
Czechoslovakian	66	0.22
Danish	96	0.32
Dutch	593	1.99
Eastern European	18	0.06
English	1,377	4.61
Estonian	10	0.03
European	188	0.63
Finnish	6	0.02
French, except Basque	594	1.99
French Canadian	195	0.65
German	2,581	8.64
Greek	160	0.54
Hawaii Native/Pacific Islander:	39	0.13
Micronesian: (7)	8	0.03
Guamanian/Chamorro (3)	4	0.01
Other Micronesian (4)	4	0.01
Polynesian: (3)	11	0.04
Native Hawaiian	4	0.01
Samoan (3)	6	0.02
Other Polynesian	1	0.00
Other Pac. Isl., not spec. (2)	20	0.07
Hispanic or Latino:	3,177	10.64
Central American:	148	0.50
Costa Rican	19	0.06
Guatemalan	44	0.15
Honduran	15	0.05
Nicaraguan	12	0.04
Panamanian	24	0.08
Salvadoran	25	0.08
Other Central American	9	0.03
Cuban	54	0.18
Dominican Republic	100	0.33
Mexican	1,616	5.41
Puerto Rican	817	2.74
South American:	114	0.38
Argentinean	3	0.01
Chilean	1	0.00

Notes: 1. Figures in the "Number" column do not add up to the total population due to: a) Ancestry/Race overlap — e.g. persons can report being both White and Irish, b) persons of Hispanic origin can report being any race, c) persons reporting two ancestries are counted in both categories. 2. Numbers in parentheses indicate the number of persons reporting this ancestry/race alone, not in combination with any other ancestry/race. 3. Refer to the Explanation of Data in the front of the book for more detailed information.

Colombian	39	0.13
Ecuadorian	28	0.09
Peruvian	12	0.04
Uruguayan	7	0.02
Venezuelan	20	0.07
Other South American	4	0.01
Other Hispanic or Latino	328	1.10
Hungarian	229	0.77
Icelander	5	0.02
Iranian	5	0.02
Irish	3,568	11.94
Israeli	16	0.05
Italian	3,693	12.36
Latvian	22	0.07
Lithuanian	13	0.04
Northern European	17	0.06
Norwegian	49	0.16
Pennsylvania German	18	0.06
Polish	1,111	3.72
Portuguese	55	0.18
Romanian	54	0.18
Russian	364	1.22
Scandinavian	26	0.09
Scotch-Irish	192	0.64
Scottish	325	1.09
Serbian	10	0.03
Slavic	5	0.02
Slovak	59	0.20
Slovene	7	0.02
Swedish	281	0.94
Swiss	61	0.20
Ukrainian	106	0.35
United States or American	873	2.92
Welsh	71	0.24
West Indian, excl. Hispanic:	1,795	6.01
Bahamian	55	0.18
Barbadian	10	0.03
British West Indian	8	0.03
Haitian	113	0.38
Jamaican	1,524	5.10
Trinidadian and Tobagonian	25	0.08
U.S. Virgin Islander	10	0.03
West Indian	50	0.17
White:	16,528	55.33
Not Hispanic (14,706)	15,298	51.21
Hispanic (1,079)	1,230	4.12
Yugoslavian	8	0.03

Poughkeepsie

Place Type: Town
County: Dutchess
Population: 42,777

Ancestry/Race	Number	%
African American/Black:	3,771	8.82
Not Hispanic (3,326)	3,590	8.39
Hispanic (127)	181	0.42
African, sub-Saharan:	273	0.64
African	30	0.07
Cape Verdean	25	0.06
Ghanian	22	0.05
Kenyan	41	0.10
Nigerian	101	0.24
Sierra Leonean	11	0.03
Somalian	24	0.06
South African	7	0.02
Ugandan	12	0.03
Am. Ind. or Alaska Nat., not spec.	95	0.22
Alsatian	7	0.02
American Indian tribes, specified:	111	0.26
Apache	2	0.00
Blackfeet (1)	13	0.03
Cherokee (13)	44	0.10
Chickasaw (1)	4	0.01
Chippewa	2	0.00
Choctaw	1	0.00
Creek	2	0.00
Delaware	1	0.00
Iroquois (5)	9	0.02
Latin American Indians (6)	12	0.03
Osage (1)	1	0.00
Pima (1)	1	0.00
Seminole (2)	2	0.00
Shoshone	3	0.01
Sioux (1)	2	0.00
All other tribes (3)	12	0.03
American Indian tribes, not spec.	8	0.02
Arab:	308	0.72
Arab/Arabic	99	0.23
Egyptian	8	0.02
Jordanian	64	0.15
Lebanese	73	0.17
Palestinian	64	0.15
Armenian	49	0.11
Asian:	2,475	5.79
Bangladeshi (26)	26	0.06
Cambodian (1)	1	0.00
Chinese, ex. Taiwanese (641)	706	1.65
Filipino (151)	203	0.47
Indian (932)	976	2.28
Indonesian (8)	12	0.03
Japanese (51)	84	0.20
Korean (168)	179	0.42
Laotian (4)	4	0.01
Malaysian	1	0.00
Pakistani (42)	53	0.12
Sri Lankan (8)	10	0.02
Taiwanese (30)	36	0.08
Thai (10)	14	0.03
Vietnamese (72)	77	0.18
Other Asian, specified (2)	7	0.02
Other Asian, not specified (28)	86	0.20
Austrian	194	0.45
Basque	9	0.02
Belgian	19	0.04
Brazilian	52	0.12
British	257	0.60
Canadian	42	0.10
Celtic	48	0.11
Croatian	34	0.08
Czech	128	0.30
Czechoslovakian	132	0.31
Danish	284	0.66
Dutch	1,114	2.61
Eastern European	79	0.18
English	4,540	10.62
European	188	0.44
Finnish	121	0.28
French, except Basque	1,112	2.60
French Canadian	465	1.09
German	6,124	14.33
Greek	407	0.95
Guyanese	39	0.09
Hawaii Native/Pacific Islander:	49	0.11
Micronesian:	4	0.01
Guamanian/Chamorro	4	0.01
Polynesian: (8)	20	0.05
Native Hawaiian (6)	15	0.04
Samoan (2)	5	0.01
Other Pac. Isl., specified	2	0.00
Other Pac. Isl., not spec. (2)	23	0.05
Hispanic or Latino:	2,254	5.27
Central American:	68	0.16
Costa Rican	8	0.02
Guatemalan	10	0.02
Honduran	6	0.01
Nicaraguan	3	0.01
Panamanian	26	0.06
Salvadoran	11	0.03
Other Central American	4	0.01
Cuban	110	0.26
Dominican Republic	92	0.22
Mexican	265	0.62
Puerto Rican	1,035	2.42
South American:	229	0.54
Argentinean	17	0.04
Chilean	16	0.04
Colombian	91	0.21
Ecuadorian	32	0.07
Paraguayan	1	0.00
Peruvian	38	0.09
Uruguayan	5	0.01
Venezuelan	21	0.05
Other South American	8	0.02
Other Hispanic or Latino	455	1.06
Hungarian	509	1.19
Iranian	114	0.27
Irish	8,334	19.50
Israeli	50	0.12
Italian	8,751	20.47
Latvian	25	0.06
Lithuanian	226	0.53
Norwegian	298	0.70
Pennsylvania German	21	0.05
Polish	2,408	5.63
Portuguese	113	0.26
Romanian	133	0.31
Russian	1,009	2.36
Scandinavian	120	0.28
Scotch-Irish	402	0.94
Scottish	767	1.79
Serbian	25	0.06
Slavic	66	0.15
Slovak	132	0.31
Swedish	498	1.17
Swiss	81	0.19
Turkish	9	0.02
Ukrainian	311	0.73
United States or American	1,380	3.23
Welsh	200	0.47
West Indian, excl. Hispanic:	933	2.18
Bahamian	25	0.06
Barbadian	10	0.02
British West Indian	10	0.02
Dutch West Indian	18	0.04
Haitian	24	0.06
Jamaican	746	1.75
Trinidadian and Tobagonian	42	0.10
U.S. Virgin Islander	13	0.03
West Indian	45	0.11
White:	36,203	84.63
Not Hispanic (34,231)	34,772	81.29
Hispanic (1,280)	1,431	3.35
Yugoslavian	58	0.14

Putnam Valley

Place Type: Town
County: Putnam
Population: 10,686

Ancestry/Race	Number	%
African American/Black:	216	2.02
Not Hispanic (149)	186	1.74
Hispanic (22)	30	0.28
African, sub-Saharan:	22	0.21
African	22	0.21
Am. Ind. or Alaska Nat., not spec.	15	0.14
Albanian	96	0.90
American Indian tribes, specified:	38	0.36
Apache (1)	1	0.01
Blackfeet	2	0.02
Cherokee (4)	16	0.15
Cheyenne (1)	1	0.01
Chippewa (1)	1	0.01
Delaware	3	0.03
Iroquois	2	0.02
Latin American Indians	4	0.04
Sioux (2)	2	0.02
All other tribes (3)	6	0.06
American Indian tribes, not spec.	5	0.05
Arab:	114	1.07
Arab/Arabic	41	0.38
Jordanian	56	0.52
Palestinian	17	0.16
Armenian	12	0.11
Asian:	142	1.33
Bangladeshi	1	0.01
Cambodian (1)	1	0.01

Notes: 1. Figures in the "Number" column do not add up to the total population due to: a) Ancestry/Race overlap — e.g. persons can report being both White and Irish, b) persons of Hispanic origin can report being any race, c) persons reporting two ancestries are counted in both categories. 2. Numbers in parentheses indicate the number of persons reporting this ancestry/race alone, not in combination with any other ancestry/race. 3. Refer to the Explanation of Data in the front of the book for more detailed information.

Ancestry/Race	Number	%
Chinese, ex. Taiwanese (26)	41	0.38
Filipino (17)	34	0.32
Indian (21)	25	0.23
Japanese (6)	8	0.07
Korean (13)	17	0.16
Pakistani	1	0.01
Thai (3)	4	0.04
Vietnamese	2	0.02
Other Asian, specified (1)	1	0.01
Other Asian, not specified	7	0.07
Australian	13	0.12
Austrian	153	1.43
Basque	46	0.43
Belgian	17	0.16
Brazilian	5	0.05
British	56	0.52
Bulgarian	12	0.11
Canadian	12	0.11
Croatian	6	0.06
Czech	81	0.76
Czechoslovakian	50	0.47
Danish	10	0.09
Dutch	194	1.82
Eastern European	66	0.62
English	728	6.81
European	80	0.75
Finnish	20	0.19
French, except Basque	249	2.33
French Canadian	50	0.47
German	1,952	18.27
Greek	104	0.97
Hawaii Native/Pacific Islander:	13	0.12
Micronesian:	5	0.05
Guamanian/Chamorro	5	0.05
Polynesian:	7	0.07
Native Hawaiian	7	0.07
Other Pac. Isl., not spec.	1	0.01
Hispanic or Latino:	671	6.28
Central American:	23	0.22
Costa Rican	6	0.06
Guatemalan	1	0.01
Honduran	3	0.03
Nicaraguan	3	0.03
Panamanian	1	0.01
Salvadoran	9	0.08
Cuban	33	0.31
Dominican Republic	23	0.22
Mexican	55	0.51
Puerto Rican	338	3.16
South American:	80	0.75
Argentinean	3	0.03
Chilean	2	0.02
Colombian	20	0.19
Ecuadorian	7	0.07
Paraguayan	2	0.02
Peruvian	21	0.20
Uruguayan	13	0.12
Other South American	12	0.11
Other Hispanic or Latino	119	1.11
Hungarian	117	1.09
Iranian	11	0.10
Irish	2,517	23.55
Italian	3,122	29.22
Lithuanian	27	0.25
Northern European	35	0.33
Norwegian	93	0.87
Polish	595	5.57
Portuguese	10	0.09
Romanian	36	0.34
Russian	377	3.53
Scandinavian	13	0.12
Scotch-Irish	261	2.44
Scottish	270	2.53
Slavic	13	0.12
Slovak	40	0.37
Slovene	13	0.12
Swedish	171	1.60
Swiss	35	0.33
Ukrainian	155	1.45
United States or American	379	3.55
Welsh	36	0.34
West Indian, excl. Hispanic:	7	0.07
Other West Indian	7	0.07
White:	10,252	95.94
Not Hispanic (9,613)	9,723	90.99
Hispanic (490)	529	4.95
Yugoslavian	35	0.33

Queensbury

Place Type: Town
County: Warren
Population: 25,441

Ancestry/Race	Number	%
African American/Black:	189	0.74
Not Hispanic (131)	175	0.69
Hispanic (10)	14	0.06
Am. Ind. or Alaska Nat., not spec.	59	0.23
Albanian	13	0.05
American Indian tribes, specified:	80	0.31
Blackfeet	12	0.05
Cherokee (2)	5	0.02
Chickasaw	1	0.00
Chippewa (2)	5	0.02
Choctaw	2	0.01
Cree	1	0.00
Iroquois (11)	21	0.08
Kiowa (1)	1	0.00
Latin American Indians (1)	2	0.01
Ottawa (2)	2	0.01
Sioux (6)	8	0.03
All other tribes (1)	20	0.08
American Indian tribes, not spec.	11	0.04
Arab:	80	0.32
Lebanese	64	0.25
Syrian	16	0.06
Asian:	218	0.86
Chinese, ex. Taiwanese (66)	70	0.28
Filipino (17)	28	0.11
Indian (46)	54	0.21
Indonesian (1)	1	0.00
Japanese (5)	9	0.04
Korean (39)	44	0.17
Pakistani (4)	4	0.02
Taiwanese (1)	1	0.00
Thai (1)	1	0.00
Other Asian, specified	1	0.00
Other Asian, not specified (1)	5	0.02
Austrian	48	0.19
Belgian	7	0.03
British	132	0.52
Bulgarian	28	0.11
Canadian	137	0.54
Cypriot	7	0.03
Czech	53	0.21
Czechoslovakian	23	0.09
Danish	64	0.25
Dutch	766	3.02
Eastern European	23	0.09
English	4,343	17.13
European	86	0.34
Finnish	48	0.19
French, except Basque	3,497	13.79
French Canadian	1,232	4.86
German	3,227	12.73
Greek	126	0.50
Guyanese	7	0.03
Hawaii Native/Pacific Islander:	8	0.03
Micronesian: (1)	4	0.02
Guamanian/Chamorro (1)	4	0.02
Polynesian: (3)	4	0.02
Native Hawaiian (2)	3	0.01
Samoan (1)	1	0.00
Hispanic or Latino:	285	1.12
Central American:	13	0.05
Costa Rican	2	0.01
Guatemalan	4	0.02
Honduran	4	0.02
Nicaraguan	1	0.00
Panamanian	1	0.00
Salvadoran	1	0.00
Cuban	9	0.04
Dominican Republic	4	0.02
Mexican	36	0.14
Puerto Rican	106	0.42
South American:	33	0.13
Argentinean	5	0.02
Bolivian	1	0.00
Colombian	13	0.05
Ecuadorian	7	0.03
Peruvian	6	0.02
Uruguayan	1	0.00
Other Hispanic or Latino	84	0.33
Hungarian	115	0.45
Icelander	16	0.06
Irish	5,793	22.85
Italian	3,063	12.08
Lithuanian	114	0.45
Northern European	9	0.04
Norwegian	125	0.49
Polish	1,182	4.66
Portuguese	43	0.17
Russian	185	0.73
Scandinavian	18	0.07
Scotch-Irish	593	2.34
Scottish	600	2.37
Slovak	60	0.24
Swedish	351	1.38
Swiss	62	0.24
Ukrainian	85	0.34
United States or American	1,414	5.58
Welsh	464	1.83
West Indian, excl. Hispanic:	7	0.03
Jamaican	7	0.03
White:	24,998	98.26
Not Hispanic (24,630)	24,787	97.43
Hispanic (186)	211	0.83
Yugoslavian	14	0.06

Ramapo

Place Type: Town
County: Rockland
Population: 108,905

Ancestry/Race	Number	%
African American/Black:	20,291	18.63
Not Hispanic (17,965)	19,508	17.91
Hispanic (590)	783	0.72
African, sub-Saharan:	940	0.86
African	524	0.48
Cape Verdean	21	0.02
Ethiopian	10	0.01
Ghanian	87	0.08
Kenyan	44	0.04
Liberian	10	0.01
Nigerian	240	0.22
Other sub-Saharan African	4	0.00
Alaska Native tribes, specified:	2	0.00
Tlingit-Haida	2	0.00
Am. Ind. or Alaska Nat., not spec.	292	0.27
Albanian	143	0.13
Alsatian	5	0.00
American Indian tribes, specified:	369	0.34
Apache (5)	8	0.01
Blackfeet	4	0.00
Cherokee (18)	63	0.06
Chippewa	1	0.00
Colville	1	0.00
Comanche (1)	2	0.00
Cree (1)	1	0.00
Creek (1)	1	0.00
Delaware (81)	142	0.13
Iroquois (4)	13	0.01
Latin American Indians (34)	108	0.10
Pueblo	2	0.00
Seminole	2	0.00
Sioux (3)	4	0.00
Tohono O'Odham (2)	5	0.00

Notes: 1. Figures in the "Number" column do not add up to the total population due to: a) Ancestry/Race overlap — e.g. persons can report being both White and Irish, b) persons of Hispanic origin can report being any race, c) persons reporting two ancestries are counted in both categories. 2. Numbers in parentheses indicate the number of persons reporting this ancestry/race alone, not in combination with any other ancestry/race. 3. Refer to the Explanation of Data in the front of the book for more detailed information.

All other tribes (2)	12	0.01
American Indian tribes, not spec.	141	0.13
Arab:	505	0.46
Arab/Arabic	79	0.07
Egyptian	40	0.04
Iraqi	9	0.01
Jordanian	38	0.03
Lebanese	57	0.05
Moroccan	56	0.05
Palestinian	108	0.10
Syrian	24	0.02
Other Arab	94	0.09
Armenian	88	0.08
Asian:	5,675	5.21
Bangladeshi (16)	19	0.02
Cambodian (65)	84	0.08
Chinese, ex. Taiwanese (531)	696	0.64
Filipino (1,366)	1,534	1.41
Indian (1,978)	2,157	1.98
Indonesian (14)	22	0.02
Japanese (96)	121	0.11
Korean (288)	314	0.29
Laotian (4)	4	0.00
Malaysian	3	0.00
Pakistani (190)	242	0.22
Sri Lankan (26)	28	0.03
Taiwanese (25)	25	0.02
Thai (53)	60	0.06
Vietnamese (159)	213	0.20
Other Asian, specified (5)	7	0.01
Other Asian, not specified (73)	146	0.13
Australian	46	0.04
Austrian	926	0.85
Belgian	41	0.04
Brazilian	159	0.15
British	159	0.15
Bulgarian	9	0.01
Canadian	297	0.27
Croatian	49	0.04
Cypriot	22	0.02
Czech	326	0.30
Czechoslovakian	277	0.25
Danish	63	0.06
Dutch	748	0.69
Eastern European	1,193	1.10
English	3,082	2.83
Estonian	7	0.01
European	1,745	1.60
Finnish	72	0.07
French, except Basque	723	0.66
French Canadian	179	0.16
German	5,711	5.24
German Russian	15	0.01
Greek	434	0.40
Guyanese	169	0.16
Hawaii Native/Pacific Islander:	254	0.23
Melanesian: (1)	1	0.00
Fijian (1)	1	0.00
Micronesian: (32)	46	0.04
Guamanian/Chamorro (32)	46	0.04
Polynesian: (25)	48	0.04
Native Hawaiian (14)	35	0.03
Samoan (11)	13	0.01
Other Pac. Isl., specified	2	0.00
Other Pac. Isl., not spec. (19)	157	0.14
Hispanic or Latino:	8,923	8.19
Central American:	1,546	1.42
Costa Rican	93	0.09
Guatemalan	1,116	1.02
Honduran	55	0.05
Nicaraguan	13	0.01
Panamanian	43	0.04
Salvadoran	182	0.17
Other Central American	44	0.04
Cuban	207	0.19
Dominican Republic	385	0.35
Mexican	1,268	1.16
Puerto Rican	2,636	2.42
South American:	1,215	1.12
Argentinean	47	0.04
Bolivian	4	0.00
Chilean	54	0.05
Colombian	261	0.24
Ecuadorian	631	0.58
Paraguayan	2	0.00
Peruvian	118	0.11
Uruguayan	6	0.01
Venezuelan	37	0.03
Other South American	55	0.05
Other Hispanic or Latino	1,666	1.53
Hungarian	2,708	2.49
Icelander	19	0.02
Iranian	215	0.20
Irish	8,638	7.93
Israeli	917	0.84
Italian	9,987	9.17
Latvian	102	0.09
Lithuanian	375	0.34
Macedonian	27	0.02
Maltese	18	0.02
Northern European	4	0.00
Norwegian	249	0.23
Polish	6,124	5.62
Portuguese	231	0.21
Romanian	823	0.76
Russian	4,997	4.59
Scandinavian	60	0.06
Scotch-Irish	336	0.31
Scottish	656	0.60
Serbian	8	0.01
Slavic	75	0.07
Slovak	153	0.14
Slovene	8	0.01
Soviet Union	5	0.00
Swedish	348	0.32
Swiss	182	0.17
Turkish	198	0.18
Ukrainian	807	0.74
United States or American	6,752	6.20
Welsh	105	0.10
West Indian, excl. Hispanic:	9,716	8.92
Barbadian	101	0.09
Belizean	30	0.03
British West Indian	80	0.07
Haitian	7,559	6.94
Jamaican	1,684	1.55
Trinidadian and Tobagonian	64	0.06
U.S. Virgin Islander	7	0.01
West Indian	185	0.17
Other West Indian	6	0.01
White:	80,491	73.91
Not Hispanic (74,199)	75,143	69.00
Hispanic (4,797)	5,348	4.91
Yugoslavian	119	0.11

Red Hook

Place Type: Town
County: Dutchess
Population: 10,408

Ancestry/Race	Number	%
African American/Black:	182	1.75
Not Hispanic (135)	162	1.56
Hispanic (15)	20	0.19
African, sub-Saharan:	24	0.23
African	22	0.21
South African	2	0.02
Am. Ind. or Alaska Nat., not spec.	21	0.20
Albanian	2	0.02
American Indian tribes, specified:	16	0.15
Apache (1)	1	0.01
Blackfeet (1)	1	0.01
Cherokee (1)	6	0.06
Creek (1)	1	0.01
Iroquois (1)	4	0.04
Sioux	2	0.02
All other tribes	1	0.01
Arab:	47	0.45
Arab/Arabic	4	0.04
Egyptian	7	0.07
Lebanese	33	0.32
Syrian	3	0.03
Armenian	5	0.05
Asian:	277	2.66
Bangladeshi (1)	1	0.01
Chinese, ex. Taiwanese (33)	45	0.43
Filipino (12)	12	0.12
Indian (54)	59	0.57
Indonesian (1)	1	0.01
Japanese (45)	62	0.60
Korean (49)	53	0.51
Malaysian (1)	3	0.03
Pakistani (1)	1	0.01
Taiwanese (4)	4	0.04
Vietnamese (2)	3	0.03
Other Asian, specified (1)	3	0.03
Other Asian, not specified (9)	30	0.29
Austrian	112	1.08
Belgian	19	0.18
Brazilian	22	0.21
British	94	0.90
Bulgarian	11	0.11
Canadian	29	0.28
Celtic	2	0.02
Croatian	32	0.31
Cypriot	4	0.04
Czech	53	0.51
Czechoslovakian	50	0.48
Danish	100	0.96
Dutch	435	4.18
Eastern European	19	0.18
English	1,638	15.74
Estonian	6	0.06
European	93	0.89
Finnish	31	0.30
French, except Basque	497	4.78
French Canadian	128	1.23
German	2,329	22.38
German Russian	6	0.06
Greek	57	0.55
Guyanese	21	0.20
Hawaii Native/Pacific Islander:	31	0.30
Micronesian: (2)	2	0.02
Guamanian/Chamorro (2)	2	0.02
Polynesian: (2)	7	0.07
Native Hawaiian (2)	7	0.07
Other Pac. Isl., specified	2	0.02
Other Pac. Isl., not spec. (7)	20	0.19
Hispanic or Latino:	276	2.65
Central American:	14	0.13
Costa Rican	6	0.06
Guatemalan	4	0.04
Nicaraguan	1	0.01
Panamanian	3	0.03
Cuban	8	0.08
Dominican Republic	6	0.06
Mexican	59	0.57
Puerto Rican	90	0.86
South American:	31	0.30
Argentinean	7	0.07
Bolivian	3	0.03
Chilean	4	0.04
Colombian	14	0.13
Ecuadorian	1	0.01
Peruvian	1	0.01
Other South American	1	0.01
Other Hispanic or Latino	68	0.65
Hungarian	152	1.46
Irish	2,192	21.06
Italian	1,755	16.86
Lithuanian	63	0.61
Norwegian	187	1.80
Polish	484	4.65
Portuguese	5	0.05
Romanian	8	0.08
Russian	144	1.38
Scandinavian	36	0.35
Scotch-Irish	202	1.94
Scottish	292	2.81

Notes: 1. Figures in the "Number" column do not add up to the total population due to: a) Ancestry/Race overlap — e.g. persons can report being both White and Irish, b) persons of Hispanic origin can report being any race, c) persons reporting two ancestries are counted in both categories. 2. Numbers in parentheses indicate the number of persons reporting this ancestry/race alone, not in combination with any other ancestry/race. 3. Refer to the Explanation of Data in the front of the book for more detailed information.

Ancestry/Race	Number	%
Serbian	6	0.06
Slavic	13	0.12
Slovak	19	0.18
Slovene	31	0.30
Swedish	161	1.55
Swiss	51	0.49
Turkish	2	0.02
Ukrainian	64	0.61
United States or American	320	3.07
Welsh	83	0.80
West Indian, excl. Hispanic:	36	0.35
Barbadian	17	0.16
Bermudan	5	0.05
Jamaican	14	0.13
White:	9,933	95.44
Not Hispanic (9,610)	9,722	93.41
Hispanic (194)	211	2.03
Yugoslavian	4	0.04

Ridge

Place Type: Census Designated Place
County: Suffolk
Population: 13,380

Ancestry/Race	Number	%
African American/Black:	563	4.21
Not Hispanic (441)	533	3.98
Hispanic (21)	30	0.22
African, sub-Saharan:	56	0.42
African	56	0.42
Am. Ind. or Alaska Nat., not spec.	38	0.28
American Indian tribes, specified:	77	0.58
Blackfeet	2	0.01
Cherokee (2)	29	0.22
Chippewa	1	0.01
Creek	1	0.01
Iroquois (3)	11	0.08
Sioux	5	0.04
All other tribes (19)	28	0.21
American Indian tribes, not spec.	1	0.01
Arab:	41	0.31
Egyptian	27	0.20
Syrian	6	0.05
Other Arab	8	0.06
Armenian	8	0.06
Asian:	180	1.35
Chinese, ex. Taiwanese (19)	30	0.22
Filipino (6)	14	0.10
Indian (49)	49	0.37
Japanese (9)	12	0.09
Korean (21)	30	0.22
Pakistani (12)	21	0.16
Vietnamese (1)	3	0.02
Other Asian, not specified (2)	21	0.16
Austrian	74	0.56
British	17	0.13
Canadian	48	0.36
Cypriot	28	0.21
Czech	70	0.53
Czechoslovakian	68	0.51
Danish	23	0.17
Dutch	129	0.97
Eastern European	9	0.07
English	898	6.77
Estonian	7	0.05
European	26	0.20
Finnish	33	0.25
French, except Basque	226	1.70
French Canadian	97	0.73
German	2,839	21.42
Greek	90	0.68
Guyanese	8	0.06
Hawaii Native/Pacific Islander:	8	0.06
Micronesian:	1	0.01
Guamanian/Chamorro	1	0.01
Polynesian: (1)	4	0.03
Native Hawaiian	3	0.02
Samoan (1)	1	0.01
Other Pac. Isl., not spec. (3)	3	0.02
Hispanic or Latino:	469	3.51
Central American:	14	0.10
Salvadoran	14	0.10
Cuban	13	0.10
Dominican Republic	25	0.19
Mexican	25	0.19
Puerto Rican	242	1.81
South American:	56	0.42
Argentinean	9	0.07
Chilean	1	0.01
Colombian	25	0.19
Ecuadorian	10	0.07
Peruvian	9	0.07
Other South American	2	0.01
Other Hispanic or Latino	94	0.70
Hungarian	57	0.43
Irish	3,736	28.18
Italian	4,399	33.18
Latvian	20	0.15
Lithuanian	81	0.61
Norwegian	275	2.07
Polish	686	5.18
Portuguese	48	0.36
Romanian	11	0.08
Russian	257	1.94
Scandinavian	14	0.11
Scotch-Irish	124	0.94
Scottish	164	1.24
Serbian	5	0.04
Slavic	8	0.06
Slovak	9	0.07
Swedish	99	0.75
Swiss	67	0.51
Turkish	34	0.26
Ukrainian	51	0.38
United States or American	602	4.54
Welsh	29	0.22
West Indian, excl. Hispanic:	56	0.42
Jamaican	10	0.08
Trinidadian and Tobagonian	14	0.11
West Indian	32	0.24
White:	12,592	94.11
Not Hispanic (12,105)	12,237	91.46
Hispanic (337)	355	2.65

Riverhead

Place Type: Town
County: Suffolk
Population: 27,680

Ancestry/Race	Number	%
African American/Black:	3,082	11.13
Not Hispanic (2,862)	3,011	10.88
Hispanic (51)	71	0.26
African, sub-Saharan:	53	0.19
African	53	0.19
Alaska Native tribes, specified:	1	0.00
Aleut (1)	1	0.00
Am. Ind. or Alaska Nat., not spec.	93	0.34
Albanian	14	0.05
Alsatian	10	0.04
American Indian tribes, specified:	116	0.42
Apache	1	0.00
Blackfeet (1)	5	0.02
Cherokee (3)	17	0.06
Chippewa (5)	6	0.02
Choctaw	1	0.00
Creek	5	0.02
Delaware	2	0.01
Iroquois	5	0.02
Latin American Indians (5)	20	0.07
Lumbee (4)	5	0.02
Seminole (1)	1	0.00
Sioux	1	0.00
All other tribes (24)	47	0.17
American Indian tribes, not spec.	10	0.04
Arab:	81	0.29
Arab/Arabic	17	0.06
Egyptian	24	0.09
Lebanese	31	0.11
Syrian	4	0.01
Other Arab	5	0.02
Armenian	15	0.05
Asian:	327	1.18
Bangladeshi	4	0.01
Chinese, ex. Taiwanese (72)	85	0.31
Filipino (13)	25	0.09
Indian (47)	56	0.20
Indonesian (1)	1	0.00
Japanese (17)	34	0.12
Korean (32)	40	0.14
Malaysian (1)	3	0.01
Pakistani (37)	42	0.15
Thai (1)	2	0.01
Vietnamese (18)	18	0.07
Other Asian, specified (1)	1	0.00
Other Asian, not specified	16	0.06
Australian	15	0.05
Austrian	144	0.52
Belgian	11	0.04
British	90	0.33
Canadian	89	0.32
Croatian	50	0.18
Czech	209	0.76
Czechoslovakian	48	0.17
Danish	108	0.39
Dutch	424	1.53
Eastern European	20	0.07
English	2,034	7.35
Estonian	16	0.06
European	58	0.21
Finnish	61	0.22
French, except Basque	603	2.18
French Canadian	205	0.74
German	5,547	20.04
Greek	297	1.07
Hawaii Native/Pacific Islander:	46	0.17
Micronesian: (13)	15	0.05
Guamanian/Chamorro (13)	15	0.05
Polynesian: (8)	11	0.04
Native Hawaiian (5)	7	0.03
Samoan (3)	4	0.01
Other Pac. Isl., not spec. (3)	20	0.07
Hispanic or Latino:	1,678	6.06
Central American:	541	1.95
Costa Rican	9	0.03
Guatemalan	292	1.05
Honduran	62	0.22
Nicaraguan	2	0.01
Salvadoran	160	0.58
Other Central American	16	0.06
Cuban	37	0.13
Dominican Republic	28	0.10
Mexican	246	0.89
Puerto Rican	414	1.50
South American:	128	0.46
Argentinean	3	0.01
Chilean	2	0.01
Colombian	63	0.23
Ecuadorian	35	0.13
Paraguayan	1	0.00
Peruvian	14	0.05
Uruguayan	3	0.01
Other South American	7	0.03
Other Hispanic or Latino	284	1.03
Hungarian	202	0.73
Irish	6,201	22.40
Italian	5,211	18.83
Latvian	7	0.03
Lithuanian	151	0.55
Luxemburger	8	0.03
Northern European	14	0.05
Norwegian	419	1.51
Polish	4,160	15.03
Portuguese	25	0.09
Romanian	12	0.04
Russian	353	1.28
Scandinavian	10	0.04
Scotch-Irish	278	1.00

Notes: 1. Figures in the "Number" column do not add up to the total population due to: a) Ancestry/Race overlap — e.g. persons can report being both White and Irish, b) persons of Hispanic origin can report being any race, c) persons reporting two ancestries are counted in both categories. 2. Numbers in parentheses indicate the number of persons reporting this ancestry/race alone, not in combination with any other ancestry/race. 3. Refer to the Explanation of Data in the front of the book for more detailed information.

Ancestry/Race	Number	%
Scottish	438	1.58
Serbian	23	0.08
Slovak	19	0.07
Slovene	19	0.07
Swedish	381	1.38
Swiss	121	0.44
Turkish	101	0.36
Ukrainian	391	1.41
United States or American	730	2.64
Welsh	78	0.28
West Indian, excl. Hispanic:	93	0.34
Haitian	25	0.09
Jamaican	11	0.04
West Indian	57	0.21
White:	23,938	86.48
Not Hispanic (22,493)	22,738	82.15
Hispanic (1,100)	1,200	4.34
Yugoslavian	13	0.05

Rochester

Place Type: City
County: Monroe
Population: 219,773

Ancestry/Race	Number	%
Acadian/Cajun	10	0.00
Afghan	38	0.02
African American/Black:	89,411	40.68
Not Hispanic (82,267)	85,922	39.10
Hispanic (2,450)	3,489	1.59
African, sub-Saharan:	4,202	1.91
African	3,286	1.50
Cape Verdean	15	0.01
Ethiopian	383	0.17
Ghanian	21	0.01
Liberian	19	0.01
Nigerian	141	0.06
Somalian	171	0.08
South African	33	0.02
Sudanese	42	0.02
Ugandan	42	0.02
Other sub-Saharan African	49	0.02
Alaska Native tribes, specified:	6	0.00
Alaska Athabascan (1)	3	0.00
Eskimo (2)	2	0.00
Tlingit-Haida (1)	1	0.00
Alaska Native tribes, not specified	9	0.00
Am. Ind. or Alaska Nat., not spec.	1,166	0.53
Albanian	221	0.10
Alsatian	11	0.01
American Indian tribes, specified:	1,467	0.67
Apache (4)	19	0.01
Blackfeet (12)	93	0.04
Cherokee (65)	377	0.17
Chickasaw (1)	9	0.00
Chippewa (12)	22	0.01
Choctaw (3)	12	0.01
Colville	2	0.00
Comanche	3	0.00
Cree (1)	2	0.00
Creek	8	0.00
Crow	1	0.00
Delaware (2)	10	0.00
Iroquois (354)	631	0.29
Latin American Indians (26)	85	0.04
Menominee (2)	2	0.00
Navajo (6)	21	0.01
Osage	1	0.00
Ottawa	1	0.00
Pima	2	0.00
Potawatomi (3)	5	0.00
Pueblo (1)	4	0.00
Seminole (3)	35	0.02
Shoshone	1	0.00
Sioux (11)	37	0.02
Tohono O'Odham	1	0.00
Yakama (1)	1	0.00
Yaqui (1)	2	0.00
Yuman	1	0.00
All other tribes (25)	79	0.04
American Indian tribes, not spec.	176	0.08
Arab:	921	0.42
Arab/Arabic	351	0.16
Egyptian	64	0.03
Iraqi	31	0.01
Lebanese	314	0.14
Moroccan	7	0.00
Palestinian	29	0.01
Syrian	105	0.05
Other Arab	20	0.01
Armenian	52	0.02
Asian:	6,174	2.81
Bangladeshi (4)	5	0.00
Cambodian (275)	311	0.14
Chinese, ex. Taiwanese (878)	1,051	0.48
Filipino (195)	312	0.14
Hmong	3	0.00
Indian (670)	843	0.38
Indonesian (6)	10	0.00
Japanese (169)	280	0.13
Korean (399)	486	0.22
Laotian (748)	933	0.42
Malaysian (2)	2	0.00
Pakistani (31)	43	0.02
Sri Lankan (18)	24	0.01
Taiwanese (41)	50	0.02
Thai (31)	46	0.02
Vietnamese (1,248)	1,390	0.63
Other Asian, specified (7)	47	0.02
Other Asian, not specified (99)	338	0.15
Assyrian/Chaldean/Syriac	6	0.00
Australian	8	0.00
Austrian	452	0.21
Belgian	161	0.07
Brazilian	98	0.04
British	636	0.29
Bulgarian	81	0.04
Canadian	492	0.22
Celtic	80	0.04
Croatian	118	0.05
Cypriot	12	0.01
Czech	197	0.09
Czechoslovakian	133	0.06
Danish	323	0.15
Dutch	3,627	1.65
Eastern European	184	0.08
English	12,677	5.77
Estonian	11	0.01
European	1,007	0.46
Finnish	82	0.04
French, except Basque	4,561	2.08
French Canadian	1,568	0.71
German	23,892	10.87
Greek	547	0.25
Guyanese	126	0.06
Hawaii Native/Pacific Islander:	396	0.18
Melanesian: (1)	1	0.00
Fijian (1)	1	0.00
Micronesian: (13)	18	0.01
Guamanian/Chamorro (13)	18	0.01
Polynesian: (55)	102	0.05
Native Hawaiian (20)	50	0.02
Samoan (35)	49	0.02
Other Polynesian	3	0.00
Other Pac. Isl., specified	38	0.02
Other Pac. Isl., not spec. (35)	237	0.11
Hispanic or Latino:	28,032	12.75
Central American:	277	0.13
Costa Rican	32	0.01
Guatemalan	29	0.01
Honduran	34	0.02
Nicaraguan	48	0.02
Panamanian	81	0.04
Salvadoran	41	0.02
Other Central American	12	0.01
Cuban	1,177	0.54
Dominican Republic	808	0.37
Mexican	851	0.39
Puerto Rican	21,897	9.96
South American:	362	0.16
Argentinean	34	0.02
Bolivian	13	0.01
Chilean	55	0.03
Colombian	118	0.05
Ecuadorian	34	0.02
Paraguayan	8	0.00
Peruvian	50	0.02
Uruguayan	3	0.00
Venezuelan	23	0.01
Other South American	24	0.01
Other Hispanic or Latino	2,660	1.21
Hungarian	442	0.20
Iranian	60	0.03
Irish	21,011	9.56
Israeli	27	0.01
Italian	22,077	10.05
Latvian	38	0.02
Lithuanian	456	0.21
Macedonian	108	0.05
Northern European	92	0.04
Norwegian	435	0.20
Pennsylvania German	55	0.03
Polish	5,985	2.72
Portuguese	267	0.12
Romanian	133	0.06
Russian	1,569	0.71
Scandinavian	145	0.07
Scotch-Irish	1,296	0.59
Scottish	2,654	1.21
Serbian	15	0.01
Slavic	76	0.03
Slovak	114	0.05
Slovene	12	0.01
Swedish	944	0.43
Swiss	347	0.16
Turkish	593	0.27
Ukrainian	2,179	0.99
United States or American	4,837	2.20
Welsh	979	0.45
West Indian, excl. Hispanic:	3,755	1.71
Bahamian	30	0.01
Barbadian	155	0.07
Belizean	195	0.09
British West Indian	81	0.04
Haitian	349	0.16
Jamaican	2,517	1.15
Trinidadian and Tobagonian	137	0.06
U.S. Virgin Islander	23	0.01
West Indian	268	0.12
White:	111,891	50.91
Not Hispanic (97,395)	101,473	46.17
Hispanic (8,766)	10,418	4.74
Yugoslavian	703	0.32

Rockville Centre

Place Type: Village
County: Nassau
Population: 24,568

Ancestry/Race	Number	%
African American/Black:	991	4.03
Not Hispanic (878)	931	3.79
Hispanic (36)	60	0.24
African, sub-Saharan:	7	0.03
African	7	0.03
Am. Ind. or Alaska Nat., not spec.	13	0.05
Albanian	31	0.13
Alsatian	33	0.13
American Indian tribes, specified:	29	0.12
Cherokee (8)	11	0.04
Choctaw	1	0.00
Creek (3)	3	0.01
Delaware	4	0.02
Iroquois	1	0.00
Latin American Indians (1)	1	0.00
Navajo	1	0.00
Sioux	2	0.01
All other tribes (1)	5	0.02

Notes: 1. Figures in the "Number" column do not add up to the total population due to: a) Ancestry/Race overlap — e.g. persons can report being both White and Irish, b) persons of Hispanic origin can report being any race, c) persons reporting two ancestries are counted in both categories. 2. Numbers in parentheses indicate the number of persons reporting this ancestry/race alone, not in combination with any other ancestry/race. 3. Refer to the Explanation of Data in the front of the book for more detailed information.

Ancestry/Race	Number	%
American Indian tribes, not spec.	5	0.02
Arab:	25	0.10
Arab/Arabic	5	0.02
Egyptian	15	0.06
Syrian	5	0.02
Armenian	42	0.17
Asian:	426	1.73
Chinese, ex. Taiwanese (85)	115	0.47
Filipino (65)	70	0.28
Indian (96)	118	0.48
Indonesian (1)	2	0.01
Japanese (23)	32	0.13
Korean (44)	52	0.21
Pakistani (2)	5	0.02
Sri Lankan (1)	1	0.00
Taiwanese (7)	7	0.03
Thai (1)	1	0.00
Vietnamese (9)	10	0.04
Other Asian, not specified (8)	13	0.05
Australian	4	0.02
Austrian	336	1.37
Belgian	18	0.07
Brazilian	17	0.07
British	59	0.24
Canadian	42	0.17
Croatian	97	0.39
Czech	108	0.44
Czechoslovakian	70	0.28
Danish	77	0.31
Dutch	232	0.94
Eastern European	177	0.72
English	1,338	5.45
Estonian	7	0.03
European	180	0.73
Finnish	27	0.11
French, except Basque	523	2.13
French Canadian	122	0.50
German	3,806	15.49
Greek	283	1.15
Guyanese	40	0.16
Hawaii Native/Pacific Islander:	13	0.05
Micronesian: (2)	2	0.01
Guamanian/Chamorro (2)	2	0.01
Polynesian: (1)	1	0.00
Native Hawaiian (1)	1	0.00
Other Pac. Isl., not spec. (7)	10	0.04
Hispanic or Latino:	1,896	7.72
Central American:	149	0.61
Costa Rican	2	0.01
Guatemalan	28	0.11
Honduran	13	0.05
Nicaraguan	1	0.00
Panamanian	4	0.02
Salvadoran	94	0.38
Other Central American	7	0.03
Cuban	152	0.62
Dominican Republic	617	2.51
Mexican	54	0.22
Puerto Rican	354	1.44
South American:	172	0.70
Argentinean	12	0.05
Bolivian	1	0.00
Chilean	14	0.06
Colombian	75	0.31
Ecuadorian	22	0.09
Paraguayan	1	0.00
Peruvian	25	0.10
Uruguayan	5	0.02
Venezuelan	4	0.02
Other South American	13	0.05
Other Hispanic or Latino	398	1.62
Hungarian	258	1.05
Iranian	14	0.06
Irish	8,214	33.43
Israeli	5	0.02
Italian	5,800	23.60
Latvian	9	0.04
Lithuanian	134	0.55
Maltese	7	0.03
New Zealander	6	0.02
Norwegian	224	0.91
Pennsylvania German	14	0.06
Polish	1,209	4.92
Portuguese	27	0.11
Romanian	224	0.91
Russian	1,588	6.46
Scandinavian	10	0.04
Scotch-Irish	229	0.93
Scottish	299	1.22
Serbian	18	0.07
Slavic	30	0.12
Slovak	20	0.08
Slovene	22	0.09
Swedish	206	0.84
Swiss	52	0.21
Turkish	4	0.02
Ukrainian	230	0.94
United States or American	783	3.19
Welsh	45	0.18
West Indian, excl. Hispanic:	162	0.66
British West Indian	12	0.05
Haitian	85	0.35
Jamaican	30	0.12
Trinidadian and Tobagonian	14	0.06
West Indian	21	0.09
White:	22,538	91.74
Not Hispanic (21,262)	21,377	87.01
Hispanic (1,065)	1,161	4.73
Yugoslavian	25	0.10

Rocky Point

Place Type: Census Designated Place
County: Suffolk
Population: 10,185

Ancestry/Race	Number	%
African American/Black:	105	1.03
Not Hispanic (60)	91	0.89
Hispanic (9)	14	0.14
Am. Ind. or Alaska Nat., not spec.	21	0.21
Albanian	15	0.15
American Indian tribes, specified:	26	0.26
Blackfeet	2	0.02
Cherokee (1)	2	0.02
Iroquois	2	0.02
Latin American Indians	3	0.03
Navajo	2	0.02
Osage	3	0.03
Paiute (1)	1	0.01
All other tribes (2)	11	0.11
American Indian tribes, not spec.	7	0.07
Arab:	25	0.24
Jordanian	20	0.20
Syrian	5	0.05
Armenian	28	0.27
Asian:	169	1.66
Chinese, ex. Taiwanese (48)	52	0.51
Filipino (11)	21	0.21
Indian (25)	33	0.32
Japanese (5)	9	0.09
Korean (19)	26	0.26
Pakistani (2)	10	0.10
Thai (2)	2	0.02
Vietnamese (2)	2	0.02
Other Asian, specified	1	0.01
Other Asian, not specified	13	0.13
Austrian	42	0.41
Brazilian	2	0.02
British	21	0.21
Canadian	70	0.68
Croatian	15	0.15
Czech	61	0.60
Czechoslovakian	37	0.36
Danish	28	0.27
Dutch	114	1.11
Eastern European	10	0.10
English	784	7.66
Finnish	28	0.27
French, except Basque	288	2.81
French Canadian	19	0.19
German	2,111	20.62
Greek	252	2.46
Hawaii Native/Pacific Islander:	1	0.01
Micronesian: (1)	1	0.01
Guamanian/Chamorro (1)	1	0.01
Hispanic or Latino:	511	5.02
Central American:	60	0.59
Guatemalan	4	0.04
Nicaraguan	2	0.02
Salvadoran	42	0.41
Other Central American	12	0.12
Cuban	14	0.14
Dominican Republic	19	0.19
Mexican	31	0.30
Puerto Rican	235	2.31
South American:	30	0.29
Argentinean	3	0.03
Chilean	4	0.04
Colombian	13	0.13
Ecuadorian	5	0.05
Paraguayan	1	0.01
Other South American	4	0.04
Other Hispanic or Latino	122	1.20
Hungarian	167	1.63
Irish	2,602	25.42
Italian	3,803	37.15
Lithuanian	72	0.70
Luxemburger	3	0.03
Maltese	41	0.40
Norwegian	263	2.57
Pennsylvania German	8	0.08
Polish	572	5.59
Portuguese	110	1.07
Romanian	18	0.18
Russian	154	1.50
Scandinavian	39	0.38
Scotch-Irish	133	1.30
Scottish	153	1.49
Slovak	8	0.08
Swedish	201	1.96
Turkish	71	0.69
Ukrainian	30	0.29
United States or American	200	1.95
Welsh	20	0.20
West Indian, excl. Hispanic:	31	0.30
Barbadian	13	0.13
Haitian	2	0.02
Trinidadian and Tobagonian	9	0.09
West Indian	7	0.07
White:	9,883	97.03
Not Hispanic (9,364)	9,470	92.98
Hispanic (373)	413	4.05
Yugoslavian	2	0.02

Rome

Place Type: City
County: Oneida
Population: 34,950

Ancestry/Race	Number	%
African American/Black:	2,984	8.54
Not Hispanic (2,495)	2,781	7.96
Hispanic (155)	203	0.58
African, sub-Saharan:	143	0.41
African	143	0.41
Alaska Native tribes, specified:	1	0.00
Tlingit-Haida (1)	1	0.00
Am. Ind. or Alaska Nat., not spec.	81	0.23
Alsatian	6	0.02
American Indian tribes, specified:	129	0.37
Apache	4	0.01
Blackfeet	4	0.01
Cherokee (6)	30	0.09
Chippewa (1)	2	0.01
Choctaw	1	0.00
Cree (3)	4	0.01
Iroquois (26)	49	0.14
Latin American Indians (2)	2	0.01

Notes: 1. Figures in the "Number" column do not add up to the total population due to: a) Ancestry/Race overlap — e.g. persons can report being both White and Irish, b) persons of Hispanic origin can report being any race, c) persons reporting two ancestries are counted in both categories. 2. Numbers in parentheses indicate the number of persons reporting this ancestry/race alone, not in combination with any other ancestry/race. 3. Refer to the Explanation of Data in the front of the book for more detailed information.

Ancestry/Race	Number	%
Menominee	1	0.00
Osage	1	0.00
Puget Sound Salish	1	0.00
Seminole	2	0.01
Shoshone	1	0.00
Sioux (4)	11	0.03
All other tribes (11)	16	0.05
American Indian tribes, not spec.	11	0.03
Arab:	118	0.34
Arab/Arabic	3	0.01
Lebanese	75	0.21
Syrian	22	0.06
Other Arab	18	0.05
Asian:	418	1.20
Cambodian (3)	7	0.02
Chinese, ex. Taiwanese (44)	56	0.16
Filipino (33)	54	0.15
Indian (65)	82	0.23
Japanese (22)	33	0.09
Korean (38)	48	0.14
Laotian (16)	18	0.05
Malaysian (1)	1	0.00
Pakistani (14)	20	0.06
Sri Lankan (4)	4	0.01
Taiwanese (11)	11	0.03
Thai (31)	46	0.13
Vietnamese (14)	17	0.05
Other Asian, specified	1	0.00
Other Asian, not specified (8)	20	0.06
Austrian	11	0.03
Belgian	12	0.03
British	72	0.21
Canadian	92	0.26
Celtic	24	0.07
Czech	22	0.06
Czechoslovakian	27	0.08
Danish	72	0.21
Dutch	639	1.83
Eastern European	6	0.02
English	3,327	9.53
European	108	0.31
Finnish	6	0.02
French, except Basque	1,744	4.99
French Canadian	544	1.56
German	5,119	14.66
Greek	33	0.09
Hawaii Native/Pacific Islander:	24	0.07
Micronesian: (1)	4	0.01
Guamanian/Chamorro (1)	3	0.01
Other Micronesian	1	0.00
Polynesian: (4)	9	0.03
Native Hawaiian (4)	8	0.02
Samoan	1	0.00
Other Pac. Isl., specified	1	0.00
Other Pac. Isl., not spec. (1)	10	0.03
Hispanic or Latino:	1,648	4.72
Central American:	42	0.12
Guatemalan	6	0.02
Honduran	7	0.02
Nicaraguan	1	0.00
Panamanian	21	0.06
Salvadoran	7	0.02
Cuban	46	0.13
Dominican Republic	151	0.43
Mexican	146	0.42
Puerto Rican	919	2.63
South American:	54	0.15
Argentinean	2	0.01
Chilean	4	0.01
Colombian	28	0.08
Ecuadorian	9	0.03
Paraguayan	1	0.00
Peruvian	4	0.01
Venezuelan	6	0.02
Other Hispanic or Latino	290	0.83
Hungarian	173	0.50
Irish	5,431	15.55
Israeli	8	0.02
Italian	8,978	25.71
Latvian	9	0.03
Lithuanian	85	0.24
New Zealander	6	0.02
Northern European	19	0.05
Norwegian	55	0.16
Pennsylvania German	27	0.08
Polish	2,516	7.20
Portuguese	70	0.20
Romanian	17	0.05
Russian	84	0.24
Scotch-Irish	188	0.54
Scottish	314	0.90
Slavic	13	0.04
Slovak	31	0.09
Slovene	6	0.02
Swedish	235	0.67
Swiss	281	0.80
Turkish	16	0.05
Ukrainian	386	1.11
United States or American	1,960	5.61
Welsh	868	2.49
West Indian, excl. Hispanic:	116	0.33
Barbadian	42	0.12
British West Indian	16	0.05
Jamaican	49	0.14
West Indian	9	0.03
White:	31,338	89.67
Not Hispanic (29,872)	30,322	86.76
Hispanic (832)	1,016	2.91
Yugoslavian	36	0.10

Ronkonkoma

Place Type: Census Designated Place
County: Suffolk
Population: 20,029

Ancestry/Race	Number	%
Acadian/Cajun	15	0.07
African American/Black:	260	1.30
Not Hispanic (153)	218	1.09
Hispanic (27)	42	0.21
Alaska Native tribes, specified:	1	0.00
Aleut	1	0.00
Am. Ind. or Alaska Nat., not spec.	32	0.16
American Indian tribes, specified:	31	0.15
Apache	1	0.00
Cherokee (3)	11	0.05
Choctaw	1	0.00
Iroquois (1)	5	0.02
Latin American Indians (1)	6	0.03
Sioux (1)	1	0.00
Ute (1)	1	0.00
All other tribes (1)	5	0.02
American Indian tribes, not spec.	5	0.02
Arab:	28	0.14
Arab/Arabic	6	0.03
Egyptian	14	0.07
Lebanese	8	0.04
Armenian	74	0.37
Asian:	583	2.91
Bangladeshi (32)	33	0.16
Chinese, ex. Taiwanese (86)	106	0.53
Filipino (53)	62	0.31
Indian (166)	201	1.00
Indonesian (1)	1	0.00
Japanese (5)	6	0.03
Korean (52)	59	0.29
Pakistani (35)	43	0.21
Taiwanese (2)	5	0.02
Thai (6)	8	0.04
Vietnamese (23)	29	0.14
Other Asian, specified	10	0.05
Other Asian, not specified (9)	20	0.10
Austrian	147	0.73
Brazilian	42	0.21
British	30	0.15
Canadian	63	0.31
Croatian	44	0.22
Czech	87	0.43
Czechoslovakian	111	0.55
Danish	84	0.42
Dutch	145	0.72
English	922	4.60
European	37	0.18
Finnish	18	0.09
French, except Basque	457	2.28
French Canadian	175	0.87
German	3,860	19.26
Greek	267	1.33
Hawaii Native/Pacific Islander:	27	0.13
Micronesian: (8)	8	0.04
Guamanian/Chamorro (8)	8	0.04
Polynesian:	2	0.01
Samoan	2	0.01
Other Pac. Isl., specified	6	0.03
Other Pac. Isl., not spec.	11	0.05
Hispanic or Latino:	1,269	6.34
Central American:	71	0.35
Costa Rican	4	0.02
Guatemalan	26	0.13
Honduran	4	0.02
Panamanian	3	0.01
Salvadoran	32	0.16
Other Central American	2	0.01
Cuban	48	0.24
Dominican Republic	54	0.27
Mexican	30	0.15
Puerto Rican	624	3.12
South American:	163	0.81
Argentinean	3	0.01
Chilean	3	0.01
Colombian	85	0.42
Ecuadorian	21	0.10
Peruvian	24	0.12
Uruguayan	6	0.03
Venezuelan	12	0.06
Other South American	9	0.04
Other Hispanic or Latino	279	1.39
Hungarian	189	0.94
Iranian	32	0.16
Irish	5,361	26.75
Israeli	19	0.09
Italian	7,963	39.73
Lithuanian	48	0.24
Maltese	102	0.51
Norwegian	140	0.70
Polish	1,369	6.83
Portuguese	295	1.47
Romanian	52	0.26
Russian	513	2.56
Scotch-Irish	213	1.06
Scottish	245	1.22
Slavic	11	0.05
Slovak	31	0.15
Soviet Union	8	0.04
Swedish	273	1.36
Swiss	31	0.15
Turkish	38	0.19
Ukrainian	60	0.30
United States or American	482	2.40
Welsh	27	0.13
West Indian, excl. Hispanic:	41	0.20
Belizean	7	0.03
Jamaican	25	0.12
Trinidadian and Tobagonian	9	0.04
White:	19,066	95.19
Not Hispanic (17,835)	18,038	90.06
Hispanic (963)	1,028	5.13
Yugoslavian	21	0.10

Roosevelt

Place Type: Census Designated Place
County: Nassau
Population: 15,854

Ancestry/Race	Number	%
African American/Black:	12,895	81.34
Not Hispanic (12,307)	12,615	79.57
Hispanic (221)	280	1.77

Notes: 1. Figures in the "Number" column do not add up to the total population due to: a) Ancestry/Race overlap — e.g. persons can report being both White and Irish, b) persons of Hispanic origin can report being any race, c) persons reporting two ancestries are counted in both categories. 2. Numbers in parentheses indicate the number of persons reporting this ancestry/race alone, not in combination with any other ancestry/race. 3. Refer to the Explanation of Data in the front of the book for more detailed information.

Ancestry/Race	Number	%
African, sub-Saharan:	314	1.98
African	297	1.87
Cape Verdean	11	0.07
Other sub-Saharan African	6	0.04
Am. Ind. or Alaska Nat., not spec.	110	0.69
American Indian tribes, specified:	134	0.85
Apache	3	0.02
Blackfeet (1)	15	0.09
Cherokee (6)	69	0.44
Creek	1	0.01
Iroquois	4	0.03
Latin American Indians (6)	6	0.04
Pueblo (4)	8	0.05
Seminole	10	0.06
All other tribes (3)	18	0.11
American Indian tribes, not spec.	15	0.09
Arab:	4	0.03
Arab/Arabic	4	0.03
Asian:	156	0.98
Chinese, ex. Taiwanese (5)	20	0.13
Filipino (8)	18	0.11
Indian (37)	61	0.38
Japanese (3)	6	0.04
Korean (13)	14	0.09
Pakistani (4)	16	0.10
Sri Lankan (4)	4	0.03
Other Asian, specified	4	0.03
Other Asian, not specified (2)	13	0.08
British	31	0.20
Danish	6	0.04
English	60	0.38
European	6	0.04
French Canadian	6	0.04
German	73	0.46
Guyanese	156	0.98
Hawaii Native/Pacific Islander:	33	0.21
Micronesian: (8)	8	0.05
Guamanian/Chamorro (7)	7	0.04
Other Micronesian (1)	1	0.01
Polynesian:	3	0.02
Native Hawaiian	2	0.01
Samoan	1	0.01
Other Pac. Isl., specified	4	0.03
Other Pac. Isl., not spec.	18	0.11
Hispanic or Latino:	2,572	16.22
Central American:	1,290	8.14
Costa Rican	9	0.06
Guatemalan	83	0.52
Honduran	79	0.50
Nicaraguan	3	0.02
Panamanian	25	0.16
Salvadoran	1,064	6.71
Other Central American	27	0.17
Cuban	44	0.28
Dominican Republic	153	0.97
Mexican	51	0.32
Puerto Rican	222	1.40
South American:	78	0.49
Argentinean	7	0.04
Chilean	2	0.01
Colombian	23	0.15
Ecuadorian	33	0.21
Peruvian	4	0.03
Other South American	9	0.06
Other Hispanic or Latino	734	4.63
Hungarian	12	0.08
Irish	110	0.69
Italian	124	0.78
Norwegian	16	0.10
Polish	13	0.08
Portuguese	8	0.05
Russian	14	0.09
Scottish	6	0.04
Ukrainian	3	0.02
United States or American	555	3.50
West Indian, excl. Hispanic:	2,343	14.78
Barbadian	50	0.32
Belizean	3	0.02
Bermudan	18	0.11
British West Indian	78	0.49
Haitian	599	3.78
Jamaican	1,187	7.49
Trinidadian and Tobagonian	272	1.72
West Indian	136	0.86
White:	1,552	9.79
Not Hispanic (461)	575	3.63
Hispanic (802)	977	6.16

Rotterdam

Place Type: Town
County: Schenectady
Population: 28,316

Ancestry/Race	Number	%
Afghan	34	0.12
African American/Black:	361	1.27
Not Hispanic (267)	345	1.22
Hispanic (2)	16	0.06
African, sub-Saharan:	2	0.01
African	2	0.01
Alaska Native tribes, specified:	4	0.01
Alaska Athabascan (2)	2	0.01
Aleut (1)	1	0.00
Eskimo	1	0.00
Am. Ind. or Alaska Nat., not spec.	43	0.15
American Indian tribes, specified:	71	0.25
Blackfeet (1)	3	0.01
Cherokee (5)	18	0.06
Chickasaw	1	0.00
Chippewa (1)	1	0.00
Cree	1	0.00
Crow	1	0.00
Iroquois (10)	30	0.11
Sioux	1	0.00
All other tribes (10)	15	0.05
American Indian tribes, not spec.	4	0.01
Arab:	97	0.34
Lebanese	55	0.19
Other Arab	42	0.15
Armenian	61	0.21
Asian:	232	0.82
Cambodian (1)	1	0.00
Chinese, ex. Taiwanese (43)	59	0.21
Filipino (12)	18	0.06
Indian (53)	62	0.22
Japanese (4)	23	0.08
Korean (24)	32	0.11
Pakistani (6)	6	0.02
Taiwanese (5)	6	0.02
Thai (3)	7	0.02
Vietnamese (3)	6	0.02
Other Asian, not specified (5)	12	0.04
Austrian	54	0.19
Belgian	10	0.04
British	64	0.23
Canadian	24	0.08
Celtic	14	0.05
Czech	107	0.38
Czechoslovakian	90	0.32
Danish	91	0.32
Dutch	1,538	5.42
Eastern European	9	0.03
English	2,752	9.69
European	76	0.27
Finnish	20	0.07
French, except Basque	2,428	8.55
French Canadian	689	2.43
German	4,879	17.19
Greek	135	0.48
Guyanese	12	0.04
Hawaii Native/Pacific Islander:	14	0.05
Polynesian: (4)	14	0.05
Native Hawaiian (3)	12	0.04
Samoan (1)	2	0.01
Hispanic or Latino:	276	0.97
Central American:	6	0.02
Guatemalan	4	0.01
Panamanian	2	0.01
Cuban	12	0.04
Dominican Republic	7	0.02
Mexican	35	0.12
Puerto Rican	132	0.47
South American:	16	0.06
Argentinean	1	0.00
Bolivian	1	0.00
Colombian	7	0.02
Ecuadorian	3	0.01
Venezuelan	2	0.01
Other South American	2	0.01
Other Hispanic or Latino	68	0.24
Hungarian	193	0.68
Irish	5,840	20.57
Italian	9,364	32.99
Lithuanian	163	0.57
Norwegian	73	0.26
Pennsylvania German	21	0.07
Polish	3,751	13.21
Portuguese	31	0.11
Romanian	25	0.09
Russian	153	0.54
Scandinavian	6	0.02
Scotch-Irish	263	0.93
Scottish	557	1.96
Slavic	58	0.20
Slovak	147	0.52
Swedish	313	1.10
Swiss	49	0.17
Turkish	7	0.02
Ukrainian	104	0.37
United States or American	863	3.04
Welsh	144	0.51
West Indian, excl. Hispanic:	29	0.10
Bahamian	7	0.02
Haitian	8	0.03
Jamaican	14	0.05
White:	27,748	97.99
Not Hispanic (27,345)	27,528	97.22
Hispanic (196)	220	0.78
Yugoslavian	24	0.08

Rye

Place Type: City
County: Westchester
Population: 14,955

Ancestry/Race	Number	%
African American/Black:	218	1.46
Not Hispanic (181)	201	1.34
Hispanic (9)	17	0.11
African, sub-Saharan:	72	0.48
African	11	0.07
South African	61	0.41
Am. Ind. or Alaska Nat., not spec.	11	0.07
American Indian tribes, specified:	19	0.13
Blackfeet	2	0.01
Cherokee (1)	2	0.01
Chippewa	1	0.01
Delaware	1	0.01
Iroquois	4	0.03
Latin American Indians (4)	4	0.03
Pueblo (1)	1	0.01
Sioux (1)	1	0.01
All other tribes (3)	3	0.02
American Indian tribes, not spec.	1	0.01
Arab:	184	1.23
Arab/Arabic	10	0.07
Iraqi	26	0.17
Jordanian	30	0.20
Lebanese	64	0.43
Palestinian	5	0.03
Syrian	49	0.33
Asian:	1,084	7.25
Chinese, ex. Taiwanese (143)	190	1.27
Filipino (52)	69	0.46
Indian (86)	93	0.62
Indonesian (1)	2	0.01
Japanese (578)	611	4.09
Korean (77)	81	0.54

Notes: 1. Figures in the "Number" column do not add up to the total population due to: a) Ancestry/Race overlap — e.g. persons can report being both White and Irish, b) persons of Hispanic origin can report being any race, c) persons reporting two ancestries are counted in both categories. 2. Numbers in parentheses indicate the number of persons reporting this ancestry/race alone, not in combination with any other ancestry/race. 3. Refer to the Explanation of Data in the front of the book for more detailed information.

Ancestry/Race	Number	%
Laotian (6)	7	0.05
Pakistani (2)	2	0.01
Sri Lankan (1)	1	0.01
Taiwanese (3)	4	0.03
Thai (3)	3	0.02
Vietnamese	2	0.01
Other Asian, specified	5	0.03
Other Asian, not specified (6)	14	0.09
Australian	43	0.29
Austrian	153	1.02
Belgian	23	0.15
Brazilian	36	0.24
British	169	1.13
Canadian	155	1.04
Carpatho Rusyn	5	0.03
Croatian	24	0.16
Czech	51	0.34
Czechoslovakian	40	0.27
Danish	75	0.50
Dutch	404	2.70
Eastern European	122	0.82
English	1,629	10.89
European	188	1.26
Finnish	13	0.09
French, except Basque	614	4.11
French Canadian	36	0.24
German	1,547	10.34
Greek	72	0.48
Hawaii Native/Pacific Islander:	14	0.09
Micronesian: (1)	1	0.01
Guamanian/Chamorro (1)	1	0.01
Polynesian:	5	0.03
Native Hawaiian	2	0.01
Samoan	3	0.02
Other Pac. Isl., specified	5	0.03
Other Pac. Isl., not spec.	3	0.02
Hispanic or Latino:	718	4.80
Central American:	38	0.25
Costa Rican	4	0.03
Guatemalan	6	0.04
Honduran	5	0.03
Nicaraguan	1	0.01
Panamanian	2	0.01
Salvadoran	19	0.13
Other Central American	1	0.01
Cuban	66	0.44
Dominican Republic	11	0.07
Mexican	91	0.61
Puerto Rican	94	0.63
South American:	220	1.47
Argentinean	20	0.13
Bolivian	10	0.07
Chilean	30	0.20
Colombian	41	0.27
Ecuadorian	16	0.11
Paraguayan	4	0.03
Peruvian	78	0.52
Uruguayan	4	0.03
Venezuelan	3	0.02
Other South American	14	0.09
Other Hispanic or Latino	198	1.32
Hungarian	73	0.49
Icelander	30	0.20
Irish	3,077	20.58
Italian	2,704	18.08
Lithuanian	92	0.62
Macedonian	16	0.11
New Zealander	19	0.13
Northern European	15	0.10
Norwegian	260	1.74
Polish	483	3.23
Portuguese	44	0.29
Romanian	30	0.20
Russian	439	2.94
Scandinavian	6	0.04
Scotch-Irish	304	2.03
Scottish	423	2.83
Slovak	38	0.25
Slovene	27	0.18
Swedish	146	0.98
Swiss	55	0.37
Turkish	26	0.17
Ukrainian	62	0.41
United States or American	762	5.10
Welsh	85	0.57
West Indian, excl. Hispanic:	73	0.49
Barbadian	20	0.13
Bermudan	16	0.11
Jamaican	23	0.15
Trinidadian and Tobagonian	14	0.09
White:	13,560	90.67
Not Hispanic (12,907)	13,034	87.15
Hispanic (494)	526	3.52

Rye

Place Type: Town
County: Westchester
Population: 43,880

Ancestry/Race	Number	%
African American/Black:	2,487	5.67
Not Hispanic (2,069)	2,221	5.06
Hispanic (187)	266	0.61
African, sub-Saharan:	85	0.19
African	23	0.05
Ethiopian	7	0.02
Other sub-Saharan African	55	0.13
Am. Ind. or Alaska Nat., not spec.	121	0.28
Albanian	8	0.02
American Indian tribes, specified:	84	0.19
Blackfeet	2	0.00
Cherokee (11)	15	0.03
Chippewa (1)	1	0.00
Cree	1	0.00
Latin American Indians (35)	59	0.13
Pueblo	1	0.00
Sioux	2	0.00
Ute (3)	3	0.01
American Indian tribes, not spec.	48	0.11
Arab:	124	0.28
Arab/Arabic	74	0.17
Egyptian	28	0.06
Lebanese	5	0.01
Syrian	10	0.02
Other Arab	7	0.02
Armenian	32	0.07
Asian:	1,440	3.28
Chinese, ex. Taiwanese (204)	244	0.56
Filipino (156)	176	0.40
Indian (348)	376	0.86
Indonesian (2)	2	0.00
Japanese (395)	420	0.96
Korean (80)	91	0.21
Laotian (11)	11	0.03
Malaysian (3)	6	0.01
Pakistani (23)	26	0.06
Taiwanese (3)	4	0.01
Thai (14)	18	0.04
Vietnamese (6)	8	0.02
Other Asian, specified (5)	13	0.03
Other Asian, not specified (8)	45	0.10
Assyrian/Chaldean/Syriac	8	0.02
Australian	36	0.08
Austrian	221	0.50
Belgian	28	0.06
Brazilian	342	0.78
British	157	0.36
Canadian	95	0.22
Celtic	9	0.02
Croatian	31	0.07
Cypriot	18	0.04
Czech	104	0.24
Czechoslovakian	68	0.15
Danish	118	0.27
Dutch	143	0.33
Eastern European	423	0.96
English	1,244	2.83
Estonian	3	0.01
European	170	0.39
Finnish	29	0.07
French, except Basque	542	1.23
French Canadian	112	0.26
German	2,395	5.46
Greek	215	0.49
Hawaii Native/Pacific Islander:	57	0.13
Micronesian: (5)	13	0.03
Guamanian/Chamorro (5)	13	0.03
Polynesian: (9)	11	0.03
Native Hawaiian (3)	4	0.01
Samoan (5)	6	0.01
Other Polynesian (1)	1	0.00
Other Pac. Isl., specified	8	0.02
Other Pac. Isl., not spec. (4)	25	0.06
Hispanic or Latino:	14,264	32.51
Central American:	2,016	4.59
Costa Rican	28	0.06
Guatemalan	1,143	2.60
Honduran	103	0.23
Nicaraguan	19	0.04
Panamanian	15	0.03
Salvadoran	622	1.42
Other Central American	86	0.20
Cuban	540	1.23
Dominican Republic	299	0.68
Mexican	3,253	7.41
Puerto Rican	1,023	2.33
South American:	3,842	8.76
Argentinean	60	0.14
Bolivian	180	0.41
Chilean	139	0.32
Colombian	739	1.68
Ecuadorian	1,394	3.18
Paraguayan	51	0.12
Peruvian	1,021	2.33
Uruguayan	122	0.28
Venezuelan	33	0.08
Other South American	103	0.23
Other Hispanic or Latino	3,291	7.50
Hungarian	239	0.54
Irish	4,080	9.30
Israeli	7	0.02
Italian	10,657	24.28
Latvian	7	0.02
Lithuanian	118	0.27
Maltese	7	0.02
Norwegian	181	0.41
Polish	1,654	3.77
Portuguese	430	0.98
Romanian	148	0.34
Russian	1,308	2.98
Scandinavian	6	0.01
Scotch-Irish	301	0.69
Scottish	195	0.44
Serbian	42	0.10
Slavic	7	0.02
Slovak	62	0.14
Slovene	16	0.04
Swedish	205	0.47
Swiss	121	0.28
Turkish	43	0.10
Ukrainian	62	0.14
United States or American	1,734	3.95
Welsh	85	0.19
West Indian, excl. Hispanic:	213	0.49
Barbadian	46	0.10
Haitian	52	0.12
Jamaican	73	0.17
Trinidadian and Tobagonian	12	0.03
West Indian	30	0.07
White:	33,253	75.78
Not Hispanic (25,404)	26,000	59.25
Hispanic (5,883)	7,253	16.53
Yugoslavian	94	0.21

Notes: 1. Figures in the "Number" column do not add up to the total population due to: a) Ancestry/Race overlap — e.g. persons can report being both White and Irish, b) persons of Hispanic origin can report being any race, c) persons reporting two ancestries are counted in both categories. 2. Numbers in parentheses indicate the number of persons reporting this ancestry/race alone, not in combination with any other ancestry/race. 3. Refer to the Explanation of Data in the front of the book for more detailed information.

Saint James

Place Type: Census Designated Place
County: Suffolk
Population: 13,268

Ancestry/Race	Number	%
African American/Black:	52	0.39
Not Hispanic (34)	48	0.36
Hispanic (2)	4	0.03
African, sub-Saharan:	5	0.04
African	5	0.04
Am. Ind. or Alaska Nat., not spec.	3	0.02
Albanian	5	0.04
Alsatian	12	0.09
American Indian tribes, specified:	11	0.08
Cherokee	2	0.02
Chippewa (1)	1	0.01
Iroquois (1)	5	0.04
Latin American Indians (1)	3	0.02
American Indian tribes, not spec.	2	0.02
Arab:	8	0.06
Lebanese	8	0.06
Asian:	186	1.40
Bangladeshi (5)	5	0.04
Chinese, ex. Taiwanese (49)	60	0.45
Filipino (20)	25	0.19
Indian (38)	40	0.30
Japanese (4)	4	0.03
Korean (28)	31	0.23
Pakistani (18)	18	0.14
Vietnamese (1)	1	0.01
Other Asian, not specified	2	0.02
Austrian	217	1.64
Belgian	4	0.03
Brazilian	6	0.05
British	88	0.66
Canadian	26	0.20
Celtic	23	0.17
Croatian	5	0.04
Czech	82	0.62
Czechoslovakian	31	0.23
Danish	81	0.61
Dutch	122	0.92
Eastern European	43	0.32
English	696	5.25
Estonian	7	0.05
European	70	0.53
Finnish	46	0.35
French, except Basque	333	2.51
French Canadian	72	0.54
German	2,445	18.43
Greek	92	0.69
Guyanese	6	0.05
Hawaii Native/Pacific Islander:	3	0.02
Polynesian: (1)	1	0.01
Native Hawaiian (1)	1	0.01
Other Pac. Isl., not spec.	2	0.02
Hispanic or Latino:	458	3.45
Central American:	50	0.38
Costa Rican	1	0.01
Guatemalan	5	0.04
Honduran	2	0.02
Panamanian	1	0.01
Salvadoran	41	0.31
Cuban	24	0.18
Dominican Republic	7	0.05
Mexican	38	0.29
Puerto Rican	193	1.45
South American:	68	0.51
Argentinean	2	0.02
Bolivian	6	0.05
Chilean	2	0.02
Colombian	30	0.23
Ecuadorian	11	0.08
Paraguayan	3	0.02
Peruvian	9	0.07
Venezuelan	2	0.02
Other South American	3	0.02
Other Hispanic or Latino	78	0.59
Hungarian	136	1.03
Irish	3,912	29.48
Italian	4,662	35.14
Latvian	12	0.09
Lithuanian	68	0.51
Maltese	19	0.14
Northern European	27	0.20
Norwegian	347	2.62
Polish	819	6.17
Portuguese	50	0.38
Romanian	20	0.15
Russian	337	2.54
Scandinavian	11	0.08
Scotch-Irish	92	0.69
Scottish	92	0.69
Slavic	20	0.15
Slovak	47	0.35
Swedish	272	2.05
Swiss	44	0.33
Turkish	49	0.37
Ukrainian	102	0.77
United States or American	427	3.22
Welsh	31	0.23
West Indian, excl. Hispanic:	41	0.31
Haitian	41	0.31
White:	12,975	97.79
Not Hispanic (12,543)	12,592	94.91
Hispanic (375)	383	2.89
Yugoslavian	21	0.16

Salina

Place Type: Town
County: Onondaga
Population: 33,290

Ancestry/Race	Number	%
African American/Black:	879	2.64
Not Hispanic (700)	852	2.56
Hispanic (18)	27	0.08
African, sub-Saharan:	53	0.16
African	22	0.07
Nigerian	6	0.02
Other sub-Saharan African	25	0.08
Am. Ind. or Alaska Nat., not spec.	80	0.24
American Indian tribes, specified:	247	0.74
Apache (1)	1	0.00
Blackfeet	1	0.00
Cherokee (6)	18	0.05
Chippewa (1)	3	0.01
Cree	1	0.00
Iroquois (129)	202	0.61
Latin American Indians	1	0.00
Navajo	1	0.00
Potawatomi	1	0.00
Shoshone	1	0.00
Sioux	1	0.00
Ute	2	0.01
All other tribes (6)	14	0.04
American Indian tribes, not spec.	2	0.01
Arab:	336	1.01
Arab/Arabic	179	0.54
Egyptian	26	0.08
Lebanese	78	0.23
Moroccan	6	0.02
Palestinian	26	0.08
Syrian	21	0.06
Armenian	42	0.13
Asian:	651	1.96
Cambodian (14)	17	0.05
Chinese, ex. Taiwanese (107)	137	0.41
Filipino (38)	56	0.17
Hmong (4)	7	0.02
Indian (126)	139	0.42
Indonesian	1	0.00
Japanese (14)	31	0.09
Korean (28)	40	0.12
Laotian (4)	5	0.02
Pakistani (4)	6	0.02
Thai (6)	9	0.03
Vietnamese (167)	182	0.55
Other Asian, specified (1)	1	0.00
Other Asian, not specified (10)	20	0.06
Austrian	76	0.23
Belgian	4	0.01
British	70	0.21
Canadian	97	0.29
Celtic	5	0.02
Croatian	25	0.08
Czech	19	0.06
Czechoslovakian	55	0.17
Danish	52	0.16
Dutch	837	2.51
Eastern European	10	0.03
English	4,114	12.36
European	121	0.36
Finnish	39	0.12
French, except Basque	2,026	6.09
French Canadian	903	2.71
German	6,950	20.88
Greek	187	0.56
Hawaii Native/Pacific Islander:	28	0.08
Micronesian: (3)	3	0.01
Guamanian/Chamorro (3)	3	0.01
Polynesian: (5)	11	0.03
Native Hawaiian (4)	9	0.03
Samoan	1	0.00
Other Polynesian (1)	1	0.00
Other Pac. Isl., not spec. (4)	14	0.04
Hispanic or Latino:	466	1.40
Central American:	18	0.05
Costa Rican	2	0.01
Guatemalan	12	0.04
Panamanian	3	0.01
Other Central American	1	0.00
Cuban	29	0.09
Dominican Republic	15	0.05
Mexican	110	0.33
Puerto Rican	170	0.51
South American:	40	0.12
Chilean	6	0.02
Colombian	21	0.06
Ecuadorian	7	0.02
Peruvian	1	0.00
Other South American	5	0.02
Other Hispanic or Latino	84	0.25
Hungarian	135	0.41
Irish	6,372	19.14
Israeli	10	0.03
Italian	9,356	28.10
Latvian	7	0.02
Lithuanian	114	0.34
Macedonian	109	0.33
Northern European	12	0.04
Norwegian	112	0.34
Pennsylvania German	28	0.08
Polish	2,646	7.95
Portuguese	22	0.07
Russian	179	0.54
Scandinavian	35	0.11
Scotch-Irish	402	1.21
Scottish	644	1.93
Slavic	8	0.02
Slovak	148	0.44
Slovene	15	0.05
Swedish	182	0.55
Swiss	158	0.47
Turkish	42	0.13
Ukrainian	368	1.11
United States or American	1,058	3.18
Welsh	334	1.00
West Indian, excl. Hispanic:	28	0.08
Jamaican	28	0.08
White:	31,680	95.16
Not Hispanic (30,951)	31,353	94.18
Hispanic (299)	327	0.98
Yugoslavian	22	0.07

Notes: 1. Figures in the "Number" column do not add up to the total population due to: a) Ancestry/Race overlap — e.g. persons can report being both White and Irish, b) persons of Hispanic origin can report being any race, c) persons reporting two ancestries are counted in both categories. 2. Numbers in parentheses indicate the number of persons reporting this ancestry/race alone, not in combination with any other ancestry/race. 3. Refer to the Explanation of Data in the front of the book for more detailed information.

Salisbury

Place Type: Census Designated Place
County: Nassau
Population: 12,341

Ancestry/Race	Number	%
African American/Black:	144	1.17
Not Hispanic (118)	133	1.08
Hispanic (9)	11	0.09
Am. Ind. or Alaska Nat., not spec.	14	0.11
Albanian	19	0.15
American Indian tribes, specified:	23	0.19
Cherokee (4)	5	0.04
Delaware (1)	3	0.02
Iroquois	3	0.02
Latin American Indians (2)	5	0.04
Navajo	1	0.01
All other tribes	6	0.05
Arab:	114	0.93
Arab/Arabic	14	0.11
Egyptian	21	0.17
Iraqi	8	0.07
Jordanian	4	0.03
Palestinian	5	0.04
Syrian	57	0.46
Other Arab	5	0.04
Armenian	55	0.45
Asian:	1,181	9.57
Bangladeshi (7)	7	0.06
Cambodian (5)	5	0.04
Chinese, ex. Taiwanese (221)	238	1.93
Filipino (188)	193	1.56
Indian (409)	439	3.56
Indonesian (2)	2	0.02
Japanese (21)	26	0.21
Korean (119)	124	1.00
Malaysian (1)	1	0.01
Pakistani (52)	56	0.45
Taiwanese (8)	8	0.06
Thai (12)	15	0.12
Vietnamese (42)	44	0.36
Other Asian, not specified (13)	23	0.19
Austrian	229	1.86
Belgian	10	0.08
Brazilian	31	0.25
British	44	0.36
Canadian	5	0.04
Croatian	33	0.27
Cypriot	51	0.41
Czech	20	0.16
Czechoslovakian	15	0.12
Danish	10	0.08
Dutch	87	0.71
Eastern European	40	0.33
English	460	3.74
European	92	0.75
Finnish	12	0.10
French, except Basque	137	1.11
French Canadian	36	0.29
German	1,687	13.71
Greek	313	2.54
Hawaii Native/Pacific Islander:	4	0.03
Polynesian: (1)	3	0.02
Native Hawaiian (1)	3	0.02
Other Pac. Isl., not spec.	1	0.01
Hispanic or Latino:	1,056	8.56
Central American:	204	1.65
Costa Rican	2	0.02
Guatemalan	11	0.09
Honduran	24	0.19
Salvadoran	143	1.16
Other Central American	24	0.19
Cuban	50	0.41
Dominican Republic	32	0.26
Mexican	42	0.34
Puerto Rican	246	1.99
South American:	242	1.96
Argentinean	14	0.11
Bolivian	19	0.15
Chilean	27	0.22
Colombian	87	0.70
Ecuadorian	37	0.30
Paraguayan	1	0.01
Peruvian	26	0.21
Uruguayan	6	0.05
Venezuelan	4	0.03
Other South American	21	0.17
Other Hispanic or Latino	240	1.94
Hungarian	168	1.37
Iranian	17	0.14
Irish	2,467	20.06
Israeli	7	0.06
Italian	3,457	28.10
Latvian	6	0.05
Lithuanian	30	0.24
Norwegian	74	0.60
Pennsylvania German	8	0.07
Polish	826	6.71
Romanian	143	1.16
Russian	572	4.65
Scotch-Irish	111	0.90
Scottish	112	0.91
Serbian	17	0.14
Slovak	11	0.09
Swedish	133	1.08
Swiss	6	0.05
Turkish	40	0.33
Ukrainian	113	0.92
United States or American	542	4.41
Welsh	10	0.08
West Indian, excl. Hispanic:	74	0.60
Haitian	38	0.31
Jamaican	25	0.20
Trinidadian and Tobagonian	6	0.05
U.S. Virgin Islander	5	0.04
White:	10,864	88.03
Not Hispanic (9,922)	10,007	81.09
Hispanic (806)	857	6.94
Yugoslavian	12	0.10

Saratoga Springs

Place Type: City
County: Saratoga
Population: 26,186

Ancestry/Race	Number	%
African American/Black:	997	3.81
Not Hispanic (777)	937	3.58
Hispanic (38)	60	0.23
African, sub-Saharan:	61	0.23
African	50	0.19
South African	11	0.04
Alaska Native tribes, specified:	1	0.00
Alaska Athabascan (1)	1	0.00
Alaska Native tribes, not specified	5	0.02
Am. Ind. or Alaska Nat., not spec.	50	0.19
Albanian	4	0.02
American Indian tribes, specified:	128	0.49
Apache	3	0.01
Blackfeet	12	0.05
Cherokee (6)	27	0.10
Cheyenne	1	0.00
Chippewa (1)	1	0.00
Cree (5)	6	0.02
Creek (1)	2	0.01
Delaware	4	0.02
Iroquois (9)	22	0.08
Latin American Indians (13)	18	0.07
Navajo (2)	3	0.01
Pueblo (2)	2	0.01
Seminole (1)	4	0.02
Sioux	3	0.01
Ute (1)	1	0.00
All other tribes (4)	19	0.07
American Indian tribes, not spec.	4	0.02
Arab:	59	0.23
Arab/Arabic	11	0.04
Egyptian	13	0.05
Syrian	29	0.11
Other Arab	6	0.02
Armenian	25	0.10
Asian:	344	1.31
Chinese, ex. Taiwanese (83)	94	0.36
Filipino (36)	47	0.18
Indian (46)	54	0.21
Indonesian (1)	2	0.01
Japanese (21)	25	0.10
Korean (40)	56	0.21
Pakistani	7	0.03
Sri Lankan (1)	5	0.02
Taiwanese (1)	2	0.01
Thai (4)	4	0.02
Vietnamese (15)	19	0.07
Other Asian, specified (4)	4	0.02
Other Asian, not specified (17)	25	0.10
Australian	9	0.03
Austrian	125	0.48
Belgian	7	0.03
British	160	0.61
Canadian	128	0.49
Croatian	36	0.14
Czech	149	0.57
Czechoslovakian	163	0.62
Danish	94	0.36
Dutch	916	3.50
Eastern European	20	0.08
English	3,590	13.71
European	169	0.65
Finnish	26	0.10
French, except Basque	2,021	7.72
French Canadian	626	2.39
German	4,479	17.10
Greek	204	0.78
Hawaii Native/Pacific Islander:	13	0.05
Micronesian: (4)	5	0.02
Guamanian/Chamorro (4)	5	0.02
Polynesian: (4)	7	0.03
Native Hawaiian (2)	4	0.02
Samoan (2)	3	0.01
Other Pac. Isl., not spec.	1	0.00
Hispanic or Latino:	485	1.85
Central American:	25	0.10
Costa Rican	1	0.00
Guatemalan	3	0.01
Honduran	1	0.00
Nicaraguan	6	0.02
Salvadoran	13	0.05
Other Central American	1	0.00
Cuban	24	0.09
Dominican Republic	33	0.13
Mexican	97	0.37
Puerto Rican	137	0.52
South American:	63	0.24
Argentinean	15	0.06
Chilean	4	0.02
Colombian	22	0.08
Ecuadorian	7	0.03
Peruvian	8	0.03
Venezuelan	5	0.02
Other South American	2	0.01
Other Hispanic or Latino	106	0.40
Hungarian	220	0.84
Icelander	3	0.01
Irish	6,708	25.62
Italian	4,665	17.81
Latvian	7	0.03
Lithuanian	100	0.38
Northern European	12	0.05
Norwegian	354	1.35
Pennsylvania German	24	0.09
Polish	1,437	5.49
Portuguese	40	0.15
Romanian	41	0.16
Russian	491	1.87
Scandinavian	33	0.13
Scotch-Irish	647	2.47
Scottish	682	2.60
Slavic	46	0.18

Notes: 1. Figures in the "Number" column do not add up to the total population due to: a) Ancestry/Race overlap — e.g. persons can report being both White and Irish, b) persons of Hispanic origin can report being any race, c) persons reporting two ancestries are counted in both categories. 2. Numbers in parentheses indicate the number of persons reporting this ancestry/race alone, not in combination with any other ancestry/race. 3. Refer to the Explanation of Data in the front of the book for more detailed information.

Ancestry/Race	Number	%
Slovak	70	0.27
Slovene	22	0.08
Swedish	337	1.29
Swiss	54	0.21
Turkish	29	0.11
Ukrainian	204	0.78
United States or American	822	3.14
Welsh	286	1.09
West Indian, excl. Hispanic:	63	0.24
Bahamian	7	0.03
Dutch West Indian	7	0.03
Jamaican	34	0.13
Trinidadian and Tobagonian	7	0.03
West Indian	8	0.03
White:	24,821	94.79
Not Hispanic (24,252)	24,525	93.66
Hispanic (241)	296	1.13

Saugerties

Place Type: Town
County: Ulster
Population: 19,868

Ancestry/Race	Number	%
African American/Black:	876	4.41
Not Hispanic (771)	831	4.18
Hispanic (35)	45	0.23
African, sub-Saharan:	5	0.03
African	5	0.03
Am. Ind. or Alaska Nat., not spec.	67	0.34
Albanian	7	0.04
American Indian tribes, specified:	75	0.38
Apache	2	0.01
Blackfeet	4	0.02
Cherokee	17	0.09
Cheyenne	1	0.01
Chippewa	1	0.01
Choctaw	2	0.01
Cree (1)	1	0.01
Iroquois (4)	16	0.08
Latin American Indians (4)	6	0.03
Sioux (3)	8	0.04
All other tribes (8)	17	0.09
American Indian tribes, not spec.	9	0.05
Arab:	49	0.25
Arab/Arabic	9	0.05
Lebanese	25	0.13
Palestinian	7	0.04
Syrian	8	0.04
Armenian	22	0.11
Asian:	213	1.07
Chinese, ex. Taiwanese (51)	70	0.35
Filipino (21)	32	0.16
Indian (33)	35	0.18
Indonesian (1)	3	0.02
Japanese (13)	24	0.12
Korean (19)	23	0.12
Malaysian (1)	1	0.01
Pakistani	1	0.01
Thai (2)	8	0.04
Vietnamese (8)	11	0.06
Other Asian, not specified (2)	5	0.03
Australian	19	0.10
Austrian	169	0.85
Basque	7	0.04
Belgian	5	0.03
Brazilian	11	0.06
British	73	0.37
Canadian	29	0.15
Croatian	32	0.16
Czech	16	0.08
Czechoslovakian	38	0.19
Danish	76	0.38
Dutch	1,508	7.63
Eastern European	31	0.16
English	1,863	9.42
European	78	0.39
Finnish	81	0.41
French, except Basque	501	2.53
French Canadian	194	0.98
German	5,092	25.76
Greek	173	0.88
Hawaii Native/Pacific Islander:	8	0.04
Micronesian: (2)	2	0.01
Guamanian/Chamorro (2)	2	0.01
Polynesian: (2)	4	0.02
Native Hawaiian (2)	3	0.02
Samoan	1	0.01
Other Pac. Isl., not spec.	2	0.01
Hispanic or Latino:	916	4.61
Central American:	76	0.38
Guatemalan	21	0.11
Honduran	3	0.02
Nicaraguan	2	0.01
Panamanian	8	0.04
Salvadoran	35	0.18
Other Central American	7	0.04
Cuban	23	0.12
Dominican Republic	84	0.42
Mexican	88	0.44
Puerto Rican	437	2.20
South American:	52	0.26
Argentinean	5	0.03
Chilean	2	0.01
Colombian	27	0.14
Ecuadorian	9	0.05
Peruvian	8	0.04
Venezuelan	1	0.01
Other Hispanic or Latino	156	0.79
Hungarian	160	0.81
Irish	4,725	23.90
Israeli	11	0.06
Italian	3,821	19.33
Latvian	54	0.27
Lithuanian	74	0.37
Norwegian	357	1.81
Pennsylvania German	11	0.06
Polish	999	5.05
Portuguese	52	0.26
Romanian	20	0.10
Russian	328	1.66
Scandinavian	44	0.22
Scotch-Irish	305	1.54
Scottish	398	2.01
Slovak	31	0.16
Swedish	218	1.10
Swiss	35	0.18
Turkish	9	0.05
Ukrainian	110	0.56
United States or American	723	3.66
Welsh	101	0.51
West Indian, excl. Hispanic:	8	0.04
Jamaican	8	0.04
White:	18,512	93.17
Not Hispanic (17,764)	17,958	90.39
Hispanic (513)	554	2.79
Yugoslavian	64	0.32

Sayville

Place Type: Census Designated Place
County: Suffolk
Population: 16,735

Ancestry/Race	Number	%
African American/Black:	166	0.99
Not Hispanic (107)	145	0.87
Hispanic (14)	21	0.13
Alaska Native tribes, specified:	1	0.01
Tlingit-Haida	1	0.01
Am. Ind. or Alaska Nat., not spec.	16	0.10
American Indian tribes, specified:	24	0.14
Cherokee	8	0.05
Cheyenne	1	0.01
Choctaw	1	0.01
Comanche	1	0.01
Cree (1)	1	0.01
Iroquois	1	0.01
Latin American Indians	3	0.02
Sioux	1	0.01
All other tribes (3)	7	0.04
American Indian tribes, not spec.	1	0.01
Arab:	16	0.10
Lebanese	6	0.04
Other Arab	10	0.06
Armenian	6	0.04
Asian:	419	2.50
Chinese, ex. Taiwanese (53)	72	0.43
Filipino (12)	24	0.14
Indian (205)	220	1.31
Indonesian (9)	9	0.05
Japanese (3)	13	0.08
Korean (40)	44	0.26
Pakistani (11)	21	0.13
Thai (1)	1	0.01
Vietnamese (1)	4	0.02
Other Asian, specified	5	0.03
Other Asian, not specified (2)	6	0.04
Austrian	116	0.69
Belgian	8	0.05
British	103	0.62
Canadian	24	0.14
Czech	193	1.15
Czechoslovakian	50	0.30
Danish	65	0.39
Dutch	231	1.38
Eastern European	33	0.20
English	1,294	7.73
European	54	0.32
Finnish	12	0.07
French, except Basque	315	1.88
French Canadian	133	0.79
German	3,909	23.35
Greek	233	1.39
Hawaii Native/Pacific Islander:	6	0.04
Micronesian:	1	0.01
Other Micronesian	1	0.01
Other Pac. Isl., specified	5	0.03
Hispanic or Latino:	505	3.02
Central American:	16	0.10
Guatemalan	1	0.01
Honduran	6	0.04
Salvadoran	7	0.04
Other Central American	2	0.01
Cuban	29	0.17
Dominican Republic	6	0.04
Mexican	21	0.13
Puerto Rican	279	1.67
South American:	46	0.27
Argentinean	4	0.02
Bolivian	1	0.01
Chilean	6	0.04
Colombian	12	0.07
Ecuadorian	10	0.06
Peruvian	4	0.02
Venezuelan	5	0.03
Other South American	4	0.02
Other Hispanic or Latino	108	0.65
Hungarian	186	1.11
Icelander	24	0.14
Iranian	8	0.05
Irish	5,967	35.65
Israeli	6	0.04
Italian	5,160	30.82
Lithuanian	94	0.56
Maltese	19	0.11
Northern European	11	0.07
Norwegian	210	1.25
Polish	844	5.04
Portuguese	49	0.29
Romanian	29	0.17
Russian	246	1.47
Scandinavian	16	0.10
Scotch-Irish	199	1.19
Scottish	211	1.26
Slavic	6	0.04
Slovak	22	0.13
Swedish	171	1.02
Swiss	70	0.42

Notes: 1. Figures in the "Number" column do not add up to the total population due to: a) Ancestry/Race overlap — e.g. persons can report being both White and Irish, b) persons of Hispanic origin can report being any race, c) persons reporting two ancestries are counted in both categories. 2. Numbers in parentheses indicate the number of persons reporting this ancestry/race alone, not in combination with any other ancestry/race. 3. Refer to the Explanation of Data in the front of the book for more detailed information.

Turkish	28	0.17
Ukrainian	79	0.47
United States or American	537	3.21
Welsh	47	0.28
West Indian, excl. Hispanic:	16	0.10
Jamaican	16	0.10
White:	16,153	96.52
Not Hispanic (15,653)	15,742	94.07
Hispanic (380)	411	2.46
Yugoslavian	16	0.10

Scarsdale

Place Type: Village
County: Westchester
Population: 17,823

Ancestry/Race	Number	%
African American/Black:	310	1.74
Not Hispanic (263)	294	1.65
Hispanic (8)	16	0.09
African, sub-Saharan:	65	0.36
African	14	0.08
Ghanian	7	0.04
South African	44	0.25
Am. Ind. or Alaska Nat., not spec.	16	0.09
Albanian	5	0.03
American Indian tribes, specified:	11	0.06
Cherokee	8	0.04
Latin American Indians (1)	2	0.01
All other tribes	1	0.01
American Indian tribes, not spec.	3	0.02
Arab:	232	1.30
Arab/Arabic	18	0.10
Egyptian	17	0.10
Iraqi	9	0.05
Lebanese	126	0.71
Moroccan	9	0.05
Palestinian	4	0.02
Syrian	49	0.27
Armenian	48	0.27
Asian:	2,431	13.64
Bangladeshi (10)	10	0.06
Chinese, ex. Taiwanese (480)	538	3.02
Filipino (113)	150	0.84
Indian (374)	394	2.21
Indonesian (4)	5	0.03
Japanese (691)	728	4.08
Korean (367)	394	2.21
Pakistani (27)	31	0.17
Sri Lankan (16)	17	0.10
Taiwanese (57)	63	0.35
Thai (36)	43	0.24
Vietnamese (4)	4	0.02
Other Asian, specified (19)	19	0.11
Other Asian, not specified (18)	35	0.20
Australian	24	0.13
Austrian	336	1.89
Basque	9	0.05
Belgian	11	0.06
Brazilian	119	0.67
British	87	0.49
Canadian	43	0.24
Celtic	6	0.03
Croatian	5	0.03
Czech	55	0.31
Czechoslovakian	31	0.17
Danish	24	0.13
Dutch	69	0.39
Eastern European	647	3.63
English	1,034	5.80
European	350	1.96
Finnish	11	0.06
French, except Basque	265	1.49
French Canadian	45	0.25
German	1,908	10.71
Greek	372	2.09
Guyanese	19	0.11
Hawaii Native/Pacific Islander:	14	0.08
Melanesian: (3)	3	0.02
Fijian (1)	1	0.01
Other Melanesian (2)	2	0.01
Polynesian:	3	0.02
Native Hawaiian	3	0.02
Other Pac. Isl., not spec.	8	0.04
Hispanic or Latino:	467	2.62
Central American:	22	0.12
Costa Rican	1	0.01
Guatemalan	10	0.06
Honduran	1	0.01
Nicaraguan	1	0.01
Panamanian	5	0.03
Salvadoran	4	0.02
Cuban	35	0.20
Dominican Republic	13	0.07
Mexican	58	0.33
Puerto Rican	77	0.43
South American:	137	0.77
Argentinean	23	0.13
Bolivian	1	0.01
Chilean	13	0.07
Colombian	34	0.19
Ecuadorian	19	0.11
Paraguayan	2	0.01
Peruvian	29	0.16
Uruguayan	4	0.02
Venezuelan	5	0.03
Other South American	7	0.04
Other Hispanic or Latino	125	0.70
Hungarian	417	2.34
Iranian	5	0.03
Irish	1,775	9.96
Israeli	105	0.59
Italian	1,741	9.77
Latvian	42	0.24
Lithuanian	89	0.50
Northern European	29	0.16
Norwegian	39	0.22
Pennsylvania German	6	0.03
Polish	1,213	6.81
Portuguese	52	0.29
Romanian	135	0.76
Russian	2,075	11.64
Scotch-Irish	151	0.85
Scottish	161	0.90
Slavic	6	0.03
Slovak	13	0.07
Swedish	88	0.49
Swiss	123	0.69
Turkish	28	0.16
Ukrainian	74	0.42
United States or American	1,136	6.37
Welsh	51	0.29
West Indian, excl. Hispanic:	75	0.42
Bahamian	4	0.02
Barbadian	10	0.06
British West Indian	4	0.02
Jamaican	44	0.25
Trinidadian and Tobagonian	6	0.03
U.S. Virgin Islander	7	0.04
White:	15,189	85.22
Not Hispanic (14,594)	14,778	82.92
Hispanic (395)	411	2.31

Schenectady

Place Type: City
County: Schenectady
Population: 61,821

Ancestry/Race	Number	%
Afghan	298	0.48
African American/Black:	10,364	16.76
Not Hispanic (8,651)	9,714	15.71
Hispanic (481)	650	1.05
African, sub-Saharan:	771	1.25
African	515	0.83
Cape Verdean	36	0.06
Ghanian	6	0.01
Kenyan	15	0.02
Nigerian	90	0.15
Sudanese	109	0.18
Alaska Native tribes, specified:	1	0.00
Eskimo	1	0.00
Am. Ind. or Alaska Nat., not spec.	286	0.46
Albanian	36	0.06
American Indian tribes, specified:	320	0.52
Apache (5)	11	0.02
Blackfeet (1)	27	0.04
Cherokee (27)	103	0.17
Cheyenne	2	0.00
Chippewa (4)	13	0.02
Choctaw (2)	5	0.01
Delaware (3)	3	0.00
Iroquois (16)	83	0.13
Latin American Indians (7)	28	0.05
Pueblo	1	0.00
Seminole (1)	9	0.01
Sioux (6)	10	0.02
All other tribes (9)	25	0.04
American Indian tribes, not spec.	23	0.04
Arab:	283	0.46
Arab/Arabic	16	0.03
Egyptian	87	0.14
Iraqi	7	0.01
Lebanese	73	0.12
Palestinian	20	0.03
Syrian	35	0.06
Other Arab	45	0.07
Armenian	99	0.16
Asian:	1,659	2.68
Bangladeshi (2)	4	0.01
Cambodian (5)	5	0.01
Chinese, ex. Taiwanese (246)	285	0.46
Filipino (75)	103	0.17
Indian (564)	661	1.07
Indonesian (4)	8	0.01
Japanese (31)	55	0.09
Korean (100)	128	0.21
Laotian (1)	1	0.00
Malaysian (2)	3	0.00
Pakistani (20)	52	0.08
Sri Lankan (1)	3	0.00
Taiwanese (4)	4	0.01
Thai (4)	6	0.01
Vietnamese (82)	95	0.15
Other Asian, specified (10)	14	0.02
Other Asian, not specified (68)	232	0.38
Assyrian/Chaldean/Syriac	7	0.01
Australian	54	0.09
Austrian	96	0.16
Belgian	8	0.01
Brazilian	5	0.01
British	122	0.20
Bulgarian	18	0.03
Canadian	79	0.13
Celtic	26	0.04
Czech	162	0.26
Czechoslovakian	105	0.17
Danish	188	0.30
Dutch	2,070	3.34
Eastern European	81	0.13
English	4,604	7.44
Estonian	6	0.01
European	307	0.50
Finnish	52	0.08
French, except Basque	3,700	5.98
French Canadian	1,077	1.74
German	7,554	12.20
Greek	261	0.42
Guyanese	355	0.57
Hawaii Native/Pacific Islander:	102	0.16
Micronesian: (3)	3	0.00
Guamanian/Chamorro (3)	3	0.00
Polynesian: (9)	36	0.06
Native Hawaiian (7)	23	0.04
Samoan (2)	7	0.01
Other Polynesian	6	0.01
Other Pac. Isl., specified	2	0.00
Other Pac. Isl., not spec. (8)	61	0.10

Notes: 1. Figures in the "Number" column do not add up to the total population due to: a) Ancestry/Race overlap — e.g. persons can report being both White and Irish, b) persons of Hispanic origin can report being any race, c) persons reporting two ancestries are counted in both categories. 2. Numbers in parentheses indicate the number of persons reporting this ancestry/race alone, not in combination with any other ancestry/race. 3. Refer to the Explanation of Data in the front of the book for more detailed information.

Ancestry/Race	Number	%
Hispanic or Latino:	3,632	5.88
Central American:	99	0.16
Costa Rican	24	0.04
Guatemalan	5	0.01
Honduran	18	0.03
Nicaraguan	3	0.00
Panamanian	15	0.02
Salvadoran	29	0.05
Other Central American	5	0.01
Cuban	96	0.16
Dominican Republic	121	0.20
Mexican	188	0.30
Puerto Rican	2,422	3.92
South American:	130	0.21
Argentinean	3	0.00
Bolivian	4	0.01
Chilean	13	0.02
Colombian	21	0.03
Ecuadorian	28	0.05
Paraguayan	1	0.00
Peruvian	47	0.08
Uruguayan	2	0.00
Venezuelan	5	0.01
Other South American	6	0.01
Other Hispanic or Latino	576	0.93
Hungarian	397	0.64
Icelander	8	0.01
Iranian	8	0.01
Irish	9,769	15.78
Israeli	12	0.02
Italian	12,168	19.65
Latvian	40	0.06
Lithuanian	265	0.43
Maltese	11	0.02
Northern European	13	0.02
Norwegian	168	0.27
Pennsylvania German	37	0.06
Polish	5,568	8.99
Portuguese	57	0.09
Romanian	62	0.10
Russian	690	1.11
Scandinavian	23	0.04
Scotch-Irish	565	0.91
Scottish	1,010	1.63
Slavic	16	0.03
Slovak	119	0.19
Slovene	4	0.01
Swedish	338	0.55
Swiss	104	0.17
Turkish	7	0.01
Ukrainian	290	0.47
United States or American	1,686	2.72
Welsh	277	0.45
West Indian, excl. Hispanic:	491	0.79
Barbadian	9	0.01
Belizean	18	0.03
Haitian	58	0.09
Jamaican	162	0.26
Trinidadian and Tobagonian	9	0.01
U.S. Virgin Islander	29	0.05
West Indian	198	0.32
Other West Indian	8	0.01
White:	49,238	79.65
Not Hispanic (46,069)	47,582	76.97
Hispanic (1,391)	1,656	2.68
Yugoslavian	6	0.01

Schodack

Place Type: Town
County: Rensselaer
Population: 12,536

Ancestry/Race	Number	%
African American/Black:	113	0.90
Not Hispanic (77)	103	0.82
Hispanic (8)	10	0.08
African, sub-Saharan:	6	0.05
African	6	0.05
Am. Ind. or Alaska Nat., not spec.	21	0.17
American Indian tribes, specified:	32	0.26
Apache (1)	1	0.01
Blackfeet	6	0.05
Cherokee (1)	2	0.02
Cree	2	0.02
Iroquois (9)	12	0.10
Latin American Indians (1)	1	0.01
Sioux (1)	1	0.01
All other tribes	7	0.06
Arab:	51	0.41
Lebanese	23	0.18
Syrian	22	0.18
Other Arab	6	0.05
Armenian	20	0.16
Asian:	87	0.69
Chinese, ex. Taiwanese (11)	17	0.14
Filipino (7)	9	0.07
Indian (15)	21	0.17
Japanese (4)	7	0.06
Korean (18)	20	0.16
Pakistani	4	0.03
Taiwanese (1)	1	0.01
Thai (2)	3	0.02
Vietnamese (1)	3	0.02
Other Asian, not specified	2	0.02
Austrian	33	0.26
Belgian	6	0.05
British	70	0.56
Canadian	38	0.30
Carpatho Rusyn	7	0.06
Croatian	7	0.06
Czech	34	0.27
Czechoslovakian	21	0.17
Danish	49	0.39
Dutch	945	7.54
Eastern European	25	0.20
English	1,720	13.72
Estonian	29	0.23
European	126	1.00
Finnish	23	0.18
French, except Basque	1,070	8.53
French Canadian	299	2.38
German	3,363	26.82
Greek	58	0.46
Hawaii Native/Pacific Islander:	5	0.04
Melanesian:	1	0.01
Fijian	1	0.01
Polynesian:	3	0.02
Native Hawaiian	3	0.02
Other Pac. Isl., not spec.	1	0.01
Hispanic or Latino:	187	1.49
Central American:	4	0.03
Costa Rican	1	0.01
Guatemalan	1	0.01
Nicaraguan	1	0.01
Other Central American	1	0.01
Cuban	5	0.04
Mexican	27	0.22
Puerto Rican	77	0.61
South American:	16	0.13
Chilean	5	0.04
Colombian	5	0.04
Ecuadorian	3	0.02
Peruvian	3	0.02
Other Hispanic or Latino	58	0.46
Hungarian	83	0.66
Irish	3,149	25.12
Italian	1,742	13.89
Latvian	6	0.05
Lithuanian	70	0.56
Northern European	36	0.29
Norwegian	43	0.34
Pennsylvania German	7	0.06
Polish	839	6.69
Portuguese	9	0.07
Romanian	8	0.06
Russian	203	1.62
Scandinavian	6	0.05
Scotch-Irish	149	1.19
Scottish	279	2.23
Slavic	9	0.07
Slovak	34	0.27
Swedish	186	1.48
Swiss	11	0.09
Ukrainian	136	1.08
United States or American	528	4.21
Welsh	104	0.83
West Indian, excl. Hispanic:	15	0.12
Barbadian	5	0.04
West Indian	10	0.08
White:	12,308	98.18
Not Hispanic (12,114)	12,179	97.15
Hispanic (114)	129	1.03

Seaford

Place Type: Census Designated Place
County: Nassau
Population: 15,791

Ancestry/Race	Number	%
African American/Black:	63	0.40
Not Hispanic (38)	49	0.31
Hispanic (11)	14	0.09
African, sub-Saharan:	10	0.06
Sierra Leonean	10	0.06
Am. Ind. or Alaska Nat., not spec.	5	0.03
Albanian	38	0.24
Alsatian	12	0.08
American Indian tribes, specified:	26	0.16
Cherokee	5	0.03
Chippewa	4	0.03
Iroquois (4)	7	0.04
Latin American Indians (1)	4	0.03
Lumbee	1	0.01
Paiute (1)	1	0.01
Sioux	3	0.02
All other tribes	1	0.01
American Indian tribes, not spec.	1	0.01
Arab:	133	0.84
Arab/Arabic	9	0.06
Egyptian	90	0.57
Lebanese	13	0.08
Moroccan	7	0.04
Syrian	14	0.09
Armenian	40	0.25
Asian:	302	1.91
Bangladeshi (4)	4	0.03
Chinese, ex. Taiwanese (114)	123	0.78
Filipino (48)	56	0.35
Indian (53)	55	0.35
Japanese (5)	11	0.07
Korean (24)	31	0.20
Pakistani	1	0.01
Thai (1)	1	0.01
Vietnamese (8)	10	0.06
Other Asian, specified (2)	2	0.01
Other Asian, not specified (5)	8	0.05
Austrian	162	1.03
Belgian	11	0.07
Brazilian	6	0.04
British	16	0.10
Bulgarian	5	0.03
Canadian	34	0.22
Croatian	54	0.34
Cypriot	39	0.25
Czech	34	0.22
Czechoslovakian	33	0.21
Danish	55	0.35
Dutch	76	0.48
Eastern European	23	0.15
English	611	3.87
European	12	0.08
Finnish	13	0.08
French, except Basque	321	2.03
French Canadian	54	0.34
German	3,015	19.09
Greek	209	1.32
Hawaii Native/Pacific Islander:	4	0.03
Polynesian: (3)	3	0.02

Notes: 1. Figures in the "Number" column do not add up to the total population due to: a) Ancestry/Race overlap — e.g. persons can report being both White and Irish, b) persons of Hispanic origin can report being any race, c) persons reporting two ancestries are counted in both categories. 2. Numbers in parentheses indicate the number of persons reporting this ancestry/race alone, not in combination with any other ancestry/race. 3. Refer to the Explanation of Data in the front of the book for more detailed information.

Native Hawaiian (2)	2	0.01
Samoan (1)	1	0.01
Other Pac. Isl., not spec.	1	0.01
Hispanic or Latino:	586	3.71
Central American:	28	0.18
Guatemalan	5	0.03
Honduran	10	0.06
Nicaraguan	2	0.01
Salvadoran	10	0.06
Other Central American	1	0.01
Cuban	24	0.15
Dominican Republic	25	0.16
Mexican	33	0.21
Puerto Rican	265	1.68
South American:	107	0.68
Argentinean	15	0.09
Chilean	2	0.01
Colombian	36	0.23
Ecuadorian	19	0.12
Paraguayan	1	0.01
Peruvian	28	0.18
Uruguayan	2	0.01
Other South American	4	0.03
Other Hispanic or Latino	104	0.66
Hungarian	112	0.71
Iranian	10	0.06
Irish	4,564	28.90
Israeli	6	0.04
Italian	5,960	37.74
Latvian	23	0.15
Lithuanian	32	0.20
Maltese	47	0.30
Norwegian	98	0.62
Polish	940	5.95
Portuguese	8	0.05
Romanian	25	0.16
Russian	552	3.50
Scandinavian	21	0.13
Scotch-Irish	215	1.36
Scottish	152	0.96
Serbian	10	0.06
Slavic	5	0.03
Slovak	30	0.19
Swedish	244	1.55
Swiss	31	0.20
Turkish	26	0.16
Ukrainian	169	1.07
United States or American	529	3.35
Welsh	28	0.18
West Indian, excl. Hispanic:	30	0.19
Dutch West Indian	7	0.04
Jamaican	16	0.10
West Indian	7	0.04
White:	15,376	97.37
Not Hispanic (14,819)	14,884	94.26
Hispanic (467)	492	3.12
Yugoslavian	10	0.06

Selden

Place Type: Census Designated Place
County: Suffolk
Population: 21,861

Ancestry/Race	Number	%
African American/Black:	506	2.31
Not Hispanic (349)	431	1.97
Hispanic (61)	75	0.34
African, sub-Saharan:	9	0.04
African	6	0.03
Other sub-Saharan African	3	0.01
Am. Ind. or Alaska Nat., not spec.	53	0.24
American Indian tribes, specified:	47	0.21
Blackfeet	4	0.02
Cherokee (7)	13	0.06
Iroquois	1	0.00
Latin American Indians (6)	7	0.03
Navajo	4	0.02
Seminole	8	0.04
All other tribes	10	0.05
American Indian tribes, not spec.	8	0.04
Arab:	118	0.54
Egyptian	90	0.41
Syrian	14	0.06
Other Arab	14	0.06
Armenian	30	0.14
Asian:	635	2.90
Bangladeshi (2)	8	0.04
Cambodian	1	0.00
Chinese, ex. Taiwanese (119)	124	0.57
Filipino (86)	112	0.51
Indian (153)	177	0.81
Japanese (14)	24	0.11
Korean (37)	44	0.20
Malaysian (2)	2	0.01
Pakistani (60)	79	0.36
Taiwanese	2	0.01
Thai (1)	2	0.01
Vietnamese (39)	39	0.18
Other Asian, specified (6)	6	0.03
Other Asian, not specified (10)	15	0.07
Austrian	165	0.76
Brazilian	13	0.06
British	21	0.10
Canadian	27	0.12
Croatian	42	0.19
Czech	109	0.50
Czechoslovakian	47	0.22
Danish	27	0.12
Dutch	101	0.46
English	978	4.48
European	86	0.39
Finnish	29	0.13
French, except Basque	477	2.19
French Canadian	143	0.66
German	4,556	20.89
Greek	288	1.32
Hawaii Native/Pacific Islander:	14	0.06
Micronesian: (1)	2	0.01
Guamanian/Chamorro (1)	1	0.00
Other Micronesian	1	0.00
Polynesian: (2)	3	0.01
Native Hawaiian	1	0.00
Samoan (2)	2	0.01
Other Pac. Isl., not spec. (1)	9	0.04
Hispanic or Latino:	1,799	8.23
Central American:	102	0.47
Guatemalan	22	0.10
Honduran	12	0.05
Nicaraguan	4	0.02
Panamanian	8	0.04
Salvadoran	53	0.24
Other Central American	3	0.01
Cuban	33	0.15
Dominican Republic	137	0.63
Mexican	115	0.53
Puerto Rican	776	3.55
South American:	244	1.12
Argentinean	18	0.08
Chilean	11	0.05
Colombian	93	0.43
Ecuadorian	72	0.33
Peruvian	34	0.16
Venezuelan	5	0.02
Other South American	11	0.05
Other Hispanic or Latino	392	1.79
Hungarian	180	0.83
Iranian	34	0.16
Irish	5,617	25.75
Italian	8,748	40.10
Lithuanian	72	0.33
Maltese	12	0.06
New Zealander	7	0.03
Northern European	6	0.03
Norwegian	252	1.16
Polish	1,209	5.54
Portuguese	421	1.93
Romanian	39	0.18
Russian	355	1.63
Scandinavian	7	0.03
Scotch-Irish	182	0.83
Scottish	110	0.50
Serbian	9	0.04
Slavic	4	0.02
Slovak	65	0.30
Swedish	247	1.13
Swiss	38	0.17
Turkish	67	0.31
Ukrainian	80	0.37
United States or American	386	1.77
Welsh	14	0.06
West Indian, excl. Hispanic:	147	0.67
Haitian	67	0.31
Jamaican	21	0.10
Trinidadian and Tobagonian	17	0.08
West Indian	42	0.19
White:	20,416	93.39
Not Hispanic (18,863)	19,077	87.26
Hispanic (1,240)	1,339	6.13
Yugoslavian	44	0.20

Setauket-East Setauket

Place Type: Census Designated Place
County: Suffolk
Population: 15,931

Ancestry/Race	Number	%
African American/Black:	268	1.68
Not Hispanic (194)	247	1.55
Hispanic (9)	21	0.13
African, sub-Saharan:	11	0.07
African	11	0.07
Am. Ind. or Alaska Nat., not spec.	27	0.17
Albanian	15	0.09
American Indian tribes, specified:	48	0.30
Blackfeet	1	0.01
Cherokee (2)	18	0.11
Chippewa	1	0.01
Creek	1	0.01
Iroquois (3)	5	0.03
Latin American Indians (2)	2	0.01
Navajo (2)	2	0.01
Sioux	1	0.01
All other tribes (4)	17	0.11
American Indian tribes, not spec.	7	0.04
Arab:	78	0.49
Arab/Arabic	25	0.16
Egyptian	10	0.06
Iraqi	18	0.11
Moroccan	8	0.05
Other Arab	17	0.11
Armenian	58	0.36
Asian:	1,500	9.42
Bangladeshi (13)	13	0.08
Chinese, ex. Taiwanese (691)	721	4.53
Filipino (72)	79	0.50
Indian (305)	330	2.07
Indonesian (2)	2	0.01
Japanese (31)	44	0.28
Korean (192)	197	1.24
Pakistani (25)	26	0.16
Sri Lankan (4)	4	0.03
Taiwanese (33)	36	0.23
Thai (4)	4	0.03
Vietnamese (7)	8	0.05
Other Asian, specified	4	0.03
Other Asian, not specified (11)	32	0.20
Australian	38	0.24
Austrian	213	1.34
Belgian	36	0.23
British	122	0.76
Canadian	23	0.14
Croatian	21	0.13
Cypriot	3	0.02
Czech	24	0.15
Czechoslovakian	108	0.68
Danish	170	1.07
Dutch	245	1.54
Eastern European	74	0.46

Notes: 1. Figures in the "Number" column do not add up to the total population due to: a) Ancestry/Race overlap — e.g. persons can report being both White and Irish, b) persons of Hispanic origin can report being any race, c) persons reporting two ancestries are counted in both categories. 2. Numbers in parentheses indicate the number of persons reporting this ancestry/race alone, not in combination with any other ancestry/race. 3. Refer to the Explanation of Data in the front of the book for more detailed information.

Ancestry/Race	Number	%
English	1,329	8.33
European	90	0.56
Finnish	44	0.28
French, except Basque	311	1.95
French Canadian	78	0.49
German	3,154	19.77
Greek	322	2.02
Guyanese	14	0.09
Hawaii Native/Pacific Islander:	14	0.09
Melanesian: (4)	4	0.03
Other Melanesian (4)	4	0.03
Polynesian:	1	0.01
Native Hawaiian	1	0.01
Other Pac. Isl., specified	4	0.03
Other Pac. Isl., not spec. (2)	5	0.03
Hispanic or Latino:	546	3.43
Central American:	42	0.26
Costa Rican	3	0.02
Guatemalan	6	0.04
Honduran	2	0.01
Nicaraguan	1	0.01
Panamanian	5	0.03
Salvadoran	25	0.16
Cuban	40	0.25
Dominican Republic	19	0.12
Mexican	33	0.21
Puerto Rican	197	1.24
South American:	67	0.42
Argentinean	7	0.04
Chilean	9	0.06
Colombian	22	0.14
Ecuadorian	9	0.06
Paraguayan	4	0.03
Peruvian	10	0.06
Venezuelan	4	0.03
Other South American	2	0.01
Other Hispanic or Latino	148	0.93
Hungarian	235	1.47
Irish	3,635	22.79
Israeli	66	0.41
Italian	3,908	24.50
Latvian	24	0.15
Lithuanian	70	0.44
Northern European	3	0.02
Norwegian	202	1.27
Polish	950	5.96
Portuguese	23	0.14
Romanian	99	0.62
Russian	1,009	6.33
Scandinavian	15	0.09
Scotch-Irish	180	1.13
Scottish	283	1.77
Slovak	32	0.20
Swedish	259	1.62
Swiss	76	0.48
Turkish	64	0.40
Ukrainian	57	0.36
United States or American	461	2.89
Welsh	50	0.31
West Indian, excl. Hispanic:	20	0.13
Dutch West Indian	12	0.08
Other West Indian	8	0.05
White:	14,145	88.79
Not Hispanic (13,563)	13,685	85.90
Hispanic (418)	460	2.89
Yugoslavian	12	0.08

Shawangunk

Place Type: Town
County: Ulster
Population: 12,022

Ancestry/Race	Number	%
African American/Black:	1,032	8.58
Not Hispanic (945)	987	8.21
Hispanic (33)	45	0.37
Alaska Native tribes, specified:	2	0.02
Aleut (1)	1	0.01
Eskimo (1)	1	0.01
Am. Ind. or Alaska Nat., not spec.	29	0.24
Albanian	26	0.22
American Indian tribes, specified:	67	0.56
Apache (5)	5	0.04
Blackfeet	5	0.04
Cherokee (8)	23	0.19
Choctaw (1)	7	0.06
Comanche (1)	1	0.01
Creek (1)	4	0.03
Delaware (1)	6	0.05
Iroquois (1)	4	0.03
Latin American Indians (1)	2	0.02
Lumbee (2)	2	0.02
Navajo	1	0.01
Sioux (2)	3	0.02
All other tribes (2)	4	0.03
American Indian tribes, not spec.	4	0.03
Arab:	29	0.24
Lebanese	15	0.12
Syrian	14	0.12
Armenian	33	0.27
Asian:	155	1.29
Chinese, ex. Taiwanese (27)	39	0.32
Filipino (14)	27	0.22
Indian (16)	23	0.19
Indonesian (1)	2	0.02
Japanese (10)	19	0.16
Korean (36)	39	0.32
Thai (1)	1	0.01
Vietnamese (1)	2	0.02
Other Asian, specified (1)	2	0.02
Other Asian, not specified (1)	1	0.01
Australian	8	0.07
Austrian	22	0.18
Belgian	32	0.27
British	10	0.08
Canadian	29	0.24
Celtic	18	0.15
Czech	41	0.34
Danish	66	0.55
Dutch	534	4.43
Eastern European	11	0.09
English	1,225	10.17
European	68	0.56
Finnish	7	0.06
French, except Basque	269	2.23
French Canadian	117	0.97
German	2,249	18.68
Greek	54	0.45
Hawaii Native/Pacific Islander:	6	0.05
Micronesian:	2	0.02
Guamanian/Chamorro	2	0.02
Polynesian: (1)	4	0.03
Native Hawaiian (1)	4	0.03
Hispanic or Latino:	837	6.96
Central American:	16	0.13
Guatemalan	7	0.06
Honduran	3	0.02
Panamanian	3	0.02
Salvadoran	1	0.01
Other Central American	2	0.02
Cuban	30	0.25
Dominican Republic	47	0.39
Mexican	137	1.14
Puerto Rican	441	3.67
South American:	24	0.20
Argentinean	2	0.02
Colombian	13	0.11
Ecuadorian	5	0.04
Peruvian	3	0.02
Venezuelan	1	0.01
Other Hispanic or Latino	142	1.18
Hungarian	51	0.42
Icelander	4	0.03
Iranian	6	0.05
Irish	2,647	21.98
Italian	1,892	15.71
Latvian	6	0.05
Lithuanian	54	0.45
Norwegian	178	1.48
Polish	526	4.37
Portuguese	37	0.31
Russian	152	1.26
Scandinavian	29	0.24
Scotch-Irish	159	1.32
Scottish	258	2.14
Slavic	7	0.06
Slovak	29	0.24
Swedish	91	0.76
Swiss	40	0.33
Ukrainian	42	0.35
United States or American	578	4.80
Welsh	83	0.69
West Indian, excl. Hispanic:	59	0.49
Jamaican	59	0.49
White:	10,543	87.70
Not Hispanic (9,975)	10,086	83.90
Hispanic (423)	457	3.80
Yugoslavian	51	0.42

Shirley

Place Type: Census Designated Place
County: Suffolk
Population: 25,395

Ancestry/Race	Number	%
Afghan	6	0.02
African American/Black:	1,110	4.37
Not Hispanic (788)	988	3.89
Hispanic (57)	122	0.48
African, sub-Saharan:	64	0.25
African	64	0.25
Am. Ind. or Alaska Nat., not spec.	84	0.33
American Indian tribes, specified:	114	0.45
Apache (1)	1	0.00
Blackfeet (5)	13	0.05
Cherokee (13)	40	0.16
Chickasaw (4)	4	0.02
Comanche	4	0.02
Creek	2	0.01
Crow	1	0.00
Iroquois (1)	7	0.03
Latin American Indians (6)	10	0.04
Lumbee	1	0.00
Pueblo (3)	3	0.01
Ute (1)	1	0.00
All other tribes (10)	27	0.11
American Indian tribes, not spec.	7	0.03
Arab:	34	0.13
Egyptian	21	0.08
Lebanese	13	0.05
Armenian	29	0.11
Asian:	444	1.75
Bangladeshi (1)	1	0.00
Chinese, ex. Taiwanese (73)	96	0.38
Filipino (21)	47	0.19
Indian (78)	104	0.41
Indonesian (1)	3	0.01
Japanese (1)	12	0.05
Korean (33)	47	0.19
Laotian (4)	9	0.04
Malaysian	1	0.00
Pakistani (35)	54	0.21
Thai (2)	5	0.02
Vietnamese (45)	47	0.19
Other Asian, not specified (2)	18	0.07
Austrian	85	0.33
Basque	8	0.03
Brazilian	26	0.10
British	29	0.11
Bulgarian	14	0.06
Canadian	46	0.18
Croatian	22	0.09
Cypriot	18	0.07
Czech	87	0.34
Czechoslovakian	67	0.26
Danish	41	0.16
Dutch	285	1.12
Eastern European	8	0.03

Notes: 1. Figures in the "Number" column do not add up to the total population due to: a) Ancestry/Race overlap — e.g. persons can report being both White and Irish, b) persons of Hispanic origin can report being any race, c) persons reporting two ancestries are counted in both categories. 2. Numbers in parentheses indicate the number of persons reporting this ancestry/race alone, not in combination with any other ancestry/race. 3. Refer to the Explanation of Data in the front of the book for more detailed information.

English	1,070	4.21
European	15	0.06
Finnish	6	0.02
French, except Basque	507	2.00
French Canadian	47	0.19
German	4,816	18.96
Greek	349	1.37
Hawaii Native/Pacific Islander:	17	0.07
Micronesian: (1)	4	0.02
Guamanian/Chamorro (1)	4	0.02
Polynesian: (6)	7	0.03
Native Hawaiian (6)	7	0.03
Other Pac. Isl., not spec. (1)	6	0.02
Hispanic or Latino:	2,749	10.82
Central American:	169	0.67
Costa Rican	5	0.02
Guatemalan	23	0.09
Honduran	7	0.03
Nicaraguan	9	0.04
Panamanian	14	0.06
Salvadoran	106	0.42
Other Central American	5	0.02
Cuban	72	0.28
Dominican Republic	93	0.37
Mexican	121	0.48
Puerto Rican	1,689	6.65
South American:	229	0.90
Argentinean	8	0.03
Bolivian	4	0.02
Chilean	14	0.06
Colombian	74	0.29
Ecuadorian	72	0.28
Peruvian	33	0.13
Uruguayan	8	0.03
Venezuelan	8	0.03
Other South American	8	0.03
Other Hispanic or Latino	376	1.48
Hungarian	133	0.52
Irish	6,459	25.43
Israeli	11	0.04
Italian	9,797	38.58
Latvian	30	0.12
Lithuanian	25	0.10
Maltese	84	0.33
Norwegian	335	1.32
Polish	1,753	6.90
Portuguese	151	0.59
Romanian	20	0.08
Russian	430	1.69
Scandinavian	81	0.32
Scotch-Irish	180	0.71
Scottish	249	0.98
Slovak	101	0.40
Swedish	259	1.02
Swiss	27	0.11
Turkish	44	0.17
Ukrainian	170	0.67
United States or American	793	3.12
Welsh	19	0.07
West Indian, excl. Hispanic:	89	0.35
Haitian	4	0.02
Jamaican	14	0.06
Trinidadian and Tobagonian	22	0.09
West Indian	49	0.19
White:	23,312	91.80
Not Hispanic (20,995)	21,349	84.07
Hispanic (1,783)	1,963	7.73
Yugoslavian	64	0.25

Smithtown

Place Type: Town
County: Suffolk
Population: 115,715

Ancestry/Race	Number	%
Afghan	112	0.10
African American/Black:	924	0.80
Not Hispanic (689)	831	0.72
Hispanic (59)	93	0.08
African, sub-Saharan:	80	0.07
African	80	0.07
Alaska Native tribes, specified:	2	0.00
Eskimo (2)	2	0.00
Am. Ind. or Alaska Nat., not spec.	90	0.08
Albanian	50	0.04
Alsatian	18	0.02
American Indian tribes, specified:	128	0.11
Apache (1)	1	0.00
Blackfeet (2)	12	0.01
Cherokee (5)	32	0.03
Cheyenne (1)	1	0.00
Chickasaw (1)	1	0.00
Chippewa (1)	1	0.00
Choctaw (2)	2	0.00
Cree (1)	1	0.00
Creek	3	0.00
Crow	1	0.00
Iroquois (7)	27	0.02
Latin American Indians (13)	15	0.01
Navajo	1	0.00
Pueblo	1	0.00
Seminole	1	0.00
Sioux (1)	5	0.00
Ute (1)	1	0.00
All other tribes (5)	22	0.02
American Indian tribes, not spec.	9	0.01
Arab:	469	0.41
Arab/Arabic	90	0.08
Egyptian	174	0.15
Jordanian	9	0.01
Lebanese	122	0.11
Palestinian	17	0.01
Syrian	32	0.03
Other Arab	25	0.02
Armenian	231	0.20
Asian:	3,198	2.76
Bangladeshi (5)	5	0.00
Cambodian (1)	1	0.00
Chinese, ex. Taiwanese (759)	866	0.75
Filipino (299)	384	0.33
Indian (797)	868	0.75
Indonesian (1)	6	0.01
Japanese (80)	109	0.09
Korean (480)	521	0.45
Laotian (3)	3	0.00
Malaysian (1)	1	0.00
Pakistani (189)	227	0.20
Sri Lankan (2)	7	0.01
Taiwanese (31)	34	0.03
Thai (16)	20	0.02
Vietnamese (24)	25	0.02
Other Asian, specified (4)	11	0.01
Other Asian, not specified (36)	110	0.10
Australian	5	0.00
Austrian	1,088	0.94
Basque	12	0.01
Belgian	83	0.07
Brazilian	50	0.04
British	377	0.33
Bulgarian	10	0.01
Canadian	241	0.21
Carpatho Rusyn	6	0.01
Celtic	29	0.03
Croatian	178	0.15
Cypriot	1	0.00
Czech	593	0.51
Czechoslovakian	318	0.27
Danish	394	0.34
Dutch	843	0.73
Eastern European	473	0.41
English	5,835	5.04
Estonian	33	0.03
European	415	0.36
Finnish	264	0.23
French, except Basque	2,007	1.73
French Canadian	483	0.42
German	21,678	18.73
Greek	1,843	1.59
Guyanese	68	0.06
Hawaii Native/Pacific Islander:	59	0.05
Micronesian: (1)	3	0.00
Guamanian/Chamorro (1)	3	0.00
Polynesian: (16)	24	0.02
Native Hawaiian (10)	18	0.02
Samoan (6)	6	0.01
Other Pac. Isl., specified	4	0.00
Other Pac. Isl., not spec. (5)	28	0.02
Hispanic or Latino:	3,855	3.33
Central American:	256	0.22
Costa Rican	4	0.00
Guatemalan	33	0.03
Honduran	46	0.04
Nicaraguan	9	0.01
Panamanian	11	0.01
Salvadoran	145	0.13
Other Central American	8	0.01
Cuban	225	0.19
Dominican Republic	117	0.10
Mexican	313	0.27
Puerto Rican	1,461	1.26
South American:	710	0.61
Argentinean	82	0.07
Bolivian	23	0.02
Chilean	55	0.05
Colombian	229	0.20
Ecuadorian	108	0.09
Paraguayan	8	0.01
Peruvian	116	0.10
Uruguayan	21	0.02
Venezuelan	20	0.02
Other South American	48	0.04
Other Hispanic or Latino	773	0.67
Hungarian	1,499	1.30
Icelander	28	0.02
Iranian	220	0.19
Irish	30,091	26.00
Israeli	136	0.12
Italian	40,891	35.34
Latvian	63	0.05
Lithuanian	583	0.50
Luxemburger	14	0.01
Macedonian	6	0.01
Maltese	149	0.13
New Zealander	6	0.01
Northern European	53	0.05
Norwegian	1,485	1.28
Pennsylvania German	21	0.02
Polish	7,970	6.89
Portuguese	319	0.28
Romanian	379	0.33
Russian	4,736	4.09
Scandinavian	73	0.06
Scotch-Irish	957	0.83
Scottish	1,317	1.14
Serbian	6	0.01
Slavic	122	0.11
Slovak	166	0.14
Slovene	43	0.04
Swedish	1,375	1.19
Swiss	289	0.25
Turkish	328	0.28
Ukrainian	1,004	0.87
United States or American	3,748	3.24
Welsh	233	0.20
West Indian, excl. Hispanic:	452	0.39
Belizean	12	0.01
Bermudan	14	0.01
British West Indian	11	0.01
Haitian	163	0.14
Jamaican	181	0.16
Trinidadian and Tobagonian	59	0.05
West Indian	12	0.01
White:	111,298	96.18
Not Hispanic (107,537)	108,125	93.44
Hispanic (3,009)	3,173	2.74
Yugoslavian	172	0.15

Notes: 1. Figures in the "Number" column do not add up to the total population due to: a) Ancestry/Race overlap — e.g. persons can report being both White and Irish, b) persons of Hispanic origin can report being any race, c) persons reporting two ancestries are counted in both categories. 2. Numbers in parentheses indicate the number of persons reporting this ancestry/race alone, not in combination with any other ancestry/race. 3. Refer to the Explanation of Data in the front of the book for more detailed information.

Somers

Place Type: Town
County: Westchester
Population: 18,346

Ancestry/Race	Number	%
African American/Black:	371	2.02
Not Hispanic (293)	334	1.82
Hispanic (20)	37	0.20
African, sub-Saharan:	15	0.08
African	6	0.03
South African	9	0.05
Am. Ind. or Alaska Nat., not spec.	19	0.10
Albanian	53	0.29
American Indian tribes, specified:	13	0.07
Apache	1	0.01
Cherokee (2)	4	0.02
Iroquois (3)	3	0.02
Latin American Indians (1)	1	0.01
All other tribes (2)	4	0.02
American Indian tribes, not spec.	1	0.01
Arab:	18	0.10
Arab/Arabic	4	0.02
Lebanese	9	0.05
Syrian	5	0.03
Armenian	54	0.29
Asian:	417	2.27
Chinese, ex. Taiwanese (120)	144	0.78
Filipino (28)	37	0.20
Indian (83)	98	0.53
Indonesian (2)	2	0.01
Japanese (29)	43	0.23
Korean (44)	49	0.27
Pakistani	2	0.01
Taiwanese (7)	7	0.04
Vietnamese (12)	15	0.08
Other Asian, specified (5)	6	0.03
Other Asian, not specified (3)	14	0.08
Australian	14	0.08
Austrian	334	1.82
Belgian	19	0.10
Brazilian	49	0.27
British	133	0.72
Canadian	122	0.66
Celtic	12	0.07
Czech	162	0.88
Czechoslovakian	50	0.27
Danish	60	0.33
Dutch	172	0.94
Eastern European	127	0.69
English	1,491	8.13
European	119	0.65
Finnish	78	0.43
French, except Basque	373	2.03
French Canadian	188	1.02
German	3,037	16.55
Greek	194	1.06
Hawaii Native/Pacific Islander:	5	0.03
Micronesian:	1	0.01
Guamanian/Chamorro	1	0.01
Other Pac. Isl., specified	1	0.01
Other Pac. Isl., not spec. (1)	3	0.02
Hispanic or Latino:	543	2.96
Central American:	9	0.05
Guatemalan	3	0.02
Honduran	1	0.01
Panamanian	2	0.01
Salvadoran	3	0.02
Cuban	43	0.23
Dominican Republic	19	0.10
Mexican	36	0.20
Puerto Rican	213	1.16
South American:	119	0.65
Argentinean	13	0.07
Chilean	11	0.06
Colombian	47	0.26
Ecuadorian	14	0.08
Paraguayan	2	0.01
Peruvian	21	0.11
Uruguayan	1	0.01
Venezuelan	1	0.01
Other South American	9	0.05
Other Hispanic or Latino	104	0.57
Hungarian	209	1.14
Icelander	36	0.20
Iranian	56	0.31
Irish	3,775	20.58
Israeli	5	0.03
Italian	5,599	30.52
Latvian	22	0.12
Lithuanian	99	0.54
Maltese	48	0.26
Northern European	23	0.13
Norwegian	304	1.66
Pennsylvania German	9	0.05
Polish	898	4.89
Portuguese	99	0.54
Romanian	47	0.26
Russian	949	5.17
Scandinavian	94	0.51
Scotch-Irish	216	1.18
Scottish	279	1.52
Serbian	27	0.15
Slovak	40	0.22
Slovene	6	0.03
Swedish	242	1.32
Swiss	96	0.52
Turkish	7	0.04
Ukrainian	103	0.56
United States or American	715	3.90
Welsh	21	0.11
West Indian, excl. Hispanic:	42	0.23
Jamaican	15	0.08
Trinidadian and Tobagonian	15	0.08
West Indian	12	0.07
White:	17,544	95.63
Not Hispanic (17,006)	17,132	93.38
Hispanic (394)	412	2.25
Yugoslavian	18	0.10

South Farmingdale

Place Type: Census Designated Place
County: Nassau
Population: 15,061

Ancestry/Race	Number	%
Afghan	12	0.08
African American/Black:	146	0.97
Not Hispanic (117)	131	0.87
Hispanic (2)	15	0.10
Am. Ind. or Alaska Nat., not spec.	22	0.15
Alsatian	6	0.04
American Indian tribes, specified:	16	0.11
Cherokee	4	0.03
Iroquois (1)	1	0.01
Latin American Indians (4)	5	0.03
Yaqui	1	0.01
All other tribes (5)	5	0.03
American Indian tribes, not spec.	5	0.03
Arab:	34	0.23
Lebanese	13	0.09
Other Arab	21	0.14
Armenian	33	0.22
Asian:	539	3.58
Chinese, ex. Taiwanese (96)	104	0.69
Filipino (107)	122	0.81
Indian (154)	167	1.11
Indonesian (1)	3	0.02
Japanese (7)	7	0.05
Korean (28)	34	0.23
Pakistani (27)	39	0.26
Taiwanese (2)	2	0.01
Thai (7)	9	0.06
Vietnamese (20)	21	0.14
Other Asian, not specified (23)	31	0.21
Austrian	98	0.65
Belgian	12	0.08
British	50	0.33
Canadian	24	0.16
Croatian	38	0.25
Cypriot	10	0.07
Czech	140	0.93
Czechoslovakian	23	0.15
Danish	24	0.16
Dutch	35	0.23
English	658	4.37
Estonian	5	0.03
European	26	0.17
Finnish	10	0.07
French, except Basque	422	2.80
French Canadian	94	0.62
German	3,096	20.56
Greek	206	1.37
Guyanese	53	0.35
Hawaii Native/Pacific Islander:	7	0.05
Micronesian: (3)	3	0.02
Guamanian/Chamorro (3)	3	0.02
Polynesian: (1)	2	0.01
Native Hawaiian (1)	1	0.01
Samoan	1	0.01
Other Pac. Isl., not spec.	2	0.01
Hispanic or Latino:	888	5.90
Central American:	104	0.69
Costa Rican	1	0.01
Guatemalan	22	0.15
Honduran	6	0.04
Panamanian	1	0.01
Salvadoran	66	0.44
Other Central American	8	0.05
Cuban	42	0.28
Dominican Republic	38	0.25
Mexican	24	0.16
Puerto Rican	299	1.99
South American:	175	1.16
Argentinean	14	0.09
Bolivian	1	0.01
Chilean	11	0.07
Colombian	67	0.44
Ecuadorian	32	0.21
Paraguayan	14	0.09
Peruvian	26	0.17
Uruguayan	3	0.02
Other South American	7	0.05
Other Hispanic or Latino	206	1.37
Hungarian	109	0.72
Icelander	11	0.07
Iranian	13	0.09
Irish	3,684	24.46
Italian	5,700	37.85
Latvian	37	0.25
Lithuanian	58	0.39
Maltese	21	0.14
Norwegian	152	1.01
Polish	846	5.62
Portuguese	5	0.03
Romanian	19	0.13
Russian	319	2.12
Scotch-Irish	175	1.16
Scottish	142	0.94
Slavic	21	0.14
Slovak	20	0.13
Swedish	128	0.85
Swiss	4	0.03
Turkish	8	0.05
Ukrainian	112	0.74
United States or American	568	3.77
Welsh	26	0.17
West Indian, excl. Hispanic:	45	0.30
British West Indian	6	0.04
Jamaican	4	0.03
West Indian	35	0.23
White:	14,133	93.84
Not Hispanic (13,437)	13,516	89.74
Hispanic (571)	617	4.10
Yugoslavian	46	0.31

Notes: 1. Figures in the "Number" column do not add up to the total population due to: a) Ancestry/Race overlap — e.g. persons can report being both White and Irish, b) persons of Hispanic origin can report being any race, c) persons reporting two ancestries are counted in both categories. 2. Numbers in parentheses indicate the number of persons reporting this ancestry/race alone, not in combination with any other ancestry/race. 3. Refer to the Explanation of Data in the front of the book for more detailed information.

Southampton

Place Type: Town
County: Suffolk
Population: 54,712

Ancestry/Race	Number	%
Afghan	28	0.05
African American/Black:	3,937	7.20
Not Hispanic (3,491)	3,744	6.84
Hispanic (133)	193	0.35
African, sub-Saharan:	193	0.35
African	190	0.35
Ethiopian	3	0.01
Alaska Native tribes, specified:	1	0.00
Eskimo (1)	1	0.00
Am. Ind. or Alaska Nat., not spec.	172	0.31
Albanian	34	0.06
Alsatian	3	0.01
American Indian tribes, specified:	251	0.46
Apache (1)	2	0.00
Blackfeet (4)	10	0.02
Cherokee (12)	48	0.09
Chippewa	1	0.00
Choctaw (1)	2	0.00
Delaware (3)	3	0.01
Iroquois (1)	7	0.01
Latin American Indians (40)	55	0.10
Navajo (1)	1	0.00
Osage	1	0.00
Pueblo	1	0.00
Seminole	1	0.00
Shoshone	4	0.01
Sioux	2	0.00
All other tribes (63)	113	0.21
American Indian tribes, not spec.	13	0.02
Arab:	120	0.22
Arab/Arabic	45	0.08
Egyptian	2	0.00
Jordanian	3	0.01
Lebanese	37	0.07
Moroccan	9	0.02
Syrian	24	0.04
Armenian	100	0.18
Asian:	664	1.21
Bangladeshi	3	0.01
Chinese, ex. Taiwanese (124)	141	0.26
Filipino (80)	124	0.23
Indian (61)	85	0.16
Indonesian (3)	5	0.01
Japanese (39)	67	0.12
Korean (38)	59	0.11
Laotian (1)	5	0.01
Malaysian (2)	9	0.02
Pakistani (36)	40	0.07
Taiwanese (8)	11	0.02
Thai (10)	10	0.02
Vietnamese (38)	39	0.07
Other Asian, specified	1	0.00
Other Asian, not specified (30)	65	0.12
Australian	22	0.04
Austrian	461	0.84
Basque	8	0.01
Belgian	39	0.07
Brazilian	127	0.23
British	270	0.49
Bulgarian	4	0.01
Canadian	138	0.25
Celtic	13	0.02
Croatian	49	0.09
Cypriot	37	0.07
Czech	418	0.76
Czechoslovakian	129	0.24
Danish	249	0.46
Dutch	884	1.62
Eastern European	88	0.16
English	6,113	11.18
Estonian	16	0.03
European	233	0.43
Finnish	154	0.28
French, except Basque	1,597	2.92
French Canadian	343	0.63
German	9,654	17.66
Greek	441	0.81
Guyanese	10	0.02
Hawaii Native/Pacific Islander:	86	0.16
Micronesian: (25)	26	0.05
Guamanian/Chamorro (25)	26	0.05
Polynesian: (9)	27	0.05
Native Hawaiian (5)	19	0.03
Samoan (4)	8	0.01
Other Pac. Isl., specified	1	0.00
Other Pac. Isl., not spec. (11)	32	0.06
Hispanic or Latino:	4,700	8.59
Central American:	1,005	1.84
Costa Rican	306	0.56
Guatemalan	446	0.82
Honduran	53	0.10
Nicaraguan	18	0.03
Panamanian	4	0.01
Salvadoran	155	0.28
Other Central American	23	0.04
Cuban	76	0.14
Dominican Republic	43	0.08
Mexican	1,058	1.93
Puerto Rican	599	1.09
South American:	799	1.46
Argentinean	29	0.05
Bolivian	11	0.02
Chilean	23	0.04
Colombian	409	0.75
Ecuadorian	218	0.40
Paraguayan	10	0.02
Peruvian	53	0.10
Uruguayan	2	0.00
Venezuelan	15	0.03
Other South American	29	0.05
Other Hispanic or Latino	1,120	2.05
Hungarian	473	0.87
Icelander	3	0.01
Iranian	5	0.01
Irish	12,036	22.02
Israeli	27	0.05
Italian	10,070	18.42
Latvian	53	0.10
Lithuanian	382	0.70
Luxemburger	14	0.03
Maltese	54	0.10
New Zealander	37	0.07
Northern European	32	0.06
Norwegian	586	1.07
Pennsylvania German	11	0.02
Polish	4,799	8.78
Portuguese	137	0.25
Romanian	150	0.27
Russian	1,338	2.45
Scandinavian	58	0.11
Scotch-Irish	728	1.33
Scottish	1,128	2.06
Serbian	20	0.04
Slavic	20	0.04
Slovak	67	0.12
Swedish	820	1.50
Swiss	230	0.42
Turkish	103	0.19
Ukrainian	438	0.80
United States or American	1,917	3.51
Welsh	271	0.50
West Indian, excl. Hispanic:	172	0.31
Barbadian	4	0.01
British West Indian	16	0.03
Jamaican	97	0.18
Trinidadian and Tobagonian	19	0.03
U.S. Virgin Islander	8	0.01
West Indian	28	0.05
White:	48,885	89.35
Not Hispanic (45,212)	45,637	83.41
Hispanic (2,921)	3,248	5.94
Yugoslavian	84	0.15

Southeast

Place Type: Town
County: Putnam
Population: 17,316

Ancestry/Race	Number	%
African American/Black:	366	2.11
Not Hispanic (304)	336	1.94
Hispanic (19)	30	0.17
African, sub-Saharan:	25	0.14
Nigerian	13	0.08
South African	12	0.07
Am. Ind. or Alaska Nat., not spec.	30	0.17
Albanian	10	0.06
American Indian tribes, specified:	20	0.12
Blackfeet	1	0.01
Cherokee	1	0.01
Chippewa	1	0.01
Choctaw	4	0.02
Iroquois (1)	2	0.01
Latin American Indians (3)	7	0.04
Lumbee (1)	1	0.01
All other tribes	3	0.02
American Indian tribes, not spec.	4	0.02
Arab:	98	0.57
Egyptian	8	0.05
Lebanese	59	0.34
Palestinian	6	0.03
Syrian	25	0.14
Armenian	19	0.11
Asian:	340	1.96
Chinese, ex. Taiwanese (84)	92	0.53
Filipino (72)	86	0.50
Indian (62)	74	0.43
Japanese (15)	31	0.18
Korean (29)	32	0.18
Pakistani (1)	1	0.01
Taiwanese (1)	1	0.01
Thai (2)	2	0.01
Vietnamese (12)	12	0.07
Other Asian, specified (2)	6	0.03
Other Asian, not specified (2)	3	0.02
Assyrian/Chaldean/Syriac	3	0.02
Australian	5	0.03
Austrian	128	0.74
Basque	10	0.06
Belgian	8	0.05
Brazilian	38	0.22
British	61	0.35
Canadian	160	0.92
Czech	30	0.17
Czechoslovakian	86	0.50
Danish	58	0.33
Dutch	271	1.57
Eastern European	38	0.22
English	1,239	7.16
European	116	0.67
Finnish	82	0.47
French, except Basque	368	2.13
French Canadian	83	0.48
German	2,789	16.11
Greek	113	0.65
Hawaii Native/Pacific Islander:	23	0.13
Polynesian: (13)	13	0.08
Native Hawaiian (9)	9	0.05
Samoan (4)	4	0.02
Other Pac. Isl., specified	4	0.02
Other Pac. Isl., not spec. (3)	6	0.03
Hispanic or Latino:	1,393	8.04
Central American:	420	2.43
Costa Rican	3	0.02
Guatemalan	361	2.08
Honduran	13	0.08
Nicaraguan	6	0.03
Panamanian	2	0.01
Salvadoran	32	0.18
Other Central American	3	0.02
Cuban	41	0.24
Dominican Republic	37	0.21

Notes: 1. Figures in the "Number" column do not add up to the total population due to: a) Ancestry/Race overlap — e.g. persons can report being both White and Irish, b) persons of Hispanic origin can report being any race, c) persons reporting two ancestries are counted in both categories. 2. Numbers in parentheses indicate the number of persons reporting this ancestry/race alone, not in combination with any other ancestry/race. 3. Refer to the Explanation of Data in the front of the book for more detailed information.

Ancestry/Race	Number	%
Mexican	98	0.57
Puerto Rican	306	1.77
South American:	188	1.09
Argentinean	12	0.07
Bolivian	1	0.01
Chilean	4	0.02
Colombian	68	0.39
Ecuadorian	84	0.49
Paraguayan	2	0.01
Peruvian	8	0.05
Uruguayan	7	0.04
Venezuelan	1	0.01
Other South American	1	0.01
Other Hispanic or Latino	303	1.75
Hungarian	145	0.84
Iranian	6	0.03
Irish	4,955	28.62
Israeli	4	0.02
Italian	5,457	31.51
Latvian	6	0.03
Lithuanian	51	0.29
Maltese	24	0.14
Northern European	23	0.13
Norwegian	206	1.19
Polish	894	5.16
Portuguese	77	0.44
Romanian	7	0.04
Russian	349	2.02
Scandinavian	11	0.06
Scotch-Irish	221	1.28
Scottish	294	1.70
Slavic	18	0.10
Slovak	122	0.70
Slovene	12	0.07
Swedish	191	1.10
Swiss	93	0.54
Ukrainian	60	0.35
United States or American	577	3.33
Welsh	15	0.09
West Indian, excl. Hispanic:	115	0.66
Haitian	31	0.18
Jamaican	84	0.49
White:	16,244	93.81
Not Hispanic (15,194)	15,300	88.36
Hispanic (889)	944	5.45
Yugoslavian	16	0.09

Southold

Place Type: Town
County: Suffolk
Population: 20,599

Ancestry/Race	Number	%
African American/Black:	698	3.39
Not Hispanic (579)	659	3.20
Hispanic (21)	39	0.19
African, sub-Saharan:	29	0.14
African	19	0.09
South African	10	0.05
Am. Ind. or Alaska Nat., not spec.	27	0.13
Albanian	9	0.04
American Indian tribes, specified:	28	0.14
Blackfeet (2)	3	0.01
Cherokee (1)	7	0.03
Chippewa	1	0.00
Cree	3	0.01
Iroquois (2)	4	0.02
Latin American Indians (1)	6	0.03
All other tribes (1)	4	0.02
American Indian tribes, not spec.	6	0.03
Arab:	45	0.22
Arab/Arabic	12	0.06
Iraqi	6	0.03
Lebanese	10	0.05
Syrian	17	0.08
Armenian	18	0.09
Asian:	136	0.66
Chinese, ex. Taiwanese (19)	25	0.12
Filipino (10)	10	0.05
Indian (24)	27	0.13
Japanese (6)	14	0.07
Korean (20)	25	0.12
Pakistani (7)	16	0.08
Vietnamese (5)	5	0.02
Other Asian, specified (1)	1	0.00
Other Asian, not specified	13	0.06
Austrian	118	0.57
Basque	9	0.04
Belgian	37	0.18
Brazilian	14	0.07
British	86	0.42
Canadian	38	0.18
Croatian	57	0.28
Cypriot	10	0.05
Czech	88	0.43
Czechoslovakian	59	0.29
Danish	72	0.35
Dutch	425	2.06
Eastern European	16	0.08
English	3,133	15.21
Estonian	11	0.05
European	134	0.65
Finnish	54	0.26
French, except Basque	856	4.16
French Canadian	120	0.58
German	4,941	23.99
Greek	338	1.64
Hawaii Native/Pacific Islander:	19	0.09
Micronesian: (7)	7	0.03
Guamanian/Chamorro (7)	7	0.03
Polynesian: (1)	1	0.00
Native Hawaiian (1)	1	0.00
Other Pac. Isl., not spec. (6)	11	0.05
Hispanic or Latino:	982	4.77
Central American:	330	1.60
Guatemalan	232	1.13
Honduran	5	0.02
Panamanian	1	0.00
Salvadoran	76	0.37
Other Central American	16	0.08
Cuban	24	0.12
Dominican Republic	19	0.09
Mexican	146	0.71
Puerto Rican	215	1.04
South American:	90	0.44
Argentinean	2	0.01
Bolivian	1	0.00
Chilean	2	0.01
Colombian	42	0.20
Ecuadorian	27	0.13
Peruvian	15	0.07
Venezuelan	1	0.00
Other Hispanic or Latino	158	0.77
Hungarian	119	0.58
Irish	5,124	24.87
Italian	3,339	16.21
Latvian	33	0.16
Lithuanian	245	1.19
Maltese	8	0.04
Northern European	15	0.07
Norwegian	259	1.26
Pennsylvania German	3	0.01
Polish	3,160	15.34
Portuguese	62	0.30
Romanian	6	0.03
Russian	405	1.97
Scandinavian	85	0.41
Scotch-Irish	282	1.37
Scottish	522	2.53
Slavic	2	0.01
Slovak	12	0.06
Slovene	2	0.01
Swedish	430	2.09
Swiss	44	0.21
Turkish	51	0.25
Ukrainian	183	0.89
United States or American	588	2.85
Welsh	161	0.78
West Indian, excl. Hispanic:	32	0.16
British West Indian	4	0.02
Jamaican	15	0.07
U.S. Virgin Islander	3	0.01
West Indian	10	0.05
White:	19,506	94.69
Not Hispanic (18,687)	18,855	91.53
Hispanic (579)	651	3.16
Yugoslavian	45	0.22

Southport

Place Type: Town
County: Chemung
Population: 11,185

Ancestry/Race	Number	%
African American/Black:	805	7.20
Not Hispanic (722)	766	6.85
Hispanic (36)	39	0.35
African, sub-Saharan:	8	0.07
African	8	0.07
Am. Ind. or Alaska Nat., not spec.	21	0.19
American Indian tribes, specified:	41	0.37
Blackfeet	1	0.01
Cherokee (4)	18	0.16
Iroquois (3)	14	0.13
Navajo	1	0.01
Pueblo	1	0.01
All other tribes (2)	6	0.05
Arab:	13	0.12
Syrian	13	0.12
Armenian	6	0.05
Asian:	34	0.30
Chinese, ex. Taiwanese (2)	3	0.03
Filipino (4)	5	0.04
Indian (6)	10	0.09
Japanese (3)	5	0.04
Korean (6)	6	0.05
Vietnamese (2)	2	0.02
Other Asian, not specified (2)	3	0.03
Austrian	69	0.62
British	42	0.38
Canadian	29	0.26
Celtic	13	0.12
Czech	29	0.26
Czechoslovakian	19	0.17
Danish	22	0.20
Dutch	219	1.96
English	1,904	17.02
European	103	0.92
Finnish	30	0.27
French, except Basque	394	3.52
French Canadian	51	0.46
German	2,209	19.75
Greek	21	0.19
Hawaii Native/Pacific Islander:	6	0.05
Polynesian: (4)	4	0.04
Native Hawaiian (3)	3	0.03
Samoan (1)	1	0.01
Other Pac. Isl., not spec.	2	0.02
Hispanic or Latino:	326	2.91
Central American:	8	0.07
Guatemalan	1	0.01
Honduran	1	0.01
Panamanian	3	0.03
Salvadoran	3	0.03
Cuban	15	0.13
Dominican Republic	39	0.35
Mexican	9	0.08
Puerto Rican	192	1.72
South American:	5	0.04
Colombian	5	0.04
Other Hispanic or Latino	58	0.52
Hungarian	31	0.28
Irish	1,824	16.31
Italian	1,003	8.97
Lithuanian	10	0.09
Pennsylvania German	189	1.69
Polish	519	4.64
Portuguese	10	0.09

Notes: 1. Figures in the "Number" column do not add up to the total population due to: a) Ancestry/Race overlap — e.g. persons can report being both White and Irish, b) persons of Hispanic origin can report being any race, c) persons reporting two ancestries are counted in both categories. 2. Numbers in parentheses indicate the number of persons reporting this ancestry/race alone, not in combination with any other ancestry/race. 3. Refer to the Explanation of Data in the front of the book for more detailed information.

Russian	135	1.21
Scotch-Irish	137	1.22
Scottish	218	1.95
Slovak	24	0.21
Swedish	118	1.05
Swiss	27	0.24
Ukrainian	94	0.84
United States or American	692	6.19
Welsh	117	1.05
West Indian, excl. Hispanic:	17	0.15
Jamaican	3	0.03
U.S. Virgin Islander	4	0.04
West Indian	10	0.09
White:	10,204	91.23
Not Hispanic (9,995)	10,066	90.00
Hispanic (133)	138	1.23

Spring Valley

Place Type: Village
County: Rockland
Population: 25,464

Ancestry/Race	Number	%
African American/Black:	12,294	48.28
Not Hispanic (10,936)	11,930	46.85
Hispanic (264)	364	1.43
African, sub-Saharan:	277	1.09
African	221	0.87
Kenyan	29	0.11
Liberian	10	0.04
Nigerian	17	0.07
Alaska Native tribes, specified:	2	0.01
Tlingit-Haida	2	0.01
Am. Ind. or Alaska Nat., not spec.	88	0.35
Albanian	61	0.24
American Indian tribes, specified:	113	0.44
Apache (4)	4	0.02
Cherokee (5)	24	0.09
Colville	1	0.00
Cree (1)	1	0.00
Delaware (11)	12	0.05
Iroquois	2	0.01
Latin American Indians (26)	62	0.24
Pueblo	1	0.00
Tohono O'Odham	3	0.01
All other tribes	3	0.01
American Indian tribes, not spec.	9	0.04
Arab:	140	0.55
Arab/Arabic	7	0.03
Jordanian	29	0.11
Lebanese	41	0.16
Palestinian	37	0.15
Other Arab	26	0.10
Asian:	1,604	6.30
Bangladeshi (2)	4	0.02
Cambodian (11)	22	0.09
Chinese, ex. Taiwanese (117)	143	0.56
Filipino (319)	346	1.36
Indian (680)	742	2.91
Indonesian (5)	9	0.04
Japanese (18)	25	0.10
Korean (44)	47	0.18
Malaysian	1	0.00
Pakistani (93)	125	0.49
Sri Lankan (18)	20	0.08
Thai (9)	9	0.04
Vietnamese (57)	61	0.24
Other Asian, specified (2)	2	0.01
Other Asian, not specified (17)	48	0.19
Austrian	77	0.30
Brazilian	63	0.25
British	5	0.02
Bulgarian	9	0.04
Canadian	53	0.21
Croatian	6	0.02
Czech	30	0.12
Danish	11	0.04
Dutch	34	0.13
Eastern European	40	0.16
English	132	0.52
European	225	0.89
French, except Basque	73	0.29
French Canadian	9	0.04
German	467	1.84
Greek	28	0.11
Guyanese	54	0.21
Hawaii Native/Pacific Islander:	175	0.69
Micronesian: (59)	73	0.29
Guamanian/Chamorro (59)	73	0.29
Polynesian:	11	0.04
Native Hawaiian	10	0.04
Samoan	1	0.00
Other Pac. Isl., not spec. (4)	91	0.36
Hispanic or Latino:	3,921	15.40
Central American:	1,193	4.69
Costa Rican	51	0.20
Guatemalan	960	3.77
Honduran	28	0.11
Nicaraguan	8	0.03
Panamanian	6	0.02
Salvadoran	125	0.49
Other Central American	15	0.06
Cuban	35	0.14
Dominican Republic	90	0.35
Mexican	464	1.82
Puerto Rican	692	2.72
South American:	638	2.51
Argentinean	8	0.03
Bolivian	2	0.01
Chilean	13	0.05
Colombian	52	0.20
Ecuadorian	500	1.96
Peruvian	37	0.15
Venezuelan	11	0.04
Other South American	15	0.06
Other Hispanic or Latino	809	3.18
Hungarian	80	0.32
Iranian	20	0.08
Irish	628	2.47
Israeli	50	0.20
Italian	758	2.99
Latvian	35	0.14
Lithuanian	40	0.16
Norwegian	35	0.14
Polish	969	3.82
Portuguese	12	0.05
Romanian	88	0.35
Russian	582	2.29
Scandinavian	8	0.03
Scotch-Irish	34	0.13
Scottish	19	0.07
Slovak	8	0.03
Swedish	16	0.06
Swiss	11	0.04
Ukrainian	297	1.17
United States or American	1,317	5.19
Welsh	16	0.06
West Indian, excl. Hispanic:	6,484	25.55
Barbadian	22	0.09
British West Indian	30	0.12
Haitian	5,349	21.08
Jamaican	974	3.84
Trinidadian and Tobagonian	20	0.08
West Indian	83	0.33
Other West Indian	6	0.02
White:	10,254	40.27
Not Hispanic (7,866)	8,128	31.92
Hispanic (1,868)	2,126	8.35
Yugoslavian	18	0.07

Stony Brook

Place Type: Census Designated Place
County: Suffolk
Population: 13,727

Ancestry/Race	Number	%
African American/Black:	204	1.49
Not Hispanic (158)	193	1.41
Hispanic (11)	11	0.08
African, sub-Saharan:	26	0.19
African	13	0.10
Sierra Leonean	13	0.10
Am. Ind. or Alaska Nat., not spec.	16	0.12
American Indian tribes, specified:	19	0.14
Cherokee (1)	8	0.06
Choctaw	2	0.01
Delaware	1	0.01
Iroquois (2)	2	0.01
Latin American Indians	3	0.02
Seminole	1	0.01
All other tribes (1)	2	0.01
American Indian tribes, not spec.	2	0.01
Arab:	14	0.10
Syrian	14	0.10
Asian:	874	6.37
Bangladeshi (4)	4	0.03
Chinese, ex. Taiwanese (411)	449	3.27
Filipino (26)	35	0.25
Indian (165)	174	1.27
Japanese (24)	30	0.22
Korean (87)	97	0.71
Laotian (2)	2	0.01
Pakistani (16)	27	0.20
Taiwanese (11)	27	0.20
Thai (7)	8	0.06
Vietnamese (11)	11	0.08
Other Asian, not specified (3)	10	0.07
Austrian	155	1.13
Belgian	20	0.15
British	78	0.57
Bulgarian	65	0.48
Canadian	49	0.36
Celtic	27	0.20
Croatian	45	0.33
Czech	43	0.31
Czechoslovakian	109	0.80
Danish	159	1.16
Dutch	188	1.37
Eastern European	104	0.76
English	1,032	7.54
Estonian	21	0.15
European	65	0.48
Finnish	90	0.66
French, except Basque	162	1.18
French Canadian	103	0.75
German	2,622	19.16
Greek	237	1.73
Hawaii Native/Pacific Islander:	17	0.12
Micronesian:	1	0.01
Guamanian/Chamorro	1	0.01
Polynesian: (3)	3	0.02
Native Hawaiian (3)	3	0.02
Other Pac. Isl., not spec.	13	0.09
Hispanic or Latino:	334	2.43
Central American:	15	0.11
Guatemalan	4	0.03
Honduran	1	0.01
Panamanian	3	0.02
Salvadoran	7	0.05
Cuban	28	0.20
Dominican Republic	5	0.04
Mexican	23	0.17
Puerto Rican	132	0.96
South American:	54	0.39
Argentinean	11	0.08
Bolivian	6	0.04
Chilean	1	0.01
Colombian	21	0.15
Ecuadorian	4	0.03
Peruvian	5	0.04
Venezuelan	1	0.01
Other South American	5	0.04
Other Hispanic or Latino	77	0.56
Hungarian	178	1.30
Iranian	79	0.58
Irish	3,131	22.88
Israeli	45	0.33
Italian	3,316	24.23

Notes: 1. Figures in the "Number" column do not add up to the total population due to: a) Ancestry/Race overlap — e.g. persons can report being both White and Irish, b) persons of Hispanic origin can report being any race, c) persons reporting two ancestries are counted in both categories. 2. Numbers in parentheses indicate the number of persons reporting this ancestry/race alone, not in combination with any other ancestry/race. 3. Refer to the Explanation of Data in the front of the book for more detailed information.

Ancestry/Race	Number	%
Latvian	33	0.24
Lithuanian	64	0.47
Maltese	15	0.11
Northern European	19	0.14
Norwegian	128	0.94
Polish	939	6.86
Portuguese	80	0.58
Romanian	54	0.39
Russian	731	5.34
Scandinavian	49	0.36
Scotch-Irish	186	1.36
Scottish	269	1.97
Slavic	9	0.07
Swedish	153	1.12
Swiss	45	0.33
Turkish	9	0.07
Ukrainian	87	0.64
United States or American	520	3.80
Welsh	28	0.20
West Indian, excl. Hispanic:	15	0.11
Jamaican	8	0.06
Trinidadian and Tobagonian	7	0.05
White:	12,697	92.50
Not Hispanic (12,320)	12,403	90.35
Hispanic (284)	294	2.14
Yugoslavian	16	0.12

Stony Point

Place Type: Town
County: Rockland
Population: 14,244

Ancestry/Race	Number	%
African American/Black:	239	1.68
Not Hispanic (163)	216	1.52
Hispanic (18)	23	0.16
African, sub-Saharan:	18	0.13
African	10	0.07
Nigerian	8	0.06
Am. Ind. or Alaska Nat., not spec.	21	0.15
American Indian tribes, specified:	46	0.32
Apache (2)	5	0.04
Blackfeet	1	0.01
Cherokee (2)	12	0.08
Creek	1	0.01
Delaware (9)	20	0.14
Iroquois (2)	3	0.02
Navajo	1	0.01
All other tribes (3)	3	0.02
American Indian tribes, not spec.	1	0.01
Arab:	37	0.26
Arab/Arabic	12	0.08
Jordanian	12	0.08
Lebanese	13	0.09
Armenian	7	0.05
Asian:	236	1.66
Chinese, ex. Taiwanese (41)	51	0.36
Filipino (34)	44	0.31
Indian (60)	70	0.49
Japanese (5)	11	0.08
Korean (35)	43	0.30
Pakistani (2)	2	0.01
Sri Lankan (1)	1	0.01
Thai (2)	3	0.02
Vietnamese (1)	2	0.01
Other Asian, specified	1	0.01
Other Asian, not specified (3)	8	0.06
Austrian	148	1.04
Belgian	19	0.13
Brazilian	7	0.05
British	91	0.64
Canadian	18	0.13
Croatian	7	0.05
Czech	40	0.28
Czechoslovakian	65	0.46
Danish	14	0.10
Dutch	163	1.14
English	898	6.30
European	54	0.38
French, except Basque	293	2.06
French Canadian	99	0.70
German	1,970	13.83
Greek	204	1.43
Guyanese	27	0.19
Hawaii Native/Pacific Islander:	5	0.04
Polynesian: (1)	2	0.01
Native Hawaiian (1)	2	0.01
Other Pac. Isl., not spec. (2)	3	0.02
Hispanic or Latino:	974	6.84
Central American:	16	0.11
Costa Rican	4	0.03
Guatemalan	2	0.01
Honduran	1	0.01
Nicaraguan	3	0.02
Salvadoran	6	0.04
Cuban	42	0.29
Dominican Republic	98	0.69
Mexican	60	0.42
Puerto Rican	557	3.91
South American:	56	0.39
Argentinean	12	0.08
Chilean	4	0.03
Colombian	26	0.18
Ecuadorian	10	0.07
Peruvian	3	0.02
Venezuelan	1	0.01
Other Hispanic or Latino	145	1.02
Hungarian	190	1.33
Irish	5,104	35.83
Italian	4,375	30.71
Latvian	19	0.13
Lithuanian	32	0.22
Maltese	5	0.04
Norwegian	110	0.77
Polish	612	4.30
Portuguese	30	0.21
Romanian	17	0.12
Russian	255	1.79
Scandinavian	21	0.15
Scotch-Irish	142	1.00
Scottish	177	1.24
Slavic	27	0.19
Slovak	105	0.74
Swedish	72	0.51
Swiss	11	0.08
Ukrainian	165	1.16
United States or American	479	3.36
Welsh	46	0.32
West Indian, excl. Hispanic:	125	0.88
Dutch West Indian	26	0.18
Haitian	27	0.19
Jamaican	72	0.51
White:	13,585	95.37
Not Hispanic (12,756)	12,863	90.30
Hispanic (681)	722	5.07
Yugoslavian	7	0.05

Suffern

Place Type: Village
County: Rockland
Population: 11,006

Ancestry/Race	Number	%
African American/Black:	450	4.09
Not Hispanic (352)	403	3.66
Hispanic (36)	47	0.43
African, sub-Saharan:	30	0.27
African	20	0.18
Cape Verdean	10	0.09
Am. Ind. or Alaska Nat., not spec.	31	0.28
Alsatian	5	0.05
American Indian tribes, specified:	57	0.52
Apache (1)	1	0.01
Blackfeet	1	0.01
Cherokee (2)	7	0.06
Chippewa	1	0.01
Comanche (1)	1	0.01
Delaware (4)	6	0.05
Iroquois (2)	5	0.05
Latin American Indians (4)	32	0.29
All other tribes	3	0.03
American Indian tribes, not spec.	4	0.04
Arab:	67	0.61
Arab/Arabic	44	0.40
Iraqi	4	0.04
Jordanian	9	0.08
Moroccan	10	0.09
Asian:	352	3.20
Bangladeshi (5)	6	0.05
Cambodian (11)	11	0.10
Chinese, ex. Taiwanese (38)	48	0.44
Filipino (35)	39	0.35
Indian (132)	145	1.32
Japanese (14)	16	0.15
Korean (35)	39	0.35
Pakistani (23)	26	0.24
Taiwanese (4)	4	0.04
Thai (2)	2	0.02
Vietnamese (6)	6	0.05
Other Asian, specified	2	0.02
Other Asian, not specified (2)	8	0.07
Australian	17	0.15
Austrian	120	1.09
Brazilian	63	0.57
Canadian	64	0.58
Croatian	14	0.13
Czech	93	0.84
Czechoslovakian	32	0.29
Danish	14	0.13
Dutch	193	1.75
Eastern European	53	0.48
English	734	6.67
European	92	0.84
Finnish	13	0.12
French, except Basque	169	1.54
French Canadian	12	0.11
German	1,164	10.58
Greek	106	0.96
Hawaii Native/Pacific Islander:	37	0.34
Polynesian:	4	0.04
Native Hawaiian	3	0.03
Samoan	1	0.01
Other Pac. Isl., specified	2	0.02
Other Pac. Isl., not spec. (10)	31	0.28
Hispanic or Latino:	1,416	12.87
Central American:	88	0.80
Costa Rican	10	0.09
Guatemalan	33	0.30
Honduran	3	0.03
Nicaraguan	1	0.01
Panamanian	6	0.05
Salvadoran	31	0.28
Other Central American	4	0.04
Cuban	26	0.24
Dominican Republic	42	0.38
Mexican	595	5.41
Puerto Rican	288	2.62
South American:	200	1.82
Argentinean	12	0.11
Bolivian	1	0.01
Chilean	9	0.08
Colombian	77	0.70
Ecuadorian	19	0.17
Peruvian	64	0.58
Venezuelan	2	0.02
Other South American	16	0.15
Other Hispanic or Latino	177	1.61
Hungarian	229	2.08
Iranian	74	0.67
Irish	2,388	21.70
Israeli	44	0.40
Italian	2,354	21.39
Latvian	10	0.09
Lithuanian	58	0.53
Northern European	4	0.04
Norwegian	46	0.42
Polish	622	5.65
Portuguese	15	0.14

Notes: 1. Figures in the "Number" column do not add up to the total population due to: a) Ancestry/Race overlap — e.g. persons can report being both White and Irish, b) persons of Hispanic origin can report being any race, c) persons reporting two ancestries are counted in both categories. 2. Numbers in parentheses indicate the number of persons reporting this ancestry/race alone, not in combination with any other ancestry/race. 3. Refer to the Explanation of Data in the front of the book for more detailed information.

Romanian	81	0.74
Russian	628	5.71
Scotch-Irish	107	0.97
Scottish	123	1.12
Serbian	6	0.05
Slavic	8	0.07
Slovak	23	0.21
Swedish	105	0.95
Swiss	31	0.28
Turkish	17	0.15
Ukrainian	90	0.82
United States or American	406	3.69
Welsh	27	0.25
West Indian, excl. Hispanic:	97	0.88
Barbadian	4	0.04
Haitian	62	0.56
Jamaican	7	0.06
West Indian	24	0.22
White:	9,701	88.14
Not Hispanic (8,777)	8,856	80.47
Hispanic (780)	845	7.68

Sullivan

Place Type: Town
County: Madison
Population: 14,991

Ancestry/Race	Number	%
African American/Black:	71	0.47
Not Hispanic (45)	67	0.45
Hispanic (4)	4	0.03
Am. Ind. or Alaska Nat., not spec.	29	0.19
American Indian tribes, specified:	83	0.55
Cherokee (5)	12	0.08
Iroquois (39)	62	0.41
Latin American Indians (1)	1	0.01
Sioux	1	0.01
Yuman	1	0.01
All other tribes	6	0.04
Arab:	67	0.45
Jordanian	67	0.45
Asian:	55	0.37
Cambodian (4)	5	0.03
Chinese, ex. Taiwanese (4)	10	0.07
Filipino (9)	17	0.11
Indian (2)	3	0.02
Japanese (1)	2	0.01
Korean (3)	6	0.04
Thai (2)	3	0.02
Vietnamese (9)	10	0.07
Austrian	46	0.31
British	36	0.24
Canadian	61	0.41
Celtic	24	0.16
Czech	49	0.33
Czechoslovakian	13	0.09
Danish	108	0.72
Dutch	721	4.81
Eastern European	17	0.11
English	2,979	19.87
European	67	0.45
French, except Basque	1,143	7.62
French Canadian	415	2.77
German	3,303	22.03
Greek	10	0.07
Hawaii Native/Pacific Islander:	8	0.05
Micronesian:	3	0.02
Guamanian/Chamorro	3	0.02
Polynesian:	5	0.03
Native Hawaiian	5	0.03
Hispanic or Latino:	81	0.54
Central American:	4	0.03
Honduran	1	0.01
Panamanian	3	0.02
Cuban	5	0.03
Dominican Republic	4	0.03
Mexican	19	0.13
Puerto Rican	16	0.11
South American:	13	0.09
Argentinean	4	0.03
Colombian	5	0.03
Ecuadorian	3	0.02
Other South American	1	0.01
Other Hispanic or Latino	20	0.13
Hungarian	46	0.31
Irish	3,267	21.79
Italian	1,652	11.02
Latvian	21	0.14
Lithuanian	5	0.03
Macedonian	6	0.04
Northern European	7	0.05
Norwegian	90	0.60
Pennsylvania German	6	0.04
Polish	1,037	6.92
Portuguese	47	0.31
Russian	68	0.45
Scandinavian	11	0.07
Scotch-Irish	185	1.23
Scottish	294	1.96
Slavic	14	0.09
Slovak	6	0.04
Swedish	123	0.82
Swiss	160	1.07
Turkish	5	0.03
Ukrainian	130	0.87
United States or American	702	4.68
Welsh	246	1.64
White:	14,827	98.91
Not Hispanic (14,677)	14,768	98.51
Hispanic (51)	59	0.39

Sweden

Place Type: Town
County: Monroe
Population: 13,716

Ancestry/Race	Number	%
Acadian/Cajun	8	0.06
African American/Black:	598	4.36
Not Hispanic (498)	574	4.18
Hispanic (12)	24	0.17
African, sub-Saharan:	64	0.47
African	31	0.23
Nigerian	33	0.24
Am. Ind. or Alaska Nat., not spec.	16	0.12
American Indian tribes, specified:	54	0.39
Blackfeet (1)	4	0.03
Cherokee (2)	11	0.08
Chickasaw	1	0.01
Chippewa	1	0.01
Creek (5)	5	0.04
Iroquois (14)	21	0.15
Latin American Indians (4)	6	0.04
Sioux	3	0.02
All other tribes	2	0.01
American Indian tribes, not spec.	9	0.07
Arab:	34	0.25
Arab/Arabic	6	0.04
Lebanese	19	0.14
Other Arab	9	0.07
Armenian	7	0.05
Asian:	177	1.29
Bangladeshi	4	0.03
Cambodian (2)	2	0.01
Chinese, ex. Taiwanese (42)	49	0.36
Filipino (8)	12	0.09
Indian (25)	31	0.23
Indonesian (2)	3	0.02
Japanese (9)	20	0.15
Korean (36)	39	0.28
Laotian (3)	3	0.02
Malaysian (1)	1	0.01
Taiwanese	1	0.01
Thai (1)	1	0.01
Vietnamese (6)	8	0.06
Other Asian, not specified	3	0.02
Australian	6	0.04
Austrian	63	0.46
Belgian	11	0.08
British	34	0.25
Canadian	75	0.55
Celtic	6	0.04
Croatian	19	0.14
Czech	70	0.51
Czechoslovakian	14	0.10
Danish	55	0.40
Dutch	450	3.28
English	2,389	17.42
European	110	0.80
Finnish	9	0.07
French, except Basque	591	4.31
French Canadian	175	1.28
German	3,178	23.17
Greek	51	0.37
Guyanese	5	0.04
Hawaii Native/Pacific Islander:	18	0.13
Micronesian: (1)	1	0.01
Guamanian/Chamorro (1)	1	0.01
Polynesian: (2)	8	0.06
Native Hawaiian (2)	5	0.04
Samoan	3	0.02
Other Pac. Isl., not spec. (5)	9	0.07
Hispanic or Latino:	395	2.88
Central American:	9	0.07
Costa Rican	1	0.01
Guatemalan	3	0.02
Honduran	1	0.01
Panamanian	1	0.01
Salvadoran	2	0.01
Other Central American	1	0.01
Cuban	9	0.07
Dominican Republic	14	0.10
Mexican	164	1.20
Puerto Rican	133	0.97
South American:	24	0.17
Bolivian	3	0.02
Chilean	4	0.03
Colombian	4	0.03
Ecuadorian	7	0.05
Paraguayan	1	0.01
Peruvian	5	0.04
Other Hispanic or Latino	42	0.31
Hungarian	105	0.77
Iranian	7	0.05
Irish	2,445	17.83
Israeli	12	0.09
Italian	1,929	14.06
Latvian	6	0.04
Lithuanian	32	0.23
Macedonian	8	0.06
Northern European	16	0.12
Norwegian	76	0.55
Pennsylvania German	10	0.07
Polish	648	4.72
Portuguese	2	0.01
Romanian	8	0.06
Russian	82	0.60
Scandinavian	10	0.07
Scotch-Irish	235	1.71
Scottish	392	2.86
Slovak	65	0.47
Swedish	206	1.50
Swiss	18	0.13
Turkish	5	0.04
Ukrainian	123	0.90
United States or American	788	5.75
Welsh	163	1.19
West Indian, excl. Hispanic:	57	0.42
Barbadian	5	0.04
Haitian	18	0.13
Jamaican	28	0.20
Trinidadian and Tobagonian	6	0.04
White:	12,857	93.74
Not Hispanic (12,494)	12,629	92.07
Hispanic (205)	228	1.66

Notes: 1. Figures in the "Number" column do not add up to the total population due to: a) Ancestry/Race overlap — e.g. persons can report being both White and Irish, b) persons of Hispanic origin can report being any race, c) persons reporting two ancestries are counted in both categories. 2. Numbers in parentheses indicate the number of persons reporting this ancestry/race alone, not in combination with any other ancestry/race. 3. Refer to the Explanation of Data in the front of the book for more detailed information.

Syosset

Place Type: Census Designated Place
County: Nassau
Population: 18,544

Ancestry/Race	Number	%
Afghan	21	0.11
African American/Black:	125	0.67
Not Hispanic (85)	109	0.59
Hispanic (8)	16	0.09
African, sub-Saharan:	12	0.06
African	12	0.06
Am. Ind. or Alaska Nat., not spec.	8	0.04
Albanian	5	0.03
American Indian tribes, specified:	21	0.11
Cherokee	3	0.02
Iroquois	6	0.03
Latin American Indians	8	0.04
Potawatomi	1	0.01
Sioux (2)	2	0.01
All other tribes (1)	1	0.01
American Indian tribes, not spec.	3	0.02
Arab:	108	0.58
Egyptian	58	0.31
Iraqi	17	0.09
Lebanese	8	0.04
Palestinian	6	0.03
Syrian	19	0.10
Armenian	108	0.58
Asian:	2,440	13.16
Bangladeshi (6)	6	0.03
Chinese, ex. Taiwanese (778)	803	4.33
Filipino (91)	105	0.57
Indian (535)	577	3.11
Indonesian (9)	9	0.05
Japanese (121)	125	0.67
Korean (676)	685	3.69
Pakistani (48)	56	0.30
Sri Lankan (5)	6	0.03
Taiwanese (33)	33	0.18
Thai	1	0.01
Vietnamese (7)	9	0.05
Other Asian, not specified (17)	25	0.13
Austrian	423	2.28
Belgian	31	0.17
Brazilian	15	0.08
British	20	0.11
Bulgarian	18	0.10
Canadian	34	0.18
Croatian	97	0.52
Cypriot	22	0.12
Czech	74	0.40
Czechoslovakian	41	0.22
Danish	21	0.11
Dutch	126	0.68
Eastern European	269	1.45
English	725	3.91
European	195	1.05
Finnish	20	0.11
French, except Basque	139	0.75
French Canadian	35	0.19
German	2,209	11.91
Greek	478	2.58
Guyanese	9	0.05
Hawaii Native/Pacific Islander:	5	0.03
Polynesian: (2)	2	0.01
Samoan (2)	2	0.01
Other Pac. Isl., not spec.	3	0.02
Hispanic or Latino:	542	2.92
Central American:	59	0.32
Costa Rican	3	0.02
Guatemalan	4	0.02
Honduran	9	0.05
Nicaraguan	1	0.01
Salvadoran	42	0.23
Cuban	30	0.16
Dominican Republic	25	0.13
Mexican	55	0.30
Puerto Rican	122	0.66
South American:	134	0.72
Argentinean	14	0.08
Bolivian	3	0.02
Chilean	9	0.05
Colombian	68	0.37
Ecuadorian	22	0.12
Paraguayan	1	0.01
Peruvian	10	0.05
Venezuelan	3	0.02
Other South American	4	0.02
Other Hispanic or Latino	117	0.63
Hungarian	238	1.28
Icelander	8	0.04
Iranian	70	0.38
Irish	2,560	13.81
Israeli	30	0.16
Italian	3,933	21.21
Latvian	44	0.24
Lithuanian	140	0.75
Maltese	38	0.20
Northern European	5	0.03
Norwegian	84	0.45
Polish	1,521	8.20
Portuguese	19	0.10
Romanian	177	0.95
Russian	1,285	6.93
Scandinavian	20	0.11
Scotch-Irish	76	0.41
Scottish	179	0.97
Slavic	16	0.09
Slovak	44	0.24
Swedish	117	0.63
Swiss	27	0.15
Turkish	41	0.22
Ukrainian	124	0.67
United States or American	927	5.00
Welsh	18	0.10
West Indian, excl. Hispanic:	12	0.06
Barbadian	7	0.04
Jamaican	5	0.03
White:	15,980	86.17
Not Hispanic (15,412)	15,531	83.75
Hispanic (398)	449	2.42
Yugoslavian	15	0.08

Syracuse

Place Type: City
County: Onondaga
Population: 147,306

Ancestry/Race	Number	%
Acadian/Cajun	8	0.01
African American/Black:	40,436	27.45
Not Hispanic (36,246)	38,929	26.43
Hispanic (1,090)	1,507	1.02
African, sub-Saharan:	2,179	1.48
African	1,780	1.21
Cape Verdean	28	0.02
Ethiopian	42	0.03
Ghanian	17	0.01
Kenyan	60	0.04
Liberian	92	0.06
Nigerian	25	0.02
Sierra Leonean	6	0.00
Somalian	31	0.02
South African	4	0.00
Zairian	20	0.01
Other sub-Saharan African	74	0.05
Alaska Native tribes, specified:	7	0.00
Alaska Athabascan	2	0.00
Aleut (1)	1	0.00
Eskimo	4	0.00
Alaska Native tribes, not specified	1	0.00
Am. Ind. or Alaska Nat., not spec.	1,081	0.73
Albanian	170	0.12
Alsatian	7	0.00
American Indian tribes, specified:	2,140	1.45
Apache (10)	29	0.02
Blackfeet (14)	91	0.06
Cherokee (33)	218	0.15
Cheyenne (3)	5	0.00
Chippewa (8)	13	0.01
Choctaw (5)	18	0.01
Comanche (1)	5	0.00
Cree (1)	4	0.00
Creek (1)	3	0.00
Crow (2)	3	0.00
Delaware	4	0.00
Houma (1)	4	0.00
Iroquois (970)	1,511	1.03
Kiowa	1	0.00
Latin American Indians (20)	47	0.03
Lumbee	1	0.00
Navajo (2)	6	0.00
Pueblo	2	0.00
Seminole (5)	14	0.01
Shoshone (1)	5	0.00
Sioux (7)	28	0.02
Ute	1	0.00
Yakama (1)	1	0.00
Yaqui	1	0.00
Yuman (2)	2	0.00
All other tribes (42)	123	0.08
American Indian tribes, not spec.	130	0.09
Arab:	1,034	0.70
Arab/Arabic	370	0.25
Egyptian	69	0.05
Iraqi	6	0.00
Jordanian	35	0.02
Lebanese	289	0.20
Moroccan	6	0.00
Palestinian	66	0.04
Syrian	147	0.10
Other Arab	46	0.03
Armenian	204	0.14
Asian:	5,766	3.91
Bangladeshi (30)	37	0.03
Cambodian (93)	108	0.07
Chinese, ex. Taiwanese (789)	920	0.62
Filipino (157)	252	0.17
Hmong (148)	174	0.12
Indian (754)	851	0.58
Indonesian (35)	43	0.03
Japanese (169)	236	0.16
Korean (687)	745	0.51
Laotian (121)	166	0.11
Malaysian (29)	32	0.02
Pakistani (51)	68	0.05
Sri Lankan (5)	7	0.00
Taiwanese (122)	155	0.11
Thai (85)	103	0.07
Vietnamese (1,475)	1,600	1.09
Other Asian, specified (11)	25	0.02
Other Asian, not specified (99)	244	0.17
Assyrian/Chaldean/Syriac	6	0.00
Australian	11	0.01
Austrian	432	0.29
Belgian	40	0.03
Brazilian	85	0.06
British	587	0.40
Bulgarian	65	0.04
Canadian	435	0.30
Celtic	106	0.07
Croatian	124	0.08
Cypriot	18	0.01
Czech	187	0.13
Czechoslovakian	137	0.09
Danish	253	0.17
Dutch	2,244	1.52
Eastern European	113	0.08
English	11,140	7.56
European	751	0.51
Finnish	106	0.07
French, except Basque	6,203	4.21
French Canadian	2,539	1.72
German	17,942	12.18
Greek	617	0.42
Guyanese	37	0.03
Hawaii Native/Pacific Islander:	203	0.14

Notes: 1. Figures in the "Number" column do not add up to the total population due to: a) Ancestry/Race overlap — e.g. persons can report being both White and Irish, b) persons of Hispanic origin can report being any race, c) persons reporting two ancestries are counted in both categories. 2. Numbers in parentheses indicate the number of persons reporting this ancestry/race alone, not in combination with any other ancestry/race. 3. Refer to the Explanation of Data in the front of the book for more detailed information.

Melanesian: (1)	1	0.00
Fijian (1)	1	0.00
Micronesian: (8)	21	0.01
Guamanian/Chamorro (6)	17	0.01
Other Micronesian (2)	4	0.00
Polynesian: (50)	99	0.07
Native Hawaiian (28)	60	0.04
Samoan (21)	35	0.02
Tongan (1)	2	0.00
Other Polynesian	2	0.00
Other Pac. Isl., specified	11	0.01
Other Pac. Isl., not spec. (13)	71	0.05
Hispanic or Latino:	7,768	5.27
Central American:	152	0.10
Costa Rican	14	0.01
Guatemalan	44	0.03
Honduran	12	0.01
Nicaraguan	11	0.01
Panamanian	49	0.03
Salvadoran	19	0.01
Other Central American	3	0.00
Cuban	552	0.37
Dominican Republic	265	0.18
Mexican	610	0.41
Puerto Rican	4,885	3.32
South American:	289	0.20
Argentinean	18	0.01
Bolivian	10	0.01
Chilean	22	0.01
Colombian	87	0.06
Ecuadorian	55	0.04
Paraguayan	2	0.00
Peruvian	47	0.03
Uruguayan	1	0.00
Venezuelan	35	0.02
Other South American	12	0.01
Other Hispanic or Latino	1,015	0.69
Hungarian	597	0.41
Iranian	63	0.04
Irish	23,375	15.87
Israeli	56	0.04
Italian	20,778	14.10
Latvian	109	0.07
Lithuanian	227	0.15
Macedonian	139	0.09
Maltese	4	0.00
New Zealander	7	0.00
Northern European	107	0.07
Norwegian	437	0.30
Pennsylvania German	46	0.03
Polish	7,424	5.04
Portuguese	249	0.17
Romanian	164	0.11
Russian	1,612	1.09
Scandinavian	89	0.06
Scotch-Irish	1,669	1.13
Scottish	2,044	1.39
Serbian	8	0.01
Slavic	60	0.04
Slovak	268	0.18
Slovene	51	0.03
Swedish	958	0.65
Swiss	282	0.19
Turkish	241	0.16
Ukrainian	1,361	0.92
United States or American	3,489	2.37
Welsh	938	0.64
West Indian, excl. Hispanic:	1,197	0.81
Bahamian	6	0.00
Barbadian	25	0.02
British West Indian	58	0.04
Haitian	134	0.09
Jamaican	729	0.49
Trinidadian and Tobagonian	51	0.03
U.S. Virgin Islander	8	0.01
West Indian	186	0.13
White:	98,899	67.14
Not Hispanic (91,928)	95,595	64.90
Hispanic (2,735)	3,304	2.24
Yugoslavian	634	0.43

Tarrytown

Place Type: Village
County: Westchester
Population: 11,090

Ancestry/Race	Number	%
African American/Black:	903	8.14
Not Hispanic (705)	790	7.12
Hispanic (76)	113	1.02
African, sub-Saharan:	56	0.50
African	26	0.23
Cape Verdean	7	0.06
Ethiopian	6	0.05
Ghanian	5	0.05
South African	6	0.05
Other sub-Saharan African	6	0.05
Am. Ind. or Alaska Nat., not spec.	31	0.28
American Indian tribes, specified:	32	0.29
Apache	1	0.01
Blackfeet	2	0.02
Cherokee	9	0.08
Chickasaw	3	0.03
Houma	1	0.01
Iroquois (1)	4	0.04
Latin American Indians (6)	9	0.08
Seminole	1	0.01
Sioux	1	0.01
All other tribes	1	0.01
American Indian tribes, not spec.	9	0.08
Arab:	71	0.64
Iraqi	62	0.56
Syrian	9	0.08
Armenian	12	0.11
Asian:	809	7.29
Bangladeshi (5)	5	0.05
Chinese, ex. Taiwanese (144)	163	1.47
Filipino (52)	59	0.53
Indian (244)	256	2.31
Indonesian (2)	2	0.02
Japanese (128)	160	1.44
Korean (117)	130	1.17
Laotian	1	0.01
Pakistani (9)	10	0.09
Sri Lankan	1	0.01
Taiwanese (4)	4	0.04
Thai (1)	2	0.02
Vietnamese (2)	3	0.03
Other Asian, not specified (3)	13	0.12
Austrian	63	0.57
Belgian	11	0.10
Brazilian	21	0.19
British	9	0.08
Bulgarian	9	0.08
Canadian	15	0.14
Celtic	20	0.18
Czech	49	0.44
Czechoslovakian	30	0.27
Danish	115	1.04
Dutch	91	0.82
Eastern European	136	1.23
English	641	5.78
European	126	1.14
Finnish	8	0.07
French, except Basque	191	1.72
French Canadian	98	0.88
German	831	7.49
Greek	61	0.55
Hawaii Native/Pacific Islander:	10	0.09
Micronesian: (3)	3	0.03
Guamanian/Chamorro (3)	3	0.03
Polynesian: (2)	3	0.03
Native Hawaiian (2)	3	0.03
Other Pac. Isl., not spec.	4	0.04
Hispanic or Latino:	1,793	16.17
Central American:	44	0.40
Costa Rican	2	0.02
Guatemalan	14	0.13
Honduran	3	0.03
Nicaraguan	2	0.02
Panamanian	6	0.05
Salvadoran	13	0.12
Other Central American	4	0.04
Cuban	213	1.92
Dominican Republic	271	2.44
Mexican	87	0.78
Puerto Rican	291	2.62
South American:	477	4.30
Argentinean	11	0.10
Chilean	54	0.49
Colombian	81	0.73
Ecuadorian	267	2.41
Paraguayan	3	0.03
Peruvian	43	0.39
Uruguayan	9	0.08
Venezuelan	2	0.02
Other South American	7	0.06
Other Hispanic or Latino	410	3.70
Hungarian	150	1.35
Icelander	8	0.07
Iranian	69	0.62
Irish	2,045	18.44
Israeli	24	0.22
Italian	2,111	19.04
Latvian	26	0.23
Lithuanian	80	0.72
Northern European	10	0.09
Norwegian	29	0.26
Pennsylvania German	6	0.05
Polish	519	4.68
Portuguese	68	0.61
Romanian	23	0.21
Russian	380	3.43
Scotch-Irish	91	0.82
Scottish	102	0.92
Slavic	28	0.25
Slovak	99	0.89
Swedish	35	0.32
Swiss	46	0.41
Turkish	24	0.22
Ukrainian	77	0.69
United States or American	364	3.28
Welsh	43	0.39
West Indian, excl. Hispanic:	58	0.52
Bahamian	8	0.07
Barbadian	16	0.14
British West Indian	6	0.05
Haitian	5	0.05
Jamaican	13	0.12
Trinidadian and Tobagonian	5	0.05
West Indian	5	0.05
White:	8,912	80.36
Not Hispanic (7,614)	7,798	70.32
Hispanic (974)	1,114	10.05

Terryville

Place Type: Census Designated Place
County: Suffolk
Population: 10,589

Ancestry/Race	Number	%
African American/Black:	210	1.98
Not Hispanic (154)	181	1.71
Hispanic (18)	29	0.27
African, sub-Saharan:	54	0.51
African	49	0.46
Nigerian	5	0.05
Am. Ind. or Alaska Nat., not spec.	15	0.14
Albanian	8	0.08
American Indian tribes, specified:	10	0.09
Apache (1)	1	0.01
Cherokee (1)	8	0.08
Latin American Indians	1	0.01
American Indian tribes, not spec.	1	0.01
Arab:	115	1.09
Egyptian	14	0.13
Lebanese	79	0.75
Palestinian	22	0.21
Armenian	27	0.25

Notes: 1. Figures in the "Number" column do not add up to the total population due to: a) Ancestry/Race overlap — e.g. persons can report being both White and Irish, b) persons of Hispanic origin can report being any race, c) persons reporting two ancestries are counted in both categories. 2. Numbers in parentheses indicate the number of persons reporting this ancestry/race alone, not in combination with any other ancestry/race. 3. Refer to the Explanation of Data in the front of the book for more detailed information.

Asian:	291	2.75
Bangladeshi (7)	8	0.08
Chinese, ex. Taiwanese (59)	67	0.63
Filipino (40)	47	0.44
Indian (82)	88	0.83
Indonesian	1	0.01
Japanese (5)	12	0.11
Korean (22)	27	0.25
Laotian (4)	4	0.04
Pakistani (12)	12	0.11
Thai (2)	4	0.04
Vietnamese (5)	6	0.06
Other Asian, not specified (3)	15	0.14
Australian	9	0.08
Austrian	106	1.00
British	47	0.44
Canadian	40	0.38
Croatian	26	0.25
Czech	25	0.24
Czechoslovakian	23	0.22
Danish	14	0.13
Dutch	49	0.46
Eastern European	29	0.27
English	520	4.91
Finnish	31	0.29
French, except Basque	259	2.45
French Canadian	42	0.40
German	1,822	17.20
Greek	453	4.28
Hawaii Native/Pacific Islander:	10	0.09
Polynesian:	5	0.05
Native Hawaiian	3	0.03
Other Polynesian	2	0.02
Other Pac. Isl., not spec. (1)	5	0.05
Hispanic or Latino:	1,007	9.51
Central American:	33	0.31
Costa Rican	1	0.01
Guatemalan	13	0.12
Honduran	9	0.08
Nicaraguan	1	0.01
Salvadoran	9	0.08
Cuban	26	0.25
Dominican Republic	335	3.16
Mexican	23	0.22
Puerto Rican	324	3.06
South American:	60	0.57
Argentinean	5	0.05
Bolivian	1	0.01
Colombian	27	0.25
Ecuadorian	9	0.08
Peruvian	6	0.06
Other South American	12	0.11
Other Hispanic or Latino	206	1.95
Hungarian	72	0.68
Irish	2,216	20.92
Italian	3,908	36.90
Lithuanian	22	0.21
Maltese	16	0.15
Norwegian	98	0.93
Pennsylvania German	13	0.12
Polish	712	6.72
Portuguese	74	0.70
Romanian	9	0.08
Russian	257	2.43
Scotch-Irish	72	0.68
Scottish	58	0.55
Slovak	27	0.25
Swedish	94	0.89
Swiss	72	0.68
Turkish	12	0.11
Ukrainian	80	0.76
United States or American	371	3.50
Welsh	65	0.61
West Indian, excl. Hispanic:	144	1.36
British West Indian	54	0.51
Haitian	15	0.14
Jamaican	11	0.10
West Indian	64	0.60
White:	9,850	93.02
Not Hispanic (9,064)	9,143	86.34
Hispanic (658)	707	6.68

Thompson

Place Type: Town
County: Sullivan
Population: 14,189

Ancestry/Race	Number	%
African American/Black:	2,604	18.35
Not Hispanic (2,268)	2,411	16.99
Hispanic (135)	193	1.36
African, sub-Saharan:	45	0.32
African	43	0.30
Nigerian	2	0.01
Am. Ind. or Alaska Nat., not spec.	39	0.27
Albanian	40	0.28
American Indian tribes, specified:	42	0.30
Apache	3	0.02
Blackfeet (3)	3	0.02
Cherokee (4)	19	0.13
Comanche	1	0.01
Creek	1	0.01
Delaware (2)	2	0.01
Iroquois (2)	3	0.02
Latin American Indians (4)	7	0.05
Navajo (1)	2	0.01
Sioux	1	0.01
American Indian tribes, not spec.	2	0.01
Arab:	24	0.17
Lebanese	24	0.17
Armenian	27	0.19
Asian:	306	2.16
Bangladeshi (1)	1	0.01
Cambodian (1)	1	0.01
Chinese, ex. Taiwanese (81)	91	0.64
Filipino (30)	34	0.24
Indian (51)	56	0.39
Indonesian	1	0.01
Japanese (11)	14	0.10
Korean (43)	48	0.34
Pakistani (20)	28	0.20
Taiwanese (2)	3	0.02
Vietnamese (1)	1	0.01
Other Asian, not specified (18)	28	0.20
Austrian	63	0.44
Belgian	12	0.08
Brazilian	35	0.25
British	35	0.25
Canadian	16	0.11
Cypriot	21	0.15
Czech	12	0.08
Czechoslovakian	15	0.11
Danish	18	0.13
Dutch	263	1.85
Eastern European	61	0.43
English	860	6.03
European	52	0.36
French, except Basque	304	2.13
French Canadian	59	0.41
German	1,561	10.95
Greek	83	0.58
Hawaii Native/Pacific Islander:	9	0.06
Polynesian: (2)	3	0.02
Native Hawaiian (1)	1	0.01
Samoan (1)	1	0.01
Other Polynesian	1	0.01
Other Pac. Isl., not spec. (2)	6	0.04
Hispanic or Latino:	2,066	14.56
Central American:	88	0.62
Costa Rican	18	0.13
Guatemalan	6	0.04
Honduran	30	0.21
Nicaraguan	5	0.04
Panamanian	14	0.10
Salvadoran	15	0.11
Cuban	60	0.42
Dominican Republic	22	0.16
Mexican	168	1.18
Puerto Rican	1,038	7.32
South American:	279	1.97
Argentinean	6	0.04
Chilean	1	0.01
Colombian	187	1.32
Ecuadorian	12	0.08
Peruvian	60	0.42
Other South American	13	0.09
Other Hispanic or Latino	411	2.90
Hungarian	98	0.69
Irish	1,634	11.46
Israeli	10	0.07
Italian	1,399	9.82
Latvian	8	0.06
Lithuanian	44	0.31
Northern European	6	0.04
Norwegian	32	0.22
Polish	945	6.63
Portuguese	7	0.05
Romanian	68	0.48
Russian	457	3.21
Scotch-Irish	162	1.14
Scottish	101	0.71
Slovak	47	0.33
Swedish	39	0.27
Swiss	44	0.31
Ukrainian	80	0.56
United States or American	962	6.75
Welsh	25	0.18
West Indian, excl. Hispanic:	117	0.82
Jamaican	80	0.56
West Indian	37	0.26
White:	10,752	75.78
Not Hispanic (9,333)	9,487	66.86
Hispanic (1,124)	1,265	8.92
Yugoslavian	7	0.05

Tonawanda

Place Type: City
County: Erie
Population: 16,136

Ancestry/Race	Number	%
African American/Black:	90	0.56
Not Hispanic (59)	80	0.50
Hispanic (8)	10	0.06
African, sub-Saharan:	19	0.12
African	19	0.12
Am. Ind. or Alaska Nat., not spec.	23	0.14
American Indian tribes, specified:	76	0.47
Blackfeet	2	0.01
Cherokee (1)	2	0.01
Chippewa (1)	2	0.01
Iroquois (48)	63	0.39
Latin American Indians	1	0.01
Navajo (1)	1	0.01
Osage (1)	1	0.01
Seminole	1	0.01
All other tribes (1)	3	0.02
American Indian tribes, not spec.	4	0.02
Arab:	115	0.71
Jordanian	8	0.05
Lebanese	34	0.21
Syrian	73	0.45
Asian:	85	0.53
Chinese, ex. Taiwanese (10)	12	0.07
Filipino (4)	8	0.05
Indian (10)	11	0.07
Indonesian (1)	1	0.01
Japanese (5)	11	0.07
Korean (18)	22	0.14
Laotian (3)	3	0.02
Thai (2)	3	0.02
Vietnamese (9)	10	0.06
Other Asian, not specified	4	0.02
Austrian	98	0.61
Brazilian	7	0.04
British	53	0.33
Canadian	135	0.84
Croatian	102	0.63

Notes: 1. Figures in the "Number" column do not add up to the total population due to: a) Ancestry/Race overlap — e.g. persons can report being both White and Irish, b) persons of Hispanic origin can report being any race, c) persons reporting two ancestries are counted in both categories. 2. Numbers in parentheses indicate the number of persons reporting this ancestry/race alone, not in combination with any other ancestry/race. 3. Refer to the Explanation of Data in the front of the book for more detailed information.

Ancestry/Race	Number	%
Czech	23	0.14
Czechoslovakian	16	0.10
Danish	44	0.27
Dutch	294	1.82
English	1,388	8.60
Estonian	19	0.12
European	16	0.10
Finnish	22	0.14
French, except Basque	1,030	6.38
French Canadian	294	1.82
German	6,090	37.74
Greek	60	0.37
Hawaii Native/Pacific Islander:	4	0.02
Micronesian:	1	0.01
Guamanian/Chamorro	1	0.01
Polynesian: (2)	2	0.01
Native Hawaiian (2)	2	0.01
Other Pac. Isl., not spec.	1	0.01
Hispanic or Latino:	144	0.89
Central American:	3	0.02
Guatemalan	2	0.01
Panamanian	1	0.01
Cuban	3	0.02
Dominican Republic	1	0.01
Mexican	23	0.14
Puerto Rican	89	0.55
South American:	5	0.03
Colombian	2	0.01
Venezuelan	3	0.02
Other Hispanic or Latino	20	0.12
Hungarian	516	3.20
Irish	3,178	19.70
Italian	2,817	17.46
Lithuanian	27	0.17
Norwegian	40	0.25
Pennsylvania German	13	0.08
Polish	2,117	13.12
Portuguese	6	0.04
Romanian	8	0.05
Russian	112	0.69
Scotch-Irish	192	1.19
Scottish	348	2.16
Serbian	16	0.10
Slavic	9	0.06
Slovak	30	0.19
Swedish	124	0.77
Swiss	38	0.24
Turkish	15	0.09
Ukrainian	65	0.40
United States or American	584	3.62
Welsh	182	1.13
White:	15,892	98.49
Not Hispanic (15,726)	15,788	97.84
Hispanic (100)	104	0.64
Yugoslavian	21	0.13

Tonawanda

Place Type: Town
County: Erie
Population: 78,155

Ancestry/Race	Number	%
Afghan	7	0.01
African American/Black:	1,314	1.68
Not Hispanic (1,075)	1,275	1.63
Hispanic (28)	39	0.05
African, sub-Saharan:	106	0.14
African	61	0.08
Ethiopian	8	0.01
Ghanian	20	0.03
Other sub-Saharan African	17	0.02
Am. Ind. or Alaska Nat., not spec.	116	0.15
Albanian	60	0.08
Alsatian	26	0.03
American Indian tribes, specified:	272	0.35
Apache	2	0.00
Blackfeet	5	0.01
Cherokee	11	0.01
Cheyenne (1)	1	0.00
Chickasaw	1	0.00
Chippewa (7)	10	0.01
Choctaw	2	0.00
Comanche	3	0.00
Cree	1	0.00
Creek	1	0.00
Delaware (3)	7	0.01
Iroquois (135)	209	0.27
Latin American Indians (3)	3	0.00
Lumbee (1)	4	0.01
Sioux (2)	2	0.00
Yuman	1	0.00
All other tribes (6)	9	0.01
American Indian tribes, not spec.	14	0.02
Arab:	550	0.70
Arab/Arabic	41	0.05
Lebanese	341	0.44
Palestinian	67	0.09
Syrian	93	0.12
Other Arab	8	0.01
Armenian	88	0.11
Asian:	1,082	1.38
Bangladeshi (1)	1	0.00
Cambodian (4)	4	0.01
Chinese, ex. Taiwanese (177)	195	0.25
Filipino (48)	65	0.08
Indian (212)	242	0.31
Indonesian (6)	16	0.02
Japanese (37)	71	0.09
Korean (232)	251	0.32
Laotian (15)	19	0.02
Malaysian (10)	10	0.01
Pakistani (9)	10	0.01
Sri Lankan (1)	1	0.00
Taiwanese (29)	30	0.04
Thai (18)	23	0.03
Vietnamese (69)	75	0.10
Other Asian, specified	1	0.00
Other Asian, not specified (19)	68	0.09
Australian	4	0.01
Austrian	343	0.44
Belgian	51	0.07
Brazilian	20	0.03
British	306	0.39
Bulgarian	69	0.09
Canadian	421	0.54
Croatian	338	0.43
Czech	183	0.23
Czechoslovakian	163	0.21
Danish	159	0.20
Dutch	1,189	1.52
Eastern European	22	0.03
English	8,311	10.63
Estonian	33	0.04
European	188	0.24
Finnish	9	0.01
French, except Basque	2,815	3.60
French Canadian	870	1.11
German	25,522	32.66
Greek	358	0.46
Hawaii Native/Pacific Islander:	42	0.05
Micronesian: (5)	13	0.02
Guamanian/Chamorro (4)	12	0.02
Other Micronesian (1)	1	0.00
Polynesian: (6)	10	0.01
Native Hawaiian (5)	9	0.01
Samoan (1)	1	0.00
Other Pac. Isl., specified	1	0.00
Other Pac. Isl., not spec. (4)	18	0.02
Hispanic or Latino:	1,015	1.30
Central American:	23	0.03
Costa Rican	3	0.00
Guatemalan	3	0.00
Honduran	1	0.00
Nicaraguan	5	0.01
Panamanian	7	0.01
Salvadoran	3	0.00
Other Central American	1	0.00
Cuban	35	0.04
Dominican Republic	15	0.02
Mexican	145	0.19
Puerto Rican	531	0.68
South American:	76	0.10
Argentinean	13	0.02
Bolivian	3	0.00
Chilean	6	0.01
Colombian	29	0.04
Ecuadorian	9	0.01
Paraguayan	1	0.00
Peruvian	3	0.00
Uruguayan	1	0.00
Venezuelan	6	0.01
Other South American	5	0.01
Other Hispanic or Latino	190	0.24
Hungarian	1,403	1.80
Iranian	36	0.05
Irish	16,819	21.52
Israeli	6	0.01
Italian	18,881	24.16
Latvian	31	0.04
Lithuanian	151	0.19
Luxemburger	5	0.01
Macedonian	24	0.03
Maltese	20	0.03
Norwegian	254	0.32
Pennsylvania German	70	0.09
Polish	10,969	14.03
Portuguese	23	0.03
Romanian	155	0.20
Russian	777	0.99
Scandinavian	51	0.07
Scotch-Irish	869	1.11
Scottish	1,895	2.42
Serbian	81	0.10
Slavic	84	0.11
Slovak	182	0.23
Slovene	21	0.03
Swedish	966	1.24
Swiss	144	0.18
Turkish	29	0.04
Ukrainian	501	0.64
United States or American	1,917	2.45
Welsh	503	0.64
West Indian, excl. Hispanic:	55	0.07
Bahamian	12	0.02
Belizean	10	0.01
Haitian	17	0.02
Jamaican	11	0.01
West Indian	5	0.01
White:	75,591	96.72
Not Hispanic (74,320)	74,843	95.76
Hispanic (688)	748	0.96
Yugoslavian	81	0.10

Troy

Place Type: City
County: Rensselaer
Population: 49,170

Ancestry/Race	Number	%
African American/Black:	6,212	12.63
Not Hispanic (5,389)	5,891	11.98
Hispanic (223)	321	0.65
African, sub-Saharan:	272	0.55
African	170	0.35
Ethiopian	48	0.10
Ghanian	7	0.01
Liberian	11	0.02
Nigerian	18	0.04
Senegalese	4	0.01
Sudanese	14	0.03
Alaska Native tribes, specified:	6	0.01
Alaska Athabascan (1)	2	0.00
Tlingit-Haida (2)	4	0.01
Alaska Native tribes, not specified	1	0.00
Am. Ind. or Alaska Nat., not spec.	143	0.29
Albanian	9	0.02
American Indian tribes, specified:	209	0.43
Apache (1)	5	0.01

Notes: 1. Figures in the "Number" column do not add up to the total population due to: a) Ancestry/Race overlap — e.g. persons can report being both White and Irish, b) persons of Hispanic origin can report being any race, c) persons reporting two ancestries are counted in both categories. 2. Numbers in parentheses indicate the number of persons reporting this ancestry/race alone, not in combination with any other ancestry/race. 3. Refer to the Explanation of Data in the front of the book for more detailed information.

Blackfeet (7)	22	0.04
Cherokee (21)	52	0.11
Cheyenne (1)	1	0.00
Chippewa (4)	4	0.01
Comanche (1)	1	0.00
Cree	2	0.00
Crow	1	0.00
Delaware	5	0.01
Iroquois (15)	48	0.10
Latin American Indians (2)	6	0.01
Navajo (1)	1	0.00
Seminole	2	0.00
Sioux	7	0.01
Tohono O'Odham (8)	8	0.02
All other tribes (16)	44	0.09
American Indian tribes, not spec.	18	0.04
Arab:	332	0.68
Arab/Arabic	5	0.01
Egyptian	7	0.01
Lebanese	271	0.55
Syrian	13	0.03
Other Arab	36	0.07
Armenian	364	0.74
Asian:	1,916	3.90
Bangladeshi (1)	1	0.00
Cambodian (5)	5	0.01
Chinese, ex. Taiwanese (729)	772	1.57
Filipino (74)	87	0.18
Indian (401)	442	0.90
Indonesian (13)	17	0.03
Japanese (50)	71	0.14
Korean (236)	244	0.50
Laotian (1)	1	0.00
Malaysian (16)	28	0.06
Pakistani (28)	38	0.08
Sri Lankan (2)	5	0.01
Taiwanese (38)	49	0.10
Thai (28)	32	0.07
Vietnamese (52)	68	0.14
Other Asian, specified (10)	12	0.02
Other Asian, not specified (15)	44	0.09
Austrian	111	0.23
Belgian	18	0.04
Brazilian	21	0.04
British	93	0.19
Bulgarian	5	0.01
Canadian	67	0.14
Carpatho Rusyn	11	0.02
Celtic	4	0.01
Croatian	5	0.01
Cypriot	8	0.02
Czech	50	0.10
Czechoslovakian	13	0.03
Danish	286	0.58
Dutch	1,183	2.41
Eastern European	42	0.09
English	3,652	7.43
Estonian	10	0.02
European	149	0.30
Finnish	32	0.07
French, except Basque	4,490	9.13
French Canadian	1,229	2.50
German	6,256	12.72
Greek	201	0.41
Guyanese	61	0.12
Hawaii Native/Pacific Islander:	51	0.10
Micronesian: (6)	7	0.01
Guamanian/Chamorro (4)	5	0.01
Other Micronesian (2)	2	0.00
Polynesian: (8)	23	0.05
Native Hawaiian (7)	17	0.03
Samoan (1)	4	0.01
Other Polynesian	2	0.00
Other Pac. Isl., not spec. (6)	21	0.04
Hispanic or Latino:	2,131	4.33
Central American:	57	0.12
Costa Rican	8	0.02
Guatemalan	5	0.01
Honduran	2	0.00
Nicaraguan	10	0.02
Panamanian	14	0.03
Salvadoran	18	0.04
Cuban	44	0.09
Dominican Republic	72	0.15
Mexican	171	0.35
Puerto Rican	1,412	2.87
South American:	82	0.17
Argentinean	4	0.01
Bolivian	2	0.00
Chilean	4	0.01
Colombian	24	0.05
Ecuadorian	11	0.02
Paraguayan	6	0.01
Peruvian	18	0.04
Venezuelan	11	0.02
Other South American	2	0.00
Other Hispanic or Latino	293	0.60
Hungarian	112	0.23
Icelander	25	0.05
Iranian	19	0.04
Irish	11,937	24.28
Israeli	7	0.01
Italian	6,981	14.20
Latvian	11	0.02
Lithuanian	152	0.31
Maltese	25	0.05
Northern European	24	0.05
Norwegian	181	0.37
Polish	2,593	5.27
Portuguese	41	0.08
Romanian	40	0.08
Russian	483	0.98
Scandinavian	30	0.06
Scotch-Irish	409	0.83
Scottish	735	1.49
Slavic	4	0.01
Slovak	60	0.12
Slovene	6	0.01
Swedish	179	0.36
Swiss	62	0.13
Turkish	42	0.09
Ukrainian	711	1.45
United States or American	1,886	3.84
Welsh	212	0.43
West Indian, excl. Hispanic:	354	0.72
Barbadian	23	0.05
Haitian	124	0.25
Jamaican	93	0.19
Trinidadian and Tobagonian	70	0.14
West Indian	44	0.09
White:	40,413	82.19
Not Hispanic (38,711)	39,538	80.41
Hispanic (732)	875	1.78
Yugoslavian	10	0.02

Ulster

Place Type: Town
County: Ulster
Population: 12,544

Ancestry/Race	Number	%
African American/Black:	435	3.47
Not Hispanic (349)	418	3.33
Hispanic (13)	17	0.14
Alaska Native tribes, specified:	1	0.01
Eskimo	1	0.01
Am. Ind. or Alaska Nat., not spec.	42	0.33
Albanian	6	0.05
American Indian tribes, specified:	38	0.30
Blackfeet	4	0.03
Cherokee (4)	9	0.07
Cheyenne	1	0.01
Chickasaw (1)	1	0.01
Chippewa	2	0.02
Cree (1)	1	0.01
Iroquois (1)	6	0.05
Latin American Indians (1)	2	0.02
Navajo (1)	2	0.02
Seminole	5	0.04
Sioux	1	0.01
All other tribes (1)	4	0.03
American Indian tribes, not spec.	9	0.07
Arab:	105	0.84
Egyptian	23	0.18
Jordanian	38	0.30
Syrian	18	0.14
Other Arab	26	0.21
Asian:	240	1.91
Chinese, ex. Taiwanese (38)	42	0.33
Filipino (11)	18	0.14
Indian (78)	90	0.72
Japanese (8)	14	0.11
Korean (8)	9	0.07
Pakistani (31)	35	0.28
Taiwanese (2)	2	0.02
Thai (3)	4	0.03
Vietnamese (2)	5	0.04
Other Asian, specified (1)	1	0.01
Other Asian, not specified (14)	20	0.16
Australian	7	0.06
Austrian	37	0.29
Belgian	9	0.07
British	4	0.03
Canadian	22	0.18
Croatian	10	0.08
Czech	55	0.44
Czechoslovakian	40	0.32
Danish	31	0.25
Dutch	749	5.97
Eastern European	52	0.41
English	956	7.62
European	24	0.19
Finnish	18	0.14
French, except Basque	439	3.50
French Canadian	101	0.81
German	2,607	20.78
Greek	113	0.90
Guyanese	7	0.06
Hawaii Native/Pacific Islander:	14	0.11
Micronesian: (7)	8	0.06
Guamanian/Chamorro (4)	4	0.03
Other Micronesian (3)	4	0.03
Polynesian:	4	0.03
Native Hawaiian	4	0.03
Other Pac. Isl., not spec. (1)	2	0.02
Hispanic or Latino:	307	2.45
Central American:	16	0.13
Guatemalan	1	0.01
Honduran	2	0.02
Panamanian	4	0.03
Salvadoran	5	0.04
Other Central American	4	0.03
Cuban	10	0.08
Dominican Republic	7	0.06
Mexican	63	0.50
Puerto Rican	150	1.20
South American:	20	0.16
Argentinean	6	0.05
Chilean	1	0.01
Colombian	3	0.02
Ecuadorian	4	0.03
Peruvian	2	0.02
Venezuelan	4	0.03
Other Hispanic or Latino	41	0.33
Hungarian	112	0.89
Irish	2,690	21.44
Israeli	5	0.04
Italian	2,370	18.89
Lithuanian	19	0.15
Northern European	9	0.07
Norwegian	91	0.73
Polish	512	4.08
Portuguese	25	0.20
Russian	109	0.87
Scotch-Irish	163	1.30
Scottish	182	1.45
Slavic	5	0.04
Slovak	8	0.06
Swedish	123	0.98

Notes: 1. Figures in the "Number" column do not add up to the total population due to: a) Ancestry/Race overlap — e.g. persons can report being both White and Irish, b) persons of Hispanic origin can report being any race, c) persons reporting two ancestries are counted in both categories. 2. Numbers in parentheses indicate the number of persons reporting this ancestry/race alone, not in combination with any other ancestry/race. 3. Refer to the Explanation of Data in the front of the book for more detailed information.

Ancestry/Race	Number	%
Swiss	33	0.26
Ukrainian	61	0.49
United States or American	539	4.30
Welsh	99	0.79
West Indian, excl. Hispanic:	29	0.23
Haitian	6	0.05
Jamaican	15	0.12
West Indian	8	0.06
White:	11,889	94.78
Not Hispanic (11,494)	11,645	92.83
Hispanic (227)	244	1.95
Yugoslavian	5	0.04

Union

Place Type: Town
County: Broome
Population: 56,298

Ancestry/Race	Number	%
Acadian/Cajun	10	0.02
African American/Black:	1,737	3.09
Not Hispanic (1,343)	1,663	2.95
Hispanic (34)	74	0.13
African, sub-Saharan:	110	0.20
African	58	0.10
Ethiopian	9	0.02
Nigerian	29	0.05
South African	6	0.01
Other sub-Saharan African	8	0.01
Am. Ind. or Alaska Nat., not spec.	133	0.24
Albanian	25	0.04
American Indian tribes, specified:	177	0.31
Apache (2)	7	0.01
Blackfeet (5)	18	0.03
Cherokee (11)	44	0.08
Chippewa (2)	5	0.01
Choctaw (2)	3	0.01
Comanche	2	0.00
Delaware (2)	7	0.01
Iroquois (11)	52	0.09
Kiowa	2	0.00
Latin American Indians (1)	1	0.00
Navajo (1)	2	0.00
Ottawa	1	0.00
Potawatomi (1)	1	0.00
Seminole (2)	2	0.00
Sioux (13)	16	0.03
All other tribes (8)	14	0.02
American Indian tribes, not spec.	14	0.02
Arab:	145	0.26
Arab/Arabic	11	0.02
Egyptian	27	0.05
Jordanian	5	0.01
Lebanese	84	0.15
Moroccan	6	0.01
Syrian	12	0.02
Armenian	77	0.14
Asian:	1,698	3.02
Bangladeshi (4)	4	0.01
Chinese, ex. Taiwanese (327)	350	0.62
Filipino (62)	97	0.17
Indian (287)	308	0.55
Indonesian (3)	6	0.01
Japanese (27)	42	0.07
Korean (156)	174	0.31
Laotian (286)	316	0.56
Malaysian (1)	1	0.00
Pakistani (50)	52	0.09
Taiwanese (24)	26	0.05
Thai (3)	7	0.01
Vietnamese (208)	233	0.41
Other Asian, specified (3)	4	0.01
Other Asian, not specified (55)	78	0.14
Australian	24	0.04
Austrian	352	0.63
Belgian	5	0.01
Brazilian	7	0.01
British	157	0.28
Canadian	107	0.19
Carpatho Rusyn	62	0.11
Celtic	42	0.07
Croatian	43	0.08
Czech	535	0.95
Czechoslovakian	709	1.26
Danish	107	0.19
Dutch	1,835	3.26
Eastern European	149	0.26
English	8,189	14.55
European	186	0.33
Finnish	77	0.14
French, except Basque	1,558	2.77
French Canadian	501	0.89
German	8,454	15.02
Greek	424	0.75
Guyanese	36	0.06
Hawaii Native/Pacific Islander:	41	0.07
Micronesian: (5)	6	0.01
Guamanian/Chamorro (5)	6	0.01
Polynesian: (8)	13	0.02
Native Hawaiian (7)	10	0.02
Samoan (1)	3	0.01
Other Pac. Isl., not spec. (5)	22	0.04
Hispanic or Latino:	863	1.53
Central American:	22	0.04
Costa Rican	9	0.02
Guatemalan	8	0.01
Nicaraguan	1	0.00
Panamanian	4	0.01
Cuban	36	0.06
Dominican Republic	22	0.04
Mexican	107	0.19
Puerto Rican	454	0.81
South American:	38	0.07
Argentinean	5	0.01
Bolivian	2	0.00
Chilean	7	0.01
Colombian	10	0.02
Ecuadorian	1	0.00
Peruvian	6	0.01
Uruguayan	3	0.01
Venezuelan	2	0.00
Other South American	2	0.00
Other Hispanic or Latino	184	0.33
Hungarian	292	0.52
Iranian	15	0.03
Irish	10,754	19.10
Israeli	9	0.02
Italian	9,693	17.22
Latvian	13	0.02
Lithuanian	394	0.70
Northern European	18	0.03
Norwegian	173	0.31
Pennsylvania German	223	0.40
Polish	4,842	8.60
Portuguese	71	0.13
Romanian	77	0.14
Russian	1,454	2.58
Scandinavian	51	0.09
Scotch-Irish	646	1.15
Scottish	941	1.67
Serbian	6	0.01
Slavic	137	0.24
Slovak	3,039	5.40
Slovene	47	0.08
Swedish	613	1.09
Swiss	184	0.33
Turkish	23	0.04
Ukrainian	1,129	2.01
United States or American	2,385	4.24
Welsh	1,281	2.28
West Indian, excl. Hispanic:	142	0.25
Barbadian	8	0.01
British West Indian	21	0.04
Jamaican	58	0.10
Trinidadian and Tobagonian	10	0.02
West Indian	45	0.08
White:	52,875	93.92
Not Hispanic (51,767)	52,366	93.02
Hispanic (431)	509	0.90
Yugoslavian	80	0.14

Uniondale

Place Type: Census Designated Place
County: Nassau
Population: 23,011

Ancestry/Race	Number	%
African American/Black:	13,411	58.28
Not Hispanic (12,384)	12,907	56.09
Hispanic (395)	504	2.19
African, sub-Saharan:	501	2.18
African	275	1.20
Liberian	129	0.56
Nigerian	97	0.42
Am. Ind. or Alaska Nat., not spec.	134	0.58
American Indian tribes, specified:	100	0.43
Blackfeet (2)	9	0.04
Cherokee (12)	43	0.19
Latin American Indians (8)	22	0.10
Seminole	1	0.00
Sioux (3)	11	0.05
All other tribes (6)	14	0.06
American Indian tribes, not spec.	30	0.13
Arab:	18	0.08
Arab/Arabic	18	0.08
Armenian	14	0.06
Asian:	635	2.76
Cambodian	1	0.00
Chinese, ex. Taiwanese (58)	86	0.37
Filipino (101)	105	0.46
Indian (265)	333	1.45
Indonesian (1)	3	0.01
Japanese (7)	12	0.05
Korean (11)	12	0.05
Malaysian	1	0.00
Sri Lankan (6)	6	0.03
Taiwanese (1)	1	0.00
Vietnamese (13)	19	0.08
Other Asian, specified	6	0.03
Other Asian, not specified (19)	50	0.22
Austrian	13	0.06
Belgian	5	0.02
Brazilian	15	0.07
British	7	0.03
Canadian	42	0.18
Czech	20	0.09
Danish	44	0.19
Dutch	73	0.32
English	182	0.79
European	10	0.04
French, except Basque	115	0.50
French Canadian	42	0.18
German	968	4.21
Greek	52	0.23
Guyanese	268	1.16
Hawaii Native/Pacific Islander:	50	0.22
Micronesian: (12)	12	0.05
Guamanian/Chamorro (12)	12	0.05
Polynesian:	13	0.06
Native Hawaiian	13	0.06
Other Pac. Isl., not spec. (6)	25	0.11
Hispanic or Latino:	5,261	22.86
Central American:	2,114	9.19
Costa Rican	43	0.19
Guatemalan	117	0.51
Honduran	120	0.52
Nicaraguan	10	0.04
Panamanian	40	0.17
Salvadoran	1,648	7.16
Other Central American	136	0.59
Cuban	75	0.33
Dominican Republic	247	1.07
Mexican	133	0.58
Puerto Rican	724	3.15
South American:	376	1.63
Argentinean	10	0.04
Bolivian	1	0.00
Chilean	16	0.07

Notes: 1. Figures in the "Number" column do not add up to the total population due to: a) Ancestry/Race overlap — e.g. persons can report being both White and Irish, b) persons of Hispanic origin can report being any race, c) persons reporting two ancestries are counted in both categories. 2. Numbers in parentheses indicate the number of persons reporting this ancestry/race alone, not in combination with any other ancestry/race. 3. Refer to the Explanation of Data in the front of the book for more detailed information.

Colombian	113	0.49
Ecuadorian	150	0.65
Peruvian	48	0.21
Venezuelan	12	0.05
Other South American	26	0.11
Other Hispanic or Latino	1,592	6.92
Hungarian	42	0.18
Iranian	24	0.10
Irish	969	4.21
Israeli	24	0.10
Italian	997	4.33
Latvian	23	0.10
Lithuanian	6	0.03
Norwegian	47	0.20
Polish	303	1.32
Portuguese	24	0.10
Russian	123	0.53
Scotch-Irish	111	0.48
Scottish	111	0.48
Slovak	8	0.03
Swedish	80	0.35
Swiss	11	0.05
Turkish	21	0.09
Ukrainian	47	0.20
United States or American	586	2.55
Welsh	7	0.03
West Indian, excl. Hispanic:	5,030	21.86
Barbadian	74	0.32
Belizean	10	0.04
British West Indian	109	0.47
Dutch West Indian	13	0.06
Haitian	1,882	8.18
Jamaican	2,430	10.56
Trinidadian and Tobagonian	242	1.05
West Indian	270	1.17
White:	6,757	29.36
Not Hispanic (4,056)	4,217	18.33
Hispanic (2,151)	2,540	11.04

Utica

Place Type: City
County: Oneida
Population: 60,651

Ancestry/Race	Number	%
African American/Black:	8,489	14.00
Not Hispanic (7,548)	8,105	13.36
Hispanic (290)	384	0.63
African, sub-Saharan:	368	0.61
African	363	0.60
Kenyan	5	0.01
Alaska Native tribes, specified:	4	0.01
Alaska Athabascan	1	0.00
Tlingit-Haida (3)	3	0.00
Am. Ind. or Alaska Nat., not spec.	199	0.33
Albanian	44	0.07
Alsatian	7	0.01
American Indian tribes, specified:	196	0.32
Apache (4)	5	0.01
Blackfeet (3)	16	0.03
Cherokee (18)	57	0.09
Chippewa (1)	2	0.00
Comanche (1)	2	0.00
Creek (1)	1	0.00
Crow (1)	2	0.00
Iroquois (33)	73	0.12
Latin American Indians (3)	3	0.00
Menominee	1	0.00
Navajo	2	0.00
Seminole	3	0.00
Shoshone	1	0.00
Sioux (8)	15	0.02
All other tribes (3)	13	0.02
American Indian tribes, not spec.	22	0.04
Arab:	1,313	2.16
Arab/Arabic	63	0.10
Egyptian	21	0.03
Iraqi	45	0.07
Lebanese	945	1.56
Moroccan	12	0.02
Syrian	146	0.24
Other Arab	81	0.13
Armenian	43	0.07
Asian:	1,621	2.67
Bangladeshi	2	0.00
Cambodian (53)	65	0.11
Chinese, ex. Taiwanese (99)	135	0.22
Filipino (17)	27	0.04
Hmong	1	0.00
Indian (156)	178	0.29
Indonesian (1)	2	0.00
Japanese (42)	59	0.10
Korean (32)	52	0.09
Laotian (34)	44	0.07
Pakistani (8)	20	0.03
Taiwanese (6)	13	0.02
Thai (7)	19	0.03
Vietnamese (825)	881	1.45
Other Asian, specified (23)	33	0.05
Other Asian, not specified (18)	90	0.15
Austrian	59	0.10
Basque	7	0.01
Belgian	11	0.02
Brazilian	28	0.05
British	63	0.10
Bulgarian	74	0.12
Canadian	82	0.14
Celtic	8	0.01
Croatian	60	0.10
Czech	62	0.10
Czechoslovakian	21	0.03
Danish	79	0.13
Dutch	778	1.28
Eastern European	14	0.02
English	3,383	5.58
Estonian	5	0.01
European	67	0.11
Finnish	11	0.02
French, except Basque	2,292	3.78
French Canadian	660	1.09
German	6,088	10.03
Greek	74	0.12
Hawaii Native/Pacific Islander:	87	0.14
Micronesian: (3)	4	0.01
Guamanian/Chamorro (3)	4	0.01
Polynesian: (18)	36	0.06
Native Hawaiian (10)	19	0.03
Samoan (8)	15	0.02
Tongan	2	0.00
Other Pac. Isl., specified	2	0.00
Other Pac. Isl., not spec. (8)	45	0.07
Hispanic or Latino:	3,510	5.79
Central American:	30	0.05
Costa Rican	2	0.00
Guatemalan	2	0.00
Honduran	6	0.01
Nicaraguan	2	0.00
Panamanian	7	0.01
Salvadoran	8	0.01
Other Central American	3	0.00
Cuban	59	0.10
Dominican Republic	102	0.17
Mexican	139	0.23
Puerto Rican	2,721	4.49
South American:	56	0.09
Argentinean	1	0.00
Bolivian	13	0.02
Chilean	3	0.00
Colombian	10	0.02
Ecuadorian	4	0.01
Peruvian	6	0.01
Venezuelan	10	0.02
Other South American	9	0.01
Other Hispanic or Latino	403	0.66
Hungarian	115	0.19
Iranian	6	0.01
Irish	7,484	12.33
Israeli	13	0.02
Italian	15,831	26.09
Lithuanian	202	0.33
Northern European	6	0.01
Norwegian	125	0.21
Pennsylvania German	6	0.01
Polish	5,225	8.61
Portuguese	38	0.06
Romanian	100	0.16
Russian	708	1.17
Scandinavian	10	0.02
Scotch-Irish	298	0.49
Scottish	450	0.74
Slavic	6	0.01
Slovak	39	0.06
Swedish	128	0.21
Swiss	119	0.20
Turkish	6	0.01
Ukrainian	790	1.30
United States or American	1,918	3.16
Welsh	1,125	1.85
West Indian, excl. Hispanic:	395	0.65
Barbadian	5	0.01
British West Indian	15	0.02
Haitian	85	0.14
Jamaican	222	0.37
Trinidadian and Tobagonian	5	0.01
U.S. Virgin Islander	6	0.01
West Indian	57	0.09
White:	49,722	81.98
Not Hispanic (46,389)	47,767	78.76
Hispanic (1,777)	1,955	3.22
Yugoslavian	2,596	4.28

Valley Stream

Place Type: Village
County: Nassau
Population: 36,368

Ancestry/Race	Number	%
Afghan	21	0.06
African American/Black:	3,008	8.27
Not Hispanic (2,603)	2,825	7.77
Hispanic (111)	183	0.50
African, sub-Saharan:	151	0.41
African	95	0.26
South African	22	0.06
Other sub-Saharan African	34	0.09
Alaska Native tribes, specified:	7	0.02
Tlingit-Haida	7	0.02
Am. Ind. or Alaska Nat., not spec.	57	0.16
Albanian	20	0.05
American Indian tribes, specified:	72	0.20
Blackfeet	1	0.00
Cherokee (2)	21	0.06
Chippewa (1)	1	0.00
Choctaw	1	0.00
Creek (1)	2	0.01
Iroquois	2	0.01
Latin American Indians (15)	30	0.08
Navajo	1	0.00
Sioux (1)	4	0.01
Yaqui (1)	1	0.00
All other tribes (7)	8	0.02
American Indian tribes, not spec.	9	0.02
Arab:	320	0.88
Arab/Arabic	9	0.02
Egyptian	226	0.62
Lebanese	64	0.18
Syrian	9	0.02
Other Arab	12	0.03
Armenian	59	0.16
Asian:	2,848	7.83
Bangladeshi (4)	5	0.01
Chinese, ex. Taiwanese (625)	669	1.84
Filipino (480)	538	1.48
Indian (731)	836	2.30
Japanese (36)	44	0.12
Korean (295)	307	0.84
Laotian (1)	1	0.00
Malaysian (1)	2	0.01

Notes: 1. Figures in the "Number" column do not add up to the total population due to: a) Ancestry/Race overlap — e.g. persons can report being both White and Irish, b) persons of Hispanic origin can report being any race, c) persons reporting two ancestries are counted in both categories. 2. Numbers in parentheses indicate the number of persons reporting this ancestry/race alone, not in combination with any other ancestry/race. 3. Refer to the Explanation of Data in the front of the book for more detailed information.

Pakistani (171)	248	0.68
Sri Lankan (1)	1	0.00
Taiwanese (51)	67	0.18
Thai (18)	31	0.09
Vietnamese (14)	23	0.06
Other Asian, specified (5)	6	0.02
Other Asian, not specified (14)	70	0.19
Austrian	289	0.79
Basque	12	0.03
Belgian	25	0.07
Brazilian	7	0.02
British	37	0.10
Bulgarian	4	0.01
Canadian	78	0.21
Croatian	13	0.04
Cypriot	12	0.03
Czech	46	0.13
Czechoslovakian	55	0.15
Danish	41	0.11
Dutch	183	0.50
Eastern European	103	0.28
English	1,093	3.00
European	70	0.19
Finnish	41	0.11
French, except Basque	325	0.89
French Canadian	44	0.12
German	4,101	11.27
Greek	668	1.84
Guyanese	185	0.51
Hawaii Native/Pacific Islander:	74	0.20
Micronesian: (5)	5	0.01
Guamanian/Chamorro (5)	5	0.01
Polynesian: (9)	17	0.05
Native Hawaiian (4)	11	0.03
Samoan (3)	4	0.01
Other Polynesian (2)	2	0.01
Other Pac. Isl., specified	1	0.00
Other Pac. Isl., not spec. (3)	51	0.14
Hispanic or Latino:	4,463	12.27
Central American:	579	1.59
Costa Rican	39	0.11
Guatemalan	65	0.18
Honduran	45	0.12
Nicaraguan	5	0.01
Panamanian	20	0.05
Salvadoran	386	1.06
Other Central American	19	0.05
Cuban	130	0.36
Dominican Republic	416	1.14
Mexican	93	0.26
Puerto Rican	1,159	3.19
South American:	1,023	2.81
Argentinean	76	0.21
Bolivian	17	0.05
Chilean	118	0.32
Colombian	345	0.95
Ecuadorian	203	0.56
Paraguayan	3	0.01
Peruvian	193	0.53
Uruguayan	20	0.05
Venezuelan	13	0.04
Other South American	35	0.10
Other Hispanic or Latino	1,063	2.92
Hungarian	213	0.59
Irish	6,247	17.16
Israeli	68	0.19
Italian	11,559	31.76
Latvian	26	0.07
Lithuanian	133	0.37
Maltese	33	0.09
Norwegian	325	0.89
Polish	1,673	4.60
Portuguese	71	0.20
Romanian	120	0.33
Russian	862	2.37
Scandinavian	28	0.08
Scotch-Irish	242	0.66
Scottish	269	0.74
Slavic	13	0.04
Slovak	153	0.42
Slovene	11	0.03
Soviet Union	19	0.05
Swedish	247	0.68
Swiss	25	0.07
Turkish	83	0.23
Ukrainian	177	0.49
United States or American	1,095	3.01
Welsh	35	0.10
West Indian, excl. Hispanic:	1,452	3.99
British West Indian	28	0.08
Haitian	582	1.60
Jamaican	542	1.49
Trinidadian and Tobagonian	221	0.61
West Indian	51	0.14
Other West Indian	28	0.08
White:	29,230	80.37
Not Hispanic (25,981)	26,284	72.27
Hispanic (2,673)	2,946	8.10

Van Buren

Place Type: Town
County: Onondaga
Population: 12,667

Ancestry/Race	Number	%
African American/Black:	142	1.12
Not Hispanic (99)	135	1.07
Hispanic (2)	7	0.06
Am. Ind. or Alaska Nat., not spec.	29	0.23
Albanian	8	0.06
American Indian tribes, specified:	84	0.66
Cherokee	9	0.07
Chippewa (1)	2	0.02
Iroquois (47)	68	0.54
Sioux (1)	3	0.02
All other tribes (1)	2	0.02
American Indian tribes, not spec.	6	0.05
Arab:	30	0.24
Arab/Arabic	5	0.04
Lebanese	25	0.20
Armenian	22	0.17
Asian:	92	0.73
Chinese, ex. Taiwanese (15)	24	0.19
Filipino (14)	22	0.17
Indian (10)	15	0.12
Japanese	7	0.06
Korean (9)	12	0.09
Malaysian	1	0.01
Vietnamese (3)	4	0.03
Other Asian, not specified	7	0.06
Australian	6	0.05
Austrian	4	0.03
British	34	0.27
Canadian	74	0.58
Croatian	6	0.05
Czech	64	0.51
Czechoslovakian	18	0.14
Danish	47	0.37
Dutch	458	3.62
English	2,120	16.74
Estonian	8	0.06
European	45	0.36
Finnish	78	0.62
French, except Basque	1,114	8.79
French Canadian	439	3.47
German	2,721	21.48
Greek	97	0.77
Hawaii Native/Pacific Islander:	3	0.02
Micronesian: (1)	2	0.02
Guamanian/Chamorro (1)	2	0.02
Polynesian: (1)	1	0.01
Samoan (1)	1	0.01
Hispanic or Latino:	95	0.75
Central American:	1	0.01
Costa Rican	1	0.01
Cuban	3	0.02
Mexican	22	0.17
Puerto Rican	34	0.27
South American:	10	0.08
Argentinean	2	0.02
Ecuadorian	5	0.04
Peruvian	2	0.02
Other South American	1	0.01
Other Hispanic or Latino	25	0.20
Hungarian	15	0.12
Iranian	5	0.04
Irish	2,654	20.95
Italian	1,792	14.15
Lithuanian	48	0.38
Norwegian	51	0.40
Pennsylvania German	36	0.28
Polish	922	7.28
Portuguese	18	0.14
Russian	54	0.43
Scotch-Irish	210	1.66
Scottish	385	3.04
Serbian	5	0.04
Slavic	15	0.12
Slovak	12	0.09
Slovene	15	0.12
Swedish	158	1.25
Swiss	24	0.19
Ukrainian	189	1.49
United States or American	615	4.86
Welsh	132	1.04
White:	12,412	97.99
Not Hispanic (12,218)	12,335	97.38
Hispanic (75)	77	0.61
Yugoslavian	9	0.07

Vestal

Place Type: Town
County: Broome
Population: 26,535

Ancestry/Race	Number	%
African American/Black:	671	2.53
Not Hispanic (555)	619	2.33
Hispanic (25)	52	0.20
African, sub-Saharan:	93	0.35
African	37	0.14
Ghanian	21	0.08
Kenyan	6	0.02
Nigerian	24	0.09
Ugandan	5	0.02
Am. Ind. or Alaska Nat., not spec.	35	0.13
American Indian tribes, specified:	56	0.21
Blackfeet (2)	4	0.02
Cherokee (2)	13	0.05
Chippewa (1)	1	0.00
Delaware	3	0.01
Iroquois (11)	18	0.07
Latin American Indians (1)	5	0.02
Sioux (4)	4	0.02
All other tribes (4)	8	0.03
American Indian tribes, not spec.	13	0.05
Arab:	251	0.95
Egyptian	11	0.04
Iraqi	12	0.05
Lebanese	148	0.56
Palestinian	8	0.03
Syrian	25	0.09
Other Arab	47	0.18
Armenian	77	0.29
Asian:	2,373	8.94
Bangladeshi (2)	2	0.01
Cambodian (1)	6	0.02
Chinese, ex. Taiwanese (832)	890	3.35
Filipino (147)	169	0.64
Indian (495)	517	1.95
Indonesian (4)	9	0.03
Japanese (48)	70	0.26
Korean (438)	453	1.71
Laotian	2	0.01
Malaysian	1	0.00
Pakistani (51)	64	0.24
Sri Lankan (7)	7	0.03
Taiwanese (86)	94	0.35

Notes: 1. Figures in the "Number" column do not add up to the total population due to: a) Ancestry/Race overlap — e.g. persons can report being both White and Irish, b) persons of Hispanic origin can report being any race, c) persons reporting two ancestries are counted in both categories. 2. Numbers in parentheses indicate the number of persons reporting this ancestry/race alone, not in combination with any other ancestry/race. 3. Refer to the Explanation of Data in the front of the book for more detailed information.

Ancestry/Race	Number	%
Thai (16)	16	0.06
Vietnamese (31)	37	0.14
Other Asian, specified (1)	2	0.01
Other Asian, not specified (14)	34	0.13
Australian	9	0.03
Austrian	196	0.74
Belgian	32	0.12
British	197	0.74
Bulgarian	8	0.03
Canadian	72	0.27
Croatian	49	0.18
Czech	274	1.03
Czechoslovakian	209	0.79
Danish	55	0.21
Dutch	629	2.37
Eastern European	63	0.24
English	3,668	13.82
Estonian	13	0.05
European	150	0.57
Finnish	36	0.14
French, except Basque	709	2.67
French Canadian	297	1.12
German	4,716	17.77
Greek	215	0.81
Guyanese	7	0.03
Hawaii Native/Pacific Islander:	15	0.06
Micronesian: (1)	2	0.01
Guamanian/Chamorro (1)	2	0.01
Polynesian:	4	0.02
Native Hawaiian	4	0.02
Other Pac. Isl., not spec.	9	0.03
Hispanic or Latino:	637	2.40
Central American:	37	0.14
Costa Rican	5	0.02
Guatemalan	8	0.03
Honduran	8	0.03
Nicaraguan	3	0.01
Panamanian	10	0.04
Salvadoran	2	0.01
Other Central American	1	0.00
Cuban	26	0.10
Dominican Republic	69	0.26
Mexican	70	0.26
Puerto Rican	218	0.82
South American:	107	0.40
Argentinean	14	0.05
Bolivian	3	0.01
Chilean	5	0.02
Colombian	31	0.12
Ecuadorian	26	0.10
Peruvian	18	0.07
Uruguayan	2	0.01
Venezuelan	6	0.02
Other South American	2	0.01
Other Hispanic or Latino	110	0.41
Hungarian	157	0.59
Iranian	34	0.13
Irish	4,850	18.28
Israeli	73	0.28
Italian	3,413	12.86
Lithuanian	261	0.98
Macedonian	6	0.02
New Zealander	14	0.05
Northern European	23	0.09
Norwegian	182	0.69
Pennsylvania German	96	0.36
Polish	1,892	7.13
Portuguese	43	0.16
Romanian	59	0.22
Russian	941	3.55
Scandinavian	20	0.08
Scotch-Irish	320	1.21
Scottish	589	2.22
Serbian	6	0.02
Slavic	20	0.08
Slovak	543	2.05
Slovene	40	0.15
Swedish	273	1.03
Swiss	141	0.53
Turkish	15	0.06
Ukrainian	381	1.44
United States or American	1,087	4.10
Welsh	538	2.03
West Indian, excl. Hispanic:	177	0.67
Belizean	7	0.03
British West Indian	8	0.03
Haitian	23	0.09
Jamaican	85	0.32
Trinidadian and Tobagonian	39	0.15
West Indian	15	0.06
White:	23,371	88.08
Not Hispanic (22,811)	23,012	86.72
Hispanic (309)	359	1.35
Yugoslavian	39	0.15

Wallkill

Place Type: Town
County: Orange
Population: 24,659

Ancestry/Race	Number	%
African American/Black:	2,668	10.82
Not Hispanic (2,145)	2,436	9.88
Hispanic (159)	232	0.94
African, sub-Saharan:	116	0.47
African	107	0.43
Nigerian	9	0.04
Alaska Native tribes, specified:	10	0.04
Eskimo (10)	10	0.04
Am. Ind. or Alaska Nat., not spec.	135	0.55
Albanian	22	0.09
Alsatian	11	0.04
American Indian tribes, specified:	108	0.44
Apache	1	0.00
Blackfeet	10	0.04
Cherokee (1)	28	0.11
Delaware (9)	18	0.07
Iroquois (6)	21	0.09
Latin American Indians (5)	8	0.03
Seminole	7	0.03
Sioux	3	0.01
Yuman (1)	1	0.00
All other tribes (1)	11	0.04
American Indian tribes, not spec.	14	0.06
Arab:	58	0.24
Arab/Arabic	6	0.02
Lebanese	28	0.11
Moroccan	5	0.02
Syrian	14	0.06
Other Arab	5	0.02
Armenian	7	0.03
Asian:	692	2.81
Bangladeshi (5)	5	0.02
Cambodian (18)	19	0.08
Chinese, ex. Taiwanese (115)	131	0.53
Filipino (66)	88	0.36
Indian (265)	288	1.17
Japanese (9)	28	0.11
Korean (35)	43	0.17
Pakistani (39)	47	0.19
Taiwanese (5)	6	0.02
Thai (8)	12	0.05
Vietnamese (13)	13	0.05
Other Asian, not specified (7)	12	0.05
Australian	5	0.02
Austrian	113	0.46
Belgian	9	0.04
Brazilian	7	0.03
British	37	0.15
Canadian	56	0.23
Celtic	29	0.12
Czech	99	0.40
Czechoslovakian	71	0.29
Danish	50	0.20
Dutch	794	3.22
Eastern European	39	0.16
English	1,701	6.90
European	318	1.29
Finnish	58	0.24
French, except Basque	635	2.57
French Canadian	137	0.56
German	3,351	13.58
Greek	139	0.56
Hawaii Native/Pacific Islander:	41	0.17
Micronesian: (7)	8	0.03
Guamanian/Chamorro (7)	8	0.03
Polynesian: (2)	8	0.03
Native Hawaiian (1)	4	0.02
Samoan (1)	4	0.02
Other Pac. Isl., not spec. (3)	25	0.10
Hispanic or Latino:	3,304	13.40
Central American:	93	0.38
Costa Rican	13	0.05
Guatemalan	13	0.05
Honduran	19	0.08
Nicaraguan	1	0.00
Panamanian	13	0.05
Salvadoran	26	0.11
Other Central American	8	0.03
Cuban	79	0.32
Dominican Republic	78	0.32
Mexican	336	1.36
Puerto Rican	2,004	8.13
South American:	257	1.04
Argentinean	10	0.04
Bolivian	2	0.01
Chilean	15	0.06
Colombian	170	0.69
Ecuadorian	14	0.06
Paraguayan	2	0.01
Peruvian	22	0.09
Uruguayan	8	0.03
Venezuelan	5	0.02
Other South American	9	0.04
Other Hispanic or Latino	457	1.85
Hungarian	255	1.03
Irish	4,607	18.67
Italian	4,862	19.71
Latvian	28	0.11
Lithuanian	74	0.30
Norwegian	108	0.44
Pennsylvania German	34	0.14
Polish	1,575	6.38
Portuguese	90	0.36
Romanian	32	0.13
Russian	272	1.10
Scandinavian	7	0.03
Scotch-Irish	307	1.24
Scottish	337	1.37
Slavic	8	0.03
Slovak	87	0.35
Slovene	24	0.10
Swedish	274	1.11
Swiss	31	0.13
Ukrainian	106	0.43
United States or American	755	3.06
Welsh	99	0.40
West Indian, excl. Hispanic:	528	2.14
Bermudan	10	0.04
British West Indian	33	0.13
Haitian	152	0.62
Jamaican	182	0.74
Trinidadian and Tobagonian	41	0.17
West Indian	110	0.45
White:	20,419	82.81
Not Hispanic (18,020)	18,377	74.52
Hispanic (1,879)	2,042	8.28
Yugoslavian	28	0.11

Wantagh

Place Type: Census Designated Place
County: Nassau
Population: 18,971

Ancestry/Race	Number	%
African American/Black:	60	0.32
Not Hispanic (35)	51	0.27
Hispanic (2)	9	0.05

Notes: 1. Figures in the "Number" column do not add up to the total population due to: a) Ancestry/Race overlap — e.g. persons can report being both White and Irish, b) persons of Hispanic origin can report being any race, c) persons reporting two ancestries are counted in both categories. 2. Numbers in parentheses indicate the number of persons reporting this ancestry/race alone, not in combination with any other ancestry/race. 3. Refer to the Explanation of Data in the front of the book for more detailed information.

Ancestry/Race	Number	%
Am. Ind. or Alaska Nat., not spec.	17	0.09
Albanian	23	0.12
American Indian tribes, specified:	15	0.08
Blackfeet	4	0.02
Cherokee	7	0.04
Iroquois	2	0.01
Pueblo (1)	1	0.01
All other tribes	1	0.01
Armenian	36	0.19
Asian:	439	2.31
Chinese, ex. Taiwanese (163)	184	0.97
Filipino (31)	45	0.24
Indian (98)	114	0.60
Japanese (7)	10	0.05
Korean (35)	42	0.22
Pakistani (8)	22	0.12
Sri Lankan (3)	3	0.02
Taiwanese (3)	3	0.02
Thai (4)	5	0.03
Vietnamese (2)	3	0.02
Other Asian, not specified (2)	8	0.04
Austrian	149	0.79
Belgian	16	0.08
Brazilian	11	0.06
Bulgarian	8	0.04
Canadian	24	0.13
Croatian	62	0.33
Czech	108	0.57
Czechoslovakian	51	0.27
Danish	57	0.30
Dutch	160	0.84
Eastern European	147	0.77
English	982	5.18
European	53	0.28
Finnish	18	0.09
French, except Basque	281	1.48
French Canadian	169	0.89
German	4,117	21.70
Greek	403	2.12
Guyanese	19	0.10
Hawaii Native/Pacific Islander:	2	0.01
Polynesian:	1	0.01
Native Hawaiian	1	0.01
Other Pac. Isl., not spec.	1	0.01
Hispanic or Latino:	619	3.26
Central American:	32	0.17
Costa Rican	1	0.01
Guatemalan	9	0.05
Honduran	6	0.03
Nicaraguan	1	0.01
Salvadoran	15	0.08
Cuban	40	0.21
Dominican Republic	17	0.09
Mexican	39	0.21
Puerto Rican	244	1.29
South American:	119	0.63
Argentinean	25	0.13
Chilean	8	0.04
Colombian	38	0.20
Ecuadorian	26	0.14
Peruvian	10	0.05
Uruguayan	4	0.02
Other South American	8	0.04
Other Hispanic or Latino	128	0.67
Hungarian	167	0.88
Iranian	25	0.13
Irish	5,222	27.53
Israeli	40	0.21
Italian	5,910	31.15
Lithuanian	39	0.21
Maltese	27	0.14
New Zealander	9	0.05
Northern European	17	0.09
Norwegian	131	0.69
Polish	1,142	6.02
Portuguese	58	0.31
Romanian	89	0.47
Russian	830	4.38
Scotch-Irish	193	1.02
Scottish	247	1.30
Slavic	13	0.07
Slovak	21	0.11
Swedish	187	0.99
Swiss	66	0.35
Turkish	13	0.07
Ukrainian	47	0.25
United States or American	777	4.10
Welsh	14	0.07
West Indian, excl. Hispanic:	41	0.22
British West Indian	6	0.03
Haitian	35	0.18
White:	18,485	97.44
Not Hispanic (17,829)	17,922	94.47
Hispanic (525)	563	2.97

Wappinger

Place Type: Town
County: Dutchess
Population: 26,274

Ancestry/Race	Number	%
Acadian/Cajun	8	0.03
Afghan	6	0.02
African American/Black:	1,504	5.72
Not Hispanic (1,235)	1,394	5.31
Hispanic (67)	110	0.42
African, sub-Saharan:	80	0.30
African	59	0.22
Ghanian	13	0.05
Ugandan	8	0.03
Alaska Native tribes, not specified	3	0.01
Am. Ind. or Alaska Nat., not spec.	81	0.31
Albanian	88	0.33
American Indian tribes, specified:	72	0.27
Apache	1	0.00
Blackfeet (2)	4	0.02
Cherokee (2)	18	0.07
Cheyenne	1	0.00
Chippewa	2	0.01
Choctaw (1)	1	0.00
Delaware	1	0.00
Iroquois (7)	18	0.07
Latin American Indians (9)	11	0.04
Menominee (1)	1	0.00
Navajo	3	0.01
Pueblo	1	0.00
Seminole	3	0.01
Sioux (1)	2	0.01
All other tribes (1)	5	0.02
American Indian tribes, not spec.	12	0.05
Arab:	243	0.92
Arab/Arabic	95	0.36
Egyptian	70	0.27
Jordanian	13	0.05
Lebanese	27	0.10
Syrian	34	0.13
Other Arab	4	0.02
Armenian	16	0.06
Asian:	1,236	4.70
Bangladeshi (20)	25	0.10
Cambodian (7)	7	0.03
Chinese, ex. Taiwanese (333)	352	1.34
Filipino (43)	54	0.21
Indian (504)	528	2.01
Indonesian (1)	5	0.02
Japanese (32)	39	0.15
Korean (69)	74	0.28
Pakistani (30)	41	0.16
Taiwanese (12)	12	0.05
Thai (8)	11	0.04
Vietnamese (46)	48	0.18
Other Asian, specified (3)	3	0.01
Other Asian, not specified (14)	37	0.14
Austrian	161	0.61
Belgian	14	0.05
British	123	0.47
Canadian	80	0.30
Czech	89	0.34
Czechoslovakian	124	0.47
Danish	88	0.33
Dutch	473	1.80
Eastern European	15	0.06
English	2,043	7.77
European	142	0.54
Finnish	46	0.17
French, except Basque	625	2.38
French Canadian	246	0.94
German	4,345	16.52
Greek	309	1.17
Guyanese	16	0.06
Hawaii Native/Pacific Islander:	12	0.05
Micronesian: (2)	5	0.02
Guamanian/Chamorro (2)	5	0.02
Polynesian: (2)	4	0.02
Native Hawaiian (2)	3	0.01
Samoan	1	0.00
Other Pac. Isl., not spec.	3	0.01
Hispanic or Latino:	2,068	7.87
Central American:	57	0.22
Guatemalan	14	0.05
Honduran	17	0.06
Nicaraguan	7	0.03
Panamanian	10	0.04
Salvadoran	7	0.03
Other Central American	2	0.01
Cuban	99	0.38
Dominican Republic	67	0.26
Mexican	278	1.06
Puerto Rican	1,020	3.88
South American:	216	0.82
Argentinean	17	0.06
Bolivian	1	0.00
Chilean	13	0.05
Colombian	43	0.16
Ecuadorian	107	0.41
Paraguayan	1	0.00
Peruvian	14	0.05
Uruguayan	6	0.02
Venezuelan	5	0.02
Other South American	9	0.03
Other Hispanic or Latino	331	1.26
Hungarian	243	0.92
Iranian	27	0.10
Irish	6,457	24.54
Israeli	12	0.05
Italian	7,488	28.46
Lithuanian	84	0.32
Maltese	17	0.06
Northern European	16	0.06
Norwegian	180	0.68
Pennsylvania German	10	0.04
Polish	1,314	4.99
Portuguese	134	0.51
Romanian	76	0.29
Russian	296	1.13
Scandinavian	15	0.06
Scotch-Irish	244	0.93
Scottish	437	1.66
Slavic	26	0.10
Slovak	89	0.34
Slovene	10	0.04
Swedish	181	0.69
Swiss	34	0.13
Ukrainian	226	0.86
United States or American	651	2.47
Welsh	126	0.48
West Indian, excl. Hispanic:	197	0.75
British West Indian	50	0.19
Jamaican	119	0.45
Trinidadian and Tobagonian	23	0.09
West Indian	5	0.02
White:	23,044	87.71
Not Hispanic (21,432)	21,697	82.58
Hispanic (1,211)	1,347	5.13
Yugoslavian	17	0.06

Notes: 1. Figures in the "Number" column do not add up to the total population due to: a) Ancestry/Race overlap — e.g. persons can report being both White and Irish, b) persons of Hispanic origin can report being any race, c) persons reporting two ancestries are counted in both categories. 2. Numbers in parentheses indicate the number of persons reporting this ancestry/race alone, not in combination with any other ancestry/race. 3. Refer to the Explanation of Data in the front of the book for more detailed information.

Warwick

Place Type: Town
County: Orange
Population: 30,764

Ancestry/Race	Number	%
African American/Black:	1,580	5.14
Not Hispanic (1,234)	1,374	4.47
Hispanic (153)	206	0.67
African, sub-Saharan:	57	0.19
African	38	0.12
South African	9	0.03
Other sub-Saharan African	10	0.03
Alaska Native tribes, specified:	1	0.00
Tlingit-Haida (1)	1	0.00
Am. Ind. or Alaska Nat., not spec.	105	0.34
American Indian tribes, specified:	141	0.46
Apache	5	0.02
Blackfeet (1)	10	0.03
Cherokee (7)	45	0.15
Cheyenne	1	0.00
Chippewa (1)	1	0.00
Choctaw (2)	5	0.02
Delaware (20)	38	0.12
Iroquois (3)	7	0.02
Latin American Indians (12)	18	0.06
Seminole	3	0.01
Sioux	1	0.00
All other tribes (3)	7	0.02
American Indian tribes, not spec.	22	0.07
Arab:	69	0.22
Iraqi	8	0.03
Lebanese	35	0.11
Syrian	7	0.02
Other Arab	19	0.06
Armenian	34	0.11
Asian:	357	1.16
Cambodian (1)	1	0.00
Chinese, ex. Taiwanese (77)	98	0.32
Filipino (57)	76	0.25
Indian (44)	50	0.16
Japanese (14)	27	0.09
Korean (44)	58	0.19
Laotian (3)	3	0.01
Malaysian (1)	1	0.00
Pakistani (9)	9	0.03
Thai (1)	1	0.00
Vietnamese (3)	6	0.02
Other Asian, specified	3	0.01
Other Asian, not specified (9)	24	0.08
Australian	42	0.14
Austrian	162	0.53
Belgian	65	0.21
Brazilian	55	0.18
British	224	0.73
Canadian	64	0.21
Celtic	21	0.07
Croatian	72	0.23
Czech	188	0.61
Czechoslovakian	55	0.18
Danish	60	0.20
Dutch	1,271	4.13
Eastern European	38	0.12
English	2,301	7.48
Estonian	26	0.08
European	227	0.74
Finnish	61	0.20
French, except Basque	679	2.21
French Canadian	141	0.46
German	5,670	18.43
Greek	270	0.88
Guyanese	19	0.06
Hawaii Native/Pacific Islander:	21	0.07
Micronesian: (2)	2	0.01
Guamanian/Chamorro (2)	2	0.01
Polynesian: (6)	8	0.03
Native Hawaiian (6)	8	0.03
Other Pac. Isl., specified	3	0.01
Other Pac. Isl., not spec. (6)	8	0.03
Hispanic or Latino:	1,991	6.47
Central American:	46	0.15
Costa Rican	5	0.02
Guatemalan	14	0.05
Honduran	3	0.01
Nicaraguan	2	0.01
Panamanian	5	0.02
Salvadoran	15	0.05
Other Central American	2	0.01
Cuban	65	0.21
Dominican Republic	48	0.16
Mexican	228	0.74
Puerto Rican	1,178	3.83
South American:	132	0.43
Argentinean	8	0.03
Bolivian	6	0.02
Chilean	8	0.03
Colombian	54	0.18
Ecuadorian	32	0.10
Peruvian	15	0.05
Uruguayan	1	0.00
Venezuelan	1	0.00
Other South American	7	0.02
Other Hispanic or Latino	294	0.96
Hungarian	418	1.36
Iranian	43	0.14
Irish	7,864	25.56
Israeli	8	0.03
Italian	6,038	19.63
Latvian	11	0.04
Lithuanian	129	0.42
Maltese	7	0.02
Northern European	63	0.20
Norwegian	414	1.35
Pennsylvania German	55	0.18
Polish	3,084	10.02
Portuguese	33	0.11
Romanian	23	0.07
Russian	567	1.84
Scandinavian	38	0.12
Scotch-Irish	396	1.29
Scottish	489	1.59
Serbian	9	0.03
Slovak	116	0.38
Slovene	21	0.07
Swedish	308	1.00
Swiss	135	0.44
Turkish	32	0.10
Ukrainian	171	0.56
United States or American	1,425	4.63
Welsh	184	0.60
West Indian, excl. Hispanic:	242	0.79
British West Indian	8	0.03
Haitian	34	0.11
Jamaican	116	0.38
Trinidadian and Tobagonian	74	0.24
West Indian	10	0.03
White:	28,435	92.43
Not Hispanic (26,825)	27,107	88.11
Hispanic (1,190)	1,328	4.32
Yugoslavian	104	0.34

Watertown

Place Type: City
County: Jefferson
Population: 26,705

Ancestry/Race	Number	%
African American/Black:	1,618	6.06
Not Hispanic (1,260)	1,516	5.68
Hispanic (61)	102	0.38
African, sub-Saharan:	31	0.12
African	31	0.12
Alaska Native tribes, specified:	6	0.02
Alaska Athabascan (3)	4	0.01
Aleut	1	0.00
Tlingit-Haida	1	0.00
Am. Ind. or Alaska Nat., not spec.	101	0.38
American Indian tribes, specified:	183	0.69
Apache (2)	2	0.01
Blackfeet (1)	19	0.07
Cherokee (7)	29	0.11
Cheyenne	1	0.00
Chippewa (4)	4	0.01
Choctaw (2)	2	0.01
Creek (4)	4	0.01
Iroquois (59)	85	0.32
Latin American Indians (7)	12	0.04
Lumbee (1)	1	0.00
Shoshone	1	0.00
Sioux (3)	8	0.03
All other tribes (7)	15	0.06
American Indian tribes, not spec.	23	0.09
Arab:	77	0.29
Arab/Arabic	4	0.01
Lebanese	67	0.25
Syrian	6	0.02
Armenian	5	0.02
Asian:	433	1.62
Cambodian (1)	1	0.00
Chinese, ex. Taiwanese (46)	54	0.20
Filipino (79)	122	0.46
Indian (37)	43	0.16
Indonesian (1)	1	0.00
Japanese (9)	20	0.07
Korean (103)	144	0.54
Pakistani (4)	8	0.03
Thai (1)	4	0.01
Vietnamese (16)	20	0.07
Other Asian, specified	1	0.00
Other Asian, not specified (6)	15	0.06
Austrian	39	0.15
Belgian	20	0.07
British	101	0.38
Canadian	289	1.08
Celtic	4	0.01
Czech	29	0.11
Czechoslovakian	31	0.12
Danish	60	0.22
Dutch	597	2.24
Eastern European	6	0.02
English	2,785	10.43
European	105	0.39
French, except Basque	2,704	10.13
French Canadian	1,365	5.11
German	3,357	12.57
Greek	102	0.38
Hawaii Native/Pacific Islander:	70	0.26
Micronesian: (13)	16	0.06
Guamanian/Chamorro (13)	16	0.06
Polynesian: (14)	35	0.13
Native Hawaiian (8)	26	0.10
Samoan (6)	9	0.03
Other Pac. Isl., not spec. (3)	19	0.07
Hispanic or Latino:	960	3.59
Central American:	62	0.23
Costa Rican	1	0.00
Honduran	1	0.00
Nicaraguan	1	0.00
Panamanian	40	0.15
Salvadoran	15	0.06
Other Central American	4	0.01
Cuban	22	0.08
Dominican Republic	36	0.13
Mexican	219	0.82
Puerto Rican	396	1.48
South American:	46	0.17
Argentinean	3	0.01
Bolivian	1	0.00
Chilean	2	0.01
Colombian	13	0.05
Ecuadorian	5	0.02
Peruvian	9	0.03
Venezuelan	5	0.02
Other South American	8	0.03
Other Hispanic or Latino	179	0.67
Hungarian	232	0.87
Icelander	22	0.08
Irish	4,895	18.33

Notes: 1. Figures in the "Number" column do not add up to the total population due to: a) Ancestry/Race overlap — e.g. persons can report being both White and Irish, b) persons of Hispanic origin can report being any race, c) persons reporting two ancestries are counted in both categories. 2. Numbers in parentheses indicate the number of persons reporting this ancestry/race alone, not in combination with any other ancestry/race. 3. Refer to the Explanation of Data in the front of the book for more detailed information.

Ancestry/Race	Number	%
Italian	3,144	11.77
Latvian	5	0.02
Lithuanian	37	0.14
Luxemburger	28	0.10
Maltese	16	0.06
Northern European	16	0.06
Norwegian	122	0.46
Pennsylvania German	27	0.10
Polish	706	2.64
Portuguese	68	0.25
Romanian	12	0.04
Russian	123	0.46
Scandinavian	6	0.02
Scotch-Irish	453	1.70
Scottish	650	2.43
Slovak	8	0.03
Swedish	191	0.72
Swiss	63	0.24
Turkish	13	0.05
Ukrainian	114	0.43
United States or American	2,124	7.95
Welsh	242	0.91
West Indian, excl. Hispanic:	136	0.51
Haitian	53	0.20
Jamaican	62	0.23
West Indian	21	0.08
White:	24,364	91.23
Not Hispanic (23,438)	23,912	89.54
Hispanic (363)	452	1.69
Yugoslavian	8	0.03

Watervliet

Place Type: City
County: Albany
Population: 10,207

Ancestry/Race	Number	%
African American/Black:	448	4.39
Not Hispanic (355)	402	3.94
Hispanic (40)	46	0.45
African, sub-Saharan:	20	0.20
African	12	0.12
Nigerian	8	0.08
Am. Ind. or Alaska Nat., not spec.	27	0.26
Alsatian	8	0.08
American Indian tribes, specified:	29	0.28
Blackfeet	2	0.02
Cherokee	5	0.05
Chippewa	1	0.01
Choctaw (1)	1	0.01
Iroquois (6)	8	0.08
Sioux	1	0.01
All other tribes (3)	11	0.11
American Indian tribes, not spec.	2	0.02
Arab:	36	0.35
Lebanese	36	0.35
Armenian	88	0.86
Asian:	166	1.63
Cambodian (5)	5	0.05
Chinese, ex. Taiwanese (19)	22	0.22
Filipino (24)	33	0.32
Hmong	1	0.01
Indian (42)	47	0.46
Japanese (5)	7	0.07
Korean (21)	24	0.24
Pakistani (7)	7	0.07
Sri Lankan (2)	2	0.02
Vietnamese (8)	10	0.10
Other Asian, not specified	8	0.08
Austrian	5	0.05
Brazilian	13	0.13
British	1	0.01
Czech	4	0.04
Czechoslovakian	42	0.41
Danish	38	0.37
Dutch	267	2.62
English	669	6.55
European	10	0.10
French, except Basque	1,269	12.43
French Canadian	415	4.07
German	1,477	14.47
Greek	80	0.78
Hawaii Native/Pacific Islander:	12	0.12
Micronesian:	1	0.01
Guamanian/Chamorro	1	0.01
Polynesian: (1)	1	0.01
Samoan (1)	1	0.01
Other Pac. Isl., not spec. (7)	10	0.10
Hispanic or Latino:	369	3.62
Cuban	3	0.03
Dominican Republic	14	0.14
Mexican	47	0.46
Puerto Rican	218	2.14
South American:	9	0.09
Bolivian	1	0.01
Colombian	1	0.01
Ecuadorian	1	0.01
Peruvian	4	0.04
Venezuelan	2	0.02
Other Hispanic or Latino	78	0.76
Hungarian	27	0.26
Irish	3,111	30.48
Italian	1,950	19.10
Lithuanian	92	0.90
Norwegian	78	0.76
Pennsylvania German	7	0.07
Polish	865	8.47
Russian	87	0.85
Scandinavian	2	0.02
Scotch-Irish	88	0.86
Scottish	158	1.55
Slovak	32	0.31
Swedish	27	0.26
Turkish	20	0.20
Ukrainian	284	2.78
United States or American	298	2.92
Welsh	84	0.82
West Indian, excl. Hispanic:	26	0.25
Jamaican	25	0.24
West Indian	1	0.01
White:	9,517	93.24
Not Hispanic (9,197)	9,304	91.15
Hispanic (193)	213	2.09

Wawarsing

Place Type: Town
County: Ulster
Population: 12,889

Ancestry/Race	Number	%
African American/Black:	1,774	13.76
Not Hispanic (1,483)	1,607	12.47
Hispanic (122)	167	1.30
African, sub-Saharan:	44	0.34
African	36	0.28
Nigerian	8	0.06
Am. Ind. or Alaska Nat., not spec.	63	0.49
American Indian tribes, specified:	101	0.78
Apache	1	0.01
Blackfeet (1)	3	0.02
Cherokee	28	0.22
Cheyenne	1	0.01
Chippewa	1	0.01
Creek (1)	1	0.01
Delaware (8)	12	0.09
Iroquois (3)	14	0.11
Kiowa (1)	1	0.01
Latin American Indians (16)	28	0.22
Navajo	1	0.01
Pueblo	2	0.02
Sioux (3)	3	0.02
All other tribes (5)	5	0.04
American Indian tribes, not spec.	7	0.05
Arab:	16	0.12
Lebanese	16	0.12
Armenian	10	0.08
Asian:	196	1.52
Bangladeshi (5)	6	0.05
Cambodian (1)	1	0.01
Chinese, ex. Taiwanese (83)	93	0.72
Filipino (6)	6	0.05
Indian (31)	45	0.35
Japanese (2)	3	0.02
Korean (8)	12	0.09
Pakistani (4)	14	0.11
Taiwanese (1)	1	0.01
Thai (1)	1	0.01
Vietnamese (2)	2	0.02
Other Asian, specified	1	0.01
Other Asian, not specified (2)	11	0.09
Australian	6	0.05
Austrian	26	0.20
Belgian	9	0.07
Brazilian	22	0.17
Canadian	10	0.08
Croatian	14	0.11
Czech	33	0.26
Czechoslovakian	19	0.15
Danish	52	0.40
Dutch	647	5.02
Eastern European	31	0.24
English	789	6.12
European	21	0.16
Finnish	38	0.29
French, except Basque	273	2.12
French Canadian	33	0.26
German	1,752	13.59
Greek	34	0.26
Hawaii Native/Pacific Islander:	6	0.05
Polynesian:	1	0.01
Samoan	1	0.01
Other Pac. Isl., specified	1	0.01
Other Pac. Isl., not spec. (1)	4	0.03
Hispanic or Latino:	2,326	18.05
Central American:	39	0.30
Costa Rican	5	0.04
Guatemalan	2	0.02
Honduran	13	0.10
Nicaraguan	5	0.04
Panamanian	4	0.03
Salvadoran	10	0.08
Cuban	35	0.27
Dominican Republic	118	0.92
Mexican	56	0.43
Puerto Rican	1,383	10.73
South American:	312	2.42
Argentinean	4	0.03
Chilean	48	0.37
Colombian	206	1.60
Ecuadorian	26	0.20
Peruvian	17	0.13
Venezuelan	4	0.03
Other South American	7	0.05
Other Hispanic or Latino	383	2.97
Hungarian	108	0.84
Irish	1,613	12.51
Italian	1,226	9.51
Lithuanian	43	0.33
Macedonian	18	0.14
Norwegian	62	0.48
Polish	598	4.64
Portuguese	53	0.41
Romanian	13	0.10
Russian	255	1.98
Scandinavian	5	0.04
Scotch-Irish	72	0.56
Scottish	144	1.12
Slovak	11	0.09
Slovene	6	0.05
Swedish	146	1.13
Swiss	21	0.16
Turkish	19	0.15
Ukrainian	279	2.16
United States or American	905	7.02
Welsh	26	0.20
West Indian, excl. Hispanic:	181	1.40
Bahamian	7	0.05
Barbadian	15	0.12

Notes: 1. Figures in the "Number" column do not add up to the total population due to: a) Ancestry/Race overlap — e.g. persons can report being both White and Irish, b) persons of Hispanic origin can report being any race, c) persons reporting two ancestries are counted in both categories. 2. Numbers in parentheses indicate the number of persons reporting this ancestry/race alone, not in combination with any other ancestry/race. 3. Refer to the Explanation of Data in the front of the book for more detailed information.

British West Indian	10	0.08
Haitian	10	0.08
Jamaican	97	0.75
West Indian	42	0.33
White:	9,964	77.31
Not Hispanic (8,602)	8,802	68.29
Hispanic (1,068)	1,162	9.02
Yugoslavian	18	0.14

Webster

Place Type: Town
County: Monroe
Population: 37,926

Ancestry/Race	Number	%
African American/Black:	731	1.93
Not Hispanic (575)	691	1.82
Hispanic (32)	40	0.11
African, sub-Saharan:	76	0.20
African	33	0.09
South African	43	0.11
Alaska Native tribes, specified:	2	0.01
Tlingit-Haida (1)	2	0.01
Am. Ind. or Alaska Nat., not spec.	48	0.13
Alsatian	8	0.02
American Indian tribes, specified:	91	0.24
Apache	3	0.01
Blackfeet (1)	4	0.01
Cherokee	12	0.03
Chippewa	3	0.01
Choctaw (1)	1	0.00
Iroquois (18)	47	0.12
Latin American Indians	6	0.02
Ottawa	1	0.00
Pueblo (1)	1	0.00
Seminole	2	0.01
Sioux (3)	4	0.01
All other tribes (3)	7	0.02
American Indian tribes, not spec.	2	0.01
Arab:	177	0.47
Arab/Arabic	32	0.08
Egyptian	13	0.03
Iraqi	10	0.03
Lebanese	47	0.12
Moroccan	7	0.02
Palestinian	7	0.02
Syrian	18	0.05
Other Arab	43	0.11
Armenian	15	0.04
Asian:	865	2.28
Cambodian (6)	9	0.02
Chinese, ex. Taiwanese (172)	190	0.50
Filipino (32)	45	0.12
Indian (229)	246	0.65
Indonesian (3)	3	0.01
Japanese (27)	47	0.12
Korean (114)	122	0.32
Laotian (64)	67	0.18
Pakistani (5)	8	0.02
Sri Lankan (6)	6	0.02
Taiwanese (8)	10	0.03
Thai (2)	4	0.01
Vietnamese (50)	57	0.15
Other Asian, not specified (15)	51	0.13
Australian	8	0.02
Austrian	144	0.38
Belgian	116	0.31
British	200	0.53
Bulgarian	22	0.06
Canadian	181	0.48
Celtic	7	0.02
Croatian	20	0.05
Czech	128	0.34
Czechoslovakian	94	0.25
Danish	109	0.29
Dutch	1,716	4.52
Eastern European	45	0.12
English	5,524	14.57
European	293	0.77
Finnish	62	0.16
French, except Basque	1,675	4.42
French Canadian	326	0.86
German	10,236	26.99
Greek	401	1.06
Hawaii Native/Pacific Islander:	19	0.05
Micronesian:	4	0.01
Guamanian/Chamorro	4	0.01
Polynesian: (1)	14	0.04
Native Hawaiian (1)	10	0.03
Samoan	4	0.01
Other Pac. Isl., not spec.	1	0.00
Hispanic or Latino:	596	1.57
Central American:	40	0.11
Costa Rican	5	0.01
Guatemalan	7	0.02
Honduran	1	0.00
Nicaraguan	8	0.02
Panamanian	5	0.01
Salvadoran	12	0.03
Other Central American	2	0.01
Cuban	29	0.08
Dominican Republic	19	0.05
Mexican	84	0.22
Puerto Rican	288	0.76
South American:	60	0.16
Argentinean	16	0.04
Chilean	11	0.03
Colombian	16	0.04
Ecuadorian	1	0.00
Paraguayan	2	0.01
Peruvian	6	0.02
Venezuelan	6	0.02
Other South American	2	0.01
Other Hispanic or Latino	76	0.20
Hungarian	163	0.43
Icelander	7	0.02
Iranian	29	0.08
Irish	7,012	18.49
Italian	9,005	23.74
Latvian	33	0.09
Lithuanian	104	0.27
Macedonian	47	0.12
Maltese	8	0.02
Northern European	31	0.08
Norwegian	170	0.45
Polish	2,903	7.65
Portuguese	11	0.03
Romanian	53	0.14
Russian	332	0.88
Scandinavian	5	0.01
Scotch-Irish	553	1.46
Scottish	862	2.27
Serbian	17	0.04
Slavic	11	0.03
Slovak	58	0.15
Slovene	13	0.03
Swedish	599	1.58
Swiss	222	0.59
Turkish	108	0.28
Ukrainian	958	2.53
United States or American	1,543	4.07
Welsh	318	0.84
West Indian, excl. Hispanic:	49	0.13
Haitian	18	0.05
Jamaican	31	0.08
White:	36,321	95.77
Not Hispanic (35,664)	35,919	94.71
Hispanic (349)	402	1.06
Yugoslavian	151	0.40

West Babylon

Place Type: Census Designated Place
County: Suffolk
Population: 43,452

Ancestry/Race	Number	%
Acadian/Cajun	6	0.01
African American/Black:	4,799	11.04
Not Hispanic (4,333)	4,597	10.58
Hispanic (150)	202	0.46
African, sub-Saharan:	223	0.51
African	133	0.31
Ghanian	25	0.06
Nigerian	61	0.14
South African	4	0.01
Alaska Native tribes, specified:	1	0.00
Tlingit-Haida	1	0.00
Am. Ind. or Alaska Nat., not spec.	120	0.28
American Indian tribes, specified:	96	0.22
Apache	3	0.01
Blackfeet	10	0.02
Cherokee (2)	25	0.06
Chippewa	1	0.00
Choctaw	1	0.00
Creek	2	0.00
Iroquois (7)	11	0.03
Latin American Indians (2)	4	0.01
Navajo (1)	2	0.00
Pima (1)	1	0.00
Pueblo	1	0.00
Seminole	2	0.00
Sioux (2)	10	0.02
All other tribes (2)	23	0.05
American Indian tribes, not spec.	11	0.03
Arab:	99	0.23
Lebanese	66	0.15
Moroccan	19	0.04
Syrian	14	0.03
Armenian	14	0.03
Asian:	1,019	2.35
Bangladeshi (11)	11	0.03
Chinese, ex. Taiwanese (161)	206	0.47
Filipino (122)	157	0.36
Indian (261)	304	0.70
Indonesian (2)	2	0.00
Japanese (12)	23	0.05
Korean (51)	60	0.14
Malaysian	1	0.00
Pakistani (60)	97	0.22
Taiwanese (3)	3	0.01
Thai (12)	15	0.03
Vietnamese (76)	90	0.21
Other Asian, not specified (25)	50	0.12
Australian	6	0.01
Austrian	229	0.53
Belgian	17	0.04
Brazilian	34	0.08
British	91	0.21
Canadian	49	0.11
Croatian	64	0.15
Cypriot	17	0.04
Czech	115	0.26
Czechoslovakian	69	0.16
Danish	194	0.45
Dutch	346	0.80
Eastern European	32	0.07
English	1,672	3.85
European	78	0.18
Finnish	85	0.20
French, except Basque	460	1.06
French Canadian	127	0.29
German	7,527	17.32
Greek	605	1.39
Guyanese	41	0.09
Hawaii Native/Pacific Islander:	35	0.08
Micronesian: (1)	2	0.00
Guamanian/Chamorro (1)	2	0.00
Polynesian: (5)	12	0.03
Native Hawaiian (4)	9	0.02
Samoan (1)	3	0.01
Other Pac. Isl., not spec. (2)	21	0.05
Hispanic or Latino:	3,344	7.70
Central American:	325	0.75
Costa Rican	14	0.03
Guatemalan	45	0.10
Honduran	31	0.07
Nicaraguan	3	0.01
Panamanian	19	0.04

Notes: 1. Figures in the "Number" column do not add up to the total population due to: a) Ancestry/Race overlap — e.g. persons can report being both White and Irish, b) persons of Hispanic origin can report being any race, c) persons reporting two ancestries are counted in both categories. 2. Numbers in parentheses indicate the number of persons reporting this ancestry/race alone, not in combination with any other ancestry/race. 3. Refer to the Explanation of Data in the front of the book for more detailed information.

Ancestry/Race	Number	%
Salvadoran	192	0.44
Other Central American	21	0.05
Cuban	91	0.21
Dominican Republic	278	0.64
Mexican	116	0.27
Puerto Rican	1,300	2.99
South American:	456	1.05
Argentinean	23	0.05
Bolivian	10	0.02
Chilean	18	0.04
Colombian	176	0.41
Ecuadorian	94	0.22
Peruvian	92	0.21
Uruguayan	19	0.04
Venezuelan	8	0.02
Other South American	16	0.04
Other Hispanic or Latino	778	1.79
Hungarian	257	0.59
Icelander	9	0.02
Iranian	7	0.02
Irish	9,597	22.09
Italian	15,785	36.33
Latvian	21	0.05
Lithuanian	83	0.19
Maltese	90	0.21
Norwegian	418	0.96
Pennsylvania German	32	0.07
Polish	2,380	5.48
Portuguese	161	0.37
Romanian	64	0.15
Russian	488	1.12
Scandinavian	17	0.04
Scotch-Irish	282	0.65
Scottish	237	0.55
Slavic	7	0.02
Slovak	11	0.03
Slovene	28	0.06
Swedish	245	0.56
Swiss	63	0.14
Turkish	154	0.35
Ukrainian	276	0.64
United States or American	1,115	2.57
Welsh	87	0.20
West Indian, excl. Hispanic:	899	2.07
Barbadian	31	0.07
Bermudan	16	0.04
British West Indian	13	0.03
Dutch West Indian	21	0.05
Haitian	326	0.75
Jamaican	310	0.71
Trinidadian and Tobagonian	72	0.17
West Indian	110	0.25
White:	36,937	85.01
Not Hispanic (34,253)	34,630	79.70
Hispanic (2,154)	2,307	5.31
Yugoslavian	8	0.02

West Haverstraw

Place Type: Village
County: Rockland
Population: 10,295

Ancestry/Race	Number	%
Afghan	62	0.60
African American/Black:	1,491	14.48
Not Hispanic (1,220)	1,339	13.01
Hispanic (98)	152	1.48
African, sub-Saharan:	27	0.26
African	27	0.26
Am. Ind. or Alaska Nat., not spec.	63	0.61
American Indian tribes, specified:	50	0.49
Blackfeet	3	0.03
Cherokee (6)	11	0.11
Chickasaw	1	0.01
Comanche (1)	1	0.01
Delaware (6)	16	0.16
Iroquois	4	0.04
Latin American Indians (1)	12	0.12
Shoshone	1	0.01
All other tribes (1)	1	0.01
American Indian tribes, not spec.	11	0.11
Arab:	48	0.47
Egyptian	24	0.23
Iraqi	4	0.04
Lebanese	20	0.19
Asian:	533	5.18
Bangladeshi (11)	18	0.17
Cambodian (11)	16	0.16
Chinese, ex. Taiwanese (36)	54	0.52
Filipino (74)	89	0.86
Indian (208)	251	2.44
Indonesian (2)	7	0.07
Japanese (1)	3	0.03
Korean (22)	23	0.22
Pakistani (15)	15	0.15
Taiwanese (4)	4	0.04
Thai (4)	6	0.06
Vietnamese (20)	23	0.22
Other Asian, not specified (14)	24	0.23
Austrian	60	0.58
Bulgarian	9	0.09
Canadian	13	0.13
Celtic	10	0.10
Croatian	18	0.17
Czech	18	0.17
Czechoslovakian	24	0.23
Danish	21	0.20
Dutch	79	0.77
English	370	3.59
European	20	0.19
Finnish	8	0.08
French, except Basque	142	1.38
French Canadian	45	0.44
German	971	9.43
German Russian	11	0.11
Greek	68	0.66
Hawaii Native/Pacific Islander:	13	0.13
Micronesian: (1)	1	0.01
Guamanian/Chamorro (1)	1	0.01
Polynesian: (7)	7	0.07
Native Hawaiian (3)	3	0.03
Samoan (4)	4	0.04
Other Pac. Isl., not spec. (2)	5	0.05
Hispanic or Latino:	3,127	30.37
Central American:	99	0.96
Costa Rican	9	0.09
Guatemalan	37	0.36
Honduran	2	0.02
Nicaraguan	11	0.11
Panamanian	2	0.02
Salvadoran	31	0.30
Other Central American	7	0.07
Cuban	36	0.35
Dominican Republic	841	8.17
Mexican	98	0.95
Puerto Rican	1,464	14.22
South American:	156	1.52
Argentinean	17	0.17
Chilean	1	0.01
Colombian	34	0.33
Ecuadorian	53	0.51
Peruvian	36	0.35
Venezuelan	11	0.11
Other South American	4	0.04
Other Hispanic or Latino	433	4.21
Hungarian	71	0.69
Icelander	28	0.27
Irish	1,700	16.51
Italian	2,045	19.86
Lithuanian	34	0.33
Norwegian	21	0.20
Polish	367	3.56
Russian	130	1.26
Scandinavian	34	0.33
Scotch-Irish	45	0.44
Scottish	99	0.96
Slavic	25	0.24
Slovak	12	0.12
Swedish	66	0.64
Swiss	26	0.25
Ukrainian	23	0.22
United States or American	313	3.04
Welsh	13	0.13
West Indian, excl. Hispanic:	597	5.80
Haitian	380	3.69
Jamaican	131	1.27
Trinidadian and Tobagonian	32	0.31
West Indian	54	0.52
White:	6,998	67.97
Not Hispanic (5,246)	5,348	51.95
Hispanic (1,430)	1,650	16.03

West Hempstead

Place Type: Census Designated Place
County: Nassau
Population: 18,713

Ancestry/Race	Number	%
Afghan	20	0.11
African American/Black:	1,251	6.69
Not Hispanic (1,012)	1,119	5.98
Hispanic (99)	132	0.71
African, sub-Saharan:	22	0.12
African	22	0.12
Alaska Native tribes, specified:	1	0.01
Tlingit-Haida (1)	1	0.01
Am. Ind. or Alaska Nat., not spec.	26	0.14
Albanian	14	0.07
American Indian tribes, specified:	45	0.24
Cherokee (1)	6	0.03
Chippewa (1)	2	0.01
Choctaw	5	0.03
Crow	1	0.01
Iroquois (1)	1	0.01
Latin American Indians (10)	23	0.12
Seminole	1	0.01
Sioux (2)	4	0.02
All other tribes	2	0.01
American Indian tribes, not spec.	5	0.03
Arab:	160	0.86
Arab/Arabic	58	0.31
Egyptian	28	0.15
Iraqi	7	0.04
Jordanian	9	0.05
Lebanese	25	0.13
Moroccan	7	0.04
Palestinian	17	0.09
Other Arab	9	0.05
Armenian	37	0.20
Asian:	1,106	5.91
Bangladeshi (2)	2	0.01
Cambodian (1)	1	0.01
Chinese, ex. Taiwanese (225)	253	1.35
Filipino (175)	191	1.02
Indian (368)	398	2.13
Indonesian (3)	7	0.04
Japanese (9)	11	0.06
Korean (70)	80	0.43
Laotian (3)	3	0.02
Pakistani (50)	71	0.38
Sri Lankan (5)	5	0.03
Taiwanese (3)	5	0.03
Thai (9)	9	0.05
Vietnamese (6)	10	0.05
Other Asian, specified (5)	5	0.03
Other Asian, not specified (6)	55	0.29
Austrian	236	1.26
Belgian	20	0.11
Brazilian	44	0.24
British	23	0.12
Canadian	71	0.38
Croatian	52	0.28
Cypriot	4	0.02
Czech	50	0.27
Czechoslovakian	90	0.48
Danish	34	0.18
Dutch	34	0.18
Eastern European	181	0.97

Notes: 1. Figures in the "Number" column do not add up to the total population due to: a) Ancestry/Race overlap — e.g. persons can report being both White and Irish, b) persons of Hispanic origin can report being any race, c) persons reporting two ancestries are counted in both categories. 2. Numbers in parentheses indicate the number of persons reporting this ancestry/race alone, not in combination with any other ancestry/race. 3. Refer to the Explanation of Data in the front of the book for more detailed information.

Ancestry/Race	Number	%
English	472	2.52
Estonian	6	0.03
European	165	0.88
Finnish	9	0.05
French, except Basque	178	0.95
French Canadian	79	0.42
German	2,339	12.50
Greek	407	2.18
Guyanese	39	0.21
Hawaii Native/Pacific Islander:	23	0.12
Other Pac. Isl., not spec. (4)	23	0.12
Hispanic or Latino:	1,860	9.94
Central American:	399	2.13
Costa Rican	2	0.01
Guatemalan	23	0.12
Honduran	46	0.25
Nicaraguan	10	0.05
Panamanian	11	0.06
Salvadoran	291	1.56
Other Central American	16	0.09
Cuban	65	0.35
Dominican Republic	121	0.65
Mexican	111	0.59
Puerto Rican	433	2.31
South American:	292	1.56
Argentinean	24	0.13
Bolivian	2	0.01
Chilean	12	0.06
Colombian	142	0.76
Ecuadorian	51	0.27
Peruvian	41	0.22
Uruguayan	9	0.05
Venezuelan	5	0.03
Other South American	6	0.03
Other Hispanic or Latino	439	2.35
Hungarian	213	1.14
Irish	2,920	15.61
Israeli	88	0.47
Italian	5,217	27.89
Lithuanian	98	0.52
Maltese	43	0.23
Norwegian	75	0.40
Polish	1,008	5.39
Portuguese	79	0.42
Romanian	78	0.42
Russian	562	3.00
Scotch-Irish	72	0.38
Scottish	51	0.27
Slovak	25	0.13
Swedish	163	0.87
Swiss	12	0.06
Turkish	64	0.34
Ukrainian	80	0.43
United States or American	1,063	5.68
Welsh	44	0.24
West Indian, excl. Hispanic:	481	2.57
Barbadian	9	0.05
British West Indian	16	0.09
Haitian	202	1.08
Jamaican	166	0.89
Trinidadian and Tobagonian	23	0.12
West Indian	65	0.35
White:	15,864	84.78
Not Hispanic (14,492)	14,699	78.55
Hispanic (981)	1,165	6.23
Yugoslavian	18	0.10

West Islip

Place Type: Census Designated Place
County: Suffolk
Population: 28,907

Ancestry/Race	Number	%
African American/Black:	145	0.50
Not Hispanic (108)	137	0.47
Hispanic (7)	8	0.03
African, sub-Saharan:	37	0.13
African	37	0.13
Alaska Native tribes, specified:	3	0.01
Eskimo (3)	3	0.01
Am. Ind. or Alaska Nat., not spec.	20	0.07
Albanian	20	0.07
American Indian tribes, specified:	30	0.10
Blackfeet	2	0.01
Cherokee	11	0.04
Chippewa (3)	3	0.01
Iroquois (3)	3	0.01
Latin American Indians	3	0.01
Sioux (1)	1	0.00
All other tribes	7	0.02
American Indian tribes, not spec.	15	0.05
Arab:	174	0.60
Arab/Arabic	77	0.26
Egyptian	23	0.08
Lebanese	51	0.18
Syrian	23	0.08
Armenian	48	0.16
Asian:	444	1.54
Chinese, ex. Taiwanese (99)	118	0.41
Filipino (56)	81	0.28
Indian (51)	74	0.26
Japanese (10)	27	0.09
Korean (47)	51	0.18
Pakistani (19)	28	0.10
Sri Lankan (3)	3	0.01
Taiwanese (5)	5	0.02
Thai (1)	1	0.00
Vietnamese (11)	16	0.06
Other Asian, specified	1	0.00
Other Asian, not specified (8)	39	0.13
Austrian	166	0.57
Belgian	28	0.10
British	30	0.10
Bulgarian	24	0.08
Canadian	37	0.13
Croatian	77	0.26
Czech	160	0.55
Czechoslovakian	171	0.59
Danish	15	0.05
Dutch	300	1.03
Eastern European	20	0.07
English	1,488	5.11
Estonian	7	0.02
European	45	0.15
Finnish	131	0.45
French, except Basque	508	1.75
French Canadian	164	0.56
German	6,045	20.77
Greek	468	1.61
Guyanese	6	0.02
Hawaii Native/Pacific Islander:	9	0.03
Polynesian: (3)	6	0.02
Native Hawaiian (2)	5	0.02
Samoan (1)	1	0.00
Other Pac. Isl., not spec.	3	0.01
Hispanic or Latino:	1,018	3.52
Central American:	53	0.18
Costa Rican	3	0.01
Guatemalan	9	0.03
Honduran	12	0.04
Nicaraguan	11	0.04
Panamanian	3	0.01
Salvadoran	15	0.05
Cuban	64	0.22
Dominican Republic	48	0.17
Mexican	55	0.19
Puerto Rican	482	1.67
South American:	149	0.52
Argentinean	21	0.07
Bolivian	5	0.02
Chilean	7	0.02
Colombian	46	0.16
Ecuadorian	28	0.10
Paraguayan	2	0.01
Peruvian	33	0.11
Uruguayan	1	0.00
Venezuelan	5	0.02
Other South American	1	0.00
Other Hispanic or Latino	167	0.58
Hungarian	131	0.45
Icelander	7	0.02
Iranian	14	0.05
Irish	8,990	30.89
Israeli	12	0.04
Italian	11,177	38.40
Latvian	60	0.21
Lithuanian	97	0.33
Maltese	10	0.03
Norwegian	440	1.51
Pennsylvania German	6	0.02
Polish	2,093	7.19
Portuguese	49	0.17
Romanian	23	0.08
Russian	691	2.37
Scandinavian	13	0.04
Scotch-Irish	319	1.10
Scottish	340	1.17
Slavic	6	0.02
Slovak	40	0.14
Swedish	332	1.14
Swiss	46	0.16
Turkish	4	0.01
Ukrainian	199	0.68
United States or American	902	3.10
Welsh	56	0.19
West Indian, excl. Hispanic:	118	0.41
Barbadian	4	0.01
Haitian	14	0.05
Jamaican	94	0.32
West Indian	6	0.02
White:	28,293	97.88
Not Hispanic (27,191)	27,415	94.84
Hispanic (818)	878	3.04
Yugoslavian	27	0.09

West Seneca

Place Type: Town
County: Erie
Population: 45,920

Ancestry/Race	Number	%
African American/Black:	262	0.57
Not Hispanic (207)	253	0.55
Hispanic (6)	9	0.02
Am. Ind. or Alaska Nat., not spec.	46	0.10
Albanian	7	0.02
Alsatian	6	0.01
American Indian tribes, specified:	117	0.25
Apache	1	0.00
Cherokee (2)	8	0.02
Chippewa (3)	3	0.01
Crow (1)	1	0.00
Iroquois (54)	85	0.19
Latin American Indians (6)	9	0.02
Ottawa	2	0.00
Pueblo	1	0.00
Sioux (1)	2	0.00
All other tribes (3)	5	0.01
American Indian tribes, not spec.	8	0.02
Arab:	266	0.58
Arab/Arabic	41	0.09
Lebanese	184	0.40
Palestinian	41	0.09
Armenian	19	0.04
Asian:	298	0.65
Chinese, ex. Taiwanese (37)	49	0.11
Filipino (44)	60	0.13
Indian (54)	69	0.15
Japanese (8)	18	0.04
Korean (40)	47	0.10
Laotian (9)	9	0.02
Pakistani (8)	8	0.02
Taiwanese (2)	2	0.00
Vietnamese (13)	21	0.05
Other Asian, not specified (6)	15	0.03
Australian	9	0.02
Austrian	177	0.38
British	69	0.15

Notes: 1. Figures in the "Number" column do not add up to the total population due to: a) Ancestry/Race overlap — e.g. persons can report being both White and Irish, b) persons of Hispanic origin can report being any race, c) persons reporting two ancestries are counted in both categories. 2. Numbers in parentheses indicate the number of persons reporting this ancestry/race alone, not in combination with any other ancestry/race. 3. Refer to the Explanation of Data in the front of the book for more detailed information.

Bulgarian	29	0.06
Canadian	101	0.22
Croatian	115	0.25
Czech	219	0.48
Czechoslovakian	56	0.12
Danish	61	0.13
Dutch	402	0.87
Eastern European	8	0.02
English	3,081	6.70
European	57	0.12
Finnish	28	0.06
French, except Basque	1,325	2.88
French Canadian	433	0.94
German	15,082	32.79
Greek	260	0.57
Hawaii Native/Pacific Islander:	9	0.02
Micronesian: (1)	1	0.00
Guamanian/Chamorro (1)	1	0.00
Polynesian: (1)	4	0.01
Native Hawaiian (1)	4	0.01
Other Pac. Isl., not spec. (2)	4	0.01
Hispanic or Latino:	405	0.88
Central American:	6	0.01
Honduran	2	0.00
Panamanian	1	0.00
Salvadoran	3	0.01
Cuban	6	0.01
Dominican Republic	5	0.01
Mexican	64	0.14
Puerto Rican	228	0.50
South American:	12	0.03
Argentinean	4	0.01
Colombian	6	0.01
Peruvian	2	0.00
Other Hispanic or Latino	84	0.18
Hungarian	459	1.00
Iranian	36	0.08
Irish	10,535	22.90
Italian	8,221	17.87
Lithuanian	94	0.20
Luxemburger	7	0.02
Macedonian	127	0.28
Norwegian	111	0.24
Pennsylvania German	12	0.03
Polish	14,236	30.95
Portuguese	5	0.01
Romanian	13	0.03
Russian	179	0.39
Scotch-Irish	284	0.62
Scottish	699	1.52
Serbian	68	0.15
Slavic	30	0.07
Slovak	84	0.18
Slovene	16	0.03
Swedish	392	0.85
Swiss	71	0.15
Ukrainian	507	1.10
United States or American	1,001	2.18
Welsh	248	0.54
West Indian, excl. Hispanic:	17	0.04
West Indian	17	0.04
White:	45,296	98.64
Not Hispanic (44,743)	44,969	97.93
Hispanic (308)	327	0.71
Yugoslavian	28	0.06

Westbury

Place Type: Village
County: Nassau
Population: 14,263

Ancestry/Race	Number	%
Afghan	7	0.05
African American/Black:	3,510	24.61
Not Hispanic (3,107)	3,327	23.33
Hispanic (123)	183	1.28
African, sub-Saharan:	188	1.32
African	50	0.35
Cape Verdean	21	0.15
Ghanian	11	0.08
Nigerian	98	0.69
Other sub-Saharan African	8	0.06
Am. Ind. or Alaska Nat., not spec.	51	0.36
Albanian	18	0.13
American Indian tribes, specified:	44	0.31
Blackfeet (1)	1	0.01
Cherokee (4)	16	0.11
Choctaw	1	0.01
Creek	2	0.01
Delaware	1	0.01
Iroquois (1)	3	0.02
Kiowa	1	0.01
Latin American Indians (2)	7	0.05
All other tribes (4)	12	0.08
American Indian tribes, not spec.	8	0.06
Arab:	82	0.57
Arab/Arabic	31	0.22
Egyptian	23	0.16
Lebanese	7	0.05
Moroccan	6	0.04
Syrian	7	0.05
Other Arab	8	0.06
Armenian	9	0.06
Asian:	762	5.34
Bangladeshi (11)	17	0.12
Chinese, ex. Taiwanese (139)	152	1.07
Filipino (133)	156	1.09
Indian (249)	281	1.97
Indonesian	1	0.01
Japanese (17)	19	0.13
Korean (34)	34	0.24
Pakistani (26)	31	0.22
Taiwanese (5)	5	0.04
Thai (4)	7	0.05
Vietnamese (33)	38	0.27
Other Asian, not specified (8)	21	0.15
Austrian	91	0.64
Brazilian	16	0.11
British	36	0.25
Canadian	45	0.32
Croatian	11	0.08
Czech	14	0.10
Czechoslovakian	35	0.25
Danish	25	0.18
Dutch	46	0.32
English	450	3.16
European	3	0.02
Finnish	6	0.04
French, except Basque	149	1.04
German	1,183	8.29
Greek	52	0.36
Guyanese	89	0.62
Hawaii Native/Pacific Islander:	32	0.22
Polynesian: (9)	9	0.06
Native Hawaiian (2)	2	0.01
Samoan (7)	7	0.05
Other Pac. Isl., not spec. (6)	23	0.16
Hispanic or Latino:	2,689	18.85
Central American:	765	5.36
Costa Rican	15	0.11
Guatemalan	10	0.07
Honduran	72	0.50
Nicaraguan	2	0.01
Panamanian	15	0.11
Salvadoran	621	4.35
Other Central American	30	0.21
Cuban	54	0.38
Dominican Republic	119	0.83
Mexican	494	3.46
Puerto Rican	285	2.00
South American:	278	1.95
Argentinean	14	0.10
Bolivian	11	0.08
Chilean	18	0.13
Colombian	111	0.78
Ecuadorian	71	0.50
Paraguayan	1	0.01
Peruvian	43	0.30
Venezuelan	5	0.04
Other South American	4	0.03
Other Hispanic or Latino	694	4.87
Hungarian	96	0.67
Iranian	35	0.25
Irish	1,716	12.03
Israeli	43	0.30
Italian	3,341	23.42
Latvian	5	0.04
Northern European	14	0.10
Norwegian	29	0.20
Polish	339	2.38
Portuguese	128	0.90
Romanian	51	0.36
Russian	152	1.07
Scandinavian	9	0.06
Scotch-Irish	60	0.42
Scottish	177	1.24
Serbian	5	0.04
Slovak	24	0.17
Slovene	7	0.05
Swedish	72	0.50
Swiss	17	0.12
Turkish	23	0.16
Ukrainian	56	0.39
United States or American	388	2.72
Welsh	39	0.27
West Indian, excl. Hispanic:	1,130	7.92
Barbadian	34	0.24
Bermudan	7	0.05
British West Indian	23	0.16
Haitian	366	2.57
Jamaican	562	3.94
Trinidadian and Tobagonian	83	0.58
U.S. Virgin Islander	7	0.05
West Indian	48	0.34
White:	9,252	64.87
Not Hispanic (7,358)	7,547	52.91
Hispanic (1,431)	1,705	11.95
Yugoslavian	9	0.06

Wheatfield

Place Type: Town
County: Niagara
Population: 14,086

Ancestry/Race	Number	%
African American/Black:	160	1.14
Not Hispanic (139)	159	1.13
Hispanic	1	0.01
Am. Ind. or Alaska Nat., not spec.	18	0.13
American Indian tribes, specified:	64	0.45
Apache (1)	1	0.01
Cherokee	3	0.02
Chippewa (4)	4	0.03
Delaware (1)	1	0.01
Iroquois (42)	54	0.38
Osage (1)	1	0.01
American Indian tribes, not spec.	5	0.04
Arab:	89	0.63
Arab/Arabic	52	0.37
Lebanese	37	0.26
Armenian	20	0.14
Asian:	87	0.62
Chinese, ex. Taiwanese (4)	5	0.04
Filipino (7)	10	0.07
Indian (34)	38	0.27
Indonesian	1	0.01
Japanese	6	0.04
Korean (8)	10	0.07
Pakistani (3)	3	0.02
Thai (2)	2	0.01
Vietnamese (10)	10	0.07
Other Asian, not specified (1)	2	0.01
Austrian	42	0.30
British	22	0.16
Canadian	37	0.26
Croatian	23	0.16
Czech	69	0.49
Danish	50	0.35

Notes: 1. Figures in the "Number" column do not add up to the total population due to: a) Ancestry/Race overlap — e.g. persons can report being both White and Irish, b) persons of Hispanic origin can report being any race, c) persons reporting two ancestries are counted in both categories. 2. Numbers in parentheses indicate the number of persons reporting this ancestry/race alone, not in combination with any other ancestry/race. 3. Refer to the Explanation of Data in the front of the book for more detailed information.

Ancestry/Race	Number	%
Dutch	131	0.93
English	1,556	11.05
European	10	0.07
French, except Basque	642	4.56
French Canadian	83	0.59
German	5,103	36.23
Greek	54	0.38
Hawaii Native/Pacific Islander:	10	0.07
Micronesian:	4	0.03
Guamanian/Chamorro	3	0.02
Other Micronesian	1	0.01
Polynesian: (4)	4	0.03
Native Hawaiian (1)	1	0.01
Samoan (3)	3	0.02
Other Pac. Isl., not spec. (1)	2	0.01
Hispanic or Latino:	82	0.58
Central American:	1	0.01
Panamanian	1	0.01
Cuban	2	0.01
Mexican	19	0.13
Puerto Rican	31	0.22
South American:	2	0.01
Colombian	2	0.01
Other Hispanic or Latino	27	0.19
Hungarian	152	1.08
Irish	1,977	14.04
Italian	3,526	25.03
Latvian	9	0.06
Lithuanian	46	0.33
Luxemburger	7	0.05
Macedonian	29	0.21
Northern European	6	0.04
Norwegian	70	0.50
Polish	2,339	16.61
Portuguese	9	0.06
Romanian	7	0.05
Russian	101	0.72
Scandinavian	21	0.15
Scotch-Irish	120	0.85
Scottish	309	2.19
Slovak	21	0.15
Slovene	9	0.06
Swedish	171	1.21
Swiss	40	0.28
Ukrainian	134	0.95
United States or American	333	2.36
Welsh	125	0.89
White:	13,796	97.94
Not Hispanic (13,654)	13,724	97.43
Hispanic (71)	72	0.51
Yugoslavian	23	0.16

White Plains

Place Type: City
County: Westchester
Population: 53,077

Ancestry/Race	Number	%
Acadian/Cajun	12	0.02
African American/Black:	9,073	17.09
Not Hispanic (8,138)	8,650	16.30
Hispanic (306)	423	0.80
African, sub-Saharan:	424	0.80
African	289	0.54
Cape Verdean	15	0.03
Ghanian	13	0.02
Liberian	10	0.02
Nigerian	40	0.08
Senegalese	5	0.01
South African	36	0.07
Sudanese	16	0.03
Am. Ind. or Alaska Nat., not spec.	187	0.35
Albanian	164	0.31
Alsatian	4	0.01
American Indian tribes, specified:	204	0.38
Apache (1)	5	0.01
Blackfeet	8	0.02
Cherokee (6)	62	0.12
Cheyenne (1)	1	0.00
Chippewa (1)	3	0.01
Choctaw	1	0.00
Crow	1	0.00
Delaware (1)	1	0.00
Iroquois (2)	5	0.01
Latin American Indians (46)	95	0.18
Osage	1	0.00
Pueblo	2	0.00
Seminole	2	0.00
Sioux	1	0.00
All other tribes (9)	16	0.03
American Indian tribes, not spec.	26	0.05
Arab:	233	0.44
Arab/Arabic	8	0.02
Egyptian	26	0.05
Iraqi	33	0.06
Jordanian	6	0.01
Lebanese	63	0.12
Moroccan	26	0.05
Syrian	7	0.01
Other Arab	64	0.12
Armenian	173	0.33
Asian:	2,721	5.13
Bangladeshi (2)	4	0.01
Cambodian (4)	4	0.01
Chinese, ex. Taiwanese (551)	621	1.17
Filipino (257)	296	0.56
Indian (946)	1,031	1.94
Indonesian (1)	3	0.01
Japanese (276)	310	0.58
Korean (186)	207	0.39
Malaysian (2)	2	0.00
Pakistani (32)	66	0.12
Sri Lankan (11)	18	0.03
Taiwanese (25)	26	0.05
Thai (14)	16	0.03
Vietnamese (27)	32	0.06
Other Asian, specified (7)	18	0.03
Other Asian, not specified (19)	67	0.13
Assyrian/Chaldean/Syriac	20	0.04
Australian	33	0.06
Austrian	488	0.92
Basque	13	0.02
Belgian	96	0.18
Brazilian	160	0.30
British	241	0.45
Bulgarian	21	0.04
Canadian	108	0.20
Celtic	7	0.01
Croatian	79	0.15
Czech	74	0.14
Czechoslovakian	69	0.13
Danish	155	0.29
Dutch	380	0.72
Eastern European	480	0.90
English	1,979	3.73
Estonian	26	0.05
European	289	0.54
Finnish	83	0.16
French, except Basque	592	1.12
French Canadian	188	0.35
German	3,675	6.92
German Russian	11	0.02
Greek	173	0.33
Guyanese	93	0.18
Hawaii Native/Pacific Islander:	267	0.50
Melanesian: (5)	5	0.01
Fijian (5)	5	0.01
Micronesian: (5)	9	0.02
Guamanian/Chamorro (4)	6	0.01
Other Micronesian (1)	3	0.01
Polynesian: (9)	13	0.02
Native Hawaiian (4)	7	0.01
Samoan (5)	6	0.01
Other Pac. Isl., specified	5	0.01
Other Pac. Isl., not spec. (18)	235	0.44
Hispanic or Latino:	12,476	23.51
Central American:	453	0.85
Costa Rican	22	0.04
Guatemalan	198	0.37
Honduran	48	0.09
Nicaraguan	22	0.04
Panamanian	23	0.04
Salvadoran	114	0.21
Other Central American	26	0.05
Cuban	299	0.56
Dominican Republic	667	1.26
Mexican	3,410	6.42
Puerto Rican	1,162	2.19
South American:	3,641	6.86
Argentinean	81	0.15
Bolivian	42	0.08
Chilean	35	0.07
Colombian	1,458	2.75
Ecuadorian	452	0.85
Paraguayan	171	0.32
Peruvian	1,266	2.39
Uruguayan	22	0.04
Venezuelan	36	0.07
Other South American	78	0.15
Other Hispanic or Latino	2,844	5.36
Hungarian	545	1.03
Icelander	10	0.02
Iranian	137	0.26
Irish	6,113	11.52
Israeli	87	0.16
Italian	8,047	15.16
Latvian	60	0.11
Lithuanian	144	0.27
Macedonian	35	0.07
Northern European	13	0.02
Norwegian	126	0.24
Polish	1,913	3.60
Portuguese	160	0.30
Romanian	273	0.51
Russian	2,194	4.13
Scandinavian	19	0.04
Scotch-Irish	362	0.68
Scottish	384	0.72
Slovak	99	0.19
Swedish	285	0.54
Swiss	164	0.31
Turkish	50	0.09
Ukrainian	222	0.42
United States or American	1,801	3.39
Welsh	131	0.25
West Indian, excl. Hispanic:	1,726	3.25
Bahamian	13	0.02
Barbadian	109	0.21
British West Indian	27	0.05
Dutch West Indian	7	0.01
Haitian	314	0.59
Jamaican	963	1.81
Trinidadian and Tobagonian	127	0.24
U.S. Virgin Islander	18	0.03
West Indian	141	0.27
Other West Indian	7	0.01
White:	35,848	67.54
Not Hispanic (28,743)	29,338	55.27
Hispanic (5,722)	6,510	12.27
Yugoslavian	43	0.08

Whitestown

Place Type: Town
County: Oneida
Population: 18,635

Ancestry/Race	Number	%
African American/Black:	249	1.34
Not Hispanic (209)	233	1.25
Hispanic (11)	16	0.09
African, sub-Saharan:	8	0.04
African	8	0.04
Am. Ind. or Alaska Nat., not spec.	18	0.10
American Indian tribes, specified:	29	0.16
Blackfeet	3	0.02
Cherokee (2)	5	0.03
Cheyenne (2)	2	0.01
Chickasaw	1	0.01

Notes: 1. Figures in the "Number" column do not add up to the total population due to: a) Ancestry/Race overlap — e.g. persons can report being both White and Irish, b) persons of Hispanic origin can report being any race, c) persons reporting two ancestries are counted in both categories. 2. Numbers in parentheses indicate the number of persons reporting this ancestry/race alone, not in combination with any other ancestry/race. 3. Refer to the Explanation of Data in the front of the book for more detailed information.

Ancestry/Race	Number	%
Iroquois (6)	16	0.09
Latin American Indians	1	0.01
All other tribes	1	0.01
American Indian tribes, not spec.	6	0.03
Arab:	358	1.92
Lebanese	301	1.62
Syrian	57	0.31
Armenian	12	0.06
Asian:	110	0.59
Bangladeshi (1)	1	0.01
Chinese, ex. Taiwanese (13)	17	0.09
Filipino (14)	17	0.09
Indian (21)	21	0.11
Japanese (6)	8	0.04
Korean (14)	16	0.09
Pakistani (6)	6	0.03
Thai (5)	5	0.03
Vietnamese (9)	14	0.08
Other Asian, not specified (1)	5	0.03
Austrian	56	0.30
Belgian	4	0.02
British	13	0.07
Bulgarian	18	0.10
Canadian	46	0.25
Croatian	6	0.03
Czech	21	0.11
Czechoslovakian	5	0.03
Danish	37	0.20
Dutch	381	2.05
English	1,961	10.54
European	69	0.37
Finnish	2	0.01
French, except Basque	910	4.89
French Canadian	350	1.88
German	3,573	19.20
Greek	35	0.19
Hawaii Native/Pacific Islander:	5	0.03
Polynesian:	2	0.01
Native Hawaiian	1	0.01
Samoan	1	0.01
Other Pac. Isl., not spec. (1)	3	0.02
Hispanic or Latino:	246	1.32
Central American:	3	0.02
Guatemalan	1	0.01
Salvadoran	2	0.01
Cuban	4	0.02
Dominican Republic	21	0.11
Mexican	37	0.20
Puerto Rican	125	0.67
South American:	4	0.02
Colombian	3	0.02
Ecuadorian	1	0.01
Other Hispanic or Latino	52	0.28
Hungarian	48	0.26
Irish	3,961	21.28
Italian	3,842	20.64
Latvian	10	0.05
Lithuanian	36	0.19
Northern European	13	0.07
Norwegian	60	0.32
Polish	3,954	21.25
Portuguese	16	0.09
Romanian	7	0.04
Russian	36	0.19
Scandinavian	8	0.04
Scotch-Irish	153	0.82
Scottish	214	1.15
Slovak	25	0.13
Slovene	13	0.07
Swedish	72	0.39
Swiss	125	0.67
Ukrainian	144	0.77
United States or American	550	2.96
Welsh	781	4.20
White:	18,241	97.89
Not Hispanic (17,973)	18,063	96.93
Hispanic (153)	178	0.96

Wilton

Place Type: Town
County: Saratoga
Population: 12,511

Ancestry/Race	Number	%
African American/Black:	171	1.37
Not Hispanic (118)	168	1.34
Hispanic (2)	3	0.02
Alaska Native tribes, specified:	1	0.01
Alaska Athabascan (1)	1	0.01
Am. Ind. or Alaska Nat., not spec.	17	0.14
American Indian tribes, specified:	44	0.35
Apache (2)	2	0.02
Blackfeet	2	0.02
Cherokee (2)	16	0.13
Chippewa (1)	1	0.01
Choctaw	2	0.02
Iroquois (6)	10	0.08
Latin American Indians	2	0.02
Pueblo	1	0.01
Sioux	1	0.01
Ute	2	0.02
All other tribes (3)	5	0.04
American Indian tribes, not spec.	2	0.02
Arab:	8	0.06
Lebanese	8	0.06
Armenian	15	0.12
Asian:	100	0.80
Cambodian (1)	1	0.01
Chinese, ex. Taiwanese (10)	15	0.12
Filipino (10)	16	0.13
Indian (11)	20	0.16
Japanese (5)	9	0.07
Korean (21)	25	0.20
Malaysian (1)	3	0.02
Vietnamese (3)	5	0.04
Other Asian, not specified (3)	6	0.05
Austrian	67	0.54
Belgian	7	0.06
British	82	0.66
Canadian	93	0.74
Czech	50	0.40
Czechoslovakian	14	0.11
Danish	52	0.42
Dutch	425	3.40
Eastern European	15	0.12
English	1,830	14.63
European	61	0.49
Finnish	6	0.05
French, except Basque	1,477	11.81
French Canadian	423	3.38
German	1,939	15.50
Greek	26	0.21
Hawaii Native/Pacific Islander:	8	0.06
Micronesian: (4)	4	0.03
Guamanian/Chamorro (4)	4	0.03
Polynesian: (3)	3	0.02
Native Hawaiian (1)	1	0.01
Samoan (2)	2	0.02
Other Pac. Isl., not spec.	1	0.01
Hispanic or Latino:	143	1.14
Central American:	4	0.03
Costa Rican	1	0.01
Honduran	3	0.02
Cuban	5	0.04
Mexican	36	0.29
Puerto Rican	70	0.56
South American:	8	0.06
Bolivian	2	0.02
Chilean	2	0.02
Colombian	2	0.02
Ecuadorian	1	0.01
Other South American	1	0.01
Other Hispanic or Latino	20	0.16
Hungarian	91	0.73
Icelander	10	0.08
Irish	2,997	23.95
Italian	1,844	14.74
Latvian	8	0.06
Lithuanian	84	0.67
Norwegian	110	0.88
Polish	889	7.11
Portuguese	18	0.14
Russian	286	2.29
Scandinavian	8	0.06
Scotch-Irish	143	1.14
Scottish	354	2.83
Slavic	20	0.16
Slovak	108	0.86
Slovene	6	0.05
Swedish	150	1.20
Swiss	21	0.17
Turkish	9	0.07
Ukrainian	70	0.56
United States or American	1,028	8.22
Welsh	188	1.50
West Indian, excl. Hispanic:	46	0.37
Haitian	11	0.09
Jamaican	28	0.22
Trinidadian and Tobagonian	7	0.06
White:	12,259	97.99
Not Hispanic (12,024)	12,134	96.99
Hispanic (118)	125	1.00

Woodmere

Place Type: Census Designated Place
County: Nassau
Population: 16,447

Ancestry/Race	Number	%
African American/Black:	310	1.88
Not Hispanic (269)	302	1.84
Hispanic (5)	8	0.05
African, sub-Saharan:	8	0.05
Zimbabwean	8	0.05
Am. Ind. or Alaska Nat., not spec.	3	0.02
Albanian	6	0.04
American Indian tribes, specified:	15	0.09
Blackfeet	1	0.01
Cherokee	1	0.01
Latin American Indians (1)	12	0.07
Sioux	1	0.01
American Indian tribes, not spec.	2	0.01
Arab:	78	0.47
Arab/Arabic	10	0.06
Moroccan	14	0.09
Palestinian	19	0.12
Syrian	20	0.12
Other Arab	15	0.09
Asian:	659	4.01
Bangladeshi (8)	9	0.05
Chinese, ex. Taiwanese (86)	95	0.58
Filipino (58)	58	0.35
Indian (225)	240	1.46
Japanese (2)	5	0.03
Korean (140)	141	0.86
Pakistani (57)	67	0.41
Taiwanese (11)	11	0.07
Thai (4)	5	0.03
Vietnamese (4)	4	0.02
Other Asian, specified (5)	5	0.03
Other Asian, not specified (10)	19	0.12
Austrian	223	1.36
Belgian	10	0.06
British	16	0.10
Canadian	18	0.11
Croatian	80	0.49
Czech	10	0.06
Czechoslovakian	77	0.47
Dutch	55	0.33
Eastern European	441	2.68
English	189	1.15
European	418	2.54
Finnish	10	0.06
French, except Basque	199	1.21
French Canadian	23	0.14
German	570	3.47

Notes: 1. Figures in the "Number" column do not add up to the total population due to: a) Ancestry/Race overlap — e.g. persons can report being both White and Irish, b) persons of Hispanic origin can report being any race, c) persons reporting two ancestries are counted in both categories. 2. Numbers in parentheses indicate the number of persons reporting this ancestry/race alone, not in combination with any other ancestry/race. 3. Refer to the Explanation of Data in the front of the book for more detailed information.

Ancestry/Race	Number	%
Greek	193	1.17
Guyanese	61	0.37
Hawaii Native/Pacific Islander:	11	0.07
Micronesian:	2	0.01
Guamanian/Chamorro	2	0.01
Polynesian:	1	0.01
Samoan	1	0.01
Other Pac. Isl., not spec. (1)	8	0.05
Hispanic or Latino:	587	3.57
Central American:	103	0.63
Costa Rican	20	0.12
Guatemalan	24	0.15
Honduran	2	0.01
Nicaraguan	12	0.07
Panamanian	3	0.02
Salvadoran	37	0.22
Other Central American	5	0.03
Cuban	29	0.18
Dominican Republic	52	0.32
Mexican	22	0.13
Puerto Rican	116	0.71
South American:	130	0.79
Argentinean	14	0.09
Bolivian	9	0.05
Chilean	17	0.10
Colombian	24	0.15
Ecuadorian	16	0.10
Peruvian	27	0.16
Uruguayan	7	0.04
Venezuelan	6	0.04
Other South American	10	0.06
Other Hispanic or Latino	135	0.82
Hungarian	399	2.43
Iranian	6	0.04
Irish	762	4.63
Israeli	450	2.74
Italian	1,148	6.98
Latvian	21	0.13
Lithuanian	70	0.43
New Zealander	9	0.05
Polish	1,990	12.10
Portuguese	9	0.05
Romanian	186	1.13
Russian	2,391	14.54
Scandinavian	15	0.09
Scotch-Irish	11	0.07
Scottish	18	0.11
Slovak	7	0.04
Swiss	4	0.02
Turkish	80	0.49
Ukrainian	128	0.78
United States or American	1,825	11.10
West Indian, excl. Hispanic:	184	1.12
British West Indian	4	0.02
Haitian	80	0.49
Jamaican	85	0.52
West Indian	15	0.09
White:	15,299	93.02
Not Hispanic (14,854)	14,914	90.68
Hispanic (356)	385	2.34
Yugoslavian	18	0.11

Wyandanch

Place Type: Census Designated Place
County: Suffolk
Population: 10,546

Ancestry/Race	Number	%
African American/Black:	8,523	80.82
Not Hispanic (7,949)	8,228	78.02
Hispanic (247)	295	2.80
African, sub-Saharan:	354	3.35
African	248	2.34
Ethiopian	106	1.00
Alaska Native tribes, specified:	1	0.01
Tlingit-Haida	1	0.01
Am. Ind. or Alaska Nat., not spec.	84	0.80
American Indian tribes, specified:	127	1.20
Apache (1)	1	0.01
Blackfeet	9	0.09
Cherokee (10)	43	0.41
Choctaw	5	0.05
Cree	1	0.01
Creek	1	0.01
Iroquois	2	0.02
Latin American Indians (11)	19	0.18
Seminole	4	0.04
Yuman (1)	1	0.01
All other tribes (13)	41	0.39
American Indian tribes, not spec.	22	0.21
Arab:	19	0.18
Arab/Arabic	15	0.14
Moroccan	4	0.04
Asian:	84	0.80
Chinese, ex. Taiwanese (14)	21	0.20
Filipino (4)	6	0.06
Indian (31)	41	0.39
Japanese (1)	2	0.02
Korean (8)	8	0.08
Thai (1)	1	0.01
Other Asian, not specified	5	0.05
British	4	0.04
Czech	6	0.06
English	35	0.33
French, except Basque	6	0.06
German	41	0.39
Guyanese	55	0.52
Hawaii Native/Pacific Islander:	10	0.09
Micronesian:	2	0.02
Guamanian/Chamorro	2	0.02
Polynesian: (3)	3	0.03
Native Hawaiian (2)	2	0.02
Other Polynesian (1)	1	0.01
Other Pac. Isl., not spec.	5	0.05
Hispanic or Latino:	1,724	16.35
Central American:	576	5.46
Costa Rican	11	0.10
Guatemalan	15	0.14
Honduran	80	0.76
Panamanian	21	0.20
Salvadoran	445	4.22
Other Central American	4	0.04
Cuban	19	0.18
Dominican Republic	124	1.18
Mexican	93	0.88
Puerto Rican	490	4.65
South American:	111	1.05
Argentinean	2	0.02
Chilean	1	0.01
Colombian	24	0.23
Ecuadorian	39	0.37
Peruvian	42	0.40
Venezuelan	3	0.03
Other Hispanic or Latino	311	2.95
Irish	63	0.60
Italian	71	0.67
Portuguese	22	0.21
Russian	3	0.03
Scottish	11	0.10
Turkish	18	0.17
Ukrainian	6	0.06
United States or American	186	1.76
West Indian, excl. Hispanic:	852	8.05
Belizean	3	0.03
British West Indian	12	0.11
Haitian	487	4.60
Jamaican	223	2.11
Trinidadian and Tobagonian	70	0.66
U.S. Virgin Islander	17	0.16
West Indian	40	0.38
White:	1,281	12.15
Not Hispanic (409)	504	4.78
Hispanic (668)	777	7.37

Yonkers

Place Type: City
County: Westchester
Population: 196,086

Ancestry/Race	Number	%
African American/Black:	35,421	18.06
Not Hispanic (30,164)	32,131	16.39
Hispanic (2,411)	3,290	1.68
African, sub-Saharan:	2,228	1.14
African	1,332	0.68
Cape Verdean	137	0.07
Ethiopian	23	0.01
Ghanian	363	0.19
Kenyan	26	0.01
Liberian	33	0.02
Nigerian	123	0.06
Senegalese	12	0.01
Sierra Leonean	33	0.02
South African	35	0.02
Zimbabwean	24	0.01
Other sub-Saharan African	87	0.04
Alaska Native tribes, specified:	4	0.00
Alaska Athabascan (1)	1	0.00
Eskimo	3	0.00
Alaska Native tribes, not specified	1	0.00
Am. Ind. or Alaska Nat., not spec.	900	0.46
Albanian	1,310	0.67
Alsatian	12	0.01
American Indian tribes, specified:	717	0.37
Apache (5)	12	0.01
Blackfeet (8)	34	0.02
Cherokee (59)	211	0.11
Cheyenne (4)	6	0.00
Chippewa (1)	4	0.00
Choctaw	3	0.00
Cree (2)	2	0.00
Creek	5	0.00
Crow	6	0.00
Delaware	4	0.00
Houma (1)	2	0.00
Iroquois (4)	38	0.02
Latin American Indians (143)	244	0.12
Lumbee (3)	3	0.00
Menominee	1	0.00
Navajo (1)	7	0.00
Paiute	1	0.00
Pueblo (10)	65	0.03
Seminole	3	0.00
Shoshone	3	0.00
Sioux (3)	10	0.01
Yaqui	7	0.00
All other tribes (17)	46	0.02
American Indian tribes, not spec.	162	0.08
Arab:	2,697	1.38
Arab/Arabic	854	0.44
Egyptian	183	0.09
Jordanian	1,093	0.56
Lebanese	171	0.09
Moroccan	44	0.02
Palestinian	177	0.09
Syrian	102	0.05
Other Arab	73	0.04
Armenian	204	0.10
Asian:	11,006	5.61
Bangladeshi (39)	55	0.03
Cambodian (17)	19	0.01
Chinese, ex. Taiwanese (938)	1,130	0.58
Filipino (1,902)	2,082	1.06
Indian (4,548)	5,008	2.55
Indonesian (20)	23	0.01
Japanese (214)	270	0.14
Korean (885)	946	0.48
Laotian (5)	10	0.01
Malaysian (1)	4	0.00
Pakistani (388)	553	0.28
Sri Lankan (17)	22	0.01
Taiwanese (17)	20	0.01
Thai (229)	246	0.13

Notes: 1. Figures in the "Number" column do not add up to the total population due to: a) Ancestry/Race overlap — e.g. persons can report being both White and Irish, b) persons of Hispanic origin can report being any race, c) persons reporting two ancestries are counted in both categories. 2. Numbers in parentheses indicate the number of persons reporting this ancestry/race alone, not in combination with any other ancestry/race. 3. Refer to the Explanation of Data in the front of the book for more detailed information.

Ancestry/Race	Number	%
Vietnamese (67)	73	0.04
Other Asian, specified (5)	32	0.02
Other Asian, not specified (120)	513	0.26
Assyrian/Chaldean/Syriac	179	0.09
Australian	78	0.04
Austrian	829	0.42
Basque	4	0.00
Belgian	83	0.04
Brazilian	155	0.08
British	294	0.15
Bulgarian	23	0.01
Canadian	351	0.18
Carpatho Rusyn	8	0.00
Celtic	28	0.01
Croatian	64	0.03
Cypriot	73	0.04
Czech	458	0.23
Czechoslovakian	453	0.23
Danish	139	0.07
Dutch	574	0.29
Eastern European	260	0.13
English	3,878	1.98
Estonian	7	0.00
European	397	0.20
Finnish	139	0.07
French, except Basque	1,351	0.69
French Canadian	384	0.20
German	9,222	4.70
Greek	1,563	0.80
Guyanese	426	0.22
Hawaii Native/Pacific Islander:	384	0.20
Micronesian: (35)	51	0.03
Guamanian/Chamorro (34)	50	0.03
Other Micronesian (1)	1	0.00
Polynesian: (34)	70	0.04
Native Hawaiian (18)	46	0.02
Samoan (16)	22	0.01
Tongan	1	0.00
Other Polynesian	1	0.00
Other Pac. Isl., specified	15	0.01
Other Pac. Isl., not spec. (29)	248	0.13
Hispanic or Latino:	50,852	25.93
Central American:	3,374	1.72
Costa Rican	135	0.07
Guatemalan	343	0.17
Honduran	736	0.38
Nicaraguan	391	0.20
Panamanian	115	0.06
Salvadoran	1,518	0.77
Other Central American	136	0.07
Cuban	1,450	0.74
Dominican Republic	7,838	4.00
Mexican	7,294	3.72
Puerto Rican	18,097	9.23
South American:	3,944	2.01
Argentinean	190	0.10
Bolivian	15	0.01
Chilean	132	0.07
Colombian	991	0.51
Ecuadorian	1,839	0.94
Paraguayan	17	0.01
Peruvian	464	0.24
Uruguayan	29	0.01
Venezuelan	126	0.06
Other South American	141	0.07
Other Hispanic or Latino	8,855	4.52
Hungarian	1,327	0.68
Icelander	20	0.01
Iranian	247	0.13
Irish	25,213	12.86
Israeli	32	0.02
Italian	36,907	18.82
Latvian	70	0.04
Lithuanian	372	0.19
Maltese	61	0.03
New Zealander	23	0.01
Northern European	30	0.02
Norwegian	367	0.19
Pennsylvania German	19	0.01
Polish	6,444	3.29
Portuguese	2,558	1.30
Romanian	456	0.23
Russian	3,150	1.61
Scandinavian	22	0.01
Scotch-Irish	856	0.44
Scottish	1,339	0.68
Serbian	6	0.00
Slavic	173	0.09
Slovak	931	0.47
Slovene	38	0.02
Swedish	675	0.34
Swiss	89	0.05
Turkish	126	0.06
Ukrainian	1,975	1.01
United States or American	5,088	2.59
Welsh	279	0.14
West Indian, excl. Hispanic:	6,418	3.27
Bahamian	37	0.02
Barbadian	160	0.08
Belizean	64	0.03
Bermudan	14	0.01
British West Indian	250	0.13
Dutch West Indian	34	0.02
Haitian	887	0.45
Jamaican	3,822	1.95
Trinidadian and Tobagonian	359	0.18
U.S. Virgin Islander	6	0.00
West Indian	785	0.40
White:	123,920	63.20
Not Hispanic (99,346)	102,650	52.35
Hispanic (18,661)	21,270	10.85
Yugoslavian	358	0.18

Yorktown

Place Type: Town
County: Westchester
Population: 36,318

Ancestry/Race	Number	%
African American/Black:	1,248	3.44
Not Hispanic (994)	1,076	2.96
Hispanic (109)	172	0.47
African, sub-Saharan:	24	0.07
African	24	0.07
Alaska Native tribes, specified:	2	0.01
Tlingit-Haida	2	0.01
Am. Ind. or Alaska Nat., not spec.	75	0.21
Albanian	138	0.38
Alsatian	6	0.02
American Indian tribes, specified:	72	0.20
Blackfeet (1)	5	0.01
Cherokee (5)	23	0.06
Chippewa	5	0.01
Comanche (2)	2	0.01
Iroquois (1)	6	0.02
Latin American Indians (4)	7	0.02
Lumbee (6)	6	0.02
Pueblo (1)	1	0.00
Seminole	1	0.00
Sioux (5)	6	0.02
All other tribes (2)	10	0.03
American Indian tribes, not spec.	18	0.05
Arab:	166	0.46
Arab/Arabic	20	0.06
Egyptian	68	0.19
Iraqi	18	0.05
Jordanian	22	0.06
Lebanese	15	0.04
Moroccan	19	0.05
Syrian	4	0.01
Armenian	44	0.12
Asian:	1,463	4.03
Chinese, ex. Taiwanese (435)	496	1.37
Filipino (149)	199	0.55
Indian (427)	465	1.28
Japanese (45)	71	0.20
Korean (77)	93	0.26
Pakistani (24)	28	0.08
Sri Lankan	4	0.01
Taiwanese (12)	18	0.05
Thai (19)	25	0.07
Vietnamese (19)	22	0.06
Other Asian, specified	2	0.01
Other Asian, not specified (13)	40	0.11
Austrian	547	1.51
Belgian	50	0.14
Brazilian	23	0.06
British	84	0.23
Canadian	65	0.18
Celtic	28	0.08
Croatian	46	0.13
Czech	113	0.31
Czechoslovakian	124	0.34
Danish	46	0.13
Dutch	616	1.70
Eastern European	239	0.66
English	2,313	6.37
Estonian	25	0.07
European	212	0.58
Finnish	78	0.21
French, except Basque	614	1.69
French Canadian	296	0.82
German	4,739	13.05
Greek	257	0.71
Guyanese	12	0.03
Hawaii Native/Pacific Islander:	17	0.05
Micronesian: (1)	1	0.00
Guamanian/Chamorro (1)	1	0.00
Other Pac. Isl., specified	1	0.00
Other Pac. Isl., not spec. (2)	15	0.04
Hispanic or Latino:	2,112	5.82
Central American:	47	0.13
Costa Rican	4	0.01
Guatemalan	14	0.04
Honduran	10	0.03
Nicaraguan	2	0.01
Panamanian	2	0.01
Salvadoran	14	0.04
Other Central American	1	0.00
Cuban	90	0.25
Dominican Republic	118	0.32
Mexican	78	0.21
Puerto Rican	1,051	2.89
South American:	308	0.85
Argentinean	34	0.09
Bolivian	3	0.01
Chilean	14	0.04
Colombian	63	0.17
Ecuadorian	95	0.26
Paraguayan	10	0.03
Peruvian	49	0.13
Uruguayan	14	0.04
Venezuelan	8	0.02
Other South American	18	0.05
Other Hispanic or Latino	420	1.16
Hungarian	504	1.39
Iranian	44	0.12
Irish	8,192	22.56
Israeli	18	0.05
Italian	12,407	34.16
Latvian	44	0.12
Lithuanian	193	0.53
New Zealander	27	0.07
Northern European	10	0.03
Norwegian	186	0.51
Polish	1,877	5.17
Portuguese	120	0.33
Romanian	263	0.72
Russian	1,478	4.07
Scandinavian	15	0.04
Scotch-Irish	292	0.80
Scottish	491	1.35
Slavic	39	0.11
Slovak	188	0.52
Swedish	336	0.93
Swiss	245	0.67
Turkish	72	0.20
Ukrainian	249	0.69
United States or American	1,342	3.70

Notes: 1. Figures in the "Number" column do not add up to the total population due to: a) Ancestry/Race overlap — e.g. persons can report being both White and Irish, b) persons of Hispanic origin can report being any race, c) persons reporting two ancestries are counted in both categories. 2. Numbers in parentheses indicate the number of persons reporting this ancestry/race alone, not in combination with any other ancestry/race. 3. Refer to the Explanation of Data in the front of the book for more detailed information.

Welsh	139	0.38
West Indian, excl. Hispanic:	273	0.75
Barbadian	40	0.11
British West Indian	36	0.10
Haitian	6	0.02
Jamaican	147	0.40
Trinidadian and Tobagonian	24	0.07
West Indian	20	0.06
White:	33,331	91.78
Not Hispanic (31,526)	31,825	87.63
Hispanic (1,393)	1,506	4.15
Yugoslavian	26	0.07

Albemarle

Place Type: City
County: Stanly
Population: 15,680

Ancestry/Race	Number	%
African American/Black:	3,300	21.05
Not Hispanic (3,207)	3,284	20.94
Hispanic (8)	16	0.10
African, sub-Saharan:	36	0.23
African	36	0.23
Am. Ind. or Alaska Nat., not spec.	24	0.15
American Indian tribes, specified:	57	0.36
Apache (2)	6	0.04
Blackfeet	2	0.01
Cherokee (9)	29	0.18
Chickasaw (1)	1	0.01
Creek (1)	1	0.01
Iroquois (1)	1	0.01
Lumbee (6)	6	0.04
Navajo (1)	1	0.01
All other tribes (5)	10	0.06
American Indian tribes, not spec.	1	0.01
Asian:	748	4.77
Bangladeshi	2	0.01
Cambodian	5	0.03
Chinese, ex. Taiwanese (23)	38	0.24
Filipino (35)	45	0.29
Hmong (370)	395	2.52
Indian (21)	38	0.24
Japanese (1)	5	0.03
Korean (24)	32	0.20
Laotian (83)	96	0.61
Pakistani	2	0.01
Thai (4)	11	0.07
Vietnamese (9)	11	0.07
Other Asian, specified	1	0.01
Other Asian, not specified (66)	67	0.43
British	15	0.10
Canadian	28	0.18
Danish	5	0.03
Dutch	173	1.11
English	1,238	7.93
European	122	0.78
French, except Basque	114	0.73
French Canadian	10	0.06
German	1,428	9.15
Greek	9	0.06
Hawaii Native/Pacific Islander:	11	0.07
Micronesian:	2	0.01
Guamanian/Chamorro	2	0.01
Polynesian: (1)	3	0.02
Native Hawaiian	2	0.01
Samoan (1)	1	0.01
Other Pac. Isl., specified	1	0.01
Other Pac. Isl., not spec. (4)	5	0.03
Hispanic or Latino:	293	1.87
Central American:	9	0.06
Guatemalan	3	0.02
Salvadoran	6	0.04
Cuban	3	0.02
Dominican Republic	1	0.01
Mexican	211	1.35
Puerto Rican	19	0.12
South American:	3	0.02
Bolivian	1	0.01
Colombian	2	0.01
Other Hispanic or Latino	47	0.30
Hungarian	19	0.12
Irish	642	4.11
Italian	258	1.65
Lithuanian	5	0.03
Norwegian	21	0.13
Pennsylvania German	5	0.03
Polish	81	0.52
Portuguese	5	0.03
Russian	9	0.06
Scandinavian	6	0.04
Scotch-Irish	425	2.72
Scottish	358	2.29
Slovak	5	0.03
Swedish	39	0.25
Swiss	8	0.05
Ukrainian	11	0.07
United States or American	3,187	20.42
Welsh	40	0.26
West Indian, excl. Hispanic:	10	0.06
West Indian	10	0.06
White:	11,543	73.62
Not Hispanic (11,328)	11,434	72.92
Hispanic (95)	109	0.70

Apex

Place Type: Town
County: Wake
Population: 20,212

Ancestry/Race	Number	%
African American/Black:	1,639	8.11
Not Hispanic (1,510)	1,599	7.91
Hispanic (16)	40	0.20
African, sub-Saharan:	169	0.84
African	59	0.29
Cape Verdean	16	0.08
Ghanian	37	0.18
Liberian	4	0.02
South African	53	0.26
Alaska Native tribes, specified:	2	0.01
Aleut (1)	1	0.00
Tlingit-Haida (1)	1	0.00
Am. Ind. or Alaska Nat., not spec.	42	0.21
American Indian tribes, specified:	98	0.48
Apache (1)	2	0.01
Blackfeet	3	0.01
Cherokee (5)	25	0.12
Chickasaw (1)	1	0.00
Chippewa	4	0.02
Creek (3)	5	0.02
Iroquois (1)	1	0.00
Latin American Indians (11)	21	0.10
Lumbee (20)	24	0.12
Pueblo (1)	1	0.00
Sioux	2	0.01
All other tribes (1)	9	0.04
American Indian tribes, not spec.	9	0.04
Arab:	87	0.43
Arab/Arabic	30	0.15
Egyptian	3	0.01
Iraqi	5	0.02
Lebanese	31	0.15
Palestinian	18	0.09
Armenian	6	0.03
Asian:	1,015	5.02
Bangladeshi (1)	1	0.00
Chinese, ex. Taiwanese (264)	295	1.46
Filipino (54)	79	0.39
Indian (341)	366	1.81
Indonesian	3	0.01
Japanese (20)	47	0.23
Korean (71)	81	0.40
Laotian (7)	9	0.04
Malaysian (5)	5	0.02
Pakistani (6)	10	0.05
Sri Lankan (12)	12	0.06
Taiwanese (5)	5	0.02
Thai (8)	8	0.04
Vietnamese (52)	67	0.33
Other Asian, specified (4)	5	0.02
Other Asian, not specified (6)	22	0.11
Assyrian/Chaldean/Syriac	5	0.02
Australian	6	0.03
Austrian	20	0.10
Belgian	15	0.07
British	250	1.25
Canadian	157	0.78
Celtic	6	0.03
Croatian	7	0.03
Czech	66	0.33
Czechoslovakian	16	0.08
Danish	45	0.22
Dutch	365	1.82
Eastern European	6	0.03
English	3,018	15.04
European	461	2.30
Finnish	10	0.05
French, except Basque	566	2.82
French Canadian	152	0.76
German	3,543	17.65
Greek	156	0.78
Guyanese	4	0.02
Hawaii Native/Pacific Islander:	53	0.26
Micronesian: (6)	19	0.09
Guamanian/Chamorro (6)	19	0.09
Polynesian: (3)	27	0.13
Native Hawaiian (3)	10	0.05
Samoan	17	0.08
Other Pac. Isl., specified	1	0.00
Other Pac. Isl., not spec. (2)	6	0.03
Hispanic or Latino:	648	3.21
Central American:	26	0.13
Costa Rican	6	0.03
Guatemalan	3	0.01
Honduran	7	0.03
Nicaraguan	4	0.02
Panamanian	5	0.02
Salvadoran	1	0.00
Cuban	53	0.26
Dominican Republic	9	0.04
Mexican	265	1.31
Puerto Rican	115	0.57
South American:	63	0.31
Argentinean	6	0.03
Chilean	8	0.04
Colombian	20	0.10
Ecuadorian	7	0.03
Peruvian	10	0.05
Venezuelan	2	0.01
Other South American	10	0.05
Other Hispanic or Latino	117	0.58
Hungarian	51	0.25
Iranian	27	0.13
Irish	2,700	13.45
Italian	1,801	8.97
Latvian	6	0.03
Lithuanian	35	0.17
Maltese	6	0.03
Northern European	23	0.11
Norwegian	181	0.90
Pennsylvania German	64	0.32
Polish	745	3.71
Portuguese	60	0.30
Romanian	20	0.10
Russian	213	1.06
Scandinavian	45	0.22
Scotch-Irish	710	3.54
Scottish	647	3.22
Serbian	19	0.09
Slavic	30	0.15
Slovak	100	0.50
Slovene	15	0.07
Swedish	297	1.48
Swiss	80	0.40
Turkish	24	0.12
Ukrainian	102	0.51
United States or American	1,676	8.35

Notes: 1. Figures in the "Number" column do not add up to the total population due to: a) Ancestry/Race overlap — e.g. persons can report being both White and Irish, b) persons of Hispanic origin can report being any race, c) persons reporting two ancestries are counted in both categories. 2. Numbers in parentheses indicate the number of persons reporting this ancestry/race alone, not in combination with any other ancestry/race. 3. Refer to the Explanation of Data in the front of the book for more detailed information.

Welsh	242	1.21
West Indian, excl. Hispanic:	128	0.64
Bahamian	21	0.10
Barbadian	46	0.23
Haitian	7	0.03
Jamaican	54	0.27
White:	17,455	86.36
Not Hispanic (16,861)	17,077	84.49
Hispanic (331)	378	1.87
Yugoslavian	26	0.13

Asheboro

Place Type: City
County: Randolph
Population: 21,672

Ancestry/Race	Number	%
African American/Black:	2,762	12.74
Not Hispanic (2,564)	2,631	12.14
Hispanic (54)	131	0.60
African, sub-Saharan:	111	0.51
African	111	0.51
Alaska Native tribes, specified:	1	0.00
Eskimo	1	0.00
Am. Ind. or Alaska Nat., not spec.	69	0.32
American Indian tribes, specified:	103	0.48
Apache (5)	6	0.03
Blackfeet (1)	8	0.04
Cherokee (14)	33	0.15
Cheyenne	1	0.00
Chippewa	2	0.01
Choctaw (4)	5	0.02
Creek (2)	2	0.01
Iroquois	3	0.01
Latin American Indians (12)	27	0.12
Lumbee (2)	8	0.04
Sioux (4)	4	0.02
All other tribes	4	0.02
American Indian tribes, not spec.	10	0.05
Armenian	4	0.02
Asian:	371	1.71
Cambodian (9)	11	0.05
Chinese, ex. Taiwanese (34)	42	0.19
Filipino (20)	24	0.11
Indian (81)	94	0.43
Japanese (4)	6	0.03
Korean (13)	15	0.07
Laotian (2)	7	0.03
Pakistani (25)	49	0.23
Taiwanese (3)	3	0.01
Thai (12)	21	0.10
Vietnamese (45)	55	0.25
Other Asian, not specified (37)	44	0.20
Austrian	14	0.06
Brazilian	9	0.04
British	120	0.55
Canadian	39	0.18
Czech	12	0.06
Czechoslovakian	6	0.03
Danish	7	0.03
Dutch	294	1.35
English	1,740	7.98
European	163	0.75
Finnish	19	0.09
French, except Basque	200	0.92
French Canadian	23	0.11
German	1,703	7.81
Greek	45	0.21
Hawaii Native/Pacific Islander:	8	0.04
Micronesian:	3	0.01
Guamanian/Chamorro	3	0.01
Polynesian: (3)	4	0.02
Native Hawaiian (1)	2	0.01
Samoan (2)	2	0.01
Other Pac. Isl., not spec.	1	0.00
Hispanic or Latino:	4,319	19.93
Central American:	238	1.10
Costa Rican	28	0.13
Guatemalan	58	0.27
Honduran	20	0.09
Nicaraguan	37	0.17
Panamanian	7	0.03
Salvadoran	77	0.36
Other Central American	11	0.05
Cuban	13	0.06
Dominican Republic	29	0.13
Mexican	3,608	16.65
Puerto Rican	41	0.19
South American:	18	0.08
Colombian	12	0.06
Ecuadorian	1	0.00
Peruvian	4	0.02
Venezuelan	1	0.00
Other Hispanic or Latino	372	1.72
Hungarian	26	0.12
Irish	1,464	6.72
Italian	372	1.71
Lithuanian	6	0.03
Northern European	64	0.29
Norwegian	127	0.58
Pennsylvania German	9	0.04
Polish	203	0.93
Portuguese	23	0.11
Romanian	10	0.05
Russian	43	0.20
Scotch-Irish	543	2.49
Scottish	443	2.03
Slovak	8	0.04
Swedish	24	0.11
Swiss	7	0.03
Ukrainian	5	0.02
United States or American	3,231	14.83
Welsh	42	0.19
West Indian, excl. Hispanic:	20	0.09
Jamaican	7	0.03
West Indian	13	0.06
White:	16,906	78.01
Not Hispanic (14,219)	14,349	66.21
Hispanic (2,358)	2,557	11.80

Asheville

Place Type: City
County: Buncombe
Population: 68,889

Ancestry/Race	Number	%
Acadian/Cajun	20	0.03
African American/Black:	12,530	18.19
Not Hispanic (12,054)	12,437	18.05
Hispanic (75)	93	0.13
African, sub-Saharan:	583	0.85
African	538	0.78
Ethiopian	26	0.04
Nigerian	19	0.03
Alaska Native tribes, specified:	3	0.00
Aleut (1)	2	0.00
Eskimo (1)	1	0.00
Alaska Native tribes, not specified	1	0.00
Am. Ind. or Alaska Nat., not spec.	175	0.25
Albanian	5	0.01
American Indian tribes, specified:	369	0.54
Apache (3)	12	0.02
Blackfeet (3)	15	0.02
Cherokee (62)	200	0.29
Cheyenne (1)	1	0.00
Chickasaw	2	0.00
Chippewa (8)	13	0.02
Choctaw (3)	8	0.01
Comanche (1)	2	0.00
Creek (3)	6	0.01
Delaware (1)	1	0.00
Houma (1)	3	0.00
Iroquois (8)	21	0.03
Latin American Indians (9)	24	0.03
Lumbee (11)	11	0.02
Navajo (5)	8	0.01
Osage	3	0.00
Pueblo	1	0.00
Shoshone	1	0.00
Sioux (10)	12	0.02
Yakama (2)	2	0.00
All other tribes (11)	23	0.03
American Indian tribes, not spec.	42	0.06
Arab:	82	0.12
Arab/Arabic	8	0.01
Egyptian	11	0.02
Lebanese	56	0.08
Other Arab	7	0.01
Armenian	13	0.02
Asian:	818	1.19
Cambodian (17)	17	0.02
Chinese, ex. Taiwanese (97)	118	0.17
Filipino (106)	142	0.21
Hmong (3)	3	0.00
Indian (175)	200	0.29
Indonesian (7)	13	0.02
Japanese (41)	68	0.10
Korean (67)	84	0.12
Laotian (2)	2	0.00
Malaysian (3)	8	0.01
Pakistani (5)	7	0.01
Sri Lankan	1	0.00
Taiwanese (2)	3	0.00
Thai (11)	17	0.02
Vietnamese (54)	63	0.09
Other Asian, specified (1)	9	0.01
Other Asian, not specified (35)	63	0.09
Australian	20	0.03
Austrian	174	0.25
Basque	2	0.00
Belgian	51	0.07
Brazilian	42	0.06
British	822	1.19
Canadian	124	0.18
Carpatho Rusyn	7	0.01
Celtic	24	0.03
Croatian	58	0.08
Czech	106	0.15
Czechoslovakian	63	0.09
Danish	106	0.15
Dutch	1,237	1.79
Eastern European	39	0.06
English	9,419	13.66
Estonian	20	0.03
European	666	0.97
Finnish	30	0.04
French, except Basque	1,479	2.14
French Canadian	335	0.49
German	7,933	11.51
Greek	267	0.39
Hawaii Native/Pacific Islander:	78	0.11
Micronesian: (23)	35	0.05
Guamanian/Chamorro (18)	25	0.04
Other Micronesian (5)	10	0.01
Polynesian: (14)	19	0.03
Native Hawaiian (7)	10	0.01
Samoan (4)	5	0.01
Tongan (3)	3	0.00
Other Polynesian	1	0.00
Other Pac. Isl., specified	8	0.01
Other Pac. Isl., not spec. (2)	16	0.02
Hispanic or Latino:	2,589	3.76
Central American:	349	0.51
Costa Rican	10	0.01
Guatemalan	65	0.09
Honduran	46	0.07
Nicaraguan	20	0.03
Panamanian	10	0.01
Salvadoran	190	0.28
Other Central American	8	0.01
Cuban	76	0.11
Dominican Republic	8	0.01
Mexican	1,488	2.16
Puerto Rican	195	0.28
South American:	147	0.21
Argentinean	11	0.02
Bolivian	2	0.00
Chilean	27	0.04

Notes: 1. Figures in the "Number" column do not add up to the total population due to: a) Ancestry/Race overlap — e.g. persons can report being both White and Irish, b) persons of Hispanic origin can report being any race, c) persons reporting two ancestries are counted in both categories. 2. Numbers in parentheses indicate the number of persons reporting this ancestry/race alone, not in combination with any other ancestry/race. 3. Refer to the Explanation of Data in the front of the book for more detailed information.

Ancestry/Race	Number	%
Colombian	36	0.05
Ecuadorian	29	0.04
Peruvian	13	0.02
Venezuelan	16	0.02
Other South American	13	0.02
Other Hispanic or Latino	326	0.47
Hungarian	275	0.40
Iranian	20	0.03
Irish	7,332	10.63
Italian	1,800	2.61
Latvian	13	0.02
Lithuanian	158	0.23
Maltese	4	0.01
Northern European	76	0.11
Norwegian	440	0.64
Pennsylvania German	18	0.03
Polish	938	1.36
Portuguese	83	0.12
Romanian	143	0.21
Russian	436	0.63
Scandinavian	116	0.17
Scotch-Irish	3,860	5.60
Scottish	2,639	3.83
Serbian	19	0.03
Slavic	21	0.03
Slovak	82	0.12
Slovene	28	0.04
Swedish	506	0.73
Swiss	252	0.37
Ukrainian	421	0.61
United States or American	6,800	9.86
Welsh	734	1.06
West Indian, excl. Hispanic:	103	0.15
Bahamian	8	0.01
Dutch West Indian	7	0.01
Jamaican	70	0.10
West Indian	18	0.03
White:	54,663	79.35
Not Hispanic (52,340)	53,142	77.14
Hispanic (1,361)	1,521	2.21
Yugoslavian	17	0.02

Boone

Place Type: Town
County: Watauga
Population: 13,472

Ancestry/Race	Number	%
African American/Black:	485	3.60
Not Hispanic (456)	479	3.56
Hispanic (5)	6	0.04
African, sub-Saharan:	19	0.14
African	19	0.14
Am. Ind. or Alaska Nat., not spec.	27	0.20
American Indian tribes, specified:	43	0.32
Blackfeet (1)	2	0.01
Cherokee (6)	16	0.12
Chickasaw (1)	1	0.01
Chippewa (2)	4	0.03
Latin American Indians (7)	8	0.06
Lumbee (3)	8	0.06
Seminole (1)	1	0.01
Yaqui	1	0.01
All other tribes	2	0.01
Arab:	25	0.19
Syrian	25	0.19
Asian:	187	1.39
Chinese, ex. Taiwanese (41)	43	0.32
Filipino (3)	11	0.08
Hmong (1)	2	0.01
Indian (46)	50	0.37
Indonesian (1)	2	0.01
Japanese (19)	22	0.16
Korean (16)	22	0.16
Laotian (1)	1	0.01
Sri Lankan (1)	1	0.01
Taiwanese (2)	2	0.01
Thai (1)	2	0.01
Vietnamese (7)	7	0.05
Other Asian, not specified (19)	22	0.16
Austrian	9	0.07
Belgian	32	0.24
Brazilian	7	0.05
British	133	0.99
Canadian	34	0.25
Celtic	5	0.04
Croatian	7	0.05
Czech	16	0.12
Czechoslovakian	11	0.08
Danish	42	0.31
Dutch	242	1.80
English	1,663	12.37
European	345	2.57
Finnish	7	0.05
French, except Basque	257	1.91
French Canadian	23	0.17
German	2,021	15.03
Greek	105	0.78
Hawaii Native/Pacific Islander:	10	0.07
Micronesian: (2)	2	0.01
Guamanian/Chamorro (2)	2	0.01
Polynesian: (5)	6	0.04
Native Hawaiian (2)	2	0.01
Samoan (2)	3	0.02
Other Polynesian (1)	1	0.01
Other Pac. Isl., not spec.	2	0.01
Hispanic or Latino:	221	1.64
Central American:	3	0.02
Guatemalan	2	0.01
Panamanian	1	0.01
Cuban	18	0.13
Dominican Republic	2	0.01
Mexican	113	0.84
Puerto Rican	20	0.15
South American:	20	0.15
Argentinean	1	0.01
Chilean	3	0.02
Colombian	12	0.09
Ecuadorian	1	0.01
Peruvian	1	0.01
Venezuelan	2	0.01
Other Hispanic or Latino	45	0.33
Hungarian	14	0.10
Icelander	8	0.06
Irish	1,264	9.40
Israeli	41	0.30
Italian	684	5.09
Norwegian	114	0.85
Polish	210	1.56
Romanian	9	0.07
Russian	35	0.26
Scandinavian	16	0.12
Scotch-Irish	1,039	7.73
Scottish	740	5.50
Slavic	8	0.06
Slovene	4	0.03
Soviet Union	7	0.05
Swedish	231	1.72
Swiss	59	0.44
Turkish	8	0.06
United States or American	1,080	8.03
Welsh	116	0.86
West Indian, excl. Hispanic:	35	0.26
Trinidadian and Tobagonian	35	0.26
White:	12,735	94.53
Not Hispanic (12,518)	12,586	93.42
Hispanic (143)	149	1.11
Yugoslavian	14	0.10

Burlington

Place Type: City
County: Alamance
Population: 44,917

Ancestry/Race	Number	%
African American/Black:	11,500	25.60
Not Hispanic (11,166)	11,399	25.38
Hispanic (86)	101	0.22
African, sub-Saharan:	599	1.32
African	588	1.30
South African	11	0.02
Alaska Native tribes, specified:	1	0.00
Alaska Athabascan	1	0.00
Am. Ind. or Alaska Nat., not spec.	112	0.25
Alsatian	6	0.01
American Indian tribes, specified:	190	0.42
Apache (1)	1	0.00
Blackfeet (4)	16	0.04
Cherokee (18)	65	0.14
Chippewa (6)	7	0.02
Choctaw	2	0.00
Colville (1)	1	0.00
Comanche	1	0.00
Creek	3	0.01
Iroquois (3)	7	0.02
Latin American Indians (21)	30	0.07
Lumbee (18)	24	0.05
Navajo	2	0.00
Pueblo (1)	1	0.00
Seminole (4)	5	0.01
Sioux (2)	7	0.02
Ute (1)	1	0.00
All other tribes (12)	17	0.04
American Indian tribes, not spec.	30	0.07
Arab:	113	0.25
Egyptian	62	0.14
Lebanese	51	0.11
Armenian	13	0.03
Asian:	916	2.04
Cambodian (1)	2	0.00
Chinese, ex. Taiwanese (83)	97	0.22
Filipino (27)	44	0.10
Indian (252)	269	0.60
Indonesian (2)	4	0.01
Japanese (13)	15	0.03
Korean (56)	71	0.16
Laotian (137)	174	0.39
Malaysian	2	0.00
Pakistani (37)	49	0.11
Thai (9)	10	0.02
Vietnamese (115)	126	0.28
Other Asian, specified	1	0.00
Other Asian, not specified (22)	52	0.12
Austrian	36	0.08
Brazilian	11	0.02
British	143	0.32
Canadian	43	0.09
Celtic	39	0.09
Czech	47	0.10
Czechoslovakian	18	0.04
Danish	26	0.06
Dutch	493	1.09
English	3,934	8.67
European	290	0.64
Finnish	29	0.06
French, except Basque	481	1.06
French Canadian	137	0.30
German	3,587	7.91
Greek	201	0.44
Guyanese	23	0.05
Hawaii Native/Pacific Islander:	37	0.08
Micronesian: (3)	3	0.01
Guamanian/Chamorro (2)	2	0.00
Other Micronesian (1)	1	0.00
Polynesian: (6)	14	0.03
Native Hawaiian (1)	7	0.02
Samoan (5)	7	0.02
Other Pac. Isl., specified	1	0.00
Other Pac. Isl., not spec. (7)	19	0.04
Hispanic or Latino:	4,525	10.07
Central American:	340	0.76
Costa Rican	11	0.02
Guatemalan	17	0.04
Honduran	63	0.14
Nicaraguan	10	0.02
Panamanian	16	0.04
Salvadoran	213	0.47
Other Central American	10	0.02

Notes: 1. Figures in the "Number" column do not add up to the total population due to: a) Ancestry/Race overlap — e.g. persons can report being both White and Irish, b) persons of Hispanic origin can report being any race, c) persons reporting two ancestries are counted in both categories. 2. Numbers in parentheses indicate the number of persons reporting this ancestry/race alone, not in combination with any other ancestry/race. 3. Refer to the Explanation of Data in the front of the book for more detailed information.

Ancestry/Race	Number	%
Cuban	30	0.07
Dominican Republic	9	0.02
Mexican	3,352	7.46
Puerto Rican	213	0.47
South American:	102	0.23
Argentinean	6	0.01
Bolivian	1	0.00
Chilean	17	0.04
Colombian	16	0.04
Ecuadorian	41	0.09
Peruvian	10	0.02
Uruguayan	6	0.01
Venezuelan	2	0.00
Other South American	3	0.01
Other Hispanic or Latino	479	1.07
Hungarian	37	0.08
Iranian	37	0.08
Irish	2,956	6.52
Israeli	10	0.02
Italian	652	1.44
Norwegian	146	0.32
Pennsylvania German	6	0.01
Polish	327	0.72
Portuguese	29	0.06
Romanian	15	0.03
Russian	26	0.06
Scandinavian	8	0.02
Scotch-Irish	1,656	3.65
Scottish	967	2.13
Slavic	11	0.02
Slovak	23	0.05
Swedish	113	0.25
Swiss	15	0.03
Ukrainian	8	0.02
United States or American	5,933	13.08
Welsh	139	0.31
West Indian, excl. Hispanic:	47	0.10
Haitian	13	0.03
Jamaican	34	0.07
White:	30,244	67.33
Not Hispanic (27,828)	28,167	62.71
Hispanic (1,938)	2,077	4.62
Yugoslavian	5	0.01

Carrboro

Place Type: Town
County: Orange
Population: 16,782

Ancestry/Race	Number	%
Acadian/Cajun	10	0.06
African American/Black:	2,388	14.23
Not Hispanic (2,231)	2,334	13.91
Hispanic (42)	54	0.32
African, sub-Saharan:	357	2.14
African	189	1.13
Ghanian	12	0.07
Nigerian	42	0.25
Senegalese	7	0.04
South African	15	0.09
Ugandan	30	0.18
Other sub-Saharan African	62	0.37
Alaska Native tribes, specified:	1	0.01
Alaska Athabascan (1)	1	0.01
Am. Ind. or Alaska Nat., not spec.	56	0.33
American Indian tribes, specified:	93	0.55
Apache	1	0.01
Blackfeet	3	0.02
Cherokee (5)	30	0.18
Chickasaw	1	0.01
Chippewa	1	0.01
Choctaw	2	0.01
Cree (1)	1	0.01
Creek (1)	2	0.01
Delaware (1)	1	0.01
Iroquois	6	0.04
Latin American Indians (17)	18	0.11
Lumbee (10)	15	0.09
Seminole	2	0.01
Shoshone	1	0.01
Sioux (2)	3	0.02
All other tribes (3)	6	0.04
American Indian tribes, not spec.	1	0.01
Arab:	58	0.35
Arab/Arabic	15	0.09
Jordanian	20	0.12
Palestinian	8	0.05
Other Arab	15	0.09
Armenian	15	0.09
Asian:	988	5.89
Bangladeshi (4)	4	0.02
Chinese, ex. Taiwanese (298)	324	1.93
Filipino (25)	40	0.24
Indian (213)	229	1.36
Indonesian (2)	2	0.01
Japanese (60)	80	0.48
Korean (126)	144	0.86
Laotian (5)	6	0.04
Malaysian (2)	2	0.01
Pakistani (11)	14	0.08
Sri Lankan (5)	5	0.03
Taiwanese (21)	28	0.17
Thai (26)	30	0.18
Vietnamese (33)	34	0.20
Other Asian, specified (18)	25	0.15
Other Asian, not specified (6)	21	0.13
Austrian	32	0.19
Belgian	11	0.07
British	202	1.21
Canadian	6	0.04
Croatian	7	0.04
Czech	44	0.26
Czechoslovakian	33	0.20
Danish	69	0.41
Dutch	176	1.05
Eastern European	48	0.29
English	2,333	13.97
European	369	2.21
Finnish	13	0.08
French, except Basque	564	3.38
French Canadian	96	0.57
German	2,344	14.03
Greek	170	1.02
Guyanese	4	0.02
Hawaii Native/Pacific Islander:	16	0.10
Micronesian:	1	0.01
Guamanian/Chamorro	1	0.01
Polynesian:	7	0.04
Native Hawaiian	3	0.02
Samoan	1	0.01
Tongan	2	0.01
Other Polynesian	1	0.01
Other Pac. Isl., specified	2	0.01
Other Pac. Isl., not spec. (1)	6	0.04
Hispanic or Latino:	2,062	12.29
Central American:	106	0.63
Costa Rican	2	0.01
Guatemalan	32	0.19
Honduran	23	0.14
Nicaraguan	4	0.02
Panamanian	7	0.04
Salvadoran	36	0.21
Other Central American	2	0.01
Cuban	41	0.24
Dominican Republic	8	0.05
Mexican	1,530	9.12
Puerto Rican	41	0.24
South American:	117	0.70
Argentinean	7	0.04
Bolivian	7	0.04
Chilean	6	0.04
Colombian	48	0.29
Paraguayan	2	0.01
Peruvian	25	0.15
Venezuelan	17	0.10
Other South American	5	0.03
Other Hispanic or Latino	219	1.30
Hungarian	71	0.43
Iranian	20	0.12
Irish	2,172	13.00
Italian	808	4.84
Latvian	40	0.24
Lithuanian	80	0.48
Northern European	47	0.28
Norwegian	100	0.60
Polish	516	3.09
Portuguese	14	0.08
Romanian	78	0.47
Russian	135	0.81
Scandinavian	7	0.04
Scotch-Irish	541	3.24
Scottish	672	4.02
Serbian	8	0.05
Slovak	17	0.10
Swedish	219	1.31
Swiss	65	0.39
Turkish	25	0.15
Ukrainian	106	0.63
United States or American	755	4.52
Welsh	108	0.65
West Indian, excl. Hispanic:	94	0.56
Barbadian	8	0.05
Haitian	12	0.07
Jamaican	25	0.15
West Indian	49	0.29
White:	12,539	74.72
Not Hispanic (11,256)	11,514	68.61
Hispanic (939)	1,025	6.11
Yugoslavian	21	0.13

Cary

Place Type: Town
County: Wake
Population: 94,536

Ancestry/Race	Number	%
Acadian/Cajun	6	0.01
Afghan	5	0.01
African American/Black:	6,232	6.59
Not Hispanic (5,744)	6,099	6.45
Hispanic (69)	133	0.14
African, sub-Saharan:	754	0.80
African	283	0.30
Ethiopian	91	0.10
Ghanian	5	0.01
Kenyan	18	0.02
Liberian	10	0.01
Nigerian	58	0.06
Sierra Leonean	8	0.01
South African	158	0.17
Ugandan	53	0.06
Zimbabwean	6	0.01
Other sub-Saharan African	64	0.07
Alaska Native tribes, specified:	4	0.00
Alaska Athabascan (3)	4	0.00
Am. Ind. or Alaska Nat., not spec.	175	0.19
Albanian	16	0.02
Alsatian	13	0.01
American Indian tribes, specified:	385	0.41
Apache (2)	6	0.01
Blackfeet (4)	12	0.01
Cherokee (27)	134	0.14
Chickasaw (1)	3	0.00
Chippewa (5)	7	0.01
Choctaw (2)	3	0.00
Comanche (1)	1	0.00
Creek (3)	7	0.01
Iroquois (7)	18	0.02
Kiowa (2)	2	0.00
Latin American Indians (28)	48	0.05
Lumbee (66)	76	0.08
Navajo (2)	5	0.01
Osage (1)	5	0.01
Ottawa (3)	3	0.00
Potawatomi (1)	3	0.00
Pueblo	3	0.00
Seminole	3	0.00
Shoshone (1)	3	0.00

Notes: 1. Figures in the "Number" column do not add up to the total population due to: a) Ancestry/Race overlap — e.g. persons can report being both White and Irish, b) persons of Hispanic origin can report being any race, c) persons reporting two ancestries are counted in both categories. 2. Numbers in parentheses indicate the number of persons reporting this ancestry/race alone, not in combination with any other ancestry/race. 3. Refer to the Explanation of Data in the front of the book for more detailed information.

Ancestry/Race	Number	%
Sioux (3)	13	0.01
Yaqui (1)	1	0.00
All other tribes (14)	29	0.03
American Indian tribes, not spec.	22	0.02
Arab:	1,001	1.06
Arab/Arabic	149	0.16
Egyptian	168	0.18
Iraqi	9	0.01
Jordanian	72	0.08
Lebanese	248	0.26
Moroccan	64	0.07
Palestinian	5	0.01
Syrian	127	0.13
Other Arab	159	0.17
Armenian	158	0.17
Asian:	8,398	8.88
Bangladeshi (29)	30	0.03
Cambodian (6)	6	0.01
Chinese, ex. Taiwanese (1,916)	2,061	2.18
Filipino (268)	358	0.38
Indian (3,268)	3,379	3.57
Indonesian (13)	17	0.02
Japanese (286)	419	0.44
Korean (596)	650	0.69
Laotian (7)	12	0.01
Malaysian (9)	12	0.01
Pakistani (206)	255	0.27
Sri Lankan (33)	34	0.04
Taiwanese (212)	229	0.24
Thai (46)	57	0.06
Vietnamese (587)	625	0.66
Other Asian, specified (10)	20	0.02
Other Asian, not specified (102)	234	0.25
Australian	123	0.13
Austrian	456	0.48
Belgian	182	0.19
Brazilian	50	0.05
British	1,302	1.38
Bulgarian	5	0.01
Canadian	518	0.55
Celtic	15	0.02
Croatian	216	0.23
Cypriot	32	0.03
Czech	309	0.33
Czechoslovakian	139	0.15
Danish	291	0.31
Dutch	1,559	1.65
Eastern European	128	0.14
English	13,498	14.28
Estonian	62	0.07
European	1,791	1.89
Finnish	222	0.23
French, except Basque	2,834	3.00
French Canadian	738	0.78
German	16,359	17.31
Greek	477	0.50
Guyanese	27	0.03
Hawaii Native/Pacific Islander:	94	0.10
Micronesian: (7)	15	0.02
Guamanian/Chamorro (7)	15	0.02
Polynesian: (14)	42	0.04
Native Hawaiian (6)	24	0.03
Samoan (8)	15	0.02
Tongan	2	0.00
Other Polynesian	1	0.00
Other Pac. Isl., specified	6	0.01
Other Pac. Isl., not spec. (7)	31	0.03
Hispanic or Latino:	4,047	4.28
Central American:	360	0.38
Costa Rican	11	0.01
Guatemalan	81	0.09
Honduran	69	0.07
Nicaraguan	30	0.03
Panamanian	31	0.03
Salvadoran	116	0.12
Other Central American	22	0.02
Cuban	199	0.21
Dominican Republic	31	0.03
Mexican	2,157	2.28
Puerto Rican	390	0.41
South American:	361	0.38
Argentinean	28	0.03
Bolivian	3	0.00
Chilean	21	0.02
Colombian	116	0.12
Ecuadorian	39	0.04
Paraguayan	4	0.00
Peruvian	59	0.06
Uruguayan	6	0.01
Venezuelan	72	0.08
Other South American	13	0.01
Other Hispanic or Latino	549	0.58
Hungarian	626	0.66
Icelander	15	0.02
Iranian	173	0.18
Irish	11,628	12.30
Israeli	17	0.02
Italian	6,100	6.45
Latvian	14	0.01
Lithuanian	323	0.34
Luxemburger	3	0.00
Macedonian	44	0.05
Maltese	6	0.01
New Zealander	47	0.05
Northern European	102	0.11
Norwegian	1,082	1.14
Pennsylvania German	13	0.01
Polish	3,423	3.62
Portuguese	130	0.14
Romanian	203	0.21
Russian	1,193	1.26
Scandinavian	154	0.16
Scotch-Irish	3,050	3.23
Scottish	3,034	3.21
Serbian	26	0.03
Slavic	51	0.05
Slovak	384	0.41
Slovene	122	0.13
Swedish	1,505	1.59
Swiss	255	0.27
Turkish	129	0.14
Ukrainian	455	0.48
United States or American	7,002	7.41
Welsh	873	0.92
West Indian, excl. Hispanic:	196	0.21
Barbadian	22	0.02
Bermudan	7	0.01
British West Indian	10	0.01
Jamaican	74	0.08
Trinidadian and Tobagonian	39	0.04
U.S. Virgin Islander	30	0.03
West Indian	14	0.01
White:	79,115	83.69
Not Hispanic (75,299)	76,467	80.89
Hispanic (2,384)	2,648	2.80
Yugoslavian	115	0.12

Chapel Hill

Place Type: Town
County: Orange
Population: 48,715

Ancestry/Race	Number	%
Acadian/Cajun	5	0.01
African American/Black:	5,898	12.11
Not Hispanic (5,517)	5,810	11.93
Hispanic (48)	88	0.18
African, sub-Saharan:	673	1.38
African	528	1.08
Ethiopian	13	0.03
Ghanian	26	0.05
Kenyan	28	0.06
Liberian	28	0.06
Nigerian	38	0.08
Other sub-Saharan African	12	0.02
Alaska Native tribes, specified:	3	0.01
Alaska Athabascan (1)	1	0.00
Eskimo (1)	1	0.00
Tlingit-Haida (1)	1	0.00
Am. Ind. or Alaska Nat., not spec.	94	0.19
Albanian	9	0.02
American Indian tribes, specified:	284	0.58
Apache (1)	1	0.00
Blackfeet (2)	7	0.01
Cherokee (24)	94	0.19
Cheyenne	1	0.00
Chickasaw (1)	1	0.00
Chippewa (10)	15	0.03
Choctaw	1	0.00
Comanche (1)	1	0.00
Cree	1	0.00
Creek	4	0.01
Delaware	2	0.00
Iroquois (3)	10	0.02
Latin American Indians (4)	12	0.02
Lumbee (52)	63	0.13
Navajo (1)	1	0.00
Osage (1)	1	0.00
Potawatomi	4	0.01
Seminole	1	0.00
Sioux (1)	6	0.01
Yaqui (6)	6	0.01
All other tribes (28)	52	0.11
American Indian tribes, not spec.	44	0.09
Arab:	295	0.60
Arab/Arabic	40	0.08
Egyptian	39	0.08
Iraqi	17	0.03
Lebanese	110	0.23
Moroccan	12	0.02
Palestinian	35	0.07
Syrian	16	0.03
Other Arab	26	0.05
Armenian	46	0.09
Asian:	3,914	8.03
Bangladeshi (9)	9	0.02
Cambodian (3)	7	0.01
Chinese, ex. Taiwanese (1,354)	1,470	3.02
Filipino (129)	175	0.36
Hmong (34)	39	0.08
Indian (799)	853	1.75
Indonesian (11)	11	0.02
Japanese (246)	326	0.67
Korean (534)	575	1.18
Laotian (8)	8	0.02
Malaysian (1)	6	0.01
Pakistani (23)	29	0.06
Sri Lankan (19)	23	0.05
Taiwanese (98)	113	0.23
Thai (48)	61	0.13
Vietnamese (106)	112	0.23
Other Asian, specified (17)	20	0.04
Other Asian, not specified (17)	77	0.16
Australian	41	0.08
Austrian	257	0.53
Belgian	36	0.07
Brazilian	40	0.08
British	816	1.67
Bulgarian	6	0.01
Canadian	142	0.29
Celtic	43	0.09
Croatian	54	0.11
Cypriot	7	0.01
Czech	231	0.47
Czechoslovakian	52	0.11
Danish	218	0.45
Dutch	736	1.51
Eastern European	177	0.36
English	7,576	15.53
Estonian	15	0.03
European	959	1.97
Finnish	88	0.18
French, except Basque	1,288	2.64
French Canadian	315	0.65
German	7,354	15.07
Greek	247	0.51
Guyanese	21	0.04
Hawaii Native/Pacific Islander:	50	0.10
Micronesian: (2)	5	0.01

Notes: 1. Figures in the "Number" column do not add up to the total population due to: a) Ancestry/Race overlap — e.g. persons can report being both White and Irish, b) persons of Hispanic origin can report being any race, c) persons reporting two ancestries are counted in both categories. 2. Numbers in parentheses indicate the number of persons reporting this ancestry/race alone, not in combination with any other ancestry/race. 3. Refer to the Explanation of Data in the front of the book for more detailed information.

Guamanian/Chamorro (2)	5	0.01
Polynesian: (8)	25	0.05
Native Hawaiian (4)	14	0.03
Samoan (4)	9	0.02
Tongan	1	0.00
Other Polynesian	1	0.00
Other Pac. Isl., specified	3	0.01
Other Pac. Isl., not spec. (2)	17	0.03
Hispanic or Latino:	1,564	3.21
Central American:	146	0.30
Costa Rican	9	0.02
Guatemalan	25	0.05
Honduran	11	0.02
Nicaraguan	12	0.02
Panamanian	15	0.03
Salvadoran	72	0.15
Other Central American	2	0.00
Cuban	80	0.16
Dominican Republic	12	0.02
Mexican	685	1.41
Puerto Rican	155	0.32
South American:	239	0.49
Argentinean	28	0.06
Bolivian	13	0.03
Chilean	31	0.06
Colombian	60	0.12
Ecuadorian	24	0.05
Paraguayan	3	0.01
Peruvian	37	0.08
Uruguayan	6	0.01
Venezuelan	30	0.06
Other South American	7	0.01
Other Hispanic or Latino	247	0.51
Hungarian	230	0.47
Icelander	8	0.02
Iranian	84	0.17
Irish	5,000	10.25
Israeli	24	0.05
Italian	2,286	4.68
Latvian	88	0.18
Lithuanian	100	0.20
Luxemburger	10	0.02
Northern European	106	0.22
Norwegian	525	1.08
Pennsylvania German	17	0.03
Polish	1,347	2.76
Portuguese	113	0.23
Romanian	65	0.13
Russian	940	1.93
Scandinavian	105	0.22
Scotch-Irish	2,365	4.85
Scottish	2,224	4.56
Serbian	13	0.03
Slavic	38	0.08
Slovak	118	0.24
Swedish	590	1.21
Swiss	207	0.42
Turkish	44	0.09
Ukrainian	80	0.16
United States or American	1,871	3.83
Welsh	648	1.33
West Indian, excl. Hispanic:	224	0.46
Bermudan	11	0.02
British West Indian	18	0.04
Haitian	19	0.04
Jamaican	71	0.15
Trinidadian and Tobagonian	56	0.11
U.S. Virgin Islander	7	0.01
West Indian	42	0.09
White:	38,681	79.40
Not Hispanic (37,073)	37,682	77.35
Hispanic (900)	999	2.05
Yugoslavian	16	0.03

Charlotte

Place Type: City
County: Mecklenburg
Population: 540,828

Ancestry/Race	Number	%
Acadian/Cajun	48	0.01
Afghan	12	0.00
African American/Black:	180,371	33.35
Not Hispanic (175,661)	178,699	33.04
Hispanic (1,303)	1,672	0.31
African, sub-Saharan:	8,902	1.64
African	5,402	1.00
Cape Verdean	35	0.01
Ethiopian	608	0.11
Ghanian	245	0.05
Kenyan	24	0.00
Liberian	546	0.10
Nigerian	591	0.11
Senegalese	6	0.00
Sierra Leonean	122	0.02
Somalian	624	0.12
South African	140	0.03
Sudanese	45	0.01
Zairian	116	0.02
Zimbabwean	98	0.02
Other sub-Saharan African	300	0.06
Alaska Native tribes, specified:	22	0.00
Aleut (11)	17	0.00
Eskimo (2)	4	0.00
Tlingit-Haida	1	0.00
Alaska Native tribes, not specified	2	0.00
Am. Ind. or Alaska Nat., not spec.	1,366	0.25
Albanian	52	0.01
Alsatian	33	0.01
American Indian tribes, specified:	2,300	0.43
Apache (11)	24	0.00
Blackfeet (17)	91	0.02
Cherokee (259)	806	0.15
Cheyenne (1)	8	0.00
Chickasaw (3)	4	0.00
Chippewa (11)	27	0.00
Choctaw (28)	45	0.01
Comanche (2)	4	0.00
Cree (1)	6	0.00
Creek (17)	32	0.01
Crow (1)	10	0.00
Delaware (1)	3	0.00
Iroquois (45)	89	0.02
Kiowa (2)	2	0.00
Latin American Indians (104)	281	0.05
Lumbee (471)	558	0.10
Menominee (4)	4	0.00
Navajo (7)	12	0.00
Osage (1)	3	0.00
Ottawa (1)	2	0.00
Potawatomi (1)	1	0.00
Pueblo (4)	9	0.00
Puget Sound Salish	1	0.00
Seminole (10)	26	0.00
Shoshone	1	0.00
Sioux (19)	28	0.01
Ute (4)	4	0.00
Yakama (1)	1	0.00
Yaqui (1)	1	0.00
All other tribes (122)	217	0.04
American Indian tribes, not spec.	186	0.03
Arab:	3,342	0.62
Arab/Arabic	783	0.14
Egyptian	303	0.06
Iraqi	52	0.01
Jordanian	42	0.01
Lebanese	1,083	0.20
Moroccan	81	0.01
Palestinian	406	0.07
Syrian	179	0.03
Other Arab	413	0.08
Armenian	132	0.02
Asian:	20,813	3.85
Bangladeshi (20)	27	0.00
Cambodian (653)	761	0.14
Chinese, ex. Taiwanese (2,356)	2,677	0.49
Filipino (780)	1,038	0.19
Hmong (702)	797	0.15
Indian (4,684)	5,017	0.93
Indonesian (61)	80	0.01
Japanese (668)	848	0.16
Korean (1,728)	1,936	0.36
Laotian (1,061)	1,211	0.22
Malaysian (19)	29	0.01
Pakistani (172)	221	0.04
Sri Lankan (20)	23	0.00
Taiwanese (79)	115	0.02
Thai (127)	193	0.04
Vietnamese (4,421)	4,709	0.87
Other Asian, specified (34)	86	0.02
Other Asian, not specified (524)	1,045	0.19
Assyrian/Chaldean/Syriac	71	0.01
Australian	190	0.04
Austrian	956	0.18
Basque	14	0.00
Belgian	343	0.06
Brazilian	260	0.05
British	2,999	0.55
Bulgarian	106	0.02
Canadian	1,269	0.23
Carpatho Rusyn	22	0.00
Celtic	99	0.02
Croatian	414	0.08
Czech	993	0.18
Czechoslovakian	480	0.09
Danish	912	0.17
Dutch	5,410	1.00
Eastern European	277	0.05
English	46,020	8.49
Estonian	48	0.01
European	4,624	0.85
Finnish	606	0.11
French, except Basque	9,675	1.78
French Canadian	1,901	0.35
German	54,861	10.12
Greek	3,612	0.67
Guyanese	166	0.03
Hawaii Native/Pacific Islander:	634	0.12
Melanesian: (2)	2	0.00
Other Melanesian (2)	2	0.00
Micronesian: (71)	111	0.02
Guamanian/Chamorro (50)	86	0.02
Other Micronesian (21)	25	0.00
Polynesian: (133)	250	0.05
Native Hawaiian (49)	110	0.02
Samoan (67)	116	0.02
Tongan (17)	21	0.00
Other Polynesian	3	0.00
Other Pac. Isl., specified	36	0.01
Other Pac. Isl., not spec. (71)	235	0.04
Hispanic or Latino:	39,800	7.36
Central American:	5,001	0.92
Costa Rican	284	0.05
Guatemalan	449	0.08
Honduran	1,577	0.29
Nicaraguan	459	0.08
Panamanian	133	0.02
Salvadoran	1,891	0.35
Other Central American	208	0.04
Cuban	1,098	0.20
Dominican Republic	472	0.09
Mexican	22,168	4.10
Puerto Rican	2,415	0.45
South American:	2,732	0.51
Argentinean	123	0.02
Bolivian	36	0.01
Chilean	140	0.03
Colombian	835	0.15
Ecuadorian	800	0.15
Paraguayan	9	0.00
Peruvian	417	0.08
Uruguayan	22	0.00
Venezuelan	230	0.04

Notes: 1. Figures in the "Number" column do not add up to the total population due to: a) Ancestry/Race overlap — e.g. persons can report being both White and Irish, b) persons of Hispanic origin can report being any race, c) persons reporting two ancestries are counted in both categories. 2. Numbers in parentheses indicate the number of persons reporting this ancestry/race alone, not in combination with any other ancestry/race. 3. Refer to the Explanation of Data in the front of the book for more detailed information.

Ancestry/Race	Number	%
Other South American	120	0.02
Other Hispanic or Latino	5,914	1.09
Hungarian	1,660	0.31
Icelander	32	0.01
Iranian	633	0.12
Irish	42,394	7.82
Israeli	77	0.01
Italian	17,676	3.26
Latvian	120	0.02
Lithuanian	735	0.14
Luxemburger	14	0.00
Macedonian	31	0.01
Maltese	25	0.00
New Zealander	26	0.00
Northern European	360	0.07
Norwegian	2,553	0.47
Pennsylvania German	79	0.01
Polish	8,090	1.49
Portuguese	567	0.10
Romanian	366	0.07
Russian	3,018	0.56
Scandinavian	424	0.08
Scotch-Irish	21,114	3.89
Scottish	12,846	2.37
Serbian	257	0.05
Slavic	169	0.03
Slovak	1,006	0.19
Slovene	236	0.04
Swedish	3,417	0.63
Swiss	987	0.18
Turkish	154	0.03
Ukrainian	1,075	0.20
United States or American	36,557	6.74
Welsh	3,208	0.59
West Indian, excl. Hispanic:	2,453	0.45
Bahamian	75	0.01
Barbadian	43	0.01
Belizean	4	0.00
Bermudan	10	0.00
British West Indian	97	0.02
Dutch West Indian	18	0.00
Haitian	422	0.08
Jamaican	1,116	0.21
Trinidadian and Tobagonian	214	0.04
U.S. Virgin Islander	40	0.01
West Indian	408	0.08
Other West Indian	6	0.00
White:	321,491	59.44
Not Hispanic (297,845)	302,363	55.91
Hispanic (17,216)	19,128	3.54
Yugoslavian	535	0.10

Clemmons

Place Type: Village
County: Forsyth
Population: 13,827

Ancestry/Race	Number	%
African American/Black:	770	5.57
Not Hispanic (703)	750	5.42
Hispanic (18)	20	0.14
African, sub-Saharan:	43	0.31
African	28	0.20
Nigerian	8	0.06
South African	7	0.05
Alaska Native tribes, specified:	1	0.01
Alaska Athabascan (1)	1	0.01
Am. Ind. or Alaska Nat., not spec.	19	0.14
Alsatian	4	0.03
American Indian tribes, specified:	19	0.14
Cherokee (2)	14	0.10
Iroquois	1	0.01
Lumbee (1)	1	0.01
Shoshone (1)	1	0.01
Sioux	1	0.01
All other tribes (1)	1	0.01
American Indian tribes, not spec.	3	0.02
Arab:	51	0.36
Egyptian	19	0.14
Lebanese	20	0.14
Other Arab	12	0.09
Asian:	329	2.38
Cambodian (4)	4	0.03
Chinese, ex. Taiwanese (90)	95	0.69
Filipino (31)	37	0.27
Indian (76)	80	0.58
Japanese (5)	19	0.14
Korean (11)	14	0.10
Malaysian	4	0.03
Taiwanese (4)	4	0.03
Vietnamese (63)	66	0.48
Other Asian, not specified (2)	6	0.04
Austrian	41	0.29
Belgian	5	0.04
Brazilian	9	0.06
British	61	0.44
Canadian	44	0.31
Croatian	13	0.09
Czech	22	0.16
Czechoslovakian	13	0.09
Danish	10	0.07
Dutch	154	1.10
Eastern European	32	0.23
English	2,468	17.64
European	274	1.96
Finnish	13	0.09
French, except Basque	336	2.40
French Canadian	49	0.35
German	2,400	17.16
Greek	122	0.87
Hawaii Native/Pacific Islander:	4	0.03
Polynesian: (1)	2	0.01
Native Hawaiian	1	0.01
Other Polynesian (1)	1	0.01
Other Pac. Isl., not spec. (2)	2	0.01
Hispanic or Latino:	490	3.54
Central American:	33	0.24
Costa Rican	2	0.01
Guatemalan	23	0.17
Nicaraguan	1	0.01
Panamanian	2	0.01
Salvadoran	5	0.04
Cuban	12	0.09
Dominican Republic	8	0.06
Mexican	298	2.16
Puerto Rican	25	0.18
South American:	57	0.41
Chilean	3	0.02
Colombian	22	0.16
Ecuadorian	10	0.07
Peruvian	2	0.01
Venezuelan	17	0.12
Other South American	3	0.02
Other Hispanic or Latino	57	0.41
Hungarian	26	0.19
Iranian	17	0.12
Irish	1,494	10.68
Italian	411	2.94
Lithuanian	38	0.27
New Zealander	6	0.04
Northern European	9	0.06
Norwegian	64	0.46
Polish	360	2.57
Romanian	8	0.06
Russian	69	0.49
Scandinavian	25	0.18
Scotch-Irish	490	3.50
Scottish	354	2.53
Slavic	6	0.04
Slovak	76	0.54
Swedish	103	0.74
Swiss	66	0.47
Ukrainian	12	0.09
United States or American	1,612	11.52
Welsh	112	0.80
West Indian, excl. Hispanic:	7	0.05
Haitian	7	0.05
White:	12,538	90.68
Not Hispanic (12,196)	12,290	88.88
Hispanic (230)	248	1.79
Yugoslavian	6	0.04

Concord

Place Type: City
County: Cabarrus
Population: 55,977

Ancestry/Race	Number	%
Acadian/Cajun	49	0.09
African American/Black:	8,669	15.49
Not Hispanic (8,304)	8,477	15.14
Hispanic (146)	192	0.34
African, sub-Saharan:	405	0.72
African	352	0.63
Ghanian	33	0.06
Liberian	12	0.02
Ugandan	8	0.01
Alaska Native tribes, not specified	2	0.00
Am. Ind. or Alaska Nat., not spec.	109	0.19
American Indian tribes, specified:	231	0.41
Apache (1)	2	0.00
Blackfeet (1)	8	0.01
Cherokee (35)	85	0.15
Chippewa (3)	3	0.01
Choctaw (4)	9	0.02
Colville (1)	1	0.00
Comanche (1)	1	0.00
Creek (1)	1	0.00
Delaware	2	0.00
Iroquois (2)	4	0.01
Latin American Indians (16)	29	0.05
Lumbee (33)	50	0.09
Navajo (3)	8	0.01
Ottawa (2)	2	0.00
Puget Sound Salish (1)	1	0.00
Seminole	3	0.01
Sioux (2)	9	0.02
All other tribes (9)	13	0.02
American Indian tribes, not spec.	6	0.01
Arab:	74	0.13
Lebanese	29	0.05
Moroccan	11	0.02
Syrian	34	0.06
Armenian	5	0.01
Asian:	810	1.45
Bangladeshi (2)	2	0.00
Cambodian (6)	7	0.01
Chinese, ex. Taiwanese (101)	110	0.20
Filipino (54)	87	0.16
Hmong (6)	6	0.01
Indian (210)	225	0.40
Indonesian (1)	3	0.01
Japanese (27)	46	0.08
Korean (152)	168	0.30
Laotian (35)	36	0.06
Pakistani (15)	16	0.03
Sri Lankan (1)	1	0.00
Taiwanese	1	0.00
Thai (9)	10	0.02
Vietnamese (47)	56	0.10
Other Asian, specified (1)	3	0.01
Other Asian, not specified (10)	33	0.06
Austrian	53	0.09
Belgian	14	0.03
British	258	0.46
Bulgarian	7	0.01
Canadian	166	0.30
Croatian	27	0.05
Czech	103	0.18
Czechoslovakian	45	0.08
Danish	135	0.24
Dutch	868	1.55
Eastern European	26	0.05
English	4,413	7.89
European	248	0.44
Finnish	47	0.08
French, except Basque	922	1.65
French Canadian	171	0.31

Notes: 1. Figures in the "Number" column do not add up to the total population due to: a) Ancestry/Race overlap — e.g. persons can report being both White and Irish, b) persons of Hispanic origin can report being any race, c) persons reporting two ancestries are counted in both categories. 2. Numbers in parentheses indicate the number of persons reporting this ancestry/race alone, not in combination with any other ancestry/race. 3. Refer to the Explanation of Data in the front of the book for more detailed information.

German	7,858	14.05
Greek	149	0.27
Hawaii Native/Pacific Islander:	36	0.06
Micronesian: (8)	10	0.02
Guamanian/Chamorro (8)	10	0.02
Polynesian: (6)	21	0.04
Native Hawaiian (5)	16	0.03
Samoan	4	0.01
Other Polynesian (1)	1	0.00
Other Pac. Isl., specified	2	0.00
Other Pac. Isl., not spec.	3	0.01
Hispanic or Latino:	4,369	7.80
Central American:	99	0.18
Costa Rican	6	0.01
Guatemalan	33	0.06
Honduran	19	0.03
Nicaraguan	10	0.02
Panamanian	12	0.02
Salvadoran	17	0.03
Other Central American	2	0.00
Cuban	73	0.13
Dominican Republic	11	0.02
Mexican	3,527	6.30
Puerto Rican	244	0.44
South American:	70	0.13
Chilean	2	0.00
Colombian	23	0.04
Ecuadorian	12	0.02
Paraguayan	1	0.00
Peruvian	17	0.03
Uruguayan	1	0.00
Venezuelan	7	0.01
Other South American	7	0.01
Other Hispanic or Latino	345	0.62
Hungarian	113	0.20
Iranian	6	0.01
Irish	4,741	8.48
Israeli	17	0.03
Italian	1,750	3.13
Latvian	18	0.03
Lithuanian	86	0.15
Northern European	17	0.03
Norwegian	151	0.27
Pennsylvania German	13	0.02
Polish	579	1.04
Portuguese	67	0.12
Russian	55	0.10
Scandinavian	38	0.07
Scotch-Irish	2,153	3.85
Scottish	1,201	2.15
Slavic	26	0.05
Slovak	42	0.08
Slovene	7	0.01
Swedish	246	0.44
Swiss	81	0.14
Ukrainian	42	0.08
United States or American	7,887	14.10
Welsh	316	0.56
West Indian, excl. Hispanic:	175	0.31
Bahamian	8	0.01
Barbadian	9	0.02
British West Indian	24	0.04
Haitian	13	0.02
Jamaican	16	0.03
Trinidadian and Tobagonian	35	0.06
U.S. Virgin Islander	15	0.03
West Indian	55	0.10
White:	44,671	79.80
Not Hispanic (41,985)	42,365	75.68
Hispanic (2,143)	2,306	4.12
Yugoslavian	7	0.01

Cornelius

Place Type: Town
County: Mecklenburg
Population: 11,969

Ancestry/Race	Number	%
Acadian/Cajun	6	0.05
African American/Black:	687	5.74
Not Hispanic (661)	669	5.59
Hispanic (12)	18	0.15
African, sub-Saharan:	14	0.12
African	6	0.05
Other sub-Saharan African	8	0.07
Alaska Native tribes, specified:	1	0.01
Aleut	1	0.01
Am. Ind. or Alaska Nat., not spec.	17	0.14
American Indian tribes, specified:	41	0.34
Apache (1)	1	0.01
Cherokee (7)	20	0.17
Chippewa (1)	1	0.01
Creek	1	0.01
Delaware (1)	1	0.01
Lumbee (8)	10	0.08
Puget Sound Salish (1)	1	0.01
Sioux	3	0.03
All other tribes (2)	3	0.03
American Indian tribes, not spec.	2	0.02
Arab:	26	0.22
Lebanese	26	0.22
Asian:	183	1.53
Chinese, ex. Taiwanese (32)	42	0.35
Filipino (10)	23	0.19
Indian (32)	33	0.28
Japanese (18)	20	0.17
Korean (14)	15	0.13
Laotian (13)	13	0.11
Thai	6	0.05
Vietnamese (23)	23	0.19
Other Asian, specified (1)	1	0.01
Other Asian, not specified (3)	7	0.06
Australian	11	0.09
Austrian	49	0.42
Basque	6	0.05
Belgian	19	0.16
British	73	0.62
Canadian	69	0.59
Croatian	4	0.03
Czech	27	0.23
Czechoslovakian	25	0.21
Danish	25	0.21
Dutch	205	1.75
Eastern European	15	0.13
English	1,639	13.99
Estonian	6	0.05
European	159	1.36
Finnish	25	0.21
French, except Basque	400	3.41
French Canadian	132	1.13
German	2,039	17.40
Greek	113	0.96
Guyanese	5	0.04
Hawaii Native/Pacific Islander:	13	0.11
Micronesian: (5)	5	0.04
Other Micronesian (5)	5	0.04
Polynesian:	5	0.04
Native Hawaiian	5	0.04
Other Pac. Isl., not spec. (1)	3	0.03
Hispanic or Latino:	334	2.79
Central American:	9	0.08
Costa Rican	2	0.02
Guatemalan	3	0.03
Honduran	1	0.01
Panamanian	1	0.01
Salvadoran	2	0.02
Cuban	13	0.11
Mexican	239	2.00
Puerto Rican	27	0.23
South American:	18	0.15
Argentinean	1	0.01
Bolivian	6	0.05
Chilean	1	0.01
Colombian	6	0.05
Ecuadorian	4	0.03
Other Hispanic or Latino	28	0.23
Hungarian	76	0.65
Icelander	37	0.32
Iranian	4	0.03
Irish	1,447	12.35
Israeli	5	0.04
Italian	575	4.91
Lithuanian	12	0.10
Norwegian	114	0.97
Pennsylvania German	22	0.19
Polish	383	3.27
Portuguese	64	0.55
Romanian	21	0.18
Russian	58	0.50
Scandinavian	9	0.08
Scotch-Irish	704	6.01
Scottish	411	3.51
Slovak	7	0.06
Swedish	182	1.55
Swiss	49	0.42
Ukrainian	13	0.11
United States or American	1,062	9.06
Welsh	71	0.61
West Indian, excl. Hispanic:	8	0.07
Jamaican	8	0.07
White:	11,045	92.28
Not Hispanic (10,741)	10,795	90.19
Hispanic (228)	250	2.09
Yugoslavian	6	0.05

Durham

Place Type: City
County: Durham
Population: 187,035

Ancestry/Race	Number	%
Acadian/Cajun	42	0.02
Afghan	41	0.02
African American/Black:	83,485	44.64
Not Hispanic (81,370)	82,750	44.24
Hispanic (567)	735	0.39
African, sub-Saharan:	3,738	2.00
African	2,767	1.48
Cape Verdean	7	0.00
Ethiopian	12	0.01
Ghanian	46	0.02
Kenyan	96	0.05
Liberian	39	0.02
Nigerian	396	0.21
Senegalese	4	0.00
Sierra Leonean	7	0.00
Somalian	50	0.03
South African	24	0.01
Sudanese	67	0.04
Zimbabwean	55	0.03
Other sub-Saharan African	168	0.09
Alaska Native tribes, specified:	4	0.00
Alaska Athabascan (1)	1	0.00
Eskimo (2)	2	0.00
Tlingit-Haida	1	0.00
Am. Ind. or Alaska Nat., not spec.	589	0.31
Albanian	13	0.01
American Indian tribes, specified:	899	0.48
Apache (4)	15	0.01
Blackfeet (9)	62	0.03
Cherokee (80)	332	0.18
Chickasaw (7)	8	0.00
Chippewa (7)	14	0.01
Choctaw (8)	22	0.01
Cree	2	0.00
Creek (1)	5	0.00
Delaware	1	0.00
Iroquois (1)	27	0.01
Latin American Indians (61)	126	0.07
Lumbee (83)	129	0.07
Navajo (1)	12	0.01
Osage (2)	5	0.00
Potawatomi (1)	1	0.00
Pueblo (1)	2	0.00
Seminole (1)	9	0.00
Shoshone	2	0.00
Sioux (7)	9	0.00
Yaqui (1)	1	0.00

Notes: 1. Figures in the "Number" column do not add up to the total population due to: a) Ancestry/Race overlap — e.g. persons can report being both White and Irish, b) persons of Hispanic origin can report being any race, c) persons reporting two ancestries are counted in both categories. 2. Numbers in parentheses indicate the number of persons reporting this ancestry/race alone, not in combination with any other ancestry/race. 3. Refer to the Explanation of Data in the front of the book for more detailed information.

Ancestry/Race	Number	%
All other tribes (48)	115	0.06
American Indian tribes, not spec.	77	0.04
Arab:	903	0.48
Arab/Arabic	292	0.16
Egyptian	157	0.08
Iraqi	8	0.00
Jordanian	29	0.02
Lebanese	181	0.10
Moroccan	32	0.02
Palestinian	69	0.04
Syrian	45	0.02
Other Arab	90	0.05
Armenian	57	0.03
Asian:	7,836	4.19
Bangladeshi (34)	42	0.02
Cambodian (24)	29	0.02
Chinese, ex. Taiwanese (1,865)	2,083	1.11
Filipino (495)	634	0.34
Hmong (16)	16	0.01
Indian (2,395)	2,551	1.36
Indonesian (11)	26	0.01
Japanese (339)	460	0.25
Korean (596)	695	0.37
Laotian (9)	9	0.00
Malaysian (23)	28	0.01
Pakistani (208)	251	0.13
Sri Lankan (17)	20	0.01
Taiwanese (139)	179	0.10
Thai (66)	77	0.04
Vietnamese (333)	367	0.20
Other Asian, specified (24)	54	0.03
Other Asian, not specified (133)	315	0.17
Assyrian/Chaldean/Syriac	10	0.01
Australian	90	0.05
Austrian	272	0.15
Basque	15	0.01
Belgian	73	0.04
Brazilian	93	0.05
British	1,340	0.72
Bulgarian	45	0.02
Canadian	628	0.34
Celtic	73	0.04
Croatian	54	0.03
Czech	247	0.13
Czechoslovakian	119	0.06
Danish	334	0.18
Dutch	1,190	0.64
Eastern European	331	0.18
English	15,222	8.13
Estonian	7	0.00
European	2,117	1.13
Finnish	152	0.08
French, except Basque	2,442	1.30
French Canadian	711	0.38
German	13,437	7.18
Greek	395	0.21
Guyanese	75	0.04
Hawaii Native/Pacific Islander:	223	0.12
Micronesian: (31)	43	0.02
Guamanian/Chamorro (9)	11	0.01
Other Micronesian (22)	32	0.02
Polynesian: (16)	64	0.03
Native Hawaiian (5)	45	0.02
Samoan (11)	19	0.01
Other Pac. Isl., specified	23	0.01
Other Pac. Isl., not spec. (24)	93	0.05
Hispanic or Latino:	16,012	8.56
Central American:	2,305	1.23
Costa Rican	24	0.01
Guatemalan	310	0.17
Honduran	1,086	0.58
Nicaraguan	17	0.01
Panamanian	60	0.03
Salvadoran	717	0.38
Other Central American	91	0.05
Cuban	236	0.13
Dominican Republic	75	0.04
Mexican	10,343	5.53
Puerto Rican	696	0.37
South American:	523	0.28
Argentinean	92	0.05
Bolivian	36	0.02
Chilean	56	0.03
Colombian	125	0.07
Ecuadorian	31	0.02
Paraguayan	3	0.00
Peruvian	71	0.04
Uruguayan	10	0.01
Venezuelan	71	0.04
Other South American	28	0.01
Other Hispanic or Latino	1,834	0.98
Hungarian	440	0.24
Icelander	47	0.03
Iranian	155	0.08
Irish	10,557	5.64
Israeli	84	0.04
Italian	3,965	2.12
Latvian	55	0.03
Lithuanian	224	0.12
Luxemburger	4	0.00
New Zealander	42	0.02
Northern European	190	0.10
Norwegian	1,038	0.55
Pennsylvania German	33	0.02
Polish	2,442	1.30
Portuguese	166	0.09
Romanian	175	0.09
Russian	1,285	0.69
Scandinavian	159	0.08
Scotch-Irish	3,778	2.02
Scottish	3,378	1.80
Serbian	39	0.02
Slavic	25	0.01
Slovak	139	0.07
Slovene	35	0.02
Soviet Union	7	0.00
Swedish	1,209	0.65
Swiss	383	0.20
Turkish	56	0.03
Ukrainian	292	0.16
United States or American	9,266	4.95
Welsh	1,030	0.55
West Indian, excl. Hispanic:	660	0.35
Bahamian	52	0.03
Barbadian	26	0.01
British West Indian	35	0.02
Haitian	59	0.03
Jamaican	323	0.17
Trinidadian and Tobagonian	84	0.04
U.S. Virgin Islander	28	0.01
West Indian	53	0.03
White:	87,608	46.84
Not Hispanic (79,277)	81,101	43.36
Hispanic (5,849)	6,507	3.48
Yugoslavian	95	0.05

Eden

Place Type: City
County: Rockingham
Population: 15,908

Ancestry/Race	Number	%
African American/Black:	3,578	22.49
Not Hispanic (3,511)	3,562	22.39
Hispanic (13)	16	0.10
African, sub-Saharan:	67	0.42
African	67	0.42
Am. Ind. or Alaska Nat., not spec.	36	0.23
American Indian tribes, specified:	45	0.28
Apache (1)	5	0.03
Cherokee (9)	21	0.13
Chickasaw	1	0.01
Latin American Indians (1)	1	0.01
Lumbee (8)	9	0.06
Pima	1	0.01
Pueblo	1	0.01
Sioux (3)	3	0.02
All other tribes (1)	3	0.02
American Indian tribes, not spec.	1	0.01
Arab:	19	0.12
Arab/Arabic	13	0.08
Lebanese	6	0.04
Asian:	69	0.43
Chinese, ex. Taiwanese (10)	11	0.07
Filipino (5)	10	0.06
Indian (14)	17	0.11
Japanese	2	0.01
Korean (3)	5	0.03
Pakistani (9)	9	0.06
Thai (2)	3	0.02
Other Asian, specified	1	0.01
Other Asian, not specified (6)	11	0.07
Austrian	79	0.49
Belgian	6	0.04
British	49	0.31
Czech	5	0.03
Czechoslovakian	9	0.06
Dutch	106	0.66
English	1,334	8.32
European	237	1.48
Finnish	36	0.22
French, except Basque	183	1.14
French Canadian	11	0.07
German	708	4.41
Hawaii Native/Pacific Islander:	10	0.06
Micronesian: (3)	3	0.02
Guamanian/Chamorro (3)	3	0.02
Polynesian: (1)	1	0.01
Native Hawaiian (1)	1	0.01
Other Pac. Isl., specified	1	0.01
Other Pac. Isl., not spec. (5)	5	0.03
Hispanic or Latino:	372	2.34
Central American:	40	0.25
Costa Rican	3	0.02
Guatemalan	22	0.14
Honduran	3	0.02
Nicaraguan	1	0.01
Panamanian	3	0.02
Salvadoran	6	0.04
Other Central American	2	0.01
Cuban	1	0.01
Mexican	258	1.62
Puerto Rican	14	0.09
South American:	7	0.04
Argentinean	1	0.01
Chilean	1	0.01
Colombian	5	0.03
Other Hispanic or Latino	52	0.33
Hungarian	9	0.06
Irish	764	4.76
Israeli	6	0.04
Italian	204	1.27
Lithuanian	8	0.05
Norwegian	49	0.31
Polish	51	0.32
Russian	14	0.09
Scotch-Irish	251	1.56
Scottish	192	1.20
Swedish	19	0.12
Swiss	20	0.12
Ukrainian	6	0.04
United States or American	3,615	22.54
Welsh	30	0.19
West Indian, excl. Hispanic:	29	0.18
Bermudan	24	0.15
West Indian	5	0.03
White:	12,117	76.17
Not Hispanic (11,819)	11,917	74.91
Hispanic (181)	200	1.26

Elizabeth City

Place Type: City
County: Pasquotank
Population: 17,188

Ancestry/Race	Number	%
African American/Black:	9,870	57.42
Not Hispanic (9,692)	9,821	57.14

Notes: 1. Figures in the "Number" column do not add up to the total population due to: a) Ancestry/Race overlap — e.g. persons can report being both White and Irish, b) persons of Hispanic origin can report being any race, c) persons reporting two ancestries are counted in both categories. 2. Numbers in parentheses indicate the number of persons reporting this ancestry/race alone, not in combination with any other ancestry/race. 3. Refer to the Explanation of Data in the front of the book for more detailed information.

Hispanic (37)	49	0.29
African, sub-Saharan:	131	0.76
African	124	0.72
Cape Verdean	7	0.04
Am. Ind. or Alaska Nat., not spec.	39	0.23
American Indian tribes, specified:	117	0.68
Apache	1	0.01
Blackfeet	3	0.02
Cherokee (13)	68	0.40
Creek (2)	2	0.01
Iroquois (4)	11	0.06
Latin American Indians (4)	5	0.03
Lumbee (4)	4	0.02
Sioux (2)	3	0.02
All other tribes (5)	20	0.12
American Indian tribes, not spec.	6	0.03
Arab:	5	0.03
Lebanese	5	0.03
Asian:	182	1.06
Chinese, ex. Taiwanese (24)	25	0.15
Filipino (28)	50	0.29
Hmong (11)	11	0.06
Indian (33)	42	0.24
Indonesian (1)	2	0.01
Japanese (1)	4	0.02
Korean (5)	8	0.05
Taiwanese (1)	1	0.01
Vietnamese (31)	32	0.19
Other Asian, not specified (1)	7	0.04
Australian	9	0.05
Austrian	7	0.04
British	76	0.44
Canadian	39	0.23
Celtic	6	0.03
Dutch	70	0.40
English	1,130	6.54
European	115	0.67
Finnish	5	0.03
French, except Basque	222	1.28
French Canadian	75	0.43
German	846	4.89
Greek	7	0.04
Hawaii Native/Pacific Islander:	10	0.06
Micronesian:	1	0.01
Guamanian/Chamorro	1	0.01
Polynesian: (2)	4	0.02
Native Hawaiian (2)	4	0.02
Other Pac. Isl., not spec.	5	0.03
Hispanic or Latino:	258	1.50
Central American:	11	0.06
Guatemalan	4	0.02
Panamanian	5	0.03
Salvadoran	2	0.01
Cuban	11	0.06
Dominican Republic	5	0.03
Mexican	112	0.65
Puerto Rican	73	0.42
South American:	5	0.03
Colombian	2	0.01
Venezuelan	3	0.02
Other Hispanic or Latino	41	0.24
Hungarian	12	0.07
Irish	753	4.36
Italian	227	1.31
Latvian	12	0.07
Lithuanian	6	0.03
Northern European	6	0.03
Norwegian	32	0.19
Polish	62	0.36
Russian	5	0.03
Scandinavian	7	0.04
Scotch-Irish	260	1.50
Scottish	180	1.04
Slovak	6	0.03
Swedish	58	0.34
Swiss	31	0.18
Ukrainian	4	0.02
United States or American	1,574	9.11
Welsh	60	0.35
West Indian, excl. Hispanic:	53	0.31
Haitian	7	0.04
Jamaican	22	0.13
U.S. Virgin Islander	20	0.12
West Indian	4	0.02
White:	7,080	41.19
Not Hispanic (6,813)	6,962	40.51
Hispanic (104)	118	0.69
Yugoslavian	3	0.02

Fayetteville

Place Type: City
County: Cumberland
Population: 121,015

Ancestry/Race	Number	%
African American/Black:	52,999	43.80
Not Hispanic (50,656)	52,045	43.01
Hispanic (682)	954	0.79
African, sub-Saharan:	1,606	1.33
African	1,319	1.09
Cape Verdean	15	0.01
Ethiopian	13	0.01
Liberian	11	0.01
Nigerian	181	0.15
Sierra Leonean	8	0.01
South African	14	0.01
Other sub-Saharan African	45	0.04
Alaska Native tribes, specified:	14	0.01
Aleut (6)	9	0.01
Eskimo (2)	2	0.00
Tlingit-Haida (3)	3	0.00
Am. Ind. or Alaska Nat., not spec.	702	0.58
Albanian	6	0.00
American Indian tribes, specified:	1,384	1.14
Apache (12)	25	0.02
Blackfeet (6)	51	0.04
Cherokee (196)	430	0.36
Cheyenne (2)	2	0.00
Chickasaw (5)	10	0.01
Chippewa (7)	11	0.01
Choctaw (8)	16	0.01
Comanche (7)	10	0.01
Cree (1)	1	0.00
Creek (10)	13	0.01
Crow (1)	1	0.00
Delaware (1)	1	0.00
Houma (1)	1	0.00
Iroquois (30)	49	0.04
Latin American Indians (25)	39	0.03
Lumbee (406)	484	0.40
Menominee (1)	2	0.00
Navajo (17)	20	0.02
Osage (7)	9	0.01
Ottawa (1)	2	0.00
Paiute	1	0.00
Pima (3)	3	0.00
Potawatomi (1)	2	0.00
Pueblo (2)	7	0.01
Puget Sound Salish (1)	1	0.00
Seminole (4)	6	0.00
Shoshone (1)	2	0.00
Sioux (29)	44	0.04
Yaqui (1)	1	0.00
All other tribes (90)	140	0.12
American Indian tribes, not spec.	90	0.07
Arab:	264	0.22
Arab/Arabic	20	0.02
Lebanese	218	0.18
Syrian	7	0.01
Other Arab	19	0.02
Asian:	3,684	3.04
Bangladeshi (8)	8	0.01
Cambodian (5)	7	0.01
Chinese, ex. Taiwanese (197)	291	0.24
Filipino (380)	594	0.49
Indian (383)	445	0.37
Indonesian	3	0.00
Japanese (251)	433	0.36
Korean (917)	1,187	0.98
Laotian (2)	11	0.01
Malaysian	2	0.00
Pakistani (11)	13	0.01
Sri Lankan (1)	1	0.00
Taiwanese (21)	34	0.03
Thai (104)	166	0.14
Vietnamese (214)	270	0.22
Other Asian, specified (11)	26	0.02
Other Asian, not specified (89)	193	0.16
Assyrian/Chaldean/Syriac	9	0.01
Australian	26	0.02
Austrian	100	0.08
Basque	54	0.04
Belgian	54	0.04
Brazilian	6	0.00
British	456	0.38
Canadian	191	0.16
Celtic	14	0.01
Croatian	37	0.03
Czech	138	0.11
Czechoslovakian	46	0.04
Danish	269	0.22
Dutch	932	0.77
Eastern European	40	0.03
English	7,663	6.34
European	1,034	0.86
Finnish	31	0.03
French, except Basque	1,995	1.65
French Canadian	405	0.34
German	10,251	8.48
German Russian	10	0.01
Greek	524	0.43
Guyanese	7	0.01
Hawaii Native/Pacific Islander:	524	0.43
Micronesian: (116)	174	0.14
Guamanian/Chamorro (110)	162	0.13
Other Micronesian (6)	12	0.01
Polynesian: (120)	245	0.20
Native Hawaiian (75)	176	0.15
Samoan (43)	65	0.05
Tongan (2)	3	0.00
Other Polynesian	1	0.00
Other Pac. Isl., specified	8	0.01
Other Pac. Isl., not spec. (26)	97	0.08
Hispanic or Latino:	6,862	5.67
Central American:	703	0.58
Costa Rican	37	0.03
Guatemalan	45	0.04
Honduran	54	0.04
Nicaraguan	13	0.01
Panamanian	483	0.40
Salvadoran	56	0.05
Other Central American	15	0.01
Cuban	133	0.11
Dominican Republic	128	0.11
Mexican	2,054	1.70
Puerto Rican	2,488	2.06
South American:	313	0.26
Argentinean	23	0.02
Bolivian	17	0.01
Chilean	25	0.02
Colombian	112	0.09
Ecuadorian	52	0.04
Paraguayan	4	0.00
Peruvian	51	0.04
Uruguayan	1	0.00
Venezuelan	22	0.02
Other South American	6	0.00
Other Hispanic or Latino	1,043	0.86
Hungarian	282	0.23
Iranian	16	0.01
Irish	7,492	6.20
Italian	3,319	2.75
Lithuanian	104	0.09
Luxemburger	5	0.00
Norwegian	449	0.37
Pennsylvania German	31	0.03
Polish	1,307	1.08
Portuguese	192	0.16
Romanian	39	0.03

Notes: 1. Figures in the "Number" column do not add up to the total population due to: a) Ancestry/Race overlap — e.g. persons can report being both White and Irish, b) persons of Hispanic origin can report being any race, c) persons reporting two ancestries are counted in both categories. 2. Numbers in parentheses indicate the number of persons reporting this ancestry/race alone, not in combination with any other ancestry/race. 3. Refer to the Explanation of Data in the front of the book for more detailed information.

Russian	292	0.24
Scandinavian	76	0.06
Scotch-Irish	3,222	2.67
Scottish	2,666	2.21
Serbian	41	0.03
Slavic	37	0.03
Slovak	86	0.07
Swedish	590	0.49
Swiss	102	0.08
Turkish	19	0.02
Ukrainian	149	0.12
United States or American	9,326	7.72
Welsh	498	0.41
West Indian, excl. Hispanic:	685	0.57
Bahamian	18	0.01
Barbadian	7	0.01
Belizean	10	0.01
British West Indian	25	0.02
Haitian	59	0.05
Jamaican	377	0.31
Trinidadian and Tobagonian	74	0.06
U.S. Virgin Islander	9	0.01
West Indian	106	0.09
White:	61,353	50.70
Not Hispanic (56,419)	58,319	48.19
Hispanic (2,588)	3,034	2.51
Yugoslavian	31	0.03

Fort Bragg

Place Type: Census Designated Place
County: Cumberland
Population: 29,183

Ancestry/Race	Number	%
African American/Black:	7,939	27.20
Not Hispanic (7,115)	7,561	25.91
Hispanic (253)	378	1.30
African, sub-Saharan:	281	0.96
African	222	0.76
Cape Verdean	20	0.07
Nigerian	30	0.10
Sudanese	9	0.03
Alaska Native tribes, specified:	12	0.04
Alaska Athabascan (3)	3	0.01
Aleut	2	0.01
Eskimo (6)	6	0.02
Tlingit-Haida (1)	1	0.00
Alaska Native tribes, not specified	2	0.01
Am. Ind. or Alaska Nat., not spec.	154	0.53
American Indian tribes, specified:	424	1.45
Apache (6)	15	0.05
Blackfeet (5)	16	0.05
Cherokee (51)	117	0.40
Cheyenne (2)	3	0.01
Chickasaw (3)	4	0.01
Chippewa (11)	15	0.05
Choctaw (19)	23	0.08
Comanche (1)	2	0.01
Cree (1)	1	0.00
Creek (2)	7	0.02
Crow (3)	3	0.01
Delaware (1)	5	0.02
Iroquois (2)	4	0.01
Latin American Indians (13)	29	0.10
Lumbee (18)	22	0.08
Navajo (42)	48	0.16
Osage	1	0.00
Ottawa (1)	4	0.01
Pima (3)	3	0.01
Potawatomi (2)	2	0.01
Pueblo (7)	12	0.04
Puget Sound Salish (1)	1	0.00
Seminole (4)	10	0.03
Shoshone (1)	2	0.01
Sioux (24)	36	0.12
Tohono O'Odham (1)	1	0.00
Ute	1	0.00
Yaqui (4)	5	0.02
Yuman (1)	1	0.00
All other tribes (12)	31	0.11
American Indian tribes, not spec.	37	0.13
Arab:	119	0.41
Arab/Arabic	35	0.12
Egyptian	23	0.08
Lebanese	8	0.03
Moroccan	7	0.02
Syrian	16	0.05
Other Arab	30	0.10
Asian:	969	3.32
Cambodian (13)	17	0.06
Chinese, ex. Taiwanese (27)	75	0.26
Filipino (189)	322	1.10
Hmong (2)	2	0.01
Indian (38)	58	0.20
Indonesian	4	0.01
Japanese (22)	71	0.24
Korean (152)	236	0.81
Laotian (11)	11	0.04
Malaysian	1	0.00
Pakistani (3)	5	0.02
Thai (7)	32	0.11
Vietnamese (34)	56	0.19
Other Asian, specified	1	0.00
Other Asian, not specified (19)	78	0.27
Australian	8	0.03
Austrian	25	0.09
Belgian	28	0.10
Brazilian	9	0.03
British	99	0.34
Canadian	55	0.19
Celtic	8	0.03
Croatian	50	0.17
Czech	34	0.12
Czechoslovakian	79	0.27
Danish	91	0.31
Dutch	184	0.63
English	1,180	4.03
European	444	1.52
Finnish	86	0.29
French, except Basque	709	2.42
French Canadian	147	0.50
German	4,432	15.15
Greek	81	0.28
Guyanese	16	0.05
Hawaii Native/Pacific Islander:	426	1.46
Melanesian: (1)	3	0.01
Fijian (1)	3	0.01
Micronesian: (121)	148	0.51
Guamanian/Chamorro (80)	101	0.35
Other Micronesian (41)	47	0.16
Polynesian: (107)	232	0.79
Native Hawaiian (35)	114	0.39
Samoan (67)	101	0.35
Tongan (3)	5	0.02
Other Polynesian (2)	12	0.04
Other Pac. Isl., not spec. (10)	43	0.15
Hispanic or Latino:	4,603	15.77
Central American:	293	1.00
Costa Rican	13	0.04
Guatemalan	26	0.09
Honduran	30	0.10
Nicaraguan	12	0.04
Panamanian	165	0.57
Salvadoran	45	0.15
Other Central American	2	0.01
Cuban	107	0.37
Dominican Republic	101	0.35
Mexican	1,668	5.72
Puerto Rican	1,711	5.86
South American:	155	0.53
Argentinean	4	0.01
Bolivian	14	0.05
Chilean	2	0.01
Colombian	73	0.25
Ecuadorian	21	0.07
Peruvian	33	0.11
Venezuelan	8	0.03
Other Hispanic or Latino	568	1.95
Hungarian	85	0.29
Iranian	8	0.03
Irish	3,150	10.77
Italian	1,213	4.15
Lithuanian	8	0.03
Luxemburger	7	0.02
Maltese	9	0.03
Northern European	16	0.05
Norwegian	360	1.23
Polish	661	2.26
Portuguese	120	0.41
Russian	114	0.39
Scandinavian	42	0.14
Scotch-Irish	369	1.26
Scottish	809	2.77
Serbian	11	0.04
Slavic	17	0.06
Slovak	31	0.11
Swedish	280	0.96
Swiss	64	0.22
Ukrainian	63	0.22
United States or American	1,485	5.08
Welsh	143	0.49
West Indian, excl. Hispanic:	572	1.96
Bahamian	8	0.03
Barbadian	22	0.08
Belizean	8	0.03
British West Indian	42	0.14
Dutch West Indian	15	0.05
Haitian	92	0.31
Jamaican	184	0.63
Trinidadian and Tobagonian	64	0.22
U.S. Virgin Islander	17	0.06
West Indian	120	0.41
White:	17,912	61.38
Not Hispanic (15,436)	16,147	55.33
Hispanic (1,506)	1,765	6.05
Yugoslavian	23	0.08

Garner

Place Type: Town
County: Wake
Population: 17,757

Ancestry/Race	Number	%
African American/Black:	4,959	27.93
Not Hispanic (4,785)	4,911	27.66
Hispanic (32)	48	0.27
African, sub-Saharan:	230	1.31
African	198	1.13
Sierra Leonean	6	0.03
South African	6	0.03
Sudanese	20	0.11
Alaska Native tribes, specified:	1	0.01
Alaska Athabascan (1)	1	0.01
Am. Ind. or Alaska Nat., not spec.	57	0.32
American Indian tribes, specified:	75	0.42
Apache	3	0.02
Blackfeet (1)	2	0.01
Cherokee (11)	23	0.13
Chippewa	1	0.01
Choctaw	1	0.01
Creek (3)	4	0.02
Delaware	1	0.01
Iroquois (5)	5	0.03
Latin American Indians (3)	4	0.02
Lumbee (16)	19	0.11
Potawatomi (3)	3	0.02
All other tribes (4)	9	0.05
American Indian tribes, not spec.	11	0.06
Arab:	53	0.30
Arab/Arabic	27	0.15
Lebanese	26	0.15
Asian:	243	1.37
Bangladeshi (3)	4	0.02
Cambodian (7)	9	0.05
Chinese, ex. Taiwanese (35)	46	0.26
Filipino (8)	13	0.07
Indian (60)	69	0.39
Japanese (7)	12	0.07

Notes: 1. Figures in the "Number" column do not add up to the total population due to: a) Ancestry/Race overlap — e.g. persons can report being both White and Irish, b) persons of Hispanic origin can report being any race, c) persons reporting two ancestries are counted in both categories. 2. Numbers in parentheses indicate the number of persons reporting this ancestry/race alone, not in combination with any other ancestry/race. 3. Refer to the Explanation of Data in the front of the book for more detailed information.

Korean (15)	17	0.10
Pakistani (2)	2	0.01
Taiwanese (1)	2	0.01
Thai (6)	6	0.03
Vietnamese (34)	43	0.24
Other Asian, specified (1)	2	0.01
Other Asian, not specified (9)	18	0.10
Australian	4	0.02
Austrian	6	0.03
Belgian	12	0.07
British	128	0.73
Canadian	64	0.36
Czechoslovakian	28	0.16
Danish	31	0.18
Dutch	94	0.53
English	2,278	12.95
European	195	1.11
French, except Basque	375	2.13
French Canadian	47	0.27
German	1,782	10.13
Greek	8	0.05
Guyanese	8	0.05
Hawaii Native/Pacific Islander:	6	0.03
Micronesian: (1)	1	0.01
Guamanian/Chamorro (1)	1	0.01
Polynesian: (3)	3	0.02
Native Hawaiian (1)	1	0.01
Samoan (1)	1	0.01
Tongan (1)	1	0.01
Other Pac. Isl., not spec.	2	0.01
Hispanic or Latino:	843	4.75
Central American:	34	0.19
Guatemalan	7	0.04
Honduran	14	0.08
Nicaraguan	3	0.02
Panamanian	1	0.01
Salvadoran	9	0.05
Cuban	10	0.06
Dominican Republic	12	0.07
Mexican	603	3.40
Puerto Rican	88	0.50
South American:	27	0.15
Argentinean	2	0.01
Colombian	1	0.01
Peruvian	16	0.09
Venezuelan	8	0.05
Other Hispanic or Latino	69	0.39
Hungarian	28	0.16
Irish	1,673	9.51
Italian	449	2.55
Lithuanian	16	0.09
Maltese	8	0.05
Norwegian	165	0.94
Polish	174	0.99
Portuguese	37	0.21
Russian	90	0.51
Scotch-Irish	624	3.55
Scottish	474	2.69
Slovene	7	0.04
Swedish	68	0.39
Swiss	88	0.50
Ukrainian	27	0.15
United States or American	1,965	11.17
Welsh	85	0.48
West Indian, excl. Hispanic:	93	0.53
Belizean	7	0.04
British West Indian	4	0.02
Haitian	28	0.16
Jamaican	36	0.20
U.S. Virgin Islander	4	0.02
West Indian	14	0.08
White:	12,100	68.14
Not Hispanic (11,622)	11,779	66.33
Hispanic (279)	321	1.81
Yugoslavian	15	0.09

Gastonia

Place Type: City
County: Gaston
Population: 66,277

Ancestry/Race	Number	%
African American/Black:	17,284	26.08
Not Hispanic (16,520)	16,787	25.33
Hispanic (461)	497	0.75
African, sub-Saharan:	791	1.19
African	725	1.09
Cape Verdean	24	0.04
Ghanian	5	0.01
Nigerian	21	0.03
South African	16	0.02
Am. Ind. or Alaska Nat., not spec.	138	0.21
American Indian tribes, specified:	201	0.30
Apache	4	0.01
Blackfeet (1)	6	0.01
Cherokee (25)	105	0.16
Chippewa	3	0.00
Choctaw (1)	1	0.00
Comanche (1)	1	0.00
Cree	2	0.00
Creek (4)	6	0.01
Delaware (1)	3	0.00
Iroquois (1)	7	0.01
Latin American Indians (6)	11	0.02
Lumbee (17)	22	0.03
Navajo	2	0.00
Potawatomi	1	0.00
Pueblo (1)	1	0.00
Sioux	6	0.01
Yaqui (3)	3	0.00
All other tribes (12)	17	0.03
American Indian tribes, not spec.	27	0.04
Arab:	166	0.25
Arab/Arabic	27	0.04
Egyptian	47	0.07
Lebanese	84	0.13
Syrian	8	0.01
Armenian	18	0.03
Asian:	921	1.39
Bangladeshi	4	0.01
Cambodian (2)	2	0.00
Chinese, ex. Taiwanese (113)	127	0.19
Filipino (30)	42	0.06
Hmong (1)	1	0.00
Indian (243)	277	0.42
Indonesian	1	0.00
Japanese (33)	44	0.07
Korean (49)	65	0.10
Laotian (35)	36	0.05
Malaysian (1)	4	0.01
Pakistani (52)	63	0.10
Sri Lankan (19)	19	0.03
Thai (1)	5	0.01
Vietnamese (165)	186	0.28
Other Asian, specified (1)	11	0.02
Other Asian, not specified (16)	34	0.05
Australian	5	0.01
Austrian	25	0.04
Belgian	5	0.01
British	174	0.26
Bulgarian	18	0.03
Canadian	105	0.16
Celtic	16	0.02
Czech	48	0.07
Czechoslovakian	12	0.02
Danish	38	0.06
Dutch	1,086	1.64
Eastern European	29	0.04
English	4,258	6.42
European	599	0.90
Finnish	14	0.02
French, except Basque	872	1.32
French Canadian	172	0.26
German	5,958	8.99
Greek	45	0.07
Hawaii Native/Pacific Islander:	55	0.08
Micronesian: (5)	9	0.01
Guamanian/Chamorro (5)	9	0.01
Polynesian: (10)	21	0.03
Native Hawaiian (1)	11	0.02
Samoan (9)	10	0.02
Other Pac. Isl., specified	9	0.01
Other Pac. Isl., not spec. (4)	16	0.02
Hispanic or Latino:	3,613	5.45
Central American:	167	0.25
Costa Rican	12	0.02
Guatemalan	33	0.05
Honduran	71	0.11
Nicaraguan	26	0.04
Panamanian	7	0.01
Salvadoran	17	0.03
Other Central American	1	0.00
Cuban	85	0.13
Dominican Republic	39	0.06
Mexican	2,343	3.54
Puerto Rican	229	0.35
South American:	337	0.51
Argentinean	4	0.01
Bolivian	1	0.00
Chilean	30	0.05
Colombian	262	0.40
Ecuadorian	3	0.00
Peruvian	21	0.03
Uruguayan	7	0.01
Venezuelan	2	0.00
Other South American	7	0.01
Other Hispanic or Latino	413	0.62
Hungarian	54	0.08
Iranian	11	0.02
Irish	4,691	7.08
Italian	930	1.40
Latvian	7	0.01
Lithuanian	33	0.05
Macedonian	7	0.01
Northern European	5	0.01
Norwegian	151	0.23
Pennsylvania German	60	0.09
Polish	400	0.60
Portuguese	36	0.05
Romanian	46	0.07
Russian	168	0.25
Scandinavian	7	0.01
Scotch-Irish	2,634	3.97
Scottish	1,198	1.81
Serbian	7	0.01
Slovak	46	0.07
Slovene	19	0.03
Swedish	212	0.32
Swiss	113	0.17
Turkish	20	0.03
Ukrainian	55	0.08
United States or American	9,128	13.77
Welsh	228	0.34
West Indian, excl. Hispanic:	66	0.10
Haitian	21	0.03
Jamaican	34	0.05
Trinidadian and Tobagonian	11	0.02
White:	47,058	71.00
Not Hispanic (44,615)	45,069	68.00
Hispanic (1,898)	1,989	3.00
Yugoslavian	13	0.02

Goldsboro

Place Type: City
County: Wayne
Population: 39,043

Ancestry/Race	Number	%
African American/Black:	20,757	53.16
Not Hispanic (20,295)	20,616	52.80
Hispanic (102)	141	0.36
African, sub-Saharan:	450	1.16
African	440	1.14
Other sub-Saharan African	10	0.03

Notes: 1. Figures in the "Number" column do not add up to the total population due to: a) Ancestry/Race overlap — e.g. persons can report being both White and Irish, b) persons of Hispanic origin can report being any race, c) persons reporting two ancestries are counted in both categories. 2. Numbers in parentheses indicate the number of persons reporting this ancestry/race alone, not in combination with any other ancestry/race. 3. Refer to the Explanation of Data in the front of the book for more detailed information.

Alaska Native tribes, specified:	3	0.01
Aleut (2)	2	0.01
Eskimo (1)	1	0.00
Alaska Native tribes, not specified	3	0.01
Am. Ind. or Alaska Nat., not spec.	118	0.30
American Indian tribes, specified:	197	0.50
Apache (2)	3	0.01
Blackfeet (3)	13	0.03
Cherokee (27)	91	0.23
Chippewa (1)	3	0.01
Choctaw (1)	4	0.01
Comanche (2)	3	0.01
Cree (1)	1	0.00
Creek (2)	4	0.01
Delaware (1)	1	0.00
Iroquois (6)	7	0.02
Latin American Indians (3)	4	0.01
Lumbee (23)	30	0.08
Menominee (2)	2	0.01
Navajo (4)	4	0.01
Pueblo (1)	1	0.00
Seminole	1	0.00
Sioux (1)	1	0.00
Tohono O'Odham (1)	1	0.00
All other tribes (20)	23	0.06
American Indian tribes, not spec.	13	0.03
Arab:	160	0.41
Arab/Arabic	69	0.18
Lebanese	33	0.09
Moroccan	8	0.02
Syrian	12	0.03
Other Arab	38	0.10
Asian:	755	1.93
Chinese, ex. Taiwanese (62)	80	0.20
Filipino (134)	191	0.49
Indian (117)	130	0.33
Japanese (41)	63	0.16
Korean (111)	139	0.36
Laotian	1	0.00
Malaysian	4	0.01
Pakistani (2)	8	0.02
Sri Lankan (2)	3	0.01
Taiwanese (1)	1	0.00
Thai (34)	53	0.14
Vietnamese (34)	36	0.09
Other Asian, specified	5	0.01
Other Asian, not specified (15)	41	0.11
Austrian	33	0.09
Belgian	15	0.04
British	104	0.27
Canadian	51	0.13
Czech	35	0.09
Czechoslovakian	35	0.09
Danish	25	0.06
Dutch	236	0.61
Eastern European	14	0.04
English	2,767	7.14
Estonian	7	0.02
European	222	0.57
Finnish	9	0.02
French, except Basque	575	1.48
French Canadian	155	0.40
German	2,293	5.92
Greek	58	0.15
Hawaii Native/Pacific Islander:	56	0.14
Micronesian: (15)	18	0.05
Guamanian/Chamorro (15)	18	0.05
Polynesian: (12)	22	0.06
Native Hawaiian (11)	18	0.05
Samoan (1)	3	0.01
Other Polynesian	1	0.00
Other Pac. Isl., specified	5	0.01
Other Pac. Isl., not spec. (2)	11	0.03
Hispanic or Latino:	1,052	2.69
Central American:	84	0.22
Costa Rican	6	0.02
Guatemalan	13	0.03
Honduran	27	0.07
Nicaraguan	1	0.00
Panamanian	29	0.07
Salvadoran	8	0.02
Cuban	23	0.06
Dominican Republic	19	0.05
Mexican	477	1.22
Puerto Rican	230	0.59
South American:	32	0.08
Argentinean	2	0.01
Bolivian	1	0.00
Chilean	2	0.01
Colombian	9	0.02
Ecuadorian	6	0.02
Peruvian	3	0.01
Venezuelan	8	0.02
Other South American	1	0.00
Other Hispanic or Latino	187	0.48
Hungarian	71	0.18
Irish	1,848	4.77
Israeli	14	0.04
Italian	675	1.74
Lithuanian	8	0.02
Northern European	36	0.09
Norwegian	239	0.62
Polish	231	0.60
Portuguese	28	0.07
Russian	36	0.09
Scandinavian	10	0.03
Scotch-Irish	748	1.93
Scottish	557	1.44
Slovak	74	0.19
Swedish	137	0.35
Turkish	15	0.04
Ukrainian	46	0.12
United States or American	2,809	7.25
Welsh	115	0.30
West Indian, excl. Hispanic:	92	0.24
Haitian	10	0.03
Jamaican	47	0.12
U.S. Virgin Islander	15	0.04
West Indian	20	0.05
White:	17,247	44.17
Not Hispanic (16,346)	16,742	42.88
Hispanic (457)	505	1.29
Yugoslavian	44	0.11

Graham

Place Type: City
County: Alamance
Population: 12,833

Ancestry/Race	Number	%
African American/Black:	2,836	22.10
Not Hispanic (2,753)	2,804	21.85
Hispanic (24)	32	0.25
African, sub-Saharan:	104	0.82
African	104	0.82
Am. Ind. or Alaska Nat., not spec.	38	0.30
American Indian tribes, specified:	43	0.34
Blackfeet (1)	2	0.02
Cherokee (4)	15	0.12
Comanche	5	0.04
Iroquois (3)	5	0.04
Lumbee (6)	7	0.05
Yaqui	1	0.01
All other tribes (3)	8	0.06
American Indian tribes, not spec.	12	0.09
Asian:	124	0.97
Bangladeshi (1)	1	0.01
Chinese, ex. Taiwanese (19)	25	0.19
Filipino (9)	13	0.10
Indian (7)	12	0.09
Japanese (3)	11	0.09
Korean (2)	5	0.04
Laotian (16)	17	0.13
Pakistani (9)	9	0.07
Taiwanese (1)	1	0.01
Thai (3)	5	0.04
Vietnamese (16)	16	0.12
Other Asian, not specified (7)	9	0.07
British	75	0.59
Canadian	8	0.06
Czech	14	0.11
Czechoslovakian	2	0.02
Dutch	203	1.60
English	1,132	8.93
European	78	0.61
Finnish	13	0.10
French, except Basque	185	1.46
French Canadian	9	0.07
German	955	7.53
Hawaii Native/Pacific Islander:	7	0.05
Polynesian:	6	0.05
Native Hawaiian	5	0.04
Samoan	1	0.01
Other Pac. Isl., not spec.	1	0.01
Hispanic or Latino:	1,301	10.14
Central American:	147	1.15
Costa Rican	3	0.02
Guatemalan	13	0.10
Honduran	2	0.02
Nicaraguan	8	0.06
Panamanian	1	0.01
Salvadoran	116	0.90
Other Central American	4	0.03
Cuban	6	0.05
Dominican Republic	3	0.02
Mexican	994	7.75
Puerto Rican	32	0.25
South American:	9	0.07
Argentinean	1	0.01
Chilean	5	0.04
Colombian	2	0.02
Venezuelan	1	0.01
Other Hispanic or Latino	110	0.86
Irish	892	7.03
Italian	209	1.65
Norwegian	39	0.31
Polish	27	0.21
Russian	25	0.20
Scandinavian	6	0.05
Scotch-Irish	377	2.97
Scottish	214	1.69
Swedish	66	0.52
Swiss	8	0.06
Turkish	10	0.08
Ukrainian	13	0.10
United States or American	2,562	20.20
Welsh	47	0.37
White:	9,470	73.79
Not Hispanic (8,530)	8,605	67.05
Hispanic (823)	865	6.74

Greensboro

Place Type: City
County: Guilford
Population: 223,891

Ancestry/Race	Number	%
Acadian/Cajun	50	0.02
Afghan	18	0.01
African American/Black:	85,634	38.25
Not Hispanic (83,041)	84,774	37.86
Hispanic (687)	860	0.38
African, sub-Saharan:	4,721	2.11
African	2,983	1.34
Ethiopian	62	0.03
Ghanian	242	0.11
Kenyan	22	0.01
Liberian	51	0.02
Nigerian	544	0.24
Senegalese	16	0.01
Sierra Leonean	65	0.03
Somalian	313	0.14
South African	42	0.02
Sudanese	196	0.09
Zimbabwean	23	0.01
Other sub-Saharan African	162	0.07
Alaska Native tribes, specified:	3	0.00
Aleut	1	0.00

Notes: 1. Figures in the "Number" column do not add up to the total population due to: a) Ancestry/Race overlap — e.g. persons can report being both White and Irish, b) persons of Hispanic origin can report being any race, c) persons reporting two ancestries are counted in both categories. 2. Numbers in parentheses indicate the number of persons reporting this ancestry/race alone, not in combination with any other ancestry/race. 3. Refer to the Explanation of Data in the front of the book for more detailed information.

Eskimo (1)	2	0.00
Alaska Native tribes, not specified	1	0.00
Am. Ind. or Alaska Nat., not spec.	725	0.32
Albanian	14	0.01
Alsatian	5	0.00
American Indian tribes, specified:	1,185	0.53
Apache (6)	10	0.00
Blackfeet (11)	47	0.02
Cherokee (121)	445	0.20
Chickasaw (1)	1	0.00
Chippewa (10)	10	0.00
Choctaw (1)	15	0.01
Comanche (1)	1	0.00
Creek (2)	6	0.00
Crow (1)	1	0.00
Delaware	3	0.00
Iroquois (12)	33	0.01
Latin American Indians (40)	62	0.03
Lumbee (301)	374	0.17
Navajo (12)	17	0.01
Pueblo (1)	5	0.00
Seminole (3)	8	0.00
Sioux (14)	32	0.01
Yaqui (1)	1	0.00
All other tribes (52)	114	0.05
American Indian tribes, not spec.	77	0.03
Arab:	1,003	0.45
Arab/Arabic	173	0.08
Egyptian	193	0.09
Jordanian	57	0.03
Lebanese	226	0.10
Moroccan	48	0.02
Palestinian	223	0.10
Syrian	40	0.02
Other Arab	43	0.02
Armenian	20	0.01
Asian:	7,394	3.30
Bangladeshi (36)	41	0.02
Cambodian (388)	474	0.21
Chinese, ex. Taiwanese (605)	706	0.32
Filipino (238)	335	0.15
Hmong (3)	9	0.00
Indian (1,249)	1,410	0.63
Indonesian (3)	4	0.00
Japanese (183)	247	0.11
Korean (509)	604	0.27
Laotian (348)	380	0.17
Malaysian (8)	9	0.00
Pakistani (67)	95	0.04
Sri Lankan (28)	28	0.01
Taiwanese (15)	24	0.01
Thai (82)	105	0.05
Vietnamese (2,166)	2,340	1.05
Other Asian, specified (27)	42	0.02
Other Asian, not specified (284)	541	0.24
Australian	50	0.02
Austrian	376	0.17
Basque	22	0.01
Belgian	86	0.04
Brazilian	54	0.02
British	1,279	0.57
Bulgarian	73	0.03
Canadian	489	0.22
Celtic	24	0.01
Croatian	123	0.06
Czech	254	0.11
Czechoslovakian	115	0.05
Danish	376	0.17
Dutch	2,395	1.07
Eastern European	149	0.07
English	21,970	9.84
Estonian	13	0.01
European	2,279	1.02
Finnish	146	0.07
French, except Basque	3,796	1.70
French Canadian	744	0.33
German	19,659	8.80
Greek	625	0.28
Guyanese	18	0.01
Hawaii Native/Pacific Islander:	215	0.10
Micronesian: (31)	45	0.02
Guamanian/Chamorro (11)	22	0.01
Other Micronesian (20)	23	0.01
Polynesian: (44)	97	0.04
Native Hawaiian (24)	56	0.03
Samoan (17)	38	0.02
Other Polynesian (3)	3	0.00
Other Pac. Isl., specified	5	0.00
Other Pac. Isl., not spec. (13)	68	0.03
Hispanic or Latino:	9,742	4.35
Central American:	600	0.27
Costa Rican	60	0.03
Guatemalan	107	0.05
Honduran	115	0.05
Nicaraguan	25	0.01
Panamanian	64	0.03
Salvadoran	203	0.09
Other Central American	26	0.01
Cuban	357	0.16
Dominican Republic	101	0.05
Mexican	6,205	2.77
Puerto Rican	785	0.35
South American:	465	0.21
Argentinean	45	0.02
Bolivian	11	0.00
Chilean	25	0.01
Colombian	186	0.08
Ecuadorian	28	0.01
Paraguayan	3	0.00
Peruvian	68	0.03
Uruguayan	1	0.00
Venezuelan	81	0.04
Other South American	17	0.01
Other Hispanic or Latino	1,229	0.55
Hungarian	528	0.24
Icelander	39	0.02
Iranian	165	0.07
Irish	14,492	6.49
Israeli	17	0.01
Italian	5,731	2.57
Latvian	28	0.01
Lithuanian	142	0.06
Maltese	16	0.01
Northern European	137	0.06
Norwegian	1,159	0.52
Pennsylvania German	47	0.02
Polish	2,585	1.16
Portuguese	210	0.09
Romanian	85	0.04
Russian	882	0.39
Scandinavian	173	0.08
Scotch-Irish	8,118	3.64
Scottish	5,151	2.31
Serbian	70	0.03
Slavic	33	0.01
Slovak	201	0.09
Slovene	9	0.00
Swedish	1,655	0.74
Swiss	482	0.22
Turkish	20	0.01
Ukrainian	305	0.14
United States or American	16,391	7.34
Welsh	1,202	0.54
West Indian, excl. Hispanic:	848	0.38
Bahamian	17	0.01
Barbadian	27	0.01
Belizean	25	0.01
Bermudan	32	0.01
British West Indian	27	0.01
Haitian	122	0.05
Jamaican	332	0.15
Trinidadian and Tobagonian	90	0.04
U.S. Virgin Islander	19	0.01
West Indian	152	0.07
Other West Indian	5	0.00
White:	126,700	56.59
Not Hispanic (120,112)	122,099	54.54
Hispanic (4,131)	4,601	2.06
Yugoslavian	304	0.14

Greenville

Place Type: City
County: Pitt
Population: 60,476

Ancestry/Race	Number	%
Acadian/Cajun	9	0.01
Afghan	18	0.03
African American/Black:	20,973	34.68
Not Hispanic (20,531)	20,815	34.42
Hispanic (118)	158	0.26
African, sub-Saharan:	570	0.94
African	511	0.85
Ghanian	12	0.02
Nigerian	16	0.03
South African	24	0.04
Ugandan	7	0.01
Alaska Native tribes, specified:	1	0.00
Aleut	1	0.00
Am. Ind. or Alaska Nat., not spec.	95	0.16
Albanian	15	0.02
American Indian tribes, specified:	239	0.40
Blackfeet (1)	6	0.01
Cherokee (24)	86	0.14
Chippewa (2)	3	0.00
Choctaw (5)	6	0.01
Comanche	1	0.00
Cree	2	0.00
Creek (5)	5	0.01
Delaware (1)	2	0.00
Iroquois (4)	12	0.02
Kiowa (1)	1	0.00
Latin American Indians (5)	11	0.02
Lumbee (47)	53	0.09
Navajo (1)	1	0.00
Osage (1)	1	0.00
Seminole	4	0.01
Sioux (1)	4	0.01
All other tribes (23)	41	0.07
American Indian tribes, not spec.	15	0.02
Arab:	436	0.72
Arab/Arabic	170	0.28
Egyptian	33	0.05
Jordanian	44	0.07
Lebanese	80	0.13
Moroccan	18	0.03
Palestinian	67	0.11
Syrian	16	0.03
Other Arab	8	0.01
Armenian	35	0.06
Asian:	1,332	2.20
Cambodian (3)	3	0.00
Chinese, ex. Taiwanese (247)	279	0.46
Filipino (88)	127	0.21
Hmong (8)	8	0.01
Indian (378)	401	0.66
Indonesian (4)	4	0.01
Japanese (86)	130	0.21
Korean (123)	163	0.27
Laotian (7)	7	0.01
Pakistani (11)	14	0.02
Sri Lankan (1)	2	0.00
Taiwanese (3)	5	0.01
Thai (5)	8	0.01
Vietnamese (69)	80	0.13
Other Asian, specified (4)	8	0.01
Other Asian, not specified (48)	93	0.15
Austrian	98	0.16
Belgian	27	0.04
Brazilian	8	0.01
British	359	0.59
Bulgarian	19	0.03
Canadian	202	0.33
Croatian	26	0.04
Czech	172	0.28
Czechoslovakian	57	0.09
Danish	74	0.12
Dutch	487	0.81
Eastern European	14	0.02

Notes: 1. Figures in the "Number" column do not add up to the total population due to: a) Ancestry/Race overlap — e.g. persons can report being both White and Irish, b) persons of Hispanic origin can report being any race, c) persons reporting two ancestries are counted in both categories. 2. Numbers in parentheses indicate the number of persons reporting this ancestry/race alone, not in combination with any other ancestry/race. 3. Refer to the Explanation of Data in the front of the book for more detailed information.

Ancestry/Race	Number	%
English	6,158	10.20
European	925	1.53
Finnish	18	0.03
French, except Basque	987	1.63
French Canadian	166	0.27
German	5,316	8.80
Greek	142	0.24
Guyanese	28	0.05
Hawaii Native/Pacific Islander:	58	0.10
Melanesian: (1)	1	0.00
Fijian (1)	1	0.00
Micronesian: (12)	13	0.02
Guamanian/Chamorro (12)	13	0.02
Polynesian: (10)	23	0.04
Native Hawaiian (6)	17	0.03
Samoan (4)	5	0.01
Other Polynesian	1	0.00
Other Pac. Isl., specified	4	0.01
Other Pac. Isl., not spec. (3)	17	0.03
Hispanic or Latino:	1,244	2.06
Central American:	65	0.11
Costa Rican	11	0.02
Guatemalan	3	0.00
Honduran	9	0.01
Nicaraguan	7	0.01
Panamanian	24	0.04
Salvadoran	11	0.02
Cuban	51	0.08
Dominican Republic	18	0.03
Mexican	589	0.97
Puerto Rican	180	0.30
South American:	137	0.23
Argentinean	14	0.02
Bolivian	9	0.01
Chilean	10	0.02
Colombian	35	0.06
Ecuadorian	7	0.01
Peruvian	15	0.02
Uruguayan	1	0.00
Venezuelan	35	0.06
Other South American	11	0.02
Other Hispanic or Latino	204	0.34
Hungarian	113	0.19
Icelander	8	0.01
Iranian	67	0.11
Irish	4,522	7.49
Israeli	10	0.02
Italian	1,515	2.51
Latvian	7	0.01
Lithuanian	80	0.13
Luxemburger	8	0.01
Maltese	9	0.01
Northern European	34	0.06
Norwegian	196	0.32
Polish	718	1.19
Portuguese	98	0.16
Romanian	16	0.03
Russian	320	0.53
Scandinavian	65	0.11
Scotch-Irish	1,674	2.77
Scottish	1,254	2.08
Serbian	13	0.02
Slavic	17	0.03
Slovak	47	0.08
Swedish	398	0.66
Swiss	108	0.18
Ukrainian	62	0.10
United States or American	4,460	7.39
Welsh	408	0.68
West Indian, excl. Hispanic:	141	0.23
Belizean	9	0.01
British West Indian	12	0.02
Haitian	16	0.03
Jamaican	72	0.12
West Indian	24	0.04
Other West Indian	8	0.01
White:	37,725	62.38
Not Hispanic (36,660)	37,174	61.47
Hispanic (473)	551	0.91
Yugoslavian	65	0.11

Havelock

Place Type: City
County: Craven
Population: 22,442

Ancestry/Race	Number	%
Acadian/Cajun	7	0.03
African American/Black:	4,473	19.93
Not Hispanic (4,043)	4,288	19.11
Hispanic (116)	185	0.82
African, sub-Saharan:	198	0.87
African	105	0.46
Cape Verdean	13	0.06
Ghanian	29	0.13
Liberian	7	0.03
Senegalese	24	0.11
Other sub-Saharan African	20	0.09
Alaska Native tribes, specified:	6	0.03
Alaska Athabascan	2	0.01
Aleut (1)	3	0.01
Eskimo	1	0.00
Am. Ind. or Alaska Nat., not spec.	88	0.39
American Indian tribes, specified:	278	1.24
Apache (2)	4	0.02
Blackfeet (2)	16	0.07
Cherokee (32)	104	0.46
Chickasaw (1)	2	0.01
Chippewa (9)	13	0.06
Choctaw (4)	8	0.04
Comanche (1)	2	0.01
Cree	1	0.00
Creek (3)	4	0.02
Delaware (1)	1	0.00
Houma (3)	4	0.02
Iroquois (2)	11	0.05
Latin American Indians (3)	8	0.04
Lumbee (10)	16	0.07
Navajo (14)	19	0.08
Ottawa (2)	2	0.01
Potawatomi	3	0.01
Pueblo (7)	7	0.03
Seminole	3	0.01
Sioux (8)	11	0.05
Tohono O'Odham (1)	1	0.00
Ute (1)	1	0.00
Yakama (4)	4	0.02
Yaqui	1	0.00
All other tribes (23)	32	0.14
American Indian tribes, not spec.	17	0.08
Arab:	14	0.06
Lebanese	7	0.03
Syrian	7	0.03
Armenian	25	0.11
Asian:	845	3.77
Cambodian (2)	2	0.01
Chinese, ex. Taiwanese (34)	61	0.27
Filipino (291)	401	1.79
Indian (31)	53	0.24
Japanese (104)	158	0.70
Korean (41)	68	0.30
Laotian (4)	4	0.02
Pakistani (3)	3	0.01
Thai (16)	27	0.12
Vietnamese (20)	32	0.14
Other Asian, specified (1)	2	0.01
Other Asian, not specified (15)	34	0.15
Austrian	46	0.20
Belgian	17	0.07
British	44	0.19
Canadian	58	0.26
Croatian	69	0.30
Czech	41	0.18
Czechoslovakian	7	0.03
Danish	44	0.19
Dutch	272	1.20
English	1,936	8.53
European	67	0.30
French, except Basque	569	2.51
French Canadian	194	0.85
German	3,585	15.79
Greek	29	0.13
Hawaii Native/Pacific Islander:	73	0.33
Micronesian: (19)	21	0.09
Guamanian/Chamorro (16)	18	0.08
Other Micronesian (3)	3	0.01
Polynesian: (7)	36	0.16
Native Hawaiian (4)	31	0.14
Samoan (2)	4	0.02
Tongan (1)	1	0.00
Other Pac. Isl., not spec. (6)	16	0.07
Hispanic or Latino:	2,022	9.01
Central American:	57	0.25
Costa Rican	2	0.01
Guatemalan	6	0.03
Honduran	12	0.05
Nicaraguan	6	0.03
Panamanian	16	0.07
Salvadoran	14	0.06
Other Central American	1	0.00
Cuban	55	0.25
Dominican Republic	64	0.29
Mexican	832	3.71
Puerto Rican	594	2.65
South American:	81	0.36
Argentinean	1	0.00
Bolivian	4	0.02
Chilean	3	0.01
Colombian	35	0.16
Ecuadorian	9	0.04
Peruvian	25	0.11
Uruguayan	2	0.01
Venezuelan	2	0.01
Other Hispanic or Latino	339	1.51
Hungarian	113	0.50
Irish	3,027	13.33
Israeli	8	0.04
Italian	1,184	5.22
Lithuanian	18	0.08
Norwegian	157	0.69
Pennsylvania German	15	0.07
Polish	674	2.97
Portuguese	61	0.27
Romanian	27	0.12
Russian	54	0.24
Scandinavian	70	0.31
Scotch-Irish	463	2.04
Scottish	374	1.65
Serbian	16	0.07
Slavic	25	0.11
Slovak	53	0.23
Slovene	9	0.04
Swedish	59	0.26
Swiss	47	0.21
Turkish	9	0.04
Ukrainian	24	0.11
United States or American	1,753	7.72
Welsh	149	0.66
West Indian, excl. Hispanic:	175	0.77
Haitian	8	0.04
Jamaican	108	0.48
Trinidadian and Tobagonian	16	0.07
West Indian	43	0.19
White:	16,442	73.26
Not Hispanic (15,002)	15,477	68.96
Hispanic (814)	965	4.30

Henderson

Place Type: City
County: Vance
Population: 16,095

Ancestry/Race	Number	%
African American/Black:	9,591	59.59
Not Hispanic (9,474)	9,519	59.14
Hispanic (50)	72	0.45
African, sub-Saharan:	123	0.76
African	123	0.76
Am. Ind. or Alaska Nat., not spec.	25	0.16

Notes: 1. Figures in the "Number" column do not add up to the total population due to: a) Ancestry/Race overlap — e.g. persons can report being both White and Irish, b) persons of Hispanic origin can report being any race, c) persons reporting two ancestries are counted in both categories. 2. Numbers in parentheses indicate the number of persons reporting this ancestry/race alone, not in combination with any other ancestry/race. 3. Refer to the Explanation of Data in the front of the book for more detailed information.

Ancestry/Race	Number	%
American Indian tribes, specified:	34	0.21
Cherokee (10)	17	0.11
Latin American Indians (1)	1	0.01
Lumbee	3	0.02
Potawatomi	1	0.01
All other tribes (10)	12	0.07
American Indian tribes, not spec.	6	0.04
Arab:	30	0.18
Jordanian	21	0.13
Lebanese	9	0.06
Asian:	119	0.74
Chinese, ex. Taiwanese (17)	18	0.11
Filipino (1)	1	0.01
Indian (47)	51	0.32
Japanese	3	0.02
Korean (11)	13	0.08
Pakistani (2)	2	0.01
Thai (1)	1	0.01
Vietnamese (20)	20	0.12
Other Asian, specified	3	0.02
Other Asian, not specified (4)	7	0.04
British	12	0.07
Czech	6	0.04
Czechoslovakian	27	0.17
Danish	7	0.04
Dutch	63	0.39
English	1,025	6.31
European	9	0.06
French, except Basque	51	0.31
French Canadian	20	0.12
German	389	2.39
Greek	29	0.18
Hawaii Native/Pacific Islander:	10	0.06
Micronesian: (3)	3	0.02
Guamanian/Chamorro (3)	3	0.02
Polynesian:	3	0.02
Native Hawaiian	3	0.02
Other Pac. Isl., specified	3	0.02
Other Pac. Isl., not spec. (1)	1	0.01
Hispanic or Latino:	826	5.13
Central American:	37	0.23
Guatemalan	2	0.01
Honduran	12	0.07
Panamanian	1	0.01
Salvadoran	21	0.13
Other Central American	1	0.01
Cuban	5	0.03
Dominican Republic	1	0.01
Mexican	689	4.28
Puerto Rican	31	0.19
South American:	4	0.02
Argentinean	4	0.02
Other Hispanic or Latino	59	0.37
Irish	459	2.82
Italian	131	0.81
Lithuanian	4	0.02
Norwegian	19	0.12
Pennsylvania German	4	0.02
Polish	31	0.19
Portuguese	6	0.04
Russian	19	0.12
Scotch-Irish	208	1.28
Scottish	128	0.79
Slovak	63	0.39
Slovene	4	0.02
Swedish	12	0.07
Swiss	10	0.06
Ukrainian	4	0.02
United States or American	1,431	8.81
Welsh	7	0.04
West Indian, excl. Hispanic:	13	0.08
Bahamian	6	0.04
Haitian	7	0.04
White:	6,002	37.29
Not Hispanic (5,562)	5,622	34.93
Hispanic (355)	380	2.36
Yugoslavian	6	0.04

Hendersonville

Place Type: City
County: Henderson
Population: 10,420

Ancestry/Race	Number	%
African American/Black:	1,371	13.16
Not Hispanic (1,294)	1,351	12.97
Hispanic (13)	20	0.19
African, sub-Saharan:	65	0.63
African	65	0.63
Am. Ind. or Alaska Nat., not spec.	28	0.27
American Indian tribes, specified:	41	0.39
Apache (1)	1	0.01
Blackfeet	2	0.02
Cherokee (7)	16	0.15
Chippewa (1)	1	0.01
Cree	1	0.01
Iroquois (1)	5	0.05
Latin American Indians (5)	10	0.10
Lumbee (1)	3	0.03
Navajo	1	0.01
All other tribes	1	0.01
American Indian tribes, not spec.	1	0.01
Asian:	103	0.99
Cambodian (9)	9	0.09
Chinese, ex. Taiwanese (13)	16	0.15
Filipino (6)	10	0.10
Indian (25)	30	0.29
Japanese (2)	10	0.10
Korean (13)	13	0.12
Pakistani (1)	3	0.03
Sri Lankan (3)	3	0.03
Thai	2	0.02
Vietnamese (1)	1	0.01
Other Asian, specified	2	0.02
Other Asian, not specified (2)	4	0.04
Austrian	47	0.45
Belgian	7	0.07
British	80	0.77
Canadian	9	0.09
Croatian	5	0.05
Czech	15	0.14
Danish	151	1.46
Dutch	122	1.18
English	1,667	16.07
European	113	1.09
Finnish	28	0.27
French, except Basque	269	2.59
French Canadian	75	0.72
German	1,253	12.08
Greek	38	0.37
Hawaii Native/Pacific Islander:	3	0.03
Micronesian: (1)	1	0.01
Guamanian/Chamorro (1)	1	0.01
Other Pac. Isl., specified	2	0.02
Hispanic or Latino:	947	9.09
Central American:	18	0.17
Costa Rican	7	0.07
Guatemalan	4	0.04
Honduran	2	0.02
Salvadoran	5	0.05
Cuban	8	0.08
Dominican Republic	4	0.04
Mexican	814	7.81
Puerto Rican	23	0.22
South American:	22	0.21
Argentinean	1	0.01
Chilean	8	0.08
Colombian	7	0.07
Venezuelan	2	0.02
Other South American	4	0.04
Other Hispanic or Latino	58	0.56
Hungarian	48	0.46
Irish	915	8.82
Israeli	6	0.06
Italian	240	2.31
Lithuanian	6	0.06
Northern European	15	0.14
Norwegian	51	0.49
Polish	139	1.34
Portuguese	15	0.14
Romanian	2	0.02
Russian	80	0.77
Scandinavian	13	0.13
Scotch-Irish	499	4.81
Scottish	341	3.29
Slovak	14	0.13
Slovene	9	0.09
Swedish	71	0.68
Swiss	32	0.31
Ukrainian	44	0.42
United States or American	1,027	9.90
Welsh	41	0.40
West Indian, excl. Hispanic:	29	0.28
Jamaican	18	0.17
West Indian	11	0.11
White:	8,620	82.73
Not Hispanic (7,957)	8,052	77.27
Hispanic (529)	568	5.45

Hickory

Place Type: City
County: Catawba
Population: 37,222

Ancestry/Race	Number	%
Acadian/Cajun	51	0.14
African American/Black:	5,424	14.57
Not Hispanic (5,181)	5,340	14.35
Hispanic (62)	84	0.23
African, sub-Saharan:	320	0.85
African	320	0.85
Am. Ind. or Alaska Nat., not spec.	68	0.18
American Indian tribes, specified:	96	0.26
Apache (1)	2	0.01
Blackfeet	1	0.00
Cherokee (16)	47	0.13
Chickasaw	1	0.00
Chippewa (4)	5	0.01
Choctaw	1	0.00
Comanche	1	0.00
Creek	4	0.01
Latin American Indians (5)	5	0.01
Lumbee (6)	10	0.03
Potawatomi (3)	3	0.01
Seminole	2	0.01
Sioux (3)	3	0.01
All other tribes (7)	11	0.03
American Indian tribes, not spec.	8	0.02
Arab:	62	0.17
Lebanese	31	0.08
Syrian	25	0.07
Other Arab	6	0.02
Armenian	8	0.02
Asian:	1,661	4.46
Cambodian (5)	5	0.01
Chinese, ex. Taiwanese (93)	100	0.27
Filipino (17)	36	0.10
Hmong (620)	705	1.89
Indian (95)	112	0.30
Indonesian (7)	7	0.02
Japanese (34)	49	0.13
Korean (25)	32	0.09
Laotian (174)	203	0.55
Pakistani (13)	13	0.03
Sri Lankan (2)	2	0.01
Taiwanese (1)	1	0.00
Thai (8)	24	0.06
Vietnamese (266)	289	0.78
Other Asian, specified	6	0.02
Other Asian, not specified (54)	77	0.21
Australian	40	0.11
Austrian	46	0.12
British	280	0.75
Canadian	71	0.19
Czech	40	0.11
Czechoslovakian	20	0.05

Notes: 1. Figures in the "Number" column do not add up to the total population due to: a) Ancestry/Race overlap — e.g. persons can report being both White and Irish, b) persons of Hispanic origin can report being any race, c) persons reporting two ancestries are counted in both categories. 2. Numbers in parentheses indicate the number of persons reporting this ancestry/race alone, not in combination with any other ancestry/race. 3. Refer to the Explanation of Data in the front of the book for more detailed information.

Ancestry/Race	Number	%
Danish	28	0.07
Dutch	922	2.46
English	3,453	9.21
European	315	0.84
French, except Basque	695	1.85
French Canadian	160	0.43
German	5,767	15.37
German Russian	6	0.02
Greek	26	0.07
Hawaii Native/Pacific Islander:	52	0.14
Micronesian: (5)	11	0.03
Guamanian/Chamorro (5)	11	0.03
Polynesian: (8)	10	0.03
Native Hawaiian (5)	7	0.02
Samoan (3)	3	0.01
Other Pac. Isl., specified	6	0.02
Other Pac. Isl., not spec. (11)	25	0.07
Hispanic or Latino:	2,863	7.69
Central American:	158	0.42
Costa Rican	43	0.12
Guatemalan	28	0.08
Honduran	32	0.09
Nicaraguan	16	0.04
Panamanian	4	0.01
Salvadoran	30	0.08
Other Central American	5	0.01
Cuban	35	0.09
Dominican Republic	22	0.06
Mexican	2,059	5.53
Puerto Rican	141	0.38
South American:	105	0.28
Bolivian	1	0.00
Chilean	5	0.01
Colombian	80	0.21
Ecuadorian	5	0.01
Peruvian	8	0.02
Venezuelan	4	0.01
Other South American	2	0.01
Other Hispanic or Latino	343	0.92
Hungarian	43	0.11
Irish	2,758	7.35
Italian	749	2.00
Latvian	22	0.06
Lithuanian	45	0.12
Luxemburger	9	0.02
Norwegian	179	0.48
Polish	312	0.83
Portuguese	64	0.17
Romanian	128	0.34
Russian	54	0.14
Scandinavian	61	0.16
Scotch-Irish	1,369	3.65
Scottish	964	2.57
Swedish	292	0.78
Swiss	81	0.22
Ukrainian	30	0.08
United States or American	4,638	12.36
Welsh	174	0.46
West Indian, excl. Hispanic:	25	0.07
Jamaican	25	0.07
White:	29,157	78.33
Not Hispanic (27,245)	27,547	74.01
Hispanic (1,502)	1,610	4.33

High Point

Place Type: City
County: Guilford
Population: 85,839

Ancestry/Race	Number	%
Acadian/Cajun	7	0.01
African American/Black:	27,753	32.33
Not Hispanic (27,064)	27,473	32.01
Hispanic (211)	280	0.33
African, sub-Saharan:	606	0.71
African	518	0.60
Ethiopian	60	0.07
Nigerian	28	0.03
Alaska Native tribes, specified:	4	0.00
Aleut	1	0.00
Eskimo (1)	2	0.00
Tlingit-Haida	1	0.00
Am. Ind. or Alaska Nat., not spec.	263	0.31
American Indian tribes, specified:	386	0.45
Apache (1)	4	0.00
Blackfeet (2)	12	0.01
Cherokee (44)	126	0.15
Cheyenne (1)	1	0.00
Chickasaw (1)	1	0.00
Chippewa (9)	10	0.01
Choctaw (1)	1	0.00
Comanche (2)	3	0.00
Cree (2)	2	0.00
Crow (1)	1	0.00
Iroquois (6)	9	0.01
Latin American Indians (19)	22	0.03
Lumbee (120)	149	0.17
Navajo (2)	2	0.00
Ottawa	1	0.00
Pima (2)	3	0.00
Seminole (1)	3	0.00
Shoshone	1	0.00
Sioux (1)	1	0.00
All other tribes (25)	34	0.04
American Indian tribes, not spec.	40	0.05
Arab:	222	0.26
Arab/Arabic	77	0.09
Jordanian	6	0.01
Lebanese	113	0.13
Palestinian	18	0.02
Other Arab	8	0.01
Armenian	9	0.01
Asian:	3,403	3.96
Bangladeshi (4)	4	0.00
Cambodian (49)	57	0.07
Chinese, ex. Taiwanese (196)	226	0.26
Filipino (82)	108	0.13
Indian (528)	621	0.72
Indonesian (1)	3	0.00
Japanese (48)	81	0.09
Korean (317)	343	0.40
Laotian (441)	502	0.58
Malaysian	3	0.00
Pakistani (357)	517	0.60
Sri Lankan (1)	1	0.00
Taiwanese (1)	1	0.00
Thai (38)	40	0.05
Vietnamese (601)	647	0.75
Other Asian, specified (23)	38	0.04
Other Asian, not specified (133)	211	0.25
Australian	29	0.03
Austrian	56	0.07
Belgian	23	0.03
Brazilian	35	0.04
British	337	0.39
Canadian	203	0.24
Celtic	21	0.02
Croatian	84	0.10
Czech	105	0.12
Czechoslovakian	93	0.11
Danish	78	0.09
Dutch	1,020	1.19
Eastern European	31	0.04
English	7,742	9.01
European	624	0.73
Finnish	24	0.03
French, except Basque	1,290	1.50
French Canadian	318	0.37
German	8,014	9.32
Greek	320	0.37
Hawaii Native/Pacific Islander:	63	0.07
Micronesian: (1)	5	0.01
Guamanian/Chamorro (1)	5	0.01
Polynesian: (16)	23	0.03
Native Hawaiian (9)	15	0.02
Samoan (7)	8	0.01
Other Pac. Isl., specified	11	0.01
Other Pac. Isl., not spec.	24	0.03
Hispanic or Latino:	4,197	4.89
Central American:	266	0.31
Costa Rican	19	0.02
Guatemalan	46	0.05
Honduran	118	0.14
Nicaraguan	1	0.00
Panamanian	13	0.02
Salvadoran	64	0.07
Other Central American	5	0.01
Cuban	120	0.14
Dominican Republic	51	0.06
Mexican	2,880	3.36
Puerto Rican	242	0.28
South American:	136	0.16
Argentinean	15	0.02
Bolivian	1	0.00
Chilean	9	0.01
Colombian	69	0.08
Ecuadorian	9	0.01
Paraguayan	1	0.00
Peruvian	12	0.01
Uruguayan	1	0.00
Venezuelan	16	0.02
Other South American	3	0.00
Other Hispanic or Latino	502	0.58
Hungarian	194	0.23
Icelander	8	0.01
Iranian	9	0.01
Irish	5,943	6.91
Israeli	7	0.01
Italian	2,008	2.34
Latvian	6	0.01
Lithuanian	17	0.02
New Zealander	33	0.04
Northern European	19	0.02
Norwegian	260	0.30
Pennsylvania German	20	0.02
Polish	931	1.08
Portuguese	65	0.08
Romanian	74	0.09
Russian	263	0.31
Scandinavian	54	0.06
Scotch-Irish	2,297	2.67
Scottish	1,676	1.95
Serbian	17	0.02
Slovak	36	0.04
Slovene	6	0.01
Swedish	280	0.33
Swiss	239	0.28
Turkish	27	0.03
Ukrainian	47	0.05
United States or American	8,482	9.87
Welsh	417	0.49
West Indian, excl. Hispanic:	250	0.29
Bahamian	40	0.05
Haitian	5	0.01
Jamaican	174	0.20
Trinidadian and Tobagonian	8	0.01
West Indian	23	0.03
White:	52,898	61.62
Not Hispanic (50,176)	50,839	59.23
Hispanic (1,809)	2,059	2.40
Yugoslavian	139	0.16

Hope Mills

Place Type: Town
County: Cumberland
Population: 11,237

Ancestry/Race	Number	%
African American/Black:	2,099	18.68
Not Hispanic (1,948)	2,047	18.22
Hispanic (31)	52	0.46
African, sub-Saharan:	51	0.45
African	51	0.45
Alaska Native tribes, specified:	2	0.02
Aleut (1)	2	0.02
Am. Ind. or Alaska Nat., not spec.	84	0.75
American Indian tribes, specified:	223	1.98
Apache	3	0.03

Notes: 1. Figures in the "Number" column do not add up to the total population due to: a) Ancestry/Race overlap — e.g. persons can report being both White and Irish, b) persons of Hispanic origin can report being any race, c) persons reporting two ancestries are counted in both categories. 2. Numbers in parentheses indicate the number of persons reporting this ancestry/race alone, not in combination with any other ancestry/race. 3. Refer to the Explanation of Data in the front of the book for more detailed information.

Blackfeet (1)	5	0.04
Cherokee (23)	56	0.50
Chickasaw (2)	3	0.03
Choctaw (5)	5	0.04
Creek (1)	1	0.01
Crow	1	0.01
Delaware (3)	6	0.05
Iroquois (3)	4	0.04
Kiowa (1)	1	0.01
Latin American Indians (3)	4	0.04
Lumbee (81)	99	0.88
Potawatomi (1)	1	0.01
Pueblo (6)	6	0.05
Seminole	3	0.03
Shoshone (1)	1	0.01
Sioux (4)	6	0.05
Yaqui (1)	2	0.02
All other tribes (12)	16	0.14
American Indian tribes, not spec.	21	0.19
Arab:	11	0.10
Arab/Arabic	11	0.10
Asian:	230	2.05
Cambodian (1)	1	0.01
Chinese, ex. Taiwanese (6)	16	0.14
Filipino (28)	43	0.38
Indian (16)	18	0.16
Japanese (9)	17	0.15
Korean (63)	99	0.88
Thai (5)	11	0.10
Vietnamese (8)	15	0.13
Other Asian, not specified (5)	10	0.09
Austrian	9	0.08
British	34	0.30
Bulgarian	11	0.10
Canadian	20	0.18
Croatian	10	0.09
Czech	29	0.26
Dutch	72	0.63
English	821	7.23
European	129	1.14
French, except Basque	264	2.32
French Canadian	60	0.53
German	1,379	12.14
Greek	23	0.20
Hawaii Native/Pacific Islander:	39	0.35
Micronesian: (8)	10	0.09
Guamanian/Chamorro (7)	7	0.06
Other Micronesian (1)	3	0.03
Polynesian: (11)	20	0.18
Native Hawaiian (8)	11	0.10
Samoan (3)	9	0.08
Other Pac. Isl., not spec. (5)	9	0.08
Hispanic or Latino:	719	6.40
Central American:	54	0.48
Costa Rican	3	0.03
Honduran	1	0.01
Nicaraguan	1	0.01
Panamanian	30	0.27
Salvadoran	16	0.14
Other Central American	3	0.03
Cuban	18	0.16
Dominican Republic	17	0.15
Mexican	200	1.78
Puerto Rican	286	2.55
South American:	21	0.19
Chilean	3	0.03
Colombian	13	0.12
Ecuadorian	2	0.02
Peruvian	3	0.03
Other Hispanic or Latino	123	1.09
Hungarian	7	0.06
Irish	1,118	9.84
Italian	381	3.35
Lithuanian	10	0.09
Norwegian	94	0.83
Polish	203	1.79
Romanian	12	0.11
Russian	6	0.05
Scotch-Irish	476	4.19
Scottish	287	2.53
Serbian	17	0.15
Slovak	9	0.08
Swedish	52	0.46
Swiss	24	0.21
Ukrainian	14	0.12
United States or American	1,550	13.65
Welsh	28	0.25
West Indian, excl. Hispanic:	90	0.79
Belizean	18	0.16
Jamaican	10	0.09
Trinidadian and Tobagonian	34	0.30
West Indian	28	0.25
White:	8,491	75.56
Not Hispanic (7,920)	8,135	72.39
Hispanic (287)	356	3.17

Huntersville

Place Type: Town
County: Mecklenburg
Population: 24,960

Ancestry/Race	Number	%
African American/Black:	1,987	7.96
Not Hispanic (1,830)	1,897	7.60
Hispanic (35)	90	0.36
African, sub-Saharan:	99	0.40
African	52	0.21
Cape Verdean	8	0.03
South African	30	0.12
Other sub-Saharan African	9	0.04
Am. Ind. or Alaska Nat., not spec.	34	0.14
Alsatian	17	0.07
American Indian tribes, specified:	95	0.38
Apache (1)	1	0.00
Cherokee (11)	27	0.11
Chickasaw (1)	1	0.00
Chippewa (1)	2	0.01
Choctaw	1	0.00
Iroquois (3)	6	0.02
Latin American Indians (1)	8	0.03
Lumbee (32)	34	0.14
Sioux (3)	5	0.02
All other tribes (8)	10	0.04
American Indian tribes, not spec.	12	0.05
Arab:	59	0.24
Arab/Arabic	7	0.03
Egyptian	7	0.03
Lebanese	7	0.03
Syrian	38	0.15
Armenian	34	0.14
Asian:	466	1.87
Chinese, ex. Taiwanese (69)	86	0.34
Filipino (25)	43	0.17
Indian (77)	86	0.34
Indonesian (1)	1	0.00
Japanese (43)	56	0.22
Korean (55)	68	0.27
Laotian (28)	32	0.13
Pakistani (6)	8	0.03
Thai (1)	1	0.00
Vietnamese (52)	58	0.23
Other Asian, specified (1)	2	0.01
Other Asian, not specified (11)	25	0.10
Australian	42	0.17
Austrian	54	0.22
Belgian	36	0.14
British	279	1.12
Canadian	64	0.26
Croatian	17	0.07
Czech	72	0.29
Czechoslovakian	86	0.35
Danish	33	0.13
Dutch	534	2.14
Eastern European	6	0.02
English	3,373	13.53
Estonian	13	0.05
European	227	0.91
Finnish	71	0.28
French, except Basque	828	3.32
French Canadian	163	0.65
German	4,497	18.04
Greek	95	0.38
Hawaii Native/Pacific Islander:	27	0.11
Micronesian: (2)	2	0.01
Guamanian/Chamorro (2)	2	0.01
Polynesian: (11)	19	0.08
Native Hawaiian (8)	15	0.06
Samoan (3)	4	0.02
Other Pac. Isl., specified	1	0.00
Other Pac. Isl., not spec.	5	0.02
Hispanic or Latino:	968	3.88
Central American:	21	0.08
Costa Rican	6	0.02
Guatemalan	2	0.01
Honduran	4	0.02
Nicaraguan	3	0.01
Panamanian	4	0.02
Salvadoran	2	0.01
Cuban	43	0.17
Dominican Republic	4	0.02
Mexican	655	2.62
Puerto Rican	77	0.31
South American:	64	0.26
Argentinean	5	0.02
Bolivian	1	0.00
Chilean	3	0.01
Colombian	17	0.07
Ecuadorian	7	0.03
Peruvian	19	0.08
Venezuelan	3	0.01
Other South American	9	0.04
Other Hispanic or Latino	104	0.42
Hungarian	59	0.24
Irish	3,488	13.99
Italian	1,528	6.13
Latvian	9	0.04
Lithuanian	83	0.33
Northern European	41	0.16
Norwegian	159	0.64
Pennsylvania German	22	0.09
Polish	673	2.70
Portuguese	34	0.14
Romanian	26	0.10
Russian	224	0.90
Scandinavian	8	0.03
Scotch-Irish	1,309	5.25
Scottish	718	2.88
Slavic	9	0.04
Slovak	120	0.48
Slovene	14	0.06
Swedish	364	1.46
Swiss	46	0.18
Turkish	7	0.03
Ukrainian	75	0.30
United States or American	2,132	8.55
Welsh	203	0.81
West Indian, excl. Hispanic:	51	0.20
Barbadian	20	0.08
Jamaican	31	0.12
White:	22,313	89.40
Not Hispanic (21,497)	21,650	86.74
Hispanic (573)	663	2.66
Yugoslavian	25	0.10

Indian Trail

Place Type: Town
County: Union
Population: 11,905

Ancestry/Race	Number	%
African American/Black:	678	5.70
Not Hispanic (634)	675	5.67
Hispanic (3)	3	0.03
African, sub-Saharan:	39	0.33
South African	39	0.33
Am. Ind. or Alaska Nat., not spec.	18	0.15
Albanian	17	0.14
American Indian tribes, specified:	95	0.80

Notes: 1. Figures in the "Number" column do not add up to the total population due to: a) Ancestry/Race overlap — e.g. persons can report being both White and Irish, b) persons of Hispanic origin can report being any race, c) persons reporting two ancestries are counted in both categories. 2. Numbers in parentheses indicate the number of persons reporting this ancestry/race alone, not in combination with any other ancestry/race. 3. Refer to the Explanation of Data in the front of the book for more detailed information.

Ancestry/Race	Number	%
Cherokee (8)	36	0.30
Choctaw (1)	1	0.01
Iroquois (2)	2	0.02
Kiowa	1	0.01
Lumbee (32)	46	0.39
All other tribes (5)	9	0.08
American Indian tribes, not spec.	5	0.04
Arab:	26	0.22
Arab/Arabic	7	0.06
Lebanese	13	0.11
Syrian	6	0.05
Armenian	13	0.11
Asian:	134	1.13
Chinese, ex. Taiwanese (6)	6	0.05
Filipino (36)	41	0.34
Indian (20)	25	0.21
Japanese (8)	9	0.08
Korean (14)	14	0.12
Laotian (1)	1	0.01
Thai	3	0.03
Vietnamese (21)	23	0.19
Other Asian, specified	2	0.02
Other Asian, not specified (8)	10	0.08
Austrian	12	0.10
British	64	0.54
Canadian	37	0.31
Czech	8	0.07
Danish	10	0.08
Dutch	222	1.88
English	1,048	8.86
European	154	1.30
Finnish	2	0.02
French, except Basque	314	2.66
French Canadian	87	0.74
German	1,915	16.20
Greek	42	0.36
Hawaii Native/Pacific Islander:	12	0.10
Micronesian: (7)	7	0.06
Guamanian/Chamorro (7)	7	0.06
Polynesian: (3)	4	0.03
Native Hawaiian	1	0.01
Samoan (3)	3	0.03
Other Pac. Isl., not spec. (1)	1	0.01
Hispanic or Latino:	295	2.48
Central American:	31	0.26
Costa Rican	8	0.07
Guatemalan	4	0.03
Honduran	6	0.05
Nicaraguan	2	0.02
Salvadoran	11	0.09
Cuban	8	0.07
Mexican	89	0.75
Puerto Rican	59	0.50
South American:	50	0.42
Argentinean	10	0.08
Bolivian	2	0.02
Chilean	4	0.03
Colombian	27	0.23
Ecuadorian	2	0.02
Peruvian	2	0.02
Venezuelan	3	0.03
Other Hispanic or Latino	58	0.49
Hungarian	44	0.37
Icelander	3	0.03
Irish	1,295	10.95
Italian	459	3.88
Norwegian	46	0.39
Polish	381	3.22
Portuguese	10	0.08
Russian	102	0.86
Scandinavian	2	0.02
Scotch-Irish	626	5.29
Scottish	191	1.62
Slovak	2	0.02
Slovene	12	0.10
Swedish	121	1.02
Swiss	10	0.08
Ukrainian	6	0.05
United States or American	1,725	14.59
Welsh	55	0.47
White:	10,962	92.08
Not Hispanic (10,654)	10,769	90.46
Hispanic (168)	193	1.62

Jacksonville

Place Type: City
County: Onslow
Population: 66,715

Ancestry/Race	Number	%
Acadian/Cajun	80	0.12
African American/Black:	17,015	25.50
Not Hispanic (15,576)	16,419	24.61
Hispanic (411)	596	0.89
African, sub-Saharan:	638	0.96
African	504	0.76
Cape Verdean	29	0.04
Ethiopian	7	0.01
Kenyan	6	0.01
Liberian	12	0.02
Nigerian	13	0.02
Senegalese	17	0.03
Sierra Leonean	25	0.04
South African	19	0.03
Other sub-Saharan African	6	0.01
Alaska Native tribes, specified:	17	0.03
Alaska Athabascan (1)	2	0.00
Aleut (4)	4	0.01
Eskimo (2)	3	0.00
Tlingit-Haida (6)	6	0.01
All other tribes (1)	2	0.00
Alaska Native tribes, not specified	1	0.00
Am. Ind. or Alaska Nat., not spec.	251	0.38
American Indian tribes, specified:	787	1.18
Apache (15)	40	0.06
Blackfeet (4)	35	0.05
Cherokee (80)	273	0.41
Cheyenne (3)	8	0.01
Chickasaw (6)	8	0.01
Chippewa (25)	35	0.05
Choctaw (9)	24	0.04
Colville (2)	4	0.01
Comanche (2)	6	0.01
Cree (1)	6	0.01
Creek (13)	29	0.04
Crow (2)	4	0.01
Delaware (4)	7	0.01
Houma (5)	5	0.01
Iroquois (10)	21	0.03
Kiowa (2)	5	0.01
Latin American Indians (19)	25	0.04
Lumbee (33)	45	0.07
Menominee (2)	2	0.00
Navajo (41)	61	0.09
Ottawa	1	0.00
Paiute (2)	2	0.00
Pima (1)	1	0.00
Potawatomi (4)	5	0.01
Pueblo (6)	9	0.01
Seminole (4)	10	0.01
Shoshone (4)	4	0.01
Sioux (26)	38	0.06
Tohono O'Odham (1)	3	0.00
Yakama (1)	1	0.00
Yaqui (1)	1	0.00
Yuman (3)	3	0.00
All other tribes (41)	66	0.10
American Indian tribes, not spec.	43	0.06
Arab:	156	0.23
Arab/Arabic	31	0.05
Iraqi	7	0.01
Lebanese	86	0.13
Moroccan	7	0.01
Palestinian	7	0.01
Syrian	7	0.01
Other Arab	11	0.02
Armenian	7	0.01
Asian:	2,156	3.23
Bangladeshi (2)	2	0.00
Cambodian (15)	21	0.03
Chinese, ex. Taiwanese (130)	194	0.29
Filipino (585)	921	1.38
Hmong (6)	9	0.01
Indian (91)	134	0.20
Indonesian	1	0.00
Japanese (186)	318	0.48
Korean (150)	225	0.34
Laotian (13)	16	0.02
Malaysian (2)	5	0.01
Pakistani (5)	7	0.01
Taiwanese	1	0.00
Thai (45)	79	0.12
Vietnamese (77)	95	0.14
Other Asian, specified (11)	16	0.02
Other Asian, not specified (40)	112	0.17
Assyrian/Chaldean/Syriac	21	0.03
Australian	90	0.13
Austrian	59	0.09
Basque	7	0.01
Belgian	63	0.09
Brazilian	25	0.04
British	305	0.46
Canadian	170	0.25
Celtic	7	0.01
Croatian	69	0.10
Cypriot	8	0.01
Czech	189	0.28
Czechoslovakian	78	0.12
Danish	57	0.09
Dutch	781	1.17
Eastern European	13	0.02
English	4,813	7.21
European	324	0.49
Finnish	90	0.13
French, except Basque	1,930	2.89
French Canadian	514	0.77
German	9,110	13.65
Greek	204	0.31
Guyanese	43	0.06
Hawaii Native/Pacific Islander:	361	0.54
Micronesian: (34)	70	0.10
Guamanian/Chamorro (28)	64	0.10
Other Micronesian (6)	6	0.01
Polynesian: (79)	202	0.30
Native Hawaiian (59)	147	0.22
Samoan (16)	45	0.07
Tongan (2)	5	0.01
Other Polynesian (2)	5	0.01
Other Pac. Isl., not spec. (6)	89	0.13
Hispanic or Latino:	6,702	10.05
Central American:	399	0.60
Costa Rican	22	0.03
Guatemalan	47	0.07
Honduran	51	0.08
Nicaraguan	66	0.10
Panamanian	107	0.16
Salvadoran	97	0.15
Other Central American	9	0.01
Cuban	216	0.32
Dominican Republic	253	0.38
Mexican	2,545	3.81
Puerto Rican	1,865	2.80
South American:	388	0.58
Argentinean	21	0.03
Bolivian	26	0.04
Chilean	23	0.03
Colombian	144	0.22
Ecuadorian	73	0.11
Peruvian	62	0.09
Uruguayan	8	0.01
Venezuelan	19	0.03
Other South American	12	0.02
Other Hispanic or Latino	1,036	1.55
Hungarian	234	0.35
Icelander	16	0.02
Irish	8,173	12.24
Italian	3,766	5.64
Latvian	7	0.01
Lithuanian	146	0.22

Notes: 1. Figures in the "Number" column do not add up to the total population due to: a) Ancestry/Race overlap — e.g. persons can report being both White and Irish, b) persons of Hispanic origin can report being any race, c) persons reporting two ancestries are counted in both categories. 2. Numbers in parentheses indicate the number of persons reporting this ancestry/race alone, not in combination with any other ancestry/race. 3. Refer to the Explanation of Data in the front of the book for more detailed information.

Luxemburger	11	0.02
Maltese	12	0.02
New Zealander	13	0.02
Northern European	36	0.05
Norwegian	693	1.04
Pennsylvania German	35	0.05
Polish	1,543	2.31
Portuguese	209	0.31
Romanian	51	0.08
Russian	291	0.44
Scandinavian	79	0.12
Scotch-Irish	1,097	1.64
Scottish	1,452	2.18
Serbian	39	0.06
Slavic	34	0.05
Slovak	34	0.05
Slovene	2	0.00
Swedish	461	0.69
Swiss	97	0.15
Ukrainian	74	0.11
United States or American	3,428	5.14
Welsh	375	0.56
West Indian, excl. Hispanic:	649	0.97
Bahamian	14	0.02
Barbadian	18	0.03
Belizean	23	0.03
British West Indian	20	0.03
Haitian	117	0.18
Jamaican	278	0.42
Trinidadian and Tobagonian	67	0.10
U.S. Virgin Islander	6	0.01
West Indian	106	0.16
White:	44,440	66.61
Not Hispanic (40,583)	41,904	62.81
Hispanic (2,072)	2,536	3.80
Yugoslavian	17	0.03

Kannapolis

Place Type: City
County: Cabarrus
Population: 36,910

Ancestry/Race	Number	%
African American/Black:	6,227	16.87
Not Hispanic (6,044)	6,179	16.74
Hispanic (28)	48	0.13
African, sub-Saharan:	300	0.82
African	218	0.59
Ghanian	21	0.06
Liberian	21	0.06
Nigerian	40	0.11
Alaska Native tribes, specified:	1	0.00
Aleut (1)	1	0.00
Am. Ind. or Alaska Nat., not spec.	95	0.26
American Indian tribes, specified:	129	0.35
Apache	1	0.00
Blackfeet (2)	7	0.02
Cherokee (25)	49	0.13
Chickasaw (2)	3	0.01
Chippewa (2)	2	0.01
Choctaw (1)	2	0.01
Creek (1)	10	0.03
Iroquois (1)	2	0.01
Latin American Indians (9)	14	0.04
Lumbee (17)	27	0.07
Navajo	1	0.00
Pima (1)	1	0.00
Potawatomi (2)	2	0.01
Puget Sound Salish (2)	2	0.01
Sioux (1)	1	0.00
All other tribes (1)	5	0.01
American Indian tribes, not spec.	15	0.04
Arab:	14	0.04
Arab/Arabic	8	0.02
Lebanese	6	0.02
Asian:	428	1.16
Chinese, ex. Taiwanese (24)	25	0.07
Filipino (16)	30	0.08
Hmong (29)	41	0.11
Indian (71)	80	0.22
Indonesian	1	0.00
Japanese (6)	12	0.03
Korean (24)	34	0.09
Laotian (104)	129	0.35
Pakistani	9	0.02
Taiwanese (1)	1	0.00
Thai (9)	18	0.05
Vietnamese (11)	13	0.04
Other Asian, specified (1)	4	0.01
Other Asian, not specified (17)	31	0.08
Australian	24	0.07
Austrian	15	0.04
Belgian	16	0.04
Brazilian	11	0.03
British	122	0.33
Celtic	7	0.02
Croatian	12	0.03
Czech	27	0.07
Czechoslovakian	9	0.02
Danish	37	0.10
Dutch	637	1.74
English	2,492	6.79
European	176	0.48
Finnish	10	0.03
French, except Basque	264	0.72
French Canadian	156	0.43
German	3,650	9.95
Greek	60	0.16
Hawaii Native/Pacific Islander:	28	0.08
Micronesian:	5	0.01
Guamanian/Chamorro	5	0.01
Polynesian: (3)	5	0.01
Native Hawaiian (3)	5	0.01
Other Pac. Isl., specified	3	0.01
Other Pac. Isl., not spec. (2)	15	0.04
Hispanic or Latino:	2,337	6.33
Central American:	105	0.28
Costa Rican	2	0.01
Guatemalan	27	0.07
Honduran	18	0.05
Nicaraguan	1	0.00
Panamanian	13	0.04
Salvadoran	42	0.11
Other Central American	2	0.01
Cuban	21	0.06
Dominican Republic	12	0.03
Mexican	1,845	5.00
Puerto Rican	105	0.28
South American:	28	0.08
Argentinean	2	0.01
Colombian	14	0.04
Ecuadorian	1	0.00
Peruvian	10	0.03
Venezuelan	1	0.00
Other Hispanic or Latino	221	0.60
Hungarian	24	0.07
Icelander	6	0.02
Iranian	9	0.02
Irish	2,495	6.80
Italian	623	1.70
Latvian	6	0.02
Lithuanian	27	0.07
Northern European	11	0.03
Norwegian	75	0.20
Pennsylvania German	15	0.04
Polish	235	0.64
Portuguese	11	0.03
Romanian	12	0.03
Russian	51	0.14
Scandinavian	5	0.01
Scotch-Irish	1,166	3.18
Scottish	644	1.75
Slavic	12	0.03
Swedish	115	0.31
Swiss	27	0.07
Ukrainian	8	0.02
United States or American	5,896	16.07
Welsh	89	0.24
West Indian, excl. Hispanic:	35	0.10
Jamaican	35	0.10
White:	29,033	78.66
Not Hispanic (27,748)	28,004	75.87
Hispanic (947)	1,029	2.79

Kernersville

Place Type: Town
County: Forsyth
Population: 17,126

Ancestry/Race	Number	%
African American/Black:	1,559	9.10
Not Hispanic (1,481)	1,535	8.96
Hispanic (16)	24	0.14
African, sub-Saharan:	57	0.34
African	10	0.06
Cape Verdean	6	0.04
Ghanian	9	0.05
Liberian	23	0.14
Other sub-Saharan African	9	0.05
Alaska Native tribes, specified:	1	0.01
Alaska Athabascan (1)	1	0.01
Am. Ind. or Alaska Nat., not spec.	34	0.20
American Indian tribes, specified:	70	0.41
Apache	1	0.01
Blackfeet (1)	1	0.01
Cherokee (7)	25	0.15
Chippewa (1)	1	0.01
Creek (1)	1	0.01
Latin American Indians (3)	3	0.02
Lumbee (16)	21	0.12
Navajo	2	0.01
Shoshone (1)	1	0.01
Sioux (4)	5	0.03
All other tribes (5)	9	0.05
American Indian tribes, not spec.	5	0.03
Arab:	39	0.23
Jordanian	16	0.10
Lebanese	7	0.04
Palestinian	16	0.10
Asian:	262	1.53
Cambodian (12)	12	0.07
Chinese, ex. Taiwanese (61)	66	0.39
Filipino (17)	31	0.18
Indian (36)	39	0.23
Indonesian (2)	2	0.01
Japanese (8)	20	0.12
Korean (11)	12	0.07
Laotian (10)	13	0.08
Malaysian (1)	2	0.01
Vietnamese (54)	57	0.33
Other Asian, not specified	8	0.05
Austrian	6	0.04
Belgian	8	0.05
British	72	0.43
Bulgarian	14	0.08
Canadian	55	0.33
Czech	29	0.17
Danish	8	0.05
Dutch	325	1.95
Eastern European	5	0.03
English	1,971	11.83
European	109	0.65
Finnish	6	0.04
French, except Basque	372	2.23
French Canadian	96	0.58
German	2,355	14.13
Greek	47	0.28
Hawaii Native/Pacific Islander:	18	0.11
Micronesian: (2)	4	0.02
Guamanian/Chamorro (2)	4	0.02
Polynesian: (7)	11	0.06
Native Hawaiian (7)	11	0.06
Other Pac. Isl., not spec.	3	0.02
Hispanic or Latino:	1,261	7.36
Central American:	65	0.38
Costa Rican	1	0.01
Guatemalan	4	0.02
Honduran	3	0.02

Notes: 1. Figures in the "Number" column do not add up to the total population due to: a) Ancestry/Race overlap — e.g. persons can report being both White and Irish, b) persons of Hispanic origin can report being any race, c) persons reporting two ancestries are counted in both categories. 2. Numbers in parentheses indicate the number of persons reporting this ancestry/race alone, not in combination with any other ancestry/race. 3. Refer to the Explanation of Data in the front of the book for more detailed information.

Salvadoran	56	0.33
Other Central American	1	0.01
Cuban	32	0.19
Dominican Republic	7	0.04
Mexican	981	5.73
Puerto Rican	57	0.33
South American:	26	0.15
Argentinean	3	0.02
Chilean	1	0.01
Colombian	7	0.04
Paraguayan	3	0.02
Peruvian	10	0.06
Venezuelan	2	0.01
Other Hispanic or Latino	93	0.54
Hungarian	49	0.29
Icelander	27	0.16
Iranian	20	0.12
Irish	1,488	8.93
Italian	539	3.23
Lithuanian	8	0.05
Northern European	21	0.13
Norwegian	73	0.44
Pennsylvania German	35	0.21
Polish	360	2.16
Portuguese	63	0.38
Russian	36	0.22
Scotch-Irish	456	2.74
Scottish	384	2.30
Serbian	9	0.05
Slavic	8	0.05
Slovak	25	0.15
Swedish	130	0.78
Swiss	20	0.12
Ukrainian	21	0.13
United States or American	2,573	15.44
Welsh	88	0.53
West Indian, excl. Hispanic:	26	0.16
Bahamian	11	0.07
Jamaican	7	0.04
U.S. Virgin Islander	2	0.01
West Indian	6	0.04
White:	14,580	85.13
Not Hispanic (13,941)	14,072	82.17
Hispanic (463)	508	2.97
Yugoslavian	10	0.06

Kinston

Place Type: City
County: Lenoir
Population: 23,688

Ancestry/Race	Number	%
African American/Black:	14,927	63.02
Not Hispanic (14,792)	14,875	62.80
Hispanic (45)	52	0.22
African, sub-Saharan:	179	0.75
African	142	0.60
Liberian	37	0.16
Am. Ind. or Alaska Nat., not spec.	47	0.20
American Indian tribes, specified:	40	0.17
Cherokee (12)	25	0.11
Choctaw (1)	5	0.02
Iroquois	1	0.00
Lumbee (2)	4	0.02
Sioux (2)	2	0.01
All other tribes	3	0.01
American Indian tribes, not spec.	6	0.03
Arab:	31	0.13
Lebanese	21	0.09
Palestinian	5	0.02
Syrian	5	0.02
Armenian	13	0.05
Asian:	173	0.73
Chinese, ex. Taiwanese (36)	42	0.18
Filipino (12)	21	0.09
Hmong (12)	12	0.05
Indian (32)	41	0.17
Japanese (2)	9	0.04
Korean (18)	25	0.11
Laotian (3)	3	0.01
Pakistani (3)	3	0.01
Taiwanese (1)	1	0.00
Thai (2)	2	0.01
Vietnamese (8)	10	0.04
Other Asian, specified	1	0.00
Other Asian, not specified (1)	3	0.01
Austrian	15	0.06
British	49	0.21
Czech	20	0.08
Danish	45	0.19
Dutch	62	0.26
English	1,703	7.15
European	21	0.09
Finnish	5	0.02
French, except Basque	232	0.97
German	608	2.55
Greek	4	0.02
Hawaii Native/Pacific Islander:	18	0.08
Micronesian: (1)	2	0.01
Guamanian/Chamorro (1)	2	0.01
Polynesian: (10)	15	0.06
Native Hawaiian	5	0.02
Samoan (10)	10	0.04
Other Pac. Isl., specified	1	0.00
Hispanic or Latino:	269	1.14
Central American:	20	0.08
Costa Rican	1	0.00
Guatemalan	2	0.01
Honduran	17	0.07
Cuban	4	0.02
Dominican Republic	1	0.00
Mexican	149	0.63
Puerto Rican	36	0.15
South American:	8	0.03
Argentinean	6	0.03
Colombian	2	0.01
Other Hispanic or Latino	51	0.22
Hungarian	16	0.07
Irish	722	3.03
Italian	117	0.49
Norwegian	14	0.06
Polish	47	0.20
Russian	24	0.10
Scotch-Irish	297	1.25
Scottish	284	1.19
Slovak	8	0.03
Swedish	34	0.14
Swiss	6	0.03
Ukrainian	26	0.11
United States or American	1,567	6.58
Welsh	83	0.35
West Indian, excl. Hispanic:	5	0.02
Jamaican	5	0.02
White:	8,465	35.74
Not Hispanic (8,290)	8,379	35.37
Hispanic (64)	86	0.36

Laurinburg

Place Type: City
County: Scotland
Population: 15,874

Ancestry/Race	Number	%
Acadian/Cajun	5	0.03
African American/Black:	6,901	43.47
Not Hispanic (6,806)	6,867	43.26
Hispanic (29)	34	0.21
African, sub-Saharan:	113	0.72
African	101	0.64
Other sub-Saharan African	12	0.08
Am. Ind. or Alaska Nat., not spec.	322	2.03
American Indian tribes, specified:	433	2.73
Apache (1)	3	0.02
Cherokee (59)	88	0.55
Chickasaw (1)	1	0.01
Iroquois (5)	5	0.03
Latin American Indians	3	0.02
Lumbee (294)	321	2.02
Menominee (4)	4	0.03
Potawatomi (3)	3	0.02
Seminole (2)	2	0.01
All other tribes (1)	3	0.02
American Indian tribes, not spec.	18	0.11
Arab:	50	0.32
Arab/Arabic	18	0.11
Lebanese	25	0.16
Moroccan	7	0.04
Asian:	137	0.86
Chinese, ex. Taiwanese (29)	32	0.20
Filipino (20)	23	0.14
Indian (37)	43	0.27
Japanese (4)	5	0.03
Korean (5)	9	0.06
Pakistani (13)	13	0.08
Vietnamese (10)	10	0.06
Other Asian, not specified	2	0.01
British	45	0.28
Canadian	32	0.20
Celtic	10	0.06
Czech	15	0.09
Dutch	111	0.70
English	926	5.86
European	44	0.28
French, except Basque	189	1.20
French Canadian	51	0.32
German	754	4.77
Greek	11	0.07
Hawaii Native/Pacific Islander:	6	0.04
Micronesian: (2)	2	0.01
Guamanian/Chamorro (2)	2	0.01
Polynesian: (3)	4	0.03
Native Hawaiian (3)	4	0.03
Hispanic or Latino:	168	1.06
Central American:	5	0.03
Honduran	3	0.02
Nicaraguan	2	0.01
Cuban	3	0.02
Mexican	64	0.40
Puerto Rican	31	0.20
South American:	9	0.06
Colombian	3	0.02
Peruvian	1	0.01
Venezuelan	5	0.03
Other Hispanic or Latino	56	0.35
Hungarian	9	0.06
Irish	567	3.59
Italian	265	1.68
Northern European	18	0.11
Norwegian	40	0.25
Pennsylvania German	10	0.06
Polish	106	0.67
Portuguese	43	0.27
Romanian	16	0.10
Russian	50	0.32
Scandinavian	14	0.09
Scotch-Irish	859	5.44
Scottish	632	4.00
Slavic	9	0.06
Slovak	23	0.15
Swedish	54	0.34
Swiss	9	0.06
Ukrainian	6	0.04
United States or American	1,438	9.11
Welsh	35	0.22
West Indian, excl. Hispanic:	18	0.11
Jamaican	10	0.06
Trinidadian and Tobagonian	8	0.05
White:	8,141	51.29
Not Hispanic (7,953)	8,067	50.82
Hispanic (70)	74	0.47

Lenoir

Place Type: City
County: Caldwell
Population: 16,793

Ancestry/Race	Number	%

Notes: 1. Figures in the "Number" column do not add up to the total population due to: a) Ancestry/Race overlap — e.g. persons can report being both White and Irish, b) persons of Hispanic origin can report being any race, c) persons reporting two ancestries are counted in both categories. 2. Numbers in parentheses indicate the number of persons reporting this ancestry/race alone, not in combination with any other ancestry/race. 3. Refer to the Explanation of Data in the front of the book for more detailed information.

Ancestry/Race	Number	%
African American/Black:	2,565	15.27
Not Hispanic (2,451)	2,543	15.14
Hispanic (19)	22	0.13
African, sub-Saharan:	101	0.61
African	100	0.60
Nigerian	1	0.01
Alaska Native tribes, specified:	1	0.01
Alaska Athabascan (1)	1	0.01
Am. Ind. or Alaska Nat., not spec.	25	0.15
American Indian tribes, specified:	52	0.31
Blackfeet (4)	8	0.05
Cherokee (13)	30	0.18
Iroquois (3)	3	0.02
Latin American Indians (4)	4	0.02
Lumbee (3)	4	0.02
Osage (1)	1	0.01
All other tribes (2)	2	0.01
American Indian tribes, not spec.	6	0.04
Asian:	141	0.84
Chinese, ex. Taiwanese (43)	47	0.28
Filipino (11)	17	0.10
Hmong (2)	3	0.02
Indian (16)	22	0.13
Japanese (4)	8	0.05
Korean (14)	14	0.08
Laotian (4)	4	0.02
Thai	2	0.01
Vietnamese (10)	12	0.07
Other Asian, not specified (7)	12	0.07
Austrian	8	0.05
British	35	0.21
Canadian	11	0.07
Czechoslovakian	4	0.02
Danish	9	0.05
Dutch	345	2.07
English	1,240	7.45
European	119	0.71
Finnish	15	0.09
French, except Basque	198	1.19
French Canadian	39	0.23
German	1,559	9.36
Greek	38	0.23
Hawaii Native/Pacific Islander:	21	0.13
Micronesian: (16)	17	0.10
Guamanian/Chamorro (16)	17	0.10
Polynesian: (3)	3	0.02
Native Hawaiian (3)	3	0.02
Other Pac. Isl., not spec.	1	0.01
Hispanic or Latino:	714	4.25
Central American:	154	0.92
Guatemalan	29	0.17
Honduran	101	0.60
Nicaraguan	1	0.01
Panamanian	2	0.01
Salvadoran	16	0.10
Other Central American	5	0.03
Cuban	30	0.18
Mexican	397	2.36
Puerto Rican	23	0.14
South American:	14	0.08
Colombian	13	0.08
Venezuelan	1	0.01
Other Hispanic or Latino	96	0.57
Hungarian	14	0.08
Irish	1,057	6.35
Italian	303	1.82
Lithuanian	9	0.05
Norwegian	46	0.28
Polish	96	0.58
Russian	21	0.13
Scotch-Irish	561	3.37
Scottish	369	2.22
Slovak	2	0.01
Swedish	37	0.22
Swiss	12	0.07
United States or American	3,826	22.97
Welsh	73	0.44
White:	13,745	81.85
Not Hispanic (13,305)	13,435	80.00
Hispanic (278)	310	1.85

Lexington

Place Type: City
County: Davidson
Population: 19,953

Ancestry/Race	Number	%
African American/Black:	6,138	30.76
Not Hispanic (5,941)	6,089	30.52
Hispanic (27)	49	0.25
African, sub-Saharan:	105	0.52
African	105	0.52
Alaska Native tribes, not specified	1	0.01
Am. Ind. or Alaska Nat., not spec.	56	0.28
American Indian tribes, specified:	143	0.72
Apache (3)	4	0.02
Blackfeet	3	0.02
Cherokee (11)	75	0.38
Chippewa (2)	2	0.01
Choctaw (2)	2	0.01
Comanche (1)	1	0.01
Iroquois (1)	1	0.01
Latin American Indians (23)	29	0.15
Lumbee (9)	17	0.09
Seminole	1	0.01
Sioux	1	0.01
All other tribes (3)	7	0.04
American Indian tribes, not spec.	9	0.05
Asian:	657	3.29
Cambodian (306)	386	1.93
Chinese, ex. Taiwanese (9)	24	0.12
Filipino (12)	17	0.09
Indian (81)	97	0.49
Japanese (11)	16	0.08
Korean (11)	21	0.11
Laotian (23)	23	0.12
Pakistani (15)	16	0.08
Taiwanese (3)	3	0.02
Thai (3)	12	0.06
Vietnamese (3)	6	0.03
Other Asian, not specified (16)	36	0.18
British	55	0.27
Canadian	39	0.19
Celtic	10	0.05
Czechoslovakian	8	0.04
Dutch	326	1.61
English	1,059	5.22
European	218	1.07
Finnish	9	0.04
French, except Basque	169	0.83
French Canadian	24	0.12
German	1,562	7.69
Greek	25	0.12
Guyanese	46	0.23
Hawaii Native/Pacific Islander:	15	0.08
Micronesian: (7)	7	0.04
Guamanian/Chamorro (7)	7	0.04
Polynesian: (1)	2	0.01
Native Hawaiian (1)	1	0.01
Samoan	1	0.01
Other Pac. Isl., not spec. (1)	6	0.03
Hispanic or Latino:	2,135	10.70
Central American:	77	0.39
Costa Rican	1	0.01
Guatemalan	11	0.06
Honduran	8	0.04
Nicaraguan	4	0.02
Salvadoran	51	0.26
Other Central American	2	0.01
Cuban	8	0.04
Dominican Republic	1	0.01
Mexican	1,785	8.95
Puerto Rican	40	0.20
South American:	23	0.12
Argentinean	3	0.02
Colombian	16	0.08
Peruvian	3	0.02
Other South American	1	0.01
Other Hispanic or Latino	201	1.01
Hungarian	17	0.08
Irish	765	3.77
Italian	168	0.83
Macedonian	10	0.05
Norwegian	46	0.23
Polish	59	0.29
Portuguese	21	0.10
Romanian	29	0.14
Russian	25	0.12
Scotch-Irish	282	1.39
Scottish	308	1.52
Slavic	29	0.14
Swedish	69	0.34
Swiss	6	0.03
United States or American	2,502	12.32
Welsh	23	0.11
West Indian, excl. Hispanic:	25	0.12
Jamaican	25	0.12
White:	12,019	60.24
Not Hispanic (10,936)	11,130	55.78
Hispanic (797)	889	4.46
Yugoslavian	20	0.10

Lumberton

Place Type: City
County: Robeson
Population: 20,795

Ancestry/Race	Number	%
African American/Black:	7,439	35.77
Not Hispanic (7,333)	7,399	35.58
Hispanic (36)	40	0.19
African, sub-Saharan:	199	0.97
African	170	0.83
Sudanese	29	0.14
Alaska Native tribes, specified:	2	0.01
Tlingit-Haida (2)	2	0.01
Am. Ind. or Alaska Nat., not spec.	897	4.31
American Indian tribes, specified:	1,755	8.44
Blackfeet	1	0.00
Cherokee (23)	34	0.16
Choctaw (1)	1	0.00
Creek (1)	1	0.00
Crow (1)	1	0.00
Iroquois (5)	7	0.03
Kiowa	1	0.00
Latin American Indians (2)	2	0.01
Lumbee (1,619)	1,686	8.11
Menominee (3)	3	0.01
Seminole	3	0.01
All other tribes (15)	15	0.07
American Indian tribes, not spec.	131	0.63
Arab:	21	0.10
Egyptian	15	0.07
Lebanese	6	0.03
Asian:	236	1.13
Chinese, ex. Taiwanese (22)	25	0.12
Filipino (24)	31	0.15
Indian (105)	121	0.58
Japanese (9)	11	0.05
Korean (8)	11	0.05
Laotian (2)	3	0.01
Pakistani (5)	5	0.02
Vietnamese (9)	15	0.07
Other Asian, not specified (3)	14	0.07
Austrian	5	0.02
Belgian	7	0.03
British	89	0.43
Canadian	5	0.02
Danish	14	0.07
Dutch	99	0.48
English	1,561	7.61
European	157	0.77
French, except Basque	129	0.63
French Canadian	70	0.34
German	648	3.16
Hawaii Native/Pacific Islander:	15	0.07
Micronesian: (2)	2	0.01
Guamanian/Chamorro (2)	2	0.01
Polynesian: (4)	8	0.04

Notes: 1. Figures in the "Number" column do not add up to the total population due to: a) Ancestry/Race overlap — e.g. persons can report being both White and Irish, b) persons of Hispanic origin can report being any race, c) persons reporting two ancestries are counted in both categories. 2. Numbers in parentheses indicate the number of persons reporting this ancestry/race alone, not in combination with any other ancestry/race. 3. Refer to the Explanation of Data in the front of the book for more detailed information.

Ancestry/Race	Number	%
Native Hawaiian (2)	4	0.02
Samoan (2)	4	0.02
Other Pac. Isl., not spec. (1)	5	0.02
Hispanic or Latino:	686	3.30
Central American:	48	0.23
Guatemalan	15	0.07
Honduran	6	0.03
Panamanian	5	0.02
Salvadoran	22	0.11
Cuban	14	0.07
Mexican	490	2.36
Puerto Rican	49	0.24
South American:	14	0.07
Chilean	2	0.01
Colombian	10	0.05
Ecuadorian	1	0.00
Peruvian	1	0.00
Other Hispanic or Latino	71	0.34
Hungarian	38	0.19
Irish	690	3.36
Italian	122	0.59
Lithuanian	16	0.08
Norwegian	21	0.10
Pennsylvania German	6	0.03
Polish	73	0.36
Russian	14	0.07
Scandinavian	8	0.04
Scotch-Irish	717	3.49
Scottish	473	2.30
Slovene	9	0.04
Swedish	116	0.57
Swiss	14	0.07
Ukrainian	5	0.02
United States or American	1,533	7.47
Welsh	94	0.46
West Indian, excl. Hispanic:	18	0.09
Jamaican	9	0.04
West Indian	9	0.04
White:	10,252	49.30
Not Hispanic (9,742)	9,861	47.42
Hispanic (352)	391	1.88

Masonboro

Place Type: Census Designated Place
County: New Hanover
Population: 11,812

Ancestry/Race	Number	%
African American/Black:	417	3.53
Not Hispanic (387)	407	3.45
Hispanic (9)	10	0.08
African, sub-Saharan:	101	0.84
African	45	0.38
Nigerian	38	0.32
Sierra Leonean	18	0.15
Alaska Native tribes, specified:	3	0.03
Eskimo (3)	3	0.03
Am. Ind. or Alaska Nat., not spec.	15	0.13
American Indian tribes, specified:	47	0.40
Apache (3)	3	0.03
Blackfeet	4	0.03
Cherokee (4)	24	0.20
Chippewa	1	0.01
Latin American Indians (1)	1	0.01
Lumbee (9)	9	0.08
All other tribes (4)	5	0.04
Arab:	108	0.90
Jordanian	12	0.10
Lebanese	28	0.23
Palestinian	49	0.41
Syrian	19	0.16
Armenian	6	0.05
Asian:	203	1.72
Cambodian	2	0.02
Chinese, ex. Taiwanese (52)	60	0.51
Filipino (7)	14	0.12
Indian (47)	54	0.46
Japanese (17)	29	0.25
Korean (16)	21	0.18
Sri Lankan (4)	4	0.03
Taiwanese (4)	7	0.06
Thai	2	0.02
Other Asian, specified	1	0.01
Other Asian, not specified (1)	9	0.08
Australian	14	0.12
Austrian	7	0.06
Belgian	8	0.07
British	91	0.76
Canadian	34	0.28
Celtic	33	0.28
Czech	26	0.22
Czechoslovakian	35	0.29
Danish	51	0.43
Dutch	153	1.28
English	2,259	18.89
European	187	1.56
Finnish	12	0.10
French, except Basque	560	4.68
French Canadian	102	0.85
German	2,143	17.92
Greek	37	0.31
Hawaii Native/Pacific Islander:	6	0.05
Micronesian: (1)	1	0.01
Guamanian/Chamorro (1)	1	0.01
Polynesian: (1)	4	0.03
Samoan (1)	4	0.03
Other Pac. Isl., specified	1	0.01
Hispanic or Latino:	138	1.17
Central American:	20	0.17
Guatemalan	1	0.01
Honduran	5	0.04
Panamanian	8	0.07
Salvadoran	6	0.05
Cuban	8	0.07
Dominican Republic	1	0.01
Mexican	57	0.48
Puerto Rican	15	0.13
South American:	19	0.16
Argentinean	5	0.04
Chilean	1	0.01
Colombian	4	0.03
Peruvian	1	0.01
Uruguayan	1	0.01
Venezuelan	2	0.02
Other South American	5	0.04
Other Hispanic or Latino	18	0.15
Hungarian	127	1.06
Irish	2,012	16.82
Israeli	9	0.08
Italian	755	6.31
Latvian	7	0.06
Lithuanian	17	0.14
Norwegian	44	0.37
Polish	347	2.90
Russian	70	0.59
Scandinavian	27	0.23
Scotch-Irish	725	6.06
Scottish	467	3.91
Slavic	8	0.07
Slovak	22	0.18
Swedish	199	1.66
Swiss	45	0.38
Ukrainian	62	0.52
United States or American	1,231	10.29
Welsh	97	0.81
White:	11,176	94.62
Not Hispanic (10,991)	11,088	93.87
Hispanic (67)	88	0.75

Matthews

Place Type: Town
County: Mecklenburg
Population: 22,127

Ancestry/Race	Number	%
African American/Black:	1,215	5.49
Not Hispanic (1,179)	1,209	5.46
Hispanic (2)	6	0.03
African, sub-Saharan:	163	0.73
African	148	0.66
Zairian	15	0.07
Am. Ind. or Alaska Nat., not spec.	25	0.11
Albanian	62	0.28
American Indian tribes, specified:	79	0.36
Apache	1	0.00
Cherokee (8)	14	0.06
Chippewa	2	0.01
Choctaw	3	0.01
Iroquois (1)	3	0.01
Latin American Indians (1)	2	0.01
Lumbee (38)	45	0.20
Osage (1)	1	0.00
All other tribes (4)	8	0.04
American Indian tribes, not spec.	6	0.03
Arab:	118	0.53
Jordanian	53	0.24
Lebanese	65	0.29
Armenian	27	0.12
Asian:	602	2.72
Cambodian	1	0.00
Chinese, ex. Taiwanese (105)	111	0.50
Filipino (44)	58	0.26
Indian (159)	161	0.73
Indonesian	4	0.02
Japanese (19)	28	0.13
Korean (85)	98	0.44
Laotian (7)	7	0.03
Pakistani (9)	10	0.05
Taiwanese (1)	1	0.00
Thai (5)	13	0.06
Vietnamese (70)	78	0.35
Other Asian, not specified (11)	32	0.14
Austrian	64	0.29
Belgian	31	0.14
British	266	1.19
Canadian	60	0.27
Croatian	14	0.06
Czech	110	0.49
Czechoslovakian	58	0.26
Danish	6	0.03
Dutch	495	2.21
Eastern European	7	0.03
English	3,456	15.42
European	310	1.38
Finnish	75	0.33
French, except Basque	583	2.60
French Canadian	295	1.32
German	3,983	17.77
Greek	123	0.55
Guyanese	59	0.26
Hawaii Native/Pacific Islander:	10	0.05
Micronesian: (2)	3	0.01
Guamanian/Chamorro (2)	3	0.01
Other Pac. Isl., not spec.	7	0.03
Hispanic or Latino:	553	2.50
Central American:	30	0.14
Guatemalan	3	0.01
Honduran	4	0.02
Nicaraguan	7	0.03
Panamanian	4	0.02
Salvadoran	12	0.05
Cuban	34	0.15
Dominican Republic	7	0.03
Mexican	219	0.99
Puerto Rican	63	0.28
South American:	88	0.40
Argentinean	6	0.03
Bolivian	5	0.02
Chilean	1	0.00
Colombian	45	0.20
Ecuadorian	9	0.04
Paraguayan	4	0.02
Peruvian	10	0.05
Venezuelan	7	0.03
Other South American	1	0.00
Other Hispanic or Latino	112	0.51
Hungarian	92	0.41
Iranian	43	0.19

Notes: 1. Figures in the "Number" column do not add up to the total population due to: a) Ancestry/Race overlap — e.g. persons can report being both White and Irish, b) persons of Hispanic origin can report being any race, c) persons reporting two ancestries are counted in both categories. 2. Numbers in parentheses indicate the number of persons reporting this ancestry/race alone, not in combination with any other ancestry/race. 3. Refer to the Explanation of Data in the front of the book for more detailed information.

Ancestry/Race	Number	%
Irish	2,734	12.20
Israeli	8	0.04
Italian	1,125	5.02
Lithuanian	15	0.07
Norwegian	172	0.77
Pennsylvania German	7	0.03
Polish	719	3.21
Portuguese	3	0.01
Romanian	32	0.14
Russian	258	1.15
Scandinavian	17	0.08
Scotch-Irish	1,201	5.36
Scottish	654	2.92
Slovak	66	0.29
Slovene	15	0.07
Swedish	315	1.41
Swiss	74	0.33
Turkish	7	0.03
Ukrainian	62	0.28
United States or American	2,336	10.42
Welsh	183	0.82
West Indian, excl. Hispanic:	154	0.69
British West Indian	66	0.29
Jamaican	29	0.13
West Indian	59	0.26
White:	20,158	91.10
Not Hispanic (19,625)	19,770	89.35
Hispanic (345)	388	1.75
Yugoslavian	7	0.03

Mint Hill

Place Type: Town
County: Mecklenburg
Population: 14,922

Ancestry/Race	Number	%
Acadian/Cajun	10	0.07
African American/Black:	907	6.08
Not Hispanic (852)	886	5.94
Hispanic (15)	21	0.14
Am. Ind. or Alaska Nat., not spec.	25	0.17
American Indian tribes, specified:	113	0.76
Blackfeet (4)	6	0.04
Cherokee (6)	21	0.14
Chippewa	1	0.01
Iroquois (3)	4	0.03
Latin American Indians (1)	1	0.01
Lumbee (56)	60	0.40
Ottawa (1)	1	0.01
Pueblo (1)	1	0.01
Seminole	1	0.01
Sioux (2)	5	0.03
All other tribes (6)	12	0.08
American Indian tribes, not spec.	5	0.03
Arab:	22	0.15
Lebanese	11	0.07
Moroccan	3	0.02
Palestinian	8	0.05
Asian:	232	1.55
Chinese, ex. Taiwanese (25)	29	0.19
Filipino (14)	27	0.18
Hmong (15)	22	0.15
Indian (21)	21	0.14
Indonesian (1)	1	0.01
Japanese (6)	13	0.09
Korean (58)	70	0.47
Laotian (6)	6	0.04
Malaysian	1	0.01
Pakistani (3)	3	0.02
Thai (3)	3	0.02
Vietnamese (14)	20	0.13
Other Asian, not specified (5)	16	0.11
Austrian	13	0.09
Belgian	29	0.20
Brazilian	5	0.03
British	152	1.03
Canadian	22	0.15
Croatian	8	0.05
Czech	55	0.37
Czechoslovakian	19	0.13
Danish	6	0.04
Dutch	222	1.51
Eastern European	36	0.24
English	2,075	14.11
European	98	0.67
Finnish	17	0.12
French, except Basque	404	2.75
French Canadian	53	0.36
German	2,070	14.08
Greek	57	0.39
Guyanese	29	0.20
Hawaii Native/Pacific Islander:	13	0.09
Micronesian: (1)	3	0.02
Guamanian/Chamorro (1)	3	0.02
Polynesian: (2)	3	0.02
Native Hawaiian (2)	3	0.02
Other Pac. Isl., not spec. (1)	7	0.05
Hispanic or Latino:	472	3.16
Central American:	44	0.29
Costa Rican	5	0.03
Guatemalan	3	0.02
Honduran	9	0.06
Nicaraguan	3	0.02
Panamanian	9	0.06
Salvadoran	13	0.09
Other Central American	2	0.01
Cuban	8	0.05
Dominican Republic	7	0.05
Mexican	199	1.33
Puerto Rican	64	0.43
South American:	63	0.42
Argentinean	10	0.07
Colombian	33	0.22
Ecuadorian	2	0.01
Peruvian	9	0.06
Venezuelan	9	0.06
Other Hispanic or Latino	87	0.58
Hungarian	41	0.28
Irish	1,621	11.02
Italian	620	4.22
Lithuanian	16	0.11
Northern European	9	0.06
Norwegian	100	0.68
Pennsylvania German	7	0.05
Polish	303	2.06
Romanian	39	0.27
Russian	109	0.74
Scotch-Irish	1,249	8.49
Scottish	468	3.18
Slavic	12	0.08
Slovak	62	0.42
Swedish	100	0.68
Swiss	21	0.14
Ukrainian	151	1.03
United States or American	1,864	12.68
Welsh	176	1.20
West Indian, excl. Hispanic:	20	0.14
Jamaican	20	0.14
White:	13,580	91.01
Not Hispanic (13,187)	13,293	89.08
Hispanic (259)	287	1.92

Monroe

Place Type: City
County: Union
Population: 26,228

Ancestry/Race	Number	%
African American/Black:	7,408	28.24
Not Hispanic (7,155)	7,247	27.63
Hispanic (132)	161	0.61
African, sub-Saharan:	216	0.83
African	216	0.83
Am. Ind. or Alaska Nat., not spec.	55	0.21
American Indian tribes, specified:	120	0.46
Apache (1)	4	0.02
Cherokee (9)	37	0.14
Choctaw	1	0.00
Iroquois (4)	4	0.02
Latin American Indians (26)	35	0.13
Lumbee (20)	25	0.10
Potawatomi	1	0.00
Shoshone	1	0.00
Sioux (2)	3	0.01
All other tribes (6)	9	0.03
American Indian tribes, not spec.	9	0.03
Arab:	54	0.21
Arab/Arabic	9	0.03
Lebanese	45	0.17
Asian:	223	0.85
Chinese, ex. Taiwanese (31)	38	0.14
Filipino (20)	29	0.11
Hmong (9)	9	0.03
Indian (63)	72	0.27
Japanese (6)	16	0.06
Korean (17)	26	0.10
Vietnamese (20)	22	0.08
Other Asian, not specified (2)	11	0.04
Austrian	34	0.13
British	71	0.27
Bulgarian	11	0.04
Canadian	29	0.11
Czech	33	0.13
Dutch	205	0.79
English	2,000	7.71
European	36	0.14
French, except Basque	264	1.02
French Canadian	35	0.13
German	1,827	7.04
Greek	42	0.16
Hawaii Native/Pacific Islander:	16	0.06
Micronesian: (4)	4	0.02
Guamanian/Chamorro (4)	4	0.02
Polynesian: (2)	7	0.03
Native Hawaiian (2)	6	0.02
Samoan	1	0.00
Other Pac. Isl., not spec. (3)	5	0.02
Hispanic or Latino:	5,611	21.39
Central American:	176	0.67
Costa Rican	17	0.06
Guatemalan	81	0.31
Honduran	24	0.09
Nicaraguan	2	0.01
Panamanian	7	0.03
Salvadoran	35	0.13
Other Central American	10	0.04
Cuban	18	0.07
Dominican Republic	2	0.01
Mexican	4,741	18.08
Puerto Rican	122	0.47
South American:	74	0.28
Argentinean	1	0.00
Colombian	48	0.18
Ecuadorian	5	0.02
Peruvian	17	0.06
Uruguayan	1	0.00
Venezuelan	2	0.01
Other Hispanic or Latino	478	1.82
Hungarian	28	0.11
Irish	1,085	4.18
Israeli	15	0.06
Italian	509	1.96
Lithuanian	67	0.26
Norwegian	50	0.19
Polish	174	0.67
Portuguese	7	0.03
Romanian	9	0.03
Russian	27	0.10
Scandinavian	20	0.08
Scotch-Irish	788	3.04
Scottish	247	0.95
Slovak	7	0.03
Swedish	71	0.27
Swiss	33	0.13
Ukrainian	36	0.14
United States or American	2,692	10.37
Welsh	98	0.38
West Indian, excl. Hispanic:	106	0.41

Notes: 1. Figures in the "Number" column do not add up to the total population due to: a) Ancestry/Race overlap — e.g. persons can report being both White and Irish, b) persons of Hispanic origin can report being any race, c) persons reporting two ancestries are counted in both categories. 2. Numbers in parentheses indicate the number of persons reporting this ancestry/race alone, not in combination with any other ancestry/race. 3. Refer to the Explanation of Data in the front of the book for more detailed information.

Bahamian	14	0.05
Bermudan	8	0.03
Jamaican	33	0.13
Trinidadian and Tobagonian	9	0.03
West Indian	42	0.16
White:	16,112	61.43
Not Hispanic (12,998)	13,136	50.08
Hispanic (2,771)	2,976	11.35
Yugoslavian	12	0.05

Mooresville

Place Type: Town
County: Iredell
Population: 18,823

Ancestry/Race	Number	%
African American/Black:	2,758	14.65
Not Hispanic (2,653)	2,732	14.51
Hispanic (26)	26	0.14
African, sub-Saharan:	44	0.23
African	44	0.23
Alaska Native tribes, specified:	1	0.01
Aleut	1	0.01
Am. Ind. or Alaska Nat., not spec.	29	0.15
American Indian tribes, specified:	89	0.47
Apache (5)	7	0.04
Blackfeet (1)	1	0.01
Cherokee (16)	43	0.23
Choctaw (2)	2	0.01
Iroquois (1)	1	0.01
Latin American Indians (5)	7	0.04
Lumbee (11)	12	0.06
Osage	1	0.01
Sioux (2)	2	0.01
All other tribes (6)	13	0.07
American Indian tribes, not spec.	11	0.06
Arab:	62	0.32
Lebanese	55	0.29
Syrian	7	0.04
Asian:	363	1.93
Chinese, ex. Taiwanese (89)	96	0.51
Filipino (32)	46	0.24
Indian (58)	64	0.34
Japanese (58)	70	0.37
Korean (22)	27	0.14
Laotian (13)	13	0.07
Thai (4)	4	0.02
Vietnamese (24)	25	0.13
Other Asian, not specified (11)	18	0.10
Austrian	6	0.03
Basque	23	0.12
British	82	0.43
Bulgarian	8	0.04
Canadian	82	0.43
Croatian	11	0.06
Czech	17	0.09
Czechoslovakian	9	0.05
Danish	30	0.16
Dutch	234	1.22
Eastern European	9	0.05
English	1,622	8.49
European	152	0.80
Finnish	6	0.03
French, except Basque	454	2.38
French Canadian	123	0.64
German	2,887	15.11
Greek	34	0.18
Guyanese	19	0.10
Hawaii Native/Pacific Islander:	16	0.09
Micronesian: (1)	2	0.01
Guamanian/Chamorro (1)	2	0.01
Polynesian: (2)	8	0.04
Native Hawaiian (2)	7	0.04
Samoan	1	0.01
Other Pac. Isl., not spec. (1)	6	0.03
Hispanic or Latino:	480	2.55
Central American:	33	0.18
Costa Rican	2	0.01
Guatemalan	1	0.01
Honduran	4	0.02
Nicaraguan	1	0.01
Panamanian	3	0.02
Salvadoran	22	0.12
Cuban	32	0.17
Dominican Republic	3	0.02
Mexican	269	1.43
Puerto Rican	61	0.32
South American:	14	0.07
Colombian	4	0.02
Ecuadorian	3	0.02
Peruvian	3	0.02
Venezuelan	1	0.01
Other South American	3	0.02
Other Hispanic or Latino	68	0.36
Hungarian	68	0.36
Irish	1,945	10.18
Italian	792	4.15
Lithuanian	13	0.07
Maltese	9	0.05
Norwegian	148	0.77
Pennsylvania German	5	0.03
Polish	343	1.80
Portuguese	21	0.11
Romanian	16	0.08
Russian	57	0.30
Scandinavian	8	0.04
Scotch-Irish	811	4.24
Scottish	375	1.96
Serbian	19	0.10
Slavic	22	0.12
Swedish	137	0.72
Swiss	38	0.20
Ukrainian	8	0.04
United States or American	2,616	13.69
Welsh	122	0.64
West Indian, excl. Hispanic:	24	0.13
West Indian	24	0.13
White:	15,509	82.39
Not Hispanic (15,129)	15,268	81.11
Hispanic (219)	241	1.28

Morganton

Place Type: City
County: Burke
Population: 17,310

Ancestry/Race	Number	%
African American/Black:	2,299	13.28
Not Hispanic (2,198)	2,274	13.14
Hispanic (10)	25	0.14
African, sub-Saharan:	178	1.04
African	168	0.98
Ethiopian	10	0.06
Am. Ind. or Alaska Nat., not spec.	37	0.21
American Indian tribes, specified:	144	0.83
Apache	1	0.01
Blackfeet	1	0.01
Cherokee (14)	35	0.20
Chippewa (2)	3	0.02
Iroquois (2)	2	0.01
Latin American Indians (47)	90	0.52
Lumbee (4)	4	0.02
Ottawa (1)	1	0.01
Sioux (3)	4	0.02
All other tribes (3)	3	0.02
American Indian tribes, not spec.	10	0.06
Arab:	7	0.04
Lebanese	7	0.04
Asian:	406	2.35
Bangladeshi (4)	5	0.03
Cambodian (1)	1	0.01
Chinese, ex. Taiwanese (77)	87	0.50
Filipino (15)	18	0.10
Hmong (82)	98	0.57
Indian (54)	68	0.39
Indonesian (2)	2	0.01
Japanese (4)	8	0.05
Korean (12)	13	0.08
Laotian (36)	43	0.25
Malaysian (6)	6	0.03
Pakistani (3)	3	0.02
Thai (4)	4	0.02
Vietnamese (22)	22	0.13
Other Asian, not specified (9)	28	0.16
Austrian	6	0.04
Belgian	5	0.03
British	56	0.33
Canadian	9	0.05
Czechoslovakian	12	0.07
Dutch	308	1.80
English	1,657	9.70
European	125	0.73
Finnish	18	0.11
French, except Basque	263	1.54
French Canadian	56	0.33
German	1,661	9.72
Greek	46	0.27
Hawaii Native/Pacific Islander:	154	0.89
Micronesian: (127)	133	0.77
Guamanian/Chamorro (127)	133	0.77
Polynesian: (9)	11	0.06
Native Hawaiian (5)	7	0.04
Samoan (4)	4	0.02
Other Pac. Isl., not spec. (5)	10	0.06
Hispanic or Latino:	1,931	11.16
Central American:	1,052	6.08
Costa Rican	19	0.11
Guatemalan	945	5.46
Honduran	35	0.20
Nicaraguan	20	0.12
Salvadoran	17	0.10
Other Central American	16	0.09
Cuban	27	0.16
Dominican Republic	2	0.01
Mexican	484	2.80
Puerto Rican	30	0.17
South American:	19	0.11
Bolivian	2	0.01
Chilean	2	0.01
Colombian	13	0.08
Peruvian	1	0.01
Uruguayan	1	0.01
Other Hispanic or Latino	317	1.83
Hungarian	19	0.11
Irish	1,246	7.29
Italian	286	1.67
Lithuanian	7	0.04
New Zealander	9	0.05
Northern European	17	0.10
Norwegian	51	0.30
Polish	209	1.22
Russian	46	0.27
Scandinavian	18	0.11
Scotch-Irish	707	4.14
Scottish	236	1.38
Serbian	3	0.02
Swedish	68	0.40
Ukrainian	47	0.27
United States or American	2,375	13.90
Welsh	18	0.11
White:	13,275	76.69
Not Hispanic (12,570)	12,687	73.29
Hispanic (528)	588	3.40
Yugoslavian	3	0.02

New Bern

Place Type: City
County: Craven
Population: 23,128

Ancestry/Race	Number	%
Acadian/Cajun	7	0.03
African American/Black:	9,462	40.91
Not Hispanic (9,260)	9,378	40.55
Hispanic (65)	84	0.36
African, sub-Saharan:	270	1.18
African	259	1.13

Notes: 1. Figures in the "Number" column do not add up to the total population due to: a) Ancestry/Race overlap — e.g. persons can report being both White and Irish, b) persons of Hispanic origin can report being any race, c) persons reporting two ancestries are counted in both categories. 2. Numbers in parentheses indicate the number of persons reporting this ancestry/race alone, not in combination with any other ancestry/race. 3. Refer to the Explanation of Data in the front of the book for more detailed information.

Ghanian	11	0.05
Alaska Native tribes, specified:	2	0.01
Eskimo	2	0.01
Alaska Native tribes, not specified	1	0.00
Am. Ind. or Alaska Nat., not spec.	50	0.22
Albanian	8	0.03
American Indian tribes, specified:	102	0.44
Apache (1)	2	0.01
Blackfeet	4	0.02
Cherokee (12)	35	0.15
Chippewa (1)	2	0.01
Choctaw	4	0.02
Creek (3)	3	0.01
Delaware	1	0.00
Iroquois (7)	11	0.05
Latin American Indians (2)	5	0.02
Lumbee (9)	19	0.08
Navajo	2	0.01
Seminole (1)	1	0.00
All other tribes (11)	13	0.06
American Indian tribes, not spec.	10	0.04
Arab:	11	0.05
Lebanese	11	0.05
Asian:	221	0.96
Cambodian	5	0.02
Chinese, ex. Taiwanese (40)	51	0.22
Filipino (27)	44	0.19
Indian (16)	26	0.11
Indonesian	2	0.01
Japanese (7)	14	0.06
Korean (21)	26	0.11
Pakistani (4)	5	0.02
Thai (1)	1	0.00
Vietnamese (16)	17	0.07
Other Asian, specified (10)	11	0.05
Other Asian, not specified (4)	19	0.08
Australian	9	0.04
Austrian	50	0.22
British	45	0.20
Canadian	14	0.06
Celtic	8	0.03
Croatian	25	0.11
Czech	4	0.02
Czechoslovakian	31	0.14
Danish	65	0.28
Dutch	156	0.68
English	2,482	10.83
European	42	0.18
Finnish	7	0.03
French, except Basque	433	1.89
French Canadian	112	0.49
German	1,941	8.47
Greek	28	0.12
Hawaii Native/Pacific Islander:	30	0.13
Micronesian: (1)	3	0.01
Guamanian/Chamorro (1)	3	0.01
Polynesian: (7)	21	0.09
Native Hawaiian (4)	17	0.07
Samoan (3)	4	0.02
Other Pac. Isl., specified	1	0.00
Other Pac. Isl., not spec. (1)	5	0.02
Hispanic or Latino:	692	2.99
Central American:	45	0.19
Guatemalan	10	0.04
Honduran	21	0.09
Panamanian	6	0.03
Salvadoran	7	0.03
Other Central American	1	0.00
Cuban	11	0.05
Dominican Republic	1	0.00
Mexican	314	1.36
Puerto Rican	125	0.54
South American:	61	0.26
Argentinean	1	0.00
Chilean	1	0.00
Colombian	49	0.21
Ecuadorian	1	0.00
Paraguayan	1	0.00
Peruvian	6	0.03
Venezuelan	2	0.01
Other Hispanic or Latino	135	0.58
Hungarian	41	0.18
Irish	1,947	8.50
Italian	417	1.82
Latvian	10	0.04
Lithuanian	7	0.03
Norwegian	137	0.60
Polish	361	1.58
Portuguese	70	0.31
Russian	38	0.17
Scandinavian	6	0.03
Scotch-Irish	330	1.44
Scottish	588	2.57
Swedish	123	0.54
Swiss	128	0.56
Ukrainian	35	0.15
United States or American	2,312	10.09
Welsh	131	0.57
West Indian, excl. Hispanic:	38	0.17
Jamaican	25	0.11
West Indian	13	0.06
White:	13,152	56.87
Not Hispanic (12,685)	12,861	55.61
Hispanic (258)	291	1.26

Newton

Place Type: City
County: Catawba
Population: 12,560

Ancestry/Race	Number	%
African American/Black:	1,625	12.94
Not Hispanic (1,540)	1,605	12.78
Hispanic (9)	20	0.16
African, sub-Saharan:	35	0.28
African	35	0.28
Alaska Native tribes, specified:	4	0.03
Aleut (4)	4	0.03
Am. Ind. or Alaska Nat., not spec.	51	0.41
Alsatian	2	0.02
American Indian tribes, specified:	39	0.31
Apache (1)	4	0.03
Blackfeet	3	0.02
Cherokee (9)	15	0.12
Chippewa (6)	6	0.05
Latin American Indians (3)	3	0.02
Lumbee (2)	2	0.02
Sioux (2)	3	0.02
All other tribes (1)	3	0.02
American Indian tribes, not spec.	4	0.03
Arab:	54	0.42
Lebanese	12	0.09
Syrian	42	0.33
Asian:	487	3.88
Chinese, ex. Taiwanese (23)	27	0.21
Filipino (7)	13	0.10
Hmong (191)	206	1.64
Indian (14)	15	0.12
Japanese (4)	7	0.06
Korean (18)	20	0.16
Laotian (131)	148	1.18
Thai (3)	3	0.02
Vietnamese (16)	21	0.17
Other Asian, specified	2	0.02
Other Asian, not specified (16)	25	0.20
British	60	0.47
Canadian	7	0.06
Celtic	10	0.08
Croatian	7	0.06
Dutch	138	1.08
English	689	5.42
European	57	0.45
French, except Basque	150	1.18
French Canadian	16	0.13
German	2,058	16.18
Greek	20	0.16
Hawaii Native/Pacific Islander:	19	0.15
Polynesian: (2)	5	0.04
Native Hawaiian	2	0.02
Samoan (2)	3	0.02
Other Pac. Isl., specified	2	0.02
Other Pac. Isl., not spec. (2)	12	0.10
Hispanic or Latino:	1,196	9.52
Central American:	131	1.04
Costa Rican	36	0.29
Guatemalan	11	0.09
Honduran	32	0.25
Nicaraguan	13	0.10
Panamanian	4	0.03
Salvadoran	35	0.28
Cuban	13	0.10
Dominican Republic	1	0.01
Mexican	784	6.24
Puerto Rican	35	0.28
South American:	67	0.53
Argentinean	1	0.01
Chilean	3	0.02
Colombian	63	0.50
Other Hispanic or Latino	165	1.31
Irish	881	6.93
Italian	151	1.19
New Zealander	7	0.06
Norwegian	5	0.04
Polish	51	0.40
Portuguese	1	0.01
Romanian	7	0.06
Scotch-Irish	255	2.00
Scottish	298	2.34
Swedish	107	0.84
Swiss	9	0.07
Ukrainian	6	0.05
United States or American	1,987	15.62
Welsh	33	0.26
White:	9,889	78.73
Not Hispanic (9,220)	9,306	74.09
Hispanic (524)	583	4.64

Piney Green

Place Type: Census Designated Place
County: Onslow
Population: 11,658

Ancestry/Race	Number	%
Acadian/Cajun	22	0.19
African American/Black:	3,053	26.19
Not Hispanic (2,806)	2,965	25.43
Hispanic (57)	88	0.75
African, sub-Saharan:	81	0.69
African	64	0.55
Cape Verdean	17	0.15
Alaska Native tribes, specified:	3	0.03
Alaska Athabascan	1	0.01
Tlingit-Haida (2)	2	0.02
Alaska Native tribes, not specified	2	0.02
Am. Ind. or Alaska Nat., not spec.	47	0.40
American Indian tribes, specified:	126	1.08
Apache	1	0.01
Blackfeet	6	0.05
Cherokee (24)	62	0.53
Chickasaw (2)	4	0.03
Chippewa (3)	3	0.03
Choctaw (1)	5	0.04
Cree	1	0.01
Delaware	1	0.01
Iroquois (7)	7	0.06
Latin American Indians (8)	15	0.13
Lumbee (4)	7	0.06
Navajo (3)	3	0.03
Sioux (1)	1	0.01
All other tribes (5)	10	0.09
American Indian tribes, not spec.	12	0.10
Arab:	5	0.04
Palestinian	5	0.04
Asian:	458	3.93
Chinese, ex. Taiwanese (18)	24	0.21
Filipino (116)	191	1.64
Indian (14)	17	0.15
Indonesian (2)	2	0.02

Notes: 1. Figures in the "Number" column do not add up to the total population due to: a) Ancestry/Race overlap — e.g. persons can report being both White and Irish, b) persons of Hispanic origin can report being any race, c) persons reporting two ancestries are counted in both categories. 2. Numbers in parentheses indicate the number of persons reporting this ancestry/race alone, not in combination with any other ancestry/race. 3. Refer to the Explanation of Data in the front of the book for more detailed information.

Japanese (92)	135	1.16
Korean (17)	26	0.22
Laotian (1)	2	0.02
Malaysian	1	0.01
Taiwanese (3)	4	0.03
Thai (1)	4	0.03
Vietnamese (18)	23	0.20
Other Asian, specified (4)	16	0.14
Other Asian, not specified (5)	13	0.11
Austrian	13	0.11
British	9	0.08
Canadian	6	0.05
Czech	26	0.22
Czechoslovakian	18	0.15
Danish	6	0.05
Dutch	217	1.85
English	933	7.96
European	11	0.09
Finnish	14	0.12
French, except Basque	486	4.15
French Canadian	88	0.75
German	1,651	14.09
Greek	76	0.65
Guyanese	11	0.09
Hawaii Native/Pacific Islander:	40	0.34
Micronesian: (4)	5	0.04
Guamanian/Chamorro (4)	5	0.04
Polynesian: (22)	30	0.26
Native Hawaiian (12)	20	0.17
Samoan (10)	10	0.09
Other Pac. Isl., not spec. (3)	5	0.04
Hispanic or Latino:	887	7.61
Central American:	72	0.62
Costa Rican	11	0.09
Guatemalan	9	0.08
Honduran	9	0.08
Panamanian	41	0.35
Salvadoran	2	0.02
Cuban	26	0.22
Dominican Republic	13	0.11
Mexican	303	2.60
Puerto Rican	301	2.58
South American:	30	0.26
Argentinean	1	0.01
Bolivian	6	0.05
Chilean	1	0.01
Colombian	11	0.09
Ecuadorian	1	0.01
Peruvian	7	0.06
Venezuelan	1	0.01
Other South American	2	0.02
Other Hispanic or Latino	142	1.22
Hungarian	24	0.20
Icelander	7	0.06
Irish	1,332	11.36
Italian	500	4.27
Lithuanian	10	0.09
Norwegian	106	0.90
Polish	246	2.10
Portuguese	58	0.49
Romanian	13	0.11
Scandinavian	15	0.13
Scotch-Irish	207	1.77
Scottish	245	2.09
Slovak	39	0.33
Swedish	82	0.70
Swiss	7	0.06
Turkish	6	0.05
Ukrainian	25	0.21
United States or American	967	8.25
Welsh	29	0.25
West Indian, excl. Hispanic:	34	0.29
Barbadian	8	0.07
Jamaican	15	0.13
Trinidadian and Tobagonian	11	0.09
White:	7,912	67.87
Not Hispanic (7,204)	7,482	64.18
Hispanic (343)	430	3.69

Raleigh

Place Type: City
County: Wake
Population: 276,093

Ancestry/Race	Number	%
Acadian/Cajun	25	0.01
Afghan	152	0.05
African American/Black:	78,844	28.56
Not Hispanic (75,931)	77,667	28.13
Hispanic (825)	1,177	0.43
African, sub-Saharan:	4,922	1.78
African	2,969	1.07
Cape Verdean	7	0.00
Ethiopian	107	0.04
Ghanian	115	0.04
Kenyan	137	0.05
Liberian	68	0.02
Nigerian	749	0.27
Senegalese	30	0.01
Sierra Leonean	72	0.03
Somalian	160	0.06
South African	55	0.02
Sudanese	62	0.02
Ugandan	20	0.01
Zairian	49	0.02
Other sub-Saharan African	322	0.12
Alaska Native tribes, specified:	5	0.00
Alaska Athabascan	1	0.00
Eskimo (1)	2	0.00
Tlingit-Haida (2)	2	0.00
Am. Ind. or Alaska Nat., not spec.	807	0.29
Albanian	8	0.00
Alsatian	9	0.00
American Indian tribes, specified:	1,221	0.44
Apache (1)	10	0.00
Blackfeet (4)	42	0.02
Cherokee (123)	469	0.17
Cheyenne (1)	2	0.00
Chickasaw (1)	6	0.00
Chippewa (7)	19	0.01
Choctaw (7)	27	0.01
Comanche (1)	2	0.00
Cree (2)	4	0.00
Creek (6)	14	0.01
Crow (1)	1	0.00
Delaware (1)	1	0.00
Iroquois (11)	41	0.01
Kiowa (2)	4	0.00
Latin American Indians (98)	144	0.05
Lumbee (188)	232	0.08
Navajo (3)	10	0.00
Osage (3)	7	0.00
Potawatomi	3	0.00
Pueblo (3)	6	0.00
Seminole (2)	11	0.00
Sioux (14)	30	0.01
Ute (1)	1	0.00
Yaqui (2)	5	0.00
All other tribes (65)	130	0.05
American Indian tribes, not spec.	108	0.04
Arab:	2,577	0.93
Arab/Arabic	523	0.19
Egyptian	348	0.13
Iraqi	33	0.01
Jordanian	119	0.04
Lebanese	711	0.26
Moroccan	112	0.04
Palestinian	404	0.15
Syrian	81	0.03
Other Arab	246	0.09
Armenian	54	0.02
Asian:	10,747	3.89
Bangladeshi (61)	73	0.03
Cambodian (15)	21	0.01
Chinese, ex. Taiwanese (1,899)	2,102	0.76
Filipino (602)	840	0.30
Hmong (15)	16	0.01
Indian (2,605)	2,813	1.02
Indonesian (35)	42	0.02
Japanese (332)	494	0.18
Korean (1,240)	1,367	0.50
Laotian (128)	171	0.06
Malaysian (14)	21	0.01
Pakistani (169)	206	0.07
Sri Lankan (50)	50	0.02
Taiwanese (136)	158	0.06
Thai (125)	158	0.06
Vietnamese (1,542)	1,627	0.59
Other Asian, specified (36)	68	0.02
Other Asian, not specified (195)	520	0.19
Australian	120	0.04
Austrian	505	0.18
Basque	22	0.01
Belgian	132	0.05
Brazilian	149	0.05
British	2,494	0.90
Bulgarian	72	0.03
Canadian	836	0.30
Celtic	30	0.01
Croatian	174	0.06
Cypriot	16	0.01
Czech	686	0.25
Czechoslovakian	410	0.15
Danish	903	0.33
Dutch	2,599	0.94
Eastern European	251	0.09
English	33,044	11.95
Estonian	22	0.01
European	3,466	1.25
Finnish	446	0.16
French, except Basque	5,891	2.13
French Canadian	1,390	0.50
German	27,737	10.03
German Russian	7	0.00
Greek	942	0.34
Guyanese	34	0.01
Hawaii Native/Pacific Islander:	302	0.11
Melanesian:	2	0.00
Fijian	2	0.00
Micronesian: (30)	53	0.02
Guamanian/Chamorro (26)	45	0.02
Other Micronesian (4)	8	0.00
Polynesian: (49)	122	0.04
Native Hawaiian (27)	88	0.03
Samoan (16)	24	0.01
Other Polynesian (6)	10	0.00
Other Pac. Isl., specified	18	0.01
Other Pac. Isl., not spec. (39)	107	0.04
Hispanic or Latino:	19,308	6.99
Central American:	1,926	0.70
Costa Rican	44	0.02
Guatemalan	282	0.10
Honduran	476	0.17
Nicaraguan	52	0.02
Panamanian	114	0.04
Salvadoran	837	0.30
Other Central American	121	0.04
Cuban	399	0.14
Dominican Republic	318	0.12
Mexican	12,227	4.43
Puerto Rican	1,306	0.47
South American:	883	0.32
Argentinean	64	0.02
Bolivian	26	0.01
Chilean	49	0.02
Colombian	322	0.12
Ecuadorian	76	0.03
Paraguayan	4	0.00
Peruvian	180	0.07
Uruguayan	7	0.00
Venezuelan	111	0.04
Other South American	44	0.02
Other Hispanic or Latino	2,249	0.81
Hungarian	737	0.27
Icelander	31	0.01
Iranian	376	0.14
Irish	23,117	8.36
Israeli	89	0.03

Notes: 1. Figures in the "Number" column do not add up to the total population due to: a) Ancestry/Race overlap — e.g. persons can report being both White and Irish, b) persons of Hispanic origin can report being any race, c) persons reporting two ancestries are counted in both categories. 2. Numbers in parentheses indicate the number of persons reporting this ancestry/race alone, not in combination with any other ancestry/race. 3. Refer to the Explanation of Data in the front of the book for more detailed information.

Italian	9,816	3.55
Latvian	74	0.03
Lithuanian	405	0.15
Luxemburger	27	0.01
Macedonian	16	0.01
Maltese	23	0.01
New Zealander	15	0.01
Northern European	198	0.07
Norwegian	1,864	0.67
Pennsylvania German	72	0.03
Polish	5,127	1.85
Portuguese	421	0.15
Romanian	182	0.07
Russian	2,135	0.77
Scandinavian	250	0.09
Scotch-Irish	9,482	3.43
Scottish	7,915	2.86
Serbian	56	0.02
Slavic	93	0.03
Slovak	419	0.15
Slovene	123	0.04
Swedish	2,207	0.80
Swiss	620	0.22
Turkish	416	0.15
Ukrainian	718	0.26
United States or American	17,282	6.25
Welsh	2,052	0.74
West Indian, excl. Hispanic:	1,381	0.50
Bahamian	133	0.05
Barbadian	48	0.02
Belizean	42	0.02
Bermudan	24	0.01
British West Indian	60	0.02
Haitian	116	0.04
Jamaican	439	0.16
Trinidadian and Tobagonian	62	0.02
U.S. Virgin Islander	16	0.01
West Indian	441	0.16
White:	178,649	64.71
Not Hispanic (166,386)	169,263	61.31
Hispanic (8,400)	9,386	3.40
Yugoslavian	130	0.05

Reidsville

Place Type: City
County: Rockingham
Population: 14,485

Ancestry/Race	Number	%
African American/Black:	5,819	40.17
Not Hispanic (5,707)	5,794	40.00
Hispanic (18)	25	0.17
African, sub-Saharan:	84	0.59
African	84	0.59
Alaska Native tribes, specified:	1	0.01
Tlingit-Haida (1)	1	0.01
Am. Ind. or Alaska Nat., not spec.	30	0.21
American Indian tribes, specified:	41	0.28
Blackfeet	1	0.01
Cherokee (4)	23	0.16
Choctaw	3	0.02
Iroquois	1	0.01
Lumbee (4)	6	0.04
All other tribes (6)	7	0.05
American Indian tribes, not spec.	5	0.03
Arab:	8	0.06
Arab/Arabic	8	0.06
Armenian	10	0.07
Asian:	112	0.77
Chinese, ex. Taiwanese (14)	21	0.14
Filipino (5)	8	0.06
Indian (43)	48	0.33
Japanese (6)	6	0.04
Korean (5)	5	0.03
Pakistani (7)	7	0.05
Thai (4)	5	0.03
Vietnamese (9)	9	0.06
Other Asian, specified	1	0.01
Other Asian, not specified	2	0.01
British	21	0.15
Canadian	10	0.07
Czech	21	0.15
Danish	9	0.06
Dutch	80	0.56
English	1,348	9.41
European	154	1.08
French, except Basque	133	0.93
French Canadian	11	0.08
German	680	4.75
Hawaii Native/Pacific Islander:	14	0.10
Polynesian: (9)	11	0.08
Native Hawaiian (5)	7	0.05
Samoan (4)	4	0.03
Other Pac. Isl., specified	1	0.01
Other Pac. Isl., not spec.	2	0.01
Hispanic or Latino:	381	2.63
Central American:	7	0.05
Guatemalan	6	0.04
Salvadoran	1	0.01
Cuban	8	0.06
Mexican	299	2.06
Puerto Rican	13	0.09
South American:	2	0.01
Colombian	1	0.01
Peruvian	1	0.01
Other Hispanic or Latino	52	0.36
Irish	991	6.92
Italian	129	0.90
Lithuanian	7	0.05
Norwegian	41	0.29
Pennsylvania German	7	0.05
Polish	49	0.34
Portuguese	6	0.04
Romanian	9	0.06
Russian	34	0.24
Scotch-Irish	392	2.74
Scottish	206	1.44
Swedish	8	0.06
Swiss	22	0.15
United States or American	1,882	13.14
Welsh	82	0.57
West Indian, excl. Hispanic:	86	0.60
Dutch West Indian	31	0.22
Jamaican	6	0.04
West Indian	49	0.34
White:	8,399	57.98
Not Hispanic (8,121)	8,221	56.76
Hispanic (139)	178	1.23

Roanoke Rapids

Place Type: City
County: Halifax
Population: 16,957

Ancestry/Race	Number	%
African American/Black:	4,269	25.18
Not Hispanic (4,203)	4,254	25.09
Hispanic (15)	15	0.09
African, sub-Saharan:	219	1.29
African	142	0.83
Kenyan	21	0.12
Nigerian	56	0.33
Am. Ind. or Alaska Nat., not spec.	59	0.35
American Indian tribes, specified:	83	0.49
Blackfeet	1	0.01
Cherokee (6)	17	0.10
Iroquois (1)	2	0.01
Lumbee (8)	8	0.05
Pueblo	1	0.01
Seminole	1	0.01
Sioux (2)	2	0.01
All other tribes (44)	51	0.30
American Indian tribes, not spec.	1	0.01
Asian:	253	1.49
Chinese, ex. Taiwanese (56)	56	0.33
Filipino (21)	23	0.14
Indian (90)	91	0.54
Japanese (5)	5	0.03
Korean (21)	22	0.13
Pakistani (4)	4	0.02
Thai	1	0.01
Vietnamese (43)	48	0.28
Other Asian, specified	2	0.01
Other Asian, not specified	1	0.01
Austrian	26	0.15
Belgian	8	0.05
British	15	0.09
Canadian	52	0.31
Dutch	97	0.57
Eastern European	33	0.19
English	2,364	13.88
European	141	0.83
French, except Basque	291	1.71
German	890	5.23
Greek	13	0.08
Hawaii Native/Pacific Islander:	8	0.05
Micronesian: (1)	1	0.01
Guamanian/Chamorro (1)	1	0.01
Polynesian: (4)	4	0.02
Native Hawaiian (4)	4	0.02
Other Pac. Isl., specified	2	0.01
Other Pac. Isl., not spec.	1	0.01
Hispanic or Latino:	179	1.06
Central American:	21	0.12
Costa Rican	2	0.01
Guatemalan	4	0.02
Honduran	6	0.04
Salvadoran	9	0.05
Cuban	1	0.01
Dominican Republic	1	0.01
Mexican	79	0.47
Puerto Rican	29	0.17
South American:	20	0.12
Argentinean	1	0.01
Chilean	1	0.01
Colombian	5	0.03
Paraguayan	1	0.01
Peruvian	7	0.04
Venezuelan	1	0.01
Other South American	4	0.02
Other Hispanic or Latino	28	0.17
Hungarian	11	0.06
Irish	993	5.83
Italian	176	1.03
Macedonian	11	0.06
Norwegian	18	0.11
Pennsylvania German	8	0.05
Polish	84	0.49
Russian	28	0.16
Scotch-Irish	313	1.84
Scottish	209	1.23
Slovak	25	0.15
Swedish	39	0.23
Swiss	45	0.26
Ukrainian	7	0.04
United States or American	2,353	13.82
Welsh	52	0.31
West Indian, excl. Hispanic:	16	0.09
Jamaican	16	0.09
White:	12,288	72.47
Not Hispanic (12,135)	12,195	71.92
Hispanic (79)	93	0.55

Rocky Mount

Place Type: City
County: Nash
Population: 55,893

Ancestry/Race	Number	%
Afghan	11	0.02
African American/Black:	31,594	56.53
Not Hispanic (31,175)	31,437	56.24
Hispanic (139)	157	0.28
African, sub-Saharan:	464	0.82
African	415	0.74
Ghanian	7	0.01
South African	32	0.06

Notes: 1. Figures in the "Number" column do not add up to the total population due to: a) Ancestry/Race overlap — e.g. persons can report being both White and Irish, b) persons of Hispanic origin can report being any race, c) persons reporting two ancestries are counted in both categories. 2. Numbers in parentheses indicate the number of persons reporting this ancestry/race alone, not in combination with any other ancestry/race. 3. Refer to the Explanation of Data in the front of the book for more detailed information.

Ancestry/Race	Number	%
Other sub-Saharan African	10	0.02
Alaska Native tribes, specified:	1	0.00
Alaska Athabascan	1	0.00
Alaska Native tribes, not specified	1	0.00
Am. Ind. or Alaska Nat., not spec.	137	0.25
American Indian tribes, specified:	193	0.35
Apache (1)	1	0.00
Blackfeet	7	0.01
Cherokee (30)	63	0.11
Chippewa (1)	1	0.00
Cree (4)	4	0.01
Iroquois (2)	7	0.01
Latin American Indians (2)	7	0.01
Lumbee (1)	6	0.01
Navajo	1	0.00
Potawatomi	1	0.00
Pueblo (1)	3	0.01
Seminole (1)	4	0.01
Sioux (1)	4	0.01
All other tribes (68)	86	0.15
American Indian tribes, not spec.	26	0.05
Arab:	349	0.62
Arab/Arabic	238	0.42
Egyptian	7	0.01
Lebanese	57	0.10
Moroccan	19	0.03
Palestinian	11	0.02
Syrian	17	0.03
Armenian	6	0.01
Asian:	541	0.97
Chinese, ex. Taiwanese (79)	91	0.16
Filipino (38)	57	0.10
Hmong (10)	10	0.02
Indian (115)	130	0.23
Indonesian (2)	2	0.00
Japanese (20)	38	0.07
Korean (36)	43	0.08
Malaysian (1)	1	0.00
Pakistani (7)	7	0.01
Sri Lankan (2)	2	0.00
Thai (5)	15	0.03
Vietnamese (57)	66	0.12
Other Asian, specified	9	0.02
Other Asian, not specified (15)	70	0.13
Australian	21	0.04
Austrian	11	0.02
Belgian	40	0.07
British	222	0.39
Canadian	47	0.08
Czech	11	0.02
Danish	21	0.04
Dutch	164	0.29
English	4,831	8.59
European	358	0.64
French, except Basque	448	0.80
French Canadian	83	0.15
German	1,651	2.94
Greek	47	0.08
Hawaii Native/Pacific Islander:	37	0.07
Micronesian: (2)	9	0.02
Guamanian/Chamorro (2)	7	0.01
Other Micronesian	2	0.00
Polynesian: (8)	15	0.03
Native Hawaiian (4)	9	0.02
Samoan (4)	6	0.01
Other Pac. Isl., specified	7	0.01
Other Pac. Isl., not spec. (2)	6	0.01
Hispanic or Latino:	1,033	1.85
Central American:	51	0.09
Costa Rican	1	0.00
Guatemalan	6	0.01
Honduran	20	0.04
Nicaraguan	1	0.00
Panamanian	11	0.02
Salvadoran	6	0.01
Other Central American	6	0.01
Cuban	32	0.06
Dominican Republic	7	0.01
Mexican	590	1.06
Puerto Rican	77	0.14
South American:	30	0.05
Argentinean	4	0.01
Bolivian	1	0.00
Chilean	5	0.01
Colombian	13	0.02
Ecuadorian	3	0.01
Paraguayan	2	0.00
Peruvian	1	0.00
Other South American	1	0.00
Other Hispanic or Latino	246	0.44
Hungarian	58	0.10
Iranian	7	0.01
Irish	1,928	3.43
Italian	681	1.21
Lithuanian	11	0.02
Norwegian	123	0.22
Pennsylvania German	7	0.01
Polish	240	0.43
Portuguese	34	0.06
Romanian	34	0.06
Russian	23	0.04
Scandinavian	48	0.09
Scotch-Irish	836	1.49
Scottish	493	0.88
Slovak	49	0.09
Swedish	153	0.27
Swiss	18	0.03
United States or American	4,745	8.44
Welsh	180	0.32
West Indian, excl. Hispanic:	82	0.15
Haitian	22	0.04
Jamaican	50	0.09
Trinidadian and Tobagonian	10	0.02
White:	23,302	41.69
Not Hispanic (22,548)	22,909	40.99
Hispanic (326)	393	0.70

Salisbury

Place Type: City
County: Rowan
Population: 26,462

Ancestry/Race	Number	%
African American/Black:	10,120	38.24
Not Hispanic (9,874)	10,045	37.96
Hispanic (66)	75	0.28
African, sub-Saharan:	476	1.78
African	389	1.46
Liberian	87	0.33
Alaska Native tribes, not specified	1	0.00
Am. Ind. or Alaska Nat., not spec.	89	0.34
American Indian tribes, specified:	79	0.30
Apache	1	0.00
Blackfeet	5	0.02
Cherokee (9)	33	0.12
Chickasaw (1)	1	0.00
Choctaw (1)	2	0.01
Creek	1	0.00
Iroquois	1	0.00
Latin American Indians (2)	4	0.02
Lumbee (12)	21	0.08
Pueblo (1)	1	0.00
Sioux (1)	4	0.02
All other tribes (2)	5	0.02
American Indian tribes, not spec.	10	0.04
Arab:	55	0.21
Egyptian	23	0.09
Lebanese	32	0.12
Armenian	8	0.03
Asian:	466	1.76
Cambodian (1)	4	0.02
Chinese, ex. Taiwanese (22)	27	0.10
Filipino (20)	39	0.15
Hmong (20)	23	0.09
Indian (141)	155	0.59
Indonesian (3)	3	0.01
Japanese (6)	9	0.03
Korean (14)	19	0.07
Laotian (24)	30	0.11
Pakistani (1)	1	0.00
Sri Lankan (1)	3	0.01
Taiwanese (2)	2	0.01
Thai (1)	3	0.01
Vietnamese (95)	100	0.38
Other Asian, not specified (10)	48	0.18
Australian	51	0.19
Austrian	12	0.04
Belgian	8	0.03
British	89	0.33
Canadian	7	0.03
Celtic	3	0.01
Danish	16	0.06
Dutch	281	1.05
English	1,951	7.31
Estonian	28	0.10
European	219	0.82
French, except Basque	443	1.66
French Canadian	56	0.21
German	2,551	9.56
Greek	37	0.14
Hawaii Native/Pacific Islander:	35	0.13
Micronesian: (1)	2	0.01
Guamanian/Chamorro (1)	2	0.01
Polynesian: (3)	10	0.04
Native Hawaiian (1)	8	0.03
Samoan (2)	2	0.01
Other Pac. Isl., not spec. (11)	23	0.09
Hispanic or Latino:	1,138	4.30
Central American:	226	0.85
Costa Rican	1	0.00
Guatemalan	8	0.03
Honduran	160	0.60
Nicaraguan	6	0.02
Panamanian	6	0.02
Salvadoran	38	0.14
Other Central American	7	0.03
Cuban	29	0.11
Dominican Republic	1	0.00
Mexican	640	2.42
Puerto Rican	77	0.29
South American:	25	0.09
Argentinean	1	0.00
Colombian	2	0.01
Ecuadorian	1	0.00
Peruvian	14	0.05
Venezuelan	2	0.01
Other South American	5	0.02
Other Hispanic or Latino	140	0.53
Hungarian	28	0.10
Irish	995	3.73
Italian	351	1.32
New Zealander	11	0.04
Northern European	19	0.07
Norwegian	110	0.41
Pennsylvania German	8	0.03
Polish	145	0.54
Portuguese	29	0.11
Romanian	11	0.04
Russian	29	0.11
Scandinavian	39	0.15
Scotch-Irish	702	2.63
Scottish	419	1.57
Slovak	42	0.16
Swedish	101	0.38
Swiss	81	0.30
Ukrainian	6	0.02
United States or American	3,390	12.71
Welsh	130	0.49
West Indian, excl. Hispanic:	101	0.38
Bahamian	11	0.04
Haitian	10	0.04
Jamaican	59	0.22
U.S. Virgin Islander	14	0.05
West Indian	7	0.03
White:	15,458	58.42
Not Hispanic (14,650)	14,894	56.28
Hispanic (513)	564	2.13
Yugoslavian	36	0.13

Notes: 1. Figures in the "Number" column do not add up to the total population due to: a) Ancestry/Race overlap — e.g. persons can report being both White and Irish, b) persons of Hispanic origin can report being any race, c) persons reporting two ancestries are counted in both categories. 2. Numbers in parentheses indicate the number of persons reporting this ancestry/race alone, not in combination with any other ancestry/race. 3. Refer to the Explanation of Data in the front of the book for more detailed information.

Sanford

Place Type: City
County: Lee
Population: 23,220

Ancestry/Race	Number	%
Acadian/Cajun	10	0.04
African American/Black:	6,895	29.69
Not Hispanic (6,741)	6,827	29.40
Hispanic (38)	68	0.29
African, sub-Saharan:	341	1.44
African	270	1.14
Nigerian	41	0.17
Sierra Leonean	30	0.13
Alaska Native tribes, specified:	1	0.00
Eskimo	1	0.00
Am. Ind. or Alaska Nat., not spec.	52	0.22
American Indian tribes, specified:	132	0.57
Apache	1	0.00
Cherokee (21)	46	0.20
Chickasaw (3)	4	0.02
Choctaw (2)	6	0.03
Creek (3)	3	0.01
Iroquois (1)	7	0.03
Latin American Indians (25)	27	0.12
Lumbee (28)	34	0.15
Seminole	1	0.00
Sioux (1)	1	0.00
All other tribes (1)	2	0.01
American Indian tribes, not spec.	12	0.05
Arab:	45	0.19
Iraqi	8	0.03
Lebanese	23	0.10
Syrian	6	0.03
Other Arab	8	0.03
Asian:	295	1.27
Cambodian	1	0.00
Chinese, ex. Taiwanese (29)	32	0.14
Filipino (69)	83	0.36
Indian (51)	52	0.22
Japanese (7)	10	0.04
Korean (11)	17	0.07
Pakistani (2)	2	0.01
Taiwanese (1)	1	0.00
Thai (2)	3	0.01
Vietnamese (69)	72	0.31
Other Asian, specified	1	0.00
Other Asian, not specified (5)	21	0.09
Austrian	8	0.03
British	35	0.15
Canadian	42	0.18
Czechoslovakian	12	0.05
Danish	25	0.11
Dutch	179	0.76
Eastern European	12	0.05
English	1,758	7.44
European	110	0.47
Finnish	11	0.05
French, except Basque	243	1.03
French Canadian	158	0.67
German	1,311	5.55
Greek	7	0.03
Hawaii Native/Pacific Islander:	26	0.11
Melanesian: (1)	1	0.00
Fijian (1)	1	0.00
Micronesian:	2	0.01
Guamanian/Chamorro	2	0.01
Polynesian: (6)	14	0.06
Native Hawaiian (5)	11	0.05
Samoan (1)	3	0.01
Other Pac. Isl., specified	1	0.00
Other Pac. Isl., not spec. (1)	8	0.03
Hispanic or Latino:	4,419	19.03
Central American:	709	3.05
Costa Rican	15	0.06
Guatemalan	158	0.68
Honduran	144	0.62
Nicaraguan	29	0.12
Panamanian	12	0.05
Salvadoran	329	1.42
Other Central American	22	0.09
Cuban	7	0.03
Dominican Republic	12	0.05
Mexican	2,965	12.77
Puerto Rican	174	0.75
South American:	49	0.21
Argentinean	1	0.00
Bolivian	3	0.01
Chilean	3	0.01
Colombian	16	0.07
Ecuadorian	3	0.01
Peruvian	9	0.04
Uruguayan	1	0.00
Venezuelan	12	0.05
Other South American	1	0.00
Other Hispanic or Latino	503	2.17
Hungarian	36	0.15
Irish	1,028	4.35
Italian	385	1.63
Lithuanian	8	0.03
Norwegian	46	0.19
Polish	45	0.19
Portuguese	28	0.12
Russian	39	0.17
Scotch-Irish	842	3.56
Scottish	717	3.03
Serbian	6	0.03
Slovak	8	0.03
Swedish	118	0.50
Swiss	27	0.11
United States or American	2,879	12.18
Welsh	42	0.18
West Indian, excl. Hispanic:	19	0.08
Bermudan	9	0.04
Jamaican	10	0.04
White:	13,219	56.93
Not Hispanic (11,511)	11,639	50.12
Hispanic (1,462)	1,580	6.80

Shelby

Place Type: City
County: Cleveland
Population: 19,477

Ancestry/Race	Number	%
African American/Black:	8,055	41.36
Not Hispanic (7,922)	7,987	41.01
Hispanic (58)	68	0.35
African, sub-Saharan:	119	0.61
African	119	0.61
Am. Ind. or Alaska Nat., not spec.	20	0.10
American Indian tribes, specified:	29	0.15
Blackfeet	2	0.01
Cherokee (2)	12	0.06
Latin American Indians (2)	2	0.01
Lumbee (3)	3	0.02
Navajo (4)	4	0.02
Seminole	1	0.01
All other tribes (2)	5	0.03
American Indian tribes, not spec.	5	0.03
Arab:	19	0.10
Syrian	19	0.10
Asian:	141	0.72
Cambodian (2)	2	0.01
Chinese, ex. Taiwanese (18)	23	0.12
Filipino (16)	18	0.09
Indian (47)	54	0.28
Japanese (6)	6	0.03
Korean (5)	10	0.05
Pakistani (5)	5	0.03
Thai (1)	6	0.03
Vietnamese (8)	8	0.04
Other Asian, specified	5	0.03
Other Asian, not specified (1)	4	0.02
Austrian	10	0.05
British	63	0.32
Canadian	40	0.21
Celtic	9	0.05
Croatian	24	0.12
Czech	40	0.21
Danish	17	0.09
Dutch	207	1.07
English	1,328	6.85
European	74	0.38
French, except Basque	269	1.39
French Canadian	12	0.06
German	1,846	9.52
Greek	52	0.27
Hawaii Native/Pacific Islander:	12	0.06
Polynesian: (3)	6	0.03
Native Hawaiian	3	0.02
Samoan (2)	2	0.01
Other Polynesian (1)	1	0.01
Other Pac. Isl., specified	5	0.03
Other Pac. Isl., not spec.	1	0.01
Hispanic or Latino:	304	1.56
Central American:	9	0.05
Guatemalan	1	0.01
Panamanian	7	0.04
Salvadoran	1	0.01
Cuban	23	0.12
Dominican Republic	5	0.03
Mexican	178	0.91
Puerto Rican	22	0.11
South American:	5	0.03
Argentinean	1	0.01
Colombian	3	0.02
Peruvian	1	0.01
Other Hispanic or Latino	62	0.32
Hungarian	5	0.03
Irish	819	4.22
Italian	166	0.86
Latvian	7	0.04
Norwegian	36	0.19
Polish	120	0.62
Romanian	4	0.02
Russian	5	0.03
Scotch-Irish	597	3.08
Scottish	389	2.01
Slavic	6	0.03
Slovak	91	0.47
Swedish	61	0.31
Swiss	25	0.13
United States or American	2,511	12.95
Welsh	25	0.13
West Indian, excl. Hispanic:	11	0.06
Trinidadian and Tobagonian	11	0.06
White:	11,194	57.47
Not Hispanic (10,985)	11,078	56.88
Hispanic (94)	116	0.60

Smithfield

Place Type: Town
County: Johnston
Population: 11,510

Ancestry/Race	Number	%
African American/Black:	3,601	31.29
Not Hispanic (3,554)	3,585	31.15
Hispanic (13)	16	0.14
African, sub-Saharan:	84	0.74
African	78	0.68
Nigerian	6	0.05
Alaska Native tribes, specified:	1	0.01
Eskimo	1	0.01
Am. Ind. or Alaska Nat., not spec.	33	0.29
Albanian	7	0.06
American Indian tribes, specified:	44	0.38
Apache	2	0.02
Cherokee (6)	15	0.13
Chippewa (1)	1	0.01
Cree	2	0.02
Iroquois	2	0.02
Latin American Indians (4)	10	0.09
Lumbee (10)	11	0.10
Sioux (1)	1	0.01
American Indian tribes, not spec.	9	0.08

Notes: 1. Figures in the "Number" column do not add up to the total population due to: a) Ancestry/Race overlap — e.g. persons can report being both White and Irish, b) persons of Hispanic origin can report being any race, c) persons reporting two ancestries are counted in both categories. 2. Numbers in parentheses indicate the number of persons reporting this ancestry/race alone, not in combination with any other ancestry/race. 3. Refer to the Explanation of Data in the front of the book for more detailed information.

Ancestry/Race	Number	%
Arab:	53	0.46
Arab/Arabic	27	0.24
Lebanese	26	0.23
Asian:	91	0.79
Chinese, ex. Taiwanese (8)	8	0.07
Filipino (1)	10	0.09
Indian (44)	45	0.39
Japanese (1)	3	0.03
Korean (6)	6	0.05
Laotian (2)	2	0.02
Thai (3)	6	0.05
Vietnamese (6)	6	0.05
Other Asian, not specified (1)	5	0.04
Brazilian	10	0.09
British	21	0.18
Danish	14	0.12
Dutch	35	0.31
English	1,239	10.85
European	113	0.99
French, except Basque	206	1.80
German	389	3.41
Greek	13	0.11
Hawaii Native/Pacific Islander:	10	0.09
Polynesian: (2)	10	0.09
Native Hawaiian (1)	9	0.08
Samoan (1)	1	0.01
Hispanic or Latino:	1,140	9.90
Central American:	149	1.29
Guatemalan	18	0.16
Honduran	106	0.92
Nicaraguan	1	0.01
Panamanian	11	0.10
Salvadoran	7	0.06
Other Central American	6	0.05
Cuban	8	0.07
Mexican	790	6.86
Puerto Rican	58	0.50
South American:	21	0.18
Argentinean	5	0.04
Colombian	6	0.05
Ecuadorian	1	0.01
Peruvian	5	0.04
Venezuelan	4	0.03
Other Hispanic or Latino	114	0.99
Hungarian	17	0.15
Irish	547	4.79
Italian	173	1.52
Norwegian	43	0.38
Polish	10	0.09
Portuguese	20	0.18
Russian	11	0.10
Scotch-Irish	146	1.28
Scottish	192	1.68
Swedish	31	0.27
Swiss	5	0.04
United States or American	1,580	13.84
Welsh	33	0.29
White:	7,324	63.63
Not Hispanic (6,611)	6,683	58.06
Hispanic (601)	641	5.57
Yugoslavian	11	0.10

Southern Pines

Place Type: Town
County: Moore
Population: 10,918

Ancestry/Race	Number	%
African American/Black:	2,940	26.93
Not Hispanic (2,888)	2,919	26.74
Hispanic (13)	21	0.19
African, sub-Saharan:	33	0.29
African	26	0.23
South African	7	0.06
Am. Ind. or Alaska Nat., not spec.	30	0.27
American Indian tribes, specified:	43	0.39
Apache	3	0.03
Blackfeet	2	0.02
Cherokee (2)	20	0.18
Latin American Indians	1	0.01
Lumbee (13)	16	0.15
Sioux	1	0.01
American Indian tribes, not spec.	3	0.03
Arab:	20	0.18
Arab/Arabic	12	0.11
Lebanese	8	0.07
Armenian	7	0.06
Asian:	91	0.83
Chinese, ex. Taiwanese (20)	21	0.19
Filipino (2)	9	0.08
Hmong (3)	4	0.04
Indian (19)	20	0.18
Japanese (8)	11	0.10
Korean (6)	8	0.07
Laotian	1	0.01
Thai (1)	4	0.04
Vietnamese (4)	8	0.07
Other Asian, specified	1	0.01
Other Asian, not specified (2)	4	0.04
Belgian	12	0.11
Brazilian	7	0.06
British	96	0.86
Canadian	50	0.45
Celtic	11	0.10
Czech	6	0.05
Danish	14	0.12
Dutch	127	1.13
English	1,500	13.38
European	114	1.02
French, except Basque	270	2.41
French Canadian	40	0.36
German	1,165	10.40
Greek	27	0.24
Hawaii Native/Pacific Islander:	10	0.09
Micronesian: (4)	6	0.05
Guamanian/Chamorro (4)	6	0.05
Polynesian: (4)	4	0.04
Native Hawaiian (3)	3	0.03
Samoan (1)	1	0.01
Hispanic or Latino:	223	2.04
Central American:	17	0.16
Costa Rican	7	0.06
Guatemalan	2	0.02
Panamanian	3	0.03
Salvadoran	5	0.05
Cuban	2	0.02
Mexican	144	1.32
Puerto Rican	22	0.20
South American:	11	0.10
Chilean	2	0.02
Colombian	7	0.06
Ecuadorian	1	0.01
Peruvian	1	0.01
Other Hispanic or Latino	27	0.25
Hungarian	20	0.18
Irish	844	7.53
Italian	400	3.57
Lithuanian	30	0.27
Norwegian	31	0.28
Polish	245	2.19
Russian	41	0.37
Scandinavian	20	0.18
Scotch-Irish	481	4.29
Scottish	579	5.17
Slavic	8	0.07
Slovene	7	0.06
Swedish	114	1.02
Swiss	48	0.43
Ukrainian	7	0.06
United States or American	964	8.60
Welsh	102	0.91
West Indian, excl. Hispanic:	44	0.39
Jamaican	44	0.39
White:	7,795	71.40
Not Hispanic (7,618)	7,670	70.25
Hispanic (111)	125	1.14
Yugoslavian	4	0.04

Statesville

Place Type: City
County: Iredell
Population: 23,320

Ancestry/Race	Number	%
African American/Black:	7,617	32.66
Not Hispanic (7,375)	7,526	32.27
Hispanic (58)	91	0.39
African, sub-Saharan:	494	2.15
African	439	1.91
Nigerian	29	0.13
Sudanese	26	0.11
Am. Ind. or Alaska Nat., not spec.	53	0.23
American Indian tribes, specified:	52	0.22
Blackfeet	4	0.02
Cherokee (3)	26	0.11
Choctaw	3	0.01
Comanche (1)	1	0.00
Iroquois (2)	3	0.01
Latin American Indians (1)	1	0.00
Lumbee (4)	4	0.02
Ottawa (1)	1	0.00
Sioux	3	0.01
All other tribes (1)	6	0.03
American Indian tribes, not spec.	11	0.05
Armenian	7	0.03
Asian:	671	2.88
Chinese, ex. Taiwanese (42)	46	0.20
Filipino (7)	9	0.04
Hmong (269)	275	1.18
Indian (110)	119	0.51
Indonesian (5)	5	0.02
Japanese (67)	72	0.31
Korean (41)	44	0.19
Laotian (24)	28	0.12
Pakistani (3)	3	0.01
Sri Lankan (7)	7	0.03
Thai (7)	7	0.03
Vietnamese (35)	36	0.15
Other Asian, specified	2	0.01
Other Asian, not specified (9)	18	0.08
Austrian	15	0.07
Belgian	10	0.04
British	45	0.20
Bulgarian	8	0.03
Canadian	34	0.15
Dutch	200	0.87
English	1,738	7.55
European	624	2.71
Finnish	5	0.02
French, except Basque	238	1.03
French Canadian	49	0.21
German	1,988	8.64
Greek	14	0.06
Hawaii Native/Pacific Islander:	10	0.04
Micronesian: (2)	2	0.01
Guamanian/Chamorro (2)	2	0.01
Polynesian: (1)	2	0.01
Native Hawaiian (1)	2	0.01
Other Pac. Isl., specified	1	0.00
Other Pac. Isl., not spec. (1)	5	0.02
Hispanic or Latino:	1,658	7.11
Central American:	67	0.29
Costa Rican	3	0.01
Guatemalan	3	0.01
Honduran	16	0.07
Nicaraguan	9	0.04
Panamanian	8	0.03
Salvadoran	27	0.12
Other Central American	1	0.00
Cuban	24	0.10
Dominican Republic	3	0.01
Mexican	982	4.21
Puerto Rican	76	0.33
South American:	258	1.11
Chilean	28	0.12
Colombian	210	0.90
Ecuadorian	12	0.05

Notes: 1. Figures in the "Number" column do not add up to the total population due to: a) Ancestry/Race overlap — e.g. persons can report being both White and Irish, b) persons of Hispanic origin can report being any race, c) persons reporting two ancestries are counted in both categories. 2. Numbers in parentheses indicate the number of persons reporting this ancestry/race alone, not in combination with any other ancestry/race. 3. Refer to the Explanation of Data in the front of the book for more detailed information.

Peruvian	1	0.00
Venezuelan	4	0.02
Other South American	3	0.01
Other Hispanic or Latino	248	1.06
Hungarian	27	0.12
Irish	1,331	5.78
Italian	330	1.43
Lithuanian	21	0.09
Norwegian	55	0.24
Polish	278	1.21
Portuguese	37	0.16
Russian	18	0.08
Scandinavian	5	0.02
Scotch-Irish	1,166	5.06
Scottish	355	1.54
Swedish	107	0.46
Swiss	51	0.22
Turkish	6	0.03
United States or American	2,021	8.78
Welsh	49	0.21
West Indian, excl. Hispanic:	212	0.92
Bermudan	10	0.04
British West Indian	8	0.03
Haitian	140	0.61
Jamaican	38	0.17
Trinidadian and Tobagonian	16	0.07
White:	14,214	60.95
Not Hispanic (13,381)	13,542	58.07
Hispanic (598)	672	2.88

Tarboro

Place Type: Town
County: Edgecombe
Population: 11,138

Ancestry/Race	Number	%
African American/Black:	4,419	39.67
Not Hispanic (4,375)	4,397	39.48
Hispanic (18)	22	0.20
African, sub-Saharan:	31	0.28
African	31	0.28
Am. Ind. or Alaska Nat., not spec.	10	0.09
American Indian tribes, specified:	16	0.14
Cherokee (1)	6	0.05
Cheyenne	4	0.04
Lumbee (1)	1	0.01
Shoshone (1)	1	0.01
All other tribes	4	0.04
American Indian tribes, not spec.	2	0.02
Arab:	5	0.04
Lebanese	5	0.04
Asian:	48	0.43
Chinese, ex. Taiwanese (6)	6	0.05
Filipino (7)	8	0.07
Indian (7)	8	0.07
Indonesian	1	0.01
Japanese	3	0.03
Korean (1)	1	0.01
Taiwanese (3)	3	0.03
Vietnamese (9)	9	0.08
Other Asian, not specified (1)	9	0.08
British	28	0.25
Canadian	10	0.09
Croatian	6	0.05
Czechoslovakian	5	0.04
Dutch	6	0.05
English	920	8.20
European	26	0.23
French, except Basque	140	1.25
German	459	4.09
Greek	6	0.05
Hawaii Native/Pacific Islander:	2	0.02
Polynesian:	2	0.02
Native Hawaiian	1	0.01
Samoan	1	0.01
Hispanic or Latino:	662	5.94
Central American:	31	0.28
Costa Rican	5	0.04
Guatemalan	15	0.13
Honduran	9	0.08
Nicaraguan	1	0.01
Salvadoran	1	0.01
Cuban	2	0.02
Dominican Republic	2	0.02
Mexican	516	4.63
Puerto Rican	21	0.19
South American:	30	0.27
Colombian	24	0.22
Ecuadorian	1	0.01
Peruvian	4	0.04
Venezuelan	1	0.01
Other Hispanic or Latino	60	0.54
Irish	384	3.42
Italian	81	0.72
Polish	73	0.65
Portuguese	10	0.09
Russian	9	0.08
Scandinavian	5	0.04
Scotch-Irish	106	0.94
Scottish	77	0.69
Swedish	10	0.09
Swiss	5	0.04
Ukrainian	5	0.04
United States or American	2,140	19.07
Welsh	13	0.12
White:	6,282	56.40
Not Hispanic (6,021)	6,047	54.29
Hispanic (220)	235	2.11

Thomasville

Place Type: City
County: Davidson
Population: 19,788

Ancestry/Race	Number	%
African American/Black:	4,820	24.36
Not Hispanic (4,711)	4,796	24.24
Hispanic (20)	24	0.12
African, sub-Saharan:	212	1.08
African	212	1.08
Am. Ind. or Alaska Nat., not spec.	59	0.30
American Indian tribes, specified:	95	0.48
Apache (1)	1	0.01
Blackfeet (1)	2	0.01
Cherokee (15)	45	0.23
Cheyenne (1)	1	0.01
Chippewa	2	0.01
Cree	1	0.01
Crow	1	0.01
Delaware (1)	1	0.01
Iroquois (4)	5	0.03
Latin American Indians (1)	5	0.03
Lumbee (19)	25	0.13
Ute (1)	3	0.02
All other tribes (3)	3	0.02
American Indian tribes, not spec.	21	0.11
Arab:	10	0.05
Lebanese	10	0.05
Asian:	232	1.17
Cambodian (3)	5	0.03
Chinese, ex. Taiwanese (11)	16	0.08
Filipino (43)	47	0.24
Indian (41)	54	0.27
Japanese (1)	2	0.01
Korean (1)	6	0.03
Laotian (1)	11	0.06
Pakistani (32)	41	0.21
Thai (2)	2	0.01
Vietnamese (20)	22	0.11
Other Asian, specified	4	0.02
Other Asian, not specified (3)	22	0.11
Austrian	10	0.05
British	52	0.26
Canadian	7	0.04
Czech	12	0.06
Dutch	88	0.45
English	1,384	7.04
European	66	0.34
French, except Basque	202	1.03
French Canadian	79	0.40
German	1,558	7.93
German Russian	9	0.05
Greek	52	0.26
Hawaii Native/Pacific Islander:	9	0.05
Polynesian:	4	0.02
Native Hawaiian	4	0.02
Other Pac. Isl., specified	4	0.02
Other Pac. Isl., not spec.	1	0.01
Hispanic or Latino:	1,371	6.93
Central American:	119	0.60
Costa Rican	1	0.01
Guatemalan	11	0.06
Honduran	21	0.11
Nicaraguan	2	0.01
Panamanian	1	0.01
Salvadoran	62	0.31
Other Central American	21	0.11
Cuban	18	0.09
Dominican Republic	4	0.02
Mexican	1,023	5.17
Puerto Rican	41	0.21
South American:	20	0.10
Argentinean	1	0.01
Chilean	1	0.01
Colombian	10	0.05
Ecuadorian	2	0.01
Peruvian	3	0.02
Venezuelan	3	0.02
Other Hispanic or Latino	146	0.74
Hungarian	7	0.04
Irish	1,177	5.99
Italian	272	1.38
Lithuanian	13	0.07
Norwegian	15	0.08
Polish	84	0.43
Russian	13	0.07
Scotch-Irish	256	1.30
Scottish	223	1.13
Slovak	24	0.12
Swedish	50	0.25
Swiss	9	0.05
United States or American	3,662	18.64
Welsh	64	0.33
West Indian, excl. Hispanic:	10	0.05
Jamaican	10	0.05
White:	13,999	70.74
Not Hispanic (13,236)	13,399	67.71
Hispanic (543)	600	3.03

Wake Forest

Place Type: Town
County: Wake
Population: 12,588

Ancestry/Race	Number	%
Afghan	14	0.11
African American/Black:	2,048	16.27
Not Hispanic (1,978)	2,032	16.14
Hispanic (9)	16	0.13
African, sub-Saharan:	132	1.05
African	27	0.22
Ethiopian	5	0.04
Ghanian	3	0.02
Kenyan	43	0.34
Liberian	13	0.10
Nigerian	14	0.11
South African	2	0.02
Other sub-Saharan African	25	0.20
Am. Ind. or Alaska Nat., not spec.	25	0.20
American Indian tribes, specified:	49	0.39
Blackfeet (1)	2	0.02
Cherokee (5)	26	0.21
Choctaw	1	0.01
Delaware	1	0.01
Lumbee (3)	5	0.04
Potawatomi (4)	4	0.03
Sioux	2	0.02

Notes: 1. Figures in the "Number" column do not add up to the total population due to: a) Ancestry/Race overlap — e.g. persons can report being both White and Irish, b) persons of Hispanic origin can report being any race, c) persons reporting two ancestries are counted in both categories. 2. Numbers in parentheses indicate the number of persons reporting this ancestry/race alone, not in combination with any other ancestry/race. 3. Refer to the Explanation of Data in the front of the book for more detailed information.

Ancestry/Race	Number	%
All other tribes (6)	8	0.06
American Indian tribes, not spec.	5	0.04
Arab:	52	0.41
Arab/Arabic	13	0.10
Egyptian	6	0.05
Lebanese	15	0.12
Other Arab	18	0.14
Asian:	328	2.61
Bangladeshi (4)	4	0.03
Chinese, ex. Taiwanese (52)	60	0.48
Filipino (27)	44	0.35
Indian (59)	72	0.57
Indonesian (1)	1	0.01
Japanese (3)	10	0.08
Korean (72)	88	0.70
Pakistani	7	0.06
Sri Lankan (3)	3	0.02
Taiwanese (1)	1	0.01
Thai (1)	3	0.02
Vietnamese (18)	20	0.16
Other Asian, not specified (8)	15	0.12
Australian	8	0.06
Austrian	33	0.26
Belgian	19	0.15
Brazilian	26	0.21
British	69	0.55
Canadian	43	0.34
Celtic	5	0.04
Croatian	30	0.24
Czech	52	0.41
Czechoslovakian	11	0.09
Danish	38	0.30
Dutch	160	1.27
English	1,687	13.44
European	153	1.22
Finnish	18	0.14
French, except Basque	371	2.96
French Canadian	63	0.50
German	1,584	12.62
Greek	48	0.38
Hawaii Native/Pacific Islander:	4	0.03
Micronesian: (1)	1	0.01
Guamanian/Chamorro (1)	1	0.01
Polynesian:	3	0.02
Native Hawaiian	3	0.02
Hispanic or Latino:	262	2.08
Central American:	28	0.22
Costa Rican	9	0.07
Guatemalan	1	0.01
Salvadoran	15	0.12
Other Central American	3	0.02
Cuban	17	0.14
Dominican Republic	12	0.10
Mexican	78	0.62
Puerto Rican	41	0.33
South American:	26	0.21
Argentinean	1	0.01
Bolivian	3	0.02
Chilean	4	0.03
Colombian	6	0.05
Ecuadorian	3	0.02
Peruvian	6	0.05
Uruguayan	1	0.01
Venezuelan	1	0.01
Other South American	1	0.01
Other Hispanic or Latino	60	0.48
Hungarian	46	0.37
Icelander	3	0.02
Iranian	8	0.06
Irish	1,336	10.65
Italian	724	5.77
Lithuanian	16	0.13
Northern European	15	0.12
Norwegian	79	0.63
Polish	306	2.44
Portuguese	17	0.14
Romanian	36	0.29
Russian	75	0.60
Scandinavian	13	0.10
Scotch-Irish	452	3.60
Scottish	366	2.92
Serbian	2	0.02
Slavic	5	0.04
Slovak	23	0.18
Slovene	6	0.05
Swedish	98	0.78
Swiss	23	0.18
Ukrainian	66	0.53
United States or American	1,687	13.44
Welsh	69	0.55
West Indian, excl. Hispanic:	65	0.52
Bahamian	7	0.06
Barbadian	8	0.06
British West Indian	8	0.06
Haitian	3	0.02
Jamaican	32	0.25
Trinidadian and Tobagonian	4	0.03
West Indian	3	0.02
White:	10,186	80.92
Not Hispanic (9,897)	10,033	79.70
Hispanic (127)	153	1.22
Yugoslavian	10	0.08

Wilmington

Place Type: City
County: New Hanover
Population: 75,838

Ancestry/Race	Number	%
Acadian/Cajun	5	0.01
African American/Black:	19,918	26.26
Not Hispanic (19,423)	19,725	26.01
Hispanic (156)	193	0.25
African, sub-Saharan:	546	0.72
African	428	0.57
Kenyan	6	0.01
Liberian	68	0.09
Nigerian	7	0.01
South African	30	0.04
Other sub-Saharan African	7	0.01
Am. Ind. or Alaska Nat., not spec.	161	0.21
American Indian tribes, specified:	362	0.48
Apache (2)	5	0.01
Blackfeet (2)	8	0.01
Cherokee (41)	169	0.22
Cheyenne (1)	1	0.00
Chippewa (4)	4	0.01
Choctaw (3)	3	0.00
Creek (4)	8	0.01
Crow	1	0.00
Delaware	1	0.00
Iroquois (2)	18	0.02
Latin American Indians (9)	14	0.02
Lumbee (40)	53	0.07
Navajo (1)	1	0.00
Osage (1)	1	0.00
Paiute (1)	2	0.00
Potawatomi (2)	2	0.00
Pueblo	1	0.00
Puget Sound Salish (2)	2	0.00
Seminole (2)	3	0.00
Sioux (6)	17	0.02
All other tribes (32)	48	0.06
American Indian tribes, not spec.	39	0.05
Arab:	342	0.45
Arab/Arabic	117	0.15
Egyptian	54	0.07
Jordanian	20	0.03
Lebanese	105	0.14
Palestinian	42	0.06
Syrian	4	0.01
Armenian	32	0.04
Asian:	844	1.11
Cambodian (5)	6	0.01
Chinese, ex. Taiwanese (187)	198	0.26
Filipino (77)	104	0.14
Indian (196)	209	0.28
Indonesian (3)	3	0.00
Japanese (47)	83	0.11
Korean (57)	69	0.09
Laotian (5)	5	0.01
Malaysian (1)	3	0.00
Pakistani (8)	8	0.01
Taiwanese (2)	4	0.01
Thai (14)	18	0.02
Vietnamese (60)	71	0.09
Other Asian, specified (2)	8	0.01
Other Asian, not specified (12)	55	0.07
Assyrian/Chaldean/Syriac	10	0.01
Australian	9	0.01
Austrian	138	0.18
Basque	25	0.03
Belgian	55	0.07
Brazilian	27	0.04
British	498	0.66
Canadian	118	0.16
Croatian	24	0.03
Cypriot	18	0.02
Czech	121	0.16
Czechoslovakian	69	0.09
Danish	176	0.23
Dutch	849	1.12
Eastern European	20	0.03
English	9,479	12.55
European	597	0.79
Finnish	84	0.11
French, except Basque	1,539	2.04
French Canadian	380	0.50
German	7,673	10.16
Greek	397	0.53
Hawaii Native/Pacific Islander:	109	0.14
Micronesian: (11)	15	0.02
Guamanian/Chamorro (11)	15	0.02
Polynesian: (51)	65	0.09
Native Hawaiian (23)	31	0.04
Samoan (27)	32	0.04
Other Polynesian (1)	2	0.00
Other Pac. Isl., specified	6	0.01
Other Pac. Isl., not spec. (5)	23	0.03
Hispanic or Latino:	1,991	2.63
Central American:	125	0.16
Costa Rican	13	0.02
Guatemalan	31	0.04
Honduran	34	0.04
Nicaraguan	6	0.01
Panamanian	13	0.02
Salvadoran	26	0.03
Other Central American	2	0.00
Cuban	75	0.10
Dominican Republic	21	0.03
Mexican	1,195	1.58
Puerto Rican	238	0.31
South American:	89	0.12
Argentinean	7	0.01
Bolivian	8	0.01
Chilean	6	0.01
Colombian	42	0.06
Ecuadorian	12	0.02
Peruvian	6	0.01
Venezuelan	6	0.01
Other South American	2	0.00
Other Hispanic or Latino	248	0.33
Hungarian	295	0.39
Icelander	20	0.03
Iranian	8	0.01
Irish	7,126	9.43
Israeli	20	0.03
Italian	2,517	3.33
Lithuanian	77	0.10
New Zealander	35	0.05
Northern European	55	0.07
Norwegian	482	0.64
Pennsylvania German	32	0.04
Polish	1,059	1.40
Portuguese	150	0.20
Romanian	33	0.04
Russian	427	0.57
Scandinavian	46	0.06
Scotch-Irish	3,248	4.30

Notes: 1. Figures in the "Number" column do not add up to the total population due to: a) Ancestry/Race overlap — e.g. persons can report being both White and Irish, b) persons of Hispanic origin can report being any race, c) persons reporting two ancestries are counted in both categories. 2. Numbers in parentheses indicate the number of persons reporting this ancestry/race alone, not in combination with any other ancestry/race. 3. Refer to the Explanation of Data in the front of the book for more detailed information.

Ancestry/Race	Number	%
Scottish	2,361	3.13
Serbian	19	0.03
Slavic	14	0.02
Slovak	58	0.08
Slovene	8	0.01
Swedish	528	0.70
Swiss	100	0.13
Turkish	7	0.01
Ukrainian	218	0.29
United States or American	6,344	8.40
Welsh	637	0.84
West Indian, excl. Hispanic:	176	0.23
Barbadian	14	0.02
British West Indian	9	0.01
Haitian	14	0.02
Jamaican	91	0.12
Trinidadian and Tobagonian	37	0.05
West Indian	11	0.01
White:	54,214	71.49
Not Hispanic (52,639)	53,206	70.16
Hispanic (877)	1,008	1.33
Yugoslavian	7	0.01

Wilson

Place Type: City
County: Wilson
Population: 44,405

Ancestry/Race	Number	%
African American/Black:	21,270	47.90
Not Hispanic (21,007)	21,152	47.63
Hispanic (99)	118	0.27
African, sub-Saharan:	300	0.68
African	294	0.66
Ethiopian	6	0.01
Alaska Native tribes, specified:	3	0.01
Eskimo (3)	3	0.01
Alaska Native tribes, not specified	1	0.00
Am. Ind. or Alaska Nat., not spec.	101	0.23
American Indian tribes, specified:	116	0.26
Blackfeet (2)	15	0.03
Cherokee (15)	42	0.09
Chickasaw	1	0.00
Iroquois (1)	3	0.01
Latin American Indians (15)	16	0.04
Lumbee (18)	20	0.05
Pueblo	1	0.00
Seminole (1)	1	0.00
Shoshone	1	0.00
All other tribes (11)	16	0.04
American Indian tribes, not spec.	18	0.04
Arab:	176	0.40
Arab/Arabic	51	0.12
Egyptian	5	0.01
Jordanian	58	0.13
Lebanese	34	0.08
Other Arab	28	0.06
Asian:	373	0.84
Cambodian (1)	2	0.00
Chinese, ex. Taiwanese (43)	57	0.13
Filipino (31)	46	0.10
Indian (86)	101	0.23
Indonesian (2)	2	0.00
Japanese (15)	34	0.08
Korean (27)	32	0.07
Pakistani (4)	4	0.01
Thai (3)	5	0.01
Vietnamese (16)	27	0.06
Other Asian, specified	4	0.01
Other Asian, not specified (20)	59	0.13
Austrian	4	0.01
Brazilian	13	0.03
British	148	0.33
Canadian	35	0.08
Czech	13	0.03
Czechoslovakian	17	0.04
Danish	13	0.03
Dutch	144	0.32
English	2,951	6.66
European	253	0.57
Finnish	16	0.04
French, except Basque	198	0.45
French Canadian	47	0.11
German	1,632	3.68
Greek	70	0.16
Guyanese	15	0.03
Hawaii Native/Pacific Islander:	26	0.06
Micronesian: (2)	6	0.01
Guamanian/Chamorro (2)	6	0.01
Polynesian: (6)	12	0.03
Native Hawaiian (4)	10	0.02
Samoan (2)	2	0.00
Other Pac. Isl., specified	4	0.01
Other Pac. Isl., not spec.	4	0.01
Hispanic or Latino:	3,237	7.29
Central American:	105	0.24
Costa Rican	12	0.03
Guatemalan	20	0.05
Honduran	24	0.05
Nicaraguan	15	0.03
Salvadoran	30	0.07
Other Central American	4	0.01
Cuban	27	0.06
Dominican Republic	7	0.02
Mexican	2,637	5.94
Puerto Rican	89	0.20
South American:	39	0.09
Argentinean	4	0.01
Chilean	6	0.01
Colombian	14	0.03
Ecuadorian	2	0.00
Peruvian	3	0.01
Uruguayan	1	0.00
Venezuelan	8	0.02
Other Hispanic or Latino	333	0.75
Hungarian	13	0.03
Iranian	88	0.20
Irish	1,529	3.45
Italian	480	1.08
Northern European	57	0.13
Norwegian	122	0.28
Pennsylvania German	7	0.02
Polish	131	0.30
Portuguese	20	0.05
Russian	7	0.02
Scandinavian	10	0.02
Scotch-Irish	698	1.58
Scottish	618	1.39
Slovak	33	0.07
Swedish	37	0.08
Swiss	39	0.09
Turkish	25	0.06
Ukrainian	53	0.12
United States or American	5,022	11.33
Welsh	129	0.29
West Indian, excl. Hispanic:	43	0.10
Barbadian	7	0.02
British West Indian	24	0.05
Jamaican	8	0.02
West Indian	4	0.01
White:	21,060	47.43
Not Hispanic (19,479)	19,698	44.36
Hispanic (1,244)	1,362	3.07

Winston-Salem

Place Type: City
County: Forsyth
Population: 185,776

Ancestry/Race	Number	%
African American/Black:	70,434	37.91
Not Hispanic (67,648)	68,671	36.96
Hispanic (1,276)	1,763	0.95
African, sub-Saharan:	1,840	0.99
African	1,539	0.83
Cape Verdean	6	0.00
Ethiopian	35	0.02
Ghanian	8	0.00
Liberian	75	0.04
Nigerian	113	0.06
Sierra Leonean	7	0.00
South African	21	0.01
Ugandan	5	0.00
Other sub-Saharan African	31	0.02
Alaska Native tribes, specified:	1	0.00
Eskimo (1)	1	0.00
Am. Ind. or Alaska Nat., not spec.	426	0.23
Albanian	40	0.02
Alsatian	17	0.01
American Indian tribes, specified:	743	0.40
Apache (4)	8	0.00
Blackfeet (3)	29	0.02
Cherokee (109)	325	0.17
Cheyenne	2	0.00
Chippewa (7)	11	0.01
Choctaw (6)	13	0.01
Creek (2)	8	0.00
Crow	2	0.00
Delaware (4)	10	0.01
Iroquois (6)	14	0.01
Latin American Indians (69)	103	0.06
Lumbee (90)	121	0.07
Navajo (8)	13	0.01
Osage (1)	3	0.00
Ottawa	1	0.00
Paiute	1	0.00
Pueblo	7	0.00
Seminole (2)	3	0.00
Shoshone (3)	6	0.00
Sioux (7)	19	0.01
Tohono O'Odham	1	0.00
Ute	2	0.00
Yaqui (2)	2	0.00
All other tribes (24)	39	0.02
American Indian tribes, not spec.	44	0.02
Arab:	550	0.30
Arab/Arabic	34	0.02
Egyptian	47	0.03
Iraqi	8	0.00
Lebanese	322	0.17
Moroccan	15	0.01
Palestinian	30	0.02
Syrian	56	0.03
Other Arab	38	0.02
Armenian	16	0.01
Asian:	2,591	1.39
Bangladeshi (1)	3	0.00
Cambodian (11)	17	0.01
Chinese, ex. Taiwanese (584)	658	0.35
Filipino (192)	273	0.15
Indian (540)	609	0.33
Indonesian (6)	6	0.00
Japanese (125)	195	0.10
Korean (186)	214	0.12
Laotian (46)	47	0.03
Malaysian (2)	2	0.00
Pakistani (46)	61	0.03
Sri Lankan (9)	10	0.01
Taiwanese (7)	10	0.01
Thai (27)	33	0.02
Vietnamese (242)	265	0.14
Other Asian, specified (7)	33	0.02
Other Asian, not specified (57)	155	0.08
Austrian	230	0.12
Basque	7	0.00
Belgian	60	0.03
Brazilian	55	0.03
British	750	0.40
Bulgarian	48	0.03
Canadian	331	0.18
Carpatho Rusyn	6	0.00
Celtic	5	0.00
Croatian	94	0.05
Cypriot	7	0.00
Czech	287	0.15
Czechoslovakian	128	0.07
Danish	291	0.16
Dutch	1,830	0.99

Notes: 1. Figures in the "Number" column do not add up to the total population due to: a) Ancestry/Race overlap — e.g. persons can report being both White and Irish, b) persons of Hispanic origin can report being any race, c) persons reporting two ancestries are counted in both categories. 2. Numbers in parentheses indicate the number of persons reporting this ancestry/race alone, not in combination with any other ancestry/race. 3. Refer to the Explanation of Data in the front of the book for more detailed information.

Eastern European	55	0.03
English	17,913	9.66
Estonian	7	0.00
European	1,773	0.96
Finnish	119	0.06
French, except Basque	2,778	1.50
French Canadian	496	0.27
German	17,161	9.25
Greek	821	0.44
Guyanese	33	0.02
Hawaii Native/Pacific Islander:	189	0.10
Micronesian: (27)	42	0.02
Guamanian/Chamorro (20)	34	0.02
Other Micronesian (7)	8	0.00
Polynesian: (30)	60	0.03
Native Hawaiian (20)	47	0.03
Samoan (9)	10	0.01
Other Polynesian (1)	3	0.00
Other Pac. Isl., specified	25	0.01
Other Pac. Isl., not spec. (10)	62	0.03
Hispanic or Latino:	16,043	8.64
Central American:	1,101	0.59
Costa Rican	24	0.01
Guatemalan	351	0.19
Honduran	102	0.05
Nicaraguan	46	0.02
Panamanian	33	0.02
Salvadoran	527	0.28
Other Central American	18	0.01
Cuban	236	0.13
Dominican Republic	105	0.06
Mexican	11,908	6.41
Puerto Rican	632	0.34
South American:	364	0.20
Argentinean	45	0.02
Bolivian	6	0.00
Chilean	35	0.02
Colombian	117	0.06
Ecuadorian	60	0.03
Peruvian	46	0.02
Uruguayan	2	0.00
Venezuelan	44	0.02
Other South American	9	0.00
Other Hispanic or Latino	1,697	0.91
Hungarian	311	0.17
Icelander	6	0.00
Iranian	42	0.02
Irish	10,971	5.91
Italian	3,678	1.98
Latvian	26	0.01
Lithuanian	137	0.07
Luxemburger	6	0.00
Macedonian	7	0.00
Maltese	23	0.01
Northern European	117	0.06
Norwegian	726	0.39
Pennsylvania German	33	0.02
Polish	2,057	1.11
Portuguese	140	0.08
Romanian	83	0.04
Russian	651	0.35
Scandinavian	155	0.08
Scotch-Irish	4,747	2.56
Scottish	3,740	2.02
Serbian	51	0.03
Slavic	31	0.02
Slovak	89	0.05
Slovene	30	0.02
Swedish	630	0.34
Swiss	261	0.14
Turkish	15	0.01
Ukrainian	327	0.18
United States or American	13,890	7.49
Welsh	1,125	0.61
West Indian, excl. Hispanic:	510	0.27
Bahamian	5	0.00
Belizean	25	0.01
Haitian	50	0.03
Jamaican	335	0.18
Trinidadian and Tobagonian	6	0.00
U.S. Virgin Islander	18	0.01
West Indian	71	0.04
White:	105,410	56.74
Not Hispanic (97,420)	98,788	53.18
Hispanic (5,823)	6,622	3.56
Yugoslavian	143	0.08

Bismarck

Place Type: City
County: Burleigh
Population: 55,532

Ancestry/Race	Number	%
African American/Black:	235	0.42
Not Hispanic (141)	218	0.39
Hispanic (15)	17	0.03
African, sub-Saharan:	19	0.03
African	11	0.02
Somalian	8	0.01
Alaska Native tribes, specified:	1	0.00
Eskimo (1)	1	0.00
Am. Ind. or Alaska Nat., not spec.	453	0.82
Alsatian	7	0.01
American Indian tribes, specified:	1,651	2.97
Apache (7)	9	0.02
Blackfeet (9)	13	0.02
Cherokee (5)	13	0.02
Cheyenne (4)	9	0.02
Chippewa (296)	352	0.63
Choctaw (1)	4	0.01
Colville (1)	1	0.00
Comanche (1)	1	0.00
Cree (1)	2	0.00
Crow (22)	22	0.04
Delaware (1)	1	0.00
Iroquois (4)	4	0.01
Latin American Indians (5)	9	0.02
Menominee	1	0.00
Navajo (4)	5	0.01
Osage (1)	1	0.00
Ottawa (1)	1	0.00
Potawatomi (1)	1	0.00
Pueblo (6)	6	0.01
Puget Sound Salish (1)	1	0.00
Seminole	1	0.00
Shoshone (8)	8	0.01
Sioux (713)	814	1.47
Tohono O'Odham (1)	1	0.00
Ute (8)	8	0.01
Yakama	1	0.00
Yaqui	1	0.00
All other tribes (271)	361	0.65
American Indian tribes, not spec.	95	0.17
Arab:	113	0.20
Arab/Arabic	12	0.02
Iraqi	9	0.02
Lebanese	83	0.15
Other Arab	9	0.02
Armenian	19	0.03
Asian:	347	0.62
Bangladeshi	1	0.00
Chinese, ex. Taiwanese (32)	41	0.07
Filipino (40)	64	0.12
Indian (75)	83	0.15
Japanese (8)	21	0.04
Korean (28)	39	0.07
Laotian (1)	1	0.00
Malaysian (3)	3	0.01
Pakistani (16)	18	0.03
Sri Lankan (3)	3	0.01
Taiwanese (1)	1	0.00
Thai (14)	18	0.03
Vietnamese (27)	34	0.06
Other Asian, not specified (1)	20	0.04
Australian	14	0.03
Austrian	113	0.20
Basque	8	0.01
Belgian	75	0.14
British	74	0.13
Bulgarian	8	0.01
Canadian	37	0.07
Celtic	5	0.01
Czech	827	1.50
Czechoslovakian	150	0.27
Danish	610	1.10
Dutch	938	1.70
English	2,768	5.01
European	148	0.27
Finnish	193	0.35
French, except Basque	1,523	2.75
French Canadian	374	0.68
German	32,138	58.13
German Russian	131	0.24
Hawaii Native/Pacific Islander:	32	0.06
Micronesian: (6)	15	0.03
Guamanian/Chamorro (1)	9	0.02
Other Micronesian (5)	6	0.01
Polynesian: (9)	12	0.02
Native Hawaiian (5)	6	0.01
Samoan (4)	5	0.01
Tongan	1	0.00
Other Pac. Isl., not spec.	5	0.01
Hispanic or Latino:	415	0.75
Central American:	22	0.04
Costa Rican	1	0.00
Guatemalan	2	0.00
Honduran	3	0.01
Nicaraguan	1	0.00
Panamanian	14	0.03
Other Central American	1	0.00
Cuban	45	0.08
Mexican	167	0.30
Puerto Rican	29	0.05
South American:	25	0.05
Chilean	1	0.00
Colombian	20	0.04
Venezuelan	2	0.00
Other South American	2	0.00
Other Hispanic or Latino	127	0.23
Hungarian	330	0.60
Icelander	87	0.16
Iranian	14	0.03
Irish	3,971	7.18
Italian	340	0.62
Latvian	11	0.02
Lithuanian	33	0.06
Luxemburger	16	0.03
Macedonian	27	0.05
Northern European	23	0.04
Norwegian	10,121	18.31
Pennsylvania German	31	0.06
Polish	1,463	2.65
Portuguese	32	0.06
Romanian	12	0.02
Russian	4,250	7.69
Scandinavian	463	0.84
Scotch-Irish	609	1.10
Scottish	589	1.07
Slavic	16	0.03
Slovak	33	0.06
Swedish	2,395	4.33
Swiss	177	0.32
Turkish	11	0.02
Ukrainian	459	0.83
United States or American	1,167	2.11
Welsh	145	0.26
West Indian, excl. Hispanic:	43	0.08
Haitian	36	0.07
Jamaican	7	0.01
White:	53,106	95.63
Not Hispanic (52,387)	52,830	95.13
Hispanic (247)	276	0.50
Yugoslavian	40	0.07

Notes: 1. Figures in the "Number" column do not add up to the total population due to: a) Ancestry/Race overlap — e.g. persons can report being both White and Irish, b) persons of Hispanic origin can report being any race, c) persons reporting two ancestries are counted in both categories. 2. Numbers in parentheses indicate the number of persons reporting this ancestry/race alone, not in combination with any other ancestry/race. 3. Refer to the Explanation of Data in the front of the book for more detailed information.

Dickinson

Place Type: City
County: Stark
Population: 16,010

Ancestry/Race	Number	%
African American/Black:	73	0.46
Not Hispanic (39)	67	0.42
Hispanic (4)	6	0.04
Am. Ind. or Alaska Nat., not spec.	86	0.54
American Indian tribes, specified:	168	1.05
Apache	1	0.01
Blackfeet (7)	9	0.06
Cherokee (1)	6	0.04
Cheyenne (4)	4	0.02
Chippewa (8)	15	0.09
Crow (2)	3	0.02
Latin American Indians (1)	1	0.01
Navajo (3)	3	0.02
Pueblo (2)	2	0.01
Seminole	2	0.01
Shoshone (1)	1	0.01
Sioux (42)	61	0.38
Tohono O'Odham (3)	3	0.02
All other tribes (51)	57	0.36
American Indian tribes, not spec.	18	0.11
Arab:	18	0.11
Arab/Arabic	18	0.11
Asian:	49	0.31
Cambodian (1)	1	0.01
Chinese, ex. Taiwanese (10)	10	0.06
Filipino (5)	7	0.04
Indian (12)	15	0.09
Japanese (2)	4	0.02
Korean (2)	2	0.01
Malaysian	1	0.01
Vietnamese	3	0.02
Other Asian, specified	1	0.01
Other Asian, not specified (5)	5	0.03
Australian	8	0.05
Austrian	25	0.16
Basque	6	0.04
Belgian	7	0.04
British	12	0.08
Canadian	27	0.17
Celtic	7	0.04
Czech	1,118	7.06
Czechoslovakian	89	0.56
Danish	110	0.69
Dutch	264	1.67
English	596	3.76
European	7	0.04
Finnish	33	0.21
French, except Basque	479	3.02
French Canadian	111	0.70
German	8,665	54.69
German Russian	88	0.56
Hawaii Native/Pacific Islander:	9	0.06
Polynesian: (4)	7	0.04
Native Hawaiian (2)	4	0.02
Samoan (2)	3	0.02
Other Pac. Isl., not spec. (1)	2	0.01
Hispanic or Latino:	168	1.05
Central American:	5	0.03
Costa Rican	1	0.01
Nicaraguan	1	0.01
Panamanian	3	0.02
Cuban	8	0.05
Dominican Republic	1	0.01
Mexican	81	0.51
Puerto Rican	4	0.02
South American:	5	0.03
Colombian	4	0.02
Other South American	1	0.01
Other Hispanic or Latino	64	0.40
Hungarian	397	2.51
Icelander	41	0.26
Irish	873	5.51
Italian	111	0.70
Lithuanian	5	0.03
Luxemburger	17	0.11
Norwegian	2,266	14.30
Pennsylvania German	9	0.06
Polish	329	2.08
Russian	1,152	7.27
Scandinavian	46	0.29
Scotch-Irish	84	0.53
Scottish	130	0.82
Slavic	9	0.06
Slovak	20	0.13
Swedish	442	2.79
Swiss	37	0.23
Turkish	33	0.21
Ukrainian	350	2.21
United States or American	540	3.41
Welsh	20	0.13
White:	15,675	97.91
Not Hispanic (15,448)	15,564	97.21
Hispanic (108)	111	0.69
Yugoslavian	9	0.06

Fargo

Place Type: City
County: Cass
Population: 90,599

Ancestry/Race	Number	%
African American/Black:	1,287	1.42
Not Hispanic (908)	1,248	1.38
Hispanic (14)	39	0.04
African, sub-Saharan:	690	0.76
African	278	0.31
Kenyan	6	0.01
Nigerian	28	0.03
Somalian	258	0.28
South African	7	0.01
Sudanese	103	0.11
Other sub-Saharan African	10	0.01
Alaska Native tribes, specified:	2	0.00
Eskimo (2)	2	0.00
Am. Ind. or Alaska Nat., not spec.	414	0.46
Albanian	54	0.06
Alsatian	5	0.01
American Indian tribes, specified:	1,098	1.21
Apache (6)	7	0.01
Blackfeet (2)	12	0.01
Cherokee (9)	29	0.03
Cheyenne (1)	3	0.00
Chickasaw	4	0.00
Chippewa (460)	589	0.65
Choctaw (5)	8	0.01
Comanche (4)	7	0.01
Cree	1	0.00
Creek (1)	3	0.00
Crow	2	0.00
Iroquois (1)	4	0.00
Latin American Indians (2)	15	0.02
Lumbee (4)	4	0.00
Menominee (2)	2	0.00
Navajo (3)	5	0.01
Osage	3	0.00
Ottawa (1)	1	0.00
Paiute	11	0.01
Potawatomi (1)	1	0.00
Pueblo	2	0.00
Shoshone	1	0.00
Sioux (209)	276	0.30
All other tribes (77)	106	0.12
American Indian tribes, not spec.	46	0.05
Arab:	335	0.37
Arab/Arabic	7	0.01
Egyptian	40	0.04
Iraqi	30	0.03
Lebanese	96	0.11
Moroccan	6	0.01
Palestinian	70	0.08
Syrian	38	0.04
Other Arab	48	0.05
Armenian	20	0.02
Asian:	1,865	2.06
Bangladeshi (49)	50	0.06
Cambodian (13)	27	0.03
Chinese, ex. Taiwanese (264)	300	0.33
Filipino (86)	156	0.17
Hmong (2)	2	0.00
Indian (388)	430	0.47
Indonesian (1)	2	0.00
Japanese (43)	65	0.07
Korean (142)	173	0.19
Laotian (8)	9	0.01
Malaysian	2	0.00
Pakistani (26)	27	0.03
Sri Lankan (5)	7	0.01
Taiwanese (14)	16	0.02
Thai (14)	20	0.02
Vietnamese (349)	389	0.43
Other Asian, specified (4)	8	0.01
Other Asian, not specified (44)	182	0.20
Australian	7	0.01
Austrian	237	0.26
Basque	19	0.02
Belgian	174	0.19
British	324	0.36
Bulgarian	44	0.05
Canadian	334	0.37
Carpatho Rusyn	6	0.01
Croatian	129	0.14
Czech	1,479	1.63
Czechoslovakian	306	0.34
Danish	1,434	1.58
Dutch	1,114	1.23
Eastern European	12	0.01
English	4,682	5.16
European	219	0.24
Finnish	705	0.78
French, except Basque	4,281	4.72
French Canadian	929	1.02
German	36,827	40.56
German Russian	103	0.11
Greek	140	0.15
Hawaii Native/Pacific Islander:	81	0.09
Micronesian: (1)	6	0.01
Guamanian/Chamorro	5	0.01
Other Micronesian (1)	1	0.00
Polynesian: (35)	52	0.06
Native Hawaiian (16)	22	0.02
Samoan (18)	29	0.03
Tongan (1)	1	0.00
Other Pac. Isl., specified	3	0.00
Other Pac. Isl., not spec. (4)	20	0.02
Hispanic or Latino:	1,167	1.29
Central American:	27	0.03
Costa Rican	3	0.00
Guatemalan	4	0.00
Honduran	2	0.00
Nicaraguan	5	0.01
Panamanian	8	0.01
Salvadoran	5	0.01
Cuban	47	0.05
Dominican Republic	4	0.00
Mexican	668	0.74
Puerto Rican	54	0.06
South American:	61	0.07
Argentinean	4	0.00
Bolivian	3	0.00
Chilean	10	0.01
Colombian	23	0.03
Ecuadorian	4	0.00
Peruvian	11	0.01
Venezuelan	1	0.00
Other South American	5	0.01
Other Hispanic or Latino	306	0.34
Hungarian	191	0.21
Icelander	265	0.29
Iranian	96	0.11
Irish	7,766	8.55
Israeli	29	0.03
Italian	941	1.04

Notes: 1. Figures in the "Number" column do not add up to the total population due to: a) Ancestry/Race overlap — e.g. persons can report being both White and Irish, b) persons of Hispanic origin can report being any race, c) persons reporting two ancestries are counted in both categories. 2. Numbers in parentheses indicate the number of persons reporting this ancestry/race alone, not in combination with any other ancestry/race. 3. Refer to the Explanation of Data in the front of the book for more detailed information.

Ancestry/Race	Number	%
Latvian	13	0.01
Lithuanian	83	0.09
Luxemburger	71	0.08
Northern European	46	0.05
Norwegian	32,515	35.81
Pennsylvania German	53	0.06
Polish	2,572	2.83
Portuguese	9	0.01
Romanian	51	0.06
Russian	1,881	2.07
Scandinavian	1,141	1.26
Scotch-Irish	900	0.99
Scottish	1,054	1.16
Serbian	39	0.04
Slavic	28	0.03
Slovak	135	0.15
Slovene	8	0.01
Swedish	5,910	6.51
Swiss	276	0.30
Turkish	13	0.01
Ukrainian	226	0.25
United States or American	1,816	2.00
Welsh	173	0.19
West Indian, excl. Hispanic:	32	0.04
Jamaican	10	0.01
West Indian	22	0.02
White:	86,430	95.40
Not Hispanic (84,660)	85,669	94.56
Hispanic (661)	761	0.84
Yugoslavian	660	0.73

Grand Forks

Place Type: City
County: Grand Forks
Population: 49,321

Ancestry/Race	Number	%
African American/Black:	605	1.23
Not Hispanic (412)	573	1.16
Hispanic (14)	32	0.06
African, sub-Saharan:	51	0.10
African	10	0.02
Nigerian	12	0.02
Somalian	29	0.06
Alaska Native tribes, specified:	6	0.01
Alaska Athabascan (1)	1	0.00
Eskimo (2)	4	0.01
Tlingit-Haida (1)	1	0.00
Am. Ind. or Alaska Nat., not spec.	379	0.77
Albanian	40	0.08
American Indian tribes, specified:	1,286	2.61
Apache (5)	8	0.02
Blackfeet (5)	7	0.01
Cherokee (19)	36	0.07
Cheyenne (7)	8	0.02
Chickasaw (1)	2	0.00
Chippewa (697)	848	1.72
Choctaw (5)	6	0.01
Colville (1)	1	0.00
Comanche (1)	1	0.00
Cree (1)	1	0.00
Creek (2)	4	0.01
Crow (5)	5	0.01
Iroquois (4)	6	0.01
Latin American Indians (1)	3	0.01
Menominee (1)	5	0.01
Navajo (1)	6	0.01
Paiute (1)	1	0.00
Pueblo (5)	6	0.01
Seminole	2	0.00
Shoshone (1)	1	0.00
Sioux (193)	222	0.45
All other tribes (87)	107	0.22
American Indian tribes, not spec.	53	0.11
Arab:	122	0.25
Arab/Arabic	6	0.01
Lebanese	71	0.14
Syrian	40	0.08
Other Arab	5	0.01
Armenian	20	0.04
Asian:	660	1.34
Bangladeshi (9)	9	0.02
Cambodian (4)	7	0.01
Chinese, ex. Taiwanese (102)	138	0.28
Filipino (77)	131	0.27
Indian (108)	119	0.24
Indonesian (4)	4	0.01
Japanese (29)	54	0.11
Korean (62)	92	0.19
Laotian (2)	4	0.01
Malaysian (1)	1	0.00
Pakistani (6)	8	0.02
Sri Lankan (2)	2	0.00
Taiwanese (1)	1	0.00
Thai (13)	24	0.05
Vietnamese (30)	36	0.07
Other Asian, specified (1)	2	0.00
Other Asian, not specified (17)	28	0.06
Austrian	104	0.21
Belgian	77	0.16
British	117	0.24
Bulgarian	9	0.02
Canadian	173	0.35
Celtic	7	0.01
Croatian	14	0.03
Czech	1,442	2.93
Czechoslovakian	282	0.57
Danish	496	1.01
Dutch	434	0.88
Eastern European	7	0.01
English	2,985	6.06
Estonian	21	0.04
European	81	0.16
Finnish	391	0.79
French, except Basque	3,182	6.46
French Canadian	618	1.25
German	17,106	34.71
German Russian	84	0.17
Greek	68	0.14
Hawaii Native/Pacific Islander:	61	0.12
Micronesian: (7)	17	0.03
Guamanian/Chamorro (6)	16	0.03
Other Micronesian (1)	1	0.00
Polynesian: (12)	23	0.05
Native Hawaiian (9)	19	0.04
Samoan (3)	4	0.01
Other Pac. Isl., specified	1	0.00
Other Pac. Isl., not spec. (9)	20	0.04
Hispanic or Latino:	921	1.87
Central American:	9	0.02
Costa Rican	2	0.00
Honduran	1	0.00
Panamanian	4	0.01
Salvadoran	1	0.00
Other Central American	1	0.00
Cuban	10	0.02
Mexican	545	1.11
Puerto Rican	58	0.12
South American:	19	0.04
Bolivian	1	0.00
Chilean	3	0.01
Colombian	5	0.01
Ecuadorian	5	0.01
Paraguayan	2	0.00
Venezuelan	3	0.01
Other Hispanic or Latino	280	0.57
Hungarian	73	0.15
Icelander	288	0.58
Iranian	47	0.10
Irish	5,235	10.62
Israeli	5	0.01
Italian	665	1.35
Latvian	12	0.02
Lithuanian	22	0.04
Luxemburger	30	0.06
Northern European	12	0.02
Norwegian	17,945	36.41
Pennsylvania German	7	0.01
Polish	3,047	6.18
Portuguese	77	0.16
Romanian	34	0.07
Russian	753	1.53
Scandinavian	416	0.84
Scotch-Irish	700	1.42
Scottish	1,121	2.27
Serbian	4	0.01
Slavic	15	0.03
Slovak	92	0.19
Slovene	18	0.04
Swedish	2,886	5.86
Swiss	116	0.24
Turkish	9	0.02
Ukrainian	202	0.41
United States or American	777	1.58
Welsh	175	0.36
West Indian, excl. Hispanic:	32	0.06
Trinidadian and Tobagonian	15	0.03
West Indian	17	0.03
White:	46,679	94.64
Not Hispanic (45,534)	46,096	93.46
Hispanic (506)	583	1.18
Yugoslavian	118	0.24

Jamestown

Place Type: City
County: Stutsman
Population: 15,527

Ancestry/Race	Number	%
African American/Black:	80	0.52
Not Hispanic (52)	74	0.48
Hispanic (4)	6	0.04
African, sub-Saharan:	12	0.08
African	12	0.08
Alaska Native tribes, specified:	1	0.01
Eskimo	1	0.01
Am. Ind. or Alaska Nat., not spec.	111	0.71
American Indian tribes, specified:	137	0.88
Apache (1)	1	0.01
Blackfeet (1)	1	0.01
Cherokee (1)	8	0.05
Cheyenne (1)	2	0.01
Chippewa (50)	69	0.44
Latin American Indians (1)	1	0.01
Navajo (1)	1	0.01
Osage (1)	1	0.01
Sioux (29)	37	0.24
Yuman (1)	1	0.01
All other tribes (10)	15	0.10
American Indian tribes, not spec.	7	0.05
Arab:	27	0.17
Iraqi	5	0.03
Lebanese	7	0.05
Syrian	15	0.10
Armenian	15	0.10
Asian:	97	0.62
Chinese, ex. Taiwanese (20)	24	0.15
Filipino (14)	20	0.13
Indian (13)	13	0.08
Japanese (3)	5	0.03
Korean (10)	10	0.06
Pakistani (4)	4	0.03
Taiwanese	1	0.01
Vietnamese (6)	9	0.06
Other Asian, specified (3)	4	0.03
Other Asian, not specified (1)	7	0.05
Austrian	20	0.13
Belgian	12	0.08
British	16	0.10
Bulgarian	5	0.03
Croatian	15	0.10
Czech	107	0.69
Czechoslovakian	21	0.14
Danish	276	1.78
Dutch	286	1.85
English	1,019	6.59
European	16	0.10
Finnish	51	0.33

Notes: 1. Figures in the "Number" column do not add up to the total population due to: a) Ancestry/Race overlap — e.g. persons can report being both White and Irish, b) persons of Hispanic origin can report being any race, c) persons reporting two ancestries are counted in both categories. 2. Numbers in parentheses indicate the number of persons reporting this ancestry/race alone, not in combination with any other ancestry/race. 3. Refer to the Explanation of Data in the front of the book for more detailed information.

French, except Basque	484	3.13
French Canadian	146	0.94
German	8,386	54.20
German Russian	49	0.32
Greek	13	0.08
Hawaii Native/Pacific Islander:	14	0.09
Micronesian: (5)	9	0.06
Guamanian/Chamorro (1)	4	0.03
Other Micronesian (4)	5	0.03
Polynesian: (2)	3	0.02
Native Hawaiian (1)	1	0.01
Samoan (1)	2	0.01
Other Pac. Isl., specified	1	0.01
Other Pac. Isl., not spec.	1	0.01
Hispanic or Latino:	185	1.19
Central American:	8	0.05
Honduran	1	0.01
Panamanian	7	0.05
Cuban	4	0.03
Dominican Republic	7	0.05
Mexican	55	0.35
Puerto Rican	17	0.11
South American:	9	0.06
Colombian	8	0.05
Peruvian	1	0.01
Other Hispanic or Latino	85	0.55
Hungarian	30	0.19
Icelander	33	0.21
Irish	1,403	9.07
Italian	141	0.91
Norwegian	3,475	22.46
Polish	478	3.09
Portuguese	7	0.05
Romanian	13	0.08
Russian	594	3.84
Scandinavian	75	0.48
Scotch-Irish	113	0.73
Scottish	233	1.51
Slovene	8	0.05
Swedish	643	4.16
Swiss	65	0.42
Ukrainian	17	0.11
United States or American	533	3.45
Welsh	55	0.36
White:	15,152	97.58
Not Hispanic (14,923)	15,020	96.73
Hispanic (114)	132	0.85

Mandan

Place Type: City
County: Morton
Population: 16,718

Ancestry/Race	Number	%
Acadian/Cajun	5	0.03
African American/Black:	72	0.43
Not Hispanic (34)	69	0.41
Hispanic	3	0.02
African, sub-Saharan:	12	0.07
African	12	0.07
Alaska Native tribes, specified:	1	0.01
Eskimo (1)	1	0.01
Am. Ind. or Alaska Nat., not spec.	100	0.60
American Indian tribes, specified:	526	3.15
Apache	1	0.01
Blackfeet	1	0.01
Cherokee (2)	7	0.04
Cheyenne	2	0.01
Chippewa (135)	156	0.93
Crow (1)	1	0.01
Latin American Indians (1)	1	0.01
Navajo (1)	3	0.02
Ottawa (1)	1	0.01
Potawatomi (5)	5	0.03
Pueblo (1)	3	0.02
Sioux (228)	287	1.72
Yuman (3)	3	0.02
All other tribes (38)	55	0.33
American Indian tribes, not spec.	27	0.16
Arab:	25	0.15
Lebanese	18	0.11
Syrian	7	0.04
Asian:	78	0.47
Chinese, ex. Taiwanese (11)	11	0.07
Filipino (10)	13	0.08
Indian (24)	25	0.15
Japanese (4)	5	0.03
Korean (2)	12	0.07
Malaysian (1)	2	0.01
Sri Lankan	2	0.01
Vietnamese (1)	1	0.01
Other Asian, not specified (2)	7	0.04
Austrian	93	0.56
Belgian	18	0.11
British	11	0.07
Canadian	7	0.04
Czech	341	2.04
Czechoslovakian	7	0.04
Danish	190	1.14
Dutch	197	1.18
English	703	4.20
European	36	0.22
Finnish	28	0.17
French, except Basque	433	2.59
French Canadian	101	0.60
German	10,244	61.20
German Russian	38	0.23
Greek	22	0.13
Hawaii Native/Pacific Islander:	5	0.03
Micronesian: (2)	3	0.02
Guamanian/Chamorro	1	0.01
Other Micronesian (2)	2	0.01
Polynesian:	1	0.01
Native Hawaiian	1	0.01
Other Pac. Isl., not spec.	1	0.01
Hispanic or Latino:	130	0.78
Central American:	2	0.01
Guatemalan	2	0.01
Cuban	2	0.01
Mexican	54	0.32
Puerto Rican	12	0.07
South American:	9	0.05
Colombian	4	0.02
Ecuadorian	3	0.02
Paraguayan	2	0.01
Other Hispanic or Latino	51	0.31
Hungarian	207	1.24
Icelander	25	0.15
Irish	1,328	7.93
Italian	85	0.51
Latvian	16	0.10
Norwegian	2,567	15.34
Pennsylvania German	10	0.06
Polish	225	1.34
Portuguese	22	0.13
Russian	2,185	13.05
Scandinavian	102	0.61
Scotch-Irish	167	1.00
Scottish	111	0.66
Slovak	7	0.04
Swedish	463	2.77
Swiss	33	0.20
Ukrainian	107	0.64
United States or American	477	2.85
Welsh	19	0.11
White:	16,089	96.24
Not Hispanic (15,801)	15,991	95.65
Hispanic (78)	98	0.59

Minot

Place Type: City
County: Ward
Population: 36,567

Ancestry/Race	Number	%
African American/Black:	670	1.83
Not Hispanic (471)	645	1.76
Hispanic (19)	25	0.07
African, sub-Saharan:	61	0.17
African	55	0.15
Somalian	6	0.02
Alaska Native tribes, specified:	5	0.01
Aleut (3)	3	0.01
Eskimo (1)	1	0.00
Tlingit-Haida (1)	1	0.00
Am. Ind. or Alaska Nat., not spec.	283	0.77
American Indian tribes, specified:	944	2.58
Apache	1	0.00
Blackfeet (4)	5	0.01
Cherokee (6)	22	0.06
Chickasaw	3	0.01
Chippewa (475)	583	1.59
Choctaw (1)	3	0.01
Comanche (1)	1	0.00
Cree (2)	2	0.01
Creek (1)	3	0.01
Crow (1)	1	0.00
Latin American Indians (2)	2	0.01
Lumbee (1)	1	0.00
Menominee (2)	2	0.01
Navajo	1	0.00
Ottawa	1	0.00
Potawatomi (7)	8	0.02
Pueblo	1	0.00
Seminole	3	0.01
Sioux (101)	127	0.35
Tohono O'Odham	1	0.00
Ute (1)	1	0.00
All other tribes (143)	172	0.47
American Indian tribes, not spec.	71	0.19
Arab:	65	0.18
Arab/Arabic	6	0.02
Lebanese	42	0.11
Syrian	17	0.05
Asian:	340	0.93
Chinese, ex. Taiwanese (38)	41	0.11
Filipino (51)	86	0.24
Indian (53)	67	0.18
Indonesian (1)	1	0.00
Japanese (21)	42	0.11
Korean (30)	51	0.14
Laotian (5)	6	0.02
Pakistani	1	0.00
Thai (8)	16	0.04
Vietnamese (8)	12	0.03
Other Asian, specified (3)	4	0.01
Other Asian, not specified (4)	13	0.04
Austrian	54	0.15
Belgian	67	0.18
Brazilian	22	0.06
British	43	0.12
Bulgarian	5	0.01
Canadian	88	0.24
Celtic	20	0.05
Czech	296	0.81
Czechoslovakian	98	0.27
Danish	533	1.46
Dutch	587	1.60
English	1,958	5.35
European	146	0.40
Finnish	146	0.40
French, except Basque	1,176	3.21
French Canadian	323	0.88
German	14,913	40.77
German Russian	10	0.03
Greek	162	0.44
Hawaii Native/Pacific Islander:	41	0.11
Micronesian: (10)	15	0.04
Guamanian/Chamorro (9)	12	0.03
Other Micronesian (1)	3	0.01
Polynesian: (11)	18	0.05
Native Hawaiian (4)	7	0.02
Samoan (7)	11	0.03
Other Pac. Isl., not spec. (4)	8	0.02
Hispanic or Latino:	539	1.47
Central American:	13	0.04
Guatemalan	2	0.01
Honduran	5	0.01

Notes: 1. Figures in the "Number" column do not add up to the total population due to: a) Ancestry/Race overlap — e.g. persons can report being both White and Irish, b) persons of Hispanic origin can report being any race, c) persons reporting two ancestries are counted in both categories. 2. Numbers in parentheses indicate the number of persons reporting this ancestry/race alone, not in combination with any other ancestry/race. 3. Refer to the Explanation of Data in the front of the book for more detailed information.

Nicaraguan	2	0.01
Panamanian	2	0.01
Salvadoran	1	0.00
Other Central American	1	0.00
Cuban	39	0.11
Dominican Republic	4	0.01
Mexican	257	0.70
Puerto Rican	102	0.28
South American:	15	0.04
Bolivian	2	0.01
Colombian	8	0.02
Ecuadorian	4	0.01
Peruvian	1	0.00
Other Hispanic or Latino	109	0.30
Hungarian	96	0.26
Icelander	97	0.27
Irish	3,159	8.64
Italian	487	1.33
Lithuanian	33	0.09
Luxemburger	18	0.05
Northern European	7	0.02
Norwegian	11,805	32.27
Pennsylvania German	50	0.14
Polish	608	1.66
Portuguese	59	0.16
Romanian	38	0.10
Russian	870	2.38
Scandinavian	378	1.03
Scotch-Irish	604	1.65
Scottish	510	1.39
Serbian	20	0.05
Slavic	7	0.02
Slovak	77	0.21
Slovene	27	0.07
Swedish	1,539	4.21
Swiss	65	0.18
Turkish	11	0.03
Ukrainian	358	0.98
United States or American	968	2.65
Welsh	180	0.49
West Indian, excl. Hispanic:	9	0.02
Haitian	9	0.02
White:	34,583	94.57
Not Hispanic (33,798)	34,270	93.72
Hispanic (276)	313	0.86
Yugoslavian	29	0.08

West Fargo

Place Type: City
County: Cass
Population: 14,940

Ancestry/Race	Number	%
African American/Black:	97	0.65
Not Hispanic (59)	86	0.58
Hispanic (4)	11	0.07
African, sub-Saharan:	7	0.05
African	7	0.05
Am. Ind. or Alaska Nat., not spec.	61	0.41
American Indian tribes, specified:	165	1.10
Cherokee (6)	8	0.05
Chippewa (81)	110	0.74
Cree (2)	2	0.01
Creek (1)	1	0.01
Crow (1)	3	0.02
Latin American Indians	3	0.02
Sioux (15)	16	0.11
Ute (1)	2	0.01
All other tribes (10)	20	0.13
American Indian tribes, not spec.	6	0.04
Arab:	14	0.10
Lebanese	8	0.05
Other Arab	6	0.04
Asian:	82	0.55
Chinese, ex. Taiwanese (6)	6	0.04
Filipino (10)	22	0.15
Indian (2)	2	0.01
Indonesian	1	0.01
Japanese	5	0.03
Korean (6)	14	0.09
Laotian (2)	2	0.01
Thai (4)	8	0.05
Vietnamese (10)	13	0.09
Other Asian, not specified (2)	9	0.06
Belgian	9	0.06
Brazilian	4	0.03
British	7	0.05
Canadian	6	0.04
Croatian	16	0.11
Czech	111	0.76
Czechoslovakian	8	0.05
Danish	249	1.70
Dutch	89	0.61
English	719	4.91
European	42	0.29
Finnish	108	0.74
French, except Basque	780	5.33
French Canadian	197	1.35
German	7,152	48.88
German Russian	6	0.04
Greek	41	0.28
Hawaii Native/Pacific Islander:	4	0.03
Micronesian: (2)	2	0.01
Guamanian/Chamorro (2)	2	0.01
Other Pac. Isl., not spec. (1)	2	0.01
Hispanic or Latino:	211	1.41
Central American:	2	0.01
Nicaraguan	1	0.01
Salvadoran	1	0.01
Cuban	6	0.04
Dominican Republic	1	0.01
Mexican	130	0.87
Puerto Rican	5	0.03
South American:	1	0.01
Colombian	1	0.01
Other Hispanic or Latino	66	0.44
Icelander	23	0.16
Irish	1,236	8.45
Italian	220	1.50
Lithuanian	12	0.08
Luxemburger	20	0.14
Norwegian	5,938	40.58
Polish	390	2.67
Portuguese	30	0.21
Russian	278	1.90
Scandinavian	214	1.46
Scotch-Irish	112	0.77
Scottish	187	1.28
Slovak	5	0.03
Swedish	1,083	7.40
Ukrainian	48	0.33
United States or American	210	1.44
Welsh	29	0.20
West Indian, excl. Hispanic:	4	0.03
Jamaican	4	0.03
White:	14,571	97.53
Not Hispanic (14,312)	14,463	96.81
Hispanic (90)	108	0.72
Yugoslavian	13	0.09

Williston

Place Type: City
County: Williams
Population: 12,512

Ancestry/Race	Number	%
African American/Black:	36	0.29
Not Hispanic (15)	29	0.23
Hispanic (6)	7	0.06
African, sub-Saharan:	1	0.01
African	1	0.01
Alaska Native tribes, specified:	2	0.02
Alaska Athabascan (1)	2	0.02
Am. Ind. or Alaska Nat., not spec.	147	1.17
American Indian tribes, specified:	514	4.11
Blackfeet (2)	2	0.02
Cherokee (3)	5	0.04
Chippewa (237)	361	2.89
Choctaw (1)	1	0.01
Cree (2)	2	0.02
Latin American Indians	4	0.03
Osage	1	0.01
Pueblo	3	0.02
Sioux (52)	65	0.52
All other tribes (53)	70	0.56
American Indian tribes, not spec.	16	0.13
Arab:	77	0.61
Lebanese	71	0.56
Syrian	6	0.05
Armenian	5	0.04
Asian:	47	0.38
Chinese, ex. Taiwanese (6)	7	0.06
Filipino (5)	9	0.07
Indian (11)	13	0.10
Japanese (3)	9	0.07
Korean (1)	2	0.02
Taiwanese (1)	2	0.01
Thai (1)	1	0.01
Vietnamese (1)	1	0.01
Other Asian, specified (1)	1	0.01
Other Asian, not specified	3	0.02
Austrian	7	0.06
British	21	0.17
Croatian	13	0.10
Czech	74	0.59
Czechoslovakian	6	0.05
Danish	274	2.18
Dutch	184	1.46
Eastern European	5	0.04
English	729	5.80
European	24	0.19
Finnish	69	0.55
French, except Basque	499	3.97
French Canadian	85	0.68
German	3,960	31.48
German Russian	11	0.09
Greek	17	0.14
Hawaii Native/Pacific Islander:	3	0.02
Polynesian: (2)	3	0.02
Native Hawaiian	1	0.01
Samoan (2)	2	0.02
Hispanic or Latino:	154	1.23
Cuban	8	0.06
Mexican	87	0.70
Puerto Rican	5	0.04
South American:	3	0.02
Peruvian	2	0.02
Other South American	1	0.01
Other Hispanic or Latino	51	0.41
Hungarian	6	0.05
Icelander	42	0.33
Irish	1,203	9.56
Italian	76	0.60
Maltese	4	0.03
Norwegian	5,978	47.52
Pennsylvania German	5	0.04
Polish	147	1.17
Romanian	15	0.12
Russian	150	1.19
Scandinavian	124	0.99
Scotch-Irish	100	0.79
Scottish	121	0.96
Swedish	559	4.44
Swiss	39	0.31
Ukrainian	152	1.21
United States or American	316	2.51
Welsh	12	0.10
West Indian, excl. Hispanic:	6	0.05
Trinidadian and Tobagonian	6	0.05
White:	11,969	95.66
Not Hispanic (11,622)	11,851	94.72
Hispanic (101)	118	0.94
Yugoslavian	6	0.05

Notes: 1. Figures in the "Number" column do not add up to the total population due to: a) Ancestry/Race overlap — e.g. persons can report being both White and Irish, b) persons of Hispanic origin can report being any race, c) persons reporting two ancestries are counted in both categories. 2. Numbers in parentheses indicate the number of persons reporting this ancestry/race alone, not in combination with any other ancestry/race. 3. Refer to the Explanation of Data in the front of the book for more detailed information.

Akron

Place Type: City
County: Summit
Population: 217,074

Ancestry/Race	Number	%
African American/Black:	64,530	29.73
Not Hispanic (61,510)	64,073	29.52
Hispanic (317)	457	0.21
African, sub-Saharan:	3,687	1.70
African	3,525	1.62
Cape Verdean	11	0.01
Ethiopian	6	0.00
Ghanian	39	0.02
Liberian	14	0.01
Nigerian	51	0.02
Sudanese	7	0.00
Zimbabwean	15	0.01
Other sub-Saharan African	19	0.01
Alaska Native tribes, specified:	14	0.01
Aleut (4)	8	0.00
Eskimo (2)	5	0.00
Tlingit-Haida (1)	1	0.00
Alaska Native tribes, not specified	3	0.00
Am. Ind. or Alaska Nat., not spec.	792	0.36
Albanian	160	0.07
Alsatian	35	0.02
American Indian tribes, specified:	1,187	0.55
Apache (1)	20	0.01
Blackfeet (28)	155	0.07
Cherokee (146)	662	0.30
Cheyenne (2)	11	0.01
Chickasaw	7	0.00
Chippewa (21)	34	0.02
Choctaw (8)	24	0.01
Comanche	5	0.00
Cree (5)	9	0.00
Creek (1)	7	0.00
Crow (1)	8	0.00
Delaware	8	0.00
Houma (1)	1	0.00
Iroquois (12)	38	0.02
Kiowa	5	0.00
Latin American Indians (4)	14	0.01
Lumbee (5)	5	0.00
Navajo (6)	18	0.01
Osage (2)	2	0.00
Ottawa (1)	2	0.00
Pueblo (3)	10	0.00
Seminole (3)	14	0.01
Shoshone (2)	6	0.00
Sioux (22)	63	0.03
Yaqui (2)	2	0.00
All other tribes (23)	57	0.03
American Indian tribes, not spec.	85	0.04
Arab:	1,453	0.67
Arab/Arabic	248	0.11
Egyptian	9	0.00
Jordanian	150	0.07
Lebanese	834	0.38
Palestinian	82	0.04
Syrian	123	0.06
Other Arab	7	0.00
Armenian	88	0.04
Asian:	3,919	1.81
Bangladeshi (15)	16	0.01
Cambodian (32)	37	0.02
Chinese, ex. Taiwanese (584)	656	0.30
Filipino (168)	252	0.12
Hmong (273)	280	0.13
Indian (647)	756	0.35
Indonesian (5)	10	0.00
Japanese (86)	151	0.07
Korean (292)	366	0.17
Laotian (469)	516	0.24
Malaysian (8)	8	0.00
Pakistani (41)	59	0.03
Sri Lankan (9)	11	0.01
Taiwanese (10)	10	0.00
Thai (57)	79	0.04
Vietnamese (398)	434	0.20
Other Asian, specified (20)	39	0.02
Other Asian, not specified (109)	239	0.11
Australian	50	0.02
Austrian	602	0.28
Belgian	117	0.05
British	663	0.31
Bulgarian	67	0.03
Canadian	218	0.10
Carpatho Rusyn	51	0.02
Celtic	38	0.02
Croatian	856	0.39
Cypriot	51	0.02
Czech	500	0.23
Czechoslovakian	563	0.26
Danish	209	0.10
Dutch	3,053	1.41
Eastern European	85	0.04
English	15,720	7.24
Estonian	7	0.00
European	933	0.43
Finnish	119	0.05
French, except Basque	3,799	1.75
French Canadian	469	0.22
German	39,203	18.06
German Russian	16	0.01
Greek	1,267	0.58
Guyanese	13	0.01
Hawaii Native/Pacific Islander:	178	0.08
Melanesian: (2)	2	0.00
Fijian (2)	2	0.00
Micronesian: (7)	23	0.01
Guamanian/Chamorro (7)	22	0.01
Other Micronesian	1	0.00
Polynesian: (23)	81	0.04
Native Hawaiian (14)	52	0.02
Samoan (5)	21	0.01
Other Polynesian (4)	8	0.00
Other Pac. Isl., specified	18	0.01
Other Pac. Isl., not spec. (16)	54	0.02
Hispanic or Latino:	2,513	1.16
Central American:	134	0.06
Costa Rican	7	0.00
Guatemalan	21	0.01
Honduran	48	0.02
Nicaraguan	9	0.00
Panamanian	18	0.01
Salvadoran	30	0.01
Other Central American	1	0.00
Cuban	74	0.03
Dominican Republic	19	0.01
Mexican	940	0.43
Puerto Rican	654	0.30
South American:	115	0.05
Argentinean	20	0.01
Bolivian	5	0.00
Chilean	5	0.00
Colombian	23	0.01
Ecuadorian	20	0.01
Peruvian	17	0.01
Uruguayan	1	0.00
Venezuelan	20	0.01
Other South American	8	0.00
Other Hispanic or Latino	577	0.27
Hungarian	4,025	1.85
Iranian	121	0.06
Irish	24,889	11.46
Israeli	10	0.00
Italian	14,705	6.77
Latvian	24	0.01
Lithuanian	423	0.19
Macedonian	214	0.10
Northern European	23	0.01
Norwegian	783	0.36
Pennsylvania German	405	0.19
Polish	5,200	2.40
Portuguese	70	0.03
Romanian	623	0.29
Russian	1,469	0.68
Scandinavian	34	0.02
Scotch-Irish	2,991	1.38
Scottish	3,134	1.44
Serbian	1,135	0.52
Slavic	100	0.05
Slovak	2,479	1.14
Slovene	535	0.25
Swedish	1,629	0.75
Swiss	976	0.45
Turkish	48	0.02
Ukrainian	844	0.39
United States or American	13,911	6.41
Welsh	2,390	1.10
West Indian, excl. Hispanic:	378	0.17
Bermudan	9	0.00
British West Indian	14	0.01
Dutch West Indian	36	0.02
Haitian	45	0.02
Jamaican	235	0.11
Trinidadian and Tobagonian	8	0.00
U.S. Virgin Islander	11	0.01
West Indian	20	0.01
White:	149,577	68.91
Not Hispanic (144,719)	148,161	68.25
Hispanic (1,205)	1,416	0.65
Yugoslavian	626	0.29

Alliance

Place Type: City
County: Stark
Population: 23,253

Ancestry/Race	Number	%
African American/Black:	2,919	12.55
Not Hispanic (2,581)	2,892	12.44
Hispanic (21)	27	0.12
African, sub-Saharan:	126	0.54
African	104	0.45
Cape Verdean	22	0.09
Am. Ind. or Alaska Nat., not spec.	45	0.19
American Indian tribes, specified:	84	0.36
Apache	2	0.01
Blackfeet	7	0.03
Cherokee (8)	44	0.19
Cheyenne (1)	1	0.00
Choctaw	1	0.00
Cree (4)	4	0.02
Crow	1	0.00
Delaware (6)	7	0.03
Latin American Indians (1)	1	0.00
Lumbee (2)	4	0.02
Pueblo (1)	1	0.00
Seminole	3	0.01
Sioux	6	0.03
All other tribes	2	0.01
American Indian tribes, not spec.	10	0.04
Arab:	27	0.12
Lebanese	13	0.06
Syrian	14	0.06
Asian:	233	1.00
Bangladeshi (1)	2	0.01
Chinese, ex. Taiwanese (46)	53	0.23
Filipino (24)	48	0.21
Indian (26)	36	0.15
Japanese (42)	46	0.20
Korean (20)	26	0.11
Malaysian (1)	2	0.01
Pakistani (6)	6	0.03
Sri Lankan (4)	4	0.02
Thai (3)	3	0.01
Vietnamese	1	0.00
Other Asian, not specified (2)	6	0.03
Austrian	67	0.29
Belgian	42	0.18
British	60	0.26
Canadian	14	0.06
Celtic	32	0.14
Croatian	38	0.16
Czech	71	0.31

Notes: 1. Figures in the "Number" column do not add up to the total population due to: a) Ancestry/Race overlap — e.g. persons can report being both White and Irish, b) persons of Hispanic origin can report being any race, c) persons reporting two ancestries are counted in both categories. 2. Numbers in parentheses indicate the number of persons reporting this ancestry/race alone, not in combination with any other ancestry/race. 3. Refer to the Explanation of Data in the front of the book for more detailed information.

Ancestry/Race	Number	%
Czechoslovakian	12	0.05
Danish	39	0.17
Dutch	567	2.44
Eastern European	7	0.03
English	2,210	9.51
European	122	0.53
Finnish	28	0.12
French, except Basque	586	2.52
French Canadian	46	0.20
German	5,238	22.55
Greek	141	0.61
Hawaii Native/Pacific Islander:	10	0.04
Micronesian: (2)	5	0.02
Guamanian/Chamorro (2)	5	0.02
Polynesian: (2)	5	0.02
Native Hawaiian	2	0.01
Samoan (2)	3	0.01
Hispanic or Latino:	271	1.17
Central American:	6	0.03
Guatemalan	2	0.01
Honduran	4	0.02
Cuban	3	0.01
Dominican Republic	1	0.00
Mexican	134	0.58
Puerto Rican	63	0.27
South American:	3	0.01
Colombian	2	0.01
Venezuelan	1	0.00
Other Hispanic or Latino	61	0.26
Hungarian	369	1.59
Irish	2,740	11.80
Italian	2,309	9.94
Latvian	7	0.03
Lithuanian	49	0.21
Northern European	16	0.07
Norwegian	74	0.32
Pennsylvania German	87	0.37
Polish	508	2.19
Romanian	406	1.75
Russian	54	0.23
Scotch-Irish	393	1.69
Scottish	380	1.64
Serbian	33	0.14
Slovak	99	0.43
Slovene	23	0.10
Swedish	161	0.69
Swiss	537	2.31
Turkish	14	0.06
Ukrainian	75	0.32
United States or American	2,087	8.98
Welsh	391	1.68
White:	20,296	87.28
Not Hispanic (19,730)	20,119	86.52
Hispanic (154)	177	0.76
Yugoslavian	12	0.05

Amherst

Place Type: City
County: Lorain
Population: 11,797

Ancestry/Race	Number	%
African American/Black:	80	0.68
Not Hispanic (52)	67	0.57
Hispanic (10)	13	0.11
Am. Ind. or Alaska Nat., not spec.	25	0.21
American Indian tribes, specified:	32	0.27
Cherokee (8)	18	0.15
Cheyenne	2	0.02
Chippewa	1	0.01
Choctaw (3)	3	0.03
Cree	1	0.01
Delaware (1)	1	0.01
Iroquois	2	0.02
Latin American Indians (1)	2	0.02
Seminole	1	0.01
All other tribes (1)	1	0.01
American Indian tribes, not spec.	4	0.03
Arab:	124	1.04
Lebanese	36	0.30
Syrian	88	0.74
Asian:	115	0.97
Chinese, ex. Taiwanese (7)	12	0.10
Filipino (32)	39	0.33
Indian (13)	14	0.12
Indonesian	1	0.01
Japanese (5)	11	0.09
Korean (20)	22	0.19
Pakistani	4	0.03
Sri Lankan (1)	1	0.01
Taiwanese (3)	5	0.04
Vietnamese (2)	2	0.02
Other Asian, not specified	4	0.03
Austrian	37	0.31
Belgian	4	0.03
British	47	0.40
Canadian	34	0.29
Carpatho Rusyn	30	0.25
Croatian	226	1.90
Czech	169	1.42
Czechoslovakian	32	0.27
Danish	47	0.40
Dutch	233	1.96
Eastern European	12	0.10
English	1,784	15.02
European	114	0.96
Finnish	59	0.50
French, except Basque	262	2.21
French Canadian	47	0.40
German	3,594	30.25
Greek	24	0.20
Hawaii Native/Pacific Islander:	6	0.05
Micronesian: (1)	1	0.01
Other Micronesian (1)	1	0.01
Polynesian:	4	0.03
Native Hawaiian	4	0.03
Other Pac. Isl., not spec.	1	0.01
Hispanic or Latino:	346	2.93
Central American:	7	0.06
Guatemalan	5	0.04
Salvadoran	2	0.02
Cuban	1	0.01
Mexican	104	0.88
Puerto Rican	169	1.43
South American:	11	0.09
Chilean	4	0.03
Peruvian	3	0.03
Venezuelan	4	0.03
Other Hispanic or Latino	54	0.46
Hungarian	711	5.98
Irish	1,742	14.66
Italian	1,101	9.27
Lithuanian	10	0.08
Macedonian	52	0.44
Norwegian	15	0.13
Pennsylvania German	19	0.16
Polish	1,557	13.10
Portuguese	6	0.05
Romanian	33	0.28
Russian	124	1.04
Scandinavian	46	0.39
Scotch-Irish	280	2.36
Scottish	208	1.75
Serbian	69	0.58
Slavic	5	0.04
Slovak	468	3.94
Slovene	159	1.34
Swedish	114	0.96
Swiss	51	0.43
Ukrainian	116	0.98
United States or American	524	4.41
Welsh	93	0.78
White:	11,532	97.75
Not Hispanic (11,206)	11,293	95.73
Hispanic (218)	239	2.03
Yugoslavian	25	0.21

Ashland

Place Type: City
County: Ashland
Population: 21,249

Ancestry/Race	Number	%
African American/Black:	311	1.46
Not Hispanic (251)	309	1.45
Hispanic (2)	2	0.01
African, sub-Saharan:	11	0.05
African	11	0.05
Alaska Native tribes, specified:	2	0.01
Alaska Athabascan (1)	1	0.00
Eskimo	1	0.00
Alaska Native tribes, not specified	1	0.00
Am. Ind. or Alaska Nat., not spec.	49	0.23
American Indian tribes, specified:	48	0.23
Apache	2	0.01
Blackfeet	9	0.04
Cherokee (3)	25	0.12
Chippewa (2)	2	0.01
Iroquois	1	0.00
Lumbee (1)	1	0.00
Potawatomi (1)	2	0.01
Sioux (2)	4	0.02
All other tribes	2	0.01
American Indian tribes, not spec.	2	0.01
Arab:	136	0.64
Arab/Arabic	44	0.21
Lebanese	51	0.24
Palestinian	32	0.15
Syrian	9	0.04
Armenian	9	0.04
Asian:	265	1.25
Cambodian (5)	6	0.03
Chinese, ex. Taiwanese (66)	74	0.35
Filipino (9)	19	0.09
Indian (47)	53	0.25
Japanese (23)	30	0.14
Korean (43)	47	0.22
Sri Lankan (5)	6	0.03
Taiwanese (7)	7	0.03
Thai (12)	12	0.06
Other Asian, not specified (7)	11	0.05
Australian	5	0.02
Austrian	25	0.12
Belgian	10	0.05
British	58	0.27
Canadian	39	0.18
Czech	76	0.36
Czechoslovakian	54	0.26
Danish	68	0.32
Dutch	435	2.05
English	2,280	10.77
Estonian	13	0.06
European	80	0.38
Finnish	5	0.02
French, except Basque	540	2.55
French Canadian	39	0.18
German	6,663	31.46
Greek	37	0.17
Hawaii Native/Pacific Islander:	22	0.10
Micronesian: (8)	10	0.05
Guamanian/Chamorro (8)	10	0.05
Polynesian: (1)	10	0.05
Native Hawaiian (1)	6	0.03
Other Polynesian	4	0.02
Other Pac. Isl., not spec. (1)	2	0.01
Hispanic or Latino:	181	0.85
Central American:	8	0.04
Costa Rican	3	0.01
Guatemalan	2	0.01
Nicaraguan	1	0.00
Salvadoran	2	0.01
Cuban	2	0.01
Mexican	102	0.48
Puerto Rican	21	0.10
South American:	11	0.05
Argentinean	2	0.01

Notes: 1. Figures in the "Number" column do not add up to the total population due to: a) Ancestry/Race overlap — e.g. persons can report being both White and Irish, b) persons of Hispanic origin can report being any race, c) persons reporting two ancestries are counted in both categories. 2. Numbers in parentheses indicate the number of persons reporting this ancestry/race alone, not in combination with any other ancestry/race. 3. Refer to the Explanation of Data in the front of the book for more detailed information.

Ancestry/Race	Number	%
Colombian	5	0.02
Ecuadorian	1	0.00
Peruvian	1	0.00
Venezuelan	1	0.00
Other South American	1	0.00
Other Hispanic or Latino	37	0.17
Hungarian	103	0.49
Irish	2,476	11.69
Italian	722	3.41
Lithuanian	43	0.20
Northern European	10	0.05
Norwegian	34	0.16
Pennsylvania German	100	0.47
Polish	447	2.11
Portuguese	2	0.01
Romanian	11	0.05
Russian	36	0.17
Scotch-Irish	419	1.98
Scottish	550	2.60
Slavic	10	0.05
Slovak	123	0.58
Slovene	25	0.12
Swedish	105	0.50
Swiss	155	0.73
Ukrainian	36	0.17
United States or American	2,397	11.32
Welsh	149	0.70
West Indian, excl. Hispanic:	4	0.02
Haitian	4	0.02
White:	20,656	97.21
Not Hispanic (20,374)	20,537	96.65
Hispanic (99)	119	0.56
Yugoslavian	41	0.19

Ashtabula

Place Type: City
County: Ashtabula
Population: 20,962

Ancestry/Race	Number	%
African American/Black:	2,340	11.16
Not Hispanic (1,998)	2,276	10.86
Hispanic (55)	64	0.31
African, sub-Saharan:	86	0.41
African	79	0.38
Nigerian	7	0.03
Am. Ind. or Alaska Nat., not spec.	64	0.31
American Indian tribes, specified:	116	0.55
Apache (1)	1	0.00
Blackfeet (2)	20	0.10
Cherokee (12)	50	0.24
Cheyenne (1)	1	0.00
Chippewa (5)	13	0.06
Choctaw (1)	1	0.00
Comanche (1)	1	0.00
Cree	2	0.01
Creek	1	0.00
Crow	3	0.01
Delaware	3	0.01
Iroquois (2)	4	0.02
Navajo (1)	1	0.00
Osage (3)	3	0.01
Seminole	1	0.00
Sioux (5)	7	0.03
Yaqui	2	0.01
All other tribes	2	0.01
American Indian tribes, not spec.	3	0.01
Arab:	88	0.42
Lebanese	80	0.38
Syrian	8	0.04
Asian:	121	0.58
Chinese, ex. Taiwanese (21)	29	0.14
Filipino (4)	7	0.03
Indian (13)	16	0.08
Indonesian (3)	4	0.02
Japanese (5)	10	0.05
Korean (23)	33	0.16
Malaysian	1	0.00
Pakistani (1)	1	0.00
Taiwanese	2	0.01
Thai (2)	2	0.01
Vietnamese (6)	6	0.03
Other Asian, not specified (4)	10	0.05
Australian	2	0.01
Austrian	35	0.17
British	27	0.13
Canadian	21	0.10
Croatian	16	0.08
Czech	51	0.24
Czechoslovakian	50	0.24
Danish	12	0.06
Dutch	432	2.07
Eastern European	7	0.03
English	1,911	9.16
European	116	0.56
Finnish	878	4.21
French, except Basque	357	1.71
French Canadian	68	0.33
German	3,522	16.89
Greek	60	0.29
Hawaii Native/Pacific Islander:	16	0.08
Micronesian: (3)	6	0.03
Guamanian/Chamorro (3)	5	0.02
Other Micronesian	1	0.00
Polynesian: (7)	9	0.04
Native Hawaiian (7)	9	0.04
Other Pac. Isl., not spec. (1)	1	0.00
Hispanic or Latino:	1,115	5.32
Central American:	4	0.02
Honduran	3	0.01
Panamanian	1	0.00
Cuban	14	0.07
Dominican Republic	5	0.02
Mexican	260	1.24
Puerto Rican	727	3.47
South American:	3	0.01
Colombian	1	0.00
Ecuadorian	1	0.00
Peruvian	1	0.00
Other Hispanic or Latino	102	0.49
Hungarian	539	2.58
Irish	2,400	11.51
Italian	3,137	15.04
Lithuanian	21	0.10
Norwegian	64	0.31
Pennsylvania German	78	0.37
Polish	666	3.19
Portuguese	133	0.64
Romanian	6	0.03
Russian	47	0.23
Scandinavian	37	0.18
Scotch-Irish	221	1.06
Scottish	401	1.92
Serbian	11	0.05
Slavic	11	0.05
Slovak	142	0.68
Slovene	133	0.64
Swedish	478	2.29
Swiss	17	0.08
Ukrainian	19	0.09
United States or American	1,492	7.15
Welsh	96	0.46
West Indian, excl. Hispanic:	12	0.06
Jamaican	12	0.06
White:	18,207	86.86
Not Hispanic (17,262)	17,658	84.24
Hispanic (491)	549	2.62
Yugoslavian	9	0.04

Athens

Place Type: City
County: Athens
Population: 21,342

Ancestry/Race	Number	%
African American/Black:	918	4.30
Not Hispanic (806)	905	4.24
Hispanic (10)	13	0.06
African, sub-Saharan:	62	0.29
African	23	0.11
Cape Verdean	16	0.08
Ghanian	7	0.03
Nigerian	7	0.03
South African	9	0.04
Am. Ind. or Alaska Nat., not spec.	45	0.21
Alsatian	9	0.04
American Indian tribes, specified:	93	0.44
Blackfeet	1	0.00
Cherokee (4)	57	0.27
Chippewa (1)	1	0.00
Choctaw (3)	6	0.03
Creek (1)	1	0.00
Delaware (1)	2	0.01
Iroquois	3	0.01
Latin American Indians (1)	4	0.02
Lumbee	1	0.00
Navajo (1)	2	0.01
Osage (1)	1	0.00
Potawatomi (1)	1	0.00
Seminole	3	0.01
Sioux	2	0.01
All other tribes (3)	8	0.04
American Indian tribes, not spec.	4	0.02
Arab:	251	1.18
Arab/Arabic	60	0.28
Lebanese	95	0.45
Syrian	27	0.13
Other Arab	69	0.33
Armenian	6	0.03
Asian:	1,080	5.06
Bangladeshi (5)	6	0.03
Cambodian (3)	3	0.01
Chinese, ex. Taiwanese (322)	339	1.59
Filipino (19)	36	0.17
Indian (210)	231	1.08
Indonesian (22)	22	0.10
Japanese (136)	146	0.68
Korean (98)	106	0.50
Malaysian (18)	25	0.12
Pakistani (6)	6	0.03
Sri Lankan (5)	7	0.03
Taiwanese (38)	47	0.22
Thai (23)	28	0.13
Vietnamese (20)	24	0.11
Other Asian, specified (6)	8	0.04
Other Asian, not specified (14)	46	0.22
Austrian	81	0.38
Belgian	15	0.07
British	156	0.74
Bulgarian	20	0.09
Canadian	69	0.33
Celtic	16	0.08
Croatian	91	0.43
Czech	98	0.46
Czechoslovakian	85	0.40
Danish	69	0.33
Dutch	279	1.32
Eastern European	32	0.15
English	2,256	10.65
Estonian	11	0.05
European	374	1.76
Finnish	25	0.12
French, except Basque	409	1.93
French Canadian	98	0.46
German	6,003	28.33
Greek	189	0.89
Guyanese	14	0.07
Hawaii Native/Pacific Islander:	28	0.13
Micronesian: (1)	4	0.02
Guamanian/Chamorro (1)	4	0.02
Polynesian: (7)	11	0.05
Native Hawaiian (5)	7	0.03
Samoan (2)	4	0.02
Other Pac. Isl., specified	2	0.01
Other Pac. Isl., not spec. (4)	11	0.05
Hispanic or Latino:	301	1.41
Central American:	26	0.12
Costa Rican	4	0.02

Notes: 1. Figures in the "Number" column do not add up to the total population due to: a) Ancestry/Race overlap — e.g. persons can report being both White and Irish, b) persons of Hispanic origin can report being any race, c) persons reporting two ancestries are counted in both categories. 2. Numbers in parentheses indicate the number of persons reporting this ancestry/race alone, not in combination with any other ancestry/race. 3. Refer to the Explanation of Data in the front of the book for more detailed information.

Guatemalan	9	0.04
Honduran	3	0.01
Nicaraguan	3	0.01
Salvadoran	4	0.02
Other Central American	3	0.01
Cuban	16	0.07
Mexican	87	0.41
Puerto Rican	45	0.21
South American:	60	0.28
Argentinean	7	0.03
Bolivian	3	0.01
Chilean	6	0.03
Colombian	9	0.04
Ecuadorian	10	0.05
Peruvian	10	0.05
Venezuelan	14	0.07
Other South American	1	0.00
Other Hispanic or Latino	67	0.31
Hungarian	333	1.57
Iranian	8	0.04
Irish	3,628	17.12
Israeli	8	0.04
Italian	1,765	8.33
Latvian	10	0.05
Lithuanian	55	0.26
Luxemburger	10	0.05
Norwegian	94	0.44
Pennsylvania German	28	0.13
Polish	1,105	5.21
Portuguese	20	0.09
Romanian	81	0.38
Russian	244	1.15
Scandinavian	20	0.09
Scotch-Irish	456	2.15
Scottish	606	2.86
Serbian	14	0.07
Slavic	12	0.06
Slovak	218	1.03
Slovene	74	0.35
Swedish	242	1.14
Swiss	216	1.02
Turkish	15	0.07
Ukrainian	198	0.93
United States or American	556	2.62
Welsh	515	2.43
West Indian, excl. Hispanic:	17	0.08
British West Indian	8	0.04
Haitian	4	0.02
Jamaican	5	0.02
White:	19,346	90.65
Not Hispanic (18,861)	19,162	89.79
Hispanic (167)	184	0.86
Yugoslavian	8	0.04

Aurora

Place Type: City
County: Portage
Population: 13,556

Ancestry/Race	Number	%
African American/Black:	317	2.34
Not Hispanic (291)	314	2.32
Hispanic (2)	3	0.02
African, sub-Saharan:	27	0.20
African	11	0.08
Ethiopian	16	0.12
Alaska Native tribes, specified:	1	0.01
Alaska Athabascan (1)	1	0.01
Am. Ind. or Alaska Nat., not spec.	19	0.14
American Indian tribes, specified:	32	0.24
Apache (2)	2	0.01
Blackfeet	2	0.01
Cherokee (5)	16	0.12
Choctaw (1)	1	0.01
Iroquois	7	0.05
Navajo	1	0.01
Sioux	2	0.01
All other tribes (1)	1	0.01
American Indian tribes, not spec.	2	0.01
Arab:	69	0.51
Lebanese	60	0.44
Syrian	9	0.07
Armenian	25	0.18
Asian:	214	1.58
Chinese, ex. Taiwanese (40)	51	0.38
Filipino (25)	43	0.32
Indian (58)	62	0.46
Japanese (11)	14	0.10
Korean (15)	16	0.12
Pakistani (3)	3	0.02
Sri Lankan (6)	6	0.04
Thai (2)	2	0.01
Vietnamese	6	0.04
Other Asian, not specified (3)	11	0.08
Assyrian/Chaldean/Syriac	7	0.05
Austrian	60	0.44
Belgian	6	0.04
British	72	0.53
Bulgarian	7	0.05
Canadian	63	0.46
Celtic	25	0.18
Croatian	99	0.73
Czech	412	3.04
Czechoslovakian	81	0.60
Danish	17	0.13
Dutch	195	1.44
Eastern European	16	0.12
English	1,840	13.57
European	71	0.52
Finnish	17	0.13
French, except Basque	424	3.13
French Canadian	28	0.21
German	3,543	26.14
Greek	114	0.84
Hawaii Native/Pacific Islander:	6	0.04
Polynesian: (2)	5	0.04
Native Hawaiian (1)	4	0.03
Samoan (1)	1	0.01
Other Pac. Isl., not spec.	1	0.01
Hispanic or Latino:	78	0.58
Cuban	11	0.08
Mexican	28	0.21
Puerto Rican	17	0.13
South American:	5	0.04
Argentinean	2	0.01
Colombian	1	0.01
Peruvian	2	0.01
Other Hispanic or Latino	17	0.13
Hungarian	626	4.62
Irish	2,229	16.44
Italian	1,884	13.90
Lithuanian	72	0.53
Luxemburger	9	0.07
Northern European	43	0.32
Norwegian	52	0.38
Pennsylvania German	16	0.12
Polish	1,335	9.85
Romanian	44	0.32
Russian	345	2.54
Scandinavian	6	0.04
Scotch-Irish	414	3.05
Scottish	481	3.55
Slavic	6	0.04
Slovak	441	3.25
Slovene	278	2.05
Swedish	126	0.93
Swiss	75	0.55
Turkish	7	0.05
Ukrainian	75	0.55
United States or American	667	4.92
Welsh	148	1.09
West Indian, excl. Hispanic:	24	0.18
Jamaican	24	0.18
White:	13,055	96.30
Not Hispanic (12,917)	12,999	95.89
Hispanic (52)	56	0.41
Yugoslavian	45	0.33

Austintown

Place Type: Census Designated Place
County: Mahoning
Population: 31,627

Ancestry/Race	Number	%
African American/Black:	1,751	5.54
Not Hispanic (1,580)	1,702	5.38
Hispanic (30)	49	0.15
African, sub-Saharan:	67	0.21
African	43	0.14
Nigerian	13	0.04
South African	11	0.03
Alaska Native tribes, not specified	1	0.00
Am. Ind. or Alaska Nat., not spec.	57	0.18
American Indian tribes, specified:	106	0.34
Apache (3)	7	0.02
Blackfeet	3	0.01
Cherokee (11)	57	0.18
Chickasaw (1)	1	0.00
Chippewa (1)	1	0.00
Crow	2	0.01
Iroquois (2)	6	0.02
Latin American Indians (1)	6	0.02
Potawatomi (2)	4	0.01
Pueblo (1)	1	0.00
Seminole	2	0.01
Sioux (3)	9	0.03
All other tribes (5)	7	0.02
American Indian tribes, not spec.	7	0.02
Arab:	167	0.53
Arab/Arabic	24	0.08
Lebanese	143	0.45
Armenian	12	0.04
Asian:	272	0.86
Cambodian (3)	3	0.01
Chinese, ex. Taiwanese (43)	47	0.15
Filipino (17)	40	0.13
Indian (55)	69	0.22
Japanese (7)	11	0.03
Korean (18)	33	0.10
Pakistani (14)	31	0.10
Taiwanese (1)	2	0.01
Thai (4)	6	0.02
Vietnamese (12)	14	0.04
Other Asian, not specified (3)	16	0.05
Austrian	78	0.25
Belgian	17	0.05
Brazilian	9	0.03
British	81	0.26
Bulgarian	9	0.03
Canadian	62	0.20
Celtic	15	0.05
Croatian	486	1.54
Czech	115	0.36
Czechoslovakian	162	0.51
Danish	14	0.04
Dutch	536	1.69
English	2,908	9.19
European	37	0.12
Finnish	33	0.10
French, except Basque	612	1.93
French Canadian	118	0.37
German	8,246	26.06
Greek	225	0.71
Guyanese	11	0.03
Hawaii Native/Pacific Islander:	17	0.05
Micronesian: (1)	1	0.00
Guamanian/Chamorro (1)	1	0.00
Polynesian: (7)	15	0.05
Native Hawaiian (4)	6	0.02
Samoan (2)	6	0.02
Other Polynesian (1)	3	0.01
Other Pac. Isl., not spec.	1	0.00
Hispanic or Latino:	578	1.83
Central American:	28	0.09
Costa Rican	8	0.03
Guatemalan	1	0.00
Honduran	6	0.02

Notes: 1. Figures in the "Number" column do not add up to the total population due to: a) Ancestry/Race overlap — e.g. persons can report being both White and Irish, b) persons of Hispanic origin can report being any race, c) persons reporting two ancestries are counted in both categories. 2. Numbers in parentheses indicate the number of persons reporting this ancestry/race alone, not in combination with any other ancestry/race. 3. Refer to the Explanation of Data in the front of the book for more detailed information.

	Number	%
Panamanian	8	0.03
Salvadoran	5	0.02
Cuban	15	0.05
Dominican Republic	15	0.05
Mexican	128	0.40
Puerto Rican	269	0.85
South American:	20	0.06
Argentinean	7	0.02
Chilean	2	0.01
Colombian	4	0.01
Peruvian	3	0.01
Venezuelan	3	0.01
Other South American	1	0.00
Other Hispanic or Latino	103	0.33
Hungarian	1,032	3.26
Irish	5,632	17.80
Italian	6,098	19.27
Latvian	6	0.02
Lithuanian	83	0.26
Macedonian	26	0.08
Norwegian	39	0.12
Pennsylvania German	179	0.57
Polish	1,557	4.92
Romanian	179	0.57
Russian	329	1.04
Scotch-Irish	647	2.04
Scottish	801	2.53
Serbian	111	0.35
Slavic	23	0.07
Slovak	2,411	7.62
Slovene	60	0.19
Swedish	334	1.06
Swiss	73	0.23
Ukrainian	651	2.06
United States or American	1,508	4.77
Welsh	990	3.13
West Indian, excl. Hispanic:	29	0.09
Barbadian	11	0.03
Dutch West Indian	18	0.06
White:	29,601	93.59
Not Hispanic (28,904)	29,198	92.32
Hispanic (354)	403	1.27
Yugoslavian	73	0.23

Avon Lake

Place Type: City
County: Lorain
Population: 18,145

Ancestry/Race	Number	%
African American/Black:	110	0.61
Not Hispanic (82)	106	0.58
Hispanic	4	0.02
African, sub-Saharan:	7	0.04
African	7	0.04
Alaska Native tribes, specified:	4	0.02
Tlingit-Haida (4)	4	0.02
Am. Ind. or Alaska Nat., not spec.	23	0.13
Albanian	19	0.10
American Indian tribes, specified:	58	0.32
Apache	5	0.03
Blackfeet (1)	8	0.04
Cherokee (6)	24	0.13
Chippewa (1)	1	0.01
Crow (1)	1	0.01
Iroquois	2	0.01
Navajo	4	0.02
Shoshone	1	0.01
Sioux (3)	3	0.02
Yaqui	1	0.01
All other tribes	8	0.04
American Indian tribes, not spec.	5	0.03
Arab:	139	0.77
Egyptian	18	0.10
Lebanese	76	0.42
Syrian	45	0.25
Armenian	46	0.25
Asian:	221	1.22
Chinese, ex. Taiwanese (36)	49	0.27
Filipino (18)	23	0.13
Indian (65)	72	0.40
Japanese (14)	26	0.14
Korean (27)	30	0.17
Pakistani (6)	6	0.03
Taiwanese (2)	2	0.01
Thai	1	0.01
Vietnamese (2)	2	0.01
Other Asian, specified (1)	1	0.01
Other Asian, not specified (4)	9	0.05
Austrian	72	0.40
Belgian	39	0.21
British	143	0.79
Bulgarian	7	0.04
Canadian	63	0.35
Croatian	115	0.63
Czech	318	1.75
Czechoslovakian	109	0.60
Danish	59	0.33
Dutch	343	1.89
Eastern European	7	0.04
English	2,522	13.90
European	33	0.18
Finnish	6	0.03
French, except Basque	549	3.03
French Canadian	78	0.43
German	6,565	36.18
Greek	87	0.48
Hawaii Native/Pacific Islander:	11	0.06
Micronesian: (6)	9	0.05
Guamanian/Chamorro (4)	7	0.04
Other Micronesian (2)	2	0.01
Polynesian: (1)	2	0.01
Native Hawaiian (1)	2	0.01
Hispanic or Latino:	226	1.25
Central American:	8	0.04
Guatemalan	4	0.02
Honduran	4	0.02
Cuban	9	0.05
Mexican	99	0.55
Puerto Rican	70	0.39
South American:	24	0.13
Argentinean	7	0.04
Colombian	7	0.04
Ecuadorian	7	0.04
Paraguayan	1	0.01
Other South American	2	0.01
Other Hispanic or Latino	16	0.09
Hungarian	852	4.70
Irish	4,116	22.68
Italian	2,072	11.42
Latvian	12	0.07
Lithuanian	48	0.26
Luxemburger	8	0.04
Macedonian	5	0.03
Norwegian	212	1.17
Pennsylvania German	17	0.09
Polish	1,316	7.25
Portuguese	40	0.22
Romanian	92	0.51
Russian	211	1.16
Scandinavian	25	0.14
Scotch-Irish	638	3.52
Scottish	794	4.38
Serbian	28	0.15
Slavic	55	0.30
Slovak	962	5.30
Slovene	226	1.25
Swedish	138	0.76
Swiss	94	0.52
Turkish	25	0.14
Ukrainian	224	1.23
United States or American	593	3.27
Welsh	289	1.59
West Indian, excl. Hispanic:	5	0.03
Jamaican	5	0.03
White:	17,801	98.10
Not Hispanic (17,484)	17,612	97.06
Hispanic (172)	189	1.04
Yugoslavian	36	0.20

Avon

Place Type: City
County: Lorain
Population: 11,446

Ancestry/Race	Number	%
African American/Black:	100	0.87
Not Hispanic (80)	97	0.85
Hispanic (2)	3	0.03
Am. Ind. or Alaska Nat., not spec.	19	0.17
Albanian	35	0.31
American Indian tribes, specified:	39	0.34
Apache (1)	1	0.01
Blackfeet	2	0.02
Cherokee (5)	18	0.16
Chippewa (4)	4	0.03
Creek	4	0.03
Iroquois	4	0.03
Paiute (3)	3	0.03
Pueblo (1)	1	0.01
Shoshone (1)	1	0.01
Sioux	1	0.01
Arab:	72	0.63
Arab/Arabic	11	0.10
Jordanian	37	0.32
Lebanese	7	0.06
Syrian	17	0.15
Asian:	156	1.36
Chinese, ex. Taiwanese (13)	16	0.14
Filipino (33)	41	0.36
Indian (44)	44	0.38
Japanese (10)	26	0.23
Korean (10)	16	0.14
Thai (1)	1	0.01
Vietnamese (1)	3	0.03
Other Asian, specified	1	0.01
Other Asian, not specified (3)	8	0.07
Austrian	103	0.90
British	30	0.26
Bulgarian	19	0.17
Canadian	30	0.26
Croatian	196	1.71
Czech	156	1.36
Czechoslovakian	96	0.84
Danish	66	0.58
Dutch	128	1.12
English	1,192	10.41
European	84	0.73
Finnish	92	0.80
French, except Basque	367	3.21
French Canadian	77	0.67
German	4,008	35.02
Greek	124	1.08
Hispanic or Latino:	147	1.28
Central American:	1	0.01
Guatemalan	1	0.01
Mexican	36	0.31
Puerto Rican	83	0.73
South American:	2	0.02
Colombian	1	0.01
Uruguayan	1	0.01
Other Hispanic or Latino	25	0.22
Hungarian	708	6.19
Irish	2,078	18.15
Italian	1,241	10.84
Latvian	17	0.15
Lithuanian	33	0.29
Macedonian	5	0.04
Norwegian	56	0.49
Pennsylvania German	18	0.16
Polish	1,106	9.66
Romanian	30	0.26
Russian	127	1.11
Scandinavian	16	0.14
Scotch-Irish	190	1.66
Scottish	247	2.16
Serbian	52	0.45
Slovak	556	4.86
Slovene	182	1.59

Notes: 1. Figures in the "Number" column do not add up to the total population due to: a) Ancestry/Race overlap — e.g. persons can report being both White and Irish, b) persons of Hispanic origin can report being any race, c) persons reporting two ancestries are counted in both categories. 2. Numbers in parentheses indicate the number of persons reporting this ancestry/race alone, not in combination with any other ancestry/race. 3. Refer to the Explanation of Data in the front of the book for more detailed information.

Ancestry/Race	Number	%
Swedish	98	0.86
Swiss	36	0.31
Ukrainian	173	1.51
United States or American	441	3.85
Welsh	210	1.83
White:	11,190	97.76
Not Hispanic (10,998)	11,075	96.76
Hispanic (107)	115	1.00
Yugoslavian	54	0.47

Barberton

Place Type: City
County: Summit
Population: 27,899

Ancestry/Race	Number	%
Acadian/Cajun	23	0.08
African American/Black:	1,658	5.94
Not Hispanic (1,482)	1,647	5.90
Hispanic (6)	11	0.04
African, sub-Saharan:	81	0.29
African	81	0.29
Am. Ind. or Alaska Nat., not spec.	71	0.25
American Indian tribes, specified:	150	0.54
Apache (1)	5	0.02
Blackfeet (1)	8	0.03
Cherokee (30)	89	0.32
Chickasaw (3)	3	0.01
Chippewa	7	0.03
Choctaw	2	0.01
Creek	1	0.00
Iroquois (2)	6	0.02
Latin American Indians (1)	1	0.00
Navajo	4	0.01
Shoshone	1	0.00
Sioux (7)	11	0.04
All other tribes (4)	11	0.04
American Indian tribes, not spec.	19	0.07
Arab:	159	0.57
Lebanese	159	0.57
Armenian	9	0.03
Asian:	148	0.53
Chinese, ex. Taiwanese (22)	26	0.09
Filipino (18)	23	0.08
Indian (22)	29	0.10
Indonesian (1)	1	0.00
Japanese (5)	9	0.03
Korean (14)	22	0.08
Laotian (1)	6	0.02
Pakistani (5)	5	0.02
Taiwanese	3	0.01
Thai (3)	4	0.01
Other Asian, specified (1)	2	0.01
Other Asian, not specified (10)	18	0.06
Austrian	100	0.36
Belgian	11	0.04
British	55	0.20
Bulgarian	13	0.05
Canadian	42	0.15
Celtic	6	0.02
Croatian	160	0.57
Czech	81	0.29
Czechoslovakian	80	0.29
Danish	36	0.13
Dutch	640	2.29
English	1,987	7.10
European	118	0.42
Finnish	14	0.05
French, except Basque	676	2.41
French Canadian	30	0.11
German	6,690	23.90
Greek	113	0.40
Hawaii Native/Pacific Islander:	5	0.02
Micronesian:	1	0.00
Guamanian/Chamorro	1	0.00
Polynesian: (1)	1	0.00
Samoan (1)	1	0.00
Other Pac. Isl., not spec. (1)	3	0.01
Hispanic or Latino:	179	0.64
Central American:	4	0.01
Honduran	1	0.00
Panamanian	2	0.01
Other Central American	1	0.00
Cuban	2	0.01
Mexican	74	0.27
Puerto Rican	53	0.19
South American:	12	0.04
Argentinean	3	0.01
Chilean	1	0.00
Colombian	4	0.01
Ecuadorian	3	0.01
Other South American	1	0.00
Other Hispanic or Latino	34	0.12
Hungarian	1,215	4.34
Irish	3,664	13.09
Italian	1,544	5.52
Lithuanian	56	0.20
Macedonian	59	0.21
Norwegian	96	0.34
Pennsylvania German	35	0.13
Polish	769	2.75
Portuguese	16	0.06
Romanian	75	0.27
Russian	59	0.21
Scandinavian	6	0.02
Scotch-Irish	366	1.31
Scottish	480	1.71
Serbian	334	1.19
Slavic	66	0.24
Slovak	817	2.92
Slovene	393	1.40
Swedish	112	0.40
Swiss	106	0.38
Ukrainian	47	0.17
United States or American	2,840	10.14
Welsh	366	1.31
West Indian, excl. Hispanic:	14	0.05
Haitian	14	0.05
White:	26,134	93.67
Not Hispanic (25,662)	25,999	93.19
Hispanic (125)	135	0.48
Yugoslavian	107	0.38

Bay Village

Place Type: City
County: Cuyahoga
Population: 16,087

Ancestry/Race	Number	%
African American/Black:	64	0.40
Not Hispanic (42)	57	0.35
Hispanic (1)	7	0.04
Am. Ind. or Alaska Nat., not spec.	9	0.06
Albanian	5	0.03
American Indian tribes, specified:	24	0.15
Blackfeet	1	0.01
Cherokee (1)	14	0.09
Chippewa	3	0.02
Creek (1)	1	0.01
Navajo (1)	1	0.01
Sioux	1	0.01
All other tribes	3	0.02
American Indian tribes, not spec.	4	0.02
Arab:	145	0.90
Jordanian	33	0.21
Lebanese	69	0.43
Palestinian	6	0.04
Syrian	37	0.23
Armenian	23	0.14
Asian:	166	1.03
Chinese, ex. Taiwanese (33)	39	0.24
Filipino (11)	18	0.11
Indian (19)	23	0.14
Indonesian	1	0.01
Japanese (15)	29	0.18
Korean (19)	23	0.14
Pakistani (9)	11	0.07
Thai (3)	4	0.02
Vietnamese (3)	8	0.05
Other Asian, not specified (1)	10	0.06
Austrian	60	0.37
Belgian	15	0.09
British	176	1.09
Bulgarian	4	0.02
Canadian	91	0.57
Carpatho Rusyn	9	0.06
Celtic	17	0.11
Croatian	96	0.60
Czech	253	1.57
Czechoslovakian	50	0.31
Danish	101	0.63
Dutch	281	1.75
Eastern European	15	0.09
English	2,493	15.50
European	85	0.53
Finnish	104	0.65
French, except Basque	487	3.03
French Canadian	96	0.60
German	5,026	31.24
Greek	88	0.55
Hawaii Native/Pacific Islander:	3	0.02
Polynesian: (1)	1	0.01
Native Hawaiian (1)	1	0.01
Other Pac. Isl., not spec.	2	0.01
Hispanic or Latino:	157	0.98
Central American:	5	0.03
Guatemalan	1	0.01
Panamanian	3	0.02
Salvadoran	1	0.01
Cuban	10	0.06
Dominican Republic	1	0.01
Mexican	54	0.34
Puerto Rican	28	0.17
South American:	11	0.07
Argentinean	1	0.01
Chilean	1	0.01
Colombian	3	0.02
Peruvian	1	0.01
Venezuelan	5	0.03
Other Hispanic or Latino	48	0.30
Hungarian	604	3.75
Irish	4,310	26.79
Israeli	5	0.03
Italian	1,542	9.59
Lithuanian	140	0.87
Macedonian	5	0.03
Norwegian	144	0.90
Pennsylvania German	5	0.03
Polish	1,126	7.00
Portuguese	8	0.05
Romanian	137	0.85
Russian	186	1.16
Scandinavian	48	0.30
Scotch-Irish	318	1.98
Scottish	633	3.93
Serbian	10	0.06
Slavic	6	0.04
Slovak	634	3.94
Slovene	177	1.10
Swedish	278	1.73
Swiss	71	0.44
Ukrainian	209	1.30
United States or American	597	3.71
Welsh	256	1.59
White:	15,875	98.68
Not Hispanic (15,655)	15,740	97.84
Hispanic (118)	135	0.84
Yugoslavian	52	0.32

Beachwood

Place Type: City
County: Cuyahoga
Population: 12,186

Ancestry/Race	Number	%
African American/Black:	1,153	9.46
Not Hispanic (1,099)	1,144	9.39

Notes: 1. Figures in the "Number" column do not add up to the total population due to: a) Ancestry/Race overlap — e.g. persons can report being both White and Irish, b) persons of Hispanic origin can report being any race, c) persons reporting two ancestries are counted in both categories. 2. Numbers in parentheses indicate the number of persons reporting this ancestry/race alone, not in combination with any other ancestry/race. 3. Refer to the Explanation of Data in the front of the book for more detailed information.

Ancestry/Race	Number	%
Hispanic (7)	9	0.07
African, sub-Saharan:	191	1.57
African	116	0.95
Senegalese	20	0.16
South African	55	0.45
Am. Ind. or Alaska Nat., not spec.	14	0.11
American Indian tribes, specified:	16	0.13
Cherokee (1)	12	0.10
Chickasaw	1	0.01
Latin American Indians	1	0.01
Navajo	2	0.02
Arab:	76	0.62
Arab/Arabic	17	0.14
Iraqi	18	0.15
Lebanese	7	0.06
Moroccan	6	0.05
Palestinian	10	0.08
Syrian	18	0.15
Asian:	437	3.59
Chinese, ex. Taiwanese (102)	113	0.93
Filipino (22)	30	0.25
Indian (146)	157	1.29
Indonesian (1)	1	0.01
Japanese (43)	48	0.39
Korean (67)	69	0.57
Taiwanese	1	0.01
Thai (4)	4	0.03
Other Asian, specified	1	0.01
Other Asian, not specified (2)	13	0.11
Australian	50	0.41
Austrian	198	1.62
Belgian	9	0.07
British	6	0.05
Canadian	20	0.16
Croatian	29	0.24
Czech	105	0.86
Czechoslovakian	74	0.61
Danish	7	0.06
Dutch	19	0.16
Eastern European	391	3.21
English	237	1.94
European	101	0.83
French, except Basque	99	0.81
French Canadian	18	0.15
German	529	4.34
Greek	23	0.19
Hawaii Native/Pacific Islander:	3	0.02
Polynesian: (1)	1	0.01
Samoan (1)	1	0.01
Other Pac. Isl., specified	1	0.01
Other Pac. Isl., not spec. (1)	1	0.01
Hispanic or Latino:	95	0.78
Central American:	1	0.01
Panamanian	1	0.01
Cuban	11	0.09
Dominican Republic	5	0.04
Mexican	26	0.21
Puerto Rican	11	0.09
South American:	21	0.17
Argentinean	7	0.06
Chilean	3	0.02
Colombian	4	0.03
Peruvian	3	0.02
Venezuelan	4	0.03
Other Hispanic or Latino	20	0.16
Hungarian	830	6.81
Iranian	37	0.30
Irish	378	3.10
Israeli	178	1.46
Italian	351	2.88
Latvian	31	0.25
Lithuanian	308	2.53
Norwegian	13	0.11
Polish	995	8.17
Portuguese	20	0.16
Romanian	154	1.26
Russian	1,894	15.54
Scotch-Irish	37	0.30
Scottish	59	0.48
Serbian	18	0.15
Slovak	66	0.54
Slovene	10	0.08
Soviet Union	9	0.07
Swedish	12	0.10
Swiss	5	0.04
Ukrainian	130	1.07
United States or American	1,207	9.90
Welsh	16	0.13
West Indian, excl. Hispanic:	4	0.03
Jamaican	4	0.03
White:	10,632	87.25
Not Hispanic (10,469)	10,554	86.61
Hispanic (72)	78	0.64
Yugoslavian	9	0.07

Beavercreek

Place Type: City
County: Greene
Population: 37,984

Ancestry/Race	Number	%
Acadian/Cajun	22	0.06
African American/Black:	615	1.62
Not Hispanic (537)	603	1.59
Hispanic (3)	12	0.03
African, sub-Saharan:	48	0.13
African	34	0.09
Nigerian	14	0.04
Am. Ind. or Alaska Nat., not spec.	35	0.09
Albanian	10	0.03
American Indian tribes, specified:	154	0.41
Apache	4	0.01
Blackfeet (2)	6	0.02
Cherokee (18)	90	0.24
Cheyenne (1)	2	0.01
Chippewa (3)	6	0.02
Choctaw (1)	4	0.01
Cree (1)	4	0.01
Iroquois (3)	10	0.03
Kiowa (1)	1	0.00
Latin American Indians (3)	4	0.01
Potawatomi (2)	2	0.01
Seminole	1	0.00
Sioux (1)	5	0.01
All other tribes (7)	15	0.04
American Indian tribes, not spec.	14	0.04
Arab:	348	0.91
Arab/Arabic	13	0.03
Lebanese	205	0.54
Palestinian	50	0.13
Syrian	57	0.15
Other Arab	23	0.06
Armenian	37	0.10
Asian:	1,549	4.08
Bangladeshi (10)	10	0.03
Cambodian (5)	5	0.01
Chinese, ex. Taiwanese (289)	322	0.85
Filipino (69)	111	0.29
Indian (454)	483	1.27
Indonesian (3)	3	0.01
Japanese (83)	121	0.32
Korean (238)	284	0.75
Laotian (1)	1	0.00
Malaysian (4)	4	0.01
Pakistani (12)	17	0.04
Sri Lankan (2)	2	0.01
Taiwanese (39)	46	0.12
Thai (11)	19	0.05
Vietnamese (71)	74	0.19
Other Asian, specified (1)	5	0.01
Other Asian, not specified (21)	42	0.11
Australian	19	0.05
Austrian	104	0.27
Belgian	48	0.13
British	247	0.65
Bulgarian	10	0.03
Canadian	67	0.18
Croatian	6	0.02
Czech	62	0.16
Czechoslovakian	54	0.14
Danish	167	0.44
Dutch	1,066	2.79
Eastern European	12	0.03
English	5,470	14.33
European	469	1.23
Finnish	56	0.15
French, except Basque	1,107	2.90
French Canadian	250	0.65
German	11,542	30.23
German Russian	10	0.03
Greek	153	0.40
Hawaii Native/Pacific Islander:	27	0.07
Polynesian: (6)	22	0.06
Native Hawaiian (5)	21	0.06
Samoan (1)	1	0.00
Other Pac. Isl., not spec. (2)	5	0.01
Hispanic or Latino:	433	1.14
Central American:	16	0.04
Guatemalan	3	0.01
Honduran	1	0.00
Nicaraguan	1	0.00
Panamanian	9	0.02
Salvadoran	1	0.00
Other Central American	1	0.00
Cuban	27	0.07
Dominican Republic	4	0.01
Mexican	151	0.40
Puerto Rican	89	0.23
South American:	25	0.07
Argentinean	4	0.01
Bolivian	2	0.01
Colombian	4	0.01
Ecuadorian	2	0.01
Paraguayan	1	0.00
Peruvian	6	0.02
Venezuelan	5	0.01
Other South American	1	0.00
Other Hispanic or Latino	121	0.32
Hungarian	278	0.73
Iranian	27	0.07
Irish	5,496	14.39
Italian	1,930	5.05
Lithuanian	96	0.25
Macedonian	15	0.04
Maltese	22	0.06
Northern European	11	0.03
Norwegian	465	1.22
Pennsylvania German	54	0.14
Polish	1,245	3.26
Portuguese	65	0.17
Romanian	8	0.02
Russian	133	0.35
Scandinavian	108	0.28
Scotch-Irish	735	1.92
Scottish	873	2.29
Serbian	21	0.05
Slovak	109	0.29
Slovene	95	0.25
Swedish	604	1.58
Swiss	112	0.29
Turkish	21	0.05
Ukrainian	76	0.20
United States or American	3,943	10.33
Welsh	647	1.69
West Indian, excl. Hispanic:	44	0.12
Jamaican	31	0.08
Trinidadian and Tobagonian	7	0.02
West Indian	6	0.02
White:	35,895	94.50
Not Hispanic (35,190)	35,552	93.60
Hispanic (305)	343	0.90
Yugoslavian	11	0.03

Notes: 1. Figures in the "Number" column do not add up to the total population due to: a) Ancestry/Race overlap — e.g. persons can report being both White and Irish, b) persons of Hispanic origin can report being any race, c) persons reporting two ancestries are counted in both categories. 2. Numbers in parentheses indicate the number of persons reporting this ancestry/race alone, not in combination with any other ancestry/race. 3. Refer to the Explanation of Data in the front of the book for more detailed information.

Bedford Heights

Place Type: City
County: Cuyahoga
Population: 11,375

Ancestry/Race	Number	%
African American/Black:	7,855	69.05
Not Hispanic (7,616)	7,793	68.51
Hispanic (53)	62	0.55
African, sub-Saharan:	137	1.20
African	124	1.09
Nigerian	13	0.11
Am. Ind. or Alaska Nat., not spec.	44	0.39
American Indian tribes, specified:	40	0.35
Blackfeet (3)	4	0.04
Cherokee (3)	18	0.16
Cheyenne	2	0.02
Chickasaw	1	0.01
Choctaw	3	0.03
Creek	1	0.01
Iroquois (1)	1	0.01
Menominee	1	0.01
Pueblo	1	0.01
Seminole	1	0.01
Sioux (1)	4	0.04
Tohono O'Odham (1)	1	0.01
All other tribes	2	0.02
American Indian tribes, not spec.	5	0.04
Asian:	246	2.16
Bangladeshi (4)	8	0.07
Chinese, ex. Taiwanese (13)	15	0.13
Filipino (45)	52	0.46
Indian (130)	138	1.21
Korean (9)	10	0.09
Thai (1)	1	0.01
Vietnamese (13)	13	0.11
Other Asian, specified	3	0.03
Other Asian, not specified (1)	6	0.05
Austrian	14	0.12
Belgian	6	0.05
Croatian	14	0.12
Czech	111	0.98
Czechoslovakian	43	0.38
Danish	4	0.04
Dutch	83	0.73
English	258	2.27
European	5	0.04
French, except Basque	69	0.61
French Canadian	16	0.14
German	526	4.62
Guyanese	7	0.06
Hawaii Native/Pacific Islander:	15	0.13
Micronesian:	2	0.02
Guamanian/Chamorro	2	0.02
Polynesian: (1)	3	0.03
Native Hawaiian	2	0.02
Samoan (1)	1	0.01
Other Pac. Isl., specified	3	0.03
Other Pac. Isl., not spec.	7	0.06
Hispanic or Latino:	182	1.60
Central American:	7	0.06
Honduran	1	0.01
Panamanian	4	0.04
Salvadoran	2	0.02
Cuban	12	0.11
Dominican Republic	6	0.05
Mexican	58	0.51
Puerto Rican	50	0.44
South American:	1	0.01
Bolivian	1	0.01
Other Hispanic or Latino	48	0.42
Hungarian	239	2.10
Irish	465	4.09
Italian	655	5.76
Lithuanian	25	0.22
Pennsylvania German	6	0.05
Polish	318	2.80
Romanian	10	0.09
Russian	30	0.26
Scotch-Irish	57	0.50
Scottish	69	0.61
Slavic	18	0.16
Slovak	203	1.78
Slovene	39	0.34
Swedish	4	0.04
Swiss	4	0.04
Ukrainian	25	0.22
United States or American	183	1.61
Welsh	33	0.29
West Indian, excl. Hispanic:	52	0.46
Belizean	5	0.04
Jamaican	42	0.37
West Indian	5	0.04
White:	3,306	29.06
Not Hispanic (3,103)	3,225	28.35
Hispanic (70)	81	0.71

Bedford

Place Type: City
County: Cuyahoga
Population: 14,214

Ancestry/Race	Number	%
African American/Black:	2,634	18.53
Not Hispanic (2,498)	2,622	18.45
Hispanic (8)	12	0.08
African, sub-Saharan:	57	0.40
African	18	0.13
Cape Verdean	8	0.06
Ethiopian	5	0.04
Ghanian	6	0.04
Nigerian	14	0.10
Other sub-Saharan African	6	0.04
Alaska Native tribes, specified:	3	0.02
Aleut	1	0.01
Eskimo (2)	2	0.01
Am. Ind. or Alaska Nat., not spec.	39	0.27
American Indian tribes, specified:	51	0.36
Apache (3)	3	0.02
Blackfeet (1)	9	0.06
Cherokee (6)	24	0.17
Choctaw (1)	1	0.01
Cree (1)	1	0.01
Iroquois	4	0.03
Latin American Indians	1	0.01
Shoshone	2	0.01
Sioux	2	0.01
All other tribes	4	0.03
American Indian tribes, not spec.	4	0.03
Arab:	46	0.32
Lebanese	39	0.27
Palestinian	7	0.05
Armenian	7	0.05
Asian:	218	1.53
Chinese, ex. Taiwanese (23)	30	0.21
Filipino (36)	58	0.41
Indian (62)	72	0.51
Japanese (7)	11	0.08
Korean (10)	21	0.15
Pakistani (3)	3	0.02
Thai (1)	1	0.01
Vietnamese (10)	14	0.10
Other Asian, not specified (2)	8	0.06
Austrian	56	0.39
Basque	5	0.04
Belgian	7	0.05
British	14	0.10
Canadian	29	0.20
Carpatho Rusyn	18	0.13
Croatian	82	0.58
Czech	396	2.79
Czechoslovakian	130	0.91
Danish	8	0.06
Dutch	186	1.31
Eastern European	28	0.20
English	1,032	7.26
Estonian	6	0.04
European	27	0.19
Finnish	12	0.08
French, except Basque	193	1.36
French Canadian	60	0.42
German	2,719	19.13
Greek	39	0.27
Hawaii Native/Pacific Islander:	8	0.06
Polynesian: (2)	3	0.02
Native Hawaiian (1)	2	0.01
Samoan (1)	1	0.01
Other Pac. Isl., not spec.	5	0.04
Hispanic or Latino:	152	1.07
Central American:	9	0.06
Guatemalan	3	0.02
Nicaraguan	3	0.02
Panamanian	3	0.02
Cuban	12	0.08
Dominican Republic	3	0.02
Mexican	41	0.29
Puerto Rican	48	0.34
South American:	7	0.05
Argentinean	1	0.01
Peruvian	5	0.04
Other South American	1	0.01
Other Hispanic or Latino	32	0.23
Hungarian	841	5.92
Irish	1,887	13.28
Italian	1,532	10.78
Lithuanian	128	0.90
Norwegian	37	0.26
Pennsylvania German	11	0.08
Polish	1,656	11.65
Romanian	5	0.04
Russian	159	1.12
Scotch-Irish	168	1.18
Scottish	296	2.08
Slavic	32	0.23
Slovak	711	5.00
Slovene	289	2.03
Swedish	147	1.03
Swiss	13	0.09
Turkish	9	0.06
Ukrainian	69	0.49
United States or American	647	4.55
Welsh	156	1.10
West Indian, excl. Hispanic:	57	0.40
Jamaican	49	0.34
Trinidadian and Tobagonian	8	0.06
White:	11,419	80.34
Not Hispanic (11,145)	11,319	79.63
Hispanic (86)	100	0.70
Yugoslavian	33	0.23

Bellefontaine

Place Type: City
County: Logan
Population: 13,069

Ancestry/Race	Number	%
African American/Black:	888	6.79
Not Hispanic (667)	882	6.75
Hispanic (3)	6	0.05
Alaska Native tribes, specified:	4	0.03
Aleut	4	0.03
Am. Ind. or Alaska Nat., not spec.	27	0.21
American Indian tribes, specified:	61	0.47
Blackfeet (1)	18	0.14
Cherokee (3)	22	0.17
Cheyenne (1)	1	0.01
Chippewa (1)	1	0.01
Creek	2	0.02
Latin American Indians (2)	2	0.02
Sioux (7)	9	0.07
All other tribes (2)	6	0.05
American Indian tribes, not spec.	5	0.04
Arab:	51	0.39
Arab/Arabic	51	0.39
Asian:	164	1.25
Chinese, ex. Taiwanese (13)	22	0.17
Filipino (11)	19	0.15

Notes: 1. Figures in the "Number" column do not add up to the total population due to: a) Ancestry/Race overlap — e.g. persons can report being both White and Irish, b) persons of Hispanic origin can report being any race, c) persons reporting two ancestries are counted in both categories. 2. Numbers in parentheses indicate the number of persons reporting this ancestry/race alone, not in combination with any other ancestry/race. 3. Refer to the Explanation of Data in the front of the book for more detailed information.

Ancestry/Race	Number	%
Indian (11)	17	0.13
Japanese (70)	73	0.56
Korean (4)	11	0.08
Pakistani	2	0.02
Taiwanese (3)	8	0.06
Vietnamese (3)	3	0.02
Other Asian, specified	1	0.01
Other Asian, not specified (2)	8	0.06
Belgian	6	0.05
British	79	0.61
Canadian	42	0.32
Croatian	11	0.08
Czechoslovakian	18	0.14
Dutch	483	3.70
English	1,088	8.34
European	165	1.26
Finnish	7	0.05
French, except Basque	370	2.84
French Canadian	50	0.38
German	2,918	22.36
Hawaii Native/Pacific Islander:	12	0.09
Micronesian: (2)	3	0.02
Other Micronesian (2)	3	0.02
Polynesian: (2)	6	0.05
Native Hawaiian (2)	6	0.05
Other Pac. Isl., specified	1	0.01
Other Pac. Isl., not spec. (1)	2	0.02
Hispanic or Latino:	146	1.12
Central American:	17	0.13
Costa Rican	8	0.06
Salvadoran	9	0.07
Cuban	3	0.02
Mexican	87	0.67
Puerto Rican	12	0.09
South American:	1	0.01
Argentinean	1	0.01
Other Hispanic or Latino	26	0.20
Hungarian	54	0.41
Irish	1,395	10.69
Italian	321	2.46
Norwegian	5	0.04
Pennsylvania German	10	0.08
Polish	124	0.95
Russian	7	0.05
Scotch-Irish	247	1.89
Scottish	215	1.65
Slovak	7	0.05
Swedish	94	0.72
Swiss	92	0.70
Turkish	15	0.11
Ukrainian	6	0.05
United States or American	2,155	16.51
Welsh	63	0.48
West Indian, excl. Hispanic:	5	0.04
West Indian	5	0.04
White:	12,159	93.04
Not Hispanic (11,807)	12,081	92.44
Hispanic (62)	78	0.60

Berea

Place Type: City
County: Cuyahoga
Population: 18,970

Ancestry/Race	Number	%
African American/Black:	1,111	5.86
Not Hispanic (965)	1,097	5.78
Hispanic (9)	14	0.07
African, sub-Saharan:	26	0.14
African	16	0.08
Nigerian	10	0.05
Alaska Native tribes, specified:	1	0.01
Eskimo (1)	1	0.01
Am. Ind. or Alaska Nat., not spec.	34	0.18
Albanian	32	0.17
Alsatian	6	0.03
American Indian tribes, specified:	103	0.54
Apache	1	0.01
Blackfeet	8	0.04
Cherokee (13)	58	0.31
Cheyenne	1	0.01
Choctaw	3	0.02
Creek	3	0.02
Delaware	1	0.01
Houma	1	0.01
Iroquois (5)	5	0.03
Navajo (7)	7	0.04
Seminole (1)	1	0.01
Sioux (3)	4	0.02
Ute (1)	1	0.01
All other tribes (6)	9	0.05
American Indian tribes, not spec.	1	0.01
Arab:	196	1.03
Arab/Arabic	7	0.04
Egyptian	25	0.13
Lebanese	139	0.73
Syrian	13	0.07
Other Arab	12	0.06
Armenian	6	0.03
Asian:	223	1.18
Bangladeshi (3)	3	0.02
Cambodian (6)	10	0.05
Chinese, ex. Taiwanese (32)	35	0.18
Filipino (24)	31	0.16
Indian (28)	39	0.21
Indonesian (1)	1	0.01
Japanese (39)	52	0.27
Korean (14)	16	0.08
Malaysian	1	0.01
Taiwanese (1)	1	0.01
Thai (8)	11	0.06
Vietnamese (6)	6	0.03
Other Asian, specified (2)	2	0.01
Other Asian, not specified (5)	15	0.08
Australian	5	0.03
Austrian	92	0.48
British	47	0.25
Bulgarian	7	0.04
Canadian	14	0.07
Croatian	158	0.83
Czech	358	1.88
Czechoslovakian	58	0.31
Danish	47	0.25
Dutch	347	1.83
Eastern European	24	0.13
English	2,567	13.51
Estonian	6	0.03
European	154	0.81
Finnish	47	0.25
French, except Basque	426	2.24
French Canadian	53	0.28
German	5,290	27.84
Greek	131	0.69
Hawaii Native/Pacific Islander:	10	0.05
Micronesian: (2)	2	0.01
Guamanian/Chamorro (2)	2	0.01
Polynesian: (4)	6	0.03
Native Hawaiian (1)	3	0.02
Samoan (2)	2	0.01
Tongan (1)	1	0.01
Other Pac. Isl., not spec.	2	0.01
Hispanic or Latino:	301	1.59
Central American:	17	0.09
Costa Rican	1	0.01
Guatemalan	3	0.02
Honduran	5	0.03
Nicaraguan	1	0.01
Salvadoran	3	0.02
Other Central American	4	0.02
Cuban	12	0.06
Dominican Republic	4	0.02
Mexican	64	0.34
Puerto Rican	161	0.85
South American:	17	0.09
Argentinean	1	0.01
Colombian	7	0.04
Ecuadorian	1	0.01
Peruvian	4	0.02
Venezuelan	4	0.02
Other Hispanic or Latino	26	0.14
Hungarian	702	3.69
Irish	3,382	17.80
Italian	1,866	9.82
Lithuanian	80	0.42
Norwegian	189	0.99
Pennsylvania German	15	0.08
Polish	2,033	10.70
Portuguese	16	0.08
Romanian	139	0.73
Russian	308	1.62
Scandinavian	13	0.07
Scotch-Irish	334	1.76
Scottish	499	2.63
Serbian	20	0.11
Slovak	838	4.41
Slovene	223	1.17
Swedish	264	1.39
Swiss	99	0.52
Turkish	11	0.06
Ukrainian	268	1.41
United States or American	709	3.73
Welsh	206	1.08
West Indian, excl. Hispanic:	31	0.16
Jamaican	10	0.05
Trinidadian and Tobagonian	6	0.03
West Indian	15	0.08
White:	17,637	92.97
Not Hispanic (17,175)	17,433	91.90
Hispanic (178)	204	1.08
Yugoslavian	11	0.06

Bexley

Place Type: City
County: Franklin
Population: 13,203

Ancestry/Race	Number	%
African American/Black:	684	5.18
Not Hispanic (584)	670	5.07
Hispanic (8)	14	0.11
African, sub-Saharan:	53	0.40
African	39	0.30
Somalian	7	0.05
South African	7	0.05
Am. Ind. or Alaska Nat., not spec.	24	0.18
Alsatian	6	0.05
American Indian tribes, specified:	35	0.27
Blackfeet	6	0.05
Cherokee (6)	19	0.14
Choctaw	3	0.02
Cree (1)	1	0.01
Creek (1)	1	0.01
Iroquois (1)	2	0.02
Seminole (1)	1	0.01
All other tribes (2)	2	0.02
American Indian tribes, not spec.	8	0.06
Arab:	104	0.79
Lebanese	23	0.17
Moroccan	69	0.52
Syrian	12	0.09
Armenian	9	0.07
Asian:	187	1.42
Cambodian (2)	2	0.02
Chinese, ex. Taiwanese (29)	45	0.34
Filipino (11)	16	0.12
Indian (21)	24	0.18
Japanese (11)	25	0.19
Korean (15)	24	0.18
Laotian (10)	10	0.08
Malaysian (1)	1	0.01
Pakistani (2)	2	0.02
Taiwanese (3)	5	0.04
Thai (1)	1	0.01
Vietnamese (6)	9	0.07
Other Asian, specified (4)	4	0.03
Other Asian, not specified (13)	19	0.14
Australian	20	0.15
Austrian	44	0.33

Notes: 1. Figures in the "Number" column do not add up to the total population due to: a) Ancestry/Race overlap — e.g. persons can report being both White and Irish, b) persons of Hispanic origin can report being any race, c) persons reporting two ancestries are counted in both categories. 2. Numbers in parentheses indicate the number of persons reporting this ancestry/race alone, not in combination with any other ancestry/race. 3. Refer to the Explanation of Data in the front of the book for more detailed information.

British	82	0.62
Canadian	50	0.38
Croatian	21	0.16
Czech	74	0.56
Czechoslovakian	7	0.05
Danish	23	0.17
Dutch	248	1.88
Eastern European	223	1.69
English	1,727	13.08
European	236	1.79
Finnish	24	0.18
French, except Basque	336	2.55
French Canadian	86	0.65
German	3,661	27.73
Greek	153	1.16
Hawaii Native/Pacific Islander:	15	0.11
Micronesian: (2)	2	0.02
Guamanian/Chamorro (2)	2	0.02
Polynesian: (3)	12	0.09
Native Hawaiian (3)	5	0.04
Samoan	7	0.05
Other Pac. Isl., not spec. (1)	1	0.01
Hispanic or Latino:	121	0.92
Central American:	7	0.05
Guatemalan	5	0.04
Panamanian	2	0.02
Cuban	11	0.08
Mexican	41	0.31
Puerto Rican	13	0.10
South American:	13	0.10
Argentinean	5	0.04
Chilean	1	0.01
Colombian	2	0.02
Ecuadorian	3	0.02
Paraguayan	1	0.01
Venezuelan	1	0.01
Other Hispanic or Latino	36	0.27
Hungarian	254	1.92
Iranian	51	0.39
Irish	1,957	14.83
Israeli	33	0.25
Italian	702	5.32
Latvian	11	0.08
Lithuanian	172	1.30
Macedonian	9	0.07
Northern European	36	0.27
Norwegian	37	0.28
Pennsylvania German	15	0.11
Polish	554	4.20
Portuguese	7	0.05
Romanian	77	0.58
Russian	967	7.33
Scandinavian	4	0.03
Scotch-Irish	283	2.14
Scottish	463	3.51
Slovak	54	0.41
Slovene	26	0.20
Swedish	282	2.14
Swiss	69	0.52
Turkish	20	0.15
Ukrainian	208	1.58
United States or American	930	7.05
Welsh	239	1.81
White:	12,369	93.68
Not Hispanic (12,134)	12,282	93.02
Hispanic (72)	87	0.66

Blue Ash

Place Type: City
County: Hamilton
Population: 12,513

Ancestry/Race	Number	%
African American/Black:	658	5.26
Not Hispanic (626)	657	5.25
Hispanic (1)	1	0.01
African, sub-Saharan:	119	0.93
African	95	0.74
Somalian	16	0.13
South African	8	0.06
Am. Ind. or Alaska Nat., not spec.	27	0.22
American Indian tribes, specified:	57	0.46
Blackfeet	2	0.02
Cherokee (9)	38	0.30
Cree	1	0.01
Iroquois	1	0.01
Kiowa	2	0.02
Latin American Indians (5)	5	0.04
Sioux (4)	7	0.06
All other tribes	1	0.01
American Indian tribes, not spec.	1	0.01
Arab:	145	1.14
Arab/Arabic	8	0.06
Egyptian	22	0.17
Lebanese	71	0.56
Moroccan	5	0.04
Palestinian	14	0.11
Other Arab	25	0.20
Asian:	845	6.75
Bangladeshi (3)	3	0.02
Cambodian (2)	2	0.02
Chinese, ex. Taiwanese (132)	141	1.13
Filipino (46)	54	0.43
Indian (368)	379	3.03
Japanese (81)	92	0.74
Korean (114)	118	0.94
Malaysian (1)	1	0.01
Pakistani (9)	10	0.08
Sri Lankan (7)	7	0.06
Taiwanese (12)	13	0.10
Thai (7)	7	0.06
Vietnamese (4)	6	0.05
Other Asian, specified (4)	5	0.04
Other Asian, not specified (4)	7	0.06
Austrian	46	0.36
Belgian	5	0.04
British	79	0.62
Bulgarian	19	0.15
Canadian	18	0.14
Croatian	9	0.07
Czech	19	0.15
Czechoslovakian	7	0.05
Danish	35	0.27
Dutch	252	1.98
Eastern European	92	0.72
English	1,473	11.55
European	192	1.51
Finnish	26	0.20
French, except Basque	352	2.76
French Canadian	40	0.31
German	3,800	29.79
Greek	73	0.57
Hawaii Native/Pacific Islander:	6	0.05
Micronesian: (1)	1	0.01
Other Micronesian (1)	1	0.01
Polynesian:	2	0.02
Native Hawaiian	2	0.02
Other Pac. Isl., not spec. (1)	3	0.02
Hispanic or Latino:	122	0.97
Central American:	1	0.01
Nicaraguan	1	0.01
Cuban	19	0.15
Dominican Republic	1	0.01
Mexican	37	0.30
Puerto Rican	13	0.10
South American:	20	0.16
Argentinean	1	0.01
Colombian	3	0.02
Ecuadorian	1	0.01
Peruvian	6	0.05
Venezuelan	9	0.07
Other Hispanic or Latino	31	0.25
Hungarian	160	1.25
Iranian	14	0.11
Irish	1,715	13.45
Israeli	23	0.18
Italian	520	4.08
Latvian	6	0.05
Lithuanian	66	0.52
Norwegian	34	0.27
Polish	359	2.81
Romanian	80	0.63
Russian	454	3.56
Scandinavian	8	0.06
Scotch-Irish	157	1.23
Scottish	276	2.16
Slavic	7	0.05
Slovak	37	0.29
Slovene	7	0.05
Swedish	104	0.82
Swiss	93	0.73
Ukrainian	110	0.86
United States or American	855	6.70
Welsh	116	0.91
White:	11,003	87.93
Not Hispanic (10,805)	10,908	87.17
Hispanic (92)	95	0.76
Yugoslavian	33	0.26

Boardman

Place Type: Census Designated Place
County: Mahoning
Population: 37,215

Ancestry/Race	Number	%
African American/Black:	1,041	2.80
Not Hispanic (936)	1,012	2.72
Hispanic (15)	29	0.08
African, sub-Saharan:	24	0.06
African	13	0.03
Nigerian	11	0.03
Alaska Native tribes, specified:	3	0.01
Aleut (1)	1	0.00
Eskimo	1	0.00
Tlingit-Haida (1)	1	0.00
Am. Ind. or Alaska Nat., not spec.	39	0.10
Albanian	13	0.03
American Indian tribes, specified:	75	0.20
Apache	1	0.00
Blackfeet (1)	2	0.01
Cherokee (9)	37	0.10
Chickasaw	1	0.00
Chippewa	1	0.00
Choctaw	1	0.00
Delaware	1	0.00
Iroquois (1)	8	0.02
Latin American Indians (3)	12	0.03
Lumbee (2)	2	0.01
Navajo (1)	1	0.00
Sioux	2	0.01
All other tribes (3)	6	0.02
American Indian tribes, not spec.	5	0.01
Arab:	516	1.38
Arab/Arabic	40	0.11
Lebanese	441	1.18
Moroccan	7	0.02
Palestinian	10	0.03
Syrian	18	0.05
Armenian	6	0.02
Asian:	366	0.98
Chinese, ex. Taiwanese (40)	55	0.15
Filipino (28)	31	0.08
Indian (133)	135	0.36
Indonesian (3)	3	0.01
Japanese (14)	29	0.08
Korean (31)	44	0.12
Pakistani (2)	5	0.01
Taiwanese	2	0.01
Thai (2)	2	0.01
Vietnamese (39)	39	0.10
Other Asian, specified	3	0.01
Other Asian, not specified (6)	18	0.05
Austrian	122	0.33
Belgian	10	0.03
British	69	0.19
Bulgarian	7	0.02
Canadian	33	0.09
Carpatho Rusyn	8	0.02

Notes: 1. Figures in the "Number" column do not add up to the total population due to: a) Ancestry/Race overlap — e.g. persons can report being both White and Irish, b) persons of Hispanic origin can report being any race, c) persons reporting two ancestries are counted in both categories. 2. Numbers in parentheses indicate the number of persons reporting this ancestry/race alone, not in combination with any other ancestry/race. 3. Refer to the Explanation of Data in the front of the book for more detailed information.

Ancestry/Race	Number	%
Celtic	13	0.03
Croatian	864	2.32
Cypriot	18	0.05
Czech	118	0.32
Czechoslovakian	68	0.18
Danish	75	0.20
Dutch	460	1.23
English	3,582	9.61
European	48	0.13
Finnish	110	0.30
French, except Basque	638	1.71
French Canadian	92	0.25
German	7,769	20.85
Greek	508	1.36
Hawaii Native/Pacific Islander:	10	0.03
Polynesian: (5)	7	0.02
Native Hawaiian (2)	4	0.01
Other Polynesian (3)	3	0.01
Other Pac. Isl., not spec. (3)	3	0.01
Hispanic or Latino:	670	1.80
Central American:	9	0.02
Honduran	3	0.01
Nicaraguan	1	0.00
Salvadoran	5	0.01
Cuban	15	0.04
Dominican Republic	10	0.03
Mexican	100	0.27
Puerto Rican	422	1.13
South American:	21	0.06
Argentinean	1	0.00
Colombian	13	0.03
Ecuadorian	3	0.01
Paraguayan	1	0.00
Venezuelan	2	0.01
Other South American	1	0.00
Other Hispanic or Latino	93	0.25
Hungarian	1,284	3.45
Iranian	28	0.08
Irish	6,593	17.69
Israeli	11	0.03
Italian	9,888	26.53
Latvian	7	0.02
Lithuanian	204	0.55
Macedonian	47	0.13
Norwegian	100	0.27
Pennsylvania German	60	0.16
Polish	2,673	7.17
Portuguese	55	0.15
Romanian	414	1.11
Russian	331	0.89
Scandinavian	6	0.02
Scotch-Irish	666	1.79
Scottish	683	1.83
Serbian	67	0.18
Slavic	18	0.05
Slovak	3,552	9.53
Slovene	35	0.09
Swedish	592	1.59
Swiss	144	0.39
Ukrainian	601	1.61
United States or American	942	2.53
Welsh	950	2.55
White:	35,737	96.03
Not Hispanic (34,986)	35,224	94.65
Hispanic (462)	513	1.38
Yugoslavian	49	0.13

Bowling Green

Place Type: City
County: Wood
Population: 29,636

Ancestry/Race	Number	%
African American/Black:	963	3.25
Not Hispanic (810)	922	3.11
Hispanic (27)	41	0.14
African, sub-Saharan:	102	0.35
African	76	0.26
Cape Verdean	12	0.04
Ghanian	8	0.03
Kenyan	6	0.02
Am. Ind. or Alaska Nat., not spec.	47	0.16
American Indian tribes, specified:	125	0.42
Apache	2	0.01
Blackfeet (2)	5	0.02
Cherokee (13)	64	0.22
Choctaw	2	0.01
Creek (1)	1	0.00
Crow (1)	1	0.00
Delaware	1	0.00
Iroquois (7)	19	0.06
Latin American Indians (2)	5	0.02
Puget Sound Salish (2)	2	0.01
Seminole	3	0.01
Sioux (3)	4	0.01
Yuman	2	0.01
All other tribes (3)	14	0.05
American Indian tribes, not spec.	23	0.08
Arab:	183	0.62
Arab/Arabic	76	0.26
Lebanese	74	0.25
Moroccan	6	0.02
Syrian	27	0.09
Armenian	24	0.08
Asian:	649	2.19
Bangladeshi (1)	1	0.00
Cambodian (2)	2	0.01
Chinese, ex. Taiwanese (201)	219	0.74
Filipino (35)	48	0.16
Indian (131)	143	0.48
Indonesian (3)	3	0.01
Japanese (36)	50	0.17
Korean (53)	70	0.24
Laotian (1)	1	0.00
Malaysian (2)	2	0.01
Pakistani (8)	9	0.03
Sri Lankan (9)	9	0.03
Taiwanese (3)	5	0.02
Thai (11)	14	0.05
Vietnamese (13)	13	0.04
Other Asian, specified (4)	7	0.02
Other Asian, not specified (24)	53	0.18
Austrian	52	0.18
Basque	12	0.04
Belgian	68	0.23
Brazilian	32	0.11
British	149	0.50
Bulgarian	8	0.03
Canadian	83	0.28
Celtic	8	0.03
Croatian	80	0.27
Cypriot	12	0.04
Czech	160	0.54
Czechoslovakian	49	0.17
Danish	104	0.35
Dutch	473	1.60
English	3,125	10.57
European	273	0.92
Finnish	65	0.22
French, except Basque	820	2.77
French Canadian	147	0.50
German	9,289	31.42
Greek	77	0.26
Hawaii Native/Pacific Islander:	30	0.10
Micronesian: (2)	3	0.01
Guamanian/Chamorro (1)	2	0.01
Other Micronesian (1)	1	0.00
Polynesian: (2)	6	0.02
Native Hawaiian (2)	4	0.01
Samoan	1	0.00
Other Polynesian	1	0.00
Other Pac. Isl., specified	2	0.01
Other Pac. Isl., not spec. (1)	19	0.06
Hispanic or Latino:	1,031	3.48
Central American:	24	0.08
Costa Rican	2	0.01
Guatemalan	1	0.00
Honduran	1	0.00
Nicaraguan	10	0.03
Panamanian	7	0.02
Salvadoran	3	0.01
Cuban	17	0.06
Dominican Republic	1	0.00
Mexican	663	2.24
Puerto Rican	74	0.25
South American:	41	0.14
Argentinean	5	0.02
Bolivian	2	0.01
Chilean	3	0.01
Colombian	6	0.02
Peruvian	9	0.03
Uruguayan	1	0.00
Venezuelan	10	0.03
Other South American	5	0.02
Other Hispanic or Latino	211	0.71
Hungarian	495	1.67
Icelander	7	0.02
Iranian	6	0.02
Irish	3,473	11.75
Italian	1,490	5.04
Latvian	7	0.02
Lithuanian	78	0.26
Luxemburger	7	0.02
Macedonian	8	0.03
Northern European	6	0.02
Norwegian	278	0.94
Pennsylvania German	52	0.18
Polish	1,299	4.39
Portuguese	32	0.11
Romanian	81	0.27
Russian	238	0.81
Scandinavian	42	0.14
Scotch-Irish	351	1.19
Scottish	827	2.80
Serbian	7	0.02
Slavic	32	0.11
Slovak	155	0.52
Slovene	101	0.34
Swedish	375	1.27
Swiss	198	0.67
Ukrainian	112	0.38
United States or American	1,510	5.11
Welsh	273	0.92
West Indian, excl. Hispanic:	40	0.14
Haitian	9	0.03
Jamaican	31	0.10
White:	27,598	93.12
Not Hispanic (26,839)	27,133	91.55
Hispanic (380)	465	1.57
Yugoslavian	7	0.02

Brecksville

Place Type: City
County: Cuyahoga
Population: 13,382

Ancestry/Race	Number	%
African American/Black:	260	1.94
Not Hispanic (254)	259	1.94
Hispanic (1)	1	0.01
African, sub-Saharan:	17	0.13
African	17	0.13
Am. Ind. or Alaska Nat., not spec.	10	0.07
American Indian tribes, specified:	19	0.14
Cherokee (2)	11	0.08
Choctaw (1)	4	0.03
Cree	2	0.01
Iroquois	1	0.01
Navajo	1	0.01
Arab:	245	1.84
Egyptian	21	0.16
Iraqi	13	0.10
Lebanese	161	1.21
Syrian	50	0.38
Armenian	33	0.25
Asian:	373	2.79
Bangladeshi (10)	10	0.07
Chinese, ex. Taiwanese (42)	53	0.40

Notes: 1. Figures in the "Number" column do not add up to the total population due to: a) Ancestry/Race overlap — e.g. persons can report being both White and Irish, b) persons of Hispanic origin can report being any race, c) persons reporting two ancestries are counted in both categories. 2. Numbers in parentheses indicate the number of persons reporting this ancestry/race alone, not in combination with any other ancestry/race. 3. Refer to the Explanation of Data in the front of the book for more detailed information.

Filipino (62)	68	0.51
Indian (128)	133	0.99
Japanese (8)	12	0.09
Korean (51)	55	0.41
Malaysian (1)	1	0.01
Pakistani (17)	17	0.13
Sri Lankan (1)	1	0.01
Taiwanese (9)	10	0.07
Thai (3)	3	0.02
Vietnamese (2)	2	0.01
Other Asian, not specified (5)	8	0.06
Austrian	120	0.90
Brazilian	10	0.08
British	92	0.69
Canadian	96	0.72
Carpatho Rusyn	6	0.05
Celtic	4	0.03
Croatian	217	1.63
Cypriot	20	0.15
Czech	568	4.26
Czechoslovakian	184	1.38
Danish	20	0.15
Dutch	143	1.07
Eastern European	11	0.08
English	1,184	8.88
European	50	0.38
Finnish	21	0.16
French, except Basque	208	1.56
French Canadian	5	0.04
German	2,950	22.13
Greek	148	1.11
Hawaii Native/Pacific Islander:	3	0.02
Polynesian:	2	0.01
Native Hawaiian	2	0.01
Other Pac. Isl., not spec. (1)	1	0.01
Hispanic or Latino:	136	1.02
Central American:	1	0.01
Panamanian	1	0.01
Cuban	15	0.11
Mexican	37	0.28
Puerto Rican	27	0.20
South American:	33	0.25
Argentinean	4	0.03
Chilean	3	0.02
Colombian	10	0.07
Ecuadorian	2	0.01
Peruvian	4	0.03
Other South American	10	0.07
Other Hispanic or Latino	23	0.17
Hungarian	601	4.51
Iranian	6	0.05
Irish	1,782	13.37
Israeli	12	0.09
Italian	1,684	12.63
Latvian	11	0.08
Lithuanian	90	0.68
Northern European	5	0.04
Norwegian	32	0.24
Pennsylvania German	6	0.05
Polish	2,436	18.27
Portuguese	14	0.11
Romanian	91	0.68
Russian	129	0.97
Scotch-Irish	203	1.52
Scottish	291	2.18
Serbian	82	0.62
Slovak	775	5.81
Slovene	283	2.12
Swedish	141	1.06
Swiss	114	0.86
Ukrainian	245	1.84
United States or American	495	3.71
Welsh	121	0.91
White:	12,766	95.40
Not Hispanic (12,578)	12,644	94.49
Hispanic (117)	122	0.91
Yugoslavian	60	0.45

Bridgetown North

Place Type: Census Designated Place
County: Hamilton
Population: 12,569

Ancestry/Race	Number	%
African American/Black:	63	0.50
Not Hispanic (38)	55	0.44
Hispanic (7)	8	0.06
Am. Ind. or Alaska Nat., not spec.	5	0.04
American Indian tribes, specified:	24	0.19
Apache (1)	1	0.01
Cherokee (2)	15	0.12
Cree	4	0.03
Creek (1)	1	0.01
Potawatomi	1	0.01
All other tribes	2	0.02
American Indian tribes, not spec.	8	0.06
Arab:	43	0.34
Lebanese	35	0.28
Syrian	8	0.06
Asian:	80	0.64
Chinese, ex. Taiwanese (39)	40	0.32
Filipino (6)	8	0.06
Indian (8)	8	0.06
Japanese (8)	16	0.13
Korean (3)	3	0.02
Other Asian, not specified (2)	5	0.04
Austrian	21	0.17
Bulgarian	5	0.04
Croatian	7	0.06
Czechoslovakian	6	0.05
Dutch	171	1.34
English	1,194	9.38
Estonian	7	0.06
European	126	0.99
French, except Basque	301	2.37
French Canadian	18	0.14
German	7,249	56.98
Greek	41	0.32
Hawaii Native/Pacific Islander:	3	0.02
Micronesian: (1)	1	0.01
Guamanian/Chamorro (1)	1	0.01
Polynesian: (2)	2	0.02
Native Hawaiian (2)	2	0.02
Hispanic or Latino:	63	0.50
Central American:	1	0.01
Panamanian	1	0.01
Cuban	4	0.03
Mexican	23	0.18
Puerto Rican	8	0.06
South American:	1	0.01
Ecuadorian	1	0.01
Other Hispanic or Latino	26	0.21
Hungarian	119	0.94
Irish	2,284	17.95
Italian	939	7.38
Macedonian	14	0.11
Norwegian	35	0.28
Pennsylvania German	7	0.06
Polish	98	0.77
Romanian	20	0.16
Russian	7	0.06
Scandinavian	13	0.10
Scotch-Irish	150	1.18
Scottish	104	0.82
Serbian	10	0.08
Slovene	5	0.04
Swedish	15	0.12
Swiss	62	0.49
Turkish	11	0.09
United States or American	722	5.67
Welsh	39	0.31
West Indian, excl. Hispanic:	12	0.09
West Indian	12	0.09
White:	12,426	98.86
Not Hispanic (12,337)	12,390	98.58
Hispanic (31)	36	0.29
Yugoslavian	5	0.04

Broadview Heights

Place Type: City
County: Cuyahoga
Population: 15,967

Ancestry/Race	Number	%
African American/Black:	147	0.92
Not Hispanic (126)	147	0.92
African, sub-Saharan:	45	0.28
African	45	0.28
Alaska Native tribes, not specified	1	0.01
Am. Ind. or Alaska Nat., not spec.	8	0.05
American Indian tribes, specified:	23	0.14
Cherokee (3)	4	0.03
Chippewa	1	0.01
Choctaw (1)	2	0.01
Delaware	1	0.01
Latin American Indians	1	0.01
Lumbee (2)	2	0.01
Ottawa	1	0.01
Seminole	1	0.01
Sioux	5	0.03
All other tribes (1)	5	0.03
American Indian tribes, not spec.	2	0.01
Arab:	180	1.13
Arab/Arabic	26	0.16
Egyptian	6	0.04
Lebanese	148	0.93
Armenian	39	0.24
Asian:	545	3.41
Cambodian (4)	6	0.04
Chinese, ex. Taiwanese (100)	112	0.70
Filipino (59)	76	0.48
Indian (168)	178	1.11
Indonesian	5	0.03
Japanese (9)	18	0.11
Korean (100)	108	0.68
Pakistani (6)	9	0.06
Taiwanese (3)	4	0.03
Thai (4)	4	0.03
Vietnamese (4)	4	0.03
Other Asian, specified (1)	1	0.01
Other Asian, not specified (9)	20	0.13
Austrian	98	0.61
Belgian	6	0.04
British	38	0.24
Bulgarian	12	0.08
Canadian	19	0.12
Croatian	63	0.39
Czech	610	3.82
Czechoslovakian	153	0.96
Danish	42	0.26
Dutch	202	1.27
Eastern European	37	0.23
English	1,162	7.28
Estonian	44	0.28
European	69	0.43
Finnish	59	0.37
French, except Basque	188	1.18
French Canadian	28	0.18
German	3,768	23.60
Greek	154	0.96
Hawaii Native/Pacific Islander:	15	0.09
Micronesian:	3	0.02
Guamanian/Chamorro	2	0.01
Other Micronesian	1	0.01
Polynesian: (1)	1	0.01
Samoan (1)	1	0.01
Other Pac. Isl., not spec.	11	0.07
Hispanic or Latino:	147	0.92
Central American:	3	0.02
Nicaraguan	1	0.01
Salvadoran	2	0.01
Cuban	9	0.06
Dominican Republic	1	0.01
Mexican	42	0.26
Puerto Rican	52	0.33
South American:	17	0.11
Argentinean	2	0.01

Notes: 1. Figures in the "Number" column do not add up to the total population due to: a) Ancestry/Race overlap — e.g. persons can report being both White and Irish, b) persons of Hispanic origin can report being any race, c) persons reporting two ancestries are counted in both categories. 2. Numbers in parentheses indicate the number of persons reporting this ancestry/race alone, not in combination with any other ancestry/race. 3. Refer to the Explanation of Data in the front of the book for more detailed information.

Chilean	2	0.01
Colombian	7	0.04
Ecuadorian	3	0.02
Venezuelan	2	0.01
Other South American	1	0.01
Other Hispanic or Latino	23	0.14
Hungarian	846	5.30
Irish	2,141	13.41
Italian	2,685	16.82
Latvian	51	0.32
Lithuanian	107	0.67
Macedonian	50	0.31
Norwegian	42	0.26
Pennsylvania German	10	0.06
Polish	2,565	16.06
Romanian	62	0.39
Russian	291	1.82
Scotch-Irish	304	1.90
Scottish	267	1.67
Serbian	314	1.97
Slavic	7	0.04
Slovak	1,177	7.37
Slovene	515	3.23
Swedish	85	0.53
Swiss	72	0.45
Ukrainian	393	2.46
United States or American	521	3.26
Welsh	144	0.90
West Indian, excl. Hispanic:	43	0.27
Jamaican	43	0.27
White:	15,281	95.70
Not Hispanic (15,069)	15,177	95.05
Hispanic (101)	104	0.65
Yugoslavian	63	0.39

Brook Park

Place Type: City
County: Cuyahoga
Population: 21,218

Ancestry/Race	Number	%
African American/Black:	492	2.32
Not Hispanic (409)	484	2.28
Hispanic (5)	8	0.04
African, sub-Saharan:	13	0.06
African	9	0.04
Nigerian	4	0.02
Alaska Native tribes, specified:	1	0.00
Eskimo	1	0.00
Am. Ind. or Alaska Nat., not spec.	37	0.17
Albanian	13	0.06
American Indian tribes, specified:	82	0.39
Apache (5)	5	0.02
Blackfeet	12	0.06
Cherokee (10)	38	0.18
Cheyenne (5)	5	0.02
Choctaw (1)	1	0.00
Cree	1	0.00
Creek	1	0.00
Delaware (1)	1	0.00
Iroquois (2)	6	0.03
Latin American Indians (2)	3	0.01
Ute (4)	4	0.02
All other tribes (4)	5	0.02
American Indian tribes, not spec.	3	0.01
Arab:	223	1.05
Arab/Arabic	28	0.13
Egyptian	13	0.06
Lebanese	113	0.53
Syrian	65	0.31
Other Arab	4	0.02
Asian:	326	1.54
Cambodian	3	0.01
Chinese, ex. Taiwanese (43)	53	0.25
Filipino (52)	62	0.29
Indian (123)	135	0.64
Indonesian (1)	1	0.00
Japanese (6)	11	0.05
Korean (6)	6	0.03
Laotian (2)	2	0.01
Malaysian (1)	1	0.00
Pakistani	2	0.01
Sri Lankan (2)	2	0.01
Taiwanese	1	0.00
Thai (3)	5	0.02
Vietnamese (22)	32	0.15
Other Asian, not specified (3)	10	0.05
Austrian	96	0.45
Belgian	5	0.02
British	35	0.16
Bulgarian	20	0.09
Canadian	66	0.31
Carpatho Rusyn	5	0.02
Croatian	155	0.73
Czech	517	2.44
Czechoslovakian	108	0.51
Danish	70	0.33
Dutch	271	1.28
Eastern European	17	0.08
English	1,537	7.24
European	49	0.23
Finnish	18	0.08
French, except Basque	431	2.03
French Canadian	50	0.24
German	5,632	26.54
Greek	270	1.27
Hawaii Native/Pacific Islander:	8	0.04
Micronesian:	2	0.01
Guamanian/Chamorro	2	0.01
Polynesian:	2	0.01
Native Hawaiian	2	0.01
Other Pac. Isl., not spec.	4	0.02
Hispanic or Latino:	423	1.99
Central American:	12	0.06
Guatemalan	2	0.01
Nicaraguan	2	0.01
Panamanian	5	0.02
Salvadoran	3	0.01
Cuban	15	0.07
Mexican	92	0.43
Puerto Rican	219	1.03
South American:	22	0.10
Bolivian	1	0.00
Chilean	1	0.00
Colombian	11	0.05
Peruvian	1	0.00
Venezuelan	4	0.02
Other South American	4	0.02
Other Hispanic or Latino	63	0.30
Hungarian	1,059	4.99
Icelander	5	0.02
Irish	3,927	18.51
Italian	2,807	13.23
Latvian	65	0.31
Lithuanian	159	0.75
Macedonian	19	0.09
Norwegian	41	0.19
Pennsylvania German	16	0.08
Polish	2,998	14.13
Romanian	159	0.75
Russian	334	1.57
Scandinavian	8	0.04
Scotch-Irish	276	1.30
Scottish	357	1.68
Serbian	121	0.57
Slavic	45	0.21
Slovak	1,444	6.81
Slovene	262	1.23
Swedish	101	0.48
Swiss	21	0.10
Ukrainian	422	1.99
United States or American	891	4.20
Welsh	185	0.87
West Indian, excl. Hispanic:	3	0.01
Jamaican	3	0.01
White:	20,294	95.65
Not Hispanic (19,811)	20,027	94.39
Hispanic (237)	267	1.26
Yugoslavian	92	0.43

Brooklyn

Place Type: City
County: Cuyahoga
Population: 11,586

Ancestry/Race	Number	%
African American/Black:	231	1.99
Not Hispanic (192)	222	1.92
Hispanic (4)	9	0.08
African, sub-Saharan:	52	0.45
African	14	0.12
Sudanese	38	0.33
Am. Ind. or Alaska Nat., not spec.	7	0.06
American Indian tribes, specified:	50	0.43
Apache	1	0.01
Blackfeet	3	0.03
Cherokee (3)	31	0.27
Chickasaw (3)	3	0.03
Choctaw (1)	2	0.02
Comanche (1)	1	0.01
Iroquois (1)	3	0.03
Sioux (2)	5	0.04
All other tribes	1	0.01
American Indian tribes, not spec.	11	0.09
Arab:	317	2.74
Egyptian	22	0.19
Jordanian	30	0.26
Lebanese	154	1.33
Palestinian	49	0.42
Other Arab	62	0.54
Asian:	294	2.54
Cambodian (17)	20	0.17
Chinese, ex. Taiwanese (66)	74	0.64
Filipino (20)	24	0.21
Indian (59)	60	0.52
Japanese (8)	14	0.12
Korean (19)	20	0.17
Laotian	1	0.01
Pakistani (2)	4	0.03
Vietnamese (66)	67	0.58
Other Asian, not specified (5)	10	0.09
Austrian	54	0.47
Brazilian	7	0.06
British	70	0.60
Canadian	8	0.07
Carpatho Rusyn	30	0.26
Croatian	130	1.12
Czech	350	3.02
Czechoslovakian	140	1.21
Danish	6	0.05
Dutch	116	1.00
Eastern European	4	0.03
English	705	6.08
European	7	0.06
Finnish	43	0.37
French, except Basque	181	1.56
French Canadian	19	0.16
German	2,729	23.55
Greek	208	1.80
Hawaii Native/Pacific Islander:	7	0.06
Polynesian: (1)	1	0.01
Native Hawaiian (1)	1	0.01
Other Pac. Isl., not spec.	6	0.05
Hispanic or Latino:	449	3.88
Central American:	12	0.10
Guatemalan	4	0.03
Honduran	2	0.02
Salvadoran	6	0.05
Cuban	6	0.05
Dominican Republic	1	0.01
Mexican	53	0.46
Puerto Rican	300	2.59
South American:	19	0.16
Argentinean	6	0.05
Bolivian	3	0.03
Chilean	4	0.03
Colombian	3	0.03
Ecuadorian	2	0.02
Venezuelan	1	0.01

Notes: 1. Figures in the "Number" column do not add up to the total population due to: a) Ancestry/Race overlap — e.g. persons can report being both White and Irish, b) persons of Hispanic origin can report being any race, c) persons reporting two ancestries are counted in both categories. 2. Numbers in parentheses indicate the number of persons reporting this ancestry/race alone, not in combination with any other ancestry/race. 3. Refer to the Explanation of Data in the front of the book for more detailed information.

Other Hispanic or Latino	58	0.50
Hungarian	576	4.97
Irish	1,581	13.65
Italian	1,437	12.40
Latvian	8	0.07
Lithuanian	71	0.61
Norwegian	41	0.35
Pennsylvania German	8	0.07
Polish	1,629	14.06
Romanian	110	0.95
Russian	227	1.96
Scotch-Irish	117	1.01
Scottish	188	1.62
Serbian	105	0.91
Slavic	46	0.40
Slovak	1,090	9.41
Slovene	208	1.80
Swedish	39	0.34
Swiss	14	0.12
Ukrainian	162	1.40
United States or American	233	2.01
Welsh	77	0.66
West Indian, excl. Hispanic:	13	0.11
Jamaican	13	0.11
White:	10,913	94.19
Not Hispanic (10,493)	10,652	91.94
Hispanic (243)	261	2.25
Yugoslavian	5	0.04

Brunswick

Place Type: City
County: Medina
Population: 33,388

Ancestry/Race	Number	%
African American/Black:	286	0.86
Not Hispanic (244)	284	0.85
Hispanic (2)	2	0.01
African, sub-Saharan:	34	0.10
African	25	0.07
Nigerian	9	0.03
Am. Ind. or Alaska Nat., not spec.	50	0.15
American Indian tribes, specified:	80	0.24
Apache	1	0.00
Blackfeet (1)	2	0.01
Cherokee (5)	43	0.13
Chippewa	4	0.01
Choctaw (3)	4	0.01
Delaware	1	0.00
Iroquois (1)	1	0.00
Latin American Indians (11)	13	0.04
Lumbee (1)	3	0.01
Menominee	1	0.00
Navajo	1	0.00
Sioux (1)	2	0.01
All other tribes (4)	4	0.01
American Indian tribes, not spec.	4	0.01
Arab:	345	1.03
Arab/Arabic	67	0.20
Egyptian	8	0.02
Iraqi	9	0.03
Lebanese	183	0.55
Palestinian	29	0.09
Syrian	31	0.09
Other Arab	18	0.05
Armenian	6	0.02
Asian:	360	1.08
Chinese, ex. Taiwanese (25)	29	0.09
Filipino (73)	95	0.28
Indian (87)	88	0.26
Japanese (19)	41	0.12
Korean (38)	51	0.15
Laotian (4)	4	0.01
Pakistani (10)	10	0.03
Taiwanese (1)	1	0.00
Thai (1)	3	0.01
Vietnamese (23)	24	0.07
Other Asian, specified	2	0.01
Other Asian, not specified (4)	12	0.04
Australian	20	0.06
Austrian	112	0.34
Belgian	6	0.02
British	34	0.10
Bulgarian	16	0.05
Canadian	109	0.33
Croatian	190	0.57
Czech	738	2.21
Czechoslovakian	152	0.46
Danish	114	0.34
Dutch	416	1.25
English	2,770	8.30
European	150	0.45
Finnish	31	0.09
French, except Basque	837	2.51
French Canadian	129	0.39
German	9,672	28.97
Greek	311	0.93
Hawaii Native/Pacific Islander:	11	0.03
Micronesian: (2)	2	0.01
Guamanian/Chamorro (2)	2	0.01
Polynesian: (6)	7	0.02
Native Hawaiian (3)	4	0.01
Samoan (3)	3	0.01
Other Pac. Isl., not spec.	2	0.01
Hispanic or Latino:	454	1.36
Central American:	13	0.04
Costa Rican	4	0.01
Guatemalan	2	0.01
Honduran	4	0.01
Panamanian	2	0.01
Salvadoran	1	0.00
Cuban	10	0.03
Mexican	136	0.41
Puerto Rican	201	0.60
South American:	19	0.06
Chilean	2	0.01
Colombian	12	0.04
Peruvian	3	0.01
Venezuelan	2	0.01
Other Hispanic or Latino	75	0.22
Hungarian	1,590	4.76
Iranian	27	0.08
Irish	6,238	18.68
Italian	3,914	11.72
Latvian	18	0.05
Lithuanian	193	0.58
Maltese	6	0.02
New Zealander	6	0.02
Norwegian	93	0.28
Pennsylvania German	36	0.11
Polish	4,204	12.59
Portuguese	10	0.03
Romanian	134	0.40
Russian	539	1.61
Scandinavian	61	0.18
Scotch-Irish	374	1.12
Scottish	519	1.55
Serbian	255	0.76
Slavic	20	0.06
Slovak	2,335	6.99
Slovene	644	1.93
Swedish	229	0.69
Swiss	105	0.31
Ukrainian	431	1.29
United States or American	1,595	4.78
Welsh	377	1.13
West Indian, excl. Hispanic:	6	0.02
Jamaican	6	0.02
White:	32,669	97.85
Not Hispanic (32,107)	32,334	96.84
Hispanic (311)	335	1.00
Yugoslavian	139	0.42

Bucyrus

Place Type: City
County: Crawford
Population: 13,224

Ancestry/Race	Number	%
African American/Black:	133	1.01
Not Hispanic (102)	131	0.99
Hispanic (1)	2	0.02
Am. Ind. or Alaska Nat., not spec.	23	0.17
American Indian tribes, specified:	67	0.51
Apache (3)	4	0.03
Blackfeet (1)	11	0.08
Cherokee (8)	32	0.24
Chippewa (3)	3	0.02
Choctaw (3)	3	0.02
Comanche (1)	1	0.01
Creek	2	0.02
Iroquois	3	0.02
Seminole (1)	1	0.01
Sioux (4)	4	0.03
All other tribes (2)	3	0.02
American Indian tribes, not spec.	5	0.04
Arab:	19	0.14
Lebanese	19	0.14
Asian:	78	0.59
Chinese, ex. Taiwanese (16)	17	0.13
Filipino (1)	1	0.01
Indian (4)	5	0.04
Japanese (36)	40	0.30
Korean (4)	7	0.05
Laotian (1)	2	0.02
Taiwanese (2)	2	0.02
Vietnamese (2)	2	0.02
Other Asian, not specified (1)	2	0.02
Austrian	12	0.09
Belgian	11	0.08
British	12	0.09
Canadian	5	0.04
Czech	28	0.21
Czechoslovakian	6	0.05
Dutch	222	1.69
English	1,241	9.42
European	30	0.23
French, except Basque	168	1.28
French Canadian	7	0.05
German	4,031	30.61
Hawaii Native/Pacific Islander:	4	0.03
Micronesian: (1)	1	0.01
Other Micronesian (1)	1	0.01
Polynesian: (1)	2	0.02
Native Hawaiian (1)	2	0.02
Other Pac. Isl., not spec.	1	0.01
Hispanic or Latino:	130	0.98
Central American:	1	0.01
Salvadoran	1	0.01
Cuban	3	0.02
Dominican Republic	2	0.02
Mexican	63	0.48
Puerto Rican	9	0.07
South American:	1	0.01
Colombian	1	0.01
Other Hispanic or Latino	51	0.39
Hungarian	82	0.62
Icelander	6	0.05
Irish	1,259	9.56
Italian	303	2.30
Lithuanian	125	0.95
Luxemburger	5	0.04
Norwegian	31	0.24
Pennsylvania German	7	0.05
Polish	89	0.68
Russian	18	0.14
Scandinavian	14	0.11
Scotch-Irish	98	0.74
Scottish	66	0.50
Slovak	7	0.05
Swedish	91	0.69
Swiss	102	0.77

Notes: 1. Figures in the "Number" column do not add up to the total population due to: a) Ancestry/Race overlap — e.g. persons can report being both White and Irish, b) persons of Hispanic origin can report being any race, c) persons reporting two ancestries are counted in both categories. 2. Numbers in parentheses indicate the number of persons reporting this ancestry/race alone, not in combination with any other ancestry/race. 3. Refer to the Explanation of Data in the front of the book for more detailed information.

Ancestry/Race	Number	%
United States or American	2,004	15.22
Welsh	92	0.70
White:	12,971	98.09
Not Hispanic (12,794)	12,873	97.35
Hispanic (83)	98	0.74

Cambridge

Place Type: City
County: Guernsey
Population: 11,520

Ancestry/Race	Number	%
African American/Black:	590	5.12
Not Hispanic (450)	587	5.10
Hispanic (1)	3	0.03
African, sub-Saharan:	36	0.31
African	36	0.31
Alaska Native tribes, not specified	3	0.03
Am. Ind. or Alaska Nat., not spec.	57	0.49
American Indian tribes, specified:	65	0.56
Apache (1)	3	0.03
Blackfeet (1)	5	0.04
Cherokee (12)	29	0.25
Chippewa (4)	4	0.03
Choctaw (1)	1	0.01
Creek	1	0.01
Iroquois (2)	2	0.02
Latin American Indians	3	0.03
Menominee	2	0.02
Navajo (1)	2	0.02
Potawatomi (1)	1	0.01
Sioux (1)	6	0.05
All other tribes	6	0.05
American Indian tribes, not spec.	3	0.03
Arab:	98	0.85
Lebanese	82	0.71
Syrian	16	0.14
Asian:	69	0.60
Chinese, ex. Taiwanese (4)	5	0.04
Filipino (11)	19	0.16
Indian (21)	24	0.21
Japanese (1)	7	0.06
Korean (6)	9	0.08
Vietnamese	1	0.01
Other Asian, specified	3	0.03
Other Asian, not specified	1	0.01
Austrian	22	0.19
Belgian	11	0.10
British	50	0.43
Canadian	45	0.39
Czech	10	0.09
Czechoslovakian	26	0.22
Dutch	355	3.07
English	1,385	11.98
European	48	0.42
French, except Basque	187	1.62
French Canadian	16	0.14
German	1,967	17.01
Greek	104	0.90
Hawaii Native/Pacific Islander:	6	0.05
Micronesian:	2	0.02
Guamanian/Chamorro	2	0.02
Polynesian:	1	0.01
Native Hawaiian	1	0.01
Other Pac. Isl., specified	3	0.03
Hispanic or Latino:	111	0.96
Central American:	7	0.06
Guatemalan	2	0.02
Panamanian	1	0.01
Other Central American	4	0.03
Cuban	1	0.01
Mexican	53	0.46
Puerto Rican	27	0.23
South American:	1	0.01
Venezuelan	1	0.01
Other Hispanic or Latino	22	0.19
Hungarian	36	0.31
Icelander	6	0.05
Iranian	31	0.27
Irish	1,665	14.40
Italian	344	2.98
Lithuanian	25	0.22
Northern European	17	0.15
Norwegian	60	0.52
Pennsylvania German	18	0.16
Polish	229	1.98
Romanian	14	0.12
Russian	24	0.21
Scandinavian	6	0.05
Scotch-Irish	197	1.70
Scottish	213	1.84
Serbian	6	0.05
Slovak	305	2.64
Slovene	19	0.16
Swedish	49	0.42
Swiss	96	0.83
Ukrainian	6	0.05
United States or American	1,050	9.08
Welsh	144	1.25
West Indian, excl. Hispanic:	13	0.11
Jamaican	13	0.11
White:	10,923	94.82
Not Hispanic (10,631)	10,846	94.15
Hispanic (64)	77	0.67
Yugoslavian	16	0.14

Canton

Place Type: City
County: Stark
Population: 80,806

Ancestry/Race	Number	%
Acadian/Cajun	8	0.01
Afghan	12	0.01
African American/Black:	18,537	22.94
Not Hispanic (16,875)	18,353	22.71
Hispanic (124)	184	0.23
African, sub-Saharan:	978	1.21
African	914	1.13
Cape Verdean	15	0.02
Kenyan	10	0.01
Nigerian	13	0.02
South African	9	0.01
Other sub-Saharan African	17	0.02
Am. Ind. or Alaska Nat., not spec.	431	0.53
Albanian	5	0.01
Alsatian	11	0.01
American Indian tribes, specified:	812	1.00
Apache (6)	33	0.04
Blackfeet (10)	49	0.06
Cherokee (111)	389	0.48
Cheyenne	1	0.00
Chickasaw	4	0.00
Chippewa (2)	19	0.02
Choctaw (1)	10	0.01
Comanche (2)	2	0.00
Cree	1	0.00
Creek	6	0.01
Crow	3	0.00
Delaware (22)	86	0.11
Houma (4)	4	0.00
Iroquois (22)	89	0.11
Latin American Indians (4)	11	0.01
Lumbee (1)	1	0.00
Menominee	1	0.00
Navajo (7)	9	0.01
Osage	1	0.00
Ottawa (7)	8	0.01
Pueblo	1	0.00
Puget Sound Salish (3)	3	0.00
Seminole (2)	11	0.01
Shoshone	2	0.00
Sioux (3)	26	0.03
Ute	3	0.00
Yakama (1)	1	0.00
Yuman (1)	1	0.00
All other tribes (11)	37	0.05
American Indian tribes, not spec.	59	0.07
Arab:	569	0.70
Arab/Arabic	41	0.05
Lebanese	250	0.31
Syrian	278	0.34
Asian:	447	0.55
Chinese, ex. Taiwanese (42)	62	0.08
Filipino (63)	102	0.13
Hmong (1)	3	0.00
Indian (53)	80	0.10
Indonesian (1)	4	0.00
Japanese (23)	43	0.05
Korean (36)	66	0.08
Malaysian (2)	6	0.01
Pakistani (1)	1	0.00
Taiwanese (1)	1	0.00
Thai (5)	16	0.02
Vietnamese (11)	22	0.03
Other Asian, specified (1)	6	0.01
Other Asian, not specified (13)	35	0.04
Austrian	226	0.28
Belgian	18	0.02
Brazilian	79	0.10
British	280	0.35
Bulgarian	10	0.01
Canadian	17	0.02
Celtic	7	0.01
Croatian	218	0.27
Czech	317	0.39
Czechoslovakian	109	0.13
Danish	151	0.19
Dutch	1,445	1.78
Eastern European	8	0.01
English	5,564	6.86
European	222	0.27
Finnish	75	0.09
French, except Basque	1,988	2.45
French Canadian	115	0.14
German	17,447	21.51
German Russian	5	0.01
Greek	1,059	1.31
Hawaii Native/Pacific Islander:	71	0.09
Micronesian: (8)	17	0.02
Guamanian/Chamorro (8)	17	0.02
Polynesian: (14)	40	0.05
Native Hawaiian (9)	30	0.04
Samoan (5)	10	0.01
Other Pac. Isl., not spec. (2)	14	0.02
Hispanic or Latino:	1,006	1.24
Central American:	62	0.08
Guatemalan	12	0.01
Honduran	34	0.04
Nicaraguan	2	0.00
Panamanian	7	0.01
Salvadoran	5	0.01
Other Central American	2	0.00
Cuban	27	0.03
Dominican Republic	5	0.01
Mexican	398	0.49
Puerto Rican	130	0.16
South American:	33	0.04
Argentinean	7	0.01
Colombian	17	0.02
Ecuadorian	1	0.00
Peruvian	2	0.00
Venezuelan	3	0.00
Other South American	3	0.00
Other Hispanic or Latino	351	0.43
Hungarian	1,032	1.27
Icelander	14	0.02
Irish	9,213	11.36
Italian	6,940	8.56
Latvian	6	0.01
Lithuanian	56	0.07
Macedonian	28	0.03
Northern European	7	0.01
Norwegian	158	0.19
Pennsylvania German	224	0.28
Polish	1,522	1.88
Portuguese	113	0.14
Romanian	517	0.64

Notes: 1. Figures in the "Number" column do not add up to the total population due to: a) Ancestry/Race overlap — e.g. persons can report being both White and Irish, b) persons of Hispanic origin can report being any race, c) persons reporting two ancestries are counted in both categories. 2. Numbers in parentheses indicate the number of persons reporting this ancestry/race alone, not in combination with any other ancestry/race. 3. Refer to the Explanation of Data in the front of the book for more detailed information.

Russian	488	0.60
Scandinavian	47	0.06
Scotch-Irish	1,114	1.37
Scottish	1,074	1.32
Serbian	172	0.21
Slavic	30	0.04
Slovak	623	0.77
Slovene	102	0.13
Swedish	389	0.48
Swiss	775	0.96
Ukrainian	255	0.31
United States or American	5,158	6.36
Welsh	1,012	1.25
West Indian, excl. Hispanic:	70	0.09
Jamaican	65	0.08
West Indian	5	0.01
White:	62,328	77.13
Not Hispanic (59,653)	61,720	76.38
Hispanic (511)	608	0.75
Yugoslavian	100	0.12

Celina

Place Type: City
County: Mercer
Population: 10,303

Ancestry/Race	Number	%
African American/Black:	38	0.37
Not Hispanic (19)	36	0.35
Hispanic	2	0.02
Am. Ind. or Alaska Nat., not spec.	40	0.39
American Indian tribes, specified:	88	0.85
Apache	7	0.07
Blackfeet	3	0.03
Cherokee (15)	46	0.45
Chippewa (1)	1	0.01
Comanche	5	0.05
Delaware	6	0.06
Iroquois (2)	2	0.02
Latin American Indians	5	0.05
Sioux	4	0.04
All other tribes (2)	9	0.09
American Indian tribes, not spec.	1	0.01
Arab:	16	0.15
Arab/Arabic	16	0.15
Asian:	84	0.82
Cambodian (11)	13	0.13
Chinese, ex. Taiwanese (3)	5	0.05
Filipino (10)	11	0.11
Indian (27)	27	0.26
Japanese (4)	12	0.12
Korean (7)	8	0.08
Vietnamese (6)	6	0.06
Other Asian, specified	1	0.01
Other Asian, not specified	1	0.01
Brazilian	16	0.15
British	23	0.22
Canadian	20	0.19
Czech	19	0.18
Czechoslovakian	14	0.13
Dutch	154	1.48
English	680	6.53
European	22	0.21
French, except Basque	371	3.56
French Canadian	9	0.09
German	5,089	48.85
Hawaii Native/Pacific Islander:	6	0.06
Micronesian:	2	0.02
Other Micronesian	2	0.02
Polynesian: (2)	2	0.02
Samoan (2)	2	0.02
Other Pac. Isl., specified	1	0.01
Other Pac. Isl., not spec.	1	0.01
Hispanic or Latino:	220	2.14
Central American:	1	0.01
Panamanian	1	0.01
Cuban	6	0.06
Mexican	158	1.53
Puerto Rican	14	0.14
South American:	6	0.06
Chilean	5	0.05
Colombian	1	0.01
Other Hispanic or Latino	35	0.34
Hungarian	58	0.56
Iranian	8	0.08
Irish	752	7.22
Italian	191	1.83
Norwegian	6	0.06
Pennsylvania German	25	0.24
Polish	72	0.69
Russian	12	0.12
Scandinavian	5	0.05
Scotch-Irish	106	1.02
Scottish	61	0.59
Serbian	5	0.05
Slovak	7	0.07
Slovene	7	0.07
Swedish	25	0.24
Swiss	59	0.57
Ukrainian	7	0.07
United States or American	890	8.54
Welsh	61	0.59
White:	10,106	98.09
Not Hispanic (9,877)	9,964	96.71
Hispanic (121)	142	1.38
Yugoslavian	6	0.06

Centerville

Place Type: City
County: Montgomery
Population: 23,024

Ancestry/Race	Number	%
African American/Black:	767	3.33
Not Hispanic (672)	754	3.27
Hispanic (6)	13	0.06
African, sub-Saharan:	34	0.15
African	27	0.12
South African	7	0.03
Am. Ind. or Alaska Nat., not spec.	19	0.08
Alsatian	18	0.08
American Indian tribes, specified:	70	0.30
Apache (3)	3	0.01
Blackfeet	3	0.01
Cherokee (9)	35	0.15
Chickasaw	3	0.01
Chippewa	1	0.00
Choctaw	1	0.00
Colville (1)	1	0.00
Comanche	1	0.00
Creek (2)	8	0.03
Delaware (1)	3	0.01
Iroquois (1)	1	0.00
Sioux (1)	1	0.00
All other tribes (5)	9	0.04
American Indian tribes, not spec.	1	0.00
Arab:	122	0.53
Arab/Arabic	38	0.16
Egyptian	14	0.06
Lebanese	64	0.28
Other Arab	6	0.03
Armenian	31	0.13
Asian:	857	3.72
Cambodian (2)	3	0.01
Chinese, ex. Taiwanese (159)	185	0.80
Filipino (49)	76	0.33
Indian (244)	268	1.16
Indonesian (2)	3	0.01
Japanese (46)	67	0.29
Korean (101)	110	0.48
Laotian (11)	11	0.05
Pakistani (17)	18	0.08
Taiwanese (22)	29	0.13
Thai (2)	3	0.01
Vietnamese (40)	42	0.18
Other Asian, not specified (16)	42	0.18
Australian	16	0.07
Austrian	35	0.15
Basque	13	0.06
Belgian	63	0.27
British	141	0.61
Canadian	39	0.17
Celtic	20	0.09
Croatian	20	0.09
Czech	106	0.46
Czechoslovakian	42	0.18
Danish	50	0.22
Dutch	495	2.13
Eastern European	20	0.09
English	3,462	14.93
Estonian	11	0.05
European	222	0.96
Finnish	27	0.12
French, except Basque	900	3.88
French Canadian	124	0.53
German	7,918	34.14
Greek	143	0.62
Hawaii Native/Pacific Islander:	28	0.12
Micronesian: (8)	13	0.06
Guamanian/Chamorro (7)	12	0.05
Other Micronesian (1)	1	0.00
Polynesian: (2)	3	0.01
Native Hawaiian (2)	3	0.01
Other Pac. Isl., not spec. (4)	12	0.05
Hispanic or Latino:	272	1.18
Central American:	2	0.01
Guatemalan	1	0.00
Other Central American	1	0.00
Cuban	13	0.06
Dominican Republic	2	0.01
Mexican	97	0.42
Puerto Rican	52	0.23
South American:	29	0.13
Bolivian	8	0.03
Colombian	8	0.03
Peruvian	10	0.04
Venezuelan	3	0.01
Other Hispanic or Latino	77	0.33
Hungarian	228	0.98
Icelander	9	0.04
Irish	4,100	17.68
Italian	1,134	4.89
Latvian	8	0.03
Lithuanian	43	0.19
Luxemburger	19	0.08
Northern European	46	0.20
Norwegian	152	0.66
Pennsylvania German	29	0.13
Polish	706	3.04
Portuguese	30	0.13
Romanian	67	0.29
Russian	188	0.81
Scandinavian	44	0.19
Scotch-Irish	550	2.37
Scottish	610	2.63
Serbian	5	0.02
Slavic	24	0.10
Slovak	165	0.71
Slovene	16	0.07
Swedish	305	1.32
Swiss	130	0.56
Turkish	30	0.13
Ukrainian	40	0.17
United States or American	1,434	6.18
Welsh	320	1.38
West Indian, excl. Hispanic:	17	0.07
Dutch West Indian	7	0.03
Haitian	10	0.04
White:	21,486	93.32
Not Hispanic (21,063)	21,276	92.41
Hispanic (195)	210	0.91
Yugoslavian	55	0.24

Notes: 1. Figures in the "Number" column do not add up to the total population due to: a) Ancestry/Race overlap — e.g. persons can report being both White and Irish, b) persons of Hispanic origin can report being any race, c) persons reporting two ancestries are counted in both categories. 2. Numbers in parentheses indicate the number of persons reporting this ancestry/race alone, not in combination with any other ancestry/race. 3. Refer to the Explanation of Data in the front of the book for more detailed information.

Chillicothe

Place Type: City
County: Ross
Population: 21,796

Ancestry/Race	Number	%
African American/Black:	1,859	8.53
Not Hispanic (1,631)	1,846	8.47
Hispanic (6)	13	0.06
African, sub-Saharan:	83	0.38
African	78	0.36
Nigerian	5	0.02
Am. Ind. or Alaska Nat., not spec.	108	0.50
Albanian	8	0.04
American Indian tribes, specified:	184	0.84
Apache	3	0.01
Blackfeet	15	0.07
Cherokee (21)	102	0.47
Chickasaw	1	0.00
Comanche	4	0.02
Crow (1)	1	0.00
Delaware	1	0.00
Iroquois	7	0.03
Kiowa	1	0.00
Latin American Indians (3)	4	0.02
Lumbee	1	0.00
Navajo (3)	4	0.02
Osage (3)	3	0.01
Seminole (1)	1	0.00
Sioux (1)	9	0.04
All other tribes (12)	27	0.12
American Indian tribes, not spec.	2	0.01
Arab:	26	0.12
Arab/Arabic	13	0.06
Lebanese	6	0.03
Syrian	7	0.03
Armenian	12	0.05
Asian:	164	0.75
Chinese, ex. Taiwanese (14)	20	0.09
Filipino (22)	42	0.19
Indian (26)	33	0.15
Japanese (24)	32	0.15
Korean (6)	8	0.04
Laotian (1)	1	0.00
Sri Lankan (1)	1	0.00
Thai (11)	11	0.05
Vietnamese (9)	13	0.06
Other Asian, not specified (2)	3	0.01
Austrian	21	0.10
Belgian	3	0.01
British	52	0.24
Canadian	38	0.17
Croatian	5	0.02
Czech	37	0.17
Danish	18	0.08
Dutch	423	1.93
English	2,299	10.48
European	179	0.82
Finnish	7	0.03
French, except Basque	492	2.24
French Canadian	18	0.08
German	4,822	21.99
Greek	29	0.13
Guyanese	5	0.02
Hawaii Native/Pacific Islander:	25	0.11
Melanesian: (1)	1	0.00
Other Melanesian (1)	1	0.00
Micronesian: (4)	4	0.02
Guamanian/Chamorro (4)	4	0.02
Polynesian: (3)	14	0.06
Native Hawaiian (1)	10	0.05
Samoan (2)	4	0.02
Other Pac. Isl., not spec.	6	0.03
Hispanic or Latino:	182	0.84
Central American:	7	0.03
Costa Rican	1	0.00
Guatemalan	1	0.00
Panamanian	4	0.02
Other Central American	1	0.00
Cuban	14	0.06
Mexican	73	0.33
Puerto Rican	33	0.15
South American:	9	0.04
Bolivian	1	0.00
Colombian	5	0.02
Ecuadorian	2	0.01
Peruvian	1	0.00
Other Hispanic or Latino	46	0.21
Hungarian	42	0.19
Icelander	6	0.03
Irish	2,589	11.81
Italian	444	2.02
Latvian	7	0.03
Lithuanian	5	0.02
Norwegian	32	0.15
Pennsylvania German	38	0.17
Polish	158	0.72
Romanian	10	0.05
Russian	21	0.10
Scandinavian	5	0.02
Scotch-Irish	309	1.41
Scottish	493	2.25
Slavic	6	0.03
Slovak	57	0.26
Slovene	8	0.04
Swedish	33	0.15
Swiss	9	0.04
Ukrainian	7	0.03
United States or American	3,041	13.87
Welsh	293	1.34
West Indian, excl. Hispanic:	26	0.12
Belizean	6	0.03
Haitian	14	0.06
U.S. Virgin Islander	6	0.03
White:	19,851	91.08
Not Hispanic (19,343)	19,722	90.48
Hispanic (102)	129	0.59

Cincinnati

Place Type: City
County: Hamilton
Population: 331,285

Ancestry/Race	Number	%
Acadian/Cajun	60	0.02
Afghan	5	0.00
African American/Black:	145,615	43.95
Not Hispanic (141,534)	144,770	43.70
Hispanic (642)	845	0.26
African, sub-Saharan:	7,196	2.18
African	6,339	1.92
Cape Verdean	27	0.01
Ethiopian	143	0.04
Ghanian	54	0.02
Kenyan	65	0.02
Liberian	9	0.00
Nigerian	232	0.07
Senegalese	26	0.01
Sierra Leonean	32	0.01
South African	13	0.00
Sudanese	36	0.01
Ugandan	8	0.00
Zimbabwean	19	0.01
Other sub-Saharan African	193	0.06
Alaska Native tribes, specified:	17	0.01
Alaska Athabascan (1)	7	0.00
Aleut (6)	6	0.00
Eskimo	1	0.00
Tlingit-Haida (2)	3	0.00
Am. Ind. or Alaska Nat., not spec.	1,033	0.31
Albanian	155	0.05
Alsatian	31	0.01
American Indian tribes, specified:	1,458	0.44
Apache (10)	36	0.01
Blackfeet (15)	143	0.04
Cherokee (173)	756	0.23
Cheyenne (1)	9	0.00
Chickasaw (3)	10	0.00
Chippewa (15)	29	0.01
Choctaw (4)	28	0.01
Comanche (3)	6	0.00
Cree (1)	4	0.00
Creek (3)	25	0.01
Crow (2)	7	0.00
Delaware (2)	8	0.00
Iroquois (10)	28	0.01
Latin American Indians (27)	136	0.04
Lumbee (1)	5	0.00
Menominee (2)	2	0.00
Navajo (6)	26	0.01
Osage	1	0.00
Ottawa	3	0.00
Paiute (3)	3	0.00
Pima	2	0.00
Potawatomi (2)	6	0.00
Pueblo	6	0.00
Seminole (1)	18	0.01
Shoshone	2	0.00
Sioux (21)	47	0.01
Tohono O'Odham (4)	4	0.00
All other tribes (44)	108	0.03
American Indian tribes, not spec.	135	0.04
Arab:	981	0.30
Arab/Arabic	105	0.03
Egyptian	82	0.02
Jordanian	6	0.00
Lebanese	559	0.17
Moroccan	30	0.01
Palestinian	67	0.02
Syrian	100	0.03
Other Arab	32	0.01
Armenian	83	0.03
Asian:	6,187	1.87
Bangladeshi (14)	17	0.01
Cambodian (183)	229	0.07
Chinese, ex. Taiwanese (1,363)	1,521	0.46
Filipino (403)	598	0.18
Hmong (3)	3	0.00
Indian (1,472)	1,633	0.49
Indonesian (25)	38	0.01
Japanese (245)	336	0.10
Korean (374)	464	0.14
Laotian (11)	12	0.00
Malaysian (2)	6	0.00
Pakistani (60)	85	0.03
Sri Lankan (47)	65	0.02
Taiwanese (73)	87	0.03
Thai (66)	88	0.03
Vietnamese (558)	620	0.19
Other Asian, specified (24)	44	0.01
Other Asian, not specified (130)	341	0.10
Assyrian/Chaldean/Syriac	6	0.00
Australian	65	0.02
Austrian	804	0.24
Belgian	167	0.05
Brazilian	54	0.02
British	1,188	0.36
Bulgarian	106	0.03
Canadian	398	0.12
Celtic	67	0.02
Croatian	247	0.07
Czech	367	0.11
Czechoslovakian	232	0.07
Danish	374	0.11
Dutch	3,032	0.92
Eastern European	262	0.08
English	18,016	5.45
Estonian	14	0.00
European	2,175	0.66
Finnish	201	0.06
French, except Basque	5,602	1.69
French Canadian	768	0.23
German	65,659	19.86
Greek	1,040	0.31
Guyanese	21	0.01
Hawaii Native/Pacific Islander:	338	0.10
Melanesian: (2)	11	0.00
Other Melanesian (2)	11	0.00

Notes: 1. Figures in the "Number" column do not add up to the total population due to: a) Ancestry/Race overlap — e.g. persons can report being both White and Irish, b) persons of Hispanic origin can report being any race, c) persons reporting two ancestries are counted in both categories. 2. Numbers in parentheses indicate the number of persons reporting this ancestry/race alone, not in combination with any other ancestry/race. 3. Refer to the Explanation of Data in the front of the book for more detailed information.

Micronesian: (49)	62	0.02
Guamanian/Chamorro (48)	59	0.02
Other Micronesian (1)	3	0.00
Polynesian: (56)	114	0.03
Native Hawaiian (25)	66	0.02
Samoan (27)	42	0.01
Other Polynesian (4)	6	0.00
Other Pac. Isl., specified	18	0.01
Other Pac. Isl., not spec. (23)	133	0.04
Hispanic or Latino:	4,230	1.28
Central American:	397	0.12
Costa Rican	38	0.01
Guatemalan	211	0.06
Honduran	47	0.01
Nicaraguan	23	0.01
Panamanian	45	0.01
Salvadoran	27	0.01
Other Central American	6	0.00
Cuban	220	0.07
Dominican Republic	51	0.02
Mexican	1,542	0.47
Puerto Rican	648	0.20
South American:	320	0.10
Argentinean	49	0.01
Bolivian	12	0.00
Chilean	21	0.01
Colombian	96	0.03
Ecuadorian	30	0.01
Paraguayan	4	0.00
Peruvian	57	0.02
Uruguayan	1	0.00
Venezuelan	36	0.01
Other South American	14	0.00
Other Hispanic or Latino	1,052	0.32
Hungarian	1,455	0.44
Icelander	22	0.01
Iranian	159	0.05
Irish	34,226	10.35
Israeli	91	0.03
Italian	10,877	3.29
Latvian	102	0.03
Lithuanian	496	0.15
Luxemburger	66	0.02
Macedonian	70	0.02
Maltese	20	0.01
Northern European	167	0.05
Norwegian	983	0.30
Pennsylvania German	114	0.03
Polish	3,638	1.10
Portuguese	158	0.05
Romanian	338	0.10
Russian	1,948	0.59
Scandinavian	168	0.05
Scotch-Irish	2,970	0.90
Scottish	4,086	1.24
Serbian	132	0.04
Slavic	106	0.03
Slovak	389	0.12
Slovene	90	0.03
Swedish	1,318	0.40
Swiss	800	0.24
Turkish	119	0.04
Ukrainian	587	0.18
United States or American	15,919	4.81
Welsh	1,745	0.53
West Indian, excl. Hispanic:	634	0.19
Bermudan	4	0.00
British West Indian	16	0.00
Haitian	70	0.02
Jamaican	437	0.13
Trinidadian and Tobagonian	14	0.00
West Indian	93	0.03
White:	179,453	54.17
Not Hispanic (173,781)	177,483	53.57
Hispanic (1,711)	1,970	0.59
Yugoslavian	213	0.06

Circleville

Place Type: City
County: Pickaway
Population: 13,485

Ancestry/Race	Number	%
African American/Black:	415	3.08
Not Hispanic (340)	408	3.03
Hispanic (2)	7	0.05
African, sub-Saharan:	11	0.08
African	11	0.08
Am. Ind. or Alaska Nat., not spec.	29	0.22
American Indian tribes, specified:	64	0.47
Apache (2)	2	0.01
Blackfeet	6	0.04
Cherokee (12)	40	0.30
Choctaw	1	0.01
Comanche (3)	4	0.03
Delaware	1	0.01
Iroquois	1	0.01
Kiowa	1	0.01
Pueblo	2	0.01
Sioux (1)	1	0.01
All other tribes (4)	5	0.04
American Indian tribes, not spec.	4	0.03
Arab:	8	0.06
Lebanese	8	0.06
Asian:	85	0.63
Chinese, ex. Taiwanese (8)	8	0.06
Filipino (15)	24	0.18
Indian (24)	26	0.19
Indonesian (1)	1	0.01
Japanese (3)	8	0.06
Korean (12)	13	0.10
Malaysian (1)	1	0.01
Other Asian, specified	1	0.01
Other Asian, not specified (2)	3	0.02
Australian	8	0.06
British	49	0.36
Bulgarian	6	0.04
Canadian	33	0.24
Czechoslovakian	6	0.04
Danish	6	0.04
Dutch	262	1.93
English	1,208	8.91
Estonian	6	0.04
European	124	0.91
Finnish	34	0.25
French, except Basque	144	1.06
French Canadian	7	0.05
German	2,593	19.12
Greek	23	0.17
Hawaii Native/Pacific Islander:	15	0.11
Polynesian: (8)	11	0.08
Native Hawaiian (8)	11	0.08
Other Pac. Isl., specified	1	0.01
Other Pac. Isl., not spec.	3	0.02
Hispanic or Latino:	111	0.82
Central American:	3	0.02
Panamanian	2	0.01
Salvadoran	1	0.01
Cuban	1	0.01
Mexican	51	0.38
Puerto Rican	16	0.12
South American:	3	0.02
Bolivian	1	0.01
Colombian	2	0.01
Other Hispanic or Latino	37	0.27
Hungarian	26	0.19
Irish	1,320	9.73
Italian	236	1.74
Northern European	7	0.05
Norwegian	23	0.17
Polish	109	0.80
Romanian	6	0.04
Russian	7	0.05
Scotch-Irish	124	0.91
Scottish	154	1.14
Slovak	4	0.03
Slovene	42	0.31
Swedish	34	0.25
Swiss	14	0.10
Turkish	8	0.06
United States or American	2,206	16.26
Welsh	94	0.69
White:	12,992	96.34
Not Hispanic (12,788)	12,915	95.77
Hispanic (71)	77	0.57

Clayton

Place Type: City
County: Montgomery
Population: 13,347

Ancestry/Race	Number	%
African American/Black:	1,385	10.38
Not Hispanic (1,315)	1,378	10.32
Hispanic (3)	7	0.05
African, sub-Saharan:	79	0.59
African	79	0.59
Am. Ind. or Alaska Nat., not spec.	19	0.14
American Indian tribes, specified:	30	0.22
Blackfeet (1)	1	0.01
Cherokee (4)	19	0.14
Choctaw	1	0.01
Creek	5	0.04
Iroquois (1)	1	0.01
Latin American Indians	2	0.01
All other tribes	1	0.01
American Indian tribes, not spec.	7	0.05
Arab:	24	0.18
Arab/Arabic	4	0.03
Iraqi	20	0.15
Asian:	240	1.80
Chinese, ex. Taiwanese (39)	47	0.35
Filipino (23)	30	0.22
Indian (77)	84	0.63
Indonesian	1	0.01
Japanese (14)	26	0.19
Korean (20)	24	0.18
Malaysian (3)	3	0.02
Pakistani	1	0.01
Taiwanese (4)	6	0.04
Thai (1)	2	0.01
Vietnamese (3)	5	0.04
Other Asian, not specified (6)	11	0.08
Austrian	55	0.41
British	41	0.31
Canadian	5	0.04
Czech	26	0.19
Czechoslovakian	14	0.10
Danish	18	0.13
Dutch	228	1.70
Eastern European	50	0.37
English	1,292	9.66
European	142	1.06
French, except Basque	528	3.95
French Canadian	54	0.40
German	4,308	32.21
Greek	172	1.29
Hawaii Native/Pacific Islander:	9	0.07
Micronesian: (2)	2	0.01
Guamanian/Chamorro (2)	2	0.01
Polynesian: (3)	5	0.04
Native Hawaiian (3)	5	0.04
Other Pac. Isl., not spec. (1)	2	0.01
Hispanic or Latino:	120	0.90
Central American:	1	0.01
Panamanian	1	0.01
Cuban	16	0.12
Mexican	63	0.47
Puerto Rican	15	0.11
South American:	4	0.03
Ecuadorian	3	0.02
Other South American	1	0.01
Other Hispanic or Latino	21	0.16
Hungarian	140	1.05
Irish	1,894	14.16

Notes: 1. Figures in the "Number" column do not add up to the total population due to: a) Ancestry/Race overlap — e.g. persons can report being both White and Irish, b) persons of Hispanic origin can report being any race, c) persons reporting two ancestries are counted in both categories. 2. Numbers in parentheses indicate the number of persons reporting this ancestry/race alone, not in combination with any other ancestry/race. 3. Refer to the Explanation of Data in the front of the book for more detailed information.

Israeli	32	0.24
Italian	542	4.05
Lithuanian	110	0.82
Northern European	20	0.15
Norwegian	77	0.58
Pennsylvania German	12	0.09
Polish	308	2.30
Portuguese	13	0.10
Romanian	42	0.31
Russian	145	1.08
Scotch-Irish	238	1.78
Scottish	360	2.69
Slavic	3	0.02
Slovak	34	0.25
Swedish	76	0.57
Swiss	75	0.56
Ukrainian	61	0.46
United States or American	1,160	8.67
Welsh	181	1.35
West Indian, excl. Hispanic:	19	0.14
Barbadian	12	0.09
British West Indian	7	0.05
White:	11,751	88.04
Not Hispanic (11,553)	11,667	87.41
Hispanic (78)	84	0.63
Yugoslavian	7	0.05

Cleveland Heights

Place Type: City
County: Cuyahoga
Population: 49,958

Ancestry/Race	Number	%
African American/Black:	21,649	43.33
Not Hispanic (20,752)	21,460	42.96
Hispanic (121)	189	0.38
African, sub-Saharan:	583	1.17
African	362	0.72
Cape Verdean	9	0.02
Ethiopian	8	0.02
Ghanian	26	0.05
Liberian	52	0.10
Nigerian	48	0.10
South African	3	0.01
Sudanese	33	0.07
Ugandan	23	0.05
Zimbabwean	13	0.03
Other sub-Saharan African	6	0.01
Alaska Native tribes, specified:	2	0.00
Alaska Athabascan (1)	1	0.00
Tlingit-Haida (1)	1	0.00
Am. Ind. or Alaska Nat., not spec.	176	0.35
Albanian	37	0.07
American Indian tribes, specified:	217	0.43
Apache	1	0.00
Blackfeet (7)	40	0.08
Cherokee (16)	82	0.16
Chickasaw	1	0.00
Chippewa (3)	7	0.01
Choctaw (2)	8	0.02
Comanche	1	0.00
Creek	9	0.02
Crow	9	0.02
Delaware	2	0.00
Iroquois (1)	5	0.01
Latin American Indians (10)	17	0.03
Navajo	2	0.00
Osage	1	0.00
Seminole	11	0.02
Sioux (1)	5	0.01
All other tribes (2)	16	0.03
American Indian tribes, not spec.	14	0.03
Arab:	298	0.60
Arab/Arabic	29	0.06
Egyptian	30	0.06
Iraqi	9	0.02
Lebanese	183	0.37
Moroccan	7	0.01
Syrian	7	0.01
Other Arab	33	0.07
Armenian	60	0.12
Asian:	1,516	3.03
Bangladeshi (7)	7	0.01
Cambodian (4)	4	0.01
Chinese, ex. Taiwanese (414)	465	0.93
Filipino (65)	98	0.20
Indian (427)	477	0.95
Indonesian (14)	16	0.03
Japanese (87)	125	0.25
Korean (121)	138	0.28
Laotian (1)	1	0.00
Malaysian (5)	6	0.01
Pakistani (10)	13	0.03
Sri Lankan (6)	7	0.01
Taiwanese (13)	19	0.04
Thai (28)	37	0.07
Vietnamese (27)	39	0.08
Other Asian, specified (11)	14	0.03
Other Asian, not specified (21)	50	0.10
Australian	31	0.06
Austrian	168	0.34
Basque	19	0.04
Belgian	95	0.19
Brazilian	6	0.01
British	247	0.49
Bulgarian	8	0.02
Canadian	198	0.40
Celtic	44	0.09
Croatian	129	0.26
Czech	355	0.71
Czechoslovakian	101	0.20
Danish	118	0.24
Dutch	495	0.99
Eastern European	323	0.65
English	3,727	7.46
Estonian	15	0.03
European	670	1.34
Finnish	94	0.19
French, except Basque	633	1.27
French Canadian	95	0.19
German	6,044	12.09
German Russian	5	0.01
Greek	289	0.58
Guyanese	18	0.04
Hawaii Native/Pacific Islander:	27	0.05
Micronesian: (2)	4	0.01
Guamanian/Chamorro (1)	3	0.01
Other Micronesian (1)	1	0.00
Polynesian: (3)	11	0.02
Native Hawaiian (1)	6	0.01
Samoan	3	0.01
Tongan (1)	1	0.00
Other Polynesian (1)	1	0.00
Other Pac. Isl., specified	2	0.00
Other Pac. Isl., not spec.	10	0.02
Hispanic or Latino:	791	1.58
Central American:	60	0.12
Costa Rican	1	0.00
Guatemalan	12	0.02
Honduran	9	0.02
Nicaraguan	3	0.01
Panamanian	8	0.02
Salvadoran	24	0.05
Other Central American	3	0.01
Cuban	43	0.09
Dominican Republic	8	0.02
Mexican	205	0.41
Puerto Rican	206	0.41
South American:	89	0.18
Argentinean	16	0.03
Bolivian	1	0.00
Chilean	6	0.01
Colombian	24	0.05
Ecuadorian	1	0.00
Paraguayan	1	0.00
Peruvian	15	0.03
Uruguayan	3	0.01
Venezuelan	17	0.03
Other South American	5	0.01
Other Hispanic or Latino	180	0.36
Hungarian	1,036	2.07
Icelander	6	0.01
Iranian	87	0.17
Irish	5,153	10.31
Israeli	49	0.10
Italian	2,910	5.82
Latvian	52	0.10
Lithuanian	296	0.59
Northern European	45	0.09
Norwegian	231	0.46
Pennsylvania German	53	0.11
Polish	1,806	3.61
Portuguese	44	0.09
Romanian	175	0.35
Russian	1,438	2.88
Scandinavian	76	0.15
Scotch-Irish	438	0.88
Scottish	892	1.78
Serbian	102	0.20
Slovak	480	0.96
Slovene	247	0.49
Swedish	418	0.84
Swiss	218	0.44
Turkish	22	0.04
Ukrainian	433	0.87
United States or American	1,085	2.17
Welsh	359	0.72
West Indian, excl. Hispanic:	322	0.64
Bahamian	7	0.01
Barbadian	5	0.01
Haitian	10	0.02
Jamaican	209	0.42
Trinidadian and Tobagonian	6	0.01
West Indian	85	0.17
White:	27,100	54.25
Not Hispanic (25,840)	26,643	53.33
Hispanic (389)	457	0.91
Yugoslavian	7	0.01

Cleveland

Place Type: City
County: Cuyahoga
Population: 478,403

Ancestry/Race	Number	%
Afghan	18	0.00
African American/Black:	249,192	52.09
Not Hispanic (241,512)	245,890	51.40
Hispanic (2,427)	3,302	0.69
African, sub-Saharan:	6,075	1.27
African	5,696	1.19
Cape Verdean	25	0.01
Ethiopian	43	0.01
Ghanian	28	0.01
Kenyan	12	0.00
Liberian	40	0.01
Nigerian	159	0.03
Senegalese	5	0.00
South African	19	0.00
Sudanese	15	0.00
Zimbabwean	4	0.00
Other sub-Saharan African	29	0.01
Alaska Native tribes, specified:	21	0.00
Alaska Athabascan	5	0.00
Aleut (2)	2	0.00
Eskimo (10)	11	0.00
Tlingit-Haida (2)	3	0.00
Am. Ind. or Alaska Nat., not spec.	1,858	0.39
Albanian	225	0.05
Alsatian	41	0.01
American Indian tribes, specified:	2,235	0.47
Apache (29)	56	0.01
Blackfeet (39)	271	0.06
Cherokee (209)	984	0.21
Cheyenne (9)	19	0.00
Chickasaw (6)	11	0.00
Chippewa (42)	77	0.02
Choctaw (31)	68	0.01

Notes: 1. Figures in the "Number" column do not add up to the total population due to: a) Ancestry/Race overlap — e.g. persons can report being both White and Irish, b) persons of Hispanic origin can report being any race, c) persons reporting two ancestries are counted in both categories. 2. Numbers in parentheses indicate the number of persons reporting this ancestry/race alone, not in combination with any other ancestry/race. 3. Refer to the Explanation of Data in the front of the book for more detailed information.

Colville	1	0.00
Comanche (1)	10	0.00
Cree (7)	13	0.00
Creek (2)	18	0.00
Crow	8	0.00
Delaware (2)	9	0.00
Iroquois (36)	91	0.02
Kiowa (6)	7	0.00
Latin American Indians (73)	155	0.03
Lumbee (1)	7	0.00
Navajo (19)	38	0.01
Osage (2)	2	0.00
Ottawa (12)	16	0.00
Paiute (2)	3	0.00
Pima (3)	8	0.00
Potawatomi (5)	5	0.00
Pueblo (9)	16	0.00
Seminole (26)	41	0.01
Shoshone (1)	2	0.00
Sioux (46)	140	0.03
Tohono O'Odham (6)	9	0.00
Ute (1)	2	0.00
Yakama (1)	2	0.00
Yaqui (1)	1	0.00
Yuman	2	0.00
All other tribes (57)	143	0.03
American Indian tribes, not spec.	238	0.05
Arab:	2,916	0.61
Arab/Arabic	805	0.17
Egyptian	329	0.07
Iraqi	27	0.01
Jordanian	135	0.03
Lebanese	1,004	0.21
Moroccan	133	0.03
Palestinian	244	0.05
Syrian	187	0.04
Other Arab	52	0.01
Armenian	56	0.01
Asian:	7,910	1.65
Bangladeshi (4)	6	0.00
Cambodian (333)	391	0.08
Chinese, ex. Taiwanese (2,039)	2,231	0.47
Filipino (725)	955	0.20
Indian (1,145)	1,445	0.30
Indonesian (63)	67	0.01
Japanese (211)	343	0.07
Korean (296)	380	0.08
Laotian (48)	70	0.01
Malaysian (17)	18	0.00
Pakistani (51)	70	0.01
Sri Lankan (7)	9	0.00
Taiwanese (44)	56	0.01
Thai (94)	121	0.03
Vietnamese (1,054)	1,186	0.25
Other Asian, specified (5)	44	0.01
Other Asian, not specified (185)	518	0.11
Australian	40	0.01
Austrian	749	0.16
Basque	16	0.00
Belgian	98	0.02
Brazilian	69	0.01
British	492	0.10
Bulgarian	79	0.02
Canadian	359	0.08
Carpatho Rusyn	48	0.01
Celtic	24	0.01
Croatian	2,219	0.46
Czech	3,580	0.75
Czechoslovakian	1,096	0.23
Danish	333	0.07
Dutch	2,847	0.60
Eastern European	66	0.01
English	13,169	2.75
Estonian	5	0.00
European	949	0.20
Finnish	475	0.10
French, except Basque	4,106	0.86
French Canadian	873	0.18
German	44,172	9.23
German Russian	13	0.00
Greek	1,385	0.29
Guyanese	159	0.03
Hawaii Native/Pacific Islander:	514	0.11
Micronesian: (43)	83	0.02
Guamanian/Chamorro (41)	78	0.02
Other Micronesian (2)	5	0.00
Polynesian: (66)	169	0.04
Native Hawaiian (40)	105	0.02
Samoan (25)	61	0.01
Other Polynesian (1)	3	0.00
Other Pac. Isl., specified	34	0.01
Other Pac. Isl., not spec. (68)	228	0.05
Hispanic or Latino:	34,728	7.26
Central American:	1,166	0.24
Costa Rican	39	0.01
Guatemalan	431	0.09
Honduran	170	0.04
Nicaraguan	91	0.02
Panamanian	47	0.01
Salvadoran	324	0.07
Other Central American	64	0.01
Cuban	512	0.11
Dominican Republic	542	0.11
Mexican	2,973	0.62
Puerto Rican	25,385	5.31
South American:	557	0.12
Argentinean	43	0.01
Bolivian	10	0.00
Chilean	61	0.01
Colombian	162	0.03
Ecuadorian	58	0.01
Paraguayan	3	0.00
Peruvian	142	0.03
Uruguayan	5	0.00
Venezuelan	47	0.01
Other South American	26	0.01
Other Hispanic or Latino	3,593	0.75
Hungarian	8,385	1.75
Icelander	25	0.01
Iranian	48	0.01
Irish	38,986	8.15
Israeli	19	0.00
Italian	22,053	4.61
Latvian	213	0.04
Lithuanian	1,444	0.30
Luxemburger	9	0.00
Macedonian	101	0.02
Maltese	6	0.00
New Zealander	6	0.00
Northern European	32	0.01
Norwegian	570	0.12
Pennsylvania German	192	0.04
Polish	22,978	4.80
Portuguese	115	0.02
Romanian	1,461	0.31
Russian	2,429	0.51
Scandinavian	72	0.02
Scotch-Irish	2,319	0.48
Scottish	2,475	0.52
Serbian	721	0.15
Slavic	189	0.04
Slovak	8,402	1.76
Slovene	3,828	0.80
Swedish	1,331	0.28
Swiss	541	0.11
Turkish	151	0.03
Ukrainian	3,224	0.67
United States or American	13,063	2.73
Welsh	1,309	0.27
West Indian, excl. Hispanic:	1,651	0.35
Bahamian	21	0.00
Barbadian	5	0.00
Belizean	16	0.00
Dutch West Indian	4	0.00
Haitian	43	0.01
Jamaican	1,194	0.25
Trinidadian and Tobagonian	184	0.04
U.S. Virgin Islander	30	0.01
West Indian	154	0.03
White:	206,487	43.16
Not Hispanic (185,641)	191,741	40.08
Hispanic (12,869)	14,746	3.08
Yugoslavian	599	0.13

Columbus

Place Type: City
County: Franklin
Population: 711,470

Ancestry/Race	Number	%
Acadian/Cajun	41	0.01
Afghan	98	0.01
African American/Black:	185,173	26.03
Not Hispanic (172,750)	183,224	25.75
Hispanic (1,315)	1,949	0.27
African, sub-Saharan:	15,914	2.24
African	8,924	1.25
Cape Verdean	59	0.01
Ethiopian	1,241	0.17
Ghanian	731	0.10
Kenyan	86	0.01
Liberian	166	0.02
Nigerian	813	0.11
Senegalese	95	0.01
Sierra Leonean	88	0.01
Somalian	2,839	0.40
South African	50	0.01
Sudanese	22	0.00
Ugandan	19	0.00
Zimbabwean	82	0.01
Other sub-Saharan African	699	0.10
Alaska Native tribes, specified:	44	0.01
Alaska Athabascan (5)	10	0.00
Aleut (2)	6	0.00
Eskimo (3)	16	0.00
Tlingit-Haida (9)	11	0.00
All other tribes	1	0.00
Alaska Native tribes, not specified	1	0.00
Am. Ind. or Alaska Nat., not spec.	2,805	0.39
Albanian	133	0.02
Alsatian	23	0.00
American Indian tribes, specified:	4,012	0.56
Apache (38)	121	0.02
Blackfeet (60)	407	0.06
Cherokee (497)	2,100	0.30
Cheyenne (8)	32	0.00
Chickasaw (10)	16	0.00
Chippewa (45)	90	0.01
Choctaw (25)	65	0.01
Comanche (8)	19	0.00
Cree (1)	14	0.00
Creek (8)	29	0.00
Crow (3)	11	0.00
Delaware (12)	32	0.00
Houma (2)	3	0.00
Iroquois (33)	118	0.02
Kiowa (1)	10	0.00
Latin American Indians (56)	160	0.02
Lumbee (39)	45	0.01
Menominee (9)	9	0.00
Navajo (35)	73	0.01
Osage (4)	15	0.00
Ottawa (3)	9	0.00
Paiute (2)	5	0.00
Pima (4)	7	0.00
Potawatomi (2)	12	0.00
Pueblo (5)	23	0.00
Puget Sound Salish	1	0.00
Seminole (7)	35	0.00
Shoshone (1)	3	0.00
Sioux (59)	178	0.03
Tohono O'Odham (4)	7	0.00
Ute	1	0.00
Yaqui (3)	9	0.00
All other tribes (156)	353	0.05
American Indian tribes, not spec.	329	0.05
Arab:	4,512	0.63
Arab/Arabic	921	0.13
Egyptian	491	0.07

Notes: 1. Figures in the "Number" column do not add up to the total population due to: a) Ancestry/Race overlap — e.g. persons can report being both White and Irish, b) persons of Hispanic origin can report being any race, c) persons reporting two ancestries are counted in both categories. 2. Numbers in parentheses indicate the number of persons reporting this ancestry/race alone, not in combination with any other ancestry/race. 3. Refer to the Explanation of Data in the front of the book for more detailed information.

Iraqi	111	0.02
Jordanian	146	0.02
Lebanese	1,291	0.18
Moroccan	121	0.02
Palestinian	510	0.07
Syrian	381	0.05
Other Arab	540	0.08
Armenian	216	0.03
Asian:	28,624	4.02
Bangladeshi (157)	194	0.03
Cambodian (1,198)	1,366	0.19
Chinese, ex. Taiwanese (5,394)	5,977	0.84
Filipino (1,271)	1,851	0.26
Hmong (13)	13	0.00
Indian (6,425)	7,025	0.99
Indonesian (419)	490	0.07
Japanese (1,955)	2,458	0.35
Korean (2,549)	2,930	0.41
Laotian (1,083)	1,290	0.18
Malaysian (47)	66	0.01
Pakistani (353)	434	0.06
Sri Lankan (99)	116	0.02
Taiwanese (352)	435	0.06
Thai (342)	472	0.07
Vietnamese (1,827)	2,089	0.29
Other Asian, specified (55)	103	0.01
Other Asian, not specified (550)	1,315	0.18
Australian	262	0.04
Austrian	1,483	0.21
Basque	37	0.01
Belgian	510	0.07
Brazilian	272	0.04
British	3,186	0.45
Bulgarian	217	0.03
Canadian	1,034	0.15
Carpatho Rusyn	41	0.01
Celtic	222	0.03
Croatian	1,117	0.16
Cypriot	27	0.00
Czech	2,232	0.31
Czechoslovakian	1,125	0.16
Danish	938	0.13
Dutch	9,831	1.38
Eastern European	428	0.06
English	55,990	7.87
Estonian	27	0.00
European	5,217	0.73
Finnish	822	0.12
French, except Basque	13,588	1.91
French Canadian	2,010	0.28
German	137,761	19.36
German Russian	23	0.00
Greek	2,702	0.38
Guyanese	61	0.01
Hawaii Native/Pacific Islander:	974	0.14
Melanesian: (3)	5	0.00
Fijian (3)	5	0.00
Micronesian: (69)	126	0.02
Guamanian/Chamorro (63)	116	0.02
Other Micronesian (6)	10	0.00
Polynesian: (188)	381	0.05
Native Hawaiian (72)	187	0.03
Samoan (112)	186	0.03
Tongan (1)	1	0.00
Other Polynesian (3)	7	0.00
Other Pac. Isl., specified	26	0.00
Other Pac. Isl., not spec. (105)	436	0.06
Hispanic or Latino:	17,471	2.46
Central American:	1,040	0.15
Costa Rican	67	0.01
Guatemalan	115	0.02
Honduran	108	0.02
Nicaraguan	73	0.01
Panamanian	173	0.02
Salvadoran	455	0.06
Other Central American	49	0.01
Cuban	627	0.09
Dominican Republic	298	0.04
Mexican	8,686	1.22
Puerto Rican	2,790	0.39
South American:	944	0.13
Argentinean	72	0.01
Bolivian	34	0.00
Chilean	51	0.01
Colombian	289	0.04
Ecuadorian	97	0.01
Paraguayan	5	0.00
Peruvian	179	0.03
Uruguayan	3	0.00
Venezuelan	180	0.03
Other South American	34	0.00
Other Hispanic or Latino	3,086	0.43
Hungarian	5,889	0.83
Icelander	36	0.01
Iranian	725	0.10
Irish	83,226	11.69
Israeli	226	0.03
Italian	35,236	4.95
Latvian	290	0.04
Lithuanian	1,028	0.14
Luxemburger	13	0.00
Macedonian	471	0.07
Maltese	29	0.00
Northern European	293	0.04
Norwegian	3,027	0.43
Pennsylvania German	487	0.07
Polish	14,510	2.04
Portuguese	549	0.08
Romanian	954	0.13
Russian	4,333	0.61
Scandinavian	596	0.08
Scotch-Irish	9,675	1.36
Scottish	11,819	1.66
Serbian	651	0.09
Slavic	374	0.05
Slovak	2,491	0.35
Slovene	733	0.10
Soviet Union	6	0.00
Swedish	4,254	0.60
Swiss	2,640	0.37
Turkish	454	0.06
Ukrainian	1,955	0.27
United States or American	51,427	7.23
Welsh	9,969	1.40
West Indian, excl. Hispanic:	1,726	0.24
Bahamian	25	0.00
Barbadian	32	0.00
Belizean	25	0.00
Bermudan	28	0.00
British West Indian	44	0.01
Dutch West Indian	33	0.00
Haitian	131	0.02
Jamaican	1,058	0.15
Trinidadian and Tobagonian	106	0.01
U.S. Virgin Islander	43	0.01
West Indian	201	0.03
White:	496,425	69.77
Not Hispanic (475,897)	487,638	68.54
Hispanic (7,435)	8,787	1.24
Yugoslavian	631	0.09

Conneaut

Place Type: City
County: Ashtabula
Population: 12,485

Ancestry/Race	Number	%
African American/Black:	203	1.63
Not Hispanic (137)	200	1.60
Hispanic (3)	3	0.02
African, sub-Saharan:	7	0.06
African	7	0.06
Alaska Native tribes, not specified	1	0.01
Am. Ind. or Alaska Nat., not spec.	36	0.29
American Indian tribes, specified:	69	0.55
Apache	1	0.01
Blackfeet (1)	14	0.11
Cherokee (2)	24	0.19
Chippewa (4)	8	0.06
Cree (4)	4	0.03
Crow	1	0.01
Iroquois (1)	6	0.05
Lumbee (1)	1	0.01
Navajo (1)	4	0.03
Sioux	5	0.04
All other tribes	1	0.01
American Indian tribes, not spec.	1	0.01
Asian:	84	0.67
Chinese, ex. Taiwanese (4)	4	0.03
Filipino (25)	39	0.31
Indian (5)	10	0.08
Indonesian	1	0.01
Japanese (2)	6	0.05
Korean (9)	11	0.09
Pakistani (5)	5	0.04
Thai (1)	1	0.01
Vietnamese (5)	6	0.05
Other Asian, not specified (1)	1	0.01
Austrian	53	0.42
British	45	0.36
Canadian	27	0.22
Celtic	8	0.06
Croatian	78	0.62
Czech	55	0.44
Czechoslovakian	16	0.13
Danish	12	0.10
Dutch	162	1.29
English	1,772	14.16
European	17	0.14
Finnish	741	5.92
French, except Basque	425	3.40
French Canadian	44	0.35
German	2,961	23.67
Greek	36	0.29
Hawaii Native/Pacific Islander:	9	0.07
Micronesian: (5)	5	0.04
Guamanian/Chamorro (5)	5	0.04
Polynesian: (1)	1	0.01
Native Hawaiian (1)	1	0.01
Other Pac. Isl., not spec.	3	0.02
Hispanic or Latino:	132	1.06
Central American:	2	0.02
Panamanian	2	0.02
Cuban	1	0.01
Mexican	49	0.39
Puerto Rican	56	0.45
South American:	1	0.01
Ecuadorian	1	0.01
Other Hispanic or Latino	23	0.18
Hungarian	498	3.98
Irish	2,054	16.42
Italian	1,824	14.58
Lithuanian	15	0.12
Norwegian	21	0.17
Pennsylvania German	25	0.20
Polish	617	4.93
Portuguese	34	0.27
Russian	86	0.69
Scotch-Irish	245	1.96
Scottish	227	1.81
Slavic	5	0.04
Slovak	121	0.97
Slovene	134	1.07
Swedish	244	1.95
Swiss	34	0.27
Ukrainian	41	0.33
United States or American	601	4.80
Welsh	111	0.89
West Indian, excl. Hispanic:	5	0.04
Jamaican	5	0.04
White:	12,222	97.89
Not Hispanic (11,950)	12,121	97.08
Hispanic (77)	101	0.81

Notes: 1. Figures in the "Number" column do not add up to the total population due to: a) Ancestry/Race overlap — e.g. persons can report being both White and Irish, b) persons of Hispanic origin can report being any race, c) persons reporting two ancestries are counted in both categories. 2. Numbers in parentheses indicate the number of persons reporting this ancestry/race alone, not in combination with any other ancestry/race. 3. Refer to the Explanation of Data in the front of the book for more detailed information.

Coshocton

Place Type: City
County: Coshocton
Population: 11,682

Ancestry/Race	Number	%
African American/Black:	266	2.28
Not Hispanic (190)	266	2.28
Alaska Native tribes, specified:	1	0.01
Alaska Athabascan	1	0.01
Am. Ind. or Alaska Nat., not spec.	16	0.14
Alsatian	8	0.07
American Indian tribes, specified:	39	0.33
Blackfeet (1)	1	0.01
Cherokee (9)	24	0.21
Chickasaw	1	0.01
Crow	1	0.01
Delaware	2	0.02
Kiowa	3	0.03
Latin American Indians (2)	2	0.02
Pueblo (1)	1	0.01
Seminole	1	0.01
Sioux (1)	3	0.03
American Indian tribes, not spec.	1	0.01
Arab:	10	0.08
Syrian	10	0.08
Asian:	101	0.86
Chinese, ex. Taiwanese (7)	9	0.08
Filipino (1)	4	0.03
Indian (14)	15	0.13
Japanese (1)	2	0.02
Korean (42)	44	0.38
Laotian (7)	7	0.06
Thai (1)	1	0.01
Vietnamese (17)	17	0.15
Other Asian, not specified (1)	2	0.02
Belgian	15	0.13
British	19	0.16
Canadian	40	0.34
Czechoslovakian	9	0.08
Danish	17	0.14
Dutch	257	2.18
English	1,328	11.26
European	63	0.53
Finnish	6	0.05
French, except Basque	320	2.71
French Canadian	10	0.08
German	2,722	23.07
Greek	22	0.19
Hawaii Native/Pacific Islander:	4	0.03
Polynesian: (2)	2	0.02
Native Hawaiian (2)	2	0.02
Other Pac. Isl., not spec.	2	0.02
Hispanic or Latino:	69	0.59
Central American:	4	0.03
Panamanian	3	0.03
Salvadoran	1	0.01
Cuban	5	0.04
Mexican	32	0.27
Puerto Rican	10	0.09
South American:	1	0.01
Bolivian	1	0.01
Other Hispanic or Latino	17	0.15
Hungarian	102	0.86
Irish	1,450	12.29
Italian	258	2.19
Northern European	16	0.14
Norwegian	22	0.19
Polish	197	1.67
Russian	38	0.32
Scotch-Irish	190	1.61
Scottish	187	1.58
Serbian	7	0.06
Slovak	12	0.10
Swedish	78	0.66
Swiss	59	0.50
Ukrainian	21	0.18
United States or American	1,696	14.37
Welsh	132	1.12
White:	11,336	97.04
Not Hispanic (11,186)	11,299	96.72
Hispanic (34)	37	0.32
Yugoslavian	7	0.06

Cuyahoga Falls

Place Type: City
County: Summit
Population: 49,374

Ancestry/Race	Number	%
African American/Black:	1,061	2.15
Not Hispanic (918)	1,054	2.13
Hispanic (5)	7	0.01
African, sub-Saharan:	4	0.01
African	4	0.01
Alaska Native tribes, specified:	2	0.00
Alaska Athabascan (1)	1	0.00
Tlingit-Haida (1)	1	0.00
Am. Ind. or Alaska Nat., not spec.	84	0.17
Albanian	44	0.09
Alsatian	14	0.03
American Indian tribes, specified:	165	0.33
Apache (1)	1	0.00
Blackfeet (13)	15	0.03
Cherokee (21)	86	0.17
Cheyenne	1	0.00
Chippewa (10)	14	0.03
Choctaw	6	0.01
Colville (1)	1	0.00
Cree (1)	1	0.00
Creek (2)	4	0.01
Delaware (1)	3	0.01
Houma	1	0.00
Iroquois (3)	9	0.02
Navajo (3)	5	0.01
Ottawa	3	0.01
Sioux (4)	4	0.01
All other tribes (2)	11	0.02
American Indian tribes, not spec.	10	0.02
Arab:	496	1.00
Arab/Arabic	59	0.12
Egyptian	15	0.03
Jordanian	31	0.06
Lebanese	273	0.55
Palestinian	36	0.07
Syrian	39	0.08
Other Arab	43	0.09
Armenian	13	0.03
Asian:	592	1.20
Cambodian	1	0.00
Chinese, ex. Taiwanese (98)	111	0.22
Filipino (38)	48	0.10
Hmong (5)	5	0.01
Indian (166)	179	0.36
Indonesian (2)	3	0.01
Japanese (30)	49	0.10
Korean (116)	128	0.26
Laotian (16)	16	0.03
Pakistani (1)	1	0.00
Taiwanese (6)	6	0.01
Thai (6)	7	0.01
Vietnamese (18)	20	0.04
Other Asian, not specified (11)	18	0.04
Australian	8	0.02
Austrian	147	0.30
Belgian	39	0.08
Brazilian	14	0.03
British	307	0.62
Bulgarian	42	0.09
Canadian	123	0.25
Croatian	352	0.71
Cypriot	8	0.02
Czech	451	0.91
Czechoslovakian	193	0.39
Danish	177	0.36
Dutch	860	1.74
Eastern European	24	0.05
English	6,410	12.99
European	220	0.45
Finnish	106	0.21
French, except Basque	1,586	3.21
French Canadian	180	0.36
German	15,305	31.01
Greek	267	0.54
Hawaii Native/Pacific Islander:	19	0.04
Polynesian: (6)	15	0.03
Native Hawaiian (6)	15	0.03
Other Pac. Isl., not spec.	4	0.01
Hispanic or Latino:	309	0.63
Central American:	18	0.04
Guatemalan	6	0.01
Honduran	2	0.00
Nicaraguan	1	0.00
Panamanian	4	0.01
Salvadoran	5	0.01
Cuban	20	0.04
Mexican	129	0.26
Puerto Rican	67	0.14
South American:	20	0.04
Argentinean	1	0.00
Bolivian	1	0.00
Chilean	1	0.00
Colombian	6	0.01
Paraguayan	3	0.01
Peruvian	4	0.01
Venezuelan	2	0.00
Other South American	2	0.00
Other Hispanic or Latino	55	0.11
Hungarian	1,211	2.45
Icelander	36	0.07
Iranian	38	0.08
Irish	8,575	17.37
Italian	6,101	12.36
Latvian	53	0.11
Lithuanian	165	0.33
Macedonian	60	0.12
New Zealander	14	0.03
Norwegian	447	0.91
Pennsylvania German	80	0.16
Polish	2,534	5.13
Portuguese	44	0.09
Romanian	219	0.44
Russian	388	0.79
Scandinavian	24	0.05
Scotch-Irish	1,446	2.93
Scottish	1,357	2.75
Serbian	192	0.39
Slavic	27	0.05
Slovak	623	1.26
Slovene	169	0.34
Swedish	597	1.21
Swiss	445	0.90
Ukrainian	216	0.44
United States or American	2,797	5.67
Welsh	1,064	2.16
White:	47,713	96.64
Not Hispanic (47,102)	47,479	96.16
Hispanic (198)	234	0.47
Yugoslavian	144	0.29

Dayton

Place Type: City
County: Montgomery
Population: 166,179

Ancestry/Race	Number	%
African American/Black:	73,552	44.26
Not Hispanic (71,291)	73,073	43.97
Hispanic (377)	479	0.29
African, sub-Saharan:	2,179	1.31
African	1,766	1.06
Cape Verdean	11	0.01
Ethiopian	65	0.04
Ghanian	43	0.03
Kenyan	23	0.01
Nigerian	147	0.09
South African	20	0.01

Notes: 1. Figures in the "Number" column do not add up to the total population due to: a) Ancestry/Race overlap — e.g. persons can report being both White and Irish, b) persons of Hispanic origin can report being any race, c) persons reporting two ancestries are counted in both categories. 2. Numbers in parentheses indicate the number of persons reporting this ancestry/race alone, not in combination with any other ancestry/race. 3. Refer to the Explanation of Data in the front of the book for more detailed information.

Ancestry/Race	Number	%
Other sub-Saharan African	104	0.06
Alaska Native tribes, specified:	8	0.00
Alaska Athabascan (2)	2	0.00
Aleut (2)	3	0.00
Eskimo (3)	3	0.00
Alaska Native tribes, not specified	4	0.00
Am. Ind. or Alaska Nat., not spec.	677	0.41
Albanian	7	0.00
Alsatian	5	0.00
American Indian tribes, specified:	869	0.52
Apache (4)	18	0.01
Blackfeet (9)	70	0.04
Cherokee (139)	490	0.29
Cheyenne	2	0.00
Chickasaw (1)	3	0.00
Chippewa (14)	18	0.01
Choctaw (10)	28	0.02
Comanche	1	0.00
Cree	5	0.00
Creek (5)	22	0.01
Crow	5	0.00
Delaware (2)	5	0.00
Iroquois (4)	21	0.01
Kiowa	1	0.00
Latin American Indians (7)	11	0.01
Lumbee	1	0.00
Menominee	2	0.00
Navajo (5)	11	0.01
Ottawa	1	0.00
Pima (3)	4	0.00
Potawatomi (4)	4	0.00
Pueblo (3)	6	0.00
Puget Sound Salish	5	0.00
Seminole (9)	16	0.01
Shoshone	1	0.00
Sioux (25)	50	0.03
Tohono O'Odham	3	0.00
Ute (1)	1	0.00
All other tribes (26)	64	0.04
American Indian tribes, not spec.	91	0.05
Arab:	542	0.33
Arab/Arabic	144	0.09
Egyptian	19	0.01
Jordanian	8	0.00
Lebanese	207	0.12
Moroccan	7	0.00
Palestinian	26	0.02
Syrian	13	0.01
Other Arab	118	0.07
Armenian	62	0.04
Asian:	1,561	0.94
Bangladeshi (21)	22	0.01
Cambodian (74)	81	0.05
Chinese, ex. Taiwanese (158)	212	0.13
Filipino (136)	242	0.15
Indian (196)	255	0.15
Indonesian (8)	15	0.01
Japanese (81)	163	0.10
Korean (112)	161	0.10
Laotian (4)	4	0.00
Malaysian (2)	5	0.00
Pakistani (17)	17	0.01
Sri Lankan (4)	4	0.00
Taiwanese (5)	11	0.01
Thai (29)	48	0.03
Vietnamese (152)	179	0.11
Other Asian, specified	13	0.01
Other Asian, not specified (58)	129	0.08
Assyrian/Chaldean/Syriac	7	0.00
Australian	15	0.01
Austrian	103	0.06
Basque	7	0.00
Belgian	56	0.03
Brazilian	42	0.03
British	483	0.29
Bulgarian	17	0.01
Canadian	119	0.07
Celtic	16	0.01
Croatian	123	0.07
Czech	212	0.13
Czechoslovakian	103	0.06
Danish	12	0.01
Dutch	1,802	1.08
Eastern European	83	0.05
English	8,170	4.92
European	894	0.54
Finnish	110	0.07
French, except Basque	2,446	1.47
French Canadian	505	0.30
German	23,990	14.44
German Russian	4	0.00
Greek	285	0.17
Guyanese	7	0.00
Hawaii Native/Pacific Islander:	149	0.09
Melanesian:	1	0.00
Fijian	1	0.00
Micronesian: (17)	29	0.02
Guamanian/Chamorro (15)	27	0.02
Other Micronesian (2)	2	0.00
Polynesian: (35)	57	0.03
Native Hawaiian (10)	24	0.01
Samoan (25)	30	0.02
Tongan	1	0.00
Other Polynesian	2	0.00
Other Pac. Isl., specified	11	0.01
Other Pac. Isl., not spec. (10)	51	0.03
Hispanic or Latino:	2,626	1.58
Central American:	72	0.04
Costa Rican	17	0.01
Guatemalan	11	0.01
Honduran	8	0.00
Nicaraguan	1	0.00
Panamanian	27	0.02
Salvadoran	4	0.00
Other Central American	4	0.00
Cuban	117	0.07
Dominican Republic	29	0.02
Mexican	1,360	0.82
Puerto Rican	456	0.27
South American:	67	0.04
Argentinean	2	0.00
Bolivian	6	0.00
Chilean	4	0.00
Colombian	27	0.02
Ecuadorian	22	0.01
Peruvian	2	0.00
Venezuelan	2	0.00
Other South American	2	0.00
Other Hispanic or Latino	525	0.32
Hungarian	1,129	0.68
Iranian	16	0.01
Irish	13,825	8.32
Italian	4,047	2.44
Latvian	14	0.01
Lithuanian	252	0.15
Northern European	41	0.02
Norwegian	494	0.30
Pennsylvania German	48	0.03
Polish	2,580	1.55
Portuguese	42	0.03
Romanian	89	0.05
Russian	247	0.15
Scandinavian	18	0.01
Scotch-Irish	1,659	1.00
Scottish	1,965	1.18
Serbian	38	0.02
Slavic	42	0.03
Slovak	199	0.12
Slovene	102	0.06
Swedish	477	0.29
Swiss	215	0.13
Ukrainian	138	0.08
United States or American	12,783	7.69
Welsh	810	0.49
West Indian, excl. Hispanic:	392	0.24
Bahamian	49	0.03
Belizean	21	0.01
Bermudan	15	0.01
British West Indian	7	0.00
Dutch West Indian	16	0.01
Haitian	52	0.03
Jamaican	170	0.10
Trinidadian and Tobagonian	15	0.01
U.S. Virgin Islander	15	0.01
West Indian	32	0.02
White:	91,049	54.79
Not Hispanic (87,487)	89,683	53.97
Hispanic (1,189)	1,366	0.82
Yugoslavian	143	0.09

Defiance

Place Type: City
County: Defiance
Population: 16,465

Ancestry/Race	Number	%
African American/Black:	674	4.09
Not Hispanic (532)	609	3.70
Hispanic (35)	65	0.39
African, sub-Saharan:	17	0.10
African	17	0.10
Am. Ind. or Alaska Nat., not spec.	61	0.37
American Indian tribes, specified:	64	0.39
Apache (1)	1	0.01
Blackfeet	2	0.01
Cherokee (13)	38	0.23
Cheyenne	1	0.01
Chippewa (4)	7	0.04
Iroquois (1)	2	0.01
Latin American Indians (5)	6	0.04
Sioux	3	0.02
All other tribes (3)	4	0.02
American Indian tribes, not spec.	17	0.10
Arab:	5	0.03
Lebanese	5	0.03
Asian:	89	0.54
Chinese, ex. Taiwanese (11)	15	0.09
Filipino (5)	9	0.05
Indian (7)	11	0.07
Indonesian (1)	1	0.01
Japanese (2)	4	0.02
Korean (18)	21	0.13
Taiwanese	3	0.02
Thai (4)	4	0.02
Vietnamese (14)	17	0.10
Other Asian, not specified (2)	4	0.02
Assyrian/Chaldean/Syriac	20	0.12
Australian	6	0.04
Austrian	28	0.17
Belgian	22	0.13
British	22	0.13
Bulgarian	23	0.14
Canadian	80	0.49
Czech	30	0.18
Czechoslovakian	40	0.25
Danish	17	0.10
Dutch	295	1.81
English	1,045	6.41
European	70	0.43
Finnish	21	0.13
French, except Basque	487	2.99
French Canadian	96	0.59
German	5,691	34.92
Greek	9	0.06
Hawaii Native/Pacific Islander:	13	0.08
Micronesian: (3)	3	0.02
Guamanian/Chamorro (3)	3	0.02
Polynesian: (5)	10	0.06
Native Hawaiian (1)	6	0.04
Samoan (4)	4	0.02
Hispanic or Latino:	2,100	12.75
Central American:	11	0.07
Costa Rican	1	0.01
Guatemalan	3	0.02
Honduran	1	0.01
Nicaraguan	4	0.02
Panamanian	1	0.01
Salvadoran	1	0.01
Cuban	1	0.01

Notes: 1. Figures in the "Number" column do not add up to the total population due to: a) Ancestry/Race overlap — e.g. persons can report being both White and Irish, b) persons of Hispanic origin can report being any race, c) persons reporting two ancestries are counted in both categories. 2. Numbers in parentheses indicate the number of persons reporting this ancestry/race alone, not in combination with any other ancestry/race. 3. Refer to the Explanation of Data in the front of the book for more detailed information.

Ancestry/Race	Number	%
Dominican Republic	1	0.01
Mexican	1,371	8.33
Puerto Rican	193	1.17
South American:	15	0.09
Argentinean	10	0.06
Colombian	1	0.01
Peruvian	2	0.01
Venezuelan	1	0.01
Other South American	1	0.01
Other Hispanic or Latino	508	3.09
Hungarian	109	0.67
Irish	1,628	9.99
Italian	409	2.51
Lithuanian	8	0.05
Norwegian	24	0.15
Pennsylvania German	12	0.07
Polish	184	1.13
Romanian	7	0.04
Russian	36	0.22
Scandinavian	7	0.04
Scotch-Irish	127	0.78
Scottish	197	1.21
Serbian	7	0.04
Slavic	6	0.04
Slovak	54	0.33
Swedish	117	0.72
Swiss	62	0.38
Ukrainian	5	0.03
United States or American	1,568	9.62
Welsh	98	0.60
White:	14,672	89.11
Not Hispanic (13,557)	13,716	83.30
Hispanic (792)	956	5.81
Yugoslavian	13	0.08

Delaware

Place Type: City
County: Delaware
Population: 25,243

Ancestry/Race	Number	%
African American/Black:	1,169	4.63
Not Hispanic (956)	1,141	4.52
Hispanic (12)	28	0.11
African, sub-Saharan:	40	0.16
African	40	0.16
Am. Ind. or Alaska Nat., not spec.	72	0.29
Alsatian	9	0.04
American Indian tribes, specified:	152	0.60
Apache (1)	3	0.01
Blackfeet (4)	18	0.07
Cherokee (11)	90	0.36
Cheyenne	1	0.00
Chickasaw	1	0.00
Chippewa (1)	1	0.00
Choctaw (1)	2	0.01
Creek (1)	2	0.01
Delaware	3	0.01
Iroquois (10)	13	0.05
Latin American Indians	3	0.01
Lumbee (3)	5	0.02
Potawatomi (1)	1	0.00
Pueblo	1	0.00
Seminole	1	0.00
Sioux	1	0.00
All other tribes (1)	6	0.02
American Indian tribes, not spec.	6	0.02
Arab:	75	0.30
Arab/Arabic	7	0.03
Egyptian	39	0.15
Lebanese	8	0.03
Syrian	21	0.08
Asian:	271	1.07
Chinese, ex. Taiwanese (32)	43	0.17
Filipino (24)	32	0.13
Indian (62)	70	0.28
Indonesian (1)	2	0.01
Japanese (14)	20	0.08
Korean (24)	34	0.13
Malaysian (1)	1	0.00
Pakistani (1)	2	0.01
Sri Lankan (4)	4	0.02
Taiwanese (1)	3	0.01
Thai (2)	5	0.02
Vietnamese (17)	22	0.09
Other Asian, specified (5)	6	0.02
Other Asian, not specified (20)	27	0.11
Australian	8	0.03
Austrian	45	0.18
Belgian	36	0.14
Brazilian	16	0.06
British	169	0.67
Canadian	59	0.23
Celtic	5	0.02
Croatian	19	0.08
Czech	107	0.42
Czechoslovakian	43	0.17
Danish	60	0.24
Dutch	423	1.68
English	2,882	11.43
Estonian	6	0.02
European	376	1.49
Finnish	20	0.08
French, except Basque	559	2.22
French Canadian	89	0.35
German	6,468	25.65
Greek	95	0.38
Hawaii Native/Pacific Islander:	36	0.14
Micronesian: (2)	3	0.01
Guamanian/Chamorro (2)	3	0.01
Polynesian: (21)	29	0.11
Native Hawaiian (20)	26	0.10
Samoan (1)	2	0.01
Other Polynesian	1	0.00
Other Pac. Isl., not spec. (1)	4	0.02
Hispanic or Latino:	312	1.24
Central American:	10	0.04
Guatemalan	3	0.01
Salvadoran	7	0.03
Cuban	11	0.04
Mexican	172	0.68
Puerto Rican	38	0.15
South American:	25	0.10
Argentinean	1	0.00
Chilean	1	0.00
Colombian	7	0.03
Ecuadorian	2	0.01
Peruvian	5	0.02
Venezuelan	9	0.04
Other Hispanic or Latino	56	0.22
Hungarian	189	0.75
Irish	2,980	11.82
Italian	1,176	4.66
Latvian	7	0.03
Lithuanian	30	0.12
Luxemburger	15	0.06
Maltese	8	0.03
New Zealander	10	0.04
Northern European	5	0.02
Norwegian	150	0.59
Pennsylvania German	34	0.13
Polish	516	2.05
Portuguese	39	0.15
Romanian	7	0.03
Russian	114	0.45
Scandinavian	15	0.06
Scotch-Irish	417	1.65
Scottish	686	2.72
Serbian	6	0.02
Slavic	11	0.04
Slovak	110	0.44
Slovene	7	0.03
Swedish	152	0.60
Swiss	122	0.48
United States or American	2,274	9.02
Welsh	543	2.15
White:	23,806	94.31
Not Hispanic (23,269)	23,611	93.53
Hispanic (166)	195	0.77
Yugoslavian	6	0.02

Dover

Place Type: City
County: Tuscarawas
Population: 12,210

Ancestry/Race	Number	%
African American/Black:	175	1.43
Not Hispanic (154)	174	1.43
Hispanic (1)	1	0.01
Alaska Native tribes, specified:	1	0.01
Eskimo (1)	1	0.01
Am. Ind. or Alaska Nat., not spec.	12	0.10
American Indian tribes, specified:	50	0.41
Blackfeet	1	0.01
Cherokee (10)	23	0.19
Cheyenne	1	0.01
Delaware	5	0.04
Iroquois	1	0.01
Latin American Indians (15)	15	0.12
Yaqui	2	0.02
All other tribes (2)	2	0.02
Armenian	10	0.08
Asian:	86	0.70
Chinese, ex. Taiwanese (8)	12	0.10
Filipino (12)	21	0.17
Indian (27)	31	0.25
Japanese	5	0.04
Korean (3)	4	0.03
Thai (1)	2	0.02
Vietnamese (4)	5	0.04
Other Asian, not specified (6)	6	0.05
Australian	6	0.05
Austrian	82	0.67
Belgian	19	0.15
British	22	0.18
Canadian	5	0.04
Croatian	29	0.24
Czech	28	0.23
Czechoslovakian	11	0.09
Danish	16	0.13
Dutch	307	2.50
Eastern European	13	0.11
English	1,434	11.69
European	90	0.73
Finnish	14	0.11
French, except Basque	237	1.93
French Canadian	19	0.15
German	4,099	33.42
Greek	23	0.19
Hawaii Native/Pacific Islander:	8	0.07
Polynesian: (3)	8	0.07
Native Hawaiian (1)	4	0.03
Samoan (2)	4	0.03
Hispanic or Latino:	73	0.60
Central American:	22	0.18
Guatemalan	19	0.16
Panamanian	3	0.02
Cuban	1	0.01
Dominican Republic	1	0.01
Mexican	26	0.21
Puerto Rican	11	0.09
South American:	3	0.02
Bolivian	2	0.02
Colombian	1	0.01
Other Hispanic or Latino	9	0.07
Hungarian	90	0.73
Irish	1,503	12.25
Italian	1,376	11.22
Luxemburger	29	0.24
Northern European	13	0.11
Norwegian	48	0.39
Pennsylvania German	59	0.48
Polish	249	2.03
Romanian	78	0.64
Russian	29	0.24
Scotch-Irish	230	1.88
Scottish	192	1.57

Notes: 1. Figures in the "Number" column do not add up to the total population due to: a) Ancestry/Race overlap — e.g. persons can report being both White and Irish, b) persons of Hispanic origin can report being any race, c) persons reporting two ancestries are counted in both categories. 2. Numbers in parentheses indicate the number of persons reporting this ancestry/race alone, not in combination with any other ancestry/race. 3. Refer to the Explanation of Data in the front of the book for more detailed information.

Serbian	14	0.11
Slavic	6	0.05
Slovak	100	0.82
Slovene	1	0.01
Swedish	49	0.40
Swiss	625	5.10
Ukrainian	49	0.40
United States or American	604	4.92
Welsh	395	3.22
White:	11,931	97.71
Not Hispanic (11,814)	11,886	97.35
Hispanic (41)	45	0.37
Yugoslavian	23	0.19

Dublin

Place Type: City
County: Franklin
Population: 31,392

Ancestry/Race	Number	%
African American/Black:	616	1.96
Not Hispanic (527)	599	1.91
Hispanic (16)	17	0.05
African, sub-Saharan:	78	0.25
African	18	0.06
Nigerian	13	0.04
South African	47	0.15
Alaska Native tribes, specified:	2	0.01
Alaska Athabascan (2)	2	0.01
Am. Ind. or Alaska Nat., not spec.	31	0.10
American Indian tribes, specified:	46	0.15
Blackfeet	3	0.01
Cherokee (8)	19	0.06
Choctaw (1)	2	0.01
Comanche (1)	1	0.00
Cree	3	0.01
Creek	1	0.00
Iroquois (2)	3	0.01
Latin American Indians (2)	2	0.01
Lumbee (1)	1	0.00
Menominee (2)	2	0.01
Sioux	5	0.02
All other tribes (1)	4	0.01
American Indian tribes, not spec.	4	0.01
Arab:	289	0.92
Egyptian	34	0.11
Jordanian	12	0.04
Lebanese	182	0.58
Palestinian	45	0.14
Syrian	16	0.05
Armenian	57	0.18
Asian:	2,527	8.05
Bangladeshi (13)	13	0.04
Chinese, ex. Taiwanese (438)	476	1.52
Filipino (44)	89	0.28
Indian (645)	678	2.16
Indonesian (3)	7	0.02
Japanese (798)	855	2.72
Korean (172)	191	0.61
Laotian (2)	2	0.01
Malaysian (1)	6	0.02
Pakistani (11)	11	0.04
Sri Lankan (4)	4	0.01
Taiwanese (65)	80	0.25
Thai (9)	16	0.05
Vietnamese (49)	59	0.19
Other Asian, specified (2)	2	0.01
Other Asian, not specified (19)	38	0.12
Australian	35	0.11
Austrian	132	0.42
Belgian	43	0.14
British	221	0.70
Bulgarian	17	0.05
Canadian	214	0.68
Croatian	116	0.37
Czech	183	0.58
Czechoslovakian	111	0.35
Danish	128	0.41
Dutch	670	2.13
Eastern European	55	0.17
English	3,869	12.29
European	414	1.32
Finnish	49	0.16
French, except Basque	836	2.66
French Canadian	213	0.68
German	9,842	31.27
Greek	270	0.86
Hawaii Native/Pacific Islander:	28	0.09
Melanesian:	2	0.01
Other Melanesian	2	0.01
Micronesian:	1	0.00
Guamanian/Chamorro	1	0.00
Polynesian: (1)	5	0.02
Native Hawaiian (1)	4	0.01
Samoan	1	0.00
Other Pac. Isl., not spec. (5)	20	0.06
Hispanic or Latino:	317	1.01
Central American:	20	0.06
Costa Rican	1	0.00
Honduran	1	0.00
Nicaraguan	3	0.01
Panamanian	2	0.01
Salvadoran	11	0.04
Other Central American	2	0.01
Cuban	11	0.04
Dominican Republic	1	0.00
Mexican	107	0.34
Puerto Rican	59	0.19
South American:	55	0.18
Argentinean	6	0.02
Bolivian	1	0.00
Colombian	18	0.06
Ecuadorian	1	0.00
Paraguayan	1	0.00
Peruvian	11	0.04
Venezuelan	16	0.05
Other South American	1	0.00
Other Hispanic or Latino	64	0.20
Hungarian	575	1.83
Icelander	32	0.10
Iranian	82	0.26
Irish	5,352	17.00
Italian	2,973	9.44
Latvian	37	0.12
Lithuanian	105	0.33
Macedonian	35	0.11
Northern European	46	0.15
Norwegian	308	0.98
Pennsylvania German	16	0.05
Polish	1,227	3.90
Portuguese	6	0.02
Romanian	43	0.14
Russian	274	0.87
Scandinavian	37	0.12
Scotch-Irish	675	2.14
Scottish	988	3.14
Serbian	18	0.06
Slavic	8	0.03
Slovak	295	0.94
Slovene	79	0.25
Swedish	720	2.29
Swiss	205	0.65
Turkish	79	0.25
Ukrainian	90	0.29
United States or American	1,729	5.49
Welsh	665	2.11
West Indian, excl. Hispanic:	24	0.08
Jamaican	24	0.08
White:	28,404	90.48
Not Hispanic (27,901)	28,149	89.67
Hispanic (245)	255	0.81
Yugoslavian	44	0.14

East Cleveland

Place Type: City
County: Cuyahoga
Population: 27,217

Ancestry/Race	Number	%
African American/Black:	25,752	94.62
Not Hispanic (25,291)	25,596	94.04
Hispanic (127)	156	0.57
African, sub-Saharan:	340	1.25
African	310	1.14
Nigerian	13	0.05
Other sub-Saharan African	17	0.06
Am. Ind. or Alaska Nat., not spec.	125	0.46
American Indian tribes, specified:	110	0.40
Apache (1)	3	0.01
Blackfeet	24	0.09
Cherokee (4)	28	0.10
Cheyenne	1	0.00
Chickasaw (3)	3	0.01
Choctaw (7)	14	0.05
Cree	1	0.00
Creek	1	0.00
Latin American Indians (3)	5	0.02
Navajo	1	0.00
Paiute	15	0.06
Seminole	1	0.00
Shoshone (2)	2	0.01
Sioux (1)	6	0.02
All other tribes	5	0.02
American Indian tribes, not spec.	17	0.06
Arab:	72	0.26
Arab/Arabic	36	0.13
Egyptian	36	0.13
Armenian	13	0.05
Asian:	103	0.38
Chinese, ex. Taiwanese (22)	26	0.10
Filipino (5)	11	0.04
Indian (17)	25	0.09
Japanese (4)	8	0.03
Korean (4)	5	0.02
Pakistani (3)	3	0.01
Sri Lankan	2	0.01
Vietnamese (1)	1	0.00
Other Asian, specified	9	0.03
Other Asian, not specified (5)	13	0.05
Australian	5	0.02
Austrian	20	0.07
British	12	0.04
Croatian	6	0.02
Czech	5	0.02
English	117	0.43
European	25	0.09
French, except Basque	25	0.09
German	196	0.72
Hawaii Native/Pacific Islander:	26	0.10
Micronesian: (1)	1	0.00
Guamanian/Chamorro (1)	1	0.00
Polynesian:	2	0.01
Native Hawaiian	2	0.01
Other Pac. Isl., specified	9	0.03
Other Pac. Isl., not spec. (3)	14	0.05
Hispanic or Latino:	207	0.76
Central American:	9	0.03
Honduran	2	0.01
Panamanian	7	0.03
Cuban	14	0.05
Dominican Republic	2	0.01
Mexican	68	0.25
Puerto Rican	62	0.23
South American:	2	0.01
Venezuelan	1	0.00
Other South American	1	0.00
Other Hispanic or Latino	50	0.18
Hungarian	42	0.15
Irish	151	0.55
Italian	151	0.55
Lithuanian	15	0.06
Norwegian	6	0.02

Notes: 1. Figures in the "Number" column do not add up to the total population due to: a) Ancestry/Race overlap — e.g. persons can report being both White and Irish, b) persons of Hispanic origin can report being any race, c) persons reporting two ancestries are counted in both categories. 2. Numbers in parentheses indicate the number of persons reporting this ancestry/race alone, not in combination with any other ancestry/race. 3. Refer to the Explanation of Data in the front of the book for more detailed information.

Pennsylvania German	8	0.03
Polish	89	0.33
Russian	137	0.50
Scotch-Irish	47	0.17
Scottish	27	0.10
Slovak	18	0.07
Slovene	4	0.01
Swedish	24	0.09
Ukrainian	94	0.35
United States or American	293	1.08
West Indian, excl. Hispanic:	145	0.53
Barbadian	9	0.03
Jamaican	118	0.43
West Indian	18	0.07
White:	1,417	5.21
Not Hispanic (1,219)	1,377	5.06
Hispanic (21)	40	0.15
Yugoslavian	27	0.10

East Liverpool

Place Type: City
County: Columbiana
Population: 13,089

Ancestry/Race	Number	%
African American/Black:	777	5.94
Not Hispanic (630)	776	5.93
Hispanic	1	0.01
African, sub-Saharan:	49	0.38
African	49	0.38
Am. Ind. or Alaska Nat., not spec.	42	0.32
American Indian tribes, specified:	39	0.30
Blackfeet	3	0.02
Cherokee (9)	26	0.20
Chippewa (1)	2	0.02
Comanche (1)	1	0.01
Creek	1	0.01
Iroquois	1	0.01
All other tribes (3)	5	0.04
American Indian tribes, not spec.	8	0.06
Asian:	24	0.18
Chinese, ex. Taiwanese (3)	3	0.02
Filipino (3)	8	0.06
Indian (2)	6	0.05
Indonesian	1	0.01
Japanese (1)	1	0.01
Korean (2)	5	0.04
Austrian	16	0.12
British	18	0.14
Croatian	28	0.22
Czech	18	0.14
Czechoslovakian	6	0.05
Danish	6	0.05
Dutch	246	1.91
English	1,603	12.47
French, except Basque	167	1.30
French Canadian	10	0.08
German	2,155	16.77
Hawaii Native/Pacific Islander:	17	0.13
Micronesian: (3)	9	0.07
Guamanian/Chamorro (1)	7	0.05
Other Micronesian (2)	2	0.02
Polynesian: (3)	3	0.02
Native Hawaiian (3)	3	0.02
Other Pac. Isl., not spec.	5	0.04
Hispanic or Latino:	94	0.72
Central American:	3	0.02
Panamanian	3	0.02
Cuban	1	0.01
Mexican	44	0.34
Puerto Rican	12	0.09
Other Hispanic or Latino	34	0.26
Hungarian	101	0.79
Irish	1,916	14.91
Italian	570	4.44
Lithuanian	22	0.17
Norwegian	8	0.06
Pennsylvania German	6	0.05
Polish	160	1.25
Portuguese	5	0.04
Russian	17	0.13
Scandinavian	7	0.05
Scotch-Irish	194	1.51
Scottish	188	1.46
Serbian	66	0.51
Slovak	31	0.24
Swedish	60	0.47
Ukrainian	5	0.04
United States or American	1,721	13.39
Welsh	134	1.04
West Indian, excl. Hispanic:	33	0.26
Haitian	5	0.04
Jamaican	28	0.22
White:	12,374	94.54
Not Hispanic (12,089)	12,297	93.95
Hispanic (64)	77	0.59
Yugoslavian	21	0.16

Eastlake

Place Type: City
County: Lake
Population: 20,255

Ancestry/Race	Number	%
African American/Black:	127	0.63
Not Hispanic (108)	125	0.62
Hispanic (2)	2	0.01
Am. Ind. or Alaska Nat., not spec.	15	0.07
American Indian tribes, specified:	67	0.33
Apache	2	0.01
Blackfeet	4	0.02
Cherokee (9)	32	0.16
Chippewa (3)	4	0.02
Creek	1	0.00
Iroquois	1	0.00
Lumbee	1	0.00
Navajo (1)	1	0.00
Seminole	2	0.01
Sioux (5)	9	0.04
Yuman	1	0.00
All other tribes (8)	9	0.04
Arab:	47	0.23
Lebanese	42	0.21
Syrian	5	0.02
Armenian	7	0.03
Asian:	253	1.25
Chinese, ex. Taiwanese (22)	31	0.15
Filipino (24)	30	0.15
Indian (102)	108	0.53
Japanese (14)	34	0.17
Korean (20)	25	0.12
Thai (3)	4	0.02
Vietnamese (6)	11	0.05
Other Asian, specified (3)	3	0.01
Other Asian, not specified (2)	7	0.03
Austrian	159	0.79
Belgian	15	0.07
British	30	0.15
Canadian	25	0.12
Croatian	901	4.47
Czech	296	1.47
Czechoslovakian	94	0.47
Danish	32	0.16
Dutch	216	1.07
Eastern European	6	0.03
English	1,971	9.77
European	72	0.36
Finnish	39	0.19
French, except Basque	471	2.34
French Canadian	158	0.78
German	4,892	24.25
Greek	73	0.36
Hawaii Native/Pacific Islander:	6	0.03
Polynesian: (2)	5	0.02
Native Hawaiian (1)	2	0.01
Samoan (1)	3	0.01
Other Pac. Isl., not spec.	1	0.00
Hispanic or Latino:	141	0.70
Central American:	4	0.02
Panamanian	2	0.01
Salvadoran	1	0.00
Other Central American	1	0.00
Cuban	7	0.03
Mexican	51	0.25
Puerto Rican	29	0.14
South American:	10	0.05
Argentinean	5	0.02
Colombian	3	0.01
Peruvian	1	0.00
Venezuelan	1	0.00
Other Hispanic or Latino	40	0.20
Hungarian	853	4.23
Irish	4,104	20.35
Italian	3,432	17.01
Latvian	18	0.09
Lithuanian	262	1.30
Maltese	6	0.03
Norwegian	54	0.27
Pennsylvania German	35	0.17
Polish	1,932	9.58
Portuguese	10	0.05
Romanian	33	0.16
Russian	198	0.98
Scotch-Irish	450	2.23
Scottish	329	1.63
Serbian	64	0.32
Slavic	16	0.08
Slovak	916	4.54
Slovene	1,558	7.72
Swedish	177	0.88
Swiss	51	0.25
Turkish	19	0.09
Ukrainian	102	0.51
United States or American	741	3.67
Welsh	194	0.96
White:	19,881	98.15
Not Hispanic (19,633)	19,766	97.59
Hispanic (104)	115	0.57
Yugoslavian	104	0.52

Elyria

Place Type: City
County: Lorain
Population: 55,953

Ancestry/Race	Number	%
African American/Black:	8,756	15.65
Not Hispanic (7,831)	8,571	15.32
Hispanic (97)	185	0.33
African, sub-Saharan:	584	1.05
African	513	0.92
Ethiopian	8	0.01
Kenyan	22	0.04
Nigerian	23	0.04
South African	18	0.03
Alaska Native tribes, specified:	2	0.00
Tlingit-Haida	2	0.00
Am. Ind. or Alaska Nat., not spec.	228	0.41
American Indian tribes, specified:	408	0.73
Apache (4)	12	0.02
Blackfeet (6)	58	0.10
Cherokee (36)	208	0.37
Cheyenne (1)	1	0.00
Chippewa (4)	5	0.01
Choctaw (7)	18	0.03
Comanche (1)	1	0.00
Cree (1)	4	0.01
Creek	5	0.01
Delaware	1	0.00
Iroquois (1)	17	0.03
Latin American Indians (4)	6	0.01
Lumbee (7)	11	0.02
Navajo (1)	5	0.01
Ottawa (1)	1	0.00
Paiute (1)	1	0.00
Potawatomi (1)	1	0.00
Pueblo (2)	3	0.01

Notes: 1. Figures in the "Number" column do not add up to the total population due to: a) Ancestry/Race overlap — e.g. persons can report being both White and Irish, b) persons of Hispanic origin can report being any race, c) persons reporting two ancestries are counted in both categories. 2. Numbers in parentheses indicate the number of persons reporting this ancestry/race alone, not in combination with any other ancestry/race. 3. Refer to the Explanation of Data in the front of the book for more detailed information.

Seminole	7	0.01
Sioux (6)	18	0.03
Tohono O'Odham	1	0.00
All other tribes (9)	24	0.04
American Indian tribes, not spec.	26	0.05
Arab:	82	0.15
Arab/Arabic	22	0.04
Egyptian	13	0.02
Lebanese	38	0.07
Moroccan	4	0.01
Palestinian	5	0.01
Asian:	495	0.88
Chinese, ex. Taiwanese (37)	51	0.09
Filipino (137)	197	0.35
Indian (76)	93	0.17
Japanese (11)	36	0.06
Korean (29)	42	0.08
Malaysian	1	0.00
Pakistani (10)	10	0.02
Sri Lankan (3)	3	0.01
Taiwanese (2)	5	0.01
Thai (8)	12	0.02
Vietnamese (10)	18	0.03
Other Asian, specified	4	0.01
Other Asian, not specified (11)	23	0.04
Australian	46	0.08
Austrian	92	0.16
Belgian	6	0.01
British	179	0.32
Bulgarian	10	0.02
Canadian	122	0.22
Croatian	203	0.36
Cypriot	9	0.02
Czech	358	0.64
Czechoslovakian	172	0.31
Danish	113	0.20
Dutch	951	1.70
Eastern European	10	0.02
English	6,114	10.94
European	215	0.38
Finnish	80	0.14
French, except Basque	1,194	2.14
French Canadian	259	0.46
German	13,308	23.81
Greek	303	0.54
Hawaii Native/Pacific Islander:	35	0.06
Micronesian: (5)	5	0.01
Guamanian/Chamorro (4)	4	0.01
Other Micronesian (1)	1	0.00
Polynesian: (6)	21	0.04
Native Hawaiian (2)	9	0.02
Samoan (4)	12	0.02
Other Pac. Isl., specified	3	0.01
Other Pac. Isl., not spec.	6	0.01
Hispanic or Latino:	1,553	2.78
Central American:	28	0.05
Costa Rican	5	0.01
Guatemalan	10	0.02
Honduran	5	0.01
Nicaraguan	1	0.00
Panamanian	6	0.01
Salvadoran	1	0.00
Cuban	20	0.04
Dominican Republic	5	0.01
Mexican	415	0.74
Puerto Rican	853	1.52
South American:	18	0.03
Chilean	2	0.00
Colombian	8	0.01
Ecuadorian	6	0.01
Peruvian	1	0.00
Other South American	1	0.00
Other Hispanic or Latino	214	0.38
Hungarian	2,342	4.19
Iranian	9	0.02
Irish	8,010	14.33
Israeli	20	0.04
Italian	3,168	5.67
Latvian	27	0.05
Lithuanian	87	0.16
Macedonian	42	0.08
Norwegian	157	0.28
Pennsylvania German	34	0.06
Polish	4,195	7.51
Portuguese	22	0.04
Romanian	161	0.29
Russian	438	0.78
Scandinavian	21	0.04
Scotch-Irish	946	1.69
Scottish	1,327	2.37
Serbian	24	0.04
Slavic	13	0.02
Slovak	1,216	2.18
Slovene	299	0.54
Swedish	294	0.53
Swiss	256	0.46
Turkish	5	0.01
Ukrainian	151	0.27
United States or American	3,324	5.95
Welsh	483	0.86
West Indian, excl. Hispanic:	54	0.10
Dutch West Indian	5	0.01
Jamaican	30	0.05
Trinidadian and Tobagonian	12	0.02
West Indian	7	0.01
White:	46,821	83.68
Not Hispanic (44,747)	45,880	82.00
Hispanic (770)	941	1.68
Yugoslavian	38	0.07

Englewood

Place Type: City
County: Montgomery
Population: 12,235

Ancestry/Race	Number	%
African American/Black:	623	5.09
Not Hispanic (556)	612	5.00
Hispanic (8)	11	0.09
African, sub-Saharan:	10	0.08
African	10	0.08
Am. Ind. or Alaska Nat., not spec.	22	0.18
American Indian tribes, specified:	48	0.39
Apache	2	0.02
Blackfeet	3	0.02
Cherokee (6)	25	0.20
Choctaw (5)	5	0.04
Comanche (3)	3	0.02
Iroquois	4	0.03
Latin American Indians (2)	2	0.02
All other tribes (2)	4	0.03
American Indian tribes, not spec.	1	0.01
Arab:	26	0.21
Lebanese	7	0.06
Moroccan	19	0.16
Armenian	9	0.07
Asian:	176	1.44
Bangladeshi (4)	4	0.03
Chinese, ex. Taiwanese (43)	44	0.36
Filipino (15)	18	0.15
Indian (18)	18	0.15
Indonesian (2)	2	0.02
Japanese (37)	43	0.35
Korean (17)	21	0.17
Taiwanese (9)	9	0.07
Thai (5)	5	0.04
Vietnamese (6)	7	0.06
Other Asian, specified (1)	1	0.01
Other Asian, not specified (2)	4	0.03
British	75	0.61
Croatian	49	0.40
Czech	30	0.25
Czechoslovakian	25	0.20
Danish	7	0.06
Dutch	374	3.06
Eastern European	10	0.08
English	1,356	11.09
European	146	1.19
French, except Basque	268	2.19
French Canadian	95	0.78
German	3,890	31.80
Greek	59	0.48
Hawaii Native/Pacific Islander:	3	0.02
Micronesian: (1)	2	0.02
Guamanian/Chamorro (1)	2	0.02
Other Pac. Isl., not spec. (1)	1	0.01
Hispanic or Latino:	106	0.87
Central American:	1	0.01
Guatemalan	1	0.01
Cuban	8	0.07
Dominican Republic	1	0.01
Mexican	57	0.47
Puerto Rican	11	0.09
South American:	4	0.03
Bolivian	1	0.01
Colombian	2	0.02
Peruvian	1	0.01
Other Hispanic or Latino	24	0.20
Hungarian	177	1.45
Irish	1,399	11.44
Italian	425	3.47
Lithuanian	33	0.27
Norwegian	57	0.47
Pennsylvania German	29	0.24
Polish	292	2.39
Portuguese	11	0.09
Russian	54	0.44
Scotch-Irish	184	1.50
Scottish	196	1.60
Slovak	28	0.23
Swedish	126	1.03
Ukrainian	102	0.83
United States or American	1,357	11.09
Welsh	138	1.13
White:	11,429	93.41
Not Hispanic (11,256)	11,360	92.85
Hispanic (62)	69	0.56

Euclid

Place Type: City
County: Cuyahoga
Population: 52,717

Ancestry/Race	Number	%
African American/Black:	16,661	31.60
Not Hispanic (16,038)	16,519	31.34
Hispanic (78)	142	0.27
African, sub-Saharan:	326	0.62
African	255	0.48
Cape Verdean	11	0.02
Ethiopian	7	0.01
Liberian	13	0.02
Nigerian	29	0.06
Sudanese	11	0.02
Am. Ind. or Alaska Nat., not spec.	136	0.26
Albanian	48	0.09
American Indian tribes, specified:	148	0.28
Apache	1	0.00
Blackfeet (2)	24	0.05
Cherokee (13)	75	0.14
Chickasaw	1	0.00
Chippewa (3)	5	0.01
Choctaw	3	0.01
Crow	1	0.00
Iroquois (1)	5	0.01
Latin American Indians (1)	6	0.01
Navajo	2	0.00
Pueblo (2)	2	0.00
Seminole	2	0.00
Sioux	5	0.01
Yaqui	2	0.00
All other tribes (4)	14	0.03
American Indian tribes, not spec.	20	0.04
Arab:	123	0.23
Arab/Arabic	4	0.01
Egyptian	15	0.03
Lebanese	89	0.17
Syrian	8	0.02

Notes: 1. Figures in the "Number" column do not add up to the total population due to: a) Ancestry/Race overlap — e.g. persons can report being both White and Irish, b) persons of Hispanic origin can report being any race, c) persons reporting two ancestries are counted in both categories. 2. Numbers in parentheses indicate the number of persons reporting this ancestry/race alone, not in combination with any other ancestry/race. 3. Refer to the Explanation of Data in the front of the book for more detailed information.

Other Arab	7	0.01
Armenian	15	0.03
Asian:	665	1.26
Chinese, ex. Taiwanese (112)	142	0.27
Filipino (65)	100	0.19
Hmong	1	0.00
Indian (85)	110	0.21
Japanese (45)	73	0.14
Korean (42)	62	0.12
Laotian (49)	50	0.09
Pakistani (12)	13	0.02
Sri Lankan (1)	1	0.00
Taiwanese (5)	5	0.01
Thai (21)	25	0.05
Vietnamese (26)	41	0.08
Other Asian, specified (2)	5	0.01
Other Asian, not specified (15)	37	0.07
Australian	4	0.01
Austrian	310	0.59
Belgian	14	0.03
British	206	0.39
Canadian	90	0.17
Carpatho Rusyn	9	0.02
Croatian	1,705	3.23
Czech	537	1.02
Czechoslovakian	174	0.33
Danish	58	0.11
Dutch	340	0.64
Eastern European	44	0.08
English	3,000	5.69
European	159	0.30
Finnish	165	0.31
French, except Basque	849	1.61
French Canadian	214	0.41
German	7,995	15.17
German Russian	20	0.04
Greek	251	0.48
Guyanese	26	0.05
Hawaii Native/Pacific Islander:	46	0.09
Micronesian: (4)	6	0.01
Guamanian/Chamorro (4)	6	0.01
Polynesian: (8)	18	0.03
Native Hawaiian (5)	11	0.02
Samoan (3)	7	0.01
Other Pac. Isl., specified	3	0.01
Other Pac. Isl., not spec. (1)	19	0.04
Hispanic or Latino:	604	1.15
Central American:	23	0.04
Guatemalan	4	0.01
Honduran	3	0.01
Nicaraguan	6	0.01
Panamanian	8	0.02
Salvadoran	2	0.00
Cuban	27	0.05
Dominican Republic	6	0.01
Mexican	142	0.27
Puerto Rican	217	0.41
South American:	32	0.06
Argentinean	9	0.02
Chilean	3	0.01
Colombian	7	0.01
Ecuadorian	1	0.00
Peruvian	6	0.01
Uruguayan	1	0.00
Venezuelan	5	0.01
Other Hispanic or Latino	157	0.30
Hungarian	1,475	2.80
Icelander	11	0.02
Iranian	49	0.09
Irish	6,638	12.59
Italian	5,064	9.61
Latvian	13	0.02
Lithuanian	811	1.54
Luxemburger	7	0.01
Maltese	10	0.02
Northern European	9	0.02
Norwegian	74	0.14
Pennsylvania German	13	0.02
Polish	3,000	5.69
Portuguese	60	0.11
Romanian	96	0.18
Russian	526	1.00
Scandinavian	14	0.03
Scotch-Irish	547	1.04
Scottish	623	1.18
Serbian	113	0.21
Slavic	44	0.08
Slovak	1,259	2.39
Slovene	4,640	8.80
Swedish	283	0.54
Swiss	134	0.25
Turkish	32	0.06
Ukrainian	271	0.51
United States or American	1,305	2.48
Welsh	391	0.74
West Indian, excl. Hispanic:	175	0.33
Barbadian	19	0.04
Belizean	7	0.01
Jamaican	140	0.27
Trinidadian and Tobagonian	9	0.02
White:	35,632	67.59
Not Hispanic (34,678)	35,284	66.93
Hispanic (307)	348	0.66
Yugoslavian	226	0.43

Fairborn

Place Type: City
County: Greene
Population: 32,052

Ancestry/Race	Number	%
African American/Black:	2,284	7.13
Not Hispanic (1,997)	2,259	7.05
Hispanic (13)	25	0.08
African, sub-Saharan:	202	0.63
African	144	0.45
Ghanian	5	0.02
Nigerian	33	0.10
Senegalese	20	0.06
Alaska Native tribes, specified:	4	0.01
Aleut (3)	3	0.01
Eskimo (1)	1	0.00
Am. Ind. or Alaska Nat., not spec.	95	0.30
American Indian tribes, specified:	241	0.75
Apache (4)	4	0.01
Blackfeet (2)	13	0.04
Cherokee (48)	145	0.45
Cheyenne	4	0.01
Chippewa (8)	11	0.03
Choctaw (5)	6	0.02
Colville (1)	1	0.00
Comanche (3)	3	0.01
Cree	2	0.01
Creek (3)	7	0.02
Iroquois (3)	5	0.02
Latin American Indians (1)	9	0.03
Lumbee	2	0.01
Pueblo (1)	2	0.01
Seminole (2)	2	0.01
Sioux (4)	9	0.03
All other tribes (15)	16	0.05
American Indian tribes, not spec.	11	0.03
Arab:	90	0.28
Egyptian	24	0.08
Jordanian	21	0.07
Lebanese	34	0.11
Moroccan	11	0.03
Armenian	7	0.02
Asian:	1,292	4.03
Bangladeshi (4)	7	0.02
Cambodian (17)	19	0.06
Chinese, ex. Taiwanese (176)	199	0.62
Filipino (107)	171	0.53
Indian (308)	322	1.00
Indonesian (3)	7	0.02
Japanese (51)	82	0.26
Korean (163)	206	0.64
Laotian (4)	4	0.01
Malaysian (6)	6	0.02
Pakistani (3)	4	0.01
Sri Lankan (11)	14	0.04
Taiwanese (8)	11	0.03
Thai (27)	41	0.13
Vietnamese (135)	145	0.45
Other Asian, not specified (29)	54	0.17
Australian	21	0.07
Austrian	30	0.09
Belgian	42	0.13
British	215	0.67
Canadian	37	0.12
Celtic	26	0.08
Croatian	25	0.08
Czech	70	0.22
Czechoslovakian	23	0.07
Danish	44	0.14
Dutch	551	1.72
Eastern European	5	0.02
English	3,261	10.19
European	709	2.22
Finnish	44	0.14
French, except Basque	748	2.34
French Canadian	167	0.52
German	6,753	21.11
Greek	116	0.36
Hawaii Native/Pacific Islander:	45	0.14
Micronesian: (10)	14	0.04
Guamanian/Chamorro (10)	13	0.04
Other Micronesian	1	0.00
Polynesian: (6)	15	0.05
Native Hawaiian (4)	11	0.03
Samoan (1)	1	0.00
Other Polynesian (1)	3	0.01
Other Pac. Isl., not spec. (4)	16	0.05
Hispanic or Latino:	542	1.69
Central American:	16	0.05
Guatemalan	1	0.00
Panamanian	11	0.03
Salvadoran	4	0.01
Cuban	12	0.04
Dominican Republic	7	0.02
Mexican	213	0.66
Puerto Rican	124	0.39
South American:	42	0.13
Argentinean	7	0.02
Bolivian	1	0.00
Chilean	2	0.01
Colombian	10	0.03
Ecuadorian	2	0.01
Peruvian	5	0.02
Venezuelan	15	0.05
Other Hispanic or Latino	128	0.40
Hungarian	167	0.52
Iranian	9	0.03
Irish	3,871	12.10
Italian	788	2.46
Lithuanian	85	0.27
New Zealander	7	0.02
Norwegian	264	0.83
Pennsylvania German	42	0.13
Polish	620	1.94
Romanian	14	0.04
Russian	86	0.27
Scandinavian	79	0.25
Scotch-Irish	496	1.55
Scottish	923	2.89
Slavic	32	0.10
Slovak	64	0.20
Slovene	7	0.02
Swedish	164	0.51
Swiss	91	0.28
Turkish	40	0.13
Ukrainian	60	0.19
United States or American	3,326	10.40
Welsh	356	1.11
West Indian, excl. Hispanic:	17	0.05
Jamaican	17	0.05
White:	28,576	89.16
Not Hispanic (27,646)	28,198	87.98
Hispanic (330)	378	1.18

Notes: 1. Figures in the "Number" column do not add up to the total population due to: a) Ancestry/Race overlap — e.g. persons can report being both White and Irish, b) persons of Hispanic origin can report being any race, c) persons reporting two ancestries are counted in both categories. 2. Numbers in parentheses indicate the number of persons reporting this ancestry/race alone, not in combination with any other ancestry/race. 3. Refer to the Explanation of Data in the front of the book for more detailed information.

Yugoslavian	13	0.04

Fairfield

Place Type: City
County: Butler
Population: 42,097

Ancestry/Race	Number	%
Acadian/Cajun	8	0.02
African American/Black:	2,765	6.57
Not Hispanic (2,526)	2,726	6.48
Hispanic (31)	39	0.09
African, sub-Saharan:	117	0.28
African	84	0.20
Ethiopian	5	0.01
Ghanian	28	0.07
Am. Ind. or Alaska Nat., not spec.	61	0.14
Albanian	12	0.03
American Indian tribes, specified:	111	0.26
Blackfeet (3)	7	0.02
Cherokee (20)	66	0.16
Cheyenne	1	0.00
Chickasaw	3	0.01
Chippewa (6)	7	0.02
Choctaw	3	0.01
Creek	2	0.00
Iroquois	1	0.00
Kiowa (1)	1	0.00
Latin American Indians	2	0.00
Lumbee (1)	1	0.00
Navajo (2)	3	0.01
Ottawa	2	0.00
Sioux (3)	5	0.01
Ute	1	0.00
All other tribes (2)	6	0.01
American Indian tribes, not spec.	3	0.01
Arab:	236	0.56
Arab/Arabic	43	0.10
Egyptian	7	0.02
Jordanian	77	0.18
Lebanese	87	0.21
Moroccan	22	0.05
Asian:	1,098	2.61
Cambodian (41)	42	0.10
Chinese, ex. Taiwanese (122)	151	0.36
Filipino (103)	146	0.35
Indian (397)	421	1.00
Japanese (33)	59	0.14
Korean (45)	52	0.12
Malaysian (2)	2	0.00
Pakistani (26)	30	0.07
Sri Lankan (1)	1	0.00
Taiwanese (4)	18	0.04
Thai (6)	9	0.02
Vietnamese (117)	120	0.29
Other Asian, specified (1)	6	0.01
Other Asian, not specified (25)	41	0.10
Austrian	25	0.06
Belgian	17	0.04
British	153	0.36
Canadian	79	0.19
Croatian	22	0.05
Czech	94	0.22
Czechoslovakian	67	0.16
Danish	98	0.23
Dutch	747	1.78
English	4,709	11.22
European	503	1.20
French, except Basque	1,052	2.51
French Canadian	126	0.30
German	13,321	31.74
Greek	267	0.64
Guyanese	6	0.01
Hawaii Native/Pacific Islander:	26	0.06
Micronesian: (9)	11	0.03
Guamanian/Chamorro (9)	11	0.03
Polynesian: (2)	5	0.01
Native Hawaiian (1)	3	0.01
Samoan (1)	2	0.00
Other Pac. Isl., specified	4	0.01
Other Pac. Isl., not spec. (3)	6	0.01
Hispanic or Latino:	646	1.53
Central American:	22	0.05
Costa Rican	1	0.00
Honduran	2	0.00
Nicaraguan	3	0.01
Panamanian	6	0.01
Salvadoran	6	0.01
Other Central American	4	0.01
Cuban	24	0.06
Dominican Republic	18	0.04
Mexican	255	0.61
Puerto Rican	121	0.29
South American:	55	0.13
Argentinean	5	0.01
Bolivian	1	0.00
Chilean	1	0.00
Colombian	22	0.05
Paraguayan	1	0.00
Peruvian	14	0.03
Venezuelan	7	0.02
Other South American	4	0.01
Other Hispanic or Latino	151	0.36
Hungarian	292	0.70
Icelander	6	0.01
Irish	6,047	14.41
Italian	2,160	5.15
Latvian	17	0.04
Lithuanian	21	0.05
Macedonian	10	0.02
Northern European	26	0.06
Norwegian	253	0.60
Pennsylvania German	12	0.03
Polish	593	1.41
Portuguese	6	0.01
Romanian	41	0.10
Russian	132	0.31
Scandinavian	34	0.08
Scotch-Irish	535	1.27
Scottish	584	1.39
Serbian	25	0.06
Slavic	69	0.16
Slovak	102	0.24
Swedish	343	0.82
Swiss	238	0.57
Ukrainian	121	0.29
United States or American	3,794	9.04
Welsh	459	1.09
West Indian, excl. Hispanic:	12	0.03
British West Indian	12	0.03
White:	38,254	90.87
Not Hispanic (37,450)	37,826	89.85
Hispanic (380)	428	1.02
Yugoslavian	25	0.06

Fairview Park

Place Type: City
County: Cuyahoga
Population: 17,572

Ancestry/Race	Number	%
African American/Black:	145	0.83
Not Hispanic (111)	143	0.81
Hispanic (2)	2	0.01
African, sub-Saharan:	14	0.08
African	14	0.08
Am. Ind. or Alaska Nat., not spec.	21	0.12
Albanian	7	0.04
Alsatian	7	0.04
American Indian tribes, specified:	28	0.16
Apache (1)	1	0.01
Blackfeet	1	0.01
Cherokee (2)	16	0.09
Iroquois (1)	3	0.02
Latin American Indians (1)	1	0.01
Sioux	5	0.03
All other tribes	1	0.01
American Indian tribes, not spec.	1	0.01
Arab:	333	1.90
Arab/Arabic	64	0.36
Egyptian	19	0.11
Jordanian	28	0.16
Lebanese	86	0.49
Moroccan	20	0.11
Palestinian	36	0.20
Syrian	60	0.34
Other Arab	20	0.11
Armenian	6	0.03
Asian:	381	2.17
Cambodian (7)	7	0.04
Chinese, ex. Taiwanese (72)	86	0.49
Filipino (27)	45	0.26
Indian (70)	92	0.52
Indonesian (7)	12	0.07
Japanese (16)	20	0.11
Korean (38)	40	0.23
Pakistani (4)	9	0.05
Taiwanese (2)	2	0.01
Thai (3)	6	0.03
Vietnamese (19)	26	0.15
Other Asian, specified (1)	1	0.01
Other Asian, not specified (1)	35	0.20
Austrian	104	0.59
Basque	5	0.03
British	41	0.23
Bulgarian	43	0.24
Canadian	45	0.26
Croatian	143	0.81
Czech	389	2.21
Czechoslovakian	88	0.50
Danish	159	0.90
Dutch	225	1.28
English	1,878	10.69
European	156	0.89
Finnish	13	0.07
French, except Basque	487	2.77
French Canadian	88	0.50
German	5,227	29.75
Greek	266	1.51
Hawaii Native/Pacific Islander:	5	0.03
Micronesian: (3)	3	0.02
Guamanian/Chamorro (3)	3	0.02
Polynesian: (1)	2	0.01
Native Hawaiian	1	0.01
Samoan (1)	1	0.01
Hispanic or Latino:	264	1.50
Central American:	11	0.06
Costa Rican	2	0.01
Guatemalan	1	0.01
Honduran	2	0.01
Salvadoran	2	0.01
Other Central American	4	0.02
Cuban	16	0.09
Mexican	64	0.36
Puerto Rican	101	0.57
South American:	27	0.15
Argentinean	2	0.01
Bolivian	3	0.02
Colombian	12	0.07
Paraguayan	2	0.01
Peruvian	2	0.01
Venezuelan	5	0.03
Other South American	1	0.01
Other Hispanic or Latino	45	0.26
Hungarian	866	4.93
Iranian	9	0.05
Irish	4,694	26.71
Italian	1,546	8.80
Latvian	26	0.15
Lithuanian	108	0.61
Macedonian	9	0.05
Northern European	13	0.07
Norwegian	92	0.52
Pennsylvania German	6	0.03
Polish	1,563	8.89
Portuguese	15	0.09
Romanian	113	0.64
Russian	141	0.80

Notes: 1. Figures in the "Number" column do not add up to the total population due to: a) Ancestry/Race overlap — e.g. persons can report being both White and Irish, b) persons of Hispanic origin can report being any race, c) persons reporting two ancestries are counted in both categories. 2. Numbers in parentheses indicate the number of persons reporting this ancestry/race alone, not in combination with any other ancestry/race. 3. Refer to the Explanation of Data in the front of the book for more detailed information.

Scotch-Irish	327	1.86
Scottish	344	1.96
Serbian	19	0.11
Slavic	12	0.07
Slovak	992	5.65
Slovene	334	1.90
Swedish	106	0.60
Swiss	114	0.65
Turkish	9	0.05
Ukrainian	306	1.74
United States or American	469	2.67
Welsh	225	1.28
West Indian, excl. Hispanic:	27	0.15
British West Indian	27	0.15
White:	17,088	97.25
Not Hispanic (16,672)	16,885	96.09
Hispanic (192)	203	1.16
Yugoslavian	73	0.42

Findlay

Place Type: City
County: Hancock
Population: 38,967

Ancestry/Race	Number	%
African American/Black:	692	1.78
Not Hispanic (521)	649	1.67
Hispanic (25)	43	0.11
African, sub-Saharan:	30	0.08
African	30	0.08
Alaska Native tribes, specified:	2	0.01
Alaska Athabascan (1)	1	0.00
Eskimo	1	0.00
Am. Ind. or Alaska Nat., not spec.	74	0.19
American Indian tribes, specified:	142	0.36
Apache	9	0.02
Blackfeet (2)	10	0.03
Cherokee (18)	60	0.15
Chickasaw (1)	1	0.00
Chippewa (2)	3	0.01
Choctaw (1)	1	0.00
Comanche	6	0.02
Cree	1	0.00
Iroquois (2)	6	0.02
Latin American Indians (3)	3	0.01
Lumbee	2	0.01
Ottawa	1	0.00
Pueblo (3)	3	0.01
Puget Sound Salish (1)	1	0.00
Shoshone	2	0.01
Sioux (5)	9	0.02
Ute	1	0.00
All other tribes (16)	23	0.06
American Indian tribes, not spec.	4	0.01
Arab:	128	0.33
Arab/Arabic	35	0.09
Lebanese	68	0.17
Palestinian	17	0.04
Other Arab	8	0.02
Armenian	25	0.06
Asian:	795	2.04
Cambodian (1)	1	0.00
Chinese, ex. Taiwanese (93)	105	0.27
Filipino (42)	69	0.18
Hmong	1	0.00
Indian (73)	81	0.21
Indonesian (3)	4	0.01
Japanese (272)	285	0.73
Korean (70)	79	0.20
Laotian (66)	67	0.17
Malaysian (3)	9	0.02
Pakistani (3)	3	0.01
Taiwanese (22)	30	0.08
Thai (3)	3	0.01
Vietnamese (9)	20	0.05
Other Asian, specified	3	0.01
Other Asian, not specified (23)	35	0.09
Australian	5	0.01
Austrian	31	0.08
Belgian	83	0.21
British	121	0.31
Bulgarian	11	0.03
Canadian	94	0.24
Carpatho Rusyn	6	0.02
Celtic	16	0.04
Croatian	45	0.11
Czech	85	0.22
Czechoslovakian	74	0.19
Danish	57	0.15
Dutch	875	2.23
English	4,141	10.55
Estonian	5	0.01
European	195	0.50
Finnish	15	0.04
French, except Basque	1,313	3.35
French Canadian	174	0.44
German	13,926	35.49
Greek	72	0.18
Hawaii Native/Pacific Islander:	27	0.07
Micronesian:	5	0.01
Guamanian/Chamorro	5	0.01
Polynesian: (3)	13	0.03
Native Hawaiian (3)	13	0.03
Other Pac. Isl., not spec. (7)	9	0.02
Hispanic or Latino:	1,539	3.95
Central American:	9	0.02
Panamanian	4	0.01
Salvadoran	5	0.01
Cuban	16	0.04
Mexican	1,215	3.12
Puerto Rican	42	0.11
South American:	29	0.07
Argentinean	1	0.00
Colombian	8	0.02
Ecuadorian	2	0.01
Paraguayan	1	0.00
Peruvian	5	0.01
Venezuelan	8	0.02
Other South American	4	0.01
Other Hispanic or Latino	228	0.59
Hungarian	348	0.89
Irish	4,194	10.69
Israeli	11	0.03
Italian	1,239	3.16
Lithuanian	14	0.04
Luxemburger	7	0.02
Northern European	21	0.05
Norwegian	122	0.31
Pennsylvania German	41	0.10
Polish	763	1.94
Portuguese	39	0.10
Romanian	25	0.06
Russian	53	0.14
Scandinavian	37	0.09
Scotch-Irish	446	1.14
Scottish	738	1.88
Serbian	9	0.02
Slavic	49	0.12
Slovak	81	0.21
Slovene	29	0.07
Swedish	227	0.58
Swiss	431	1.10
Ukrainian	25	0.06
United States or American	3,739	9.53
Welsh	356	0.91
West Indian, excl. Hispanic:	30	0.08
Bahamian	10	0.03
Jamaican	20	0.05
White:	36,958	94.84
Not Hispanic (35,763)	36,086	92.61
Hispanic (750)	872	2.24
Yugoslavian	15	0.04

Finneytown

Place Type: Census Designated Place
County: Hamilton
Population: 13,492

Ancestry/Race	Number	%
African American/Black:	3,342	24.77
Not Hispanic (3,205)	3,326	24.65
Hispanic (10)	16	0.12
African, sub-Saharan:	138	1.01
African	129	0.94
South African	9	0.07
Am. Ind. or Alaska Nat., not spec.	10	0.07
American Indian tribes, specified:	49	0.36
Blackfeet	6	0.04
Cherokee (1)	26	0.19
Chippewa (1)	2	0.01
Iroquois (1)	2	0.01
Kiowa (2)	2	0.01
Latin American Indians (1)	2	0.01
Lumbee (1)	1	0.01
Navajo (1)	1	0.01
Sioux (1)	6	0.04
All other tribes (1)	2	0.01
American Indian tribes, not spec.	8	0.06
Arab:	43	0.31
Lebanese	43	0.31
Asian:	195	1.45
Chinese, ex. Taiwanese (31)	38	0.28
Filipino (15)	23	0.17
Indian (46)	55	0.41
Indonesian	1	0.01
Japanese (7)	12	0.09
Korean (17)	26	0.19
Sri Lankan (1)	1	0.01
Taiwanese (1)	1	0.01
Thai (2)	3	0.02
Vietnamese (24)	24	0.18
Other Asian, specified (1)	5	0.04
Other Asian, not specified (1)	6	0.04
Austrian	33	0.24
Belgian	25	0.18
British	60	0.44
Canadian	27	0.20
Celtic	9	0.07
Czech	7	0.05
Czechoslovakian	5	0.04
Danish	11	0.08
Dutch	149	1.09
Eastern European	27	0.20
English	1,383	10.08
European	63	0.46
Finnish	21	0.15
French, except Basque	305	2.22
French Canadian	30	0.22
German	4,524	32.97
Greek	134	0.98
Hawaii Native/Pacific Islander:	13	0.10
Micronesian:	1	0.01
Guamanian/Chamorro	1	0.01
Polynesian: (2)	9	0.07
Native Hawaiian (2)	8	0.06
Samoan	1	0.01
Other Pac. Isl., not spec.	3	0.02
Hispanic or Latino:	108	0.80
Central American:	12	0.09
Guatemalan	2	0.01
Panamanian	5	0.04
Other Central American	5	0.04
Cuban	9	0.07
Mexican	30	0.22
Puerto Rican	28	0.21
South American:	10	0.07
Chilean	1	0.01
Colombian	1	0.01
Ecuadorian	8	0.06
Other Hispanic or Latino	19	0.14
Hungarian	67	0.49
Irish	1,808	13.17

Notes: 1. Figures in the "Number" column do not add up to the total population due to: a) Ancestry/Race overlap — e.g. persons can report being both White and Irish, b) persons of Hispanic origin can report being any race, c) persons reporting two ancestries are counted in both categories. 2. Numbers in parentheses indicate the number of persons reporting this ancestry/race alone, not in combination with any other ancestry/race. 3. Refer to the Explanation of Data in the front of the book for more detailed information.

Italian	543	3.96
Lithuanian	29	0.21
Norwegian	80	0.58
Pennsylvania German	15	0.11
Polish	239	1.74
Portuguese	8	0.06
Romanian	43	0.31
Russian	105	0.77
Scandinavian	6	0.04
Scotch-Irish	309	2.25
Scottish	317	2.31
Slovak	8	0.06
Slovene	17	0.12
Swedish	123	0.90
Swiss	45	0.33
Ukrainian	24	0.17
United States or American	754	5.49
Welsh	162	1.18
White:	10,017	74.24
Not Hispanic (9,782)	9,947	73.73
Hispanic (61)	70	0.52

Forest Park

Place Type: City
County: Hamilton
Population: 19,463

Ancestry/Race	Number	%
African American/Black:	11,269	57.90
Not Hispanic (10,911)	11,216	57.63
Hispanic (38)	53	0.27
African, sub-Saharan:	539	2.78
African	299	1.54
Ethiopian	8	0.04
Nigerian	132	0.68
South African	51	0.26
Other sub-Saharan African	49	0.25
Am. Ind. or Alaska Nat., not spec.	58	0.30
American Indian tribes, specified:	81	0.42
Apache	1	0.01
Blackfeet (2)	6	0.03
Cherokee (7)	46	0.24
Choctaw	2	0.01
Comanche (1)	1	0.01
Creek	6	0.03
Iroquois	1	0.01
Latin American Indians	1	0.01
Paiute	4	0.02
Pueblo	1	0.01
Seminole	2	0.01
Yuman	1	0.01
All other tribes (6)	9	0.05
American Indian tribes, not spec.	4	0.02
Arab:	75	0.39
Egyptian	15	0.08
Lebanese	51	0.26
Other Arab	9	0.05
Asian:	802	4.12
Bangladeshi (8)	8	0.04
Cambodian (35)	39	0.20
Chinese, ex. Taiwanese (50)	58	0.30
Filipino (86)	112	0.58
Indian (353)	364	1.87
Indonesian (1)	1	0.01
Japanese (16)	30	0.15
Korean (12)	32	0.16
Pakistani (42)	42	0.22
Taiwanese (3)	3	0.02
Thai (4)	6	0.03
Vietnamese (92)	93	0.48
Other Asian, not specified (10)	14	0.07
Austrian	7	0.04
Belgian	8	0.04
British	62	0.32
Canadian	23	0.12
Croatian	6	0.03
Czech	28	0.14
Czechoslovakian	17	0.09
Dutch	181	0.93
English	1,131	5.84
European	83	0.43
Finnish	17	0.09
French, except Basque	330	1.70
French Canadian	15	0.08
German	2,829	14.60
Greek	27	0.14
Hawaii Native/Pacific Islander:	26	0.13
Micronesian: (1)	3	0.02
Guamanian/Chamorro	1	0.01
Other Micronesian (1)	2	0.01
Polynesian: (7)	13	0.07
Native Hawaiian (2)	8	0.04
Samoan (5)	5	0.03
Other Pac. Isl., not spec. (7)	10	0.05
Hispanic or Latino:	289	1.48
Central American:	19	0.10
Guatemalan	5	0.03
Honduran	2	0.01
Panamanian	7	0.04
Salvadoran	4	0.02
Other Central American	1	0.01
Cuban	9	0.05
Dominican Republic	6	0.03
Mexican	146	0.75
Puerto Rican	41	0.21
South American:	15	0.08
Argentinean	3	0.02
Colombian	6	0.03
Ecuadorian	1	0.01
Peruvian	1	0.01
Venezuelan	1	0.01
Other South American	3	0.02
Other Hispanic or Latino	53	0.27
Hungarian	50	0.26
Irish	1,276	6.58
Italian	213	1.10
Latvian	8	0.04
Lithuanian	27	0.14
Luxemburger	4	0.02
Northern European	6	0.03
Norwegian	37	0.19
Polish	75	0.39
Romanian	16	0.08
Russian	16	0.08
Scandinavian	7	0.04
Scotch-Irish	193	1.00
Scottish	227	1.17
Serbian	8	0.04
Slavic	10	0.05
Slovak	73	0.38
Slovene	12	0.06
Swedish	77	0.40
Swiss	22	0.11
Ukrainian	43	0.22
United States or American	718	3.70
Welsh	127	0.66
West Indian, excl. Hispanic:	104	0.54
Barbadian	22	0.11
Jamaican	57	0.29
Trinidadian and Tobagonian	7	0.04
West Indian	18	0.09
White:	7,464	38.35
Not Hispanic (7,035)	7,342	37.72
Hispanic (107)	122	0.63
Yugoslavian	18	0.09

Forestville

Place Type: Census Designated Place
County: Hamilton
Population: 10,978

Ancestry/Race	Number	%
African American/Black:	118	1.07
Not Hispanic (96)	115	1.05
Hispanic	3	0.03
African, sub-Saharan:	55	0.50
Nigerian	55	0.50
Am. Ind. or Alaska Nat., not spec.	17	0.15
American Indian tribes, specified:	18	0.16
Blackfeet	2	0.02
Cherokee (1)	6	0.05
Chippewa (1)	2	0.02
Creek	1	0.01
Shoshone (1)	3	0.03
All other tribes (1)	4	0.04
American Indian tribes, not spec.	1	0.01
Arab:	107	0.97
Lebanese	100	0.90
Syrian	7	0.06
Asian:	287	2.61
Cambodian	2	0.02
Chinese, ex. Taiwanese (75)	85	0.77
Filipino (15)	18	0.16
Indian (86)	91	0.83
Indonesian (2)	2	0.02
Japanese (17)	29	0.26
Korean (3)	4	0.04
Pakistani (8)	10	0.09
Taiwanese (12)	13	0.12
Thai (4)	4	0.04
Vietnamese (2)	7	0.06
Other Asian, not specified (16)	22	0.20
Austrian	30	0.27
Brazilian	10	0.09
British	26	0.24
Canadian	46	0.42
Celtic	12	0.11
Croatian	21	0.19
Czech	33	0.30
Czechoslovakian	11	0.10
Danish	11	0.10
Dutch	228	2.06
English	1,510	13.65
European	120	1.08
French, except Basque	270	2.44
French Canadian	22	0.20
German	4,281	38.70
Hawaii Native/Pacific Islander:	5	0.05
Micronesian: (1)	1	0.01
Guamanian/Chamorro (1)	1	0.01
Polynesian:	1	0.01
Native Hawaiian	1	0.01
Other Pac. Isl., not spec.	3	0.03
Hispanic or Latino:	116	1.06
Central American:	5	0.05
Costa Rican	2	0.02
Guatemalan	2	0.02
Salvadoran	1	0.01
Cuban	3	0.03
Dominican Republic	5	0.05
Mexican	48	0.44
Puerto Rican	20	0.18
South American:	7	0.06
Argentinean	4	0.04
Bolivian	1	0.01
Chilean	1	0.01
Venezuelan	1	0.01
Other Hispanic or Latino	28	0.26
Hungarian	64	0.58
Iranian	30	0.27
Irish	2,455	22.20
Italian	606	5.48
Lithuanian	19	0.17
Macedonian	20	0.18
Norwegian	104	0.94
Polish	248	2.24
Portuguese	34	0.31
Romanian	29	0.26
Russian	46	0.42
Scandinavian	9	0.08
Scotch-Irish	182	1.65
Scottish	257	2.32
Serbian	7	0.06
Slovene	16	0.14
Swedish	107	0.97
Swiss	95	0.86
Turkish	37	0.33
United States or American	658	5.95

Notes: 1. Figures in the "Number" column do not add up to the total population due to: a) Ancestry/Race overlap — e.g. persons can report being both White and Irish, b) persons of Hispanic origin can report being any race, c) persons reporting two ancestries are counted in both categories. 2. Numbers in parentheses indicate the number of persons reporting this ancestry/race alone, not in combination with any other ancestry/race. 3. Refer to the Explanation of Data in the front of the book for more detailed information.

	Number	%
Welsh	44	0.40
White:	10,588	96.45
Not Hispanic (10,430)	10,498	95.63
Hispanic (78)	90	0.82
Yugoslavian	34	0.31

Fostoria

Place Type: City
County: Seneca
Population: 13,931

Ancestry/Race	Number	%
African American/Black:	993	7.13
Not Hispanic (788)	957	6.87
Hispanic (13)	36	0.26
African, sub-Saharan:	83	0.59
African	56	0.40
South African	27	0.19
Alaska Native tribes, specified:	1	0.01
Alaska Athabascan (1)	1	0.01
Am. Ind. or Alaska Nat., not spec.	41	0.29
American Indian tribes, specified:	62	0.45
Apache (5)	5	0.04
Blackfeet	1	0.01
Cherokee (3)	28	0.20
Cree (1)	1	0.01
Crow	1	0.01
Iroquois (1)	2	0.01
Latin American Indians (1)	1	0.01
Lumbee	8	0.06
Menominee (3)	3	0.02
Seminole	3	0.02
Sioux	1	0.01
All other tribes (2)	8	0.06
American Indian tribes, not spec.	1	0.01
Arab:	14	0.10
Arab/Arabic	9	0.06
Lebanese	5	0.04
Armenian	23	0.16
Asian:	83	0.60
Cambodian (1)	1	0.01
Chinese, ex. Taiwanese (7)	8	0.06
Filipino (8)	17	0.12
Indian (24)	27	0.19
Japanese (1)	1	0.01
Korean (3)	4	0.03
Laotian (18)	18	0.13
Pakistani (4)	4	0.03
Other Asian, not specified (1)	3	0.02
Belgian	37	0.26
British	51	0.36
Canadian	7	0.05
Czech	4	0.03
Danish	6	0.04
Dutch	251	1.79
English	1,066	7.62
European	34	0.24
French, except Basque	391	2.79
French Canadian	8	0.06
German	4,644	33.20
Greek	6	0.04
Hawaii Native/Pacific Islander:	1	0.01
Other Pac. Isl., not spec.	1	0.01
Hispanic or Latino:	1,104	7.92
Central American:	1	0.01
Honduran	1	0.01
Cuban	1	0.01
Mexican	948	6.80
Puerto Rican	14	0.10
Other Hispanic or Latino	140	1.00
Hungarian	54	0.39
Irish	1,350	9.65
Italian	331	2.37
Lithuanian	7	0.05
Luxemburger	21	0.15
Norwegian	27	0.19
Pennsylvania German	5	0.04
Polish	252	1.80
Portuguese	9	0.06
Russian	30	0.21
Scotch-Irish	102	0.73
Scottish	141	1.01
Slovene	11	0.08
Swedish	54	0.39
Swiss	47	0.34
Ukrainian	8	0.06
United States or American	915	6.54
Welsh	45	0.32
White:	12,508	89.79
Not Hispanic (11,681)	11,916	85.54
Hispanic (484)	592	4.25

Franklin

Place Type: City
County: Warren
Population: 11,396

Ancestry/Race	Number	%
African American/Black:	115	1.01
Not Hispanic (84)	106	0.93
Hispanic (9)	9	0.08
Am. Ind. or Alaska Nat., not spec.	23	0.20
American Indian tribes, specified:	44	0.39
Apache	3	0.03
Blackfeet	2	0.02
Cherokee (10)	28	0.25
Choctaw	1	0.01
Cree	1	0.01
Iroquois (1)	3	0.03
Latin American Indians (1)	1	0.01
Navajo	5	0.04
American Indian tribes, not spec.	4	0.04
Arab:	9	0.08
Arab/Arabic	9	0.08
Armenian	11	0.10
Asian:	71	0.62
Chinese, ex. Taiwanese (2)	3	0.03
Filipino (1)	3	0.03
Indian (20)	20	0.18
Japanese (5)	14	0.12
Korean (3)	11	0.10
Vietnamese (5)	5	0.04
Other Asian, specified (8)	11	0.10
Other Asian, not specified (2)	4	0.04
Austrian	11	0.10
British	41	0.36
Bulgarian	5	0.04
Canadian	5	0.04
Czech	6	0.05
Danish	7	0.06
Dutch	186	1.61
English	1,036	8.98
European	112	0.97
Finnish	13	0.11
French, except Basque	424	3.68
French Canadian	12	0.10
German	1,729	14.99
Hispanic or Latino:	81	0.71
Central American:	1	0.01
Guatemalan	1	0.01
Cuban	4	0.04
Mexican	26	0.23
Puerto Rican	15	0.13
South American:	6	0.05
Colombian	1	0.01
Ecuadorian	5	0.04
Other Hispanic or Latino	29	0.25
Hungarian	96	0.83
Irish	1,197	10.38
Italian	157	1.36
Norwegian	38	0.33
Polish	94	0.81
Portuguese	21	0.18
Scotch-Irish	157	1.36
Scottish	194	1.68
Swedish	27	0.23
Swiss	6	0.05
Ukrainian	10	0.09
United States or American	2,482	21.51
Welsh	49	0.42
White:	11,204	98.32
Not Hispanic (11,068)	11,156	97.89
Hispanic (44)	48	0.42
Yugoslavian	5	0.04

Fremont

Place Type: City
County: Sandusky
Population: 17,375

Ancestry/Race	Number	%
African American/Black:	1,718	9.89
Not Hispanic (1,414)	1,646	9.47
Hispanic (27)	72	0.41
African, sub-Saharan:	92	0.53
African	75	0.43
Other sub-Saharan African	17	0.10
Am. Ind. or Alaska Nat., not spec.	37	0.21
Alsatian	10	0.06
American Indian tribes, specified:	78	0.45
Apache (1)	1	0.01
Blackfeet	5	0.03
Cherokee (4)	40	0.23
Chippewa (1)	4	0.02
Choctaw	2	0.01
Creek (3)	4	0.02
Iroquois	3	0.02
Latin American Indians (3)	9	0.05
Navajo (1)	2	0.01
Ottawa (1)	1	0.01
Potawatomi	1	0.01
Seminole	3	0.02
Sioux (1)	2	0.01
Yaqui (1)	1	0.01
All other tribes	1	0.01
American Indian tribes, not spec.	3	0.02
Arab:	59	0.34
Lebanese	30	0.17
Syrian	29	0.17
Asian:	67	0.39
Chinese, ex. Taiwanese (6)	6	0.03
Filipino (11)	23	0.13
Indian (10)	14	0.08
Japanese (1)	5	0.03
Korean (7)	11	0.06
Laotian	1	0.01
Malaysian (3)	3	0.02
Taiwanese	1	0.01
Thai	1	0.01
Vietnamese (1)	1	0.01
Other Asian, not specified (1)	1	0.01
Austrian	13	0.07
Belgian	19	0.11
British	42	0.24
Canadian	27	0.16
Croatian	11	0.06
Czech	59	0.34
Czechoslovakian	30	0.17
Danish	12	0.07
Dutch	261	1.50
English	1,072	6.18
European	134	0.77
Finnish	10	0.06
French, except Basque	422	2.43
French Canadian	91	0.52
German	5,876	33.86
Greek	22	0.13
Hawaii Native/Pacific Islander:	7	0.04
Micronesian:	2	0.01
Guamanian/Chamorro	2	0.01
Polynesian:	3	0.02
Native Hawaiian	2	0.01
Samoan	1	0.01
Other Pac. Isl., not spec.	2	0.01
Hispanic or Latino:	2,140	12.32
Central American:	3	0.02
Guatemalan	2	0.01

Notes: 1. Figures in the "Number" column do not add up to the total population due to: a) Ancestry/Race overlap — e.g. persons can report being both White and Irish, b) persons of Hispanic origin can report being any race, c) persons reporting two ancestries are counted in both categories. 2. Numbers in parentheses indicate the number of persons reporting this ancestry/race alone, not in combination with any other ancestry/race. 3. Refer to the Explanation of Data in the front of the book for more detailed information.

Ancestry/Race	Number	%
Honduran	1	0.01
Cuban	6	0.03
Mexican	1,584	9.12
Puerto Rican	137	0.79
South American:	4	0.02
Colombian	1	0.01
Ecuadorian	1	0.01
Other South American	2	0.01
Other Hispanic or Latino	406	2.34
Hungarian	153	0.88
Iranian	21	0.12
Irish	1,626	9.37
Italian	472	2.72
Lithuanian	6	0.03
Norwegian	41	0.24
Polish	702	4.05
Portuguese	9	0.05
Romanian	7	0.04
Scotch-Irish	121	0.70
Scottish	208	1.20
Slavic	13	0.07
Slovak	47	0.27
Slovene	20	0.12
Swedish	115	0.66
Swiss	69	0.40
Ukrainian	6	0.03
United States or American	1,035	5.96
Welsh	79	0.46
West Indian, excl. Hispanic:	5	0.03
British West Indian	5	0.03
White:	14,798	85.17
Not Hispanic (13,407)	13,708	78.89
Hispanic (883)	1,090	6.27

Gahanna

Place Type: City
County: Franklin
Population: 32,636

Ancestry/Race	Number	%
African American/Black:	2,860	8.76
Not Hispanic (2,636)	2,832	8.68
Hispanic (21)	28	0.09
African, sub-Saharan:	181	0.56
African	173	0.53
South African	8	0.02
Alaska Native tribes, specified:	1	0.00
Aleut (1)	1	0.00
Am. Ind. or Alaska Nat., not spec.	68	0.21
Alsatian	7	0.02
American Indian tribes, specified:	105	0.32
Apache (2)	4	0.01
Blackfeet	9	0.03
Cherokee (23)	55	0.17
Chickasaw	1	0.00
Chippewa (1)	3	0.01
Choctaw (3)	3	0.01
Comanche	1	0.00
Creek	1	0.00
Crow	1	0.00
Delaware (1)	1	0.00
Iroquois	1	0.00
Latin American Indians (4)	8	0.02
Navajo (1)	3	0.01
Seminole	1	0.00
Sioux (5)	5	0.02
Yaqui	1	0.00
All other tribes (2)	7	0.02
American Indian tribes, not spec.	9	0.03
Arab:	65	0.20
Egyptian	18	0.06
Lebanese	8	0.02
Palestinian	9	0.03
Syrian	14	0.04
Other Arab	16	0.05
Asian:	1,226	3.76
Bangladeshi (7)	7	0.02
Cambodian (38)	38	0.12
Chinese, ex. Taiwanese (247)	275	0.84
Filipino (69)	100	0.31
Indian (381)	407	1.25
Indonesian (8)	8	0.02
Japanese (50)	81	0.25
Korean (117)	141	0.43
Laotian (13)	14	0.04
Malaysian (4)	4	0.01
Pakistani (12)	12	0.04
Taiwanese (7)	8	0.02
Thai (11)	23	0.07
Vietnamese (78)	82	0.25
Other Asian, specified (1)	1	0.00
Other Asian, not specified (12)	25	0.08
Assyrian/Chaldean/Syriac	6	0.02
Austrian	113	0.35
Belgian	92	0.28
Brazilian	23	0.07
British	215	0.66
Canadian	20	0.06
Carpatho Rusyn	7	0.02
Croatian	100	0.31
Czech	159	0.49
Czechoslovakian	62	0.19
Danish	100	0.31
Dutch	641	1.97
Eastern European	140	0.43
English	4,189	12.88
Estonian	11	0.03
European	268	0.82
Finnish	28	0.09
French, except Basque	856	2.63
French Canadian	129	0.40
German	8,554	26.30
Greek	131	0.40
Hawaii Native/Pacific Islander:	21	0.06
Micronesian: (2)	2	0.01
Guamanian/Chamorro (2)	2	0.01
Polynesian: (7)	13	0.04
Native Hawaiian (3)	8	0.02
Samoan (4)	5	0.02
Other Pac. Isl., not spec.	6	0.02
Hispanic or Latino:	430	1.32
Central American:	15	0.05
Costa Rican	3	0.01
Guatemalan	3	0.01
Panamanian	3	0.01
Salvadoran	3	0.01
Other Central American	3	0.01
Cuban	19	0.06
Dominican Republic	6	0.02
Mexican	176	0.54
Puerto Rican	66	0.20
South American:	67	0.21
Argentinean	24	0.07
Bolivian	2	0.01
Chilean	2	0.01
Colombian	5	0.02
Ecuadorian	5	0.02
Peruvian	19	0.06
Venezuelan	3	0.01
Other South American	7	0.02
Other Hispanic or Latino	81	0.25
Hungarian	420	1.29
Iranian	14	0.04
Irish	4,696	14.44
Italian	2,069	6.36
Latvian	21	0.06
Lithuanian	88	0.27
Macedonian	284	0.87
Maltese	16	0.05
Norwegian	199	0.61
Pennsylvania German	16	0.05
Polish	1,127	3.47
Portuguese	26	0.08
Romanian	72	0.22
Russian	349	1.07
Scandinavian	28	0.09
Scotch-Irish	748	2.30
Scottish	882	2.71
Serbian	29	0.09
Slavic	29	0.09
Slovak	173	0.53
Slovene	81	0.25
Swedish	401	1.23
Swiss	189	0.58
Turkish	15	0.05
Ukrainian	129	0.40
United States or American	2,533	7.79
Welsh	655	2.01
West Indian, excl. Hispanic:	77	0.24
British West Indian	14	0.04
Dutch West Indian	7	0.02
Jamaican	36	0.11
West Indian	20	0.06
White:	28,635	87.74
Not Hispanic (27,966)	28,365	86.91
Hispanic (250)	270	0.83
Yugoslavian	67	0.21

Galion

Place Type: City
County: Crawford
Population: 11,341

Ancestry/Race	Number	%
African American/Black:	41	0.36
Not Hispanic (25)	41	0.36
Am. Ind. or Alaska Nat., not spec.	31	0.27
American Indian tribes, specified:	41	0.36
Apache (1)	1	0.01
Blackfeet (1)	2	0.02
Cherokee (5)	23	0.20
Chickasaw (5)	5	0.04
Comanche	1	0.01
Delaware (2)	2	0.02
Iroquois	1	0.01
Sioux (5)	5	0.04
All other tribes	1	0.01
American Indian tribes, not spec.	5	0.04
Arab:	5	0.04
Lebanese	5	0.04
Asian:	35	0.31
Chinese, ex. Taiwanese (9)	10	0.09
Filipino (1)	2	0.02
Indian (3)	4	0.04
Japanese (3)	5	0.04
Korean (3)	3	0.03
Taiwanese (3)	3	0.03
Vietnamese (8)	8	0.07
Austrian	39	0.34
Belgian	15	0.13
Canadian	15	0.13
Celtic	5	0.04
Czech	40	0.35
Danish	11	0.10
Dutch	188	1.64
English	1,074	9.35
European	36	0.31
French, except Basque	245	2.13
French Canadian	36	0.31
German	3,226	28.07
Greek	12	0.10
Hawaii Native/Pacific Islander:	1	0.01
Micronesian: (1)	1	0.01
Guamanian/Chamorro (1)	1	0.01
Hispanic or Latino:	105	0.93
Mexican	82	0.72
Puerto Rican	2	0.02
South American:	1	0.01
Peruvian	1	0.01
Other Hispanic or Latino	20	0.18
Hungarian	27	0.23
Irish	1,244	10.82
Italian	329	2.86
Lithuanian	8	0.07
Norwegian	40	0.35
Pennsylvania German	52	0.45
Polish	145	1.26
Romanian	21	0.18

Notes: 1. Figures in the "Number" column do not add up to the total population due to: a) Ancestry/Race overlap — e.g. persons can report being both White and Irish, b) persons of Hispanic origin can report being any race, c) persons reporting two ancestries are counted in both categories. 2. Numbers in parentheses indicate the number of persons reporting this ancestry/race alone, not in combination with any other ancestry/race. 3. Refer to the Explanation of Data in the front of the book for more detailed information.

Ancestry/Race	Number	%
Russian	21	0.18
Scotch-Irish	197	1.71
Scottish	154	1.34
Slovak	22	0.19
Slovene	6	0.05
Swedish	10	0.09
Swiss	58	0.50
Ukrainian	22	0.19
United States or American	1,879	16.35
Welsh	77	0.67
West Indian, excl. Hispanic:	6	0.05
Jamaican	6	0.05
White:	11,206	98.81
Not Hispanic (11,071)	11,130	98.14
Hispanic (75)	76	0.67

Garfield Heights

Place Type: City
County: Cuyahoga
Population: 30,734

Ancestry/Race	Number	%
African American/Black:	5,301	17.25
Not Hispanic (5,143)	5,270	17.15
Hispanic (21)	31	0.10
African, sub-Saharan:	202	0.66
African	175	0.57
Ghanian	6	0.02
Liberian	6	0.02
Nigerian	9	0.03
Other sub-Saharan African	6	0.02
Am. Ind. or Alaska Nat., not spec.	61	0.20
American Indian tribes, specified:	81	0.26
Apache (3)	3	0.01
Blackfeet	3	0.01
Cherokee (3)	29	0.09
Chickasaw	3	0.01
Chippewa (3)	6	0.02
Choctaw (1)	3	0.01
Creek (1)	1	0.00
Iroquois (3)	10	0.03
Latin American Indians	2	0.01
Navajo (4)	4	0.01
Ottawa (1)	1	0.00
Pueblo (3)	4	0.01
Shoshone	2	0.01
Sioux (4)	4	0.01
All other tribes (2)	6	0.02
American Indian tribes, not spec.	15	0.05
Arab:	73	0.24
Arab/Arabic	26	0.08
Jordanian	7	0.02
Lebanese	40	0.13
Armenian	52	0.17
Asian:	340	1.11
Chinese, ex. Taiwanese (42)	50	0.16
Filipino (80)	94	0.31
Indian (141)	154	0.50
Indonesian	1	0.00
Japanese (2)	9	0.03
Korean (7)	11	0.04
Laotian (5)	5	0.02
Malaysian	1	0.00
Thai (1)	3	0.01
Vietnamese (2)	2	0.01
Other Asian, not specified (4)	10	0.03
Austrian	93	0.30
Belgian	18	0.06
British	71	0.23
Canadian	40	0.13
Carpatho Rusyn	12	0.04
Croatian	301	0.98
Czech	1,445	4.72
Czechoslovakian	160	0.52
Danish	29	0.09
Dutch	278	0.91
Eastern European	15	0.05
English	1,268	4.14
European	121	0.40
Finnish	5	0.02
French, except Basque	256	0.84
French Canadian	78	0.25
German	4,563	14.90
Greek	144	0.47
Hawaii Native/Pacific Islander:	13	0.04
Polynesian: (3)	3	0.01
Native Hawaiian (3)	3	0.01
Other Pac. Isl., not spec.	10	0.03
Hispanic or Latino:	388	1.26
Central American:	21	0.07
Guatemalan	4	0.01
Honduran	2	0.01
Nicaraguan	4	0.01
Panamanian	5	0.02
Salvadoran	6	0.02
Cuban	5	0.02
Dominican Republic	4	0.01
Mexican	124	0.40
Puerto Rican	168	0.55
South American:	9	0.03
Argentinean	3	0.01
Colombian	1	0.00
Peruvian	4	0.01
Venezuelan	1	0.00
Other Hispanic or Latino	57	0.19
Hungarian	1,310	4.28
Irish	3,138	10.25
Italian	4,294	14.02
Latvian	15	0.05
Lithuanian	64	0.21
Maltese	16	0.05
Norwegian	40	0.13
Polish	7,983	26.07
Portuguese	15	0.05
Romanian	19	0.06
Russian	365	1.19
Scotch-Irish	207	0.68
Scottish	339	1.11
Serbian	39	0.13
Slavic	33	0.11
Slovak	1,485	4.85
Slovene	720	2.35
Swedish	76	0.25
Swiss	75	0.24
Ukrainian	213	0.70
United States or American	889	2.90
Welsh	276	0.90
West Indian, excl. Hispanic:	78	0.25
Haitian	6	0.02
Jamaican	66	0.22
West Indian	6	0.02
White:	25,053	81.52
Not Hispanic (24,577)	24,796	80.68
Hispanic (230)	257	0.84
Yugoslavian	56	0.18

Girard

Place Type: City
County: Trumbull
Population: 10,902

Ancestry/Race	Number	%
African American/Black:	316	2.90
Not Hispanic (261)	309	2.83
Hispanic (5)	7	0.06
African, sub-Saharan:	10	0.09
African	10	0.09
Am. Ind. or Alaska Nat., not spec.	28	0.26
Albanian	13	0.12
American Indian tribes, specified:	40	0.37
Apache (1)	2	0.02
Blackfeet	5	0.05
Cherokee (3)	14	0.13
Chickasaw	1	0.01
Choctaw	1	0.01
Iroquois (3)	5	0.05
Latin American Indians	4	0.04
Potawatomi (1)	1	0.01
Seminole (1)	2	0.02
Sioux	3	0.03
All other tribes (2)	2	0.02
Arab:	14	0.13
Lebanese	6	0.05
Syrian	8	0.07
Asian:	56	0.51
Chinese, ex. Taiwanese (2)	2	0.02
Filipino (8)	17	0.16
Indian (16)	17	0.16
Japanese (3)	3	0.03
Korean (6)	7	0.06
Thai (2)	2	0.02
Vietnamese (1)	1	0.01
Other Asian, not specified	7	0.06
Austrian	36	0.32
British	14	0.13
Canadian	6	0.05
Croatian	147	1.32
Czech	55	0.49
Czechoslovakian	64	0.57
Dutch	158	1.42
English	954	8.56
European	18	0.16
Finnish	51	0.46
French, except Basque	226	2.03
French Canadian	13	0.12
German	2,430	21.79
Greek	28	0.25
Hawaii Native/Pacific Islander:	21	0.19
Micronesian:	8	0.07
Guamanian/Chamorro	8	0.07
Polynesian: (1)	3	0.03
Native Hawaiian	2	0.02
Samoan (1)	1	0.01
Other Pac. Isl., not spec. (1)	10	0.09
Hispanic or Latino:	79	0.72
Central American:	2	0.02
Honduran	2	0.02
Cuban	1	0.01
Mexican	38	0.35
Puerto Rican	25	0.23
Other Hispanic or Latino	13	0.12
Hungarian	231	2.07
Irish	2,273	20.39
Italian	3,285	29.46
Macedonian	7	0.06
Norwegian	19	0.17
Pennsylvania German	20	0.18
Polish	401	3.60
Portuguese	6	0.05
Romanian	38	0.34
Russian	126	1.13
Scandinavian	10	0.09
Scotch-Irish	212	1.90
Scottish	120	1.08
Serbian	72	0.65
Slavic	13	0.12
Slovak	399	3.58
Slovene	127	1.14
Swedish	86	0.77
Swiss	43	0.39
Ukrainian	233	2.09
United States or American	641	5.75
Welsh	303	2.72
White:	10,531	96.60
Not Hispanic (10,377)	10,478	96.11
Hispanic (44)	53	0.49

Green

Place Type: City
County: Summit
Population: 22,817

Ancestry/Race	Number	%
African American/Black:	206	0.90
Not Hispanic (165)	206	0.90
African, sub-Saharan:	7	0.03
Liberian	7	0.03

Notes: 1. Figures in the "Number" column do not add up to the total population due to: a) Ancestry/Race overlap — e.g. persons can report being both White and Irish, b) persons of Hispanic origin can report being any race, c) persons reporting two ancestries are counted in both categories. 2. Numbers in parentheses indicate the number of persons reporting this ancestry/race alone, not in combination with any other ancestry/race. 3. Refer to the Explanation of Data in the front of the book for more detailed information.

Am. Ind. or Alaska Nat., not spec.	42	0.18
Alsatian	6	0.03
American Indian tribes, specified:	59	0.26
Apache	4	0.02
Blackfeet	3	0.01
Cherokee (16)	33	0.14
Creek	1	0.00
Iroquois (2)	10	0.04
Latin American Indians (1)	1	0.00
Sioux	2	0.01
All other tribes (2)	5	0.02
American Indian tribes, not spec.	1	0.00
Arab:	118	0.52
Arab/Arabic	14	0.06
Lebanese	104	0.46
Armenian	25	0.11
Asian:	222	0.97
Bangladeshi (1)	1	0.00
Chinese, ex. Taiwanese (49)	56	0.25
Filipino (12)	17	0.07
Indian (66)	70	0.31
Indonesian (1)	3	0.01
Japanese (6)	16	0.07
Korean (21)	26	0.11
Malaysian	1	0.00
Pakistani (2)	6	0.03
Thai (2)	2	0.01
Vietnamese (9)	9	0.04
Other Asian, specified (1)	1	0.00
Other Asian, not specified (7)	14	0.06
Austrian	84	0.37
British	104	0.46
Canadian	71	0.31
Celtic	17	0.07
Croatian	231	1.01
Czech	193	0.85
Czechoslovakian	81	0.35
Danish	39	0.17
Dutch	386	1.69
Eastern European	7	0.03
English	2,485	10.89
European	213	0.93
Finnish	28	0.12
French, except Basque	636	2.79
French Canadian	28	0.12
German	6,467	28.34
Greek	199	0.87
Hawaii Native/Pacific Islander:	7	0.03
Micronesian: (1)	1	0.00
Guamanian/Chamorro (1)	1	0.00
Polynesian: (4)	5	0.02
Native Hawaiian (3)	4	0.02
Samoan (1)	1	0.00
Other Pac. Isl., not spec.	1	0.00
Hispanic or Latino:	111	0.49
Central American:	5	0.02
Guatemalan	4	0.02
Salvadoran	1	0.00
Mexican	38	0.17
Puerto Rican	25	0.11
South American:	10	0.04
Chilean	1	0.00
Colombian	5	0.02
Peruvian	3	0.01
Other South American	1	0.00
Other Hispanic or Latino	33	0.14
Hungarian	948	4.15
Irish	3,738	16.38
Italian	1,786	7.83
Lithuanian	52	0.23
Macedonian	79	0.35
Norwegian	54	0.24
Pennsylvania German	28	0.12
Polish	809	3.55
Portuguese	12	0.05
Romanian	226	0.99
Russian	289	1.27
Scotch-Irish	356	1.56
Scottish	651	2.85
Serbian	135	0.59
Slavic	31	0.14
Slovak	532	2.33
Slovene	75	0.33
Swedish	205	0.90
Swiss	188	0.82
Ukrainian	243	1.06
United States or American	2,073	9.09
Welsh	217	0.95
West Indian, excl. Hispanic:	6	0.03
Dutch West Indian	6	0.03
White:	22,399	98.17
Not Hispanic (22,164)	22,305	97.76
Hispanic (86)	94	0.41
Yugoslavian	168	0.74

Greenville

Place Type: City
County: Darke
Population: 13,294

Ancestry/Race	Number	%
African American/Black:	136	1.02
Not Hispanic (75)	135	1.02
Hispanic	1	0.01
African, sub-Saharan:	7	0.05
African	7	0.05
Am. Ind. or Alaska Nat., not spec.	20	0.15
American Indian tribes, specified:	41	0.31
Blackfeet (1)	4	0.03
Cherokee (9)	19	0.14
Chickasaw	1	0.01
Chippewa (6)	7	0.05
Comanche	1	0.01
Latin American Indians (1)	3	0.02
Navajo (1)	1	0.01
Shoshone (1)	1	0.01
All other tribes	4	0.03
American Indian tribes, not spec.	1	0.01
Arab:	35	0.27
Arab/Arabic	10	0.08
Lebanese	25	0.19
Asian:	78	0.59
Chinese, ex. Taiwanese (3)	3	0.02
Filipino (18)	18	0.14
Indian (8)	8	0.06
Indonesian (1)	1	0.01
Japanese (35)	40	0.30
Korean (3)	3	0.02
Thai (1)	4	0.03
Other Asian, not specified (1)	1	0.01
Australian	10	0.08
Austrian	19	0.14
Belgian	9	0.07
British	54	0.41
Canadian	6	0.05
Czechoslovakian	16	0.12
Danish	10	0.08
Dutch	444	3.36
English	1,317	9.97
European	94	0.71
French, except Basque	424	3.21
French Canadian	41	0.31
German	4,084	30.92
Greek	5	0.04
Hawaii Native/Pacific Islander:	5	0.04
Polynesian: (2)	5	0.04
Native Hawaiian (2)	4	0.03
Samoan	1	0.01
Hispanic or Latino:	152	1.14
Central American:	6	0.05
Guatemalan	3	0.02
Panamanian	2	0.02
Salvadoran	1	0.01
Cuban	5	0.04
Mexican	83	0.62
Puerto Rican	9	0.07
South American:	4	0.03
Ecuadorian	4	0.03
Other Hispanic or Latino	45	0.34
Hungarian	92	0.70
Irish	1,428	10.81
Italian	293	2.22
Lithuanian	8	0.06
Norwegian	41	0.31
Pennsylvania German	15	0.11
Polish	56	0.42
Russian	23	0.17
Scandinavian	7	0.05
Scotch-Irish	132	1.00
Scottish	170	1.29
Serbian	24	0.18
Slovene	4	0.03
Swedish	41	0.31
Swiss	26	0.20
Ukrainian	4	0.03
United States or American	1,924	14.57
Welsh	76	0.58
White:	13,064	98.27
Not Hispanic (12,853)	12,964	97.52
Hispanic (84)	100	0.75

Grove City

Place Type: City
County: Franklin
Population: 27,075

Ancestry/Race	Number	%
African American/Black:	527	1.95
Not Hispanic (405)	507	1.87
Hispanic (13)	20	0.07
African, sub-Saharan:	17	0.06
African	17	0.06
Alaska Native tribes, specified:	2	0.01
Tlingit-Haida	1	0.00
All other tribes	1	0.00
Alaska Native tribes, not specified	1	0.00
Am. Ind. or Alaska Nat., not spec.	55	0.20
American Indian tribes, specified:	110	0.41
Apache (1)	5	0.02
Blackfeet (2)	9	0.03
Cherokee (19)	61	0.23
Cheyenne (1)	1	0.00
Chippewa (5)	5	0.02
Choctaw	1	0.00
Crow	4	0.01
Iroquois	1	0.00
Latin American Indians (2)	2	0.01
Navajo (1)	3	0.01
Sioux (2)	5	0.02
All other tribes (3)	13	0.05
American Indian tribes, not spec.	17	0.06
Arab:	39	0.14
Lebanese	14	0.05
Palestinian	13	0.05
Syrian	12	0.04
Asian:	238	0.88
Cambodian (9)	14	0.05
Chinese, ex. Taiwanese (30)	39	0.14
Filipino (21)	30	0.11
Indian (54)	74	0.27
Indonesian	4	0.01
Japanese (7)	19	0.07
Korean (10)	15	0.06
Laotian (3)	6	0.02
Thai (2)	4	0.01
Vietnamese (22)	24	0.09
Other Asian, not specified	9	0.03
Austrian	7	0.03
Belgian	26	0.10
British	179	0.66
Canadian	70	0.26
Croatian	41	0.15
Czech	23	0.09
Czechoslovakian	37	0.14
Danish	15	0.06
Dutch	688	2.55
Eastern European	40	0.15
English	3,049	11.28

Notes: 1. Figures in the "Number" column do not add up to the total population due to: a) Ancestry/Race overlap — e.g. persons can report being both White and Irish, b) persons of Hispanic origin can report being any race, c) persons reporting two ancestries are counted in both categories. 2. Numbers in parentheses indicate the number of persons reporting this ancestry/race alone, not in combination with any other ancestry/race. 3. Refer to the Explanation of Data in the front of the book for more detailed information.

European	181	0.67
Finnish	9	0.03
French, except Basque	829	3.07
French Canadian	65	0.24
German	8,000	29.61
Greek	182	0.67
Hawaii Native/Pacific Islander:	9	0.03
Micronesian: (2)	2	0.01
Guamanian/Chamorro (1)	1	0.00
Other Micronesian (1)	1	0.00
Polynesian: (1)	2	0.01
Samoan (1)	1	0.00
Other Polynesian	1	0.00
Other Pac. Isl., not spec.	5	0.02
Hispanic or Latino:	318	1.17
Central American:	8	0.03
Guatemalan	2	0.01
Honduran	1	0.00
Panamanian	3	0.01
Salvadoran	1	0.00
Other Central American	1	0.00
Cuban	25	0.09
Dominican Republic	4	0.01
Mexican	137	0.51
Puerto Rican	74	0.27
South American:	11	0.04
Bolivian	1	0.00
Chilean	6	0.02
Colombian	4	0.01
Other Hispanic or Latino	59	0.22
Hungarian	206	0.76
Iranian	18	0.07
Irish	4,543	16.81
Italian	1,650	6.11
Lithuanian	49	0.18
Macedonian	13	0.05
Norwegian	135	0.50
Pennsylvania German	45	0.17
Polish	332	1.23
Portuguese	19	0.07
Romanian	6	0.02
Russian	99	0.37
Scotch-Irish	497	1.84
Scottish	579	2.14
Serbian	51	0.19
Slavic	42	0.16
Slovak	100	0.37
Swedish	149	0.55
Swiss	132	0.49
Turkish	14	0.05
Ukrainian	53	0.20
United States or American	3,250	12.03
Welsh	856	3.17
West Indian, excl. Hispanic:	8	0.03
Jamaican	8	0.03
White:	26,308	97.17
Not Hispanic (25,836)	26,087	96.35
Hispanic (203)	221	0.82
Yugoslavian	35	0.13

Hamilton

Place Type: City
County: Butler
Population: 60,690

Ancestry/Race	Number	%
Acadian/Cajun	20	0.03
African American/Black:	4,842	7.98
Not Hispanic (4,562)	4,813	7.93
Hispanic (19)	29	0.05
African, sub-Saharan:	145	0.24
African	109	0.18
Kenyan	8	0.01
South African	9	0.01
Ugandan	19	0.03
Alaska Native tribes, specified:	6	0.01
Aleut	1	0.00
Tlingit-Haida	2	0.00
All other tribes (3)	3	0.00
Am. Ind. or Alaska Nat., not spec.	168	0.28
American Indian tribes, specified:	313	0.52
Blackfeet (2)	11	0.02
Cherokee (73)	233	0.38
Chickasaw (3)	5	0.01
Chippewa (3)	12	0.02
Choctaw (1)	3	0.00
Comanche (1)	1	0.00
Cree (2)	2	0.00
Creek	1	0.00
Delaware	1	0.00
Iroquois (6)	13	0.02
Latin American Indians (5)	6	0.01
Navajo (2)	3	0.00
Ottawa	1	0.00
Potawatomi	2	0.00
Seminole (1)	1	0.00
Sioux (2)	8	0.01
All other tribes (4)	10	0.02
American Indian tribes, not spec.	31	0.05
Arab:	21	0.03
Lebanese	11	0.02
Moroccan	10	0.02
Armenian	8	0.01
Asian:	405	0.67
Cambodian (7)	8	0.01
Chinese, ex. Taiwanese (20)	26	0.04
Filipino (104)	141	0.23
Indian (25)	46	0.08
Indonesian (2)	3	0.00
Japanese (22)	34	0.06
Korean (17)	34	0.06
Malaysian (1)	4	0.01
Pakistani (1)	1	0.00
Taiwanese (1)	2	0.00
Thai (4)	10	0.02
Vietnamese (45)	48	0.08
Other Asian, specified	15	0.02
Other Asian, not specified (21)	33	0.05
Australian	7	0.01
Austrian	49	0.08
Belgian	16	0.03
British	220	0.36
Bulgarian	10	0.02
Canadian	29	0.05
Celtic	4	0.01
Croatian	7	0.01
Czech	56	0.09
Czechoslovakian	46	0.08
Danish	61	0.10
Dutch	616	1.02
English	5,211	8.59
European	395	0.65
Finnish	12	0.02
French, except Basque	1,093	1.80
French Canadian	149	0.25
German	13,113	21.62
Greek	133	0.22
Hawaii Native/Pacific Islander:	57	0.09
Micronesian: (3)	9	0.01
Guamanian/Chamorro (2)	8	0.01
Other Micronesian (1)	1	0.00
Polynesian: (20)	28	0.05
Native Hawaiian (5)	10	0.02
Samoan (14)	17	0.03
Tongan (1)	1	0.00
Other Pac. Isl., specified	12	0.02
Other Pac. Isl., not spec.	8	0.01
Hispanic or Latino:	1,566	2.58
Central American:	22	0.04
Costa Rican	1	0.00
Guatemalan	8	0.01
Honduran	8	0.01
Nicaraguan	3	0.00
Panamanian	2	0.00
Cuban	56	0.09
Dominican Republic	91	0.15
Mexican	1,073	1.77
Puerto Rican	66	0.11
South American:	25	0.04
Chilean	2	0.00
Colombian	2	0.00
Ecuadorian	15	0.02
Peruvian	4	0.01
Venezuelan	2	0.00
Other Hispanic or Latino	233	0.38
Hungarian	140	0.23
Irish	7,139	11.77
Italian	1,868	3.08
Luxemburger	5	0.01
Northern European	17	0.03
Norwegian	67	0.11
Pennsylvania German	20	0.03
Polish	540	0.89
Portuguese	36	0.06
Romanian	5	0.01
Russian	122	0.20
Scandinavian	16	0.03
Scotch-Irish	758	1.25
Scottish	773	1.27
Serbian	8	0.01
Slavic	15	0.02
Slovak	70	0.12
Swedish	243	0.40
Swiss	173	0.29
Ukrainian	26	0.04
United States or American	9,129	15.05
Welsh	275	0.45
West Indian, excl. Hispanic:	16	0.03
Dutch West Indian	7	0.01
Jamaican	9	0.01
White:	54,699	90.13
Not Hispanic (53,386)	53,999	88.98
Hispanic (589)	700	1.15

Hilliard

Place Type: City
County: Franklin
Population: 24,230

Ancestry/Race	Number	%
African American/Black:	457	1.89
Not Hispanic (339)	432	1.78
Hispanic (18)	25	0.10
African, sub-Saharan:	26	0.11
African	26	0.11
Am. Ind. or Alaska Nat., not spec.	49	0.20
American Indian tribes, specified:	68	0.28
Blackfeet (5)	7	0.03
Cherokee (12)	35	0.14
Chippewa (1)	1	0.00
Choctaw (1)	5	0.02
Comanche	1	0.00
Creek	4	0.02
Iroquois	3	0.01
Latin American Indians (1)	1	0.00
Osage	1	0.00
Potawatomi	1	0.00
Seminole	1	0.00
Sioux (3)	3	0.01
All other tribes (3)	5	0.02
American Indian tribes, not spec.	6	0.02
Arab:	219	0.91
Arab/Arabic	72	0.30
Egyptian	35	0.14
Lebanese	101	0.42
Syrian	11	0.05
Asian:	982	4.05
Bangladeshi (5)	5	0.02
Cambodian (7)	19	0.08
Chinese, ex. Taiwanese (186)	212	0.87
Filipino (56)	75	0.31
Indian (252)	277	1.14
Indonesian (12)	12	0.05
Japanese (147)	174	0.72
Korean (63)	72	0.30
Laotian (1)	1	0.00
Malaysian	1	0.00
Pakistani (6)	10	0.04

Notes: 1. Figures in the "Number" column do not add up to the total population due to: a) Ancestry/Race overlap — e.g. persons can report being both White and Irish, b) persons of Hispanic origin can report being any race, c) persons reporting two ancestries are counted in both categories. 2. Numbers in parentheses indicate the number of persons reporting this ancestry/race alone, not in combination with any other ancestry/race. 3. Refer to the Explanation of Data in the front of the book for more detailed information.

Ancestry/Race	Number	%
Sri Lankan (14)	15	0.06
Taiwanese (29)	32	0.13
Thai (8)	9	0.04
Vietnamese (36)	44	0.18
Other Asian, not specified (13)	24	0.10
Austrian	37	0.15
Basque	8	0.03
Belgian	18	0.07
British	202	0.84
Canadian	79	0.33
Croatian	65	0.27
Czech	106	0.44
Czechoslovakian	128	0.53
Danish	72	0.30
Dutch	556	2.30
English	3,065	12.67
European	254	1.05
Finnish	64	0.26
French, except Basque	861	3.56
French Canadian	63	0.26
German	7,278	30.09
Greek	156	0.65
Hawaii Native/Pacific Islander:	9	0.04
Micronesian: (1)	1	0.00
Guamanian/Chamorro (1)	1	0.00
Polynesian: (1)	4	0.02
Native Hawaiian	3	0.01
Samoan (1)	1	0.00
Other Pac. Isl., not spec. (2)	4	0.02
Hispanic or Latino:	426	1.76
Central American:	21	0.09
Costa Rican	1	0.00
Guatemalan	10	0.04
Honduran	1	0.00
Nicaraguan	1	0.00
Panamanian	6	0.02
Salvadoran	2	0.01
Cuban	20	0.08
Dominican Republic	5	0.02
Mexican	171	0.71
Puerto Rican	85	0.35
South American:	21	0.09
Argentinean	4	0.02
Chilean	4	0.02
Colombian	4	0.02
Peruvian	3	0.01
Venezuelan	1	0.00
Other South American	5	0.02
Other Hispanic or Latino	103	0.43
Hungarian	335	1.39
Irish	4,167	17.23
Italian	1,897	7.84
Lithuanian	29	0.12
Macedonian	22	0.09
Norwegian	195	0.81
Pennsylvania German	22	0.09
Polish	915	3.78
Portuguese	23	0.10
Romanian	29	0.12
Russian	103	0.43
Scandinavian	16	0.07
Scotch-Irish	560	2.32
Scottish	698	2.89
Serbian	18	0.07
Slavic	42	0.17
Slovak	182	0.75
Slovene	52	0.22
Swedish	228	0.94
Swiss	146	0.60
Turkish	8	0.03
Ukrainian	80	0.33
United States or American	1,998	8.26
Welsh	509	2.10
White:	22,759	93.93
Not Hispanic (22,268)	22,516	92.93
Hispanic (221)	243	1.00
Yugoslavian	23	0.10

Huber Heights

Place Type: City
County: Montgomery
Population: 38,212

Ancestry/Race	Number	%
African American/Black:	4,182	10.94
Not Hispanic (3,703)	4,117	10.77
Hispanic (34)	65	0.17
African, sub-Saharan:	140	0.37
African	125	0.33
Nigerian	15	0.04
Am. Ind. or Alaska Nat., not spec.	95	0.25
American Indian tribes, specified:	201	0.53
Apache (5)	10	0.03
Blackfeet (5)	16	0.04
Cherokee (25)	113	0.30
Cheyenne	1	0.00
Chippewa (1)	1	0.00
Choctaw (7)	8	0.02
Creek (1)	3	0.01
Delaware (3)	3	0.01
Iroquois	4	0.01
Kiowa	1	0.00
Latin American Indians (1)	2	0.01
Lumbee	1	0.00
Navajo (4)	7	0.02
Potawatomi (1)	1	0.00
Seminole	2	0.01
Sioux (5)	9	0.02
All other tribes (6)	19	0.05
American Indian tribes, not spec.	26	0.07
Arab:	219	0.57
Arab/Arabic	108	0.28
Egyptian	15	0.04
Iraqi	5	0.01
Jordanian	46	0.12
Lebanese	9	0.02
Palestinian	16	0.04
Syrian	20	0.05
Asian:	1,097	2.87
Bangladeshi (3)	3	0.01
Cambodian (6)	6	0.02
Chinese, ex. Taiwanese (56)	73	0.19
Filipino (140)	218	0.57
Indian (105)	120	0.31
Indonesian (1)	1	0.00
Japanese (107)	169	0.44
Korean (98)	146	0.38
Laotian (17)	17	0.04
Malaysian	2	0.01
Pakistani (12)	12	0.03
Taiwanese (2)	3	0.01
Thai (33)	40	0.10
Vietnamese (226)	245	0.64
Other Asian, specified (2)	4	0.01
Other Asian, not specified (15)	38	0.10
Assyrian/Chaldean/Syriac	5	0.01
Australian	7	0.02
Austrian	97	0.25
Belgian	45	0.12
Brazilian	7	0.02
British	116	0.30
Canadian	40	0.10
Celtic	5	0.01
Croatian	14	0.04
Czech	79	0.21
Czechoslovakian	40	0.10
Danish	87	0.23
Dutch	709	1.85
Eastern European	6	0.02
English	3,929	10.27
European	331	0.86
Finnish	42	0.11
French, except Basque	1,030	2.69
French Canadian	230	0.60
German	9,511	24.85
German Russian	11	0.03
Greek	98	0.26
Hawaii Native/Pacific Islander:	40	0.10
Micronesian: (2)	12	0.03
Guamanian/Chamorro (1)	9	0.02
Other Micronesian (1)	3	0.01
Polynesian: (14)	18	0.05
Native Hawaiian (14)	18	0.05
Other Pac. Isl., not spec. (7)	10	0.03
Hispanic or Latino:	635	1.66
Central American:	24	0.06
Guatemalan	1	0.00
Honduran	3	0.01
Panamanian	18	0.05
Salvadoran	2	0.01
Cuban	23	0.06
Dominican Republic	4	0.01
Mexican	237	0.62
Puerto Rican	141	0.37
South American:	41	0.11
Argentinean	6	0.02
Chilean	6	0.02
Colombian	2	0.01
Ecuadorian	6	0.02
Peruvian	5	0.01
Uruguayan	4	0.01
Venezuelan	12	0.03
Other Hispanic or Latino	165	0.43
Hungarian	466	1.22
Irish	4,412	11.53
Italian	1,404	3.67
Lithuanian	100	0.26
Norwegian	245	0.64
Pennsylvania German	27	0.07
Polish	934	2.44
Portuguese	24	0.06
Romanian	73	0.19
Russian	58	0.15
Scandinavian	74	0.19
Scotch-Irish	628	1.64
Scottish	875	2.29
Slavic	13	0.03
Slovak	93	0.24
Slovene	44	0.11
Swedish	282	0.74
Swiss	121	0.32
Turkish	22	0.06
Ukrainian	22	0.06
United States or American	3,720	9.72
Welsh	355	0.93
West Indian, excl. Hispanic:	104	0.27
British West Indian	7	0.02
Jamaican	42	0.11
Trinidadian and Tobagonian	44	0.11
West Indian	11	0.03
White:	33,170	86.81
Not Hispanic (32,075)	32,760	85.73
Hispanic (358)	410	1.07
Yugoslavian	15	0.04

Hudson

Place Type: City
County: Summit
Population: 22,439

Ancestry/Race	Number	%
African American/Black:	364	1.62
Not Hispanic (331)	361	1.61
Hispanic (2)	3	0.01
Am. Ind. or Alaska Nat., not spec.	14	0.06
Alsatian	22	0.10
American Indian tribes, specified:	38	0.17
Cherokee (2)	12	0.05
Chippewa (4)	5	0.02
Choctaw (2)	4	0.02
Iroquois (4)	8	0.04
Latin American Indians (1)	5	0.02
Seminole	1	0.00
Ute (3)	3	0.01
American Indian tribes, not spec.	3	0.01
Arab:	109	0.49

Notes: 1. Figures in the "Number" column do not add up to the total population due to: a) Ancestry/Race overlap — e.g. persons can report being both White and Irish, b) persons of Hispanic origin can report being any race, c) persons reporting two ancestries are counted in both categories. 2. Numbers in parentheses indicate the number of persons reporting this ancestry/race alone, not in combination with any other ancestry/race. 3. Refer to the Explanation of Data in the front of the book for more detailed information.

Ancestry/Race	Number	%
Arab/Arabic	9	0.04
Lebanese	89	0.40
Palestinian	3	0.01
Syrian	8	0.04
Armenian	36	0.16
Asian:	751	3.35
Chinese, ex. Taiwanese (245)	263	1.17
Filipino (33)	55	0.25
Indian (178)	190	0.85
Indonesian (5)	5	0.02
Japanese (68)	91	0.41
Korean (64)	83	0.37
Pakistani (2)	3	0.01
Sri Lankan (2)	2	0.01
Taiwanese (16)	21	0.09
Thai (5)	9	0.04
Vietnamese (4)	11	0.05
Other Asian, not specified (2)	18	0.08
Australian	26	0.12
Austrian	102	0.46
Belgian	55	0.25
British	285	1.27
Canadian	114	0.51
Croatian	220	0.98
Czech	240	1.07
Czechoslovakian	120	0.54
Danish	132	0.59
Dutch	434	1.94
Eastern European	17	0.08
English	3,899	17.42
Estonian	7	0.03
European	200	0.89
Finnish	61	0.27
French, except Basque	431	1.93
French Canadian	142	0.63
German	6,727	30.06
Greek	118	0.53
Hawaii Native/Pacific Islander:	2	0.01
Polynesian: (1)	1	0.00
Samoan (1)	1	0.00
Other Pac. Isl., not spec.	1	0.00
Hispanic or Latino:	184	0.82
Central American:	7	0.03
Costa Rican	1	0.00
Guatemalan	3	0.01
Honduran	2	0.01
Nicaraguan	1	0.00
Cuban	18	0.08
Dominican Republic	1	0.00
Mexican	61	0.27
Puerto Rican	15	0.07
South American:	39	0.17
Argentinean	4	0.02
Bolivian	2	0.01
Chilean	6	0.03
Colombian	9	0.04
Ecuadorian	1	0.00
Paraguayan	1	0.00
Peruvian	4	0.02
Venezuelan	12	0.05
Other Hispanic or Latino	43	0.19
Hungarian	524	2.34
Iranian	19	0.08
Irish	4,431	19.80
Italian	2,377	10.62
Lithuanian	115	0.51
Maltese	23	0.10
Northern European	21	0.09
Norwegian	339	1.51
Pennsylvania German	8	0.04
Polish	1,624	7.26
Portuguese	19	0.08
Romanian	61	0.27
Russian	451	2.02
Scandinavian	71	0.32
Scotch-Irish	554	2.48
Scottish	679	3.03
Serbian	32	0.14
Slavic	52	0.23
Slovak	558	2.49
Slovene	299	1.34
Swedish	485	2.17
Swiss	192	0.86
Ukrainian	217	0.97
United States or American	821	3.67
Welsh	351	1.57
White:	21,390	95.33
Not Hispanic (21,102)	21,237	94.64
Hispanic (137)	153	0.68
Yugoslavian	16	0.07

Ironton

Place Type: City
County: Lawrence
Population: 11,211

Ancestry/Race	Number	%
African American/Black:	651	5.81
Not Hispanic (584)	646	5.76
Hispanic (3)	5	0.04
African, sub-Saharan:	21	0.19
African	21	0.19
Am. Ind. or Alaska Nat., not spec.	16	0.14
American Indian tribes, specified:	30	0.27
Apache	2	0.02
Blackfeet	1	0.01
Cherokee (6)	25	0.22
Navajo	2	0.02
American Indian tribes, not spec.	2	0.02
Arab:	26	0.23
Lebanese	26	0.23
Asian:	42	0.37
Chinese, ex. Taiwanese (4)	5	0.04
Filipino (13)	18	0.16
Indian (5)	5	0.04
Japanese (1)	2	0.02
Korean	1	0.01
Taiwanese (1)	1	0.01
Vietnamese (1)	2	0.02
Other Asian, specified (2)	2	0.02
Other Asian, not specified (1)	6	0.05
British	14	0.12
Canadian	12	0.11
Czech	11	0.10
Czechoslovakian	7	0.06
Dutch	137	1.21
English	1,089	9.65
European	26	0.23
French, except Basque	126	1.12
French Canadian	38	0.34
German	1,561	13.83
Greek	11	0.10
Hawaii Native/Pacific Islander:	10	0.09
Micronesian: (1)	2	0.02
Guamanian/Chamorro (1)	2	0.02
Polynesian:	2	0.02
Native Hawaiian	1	0.01
Samoan	1	0.01
Other Pac. Isl., not spec. (1)	6	0.05
Hispanic or Latino:	57	0.51
Central American:	2	0.02
Guatemalan	2	0.02
Cuban	5	0.04
Mexican	10	0.09
Puerto Rican	10	0.09
South American:	1	0.01
Venezuelan	1	0.01
Other Hispanic or Latino	29	0.26
Hungarian	14	0.12
Irish	1,312	11.63
Italian	87	0.77
Norwegian	15	0.13
Polish	37	0.33
Scandinavian	10	0.09
Scotch-Irish	99	0.88
Scottish	121	1.07
Slovak	22	0.19
Swedish	24	0.21
Swiss	16	0.14
United States or American	2,042	18.09
Welsh	205	1.82
White:	10,570	94.28
Not Hispanic (10,435)	10,527	93.90
Hispanic (28)	43	0.38

Kent

Place Type: City
County: Portage
Population: 27,906

Ancestry/Race	Number	%
African American/Black:	2,838	10.17
Not Hispanic (2,533)	2,814	10.08
Hispanic (8)	24	0.09
African, sub-Saharan:	273	0.98
African	210	0.75
Ethiopian	7	0.03
Kenyan	11	0.04
Liberian	37	0.13
Zimbabwean	8	0.03
Am. Ind. or Alaska Nat., not spec.	67	0.24
Albanian	18	0.06
Alsatian	10	0.04
American Indian tribes, specified:	129	0.46
Blackfeet	11	0.04
Cherokee (10)	52	0.19
Cheyenne	1	0.00
Chickasaw (1)	3	0.01
Chippewa (6)	7	0.03
Choctaw (1)	3	0.01
Creek	1	0.00
Crow	1	0.00
Delaware (1)	6	0.02
Iroquois (1)	10	0.04
Latin American Indians	4	0.01
Lumbee (1)	1	0.00
Navajo (1)	1	0.00
Potawatomi (3)	3	0.01
Seminole (1)	5	0.02
Sioux (3)	15	0.05
All other tribes (1)	5	0.02
American Indian tribes, not spec.	17	0.06
Arab:	267	0.95
Arab/Arabic	108	0.39
Lebanese	96	0.34
Syrian	63	0.23
Asian:	709	2.54
Bangladeshi (4)	4	0.01
Cambodian (1)	3	0.01
Chinese, ex. Taiwanese (222)	239	0.86
Filipino (25)	42	0.15
Indian (139)	160	0.57
Indonesian (1)	3	0.01
Japanese (47)	63	0.23
Korean (78)	86	0.31
Laotian (5)	5	0.02
Malaysian (3)	3	0.01
Pakistani (15)	15	0.05
Sri Lankan (8)	9	0.03
Taiwanese (4)	12	0.04
Thai (7)	10	0.04
Vietnamese (11)	14	0.05
Other Asian, specified (7)	8	0.03
Other Asian, not specified (10)	33	0.12
Australian	26	0.09
Austrian	53	0.19
Belgian	58	0.21
British	239	0.85
Bulgarian	8	0.03
Canadian	46	0.16
Carpatho Rusyn	6	0.02
Celtic	19	0.07
Croatian	149	0.53
Czech	205	0.73
Czechoslovakian	112	0.40
Danish	68	0.24
Dutch	503	1.80
Eastern European	6	0.02

Notes: 1. Figures in the "Number" column do not add up to the total population due to: a) Ancestry/Race overlap — e.g. persons can report being both White and Irish, b) persons of Hispanic origin can report being any race, c) persons reporting two ancestries are counted in both categories. 2. Numbers in parentheses indicate the number of persons reporting this ancestry/race alone, not in combination with any other ancestry/race. 3. Refer to the Explanation of Data in the front of the book for more detailed information.

English	3,085	11.02
Estonian	10	0.04
European	183	0.65
Finnish	126	0.45
French, except Basque	851	3.04
French Canadian	179	0.64
German	7,271	25.97
Greek	200	0.71
Hawaii Native/Pacific Islander:	22	0.08
Micronesian: (2)	6	0.02
Guamanian/Chamorro (2)	6	0.02
Polynesian: (5)	7	0.03
Native Hawaiian (4)	6	0.02
Samoan (1)	1	0.00
Other Pac. Isl., not spec. (2)	9	0.03
Hispanic or Latino:	357	1.28
Central American:	10	0.04
Guatemalan	1	0.00
Panamanian	3	0.01
Salvadoran	5	0.02
Other Central American	1	0.00
Cuban	20	0.07
Dominican Republic	1	0.00
Mexican	131	0.47
Puerto Rican	76	0.27
South American:	37	0.13
Argentinean	10	0.04
Chilean	8	0.03
Colombian	8	0.03
Ecuadorian	3	0.01
Peruvian	5	0.02
Venezuelan	3	0.01
Other Hispanic or Latino	82	0.29
Hungarian	748	2.67
Iranian	10	0.04
Irish	4,188	14.96
Israeli	7	0.03
Italian	3,016	10.77
Lithuanian	79	0.28
Macedonian	10	0.04
New Zealander	7	0.03
Northern European	25	0.09
Norwegian	165	0.59
Pennsylvania German	24	0.09
Polish	1,470	5.25
Portuguese	21	0.08
Romanian	87	0.31
Russian	254	0.91
Scandinavian	31	0.11
Scotch-Irish	444	1.59
Scottish	795	2.84
Serbian	53	0.19
Slavic	22	0.08
Slovak	395	1.41
Slovene	184	0.66
Swedish	364	1.30
Swiss	155	0.55
Turkish	81	0.29
Ukrainian	193	0.69
United States or American	1,253	4.48
Welsh	411	1.47
West Indian, excl. Hispanic:	39	0.14
Barbadian	4	0.01
Jamaican	24	0.09
Trinidadian and Tobagonian	11	0.04
White:	24,523	87.88
Not Hispanic (23,807)	24,270	86.97
Hispanic (211)	253	0.91
Yugoslavian	15	0.05

Kettering

Place Type: City
County: Montgomery
Population: 57,502

Ancestry/Race	Number	%
Acadian/Cajun	4	0.01
African American/Black:	1,162	2.02
Not Hispanic (942)	1,133	1.97
Hispanic (13)	29	0.05
African, sub-Saharan:	39	0.07
African	17	0.03
Kenyan	6	0.01
Nigerian	16	0.03
Alaska Native tribes, specified:	2	0.00
Aleut (1)	1	0.00
Eskimo (1)	1	0.00
Am. Ind. or Alaska Nat., not spec.	110	0.19
Albanian	20	0.03
American Indian tribes, specified:	191	0.33
Apache	1	0.00
Blackfeet (2)	3	0.01
Cherokee (42)	125	0.22
Chickasaw	2	0.00
Chippewa (4)	6	0.01
Choctaw	1	0.00
Comanche	2	0.00
Delaware	1	0.00
Iroquois (2)	13	0.02
Latin American Indians	3	0.01
Lumbee (1)	1	0.00
Navajo (1)	2	0.00
Ottawa (1)	1	0.00
Pima (1)	1	0.00
Potawatomi (2)	2	0.00
Pueblo (1)	1	0.00
Seminole (1)	1	0.00
Yuman (1)	1	0.00
All other tribes (14)	24	0.04
American Indian tribes, not spec.	10	0.02
Arab:	194	0.34
Arab/Arabic	35	0.06
Egyptian	28	0.05
Jordanian	37	0.06
Lebanese	66	0.11
Syrian	22	0.04
Other Arab	6	0.01
Armenian	19	0.03
Asian:	1,032	1.79
Bangladeshi (4)	4	0.01
Chinese, ex. Taiwanese (158)	184	0.32
Filipino (108)	157	0.27
Indian (182)	215	0.37
Indonesian (6)	18	0.03
Japanese (57)	108	0.19
Korean (79)	104	0.18
Laotian (8)	8	0.01
Malaysian (3)	5	0.01
Pakistani (19)	25	0.04
Sri Lankan (2)	2	0.00
Taiwanese (16)	20	0.03
Thai (9)	15	0.03
Vietnamese (107)	120	0.21
Other Asian, specified	1	0.00
Other Asian, not specified (23)	46	0.08
Assyrian/Chaldean/Syriac	6	0.01
Austrian	129	0.22
Belgian	38	0.07
British	251	0.44
Canadian	121	0.21
Celtic	6	0.01
Croatian	29	0.05
Czech	161	0.28
Czechoslovakian	152	0.26
Danish	117	0.20
Dutch	1,366	2.37
Eastern European	67	0.12
English	7,303	12.69
European	627	1.09
Finnish	37	0.06
French, except Basque	2,086	3.63
French Canadian	365	0.63
German	19,450	33.81
Greek	350	0.61
Hawaii Native/Pacific Islander:	43	0.07
Micronesian: (2)	9	0.02
Guamanian/Chamorro (2)	9	0.02
Polynesian: (9)	20	0.03
Native Hawaiian (8)	19	0.03
Samoan (1)	1	0.00
Other Pac. Isl., specified	1	0.00
Other Pac. Isl., not spec. (3)	13	0.02
Hispanic or Latino:	640	1.11
Central American:	24	0.04
Costa Rican	8	0.01
Guatemalan	5	0.01
Honduran	3	0.01
Nicaraguan	1	0.00
Panamanian	5	0.01
Salvadoran	1	0.00
Other Central American	1	0.00
Cuban	61	0.11
Dominican Republic	3	0.01
Mexican	239	0.42
Puerto Rican	112	0.19
South American:	59	0.10
Argentinean	7	0.01
Bolivian	9	0.02
Chilean	1	0.00
Colombian	24	0.04
Ecuadorian	3	0.01
Peruvian	7	0.01
Uruguayan	1	0.00
Venezuelan	7	0.01
Other Hispanic or Latino	142	0.25
Hungarian	763	1.33
Iranian	46	0.08
Irish	8,909	15.49
Italian	2,695	4.68
Lithuanian	157	0.27
Macedonian	18	0.03
Maltese	6	0.01
Northern European	66	0.11
Norwegian	366	0.64
Pennsylvania German	78	0.14
Polish	1,357	2.36
Portuguese	84	0.15
Romanian	39	0.07
Russian	250	0.43
Scandinavian	41	0.07
Scotch-Irish	1,267	2.20
Scottish	1,563	2.72
Serbian	22	0.04
Slavic	27	0.05
Slovak	226	0.39
Slovene	68	0.12
Swedish	441	0.77
Swiss	358	0.62
Turkish	3	0.01
Ukrainian	123	0.21
United States or American	4,970	8.64
Welsh	686	1.19
West Indian, excl. Hispanic:	55	0.10
Barbadian	11	0.02
Jamaican	34	0.06
West Indian	10	0.02
White:	55,389	96.33
Not Hispanic (54,338)	54,906	95.49
Hispanic (419)	483	0.84
Yugoslavian	12	0.02

Lakewood

Place Type: City
County: Cuyahoga
Population: 56,646

Ancestry/Race	Number	%
Afghan	6	0.01
African American/Black:	1,413	2.49
Not Hispanic (1,088)	1,355	2.39
Hispanic (28)	58	0.10
African, sub-Saharan:	104	0.18
African	40	0.07
Ethiopian	7	0.01
Liberian	37	0.07
South African	9	0.02
Other sub-Saharan African	11	0.02
Alaska Native tribes, specified:	4	0.01

Notes: 1. Figures in the "Number" column do not add up to the total population due to: a) Ancestry/Race overlap — e.g. persons can report being both White and Irish, b) persons of Hispanic origin can report being any race, c) persons reporting two ancestries are counted in both categories. 2. Numbers in parentheses indicate the number of persons reporting this ancestry/race alone, not in combination with any other ancestry/race. 3. Refer to the Explanation of Data in the front of the book for more detailed information.

Aleut (1)	1	0.00
Tlingit-Haida (3)	3	0.01
Alaska Native tribes, not specified	2	0.00
Am. Ind. or Alaska Nat., not spec.	130	0.23
Albanian	593	1.05
American Indian tribes, specified:	259	0.46
Apache (1)	4	0.01
Blackfeet (4)	15	0.03
Cherokee (25)	122	0.22
Chickasaw (3)	3	0.01
Chippewa (9)	11	0.02
Choctaw (1)	7	0.01
Comanche (1)	3	0.01
Cree (2)	5	0.01
Creek	1	0.00
Iroquois	18	0.03
Latin American Indians (8)	10	0.02
Lumbee	3	0.01
Navajo (2)	7	0.01
Osage (1)	2	0.00
Ottawa (1)	1	0.00
Pueblo	1	0.00
Sioux (15)	26	0.05
Tohono O'Odham	1	0.00
All other tribes (5)	19	0.03
American Indian tribes, not spec.	18	0.03
Arab:	2,371	4.19
Arab/Arabic	721	1.27
Egyptian	118	0.21
Iraqi	7	0.01
Jordanian	106	0.19
Lebanese	645	1.14
Moroccan	26	0.05
Palestinian	473	0.84
Syrian	213	0.38
Other Arab	62	0.11
Armenian	45	0.08
Asian:	1,058	1.87
Bangladeshi (1)	1	0.00
Cambodian	1	0.00
Chinese, ex. Taiwanese (126)	155	0.27
Filipino (58)	111	0.20
Indian (289)	322	0.57
Indonesian (43)	46	0.08
Japanese (61)	98	0.17
Korean (50)	59	0.10
Malaysian (5)	7	0.01
Pakistani (25)	48	0.08
Sri Lankan (3)	3	0.01
Taiwanese (10)	11	0.02
Thai (24)	30	0.05
Vietnamese (58)	71	0.13
Other Asian, specified (6)	10	0.02
Other Asian, not specified (28)	85	0.15
Assyrian/Chaldean/Syriac	6	0.01
Australian	30	0.05
Austrian	385	0.68
Belgian	75	0.13
Brazilian	20	0.04
British	252	0.44
Bulgarian	15	0.03
Canadian	88	0.16
Carpatho Rusyn	15	0.03
Celtic	5	0.01
Croatian	536	0.95
Cypriot	7	0.01
Czech	1,014	1.79
Czechoslovakian	446	0.79
Danish	152	0.27
Dutch	748	1.32
Eastern European	43	0.08
English	5,544	9.79
Estonian	39	0.07
European	351	0.62
Finnish	214	0.38
French, except Basque	1,574	2.78
French Canadian	339	0.60
German	14,269	25.19
Greek	703	1.24
Hawaii Native/Pacific Islander:	41	0.07
Micronesian: (5)	5	0.01
Guamanian/Chamorro (5)	5	0.01
Polynesian: (8)	18	0.03
Native Hawaiian (2)	10	0.02
Samoan (6)	7	0.01
Other Polynesian	1	0.00
Other Pac. Isl., specified	2	0.00
Other Pac. Isl., not spec. (2)	16	0.03
Hispanic or Latino:	1,269	2.24
Central American:	52	0.09
Costa Rican	5	0.01
Guatemalan	21	0.04
Honduran	1	0.00
Nicaraguan	6	0.01
Panamanian	4	0.01
Salvadoran	11	0.02
Other Central American	4	0.01
Cuban	50	0.09
Dominican Republic	20	0.04
Mexican	270	0.48
Puerto Rican	538	0.95
South American:	116	0.20
Argentinean	16	0.03
Chilean	11	0.02
Colombian	32	0.06
Ecuadorian	6	0.01
Paraguayan	1	0.00
Peruvian	21	0.04
Venezuelan	24	0.04
Other South American	5	0.01
Other Hispanic or Latino	223	0.39
Hungarian	2,674	4.72
Iranian	23	0.04
Irish	13,379	23.62
Israeli	9	0.02
Italian	5,066	8.94
Latvian	141	0.25
Lithuanian	299	0.53
Luxemburger	9	0.02
Macedonian	92	0.16
Maltese	5	0.01
Northern European	9	0.02
Norwegian	366	0.65
Pennsylvania German	46	0.08
Polish	4,406	7.78
Portuguese	35	0.06
Romanian	582	1.03
Russian	733	1.29
Scandinavian	12	0.02
Scotch-Irish	1,014	1.79
Scottish	1,393	2.46
Serbian	296	0.52
Slavic	91	0.16
Slovak	3,006	5.31
Slovene	662	1.17
Swedish	572	1.01
Swiss	338	0.60
Turkish	18	0.03
Ukrainian	663	1.17
United States or American	1,642	2.90
Welsh	696	1.23
West Indian, excl. Hispanic:	45	0.08
Bermudan	6	0.01
Haitian	4	0.01
Jamaican	35	0.06
White:	54,128	95.55
Not Hispanic (51,921)	53,217	93.95
Hispanic (802)	911	1.61
Yugoslavian	254	0.45

Lancaster

Place Type: City
County: Fairfield
Population: 35,335

Ancestry/Race	Number	%
African American/Black:	356	1.01
Not Hispanic (214)	350	0.99
Hispanic	6	0.02
African, sub-Saharan:	7	0.02
Ugandan	7	0.02
Am. Ind. or Alaska Nat., not spec.	89	0.25
American Indian tribes, specified:	190	0.54
Apache (2)	4	0.01
Blackfeet (4)	9	0.03
Cherokee (49)	117	0.33
Cheyenne	3	0.01
Chippewa (3)	3	0.01
Cree	1	0.00
Creek	3	0.01
Iroquois (3)	5	0.01
Latin American Indians (1)	2	0.01
Lumbee	1	0.00
Navajo (5)	9	0.03
Pueblo	1	0.00
Seminole (1)	6	0.02
Sioux (3)	9	0.03
Ute	4	0.01
All other tribes (10)	13	0.04
American Indian tribes, not spec.	9	0.03
Arab:	36	0.10
Egyptian	10	0.03
Lebanese	5	0.01
Palestinian	6	0.02
Other Arab	15	0.04
Armenian	12	0.03
Asian:	226	0.64
Cambodian (4)	4	0.01
Chinese, ex. Taiwanese (25)	32	0.09
Filipino (23)	31	0.09
Indian (27)	40	0.11
Indonesian (3)	5	0.01
Japanese (15)	23	0.07
Korean (21)	32	0.09
Pakistani (12)	12	0.03
Taiwanese (1)	1	0.00
Thai (3)	6	0.02
Vietnamese (25)	25	0.07
Other Asian, not specified (5)	15	0.04
Australian	22	0.06
Austrian	100	0.28
Belgian	50	0.14
British	95	0.27
Canadian	15	0.04
Czech	84	0.24
Czechoslovakian	10	0.03
Danish	55	0.16
Dutch	1,025	2.91
Eastern European	28	0.08
English	3,091	8.76
European	83	0.24
Finnish	6	0.02
French, except Basque	902	2.56
French Canadian	79	0.22
German	9,738	27.61
Greek	64	0.18
Hawaii Native/Pacific Islander:	24	0.07
Micronesian: (2)	2	0.01
Guamanian/Chamorro (1)	1	0.00
Other Micronesian (1)	1	0.00
Polynesian: (9)	19	0.05
Native Hawaiian (7)	16	0.05
Samoan (2)	3	0.01
Other Pac. Isl., not spec. (2)	3	0.01
Hispanic or Latino:	291	0.82
Central American:	15	0.04
Costa Rican	3	0.01
Guatemalan	6	0.02
Honduran	1	0.00
Panamanian	2	0.01
Salvadoran	3	0.01
Cuban	8	0.02
Dominican Republic	1	0.00
Mexican	112	0.32
Puerto Rican	57	0.16
South American:	12	0.03
Colombian	1	0.00
Ecuadorian	6	0.02
Venezuelan	4	0.01

Notes: 1. Figures in the "Number" column do not add up to the total population due to: a) Ancestry/Race overlap — e.g. persons can report being both White and Irish, b) persons of Hispanic origin can report being any race, c) persons reporting two ancestries are counted in both categories. 2. Numbers in parentheses indicate the number of persons reporting this ancestry/race alone, not in combination with any other ancestry/race. 3. Refer to the Explanation of Data in the front of the book for more detailed information.

Other South American	1	0.00
Other Hispanic or Latino	86	0.24
Hungarian	144	0.41
Irish	4,736	13.43
Italian	1,092	3.10
Lithuanian	16	0.05
Northern European	23	0.07
Norwegian	130	0.37
Pennsylvania German	72	0.20
Polish	294	0.83
Portuguese	7	0.02
Romanian	22	0.06
Russian	38	0.11
Scotch-Irish	495	1.40
Scottish	621	1.76
Serbian	6	0.02
Slavic	5	0.01
Slovak	18	0.05
Slovene	44	0.12
Swedish	116	0.33
Swiss	120	0.34
Turkish	33	0.09
United States or American	5,372	15.23
Welsh	540	1.53
West Indian, excl. Hispanic:	7	0.02
Dutch West Indian	7	0.02
White:	34,748	98.34
Not Hispanic (34,220)	34,522	97.70
Hispanic (189)	226	0.64
Yugoslavian	9	0.03

Landen

Place Type: Census Designated Place
County: Warren
Population: 12,766

Ancestry/Race	Number	%
African American/Black:	236	1.85
Not Hispanic (182)	223	1.75
Hispanic (7)	13	0.10
African, sub-Saharan:	31	0.25
South African	31	0.25
Am. Ind. or Alaska Nat., not spec.	8	0.06
American Indian tribes, specified:	39	0.31
Blackfeet (1)	4	0.03
Cherokee (3)	24	0.19
Chippewa (1)	2	0.02
Choctaw (1)	4	0.03
Lumbee (3)	4	0.03
All other tribes	1	0.01
Arab:	73	0.58
Jordanian	35	0.28
Lebanese	8	0.06
Palestinian	30	0.24
Armenian	11	0.09
Asian:	405	3.17
Chinese, ex. Taiwanese (37)	52	0.41
Filipino (33)	46	0.36
Indian (133)	139	1.09
Japanese (62)	78	0.61
Korean (43)	45	0.35
Malaysian	1	0.01
Pakistani (6)	6	0.05
Taiwanese (4)	4	0.03
Thai (2)	2	0.02
Vietnamese (14)	17	0.13
Other Asian, specified	8	0.06
Other Asian, not specified (3)	7	0.05
Austrian	29	0.23
British	107	0.85
Bulgarian	8	0.06
Canadian	16	0.13
Croatian	52	0.41
Czech	62	0.49
Czechoslovakian	50	0.40
Danish	65	0.51
Dutch	263	2.08
Eastern European	20	0.16
English	1,574	12.45
European	143	1.13
Finnish	37	0.29
French, except Basque	282	2.23
French Canadian	52	0.41
German	4,604	36.41
Greek	94	0.74
Hawaii Native/Pacific Islander:	30	0.23
Micronesian: (8)	8	0.06
Guamanian/Chamorro (8)	8	0.06
Polynesian: (5)	14	0.11
Native Hawaiian (1)	9	0.07
Samoan (4)	5	0.04
Other Pac. Isl., not spec.	8	0.06
Hispanic or Latino:	278	2.18
Central American:	20	0.16
Costa Rican	1	0.01
Guatemalan	5	0.04
Honduran	1	0.01
Nicaraguan	1	0.01
Panamanian	2	0.02
Salvadoran	5	0.04
Other Central American	5	0.04
Cuban	30	0.23
Mexican	150	1.17
Puerto Rican	15	0.12
South American:	27	0.21
Argentinean	1	0.01
Bolivian	1	0.01
Colombian	9	0.07
Ecuadorian	2	0.02
Paraguayan	1	0.01
Peruvian	11	0.09
Uruguayan	1	0.01
Other South American	1	0.01
Other Hispanic or Latino	36	0.28
Hungarian	174	1.38
Icelander	11	0.09
Iranian	7	0.06
Irish	2,336	18.47
Italian	842	6.66
Latvian	10	0.08
Lithuanian	42	0.33
Luxemburger	23	0.18
Macedonian	9	0.07
Northern European	18	0.14
Norwegian	103	0.81
Polish	247	1.95
Portuguese	30	0.24
Romanian	63	0.50
Russian	215	1.70
Scotch-Irish	212	1.68
Scottish	273	2.16
Slavic	8	0.06
Slovak	65	0.51
Swedish	121	0.96
Swiss	67	0.53
Ukrainian	9	0.07
United States or American	793	6.27
Welsh	64	0.51
White:	12,099	94.78
Not Hispanic (11,823)	11,921	93.38
Hispanic (159)	178	1.39
Yugoslavian	6	0.05

Lebanon

Place Type: City
County: Warren
Population: 16,962

Ancestry/Race	Number	%
Acadian/Cajun	7	0.04
African American/Black:	1,159	6.83
Not Hispanic (1,070)	1,150	6.78
Hispanic (9)	9	0.05
African, sub-Saharan:	9	0.05
African	9	0.05
Am. Ind. or Alaska Nat., not spec.	49	0.29
American Indian tribes, specified:	69	0.41
Apache (1)	4	0.02
Blackfeet	3	0.02
Cherokee (18)	42	0.25
Chippewa (4)	4	0.02
Choctaw (2)	3	0.02
Creek (2)	2	0.01
Iroquois	4	0.02
Kiowa (2)	2	0.01
Navajo (1)	1	0.01
Pueblo (1)	1	0.01
Seminole	1	0.01
Sioux	1	0.01
All other tribes	1	0.01
American Indian tribes, not spec.	16	0.09
Arab:	9	0.05
Lebanese	9	0.05
Asian:	148	0.87
Chinese, ex. Taiwanese (5)	7	0.04
Filipino (14)	19	0.11
Indian (18)	35	0.21
Japanese (21)	26	0.15
Korean (15)	25	0.15
Vietnamese (27)	28	0.17
Other Asian, not specified (8)	8	0.05
Austrian	53	0.31
British	90	0.53
Bulgarian	45	0.27
Croatian	4	0.02
Czech	41	0.24
Czechoslovakian	17	0.10
Danish	128	0.76
Dutch	203	1.20
English	1,508	8.95
European	98	0.58
Finnish	28	0.17
French, except Basque	380	2.26
French Canadian	36	0.21
German	3,453	20.50
Greek	40	0.24
Hawaii Native/Pacific Islander:	21	0.12
Polynesian: (3)	6	0.04
Native Hawaiian (2)	5	0.03
Samoan (1)	1	0.01
Other Pac. Isl., not spec.	15	0.09
Hispanic or Latino:	191	1.13
Central American:	20	0.12
Costa Rican	12	0.07
Guatemalan	2	0.01
Honduran	1	0.01
Panamanian	2	0.01
Salvadoran	2	0.01
Other Central American	1	0.01
Cuban	3	0.02
Mexican	111	0.65
Puerto Rican	15	0.09
South American:	7	0.04
Colombian	3	0.02
Peruvian	2	0.01
Venezuelan	1	0.01
Other South American	1	0.01
Other Hispanic or Latino	35	0.21
Hungarian	144	0.85
Irish	1,932	11.47
Italian	535	3.18
Lithuanian	26	0.15
Norwegian	53	0.31
Pennsylvania German	18	0.11
Polish	284	1.69
Portuguese	5	0.03
Russian	92	0.55
Scandinavian	47	0.28
Scotch-Irish	240	1.42
Scottish	254	1.51
Slavic	7	0.04
Slovak	41	0.24
Swedish	59	0.35
Swiss	56	0.33
Ukrainian	11	0.07
United States or American	2,616	15.53
Welsh	93	0.55
West Indian, excl. Hispanic:	8	0.05

Notes: 1. Figures in the "Number" column do not add up to the total population due to: a) Ancestry/Race overlap — e.g. persons can report being both White and Irish, b) persons of Hispanic origin can report being any race, c) persons reporting two ancestries are counted in both categories. 2. Numbers in parentheses indicate the number of persons reporting this ancestry/race alone, not in combination with any other ancestry/race. 3. Refer to the Explanation of Data in the front of the book for more detailed information.

Ancestry/Race	Number	%
Jamaican	8	0.05
White:	15,624	92.11
Not Hispanic (15,315)	15,496	91.36
Hispanic (117)	128	0.75

Lima

Place Type: City
County: Allen
Population: 40,081

Ancestry/Race	Number	%
African American/Black:	11,303	28.20
Not Hispanic (10,533)	11,197	27.94
Hispanic (81)	106	0.26
African, sub-Saharan:	589	1.46
African	575	1.43
Nigerian	7	0.02
Sudanese	7	0.02
Am. Ind. or Alaska Nat., not spec.	155	0.39
American Indian tribes, specified:	206	0.51
Apache (2)	7	0.02
Blackfeet (1)	20	0.05
Cherokee (42)	110	0.27
Cheyenne (1)	2	0.00
Chippewa (5)	8	0.02
Choctaw (3)	4	0.01
Creek (1)	3	0.01
Crow	1	0.00
Iroquois	1	0.00
Latin American Indians (3)	7	0.02
Menominee (2)	6	0.01
Osage	1	0.00
Potawatomi	1	0.00
Pueblo	1	0.00
Seminole (2)	4	0.01
Shoshone (1)	2	0.00
Sioux (5)	10	0.02
All other tribes (5)	18	0.04
American Indian tribes, not spec.	20	0.05
Arab:	58	0.14
Lebanese	52	0.13
Syrian	6	0.01
Armenian	14	0.03
Asian:	292	0.73
Chinese, ex. Taiwanese (11)	26	0.06
Filipino (60)	80	0.20
Indian (46)	55	0.14
Japanese (13)	21	0.05
Korean (24)	45	0.11
Laotian (15)	21	0.05
Pakistani	3	0.01
Taiwanese	3	0.01
Thai (3)	4	0.01
Vietnamese (21)	24	0.06
Other Asian, specified (1)	1	0.00
Other Asian, not specified (4)	9	0.02
Austrian	84	0.21
Belgian	18	0.04
British	50	0.12
Canadian	23	0.06
Celtic	16	0.04
Croatian	36	0.09
Czech	59	0.15
Czechoslovakian	12	0.03
Dutch	665	1.65
English	2,085	5.18
European	84	0.21
Finnish	8	0.02
French, except Basque	660	1.64
French Canadian	162	0.40
German	8,405	20.88
Greek	50	0.12
Hawaii Native/Pacific Islander:	8	0.02
Micronesian: (1)	1	0.00
Guamanian/Chamorro (1)	1	0.00
Polynesian: (3)	4	0.01
Native Hawaiian (2)	3	0.01
Samoan (1)	1	0.00
Other Pac. Isl., not spec.	3	0.01
Hispanic or Latino:	789	1.97
Central American:	8	0.02
Costa Rican	1	0.00
Guatemalan	2	0.00
Honduran	1	0.00
Panamanian	3	0.01
Salvadoran	1	0.00
Cuban	13	0.03
Mexican	521	1.30
Puerto Rican	58	0.14
South American:	17	0.04
Bolivian	4	0.01
Chilean	1	0.00
Colombian	4	0.01
Peruvian	7	0.02
Other South American	1	0.00
Other Hispanic or Latino	172	0.43
Hungarian	81	0.20
Iranian	16	0.04
Irish	4,421	10.98
Italian	1,182	2.94
Lithuanian	35	0.09
Macedonian	23	0.06
Northern European	6	0.01
Norwegian	47	0.12
Pennsylvania German	37	0.09
Polish	311	0.77
Portuguese	19	0.05
Romanian	14	0.03
Russian	71	0.18
Scotch-Irish	355	0.88
Scottish	490	1.22
Serbian	9	0.02
Slavic	37	0.09
Slovak	15	0.04
Slovene	14	0.03
Swedish	153	0.38
Swiss	162	0.40
Ukrainian	40	0.10
United States or American	3,876	9.63
Welsh	472	1.17
West Indian, excl. Hispanic:	31	0.08
Jamaican	5	0.01
Trinidadian and Tobagonian	9	0.02
West Indian	17	0.04
White:	28,641	71.46
Not Hispanic (27,408)	28,202	70.36
Hispanic (368)	439	1.10
Yugoslavian	38	0.09

Lorain

Place Type: City
County: Lorain
Population: 68,652

Ancestry/Race	Number	%
African American/Black:	12,220	17.80
Not Hispanic (10,286)	11,181	16.29
Hispanic (657)	1,039	1.51
African, sub-Saharan:	331	0.48
African	331	0.48
Alaska Native tribes, specified:	3	0.00
Aleut	1	0.00
Eskimo	2	0.00
Am. Ind. or Alaska Nat., not spec.	308	0.45
Albanian	15	0.02
American Indian tribes, specified:	504	0.73
Apache (5)	15	0.02
Blackfeet (7)	48	0.07
Cherokee (69)	262	0.38
Cheyenne (1)	6	0.01
Chickasaw	3	0.00
Chippewa (5)	11	0.02
Choctaw	6	0.01
Cree	4	0.01
Creek	3	0.00
Crow (3)	3	0.00
Delaware (6)	9	0.01
Iroquois (9)	38	0.06
Latin American Indians (30)	46	0.07
Navajo (3)	7	0.01
Ottawa (1)	4	0.01
Pueblo (4)	7	0.01
Seminole	5	0.01
Shoshone (3)	3	0.00
Sioux (1)	6	0.01
All other tribes (9)	18	0.03
American Indian tribes, not spec.	44	0.06
Arab:	192	0.28
Arab/Arabic	25	0.04
Lebanese	95	0.14
Moroccan	6	0.01
Syrian	66	0.10
Armenian	6	0.01
Asian:	384	0.56
Cambodian	3	0.00
Chinese, ex. Taiwanese (61)	83	0.12
Filipino (58)	92	0.13
Indian (46)	61	0.09
Indonesian	2	0.00
Japanese (8)	26	0.04
Korean (24)	52	0.08
Pakistani (4)	4	0.01
Taiwanese	1	0.00
Thai (4)	6	0.01
Vietnamese (11)	21	0.03
Other Asian, specified	1	0.00
Other Asian, not specified (8)	32	0.05
Australian	6	0.01
Austrian	104	0.15
Belgian	4	0.01
Brazilian	5	0.01
British	116	0.17
Bulgarian	43	0.06
Canadian	51	0.07
Celtic	12	0.02
Croatian	830	1.21
Czech	244	0.36
Czechoslovakian	157	0.23
Danish	38	0.06
Dutch	721	1.05
English	4,174	6.08
European	116	0.17
Finnish	7	0.01
French, except Basque	1,054	1.54
French Canadian	181	0.26
German	10,993	16.01
German Russian	18	0.03
Greek	412	0.60
Hawaii Native/Pacific Islander:	61	0.09
Micronesian: (4)	10	0.01
Guamanian/Chamorro (4)	10	0.01
Polynesian: (6)	13	0.02
Native Hawaiian (5)	11	0.02
Samoan (1)	2	0.00
Other Pac. Isl., not spec. (14)	38	0.06
Hispanic or Latino:	14,438	21.03
Central American:	48	0.07
Costa Rican	2	0.00
Guatemalan	15	0.02
Honduran	5	0.01
Nicaraguan	1	0.00
Panamanian	13	0.02
Salvadoran	10	0.01
Other Central American	2	0.00
Cuban	64	0.09
Dominican Republic	69	0.10
Mexican	2,437	3.55
Puerto Rican	10,536	15.35
South American:	55	0.08
Argentinean	2	0.00
Chilean	2	0.00
Colombian	11	0.02
Ecuadorian	17	0.02
Peruvian	17	0.02
Uruguayan	1	0.00
Venezuelan	3	0.00
Other South American	2	0.00
Other Hispanic or Latino	1,229	1.79

Notes: 1. Figures in the "Number" column do not add up to the total population due to: a) Ancestry/Race overlap — e.g. persons can report being both White and Irish, b) persons of Hispanic origin can report being any race, c) persons reporting two ancestries are counted in both categories. 2. Numbers in parentheses indicate the number of persons reporting this ancestry/race alone, not in combination with any other ancestry/race. 3. Refer to the Explanation of Data in the front of the book for more detailed information.

Ancestry/Race	Number	%
Hungarian	3,078	4.48
Iranian	5	0.01
Irish	7,569	11.02
Italian	4,595	6.69
Latvian	5	0.01
Lithuanian	96	0.14
Macedonian	105	0.15
Northern European	24	0.03
Norwegian	157	0.23
Pennsylvania German	27	0.04
Polish	5,386	7.85
Portuguese	19	0.03
Romanian	113	0.16
Russian	587	0.85
Scandinavian	11	0.02
Scotch-Irish	723	1.05
Scottish	829	1.21
Serbian	324	0.47
Slavic	45	0.07
Slovak	2,618	3.81
Slovene	544	0.79
Swedish	314	0.46
Swiss	147	0.21
Turkish	12	0.02
Ukrainian	440	0.64
United States or American	2,925	4.26
Welsh	444	0.65
West Indian, excl. Hispanic:	96	0.14
Dutch West Indian	44	0.06
Haitian	12	0.02
Jamaican	19	0.03
West Indian	21	0.03
White:	50,246	73.19
Not Hispanic (41,935)	43,317	63.10
Hispanic (5,913)	6,929	10.09
Yugoslavian	103	0.15

Loveland

Place Type: City
County: Hamilton
Population: 11,677

Ancestry/Race	Number	%
Acadian/Cajun	29	0.24
African American/Black:	249	2.13
Not Hispanic (180)	243	2.08
Hispanic (2)	6	0.05
African, sub-Saharan:	34	0.28
South African	34	0.28
Am. Ind. or Alaska Nat., not spec.	12	0.10
Alsatian	10	0.08
American Indian tribes, specified:	31	0.27
Blackfeet	3	0.03
Cherokee (3)	23	0.20
Chippewa (1)	1	0.01
Iroquois	1	0.01
Latin American Indians	1	0.01
Sioux	1	0.01
All other tribes	1	0.01
American Indian tribes, not spec.	2	0.02
Arab:	36	0.30
Lebanese	36	0.30
Armenian	23	0.19
Asian:	158	1.35
Bangladeshi (4)	4	0.03
Chinese, ex. Taiwanese (22)	30	0.26
Filipino (8)	14	0.12
Indian (42)	43	0.37
Indonesian	1	0.01
Japanese (9)	15	0.13
Korean (18)	26	0.22
Pakistani (1)	2	0.02
Sri Lankan (4)	4	0.03
Thai	1	0.01
Vietnamese (8)	8	0.07
Other Asian, specified	1	0.01
Other Asian, not specified (7)	9	0.08
Australian	29	0.24
Austrian	50	0.42
Belgian	38	0.32
Brazilian	21	0.18
British	24	0.20
Canadian	55	0.46
Celtic	9	0.08
Czech	56	0.47
Czechoslovakian	37	0.31
Danish	25	0.21
Dutch	109	0.91
Eastern European	10	0.08
English	1,478	12.37
European	66	0.55
Finnish	18	0.15
French, except Basque	271	2.27
French Canadian	51	0.43
German	3,762	31.49
Greek	36	0.30
Hawaii Native/Pacific Islander:	5	0.04
Polynesian:	3	0.03
Native Hawaiian	3	0.03
Other Pac. Isl., specified	1	0.01
Other Pac. Isl., not spec.	1	0.01
Hispanic or Latino:	131	1.12
Central American:	7	0.06
Guatemalan	1	0.01
Nicaraguan	4	0.03
Salvadoran	2	0.02
Cuban	2	0.02
Mexican	62	0.53
Puerto Rican	15	0.13
South American:	16	0.14
Argentinean	3	0.03
Bolivian	1	0.01
Chilean	2	0.02
Colombian	7	0.06
Peruvian	1	0.01
Uruguayan	1	0.01
Venezuelan	1	0.01
Other Hispanic or Latino	29	0.25
Hungarian	207	1.73
Iranian	9	0.08
Irish	2,085	17.45
Israeli	7	0.06
Italian	589	4.93
Lithuanian	8	0.07
Norwegian	69	0.58
Pennsylvania German	10	0.08
Polish	301	2.52
Romanian	81	0.68
Russian	196	1.64
Scandinavian	14	0.12
Scotch-Irish	190	1.59
Scottish	192	1.61
Slavic	39	0.33
Slovak	98	0.82
Slovene	41	0.34
Swedish	118	0.99
Swiss	57	0.48
Turkish	23	0.19
Ukrainian	14	0.12
United States or American	1,016	8.50
Welsh	179	1.50
White:	11,309	96.85
Not Hispanic (11,087)	11,212	96.02
Hispanic (83)	97	0.83

Lyndhurst

Place Type: City
County: Cuyahoga
Population: 15,279

Ancestry/Race	Number	%
African American/Black:	223	1.46
Not Hispanic (196)	222	1.45
Hispanic	1	0.01
African, sub-Saharan:	11	0.07
African	11	0.07
Am. Ind. or Alaska Nat., not spec.	11	0.07
American Indian tribes, specified:	12	0.08
Cherokee	11	0.07
Osage (1)	1	0.01
American Indian tribes, not spec.	1	0.01
Arab:	148	0.97
Arab/Arabic	14	0.09
Egyptian	28	0.18
Lebanese	100	0.65
Syrian	6	0.04
Armenian	32	0.21
Asian:	218	1.43
Bangladeshi (5)	5	0.03
Chinese, ex. Taiwanese (85)	96	0.63
Filipino (16)	22	0.14
Indian (38)	48	0.31
Japanese (8)	10	0.07
Korean (9)	9	0.06
Sri Lankan (1)	3	0.02
Taiwanese (10)	12	0.08
Vietnamese	7	0.05
Other Asian, not specified	6	0.04
Austrian	159	1.04
British	38	0.25
Bulgarian	9	0.06
Canadian	28	0.18
Croatian	133	0.87
Czech	179	1.17
Czechoslovakian	63	0.41
Danish	77	0.50
Dutch	222	1.45
Eastern European	18	0.12
English	1,443	9.44
European	62	0.41
Finnish	40	0.26
French, except Basque	180	1.18
French Canadian	25	0.16
German	2,815	18.42
Greek	74	0.48
Hawaii Native/Pacific Islander:	6	0.04
Micronesian: (1)	2	0.01
Guamanian/Chamorro (1)	1	0.01
Other Micronesian	1	0.01
Polynesian: (1)	2	0.01
Native Hawaiian (1)	2	0.01
Other Pac. Isl., not spec.	2	0.01
Hispanic or Latino:	104	0.68
Central American:	5	0.03
Salvadoran	5	0.03
Cuban	5	0.03
Dominican Republic	2	0.01
Mexican	27	0.18
Puerto Rican	13	0.09
South American:	24	0.16
Argentinean	1	0.01
Chilean	4	0.03
Colombian	5	0.03
Peruvian	8	0.05
Venezuelan	3	0.02
Other South American	3	0.02
Other Hispanic or Latino	28	0.18
Hungarian	1,127	7.38
Irish	2,431	15.91
Italian	3,646	23.86
Latvian	7	0.05
Lithuanian	167	1.09
Macedonian	15	0.10
Norwegian	28	0.18
Pennsylvania German	14	0.09
Polish	1,226	8.02
Romanian	101	0.66
Russian	893	5.84
Scandinavian	19	0.12
Scotch-Irish	182	1.19
Scottish	298	1.95
Serbian	33	0.22
Slavic	13	0.09
Slovak	538	3.52
Slovene	583	3.82
Swedish	149	0.98
Swiss	54	0.35
Ukrainian	160	1.05

Notes: 1. Figures in the "Number" column do not add up to the total population due to: a) Ancestry/Race overlap — e.g. persons can report being both White and Irish, b) persons of Hispanic origin can report being any race, c) persons reporting two ancestries are counted in both categories. 2. Numbers in parentheses indicate the number of persons reporting this ancestry/race alone, not in combination with any other ancestry/race. 3. Refer to the Explanation of Data in the front of the book for more detailed information.

United States or American	587	3.84
Welsh	158	1.03
White:	14,863	97.28
Not Hispanic (14,707)	14,782	96.75
Hispanic (71)	81	0.53
Yugoslavian	18	0.12

Mansfield

Place Type: City
County: Richland
Population: 49,346

Ancestry/Race	Number	%
Acadian/Cajun	27	0.05
Afghan	7	0.01
African American/Black:	10,321	20.92
Not Hispanic (9,655)	10,258	20.79
Hispanic (40)	63	0.13
African, sub-Saharan:	613	1.24
African	543	1.10
Ethiopian	35	0.07
Ghanian	15	0.03
Nigerian	8	0.02
Senegalese	12	0.02
Am. Ind. or Alaska Nat., not spec.	163	0.33
Albanian	149	0.30
American Indian tribes, specified:	325	0.66
Apache (1)	10	0.02
Blackfeet (2)	35	0.07
Cherokee (41)	206	0.42
Chickasaw (1)	1	0.00
Chippewa	2	0.00
Choctaw (1)	4	0.01
Cree	1	0.00
Crow	4	0.01
Iroquois (6)	13	0.03
Latin American Indians (3)	4	0.01
Lumbee	1	0.00
Navajo (3)	4	0.01
Potawatomi (1)	2	0.00
Pueblo	1	0.00
Shoshone (1)	1	0.00
Sioux	14	0.03
Yuman	1	0.00
All other tribes (10)	21	0.04
American Indian tribes, not spec.	39	0.08
Arab:	12	0.02
Lebanese	12	0.02
Armenian	15	0.03
Asian:	420	0.85
Bangladeshi (3)	4	0.01
Chinese, ex. Taiwanese (28)	45	0.09
Filipino (30)	54	0.11
Indian (118)	128	0.26
Indonesian	1	0.00
Japanese (32)	44	0.09
Korean (34)	55	0.11
Laotian (2)	2	0.00
Pakistani (3)	4	0.01
Taiwanese (9)	9	0.02
Thai (2)	6	0.01
Vietnamese (28)	39	0.08
Other Asian, specified (2)	2	0.00
Other Asian, not specified (17)	27	0.05
Australian	33	0.07
Austrian	166	0.34
Belgian	54	0.11
British	143	0.29
Bulgarian	29	0.06
Canadian	52	0.11
Croatian	74	0.15
Czech	48	0.10
Czechoslovakian	54	0.11
Danish	105	0.21
Dutch	1,082	2.19
Eastern European	51	0.10
English	3,906	7.91
European	149	0.30
Finnish	49	0.10
French, except Basque	804	1.63
French Canadian	178	0.36
German	11,067	22.40
Greek	183	0.37
Guyanese	8	0.02
Hawaii Native/Pacific Islander:	43	0.09
Melanesian: (1)	1	0.00
Fijian (1)	1	0.00
Micronesian: (12)	18	0.04
Guamanian/Chamorro (12)	18	0.04
Polynesian: (7)	16	0.03
Native Hawaiian (5)	9	0.02
Samoan (1)	4	0.01
Other Polynesian (1)	3	0.01
Other Pac. Isl., not spec.	8	0.02
Hispanic or Latino:	605	1.23
Central American:	25	0.05
Guatemalan	4	0.01
Nicaraguan	4	0.01
Panamanian	17	0.03
Cuban	15	0.03
Mexican	357	0.72
Puerto Rican	86	0.17
South American:	13	0.03
Argentinean	2	0.00
Colombian	4	0.01
Ecuadorian	1	0.00
Peruvian	3	0.01
Venezuelan	3	0.01
Other Hispanic or Latino	109	0.22
Hungarian	637	1.29
Irish	4,930	9.98
Israeli	6	0.01
Italian	1,736	3.51
Latvian	7	0.01
Lithuanian	73	0.15
Macedonian	36	0.07
Maltese	10	0.02
Northern European	15	0.03
Norwegian	190	0.38
Pennsylvania German	99	0.20
Polish	975	1.97
Portuguese	16	0.03
Romanian	103	0.21
Russian	121	0.24
Scandinavian	38	0.08
Scotch-Irish	727	1.47
Scottish	942	1.91
Serbian	55	0.11
Slavic	58	0.12
Slovak	206	0.42
Slovene	24	0.05
Swedish	175	0.35
Swiss	322	0.65
Ukrainian	98	0.20
United States or American	4,427	8.96
Welsh	480	0.97
West Indian, excl. Hispanic:	46	0.09
Haitian	10	0.02
Jamaican	17	0.03
Other West Indian	19	0.04
White:	38,760	78.55
Not Hispanic (37,547)	38,391	77.80
Hispanic (338)	369	0.75
Yugoslavian	164	0.33

Maple Heights

Place Type: City
County: Cuyahoga
Population: 26,156

Ancestry/Race	Number	%
African American/Black:	11,879	45.42
Not Hispanic (11,547)	11,798	45.11
Hispanic (51)	81	0.31
African, sub-Saharan:	288	1.10
African	288	1.10
Am. Ind. or Alaska Nat., not spec.	75	0.29
American Indian tribes, specified:	72	0.28
Blackfeet (1)	10	0.04
Cherokee (6)	35	0.13
Chippewa (1)	5	0.02
Choctaw	1	0.00
Iroquois (3)	4	0.02
Latin American Indians (2)	2	0.01
Navajo (2)	4	0.02
Seminole	2	0.01
Sioux	2	0.01
All other tribes (1)	7	0.03
American Indian tribes, not spec.	4	0.02
Arab:	77	0.29
Lebanese	49	0.19
Palestinian	21	0.08
Syrian	7	0.03
Armenian	12	0.05
Asian:	558	2.13
Cambodian (4)	4	0.02
Chinese, ex. Taiwanese (34)	39	0.15
Filipino (67)	97	0.37
Indian (300)	341	1.30
Japanese (7)	23	0.09
Korean (19)	23	0.09
Thai (4)	6	0.02
Vietnamese (14)	16	0.06
Other Asian, not specified (3)	9	0.03
Austrian	48	0.18
Belgian	5	0.02
British	39	0.15
Canadian	19	0.07
Croatian	135	0.52
Czech	964	3.69
Czechoslovakian	117	0.45
Danish	44	0.17
Dutch	113	0.43
Eastern European	7	0.03
English	852	3.26
European	47	0.18
Finnish	10	0.04
French, except Basque	174	0.67
French Canadian	54	0.21
German	2,259	8.64
Greek	7	0.03
Guyanese	8	0.03
Hawaii Native/Pacific Islander:	13	0.05
Micronesian: (3)	3	0.01
Guamanian/Chamorro (3)	3	0.01
Polynesian: (2)	6	0.02
Native Hawaiian (1)	5	0.02
Samoan (1)	1	0.00
Other Pac. Isl., not spec. (1)	4	0.02
Hispanic or Latino:	316	1.21
Central American:	14	0.05
Guatemalan	3	0.01
Honduran	3	0.01
Nicaraguan	1	0.00
Panamanian	7	0.03
Cuban	5	0.02
Mexican	69	0.26
Puerto Rican	126	0.48
South American:	29	0.11
Argentinean	3	0.01
Colombian	2	0.01
Ecuadorian	1	0.00
Peruvian	19	0.07
Venezuelan	4	0.02
Other Hispanic or Latino	73	0.28
Hungarian	992	3.79
Icelander	17	0.06
Irish	1,687	6.45
Italian	2,610	9.98
Latvian	11	0.04
Lithuanian	80	0.31
Norwegian	20	0.08
Pennsylvania German	12	0.05
Polish	2,578	9.86
Romanian	64	0.24
Russian	181	0.69
Scandinavian	8	0.03
Scotch-Irish	100	0.38

Notes: 1. Figures in the "Number" column do not add up to the total population due to: a) Ancestry/Race overlap — e.g. persons can report being both White and Irish, b) persons of Hispanic origin can report being any race, c) persons reporting two ancestries are counted in both categories. 2. Numbers in parentheses indicate the number of persons reporting this ancestry/race alone, not in combination with any other ancestry/race. 3. Refer to the Explanation of Data in the front of the book for more detailed information.

Ancestry/Race	Number	%
Scottish	189	0.72
Serbian	58	0.22
Slavic	31	0.12
Slovak	1,179	4.51
Slovene	424	1.62
Swedish	59	0.23
Swiss	30	0.11
Turkish	6	0.02
Ukrainian	75	0.29
United States or American	787	3.01
Welsh	142	0.54
West Indian, excl. Hispanic:	53	0.20
Barbadian	6	0.02
Jamaican	43	0.16
West Indian	4	0.02
White:	13,809	52.79
Not Hispanic (13,382)	13,660	52.23
Hispanic (127)	149	0.57
Yugoslavian	21	0.08

Marietta

Place Type: City
County: Washington
Population: 14,515

Ancestry/Race	Number	%
African American/Black:	211	1.45
Not Hispanic (156)	209	1.44
Hispanic (1)	2	0.01
African, sub-Saharan:	28	0.19
African	28	0.19
Alaska Native tribes, specified:	1	0.01
Aleut (1)	1	0.01
Alaska Native tribes, not specified	1	0.01
Am. Ind. or Alaska Nat., not spec.	57	0.39
American Indian tribes, specified:	89	0.61
Apache (1)	2	0.01
Blackfeet (4)	9	0.06
Cherokee (19)	42	0.29
Cheyenne (1)	3	0.02
Chippewa (3)	8	0.06
Choctaw	1	0.01
Iroquois (3)	8	0.06
Latin American Indians (1)	3	0.02
Osage (1)	1	0.01
Sioux (1)	2	0.01
Ute	1	0.01
All other tribes (2)	9	0.06
American Indian tribes, not spec.	4	0.03
Arab:	14	0.10
Lebanese	6	0.04
Syrian	8	0.06
Asian:	133	0.92
Chinese, ex. Taiwanese (57)	59	0.41
Filipino (11)	12	0.08
Indian (11)	15	0.10
Japanese (5)	11	0.08
Korean (7)	11	0.08
Sri Lankan (4)	4	0.03
Vietnamese (2)	2	0.01
Other Asian, specified	1	0.01
Other Asian, not specified (5)	18	0.12
Austrian	43	0.30
Belgian	51	0.35
Brazilian	21	0.14
British	41	0.28
Canadian	13	0.09
Croatian	26	0.18
Czech	8	0.06
Danish	33	0.23
Dutch	215	1.48
English	2,033	14.01
European	117	0.81
Finnish	9	0.06
French, except Basque	277	1.91
French Canadian	100	0.69
German	3,879	26.73
Greek	38	0.26
Hawaii Native/Pacific Islander:	27	0.19
Micronesian: (3)	6	0.04
Guamanian/Chamorro (3)	6	0.04
Polynesian: (3)	4	0.03
Native Hawaiian (1)	1	0.01
Samoan (2)	3	0.02
Other Pac. Isl., specified	1	0.01
Other Pac. Isl., not spec. (2)	16	0.11
Hispanic or Latino:	114	0.79
Central American:	3	0.02
Guatemalan	1	0.01
Honduran	2	0.01
Cuban	11	0.08
Mexican	60	0.41
Puerto Rican	7	0.05
South American:	2	0.01
Colombian	1	0.01
Venezuelan	1	0.01
Other Hispanic or Latino	31	0.21
Hungarian	72	0.50
Iranian	42	0.29
Irish	2,032	14.00
Italian	403	2.78
Lithuanian	15	0.10
Macedonian	8	0.06
Norwegian	17	0.12
Pennsylvania German	5	0.03
Polish	165	1.14
Romanian	24	0.17
Russian	37	0.25
Scandinavian	29	0.20
Scotch-Irish	290	2.00
Scottish	332	2.29
Slovak	70	0.48
Swedish	48	0.33
Swiss	64	0.44
Ukrainian	42	0.29
United States or American	1,418	9.77
Welsh	157	1.08
White:	14,123	97.30
Not Hispanic (13,898)	14,036	96.70
Hispanic (81)	87	0.60
Yugoslavian	8	0.06

Marion

Place Type: City
County: Marion
Population: 35,318

Ancestry/Race	Number	%
African American/Black:	2,681	7.59
Not Hispanic (2,465)	2,666	7.55
Hispanic (10)	15	0.04
African, sub-Saharan:	191	0.54
African	186	0.53
Nigerian	5	0.01
Am. Ind. or Alaska Nat., not spec.	86	0.24
American Indian tribes, specified:	138	0.39
Apache (2)	4	0.01
Blackfeet (4)	11	0.03
Cherokee (25)	87	0.25
Cheyenne	2	0.01
Chippewa (1)	1	0.00
Choctaw (1)	1	0.00
Crow	1	0.00
Iroquois (1)	5	0.01
Lumbee (1)	1	0.00
Navajo (1)	4	0.01
Pueblo (1)	2	0.01
Seminole	3	0.01
Sioux (2)	9	0.03
All other tribes (3)	7	0.02
American Indian tribes, not spec.	7	0.02
Arab:	35	0.10
Arab/Arabic	5	0.01
Lebanese	11	0.03
Other Arab	19	0.05
Armenian	9	0.03
Asian:	271	0.77
Chinese, ex. Taiwanese (40)	43	0.12
Filipino (33)	54	0.15
Indian (55)	70	0.20
Indonesian (1)	1	0.00
Japanese (17)	22	0.06
Korean (11)	15	0.04
Laotian (5)	5	0.01
Pakistani (3)	4	0.01
Taiwanese	12	0.03
Thai (5)	5	0.01
Vietnamese (16)	16	0.05
Other Asian, specified (1)	4	0.01
Other Asian, not specified (5)	20	0.06
Austrian	29	0.08
Belgian	8	0.02
British	29	0.08
Canadian	24	0.07
Celtic	12	0.03
Czech	22	0.06
Czechoslovakian	9	0.03
Danish	38	0.11
Dutch	529	1.50
English	2,734	7.75
European	238	0.67
Finnish	12	0.03
French, except Basque	550	1.56
French Canadian	62	0.18
German	6,160	17.45
Greek	57	0.16
Hawaii Native/Pacific Islander:	19	0.05
Micronesian:	4	0.01
Guamanian/Chamorro	4	0.01
Polynesian: (3)	11	0.03
Native Hawaiian	5	0.01
Samoan (3)	6	0.02
Other Pac. Isl., specified	3	0.01
Other Pac. Isl., not spec. (1)	1	0.00
Hispanic or Latino:	474	1.34
Central American:	5	0.01
Panamanian	1	0.00
Salvadoran	2	0.01
Other Central American	2	0.01
Cuban	6	0.02
Dominican Republic	5	0.01
Mexican	272	0.77
Puerto Rican	100	0.28
South American:	1	0.00
Peruvian	1	0.00
Other Hispanic or Latino	85	0.24
Hungarian	61	0.17
Irish	3,358	9.51
Italian	943	2.67
Lithuanian	7	0.02
Northern European	6	0.02
Norwegian	82	0.23
Pennsylvania German	103	0.29
Polish	251	0.71
Portuguese	14	0.04
Romanian	29	0.08
Russian	34	0.10
Scotch-Irish	345	0.98
Scottish	378	1.07
Slavic	21	0.06
Slovak	25	0.07
Swedish	72	0.20
Swiss	127	0.36
United States or American	6,571	18.62
Welsh	335	0.95
White:	32,284	91.41
Not Hispanic (31,658)	31,997	90.60
Hispanic (268)	287	0.81

Marysville

Place Type: City
County: Union
Population: 15,942

Ancestry/Race	Number	%
African American/Black:	1,047	6.57
Not Hispanic (976)	1,033	6.48

Notes: 1. Figures in the "Number" column do not add up to the total population due to: a) Ancestry/Race overlap — e.g. persons can report being both White and Irish, b) persons of Hispanic origin can report being any race, c) persons reporting two ancestries are counted in both categories. 2. Numbers in parentheses indicate the number of persons reporting this ancestry/race alone, not in combination with any other ancestry/race. 3. Refer to the Explanation of Data in the front of the book for more detailed information.

Hispanic (5)	14	0.09
African, sub-Saharan:	31	0.20
African	31	0.20
Am. Ind. or Alaska Nat., not spec.	32	0.20
American Indian tribes, specified:	69	0.43
Apache	1	0.01
Blackfeet (1)	10	0.06
Cherokee (6)	36	0.23
Iroquois (1)	2	0.01
Latin American Indians (1)	1	0.01
Navajo (1)	1	0.01
Potawatomi (1)	1	0.01
Seminole (1)	1	0.01
Sioux (1)	14	0.09
All other tribes	2	0.01
American Indian tribes, not spec.	5	0.03
Arab:	50	0.32
Arab/Arabic	8	0.05
Lebanese	37	0.24
Moroccan	5	0.03
Asian:	186	1.17
Cambodian (4)	4	0.03
Chinese, ex. Taiwanese (32)	35	0.22
Filipino (31)	34	0.21
Indian (25)	27	0.17
Japanese (22)	30	0.19
Korean (24)	33	0.21
Thai (3)	6	0.04
Vietnamese (6)	6	0.04
Other Asian, specified (1)	1	0.01
Other Asian, not specified (6)	10	0.06
Austrian	27	0.17
Belgian	27	0.17
Brazilian	21	0.13
British	17	0.11
Canadian	55	0.35
Croatian	63	0.40
Czech	20	0.13
Czechoslovakian	29	0.18
Danish	44	0.28
Dutch	324	2.06
English	1,622	10.31
European	101	0.64
Finnish	8	0.05
French, except Basque	359	2.28
French Canadian	17	0.11
German	4,436	28.20
Greek	101	0.64
Hawaii Native/Pacific Islander:	12	0.08
Micronesian: (2)	5	0.03
Guamanian/Chamorro (2)	5	0.03
Polynesian: (1)	4	0.03
Native Hawaiian (1)	2	0.01
Samoan	2	0.01
Other Pac. Isl., not spec. (1)	3	0.02
Hispanic or Latino:	167	1.05
Central American:	19	0.12
Costa Rican	6	0.04
Guatemalan	3	0.02
Nicaraguan	2	0.01
Panamanian	6	0.04
Salvadoran	2	0.01
Cuban	6	0.04
Dominican Republic	1	0.01
Mexican	81	0.51
Puerto Rican	20	0.13
South American:	15	0.09
Argentinean	2	0.01
Peruvian	6	0.04
Venezuelan	6	0.04
Other South American	1	0.01
Other Hispanic or Latino	25	0.16
Hungarian	106	0.67
Irish	2,087	13.27
Italian	513	3.26
Lithuanian	8	0.05
Northern European	33	0.21
Norwegian	66	0.42
Pennsylvania German	5	0.03
Polish	456	2.90
Portuguese	19	0.12
Romanian	18	0.11
Russian	41	0.26
Scandinavian	8	0.05
Scotch-Irish	296	1.88
Scottish	326	2.07
Slavic	9	0.06
Slovak	40	0.25
Slovene	26	0.17
Swedish	85	0.54
Swiss	108	0.69
Ukrainian	47	0.30
United States or American	1,605	10.20
Welsh	158	1.00
West Indian, excl. Hispanic:	15	0.10
Jamaican	8	0.05
West Indian	7	0.04
White:	14,719	92.33
Not Hispanic (14,459)	14,597	91.56
Hispanic (100)	122	0.77

Mason

Place Type: City
County: Warren
Population: 22,016

Ancestry/Race	Number	%
African American/Black:	392	1.78
Not Hispanic (353)	391	1.78
Hispanic (1)	1	0.00
African, sub-Saharan:	68	0.31
African	68	0.31
Am. Ind. or Alaska Nat., not spec.	29	0.13
Albanian	58	0.26
Alsatian	8	0.04
American Indian tribes, specified:	73	0.33
Blackfeet (1)	1	0.00
Cherokee (18)	52	0.24
Chickasaw (3)	3	0.01
Choctaw (3)	4	0.02
Delaware	1	0.00
Navajo (1)	1	0.00
Osage (1)	1	0.00
Seminole	4	0.02
Sioux (2)	2	0.01
All other tribes (1)	4	0.02
American Indian tribes, not spec.	6	0.03
Arab:	13	0.06
Jordanian	13	0.06
Asian:	579	2.63
Chinese, ex. Taiwanese (126)	136	0.62
Filipino (19)	54	0.25
Indian (195)	212	0.96
Indonesian (3)	3	0.01
Japanese (46)	56	0.25
Korean (45)	60	0.27
Malaysian	2	0.01
Pakistani (16)	19	0.09
Sri Lankan (4)	4	0.02
Taiwanese (2)	3	0.01
Thai (3)	3	0.01
Vietnamese (15)	16	0.07
Other Asian, not specified (5)	11	0.05
Australian	5	0.02
Austrian	29	0.13
Brazilian	8	0.04
British	105	0.48
Bulgarian	28	0.13
Canadian	101	0.46
Croatian	46	0.21
Czech	66	0.30
Czechoslovakian	53	0.24
Danish	27	0.12
Dutch	244	1.11
Eastern European	14	0.06
English	3,076	14.02
European	71	0.32
Finnish	8	0.04
French, except Basque	822	3.75
French Canadian	124	0.57
German	7,359	33.53
Greek	56	0.26
Hawaii Native/Pacific Islander:	14	0.06
Micronesian: (2)	5	0.02
Guamanian/Chamorro (2)	5	0.02
Polynesian:	3	0.01
Native Hawaiian	3	0.01
Other Pac. Isl., not spec.	6	0.03
Hispanic or Latino:	213	0.97
Central American:	3	0.01
Guatemalan	1	0.00
Panamanian	1	0.00
Other Central American	1	0.00
Cuban	14	0.06
Mexican	96	0.44
Puerto Rican	51	0.23
South American:	11	0.05
Argentinean	2	0.01
Colombian	2	0.01
Peruvian	3	0.01
Venezuelan	4	0.02
Other Hispanic or Latino	38	0.17
Hungarian	100	0.46
Irish	4,014	18.29
Italian	1,073	4.89
Lithuanian	75	0.34
Luxemburger	19	0.09
Macedonian	11	0.05
Northern European	7	0.03
Norwegian	190	0.87
Pennsylvania German	13	0.06
Polish	729	3.32
Portuguese	44	0.20
Romanian	24	0.11
Russian	206	0.94
Scotch-Irish	535	2.44
Scottish	413	1.88
Slovak	50	0.23
Slovene	6	0.03
Swedish	164	0.75
Swiss	14	0.06
Ukrainian	48	0.22
United States or American	1,791	8.16
Welsh	274	1.25
West Indian, excl. Hispanic:	17	0.08
Jamaican	17	0.08
White:	21,049	95.61
Not Hispanic (20,705)	20,884	94.86
Hispanic (163)	165	0.75

Massillon

Place Type: City
County: Stark
Population: 31,325

Ancestry/Race	Number	%
African American/Black:	3,244	10.36
Not Hispanic (2,934)	3,231	10.31
Hispanic (8)	13	0.04
African, sub-Saharan:	289	0.92
African	289	0.92
Alaska Native tribes, specified:	2	0.01
Alaska Athabascan	2	0.01
Am. Ind. or Alaska Nat., not spec.	102	0.33
Albanian	87	0.28
American Indian tribes, specified:	156	0.50
Apache (1)	2	0.01
Blackfeet (8)	20	0.06
Cherokee (12)	73	0.23
Cheyenne	3	0.01
Chippewa	6	0.02
Choctaw	3	0.01
Comanche	3	0.01
Creek	6	0.02
Crow (2)	3	0.01
Iroquois (2)	6	0.02
Latin American Indians	5	0.02
Ottawa (2)	2	0.01

Notes: 1. Figures in the "Number" column do not add up to the total population due to: a) Ancestry/Race overlap — e.g. persons can report being both White and Irish, b) persons of Hispanic origin can report being any race, c) persons reporting two ancestries are counted in both categories. 2. Numbers in parentheses indicate the number of persons reporting this ancestry/race alone, not in combination with any other ancestry/race. 3. Refer to the Explanation of Data in the front of the book for more detailed information.

Paiute (1)	1	0.00
Potawatomi (3)	6	0.02
Sioux (2)	10	0.03
Yuman	1	0.00
All other tribes (1)	6	0.02
American Indian tribes, not spec.	9	0.03
Arab:	145	0.46
Arab/Arabic	12	0.04
Lebanese	81	0.26
Syrian	42	0.13
Other Arab	10	0.03
Asian:	113	0.36
Chinese, ex. Taiwanese (20)	25	0.08
Filipino (16)	24	0.08
Indian (9)	14	0.04
Japanese (10)	13	0.04
Korean (19)	22	0.07
Taiwanese (2)	2	0.01
Vietnamese (2)	6	0.02
Other Asian, specified	3	0.01
Other Asian, not specified (1)	4	0.01
Austrian	90	0.29
Belgian	5	0.02
British	46	0.15
Bulgarian	56	0.18
Canadian	16	0.05
Croatian	239	0.76
Czech	66	0.21
Czechoslovakian	139	0.44
Danish	29	0.09
Dutch	704	2.24
English	2,607	8.31
Estonian	7	0.02
European	175	0.56
Finnish	19	0.06
French, except Basque	1,109	3.53
French Canadian	78	0.25
German	10,557	33.64
Greek	234	0.75
Hawaii Native/Pacific Islander:	7	0.02
Polynesian: (1)	1	0.00
Samoan (1)	1	0.00
Other Pac. Isl., specified	3	0.01
Other Pac. Isl., not spec.	3	0.01
Hispanic or Latino:	301	0.96
Central American:	13	0.04
Costa Rican	2	0.01
Guatemalan	4	0.01
Honduran	3	0.01
Panamanian	1	0.00
Salvadoran	3	0.01
Cuban	11	0.04
Mexican	111	0.35
Puerto Rican	45	0.14
South American:	18	0.06
Argentinean	1	0.00
Colombian	4	0.01
Ecuadorian	2	0.01
Peruvian	6	0.02
Uruguayan	5	0.02
Other Hispanic or Latino	103	0.33
Hungarian	453	1.44
Irish	4,245	13.53
Italian	2,240	7.14
Lithuanian	22	0.07
Macedonian	92	0.29
Northern European	10	0.03
Norwegian	48	0.15
Pennsylvania German	95	0.30
Polish	706	2.25
Portuguese	29	0.09
Romanian	278	0.89
Russian	93	0.30
Scotch-Irish	533	1.70
Scottish	456	1.45
Serbian	222	0.71
Slavic	43	0.14
Slovak	379	1.21
Slovene	34	0.11
Swedish	296	0.94
Swiss	495	1.58
Turkish	21	0.07
Ukrainian	30	0.10
United States or American	1,871	5.96
Welsh	675	2.15
West Indian, excl. Hispanic:	41	0.13
Jamaican	30	0.10
West Indian	11	0.04
White:	28,074	89.62
Not Hispanic (27,422)	27,853	88.92
Hispanic (200)	221	0.71
Yugoslavian	105	0.33

Maumee

Place Type: City
County: Lucas
Population: 15,237

Ancestry/Race	Number	%
African American/Black:	202	1.33
Not Hispanic (146)	184	1.21
Hispanic (14)	18	0.12
Alaska Native tribes, specified:	1	0.01
Eskimo (1)	1	0.01
Am. Ind. or Alaska Nat., not spec.	18	0.12
American Indian tribes, specified:	30	0.20
Blackfeet	3	0.02
Cherokee	9	0.06
Iroquois (1)	10	0.07
Latin American Indians (1)	1	0.01
Sioux	1	0.01
All other tribes (3)	6	0.04
Arab:	154	1.01
Arab/Arabic	34	0.22
Egyptian	18	0.12
Lebanese	102	0.67
Armenian	24	0.16
Asian:	148	0.97
Chinese, ex. Taiwanese (29)	46	0.30
Filipino (11)	14	0.09
Indian (30)	31	0.20
Japanese (8)	16	0.11
Korean (7)	10	0.07
Malaysian	6	0.04
Pakistani (4)	6	0.04
Thai (1)	3	0.02
Vietnamese (10)	12	0.08
Other Asian, not specified (1)	4	0.03
Australian	5	0.03
Austrian	22	0.14
Belgian	72	0.47
British	82	0.54
Bulgarian	7	0.05
Canadian	17	0.11
Croatian	15	0.10
Czech	80	0.53
Czechoslovakian	75	0.49
Danish	38	0.25
Dutch	359	2.36
Eastern European	14	0.09
English	1,522	10.00
European	34	0.22
Finnish	5	0.03
French, except Basque	814	5.35
French Canadian	174	1.14
German	6,330	41.57
Greek	98	0.64
Hawaii Native/Pacific Islander:	6	0.04
Polynesian: (2)	3	0.02
Native Hawaiian (1)	1	0.01
Samoan (1)	2	0.01
Other Pac. Isl., not spec. (3)	3	0.02
Hispanic or Latino:	277	1.82
Central American:	6	0.04
Guatemalan	4	0.03
Panamanian	2	0.01
Cuban	2	0.01
Mexican	229	1.50
Puerto Rican	5	0.03
South American:	2	0.01
Chilean	1	0.01
Paraguayan	1	0.01
Other Hispanic or Latino	33	0.22
Hungarian	321	2.11
Irish	2,366	15.54
Italian	688	4.52
Lithuanian	40	0.26
Northern European	29	0.19
Norwegian	69	0.45
Pennsylvania German	30	0.20
Polish	1,861	12.22
Russian	83	0.55
Scandinavian	41	0.27
Scotch-Irish	285	1.87
Scottish	307	2.02
Serbian	7	0.05
Slovak	87	0.57
Slovene	66	0.43
Swedish	208	1.37
Swiss	179	1.18
Turkish	15	0.10
Ukrainian	59	0.39
United States or American	784	5.15
Welsh	264	1.73
West Indian, excl. Hispanic:	5	0.03
Bahamian	5	0.03
White:	14,856	97.50
Not Hispanic (14,568)	14,680	96.34
Hispanic (152)	176	1.16

Mayfield Heights

Place Type: City
County: Cuyahoga
Population: 19,386

Ancestry/Race	Number	%
African American/Black:	624	3.22
Not Hispanic (572)	616	3.18
Hispanic (5)	8	0.04
African, sub-Saharan:	49	0.25
African	21	0.11
Ethiopian	15	0.08
Nigerian	13	0.07
Am. Ind. or Alaska Nat., not spec.	7	0.04
American Indian tribes, specified:	27	0.14
Apache	1	0.01
Blackfeet	1	0.01
Cherokee (1)	17	0.09
Iroquois (1)	4	0.02
Sioux (2)	3	0.02
All other tribes	1	0.01
Arab:	274	1.41
Arab/Arabic	7	0.04
Egyptian	71	0.37
Iraqi	46	0.24
Jordanian	5	0.03
Lebanese	131	0.68
Syrian	14	0.07
Armenian	28	0.14
Asian:	878	4.53
Bangladeshi (2)	2	0.01
Chinese, ex. Taiwanese (195)	210	1.08
Filipino (21)	34	0.18
Indian (326)	346	1.78
Indonesian (3)	4	0.02
Japanese (123)	136	0.70
Korean (81)	89	0.46
Laotian (3)	3	0.02
Pakistani (3)	5	0.03
Taiwanese (1)	5	0.03
Thai (3)	4	0.02
Vietnamese (7)	7	0.04
Other Asian, specified	2	0.01
Other Asian, not specified (6)	31	0.16
Austrian	203	1.05
Belgian	13	0.07
Brazilian	26	0.13
British	36	0.19

Notes: 1. Figures in the "Number" column do not add up to the total population due to: a) Ancestry/Race overlap — e.g. persons can report being both White and Irish, b) persons of Hispanic origin can report being any race, c) persons reporting two ancestries are counted in both categories. 2. Numbers in parentheses indicate the number of persons reporting this ancestry/race alone, not in combination with any other ancestry/race. 3. Refer to the Explanation of Data in the front of the book for more detailed information.

Ancestry/Race	Number	%
Canadian	57	0.29
Croatian	183	0.94
Czech	181	0.93
Czechoslovakian	86	0.44
Danish	15	0.08
Dutch	90	0.46
Eastern European	7	0.04
English	916	4.73
European	41	0.21
Finnish	34	0.18
French, except Basque	214	1.10
French Canadian	29	0.15
German	2,992	15.43
Greek	147	0.76
Hawaii Native/Pacific Islander:	12	0.06
Micronesian:	5	0.03
Guamanian/Chamorro	2	0.01
Other Micronesian	3	0.02
Polynesian:	3	0.02
Native Hawaiian	3	0.02
Other Pac. Isl., specified	2	0.01
Other Pac. Isl., not spec. (1)	2	0.01
Hispanic or Latino:	201	1.04
Central American:	10	0.05
Costa Rican	1	0.01
Guatemalan	4	0.02
Panamanian	1	0.01
Salvadoran	4	0.02
Cuban	6	0.03
Dominican Republic	1	0.01
Mexican	54	0.28
Puerto Rican	40	0.21
South American:	27	0.14
Argentinean	6	0.03
Chilean	5	0.03
Colombian	2	0.01
Paraguayan	4	0.02
Peruvian	9	0.05
Venezuelan	1	0.01
Other Hispanic or Latino	63	0.32
Hungarian	957	4.94
Iranian	117	0.60
Irish	1,741	8.98
Israeli	23	0.12
Italian	5,061	26.11
Latvian	38	0.20
Lithuanian	146	0.75
Norwegian	44	0.23
Pennsylvania German	12	0.06
Polish	1,146	5.91
Portuguese	29	0.15
Romanian	188	0.97
Russian	1,318	6.80
Scandinavian	7	0.04
Scotch-Irish	216	1.11
Scottish	238	1.23
Serbian	31	0.16
Slavic	17	0.09
Slovak	507	2.62
Slovene	507	2.62
Swedish	225	1.16
Swiss	16	0.08
Turkish	24	0.12
Ukrainian	416	2.15
United States or American	798	4.12
Welsh	200	1.03
West Indian, excl. Hispanic:	16	0.08
Bahamian	9	0.05
Dutch West Indian	7	0.04
White:	17,966	92.68
Not Hispanic (17,648)	17,802	91.83
Hispanic (158)	164	0.85
Yugoslavian	131	0.68

Medina

Place Type: City
County: Medina
Population: 25,139

Ancestry/Race	Number	%
African American/Black:	890	3.54
Not Hispanic (687)	878	3.49
Hispanic (10)	12	0.05
African, sub-Saharan:	41	0.16
African	41	0.16
Alaska Native tribes, specified:	1	0.00
Eskimo (1)	1	0.00
Am. Ind. or Alaska Nat., not spec.	64	0.25
Alsatian	6	0.02
American Indian tribes, specified:	90	0.36
Apache	4	0.02
Blackfeet (2)	3	0.01
Cherokee (14)	52	0.21
Chippewa (1)	6	0.02
Choctaw (1)	6	0.02
Creek	1	0.00
Iroquois	3	0.01
Lumbee (1)	1	0.00
Navajo	1	0.00
Pueblo (1)	1	0.00
Sioux (2)	4	0.02
All other tribes (1)	8	0.03
American Indian tribes, not spec.	7	0.03
Arab:	111	0.44
Egyptian	24	0.10
Lebanese	87	0.35
Armenian	8	0.03
Asian:	243	0.97
Chinese, ex. Taiwanese (30)	38	0.15
Filipino (25)	44	0.18
Hmong (6)	6	0.02
Indian (60)	66	0.26
Indonesian (1)	1	0.00
Japanese (14)	23	0.09
Korean (23)	32	0.13
Laotian (2)	2	0.01
Taiwanese (8)	8	0.03
Thai (3)	4	0.02
Vietnamese (7)	8	0.03
Other Asian, not specified (4)	11	0.04
Australian	10	0.04
Austrian	62	0.25
Belgian	17	0.07
Brazilian	10	0.04
British	57	0.23
Bulgarian	7	0.03
Canadian	53	0.21
Croatian	133	0.53
Czech	415	1.66
Czechoslovakian	108	0.43
Danish	33	0.13
Dutch	491	1.96
English	2,982	11.89
European	194	0.77
Finnish	24	0.10
French, except Basque	593	2.37
French Canadian	60	0.24
German	8,209	32.74
German Russian	3	0.01
Greek	182	0.73
Hawaii Native/Pacific Islander:	20	0.08
Micronesian: (4)	7	0.03
Guamanian/Chamorro	2	0.01
Other Micronesian (4)	5	0.02
Polynesian: (1)	12	0.05
Native Hawaiian	9	0.04
Samoan (1)	3	0.01
Other Pac. Isl., not spec. (1)	1	0.00
Hispanic or Latino:	252	1.00
Central American:	12	0.05
Honduran	3	0.01
Nicaraguan	5	0.02
Panamanian	2	0.01
Salvadoran	2	0.01
Cuban	4	0.02
Dominican Republic	1	0.00
Mexican	104	0.41
Puerto Rican	64	0.25
South American:	15	0.06
Argentinean	2	0.01
Colombian	4	0.02
Peruvian	3	0.01
Venezuelan	6	0.02
Other Hispanic or Latino	52	0.21
Hungarian	872	3.48
Irish	4,190	16.71
Italian	2,396	9.56
Latvian	7	0.03
Lithuanian	117	0.47
Macedonian	10	0.04
Northern European	18	0.07
Norwegian	105	0.42
Pennsylvania German	8	0.03
Polish	2,201	8.78
Portuguese	35	0.14
Romanian	35	0.14
Russian	277	1.10
Scandinavian	42	0.17
Scotch-Irish	493	1.97
Scottish	573	2.29
Serbian	70	0.28
Slavic	58	0.23
Slovak	845	3.37
Slovene	228	0.91
Swedish	223	0.89
Swiss	221	0.88
Turkish	10	0.04
Ukrainian	167	0.67
United States or American	1,462	5.83
Welsh	284	1.13
West Indian, excl. Hispanic:	20	0.08
Dutch West Indian	13	0.05
Jamaican	7	0.03
White:	24,121	95.95
Not Hispanic (23,607)	23,922	95.16
Hispanic (174)	199	0.79
Yugoslavian	34	0.14

Mentor

Place Type: City
County: Lake
Population: 50,278

Ancestry/Race	Number	%
African American/Black:	412	0.82
Not Hispanic (324)	412	0.82
African, sub-Saharan:	34	0.07
African	17	0.03
South African	17	0.03
Am. Ind. or Alaska Nat., not spec.	45	0.09
Albanian	6	0.01
American Indian tribes, specified:	77	0.15
Apache	3	0.01
Blackfeet	9	0.02
Cherokee (7)	42	0.08
Chippewa (1)	4	0.01
Comanche (2)	2	0.00
Cree	2	0.00
Houma	2	0.00
Iroquois	1	0.00
Latin American Indians (2)	2	0.00
Navajo (1)	4	0.01
Seminole	3	0.01
Sioux	1	0.00
All other tribes (1)	2	0.00
American Indian tribes, not spec.	2	0.00
Arab:	218	0.43
Arab/Arabic	6	0.01
Egyptian	17	0.03
Lebanese	170	0.34
Palestinian	18	0.04
Syrian	7	0.01

Notes: 1. Figures in the "Number" column do not add up to the total population due to: a) Ancestry/Race overlap — e.g. persons can report being both White and Irish, b) persons of Hispanic origin can report being any race, c) persons reporting two ancestries are counted in both categories. 2. Numbers in parentheses indicate the number of persons reporting this ancestry/race alone, not in combination with any other ancestry/race. 3. Refer to the Explanation of Data in the front of the book for more detailed information.

Asian:	705	1.40
Bangladeshi	1	0.00
Chinese, ex. Taiwanese (145)	166	0.33
Filipino (43)	62	0.12
Indian (218)	232	0.46
Indonesian	1	0.00
Japanese (45)	78	0.16
Korean (69)	79	0.16
Laotian (3)	3	0.01
Pakistani (16)	20	0.04
Taiwanese (3)	7	0.01
Thai (5)	8	0.02
Vietnamese (35)	35	0.07
Other Asian, specified (2)	2	0.00
Other Asian, not specified (5)	11	0.02
Austrian	233	0.46
Belgian	42	0.08
British	207	0.41
Bulgarian	8	0.02
Canadian	154	0.31
Carpatho Rusyn	7	0.01
Croatian	1,173	2.33
Czech	990	1.97
Czechoslovakian	218	0.43
Danish	215	0.43
Dutch	677	1.35
Eastern European	9	0.02
English	6,457	12.84
Estonian	18	0.04
European	184	0.37
Finnish	508	1.01
French, except Basque	1,035	2.06
French Canadian	202	0.40
German	13,362	26.58
Greek	219	0.44
Hawaii Native/Pacific Islander:	22	0.04
Polynesian: (7)	11	0.02
Native Hawaiian (2)	4	0.01
Samoan (5)	7	0.01
Other Pac. Isl., not spec. (9)	11	0.02
Hispanic or Latino:	363	0.72
Central American:	21	0.04
Honduran	2	0.00
Nicaraguan	8	0.02
Panamanian	3	0.01
Salvadoran	7	0.01
Other Central American	1	0.00
Cuban	20	0.04
Mexican	93	0.18
Puerto Rican	117	0.23
South American:	34	0.07
Argentinean	3	0.01
Bolivian	1	0.00
Chilean	5	0.01
Colombian	10	0.02
Ecuadorian	1	0.00
Peruvian	9	0.02
Venezuelan	5	0.01
Other Hispanic or Latino	78	0.16
Hungarian	2,253	4.48
Iranian	17	0.03
Irish	9,804	19.50
Italian	8,167	16.24
Latvian	14	0.03
Lithuanian	426	0.85
Macedonian	8	0.02
Northern European	55	0.11
Norwegian	297	0.59
Pennsylvania German	39	0.08
Polish	4,209	8.37
Portuguese	25	0.05
Romanian	213	0.42
Russian	477	0.95
Scandinavian	8	0.02
Scotch-Irish	822	1.63
Scottish	1,101	2.19
Serbian	145	0.29
Slavic	66	0.13
Slovak	1,851	3.68
Slovene	3,652	7.26
Swedish	521	1.04
Swiss	159	0.32
Ukrainian	475	0.94
United States or American	2,352	4.68
Welsh	704	1.40
White:	49,208	97.87
Not Hispanic (48,650)	48,919	97.30
Hispanic (270)	289	0.57
Yugoslavian	66	0.13

Miamisburg

Place Type: City
County: Montgomery
Population: 19,489

Ancestry/Race	Number	%
African American/Black:	354	1.82
Not Hispanic (309)	352	1.81
Hispanic (1)	2	0.01
African, sub-Saharan:	96	0.48
African	96	0.48
Alaska Native tribes, specified:	1	0.01
Aleut	1	0.01
Am. Ind. or Alaska Nat., not spec.	29	0.15
American Indian tribes, specified:	65	0.33
Blackfeet	7	0.04
Cherokee (11)	37	0.19
Chippewa (2)	2	0.01
Choctaw (1)	1	0.01
Crow	3	0.02
Delaware	1	0.01
Iroquois	2	0.01
Latin American Indians	4	0.02
Sioux (2)	5	0.03
All other tribes (1)	3	0.02
American Indian tribes, not spec.	1	0.01
Arab:	137	0.69
Jordanian	91	0.46
Lebanese	5	0.03
Palestinian	13	0.07
Other Arab	28	0.14
Armenian	4	0.02
Asian:	239	1.23
Cambodian	2	0.01
Chinese, ex. Taiwanese (19)	32	0.16
Filipino (23)	40	0.21
Indian (47)	50	0.26
Japanese (13)	18	0.09
Korean (19)	28	0.14
Laotian (3)	6	0.03
Taiwanese (3)	4	0.02
Vietnamese (9)	13	0.07
Other Asian, not specified (5)	46	0.24
Brazilian	10	0.05
British	28	0.14
Bulgarian	19	0.10
Canadian	35	0.18
Croatian	8	0.04
Czech	25	0.13
Danish	9	0.05
Dutch	499	2.52
English	2,172	10.95
European	219	1.10
French, except Basque	391	1.97
French Canadian	50	0.25
German	5,253	26.49
Greek	59	0.30
Guyanese	10	0.05
Hawaii Native/Pacific Islander:	16	0.08
Micronesian:	2	0.01
Guamanian/Chamorro	2	0.01
Polynesian: (7)	13	0.07
Native Hawaiian (1)	7	0.04
Samoan (6)	6	0.03
Other Pac. Isl., not spec.	1	0.01
Hispanic or Latino:	165	0.85
Central American:	10	0.05
Costa Rican	3	0.02
Guatemalan	1	0.01
Nicaraguan	4	0.02
Panamanian	1	0.01
Salvadoran	1	0.01
Cuban	3	0.02
Dominican Republic	1	0.01
Mexican	74	0.38
Puerto Rican	23	0.12
South American:	17	0.09
Bolivian	8	0.04
Colombian	5	0.03
Ecuadorian	2	0.01
Paraguayan	2	0.01
Other Hispanic or Latino	37	0.19
Hungarian	98	0.49
Irish	2,457	12.39
Italian	653	3.29
Lithuanian	20	0.10
Norwegian	60	0.30
Pennsylvania German	11	0.06
Polish	357	1.80
Russian	32	0.16
Scotch-Irish	329	1.66
Scottish	265	1.34
Slovak	29	0.15
Slovene	31	0.16
Swedish	164	0.83
Swiss	22	0.11
United States or American	2,550	12.86
Welsh	132	0.67
West Indian, excl. Hispanic:	11	0.06
West Indian	11	0.06
White:	18,928	97.12
Not Hispanic (18,600)	18,814	96.54
Hispanic (99)	114	0.58
Yugoslavian	9	0.05

Middleburg Heights

Place Type: City
County: Cuyahoga
Population: 15,542

Ancestry/Race	Number	%
African American/Black:	258	1.66
Not Hispanic (206)	253	1.63
Hispanic	5	0.03
Am. Ind. or Alaska Nat., not spec.	29	0.19
American Indian tribes, specified:	35	0.23
Blackfeet (1)	1	0.01
Cherokee (3)	12	0.08
Chippewa (1)	1	0.01
Cree	2	0.01
Iroquois (6)	8	0.05
Kiowa (3)	3	0.02
Latin American Indians (1)	1	0.01
Navajo (3)	4	0.03
Pueblo	1	0.01
All other tribes	2	0.01
American Indian tribes, not spec.	2	0.01
Arab:	227	1.46
Arab/Arabic	66	0.42
Lebanese	127	0.82
Moroccan	8	0.05
Palestinian	26	0.17
Armenian	47	0.30
Asian:	397	2.55
Bangladeshi (2)	2	0.01
Cambodian (4)	4	0.03
Chinese, ex. Taiwanese (60)	63	0.41
Filipino (35)	43	0.28
Indian (198)	212	1.36
Japanese (6)	7	0.05
Korean (14)	21	0.14
Pakistani (15)	20	0.13
Taiwanese (3)	4	0.03
Thai (1)	1	0.01
Vietnamese (2)	2	0.01
Other Asian, specified (4)	5	0.03
Other Asian, not specified (1)	13	0.08
Austrian	75	0.48

Notes: 1. Figures in the "Number" column do not add up to the total population due to: a) Ancestry/Race overlap — e.g. persons can report being both White and Irish, b) persons of Hispanic origin can report being any race, c) persons reporting two ancestries are counted in both categories. 2. Numbers in parentheses indicate the number of persons reporting this ancestry/race alone, not in combination with any other ancestry/race. 3. Refer to the Explanation of Data in the front of the book for more detailed information.

Belgian	8	0.05
Brazilian	7	0.05
British	33	0.21
Canadian	58	0.37
Celtic	7	0.05
Croatian	150	0.97
Czech	484	3.11
Czechoslovakian	121	0.78
Danish	29	0.19
Dutch	127	0.82
Eastern European	7	0.05
English	1,155	7.43
European	32	0.21
Finnish	58	0.37
French, except Basque	241	1.55
French Canadian	83	0.53
German	4,130	26.57
Greek	236	1.52
Guyanese	3	0.02
Hawaii Native/Pacific Islander:	21	0.14
Micronesian: (3)	3	0.02
Guamanian/Chamorro (3)	3	0.02
Polynesian: (7)	17	0.11
Native Hawaiian (1)	2	0.01
Samoan (4)	4	0.03
Tongan (2)	7	0.05
Other Polynesian	4	0.03
Other Pac. Isl., specified	1	0.01
Hispanic or Latino:	197	1.27
Central American:	11	0.07
Costa Rican	1	0.01
Guatemalan	1	0.01
Nicaraguan	2	0.01
Panamanian	1	0.01
Salvadoran	6	0.04
Cuban	10	0.06
Dominican Republic	1	0.01
Mexican	51	0.33
Puerto Rican	76	0.49
South American:	15	0.10
Chilean	3	0.02
Colombian	2	0.01
Peruvian	1	0.01
Venezuelan	4	0.03
Other South American	5	0.03
Other Hispanic or Latino	33	0.21
Hungarian	875	5.63
Icelander	9	0.06
Irish	2,500	16.09
Italian	2,217	14.26
Latvian	20	0.13
Lithuanian	46	0.30
Macedonian	24	0.15
Norwegian	34	0.22
Pennsylvania German	22	0.14
Polish	1,845	11.87
Portuguese	6	0.04
Romanian	249	1.60
Russian	229	1.47
Scandinavian	7	0.05
Scotch-Irish	154	0.99
Scottish	201	1.29
Serbian	35	0.23
Slovak	1,226	7.89
Slovene	300	1.93
Swedish	217	1.40
Swiss	58	0.37
Ukrainian	473	3.04
United States or American	357	2.30
Welsh	208	1.34
West Indian, excl. Hispanic:	37	0.24
Haitian	4	0.03
Trinidadian and Tobagonian	33	0.21
White:	14,888	95.79
Not Hispanic (14,587)	14,742	94.85
Hispanic (121)	146	0.94
Yugoslavian	34	0.22

Middletown

Place Type: City
County: Butler
Population: 51,605

Ancestry/Race	Number	%
African American/Black:	5,892	11.42
Not Hispanic (5,447)	5,860	11.36
Hispanic (20)	32	0.06
African, sub-Saharan:	183	0.35
African	171	0.33
Nigerian	3	0.01
South African	9	0.02
Alaska Native tribes, specified:	2	0.00
Tlingit-Haida (1)	2	0.00
Am. Ind. or Alaska Nat., not spec.	134	0.26
American Indian tribes, specified:	204	0.40
Apache	3	0.01
Blackfeet (11)	28	0.05
Cherokee (39)	113	0.22
Chippewa (2)	5	0.01
Choctaw (2)	2	0.00
Creek	3	0.01
Crow	1	0.00
Delaware (1)	1	0.00
Iroquois (6)	7	0.01
Lumbee (2)	2	0.00
Navajo	1	0.00
Osage	3	0.01
Pueblo	1	0.00
Sioux (1)	7	0.01
Yaqui (1)	2	0.00
All other tribes (14)	25	0.05
American Indian tribes, not spec.	25	0.05
Arab:	70	0.14
Arab/Arabic	20	0.04
Egyptian	4	0.01
Lebanese	20	0.04
Palestinian	14	0.03
Syrian	12	0.02
Armenian	4	0.01
Asian:	273	0.53
Bangladeshi (9)	9	0.02
Cambodian	10	0.02
Chinese, ex. Taiwanese (26)	43	0.08
Filipino (23)	39	0.08
Indian (47)	56	0.11
Indonesian (1)	1	0.00
Japanese (15)	19	0.04
Korean (29)	34	0.07
Malaysian (1)	1	0.00
Pakistani (3)	3	0.01
Taiwanese (3)	3	0.01
Thai	4	0.01
Vietnamese (11)	18	0.03
Other Asian, specified (4)	6	0.01
Other Asian, not specified (7)	27	0.05
Austrian	62	0.12
Belgian	8	0.02
British	224	0.43
Bulgarian	20	0.04
Canadian	49	0.09
Celtic	7	0.01
Croatian	38	0.07
Czech	82	0.16
Czechoslovakian	75	0.14
Danish	40	0.08
Dutch	753	1.45
English	5,192	10.02
European	232	0.45
Finnish	53	0.10
French, except Basque	1,128	2.18
French Canadian	89	0.17
German	8,761	16.91
German Russian	16	0.03
Greek	276	0.53
Hawaii Native/Pacific Islander:	44	0.09
Micronesian: (1)	4	0.01
Guamanian/Chamorro (1)	4	0.01
Polynesian: (11)	23	0.04
Native Hawaiian (4)	15	0.03
Samoan (7)	8	0.02
Other Pac. Isl., specified	1	0.00
Other Pac. Isl., not spec. (6)	16	0.03
Hispanic or Latino:	460	0.89
Central American:	48	0.09
Costa Rican	4	0.01
Guatemalan	2	0.00
Honduran	8	0.02
Nicaraguan	9	0.02
Panamanian	7	0.01
Salvadoran	14	0.03
Other Central American	4	0.01
Cuban	17	0.03
Dominican Republic	10	0.02
Mexican	174	0.34
Puerto Rican	82	0.16
South American:	15	0.03
Bolivian	2	0.00
Chilean	3	0.01
Colombian	8	0.02
Peruvian	1	0.00
Venezuelan	1	0.00
Other Hispanic or Latino	114	0.22
Hungarian	311	0.60
Irish	5,969	11.52
Italian	1,257	2.43
Lithuanian	26	0.05
Macedonian	7	0.01
Norwegian	233	0.45
Pennsylvania German	7	0.01
Polish	312	0.60
Portuguese	36	0.07
Romanian	21	0.04
Russian	54	0.10
Scandinavian	6	0.01
Scotch-Irish	728	1.41
Scottish	883	1.70
Serbian	10	0.02
Slavic	10	0.02
Slovak	116	0.22
Swedish	183	0.35
Swiss	35	0.07
Ukrainian	6	0.01
United States or American	7,955	15.36
Welsh	408	0.79
West Indian, excl. Hispanic:	17	0.03
Jamaican	17	0.03
White:	45,534	88.24
Not Hispanic (44,658)	45,264	87.71
Hispanic (228)	270	0.52
Yugoslavian	42	0.08

Montgomery

Place Type: City
County: Hamilton
Population: 10,163

Ancestry/Race	Number	%
African American/Black:	193	1.90
Not Hispanic (160)	192	1.89
Hispanic	1	0.01
African, sub-Saharan:	10	0.10
South African	10	0.10
Am. Ind. or Alaska Nat., not spec.	10	0.10
Alsatian	10	0.10
American Indian tribes, specified:	13	0.13
Cherokee	11	0.11
Creek (2)	2	0.02
American Indian tribes, not spec.	1	0.01
Arab:	165	1.64
Jordanian	35	0.35
Lebanese	57	0.57
Palestinian	35	0.35
Syrian	38	0.38
Armenian	10	0.10
Asian:	384	3.78
Chinese, ex. Taiwanese (78)	92	0.91

Notes: 1. Figures in the "Number" column do not add up to the total population due to: a) Ancestry/Race overlap — e.g. persons can report being both White and Irish, b) persons of Hispanic origin can report being any race, c) persons reporting two ancestries are counted in both categories. 2. Numbers in parentheses indicate the number of persons reporting this ancestry/race alone, not in combination with any other ancestry/race. 3. Refer to the Explanation of Data in the front of the book for more detailed information.

Ancestry/Race	Number	%
Filipino (9)	15	0.15
Indian (103)	115	1.13
Japanese (67)	77	0.76
Korean (55)	55	0.54
Malaysian (1)	1	0.01
Pakistani	3	0.03
Taiwanese (12)	16	0.16
Vietnamese (1)	1	0.01
Other Asian, not specified (2)	9	0.09
Australian	10	0.10
Austrian	68	0.68
Belgian	46	0.46
British	121	1.20
Canadian	22	0.22
Celtic	9	0.09
Czech	40	0.40
Czechoslovakian	16	0.16
Danish	14	0.14
Dutch	263	2.62
Eastern European	47	0.47
English	1,494	14.88
European	191	1.90
French, except Basque	535	5.33
French Canadian	45	0.45
German	3,432	34.17
Greek	19	0.19
Hawaii Native/Pacific Islander:	9	0.09
Other Pac. Isl., not spec.	9	0.09
Hispanic or Latino:	78	0.77
Central American:	1	0.01
Honduran	1	0.01
Cuban	13	0.13
Mexican	22	0.22
Puerto Rican	8	0.08
South American:	18	0.18
Argentinean	3	0.03
Colombian	4	0.04
Ecuadorian	1	0.01
Peruvian	6	0.06
Venezuelan	2	0.02
Other South American	2	0.02
Other Hispanic or Latino	16	0.16
Hungarian	64	0.64
Iranian	18	0.18
Irish	1,682	16.75
Israeli	24	0.24
Italian	417	4.15
Lithuanian	72	0.72
Northern European	6	0.06
Norwegian	160	1.59
Pennsylvania German	6	0.06
Polish	443	4.41
Romanian	7	0.07
Russian	221	2.20
Scotch-Irish	215	2.14
Scottish	285	2.84
Slavic	19	0.19
Slovak	79	0.79
Swedish	87	0.87
Swiss	71	0.71
Turkish	59	0.59
Ukrainian	26	0.26
United States or American	597	5.94
Welsh	87	0.87
White:	9,636	94.81
Not Hispanic (9,494)	9,571	94.17
Hispanic (59)	65	0.64

Mount Vernon

Place Type: City
County: Knox
Population: 14,375

Ancestry/Race	Number	%
Acadian/Cajun	6	0.04
African American/Black:	226	1.57
Not Hispanic (163)	221	1.54
Hispanic (3)	5	0.03
Am. Ind. or Alaska Nat., not spec.	52	0.36
American Indian tribes, specified:	68	0.47
Apache (1)	2	0.01
Blackfeet	3	0.02
Cherokee (15)	41	0.29
Chippewa	1	0.01
Choctaw (1)	1	0.01
Cree (1)	1	0.01
Iroquois	1	0.01
Latin American Indians (2)	3	0.02
Osage	1	0.01
Seminole (1)	1	0.01
Sioux (1)	4	0.03
Ute	1	0.01
Yaqui	1	0.01
All other tribes (3)	7	0.05
American Indian tribes, not spec.	4	0.03
Arab:	33	0.23
Egyptian	11	0.08
Lebanese	11	0.08
Syrian	11	0.08
Asian:	87	0.61
Chinese, ex. Taiwanese (25)	25	0.17
Filipino (7)	10	0.07
Indian (13)	14	0.10
Japanese (7)	7	0.05
Korean (9)	11	0.08
Sri Lankan (1)	1	0.01
Taiwanese (4)	4	0.03
Thai (1)	3	0.02
Vietnamese (6)	6	0.04
Other Asian, specified (3)	3	0.02
Other Asian, not specified (1)	3	0.02
Australian	50	0.34
Austrian	9	0.06
Belgian	65	0.45
British	35	0.24
Bulgarian	34	0.23
Canadian	28	0.19
Croatian	6	0.04
Czech	13	0.09
Czechoslovakian	28	0.19
Danish	10	0.07
Dutch	374	2.57
English	1,500	10.30
European	118	0.81
Finnish	7	0.05
French, except Basque	428	2.94
French Canadian	22	0.15
German	2,866	19.68
Greek	80	0.55
Hawaii Native/Pacific Islander:	4	0.03
Micronesian:	2	0.01
Guamanian/Chamorro	2	0.01
Polynesian:	2	0.01
Native Hawaiian	2	0.01
Hispanic or Latino:	125	0.87
Central American:	3	0.02
Guatemalan	1	0.01
Nicaraguan	1	0.01
Salvadoran	1	0.01
Cuban	1	0.01
Dominican Republic	3	0.02
Mexican	65	0.45
Puerto Rican	11	0.08
South American:	8	0.06
Chilean	5	0.03
Peruvian	1	0.01
Venezuelan	2	0.01
Other Hispanic or Latino	34	0.24
Hungarian	88	0.60
Irish	1,819	12.49
Italian	406	2.79
Lithuanian	5	0.03
Northern European	21	0.14
Norwegian	65	0.45
Pennsylvania German	6	0.04
Polish	136	0.93
Romanian	4	0.03
Russian	71	0.49
Scandinavian	18	0.12
Scotch-Irish	147	1.01
Scottish	163	1.12
Serbian	10	0.07
Slovak	27	0.19
Slovene	10	0.07
Swedish	90	0.62
Swiss	94	0.65
Turkish	8	0.05
Ukrainian	21	0.14
United States or American	2,275	15.62
Welsh	152	1.04
White:	14,043	97.69
Not Hispanic (13,818)	13,957	97.09
Hispanic (77)	86	0.60

New Philadelphia

Place Type: City
County: Tuscarawas
Population: 17,056

Ancestry/Race	Number	%
African American/Black:	220	1.29
Not Hispanic (165)	216	1.27
Hispanic	4	0.02
African, sub-Saharan:	6	0.04
African	6	0.04
Am. Ind. or Alaska Nat., not spec.	41	0.24
American Indian tribes, specified:	58	0.34
Apache	1	0.01
Blackfeet	1	0.01
Cherokee (5)	28	0.16
Choctaw (2)	3	0.02
Crow (4)	7	0.04
Delaware	5	0.03
Iroquois	1	0.01
Latin American Indians (1)	1	0.01
Navajo	1	0.01
Seminole (1)	1	0.01
Sioux (1)	1	0.01
All other tribes (6)	8	0.05
American Indian tribes, not spec.	3	0.02
Arab:	53	0.31
Arab/Arabic	15	0.09
Lebanese	38	0.23
Asian:	109	0.64
Chinese, ex. Taiwanese (24)	26	0.15
Filipino (13)	19	0.11
Indian (32)	36	0.21
Japanese (2)	4	0.02
Korean (6)	13	0.08
Thai (1)	3	0.02
Other Asian, specified (4)	5	0.03
Other Asian, not specified	3	0.02
Austrian	143	0.85
Belgian	6	0.04
Brazilian	4	0.02
British	78	0.46
Canadian	16	0.09
Celtic	9	0.05
Croatian	13	0.08
Czech	73	0.43
Czechoslovakian	30	0.18
Danish	14	0.08
Dutch	372	2.20
English	1,813	10.74
European	80	0.47
French, except Basque	333	1.97
French Canadian	66	0.39
German	5,038	29.83
Greek	46	0.27
Hawaii Native/Pacific Islander:	17	0.10
Micronesian: (2)	2	0.01
Guamanian/Chamorro (2)	2	0.01
Polynesian: (4)	8	0.05
Native Hawaiian (1)	3	0.02
Samoan (3)	5	0.03
Other Pac. Isl., not spec. (4)	7	0.04
Hispanic or Latino:	227	1.33
Central American:	67	0.39

Notes: 1. Figures in the "Number" column do not add up to the total population due to: a) Ancestry/Race overlap — e.g. persons can report being both White and Irish, b) persons of Hispanic origin can report being any race, c) persons reporting two ancestries are counted in both categories. 2. Numbers in parentheses indicate the number of persons reporting this ancestry/race alone, not in combination with any other ancestry/race. 3. Refer to the Explanation of Data in the front of the book for more detailed information.

Ancestry/Race	Number	%
Guatemalan	65	0.38
Honduran	1	0.01
Panamanian	1	0.01
Cuban	2	0.01
Dominican Republic	4	0.02
Mexican	92	0.54
Puerto Rican	29	0.17
South American:	6	0.04
Colombian	6	0.04
Other Hispanic or Latino	27	0.16
Hungarian	206	1.22
Irish	2,411	14.28
Italian	1,321	7.82
Lithuanian	10	0.06
Northern European	9	0.05
Norwegian	15	0.09
Pennsylvania German	54	0.32
Polish	408	2.42
Portuguese	27	0.16
Romanian	58	0.34
Russian	77	0.46
Scandinavian	7	0.04
Scotch-Irish	292	1.73
Scottish	489	2.90
Serbian	7	0.04
Slovak	203	1.20
Slovene	6	0.04
Swedish	98	0.58
Swiss	418	2.48
Ukrainian	15	0.09
United States or American	1,334	7.90
Welsh	320	1.89
White:	16,679	97.79
Not Hispanic (16,384)	16,521	96.86
Hispanic (141)	158	0.93

Newark

Place Type: City
County: Licking
Population: 46,279

Ancestry/Race	Number	%
African American/Black:	1,785	3.86
Not Hispanic (1,422)	1,753	3.79
Hispanic (13)	32	0.07
African, sub-Saharan:	108	0.23
African	108	0.23
Alaska Native tribes, not specified	1	0.00
Am. Ind. or Alaska Nat., not spec.	136	0.29
American Indian tribes, specified:	221	0.48
Apache (7)	9	0.02
Blackfeet (4)	24	0.05
Cherokee (40)	117	0.25
Cheyenne	3	0.01
Chippewa (1)	2	0.00
Choctaw	3	0.01
Comanche (1)	1	0.00
Delaware (4)	4	0.01
Iroquois (5)	12	0.03
Latin American Indians	1	0.00
Lumbee (1)	1	0.00
Navajo (5)	5	0.01
Paiute (1)	2	0.00
Pima (1)	1	0.00
Pueblo (1)	1	0.00
Sioux (10)	20	0.04
All other tribes (5)	15	0.03
American Indian tribes, not spec.	15	0.03
Arab:	70	0.15
Lebanese	55	0.12
Syrian	15	0.03
Armenian	7	0.02
Asian:	381	0.82
Cambodian (9)	9	0.02
Chinese, ex. Taiwanese (71)	78	0.17
Filipino (41)	55	0.12
Indian (28)	42	0.09
Indonesian (4)	5	0.01
Japanese (18)	33	0.07
Korean (45)	57	0.12
Laotian (1)	1	0.00
Malaysian (1)	1	0.00
Pakistani (2)	3	0.01
Taiwanese (14)	16	0.03
Thai (9)	21	0.05
Vietnamese (18)	30	0.06
Other Asian, specified (1)	5	0.01
Other Asian, not specified (14)	25	0.05
Austrian	41	0.09
Belgian	27	0.06
Brazilian	5	0.01
British	215	0.47
Bulgarian	22	0.05
Canadian	91	0.20
Celtic	29	0.06
Croatian	46	0.10
Czech	44	0.10
Czechoslovakian	73	0.16
Danish	65	0.14
Dutch	1,072	2.32
Eastern European	23	0.05
English	4,991	10.82
European	326	0.71
Finnish	27	0.06
French, except Basque	985	2.14
French Canadian	76	0.16
German	10,651	23.10
Greek	112	0.24
Hawaii Native/Pacific Islander:	36	0.08
Micronesian: (4)	9	0.02
Guamanian/Chamorro (4)	9	0.02
Polynesian: (8)	21	0.05
Native Hawaiian (2)	11	0.02
Samoan (5)	6	0.01
Tongan (1)	4	0.01
Other Pac. Isl., specified	2	0.00
Other Pac. Isl., not spec. (1)	4	0.01
Hispanic or Latino:	390	0.84
Central American:	13	0.03
Costa Rican	4	0.01
Guatemalan	1	0.00
Panamanian	4	0.01
Salvadoran	4	0.01
Cuban	6	0.01
Dominican Republic	5	0.01
Mexican	168	0.36
Puerto Rican	49	0.11
South American:	21	0.05
Argentinean	2	0.00
Chilean	1	0.00
Colombian	14	0.03
Peruvian	2	0.00
Venezuelan	2	0.00
Other Hispanic or Latino	128	0.28
Hungarian	279	0.61
Icelander	6	0.01
Irish	6,647	14.41
Italian	1,992	4.32
Lithuanian	36	0.08
Macedonian	13	0.03
Northern European	26	0.06
Norwegian	94	0.20
Pennsylvania German	66	0.14
Polish	538	1.17
Portuguese	47	0.10
Romanian	25	0.05
Russian	62	0.13
Scandinavian	33	0.07
Scotch-Irish	813	1.76
Scottish	793	1.72
Serbian	9	0.02
Slavic	11	0.02
Slovak	69	0.15
Slovene	5	0.01
Swedish	205	0.44
Swiss	151	0.33
Turkish	13	0.03
Ukrainian	34	0.07
United States or American	6,265	13.59
Welsh	975	2.11
West Indian, excl. Hispanic:	18	0.04
Jamaican	18	0.04
White:	44,220	95.55
Not Hispanic (43,312)	43,926	94.92
Hispanic (248)	294	0.64
Yugoslavian	6	0.01

Niles

Place Type: City
County: Trumbull
Population: 20,932

Ancestry/Race	Number	%
African American/Black:	563	2.69
Not Hispanic (463)	543	2.59
Hispanic (12)	20	0.10
African, sub-Saharan:	87	0.42
African	87	0.42
Alaska Native tribes, specified:	2	0.01
Alaska Athabascan (1)	1	0.00
Eskimo	1	0.00
Am. Ind. or Alaska Nat., not spec.	48	0.23
Albanian	74	0.35
American Indian tribes, specified:	80	0.38
Apache (1)	1	0.00
Blackfeet	7	0.03
Cherokee (12)	43	0.21
Chippewa	6	0.03
Choctaw (1)	1	0.00
Delaware	1	0.00
Iroquois	1	0.00
Navajo (1)	1	0.00
Pueblo (1)	4	0.02
Sioux	5	0.02
All other tribes	10	0.05
American Indian tribes, not spec.	10	0.05
Arab:	117	0.56
Arab/Arabic	6	0.03
Lebanese	45	0.22
Palestinian	31	0.15
Syrian	35	0.17
Armenian	11	0.05
Asian:	113	0.54
Bangladeshi	1	0.00
Chinese, ex. Taiwanese (11)	15	0.07
Filipino (6)	9	0.04
Indian (12)	19	0.09
Indonesian (1)	1	0.00
Japanese (10)	17	0.08
Korean (15)	22	0.11
Thai (1)	1	0.00
Vietnamese (8)	8	0.04
Other Asian, not specified (3)	20	0.10
Australian	4	0.02
Austrian	29	0.14
British	43	0.21
Canadian	22	0.11
Croatian	337	1.61
Czech	28	0.13
Czechoslovakian	54	0.26
Dutch	257	1.23
English	2,226	10.64
Finnish	134	0.64
French, except Basque	365	1.74
French Canadian	39	0.19
German	4,473	21.37
Greek	170	0.81
Hawaii Native/Pacific Islander:	13	0.06
Polynesian: (2)	6	0.03
Native Hawaiian (2)	5	0.02
Samoan	1	0.00
Other Pac. Isl., not spec.	7	0.03
Hispanic or Latino:	174	0.83
Central American:	2	0.01
Guatemalan	1	0.00
Salvadoran	1	0.00
Cuban	6	0.03
Dominican Republic	1	0.00

Notes: 1. Figures in the "Number" column do not add up to the total population due to: a) Ancestry/Race overlap — e.g. persons can report being both White and Irish, b) persons of Hispanic origin can report being any race, c) persons reporting two ancestries are counted in both categories. 2. Numbers in parentheses indicate the number of persons reporting this ancestry/race alone, not in combination with any other ancestry/race. 3. Refer to the Explanation of Data in the front of the book for more detailed information.

Mexican	73	0.35
Puerto Rican	51	0.24
South American:	4	0.02
Argentinean	1	0.00
Colombian	3	0.01
Other Hispanic or Latino	37	0.18
Hungarian	692	3.31
Irish	3,658	17.48
Italian	5,011	23.94
Latvian	10	0.05
Lithuanian	35	0.17
Luxemburger	8	0.04
Macedonian	9	0.04
Northern European	8	0.04
Norwegian	33	0.16
Pennsylvania German	70	0.33
Polish	885	4.23
Portuguese	16	0.08
Romanian	220	1.05
Russian	121	0.58
Scandinavian	6	0.03
Scotch-Irish	379	1.81
Scottish	411	1.96
Serbian	23	0.11
Slavic	21	0.10
Slovak	1,003	4.79
Slovene	72	0.34
Swedish	92	0.44
Swiss	57	0.27
Ukrainian	291	1.39
United States or American	1,125	5.38
Welsh	819	3.91
White:	20,288	96.92
Not Hispanic (19,981)	20,161	96.32
Hispanic (109)	127	0.61
Yugoslavian	44	0.21

North Canton

Place Type: City
County: Stark
Population: 16,369

Ancestry/Race	Number	%
African American/Black:	221	1.35
Not Hispanic (179)	213	1.30
Hispanic (4)	8	0.05
Am. Ind. or Alaska Nat., not spec.	25	0.15
American Indian tribes, specified:	27	0.16
Cherokee (2)	9	0.05
Cheyenne	1	0.01
Cree	1	0.01
Iroquois	3	0.02
Latin American Indians	2	0.01
Navajo	1	0.01
Shoshone	1	0.01
Sioux (3)	4	0.02
All other tribes (1)	5	0.03
American Indian tribes, not spec.	2	0.01
Arab:	185	1.13
Lebanese	120	0.73
Syrian	48	0.29
Other Arab	17	0.10
Armenian	22	0.13
Asian:	203	1.24
Chinese, ex. Taiwanese (38)	45	0.27
Filipino (17)	31	0.19
Indian (43)	46	0.28
Indonesian	2	0.01
Japanese (11)	15	0.09
Korean (26)	27	0.16
Pakistani (1)	1	0.01
Taiwanese (4)	4	0.02
Thai (1)	1	0.01
Vietnamese (21)	21	0.13
Other Asian, specified (5)	5	0.03
Other Asian, not specified (1)	5	0.03
Austrian	95	0.58
Belgian	33	0.20
Brazilian	31	0.19
British	86	0.52
Canadian	21	0.13
Croatian	110	0.67
Czech	109	0.67
Czechoslovakian	32	0.20
Danish	61	0.37
Dutch	311	1.90
English	2,123	12.96
European	177	1.08
Finnish	13	0.08
French, except Basque	518	3.16
French Canadian	46	0.28
German	5,592	34.14
Greek	260	1.59
Hawaii Native/Pacific Islander:	6	0.04
Polynesian:	3	0.02
Native Hawaiian	3	0.02
Other Pac. Isl., not spec.	3	0.02
Hispanic or Latino:	134	0.82
Central American:	17	0.10
Costa Rican	1	0.01
Honduran	13	0.08
Panamanian	1	0.01
Salvadoran	2	0.01
Cuban	3	0.02
Dominican Republic	2	0.01
Mexican	39	0.24
Puerto Rican	16	0.10
South American:	7	0.04
Argentinean	1	0.01
Colombian	5	0.03
Peruvian	1	0.01
Other Hispanic or Latino	50	0.31
Hungarian	217	1.32
Iranian	3	0.02
Irish	2,260	13.80
Italian	1,707	10.42
Latvian	8	0.05
Lithuanian	27	0.16
Macedonian	35	0.21
Norwegian	91	0.56
Pennsylvania German	45	0.27
Polish	515	3.14
Portuguese	10	0.06
Romanian	177	1.08
Russian	104	0.63
Scandinavian	17	0.10
Scotch-Irish	309	1.89
Scottish	557	3.40
Serbian	48	0.29
Slavic	11	0.07
Slovak	215	1.31
Slovene	31	0.19
Swedish	194	1.18
Swiss	291	1.78
Turkish	8	0.05
Ukrainian	70	0.43
United States or American	853	5.21
Welsh	406	2.48
West Indian, excl. Hispanic:	6	0.04
Haitian	6	0.04
White:	15,960	97.50
Not Hispanic (15,762)	15,854	96.85
Hispanic (100)	106	0.65
Yugoslavian	56	0.34

North College Hill

Place Type: City
County: Hamilton
Population: 10,082

Ancestry/Race	Number	%
African American/Black:	2,265	22.47
Not Hispanic (2,182)	2,260	22.42
Hispanic (5)	5	0.05
African, sub-Saharan:	111	1.10
African	98	0.97
Nigerian	13	0.13
Am. Ind. or Alaska Nat., not spec.	25	0.25
American Indian tribes, specified:	35	0.35
Blackfeet (1)	1	0.01
Cherokee (7)	21	0.21
Chippewa	5	0.05
Iroquois	1	0.01
Latin American Indians (1)	1	0.01
Pueblo	1	0.01
Sioux (1)	3	0.03
All other tribes (2)	2	0.02
American Indian tribes, not spec.	1	0.01
Asian:	48	0.48
Chinese, ex. Taiwanese (16)	18	0.18
Filipino (2)	3	0.03
Indian (5)	7	0.07
Japanese	1	0.01
Korean (2)	5	0.05
Vietnamese	2	0.02
Other Asian, not specified (1)	12	0.12
Austrian	46	0.46
Belgian	5	0.05
British	23	0.23
Canadian	11	0.11
Croatian	7	0.07
Czech	6	0.06
Danish	40	0.40
Dutch	137	1.36
English	721	7.16
European	73	0.72
Finnish	8	0.08
French, except Basque	155	1.54
French Canadian	6	0.06
German	3,517	34.91
Greek	44	0.44
Hawaii Native/Pacific Islander:	1	0.01
Micronesian: (1)	1	0.01
Guamanian/Chamorro (1)	1	0.01
Hispanic or Latino:	59	0.59
Central American:	1	0.01
Salvadoran	1	0.01
Cuban	10	0.10
Mexican	21	0.21
Puerto Rican	8	0.08
South American:	1	0.01
Colombian	1	0.01
Other Hispanic or Latino	18	0.18
Hungarian	57	0.57
Icelander	11	0.11
Irish	1,078	10.70
Italian	193	1.92
Lithuanian	9	0.09
Polish	111	1.10
Portuguese	11	0.11
Romanian	22	0.22
Russian	25	0.25
Scotch-Irish	92	0.91
Scottish	74	0.73
Serbian	60	0.60
Slavic	15	0.15
Slovak	10	0.10
Slovene	10	0.10
Swedish	22	0.22
Swiss	70	0.69
United States or American	1,363	13.53
Welsh	123	1.22
West Indian, excl. Hispanic:	9	0.09
West Indian	9	0.09
White:	7,785	77.22
Not Hispanic (7,647)	7,747	76.84
Hispanic (35)	38	0.38
Yugoslavian	14	0.14

North Olmsted

Place Type: City
County: Cuyahoga
Population: 34,113

Ancestry/Race	Number	%
African American/Black:	414	1.21
Not Hispanic (341)	399	1.17

Notes: 1. Figures in the "Number" column do not add up to the total population due to: a) Ancestry/Race overlap — e.g. persons can report being both White and Irish, b) persons of Hispanic origin can report being any race, c) persons reporting two ancestries are counted in both categories. 2. Numbers in parentheses indicate the number of persons reporting this ancestry/race alone, not in combination with any other ancestry/race. 3. Refer to the Explanation of Data in the front of the book for more detailed information.

Ancestry/Race	Number	%
Hispanic (5)	15	0.04
African, sub-Saharan:	66	0.19
African	40	0.12
Ghanian	11	0.03
Liberian	7	0.02
South African	8	0.02
Alaska Native tribes, specified:	2	0.01
Eskimo (2)	2	0.01
Am. Ind. or Alaska Nat., not spec.	44	0.13
Albanian	17	0.05
American Indian tribes, specified:	75	0.22
Apache (1)	1	0.00
Blackfeet (3)	9	0.03
Cherokee (7)	43	0.13
Chickasaw	1	0.00
Chippewa (2)	3	0.01
Choctaw (1)	1	0.00
Cree	1	0.00
Creek (1)	1	0.00
Latin American Indians (3)	4	0.01
Lumbee (1)	1	0.00
Navajo	2	0.01
Pueblo (1)	1	0.00
Seminole (2)	2	0.01
Sioux	1	0.00
All other tribes	4	0.01
American Indian tribes, not spec.	5	0.01
Arab:	1,050	3.08
Arab/Arabic	335	0.98
Egyptian	7	0.02
Jordanian	23	0.07
Lebanese	282	0.83
Moroccan	15	0.04
Palestinian	354	1.04
Syrian	34	0.10
Asian:	1,106	3.24
Bangladeshi (4)	4	0.01
Cambodian (17)	17	0.05
Chinese, ex. Taiwanese (216)	236	0.69
Filipino (68)	92	0.27
Indian (408)	425	1.25
Japanese (50)	62	0.18
Korean (59)	72	0.21
Malaysian (2)	2	0.01
Pakistani (8)	12	0.04
Sri Lankan (5)	5	0.01
Taiwanese (5)	7	0.02
Thai (8)	10	0.03
Vietnamese (55)	68	0.20
Other Asian, specified (3)	3	0.01
Other Asian, not specified (16)	91	0.27
Australian	10	0.03
Austrian	192	0.56
Belgian	30	0.09
Brazilian	18	0.05
British	104	0.30
Bulgarian	28	0.08
Canadian	24	0.07
Celtic	13	0.04
Croatian	400	1.17
Czech	452	1.33
Czechoslovakian	210	0.62
Danish	53	0.16
Dutch	590	1.73
English	3,264	9.57
European	111	0.33
Finnish	39	0.11
French, except Basque	907	2.66
French Canadian	169	0.50
German	10,200	29.90
Greek	365	1.07
Guyanese	8	0.02
Hawaii Native/Pacific Islander:	7	0.02
Polynesian: (3)	5	0.01
Native Hawaiian (1)	3	0.01
Samoan (2)	2	0.01
Other Pac. Isl., not spec. (1)	2	0.01
Hispanic or Latino:	575	1.69
Central American:	38	0.11
Costa Rican	6	0.02
Guatemalan	10	0.03
Honduran	2	0.01
Nicaraguan	7	0.02
Salvadoran	12	0.04
Other Central American	1	0.00
Cuban	13	0.04
Dominican Republic	7	0.02
Mexican	149	0.44
Puerto Rican	237	0.69
South American:	45	0.13
Chilean	1	0.00
Colombian	24	0.07
Peruvian	16	0.05
Venezuelan	1	0.00
Other South American	3	0.01
Other Hispanic or Latino	86	0.25
Hungarian	1,815	5.32
Icelander	10	0.03
Iranian	7	0.02
Irish	7,761	22.75
Italian	3,637	10.66
Latvian	45	0.13
Lithuanian	185	0.54
Macedonian	18	0.05
Northern European	6	0.02
Norwegian	271	0.79
Pennsylvania German	20	0.06
Polish	3,376	9.90
Portuguese	64	0.19
Romanian	453	1.33
Russian	388	1.14
Scandinavian	12	0.04
Scotch-Irish	566	1.66
Scottish	653	1.91
Serbian	26	0.08
Slavic	59	0.17
Slovak	1,990	5.83
Slovene	657	1.93
Swedish	205	0.60
Swiss	120	0.35
Turkish	29	0.09
Ukrainian	440	1.29
United States or American	1,104	3.24
Welsh	408	1.20
White:	32,601	95.57
Not Hispanic (31,666)	32,168	94.30
Hispanic (389)	433	1.27
Yugoslavian	57	0.17

North Ridgeville

Place Type: City
County: Lorain
Population: 22,338

Ancestry/Race	Number	%
African American/Black:	256	1.15
Not Hispanic (191)	254	1.14
Hispanic (1)	2	0.01
Alaska Native tribes, specified:	2	0.01
Tlingit-Haida (2)	2	0.01
Am. Ind. or Alaska Nat., not spec.	57	0.26
American Indian tribes, specified:	81	0.36
Apache (1)	1	0.00
Blackfeet	3	0.01
Cherokee (17)	44	0.20
Cheyenne	2	0.01
Chickasaw	1	0.00
Creek (1)	2	0.01
Crow (2)	5	0.02
Iroquois (1)	4	0.02
Kiowa (3)	6	0.03
Latin American Indians (1)	1	0.00
Pueblo	1	0.00
Sioux (6)	7	0.03
All other tribes	4	0.02
American Indian tribes, not spec.	6	0.03
Arab:	134	0.60
Arab/Arabic	9	0.04
Jordanian	27	0.12
Lebanese	87	0.39
Syrian	11	0.05
Asian:	289	1.29
Chinese, ex. Taiwanese (25)	37	0.17
Filipino (36)	55	0.25
Indian (72)	79	0.35
Indonesian	1	0.00
Japanese (14)	21	0.09
Korean (18)	36	0.16
Pakistani (5)	5	0.02
Taiwanese	3	0.01
Thai (4)	5	0.02
Vietnamese (29)	30	0.13
Other Asian, specified	1	0.00
Other Asian, not specified (3)	16	0.07
Australian	7	0.03
Austrian	50	0.22
Belgian	16	0.07
Brazilian	20	0.09
British	118	0.53
Bulgarian	12	0.05
Canadian	43	0.19
Croatian	193	0.86
Czech	335	1.50
Czechoslovakian	89	0.40
Danish	89	0.40
Dutch	415	1.86
English	2,809	12.57
Estonian	7	0.03
European	35	0.16
Finnish	66	0.30
French, except Basque	664	2.97
French Canadian	127	0.57
German	7,347	32.89
Greek	174	0.78
Guyanese	16	0.07
Hawaii Native/Pacific Islander:	11	0.05
Micronesian: (1)	1	0.00
Guamanian/Chamorro (1)	1	0.00
Polynesian:	6	0.03
Native Hawaiian	2	0.01
Samoan	4	0.02
Other Pac. Isl., specified	1	0.00
Other Pac. Isl., not spec.	3	0.01
Hispanic or Latino:	445	1.99
Central American:	8	0.04
Costa Rican	1	0.00
Guatemalan	3	0.01
Honduran	2	0.01
Salvadoran	2	0.01
Cuban	11	0.05
Mexican	154	0.69
Puerto Rican	199	0.89
South American:	15	0.07
Argentinean	3	0.01
Chilean	3	0.01
Colombian	7	0.03
Ecuadorian	1	0.00
Venezuelan	1	0.00
Other Hispanic or Latino	58	0.26
Hungarian	1,183	5.30
Irish	4,296	19.23
Italian	2,005	8.98
Latvian	8	0.04
Lithuanian	123	0.55
Macedonian	29	0.13
Norwegian	82	0.37
Pennsylvania German	33	0.15
Polish	2,384	10.67
Portuguese	7	0.03
Romanian	84	0.38
Russian	303	1.36
Scotch-Irish	474	2.12
Scottish	573	2.57
Serbian	82	0.37
Slavic	6	0.03
Slovak	1,004	4.49
Slovene	213	0.95
Swedish	173	0.77
Swiss	122	0.55

Notes: 1. Figures in the "Number" column do not add up to the total population due to: a) Ancestry/Race overlap — e.g. persons can report being both White and Irish, b) persons of Hispanic origin can report being any race, c) persons reporting two ancestries are counted in both categories. 2. Numbers in parentheses indicate the number of persons reporting this ancestry/race alone, not in combination with any other ancestry/race. 3. Refer to the Explanation of Data in the front of the book for more detailed information.

Ukrainian	239	1.07
United States or American	740	3.31
Welsh	241	1.08
White:	21,769	97.45
Not Hispanic (21,226)	21,439	95.98
Hispanic (300)	330	1.48
Yugoslavian	81	0.36

North Royalton

Place Type: City
County: Cuyahoga
Population: 28,648

Ancestry/Race	Number	%
African American/Black:	237	0.83
Not Hispanic (200)	230	0.80
Hispanic (3)	7	0.02
Am. Ind. or Alaska Nat., not spec.	14	0.05
American Indian tribes, specified:	54	0.19
Blackfeet	2	0.01
Cherokee (12)	27	0.09
Chippewa	1	0.00
Choctaw (2)	2	0.01
Cree (6)	6	0.02
Lumbee	3	0.01
Potawatomi (1)	1	0.00
Seminole	1	0.00
Sioux (4)	8	0.03
All other tribes (1)	3	0.01
American Indian tribes, not spec.	1	0.00
Arab:	295	1.03
Arab/Arabic	38	0.13
Lebanese	226	0.79
Syrian	7	0.02
Other Arab	24	0.08
Armenian	87	0.30
Asian:	680	2.37
Cambodian (5)	5	0.02
Chinese, ex. Taiwanese (76)	84	0.29
Filipino (125)	170	0.59
Indian (252)	264	0.92
Indonesian (1)	2	0.01
Japanese (12)	21	0.07
Korean (55)	74	0.26
Pakistani (14)	18	0.06
Taiwanese (1)	3	0.01
Thai (3)	4	0.01
Vietnamese (11)	12	0.04
Other Asian, specified	3	0.01
Other Asian, not specified (7)	20	0.07
Austrian	114	0.40
Belgian	30	0.10
British	11	0.04
Bulgarian	8	0.03
Canadian	33	0.12
Carpatho Rusyn	34	0.12
Croatian	390	1.36
Czech	949	3.31
Czechoslovakian	210	0.73
Danish	56	0.20
Dutch	340	1.19
Eastern European	22	0.08
English	2,385	8.33
European	122	0.43
Finnish	16	0.06
French, except Basque	563	1.97
French Canadian	85	0.30
German	7,275	25.39
Greek	406	1.42
Hawaii Native/Pacific Islander:	20	0.07
Polynesian: (6)	7	0.02
Native Hawaiian (6)	7	0.02
Other Pac. Isl., specified	3	0.01
Other Pac. Isl., not spec.	10	0.03
Hispanic or Latino:	273	0.95
Central American:	14	0.05
Costa Rican	2	0.01
Guatemalan	5	0.02
Honduran	4	0.01
Nicaraguan	1	0.00
Salvadoran	2	0.01
Cuban	6	0.02
Mexican	92	0.32
Puerto Rican	107	0.37
South American:	16	0.06
Chilean	2	0.01
Colombian	8	0.03
Ecuadorian	1	0.00
Peruvian	4	0.01
Uruguayan	1	0.00
Other Hispanic or Latino	38	0.13
Hungarian	1,372	4.79
Irish	4,008	13.99
Italian	3,519	12.28
Latvian	50	0.17
Lithuanian	240	0.84
Macedonian	28	0.10
Norwegian	172	0.60
Pennsylvania German	36	0.13
Polish	5,278	18.42
Romanian	191	0.67
Russian	573	2.00
Scandinavian	11	0.04
Scotch-Irish	500	1.75
Scottish	399	1.39
Serbian	229	0.80
Slavic	126	0.44
Slovak	2,276	7.94
Slovene	555	1.94
Swedish	271	0.95
Swiss	68	0.24
Turkish	6	0.02
Ukrainian	836	2.92
United States or American	880	3.07
Welsh	223	0.78
West Indian, excl. Hispanic:	17	0.06
Jamaican	12	0.04
West Indian	5	0.02
White:	27,771	96.94
Not Hispanic (27,356)	27,535	96.11
Hispanic (197)	236	0.82
Yugoslavian	155	0.54

Northbrook

Place Type: Census Designated Place
County: Hamilton
Population: 11,076

Ancestry/Race	Number	%
African American/Black:	1,670	15.08
Not Hispanic (1,557)	1,658	14.97
Hispanic (11)	12	0.11
African, sub-Saharan:	105	0.93
African	105	0.93
Am. Ind. or Alaska Nat., not spec.	24	0.22
American Indian tribes, specified:	68	0.61
Apache	4	0.04
Blackfeet	2	0.02
Cherokee (12)	35	0.32
Chippewa (2)	2	0.02
Choctaw	1	0.01
Cree	2	0.02
Creek	2	0.02
Latin American Indians	3	0.03
Navajo (4)	7	0.06
Pueblo (4)	4	0.04
Sioux (2)	2	0.02
All other tribes (3)	4	0.04
American Indian tribes, not spec.	4	0.04
Arab:	73	0.65
Arab/Arabic	38	0.34
Lebanese	27	0.24
Syrian	8	0.07
Asian:	142	1.28
Cambodian (7)	7	0.06
Chinese, ex. Taiwanese (13)	13	0.12
Filipino (37)	58	0.52
Indian (26)	27	0.24
Indonesian (3)	3	0.03
Japanese (1)	7	0.06
Korean (5)	9	0.08
Thai (2)	3	0.03
Vietnamese (7)	7	0.06
Other Asian, specified (3)	3	0.03
Other Asian, not specified (2)	5	0.05
Austrian	7	0.06
British	48	0.43
Canadian	38	0.34
Czech	20	0.18
Czechoslovakian	6	0.05
Dutch	289	2.57
English	999	8.88
European	21	0.19
French, except Basque	295	2.62
French Canadian	106	0.94
German	3,581	31.85
Greek	11	0.10
Hawaii Native/Pacific Islander:	15	0.14
Micronesian: (5)	5	0.05
Guamanian/Chamorro (5)	5	0.05
Polynesian: (2)	7	0.06
Native Hawaiian (1)	6	0.05
Samoan (1)	1	0.01
Other Pac. Isl., not spec. (3)	3	0.03
Hispanic or Latino:	173	1.56
Central American:	4	0.04
Costa Rican	2	0.02
Honduran	2	0.02
Mexican	88	0.79
Puerto Rican	31	0.28
South American:	6	0.05
Chilean	1	0.01
Colombian	2	0.02
Ecuadorian	2	0.02
Peruvian	1	0.01
Other Hispanic or Latino	44	0.40
Hungarian	39	0.35
Irish	1,438	12.79
Italian	343	3.05
Norwegian	55	0.49
Polish	100	0.89
Romanian	6	0.05
Russian	24	0.21
Scotch-Irish	153	1.36
Scottish	146	1.30
Slovak	6	0.05
Swedish	63	0.56
Swiss	25	0.22
United States or American	989	8.80
Welsh	28	0.25
West Indian, excl. Hispanic:	5	0.04
Jamaican	5	0.04
White:	9,255	83.56
Not Hispanic (9,014)	9,155	82.66
Hispanic (85)	100	0.90

Norton

Place Type: City
County: Summit
Population: 11,523

Ancestry/Race	Number	%
African American/Black:	177	1.54
Not Hispanic (153)	176	1.53
Hispanic (1)	1	0.01
Am. Ind. or Alaska Nat., not spec.	25	0.22
American Indian tribes, specified:	38	0.33
Apache (1)	1	0.01
Blackfeet	2	0.02
Cherokee (4)	19	0.16
Cheyenne	4	0.03
Choctaw (2)	2	0.02
Creek (3)	3	0.03
Latin American Indians	1	0.01
Seminole	1	0.01
Sioux	2	0.02
Tohono O'Odham (1)	1	0.01

Notes: 1. Figures in the "Number" column do not add up to the total population due to: a) Ancestry/Race overlap — e.g. persons can report being both White and Irish, b) persons of Hispanic origin can report being any race, c) persons reporting two ancestries are counted in both categories. 2. Numbers in parentheses indicate the number of persons reporting this ancestry/race alone, not in combination with any other ancestry/race. 3. Refer to the Explanation of Data in the front of the book for more detailed information.

Ancestry/Race	Number	%
All other tribes	2	0.02
American Indian tribes, not spec.	1	0.01
Arab:	24	0.21
Lebanese	24	0.21
Asian:	36	0.31
Filipino (5)	7	0.06
Indian (5)	5	0.04
Japanese (2)	4	0.03
Korean (4)	4	0.03
Pakistani (1)	1	0.01
Vietnamese (12)	12	0.10
Other Asian, not specified (3)	3	0.03
Austrian	74	0.64
Belgian	20	0.17
British	26	0.23
Bulgarian	9	0.08
Canadian	17	0.15
Croatian	55	0.48
Czech	25	0.22
Czechoslovakian	79	0.69
Danish	9	0.08
Dutch	274	2.38
English	1,574	13.66
European	111	0.96
Finnish	33	0.29
French, except Basque	288	2.50
French Canadian	10	0.09
German	3,318	28.80
Greek	89	0.77
Hawaii Native/Pacific Islander:	5	0.04
Polynesian: (3)	4	0.03
Native Hawaiian (3)	4	0.03
Other Pac. Isl., not spec. (1)	1	0.01
Hispanic or Latino:	47	0.41
Central American:	4	0.03
Panamanian	4	0.03
Mexican	28	0.24
Puerto Rican	8	0.07
South American:	3	0.03
Chilean	3	0.03
Other Hispanic or Latino	4	0.03
Hungarian	454	3.94
Irish	1,566	13.59
Italian	846	7.34
Latvian	23	0.20
Macedonian	20	0.17
Northern European	11	0.10
Norwegian	52	0.45
Pennsylvania German	18	0.16
Polish	397	3.45
Portuguese	24	0.21
Romanian	10	0.09
Russian	79	0.69
Scotch-Irish	176	1.53
Scottish	212	1.84
Serbian	158	1.37
Slovak	432	3.75
Slovene	168	1.46
Swedish	70	0.61
Swiss	69	0.60
Ukrainian	38	0.33
United States or American	990	8.59
Welsh	127	1.10
White:	11,297	98.04
Not Hispanic (11,185)	11,260	97.72
Hispanic (33)	37	0.32
Yugoslavian	37	0.32

Norwalk

Place Type: City
County: Huron
Population: 16,238

Ancestry/Race	Number	%
African American/Black:	396	2.44
Not Hispanic (307)	375	2.31
Hispanic (9)	21	0.13
African, sub-Saharan:	53	0.33
African	53	0.33
Am. Ind. or Alaska Nat., not spec.	31	0.19
American Indian tribes, specified:	59	0.36
Blackfeet (4)	7	0.04
Cherokee (7)	27	0.17
Chippewa (3)	3	0.02
Comanche	1	0.01
Iroquois (1)	1	0.01
Latin American Indians (4)	4	0.02
Lumbee (1)	2	0.01
Menominee (3)	3	0.02
Seminole	1	0.01
Shoshone (1)	1	0.01
Sioux	4	0.02
Ute	1	0.01
All other tribes (1)	4	0.02
American Indian tribes, not spec.	3	0.02
Arab:	5	0.03
Lebanese	5	0.03
Armenian	10	0.06
Asian:	67	0.41
Chinese, ex. Taiwanese (7)	9	0.06
Filipino (10)	16	0.10
Indian (20)	21	0.13
Japanese (1)	2	0.01
Korean (8)	12	0.07
Vietnamese (3)	3	0.02
Other Asian, not specified (3)	4	0.02
Australian	8	0.05
Austrian	42	0.26
Belgian	5	0.03
British	16	0.10
Bulgarian	14	0.09
Canadian	46	0.28
Croatian	15	0.09
Czech	117	0.72
Czechoslovakian	47	0.29
Danish	39	0.24
Dutch	509	3.13
Eastern European	12	0.07
English	1,821	11.18
European	53	0.33
French, except Basque	409	2.51
French Canadian	87	0.53
German	5,569	34.20
Greek	74	0.45
Hawaii Native/Pacific Islander:	4	0.02
Polynesian:	2	0.01
Native Hawaiian	2	0.01
Other Pac. Isl., not spec.	2	0.01
Hispanic or Latino:	620	3.82
Central American:	5	0.03
Guatemalan	1	0.01
Honduran	1	0.01
Panamanian	3	0.02
Cuban	3	0.02
Mexican	469	2.89
Puerto Rican	46	0.28
South American:	4	0.02
Peruvian	1	0.01
Venezuelan	3	0.02
Other Hispanic or Latino	93	0.57
Hungarian	176	1.08
Irish	1,764	10.83
Italian	946	5.81
Latvian	11	0.07
Macedonian	11	0.07
Maltese	12	0.07
Norwegian	72	0.44
Pennsylvania German	5	0.03
Polish	361	2.22
Portuguese	9	0.06
Russian	24	0.15
Scandinavian	7	0.04
Scotch-Irish	131	0.80
Scottish	353	2.17
Slavic	7	0.04
Slovak	10	0.06
Slovene	10	0.06
Swedish	84	0.52
Swiss	73	0.45
Ukrainian	32	0.20
United States or American	1,490	9.15
Welsh	256	1.57
White:	15,519	95.57
Not Hispanic (15,079)	15,206	93.64
Hispanic (271)	313	1.93
Yugoslavian	45	0.28

Norwood

Place Type: City
County: Hamilton
Population: 21,675

Ancestry/Race	Number	%
Acadian/Cajun	15	0.07
African American/Black:	596	2.75
Not Hispanic (502)	586	2.70
Hispanic (7)	10	0.05
African, sub-Saharan:	64	0.30
African	58	0.27
Ethiopian	6	0.03
Alaska Native tribes, specified:	13	0.06
Alaska Athabascan (1)	1	0.00
Aleut (7)	11	0.05
All other tribes (1)	1	0.00
Alaska Native tribes, not specified	1	0.00
Am. Ind. or Alaska Nat., not spec.	53	0.24
American Indian tribes, specified:	149	0.69
Apache (1)	2	0.01
Blackfeet (1)	2	0.01
Cherokee (25)	95	0.44
Cheyenne (1)	6	0.03
Chippewa (1)	2	0.01
Choctaw	1	0.00
Cree	2	0.01
Creek (2)	2	0.01
Crow	2	0.01
Delaware	1	0.00
Iroquois	2	0.01
Latin American Indians (14)	14	0.06
Menominee (2)	2	0.01
Navajo (5)	5	0.02
Sioux (1)	7	0.03
All other tribes (1)	4	0.02
American Indian tribes, not spec.	8	0.04
Arab:	71	0.33
Arab/Arabic	9	0.04
Egyptian	11	0.05
Lebanese	43	0.20
Palestinian	8	0.04
Asian:	202	0.93
Cambodian (19)	19	0.09
Chinese, ex. Taiwanese (25)	32	0.15
Filipino (19)	31	0.14
Indian (28)	33	0.15
Japanese (3)	8	0.04
Korean (20)	22	0.10
Taiwanese (1)	2	0.01
Thai (7)	7	0.03
Vietnamese (41)	41	0.19
Other Asian, not specified (3)	7	0.03
Australian	5	0.02
Austrian	39	0.18
Belgian	5	0.02
Brazilian	7	0.03
British	46	0.21
Bulgarian	15	0.07
Canadian	6	0.03
Croatian	17	0.08
Czech	20	0.09
Danish	24	0.11
Dutch	390	1.80
English	2,120	9.78
European	142	0.66
French, except Basque	580	2.68
French Canadian	24	0.11
German	6,115	28.21
Greek	79	0.36
Hawaii Native/Pacific Islander:	14	0.06

Notes: 1. Figures in the "Number" column do not add up to the total population due to: a) Ancestry/Race overlap — e.g. persons can report being both White and Irish, b) persons of Hispanic origin can report being any race, c) persons reporting two ancestries are counted in both categories. 2. Numbers in parentheses indicate the number of persons reporting this ancestry/race alone, not in combination with any other ancestry/race. 3. Refer to the Explanation of Data in the front of the book for more detailed information.

Ancestry/Race	Number	%
Melanesian: (1)	1	0.00
Other Melanesian (1)	1	0.00
Polynesian: (3)	7	0.03
Native Hawaiian (3)	6	0.03
Samoan	1	0.00
Other Pac. Isl., not spec.	6	0.03
Hispanic or Latino:	401	1.85
Central American:	31	0.14
Honduran	17	0.08
Nicaraguan	3	0.01
Panamanian	7	0.03
Salvadoran	4	0.02
Cuban	8	0.04
Dominican Republic	9	0.04
Mexican	235	1.08
Puerto Rican	24	0.11
South American:	11	0.05
Argentinean	4	0.02
Chilean	1	0.00
Peruvian	3	0.01
Venezuelan	2	0.01
Other South American	1	0.00
Other Hispanic or Latino	83	0.38
Hungarian	51	0.24
Irish	4,123	19.02
Israeli	15	0.07
Italian	1,075	4.96
Latvian	9	0.04
Lithuanian	17	0.08
Norwegian	52	0.24
Pennsylvania German	22	0.10
Polish	207	0.96
Romanian	7	0.03
Russian	17	0.08
Scandinavian	52	0.24
Scotch-Irish	394	1.82
Scottish	223	1.03
Serbian	35	0.16
Slovak	7	0.03
Swedish	71	0.33
Swiss	104	0.48
Turkish	31	0.14
United States or American	2,270	10.47
Welsh	206	0.95
West Indian, excl. Hispanic:	27	0.12
Dutch West Indian	11	0.05
Jamaican	9	0.04
Trinidadian and Tobagonian	7	0.03
White:	20,701	95.51
Not Hispanic (20,249)	20,478	94.48
Hispanic (180)	223	1.03

Oregon

Place Type: City
County: Lucas
Population: 19,355

Ancestry/Race	Number	%
African American/Black:	249	1.29
Not Hispanic (184)	232	1.20
Hispanic (9)	17	0.09
African, sub-Saharan:	15	0.08
African	15	0.08
Am. Ind. or Alaska Nat., not spec.	39	0.20
American Indian tribes, specified:	59	0.30
Blackfeet	4	0.02
Cherokee (12)	32	0.17
Chippewa (1)	4	0.02
Cree (1)	1	0.01
Delaware	2	0.01
Iroquois	1	0.01
Latin American Indians (2)	2	0.01
Navajo (1)	1	0.01
Ottawa (2)	3	0.02
Seminole	1	0.01
Sioux (1)	1	0.01
All other tribes	7	0.04
American Indian tribes, not spec.	1	0.01
Arab:	172	0.89
Lebanese	136	0.70
Syrian	36	0.19
Armenian	11	0.06
Asian:	179	0.92
Cambodian (1)	1	0.01
Chinese, ex. Taiwanese (43)	48	0.25
Filipino (22)	34	0.18
Indian (29)	34	0.18
Japanese (3)	8	0.04
Korean (6)	9	0.05
Laotian (9)	15	0.08
Pakistani	2	0.01
Thai (2)	2	0.01
Vietnamese (14)	14	0.07
Other Asian, specified	1	0.01
Other Asian, not specified (5)	11	0.06
Assyrian/Chaldean/Syriac	6	0.03
Australian	12	0.06
Austrian	19	0.10
Belgian	6	0.03
British	21	0.11
Bulgarian	63	0.33
Canadian	37	0.19
Croatian	6	0.03
Czech	171	0.88
Czechoslovakian	72	0.37
Danish	33	0.17
Dutch	475	2.45
English	1,513	7.82
Estonian	14	0.07
European	101	0.52
French, except Basque	1,445	7.47
French Canadian	178	0.92
German	6,550	33.84
Greek	181	0.94
Hawaii Native/Pacific Islander:	4	0.02
Polynesian: (2)	3	0.02
Native Hawaiian (2)	2	0.01
Samoan	1	0.01
Other Pac. Isl., not spec.	1	0.01
Hispanic or Latino:	922	4.76
Central American:	4	0.02
Guatemalan	3	0.02
Other Central American	1	0.01
Cuban	14	0.07
Dominican Republic	3	0.02
Mexican	689	3.56
Puerto Rican	44	0.23
South American:	5	0.03
Argentinean	1	0.01
Chilean	1	0.01
Colombian	3	0.02
Other Hispanic or Latino	163	0.84
Hungarian	1,412	7.29
Irish	2,118	10.94
Italian	867	4.48
Lithuanian	5	0.03
Macedonian	23	0.12
Norwegian	36	0.19
Pennsylvania German	15	0.08
Polish	1,724	8.91
Romanian	15	0.08
Russian	43	0.22
Scotch-Irish	158	0.82
Scottish	260	1.34
Serbian	5	0.03
Slavic	8	0.04
Slovak	120	0.62
Slovene	61	0.32
Swedish	97	0.50
Swiss	112	0.58
Turkish	7	0.04
United States or American	835	4.31
Welsh	92	0.48
West Indian, excl. Hispanic:	5	0.03
Jamaican	5	0.03
White:	18,642	96.32
Not Hispanic (17,871)	18,067	93.35
Hispanic (498)	575	2.97
Yugoslavian	5	0.03

Oxford

Place Type: City
County: Butler
Population: 21,943

Ancestry/Race	Number	%
Acadian/Cajun	6	0.03
African American/Black:	1,069	4.87
Not Hispanic (938)	1,055	4.81
Hispanic (9)	14	0.06
African, sub-Saharan:	86	0.39
African	71	0.32
South African	9	0.04
Other sub-Saharan African	6	0.03
Alaska Native tribes, specified:	2	0.01
Aleut	1	0.00
Eskimo	1	0.00
Am. Ind. or Alaska Nat., not spec.	38	0.17
Albanian	13	0.06
American Indian tribes, specified:	83	0.38
Apache (1)	1	0.00
Blackfeet	2	0.01
Cherokee (6)	40	0.18
Chickasaw (3)	4	0.02
Chippewa (1)	1	0.00
Choctaw (1)	3	0.01
Creek	1	0.00
Delaware	1	0.00
Iroquois (2)	3	0.01
Latin American Indians (1)	2	0.01
Lumbee (1)	2	0.01
Navajo (1)	1	0.00
Osage	1	0.00
Seminole	1	0.00
Sioux (1)	2	0.01
All other tribes (10)	18	0.08
American Indian tribes, not spec.	2	0.01
Arab:	84	0.38
Lebanese	84	0.38
Armenian	20	0.09
Asian:	662	3.02
Bangladeshi (1)	1	0.00
Cambodian (6)	17	0.08
Chinese, ex. Taiwanese (143)	168	0.77
Filipino (27)	52	0.24
Indian (151)	171	0.78
Indonesian (4)	4	0.02
Japanese (54)	74	0.34
Korean (68)	84	0.38
Pakistani (10)	11	0.05
Sri Lankan (2)	4	0.02
Taiwanese (8)	11	0.05
Thai (6)	8	0.04
Vietnamese (18)	24	0.11
Other Asian, specified (9)	10	0.05
Other Asian, not specified (8)	23	0.10
Austrian	108	0.49
Belgian	15	0.07
British	223	1.01
Bulgarian	11	0.05
Canadian	41	0.19
Croatian	51	0.23
Czech	196	0.89
Czechoslovakian	86	0.39
Danish	115	0.52
Dutch	386	1.75
Eastern European	13	0.06
English	2,390	10.82
Estonian	4	0.02
European	214	0.97
Finnish	41	0.19
French, except Basque	655	2.97
French Canadian	98	0.44
German	6,986	31.63
Greek	151	0.68
Hawaii Native/Pacific Islander:	14	0.06
Micronesian:	1	0.00
Guamanian/Chamorro	1	0.00
Polynesian: (1)	5	0.02

Notes: 1. Figures in the "Number" column do not add up to the total population due to: a) Ancestry/Race overlap — e.g. persons can report being both White and Irish, b) persons of Hispanic origin can report being any race, c) persons reporting two ancestries are counted in both categories. 2. Numbers in parentheses indicate the number of persons reporting this ancestry/race alone, not in combination with any other ancestry/race. 3. Refer to the Explanation of Data in the front of the book for more detailed information.

Ancestry/Race	Number	%
Native Hawaiian (1)	4	0.02
Samoan	1	0.00
Other Pac. Isl., specified	1	0.00
Other Pac. Isl., not spec. (4)	7	0.03
Hispanic or Latino:	317	1.44
Central American:	14	0.06
Costa Rican	5	0.02
Guatemalan	1	0.00
Honduran	4	0.02
Nicaraguan	1	0.00
Panamanian	1	0.00
Salvadoran	2	0.01
Cuban	34	0.15
Dominican Republic	8	0.04
Mexican	97	0.44
Puerto Rican	45	0.21
South American:	66	0.30
Argentinean	7	0.03
Bolivian	2	0.01
Chilean	4	0.02
Colombian	26	0.12
Ecuadorian	11	0.05
Peruvian	8	0.04
Uruguayan	3	0.01
Venezuelan	4	0.02
Other South American	1	0.00
Other Hispanic or Latino	53	0.24
Hungarian	289	1.31
Iranian	6	0.03
Irish	3,516	15.92
Israeli	15	0.07
Italian	1,803	8.16
Lithuanian	80	0.36
Luxemburger	7	0.03
Macedonian	23	0.10
Norwegian	242	1.10
Pennsylvania German	3	0.01
Polish	1,002	4.54
Portuguese	27	0.12
Romanian	30	0.14
Russian	290	1.31
Scandinavian	31	0.14
Scotch-Irish	508	2.30
Scottish	651	2.95
Serbian	38	0.17
Slavic	6	0.03
Slovak	137	0.62
Slovene	51	0.23
Swedish	298	1.35
Swiss	100	0.45
Turkish	29	0.13
Ukrainian	88	0.40
United States or American	944	4.27
Welsh	248	1.12
White:	20,278	92.41
Not Hispanic (19,813)	20,056	91.40
Hispanic (200)	222	1.01
Yugoslavian	50	0.23

Painesville

Place Type: City
County: Lake
Population: 17,503

Ancestry/Race	Number	%
African American/Black:	2,616	14.95
Not Hispanic (2,202)	2,519	14.39
Hispanic (62)	97	0.55
African, sub-Saharan:	166	0.95
African	166	0.95
Am. Ind. or Alaska Nat., not spec.	71	0.41
American Indian tribes, specified:	89	0.51
Apache	1	0.01
Blackfeet (5)	21	0.12
Cherokee (5)	38	0.22
Chickasaw	1	0.01
Choctaw	4	0.02
Cree (1)	1	0.01
Creek (2)	2	0.01
Iroquois	2	0.01
Latin American Indians (1)	1	0.01
Lumbee (1)	1	0.01
Navajo (1)	3	0.02
Sioux (1)	5	0.03
All other tribes (1)	9	0.05
American Indian tribes, not spec.	12	0.07
Arab:	50	0.29
Lebanese	36	0.21
Syrian	14	0.08
Armenian	6	0.03
Asian:	111	0.63
Chinese, ex. Taiwanese (6)	6	0.03
Filipino (9)	23	0.13
Indian (22)	28	0.16
Japanese (10)	13	0.07
Korean (6)	12	0.07
Pakistani (1)	1	0.01
Thai (1)	1	0.01
Vietnamese (18)	19	0.11
Other Asian, not specified (1)	8	0.05
Austrian	60	0.34
Belgian	13	0.07
British	51	0.29
Canadian	5	0.03
Celtic	8	0.05
Croatian	93	0.53
Czech	66	0.38
Czechoslovakian	41	0.23
Dutch	326	1.86
Eastern European	18	0.10
English	1,838	10.51
Estonian	14	0.08
European	10	0.06
Finnish	289	1.65
French, except Basque	331	1.89
French Canadian	29	0.17
German	3,264	18.66
Hawaii Native/Pacific Islander:	19	0.11
Polynesian: (1)	9	0.05
Native Hawaiian (1)	9	0.05
Other Pac. Isl., not spec.	10	0.06
Hispanic or Latino:	2,256	12.89
Central American:	22	0.13
Costa Rican	4	0.02
Honduran	6	0.03
Nicaraguan	11	0.06
Salvadoran	1	0.01
Cuban	10	0.06
Dominican Republic	1	0.01
Mexican	1,869	10.68
Puerto Rican	245	1.40
South American:	13	0.07
Argentinean	5	0.03
Chilean	4	0.02
Peruvian	2	0.01
Venezuelan	2	0.01
Other Hispanic or Latino	96	0.55
Hungarian	796	4.55
Irish	2,398	13.71
Italian	1,634	9.34
Lithuanian	42	0.24
Norwegian	113	0.65
Pennsylvania German	21	0.12
Polish	627	3.59
Portuguese	8	0.05
Romanian	36	0.21
Russian	111	0.63
Scandinavian	6	0.03
Scotch-Irish	188	1.08
Scottish	401	2.29
Slavic	59	0.34
Slovak	187	1.07
Slovene	336	1.92
Swedish	183	1.05
Swiss	23	0.13
Ukrainian	58	0.33
United States or American	767	4.39
Welsh	99	0.57
West Indian, excl. Hispanic:	28	0.16
Jamaican	6	0.03
West Indian	22	0.13
White:	13,909	79.47
Not Hispanic (12,502)	12,857	73.46
Hispanic (973)	1,052	6.01
Yugoslavian	21	0.12

Parma Heights

Place Type: City
County: Cuyahoga
Population: 21,659

Ancestry/Race	Number	%
African American/Black:	298	1.38
Not Hispanic (243)	285	1.32
Hispanic (10)	13	0.06
African, sub-Saharan:	36	0.17
African	36	0.17
Alaska Native tribes, specified:	1	0.00
Eskimo (1)	1	0.00
Am. Ind. or Alaska Nat., not spec.	32	0.15
Albanian	10	0.05
American Indian tribes, specified:	43	0.20
Blackfeet	3	0.01
Cherokee (1)	13	0.06
Chickasaw	1	0.00
Chippewa (4)	8	0.04
Choctaw	2	0.01
Delaware	2	0.01
Iroquois (4)	6	0.03
Potawatomi (1)	1	0.00
Pueblo (2)	2	0.01
Sioux	2	0.01
All other tribes (1)	3	0.01
American Indian tribes, not spec.	1	0.00
Arab:	389	1.80
Egyptian	98	0.45
Iraqi	31	0.14
Lebanese	233	1.08
Moroccan	5	0.02
Palestinian	9	0.04
Syrian	13	0.06
Asian:	592	2.73
Bangladeshi (7)	7	0.03
Cambodian (7)	7	0.03
Chinese, ex. Taiwanese (84)	87	0.40
Filipino (60)	81	0.37
Indian (217)	230	1.06
Indonesian (1)	1	0.00
Japanese (18)	27	0.12
Korean (31)	39	0.18
Malaysian (1)	1	0.00
Pakistani (9)	14	0.06
Thai (4)	4	0.02
Vietnamese (45)	59	0.27
Other Asian, specified (1)	1	0.00
Other Asian, not specified (15)	34	0.16
Assyrian/Chaldean/Syriac	5	0.02
Austrian	137	0.63
Belgian	11	0.05
British	23	0.11
Canadian	75	0.35
Carpatho Rusyn	21	0.10
Croatian	183	0.84
Czech	561	2.59
Czechoslovakian	170	0.78
Danish	42	0.19
Dutch	152	0.70
English	1,408	6.50
Estonian	19	0.09
European	34	0.16
Finnish	62	0.29
French, except Basque	384	1.77
French Canadian	87	0.40
German	5,417	25.01
Greek	230	1.06
Guyanese	8	0.04
Hawaii Native/Pacific Islander:	15	0.07
Polynesian: (2)	3	0.01

Notes: 1. Figures in the "Number" column do not add up to the total population due to: a) Ancestry/Race overlap — e.g. persons can report being both White and Irish, b) persons of Hispanic origin can report being any race, c) persons reporting two ancestries are counted in both categories. 2. Numbers in parentheses indicate the number of persons reporting this ancestry/race alone, not in combination with any other ancestry/race. 3. Refer to the Explanation of Data in the front of the book for more detailed information.

Ancestry/Race	Number	%
Native Hawaiian (1)	2	0.01
Samoan (1)	1	0.00
Other Pac. Isl., not spec. (1)	12	0.06
Hispanic or Latino:	351	1.62
Central American:	3	0.01
Guatemalan	1	0.00
Nicaraguan	1	0.00
Salvadoran	1	0.00
Cuban	1	0.00
Dominican Republic	9	0.04
Mexican	83	0.38
Puerto Rican	158	0.73
South American:	26	0.12
Argentinean	6	0.03
Chilean	3	0.01
Colombian	5	0.02
Ecuadorian	1	0.00
Peruvian	6	0.03
Venezuelan	4	0.02
Other South American	1	0.00
Other Hispanic or Latino	71	0.33
Hungarian	1,123	5.18
Irish	3,540	16.34
Italian	2,590	11.96
Latvian	12	0.06
Lithuanian	121	0.56
Macedonian	57	0.26
Norwegian	20	0.09
Pennsylvania German	7	0.03
Polish	2,827	13.05
Romanian	327	1.51
Russian	298	1.38
Scandinavian	5	0.02
Scotch-Irish	296	1.37
Scottish	307	1.42
Serbian	146	0.67
Slavic	66	0.30
Slovak	1,690	7.80
Slovene	306	1.41
Swedish	108	0.50
Swiss	80	0.37
Ukrainian	622	2.87
United States or American	816	3.77
Welsh	145	0.67
White:	20,750	95.80
Not Hispanic (20,300)	20,508	94.69
Hispanic (223)	242	1.12
Yugoslavian	182	0.84

Parma

Place Type: City
County: Cuyahoga
Population: 85,655

Ancestry/Race	Number	%
African American/Black:	1,073	1.25
Not Hispanic (901)	1,042	1.22
Hispanic (4)	31	0.04
African, sub-Saharan:	61	0.07
African	41	0.05
Nigerian	8	0.01
Other sub-Saharan African	12	0.01
Alaska Native tribes, specified:	10	0.01
Eskimo (1)	1	0.00
Tlingit-Haida (2)	6	0.01
All other tribes	3	0.00
Am. Ind. or Alaska Nat., not spec.	77	0.09
Albanian	70	0.08
American Indian tribes, specified:	225	0.26
Apache (9)	14	0.02
Blackfeet (5)	24	0.03
Cherokee (14)	82	0.10
Chippewa (3)	9	0.01
Choctaw (8)	14	0.02
Cree	2	0.00
Iroquois (3)	17	0.02
Latin American Indians (4)	8	0.01
Lumbee (1)	17	0.02
Menominee (2)	2	0.00
Navajo (3)	6	0.01
Potawatomi	1	0.00
Pueblo (4)	4	0.00
Seminole	2	0.00
Sioux (5)	6	0.01
All other tribes (11)	17	0.02
American Indian tribes, not spec.	12	0.01
Arab:	1,381	1.61
Arab/Arabic	120	0.14
Egyptian	103	0.12
Jordanian	34	0.04
Lebanese	958	1.12
Palestinian	87	0.10
Syrian	74	0.09
Other Arab	5	0.01
Armenian	39	0.05
Asian:	1,634	1.91
Bangladeshi (4)	6	0.01
Cambodian (37)	40	0.05
Chinese, ex. Taiwanese (199)	217	0.25
Filipino (280)	340	0.40
Indian (554)	603	0.70
Japanese (50)	90	0.11
Korean (79)	100	0.12
Laotian (11)	11	0.01
Malaysian (1)	1	0.00
Pakistani (6)	7	0.01
Sri Lankan (4)	4	0.00
Taiwanese (4)	4	0.00
Thai (5)	5	0.01
Vietnamese (88)	96	0.11
Other Asian, specified (2)	3	0.00
Other Asian, not specified (18)	107	0.12
Australian	26	0.03
Austrian	473	0.55
Belgian	51	0.06
British	132	0.15
Bulgarian	21	0.02
Canadian	140	0.16
Carpatho Rusyn	34	0.04
Croatian	851	0.99
Czech	2,554	2.98
Czechoslovakian	766	0.89
Danish	107	0.12
Dutch	657	0.77
Eastern European	16	0.02
English	4,919	5.74
Estonian	34	0.04
European	278	0.32
Finnish	209	0.24
French, except Basque	1,266	1.48
French Canadian	277	0.32
German	21,013	24.53
Greek	867	1.01
Guyanese	35	0.04
Hawaii Native/Pacific Islander:	55	0.06
Micronesian:	6	0.01
Guamanian/Chamorro	2	0.00
Other Micronesian	4	0.00
Polynesian: (16)	27	0.03
Native Hawaiian (11)	20	0.02
Samoan (4)	5	0.01
Tongan (1)	2	0.00
Other Pac. Isl., specified	1	0.00
Other Pac. Isl., not spec. (1)	21	0.02
Hispanic or Latino:	1,323	1.54
Central American:	36	0.04
Guatemalan	11	0.01
Honduran	10	0.01
Nicaraguan	2	0.00
Panamanian	10	0.01
Salvadoran	2	0.00
Other Central American	1	0.00
Cuban	30	0.04
Dominican Republic	4	0.00
Mexican	236	0.28
Puerto Rican	695	0.81
South American:	77	0.09
Argentinean	9	0.01
Chilean	5	0.01
Colombian	12	0.01
Ecuadorian	2	0.00
Peruvian	44	0.05
Uruguayan	1	0.00
Venezuelan	3	0.00
Other South American	1	0.00
Other Hispanic or Latino	245	0.29
Hungarian	4,514	5.27
Icelander	18	0.02
Irish	12,466	14.55
Italian	11,603	13.55
Latvian	131	0.15
Lithuanian	527	0.62
Macedonian	46	0.05
Northern European	13	0.02
Norwegian	211	0.25
Pennsylvania German	48	0.06
Polish	15,503	18.10
Portuguese	32	0.04
Romanian	506	0.59
Russian	1,125	1.31
Scandinavian	7	0.01
Scotch-Irish	981	1.15
Scottish	1,168	1.36
Serbian	941	1.10
Slavic	112	0.13
Slovak	7,940	9.27
Slovene	1,477	1.72
Swedish	597	0.70
Swiss	180	0.21
Turkish	42	0.05
Ukrainian	3,692	4.31
United States or American	2,635	3.08
Welsh	547	0.64
West Indian, excl. Hispanic:	55	0.06
Belizean	6	0.01
Jamaican	49	0.06
White:	82,806	96.67
Not Hispanic (81,102)	81,853	95.56
Hispanic (846)	953	1.11
Yugoslavian	383	0.45

Pataskala

Place Type: City
County: Licking
Population: 10,249

Ancestry/Race	Number	%
African American/Black:	343	3.35
Not Hispanic (301)	337	3.29
Hispanic (2)	6	0.06
African, sub-Saharan:	5	0.05
African	5	0.05
Am. Ind. or Alaska Nat., not spec.	20	0.20
American Indian tribes, specified:	60	0.59
Blackfeet	2	0.02
Cherokee (14)	39	0.38
Chippewa (3)	3	0.03
Delaware (4)	4	0.04
Iroquois	1	0.01
Latin American Indians	1	0.01
Lumbee (1)	1	0.01
Navajo (4)	6	0.06
Sioux	1	0.01
All other tribes (1)	2	0.02
American Indian tribes, not spec.	2	0.02
Asian:	82	0.80
Chinese, ex. Taiwanese (7)	10	0.10
Filipino (14)	25	0.24
Indian (13)	17	0.17
Japanese (8)	13	0.13
Korean (5)	7	0.07
Pakistani (4)	4	0.04
Taiwanese (1)	3	0.03
Other Asian, not specified (2)	3	0.03
Australian	8	0.08
Austrian	4	0.04
British	30	0.29
Canadian	15	0.15

Notes: 1. Figures in the "Number" column do not add up to the total population due to: a) Ancestry/Race overlap — e.g. persons can report being both White and Irish, b) persons of Hispanic origin can report being any race, c) persons reporting two ancestries are counted in both categories. 2. Numbers in parentheses indicate the number of persons reporting this ancestry/race alone, not in combination with any other ancestry/race. 3. Refer to the Explanation of Data in the front of the book for more detailed information.

Ancestry/Race	Number	%
Croatian	16	0.16
Czech	8	0.08
Czechoslovakian	22	0.21
Danish	11	0.11
Dutch	182	1.78
Eastern European	27	0.26
English	1,250	12.19
European	169	1.65
Finnish	10	0.10
French, except Basque	339	3.31
French Canadian	52	0.51
German	2,704	26.37
Greek	76	0.74
Hawaii Native/Pacific Islander:	1	0.01
Polynesian: (1)	1	0.01
Samoan (1)	1	0.01
Hispanic or Latino:	104	1.01
Central American:	5	0.05
Panamanian	5	0.05
Cuban	4	0.04
Dominican Republic	6	0.06
Mexican	42	0.41
Puerto Rican	13	0.13
South American:	2	0.02
Venezuelan	2	0.02
Other Hispanic or Latino	32	0.31
Hungarian	93	0.91
Irish	1,737	16.94
Italian	484	4.72
Macedonian	11	0.11
Northern European	19	0.19
Norwegian	44	0.43
Pennsylvania German	6	0.06
Polish	243	2.37
Russian	18	0.18
Scandinavian	8	0.08
Scotch-Irish	91	0.89
Scottish	239	2.33
Serbian	6	0.06
Slavic	7	0.07
Slovak	14	0.14
Slovene	14	0.14
Swedish	25	0.24
Swiss	11	0.11
Ukrainian	23	0.22
United States or American	1,013	9.88
Welsh	211	2.06
White:	9,786	95.48
Not Hispanic (9,648)	9,733	94.97
Hispanic (45)	53	0.52
Yugoslavian	4	0.04

Perrysburg

Place Type: City
County: Wood
Population: 16,945

Ancestry/Race	Number	%
African American/Black:	203	1.20
Not Hispanic (165)	193	1.14
Hispanic (9)	10	0.06
Am. Ind. or Alaska Nat., not spec.	19	0.11
Alsatian	6	0.04
American Indian tribes, specified:	31	0.18
Cherokee (3)	16	0.09
Chickasaw (1)	1	0.01
Chippewa (2)	2	0.01
Choctaw	1	0.01
Creek	2	0.01
Delaware	1	0.01
Iroquois	1	0.01
Latin American Indians (1)	2	0.01
Navajo (1)	2	0.01
Potawatomi (2)	2	0.01
All other tribes	1	0.01
American Indian tribes, not spec.	2	0.01
Arab:	145	0.85
Arab/Arabic	53	0.31
Lebanese	84	0.49
Syrian	8	0.05
Armenian	13	0.08
Asian:	352	2.08
Bangladeshi (4)	4	0.02
Cambodian (1)	3	0.02
Chinese, ex. Taiwanese (89)	97	0.57
Filipino (21)	24	0.14
Indian (89)	102	0.60
Indonesian (1)	1	0.01
Japanese (13)	19	0.11
Korean (43)	49	0.29
Laotian (4)	4	0.02
Malaysian (1)	1	0.01
Pakistani (4)	13	0.08
Sri Lankan (3)	3	0.02
Taiwanese (1)	1	0.01
Thai (6)	6	0.04
Vietnamese (8)	8	0.05
Other Asian, not specified (4)	17	0.10
Australian	7	0.04
Austrian	113	0.66
Belgian	55	0.32
Brazilian	8	0.05
British	66	0.39
Bulgarian	8	0.05
Canadian	79	0.46
Carpatho Rusyn	21	0.12
Croatian	29	0.17
Czech	162	0.95
Czechoslovakian	96	0.56
Danish	88	0.51
Dutch	350	2.05
English	2,404	14.05
European	55	0.32
Finnish	22	0.13
French, except Basque	832	4.86
French Canadian	176	1.03
German	6,774	39.59
Greek	98	0.57
Hawaii Native/Pacific Islander:	10	0.06
Micronesian: (2)	2	0.01
Other Micronesian (2)	2	0.01
Polynesian: (2)	7	0.04
Native Hawaiian (1)	5	0.03
Samoan (1)	2	0.01
Other Pac. Isl., not spec.	1	0.01
Hispanic or Latino:	348	2.05
Central American:	8	0.05
Costa Rican	7	0.04
Salvadoran	1	0.01
Cuban	4	0.02
Mexican	226	1.33
Puerto Rican	22	0.13
South American:	33	0.19
Argentinean	1	0.01
Colombian	16	0.09
Ecuadorian	4	0.02
Paraguayan	2	0.01
Peruvian	1	0.01
Venezuelan	6	0.04
Other South American	3	0.02
Other Hispanic or Latino	55	0.32
Hungarian	554	3.24
Iranian	10	0.06
Irish	2,314	13.53
Italian	873	5.10
Lithuanian	23	0.13
Luxemburger	18	0.11
Norwegian	178	1.04
Pennsylvania German	34	0.20
Polish	1,373	8.03
Portuguese	41	0.24
Romanian	48	0.28
Russian	113	0.66
Scandinavian	53	0.31
Scotch-Irish	310	1.81
Scottish	573	3.35
Serbian	7	0.04
Slavic	11	0.06
Slovak	177	1.03
Slovene	6	0.04
Swedish	198	1.16
Swiss	186	1.09
Ukrainian	59	0.34
United States or American	788	4.61
Welsh	188	1.10
West Indian, excl. Hispanic:	9	0.05
Jamaican	9	0.05
White:	16,286	96.11
Not Hispanic (15,979)	16,079	94.89
Hispanic (177)	207	1.22

Piqua

Place Type: City
County: Miami
Population: 20,738

Ancestry/Race	Number	%
African American/Black:	881	4.25
Not Hispanic (697)	873	4.21
Hispanic (3)	8	0.04
Alaska Native tribes, specified:	1	0.00
Eskimo (1)	1	0.00
Am. Ind. or Alaska Nat., not spec.	45	0.22
American Indian tribes, specified:	88	0.42
Blackfeet	1	0.00
Cherokee (16)	41	0.20
Chippewa (2)	3	0.01
Choctaw (1)	1	0.00
Iroquois (6)	7	0.03
Kiowa (1)	1	0.00
Latin American Indians (1)	2	0.01
Lumbee	3	0.01
Navajo	1	0.00
Seminole	3	0.01
Shoshone	1	0.00
Sioux (5)	5	0.02
Ute	1	0.00
Yaqui (1)	1	0.00
All other tribes (16)	17	0.08
American Indian tribes, not spec.	12	0.06
Arab:	26	0.12
Lebanese	26	0.12
Asian:	127	0.61
Cambodian (1)	1	0.00
Chinese, ex. Taiwanese (5)	7	0.03
Filipino (27)	41	0.20
Indian (16)	19	0.09
Indonesian (1)	2	0.01
Japanese (22)	34	0.16
Korean (7)	9	0.04
Pakistani (1)	1	0.00
Sri Lankan (1)	1	0.00
Taiwanese (2)	2	0.01
Vietnamese (5)	5	0.02
Other Asian, not specified (4)	5	0.02
British	79	0.38
Croatian	7	0.03
Czech	9	0.04
Czechoslovakian	29	0.14
Danish	6	0.03
Dutch	586	2.81
English	1,707	8.20
European	136	0.65
French, except Basque	880	4.23
French Canadian	33	0.16
German	5,855	28.12
Greek	17	0.08
Hawaii Native/Pacific Islander:	6	0.03
Polynesian:	4	0.02
Native Hawaiian	4	0.02
Other Pac. Isl., not spec.	2	0.01
Hispanic or Latino:	153	0.74
Central American:	4	0.02
Costa Rican	1	0.00
Guatemalan	2	0.01
Nicaraguan	1	0.00
Cuban	2	0.01
Mexican	80	0.39

Notes: 1. Figures in the "Number" column do not add up to the total population due to: a) Ancestry/Race overlap — e.g. persons can report being both White and Irish, b) persons of Hispanic origin can report being any race, c) persons reporting two ancestries are counted in both categories. 2. Numbers in parentheses indicate the number of persons reporting this ancestry/race alone, not in combination with any other ancestry/race. 3. Refer to the Explanation of Data in the front of the book for more detailed information.

Ancestry/Race	Number	%
Puerto Rican	10	0.05
South American:	4	0.02
Bolivian	2	0.01
Chilean	1	0.00
Ecuadorian	1	0.00
Other Hispanic or Latino	53	0.26
Hungarian	41	0.20
Irish	2,225	10.69
Italian	321	1.54
Lithuanian	23	0.11
Macedonian	11	0.05
Norwegian	61	0.29
Pennsylvania German	41	0.20
Polish	125	0.60
Portuguese	12	0.06
Romanian	15	0.07
Russian	60	0.29
Scotch-Irish	203	0.97
Scottish	253	1.22
Serbian	16	0.08
Swedish	32	0.15
Swiss	6	0.03
Turkish	11	0.05
United States or American	3,047	14.63
Welsh	175	0.84
West Indian, excl. Hispanic:	29	0.14
Barbadian	12	0.06
Jamaican	17	0.08
White:	19,804	95.50
Not Hispanic (19,445)	19,696	94.98
Hispanic (92)	108	0.52
Yugoslavian	7	0.03

Portsmouth

Place Type: City
County: Scioto
Population: 20,909

Ancestry/Race	Number	%
African American/Black:	1,189	5.69
Not Hispanic (1,034)	1,174	5.61
Hispanic (12)	15	0.07
Alaska Native tribes, specified:	2	0.01
Alaska Athabascan	2	0.01
Alaska Native tribes, not specified	2	0.01
Am. Ind. or Alaska Nat., not spec.	132	0.63
American Indian tribes, specified:	225	1.08
Apache	3	0.01
Blackfeet (5)	20	0.10
Cherokee (43)	126	0.60
Cheyenne (1)	4	0.02
Chippewa	4	0.02
Choctaw	4	0.02
Cree	2	0.01
Iroquois (6)	6	0.03
Kiowa (1)	1	0.00
Latin American Indians (6)	6	0.03
Menominee (1)	1	0.00
Ottawa (3)	3	0.01
Pueblo	3	0.01
Seminole	4	0.02
Sioux	10	0.05
All other tribes (7)	28	0.13
American Indian tribes, not spec.	11	0.05
Arab:	14	0.07
Lebanese	6	0.03
Syrian	8	0.04
Asian:	169	0.81
Bangladeshi	1	0.00
Chinese, ex. Taiwanese (27)	35	0.17
Filipino (26)	42	0.20
Indian (35)	40	0.19
Indonesian (5)	6	0.03
Japanese (4)	10	0.05
Korean (14)	22	0.11
Pakistani (3)	4	0.02
Taiwanese (2)	2	0.01
Thai (1)	1	0.00
Vietnamese (4)	4	0.02
Other Asian, not specified (2)	2	0.01
Austrian	6	0.03
Belgian	5	0.02
British	133	0.64
Canadian	7	0.03
Croatian	7	0.03
Danish	8	0.04
Dutch	302	1.45
English	2,079	9.98
European	141	0.68
French, except Basque	532	2.55
French Canadian	8	0.04
German	3,483	16.72
Greek	32	0.15
Hawaii Native/Pacific Islander:	13	0.06
Polynesian: (3)	9	0.04
Native Hawaiian (2)	8	0.04
Samoan (1)	1	0.00
Other Pac. Isl., not spec. (1)	4	0.02
Hispanic or Latino:	195	0.93
Central American:	6	0.03
Nicaraguan	2	0.01
Panamanian	2	0.01
Other Central American	2	0.01
Cuban	5	0.02
Mexican	99	0.47
Puerto Rican	19	0.09
South American:	1	0.00
Colombian	1	0.00
Other Hispanic or Latino	65	0.31
Hungarian	8	0.04
Irish	2,602	12.49
Italian	317	1.52
Latvian	9	0.04
Lithuanian	4	0.02
Norwegian	30	0.14
Polish	147	0.71
Portuguese	2	0.01
Romanian	7	0.03
Russian	64	0.31
Scandinavian	5	0.02
Scotch-Irish	242	1.16
Scottish	260	1.25
Slavic	8	0.04
Slovak	9	0.04
Swedish	68	0.33
Swiss	52	0.25
United States or American	3,315	15.91
Welsh	307	1.47
West Indian, excl. Hispanic:	14	0.07
Haitian	14	0.07
White:	19,505	93.29
Not Hispanic (19,027)	19,384	92.71
Hispanic (104)	121	0.58

Ravenna

Place Type: City
County: Portage
Population: 11,771

Ancestry/Race	Number	%
African American/Black:	615	5.22
Not Hispanic (520)	613	5.21
Hispanic	2	0.02
African, sub-Saharan:	12	0.10
African	12	0.10
Am. Ind. or Alaska Nat., not spec.	45	0.38
American Indian tribes, specified:	62	0.53
Blackfeet (6)	9	0.08
Cherokee (8)	34	0.29
Cheyenne	1	0.01
Chickasaw	1	0.01
Comanche (2)	2	0.02
Houma (1)	1	0.01
Iroquois (3)	5	0.04
Navajo	3	0.03
All other tribes (3)	6	0.05
American Indian tribes, not spec.	13	0.11
Asian:	67	0.57
Chinese, ex. Taiwanese (11)	18	0.15
Filipino (9)	12	0.10
Indian (8)	10	0.08
Japanese (7)	7	0.06
Korean (4)	9	0.08
Pakistani (2)	2	0.02
Thai (2)	3	0.03
Vietnamese (1)	4	0.03
Other Asian, not specified (2)	2	0.02
Austrian	38	0.32
British	69	0.57
Canadian	17	0.14
Croatian	6	0.05
Czech	71	0.59
Czechoslovakian	37	0.31
Dutch	325	2.70
English	1,263	10.48
European	77	0.64
French, except Basque	234	1.94
French Canadian	10	0.08
German	3,387	28.12
Greek	26	0.22
Hawaii Native/Pacific Islander:	7	0.06
Micronesian:	2	0.02
Guamanian/Chamorro	2	0.02
Polynesian: (1)	3	0.03
Native Hawaiian (1)	2	0.02
Samoan	1	0.01
Other Pac. Isl., not spec. (1)	2	0.02
Hispanic or Latino:	107	0.91
Central American:	1	0.01
Honduran	1	0.01
Cuban	10	0.08
Mexican	43	0.37
Puerto Rican	31	0.26
Other Hispanic or Latino	22	0.19
Hungarian	425	3.53
Irish	2,072	17.20
Italian	1,313	10.90
Lithuanian	27	0.22
Northern European	14	0.12
Norwegian	45	0.37
Pennsylvania German	35	0.29
Polish	401	3.33
Romanian	13	0.11
Russian	31	0.26
Scotch-Irish	153	1.27
Scottish	256	2.13
Slovak	223	1.85
Slovene	38	0.32
Swedish	158	1.31
Swiss	64	0.53
Ukrainian	32	0.27
United States or American	969	8.04
Welsh	290	2.41
West Indian, excl. Hispanic:	11	0.09
British West Indian	4	0.03
Dutch West Indian	7	0.06
White:	11,127	94.53
Not Hispanic (10,873)	11,046	93.84
Hispanic (77)	81	0.69

Reading

Place Type: City
County: Hamilton
Population: 11,292

Ancestry/Race	Number	%
African American/Black:	388	3.44
Not Hispanic (353)	379	3.36
Hispanic (8)	9	0.08
Alaska Native tribes, specified:	1	0.01
Alaska Athabascan (1)	1	0.01
Am. Ind. or Alaska Nat., not spec.	16	0.14
Albanian	35	0.31
American Indian tribes, specified:	37	0.33
Blackfeet	3	0.03
Cherokee (7)	23	0.20
Latin American Indians (1)	2	0.02

Notes: 1. Figures in the "Number" column do not add up to the total population due to: a) Ancestry/Race overlap — e.g. persons can report being both White and Irish, b) persons of Hispanic origin can report being any race, c) persons reporting two ancestries are counted in both categories. 2. Numbers in parentheses indicate the number of persons reporting this ancestry/race alone, not in combination with any other ancestry/race. 3. Refer to the Explanation of Data in the front of the book for more detailed information.

Navajo (1)	4	0.04
Sioux (1)	4	0.04
All other tribes	1	0.01
American Indian tribes, not spec.	4	0.04
Arab:	16	0.14
Lebanese	8	0.07
Syrian	8	0.07
Asian:	154	1.36
Chinese, ex. Taiwanese (33)	34	0.30
Filipino (10)	14	0.12
Indian (54)	56	0.50
Japanese (1)	6	0.05
Korean (10)	12	0.11
Laotian (1)	1	0.01
Malaysian (3)	3	0.03
Pakistani (9)	9	0.08
Sri Lankan (1)	1	0.01
Thai (3)	3	0.03
Vietnamese (8)	10	0.09
Other Asian, not specified	5	0.04
Australian	9	0.08
Austrian	17	0.15
Basque	15	0.13
British	40	0.36
Canadian	5	0.04
Croatian	40	0.36
Czech	28	0.25
Czechoslovakian	6	0.05
Danish	8	0.07
Dutch	119	1.06
Eastern European	5	0.04
English	1,014	9.05
European	84	0.75
Finnish	9	0.08
French, except Basque	356	3.18
French Canadian	24	0.21
German	4,432	39.56
Hawaii Native/Pacific Islander:	2	0.02
Polynesian: (2)	2	0.02
Native Hawaiian (2)	2	0.02
Hispanic or Latino:	89	0.79
Central American:	3	0.03
Honduran	2	0.02
Panamanian	1	0.01
Dominican Republic	9	0.08
Mexican	37	0.33
Puerto Rican	12	0.11
South American:	10	0.09
Colombian	3	0.03
Ecuadorian	3	0.03
Venezuelan	4	0.04
Other Hispanic or Latino	18	0.16
Hungarian	99	0.88
Irish	1,995	17.81
Italian	412	3.68
Luxemburger	7	0.06
Norwegian	8	0.07
Polish	54	0.48
Portuguese	8	0.07
Romanian	64	0.57
Russian	55	0.49
Scandinavian	8	0.07
Scotch-Irish	96	0.86
Scottish	75	0.67
Serbian	31	0.28
Slovak	27	0.24
Swedish	31	0.28
Ukrainian	61	0.54
United States or American	954	8.52
Welsh	75	0.67
White:	10,713	94.87
Not Hispanic (10,539)	10,669	94.48
Hispanic (40)	44	0.39
Yugoslavian	32	0.29

Reynoldsburg

Place Type: City
County: Franklin
Population: 32,069

Ancestry/Race	Number	%
African American/Black:	3,606	11.24
Not Hispanic (3,325)	3,570	11.13
Hispanic (22)	36	0.11
African, sub-Saharan:	353	1.10
African	154	0.48
Ethiopian	6	0.02
Kenyan	45	0.14
Liberian	6	0.02
Nigerian	25	0.08
Somalian	9	0.03
South African	108	0.34
Am. Ind. or Alaska Nat., not spec.	74	0.23
Albanian	18	0.06
American Indian tribes, specified:	143	0.45
Apache (2)	4	0.01
Blackfeet (7)	14	0.04
Cherokee (28)	76	0.24
Chickasaw	1	0.00
Chippewa (1)	2	0.01
Choctaw	1	0.00
Comanche	2	0.01
Cree	1	0.00
Delaware	1	0.00
Houma (1)	1	0.00
Iroquois (4)	11	0.03
Latin American Indians	1	0.00
Lumbee (6)	6	0.02
Seminole	3	0.01
Shoshone	1	0.00
Sioux (4)	12	0.04
Ute (1)	1	0.00
All other tribes	5	0.02
American Indian tribes, not spec.	12	0.04
Arab:	165	0.51
Arab/Arabic	106	0.33
Lebanese	34	0.11
Palestinian	25	0.08
Armenian	24	0.07
Asian:	716	2.23
Cambodian (8)	8	0.02
Chinese, ex. Taiwanese (146)	169	0.53
Filipino (31)	73	0.23
Indian (154)	171	0.53
Indonesian (2)	2	0.01
Japanese (38)	66	0.21
Korean (56)	82	0.26
Laotian (12)	15	0.05
Malaysian (1)	1	0.00
Pakistani (16)	17	0.05
Taiwanese (7)	8	0.02
Thai (6)	13	0.04
Vietnamese (43)	49	0.15
Other Asian, specified	1	0.00
Other Asian, not specified (15)	41	0.13
Austrian	84	0.26
British	150	0.47
Canadian	18	0.06
Celtic	14	0.04
Croatian	36	0.11
Czech	118	0.37
Czechoslovakian	93	0.29
Danish	87	0.27
Dutch	831	2.58
English	3,439	10.67
European	198	0.61
Finnish	64	0.20
French, except Basque	774	2.40
French Canadian	114	0.35
German	8,637	26.80
Greek	112	0.35
Guyanese	7	0.02
Hawaii Native/Pacific Islander:	31	0.10
Micronesian: (6)	10	0.03
Guamanian/Chamorro (6)	10	0.03
Polynesian: (3)	9	0.03
Native Hawaiian (3)	9	0.03
Other Pac. Isl., not spec. (4)	12	0.04
Hispanic or Latino:	578	1.80
Central American:	25	0.08
Guatemalan	9	0.03
Honduran	2	0.01
Nicaraguan	4	0.01
Panamanian	5	0.02
Salvadoran	5	0.02
Cuban	19	0.06
Dominican Republic	17	0.05
Mexican	231	0.72
Puerto Rican	111	0.35
South American:	45	0.14
Argentinean	5	0.02
Bolivian	4	0.01
Chilean	5	0.02
Colombian	10	0.03
Ecuadorian	5	0.02
Paraguayan	1	0.00
Peruvian	8	0.02
Venezuelan	4	0.01
Other South American	3	0.01
Other Hispanic or Latino	130	0.41
Hungarian	342	1.06
Irish	4,659	14.46
Israeli	12	0.04
Italian	1,643	5.10
Lithuanian	45	0.14
Northern European	15	0.05
Norwegian	128	0.40
Pennsylvania German	77	0.24
Polish	809	2.51
Portuguese	54	0.17
Romanian	69	0.21
Russian	247	0.77
Scandinavian	21	0.07
Scotch-Irish	571	1.77
Scottish	882	2.74
Serbian	35	0.11
Slavic	20	0.06
Slovak	218	0.68
Slovene	39	0.12
Swedish	188	0.58
Swiss	181	0.56
Ukrainian	100	0.31
United States or American	2,759	8.56
Welsh	607	1.88
West Indian, excl. Hispanic:	30	0.09
West Indian	30	0.09
White:	27,773	86.60
Not Hispanic (26,946)	27,413	85.48
Hispanic (315)	360	1.12
Yugoslavian	118	0.37

Richmond Heights

Place Type: City
County: Cuyahoga
Population: 10,944

Ancestry/Race	Number	%
African American/Black:	2,712	24.78
Not Hispanic (2,582)	2,679	24.48
Hispanic (30)	33	0.30
African, sub-Saharan:	100	0.91
African	73	0.67
South African	27	0.25
Am. Ind. or Alaska Nat., not spec.	14	0.13
American Indian tribes, specified:	28	0.26
Apache	3	0.03
Blackfeet	4	0.04
Cherokee	17	0.16
Latin American Indians (1)	1	0.01
Lumbee	1	0.01
Seminole	1	0.01
Yuman	1	0.01
American Indian tribes, not spec.	5	0.05

Notes: 1. Figures in the "Number" column do not add up to the total population due to: a) Ancestry/Race overlap — e.g. persons can report being both White and Irish, b) persons of Hispanic origin can report being any race, c) persons reporting two ancestries are counted in both categories. 2. Numbers in parentheses indicate the number of persons reporting this ancestry/race alone, not in combination with any other ancestry/race. 3. Refer to the Explanation of Data in the front of the book for more detailed information.

Ancestry/Race	Number	%
Arab:	109	1.00
Egyptian	27	0.25
Lebanese	62	0.57
Syrian	20	0.18
Asian:	582	5.32
Bangladeshi (2)	2	0.02
Chinese, ex. Taiwanese (139)	144	1.32
Filipino (33)	48	0.44
Indian (225)	240	2.19
Japanese (23)	27	0.25
Korean (32)	35	0.32
Laotian (10)	10	0.09
Pakistani (19)	20	0.18
Taiwanese (9)	9	0.08
Thai (4)	4	0.04
Vietnamese (14)	19	0.17
Other Asian, specified (3)	5	0.05
Other Asian, not specified (6)	19	0.17
Austrian	17	0.16
Belgian	16	0.15
British	41	0.37
Croatian	252	2.30
Czech	130	1.19
Czechoslovakian	75	0.69
Danish	10	0.09
Dutch	43	0.39
Eastern European	3	0.03
English	472	4.31
European	84	0.77
Finnish	12	0.11
French, except Basque	66	0.60
French Canadian	56	0.51
German	1,363	12.45
Greek	92	0.84
Guyanese	14	0.13
Hawaii Native/Pacific Islander:	9	0.08
Other Pac. Isl., specified	1	0.01
Other Pac. Isl., not spec. (4)	8	0.07
Hispanic or Latino:	173	1.58
Central American:	4	0.04
Panamanian	4	0.04
Cuban	5	0.05
Dominican Republic	1	0.01
Mexican	43	0.39
Puerto Rican	46	0.42
South American:	30	0.27
Argentinean	6	0.05
Colombian	10	0.09
Ecuadorian	1	0.01
Peruvian	5	0.05
Uruguayan	7	0.06
Venezuelan	1	0.01
Other Hispanic or Latino	44	0.40
Hungarian	289	2.64
Irish	694	6.34
Italian	1,270	11.60
Lithuanian	173	1.58
Northern European	8	0.07
Norwegian	29	0.26
Polish	725	6.62
Portuguese	17	0.16
Romanian	7	0.06
Russian	496	4.53
Scandinavian	15	0.14
Scotch-Irish	126	1.15
Scottish	99	0.90
Serbian	4	0.04
Slavic	5	0.05
Slovak	216	1.97
Slovene	613	5.60
Swedish	18	0.16
Swiss	23	0.21
Ukrainian	173	1.58
United States or American	178	1.63
Welsh	43	0.39
West Indian, excl. Hispanic:	6	0.05
Jamaican	6	0.05
White:	7,682	70.19
Not Hispanic (7,472)	7,598	69.43
Hispanic (77)	84	0.77

Riverside

Place Type: City
County: Montgomery
Population: 23,545

Ancestry/Race	Number	%
African American/Black:	1,149	4.88
Not Hispanic (990)	1,126	4.78
Hispanic (13)	23	0.10
African, sub-Saharan:	16	0.07
African	12	0.05
Nigerian	4	0.02
Am. Ind. or Alaska Nat., not spec.	56	0.24
American Indian tribes, specified:	118	0.50
Apache	2	0.01
Blackfeet (3)	12	0.05
Cherokee (20)	70	0.30
Cheyenne (1)	3	0.01
Chippewa (1)	5	0.02
Choctaw (2)	2	0.01
Cree	1	0.00
Iroquois	2	0.01
Latin American Indians (1)	3	0.01
Navajo	1	0.00
Pima (1)	1	0.00
Potawatomi (1)	1	0.00
Pueblo (4)	4	0.02
Seminole	3	0.01
All other tribes (5)	8	0.03
American Indian tribes, not spec.	4	0.02
Arab:	63	0.27
Iraqi	7	0.03
Lebanese	38	0.16
Moroccan	18	0.08
Asian:	540	2.29
Bangladeshi (9)	9	0.04
Cambodian (1)	1	0.00
Chinese, ex. Taiwanese (49)	55	0.23
Filipino (63)	96	0.41
Indian (110)	119	0.51
Indonesian (1)	5	0.02
Japanese (54)	85	0.36
Korean (30)	51	0.22
Laotian (1)	1	0.00
Malaysian	4	0.02
Pakistani (4)	4	0.02
Taiwanese (1)	1	0.00
Thai (16)	22	0.09
Vietnamese (65)	68	0.29
Other Asian, not specified (6)	19	0.08
Austrian	46	0.19
Belgian	19	0.08
British	77	0.33
Canadian	24	0.10
Croatian	8	0.03
Czech	74	0.31
Czechoslovakian	14	0.06
Danish	49	0.21
Dutch	318	1.34
English	2,159	9.13
European	170	0.72
Finnish	13	0.05
French, except Basque	682	2.88
French Canadian	32	0.14
German	5,276	22.31
Greek	31	0.13
Guyanese	7	0.03
Hawaii Native/Pacific Islander:	25	0.11
Micronesian: (1)	2	0.01
Guamanian/Chamorro (1)	2	0.01
Polynesian: (6)	13	0.06
Native Hawaiian (5)	10	0.04
Samoan (1)	2	0.01
Tongan	1	0.00
Other Pac. Isl., not spec. (3)	10	0.04
Hispanic or Latino:	364	1.55
Central American:	7	0.03
Costa Rican	2	0.01
Honduran	2	0.01
Nicaraguan	2	0.01
Panamanian	1	0.00
Cuban	16	0.07
Dominican Republic	4	0.02
Mexican	153	0.65
Puerto Rican	76	0.32
South American:	17	0.07
Chilean	3	0.01
Peruvian	4	0.02
Venezuelan	10	0.04
Other Hispanic or Latino	91	0.39
Hungarian	206	0.87
Irish	3,170	13.41
Italian	822	3.48
Latvian	6	0.03
Lithuanian	58	0.25
Norwegian	203	0.86
Polish	493	2.09
Portuguese	8	0.03
Russian	47	0.20
Scandinavian	25	0.11
Scotch-Irish	360	1.52
Scottish	266	1.12
Slovak	57	0.24
Slovene	28	0.12
Swedish	83	0.35
Turkish	24	0.10
Ukrainian	15	0.06
United States or American	3,408	14.41
Welsh	120	0.51
White:	21,872	92.89
Not Hispanic (21,321)	21,637	91.90
Hispanic (211)	235	1.00
Yugoslavian	31	0.13

Rocky River

Place Type: City
County: Cuyahoga
Population: 20,735

Ancestry/Race	Number	%
African American/Black:	127	0.61
Not Hispanic (80)	118	0.57
Hispanic (4)	9	0.04
African, sub-Saharan:	8	0.04
African	8	0.04
Alaska Native tribes, specified:	1	0.00
Tlingit-Haida	1	0.00
Am. Ind. or Alaska Nat., not spec.	20	0.10
Albanian	51	0.25
Alsatian	7	0.03
American Indian tribes, specified:	36	0.17
Cherokee (3)	9	0.04
Cheyenne (3)	3	0.01
Chippewa (1)	7	0.03
Choctaw	2	0.01
Iroquois	1	0.00
Latin American Indians (1)	1	0.00
Navajo	3	0.01
Pueblo	4	0.02
Seminole	1	0.00
All other tribes (5)	5	0.02
American Indian tribes, not spec.	2	0.01
Arab:	444	2.14
Arab/Arabic	69	0.33
Egyptian	23	0.11
Lebanese	180	0.87
Palestinian	106	0.51
Syrian	52	0.25
Other Arab	14	0.07
Asian:	339	1.63
Bangladeshi (1)	1	0.00
Cambodian (2)	2	0.01
Chinese, ex. Taiwanese (96)	105	0.51
Filipino (35)	47	0.23
Indian (78)	91	0.44
Indonesian (2)	2	0.01
Japanese (17)	24	0.12
Korean (9)	11	0.05

Notes: 1. Figures in the "Number" column do not add up to the total population due to: a) Ancestry/Race overlap — e.g. persons can report being both White and Irish, b) persons of Hispanic origin can report being any race, c) persons reporting two ancestries are counted in both categories. 2. Numbers in parentheses indicate the number of persons reporting this ancestry/race alone, not in combination with any other ancestry/race. 3. Refer to the Explanation of Data in the front of the book for more detailed information.

Pakistani (4)	7	0.03
Sri Lankan (4)	4	0.02
Taiwanese (4)	6	0.03
Vietnamese (20)	21	0.10
Other Asian, specified	2	0.01
Other Asian, not specified	16	0.08
Assyrian/Chaldean/Syriac	39	0.19
Austrian	176	0.85
Basque	5	0.02
Belgian	9	0.04
Brazilian	9	0.04
British	220	1.06
Bulgarian	51	0.25
Canadian	118	0.57
Croatian	152	0.73
Czech	373	1.80
Czechoslovakian	78	0.38
Danish	60	0.29
Dutch	216	1.04
Eastern European	7	0.03
English	2,574	12.41
European	29	0.14
Finnish	39	0.19
French, except Basque	525	2.53
French Canadian	119	0.57
German	5,825	28.09
Greek	211	1.02
Hawaii Native/Pacific Islander:	13	0.06
Polynesian: (2)	9	0.04
Native Hawaiian	3	0.01
Samoan (2)	6	0.03
Other Pac. Isl., specified	2	0.01
Other Pac. Isl., not spec. (2)	2	0.01
Hispanic or Latino:	248	1.20
Central American:	3	0.01
Costa Rican	1	0.00
Panamanian	1	0.00
Other Central American	1	0.00
Cuban	24	0.12
Dominican Republic	2	0.01
Mexican	64	0.31
Puerto Rican	72	0.35
South American:	42	0.20
Argentinean	4	0.02
Chilean	5	0.02
Colombian	9	0.04
Paraguayan	4	0.02
Peruvian	7	0.03
Venezuelan	13	0.06
Other Hispanic or Latino	41	0.20
Hungarian	1,039	5.01
Iranian	25	0.12
Irish	5,580	26.91
Italian	1,957	9.44
Latvian	17	0.08
Lithuanian	79	0.38
Macedonian	23	0.11
Northern European	8	0.04
Norwegian	190	0.92
Pennsylvania German	9	0.04
Polish	1,366	6.59
Portuguese	11	0.05
Romanian	237	1.14
Russian	173	0.83
Scotch-Irish	331	1.60
Scottish	566	2.73
Serbian	56	0.27
Slavic	14	0.07
Slovak	991	4.78
Slovene	268	1.29
Swedish	306	1.48
Swiss	90	0.43
Turkish	5	0.02
Ukrainian	182	0.88
United States or American	689	3.32
Welsh	343	1.65
West Indian, excl. Hispanic:	9	0.04
Haitian	9	0.04
White:	20,288	97.84
Not Hispanic (19,891)	20,091	96.89
Hispanic (186)	197	0.95
Yugoslavian	37	0.18

Salem

Place Type: City
County: Columbiana
Population: 12,197

Ancestry/Race	Number	%
African American/Black:	89	0.73
Not Hispanic (62)	88	0.72
Hispanic (1)	1	0.01
Am. Ind. or Alaska Nat., not spec.	16	0.13
American Indian tribes, specified:	21	0.17
Blackfeet	4	0.03
Cherokee	7	0.06
Choctaw	1	0.01
Iroquois	2	0.02
Latin American Indians	1	0.01
Sioux (6)	6	0.05
American Indian tribes, not spec.	2	0.02
Arab:	36	0.30
Lebanese	27	0.22
Other Arab	9	0.07
Asian:	61	0.50
Chinese, ex. Taiwanese (11)	15	0.12
Filipino (7)	9	0.07
Indian	3	0.02
Japanese (12)	17	0.14
Korean (2)	7	0.06
Laotian (3)	3	0.02
Thai (2)	4	0.03
Other Asian, specified (1)	2	0.02
Other Asian, not specified	1	0.01
Austrian	75	0.62
Belgian	14	0.12
British	63	0.52
Canadian	56	0.46
Croatian	42	0.35
Czech	89	0.74
Czechoslovakian	13	0.11
Dutch	350	2.90
English	1,506	12.48
European	9	0.07
Finnish	20	0.17
French, except Basque	292	2.42
French Canadian	7	0.06
German	3,411	28.27
Greek	92	0.76
Hawaii Native/Pacific Islander:	6	0.05
Micronesian: (1)	1	0.01
Guamanian/Chamorro (1)	1	0.01
Polynesian: (2)	4	0.03
Native Hawaiian (2)	4	0.03
Other Pac. Isl., not spec.	1	0.01
Hispanic or Latino:	66	0.54
Central American:	1	0.01
Guatemalan	1	0.01
Cuban	2	0.02
Mexican	24	0.20
Puerto Rican	21	0.17
South American:	4	0.03
Argentinean	2	0.02
Colombian	1	0.01
Other South American	1	0.01
Other Hispanic or Latino	14	0.11
Hungarian	159	1.32
Irish	2,015	16.70
Italian	1,279	10.60
Latvian	18	0.15
Lithuanian	25	0.21
Norwegian	42	0.35
Pennsylvania German	54	0.45
Polish	275	2.28
Romanian	96	0.80
Russian	22	0.18
Scandinavian	10	0.08
Scotch-Irish	173	1.43
Scottish	289	2.39
Serbian	20	0.17
Slavic	24	0.20
Slovak	232	1.92
Slovene	15	0.12
Swedish	112	0.93
Swiss	80	0.66
Ukrainian	7	0.06
United States or American	793	6.57
Welsh	154	1.28
West Indian, excl. Hispanic:	10	0.08
Jamaican	10	0.08
White:	12,068	98.94
Not Hispanic (11,945)	12,015	98.51
Hispanic (51)	53	0.43
Yugoslavian	7	0.06

Sandusky

Place Type: City
County: Erie
Population: 27,844

Ancestry/Race	Number	%
African American/Black:	6,422	23.06
Not Hispanic (5,833)	6,356	22.83
Hispanic (37)	66	0.24
African, sub-Saharan:	447	1.60
African	447	1.60
Am. Ind. or Alaska Nat., not spec.	108	0.39
American Indian tribes, specified:	121	0.43
Apache (4)	13	0.05
Blackfeet (6)	24	0.09
Cherokee (15)	42	0.15
Chickasaw	1	0.00
Chippewa (1)	8	0.03
Cree	4	0.01
Iroquois (2)	6	0.02
Latin American Indians (7)	10	0.04
Lumbee (1)	2	0.01
Navajo	4	0.01
Ottawa (3)	5	0.02
Potawatomi	1	0.00
Sioux (1)	1	0.00
Yaqui (1)	1	0.00
American Indian tribes, not spec.	12	0.04
Arab:	50	0.18
Lebanese	13	0.05
Syrian	27	0.10
Other Arab	10	0.04
Asian:	131	0.47
Chinese, ex. Taiwanese (14)	18	0.06
Filipino (12)	25	0.09
Indian (11)	24	0.09
Japanese (5)	11	0.04
Korean (12)	19	0.07
Laotian (2)	2	0.01
Taiwanese	1	0.00
Thai (1)	1	0.00
Vietnamese (13)	15	0.05
Other Asian, specified	4	0.01
Other Asian, not specified (2)	11	0.04
Austrian	59	0.21
Belgian	24	0.09
British	60	0.21
Bulgarian	24	0.09
Canadian	20	0.07
Croatian	17	0.06
Czech	50	0.18
Czechoslovakian	18	0.06
Danish	186	0.66
Dutch	368	1.31
English	2,197	7.85
European	8	0.03
Finnish	29	0.10
French, except Basque	612	2.19
French Canadian	133	0.48
German	8,981	32.08
German Russian	7	0.03
Greek	74	0.26
Hawaii Native/Pacific Islander:	15	0.05

Notes: 1. Figures in the "Number" column do not add up to the total population due to: a) Ancestry/Race overlap — e.g. persons can report being both White and Irish, b) persons of Hispanic origin can report being any race, c) persons reporting two ancestries are counted in both categories. 2. Numbers in parentheses indicate the number of persons reporting this ancestry/race alone, not in combination with any other ancestry/race. 3. Refer to the Explanation of Data in the front of the book for more detailed information.

Ancestry/Race	Number	%
Micronesian: (3)	5	0.02
Guamanian/Chamorro (3)	5	0.02
Polynesian: (1)	1	0.00
Samoan (1)	1	0.00
Other Pac. Isl., specified	4	0.01
Other Pac. Isl., not spec.	5	0.02
Hispanic or Latino:	859	3.09
Cuban	6	0.02
Mexican	559	2.01
Puerto Rican	116	0.42
South American:	9	0.03
Chilean	3	0.01
Colombian	6	0.02
Other Hispanic or Latino	169	0.61
Hungarian	293	1.05
Icelander	13	0.05
Irish	3,460	12.36
Italian	2,079	7.43
Latvian	29	0.10
Lithuanian	5	0.02
Luxemburger	9	0.03
Macedonian	37	0.13
Norwegian	96	0.34
Pennsylvania German	30	0.11
Polish	548	1.96
Portuguese	6	0.02
Romanian	14	0.05
Russian	70	0.25
Scandinavian	5	0.02
Scotch-Irish	235	0.84
Scottish	248	0.89
Serbian	7	0.03
Slovak	97	0.35
Slovene	21	0.08
Swedish	193	0.69
Swiss	61	0.22
Ukrainian	7	0.03
United States or American	1,863	6.65
Welsh	89	0.32
West Indian, excl. Hispanic:	4	0.01
Jamaican	4	0.01
White:	21,441	77.00
Not Hispanic (20,317)	20,901	75.06
Hispanic (428)	540	1.94

Seven Hills

Place Type: City
County: Cuyahoga
Population: 12,080

Ancestry/Race	Number	%
African American/Black:	22	0.18
Not Hispanic (18)	22	0.18
Am. Ind. or Alaska Nat., not spec.	6	0.05
Alsatian	7	0.06
American Indian tribes, specified:	11	0.09
Blackfeet	3	0.02
Cherokee	3	0.02
Sioux (1)	4	0.03
All other tribes (1)	1	0.01
American Indian tribes, not spec.	3	0.02
Arab:	129	1.07
Egyptian	20	0.17
Lebanese	98	0.81
Syrian	11	0.09
Asian:	279	2.31
Chinese, ex. Taiwanese (55)	59	0.49
Filipino (69)	81	0.67
Indian (69)	74	0.61
Japanese (3)	6	0.05
Korean (29)	29	0.24
Pakistani	1	0.01
Vietnamese (19)	22	0.18
Other Asian, not specified (4)	7	0.06
Austrian	56	0.46
British	23	0.19
Canadian	13	0.11
Carpatho Rusyn	4	0.03
Croatian	329	2.72
Czech	704	5.83
Czechoslovakian	127	1.05
Danish	9	0.07
Dutch	61	0.50
English	634	5.25
European	13	0.11
Finnish	7	0.06
French, except Basque	186	1.54
French Canadian	25	0.21
German	2,306	19.09
Greek	310	2.57
Hawaii Native/Pacific Islander:	2	0.02
Micronesian:	1	0.01
Guamanian/Chamorro	1	0.01
Other Pac. Isl., not spec.	1	0.01
Hispanic or Latino:	92	0.76
Central American:	2	0.02
Guatemalan	1	0.01
Honduran	1	0.01
Cuban	1	0.01
Mexican	17	0.14
Puerto Rican	33	0.27
South American:	7	0.06
Argentinean	4	0.03
Colombian	1	0.01
Peruvian	2	0.02
Other Hispanic or Latino	32	0.26
Hungarian	592	4.90
Irish	1,110	9.19
Italian	1,976	16.36
Lithuanian	57	0.47
Norwegian	43	0.36
Polish	2,732	22.62
Romanian	93	0.77
Russian	211	1.75
Scandinavian	7	0.06
Scotch-Irish	105	0.87
Scottish	88	0.73
Serbian	135	1.12
Slovak	1,081	8.95
Slovene	240	1.99
Swedish	55	0.46
Swiss	32	0.26
Turkish	5	0.04
Ukrainian	501	4.15
United States or American	372	3.08
Welsh	27	0.22
West Indian, excl. Hispanic:	8	0.07
Jamaican	8	0.07
White:	11,790	97.60
Not Hispanic (11,668)	11,710	96.94
Hispanic (71)	80	0.66
Yugoslavian	57	0.47

Shaker Heights

Place Type: City
County: Cuyahoga
Population: 29,405

Ancestry/Race	Number	%
African American/Black:	10,420	35.44
Not Hispanic (9,985)	10,358	35.23
Hispanic (45)	62	0.21
African, sub-Saharan:	431	1.47
African	324	1.10
Ethiopian	18	0.06
Ghanian	12	0.04
Kenyan	41	0.14
Nigerian	7	0.02
South African	16	0.05
Other sub-Saharan African	13	0.04
Alaska Native tribes, specified:	3	0.01
Aleut	1	0.00
Eskimo	2	0.01
Am. Ind. or Alaska Nat., not spec.	96	0.33
Albanian	6	0.02
American Indian tribes, specified:	101	0.34
Apache	4	0.01
Blackfeet (1)	5	0.02
Cherokee (6)	58	0.20
Chippewa	2	0.01
Choctaw	3	0.01
Cree	1	0.00
Creek	2	0.01
Iroquois	5	0.02
Latin American Indians (1)	3	0.01
Navajo	5	0.02
Pueblo	3	0.01
Seminole	5	0.02
Sioux	1	0.00
All other tribes (1)	4	0.01
American Indian tribes, not spec.	10	0.03
Arab:	165	0.56
Arab/Arabic	24	0.08
Egyptian	7	0.02
Iraqi	7	0.02
Lebanese	92	0.31
Palestinian	5	0.02
Syrian	21	0.07
Other Arab	9	0.03
Asian:	1,122	3.82
Bangladeshi (1)	2	0.01
Cambodian (1)	1	0.00
Chinese, ex. Taiwanese (318)	371	1.26
Filipino (43)	74	0.25
Hmong (2)	2	0.01
Indian (291)	332	1.13
Indonesian (9)	9	0.03
Japanese (61)	84	0.29
Korean (122)	134	0.46
Laotian (2)	2	0.01
Malaysian (1)	1	0.00
Pakistani (9)	10	0.03
Sri Lankan (11)	11	0.04
Taiwanese (10)	12	0.04
Thai (8)	11	0.04
Vietnamese (8)	12	0.04
Other Asian, specified (1)	7	0.02
Other Asian, not specified (21)	47	0.16
Australian	54	0.18
Austrian	183	0.62
Basque	6	0.02
Belgian	55	0.19
Brazilian	18	0.06
British	68	0.23
Canadian	93	0.32
Celtic	6	0.02
Croatian	77	0.26
Czech	279	0.95
Czechoslovakian	65	0.22
Danish	142	0.48
Dutch	228	0.78
Eastern European	372	1.26
English	2,704	9.19
European	197	0.67
Finnish	65	0.22
French, except Basque	379	1.29
French Canadian	80	0.27
German	3,885	13.21
Greek	71	0.24
Guyanese	9	0.03
Hawaii Native/Pacific Islander:	19	0.06
Micronesian: (1)	2	0.01
Guamanian/Chamorro (1)	1	0.00
Other Micronesian	1	0.00
Polynesian: (3)	6	0.02
Native Hawaiian	1	0.00
Samoan (3)	4	0.01
Other Polynesian	1	0.00
Other Pac. Isl., specified	2	0.01
Other Pac. Isl., not spec.	9	0.03
Hispanic or Latino:	339	1.15
Central American:	21	0.07
Guatemalan	9	0.03
Honduran	6	0.02
Panamanian	6	0.02
Cuban	11	0.04
Dominican Republic	2	0.01
Mexican	80	0.27

Notes: 1. Figures in the "Number" column do not add up to the total population due to: a) Ancestry/Race overlap — e.g. persons can report being both White and Irish, b) persons of Hispanic origin can report being any race, c) persons reporting two ancestries are counted in both categories. 2. Numbers in parentheses indicate the number of persons reporting this ancestry/race alone, not in combination with any other ancestry/race. 3. Refer to the Explanation of Data in the front of the book for more detailed information.

Puerto Rican	87	0.30
South American:	78	0.27
Argentinean	18	0.06
Bolivian	4	0.01
Chilean	10	0.03
Colombian	12	0.04
Ecuadorian	3	0.01
Peruvian	7	0.02
Uruguayan	3	0.01
Venezuelan	17	0.06
Other South American	4	0.01
Other Hispanic or Latino	60	0.20
Hungarian	768	2.61
Icelander	8	0.03
Iranian	10	0.03
Irish	2,756	9.37
Israeli	19	0.06
Italian	1,345	4.57
Latvian	36	0.12
Lithuanian	190	0.65
Northern European	71	0.24
Norwegian	191	0.65
Pennsylvania German	7	0.02
Polish	1,099	3.74
Portuguese	9	0.03
Romanian	159	0.54
Russian	1,509	5.13
Scandinavian	56	0.19
Scotch-Irish	522	1.77
Scottish	622	2.11
Serbian	39	0.13
Slavic	35	0.12
Slovak	239	0.81
Slovene	97	0.33
Swedish	232	0.79
Swiss	116	0.39
Turkish	18	0.06
Ukrainian	120	0.41
United States or American	1,217	4.14
Welsh	199	0.68
West Indian, excl. Hispanic:	92	0.31
Belizean	6	0.02
Jamaican	62	0.21
Trinidadian and Tobagonian	12	0.04
West Indian	12	0.04
White:	18,129	61.65
Not Hispanic (17,434)	17,917	60.93
Hispanic (190)	212	0.72
Yugoslavian	6	0.02

Sharonville

Place Type: City
County: Hamilton
Population: 13,804

Ancestry/Race	Number	%
African American/Black:	756	5.48
Not Hispanic (666)	752	5.45
Hispanic	4	0.03
African, sub-Saharan:	95	0.69
African	61	0.45
Nigerian	25	0.18
South African	9	0.07
Am. Ind. or Alaska Nat., not spec.	24	0.17
American Indian tribes, specified:	41	0.30
Apache (1)	3	0.02
Blackfeet	1	0.01
Cherokee (5)	29	0.21
Choctaw	1	0.01
Latin American Indians (1)	1	0.01
Seminole	1	0.01
Sioux (1)	2	0.01
All other tribes (1)	3	0.02
American Indian tribes, not spec.	5	0.04
Arab:	8	0.06
Egyptian	8	0.06
Armenian	34	0.25
Asian:	579	4.19
Bangladeshi (3)	4	0.03
Cambodian (2)	3	0.02
Chinese, ex. Taiwanese (85)	104	0.75
Filipino (21)	34	0.25
Hmong (1)	1	0.01
Indian (289)	290	2.10
Indonesian	1	0.01
Japanese (18)	24	0.17
Korean (19)	23	0.17
Laotian (1)	1	0.01
Malaysian (1)	2	0.01
Pakistani (3)	3	0.02
Taiwanese (14)	21	0.15
Vietnamese (46)	47	0.34
Other Asian, specified	1	0.01
Other Asian, not specified (11)	20	0.14
Austrian	17	0.12
British	144	1.05
Canadian	52	0.38
Croatian	13	0.09
Czech	34	0.25
Czechoslovakian	8	0.06
Danish	24	0.18
Dutch	267	1.95
Eastern European	8	0.06
English	1,462	10.67
European	151	1.10
French, except Basque	364	2.66
French Canadian	60	0.44
German	5,145	37.55
Greek	48	0.35
Hawaii Native/Pacific Islander:	21	0.15
Micronesian: (2)	4	0.03
Guamanian/Chamorro (2)	4	0.03
Polynesian: (1)	7	0.05
Native Hawaiian (1)	7	0.05
Other Pac. Isl., not spec.	10	0.07
Hispanic or Latino:	317	2.30
Central American:	32	0.23
Costa Rican	11	0.08
Guatemalan	1	0.01
Honduran	8	0.06
Panamanian	1	0.01
Salvadoran	11	0.08
Cuban	13	0.09
Dominican Republic	8	0.06
Mexican	186	1.35
Puerto Rican	15	0.11
South American:	9	0.07
Bolivian	1	0.01
Colombian	3	0.02
Ecuadorian	1	0.01
Venezuelan	4	0.03
Other Hispanic or Latino	54	0.39
Hungarian	35	0.26
Icelander	7	0.05
Irish	1,742	12.71
Italian	504	3.68
Lithuanian	13	0.09
Norwegian	58	0.42
Polish	291	2.12
Russian	114	0.83
Scandinavian	23	0.17
Scotch-Irish	264	1.93
Scottish	275	2.01
Serbian	21	0.15
Slavic	11	0.08
Slovak	10	0.07
Slovene	18	0.13
Swedish	113	0.82
Swiss	57	0.42
Turkish	7	0.05
Ukrainian	42	0.31
United States or American	1,220	8.90
Welsh	169	1.23
West Indian, excl. Hispanic:	9	0.07
Trinidadian and Tobagonian	5	0.04
West Indian	4	0.03
White:	12,431	90.05
Not Hispanic (12,081)	12,238	88.66
Hispanic (169)	193	1.40
Yugoslavian	7	0.05

Shiloh

Place Type: Census Designated Place
County: Montgomery
Population: 11,272

Ancestry/Race	Number	%
Acadian/Cajun	6	0.05
African American/Black:	4,079	36.19
Not Hispanic (3,923)	4,062	36.04
Hispanic (14)	17	0.15
African, sub-Saharan:	178	1.58
African	142	1.26
Ethiopian	14	0.12
Kenyan	9	0.08
Nigerian	13	0.12
Am. Ind. or Alaska Nat., not spec.	28	0.25
American Indian tribes, specified:	57	0.51
Apache (3)	4	0.04
Blackfeet	5	0.04
Cherokee (3)	25	0.22
Cheyenne	1	0.01
Chickasaw	1	0.01
Chippewa	1	0.01
Choctaw	3	0.03
Cree (1)	1	0.01
Creek	1	0.01
Iroquois (1)	1	0.01
Navajo (1)	1	0.01
Sioux	3	0.03
All other tribes (5)	10	0.09
American Indian tribes, not spec.	6	0.05
Arab:	25	0.22
Arab/Arabic	7	0.06
Iraqi	4	0.04
Lebanese	14	0.12
Asian:	131	1.16
Bangladeshi	1	0.01
Chinese, ex. Taiwanese (6)	8	0.07
Filipino (11)	20	0.18
Indian (23)	38	0.34
Japanese (10)	16	0.14
Korean (9)	14	0.12
Pakistani (2)	5	0.04
Taiwanese (1)	1	0.01
Thai (2)	3	0.03
Vietnamese (9)	11	0.10
Other Asian, specified (1)	3	0.03
Other Asian, not specified (2)	11	0.10
Australian	10	0.09
Austrian	33	0.29
British	72	0.64
Czechoslovakian	9	0.08
Danish	6	0.05
Dutch	90	0.80
Eastern European	17	0.15
English	777	6.89
European	160	1.42
French, except Basque	272	2.41
French Canadian	33	0.29
German	2,101	18.63
Greek	41	0.36
Guyanese	19	0.17
Hawaii Native/Pacific Islander:	15	0.13
Micronesian: (1)	2	0.02
Guamanian/Chamorro (1)	2	0.02
Polynesian: (4)	5	0.04
Native Hawaiian	1	0.01
Samoan (4)	4	0.04
Other Pac. Isl., specified	2	0.02
Other Pac. Isl., not spec.	6	0.05
Hispanic or Latino:	130	1.15
Central American:	6	0.05
Honduran	1	0.01
Panamanian	5	0.04
Cuban	2	0.02
Dominican Republic	1	0.01
Mexican	73	0.65

Notes: 1. Figures in the "Number" column do not add up to the total population due to: a) Ancestry/Race overlap — e.g. persons can report being both White and Irish, b) persons of Hispanic origin can report being any race, c) persons reporting two ancestries are counted in both categories. 2. Numbers in parentheses indicate the number of persons reporting this ancestry/race alone, not in combination with any other ancestry/race. 3. Refer to the Explanation of Data in the front of the book for more detailed information.

Puerto Rican	23	0.20
South American:	5	0.04
Colombian	2	0.02
Ecuadorian	1	0.01
Other South American	2	0.02
Other Hispanic or Latino	20	0.18
Hungarian	155	1.37
Irish	819	7.26
Italian	224	1.99
Latvian	6	0.05
Lithuanian	23	0.20
Norwegian	18	0.16
Pennsylvania German	7	0.06
Polish	242	2.15
Portuguese	11	0.10
Romanian	47	0.42
Russian	155	1.37
Scotch-Irish	128	1.13
Scottish	96	0.85
Serbian	6	0.05
Slovak	6	0.05
Slovene	8	0.07
Swedish	12	0.11
Swiss	48	0.43
Ukrainian	14	0.12
United States or American	723	6.41
Welsh	68	0.60
West Indian, excl. Hispanic:	88	0.78
Jamaican	88	0.78
White:	7,111	63.09
Not Hispanic (6,873)	7,025	62.32
Hispanic (76)	86	0.76
Yugoslavian	7	0.06

Sidney

Place Type: City
County: Shelby
Population: 20,211

Ancestry/Race	Number	%
African American/Black:	798	3.95
Not Hispanic (614)	788	3.90
Hispanic (4)	10	0.05
African, sub-Saharan:	142	0.70
African	25	0.12
Nigerian	63	0.31
Other sub-Saharan African	54	0.27
Alaska Native tribes, specified:	3	0.01
Aleut	3	0.01
Am. Ind. or Alaska Nat., not spec.	54	0.27
American Indian tribes, specified:	88	0.44
Apache	6	0.03
Blackfeet (1)	5	0.02
Cherokee (13)	32	0.16
Chickasaw	1	0.00
Chippewa (3)	5	0.02
Choctaw	1	0.00
Creek	1	0.00
Crow	4	0.02
Iroquois (3)	6	0.03
Latin American Indians (5)	7	0.03
Pueblo (1)	3	0.01
Seminole	1	0.00
Sioux (7)	7	0.03
All other tribes (2)	9	0.04
American Indian tribes, not spec.	8	0.04
Arab:	12	0.06
Lebanese	12	0.06
Asian:	443	2.19
Chinese, ex. Taiwanese (35)	37	0.18
Filipino (28)	36	0.18
Indian (55)	62	0.31
Indonesian (1)	1	0.00
Japanese (226)	239	1.18
Korean (11)	26	0.13
Laotian (9)	9	0.04
Malaysian (1)	3	0.01
Pakistani (2)	2	0.01
Thai (1)	4	0.02
Vietnamese (2)	3	0.01
Other Asian, specified (1)	3	0.01
Other Asian, not specified (2)	18	0.09
Austrian	33	0.16
British	106	0.52
Canadian	38	0.19
Czechoslovakian	43	0.21
Danish	39	0.19
Dutch	466	2.30
English	1,836	9.06
European	187	0.92
French, except Basque	727	3.59
French Canadian	24	0.12
German	6,373	31.45
Greek	24	0.12
Hawaii Native/Pacific Islander:	31	0.15
Micronesian: (17)	21	0.10
Guamanian/Chamorro (16)	18	0.09
Other Micronesian (1)	3	0.01
Polynesian: (2)	7	0.03
Native Hawaiian (2)	5	0.02
Tongan	2	0.01
Other Pac. Isl., specified	1	0.00
Other Pac. Isl., not spec. (1)	2	0.01
Hispanic or Latino:	262	1.30
Central American:	2	0.01
Costa Rican	1	0.00
Honduran	1	0.00
Cuban	2	0.01
Mexican	167	0.83
Puerto Rican	34	0.17
South American:	1	0.00
Chilean	1	0.00
Other Hispanic or Latino	56	0.28
Hungarian	49	0.24
Icelander	7	0.03
Irish	2,203	10.87
Italian	386	1.90
Macedonian	11	0.05
Norwegian	94	0.46
Pennsylvania German	17	0.08
Polish	244	1.20
Portuguese	31	0.15
Russian	11	0.05
Scandinavian	13	0.06
Scotch-Irish	232	1.14
Scottish	360	1.78
Slavic	15	0.07
Slovak	26	0.13
Swedish	127	0.63
Swiss	62	0.31
Ukrainian	5	0.02
United States or American	3,158	15.58
Welsh	180	0.89
West Indian, excl. Hispanic:	36	0.18
Haitian	28	0.14
Trinidadian and Tobagonian	8	0.04
White:	19,046	94.24
Not Hispanic (18,544)	18,852	93.28
Hispanic (173)	194	0.96

Solon

Place Type: City
County: Cuyahoga
Population: 21,802

Ancestry/Race	Number	%
African American/Black:	1,409	6.46
Not Hispanic (1,319)	1,392	6.38
Hispanic (15)	17	0.08
African, sub-Saharan:	132	0.61
African	22	0.10
Nigerian	82	0.38
South African	28	0.13
Am. Ind. or Alaska Nat., not spec.	23	0.11
Albanian	5	0.02
Alsatian	8	0.04
American Indian tribes, specified:	23	0.11
Cherokee (1)	9	0.04
Chippewa (3)	3	0.01
Choctaw (1)	1	0.00
Potawatomi	3	0.01
Seminole	1	0.00
Sioux	4	0.02
All other tribes (1)	2	0.01
American Indian tribes, not spec.	5	0.02
Arab:	205	0.94
Arab/Arabic	49	0.22
Egyptian	9	0.04
Iraqi	20	0.09
Lebanese	127	0.58
Armenian	16	0.07
Asian:	1,168	5.36
Bangladeshi (1)	1	0.00
Chinese, ex. Taiwanese (319)	355	1.63
Filipino (68)	88	0.40
Indian (495)	510	2.34
Japanese (21)	26	0.12
Korean (86)	97	0.44
Pakistani (12)	17	0.08
Sri Lankan (9)	9	0.04
Taiwanese (32)	39	0.18
Thai (3)	3	0.01
Vietnamese (10)	12	0.06
Other Asian, not specified (3)	11	0.05
Australian	51	0.23
Austrian	159	0.73
Belgian	6	0.03
British	107	0.49
Canadian	64	0.29
Carpatho Rusyn	14	0.06
Croatian	133	0.61
Czech	757	3.47
Czechoslovakian	155	0.71
Danish	93	0.43
Dutch	138	0.63
Eastern European	198	0.91
English	2,075	9.52
European	118	0.54
Finnish	105	0.48
French, except Basque	365	1.67
French Canadian	44	0.20
German	3,671	16.84
Greek	89	0.41
Guyanese	7	0.03
Hawaii Native/Pacific Islander:	12	0.06
Micronesian: (1)	1	0.00
Guamanian/Chamorro (1)	1	0.00
Polynesian: (1)	4	0.02
Native Hawaiian	3	0.01
Samoan (1)	1	0.00
Other Pac. Isl., not spec.	7	0.03
Hispanic or Latino:	153	0.70
Central American:	7	0.03
Honduran	2	0.01
Panamanian	3	0.01
Salvadoran	2	0.01
Cuban	10	0.05
Dominican Republic	1	0.00
Mexican	52	0.24
Puerto Rican	25	0.11
South American:	21	0.10
Argentinean	3	0.01
Bolivian	2	0.01
Chilean	2	0.01
Colombian	8	0.04
Peruvian	2	0.01
Venezuelan	4	0.02
Other Hispanic or Latino	37	0.17
Hungarian	1,325	6.08
Iranian	25	0.11
Irish	2,534	11.62
Italian	3,169	14.54
Latvian	6	0.03
Lithuanian	168	0.77
Macedonian	9	0.04
Norwegian	101	0.46
Pennsylvania German	10	0.05
Polish	2,171	9.96

Notes: 1. Figures in the "Number" column do not add up to the total population due to: a) Ancestry/Race overlap — e.g. persons can report being both White and Irish, b) persons of Hispanic origin can report being any race, c) persons reporting two ancestries are counted in both categories. 2. Numbers in parentheses indicate the number of persons reporting this ancestry/race alone, not in combination with any other ancestry/race. 3. Refer to the Explanation of Data in the front of the book for more detailed information.

Ancestry/Race	Number	%
Romanian	85	0.39
Russian	1,464	6.71
Scotch-Irish	183	0.84
Scottish	426	1.95
Serbian	33	0.15
Slavic	36	0.17
Slovak	878	4.03
Slovene	395	1.81
Swedish	231	1.06
Swiss	68	0.31
Turkish	49	0.22
Ukrainian	230	1.05
United States or American	991	4.55
Welsh	207	0.95
West Indian, excl. Hispanic:	46	0.21
Jamaican	46	0.21
White:	19,318	88.61
Not Hispanic (19,046)	19,205	88.09
Hispanic (94)	113	0.52
Yugoslavian	7	0.03

South Euclid

Place Type: City
County: Cuyahoga
Population: 23,537

Ancestry/Race	Number	%
African American/Black:	5,207	22.12
Not Hispanic (5,005)	5,163	21.94
Hispanic (27)	44	0.19
African, sub-Saharan:	225	0.96
African	198	0.84
Ethiopian	7	0.03
Ghanian	8	0.03
South African	12	0.05
Am. Ind. or Alaska Nat., not spec.	50	0.21
Albanian	11	0.05
Alsatian	11	0.05
American Indian tribes, specified:	58	0.25
Apache	1	0.00
Blackfeet	5	0.02
Cherokee (9)	22	0.09
Chippewa (1)	1	0.00
Comanche	2	0.01
Creek (1)	4	0.02
Iroquois	1	0.00
Latin American Indians	6	0.03
Navajo	1	0.00
Paiute	1	0.00
Pueblo (1)	1	0.00
Seminole	1	0.00
Sioux	2	0.01
All other tribes (1)	10	0.04
American Indian tribes, not spec.	3	0.01
Arab:	170	0.72
Lebanese	124	0.53
Moroccan	35	0.15
Other Arab	11	0.05
Armenian	8	0.03
Asian:	407	1.73
Cambodian (7)	7	0.03
Chinese, ex. Taiwanese (117)	124	0.53
Filipino (26)	33	0.14
Indian (98)	104	0.44
Indonesian (1)	1	0.00
Japanese (24)	39	0.17
Korean (31)	38	0.16
Malaysian (1)	1	0.00
Pakistani (1)	1	0.00
Sri Lankan (3)	4	0.02
Taiwanese (6)	7	0.03
Thai (2)	2	0.01
Vietnamese (22)	25	0.11
Other Asian, not specified (12)	21	0.09
Austrian	187	0.79
British	73	0.31
Canadian	23	0.10
Croatian	249	1.06
Czech	355	1.51
Czechoslovakian	97	0.41
Danish	11	0.05
Dutch	208	0.88
Eastern European	124	0.53
English	1,387	5.89
Estonian	9	0.04
European	174	0.74
Finnish	27	0.11
French, except Basque	358	1.52
French Canadian	24	0.10
German	3,273	13.91
Greek	40	0.17
Hawaii Native/Pacific Islander:	10	0.04
Polynesian: (1)	4	0.02
Native Hawaiian (1)	4	0.02
Other Pac. Isl., not spec. (2)	6	0.03
Hispanic or Latino:	241	1.02
Central American:	18	0.08
Costa Rican	1	0.00
Guatemalan	10	0.04
Panamanian	4	0.02
Salvadoran	3	0.01
Cuban	20	0.08
Dominican Republic	10	0.04
Mexican	50	0.21
Puerto Rican	53	0.23
South American:	47	0.20
Argentinean	8	0.03
Chilean	8	0.03
Colombian	8	0.03
Peruvian	12	0.05
Venezuelan	7	0.03
Other South American	4	0.02
Other Hispanic or Latino	43	0.18
Hungarian	1,039	4.41
Iranian	38	0.16
Irish	3,215	13.66
Israeli	119	0.51
Italian	3,616	15.36
Latvian	24	0.10
Lithuanian	208	0.88
Macedonian	12	0.05
Norwegian	98	0.42
Pennsylvania German	14	0.06
Polish	1,363	5.79
Portuguese	32	0.14
Romanian	111	0.47
Russian	1,439	6.11
Scandinavian	14	0.06
Scotch-Irish	279	1.19
Scottish	341	1.45
Serbian	18	0.08
Slavic	19	0.08
Slovak	543	2.31
Slovene	459	1.95
Swedish	249	1.06
Swiss	64	0.27
Turkish	43	0.18
Ukrainian	303	1.29
United States or American	599	2.54
Welsh	171	0.73
West Indian, excl. Hispanic:	156	0.66
Barbadian	3	0.01
Jamaican	124	0.53
Trinidadian and Tobagonian	29	0.12
White:	17,978	76.38
Not Hispanic (17,569)	17,818	75.70
Hispanic (140)	160	0.68
Yugoslavian	41	0.17

Springboro

Place Type: City
County: Warren
Population: 12,380

Ancestry/Race	Number	%
African American/Black:	153	1.24
Not Hispanic (123)	147	1.19
Hispanic	6	0.05
Am. Ind. or Alaska Nat., not spec.	17	0.14
American Indian tribes, specified:	41	0.33
Apache	1	0.01
Cherokee (8)	28	0.23
Choctaw	4	0.03
Colville (1)	1	0.01
Creek	2	0.02
Iroquois (4)	4	0.03
Shoshone	1	0.01
American Indian tribes, not spec.	1	0.01
Arab:	84	0.69
Egyptian	18	0.15
Lebanese	29	0.24
Syrian	37	0.30
Asian:	251	2.03
Bangladeshi (3)	3	0.02
Chinese, ex. Taiwanese (39)	46	0.37
Filipino (22)	37	0.30
Indian (64)	64	0.52
Japanese (9)	19	0.15
Korean (27)	38	0.31
Pakistani (4)	4	0.03
Taiwanese (6)	8	0.06
Thai (1)	1	0.01
Vietnamese (14)	14	0.11
Other Asian, specified (3)	11	0.09
Other Asian, not specified (4)	6	0.05
Austrian	69	0.57
Belgian	33	0.27
Brazilian	7	0.06
British	17	0.14
Canadian	10	0.08
Croatian	18	0.15
Czech	32	0.26
Czechoslovakian	14	0.11
Danish	28	0.23
Dutch	202	1.65
English	1,870	15.32
European	100	0.82
Finnish	30	0.25
French, except Basque	282	2.31
French Canadian	50	0.41
German	3,793	31.07
Greek	118	0.97
Hawaii Native/Pacific Islander:	12	0.10
Polynesian: (3)	3	0.02
Samoan (3)	3	0.02
Other Pac. Isl., specified	8	0.06
Other Pac. Isl., not spec. (1)	1	0.01
Hispanic or Latino:	124	1.00
Central American:	2	0.02
Guatemalan	1	0.01
Salvadoran	1	0.01
Cuban	8	0.06
Dominican Republic	3	0.02
Mexican	32	0.26
Puerto Rican	31	0.25
South American:	11	0.09
Argentinean	1	0.01
Chilean	1	0.01
Colombian	5	0.04
Ecuadorian	3	0.02
Peruvian	1	0.01
Other Hispanic or Latino	37	0.30
Hungarian	172	1.41
Iranian	26	0.21
Irish	2,123	17.39
Israeli	7	0.06
Italian	460	3.77
Lithuanian	18	0.15
Norwegian	113	0.93
Polish	255	2.09
Portuguese	11	0.09
Romanian	6	0.05
Russian	19	0.16
Scandinavian	43	0.35
Scotch-Irish	180	1.47
Scottish	242	1.98
Slovak	34	0.28
Slovene	43	0.35

Notes: 1. Figures in the "Number" column do not add up to the total population due to: a) Ancestry/Race overlap — e.g. persons can report being both White and Irish, b) persons of Hispanic origin can report being any race, c) persons reporting two ancestries are counted in both categories. 2. Numbers in parentheses indicate the number of persons reporting this ancestry/race alone, not in combination with any other ancestry/race. 3. Refer to the Explanation of Data in the front of the book for more detailed information.

Swedish	199	1.63
Swiss	98	0.80
Turkish	29	0.24
Ukrainian	17	0.14
United States or American	1,347	11.03
Welsh	119	0.97
White:	11,990	96.85
Not Hispanic (11,800)	11,891	96.05
Hispanic (85)	99	0.80

Springdale

Place Type: City
County: Hamilton
Population: 10,563

Ancestry/Race	Number	%
African American/Black:	2,811	26.61
Not Hispanic (2,692)	2,794	26.45
Hispanic (15)	17	0.16
African, sub-Saharan:	178	1.68
African	158	1.49
Nigerian	8	0.08
Other sub-Saharan African	12	0.11
Am. Ind. or Alaska Nat., not spec.	19	0.18
American Indian tribes, specified:	44	0.42
Cherokee (6)	23	0.22
Cheyenne	4	0.04
Chippewa	4	0.04
Crow (1)	2	0.02
Iroquois	1	0.01
Navajo	2	0.02
Sioux	3	0.03
All other tribes	5	0.05
American Indian tribes, not spec.	2	0.02
Arab:	72	0.68
Arab/Arabic	18	0.17
Lebanese	54	0.51
Asian:	307	2.91
Bangladeshi (2)	2	0.02
Cambodian (2)	2	0.02
Chinese, ex. Taiwanese (31)	38	0.36
Filipino (12)	17	0.16
Indian (97)	103	0.98
Japanese (19)	27	0.26
Korean (9)	15	0.14
Pakistani (8)	8	0.08
Taiwanese (17)	19	0.18
Thai (1)	1	0.01
Vietnamese (67)	74	0.70
Other Asian, not specified	1	0.01
Austrian	4	0.04
Belgian	6	0.06
British	23	0.22
Canadian	34	0.32
Czech	10	0.09
Czechoslovakian	18	0.17
Danish	21	0.20
Dutch	92	0.87
English	874	8.26
European	115	1.09
Finnish	10	0.09
French, except Basque	268	2.53
French Canadian	42	0.40
German	2,243	21.20
Greek	18	0.17
Hawaii Native/Pacific Islander:	12	0.11
Micronesian: (2)	8	0.08
Guamanian/Chamorro (2)	8	0.08
Polynesian:	4	0.04
Native Hawaiian	4	0.04
Hispanic or Latino:	384	3.64
Central American:	27	0.26
Guatemalan	13	0.12
Honduran	1	0.01
Nicaraguan	7	0.07
Panamanian	1	0.01
Salvadoran	5	0.05
Cuban	11	0.10
Dominican Republic	5	0.05
Mexican	255	2.41
Puerto Rican	38	0.36
South American:	10	0.09
Argentinean	2	0.02
Colombian	6	0.06
Peruvian	1	0.01
Venezuelan	1	0.01
Other Hispanic or Latino	38	0.36
Hungarian	77	0.73
Irish	995	9.41
Italian	146	1.38
Lithuanian	6	0.06
Macedonian	7	0.07
Northern European	19	0.18
Norwegian	115	1.09
Polish	98	0.93
Russian	16	0.15
Scotch-Irish	148	1.40
Scottish	136	1.29
Slovak	54	0.51
Swedish	31	0.29
Swiss	7	0.07
Turkish	16	0.15
Ukrainian	15	0.14
United States or American	831	7.86
Welsh	70	0.66
West Indian, excl. Hispanic:	58	0.55
Haitian	31	0.29
Jamaican	27	0.26
White:	7,379	69.86
Not Hispanic (6,999)	7,136	67.56
Hispanic (224)	243	2.30

Springfield

Place Type: City
County: Clark
Population: 65,358

Ancestry/Race	Number	%
African American/Black:	12,781	19.56
Not Hispanic (11,832)	12,668	19.38
Hispanic (77)	113	0.17
African, sub-Saharan:	424	0.65
African	377	0.58
Ghanian	10	0.02
Nigerian	37	0.06
Alaska Native tribes, specified:	2	0.00
Alaska Athabascan	1	0.00
All other tribes (1)	1	0.00
Am. Ind. or Alaska Nat., not spec.	299	0.46
American Indian tribes, specified:	430	0.66
Apache (4)	15	0.02
Blackfeet (13)	38	0.06
Cherokee (60)	249	0.38
Cheyenne (5)	5	0.01
Chippewa (5)	8	0.01
Choctaw (1)	1	0.00
Creek (1)	4	0.01
Delaware	1	0.00
Iroquois (1)	7	0.01
Latin American Indians (6)	8	0.01
Menominee	1	0.00
Navajo (1)	7	0.01
Osage	1	0.00
Ottawa (1)	3	0.00
Potawatomi (2)	8	0.01
Pueblo	2	0.00
Seminole (1)	1	0.00
Sioux (3)	10	0.02
Yaqui (1)	3	0.00
All other tribes (26)	58	0.09
American Indian tribes, not spec.	38	0.06
Arab:	23	0.04
Egyptian	17	0.03
Lebanese	6	0.01
Armenian	5	0.01
Asian:	587	0.90
Cambodian	1	0.00
Chinese, ex. Taiwanese (54)	67	0.10
Filipino (31)	47	0.07
Indian (203)	221	0.34
Indonesian (1)	6	0.01
Japanese (56)	81	0.12
Korean (27)	48	0.07
Laotian	2	0.00
Malaysian (2)	4	0.01
Pakistani (28)	30	0.05
Taiwanese (1)	2	0.00
Thai (5)	10	0.02
Vietnamese (13)	18	0.03
Other Asian, specified (4)	7	0.01
Other Asian, not specified (24)	43	0.07
Austrian	44	0.07
Belgian	91	0.14
British	137	0.21
Bulgarian	5	0.01
Canadian	57	0.09
Celtic	9	0.01
Croatian	20	0.03
Czech	71	0.11
Czechoslovakian	32	0.05
Danish	82	0.13
Dutch	1,414	2.16
Eastern European	10	0.02
English	4,220	6.46
European	277	0.42
Finnish	33	0.05
French, except Basque	1,216	1.86
French Canadian	156	0.24
German	11,683	17.89
German Russian	12	0.02
Greek	124	0.19
Hawaii Native/Pacific Islander:	36	0.06
Micronesian: (5)	7	0.01
Guamanian/Chamorro (5)	7	0.01
Polynesian: (8)	17	0.03
Native Hawaiian (2)	4	0.01
Samoan (5)	11	0.02
Other Polynesian (1)	2	0.00
Other Pac. Isl., specified	2	0.00
Other Pac. Isl., not spec. (1)	10	0.02
Hispanic or Latino:	770	1.18
Central American:	9	0.01
Guatemalan	2	0.00
Honduran	1	0.00
Panamanian	5	0.01
Salvadoran	2	0.00
Cuban	28	0.04
Dominican Republic	6	0.01
Mexican	428	0.65
Puerto Rican	74	0.11
South American:	18	0.03
Argentinean	2	0.00
Colombian	10	0.02
Ecuadorian	1	0.00
Peruvian	4	0.01
Venezuelan	2	0.00
Other Hispanic or Latino	207	0.32
Hungarian	174	0.27
Irish	6,773	10.37
Italian	1,394	2.13
Latvian	51	0.08
Lithuanian	26	0.04
Macedonian	50	0.08
Northern European	10	0.02
Norwegian	161	0.25
Pennsylvania German	58	0.09
Polish	716	1.10
Portuguese	37	0.06
Romanian	11	0.02
Russian	107	0.16
Scandinavian	50	0.08
Scotch-Irish	883	1.35
Scottish	792	1.21
Serbian	9	0.01
Slovak	122	0.19
Slovene	32	0.05
Swedish	304	0.47
Swiss	143	0.22

Notes: 1. Figures in the "Number" column do not add up to the total population due to: a) Ancestry/Race overlap — e.g. persons can report being both White and Irish, b) persons of Hispanic origin can report being any race, c) persons reporting two ancestries are counted in both categories. 2. Numbers in parentheses indicate the number of persons reporting this ancestry/race alone, not in combination with any other ancestry/race. 3. Refer to the Explanation of Data in the front of the book for more detailed information.

Turkish	16	0.02
Ukrainian	74	0.11
United States or American	9,036	13.83
Welsh	751	1.15
West Indian, excl. Hispanic:	40	0.06
Dutch West Indian	6	0.01
Haitian	9	0.01
Jamaican	25	0.04
White:	52,229	79.91
Not Hispanic (50,663)	51,805	79.26
Hispanic (344)	424	0.65
Yugoslavian	8	0.01

Steubenville

Place Type: City
County: Jefferson
Population: 19,015

Ancestry/Race	Number	%
Acadian/Cajun	11	0.06
African American/Black:	3,508	18.45
Not Hispanic (3,273)	3,497	18.39
Hispanic (8)	11	0.06
African, sub-Saharan:	73	0.38
African	62	0.32
Nigerian	11	0.06
Am. Ind. or Alaska Nat., not spec.	50	0.26
Alsatian	8	0.04
American Indian tribes, specified:	71	0.37
Blackfeet (5)	11	0.06
Cherokee (6)	34	0.18
Chickasaw	1	0.01
Chippewa (1)	4	0.02
Comanche	1	0.01
Creek (2)	2	0.01
Crow (3)	4	0.02
Iroquois	1	0.01
Navajo	1	0.01
Pueblo (2)	4	0.02
Seminole	6	0.03
Sioux	1	0.01
All other tribes (1)	1	0.01
American Indian tribes, not spec.	11	0.06
Arab:	56	0.29
Lebanese	22	0.12
Syrian	16	0.08
Other Arab	18	0.09
Asian:	191	1.00
Chinese, ex. Taiwanese (20)	32	0.17
Filipino (52)	68	0.36
Indian (32)	43	0.23
Indonesian (1)	2	0.01
Japanese (5)	10	0.05
Korean (12)	15	0.08
Malaysian (1)	1	0.01
Pakistani (4)	4	0.02
Sri Lankan (1)	1	0.01
Taiwanese (1)	2	0.01
Thai (3)	4	0.02
Vietnamese (1)	1	0.01
Other Asian, specified	2	0.01
Other Asian, not specified	6	0.03
Austrian	32	0.17
Belgian	17	0.09
British	52	0.27
Celtic	26	0.14
Croatian	54	0.28
Czech	9	0.05
Czechoslovakian	32	0.17
Dutch	225	1.18
English	1,089	5.70
European	46	0.24
Finnish	34	0.18
French, except Basque	237	1.24
French Canadian	59	0.31
German	2,457	12.87
Greek	227	1.19
Hawaii Native/Pacific Islander:	7	0.04
Polynesian: (2)	4	0.02
Native Hawaiian (1)	3	0.02
Samoan (1)	1	0.01
Other Pac. Isl., specified	2	0.01
Other Pac. Isl., not spec.	1	0.01
Hispanic or Latino:	185	0.97
Central American:	7	0.04
Costa Rican	2	0.01
Guatemalan	3	0.02
Honduran	2	0.01
Cuban	8	0.04
Dominican Republic	4	0.02
Mexican	79	0.42
Puerto Rican	30	0.16
South American:	3	0.02
Chilean	2	0.01
Colombian	1	0.01
Other Hispanic or Latino	54	0.28
Hungarian	264	1.38
Irish	2,417	12.66
Italian	3,613	18.92
Lithuanian	74	0.39
Norwegian	5	0.03
Pennsylvania German	19	0.10
Polish	1,309	6.86
Portuguese	15	0.08
Romanian	20	0.10
Russian	113	0.59
Scotch-Irish	491	2.57
Scottish	317	1.66
Serbian	192	1.01
Slavic	69	0.36
Slovak	472	2.47
Slovene	14	0.07
Swedish	83	0.43
Swiss	68	0.36
Turkish	13	0.07
Ukrainian	58	0.30
United States or American	843	4.41
Welsh	285	1.49
West Indian, excl. Hispanic:	27	0.14
Bahamian	8	0.04
Dutch West Indian	6	0.03
Jamaican	13	0.07
White:	15,398	80.98
Not Hispanic (15,013)	15,273	80.32
Hispanic (114)	125	0.66
Yugoslavian	8	0.04

Stow

Place Type: City
County: Summit
Population: 32,139

Ancestry/Race	Number	%
African American/Black:	578	1.80
Not Hispanic (492)	572	1.78
Hispanic (3)	6	0.02
African, sub-Saharan:	34	0.11
African	15	0.05
South African	19	0.06
Am. Ind. or Alaska Nat., not spec.	44	0.14
Albanian	18	0.06
American Indian tribes, specified:	79	0.25
Apache (1)	4	0.01
Blackfeet	5	0.02
Cherokee (11)	36	0.11
Cheyenne (2)	2	0.01
Chickasaw	2	0.01
Chippewa (3)	3	0.01
Choctaw (1)	5	0.02
Colville (1)	1	0.00
Comanche (1)	1	0.00
Iroquois (2)	4	0.01
Latin American Indians	1	0.00
Lumbee (1)	1	0.00
Ottawa (1)	1	0.00
Paiute (1)	1	0.00
Seminole	1	0.00
Shoshone	1	0.00
Sioux (1)	5	0.02
All other tribes (1)	5	0.02
American Indian tribes, not spec.	4	0.01
Arab:	312	0.97
Arab/Arabic	40	0.12
Lebanese	162	0.50
Palestinian	27	0.08
Syrian	57	0.18
Other Arab	26	0.08
Armenian	15	0.05
Asian:	730	2.27
Bangladeshi (1)	3	0.01
Cambodian (8)	9	0.03
Chinese, ex. Taiwanese (227)	245	0.76
Filipino (45)	68	0.21
Indian (180)	193	0.60
Indonesian (6)	10	0.03
Japanese (30)	50	0.16
Korean (66)	81	0.25
Laotian (7)	7	0.02
Malaysian	1	0.00
Pakistani (2)	3	0.01
Sri Lankan (1)	1	0.00
Taiwanese (8)	8	0.02
Thai (8)	12	0.04
Vietnamese (13)	15	0.05
Other Asian, specified	5	0.02
Other Asian, not specified (10)	19	0.06
Australian	7	0.02
Austrian	121	0.38
Belgian	35	0.11
Brazilian	5	0.02
British	135	0.42
Canadian	70	0.22
Croatian	209	0.65
Czech	409	1.27
Czechoslovakian	129	0.40
Danish	120	0.37
Dutch	659	2.05
Eastern European	21	0.07
English	4,595	14.30
Estonian	16	0.05
European	205	0.64
Finnish	65	0.20
French, except Basque	1,061	3.30
French Canadian	65	0.20
German	9,555	29.73
Greek	196	0.61
Hawaii Native/Pacific Islander:	14	0.04
Micronesian: (3)	4	0.01
Guamanian/Chamorro (3)	4	0.01
Polynesian: (1)	5	0.02
Native Hawaiian (1)	5	0.02
Other Pac. Isl., specified	5	0.02
Hispanic or Latino:	291	0.91
Central American:	10	0.03
Costa Rican	2	0.01
Guatemalan	1	0.00
Honduran	1	0.00
Nicaraguan	1	0.00
Panamanian	1	0.00
Salvadoran	3	0.01
Other Central American	1	0.00
Cuban	15	0.05
Dominican Republic	1	0.00
Mexican	131	0.41
Puerto Rican	51	0.16
South American:	27	0.08
Argentinean	1	0.00
Chilean	1	0.00
Colombian	4	0.01
Paraguayan	1	0.00
Peruvian	9	0.03
Uruguayan	2	0.01
Venezuelan	8	0.02
Other South American	1	0.00
Other Hispanic or Latino	56	0.17
Hungarian	1,159	3.61
Iranian	39	0.12
Irish	5,699	17.73

Notes: 1. Figures in the "Number" column do not add up to the total population due to: a) Ancestry/Race overlap — e.g. persons can report being both White and Irish, b) persons of Hispanic origin can report being any race, c) persons reporting two ancestries are counted in both categories. 2. Numbers in parentheses indicate the number of persons reporting this ancestry/race alone, not in combination with any other ancestry/race. 3. Refer to the Explanation of Data in the front of the book for more detailed information.

Ancestry/Race	Number	%
Italian	3,860	12.01
Lithuanian	162	0.50
Northern European	8	0.02
Norwegian	133	0.41
Pennsylvania German	85	0.26
Polish	2,076	6.46
Portuguese	59	0.18
Romanian	127	0.40
Russian	252	0.78
Scandinavian	49	0.15
Scotch-Irish	662	2.06
Scottish	904	2.81
Serbian	140	0.44
Slavic	61	0.19
Slovak	903	2.81
Slovene	320	1.00
Swedish	459	1.43
Swiss	165	0.51
Ukrainian	188	0.58
United States or American	1,366	4.25
Welsh	793	2.47
White:	30,873	96.06
Not Hispanic (30,415)	30,662	95.40
Hispanic (181)	211	0.66
Yugoslavian	55	0.17

Streetsboro

Place Type: City
County: Portage
Population: 12,311

Ancestry/Race	Number	%
African American/Black:	277	2.25
Not Hispanic (241)	273	2.22
Hispanic	4	0.03
African, sub-Saharan:	20	0.16
African	20	0.16
Am. Ind. or Alaska Nat., not spec.	11	0.09
American Indian tribes, specified:	47	0.38
Apache	1	0.01
Blackfeet	5	0.04
Cherokee (5)	26	0.21
Choctaw (2)	2	0.02
Iroquois	1	0.01
Latin American Indians (2)	2	0.02
Pima	3	0.02
Sioux (1)	3	0.02
Ute	3	0.02
All other tribes	1	0.01
American Indian tribes, not spec.	2	0.02
Arab:	48	0.39
Egyptian	13	0.11
Lebanese	35	0.28
Asian:	205	1.67
Chinese, ex. Taiwanese (19)	19	0.15
Filipino (47)	50	0.41
Indian (67)	77	0.63
Japanese (7)	24	0.19
Korean (10)	13	0.11
Pakistani (2)	2	0.02
Sri Lankan (2)	2	0.02
Taiwanese (3)	4	0.03
Thai (2)	4	0.03
Vietnamese (6)	6	0.05
Other Asian, not specified (4)	4	0.03
Austrian	40	0.32
Belgian	12	0.10
British	30	0.24
Canadian	16	0.13
Croatian	102	0.83
Czech	275	2.23
Czechoslovakian	62	0.50
Danish	17	0.14
Dutch	265	2.15
Eastern European	4	0.03
English	1,104	8.96
European	25	0.20
Finnish	20	0.16
French, except Basque	261	2.12
French Canadian	44	0.36
German	3,426	27.79
Hawaii Native/Pacific Islander:	3	0.02
Micronesian: (2)	2	0.02
Guamanian/Chamorro (2)	2	0.02
Polynesian:	1	0.01
Native Hawaiian	1	0.01
Hispanic or Latino:	96	0.78
Central American:	4	0.03
Honduran	1	0.01
Salvadoran	3	0.02
Cuban	3	0.02
Dominican Republic	1	0.01
Mexican	34	0.28
Puerto Rican	24	0.19
South American:	2	0.02
Venezuelan	2	0.02
Other Hispanic or Latino	28	0.23
Hungarian	721	5.85
Icelander	10	0.08
Irish	1,965	15.94
Italian	1,414	11.47
Lithuanian	65	0.53
Macedonian	6	0.05
Norwegian	50	0.41
Pennsylvania German	15	0.12
Polish	1,181	9.58
Portuguese	28	0.23
Romanian	37	0.30
Russian	154	1.25
Scotch-Irish	209	1.70
Scottish	214	1.74
Serbian	45	0.37
Slovak	320	2.60
Slovene	174	1.41
Swedish	105	0.85
Swiss	100	0.81
Turkish	4	0.03
Ukrainian	67	0.54
United States or American	540	4.38
Welsh	186	1.51
White:	11,858	96.32
Not Hispanic (11,674)	11,780	95.69
Hispanic (70)	78	0.63
Yugoslavian	34	0.28

Strongsville

Place Type: City
County: Cuyahoga
Population: 43,858

Ancestry/Race	Number	%
African American/Black:	643	1.47
Not Hispanic (533)	610	1.39
Hispanic (18)	33	0.08
African, sub-Saharan:	58	0.13
African	49	0.11
South African	9	0.02
Am. Ind. or Alaska Nat., not spec.	32	0.07
Albanian	20	0.05
American Indian tribes, specified:	70	0.16
Apache	1	0.00
Blackfeet (1)	6	0.01
Cherokee (4)	37	0.08
Creek	1	0.00
Iroquois	7	0.02
Latin American Indians	2	0.00
Pueblo	1	0.00
Sioux (1)	8	0.02
All other tribes (2)	7	0.02
American Indian tribes, not spec.	3	0.01
Arab:	623	1.42
Arab/Arabic	68	0.16
Egyptian	6	0.01
Lebanese	478	1.09
Syrian	71	0.16
Armenian	35	0.08
Asian:	1,594	3.63
Bangladeshi (14)	14	0.03
Cambodian (6)	6	0.01
Chinese, ex. Taiwanese (229)	262	0.60
Filipino (160)	211	0.48
Indian (699)	738	1.68
Indonesian	1	0.00
Japanese (27)	40	0.09
Korean (84)	102	0.23
Malaysian (2)	5	0.01
Pakistani (42)	46	0.10
Sri Lankan (1)	7	0.02
Taiwanese (31)	32	0.07
Thai (2)	2	0.00
Vietnamese (73)	81	0.18
Other Asian, specified (6)	8	0.02
Other Asian, not specified (11)	39	0.09
Austrian	312	0.71
Belgian	39	0.09
Brazilian	19	0.04
British	121	0.28
Bulgarian	45	0.10
Canadian	145	0.33
Celtic	17	0.04
Croatian	446	1.02
Czech	1,180	2.69
Czechoslovakian	334	0.76
Danish	184	0.42
Dutch	588	1.34
Eastern European	53	0.12
English	4,685	10.68
European	287	0.65
Finnish	119	0.27
French, except Basque	912	2.08
French Canadian	109	0.25
German	12,749	29.07
Greek	349	0.80
Hawaii Native/Pacific Islander:	16	0.04
Micronesian: (1)	1	0.00
Guamanian/Chamorro (1)	1	0.00
Polynesian: (2)	11	0.03
Native Hawaiian (1)	6	0.01
Tongan (1)	4	0.01
Other Polynesian	1	0.00
Other Pac. Isl., specified	1	0.00
Other Pac. Isl., not spec. (1)	3	0.01
Hispanic or Latino:	557	1.27
Central American:	21	0.05
Guatemalan	3	0.01
Honduran	5	0.01
Nicaraguan	6	0.01
Panamanian	3	0.01
Salvadoran	3	0.01
Other Central American	1	0.00
Cuban	9	0.02
Dominican Republic	3	0.01
Mexican	129	0.29
Puerto Rican	276	0.63
South American:	40	0.09
Argentinean	1	0.00
Chilean	4	0.01
Colombian	12	0.03
Ecuadorian	5	0.01
Peruvian	8	0.02
Venezuelan	6	0.01
Other South American	4	0.01
Other Hispanic or Latino	79	0.18
Hungarian	1,885	4.30
Iranian	64	0.15
Irish	7,894	18.00
Italian	5,879	13.40
Latvian	60	0.14
Lithuanian	236	0.54
Macedonian	33	0.08
Norwegian	183	0.42
Pennsylvania German	23	0.05
Polish	5,536	12.62
Romanian	337	0.77
Russian	546	1.24
Scandinavian	39	0.09
Scotch-Irish	492	1.12
Scottish	949	2.16

Notes: 1. Figures in the "Number" column do not add up to the total population due to: a) Ancestry/Race overlap — e.g. persons can report being both White and Irish, b) persons of Hispanic origin can report being any race, c) persons reporting two ancestries are counted in both categories. 2. Numbers in parentheses indicate the number of persons reporting this ancestry/race alone, not in combination with any other ancestry/race. 3. Refer to the Explanation of Data in the front of the book for more detailed information.

Serbian	266	0.61
Slavic	24	0.05
Slovak	2,467	5.62
Slovene	979	2.23
Swedish	284	0.65
Swiss	266	0.61
Turkish	37	0.08
Ukrainian	1,019	2.32
United States or American	1,538	3.51
Welsh	526	1.20
West Indian, excl. Hispanic:	33	0.08
Bahamian	33	0.08
White:	41,717	95.12
Not Hispanic (40,929)	41,298	94.16
Hispanic (375)	419	0.96
Yugoslavian	90	0.21

Struthers

Place Type: City
County: Mahoning
Population: 11,756

Ancestry/Race	Number	%
African American/Black:	238	2.02
Not Hispanic (203)	231	1.96
Hispanic (6)	7	0.06
African, sub-Saharan:	8	0.07
African	4	0.03
Cape Verdean	4	0.03
Am. Ind. or Alaska Nat., not spec.	19	0.16
American Indian tribes, specified:	47	0.40
Blackfeet	4	0.03
Cherokee (5)	18	0.15
Chippewa	1	0.01
Choctaw	1	0.01
Creek	2	0.02
Houma (3)	3	0.03
Iroquois	2	0.02
Latin American Indians	7	0.06
Navajo (1)	1	0.01
All other tribes (1)	8	0.07
American Indian tribes, not spec.	3	0.03
Arab:	44	0.37
Arab/Arabic	27	0.23
Lebanese	10	0.09
Syrian	7	0.06
Asian:	29	0.25
Chinese, ex. Taiwanese	1	0.01
Filipino (4)	5	0.04
Indian (1)	4	0.03
Japanese (2)	3	0.03
Korean (1)	1	0.01
Vietnamese (14)	15	0.13
Austrian	23	0.20
Canadian	9	0.08
Croatian	506	4.30
Czech	38	0.32
Czechoslovakian	68	0.58
Danish	15	0.13
Dutch	155	1.32
English	710	6.04
European	20	0.17
French, except Basque	190	1.62
French Canadian	17	0.14
German	2,354	20.02
Greek	41	0.35
Hawaii Native/Pacific Islander:	1	0.01
Other Pac. Isl., not spec. (1)	1	0.01
Hispanic or Latino:	237	2.02
Central American:	1	0.01
Salvadoran	1	0.01
Cuban	1	0.01
Dominican Republic	1	0.01
Mexican	54	0.46
Puerto Rican	130	1.11
South American:	3	0.03
Colombian	3	0.03
Other Hispanic or Latino	47	0.40
Hungarian	285	2.42
Irish	1,863	15.85
Italian	3,332	28.34
Lithuanian	40	0.34
Norwegian	7	0.06
Pennsylvania German	32	0.27
Polish	751	6.39
Portuguese	9	0.08
Romanian	90	0.77
Russian	180	1.53
Scotch-Irish	231	1.96
Scottish	95	0.81
Serbian	53	0.45
Slavic	17	0.14
Slovak	1,887	16.05
Slovene	45	0.38
Swedish	205	1.74
Ukrainian	132	1.12
United States or American	473	4.02
Welsh	135	1.15
White:	11,438	97.29
Not Hispanic (11,214)	11,270	95.87
Hispanic (146)	168	1.43
Yugoslavian	15	0.13

Sylvania

Place Type: City
County: Lucas
Population: 18,670

Ancestry/Race	Number	%
African American/Black:	221	1.18
Not Hispanic (178)	211	1.13
Hispanic (8)	10	0.05
African, sub-Saharan:	50	0.27
African	4	0.02
Kenyan	15	0.08
Nigerian	31	0.17
Am. Ind. or Alaska Nat., not spec.	13	0.07
Albanian	21	0.11
American Indian tribes, specified:	43	0.23
Apache (1)	1	0.01
Blackfeet (1)	1	0.01
Cherokee (2)	21	0.11
Chippewa (2)	3	0.02
Choctaw (1)	1	0.01
Crow	3	0.02
Iroquois	2	0.01
Latin American Indians	1	0.01
Ottawa (2)	6	0.03
Seminole	2	0.01
All other tribes (2)	2	0.01
American Indian tribes, not spec.	2	0.01
Arab:	277	1.48
Egyptian	7	0.04
Jordanian	7	0.04
Lebanese	201	1.07
Syrian	62	0.33
Armenian	13	0.07
Asian:	451	2.42
Chinese, ex. Taiwanese (108)	123	0.66
Filipino (15)	23	0.12
Indian (130)	136	0.73
Indonesian (2)	2	0.01
Japanese (22)	34	0.18
Korean (55)	65	0.35
Laotian	2	0.01
Malaysian	1	0.01
Pakistani (12)	15	0.08
Taiwanese (6)	6	0.03
Thai (6)	6	0.03
Vietnamese (12)	13	0.07
Other Asian, specified (2)	2	0.01
Other Asian, not specified (10)	23	0.12
Austrian	26	0.14
Belgian	82	0.44
British	68	0.36
Bulgarian	42	0.22
Canadian	59	0.31
Celtic	9	0.05
Czech	136	0.73
Czechoslovakian	66	0.35
Danish	34	0.18
Dutch	340	1.81
English	2,138	11.41
European	139	0.74
Finnish	34	0.18
French, except Basque	805	4.30
French Canadian	249	1.33
German	6,143	32.79
Greek	223	1.19
Hawaii Native/Pacific Islander:	6	0.03
Polynesian: (1)	1	0.01
Native Hawaiian (1)	1	0.01
Other Pac. Isl., not spec.	5	0.03
Hispanic or Latino:	304	1.63
Central American:	4	0.02
Guatemalan	1	0.01
Panamanian	1	0.01
Salvadoran	2	0.01
Cuban	9	0.05
Mexican	212	1.14
Puerto Rican	18	0.10
South American:	13	0.07
Argentinean	1	0.01
Chilean	7	0.04
Paraguayan	3	0.02
Venezuelan	1	0.01
Other South American	1	0.01
Other Hispanic or Latino	48	0.26
Hungarian	370	1.97
Iranian	14	0.07
Irish	2,932	15.65
Italian	1,159	6.19
Lithuanian	39	0.21
Maltese	7	0.04
Norwegian	86	0.46
Pennsylvania German	40	0.21
Polish	1,998	10.66
Romanian	14	0.07
Russian	241	1.29
Scandinavian	26	0.14
Scotch-Irish	341	1.82
Scottish	447	2.39
Slavic	19	0.10
Slovak	65	0.35
Slovene	19	0.10
Swedish	170	0.91
Swiss	192	1.02
Turkish	32	0.17
Ukrainian	135	0.72
United States or American	912	4.87
Welsh	146	0.78
White:	17,944	96.11
Not Hispanic (17,588)	17,744	95.04
Hispanic (186)	200	1.07
Yugoslavian	8	0.04

Tallmadge

Place Type: City
County: Summit
Population: 16,390

Ancestry/Race	Number	%
African American/Black:	393	2.40
Not Hispanic (333)	379	2.31
Hispanic (8)	14	0.09
African, sub-Saharan:	1	0.01
African	1	0.01
Am. Ind. or Alaska Nat., not spec.	31	0.19
Albanian	9	0.05
American Indian tribes, specified:	37	0.23
Apache (1)	1	0.01
Blackfeet	1	0.01
Cherokee (2)	18	0.11
Chippewa (2)	2	0.01
Comanche	1	0.01
Iroquois	1	0.01
Lumbee (4)	4	0.02

Notes: 1. Figures in the "Number" column do not add up to the total population due to: a) Ancestry/Race overlap — e.g. persons can report being both White and Irish, b) persons of Hispanic origin can report being any race, c) persons reporting two ancestries are counted in both categories. 2. Numbers in parentheses indicate the number of persons reporting this ancestry/race alone, not in combination with any other ancestry/race. 3. Refer to the Explanation of Data in the front of the book for more detailed information.

Ancestry/Race	Number	%
Sioux (1)	1	0.01
All other tribes	8	0.05
American Indian tribes, not spec.	2	0.01
Arab:	119	0.73
Egyptian	18	0.11
Jordanian	13	0.08
Lebanese	47	0.29
Palestinian	35	0.21
Syrian	6	0.04
Armenian	34	0.21
Asian:	203	1.24
Chinese, ex. Taiwanese (50)	53	0.32
Filipino (13)	32	0.20
Indian (42)	51	0.31
Japanese (6)	14	0.09
Korean (9)	10	0.06
Laotian (5)	5	0.03
Taiwanese (4)	4	0.02
Thai (2)	3	0.02
Vietnamese (5)	5	0.03
Other Asian, specified (4)	4	0.02
Other Asian, not specified (1)	22	0.13
Austrian	38	0.23
Belgian	26	0.16
British	82	0.50
Bulgarian	9	0.05
Canadian	21	0.13
Celtic	9	0.05
Croatian	84	0.51
Czech	68	0.42
Czechoslovakian	86	0.53
Danish	26	0.16
Dutch	474	2.90
Eastern European	16	0.10
English	2,139	13.06
European	116	0.71
French, except Basque	487	2.97
French Canadian	42	0.26
German	4,743	28.97
Greek	172	1.05
Hawaii Native/Pacific Islander:	22	0.13
Polynesian: (5)	22	0.13
Native Hawaiian (5)	22	0.13
Hispanic or Latino:	94	0.57
Central American:	4	0.02
Costa Rican	1	0.01
Honduran	3	0.02
Cuban	8	0.05
Mexican	18	0.11
Puerto Rican	27	0.16
South American:	13	0.08
Bolivian	4	0.02
Chilean	5	0.03
Colombian	1	0.01
Uruguayan	1	0.01
Other South American	2	0.01
Other Hispanic or Latino	24	0.15
Hungarian	405	2.47
Irish	2,680	16.37
Italian	1,958	11.96
Lithuanian	52	0.32
Macedonian	6	0.04
Norwegian	148	0.90
Pennsylvania German	33	0.20
Polish	877	5.36
Portuguese	23	0.14
Romanian	50	0.31
Russian	85	0.52
Scandinavian	6	0.04
Scotch-Irish	274	1.67
Scottish	355	2.17
Serbian	110	0.67
Slavic	26	0.16
Slovak	314	1.92
Slovene	31	0.19
Swedish	142	0.87
Swiss	114	0.70
Turkish	12	0.07
Ukrainian	113	0.69
United States or American	1,302	7.95
Welsh	250	1.53
West Indian, excl. Hispanic:	14	0.09
Jamaican	14	0.09
White:	15,858	96.75
Not Hispanic (15,628)	15,781	96.28
Hispanic (70)	77	0.47
Yugoslavian	42	0.26

Tiffin

Place Type: City
County: Seneca
Population: 18,135

Ancestry/Race	Number	%
African American/Black:	340	1.87
Not Hispanic (258)	327	1.80
Hispanic (6)	13	0.07
African, sub-Saharan:	42	0.23
African	37	0.20
Ethiopian	5	0.03
Am. Ind. or Alaska Nat., not spec.	25	0.14
American Indian tribes, specified:	63	0.35
Apache (1)	7	0.04
Blackfeet	2	0.01
Cherokee (9)	31	0.17
Chippewa	5	0.03
Creek	1	0.01
Iroquois (2)	4	0.02
Latin American Indians (2)	7	0.04
Navajo (1)	2	0.01
Seminole	1	0.01
Yaqui	1	0.01
All other tribes	2	0.01
American Indian tribes, not spec.	4	0.02
Arab:	21	0.12
Arab/Arabic	7	0.04
Lebanese	14	0.08
Asian:	129	0.71
Cambodian (1)	1	0.01
Chinese, ex. Taiwanese (9)	11	0.06
Filipino (31)	36	0.20
Indian (18)	32	0.18
Indonesian (1)	1	0.01
Japanese (18)	21	0.12
Korean (4)	13	0.07
Pakistani (3)	3	0.02
Thai (2)	2	0.01
Vietnamese (2)	2	0.01
Other Asian, specified (1)	1	0.01
Other Asian, not specified (2)	6	0.03
Austrian	49	0.27
Belgian	29	0.16
British	87	0.48
Canadian	64	0.35
Czech	24	0.13
Czechoslovakian	16	0.09
Danish	22	0.12
Dutch	348	1.92
English	1,641	9.05
European	24	0.13
Finnish	14	0.08
French, except Basque	597	3.29
French Canadian	11	0.06
German	8,025	44.25
Greek	21	0.12
Hawaii Native/Pacific Islander:	8	0.04
Micronesian: (1)	1	0.01
Guamanian/Chamorro (1)	1	0.01
Polynesian: (1)	4	0.02
Native Hawaiian (1)	4	0.02
Other Pac. Isl., not spec. (1)	3	0.02
Hispanic or Latino:	380	2.10
Central American:	11	0.06
Honduran	1	0.01
Panamanian	1	0.01
Salvadoran	3	0.02
Other Central American	6	0.03
Cuban	10	0.06
Mexican	248	1.37
Puerto Rican	36	0.20
South American:	1	0.01
Colombian	1	0.01
Other Hispanic or Latino	74	0.41
Hungarian	83	0.46
Icelander	7	0.04
Iranian	19	0.10
Irish	2,000	11.03
Italian	796	4.39
Latvian	25	0.14
Lithuanian	5	0.03
Norwegian	46	0.25
Pennsylvania German	28	0.15
Polish	409	2.26
Portuguese	4	0.02
Romanian	6	0.03
Russian	41	0.23
Scandinavian	6	0.03
Scotch-Irish	194	1.07
Scottish	162	0.89
Slovak	32	0.18
Slovene	16	0.09
Swedish	49	0.27
Swiss	138	0.76
Ukrainian	5	0.03
United States or American	1,748	9.64
Welsh	122	0.67
White:	17,619	97.15
Not Hispanic (17,220)	17,362	95.74
Hispanic (237)	257	1.42

Toledo

Place Type: City
County: Lucas
Population: 313,619

Ancestry/Race	Number	%
Acadian/Cajun	12	0.00
African American/Black:	77,765	24.80
Not Hispanic (73,134)	76,563	24.41
Hispanic (720)	1,202	0.38
African, sub-Saharan:	2,947	0.94
African	2,668	0.85
Cape Verdean	7	0.00
Ghanian	12	0.00
Kenyan	19	0.01
Liberian	64	0.02
Nigerian	135	0.04
Sierra Leonean	5	0.00
Somalian	12	0.00
South African	12	0.00
Sudanese	5	0.00
Other sub-Saharan African	8	0.00
Alaska Native tribes, specified:	11	0.00
Alaska Athabascan (1)	5	0.00
Aleut	4	0.00
Eskimo (1)	1	0.00
Tlingit-Haida	1	0.00
Alaska Native tribes, not specified	4	0.00
Am. Ind. or Alaska Nat., not spec.	1,213	0.39
Alsatian	28	0.01
American Indian tribes, specified:	1,665	0.53
Apache (15)	53	0.02
Blackfeet (39)	175	0.06
Cherokee (189)	763	0.24
Cheyenne (4)	10	0.00
Chickasaw	2	0.00
Chippewa (67)	105	0.03
Choctaw (8)	40	0.01
Comanche (3)	6	0.00
Cree (5)	7	0.00
Creek (1)	7	0.00
Crow (6)	17	0.01
Delaware (2)	6	0.00
Houma (1)	1	0.00
Iroquois (17)	41	0.01
Kiowa (1)	3	0.00
Latin American Indians (55)	118	0.04
Lumbee (4)	12	0.00

Notes: 1. Figures in the "Number" column do not add up to the total population due to: a) Ancestry/Race overlap — e.g. persons can report being both White and Irish, b) persons of Hispanic origin can report being any race, c) persons reporting two ancestries are counted in both categories. 2. Numbers in parentheses indicate the number of persons reporting this ancestry/race alone, not in combination with any other ancestry/race. 3. Refer to the Explanation of Data in the front of the book for more detailed information.

Ancestry/Race	Number	%
Menominee (3)	6	0.00
Navajo (4)	22	0.01
Osage (1)	6	0.00
Ottawa (10)	20	0.01
Paiute (2)	2	0.00
Potawatomi (2)	18	0.01
Pueblo (12)	17	0.01
Seminole (1)	27	0.01
Shoshone	1	0.00
Sioux (20)	60	0.02
Ute	1	0.00
Yakama (1)	1	0.00
Yaqui	1	0.00
All other tribes (47)	117	0.04
American Indian tribes, not spec.	179	0.06
Arab:	3,668	1.17
Arab/Arabic	359	0.11
Egyptian	95	0.03
Iraqi	121	0.04
Jordanian	174	0.06
Lebanese	2,048	0.65
Moroccan	17	0.01
Palestinian	322	0.10
Syrian	304	0.10
Other Arab	228	0.07
Armenian	102	0.03
Asian:	4,293	1.37
Bangladeshi (13)	14	0.00
Cambodian (3)	5	0.00
Chinese, ex. Taiwanese (919)	1,040	0.33
Filipino (349)	529	0.17
Hmong (8)	8	0.00
Indian (782)	908	0.29
Indonesian (32)	39	0.01
Japanese (149)	291	0.09
Korean (274)	370	0.12
Laotian (103)	146	0.05
Malaysian (31)	43	0.01
Pakistani (59)	68	0.02
Sri Lankan (10)	10	0.00
Taiwanese (24)	27	0.01
Thai (58)	76	0.02
Vietnamese (254)	298	0.10
Other Asian, specified (2)	22	0.01
Other Asian, not specified (115)	399	0.13
Assyrian/Chaldean/Syriac	15	0.00
Australian	107	0.03
Austrian	396	0.13
Basque	10	0.00
Belgian	458	0.15
Brazilian	25	0.01
British	689	0.22
Bulgarian	167	0.05
Canadian	682	0.22
Celtic	46	0.01
Croatian	186	0.06
Cypriot	24	0.01
Czech	550	0.18
Czechoslovakian	569	0.18
Danish	467	0.15
Dutch	4,309	1.37
Eastern European	50	0.02
English	18,854	6.01
European	785	0.25
Finnish	215	0.07
French, except Basque	14,382	4.59
French Canadian	2,604	0.83
German	73,482	23.43
Greek	1,554	0.50
Guyanese	77	0.02
Hawaii Native/Pacific Islander:	197	0.06
Micronesian: (12)	19	0.01
Guamanian/Chamorro (12)	19	0.01
Polynesian: (47)	110	0.04
Native Hawaiian (21)	51	0.02
Samoan (23)	49	0.02
Tongan (1)	5	0.00
Other Polynesian (2)	5	0.00
Other Pac. Isl., specified	15	0.00
Other Pac. Isl., not spec. (17)	53	0.02
Hispanic or Latino:	17,141	5.47
Central American:	151	0.05
Costa Rican	5	0.00
Guatemalan	23	0.01
Honduran	15	0.00
Nicaraguan	69	0.02
Panamanian	33	0.01
Salvadoran	2	0.00
Other Central American	4	0.00
Cuban	181	0.06
Dominican Republic	23	0.01
Mexican	13,320	4.25
Puerto Rican	742	0.24
South American:	159	0.05
Argentinean	11	0.00
Bolivian	8	0.00
Chilean	17	0.01
Colombian	44	0.01
Ecuadorian	11	0.00
Paraguayan	7	0.00
Peruvian	18	0.01
Venezuelan	27	0.01
Other South American	16	0.01
Other Hispanic or Latino	2,565	0.82
Hungarian	6,188	1.97
Icelander	25	0.01
Iranian	10	0.00
Irish	33,738	10.76
Israeli	69	0.02
Italian	9,383	2.99
Latvian	65	0.02
Lithuanian	252	0.08
Luxemburger	40	0.01
Macedonian	61	0.02
Maltese	11	0.00
New Zealander	27	0.01
Northern European	71	0.02
Norwegian	961	0.31
Pennsylvania German	223	0.07
Polish	31,802	10.14
Portuguese	157	0.05
Romanian	290	0.09
Russian	1,291	0.41
Scandinavian	122	0.04
Scotch-Irish	2,923	0.93
Scottish	3,419	1.09
Serbian	87	0.03
Slavic	87	0.03
Slovak	1,001	0.32
Slovene	238	0.08
Swedish	1,640	0.52
Swiss	1,245	0.40
Turkish	66	0.02
Ukrainian	561	0.18
United States or American	12,242	3.90
Welsh	1,611	0.51
West Indian, excl. Hispanic:	562	0.18
Bahamian	6	0.00
Barbadian	5	0.00
Bermudan	15	0.00
British West Indian	11	0.00
Dutch West Indian	6	0.00
Haitian	17	0.01
Jamaican	480	0.15
Trinidadian and Tobagonian	17	0.01
West Indian	5	0.00
White:	227,094	72.41
Not Hispanic (212,658)	217,906	69.48
Hispanic (7,603)	9,188	2.93
Yugoslavian	163	0.05

Trotwood

Place Type: City
County: Montgomery
Population: 27,420

Ancestry/Race	Number	%
African American/Black:	16,405	59.83
Not Hispanic (15,953)	16,342	59.60
Hispanic (45)	63	0.23
African, sub-Saharan:	638	2.32
African	478	1.74
Liberian	27	0.10
Nigerian	133	0.48
Alaska Native tribes, specified:	3	0.01
Alaska Athabascan (2)	3	0.01
Am. Ind. or Alaska Nat., not spec.	120	0.44
American Indian tribes, specified:	150	0.55
Apache (1)	6	0.02
Blackfeet (1)	14	0.05
Cherokee (20)	86	0.31
Choctaw	4	0.01
Iroquois	2	0.01
Latin American Indians (2)	4	0.01
Navajo (2)	2	0.01
Osage (2)	2	0.01
Seminole (1)	3	0.01
Sioux (3)	7	0.03
All other tribes (18)	20	0.07
American Indian tribes, not spec.	10	0.04
Arab:	7	0.03
Lebanese	7	0.03
Asian:	123	0.45
Cambodian	2	0.01
Chinese, ex. Taiwanese (6)	13	0.05
Filipino (12)	24	0.09
Indian (16)	21	0.08
Japanese (15)	32	0.12
Korean (8)	10	0.04
Pakistani (1)	3	0.01
Thai (5)	8	0.03
Vietnamese (4)	4	0.01
Other Asian, not specified	6	0.02
Austrian	21	0.08
Belgian	22	0.08
Brazilian	7	0.03
British	47	0.17
Canadian	8	0.03
Croatian	7	0.03
Czech	21	0.08
Dutch	175	0.64
English	941	3.42
European	113	0.41
Finnish	5	0.02
French, except Basque	302	1.10
French Canadian	40	0.15
German	2,252	8.18
Greek	13	0.05
Hawaii Native/Pacific Islander:	19	0.07
Micronesian: (2)	3	0.01
Guamanian/Chamorro (2)	3	0.01
Polynesian: (1)	8	0.03
Native Hawaiian (1)	8	0.03
Other Pac. Isl., not spec. (1)	8	0.03
Hispanic or Latino:	224	0.82
Central American:	4	0.01
Guatemalan	2	0.01
Panamanian	2	0.01
Cuban	6	0.02
Mexican	112	0.41
Puerto Rican	57	0.21
South American:	9	0.03
Argentinean	1	0.00
Chilean	1	0.00
Colombian	3	0.01
Ecuadorian	1	0.00
Peruvian	2	0.01
Other South American	1	0.00
Other Hispanic or Latino	36	0.13
Hungarian	102	0.37
Irish	1,265	4.59
Italian	172	0.62
Lithuanian	43	0.16
Norwegian	18	0.07
Polish	36	0.13
Romanian	23	0.08
Russian	112	0.41
Scotch-Irish	174	0.63
Scottish	147	0.53

Notes: 1. Figures in the "Number" column do not add up to the total population due to: a) Ancestry/Race overlap — e.g. persons can report being both White and Irish, b) persons of Hispanic origin can report being any race, c) persons reporting two ancestries are counted in both categories. 2. Numbers in parentheses indicate the number of persons reporting this ancestry/race alone, not in combination with any other ancestry/race. 3. Refer to the Explanation of Data in the front of the book for more detailed information.

Ancestry/Race	Number	%
Swedish	9	0.03
Swiss	42	0.15
Ukrainian	47	0.17
United States or American	2,107	7.65
Welsh	126	0.46
West Indian, excl. Hispanic:	31	0.11
Jamaican	25	0.09
West Indian	6	0.02
White:	10,991	40.08
Not Hispanic (10,501)	10,877	39.67
Hispanic (99)	114	0.42
Yugoslavian	47	0.17

Troy

Place Type: City
County: Miami
Population: 21,999

Ancestry/Race	Number	%
African American/Black:	1,270	5.77
Not Hispanic (1,046)	1,258	5.72
Hispanic (5)	12	0.05
African, sub-Saharan:	179	0.81
African	164	0.74
Cape Verdean	9	0.04
Nigerian	6	0.03
Alaska Native tribes, specified:	3	0.01
Alaska Athabascan (1)	3	0.01
Am. Ind. or Alaska Nat., not spec.	25	0.11
American Indian tribes, specified:	87	0.40
Apache	1	0.00
Blackfeet	6	0.03
Cherokee (12)	49	0.22
Chippewa (3)	4	0.02
Choctaw	2	0.01
Navajo	5	0.02
Pueblo	1	0.00
Sioux	1	0.00
All other tribes (17)	18	0.08
American Indian tribes, not spec.	22	0.10
Arab:	52	0.23
Lebanese	52	0.23
Asian:	391	1.78
Chinese, ex. Taiwanese (46)	47	0.21
Filipino (17)	27	0.12
Indian (54)	58	0.26
Japanese (167)	172	0.78
Korean (34)	34	0.15
Malaysian	1	0.00
Pakistani (6)	6	0.03
Sri Lankan (2)	2	0.01
Taiwanese (4)	5	0.02
Thai (1)	3	0.01
Vietnamese (27)	29	0.13
Other Asian, specified (1)	1	0.00
Other Asian, not specified (6)	6	0.03
Australian	8	0.04
Austrian	22	0.10
Belgian	30	0.14
British	109	0.49
Canadian	138	0.62
Croatian	8	0.04
Czech	31	0.14
Czechoslovakian	8	0.04
Danish	38	0.17
Dutch	425	1.92
English	1,776	8.02
European	222	1.00
Finnish	20	0.09
French, except Basque	749	3.38
French Canadian	97	0.44
German	5,604	25.32
Greek	26	0.12
Hawaii Native/Pacific Islander:	7	0.03
Polynesian: (2)	7	0.03
Native Hawaiian (2)	5	0.02
Samoan	2	0.01
Hispanic or Latino:	170	0.77
Central American:	2	0.01
Guatemalan	1	0.00
Nicaraguan	1	0.00
Cuban	6	0.03
Mexican	78	0.35
Puerto Rican	25	0.11
South American:	6	0.03
Bolivian	2	0.01
Colombian	2	0.01
Ecuadorian	1	0.00
Peruvian	1	0.00
Other Hispanic or Latino	53	0.24
Hungarian	109	0.49
Irish	2,534	11.45
Italian	296	1.34
Macedonian	7	0.03
Norwegian	169	0.76
Pennsylvania German	26	0.12
Polish	257	1.16
Portuguese	21	0.09
Romanian	10	0.05
Russian	31	0.14
Scandinavian	21	0.09
Scotch-Irish	328	1.48
Scottish	397	1.79
Slovak	8	0.04
Swedish	148	0.67
Swiss	79	0.36
Ukrainian	61	0.28
United States or American	3,234	14.61
Welsh	130	0.59
White:	20,439	92.91
Not Hispanic (20,036)	20,315	92.35
Hispanic (104)	124	0.56

Twinsburg

Place Type: City
County: Summit
Population: 17,006

Ancestry/Race	Number	%
African American/Black:	1,552	9.13
Not Hispanic (1,468)	1,530	9.00
Hispanic (16)	22	0.13
African, sub-Saharan:	92	0.54
African	92	0.54
Am. Ind. or Alaska Nat., not spec.	28	0.16
Albanian	13	0.08
American Indian tribes, specified:	22	0.13
Blackfeet	1	0.01
Cherokee (1)	9	0.05
Creek	1	0.01
Latin American Indians (1)	1	0.01
Ottawa (1)	1	0.01
Sioux	1	0.01
All other tribes (7)	8	0.05
Arab:	43	0.25
Lebanese	43	0.25
Asian:	560	3.29
Bangladeshi (9)	9	0.05
Chinese, ex. Taiwanese (120)	125	0.74
Filipino (66)	75	0.44
Indian (249)	265	1.56
Indonesian (2)	6	0.04
Japanese (19)	26	0.15
Korean (19)	26	0.15
Laotian (1)	2	0.01
Malaysian	1	0.01
Pakistani (2)	3	0.02
Sri Lankan	1	0.01
Vietnamese (9)	10	0.06
Other Asian, not specified (3)	11	0.06
Austrian	37	0.22
Belgian	9	0.05
British	69	0.41
Canadian	87	0.52
Croatian	177	1.05
Czech	417	2.47
Czechoslovakian	109	0.65
Danish	26	0.15
Dutch	232	1.37
Eastern European	25	0.15
English	1,787	10.58
European	106	0.63
Finnish	70	0.41
French, except Basque	368	2.18
French Canadian	84	0.50
German	3,896	23.07
Greek	96	0.57
Hawaii Native/Pacific Islander:	2	0.01
Micronesian: (1)	1	0.01
Guamanian/Chamorro (1)	1	0.01
Polynesian: (1)	1	0.01
Samoan (1)	1	0.01
Hispanic or Latino:	176	1.03
Central American:	4	0.02
Costa Rican	1	0.01
Honduran	2	0.01
Nicaraguan	1	0.01
Cuban	5	0.03
Dominican Republic	1	0.01
Mexican	65	0.38
Puerto Rican	35	0.21
South American:	27	0.16
Argentinean	7	0.04
Chilean	3	0.02
Colombian	12	0.07
Ecuadorian	2	0.01
Paraguayan	1	0.01
Peruvian	2	0.01
Other Hispanic or Latino	39	0.23
Hungarian	1,012	5.99
Irish	2,379	14.09
Italian	2,527	14.96
Lithuanian	36	0.21
Norwegian	79	0.47
Pennsylvania German	5	0.03
Polish	1,924	11.39
Romanian	29	0.17
Russian	251	1.49
Scandinavian	24	0.14
Scotch-Irish	333	1.97
Scottish	391	2.32
Serbian	60	0.36
Slovak	815	4.83
Slovene	407	2.41
Swedish	206	1.22
Swiss	35	0.21
Ukrainian	94	0.56
United States or American	462	2.74
Welsh	121	0.72
West Indian, excl. Hispanic:	12	0.07
Jamaican	12	0.07
White:	14,926	87.77
Not Hispanic (14,686)	14,811	87.09
Hispanic (97)	115	0.68
Yugoslavian	25	0.15

University Heights

Place Type: City
County: Cuyahoga
Population: 14,146

Ancestry/Race	Number	%
African American/Black:	3,014	21.31
Not Hispanic (2,901)	2,993	21.16
Hispanic (15)	21	0.15
African, sub-Saharan:	177	1.25
African	51	0.36
Ethiopian	33	0.23
Nigerian	93	0.66
Am. Ind. or Alaska Nat., not spec.	24	0.17
American Indian tribes, specified:	42	0.30
Blackfeet (1)	2	0.01
Cherokee (5)	15	0.11
Choctaw	3	0.02
Creek	3	0.02
Iroquois	9	0.06
Pueblo	5	0.04

Notes: 1. Figures in the "Number" column do not add up to the total population due to: a) Ancestry/Race overlap — e.g. persons can report being both White and Irish, b) persons of Hispanic origin can report being any race, c) persons reporting two ancestries are counted in both categories. 2. Numbers in parentheses indicate the number of persons reporting this ancestry/race alone, not in combination with any other ancestry/race. 3. Refer to the Explanation of Data in the front of the book for more detailed information.

Seminole	2	0.01
Sioux (1)	1	0.01
All other tribes (1)	2	0.01
Arab:	96	0.68
Arab/Arabic	17	0.12
Lebanese	70	0.49
Other Arab	9	0.06
Armenian	10	0.07
Asian:	316	2.23
Chinese, ex. Taiwanese (59)	72	0.51
Filipino (22)	38	0.27
Indian (79)	87	0.62
Indonesian	2	0.01
Japanese (22)	36	0.25
Korean (16)	18	0.13
Pakistani (2)	2	0.01
Sri Lankan (2)	2	0.01
Taiwanese (5)	5	0.04
Thai (3)	5	0.04
Vietnamese (18)	18	0.13
Other Asian, specified (1)	10	0.07
Other Asian, not specified (7)	21	0.15
Austrian	114	0.81
Belgian	4	0.03
British	61	0.43
Bulgarian	12	0.08
Canadian	28	0.20
Croatian	61	0.43
Czech	173	1.22
Czechoslovakian	89	0.63
Danish	32	0.23
Dutch	91	0.64
Eastern European	198	1.40
English	783	5.54
Estonian	4	0.03
European	236	1.67
Finnish	24	0.17
French, except Basque	248	1.75
French Canadian	34	0.24
German	2,274	16.08
Greek	91	0.64
Hawaii Native/Pacific Islander:	28	0.20
Polynesian: (1)	3	0.02
Native Hawaiian (1)	3	0.02
Other Pac. Isl., specified	7	0.05
Other Pac. Isl., not spec. (5)	18	0.13
Hispanic or Latino:	221	1.56
Central American:	18	0.13
Costa Rican	2	0.01
Guatemalan	1	0.01
Nicaraguan	5	0.04
Salvadoran	10	0.07
Cuban	4	0.03
Dominican Republic	4	0.03
Mexican	62	0.44
Puerto Rican	36	0.25
South American:	41	0.29
Argentinean	7	0.05
Chilean	8	0.06
Colombian	12	0.08
Ecuadorian	9	0.06
Paraguayan	3	0.02
Peruvian	2	0.01
Other Hispanic or Latino	56	0.40
Hungarian	603	4.26
Irish	2,234	15.79
Israeli	33	0.23
Italian	1,478	10.45
Latvian	13	0.09
Lithuanian	126	0.89
Norwegian	30	0.21
Polish	1,222	8.64
Portuguese	4	0.03
Romanian	66	0.47
Russian	880	6.22
Scotch-Irish	155	1.10
Scottish	175	1.24
Serbian	14	0.10
Slovak	261	1.85
Slovene	135	0.95
Swedish	96	0.68
Swiss	63	0.45
Ukrainian	132	0.93
United States or American	446	3.15
Welsh	137	0.97
West Indian, excl. Hispanic:	82	0.58
British West Indian	15	0.11
Jamaican	67	0.47
White:	10,841	76.64
Not Hispanic (10,532)	10,695	75.60
Hispanic (139)	146	1.03
Yugoslavian	24	0.17

Upper Arlington

Place Type: City
County: Franklin
Population: 33,686

Ancestry/Race	Number	%
Afghan	26	0.08
African American/Black:	261	0.77
Not Hispanic (198)	253	0.75
Hispanic (2)	8	0.02
African, sub-Saharan:	58	0.17
African	46	0.14
Cape Verdean	5	0.01
Senegalese	7	0.02
Alaska Native tribes, specified:	1	0.00
Tlingit-Haida (1)	1	0.00
Am. Ind. or Alaska Nat., not spec.	25	0.07
Albanian	18	0.05
American Indian tribes, specified:	64	0.19
Apache (1)	1	0.00
Blackfeet (1)	6	0.02
Cherokee (8)	26	0.08
Choctaw	5	0.01
Creek (1)	2	0.01
Iroquois (2)	2	0.01
Latin American Indians (2)	4	0.01
Lumbee (3)	3	0.01
Navajo	2	0.01
Sioux (1)	2	0.01
All other tribes (4)	11	0.03
American Indian tribes, not spec.	6	0.02
Arab:	360	1.07
Arab/Arabic	4	0.01
Egyptian	101	0.30
Lebanese	182	0.54
Palestinian	30	0.09
Syrian	43	0.13
Armenian	90	0.27
Asian:	1,322	3.92
Bangladeshi (5)	5	0.01
Cambodian (6)	6	0.02
Chinese, ex. Taiwanese (464)	502	1.49
Filipino (36)	51	0.15
Indian (261)	279	0.83
Indonesian (12)	13	0.04
Japanese (85)	116	0.34
Korean (110)	121	0.36
Laotian (2)	2	0.01
Malaysian (2)	3	0.01
Pakistani (19)	19	0.06
Sri Lankan (11)	12	0.04
Taiwanese (98)	103	0.31
Thai (16)	18	0.05
Vietnamese (30)	33	0.10
Other Asian, specified (6)	6	0.02
Other Asian, not specified (9)	33	0.10
Australian	12	0.04
Austrian	144	0.43
Basque	5	0.01
Belgian	28	0.08
British	346	1.03
Bulgarian	20	0.06
Canadian	156	0.46
Carpatho Rusyn	6	0.02
Celtic	15	0.04
Croatian	58	0.17
Czech	146	0.43
Czechoslovakian	50	0.15
Danish	114	0.34
Dutch	663	1.97
Eastern European	94	0.28
English	6,462	19.23
European	394	1.17
Finnish	40	0.12
French, except Basque	1,116	3.32
French Canadian	80	0.24
German	10,290	30.62
Greek	588	1.75
Hawaii Native/Pacific Islander:	12	0.04
Polynesian: (1)	6	0.02
Native Hawaiian (1)	3	0.01
Samoan	3	0.01
Other Pac. Isl., not spec. (2)	6	0.02
Hispanic or Latino:	330	0.98
Central American:	7	0.02
Costa Rican	4	0.01
Guatemalan	1	0.00
Honduran	1	0.00
Nicaraguan	1	0.00
Cuban	11	0.03
Dominican Republic	2	0.01
Mexican	119	0.35
Puerto Rican	45	0.13
South American:	69	0.20
Argentinean	5	0.01
Bolivian	5	0.01
Chilean	2	0.01
Colombian	13	0.04
Ecuadorian	4	0.01
Peruvian	17	0.05
Uruguayan	1	0.00
Venezuelan	22	0.07
Other Hispanic or Latino	77	0.23
Hungarian	527	1.57
Icelander	10	0.03
Iranian	105	0.31
Irish	5,091	15.15
Italian	2,278	6.78
Latvian	27	0.08
Lithuanian	75	0.22
Luxemburger	6	0.02
Macedonian	6	0.02
Northern European	30	0.09
Norwegian	342	1.02
Pennsylvania German	18	0.05
Polish	1,056	3.14
Portuguese	19	0.06
Romanian	72	0.21
Russian	394	1.17
Scandinavian	62	0.18
Scotch-Irish	1,153	3.43
Scottish	1,326	3.95
Serbian	35	0.10
Slavic	36	0.11
Slovak	259	0.77
Slovene	73	0.22
Swedish	374	1.11
Swiss	365	1.09
Turkish	97	0.29
Ukrainian	120	0.36
United States or American	2,087	6.21
Welsh	1,060	3.15
West Indian, excl. Hispanic:	5	0.01
Jamaican	5	0.01
White:	32,151	95.44
Not Hispanic (31,647)	31,880	94.64
Hispanic (259)	271	0.80
Yugoslavian	6	0.02

Urbana

Place Type: City
County: Champaign
Population: 11,613

Ancestry/Race	Number	%

Notes: 1. Figures in the "Number" column do not add up to the total population due to: a) Ancestry/Race overlap — e.g. persons can report being both White and Irish, b) persons of Hispanic origin can report being any race, c) persons reporting two ancestries are counted in both categories. 2. Numbers in parentheses indicate the number of persons reporting this ancestry/race alone, not in combination with any other ancestry/race. 3. Refer to the Explanation of Data in the front of the book for more detailed information.

Ancestry/Race	Number	%
African American/Black:	837	7.21
Not Hispanic (688)	830	7.15
Hispanic (3)	7	0.06
African, sub-Saharan:	25	0.22
African	25	0.22
Am. Ind. or Alaska Nat., not spec.	35	0.30
American Indian tribes, specified:	80	0.69
Apache	6	0.05
Blackfeet (1)	6	0.05
Cherokee (3)	22	0.19
Cheyenne	1	0.01
Chippewa (2)	2	0.02
Comanche (3)	7	0.06
Delaware	1	0.01
Latin American Indians (2)	2	0.02
Ottawa (1)	2	0.02
Sioux (2)	3	0.03
All other tribes (15)	28	0.24
American Indian tribes, not spec.	3	0.03
Arab:	7	0.06
Lebanese	7	0.06
Asian:	50	0.43
Bangladeshi (1)	1	0.01
Chinese, ex. Taiwanese (18)	20	0.17
Filipino (2)	4	0.03
Indian (2)	3	0.03
Japanese (2)	4	0.03
Korean (7)	12	0.10
Malaysian (2)	2	0.02
Pakistani	1	0.01
Vietnamese (1)	1	0.01
Other Asian, not specified	2	0.02
British	8	0.07
Canadian	6	0.05
Dutch	282	2.43
English	953	8.20
European	44	0.38
French, except Basque	173	1.49
French Canadian	15	0.13
German	2,244	19.31
Greek	17	0.15
Hawaii Native/Pacific Islander:	4	0.03
Melanesian: (1)	1	0.01
Fijian (1)	1	0.01
Polynesian:	1	0.01
Native Hawaiian	1	0.01
Other Pac. Isl., not spec. (2)	2	0.02
Hispanic or Latino:	126	1.08
Mexican	95	0.82
Puerto Rican	11	0.09
Other Hispanic or Latino	20	0.17
Hungarian	40	0.34
Irish	1,478	12.72
Italian	222	1.91
Macedonian	17	0.15
Maltese	6	0.05
Norwegian	20	0.17
Pennsylvania German	34	0.29
Polish	99	0.85
Scotch-Irish	129	1.11
Scottish	241	2.07
Serbian	17	0.15
Slovak	11	0.09
Slovene	20	0.17
Swedish	44	0.38
Swiss	18	0.15
Turkish	8	0.07
Ukrainian	16	0.14
United States or American	1,889	16.26
Welsh	161	1.39
White:	10,762	92.67
Not Hispanic (10,506)	10,680	91.97
Hispanic (65)	82	0.71

Van Wert

Place Type: City
County: Van Wert
Population: 10,690

Ancestry/Race	Number	%
African American/Black:	190	1.78
Not Hispanic (160)	189	1.77
Hispanic	1	0.01
Am. Ind. or Alaska Nat., not spec.	10	0.09
American Indian tribes, specified:	18	0.17
Cherokee (7)	13	0.12
Chippewa (1)	2	0.02
Latin American Indians	1	0.01
Potawatomi (1)	1	0.01
Sioux	1	0.01
American Indian tribes, not spec.	1	0.01
Asian:	61	0.57
Chinese, ex. Taiwanese (10)	14	0.13
Filipino (6)	14	0.13
Indian (9)	11	0.10
Japanese (3)	4	0.04
Korean (4)	6	0.06
Taiwanese (3)	3	0.03
Vietnamese (2)	2	0.02
Other Asian, not specified	7	0.07
Austrian	5	0.05
Belgian	4	0.04
British	27	0.25
Canadian	7	0.07
Celtic	22	0.21
Croatian	6	0.06
Czechoslovakian	10	0.09
Danish	5	0.05
Dutch	295	2.75
English	801	7.48
European	36	0.34
French, except Basque	284	2.65
French Canadian	68	0.63
German	3,586	33.48
Greek	14	0.13
Hawaii Native/Pacific Islander:	2	0.02
Micronesian:	2	0.02
Guamanian/Chamorro	2	0.02
Hispanic or Latino:	241	2.25
Central American:	1	0.01
Panamanian	1	0.01
Cuban	2	0.02
Mexican	167	1.56
Puerto Rican	11	0.10
South American:	1	0.01
Argentinean	1	0.01
Other Hispanic or Latino	59	0.55
Hungarian	29	0.27
Iranian	15	0.14
Irish	1,195	11.16
Italian	135	1.26
Norwegian	6	0.06
Pennsylvania German	19	0.18
Polish	120	1.12
Romanian	11	0.10
Russian	21	0.20
Scotch-Irish	117	1.09
Scottish	116	1.08
Slovak	15	0.14
Swedish	18	0.17
Swiss	100	0.93
Ukrainian	6	0.06
United States or American	1,132	10.57
Welsh	252	2.35
White:	10,356	96.88
Not Hispanic (10,157)	10,219	95.59
Hispanic (113)	137	1.28

Vandalia

Place Type: City
County: Montgomery
Population: 14,603

Ancestry/Race	Number	%
Acadian/Cajun	8	0.05
African American/Black:	220	1.51
Not Hispanic (186)	218	1.49
Hispanic (1)	2	0.01
African, sub-Saharan:	29	0.20
African	29	0.20
Alaska Native tribes, not specified	1	0.01
Am. Ind. or Alaska Nat., not spec.	26	0.18
American Indian tribes, specified:	60	0.41
Apache (3)	4	0.03
Blackfeet	1	0.01
Cherokee (9)	44	0.30
Chippewa	2	0.01
Choctaw (2)	2	0.01
Crow	3	0.02
Latin American Indians	1	0.01
Osage	1	0.01
All other tribes (2)	2	0.01
American Indian tribes, not spec.	2	0.01
Arab:	5	0.03
Lebanese	5	0.03
Armenian	17	0.12
Asian:	213	1.46
Chinese, ex. Taiwanese (37)	40	0.27
Filipino (19)	24	0.16
Indian (66)	74	0.51
Indonesian (1)	1	0.01
Japanese (7)	11	0.08
Korean (20)	28	0.19
Laotian (2)	4	0.03
Pakistani (5)	5	0.03
Thai (2)	3	0.02
Vietnamese (12)	13	0.09
Other Asian, not specified (7)	10	0.07
British	143	0.98
Canadian	16	0.11
Croatian	7	0.05
Czech	28	0.19
Czechoslovakian	14	0.10
Danish	47	0.32
Dutch	403	2.75
English	1,574	10.75
European	135	0.92
Finnish	8	0.05
French, except Basque	382	2.61
French Canadian	32	0.22
German	4,436	30.30
Greek	122	0.83
Hawaii Native/Pacific Islander:	6	0.04
Micronesian: (1)	2	0.01
Guamanian/Chamorro (1)	2	0.01
Polynesian: (2)	2	0.01
Native Hawaiian (1)	1	0.01
Samoan (1)	1	0.01
Other Pac. Isl., not spec. (1)	2	0.01
Hispanic or Latino:	130	0.89
Central American:	3	0.02
Costa Rican	2	0.01
Panamanian	1	0.01
Cuban	2	0.01
Mexican	74	0.51
Puerto Rican	14	0.10
South American:	9	0.06
Bolivian	1	0.01
Colombian	5	0.03
Ecuadorian	2	0.01
Peruvian	1	0.01
Other Hispanic or Latino	28	0.19
Hungarian	271	1.85
Irish	1,874	12.80
Italian	386	2.64
Lithuanian	98	0.67
Macedonian	11	0.08

Notes: 1. Figures in the "Number" column do not add up to the total population due to: a) Ancestry/Race overlap — e.g. persons can report being both White and Irish, b) persons of Hispanic origin can report being any race, c) persons reporting two ancestries are counted in both categories. 2. Numbers in parentheses indicate the number of persons reporting this ancestry/race alone, not in combination with any other ancestry/race. 3. Refer to the Explanation of Data in the front of the book for more detailed information.

Ancestry/Race	Number	%
Northern European	20	0.14
Norwegian	37	0.25
Pennsylvania German	16	0.11
Polish	288	1.97
Portuguese	7	0.05
Romanian	11	0.08
Russian	93	0.64
Scandinavian	19	0.13
Scotch-Irish	214	1.46
Scottish	289	1.97
Slovak	44	0.30
Slovene	11	0.08
Swedish	149	1.02
Swiss	50	0.34
Ukrainian	49	0.33
United States or American	1,434	9.80
Welsh	194	1.33
West Indian, excl. Hispanic:	38	0.26
Jamaican	19	0.13
Trinidadian and Tobagonian	19	0.13
White:	14,155	96.93
Not Hispanic (13,942)	14,055	96.25
Hispanic (89)	100	0.68
Yugoslavian	11	0.08

Vermilion

Place Type: City
County: Lorain
Population: 10,927

Ancestry/Race	Number	%
African American/Black:	40	0.37
Not Hispanic (19)	38	0.35
Hispanic	2	0.02
Am. Ind. or Alaska Nat., not spec.	19	0.17
American Indian tribes, specified:	36	0.33
Blackfeet	2	0.02
Cherokee	29	0.27
Iroquois (2)	3	0.03
All other tribes	2	0.02
American Indian tribes, not spec.	2	0.02
Arab:	14	0.13
Lebanese	6	0.06
Moroccan	8	0.07
Asian:	39	0.36
Cambodian (4)	5	0.05
Chinese, ex. Taiwanese (1)	1	0.01
Filipino (4)	5	0.05
Indian	3	0.03
Japanese	1	0.01
Korean (9)	14	0.13
Vietnamese (4)	6	0.05
Other Asian, not specified (1)	4	0.04
Austrian	44	0.40
Belgian	24	0.22
British	38	0.35
Bulgarian	8	0.07
Canadian	48	0.44
Carpatho Rusyn	7	0.06
Celtic	8	0.07
Croatian	80	0.74
Czech	123	1.13
Czechoslovakian	97	0.89
Danish	27	0.25
Dutch	335	3.08
English	1,495	13.76
Finnish	7	0.06
French, except Basque	355	3.27
French Canadian	114	1.05
German	3,691	33.96
Greek	81	0.75
Hawaii Native/Pacific Islander:	1	0.01
Other Pac. Isl., not spec.	1	0.01
Hispanic or Latino:	190	1.74
Central American:	3	0.03
Panamanian	1	0.01
Salvadoran	2	0.02
Cuban	2	0.02
Mexican	83	0.76
Puerto Rican	77	0.70
South American:	1	0.01
Colombian	1	0.01
Other Hispanic or Latino	24	0.22
Hungarian	340	3.13
Icelander	31	0.29
Irish	1,859	17.11
Italian	809	7.44
Latvian	13	0.12
Lithuanian	44	0.40
Luxemburger	21	0.19
Norwegian	89	0.82
Pennsylvania German	24	0.22
Polish	667	6.14
Romanian	19	0.17
Russian	41	0.38
Scotch-Irish	247	2.27
Scottish	216	1.99
Slavic	5	0.05
Slovak	272	2.50
Slovene	72	0.66
Swedish	93	0.86
Swiss	38	0.35
Ukrainian	59	0.54
United States or American	653	6.01
Welsh	221	2.03
White:	10,831	99.12
Not Hispanic (10,594)	10,672	97.67
Hispanic (130)	159	1.46
Yugoslavian	10	0.09

Wadsworth

Place Type: City
County: Medina
Population: 18,437

Ancestry/Race	Number	%
African American/Black:	106	0.57
Not Hispanic (71)	105	0.57
Hispanic (1)	1	0.01
Am. Ind. or Alaska Nat., not spec.	24	0.13
American Indian tribes, specified:	93	0.50
Apache (1)	4	0.02
Blackfeet (1)	6	0.03
Cherokee (18)	56	0.30
Chippewa (4)	8	0.04
Choctaw	5	0.03
Comanche	1	0.01
Cree	1	0.01
Crow	1	0.01
Delaware	1	0.01
Iroquois	2	0.01
Latin American Indians (2)	3	0.02
Sioux (1)	1	0.01
All other tribes	4	0.02
Arab:	89	0.48
Arab/Arabic	33	0.18
Lebanese	49	0.26
Moroccan	7	0.04
Asian:	150	0.81
Chinese, ex. Taiwanese (39)	39	0.21
Filipino (7)	20	0.11
Indian (18)	26	0.14
Japanese (8)	16	0.09
Korean (20)	22	0.12
Laotian (11)	11	0.06
Thai (3)	5	0.03
Vietnamese (3)	4	0.02
Other Asian, not specified (1)	7	0.04
Austrian	59	0.32
Belgian	32	0.17
British	37	0.20
Canadian	35	0.19
Croatian	72	0.39
Czech	154	0.83
Czechoslovakian	69	0.37
Danish	8	0.04
Dutch	273	1.47
English	2,168	11.70
European	155	0.84
Finnish	79	0.43
French, except Basque	435	2.35
French Canadian	58	0.31
German	6,395	34.51
Greek	114	0.62
Hawaii Native/Pacific Islander:	8	0.04
Micronesian: (1)	1	0.01
Other Micronesian (1)	1	0.01
Polynesian:	5	0.03
Native Hawaiian	5	0.03
Other Pac. Isl., not spec. (1)	2	0.01
Hispanic or Latino:	125	0.68
Central American:	5	0.03
Guatemalan	1	0.01
Honduran	2	0.01
Panamanian	1	0.01
Salvadoran	1	0.01
Cuban	5	0.03
Dominican Republic	1	0.01
Mexican	45	0.24
Puerto Rican	29	0.16
South American:	5	0.03
Argentinean	2	0.01
Colombian	1	0.01
Peruvian	1	0.01
Other South American	1	0.01
Other Hispanic or Latino	35	0.19
Hungarian	567	3.06
Irish	2,926	15.79
Italian	1,617	8.73
Latvian	9	0.05
Lithuanian	15	0.08
Maltese	7	0.04
Norwegian	89	0.48
Pennsylvania German	154	0.83
Polish	731	3.94
Romanian	13	0.07
Russian	173	0.93
Scandinavian	17	0.09
Scotch-Irish	345	1.86
Scottish	658	3.55
Serbian	94	0.51
Slavic	29	0.16
Slovak	342	1.85
Slovene	157	0.85
Swedish	204	1.10
Swiss	432	2.33
Turkish	18	0.10
Ukrainian	84	0.45
United States or American	1,387	7.49
Welsh	298	1.61
West Indian, excl. Hispanic:	25	0.13
Jamaican	25	0.13
White:	18,164	98.52
Not Hispanic (17,954)	18,072	98.02
Hispanic (86)	92	0.50
Yugoslavian	23	0.12

Warren

Place Type: City
County: Trumbull
Population: 46,832

Ancestry/Race	Number	%
Acadian/Cajun	4	0.01
African American/Black:	12,424	26.53
Not Hispanic (11,730)	12,330	26.33
Hispanic (72)	94	0.20
African, sub-Saharan:	378	0.81
African	378	0.81
Am. Ind. or Alaska Nat., not spec.	176	0.38
Albanian	26	0.06
American Indian tribes, specified:	161	0.34
Apache (2)	5	0.01
Blackfeet (2)	12	0.03
Cherokee (20)	103	0.22
Chippewa	5	0.01
Choctaw (1)	3	0.01

Notes: 1. Figures in the "Number" column do not add up to the total population due to: a) Ancestry/Race overlap — e.g. persons can report being both White and Irish, b) persons of Hispanic origin can report being any race, c) persons reporting two ancestries are counted in both categories. 2. Numbers in parentheses indicate the number of persons reporting this ancestry/race alone, not in combination with any other ancestry/race. 3. Refer to the Explanation of Data in the front of the book for more detailed information.

Comanche (1)	1	0.00
Crow	1	0.00
Iroquois (1)	8	0.02
Latin American Indians	1	0.00
Lumbee (1)	1	0.00
Paiute	1	0.00
Seminole	2	0.00
Shoshone (1)	1	0.00
Sioux (1)	7	0.01
All other tribes (3)	10	0.02
American Indian tribes, not spec.	17	0.04
Arab:	99	0.21
Arab/Arabic	12	0.03
Lebanese	46	0.10
Syrian	32	0.07
Other Arab	9	0.02
Asian:	284	0.61
Chinese, ex. Taiwanese (56)	65	0.14
Filipino (30)	40	0.09
Indian (40)	60	0.13
Indonesian (1)	1	0.00
Japanese (19)	47	0.10
Korean (24)	28	0.06
Taiwanese (3)	3	0.01
Thai (6)	7	0.01
Vietnamese (14)	17	0.04
Other Asian, not specified (2)	16	0.03
Australian	5	0.01
Austrian	80	0.17
Belgian	40	0.09
British	74	0.16
Bulgarian	6	0.01
Canadian	32	0.07
Carpatho Rusyn	21	0.04
Croatian	217	0.46
Czech	90	0.19
Czechoslovakian	135	0.29
Danish	22	0.05
Dutch	733	1.56
English	3,504	7.47
European	132	0.28
Finnish	195	0.42
French, except Basque	681	1.45
French Canadian	117	0.25
German	7,143	15.23
German Russian	11	0.02
Greek	1,033	2.20
Hawaii Native/Pacific Islander:	32	0.07
Micronesian: (5)	8	0.02
Guamanian/Chamorro (5)	8	0.02
Polynesian: (8)	16	0.03
Native Hawaiian (4)	11	0.02
Samoan (4)	5	0.01
Other Pac. Isl., not spec. (3)	8	0.02
Hispanic or Latino:	485	1.04
Central American:	2	0.00
Panamanian	1	0.00
Salvadoran	1	0.00
Cuban	11	0.02
Mexican	198	0.42
Puerto Rican	151	0.32
South American:	8	0.02
Colombian	1	0.00
Ecuadorian	2	0.00
Peruvian	4	0.01
Venezuelan	1	0.00
Other Hispanic or Latino	115	0.25
Hungarian	1,044	2.23
Icelander	5	0.01
Iranian	5	0.01
Irish	5,438	11.60
Italian	4,835	10.31
Latvian	6	0.01
Lithuanian	54	0.12
Norwegian	80	0.17
Pennsylvania German	181	0.39
Polish	2,011	4.29
Portuguese	6	0.01
Romanian	487	1.04
Russian	334	0.71
Scandinavian	18	0.04
Scotch-Irish	740	1.58
Scottish	473	1.01
Serbian	46	0.10
Slavic	18	0.04
Slovak	1,594	3.40
Slovene	133	0.28
Swedish	251	0.54
Swiss	42	0.09
Ukrainian	272	0.58
United States or American	3,221	6.87
Welsh	782	1.67
West Indian, excl. Hispanic:	25	0.05
Haitian	8	0.02
Jamaican	13	0.03
Trinidadian and Tobagonian	4	0.01
White:	34,482	73.63
Not Hispanic (33,420)	34,184	72.99
Hispanic (270)	298	0.64
Yugoslavian	32	0.07

Warrensville Heights

Place Type: City
County: Cuyahoga
Population: 15,109

Ancestry/Race	Number	%
African American/Black:	13,863	91.75
Not Hispanic (13,600)	13,799	91.33
Hispanic (60)	64	0.42
African, sub-Saharan:	363	2.36
African	329	2.13
Liberian	13	0.08
Nigerian	9	0.06
Other sub-Saharan African	12	0.08
Am. Ind. or Alaska Nat., not spec.	74	0.49
American Indian tribes, specified:	57	0.38
Apache	1	0.01
Blackfeet	8	0.05
Cherokee (8)	33	0.22
Chippewa	1	0.01
Choctaw	2	0.01
Creek	1	0.01
Crow (1)	2	0.01
Navajo	2	0.01
Pueblo	1	0.01
Seminole	3	0.02
Sioux	1	0.01
All other tribes (1)	2	0.01
American Indian tribes, not spec.	3	0.02
Arab:	35	0.23
Arab/Arabic	30	0.19
Lebanese	5	0.03
Asian:	172	1.14
Chinese, ex. Taiwanese (9)	12	0.08
Filipino (13)	19	0.13
Indian (88)	100	0.66
Japanese (4)	6	0.04
Korean (8)	11	0.07
Pakistani (3)	5	0.03
Taiwanese (4)	4	0.03
Thai (3)	3	0.02
Vietnamese (3)	3	0.02
Other Asian, specified	1	0.01
Other Asian, not specified (2)	8	0.05
Austrian	17	0.11
Canadian	17	0.11
Croatian	13	0.08
Czech	86	0.56
Czechoslovakian	6	0.04
Dutch	21	0.14
English	72	0.47
Estonian	4	0.03
French, except Basque	34	0.22
French Canadian	14	0.09
German	142	0.92
Greek	8	0.05
Guyanese	8	0.05
Hawaii Native/Pacific Islander:	14	0.09
Polynesian:	10	0.07
Samoan	5	0.03
Other Polynesian	5	0.03
Other Pac. Isl., specified	1	0.01
Other Pac. Isl., not spec. (2)	3	0.02
Hispanic or Latino:	113	0.75
Central American:	6	0.04
Panamanian	2	0.01
Other Central American	4	0.03
Cuban	14	0.09
Mexican	34	0.23
Puerto Rican	36	0.24
South American:	3	0.02
Colombian	3	0.02
Other Hispanic or Latino	20	0.13
Hungarian	43	0.28
Irish	208	1.35
Italian	144	0.93
Lithuanian	7	0.05
Polish	145	0.94
Portuguese	12	0.08
Russian	6	0.04
Scandinavian	2	0.01
Scotch-Irish	10	0.06
Scottish	27	0.18
Slovak	39	0.25
Slovene	21	0.14
Swedish	35	0.23
Swiss	21	0.14
Ukrainian	35	0.23
United States or American	161	1.04
Welsh	16	0.10
West Indian, excl. Hispanic:	194	1.26
Barbadian	5	0.03
Bermudan	11	0.07
Haitian	8	0.05
Jamaican	108	0.70
Trinidadian and Tobagonian	51	0.33
West Indian	11	0.07
White:	1,141	7.55
Not Hispanic (969)	1,112	7.36
Hispanic (24)	29	0.19

Washington

Place Type: City
County: Fayette
Population: 13,524

Ancestry/Race	Number	%
African American/Black:	443	3.28
Not Hispanic (361)	432	3.19
Hispanic (6)	11	0.08
African, sub-Saharan:	34	0.25
African	34	0.25
Am. Ind. or Alaska Nat., not spec.	19	0.14
Alsatian	13	0.10
American Indian tribes, specified:	57	0.42
Apache (1)	1	0.01
Blackfeet	4	0.03
Cherokee (7)	35	0.26
Chippewa (2)	6	0.04
Choctaw	1	0.01
Iroquois	1	0.01
Latin American Indians	1	0.01
Navajo	1	0.01
Pueblo	1	0.01
Sioux (1)	1	0.01
All other tribes	5	0.04
American Indian tribes, not spec.	3	0.02
Arab:	15	0.11
Other Arab	15	0.11
Armenian	4	0.03
Asian:	137	1.01
Chinese, ex. Taiwanese (7)	8	0.06
Filipino (5)	10	0.07
Indian (11)	19	0.14
Japanese (69)	73	0.54
Korean (6)	9	0.07
Laotian (2)	4	0.03

Notes: 1. Figures in the "Number" column do not add up to the total population due to: a) Ancestry/Race overlap — e.g. persons can report being both White and Irish, b) persons of Hispanic origin can report being any race, c) persons reporting two ancestries are counted in both categories. 2. Numbers in parentheses indicate the number of persons reporting this ancestry/race alone, not in combination with any other ancestry/race. 3. Refer to the Explanation of Data in the front of the book for more detailed information.

Thai (1)	1	0.01
Vietnamese (4)	4	0.03
Other Asian, not specified (4)	9	0.07
Belgian	5	0.04
British	38	0.28
Canadian	4	0.03
Croatian	8	0.06
Czechoslovakian	22	0.16
Danish	6	0.04
Dutch	294	2.19
English	1,281	9.53
European	90	0.67
French, except Basque	221	1.64
French Canadian	5	0.04
German	2,570	19.12
Greek	5	0.04
Hawaii Native/Pacific Islander:	8	0.06
Polynesian: (2)	4	0.03
Native Hawaiian (1)	3	0.02
Samoan (1)	1	0.01
Other Pac. Isl., not spec.	4	0.03
Hispanic or Latino:	187	1.38
Central American:	6	0.04
Honduran	3	0.02
Nicaraguan	3	0.02
Cuban	18	0.13
Mexican	36	0.27
Puerto Rican	10	0.07
South American:	9	0.07
Ecuadorian	6	0.04
Peruvian	2	0.01
Other South American	1	0.01
Other Hispanic or Latino	108	0.80
Hungarian	9	0.07
Irish	1,665	12.39
Italian	304	2.26
Norwegian	20	0.15
Polish	62	0.46
Russian	7	0.05
Scandinavian	13	0.10
Scotch-Irish	154	1.15
Scottish	157	1.17
Slavic	14	0.10
Swedish	50	0.37
Swiss	19	0.14
Ukrainian	14	0.10
United States or American	2,420	18.00
Welsh	88	0.65
White:	12,919	95.53
Not Hispanic (12,691)	12,818	94.78
Hispanic (92)	101	0.75

West Carrollton City

Place Type: City
County: Montgomery
Population: 13,818

Ancestry/Race	Number	%
African American/Black:	655	4.74
Not Hispanic (578)	647	4.68
Hispanic (4)	8	0.06
Am. Ind. or Alaska Nat., not spec.	20	0.14
American Indian tribes, specified:	59	0.43
Apache	4	0.03
Cherokee (14)	37	0.27
Chippewa (1)	1	0.01
Choctaw (1)	1	0.01
Delaware	1	0.01
Kiowa (1)	1	0.01
All other tribes (9)	14	0.10
Arab:	161	1.15
Arab/Arabic	92	0.66
Jordanian	16	0.11
Lebanese	44	0.31
Moroccan	9	0.06
Asian:	201	1.45
Cambodian	2	0.01
Chinese, ex. Taiwanese (20)	21	0.15
Filipino (18)	24	0.17
Indian (42)	47	0.34
Indonesian (1)	1	0.01
Japanese (5)	10	0.07
Korean (27)	35	0.25
Laotian (1)	1	0.01
Pakistani (3)	3	0.02
Taiwanese (10)	10	0.07
Thai (4)	8	0.06
Vietnamese (30)	30	0.22
Other Asian, not specified	9	0.07
Austrian	93	0.66
British	103	0.73
Croatian	7	0.05
Czech	34	0.24
Czechoslovakian	21	0.15
Danish	5	0.04
Dutch	232	1.65
English	1,498	10.68
European	189	1.35
Finnish	16	0.11
French, except Basque	302	2.15
French Canadian	66	0.47
German	3,203	22.84
Greek	7	0.05
Hawaii Native/Pacific Islander:	5	0.04
Polynesian: (1)	2	0.01
Native Hawaiian (1)	2	0.01
Other Pac. Isl., not spec.	3	0.02
Hispanic or Latino:	199	1.44
Central American:	4	0.03
Guatemalan	2	0.01
Panamanian	2	0.01
Cuban	11	0.08
Dominican Republic	10	0.07
Mexican	85	0.62
Puerto Rican	31	0.22
South American:	10	0.07
Argentinean	1	0.01
Colombian	4	0.03
Venezuelan	4	0.03
Other South American	1	0.01
Other Hispanic or Latino	48	0.35
Hungarian	281	2.00
Irish	1,475	10.52
Italian	334	2.38
Lithuanian	10	0.07
Norwegian	106	0.76
Pennsylvania German	27	0.19
Polish	208	1.48
Portuguese	22	0.16
Romanian	8	0.06
Russian	10	0.07
Scandinavian	21	0.15
Scotch-Irish	183	1.31
Scottish	118	0.84
Serbian	7	0.05
Slovene	8	0.06
Swedish	142	1.01
Swiss	25	0.18
Ukrainian	13	0.09
United States or American	2,003	14.28
Welsh	149	1.06
West Indian, excl. Hispanic:	9	0.06
Jamaican	9	0.06
White:	12,964	93.82
Not Hispanic (12,675)	12,832	92.86
Hispanic (119)	132	0.96
Yugoslavian	7	0.05

Westerville

Place Type: City
County: Franklin
Population: 35,318

Ancestry/Race	Number	%
African American/Black:	1,319	3.73
Not Hispanic (1,115)	1,290	3.65
Hispanic (16)	29	0.08
African, sub-Saharan:	46	0.13
African	42	0.12
Nigerian	4	0.01
Am. Ind. or Alaska Nat., not spec.	58	0.16
Alsatian	9	0.03
American Indian tribes, specified:	97	0.27
Apache (2)	4	0.01
Blackfeet	2	0.01
Cherokee (15)	52	0.15
Cheyenne (1)	1	0.00
Choctaw (3)	4	0.01
Delaware	3	0.01
Iroquois	7	0.02
Latin American Indians (1)	1	0.00
Lumbee	2	0.01
Menominee (1)	1	0.00
Navajo	2	0.01
Ottawa (1)	1	0.00
Seminole	1	0.00
Sioux	3	0.01
Ute	1	0.00
Yakama (1)	1	0.00
All other tribes (6)	11	0.03
American Indian tribes, not spec.	2	0.01
Arab:	297	0.84
Arab/Arabic	159	0.45
Jordanian	2	0.01
Lebanese	116	0.33
Moroccan	12	0.03
Syrian	8	0.02
Armenian	81	0.23
Asian:	660	1.87
Bangladeshi (8)	8	0.02
Cambodian (1)	1	0.00
Chinese, ex. Taiwanese (190)	216	0.61
Filipino (34)	53	0.15
Indian (143)	151	0.43
Japanese (39)	60	0.17
Korean (52)	66	0.19
Laotian (6)	9	0.03
Pakistani (6)	6	0.02
Sri Lankan (1)	1	0.00
Taiwanese (4)	4	0.01
Thai (6)	11	0.03
Vietnamese (41)	48	0.14
Other Asian, specified (4)	8	0.02
Other Asian, not specified (7)	18	0.05
Austrian	152	0.43
Belgian	77	0.22
Brazilian	15	0.04
British	279	0.79
Canadian	170	0.48
Croatian	207	0.58
Czech	163	0.46
Czechoslovakian	103	0.29
Danish	170	0.48
Dutch	824	2.33
Eastern European	18	0.05
English	5,075	14.33
Estonian	11	0.03
European	316	0.89
Finnish	73	0.21
French, except Basque	1,268	3.58
French Canadian	123	0.35
German	10,464	29.55
Greek	227	0.64
Guyanese	8	0.02
Hawaii Native/Pacific Islander:	28	0.08
Micronesian: (3)	7	0.02
Guamanian/Chamorro (3)	7	0.02
Polynesian: (6)	9	0.03
Native Hawaiian (2)	4	0.01
Samoan (4)	5	0.01
Other Pac. Isl., specified	4	0.01
Other Pac. Isl., not spec. (1)	8	0.02
Hispanic or Latino:	379	1.07
Central American:	15	0.04
Costa Rican	1	0.00
Guatemalan	2	0.01
Honduran	3	0.01
Nicaraguan	1	0.00

Notes: 1. Figures in the "Number" column do not add up to the total population due to: a) Ancestry/Race overlap — e.g. persons can report being both White and Irish, b) persons of Hispanic origin can report being any race, c) persons reporting two ancestries are counted in both categories. 2. Numbers in parentheses indicate the number of persons reporting this ancestry/race alone, not in combination with any other ancestry/race. 3. Refer to the Explanation of Data in the front of the book for more detailed information.

Ancestry/Race	Number	%
Panamanian	5	0.01
Salvadoran	1	0.00
Other Central American	2	0.01
Cuban	29	0.08
Dominican Republic	1	0.00
Mexican	104	0.29
Puerto Rican	79	0.22
South American:	51	0.14
Argentinean	2	0.01
Bolivian	3	0.01
Chilean	15	0.04
Colombian	13	0.04
Ecuadorian	2	0.01
Paraguayan	1	0.00
Peruvian	9	0.03
Uruguayan	1	0.00
Venezuelan	4	0.01
Other South American	1	0.00
Other Hispanic or Latino	100	0.28
Hungarian	326	0.92
Icelander	8	0.02
Iranian	38	0.11
Irish	5,446	15.38
Italian	2,243	6.33
Latvian	27	0.08
Lithuanian	80	0.23
Macedonian	9	0.03
Northern European	15	0.04
Norwegian	208	0.59
Pennsylvania German	42	0.12
Polish	1,145	3.23
Portuguese	16	0.05
Romanian	80	0.23
Russian	217	0.61
Scandinavian	61	0.17
Scotch-Irish	835	2.36
Scottish	1,368	3.86
Slavic	31	0.09
Slovak	324	0.92
Slovene	126	0.36
Swedish	445	1.26
Swiss	221	0.62
Turkish	15	0.04
Ukrainian	159	0.45
United States or American	3,205	9.05
Welsh	956	2.70
West Indian, excl. Hispanic:	16	0.05
Haitian	16	0.05
White:	33,413	94.61
Not Hispanic (32,803)	33,150	93.86
Hispanic (232)	263	0.74
Yugoslavian	72	0.20

Westlake

Place Type: City
County: Cuyahoga
Population: 31,719

Ancestry/Race	Number	%
African American/Black:	359	1.13
Not Hispanic (299)	351	1.11
Hispanic (2)	8	0.03
African, sub-Saharan:	12	0.04
African	3	0.01
South African	9	0.03
Alaska Native tribes, specified:	1	0.00
Aleut (1)	1	0.00
Am. Ind. or Alaska Nat., not spec.	32	0.10
Albanian	26	0.08
Alsatian	8	0.03
American Indian tribes, specified:	42	0.13
Apache (1)	1	0.00
Blackfeet	1	0.00
Cherokee (4)	26	0.08
Chippewa	1	0.00
Choctaw (1)	1	0.00
Delaware	1	0.00
Iroquois	2	0.01
Lumbee (1)	4	0.01
Potawatomi	3	0.01
Sioux (1)	1	0.00
All other tribes	1	0.00
American Indian tribes, not spec.	4	0.01
Arab:	926	2.91
Arab/Arabic	237	0.74
Egyptian	70	0.22
Lebanese	304	0.95
Palestinian	98	0.31
Syrian	156	0.49
Other Arab	61	0.19
Armenian	94	0.30
Asian:	1,506	4.75
Bangladeshi (7)	7	0.02
Cambodian (14)	15	0.05
Chinese, ex. Taiwanese (224)	263	0.83
Filipino (100)	126	0.40
Indian (593)	611	1.93
Indonesian (5)	7	0.02
Japanese (76)	85	0.27
Korean (178)	193	0.61
Malaysian (1)	3	0.01
Pakistani (43)	50	0.16
Taiwanese (33)	37	0.12
Thai (6)	6	0.02
Vietnamese (21)	25	0.08
Other Asian, specified (2)	3	0.01
Other Asian, not specified (21)	75	0.24
Australian	20	0.06
Austrian	269	0.84
Basque	9	0.03
Belgian	51	0.16
Brazilian	35	0.11
British	72	0.23
Bulgarian	7	0.02
Canadian	75	0.24
Celtic	5	0.02
Croatian	197	0.62
Czech	483	1.52
Czechoslovakian	281	0.88
Danish	143	0.45
Dutch	393	1.23
Eastern European	14	0.04
English	3,178	9.98
European	155	0.49
Finnish	69	0.22
French, except Basque	824	2.59
French Canadian	109	0.34
German	8,352	26.22
Greek	647	2.03
Guyanese	18	0.06
Hawaii Native/Pacific Islander:	11	0.03
Micronesian: (5)	5	0.02
Guamanian/Chamorro (5)	5	0.02
Polynesian:	1	0.00
Native Hawaiian	1	0.00
Other Pac. Isl., not spec.	5	0.02
Hispanic or Latino:	402	1.27
Central American:	19	0.06
Costa Rican	2	0.01
Guatemalan	1	0.00
Honduran	3	0.01
Nicaraguan	3	0.01
Panamanian	4	0.01
Salvadoran	6	0.02
Cuban	19	0.06
Dominican Republic	2	0.01
Mexican	99	0.31
Puerto Rican	130	0.41
South American:	44	0.14
Argentinean	5	0.02
Bolivian	1	0.00
Chilean	8	0.03
Colombian	14	0.04
Ecuadorian	2	0.01
Paraguayan	1	0.00
Peruvian	6	0.02
Uruguayan	1	0.00
Venezuelan	5	0.02
Other South American	1	0.00
Other Hispanic or Latino	89	0.28
Hungarian	1,348	4.23
Iranian	56	0.18
Irish	7,433	23.33
Italian	3,703	11.62
Latvian	37	0.12
Lithuanian	177	0.56
Macedonian	4	0.01
Northern European	20	0.06
Norwegian	226	0.71
Pennsylvania German	28	0.09
Polish	2,346	7.36
Portuguese	37	0.12
Romanian	211	0.66
Russian	421	1.32
Scandinavian	32	0.10
Scotch-Irish	543	1.70
Scottish	648	2.03
Serbian	41	0.13
Slavic	16	0.05
Slovak	1,551	4.87
Slovene	498	1.56
Swedish	390	1.22
Swiss	164	0.51
Turkish	39	0.12
Ukrainian	426	1.34
United States or American	840	2.64
Welsh	417	1.31
West Indian, excl. Hispanic:	13	0.04
British West Indian	6	0.02
Trinidadian and Tobagonian	7	0.02
White:	29,927	94.35
Not Hispanic (29,199)	29,623	93.39
Hispanic (278)	304	0.96
Yugoslavian	29	0.09

White Oak

Place Type: Census Designated Place
County: Hamilton
Population: 13,277

Ancestry/Race	Number	%
African American/Black:	510	3.84
Not Hispanic (467)	504	3.80
Hispanic (4)	6	0.05
African, sub-Saharan:	29	0.22
African	29	0.22
Am. Ind. or Alaska Nat., not spec.	17	0.13
American Indian tribes, specified:	49	0.37
Blackfeet (4)	6	0.05
Cherokee (6)	26	0.20
Cheyenne (1)	1	0.01
Cree (1)	1	0.01
Creek (2)	2	0.02
Iroquois	1	0.01
Pueblo	1	0.01
Sioux (1)	1	0.01
All other tribes (4)	10	0.08
American Indian tribes, not spec.	3	0.02
Arab:	44	0.33
Arab/Arabic	25	0.19
Lebanese	19	0.14
Asian:	170	1.28
Cambodian (4)	4	0.03
Chinese, ex. Taiwanese (28)	30	0.23
Filipino (37)	40	0.30
Indian (27)	32	0.24
Indonesian	1	0.01
Japanese (3)	8	0.06
Korean (4)	12	0.09
Malaysian (2)	2	0.02
Pakistani (8)	9	0.07
Thai (6)	6	0.05
Vietnamese (18)	18	0.14
Other Asian, specified (1)	1	0.01
Other Asian, not specified (6)	7	0.05
Austrian	49	0.37
Belgian	16	0.12
British	9	0.07

Notes: 1. Figures in the "Number" column do not add up to the total population due to: a) Ancestry/Race overlap — e.g. persons can report being both White and Irish, b) persons of Hispanic origin can report being any race, c) persons reporting two ancestries are counted in both categories. 2. Numbers in parentheses indicate the number of persons reporting this ancestry/race alone, not in combination with any other ancestry/race. 3. Refer to the Explanation of Data in the front of the book for more detailed information.

Ancestry/Race	Number	%
Canadian	13	0.10
Czech	52	0.39
Czechoslovakian	9	0.07
Dutch	176	1.33
English	938	7.08
European	130	0.98
Finnish	26	0.20
French, except Basque	373	2.81
French Canadian	15	0.11
German	6,375	48.11
Greek	36	0.27
Hispanic or Latino:	143	1.08
Central American:	4	0.03
Panamanian	4	0.03
Mexican	73	0.55
Puerto Rican	13	0.10
South American:	6	0.05
Peruvian	6	0.05
Other Hispanic or Latino	47	0.35
Hungarian	76	0.57
Irish	2,184	16.48
Israeli	7	0.05
Italian	612	4.62
Macedonian	20	0.15
Northern European	22	0.17
Norwegian	83	0.63
Polish	119	0.90
Portuguese	6	0.05
Romanian	7	0.05
Russian	61	0.46
Scandinavian	26	0.20
Scotch-Irish	151	1.14
Scottish	114	0.86
Serbian	5	0.04
Slavic	6	0.05
Slovak	19	0.14
Swedish	51	0.38
Swiss	52	0.39
United States or American	1,171	8.84
Welsh	20	0.15
West Indian, excl. Hispanic:	7	0.05
Trinidadian and Tobagonian	7	0.05
White:	12,578	94.74
Not Hispanic (12,377)	12,486	94.04
Hispanic (87)	92	0.69

Whitehall

Place Type: City
County: Franklin
Population: 19,201

Ancestry/Race	Number	%
African American/Black:	3,977	20.71
Not Hispanic (3,636)	3,916	20.39
Hispanic (42)	61	0.32
African, sub-Saharan:	514	2.67
African	192	1.00
Ethiopian	162	0.84
Nigerian	21	0.11
South African	4	0.02
Sudanese	97	0.50
Other sub-Saharan African	38	0.20
Am. Ind. or Alaska Nat., not spec.	97	0.51
American Indian tribes, specified:	116	0.60
Apache (2)	3	0.02
Blackfeet	11	0.06
Cherokee (22)	58	0.30
Cheyenne (3)	3	0.02
Chickasaw	2	0.01
Chippewa (2)	3	0.02
Choctaw (3)	5	0.03
Cree (1)	1	0.01
Crow	3	0.02
Delaware	1	0.01
Iroquois (1)	3	0.02
Latin American Indians (4)	7	0.04
Lumbee (1)	1	0.01
Navajo (1)	3	0.02
Sioux	2	0.01
All other tribes (7)	10	0.05
American Indian tribes, not spec.	4	0.02
Arab:	24	0.12
Arab/Arabic	12	0.06
Lebanese	6	0.03
Syrian	6	0.03
Asian:	474	2.47
Bangladeshi (1)	1	0.01
Cambodian (6)	11	0.06
Chinese, ex. Taiwanese (144)	150	0.78
Filipino (17)	34	0.18
Indian (54)	58	0.30
Indonesian (2)	4	0.02
Japanese (15)	30	0.16
Korean (19)	29	0.15
Laotian (59)	75	0.39
Malaysian (1)	1	0.01
Pakistani (10)	12	0.06
Sri Lankan (2)	2	0.01
Taiwanese (1)	1	0.01
Thai (11)	13	0.07
Vietnamese (33)	36	0.19
Other Asian, not specified (10)	17	0.09
Austrian	14	0.07
Belgian	7	0.04
British	95	0.49
Canadian	9	0.05
Croatian	33	0.17
Czech	30	0.16
Czechoslovakian	30	0.16
Danish	8	0.04
Dutch	360	1.87
English	1,425	7.41
European	146	0.76
French, except Basque	361	1.88
French Canadian	60	0.31
German	3,566	18.55
Greek	13	0.07
Hawaii Native/Pacific Islander:	14	0.07
Micronesian: (2)	3	0.02
Guamanian/Chamorro (2)	3	0.02
Polynesian: (4)	9	0.05
Native Hawaiian (2)	2	0.01
Samoan (2)	6	0.03
Other Polynesian	1	0.01
Other Pac. Isl., not spec.	2	0.01
Hispanic or Latino:	566	2.95
Central American:	40	0.21
Honduran	6	0.03
Nicaraguan	2	0.01
Panamanian	1	0.01
Salvadoran	28	0.15
Other Central American	3	0.02
Cuban	13	0.07
Dominican Republic	22	0.11
Mexican	295	1.54
Puerto Rican	96	0.50
South American:	6	0.03
Colombian	3	0.02
Peruvian	2	0.01
Other South American	1	0.01
Other Hispanic or Latino	94	0.49
Hungarian	212	1.10
Irish	2,396	12.46
Italian	591	3.07
Lithuanian	11	0.06
Macedonian	75	0.39
Norwegian	43	0.22
Pennsylvania German	5	0.03
Polish	222	1.15
Russian	70	0.36
Scandinavian	8	0.04
Scotch-Irish	215	1.12
Scottish	231	1.20
Serbian	17	0.09
Slavic	7	0.04
Slovak	54	0.28
Slovene	6	0.03
Swedish	92	0.48
Swiss	31	0.16
Ukrainian	60	0.31
United States or American	2,325	12.09
Welsh	279	1.45
West Indian, excl. Hispanic:	26	0.14
Dutch West Indian	10	0.05
Jamaican	16	0.08
White:	14,705	76.58
Not Hispanic (14,036)	14,403	75.01
Hispanic (249)	302	1.57
Yugoslavian	42	0.22

Wickliffe

Place Type: City
County: Lake
Population: 13,484

Ancestry/Race	Number	%
African American/Black:	431	3.20
Not Hispanic (381)	427	3.17
Hispanic (3)	4	0.03
African, sub-Saharan:	18	0.13
African	12	0.09
Nigerian	6	0.04
Am. Ind. or Alaska Nat., not spec.	11	0.08
Albanian	16	0.12
American Indian tribes, specified:	35	0.26
Cherokee (4)	20	0.15
Cheyenne	1	0.01
Chickasaw (1)	1	0.01
Chippewa	1	0.01
Iroquois	2	0.01
Latin American Indians (1)	2	0.01
Shoshone	1	0.01
Sioux	4	0.03
All other tribes	3	0.02
American Indian tribes, not spec.	2	0.01
Armenian	6	0.04
Asian:	133	0.99
Cambodian (1)	2	0.01
Chinese, ex. Taiwanese (19)	21	0.16
Filipino (9)	14	0.10
Indian (34)	35	0.26
Japanese (25)	35	0.26
Korean (7)	8	0.06
Thai (1)	1	0.01
Vietnamese (9)	10	0.07
Other Asian, specified	4	0.03
Other Asian, not specified	3	0.02
Australian	3	0.02
Austrian	78	0.58
British	7	0.05
Bulgarian	8	0.06
Canadian	11	0.08
Croatian	260	1.93
Czech	166	1.23
Czechoslovakian	22	0.16
Dutch	92	0.68
Eastern European	6	0.04
English	1,208	8.96
European	20	0.15
Finnish	55	0.41
French, except Basque	235	1.74
French Canadian	77	0.57
German	2,856	21.18
Greek	29	0.22
Hawaii Native/Pacific Islander:	4	0.03
Polynesian:	2	0.01
Native Hawaiian	2	0.01
Other Pac. Isl., not spec. (2)	2	0.01
Hispanic or Latino:	72	0.53
Central American:	2	0.01
Guatemalan	2	0.01
Cuban	8	0.06
Dominican Republic	1	0.01
Mexican	18	0.13
Puerto Rican	19	0.14
South American:	1	0.01
Venezuelan	1	0.01
Other Hispanic or Latino	23	0.17

Notes: 1. Figures in the "Number" column do not add up to the total population due to: a) Ancestry/Race overlap — e.g. persons can report being both White and Irish, b) persons of Hispanic origin can report being any race, c) persons reporting two ancestries are counted in both categories. 2. Numbers in parentheses indicate the number of persons reporting this ancestry/race alone, not in combination with any other ancestry/race. 3. Refer to the Explanation of Data in the front of the book for more detailed information.

Hungarian	611	4.53
Irish	2,433	18.04
Italian	2,741	20.33
Latvian	12	0.09
Lithuanian	147	1.09
Norwegian	24	0.18
Pennsylvania German	16	0.12
Polish	1,452	10.77
Russian	127	0.94
Scotch-Irish	169	1.25
Scottish	170	1.26
Serbian	22	0.16
Slavic	31	0.23
Slovak	826	6.13
Slovene	1,336	9.91
Swedish	132	0.98
Swiss	42	0.31
Ukrainian	65	0.48
United States or American	415	3.08
Welsh	130	0.96
White:	12,969	96.18
Not Hispanic (12,810)	12,909	95.74
Hispanic (50)	60	0.44
Yugoslavian	29	0.22

Willoughby

Place Type: City
County: Lake
Population: 22,621

Ancestry/Race	Number	%
African American/Black:	324	1.43
Not Hispanic (258)	321	1.42
Hispanic	3	0.01
African, sub-Saharan:	10	0.04
African	10	0.04
Am. Ind. or Alaska Nat., not spec.	31	0.14
Albanian	5	0.02
American Indian tribes, specified:	64	0.28
Apache	1	0.00
Blackfeet (2)	6	0.03
Cherokee (15)	34	0.15
Iroquois (4)	11	0.05
Latin American Indians	2	0.01
Navajo	1	0.00
Sioux (2)	3	0.01
All other tribes	6	0.03
American Indian tribes, not spec.	8	0.04
Arab:	94	0.42
Jordanian	10	0.04
Lebanese	70	0.31
Syrian	8	0.04
Other Arab	6	0.03
Asian:	313	1.38
Bangladeshi (2)	2	0.01
Chinese, ex. Taiwanese (55)	68	0.30
Filipino (20)	32	0.14
Indian (110)	114	0.50
Japanese (25)	35	0.15
Korean (18)	23	0.10
Laotian (1)	1	0.00
Pakistani (4)	5	0.02
Taiwanese	4	0.02
Thai (1)	1	0.00
Vietnamese (12)	19	0.08
Other Asian, not specified (3)	9	0.04
Austrian	88	0.39
Belgian	8	0.04
British	77	0.34
Bulgarian	9	0.04
Canadian	63	0.28
Carpatho Rusyn	15	0.07
Croatian	425	1.88
Czech	278	1.23
Czechoslovakian	44	0.19
Dutch	353	1.56
English	2,558	11.33
European	6	0.03
Finnish	72	0.32
French, except Basque	650	2.88
French Canadian	154	0.68
German	5,961	26.39
Greek	53	0.23
Hawaii Native/Pacific Islander:	22	0.10
Micronesian: (1)	4	0.02
Guamanian/Chamorro (1)	3	0.01
Other Micronesian	1	0.00
Polynesian: (9)	12	0.05
Native Hawaiian	1	0.00
Samoan (9)	11	0.05
Other Pac. Isl., not spec. (4)	6	0.03
Hispanic or Latino:	161	0.71
Central American:	10	0.04
Guatemalan	1	0.00
Honduran	1	0.00
Nicaraguan	4	0.02
Panamanian	1	0.00
Salvadoran	3	0.01
Cuban	4	0.02
Mexican	51	0.23
Puerto Rican	42	0.19
South American:	17	0.08
Argentinean	7	0.03
Chilean	1	0.00
Colombian	4	0.02
Ecuadorian	1	0.00
Peruvian	4	0.02
Other Hispanic or Latino	37	0.16
Hungarian	1,190	5.27
Irish	4,274	18.92
Israeli	7	0.03
Italian	3,521	15.59
Latvian	13	0.06
Lithuanian	228	1.01
Macedonian	8	0.04
Northern European	10	0.04
Norwegian	128	0.57
Pennsylvania German	39	0.17
Polish	1,468	6.50
Portuguese	23	0.10
Romanian	102	0.45
Russian	170	0.75
Scandinavian	7	0.03
Scotch-Irish	474	2.10
Scottish	598	2.65
Serbian	36	0.16
Slavic	31	0.14
Slovak	976	4.32
Slovene	1,346	5.96
Swedish	294	1.30
Swiss	88	0.39
Turkish	24	0.11
Ukrainian	151	0.67
United States or American	1,074	4.76
Welsh	353	1.56
White:	22,021	97.35
Not Hispanic (21,695)	21,879	96.72
Hispanic (127)	142	0.63
Yugoslavian	61	0.27

Willowick

Place Type: City
County: Lake
Population: 14,361

Ancestry/Race	Number	%
African American/Black:	139	0.97
Not Hispanic (106)	136	0.95
Hispanic (1)	3	0.02
Alaska Native tribes, specified:	1	0.01
Eskimo (1)	1	0.01
Am. Ind. or Alaska Nat., not spec.	8	0.06
American Indian tribes, specified:	9	0.06
Blackfeet	1	0.01
Cherokee	2	0.01
Chippewa (1)	1	0.01
Tohono O'Odham (1)	1	0.01
All other tribes	4	0.03
American Indian tribes, not spec.	1	0.01
Arab:	24	0.17
Lebanese	24	0.17
Armenian	9	0.06
Asian:	134	0.93
Chinese, ex. Taiwanese (26)	28	0.19
Filipino (8)	17	0.12
Indian (22)	23	0.16
Japanese (14)	31	0.22
Korean (10)	15	0.10
Laotian (2)	9	0.06
Thai (1)	1	0.01
Vietnamese	3	0.02
Other Asian, specified (1)	1	0.01
Other Asian, not specified	6	0.04
Austrian	76	0.53
Belgian	33	0.23
British	7	0.05
Canadian	26	0.18
Celtic	11	0.08
Croatian	555	3.85
Czech	271	1.88
Czechoslovakian	59	0.41
Danish	33	0.23
Dutch	174	1.21
English	1,279	8.88
European	45	0.31
Finnish	65	0.45
French, except Basque	206	1.43
French Canadian	56	0.39
German	3,430	23.81
German Russian	7	0.05
Greek	27	0.19
Hispanic or Latino:	102	0.71
Central American:	3	0.02
Panamanian	1	0.01
Other Central American	2	0.01
Cuban	4	0.03
Mexican	36	0.25
Puerto Rican	25	0.17
South American:	13	0.09
Argentinean	1	0.01
Colombian	4	0.03
Venezuelan	1	0.01
Other South American	7	0.05
Other Hispanic or Latino	21	0.15
Hungarian	652	4.53
Irish	2,534	17.59
Italian	2,780	19.30
Latvian	7	0.05
Lithuanian	270	1.87
Macedonian	6	0.04
Norwegian	49	0.34
Pennsylvania German	17	0.12
Polish	1,719	11.93
Portuguese	8	0.06
Romanian	34	0.24
Russian	156	1.08
Scandinavian	7	0.05
Scotch-Irish	237	1.65
Scottish	245	1.70
Serbian	33	0.23
Slavic	37	0.26
Slovak	805	5.59
Slovene	1,387	9.63
Swedish	126	0.87
Swiss	41	0.28
Ukrainian	116	0.81
United States or American	553	3.84
Welsh	80	0.56
White:	14,147	98.51
Not Hispanic (13,963)	14,050	97.83
Hispanic (89)	97	0.68
Yugoslavian	41	0.28

Notes: 1. Figures in the "Number" column do not add up to the total population due to: a) Ancestry/Race overlap — e.g. persons can report being both White and Irish, b) persons of Hispanic origin can report being any race, c) persons reporting two ancestries are counted in both categories. 2. Numbers in parentheses indicate the number of persons reporting this ancestry/race alone, not in combination with any other ancestry/race. 3. Refer to the Explanation of Data in the front of the book for more detailed information.

Wilmington

Place Type: City
County: Clinton
Population: 11,921

Ancestry/Race	Number	%
African American/Black:	910	7.63
Not Hispanic (796)	905	7.59
Hispanic (5)	5	0.04
Am. Ind. or Alaska Nat., not spec.	40	0.34
American Indian tribes, specified:	34	0.29
Apache (2)	2	0.02
Blackfeet	2	0.02
Cherokee (7)	23	0.19
Chippewa (1)	1	0.01
Iroquois (1)	1	0.01
Sioux	2	0.02
Tohono O'Odham (1)	1	0.01
All other tribes (1)	2	0.02
American Indian tribes, not spec.	7	0.06
Arab:	9	0.08
Moroccan	9	0.08
Armenian	9	0.08
Asian:	109	0.91
Chinese, ex. Taiwanese (16)	18	0.15
Filipino (9)	16	0.13
Indian (11)	18	0.15
Japanese (21)	28	0.23
Korean (3)	4	0.03
Thai (3)	3	0.03
Vietnamese (10)	16	0.13
Other Asian, not specified (4)	6	0.05
Australian	4	0.03
Austrian	38	0.32
Belgian	11	0.09
British	83	0.69
Canadian	26	0.22
Czech	9	0.08
Czechoslovakian	8	0.07
Danish	17	0.14
Dutch	177	1.48
Eastern European	11	0.09
English	1,219	10.19
European	25	0.21
Finnish	10	0.08
French, except Basque	276	2.31
French Canadian	17	0.14
German	2,464	20.60
Hawaii Native/Pacific Islander:	2	0.02
Polynesian: (1)	2	0.02
Native Hawaiian	1	0.01
Other Polynesian (1)	1	0.01
Hispanic or Latino:	100	0.84
Central American:	5	0.04
Nicaraguan	5	0.04
Cuban	9	0.08
Dominican Republic	1	0.01
Mexican	41	0.34
Puerto Rican	14	0.12
Other Hispanic or Latino	30	0.25
Hungarian	91	0.76
Irish	1,595	13.33
Italian	123	1.03
Lithuanian	18	0.15
Norwegian	82	0.69
Pennsylvania German	17	0.14
Polish	96	0.80
Romanian	44	0.37
Russian	3	0.03
Scandinavian	19	0.16
Scotch-Irish	224	1.87
Scottish	290	2.42
Slovak	9	0.08
Slovene	10	0.08
Swedish	67	0.56
Swiss	33	0.28
Ukrainian	17	0.14
United States or American	1,771	14.81
Welsh	108	0.90
West Indian, excl. Hispanic:	24	0.20
Haitian	24	0.20
White:	10,975	92.06
Not Hispanic (10,739)	10,903	91.46
Hispanic (68)	72	0.60

Wooster

Place Type: City
County: Wayne
Population: 24,811

Ancestry/Race	Number	%
Acadian/Cajun	7	0.03
African American/Black:	1,122	4.52
Not Hispanic (933)	1,104	4.45
Hispanic (14)	18	0.07
African, sub-Saharan:	140	0.56
African	92	0.37
Ghanian	25	0.10
Nigerian	8	0.03
Somalian	7	0.03
Sudanese	8	0.03
Am. Ind. or Alaska Nat., not spec.	57	0.23
American Indian tribes, specified:	128	0.52
Apache (1)	4	0.02
Blackfeet	6	0.02
Cherokee (29)	75	0.30
Chickasaw	3	0.01
Chippewa (1)	7	0.03
Choctaw (1)	2	0.01
Colville	1	0.00
Creek (2)	3	0.01
Iroquois (4)	7	0.03
Latin American Indians (2)	3	0.01
Lumbee (1)	1	0.00
Navajo (5)	5	0.02
Sioux	6	0.02
All other tribes (4)	5	0.02
American Indian tribes, not spec.	5	0.02
Arab:	115	0.46
Arab/Arabic	10	0.04
Egyptian	10	0.04
Lebanese	88	0.35
Palestinian	7	0.03
Armenian	7	0.03
Asian:	447	1.80
Cambodian (2)	2	0.01
Chinese, ex. Taiwanese (89)	97	0.39
Filipino (26)	40	0.16
Indian (177)	188	0.76
Indonesian (1)	3	0.01
Japanese (12)	22	0.09
Korean (27)	31	0.12
Pakistani (10)	10	0.04
Sri Lankan (4)	4	0.02
Thai (2)	2	0.01
Vietnamese (23)	27	0.11
Other Asian, specified (1)	2	0.01
Other Asian, not specified (6)	19	0.08
Australian	13	0.05
Austrian	165	0.66
Belgian	20	0.08
Brazilian	10	0.04
British	162	0.65
Canadian	33	0.13
Celtic	18	0.07
Croatian	49	0.20
Czech	62	0.25
Czechoslovakian	58	0.23
Danish	50	0.20
Dutch	505	2.01
Eastern European	11	0.04
English	2,978	11.88
European	253	1.01
Finnish	6	0.02
French, except Basque	779	3.11
French Canadian	65	0.26
German	7,613	30.37
Greek	68	0.27
Hawaii Native/Pacific Islander:	10	0.04
Micronesian: (2)	5	0.02
Guamanian/Chamorro (2)	5	0.02
Other Pac. Isl., not spec.	5	0.02
Hispanic or Latino:	266	1.07
Central American:	8	0.03
Costa Rican	1	0.00
Guatemalan	6	0.02
Honduran	1	0.00
Cuban	23	0.09
Dominican Republic	3	0.01
Mexican	91	0.37
Puerto Rican	33	0.13
South American:	30	0.12
Argentinean	3	0.01
Chilean	9	0.04
Colombian	6	0.02
Ecuadorian	1	0.00
Peruvian	1	0.00
Venezuelan	8	0.03
Other South American	2	0.01
Other Hispanic or Latino	78	0.31
Hungarian	266	1.06
Icelander	5	0.02
Iranian	31	0.12
Irish	3,420	13.64
Italian	1,605	6.40
Latvian	12	0.05
Lithuanian	70	0.28
Macedonian	5	0.02
Northern European	14	0.06
Norwegian	164	0.65
Pennsylvania German	100	0.40
Polish	629	2.51
Romanian	24	0.10
Russian	187	0.75
Scandinavian	20	0.08
Scotch-Irish	530	2.11
Scottish	590	2.35
Serbian	56	0.22
Slavic	2	0.01
Slovak	152	0.61
Slovene	103	0.41
Swedish	309	1.23
Swiss	573	2.29
Ukrainian	38	0.15
United States or American	2,038	8.13
Welsh	392	1.56
West Indian, excl. Hispanic:	28	0.11
Jamaican	28	0.11
White:	23,295	93.89
Not Hispanic (22,802)	23,108	93.14
Hispanic (170)	187	0.75

Worthington

Place Type: City
County: Franklin
Population: 14,125

Ancestry/Race	Number	%
African American/Black:	304	2.15
Not Hispanic (239)	293	2.07
Hispanic (2)	11	0.08
African, sub-Saharan:	38	0.27
African	17	0.12
Nigerian	11	0.08
Other sub-Saharan African	10	0.07
Am. Ind. or Alaska Nat., not spec.	30	0.21
Albanian	4	0.03
Alsatian	16	0.11
American Indian tribes, specified:	48	0.34
Blackfeet	2	0.01
Cherokee (7)	27	0.19
Chippewa (1)	1	0.01
Creek	1	0.01
Iroquois	3	0.02
Latin American Indians (4)	5	0.04
Pueblo	2	0.01
Seminole	1	0.01

Notes: 1. Figures in the "Number" column do not add up to the total population due to: a) Ancestry/Race overlap — e.g. persons can report being both White and Irish, b) persons of Hispanic origin can report being any race, c) persons reporting two ancestries are counted in both categories. 2. Numbers in parentheses indicate the number of persons reporting this ancestry/race alone, not in combination with any other ancestry/race. 3. Refer to the Explanation of Data in the front of the book for more detailed information.

Ancestry/Race	Number	%
Sioux (1)	3	0.02
Yuman	1	0.01
All other tribes (1)	2	0.01
American Indian tribes, not spec.	2	0.01
Arab:	55	0.38
Egyptian	37	0.26
Lebanese	14	0.10
Palestinian	4	0.03
Armenian	15	0.10
Asian:	452	3.20
Cambodian (9)	9	0.06
Chinese, ex. Taiwanese (120)	138	0.98
Filipino (19)	24	0.17
Indian (85)	97	0.69
Indonesian (1)	4	0.03
Japanese (56)	73	0.52
Korean (65)	70	0.50
Pakistani (1)	1	0.01
Taiwanese (12)	14	0.10
Thai (8)	9	0.06
Vietnamese (6)	6	0.04
Other Asian, specified (1)	4	0.03
Other Asian, not specified (3)	3	0.02
Australian	30	0.21
Austrian	59	0.41
Belgian	28	0.20
British	157	1.10
Canadian	29	0.20
Celtic	3	0.02
Croatian	35	0.24
Czech	125	0.87
Czechoslovakian	46	0.32
Danish	54	0.38
Dutch	340	2.37
Eastern European	11	0.08
English	2,728	19.05
European	239	1.67
Finnish	48	0.34
French, except Basque	408	2.85
French Canadian	60	0.42
German	4,796	33.49
Greek	83	0.58
Hawaii Native/Pacific Islander:	9	0.06
Polynesian:	3	0.02
Native Hawaiian	3	0.02
Other Pac. Isl., specified	3	0.02
Other Pac. Isl., not spec. (1)	3	0.02
Hispanic or Latino:	138	0.98
Central American:	3	0.02
Costa Rican	2	0.01
Guatemalan	1	0.01
Cuban	8	0.06
Dominican Republic	1	0.01
Mexican	44	0.31
Puerto Rican	19	0.13
South American:	42	0.30
Argentinean	4	0.03
Bolivian	3	0.02
Chilean	7	0.05
Colombian	12	0.08
Ecuadorian	7	0.05
Paraguayan	1	0.01
Peruvian	2	0.01
Venezuelan	3	0.02
Other South American	3	0.02
Other Hispanic or Latino	21	0.15
Hungarian	240	1.68
Iranian	6	0.04
Irish	2,252	15.73
Italian	899	6.28
Latvian	23	0.16
Lithuanian	32	0.22
Macedonian	2	0.01
Northern European	6	0.04
Norwegian	170	1.19
Pennsylvania German	21	0.15
Polish	426	2.97
Portuguese	33	0.23
Romanian	26	0.18
Russian	177	1.24
Scandinavian	7	0.05
Scotch-Irish	443	3.09
Scottish	511	3.57
Serbian	19	0.13
Slavic	35	0.24
Slovak	55	0.38
Slovene	25	0.17
Swedish	161	1.12
Swiss	88	0.61
Ukrainian	84	0.59
United States or American	985	6.88
Welsh	448	3.13
White:	13,433	95.10
Not Hispanic (13,172)	13,318	94.29
Hispanic (101)	115	0.81
Yugoslavian	6	0.04

Xenia

Place Type: City
County: Greene
Population: 24,164

Ancestry/Race	Number	%
Acadian/Cajun	5	0.02
African American/Black:	3,555	14.71
Not Hispanic (3,224)	3,503	14.50
Hispanic (41)	52	0.22
African, sub-Saharan:	171	0.70
African	134	0.55
Nigerian	13	0.05
Sudanese	24	0.10
Am. Ind. or Alaska Nat., not spec.	82	0.34
American Indian tribes, specified:	167	0.69
Apache	3	0.01
Blackfeet (4)	15	0.06
Cherokee (30)	93	0.38
Cheyenne	2	0.01
Cree (1)	1	0.00
Creek (3)	6	0.02
Crow	1	0.00
Delaware	2	0.01
Iroquois (5)	9	0.04
Latin American Indians	2	0.01
Potawatomi (3)	5	0.02
Seminole (1)	1	0.00
Sioux	3	0.01
All other tribes (9)	24	0.10
American Indian tribes, not spec.	16	0.07
Arab:	48	0.20
Arab/Arabic	27	0.11
Lebanese	8	0.03
Syrian	5	0.02
Other Arab	8	0.03
Armenian	4	0.02
Asian:	121	0.50
Chinese, ex. Taiwanese (11)	15	0.06
Filipino (22)	37	0.15
Indian (4)	16	0.07
Japanese (5)	10	0.04
Korean (18)	27	0.11
Laotian (1)	1	0.00
Sri Lankan (1)	1	0.00
Thai (2)	3	0.01
Vietnamese (2)	3	0.01
Other Asian, not specified (4)	8	0.03
Austrian	7	0.03
Belgian	4	0.02
Brazilian	5	0.02
British	135	0.56
Canadian	52	0.21
Celtic	10	0.04
Czech	5	0.02
Czechoslovakian	10	0.04
Dutch	418	1.72
English	2,128	8.77
European	170	0.70
French, except Basque	376	1.55
French Canadian	113	0.47
German	4,087	16.84
Greek	50	0.21
Hawaii Native/Pacific Islander:	23	0.10
Micronesian: (5)	7	0.03
Guamanian/Chamorro (5)	7	0.03
Polynesian: (5)	11	0.05
Native Hawaiian (1)	4	0.02
Other Polynesian (4)	7	0.03
Other Pac. Isl., not spec. (2)	5	0.02
Hispanic or Latino:	264	1.09
Central American:	7	0.03
Panamanian	5	0.02
Salvadoran	2	0.01
Cuban	6	0.02
Mexican	125	0.52
Puerto Rican	26	0.11
South American:	15	0.06
Colombian	7	0.03
Ecuadorian	1	0.00
Peruvian	4	0.02
Venezuelan	3	0.01
Other Hispanic or Latino	85	0.35
Hungarian	50	0.21
Irish	2,523	10.40
Italian	302	1.24
Lithuanian	5	0.02
Norwegian	147	0.61
Pennsylvania German	11	0.05
Polish	135	0.56
Portuguese	15	0.06
Romanian	7	0.03
Scandinavian	20	0.08
Scotch-Irish	437	1.80
Scottish	348	1.43
Slovak	13	0.05
Slovene	5	0.02
Swedish	103	0.42
Swiss	39	0.16
Turkish	7	0.03
United States or American	3,460	14.26
Welsh	233	0.96
West Indian, excl. Hispanic:	38	0.16
Bermudan	7	0.03
Jamaican	18	0.07
Trinidadian and Tobagonian	7	0.03
West Indian	6	0.02
White:	20,546	85.03
Not Hispanic (20,008)	20,401	84.43
Hispanic (120)	145	0.60

Youngstown

Place Type: City
County: Mahoning
Population: 82,026

Ancestry/Race	Number	%
African American/Black:	37,301	45.47
Not Hispanic (35,440)	36,561	44.57
Hispanic (497)	740	0.90
African, sub-Saharan:	1,031	1.26
African	960	1.17
Nigerian	71	0.09
Alaska Native tribes, specified:	3	0.00
Eskimo (1)	3	0.00
Alaska Native tribes, not specified	1	0.00
Am. Ind. or Alaska Nat., not spec.	361	0.44
Albanian	11	0.01
American Indian tribes, specified:	484	0.59
Apache (2)	14	0.02
Blackfeet (5)	36	0.04
Cherokee (62)	295	0.36
Cheyenne	10	0.01
Chickasaw	2	0.00
Chippewa	11	0.01
Choctaw	9	0.01
Creek (1)	2	0.00
Crow	1	0.00
Delaware	2	0.00
Iroquois (4)	8	0.01
Latin American Indians (4)	15	0.02

Notes: 1. Figures in the "Number" column do not add up to the total population due to: a) Ancestry/Race overlap — e.g. persons can report being both White and Irish, b) persons of Hispanic origin can report being any race, c) persons reporting two ancestries are counted in both categories. 2. Numbers in parentheses indicate the number of persons reporting this ancestry/race alone, not in combination with any other ancestry/race. 3. Refer to the Explanation of Data in the front of the book for more detailed information.

Ancestry/Race	Number	%
Lumbee (1)	4	0.00
Navajo (1)	5	0.01
Osage (1)	1	0.00
Potawatomi	4	0.00
Seminole (3)	14	0.02
Sioux (3)	13	0.02
Tohono O'Odham	2	0.00
All other tribes (21)	36	0.04
American Indian tribes, not spec.	42	0.05
Arab:	525	0.64
Arab/Arabic	108	0.13
Jordanian	19	0.02
Lebanese	196	0.24
Moroccan	92	0.11
Palestinian	29	0.04
Other Arab	81	0.10
Armenian	5	0.01
Asian:	428	0.52
Bangladeshi (2)	2	0.00
Cambodian (5)	5	0.01
Chinese, ex. Taiwanese (17)	37	0.05
Filipino (42)	60	0.07
Indian (57)	87	0.11
Indonesian	2	0.00
Japanese (14)	33	0.04
Korean (32)	42	0.05
Malaysian (1)	2	0.00
Pakistani (3)	3	0.00
Sri Lankan	1	0.00
Taiwanese (8)	8	0.01
Thai (1)	2	0.00
Vietnamese (54)	63	0.08
Other Asian, specified (1)	10	0.01
Other Asian, not specified (27)	71	0.09
Australian	15	0.02
Austrian	82	0.10
Belgian	9	0.01
British	67	0.08
Bulgarian	54	0.07
Canadian	57	0.07
Croatian	1,013	1.23
Czech	150	0.18
Czechoslovakian	193	0.24
Danish	32	0.04
Dutch	603	0.74
Eastern European	12	0.01
English	3,495	4.26
European	80	0.10
Finnish	108	0.13
French, except Basque	638	0.78
French Canadian	97	0.12
German	8,479	10.34
German Russian	6	0.01
Greek	425	0.52
Hawaii Native/Pacific Islander:	63	0.08
Micronesian: (5)	8	0.01
Guamanian/Chamorro (3)	6	0.01
Other Micronesian (2)	2	0.00
Polynesian: (10)	19	0.02
Native Hawaiian (3)	9	0.01
Samoan (7)	10	0.01
Other Pac. Isl., specified	7	0.01
Other Pac. Isl., not spec. (14)	29	0.04
Hispanic or Latino:	4,282	5.22
Central American:	58	0.07
Costa Rican	2	0.00
Guatemalan	11	0.01
Honduran	4	0.00
Nicaraguan	1	0.00
Panamanian	20	0.02
Salvadoran	20	0.02
Cuban	68	0.08
Dominican Republic	19	0.02
Mexican	438	0.53
Puerto Rican	3,222	3.93
South American:	36	0.04
Argentinean	2	0.00
Chilean	4	0.00
Colombian	8	0.01
Ecuadorian	5	0.01
Paraguayan	1	0.00
Peruvian	15	0.02
Other South American	1	0.00
Other Hispanic or Latino	441	0.54
Hungarian	1,692	2.06
Irish	7,716	9.41
Israeli	24	0.03
Italian	9,210	11.23
Lithuanian	86	0.10
Luxemburger	5	0.01
Macedonian	10	0.01
Norwegian	93	0.11
Pennsylvania German	175	0.21
Polish	2,492	3.04
Portuguese	15	0.02
Romanian	350	0.43
Russian	476	0.58
Scandinavian	7	0.01
Scotch-Irish	654	0.80
Scottish	597	0.73
Serbian	253	0.31
Slavic	80	0.10
Slovak	4,345	5.30
Slovene	84	0.10
Swedish	303	0.37
Swiss	93	0.11
Ukrainian	1,111	1.35
United States or American	2,384	2.91
Welsh	983	1.20
West Indian, excl. Hispanic:	125	0.15
Bahamian	14	0.02
Barbadian	14	0.02
Jamaican	77	0.09
West Indian	20	0.02
White:	43,185	52.65
Not Hispanic (40,100)	41,277	50.32
Hispanic (1,637)	1,908	2.33
Yugoslavian	92	0.11

Zanesville

Place Type: City
County: Muskingum
Population: 25,586

Ancestry/Race	Number	%
African American/Black:	3,252	12.71
Not Hispanic (2,731)	3,227	12.61
Hispanic (22)	25	0.10
African, sub-Saharan:	110	0.43
African	110	0.43
Am. Ind. or Alaska Nat., not spec.	149	0.58
American Indian tribes, specified:	180	0.70
Apache (5)	11	0.04
Blackfeet (4)	16	0.06
Cherokee (26)	103	0.40
Cheyenne (1)	3	0.01
Chickasaw (1)	1	0.00
Chippewa	4	0.02
Choctaw	1	0.00
Creek	6	0.02
Delaware (5)	8	0.03
Iroquois	1	0.00
Latin American Indians	1	0.00
Lumbee (3)	3	0.01
Navajo	1	0.00
Osage	5	0.02
Sioux (1)	3	0.01
All other tribes (5)	13	0.05
American Indian tribes, not spec.	10	0.04
Arab:	93	0.36
Jordanian	10	0.04
Lebanese	83	0.32
Asian:	104	0.41
Chinese, ex. Taiwanese (10)	13	0.05
Filipino (10)	20	0.08
Indian (13)	23	0.09
Japanese (7)	14	0.05
Korean (1)	7	0.03
Laotian (1)	1	0.00
Vietnamese (11)	19	0.07
Other Asian, not specified (5)	7	0.03
Austrian	25	0.10
British	54	0.21
Celtic	13	0.05
Croatian	14	0.05
Czech	47	0.18
Czechoslovakian	7	0.03
Danish	31	0.12
Dutch	362	1.41
English	1,913	7.45
European	68	0.26
French, except Basque	315	1.23
French Canadian	33	0.13
German	3,750	14.60
Greek	87	0.34
Hawaii Native/Pacific Islander:	10	0.04
Micronesian: (2)	5	0.02
Guamanian/Chamorro (2)	4	0.02
Other Micronesian	1	0.00
Polynesian: (2)	2	0.01
Samoan (2)	2	0.01
Other Pac. Isl., not spec. (1)	3	0.01
Hispanic or Latino:	202	0.79
Central American:	1	0.00
Nicaraguan	1	0.00
Cuban	7	0.03
Mexican	68	0.27
Puerto Rican	45	0.18
South American:	7	0.03
Colombian	6	0.02
Uruguayan	1	0.00
Other Hispanic or Latino	74	0.29
Hungarian	75	0.29
Irish	2,665	10.37
Italian	589	2.29
Lithuanian	34	0.13
Norwegian	188	0.73
Pennsylvania German	6	0.02
Polish	201	0.78
Portuguese	24	0.09
Romanian	48	0.19
Russian	23	0.09
Scotch-Irish	354	1.38
Scottish	314	1.22
Serbian	12	0.05
Slovak	39	0.15
Slovene	16	0.06
Swedish	80	0.31
Swiss	57	0.22
Ukrainian	13	0.05
United States or American	3,884	15.12
Welsh	233	0.91
White:	22,507	87.97
Not Hispanic (21,740)	22,352	87.36
Hispanic (130)	155	0.61
Yugoslavian	10	0.04

Ada

Place Type: City
County: Pontotoc
Population: 15,691

Ancestry/Race	Number	%
African American/Black:	765	4.88
Not Hispanic (548)	755	4.81
Hispanic (7)	10	0.06
African, sub-Saharan:	34	0.22
African	34	0.22
Alaska Native tribes, specified:	3	0.02
Eskimo (2)	2	0.01
Tlingit-Haida	1	0.01
Alaska Native tribes, not specified	1	0.01
Am. Ind. or Alaska Nat., not spec.	284	1.81
American Indian tribes, specified:	3,029	19.30
Apache (7)	8	0.05
Blackfeet (1)	3	0.02
Cherokee (161)	341	2.17
Cheyenne (8)	10	0.06

Notes: 1. Figures in the "Number" column do not add up to the total population due to: a) Ancestry/Race overlap — e.g. persons can report being both White and Irish, b) persons of Hispanic origin can report being any race, c) persons reporting two ancestries are counted in both categories. 2. Numbers in parentheses indicate the number of persons reporting this ancestry/race alone, not in combination with any other ancestry/race. 3. Refer to the Explanation of Data in the front of the book for more detailed information.

Ancestry/Race	Number	%
Chickasaw (865)	1,189	7.58
Chippewa (2)	4	0.03
Choctaw (475)	837	5.33
Comanche (5)	7	0.04
Cree (4)	4	0.03
Creek (87)	182	1.16
Delaware (4)	4	0.03
Iroquois (1)	7	0.04
Kiowa (17)	22	0.14
Latin American Indians (3)	11	0.07
Navajo (19)	25	0.16
Osage (1)	8	0.05
Pima	1	0.01
Potawatomi (45)	53	0.34
Pueblo (1)	1	0.01
Seminole (124)	223	1.42
Shoshone (3)	4	0.03
Sioux (23)	25	0.16
Tohono O'Odham	1	0.01
Ute	1	0.01
All other tribes (36)	58	0.37
American Indian tribes, not spec.	94	0.60
Arab:	36	0.23
Arab/Arabic	17	0.11
Lebanese	8	0.05
Syrian	11	0.07
Asian:	163	1.04
Bangladeshi (1)	1	0.01
Chinese, ex. Taiwanese (25)	27	0.17
Filipino (27)	36	0.23
Indian (26)	30	0.19
Indonesian	1	0.01
Japanese (15)	16	0.10
Korean (22)	27	0.17
Laotian (1)	1	0.01
Pakistani (4)	4	0.03
Thai (1)	1	0.01
Vietnamese (4)	6	0.04
Other Asian, specified (2)	2	0.01
Other Asian, not specified (2)	11	0.07
Australian	9	0.06
Austrian	5	0.03
Basque	5	0.03
Belgian	5	0.03
British	17	0.11
Canadian	12	0.08
Croatian	7	0.04
Czech	10	0.06
Czechoslovakian	8	0.05
Danish	13	0.08
Dutch	212	1.36
English	1,109	7.09
European	119	0.76
French, except Basque	357	2.28
French Canadian	17	0.11
German	1,309	8.37
Greek	22	0.14
Hawaii Native/Pacific Islander:	9	0.06
Polynesian: (2)	2	0.01
Native Hawaiian (1)	1	0.01
Samoan (1)	1	0.01
Other Pac. Isl., not spec.	7	0.04
Hispanic or Latino:	453	2.89
Central American:	5	0.03
Honduran	1	0.01
Nicaraguan	1	0.01
Other Central American	3	0.02
Cuban	8	0.05
Mexican	338	2.15
Puerto Rican	17	0.11
South American:	2	0.01
Bolivian	1	0.01
Ecuadorian	1	0.01
Other Hispanic or Latino	83	0.53
Hungarian	25	0.16
Irish	1,551	9.91
Italian	171	1.09
Norwegian	75	0.48
Pennsylvania German	8	0.05
Polish	62	0.40
Portuguese	5	0.03
Russian	26	0.17
Scotch-Irish	160	1.02
Scottish	211	1.35
Swedish	55	0.35
Swiss	13	0.08
United States or American	1,955	12.50
Welsh	63	0.40
West Indian, excl. Hispanic:	214	1.37
Dutch West Indian	214	1.37
White:	12,356	78.75
Not Hispanic (11,379)	12,111	77.18
Hispanic (203)	245	1.56
Yugoslavian	5	0.03

Altus

Place Type: City
County: Jackson
Population: 21,447

Ancestry/Race	Number	%
African American/Black:	2,445	11.40
Not Hispanic (2,194)	2,342	10.92
Hispanic (39)	103	0.48
African, sub-Saharan:	30	0.14
African	30	0.14
Alaska Native tribes, specified:	1	0.00
Alaska Athabascan (1)	1	0.00
Am. Ind. or Alaska Nat., not spec.	104	0.48
American Indian tribes, specified:	471	2.20
Apache (5)	17	0.08
Blackfeet	5	0.02
Cherokee (60)	159	0.74
Cheyenne (1)	1	0.00
Chickasaw (16)	26	0.12
Chippewa (2)	2	0.01
Choctaw (53)	87	0.41
Comanche (10)	20	0.09
Cree (1)	1	0.00
Creek (16)	37	0.17
Crow	2	0.01
Delaware	1	0.00
Iroquois (4)	8	0.04
Kiowa (11)	21	0.10
Latin American Indians (5)	11	0.05
Lumbee	1	0.00
Navajo (6)	8	0.04
Osage (7)	7	0.03
Potawatomi	3	0.01
Pueblo (1)	2	0.01
Seminole (5)	8	0.04
Sioux (1)	3	0.01
Yaqui	1	0.00
All other tribes (30)	40	0.19
American Indian tribes, not spec.	19	0.09
Arab:	74	0.34
Arab/Arabic	6	0.03
Egyptian	32	0.15
Lebanese	27	0.13
Other Arab	9	0.04
Armenian	8	0.04
Asian:	440	2.05
Cambodian (4)	4	0.02
Chinese, ex. Taiwanese (14)	31	0.14
Filipino (105)	143	0.67
Indian (22)	25	0.12
Japanese (36)	60	0.28
Korean (34)	53	0.25
Laotian (10)	19	0.09
Pakistani (9)	15	0.07
Sri Lankan (1)	1	0.00
Taiwanese (3)	8	0.04
Thai (32)	42	0.20
Vietnamese (7)	12	0.06
Other Asian, specified (2)	2	0.01
Other Asian, not specified (12)	25	0.12
Austrian	52	0.24
Belgian	6	0.03
British	119	0.55
Bulgarian	7	0.03
Canadian	67	0.31
Czech	40	0.19
Czechoslovakian	32	0.15
Danish	98	0.46
Dutch	287	1.34
English	1,935	9.00
European	84	0.39
Finnish	10	0.05
French, except Basque	441	2.05
French Canadian	125	0.58
German	2,700	12.56
Greek	41	0.19
Hawaii Native/Pacific Islander:	82	0.38
Micronesian: (25)	45	0.21
Guamanian/Chamorro (19)	34	0.16
Other Micronesian (6)	11	0.05
Polynesian: (8)	24	0.11
Native Hawaiian (2)	17	0.08
Samoan (6)	7	0.03
Other Pac. Isl., not spec. (9)	13	0.06
Hispanic or Latino:	3,699	17.25
Central American:	42	0.20
Guatemalan	1	0.00
Honduran	2	0.01
Nicaraguan	1	0.00
Panamanian	35	0.16
Salvadoran	3	0.01
Cuban	14	0.07
Dominican Republic	3	0.01
Mexican	2,706	12.62
Puerto Rican	102	0.48
South American:	23	0.11
Bolivian	1	0.00
Colombian	8	0.04
Ecuadorian	4	0.02
Peruvian	5	0.02
Venezuelan	4	0.02
Other South American	1	0.00
Other Hispanic or Latino	809	3.77
Hungarian	20	0.09
Irish	2,141	9.96
Italian	423	1.97
Lithuanian	10	0.05
Northern European	6	0.03
Norwegian	133	0.62
Pennsylvania German	5	0.02
Polish	213	0.99
Portuguese	32	0.15
Romanian	12	0.06
Russian	33	0.15
Scandinavian	43	0.20
Scotch-Irish	336	1.56
Scottish	311	1.45
Slovak	4	0.02
Slovene	5	0.02
Swedish	142	0.66
Swiss	38	0.18
Turkish	28	0.13
Ukrainian	8	0.04
United States or American	2,088	9.72
Welsh	66	0.31
West Indian, excl. Hispanic:	34	0.16
Dutch West Indian	22	0.10
Jamaican	9	0.04
Other West Indian	3	0.01
White:	16,180	75.44
Not Hispanic (14,461)	14,828	69.14
Hispanic (1,113)	1,352	6.30
Yugoslavian	4	0.02

Ardmore

Place Type: City
County: Carter
Population: 23,711

Ancestry/Race	Number	%
Acadian/Cajun	19	0.08
African American/Black:	2,940	12.40

Notes: 1. Figures in the "Number" column do not add up to the total population due to: a) Ancestry/Race overlap — e.g. persons can report being both White and Irish, b) persons of Hispanic origin can report being any race, c) persons reporting two ancestries are counted in both categories. 2. Numbers in parentheses indicate the number of persons reporting this ancestry/race alone, not in combination with any other ancestry/race. 3. Refer to the Explanation of Data in the front of the book for more detailed information.

Not Hispanic (2,641)	2,897	12.22
Hispanic (31)	43	0.18
African, sub-Saharan:	94	0.40
African	83	0.35
Liberian	11	0.05
Alaska Native tribes, specified:	6	0.03
Aleut (3)	5	0.02
Eskimo	1	0.00
Alaska Native tribes, not specified	6	0.03
Am. Ind. or Alaska Nat., not spec.	240	1.01
American Indian tribes, specified:	2,887	12.18
Apache (8)	16	0.07
Blackfeet (3)	5	0.02
Cherokee (136)	297	1.25
Cheyenne (5)	13	0.05
Chickasaw (521)	978	4.12
Chippewa (2)	2	0.01
Choctaw (849)	1,294	5.46
Comanche (7)	8	0.03
Creek (31)	60	0.25
Crow (1)	1	0.00
Delaware (4)	5	0.02
Iroquois (2)	3	0.01
Kiowa (7)	10	0.04
Latin American Indians (1)	1	0.00
Navajo (7)	8	0.03
Osage (11)	20	0.08
Potawatomi (19)	22	0.09
Pueblo (1)	1	0.00
Puget Sound Salish	1	0.00
Seminole (34)	55	0.23
Shoshone (2)	2	0.01
Sioux (3)	9	0.04
All other tribes (52)	76	0.32
American Indian tribes, not spec.	58	0.24
Arab:	33	0.14
Lebanese	33	0.14
Asian:	282	1.19
Bangladcshi (4)	4	0.02
Chinese, ex. Taiwanese (65)	66	0.28
Filipino (11)	19	0.08
Indian (48)	54	0.23
Japanese (9)	13	0.05
Korean (20)	27	0.11
Pakistani (8)	8	0.03
Taiwanese (4)	6	0.03
Thai (8)	13	0.05
Vietnamese (52)	55	0.23
Other Asian, not specified (5)	17	0.07
Basque	4	0.02
Belgian	9	0.04
British	104	0.44
Canadian	42	0.18
Czech	26	0.11
Czechoslovakian	11	0.05
Danish	68	0.29
Dutch	437	1.86
English	2,168	9.22
European	140	0.60
Finnish	11	0.05
French, except Basque	446	1.90
French Canadian	60	0.26
German	1,996	8.49
Hawaii Native/Pacific Islander:	14	0.06
Micronesian: (3)	5	0.02
Guamanian/Chamorro (2)	4	0.02
Other Micronesian (1)	1	0.00
Polynesian: (1)	6	0.03
Native Hawaiian (1)	6	0.03
Other Pac. Isl., not spec.	3	0.01
Hispanic or Latino:	877	3.70
Central American:	20	0.08
Costa Rican	1	0.00
Honduran	4	0.02
Nicaraguan	6	0.03
Panamanian	2	0.01
Salvadoran	6	0.03
Other Central American	1	0.00
Cuban	9	0.04
Dominican Republic	5	0.02
Mexican	646	2.72
Puerto Rican	18	0.08
South American:	2	0.01
Venezuelan	2	0.01
Other Hispanic or Latino	177	0.75
Hungarian	7	0.03
Icelander	16	0.07
Irish	2,264	9.63
Italian	256	1.09
Northern European	7	0.03
Norwegian	118	0.50
Pennsylvania German	7	0.03
Polish	76	0.32
Portuguese	15	0.06
Russian	18	0.08
Scotch-Irish	349	1.48
Scottish	269	1.14
Serbian	8	0.03
Swedish	88	0.37
Swiss	61	0.26
United States or American	2,547	10.83
Welsh	61	0.26
West Indian, excl. Hispanic:	233	0.99
Dutch West Indian	227	0.97
Jamaican	6	0.03
White:	18,151	76.55
Not Hispanic (16,986)	17,753	74.87
Hispanic (327)	398	1.68

Bartlesville

Place Type: City
County: Washington
Population: 34,748

Ancestry/Race	Number	%
Acadian/Cajun	9	0.03
African American/Black:	1,304	3.75
Not Hispanic (1,103)	1,271	3.66
Hispanic (9)	33	0.09
African, sub-Saharan:	113	0.33
African	104	0.30
South African	9	0.03
Alaska Native tribes, specified:	2	0.01
Alaska Athabascan (1)	1	0.00
Aleut (1)	1	0.00
Alaska Native tribes, not specified	8	0.02
Am. Ind. or Alaska Nat., not spec.	374	1.08
American Indian tribes, specified:	3,822	11.00
Apache (10)	33	0.09
Blackfeet (4)	41	0.12
Cherokee (1,264)	2,313	6.66
Cheyenne (6)	11	0.03
Chickasaw (47)	67	0.19
Chippewa (2)	7	0.02
Choctaw (89)	169	0.49
Comanche (3)	15	0.04
Creek (75)	114	0.33
Delaware (273)	396	1.14
Iroquois (22)	38	0.11
Kiowa (7)	15	0.04
Latin American Indians (8)	10	0.03
Menominee (2)	2	0.01
Navajo (7)	12	0.03
Osage (194)	342	0.98
Ottawa (1)	1	0.00
Pima	3	0.01
Potawatomi (12)	34	0.10
Pueblo (4)	5	0.01
Seminole (14)	24	0.07
Shoshone	1	0.00
Sioux (21)	32	0.09
All other tribes (79)	137	0.39
American Indian tribes, not spec.	95	0.27
Arab:	93	0.27
Arab/Arabic	10	0.03
Iraqi	24	0.07
Lebanese	59	0.17
Asian:	441	1.27
Chinese, ex. Taiwanese (115)	128	0.37
Filipino (22)	49	0.14
Indian (80)	87	0.25
Indonesian	3	0.01
Japanese (27)	47	0.14
Korean (36)	42	0.12
Laotian	2	0.01
Malaysian (1)	1	0.00
Pakistani (5)	5	0.01
Sri Lankan (1)	1	0.00
Taiwanese (10)	11	0.03
Thai (1)	5	0.01
Vietnamese (26)	36	0.10
Other Asian, specified (2)	11	0.03
Other Asian, not specified (4)	13	0.04
Austrian	68	0.20
Belgian	8	0.02
Brazilian	11	0.03
British	131	0.38
Canadian	32	0.09
Croatian	37	0.11
Czech	49	0.14
Czechoslovakian	19	0.05
Danish	90	0.26
Dutch	820	2.36
English	4,534	13.05
European	490	1.41
Finnish	7	0.02
French, except Basque	631	1.82
French Canadian	57	0.16
German	5,965	17.17
Greek	59	0.17
Hawaii Native/Pacific Islander:	19	0.05
Micronesian: (1)	1	0.00
Guamanian/Chamorro (1)	1	0.00
Polynesian: (4)	4	0.01
Native Hawaiian (2)	2	0.01
Tongan (2)	2	0.01
Other Pac. Isl., specified	9	0.03
Other Pac. Isl., not spec. (1)	5	0.01
Hispanic or Latino:	1,049	3.02
Central American:	34	0.10
Costa Rican	7	0.02
Guatemalan	2	0.01
Honduran	9	0.03
Nicaraguan	1	0.00
Panamanian	2	0.01
Salvadoran	13	0.04
Cuban	14	0.04
Mexican	732	2.11
Puerto Rican	25	0.07
South American:	54	0.16
Argentinean	13	0.04
Bolivian	2	0.01
Ecuadorian	11	0.03
Peruvian	6	0.02
Venezuelan	22	0.06
Other Hispanic or Latino	190	0.55
Hungarian	48	0.14
Irish	4,001	11.52
Italian	554	1.60
Lithuanian	9	0.03
Northern European	23	0.07
Norwegian	217	0.62
Polish	484	1.39
Portuguese	27	0.08
Romanian	4	0.01
Russian	36	0.10
Scandinavian	75	0.22
Scotch-Irish	905	2.61
Scottish	786	2.26
Slovak	11	0.03
Swedish	588	1.69
Swiss	134	0.39
Ukrainian	10	0.03
United States or American	3,811	10.97
Welsh	228	0.66
West Indian, excl. Hispanic:	84	0.24
British West Indian	5	0.01
Dutch West Indian	79	0.23
White:	30,370	87.40

Notes: 1. Figures in the "Number" column do not add up to the total population due to: a) Ancestry/Race overlap — e.g. persons can report being both White and Irish, b) persons of Hispanic origin can report being any race, c) persons reporting two ancestries are counted in both categories. 2. Numbers in parentheses indicate the number of persons reporting this ancestry/race alone, not in combination with any other ancestry/race. 3. Refer to the Explanation of Data in the front of the book for more detailed information.

Not Hispanic (28,003)	29,733	85.57
Hispanic (521)	637	1.83

Bethany

Place Type: City
County: Oklahoma
Population: 20,307

Ancestry/Race	Number	%
African American/Black:	1,029	5.07
Not Hispanic (872)	1,005	4.95
Hispanic (14)	24	0.12
African, sub-Saharan:	187	0.91
African	153	0.75
Nigerian	24	0.12
Other sub-Saharan African	10	0.05
Am. Ind. or Alaska Nat., not spec.	151	0.74
American Indian tribes, specified:	892	4.39
Apache (6)	14	0.07
Blackfeet	4	0.02
Cherokee (117)	264	1.30
Cheyenne (10)	16	0.08
Chickasaw (26)	67	0.33
Chippewa	4	0.02
Choctaw (101)	186	0.92
Comanche (21)	27	0.13
Cree (1)	1	0.00
Creek (45)	73	0.36
Delaware (6)	7	0.03
Iroquois (3)	5	0.02
Kiowa (12)	23	0.11
Latin American Indians (2)	3	0.01
Navajo (3)	4	0.02
Osage (12)	16	0.08
Ottawa (2)	4	0.02
Paiute (3)	3	0.01
Potawatomi (19)	26	0.13
Pueblo (2)	2	0.01
Seminole (13)	25	0.12
Sioux (10)	16	0.08
All other tribes (74)	102	0.50
American Indian tribes, not spec.	48	0.24
Arab:	26	0.13
Lebanese	26	0.13
Asian:	356	1.75
Bangladeshi (1)	1	0.00
Cambodian (2)	2	0.01
Chinese, ex. Taiwanese (24)	34	0.17
Filipino (25)	35	0.17
Indian (66)	76	0.37
Indonesian (4)	9	0.04
Japanese (8)	27	0.13
Korean (13)	16	0.08
Laotian (1)	1	0.00
Pakistani (1)	1	0.00
Thai (6)	6	0.03
Vietnamese (121)	132	0.65
Other Asian, not specified (3)	16	0.08
Austrian	18	0.09
British	98	0.48
Canadian	12	0.06
Croatian	38	0.19
Czech	104	0.51
Czechoslovakian	107	0.52
Danish	71	0.35
Dutch	343	1.68
Eastern European	19	0.09
English	2,407	11.76
European	238	1.16
Finnish	5	0.02
French, except Basque	551	2.69
French Canadian	105	0.51
German	3,024	14.78
German Russian	6	0.03
Greek	12	0.06
Hawaii Native/Pacific Islander:	25	0.12
Micronesian:	4	0.02
Guamanian/Chamorro	4	0.02
Polynesian: (11)	13	0.06
Native Hawaiian (5)	7	0.03
Samoan (6)	6	0.03
Other Pac. Isl., not spec.	8	0.04
Hispanic or Latino:	1,178	5.80
Central American:	30	0.15
Costa Rican	8	0.04
Guatemalan	10	0.05
Honduran	2	0.01
Panamanian	7	0.03
Salvadoran	3	0.01
Cuban	18	0.09
Mexican	903	4.45
Puerto Rican	44	0.22
South American:	13	0.06
Argentinean	1	0.00
Colombian	1	0.00
Ecuadorian	7	0.03
Peruvian	3	0.01
Venezuelan	1	0.00
Other Hispanic or Latino	170	0.84
Iranian	20	0.10
Irish	2,359	11.53
Italian	252	1.23
Luxemburger	11	0.05
Northern European	14	0.07
Norwegian	251	1.23
Polish	143	0.70
Portuguese	5	0.02
Romanian	11	0.05
Russian	4	0.02
Scandinavian	25	0.12
Scotch-Irish	514	2.51
Scottish	488	2.39
Serbian	11	0.05
Swedish	325	1.59
Swiss	25	0.12
Ukrainian	6	0.03
United States or American	2,245	10.97
Welsh	143	0.70
West Indian, excl. Hispanic:	58	0.28
Dutch West Indian	51	0.25
Jamaican	7	0.03
White:	18,022	88.75
Not Hispanic (16,822)	17,333	85.35
Hispanic (600)	689	3.39
Yugoslavian	13	0.06

Bixby

Place Type: City
County: Tulsa
Population: 13,336

Ancestry/Race	Number	%
African American/Black:	148	1.11
Not Hispanic (123)	141	1.06
Hispanic (2)	7	0.05
Am. Ind. or Alaska Nat., not spec.	107	0.80
American Indian tribes, specified:	1,134	8.50
Apache (1)	6	0.04
Blackfeet	3	0.02
Cherokee (309)	524	3.93
Chickasaw (7)	12	0.09
Chippewa	2	0.01
Choctaw (78)	148	1.11
Comanche (9)	9	0.07
Creek (186)	289	2.17
Delaware (1)	2	0.01
Iroquois (10)	13	0.10
Kiowa (5)	8	0.06
Latin American Indians (2)	5	0.04
Navajo (1)	1	0.01
Osage (17)	34	0.25
Ottawa	2	0.01
Potawatomi (6)	8	0.06
Pueblo (1)	1	0.01
Seminole (13)	14	0.10
Shoshone	1	0.01
Sioux (3)	7	0.05
All other tribes (28)	45	0.34
American Indian tribes, not spec.	28	0.21
Arab:	31	0.24
Lebanese	25	0.19
Moroccan	6	0.05
Asian:	94	0.70
Chinese, ex. Taiwanese (13)	16	0.12
Filipino (8)	13	0.10
Indian (7)	14	0.10
Japanese (13)	15	0.11
Korean (10)	11	0.08
Pakistani (5)	5	0.04
Sri Lankan (1)	3	0.02
Vietnamese (8)	9	0.07
Other Asian, specified	4	0.03
Other Asian, not specified	4	0.03
Austrian	7	0.05
Belgian	67	0.51
British	73	0.55
Canadian	16	0.12
Czech	76	0.58
Czechoslovakian	76	0.58
Danish	40	0.30
Dutch	315	2.39
English	1,538	11.67
European	108	0.82
Finnish	11	0.08
French, except Basque	508	3.85
French Canadian	54	0.41
German	2,254	17.10
Hawaii Native/Pacific Islander:	14	0.10
Polynesian: (2)	10	0.07
Native Hawaiian (2)	9	0.07
Other Polynesian	1	0.01
Other Pac. Isl., specified	4	0.03
Hispanic or Latino:	530	3.97
Central American:	6	0.04
Salvadoran	6	0.04
Cuban	12	0.09
Dominican Republic	2	0.01
Mexican	374	2.80
Puerto Rican	33	0.25
South American:	8	0.06
Argentinean	1	0.01
Chilean	1	0.01
Colombian	5	0.04
Venezuelan	1	0.01
Other Hispanic or Latino	95	0.71
Hungarian	38	0.29
Irish	1,802	13.67
Italian	412	3.13
Norwegian	193	1.46
Polish	142	1.08
Romanian	14	0.11
Russian	13	0.10
Scandinavian	17	0.13
Scotch-Irish	282	2.14
Scottish	266	2.02
Slovene	7	0.05
Swedish	132	1.00
Swiss	33	0.25
Ukrainian	11	0.08
United States or American	1,016	7.71
Welsh	144	1.09
West Indian, excl. Hispanic:	27	0.20
Dutch West Indian	27	0.20
White:	12,104	90.76
Not Hispanic (11,377)	11,849	88.85
Hispanic (213)	255	1.91

Broken Arrow

Place Type: City
County: Tulsa
Population: 74,859

Ancestry/Race	Number	%
African American/Black:	3,153	4.21
Not Hispanic (2,728)	3,051	4.08
Hispanic (65)	102	0.14
African, sub-Saharan:	298	0.40

Notes: 1. Figures in the "Number" column do not add up to the total population due to: a) Ancestry/Race overlap — e.g. persons can report being both White and Irish, b) persons of Hispanic origin can report being any race, c) persons reporting two ancestries are counted in both categories. 2. Numbers in parentheses indicate the number of persons reporting this ancestry/race alone, not in combination with any other ancestry/race. 3. Refer to the Explanation of Data in the front of the book for more detailed information.

Ancestry/Race	Number	%
African	140	0.19
Ethiopian	77	0.10
Ghanian	13	0.02
Nigerian	12	0.02
South African	35	0.05
Other sub-Saharan African	21	0.03
Alaska Native tribes, specified:	13	0.02
Aleut (6)	6	0.01
Eskimo (3)	3	0.00
Tlingit-Haida (4)	4	0.01
Am. Ind. or Alaska Nat., not spec.	450	0.60
Albanian	9	0.01
Alsatian	6	0.01
American Indian tribes, specified:	4,563	6.10
Apache (8)	15	0.02
Blackfeet (3)	15	0.02
Cherokee (1,399)	2,538	3.39
Cheyenne (14)	14	0.02
Chickasaw (67)	122	0.16
Chippewa (12)	23	0.03
Choctaw (270)	441	0.59
Comanche (21)	29	0.04
Cree	1	0.00
Creek (476)	671	0.90
Crow (1)	5	0.01
Delaware (36)	61	0.08
Houma (1)	1	0.00
Iroquois (25)	50	0.07
Kiowa (10)	15	0.02
Latin American Indians (12)	20	0.03
Lumbee	2	0.00
Menominee (2)	2	0.00
Navajo (6)	15	0.02
Osage (55)	119	0.16
Ottawa (11)	13	0.02
Paiute (2)	4	0.01
Pima (1)	2	0.00
Potawatomi (28)	56	0.07
Pueblo (5)	11	0.01
Seminole (29)	40	0.05
Shoshone (2)	7	0.01
Sioux (17)	36	0.05
Tohono O'Odham (1)	2	0.00
Yaqui (1)	2	0.00
All other tribes (142)	231	0.31
American Indian tribes, not spec.	47	0.06
Arab:	243	0.32
Arab/Arabic	47	0.06
Egyptian	17	0.02
Jordanian	9	0.01
Lebanese	97	0.13
Palestinian	9	0.01
Syrian	20	0.03
Other Arab	44	0.06
Armenian	57	0.08
Asian:	1,796	2.40
Bangladeshi (6)	6	0.01
Cambodian (35)	40	0.05
Chinese, ex. Taiwanese (228)	276	0.37
Filipino (103)	168	0.22
Hmong (31)	31	0.04
Indian (329)	372	0.50
Indonesian (1)	7	0.01
Japanese (47)	114	0.15
Korean (149)	219	0.29
Laotian (13)	13	0.02
Malaysian (2)	2	0.00
Pakistani (60)	77	0.10
Taiwanese (1)	3	0.00
Thai (16)	28	0.04
Vietnamese (326)	354	0.47
Other Asian, specified (12)	14	0.02
Other Asian, not specified (37)	72	0.10
Austrian	121	0.16
Belgian	79	0.11
Brazilian	40	0.05
British	383	0.51
Bulgarian	14	0.02
Canadian	168	0.22
Celtic	6	0.01
Croatian	32	0.04
Czech	204	0.27
Czechoslovakian	118	0.16
Danish	195	0.26
Dutch	1,864	2.49
Eastern European	8	0.01
English	8,671	11.57
European	667	0.89
Finnish	180	0.24
French, except Basque	2,015	2.69
French Canadian	291	0.39
German	13,719	18.30
Greek	169	0.23
Hawaii Native/Pacific Islander:	87	0.12
Micronesian: (4)	14	0.02
Guamanian/Chamorro (3)	13	0.02
Other Micronesian (1)	1	0.00
Polynesian: (34)	58	0.08
Native Hawaiian (15)	31	0.04
Samoan (18)	26	0.03
Other Polynesian (1)	1	0.00
Other Pac. Isl., specified	1	0.00
Other Pac. Isl., not spec.	14	0.02
Hispanic or Latino:	2,664	3.56
Central American:	93	0.12
Costa Rican	18	0.02
Guatemalan	15	0.02
Honduran	9	0.01
Nicaraguan	4	0.01
Panamanian	11	0.01
Salvadoran	27	0.04
Other Central American	9	0.01
Cuban	92	0.12
Dominican Republic	10	0.01
Mexican	1,547	2.07
Puerto Rican	254	0.34
South American:	129	0.17
Argentinean	10	0.01
Bolivian	4	0.01
Chilean	10	0.01
Colombian	22	0.03
Ecuadorian	11	0.01
Peruvian	31	0.04
Uruguayan	2	0.00
Venezuelan	26	0.03
Other South American	13	0.02
Other Hispanic or Latino	539	0.72
Hungarian	270	0.36
Iranian	49	0.07
Irish	9,256	12.35
Israeli	6	0.01
Italian	1,813	2.42
Latvian	15	0.02
Lithuanian	90	0.12
Maltese	10	0.01
Northern European	8	0.01
Norwegian	1,225	1.63
Pennsylvania German	11	0.01
Polish	1,193	1.59
Portuguese	104	0.14
Romanian	17	0.02
Russian	271	0.36
Scandinavian	37	0.05
Scotch-Irish	1,779	2.37
Scottish	1,426	1.90
Serbian	29	0.04
Slavic	16	0.02
Slovak	34	0.05
Slovene	46	0.06
Swedish	859	1.15
Swiss	207	0.28
Ukrainian	80	0.11
United States or American	7,742	10.33
Welsh	469	0.63
West Indian, excl. Hispanic:	375	0.50
Bahamian	10	0.01
Belizean	18	0.02
Dutch West Indian	196	0.26
Haitian	18	0.02
Jamaican	76	0.10
Trinidadian and Tobagonian	37	0.05
West Indian	20	0.03
White:	66,501	88.84
Not Hispanic (62,485)	64,868	86.65
Hispanic (1,401)	1,633	2.18
Yugoslavian	71	0.09

Chickasha

Place Type: City
County: Grady
Population: 15,850

Ancestry/Race	Number	%
African American/Black:	1,448	9.14
Not Hispanic (1,329)	1,432	9.03
Hispanic (10)	16	0.10
African, sub-Saharan:	9	0.06
African	9	0.06
Alaska Native tribes, specified:	8	0.05
Aleut (3)	3	0.02
Eskimo (1)	1	0.01
Tlingit-Haida	4	0.03
Alaska Native tribes, not specified	2	0.01
Am. Ind. or Alaska Nat., not spec.	151	0.95
American Indian tribes, specified:	972	6.13
Apache (22)	27	0.17
Cherokee (151)	262	1.65
Cheyenne (6)	8	0.05
Chickasaw (55)	76	0.48
Chippewa (1)	2	0.01
Choctaw (148)	236	1.49
Comanche (36)	60	0.38
Creek (30)	49	0.31
Delaware (15)	18	0.11
Iroquois (1)	2	0.01
Kiowa (62)	90	0.57
Latin American Indians (5)	6	0.04
Navajo (3)	7	0.04
Osage (3)	8	0.05
Ottawa (1)	1	0.01
Potawatomi (16)	17	0.11
Pueblo (2)	2	0.01
Seminole (6)	9	0.06
Sioux (5)	8	0.05
Ute (1)	1	0.01
Yuman (1)	2	0.01
All other tribes (58)	81	0.51
American Indian tribes, not spec.	17	0.11
Arab:	16	0.10
Lebanese	8	0.05
Other Arab	8	0.05
Asian:	155	0.98
Chinese, ex. Taiwanese (22)	27	0.17
Filipino (9)	15	0.09
Indian (37)	44	0.28
Japanese (10)	18	0.11
Korean (16)	16	0.10
Laotian (4)	5	0.03
Malaysian	2	0.01
Pakistani (2)	2	0.01
Taiwanese (2)	2	0.01
Thai (2)	3	0.02
Vietnamese (5)	9	0.06
Other Asian, specified	1	0.01
Other Asian, not specified (4)	11	0.07
Austrian	6	0.04
Belgian	10	0.06
Brazilian	22	0.14
British	88	0.55
Canadian	6	0.04
Czech	38	0.24
Czechoslovakian	9	0.06
Dutch	292	1.84
English	1,182	7.44
European	33	0.21
Finnish	8	0.05
French, except Basque	229	1.44
French Canadian	19	0.12
German	1,559	9.82

Notes: 1. Figures in the "Number" column do not add up to the total population due to: a) Ancestry/Race overlap — e.g. persons can report being both White and Irish, b) persons of Hispanic origin can report being any race, c) persons reporting two ancestries are counted in both categories. 2. Numbers in parentheses indicate the number of persons reporting this ancestry/race alone, not in combination with any other ancestry/race. 3. Refer to the Explanation of Data in the front of the book for more detailed information.

Ancestry/Race	Number	%
Greek	18	0.11
Hawaii Native/Pacific Islander:	11	0.07
Micronesian:	1	0.01
Guamanian/Chamorro	1	0.01
Polynesian: (1)	8	0.05
Native Hawaiian (1)	8	0.05
Other Pac. Isl., specified	1	0.01
Other Pac. Isl., not spec.	1	0.01
Hispanic or Latino:	596	3.76
Cuban	4	0.03
Mexican	406	2.56
Puerto Rican	14	0.09
South American:	3	0.02
Colombian	2	0.01
Venezuelan	1	0.01
Other Hispanic or Latino	169	1.07
Iranian	24	0.15
Irish	1,461	9.20
Italian	307	1.93
Lithuanian	7	0.04
Norwegian	93	0.59
Polish	32	0.20
Portuguese	19	0.12
Russian	19	0.12
Scotch-Irish	216	1.36
Scottish	169	1.06
Swedish	119	0.75
Swiss	6	0.04
Ukrainian	8	0.05
United States or American	2,677	16.86
Welsh	108	0.68
West Indian, excl. Hispanic:	67	0.42
Dutch West Indian	56	0.35
Haitian	9	0.06
Jamaican	2	0.01
White:	13,348	84.21
Not Hispanic (12,640)	13,051	82.34
Hispanic (230)	297	1.87

Claremore

Place Type: City
County: Rogers
Population: 15,873

Ancestry/Race	Number	%
African American/Black:	387	2.44
Not Hispanic (313)	378	2.38
Hispanic (3)	9	0.06
Am. Ind. or Alaska Nat., not spec.	277	1.75
American Indian tribes, specified:	2,894	18.23
Apache (12)	20	0.13
Blackfeet (3)	5	0.03
Cherokee (1,359)	2,048	12.90
Cheyenne (1)	1	0.01
Chickasaw (18)	43	0.27
Chippewa (1)	4	0.03
Choctaw (96)	141	0.89
Comanche (16)	22	0.14
Creek (126)	188	1.18
Crow (1)	1	0.01
Delaware (51)	77	0.49
Iroquois (13)	22	0.14
Kiowa (19)	26	0.16
Latin American Indians (2)	2	0.01
Navajo (8)	9	0.06
Osage (23)	43	0.27
Ottawa (4)	5	0.03
Potawatomi (7)	10	0.06
Pueblo (2)	7	0.04
Seminole (12)	32	0.20
Sioux (10)	18	0.11
Ute (1)	1	0.01
Yakama (3)	3	0.02
All other tribes (118)	166	1.05
American Indian tribes, not spec.	109	0.69
Arab:	48	0.30
Arab/Arabic	17	0.11
Lebanese	31	0.20
Asian:	120	0.76
Chinese, ex. Taiwanese (3)	7	0.04
Filipino (15)	39	0.25
Indian (9)	9	0.06
Indonesian (1)	1	0.01
Japanese (8)	20	0.13
Korean (11)	16	0.10
Pakistani (4)	4	0.03
Thai	1	0.01
Vietnamese (11)	15	0.09
Other Asian, specified	1	0.01
Other Asian, not specified (7)	7	0.04
Austrian	5	0.03
British	17	0.11
Canadian	20	0.13
Czech	6	0.04
Danish	23	0.15
Dutch	339	2.14
English	1,429	9.01
European	30	0.19
French, except Basque	343	2.16
French Canadian	41	0.26
German	2,048	12.92
Greek	25	0.16
Hawaii Native/Pacific Islander:	11	0.07
Micronesian: (1)	2	0.01
Guamanian/Chamorro (1)	2	0.01
Polynesian: (3)	7	0.04
Native Hawaiian	4	0.03
Samoan (3)	3	0.02
Other Pac. Isl., specified	1	0.01
Other Pac. Isl., not spec.	1	0.01
Hispanic or Latino:	479	3.02
Central American:	7	0.04
Honduran	5	0.03
Panamanian	1	0.01
Salvadoran	1	0.01
Cuban	1	0.01
Dominican Republic	10	0.06
Mexican	235	1.48
Puerto Rican	99	0.62
South American:	11	0.07
Colombian	1	0.01
Peruvian	9	0.06
Venezuelan	1	0.01
Other Hispanic or Latino	116	0.73
Hungarian	7	0.04
Iranian	8	0.05
Irish	1,794	11.31
Italian	330	2.08
Lithuanian	32	0.20
Norwegian	127	0.80
Pennsylvania German	9	0.06
Polish	217	1.37
Portuguese	9	0.06
Russian	12	0.08
Scotch-Irish	242	1.53
Scottish	403	2.54
Slovak	8	0.05
Swedish	124	0.78
United States or American	2,016	12.71
Welsh	46	0.29
West Indian, excl. Hispanic:	129	0.81
Belizean	9	0.06
Dutch West Indian	99	0.62
Haitian	21	0.13
White:	13,015	81.99
Not Hispanic (11,786)	12,745	80.29
Hispanic (229)	270	1.70

Del City

Place Type: City
County: Oklahoma
Population: 22,128

Ancestry/Race	Number	%
Acadian/Cajun	7	0.03
African American/Black:	3,351	15.14
Not Hispanic (3,057)	3,287	14.85
Hispanic (49)	64	0.29
African, sub-Saharan:	102	0.46
African	69	0.31
Ghanian	33	0.15
Alaska Native tribes, specified:	5	0.02
Alaska Athabascan	1	0.00
Eskimo (2)	4	0.02
Am. Ind. or Alaska Nat., not spec.	172	0.78
American Indian tribes, specified:	1,303	5.89
Apache (3)	10	0.05
Blackfeet (1)	1	0.00
Cherokee (165)	341	1.54
Cheyenne (11)	15	0.07
Chickasaw (57)	95	0.43
Chippewa (1)	3	0.01
Choctaw (190)	275	1.24
Comanche (18)	22	0.10
Creek (72)	145	0.66
Crow	1	0.00
Delaware (14)	15	0.07
Houma	1	0.00
Iroquois	2	0.01
Kiowa (44)	59	0.27
Latin American Indians (5)	10	0.05
Navajo (2)	2	0.01
Osage (4)	7	0.03
Pima	2	0.01
Potawatomi (28)	33	0.15
Pueblo (12)	14	0.06
Seminole (69)	107	0.48
Shoshone	1	0.00
Sioux (6)	7	0.03
Yaqui	1	0.00
All other tribes (102)	134	0.61
American Indian tribes, not spec.	17	0.08
Arab:	37	0.17
Arab/Arabic	8	0.04
Lebanese	29	0.13
Asian:	524	2.37
Cambodian (3)	3	0.01
Chinese, ex. Taiwanese (40)	55	0.25
Filipino (102)	159	0.72
Indian (15)	25	0.11
Indonesian (1)	1	0.00
Japanese (36)	72	0.33
Korean (56)	81	0.37
Laotian (3)	3	0.01
Taiwanese (1)	3	0.01
Thai (15)	28	0.13
Vietnamese (71)	76	0.34
Other Asian, specified	2	0.01
Other Asian, not specified (2)	16	0.07
Austrian	25	0.11
Belgian	28	0.13
British	42	0.19
Canadian	11	0.05
Celtic	6	0.03
Croatian	7	0.03
Czech	15	0.07
Czechoslovakian	7	0.03
Danish	11	0.05
Dutch	481	2.18
Eastern European	9	0.04
English	1,756	7.96
European	265	1.20
Finnish	22	0.10
French, except Basque	556	2.52
French Canadian	107	0.48
German	2,930	13.28
Greek	16	0.07
Hawaii Native/Pacific Islander:	52	0.23
Micronesian: (16)	24	0.11
Guamanian/Chamorro (16)	24	0.11
Polynesian: (8)	22	0.10
Native Hawaiian (7)	20	0.09
Samoan (1)	2	0.01
Other Pac. Isl., not spec. (1)	6	0.03
Hispanic or Latino:	1,043	4.71
Central American:	38	0.17
Guatemalan	3	0.01
Honduran	14	0.06

Notes: 1. Figures in the "Number" column do not add up to the total population due to: a) Ancestry/Race overlap — e.g. persons can report being both White and Irish, b) persons of Hispanic origin can report being any race, c) persons reporting two ancestries are counted in both categories. 2. Numbers in parentheses indicate the number of persons reporting this ancestry/race alone, not in combination with any other ancestry/race. 3. Refer to the Explanation of Data in the front of the book for more detailed information.

Ancestry/Race	Number	%
Nicaraguan	3	0.01
Panamanian	14	0.06
Salvadoran	3	0.01
Other Central American	1	0.00
Cuban	15	0.07
Dominican Republic	1	0.00
Mexican	703	3.18
Puerto Rican	68	0.31
South American:	9	0.04
Colombian	4	0.02
Ecuadorian	4	0.02
Peruvian	1	0.00
Other Hispanic or Latino	209	0.94
Hungarian	61	0.28
Iranian	14	0.06
Irish	2,382	10.79
Italian	358	1.62
Norwegian	140	0.63
Pennsylvania German	17	0.08
Polish	166	0.75
Portuguese	25	0.11
Romanian	18	0.08
Russian	25	0.11
Scandinavian	16	0.07
Scotch-Irish	374	1.69
Scottish	338	1.53
Slovak	8	0.04
Swedish	136	0.62
Swiss	27	0.12
Ukrainian	29	0.13
United States or American	2,349	10.64
Welsh	64	0.29
West Indian, excl. Hispanic:	95	0.43
Dutch West Indian	89	0.40
Jamaican	6	0.03
White:	17,191	77.69
Not Hispanic (15,959)	16,631	75.16
Hispanic (468)	560	2.53
Yugoslavian	6	0.03

Duncan

Place Type: City
County: Stephens
Population: 22,505

Ancestry/Race	Number	%
African American/Black:	1,005	4.47
Not Hispanic (902)	983	4.37
Hispanic (13)	22	0.10
African, sub-Saharan:	24	0.11
African	24	0.11
Am. Ind. or Alaska Nat., not spec.	134	0.60
American Indian tribes, specified:	1,218	5.41
Apache (13)	28	0.12
Blackfeet	4	0.02
Cherokee (138)	259	1.15
Cheyenne (2)	3	0.01
Chickasaw (123)	211	0.94
Chippewa (1)	3	0.01
Choctaw (335)	496	2.20
Comanche (29)	38	0.17
Cree	1	0.00
Creek (26)	35	0.16
Delaware (3)	4	0.02
Iroquois (1)	3	0.01
Kiowa (15)	19	0.08
Latin American Indians (1)	7	0.03
Navajo (4)	6	0.03
Osage (4)	5	0.02
Potawatomi (14)	20	0.09
Pueblo	1	0.00
Seminole (9)	13	0.06
Sioux (3)	5	0.02
Ute (1)	1	0.00
Yuman (1)	1	0.00
All other tribes (35)	55	0.24
American Indian tribes, not spec.	32	0.14
Arab:	4	0.02
Arab/Arabic	4	0.02
Asian:	154	0.68
Chinese, ex. Taiwanese (13)	24	0.11
Filipino (18)	38	0.17
Indian (23)	24	0.11
Indonesian (3)	6	0.03
Japanese (3)	10	0.04
Korean (11)	15	0.07
Laotian	1	0.00
Thai (2)	2	0.01
Vietnamese (22)	23	0.10
Other Asian, specified	1	0.00
Other Asian, not specified (3)	10	0.04
Austrian	9	0.04
Belgian	38	0.17
British	48	0.21
Canadian	10	0.04
Czech	86	0.38
Czechoslovakian	18	0.08
Danish	10	0.04
Dutch	421	1.87
English	1,945	8.65
European	322	1.43
French, except Basque	480	2.14
French Canadian	58	0.26
German	2,280	10.14
German Russian	27	0.12
Greek	61	0.27
Hawaii Native/Pacific Islander:	19	0.08
Micronesian: (5)	5	0.02
Guamanian/Chamorro (5)	5	0.02
Polynesian: (1)	7	0.03
Native Hawaiian (1)	6	0.03
Samoan	1	0.00
Other Pac. Isl., specified	1	0.00
Other Pac. Isl., not spec. (4)	6	0.03
Hispanic or Latino:	1,349	5.99
Central American:	11	0.05
Guatemalan	6	0.03
Panamanian	4	0.02
Salvadoran	1	0.00
Cuban	8	0.04
Mexican	1,095	4.87
Puerto Rican	28	0.12
South American:	16	0.07
Colombian	5	0.02
Peruvian	10	0.04
Other South American	1	0.00
Other Hispanic or Latino	191	0.85
Hungarian	16	0.07
Irish	2,534	11.27
Italian	236	1.05
Norwegian	59	0.26
Polish	120	0.53
Portuguese	8	0.04
Russian	57	0.25
Scandinavian	7	0.03
Scotch-Irish	390	1.73
Scottish	297	1.32
Slovak	21	0.09
Swedish	165	0.73
Swiss	60	0.27
United States or American	3,271	14.55
Welsh	101	0.45
West Indian, excl. Hispanic:	146	0.65
Dutch West Indian	146	0.65
White:	20,020	88.96
Not Hispanic (18,752)	19,245	85.51
Hispanic (710)	775	3.44

Durant

Place Type: City
County: Bryan
Population: 13,549

Ancestry/Race	Number	%
African American/Black:	249	1.84
Not Hispanic (208)	247	1.82
Hispanic (1)	2	0.01
African, sub-Saharan:	23	0.17
African	23	0.17
Alaska Native tribes, specified:	1	0.01
Aleut (1)	1	0.01
Am. Ind. or Alaska Nat., not spec.	173	1.28
American Indian tribes, specified:	2,115	15.61
Apache (3)	7	0.05
Blackfeet	7	0.05
Cherokee (118)	280	2.07
Cheyenne (5)	5	0.04
Chickasaw (151)	263	1.94
Chippewa (1)	1	0.01
Choctaw (1,106)	1,411	10.41
Comanche (2)	3	0.02
Creek (30)	44	0.32
Crow (1)	1	0.01
Delaware (3)	3	0.02
Iroquois (4)	4	0.03
Kiowa (1)	4	0.03
Menominee	8	0.06
Navajo (6)	12	0.09
Osage (2)	3	0.02
Potawatomi (7)	13	0.10
Pueblo	1	0.01
Seminole (6)	10	0.07
Shoshone (1)	1	0.01
Sioux (4)	5	0.04
All other tribes (18)	29	0.21
American Indian tribes, not spec.	16	0.12
Asian:	152	1.12
Bangladeshi (10)	10	0.07
Chinese, ex. Taiwanese (13)	17	0.13
Filipino (19)	26	0.19
Indian (49)	52	0.38
Japanese (5)	9	0.07
Korean (2)	8	0.06
Taiwanese	1	0.01
Vietnamese (14)	15	0.11
Other Asian, specified (3)	6	0.04
Other Asian, not specified (6)	8	0.06
British	30	0.22
Canadian	10	0.07
Czech	11	0.08
Danish	28	0.21
Dutch	324	2.39
English	747	5.51
European	67	0.49
Finnish	6	0.04
French, except Basque	206	1.52
French Canadian	25	0.18
German	1,035	7.64
Greek	11	0.08
Hawaii Native/Pacific Islander:	14	0.10
Micronesian: (1)	3	0.02
Guamanian/Chamorro (1)	3	0.02
Polynesian: (3)	5	0.04
Native Hawaiian (3)	5	0.04
Other Pac. Isl., not spec. (2)	6	0.04
Hispanic or Latino:	483	3.56
Central American:	5	0.04
Guatemalan	2	0.01
Honduran	1	0.01
Salvadoran	2	0.01
Cuban	1	0.01
Dominican Republic	2	0.01
Mexican	391	2.89
Puerto Rican	5	0.04
South American:	8	0.06
Colombian	2	0.01
Venezuelan	2	0.01
Other South American	4	0.03
Other Hispanic or Latino	71	0.52
Hungarian	6	0.04
Iranian	13	0.10
Irish	1,333	9.83
Italian	70	0.52
Northern European	7	0.05
Norwegian	33	0.24
Polish	27	0.20
Portuguese	6	0.04
Russian	4	0.03

Notes: 1. Figures in the "Number" column do not add up to the total population due to: a) Ancestry/Race overlap — e.g. persons can report being both White and Irish, b) persons of Hispanic origin can report being any race, c) persons reporting two ancestries are counted in both categories. 2. Numbers in parentheses indicate the number of persons reporting this ancestry/race alone, not in combination with any other ancestry/race. 3. Refer to the Explanation of Data in the front of the book for more detailed information.

Ancestry/Race	Number	%
Scotch-Irish	205	1.51
Scottish	98	0.72
Serbian	7	0.05
Swedish	36	0.27
Swiss	6	0.04
Turkish	5	0.04
Ukrainian	10	0.07
United States or American	2,583	19.06
Welsh	60	0.44
West Indian, excl. Hispanic:	55	0.41
Dutch West Indian	55	0.41
White:	11,308	83.46
Not Hispanic (10,497)	11,072	81.72
Hispanic (205)	236	1.74
Yugoslavian	9	0.07

Edmond

Place Type: City
County: Oklahoma
Population: 68,315

Ancestry/Race	Number	%
Acadian/Cajun	31	0.05
African American/Black:	3,069	4.49
Not Hispanic (2,721)	3,007	4.40
Hispanic (39)	62	0.09
African, sub-Saharan:	462	0.67
African	239	0.35
Ghanian	37	0.05
Nigerian	50	0.07
South African	74	0.11
Sudanese	7	0.01
Zimbabwean	23	0.03
Other sub-Saharan African	32	0.05
Alaska Native tribes, specified:	5	0.01
Alaska Athabascan (2)	2	0.00
Aleut (3)	3	0.00
Am. Ind. or Alaska Nat., not spec.	264	0.39
Albanian	16	0.02
American Indian tribes, specified:	2,479	3.63
Apache (4)	13	0.02
Blackfeet (4)	15	0.02
Cherokee (422)	900	1.32
Cheyenne (6)	11	0.02
Chickasaw (123)	230	0.34
Chippewa (8)	11	0.02
Choctaw (299)	554	0.81
Comanche (19)	29	0.04
Cree	2	0.00
Creek (125)	198	0.29
Crow (2)	3	0.00
Delaware (19)	33	0.05
Iroquois (10)	14	0.02
Kiowa (23)	38	0.06
Latin American Indians (4)	5	0.01
Lumbee (4)	5	0.01
Menominee (1)	1	0.00
Navajo (11)	12	0.02
Osage (40)	51	0.07
Paiute	3	0.00
Potawatomi (70)	99	0.14
Pueblo (8)	10	0.01
Seminole (30)	57	0.08
Shoshone	4	0.01
Sioux (2)	6	0.01
Tohono O'Odham (2)	2	0.00
Ute (2)	2	0.00
All other tribes (132)	171	0.25
American Indian tribes, not spec.	60	0.09
Arab:	280	0.41
Arab/Arabic	45	0.07
Egyptian	33	0.05
Lebanese	189	0.28
Syrian	6	0.01
Other Arab	7	0.01
Armenian	7	0.01
Asian:	2,651	3.88
Bangladeshi (54)	59	0.09
Cambodian (1)	3	0.00
Chinese, ex. Taiwanese (619)	692	1.01
Filipino (67)	133	0.19
Indian (430)	474	0.69
Indonesian (47)	52	0.08
Japanese (295)	353	0.52
Korean (186)	225	0.33
Laotian (4)	5	0.01
Malaysian (56)	80	0.12
Pakistani (86)	102	0.15
Sri Lankan (11)	13	0.02
Taiwanese (88)	112	0.16
Thai (47)	64	0.09
Vietnamese (113)	127	0.19
Other Asian, specified (45)	55	0.08
Other Asian, not specified (36)	102	0.15
Australian	18	0.03
Austrian	205	0.30
Belgian	24	0.04
Brazilian	9	0.01
British	374	0.55
Bulgarian	13	0.02
Canadian	186	0.27
Celtic	17	0.02
Croatian	25	0.04
Czech	613	0.89
Czechoslovakian	172	0.25
Danish	253	0.37
Dutch	1,312	1.91
English	9,619	14.04
European	1,057	1.54
Finnish	4	0.01
French, except Basque	2,499	3.65
French Canadian	266	0.39
German	13,015	19.00
German Russian	12	0.02
Greek	123	0.18
Hawaii Native/Pacific Islander:	119	0.17
Micronesian: (26)	38	0.06
Guamanian/Chamorro (7)	12	0.02
Other Micronesian (19)	26	0.04
Polynesian: (19)	49	0.07
Native Hawaiian (9)	26	0.04
Samoan (10)	17	0.02
Other Polynesian	6	0.01
Other Pac. Isl., specified	4	0.01
Other Pac. Isl., not spec. (4)	28	0.04
Hispanic or Latino:	1,881	2.75
Central American:	57	0.08
Costa Rican	3	0.00
Guatemalan	16	0.02
Honduran	8	0.01
Nicaraguan	4	0.01
Panamanian	26	0.04
Cuban	49	0.07
Dominican Republic	2	0.00
Mexican	1,235	1.81
Puerto Rican	108	0.16
South American:	97	0.14
Argentinean	9	0.01
Bolivian	1	0.00
Chilean	1	0.00
Colombian	18	0.03
Ecuadorian	9	0.01
Peruvian	32	0.05
Venezuelan	21	0.03
Other South American	6	0.01
Other Hispanic or Latino	333	0.49
Hungarian	93	0.14
Iranian	363	0.53
Irish	8,168	11.92
Israeli	5	0.01
Italian	1,707	2.49
Latvian	17	0.02
Lithuanian	43	0.06
Luxemburger	46	0.07
Macedonian	33	0.05
Maltese	7	0.01
Northern European	33	0.05
Norwegian	824	1.20
Pennsylvania German	12	0.02
Polish	1,035	1.51
Portuguese	30	0.04
Romanian	61	0.09
Russian	376	0.55
Scandinavian	152	0.22
Scotch-Irish	1,936	2.83
Scottish	1,917	2.80
Slavic	24	0.04
Slovak	54	0.08
Swedish	771	1.13
Swiss	144	0.21
Turkish	16	0.02
Ukrainian	70	0.10
United States or American	6,756	9.86
Welsh	547	0.80
West Indian, excl. Hispanic:	145	0.21
Bahamian	24	0.04
British West Indian	7	0.01
Dutch West Indian	107	0.16
Jamaican	7	0.01
White:	60,928	89.19
Not Hispanic (58,104)	59,710	87.40
Hispanic (1,040)	1,218	1.78
Yugoslavian	68	0.10

El Reno

Place Type: City
County: Canadian
Population: 16,212

Ancestry/Race	Number	%
African American/Black:	1,385	8.54
Not Hispanic (1,232)	1,333	8.22
Hispanic (41)	52	0.32
African, sub-Saharan:	45	0.28
African	45	0.28
Alaska Native tribes, specified:	4	0.02
Aleut	1	0.01
Tlingit-Haida (3)	3	0.02
Am. Ind. or Alaska Nat., not spec.	161	0.99
American Indian tribes, specified:	1,811	11.17
Apache (11)	18	0.11
Blackfeet (4)	4	0.02
Cherokee (79)	166	1.02
Cheyenne (276)	318	1.96
Chickasaw (17)	34	0.21
Chippewa (3)	4	0.02
Choctaw (76)	131	0.81
Comanche (8)	12	0.07
Cree (1)	1	0.01
Creek (39)	53	0.33
Crow (1)	2	0.01
Delaware (8)	12	0.07
Iroquois (3)	3	0.02
Kiowa (64)	78	0.48
Latin American Indians (9)	10	0.06
Navajo (16)	20	0.12
Osage (3)	4	0.02
Potawatomi (22)	34	0.21
Pueblo (3)	4	0.02
Seminole (16)	36	0.22
Shoshone (1)	3	0.02
Sioux (24)	39	0.24
Ute (5)	5	0.03
Yaqui (1)	1	0.01
All other tribes (712)	819	5.05
American Indian tribes, not spec.	15	0.09
Arab:	7	0.04
Arab/Arabic	7	0.04
Asian:	134	0.83
Chinese, ex. Taiwanese (4)	7	0.04
Filipino (12)	18	0.11
Indian (29)	39	0.24
Japanese (10)	11	0.07
Korean (5)	7	0.04
Pakistani (4)	8	0.05
Thai (1)	5	0.03
Vietnamese (33)	34	0.21
Other Asian, not specified (5)	5	0.03

Notes: 1. Figures in the "Number" column do not add up to the total population due to: a) Ancestry/Race overlap — e.g. persons can report being both White and Irish, b) persons of Hispanic origin can report being any race, c) persons reporting two ancestries are counted in both categories. 2. Numbers in parentheses indicate the number of persons reporting this ancestry/race alone, not in combination with any other ancestry/race. 3. Refer to the Explanation of Data in the front of the book for more detailed information.

Ancestry/Race	Number	%
Austrian	16	0.10
British	39	0.24
Celtic	10	0.06
Czech	97	0.60
Czechoslovakian	26	0.16
Danish	31	0.19
Dutch	358	2.20
English	1,295	7.96
European	71	0.44
French, except Basque	246	1.51
French Canadian	46	0.28
German	2,633	16.18
Greek	46	0.28
Hawaii Native/Pacific Islander:	17	0.10
Polynesian: (2)	17	0.10
Native Hawaiian (2)	10	0.06
Samoan	3	0.02
Tongan	1	0.01
Other Polynesian	3	0.02
Hispanic or Latino:	1,219	7.52
Central American:	6	0.04
Costa Rican	3	0.02
Salvadoran	3	0.02
Cuban	42	0.26
Mexican	941	5.80
Puerto Rican	77	0.47
South American:	4	0.02
Venezuelan	4	0.02
Other Hispanic or Latino	149	0.92
Hungarian	2	0.01
Irish	1,404	8.63
Italian	152	0.93
Northern European	3	0.02
Norwegian	52	0.32
Pennsylvania German	12	0.07
Polish	53	0.33
Portuguese	9	0.06
Romanian	3	0.02
Russian	1	0.01
Scotch-Irish	232	1.43
Scottish	141	0.87
Slovak	35	0.22
Swedish	48	0.29
Swiss	27	0.17
Ukrainian	7	0.04
United States or American	1,730	10.63
Welsh	94	0.58
West Indian, excl. Hispanic:	34	0.21
Dutch West Indian	34	0.21
White:	12,795	78.92
Not Hispanic (11,729)	12,081	74.52
Hispanic (655)	714	4.40
Yugoslavian	2	0.01

Elk City

Place Type: City
County: Beckham
Population: 10,510

Ancestry/Race	Number	%
African American/Black:	355	3.38
Not Hispanic (312)	340	3.24
Hispanic (10)	15	0.14
African, sub-Saharan:	32	0.30
African	7	0.07
South African	25	0.24
Am. Ind. or Alaska Nat., not spec.	60	0.57
American Indian tribes, specified:	414	3.94
Apache (3)	5	0.05
Blackfeet	2	0.02
Cherokee (33)	91	0.87
Cheyenne (57)	70	0.67
Chickasaw (22)	29	0.28
Chippewa	2	0.02
Choctaw (37)	57	0.54
Colville (7)	8	0.08
Comanche (2)	3	0.03
Creek (15)	30	0.29
Crow	1	0.01
Iroquois (3)	3	0.03
Kiowa (1)	4	0.04
Latin American Indians (1)	3	0.03
Navajo (6)	10	0.10
Osage (5)	5	0.05
Potawatomi (4)	6	0.06
Sioux (5)	7	0.07
Ute (3)	3	0.03
All other tribes (60)	75	0.71
American Indian tribes, not spec.	6	0.06
Arab:	77	0.73
Lebanese	57	0.54
Syrian	20	0.19
Asian:	67	0.64
Bangladeshi (3)	3	0.03
Chinese, ex. Taiwanese (3)	4	0.04
Filipino (4)	7	0.07
Indian (29)	31	0.29
Japanese (1)	2	0.02
Korean (5)	7	0.07
Laotian (3)	3	0.03
Pakistani (4)	4	0.04
Vietnamese (3)	3	0.03
Other Asian, not specified (2)	3	0.03
British	15	0.14
Czech	23	0.22
Czechoslovakian	7	0.07
Danish	29	0.27
Dutch	228	2.15
English	998	9.42
European	14	0.13
French, except Basque	341	3.22
French Canadian	19	0.18
German	1,679	15.85
Greek	3	0.03
Hawaii Native/Pacific Islander:	4	0.04
Micronesian:	1	0.01
Guamanian/Chamorro	1	0.01
Polynesian: (3)	3	0.03
Native Hawaiian (3)	3	0.03
Hispanic or Latino:	626	5.96
Central American:	5	0.05
Nicaraguan	1	0.01
Salvadoran	4	0.04
Cuban	1	0.01
Mexican	424	4.03
Puerto Rican	13	0.12
South American:	4	0.04
Colombian	1	0.01
Peruvian	1	0.01
Venezuelan	2	0.02
Other Hispanic or Latino	179	1.70
Hungarian	8	0.08
Irish	1,263	11.92
Italian	79	0.75
Norwegian	17	0.16
Polish	65	0.61
Portuguese	10	0.09
Russian	18	0.17
Scandinavian	5	0.05
Scotch-Irish	157	1.48
Scottish	92	0.87
Slavic	8	0.08
Swedish	63	0.59
Swiss	14	0.13
United States or American	1,495	14.11
Welsh	14	0.13
West Indian, excl. Hispanic:	29	0.27
Dutch West Indian	29	0.27
White:	9,562	90.98
Not Hispanic (9,049)	9,203	87.56
Hispanic (300)	359	3.42

Enid

Place Type: City
County: Garfield
Population: 47,045

Ancestry/Race	Number	%
African American/Black:	2,121	4.51
Not Hispanic (1,815)	2,075	4.41
Hispanic (25)	46	0.10
African, sub-Saharan:	49	0.10
African	44	0.09
Other sub-Saharan African	5	0.01
Alaska Native tribes, specified:	18	0.04
Aleut (4)	4	0.01
Eskimo (3)	14	0.03
Am. Ind. or Alaska Nat., not spec.	247	0.53
Albanian	17	0.04
American Indian tribes, specified:	1,509	3.21
Apache (29)	46	0.10
Blackfeet (4)	15	0.03
Cherokee (248)	556	1.18
Cheyenne (28)	46	0.10
Chickasaw (42)	68	0.14
Chippewa (5)	12	0.03
Choctaw (100)	181	0.38
Comanche (11)	14	0.03
Cree (2)	2	0.00
Creek (64)	94	0.20
Crow	1	0.00
Delaware (7)	12	0.03
Iroquois (8)	14	0.03
Kiowa (4)	8	0.02
Latin American Indians (6)	25	0.05
Lumbee (1)	1	0.00
Navajo (9)	11	0.02
Osage (15)	45	0.10
Paiute (1)	1	0.00
Potawatomi (26)	35	0.07
Pueblo (3)	5	0.01
Seminole (10)	19	0.04
Shoshone (1)	1	0.00
Sioux (18)	40	0.09
Tohono O'Odham (1)	1	0.00
Ute (1)	1	0.00
Yaqui	1	0.00
All other tribes (193)	254	0.54
American Indian tribes, not spec.	45	0.10
Arab:	116	0.25
Lebanese	114	0.24
Syrian	2	0.00
Asian:	690	1.47
Bangladeshi (1)	1	0.00
Chinese, ex. Taiwanese (54)	78	0.17
Filipino (88)	139	0.30
Indian (89)	111	0.24
Indonesian (4)	7	0.01
Japanese (29)	74	0.16
Korean (109)	134	0.28
Laotian (12)	18	0.04
Pakistani (4)	4	0.01
Sri Lankan (1)	3	0.01
Taiwanese (4)	5	0.01
Thai (21)	35	0.07
Vietnamese (39)	43	0.09
Other Asian, specified	5	0.01
Other Asian, not specified (10)	33	0.07
Austrian	19	0.04
Belgian	17	0.04
British	153	0.32
Canadian	9	0.02
Celtic	13	0.03
Croatian	11	0.02
Czech	441	0.94
Czechoslovakian	194	0.41
Danish	96	0.20
Dutch	1,423	3.02
English	4,261	9.05
European	276	0.59
Finnish	19	0.04
French, except Basque	1,252	2.66
French Canadian	150	0.32
German	9,142	19.41
German Russian	2	0.00
Greek	68	0.14
Hawaii Native/Pacific Islander:	348	0.74
Micronesian: (239)	268	0.57

Notes: 1. Figures in the "Number" column do not add up to the total population due to: a) Ancestry/Race overlap — e.g. persons can report being both White and Irish, b) persons of Hispanic origin can report being any race, c) persons reporting two ancestries are counted in both categories. 2. Numbers in parentheses indicate the number of persons reporting this ancestry/race alone, not in combination with any other ancestry/race. 3. Refer to the Explanation of Data in the front of the book for more detailed information.

Guamanian/Chamorro (8)	12	0.03
Other Micronesian (231)	256	0.54
Polynesian: (10)	38	0.08
Native Hawaiian (9)	32	0.07
Samoan (1)	2	0.00
Tongan	4	0.01
Other Pac. Isl., not spec. (22)	42	0.09
Hispanic or Latino:	2,232	4.74
Central American:	12	0.03
Costa Rican	2	0.00
Guatemalan	1	0.00
Honduran	2	0.00
Nicaraguan	1	0.00
Panamanian	5	0.01
Salvadoran	1	0.00
Cuban	13	0.03
Dominican Republic	3	0.01
Mexican	1,705	3.62
Puerto Rican	72	0.15
South American:	40	0.09
Argentinean	5	0.01
Bolivian	3	0.01
Chilean	2	0.00
Colombian	8	0.02
Ecuadorian	3	0.01
Peruvian	14	0.03
Venezuelan	3	0.01
Other South American	2	0.00
Other Hispanic or Latino	387	0.82
Hungarian	50	0.11
Iranian	51	0.11
Irish	5,074	10.77
Israeli	11	0.02
Italian	677	1.44
Lithuanian	6	0.01
Maltese	10	0.02
Northern European	5	0.01
Norwegian	574	1.22
Pennsylvania German	32	0.07
Polish	376	0.80
Portuguese	69	0.15
Romanian	8	0.02
Russian	150	0.32
Scandinavian	28	0.06
Scotch-Irish	1,009	2.14
Scottish	704	1.49
Slovak	7	0.01
Swedish	406	0.86
Swiss	113	0.24
Ukrainian	14	0.03
United States or American	4,939	10.49
Welsh	439	0.93
West Indian, excl. Hispanic:	73	0.16
Dutch West Indian	73	0.16
White:	42,199	89.70
Not Hispanic (40,109)	41,114	87.39
Hispanic (906)	1,085	2.31

Guymon

Place Type: City
County: Texas
Population: 10,472

Ancestry/Race	Number	%
African American/Black:	113	1.08
Not Hispanic (65)	79	0.75
Hispanic (23)	34	0.32
African, sub-Saharan:	4	0.04
African	4	0.04
Am. Ind. or Alaska Nat., not spec.	50	0.48
American Indian tribes, specified:	174	1.66
Apache (9)	16	0.15
Blackfeet	1	0.01
Cherokee (19)	56	0.53
Cheyenne (3)	13	0.12
Choctaw (18)	24	0.23
Creek (6)	7	0.07
Iroquois	2	0.02
Latin American Indians (8)	10	0.10
Navajo (1)	3	0.03
Osage (3)	7	0.07
Pueblo (12)	13	0.12
Seminole	1	0.01
Sioux	2	0.02
Ute	1	0.01
All other tribes (12)	18	0.17
American Indian tribes, not spec.	8	0.08
Arab:	26	0.25
Lebanese	26	0.25
Asian:	102	0.97
Chinese, ex. Taiwanese (10)	10	0.10
Filipino (24)	25	0.24
Indian (9)	14	0.13
Japanese (5)	7	0.07
Korean (12)	13	0.12
Laotian (11)	11	0.11
Taiwanese	1	0.01
Vietnamese (15)	18	0.17
Other Asian, not specified (2)	3	0.03
British	18	0.17
Canadian	17	0.16
Czech	83	0.79
Czechoslovakian	12	0.11
Danish	17	0.16
Dutch	159	1.51
Eastern European	18	0.17
English	575	5.45
European	46	0.44
French, except Basque	175	1.66
German	1,570	14.87
Hawaii Native/Pacific Islander:	23	0.22
Micronesian: (18)	21	0.20
Guamanian/Chamorro (18)	21	0.20
Polynesian:	1	0.01
Samoan	1	0.01
Other Pac. Isl., not spec.	1	0.01
Hispanic or Latino:	4,018	38.37
Central American:	199	1.90
Guatemalan	177	1.69
Honduran	19	0.18
Panamanian	1	0.01
Salvadoran	2	0.02
Cuban	14	0.13
Mexican	2,942	28.09
Puerto Rican	42	0.40
South American:	1	0.01
Colombian	1	0.01
Other Hispanic or Latino	820	7.83
Hungarian	19	0.18
Irish	764	7.23
Italian	111	1.05
Norwegian	56	0.53
Pennsylvania German	8	0.08
Polish	66	0.63
Portuguese	9	0.09
Scotch-Irish	120	1.14
Scottish	110	1.04
Swedish	28	0.27
Swiss	17	0.16
United States or American	861	8.15
Welsh	58	0.55
West Indian, excl. Hispanic:	55	0.52
Dutch West Indian	55	0.52
White:	7,664	73.19
Not Hispanic (6,071)	6,187	59.08
Hispanic (1,305)	1,477	14.10

Lawton

Place Type: City
County: Comanche
Population: 92,757

Ancestry/Race	Number	%
Acadian/Cajun	13	0.01
African American/Black:	23,194	25.01
Not Hispanic (20,937)	22,446	24.20
Hispanic (451)	748	0.81
African, sub-Saharan:	853	0.92
African	793	0.85
Cape Verdean	23	0.02
Nigerian	26	0.03
Other sub-Saharan African	11	0.01
Alaska Native tribes, specified:	37	0.04
Alaska Athabascan (1)	1	0.00
Aleut (4)	6	0.01
Eskimo (8)	11	0.01
Tlingit-Haida (10)	15	0.02
All other tribes (4)	4	0.00
Alaska Native tribes, not specified	5	0.01
Am. Ind. or Alaska Nat., not spec.	730	0.79
American Indian tribes, specified:	4,409	4.75
Apache (108)	177	0.19
Blackfeet (14)	42	0.05
Cherokee (257)	596	0.64
Cheyenne (28)	46	0.05
Chickasaw (86)	158	0.17
Chippewa (15)	28	0.03
Choctaw (278)	424	0.46
Comanche (1,002)	1,301	1.40
Cree (4)	9	0.01
Creek (75)	139	0.15
Delaware (24)	30	0.03
Houma (2)	3	0.00
Iroquois (9)	25	0.03
Kiowa (520)	721	0.78
Latin American Indians (40)	57	0.06
Lumbee (7)	8	0.01
Menominee (1)	1	0.00
Navajo (49)	66	0.07
Osage (16)	25	0.03
Ottawa (4)	7	0.01
Pima (3)	5	0.01
Potawatomi (18)	31	0.03
Pueblo (12)	13	0.01
Puget Sound Salish	1	0.00
Seminole (37)	71	0.08
Shoshone (5)	11	0.01
Sioux (31)	61	0.07
Tohono O'Odham (1)	1	0.00
Ute (1)	1	0.00
Yakama (4)	4	0.00
Yaqui (2)	2	0.00
Yuman (3)	7	0.01
All other tribes (227)	338	0.36
American Indian tribes, not spec.	105	0.11
Arab:	159	0.17
Arab/Arabic	11	0.01
Egyptian	26	0.03
Jordanian	49	0.05
Lebanese	39	0.04
Other Arab	34	0.04
Armenian	18	0.02
Asian:	3,550	3.83
Cambodian (37)	53	0.06
Chinese, ex. Taiwanese (154)	234	0.25
Filipino (401)	622	0.67
Hmong (5)	5	0.01
Indian (135)	189	0.20
Indonesian (1)	4	0.00
Japanese (190)	436	0.47
Korean (1,009)	1,499	1.62
Laotian (12)	14	0.02
Malaysian	2	0.00
Pakistani (6)	9	0.01
Sri Lankan (1)	1	0.00
Taiwanese (2)	4	0.00
Thai (65)	117	0.13
Vietnamese (149)	195	0.21
Other Asian, specified (3)	19	0.02
Other Asian, not specified (69)	147	0.16
Assyrian/Chaldean/Syriac	1	0.00
Australian	28	0.03
Austrian	117	0.13
Belgian	55	0.06
Brazilian	10	0.01
British	319	0.34
Canadian	94	0.10
Celtic	6	0.01

Notes: 1. Figures in the "Number" column do not add up to the total population due to: a) Ancestry/Race overlap — e.g. persons can report being both White and Irish, b) persons of Hispanic origin can report being any race, c) persons reporting two ancestries are counted in both categories. 2. Numbers in parentheses indicate the number of persons reporting this ancestry/race alone, not in combination with any other ancestry/race. 3. Refer to the Explanation of Data in the front of the book for more detailed information.

Ancestry/Race	Number	%
Croatian	49	0.05
Czech	238	0.26
Czechoslovakian	100	0.11
Danish	202	0.22
Dutch	1,027	1.10
English	5,899	6.34
European	633	0.68
Finnish	80	0.09
French, except Basque	2,123	2.28
French Canadian	363	0.39
German	12,229	13.15
Greek	85	0.09
Guyanese	23	0.02
Hawaii Native/Pacific Islander:	724	0.78
Micronesian: (134)	183	0.20
Guamanian/Chamorro (108)	149	0.16
Other Micronesian (26)	34	0.04
Polynesian: (239)	436	0.47
Native Hawaiian (88)	219	0.24
Samoan (147)	206	0.22
Tongan (2)	5	0.01
Other Polynesian (2)	6	0.01
Other Pac. Isl., specified	5	0.01
Other Pac. Isl., not spec. (24)	100	0.11
Hispanic or Latino:	8,719	9.40
Central American:	329	0.35
Costa Rican	13	0.01
Guatemalan	15	0.02
Honduran	22	0.02
Nicaraguan	20	0.02
Panamanian	220	0.24
Salvadoran	32	0.03
Other Central American	7	0.01
Cuban	103	0.11
Dominican Republic	62	0.07
Mexican	4,521	4.87
Puerto Rican	2,262	2.44
South American:	106	0.11
Argentinean	3	0.00
Bolivian	2	0.00
Chilean	2	0.00
Colombian	47	0.05
Ecuadorian	13	0.01
Peruvian	27	0.03
Uruguayan	1	0.00
Venezuelan	7	0.01
Other South American	4	0.00
Other Hispanic or Latino	1,336	1.44
Hungarian	205	0.22
Icelander	12	0.01
Iranian	23	0.02
Irish	7,918	8.51
Israeli	17	0.02
Italian	2,006	2.16
Latvian	29	0.03
Lithuanian	68	0.07
Macedonian	5	0.01
Norwegian	680	0.73
Pennsylvania German	64	0.07
Polish	989	1.06
Portuguese	186	0.20
Romanian	22	0.02
Russian	308	0.33
Scandinavian	110	0.12
Scotch-Irish	1,374	1.48
Scottish	1,276	1.37
Serbian	7	0.01
Slovak	60	0.06
Slovene	5	0.01
Swedish	607	0.65
Swiss	71	0.08
Turkish	57	0.06
Ukrainian	46	0.05
United States or American	8,122	8.73
Welsh	416	0.45
West Indian, excl. Hispanic:	659	0.71
Bahamian	6	0.01
Barbadian	19	0.02
Belizean	40	0.04
British West Indian	66	0.07
Dutch West Indian	91	0.10
Haitian	54	0.06
Jamaican	249	0.27
Trinidadian and Tobagonian	66	0.07
U.S. Virgin Islander	8	0.01
West Indian	60	0.06
White:	60,433	65.15
Not Hispanic (53,605)	56,429	60.84
Hispanic (3,292)	4,004	4.32
Yugoslavian	12	0.01

McAlester

Place Type: City
County: Pittsburg
Population: 17,783

Ancestry/Race	Number	%
Acadian/Cajun	11	0.06
African American/Black:	1,695	9.53
Not Hispanic (1,529)	1,666	9.37
Hispanic (15)	29	0.16
African, sub-Saharan:	45	0.25
African	15	0.08
Nigerian	2	0.01
South African	28	0.16
Alaska Native tribes, specified:	10	0.06
Alaska Athabascan	2	0.01
Aleut (2)	4	0.02
Eskimo (2)	4	0.02
Alaska Native tribes, not specified	1	0.01
Am. Ind. or Alaska Nat., not spec.	176	0.99
American Indian tribes, specified:	2,374	13.35
Apache (10)	18	0.10
Blackfeet	1	0.01
Cherokee (226)	438	2.46
Cheyenne (6)	7	0.04
Chickasaw (74)	116	0.65
Chippewa (3)	4	0.02
Choctaw (1,054)	1,422	8.00
Colville	1	0.01
Comanche (11)	14	0.08
Cree (1)	1	0.01
Creek (110)	163	0.92
Delaware (5)	5	0.03
Iroquois (1)	6	0.03
Kiowa (12)	16	0.09
Latin American Indians (8)	10	0.06
Navajo (2)	8	0.04
Osage (14)	15	0.08
Potawatomi (5)	7	0.04
Seminole (32)	44	0.25
Sioux (6)	11	0.06
All other tribes (51)	67	0.38
American Indian tribes, not spec.	50	0.28
Arab:	9	0.05
Lebanese	9	0.05
Asian:	131	0.74
Chinese, ex. Taiwanese (13)	21	0.12
Filipino (6)	18	0.10
Indian (10)	20	0.11
Japanese (6)	14	0.08
Korean (22)	31	0.17
Malaysian	5	0.03
Pakistani (4)	4	0.02
Taiwanese	2	0.01
Thai (2)	2	0.01
Vietnamese (6)	8	0.04
Other Asian, not specified	6	0.03
Australian	8	0.04
Austrian	18	0.10
Belgian	4	0.02
British	30	0.17
Bulgarian	9	0.05
Canadian	24	0.13
Czechoslovakian	23	0.13
Danish	18	0.10
Dutch	268	1.50
English	1,301	7.30
European	48	0.27
Finnish	5	0.03
French, except Basque	233	1.31
French Canadian	18	0.10
German	1,623	9.11
Greek	2	0.01
Hawaii Native/Pacific Islander:	15	0.08
Micronesian: (2)	2	0.01
Guamanian/Chamorro (2)	2	0.01
Polynesian: (5)	8	0.04
Native Hawaiian (4)	4	0.02
Samoan (1)	4	0.02
Other Pac. Isl., not spec. (2)	5	0.03
Hispanic or Latino:	541	3.04
Central American:	5	0.03
Guatemalan	4	0.02
Panamanian	1	0.01
Cuban	6	0.03
Dominican Republic	2	0.01
Mexican	413	2.32
Puerto Rican	19	0.11
South American:	5	0.03
Argentinean	1	0.01
Bolivian	4	0.02
Other Hispanic or Latino	91	0.51
Hungarian	15	0.08
Irish	1,658	9.31
Italian	620	3.48
Lithuanian	1	0.01
Northern European	2	0.01
Norwegian	89	0.50
Pennsylvania German	7	0.04
Polish	152	0.85
Russian	47	0.26
Scotch-Irish	231	1.30
Scottish	149	0.84
Slovak	2	0.01
Slovene	46	0.26
Swedish	138	0.77
Swiss	6	0.03
Turkish	9	0.05
Ukrainian	8	0.04
United States or American	1,486	8.34
Welsh	56	0.31
West Indian, excl. Hispanic:	110	0.62
Dutch West Indian	109	0.61
West Indian	1	0.01
White:	13,976	78.59
Not Hispanic (13,088)	13,724	77.17
Hispanic (200)	252	1.42
Yugoslavian	8	0.04

Miami

Place Type: City
County: Ottawa
Population: 13,704

Ancestry/Race	Number	%
African American/Black:	195	1.42
Not Hispanic (164)	193	1.41
Hispanic	2	0.01
African, sub-Saharan:	18	0.13
African	5	0.04
Kenyan	13	0.10
Alaska Native tribes, specified:	3	0.02
Eskimo (1)	3	0.02
Alaska Native tribes, not specified	1	0.01
Am. Ind. or Alaska Nat., not spec.	213	1.55
Albanian	13	0.10
American Indian tribes, specified:	2,695	19.67
Apache (5)	6	0.04
Blackfeet (4)	10	0.07
Cherokee (983)	1,545	11.27
Cheyenne (4)	10	0.07
Chickasaw (6)	14	0.10
Choctaw (43)	70	0.51
Comanche (5)	7	0.05
Creek (43)	62	0.45
Crow	1	0.01
Delaware (25)	40	0.29

Notes: 1. Figures in the "Number" column do not add up to the total population due to: a) Ancestry/Race overlap — e.g. persons can report being both White and Irish, b) persons of Hispanic origin can report being any race, c) persons reporting two ancestries are counted in both categories. 2. Numbers in parentheses indicate the number of persons reporting this ancestry/race alone, not in combination with any other ancestry/race. 3. Refer to the Explanation of Data in the front of the book for more detailed information.

Iroquois (205)	270	1.97
Kiowa (7)	10	0.07
Latin American Indians (1)	1	0.01
Menominee	2	0.01
Navajo (8)	13	0.09
Osage (20)	25	0.18
Ottawa (58)	78	0.57
Potawatomi (7)	9	0.07
Pueblo	1	0.01
Seminole (7)	7	0.05
Shoshone	1	0.01
Sioux (3)	6	0.04
Ute	1	0.01
All other tribes (396)	506	3.69
American Indian tribes, not spec.	86	0.63
Armenian	7	0.05
Asian:	103	0.75
Chinese, ex. Taiwanese (22)	27	0.20
Filipino (3)	7	0.05
Indian (4)	14	0.10
Japanese (7)	18	0.13
Korean (10)	15	0.11
Pakistani (1)	1	0.01
Thai (1)	2	0.01
Vietnamese (12)	13	0.09
Other Asian, specified (3)	3	0.02
Other Asian, not specified (1)	3	0.02
Australian	5	0.04
Austrian	21	0.15
British	41	0.30
Canadian	13	0.10
Czech	48	0.35
Czechoslovakian	19	0.14
Danish	25	0.18
Dutch	426	3.11
English	1,310	9.58
European	33	0.24
Finnish	6	0.04
French, except Basque	336	2.46
French Canadian	42	0.31
German	2,000	14.62
Hawaii Native/Pacific Islander:	43	0.31
Micronesian: (18)	34	0.25
Guamanian/Chamorro	8	0.06
Other Micronesian (18)	26	0.19
Polynesian: (4)	8	0.06
Native Hawaiian (3)	7	0.05
Samoan (1)	1	0.01
Other Pac. Isl., not spec.	1	0.01
Hispanic or Latino:	322	2.35
Central American:	3	0.02
Guatemalan	3	0.02
Cuban	6	0.04
Mexican	239	1.74
Puerto Rican	7	0.05
South American:	7	0.05
Chilean	2	0.01
Ecuadorian	1	0.01
Peruvian	4	0.03
Other Hispanic or Latino	60	0.44
Hungarian	8	0.06
Icelander	21	0.15
Irish	1,460	10.67
Italian	209	1.53
Lithuanian	6	0.04
Norwegian	49	0.36
Polish	80	0.58
Russian	14	0.10
Scotch-Irish	220	1.61
Scottish	171	1.25
Slovak	10	0.07
Swedish	73	0.53
Swiss	53	0.39
United States or American	1,157	8.46
Welsh	77	0.56
West Indian, excl. Hispanic:	46	0.34
Bahamian	6	0.04
Dutch West Indian	40	0.29
White:	11,200	81.73
Not Hispanic (10,180)	11,026	80.46
Hispanic (149)	174	1.27

Midwest City

Place Type: City
County: Oklahoma
Population: 54,088

Ancestry/Race	Number	%
Acadian/Cajun	57	0.11
African American/Black:	11,295	20.88
Not Hispanic (10,492)	11,157	20.63
Hispanic (81)	138	0.26
African, sub-Saharan:	414	0.76
African	391	0.72
Ethiopian	6	0.01
Ghanian	9	0.02
Other sub-Saharan African	8	0.01
Alaska Native tribes, specified:	9	0.02
Aleut (5)	5	0.01
Eskimo	3	0.01
All other tribes	1	0.00
Alaska Native tribes, not specified	1	0.00
Am. Ind. or Alaska Nat., not spec.	369	0.68
Albanian	7	0.01
American Indian tribes, specified:	2,960	5.47
Apache (12)	25	0.05
Blackfeet (8)	31	0.06
Cherokee (344)	846	1.56
Cheyenne (19)	32	0.06
Chickasaw (155)	270	0.50
Chippewa (27)	43	0.08
Choctaw (393)	652	1.21
Comanche (28)	37	0.07
Cree	4	0.01
Creek (157)	262	0.48
Crow (2)	3	0.01
Delaware (28)	38	0.07
Houma	2	0.00
Iroquois (5)	10	0.02
Kiowa (60)	83	0.15
Latin American Indians (15)	21	0.04
Lumbee (8)	8	0.01
Navajo (15)	19	0.04
Osage (13)	17	0.03
Ottawa (5)	8	0.01
Potawatomi (59)	104	0.19
Pueblo (7)	19	0.04
Puget Sound Salish	2	0.00
Seminole (63)	152	0.28
Shoshone (3)	3	0.01
Sioux (5)	24	0.04
Tohono O'Odham (1)	1	0.00
Yakama (1)	2	0.00
All other tribes (163)	242	0.45
American Indian tribes, not spec.	59	0.11
Arab:	63	0.12
Jordanian	7	0.01
Lebanese	49	0.09
Syrian	7	0.01
Armenian	5	0.01
Asian:	1,318	2.44
Chinese, ex. Taiwanese (25)	53	0.10
Filipino (253)	406	0.75
Indian (55)	70	0.13
Indonesian (4)	10	0.02
Japanese (98)	200	0.37
Korean (126)	174	0.32
Laotian (4)	4	0.01
Malaysian (2)	2	0.00
Pakistani (13)	16	0.03
Sri Lankan	1	0.00
Taiwanese (6)	8	0.01
Thai (41)	64	0.12
Vietnamese (225)	247	0.46
Other Asian, specified (4)	12	0.02
Other Asian, not specified (15)	51	0.09
Australian	6	0.01
Austrian	16	0.03
Belgian	36	0.07
Brazilian	19	0.04
British	298	0.55
Canadian	68	0.13
Celtic	12	0.02
Croatian	40	0.07
Czech	135	0.25
Czechoslovakian	78	0.14
Danish	133	0.25
Dutch	926	1.71
English	4,606	8.50
European	332	0.61
Finnish	100	0.18
French, except Basque	1,339	2.47
French Canadian	292	0.54
German	6,683	12.33
Greek	43	0.08
Guyanese	6	0.01
Hawaii Native/Pacific Islander:	166	0.31
Micronesian: (27)	40	0.07
Guamanian/Chamorro (27)	40	0.07
Polynesian: (30)	94	0.17
Native Hawaiian (18)	72	0.13
Samoan (8)	10	0.02
Tongan (1)	5	0.01
Other Polynesian (3)	7	0.01
Other Pac. Isl., specified	5	0.01
Other Pac. Isl., not spec. (4)	27	0.05
Hispanic or Latino:	2,192	4.05
Central American:	60	0.11
Costa Rican	4	0.01
Guatemalan	4	0.01
Honduran	5	0.01
Nicaraguan	5	0.01
Panamanian	28	0.05
Salvadoran	7	0.01
Other Central American	7	0.01
Cuban	21	0.04
Dominican Republic	5	0.01
Mexican	1,386	2.56
Puerto Rican	190	0.35
South American:	41	0.08
Argentinean	3	0.01
Bolivian	3	0.01
Colombian	21	0.04
Peruvian	10	0.02
Venezuelan	1	0.00
Other South American	3	0.01
Other Hispanic or Latino	489	0.90
Hungarian	57	0.11
Iranian	42	0.08
Irish	5,136	9.48
Italian	981	1.81
Latvian	53	0.10
Lithuanian	19	0.04
Northern European	23	0.04
Norwegian	461	0.85
Pennsylvania German	17	0.03
Polish	714	1.32
Portuguese	63	0.12
Romanian	22	0.04
Russian	108	0.20
Scandinavian	25	0.05
Scotch-Irish	889	1.64
Scottish	775	1.43
Serbian	9	0.02
Slovene	21	0.04
Swedish	316	0.58
Swiss	55	0.10
Turkish	35	0.06
Ukrainian	23	0.04
United States or American	5,686	10.49
Welsh	255	0.47
West Indian, excl. Hispanic:	124	0.23
Dutch West Indian	76	0.14
Jamaican	29	0.05
West Indian	19	0.04
White:	39,472	72.98
Not Hispanic (36,575)	38,269	70.75
Hispanic (993)	1,203	2.22

Notes: 1. Figures in the "Number" column do not add up to the total population due to: a) Ancestry/Race overlap — e.g. persons can report being both White and Irish, b) persons of Hispanic origin can report being any race, c) persons reporting two ancestries are counted in both categories. 2. Numbers in parentheses indicate the number of persons reporting this ancestry/race alone, not in combination with any other ancestry/race. 3. Refer to the Explanation of Data in the front of the book for more detailed information.

Moore

Place Type: City
County: Cleveland
Population: 41,138

Ancestry/Race	Number	%
African American/Black:	1,473	3.58
Not Hispanic (1,181)	1,439	3.50
Hispanic (20)	34	0.08
African, sub-Saharan:	27	0.07
African	13	0.03
South African	14	0.03
Alaska Native tribes, specified:	13	0.03
Alaska Athabascan (1)	5	0.01
Eskimo (2)	5	0.01
Tlingit-Haida	3	0.01
Am. Ind. or Alaska Nat., not spec.	376	0.91
Albanian	6	0.01
American Indian tribes, specified:	2,856	6.94
Apache (5)	22	0.05
Blackfeet (8)	24	0.06
Cherokee (329)	824	2.00
Cheyenne (7)	15	0.04
Chickasaw (150)	300	0.73
Chippewa (4)	10	0.02
Choctaw (404)	717	1.74
Comanche (20)	42	0.10
Creek (112)	225	0.55
Crow	1	0.00
Delaware (13)	28	0.07
Iroquois (19)	29	0.07
Kiowa (54)	73	0.18
Latin American Indians (7)	22	0.05
Navajo (17)	30	0.07
Osage (21)	34	0.08
Ottawa	4	0.01
Pima (3)	3	0.01
Potawatomi (64)	106	0.26
Pueblo (10)	10	0.02
Seminole (59)	114	0.28
Sioux (11)	33	0.08
Yakama (2)	2	0.00
All other tribes (118)	188	0.46
American Indian tribes, not spec.	35	0.09
Arab:	49	0.12
Lebanese	6	0.01
Moroccan	22	0.05
Syrian	14	0.03
Other Arab	7	0.02
Asian:	931	2.26
Cambodian (5)	6	0.01
Chinese, ex. Taiwanese (24)	51	0.12
Filipino (84)	151	0.37
Indian (54)	65	0.16
Japanese (37)	108	0.26
Korean (193)	241	0.59
Laotian (10)	11	0.03
Malaysian (1)	1	0.00
Pakistani (4)	4	0.01
Taiwanese	5	0.01
Thai (12)	32	0.08
Vietnamese (211)	223	0.54
Other Asian, specified (1)	1	0.00
Other Asian, not specified (16)	32	0.08
Australian	7	0.02
Belgian	26	0.06
British	61	0.15
Bulgarian	62	0.15
Canadian	31	0.08
Czech	151	0.37
Czechoslovakian	124	0.30
Danish	52	0.13
Dutch	748	1.83
English	3,635	8.89
European	392	0.96
Finnish	6	0.01
French, except Basque	1,186	2.90
French Canadian	198	0.48
German	5,820	14.24
Greek	15	0.04
Hawaii Native/Pacific Islander:	65	0.16
Micronesian: (9)	29	0.07
Guamanian/Chamorro (4)	21	0.05
Other Micronesian (5)	8	0.02
Polynesian: (9)	29	0.07
Native Hawaiian (7)	24	0.06
Samoan (1)	3	0.01
Other Polynesian (1)	2	0.00
Other Pac. Isl., not spec. (1)	7	0.02
Hispanic or Latino:	2,098	5.10
Central American:	68	0.17
Costa Rican	4	0.01
Guatemalan	39	0.09
Honduran	2	0.00
Panamanian	12	0.03
Salvadoran	8	0.02
Other Central American	3	0.01
Cuban	18	0.04
Dominican Republic	1	0.00
Mexican	1,381	3.36
Puerto Rican	130	0.32
South American:	76	0.18
Argentinean	15	0.04
Bolivian	1	0.00
Chilean	1	0.00
Colombian	35	0.09
Ecuadorian	4	0.01
Peruvian	7	0.02
Uruguayan	1	0.00
Venezuelan	11	0.03
Other South American	1	0.00
Other Hispanic or Latino	424	1.03
Hungarian	96	0.23
Icelander	6	0.01
Iranian	49	0.12
Irish	4,975	12.17
Italian	941	2.30
Lithuanian	15	0.04
Maltese	18	0.04
Northern European	13	0.03
Norwegian	345	0.84
Polish	521	1.27
Portuguese	60	0.15
Romanian	32	0.08
Russian	97	0.24
Scandinavian	35	0.09
Scotch-Irish	749	1.83
Scottish	681	1.67
Serbian	6	0.01
Slavic	6	0.01
Slovak	7	0.02
Swedish	167	0.41
Swiss	100	0.24
Turkish	19	0.05
Ukrainian	48	0.12
United States or American	5,742	14.05
Welsh	179	0.44
West Indian, excl. Hispanic:	216	0.53
Dutch West Indian	201	0.49
West Indian	15	0.04
White:	36,706	89.23
Not Hispanic (33,765)	35,446	86.16
Hispanic (1,049)	1,260	3.06

Muskogee

Place Type: City
County: Muskogee
Population: 38,310

Ancestry/Race	Number	%
African American/Black:	7,394	19.30
Not Hispanic (6,813)	7,327	19.13
Hispanic (43)	67	0.17
African, sub-Saharan:	150	0.39
African	150	0.39
Alaska Native tribes, specified:	3	0.01
Alaska Athabascan (1)	2	0.01
All other tribes (1)	1	0.00
Am. Ind. or Alaska Nat., not spec.	483	1.26
American Indian tribes, specified:	6,410	16.73
Apache (16)	25	0.07
Blackfeet (10)	24	0.06
Cherokee (2,817)	4,229	11.04
Cheyenne (11)	15	0.04
Chickasaw (54)	89	0.23
Chippewa (15)	19	0.05
Choctaw (289)	511	1.33
Comanche (15)	24	0.06
Cree (1)	5	0.01
Creek (688)	1,085	2.83
Crow (4)	5	0.01
Delaware (6)	7	0.02
Iroquois (4)	12	0.03
Kiowa (23)	36	0.09
Latin American Indians (6)	7	0.02
Lumbee (3)	5	0.01
Navajo (21)	27	0.07
Osage (18)	26	0.07
Ottawa (1)	1	0.00
Paiute (2)	2	0.01
Potawatomi (22)	30	0.08
Pueblo (4)	5	0.01
Seminole (27)	66	0.17
Shoshone (7)	8	0.02
Sioux (11)	17	0.04
Yaqui (1)	1	0.00
All other tribes (82)	129	0.34
American Indian tribes, not spec.	152	0.40
Arab:	6	0.02
Syrian	6	0.02
Asian:	446	1.16
Chinese, ex. Taiwanese (42)	66	0.17
Filipino (30)	56	0.15
Indian (68)	76	0.20
Indonesian (1)	1	0.00
Japanese (17)	37	0.10
Korean (21)	27	0.07
Pakistani	1	0.00
Sri Lankan (1)	1	0.00
Thai (9)	14	0.04
Vietnamese (129)	148	0.39
Other Asian, specified (9)	13	0.03
Other Asian, not specified (2)	6	0.02
Austrian	42	0.11
Belgian	32	0.08
British	49	0.13
Celtic	7	0.02
Czech	16	0.04
Czechoslovakian	16	0.04
Danish	13	0.03
Dutch	480	1.25
English	2,306	6.02
European	176	0.46
Finnish	10	0.03
French, except Basque	857	2.24
French Canadian	97	0.25
German	3,209	8.37
Greek	9	0.02
Hawaii Native/Pacific Islander:	40	0.10
Micronesian: (2)	8	0.02
Guamanian/Chamorro (2)	6	0.02
Other Micronesian	2	0.01
Polynesian: (6)	25	0.07
Native Hawaiian (4)	15	0.04
Samoan (2)	9	0.02
Other Polynesian	1	0.00
Other Pac. Isl., specified	3	0.01
Other Pac. Isl., not spec.	4	0.01
Hispanic or Latino:	1,258	3.28
Central American:	25	0.07
Guatemalan	18	0.05
Nicaraguan	2	0.01
Salvadoran	4	0.01
Other Central American	1	0.00
Cuban	18	0.05
Dominican Republic	3	0.01
Mexican	913	2.38
Puerto Rican	56	0.15

Notes: 1. Figures in the "Number" column do not add up to the total population due to: a) Ancestry/Race overlap — e.g. persons can report being both White and Irish, b) persons of Hispanic origin can report being any race, c) persons reporting two ancestries are counted in both categories. 2. Numbers in parentheses indicate the number of persons reporting this ancestry/race alone, not in combination with any other ancestry/race. 3. Refer to the Explanation of Data in the front of the book for more detailed information.

Ancestry/Race	Number	%
South American:	9	0.02
Argentinean	2	0.01
Colombian	3	0.01
Peruvian	3	0.01
Other South American	1	0.00
Other Hispanic or Latino	234	0.61
Hungarian	21	0.05
Irish	3,227	8.42
Italian	398	1.04
Lithuanian	21	0.05
Luxemburger	9	0.02
Northern European	8	0.02
Norwegian	124	0.32
Pennsylvania German	21	0.05
Polish	121	0.32
Portuguese	20	0.05
Russian	40	0.10
Scandinavian	19	0.05
Scotch-Irish	424	1.11
Scottish	346	0.90
Slovak	6	0.02
Slovene	29	0.08
Swedish	125	0.33
Swiss	16	0.04
United States or American	2,986	7.79
Welsh	163	0.43
West Indian, excl. Hispanic:	144	0.38
Dutch West Indian	144	0.38
White:	25,400	66.30
Not Hispanic (22,983)	24,886	64.96
Hispanic (431)	514	1.34

Mustang

Place Type: City
County: Canadian
Population: 13,156

Ancestry/Race	Number	%
Acadian/Cajun	22	0.17
African American/Black:	109	0.83
Not Hispanic (71)	103	0.78
Hispanic (6)	6	0.05
African, sub-Saharan:	12	0.09
African	12	0.09
Alaska Native tribes, not specified	2	0.02
Am. Ind. or Alaska Nat., not spec.	59	0.45
American Indian tribes, specified:	694	5.28
Cherokee (92)	221	1.68
Cheyenne (3)	6	0.05
Chickasaw (56)	76	0.58
Chippewa (3)	3	0.02
Choctaw (139)	218	1.66
Comanche (4)	5	0.04
Creek (31)	59	0.45
Delaware (2)	4	0.03
Houma (1)	1	0.01
Iroquois (1)	1	0.01
Kiowa (5)	11	0.08
Navajo (4)	6	0.05
Osage (1)	5	0.04
Potawatomi (10)	22	0.17
Pueblo (4)	4	0.03
Seminole (11)	21	0.16
Sioux (1)	1	0.01
All other tribes (21)	30	0.23
American Indian tribes, not spec.	9	0.07
Arab:	6	0.05
Lebanese	6	0.05
Asian:	105	0.80
Chinese, ex. Taiwanese	1	0.01
Filipino (9)	30	0.23
Indian (18)	21	0.16
Japanese (2)	7	0.05
Korean (9)	13	0.10
Taiwanese (3)	3	0.02
Thai (1)	1	0.01
Vietnamese (22)	28	0.21
Other Asian, not specified	1	0.01
Austrian	6	0.05
Belgian	10	0.08
British	128	0.97
Canadian	42	0.32
Czech	117	0.89
Czechoslovakian	60	0.45
Danish	41	0.31
Dutch	352	2.67
English	1,511	11.45
European	48	0.36
French, except Basque	449	3.40
French Canadian	89	0.67
German	2,425	18.38
Greek	16	0.12
Hawaii Native/Pacific Islander:	16	0.12
Polynesian: (12)	16	0.12
Native Hawaiian (6)	10	0.08
Samoan (6)	6	0.05
Hispanic or Latino:	396	3.01
Central American:	11	0.08
Guatemalan	1	0.01
Honduran	2	0.02
Panamanian	7	0.05
Salvadoran	1	0.01
Cuban	10	0.08
Mexican	266	2.02
Puerto Rican	24	0.18
South American:	12	0.09
Bolivian	1	0.01
Colombian	4	0.03
Peruvian	7	0.05
Other Hispanic or Latino	73	0.55
Hungarian	16	0.12
Irish	1,489	11.29
Italian	243	1.84
Lithuanian	6	0.05
Luxemburger	9	0.07
Norwegian	130	0.99
Pennsylvania German	15	0.11
Polish	179	1.36
Portuguese	9	0.07
Romanian	15	0.11
Russian	22	0.17
Scotch-Irish	266	2.02
Scottish	300	2.27
Swedish	92	0.70
Ukrainian	5	0.04
United States or American	1,866	14.15
Welsh	78	0.59
West Indian, excl. Hispanic:	39	0.30
Dutch West Indian	32	0.24
Jamaican	7	0.05
White:	12,454	94.66
Not Hispanic (11,824)	12,166	92.47
Hispanic (231)	288	2.19

Norman

Place Type: City
County: Cleveland
Population: 95,694

Ancestry/Race	Number	%
Acadian/Cajun	26	0.03
African American/Black:	4,807	5.02
Not Hispanic (4,022)	4,704	4.92
Hispanic (58)	103	0.11
African, sub-Saharan:	549	0.57
African	258	0.27
Ethiopian	11	0.01
Ghanian	18	0.02
Kenyan	32	0.03
Nigerian	185	0.19
South African	17	0.02
Other sub-Saharan African	28	0.03
Alaska Native tribes, specified:	16	0.02
Alaska Athabascan (1)	2	0.00
Aleut (4)	4	0.00
Eskimo (3)	5	0.01
Tlingit-Haida (4)	5	0.01
Alaska Native tribes, not specified	2	0.00
Am. Ind. or Alaska Nat., not spec.	631	0.66
American Indian tribes, specified:	6,089	6.36
Apache (31)	49	0.05
Blackfeet	21	0.02
Cherokee (745)	1,560	1.63
Cheyenne (43)	66	0.07
Chickasaw (333)	577	0.60
Chippewa (20)	43	0.04
Choctaw (775)	1,285	1.34
Colville (1)	1	0.00
Comanche (108)	160	0.17
Cree (1)	2	0.00
Creek (269)	432	0.45
Crow (6)	6	0.01
Delaware (45)	77	0.08
Iroquois (33)	61	0.06
Kiowa (183)	237	0.25
Latin American Indians (4)	15	0.02
Lumbee (5)	5	0.01
Menominee (1)	1	0.00
Navajo (50)	58	0.06
Osage (74)	107	0.11
Ottawa (3)	7	0.01
Pima (1)	1	0.00
Potawatomi (145)	240	0.25
Pueblo (19)	34	0.04
Seminole (158)	231	0.24
Shoshone (3)	3	0.00
Sioux (9)	33	0.03
Ute (1)	1	0.00
Yakama (3)	3	0.00
All other tribes (612)	773	0.81
American Indian tribes, not spec.	200	0.21
Arab:	516	0.54
Arab/Arabic	52	0.05
Egyptian	14	0.01
Jordanian	18	0.02
Lebanese	234	0.24
Moroccan	7	0.01
Palestinian	21	0.02
Syrian	27	0.03
Other Arab	143	0.15
Armenian	12	0.01
Asian:	4,020	4.20
Bangladeshi (39)	39	0.04
Cambodian (13)	14	0.01
Chinese, ex. Taiwanese (872)	958	1.00
Filipino (235)	332	0.35
Hmong (13)	13	0.01
Indian (675)	735	0.77
Indonesian (59)	68	0.07
Japanese (166)	287	0.30
Korean (415)	494	0.52
Laotian (30)	32	0.03
Malaysian (61)	75	0.08
Pakistani (77)	93	0.10
Sri Lankan (10)	11	0.01
Taiwanese (66)	81	0.08
Thai (74)	108	0.11
Vietnamese (382)	445	0.47
Other Asian, specified (17)	25	0.03
Other Asian, not specified (82)	210	0.22
Assyrian/Chaldean/Syriac	6	0.01
Australian	32	0.03
Austrian	177	0.18
Basque	21	0.02
Belgian	102	0.11
Brazilian	62	0.06
British	716	0.75
Bulgarian	47	0.05
Canadian	200	0.21
Celtic	37	0.04
Croatian	32	0.03
Czech	582	0.61
Czechoslovakian	241	0.25
Danish	374	0.39
Dutch	1,860	1.94
Eastern European	44	0.05
English	12,221	12.77
European	1,441	1.51

Notes: 1. Figures in the "Number" column do not add up to the total population due to: a) Ancestry/Race overlap — e.g. persons can report being both White and Irish, b) persons of Hispanic origin can report being any race, c) persons reporting two ancestries are counted in both categories. 2. Numbers in parentheses indicate the number of persons reporting this ancestry/race alone, not in combination with any other ancestry/race. 3. Refer to the Explanation of Data in the front of the book for more detailed information.

Ancestry/Race	Number	%
Finnish	153	0.16
French, except Basque	2,902	3.03
French Canadian	448	0.47
German	15,733	16.44
Greek	230	0.24
Hawaii Native/Pacific Islander:	137	0.14
Micronesian: (22)	43	0.04
Guamanian/Chamorro (22)	43	0.04
Polynesian: (25)	63	0.07
Native Hawaiian (11)	38	0.04
Samoan (13)	24	0.03
Other Polynesian (1)	1	0.00
Other Pac. Isl., specified	5	0.01
Other Pac. Isl., not spec. (1)	26	0.03
Hispanic or Latino:	3,723	3.89
Central American:	190	0.20
Costa Rican	21	0.02
Guatemalan	84	0.09
Honduran	16	0.02
Nicaraguan	6	0.01
Panamanian	30	0.03
Salvadoran	27	0.03
Other Central American	6	0.01
Cuban	85	0.09
Dominican Republic	7	0.01
Mexican	2,150	2.25
Puerto Rican	279	0.29
South American:	299	0.31
Argentinean	29	0.03
Bolivian	15	0.02
Chilean	8	0.01
Colombian	92	0.10
Ecuadorian	15	0.02
Paraguayan	5	0.01
Peruvian	32	0.03
Venezuelan	94	0.10
Other South American	9	0.01
Other Hispanic or Latino	713	0.75
Hungarian	199	0.21
Iranian	234	0.24
Irish	12,019	12.56
Israeli	9	0.01
Italian	2,290	2.39
Latvian	6	0.01
Lithuanian	46	0.05
Macedonian	8	0.01
New Zealander	10	0.01
Northern European	138	0.14
Norwegian	921	0.96
Pennsylvania German	23	0.02
Polish	1,268	1.33
Portuguese	113	0.12
Romanian	99	0.10
Russian	414	0.43
Scandinavian	121	0.13
Scotch-Irish	2,615	2.73
Scottish	2,718	2.84
Serbian	43	0.04
Slavic	11	0.01
Slovak	94	0.10
Slovene	16	0.02
Swedish	1,097	1.15
Swiss	205	0.21
Turkish	73	0.08
Ukrainian	98	0.10
United States or American	8,354	8.73
Welsh	755	0.79
West Indian, excl. Hispanic:	391	0.41
Bahamian	26	0.03
Belizean	10	0.01
British West Indian	17	0.02
Dutch West Indian	272	0.28
Haitian	15	0.02
Jamaican	51	0.05
White:	82,336	86.04
Not Hispanic (76,852)	80,066	83.67
Hispanic (1,960)	2,270	2.37
Yugoslavian	37	0.04

Oklahoma City

Place Type: City
County: Oklahoma
Population: 506,132

Ancestry/Race	Number	%
Acadian/Cajun	110	0.02
African American/Black:	83,034	16.41
Not Hispanic (76,994)	81,714	16.14
Hispanic (816)	1,320	0.26
African, sub-Saharan:	3,584	0.71
African	2,628	0.52
Cape Verdean	36	0.01
Ethiopian	29	0.01
Ghanian	152	0.03
Kenyan	74	0.01
Liberian	80	0.02
Nigerian	400	0.08
Senegalese	8	0.00
Sierra Leonean	10	0.00
South African	59	0.01
Sudanese	9	0.00
Ugandan	6	0.00
Zimbabwean	10	0.00
Other sub-Saharan African	83	0.02
Alaska Native tribes, specified:	71	0.01
Alaska Athabascan (8)	12	0.00
Aleut (22)	23	0.00
Eskimo (16)	26	0.01
Tlingit-Haida (8)	10	0.00
Alaska Native tribes, not specified	10	0.00
Am. Ind. or Alaska Nat., not spec.	4,355	0.86
Albanian	17	0.00
Alsatian	24	0.00
American Indian tribes, specified:	25,562	5.05
Apache (175)	345	0.07
Blackfeet (29)	169	0.03
Cherokee (2,608)	6,366	1.26
Cheyenne (311)	459	0.09
Chickasaw (1,067)	1,949	0.39
Chippewa (71)	105	0.02
Choctaw (3,287)	5,576	1.10
Colville (2)	2	0.00
Comanche (358)	503	0.10
Cree (1)	10	0.00
Creek (1,339)	2,361	0.47
Crow (10)	20	0.00
Delaware (160)	281	0.06
Houma (1)	3	0.00
Iroquois (92)	177	0.03
Kiowa (703)	1,001	0.20
Latin American Indians (175)	309	0.06
Lumbee (16)	21	0.00
Navajo (142)	214	0.04
Osage (128)	269	0.05
Ottawa (7)	9	0.00
Paiute (1)	4	0.00
Pima (24)	36	0.01
Potawatomi (480)	758	0.15
Pueblo (60)	103	0.02
Puget Sound Salish (3)	7	0.00
Seminole (843)	1,486	0.29
Shoshone (11)	21	0.00
Sioux (122)	237	0.05
Tohono O'Odham (6)	13	0.00
Ute (9)	11	0.00
Yakama (1)	5	0.00
Yaqui (11)	15	0.00
Yuman (10)	14	0.00
All other tribes (1,928)	2,703	0.53
American Indian tribes, not spec.	608	0.12
Arab:	2,404	0.48
Arab/Arabic	523	0.10
Egyptian	67	0.01
Iraqi	50	0.01
Jordanian	78	0.02
Lebanese	1,287	0.25
Moroccan	198	0.04
Palestinian	17	0.00
Syrian	106	0.02
Other Arab	78	0.02
Armenian	100	0.02
Asian:	20,661	4.08
Bangladeshi (120)	146	0.03
Cambodian (101)	128	0.03
Chinese, ex. Taiwanese (1,699)	2,173	0.43
Filipino (844)	1,370	0.27
Hmong (8)	16	0.00
Indian (2,918)	3,249	0.64
Indonesian (117)	162	0.03
Japanese (492)	878	0.17
Korean (1,020)	1,342	0.27
Laotian (592)	686	0.14
Malaysian (85)	101	0.02
Pakistani (212)	265	0.05
Sri Lankan (10)	13	0.00
Taiwanese (117)	150	0.03
Thai (303)	438	0.09
Vietnamese (8,161)	8,652	1.71
Other Asian, specified (34)	53	0.01
Other Asian, not specified (359)	839	0.17
Assyrian/Chaldean/Syriac	7	0.00
Australian	141	0.03
Austrian	415	0.08
Basque	15	0.00
Belgian	250	0.05
Brazilian	70	0.01
British	1,433	0.28
Bulgarian	39	0.01
Canadian	593	0.12
Celtic	161	0.03
Croatian	90	0.02
Czech	2,021	0.40
Czechoslovakian	957	0.19
Danish	1,373	0.27
Dutch	8,567	1.69
Eastern European	89	0.02
English	43,049	8.51
Estonian	24	0.00
European	3,528	0.70
Finnish	189	0.04
French, except Basque	11,253	2.22
French Canadian	1,292	0.26
German	59,379	11.74
German Russian	9	0.00
Greek	1,021	0.20
Guyanese	5	0.00
Hawaii Native/Pacific Islander:	811	0.16
Melanesian: (2)	3	0.00
Fijian (1)	2	0.00
Other Melanesian (1)	1	0.00
Micronesian: (168)	237	0.05
Guamanian/Chamorro (158)	225	0.04
Other Micronesian (10)	12	0.00
Polynesian: (158)	343	0.07
Native Hawaiian (113)	273	0.05
Samoan (33)	55	0.01
Tongan (12)	14	0.00
Other Polynesian	1	0.00
Other Pac. Isl., specified	8	0.00
Other Pac. Isl., not spec. (29)	220	0.04
Hispanic or Latino:	51,368	10.15
Central American:	1,767	0.35
Costa Rican	42	0.01
Guatemalan	1,068	0.21
Honduran	298	0.06
Nicaraguan	54	0.01
Panamanian	134	0.03
Salvadoran	129	0.03
Other Central American	42	0.01
Cuban	365	0.07
Dominican Republic	40	0.01
Mexican	40,997	8.10
Puerto Rican	1,205	0.24
South American:	716	0.14
Argentinean	54	0.01
Bolivian	26	0.01
Chilean	27	0.01
Colombian	207	0.04

Notes: 1. Figures in the "Number" column do not add up to the total population due to: a) Ancestry/Race overlap — e.g. persons can report being both White and Irish, b) persons of Hispanic origin can report being any race, c) persons reporting two ancestries are counted in both categories. 2. Numbers in parentheses indicate the number of persons reporting this ancestry/race alone, not in combination with any other ancestry/race. 3. Refer to the Explanation of Data in the front of the book for more detailed information.

Ecuadorian	62	0.01
Paraguayan	8	0.00
Peruvian	200	0.04
Uruguayan	8	0.00
Venezuelan	99	0.02
Other South American	25	0.00
Other Hispanic or Latino	6,278	1.24
Hungarian	532	0.11
Icelander	16	0.00
Iranian	1,014	0.20
Irish	46,591	9.21
Israeli	38	0.01
Italian	7,326	1.45
Latvian	43	0.01
Lithuanian	185	0.04
Luxemburger	36	0.01
Macedonian	8	0.00
Maltese	17	0.00
New Zealander	31	0.01
Northern European	222	0.04
Norwegian	3,169	0.63
Pennsylvania German	142	0.03
Polish	4,180	0.83
Portuguese	326	0.06
Romanian	137	0.03
Russian	1,252	0.25
Scandinavian	339	0.07
Scotch-Irish	8,918	1.76
Scottish	7,985	1.58
Serbian	36	0.01
Slavic	57	0.01
Slovak	160	0.03
Slovene	43	0.01
Swedish	3,841	0.76
Swiss	783	0.15
Turkish	87	0.02
Ukrainian	325	0.06
United States or American	45,589	9.01
Welsh	2,463	0.49
West Indian, excl. Hispanic:	1,483	0.29
Bahamian	7	0.00
Belizean	13	0.00
British West Indian	22	0.00
Dutch West Indian	1,092	0.22
Haitian	17	0.00
Jamaican	237	0.05
Trinidadian and Tobagonian	50	0.01
U.S. Virgin Islander	9	0.00
West Indian	36	0.01
White:	362,788	71.68
Not Hispanic (327,225)	340,685	67.31
Hispanic (19,001)	22,103	4.37
Yugoslavian	140	0.03

Okmulgee

Place Type: City
County: Okmulgee
Population: 13,022

Ancestry/Race	Number	%
African American/Black:	2,966	22.78
Not Hispanic (2,760)	2,942	22.59
Hispanic (13)	24	0.18
African, sub-Saharan:	34	0.26
African	34	0.26
Alaska Native tribes, specified:	1	0.01
Alaska Athabascan (1)	1	0.01
Am. Ind. or Alaska Nat., not spec.	235	1.80
American Indian tribes, specified:	2,185	16.78
Apache	7	0.05
Blackfeet	5	0.04
Cherokee (190)	389	2.99
Cheyenne (12)	15	0.12
Chickasaw (20)	40	0.31
Chippewa (4)	6	0.05
Choctaw (84)	155	1.19
Colville	2	0.02
Comanche (6)	6	0.05
Cree (3)	3	0.02
Creek (1,035)	1,330	10.21
Crow	1	0.01
Delaware (4)	4	0.03
Iroquois	2	0.02
Kiowa (16)	19	0.15
Latin American Indians (1)	2	0.02
Navajo (8)	8	0.06
Osage (5)	7	0.05
Ottawa (1)	1	0.01
Potawatomi (6)	8	0.06
Pueblo (1)	1	0.01
Seminole (37)	74	0.57
Sioux (10)	14	0.11
Tohono O'Odham (2)	2	0.02
Ute (1)	1	0.01
Yuman (1)	1	0.01
All other tribes (58)	82	0.63
American Indian tribes, not spec.	38	0.29
Arab:	47	0.36
Egyptian	23	0.18
Lebanese	10	0.08
Syrian	14	0.11
Asian:	64	0.49
Chinese, ex. Taiwanese (10)	12	0.09
Filipino (6)	13	0.10
Indian (2)	8	0.06
Japanese (6)	11	0.08
Korean (5)	6	0.05
Pakistani (1)	1	0.01
Vietnamese (3)	3	0.02
Other Asian, not specified (4)	10	0.08
Austrian	24	0.18
Belgian	29	0.22
British	12	0.09
Canadian	5	0.04
Croatian	5	0.04
Czech	7	0.05
Czechoslovakian	19	0.14
Dutch	260	1.98
English	705	5.38
European	65	0.50
French, except Basque	190	1.45
French Canadian	30	0.23
German	1,122	8.56
Greek	5	0.04
Hawaii Native/Pacific Islander:	18	0.14
Micronesian: (2)	5	0.04
Guamanian/Chamorro (2)	5	0.04
Polynesian: (1)	12	0.09
Native Hawaiian (1)	11	0.08
Samoan	1	0.01
Other Pac. Isl., not spec.	1	0.01
Hispanic or Latino:	238	1.83
Central American:	1	0.01
Salvadoran	1	0.01
Cuban	4	0.03
Mexican	135	1.04
Puerto Rican	17	0.13
South American:	5	0.04
Colombian	1	0.01
Ecuadorian	2	0.02
Peruvian	1	0.01
Venezuelan		0.01
Other Hispanic or Latino	76	0.58
Hungarian	6	0.05
Irish	925	7.06
Italian	122	0.93
Lithuanian	7	0.05
Norwegian	37	0.28
Polish	40	0.31
Romanian	16	0.12
Russian	26	0.20
Scandinavian	9	0.07
Scotch-Irish	236	1.80
Scottish	137	1.05
Slovak	4	0.03
Swedish	25	0.19
Swiss	10	0.08
United States or American	1,241	9.47
Welsh	14	0.11
West Indian, excl. Hispanic:	25	0.19
Dutch West Indian	17	0.13
U.S. Virgin Islander	8	0.06
White:	8,231	63.21
Not Hispanic (7,589)	8,120	62.36
Hispanic (74)	111	0.85

Owasso

Place Type: City
County: Tulsa
Population: 18,502

Ancestry/Race	Number	%
Acadian/Cajun	16	0.09
African American/Black:	365	1.97
Not Hispanic (276)	341	1.84
Hispanic (20)	24	0.13
Am. Ind. or Alaska Nat., not spec.	151	0.82
American Indian tribes, specified:	1,372	7.42
Apache (1)	6	0.03
Blackfeet (1)	1	0.01
Cherokee (488)	886	4.79
Cheyenne	3	0.02
Chickasaw (17)	39	0.21
Chippewa (4)	9	0.05
Choctaw (57)	98	0.53
Comanche (5)	12	0.06
Creek (93)	132	0.71
Crow (1)	1	0.01
Delaware (21)	27	0.15
Iroquois (6)	13	0.07
Kiowa (4)	10	0.05
Navajo (5)	6	0.03
Osage (21)	45	0.24
Potawatomi (3)	7	0.04
Seminole (9)	13	0.07
Shoshone (3)	3	0.02
Sioux (6)	9	0.05
Yaqui (1)	1	0.01
All other tribes (40)	51	0.28
American Indian tribes, not spec.	35	0.19
Arab:	30	0.16
Syrian	30	0.16
Asian:	275	1.49
Chinese, ex. Taiwanese (33)	41	0.22
Filipino (38)	57	0.31
Hmong (12)	12	0.06
Indian (13)	27	0.15
Indonesian (1)	1	0.01
Japanese (6)	15	0.08
Korean (17)	25	0.14
Laotian (42)	43	0.23
Thai (13)	25	0.14
Vietnamese (16)	18	0.10
Other Asian, not specified (1)	11	0.06
Austrian	26	0.14
British	70	0.38
Canadian	29	0.16
Celtic	4	0.02
Czech	41	0.22
Czechoslovakian	59	0.32
Danish	52	0.28
Dutch	519	2.80
English	1,977	10.66
European	112	0.60
French, except Basque	449	2.42
French Canadian	82	0.44
German	2,959	15.95
German Russian	9	0.05
Greek	59	0.32
Hawaii Native/Pacific Islander:	13	0.07
Micronesian: (1)	2	0.01
Guamanian/Chamorro		0.01
Other Micronesian (1)	1	0.01
Polynesian:	7	0.04
Native Hawaiian	6	0.03
Other Polynesian	1	0.01
Other Pac. Isl., not spec.	4	0.02
Hispanic or Latino:	729	3.94

Notes: 1. Figures in the "Number" column do not add up to the total population due to: a) Ancestry/Race overlap — e.g. persons can report being both White and Irish, b) persons of Hispanic origin can report being any race, c) persons reporting two ancestries are counted in both categories. 2. Numbers in parentheses indicate the number of persons reporting this ancestry/race alone, not in combination with any other ancestry/race. 3. Refer to the Explanation of Data in the front of the book for more detailed information.

Central American:	22	0.12
Costa Rican	3	0.02
Guatemalan	12	0.06
Honduran	1	0.01
Panamanian	6	0.03
Cuban	10	0.05
Mexican	527	2.85
Puerto Rican	39	0.21
South American:	15	0.08
Argentinean	1	0.01
Colombian	7	0.04
Venezuelan	6	0.03
Other South American	1	0.01
Other Hispanic or Latino	116	0.63
Hungarian	10	0.05
Irish	2,618	14.11
Italian	410	2.21
Norwegian	82	0.44
Pennsylvania German	10	0.05
Polish	111	0.60
Portuguese	37	0.20
Romanian	15	0.08
Russian	82	0.44
Scandinavian	52	0.28
Scotch-Irish	351	1.89
Scottish	258	1.39
Slavic	21	0.11
Slovak	34	0.18
Swedish	292	1.57
Ukrainian	10	0.05
United States or American	2,058	11.10
Welsh	185	1.00
West Indian, excl. Hispanic:	98	0.53
Dutch West Indian	98	0.53
White:	16,721	90.37
Not Hispanic (15,688)	16,337	88.30
Hispanic (345)	384	2.08

Ponca City

Place Type: City
County: Kay
Population: 25,919

Ancestry/Race	Number	%
Acadian/Cajun	4	0.02
African American/Black:	862	3.33
Not Hispanic (767)	850	3.28
Hispanic (7)	12	0.05
African, sub-Saharan:	22	0.08
African	7	0.03
South African	6	0.02
Ugandan	9	0.03
Alaska Native tribes, specified:	5	0.02
Alaska Athabascan	1	0.00
Eskimo (2)	3	0.01
Tlingit-Haida (1)	1	0.00
Alaska Native tribes, not specified	2	0.01
Am. Ind. or Alaska Nat., not spec.	253	0.98
Alsatian	2	0.01
American Indian tribes, specified:	2,169	8.37
Apache (13)	20	0.08
Blackfeet (1)	3	0.01
Cherokee (250)	538	2.08
Cheyenne (35)	37	0.14
Chickasaw (26)	49	0.19
Chippewa (3)	5	0.02
Choctaw (46)	114	0.44
Comanche (5)	16	0.06
Creek (29)	67	0.26
Crow (2)	3	0.01
Delaware (15)	18	0.07
Iroquois (16)	29	0.11
Kiowa (17)	23	0.09
Latin American Indians	3	0.01
Navajo (13)	20	0.08
Osage (73)	162	0.63
Potawatomi (13)	22	0.08
Pueblo (2)	3	0.01
Puget Sound Salish (6)	6	0.02
Seminole (10)	22	0.08
Shoshone (4)	4	0.02
Sioux (24)	32	0.12
Tohono O'Odham	1	0.00
Ute (1)	1	0.00
All other tribes (775)	971	3.75
American Indian tribes, not spec.	66	0.25
Arab:	24	0.09
Arab/Arabic	2	0.01
Lebanese	15	0.06
Palestinian	7	0.03
Asian:	256	0.99
Chinese, ex. Taiwanese (31)	39	0.15
Filipino (33)	52	0.20
Indian (49)	56	0.22
Japanese (12)	31	0.12
Korean (17)	27	0.10
Pakistani (4)	4	0.02
Taiwanese (9)	10	0.04
Thai (5)	5	0.02
Vietnamese (13)	17	0.07
Other Asian, not specified (3)	15	0.06
Austrian	46	0.18
Belgian	7	0.03
Brazilian	2	0.01
British	117	0.45
Croatian	9	0.03
Czech	133	0.51
Czechoslovakian	32	0.12
Danish	72	0.28
Dutch	571	2.20
English	3,061	11.79
European	367	1.41
Finnish	4	0.02
French, except Basque	823	3.17
French Canadian	105	0.40
German	4,260	16.41
German Russian	5	0.02
Greek	37	0.14
Hawaii Native/Pacific Islander:	32	0.12
Micronesian:	4	0.02
Guamanian/Chamorro	4	0.02
Polynesian: (7)	13	0.05
Native Hawaiian (3)	8	0.03
Samoan (4)	5	0.02
Other Pac. Isl., not spec. (1)	15	0.06
Hispanic or Latino:	1,149	4.43
Central American:	17	0.07
Costa Rican	1	0.00
Guatemalan	11	0.04
Honduran	2	0.01
Nicaraguan	1	0.00
Salvadoran	2	0.01
Cuban	14	0.05
Mexican	873	3.37
Puerto Rican	17	0.07
South American:	6	0.02
Argentinean	1	0.00
Peruvian	4	0.02
Venezuelan	1	0.00
Other Hispanic or Latino	222	0.86
Hungarian	36	0.14
Irish	2,777	10.70
Italian	459	1.77
Lithuanian	23	0.09
Northern European	6	0.02
Norwegian	175	0.67
Pennsylvania German	13	0.05
Polish	294	1.13
Portuguese	38	0.15
Romanian	2	0.01
Russian	32	0.12
Scandinavian	9	0.03
Scotch-Irish	727	2.80
Scottish	502	1.93
Slavic	2	0.01
Slovak	13	0.05
Swedish	320	1.23
Swiss	49	0.19
Ukrainian	20	0.08
United States or American	2,973	11.45
Welsh	178	0.69
West Indian, excl. Hispanic:	87	0.34
Barbadian	2	0.01
Dutch West Indian	85	0.33
White:	22,731	87.70
Not Hispanic (21,374)	22,210	85.69
Hispanic (444)	521	2.01

Sand Springs

Place Type: City
County: Tulsa
Population: 17,451

Ancestry/Race	Number	%
Acadian/Cajun	6	0.03
African American/Black:	377	2.16
Not Hispanic (321)	370	2.12
Hispanic (2)	7	0.04
African, sub-Saharan:	17	0.10
African	17	0.10
Alaska Native tribes, not specified	1	0.01
Am. Ind. or Alaska Nat., not spec.	152	0.87
American Indian tribes, specified:	1,718	9.84
Apache (3)	11	0.06
Blackfeet (1)	2	0.01
Cherokee (622)	993	5.69
Cheyenne (1)	4	0.02
Chickasaw (32)	49	0.28
Chippewa (2)	2	0.01
Choctaw (115)	184	1.05
Colville (2)	3	0.02
Comanche (1)	2	0.01
Creek (170)	256	1.47
Crow (1)	1	0.01
Delaware (9)	15	0.09
Iroquois (5)	5	0.03
Kiowa (7)	8	0.05
Latin American Indians	1	0.01
Lumbee	3	0.02
Navajo (1)	4	0.02
Osage (36)	62	0.36
Potawatomi (13)	16	0.09
Pueblo	3	0.02
Seminole (1)	5	0.03
Shoshone (1)	1	0.01
Sioux (5)	9	0.05
Tohono O'Odham	1	0.01
Yakama (1)	1	0.01
Yaqui	1	0.01
All other tribes (61)	76	0.44
American Indian tribes, not spec.	35	0.20
Arab:	8	0.05
Lebanese	8	0.05
Asian:	117	0.67
Cambodian (1)	1	0.01
Chinese, ex. Taiwanese (24)	29	0.17
Filipino (15)	22	0.13
Indian (2)	6	0.03
Indonesian	1	0.01
Japanese (11)	27	0.15
Korean (19)	24	0.14
Thai (1)	1	0.01
Vietnamese (2)	2	0.01
Other Asian, specified (1)	3	0.02
Other Asian, not specified	1	0.01
Austrian	5	0.03
Belgian	6	0.03
British	45	0.25
Canadian	19	0.11
Celtic	36	0.20
Czech	23	0.13
Czechoslovakian	42	0.24
Danish	9	0.05
Dutch	529	2.99
English	1,649	9.32
European	49	0.28
French, except Basque	517	2.92
French Canadian	69	0.39

Notes: 1. Figures in the "Number" column do not add up to the total population due to: a) Ancestry/Race overlap — e.g. persons can report being both White and Irish, b) persons of Hispanic origin can report being any race, c) persons reporting two ancestries are counted in both categories. 2. Numbers in parentheses indicate the number of persons reporting this ancestry/race alone, not in combination with any other ancestry/race. 3. Refer to the Explanation of Data in the front of the book for more detailed information.

Ancestry/Race	Number	%
German	2,340	13.23
Greek	12	0.07
Hawaii Native/Pacific Islander:	11	0.06
Micronesian: (1)	3	0.02
Guamanian/Chamorro (1)	3	0.02
Polynesian: (1)	5	0.03
Native Hawaiian (1)	4	0.02
Other Polynesian	1	0.01
Other Pac. Isl., not spec. (1)	3	0.02
Hispanic or Latino:	360	2.06
Central American:	5	0.03
Honduran	2	0.01
Nicaraguan	2	0.01
Panamanian	1	0.01
Mexican	221	1.27
Puerto Rican	28	0.16
South American:	14	0.08
Argentinean	3	0.02
Bolivian	1	0.01
Peruvian	2	0.01
Venezuelan	7	0.04
Other South American	1	0.01
Other Hispanic or Latino	92	0.53
Hungarian	8	0.05
Iranian	15	0.08
Irish	2,018	11.41
Italian	300	1.70
Latvian	8	0.05
Lithuanian	9	0.05
Norwegian	78	0.44
Pennsylvania German	15	0.08
Polish	193	1.09
Portuguese	8	0.05
Russian	46	0.26
Scandinavian	19	0.11
Scotch-Irish	253	1.43
Scottish	325	1.84
Slovak	6	0.03
Swedish	87	0.49
Swiss	30	0.17
Ukrainian	25	0.14
United States or American	2,583	14.60
Welsh	80	0.45
West Indian, excl. Hispanic:	103	0.58
Dutch West Indian	92	0.52
Jamaican	11	0.06
White:	15,708	90.01
Not Hispanic (14,772)	15,463	88.61
Hispanic (209)	245	1.40
Yugoslavian	7	0.04

Sapulpa

Place Type: City
County: Creek
Population: 19,166

Ancestry/Race	Number	%
African American/Black:	803	4.19
Not Hispanic (716)	797	4.16
Hispanic (3)	6	0.03
African, sub-Saharan:	43	0.23
African	43	0.23
Alaska Native tribes, specified:	2	0.01
Aleut (1)	1	0.01
Eskimo	1	0.01
Am. Ind. or Alaska Nat., not spec.	243	1.27
American Indian tribes, specified:	2,343	12.22
Apache (3)	4	0.02
Blackfeet (1)	4	0.02
Cherokee (497)	963	5.02
Cheyenne (2)	5	0.03
Chickasaw (23)	44	0.23
Chippewa (10)	14	0.07
Choctaw (84)	157	0.82
Comanche (2)	2	0.01
Cree (2)	2	0.01
Creek (591)	857	4.47
Delaware (5)	10	0.05
Houma (1)	1	0.01
Iroquois (6)	15	0.08
Kiowa (3)	8	0.04
Latin American Indians (1)	2	0.01
Menominee (2)	2	0.01
Navajo (3)	4	0.02
Osage (8)	22	0.11
Ottawa (1)	1	0.01
Potawatomi (9)	10	0.05
Pueblo (1)	1	0.01
Seminole (25)	34	0.18
Sioux (6)	21	0.11
Yakama	1	0.01
All other tribes (112)	159	0.83
American Indian tribes, not spec.	44	0.23
Arab:	90	0.48
Lebanese	90	0.48
Asian:	131	0.68
Bangladeshi	1	0.01
Chinese, ex. Taiwanese (21)	27	0.14
Filipino (10)	20	0.10
Indian (13)	20	0.10
Japanese (7)	16	0.08
Korean (11)	17	0.09
Pakistani (1)	6	0.03
Sri Lankan (1)	2	0.01
Thai (3)	4	0.02
Vietnamese (7)	13	0.07
Other Asian, specified	2	0.01
Other Asian, not specified	3	0.02
Austrian	12	0.06
British	46	0.24
Canadian	9	0.05
Celtic	7	0.04
Czech	39	0.21
Czechoslovakian	41	0.22
Dutch	360	1.91
English	1,360	7.22
European	110	0.58
French, except Basque	319	1.69
French Canadian	7	0.04
German	2,259	11.99
Greek	3	0.02
Hawaii Native/Pacific Islander:	19	0.10
Micronesian: (3)	3	0.02
Other Micronesian (3)	3	0.02
Polynesian: (2)	13	0.07
Native Hawaiian (2)	11	0.06
Samoan	2	0.01
Other Pac. Isl., specified	2	0.01
Other Pac. Isl., not spec.	1	0.01
Hispanic or Latino:	470	2.45
Central American:	12	0.06
Costa Rican	4	0.02
Guatemalan	6	0.03
Honduran	1	0.01
Panamanian	1	0.01
Cuban	11	0.06
Mexican	324	1.69
Puerto Rican	29	0.15
South American:	3	0.02
Argentinean	1	0.01
Peruvian	2	0.01
Other Hispanic or Latino	91	0.47
Hungarian	2	0.01
Irish	2,016	10.70
Italian	197	1.05
Northern European	18	0.10
Norwegian	82	0.44
Polish	97	0.51
Portuguese	25	0.13
Russian	22	0.12
Scandinavian	24	0.13
Scotch-Irish	343	1.82
Scottish	249	1.32
Slovak	7	0.04
Swedish	127	0.67
Swiss	10	0.05
Ukrainian	16	0.08
United States or American	2,772	14.71
Welsh	65	0.34
West Indian, excl. Hispanic:	137	0.73
Dutch West Indian	137	0.73
White:	16,463	85.90
Not Hispanic (15,330)	16,209	84.57
Hispanic (184)	254	1.33

Shawnee

Place Type: City
County: Pottawatomie
Population: 28,692

Ancestry/Race	Number	%
Acadian/Cajun	8	0.03
African American/Black:	1,384	4.82
Not Hispanic (1,160)	1,360	4.74
Hispanic (4)	24	0.08
African, sub-Saharan:	133	0.46
African	73	0.25
Kenyan	21	0.07
Zimbabwean	39	0.14
Alaska Native tribes, specified:	3	0.01
Aleut (1)	1	0.00
Eskimo (1)	2	0.01
Alaska Native tribes, not specified	1	0.00
Am. Ind. or Alaska Nat., not spec.	423	1.47
American Indian tribes, specified:	4,338	15.12
Apache (7)	13	0.05
Blackfeet	4	0.01
Cherokee (234)	517	1.80
Cheyenne (24)	26	0.09
Chickasaw (89)	144	0.50
Chippewa (3)	18	0.06
Choctaw (247)	382	1.33
Colville (2)	2	0.01
Comanche (37)	49	0.17
Creek (274)	456	1.59
Crow	7	0.02
Delaware (12)	17	0.06
Iroquois (13)	15	0.05
Kiowa (42)	53	0.18
Latin American Indians	2	0.01
Navajo (24)	26	0.09
Osage (5)	8	0.03
Pima (3)	3	0.01
Potawatomi (364)	482	1.68
Pueblo (8)	8	0.03
Seminole (484)	656	2.29
Shoshone (4)	4	0.01
Sioux (29)	32	0.11
Yuman (1)	1	0.00
All other tribes (1,233)	1,413	4.92
American Indian tribes, not spec.	118	0.41
Arab:	31	0.11
Lebanese	31	0.11
Armenian	21	0.07
Asian:	361	1.26
Chinese, ex. Taiwanese (32)	44	0.15
Filipino (27)	40	0.14
Indian (28)	43	0.15
Indonesian (1)	3	0.01
Japanese (92)	106	0.37
Korean (21)	39	0.14
Pakistani (1)	2	0.01
Thai (3)	4	0.01
Vietnamese (23)	28	0.10
Other Asian, not specified (44)	52	0.18
Austrian	21	0.07
Belgian	7	0.02
British	30	0.10
Bulgarian	5	0.02
Canadian	20	0.07
Croatian	4	0.01
Czech	112	0.39
Czechoslovakian	58	0.20
Danish	15	0.05
Dutch	545	1.90
English	2,319	8.08
European	203	0.71
Finnish	3	0.01

Notes: 1. Figures in the "Number" column do not add up to the total population due to: a) Ancestry/Race overlap — e.g. persons can report being both White and Irish, b) persons of Hispanic origin can report being any race, c) persons reporting two ancestries are counted in both categories. 2. Numbers in parentheses indicate the number of persons reporting this ancestry/race alone, not in combination with any other ancestry/race. 3. Refer to the Explanation of Data in the front of the book for more detailed information.

Ancestry/Race	Number	%
French, except Basque	746	2.60
French Canadian	79	0.28
German	3,108	10.83
Greek	12	0.04
Hawaii Native/Pacific Islander:	33	0.12
Micronesian: (4)	11	0.04
Guamanian/Chamorro (4)	11	0.04
Polynesian: (7)	15	0.05
Native Hawaiian (5)	13	0.05
Samoan (2)	2	0.01
Other Pac. Isl., not spec. (3)	7	0.02
Hispanic or Latino:	781	2.72
Central American:	7	0.02
Guatemalan	1	0.00
Panamanian	6	0.02
Cuban	16	0.06
Mexican	556	1.94
Puerto Rican	14	0.05
South American:	9	0.03
Chilean	1	0.00
Colombian	6	0.02
Ecuadorian	1	0.00
Venezuelan	1	0.00
Other Hispanic or Latino	179	0.62
Hungarian	35	0.12
Icelander	4	0.01
Iranian	9	0.03
Irish	3,034	10.58
Italian	393	1.37
Northern European	17	0.06
Norwegian	211	0.74
Pennsylvania German	5	0.02
Polish	247	0.86
Portuguese	42	0.15
Romanian	8	0.03
Russian	57	0.20
Scandinavian	13	0.05
Scotch-Irish	545	1.90
Scottish	463	1.61
Slovak	6	0.02
Swedish	215	0.75
Swiss	17	0.06
Ukrainian	15	0.05
United States or American	2,815	9.81
Welsh	100	0.35
West Indian, excl. Hispanic:	145	0.51
Bermudan	5	0.02
Dutch West Indian	130	0.45
Haitian	5	0.02
Jamaican	5	0.02
White:	23,209	80.89
Not Hispanic (21,742)	22,760	79.33
Hispanic (359)	449	1.56
Yugoslavian	16	0.06

Stillwater

Place Type: City
County: Payne
Population: 39,065

Ancestry/Race	Number	%
African American/Black:	1,882	4.82
Not Hispanic (1,666)	1,848	4.73
Hispanic (15)	34	0.09
African, sub-Saharan:	366	0.94
African	213	0.55
Ethiopian	76	0.20
Ghanian	8	0.02
Nigerian	12	0.03
Sudanese	6	0.02
Other sub-Saharan African	51	0.13
Alaska Native tribes, specified:	1	0.00
Aleut (1)	1	0.00
Am. Ind. or Alaska Nat., not spec.	245	0.63
Alsatian	9	0.02
American Indian tribes, specified:	2,027	5.19
Apache (7)	13	0.03
Blackfeet (4)	12	0.03
Cherokee (456)	807	2.07
Cheyenne (14)	16	0.04
Chickasaw (49)	75	0.19
Chippewa (3)	7	0.02
Choctaw (207)	308	0.79
Comanche (7)	12	0.03
Creek (114)	180	0.46
Delaware (12)	19	0.05
Houma (3)	3	0.01
Iroquois (10)	12	0.03
Kiowa (10)	25	0.06
Latin American Indians (7)	12	0.03
Navajo (21)	26	0.07
Osage (46)	72	0.18
Ottawa (2)	2	0.01
Paiute (1)	1	0.00
Potawatomi (34)	40	0.10
Pueblo (7)	7	0.02
Seminole (19)	36	0.09
Sioux (20)	34	0.09
Yakama (2)	2	0.01
Yuman (1)	1	0.00
All other tribes (239)	305	0.78
American Indian tribes, not spec.	70	0.18
Arab:	260	0.67
Arab/Arabic	76	0.20
Egyptian	36	0.09
Jordanian	11	0.03
Lebanese	68	0.17
Moroccan	18	0.05
Syrian	12	0.03
Other Arab	39	0.10
Armenian	9	0.02
Asian:	2,284	5.85
Bangladeshi (16)	18	0.05
Cambodian (2)	5	0.01
Chinese, ex. Taiwanese (659)	725	1.86
Filipino (34)	63	0.16
Indian (436)	467	1.20
Indonesian (97)	103	0.26
Japanese (96)	129	0.33
Korean (225)	238	0.61
Laotian (4)	4	0.01
Malaysian (85)	100	0.26
Pakistani (43)	59	0.15
Sri Lankan (19)	23	0.06
Taiwanese (24)	30	0.08
Thai (37)	43	0.11
Vietnamese (101)	114	0.29
Other Asian, specified (6)	12	0.03
Other Asian, not specified (41)	151	0.39
Australian	15	0.04
Austrian	55	0.14
Basque	27	0.07
Belgian	51	0.13
Brazilian	12	0.03
British	148	0.38
Bulgarian	10	0.03
Canadian	79	0.20
Celtic	21	0.05
Croatian	8	0.02
Czech	311	0.80
Czechoslovakian	75	0.19
Danish	130	0.33
Dutch	733	1.88
Eastern European	9	0.02
English	4,294	11.02
European	809	2.08
Finnish	12	0.03
French, except Basque	1,138	2.92
French Canadian	134	0.34
German	7,490	19.22
Greek	73	0.19
Hawaii Native/Pacific Islander:	51	0.13
Micronesian: (3)	12	0.03
Guamanian/Chamorro (3)	10	0.03
Other Micronesian	2	0.01
Polynesian: (6)	14	0.04
Native Hawaiian (2)	10	0.03
Samoan (1)	1	0.00
Tongan (2)	2	0.01
Other Polynesian (1)	1	0.00
Other Pac. Isl., specified	4	0.01
Other Pac. Isl., not spec. (5)	21	0.05
Hispanic or Latino:	976	2.50
Central American:	36	0.09
Costa Rican	6	0.02
Guatemalan	1	0.00
Honduran	8	0.02
Nicaraguan	6	0.02
Panamanian	4	0.01
Salvadoran	11	0.03
Cuban	17	0.04
Dominican Republic	4	0.01
Mexican	547	1.40
Puerto Rican	82	0.21
South American:	101	0.26
Argentinean	13	0.03
Bolivian	12	0.03
Colombian	11	0.03
Ecuadorian	14	0.04
Paraguayan	1	0.00
Peruvian	7	0.02
Venezuelan	42	0.11
Other South American	1	0.00
Other Hispanic or Latino	189	0.48
Hungarian	112	0.29
Iranian	109	0.28
Irish	4,538	11.65
Israeli	8	0.02
Italian	793	2.04
Lithuanian	21	0.05
Northern European	41	0.11
Norwegian	611	1.57
Polish	349	0.90
Portuguese	21	0.05
Romanian	35	0.09
Russian	128	0.33
Scandinavian	95	0.24
Scotch-Irish	894	2.29
Scottish	902	2.31
Slavic	7	0.02
Slovak	32	0.08
Slovene	6	0.02
Swedish	603	1.55
Swiss	77	0.20
Turkish	117	0.30
Ukrainian	21	0.05
United States or American	3,040	7.80
Welsh	271	0.70
West Indian, excl. Hispanic:	72	0.18
Bahamian	31	0.08
Belizean	11	0.03
Dutch West Indian	13	0.03
Jamaican	5	0.01
West Indian	12	0.03
White:	33,416	85.54
Not Hispanic (31,745)	32,832	84.04
Hispanic (475)	584	1.49

Tahlequah

Place Type: City
County: Cherokee
Population: 14,458

Ancestry/Race	Number	%
African American/Black:	451	3.12
Not Hispanic (361)	438	3.03
Hispanic (5)	13	0.09
African, sub-Saharan:	24	0.17
African	24	0.17
Alaska Native tribes, specified:	2	0.01
Eskimo (1)	2	0.01
Am. Ind. or Alaska Nat., not spec.	346	2.39
American Indian tribes, specified:	4,273	29.55
Apache (12)	12	0.08
Blackfeet (1)	1	0.01
Cherokee (2,685)	3,426	23.70
Cheyenne (10)	11	0.08
Chickasaw (19)	32	0.22

Notes: 1. Figures in the "Number" column do not add up to the total population due to: a) Ancestry/Race overlap — e.g. persons can report being both White and Irish, b) persons of Hispanic origin can report being any race, c) persons reporting two ancestries are counted in both categories. 2. Numbers in parentheses indicate the number of persons reporting this ancestry/race alone, not in combination with any other ancestry/race. 3. Refer to the Explanation of Data in the front of the book for more detailed information.

Chippewa (2)	2	0.01
Choctaw (152)	224	1.55
Colville (2)	2	0.01
Comanche (6)	7	0.05
Creek (153)	218	1.51
Crow	2	0.01
Delaware (22)	26	0.18
Iroquois (13)	18	0.12
Kiowa (26)	28	0.19
Latin American Indians (2)	3	0.02
Lumbee (1)	2	0.01
Navajo (17)	18	0.12
Osage (26)	38	0.26
Ottawa (1)	1	0.01
Paiute (4)	5	0.03
Potawatomi (7)	8	0.06
Pueblo (7)	7	0.05
Seminole (22)	37	0.26
Sioux (9)	19	0.13
Yuman (3)	3	0.02
All other tribes (95)	123	0.85
American Indian tribes, not spec.	247	1.71
Arab:	16	0.11
Arab/Arabic	6	0.04
Lebanese	10	0.07
Asian:	127	0.88
Chinese, ex. Taiwanese (10)	14	0.10
Filipino (6)	18	0.12
Indian (21)	29	0.20
Japanese (4)	13	0.09
Korean (10)	13	0.09
Pakistani (8)	8	0.06
Thai (7)	10	0.07
Vietnamese (3)	3	0.02
Other Asian, specified (2)	5	0.03
Other Asian, not specified (4)	14	0.10
Australian	11	0.08
Austrian	7	0.05
Belgian	12	0.08
British	40	0.28
Canadian	21	0.14
Czech	7	0.05
Czechoslovakian	13	0.09
Danish	22	0.15
Dutch	287	1.98
Eastern European	11	0.08
English	1,072	7.39
Estonian	7	0.05
European	63	0.43
Finnish	12	0.08
French, except Basque	325	2.24
French Canadian	24	0.17
German	1,717	11.83
Greek	7	0.05
Hawaii Native/Pacific Islander:	21	0.15
Micronesian:	2	0.01
Guamanian/Chamorro	1	0.01
Other Micronesian	1	0.01
Polynesian: (5)	11	0.08
Native Hawaiian (4)	8	0.06
Samoan (1)	2	0.01
Other Polynesian	1	0.01
Other Pac. Isl., specified	3	0.02
Other Pac. Isl., not spec.	5	0.03
Hispanic or Latino:	1,049	7.26
Central American:	4	0.03
Costa Rican	1	0.01
Honduran	1	0.01
Nicaraguan	1	0.01
Panamanian	1	0.01
Cuban	3	0.02
Dominican Republic	2	0.01
Mexican	915	6.33
Puerto Rican	39	0.27
South American:	6	0.04
Argentinean	1	0.01
Colombian	1	0.01
Ecuadorian	1	0.01
Venezuelan	3	0.02
Other Hispanic or Latino	80	0.55
Hungarian	11	0.08
Irish	1,131	7.80
Italian	196	1.35
Northern European	5	0.03
Norwegian	157	1.08
Polish	59	0.41
Portuguese	16	0.11
Russian	24	0.17
Scandinavian	42	0.29
Scotch-Irish	212	1.46
Scottish	367	2.53
Swedish	207	1.43
Swiss	23	0.16
Ukrainian	3	0.02
United States or American	1,062	7.32
Welsh	20	0.14
West Indian, excl. Hispanic:	63	0.43
Dutch West Indian	63	0.43
White:	9,457	65.41
Not Hispanic (8,238)	9,103	62.96
Hispanic (294)	354	2.45
Yugoslavian	7	0.05

The Village

Place Type: City
County: Oklahoma
Population: 10,157

Ancestry/Race	Number	%
African American/Black:	1,169	11.51
Not Hispanic (1,044)	1,141	11.23
Hispanic (19)	28	0.28
African, sub-Saharan:	174	1.71
African	130	1.28
Nigerian	13	0.13
Senegalese	31	0.30
Am. Ind. or Alaska Nat., not spec.	56	0.55
Albanian	5	0.05
American Indian tribes, specified:	440	4.33
Apache (1)	6	0.06
Blackfeet	6	0.06
Cherokee (49)	134	1.32
Chickasaw (15)	28	0.28
Choctaw (45)	93	0.92
Comanche (8)	11	0.11
Creek (17)	36	0.35
Crow	1	0.01
Delaware (4)	4	0.04
Iroquois (5)	8	0.08
Kiowa (20)	25	0.25
Osage (1)	5	0.05
Potawatomi (9)	17	0.17
Pueblo (3)	3	0.03
Seminole (14)	19	0.19
Sioux (2)	2	0.02
Tohono O'Odham (3)	3	0.03
Ute (1)	1	0.01
All other tribes (22)	38	0.37
American Indian tribes, not spec.	12	0.12
Arab:	67	0.66
Arab/Arabic	7	0.07
Lebanese	49	0.48
Syrian	11	0.11
Asian:	254	2.50
Bangladeshi (4)	4	0.04
Chinese, ex. Taiwanese (33)	37	0.36
Filipino (14)	23	0.23
Indian (18)	21	0.21
Indonesian (3)	4	0.04
Japanese (14)	28	0.28
Korean (7)	16	0.16
Laotian (9)	10	0.10
Malaysian (3)	3	0.03
Pakistani (1)	1	0.01
Sri Lankan (1)	2	0.02
Taiwanese (5)	5	0.05
Thai (5)	6	0.06
Vietnamese (73)	73	0.72
Other Asian, specified	1	0.01
Other Asian, not specified (1)	20	0.20
Australian	7	0.07
Austrian	17	0.17
Brazilian	13	0.13
British	76	0.75
Canadian	19	0.19
Celtic	16	0.16
Czech	113	1.11
Czechoslovakian	38	0.37
Danish	43	0.42
Dutch	219	2.15
English	1,243	12.19
European	65	0.64
Finnish	16	0.16
French, except Basque	248	2.43
French Canadian	62	0.61
German	1,543	15.13
Greek	16	0.16
Hawaii Native/Pacific Islander:	7	0.07
Micronesian:	2	0.02
Other Micronesian	2	0.02
Polynesian: (3)	4	0.04
Native Hawaiian (2)	3	0.03
Samoan (1)	1	0.01
Other Pac. Isl., not spec.	1	0.01
Hispanic or Latino:	383	3.77
Central American:	13	0.13
Guatemalan	1	0.01
Honduran	8	0.08
Other Central American	4	0.04
Cuban	8	0.08
Mexican	258	2.54
Puerto Rican	23	0.23
South American:	21	0.21
Bolivian	2	0.02
Colombian	5	0.05
Peruvian	6	0.06
Venezuelan	6	0.06
Other South American	2	0.02
Other Hispanic or Latino	60	0.59
Iranian	12	0.12
Irish	1,203	11.80
Italian	375	3.68
Norwegian	81	0.79
Pennsylvania German	12	0.12
Polish	132	1.29
Romanian	14	0.14
Russian	12	0.12
Scandinavian	17	0.17
Scotch-Irish	332	3.26
Scottish	240	2.35
Swedish	136	1.33
Swiss	27	0.26
Ukrainian	13	0.13
United States or American	857	8.41
Welsh	92	0.90
West Indian, excl. Hispanic:	56	0.55
Dutch West Indian	18	0.18
Jamaican	6	0.06
Trinidadian and Tobagonian	32	0.31
White:	8,481	83.50
Not Hispanic (7,934)	8,234	81.07
Hispanic (211)	247	2.43
Yugoslavian	8	0.08

Tulsa

Place Type: City
County: Tulsa
Population: 393,049

Ancestry/Race	Number	%
Acadian/Cajun	88	0.02
African American/Black:	64,936	16.52
Not Hispanic (60,297)	64,132	16.32
Hispanic (497)	804	0.20
African, sub-Saharan:	2,513	0.64
African	2,063	0.52
Cape Verdean	14	0.00
Ethiopian	22	0.01

Notes: 1. Figures in the "Number" column do not add up to the total population due to: a) Ancestry/Race overlap — e.g. persons can report being both White and Irish, b) persons of Hispanic origin can report being any race, c) persons reporting two ancestries are counted in both categories. 2. Numbers in parentheses indicate the number of persons reporting this ancestry/race alone, not in combination with any other ancestry/race. 3. Refer to the Explanation of Data in the front of the book for more detailed information.

Liberian	22	0.01
Nigerian	216	0.05
South African	46	0.01
Sudanese	22	0.01
Ugandan	21	0.01
Other sub-Saharan African	87	0.02
Alaska Native tribes, specified:	39	0.01
Alaska Athabascan (4)	6	0.00
Aleut (5)	9	0.00
Eskimo (7)	14	0.00
Tlingit-Haida (5)	7	0.00
All other tribes (3)	3	0.00
Alaska Native tribes, not specified	14	0.00
Am. Ind. or Alaska Nat., not spec.	3,542	0.90
Albanian	41	0.01
Alsatian	30	0.01
American Indian tribes, specified:	27,263	6.94
Apache (77)	181	0.05
Blackfeet (36)	141	0.04
Cherokee (7,903)	14,453	3.68
Cheyenne (91)	141	0.04
Chickasaw (256)	444	0.11
Chippewa (59)	105	0.03
Choctaw (1,504)	2,595	0.66
Colville (9)	9	0.00
Comanche (81)	135	0.03
Cree (8)	14	0.00
Creek (2,576)	4,358	1.11
Crow (6)	20	0.01
Delaware (208)	339	0.09
Houma (5)	6	0.00
Iroquois (149)	268	0.07
Kiowa (221)	327	0.08
Latin American Indians (100)	174	0.04
Lumbee (7)	12	0.00
Menominee (5)	10	0.00
Navajo (135)	180	0.05
Osage (474)	804	0.20
Ottawa (24)	56	0.01
Paiute	5	0.00
Pima (8)	9	0.00
Potawatomi (145)	240	0.06
Pueblo (30)	46	0.01
Puget Sound Salish (10)	15	0.00
Seminole (251)	469	0.12
Shoshone (5)	9	0.00
Sioux (145)	278	0.07
Tohono O'Odham (1)	1	0.00
Ute (4)	15	0.00
Yakama (3)	3	0.00
Yaqui (2)	7	0.00
Yuman (1)	3	0.00
All other tribes (914)	1,391	0.35
American Indian tribes, not spec.	704	0.18
Arab:	1,991	0.51
Arab/Arabic	391	0.10
Egyptian	54	0.01
Iraqi	39	0.01
Jordanian	101	0.03
Lebanese	921	0.23
Moroccan	19	0.00
Palestinian	226	0.06
Syrian	131	0.03
Other Arab	109	0.03
Armenian	119	0.03
Asian:	9,025	2.30
Bangladeshi (47)	63	0.02
Cambodian (31)	42	0.01
Chinese, ex. Taiwanese (1,075)	1,336	0.34
Filipino (425)	728	0.19
Hmong (392)	407	0.10
Indian (1,668)	1,933	0.49
Indonesian (94)	112	0.03
Japanese (246)	503	0.13
Korean (674)	864	0.22
Laotian (100)	127	0.03
Malaysian (26)	34	0.01
Pakistani (229)	299	0.08
Sri Lankan (13)	13	0.00
Taiwanese (49)	66	0.02
Thai (89)	136	0.03
Vietnamese (1,631)	1,771	0.45
Other Asian, specified (67)	107	0.03
Other Asian, not specified (146)	484	0.12
Australian	67	0.02
Austrian	574	0.15
Basque	8	0.00
Belgian	228	0.06
Brazilian	75	0.02
British	1,881	0.48
Bulgarian	103	0.03
Canadian	507	0.13
Carpatho Rusyn	9	0.00
Celtic	54	0.01
Croatian	265	0.07
Czech	945	0.24
Czechoslovakian	521	0.13
Danish	1,164	0.30
Dutch	7,616	1.94
Eastern European	46	0.01
English	39,603	10.08
Estonian	53	0.01
European	3,739	0.95
Finnish	212	0.05
French, except Basque	10,718	2.73
French Canadian	1,241	0.32
German	51,994	13.23
German Russian	6	0.00
Greek	793	0.20
Guyanese	27	0.01
Hawaii Native/Pacific Islander:	498	0.13
Melanesian: (11)	12	0.00
Fijian (1)	1	0.00
Other Melanesian (10)	11	0.00
Micronesian: (59)	87	0.02
Guamanian/Chamorro (56)	84	0.02
Other Micronesian (3)	3	0.00
Polynesian: (96)	234	0.06
Native Hawaiian (71)	170	0.04
Samoan (17)	47	0.01
Tongan	2	0.00
Other Polynesian (8)	15	0.00
Other Pac. Isl., specified	31	0.01
Other Pac. Isl., not spec. (35)	134	0.03
Hispanic or Latino:	28,111	7.15
Central American:	723	0.18
Costa Rican	68	0.02
Guatemalan	241	0.06
Honduran	152	0.04
Nicaraguan	31	0.01
Panamanian	64	0.02
Salvadoran	140	0.04
Other Central American	27	0.01
Cuban	324	0.08
Dominican Republic	54	0.01
Mexican	21,110	5.37
Puerto Rican	1,148	0.29
South American:	896	0.23
Argentinean	60	0.02
Bolivian	43	0.01
Chilean	27	0.01
Colombian	211	0.05
Ecuadorian	51	0.01
Paraguayan	1	0.00
Peruvian	208	0.05
Uruguayan	10	0.00
Venezuelan	261	0.07
Other South American	24	0.01
Other Hispanic or Latino	3,856	0.98
Hungarian	543	0.14
Icelander	221	0.06
Iranian	432	0.11
Irish	40,850	10.39
Israeli	108	0.03
Italian	7,074	1.80
Latvian	45	0.01
Lithuanian	221	0.06
Luxemburger	28	0.01
New Zealander	45	0.01
Northern European	219	0.06
Norwegian	3,259	0.83
Pennsylvania German	93	0.02
Polish	3,745	0.95
Portuguese	259	0.07
Romanian	153	0.04
Russian	1,365	0.35
Scandinavian	478	0.12
Scotch-Irish	8,601	2.19
Scottish	8,035	2.04
Serbian	67	0.02
Slavic	54	0.01
Slovak	296	0.08
Slovene	28	0.01
Swedish	4,032	1.03
Swiss	920	0.23
Turkish	260	0.07
Ukrainian	531	0.14
United States or American	31,397	7.99
Welsh	2,705	0.69
West Indian, excl. Hispanic:	1,487	0.38
Bahamian	38	0.01
Barbadian	19	0.00
British West Indian	46	0.01
Dutch West Indian	870	0.22
Haitian	40	0.01
Jamaican	331	0.08
Trinidadian and Tobagonian	68	0.02
U.S. Virgin Islander	15	0.00
West Indian	60	0.02
White:	290,292	73.86
Not Hispanic (263,782)	276,741	70.41
Hispanic (11,706)	13,551	3.45
Yugoslavian	233	0.06

Woodward

Place Type: City
County: Woodward
Population: 11,853

Ancestry/Race	Number	%
African American/Black:	44	0.37
Not Hispanic (29)	38	0.32
Hispanic (1)	6	0.05
African, sub-Saharan:	11	0.09
African	11	0.09
Alaska Native tribes, specified:	2	0.02
Alaska Athabascan (2)	2	0.02
Am. Ind. or Alaska Nat., not spec.	76	0.64
American Indian tribes, specified:	319	2.69
Apache (1)	5	0.04
Blackfeet (1)	3	0.03
Cherokee (47)	97	0.82
Cheyenne (22)	30	0.25
Chickasaw (12)	21	0.18
Chippewa	1	0.01
Choctaw (26)	51	0.43
Cree	1	0.01
Creek (13)	21	0.18
Delaware (1)	5	0.04
Iroquois	2	0.02
Kiowa	1	0.01
Latin American Indians (2)	2	0.02
Navajo (4)	7	0.06
Osage	3	0.03
Ottawa	1	0.01
Potawatomi (5)	7	0.06
Seminole (4)	4	0.03
Sioux (2)	3	0.03
Ute	1	0.01
All other tribes (40)	53	0.45
American Indian tribes, not spec.	16	0.13
Arab:	29	0.25
Lebanese	29	0.25
Asian:	99	0.84
Chinese, ex. Taiwanese (21)	24	0.20
Filipino (16)	19	0.16
Indian (12)	14	0.12
Japanese (4)	6	0.05
Korean (11)	12	0.10

Notes: 1. Figures in the "Number" column do not add up to the total population due to: a) Ancestry/Race overlap — e.g. persons can report being both White and Irish, b) persons of Hispanic origin can report being any race, c) persons reporting two ancestries are counted in both categories. 2. Numbers in parentheses indicate the number of persons reporting this ancestry/race alone, not in combination with any other ancestry/race. 3. Refer to the Explanation of Data in the front of the book for more detailed information.

Ancestry/Race	Number	%
Pakistani (1)	1	0.01
Taiwanese (3)	3	0.03
Thai (3)	3	0.03
Vietnamese (3)	5	0.04
Other Asian, not specified (6)	12	0.10
Austrian	26	0.22
British	8	0.07
Celtic	7	0.06
Czech	59	0.51
Czechoslovakian	7	0.06
Danish	20	0.17
Dutch	365	3.13
English	966	8.27
European	71	0.61
French, except Basque	227	1.94
French Canadian	30	0.26
German	1,946	16.66
Hawaii Native/Pacific Islander:	6	0.05
Micronesian: (1)	3	0.03
Guamanian/Chamorro (1)	3	0.03
Polynesian: (1)	1	0.01
Native Hawaiian (1)	1	0.01
Other Pac. Isl., not spec.	2	0.02
Hispanic or Latino:	718	6.06
Central American:	6	0.05
Costa Rican	1	0.01
Guatemalan	3	0.03
Honduran	2	0.02
Cuban	1	0.01
Mexican	575	4.85
Puerto Rican	19	0.16
South American:	5	0.04
Colombian	1	0.01
Venezuelan	4	0.03
Other Hispanic or Latino	112	0.94
Irish	1,139	9.75
Italian	126	1.08
Latvian	5	0.04
Norwegian	85	0.73
Pennsylvania German	5	0.04
Polish	66	0.57
Portuguese	6	0.05
Russian	22	0.19
Scotch-Irish	192	1.64
Scottish	204	1.75
Serbian	6	0.05
Swedish	115	0.98
Swiss	45	0.39
Ukrainian	6	0.05
United States or American	1,785	15.29
Welsh	79	0.68
West Indian, excl. Hispanic:	5	0.04
Dutch West Indian	5	0.04
White:	11,099	93.64
Not Hispanic (10,627)	10,786	91.00
Hispanic (275)	313	2.64
Yugoslavian	15	0.13

Yukon

Place Type: City
County: Canadian
Population: 21,043

Ancestry/Race	Number	%
African American/Black:	241	1.15
Not Hispanic (171)	233	1.11
Hispanic (5)	8	0.04
African, sub-Saharan:	10	0.05
African	10	0.05
Alaska Native tribes, not specified	1	0.00
Am. Ind. or Alaska Nat., not spec.	112	0.53
American Indian tribes, specified:	811	3.85
Apache (3)	5	0.02
Cherokee (109)	263	1.25
Cheyenne (7)	9	0.04
Chickasaw (27)	47	0.22
Chippewa (6)	7	0.03
Choctaw (103)	189	0.90
Comanche (15)	17	0.08
Creek (32)	60	0.29
Delaware (7)	8	0.04
Iroquois (4)	4	0.02
Kiowa (23)	34	0.16
Latin American Indians (3)	4	0.02
Navajo (1)	1	0.00
Osage (7)	14	0.07
Potawatomi (19)	24	0.11
Pueblo (1)	1	0.00
Seminole (22)	35	0.17
Sioux (7)	10	0.05
All other tribes (65)	79	0.38
American Indian tribes, not spec.	20	0.10
Arab:	24	0.11
Lebanese	24	0.11
Asian:	444	2.11
Chinese, ex. Taiwanese (20)	20	0.10
Filipino (17)	26	0.12
Indian (237)	257	1.22
Japanese (8)	14	0.07
Korean (15)	21	0.10
Laotian (7)	10	0.05
Sri Lankan (1)	2	0.01
Thai (2)	2	0.01
Vietnamese (77)	81	0.38
Other Asian, specified	2	0.01
Other Asian, not specified (8)	9	0.04
Austrian	35	0.17
British	89	0.42
Czech	319	1.51
Czechoslovakian	97	0.46
Danish	45	0.21
Dutch	565	2.67
English	2,325	10.98
European	121	0.57
Finnish	20	0.09
French, except Basque	514	2.43
French Canadian	75	0.35
German	3,915	18.49
German Russian	8	0.04
Greek	6	0.03
Hawaii Native/Pacific Islander:	28	0.13
Polynesian: (6)	18	0.09
Native Hawaiian (1)	9	0.04
Samoan (5)	9	0.04
Other Pac. Isl., specified	2	0.01
Other Pac. Isl., not spec. (4)	8	0.04
Hispanic or Latino:	633	3.01
Central American:	9	0.04
Guatemalan	4	0.02
Salvadoran	4	0.02
Other Central American	1	0.00
Cuban	6	0.03
Mexican	422	2.01
Puerto Rican	39	0.19
South American:	11	0.05
Colombian	7	0.03
Peruvian	2	0.01
Uruguayan	1	0.00
Venezuelan	1	0.00
Other Hispanic or Latino	146	0.69
Hungarian	5	0.02
Iranian	5	0.02
Irish	2,673	12.62
Italian	435	2.05
Northern European	7	0.03
Norwegian	206	0.97
Polish	278	1.31
Portuguese	16	0.08
Russian	43	0.20
Scandinavian	5	0.02
Scotch-Irish	531	2.51
Scottish	488	2.30
Slavic	2	0.01
Slovak	14	0.07
Swedish	110	0.52
Swiss	93	0.44
Ukrainian	6	0.03
United States or American	2,743	12.95
Welsh	138	0.65
West Indian, excl. Hispanic:	60	0.28
Dutch West Indian	52	0.25
Jamaican	8	0.04
White:	19,614	93.21
Not Hispanic (18,822)	19,245	91.46
Hispanic (313)	369	1.75

Albany

Place Type: City
County: Linn
Population: 40,852

Ancestry/Race	Number	%
African American/Black:	334	0.82
Not Hispanic (192)	293	0.72
Hispanic (25)	41	0.10
African, sub-Saharan:	26	0.06
African	18	0.04
South African	8	0.02
Alaska Native tribes, specified:	14	0.03
Alaska Athabascan	1	0.00
Aleut (1)	1	0.00
Eskimo (7)	7	0.02
Tlingit-Haida (2)	5	0.01
Alaska Native tribes, not specified	2	0.00
Am. Ind. or Alaska Nat., not spec.	233	0.57
American Indian tribes, specified:	711	1.74
Apache (5)	18	0.04
Blackfeet (8)	36	0.09
Cherokee (70)	233	0.57
Cheyenne (1)	3	0.01
Chickasaw (2)	9	0.02
Chippewa (21)	29	0.07
Choctaw (24)	51	0.12
Comanche (3)	6	0.01
Cree (1)	1	0.00
Creek (9)	16	0.04
Crow (4)	6	0.01
Delaware (3)	4	0.01
Houma	1	0.00
Iroquois (4)	14	0.03
Kiowa (3)	4	0.01
Latin American Indians (15)	21	0.05
Lumbee (1)	1	0.00
Navajo (14)	17	0.04
Osage (3)	7	0.02
Ottawa (2)	2	0.00
Paiute	3	0.01
Pima (1)	1	0.00
Potawatomi (6)	6	0.01
Pueblo	3	0.01
Puget Sound Salish (1)	2	0.00
Seminole (3)	3	0.01
Shoshone (4)	6	0.01
Sioux (15)	35	0.09
Tohono O'Odham	1	0.00
Yakama (3)	4	0.01
Yaqui (1)	1	0.00
Yuman (1)	1	0.00
All other tribes (108)	166	0.41
American Indian tribes, not spec.	37	0.09
Arab:	42	0.10
Arab/Arabic	29	0.07
Lebanese	13	0.03
Armenian	43	0.11
Asian:	747	1.83
Cambodian (21)	35	0.09
Chinese, ex. Taiwanese (102)	143	0.35
Filipino (70)	138	0.34
Hmong	1	0.00
Indian (40)	55	0.13
Indonesian (11)	20	0.05
Japanese (37)	100	0.24
Korean (85)	120	0.29
Laotian (6)	8	0.02
Sri Lankan	1	0.00
Taiwanese (7)	8	0.02
Thai (4)	6	0.01
Vietnamese (51)	62	0.15

Notes: 1. Figures in the "Number" column do not add up to the total population due to: a) Ancestry/Race overlap — e.g. persons can report being both White and Irish, b) persons of Hispanic origin can report being any race, c) persons reporting two ancestries are counted in both categories. 2. Numbers in parentheses indicate the number of persons reporting this ancestry/race alone, not in combination with any other ancestry/race. 3. Refer to the Explanation of Data in the front of the book for more detailed information.

Other Asian, specified (2)	14	0.03
Other Asian, not specified (11)	36	0.09
Australian	17	0.04
Austrian	29	0.07
Basque	27	0.07
Belgian	31	0.08
British	303	0.74
Canadian	142	0.35
Celtic	14	0.03
Croatian	6	0.01
Czech	230	0.56
Czechoslovakian	114	0.28
Danish	441	1.08
Dutch	1,241	3.04
English	5,365	13.13
Estonian	9	0.02
European	635	1.55
Finnish	319	0.78
French, except Basque	1,540	3.77
French Canadian	420	1.03
German	9,023	22.09
Greek	208	0.51
Hawaii Native/Pacific Islander:	186	0.46
Melanesian: (1)	4	0.01
Fijian (1)	4	0.01
Micronesian: (33)	40	0.10
Guamanian/Chamorro (27)	33	0.08
Other Micronesian (6)	7	0.02
Polynesian: (49)	104	0.25
Native Hawaiian (34)	83	0.20
Samoan (8)	12	0.03
Tongan (7)	9	0.02
Other Pac. Isl., specified	12	0.03
Other Pac. Isl., not spec. (2)	26	0.06
Hispanic or Latino:	2,489	6.09
Central American:	70	0.17
Costa Rican	6	0.01
Guatemalan	15	0.04
Honduran	2	0.00
Nicaraguan	2	0.00
Panamanian	9	0.02
Salvadoran	34	0.08
Other Central American	2	0.00
Cuban	16	0.04
Mexican	1,898	4.65
Puerto Rican	52	0.13
South American:	17	0.04
Chilean	1	0.00
Colombian	8	0.02
Ecuadorian	1	0.00
Paraguayan	1	0.00
Peruvian	3	0.01
Venezuelan	3	0.01
Other Hispanic or Latino	436	1.07
Hungarian	69	0.17
Icelander	11	0.03
Iranian	10	0.02
Irish	4,381	10.73
Italian	790	1.93
Lithuanian	48	0.12
Luxemburger	6	0.01
New Zealander	6	0.01
Northern European	26	0.06
Norwegian	1,950	4.77
Pennsylvania German	26	0.06
Polish	376	0.92
Portuguese	186	0.46
Romanian	7	0.02
Russian	172	0.42
Scandinavian	212	0.52
Scotch-Irish	983	2.41
Scottish	1,018	2.49
Serbian	14	0.03
Slavic	15	0.04
Slovak	2	0.00
Swedish	1,057	2.59
Swiss	260	0.64
Ukrainian	31	0.08
United States or American	3,231	7.91
Welsh	612	1.50
West Indian, excl. Hispanic:	44	0.11
Dutch West Indian	7	0.02
Haitian	9	0.02
Jamaican	16	0.04
U.S. Virgin Islander	12	0.03
White:	38,420	94.05
Not Hispanic (36,361)	37,111	90.84
Hispanic (1,092)	1,309	3.20
Yugoslavian	14	0.03

Aloha

Place Type: Census Designated Place
County: Washington
Population: 41,741

Ancestry/Race	Number	%
Acadian/Cajun	7	0.02
African American/Black:	822	1.97
Not Hispanic (532)	755	1.81
Hispanic (31)	67	0.16
African, sub-Saharan:	140	0.33
African	88	0.21
Cape Verdean	9	0.02
Ethiopian	8	0.02
Ghanian	7	0.02
Nigerian	6	0.01
South African	22	0.05
Alaska Native tribes, specified:	19	0.05
Alaska Athabascan (3)	4	0.01
Aleut (3)	4	0.01
Eskimo (1)	3	0.01
Tlingit-Haida (3)	8	0.02
Alaska Native tribes, not specified	4	0.01
Am. Ind. or Alaska Nat., not spec.	153	0.37
Albanian	55	0.13
American Indian tribes, specified:	543	1.30
Apache (6)	26	0.06
Blackfeet (7)	17	0.04
Cherokee (45)	138	0.33
Cheyenne (1)	2	0.00
Chickasaw (1)	7	0.02
Chippewa (9)	26	0.06
Choctaw (10)	22	0.05
Colville (3)	3	0.01
Crow	1	0.00
Delaware (1)	1	0.00
Iroquois (1)	4	0.01
Latin American Indians (32)	93	0.22
Lumbee	1	0.00
Menominee (1)	1	0.00
Navajo (4)	14	0.03
Osage	1	0.00
Ottawa	3	0.01
Paiute (6)	8	0.02
Potawatomi	1	0.00
Pueblo (8)	11	0.03
Puget Sound Salish (10)	10	0.02
Seminole (1)	4	0.01
Shoshone (1)	1	0.00
Sioux (13)	30	0.07
Tohono O'Odham	1	0.00
Yakama	6	0.01
Yaqui	3	0.01
Yuman (1)	2	0.00
All other tribes (66)	106	0.25
American Indian tribes, not spec.	32	0.08
Arab:	51	0.12
Egyptian	9	0.02
Lebanese	5	0.01
Syrian	28	0.07
Other Arab	9	0.02
Armenian	8	0.02
Asian:	3,966	9.50
Bangladeshi (1)	1	0.00
Cambodian (307)	334	0.80
Chinese, ex. Taiwanese (326)	449	1.08
Filipino (483)	704	1.69
Hmong (75)	76	0.18
Indian (176)	224	0.54
Indonesian (11)	20	0.05
Japanese (149)	303	0.73
Korean (304)	364	0.87
Laotian (245)	276	0.66
Pakistani (8)	9	0.02
Sri Lankan (24)	26	0.06
Taiwanese (12)	24	0.06
Thai (42)	54	0.13
Vietnamese (922)	984	2.36
Other Asian, specified (4)	7	0.02
Other Asian, not specified (41)	111	0.27
Australian	10	0.02
Austrian	104	0.25
Basque	23	0.05
Belgian	30	0.07
British	145	0.34
Canadian	188	0.45
Celtic	14	0.03
Croatian	13	0.03
Czech	196	0.47
Czechoslovakian	71	0.17
Danish	727	1.73
Dutch	1,109	2.63
Eastern European	28	0.07
English	4,731	11.24
Estonian	23	0.05
European	848	2.01
Finnish	245	0.58
French, except Basque	1,462	3.47
French Canadian	253	0.60
German	8,479	20.14
German Russian	7	0.02
Greek	115	0.27
Hawaii Native/Pacific Islander:	350	0.84
Melanesian: (17)	28	0.07
Fijian (16)	26	0.06
Other Melanesian (1)	2	0.00
Micronesian: (23)	33	0.08
Guamanian/Chamorro (16)	26	0.06
Other Micronesian (7)	7	0.02
Polynesian: (93)	215	0.52
Native Hawaiian (72)	172	0.41
Samoan (18)	32	0.08
Tongan (3)	7	0.02
Other Polynesian	4	0.01
Other Pac. Isl., not spec. (13)	74	0.18
Hispanic or Latino:	5,396	12.93
Central American:	258	0.62
Costa Rican	9	0.02
Guatemalan	138	0.33
Honduran	7	0.02
Nicaraguan	10	0.02
Panamanian	5	0.01
Salvadoran	71	0.17
Other Central American	18	0.04
Cuban	43	0.10
Dominican Republic	1	0.00
Mexican	4,047	9.70
Puerto Rican	108	0.26
South American:	80	0.19
Argentinean	2	0.00
Chilean	19	0.05
Colombian	10	0.02
Peruvian	35	0.08
Venezuelan	12	0.03
Other South American	2	0.00
Other Hispanic or Latino	859	2.06
Hungarian	116	0.28
Iranian	103	0.24
Irish	4,527	10.75
Italian	1,163	2.76
Latvian	14	0.03
Lithuanian	41	0.10
Luxemburger	8	0.02
Northern European	82	0.19
Norwegian	1,834	4.36
Pennsylvania German	15	0.04
Polish	578	1.37
Portuguese	170	0.40
Romanian	44	0.10

Notes: 1. Figures in the "Number" column do not add up to the total population due to: a) Ancestry/Race overlap — e.g. persons can report being both White and Irish, b) persons of Hispanic origin can report being any race, c) persons reporting two ancestries are counted in both categories. 2. Numbers in parentheses indicate the number of persons reporting this ancestry/race alone, not in combination with any other ancestry/race. 3. Refer to the Explanation of Data in the front of the book for more detailed information.

Russian	405	0.96
Scandinavian	256	0.61
Scotch-Irish	716	1.70
Scottish	1,100	2.61
Serbian	9	0.02
Slavic	9	0.02
Slovak	6	0.01
Slovene	15	0.04
Swedish	1,431	3.40
Swiss	375	0.89
Turkish	15	0.04
Ukrainian	226	0.54
United States or American	2,842	6.75
Welsh	550	1.31
West Indian, excl. Hispanic:	47	0.11
Haitian	37	0.09
Jamaican	6	0.01
West Indian	4	0.01
White:	34,429	82.48
Not Hispanic (31,019)	31,994	76.65
Hispanic (2,124)	2,435	5.83
Yugoslavian	84	0.20

Altamont

Place Type: Census Designated Place
County: Klamath
Population: 19,603

Ancestry/Race	Number	%
African American/Black:	199	1.02
Not Hispanic (111)	173	0.88
Hispanic (14)	26	0.13
Alaska Native tribes, specified:	18	0.09
Alaska Athabascan (1)	1	0.01
Aleut (1)	5	0.03
Eskimo (4)	7	0.04
Tlingit-Haida (1)	4	0.02
All other tribes	1	0.01
Alaska Native tribes, not specified	1	0.01
Am. Ind. or Alaska Nat., not spec.	179	0.91
American Indian tribes, specified:	847	4.32
Apache (6)	8	0.04
Blackfeet (1)	14	0.07
Cherokee (34)	119	0.61
Chickasaw (4)	5	0.03
Chippewa (8)	17	0.09
Choctaw (10)	26	0.13
Comanche	1	0.01
Cree (1)	1	0.01
Delaware (3)	3	0.02
Iroquois (8)	11	0.06
Kiowa (1)	1	0.01
Latin American Indians (4)	5	0.03
Lumbee	5	0.03
Navajo (4)	5	0.03
Osage (1)	1	0.01
Paiute (17)	28	0.14
Pima (2)	3	0.02
Potawatomi (4)	7	0.04
Pueblo (1)	1	0.01
Puget Sound Salish (5)	5	0.03
Seminole	1	0.01
Sioux (4)	13	0.07
Tohono O'Odham (6)	7	0.04
Ute	1	0.01
Yakama (2)	3	0.02
Yaqui (2)	4	0.02
All other tribes (418)	552	2.82
American Indian tribes, not spec.	71	0.36
Arab:	3	0.02
Arab/Arabic	3	0.02
Asian:	265	1.35
Chinese, ex. Taiwanese (24)	38	0.19
Filipino (37)	74	0.38
Indian (12)	31	0.16
Indonesian (5)	6	0.03
Japanese (19)	37	0.19
Korean (11)	15	0.08
Laotian (11)	12	0.06
Pakistani (5)	6	0.03
Taiwanese	1	0.01
Thai (1)	1	0.01
Vietnamese (15)	17	0.09
Other Asian, specified	5	0.03
Other Asian, not specified (7)	22	0.11
Austrian	42	0.21
Basque	9	0.05
Belgian	13	0.07
British	93	0.47
Canadian	24	0.12
Celtic	45	0.23
Croatian	34	0.17
Czech	199	1.01
Czechoslovakian	45	0.23
Danish	204	1.03
Dutch	468	2.37
English	2,397	12.13
Estonian	6	0.03
European	183	0.93
Finnish	37	0.19
French, except Basque	773	3.91
French Canadian	282	1.43
German	3,667	18.55
Greek	28	0.14
Hawaii Native/Pacific Islander:	62	0.32
Micronesian: (1)	7	0.04
Guamanian/Chamorro (1)	7	0.04
Polynesian: (24)	47	0.24
Native Hawaiian (20)	38	0.19
Samoan (2)	7	0.04
Other Polynesian (2)	2	0.01
Other Pac. Isl., specified	2	0.01
Other Pac. Isl., not spec. (1)	6	0.03
Hispanic or Latino:	1,326	6.76
Central American:	20	0.10
Guatemalan	2	0.01
Nicaraguan	6	0.03
Panamanian	5	0.03
Salvadoran	4	0.02
Other Central American	3	0.02
Cuban	10	0.05
Dominican Republic	4	0.02
Mexican	1,018	5.19
Puerto Rican	37	0.19
South American:	18	0.09
Chilean	1	0.01
Colombian	6	0.03
Peruvian	5	0.03
Venezuelan	2	0.01
Other South American	4	0.02
Other Hispanic or Latino	219	1.12
Hungarian	32	0.16
Icelander	6	0.03
Irish	2,615	13.23
Italian	769	3.89
Lithuanian	17	0.09
Norwegian	795	4.02
Polish	258	1.31
Portuguese	200	1.01
Russian	38	0.19
Scandinavian	78	0.39
Scotch-Irish	412	2.08
Scottish	535	2.71
Serbian	8	0.04
Slavic	11	0.06
Slovak	15	0.08
Swedish	642	3.25
Swiss	44	0.22
Ukrainian	38	0.19
United States or American	1,393	7.05
Welsh	280	1.42
White:	18,026	91.96
Not Hispanic (16,830)	17,346	88.49
Hispanic (548)	680	3.47
Yugoslavian	50	0.25

Ashland

Place Type: City
County: Jackson
Population: 19,522

Ancestry/Race	Number	%
African American/Black:	228	1.17
Not Hispanic (110)	211	1.08
Hispanic (8)	17	0.09
African, sub-Saharan:	70	0.36
African	57	0.29
Nigerian	5	0.03
South African	8	0.04
Alaska Native tribes, specified:	15	0.08
Alaska Athabascan (2)	2	0.01
Aleut	2	0.01
Eskimo (4)	6	0.03
Tlingit-Haida (3)	5	0.03
Am. Ind. or Alaska Nat., not spec.	84	0.43
Albanian	15	0.08
Alsatian	9	0.05
American Indian tribes, specified:	332	1.70
Apache (1)	5	0.03
Blackfeet (4)	17	0.09
Cherokee (36)	103	0.53
Cheyenne	2	0.01
Chickasaw	2	0.01
Chippewa (7)	7	0.04
Choctaw (3)	12	0.06
Colville (1)	1	0.01
Comanche (1)	2	0.01
Creek (3)	3	0.02
Crow (1)	1	0.01
Iroquois (3)	11	0.06
Kiowa (3)	3	0.02
Latin American Indians	9	0.05
Menominee	2	0.01
Navajo (4)	8	0.04
Osage	3	0.02
Ottawa (1)	1	0.01
Paiute (1)	1	0.01
Pima (2)	2	0.01
Pueblo	1	0.01
Puget Sound Salish	1	0.01
Seminole (2)	3	0.02
Sioux (11)	19	0.10
Yakama (1)	1	0.01
Yaqui	6	0.03
All other tribes (75)	106	0.54
American Indian tribes, not spec.	20	0.10
Arab:	60	0.31
Egyptian	7	0.04
Lebanese	14	0.07
Syrian	5	0.03
Other Arab	34	0.17
Armenian	5	0.03
Asian:	572	2.93
Bangladeshi	1	0.01
Cambodian (3)	3	0.02
Chinese, ex. Taiwanese (55)	108	0.55
Filipino (36)	78	0.40
Indian (24)	38	0.19
Indonesian (6)	10	0.05
Japanese (125)	194	0.99
Korean (50)	70	0.36
Laotian (4)	4	0.02
Malaysian (2)	2	0.01
Pakistani	1	0.01
Sri Lankan (1)	1	0.01
Taiwanese (9)	9	0.05
Thai (10)	10	0.05
Vietnamese (10)	16	0.08
Other Asian, specified (1)	4	0.02
Other Asian, not specified (8)	23	0.12
Australian	15	0.08
Austrian	135	0.69
Basque	10	0.05
Belgian	14	0.07
Brazilian	36	0.18

Notes: 1. Figures in the "Number" column do not add up to the total population due to: a) Ancestry/Race overlap — e.g. persons can report being both White and Irish, b) persons of Hispanic origin can report being any race, c) persons reporting two ancestries are counted in both categories. 2. Numbers in parentheses indicate the number of persons reporting this ancestry/race alone, not in combination with any other ancestry/race. 3. Refer to the Explanation of Data in the front of the book for more detailed information.

British	185	0.95
Bulgarian	13	0.07
Canadian	84	0.43
Carpatho Rusyn	15	0.08
Celtic	24	0.12
Croatian	31	0.16
Czech	102	0.52
Czechoslovakian	69	0.35
Danish	278	1.42
Dutch	577	2.96
Eastern European	89	0.46
English	3,148	16.13
Estonian	11	0.06
European	725	3.72
Finnish	118	0.60
French, except Basque	896	4.59
French Canadian	212	1.09
German	3,809	19.52
German Russian	6	0.03
Greek	85	0.44
Hawaii Native/Pacific Islander:	76	0.39
Micronesian: (7)	9	0.05
Guamanian/Chamorro (5)	7	0.04
Other Micronesian (2)	2	0.01
Polynesian: (16)	61	0.31
Native Hawaiian (11)	43	0.22
Samoan (3)	7	0.04
Tongan (1)	4	0.02
Other Polynesian (1)	7	0.04
Other Pac. Isl., specified	1	0.01
Other Pac. Isl., not spec. (3)	5	0.03
Hispanic or Latino:	695	3.56
Central American:	32	0.16
Costa Rican	2	0.01
Guatemalan	21	0.11
Nicaraguan	2	0.01
Panamanian	2	0.01
Salvadoran	1	0.01
Other Central American	4	0.02
Cuban	11	0.06
Dominican Republic	4	0.02
Mexican	443	2.27
Puerto Rican	34	0.17
South American:	37	0.19
Argentinean	8	0.04
Chilean	5	0.03
Colombian	3	0.02
Ecuadorian	7	0.04
Paraguayan	3	0.02
Peruvian	8	0.04
Other South American	3	0.02
Other Hispanic or Latino	134	0.69
Hungarian	194	0.99
Icelander	24	0.12
Iranian	10	0.05
Irish	2,716	13.92
Israeli	9	0.05
Italian	836	4.28
Latvian	24	0.12
Lithuanian	71	0.36
Luxemburger	6	0.03
Northern European	99	0.51
Norwegian	785	4.02
Pennsylvania German	8	0.04
Polish	569	2.92
Portuguese	124	0.64
Romanian	36	0.18
Russian	610	3.13
Scandinavian	93	0.48
Scotch-Irish	722	3.70
Scottish	954	4.89
Serbian	11	0.06
Slavic	8	0.04
Slovak	21	0.11
Slovene	11	0.06
Swedish	542	2.78
Swiss	144	0.74
Ukrainian	50	0.26
United States or American	1,050	5.38
Welsh	191	0.98
White:	18,434	94.43
Not Hispanic (17,566)	18,046	92.44
Hispanic (307)	388	1.99
Yugoslavian	20	0.10

Beaverton

Place Type: City
County: Washington
Population: 76,129

Ancestry/Race	Number	%
Acadian/Cajun	36	0.05
African American/Black:	1,864	2.45
Not Hispanic (1,243)	1,722	2.26
Hispanic (81)	142	0.19
African, sub-Saharan:	182	0.24
African	48	0.06
Ethiopian	64	0.08
Ghanian	7	0.01
South African	8	0.01
Zimbabwean	55	0.07
Alaska Native tribes, specified:	33	0.04
Alaska Athabascan (3)	3	0.00
Aleut (9)	15	0.02
Eskimo	1	0.00
Tlingit-Haida (9)	14	0.02
Alaska Native tribes, not specified	4	0.01
Am. Ind. or Alaska Nat., not spec.	332	0.44
Albanian	75	0.10
American Indian tribes, specified:	698	0.92
Apache (5)	13	0.02
Blackfeet (9)	28	0.04
Cherokee (63)	192	0.25
Cheyenne (2)	3	0.00
Chickasaw (2)	5	0.01
Chippewa (20)	34	0.04
Choctaw (11)	40	0.05
Colville (1)	1	0.00
Comanche (2)	2	0.00
Cree (1)	2	0.00
Creek (8)	18	0.02
Crow (5)	8	0.01
Delaware	2	0.00
Houma	1	0.00
Iroquois (3)	22	0.03
Kiowa (1)	2	0.00
Latin American Indians (54)	74	0.10
Lumbee	2	0.00
Navajo (9)	14	0.02
Osage (3)	5	0.01
Ottawa	6	0.01
Paiute (1)	2	0.00
Potawatomi	2	0.00
Pueblo (3)	4	0.01
Puget Sound Salish (4)	5	0.01
Seminole (1)	11	0.01
Shoshone (1)	4	0.01
Sioux (9)	29	0.04
Ute (1)	1	0.00
Yakama (3)	3	0.00
Yaqui (1)	1	0.00
All other tribes (92)	162	0.21
American Indian tribes, not spec.	51	0.07
Arab:	689	0.91
Arab/Arabic	137	0.18
Egyptian	77	0.10
Iraqi	43	0.06
Lebanese	216	0.28
Palestinian	69	0.09
Syrian	29	0.04
Other Arab	118	0.16
Armenian	57	0.08
Asian:	8,813	11.58
Bangladeshi (2)	3	0.00
Cambodian (263)	322	0.42
Chinese, ex. Taiwanese (1,163)	1,440	1.89
Filipino (649)	954	1.25
Hmong (19)	24	0.03
Indian (1,460)	1,553	2.04
Indonesian (58)	94	0.12
Japanese (805)	1,155	1.52
Korean (1,279)	1,393	1.83
Laotian (152)	169	0.22
Malaysian (3)	7	0.01
Pakistani (55)	83	0.11
Sri Lankan (22)	29	0.04
Taiwanese (62)	76	0.10
Thai (90)	113	0.15
Vietnamese (1,016)	1,121	1.47
Other Asian, specified (15)	34	0.04
Other Asian, not specified (93)	243	0.32
Australian	38	0.05
Austrian	252	0.33
Basque	40	0.05
Belgian	89	0.12
Brazilian	11	0.01
British	476	0.63
Bulgarian	32	0.04
Canadian	530	0.70
Celtic	67	0.09
Croatian	160	0.21
Czech	354	0.47
Czechoslovakian	203	0.27
Danish	1,153	1.52
Dutch	1,523	2.01
Eastern European	42	0.06
English	9,135	12.03
Estonian	7	0.01
European	1,220	1.61
Finnish	413	0.54
French, except Basque	2,413	3.18
French Canadian	587	0.77
German	15,140	19.94
Greek	190	0.25
Hawaii Native/Pacific Islander:	612	0.80
Melanesian: (28)	29	0.04
Fijian (27)	28	0.04
Other Melanesian (1)	1	0.00
Micronesian: (52)	85	0.11
Guamanian/Chamorro (32)	51	0.07
Other Micronesian (20)	34	0.04
Polynesian: (146)	365	0.48
Native Hawaiian (96)	272	0.36
Samoan (26)	53	0.07
Tongan (16)	19	0.02
Other Polynesian (8)	21	0.03
Other Pac. Isl., specified	3	0.00
Other Pac. Isl., not spec. (40)	130	0.17
Hispanic or Latino:	8,463	11.12
Central American:	499	0.66
Costa Rican	16	0.02
Guatemalan	353	0.46
Honduran	22	0.03
Nicaraguan	12	0.02
Panamanian	18	0.02
Salvadoran	61	0.08
Other Central American	17	0.02
Cuban	88	0.12
Dominican Republic	8	0.01
Mexican	6,184	8.12
Puerto Rican	177	0.23
South American:	214	0.28
Argentinean	17	0.02
Bolivian	10	0.01
Chilean	28	0.04
Colombian	36	0.05
Ecuadorian	17	0.02
Peruvian	55	0.07
Uruguayan	5	0.01
Venezuelan	36	0.05
Other South American	10	0.01
Other Hispanic or Latino	1,293	1.70
Hungarian	303	0.40
Icelander	26	0.03
Iranian	700	0.92
Irish	7,953	10.48
Israeli	14	0.02
Italian	2,495	3.29
Latvian	57	0.08

Notes: 1. Figures in the "Number" column do not add up to the total population due to: a) Ancestry/Race overlap — e.g. persons can report being both White and Irish, b) persons of Hispanic origin can report being any race, c) persons reporting two ancestries are counted in both categories. 2. Numbers in parentheses indicate the number of persons reporting this ancestry/race alone, not in combination with any other ancestry/race. 3. Refer to the Explanation of Data in the front of the book for more detailed information.

Lithuanian	144	0.19
Macedonian	24	0.03
New Zealander	33	0.04
Northern European	256	0.34
Norwegian	3,592	4.73
Pennsylvania German	68	0.09
Polish	1,424	1.88
Portuguese	285	0.38
Romanian	399	0.53
Russian	862	1.14
Scandinavian	444	0.58
Scotch-Irish	1,512	1.99
Scottish	2,178	2.87
Serbian	28	0.04
Slavic	58	0.08
Slovak	36	0.05
Slovene	38	0.05
Swedish	2,162	2.85
Swiss	588	0.77
Turkish	150	0.20
Ukrainian	301	0.40
United States or American	3,593	4.73
Welsh	797	1.05
West Indian, excl. Hispanic:	148	0.19
Belizean	26	0.03
Dutch West Indian	10	0.01
Haitian	63	0.08
Jamaican	40	0.05
West Indian	9	0.01
White:	62,065	81.53
Not Hispanic (56,035)	58,013	76.20
Hispanic (3,580)	4,052	5.32
Yugoslavian	85	0.11

Bend

Place Type: City
County: Deschutes
Population: 52,029

Ancestry/Race	Number	%
African American/Black:	281	0.54
Not Hispanic (139)	263	0.51
Hispanic (6)	18	0.03
African, sub-Saharan:	31	0.06
African	9	0.02
South African	22	0.04
Alaska Native tribes, specified:	31	0.06
Alaska Athabascan (2)	3	0.01
Aleut (1)	4	0.01
Eskimo (2)	3	0.01
Tlingit-Haida (12)	21	0.04
Alaska Native tribes, not specified	3	0.01
Am. Ind. or Alaska Nat., not spec.	218	0.42
Albanian	10	0.02
American Indian tribes, specified:	621	1.19
Apache (7)	13	0.02
Blackfeet (2)	14	0.03
Cherokee (49)	174	0.33
Cheyenne (1)	4	0.01
Chickasaw (4)	4	0.01
Chippewa (8)	14	0.03
Choctaw (7)	28	0.05
Colville (1)	3	0.01
Comanche	1	0.00
Cree (1)	4	0.01
Creek (1)	4	0.01
Crow (2)	6	0.01
Iroquois (2)	7	0.01
Latin American Indians (14)	25	0.05
Lumbee (1)	2	0.00
Navajo (18)	27	0.05
Osage (1)	5	0.01
Paiute (1)	7	0.01
Pima (2)	2	0.00
Potawatomi (4)	4	0.01
Pueblo (6)	10	0.02
Puget Sound Salish (1)	6	0.01
Seminole (4)	5	0.01
Shoshone (2)	7	0.01
Sioux (16)	38	0.07
Ute (1)	6	0.01
Yakama (5)	10	0.02
Yaqui (5)	5	0.01
Yuman	1	0.00
All other tribes (112)	185	0.36
American Indian tribes, not spec.	52	0.10
Arab:	112	0.22
Arab/Arabic	16	0.03
Egyptian	26	0.05
Lebanese	7	0.01
Syrian	63	0.12
Armenian	82	0.16
Asian:	819	1.57
Cambodian (4)	4	0.01
Chinese, ex. Taiwanese (127)	183	0.35
Filipino (59)	139	0.27
Indian (63)	77	0.15
Indonesian (11)	16	0.03
Japanese (120)	208	0.40
Korean (59)	84	0.16
Malaysian (2)	3	0.01
Pakistani	5	0.01
Taiwanese (4)	9	0.02
Thai (10)	15	0.03
Vietnamese (47)	52	0.10
Other Asian, specified	8	0.02
Other Asian, not specified (6)	16	0.03
Australian	23	0.04
Austrian	112	0.22
Basque	56	0.11
Belgian	98	0.19
Brazilian	20	0.04
British	412	0.80
Bulgarian	51	0.10
Canadian	247	0.48
Celtic	92	0.18
Croatian	88	0.17
Czech	206	0.40
Czechoslovakian	124	0.24
Danish	700	1.35
Dutch	1,459	2.82
Eastern European	9	0.02
English	7,723	14.91
European	776	1.50
Finnish	272	0.53
French, except Basque	2,201	4.25
French Canadian	522	1.01
German	10,839	20.92
Greek	281	0.54
Hawaii Native/Pacific Islander:	143	0.27
Micronesian:	6	0.01
Guamanian/Chamorro	6	0.01
Polynesian: (36)	113	0.22
Native Hawaiian (32)	100	0.19
Samoan (4)	10	0.02
Other Polynesian	3	0.01
Other Pac. Isl., specified	4	0.01
Other Pac. Isl., not spec. (6)	20	0.04
Hispanic or Latino:	2,396	4.61
Central American:	102	0.20
Costa Rican	7	0.01
Guatemalan	23	0.04
Honduran	23	0.04
Nicaraguan	5	0.01
Panamanian	7	0.01
Salvadoran	30	0.06
Other Central American	7	0.01
Cuban	22	0.04
Dominican Republic	2	0.00
Mexican	1,725	3.32
Puerto Rican	64	0.12
South American:	49	0.09
Argentinean	1	0.00
Bolivian	1	0.00
Chilean	7	0.01
Colombian	8	0.02
Ecuadorian	5	0.01
Paraguayan	13	0.02
Peruvian	7	0.01
Venezuelan	2	0.00
Other South American	5	0.01
Other Hispanic or Latino	432	0.83
Hungarian	152	0.29
Icelander	12	0.02
Iranian	11	0.02
Irish	7,036	13.58
Italian	2,225	4.29
Latvian	10	0.02
Lithuanian	110	0.21
Macedonian	7	0.01
New Zealander	33	0.06
Northern European	66	0.13
Norwegian	2,747	5.30
Pennsylvania German	20	0.04
Polish	1,076	2.08
Portuguese	266	0.51
Romanian	24	0.05
Russian	470	0.91
Scandinavian	246	0.47
Scotch-Irish	1,239	2.39
Scottish	2,222	4.29
Serbian	10	0.02
Slavic	60	0.12
Slovak	31	0.06
Swedish	1,581	3.05
Swiss	485	0.94
Ukrainian	89	0.17
United States or American	3,500	6.76
Welsh	789	1.52
West Indian, excl. Hispanic:	15	0.03
Dutch West Indian	10	0.02
Jamaican	5	0.01
White:	49,964	96.03
Not Hispanic (47,660)	48,504	93.22
Hispanic (1,237)	1,460	2.81
Yugoslavian	246	0.47

Canby

Place Type: City
County: Clackamas
Population: 12,790

Ancestry/Race	Number	%
African American/Black:	80	0.63
Not Hispanic (35)	53	0.41
Hispanic (25)	27	0.21
Alaska Native tribes, specified:	10	0.08
Aleut (1)	1	0.01
Tlingit-Haida (9)	9	0.07
Alaska Native tribes, not specified	1	0.01
Am. Ind. or Alaska Nat., not spec.	52	0.41
American Indian tribes, specified:	124	0.97
Apache (3)	11	0.09
Blackfeet (2)	4	0.03
Cherokee (3)	27	0.21
Chippewa (8)	12	0.09
Choctaw (8)	12	0.09
Creek (2)	3	0.02
Delaware (2)	2	0.02
Iroquois (1)	3	0.02
Latin American Indians (9)	9	0.07
Lumbee (1)	1	0.01
Osage	1	0.01
Ottawa (1)	1	0.01
Paiute (1)	4	0.03
Seminole	1	0.01
Shoshone	1	0.01
Sioux (3)	7	0.05
Yakama	2	0.02
All other tribes (16)	23	0.18
Asian:	198	1.55
Cambodian (1)	1	0.01
Chinese, ex. Taiwanese (23)	38	0.30
Filipino (5)	19	0.15
Hmong (4)	4	0.03
Indian (16)	21	0.16
Indonesian (1)	2	0.02
Japanese (11)	34	0.27

Notes: 1. Figures in the "Number" column do not add up to the total population due to: a) Ancestry/Race overlap — e.g. persons can report being both White and Irish, b) persons of Hispanic origin can report being any race, c) persons reporting two ancestries are counted in both categories. 2. Numbers in parentheses indicate the number of persons reporting this ancestry/race alone, not in combination with any other ancestry/race. 3. Refer to the Explanation of Data in the front of the book for more detailed information.

Ancestry/Race	Number	%
Korean (20)	26	0.20
Laotian (7)	7	0.05
Malaysian	1	0.01
Thai (1)	2	0.02
Vietnamese (34)	36	0.28
Other Asian, not specified (3)	7	0.05
Austrian	44	0.34
British	37	0.29
Canadian	48	0.37
Celtic	22	0.17
Czech	55	0.42
Czechoslovakian	15	0.12
Danish	182	1.41
Dutch	284	2.19
English	1,689	13.04
European	230	1.78
Finnish	36	0.28
French, except Basque	363	2.80
French Canadian	37	0.29
German	3,057	23.61
Greek	21	0.16
Hawaii Native/Pacific Islander:	35	0.27
Micronesian: (2)	5	0.04
Guamanian/Chamorro	2	0.02
Other Micronesian (2)	3	0.02
Polynesian: (4)	17	0.13
Native Hawaiian (4)	14	0.11
Samoan	3	0.02
Other Pac. Isl., not spec. (10)	13	0.10
Hispanic or Latino:	1,985	15.52
Central American:	30	0.23
Guatemalan	9	0.07
Honduran	3	0.02
Nicaraguan	3	0.02
Panamanian	4	0.03
Salvadoran	11	0.09
Cuban	3	0.02
Mexican	1,730	13.53
Puerto Rican	19	0.15
South American:	8	0.06
Chilean	1	0.01
Colombian	3	0.02
Ecuadorian	2	0.02
Peruvian	2	0.02
Other Hispanic or Latino	195	1.52
Hungarian	21	0.16
Iranian	8	0.06
Irish	1,247	9.63
Italian	610	4.71
Lithuanian	7	0.05
New Zealander	17	0.13
Northern European	21	0.16
Norwegian	839	6.48
Polish	102	0.79
Romanian	18	0.14
Russian	48	0.37
Scandinavian	93	0.72
Scotch-Irish	295	2.28
Scottish	384	2.97
Swedish	548	4.23
Swiss	54	0.42
Ukrainian	26	0.20
United States or American	682	5.27
Welsh	143	1.10
White:	11,511	90.00
Not Hispanic (10,404)	10,541	82.42
Hispanic (905)	970	7.58

Cedar Mill

Place Type: Census Designated Place
County: Washington
Population: 12,597

Ancestry/Race	Number	%
African American/Black:	163	1.29
Not Hispanic (104)	157	1.25
Hispanic (4)	6	0.05
African, sub-Saharan:	35	0.27
African	35	0.27
Alaska Native tribes, specified:	7	0.06
Eskimo (4)	7	0.06
Am. Ind. or Alaska Nat., not spec.	38	0.30
American Indian tribes, specified:	84	0.67
Apache	1	0.01
Blackfeet (1)	3	0.02
Cherokee (13)	27	0.21
Chickasaw	1	0.01
Chippewa (1)	1	0.01
Choctaw	2	0.02
Iroquois (2)	4	0.03
Latin American Indians (3)	11	0.09
Pima	1	0.01
Potawatomi (1)	2	0.02
Pueblo	1	0.01
Seminole (1)	1	0.01
Sioux (4)	11	0.09
Yakama (1)	2	0.02
All other tribes (9)	16	0.13
American Indian tribes, not spec.	4	0.03
Arab:	65	0.51
Arab/Arabic	6	0.05
Egyptian	21	0.16
Lebanese	15	0.12
Palestinian	6	0.05
Other Arab	17	0.13
Armenian	46	0.36
Asian:	1,146	9.10
Bangladeshi (1)	1	0.01
Cambodian (8)	12	0.10
Chinese, ex. Taiwanese (279)	348	2.76
Filipino (51)	75	0.60
Indian (182)	201	1.60
Indonesian (3)	11	0.09
Japanese (84)	120	0.95
Korean (214)	229	1.82
Laotian (3)	10	0.08
Pakistani (3)	3	0.02
Taiwanese (16)	23	0.18
Thai (2)	6	0.05
Vietnamese (67)	76	0.60
Other Asian, specified (1)	2	0.02
Other Asian, not specified (3)	29	0.23
Austrian	50	0.39
Brazilian	9	0.07
British	182	1.42
Canadian	19	0.15
Croatian	6	0.05
Czech	162	1.27
Czechoslovakian	84	0.66
Danish	172	1.35
Dutch	237	1.86
English	1,826	14.29
European	352	2.76
Finnish	106	0.83
French, except Basque	594	4.65
French Canadian	77	0.60
German	2,977	23.30
Greek	35	0.27
Hawaii Native/Pacific Islander:	60	0.48
Micronesian: (6)	9	0.07
Guamanian/Chamorro (6)	9	0.07
Polynesian: (12)	32	0.25
Native Hawaiian (11)	31	0.25
Other Polynesian (1)	1	0.01
Other Pac. Isl., not spec. (8)	19	0.15
Hispanic or Latino:	767	6.09
Central American:	72	0.57
Costa Rican	4	0.03
Guatemalan	62	0.49
Honduran	1	0.01
Panamanian	1	0.01
Salvadoran	4	0.03
Cuban	6	0.05
Mexican	514	4.08
Puerto Rican	18	0.14
South American:	20	0.16
Argentinean	1	0.01
Bolivian	2	0.02
Chilean	6	0.05
Colombian	5	0.04
Paraguayan	2	0.02
Peruvian	4	0.03
Other Hispanic or Latino	137	1.09
Hungarian	119	0.93
Iranian	105	0.82
Irish	1,699	13.30
Italian	437	3.42
Latvian	12	0.09
Lithuanian	13	0.10
Northern European	96	0.75
Norwegian	402	3.15
Pennsylvania German	16	0.13
Polish	352	2.76
Portuguese	62	0.49
Romanian	9	0.07
Russian	170	1.33
Scandinavian	30	0.23
Scotch-Irish	308	2.41
Scottish	364	2.85
Slovak	9	0.07
Swedish	543	4.25
Swiss	117	0.92
Turkish	6	0.05
Ukrainian	102	0.80
United States or American	773	6.05
Welsh	198	1.55
West Indian, excl. Hispanic:	28	0.22
British West Indian	28	0.22
White:	11,094	88.07
Not Hispanic (10,384)	10,654	84.58
Hispanic (376)	440	3.49
Yugoslavian	74	0.58

Central Point

Place Type: City
County: Jackson
Population: 12,493

Ancestry/Race	Number	%
African American/Black:	52	0.42
Not Hispanic (30)	51	0.41
Hispanic (1)	1	0.01
African, sub-Saharan:	10	0.08
Kenyan	10	0.08
Alaska Native tribes, specified:	2	0.02
Aleut	1	0.01
Eskimo (1)	1	0.01
Alaska Native tribes, not specified	1	0.01
Am. Ind. or Alaska Nat., not spec.	54	0.43
American Indian tribes, specified:	211	1.69
Apache (2)	3	0.02
Blackfeet (1)	9	0.07
Cherokee (17)	70	0.56
Cheyenne	1	0.01
Chickasaw (1)	3	0.02
Chippewa	1	0.01
Choctaw (6)	15	0.12
Comanche (1)	2	0.02
Creek (1)	3	0.02
Iroquois (2)	5	0.04
Latin American Indians (6)	21	0.17
Lumbee	1	0.01
Navajo (1)	4	0.03
Osage	1	0.01
Potawatomi (1)	1	0.01
Pueblo (5)	7	0.06
Seminole	1	0.01
Sioux (3)	8	0.06
Yaqui (1)	1	0.01
All other tribes (26)	54	0.43
American Indian tribes, not spec.	17	0.14
Arab:	5	0.04
Lebanese	5	0.04
Armenian	11	0.09
Asian:	135	1.08
Cambodian (1)	1	0.01
Chinese, ex. Taiwanese (14)	17	0.14
Filipino (37)	55	0.44

Notes: 1. Figures in the "Number" column do not add up to the total population due to: a) Ancestry/Race overlap — e.g. persons can report being both White and Irish, b) persons of Hispanic origin can report being any race, c) persons reporting two ancestries are counted in both categories. 2. Numbers in parentheses indicate the number of persons reporting this ancestry/race alone, not in combination with any other ancestry/race. 3. Refer to the Explanation of Data in the front of the book for more detailed information.

Ancestry/Race	Number	%
Indian (1)	4	0.03
Japanese (13)	23	0.18
Korean (13)	18	0.14
Thai (9)	13	0.10
Vietnamese (2)	2	0.02
Other Asian, not specified (1)	2	0.02
Australian	5	0.04
Austrian	22	0.18
Basque	32	0.26
Belgian	8	0.06
British	27	0.22
Canadian	20	0.16
Czech	30	0.24
Czechoslovakian	54	0.43
Danish	282	2.27
Dutch	393	3.16
English	1,940	15.60
European	146	1.17
Finnish	20	0.16
French, except Basque	424	3.41
French Canadian	116	0.93
German	2,341	18.82
Greek	47	0.38
Hawaii Native/Pacific Islander:	46	0.37
Micronesian: (10)	17	0.14
Guamanian/Chamorro (10)	17	0.14
Polynesian: (14)	25	0.20
Native Hawaiian (2)	9	0.07
Samoan (11)	15	0.12
Tongan (1)	1	0.01
Other Pac. Isl., not spec.	4	0.03
Hispanic or Latino:	527	4.22
Central American:	1	0.01
Costa Rican	1	0.01
Cuban	2	0.02
Mexican	405	3.24
Puerto Rican	9	0.07
South American:	7	0.06
Argentinean	3	0.02
Chilean	1	0.01
Colombian	1	0.01
Peruvian	2	0.02
Other Hispanic or Latino	103	0.82
Hungarian	40	0.32
Irish	1,656	13.31
Italian	482	3.88
Lithuanian	63	0.51
Luxemburger	8	0.06
New Zealander	8	0.06
Northern European	24	0.19
Norwegian	450	3.62
Pennsylvania German	9	0.07
Polish	269	2.16
Portuguese	118	0.95
Russian	51	0.41
Scandinavian	39	0.31
Scotch-Irish	239	1.92
Scottish	369	2.97
Slavic	17	0.14
Swedish	392	3.15
Swiss	25	0.20
Ukrainian	14	0.11
United States or American	709	5.70
Welsh	117	0.94
White:	12,075	96.65
Not Hispanic (11,490)	11,731	93.90
Hispanic (253)	344	2.75
Yugoslavian	13	0.10

City of The Dalles

Place Type: City
County: Wasco
Population: 12,156

Ancestry/Race	Number	%
African American/Black:	95	0.78
Not Hispanic (45)	87	0.72
Hispanic (3)	8	0.07
Alaska Native tribes, specified:	9	0.07
Aleut (2)	7	0.06
Eskimo (1)	1	0.01
Tlingit-Haida	1	0.01
Am. Ind. or Alaska Nat., not spec.	66	0.54
American Indian tribes, specified:	172	1.41
Apache (1)	2	0.02
Blackfeet (4)	6	0.05
Cherokee (8)	22	0.18
Chickasaw (1)	3	0.02
Chippewa (5)	13	0.11
Choctaw (1)	5	0.04
Colville	1	0.01
Cree	1	0.01
Creek (1)	3	0.02
Latin American Indians (1)	5	0.04
Navajo (8)	8	0.07
Paiute	4	0.03
Pima (6)	6	0.05
Potawatomi (2)	4	0.03
Shoshone (1)	1	0.01
Sioux (4)	8	0.07
Yakama (30)	33	0.27
All other tribes (32)	47	0.39
American Indian tribes, not spec.	10	0.08
Arab:	18	0.15
Arab/Arabic	4	0.03
Lebanese	14	0.11
Asian:	172	1.41
Cambodian (1)	2	0.02
Chinese, ex. Taiwanese (11)	16	0.13
Filipino (12)	33	0.27
Indian (17)	20	0.16
Indonesian (2)	2	0.02
Japanese (28)	40	0.33
Korean (20)	32	0.26
Laotian (1)	1	0.01
Sri Lankan (3)	3	0.02
Taiwanese (1)	1	0.01
Vietnamese (16)	18	0.15
Other Asian, specified (1)	2	0.02
Other Asian, not specified (1)	2	0.02
Australian	7	0.06
Belgian	8	0.07
British	43	0.35
Canadian	27	0.22
Celtic	4	0.03
Croatian	10	0.08
Czech	90	0.74
Czechoslovakian	6	0.05
Danish	194	1.59
Dutch	312	2.55
Eastern European	16	0.13
English	1,692	13.83
European	167	1.37
Finnish	50	0.41
French, except Basque	620	5.07
French Canadian	79	0.65
German	2,525	20.65
German Russian	6	0.05
Greek	46	0.38
Hawaii Native/Pacific Islander:	121	1.00
Micronesian: (7)	9	0.07
Guamanian/Chamorro (7)	8	0.07
Other Micronesian	1	0.01
Polynesian: (83)	103	0.85
Native Hawaiian (2)	11	0.09
Samoan (81)	91	0.75
Other Polynesian	1	0.01
Other Pac. Isl., not spec. (3)	9	0.07
Hispanic or Latino:	1,276	10.50
Central American:	17	0.14
Guatemalan	3	0.02
Honduran	2	0.02
Panamanian	6	0.05
Salvadoran	6	0.05
Cuban	8	0.07
Mexican	1,081	8.89
Puerto Rican	8	0.07
South American:	6	0.05
Chilean	2	0.02
Colombian	1	0.01
Ecuadorian	1	0.01
Peruvian	2	0.02
Other Hispanic or Latino	156	1.28
Hungarian	19	0.16
Icelander	5	0.04
Irish	1,474	12.05
Italian	268	2.19
Northern European	27	0.22
Norwegian	702	5.74
Pennsylvania German	14	0.11
Polish	147	1.20
Portuguese	74	0.61
Romanian	13	0.11
Russian	57	0.47
Scandinavian	47	0.38
Scotch-Irish	293	2.40
Scottish	309	2.53
Slavic	5	0.04
Swedish	448	3.66
Swiss	61	0.50
Ukrainian	28	0.23
United States or American	698	5.71
Welsh	167	1.37
White:	10,975	90.28
Not Hispanic (10,271)	10,473	86.15
Hispanic (406)	502	4.13

Coos Bay

Place Type: City
County: Coos
Population: 15,374

Ancestry/Race	Number	%
African American/Black:	98	0.64
Not Hispanic (50)	78	0.51
Hispanic (7)	20	0.13
African, sub-Saharan:	43	0.28
African	36	0.23
Nigerian	7	0.05
Alaska Native tribes, specified:	28	0.18
Alaska Athabascan (2)	2	0.01
Aleut (7)	12	0.08
Eskimo (4)	4	0.03
Tlingit-Haida (8)	9	0.06
All other tribes	1	0.01
Alaska Native tribes, not specified	1	0.01
Am. Ind. or Alaska Nat., not spec.	151	0.98
American Indian tribes, specified:	508	3.30
Apache (6)	21	0.14
Blackfeet (4)	25	0.16
Cherokee (44)	146	0.95
Chippewa (15)	24	0.16
Choctaw (4)	14	0.09
Colville (1)	1	0.01
Comanche (6)	6	0.04
Cree	1	0.01
Creek	2	0.01
Delaware (1)	2	0.01
Iroquois (1)	4	0.03
Latin American Indians (7)	11	0.07
Lumbee (2)	2	0.01
Menominee (3)	4	0.03
Navajo	4	0.03
Osage	2	0.01
Paiute (1)	1	0.01
Pima	1	0.01
Potawatomi	1	0.01
Pueblo (1)	3	0.02
Puget Sound Salish (1)	1	0.01
Seminole (2)	4	0.03
Shoshone (2)	4	0.03
Sioux (11)	33	0.21
Yakama	1	0.01
Yaqui	1	0.01
All other tribes (123)	189	1.23
American Indian tribes, not spec.	38	0.25
Arab:	13	0.08
Arab/Arabic	4	0.03

Notes: 1. Figures in the "Number" column do not add up to the total population due to: a) Ancestry/Race overlap — e.g. persons can report being both White and Irish, b) persons of Hispanic origin can report being any race, c) persons reporting two ancestries are counted in both categories. 2. Numbers in parentheses indicate the number of persons reporting this ancestry/race alone, not in combination with any other ancestry/race. 3. Refer to the Explanation of Data in the front of the book for more detailed information.

Jordanian	9	0.06
Asian:	312	2.03
Chinese, ex. Taiwanese (29)	40	0.26
Filipino (36)	57	0.37
Indian (25)	41	0.27
Indonesian (1)	2	0.01
Japanese (45)	61	0.40
Korean (47)	63	0.41
Malaysian (1)	1	0.01
Taiwanese (2)	2	0.01
Thai (4)	6	0.04
Vietnamese (26)	26	0.17
Other Asian, specified	8	0.05
Other Asian, not specified (2)	5	0.03
Australian	4	0.03
Austrian	33	0.21
British	36	0.23
Bulgarian	10	0.06
Canadian	64	0.41
Celtic	28	0.18
Croatian	16	0.10
Cypriot	7	0.05
Czech	114	0.74
Czechoslovakian	41	0.27
Danish	159	1.03
Dutch	538	3.48
English	1,994	12.91
European	157	1.02
Finnish	92	0.60
French, except Basque	641	4.15
French Canadian	118	0.76
German	3,107	20.12
Hawaii Native/Pacific Islander:	96	0.62
Melanesian: (8)	8	0.05
Fijian (8)	8	0.05
Micronesian: (3)	10	0.07
Guamanian/Chamorro (2)	3	0.02
Other Micronesian (1)	7	0.05
Polynesian: (27)	51	0.33
Native Hawaiian (21)	40	0.26
Samoan (6)	11	0.07
Other Pac. Isl., specified	4	0.03
Other Pac. Isl., not spec. (10)	23	0.15
Hispanic or Latino:	691	4.49
Central American:	5	0.03
Guatemalan	3	0.02
Honduran	1	0.01
Salvadoran	1	0.01
Cuban	7	0.05
Mexican	535	3.48
Puerto Rican	15	0.10
South American:	9	0.06
Chilean	4	0.03
Colombian	4	0.03
Venezuelan	1	0.01
Other Hispanic or Latino	120	0.78
Hungarian	33	0.21
Iranian	12	0.08
Irish	2,111	13.67
Italian	343	2.22
Lithuanian	15	0.10
Northern European	116	0.75
Norwegian	774	5.01
Pennsylvania German	7	0.05
Polish	305	1.98
Portuguese	62	0.40
Romanian	17	0.11
Russian	78	0.51
Scandinavian	32	0.21
Scotch-Irish	303	1.96
Scottish	521	3.37
Slovene	7	0.05
Swedish	528	3.42
Swiss	94	0.61
Ukrainian	19	0.12
United States or American	1,082	7.01
Welsh	156	1.01
West Indian, excl. Hispanic:	36	0.23
Dutch West Indian	32	0.21
Jamaican	4	0.03
White:	14,457	94.04
Not Hispanic (13,593)	14,002	91.08
Hispanic (359)	455	2.96

Corvallis

Place Type: City
County: Benton
Population: 49,322

Ancestry/Race	Number	%
Acadian/Cajun	11	0.02
African American/Black:	788	1.60
Not Hispanic (549)	753	1.53
Hispanic (21)	35	0.07
African, sub-Saharan:	150	0.30
African	14	0.03
Cape Verdean	11	0.02
Ethiopian	46	0.09
Ghanian	24	0.05
Liberian	22	0.04
Ugandan	8	0.02
Other sub-Saharan African	25	0.05
Alaska Native tribes, specified:	34	0.07
Alaska Athabascan (1)	1	0.00
Aleut (2)	4	0.01
Eskimo (5)	7	0.01
Tlingit-Haida (18)	20	0.04
All other tribes	2	0.00
Alaska Native tribes, not specified	1	0.00
Am. Ind. or Alaska Nat., not spec.	216	0.44
American Indian tribes, specified:	499	1.01
Apache (2)	12	0.02
Blackfeet (6)	19	0.04
Cherokee (38)	132	0.27
Cheyenne (2)	4	0.01
Chickasaw (2)	3	0.01
Chippewa (18)	24	0.05
Choctaw (17)	36	0.07
Colville (2)	4	0.01
Comanche (2)	4	0.01
Cree (1)	4	0.01
Creek (3)	3	0.01
Crow	1	0.00
Delaware	1	0.00
Houma (1)	1	0.00
Iroquois (2)	4	0.01
Kiowa (3)	3	0.01
Latin American Indians (11)	23	0.05
Navajo (6)	12	0.02
Osage (3)	4	0.01
Ottawa	1	0.00
Paiute (3)	4	0.01
Pima (2)	2	0.00
Potawatomi (5)	5	0.01
Pueblo (2)	4	0.01
Puget Sound Salish (3)	3	0.01
Seminole (4)	7	0.01
Sioux (14)	28	0.06
Ute	3	0.01
Yakama (3)	3	0.01
All other tribes (87)	145	0.29
American Indian tribes, not spec.	42	0.09
Arab:	121	0.25
Arab/Arabic	8	0.02
Egyptian	11	0.02
Jordanian	27	0.05
Lebanese	15	0.03
Other Arab	60	0.12
Armenian	17	0.03
Asian:	3,840	7.79
Bangladeshi (2)	7	0.01
Cambodian (45)	54	0.11
Chinese, ex. Taiwanese (816)	1,007	2.04
Filipino (124)	254	0.51
Hmong (10)	10	0.02
Indian (361)	393	0.80
Indonesian (91)	121	0.25
Japanese (444)	622	1.26
Korean (443)	495	1.00
Laotian (40)	50	0.10
Malaysian (3)	5	0.01
Pakistani (14)	16	0.03
Sri Lankan (10)	11	0.02
Taiwanese (46)	50	0.10
Thai (154)	170	0.34
Vietnamese (286)	315	0.64
Other Asian, specified (8)	20	0.04
Other Asian, not specified (190)	240	0.49
Australian	67	0.14
Austrian	130	0.26
Basque	70	0.14
Belgian	108	0.22
Brazilian	15	0.03
British	504	1.02
Bulgarian	10	0.02
Canadian	197	0.40
Celtic	49	0.10
Croatian	38	0.08
Czech	335	0.68
Czechoslovakian	203	0.41
Danish	776	1.58
Dutch	1,121	2.28
Eastern European	53	0.11
English	6,986	14.20
Estonian	6	0.01
European	1,354	2.75
Finnish	269	0.55
French, except Basque	1,686	3.43
French Canadian	409	0.83
German	10,688	21.73
Greek	281	0.57
Hawaii Native/Pacific Islander:	318	0.64
Melanesian: (4)	5	0.01
Fijian (4)	5	0.01
Micronesian: (22)	26	0.05
Guamanian/Chamorro (19)	23	0.05
Other Micronesian (3)	3	0.01
Polynesian: (69)	201	0.41
Native Hawaiian (41)	157	0.32
Samoan (20)	31	0.06
Tongan (6)	9	0.02
Other Polynesian (2)	4	0.01
Other Pac. Isl., specified	8	0.02
Other Pac. Isl., not spec. (44)	78	0.16
Hispanic or Latino:	2,820	5.72
Central American:	82	0.17
Costa Rican	15	0.03
Guatemalan	26	0.05
Honduran	4	0.01
Nicaraguan	7	0.01
Panamanian	7	0.01
Salvadoran	23	0.05
Cuban	45	0.09
Dominican Republic	10	0.02
Mexican	1,949	3.95
Puerto Rican	105	0.21
South American:	128	0.26
Argentinean	27	0.05
Bolivian	5	0.01
Chilean	30	0.06
Colombian	23	0.05
Ecuadorian	16	0.03
Paraguayan	3	0.01
Peruvian	13	0.03
Uruguayan	2	0.00
Venezuelan	5	0.01
Other South American	4	0.01
Other Hispanic or Latino	501	1.02
Hungarian	260	0.53
Iranian	59	0.12
Irish	6,111	12.42
Israeli	10	0.02
Italian	1,392	2.83
Latvian	38	0.08
Lithuanian	53	0.11
Luxemburger	15	0.03
Maltese	6	0.01
New Zealander	6	0.01
Northern European	204	0.41

Notes: 1. Figures in the "Number" column do not add up to the total population due to: a) Ancestry/Race overlap — e.g. persons can report being both White and Irish, b) persons of Hispanic origin can report being any race, c) persons reporting two ancestries are counted in both categories. 2. Numbers in parentheses indicate the number of persons reporting this ancestry/race alone, not in combination with any other ancestry/race. 3. Refer to the Explanation of Data in the front of the book for more detailed information.

Norwegian	2,418	4.92
Pennsylvania German	49	0.10
Polish	1,086	2.21
Portuguese	347	0.71
Romanian	60	0.12
Russian	505	1.03
Scandinavian	380	0.77
Scotch-Irish	1,286	2.61
Scottish	2,067	4.20
Serbian	18	0.04
Slavic	55	0.11
Slovak	43	0.09
Slovene	36	0.07
Swedish	2,078	4.22
Swiss	561	1.14
Turkish	61	0.12
Ukrainian	92	0.19
United States or American	2,263	4.60
Welsh	616	1.25
West Indian, excl. Hispanic:	36	0.07
Bahamian	6	0.01
Dutch West Indian	14	0.03
Haitian	6	0.01
Jamaican	10	0.02
White:	43,685	88.57
Not Hispanic (41,093)	42,105	85.37
Hispanic (1,340)	1,580	3.20
Yugoslavian	170	0.35

Dallas

Place Type: City
County: Polk
Population: 12,459

Ancestry/Race	Number	%
African American/Black:	56	0.45
Not Hispanic (12)	45	0.36
Hispanic (10)	11	0.09
African, sub-Saharan:	42	0.34
African	36	0.29
Other sub-Saharan African	6	0.05
Alaska Native tribes, specified:	23	0.18
Alaska Athabascan (2)	3	0.02
Eskimo (1)	2	0.02
Tlingit-Haida (10)	15	0.12
All other tribes (3)	3	0.02
Am. Ind. or Alaska Nat., not spec.	83	0.67
American Indian tribes, specified:	307	2.46
Apache (6)	15	0.12
Blackfeet (2)	6	0.05
Cherokee (21)	71	0.57
Chickasaw (5)	5	0.04
Chippewa (5)	6	0.05
Choctaw (9)	24	0.19
Comanche	2	0.02
Creek (3)	4	0.03
Iroquois (3)	6	0.05
Latin American Indians (3)	3	0.02
Lumbee	3	0.02
Menominee (1)	1	0.01
Navajo	1	0.01
Osage (3)	4	0.03
Ottawa	1	0.01
Paiute	2	0.02
Pima	1	0.01
Potawatomi (2)	3	0.02
Pueblo	1	0.01
Puget Sound Salish (12)	12	0.10
Shoshone	1	0.01
Sioux (22)	38	0.31
Ute (6)	6	0.05
Yakama (2)	2	0.02
Yuman (1)	4	0.03
All other tribes (57)	85	0.68
American Indian tribes, not spec.	8	0.06
Armenian	26	0.21
Asian:	127	1.02
Cambodian (7)	7	0.06
Chinese, ex. Taiwanese (11)	21	0.17
Filipino (6)	19	0.15
Indian (10)	14	0.11
Indonesian	6	0.05
Japanese (13)	18	0.14
Korean (13)	27	0.22
Laotian (2)	4	0.03
Thai (1)	3	0.02
Vietnamese (1)	2	0.02
Other Asian, not specified (5)	6	0.05
Australian	11	0.09
Austrian	31	0.25
Belgian	49	0.39
Brazilian	9	0.07
British	55	0.44
Czech	93	0.75
Czechoslovakian	27	0.22
Danish	151	1.22
Dutch	645	5.19
English	1,766	14.21
European	208	1.67
Finnish	97	0.78
French, except Basque	437	3.52
French Canadian	93	0.75
German	3,163	25.45
Greek	26	0.21
Hawaii Native/Pacific Islander:	39	0.31
Melanesian:	1	0.01
Fijian	1	0.01
Micronesian: (8)	14	0.11
Guamanian/Chamorro (2)	5	0.04
Other Micronesian (6)	9	0.07
Polynesian: (5)	15	0.12
Native Hawaiian (4)	13	0.10
Samoan (1)	1	0.01
Other Polynesian	1	0.01
Other Pac. Isl., not spec.	9	0.07
Hispanic or Latino:	500	4.01
Central American:	11	0.09
Guatemalan	2	0.02
Honduran	4	0.03
Panamanian	2	0.02
Salvadoran	3	0.02
Cuban	4	0.03
Mexican	362	2.91
Puerto Rican	29	0.23
South American:	6	0.05
Bolivian	1	0.01
Colombian	1	0.01
Ecuadorian	1	0.01
Peruvian	1	0.01
Other South American	2	0.02
Other Hispanic or Latino	88	0.71
Hungarian	88	0.71
Iranian	7	0.06
Irish	1,251	10.07
Italian	361	2.90
Lithuanian	29	0.23
Norwegian	593	4.77
Pennsylvania German	56	0.45
Polish	76	0.61
Portuguese	16	0.13
Russian	81	0.65
Scandinavian	47	0.38
Scotch-Irish	360	2.90
Scottish	372	2.99
Swedish	328	2.64
Swiss	160	1.29
United States or American	890	7.16
Welsh	147	1.18
White:	11,945	95.87
Not Hispanic (11,377)	11,635	93.39
Hispanic (244)	310	2.49
Yugoslavian	7	0.06

Eugene

Place Type: City
County: Lane
Population: 137,893

Ancestry/Race	Number	%
Acadian/Cajun	47	0.03
African American/Black:	2,743	1.99
Not Hispanic (1,644)	2,560	1.86
Hispanic (85)	183	0.13
African, sub-Saharan:	423	0.31
African	301	0.22
Cape Verdean	9	0.01
Ethiopian	21	0.02
Ghanian	11	0.01
Nigerian	37	0.03
Somalian	7	0.01
South African	9	0.01
Other sub-Saharan African	28	0.02
Alaska Native tribes, specified:	112	0.08
Alaska Athabascan (8)	8	0.01
Aleut (18)	32	0.02
Eskimo (14)	24	0.02
Tlingit-Haida (30)	46	0.03
All other tribes (1)	2	0.00
Alaska Native tribes, not specified	7	0.01
Am. Ind. or Alaska Nat., not spec.	876	0.64
Albanian	25	0.02
Alsatian	41	0.03
American Indian tribes, specified:	2,149	1.56
Apache (17)	63	0.05
Blackfeet (16)	75	0.05
Cherokee (148)	633	0.46
Cheyenne (5)	19	0.01
Chickasaw (13)	31	0.02
Chippewa (46)	98	0.07
Choctaw (34)	103	0.07
Colville (11)	12	0.01
Comanche (10)	15	0.01
Cree (1)	20	0.01
Creek (8)	20	0.01
Crow (2)	9	0.01
Delaware (3)	9	0.01
Houma (1)	4	0.00
Iroquois (9)	55	0.04
Kiowa (5)	12	0.01
Latin American Indians (31)	83	0.06
Lumbee (1)	1	0.00
Menominee	3	0.00
Navajo (23)	42	0.03
Osage (6)	29	0.02
Ottawa	5	0.00
Paiute (11)	29	0.02
Pima (2)	2	0.00
Potawatomi (13)	29	0.02
Pueblo (14)	29	0.02
Puget Sound Salish (4)	9	0.01
Seminole (8)	21	0.02
Shoshone (2)	16	0.01
Sioux (36)	104	0.08
Tohono O'Odham (1)	1	0.00
Ute (2)	8	0.01
Yakama (7)	14	0.01
Yaqui (8)	21	0.02
Yuman (2)	2	0.00
All other tribes (306)	523	0.38
American Indian tribes, not spec.	138	0.10
Arab:	575	0.42
Arab/Arabic	125	0.09
Egyptian	50	0.04
Lebanese	263	0.19
Moroccan	21	0.02
Palestinian	7	0.01
Syrian	65	0.05
Other Arab	44	0.03
Armenian	83	0.06
Asian:	6,634	4.81
Bangladeshi (1)	3	0.00
Cambodian (26)	39	0.03

Notes: 1. Figures in the "Number" column do not add up to the total population due to: a) Ancestry/Race overlap — e.g. persons can report being both White and Irish, b) persons of Hispanic origin can report being any race, c) persons reporting two ancestries are counted in both categories. 2. Numbers in parentheses indicate the number of persons reporting this ancestry/race alone, not in combination with any other ancestry/race. 3. Refer to the Explanation of Data in the front of the book for more detailed information.

Chinese, ex. Taiwanese (1,315)	1,744	1.26
Filipino (286)	595	0.43
Hmong (6)	6	0.00
Indian (370)	477	0.35
Indonesian (124)	180	0.13
Japanese (1,044)	1,549	1.12
Korean (1,038)	1,179	0.86
Laotian (35)	60	0.04
Malaysian (7)	12	0.01
Pakistani (16)	24	0.02
Sri Lankan (4)	4	0.00
Taiwanese (104)	139	0.10
Thai (119)	155	0.11
Vietnamese (191)	237	0.17
Other Asian, specified (16)	35	0.03
Other Asian, not specified (104)	196	0.14
Australian	74	0.05
Austrian	442	0.32
Basque	96	0.07
Belgian	218	0.16
Brazilian	44	0.03
British	1,231	0.89
Bulgarian	70	0.05
Canadian	700	0.51
Celtic	108	0.08
Croatian	150	0.11
Cypriot	13	0.01
Czech	863	0.63
Czechoslovakian	275	0.20
Danish	2,269	1.65
Dutch	3,809	2.76
Eastern European	144	0.10
English	20,348	14.77
Estonian	33	0.02
European	2,822	2.05
Finnish	836	0.61
French, except Basque	5,606	4.07
French Canadian	1,244	0.90
German	27,948	20.28
Greek	457	0.33
Guyanese	6	0.00
Hawaii Native/Pacific Islander:	703	0.51
Melanesian: (13)	16	0.01
Fijian (13)	15	0.01
Other Melanesian	1	0.00
Micronesian: (65)	120	0.09
Guamanian/Chamorro (49)	85	0.06
Other Micronesian (16)	35	0.03
Polynesian: (171)	419	0.30
Native Hawaiian (109)	316	0.23
Samoan (57)	84	0.06
Tongan	5	0.00
Other Polynesian (5)	14	0.01
Other Pac. Isl., specified	12	0.01
Other Pac. Isl., not spec. (42)	136	0.10
Hispanic or Latino:	6,843	4.96
Central American:	243	0.18
Costa Rican	18	0.01
Guatemalan	62	0.04
Honduran	30	0.02
Nicaraguan	14	0.01
Panamanian	22	0.02
Salvadoran	86	0.06
Other Central American	11	0.01
Cuban	94	0.07
Dominican Republic	11	0.01
Mexican	4,712	3.42
Puerto Rican	245	0.18
South American:	252	0.18
Argentinean	42	0.03
Bolivian	15	0.01
Chilean	47	0.03
Colombian	39	0.03
Ecuadorian	23	0.02
Paraguayan	1	0.00
Peruvian	52	0.04
Uruguayan	1	0.00
Venezuelan	9	0.01
Other South American	23	0.02
Other Hispanic or Latino	1,286	0.93
Hungarian	631	0.46
Icelander	62	0.04
Iranian	127	0.09
Irish	17,938	13.02
Israeli	61	0.04
Italian	5,074	3.68
Latvian	66	0.05
Lithuanian	236	0.17
Luxemburger	76	0.06
Maltese	8	0.01
New Zealander	14	0.01
Northern European	626	0.45
Norwegian	6,676	4.84
Pennsylvania German	138	0.10
Polish	2,765	2.01
Portuguese	575	0.42
Romanian	139	0.10
Russian	2,167	1.57
Scandinavian	726	0.53
Scotch-Irish	4,064	2.95
Scottish	5,172	3.75
Serbian	73	0.05
Slavic	54	0.04
Slovak	96	0.07
Slovene	101	0.07
Swedish	4,396	3.19
Swiss	946	0.69
Turkish	48	0.03
Ukrainian	469	0.34
United States or American	6,625	4.81
Welsh	1,990	1.44
West Indian, excl. Hispanic:	106	0.08
Belizean	10	0.01
British West Indian	8	0.01
Dutch West Indian	16	0.01
Haitian	11	0.01
Jamaican	61	0.04
White:	126,225	91.54
Not Hispanic (118,563)	122,465	88.81
Hispanic (2,983)	3,760	2.73
Yugoslavian	199	0.14

Forest Grove

Place Type: City
County: Washington
Population: 17,708

Ancestry/Race	Number	%
Acadian/Cajun	12	0.07
African American/Black:	124	0.70
Not Hispanic (65)	107	0.60
Hispanic (12)	17	0.10
Alaska Native tribes, specified:	5	0.03
Eskimo (5)	5	0.03
Am. Ind. or Alaska Nat., not spec.	92	0.52
American Indian tribes, specified:	202	1.14
Apache (3)	7	0.04
Blackfeet (3)	9	0.05
Cherokee (21)	46	0.26
Chippewa (4)	8	0.05
Choctaw (4)	11	0.06
Colville (3)	5	0.03
Comanche	2	0.01
Houma (1)	1	0.01
Iroquois (1)	4	0.02
Latin American Indians (16)	35	0.20
Navajo (2)	2	0.01
Ottawa (3)	4	0.02
Potawatomi (2)	3	0.02
Pueblo (4)	4	0.02
Puget Sound Salish (1)	1	0.01
Sioux (6)	17	0.10
Yakama (2)	2	0.01
Yaqui (2)	2	0.01
All other tribes (15)	39	0.22
American Indian tribes, not spec.	11	0.06
Arab:	10	0.06
Palestinian	10	0.06
Armenian	8	0.05
Asian:	620	3.50
Cambodian (7)	7	0.04
Chinese, ex. Taiwanese (40)	122	0.69
Filipino (59)	126	0.71
Indian (17)	27	0.15
Indonesian (2)	2	0.01
Japanese (126)	201	1.14
Korean (42)	57	0.32
Laotian (1)	1	0.01
Pakistani	2	0.01
Sri Lankan (3)	3	0.02
Taiwanese (5)	5	0.03
Thai (3)	4	0.02
Vietnamese (17)	18	0.10
Other Asian, specified (5)	15	0.08
Other Asian, not specified (11)	30	0.17
Australian	28	0.16
Austrian	35	0.20
Basque	7	0.04
Belgian	67	0.38
British	136	0.78
Canadian	81	0.46
Celtic	14	0.08
Croatian	16	0.09
Czech	7	0.04
Czechoslovakian	37	0.21
Danish	246	1.40
Dutch	742	4.23
Eastern European	8	0.05
English	1,967	11.22
European	429	2.45
Finnish	67	0.38
French, except Basque	530	3.02
French Canadian	201	1.15
German	3,699	21.11
German Russian	9	0.05
Greek	53	0.30
Hawaii Native/Pacific Islander:	144	0.81
Melanesian:	3	0.02
Fijian	3	0.02
Micronesian: (8)	12	0.07
Guamanian/Chamorro (8)	11	0.06
Other Micronesian	1	0.01
Polynesian: (31)	115	0.65
Native Hawaiian (27)	105	0.59
Samoan (3)	6	0.03
Tongan (1)	4	0.02
Other Pac. Isl., specified	1	0.01
Other Pac. Isl., not spec. (3)	13	0.07
Hispanic or Latino:	3,065	17.31
Central American:	79	0.45
Costa Rican	3	0.02
Guatemalan	61	0.34
Honduran	5	0.03
Panamanian	7	0.04
Salvadoran	2	0.01
Other Central American	1	0.01
Cuban	12	0.07
Dominican Republic	1	0.01
Mexican	2,497	14.10
Puerto Rican	17	0.10
South American:	19	0.11
Chilean	3	0.02
Colombian	1	0.01
Ecuadorian	8	0.05
Peruvian	3	0.02
Venezuelan	2	0.01
Other South American	2	0.01
Other Hispanic or Latino	440	2.48
Hungarian	9	0.05
Irish	1,993	11.37
Italian	469	2.68
Lithuanian	9	0.05
Northern European	8	0.05
Norwegian	641	3.66
Pennsylvania German	16	0.09
Polish	228	1.30
Portuguese	10	0.06
Romanian	10	0.06
Russian	106	0.60

Notes: 1. Figures in the "Number" column do not add up to the total population due to: a) Ancestry/Race overlap — e.g. persons can report being both White and Irish, b) persons of Hispanic origin can report being any race, c) persons reporting two ancestries are counted in both categories. 2. Numbers in parentheses indicate the number of persons reporting this ancestry/race alone, not in combination with any other ancestry/race. 3. Refer to the Explanation of Data in the front of the book for more detailed information.

Scandinavian	12	0.07
Scotch-Irish	373	2.13
Scottish	430	2.45
Slovak	17	0.10
Swedish	424	2.42
Swiss	172	0.98
Ukrainian	43	0.25
United States or American	1,232	7.03
Welsh	146	0.83
White:	14,957	84.46
Not Hispanic (13,669)	13,994	79.03
Hispanic (756)	963	5.44
Yugoslavian	9	0.05

Four Corners

Place Type: Census Designated Place
County: Marion
Population: 13,922

Ancestry/Race	Number	%
African American/Black:	249	1.79
Not Hispanic (161)	218	1.57
Hispanic (23)	31	0.22
Alaska Native tribes, specified:	22	0.16
Aleut (5)	5	0.04
Eskimo (4)	12	0.09
Tlingit-Haida	5	0.04
Alaska Native tribes, not specified	1	0.01
Am. Ind. or Alaska Nat., not spec.	100	0.72
American Indian tribes, specified:	348	2.50
Apache (2)	10	0.07
Blackfeet (6)	22	0.16
Cherokee (19)	71	0.51
Chickasaw (1)	1	0.01
Chippewa (9)	19	0.14
Choctaw (13)	14	0.10
Comanche (1)	1	0.01
Cree (1)	1	0.01
Creek (1)	1	0.01
Crow (1)	1	0.01
Iroquois	1	0.01
Kiowa (5)	5	0.04
Latin American Indians (10)	14	0.10
Navajo (2)	6	0.04
Paiute	1	0.01
Potawatomi (1)	1	0.01
Pueblo (5)	6	0.04
Seminole (2)	2	0.01
Shoshone (1)	8	0.06
Sioux (9)	22	0.16
Yakama (1)	4	0.03
Yuman	2	0.01
All other tribes (109)	135	0.97
American Indian tribes, not spec.	12	0.09
Arab:	8	0.06
Egyptian	8	0.06
Asian:	343	2.46
Cambodian (6)	9	0.06
Chinese, ex. Taiwanese (27)	38	0.27
Filipino (54)	84	0.60
Hmong (42)	42	0.30
Indian (6)	13	0.09
Indonesian (7)	7	0.05
Japanese (18)	33	0.24
Korean (24)	26	0.19
Laotian (24)	29	0.21
Pakistani (1)	2	0.01
Thai (13)	16	0.11
Vietnamese (28)	32	0.23
Other Asian, specified	1	0.01
Other Asian, not specified (7)	11	0.08
Austrian	28	0.20
British	87	0.62
Canadian	54	0.39
Czech	96	0.68
Czechoslovakian	15	0.11
Danish	82	0.58
Dutch	332	2.37
English	1,358	9.69
Estonian	11	0.08
European	135	0.96
Finnish	20	0.14
French, except Basque	627	4.47
French Canadian	141	1.01
German	2,639	18.82
German Russian	8	0.06
Hawaii Native/Pacific Islander:	171	1.23
Melanesian: (1)	1	0.01
Other Melanesian (1)	1	0.01
Micronesian: (93)	106	0.76
Guamanian/Chamorro (5)	9	0.06
Other Micronesian (88)	97	0.70
Polynesian: (28)	41	0.29
Native Hawaiian (12)	25	0.18
Samoan (15)	15	0.11
Other Polynesian (1)	1	0.01
Other Pac. Isl., not spec. (11)	23	0.17
Hispanic or Latino:	2,513	18.05
Central American:	35	0.25
Guatemalan	17	0.12
Honduran	5	0.04
Nicaraguan	3	0.02
Panamanian	2	0.01
Salvadoran	6	0.04
Other Central American	2	0.01
Cuban	5	0.04
Mexican	2,105	15.12
Puerto Rican	28	0.20
South American:	6	0.04
Colombian	6	0.04
Other Hispanic or Latino	334	2.40
Hungarian	15	0.11
Irish	1,400	9.99
Italian	313	2.23
Lithuanian	9	0.06
Norwegian	613	4.37
Polish	137	0.98
Portuguese	32	0.23
Romanian	14	0.10
Russian	189	1.35
Scandinavian	55	0.39
Scotch-Irish	115	0.82
Scottish	230	1.64
Swedish	317	2.26
Swiss	63	0.45
Ukrainian	47	0.34
United States or American	997	7.11
Welsh	103	0.73
West Indian, excl. Hispanic:	24	0.17
Dutch West Indian	24	0.17
White:	11,432	82.11
Not Hispanic (10,293)	10,603	76.16
Hispanic (675)	829	5.95
Yugoslavian	36	0.26

Gladstone

Place Type: City
County: Clackamas
Population: 11,438

Ancestry/Race	Number	%
African American/Black:	145	1.27
Not Hispanic (70)	123	1.08
Hispanic (12)	22	0.19
African, sub-Saharan:	24	0.21
African	24	0.21
Alaska Native tribes, specified:	3	0.03
Tlingit-Haida (1)	3	0.03
Am. Ind. or Alaska Nat., not spec.	39	0.34
American Indian tribes, specified:	114	1.00
Apache (2)	2	0.02
Blackfeet	1	0.01
Cherokee (2)	24	0.21
Cheyenne	1	0.01
Chippewa (2)	8	0.07
Choctaw (1)	4	0.03
Kiowa (1)	1	0.01
Navajo (3)	6	0.05
Osage	3	0.03
Paiute	1	0.01
Potawatomi (3)	3	0.03
Sioux (7)	19	0.17
Yakama (1)	1	0.01
All other tribes (27)	40	0.35
American Indian tribes, not spec.	5	0.04
Arab:	10	0.09
Syrian	10	0.09
Asian:	336	2.94
Cambodian (26)	30	0.26
Chinese, ex. Taiwanese (34)	52	0.45
Filipino (36)	59	0.52
Indian (42)	45	0.39
Indonesian (4)	4	0.03
Japanese (26)	51	0.45
Korean (26)	33	0.29
Laotian (15)	15	0.13
Malaysian (1)	3	0.03
Pakistani	1	0.01
Taiwanese	1	0.01
Thai (1)	1	0.01
Vietnamese (19)	21	0.18
Other Asian, specified	1	0.01
Other Asian, not specified (6)	19	0.17
Australian	8	0.07
Austrian	30	0.26
Belgian	37	0.33
British	107	0.94
Canadian	28	0.25
Croatian	16	0.14
Czech	42	0.37
Czechoslovakian	30	0.26
Danish	134	1.18
Dutch	247	2.18
English	1,439	12.70
European	145	1.28
Finnish	48	0.42
French, except Basque	432	3.81
French Canadian	94	0.83
German	2,877	25.39
Greek	34	0.30
Hawaii Native/Pacific Islander:	62	0.54
Micronesian: (12)	24	0.21
Guamanian/Chamorro (3)	12	0.10
Other Micronesian (9)	12	0.10
Polynesian: (13)	27	0.24
Native Hawaiian (7)	17	0.15
Samoan (4)	8	0.07
Tongan (1)	1	0.01
Other Polynesian (1)	1	0.01
Other Pac. Isl., not spec. (8)	11	0.10
Hispanic or Latino:	700	6.12
Central American:	28	0.24
Guatemalan	15	0.13
Honduran	6	0.05
Nicaraguan	1	0.01
Panamanian	1	0.01
Salvadoran	3	0.03
Other Central American	2	0.02
Cuban	4	0.03
Mexican	536	4.69
Puerto Rican	17	0.15
South American:	8	0.07
Chilean	2	0.02
Colombian	1	0.01
Ecuadorian	1	0.01
Peruvian	3	0.03
Other South American	1	0.01
Other Hispanic or Latino	107	0.94
Hungarian	71	0.63
Icelander	9	0.08
Irish	1,270	11.21
Italian	424	3.74
Lithuanian	8	0.07
Northern European	16	0.14
Norwegian	700	6.18
Pennsylvania German	19	0.17
Polish	300	2.65
Portuguese	14	0.12

Notes: 1. Figures in the "Number" column do not add up to the total population due to: a) Ancestry/Race overlap — e.g. persons can report being both White and Irish, b) persons of Hispanic origin can report being any race, c) persons reporting two ancestries are counted in both categories. 2. Numbers in parentheses indicate the number of persons reporting this ancestry/race alone, not in combination with any other ancestry/race. 3. Refer to the Explanation of Data in the front of the book for more detailed information.

Romanian	8	0.07
Russian	224	1.98
Scandinavian	43	0.38
Scotch-Irish	364	3.21
Scottish	405	3.57
Slavic	5	0.04
Swedish	378	3.34
Swiss	134	1.18
Ukrainian	27	0.24
United States or American	643	5.67
Welsh	114	1.01
White:	10,642	93.04
Not Hispanic (10,086)	10,315	90.18
Hispanic (256)	327	2.86
Yugoslavian	16	0.14

Grants Pass

Place Type: City
County: Josephine
Population: 23,003

Ancestry/Race	Number	%
Acadian/Cajun	6	0.03
African American/Black:	141	0.61
Not Hispanic (70)	122	0.53
Hispanic (6)	19	0.08
Alaska Native tribes, specified:	6	0.03
Aleut	1	0.00
Eskimo (1)	1	0.00
Tlingit-Haida (1)	2	0.01
All other tribes (2)	2	0.01
Am. Ind. or Alaska Nat., not spec.	170	0.74
American Indian tribes, specified:	391	1.70
Apache (10)	19	0.08
Blackfeet (4)	14	0.06
Cherokee (32)	112	0.49
Cheyenne	1	0.00
Chickasaw (4)	9	0.04
Chippewa (5)	10	0.04
Choctaw (10)	25	0.11
Comanche	1	0.00
Cree (1)	2	0.01
Creek (5)	8	0.03
Crow	4	0.02
Iroquois (1)	6	0.03
Latin American Indians (2)	4	0.02
Lumbee (1)	1	0.00
Menominee (1)	1	0.00
Navajo (4)	11	0.05
Osage (7)	7	0.03
Ottawa	1	0.00
Paiute (4)	5	0.02
Potawatomi	1	0.00
Pueblo (3)	4	0.02
Puget Sound Salish (1)	4	0.02
Seminole	2	0.01
Shoshone (4)	5	0.02
Sioux (5)	26	0.11
Yaqui (1)	6	0.03
All other tribes (62)	102	0.44
American Indian tribes, not spec.	34	0.15
Arab:	89	0.39
Arab/Arabic	9	0.04
Lebanese	80	0.35
Armenian	8	0.03
Asian:	365	1.59
Cambodian (1)	1	0.00
Chinese, ex. Taiwanese (50)	69	0.30
Filipino (33)	70	0.30
Indian (28)	37	0.16
Indonesian (2)	15	0.07
Japanese (30)	61	0.27
Korean (20)	36	0.16
Laotian (3)	5	0.02
Pakistani	1	0.00
Sri Lankan (1)	1	0.00
Taiwanese (5)	5	0.02
Thai (21)	22	0.10
Vietnamese (24)	31	0.13
Other Asian, specified	4	0.02
Other Asian, not specified (2)	7	0.03
Australian	16	0.07
Austrian	29	0.13
Basque	49	0.21
British	156	0.68
Bulgarian	11	0.05
Canadian	106	0.46
Celtic	17	0.07
Czech	70	0.31
Czechoslovakian	30	0.13
Danish	264	1.15
Dutch	543	2.37
English	3,395	14.85
European	154	0.67
Finnish	58	0.25
French, except Basque	1,091	4.77
French Canadian	258	1.13
German	4,680	20.47
Greek	66	0.29
Hawaii Native/Pacific Islander:	68	0.30
Melanesian: (15)	15	0.07
Fijian (15)	15	0.07
Micronesian: (2)	8	0.03
Guamanian/Chamorro (2)	8	0.03
Polynesian: (10)	36	0.16
Native Hawaiian (7)	27	0.12
Samoan (2)	7	0.03
Other Polynesian (1)	2	0.01
Other Pac. Isl., not spec.	9	0.04
Hispanic or Latino:	1,236	5.37
Central American:	25	0.11
Costa Rican	5	0.02
Guatemalan	1	0.00
Honduran	8	0.03
Nicaraguan	1	0.00
Panamanian	3	0.01
Salvadoran	6	0.03
Other Central American	1	0.00
Cuban	5	0.02
Dominican Republic	1	0.00
Mexican	923	4.01
Puerto Rican	48	0.21
South American:	21	0.09
Argentinean	1	0.00
Chilean	2	0.01
Colombian	8	0.03
Ecuadorian	4	0.02
Peruvian	5	0.02
Other South American	1	0.00
Other Hispanic or Latino	213	0.93
Hungarian	117	0.51
Irish	3,495	15.29
Israeli	11	0.05
Italian	1,033	4.52
Lithuanian	33	0.14
Maltese	11	0.05
Northern European	31	0.14
Norwegian	637	2.79
Pennsylvania German	14	0.06
Polish	189	0.83
Portuguese	220	0.96
Russian	158	0.69
Scandinavian	102	0.45
Scotch-Irish	505	2.21
Scottish	430	1.88
Serbian	5	0.02
Slavic	29	0.13
Slovak	68	0.30
Slovene	18	0.08
Swedish	574	2.51
Swiss	121	0.53
Ukrainian	9	0.04
United States or American	1,296	5.67
Welsh	178	0.78
White:	22,004	95.66
Not Hispanic (20,737)	21,188	92.11
Hispanic (649)	816	3.55
Yugoslavian	26	0.11

Gresham

Place Type: City
County: Multnomah
Population: 90,205

Ancestry/Race	Number	%
Acadian/Cajun	19	0.02
Afghan	22	0.02
African American/Black:	2,346	2.60
Not Hispanic (1,618)	2,167	2.40
Hispanic (89)	179	0.20
African, sub-Saharan:	297	0.33
African	197	0.22
Ethiopian	23	0.03
Ghanian	20	0.02
South African	17	0.02
Other sub-Saharan African	40	0.04
Alaska Native tribes, specified:	70	0.08
Alaska Athabascan (12)	17	0.02
Aleut (2)	6	0.01
Eskimo (14)	19	0.02
Tlingit-Haida (12)	20	0.02
All other tribes (6)	8	0.01
Alaska Native tribes, not specified	4	0.00
Am. Ind. or Alaska Nat., not spec.	509	0.56
Alsatian	8	0.01
American Indian tribes, specified:	1,234	1.37
Apache (12)	45	0.05
Blackfeet (14)	38	0.04
Cherokee (64)	258	0.29
Cheyenne (3)	13	0.01
Chickasaw (5)	7	0.01
Chippewa (61)	125	0.14
Choctaw (14)	51	0.06
Colville (7)	8	0.01
Comanche (1)	7	0.01
Cree (3)	6	0.01
Creek (5)	13	0.01
Crow	1	0.00
Delaware (6)	10	0.01
Iroquois (18)	28	0.03
Kiowa (2)	7	0.01
Latin American Indians (56)	102	0.11
Lumbee (1)	1	0.00
Menominee (1)	1	0.00
Navajo (27)	49	0.05
Osage	11	0.01
Ottawa (4)	5	0.01
Paiute	1	0.00
Potawatomi (2)	5	0.01
Pueblo (2)	9	0.01
Puget Sound Salish (3)	5	0.01
Seminole (2)	7	0.01
Shoshone (2)	5	0.01
Sioux (39)	85	0.09
Tohono O'Odham	8	0.01
Ute	5	0.01
Yakama (8)	10	0.01
Yaqui (1)	2	0.00
All other tribes (181)	306	0.34
American Indian tribes, not spec.	49	0.05
Arab:	462	0.51
Arab/Arabic	47	0.05
Egyptian	100	0.11
Lebanese	123	0.14
Moroccan	22	0.02
Syrian	170	0.19
Armenian	72	0.08
Asian:	4,109	4.56
Bangladeshi (1)	1	0.00
Cambodian (75)	87	0.10
Chinese, ex. Taiwanese (447)	653	0.72
Filipino (485)	764	0.85
Hmong (235)	249	0.28
Indian (198)	275	0.30
Indonesian (40)	82	0.09
Japanese (422)	667	0.74
Korean (328)	396	0.44
Laotian (242)	312	0.35

Notes: 1. Figures in the "Number" column do not add up to the total population due to: a) Ancestry/Race overlap — e.g. persons can report being both White and Irish, b) persons of Hispanic origin can report being any race, c) persons reporting two ancestries are counted in both categories. 2. Numbers in parentheses indicate the number of persons reporting this ancestry/race alone, not in combination with any other ancestry/race. 3. Refer to the Explanation of Data in the front of the book for more detailed information.

Ancestry/Race	Number	%
Malaysian (2)	4	0.00
Pakistani (11)	20	0.02
Sri Lankan (4)	7	0.01
Taiwanese (3)	5	0.01
Thai (34)	50	0.06
Vietnamese (331)	383	0.42
Other Asian, specified (5)	32	0.04
Other Asian, not specified (45)	122	0.14
Assyrian/Chaldean/Syriac	5	0.01
Australian	92	0.10
Austrian	147	0.16
Basque	20	0.02
Belgian	78	0.09
Brazilian	18	0.02
British	434	0.48
Bulgarian	6	0.01
Canadian	332	0.37
Celtic	19	0.02
Croatian	158	0.18
Czech	331	0.37
Czechoslovakian	162	0.18
Danish	939	1.04
Dutch	1,796	1.99
Eastern European	42	0.05
English	10,341	11.47
Estonian	6	0.01
European	1,038	1.15
Finnish	610	0.68
French, except Basque	3,567	3.96
French Canadian	1,126	1.25
German	18,281	20.28
German Russian	17	0.02
Greek	205	0.23
Hawaii Native/Pacific Islander:	553	0.61
Melanesian: (7)	7	0.01
Fijian (7)	7	0.01
Micronesian: (84)	129	0.14
Guamanian/Chamorro (44)	80	0.09
Other Micronesian (40)	49	0.05
Polynesian: (122)	301	0.33
Native Hawaiian (77)	226	0.25
Samoan (36)	62	0.07
Tongan (7)	7	0.01
Other Polynesian (2)	6	0.01
Other Pac. Isl., specified	9	0.01
Other Pac. Isl., not spec. (21)	107	0.12
Hispanic or Latino:	10,732	11.90
Central American:	324	0.36
Costa Rican	12	0.01
Guatemalan	128	0.14
Honduran	27	0.03
Nicaraguan	3	0.00
Panamanian	29	0.03
Salvadoran	104	0.12
Other Central American	21	0.02
Cuban	139	0.15
Dominican Republic	1	0.00
Mexican	8,666	9.61
Puerto Rican	148	0.16
South American:	146	0.16
Argentinean	26	0.03
Bolivian	1	0.00
Chilean	17	0.02
Colombian	30	0.03
Ecuadorian	10	0.01
Peruvian	38	0.04
Uruguayan	9	0.01
Venezuelan	8	0.01
Other South American	7	0.01
Other Hispanic or Latino	1,308	1.45
Hungarian	373	0.41
Icelander	27	0.03
Iranian	54	0.06
Irish	9,753	10.82
Israeli	6	0.01
Italian	3,644	4.04
Latvian	9	0.01
Lithuanian	150	0.17
Luxemburger	15	0.02
Northern European	132	0.15
Norwegian	4,277	4.74
Pennsylvania German	64	0.07
Polish	1,208	1.34
Portuguese	231	0.26
Romanian	1,018	1.13
Russian	1,188	1.32
Scandinavian	707	0.78
Scotch-Irish	1,651	1.83
Scottish	2,021	2.24
Serbian	28	0.03
Slavic	65	0.07
Slovak	19	0.02
Slovene	17	0.02
Swedish	3,212	3.56
Swiss	586	0.65
Turkish	8	0.01
Ukrainian	728	0.81
United States or American	5,119	5.68
Welsh	986	1.09
West Indian, excl. Hispanic:	55	0.06
Barbadian	21	0.02
British West Indian	7	0.01
Haitian	9	0.01
Jamaican	4	0.00
West Indian	14	0.02
White:	77,652	86.08
Not Hispanic (71,194)	73,562	81.55
Hispanic (3,425)	4,090	4.53
Yugoslavian	201	0.22

Hayesville

Place Type: Census Designated Place
County: Marion
Population: 18,222

Ancestry/Race	Number	%
African American/Black:	273	1.50
Not Hispanic (158)	230	1.26
Hispanic (15)	43	0.24
African, sub-Saharan:	6	0.03
Ethiopian	6	0.03
Alaska Native tribes, specified:	15	0.08
Alaska Athabascan (3)	3	0.02
Aleut (4)	5	0.03
Eskimo (3)	6	0.03
Tlingit-Haida (1)	1	0.01
Alaska Native tribes, not specified	4	0.02
Am. Ind. or Alaska Nat., not spec.	116	0.64
American Indian tribes, specified:	361	1.98
Apache (4)	4	0.02
Blackfeet (11)	23	0.13
Cherokee (20)	72	0.40
Cheyenne	2	0.01
Chickasaw (1)	1	0.01
Chippewa (4)	6	0.03
Choctaw	6	0.03
Colville (1)	1	0.01
Cree (1)	1	0.01
Creek (7)	7	0.04
Crow (1)	1	0.01
Delaware (1)	2	0.01
Iroquois (2)	5	0.03
Latin American Indians (23)	31	0.17
Navajo (10)	16	0.09
Paiute (4)	4	0.02
Pima (3)	3	0.02
Potawatomi (1)	2	0.01
Pueblo (2)	2	0.01
Sioux (20)	27	0.15
Tohono O'Odham (1)	1	0.01
Yakama (5)	5	0.03
All other tribes (97)	139	0.76
American Indian tribes, not spec.	33	0.18
Arab:	70	0.39
Arab/Arabic	52	0.29
Moroccan	7	0.04
Syrian	11	0.06
Armenian	20	0.11
Asian:	798	4.38
Cambodian (58)	80	0.44
Chinese, ex. Taiwanese (69)	89	0.49
Filipino (63)	126	0.69
Hmong (12)	12	0.07
Indian (39)	43	0.24
Indonesian (6)	9	0.05
Japanese (67)	80	0.44
Korean (55)	62	0.34
Laotian (18)	30	0.16
Pakistani	1	0.01
Taiwanese (2)	2	0.01
Thai (3)	14	0.08
Vietnamese (202)	220	1.21
Other Asian, specified	1	0.01
Other Asian, not specified (17)	29	0.16
Austrian	66	0.37
Basque	8	0.04
British	94	0.52
Canadian	45	0.25
Czech	70	0.39
Czechoslovakian	13	0.07
Danish	201	1.12
Dutch	544	3.02
Eastern European	21	0.12
English	1,825	10.14
European	378	2.10
Finnish	61	0.34
French, except Basque	586	3.26
French Canadian	254	1.41
German	3,264	18.13
Greek	73	0.41
Hawaii Native/Pacific Islander:	201	1.10
Micronesian: (83)	97	0.53
Guamanian/Chamorro (22)	27	0.15
Other Micronesian (61)	70	0.38
Polynesian: (29)	65	0.36
Native Hawaiian (23)	49	0.27
Samoan (6)	16	0.09
Other Pac. Isl., not spec. (16)	39	0.21
Hispanic or Latino:	3,601	19.76
Central American:	72	0.40
Guatemalan	30	0.16
Honduran	1	0.01
Nicaraguan	4	0.02
Salvadoran	30	0.16
Other Central American	7	0.04
Cuban	15	0.08
Dominican Republic	1	0.01
Mexican	2,895	15.89
Puerto Rican	15	0.08
South American:	24	0.13
Argentinean	5	0.03
Bolivian	4	0.02
Chilean	4	0.02
Colombian	1	0.01
Ecuadorian	2	0.01
Peruvian	6	0.03
Other South American	2	0.01
Other Hispanic or Latino	579	3.18
Hungarian	26	0.14
Iranian	50	0.28
Irish	1,658	9.21
Italian	421	2.34
Lithuanian	7	0.04
Northern European	13	0.07
Norwegian	532	2.96
Pennsylvania German	18	0.10
Polish	143	0.79
Portuguese	21	0.12
Romanian	11	0.06
Russian	108	0.60
Scandinavian	114	0.63
Scotch-Irish	236	1.31
Scottish	325	1.81
Swedish	434	2.41
Swiss	123	0.68
Turkish	37	0.21
Ukrainian	96	0.53
United States or American	1,237	6.87
Welsh	185	1.03

Notes: 1. Figures in the "Number" column do not add up to the total population due to: a) Ancestry/Race overlap — e.g. persons can report being both White and Irish, b) persons of Hispanic origin can report being any race, c) persons reporting two ancestries are counted in both categories. 2. Numbers in parentheses indicate the number of persons reporting this ancestry/race alone, not in combination with any other ancestry/race. 3. Refer to the Explanation of Data in the front of the book for more detailed information.

West Indian, excl. Hispanic:	10	0.06
Dutch West Indian	10	0.06
White:	14,590	80.07
Not Hispanic (12,991)	13,361	73.32
Hispanic (1,006)	1,229	6.74
Yugoslavian	32	0.18

Hermiston

Place Type: City
County: Umatilla
Population: 13,154

Ancestry/Race	Number	%
African American/Black:	192	1.46
Not Hispanic (102)	168	1.28
Hispanic (20)	24	0.18
African, sub-Saharan:	14	0.10
African	14	0.10
Alaska Native tribes, specified:	2	0.02
Alaska Athabascan (1)	1	0.01
Tlingit-Haida (1)	1	0.01
Am. Ind. or Alaska Nat., not spec.	69	0.52
American Indian tribes, specified:	144	1.09
Apache	1	0.01
Blackfeet (1)	8	0.06
Cherokee (14)	38	0.29
Chippewa (7)	8	0.06
Choctaw (2)	2	0.02
Comanche (1)	2	0.02
Cree	1	0.01
Crow (2)	2	0.02
Iroquois	1	0.01
Kiowa (1)	1	0.01
Latin American Indians (2)	4	0.03
Navajo (2)	7	0.05
Puget Sound Salish (3)	3	0.02
Shoshone	1	0.01
Sioux (11)	23	0.17
Yakama	1	0.01
Yaqui (1)	1	0.01
All other tribes (25)	40	0.30
American Indian tribes, not spec.	8	0.06
Arab:	4	0.03
Arab/Arabic	4	0.03
Asian:	270	2.05
Cambodian (15)	15	0.11
Chinese, ex. Taiwanese (43)	57	0.43
Filipino (31)	38	0.29
Indian (5)	9	0.07
Indonesian (3)	11	0.08
Japanese (21)	35	0.27
Korean (21)	26	0.20
Laotian (22)	28	0.21
Taiwanese (1)	1	0.01
Thai (8)	8	0.06
Vietnamese (33)	34	0.26
Other Asian, not specified (4)	8	0.06
Austrian	36	0.27
British	55	0.41
Bulgarian	8	0.06
Celtic	13	0.10
Czech	29	0.22
Danish	334	2.49
Dutch	323	2.41
English	1,436	10.70
European	128	0.95
French, except Basque	429	3.20
French Canadian	77	0.57
German	1,856	13.83
Greek	4	0.03
Hawaii Native/Pacific Islander:	18	0.14
Micronesian: (1)	3	0.02
Guamanian/Chamorro (1)	3	0.02
Polynesian: (4)	13	0.10
Native Hawaiian (3)	11	0.08
Samoan (1)	2	0.02
Other Pac. Isl., not spec.	2	0.02
Hispanic or Latino:	3,168	24.08
Central American:	40	0.30
Guatemalan	8	0.06
Honduran	9	0.07
Panamanian	4	0.03
Salvadoran	19	0.14
Cuban	1	0.01
Mexican	2,720	20.68
Puerto Rican	19	0.14
South American:	2	0.02
Colombian	1	0.01
Peruvian	1	0.01
Other Hispanic or Latino	386	2.93
Hungarian	31	0.23
Icelander	14	0.10
Irish	1,085	8.09
Italian	217	1.62
Lithuanian	8	0.06
Northern European	6	0.04
Norwegian	241	1.80
Pennsylvania German	13	0.10
Polish	145	1.08
Portuguese	11	0.08
Russian	47	0.35
Scandinavian	46	0.34
Scotch-Irish	208	1.55
Scottish	320	2.39
Slovak	13	0.10
Swedish	188	1.40
Swiss	61	0.45
United States or American	996	7.42
Welsh	119	0.89
White:	10,683	81.21
Not Hispanic (9,365)	9,560	72.68
Hispanic (1,017)	1,123	8.54
Yugoslavian	16	0.12

Hillsboro

Place Type: City
County: Washington
Population: 70,186

Ancestry/Race	Number	%
Acadian/Cajun	9	0.01
Afghan	8	0.01
African American/Black:	1,202	1.71
Not Hispanic (745)	1,034	1.47
Hispanic (113)	168	0.24
African, sub-Saharan:	160	0.23
African	52	0.07
Ghanian	10	0.01
Somalian	32	0.05
South African	53	0.08
Other sub-Saharan African	13	0.02
Alaska Native tribes, specified:	50	0.07
Alaska Athabascan (9)	9	0.01
Aleut (1)	6	0.01
Eskimo (11)	17	0.02
Tlingit-Haida (6)	16	0.02
All other tribes (1)	2	0.00
Alaska Native tribes, not specified	4	0.01
Am. Ind. or Alaska Nat., not spec.	312	0.44
Alsatian	8	0.01
American Indian tribes, specified:	731	1.04
Apache (6)	24	0.03
Blackfeet (7)	27	0.04
Cherokee (73)	194	0.28
Cheyenne (2)	2	0.00
Chickasaw (2)	2	0.00
Chippewa (12)	33	0.05
Choctaw (16)	35	0.05
Colville (2)	2	0.00
Comanche (4)	5	0.01
Cree (5)	18	0.03
Creek (7)	11	0.02
Crow (1)	2	0.00
Delaware (2)	3	0.00
Iroquois (2)	12	0.02
Kiowa	4	0.01
Latin American Indians (42)	70	0.10
Lumbee	2	0.00
Navajo (10)	25	0.04
Osage (1)	7	0.01
Ottawa (4)	4	0.01
Paiute (4)	5	0.01
Potawatomi (5)	12	0.02
Pueblo (11)	18	0.03
Puget Sound Salish	1	0.00
Seminole (1)	3	0.00
Shoshone (2)	4	0.01
Sioux (25)	52	0.07
Tohono O'Odham (1)	1	0.00
Ute (1)	3	0.00
Yakama (1)	3	0.00
Yaqui (3)	3	0.00
All other tribes (80)	144	0.21
American Indian tribes, not spec.	51	0.07
Arab:	266	0.38
Arab/Arabic	44	0.06
Egyptian	34	0.05
Iraqi	9	0.01
Lebanese	100	0.14
Palestinian	39	0.06
Other Arab	40	0.06
Armenian	10	0.01
Asian:	5,514	7.86
Bangladeshi (24)	26	0.04
Cambodian (164)	192	0.27
Chinese, ex. Taiwanese (704)	909	1.30
Filipino (438)	672	0.96
Hmong (56)	56	0.08
Indian (1,244)	1,312	1.87
Indonesian (20)	37	0.05
Japanese (328)	514	0.73
Korean (461)	562	0.80
Laotian (131)	154	0.22
Malaysian (7)	16	0.02
Pakistani (18)	18	0.03
Sri Lankan (8)	8	0.01
Taiwanese (30)	35	0.05
Thai (25)	41	0.06
Vietnamese (754)	808	1.15
Other Asian, specified (7)	27	0.04
Other Asian, not specified (73)	127	0.18
Assyrian/Chaldean/Syriac	6	0.01
Austrian	201	0.29
Basque	34	0.05
Belgian	109	0.16
Brazilian	18	0.03
British	323	0.46
Bulgarian	78	0.11
Canadian	326	0.47
Celtic	79	0.11
Croatian	71	0.10
Cypriot	34	0.05
Czech	221	0.32
Czechoslovakian	79	0.11
Danish	608	0.87
Dutch	1,502	2.15
Eastern European	11	0.02
English	7,260	10.39
European	1,410	2.02
Finnish	376	0.54
French, except Basque	2,001	2.86
French Canadian	593	0.85
German	12,639	18.09
German Russian	17	0.02
Greek	209	0.30
Hawaii Native/Pacific Islander:	412	0.59
Melanesian: (15)	17	0.02
Fijian (15)	17	0.02
Micronesian: (67)	91	0.13
Guamanian/Chamorro (62)	84	0.12
Other Micronesian (5)	7	0.01
Polynesian: (80)	234	0.33
Native Hawaiian (67)	204	0.29
Samoan (6)	12	0.02
Tongan (7)	9	0.01
Other Polynesian	9	0.01
Other Pac. Isl., specified	2	0.00
Other Pac. Isl., not spec. (13)	68	0.10

Notes: 1. Figures in the "Number" column do not add up to the total population due to: a) Ancestry/Race overlap — e.g. persons can report being both White and Irish, b) persons of Hispanic origin can report being any race, c) persons reporting two ancestries are counted in both categories. 2. Numbers in parentheses indicate the number of persons reporting this ancestry/race alone, not in combination with any other ancestry/race. 3. Refer to the Explanation of Data in the front of the book for more detailed information.

Ancestry/Race	Number	%
Hispanic or Latino:	13,262	18.90
Central American:	585	0.83
Costa Rican	32	0.05
Guatemalan	412	0.59
Honduran	24	0.03
Nicaraguan	17	0.02
Panamanian	11	0.02
Salvadoran	86	0.12
Other Central American	3	0.00
Cuban	55	0.08
Dominican Republic	7	0.01
Mexican	10,924	15.56
Puerto Rican	191	0.27
South American:	96	0.14
Argentinean	10	0.01
Bolivian	4	0.01
Chilean	11	0.02
Colombian	23	0.03
Ecuadorian	6	0.01
Peruvian	22	0.03
Venezuelan	18	0.03
Other South American	2	0.00
Other Hispanic or Latino	1,404	2.00
Hungarian	259	0.37
Icelander	18	0.03
Iranian	18	0.03
Irish	6,901	9.88
Israeli	20	0.03
Italian	2,360	3.38
Latvian	41	0.06
Lithuanian	31	0.04
Luxemburger	6	0.01
New Zealander	18	0.03
Northern European	337	0.48
Norwegian	2,904	4.16
Pennsylvania German	33	0.05
Polish	1,026	1.47
Portuguese	204	0.29
Romanian	98	0.14
Russian	328	0.47
Scandinavian	410	0.59
Scotch-Irish	1,041	1.49
Scottish	2,153	3.08
Serbian	17	0.02
Slavic	36	0.05
Slovak	19	0.03
Swedish	1,966	2.81
Swiss	576	0.82
Turkish	70	0.10
Ukrainian	91	0.13
United States or American	3,690	5.28
Welsh	767	1.10
West Indian, excl. Hispanic:	9	0.01
Dutch West Indian	9	0.01
White:	56,417	80.38
Not Hispanic (49,339)	50,701	72.24
Hispanic (5,052)	5,716	8.14
Yugoslavian	157	0.22

Keizer

Place Type: City
County: Marion
Population: 32,203

Ancestry/Race	Number	%
African American/Black:	397	1.23
Not Hispanic (216)	328	1.02
Hispanic (26)	69	0.21
Alaska Native tribes, specified:	39	0.12
Alaska Athabascan (1)	3	0.01
Aleut (6)	6	0.02
Eskimo (6)	9	0.03
Tlingit-Haida (9)	18	0.06
All other tribes (3)	3	0.01
Alaska Native tribes, not specified	3	0.01
Am. Ind. or Alaska Nat., not spec.	152	0.47
American Indian tribes, specified:	601	1.87
Apache (4)	8	0.02
Blackfeet (19)	30	0.09
Cherokee (29)	113	0.35
Cheyenne (3)	3	0.01
Chickasaw (1)	4	0.01
Chippewa (15)	24	0.07
Choctaw (22)	42	0.13
Comanche (2)	3	0.01
Cree	1	0.00
Creek (7)	11	0.03
Crow	2	0.01
Iroquois (2)	7	0.02
Latin American Indians (12)	30	0.09
Navajo (4)	9	0.03
Osage (9)	9	0.03
Ottawa	4	0.01
Paiute (4)	4	0.01
Pueblo (1)	2	0.01
Puget Sound Salish (5)	8	0.02
Seminole	1	0.00
Shoshone (2)	3	0.01
Sioux (31)	45	0.14
Yakama (2)	4	0.01
Yaqui	1	0.00
All other tribes (162)	233	0.72
American Indian tribes, not spec.	22	0.07
Arab:	57	0.18
Lebanese	13	0.04
Syrian	32	0.10
Other Arab	12	0.04
Armenian	7	0.02
Asian:	721	2.24
Bangladeshi	1	0.00
Cambodian (27)	33	0.10
Chinese, ex. Taiwanese (93)	111	0.34
Filipino (103)	205	0.64
Hmong (9)	10	0.03
Indian (15)	22	0.07
Indonesian	1	0.00
Japanese (84)	145	0.45
Korean (82)	94	0.29
Laotian (3)	4	0.01
Pakistani	3	0.01
Thai (10)	15	0.05
Vietnamese (36)	48	0.15
Other Asian, specified	2	0.01
Other Asian, not specified (8)	27	0.08
Australian	8	0.02
Austrian	46	0.14
Basque	18	0.06
Belgian	7	0.02
British	243	0.75
Canadian	46	0.14
Carpatho Rusyn	10	0.03
Celtic	7	0.02
Czech	182	0.56
Czechoslovakian	9	0.03
Danish	419	1.29
Dutch	812	2.50
English	4,073	12.53
Estonian	9	0.03
European	388	1.19
Finnish	254	0.78
French, except Basque	1,342	4.13
French Canadian	265	0.82
German	8,100	24.93
German Russian	8	0.02
Greek	89	0.27
Hawaii Native/Pacific Islander:	147	0.46
Melanesian:	1	0.00
Fijian	1	0.00
Micronesian: (17)	32	0.10
Guamanian/Chamorro (2)	8	0.02
Other Micronesian (15)	24	0.07
Polynesian: (40)	86	0.27
Native Hawaiian (24)	60	0.19
Samoan (12)	19	0.06
Other Polynesian (4)	7	0.02
Other Pac. Isl., specified	2	0.01
Other Pac. Isl., not spec. (7)	26	0.08
Hispanic or Latino:	3,950	12.27
Central American:	89	0.28
Costa Rican	3	0.01
Guatemalan	27	0.08
Honduran	2	0.01
Panamanian	9	0.03
Salvadoran	41	0.13
Other Central American	7	0.02
Cuban	18	0.06
Dominican Republic	2	0.01
Mexican	3,230	10.03
Puerto Rican	48	0.15
South American:	30	0.09
Argentinean	2	0.01
Chilean	5	0.02
Colombian	6	0.02
Ecuadorian	1	0.00
Paraguayan	2	0.01
Peruvian	11	0.03
Uruguayan	1	0.00
Other South American	2	0.01
Other Hispanic or Latino	533	1.66
Hungarian	61	0.19
Irish	3,720	11.45
Italian	828	2.55
Latvian	10	0.03
Lithuanian	8	0.02
Northern European	88	0.27
Norwegian	1,893	5.83
Pennsylvania German	8	0.02
Polish	371	1.14
Portuguese	174	0.54
Romanian	20	0.06
Russian	506	1.56
Scandinavian	162	0.50
Scotch-Irish	609	1.87
Scottish	892	2.75
Slavic	13	0.04
Slovak	7	0.02
Slovene	9	0.03
Swedish	871	2.68
Swiss	246	0.76
Turkish	31	0.10
Ukrainian	184	0.57
United States or American	2,540	7.82
Welsh	460	1.42
White:	28,531	88.60
Not Hispanic (26,324)	27,026	83.92
Hispanic (1,215)	1,505	4.67
Yugoslavian	7	0.02

Klamath Falls

Place Type: City
County: Klamath
Population: 19,462

Ancestry/Race	Number	%
African American/Black:	300	1.54
Not Hispanic (188)	273	1.40
Hispanic (10)	27	0.14
African, sub-Saharan:	23	0.12
African	14	0.07
Kenyan	9	0.05
Alaska Native tribes, specified:	11	0.06
Aleut (3)	4	0.02
Eskimo (3)	3	0.02
Tlingit-Haida (2)	4	0.02
Am. Ind. or Alaska Nat., not spec.	274	1.41
American Indian tribes, specified:	946	4.86
Apache (3)	8	0.04
Blackfeet (10)	19	0.10
Cherokee (35)	133	0.68
Cheyenne (3)	4	0.02
Chickasaw (1)	2	0.01
Chippewa (6)	11	0.06
Choctaw (10)	22	0.11
Colville (3)	3	0.02
Comanche (1)	2	0.01
Creek (1)	3	0.02
Iroquois (2)	9	0.05
Latin American Indians (7)	14	0.07

Notes: 1. Figures in the "Number" column do not add up to the total population due to: a) Ancestry/Race overlap — e.g. persons can report being both White and Irish, b) persons of Hispanic origin can report being any race, c) persons reporting two ancestries are counted in both categories. 2. Numbers in parentheses indicate the number of persons reporting this ancestry/race alone, not in combination with any other ancestry/race. 3. Refer to the Explanation of Data in the front of the book for more detailed information.

Ancestry/Race	Number	%
Navajo (3)	4	0.02
Osage (3)	8	0.04
Paiute (15)	35	0.18
Potawatomi (4)	4	0.02
Pueblo (4)	4	0.02
Puget Sound Salish (16)	18	0.09
Seminole	4	0.02
Shoshone (1)	3	0.02
Sioux (10)	25	0.13
Yaqui (1)	1	0.01
All other tribes (498)	610	3.13
American Indian tribes, not spec.	53	0.27
Arab:	19	0.10
Egyptian	9	0.05
Other Arab	10	0.05
Armenian	38	0.20
Asian:	378	1.94
Bangladeshi (5)	5	0.03
Chinese, ex. Taiwanese (54)	65	0.33
Filipino (59)	93	0.48
Indian (35)	38	0.20
Indonesian (2)	3	0.02
Japanese (23)	59	0.30
Korean (18)	22	0.11
Laotian (23)	31	0.16
Malaysian (2)	2	0.01
Taiwanese (4)	5	0.03
Thai (3)	3	0.02
Vietnamese (18)	23	0.12
Other Asian, specified (2)	4	0.02
Other Asian, not specified (6)	25	0.13
Austrian	31	0.16
Basque	8	0.04
Belgian	47	0.24
British	120	0.62
Canadian	90	0.47
Celtic	11	0.06
Croatian	28	0.14
Czech	83	0.43
Czechoslovakian	35	0.18
Danish	123	0.64
Dutch	448	2.32
English	2,104	10.88
Estonian	8	0.04
European	275	1.42
Finnish	72	0.37
French, except Basque	717	3.71
French Canadian	222	1.15
German	3,760	19.45
Greek	5	0.03
Hawaii Native/Pacific Islander:	56	0.29
Melanesian: (2)	2	0.01
Fijian (2)	2	0.01
Micronesian: (1)	2	0.01
Other Micronesian (1)	2	0.01
Polynesian: (15)	36	0.18
Native Hawaiian (11)	24	0.12
Samoan (3)	11	0.06
Tongan (1)	1	0.01
Other Pac. Isl., specified	1	0.01
Other Pac. Isl., not spec. (7)	15	0.08
Hispanic or Latino:	1,814	9.32
Central American:	10	0.05
Costa Rican	2	0.01
Guatemalan	1	0.01
Panamanian	1	0.01
Salvadoran	5	0.03
Other Central American	1	0.01
Cuban	17	0.09
Mexican	1,469	7.55
Puerto Rican	32	0.16
South American:	17	0.09
Argentinean	1	0.01
Bolivian	1	0.01
Colombian	6	0.03
Ecuadorian	3	0.02
Peruvian	5	0.03
Venezuelan	1	0.01
Other Hispanic or Latino	269	1.38
Hungarian	93	0.48
Icelander	19	0.10
Iranian	21	0.11
Irish	2,406	12.44
Israeli	4	0.02
Italian	632	3.27
Latvian	9	0.05
Lithuanian	23	0.12
Luxemburger	6	0.03
Northern European	54	0.28
Norwegian	608	3.14
Polish	222	1.15
Portuguese	91	0.47
Russian	77	0.40
Scandinavian	95	0.49
Scotch-Irish	410	2.12
Scottish	496	2.57
Serbian	8	0.04
Slovak	14	0.07
Swedish	462	2.39
Swiss	107	0.55
Ukrainian	42	0.22
United States or American	1,311	6.78
Welsh	236	1.22
White:	17,253	88.65
Not Hispanic (15,803)	16,356	84.04
Hispanic (763)	897	4.61
Yugoslavian	21	0.11

La Grande

Place Type: City
County: Union
Population: 12,327

Ancestry/Race	Number	%
Acadian/Cajun	7	0.06
African American/Black:	119	0.97
Not Hispanic (77)	110	0.89
Hispanic (7)	9	0.07
Alaska Native tribes, specified:	5	0.04
Aleut (1)	1	0.01
Eskimo (2)	2	0.02
Tlingit-Haida (1)	1	0.01
All other tribes	1	0.01
Am. Ind. or Alaska Nat., not spec.	34	0.28
Albanian	12	0.10
American Indian tribes, specified:	145	1.18
Apache (1)	3	0.02
Blackfeet (3)	3	0.02
Cherokee (15)	42	0.34
Chickasaw (1)	2	0.02
Chippewa (2)	5	0.04
Choctaw (1)	7	0.06
Colville (1)	1	0.01
Creek (2)	2	0.02
Latin American Indians (1)	3	0.02
Osage	2	0.02
Paiute	1	0.01
Potawatomi	2	0.02
Pueblo	2	0.02
Puget Sound Salish (2)	3	0.02
Seminole	1	0.01
Sioux (3)	9	0.07
All other tribes (41)	57	0.46
American Indian tribes, not spec.	4	0.03
Arab:	30	0.24
Arab/Arabic	7	0.06
Lebanese	23	0.19
Asian:	218	1.77
Bangladeshi (1)	1	0.01
Cambodian (3)	3	0.02
Chinese, ex. Taiwanese (43)	55	0.45
Filipino (19)	38	0.31
Indian (7)	8	0.06
Indonesian (1)	3	0.02
Japanese (49)	63	0.51
Korean (21)	33	0.27
Laotian (1)	1	0.01
Vietnamese (1)	5	0.04
Other Asian, specified	1	0.01
Other Asian, not specified (7)	7	0.06
Austrian	25	0.20
Basque	40	0.33
Belgian	6	0.05
Brazilian	5	0.04
British	52	0.42
Canadian	48	0.39
Celtic	4	0.03
Croatian	15	0.12
Czech	48	0.39
Czechoslovakian	34	0.28
Danish	197	1.61
Dutch	363	2.96
English	1,679	13.70
European	223	1.82
Finnish	55	0.45
French, except Basque	521	4.25
French Canadian	101	0.82
German	2,542	20.75
Greek	103	0.84
Hawaii Native/Pacific Islander:	145	1.18
Micronesian: (73)	97	0.79
Guamanian/Chamorro (11)	19	0.15
Other Micronesian (62)	78	0.63
Polynesian: (19)	33	0.27
Native Hawaiian (8)	19	0.15
Samoan (8)	11	0.09
Other Polynesian (3)	3	0.02
Other Pac. Isl., not spec. (13)	15	0.12
Hispanic or Latino:	342	2.77
Central American:	10	0.08
Costa Rican	4	0.03
Guatemalan	3	0.02
Nicaraguan	1	0.01
Salvadoran	2	0.02
Mexican	244	1.98
Puerto Rican	4	0.03
South American:	5	0.04
Colombian	4	0.03
Ecuadorian	1	0.01
Other Hispanic or Latino	79	0.64
Hungarian	5	0.04
Irish	1,532	12.50
Italian	336	2.74
Lithuanian	7	0.06
Northern European	14	0.11
Norwegian	338	2.76
Pennsylvania German	13	0.11
Polish	142	1.16
Portuguese	16	0.13
Russian	69	0.56
Scandinavian	63	0.51
Scotch-Irish	479	3.91
Scottish	353	2.88
Serbian	6	0.05
Slavic	9	0.07
Swedish	361	2.95
Swiss	100	0.82
Ukrainian	31	0.25
United States or American	1,134	9.25
Welsh	160	1.31
White:	11,691	94.84
Not Hispanic (11,312)	11,506	93.34
Hispanic (142)	185	1.50
Yugoslavian	24	0.20

Lake Oswego

Place Type: City
County: Clackamas
Population: 35,278

Ancestry/Race	Number	%
Acadian/Cajun	7	0.02
African American/Black:	335	0.95
Not Hispanic (216)	313	0.89
Hispanic (10)	22	0.06
African, sub-Saharan:	104	0.30
Nigerian	12	0.03
South African	92	0.26

Notes: 1. Figures in the "Number" column do not add up to the total population due to: a) Ancestry/Race overlap — e.g. persons can report being both White and Irish, b) persons of Hispanic origin can report being any race, c) persons reporting two ancestries are counted in both categories. 2. Numbers in parentheses indicate the number of persons reporting this ancestry/race alone, not in combination with any other ancestry/race. 3. Refer to the Explanation of Data in the front of the book for more detailed information.

Ancestry/Race	Number	%
Alaska Native tribes, specified:	4	0.01
Alaska Athabascan (3)	3	0.01
Tlingit-Haida	1	0.00
Am. Ind. or Alaska Nat., not spec.	71	0.20
Albanian	22	0.06
American Indian tribes, specified:	211	0.60
Apache	8	0.02
Blackfeet (1)	3	0.01
Cherokee (16)	58	0.16
Cheyenne (2)	3	0.01
Chickasaw (1)	2	0.01
Chippewa (3)	9	0.03
Choctaw (2)	3	0.01
Colville (2)	2	0.01
Creek (1)	2	0.01
Delaware (1)	1	0.00
Iroquois (5)	10	0.03
Kiowa	1	0.00
Latin American Indians (6)	14	0.04
Menominee (1)	1	0.00
Navajo (2)	2	0.01
Osage	1	0.00
Ottawa (1)	1	0.00
Pueblo (1)	3	0.01
Seminole	1	0.00
Sioux (8)	11	0.03
Ute	1	0.00
Yakama (1)	2	0.01
All other tribes (37)	72	0.20
American Indian tribes, not spec.	5	0.01
Arab:	426	1.21
Arab/Arabic	116	0.33
Egyptian	65	0.18
Jordanian	26	0.07
Lebanese	121	0.34
Palestinian	38	0.11
Syrian	41	0.12
Other Arab	19	0.05
Armenian	57	0.16
Asian:	2,089	5.92
Cambodian (6)	6	0.02
Chinese, ex. Taiwanese (483)	601	1.70
Filipino (128)	184	0.52
Hmong	2	0.01
Indian (159)	182	0.52
Indonesian (9)	15	0.04
Japanese (293)	429	1.22
Korean (373)	408	1.16
Malaysian (2)	2	0.01
Pakistani (13)	14	0.04
Sri Lankan (1)	1	0.00
Taiwanese (37)	43	0.12
Thai (26)	29	0.08
Vietnamese (21)	43	0.12
Other Asian, specified (6)	9	0.03
Other Asian, not specified (32)	121	0.34
Australian	60	0.17
Austrian	228	0.65
Basque	20	0.06
Belgian	25	0.07
Brazilian	16	0.05
British	526	1.49
Canadian	215	0.61
Celtic	27	0.08
Croatian	136	0.39
Czech	191	0.54
Czechoslovakian	86	0.24
Danish	556	1.58
Dutch	932	2.65
Eastern European	65	0.18
English	6,147	17.45
Estonian	12	0.03
European	949	2.69
Finnish	165	0.47
French, except Basque	1,336	3.79
French Canadian	175	0.50
German	7,643	21.70
Greek	254	0.72
Hawaii Native/Pacific Islander:	147	0.42
Micronesian: (10)	18	0.05
Guamanian/Chamorro (10)	17	0.05
Other Micronesian	1	0.00
Polynesian: (43)	113	0.32
Native Hawaiian (27)	88	0.25
Samoan (1)	10	0.03
Tongan (9)	9	0.03
Other Polynesian (6)	6	0.02
Other Pac. Isl., not spec. (3)	16	0.05
Hispanic or Latino:	820	2.32
Central American:	36	0.10
Costa Rican	16	0.05
Guatemalan	3	0.01
Nicaraguan	1	0.00
Panamanian	2	0.01
Salvadoran	9	0.03
Other Central American	5	0.01
Cuban	30	0.09
Dominican Republic	1	0.00
Mexican	435	1.23
Puerto Rican	40	0.11
South American:	70	0.20
Argentinean	1	0.00
Bolivian	2	0.01
Chilean	10	0.03
Colombian	20	0.06
Ecuadorian	3	0.01
Paraguayan	1	0.00
Peruvian	21	0.06
Venezuelan	2	0.01
Other South American	10	0.03
Other Hispanic or Latino	208	0.59
Hungarian	232	0.66
Icelander	9	0.03
Iranian	308	0.87
Irish	4,969	14.11
Israeli	34	0.10
Italian	1,670	4.74
Latvian	20	0.06
Lithuanian	77	0.22
Luxemburger	15	0.04
Northern European	181	0.51
Norwegian	2,037	5.78
Pennsylvania German	33	0.09
Polish	780	2.21
Portuguese	206	0.58
Romanian	84	0.24
Russian	696	1.98
Scandinavian	138	0.39
Scotch-Irish	831	2.36
Scottish	1,884	5.35
Serbian	7	0.02
Slavic	46	0.13
Slovak	136	0.39
Slovene	29	0.08
Swedish	1,594	4.53
Swiss	421	1.20
Ukrainian	244	0.69
United States or American	1,690	4.80
Welsh	445	1.26
West Indian, excl. Hispanic:	28	0.08
British West Indian	7	0.02
Jamaican	14	0.04
Trinidadian and Tobagonian	7	0.02
White:	32,959	93.43
Not Hispanic (31,642)	32,353	91.71
Hispanic (507)	606	1.72
Yugoslavian	159	0.45

Lebanon

Place Type: City
County: Linn
Population: 12,950

Ancestry/Race	Number	%
African American/Black:	62	0.48
Not Hispanic (20)	51	0.39
Hispanic (2)	11	0.08
African, sub-Saharan:	24	0.19
African	11	0.09
Ethiopian	13	0.10
Alaska Native tribes, specified:	9	0.07
Eskimo (2)	3	0.02
Tlingit-Haida (5)	6	0.05
Alaska Native tribes, not specified	4	0.03
Am. Ind. or Alaska Nat., not spec.	61	0.47
American Indian tribes, specified:	216	1.67
Apache (2)	7	0.05
Blackfeet (1)	8	0.06
Cherokee (18)	61	0.47
Chickasaw	1	0.01
Chippewa (1)	7	0.05
Choctaw (2)	10	0.08
Creek (1)	1	0.01
Iroquois (1)	4	0.03
Latin American Indians (1)	2	0.02
Navajo (1)	2	0.02
Osage (1)	2	0.02
Ottawa (1)	1	0.01
Paiute	1	0.01
Potawatomi (1)	3	0.02
Pueblo (1)	4	0.03
Sioux (11)	15	0.12
Ute	3	0.02
All other tribes (52)	84	0.65
American Indian tribes, not spec.	7	0.05
Arab:	6	0.05
Lebanese	6	0.05
Asian:	179	1.38
Cambodian (5)	5	0.04
Chinese, ex. Taiwanese (39)	50	0.39
Filipino (11)	27	0.21
Indian (24)	24	0.19
Japanese (5)	12	0.09
Korean (20)	34	0.26
Laotian (4)	4	0.03
Thai (3)	6	0.05
Vietnamese (8)	10	0.08
Other Asian, specified	1	0.01
Other Asian, not specified (5)	6	0.05
Australian	25	0.19
Austrian	37	0.29
British	86	0.67
Canadian	10	0.08
Czech	84	0.65
Czechoslovakian	49	0.38
Danish	103	0.80
Dutch	421	3.27
Eastern European	8	0.06
English	1,366	10.60
European	93	0.72
Finnish	50	0.39
French, except Basque	447	3.47
French Canadian	92	0.71
German	3,086	23.96
Greek	5	0.04
Hawaii Native/Pacific Islander:	34	0.26
Micronesian:	6	0.05
Guamanian/Chamorro	6	0.05
Polynesian: (11)	21	0.16
Native Hawaiian (10)	19	0.15
Samoan (1)	2	0.02
Other Pac. Isl., specified	1	0.01
Other Pac. Isl., not spec.	6	0.05
Hispanic or Latino:	478	3.69
Central American:	9	0.07
Guatemalan	7	0.05
Nicaraguan	1	0.01
Salvadoran	1	0.01
Cuban	4	0.03
Mexican	326	2.52
Puerto Rican	21	0.16
South American:	4	0.03
Chilean	3	0.02
Peruvian	1	0.01
Other Hispanic or Latino	114	0.88
Hungarian	78	0.61
Irish	1,454	11.29
Italian	312	2.42
Lithuanian	42	0.33

Notes: 1. Figures in the "Number" column do not add up to the total population due to: a) Ancestry/Race overlap — e.g. persons can report being both White and Irish, b) persons of Hispanic origin can report being any race, c) persons reporting two ancestries are counted in both categories. 2. Numbers in parentheses indicate the number of persons reporting this ancestry/race alone, not in combination with any other ancestry/race. 3. Refer to the Explanation of Data in the front of the book for more detailed information.

Norwegian	502	3.90
Pennsylvania German	25	0.19
Polish	164	1.27
Portuguese	43	0.33
Russian	106	0.82
Scandinavian	60	0.47
Scotch-Irish	212	1.65
Scottish	401	3.11
Slavic	8	0.06
Slovak	8	0.06
Swedish	402	3.12
Swiss	173	1.34
Ukrainian	42	0.33
United States or American	1,583	12.29
Welsh	44	0.34
White:	12,455	96.18
Not Hispanic (11,956)	12,177	94.03
Hispanic (214)	278	2.15
Yugoslavian	51	0.40

McMinnville

Place Type: City
County: Yamhill
Population: 26,499

Ancestry/Race	Number	%
African American/Black:	267	1.01
Not Hispanic (103)	167	0.63
Hispanic (76)	100	0.38
African, sub-Saharan:	24	0.09
African	24	0.09
Alaska Native tribes, specified:	31	0.12
Alaska Athabascan (2)	2	0.01
Aleut (2)	4	0.02
Eskimo (4)	5	0.02
Tlingit-Haida (9)	20	0.08
Am. Ind. or Alaska Nat., not spec.	128	0.48
American Indian tribes, specified:	444	1.68
Apache (4)	10	0.04
Blackfeet (6)	17	0.06
Cherokee (39)	106	0.40
Cheyenne (1)	3	0.01
Chickasaw (10)	20	0.08
Chippewa (2)	7	0.03
Choctaw (13)	19	0.07
Creek (3)	3	0.01
Delaware (1)	2	0.01
Iroquois (1)	9	0.03
Kiowa (1)	1	0.00
Latin American Indians (7)	16	0.06
Navajo (4)	6	0.02
Osage (4)	5	0.02
Pima (1)	1	0.00
Potawatomi (8)	13	0.05
Puget Sound Salish (1)	2	0.01
Seminole (1)	9	0.03
Shoshone	1	0.00
Sioux (9)	26	0.10
Tohono O'Odham	2	0.01
Yakama (5)	7	0.03
All other tribes (121)	159	0.60
American Indian tribes, not spec.	38	0.14
Armenian	8	0.03
Asian:	560	2.11
Bangladeshi (1)	5	0.02
Cambodian (5)	5	0.02
Chinese, ex. Taiwanese (57)	81	0.31
Filipino (46)	101	0.38
Indian (16)	34	0.13
Indonesian (2)	2	0.01
Japanese (62)	132	0.50
Korean (71)	99	0.37
Laotian (24)	30	0.11
Malaysian (1)	1	0.00
Pakistani (3)	6	0.02
Sri Lankan (3)	3	0.01
Taiwanese (3)	3	0.01
Thai (5)	9	0.03
Vietnamese (10)	14	0.05
Other Asian, specified (4)	9	0.03
Other Asian, not specified (9)	26	0.10
Austrian	103	0.39
Basque	50	0.19
Belgian	30	0.11
British	120	0.45
Canadian	52	0.20
Celtic	32	0.12
Czech	104	0.39
Czechoslovakian	64	0.24
Danish	304	1.14
Dutch	821	3.09
English	3,570	13.45
European	289	1.09
Finnish	260	0.98
French, except Basque	909	3.42
French Canadian	153	0.58
German	4,854	18.28
Greek	17	0.06
Hawaii Native/Pacific Islander:	112	0.42
Micronesian: (7)	9	0.03
Guamanian/Chamorro (7)	9	0.03
Polynesian: (39)	94	0.35
Native Hawaiian (33)	78	0.29
Samoan (4)	10	0.04
Tongan (1)	2	0.01
Other Polynesian (1)	4	0.02
Other Pac. Isl., specified	1	0.00
Other Pac. Isl., not spec.	8	0.03
Hispanic or Latino:	3,879	14.64
Central American:	64	0.24
Costa Rican	1	0.00
Guatemalan	17	0.06
Honduran	6	0.02
Nicaraguan	1	0.00
Panamanian	1	0.00
Salvadoran	33	0.12
Other Central American	5	0.02
Cuban	22	0.08
Dominican Republic	1	0.00
Mexican	3,156	11.91
Puerto Rican	37	0.14
South American:	27	0.10
Argentinean	2	0.01
Bolivian	1	0.00
Chilean	8	0.03
Colombian	8	0.03
Ecuadorian	3	0.01
Paraguayan	1	0.00
Peruvian	5	0.02
Other Hispanic or Latino	572	2.16
Hungarian	51	0.19
Icelander	19	0.07
Iranian	24	0.09
Irish	2,694	10.15
Italian	574	2.16
Lithuanian	36	0.14
New Zealander	7	0.03
Northern European	8	0.03
Norwegian	1,053	3.97
Pennsylvania German	19	0.07
Polish	393	1.48
Portuguese	81	0.31
Romanian	17	0.06
Russian	63	0.24
Scandinavian	39	0.15
Scotch-Irish	615	2.32
Scottish	739	2.78
Slavic	7	0.03
Swedish	642	2.42
Swiss	170	0.64
Turkish	38	0.14
Ukrainian	44	0.17
United States or American	1,627	6.13
Welsh	307	1.16
White:	23,589	89.02
Not Hispanic (21,294)	21,757	82.10
Hispanic (1,598)	1,832	6.91
Yugoslavian	28	0.11

Medford

Place Type: City
County: Jackson
Population: 63,154

Ancestry/Race	Number	%
African American/Black:	505	0.80
Not Hispanic (291)	446	0.71
Hispanic (22)	59	0.09
African, sub-Saharan:	24	0.04
African	15	0.02
Other sub-Saharan African	9	0.01
Alaska Native tribes, specified:	24	0.04
Alaska Athabascan (2)	4	0.01
Aleut (5)	7	0.01
Eskimo (8)	8	0.01
Tlingit-Haida (1)	5	0.01
Alaska Native tribes, not specified	3	0.00
Am. Ind. or Alaska Nat., not spec.	368	0.58
Alsatian	10	0.02
American Indian tribes, specified:	978	1.55
Apache (7)	31	0.05
Blackfeet (24)	57	0.09
Cherokee (84)	290	0.46
Cheyenne (1)	4	0.01
Chickasaw (1)	3	0.00
Chippewa (19)	36	0.06
Choctaw (22)	55	0.09
Colville (1)	2	0.00
Comanche (3)	4	0.01
Cree	4	0.01
Creek (4)	7	0.01
Crow (1)	2	0.00
Delaware (6)	7	0.01
Iroquois (6)	15	0.02
Kiowa (6)	7	0.01
Latin American Indians (22)	35	0.06
Lumbee	1	0.00
Navajo (6)	10	0.02
Osage (3)	7	0.01
Ottawa (3)	4	0.01
Paiute	5	0.01
Potawatomi (1)	3	0.00
Pueblo (3)	8	0.01
Puget Sound Salish (6)	7	0.01
Seminole (2)	9	0.01
Shoshone (3)	7	0.01
Sioux (13)	40	0.06
Tohono O'Odham	1	0.00
Ute (2)	5	0.01
Yakama (1)	1	0.00
Yaqui (5)	6	0.01
Yuman (1)	1	0.00
All other tribes (203)	304	0.48
American Indian tribes, not spec.	48	0.08
Arab:	77	0.12
Arab/Arabic	11	0.02
Egyptian	9	0.01
Lebanese	49	0.08
Syrian	8	0.01
Armenian	68	0.11
Asian:	1,129	1.79
Cambodian (16)	16	0.03
Chinese, ex. Taiwanese (124)	182	0.29
Filipino (209)	356	0.56
Indian (56)	79	0.13
Indonesian (15)	30	0.05
Japanese (86)	191	0.30
Korean (103)	132	0.21
Laotian (2)	3	0.00
Sri Lankan (1)	1	0.00
Taiwanese (4)	9	0.01
Thai (29)	34	0.05
Vietnamese (54)	60	0.10
Other Asian, specified (1)	2	0.00
Other Asian, not specified (10)	34	0.05
Australian	10	0.02
Austrian	169	0.27
Basque	56	0.09

Notes: 1. Figures in the "Number" column do not add up to the total population due to: a) Ancestry/Race overlap — e.g. persons can report being both White and Irish, b) persons of Hispanic origin can report being any race, c) persons reporting two ancestries are counted in both categories. 2. Numbers in parentheses indicate the number of persons reporting this ancestry/race alone, not in combination with any other ancestry/race. 3. Refer to the Explanation of Data in the front of the book for more detailed information.

Ancestry/Race	Number	%
Belgian	38	0.06
Brazilian	8	0.01
British	413	0.65
Canadian	241	0.38
Celtic	27	0.04
Croatian	74	0.12
Czech	242	0.38
Czechoslovakian	134	0.21
Danish	721	1.14
Dutch	1,789	2.82
Eastern European	25	0.04
English	9,126	14.39
European	1,045	1.65
Finnish	244	0.38
French, except Basque	2,266	3.57
French Canadian	597	0.94
German	12,361	19.49
Greek	139	0.22
Hawaii Native/Pacific Islander:	287	0.45
Micronesian: (31)	47	0.07
Guamanian/Chamorro (23)	37	0.06
Other Micronesian (8)	10	0.02
Polynesian: (115)	187	0.30
Native Hawaiian (30)	87	0.14
Samoan (79)	93	0.15
Other Polynesian (6)	7	0.01
Other Pac. Isl., not spec. (16)	53	0.08
Hispanic or Latino:	5,841	9.25
Central American:	152	0.24
Costa Rican	8	0.01
Guatemalan	93	0.15
Honduran	12	0.02
Nicaraguan	5	0.01
Salvadoran	31	0.05
Other Central American	3	0.00
Cuban	40	0.06
Dominican Republic	15	0.02
Mexican	4,715	7.47
Puerto Rican	79	0.13
South American:	72	0.11
Argentinean	5	0.01
Bolivian	4	0.01
Chilean	5	0.01
Colombian	18	0.03
Ecuadorian	4	0.01
Peruvian	19	0.03
Venezuelan	9	0.01
Other South American	8	0.01
Other Hispanic or Latino	768	1.22
Hungarian	181	0.29
Icelander	7	0.01
Iranian	10	0.02
Irish	8,403	13.25
Italian	2,608	4.11
Latvian	51	0.08
Lithuanian	104	0.16
New Zealander	6	0.01
Northern European	28	0.04
Norwegian	2,170	3.42
Pennsylvania German	64	0.10
Polish	983	1.55
Portuguese	688	1.08
Romanian	55	0.09
Russian	435	0.69
Scandinavian	338	0.53
Scotch-Irish	1,465	2.31
Scottish	1,886	2.97
Serbian	52	0.08
Slavic	16	0.03
Slovak	15	0.02
Slovene	13	0.02
Swedish	1,808	2.85
Swiss	330	0.52
Turkish	11	0.02
Ukrainian	45	0.07
United States or American	4,234	6.67
Welsh	728	1.15
West Indian, excl. Hispanic:	41	0.06
Barbadian	9	0.01
Dutch West Indian	19	0.03
Jamaican	13	0.02
White:	58,744	93.02
Not Hispanic (54,299)	55,473	87.84
Hispanic (2,535)	3,271	5.18
Yugoslavian	46	0.07

Milwaukie

Place Type: City
County: Clackamas
Population: 20,490

Ancestry/Race	Number	%
African American/Black:	315	1.54
Not Hispanic (182)	291	1.42
Hispanic (12)	24	0.12
African, sub-Saharan:	9	0.04
African	9	0.04
Alaska Native tribes, specified:	7	0.03
Alaska Athabascan	2	0.01
Eskimo (1)	1	0.00
Tlingit-Haida (4)	4	0.02
Alaska Native tribes, not specified	2	0.01
Am. Ind. or Alaska Nat., not spec.	93	0.45
Alsatian	8	0.04
American Indian tribes, specified:	290	1.42
Apache (3)	9	0.04
Blackfeet (1)	10	0.05
Cherokee (19)	78	0.38
Cheyenne (1)	1	0.00
Chickasaw	1	0.00
Chippewa (17)	23	0.11
Choctaw (6)	9	0.04
Comanche (1)	1	0.00
Cree	2	0.01
Creek (1)	5	0.02
Delaware (1)	1	0.00
Iroquois (3)	5	0.02
Kiowa	3	0.01
Latin American Indians (7)	11	0.05
Navajo (6)	9	0.04
Osage	2	0.01
Ottawa (2)	3	0.01
Potawatomi (7)	12	0.06
Puget Sound Salish (1)	4	0.02
Seminole (1)	1	0.00
Sioux (11)	20	0.10
Tohono O'Odham	2	0.01
Ute (7)	7	0.03
Yakama (1)	3	0.01
Yaqui (1)	2	0.01
All other tribes (36)	66	0.32
American Indian tribes, not spec.	12	0.06
Arab:	90	0.43
Arab/Arabic	10	0.05
Egyptian	8	0.04
Lebanese	38	0.18
Palestinian	34	0.16
Armenian	48	0.23
Asian:	670	3.27
Cambodian (18)	23	0.11
Chinese, ex. Taiwanese (94)	136	0.66
Filipino (70)	121	0.59
Hmong (4)	4	0.02
Indian (25)	34	0.17
Indonesian (2)	7	0.03
Japanese (61)	96	0.47
Korean (60)	71	0.35
Laotian (30)	32	0.16
Pakistani	9	0.04
Sri Lankan (2)	8	0.04
Taiwanese (1)	2	0.01
Thai (7)	8	0.04
Vietnamese (91)	106	0.52
Other Asian, not specified (3)	13	0.06
Austrian	32	0.15
Basque	30	0.14
Belgian	44	0.21
British	132	0.63
Canadian	49	0.23
Celtic	5	0.02
Croatian	58	0.28
Czech	69	0.33
Czechoslovakian	30	0.14
Danish	486	2.33
Dutch	579	2.77
English	2,982	14.28
Estonian	13	0.06
European	206	0.99
Finnish	169	0.81
French, except Basque	948	4.54
French Canadian	183	0.88
German	5,052	24.19
Greek	36	0.17
Guyanese	7	0.03
Hawaii Native/Pacific Islander:	128	0.62
Melanesian: (3)	9	0.04
Fijian (3)	9	0.04
Micronesian: (7)	19	0.09
Guamanian/Chamorro (4)	16	0.08
Other Micronesian (3)	3	0.01
Polynesian: (35)	73	0.36
Native Hawaiian (15)	41	0.20
Samoan (19)	31	0.15
Other Polynesian (1)	1	0.00
Other Pac. Isl., not spec. (7)	27	0.13
Hispanic or Latino:	813	3.97
Central American:	25	0.12
Guatemalan	3	0.01
Honduran	2	0.01
Panamanian	4	0.02
Salvadoran	14	0.07
Other Central American	2	0.01
Cuban	12	0.06
Dominican Republic	1	0.00
Mexican	526	2.57
Puerto Rican	32	0.16
South American:	19	0.09
Argentinean	4	0.02
Bolivian	3	0.01
Chilean	8	0.04
Colombian	1	0.00
Ecuadorian	3	0.01
Other Hispanic or Latino	198	0.97
Hungarian	42	0.20
Icelander	11	0.05
Iranian	6	0.03
Irish	2,879	13.79
Italian	982	4.70
Latvian	5	0.02
Northern European	22	0.11
Norwegian	1,142	5.47
Pennsylvania German	8	0.04
Polish	260	1.24
Portuguese	52	0.25
Romanian	80	0.38
Russian	359	1.72
Scandinavian	104	0.50
Scotch-Irish	561	2.69
Scottish	776	3.72
Serbian	10	0.05
Slavic	7	0.03
Slovak	10	0.05
Swedish	820	3.93
Swiss	194	0.93
Turkish	32	0.15
Ukrainian	81	0.39
United States or American	883	4.23
Welsh	258	1.24
West Indian, excl. Hispanic:	6	0.03
Haitian	6	0.03
White:	19,178	93.60
Not Hispanic (18,271)	18,726	91.39
Hispanic (366)	452	2.21
Yugoslavian	92	0.44

Notes: 1. Figures in the "Number" column do not add up to the total population due to: a) Ancestry/Race overlap — e.g. persons can report being both White and Irish, b) persons of Hispanic origin can report being any race, c) persons reporting two ancestries are counted in both categories. 2. Numbers in parentheses indicate the number of persons reporting this ancestry/race alone, not in combination with any other ancestry/race. 3. Refer to the Explanation of Data in the front of the book for more detailed information.

Newberg

Place Type: City
County: Yamhill
Population: 18,064

Ancestry/Race	Number	%
Afghan	9	0.05
African American/Black:	119	0.66
Not Hispanic (59)	107	0.59
Hispanic (5)	12	0.07
African, sub-Saharan:	13	0.07
African	13	0.07
Alaska Native tribes, specified:	6	0.03
Alaska Athabascan	1	0.01
Aleut	1	0.01
Tlingit-Haida (3)	4	0.02
Alaska Native tribes, not specified	1	0.01
Am. Ind. or Alaska Nat., not spec.	77	0.43
American Indian tribes, specified:	168	0.93
Blackfeet (2)	9	0.05
Cherokee (8)	29	0.16
Cheyenne	1	0.01
Chippewa (1)	3	0.02
Choctaw (8)	15	0.08
Cree	4	0.02
Crow	3	0.02
Delaware	5	0.03
Iroquois (2)	2	0.01
Latin American Indians (6)	8	0.04
Navajo (2)	3	0.02
Osage (1)	2	0.01
Paiute (5)	5	0.03
Pima	4	0.02
Pueblo (1)	1	0.01
Puget Sound Salish (1)	3	0.02
Sioux (9)	25	0.14
Ute	1	0.01
Yakama (1)	1	0.01
Yaqui	5	0.03
All other tribes (22)	39	0.22
American Indian tribes, not spec.	7	0.04
Armenian	7	0.04
Asian:	311	1.72
Chinese, ex. Taiwanese (46)	72	0.40
Filipino (11)	40	0.22
Indian (17)	25	0.14
Indonesian (2)	7	0.04
Japanese (40)	71	0.39
Korean (37)	54	0.30
Malaysian (1)	1	0.01
Taiwanese (1)	2	0.01
Thai (2)	2	0.01
Vietnamese (24)	29	0.16
Other Asian, specified	2	0.01
Other Asian, not specified (1)	6	0.03
Austrian	8	0.04
Belgian	19	0.10
British	89	0.49
Canadian	83	0.46
Celtic	7	0.04
Czech	184	1.02
Czechoslovakian	24	0.13
Danish	216	1.19
Dutch	596	3.29
English	2,269	12.53
European	462	2.55
Finnish	95	0.52
French, except Basque	667	3.68
French Canadian	122	0.67
German	4,005	22.11
Greek	31	0.17
Hawaii Native/Pacific Islander:	85	0.47
Micronesian: (7)	13	0.07
Guamanian/Chamorro (1)	6	0.03
Other Micronesian (6)	7	0.04
Polynesian: (17)	52	0.29
Native Hawaiian (7)	35	0.19
Samoan (6)	6	0.03
Tongan (3)	10	0.06
Other Polynesian (1)	1	0.01
Other Pac. Isl., not spec. (7)	20	0.11
Hispanic or Latino:	1,901	10.52
Central American:	19	0.11
Costa Rican	1	0.01
Guatemalan	8	0.04
Panamanian	1	0.01
Salvadoran	9	0.05
Cuban	12	0.07
Dominican Republic	3	0.02
Mexican	1,603	8.87
Puerto Rican	27	0.15
South American:	20	0.11
Bolivian	1	0.01
Chilean	5	0.03
Colombian	6	0.03
Ecuadorian	1	0.01
Peruvian	2	0.01
Venezuelan	4	0.02
Other South American	1	0.01
Other Hispanic or Latino	217	1.20
Hungarian	19	0.10
Irish	1,736	9.58
Italian	497	2.74
Latvian	7	0.04
Lithuanian	17	0.09
Luxemburger	7	0.04
Northern European	7	0.04
Norwegian	734	4.05
Pennsylvania German	16	0.09
Polish	401	2.21
Portuguese	98	0.54
Romanian	12	0.07
Russian	85	0.47
Scandinavian	72	0.40
Scotch-Irish	379	2.09
Scottish	886	4.89
Serbian	32	0.18
Slovene	8	0.04
Swedish	588	3.25
Swiss	174	0.96
Ukrainian	27	0.15
United States or American	1,193	6.59
Welsh	281	1.55
West Indian, excl. Hispanic:	17	0.09
Belizean	17	0.09
White:	16,725	92.59
Not Hispanic (15,499)	15,765	87.27
Hispanic (848)	960	5.31
Yugoslavian	13	0.07

Oak Grove

Place Type: Census Designated Place
County: Clackamas
Population: 12,808

Ancestry/Race	Number	%
African American/Black:	149	1.16
Not Hispanic (68)	130	1.01
Hispanic (4)	19	0.15
African, sub-Saharan:	39	0.31
African	16	0.13
Cape Verdean	20	0.16
South African	3	0.02
Alaska Native tribes, specified:	10	0.08
Alaska Athabascan	2	0.02
Aleut (5)	5	0.04
Eskimo (2)	2	0.02
Tlingit-Haida (1)	1	0.01
Am. Ind. or Alaska Nat., not spec.	64	0.50
American Indian tribes, specified:	138	1.08
Apache (2)	4	0.03
Blackfeet	6	0.05
Cherokee (7)	34	0.27
Chippewa (9)	11	0.09
Choctaw (1)	1	0.01
Colville (1)	1	0.01
Comanche	1	0.01
Cree	1	0.01
Creek	3	0.02
Iroquois (1)	7	0.05
Latin American Indians (1)	4	0.03
Navajo	2	0.02
Osage	1	0.01
Shoshone (1)	3	0.02
Sioux (1)	5	0.04
Tohono O'Odham (1)	1	0.01
Yakama (5)	7	0.05
Yaqui	1	0.01
All other tribes (25)	45	0.35
American Indian tribes, not spec.	6	0.05
Arab:	14	0.11
Jordanian	14	0.11
Armenian	26	0.21
Asian:	321	2.51
Cambodian (10)	11	0.09
Chinese, ex. Taiwanese (41)	53	0.41
Filipino (41)	70	0.55
Indian (23)	29	0.23
Indonesian (3)	8	0.06
Japanese (31)	50	0.39
Korean (44)	51	0.40
Malaysian	1	0.01
Thai (8)	11	0.09
Vietnamese (27)	31	0.24
Other Asian, specified	3	0.02
Other Asian, not specified (1)	3	0.02
Austrian	49	0.39
Belgian	28	0.22
British	73	0.58
Bulgarian	6	0.05
Canadian	27	0.21
Celtic	7	0.06
Croatian	65	0.52
Czech	56	0.45
Czechoslovakian	25	0.20
Danish	194	1.54
Dutch	347	2.76
Eastern European	8	0.06
English	1,916	15.24
European	301	2.39
Finnish	89	0.71
French, except Basque	526	4.18
French Canadian	159	1.26
German	3,139	24.97
Greek	15	0.12
Hawaii Native/Pacific Islander:	65	0.51
Melanesian: (2)	6	0.05
Fijian (2)	6	0.05
Micronesian:	7	0.05
Guamanian/Chamorro	7	0.05
Polynesian: (8)	32	0.25
Native Hawaiian (7)	25	0.20
Samoan (1)	7	0.05
Other Pac. Isl., specified	3	0.02
Other Pac. Isl., not spec. (2)	17	0.13
Hispanic or Latino:	755	5.89
Central American:	32	0.25
Costa Rican	1	0.01
Guatemalan	2	0.02
Honduran	4	0.03
Nicaraguan	1	0.01
Panamanian	3	0.02
Salvadoran	16	0.12
Other Central American	5	0.04
Cuban	3	0.02
Dominican Republic	1	0.01
Mexican	564	4.40
Puerto Rican	12	0.09
South American:	31	0.24
Bolivian	4	0.03
Chilean	7	0.05
Colombian	5	0.04
Peruvian	13	0.10
Venezuelan	2	0.02
Other Hispanic or Latino	112	0.87
Hungarian	77	0.61
Icelander	9	0.07
Iranian	6	0.05

Notes: 1. Figures in the "Number" column do not add up to the total population due to: a) Ancestry/Race overlap — e.g. persons can report being both White and Irish, b) persons of Hispanic origin can report being any race, c) persons reporting two ancestries are counted in both categories. 2. Numbers in parentheses indicate the number of persons reporting this ancestry/race alone, not in combination with any other ancestry/race. 3. Refer to the Explanation of Data in the front of the book for more detailed information.

Ancestry/Race	Number	%
Irish	1,564	12.44
Italian	395	3.14
Lithuanian	11	0.09
Luxemburger	10	0.08
Northern European	11	0.09
Norwegian	626	4.98
Pennsylvania German	27	0.21
Polish	154	1.23
Portuguese	22	0.18
Romanian	68	0.54
Russian	134	1.07
Scandinavian	88	0.70
Scotch-Irish	251	2.00
Scottish	458	3.64
Serbian	6	0.05
Slovak	25	0.20
Slovene	16	0.13
Swedish	424	3.37
Swiss	58	0.46
United States or American	658	5.23
Welsh	161	1.28
White:	12,032	93.94
Not Hispanic (11,375)	11,638	90.87
Hispanic (340)	394	3.08
Yugoslavian	41	0.33

Oatfield

Place Type: Census Designated Place
County: Clackamas
Population: 15,750

Ancestry/Race	Number	%
African American/Black:	152	0.97
Not Hispanic (71)	146	0.93
Hispanic (3)	6	0.04
African, sub-Saharan:	42	0.27
African	1	0.01
South African	41	0.26
Alaska Native tribes, specified:	15	0.10
Alaska Athabascan (3)	6	0.04
Aleut (1)	1	0.01
Tlingit-Haida (2)	6	0.04
All other tribes	2	0.01
Am. Ind. or Alaska Nat., not spec.	44	0.28
American Indian tribes, specified:	137	0.87
Apache	1	0.01
Blackfeet (1)	7	0.04
Cherokee (21)	56	0.36
Chippewa (6)	9	0.06
Choctaw	8	0.05
Creek (6)	6	0.04
Kiowa (2)	2	0.01
Latin American Indians (3)	5	0.03
Potawatomi	2	0.01
Shoshone	1	0.01
Sioux (4)	10	0.06
All other tribes (9)	30	0.19
American Indian tribes, not spec.	6	0.04
Arab:	69	0.44
Arab/Arabic	38	0.24
Lebanese	5	0.03
Palestinian	2	0.01
Syrian	24	0.15
Asian:	460	2.92
Cambodian (18)	25	0.16
Chinese, ex. Taiwanese (55)	82	0.52
Filipino (33)	66	0.42
Indian (27)	39	0.25
Indonesian (3)	10	0.06
Japanese (57)	97	0.62
Korean (51)	60	0.38
Laotian (13)	15	0.10
Thai (5)	12	0.08
Vietnamese (44)	46	0.29
Other Asian, specified	2	0.01
Other Asian, not specified (6)	6	0.04
Australian	2	0.01
Austrian	46	0.29
Basque	1	0.01
Belgian	13	0.08
Brazilian	24	0.15
British	122	0.78
Bulgarian	19	0.12
Canadian	84	0.54
Croatian	16	0.10
Czech	83	0.53
Czechoslovakian	43	0.27
Danish	276	1.76
Dutch	428	2.73
Eastern European	2	0.01
English	2,279	14.52
Estonian	4	0.03
European	242	1.54
Finnish	205	1.31
French, except Basque	640	4.08
French Canadian	157	1.00
German	4,293	27.36
German Russian	13	0.08
Greek	31	0.20
Hawaii Native/Pacific Islander:	69	0.44
Melanesian: (2)	2	0.01
Fijian (2)	2	0.01
Micronesian: (4)	9	0.06
Guamanian/Chamorro	4	0.03
Other Micronesian (4)	5	0.03
Polynesian: (9)	35	0.22
Native Hawaiian (4)	25	0.16
Samoan (5)	10	0.06
Other Pac. Isl., not spec. (4)	23	0.15
Hispanic or Latino:	416	2.64
Central American:	20	0.13
Costa Rican	8	0.05
Guatemalan	6	0.04
Panamanian	3	0.02
Salvadoran	3	0.02
Cuban	13	0.08
Mexican	273	1.73
Puerto Rican	18	0.11
South American:	17	0.11
Chilean	7	0.04
Colombian	5	0.03
Ecuadorian	1	0.01
Peruvian	1	0.01
Venezuelan	2	0.01
Other South American	1	0.01
Other Hispanic or Latino	75	0.48
Hungarian	18	0.11
Irish	2,196	13.99
Italian	814	5.19
Latvian	10	0.06
Lithuanian	4	0.03
Luxemburger	5	0.03
Northern European	31	0.20
Norwegian	791	5.04
Pennsylvania German	1	0.01
Polish	352	2.24
Portuguese	62	0.40
Romanian	27	0.17
Russian	133	0.85
Scandinavian	84	0.54
Scotch-Irish	398	2.54
Scottish	564	3.59
Slovak	16	0.10
Slovene	7	0.04
Swedish	640	4.08
Swiss	240	1.53
Ukrainian	99	0.63
United States or American	863	5.50
Welsh	212	1.35
West Indian, excl. Hispanic:	6	0.04
Jamaican	6	0.04
White:	15,085	95.78
Not Hispanic (14,489)	14,813	94.05
Hispanic (227)	272	1.73
Yugoslavian	33	0.21

Ontario

Place Type: City
County: Malheur
Population: 10,985

Ancestry/Race	Number	%
African American/Black:	91	0.83
Not Hispanic (51)	68	0.62
Hispanic (9)	23	0.21
African, sub-Saharan:	23	0.21
African	23	0.21
Alaska Native tribes, specified:	1	0.01
Eskimo (1)	1	0.01
Am. Ind. or Alaska Nat., not spec.	44	0.40
American Indian tribes, specified:	181	1.65
Apache (1)	8	0.07
Blackfeet (4)	8	0.07
Cherokee (15)	50	0.46
Cheyenne	1	0.01
Chickasaw (1)	1	0.01
Chippewa (18)	21	0.19
Comanche	1	0.01
Cree	3	0.03
Creek	1	0.01
Delaware	2	0.02
Iroquois	2	0.02
Latin American Indians (8)	12	0.11
Lumbee	1	0.01
Navajo (3)	3	0.03
Osage	3	0.03
Paiute (1)	5	0.05
Pueblo	2	0.02
Shoshone (4)	4	0.04
Sioux (2)	14	0.13
Yakama (1)	1	0.01
All other tribes (17)	38	0.35
American Indian tribes, not spec.	3	0.03
Asian:	364	3.31
Chinese, ex. Taiwanese (22)	28	0.25
Filipino (17)	22	0.20
Indian (14)	26	0.24
Indonesian	1	0.01
Japanese (228)	265	2.41
Korean (5)	7	0.06
Thai	1	0.01
Vietnamese (2)	5	0.05
Other Asian, not specified (2)	9	0.08
Austrian	6	0.05
Basque	145	1.30
Belgian	5	0.04
British	14	0.13
Canadian	6	0.05
Czech	41	0.37
Czechoslovakian	9	0.08
Danish	116	1.04
Dutch	194	1.74
English	1,010	9.08
European	84	0.75
Finnish	12	0.11
French, except Basque	239	2.15
French Canadian	83	0.75
German	1,530	13.75
Hawaii Native/Pacific Islander:	35	0.32
Micronesian: (1)	6	0.05
Guamanian/Chamorro (1)	2	0.02
Other Micronesian	4	0.04
Polynesian: (8)	16	0.15
Native Hawaiian (8)	15	0.14
Samoan	1	0.01
Other Pac. Isl., not spec. (7)	13	0.12
Hispanic or Latino:	3,521	32.05
Central American:	5	0.05
Costa Rican	1	0.01
Salvadoran	4	0.04
Cuban	8	0.07
Mexican	2,749	25.03
Puerto Rican	13	0.12
South American:	15	0.14
Argentinean	3	0.03

Notes: 1. Figures in the "Number" column do not add up to the total population due to: a) Ancestry/Race overlap — e.g. persons can report being both White and Irish, b) persons of Hispanic origin can report being any race, c) persons reporting two ancestries are counted in both categories. 2. Numbers in parentheses indicate the number of persons reporting this ancestry/race alone, not in combination with any other ancestry/race. 3. Refer to the Explanation of Data in the front of the book for more detailed information.

Ancestry/Race	Number	%
Chilean	7	0.06
Colombian	2	0.02
Peruvian	3	0.03
Other Hispanic or Latino	731	6.65
Irish	847	7.61
Italian	144	1.29
Northern European	17	0.15
Norwegian	210	1.89
Polish	109	0.98
Portuguese	6	0.05
Russian	45	0.40
Scandinavian	97	0.87
Scotch-Irish	218	1.96
Scottish	221	1.99
Swedish	114	1.02
Swiss	96	0.86
United States or American	672	6.04
Welsh	90	0.81
White:	7,941	72.29
Not Hispanic (6,826)	7,004	63.76
Hispanic (783)	937	8.53

Oregon City

Place Type: City
County: Clackamas
Population: 25,754

Ancestry/Race	Number	%
African American/Black:	280	1.09
Not Hispanic (143)	262	1.02
Hispanic (7)	18	0.07
African, sub-Saharan:	22	0.09
African	22	0.09
Alaska Native tribes, specified:	34	0.13
Aleut (9)	12	0.05
Eskimo (1)	1	0.00
Tlingit-Haida (6)	11	0.04
All other tribes (4)	10	0.04
Alaska Native tribes, not specified	2	0.01
Am. Ind. or Alaska Nat., not spec.	138	0.54
American Indian tribes, specified:	351	1.36
Apache (8)	14	0.05
Blackfeet (10)	23	0.09
Cherokee (34)	95	0.37
Cheyenne (1)	2	0.01
Chickasaw	1	0.00
Chippewa (9)	13	0.05
Choctaw (4)	13	0.05
Colville (5)	6	0.02
Comanche (2)	2	0.01
Cree (3)	3	0.01
Creek (2)	8	0.03
Delaware (2)	2	0.01
Iroquois (7)	9	0.03
Kiowa	1	0.00
Latin American Indians (18)	22	0.09
Menominee	1	0.00
Navajo (9)	9	0.03
Osage	1	0.00
Paiute (1)	1	0.00
Pima (7)	9	0.03
Pueblo (2)	5	0.02
Puget Sound Salish	1	0.00
Seminole	3	0.01
Sioux (8)	17	0.07
Yakama	4	0.02
Yaqui	1	0.00
All other tribes (53)	85	0.33
American Indian tribes, not spec.	22	0.09
Arab:	27	0.11
Lebanese	16	0.06
Syrian	11	0.04
Asian:	475	1.84
Cambodian (3)	7	0.03
Chinese, ex. Taiwanese (48)	74	0.29
Filipino (51)	89	0.35
Hmong (4)	4	0.02
Indian (21)	32	0.12
Indonesian (10)	24	0.09
Japanese (37)	78	0.30
Korean (43)	58	0.23
Laotian (1)	2	0.01
Malaysian	2	0.01
Pakistani (6)	10	0.04
Sri Lankan (1)	2	0.01
Taiwanese (1)	1	0.00
Thai (10)	25	0.10
Vietnamese (38)	46	0.18
Other Asian, specified (1)	4	0.02
Other Asian, not specified (5)	17	0.07
Austrian	47	0.18
Basque	22	0.09
Belgian	67	0.26
British	102	0.40
Canadian	53	0.21
Celtic	24	0.09
Croatian	15	0.06
Czech	169	0.66
Czechoslovakian	46	0.18
Danish	292	1.14
Dutch	638	2.50
Eastern European	9	0.04
English	3,352	13.13
European	470	1.84
Finnish	119	0.47
French, except Basque	916	3.59
French Canadian	319	1.25
German	5,950	23.30
Greek	102	0.40
Hawaii Native/Pacific Islander:	89	0.35
Melanesian:	1	0.00
Fijian	1	0.00
Micronesian: (9)	14	0.05
Guamanian/Chamorro (2)	7	0.03
Other Micronesian (7)	7	0.03
Polynesian: (11)	47	0.18
Native Hawaiian (9)	38	0.15
Samoan (1)	7	0.03
Other Polynesian (1)	2	0.01
Other Pac. Isl., not spec. (8)	27	0.10
Hispanic or Latino:	1,283	4.98
Central American:	46	0.18
Costa Rican	3	0.01
Guatemalan	12	0.05
Nicaraguan	6	0.02
Panamanian	4	0.02
Salvadoran	15	0.06
Other Central American	6	0.02
Cuban	7	0.03
Mexican	970	3.77
Puerto Rican	30	0.12
South American:	23	0.09
Argentinean	3	0.01
Chilean	3	0.01
Colombian	6	0.02
Peruvian	3	0.01
Uruguayan	3	0.01
Other South American	5	0.02
Other Hispanic or Latino	207	0.80
Hungarian	121	0.47
Icelander	9	0.04
Iranian	8	0.03
Irish	3,232	12.66
Italian	1,063	4.16
Lithuanian	24	0.09
Northern European	5	0.02
Norwegian	1,044	4.09
Polish	365	1.43
Portuguese	57	0.22
Romanian	65	0.25
Russian	371	1.45
Scandinavian	99	0.39
Scotch-Irish	514	2.01
Scottish	778	3.05
Serbian	22	0.09
Slavic	7	0.03
Slovak	9	0.04
Swedish	953	3.73
Swiss	91	0.36
Ukrainian	248	0.97
United States or American	1,903	7.45
Welsh	418	1.64
White:	24,412	94.79
Not Hispanic (23,212)	23,733	92.15
Hispanic (595)	679	2.64
Yugoslavian	60	0.23

Pendleton

Place Type: City
County: Umatilla
Population: 16,354

Ancestry/Race	Number	%
Acadian/Cajun	6	0.04
African American/Black:	306	1.87
Not Hispanic (244)	299	1.83
Hispanic (6)	7	0.04
African, sub-Saharan:	13	0.08
South African	13	0.08
Alaska Native tribes, specified:	15	0.09
Alaska Athabascan (1)	1	0.01
Tlingit-Haida (5)	12	0.07
All other tribes (1)	2	0.01
Alaska Native tribes, not specified	3	0.02
Am. Ind. or Alaska Nat., not spec.	144	0.88
Albanian	23	0.14
American Indian tribes, specified:	379	2.32
Apache (2)	5	0.03
Blackfeet (2)	9	0.06
Cherokee (11)	44	0.27
Cheyenne (2)	5	0.03
Chickasaw (2)	2	0.01
Chippewa (18)	23	0.14
Choctaw (2)	4	0.02
Colville (4)	6	0.04
Cree (1)	2	0.01
Iroquois (2)	3	0.02
Latin American Indians (5)	7	0.04
Lumbee (2)	2	0.01
Navajo (2)	2	0.01
Osage	1	0.01
Paiute (4)	7	0.04
Pima (1)	1	0.01
Pueblo (5)	5	0.03
Puget Sound Salish (1)	1	0.01
Seminole (1)	2	0.01
Shoshone (3)	4	0.02
Sioux (16)	18	0.11
Yakama (18)	18	0.11
Yaqui (2)	3	0.02
All other tribes (159)	205	1.25
American Indian tribes, not spec.	35	0.21
Asian:	210	1.28
Bangladeshi (4)	4	0.02
Cambodian (14)	14	0.09
Chinese, ex. Taiwanese (37)	45	0.28
Filipino (18)	30	0.18
Indian (19)	23	0.14
Japanese (14)	35	0.21
Korean (11)	13	0.08
Laotian	2	0.01
Thai (3)	4	0.02
Vietnamese (9)	12	0.07
Other Asian, not specified (23)	28	0.17
Austrian	39	0.24
Basque	10	0.06
Belgian	34	0.21
British	67	0.41
Canadian	74	0.46
Croatian	5	0.03
Czech	53	0.33
Czechoslovakian	42	0.26
Danish	232	1.43
Dutch	399	2.45
English	1,924	11.83
European	401	2.47
Finnish	42	0.26
French, except Basque	506	3.11

Notes: 1. Figures in the "Number" column do not add up to the total population due to: a) Ancestry/Race overlap — e.g. persons can report being both White and Irish, b) persons of Hispanic origin can report being any race, c) persons reporting two ancestries are counted in both categories. 2. Numbers in parentheses indicate the number of persons reporting this ancestry/race alone, not in combination with any other ancestry/race. 3. Refer to the Explanation of Data in the front of the book for more detailed information.

Ancestry/Race	Number	%
French Canadian	146	0.90
German	2,799	17.21
Greek	38	0.23
Hawaii Native/Pacific Islander:	37	0.23
Micronesian:	2	0.01
Guamanian/Chamorro	2	0.01
Polynesian: (5)	29	0.18
Native Hawaiian (3)	22	0.13
Samoan (2)	6	0.04
Tongan	1	0.01
Other Pac. Isl., not spec. (4)	6	0.04
Hispanic or Latino:	981	6.00
Central American:	10	0.06
Costa Rican	2	0.01
Honduran	2	0.01
Panamanian	1	0.01
Salvadoran	5	0.03
Cuban	2	0.01
Mexican	763	4.67
Puerto Rican	16	0.10
South American:	17	0.10
Argentinean	2	0.01
Chilean	1	0.01
Ecuadorian	4	0.02
Peruvian	6	0.04
Venezuelan	4	0.02
Other Hispanic or Latino	173	1.06
Irish	1,535	9.44
Italian	313	1.92
Lithuanian	8	0.05
Luxemburger	14	0.09
New Zealander	6	0.04
Northern European	49	0.30
Norwegian	509	3.13
Pennsylvania German	11	0.07
Polish	97	0.60
Portuguese	31	0.19
Romanian	21	0.13
Russian	44	0.27
Scandinavian	52	0.32
Scotch-Irish	427	2.63
Scottish	410	2.52
Serbian	8	0.05
Slovak	14	0.09
Swedish	374	2.30
Swiss	23	0.14
Turkish	9	0.06
Ukrainian	15	0.09
United States or American	1,790	11.01
Welsh	96	0.59
West Indian, excl. Hispanic:	53	0.33
Haitian	11	0.07
Other West Indian	42	0.26
White:	14,903	91.13
Not Hispanic (14,247)	14,516	88.76
Hispanic (333)	387	2.37

Portland

Place Type: City
County: Multnomah
Population: 529,121

Ancestry/Race	Number	%
Acadian/Cajun	82	0.02
Afghan	78	0.01
African American/Black:	41,589	7.86
Not Hispanic (34,395)	40,209	7.60
Hispanic (720)	1,380	0.26
African, sub-Saharan:	4,326	0.82
African	2,205	0.42
Cape Verdean	6	0.00
Ethiopian	825	0.16
Ghanian	25	0.00
Kenyan	82	0.02
Liberian	31	0.01
Nigerian	303	0.06
Senegalese	12	0.00
Sierra Leonean	69	0.01
Somalian	390	0.07
South African	86	0.02
Sudanese	22	0.00
Zairian	5	0.00
Other sub-Saharan African	265	0.05
Alaska Native tribes, specified:	391	0.07
Alaska Athabascan (38)	76	0.01
Aleut (44)	69	0.01
Eskimo (54)	84	0.02
Tlingit-Haida (84)	138	0.03
All other tribes (15)	24	0.00
Alaska Native tribes, not specified	23	0.00
Am. Ind. or Alaska Nat., not spec.	3,424	0.65
Albanian	180	0.03
Alsatian	70	0.01
American Indian tribes, specified:	8,272	1.56
Apache (99)	233	0.04
Blackfeet (152)	529	0.10
Cherokee (395)	1,702	0.32
Cheyenne (43)	74	0.01
Chickasaw (23)	59	0.01
Chippewa (282)	539	0.10
Choctaw (85)	311	0.06
Colville (43)	53	0.01
Comanche (5)	32	0.01
Cree (13)	54	0.01
Creek (39)	110	0.02
Crow (8)	16	0.00
Delaware (11)	23	0.00
Houma (9)	10	0.00
Iroquois (70)	171	0.03
Kiowa (13)	26	0.00
Latin American Indians (311)	598	0.11
Lumbee (9)	15	0.00
Menominee (7)	11	0.00
Navajo (103)	184	0.03
Osage (10)	52	0.01
Ottawa (10)	20	0.00
Paiute (21)	48	0.01
Pima (9)	19	0.00
Potawatomi (14)	36	0.01
Pueblo (58)	89	0.02
Puget Sound Salish (60)	87	0.02
Seminole (13)	53	0.01
Shoshone (23)	45	0.01
Sioux (385)	740	0.14
Tohono O'Odham (10)	24	0.00
Ute (14)	31	0.01
Yakama (79)	150	0.03
Yaqui (16)	40	0.01
Yuman (6)	8	0.00
All other tribes (1,221)	2,080	0.39
American Indian tribes, not spec.	468	0.09
Arab:	2,144	0.41
Arab/Arabic	467	0.09
Egyptian	130	0.02
Iraqi	72	0.01
Jordanian	13	0.00
Lebanese	730	0.14
Moroccan	40	0.01
Palestinian	179	0.03
Syrian	353	0.07
Other Arab	160	0.03
Armenian	407	0.08
Asian:	40,844	7.72
Bangladeshi (9)	11	0.00
Cambodian (755)	975	0.18
Chinese, ex. Taiwanese (7,099)	8,613	1.63
Filipino (2,747)	4,262	0.81
Hmong (1,191)	1,342	0.25
Indian (1,479)	2,151	0.41
Indonesian (148)	292	0.06
Japanese (2,731)	4,207	0.80
Korean (1,897)	2,398	0.45
Laotian (2,635)	2,999	0.57
Malaysian (25)	50	0.01
Pakistani (84)	125	0.02
Sri Lankan (42)	58	0.01
Taiwanese (82)	136	0.03
Thai (346)	495	0.09
Vietnamese (10,641)	11,404	2.16
Other Asian, specified (120)	217	0.04
Other Asian, not specified (526)	1,109	0.21
Australian	375	0.07
Austrian	1,985	0.38
Basque	290	0.05
Belgian	644	0.12
Brazilian	227	0.04
British	4,122	0.78
Bulgarian	150	0.03
Canadian	2,088	0.39
Carpatho Rusyn	8	0.00
Celtic	475	0.09
Croatian	1,079	0.20
Cypriot	6	0.00
Czech	2,786	0.53
Czechoslovakian	1,048	0.20
Danish	5,786	1.09
Dutch	10,986	2.08
Eastern European	827	0.16
English	61,707	11.66
Estonian	143	0.03
European	11,371	2.15
Finnish	3,894	0.74
French, except Basque	18,441	3.49
French Canadian	4,456	0.84
German	99,715	18.85
German Russian	176	0.03
Greek	2,452	0.46
Hawaii Native/Pacific Islander:	3,732	0.71
Melanesian: (134)	177	0.03
Fijian (133)	174	0.03
Other Melanesian (1)	3	0.00
Micronesian: (667)	909	0.17
Guamanian/Chamorro (203)	321	0.06
Other Micronesian (464)	588	0.11
Polynesian: (915)	1,740	0.33
Native Hawaiian (326)	944	0.18
Samoan (235)	352	0.07
Tongan (317)	378	0.07
Other Polynesian (37)	66	0.01
Other Pac. Isl., specified	39	0.01
Other Pac. Isl., not spec. (236)	867	0.16
Hispanic or Latino:	36,058	6.81
Central American:	2,051	0.39
Costa Rican	92	0.02
Guatemalan	1,014	0.19
Honduran	203	0.04
Nicaraguan	118	0.02
Panamanian	69	0.01
Salvadoran	469	0.09
Other Central American	86	0.02
Cuban	1,329	0.25
Dominican Republic	47	0.01
Mexican	25,136	4.75
Puerto Rican	1,015	0.19
South American:	935	0.18
Argentinean	97	0.02
Bolivian	42	0.01
Chilean	124	0.02
Colombian	230	0.04
Ecuadorian	85	0.02
Paraguayan	5	0.00
Peruvian	225	0.04
Uruguayan	17	0.00
Venezuelan	55	0.01
Other South American	55	0.01
Other Hispanic or Latino	5,545	1.05
Hungarian	2,231	0.42
Icelander	210	0.04
Iranian	586	0.11
Irish	64,086	12.11
Israeli	129	0.02
Italian	19,810	3.74
Latvian	428	0.08
Lithuanian	1,034	0.20
Luxemburger	216	0.04
Macedonian	111	0.02
Maltese	23	0.00
New Zealander	66	0.01
Northern European	1,466	0.28

Notes: 1. Figures in the "Number" column do not add up to the total population due to: a) Ancestry/Race overlap — e.g. persons can report being both White and Irish, b) persons of Hispanic origin can report being any race, c) persons reporting two ancestries are counted in both categories. 2. Numbers in parentheses indicate the number of persons reporting this ancestry/race alone, not in combination with any other ancestry/race. 3. Refer to the Explanation of Data in the front of the book for more detailed information.

Norwegian	24,064	4.55
Pennsylvania German	299	0.06
Polish	10,042	1.90
Portuguese	1,618	0.31
Romanian	3,711	0.70
Russian	10,303	1.95
Scandinavian	2,471	0.47
Scotch-Irish	11,032	2.09
Scottish	17,002	3.21
Serbian	185	0.03
Slavic	344	0.07
Slovak	544	0.10
Slovene	240	0.05
Swedish	17,378	3.28
Swiss	4,102	0.78
Turkish	149	0.03
Ukrainian	5,867	1.11
United States or American	20,367	3.85
Welsh	6,701	1.27
West Indian, excl. Hispanic:	797	0.15
Bahamian	5	0.00
Barbadian	7	0.00
Belizean	22	0.00
British West Indian	30	0.01
Dutch West Indian	20	0.00
Haitian	219	0.04
Jamaican	305	0.06
Trinidadian and Tobagonian	30	0.01
U.S. Virgin Islander	29	0.01
West Indian	118	0.02
Other West Indian	12	0.00
White:	430,350	81.33
Not Hispanic (399,351)	414,564	78.35
Hispanic (12,890)	15,786	2.98
Yugoslavian	1,286	0.24

Redmond

Place Type: City
County: Deschutes
Population: 13,481

Ancestry/Race	Number	%
African American/Black:	41	0.30
Not Hispanic (11)	33	0.24
Hispanic (1)	8	0.06
Alaska Native tribes, specified:	15	0.11
Alaska Athabascan (1)	2	0.01
Aleut	3	0.02
Tlingit-Haida (10)	10	0.07
Am. Ind. or Alaska Nat., not spec.	66	0.49
American Indian tribes, specified:	213	1.58
Apache	3	0.02
Blackfeet (2)	7	0.05
Cherokee (17)	68	0.50
Chickasaw	2	0.01
Chippewa (1)	5	0.04
Choctaw (2)	6	0.04
Colville (6)	7	0.05
Cree	3	0.02
Creek (1)	3	0.02
Iroquois	1	0.01
Latin American Indians (2)	6	0.04
Navajo (7)	7	0.05
Osage (1)	2	0.01
Seminole	1	0.01
Shoshone	4	0.03
Sioux (6)	12	0.09
Yakama (7)	8	0.06
All other tribes (54)	68	0.50
American Indian tribes, not spec.	10	0.07
Arab:	6	0.04
Other Arab	6	0.04
Asian:	138	1.02
Cambodian	1	0.01
Chinese, ex. Taiwanese (15)	22	0.16
Filipino (24)	46	0.34
Indian (16)	19	0.14
Indonesian	4	0.03
Japanese (14)	20	0.15
Korean (13)	17	0.13
Thai (1)	3	0.02
Vietnamese (2)	3	0.02
Other Asian, not specified (1)	3	0.02
Austrian	25	0.18
Basque	17	0.12
Belgian	16	0.12
Brazilian	14	0.10
British	88	0.64
Canadian	13	0.09
Celtic	12	0.09
Croatian	22	0.16
Czech	75	0.54
Czechoslovakian	21	0.15
Danish	220	1.59
Dutch	484	3.50
English	1,543	11.17
European	116	0.84
Finnish	116	0.84
French, except Basque	709	5.13
French Canadian	288	2.08
German	2,639	19.10
Greek	11	0.08
Guyanese	6	0.04
Hawaii Native/Pacific Islander:	55	0.41
Micronesian: (2)	3	0.02
Guamanian/Chamorro (2)	3	0.02
Polynesian: (9)	41	0.30
Native Hawaiian (6)	25	0.19
Samoan (3)	16	0.12
Other Pac. Isl., not spec. (7)	11	0.08
Hispanic or Latino:	739	5.48
Central American:	8	0.06
Costa Rican	1	0.01
Guatemalan	1	0.01
Nicaraguan	2	0.01
Salvadoran	4	0.03
Dominican Republic	1	0.01
Mexican	574	4.26
Puerto Rican	13	0.10
South American:	6	0.04
Ecuadorian	3	0.02
Peruvian	3	0.02
Other Hispanic or Latino	137	1.02
Hungarian	40	0.29
Irish	1,765	12.78
Italian	611	4.42
Northern European	9	0.07
Norwegian	688	4.98
Pennsylvania German	33	0.24
Polish	174	1.26
Portuguese	62	0.45
Romanian	8	0.06
Russian	62	0.45
Scandinavian	87	0.63
Scotch-Irish	353	2.56
Scottish	600	4.34
Serbian	35	0.25
Slovak	24	0.17
Swedish	339	2.45
Swiss	117	0.85
Ukrainian	9	0.07
United States or American	1,158	8.38
Welsh	87	0.63
West Indian, excl. Hispanic:	6	0.04
West Indian	6	0.04
White:	12,901	95.70
Not Hispanic (12,272)	12,470	92.50
Hispanic (362)	431	3.20

Roseburg

Place Type: City
County: Douglas
Population: 20,017

Ancestry/Race	Number	%
African American/Black:	114	0.57
Not Hispanic (61)	109	0.54
Hispanic	5	0.02
African, sub-Saharan:	6	0.03
Zimbabwean	6	0.03
Alaska Native tribes, specified:	11	0.05
Aleut (3)	3	0.01
Eskimo (5)	5	0.02
Tlingit-Haida	1	0.00
All other tribes	2	0.01
Am. Ind. or Alaska Nat., not spec.	155	0.77
American Indian tribes, specified:	368	1.84
Apache	8	0.04
Blackfeet (4)	12	0.06
Cherokee (43)	139	0.69
Cheyenne	2	0.01
Chickasaw (4)	4	0.02
Chippewa (6)	17	0.08
Choctaw (9)	19	0.09
Comanche	4	0.02
Crow	1	0.00
Delaware (2)	2	0.01
Iroquois	2	0.01
Latin American Indians (3)	8	0.04
Navajo (5)	10	0.05
Osage (1)	2	0.01
Paiute	3	0.01
Potawatomi (4)	7	0.03
Pueblo (2)	2	0.01
Puget Sound Salish (1)	2	0.01
Seminole	1	0.00
Sioux (4)	15	0.07
Yaqui	2	0.01
All other tribes (80)	106	0.53
American Indian tribes, not spec.	24	0.12
Arab:	28	0.14
Syrian	28	0.14
Armenian	8	0.04
Asian:	326	1.63
Cambodian (5)	5	0.02
Chinese, ex. Taiwanese (40)	62	0.31
Filipino (25)	71	0.35
Indian (24)	32	0.16
Japanese (25)	44	0.22
Korean (37)	53	0.26
Pakistani (3)	3	0.01
Sri Lankan (1)	1	0.00
Thai (6)	11	0.05
Vietnamese (25)	27	0.13
Other Asian, specified (1)	2	0.01
Other Asian, not specified (2)	15	0.07
Austrian	46	0.23
Basque	12	0.06
Belgian	27	0.13
British	35	0.17
Canadian	30	0.15
Czech	88	0.44
Czechoslovakian	48	0.24
Danish	219	1.09
Dutch	613	3.06
English	3,100	15.47
European	260	1.30
Finnish	79	0.39
French, except Basque	843	4.21
French Canadian	148	0.74
German	4,017	20.05
German Russian	11	0.05
Greek	96	0.48
Hawaii Native/Pacific Islander:	64	0.32
Micronesian: (2)	11	0.05
Guamanian/Chamorro (2)	10	0.05
Other Micronesian	1	0.00
Polynesian: (16)	43	0.21
Native Hawaiian (10)	34	0.17
Samoan (4)	7	0.03
Other Polynesian (2)	2	0.01
Other Pac. Isl., specified	1	0.00
Other Pac. Isl., not spec. (2)	9	0.04
Hispanic or Latino:	746	3.73
Central American:	12	0.06
Costa Rican	1	0.00
Guatemalan	3	0.01
Honduran	2	0.01

Notes: 1. Figures in the "Number" column do not add up to the total population due to: a) Ancestry/Race overlap — e.g. persons can report being both White and Irish, b) persons of Hispanic origin can report being any race, c) persons reporting two ancestries are counted in both categories. 2. Numbers in parentheses indicate the number of persons reporting this ancestry/race alone, not in combination with any other ancestry/race. 3. Refer to the Explanation of Data in the front of the book for more detailed information.

Ancestry/Race	Number	%
Panamanian	2	0.01
Salvadoran	2	0.01
Other Central American	2	0.01
Cuban	4	0.02
Mexican	524	2.62
Puerto Rican	20	0.10
South American:	11	0.05
Bolivian	1	0.00
Chilean	1	0.00
Colombian	5	0.02
Ecuadorian	2	0.01
Peruvian	1	0.00
Other South American	1	0.00
Other Hispanic or Latino	175	0.87
Hungarian	64	0.32
Irish	2,136	10.66
Italian	490	2.45
Lithuanian	6	0.03
Northern European	12	0.06
Norwegian	931	4.65
Polish	352	1.76
Portuguese	29	0.14
Russian	105	0.52
Scandinavian	115	0.57
Scotch-Irish	562	2.80
Scottish	515	2.57
Slovak	5	0.02
Slovene	9	0.04
Swedish	653	3.26
Swiss	66	0.33
Ukrainian	21	0.10
United States or American	1,404	7.01
Welsh	189	0.94
West Indian, excl. Hispanic:	25	0.12
Dutch West Indian	25	0.12
White:	19,190	95.87
Not Hispanic (18,312)	18,721	93.53
Hispanic (416)	469	2.34
Yugoslavian	36	0.18

Saint Helens

Place Type: City
County: Columbia
Population: 10,019

Ancestry/Race	Number	%
African American/Black:	64	0.64
Not Hispanic (30)	56	0.56
Hispanic (4)	8	0.08
African, sub-Saharan:	10	0.10
African	10	0.10
Alaska Native tribes, specified:	14	0.14
Alaska Athabascan (1)	2	0.02
Aleut (2)	5	0.05
Tlingit-Haida (2)	7	0.07
Alaska Native tribes, not specified	2	0.02
Am. Ind. or Alaska Nat., not spec.	96	0.96
American Indian tribes, specified:	217	2.17
Apache (1)	4	0.04
Blackfeet (4)	9	0.09
Cherokee (17)	54	0.54
Chickasaw (3)	3	0.03
Chippewa (8)	17	0.17
Choctaw (3)	4	0.04
Colville (1)	1	0.01
Creek	1	0.01
Crow	1	0.01
Delaware	2	0.02
Iroquois	1	0.01
Latin American Indians (1)	6	0.06
Navajo (8)	10	0.10
Ottawa	1	0.01
Potawatomi	1	0.01
Pueblo (1)	1	0.01
Puget Sound Salish (1)	5	0.05
Seminole	2	0.02
Shoshone (2)	2	0.02
Sioux (11)	18	0.18
Yakama (1)	3	0.03
All other tribes (49)	71	0.71
American Indian tribes, not spec.	14	0.14
Arab:	13	0.13
Egyptian	5	0.05
Lebanese	8	0.08
Asian:	130	1.30
Cambodian (4)	5	0.05
Chinese, ex. Taiwanese (21)	28	0.28
Filipino (16)	44	0.44
Indian (4)	8	0.08
Japanese (9)	23	0.23
Korean (4)	10	0.10
Thai (2)	7	0.07
Vietnamese (1)	4	0.04
Other Asian, not specified	1	0.01
Basque	7	0.07
Belgian	9	0.09
British	33	0.33
Canadian	22	0.22
Croatian	17	0.17
Czech	37	0.37
Danish	131	1.29
Dutch	375	3.70
Eastern European	6	0.06
English	1,157	11.42
European	65	0.64
Finnish	70	0.69
French, except Basque	518	5.11
French Canadian	124	1.22
German	2,270	22.40
Greek	9	0.09
Hawaii Native/Pacific Islander:	29	0.29
Micronesian: (1)	2	0.02
Guamanian/Chamorro (1)	2	0.02
Polynesian: (9)	19	0.19
Native Hawaiian (8)	16	0.16
Samoan (1)	3	0.03
Other Pac. Isl., not spec. (5)	8	0.08
Hispanic or Latino:	406	4.05
Central American:	9	0.09
Guatemalan	2	0.02
Nicaraguan	1	0.01
Salvadoran	6	0.06
Cuban	8	0.08
Mexican	257	2.57
Puerto Rican	14	0.14
South American:	5	0.05
Chilean	1	0.01
Colombian	3	0.03
Ecuadorian	1	0.01
Other Hispanic or Latino	113	1.13
Hungarian	6	0.06
Irish	1,175	11.59
Italian	268	2.64
Lithuanian	10	0.10
Northern European	7	0.07
Norwegian	499	4.92
Polish	175	1.73
Portuguese	33	0.33
Russian	70	0.69
Scandinavian	116	1.14
Scotch-Irish	210	2.07
Scottish	323	3.19
Slovak	7	0.07
Swedish	450	4.44
Swiss	58	0.57
Ukrainian	2	0.02
United States or American	690	6.81
Welsh	111	1.10
West Indian, excl. Hispanic:	15	0.15
Dutch West Indian	8	0.08
Haitian	7	0.07
White:	9,594	95.76
Not Hispanic (9,107)	9,349	93.31
Hispanic (185)	245	2.45
Yugoslavian	14	0.14

Salem

Place Type: City
County: Marion
Population: 136,924

Ancestry/Race	Number	%
Acadian/Cajun	6	0.00
African American/Black:	2,455	1.79
Not Hispanic (1,621)	2,201	1.61
Hispanic (129)	254	0.19
African, sub-Saharan:	369	0.27
African	273	0.20
Cape Verdean	15	0.01
Ethiopian	29	0.02
Kenyan	10	0.01
Nigerian	36	0.03
Other sub-Saharan African	6	0.00
Alaska Native tribes, specified:	127	0.09
Alaska Athabascan (26)	28	0.02
Aleut (21)	25	0.02
Eskimo (8)	29	0.02
Tlingit-Haida (29)	42	0.03
All other tribes (2)	3	0.00
Alaska Native tribes, not specified	12	0.01
Am. Ind. or Alaska Nat., not spec.	984	0.72
Alsatian	17	0.01
American Indian tribes, specified:	2,568	1.88
Apache (47)	80	0.06
Blackfeet (43)	116	0.08
Cherokee (153)	543	0.40
Cheyenne (10)	28	0.02
Chickasaw (14)	24	0.02
Chippewa (79)	146	0.11
Choctaw (52)	113	0.08
Colville (4)	6	0.00
Comanche (7)	15	0.01
Cree (3)	9	0.01
Creek (23)	37	0.03
Crow (7)	19	0.01
Delaware (3)	8	0.01
Iroquois (18)	53	0.04
Kiowa (6)	15	0.01
Latin American Indians (124)	202	0.15
Lumbee (1)	1	0.00
Menominee (1)	4	0.00
Navajo (30)	42	0.03
Osage (12)	19	0.01
Ottawa	2	0.00
Paiute (5)	11	0.01
Pima (5)	5	0.00
Potawatomi (12)	17	0.01
Pueblo (8)	16	0.01
Puget Sound Salish (2)	6	0.00
Seminole (10)	13	0.01
Shoshone (10)	21	0.02
Sioux (93)	175	0.13
Tohono O'Odham	1	0.00
Yakama (10)	14	0.01
Yaqui (1)	1	0.00
Yuman (1)	1	0.00
All other tribes (575)	805	0.59
American Indian tribes, not spec.	148	0.11
Arab:	325	0.24
Arab/Arabic	91	0.07
Egyptian	35	0.03
Lebanese	43	0.03
Moroccan	8	0.01
Palestinian	14	0.01
Syrian	106	0.08
Other Arab	28	0.02
Armenian	21	0.02
Asian:	4,455	3.25
Bangladeshi (3)	3	0.00
Cambodian (126)	159	0.12
Chinese, ex. Taiwanese (605)	769	0.56
Filipino (392)	730	0.53
Hmong (88)	101	0.07
Indian (273)	344	0.25
Indonesian (12)	20	0.01

Notes: 1. Figures in the "Number" column do not add up to the total population due to: a) Ancestry/Race overlap — e.g. persons can report being both White and Irish, b) persons of Hispanic origin can report being any race, c) persons reporting two ancestries are counted in both categories. 2. Numbers in parentheses indicate the number of persons reporting this ancestry/race alone, not in combination with any other ancestry/race. 3. Refer to the Explanation of Data in the front of the book for more detailed information.

Japanese (464)	732	0.53
Korean (354)	461	0.34
Laotian (148)	181	0.13
Malaysian (3)	10	0.01
Pakistani (2)	4	0.00
Sri Lankan (16)	19	0.01
Taiwanese (14)	15	0.01
Thai (30)	54	0.04
Vietnamese (608)	680	0.50
Other Asian, specified (13)	24	0.02
Other Asian, not specified (66)	149	0.11
Australian	87	0.06
Austrian	292	0.21
Basque	68	0.05
Belgian	131	0.10
Brazilian	7	0.01
British	910	0.67
Bulgarian	94	0.07
Canadian	488	0.36
Celtic	89	0.07
Croatian	159	0.12
Czech	483	0.35
Czechoslovakian	178	0.13
Danish	2,130	1.56
Dutch	3,346	2.45
Eastern European	19	0.01
English	16,443	12.03
European	1,918	1.40
Finnish	491	0.36
French, except Basque	4,672	3.42
French Canadian	927	0.68
German	26,477	19.37
Greek	321	0.23
Hawaii Native/Pacific Islander:	987	0.72
Melanesian: (7)	9	0.01
Fijian (7)	9	0.01
Micronesian: (405)	491	0.36
Guamanian/Chamorro (42)	73	0.05
Other Micronesian (363)	418	0.31
Polynesian: (158)	336	0.25
Native Hawaiian (78)	214	0.16
Samoan (69)	95	0.07
Tongan (7)	14	0.01
Other Polynesian (4)	13	0.01
Other Pac. Isl., specified	4	0.00
Other Pac. Isl., not spec. (61)	147	0.11
Hispanic or Latino:	19,973	14.59
Central American:	310	0.23
Costa Rican	21	0.02
Guatemalan	99	0.07
Honduran	21	0.02
Nicaraguan	26	0.02
Panamanian	6	0.00
Salvadoran	122	0.09
Other Central American	15	0.01
Cuban	102	0.07
Dominican Republic	7	0.01
Mexican	16,636	12.15
Puerto Rican	251	0.18
South American:	125	0.09
Argentinean	14	0.01
Bolivian	11	0.01
Chilean	9	0.01
Colombian	29	0.02
Ecuadorian	12	0.01
Paraguayan	1	0.00
Peruvian	35	0.03
Uruguayan	1	0.00
Venezuelan	6	0.00
Other South American	7	0.01
Other Hispanic or Latino	2,542	1.86
Hungarian	351	0.26
Icelander	19	0.01
Iranian	101	0.07
Irish	13,777	10.08
Israeli	17	0.01
Italian	4,242	3.10
Latvian	52	0.04
Lithuanian	114	0.08
Luxemburger	27	0.02
Maltese	6	0.00
New Zealander	30	0.02
Northern European	213	0.16
Norwegian	5,282	3.86
Pennsylvania German	188	0.14
Polish	2,173	1.59
Portuguese	699	0.51
Romanian	246	0.18
Russian	1,501	1.10
Scandinavian	658	0.48
Scotch-Irish	2,813	2.06
Scottish	3,894	2.85
Serbian	50	0.04
Slavic	68	0.05
Slovak	128	0.09
Slovene	19	0.01
Swedish	3,690	2.70
Swiss	891	0.65
Ukrainian	566	0.41
United States or American	7,837	5.73
Welsh	1,612	1.18
West Indian, excl. Hispanic:	68	0.05
Barbadian	6	0.00
Dutch West Indian	17	0.01
Haitian	19	0.01
Jamaican	26	0.02
White:	117,898	86.10
Not Hispanic (106,331)	109,272	79.80
Hispanic (7,415)	8,626	6.30
Yugoslavian	152	0.11

Sherwood

Place Type: City
County: Washington
Population: 11,791

Ancestry/Race	Number	%
African American/Black:	92	0.78
Not Hispanic (47)	86	0.73
Hispanic (4)	6	0.05
African, sub-Saharan:	5	0.04
South African	5	0.04
Alaska Native tribes, specified:	1	0.01
Aleut (1)	1	0.01
Alaska Native tribes, not specified	1	0.01
Am. Ind. or Alaska Nat., not spec.	39	0.33
American Indian tribes, specified:	95	0.81
Apache	1	0.01
Blackfeet	5	0.04
Cherokee (11)	32	0.27
Chickasaw	1	0.01
Chippewa (4)	6	0.05
Choctaw (7)	8	0.07
Iroquois (1)	2	0.02
Latin American Indians (1)	7	0.06
Navajo (1)	1	0.01
Ottawa (1)	1	0.01
Sioux (3)	8	0.07
Tohono O'Odham (1)	1	0.01
Yakama (1)	1	0.01
Yaqui	1	0.01
All other tribes (5)	20	0.17
American Indian tribes, not spec.	4	0.03
Arab:	49	0.41
Lebanese	49	0.41
Armenian	7	0.06
Asian:	408	3.46
Chinese, ex. Taiwanese (39)	72	0.61
Filipino (42)	73	0.62
Hmong (2)	2	0.02
Indian (27)	37	0.31
Indonesian (2)	2	0.02
Japanese (34)	86	0.73
Korean (43)	57	0.48
Laotian (7)	8	0.07
Pakistani (4)	4	0.03
Sri Lankan (2)	2	0.02
Taiwanese (1)	1	0.01
Thai (1)	1	0.01
Vietnamese (45)	46	0.39
Other Asian, specified (6)	7	0.06
Other Asian, not specified (2)	10	0.08
Austrian	6	0.05
Belgian	23	0.19
British	59	0.49
Canadian	103	0.86
Czech	34	0.28
Czechoslovakian	42	0.35
Danish	98	0.82
Dutch	285	2.38
English	1,992	16.65
European	146	1.22
Finnish	17	0.14
French, except Basque	512	4.28
French Canadian	111	0.93
German	3,207	26.81
Greek	81	0.68
Hawaii Native/Pacific Islander:	32	0.27
Micronesian: (1)	1	0.01
Guamanian/Chamorro (1)	1	0.01
Polynesian: (4)	27	0.23
Native Hawaiian (2)	22	0.19
Samoan (1)	2	0.02
Tongan (1)	3	0.03
Other Pac. Isl., not spec.	4	0.03
Hispanic or Latino:	557	4.72
Central American:	22	0.19
Costa Rican	4	0.03
Guatemalan	6	0.05
Nicaraguan	2	0.02
Panamanian	1	0.01
Salvadoran	7	0.06
Other Central American	2	0.02
Cuban	10	0.08
Mexican	376	3.19
Puerto Rican	18	0.15
South American:	7	0.06
Chilean	1	0.01
Peruvian	2	0.02
Uruguayan	2	0.02
Venezuelan	2	0.02
Other Hispanic or Latino	124	1.05
Hungarian	31	0.26
Irish	2,155	18.01
Italian	744	6.22
Lithuanian	27	0.23
Northern European	51	0.43
Norwegian	625	5.22
Polish	164	1.37
Portuguese	10	0.08
Romanian	39	0.33
Russian	103	0.86
Scandinavian	73	0.61
Scotch-Irish	301	2.52
Scottish	422	3.53
Slovene	25	0.21
Swedish	433	3.62
Swiss	127	1.06
Turkish	5	0.04
Ukrainian	53	0.44
United States or American	866	7.24
Welsh	112	0.94
West Indian, excl. Hispanic:	29	0.24
Dutch West Indian	11	0.09
Jamaican	18	0.15
White:	11,192	94.92
Not Hispanic (10,626)	10,856	92.07
Hispanic (264)	336	2.85
Yugoslavian	17	0.14

Springfield

Place Type: City
County: Lane
Population: 52,864

Ancestry/Race	Number	%
Afghan	6	0.01
African American/Black:	710	1.34

Notes: 1. Figures in the "Number" column do not add up to the total population due to: a) Ancestry/Race overlap — e.g. persons can report being both White and Irish, b) persons of Hispanic origin can report being any race, c) persons reporting two ancestries are counted in both categories. 2. Numbers in parentheses indicate the number of persons reporting this ancestry/race alone, not in combination with any other ancestry/race. 3. Refer to the Explanation of Data in the front of the book for more detailed information.

Ancestry/Race	Number	%
Not Hispanic (356)	642	1.21
Hispanic (18)	68	0.13
African, sub-Saharan:	80	0.15
African	34	0.06
Cape Verdean	32	0.06
South African	6	0.01
Other sub-Saharan African	8	0.02
Alaska Native tribes, specified:	47	0.09
Alaska Athabascan (5)	11	0.02
Aleut (9)	12	0.02
Eskimo (1)	2	0.00
Tlingit-Haida (12)	22	0.04
Alaska Native tribes, not specified	13	0.02
Am. Ind. or Alaska Nat., not spec.	397	0.75
Albanian	20	0.04
American Indian tribes, specified:	1,263	2.39
Apache (9)	32	0.06
Blackfeet (13)	58	0.11
Cherokee (101)	405	0.77
Cheyenne (3)	11	0.02
Chickasaw (2)	11	0.02
Chippewa (15)	52	0.10
Choctaw (28)	74	0.14
Colville	2	0.00
Comanche (4)	10	0.02
Cree (1)	5	0.01
Creek (2)	9	0.02
Crow (1)	1	0.00
Delaware (8)	10	0.02
Iroquois (2)	15	0.03
Kiowa (1)	4	0.01
Latin American Indians (10)	31	0.06
Navajo (9)	10	0.02
Osage (8)	22	0.04
Ottawa (1)	1	0.00
Paiute	6	0.01
Potawatomi (7)	15	0.03
Pueblo (5)	5	0.01
Puget Sound Salish (3)	8	0.02
Seminole (1)	6	0.01
Shoshone (1)	7	0.01
Sioux (16)	48	0.09
Yakama	4	0.01
Yaqui	3	0.01
All other tribes (245)	398	0.75
American Indian tribes, not spec.	64	0.12
Arab:	105	0.20
Arab/Arabic	46	0.09
Jordanian	9	0.02
Lebanese	15	0.03
Moroccan	18	0.03
Palestinian	9	0.02
Other Arab	8	0.02
Asian:	1,033	1.95
Cambodian (11)	16	0.03
Chinese, ex. Taiwanese (74)	122	0.23
Filipino (125)	255	0.48
Indian (67)	116	0.22
Indonesian (7)	23	0.04
Japanese (64)	144	0.27
Korean (81)	120	0.23
Laotian (55)	67	0.13
Malaysian (1)	3	0.01
Pakistani (3)	17	0.03
Taiwanese (2)	2	0.00
Thai (12)	27	0.05
Vietnamese (57)	76	0.14
Other Asian, specified (1)	9	0.02
Other Asian, not specified (15)	36	0.07
Australian	26	0.05
Austrian	87	0.16
Basque	7	0.01
Belgian	62	0.12
Brazilian	29	0.05
British	159	0.30
Canadian	201	0.38
Croatian	30	0.06
Czech	228	0.43
Czechoslovakian	154	0.29
Danish	632	1.20
Dutch	1,328	2.52
English	6,337	12.02
European	805	1.53
Finnish	229	0.43
French, except Basque	2,069	3.92
French Canadian	404	0.77
German	9,830	18.64
Greek	84	0.16
Hawaii Native/Pacific Islander:	295	0.56
Melanesian: (3)	5	0.01
Fijian (3)	5	0.01
Micronesian: (69)	81	0.15
Guamanian/Chamorro (14)	24	0.05
Other Micronesian (55)	57	0.11
Polynesian: (48)	104	0.20
Native Hawaiian (28)	66	0.12
Samoan (13)	31	0.06
Tongan (6)	6	0.01
Other Polynesian (1)	1	0.00
Other Pac. Isl., specified	3	0.01
Other Pac. Isl., not spec. (42)	102	0.19
Hispanic or Latino:	3,651	6.91
Central American:	98	0.19
Costa Rican	7	0.01
Guatemalan	23	0.04
Honduran	9	0.02
Nicaraguan	9	0.02
Panamanian	6	0.01
Salvadoran	41	0.08
Other Central American	3	0.01
Cuban	27	0.05
Dominican Republic	1	0.00
Mexican	2,853	5.40
Puerto Rican	99	0.19
South American:	41	0.08
Argentinean	4	0.01
Chilean	2	0.00
Colombian	12	0.02
Ecuadorian	4	0.01
Peruvian	17	0.03
Venezuelan	2	0.00
Other Hispanic or Latino	532	1.01
Hungarian	96	0.18
Icelander	6	0.01
Iranian	54	0.10
Irish	6,386	12.11
Italian	1,528	2.90
Latvian	32	0.06
Lithuanian	48	0.09
Luxemburger	6	0.01
Northern European	83	0.16
Norwegian	1,773	3.36
Pennsylvania German	45	0.09
Polish	800	1.52
Portuguese	192	0.36
Romanian	37	0.07
Russian	316	0.60
Scandinavian	248	0.47
Scotch-Irish	1,360	2.58
Scottish	1,494	2.83
Slavic	52	0.10
Slovak	36	0.07
Slovene	30	0.06
Swedish	1,403	2.66
Swiss	251	0.48
Ukrainian	171	0.32
United States or American	4,645	8.81
Welsh	621	1.18
West Indian, excl. Hispanic:	64	0.12
Dutch West Indian	22	0.04
Jamaican	40	0.08
West Indian	2	0.00
White:	49,231	93.13
Not Hispanic (45,827)	47,305	89.48
Hispanic (1,559)	1,926	3.64
Yugoslavian	25	0.05

Tigard

Place Type: City
County: Washington
Population: 41,223

Ancestry/Race	Number	%
Acadian/Cajun	20	0.05
African American/Black:	687	1.67
Not Hispanic (443)	629	1.53
Hispanic (25)	58	0.14
African, sub-Saharan:	126	0.31
African	79	0.19
Nigerian	10	0.02
Somalian	28	0.07
South African	9	0.02
Alaska Native tribes, specified:	33	0.08
Alaska Athabascan (5)	5	0.01
Aleut (2)	3	0.01
Eskimo (6)	15	0.04
Tlingit-Haida (3)	6	0.01
All other tribes (2)	4	0.01
Alaska Native tribes, not specified	1	0.00
Am. Ind. or Alaska Nat., not spec.	139	0.34
Albanian	8	0.02
American Indian tribes, specified:	394	0.96
Apache (3)	10	0.02
Blackfeet (1)	18	0.04
Cherokee (26)	84	0.20
Cheyenne	1	0.00
Chickasaw (1)	1	0.00
Chippewa (12)	29	0.07
Choctaw (8)	15	0.04
Colville (4)	6	0.01
Comanche	1	0.00
Creek (2)	3	0.01
Houma (3)	3	0.01
Iroquois (8)	11	0.03
Kiowa	2	0.00
Latin American Indians (9)	21	0.05
Navajo (7)	12	0.03
Osage	8	0.02
Ottawa (3)	3	0.01
Paiute	1	0.00
Pima (1)	1	0.00
Pueblo (2)	3	0.01
Puget Sound Salish (5)	11	0.03
Shoshone (1)	9	0.02
Sioux (5)	10	0.02
Ute	1	0.00
Yakama (1)	9	0.02
Yaqui	12	0.03
All other tribes (63)	109	0.26
American Indian tribes, not spec.	15	0.04
Arab:	221	0.54
Arab/Arabic	38	0.09
Lebanese	89	0.22
Palestinian	37	0.09
Syrian	19	0.05
Other Arab	38	0.09
Armenian	99	0.24
Asian:	2,871	6.96
Cambodian (73)	84	0.20
Chinese, ex. Taiwanese (575)	683	1.66
Filipino (215)	360	0.87
Hmong (5)	7	0.02
Indian (164)	188	0.46
Indonesian (18)	24	0.06
Japanese (252)	412	1.00
Korean (310)	370	0.90
Laotian (23)	34	0.08
Pakistani (2)	2	0.00
Sri Lankan (4)	8	0.02
Taiwanese (16)	20	0.05
Thai (24)	34	0.08
Vietnamese (521)	578	1.40
Other Asian, specified (9)	14	0.03
Other Asian, not specified (19)	53	0.13
Assyrian/Chaldean/Syriac	17	0.04
Australian	42	0.10

Notes: 1. Figures in the "Number" column do not add up to the total population due to: a) Ancestry/Race overlap — e.g. persons can report being both White and Irish, b) persons of Hispanic origin can report being any race, c) persons reporting two ancestries are counted in both categories. 2. Numbers in parentheses indicate the number of persons reporting this ancestry/race alone, not in combination with any other ancestry/race. 3. Refer to the Explanation of Data in the front of the book for more detailed information.

Ancestry/Race	Number	%
Austrian	176	0.43
Basque	22	0.05
Belgian	58	0.14
Brazilian	8	0.02
British	365	0.88
Bulgarian	7	0.02
Canadian	140	0.34
Croatian	22	0.05
Czech	292	0.71
Czechoslovakian	149	0.36
Danish	486	1.18
Dutch	971	2.35
Eastern European	10	0.02
English	5,928	14.37
European	742	1.80
Finnish	220	0.53
French, except Basque	1,423	3.45
French Canadian	288	0.70
German	9,100	22.05
Greek	161	0.39
Hawaii Native/Pacific Islander:	400	0.97
Melanesian: (3)	8	0.02
Fijian (3)	8	0.02
Micronesian: (130)	179	0.43
Guamanian/Chamorro (16)	43	0.10
Other Micronesian (114)	136	0.33
Polynesian: (54)	153	0.37
Native Hawaiian (29)	102	0.25
Samoan (15)	31	0.08
Tongan (7)	12	0.03
Other Polynesian (3)	8	0.02
Other Pac. Isl., not spec. (22)	60	0.15
Hispanic or Latino:	3,686	8.94
Central American:	192	0.47
Costa Rican	14	0.03
Guatemalan	73	0.18
Honduran	11	0.03
Nicaraguan	6	0.01
Panamanian	2	0.00
Salvadoran	79	0.19
Other Central American	7	0.02
Cuban	57	0.14
Dominican Republic	2	0.00
Mexican	2,849	6.91
Puerto Rican	82	0.20
South American:	73	0.18
Argentinean	13	0.03
Bolivian	3	0.01
Chilean	7	0.02
Colombian	9	0.02
Ecuadorian	9	0.02
Peruvian	17	0.04
Venezuelan	14	0.03
Other South American	1	0.00
Other Hispanic or Latino	431	1.05
Hungarian	149	0.36
Iranian	62	0.15
Irish	5,022	12.17
Israeli	7	0.02
Italian	1,399	3.39
Latvian	44	0.11
Lithuanian	42	0.10
Luxemburger	5	0.01
New Zealander	6	0.01
Northern European	190	0.46
Norwegian	1,887	4.57
Pennsylvania German	18	0.04
Polish	774	1.88
Portuguese	360	0.87
Romanian	123	0.30
Russian	390	0.95
Scandinavian	284	0.69
Scotch-Irish	806	1.95
Scottish	1,300	3.15
Serbian	13	0.03
Slavic	7	0.02
Slovak	88	0.21
Slovene	22	0.05
Swedish	1,294	3.14
Swiss	313	0.76
Turkish	28	0.07
Ukrainian	110	0.27
United States or American	2,327	5.64
Welsh	723	1.75
West Indian, excl. Hispanic:	75	0.18
Dutch West Indian	6	0.01
Haitian	17	0.04
Jamaican	31	0.08
West Indian	21	0.05
White:	36,261	87.96
Not Hispanic (33,317)	34,197	82.96
Hispanic (1,878)	2,064	5.01
Yugoslavian	39	0.09

Troutdale

Place Type: City
County: Multnomah
Population: 13,777

Ancestry/Race	Number	%
African American/Black:	358	2.60
Not Hispanic (247)	337	2.45
Hispanic (15)	21	0.15
African, sub-Saharan:	19	0.14
African	5	0.04
Ethiopian	6	0.04
South African	8	0.06
Alaska Native tribes, specified:	19	0.14
Alaska Athabascan (1)	4	0.03
Aleut (3)	7	0.05
Eskimo (1)	5	0.04
Tlingit-Haida (1)	1	0.01
All other tribes	2	0.01
Am. Ind. or Alaska Nat., not spec.	79	0.57
Alsatian	6	0.04
American Indian tribes, specified:	162	1.18
Apache (6)	17	0.12
Blackfeet	7	0.05
Cherokee (8)	26	0.19
Cheyenne (1)	2	0.01
Chippewa (11)	15	0.11
Choctaw	5	0.04
Comanche	6	0.04
Creek	1	0.01
Iroquois (2)	3	0.02
Kiowa (1)	1	0.01
Latin American Indians	7	0.05
Lumbee (1)	1	0.01
Menominee (1)	1	0.01
Navajo (3)	3	0.02
Ottawa	2	0.01
Puget Sound Salish (1)	1	0.01
Seminole	1	0.01
Sioux (7)	16	0.12
All other tribes (35)	47	0.34
American Indian tribes, not spec.	4	0.03
Arab:	29	0.21
Arab/Arabic	8	0.06
Syrian	21	0.15
Asian:	805	5.84
Cambodian (21)	30	0.22
Chinese, ex. Taiwanese (65)	120	0.87
Filipino (46)	103	0.75
Hmong (66)	66	0.48
Indian (23)	25	0.18
Indonesian (2)	3	0.02
Japanese (67)	136	0.99
Korean (50)	59	0.43
Laotian (81)	99	0.72
Malaysian (28)	28	0.20
Pakistani (1)	1	0.01
Taiwanese	1	0.01
Thai (3)	7	0.05
Vietnamese (57)	75	0.54
Other Asian, specified	12	0.09
Other Asian, not specified (31)	40	0.29
Australian	7	0.05
Austrian	72	0.53
Belgian	27	0.20
British	58	0.42
Canadian	35	0.26
Croatian	20	0.15
Czech	111	0.81
Czechoslovakian	70	0.51
Danish	189	1.38
Dutch	288	2.11
English	1,583	11.60
Estonian	28	0.21
European	293	2.15
Finnish	200	1.47
French, except Basque	400	2.93
French Canadian	114	0.84
German	3,453	25.30
Greek	87	0.64
Hawaii Native/Pacific Islander:	95	0.69
Melanesian: (1)	2	0.01
Fijian (1)	2	0.01
Micronesian: (7)	11	0.08
Guamanian/Chamorro (6)	10	0.07
Other Micronesian (1)	1	0.01
Polynesian: (22)	71	0.52
Native Hawaiian (17)	53	0.38
Samoan (4)	13	0.09
Tongan (1)	4	0.03
Other Polynesian	1	0.01
Other Pac. Isl., specified	2	0.01
Other Pac. Isl., not spec. (1)	9	0.07
Hispanic or Latino:	636	4.62
Central American:	27	0.20
Costa Rican	6	0.04
Guatemalan	16	0.12
Honduran	1	0.01
Panamanian	3	0.02
Other Central American	1	0.01
Cuban	7	0.05
Dominican Republic	1	0.01
Mexican	459	3.33
Puerto Rican	22	0.16
South American:	24	0.17
Chilean	4	0.03
Colombian	11	0.08
Ecuadorian	2	0.01
Peruvian	1	0.01
Venezuelan	2	0.01
Other South American	4	0.03
Other Hispanic or Latino	96	0.70
Hungarian	23	0.17
Icelander	7	0.05
Iranian	37	0.27
Irish	1,688	12.37
Italian	581	4.26
Lithuanian	6	0.04
Northern European	49	0.36
Norwegian	715	5.24
Pennsylvania German	6	0.04
Polish	278	2.04
Portuguese	32	0.23
Romanian	64	0.47
Russian	125	0.92
Scandinavian	56	0.41
Scotch-Irish	235	1.72
Scottish	453	3.32
Slovak	8	0.06
Swedish	689	5.05
Swiss	45	0.33
Ukrainian	11	0.08
United States or American	678	4.97
Welsh	146	1.07
White:	12,499	90.72
Not Hispanic (11,752)	12,121	87.98
Hispanic (309)	378	2.74
Yugoslavian	28	0.21

Notes: 1. Figures in the "Number" column do not add up to the total population due to: a) Ancestry/Race overlap — e.g. persons can report being both White and Irish, b) persons of Hispanic origin can report being any race, c) persons reporting two ancestries are counted in both categories. 2. Numbers in parentheses indicate the number of persons reporting this ancestry/race alone, not in combination with any other ancestry/race. 3. Refer to the Explanation of Data in the front of the book for more detailed information.

Tualatin

Place Type: City
County: Washington
Population: 22,791

Ancestry/Race	Number	%
African American/Black:	274	1.20
Not Hispanic (175)	257	1.13
Hispanic (6)	17	0.07
African, sub-Saharan:	8	0.04
African	8	0.04
Alaska Native tribes, specified:	6	0.03
Aleut (3)	3	0.01
Eskimo (1)	2	0.01
Tlingit-Haida	1	0.00
Alaska Native tribes, not specified	2	0.01
Am. Ind. or Alaska Nat., not spec.	62	0.27
Albanian	42	0.19
American Indian tribes, specified:	278	1.22
Apache (1)	2	0.01
Blackfeet (4)	15	0.07
Cherokee (18)	65	0.29
Cheyenne (6)	6	0.03
Chickasaw (3)	8	0.04
Chippewa (5)	11	0.05
Choctaw (4)	18	0.08
Colville	1	0.00
Cree	2	0.01
Delaware	1	0.00
Iroquois (5)	13	0.06
Kiowa (1)	1	0.00
Latin American Indians (20)	32	0.14
Menominee	1	0.00
Navajo (12)	14	0.06
Pima	5	0.02
Pueblo (1)	1	0.00
Puget Sound Salish (1)	3	0.01
Sioux (3)	13	0.06
All other tribes (40)	66	0.29
American Indian tribes, not spec.	13	0.06
Arab:	47	0.21
Arab/Arabic	8	0.04
Lebanese	34	0.15
Palestinian	5	0.02
Asian:	1,113	4.88
Bangladeshi (2)	2	0.01
Cambodian (23)	28	0.12
Chinese, ex. Taiwanese (160)	229	1.00
Filipino (99)	178	0.78
Hmong (13)	16	0.07
Indian (83)	98	0.43
Indonesian (5)	8	0.04
Japanese (137)	199	0.87
Korean (108)	146	0.64
Laotian (16)	20	0.09
Malaysian (1)	2	0.01
Pakistani (7)	11	0.05
Sri Lankan (5)	6	0.03
Taiwanese (11)	15	0.07
Thai (9)	18	0.08
Vietnamese (95)	107	0.47
Other Asian, specified (1)	2	0.01
Other Asian, not specified (18)	28	0.12
Austrian	26	0.12
Basque	11	0.05
Belgian	51	0.23
Brazilian	9	0.04
British	103	0.46
Canadian	110	0.49
Celtic	7	0.03
Croatian	15	0.07
Czech	92	0.41
Czechoslovakian	25	0.11
Danish	344	1.52
Dutch	411	1.82
Eastern European	44	0.19
English	2,867	12.69
European	536	2.37
Finnish	127	0.56
French, except Basque	972	4.30
French Canadian	202	0.89
German	4,600	20.37
Greek	80	0.35
Hawaii Native/Pacific Islander:	146	0.64
Melanesian: (4)	4	0.02
Fijian (4)	4	0.02
Micronesian: (35)	39	0.17
Guamanian/Chamorro (14)	18	0.08
Other Micronesian (21)	21	0.09
Polynesian: (33)	75	0.33
Native Hawaiian (18)	55	0.24
Samoan (13)	17	0.07
Tongan (1)	1	0.00
Other Polynesian (1)	2	0.01
Other Pac. Isl., not spec. (12)	28	0.12
Hispanic or Latino:	2,701	11.85
Central American:	53	0.23
Costa Rican	3	0.01
Guatemalan	15	0.07
Honduran	4	0.02
Nicaraguan	2	0.01
Panamanian	7	0.03
Salvadoran	21	0.09
Other Central American	1	0.00
Cuban	16	0.07
Dominican Republic	2	0.01
Mexican	2,228	9.78
Puerto Rican	48	0.21
South American:	42	0.18
Argentinean	10	0.04
Bolivian	1	0.00
Chilean	18	0.08
Colombian	7	0.03
Ecuadorian	1	0.00
Peruvian	4	0.02
Other South American	1	0.00
Other Hispanic or Latino	312	1.37
Hungarian	87	0.39
Iranian	76	0.34
Irish	2,584	11.44
Italian	812	3.59
Latvian	16	0.07
Lithuanian	17	0.08
Northern European	32	0.14
Norwegian	1,340	5.93
Pennsylvania German	7	0.03
Polish	305	1.35
Portuguese	190	0.84
Romanian	57	0.25
Russian	254	1.12
Scandinavian	198	0.88
Scotch-Irish	615	2.72
Scottish	901	3.99
Serbian	10	0.04
Slavic	7	0.03
Slovak	14	0.06
Slovene	7	0.03
Swedish	765	3.39
Swiss	126	0.56
Turkish	14	0.06
Ukrainian	100	0.44
United States or American	1,129	5.00
Welsh	180	0.80
West Indian, excl. Hispanic:	19	0.08
Dutch West Indian	19	0.08
White:	20,382	89.43
Not Hispanic (18,431)	18,842	82.67
Hispanic (1,372)	1,540	6.76
Yugoslavian	43	0.19

West Linn

Place Type: City
County: Clackamas
Population: 22,261

Ancestry/Race	Number	%
Afghan	9	0.04
African American/Black:	182	0.82
Not Hispanic (118)	177	0.80
Hispanic (2)	5	0.02
African, sub-Saharan:	36	0.16
African	23	0.10
Ghanian	13	0.06
Alaska Native tribes, specified:	9	0.04
Alaska Athabascan (1)	1	0.00
Aleut (2)	2	0.01
Eskimo	3	0.01
Tlingit-Haida (3)	3	0.01
Alaska Native tribes, not specified	1	0.00
Am. Ind. or Alaska Nat., not spec.	29	0.13
Albanian	17	0.08
American Indian tribes, specified:	132	0.59
Blackfeet	3	0.01
Cherokee (10)	35	0.16
Cheyenne	1	0.00
Chickasaw	6	0.03
Chippewa (9)	14	0.06
Choctaw	2	0.01
Colville (1)	1	0.00
Comanche (1)	2	0.01
Cree	2	0.01
Creek (2)	3	0.01
Iroquois	7	0.03
Latin American Indians (1)	1	0.00
Menominee (1)	1	0.00
Navajo (2)	2	0.01
Osage (2)	8	0.04
Paiute (3)	3	0.01
Pueblo	2	0.01
Puget Sound Salish (1)	2	0.01
Sioux (4)	10	0.04
All other tribes (14)	27	0.12
American Indian tribes, not spec.	13	0.06
Arab:	285	1.28
Arab/Arabic	115	0.52
Egyptian	35	0.16
Jordanian	3	0.01
Lebanese	28	0.13
Syrian	77	0.35
Other Arab	27	0.12
Armenian	13	0.06
Asian:	910	4.09
Bangladeshi (3)	3	0.01
Cambodian (7)	9	0.04
Chinese, ex. Taiwanese (146)	220	0.99
Filipino (55)	101	0.45
Indian (60)	71	0.32
Indonesian (4)	13	0.06
Japanese (136)	212	0.95
Korean (128)	163	0.73
Laotian (5)	7	0.03
Malaysian (1)	1	0.00
Pakistani (3)	3	0.01
Sri Lankan (1)	1	0.00
Taiwanese (17)	24	0.11
Thai (21)	21	0.09
Vietnamese (33)	33	0.15
Other Asian, specified (1)	6	0.03
Other Asian, not specified (5)	22	0.10
Assyrian/Chaldean/Syriac	11	0.05
Australian	6	0.03
Austrian	61	0.27
Basque	6	0.03
Belgian	44	0.20
British	260	1.17
Bulgarian	9	0.04
Canadian	100	0.45
Celtic	7	0.03
Croatian	120	0.54
Czech	139	0.62
Czechoslovakian	51	0.23
Danish	241	1.08
Dutch	440	1.97
Eastern European	26	0.12
English	3,507	15.73
European	465	2.09
Finnish	82	0.37
French, except Basque	1,046	4.69

Notes: 1. Figures in the "Number" column do not add up to the total population due to: a) Ancestry/Race overlap — e.g. persons can report being both White and Irish, b) persons of Hispanic origin can report being any race, c) persons reporting two ancestries are counted in both categories. 2. Numbers in parentheses indicate the number of persons reporting this ancestry/race alone, not in combination with any other ancestry/race. 3. Refer to the Explanation of Data in the front of the book for more detailed information.

French Canadian	312	1.40
German	5,954	26.71
German Russian	9	0.04
Greek	172	0.77
Hawaii Native/Pacific Islander:	83	0.37
Micronesian:	5	0.02
Guamanian/Chamorro	4	0.02
Other Micronesian	1	0.00
Polynesian: (11)	44	0.20
Native Hawaiian (6)	33	0.15
Samoan (2)	6	0.03
Tongan (3)	4	0.02
Other Polynesian	1	0.00
Other Pac. Isl., specified	5	0.02
Other Pac. Isl., not spec. (5)	29	0.13
Hispanic or Latino:	638	2.87
Central American:	32	0.14
Costa Rican	3	0.01
Guatemalan	11	0.05
Honduran	4	0.02
Nicaraguan	6	0.03
Panamanian	5	0.02
Salvadoran	3	0.01
Cuban	22	0.10
Mexican	390	1.75
Puerto Rican	25	0.11
South American:	17	0.08
Argentinean	2	0.01
Bolivian	1	0.00
Chilean	2	0.01
Colombian	6	0.03
Ecuadorian	4	0.02
Peruvian	1	0.00
Other South American	1	0.00
Other Hispanic or Latino	152	0.68
Hungarian	64	0.29
Icelander	10	0.04
Iranian	100	0.45
Irish	2,973	13.34
Israeli	32	0.14
Italian	1,245	5.59
Lithuanian	60	0.27
Luxemburger	7	0.03
New Zealander	6	0.03
Northern European	129	0.58
Norwegian	1,194	5.36
Polish	451	2.02
Portuguese	91	0.41
Romanian	26	0.12
Russian	194	0.87
Scandinavian	192	0.86
Scotch-Irish	751	3.37
Scottish	890	3.99
Serbian	8	0.04
Slavic	19	0.09
Slovak	26	0.12
Slovene	14	0.06
Swedish	1,013	4.54
Swiss	218	0.98
Turkish	41	0.18
Ukrainian	46	0.21
United States or American	1,122	5.03
Welsh	323	1.45
West Indian, excl. Hispanic:	30	0.13
Haitian	11	0.05
Jamaican	12	0.05
West Indian	7	0.03
White:	21,196	95.22
Not Hispanic (20,362)	20,718	93.07
Hispanic (413)	478	2.15
Yugoslavian	72	0.32

Wilsonville

Place Type: City
County: Clackamas
Population: 13,991

Ancestry/Race	Number	%
Acadian/Cajun	7	0.05
Afghan	20	0.14
African American/Black:	150	1.07
Not Hispanic (90)	144	1.03
Hispanic (2)	6	0.04
African, sub-Saharan:	10	0.07
African	10	0.07
Alaska Native tribes, specified:	4	0.03
Eskimo (1)	1	0.01
Tlingit-Haida (2)	2	0.01
All other tribes (1)	1	0.01
Am. Ind. or Alaska Nat., not spec.	54	0.39
American Indian tribes, specified:	147	1.05
Apache (3)	3	0.02
Blackfeet	4	0.03
Cherokee (8)	39	0.28
Cheyenne (1)	5	0.04
Chippewa (2)	14	0.10
Choctaw	6	0.04
Colville (2)	2	0.01
Comanche	2	0.01
Creek (1)	1	0.01
Iroquois (2)	8	0.06
Kiowa (1)	1	0.01
Latin American Indians (1)	1	0.01
Navajo (1)	3	0.02
Osage (1)	1	0.01
Pima (2)	2	0.01
Potawatomi (5)	5	0.04
Shoshone	2	0.01
Sioux (7)	15	0.11
Yakama	2	0.01
Yaqui	3	0.02
All other tribes (22)	28	0.20
American Indian tribes, not spec.	6	0.04
Arab:	63	0.45
Arab/Arabic	22	0.16
Lebanese	41	0.29
Armenian	25	0.18
Asian:	449	3.21
Cambodian (3)	4	0.03
Chinese, ex. Taiwanese (69)	103	0.74
Filipino (25)	62	0.44
Hmong (7)	7	0.05
Indian (53)	67	0.48
Indonesian	3	0.02
Japanese (36)	61	0.44
Korean (57)	67	0.48
Laotian (6)	7	0.05
Taiwanese (2)	8	0.06
Thai (5)	6	0.04
Vietnamese (36)	40	0.29
Other Asian, specified (1)	2	0.01
Other Asian, not specified (3)	12	0.09
Austrian	35	0.25
Belgian	8	0.06
British	97	0.70
Canadian	99	0.71
Celtic	11	0.08
Croatian	16	0.12
Czech	94	0.68
Czechoslovakian	31	0.22
Danish	185	1.33
Dutch	349	2.51
English	2,107	15.15
European	246	1.77
Finnish	39	0.28
French, except Basque	549	3.95
French Canadian	76	0.55
German	2,917	20.98
Greek	33	0.24
Hawaii Native/Pacific Islander:	55	0.39
Micronesian: (12)	13	0.09
Guamanian/Chamorro (12)	13	0.09
Polynesian: (9)	29	0.21
Native Hawaiian (7)	24	0.17
Samoan (2)	5	0.04
Other Pac. Isl., not spec. (2)	13	0.09
Hispanic or Latino:	971	6.94
Central American:	47	0.34
Costa Rican	1	0.01
Guatemalan	14	0.10
Nicaraguan	8	0.06
Panamanian	2	0.01
Salvadoran	17	0.12
Other Central American	5	0.04
Cuban	5	0.04
Mexican	717	5.12
Puerto Rican	29	0.21
South American:	24	0.17
Bolivian	2	0.01
Chilean	6	0.04
Colombian	7	0.05
Ecuadorian	2	0.01
Peruvian	5	0.04
Venezuelan	1	0.01
Other South American	1	0.01
Other Hispanic or Latino	149	1.06
Hungarian	36	0.26
Iranian	32	0.23
Irish	1,760	12.66
Italian	701	5.04
Lithuanian	21	0.15
New Zealander	7	0.05
Northern European	22	0.16
Norwegian	608	4.37
Pennsylvania German	8	0.06
Polish	298	2.14
Portuguese	90	0.65
Russian	114	0.82
Scandinavian	76	0.55
Scotch-Irish	361	2.60
Scottish	547	3.93
Swedish	369	2.65
Swiss	101	0.73
Ukrainian	55	0.40
United States or American	960	6.90
Welsh	173	1.24
West Indian, excl. Hispanic:	22	0.16
Jamaican	22	0.16
White:	12,984	92.80
Not Hispanic (12,230)	12,474	89.16
Hispanic (425)	510	3.65

Woodburn

Place Type: City
County: Marion
Population: 20,100

Ancestry/Race	Number	%
African American/Black:	139	0.69
Not Hispanic (60)	90	0.45
Hispanic (30)	49	0.24
African, sub-Saharan:	8	0.04
African	8	0.04
Alaska Native tribes, specified:	9	0.04
Alaska Athabascan (1)	4	0.02
Aleut (1)	1	0.00
Eskimo (2)	2	0.01
Tlingit-Haida (1)	2	0.01
Am. Ind. or Alaska Nat., not spec.	98	0.49
Alsatian	10	0.05
American Indian tribes, specified:	348	1.73
Apache (9)	10	0.05
Blackfeet (2)	11	0.05
Cherokee (13)	35	0.17
Cheyenne (1)	1	0.00
Chippewa (1)	2	0.01
Choctaw (1)	13	0.06
Creek (1)	1	0.00
Iroquois (5)	10	0.05
Latin American Indians (72)	159	0.79
Lumbee (2)	2	0.01
Menominee (1)	1	0.00
Navajo (1)	1	0.00
Osage (2)	3	0.01
Paiute (2)	2	0.01
Pima	1	0.00
Potawatomi	1	0.00
Pueblo (1)	3	0.01

Notes: 1. Figures in the "Number" column do not add up to the total population due to: a) Ancestry/Race overlap — e.g. persons can report being both White and Irish, b) persons of Hispanic origin can report being any race, c) persons reporting two ancestries are counted in both categories. 2. Numbers in parentheses indicate the number of persons reporting this ancestry/race alone, not in combination with any other ancestry/race. 3. Refer to the Explanation of Data in the front of the book for more detailed information.

Puget Sound Salish (2)	7	0.03
Shoshone (2)	2	0.01
Sioux (1)	11	0.05
Tohono O'Odham (12)	14	0.07
Yakama (1)	1	0.00
All other tribes (34)	57	0.28
American Indian tribes, not spec.	10	0.05
Arab:	23	0.11
Arab/Arabic	6	0.03
Lebanese	9	0.04
Other Arab	8	0.04
Asian:	229	1.14
Cambodian	3	0.01
Chinese, ex. Taiwanese (27)	54	0.27
Filipino (17)	42	0.21
Hmong (2)	2	0.01
Indian (19)	26	0.13
Indonesian (1)	2	0.01
Japanese (14)	31	0.15
Korean (16)	18	0.09
Laotian (2)	3	0.01
Malaysian	1	0.00
Taiwanese (1)	1	0.00
Thai (1)	1	0.00
Vietnamese (3)	4	0.02
Other Asian, not specified (2)	41	0.20
Austrian	18	0.09
Basque	31	0.15
Belgian	22	0.11
British	53	0.26
Canadian	11	0.05
Croatian	9	0.04
Czech	23	0.11
Czechoslovakian	21	0.10
Danish	100	0.50
Dutch	283	1.41
English	1,467	7.31
European	121	0.60
Finnish	8	0.04
French, except Basque	345	1.72
French Canadian	127	0.63
German	2,430	12.10
Greek	7	0.03
Hawaii Native/Pacific Islander:	46	0.23
Micronesian: (8)	10	0.05
Guamanian/Chamorro (5)	5	0.02
Other Micronesian (3)	5	0.02
Polynesian: (6)	33	0.16
Native Hawaiian (4)	27	0.13
Samoan (2)	5	0.02
Other Polynesian	1	0.00
Other Pac. Isl., not spec.	3	0.01
Hispanic or Latino:	10,064	50.07
Central American:	81	0.40
Costa Rican	5	0.02
Guatemalan	23	0.11
Honduran	10	0.05
Nicaraguan	2	0.01
Salvadoran	36	0.18
Other Central American	5	0.02
Cuban	11	0.05
Mexican	8,945	44.50
Puerto Rican	26	0.13
South American:	22	0.11
Argentinean	8	0.04
Chilean	6	0.03
Colombian	1	0.00
Ecuadorian	1	0.00
Paraguayan	1	0.00
Peruvian	3	0.01
Uruguayan	1	0.00
Venezuelan	1	0.00
Other Hispanic or Latino	979	4.87
Hungarian	10	0.05
Irish	963	4.80
Italian	180	0.90
Luxemburger	6	0.03
Northern European	63	0.31
Norwegian	346	1.72
Pennsylvania German	18	0.09
Polish	263	1.31
Portuguese	19	0.09
Romanian	4	0.02
Russian	1,006	5.01
Scandinavian	22	0.11
Scotch-Irish	351	1.75
Scottish	172	0.86
Slavic	80	0.40
Swedish	216	1.08
Swiss	149	0.74
Ukrainian	359	1.79
United States or American	838	4.17
Welsh	67	0.33
White:	12,347	61.43
Not Hispanic (9,342)	9,683	48.17
Hispanic (2,340)	2,664	13.25

Abington

Place Type: Township
County: Montgomery
Population: 56,103

Ancestry/Race	Number	%
African American/Black:	6,431	11.46
Not Hispanic (5,992)	6,314	11.25
Hispanic (80)	117	0.21
African, sub-Saharan:	166	0.30
African	139	0.25
Cape Verdean	3	0.01
Nigerian	7	0.01
Sierra Leonean	10	0.02
Somalian	7	0.01
Am. Ind. or Alaska Nat., not spec.	75	0.13
American Indian tribes, specified:	117	0.21
Apache (1)	2	0.00
Blackfeet (2)	5	0.01
Cherokee (5)	52	0.09
Chippewa	1	0.00
Choctaw	1	0.00
Comanche (1)	1	0.00
Cree	5	0.01
Creek	1	0.00
Delaware (1)	15	0.03
Iroquois (1)	4	0.01
Latin American Indians (1)	6	0.01
Lumbee (3)	3	0.01
Seminole (1)	1	0.00
Sioux	4	0.01
Ute	1	0.00
All other tribes (10)	15	0.03
American Indian tribes, not spec.	14	0.02
Arab:	82	0.15
Arab/Arabic	7	0.01
Iraqi	12	0.02
Lebanese	31	0.06
Syrian	7	0.01
Other Arab	25	0.04
Armenian	55	0.10
Asian:	2,038	3.63
Cambodian (14)	15	0.03
Chinese, ex. Taiwanese (297)	328	0.58
Filipino (126)	172	0.31
Indian (194)	220	0.39
Indonesian	2	0.00
Japanese (43)	64	0.11
Korean (943)	988	1.76
Laotian (11)	15	0.03
Malaysian (2)	3	0.01
Pakistani (22)	30	0.05
Taiwanese (10)	10	0.02
Thai (22)	31	0.06
Vietnamese (115)	120	0.21
Other Asian, specified (3)	3	0.01
Other Asian, not specified (20)	37	0.07
Assyrian/Chaldean/Syriac	42	0.07
Australian	25	0.04
Austrian	451	0.80
Basque	18	0.03
Belgian	20	0.04
Brazilian	4	0.01
British	139	0.25
Bulgarian	18	0.03
Canadian	70	0.12
Croatian	40	0.07
Czech	56	0.10
Czechoslovakian	48	0.09
Danish	96	0.17
Dutch	514	0.92
Eastern European	288	0.51
English	5,538	9.87
Estonian	17	0.03
European	411	0.73
Finnish	32	0.06
French, except Basque	762	1.36
French Canadian	182	0.32
German	12,077	21.53
Greek	186	0.33
Guyanese	22	0.04
Hawaii Native/Pacific Islander:	39	0.07
Polynesian: (24)	27	0.05
Native Hawaiian (7)	10	0.02
Samoan (17)	17	0.03
Other Pac. Isl., not spec. (4)	12	0.02
Hispanic or Latino:	883	1.57
Central American:	46	0.08
Costa Rican	1	0.00
Guatemalan	10	0.02
Honduran	8	0.01
Nicaraguan	9	0.02
Panamanian	8	0.01
Salvadoran	10	0.02
Cuban	58	0.10
Dominican Republic	10	0.02
Mexican	114	0.20
Puerto Rican	367	0.65
South American:	134	0.24
Argentinean	35	0.06
Bolivian	1	0.00
Chilean	11	0.02
Colombian	42	0.07
Ecuadorian	8	0.01
Paraguayan	3	0.01
Peruvian	22	0.04
Venezuelan	9	0.02
Other South American	3	0.01
Other Hispanic or Latino	154	0.27
Hungarian	674	1.20
Icelander	8	0.01
Iranian	54	0.10
Irish	14,558	25.95
Israeli	58	0.10
Italian	7,233	12.89
Latvian	85	0.15
Lithuanian	477	0.85
New Zealander	24	0.04
Northern European	23	0.04
Norwegian	236	0.42
Pennsylvania German	194	0.35
Polish	2,809	5.01
Portuguese	111	0.20
Romanian	227	0.40
Russian	2,409	4.29
Scandinavian	20	0.04
Scotch-Irish	988	1.76
Scottish	1,141	2.03
Serbian	6	0.01
Slavic	21	0.04
Slovak	211	0.38
Slovene	16	0.03
Swedish	328	0.58
Swiss	165	0.29
Turkish	10	0.02
Ukrainian	742	1.32
United States or American	2,283	4.07
Welsh	736	1.31
West Indian, excl. Hispanic:	374	0.67
Bahamian	8	0.01
Barbadian	8	0.01
British West Indian	6	0.01

Notes: 1. Figures in the "Number" column do not add up to the total population due to: a) Ancestry/Race overlap — e.g. persons can report being both White and Irish, b) persons of Hispanic origin can report being any race, c) persons reporting two ancestries are counted in both categories. 2. Numbers in parentheses indicate the number of persons reporting this ancestry/race alone, not in combination with any other ancestry/race. 3. Refer to the Explanation of Data in the front of the book for more detailed information.

Haitian	83	0.15
Jamaican	151	0.27
Trinidadian and Tobagonian	118	0.21
White:	47,700	85.02
Not Hispanic (46,689)	47,146	84.03
Hispanic (505)	554	0.99
Yugoslavian	22	0.04

Aliquippa

Place Type: City
County: Beaver
Population: 11,734

Ancestry/Race	Number	%
African American/Black:	4,302	36.66
Not Hispanic (4,151)	4,275	36.43
Hispanic (17)	27	0.23
African, sub-Saharan:	54	0.46
African	54	0.46
Am. Ind. or Alaska Nat., not spec.	31	0.26
Alsatian	8	0.07
American Indian tribes, specified:	18	0.15
Apache (1)	1	0.01
Blackfeet	2	0.02
Cherokee (2)	11	0.09
Iroquois	1	0.01
Latin American Indians	1	0.01
Osage	1	0.01
Seminole	1	0.01
American Indian tribes, not spec.	1	0.01
Arab:	249	2.13
Lebanese	179	1.53
Moroccan	7	0.06
Palestinian	36	0.31
Syrian	16	0.14
Other Arab	11	0.09
Asian:	31	0.26
Chinese, ex. Taiwanese (7)	7	0.06
Filipino (7)	10	0.09
Indian (1)	1	0.01
Japanese (1)	3	0.03
Korean (1)	3	0.03
Malaysian	1	0.01
Vietnamese (4)	4	0.03
Other Asian, not specified	2	0.02
Austrian	26	0.22
British	15	0.13
Canadian	6	0.05
Croatian	181	1.55
Czech	6	0.05
Czechoslovakian	50	0.43
Dutch	54	0.46
English	519	4.45
Finnish	6	0.05
French, except Basque	58	0.50
French Canadian	11	0.09
German	1,491	12.78
Greek	174	1.49
Hawaii Native/Pacific Islander:	8	0.07
Micronesian: (1)	1	0.01
Guamanian/Chamorro (1)	1	0.01
Polynesian: (2)	5	0.04
Native Hawaiian (2)	5	0.04
Other Pac. Isl., not spec. (1)	2	0.02
Hispanic or Latino:	117	1.00
Cuban	12	0.10
Mexican	42	0.36
Puerto Rican	16	0.14
South American:	4	0.03
Peruvian	1	0.01
Venezuelan	2	0.02
Other South American	1	0.01
Other Hispanic or Latino	43	0.37
Hungarian	61	0.52
Irish	1,168	10.01
Italian	2,119	18.16
Lithuanian	19	0.16
Macedonian	7	0.06
New Zealander	4	0.03
Northern European	18	0.15
Norwegian	14	0.12
Pennsylvania German	35	0.30
Polish	465	3.98
Romanian	21	0.18
Russian	89	0.76
Scandinavian	10	0.09
Scotch-Irish	232	1.99
Scottish	91	0.78
Serbian	378	3.24
Slavic	19	0.16
Slovak	527	4.52
Slovene	29	0.25
Swedish	39	0.33
Swiss	20	0.17
Ukrainian	108	0.93
United States or American	356	3.05
Welsh	110	0.94
West Indian, excl. Hispanic:	13	0.11
Jamaican	13	0.11
White:	7,474	63.70
Not Hispanic (7,274)	7,391	62.99
Hispanic (70)	83	0.71
Yugoslavian	31	0.27

Allentown

Place Type: City
County: Lehigh
Population: 106,632

Ancestry/Race	Number	%
Acadian/Cajun	8	0.01
Afghan	4	0.00
African American/Black:	9,901	9.29
Not Hispanic (7,284)	8,200	7.69
Hispanic (1,086)	1,701	1.60
African, sub-Saharan:	583	0.55
African	496	0.47
Ethiopian	15	0.01
Kenyan	18	0.02
Nigerian	26	0.02
Other sub-Saharan African	28	0.03
Alaska Native tribes, specified:	4	0.00
Aleut	3	0.00
Tlingit-Haida	1	0.00
Am. Ind. or Alaska Nat., not spec.	373	0.35
Albanian	116	0.11
Alsatian	6	0.01
American Indian tribes, specified:	311	0.29
Apache (1)	5	0.00
Blackfeet (2)	25	0.02
Cherokee (25)	108	0.10
Chickasaw	3	0.00
Chippewa (2)	5	0.00
Choctaw	2	0.00
Creek	2	0.00
Crow	4	0.00
Delaware (14)	25	0.02
Iroquois (7)	9	0.01
Latin American Indians (28)	53	0.05
Lumbee (3)	3	0.00
Navajo (1)	7	0.01
Ottawa	1	0.00
Pueblo (10)	21	0.02
Seminole	1	0.00
Sioux (7)	16	0.02
Tohono O'Odham (2)	2	0.00
Yaqui	2	0.00
All other tribes (4)	17	0.02
American Indian tribes, not spec.	45	0.04
Arab:	2,638	2.47
Arab/Arabic	524	0.49
Egyptian	167	0.16
Lebanese	239	0.22
Syrian	1,708	1.60
Asian:	2,808	2.63
Bangladeshi (1)	2	0.00
Cambodian (46)	54	0.05
Chinese, ex. Taiwanese (361)	408	0.38
Filipino (120)	177	0.17
Indian (542)	598	0.56
Indonesian (16)	17	0.02
Japanese (37)	70	0.07
Korean (179)	210	0.20
Laotian (4)	6	0.01
Malaysian	3	0.00
Pakistani (35)	47	0.04
Sri Lankan (3)	3	0.00
Taiwanese (10)	12	0.01
Thai (11)	11	0.01
Vietnamese (980)	1,044	0.98
Other Asian, specified (2)	4	0.00
Other Asian, not specified (44)	142	0.13
Austrian	1,461	1.37
Belgian	39	0.04
Brazilian	15	0.01
British	299	0.28
Bulgarian	15	0.01
Canadian	133	0.12
Carpatho Rusyn	14	0.01
Celtic	18	0.02
Croatian	49	0.05
Cypriot	36	0.03
Czech	323	0.30
Czechoslovakian	338	0.32
Danish	64	0.06
Dutch	2,614	2.45
Eastern European	139	0.13
English	3,760	3.53
European	216	0.20
Finnish	24	0.02
French, except Basque	1,318	1.24
French Canadian	278	0.26
German	22,715	21.30
Greek	577	0.54
Guyanese	5	0.00
Hawaii Native/Pacific Islander:	197	0.18
Micronesian: (21)	28	0.03
Guamanian/Chamorro (18)	24	0.02
Other Micronesian (3)	4	0.00
Polynesian: (39)	63	0.06
Native Hawaiian (10)	23	0.02
Samoan (21)	32	0.03
Tongan (7)	7	0.01
Other Polynesian (1)	1	0.00
Other Pac. Isl., specified	1	0.00
Other Pac. Isl., not spec. (18)	105	0.10
Hispanic or Latino:	26,058	24.44
Central American:	498	0.47
Costa Rican	18	0.02
Guatemalan	95	0.09
Honduran	226	0.21
Nicaraguan	12	0.01
Panamanian	40	0.04
Salvadoran	68	0.06
Other Central American	39	0.04
Cuban	237	0.22
Dominican Republic	1,729	1.62
Mexican	1,033	0.97
Puerto Rican	17,682	16.58
South American:	1,185	1.11
Argentinean	9	0.01
Bolivian	11	0.01
Chilean	169	0.16
Colombian	319	0.30
Ecuadorian	349	0.33
Peruvian	234	0.22
Uruguayan	7	0.01
Venezuelan	29	0.03
Other South American	58	0.05
Other Hispanic or Latino	3,694	3.46
Hungarian	2,216	2.08
Iranian	5	0.00
Irish	8,988	8.43
Italian	6,458	6.06
Latvian	19	0.02
Lithuanian	308	0.29
Northern European	14	0.01
Norwegian	269	0.25

Notes: 1. Figures in the "Number" column do not add up to the total population due to: a) Ancestry/Race overlap — e.g. persons can report being both White and Irish, b) persons of Hispanic origin can report being any race, c) persons reporting two ancestries are counted in both categories. 2. Numbers in parentheses indicate the number of persons reporting this ancestry/race alone, not in combination with any other ancestry/race. 3. Refer to the Explanation of Data in the front of the book for more detailed information.

Ancestry/Race	Number	%
Pennsylvania German	5,614	5.26
Polish	3,083	2.89
Portuguese	104	0.10
Romanian	47	0.04
Russian	1,111	1.04
Scandinavian	35	0.03
Scotch-Irish	554	0.52
Scottish	845	0.79
Serbian	33	0.03
Slavic	110	0.10
Slovak	2,639	2.47
Slovene	49	0.05
Swedish	354	0.33
Swiss	239	0.22
Turkish	6	0.01
Ukrainian	1,442	1.35
United States or American	4,617	4.33
Welsh	1,613	1.51
West Indian, excl. Hispanic:	759	0.71
British West Indian	26	0.02
Dutch West Indian	22	0.02
Haitian	37	0.03
Jamaican	502	0.47
Trinidadian and Tobagonian	19	0.02
U.S. Virgin Islander	11	0.01
West Indian	110	0.10
Other West Indian	32	0.03
White:	80,531	75.52
Not Hispanic (68,621)	70,340	65.97
Hispanic (8,740)	10,191	9.56
Yugoslavian	115	0.11

Altoona

Place Type: City
County: Blair
Population: 49,523

Ancestry/Race	Number	%
Acadian/Cajun	11	0.02
African American/Black:	1,464	2.96
Not Hispanic (1,202)	1,419	2.87
Hispanic (29)	45	0.09
African, sub-Saharan:	70	0.14
African	36	0.07
Ethiopian	4	0.01
Nigerian	15	0.03
Other sub-Saharan African	15	0.03
Am. Ind. or Alaska Nat., not spec.	55	0.11
American Indian tribes, specified:	107	0.22
Apache (1)	1	0.00
Blackfeet (1)	16	0.03
Cherokee (11)	36	0.07
Cheyenne	2	0.00
Chippewa (2)	2	0.00
Choctaw	3	0.01
Cree	1	0.00
Delaware	7	0.01
Iroquois (6)	18	0.04
Latin American Indians (1)	1	0.00
Lumbee (1)	1	0.00
Navajo (1)	2	0.00
Pueblo (1)	1	0.00
Sioux (5)	12	0.02
All other tribes (1)	4	0.01
American Indian tribes, not spec.	11	0.02
Arab:	259	0.52
Lebanese	176	0.36
Syrian	83	0.17
Asian:	218	0.44
Cambodian (1)	1	0.00
Chinese, ex. Taiwanese (34)	41	0.08
Filipino (16)	34	0.07
Indian (33)	40	0.08
Japanese (11)	16	0.03
Korean (32)	48	0.10
Laotian (1)	2	0.00
Pakistani (5)	5	0.01
Sri Lankan (2)	2	0.00
Taiwanese	1	0.00
Thai (4)	5	0.01
Vietnamese (7)	9	0.02
Other Asian, specified	1	0.00
Other Asian, not specified (8)	13	0.03
Australian	9	0.02
Austrian	103	0.21
Belgian	11	0.02
Brazilian	16	0.03
British	104	0.21
Bulgarian	9	0.02
Canadian	5	0.01
Celtic	8	0.02
Croatian	62	0.13
Czech	83	0.17
Czechoslovakian	57	0.12
Danish	64	0.13
Dutch	1,137	2.30
English	3,601	7.27
European	93	0.19
Finnish	12	0.02
French, except Basque	883	1.78
French Canadian	76	0.15
German	18,758	37.88
Greek	158	0.32
Hawaii Native/Pacific Islander:	25	0.05
Melanesian: (1)	1	0.00
Other Melanesian (1)	1	0.00
Micronesian: (5)	9	0.02
Guamanian/Chamorro (5)	9	0.02
Polynesian: (1)	5	0.01
Native Hawaiian (1)	3	0.01
Samoan	2	0.00
Other Pac. Isl., specified	1	0.00
Other Pac. Isl., not spec. (1)	9	0.02
Hispanic or Latino:	367	0.74
Central American:	14	0.03
Costa Rican	2	0.00
Guatemalan	2	0.00
Honduran	2	0.00
Nicaraguan	1	0.00
Panamanian	6	0.01
Salvadoran	1	0.00
Cuban	5	0.01
Dominican Republic	9	0.02
Mexican	96	0.19
Puerto Rican	100	0.20
South American:	20	0.04
Argentinean	1	0.00
Chilean	2	0.00
Colombian	3	0.01
Ecuadorian	2	0.00
Peruvian	9	0.02
Uruguayan	1	0.00
Venezuelan	1	0.00
Other South American	1	0.00
Other Hispanic or Latino	123	0.25
Hungarian	189	0.38
Irish	9,031	18.24
Italian	6,589	13.30
Lithuanian	41	0.08
Macedonian	22	0.04
Northern European	12	0.02
Norwegian	80	0.16
Pennsylvania German	557	1.12
Polish	2,262	4.57
Portuguese	5	0.01
Romanian	7	0.01
Russian	177	0.36
Scandinavian	17	0.03
Scotch-Irish	899	1.82
Scottish	722	1.46
Serbian	28	0.06
Slavic	110	0.22
Slovak	268	0.54
Slovene	38	0.08
Swedish	461	0.93
Swiss	86	0.17
Turkish	5	0.01
Ukrainian	100	0.20
United States or American	2,913	5.88
Welsh	495	1.00
West Indian, excl. Hispanic:	21	0.04
Bahamian	7	0.01
Jamaican	14	0.03
White:	47,921	96.77
Not Hispanic (47,342)	47,685	96.29
Hispanic (203)	236	0.48
Yugoslavian	12	0.02

Antrim

Place Type: Township
County: Franklin
Population: 12,504

Ancestry/Race	Number	%
African American/Black:	122	0.98
Not Hispanic (92)	112	0.90
Hispanic (5)	10	0.08
African, sub-Saharan:	4	0.03
African	4	0.03
Am. Ind. or Alaska Nat., not spec.	21	0.17
American Indian tribes, specified:	24	0.19
Blackfeet	2	0.02
Cherokee (4)	6	0.05
Chippewa (1)	1	0.01
Creek (1)	1	0.01
Crow (1)	4	0.03
Iroquois (1)	2	0.02
Latin American Indians (5)	5	0.04
Menominee (1)	1	0.01
Sioux (1)	1	0.01
Ute (1)	1	0.01
American Indian tribes, not spec.	7	0.06
Asian:	61	0.49
Chinese, ex. Taiwanese (1)	3	0.02
Filipino (3)	7	0.06
Indian (8)	8	0.06
Indonesian (2)	2	0.02
Japanese (4)	7	0.06
Korean (12)	17	0.14
Thai (2)	7	0.06
Vietnamese (4)	6	0.05
Other Asian, not specified	4	0.03
Austrian	10	0.08
British	153	1.22
Canadian	15	0.12
Croatian	25	0.20
Czech	25	0.20
Czechoslovakian	22	0.18
Dutch	145	1.16
English	710	5.68
European	55	0.44
French, except Basque	121	0.97
French Canadian	32	0.26
German	4,994	39.94
Hispanic or Latino:	98	0.78
Central American:	5	0.04
Costa Rican	1	0.01
Guatemalan	3	0.02
Honduran	1	0.01
Cuban	1	0.01
Dominican Republic	1	0.01
Mexican	33	0.26
Puerto Rican	36	0.29
South American:	4	0.03
Argentinean	2	0.02
Ecuadorian	2	0.02
Other Hispanic or Latino	18	0.14
Hungarian	35	0.28
Irish	1,383	11.06
Italian	380	3.04
Lithuanian	7	0.06
Norwegian	7	0.06
Pennsylvania German	15	0.12
Polish	164	1.31
Portuguese	15	0.12
Russian	10	0.08
Scotch-Irish	283	2.26
Scottish	234	1.87

Notes: 1. Figures in the "Number" column do not add up to the total population due to: a) Ancestry/Race overlap — e.g. persons can report being both White and Irish, b) persons of Hispanic origin can report being any race, c) persons reporting two ancestries are counted in both categories. 2. Numbers in parentheses indicate the number of persons reporting this ancestry/race alone, not in combination with any other ancestry/race. 3. Refer to the Explanation of Data in the front of the book for more detailed information.

Slovak	41	0.33
Swedish	120	0.96
Swiss	243	1.94
Ukrainian	7	0.06
United States or American	1,689	13.51
Welsh	21	0.17
West Indian, excl. Hispanic:	28	0.22
Haitian	28	0.22
White:	12,306	98.42
Not Hispanic (12,190)	12,246	97.94
Hispanic (53)	60	0.48

Ardmore

Place Type: Census Designated Place
County: Montgomery
Population: 12,616

Ancestry/Race	Number	%
African American/Black:	1,556	12.33
Not Hispanic (1,438)	1,542	12.22
Hispanic (9)	14	0.11
African, sub-Saharan:	158	1.26
African	151	1.20
Nigerian	7	0.06
Am. Ind. or Alaska Nat., not spec.	30	0.24
Albanian	8	0.06
American Indian tribes, specified:	29	0.23
Apache	1	0.01
Blackfeet	1	0.01
Cherokee (2)	11	0.09
Cheyenne	1	0.01
Creek	2	0.02
Delaware	1	0.01
Iroquois	1	0.01
Latin American Indians (4)	7	0.06
Pueblo	1	0.01
Sioux (1)	2	0.02
All other tribes (1)	1	0.01
American Indian tribes, not spec.	1	0.01
Arab:	63	0.50
Egyptian	40	0.32
Lebanese	9	0.07
Palestinian	14	0.11
Armenian	71	0.56
Asian:	366	2.90
Cambodian (4)	4	0.03
Chinese, ex. Taiwanese (118)	131	1.04
Filipino (27)	40	0.32
Indian (71)	75	0.59
Japanese (25)	27	0.21
Korean (45)	49	0.39
Pakistani (1)	1	0.01
Sri Lankan (1)	1	0.01
Taiwanese (4)	5	0.04
Thai (4)	4	0.03
Vietnamese (13)	14	0.11
Other Asian, specified (3)	3	0.02
Other Asian, not specified (7)	12	0.10
Australian	32	0.25
Austrian	91	0.72
British	137	1.09
Canadian	41	0.33
Celtic	11	0.09
Croatian	15	0.12
Czech	50	0.40
Danish	29	0.23
Dutch	175	1.39
Eastern European	108	0.86
English	1,309	10.42
European	196	1.56
Finnish	8	0.06
French, except Basque	307	2.44
French Canadian	21	0.17
German	1,638	13.03
Greek	91	0.72
Hawaii Native/Pacific Islander:	34	0.27
Polynesian: (12)	16	0.13
Native Hawaiian	4	0.03
Samoan (1)	1	0.01
Tongan (11)	11	0.09
Other Pac. Isl., not spec. (4)	18	0.14
Hispanic or Latino:	259	2.05
Central American:	35	0.28
Costa Rican	1	0.01
Guatemalan	5	0.04
Honduran	7	0.06
Panamanian	7	0.06
Salvadoran	11	0.09
Other Central American	4	0.03
Cuban	14	0.11
Dominican Republic	5	0.04
Mexican	53	0.42
Puerto Rican	39	0.31
South American:	52	0.41
Argentinean	12	0.10
Chilean	5	0.04
Colombian	7	0.06
Ecuadorian	5	0.04
Paraguayan	4	0.03
Peruvian	10	0.08
Uruguayan	1	0.01
Venezuelan	3	0.02
Other South American	5	0.04
Other Hispanic or Latino	61	0.48
Hungarian	149	1.19
Iranian	22	0.18
Irish	2,670	21.24
Israeli	41	0.33
Italian	2,304	18.33
Lithuanian	128	1.02
New Zealander	5	0.04
Northern European	70	0.56
Norwegian	147	1.17
Pennsylvania German	34	0.27
Polish	450	3.58
Portuguese	14	0.11
Romanian	59	0.47
Russian	512	4.07
Scandinavian	26	0.21
Scotch-Irish	195	1.55
Scottish	305	2.43
Slavic	17	0.14
Slovak	103	0.82
Slovene	7	0.06
Swedish	248	1.97
Swiss	48	0.38
Turkish	78	0.62
Ukrainian	93	0.74
United States or American	335	2.67
Welsh	241	1.92
West Indian, excl. Hispanic:	220	1.75
British West Indian	18	0.14
Haitian	7	0.06
Jamaican	150	1.19
Trinidadian and Tobagonian	45	0.36
White:	10,669	84.57
Not Hispanic (10,377)	10,480	83.07
Hispanic (159)	189	1.50

Aston

Place Type: Township
County: Delaware
Population: 16,203

Ancestry/Race	Number	%
African American/Black:	265	1.64
Not Hispanic (236)	257	1.59
Hispanic (3)	8	0.05
Am. Ind. or Alaska Nat., not spec.	7	0.04
American Indian tribes, specified:	42	0.26
Apache	1	0.01
Blackfeet	4	0.02
Cherokee	15	0.09
Comanche (1)	1	0.01
Delaware (2)	8	0.05
Iroquois	2	0.01
Latin American Indians	1	0.01
Lumbee (2)	3	0.02
Sioux	1	0.01
All other tribes	6	0.04
American Indian tribes, not spec.	8	0.05
Arab:	41	0.25
Lebanese	41	0.25
Armenian	28	0.17
Asian:	170	1.05
Cambodian	2	0.01
Chinese, ex. Taiwanese (18)	22	0.14
Filipino (16)	32	0.20
Indian (23)	28	0.17
Japanese (9)	19	0.12
Korean (39)	42	0.26
Malaysian	1	0.01
Pakistani (6)	6	0.04
Thai (1)	3	0.02
Vietnamese (7)	8	0.05
Other Asian, not specified (5)	7	0.04
Austrian	59	0.36
Belgian	27	0.17
British	53	0.33
Canadian	9	0.06
Croatian	7	0.04
Czech	35	0.22
Czechoslovakian	13	0.08
Danish	27	0.17
Dutch	211	1.30
English	2,227	13.74
Estonian	6	0.04
European	91	0.56
Finnish	12	0.07
French, except Basque	488	3.01
French Canadian	66	0.41
German	3,507	21.64
Greek	188	1.16
Hawaii Native/Pacific Islander:	8	0.05
Micronesian:	1	0.01
Guamanian/Chamorro	1	0.01
Polynesian: (3)	5	0.03
Native Hawaiian (1)	1	0.01
Samoan (2)	4	0.02
Other Pac. Isl., not spec.	2	0.01
Hispanic or Latino:	163	1.01
Central American:	5	0.03
Honduran	2	0.01
Panamanian	3	0.02
Cuban	20	0.12
Dominican Republic	3	0.02
Mexican	45	0.28
Puerto Rican	51	0.31
South American:	15	0.09
Argentinean	5	0.03
Chilean	1	0.01
Peruvian	5	0.03
Other South American	4	0.02
Other Hispanic or Latino	24	0.15
Hungarian	82	0.51
Iranian	21	0.13
Irish	5,234	32.30
Italian	3,725	22.99
Lithuanian	143	0.88
Norwegian	111	0.69
Pennsylvania German	83	0.51
Polish	1,732	10.69
Romanian	58	0.36
Russian	125	0.77
Scandinavian	13	0.08
Scotch-Irish	218	1.35
Scottish	170	1.05
Serbian	28	0.17
Slavic	14	0.09
Slovak	166	1.02
Swedish	141	0.87
Swiss	59	0.36
Ukrainian	312	1.93
United States or American	541	3.34
Welsh	296	1.83
West Indian, excl. Hispanic:	8	0.05
West Indian	8	0.05
White:	15,770	97.33

Notes: 1. Figures in the "Number" column do not add up to the total population due to: a) Ancestry/Race overlap — e.g. persons can report being both White and Irish, b) persons of Hispanic origin can report being any race, c) persons reporting two ancestries are counted in both categories. 2. Numbers in parentheses indicate the number of persons reporting this ancestry/race alone, not in combination with any other ancestry/race. 3. Refer to the Explanation of Data in the front of the book for more detailed information.

Ancestry/Race	Number	%
Not Hispanic (15,561)	15,662	96.66
Hispanic (101)	108	0.67
Yugoslavian	57	0.35

Back Mountain

Place Type: Census Designated Place
County: Luzerne
Population: 26,690

Ancestry/Race	Number	%
African American/Black:	1,170	4.38
Not Hispanic (1,133)	1,153	4.32
Hispanic (15)	17	0.06
African, sub-Saharan:	13	0.05
Kenyan	13	0.05
Am. Ind. or Alaska Nat., not spec.	24	0.09
American Indian tribes, specified:	28	0.10
Apache	1	0.00
Cherokee (2)	9	0.03
Cheyenne (2)	2	0.01
Chippewa	1	0.00
Creek (1)	1	0.00
Delaware (2)	2	0.01
Iroquois	1	0.00
Osage	1	0.00
Puget Sound Salish (3)	3	0.01
All other tribes (4)	7	0.03
American Indian tribes, not spec.	2	0.01
Arab:	262	0.98
Arab/Arabic	5	0.02
Egyptian	15	0.06
Lebanese	130	0.49
Syrian	112	0.42
Asian:	171	0.64
Cambodian (1)	1	0.00
Chinese, ex. Taiwanese (19)	25	0.09
Filipino (14)	17	0.06
Indian (48)	57	0.21
Indonesian	1	0.00
Japanese (4)	9	0.03
Korean (32)	34	0.13
Laotian (7)	7	0.03
Malaysian (2)	2	0.01
Thai (1)	1	0.00
Vietnamese (3)	4	0.01
Other Asian, not specified (8)	13	0.05
Austrian	252	0.94
Brazilian	3	0.01
British	60	0.22
Canadian	1	0.00
Carpatho Rusyn	8	0.03
Celtic	32	0.12
Croatian	55	0.21
Czech	78	0.29
Czechoslovakian	43	0.16
Danish	23	0.09
Dutch	589	2.21
Eastern European	17	0.06
English	2,829	10.60
European	35	0.13
French, except Basque	470	1.76
French Canadian	36	0.13
German	4,961	18.59
Greek	130	0.49
Guyanese	2	0.01
Hawaii Native/Pacific Islander:	8	0.03
Polynesian: (4)	5	0.02
Native Hawaiian (4)	5	0.02
Other Pac. Isl., not spec. (1)	3	0.01
Hispanic or Latino:	281	1.05
Central American:	2	0.01
Panamanian	2	0.01
Cuban	16	0.06
Dominican Republic	1	0.00
Mexican	27	0.10
Puerto Rican	107	0.40
South American:	6	0.02
Chilean	1	0.00
Colombian	4	0.01
Ecuadorian	1	0.00
Other Hispanic or Latino	122	0.46
Hungarian	155	0.58
Iranian	32	0.12
Irish	4,109	15.39
Italian	2,774	10.39
Latvian	14	0.05
Lithuanian	775	2.90
New Zealander	8	0.03
Northern European	28	0.10
Norwegian	115	0.43
Pennsylvania German	317	1.19
Polish	4,970	18.62
Portuguese	20	0.07
Romanian	12	0.04
Russian	647	2.42
Scotch-Irish	242	0.91
Scottish	456	1.71
Serbian	24	0.09
Slavic	48	0.18
Slovak	1,135	4.25
Slovene	19	0.07
Swedish	135	0.51
Swiss	52	0.19
Ukrainian	344	1.29
United States or American	922	3.45
Welsh	2,247	8.42
White:	25,322	94.87
Not Hispanic (25,012)	25,101	94.05
Hispanic (197)	221	0.83
Yugoslavian	2	0.01

Baldwin

Place Type: Borough
County: Allegheny
Population: 19,999

Ancestry/Race	Number	%
African American/Black:	540	2.70
Not Hispanic (474)	527	2.64
Hispanic (9)	13	0.07
African, sub-Saharan:	144	0.72
African	60	0.30
Ghanian	10	0.05
Other sub-Saharan African	74	0.37
Am. Ind. or Alaska Nat., not spec.	12	0.06
Albanian	28	0.14
American Indian tribes, specified:	18	0.09
Blackfeet (1)	6	0.03
Cherokee (3)	4	0.02
Cheyenne	1	0.01
Delaware	1	0.01
Iroquois (1)	1	0.01
Latin American Indians (1)	2	0.01
Pima	1	0.01
Seminole	1	0.01
Sioux (1)	1	0.01
American Indian tribes, not spec.	3	0.02
Arab:	97	0.49
Lebanese	31	0.16
Syrian	66	0.33
Asian:	136	0.68
Chinese, ex. Taiwanese (36)	41	0.21
Filipino (16)	24	0.12
Indian (12)	17	0.09
Japanese (2)	4	0.02
Korean (5)	6	0.03
Pakistani (1)	1	0.01
Thai (1)	1	0.01
Vietnamese (35)	41	0.21
Other Asian, not specified	1	0.01
Australian	4	0.02
Austrian	86	0.43
Belgian	12	0.06
British	31	0.16
Canadian	14	0.07
Croatian	239	1.20
Czech	88	0.44
Czechoslovakian	86	0.43
Dutch	127	0.64
English	1,372	6.86
European	77	0.39
French, except Basque	358	1.79
German	7,125	35.63
Greek	102	0.51
Guyanese	10	0.05
Hawaii Native/Pacific Islander:	1	0.01
Polynesian: (1)	1	0.01
Samoan (1)	1	0.01
Hispanic or Latino:	129	0.65
Central American:	4	0.02
Guatemalan	1	0.01
Honduran	2	0.01
Salvadoran	1	0.01
Cuban	7	0.04
Dominican Republic	3	0.02
Mexican	58	0.29
Puerto Rican	10	0.05
South American:	11	0.06
Argentinean	1	0.01
Chilean	2	0.01
Ecuadorian	1	0.01
Uruguayan	1	0.01
Venezuelan	6	0.03
Other Hispanic or Latino	36	0.18
Hungarian	445	2.23
Iranian	16	0.08
Irish	4,237	21.19
Italian	3,395	16.98
Lithuanian	153	0.77
Norwegian	6	0.03
Pennsylvania German	14	0.07
Polish	2,777	13.89
Romanian	7	0.04
Russian	237	1.19
Scandinavian	21	0.11
Scotch-Irish	402	2.01
Scottish	209	1.05
Serbian	142	0.71
Slavic	35	0.18
Slovak	1,017	5.09
Slovene	122	0.61
Swedish	151	0.76
Swiss	60	0.30
Ukrainian	355	1.78
United States or American	717	3.59
Welsh	337	1.69
White:	19,351	96.76
Not Hispanic (19,159)	19,247	96.24
Hispanic (80)	104	0.52
Yugoslavian	48	0.24

Bensalem

Place Type: Township
County: Bucks
Population: 58,434

Ancestry/Race	Number	%
African American/Black:	4,337	7.42
Not Hispanic (3,937)	4,195	7.18
Hispanic (110)	142	0.24
African, sub-Saharan:	653	1.12
African	414	0.71
Ethiopian	6	0.01
Ghanian	21	0.04
Liberian	165	0.28
Nigerian	47	0.08
Alaska Native tribes, specified:	1	0.00
Alaska Athabascan (1)	1	0.00
Am. Ind. or Alaska Nat., not spec.	142	0.24
Albanian	51	0.09
American Indian tribes, specified:	192	0.33
Apache (2)	3	0.01
Blackfeet (2)	8	0.01
Cherokee (20)	66	0.11
Chickasaw (1)	1	0.00
Choctaw	1	0.00
Comanche	1	0.00

Notes: 1. Figures in the "Number" column do not add up to the total population due to: a) Ancestry/Race overlap — e.g. persons can report being both White and Irish, b) persons of Hispanic origin can report being any race, c) persons reporting two ancestries are counted in both categories. 2. Numbers in parentheses indicate the number of persons reporting this ancestry/race alone, not in combination with any other ancestry/race. 3. Refer to the Explanation of Data in the front of the book for more detailed information.

Ancestry/Race	Number	%
Creek (1)	1	0.00
Delaware (6)	14	0.02
Iroquois (4)	15	0.03
Latin American Indians (3)	9	0.02
Lumbee (7)	15	0.03
Menominee	1	0.00
Navajo (2)	2	0.00
Osage (1)	1	0.00
Paiute (1)	1	0.00
Pueblo (2)	6	0.01
Seminole (1)	1	0.00
Shoshone	1	0.00
Sioux (3)	19	0.03
All other tribes (17)	26	0.04
American Indian tribes, not spec.	11	0.02
Arab:	242	0.41
Arab/Arabic	81	0.14
Egyptian	82	0.14
Iraqi	31	0.05
Jordanian	8	0.01
Lebanese	21	0.04
Palestinian	8	0.01
Syrian	11	0.02
Armenian	136	0.23
Asian:	4,230	7.24
Bangladeshi (13)	18	0.03
Cambodian (13)	17	0.03
Chinese, ex. Taiwanese (305)	359	0.61
Filipino (277)	337	0.58
Indian (2,438)	2,570	4.40
Indonesian (2)	5	0.01
Japanese (44)	69	0.12
Korean (432)	461	0.79
Laotian (1)	1	0.00
Pakistani (104)	121	0.21
Sri Lankan (5)	5	0.01
Taiwanese (12)	20	0.03
Thai (17)	24	0.04
Vietnamese (120)	139	0.24
Other Asian, specified (1)	4	0.01
Other Asian, not specified (36)	80	0.14
Assyrian/Chaldean/Syriac	10	0.02
Australian	10	0.02
Austrian	375	0.64
Basque	35	0.06
Brazilian	8	0.01
British	116	0.20
Bulgarian	15	0.03
Canadian	99	0.17
Celtic	20	0.03
Croatian	32	0.05
Czech	135	0.23
Czechoslovakian	106	0.18
Danish	60	0.10
Dutch	504	0.86
Eastern European	197	0.34
English	4,823	8.25
Estonian	6	0.01
European	218	0.37
French, except Basque	950	1.63
French Canadian	82	0.14
German	11,903	20.37
Greek	274	0.47
Guyanese	61	0.10
Hawaii Native/Pacific Islander:	62	0.11
Micronesian: (10)	11	0.02
Guamanian/Chamorro (9)	10	0.02
Other Micronesian (1)	1	0.00
Polynesian: (10)	25	0.04
Native Hawaiian (9)	18	0.03
Samoan (1)	7	0.01
Other Pac. Isl., specified	3	0.01
Other Pac. Isl., not spec. (10)	23	0.04
Hispanic or Latino:	2,505	4.29
Central American:	157	0.27
Costa Rican	21	0.04
Guatemalan	99	0.17
Honduran	3	0.01
Nicaraguan	1	0.00
Panamanian	9	0.02
Salvadoran	21	0.04
Other Central American	3	0.01
Cuban	77	0.13
Dominican Republic	39	0.07
Mexican	911	1.56
Puerto Rican	739	1.26
South American:	205	0.35
Argentinean	12	0.02
Colombian	52	0.09
Ecuadorian	87	0.15
Peruvian	33	0.06
Uruguayan	2	0.00
Venezuelan	10	0.02
Other South American	9	0.02
Other Hispanic or Latino	377	0.65
Hungarian	410	0.70
Iranian	32	0.05
Irish	14,153	24.22
Israeli	36	0.06
Italian	8,186	14.01
Latvian	49	0.08
Lithuanian	444	0.76
New Zealander	14	0.02
Norwegian	167	0.29
Pennsylvania German	310	0.53
Polish	5,149	8.81
Portuguese	233	0.40
Romanian	163	0.28
Russian	1,874	3.21
Scandinavian	8	0.01
Scotch-Irish	590	1.01
Scottish	986	1.69
Serbian	7	0.01
Slavic	42	0.07
Slovak	192	0.33
Slovene	5	0.01
Swedish	219	0.37
Swiss	84	0.14
Turkish	58	0.10
Ukrainian	1,487	2.54
United States or American	1,998	3.42
Welsh	486	0.83
West Indian, excl. Hispanic:	224	0.38
Barbadian	29	0.05
Jamaican	151	0.26
U.S. Virgin Islander	6	0.01
West Indian	38	0.07
White:	49,180	84.16
Not Hispanic (47,165)	47,751	81.72
Hispanic (1,278)	1,429	2.45
Yugoslavian	49	0.08

Berwick

Place Type: Borough
County: Columbia
Population: 10,774

Ancestry/Race	Number	%
African American/Black:	131	1.22
Not Hispanic (88)	117	1.09
Hispanic (7)	14	0.13
Am. Ind. or Alaska Nat., not spec.	32	0.30
American Indian tribes, specified:	17	0.16
Apache	1	0.01
Blackfeet (1)	1	0.01
Cherokee (6)	7	0.06
Chickasaw (1)	1	0.01
Delaware	1	0.01
Iroquois	3	0.03
Latin American Indians	2	0.02
All other tribes (1)	1	0.01
American Indian tribes, not spec.	6	0.06
Arab:	17	0.16
Lebanese	17	0.16
Asian:	62	0.58
Chinese, ex. Taiwanese (7)	7	0.06
Filipino (7)	8	0.07
Indian (17)	18	0.17
Japanese	6	0.06
Korean (3)	3	0.03
Laotian (1)	1	0.01
Vietnamese (10)	10	0.09
Other Asian, specified	7	0.06
Other Asian, not specified	2	0.02
Australian	7	0.07
Austrian	24	0.22
British	71	0.66
Celtic	8	0.07
Croatian	17	0.16
Czech	50	0.47
Czechoslovakian	35	0.33
Dutch	1,035	9.67
English	543	5.07
French, except Basque	139	1.30
French Canadian	7	0.07
German	2,716	25.38
Greek	21	0.20
Hawaii Native/Pacific Islander:	13	0.12
Polynesian: (4)	4	0.04
Native Hawaiian (1)	1	0.01
Samoan (3)	3	0.03
Other Pac. Isl., specified	7	0.06
Other Pac. Isl., not spec. (1)	2	0.02
Hispanic or Latino:	175	1.62
Central American:	28	0.26
Costa Rican	2	0.02
Guatemalan	1	0.01
Panamanian	1	0.01
Salvadoran	24	0.22
Cuban	2	0.02
Mexican	23	0.21
Puerto Rican	73	0.68
South American:	7	0.06
Colombian	3	0.03
Peruvian	4	0.04
Other Hispanic or Latino	42	0.39
Hungarian	103	0.96
Irish	1,136	10.62
Italian	1,447	13.52
Lithuanian	9	0.08
Norwegian	37	0.35
Pennsylvania German	556	5.20
Polish	613	5.73
Romanian	12	0.11
Russian	110	1.03
Scotch-Irish	55	0.51
Scottish	93	0.87
Serbian	24	0.22
Slavic	32	0.30
Slovak	140	1.31
Swedish	58	0.54
Swiss	7	0.07
Ukrainian	387	3.62
United States or American	938	8.77
Welsh	223	2.08
White:	10,520	97.64
Not Hispanic (10,379)	10,432	96.83
Hispanic (83)	88	0.82
Yugoslavian	8	0.07

Bethel Park

Place Type: Borough
County: Allegheny
Population: 33,556

Ancestry/Race	Number	%
African American/Black:	417	1.24
Not Hispanic (340)	412	1.23
Hispanic (3)	5	0.01
African, sub-Saharan:	28	0.08
African	28	0.08
Alaska Native tribes, specified:	1	0.00
Aleut (1)	1	0.00
Am. Ind. or Alaska Nat., not spec.	24	0.07
American Indian tribes, specified:	29	0.09
Blackfeet	2	0.01
Cherokee	12	0.04
Chippewa (1)	1	0.00

Notes: 1. Figures in the "Number" column do not add up to the total population due to: a) Ancestry/Race overlap — e.g. persons can report being both White and Irish, b) persons of Hispanic origin can report being any race, c) persons reporting two ancestries are counted in both categories. 2. Numbers in parentheses indicate the number of persons reporting this ancestry/race alone, not in combination with any other ancestry/race. 3. Refer to the Explanation of Data in the front of the book for more detailed information.

Choctaw (2)	2	0.01
Creek (1)	1	0.00
Iroquois	3	0.01
Latin American Indians	1	0.00
Sioux (1)	2	0.01
All other tribes (3)	5	0.01
American Indian tribes, not spec.	3	0.01
Arab:	265	0.79
Egyptian	13	0.04
Lebanese	110	0.33
Syrian	136	0.41
Other Arab	6	0.02
Armenian	18	0.05
Asian:	475	1.42
Bangladeshi (5)	5	0.01
Chinese, ex. Taiwanese (80)	107	0.32
Filipino (14)	28	0.08
Indian (181)	205	0.61
Indonesian (1)	1	0.00
Japanese (20)	22	0.07
Korean (43)	47	0.14
Pakistani (6)	8	0.02
Thai (3)	9	0.03
Vietnamese (11)	23	0.07
Other Asian, specified (1)	3	0.01
Other Asian, not specified	17	0.05
Assyrian/Chaldean/Syriac	6	0.02
Austrian	268	0.80
Belgian	38	0.11
Brazilian	6	0.02
British	132	0.39
Bulgarian	32	0.10
Canadian	14	0.04
Carpatho Rusyn	20	0.06
Croatian	374	1.11
Czech	251	0.75
Czechoslovakian	150	0.45
Danish	25	0.07
Dutch	154	0.46
Eastern European	20	0.06
English	3,404	10.14
European	136	0.41
Finnish	39	0.12
French, except Basque	775	2.31
French Canadian	33	0.10
German	10,717	31.94
Greek	274	0.82
Hawaii Native/Pacific Islander:	19	0.06
Micronesian:	2	0.01
Guamanian/Chamorro	1	0.00
Other Micronesian	1	0.00
Polynesian: (6)	8	0.02
Native Hawaiian (5)	6	0.02
Samoan (1)	2	0.01
Other Pac. Isl., specified	1	0.00
Other Pac. Isl., not spec. (3)	8	0.02
Hispanic or Latino:	164	0.49
Central American:	17	0.05
Costa Rican	3	0.01
Guatemalan	4	0.01
Honduran	1	0.00
Panamanian	5	0.01
Salvadoran	1	0.00
Other Central American	3	0.01
Cuban	15	0.04
Dominican Republic	2	0.01
Mexican	56	0.17
Puerto Rican	19	0.06
South American:	17	0.05
Bolivian	4	0.01
Chilean	1	0.00
Colombian	2	0.01
Peruvian	9	0.03
Venezuelan	1	0.00
Other Hispanic or Latino	38	0.11
Hungarian	582	1.73
Irish	7,599	22.65
Italian	5,705	17.00
Latvian	6	0.02
Lithuanian	358	1.07
Northern European	15	0.04
Norwegian	83	0.25
Pennsylvania German	40	0.12
Polish	3,162	9.42
Portuguese	59	0.18
Romanian	42	0.13
Russian	466	1.39
Scandinavian	43	0.13
Scotch-Irish	1,069	3.19
Scottish	731	2.18
Serbian	310	0.92
Slavic	66	0.20
Slovak	1,398	4.17
Slovene	159	0.47
Swedish	245	0.73
Swiss	99	0.30
Ukrainian	438	1.31
United States or American	1,117	3.33
Welsh	567	1.69
West Indian, excl. Hispanic:	7	0.02
Jamaican	7	0.02
White:	32,758	97.62
Not Hispanic (32,463)	32,628	97.23
Hispanic (121)	130	0.39
Yugoslavian	56	0.17

Bethlehem

Place Type: City
County: Northampton
Population: 71,329

Ancestry/Race	Number	%
African American/Black:	3,207	4.50
Not Hispanic (2,244)	2,627	3.68
Hispanic (352)	580	0.81
African, sub-Saharan:	222	0.31
African	138	0.19
Ethiopian	9	0.01
Nigerian	28	0.04
Sudanese	5	0.01
Other sub-Saharan African	42	0.06
Alaska Native tribes, specified:	1	0.00
Eskimo (1)	1	0.00
Am. Ind. or Alaska Nat., not spec.	223	0.31
Albanian	32	0.04
Alsatian	7	0.01
American Indian tribes, specified:	188	0.26
Apache	2	0.00
Blackfeet (7)	21	0.03
Cherokee (9)	52	0.07
Chippewa	2	0.00
Choctaw	1	0.00
Comanche	1	0.00
Cree (1)	1	0.00
Creek	2	0.00
Delaware (3)	15	0.02
Iroquois (3)	6	0.01
Kiowa	2	0.00
Latin American Indians (35)	58	0.08
Lumbee (3)	3	0.00
Navajo	2	0.00
Pueblo (1)	2	0.00
Sioux (4)	6	0.01
Ute	2	0.00
All other tribes (6)	10	0.01
American Indian tribes, not spec.	27	0.04
Arab:	559	0.78
Arab/Arabic	105	0.15
Egyptian	43	0.06
Jordanian	8	0.01
Lebanese	199	0.28
Moroccan	4	0.01
Syrian	150	0.21
Other Arab	50	0.07
Armenian	24	0.03
Asian:	1,835	2.57
Cambodian (2)	2	0.00
Chinese, ex. Taiwanese (441)	483	0.68
Filipino (98)	119	0.17
Indian (440)	483	0.68
Indonesian (6)	16	0.02
Japanese (43)	78	0.11
Korean (210)	231	0.32
Laotian (1)	1	0.00
Malaysian (1)	1	0.00
Pakistani (18)	25	0.04
Sri Lankan (11)	12	0.02
Taiwanese (21)	31	0.04
Thai (39)	47	0.07
Vietnamese (200)	219	0.31
Other Asian, specified (3)	7	0.01
Other Asian, not specified (27)	80	0.11
Australian	68	0.10
Austrian	758	1.06
Basque	4	0.01
Belgian	25	0.04
Brazilian	92	0.13
British	334	0.47
Canadian	114	0.16
Carpatho Rusyn	4	0.01
Celtic	63	0.09
Croatian	114	0.16
Czech	274	0.38
Czechoslovakian	210	0.29
Danish	93	0.13
Dutch	1,878	2.63
Eastern European	61	0.09
English	3,830	5.37
Estonian	30	0.04
European	361	0.51
Finnish	42	0.06
French, except Basque	1,121	1.57
French Canadian	194	0.27
German	15,846	22.22
Greek	625	0.88
Guyanese	25	0.04
Hawaii Native/Pacific Islander:	103	0.14
Micronesian: (1)	3	0.00
Guamanian/Chamorro (1)	3	0.00
Polynesian: (10)	20	0.03
Native Hawaiian (5)	13	0.02
Samoan (5)	7	0.01
Other Pac. Isl., specified	4	0.01
Other Pac. Isl., not spec. (13)	76	0.11
Hispanic or Latino:	13,002	18.23
Central American:	180	0.25
Costa Rican	6	0.01
Guatemalan	74	0.10
Honduran	11	0.02
Nicaraguan	27	0.04
Panamanian	15	0.02
Salvadoran	42	0.06
Other Central American	5	0.01
Cuban	118	0.17
Dominican Republic	231	0.32
Mexican	728	1.02
Puerto Rican	10,096	14.15
South American:	340	0.48
Argentinean	19	0.03
Bolivian	5	0.01
Chilean	29	0.04
Colombian	145	0.20
Ecuadorian	78	0.11
Paraguayan	1	0.00
Peruvian	37	0.05
Uruguayan	1	0.00
Venezuelan	15	0.02
Other South American	10	0.01
Other Hispanic or Latino	1,309	1.84
Hungarian	2,907	4.08
Iranian	8	0.01
Irish	8,556	12.00
Israeli	24	0.03
Italian	6,705	9.40
Latvian	14	0.02
Lithuanian	256	0.36
Northern European	18	0.03
Norwegian	306	0.43
Pennsylvania German	2,437	3.42

Notes: 1. Figures in the "Number" column do not add up to the total population due to: a) Ancestry/Race overlap — e.g. persons can report being both White and Irish, b) persons of Hispanic origin can report being any race, c) persons reporting two ancestries are counted in both categories. 2. Numbers in parentheses indicate the number of persons reporting this ancestry/race alone, not in combination with any other ancestry/race. 3. Refer to the Explanation of Data in the front of the book for more detailed information.

Ancestry/Race	Number	%
Polish	3,260	4.57
Portuguese	658	0.92
Romanian	93	0.13
Russian	604	0.85
Scandinavian	19	0.03
Scotch-Irish	809	1.13
Scottish	782	1.10
Serbian	57	0.08
Slavic	120	0.17
Slovak	2,830	3.97
Slovene	264	0.37
Swedish	528	0.74
Swiss	206	0.29
Turkish	214	0.30
Ukrainian	947	1.33
United States or American	2,250	3.15
Welsh	1,411	1.98
West Indian, excl. Hispanic:	99	0.14
Bahamian	9	0.01
Barbadian	4	0.01
British West Indian	7	0.01
Haitian	9	0.01
Jamaican	41	0.06
Trinidadian and Tobagonian	25	0.04
U.S. Virgin Islander	4	0.01
White:	59,866	83.93
Not Hispanic (53,408)	54,147	75.91
Hispanic (4,974)	5,719	8.02
Yugoslavian	262	0.37

Bethlehem

Place Type: Township
County: Northampton
Population: 21,171

Ancestry/Race	Number	%
African American/Black:	569	2.69
Not Hispanic (496)	540	2.55
Hispanic (20)	29	0.14
African, sub-Saharan:	8	0.04
African	8	0.04
Am. Ind. or Alaska Nat., not spec.	14	0.07
Albanian	7	0.03
American Indian tribes, specified:	30	0.14
Cherokee (4)	15	0.07
Choctaw	2	0.01
Creek	1	0.00
Delaware (1)	1	0.00
Iroquois	2	0.01
Latin American Indians (1)	1	0.00
Lumbee (4)	4	0.02
Navajo (1)	1	0.00
Sioux (1)	2	0.01
All other tribes (1)	1	0.00
American Indian tribes, not spec.	4	0.02
Arab:	170	0.80
Arab/Arabic	15	0.07
Egyptian	17	0.08
Lebanese	84	0.40
Syrian	54	0.26
Armenian	13	0.06
Asian:	523	2.47
Cambodian (1)	1	0.00
Chinese, ex. Taiwanese (62)	64	0.30
Filipino (41)	47	0.22
Indian (207)	226	1.07
Indonesian (2)	2	0.01
Japanese (15)	24	0.11
Korean (33)	36	0.17
Pakistani (4)	7	0.03
Sri Lankan	1	0.00
Taiwanese (13)	13	0.06
Thai (4)	6	0.03
Vietnamese (76)	80	0.38
Other Asian, not specified (4)	16	0.08
Austrian	203	0.96
Belgian	7	0.03
Brazilian	11	0.05
British	64	0.30
Canadian	53	0.25
Croatian	63	0.30
Czech	92	0.43
Czechoslovakian	109	0.51
Danish	38	0.18
Dutch	746	3.52
Eastern European	18	0.09
English	1,610	7.60
European	76	0.36
Finnish	7	0.03
French, except Basque	395	1.87
French Canadian	169	0.80
German	5,758	27.20
Greek	236	1.11
Guyanese	8	0.04
Hawaii Native/Pacific Islander:	7	0.03
Polynesian: (1)	2	0.01
Samoan (1)	2	0.01
Other Pac. Isl., not spec. (1)	5	0.02
Hispanic or Latino:	840	3.97
Central American:	31	0.15
Costa Rican	6	0.03
Guatemalan	12	0.06
Honduran	3	0.01
Nicaraguan	4	0.02
Panamanian	1	0.00
Salvadoran	2	0.01
Other Central American	3	0.01
Cuban	48	0.23
Dominican Republic	20	0.09
Mexican	67	0.32
Puerto Rican	498	2.35
South American:	62	0.29
Argentinean	4	0.02
Chilean	5	0.02
Colombian	32	0.15
Ecuadorian	10	0.05
Paraguayan	2	0.01
Peruvian	1	0.00
Venezuelan	3	0.01
Other South American	5	0.02
Other Hispanic or Latino	114	0.54
Hungarian	1,262	5.96
Iranian	72	0.34
Irish	3,236	15.29
Italian	3,778	17.85
Lithuanian	189	0.89
Norwegian	135	0.64
Pennsylvania German	550	2.60
Polish	1,616	7.63
Portuguese	177	0.84
Russian	284	1.34
Scandinavian	29	0.14
Scotch-Irish	156	0.74
Scottish	346	1.63
Slavic	75	0.35
Slovak	870	4.11
Slovene	43	0.20
Swedish	80	0.38
Swiss	39	0.18
Turkish	48	0.23
Ukrainian	321	1.52
United States or American	768	3.63
Welsh	338	1.60
White:	19,907	94.03
Not Hispanic (19,195)	19,326	91.29
Hispanic (552)	581	2.74
Yugoslavian	50	0.24

Bloomsburg

Place Type: Town
County: Columbia
Population: 12,375

Ancestry/Race	Number	%
African American/Black:	374	3.02
Not Hispanic (299)	345	2.79
Hispanic (23)	29	0.23
African, sub-Saharan:	55	0.44
African	55	0.44
Am. Ind. or Alaska Nat., not spec.	27	0.22
American Indian tribes, specified:	27	0.22
Blackfeet	3	0.02
Cherokee (3)	8	0.06
Chippewa (2)	2	0.02
Choctaw	2	0.02
Creek	3	0.02
Delaware (1)	1	0.01
Iroquois (2)	3	0.02
Latin American Indians (1)	2	0.02
Navajo	1	0.01
All other tribes (1)	2	0.02
American Indian tribes, not spec.	7	0.06
Arab:	28	0.22
Lebanese	12	0.10
Syrian	16	0.13
Asian:	168	1.36
Bangladeshi (1)	1	0.01
Chinese, ex. Taiwanese (28)	29	0.23
Filipino (18)	21	0.17
Indian (25)	32	0.26
Japanese (7)	8	0.06
Korean (15)	17	0.14
Pakistani (1)	6	0.05
Thai (1)	5	0.04
Vietnamese (21)	22	0.18
Other Asian, specified (4)	4	0.03
Other Asian, not specified (9)	23	0.19
Austrian	66	0.53
Belgian	32	0.26
British	42	0.34
Canadian	77	0.62
Celtic	9	0.07
Czech	5	0.04
Czechoslovakian	24	0.19
Danish	6	0.05
Dutch	574	4.61
Eastern European	14	0.11
English	825	6.63
Finnish	16	0.13
French, except Basque	200	1.61
French Canadian	9	0.07
German	3,602	28.94
Greek	28	0.22
Hawaii Native/Pacific Islander:	19	0.15
Polynesian: (4)	6	0.05
Native Hawaiian (1)	1	0.01
Samoan (3)	5	0.04
Other Pac. Isl., not spec. (1)	13	0.11
Hispanic or Latino:	215	1.74
Central American:	4	0.03
Costa Rican	3	0.02
Other Central American	1	0.01
Cuban	6	0.05
Dominican Republic	2	0.02
Mexican	30	0.24
Puerto Rican	81	0.65
South American:	19	0.15
Bolivian	1	0.01
Chilean	4	0.03
Colombian	4	0.03
Ecuadorian	2	0.02
Peruvian	7	0.06
Venezuelan	1	0.01
Other Hispanic or Latino	73	0.59
Hungarian	63	0.51
Irish	1,998	16.05
Italian	951	7.64
Lithuanian	120	0.96
Northern European	11	0.09
Norwegian	52	0.42
Pennsylvania German	194	1.56
Polish	918	7.37
Romanian	26	0.21
Russian	92	0.74
Scandinavian	6	0.05
Scotch-Irish	119	0.96
Scottish	195	1.57
Slovak	153	1.23

Notes: 1. Figures in the "Number" column do not add up to the total population due to: a) Ancestry/Race overlap — e.g. persons can report being both White and Irish, b) persons of Hispanic origin can report being any race, c) persons reporting two ancestries are counted in both categories. 2. Numbers in parentheses indicate the number of persons reporting this ancestry/race alone, not in combination with any other ancestry/race. 3. Refer to the Explanation of Data in the front of the book for more detailed information.

Swedish	80	0.64
Swiss	22	0.18
Ukrainian	38	0.31
United States or American	640	5.14
Welsh	178	1.43
West Indian, excl. Hispanic:	41	0.33
Dutch West Indian	7	0.06
Jamaican	24	0.19
Trinidadian and Tobagonian	10	0.08
White:	11,764	95.06
Not Hispanic (11,583)	11,653	94.17
Hispanic (101)	111	0.90
Yugoslavian	9	0.07

Brentwood

Place Type: Borough
County: Allegheny
Population: 10,466

Ancestry/Race	Number	%
African American/Black:	75	0.72
Not Hispanic (54)	72	0.69
Hispanic (2)	3	0.03
Am. Ind. or Alaska Nat., not spec.	9	0.09
American Indian tribes, specified:	32	0.31
Blackfeet	4	0.04
Cherokee (8)	15	0.14
Cheyenne (1)	1	0.01
Chippewa (1)	1	0.01
Houma (3)	3	0.03
Iroquois (1)	2	0.02
Pueblo (4)	4	0.04
All other tribes (2)	2	0.02
American Indian tribes, not spec.	2	0.02
Arab:	63	0.60
Jordanian	16	0.15
Lebanese	38	0.36
Syrian	9	0.09
Asian:	70	0.67
Chinese, ex. Taiwanese (14)	19	0.18
Filipino (8)	12	0.11
Indian (11)	12	0.11
Japanese (2)	2	0.02
Korean (10)	11	0.11
Malaysian (1)	2	0.02
Vietnamese (11)	11	0.11
Other Asian, not specified	1	0.01
Austrian	76	0.73
Belgian	8	0.08
Carpatho Rusyn	9	0.09
Croatian	90	0.86
Czech	14	0.13
Czechoslovakian	23	0.22
Dutch	16	0.15
Eastern European	21	0.20
English	512	4.89
French, except Basque	207	1.98
German	4,205	40.18
Greek	57	0.54
Hawaii Native/Pacific Islander:	6	0.06
Micronesian: (1)	1	0.01
Other Micronesian (1)	1	0.01
Polynesian:	5	0.05
Native Hawaiian	5	0.05
Hispanic or Latino:	72	0.69
Central American:	7	0.07
Guatemalan	1	0.01
Honduran	1	0.01
Other Central American	5	0.05
Cuban	3	0.03
Mexican	16	0.15
Puerto Rican	11	0.11
South American:	9	0.09
Bolivian	1	0.01
Colombian	5	0.05
Peruvian	2	0.02
Uruguayan	1	0.01
Other Hispanic or Latino	26	0.25
Hungarian	197	1.88
Irish	2,933	28.02
Italian	1,611	15.39
Lithuanian	113	1.08
Norwegian	25	0.24
Pennsylvania German	17	0.16
Polish	1,310	12.52
Russian	77	0.74
Scotch-Irish	325	3.11
Scottish	151	1.44
Serbian	95	0.91
Slavic	23	0.22
Slovak	433	4.14
Slovene	45	0.43
Swedish	57	0.54
Swiss	31	0.30
Ukrainian	249	2.38
United States or American	288	2.75
Welsh	174	1.66
White:	10,299	98.40
Not Hispanic (10,192)	10,237	97.81
Hispanic (59)	62	0.59

Bristol

Place Type: Township
County: Bucks
Population: 55,521

Ancestry/Race	Number	%
African American/Black:	5,035	9.07
Not Hispanic (4,562)	4,865	8.76
Hispanic (128)	170	0.31
African, sub-Saharan:	408	0.73
African	296	0.53
Liberian	72	0.13
Sierra Leonean	12	0.02
Other sub-Saharan African	28	0.05
Alaska Native tribes, specified:	6	0.01
Alaska Athabascan (2)	6	0.01
Am. Ind. or Alaska Nat., not spec.	141	0.25
Albanian	15	0.03
American Indian tribes, specified:	162	0.29
Apache	4	0.01
Blackfeet (4)	17	0.03
Cherokee (23)	47	0.08
Chickasaw	1	0.00
Chippewa	1	0.00
Choctaw	3	0.01
Creek (4)	4	0.01
Delaware (3)	10	0.02
Iroquois (14)	32	0.06
Latin American Indians (6)	11	0.02
Lumbee (1)	3	0.01
Navajo (1)	5	0.01
Pueblo	1	0.00
Seminole (2)	6	0.01
Sioux (6)	10	0.02
All other tribes (2)	7	0.01
American Indian tribes, not spec.	22	0.04
Arab:	75	0.14
Lebanese	10	0.02
Moroccan	38	0.07
Syrian	17	0.03
Other Arab	10	0.02
Armenian	34	0.06
Asian:	1,437	2.59
Bangladeshi (3)	4	0.01
Cambodian (44)	48	0.09
Chinese, ex. Taiwanese (111)	142	0.26
Filipino (186)	257	0.46
Indian (618)	670	1.21
Indonesian	1	0.00
Japanese (19)	43	0.08
Korean (126)	156	0.28
Laotian	1	0.00
Malaysian	2	0.00
Pakistani (8)	9	0.02
Sri Lankan (2)	3	0.01
Taiwanese (5)	5	0.01
Thai (7)	16	0.03
Vietnamese (39)	43	0.08
Other Asian, specified (3)	3	0.01
Other Asian, not specified (10)	34	0.06
Austrian	175	0.32
Belgian	9	0.02
British	234	0.42
Bulgarian	19	0.03
Canadian	22	0.04
Carpatho Rusyn	23	0.04
Celtic	19	0.03
Croatian	38	0.07
Czech	178	0.32
Czechoslovakian	97	0.17
Danish	66	0.12
Dutch	775	1.40
Eastern European	13	0.02
English	5,153	9.28
Estonian	20	0.04
European	137	0.25
Finnish	12	0.02
French, except Basque	1,129	2.03
French Canadian	163	0.29
German	13,502	24.31
Greek	193	0.35
Guyanese	25	0.05
Hawaii Native/Pacific Islander:	42	0.08
Micronesian: (13)	19	0.03
Guamanian/Chamorro (13)	19	0.03
Polynesian: (3)	6	0.01
Native Hawaiian (1)	4	0.01
Samoan (2)	2	0.00
Other Pac. Isl., not spec. (5)	17	0.03
Hispanic or Latino:	2,139	3.85
Central American:	52	0.09
Costa Rican	30	0.05
Guatemalan	6	0.01
Honduran	3	0.01
Nicaraguan	6	0.01
Panamanian	5	0.01
Salvadoran	2	0.00
Cuban	41	0.07
Dominican Republic	28	0.05
Mexican	440	0.79
Puerto Rican	1,203	2.17
South American:	87	0.16
Argentinean	11	0.02
Bolivian	1	0.00
Chilean	2	0.00
Colombian	44	0.08
Ecuadorian	8	0.01
Peruvian	9	0.02
Venezuelan	1	0.00
Other South American	11	0.02
Other Hispanic or Latino	288	0.52
Hungarian	573	1.03
Iranian	46	0.08
Irish	15,737	28.33
Italian	8,685	15.64
Latvian	16	0.03
Lithuanian	453	0.82
Luxemburger	8	0.01
Norwegian	129	0.23
Pennsylvania German	235	0.42
Polish	4,974	8.96
Portuguese	69	0.12
Romanian	88	0.16
Russian	674	1.21
Scandinavian	11	0.02
Scotch-Irish	903	1.63
Scottish	989	1.78
Serbian	13	0.02
Slavic	82	0.15
Slovak	417	0.75
Slovene	38	0.07
Swedish	366	0.66
Swiss	77	0.14
Turkish	108	0.19
Ukrainian	679	1.22
United States or American	1,709	3.08
Welsh	634	1.14

Notes: 1. Figures in the "Number" column do not add up to the total population due to: a) Ancestry/Race overlap — e.g. persons can report being both White and Irish, b) persons of Hispanic origin can report being any race, c) persons reporting two ancestries are counted in both categories. 2. Numbers in parentheses indicate the number of persons reporting this ancestry/race alone, not in combination with any other ancestry/race. 3. Refer to the Explanation of Data in the front of the book for more detailed information.

West Indian, excl. Hispanic:	112	0.20
Belizean	9	0.02
British West Indian	24	0.04
Haitian	16	0.03
Jamaican	31	0.06
West Indian	32	0.06
White:	48,483	87.32
Not Hispanic (46,737)	47,297	85.19
Hispanic (1,081)	1,186	2.14
Yugoslavian	30	0.05

Broomall

Place Type: Census Designated Place
County: Delaware
Population: 11,046

Ancestry/Race	Number	%
Afghan	9	0.08
African American/Black:	81	0.73
Not Hispanic (70)	81	0.73
African, sub-Saharan:	5	0.04
Ethiopian	5	0.04
Am. Ind. or Alaska Nat., not spec.	6	0.05
American Indian tribes, specified:	17	0.15
Blackfeet	3	0.03
Cherokee	8	0.07
Iroquois (1)	1	0.01
All other tribes (2)	5	0.05
American Indian tribes, not spec.	3	0.03
Arab:	70	0.63
Lebanese	38	0.34
Syrian	32	0.29
Armenian	109	0.98
Asian:	826	7.48
Bangladeshi (5)	5	0.05
Chinese, ex. Taiwanese (164)	176	1.59
Filipino (12)	18	0.16
Indian (135)	138	1.25
Indonesian	4	0.04
Japanese (3)	5	0.05
Korean (418)	426	3.86
Laotian	1	0.01
Pakistani (5)	5	0.05
Sri Lankan (1)	1	0.01
Taiwanese	4	0.04
Thai (5)	5	0.05
Vietnamese (25)	26	0.24
Other Asian, not specified (8)	12	0.11
Australian	6	0.05
Austrian	65	0.58
British	25	0.22
Canadian	6	0.05
Celtic	6	0.05
Croatian	6	0.05
Czech	38	0.34
Czechoslovakian	27	0.24
Danish	7	0.06
Dutch	152	1.36
English	983	8.80
Estonian	7	0.06
European	48	0.43
French, except Basque	234	2.09
French Canadian	11	0.10
German	1,706	15.27
Greek	475	4.25
Hawaii Native/Pacific Islander:	5	0.05
Other Pac. Isl., not spec.	5	0.05
Hispanic or Latino:	69	0.62
Cuban	5	0.05
Mexican	6	0.05
Puerto Rican	20	0.18
South American:	20	0.18
Argentinean	5	0.05
Bolivian	2	0.02
Colombian	1	0.01
Ecuadorian	3	0.03
Peruvian	1	0.01
Uruguayan	5	0.05
Venezuelan	3	0.03
Other Hispanic or Latino	18	0.16
Hungarian	111	0.99
Iranian	32	0.29
Irish	3,186	28.51
Italian	3,064	27.42
Latvian	15	0.13
Lithuanian	65	0.58
Norwegian	17	0.15
Pennsylvania German	23	0.21
Polish	357	3.19
Portuguese	13	0.12
Romanian	58	0.52
Russian	260	2.33
Scotch-Irish	106	0.95
Scottish	50	0.45
Serbian	12	0.11
Slovak	59	0.53
Slovene	9	0.08
Swedish	37	0.33
Swiss	34	0.30
Ukrainian	74	0.66
United States or American	434	3.88
Welsh	60	0.54
West Indian, excl. Hispanic:	3	0.03
Jamaican	3	0.03
White:	10,149	91.88
Not Hispanic (10,041)	10,093	91.37
Hispanic (56)	56	0.51

Buckingham

Place Type: Township
County: Bucks
Population: 16,442

Ancestry/Race	Number	%
Afghan	6	0.04
African American/Black:	207	1.26
Not Hispanic (166)	197	1.20
Hispanic (5)	10	0.06
African, sub-Saharan:	27	0.16
Nigerian	27	0.16
Am. Ind. or Alaska Nat., not spec.	19	0.12
Albanian	7	0.04
American Indian tribes, specified:	27	0.16
Blackfeet	2	0.01
Cherokee (3)	6	0.04
Delaware (4)	5	0.03
Iroquois (1)	1	0.01
Latin American Indians	1	0.01
Puget Sound Salish (3)	3	0.02
Sioux	2	0.01
All other tribes (3)	7	0.04
Arab:	45	0.27
Arab/Arabic	24	0.15
Iraqi	9	0.05
Lebanese	12	0.07
Armenian	107	0.65
Asian:	234	1.42
Cambodian (1)	1	0.01
Chinese, ex. Taiwanese (70)	80	0.49
Filipino (22)	30	0.18
Indian (46)	51	0.31
Indonesian (1)	1	0.01
Japanese (2)	3	0.02
Korean (25)	28	0.17
Taiwanese (10)	10	0.06
Thai (1)	1	0.01
Vietnamese (10)	11	0.07
Other Asian, specified	4	0.02
Other Asian, not specified (6)	14	0.09
Assyrian/Chaldean/Syriac	37	0.23
Austrian	197	1.20
British	94	0.57
Canadian	76	0.46
Croatian	7	0.04
Czech	105	0.64
Czechoslovakian	61	0.37
Danish	41	0.25
Dutch	214	1.30
Eastern European	101	0.61
English	2,420	14.72
European	177	1.08
Finnish	36	0.22
French, except Basque	368	2.24
French Canadian	55	0.33
German	4,059	24.69
Greek	191	1.16
Hawaii Native/Pacific Islander:	11	0.07
Micronesian: (1)	1	0.01
Guamanian/Chamorro (1)	1	0.01
Polynesian: (1)	2	0.01
Native Hawaiian	1	0.01
Samoan (1)	1	0.01
Other Pac. Isl., specified	4	0.02
Other Pac. Isl., not spec.	4	0.02
Hispanic or Latino:	220	1.34
Central American:	7	0.04
Guatemalan	1	0.01
Salvadoran	6	0.04
Cuban	35	0.21
Dominican Republic	1	0.01
Mexican	41	0.25
Puerto Rican	56	0.34
South American:	25	0.15
Argentinean	8	0.05
Colombian	8	0.05
Ecuadorian	5	0.03
Peruvian	1	0.01
Venezuelan	2	0.01
Other South American	1	0.01
Other Hispanic or Latino	55	0.33
Hungarian	205	1.25
Iranian	24	0.15
Irish	4,194	25.51
Italian	2,920	17.76
Latvian	5	0.03
Lithuanian	107	0.65
Norwegian	91	0.55
Pennsylvania German	109	0.66
Polish	1,272	7.74
Romanian	14	0.09
Russian	374	2.27
Scandinavian	26	0.16
Scotch-Irish	255	1.55
Scottish	553	3.36
Slovak	101	0.61
Swedish	286	1.74
Swiss	80	0.49
Turkish	32	0.19
Ukrainian	309	1.88
United States or American	752	4.57
Welsh	237	1.44
West Indian, excl. Hispanic:	44	0.27
Haitian	13	0.08
Trinidadian and Tobagonian	15	0.09
West Indian	16	0.10
White:	16,002	97.32
Not Hispanic (15,741)	15,823	96.24
Hispanic (166)	179	1.09
Yugoslavian	36	0.22

Butler

Place Type: City
County: Butler
Population: 15,121

Ancestry/Race	Number	%
African American/Black:	423	2.80
Not Hispanic (332)	415	2.74
Hispanic (3)	8	0.05
African, sub-Saharan:	44	0.29
African	44	0.29
Alaska Native tribes, specified:	1	0.01
Eskimo	1	0.01
Am. Ind. or Alaska Nat., not spec.	16	0.11
Alsatian	33	0.22
American Indian tribes, specified:	55	0.36
Blackfeet (1)	3	0.02

Notes: 1. Figures in the "Number" column do not add up to the total population due to: a) Ancestry/Race overlap — e.g. persons can report being both White and Irish, b) persons of Hispanic origin can report being any race, c) persons reporting two ancestries are counted in both categories. 2. Numbers in parentheses indicate the number of persons reporting this ancestry/race alone, not in combination with any other ancestry/race. 3. Refer to the Explanation of Data in the front of the book for more detailed information.

Ancestry/Race	Number	%
Cherokee (5)	23	0.15
Chippewa (1)	1	0.01
Choctaw	4	0.03
Comanche (1)	1	0.01
Creek	3	0.02
Iroquois (5)	10	0.07
Latin American Indians (1)	1	0.01
Sioux (1)	3	0.02
Tohono O'Odham (1)	1	0.01
All other tribes (1)	5	0.03
Arab:	19	0.13
Syrian	19	0.13
Asian:	83	0.55
Chinese, ex. Taiwanese (20)	24	0.16
Filipino (9)	15	0.10
Indian (6)	6	0.04
Japanese (13)	14	0.09
Korean (9)	14	0.09
Malaysian (1)	1	0.01
Thai (3)	4	0.03
Vietnamese (3)	3	0.02
Other Asian, not specified (1)	2	0.01
Austrian	96	0.64
Belgian	26	0.17
British	9	0.06
Canadian	14	0.09
Croatian	24	0.16
Czech	145	0.96
Czechoslovakian	80	0.53
Danish	29	0.19
Dutch	302	2.01
Eastern European	8	0.05
English	1,290	8.57
European	125	0.83
Finnish	27	0.18
French, except Basque	378	2.51
French Canadian	35	0.23
German	4,691	31.17
Greek	40	0.27
Hawaii Native/Pacific Islander:	7	0.05
Melanesian:	1	0.01
Other Melanesian	1	0.01
Micronesian: (4)	4	0.03
Guamanian/Chamorro (4)	4	0.03
Polynesian:	1	0.01
Native Hawaiian	1	0.01
Other Pac. Isl., not spec.	1	0.01
Hispanic or Latino:	215	1.42
Central American:	2	0.01
Salvadoran	2	0.01
Cuban	7	0.05
Dominican Republic	1	0.01
Mexican	82	0.54
Puerto Rican	73	0.48
South American:	1	0.01
Colombian	1	0.01
Other Hispanic or Latino	49	0.32
Hungarian	127	0.84
Irish	2,648	17.59
Italian	1,868	12.41
Lithuanian	16	0.11
Northern European	18	0.12
Norwegian	11	0.07
Pennsylvania German	70	0.47
Polish	700	4.65
Portuguese	37	0.25
Romanian	16	0.11
Russian	137	0.91
Scotch-Irish	651	4.33
Scottish	262	1.74
Serbian	27	0.18
Slavic	14	0.09
Slovak	208	1.38
Slovene	21	0.14
Swedish	58	0.39
Swiss	76	0.50
Ukrainian	320	2.13
United States or American	675	4.48
Welsh	162	1.08
White:	14,611	96.63
Not Hispanic (14,319)	14,466	95.67
Hispanic (125)	145	0.96
Yugoslavian	14	0.09

Butler

Place Type: Township
County: Butler
Population: 17,185

Ancestry/Race	Number	%
African American/Black:	116	0.68
Not Hispanic (92)	116	0.68
African, sub-Saharan:	6	0.03
African	6	0.03
Am. Ind. or Alaska Nat., not spec.	14	0.08
Alsatian	10	0.06
American Indian tribes, specified:	16	0.09
Blackfeet	1	0.01
Cherokee (3)	8	0.05
Chippewa (2)	2	0.01
Comanche (1)	1	0.01
Iroquois	1	0.01
Sioux (1)	1	0.01
All other tribes (2)	2	0.01
American Indian tribes, not spec.	1	0.01
Arab:	96	0.56
Arab/Arabic	18	0.10
Lebanese	11	0.06
Syrian	67	0.39
Armenian	19	0.11
Asian:	104	0.61
Chinese, ex. Taiwanese (15)	16	0.09
Filipino (10)	16	0.09
Indian (27)	30	0.17
Indonesian (1)	1	0.01
Japanese (4)	12	0.07
Korean (10)	16	0.09
Pakistani (3)	3	0.02
Vietnamese (5)	5	0.03
Other Asian, not specified (3)	5	0.03
Austrian	107	0.62
Belgian	31	0.18
Brazilian	4	0.02
British	7	0.04
Canadian	11	0.06
Carpatho Rusyn	24	0.14
Celtic	6	0.03
Croatian	118	0.68
Czech	119	0.69
Czechoslovakian	50	0.29
Danish	6	0.03
Dutch	239	1.39
Eastern European	7	0.04
English	1,337	7.76
European	26	0.15
French, except Basque	416	2.41
French Canadian	42	0.24
German	5,517	32.01
Greek	52	0.30
Hawaii Native/Pacific Islander:	13	0.08
Micronesian: (5)	9	0.05
Guamanian/Chamorro (1)	5	0.03
Other Micronesian (4)	4	0.02
Polynesian: (3)	3	0.02
Samoan (3)	3	0.02
Other Pac. Isl., not spec. (1)	1	0.01
Hispanic or Latino:	67	0.39
Central American:	2	0.01
Costa Rican	1	0.01
Salvadoran	1	0.01
Cuban	2	0.01
Mexican	28	0.16
Puerto Rican	12	0.07
South American:	10	0.06
Colombian	4	0.02
Ecuadorian	1	0.01
Paraguayan	1	0.01
Peruvian	3	0.02
Venezuelan	1	0.01
Other Hispanic or Latino	13	0.08
Hungarian	215	1.25
Irish	2,550	14.80
Italian	1,807	10.49
Lithuanian	90	0.52
Northern European	26	0.15
Norwegian	37	0.21
Pennsylvania German	24	0.14
Polish	1,095	6.35
Romanian	30	0.17
Russian	296	1.72
Scandinavian	9	0.05
Scotch-Irish	804	4.67
Scottish	340	1.97
Serbian	48	0.28
Slavic	54	0.31
Slovak	526	3.05
Slovene	37	0.21
Swedish	169	0.98
Swiss	54	0.31
Ukrainian	600	3.48
United States or American	571	3.31
Welsh	227	1.32
West Indian, excl. Hispanic:	22	0.13
Jamaican	9	0.05
West Indian	13	0.08
White:	16,974	98.77
Not Hispanic (16,858)	16,921	98.46
Hispanic (46)	53	0.31
Yugoslavian	10	0.06

Caln

Place Type: Township
County: Chester
Population: 11,916

Ancestry/Race	Number	%
African American/Black:	2,009	16.86
Not Hispanic (1,854)	1,966	16.50
Hispanic (24)	43	0.36
African, sub-Saharan:	62	0.52
African	28	0.24
Nigerian	34	0.29
Alaska Native tribes, not specified	1	0.01
Am. Ind. or Alaska Nat., not spec.	41	0.34
American Indian tribes, specified:	33	0.28
Blackfeet (1)	3	0.03
Cherokee (5)	12	0.10
Chippewa	1	0.01
Cree (1)	1	0.01
Delaware (1)	2	0.02
Latin American Indians	1	0.01
Osage	1	0.01
Seminole (3)	3	0.03
Sioux	3	0.03
All other tribes (6)	6	0.05
Arab:	73	0.61
Arab/Arabic	30	0.25
Egyptian	20	0.17
Lebanese	23	0.19
Armenian	9	0.08
Asian:	317	2.66
Chinese, ex. Taiwanese (49)	52	0.44
Filipino (39)	46	0.39
Indian (78)	87	0.73
Japanese (6)	6	0.05
Korean (35)	37	0.31
Laotian (9)	14	0.12
Pakistani (14)	14	0.12
Taiwanese (2)	2	0.02
Thai (1)	1	0.01
Vietnamese (57)	57	0.48
Other Asian, not specified (1)	1	0.01
Austrian	66	0.55
Belgian	9	0.08
British	17	0.14
Canadian	13	0.11
Celtic	13	0.11
Czech	67	0.56

Notes: 1. Figures in the "Number" column do not add up to the total population due to: a) Ancestry/Race overlap — e.g. persons can report being both White and Irish, b) persons of Hispanic origin can report being any race, c) persons reporting two ancestries are counted in both categories. 2. Numbers in parentheses indicate the number of persons reporting this ancestry/race alone, not in combination with any other ancestry/race. 3. Refer to the Explanation of Data in the front of the book for more detailed information.

Czechoslovakian	6	0.05
Danish	11	0.09
Dutch	291	2.45
Eastern European	28	0.24
English	1,125	9.46
European	17	0.14
Finnish	16	0.13
French, except Basque	294	2.47
French Canadian	34	0.29
German	2,566	21.58
Greek	24	0.20
Hawaii Native/Pacific Islander:	12	0.10
Polynesian: (6)	8	0.07
Native Hawaiian (3)	5	0.04
Samoan (2)	2	0.02
Tongan (1)	1	0.01
Other Pac. Isl., not spec.	4	0.03
Hispanic or Latino:	386	3.24
Central American:	6	0.05
Guatemalan	4	0.03
Panamanian	1	0.01
Salvadoran	1	0.01
Cuban	14	0.12
Dominican Republic	2	0.02
Mexican	76	0.64
Puerto Rican	204	1.71
South American:	30	0.25
Argentinean	1	0.01
Chilean	2	0.02
Colombian	8	0.07
Ecuadorian	16	0.13
Venezuelan	2	0.02
Other South American	1	0.01
Other Hispanic or Latino	54	0.45
Hungarian	155	1.30
Irish	2,720	22.87
Italian	1,958	16.46
Latvian	9	0.08
Lithuanian	60	0.50
Northern European	11	0.09
Norwegian	63	0.53
Pennsylvania German	55	0.46
Polish	352	2.96
Portuguese	63	0.53
Romanian	16	0.13
Russian	32	0.27
Scotch-Irish	155	1.30
Scottish	252	2.12
Slavic	16	0.13
Slovak	48	0.40
Slovene	8	0.07
Swedish	258	2.17
Swiss	16	0.13
Ukrainian	273	2.30
United States or American	424	3.57
Welsh	222	1.87
West Indian, excl. Hispanic:	95	0.80
Bahamian	8	0.07
British West Indian	8	0.07
Jamaican	7	0.06
West Indian	72	0.61
White:	9,544	80.09
Not Hispanic (9,192)	9,325	78.26
Hispanic (195)	219	1.84

Carlisle

Place Type: Borough
County: Cumberland
Population: 17,970

Ancestry/Race	Number	%
African American/Black:	1,428	7.95
Not Hispanic (1,222)	1,389	7.73
Hispanic (21)	39	0.22
African, sub-Saharan:	114	0.63
African	91	0.51
Ghanian	23	0.13
Alaska Native tribes, specified:	1	0.01
Eskimo	1	0.01
Am. Ind. or Alaska Nat., not spec.	49	0.27
American Indian tribes, specified:	35	0.19
Blackfeet	3	0.02
Cherokee (1)	8	0.04
Creek	2	0.01
Delaware	3	0.02
Houma	1	0.01
Iroquois (2)	4	0.02
Latin American Indians (2)	2	0.01
Lumbee (2)	2	0.01
Navajo	1	0.01
Sioux (3)	4	0.02
All other tribes (1)	5	0.03
American Indian tribes, not spec.	2	0.01
Arab:	31	0.17
Egyptian	7	0.04
Jordanian	7	0.04
Lebanese	17	0.09
Asian:	357	1.99
Chinese, ex. Taiwanese (58)	67	0.37
Filipino (18)	28	0.16
Indian (37)	37	0.21
Indonesian (1)	1	0.01
Japanese (25)	31	0.17
Korean (51)	68	0.38
Laotian (2)	2	0.01
Taiwanese (10)	12	0.07
Thai	1	0.01
Vietnamese (65)	68	0.38
Other Asian, specified (5)	12	0.07
Other Asian, not specified (12)	30	0.17
Australian	7	0.04
Austrian	67	0.37
Belgian	9	0.05
Brazilian	25	0.14
British	130	0.72
Canadian	74	0.41
Carpatho Rusyn	8	0.04
Croatian	26	0.14
Czech	41	0.23
Czechoslovakian	47	0.26
Danish	71	0.40
Dutch	394	2.19
Eastern European	23	0.13
English	1,608	8.95
European	72	0.40
Finnish	9	0.05
French, except Basque	442	2.46
French Canadian	41	0.23
German	5,373	29.90
Greek	138	0.77
Hawaii Native/Pacific Islander:	15	0.08
Micronesian: (1)	1	0.01
Guamanian/Chamorro (1)	1	0.01
Polynesian: (2)	4	0.02
Native Hawaiian (2)	4	0.02
Other Pac. Isl., specified	7	0.04
Other Pac. Isl., not spec.	3	0.02
Hispanic or Latino:	352	1.96
Central American:	15	0.08
Guatemalan	3	0.02
Honduran	3	0.02
Nicaraguan	2	0.01
Panamanian	4	0.02
Salvadoran	2	0.01
Other Central American	1	0.01
Cuban	27	0.15
Dominican Republic	2	0.01
Mexican	102	0.57
Puerto Rican	118	0.66
South American:	31	0.17
Argentinean	4	0.02
Chilean	7	0.04
Colombian	9	0.05
Ecuadorian	1	0.01
Peruvian	2	0.01
Venezuelan	1	0.01
Other South American	7	0.04
Other Hispanic or Latino	57	0.32
Hungarian	127	0.71
Iranian	7	0.04
Irish	2,191	12.19
Italian	860	4.79
Lithuanian	74	0.41
Northern European	23	0.13
Norwegian	91	0.51
Pennsylvania German	76	0.42
Polish	485	2.70
Portuguese	30	0.17
Romanian	13	0.07
Russian	275	1.53
Scandinavian	13	0.07
Scotch-Irish	729	4.06
Scottish	458	2.55
Serbian	17	0.09
Slavic	24	0.13
Slovak	58	0.32
Slovene	14	0.08
Swedish	151	0.84
Swiss	127	0.71
Ukrainian	132	0.73
United States or American	1,389	7.73
Welsh	222	1.24
West Indian, excl. Hispanic:	44	0.24
Bahamian	7	0.04
Haitian	9	0.05
Jamaican	20	0.11
Trinidadian and Tobagonian	8	0.04
White:	16,250	90.43
Not Hispanic (15,795)	16,043	89.28
Hispanic (185)	207	1.15
Yugoslavian	190	1.06

Carnot-Moon

Place Type: Census Designated Place
County: Allegheny
Population: 10,637

Ancestry/Race	Number	%
African American/Black:	627	5.89
Not Hispanic (561)	618	5.81
Hispanic (4)	9	0.08
African, sub-Saharan:	69	0.66
African	44	0.42
Kenyan	13	0.12
Other sub-Saharan African	12	0.11
Am. Ind. or Alaska Nat., not spec.	23	0.22
American Indian tribes, specified:	22	0.21
Apache (1)	1	0.01
Blackfeet	1	0.01
Cherokee (5)	16	0.15
Choctaw	1	0.01
Creek	1	0.01
Iroquois	1	0.01
Navajo	1	0.01
Arab:	52	0.50
Lebanese	35	0.33
Syrian	17	0.16
Asian:	329	3.09
Chinese, ex. Taiwanese (43)	52	0.49
Filipino (48)	58	0.55
Indian (99)	104	0.98
Indonesian (2)	2	0.02
Japanese (3)	13	0.12
Korean (31)	36	0.34
Malaysian (1)	1	0.01
Pakistani (18)	19	0.18
Sri Lankan (1)	1	0.01
Taiwanese (15)	15	0.14
Thai (2)	2	0.02
Vietnamese (14)	20	0.19
Other Asian, not specified (5)	6	0.06
Austrian	55	0.52
Belgian	18	0.17
British	15	0.14
Canadian	13	0.12
Carpatho Rusyn	7	0.07
Croatian	66	0.63
Czech	70	0.67

Notes: 1. Figures in the "Number" column do not add up to the total population due to: a) Ancestry/Race overlap — e.g. persons can report being both White and Irish, b) persons of Hispanic origin can report being any race, c) persons reporting two ancestries are counted in both categories. 2. Numbers in parentheses indicate the number of persons reporting this ancestry/race alone, not in combination with any other ancestry/race. 3. Refer to the Explanation of Data in the front of the book for more detailed information.

Czechoslovakian	30	0.29
Dutch	99	0.94
English	975	9.29
European	144	1.37
Finnish	23	0.22
French, except Basque	339	3.23
French Canadian	22	0.21
German	2,579	24.58
Greek	104	0.99
Hawaii Native/Pacific Islander:	19	0.18
Micronesian: (1)	1	0.01
Guamanian/Chamorro (1)	1	0.01
Polynesian: (3)	17	0.16
Native Hawaiian (2)	13	0.12
Samoan (1)	4	0.04
Other Pac. Isl., not spec.	1	0.01
Hispanic or Latino:	112	1.05
Central American:	1	0.01
Salvadoran	1	0.01
Cuban	7	0.07
Dominican Republic	2	0.02
Mexican	28	0.26
Puerto Rican	23	0.22
South American:	14	0.13
Argentinean	2	0.02
Chilean	4	0.04
Colombian	3	0.03
Peruvian	4	0.04
Other South American	1	0.01
Other Hispanic or Latino	37	0.35
Hungarian	148	1.41
Iranian	7	0.07
Irish	1,727	16.46
Italian	1,890	18.01
Lithuanian	29	0.28
Norwegian	27	0.26
Pennsylvania German	5	0.05
Polish	985	9.39
Portuguese	22	0.21
Romanian	18	0.17
Russian	103	0.98
Scandinavian	30	0.29
Scotch-Irish	359	3.42
Scottish	197	1.88
Serbian	15	0.14
Slavic	17	0.16
Slovak	250	2.38
Slovene	13	0.12
Swedish	138	1.32
Swiss	29	0.28
Turkish	9	0.09
Ukrainian	149	1.42
United States or American	363	3.46
Welsh	72	0.69
White:	9,721	91.39
Not Hispanic (9,526)	9,628	90.51
Hispanic (81)	93	0.87

Center

Place Type: Township
County: Beaver
Population: 11,492

Ancestry/Race	Number	%
African American/Black:	362	3.15
Not Hispanic (334)	354	3.08
Hispanic (7)	8	0.07
African, sub-Saharan:	25	0.22
Ethiopian	25	0.22
Am. Ind. or Alaska Nat., not spec.	10	0.09
American Indian tribes, specified:	14	0.12
Blackfeet	2	0.02
Cherokee	7	0.06
Chippewa	1	0.01
Crow	1	0.01
Iroquois (1)	1	0.01
Navajo (1)	1	0.01
Sioux (1)	1	0.01
American Indian tribes, not spec.	1	0.01
Arab:	199	1.73
Lebanese	162	1.41
Syrian	17	0.15
Other Arab	20	0.17
Asian:	54	0.47
Chinese, ex. Taiwanese (7)	10	0.09
Filipino (4)	7	0.06
Indian (18)	18	0.16
Japanese (1)	1	0.01
Korean (9)	9	0.08
Pakistani	1	0.01
Thai (2)	3	0.03
Vietnamese (1)	1	0.01
Other Asian, not specified (4)	4	0.03
Austrian	63	0.55
Belgian	7	0.06
British	11	0.10
Canadian	2	0.02
Croatian	373	3.25
Czech	68	0.59
Czechoslovakian	13	0.11
Dutch	181	1.58
English	1,000	8.70
European	37	0.32
French, except Basque	185	1.61
French Canadian	52	0.45
German	2,956	25.72
Greek	182	1.58
Hawaii Native/Pacific Islander:	5	0.04
Other Pac. Isl., not spec.	5	0.04
Hispanic or Latino:	80	0.70
Central American:	3	0.03
Honduran	2	0.02
Panamanian	1	0.01
Cuban	4	0.03
Mexican	22	0.19
Puerto Rican	24	0.21
South American:	5	0.04
Colombian	5	0.04
Other Hispanic or Latino	22	0.19
Hungarian	168	1.46
Iranian	6	0.05
Irish	1,617	14.07
Italian	2,609	22.70
Lithuanian	36	0.31
Norwegian	56	0.49
Polish	772	6.72
Portuguese	13	0.11
Romanian	56	0.49
Russian	132	1.15
Scotch-Irish	423	3.68
Scottish	151	1.31
Serbian	362	3.15
Slavic	72	0.63
Slovak	734	6.39
Slovene	72	0.63
Swedish	132	1.15
Swiss	21	0.18
Ukrainian	117	1.02
United States or American	461	4.01
Welsh	205	1.78
White:	11,075	96.37
Not Hispanic (10,962)	11,016	95.86
Hispanic (55)	59	0.51
Yugoslavian	38	0.33

Chambersburg

Place Type: Borough
County: Franklin
Population: 17,862

Ancestry/Race	Number	%
African American/Black:	1,523	8.53
Not Hispanic (1,298)	1,444	8.08
Hispanic (52)	79	0.44
African, sub-Saharan:	60	0.34
African	47	0.26
Other sub-Saharan African	13	0.07
Alaska Native tribes, specified:	3	0.02
Alaska Athabascan (1)	3	0.02
Am. Ind. or Alaska Nat., not spec.	30	0.17
American Indian tribes, specified:	65	0.36
Apache (1)	1	0.01
Blackfeet	6	0.03
Cherokee (4)	24	0.13
Choctaw	1	0.01
Cree	1	0.01
Iroquois (3)	4	0.02
Latin American Indians (4)	5	0.03
Navajo (2)	10	0.06
Osage (1)	1	0.01
Pueblo	1	0.01
Sioux	1	0.01
Tohono O'Odham (1)	2	0.01
All other tribes (1)	8	0.04
American Indian tribes, not spec.	7	0.04
Arab:	8	0.04
Arab/Arabic	8	0.04
Asian:	200	1.12
Bangladeshi	1	0.01
Chinese, ex. Taiwanese (33)	38	0.21
Filipino (22)	32	0.18
Indian (32)	36	0.20
Indonesian (3)	3	0.02
Japanese (11)	23	0.13
Korean (23)	27	0.15
Laotian	2	0.01
Pakistani (5)	5	0.03
Taiwanese	2	0.01
Thai (1)	1	0.01
Vietnamese (21)	23	0.13
Other Asian, specified (3)	3	0.02
Other Asian, not specified	4	0.02
Australian	6	0.03
Austrian	78	0.44
Belgian	6	0.03
British	42	0.24
Canadian	10	0.06
Croatian	16	0.09
Czech	21	0.12
Czechoslovakian	14	0.08
Dutch	258	1.44
English	1,228	6.87
European	61	0.34
French, except Basque	196	1.10
French Canadian	76	0.43
German	5,491	30.74
Greek	107	0.60
Hawaii Native/Pacific Islander:	20	0.11
Micronesian: (5)	6	0.03
Guamanian/Chamorro (5)	6	0.03
Polynesian: (3)	10	0.06
Native Hawaiian (1)	5	0.03
Samoan (2)	5	0.03
Other Pac. Isl., not spec. (1)	4	0.02
Hispanic or Latino:	1,140	6.38
Central American:	155	0.87
Costa Rican	1	0.01
Guatemalan	124	0.69
Honduran	14	0.08
Panamanian	1	0.01
Salvadoran	11	0.06
Other Central American	4	0.02
Cuban	16	0.09
Dominican Republic	34	0.19
Mexican	563	3.15
Puerto Rican	196	1.10
South American:	16	0.09
Bolivian	3	0.02
Chilean	2	0.01
Colombian	2	0.01
Ecuadorian	2	0.01
Venezuelan	4	0.02
Other South American	3	0.02
Other Hispanic or Latino	160	0.90
Hungarian	49	0.27
Irish	1,680	9.41
Italian	678	3.80
Latvian	6	0.03

Notes: 1. Figures in the "Number" column do not add up to the total population due to: a) Ancestry/Race overlap — e.g. persons can report being both White and Irish, b) persons of Hispanic origin can report being any race, c) persons reporting two ancestries are counted in both categories. 2. Numbers in parentheses indicate the number of persons reporting this ancestry/race alone, not in combination with any other ancestry/race. 3. Refer to the Explanation of Data in the front of the book for more detailed information.

Lithuanian	31	0.17
Norwegian	42	0.24
Pennsylvania German	43	0.24
Polish	237	1.33
Russian	40	0.22
Scandinavian	26	0.15
Scotch-Irish	528	2.96
Scottish	360	2.02
Slovak	74	0.41
Slovene	6	0.03
Swedish	96	0.54
Swiss	91	0.51
Ukrainian	70	0.39
United States or American	1,936	10.84
Welsh	153	0.86
West Indian, excl. Hispanic:	80	0.45
Barbadian	14	0.08
Jamaican	47	0.26
Trinidadian and Tobagonian	19	0.11
White:	15,738	88.11
Not Hispanic (14,954)	15,196	85.07
Hispanic (485)	542	3.03

Cheltenham

Place Type: Township
County: Montgomery
Population: 36,875

Ancestry/Race	Number	%
Acadian/Cajun	9	0.02
African American/Black:	9,420	25.55
Not Hispanic (9,010)	9,323	25.28
Hispanic (64)	97	0.26
African, sub-Saharan:	433	1.17
African	358	0.97
Cape Verdean	4	0.01
Ghanian	8	0.02
Kenyan	4	0.01
Liberian	24	0.07
Nigerian	25	0.07
Other sub-Saharan African	10	0.03
Alaska Native tribes, specified:	1	0.00
Alaska Athabascan (1)	1	0.00
Am. Ind. or Alaska Nat., not spec.	82	0.22
American Indian tribes, specified:	117	0.32
Apache	2	0.01
Blackfeet (1)	6	0.02
Cherokee (4)	55	0.15
Chickasaw	1	0.00
Chippewa (1)	2	0.01
Choctaw	1	0.00
Delaware (1)	2	0.01
Iroquois	3	0.01
Latin American Indians (7)	10	0.03
Lumbee (1)	5	0.01
Navajo	3	0.01
Seminole (1)	1	0.00
Sioux	5	0.01
Ute (1)	1	0.00
All other tribes (10)	20	0.05
American Indian tribes, not spec.	6	0.02
Arab:	111	0.30
Arab/Arabic	22	0.06
Egyptian	34	0.09
Lebanese	32	0.09
Other Arab	23	0.06
Armenian	30	0.08
Asian:	2,572	6.97
Cambodian (23)	50	0.14
Chinese, ex. Taiwanese (371)	426	1.16
Filipino (114)	133	0.36
Indian (281)	315	0.85
Indonesian (2)	2	0.01
Japanese (27)	51	0.14
Korean (1,317)	1,346	3.65
Laotian (6)	10	0.03
Pakistani (11)	14	0.04
Sri Lankan (4)	4	0.01
Taiwanese (13)	18	0.05
Thai (3)	5	0.01
Vietnamese (144)	151	0.41
Other Asian, specified (5)	12	0.03
Other Asian, not specified (14)	35	0.09
Australian	16	0.04
Austrian	331	0.90
Basque	14	0.04
Belgian	19	0.05
British	122	0.33
Bulgarian	10	0.03
Canadian	147	0.40
Croatian	56	0.15
Czech	29	0.08
Czechoslovakian	6	0.02
Danish	25	0.07
Dutch	168	0.46
Eastern European	484	1.31
English	1,615	4.38
European	342	0.93
Finnish	11	0.03
French, except Basque	370	1.00
French Canadian	46	0.12
German	4,586	12.44
Greek	89	0.24
Hawaii Native/Pacific Islander:	44	0.12
Micronesian: (4)	6	0.02
Guamanian/Chamorro (4)	6	0.02
Polynesian: (2)	4	0.01
Native Hawaiian	2	0.01
Samoan (1)	1	0.00
Other Polynesian (1)	1	0.00
Other Pac. Isl., specified	3	0.01
Other Pac. Isl., not spec. (17)	31	0.08
Hispanic or Latino:	732	1.99
Central American:	31	0.08
Costa Rican	2	0.01
Guatemalan	10	0.03
Honduran	5	0.01
Panamanian	9	0.02
Salvadoran	5	0.01
Cuban	47	0.13
Dominican Republic	9	0.02
Mexican	71	0.19
Puerto Rican	322	0.87
South American:	92	0.25
Argentinean	17	0.05
Bolivian	3	0.01
Chilean	1	0.00
Colombian	40	0.11
Ecuadorian	7	0.02
Paraguayan	1	0.00
Peruvian	9	0.02
Uruguayan	2	0.01
Venezuelan	9	0.02
Other South American	3	0.01
Other Hispanic or Latino	160	0.43
Hungarian	358	0.97
Iranian	57	0.15
Irish	5,423	14.71
Israeli	73	0.20
Italian	2,567	6.96
Latvian	73	0.20
Lithuanian	231	0.63
Macedonian	6	0.02
Northern European	49	0.13
Norwegian	175	0.47
Pennsylvania German	55	0.15
Polish	1,617	4.39
Portuguese	8	0.02
Romanian	165	0.45
Russian	3,236	8.78
Scandinavian	7	0.02
Scotch-Irish	337	0.91
Scottish	282	0.76
Slavic	32	0.09
Slovak	133	0.36
Slovene	12	0.03
Swedish	186	0.50
Swiss	137	0.37
Turkish	31	0.08
Ukrainian	522	1.42
United States or American	1,255	3.40
Welsh	157	0.43
West Indian, excl. Hispanic:	595	1.61
Barbadian	58	0.16
Belizean	6	0.02
Haitian	100	0.27
Jamaican	276	0.75
Trinidadian and Tobagonian	88	0.24
West Indian	67	0.18
White:	24,878	67.47
Not Hispanic (24,141)	24,473	66.37
Hispanic (362)	405	1.10
Yugoslavian	23	0.06

Chester

Place Type: City
County: Delaware
Population: 36,854

Ancestry/Race	Number	%
African American/Black:	28,329	76.87
Not Hispanic (27,500)	27,855	75.58
Hispanic (397)	474	1.29
African, sub-Saharan:	1,021	2.77
African	867	2.35
Ghanian	46	0.12
Kenyan	18	0.05
Nigerian	83	0.23
Other sub-Saharan African	7	0.02
Alaska Native tribes, specified:	2	0.01
Tlingit-Haida	2	0.01
Am. Ind. or Alaska Nat., not spec.	126	0.34
American Indian tribes, specified:	82	0.22
Apache	1	0.00
Blackfeet (1)	3	0.01
Cherokee (5)	44	0.12
Delaware	2	0.01
Iroquois (2)	6	0.02
Latin American Indians (2)	5	0.01
Pima	1	0.00
Seminole (2)	4	0.01
Sioux	9	0.02
All other tribes (4)	7	0.02
American Indian tribes, not spec.	19	0.05
Arab:	109	0.30
Lebanese	4	0.01
Moroccan	48	0.13
Other Arab	57	0.15
Armenian	11	0.03
Asian:	309	0.84
Cambodian (2)	3	0.01
Chinese, ex. Taiwanese (47)	53	0.14
Filipino (24)	45	0.12
Indian (57)	73	0.20
Japanese (31)	34	0.09
Korean (30)	33	0.09
Pakistani (6)	6	0.02
Sri Lankan	2	0.01
Taiwanese (1)	1	0.00
Thai (2)	3	0.01
Vietnamese (10)	10	0.03
Other Asian, specified	4	0.01
Other Asian, not specified (15)	42	0.11
British	13	0.04
Canadian	9	0.02
Croatian	10	0.03
Czech	6	0.02
Danish	6	0.02
Dutch	149	0.40
English	437	1.19
European	17	0.05
French, except Basque	120	0.33
French Canadian	10	0.03
German	1,024	2.78
Greek	29	0.08
Guyanese	21	0.06
Hawaii Native/Pacific Islander:	28	0.08
Micronesian: (1)	1	0.00

Notes: 1. Figures in the "Number" column do not add up to the total population due to: a) Ancestry/Race overlap — e.g. persons can report being both White and Irish, b) persons of Hispanic origin can report being any race, c) persons reporting two ancestries are counted in both categories. 2. Numbers in parentheses indicate the number of persons reporting this ancestry/race alone, not in combination with any other ancestry/race. 3. Refer to the Explanation of Data in the front of the book for more detailed information.

Ancestry/Race	Number	%
Guamanian/Chamorro (1)	1	0.00
Polynesian: (3)	6	0.02
Native Hawaiian (3)	4	0.01
Samoan	2	0.01
Other Pac. Isl., specified	3	0.01
Other Pac. Isl., not spec.	18	0.05
Hispanic or Latino:	1,986	5.39
Central American:	23	0.06
Guatemalan	16	0.04
Nicaraguan	1	0.00
Panamanian	1	0.00
Salvadoran	5	0.01
Cuban	42	0.11
Dominican Republic	12	0.03
Mexican	92	0.25
Puerto Rican	1,464	3.97
South American:	18	0.05
Argentinean	4	0.01
Chilean	1	0.00
Colombian	2	0.01
Peruvian	6	0.02
Venezuelan	2	0.01
Other South American	3	0.01
Other Hispanic or Latino	335	0.91
Hungarian	37	0.10
Irish	1,911	5.19
Italian	1,097	2.98
Lithuanian	33	0.09
Norwegian	7	0.02
Pennsylvania German	66	0.18
Polish	500	1.36
Portuguese	3	0.01
Russian	46	0.12
Scandinavian	8	0.02
Scotch-Irish	81	0.22
Scottish	99	0.27
Slovak	5	0.01
Swedish	76	0.21
Ukrainian	158	0.43
United States or American	494	1.34
Welsh	51	0.14
West Indian, excl. Hispanic:	210	0.57
Barbadian	14	0.04
Haitian	14	0.04
Jamaican	125	0.34
Trinidadian and Tobagonian	31	0.08
West Indian	26	0.07
White:	7,262	19.70
Not Hispanic (6,582)	6,819	18.50
Hispanic (398)	443	1.20

Chestnuthill

Place Type: Township
County: Monroe
Population: 14,418

Ancestry/Race	Number	%
African American/Black:	674	4.67
Not Hispanic (545)	614	4.26
Hispanic (41)	60	0.42
African, sub-Saharan:	25	0.17
African	25	0.17
Alaska Native tribes, specified:	1	0.01
Tlingit-Haida (1)	1	0.01
Am. Ind. or Alaska Nat., not spec.	34	0.24
Albanian	39	0.27
American Indian tribes, specified:	53	0.37
Blackfeet (5)	10	0.07
Cherokee (5)	21	0.15
Comanche	2	0.01
Delaware (1)	2	0.01
Iroquois	2	0.01
Latin American Indians	3	0.02
Navajo	3	0.02
Osage	1	0.01
Seminole	3	0.02
Sioux	3	0.02
All other tribes (1)	3	0.02
American Indian tribes, not spec.	7	0.05
Arab:	22	0.15
Arab/Arabic	13	0.09
Egyptian	9	0.06
Armenian	27	0.19
Asian:	195	1.35
Bangladeshi (5)	5	0.03
Chinese, ex. Taiwanese (30)	38	0.26
Filipino (22)	35	0.24
Indian (40)	54	0.37
Japanese (9)	19	0.13
Korean (14)	14	0.10
Pakistani (4)	15	0.10
Vietnamese (2)	6	0.04
Other Asian, not specified (4)	9	0.06
Australian	4	0.03
Austrian	185	1.28
Belgian	15	0.10
British	10	0.07
Canadian	48	0.33
Celtic	15	0.10
Croatian	9	0.06
Czech	123	0.85
Czechoslovakian	22	0.15
Danish	43	0.30
Dutch	666	4.62
English	1,279	8.87
European	29	0.20
French, except Basque	417	2.89
French Canadian	63	0.44
German	3,604	25.00
Greek	102	0.71
Hawaii Native/Pacific Islander:	5	0.03
Polynesian: (3)	4	0.03
Native Hawaiian	1	0.01
Samoan (3)	3	0.02
Other Pac. Isl., not spec.	1	0.01
Hispanic or Latino:	703	4.88
Central American:	19	0.13
Costa Rican	7	0.05
Guatemalan	2	0.01
Honduran	9	0.06
Nicaraguan	1	0.01
Cuban	46	0.32
Dominican Republic	13	0.09
Mexican	30	0.21
Puerto Rican	427	2.96
South American:	49	0.34
Argentinean	1	0.01
Bolivian	1	0.01
Chilean	3	0.02
Colombian	9	0.06
Ecuadorian	13	0.09
Peruvian	18	0.12
Other South American	4	0.03
Other Hispanic or Latino	119	0.83
Hungarian	180	1.25
Icelander	14	0.10
Irish	2,946	20.43
Italian	3,005	20.84
Lithuanian	144	1.00
Northern European	9	0.06
Norwegian	67	0.46
Pennsylvania German	256	1.78
Polish	943	6.54
Portuguese	66	0.46
Romanian	18	0.12
Russian	285	1.98
Scandinavian	83	0.58
Scotch-Irish	157	1.09
Scottish	137	0.95
Slavic	31	0.22
Slovak	58	0.40
Swedish	165	1.14
Swiss	85	0.59
Turkish	27	0.19
Ukrainian	156	1.08
United States or American	587	4.07
Welsh	115	0.80
West Indian, excl. Hispanic:	72	0.50
Barbadian	9	0.06
Jamaican	32	0.22
Trinidadian and Tobagonian	12	0.08
West Indian	19	0.13
White:	13,480	93.49
Not Hispanic (12,841)	12,969	89.95
Hispanic (472)	511	3.54
Yugoslavian	19	0.13

Coal

Place Type: Township
County: Northumberland
Population: 10,628

Ancestry/Race	Number	%
African American/Black:	982	9.24
Not Hispanic (945)	963	9.06
Hispanic (14)	19	0.18
Am. Ind. or Alaska Nat., not spec.	20	0.19
American Indian tribes, specified:	20	0.19
Apache	1	0.01
Blackfeet	1	0.01
Cherokee	10	0.09
Cheyenne	1	0.01
Delaware	1	0.01
Iroquois	1	0.01
Latin American Indians	3	0.03
Navajo	1	0.01
All other tribes (1)	1	0.01
American Indian tribes, not spec.	1	0.01
Arab:	13	0.12
Egyptian	13	0.12
Asian:	39	0.37
Chinese, ex. Taiwanese	1	0.01
Filipino (4)	5	0.05
Indian (4)	4	0.04
Japanese (2)	6	0.06
Korean (2)	3	0.03
Vietnamese (1)	1	0.01
Other Asian, not specified (15)	19	0.18
Austrian	127	1.19
Czech	22	0.21
Czechoslovakian	12	0.11
Dutch	1,159	10.91
English	443	4.17
French, except Basque	38	0.36
French Canadian	19	0.18
German	1,959	18.43
Hawaii Native/Pacific Islander:	2	0.02
Polynesian:	1	0.01
Native Hawaiian	1	0.01
Other Pac. Isl., not spec.	1	0.01
Hispanic or Latino:	223	2.10
Central American:	2	0.02
Other Central American	2	0.02
Cuban	7	0.07
Mexican	8	0.08
Puerto Rican	104	0.98
South American:	1	0.01
Venezuelan	1	0.01
Other Hispanic or Latino	101	0.95
Hungarian	56	0.53
Irish	1,341	12.62
Italian	1,068	10.05
Lithuanian	145	1.36
Norwegian	5	0.05
Pennsylvania German	197	1.85
Polish	2,626	24.71
Russian	94	0.88
Scotch-Irish	41	0.39
Scottish	33	0.31
Serbian	18	0.17
Slavic	21	0.20
Slovak	276	2.60
Swedish	13	0.12
Swiss	45	0.42
Ukrainian	395	3.72
United States or American	439	4.13
Welsh	223	2.10
West Indian, excl. Hispanic:	4	0.04

Notes: 1. Figures in the "Number" column do not add up to the total population due to: a) Ancestry/Race overlap — e.g. persons can report being both White and Irish, b) persons of Hispanic origin can report being any race, c) persons reporting two ancestries are counted in both categories. 2. Numbers in parentheses indicate the number of persons reporting this ancestry/race alone, not in combination with any other ancestry/race. 3. Refer to the Explanation of Data in the front of the book for more detailed information.

Ancestry/Race	Number	%
British West Indian	4	0.04
White:	9,557	89.92
Not Hispanic (9,377)	9,422	88.65
Hispanic (129)	135	1.27
Yugoslavian	5	0.05

Coatesville

Place Type: City
County: Chester
Population: 10,838

Ancestry/Race	Number	%
African American/Black:	5,612	51.78
Not Hispanic (5,235)	5,487	50.63
Hispanic (92)	125	1.15
African, sub-Saharan:	332	3.04
African	305	2.79
Liberian	27	0.25
Am. Ind. or Alaska Nat., not spec.	76	0.70
American Indian tribes, specified:	56	0.52
Blackfeet (5)	14	0.13
Cherokee (4)	24	0.22
Choctaw	3	0.03
Delaware	1	0.01
Iroquois	1	0.01
Latin American Indians (2)	3	0.03
Osage (1)	1	0.01
Seminole	4	0.04
Sioux	1	0.01
All other tribes (3)	4	0.04
American Indian tribes, not spec.	4	0.04
Arab:	63	0.58
Arab/Arabic	6	0.05
Lebanese	57	0.52
Asian:	84	0.78
Chinese, ex. Taiwanese (19)	24	0.22
Filipino (5)	12	0.11
Indian (13)	22	0.20
Japanese (6)	8	0.07
Korean (1)	3	0.03
Laotian (3)	3	0.03
Pakistani (2)	2	0.02
Thai (4)	4	0.04
Vietnamese (2)	2	0.02
Other Asian, not specified (1)	4	0.04
Australian	15	0.14
Austrian	38	0.35
Czechoslovakian	37	0.34
Danish	15	0.14
Dutch	146	1.34
English	365	3.34
French, except Basque	75	0.69
French Canadian	35	0.32
German	711	6.51
Greek	29	0.27
Hawaii Native/Pacific Islander:	10	0.09
Polynesian: (3)	9	0.08
Native Hawaiian (1)	4	0.04
Samoan (1)	1	0.01
Other Polynesian (1)	4	0.04
Other Pac. Isl., not spec.	1	0.01
Hispanic or Latino:	1,165	10.75
Central American:	4	0.04
Panamanian	4	0.04
Cuban	9	0.08
Dominican Republic	2	0.02
Mexican	471	4.35
Puerto Rican	528	4.87
South American:	29	0.27
Colombian	7	0.06
Ecuadorian	14	0.13
Venezuelan	3	0.03
Other South American	5	0.05
Other Hispanic or Latino	122	1.13
Hungarian	24	0.22
Irish	706	6.47
Italian	626	5.73
Northern European	15	0.14
Pennsylvania German	29	0.27
Polish	330	3.02
Russian	69	0.63
Scotch-Irish	133	1.22
Scottish	30	0.27
Slavic	5	0.05
Slovak	117	1.07
Swedish	27	0.25
Ukrainian	96	0.88
United States or American	525	4.81
Welsh	40	0.37
West Indian, excl. Hispanic:	17	0.16
Barbadian	11	0.10
West Indian	6	0.05
White:	4,797	44.26
Not Hispanic (4,040)	4,254	39.25
Hispanic (502)	543	5.01

Colonial Park

Place Type: Census Designated Place
County: Dauphin
Population: 13,259

Ancestry/Race	Number	%
African American/Black:	1,408	10.62
Not Hispanic (1,254)	1,361	10.26
Hispanic (39)	47	0.35
African, sub-Saharan:	94	0.71
African	58	0.44
Nigerian	36	0.27
Am. Ind. or Alaska Nat., not spec.	22	0.17
American Indian tribes, specified:	31	0.23
Blackfeet	1	0.01
Cherokee (1)	11	0.08
Choctaw	1	0.01
Kiowa (1)	1	0.01
Latin American Indians	1	0.01
Lumbee	1	0.01
Navajo (1)	1	0.01
Seminole	5	0.04
Sioux (1)	3	0.02
Yakama (1)	1	0.01
All other tribes (3)	5	0.04
American Indian tribes, not spec.	1	0.01
Arab:	116	0.88
Arab/Arabic	20	0.15
Egyptian	47	0.36
Lebanese	22	0.17
Moroccan	18	0.14
Syrian	9	0.07
Armenian	8	0.06
Asian:	551	4.16
Bangladeshi (1)	1	0.01
Cambodian (4)	4	0.03
Chinese, ex. Taiwanese (50)	56	0.42
Filipino (19)	27	0.20
Indian (278)	283	2.13
Japanese (12)	17	0.13
Korean (24)	28	0.21
Laotian (4)	4	0.03
Pakistani (31)	36	0.27
Taiwanese	1	0.01
Thai (1)	3	0.02
Vietnamese (73)	77	0.58
Other Asian, specified (1)	1	0.01
Other Asian, not specified (7)	13	0.10
Austrian	60	0.46
British	67	0.51
Bulgarian	9	0.07
Canadian	7	0.05
Carpatho Rusyn	22	0.17
Croatian	118	0.90
Czech	16	0.12
Czechoslovakian	40	0.30
Danish	16	0.12
Dutch	382	2.91
Eastern European	15	0.11
English	973	7.40
Estonian	8	0.06
European	52	0.40
French, except Basque	251	1.91
French Canadian	12	0.09
German	3,905	29.70
Greek	34	0.26
Hawaii Native/Pacific Islander:	4	0.03
Polynesian: (1)	1	0.01
Native Hawaiian (1)	1	0.01
Other Pac. Isl., not spec. (1)	3	0.02
Hispanic or Latino:	414	3.12
Central American:	8	0.06
Costa Rican	1	0.01
Honduran	4	0.03
Panamanian	3	0.02
Cuban	31	0.23
Dominican Republic	13	0.10
Mexican	83	0.63
Puerto Rican	190	1.43
South American:	21	0.16
Colombian	7	0.05
Ecuadorian	11	0.08
Peruvian	3	0.02
Other Hispanic or Latino	68	0.51
Hungarian	52	0.40
Irish	1,598	12.15
Italian	1,139	8.66
Lithuanian	87	0.66
Northern European	38	0.29
Norwegian	86	0.65
Pennsylvania German	61	0.46
Polish	557	4.24
Romanian	17	0.13
Russian	90	0.68
Scandinavian	8	0.06
Scotch-Irish	180	1.37
Scottish	170	1.29
Serbian	49	0.37
Slavic	24	0.18
Slovak	149	1.13
Swedish	38	0.29
Swiss	95	0.72
Ukrainian	134	1.02
United States or American	869	6.61
Welsh	270	2.05
West Indian, excl. Hispanic:	23	0.17
British West Indian	6	0.05
Jamaican	17	0.13
White:	11,209	84.54
Not Hispanic (10,863)	11,014	83.07
Hispanic (167)	195	1.47

Columbia

Place Type: Borough
County: Lancaster
Population: 10,311

Ancestry/Race	Number	%
African American/Black:	566	5.49
Not Hispanic (414)	511	4.96
Hispanic (42)	55	0.53
African, sub-Saharan:	71	0.69
African	71	0.69
Am. Ind. or Alaska Nat., not spec.	16	0.16
American Indian tribes, specified:	32	0.31
Cherokee (2)	8	0.08
Chippewa (1)	1	0.01
Choctaw (3)	3	0.03
Cree	3	0.03
Iroquois (3)	5	0.05
Latin American Indians	4	0.04
All other tribes (6)	8	0.08
American Indian tribes, not spec.	2	0.02
Arab:	14	0.14
Egyptian	7	0.07
Lebanese	7	0.07
Asian:	62	0.60
Cambodian (2)	2	0.02
Chinese, ex. Taiwanese (5)	7	0.07
Filipino (5)	6	0.06
Indian (4)	9	0.09

Notes: 1. Figures in the "Number" column do not add up to the total population due to: a) Ancestry/Race overlap — e.g. persons can report being both White and Irish, b) persons of Hispanic origin can report being any race, c) persons reporting two ancestries are counted in both categories. 2. Numbers in parentheses indicate the number of persons reporting this ancestry/race alone, not in combination with any other ancestry/race. 3. Refer to the Explanation of Data in the front of the book for more detailed information.

Japanese (1)	1	0.01
Korean (8)	11	0.11
Thai	1	0.01
Vietnamese (14)	16	0.16
Other Asian, not specified (3)	9	0.09
Australian	7	0.07
Canadian	12	0.12
Czech	8	0.08
Dutch	203	1.97
English	595	5.77
Finnish	11	0.11
French, except Basque	206	2.00
French Canadian	21	0.20
German	4,125	40.03
Hawaii Native/Pacific Islander:	5	0.05
Other Pac. Isl., not spec. (5)	5	0.05
Hispanic or Latino:	463	4.49
Central American:	3	0.03
Honduran	3	0.03
Cuban	17	0.16
Dominican Republic	2	0.02
Mexican	32	0.31
Puerto Rican	342	3.32
South American:	1	0.01
Peruvian	1	0.01
Other Hispanic or Latino	66	0.64
Hungarian	11	0.11
Irish	1,304	12.65
Italian	422	4.09
Lithuanian	11	0.11
Norwegian	45	0.44
Pennsylvania German	47	0.46
Polish	178	1.73
Portuguese	22	0.21
Romanian	7	0.07
Russian	11	0.11
Scandinavian	6	0.06
Scotch-Irish	178	1.73
Scottish	123	1.19
Serbian	7	0.07
Slovak	10	0.10
Swedish	32	0.31
Swiss	75	0.73
United States or American	1,102	10.69
Welsh	181	1.76
White:	9,585	92.96
Not Hispanic (9,225)	9,345	90.63
Hispanic (193)	240	2.33

Coolbaugh

Place Type: Township
County: Monroe
Population: 15,205

Ancestry/Race	Number	%
African American/Black:	2,696	17.73
Not Hispanic (2,255)	2,474	16.27
Hispanic (129)	222	1.46
African, sub-Saharan:	141	0.93
African	120	0.79
Ghanian	21	0.14
Alaska Native tribes, specified:	2	0.01
Eskimo	2	0.01
Alaska Native tribes, not specified	1	0.01
Am. Ind. or Alaska Nat., not spec.	57	0.37
American Indian tribes, specified:	91	0.60
Apache	3	0.02
Blackfeet (2)	9	0.06
Cherokee (7)	37	0.24
Chippewa	3	0.02
Delaware (1)	1	0.01
Iroquois (2)	7	0.05
Latin American Indians (3)	11	0.07
Lumbee	3	0.02
Navajo	4	0.03
Pueblo (1)	1	0.01
Sioux (1)	3	0.02
All other tribes (6)	9	0.06
American Indian tribes, not spec.	7	0.05
Arab:	56	0.37
Egyptian	47	0.31
Lebanese	9	0.06
Armenian	19	0.12
Asian:	224	1.47
Chinese, ex. Taiwanese (35)	60	0.39
Filipino (33)	44	0.29
Indian (37)	44	0.29
Indonesian	6	0.04
Japanese (2)	4	0.03
Korean (20)	26	0.17
Laotian (6)	6	0.04
Pakistani (1)	1	0.01
Sri Lankan (1)	1	0.01
Thai (6)	6	0.04
Vietnamese (7)	9	0.06
Other Asian, specified (5)	6	0.04
Other Asian, not specified (1)	11	0.07
Austrian	41	0.27
Belgian	7	0.05
British	80	0.53
Canadian	13	0.09
Croatian	72	0.47
Czech	68	0.45
Czechoslovakian	68	0.45
Danish	32	0.21
Dutch	171	1.12
English	620	4.08
Estonian	7	0.05
European	57	0.37
Finnish	5	0.03
French, except Basque	154	1.01
French Canadian	24	0.16
German	2,857	18.79
Greek	54	0.36
Guyanese	131	0.86
Hawaii Native/Pacific Islander:	30	0.20
Micronesian: (1)	1	0.01
Guamanian/Chamorro (1)	1	0.01
Polynesian: (8)	8	0.05
Native Hawaiian (2)	2	0.01
Samoan (6)	6	0.04
Other Pac. Isl., not spec. (2)	21	0.14
Hispanic or Latino:	2,327	15.30
Central American:	97	0.64
Costa Rican	5	0.03
Guatemalan	17	0.11
Honduran	28	0.18
Nicaraguan	8	0.05
Panamanian	24	0.16
Salvadoran	15	0.10
Cuban	55	0.36
Dominican Republic	111	0.73
Mexican	52	0.34
Puerto Rican	1,431	9.41
South American:	163	1.07
Argentinean	6	0.04
Colombian	38	0.25
Ecuadorian	39	0.26
Paraguayan	1	0.01
Peruvian	54	0.36
Uruguayan	4	0.03
Venezuelan	15	0.10
Other South American	6	0.04
Other Hispanic or Latino	418	2.75
Hungarian	205	1.35
Irish	2,897	19.05
Italian	3,017	19.84
Lithuanian	21	0.14
Maltese	9	0.06
Norwegian	13	0.09
Pennsylvania German	68	0.45
Polish	1,077	7.08
Portuguese	11	0.07
Russian	235	1.55
Scotch-Irish	142	0.93
Scottish	211	1.39
Slovak	44	0.29
Swedish	193	1.27
Swiss	5	0.03
Ukrainian	60	0.39
United States or American	345	2.27
Welsh	225	1.48
West Indian, excl. Hispanic:	382	2.51
Haitian	68	0.45
Jamaican	124	0.82
Trinidadian and Tobagonian	175	1.15
West Indian	15	0.10
White:	11,271	74.13
Not Hispanic (9,988)	10,229	67.27
Hispanic (895)	1,042	6.85
Yugoslavian	18	0.12

Cranberry

Place Type: Township
County: Butler
Population: 23,625

Ancestry/Race	Number	%
African American/Black:	251	1.06
Not Hispanic (195)	234	0.99
Hispanic (13)	17	0.07
African, sub-Saharan:	6	0.03
Ethiopian	6	0.03
Am. Ind. or Alaska Nat., not spec.	17	0.07
Albanian	16	0.07
American Indian tribes, specified:	31	0.13
Apache	2	0.01
Blackfeet	1	0.00
Cherokee (8)	20	0.08
Chippewa (1)	1	0.00
Creek (1)	1	0.00
Iroquois	1	0.00
Potawatomi (2)	2	0.01
Sioux	2	0.01
All other tribes (1)	1	0.00
American Indian tribes, not spec.	3	0.01
Arab:	117	0.50
Egyptian	17	0.07
Lebanese	41	0.17
Moroccan	9	0.04
Syrian	50	0.21
Armenian	64	0.27
Asian:	393	1.66
Bangladeshi (1)	1	0.00
Cambodian (4)	4	0.02
Chinese, ex. Taiwanese (64)	67	0.28
Filipino (19)	39	0.17
Indian (138)	143	0.61
Japanese (13)	17	0.07
Korean (43)	60	0.25
Laotian (1)	2	0.01
Malaysian (1)	1	0.00
Pakistani (12)	12	0.05
Sri Lankan (3)	3	0.01
Taiwanese (2)	2	0.01
Thai	2	0.01
Vietnamese (16)	17	0.07
Other Asian, not specified (3)	23	0.10
Australian	41	0.17
Austrian	90	0.38
Belgian	15	0.06
British	113	0.48
Canadian	14	0.06
Carpatho Rusyn	30	0.13
Croatian	396	1.68
Czech	167	0.71
Czechoslovakian	125	0.53
Danish	77	0.33
Dutch	290	1.23
Eastern European	10	0.04
English	2,408	10.19
European	171	0.72
Finnish	28	0.12
French, except Basque	519	2.20
French Canadian	42	0.18
German	8,105	34.30
Greek	233	0.99
Hawaii Native/Pacific Islander:	8	0.03

Notes: 1. Figures in the "Number" column do not add up to the total population due to: a) Ancestry/Race overlap — e.g. persons can report being both White and Irish, b) persons of Hispanic origin can report being any race, c) persons reporting two ancestries are counted in both categories. 2. Numbers in parentheses indicate the number of persons reporting this ancestry/race alone, not in combination with any other ancestry/race. 3. Refer to the Explanation of Data in the front of the book for more detailed information.

Ancestry/Race	Number	%
Polynesian: (3)	6	0.03
Native Hawaiian (2)	4	0.02
Samoan	1	0.00
Tongan (1)	1	0.00
Other Pac. Isl., not spec. (2)	2	0.01
Hispanic or Latino:	166	0.70
Central American:	6	0.03
Guatemalan	1	0.00
Honduran	2	0.01
Salvadoran	3	0.01
Cuban	9	0.04
Dominican Republic	4	0.02
Mexican	59	0.25
Puerto Rican	39	0.17
South American:	13	0.06
Argentinean	3	0.01
Bolivian	1	0.00
Chilean	2	0.01
Colombian	3	0.01
Ecuadorian	2	0.01
Peruvian	1	0.00
Venezuelan	1	0.00
Other Hispanic or Latino	36	0.15
Hungarian	328	1.39
Irish	5,059	21.41
Italian	4,019	17.01
Lithuanian	103	0.44
Maltese	8	0.03
Norwegian	126	0.53
Pennsylvania German	6	0.03
Polish	2,027	8.58
Romanian	57	0.24
Russian	235	0.99
Scandinavian	16	0.07
Scotch-Irish	586	2.48
Scottish	623	2.64
Serbian	150	0.63
Slavic	59	0.25
Slovak	814	3.44
Slovene	72	0.30
Swedish	235	0.99
Swiss	241	1.02
Turkish	9	0.04
Ukrainian	292	1.24
United States or American	1,112	4.71
Welsh	449	1.90
White:	23,012	97.41
Not Hispanic (22,761)	22,895	96.91
Hispanic (108)	117	0.50
Yugoslavian	24	0.10

Cumru

Place Type: Township
County: Berks
Population: 13,816

Ancestry/Race	Number	%
African American/Black:	306	2.21
Not Hispanic (254)	286	2.07
Hispanic (11)	20	0.14
African, sub-Saharan:	29	0.21
African	29	0.21
Am. Ind. or Alaska Nat., not spec.	8	0.06
American Indian tribes, specified:	23	0.17
Blackfeet (1)	1	0.01
Cherokee (3)	8	0.06
Chickasaw	1	0.01
Chippewa (2)	5	0.04
Delaware	1	0.01
Iroquois (1)	2	0.01
All other tribes (1)	5	0.04
Arab:	7	0.05
Palestinian	7	0.05
Asian:	301	2.18
Bangladeshi (2)	2	0.01
Chinese, ex. Taiwanese (29)	40	0.29
Filipino (25)	33	0.24
Hmong (10)	10	0.07
Indian (119)	128	0.93
Indonesian (1)	1	0.01
Japanese (11)	15	0.11
Korean (28)	29	0.21
Laotian (11)	11	0.08
Pakistani (6)	6	0.04
Thai (1)	1	0.01
Vietnamese (16)	17	0.12
Other Asian, not specified (1)	8	0.06
Austrian	103	0.75
Brazilian	14	0.10
British	25	0.18
Canadian	14	0.10
Czech	40	0.29
Czechoslovakian	64	0.46
Danish	9	0.07
Dutch	323	2.34
English	777	5.62
European	64	0.46
French, except Basque	366	2.65
French Canadian	27	0.20
German	5,174	37.43
Greek	134	0.97
Hawaii Native/Pacific Islander:	10	0.07
Micronesian: (1)	1	0.01
Other Micronesian (1)	1	0.01
Polynesian: (1)	3	0.02
Native Hawaiian	2	0.01
Samoan (1)	1	0.01
Other Pac. Isl., not spec. (4)	6	0.04
Hispanic or Latino:	389	2.82
Central American:	8	0.06
Honduran	7	0.05
Panamanian	1	0.01
Cuban	22	0.16
Dominican Republic	13	0.09
Mexican	28	0.20
Puerto Rican	258	1.87
South American:	12	0.09
Argentinean	1	0.01
Colombian	7	0.05
Ecuadorian	1	0.01
Venezuelan	3	0.02
Other Hispanic or Latino	48	0.35
Hungarian	88	0.64
Irish	1,483	10.73
Italian	1,935	14.00
Lithuanian	118	0.85
Norwegian	36	0.26
Pennsylvania German	529	3.83
Polish	1,383	10.01
Portuguese	8	0.06
Romanian	18	0.13
Russian	86	0.62
Scandinavian	17	0.12
Scotch-Irish	198	1.43
Scottish	179	1.30
Slavic	12	0.09
Slovak	207	1.50
Swedish	87	0.63
Swiss	140	1.01
Ukrainian	269	1.95
United States or American	517	3.74
Welsh	250	1.81
West Indian, excl. Hispanic:	28	0.20
Bermudan	8	0.06
Jamaican	20	0.14
White:	13,081	94.68
Not Hispanic (12,783)	12,873	93.17
Hispanic (182)	208	1.51
Yugoslavian	7	0.05

Darby

Place Type: Borough
County: Delaware
Population: 10,299

Ancestry/Race	Number	%
African American/Black:	6,338	61.54
Not Hispanic (6,143)	6,300	61.17
Hispanic (36)	38	0.37
African, sub-Saharan:	310	3.01
African	251	2.44
Ethiopian	20	0.19
Liberian	21	0.20
Nigerian	5	0.05
Other sub-Saharan African	13	0.13
Am. Ind. or Alaska Nat., not spec.	31	0.30
American Indian tribes, specified:	25	0.24
Blackfeet	2	0.02
Cherokee (3)	12	0.12
Choctaw	3	0.03
Iroquois	5	0.05
Latin American Indians (1)	1	0.01
Sioux (1)	1	0.01
All other tribes	1	0.01
American Indian tribes, not spec.	4	0.04
Arab:	6	0.06
Lebanese	6	0.06
Armenian	6	0.06
Asian:	118	1.15
Bangladeshi (4)	7	0.07
Chinese, ex. Taiwanese (16)	28	0.27
Filipino (7)	9	0.09
Indian (19)	19	0.18
Japanese (1)	8	0.08
Korean (3)	3	0.03
Laotian (4)	4	0.04
Malaysian	1	0.01
Thai (2)	2	0.02
Vietnamese (27)	34	0.33
Other Asian, not specified	3	0.03
Austrian	8	0.08
British	6	0.06
Celtic	6	0.06
Czech	33	0.32
Danish	7	0.07
Dutch	104	1.01
English	404	3.92
European	5	0.05
French, except Basque	60	0.58
German	803	7.80
Greek	24	0.23
Hawaii Native/Pacific Islander:	19	0.18
Polynesian: (1)	6	0.06
Native Hawaiian	3	0.03
Samoan (1)	3	0.03
Other Pac. Isl., not spec. (6)	13	0.13
Hispanic or Latino:	98	0.95
Central American:	4	0.04
Panamanian	4	0.04
Cuban	1	0.01
Mexican	15	0.15
Puerto Rican	46	0.45
South American:	7	0.07
Argentinean	2	0.02
Bolivian	1	0.01
Chilean	2	0.02
Ecuadorian	2	0.02
Other Hispanic or Latino	25	0.24
Hungarian	32	0.31
Irish	1,519	14.75
Israeli	26	0.25
Italian	730	7.09
Latvian	8	0.08
Lithuanian	23	0.22
Norwegian	9	0.09
Pennsylvania German	10	0.10
Polish	154	1.50
Portuguese	35	0.34
Scotch-Irish	84	0.82
Scottish	48	0.47
Slovak	7	0.07
Swedish	48	0.47
Swiss	8	0.08
Ukrainian	11	0.11
United States or American	118	1.15
Welsh	19	0.18
West Indian, excl. Hispanic:	188	1.83
Belizean	18	0.17

Notes: 1. Figures in the "Number" column do not add up to the total population due to: a) Ancestry/Race overlap — e.g. persons can report being both White and Irish, b) persons of Hispanic origin can report being any race, c) persons reporting two ancestries are counted in both categories. 2. Numbers in parentheses indicate the number of persons reporting this ancestry/race alone, not in combination with any other ancestry/race. 3. Refer to the Explanation of Data in the front of the book for more detailed information.

Ancestry/Race	Number	%
Haitian	25	0.24
Jamaican	136	1.32
Trinidadian and Tobagonian	9	0.09
White:	3,873	37.61
Not Hispanic (3,722)	3,844	37.32
Hispanic (24)	29	0.28

Derry

Place Type: Township
County: Dauphin
Population: 21,273

Ancestry/Race	Number	%
African American/Black:	433	2.04
Not Hispanic (348)	416	1.96
Hispanic (7)	17	0.08
African, sub-Saharan:	74	0.35
African	43	0.20
Liberian	13	0.06
South African	18	0.08
Am. Ind. or Alaska Nat., not spec.	16	0.08
American Indian tribes, specified:	52	0.24
Blackfeet	13	0.06
Cherokee (4)	7	0.03
Chippewa	2	0.01
Comanche	1	0.00
Creek (2)	2	0.01
Iroquois	3	0.01
Latin American Indians (4)	6	0.03
Sioux (1)	12	0.06
All other tribes (1)	6	0.03
American Indian tribes, not spec.	5	0.02
Arab:	37	0.17
Arab/Arabic	12	0.06
Lebanese	25	0.12
Armenian	18	0.08
Asian:	923	4.34
Bangladeshi (15)	17	0.08
Cambodian (60)	63	0.30
Chinese, ex. Taiwanese (324)	337	1.58
Filipino (30)	47	0.22
Indian (226)	235	1.10
Indonesian	2	0.01
Japanese (33)	45	0.21
Korean (58)	62	0.29
Malaysian (1)	3	0.01
Pakistani (12)	13	0.06
Sri Lankan (5)	7	0.03
Taiwanese (16)	16	0.08
Thai (5)	8	0.04
Vietnamese (49)	53	0.25
Other Asian, specified (2)	2	0.01
Other Asian, not specified (2)	13	0.06
Australian	7	0.03
Austrian	69	0.32
Basque	11	0.05
Belgian	40	0.19
British	74	0.35
Bulgarian	6	0.03
Canadian	59	0.28
Croatian	136	0.64
Czech	75	0.35
Czechoslovakian	83	0.39
Danish	134	0.63
Dutch	568	2.67
Eastern European	57	0.27
English	2,636	12.39
European	195	0.92
Finnish	26	0.12
French, except Basque	480	2.26
French Canadian	68	0.32
German	7,781	36.58
Greek	106	0.50
Hawaii Native/Pacific Islander:	13	0.06
Melanesian:	1	0.00
Other Melanesian	1	0.00
Micronesian: (2)	2	0.01
Guamanian/Chamorro (2)	2	0.01
Polynesian: (3)	4	0.02
Native Hawaiian (1)	2	0.01
Samoan (2)	2	0.01
Other Pac. Isl., not spec.	6	0.03
Hispanic or Latino:	297	1.40
Central American:	14	0.07
Guatemalan	1	0.00
Panamanian	12	0.06
Salvadoran	1	0.00
Cuban	23	0.11
Dominican Republic	6	0.03
Mexican	64	0.30
Puerto Rican	107	0.50
South American:	36	0.17
Argentinean	13	0.06
Colombian	13	0.06
Ecuadorian	3	0.01
Peruvian	2	0.01
Other South American	5	0.02
Other Hispanic or Latino	47	0.22
Hungarian	269	1.26
Iranian	21	0.10
Irish	3,040	14.29
Italian	2,713	12.75
Lithuanian	111	0.52
Norwegian	172	0.81
Pennsylvania German	168	0.79
Polish	1,046	4.92
Portuguese	38	0.18
Romanian	17	0.08
Russian	302	1.42
Scandinavian	39	0.18
Scotch-Irish	461	2.17
Scottish	551	2.59
Serbian	80	0.38
Slavic	24	0.11
Slovak	170	0.80
Slovene	15	0.07
Swedish	270	1.27
Swiss	192	0.90
Ukrainian	221	1.04
United States or American	696	3.27
Welsh	495	2.33
West Indian, excl. Hispanic:	28	0.13
Haitian	7	0.03
Jamaican	12	0.06
West Indian	9	0.04
White:	19,935	93.71
Not Hispanic (19,531)	19,731	92.75
Hispanic (179)	204	0.96
Yugoslavian	93	0.44

Derry

Place Type: Township
County: Westmoreland
Population: 14,726

Ancestry/Race	Number	%
African American/Black:	189	1.28
Not Hispanic (173)	188	1.28
Hispanic (1)	1	0.01
Am. Ind. or Alaska Nat., not spec.	6	0.04
American Indian tribes, specified:	28	0.19
Blackfeet	3	0.02
Cherokee (1)	7	0.05
Delaware (1)	1	0.01
Iroquois (1)	12	0.08
Sioux	2	0.01
All other tribes (1)	3	0.02
Arab:	56	0.38
Syrian	56	0.38
Asian:	27	0.18
Chinese, ex. Taiwanese (1)	1	0.01
Filipino (8)	8	0.05
Indian (1)	1	0.01
Indonesian (1)	1	0.01
Japanese (3)	4	0.03
Korean (4)	4	0.03
Thai (2)	4	0.03
Vietnamese (1)	1	0.01
Other Asian, not specified	3	0.02
Australian	45	0.31
Austrian	49	0.33
Belgian	9	0.06
British	14	0.10
Canadian	8	0.05
Carpatho Rusyn	14	0.10
Croatian	188	1.28
Czech	128	0.87
Czechoslovakian	63	0.43
Dutch	293	1.99
English	994	6.75
European	18	0.12
French, except Basque	192	1.30
French Canadian	24	0.16
German	3,737	25.38
Greek	50	0.34
Hawaii Native/Pacific Islander:	3	0.02
Other Pac. Isl., not spec. (1)	3	0.02
Hispanic or Latino:	69	0.47
Central American:	2	0.01
Costa Rican	1	0.01
Panamanian	1	0.01
Mexican	31	0.21
Puerto Rican	10	0.07
Other Hispanic or Latino	26	0.18
Hungarian	282	1.91
Irish	2,312	15.70
Italian	2,266	15.39
Norwegian	5	0.03
Pennsylvania German	83	0.56
Polish	1,486	10.09
Romanian	9	0.06
Russian	105	0.71
Scotch-Irish	379	2.57
Scottish	133	0.90
Serbian	22	0.15
Slavic	86	0.58
Slovak	958	6.51
Slovene	90	0.61
Swedish	34	0.23
Ukrainian	320	2.17
United States or American	621	4.22
Welsh	197	1.34
West Indian, excl. Hispanic:	8	0.05
Jamaican	8	0.05
White:	14,516	98.57
Not Hispanic (14,404)	14,453	98.15
Hispanic (59)	63	0.43
Yugoslavian	6	0.04

Dover

Place Type: Township
County: York
Population: 18,074

Ancestry/Race	Number	%
African American/Black:	215	1.19
Not Hispanic (160)	205	1.13
Hispanic (6)	10	0.06
African, sub-Saharan:	30	0.17
African	30	0.17
Am. Ind. or Alaska Nat., not spec.	15	0.08
American Indian tribes, specified:	48	0.27
Cherokee (8)	25	0.14
Chippewa	1	0.01
Choctaw	4	0.02
Creek (6)	6	0.03
Delaware (1)	1	0.01
Iroquois (3)	4	0.02
Latin American Indians (1)	1	0.01
Lumbee (1)	1	0.01
Sioux (1)	3	0.02
All other tribes (1)	2	0.01
American Indian tribes, not spec.	1	0.01
Asian:	104	0.58
Bangladeshi (2)	3	0.02
Cambodian	4	0.02
Chinese, ex. Taiwanese (5)	8	0.04

Notes: 1. Figures in the "Number" column do not add up to the total population due to: a) Ancestry/Race overlap — e.g. persons can report being both White and Irish, b) persons of Hispanic origin can report being any race, c) persons reporting two ancestries are counted in both categories. 2. Numbers in parentheses indicate the number of persons reporting this ancestry/race alone, not in combination with any other ancestry/race. 3. Refer to the Explanation of Data in the front of the book for more detailed information.

Ancestry/Race	Number	%
Filipino (12)	19	0.11
Indian (16)	17	0.09
Japanese (3)	7	0.04
Korean (18)	19	0.11
Thai	1	0.01
Vietnamese (16)	18	0.10
Other Asian, not specified (4)	8	0.04
Austrian	41	0.23
British	15	0.08
Canadian	6	0.03
Croatian	13	0.07
Czech	13	0.07
Danish	6	0.03
Dutch	527	2.92
Eastern European	11	0.06
English	1,228	6.79
European	48	0.27
French, except Basque	420	2.32
French Canadian	55	0.30
German	8,008	44.31
Greek	99	0.55
Hawaii Native/Pacific Islander:	15	0.08
Micronesian: (1)	12	0.07
Guamanian/Chamorro (1)	12	0.07
Polynesian:	3	0.02
Native Hawaiian	3	0.02
Hispanic or Latino:	187	1.03
Central American:	8	0.04
Nicaraguan	4	0.02
Panamanian	2	0.01
Salvadoran	2	0.01
Cuban	3	0.02
Mexican	31	0.17
Puerto Rican	113	0.63
South American:	6	0.03
Argentinean	1	0.01
Chilean	1	0.01
Ecuadorian	4	0.02
Other Hispanic or Latino	26	0.14
Hungarian	25	0.14
Irish	1,571	8.69
Italian	672	3.72
Lithuanian	19	0.11
New Zealander	9	0.05
Norwegian	62	0.34
Pennsylvania German	61	0.34
Polish	322	1.78
Portuguese	8	0.04
Russian	23	0.13
Scotch-Irish	255	1.41
Scottish	174	0.96
Slavic	19	0.11
Slovak	70	0.39
Swedish	113	0.63
Swiss	130	0.72
Ukrainian	103	0.57
United States or American	2,149	11.89
Welsh	139	0.77
West Indian, excl. Hispanic:	9	0.05
Jamaican	9	0.05
White:	17,689	97.87
Not Hispanic (17,507)	17,609	97.43
Hispanic (70)	80	0.44
Yugoslavian	9	0.05

Doylestown

Place Type: Township
County: Bucks
Population: 17,619

Ancestry/Race	Number	%
Acadian/Cajun	8	0.05
African American/Black:	490	2.78
Not Hispanic (437)	465	2.64
Hispanic (20)	25	0.14
African, sub-Saharan:	6	0.03
African	6	0.03
Alaska Native tribes, specified:	1	0.01
Alaska Athabascan (1)	1	0.01
Am. Ind. or Alaska Nat., not spec.	15	0.09
Albanian	6	0.03
Alsatian	6	0.03
American Indian tribes, specified:	19	0.11
Apache (1)	1	0.01
Cherokee (3)	8	0.05
Chickasaw	2	0.01
Choctaw	1	0.01
Delaware (1)	2	0.01
Iroquois	1	0.01
Sioux	1	0.01
All other tribes	3	0.02
American Indian tribes, not spec.	1	0.01
Arab:	33	0.19
Egyptian	11	0.06
Iraqi	7	0.04
Lebanese	15	0.09
Armenian	15	0.09
Asian:	282	1.60
Cambodian (1)	1	0.01
Chinese, ex. Taiwanese (55)	62	0.35
Filipino (12)	23	0.13
Indian (56)	66	0.37
Japanese (16)	32	0.18
Korean (35)	41	0.23
Sri Lankan	1	0.01
Taiwanese (1)	4	0.02
Thai (6)	10	0.06
Vietnamese (25)	33	0.19
Other Asian, specified	2	0.01
Other Asian, not specified (5)	7	0.04
Assyrian/Chaldean/Syriac	7	0.04
Australian	40	0.23
Austrian	118	0.67
Belgian	7	0.04
Brazilian	31	0.18
British	133	0.75
Canadian	58	0.33
Croatian	22	0.12
Czech	95	0.54
Czechoslovakian	69	0.39
Danish	44	0.25
Dutch	228	1.29
Eastern European	101	0.57
English	2,682	15.22
European	163	0.93
French, except Basque	432	2.45
French Canadian	131	0.74
German	4,575	25.96
Greek	110	0.62
Hawaii Native/Pacific Islander:	13	0.07
Micronesian:	1	0.01
Guamanian/Chamorro	1	0.01
Polynesian: (4)	8	0.05
Native Hawaiian (4)	5	0.03
Other Polynesian	3	0.02
Other Pac. Isl., not spec.	4	0.02
Hispanic or Latino:	247	1.40
Central American:	14	0.08
Costa Rican	1	0.01
Honduran	2	0.01
Panamanian	8	0.05
Salvadoran	3	0.02
Cuban	13	0.07
Dominican Republic	5	0.03
Mexican	30	0.17
Puerto Rican	94	0.53
South American:	40	0.23
Argentinean	3	0.02
Colombian	11	0.06
Ecuadorian	12	0.07
Peruvian	7	0.04
Uruguayan	1	0.01
Venezuelan	1	0.01
Other South American	5	0.03
Other Hispanic or Latino	51	0.29
Hungarian	282	1.60
Iranian	17	0.10
Irish	4,101	23.27
Italian	2,147	12.19
Latvian	16	0.09
Lithuanian	68	0.39
Northern European	39	0.22
Norwegian	141	0.80
Pennsylvania German	39	0.22
Polish	927	5.26
Portuguese	60	0.34
Romanian	60	0.34
Russian	408	2.32
Scandinavian	64	0.36
Scotch-Irish	388	2.20
Scottish	347	1.97
Serbian	30	0.17
Slavic	8	0.05
Slovak	101	0.57
Slovene	27	0.15
Swedish	106	0.60
Swiss	127	0.72
Turkish	6	0.03
Ukrainian	170	0.96
United States or American	878	4.98
Welsh	425	2.41
West Indian, excl. Hispanic:	60	0.34
Jamaican	33	0.19
Trinidadian and Tobagonian	14	0.08
West Indian	13	0.07
White:	16,880	95.81
Not Hispanic (16,594)	16,683	94.69
Hispanic (183)	197	1.12
Yugoslavian	6	0.03

Drexel Hill

Place Type: Census Designated Place
County: Delaware
Population: 29,364

Ancestry/Race	Number	%
African American/Black:	660	2.25
Not Hispanic (560)	635	2.16
Hispanic (21)	25	0.09
African, sub-Saharan:	128	0.44
African	17	0.06
Cape Verdean	12	0.04
Ethiopian	19	0.06
Kenyan	6	0.02
Nigerian	17	0.06
South African	52	0.18
Other sub-Saharan African	5	0.02
Am. Ind. or Alaska Nat., not spec.	35	0.12
Albanian	11	0.04
American Indian tribes, specified:	28	0.10
Blackfeet	3	0.01
Cherokee (2)	12	0.04
Chippewa (1)	1	0.00
Creek	1	0.00
Iroquois	1	0.00
Latin American Indians (5)	6	0.02
Osage	1	0.00
All other tribes (2)	3	0.01
American Indian tribes, not spec.	8	0.03
Arab:	88	0.30
Arab/Arabic	8	0.03
Jordanian	16	0.05
Lebanese	32	0.11
Moroccan	6	0.02
Syrian	19	0.06
Other Arab	7	0.02
Armenian	275	0.94
Asian:	1,235	4.21
Bangladeshi (2)	2	0.01
Cambodian (15)	16	0.05
Chinese, ex. Taiwanese (393)	439	1.50
Filipino (56)	81	0.28
Indian (128)	139	0.47
Indonesian (3)	3	0.01
Japanese (84)	104	0.35
Korean (284)	288	0.98
Laotian (1)	3	0.01
Pakistani (23)	27	0.09

Notes: 1. Figures in the "Number" column do not add up to the total population due to: a) Ancestry/Race overlap — e.g. persons can report being both White and Irish, b) persons of Hispanic origin can report being any race, c) persons reporting two ancestries are counted in both categories. 2. Numbers in parentheses indicate the number of persons reporting this ancestry/race alone, not in combination with any other ancestry/race. 3. Refer to the Explanation of Data in the front of the book for more detailed information.

Ancestry/Race	Number	%
Sri Lankan (1)	1	0.00
Taiwanese (16)	17	0.06
Thai (3)	3	0.01
Vietnamese (62)	76	0.26
Other Asian, specified (4)	4	0.01
Other Asian, not specified (23)	32	0.11
Austrian	112	0.38
Belgian	24	0.08
British	90	0.31
Canadian	57	0.19
Croatian	6	0.02
Czech	52	0.18
Czechoslovakian	24	0.08
Danish	36	0.12
Dutch	269	0.92
Eastern European	16	0.05
English	2,906	9.92
European	100	0.34
Finnish	19	0.06
French, except Basque	495	1.69
French Canadian	117	0.40
German	4,901	16.73
Greek	473	1.61
Hawaii Native/Pacific Islander:	14	0.05
Micronesian: (3)	4	0.01
Guamanian/Chamorro (3)	4	0.01
Polynesian: (1)	4	0.01
Native Hawaiian (1)	1	0.00
Samoan	3	0.01
Other Pac. Isl., not spec.	6	0.02
Hispanic or Latino:	285	0.97
Central American:	24	0.08
Guatemalan	8	0.03
Honduran	10	0.03
Salvadoran	6	0.02
Cuban	23	0.08
Mexican	55	0.19
Puerto Rican	57	0.19
South American:	45	0.15
Argentinean	3	0.01
Bolivian	3	0.01
Chilean	1	0.00
Colombian	8	0.03
Ecuadorian	8	0.03
Paraguayan	2	0.01
Peruvian	15	0.05
Venezuelan	3	0.01
Other South American	2	0.01
Other Hispanic or Latino	81	0.28
Hungarian	112	0.38
Irish	12,267	41.87
Italian	7,196	24.56
Latvian	18	0.06
Lithuanian	139	0.47
Macedonian	7	0.02
New Zealander	8	0.03
Northern European	7	0.02
Norwegian	159	0.54
Pennsylvania German	50	0.17
Polish	1,231	4.20
Portuguese	17	0.06
Romanian	57	0.19
Russian	168	0.57
Scandinavian	7	0.02
Scotch-Irish	689	2.35
Scottish	330	1.13
Serbian	14	0.05
Slavic	7	0.02
Slovak	132	0.45
Slovene	10	0.03
Swedish	193	0.66
Swiss	78	0.27
Ukrainian	209	0.71
United States or American	812	2.77
Welsh	209	0.71
West Indian, excl. Hispanic:	13	0.04
Haitian	7	0.02
West Indian	6	0.02
White:	27,511	93.69
Not Hispanic (27,143)	27,312	93.01
Hispanic (179)	199	0.68
Yugoslavian	6	0.02

Dunmore

Place Type: Borough
County: Lackawanna
Population: 14,018

Ancestry/Race	Number	%
African American/Black:	89	0.63
Not Hispanic (59)	73	0.52
Hispanic (10)	16	0.11
Am. Ind. or Alaska Nat., not spec.	5	0.04
American Indian tribes, specified:	13	0.09
Cherokee	1	0.01
Delaware (1)	1	0.01
Iroquois (2)	2	0.01
Navajo (1)	1	0.01
Seminole (2)	2	0.01
All other tribes	6	0.04
American Indian tribes, not spec.	1	0.01
Arab:	22	0.16
Arab/Arabic	6	0.04
Lebanese	16	0.11
Armenian	12	0.09
Asian:	77	0.55
Chinese, ex. Taiwanese (9)	12	0.09
Filipino (8)	10	0.07
Indian (25)	25	0.18
Japanese (2)	5	0.04
Korean (5)	6	0.04
Laotian (1)	1	0.01
Taiwanese	1	0.01
Thai (2)	3	0.02
Vietnamese (8)	8	0.06
Other Asian, not specified (2)	6	0.04
Austrian	72	0.51
British	5	0.04
Canadian	8	0.06
Carpatho Rusyn	17	0.12
Celtic	6	0.04
Czech	29	0.21
Czechoslovakian	11	0.08
Dutch	84	0.60
Eastern European	26	0.19
English	584	4.17
European	13	0.09
Finnish	9	0.06
French, except Basque	63	0.45
German	2,040	14.55
Greek	43	0.31
Hawaii Native/Pacific Islander:	3	0.02
Micronesian: (1)	1	0.01
Guamanian/Chamorro (1)	1	0.01
Other Pac. Isl., not spec. (1)	2	0.01
Hispanic or Latino:	123	0.88
Central American:	4	0.03
Honduran	2	0.01
Salvadoran	1	0.01
Other Central American	1	0.01
Cuban	7	0.05
Dominican Republic	2	0.01
Mexican	15	0.11
Puerto Rican	60	0.43
South American:	9	0.06
Colombian	2	0.01
Paraguayan	1	0.01
Peruvian	2	0.01
Venezuelan	3	0.02
Other South American	1	0.01
Other Hispanic or Latino	26	0.19
Hungarian	105	0.75
Irish	4,028	28.73
Italian	5,501	39.24
Lithuanian	227	1.62
Macedonian	7	0.05
Norwegian	8	0.06
Pennsylvania German	19	0.14
Polish	1,668	11.90
Portuguese	17	0.12
Romanian	7	0.05
Russian	568	4.05
Scotch-Irish	60	0.43
Scottish	132	0.94
Slavic	38	0.27
Slovak	443	3.16
Slovene	18	0.13
Swedish	61	0.44
Swiss	19	0.14
Ukrainian	251	1.79
United States or American	349	2.49
Welsh	480	3.42
White:	13,842	98.74
Not Hispanic (13,729)	13,759	98.15
Hispanic (72)	83	0.59
Yugoslavian	8	0.06

East Goshen

Place Type: Township
County: Chester
Population: 16,824

Ancestry/Race	Number	%
African American/Black:	498	2.96
Not Hispanic (446)	487	2.89
Hispanic (6)	11	0.07
African, sub-Saharan:	76	0.45
African	46	0.27
Sierra Leonean	30	0.18
Am. Ind. or Alaska Nat., not spec.	11	0.07
American Indian tribes, specified:	18	0.11
Cherokee (2)	7	0.04
Creek	1	0.01
Delaware	1	0.01
Iroquois (2)	2	0.01
Latin American Indians (2)	2	0.01
Shoshone	2	0.01
All other tribes (3)	3	0.02
Arab:	87	0.52
Arab/Arabic	9	0.05
Lebanese	34	0.20
Moroccan	7	0.04
Palestinian	14	0.08
Syrian	7	0.04
Other Arab	16	0.10
Armenian	69	0.41
Asian:	365	2.17
Cambodian (3)	3	0.02
Chinese, ex. Taiwanese (97)	105	0.62
Filipino (16)	23	0.14
Indian (114)	120	0.71
Japanese (10)	17	0.10
Korean (50)	51	0.30
Malaysian (1)	3	0.02
Pakistani (10)	10	0.06
Taiwanese (7)	9	0.05
Thai (2)	5	0.03
Vietnamese (15)	15	0.09
Other Asian, specified (1)	1	0.01
Other Asian, not specified (3)	3	0.02
Australian	6	0.04
Austrian	70	0.42
Belgian	7	0.04
British	114	0.68
Canadian	36	0.21
Celtic	6	0.04
Czech	20	0.12
Czechoslovakian	135	0.80
Danish	27	0.16
Dutch	268	1.59
Eastern European	58	0.34
English	3,163	18.80
Estonian	44	0.26
European	142	0.84
Finnish	24	0.14
French, except Basque	389	2.31
French Canadian	105	0.62
German	3,917	23.28

Notes: 1. Figures in the "Number" column do not add up to the total population due to: a) Ancestry/Race overlap — e.g. persons can report being both White and Irish, b) persons of Hispanic origin can report being any race, c) persons reporting two ancestries are counted in both categories. 2. Numbers in parentheses indicate the number of persons reporting this ancestry/race alone, not in combination with any other ancestry/race. 3. Refer to the Explanation of Data in the front of the book for more detailed information.

Ancestry/Race	Number	%
Greek	141	0.84
Hawaii Native/Pacific Islander:	9	0.05
Polynesian:	3	0.02
Native Hawaiian	3	0.02
Other Pac. Isl., not spec. (6)	6	0.04
Hispanic or Latino:	197	1.17
Central American:	4	0.02
Guatemalan	2	0.01
Honduran	1	0.01
Panamanian	1	0.01
Cuban	17	0.10
Dominican Republic	4	0.02
Mexican	29	0.17
Puerto Rican	67	0.40
South American:	35	0.21
Bolivian	1	0.01
Chilean	7	0.04
Colombian	9	0.05
Ecuadorian	2	0.01
Peruvian	5	0.03
Venezuelan	9	0.05
Other South American	2	0.01
Other Hispanic or Latino	41	0.24
Hungarian	172	1.02
Irish	4,947	29.40
Israeli	10	0.06
Italian	2,440	14.50
Latvian	6	0.04
Lithuanian	108	0.64
Northern European	6	0.04
Norwegian	103	0.61
Pennsylvania German	51	0.30
Polish	1,002	5.96
Portuguese	24	0.14
Romanian	30	0.18
Russian	322	1.91
Scandinavian	9	0.05
Scotch-Irish	282	1.68
Scottish	491	2.92
Slovak	94	0.56
Swedish	203	1.21
Swiss	60	0.36
Turkish	14	0.08
Ukrainian	215	1.28
United States or American	515	3.06
Welsh	306	1.82
West Indian, excl. Hispanic:	16	0.10
Haitian	11	0.07
Jamaican	5	0.03
White:	15,965	94.89
Not Hispanic (15,743)	15,817	94.01
Hispanic (137)	148	0.88
Yugoslavian	18	0.11

East Hempfield

Place Type: Township
County: Lancaster
Population: 21,399

Ancestry/Race	Number	%
African American/Black:	395	1.85
Not Hispanic (311)	378	1.77
Hispanic (13)	17	0.08
African, sub-Saharan:	60	0.28
African	24	0.11
Kenyan	19	0.09
South African	17	0.08
Alaska Native tribes, specified:	1	0.00
Aleut (1)	1	0.00
Am. Ind. or Alaska Nat., not spec.	30	0.14
American Indian tribes, specified:	37	0.17
Apache (1)	1	0.00
Blackfeet	1	0.00
Cherokee (1)	9	0.04
Choctaw (1)	1	0.00
Delaware	5	0.02
Iroquois (3)	4	0.02
Latin American Indians	2	0.01
Seminole (5)	5	0.02
Sioux	2	0.01
Yuman (1)	1	0.00
All other tribes (1)	6	0.03
Arab:	26	0.12
Lebanese	18	0.08
Syrian	8	0.04
Asian:	618	2.89
Cambodian (8)	16	0.07
Chinese, ex. Taiwanese (133)	142	0.66
Filipino (14)	32	0.15
Indian (102)	109	0.51
Indonesian (5)	6	0.03
Japanese (12)	19	0.09
Korean (76)	81	0.38
Laotian (7)	7	0.03
Pakistani	2	0.01
Taiwanese (3)	3	0.01
Vietnamese (169)	184	0.86
Other Asian, specified (1)	2	0.01
Other Asian, not specified (2)	15	0.07
Austrian	92	0.43
Belgian	22	0.10
British	47	0.22
Canadian	6	0.03
Carpatho Rusyn	9	0.04
Croatian	23	0.11
Czech	113	0.53
Czechoslovakian	43	0.20
Danish	43	0.20
Dutch	395	1.86
Eastern European	13	0.06
English	1,895	8.91
European	144	0.68
Finnish	27	0.13
French, except Basque	455	2.14
French Canadian	86	0.40
German	8,667	40.76
Greek	179	0.84
Hawaii Native/Pacific Islander:	2	0.01
Micronesian:	1	0.00
Guamanian/Chamorro	1	0.00
Other Pac. Isl., not spec. (1)	1	0.00
Hispanic or Latino:	595	2.78
Central American:	13	0.06
Costa Rican	2	0.01
Guatemalan	2	0.01
Honduran	5	0.02
Nicaraguan	2	0.01
Salvadoran	2	0.01
Cuban	17	0.08
Dominican Republic	35	0.16
Mexican	51	0.24
Puerto Rican	372	1.74
South American:	30	0.14
Argentinean	1	0.00
Bolivian	2	0.01
Chilean	2	0.01
Colombian	12	0.06
Ecuadorian	2	0.01
Peruvian	9	0.04
Venezuelan	1	0.00
Other South American	1	0.00
Other Hispanic or Latino	77	0.36
Hungarian	132	0.62
Iranian	7	0.03
Irish	2,986	14.04
Italian	1,305	6.14
Latvian	57	0.27
Lithuanian	84	0.40
Macedonian	8	0.04
Norwegian	111	0.52
Pennsylvania German	48	0.23
Polish	783	3.68
Portuguese	32	0.15
Romanian	18	0.08
Russian	129	0.61
Scandinavian	20	0.09
Scotch-Irish	372	1.75
Scottish	410	1.93
Serbian	10	0.05
Slavic	8	0.04
Slovak	119	0.56
Swedish	341	1.60
Swiss	525	2.47
Ukrainian	135	0.63
United States or American	1,876	8.82
Welsh	238	1.12
West Indian, excl. Hispanic:	5	0.02
Haitian	5	0.02
White:	20,153	94.18
Not Hispanic (19,756)	19,887	92.93
Hispanic (241)	266	1.24
Yugoslavian	45	0.21

East Lampeter

Place Type: Township
County: Lancaster
Population: 13,556

Ancestry/Race	Number	%
African American/Black:	345	2.54
Not Hispanic (263)	307	2.26
Hispanic (23)	38	0.28
African, sub-Saharan:	18	0.13
African	10	0.07
Kenyan	8	0.06
Am. Ind. or Alaska Nat., not spec.	15	0.11
American Indian tribes, specified:	29	0.21
Cherokee (6)	17	0.13
Choctaw	2	0.01
Iroquois	1	0.01
Sioux (1)	1	0.01
Yaqui (1)	1	0.01
All other tribes (1)	7	0.05
Arab:	64	0.47
Arab/Arabic	19	0.14
Egyptian	14	0.10
Jordanian	4	0.03
Palestinian	23	0.17
Other Arab	4	0.03
Asian:	419	3.09
Cambodian (14)	24	0.18
Chinese, ex. Taiwanese (82)	83	0.61
Filipino (8)	19	0.14
Indian (94)	96	0.71
Indonesian (2)	2	0.01
Japanese (9)	20	0.15
Korean (21)	23	0.17
Laotian (5)	5	0.04
Malaysian (1)	1	0.01
Pakistani (11)	11	0.08
Thai (7)	7	0.05
Vietnamese (110)	113	0.83
Other Asian, specified (1)	5	0.04
Other Asian, not specified	10	0.07
Austrian	45	0.33
British	42	0.31
Canadian	29	0.21
Croatian	13	0.10
Czech	76	0.56
Czechoslovakian	41	0.30
Danish	27	0.20
Dutch	172	1.27
Eastern European	18	0.13
English	1,206	8.89
European	86	0.63
Finnish	8	0.06
French, except Basque	352	2.59
French Canadian	43	0.32
German	4,916	36.23
Greek	59	0.43
Hawaii Native/Pacific Islander:	14	0.10
Micronesian: (1)	1	0.01
Guamanian/Chamorro (1)	1	0.01
Polynesian: (3)	6	0.04
Native Hawaiian (2)	5	0.04
Samoan (1)	1	0.01
Other Pac. Isl., specified	2	0.01
Other Pac. Isl., not spec.	5	0.04

Notes: 1. Figures in the "Number" column do not add up to the total population due to: a) Ancestry/Race overlap — e.g. persons can report being both White and Irish, b) persons of Hispanic origin can report being any race, c) persons reporting two ancestries are counted in both categories. 2. Numbers in parentheses indicate the number of persons reporting this ancestry/race alone, not in combination with any other ancestry/race. 3. Refer to the Explanation of Data in the front of the book for more detailed information.

Ancestry/Race	Number	%
Hispanic or Latino:	524	3.87
Central American:	16	0.12
Guatemalan	5	0.04
Salvadoran	8	0.06
Other Central American	3	0.02
Cuban	31	0.23
Dominican Republic	12	0.09
Mexican	44	0.32
Puerto Rican	307	2.26
South American:	30	0.22
Colombian	27	0.20
Ecuadorian	1	0.01
Venezuelan	1	0.01
Other South American	1	0.01
Other Hispanic or Latino	84	0.62
Hungarian	30	0.22
Iranian	11	0.08
Irish	1,144	8.43
Italian	813	5.99
Latvian	16	0.12
Lithuanian	20	0.15
Norwegian	53	0.39
Pennsylvania German	303	2.23
Polish	280	2.06
Portuguese	46	0.34
Romanian	35	0.26
Russian	69	0.51
Scotch-Irish	282	2.08
Scottish	212	1.56
Slavic	8	0.06
Slovak	46	0.34
Swedish	71	0.52
Swiss	674	4.97
Ukrainian	21	0.15
United States or American	1,023	7.54
Welsh	122	0.90
West Indian, excl. Hispanic:	18	0.13
Dutch West Indian	18	0.13
White:	12,602	92.96
Not Hispanic (12,266)	12,347	91.08
Hispanic (223)	255	1.88

East Norriton

Place Type: Census Designated Place
County: Montgomery
Population: 13,211

Ancestry/Race	Number	%
African American/Black:	851	6.44
Not Hispanic (791)	841	6.37
Hispanic (9)	10	0.08
African, sub-Saharan:	128	0.97
African	56	0.43
Liberian	13	0.10
Nigerian	59	0.45
Am. Ind. or Alaska Nat., not spec.	16	0.12
Albanian	7	0.05
American Indian tribes, specified:	12	0.09
Blackfeet	1	0.01
Cherokee	2	0.02
Delaware (1)	1	0.01
Iroquois (3)	3	0.02
Tohono O'Odham (4)	4	0.03
All other tribes (1)	1	0.01
Arab:	17	0.13
Lebanese	6	0.05
Syrian	6	0.05
Other Arab	5	0.04
Armenian	17	0.13
Asian:	554	4.19
Cambodian (4)	4	0.03
Chinese, ex. Taiwanese (48)	55	0.42
Filipino (34)	45	0.34
Indian (241)	249	1.88
Indonesian (1)	2	0.02
Japanese (11)	14	0.11
Korean (122)	125	0.95
Pakistani (5)	5	0.04
Sri Lankan (4)	4	0.03
Taiwanese (3)	3	0.02
Thai (1)	2	0.02
Vietnamese (23)	29	0.22
Other Asian, not specified (4)	17	0.13
Australian	5	0.04
Austrian	35	0.27
Belgian	4	0.03
British	111	0.84
Canadian	6	0.05
Czech	11	0.08
Czechoslovakian	34	0.26
Danish	39	0.30
Dutch	190	1.45
Eastern European	15	0.11
English	874	6.65
European	6	0.05
Finnish	39	0.30
French, except Basque	194	1.48
French Canadian	11	0.08
German	2,279	17.34
Greek	113	0.86
Guyanese	8	0.06
Hawaii Native/Pacific Islander:	1	0.01
Other Pac. Isl., not spec.	1	0.01
Hispanic or Latino:	154	1.17
Central American:	12	0.09
Costa Rican	7	0.05
Guatemalan	1	0.01
Nicaraguan	1	0.01
Salvadoran	3	0.02
Cuban	3	0.02
Dominican Republic	4	0.03
Mexican	22	0.17
Puerto Rican	57	0.43
South American:	17	0.13
Argentinean	12	0.09
Bolivian	1	0.01
Colombian	1	0.01
Ecuadorian	1	0.01
Peruvian	2	0.02
Other Hispanic or Latino	39	0.30
Hungarian	144	1.10
Irish	2,651	20.18
Italian	3,895	29.64
Lithuanian	92	0.70
Luxemburger	7	0.05
Northern European	7	0.05
Norwegian	56	0.43
Pennsylvania German	62	0.47
Polish	1,063	8.09
Portuguese	6	0.05
Romanian	12	0.09
Russian	234	1.78
Scandinavian	9	0.07
Scotch-Irish	96	0.73
Scottish	227	1.73
Serbian	36	0.27
Slavic	12	0.09
Slovak	42	0.32
Swedish	55	0.42
Swiss	16	0.12
Ukrainian	112	0.85
United States or American	401	3.05
Welsh	135	1.03
West Indian, excl. Hispanic:	40	0.30
Haitian	4	0.03
Jamaican	36	0.27
White:	11,818	89.46
Not Hispanic (11,644)	11,725	88.75
Hispanic (86)	93	0.70
Yugoslavian	25	0.19

East Pennsboro

Place Type: Township
County: Cumberland
Population: 18,254

Ancestry/Race	Number	%
African American/Black:	358	1.96
Not Hispanic (262)	349	1.91
Hispanic (6)	9	0.05
African, sub-Saharan:	12	0.07
Nigerian	12	0.07
Am. Ind. or Alaska Nat., not spec.	34	0.19
American Indian tribes, specified:	21	0.12
Apache (3)	3	0.02
Cherokee (3)	9	0.05
Iroquois (2)	3	0.02
Paiute	1	0.01
Seminole	1	0.01
Sioux	1	0.01
All other tribes (3)	3	0.02
American Indian tribes, not spec.	2	0.01
Arab:	35	0.19
Egyptian	6	0.03
Iraqi	17	0.09
Lebanese	5	0.03
Syrian	7	0.04
Armenian	12	0.07
Asian:	516	2.83
Cambodian (1)	1	0.01
Chinese, ex. Taiwanese (57)	61	0.33
Filipino (43)	59	0.32
Hmong (2)	2	0.01
Indian (178)	185	1.01
Japanese (8)	16	0.09
Korean (41)	46	0.25
Laotian (1)	2	0.01
Pakistani (13)	13	0.07
Sri Lankan (1)	1	0.01
Taiwanese (2)	2	0.01
Thai (4)	4	0.02
Vietnamese (95)	102	0.56
Other Asian, specified	2	0.01
Other Asian, not specified (11)	20	0.11
Austrian	89	0.49
Belgian	6	0.03
British	15	0.08
Canadian	40	0.22
Croatian	90	0.49
Czech	56	0.31
Czechoslovakian	26	0.14
Dutch	661	3.63
Eastern European	7	0.04
English	1,345	7.39
European	122	0.67
French, except Basque	625	3.44
French Canadian	31	0.17
German	6,263	34.43
Greek	102	0.56
Hawaii Native/Pacific Islander:	14	0.08
Micronesian: (5)	6	0.03
Guamanian/Chamorro (1)	2	0.01
Other Micronesian (4)	4	0.02
Polynesian:	7	0.04
Native Hawaiian	6	0.03
Samoan	1	0.01
Other Pac. Isl., specified	1	0.01
Hispanic or Latino:	281	1.54
Central American:	2	0.01
Panamanian	2	0.01
Cuban	8	0.04
Dominican Republic	1	0.01
Mexican	75	0.41
Puerto Rican	151	0.83
South American:	11	0.06
Argentinean	1	0.01
Colombian	5	0.03
Ecuadorian	3	0.02
Peruvian	1	0.01
Other South American	1	0.01
Other Hispanic or Latino	33	0.18
Hungarian	119	0.65
Irish	2,820	15.50
Italian	1,507	8.28
Lithuanian	151	0.83
Macedonian	19	0.10
Norwegian	91	0.50
Pennsylvania German	302	1.66

Notes: 1. Figures in the "Number" column do not add up to the total population due to: a) Ancestry/Race overlap — e.g. persons can report being both White and Irish, b) persons of Hispanic origin can report being any race, c) persons reporting two ancestries are counted in both categories. 2. Numbers in parentheses indicate the number of persons reporting this ancestry/race alone, not in combination with any other ancestry/race. 3. Refer to the Explanation of Data in the front of the book for more detailed information.

Ancestry/Race	Number	%
Polish	720	3.96
Portuguese	16	0.09
Romanian	97	0.53
Russian	183	1.01
Scotch-Irish	308	1.69
Scottish	317	1.74
Serbian	15	0.08
Slavic	6	0.03
Slovak	133	0.73
Slovene	20	0.11
Swedish	172	0.95
Swiss	37	0.20
Ukrainian	102	0.56
United States or American	1,204	6.62
Welsh	311	1.71
West Indian, excl. Hispanic:	25	0.14
Jamaican	25	0.14
White:	17,359	95.10
Not Hispanic (16,971)	17,195	94.20
Hispanic (140)	164	0.90
Yugoslavian	92	0.51

Easton

Place Type: City
County: Northampton
Population: 26,263

Ancestry/Race	Number	%
African American/Black:	3,783	14.40
Not Hispanic (3,221)	3,611	13.75
Hispanic (117)	172	0.65
African, sub-Saharan:	212	0.81
African	165	0.63
Ethiopian	9	0.03
Ghanian	9	0.03
Ugandan	16	0.06
Zimbabwean	13	0.05
Am. Ind. or Alaska Nat., not spec.	97	0.37
Albanian	18	0.07
American Indian tribes, specified:	130	0.49
Apache (1)	3	0.01
Blackfeet (3)	13	0.05
Cherokee (12)	52	0.20
Chippewa (1)	3	0.01
Choctaw (1)	2	0.01
Creek	1	0.00
Delaware (5)	12	0.05
Iroquois	8	0.03
Latin American Indians (10)	17	0.06
Lumbee	1	0.00
Navajo	1	0.00
Pueblo	1	0.00
Sioux (2)	7	0.03
Ute	3	0.01
All other tribes (1)	6	0.02
American Indian tribes, not spec.	13	0.05
Arab:	455	1.73
Egyptian	28	0.11
Lebanese	348	1.33
Syrian	73	0.28
Other Arab	6	0.02
Armenian	16	0.06
Asian:	540	2.06
Bangladeshi (2)	2	0.01
Cambodian (4)	4	0.02
Chinese, ex. Taiwanese (34)	51	0.19
Filipino (31)	44	0.17
Indian (122)	139	0.53
Japanese (14)	26	0.10
Korean (17)	25	0.10
Pakistani (6)	7	0.03
Sri Lankan (2)	3	0.01
Thai (1)	2	0.01
Vietnamese (187)	207	0.79
Other Asian, specified (3)	3	0.01
Other Asian, not specified (8)	27	0.10
Australian	17	0.06
Austrian	69	0.26
British	105	0.40
Bulgarian	14	0.05
Canadian	35	0.13
Celtic	4	0.02
Croatian	4	0.02
Czech	46	0.18
Czechoslovakian	48	0.18
Danish	60	0.23
Dutch	1,125	4.28
Eastern European	26	0.10
English	1,527	5.81
European	106	0.40
Finnish	9	0.03
French, except Basque	435	1.66
French Canadian	78	0.30
German	5,494	20.92
Greek	175	0.67
Hawaii Native/Pacific Islander:	52	0.20
Micronesian: (17)	18	0.07
Guamanian/Chamorro (17)	18	0.07
Polynesian: (2)	5	0.02
Native Hawaiian (2)	4	0.02
Samoan	1	0.00
Other Pac. Isl., not spec. (9)	29	0.11
Hispanic or Latino:	2,570	9.79
Central American:	145	0.55
Costa Rican	13	0.05
Guatemalan	38	0.14
Honduran	19	0.07
Nicaraguan	15	0.06
Panamanian	25	0.10
Salvadoran	29	0.11
Other Central American	6	0.02
Cuban	45	0.17
Dominican Republic	35	0.13
Mexican	622	2.37
Puerto Rican	1,127	4.29
South American:	185	0.70
Argentinean	15	0.06
Bolivian	1	0.00
Chilean	5	0.02
Colombian	110	0.42
Ecuadorian	20	0.08
Paraguayan	1	0.00
Peruvian	23	0.09
Venezuelan	10	0.04
Other Hispanic or Latino	411	1.56
Hungarian	491	1.87
Icelander	5	0.02
Irish	3,052	11.62
Israeli	14	0.05
Italian	3,701	14.09
Lithuanian	119	0.45
Macedonian	17	0.06
Northern European	5	0.02
Norwegian	76	0.29
Pennsylvania German	741	2.82
Polish	943	3.59
Portuguese	56	0.21
Romanian	58	0.22
Russian	198	0.75
Scandinavian	12	0.05
Scotch-Irish	234	0.89
Scottish	397	1.51
Slavic	6	0.02
Slovak	211	0.80
Slovene	13	0.05
Swedish	127	0.48
Swiss	67	0.26
Turkish	39	0.15
Ukrainian	136	0.52
United States or American	906	3.45
Welsh	397	1.51
West Indian, excl. Hispanic:	306	1.17
Bahamian	5	0.02
Barbadian	25	0.10
Haitian	62	0.24
Jamaican	171	0.65
Trinidadian and Tobagonian	21	0.08
West Indian	22	0.08
White:	21,272	81.00
Not Hispanic (19,302)	19,808	75.42
Hispanic (1,308)	1,464	5.57

Easttown

Place Type: Township
County: Chester
Population: 10,270

Ancestry/Race	Number	%
African American/Black:	274	2.67
Not Hispanic (254)	270	2.63
Hispanic (4)	4	0.04
African, sub-Saharan:	62	0.60
African	55	0.54
South African	7	0.07
Alaska Native tribes, specified:	3	0.03
Tlingit-Haida (3)	3	0.03
Am. Ind. or Alaska Nat., not spec.	14	0.14
Alsatian	18	0.18
American Indian tribes, specified:	4	0.04
Cherokee (1)	1	0.01
Latin American Indians (1)	1	0.01
Sioux (1)	1	0.01
All other tribes (1)	1	0.01
Arab:	43	0.42
Jordanian	16	0.16
Lebanese	27	0.26
Armenian	33	0.32
Asian:	317	3.09
Cambodian (5)	5	0.05
Chinese, ex. Taiwanese (123)	131	1.28
Filipino (16)	20	0.19
Indian (82)	90	0.88
Japanese (7)	16	0.16
Korean (29)	30	0.29
Pakistani (6)	7	0.07
Taiwanese (3)	3	0.03
Vietnamese (11)	12	0.12
Other Asian, not specified	3	0.03
Australian	14	0.14
Austrian	89	0.87
Belgian	12	0.12
British	163	1.59
Canadian	70	0.68
Czech	48	0.47
Czechoslovakian	18	0.18
Danish	5	0.05
Dutch	149	1.45
Eastern European	41	0.40
English	1,888	18.38
European	107	1.04
Finnish	48	0.47
French, except Basque	463	4.51
French Canadian	78	0.76
German	1,918	18.68
Greek	96	0.93
Hawaii Native/Pacific Islander:	4	0.04
Polynesian: (1)	3	0.03
Native Hawaiian	2	0.02
Samoan (1)	1	0.01
Other Pac. Isl., not spec.	1	0.01
Hispanic or Latino:	111	1.08
Central American:	7	0.07
Costa Rican	1	0.01
Guatemalan	2	0.02
Nicaraguan	1	0.01
Salvadoran	2	0.02
Other Central American	1	0.01
Cuban	23	0.22
Mexican	22	0.21
Puerto Rican	20	0.19
South American:	24	0.23
Argentinean	5	0.05
Chilean	4	0.04
Colombian	5	0.05
Ecuadorian	2	0.02
Peruvian	4	0.04
Venezuelan	1	0.01
Other South American	3	0.03

Notes: 1. Figures in the "Number" column do not add up to the total population due to: a) Ancestry/Race overlap — e.g. persons can report being both White and Irish, b) persons of Hispanic origin can report being any race, c) persons reporting two ancestries are counted in both categories. 2. Numbers in parentheses indicate the number of persons reporting this ancestry/race alone, not in combination with any other ancestry/race. 3. Refer to the Explanation of Data in the front of the book for more detailed information.

Ancestry/Race	Number	%
Other Hispanic or Latino	15	0.15
Hungarian	184	1.79
Irish	2,437	23.73
Italian	1,466	14.27
Lithuanian	38	0.37
Norwegian	136	1.32
Pennsylvania German	9	0.09
Polish	524	5.10
Russian	135	1.31
Scandinavian	32	0.31
Scotch-Irish	265	2.58
Scottish	330	3.21
Slovak	37	0.36
Swedish	215	2.09
Swiss	6	0.06
Ukrainian	52	0.51
United States or American	396	3.86
Welsh	248	2.41
West Indian, excl. Hispanic:	55	0.54
Bahamian	9	0.09
Jamaican	46	0.45
White:	9,690	94.35
Not Hispanic (9,542)	9,595	93.43
Hispanic (88)	95	0.93
Yugoslavian	15	0.15

Elizabeth

Place Type: Township
County: Allegheny
Population: 13,839

Ancestry/Race	Number	%
African American/Black:	258	1.86
Not Hispanic (232)	256	1.85
Hispanic (2)	2	0.01
Am. Ind. or Alaska Nat., not spec.	11	0.08
American Indian tribes, specified:	21	0.15
Cherokee (1)	9	0.07
Chippewa (4)	4	0.03
Delaware	1	0.01
Iroquois	3	0.02
Latin American Indians (1)	1	0.01
Shoshone	3	0.02
Arab:	82	0.59
Lebanese	34	0.25
Palestinian	9	0.07
Syrian	39	0.28
Asian:	55	0.40
Bangladeshi (2)	2	0.01
Chinese, ex. Taiwanese (1)	1	0.01
Filipino (10)	11	0.08
Indian (8)	12	0.09
Japanese (3)	6	0.04
Korean (9)	13	0.09
Taiwanese (2)	3	0.02
Vietnamese (1)	1	0.01
Other Asian, specified	5	0.04
Other Asian, not specified	1	0.01
Australian	6	0.04
Austrian	18	0.13
Belgian	14	0.10
British	62	0.45
Carpatho Rusyn	7	0.05
Celtic	14	0.10
Croatian	377	2.72
Czech	97	0.70
Czechoslovakian	15	0.11
Dutch	181	1.31
Eastern European	13	0.09
English	1,616	11.68
European	18	0.13
Finnish	26	0.19
French, except Basque	223	1.61
French Canadian	10	0.07
German	3,311	23.93
Greek	138	1.00
Hawaii Native/Pacific Islander:	12	0.09
Micronesian: (1)	1	0.01
Guamanian/Chamorro (1)	1	0.01
Polynesian: (1)	6	0.04
Native Hawaiian (1)	6	0.04
Other Pac. Isl., specified	5	0.04
Hispanic or Latino:	51	0.37
Central American:	3	0.02
Costa Rican	2	0.01
Nicaraguan	1	0.01
Cuban	2	0.01
Mexican	16	0.12
Puerto Rican	8	0.06
Other Hispanic or Latino	22	0.16
Hungarian	623	4.50
Irish	2,496	18.04
Italian	2,042	14.76
Lithuanian	92	0.66
Norwegian	77	0.56
Pennsylvania German	8	0.06
Polish	1,419	10.25
Romanian	23	0.17
Russian	382	2.76
Scotch-Irish	390	2.82
Scottish	295	2.13
Serbian	110	0.79
Slavic	67	0.48
Slovak	1,145	8.27
Slovene	8	0.06
Swedish	289	2.09
Swiss	40	0.29
Ukrainian	144	1.04
United States or American	763	5.51
Welsh	130	0.94
White:	13,534	97.80
Not Hispanic (13,436)	13,497	97.53
Hispanic (37)	37	0.27
Yugoslavian	9	0.07

Elizabethtown

Place Type: Borough
County: Lancaster
Population: 11,887

Ancestry/Race	Number	%
African American/Black:	136	1.14
Not Hispanic (105)	134	1.13
Hispanic (2)	2	0.02
African, sub-Saharan:	14	0.12
African	4	0.03
Zimbabwean	10	0.08
Alaska Native tribes, specified:	1	0.01
Eskimo (1)	1	0.01
Am. Ind. or Alaska Nat., not spec.	11	0.09
American Indian tribes, specified:	41	0.34
Blackfeet	1	0.01
Cherokee (3)	12	0.10
Cree (1)	1	0.01
Iroquois (1)	3	0.03
Navajo	3	0.03
Pueblo	3	0.03
Seminole	1	0.01
Shoshone (9)	9	0.08
Sioux	1	0.01
Tohono O'Odham	1	0.01
All other tribes (2)	6	0.05
American Indian tribes, not spec.	4	0.03
Arab:	34	0.29
Arab/Arabic	5	0.04
Lebanese	12	0.10
Syrian	17	0.14
Asian:	175	1.47
Cambodian (12)	14	0.12
Chinese, ex. Taiwanese (12)	12	0.10
Filipino (13)	15	0.13
Hmong (5)	5	0.04
Indian (36)	39	0.33
Indonesian (1)	1	0.01
Japanese (10)	14	0.12
Korean (8)	11	0.09
Malaysian (1)	1	0.01
Pakistani (4)	4	0.03
Taiwanese (1)	1	0.01
Thai (6)	10	0.08
Vietnamese (31)	35	0.29
Other Asian, specified (3)	4	0.03
Other Asian, not specified (2)	9	0.08
Austrian	37	0.31
Brazilian	6	0.05
British	87	0.73
Canadian	31	0.26
Czech	7	0.06
Czechoslovakian	21	0.18
Danish	37	0.31
Dutch	204	1.72
English	846	7.12
European	65	0.55
Finnish	13	0.11
French, except Basque	266	2.24
French Canadian	78	0.66
German	4,908	41.31
Greek	32	0.27
Guyanese	52	0.44
Hawaii Native/Pacific Islander:	15	0.13
Polynesian: (5)	7	0.06
Native Hawaiian (3)	5	0.04
Samoan (2)	2	0.02
Other Pac. Isl., specified	1	0.01
Other Pac. Isl., not spec.	7	0.06
Hispanic or Latino:	172	1.45
Central American:	5	0.04
Costa Rican	1	0.01
Guatemalan	1	0.01
Honduran	1	0.01
Salvadoran	1	0.01
Other Central American	1	0.01
Cuban	5	0.04
Dominican Republic	3	0.03
Mexican	62	0.52
Puerto Rican	61	0.51
South American:	13	0.11
Argentinean	3	0.03
Bolivian	3	0.03
Colombian	1	0.01
Ecuadorian	4	0.03
Peruvian	1	0.01
Venezuelan	1	0.01
Other Hispanic or Latino	23	0.19
Hungarian	55	0.46
Irish	1,433	12.06
Italian	639	5.38
Lithuanian	49	0.41
Luxemburger	5	0.04
Northern European	15	0.13
Norwegian	88	0.74
Pennsylvania German	117	0.98
Polish	669	5.63
Romanian	5	0.04
Russian	61	0.51
Scandinavian	27	0.23
Scotch-Irish	221	1.86
Scottish	341	2.87
Serbian	12	0.10
Slovak	36	0.30
Swedish	205	1.73
Swiss	160	1.35
Turkish	18	0.15
Ukrainian	36	0.30
United States or American	687	5.78
Welsh	241	2.03
White:	11,545	97.12
Not Hispanic (11,349)	11,432	96.17
Hispanic (101)	113	0.95
Yugoslavian	7	0.06

Emmaus

Place Type: Borough
County: Lehigh
Population: 11,313

Ancestry/Race	Number	%

Notes: 1. Figures in the "Number" column do not add up to the total population due to: a) Ancestry/Race overlap — e.g. persons can report being both White and Irish, b) persons of Hispanic origin can report being any race, c) persons reporting two ancestries are counted in both categories. 2. Numbers in parentheses indicate the number of persons reporting this ancestry/race alone, not in combination with any other ancestry/race. 3. Refer to the Explanation of Data in the front of the book for more detailed information.

African American/Black:	101	0.89
Not Hispanic (75)	97	0.86
Hispanic (4)	4	0.04
Am. Ind. or Alaska Nat., not spec.	11	0.10
American Indian tribes, specified:	14	0.12
Cherokee	7	0.06
Delaware (1)	3	0.03
Iroquois	1	0.01
All other tribes (3)	3	0.03
Arab:	8	0.07
Egyptian	8	0.07
Asian:	219	1.94
Chinese, ex. Taiwanese (43)	43	0.38
Filipino (17)	19	0.17
Indian (81)	83	0.73
Japanese (16)	18	0.16
Korean (35)	37	0.33
Pakistani	1	0.01
Thai (1)	1	0.01
Vietnamese (5)	5	0.04
Other Asian, not specified (6)	12	0.11
Austrian	263	2.34
British	48	0.43
Czech	7	0.06
Czechoslovakian	45	0.40
Danish	14	0.12
Dutch	348	3.10
Eastern European	15	0.13
English	795	7.07
European	61	0.54
French, except Basque	278	2.47
French Canadian	96	0.85
German	4,115	36.60
Greek	51	0.45
Hawaii Native/Pacific Islander:	4	0.04
Polynesian: (2)	3	0.03
Native Hawaiian (1)	2	0.02
Other Polynesian (1)	1	0.01
Other Pac. Isl., not spec. (1)	1	0.01
Hispanic or Latino:	171	1.51
Central American:	25	0.22
Guatemalan	9	0.08
Salvadoran	16	0.14
Cuban	1	0.01
Dominican Republic	13	0.11
Mexican	15	0.13
Puerto Rican	82	0.72
South American:	10	0.09
Colombian	2	0.02
Ecuadorian	2	0.02
Peruvian	3	0.03
Venezuelan	3	0.03
Other Hispanic or Latino	25	0.22
Hungarian	276	2.46
Iranian	8	0.07
Irish	1,110	9.87
Israeli	9	0.08
Italian	778	6.92
Lithuanian	72	0.64
Norwegian	41	0.36
Pennsylvania German	988	8.79
Polish	466	4.15
Portuguese	14	0.12
Romanian	8	0.07
Russian	172	1.53
Scandinavian	8	0.07
Scotch-Irish	91	0.81
Scottish	158	1.41
Slovak	507	4.51
Slovene	11	0.10
Swedish	14	0.12
Ukrainian	210	1.87
United States or American	653	5.81
Welsh	206	1.83
White:	10,919	96.52
Not Hispanic (10,785)	10,847	95.88
Hispanic (63)	72	0.64
Yugoslavian	13	0.12

Ephrata

Place Type: Borough
County: Lancaster
Population: 13,213

Ancestry/Race	Number	%
African American/Black:	117	0.89
Not Hispanic (80)	109	0.82
Hispanic (4)	8	0.06
African, sub-Saharan:	10	0.08
Ethiopian	10	0.08
Am. Ind. or Alaska Nat., not spec.	35	0.26
American Indian tribes, specified:	31	0.23
Blackfeet (3)	3	0.02
Cherokee (3)	10	0.08
Comanche	2	0.02
Delaware (1)	2	0.02
Iroquois	1	0.01
Kiowa (1)	1	0.01
Latin American Indians (4)	4	0.03
Sioux (2)	2	0.02
All other tribes	6	0.05
American Indian tribes, not spec.	5	0.04
Arab:	7	0.05
Lebanese	7	0.05
Armenian	14	0.11
Asian:	179	1.35
Cambodian (6)	6	0.05
Chinese, ex. Taiwanese (19)	26	0.20
Filipino (8)	12	0.09
Hmong (25)	25	0.19
Indian (18)	22	0.17
Japanese (4)	7	0.05
Korean (16)	19	0.14
Laotian (16)	17	0.13
Pakistani (1)	2	0.02
Vietnamese (20)	31	0.23
Other Asian, not specified (2)	12	0.09
Austrian	20	0.15
British	21	0.16
Bulgarian	23	0.17
Canadian	12	0.09
Croatian	6	0.05
Czechoslovakian	9	0.07
Danish	17	0.13
Dutch	285	2.16
English	610	4.62
European	126	0.95
French, except Basque	179	1.36
French Canadian	48	0.36
German	5,721	43.36
Greek	20	0.15
Hawaii Native/Pacific Islander:	28	0.21
Micronesian: (1)	1	0.01
Guamanian/Chamorro (1)	1	0.01
Polynesian: (9)	16	0.12
Native Hawaiian (5)	12	0.09
Samoan (4)	4	0.03
Other Pac. Isl., not spec. (8)	11	0.08
Hispanic or Latino:	364	2.75
Central American:	6	0.05
Guatemalan	1	0.01
Nicaraguan	1	0.01
Salvadoran	4	0.03
Cuban	12	0.09
Dominican Republic	6	0.05
Mexican	41	0.31
Puerto Rican	145	1.10
South American:	90	0.68
Argentinean	1	0.01
Bolivian	4	0.03
Colombian	72	0.54
Ecuadorian	2	0.02
Paraguayan	1	0.01
Peruvian	3	0.02
Venezuelan	4	0.03
Other South American	3	0.02
Other Hispanic or Latino	64	0.48
Hungarian	38	0.29
Irish	1,470	11.14
Italian	539	4.09
Latvian	5	0.04
Lithuanian	61	0.46
Northern European	5	0.04
Norwegian	24	0.18
Pennsylvania German	126	0.95
Polish	426	3.23
Portuguese	5	0.04
Russian	286	2.17
Scotch-Irish	212	1.61
Scottish	119	0.90
Slovak	26	0.20
Swedish	80	0.61
Swiss	260	1.97
Ukrainian	85	0.64
United States or American	1,306	9.90
Welsh	141	1.07
White:	12,817	97.00
Not Hispanic (12,477)	12,572	95.15
Hispanic (221)	245	1.85

Erie

Place Type: City
County: Erie
Population: 103,717

Ancestry/Race	Number	%
Acadian/Cajun	9	0.01
African American/Black:	16,055	15.48
Not Hispanic (14,420)	15,611	15.05
Hispanic (304)	444	0.43
African, sub-Saharan:	798	0.77
African	716	0.69
Somalian	31	0.03
South African	20	0.02
Sudanese	31	0.03
Alaska Native tribes, specified:	4	0.00
Aleut	1	0.00
Eskimo	1	0.00
Tlingit-Haida (2)	2	0.00
Am. Ind. or Alaska Nat., not spec.	311	0.30
Albanian	31	0.03
Alsatian	7	0.01
American Indian tribes, specified:	385	0.37
Apache (7)	22	0.02
Blackfeet (6)	31	0.03
Cherokee (30)	135	0.13
Chickasaw	1	0.00
Chippewa (5)	7	0.01
Choctaw (1)	8	0.01
Cree	2	0.00
Creek	2	0.00
Crow	1	0.00
Delaware (1)	7	0.01
Iroquois (36)	85	0.08
Latin American Indians (15)	27	0.03
Lumbee	1	0.00
Menominee	1	0.00
Navajo (2)	6	0.01
Potawatomi	1	0.00
Seminole (2)	6	0.01
Shoshone	1	0.00
Sioux (6)	17	0.02
Tohono O'Odham (1)	2	0.00
Ute (1)	1	0.00
Yakama (1)	1	0.00
All other tribes (14)	20	0.02
American Indian tribes, not spec.	20	0.02
Arab:	434	0.42
Arab/Arabic	118	0.11
Egyptian	11	0.01
Iraqi	109	0.11
Lebanese	103	0.10
Syrian	31	0.03
Other Arab	62	0.06
Armenian	166	0.16
Asian:	1,052	1.01
Chinese, ex. Taiwanese (90)	109	0.11

Notes: 1. Figures in the "Number" column do not add up to the total population due to: a) Ancestry/Race overlap — e.g. persons can report being both White and Irish, b) persons of Hispanic origin can report being any race, c) persons reporting two ancestries are counted in both categories. 2. Numbers in parentheses indicate the number of persons reporting this ancestry/race alone, not in combination with any other ancestry/race. 3. Refer to the Explanation of Data in the front of the book for more detailed information.

Filipino (80)	141	0.14
Hmong (1)	1	0.00
Indian (160)	197	0.19
Indonesian (4)	5	0.00
Japanese (20)	51	0.05
Korean (59)	86	0.08
Laotian (9)	9	0.01
Pakistani (10)	15	0.01
Taiwanese	2	0.00
Thai (18)	31	0.03
Vietnamese (283)	309	0.30
Other Asian, specified (2)	2	0.00
Other Asian, not specified (20)	94	0.09
Australian	41	0.04
Austrian	306	0.30
Belgian	46	0.04
Brazilian	6	0.01
British	205	0.20
Canadian	133	0.13
Carpatho Rusyn	12	0.01
Celtic	40	0.04
Croatian	200	0.19
Czech	248	0.24
Czechoslovakian	233	0.22
Danish	256	0.25
Dutch	948	0.91
Eastern European	24	0.02
English	6,021	5.80
Estonian	34	0.03
European	231	0.22
Finnish	192	0.19
French, except Basque	1,742	1.68
French Canadian	346	0.33
German	25,279	24.37
German Russian	10	0.01
Greek	338	0.33
Guyanese	6	0.01
Hawaii Native/Pacific Islander:	113	0.11
Micronesian: (10)	21	0.02
Guamanian/Chamorro (7)	18	0.02
Other Micronesian (3)	3	0.00
Polynesian: (28)	53	0.05
Native Hawaiian (13)	28	0.03
Samoan (11)	15	0.01
Tongan (4)	10	0.01
Other Pac. Isl., not spec. (4)	39	0.04
Hispanic or Latino:	4,572	4.41
Central American:	128	0.12
Costa Rican	14	0.01
Guatemalan	16	0.02
Honduran	14	0.01
Nicaraguan	12	0.01
Panamanian	13	0.01
Salvadoran	57	0.05
Other Central American	2	0.00
Cuban	44	0.04
Dominican Republic	48	0.05
Mexican	840	0.81
Puerto Rican	2,911	2.81
South American:	76	0.07
Bolivian	1	0.00
Chilean	4	0.00
Colombian	38	0.04
Ecuadorian	8	0.01
Peruvian	16	0.02
Venezuelan	6	0.01
Other South American	3	0.00
Other Hispanic or Latino	525	0.51
Hungarian	992	0.96
Iranian	26	0.03
Irish	14,509	13.99
Italian	13,937	13.44
Latvian	13	0.01
Lithuanian	216	0.21
Macedonian	41	0.04
Maltese	17	0.02
Northern European	6	0.01
Norwegian	225	0.22
Pennsylvania German	128	0.12
Polish	14,718	14.19
Portuguese	289	0.28
Romanian	190	0.18
Russian	1,464	1.41
Scandinavian	31	0.03
Scotch-Irish	1,653	1.59
Scottish	1,238	1.19
Serbian	21	0.02
Slavic	344	0.33
Slovak	1,235	1.19
Slovene	35	0.03
Swedish	1,749	1.69
Swiss	181	0.17
Ukrainian	690	0.67
United States or American	3,875	3.74
Welsh	760	0.73
West Indian, excl. Hispanic:	108	0.10
British West Indian	6	0.01
Haitian	41	0.04
Jamaican	61	0.06
White:	85,647	82.58
Not Hispanic (81,605)	83,340	80.35
Hispanic (1,945)	2,307	2.22
Yugoslavian	718	0.69

Exeter

Place Type: Township
County: Berks
Population: 21,161

Ancestry/Race	Number	%
African American/Black:	477	2.25
Not Hispanic (424)	463	2.19
Hispanic (9)	14	0.07
African, sub-Saharan:	44	0.21
African	30	0.14
South African	14	0.07
Am. Ind. or Alaska Nat., not spec.	21	0.10
American Indian tribes, specified:	31	0.15
Cherokee (2)	8	0.04
Chippewa (4)	4	0.02
Comanche (1)	1	0.00
Delaware	2	0.01
Iroquois	1	0.00
Latin American Indians (2)	2	0.01
Navajo	1	0.00
Potawatomi (1)	1	0.00
Seminole (1)	1	0.00
Sioux (4)	5	0.02
All other tribes (2)	5	0.02
American Indian tribes, not spec.	6	0.03
Arab:	100	0.47
Egyptian	58	0.27
Lebanese	42	0.20
Armenian	10	0.05
Asian:	297	1.40
Chinese, ex. Taiwanese (47)	65	0.31
Filipino (36)	47	0.22
Indian (70)	77	0.36
Indonesian	3	0.01
Japanese (10)	14	0.07
Korean (30)	35	0.17
Laotian (5)	5	0.02
Malaysian	1	0.00
Pakistani (2)	2	0.01
Taiwanese (4)	4	0.02
Thai (7)	7	0.03
Vietnamese (25)	28	0.13
Other Asian, specified (3)	3	0.01
Other Asian, not specified (3)	6	0.03
Australian	9	0.04
Austrian	63	0.30
Belgian	12	0.06
Brazilian	10	0.05
British	34	0.16
Canadian	25	0.12
Croatian	10	0.05
Czech	93	0.44
Czechoslovakian	19	0.09
Dutch	903	4.26
Eastern European	16	0.08
English	1,844	8.70
European	80	0.38
Finnish	9	0.04
French, except Basque	382	1.80
French Canadian	87	0.41
German	7,847	37.04
Greek	187	0.88
Hawaii Native/Pacific Islander:	10	0.05
Micronesian:	1	0.00
Guamanian/Chamorro	1	0.00
Polynesian: (3)	7	0.03
Native Hawaiian (1)	2	0.01
Samoan (2)	2	0.01
Other Polynesian	3	0.01
Other Pac. Isl., not spec.	2	0.01
Hispanic or Latino:	374	1.77
Central American:	6	0.03
Honduran	2	0.01
Nicaraguan	2	0.01
Panamanian	2	0.01
Cuban	18	0.09
Dominican Republic	1	0.00
Mexican	42	0.20
Puerto Rican	227	1.07
South American:	24	0.11
Chilean	3	0.01
Colombian	8	0.04
Ecuadorian	1	0.00
Peruvian	11	0.05
Venezuelan	1	0.00
Other Hispanic or Latino	56	0.26
Hungarian	174	0.82
Irish	3,048	14.39
Italian	2,801	13.22
Lithuanian	122	0.58
New Zealander	8	0.04
Norwegian	81	0.38
Pennsylvania German	664	3.13
Polish	2,269	10.71
Romanian	22	0.10
Russian	259	1.22
Scandinavian	25	0.12
Scotch-Irish	252	1.19
Scottish	319	1.51
Slavic	7	0.03
Slovak	360	1.70
Swedish	119	0.56
Swiss	73	0.34
Ukrainian	193	0.91
United States or American	860	4.06
Welsh	429	2.02
West Indian, excl. Hispanic:	52	0.25
Haitian	30	0.14
Jamaican	22	0.10
White:	20,325	96.05
Not Hispanic (19,953)	20,069	94.84
Hispanic (228)	256	1.21
Yugoslavian	17	0.08

Fairview

Place Type: Township
County: Erie
Population: 10,140

Ancestry/Race	Number	%
African American/Black:	71	0.70
Not Hispanic (54)	70	0.69
Hispanic	1	0.01
Am. Ind. or Alaska Nat., not spec.	3	0.03
American Indian tribes, specified:	18	0.18
Blackfeet (1)	1	0.01
Cherokee	5	0.05
Iroquois	3	0.03
Latin American Indians	1	0.01
Potawatomi	1	0.01
All other tribes (4)	7	0.07
Arab:	15	0.15
Lebanese	6	0.06

Notes: 1. Figures in the "Number" column do not add up to the total population due to: a) Ancestry/Race overlap — e.g. persons can report being both White and Irish, b) persons of Hispanic origin can report being any race, c) persons reporting two ancestries are counted in both categories. 2. Numbers in parentheses indicate the number of persons reporting this ancestry/race alone, not in combination with any other ancestry/race. 3. Refer to the Explanation of Data in the front of the book for more detailed information.

Other Arab	9	0.09
Asian:	77	0.76
Chinese, ex. Taiwanese (5)	9	0.09
Indian (29)	31	0.31
Japanese (3)	7	0.07
Korean (9)	15	0.15
Thai (1)	1	0.01
Vietnamese (6)	9	0.09
Other Asian, not specified	5	0.05
Austrian	30	0.30
Belgian	13	0.13
British	23	0.23
Canadian	36	0.36
Croatian	81	0.80
Czech	55	0.54
Czechoslovakian	34	0.34
Danish	31	0.31
Dutch	140	1.38
English	1,209	11.92
European	69	0.68
Finnish	31	0.31
French, except Basque	142	1.40
French Canadian	37	0.36
German	3,647	35.97
Greek	52	0.51
Hawaii Native/Pacific Islander:	1	0.01
Polynesian:	1	0.01
Native Hawaiian	1	0.01
Hispanic or Latino:	69	0.68
Central American:	6	0.06
Honduran	2	0.02
Panamanian	1	0.01
Salvadoran	3	0.03
Dominican Republic	1	0.01
Mexican	13	0.13
Puerto Rican	21	0.21
South American:	9	0.09
Argentinean	3	0.03
Bolivian	2	0.02
Colombian	1	0.01
Ecuadorian	1	0.01
Venezuelan	2	0.02
Other Hispanic or Latino	19	0.19
Hungarian	151	1.49
Irish	1,845	18.20
Italian	1,402	13.83
Lithuanian	57	0.56
Norwegian	32	0.32
Pennsylvania German	27	0.27
Polish	1,113	10.98
Portuguese	17	0.17
Romanian	7	0.07
Russian	188	1.85
Scotch-Irish	273	2.69
Scottish	205	2.02
Serbian	5	0.05
Slavic	24	0.24
Slovak	160	1.58
Slovene	11	0.11
Swedish	324	3.20
Swiss	43	0.42
Ukrainian	57	0.56
United States or American	399	3.93
Welsh	155	1.53
West Indian, excl. Hispanic:	14	0.14
Jamaican	14	0.14
White:	10,005	98.67
Not Hispanic (9,902)	9,947	98.10
Hispanic (51)	58	0.57
Yugoslavian	12	0.12

Fairview

Place Type: Township
County: York
Population: 14,321

Ancestry/Race	Number	%
African American/Black:	157	1.10
Not Hispanic (125)	150	1.05
Hispanic	7	0.05
African, sub-Saharan:	7	0.05
African	7	0.05
Am. Ind. or Alaska Nat., not spec.	17	0.12
American Indian tribes, specified:	57	0.40
Apache	1	0.01
Blackfeet	7	0.05
Cherokee (2)	17	0.12
Chippewa	1	0.01
Choctaw (1)	1	0.01
Crow	3	0.02
Iroquois (2)	5	0.03
Navajo (1)	1	0.01
Sioux	7	0.05
All other tribes (7)	14	0.10
American Indian tribes, not spec.	1	0.01
Arab:	19	0.13
Lebanese	12	0.08
Syrian	7	0.05
Asian:	180	1.26
Bangladeshi (1)	1	0.01
Cambodian (1)	1	0.01
Chinese, ex. Taiwanese (11)	14	0.10
Filipino (22)	29	0.20
Indian (17)	18	0.13
Japanese (7)	13	0.09
Korean (43)	52	0.36
Laotian	4	0.03
Sri Lankan (1)	1	0.01
Thai	1	0.01
Vietnamese (38)	38	0.27
Other Asian, not specified (2)	8	0.06
Australian	6	0.04
Austrian	15	0.10
Belgian	6	0.04
British	102	0.71
Canadian	28	0.20
Croatian	97	0.68
Czech	31	0.22
Czechoslovakian	17	0.12
Danish	24	0.17
Dutch	302	2.11
Eastern European	26	0.18
English	1,332	9.30
European	99	0.69
French, except Basque	295	2.06
French Canadian	49	0.34
German	5,417	37.83
Greek	48	0.34
Guyanese	8	0.06
Hawaii Native/Pacific Islander:	24	0.17
Micronesian: (3)	3	0.02
Guamanian/Chamorro (3)	3	0.02
Polynesian: (7)	13	0.09
Native Hawaiian (7)	13	0.09
Other Pac. Isl., not spec. (2)	8	0.06
Hispanic or Latino:	186	1.30
Central American:	7	0.05
Guatemalan	2	0.01
Honduran	1	0.01
Nicaraguan	1	0.01
Panamanian	3	0.02
Cuban	6	0.04
Mexican	38	0.27
Puerto Rican	105	0.73
South American:	4	0.03
Ecuadorian	3	0.02
Other South American	1	0.01
Other Hispanic or Latino	26	0.18
Hungarian	92	0.64
Irish	2,270	15.85
Israeli	7	0.05
Italian	1,120	7.82
Lithuanian	104	0.73
Norwegian	57	0.40
Pennsylvania German	221	1.54
Polish	568	3.97
Portuguese	21	0.15
Russian	77	0.54
Scandinavian	8	0.06
Scotch-Irish	318	2.22
Scottish	496	3.46
Serbian	37	0.26
Slavic	50	0.35
Slovak	82	0.57
Slovene	27	0.19
Swedish	180	1.26
Swiss	92	0.64
Turkish	7	0.05
Ukrainian	130	0.91
United States or American	1,097	7.66
Welsh	258	1.80
West Indian, excl. Hispanic:	46	0.32
British West Indian	38	0.27
Jamaican	8	0.06
White:	13,940	97.34
Not Hispanic (13,720)	13,827	96.55
Hispanic (98)	113	0.79
Yugoslavian	7	0.05

Falls

Place Type: Township
County: Bucks
Population: 34,865

Ancestry/Race	Number	%
African American/Black:	1,872	5.37
Not Hispanic (1,673)	1,821	5.22
Hispanic (31)	51	0.15
African, sub-Saharan:	140	0.40
African	102	0.29
Nigerian	38	0.11
Am. Ind. or Alaska Nat., not spec.	47	0.13
Albanian	23	0.07
American Indian tribes, specified:	84	0.24
Apache	2	0.01
Blackfeet	2	0.01
Cherokee (16)	45	0.13
Comanche (1)	4	0.01
Creek (1)	1	0.00
Delaware (2)	6	0.02
Iroquois (6)	7	0.02
Latin American Indians (3)	4	0.01
Lumbee (1)	2	0.01
Navajo (1)	1	0.00
Sioux (1)	2	0.01
All other tribes (4)	8	0.02
American Indian tribes, not spec.	7	0.02
Arab:	92	0.26
Egyptian	51	0.15
Lebanese	41	0.12
Armenian	36	0.10
Asian:	1,061	3.04
Bangladeshi	3	0.01
Cambodian (1)	1	0.00
Chinese, ex. Taiwanese (146)	165	0.47
Filipino (98)	143	0.41
Indian (379)	406	1.16
Indonesian (1)	5	0.01
Japanese (23)	37	0.11
Korean (143)	164	0.47
Malaysian (1)	4	0.01
Pakistani (19)	39	0.11
Taiwanese	1	0.00
Thai (6)	9	0.03
Vietnamese (44)	50	0.14
Other Asian, not specified (18)	34	0.10
Austrian	175	0.50
Belgian	13	0.04
British	198	0.57
Canadian	50	0.14
Carpatho Rusyn	9	0.03
Celtic	34	0.10
Croatian	59	0.17
Czech	106	0.30
Czechoslovakian	28	0.08
Danish	91	0.26
Dutch	551	1.58
Eastern European	12	0.03

Notes: 1. Figures in the "Number" column do not add up to the total population due to: a) Ancestry/Race overlap — e.g. persons can report being both White and Irish, b) persons of Hispanic origin can report being any race, c) persons reporting two ancestries are counted in both categories. 2. Numbers in parentheses indicate the number of persons reporting this ancestry/race alone, not in combination with any other ancestry/race. 3. Refer to the Explanation of Data in the front of the book for more detailed information.

Ancestry/Race	Number	%
English	4,099	11.76
European	98	0.28
Finnish	30	0.09
French, except Basque	679	1.95
French Canadian	249	0.71
German	8,790	25.21
Greek	46	0.13
Hawaii Native/Pacific Islander:	26	0.07
Micronesian: (5)	8	0.02
Guamanian/Chamorro (5)	8	0.02
Polynesian: (2)	12	0.03
Native Hawaiian (1)	8	0.02
Samoan (1)	4	0.01
Other Pac. Isl., not spec.	6	0.02
Hispanic or Latino:	818	2.35
Central American:	29	0.08
Costa Rican	10	0.03
Guatemalan	12	0.03
Honduran	3	0.01
Nicaraguan	1	0.00
Panamanian	3	0.01
Cuban	32	0.09
Dominican Republic	14	0.04
Mexican	83	0.24
Puerto Rican	450	1.29
South American:	59	0.17
Argentinean	3	0.01
Chilean	2	0.01
Colombian	26	0.07
Ecuadorian	7	0.02
Peruvian	10	0.03
Uruguayan	3	0.01
Venezuelan	6	0.02
Other South American	2	0.01
Other Hispanic or Latino	151	0.43
Hungarian	612	1.76
Icelander	9	0.03
Iranian	8	0.02
Irish	9,595	27.52
Israeli	9	0.03
Italian	5,312	15.23
Lithuanian	285	0.82
Norwegian	120	0.34
Pennsylvania German	232	0.67
Polish	3,340	9.58
Portuguese	20	0.06
Romanian	99	0.28
Russian	593	1.70
Scandinavian	9	0.03
Scotch-Irish	521	1.49
Scottish	661	1.90
Slavic	87	0.25
Slovak	633	1.82
Slovene	12	0.03
Swedish	372	1.07
Swiss	49	0.14
Turkish	29	0.08
Ukrainian	471	1.35
United States or American	1,362	3.91
Welsh	533	1.53
West Indian, excl. Hispanic:	47	0.13
Jamaican	21	0.06
West Indian	26	0.07
White:	31,859	91.38
Not Hispanic (31,003)	31,335	89.88
Hispanic (451)	524	1.50

Ferguson

Place Type: Township
County: Centre
Population: 14,063

Ancestry/Race	Number	%
Acadian/Cajun	17	0.12
African American/Black:	405	2.88
Not Hispanic (328)	384	2.73
Hispanic (10)	21	0.15
African, sub-Saharan:	46	0.33
African	8	0.06
Kenyan	8	0.06
Nigerian	7	0.05
Ugandan	23	0.16
Alaska Native tribes, specified:	1	0.01
Eskimo (1)	1	0.01
Am. Ind. or Alaska Nat., not spec.	34	0.24
American Indian tribes, specified:	27	0.19
Apache	1	0.01
Blackfeet (1)	2	0.01
Cherokee	7	0.05
Choctaw	2	0.01
Comanche (1)	1	0.01
Creek	1	0.01
Delaware	1	0.01
Iroquois	2	0.01
Latin American Indians (4)	4	0.03
Potawatomi (1)	1	0.01
Seminole	1	0.01
Sioux (1)	1	0.01
Yaqui (2)	2	0.01
All other tribes	1	0.01
American Indian tribes, not spec.	7	0.05
Arab:	73	0.52
Arab/Arabic	30	0.21
Lebanese	36	0.26
Other Arab	7	0.05
Asian:	1,135	8.07
Cambodian	1	0.01
Chinese, ex. Taiwanese (430)	460	3.27
Filipino (25)	29	0.21
Indian (190)	201	1.43
Indonesian	1	0.01
Japanese (46)	58	0.41
Korean (289)	297	2.11
Malaysian (11)	11	0.08
Pakistani (1)	2	0.01
Taiwanese (10)	12	0.09
Thai (11)	13	0.09
Vietnamese (13)	13	0.09
Other Asian, specified	1	0.01
Other Asian, not specified (11)	36	0.26
Austrian	104	0.74
Belgian	9	0.06
Brazilian	44	0.31
British	137	0.97
Bulgarian	7	0.05
Canadian	64	0.46
Croatian	46	0.33
Czech	79	0.56
Czechoslovakian	40	0.28
Danish	14	0.10
Dutch	299	2.13
English	1,659	11.80
European	152	1.08
Finnish	9	0.06
French, except Basque	190	1.35
French Canadian	63	0.45
German	3,836	27.28
Greek	54	0.38
Hawaii Native/Pacific Islander:	5	0.04
Polynesian: (4)	4	0.03
Native Hawaiian (3)	3	0.02
Samoan (1)	1	0.01
Other Pac. Isl., not spec.	1	0.01
Hispanic or Latino:	256	1.82
Central American:	7	0.05
Costa Rican	2	0.01
Guatemalan	1	0.01
Nicaraguan	1	0.01
Panamanian	2	0.01
Salvadoran	1	0.01
Cuban	18	0.13
Dominican Republic	10	0.07
Mexican	53	0.38
Puerto Rican	78	0.55
South American:	40	0.28
Argentinean	6	0.04
Bolivian	2	0.01
Chilean	4	0.03
Colombian	13	0.09
Ecuadorian	6	0.04
Peruvian	2	0.01
Venezuelan	5	0.04
Other South American	2	0.01
Other Hispanic or Latino	50	0.36
Hungarian	136	0.97
Icelander	21	0.15
Iranian	82	0.58
Irish	1,631	11.60
Italian	1,236	8.79
Latvian	13	0.09
Lithuanian	60	0.43
Northern European	7	0.05
Norwegian	174	1.24
Pennsylvania German	132	0.94
Polish	739	5.25
Portuguese	7	0.05
Romanian	7	0.05
Russian	231	1.64
Scandinavian	24	0.17
Scotch-Irish	406	2.89
Scottish	448	3.19
Slavic	29	0.21
Slovak	260	1.85
Slovene	36	0.26
Swedish	271	1.93
Swiss	50	0.36
Turkish	70	0.50
Ukrainian	85	0.60
United States or American	960	6.83
Welsh	240	1.71
West Indian, excl. Hispanic:	10	0.07
West Indian	10	0.07
White:	12,563	89.33
Not Hispanic (12,212)	12,384	88.06
Hispanic (147)	179	1.27

Fernway

Place Type: Census Designated Place
County: Butler
Population: 12,188

Ancestry/Race	Number	%
African American/Black:	146	1.20
Not Hispanic (117)	130	1.07
Hispanic (12)	16	0.13
Am. Ind. or Alaska Nat., not spec.	8	0.07
American Indian tribes, specified:	11	0.09
Cherokee (1)	5	0.04
Chippewa (1)	1	0.01
Creek (1)	1	0.01
Iroquois	1	0.01
Sioux	2	0.02
All other tribes (1)	1	0.01
American Indian tribes, not spec.	1	0.01
Arab:	33	0.27
Lebanese	33	0.27
Armenian	64	0.53
Asian:	167	1.37
Chinese, ex. Taiwanese (30)	31	0.25
Filipino (9)	22	0.18
Indian (42)	46	0.38
Japanese (6)	7	0.06
Korean (21)	32	0.26
Laotian (1)	2	0.02
Malaysian (1)	1	0.01
Pakistani (6)	6	0.05
Taiwanese (2)	2	0.02
Thai	2	0.02
Vietnamese (10)	11	0.09
Other Asian, not specified (2)	5	0.04
Austrian	28	0.23
Belgian	7	0.06
British	99	0.81
Croatian	291	2.39
Czech	147	1.21
Czechoslovakian	113	0.93
Danish	17	0.14
Dutch	127	1.04

Notes: 1. Figures in the "Number" column do not add up to the total population due to: a) Ancestry/Race overlap — e.g. persons can report being both White and Irish, b) persons of Hispanic origin can report being any race, c) persons reporting two ancestries are counted in both categories. 2. Numbers in parentheses indicate the number of persons reporting this ancestry/race alone, not in combination with any other ancestry/race. 3. Refer to the Explanation of Data in the front of the book for more detailed information.

English	1,116	9.16
European	109	0.89
French, except Basque	301	2.47
German	4,664	38.29
Greek	130	1.07
Hawaii Native/Pacific Islander:	2	0.02
Polynesian: (1)	2	0.02
Native Hawaiian	1	0.01
Tongan (1)	1	0.01
Hispanic or Latino:	77	0.63
Central American:	1	0.01
Salvadoran	1	0.01
Cuban	5	0.04
Mexican	32	0.26
Puerto Rican	24	0.20
South American:	5	0.04
Chilean	2	0.02
Ecuadorian	1	0.01
Peruvian	1	0.01
Venezuelan	1	0.01
Other Hispanic or Latino	10	0.08
Hungarian	104	0.85
Irish	2,859	23.47
Italian	2,131	17.49
Lithuanian	28	0.23
Norwegian	72	0.59
Polish	1,116	9.16
Romanian	44	0.36
Russian	117	0.96
Scotch-Irish	286	2.35
Scottish	338	2.77
Serbian	109	0.89
Slavic	50	0.41
Slovak	442	3.63
Slovene	47	0.39
Swedish	131	1.08
Swiss	65	0.53
Ukrainian	119	0.98
United States or American	387	3.18
Welsh	193	1.58
White:	11,896	97.60
Not Hispanic (11,786)	11,849	97.22
Hispanic (43)	47	0.39
Yugoslavian	15	0.12

Franconia

Place Type: Township
County: Montgomery
Population: 11,523

Ancestry/Race	Number	%
African American/Black:	114	0.99
Not Hispanic (97)	112	0.97
Hispanic (2)	2	0.02
Am. Ind. or Alaska Nat., not spec.	3	0.03
American Indian tribes, specified:	14	0.12
Blackfeet	3	0.03
Cherokee	2	0.02
Iroquois (1)	2	0.02
Latin American Indians (2)	2	0.02
Lumbee (1)	2	0.02
All other tribes (2)	3	0.03
Arab:	22	0.19
Arab/Arabic	8	0.07
Jordanian	9	0.08
Palestinian	5	0.04
Asian:	217	1.88
Cambodian (10)	10	0.09
Chinese, ex. Taiwanese (13)	18	0.16
Filipino (6)	6	0.05
Indian (7)	9	0.08
Japanese (5)	7	0.06
Korean (18)	27	0.23
Laotian (5)	5	0.04
Pakistani	1	0.01
Vietnamese (128)	132	1.15
Other Asian, not specified (2)	2	0.02
Austrian	71	0.62
British	34	0.30
Canadian	11	0.10
Czech	32	0.28
Czechoslovakian	4	0.03
Danish	17	0.15
Dutch	263	2.28
Eastern European	8	0.07
English	1,053	9.14
Estonian	15	0.13
European	65	0.56
Finnish	17	0.15
French, except Basque	251	2.18
French Canadian	41	0.36
German	4,414	38.31
Greek	37	0.32
Hawaii Native/Pacific Islander:	2	0.02
Micronesian: (1)	1	0.01
Guamanian/Chamorro (1)	1	0.01
Polynesian:	1	0.01
Native Hawaiian	1	0.01
Hispanic or Latino:	103	0.89
Central American:	8	0.07
Guatemalan	2	0.02
Honduran	2	0.02
Nicaraguan	4	0.03
Cuban	10	0.09
Mexican	17	0.15
Puerto Rican	47	0.41
South American:	8	0.07
Colombian	5	0.04
Ecuadorian	1	0.01
Venezuelan	1	0.01
Other South American	1	0.01
Other Hispanic or Latino	13	0.11
Hungarian	96	0.83
Iranian	45	0.39
Irish	1,806	15.67
Italian	1,329	11.53
Lithuanian	100	0.87
Norwegian	52	0.45
Pennsylvania German	404	3.51
Polish	627	5.44
Portuguese	15	0.13
Romanian	9	0.08
Russian	163	1.41
Scandinavian	17	0.15
Scotch-Irish	151	1.31
Scottish	198	1.72
Slovak	77	0.67
Swedish	105	0.91
Swiss	360	3.12
Ukrainian	125	1.08
United States or American	466	4.04
Welsh	178	1.54
West Indian, excl. Hispanic:	7	0.06
Jamaican	7	0.06
White:	11,174	96.97
Not Hispanic (11,066)	11,104	96.36
Hispanic (62)	70	0.61

Franklin Park

Place Type: Borough
County: Allegheny
Population: 11,364

Ancestry/Race	Number	%
African American/Black:	134	1.18
Not Hispanic (115)	131	1.15
Hispanic (1)	3	0.03
Am. Ind. or Alaska Nat., not spec.	3	0.03
American Indian tribes, specified:	27	0.24
Cherokee (1)	12	0.11
Chickasaw (3)	3	0.03
Chippewa	1	0.01
Iroquois (1)	8	0.07
Sioux	2	0.02
All other tribes	1	0.01
Arab:	79	0.70
Lebanese	42	0.37
Syrian	37	0.33
Asian:	353	3.11
Chinese, ex. Taiwanese (119)	126	1.11
Filipino (6)	9	0.08
Indian (126)	134	1.18
Japanese (12)	15	0.13
Korean (34)	38	0.33
Pakistani (11)	11	0.10
Taiwanese (9)	11	0.10
Thai (2)	2	0.02
Vietnamese (4)	4	0.04
Other Asian, not specified (3)	3	0.03
Austrian	107	0.94
Belgian	13	0.11
British	30	0.26
Canadian	25	0.22
Carpatho Rusyn	7	0.06
Croatian	195	1.72
Czech	92	0.81
Czechoslovakian	62	0.55
Danish	29	0.26
Dutch	147	1.29
Eastern European	5	0.04
English	1,484	13.06
European	64	0.56
Finnish	9	0.08
French, except Basque	336	2.96
French Canadian	56	0.49
German	3,730	32.82
German Russian	12	0.11
Greek	98	0.86
Hawaii Native/Pacific Islander:	31	0.27
Polynesian: (11)	25	0.22
Native Hawaiian (6)	11	0.10
Samoan (1)	1	0.01
Tongan (4)	13	0.11
Other Pac. Isl., not spec. (6)	6	0.05
Hispanic or Latino:	61	0.54
Central American:	2	0.02
Costa Rican	1	0.01
Nicaraguan	1	0.01
Cuban	4	0.04
Mexican	13	0.11
Puerto Rican	24	0.21
South American:	8	0.07
Argentinean	5	0.04
Chilean	1	0.01
Venezuelan	2	0.02
Other Hispanic or Latino	10	0.09
Hungarian	133	1.17
Icelander	9	0.08
Iranian	12	0.11
Irish	2,187	19.24
Israeli	8	0.07
Italian	1,678	14.77
Latvian	24	0.21
Lithuanian	35	0.31
Northern European	8	0.07
Norwegian	62	0.55
Pennsylvania German	31	0.27
Polish	874	7.69
Romanian	8	0.07
Russian	317	2.79
Scotch-Irish	238	2.09
Scottish	321	2.82
Serbian	58	0.51
Slavic	31	0.27
Slovak	342	3.01
Slovene	4	0.04
Swedish	156	1.37
Swiss	67	0.59
Ukrainian	67	0.59
United States or American	370	3.26
Welsh	146	1.28
White:	10,868	95.64
Not Hispanic (10,753)	10,820	95.21
Hispanic (48)	48	0.42
Yugoslavian	6	0.05

Notes: 1. Figures in the "Number" column do not add up to the total population due to: a) Ancestry/Race overlap — e.g. persons can report being both White and Irish, b) persons of Hispanic origin can report being any race, c) persons reporting two ancestries are counted in both categories. 2. Numbers in parentheses indicate the number of persons reporting this ancestry/race alone, not in combination with any other ancestry/race. 3. Refer to the Explanation of Data in the front of the book for more detailed information.

Fullerton

Place Type: Census Designated Place
County: Lehigh
Population: 14,268

Ancestry/Race	Number	%
African American/Black:	623	4.37
Not Hispanic (507)	562	3.94
Hispanic (47)	61	0.43
African, sub-Saharan:	23	0.16
African	23	0.16
Am. Ind. or Alaska Nat., not spec.	17	0.12
Albanian	6	0.04
American Indian tribes, specified:	28	0.20
Blackfeet	1	0.01
Cherokee (6)	11	0.08
Chippewa	1	0.01
Choctaw (4)	5	0.04
Delaware	3	0.02
Iroquois (2)	2	0.01
Lumbee	1	0.01
Navajo (1)	1	0.01
Pueblo	1	0.01
All other tribes (2)	2	0.01
American Indian tribes, not spec.	8	0.06
Arab:	793	5.58
Arab/Arabic	124	0.87
Egyptian	23	0.16
Lebanese	213	1.50
Moroccan	19	0.13
Syrian	414	2.91
Asian:	856	6.00
Bangladeshi (9)	10	0.07
Chinese, ex. Taiwanese (114)	120	0.84
Filipino (34)	45	0.32
Hmong (1)	1	0.01
Indian (333)	358	2.51
Indonesian (4)	4	0.03
Japanese (8)	12	0.08
Korean (85)	88	0.62
Laotian (1)	1	0.01
Malaysian (6)	6	0.04
Pakistani (18)	23	0.16
Sri Lankan (3)	3	0.02
Taiwanese	2	0.01
Thai (4)	4	0.03
Vietnamese (155)	155	1.09
Other Asian, specified (1)	1	0.01
Other Asian, not specified (3)	23	0.16
Austrian	507	3.57
British	30	0.21
Canadian	6	0.04
Croatian	41	0.29
Czech	23	0.16
Czechoslovakian	51	0.36
Danish	17	0.12
Dutch	425	2.99
Eastern European	15	0.11
English	718	5.05
European	45	0.32
French, except Basque	218	1.53
French Canadian	27	0.19
German	4,033	28.38
Greek	49	0.34
Guyanese	21	0.15
Hawaii Native/Pacific Islander:	12	0.08
Micronesian: (2)	2	0.01
Guamanian/Chamorro (1)	1	0.01
Other Micronesian (1)	1	0.01
Polynesian: (7)	10	0.07
Native Hawaiian (1)	1	0.01
Samoan (6)	8	0.06
Other Polynesian	1	0.01
Hispanic or Latino:	878	6.15
Central American:	28	0.20
Costa Rican	1	0.01
Guatemalan	11	0.08
Honduran	9	0.06
Panamanian	3	0.02
Salvadoran	3	0.02
Other Central American	1	0.01
Cuban	23	0.16
Dominican Republic	75	0.53
Mexican	63	0.44
Puerto Rican	461	3.23
South American:	79	0.55
Argentinean	4	0.03
Chilean	3	0.02
Colombian	46	0.32
Ecuadorian	9	0.06
Peruvian	13	0.09
Venezuelan	3	0.02
Other South American	1	0.01
Other Hispanic or Latino	149	1.04
Hungarian	379	2.67
Irish	1,535	10.80
Italian	1,690	11.89
Lithuanian	49	0.34
Macedonian	15	0.11
Norwegian	101	0.71
Pennsylvania German	704	4.95
Polish	644	4.53
Portuguese	45	0.32
Romanian	9	0.06
Russian	113	0.80
Scandinavian	11	0.08
Scotch-Irish	134	0.94
Scottish	92	0.65
Serbian	9	0.06
Slovak	758	5.33
Slovene	11	0.08
Swedish	22	0.15
Swiss	13	0.09
Ukrainian	337	2.37
United States or American	546	3.84
Welsh	275	1.93
West Indian, excl. Hispanic:	42	0.30
Jamaican	37	0.26
West Indian	5	0.04
White:	12,488	87.52
Not Hispanic (11,868)	12,020	84.24
Hispanic (416)	468	3.28
Yugoslavian	17	0.12

Greene

Place Type: Township
County: Franklin
Population: 12,284

Ancestry/Race	Number	%
African American/Black:	221	1.80
Not Hispanic (173)	203	1.65
Hispanic (16)	18	0.15
African, sub-Saharan:	6	0.05
African	6	0.05
Am. Ind. or Alaska Nat., not spec.	9	0.07
Alsatian	7	0.06
American Indian tribes, specified:	24	0.20
Blackfeet (1)	1	0.01
Cherokee (1)	9	0.07
Chickasaw	1	0.01
Iroquois (3)	5	0.04
Lumbee (1)	1	0.01
Potawatomi (1)	1	0.01
Puget Sound Salish (1)	1	0.01
Sioux	4	0.03
All other tribes	1	0.01
American Indian tribes, not spec.	1	0.01
Arab:	34	0.28
Moroccan	26	0.21
Syrian	8	0.07
Asian:	100	0.81
Chinese, ex. Taiwanese (13)	14	0.11
Filipino (8)	11	0.09
Indian (14)	19	0.15
Japanese (7)	8	0.07
Korean (20)	24	0.20
Taiwanese (4)	4	0.03
Thai (5)	5	0.04
Vietnamese (11)	11	0.09
Other Asian, specified (3)	3	0.02
Other Asian, not specified (1)	1	0.01
Australian	11	0.09
Austrian	7	0.06
Belgian	29	0.24
British	10	0.08
Canadian	8	0.07
Croatian	59	0.48
Czech	17	0.14
Danish	9	0.07
Dutch	263	2.14
Eastern European	4	0.03
English	1,053	8.57
Estonian	8	0.07
European	200	1.63
French, except Basque	192	1.56
French Canadian	27	0.22
German	4,175	33.99
Greek	82	0.67
Hawaii Native/Pacific Islander:	16	0.13
Melanesian: (1)	4	0.03
Fijian (1)	4	0.03
Micronesian: (1)	1	0.01
Guamanian/Chamorro (1)	1	0.01
Polynesian: (6)	6	0.05
Native Hawaiian (6)	6	0.05
Other Pac. Isl., not spec. (4)	5	0.04
Hispanic or Latino:	161	1.31
Central American:	5	0.04
Costa Rican	1	0.01
Guatemalan	3	0.02
Panamanian	1	0.01
Cuban	4	0.03
Dominican Republic	1	0.01
Mexican	68	0.55
Puerto Rican	71	0.58
South American:	4	0.03
Colombian	3	0.02
Peruvian	1	0.01
Other Hispanic or Latino	8	0.07
Hungarian	36	0.29
Iranian	8	0.07
Irish	1,189	9.68
Italian	286	2.33
Lithuanian	15	0.12
Norwegian	9	0.07
Pennsylvania German	85	0.69
Polish	268	2.18
Portuguese	9	0.07
Russian	8	0.07
Scotch-Irish	317	2.58
Scottish	339	2.76
Slovak	40	0.33
Swedish	27	0.22
Swiss	83	0.68
Ukrainian	29	0.24
United States or American	1,595	12.98
Welsh	93	0.76
West Indian, excl. Hispanic:	8	0.07
Jamaican	8	0.07
White:	11,922	97.05
Not Hispanic (11,765)	11,830	96.30
Hispanic (76)	92	0.75

Greensburg

Place Type: City
County: Westmoreland
Population: 15,889

Ancestry/Race	Number	%
Acadian/Cajun	23	0.14
African American/Black:	781	4.92
Not Hispanic (608)	759	4.78
Hispanic (13)	22	0.14
African, sub-Saharan:	35	0.22
African	35	0.22
Am. Ind. or Alaska Nat., not spec.	39	0.25

Notes: 1. Figures in the "Number" column do not add up to the total population due to: a) Ancestry/Race overlap — e.g. persons can report being both White and Irish, b) persons of Hispanic origin can report being any race, c) persons reporting two ancestries are counted in both categories. 2. Numbers in parentheses indicate the number of persons reporting this ancestry/race alone, not in combination with any other ancestry/race. 3. Refer to the Explanation of Data in the front of the book for more detailed information.

Alsatian	10	0.06
American Indian tribes, specified:	45	0.28
Apache (1)	2	0.01
Blackfeet	3	0.02
Cherokee (2)	26	0.16
Chippewa	2	0.01
Creek	1	0.01
Iroquois	4	0.03
Menominee (1)	1	0.01
Seminole	2	0.01
Sioux	3	0.02
All other tribes	1	0.01
American Indian tribes, not spec.	2	0.01
Arab:	80	0.50
Arab/Arabic	5	0.03
Lebanese	12	0.08
Moroccan	6	0.04
Syrian	57	0.36
Asian:	134	0.84
Chinese, ex. Taiwanese (28)	30	0.19
Filipino (3)	7	0.04
Indian (9)	12	0.08
Japanese (26)	30	0.19
Korean (27)	30	0.19
Thai (3)	3	0.02
Vietnamese (13)	13	0.08
Other Asian, specified (1)	3	0.02
Other Asian, not specified (2)	6	0.04
Austrian	34	0.21
Belgian	12	0.08
British	77	0.48
Canadian	21	0.13
Carpatho Rusyn	7	0.04
Celtic	13	0.08
Croatian	116	0.73
Czech	119	0.75
Czechoslovakian	71	0.45
Danish	17	0.11
Dutch	226	1.42
Eastern European	22	0.14
English	1,336	8.40
European	77	0.48
French, except Basque	295	1.86
French Canadian	7	0.04
German	4,641	29.19
Greek	32	0.20
Hawaii Native/Pacific Islander:	2	0.01
Polynesian: (1)	1	0.01
Native Hawaiian (1)	1	0.01
Other Pac. Isl., not spec. (1)	1	0.01
Hispanic or Latino:	172	1.08
Central American:	2	0.01
Guatemalan	1	0.01
Panamanian	1	0.01
Cuban	10	0.06
Dominican Republic	2	0.01
Mexican	76	0.48
Puerto Rican	40	0.25
South American:	9	0.06
Argentinean	1	0.01
Chilean	1	0.01
Colombian	2	0.01
Ecuadorian	1	0.01
Peruvian	3	0.02
Venezuelan	1	0.01
Other Hispanic or Latino	33	0.21
Hungarian	188	1.18
Irish	2,428	15.27
Italian	3,321	20.89
Lithuanian	50	0.31
Norwegian	48	0.30
Pennsylvania German	78	0.49
Polish	1,247	7.84
Romanian	9	0.06
Russian	94	0.59
Scotch-Irish	416	2.62
Scottish	462	2.91
Serbian	23	0.14
Slavic	24	0.15
Slovak	628	3.95
Slovene	97	0.61
Swedish	99	0.62
Swiss	98	0.62
Ukrainian	126	0.79
United States or American	445	2.80
Welsh	166	1.04
White:	15,065	94.81
Not Hispanic (14,732)	14,937	94.01
Hispanic (113)	128	0.81

Guilford

Place Type: Township
County: Franklin
Population: 13,100

Ancestry/Race	Number	%
African American/Black:	309	2.36
Not Hispanic (228)	301	2.30
Hispanic (4)	8	0.06
Am. Ind. or Alaska Nat., not spec.	26	0.20
American Indian tribes, specified:	40	0.31
Apache (1)	2	0.02
Blackfeet	3	0.02
Cherokee (2)	8	0.06
Comanche	1	0.01
Iroquois (2)	5	0.04
Latin American Indians (4)	5	0.04
Lumbee (4)	4	0.03
Navajo (1)	1	0.01
Potawatomi (1)	1	0.01
Pueblo	1	0.01
Puget Sound Salish (1)	1	0.01
Sioux (1)	2	0.02
Tohono O'Odham (2)	2	0.02
All other tribes (3)	4	0.03
Arab:	12	0.09
Lebanese	12	0.09
Asian:	104	0.79
Cambodian (1)	1	0.01
Chinese, ex. Taiwanese (16)	22	0.17
Filipino (4)	14	0.11
Indian (13)	16	0.12
Japanese (4)	5	0.04
Korean (16)	22	0.17
Taiwanese (3)	3	0.02
Thai (3)	3	0.02
Vietnamese (12)	14	0.11
Other Asian, not specified (2)	4	0.03
Austrian	8	0.06
Canadian	12	0.09
Croatian	6	0.05
Czech	14	0.11
Czechoslovakian	22	0.17
Danish	9	0.07
Dutch	169	1.29
English	1,082	8.26
European	110	0.84
French, except Basque	376	2.87
French Canadian	29	0.22
German	4,799	36.63
Greek	20	0.15
Hawaii Native/Pacific Islander:	4	0.03
Micronesian: (1)	2	0.02
Guamanian/Chamorro (1)	2	0.02
Polynesian:	2	0.02
Native Hawaiian	1	0.01
Samoan	1	0.01
Hispanic or Latino:	164	1.25
Central American:	14	0.11
Costa Rican	2	0.02
Guatemalan	10	0.08
Panamanian	1	0.01
Salvadoran	1	0.01
Cuban	5	0.04
Mexican	52	0.40
Puerto Rican	53	0.40
South American:	5	0.04
Colombian	3	0.02
Venezuelan	1	0.01
Other South American	1	0.01
Other Hispanic or Latino	35	0.27
Hungarian	45	0.34
Irish	1,523	11.63
Italian	500	3.82
Lithuanian	16	0.12
Norwegian	53	0.40
Pennsylvania German	95	0.73
Polish	305	2.33
Portuguese	70	0.53
Russian	46	0.35
Scandinavian	10	0.08
Scotch-Irish	363	2.77
Scottish	250	1.91
Slovak	55	0.42
Swiss	211	1.61
Ukrainian	13	0.10
United States or American	1,553	11.85
Welsh	143	1.09
West Indian, excl. Hispanic:	17	0.13
Haitian	17	0.13
White:	12,701	96.95
Not Hispanic (12,463)	12,584	96.06
Hispanic (102)	117	0.89

Hampden

Place Type: Township
County: Cumberland
Population: 24,135

Ancestry/Race	Number	%
African American/Black:	250	1.04
Not Hispanic (201)	243	1.01
Hispanic (7)	7	0.03
African, sub-Saharan:	53	0.22
African	19	0.08
South African	34	0.14
Alaska Native tribes, specified:	3	0.01
Alaska Athabascan (2)	2	0.01
Tlingit-Haida (1)	1	0.00
Am. Ind. or Alaska Nat., not spec.	25	0.10
Albanian	21	0.09
American Indian tribes, specified:	41	0.17
Blackfeet	3	0.01
Cherokee (7)	19	0.08
Cheyenne (1)	1	0.00
Chippewa	1	0.00
Comanche	1	0.00
Iroquois (2)	4	0.02
Latin American Indians (2)	2	0.01
Osage (1)	1	0.00
Sioux (2)	3	0.01
Tohono O'Odham (3)	3	0.01
All other tribes	3	0.01
American Indian tribes, not spec.	10	0.04
Arab:	134	0.55
Arab/Arabic	20	0.08
Lebanese	26	0.11
Palestinian	13	0.05
Syrian	22	0.09
Other Arab	53	0.22
Armenian	17	0.07
Asian:	1,010	4.18
Cambodian (6)	6	0.02
Chinese, ex. Taiwanese (156)	170	0.70
Filipino (38)	50	0.21
Hmong (1)	4	0.02
Indian (335)	347	1.44
Indonesian (1)	2	0.01
Japanese (22)	43	0.18
Korean (172)	195	0.81
Laotian (10)	15	0.06
Pakistani (6)	10	0.04
Sri Lankan (4)	4	0.02
Taiwanese (6)	6	0.02
Thai (3)	3	0.01
Vietnamese (111)	120	0.50
Other Asian, specified (4)	6	0.02
Other Asian, not specified (22)	29	0.12

Notes: 1. Figures in the "Number" column do not add up to the total population due to: a) Ancestry/Race overlap — e.g. persons can report being both White and Irish, b) persons of Hispanic origin can report being any race, c) persons reporting two ancestries are counted in both categories. 2. Numbers in parentheses indicate the number of persons reporting this ancestry/race alone, not in combination with any other ancestry/race. 3. Refer to the Explanation of Data in the front of the book for more detailed information.

Austrian	132	0.55
Belgian	20	0.08
British	61	0.25
Canadian	24	0.10
Croatian	159	0.66
Czech	198	0.82
Czechoslovakian	59	0.24
Danish	14	0.06
Dutch	716	2.96
Eastern European	14	0.06
English	2,872	11.87
European	126	0.52
Finnish	37	0.15
French, except Basque	554	2.29
French Canadian	144	0.60
German	8,477	35.04
Greek	331	1.37
Guyanese	20	0.08
Hawaii Native/Pacific Islander:	23	0.10
Micronesian: (3)	8	0.03
Guamanian/Chamorro (2)	6	0.02
Other Micronesian (1)	2	0.01
Polynesian: (7)	14	0.06
Native Hawaiian (7)	14	0.06
Other Pac. Isl., not spec.	1	0.00
Hispanic or Latino:	289	1.20
Central American:	9	0.04
Guatemalan	4	0.02
Honduran	3	0.01
Panamanian	2	0.01
Cuban	12	0.05
Dominican Republic	2	0.01
Mexican	88	0.36
Puerto Rican	104	0.43
South American:	22	0.09
Argentinean	3	0.01
Colombian	6	0.02
Ecuadorian	3	0.01
Paraguayan	2	0.01
Peruvian	7	0.03
Venezuelan	1	0.00
Other Hispanic or Latino	52	0.22
Hungarian	301	1.24
Irish	4,232	17.49
Israeli	13	0.05
Italian	2,032	8.40
Lithuanian	188	0.78
Macedonian	18	0.07
New Zealander	34	0.14
Northern European	9	0.04
Norwegian	121	0.50
Pennsylvania German	142	0.59
Polish	1,037	4.29
Portuguese	36	0.15
Romanian	33	0.14
Russian	255	1.05
Scandinavian	8	0.03
Scotch-Irish	543	2.24
Scottish	522	2.16
Serbian	45	0.19
Slavic	33	0.14
Slovak	401	1.66
Slovene	42	0.17
Swedish	350	1.45
Swiss	131	0.54
Ukrainian	127	0.52
United States or American	1,532	6.33
Welsh	557	2.30
West Indian, excl. Hispanic:	10	0.04
Belizean	5	0.02
Jamaican	5	0.02
White:	22,860	94.72
Not Hispanic (22,498)	22,657	93.88
Hispanic (182)	203	0.84
Yugoslavian	60	0.25

Hampton Township

Place Type: Census Designated Place
County: Allegheny
Population: 17,526

Ancestry/Race	Number	%
African American/Black:	139	0.79
Not Hispanic (116)	134	0.76
Hispanic (2)	5	0.03
Alaska Native tribes, specified:	1	0.01
Alaska Athabascan (1)	1	0.01
Am. Ind. or Alaska Nat., not spec.	3	0.02
American Indian tribes, specified:	15	0.09
Blackfeet	2	0.01
Cherokee (6)	8	0.05
Choctaw	1	0.01
Crow (1)	1	0.01
Iroquois	3	0.02
Arab:	21	0.12
Lebanese	21	0.12
Armenian	8	0.05
Asian:	232	1.32
Bangladeshi (1)	1	0.01
Chinese, ex. Taiwanese (59)	64	0.37
Filipino (5)	9	0.05
Indian (117)	119	0.68
Japanese (5)	7	0.04
Korean (17)	18	0.10
Laotian (1)	1	0.01
Pakistani (4)	4	0.02
Thai (1)	1	0.01
Vietnamese (3)	3	0.02
Other Asian, not specified (1)	5	0.03
Austrian	124	0.71
Belgian	21	0.12
British	41	0.23
Canadian	17	0.10
Carpatho Rusyn	7	0.04
Croatian	546	3.12
Czech	197	1.12
Czechoslovakian	30	0.17
Danish	7	0.04
Dutch	89	0.51
Eastern European	11	0.06
English	1,662	9.48
European	93	0.53
Finnish	22	0.13
French, except Basque	353	2.01
French Canadian	29	0.17
German	6,001	34.24
Greek	50	0.29
Hawaii Native/Pacific Islander:	1	0.01
Micronesian: (1)	1	0.01
Guamanian/Chamorro (1)	1	0.01
Hispanic or Latino:	93	0.53
Central American:	3	0.02
Guatemalan	1	0.01
Panamanian	1	0.01
Salvadoran	1	0.01
Cuban	1	0.01
Mexican	38	0.22
Puerto Rican	24	0.14
South American:	13	0.07
Argentinean	2	0.01
Chilean	3	0.02
Paraguayan	1	0.01
Peruvian	1	0.01
Uruguayan	1	0.01
Venezuelan	4	0.02
Other South American	1	0.01
Other Hispanic or Latino	14	0.08
Hungarian	292	1.67
Irish	3,785	21.60
Italian	2,887	16.47
Lithuanian	124	0.71
Luxemburger	11	0.06
Northern European	25	0.14
Norwegian	68	0.39
Pennsylvania German	38	0.22
Polish	1,322	7.54
Romanian	5	0.03
Russian	236	1.35
Scotch-Irish	502	2.86
Scottish	508	2.90
Serbian	38	0.22
Slavic	7	0.04
Slovak	436	2.49
Slovene	90	0.51
Swedish	207	1.18
Swiss	176	1.00
Ukrainian	110	0.63
United States or American	779	4.44
Welsh	217	1.24
West Indian, excl. Hispanic:	14	0.08
Jamaican	14	0.08
White:	17,160	97.91
Not Hispanic (17,046)	17,084	97.48
Hispanic (70)	76	0.43
Yugoslavian	36	0.21

Hanover

Place Type: Borough
County: York
Population: 14,535

Ancestry/Race	Number	%
African American/Black:	109	0.75
Not Hispanic (70)	104	0.72
Hispanic (5)	5	0.03
African, sub-Saharan:	3	0.02
African	3	0.02
Alaska Native tribes, specified:	2	0.01
Aleut (2)	2	0.01
Am. Ind. or Alaska Nat., not spec.	28	0.19
American Indian tribes, specified:	30	0.21
Blackfeet (1)	2	0.01
Cherokee (6)	15	0.10
Cheyenne (1)	1	0.01
Choctaw	4	0.03
Crow (1)	1	0.01
Iroquois (1)	1	0.01
Latin American Indians (2)	2	0.01
Lumbee	2	0.01
Sioux	1	0.01
All other tribes	1	0.01
Asian:	140	0.96
Bangladeshi (4)	4	0.03
Chinese, ex. Taiwanese (9)	10	0.07
Filipino (8)	12	0.08
Indian (39)	42	0.29
Japanese (9)	9	0.06
Korean (23)	25	0.17
Pakistani (1)	2	0.01
Thai (1)	1	0.01
Vietnamese (26)	27	0.19
Other Asian, not specified (7)	8	0.06
Austrian	50	0.34
Belgian	13	0.09
British	74	0.51
Czech	18	0.12
Danish	16	0.11
Dutch	245	1.69
English	1,191	8.19
European	109	0.75
Finnish	7	0.05
French, except Basque	163	1.12
German	6,130	42.17
Greek	12	0.08
Hawaii Native/Pacific Islander:	10	0.07
Micronesian: (3)	3	0.02
Guamanian/Chamorro (3)	3	0.02
Polynesian: (2)	4	0.03
Native Hawaiian (1)	3	0.02
Samoan (1)	1	0.01
Other Pac. Isl., not spec. (3)	3	0.02
Hispanic or Latino:	298	2.05
Central American:	27	0.19
Guatemalan	18	0.12

Notes: 1. Figures in the "Number" column do not add up to the total population due to: a) Ancestry/Race overlap — e.g. persons can report being both White and Irish, b) persons of Hispanic origin can report being any race, c) persons reporting two ancestries are counted in both categories. 2. Numbers in parentheses indicate the number of persons reporting this ancestry/race alone, not in combination with any other ancestry/race. 3. Refer to the Explanation of Data in the front of the book for more detailed information.

Panamanian	2	0.01
Salvadoran	7	0.05
Cuban	2	0.01
Dominican Republic	5	0.03
Mexican	166	1.14
Puerto Rican	58	0.40
South American:	11	0.08
Colombian	7	0.05
Peruvian	4	0.03
Other Hispanic or Latino	29	0.20
Hungarian	81	0.56
Irish	1,624	11.17
Italian	490	3.37
Latvian	23	0.16
Lithuanian	25	0.17
Norwegian	28	0.19
Pennsylvania German	42	0.29
Polish	216	1.49
Portuguese	15	0.10
Romanian	34	0.23
Russian	14	0.10
Scandinavian	9	0.06
Scotch-Irish	163	1.12
Scottish	129	0.89
Serbian	10	0.07
Slavic	14	0.10
Slovak	5	0.03
Swedish	66	0.45
Swiss	73	0.50
Ukrainian	14	0.10
United States or American	1,506	10.36
Welsh	93	0.64
White:	14,187	97.61
Not Hispanic (13,912)	13,998	96.31
Hispanic (180)	189	1.30

Hanover

Place Type: Township
County: Luzerne
Population: 11,488

Ancestry/Race	Number	%
African American/Black:	143	1.24
Not Hispanic (110)	141	1.23
Hispanic	2	0.02
African, sub-Saharan:	19	0.17
African	19	0.17
Am. Ind. or Alaska Nat., not spec.	9	0.08
American Indian tribes, specified:	11	0.10
Cherokee	2	0.02
Comanche	1	0.01
Iroquois (1)	1	0.01
Latin American Indians	2	0.02
Shoshone	2	0.02
All other tribes	3	0.03
American Indian tribes, not spec.	3	0.03
Arab:	372	3.25
Lebanese	130	1.13
Palestinian	43	0.38
Syrian	199	1.74
Asian:	31	0.27
Filipino (7)	10	0.09
Indian (1)	2	0.02
Japanese (2)	5	0.04
Korean (1)	3	0.03
Thai	1	0.01
Vietnamese (8)	8	0.07
Other Asian, not specified	2	0.02
Austrian	30	0.26
Canadian	13	0.11
Croatian	15	0.13
Czechoslovakian	25	0.22
Danish	18	0.16
Dutch	345	3.01
English	493	4.30
European	12	0.10
French, except Basque	130	1.13
French Canadian	10	0.09
German	1,493	13.03
Greek	73	0.64
Hispanic or Latino:	69	0.60
Central American:	5	0.04
Honduran	3	0.03
Panamanian	2	0.02
Cuban	1	0.01
Dominican Republic	1	0.01
Mexican	4	0.03
Puerto Rican	37	0.32
Other Hispanic or Latino	21	0.18
Hungarian	9	0.08
Irish	2,372	20.69
Italian	1,143	9.97
Lithuanian	682	5.95
Norwegian	8	0.07
Pennsylvania German	134	1.17
Polish	3,450	30.10
Romanian	11	0.10
Russian	410	3.58
Scotch-Irish	33	0.29
Scottish	22	0.19
Slavic	7	0.06
Slovak	720	6.28
Swedish	74	0.65
Swiss	52	0.45
Ukrainian	349	3.04
United States or American	315	2.75
Welsh	764	6.67
White:	11,340	98.71
Not Hispanic (11,222)	11,282	98.21
Hispanic (46)	58	0.50
Yugoslavian	10	0.09

Harborcreek

Place Type: Township
County: Erie
Population: 15,178

Ancestry/Race	Number	%
African American/Black:	221	1.46
Not Hispanic (180)	218	1.44
Hispanic (3)	3	0.02
African, sub-Saharan:	20	0.13
African	14	0.09
Nigerian	6	0.04
Am. Ind. or Alaska Nat., not spec.	17	0.11
American Indian tribes, specified:	12	0.08
Blackfeet (1)	2	0.01
Cherokee (3)	6	0.04
Iroquois (3)	3	0.02
Seminole (1)	1	0.01
American Indian tribes, not spec.	2	0.01
Arab:	14	0.09
Lebanese	7	0.05
Syrian	7	0.05
Armenian	31	0.20
Asian:	91	0.60
Chinese, ex. Taiwanese (15)	16	0.11
Filipino (6)	9	0.06
Indian (10)	10	0.07
Japanese (2)	3	0.02
Korean (21)	26	0.17
Laotian (9)	9	0.06
Malaysian (1)	1	0.01
Taiwanese (1)	1	0.01
Vietnamese (11)	12	0.08
Other Asian, not specified (2)	4	0.03
Australian	5	0.03
Austrian	44	0.29
British	61	0.40
Canadian	36	0.24
Celtic	5	0.03
Croatian	37	0.24
Czech	35	0.23
Czechoslovakian	45	0.30
Danish	46	0.30
Dutch	293	1.93
English	1,650	10.87
European	54	0.36
Finnish	5	0.03
French, except Basque	415	2.73
French Canadian	5	0.03
German	5,011	33.01
Greek	14	0.09
Hawaii Native/Pacific Islander:	5	0.03
Micronesian: (2)	2	0.01
Other Micronesian (2)	2	0.01
Polynesian:	1	0.01
Native Hawaiian	1	0.01
Other Pac. Isl., not spec.	2	0.01
Hispanic or Latino:	86	0.57
Central American:	3	0.02
Guatemalan	1	0.01
Salvadoran	2	0.01
Cuban	1	0.01
Mexican	20	0.13
Puerto Rican	46	0.30
South American:	6	0.04
Argentinean	3	0.02
Colombian	2	0.01
Ecuadorian	1	0.01
Other Hispanic or Latino	10	0.07
Hungarian	189	1.25
Irish	2,597	17.11
Italian	1,479	9.74
Lithuanian	42	0.28
Norwegian	76	0.50
Pennsylvania German	34	0.22
Polish	2,774	18.28
Portuguese	16	0.11
Romanian	13	0.09
Russian	186	1.23
Scandinavian	17	0.11
Scotch-Irish	407	2.68
Scottish	293	1.93
Slavic	38	0.25
Slovak	290	1.91
Slovene	13	0.09
Swedish	613	4.04
Swiss	15	0.10
Ukrainian	74	0.49
United States or American	777	5.12
Welsh	130	0.86
West Indian, excl. Hispanic:	8	0.05
British West Indian	8	0.05
White:	14,870	97.97
Not Hispanic (14,742)	14,804	97.54
Hispanic (60)	66	0.43
Yugoslavian	7	0.05

Harrisburg

Place Type: City
County: Dauphin
Population: 48,950

Ancestry/Race	Number	%
African American/Black:	28,123	57.45
Not Hispanic (26,292)	27,317	55.81
Hispanic (549)	806	1.65
African, sub-Saharan:	1,032	2.10
African	802	1.63
Ethiopian	129	0.26
Ghanian	23	0.05
Liberian	42	0.09
Nigerian	16	0.03
Other sub-Saharan African	20	0.04
Alaska Native tribes, specified:	2	0.00
Alaska Athabascan (1)	1	0.00
Eskimo	1	0.00
Am. Ind. or Alaska Nat., not spec.	253	0.52
Albanian	14	0.03
American Indian tribes, specified:	248	0.51
Apache (2)	4	0.01
Blackfeet (9)	42	0.09
Cherokee (23)	106	0.22
Cheyenne (2)	2	0.00
Chippewa (2)	3	0.01
Choctaw	1	0.00

Notes: 1. Figures in the "Number" column do not add up to the total population due to: a) Ancestry/Race overlap — e.g. persons can report being both White and Irish, b) persons of Hispanic origin can report being any race, c) persons reporting two ancestries are counted in both categories. 2. Numbers in parentheses indicate the number of persons reporting this ancestry/race alone, not in combination with any other ancestry/race. 3. Refer to the Explanation of Data in the front of the book for more detailed information.

Cree (1)	2	0.00
Delaware (1)	2	0.00
Iroquois (5)	17	0.03
Latin American Indians (8)	17	0.03
Lumbee (2)	2	0.00
Menominee	1	0.00
Navajo (4)	12	0.02
Osage (1)	1	0.00
Paiute (1)	3	0.01
Pueblo	2	0.00
Seminole	2	0.00
Sioux (5)	5	0.01
All other tribes (8)	24	0.05
American Indian tribes, not spec.	32	0.07
Arab:	129	0.26
Arab/Arabic	28	0.06
Lebanese	13	0.03
Moroccan	83	0.17
Syrian	5	0.01
Armenian	8	0.02
Asian:	1,609	3.29
Cambodian (58)	86	0.18
Chinese, ex. Taiwanese (102)	113	0.23
Filipino (26)	36	0.07
Hmong	1	0.00
Indian (97)	140	0.29
Indonesian (12)	13	0.03
Japanese (22)	42	0.09
Korean (60)	82	0.17
Laotian (20)	23	0.05
Pakistani (10)	11	0.02
Sri Lankan (1)	1	0.00
Taiwanese (1)	1	0.00
Thai (5)	11	0.02
Vietnamese (915)	972	1.99
Other Asian, specified	11	0.02
Other Asian, not specified (31)	66	0.13
Austrian	64	0.13
Belgian	7	0.01
British	66	0.13
Bulgarian	27	0.05
Canadian	34	0.07
Carpatho Rusyn	15	0.03
Celtic	35	0.07
Croatian	160	0.33
Czech	57	0.12
Czechoslovakian	48	0.10
Danish	45	0.09
Dutch	413	0.84
Eastern European	12	0.02
English	1,079	2.20
European	129	0.26
Finnish	7	0.01
French, except Basque	260	0.53
French Canadian	13	0.03
German	4,700	9.57
Greek	47	0.10
Hawaii Native/Pacific Islander:	99	0.20
Melanesian:	2	0.00
Other Melanesian	2	0.00
Micronesian: (6)	24	0.05
Guamanian/Chamorro (6)	24	0.05
Polynesian: (12)	20	0.04
Native Hawaiian (9)	13	0.03
Samoan (3)	7	0.01
Other Pac. Isl., specified	10	0.02
Other Pac. Isl., not spec. (14)	43	0.09
Hispanic or Latino:	5,724	11.69
Central American:	76	0.16
Costa Rican	2	0.00
Guatemalan	12	0.02
Honduran	21	0.04
Nicaraguan	5	0.01
Panamanian	22	0.04
Salvadoran	6	0.01
Other Central American	8	0.02
Cuban	186	0.38
Dominican Republic	123	0.25
Mexican	461	0.94
Puerto Rican	3,984	8.14
South American:	133	0.27
Argentinean	5	0.01
Bolivian	1	0.00
Chilean	2	0.00
Colombian	5	0.01
Ecuadorian	80	0.16
Paraguayan	4	0.01
Peruvian	17	0.03
Uruguayan	1	0.00
Venezuelan	8	0.02
Other South American	10	0.02
Other Hispanic or Latino	761	1.55
Hungarian	145	0.30
Iranian	11	0.02
Irish	2,199	4.48
Italian	1,824	3.71
Latvian	13	0.03
Lithuanian	80	0.16
Macedonian	9	0.02
Northern European	20	0.04
Norwegian	77	0.16
Pennsylvania German	211	0.43
Polish	441	0.90
Portuguese	36	0.07
Romanian	25	0.05
Russian	183	0.37
Scandinavian	5	0.01
Scotch-Irish	292	0.59
Scottish	248	0.51
Serbian	17	0.03
Slavic	61	0.12
Slovak	199	0.41
Slovene	7	0.01
Swedish	144	0.29
Swiss	124	0.25
Ukrainian	143	0.29
United States or American	1,701	3.46
Welsh	354	0.72
West Indian, excl. Hispanic:	322	0.66
Bahamian	19	0.04
Barbadian	8	0.02
British West Indian	6	0.01
Haitian	59	0.12
Jamaican	162	0.33
Trinidadian and Tobagonian	20	0.04
West Indian	48	0.10
White:	16,782	34.28
Not Hispanic (13,988)	14,938	30.52
Hispanic (1,539)	1,844	3.77
Yugoslavian	65	0.13

Harrison Township

Place Type: Census Designated Place
County: Allegheny
Population: 10,934

Ancestry/Race	Number	%
African American/Black:	469	4.29
Not Hispanic (399)	463	4.23
Hispanic (5)	6	0.05
African, sub-Saharan:	7	0.06
African	7	0.06
Am. Ind. or Alaska Nat., not spec.	7	0.06
American Indian tribes, specified:	16	0.15
Blackfeet	1	0.01
Cherokee	5	0.05
Iroquois (1)	2	0.02
Sioux (1)	4	0.04
All other tribes (3)	4	0.04
Arab:	28	0.26
Arab/Arabic	13	0.12
Lebanese	15	0.14
Asian:	64	0.59
Chinese, ex. Taiwanese (11)	11	0.10
Filipino (1)	3	0.03
Indian (10)	17	0.16
Japanese	5	0.05
Korean (2)	6	0.05
Malaysian (1)	1	0.01
Vietnamese (18)	20	0.18
Other Asian, not specified (1)	1	0.01
Austrian	10	0.09
Belgian	101	0.92
British	58	0.53
Croatian	75	0.69
Czech	62	0.57
Czechoslovakian	114	1.04
Dutch	196	1.79
Eastern European	19	0.17
English	677	6.19
European	38	0.35
French, except Basque	230	2.10
French Canadian	8	0.07
German	2,978	27.24
Greek	24	0.22
Hawaii Native/Pacific Islander:	2	0.02
Polynesian:	1	0.01
Native Hawaiian	1	0.01
Other Pac. Isl., not spec.	1	0.01
Hispanic or Latino:	60	0.55
Central American:	1	0.01
Guatemalan	1	0.01
Cuban	1	0.01
Mexican	26	0.24
Puerto Rican	9	0.08
South American:	2	0.02
Ecuadorian	2	0.02
Other Hispanic or Latino	21	0.19
Hungarian	119	1.09
Iranian	5	0.05
Irish	1,798	16.44
Italian	1,397	12.78
Lithuanian	37	0.34
Norwegian	32	0.29
Pennsylvania German	51	0.47
Polish	2,246	20.54
Romanian	5	0.05
Russian	146	1.34
Scotch-Irish	307	2.81
Scottish	116	1.06
Serbian	14	0.13
Slavic	55	0.50
Slovak	1,150	10.52
Slovene	19	0.17
Swedish	128	1.17
Swiss	17	0.16
Ukrainian	86	0.79
United States or American	378	3.46
Welsh	82	0.75
White:	10,464	95.70
Not Hispanic (10,328)	10,414	95.24
Hispanic (39)	50	0.46

Hatfield

Place Type: Township
County: Montgomery
Population: 16,712

Ancestry/Race	Number	%
African American/Black:	697	4.17
Not Hispanic (588)	665	3.98
Hispanic (22)	32	0.19
African, sub-Saharan:	28	0.17
African	12	0.07
Ethiopian	16	0.10
Am. Ind. or Alaska Nat., not spec.	41	0.25
Albanian	30	0.18
American Indian tribes, specified:	63	0.38
Apache	3	0.02
Blackfeet	3	0.02
Cherokee (5)	38	0.23
Choctaw (3)	3	0.02
Cree	3	0.02
Delaware	2	0.01
Iroquois (1)	6	0.04
Kiowa	1	0.01
Lumbee (1)	1	0.01
Sioux	1	0.01

Notes: 1. Figures in the "Number" column do not add up to the total population due to: a) Ancestry/Race overlap — e.g. persons can report being both White and Irish, b) persons of Hispanic origin can report being any race, c) persons reporting two ancestries are counted in both categories. 2. Numbers in parentheses indicate the number of persons reporting this ancestry/race alone, not in combination with any other ancestry/race. 3. Refer to the Explanation of Data in the front of the book for more detailed information.

All other tribes (1)	2	0.01
American Indian tribes, not spec.	10	0.06
Arab:	153	0.92
Arab/Arabic	60	0.36
Egyptian	36	0.22
Lebanese	15	0.09
Syrian	7	0.04
Other Arab	35	0.21
Armenian	15	0.09
Asian:	1,917	11.47
Bangladeshi (88)	126	0.75
Cambodian (23)	23	0.14
Chinese, ex. Taiwanese (93)	112	0.67
Filipino (29)	37	0.22
Hmong (2)	2	0.01
Indian (813)	892	5.34
Japanese (14)	20	0.12
Korean (257)	267	1.60
Laotian (16)	16	0.10
Pakistani (5)	10	0.06
Sri Lankan (3)	3	0.02
Taiwanese (3)	6	0.04
Thai	1	0.01
Vietnamese (348)	362	2.17
Other Asian, specified (4)	10	0.06
Other Asian, not specified (21)	30	0.18
Australian	10	0.06
Austrian	47	0.28
British	78	0.47
Canadian	37	0.22
Croatian	19	0.11
Czech	92	0.55
Czechoslovakian	60	0.36
Danish	32	0.19
Dutch	448	2.69
Eastern European	6	0.04
English	1,447	8.70
European	46	0.28
French, except Basque	414	2.49
German	4,431	26.63
Greek	119	0.72
Hawaii Native/Pacific Islander:	13	0.08
Polynesian: (5)	6	0.04
Samoan (5)	6	0.04
Other Pac. Isl., specified	3	0.02
Other Pac. Isl., not spec. (1)	4	0.02
Hispanic or Latino:	400	2.39
Central American:	31	0.19
Costa Rican	3	0.02
Guatemalan	11	0.07
Honduran	6	0.04
Salvadoran	4	0.02
Other Central American	7	0.04
Cuban	15	0.09
Dominican Republic	4	0.02
Mexican	46	0.28
Puerto Rican	187	1.12
South American:	53	0.32
Argentinean	6	0.04
Bolivian	3	0.02
Chilean	11	0.07
Colombian	10	0.06
Ecuadorian	4	0.02
Peruvian	15	0.09
Venezuelan	1	0.01
Other South American	3	0.02
Other Hispanic or Latino	64	0.38
Hungarian	228	1.37
Irish	3,374	20.28
Italian	2,344	14.09
Latvian	12	0.07
Lithuanian	108	0.65
Northern European	20	0.12
Norwegian	62	0.37
Pennsylvania German	178	1.07
Polish	1,141	6.86
Portuguese	8	0.05
Romanian	34	0.20
Russian	185	1.11
Scandinavian	35	0.21
Scotch-Irish	315	1.89
Scottish	386	2.32
Serbian	5	0.03
Slavic	20	0.12
Slovak	58	0.35
Swedish	87	0.52
Swiss	109	0.66
Ukrainian	159	0.96
United States or American	608	3.65
Welsh	225	1.35
West Indian, excl. Hispanic:	71	0.43
British West Indian	31	0.19
Haitian	7	0.04
Jamaican	33	0.20
White:	14,065	84.16
Not Hispanic (13,675)	13,850	82.87
Hispanic (184)	215	1.29
Yugoslavian	6	0.04

Haverford

Place Type: Township
County: Delaware
Population: 48,498

Ancestry/Race	Number	%
Afghan	6	0.01
African American/Black:	1,179	2.43
Not Hispanic (1,018)	1,158	2.39
Hispanic (10)	21	0.04
African, sub-Saharan:	189	0.39
African	130	0.27
South African	54	0.11
Zairian	5	0.01
Alaska Native tribes, specified:	5	0.01
Eskimo (1)	5	0.01
Alaska Native tribes, not specified	9	0.02
Am. Ind. or Alaska Nat., not spec.	47	0.10
Albanian	33	0.07
American Indian tribes, specified:	89	0.18
Blackfeet	2	0.00
Cherokee (4)	44	0.09
Chippewa	6	0.01
Choctaw (1)	4	0.01
Delaware (3)	12	0.02
Iroquois	5	0.01
Latin American Indians (3)	7	0.01
Pueblo	1	0.00
Sioux	1	0.00
All other tribes (3)	7	0.01
American Indian tribes, not spec.	13	0.03
Arab:	324	0.67
Arab/Arabic	23	0.05
Egyptian	78	0.16
Jordanian	7	0.01
Lebanese	185	0.38
Moroccan	9	0.02
Palestinian	22	0.05
Armenian	333	0.69
Asian:	1,492	3.08
Cambodian (22)	25	0.05
Chinese, ex. Taiwanese (386)	413	0.85
Filipino (62)	93	0.19
Indian (188)	214	0.44
Indonesian (5)	5	0.01
Japanese (41)	58	0.12
Korean (437)	455	0.94
Laotian (2)	4	0.01
Malaysian (1)	1	0.00
Pakistani (26)	46	0.09
Taiwanese (7)	10	0.02
Thai (6)	12	0.02
Vietnamese (89)	92	0.19
Other Asian, specified (4)	6	0.01
Other Asian, not specified (38)	58	0.12
Australian	12	0.02
Austrian	294	0.61
Belgian	45	0.09
British	298	0.61
Canadian	136	0.28
Carpatho Rusyn	5	0.01
Croatian	44	0.09
Czech	119	0.25
Czechoslovakian	47	0.10
Danish	140	0.29
Dutch	438	0.90
Eastern European	488	1.01
English	4,601	9.49
Estonian	5	0.01
European	397	0.82
Finnish	13	0.03
French, except Basque	905	1.87
French Canadian	106	0.22
German	8,056	16.61
Greek	413	0.85
Hawaii Native/Pacific Islander:	31	0.06
Melanesian: (1)	5	0.01
Fijian (1)	5	0.01
Micronesian: (2)	2	0.00
Guamanian/Chamorro (2)	2	0.00
Polynesian: (2)	8	0.02
Native Hawaiian	5	0.01
Samoan (2)	3	0.01
Other Pac. Isl., not spec. (1)	16	0.03
Hispanic or Latino:	431	0.89
Central American:	27	0.06
Costa Rican	5	0.01
Guatemalan	4	0.01
Honduran	4	0.01
Panamanian	6	0.01
Salvadoran	4	0.01
Other Central American	4	0.01
Cuban	54	0.11
Dominican Republic	9	0.02
Mexican	82	0.17
Puerto Rican	87	0.18
South American:	62	0.13
Argentinean	8	0.02
Chilean	10	0.02
Colombian	15	0.03
Ecuadorian	6	0.01
Peruvian	10	0.02
Uruguayan	1	0.00
Venezuelan	6	0.01
Other South American	6	0.01
Other Hispanic or Latino	110	0.23
Hungarian	246	0.51
Iranian	74	0.15
Irish	17,096	35.25
Israeli	14	0.03
Italian	11,494	23.70
Latvian	62	0.13
Lithuanian	306	0.63
Macedonian	3	0.01
Northern European	41	0.08
Norwegian	298	0.61
Pennsylvania German	96	0.20
Polish	1,909	3.94
Portuguese	33	0.07
Romanian	173	0.36
Russian	1,499	3.09
Scandinavian	42	0.09
Scotch-Irish	985	2.03
Scottish	1,021	2.11
Slavic	42	0.09
Slovak	223	0.46
Slovene	19	0.04
Swedish	385	0.79
Swiss	84	0.17
Turkish	109	0.22
Ukrainian	216	0.45
United States or American	1,341	2.77
Welsh	717	1.48
West Indian, excl. Hispanic:	114	0.24
Barbadian	6	0.01
Jamaican	85	0.18
Trinidadian and Tobagonian	23	0.05
White:	45,907	94.66
Not Hispanic (45,276)	45,571	93.96
Hispanic (309)	336	0.69

Notes: 1. Figures in the "Number" column do not add up to the total population due to: a) Ancestry/Race overlap — e.g. persons can report being both White and Irish, b) persons of Hispanic origin can report being any race, c) persons reporting two ancestries are counted in both categories. 2. Numbers in parentheses indicate the number of persons reporting this ancestry/race alone, not in combination with any other ancestry/race. 3. Refer to the Explanation of Data in the front of the book for more detailed information.

Yugoslavian	8	0.02

Hazleton

Place Type: City
County: Luzerne
Population: 23,329

Ancestry/Race	Number	%
African American/Black:	248	1.06
Not Hispanic (135)	177	0.76
Hispanic (57)	71	0.30
African, sub-Saharan:	5	0.02
African	5	0.02
Am. Ind. or Alaska Nat., not spec.	31	0.13
American Indian tribes, specified:	45	0.19
Apache (2)	4	0.02
Blackfeet	9	0.04
Cherokee (10)	10	0.04
Choctaw (1)	2	0.01
Comanche	1	0.00
Creek	1	0.00
Delaware (4)	4	0.02
Iroquois (2)	5	0.02
Latin American Indians (1)	1	0.00
Navajo (1)	4	0.02
Sioux (1)	1	0.00
All other tribes (2)	3	0.01
American Indian tribes, not spec.	4	0.02
Arab:	102	0.44
Egyptian	4	0.02
Lebanese	68	0.29
Syrian	30	0.13
Asian:	186	0.80
Cambodian (6)	6	0.03
Chinese, ex. Taiwanese (21)	21	0.09
Filipino (26)	35	0.15
Indian (37)	45	0.19
Indonesian (1)	1	0.00
Japanese (7)	11	0.05
Korean (16)	18	0.08
Taiwanese (1)	1	0.00
Thai (2)	4	0.02
Vietnamese (26)	29	0.12
Other Asian, specified	6	0.03
Other Asian, not specified (8)	9	0.04
Australian	6	0.03
Austrian	450	1.93
Brazilian	5	0.02
British	22	0.09
Canadian	16	0.07
Carpatho Rusyn	6	0.03
Czech	63	0.27
Czechoslovakian	181	0.78
Danish	23	0.10
Dutch	1,271	5.46
Eastern European	32	0.14
English	790	3.40
European	27	0.12
Finnish	7	0.03
French, except Basque	142	0.61
French Canadian	18	0.08
German	3,223	13.85
Greek	521	2.24
Hawaii Native/Pacific Islander:	25	0.11
Micronesian: (2)	2	0.01
Guamanian/Chamorro (2)	2	0.01
Other Pac. Isl., specified	6	0.03
Other Pac. Isl., not spec. (1)	17	0.07
Hispanic or Latino:	1,132	4.85
Central American:	33	0.14
Guatemalan	12	0.05
Honduran	13	0.06
Nicaraguan	1	0.00
Panamanian	1	0.00
Salvadoran	5	0.02
Other Central American	1	0.00
Cuban	11	0.05
Dominican Republic	329	1.41
Mexican	159	0.68
Puerto Rican	271	1.16
South American:	54	0.23
Argentinean	3	0.01
Chilean	1	0.00
Colombian	3	0.01
Ecuadorian	13	0.06
Peruvian	27	0.12
Other South American	7	0.03
Other Hispanic or Latino	275	1.18
Hungarian	224	0.96
Iranian	9	0.04
Irish	3,064	13.17
Italian	7,477	32.14
Latvian	19	0.08
Lithuanian	279	1.20
Macedonian	5	0.02
Northern European	4	0.02
Norwegian	32	0.14
Pennsylvania German	167	0.72
Polish	3,277	14.09
Portuguese	43	0.18
Romanian	105	0.45
Russian	167	0.72
Scotch-Irish	66	0.28
Scottish	78	0.34
Serbian	11	0.05
Slavic	95	0.41
Slovak	2,662	11.44
Slovene	5	0.02
Swedish	76	0.33
Ukrainian	358	1.54
United States or American	643	2.76
Welsh	322	1.38
White:	22,273	95.47
Not Hispanic (21,741)	21,862	93.71
Hispanic (351)	411	1.76
Yugoslavian	54	0.23

Hempfield

Place Type: Township
County: Westmoreland
Population: 40,721

Ancestry/Race	Number	%
African American/Black:	503	1.24
Not Hispanic (447)	498	1.22
Hispanic (4)	5	0.01
African, sub-Saharan:	13	0.03
African	13	0.03
Alaska Native tribes, specified:	3	0.01
Alaska Athabascan (3)	3	0.01
Am. Ind. or Alaska Nat., not spec.	33	0.08
Albanian	8	0.02
American Indian tribes, specified:	46	0.11
Blackfeet	4	0.01
Cherokee (8)	23	0.06
Choctaw (1)	1	0.00
Iroquois (2)	4	0.01
Latin American Indians (1)	1	0.00
Navajo (1)	4	0.01
Sioux	4	0.01
All other tribes (2)	5	0.01
American Indian tribes, not spec.	6	0.01
Arab:	324	0.80
Arab/Arabic	45	0.11
Lebanese	113	0.28
Syrian	166	0.41
Armenian	24	0.06
Asian:	389	0.96
Chinese, ex. Taiwanese (47)	55	0.14
Filipino (36)	43	0.11
Indian (88)	96	0.24
Indonesian	1	0.00
Japanese (71)	79	0.19
Korean (39)	44	0.11
Malaysian	1	0.00
Sri Lankan	1	0.00
Taiwanese (13)	13	0.03
Thai (6)	7	0.02
Vietnamese (21)	25	0.06
Other Asian, specified (4)	4	0.01
Other Asian, not specified (13)	20	0.05
Austrian	294	0.72
Belgian	63	0.15
British	44	0.11
Bulgarian	7	0.02
Canadian	16	0.04
Carpatho Rusyn	7	0.02
Croatian	417	1.02
Cypriot	5	0.01
Czech	215	0.53
Czechoslovakian	248	0.61
Danish	69	0.17
Dutch	668	1.64
Eastern European	29	0.07
English	4,191	10.29
European	163	0.40
Finnish	16	0.04
French, except Basque	710	1.74
French Canadian	77	0.19
German	12,053	29.61
Greek	106	0.26
Hawaii Native/Pacific Islander:	23	0.06
Micronesian: (9)	9	0.02
Guamanian/Chamorro (9)	9	0.02
Polynesian: (9)	11	0.03
Native Hawaiian	2	0.00
Samoan (6)	6	0.01
Other Polynesian (3)	3	0.01
Other Pac. Isl., not spec.	3	0.01
Hispanic or Latino:	154	0.38
Central American:	8	0.02
Costa Rican	1	0.00
Guatemalan	1	0.00
Panamanian	4	0.01
Salvadoran	2	0.00
Cuban	6	0.01
Mexican	45	0.11
Puerto Rican	36	0.09
South American:	7	0.02
Bolivian	1	0.00
Colombian	1	0.00
Ecuadorian	1	0.00
Peruvian	3	0.01
Other South American	1	0.00
Other Hispanic or Latino	52	0.13
Hungarian	584	1.43
Icelander	10	0.02
Irish	5,539	13.61
Italian	7,739	19.01
Lithuanian	184	0.45
Luxemburger	7	0.02
Norwegian	168	0.41
Pennsylvania German	500	1.23
Polish	3,296	8.10
Portuguese	20	0.05
Romanian	23	0.06
Russian	435	1.07
Scotch-Irish	1,099	2.70
Scottish	885	2.17
Serbian	265	0.65
Slavic	118	0.29
Slovak	2,261	5.55
Slovene	387	0.95
Swedish	708	1.74
Swiss	23	0.06
Ukrainian	571	1.40
United States or American	1,432	3.52
Welsh	537	1.32
West Indian, excl. Hispanic:	26	0.06
West Indian	26	0.06
White:	39,824	97.80
Not Hispanic (39,568)	39,715	97.53
Hispanic (102)	109	0.27
Yugoslavian	133	0.33

Notes: 1. Figures in the "Number" column do not add up to the total population due to: a) Ancestry/Race overlap — e.g. persons can report being both White and Irish, b) persons of Hispanic origin can report being any race, c) persons reporting two ancestries are counted in both categories. 2. Numbers in parentheses indicate the number of persons reporting this ancestry/race alone, not in combination with any other ancestry/race. 3. Refer to the Explanation of Data in the front of the book for more detailed information.

Hermitage

Place Type: City
County: Mercer
Population: 16,157

Ancestry/Race	Number	%
African American/Black:	571	3.53
Not Hispanic (495)	565	3.50
Hispanic (5)	6	0.04
African, sub-Saharan:	12	0.07
African	12	0.07
Am. Ind. or Alaska Nat., not spec.	22	0.14
American Indian tribes, specified:	22	0.14
Blackfeet	2	0.01
Cherokee (2)	5	0.03
Chippewa	2	0.01
Delaware (2)	3	0.02
Iroquois	7	0.04
Latin American Indians (1)	2	0.01
All other tribes	1	0.01
American Indian tribes, not spec.	1	0.01
Arab:	110	0.68
Arab/Arabic	13	0.08
Egyptian	11	0.07
Lebanese	61	0.38
Syrian	25	0.15
Armenian	15	0.09
Asian:	155	0.96
Chinese, ex. Taiwanese (30)	31	0.19
Filipino (5)	11	0.07
Indian (47)	56	0.35
Japanese (1)	3	0.02
Korean (19)	24	0.15
Pakistani (9)	11	0.07
Sri Lankan (1)	1	0.01
Vietnamese (16)	16	0.10
Other Asian, not specified (1)	2	0.01
Austrian	74	0.46
Belgian	26	0.16
British	60	0.37
Canadian	54	0.33
Carpatho Rusyn	14	0.09
Croatian	473	2.93
Czech	118	0.73
Czechoslovakian	49	0.30
Danish	20	0.12
Dutch	328	2.03
English	1,805	11.19
European	72	0.45
Finnish	27	0.17
French, except Basque	245	1.52
French Canadian	43	0.27
German	3,737	23.17
Greek	53	0.33
Hawaii Native/Pacific Islander:	12	0.07
Polynesian: (1)	7	0.04
Native Hawaiian	6	0.04
Samoan (1)	1	0.01
Other Pac. Isl., not spec.	5	0.03
Hispanic or Latino:	107	0.66
Central American:	1	0.01
Guatemalan	1	0.01
Cuban	6	0.04
Dominican Republic	2	0.01
Mexican	24	0.15
Puerto Rican	44	0.27
South American:	1	0.01
Venezuelan	1	0.01
Other Hispanic or Latino	29	0.18
Hungarian	503	3.12
Irish	2,428	15.05
Israeli	31	0.19
Italian	3,042	18.86
Lithuanian	33	0.20
Norwegian	42	0.26
Pennsylvania German	61	0.38
Polish	1,122	6.96
Portuguese	1	0.01
Romanian	163	1.01
Russian	92	0.57
Scandinavian	70	0.43
Scotch-Irish	658	4.08
Scottish	274	1.70
Serbian	65	0.40
Slavic	32	0.20
Slovak	1,470	9.11
Slovene	128	0.79
Swedish	185	1.15
Swiss	28	0.17
Ukrainian	128	0.79
United States or American	614	3.81
Welsh	464	2.88
West Indian, excl. Hispanic:	4	0.02
Jamaican	4	0.02
White:	15,470	95.75
Not Hispanic (15,284)	15,398	95.30
Hispanic (60)	72	0.45
Yugoslavian	89	0.55

Hershey

Place Type: Census Designated Place
County: Dauphin
Population: 12,771

Ancestry/Race	Number	%
African American/Black:	326	2.55
Not Hispanic (264)	310	2.43
Hispanic (7)	16	0.13
African, sub-Saharan:	43	0.34
African	30	0.23
Liberian	13	0.10
Am. Ind. or Alaska Nat., not spec.	11	0.09
American Indian tribes, specified:	33	0.26
Blackfeet	11	0.09
Cherokee (2)	4	0.03
Chippewa	1	0.01
Comanche	1	0.01
Iroquois	1	0.01
Latin American Indians (4)	4	0.03
Sioux	8	0.06
All other tribes	3	0.02
American Indian tribes, not spec.	3	0.02
Arab:	24	0.19
Arab/Arabic	12	0.09
Lebanese	12	0.09
Armenian	9	0.07
Asian:	674	5.28
Bangladeshi (8)	10	0.08
Cambodian (41)	42	0.33
Chinese, ex. Taiwanese (261)	271	2.12
Filipino (24)	35	0.27
Indian (154)	160	1.25
Indonesian	2	0.02
Japanese (30)	36	0.28
Korean (39)	43	0.34
Malaysian	2	0.02
Pakistani (9)	10	0.08
Sri Lankan (3)	5	0.04
Taiwanese (11)	11	0.09
Thai (2)	2	0.02
Vietnamese (32)	32	0.25
Other Asian, specified (2)	2	0.02
Other Asian, not specified (1)	11	0.09
Australian	7	0.05
Austrian	63	0.49
Basque	11	0.09
Belgian	9	0.07
British	47	0.37
Bulgarian	6	0.05
Canadian	29	0.23
Croatian	105	0.82
Czech	33	0.26
Czechoslovakian	23	0.18
Danish	95	0.74
Dutch	311	2.43
Eastern European	28	0.22
English	1,609	12.59
European	112	0.88
Finnish	26	0.20
French, except Basque	244	1.91
French Canadian	41	0.32
German	4,587	35.90
Greek	91	0.71
Hawaii Native/Pacific Islander:	9	0.07
Melanesian:	1	0.01
Other Melanesian	1	0.01
Micronesian: (1)	1	0.01
Guamanian/Chamorro (1)	1	0.01
Polynesian:	1	0.01
Native Hawaiian	1	0.01
Other Pac. Isl., not spec.	6	0.05
Hispanic or Latino:	198	1.55
Central American:	9	0.07
Panamanian	9	0.07
Cuban	16	0.13
Dominican Republic	6	0.05
Mexican	34	0.27
Puerto Rican	77	0.60
South American:	28	0.22
Argentinean	9	0.07
Colombian	10	0.08
Ecuadorian	2	0.02
Peruvian	2	0.02
Other South American	5	0.04
Other Hispanic or Latino	28	0.22
Hungarian	177	1.39
Irish	1,728	13.52
Italian	1,738	13.60
Lithuanian	80	0.63
Norwegian	133	1.04
Pennsylvania German	91	0.71
Polish	648	5.07
Romanian	17	0.13
Russian	189	1.48
Scandinavian	31	0.24
Scotch-Irish	270	2.11
Scottish	359	2.81
Serbian	25	0.20
Slavic	6	0.05
Slovak	90	0.70
Slovene	8	0.06
Swedish	161	1.26
Swiss	118	0.92
Ukrainian	124	0.97
United States or American	440	3.44
Welsh	344	2.69
West Indian, excl. Hispanic:	28	0.22
Haitian	7	0.05
Jamaican	12	0.09
West Indian	9	0.07
White:	11,781	92.25
Not Hispanic (11,512)	11,648	91.21
Hispanic (119)	133	1.04
Yugoslavian	86	0.67

Hilltown

Place Type: Township
County: Bucks
Population: 12,102

Ancestry/Race	Number	%
African American/Black:	252	2.08
Not Hispanic (184)	247	2.04
Hispanic (2)	5	0.04
African, sub-Saharan:	26	0.21
African	21	0.17
South African	5	0.04
Am. Ind. or Alaska Nat., not spec.	17	0.14
American Indian tribes, specified:	29	0.24
Cherokee (3)	16	0.13
Choctaw	5	0.04
Delaware (1)	5	0.04
Sioux (3)	3	0.02
American Indian tribes, not spec.	10	0.08
Arab:	35	0.29
Arab/Arabic	18	0.15
Palestinian	6	0.05

Notes: 1. Figures in the "Number" column do not add up to the total population due to: a) Ancestry/Race overlap — e.g. persons can report being both White and Irish, b) persons of Hispanic origin can report being any race, c) persons reporting two ancestries are counted in both categories. 2. Numbers in parentheses indicate the number of persons reporting this ancestry/race alone, not in combination with any other ancestry/race. 3. Refer to the Explanation of Data in the front of the book for more detailed information.

Ancestry/Race	Number	%
Syrian	11	0.09
Armenian	10	0.08
Asian:	154	1.27
Cambodian (5)	5	0.04
Chinese, ex. Taiwanese (12)	13	0.11
Filipino (7)	12	0.10
Indian (18)	19	0.16
Japanese (3)	10	0.08
Korean (22)	27	0.22
Laotian (1)	5	0.04
Vietnamese (57)	57	0.47
Other Asian, not specified (2)	6	0.05
Austrian	54	0.45
Basque	14	0.12
Belgian	8	0.07
Brazilian	14	0.12
British	136	1.12
Canadian	34	0.28
Carpatho Rusyn	7	0.06
Czech	41	0.34
Czechoslovakian	26	0.21
Danish	10	0.08
Dutch	242	2.00
Eastern European	9	0.07
English	1,163	9.61
European	78	0.64
Finnish	6	0.05
French, except Basque	111	0.92
French Canadian	121	1.00
German	4,650	38.42
Greek	38	0.31
Hawaii Native/Pacific Islander:	6	0.05
Micronesian: (1)	1	0.01
Other Micronesian (1)	1	0.01
Polynesian:	1	0.01
Samoan	1	0.01
Other Pac. Isl., not spec. (2)	4	0.03
Hispanic or Latino:	177	1.46
Central American:	5	0.04
Costa Rican	3	0.02
Honduran	1	0.01
Panamanian	1	0.01
Cuban	6	0.05
Dominican Republic	1	0.01
Mexican	22	0.18
Puerto Rican	118	0.98
South American:	3	0.02
Colombian	1	0.01
Ecuadorian	2	0.02
Other Hispanic or Latino	22	0.18
Hungarian	148	1.22
Irish	2,329	19.24
Italian	1,445	11.94
Lithuanian	86	0.71
Norwegian	32	0.26
Pennsylvania German	162	1.34
Polish	699	5.78
Portuguese	26	0.21
Romanian	5	0.04
Russian	119	0.98
Scandinavian	8	0.07
Scotch-Irish	179	1.48
Scottish	169	1.40
Slovak	51	0.42
Swedish	61	0.50
Swiss	346	2.86
Turkish	32	0.26
Ukrainian	91	0.75
United States or American	401	3.31
Welsh	162	1.34
White:	11,718	96.83
Not Hispanic (11,494)	11,587	95.74
Hispanic (117)	131	1.08

Hopewell

Place Type: Township
County: Beaver
Population: 13,254

Ancestry/Race	Number	%
African American/Black:	260	1.96
Not Hispanic (236)	256	1.93
Hispanic (4)	4	0.03
Am. Ind. or Alaska Nat., not spec.	4	0.03
American Indian tribes, specified:	16	0.12
Blackfeet	5	0.04
Cherokee (1)	8	0.06
Latin American Indians	2	0.02
Sioux	1	0.01
Arab:	201	1.51
Lebanese	93	0.70
Syrian	108	0.81
Asian:	49	0.37
Chinese, ex. Taiwanese (8)	8	0.06
Filipino (7)	8	0.06
Indian (11)	11	0.08
Japanese (1)	3	0.02
Korean (2)	3	0.02
Thai (1)	1	0.01
Vietnamese (7)	7	0.05
Other Asian, not specified (5)	8	0.06
Austrian	90	0.68
British	47	0.35
Canadian	60	0.45
Croatian	512	3.84
Czech	80	0.60
Czechoslovakian	42	0.32
Danish	5	0.04
Dutch	316	2.37
Eastern European	15	0.11
English	1,266	9.51
European	35	0.26
French, except Basque	165	1.24
French Canadian	10	0.08
German	3,029	22.75
Greek	212	1.59
Hawaii Native/Pacific Islander:	3	0.02
Polynesian: (1)	1	0.01
Native Hawaiian (1)	1	0.01
Other Pac. Isl., not spec. (1)	2	0.02
Hispanic or Latino:	65	0.49
Central American:	1	0.01
Honduran	1	0.01
Cuban	2	0.02
Mexican	31	0.23
Puerto Rican	5	0.04
Other Hispanic or Latino	26	0.20
Hungarian	125	0.94
Irish	2,341	17.58
Italian	3,233	24.28
Lithuanian	32	0.24
Norwegian	42	0.32
Pennsylvania German	7	0.05
Polish	1,165	8.75
Portuguese	10	0.08
Romanian	42	0.32
Russian	111	0.83
Scandinavian	31	0.23
Scotch-Irish	436	3.27
Scottish	158	1.19
Serbian	466	3.50
Slavic	18	0.14
Slovak	668	5.02
Slovene	40	0.30
Swedish	59	0.44
Swiss	7	0.05
Ukrainian	257	1.93
United States or American	498	3.74
Welsh	172	1.29
White:	12,954	97.74
Not Hispanic (12,852)	12,902	97.34
Hispanic (50)	52	0.39
Yugoslavian	36	0.27

Horsham

Place Type: Township
County: Montgomery
Population: 24,232

Ancestry/Race	Number	%
African American/Black:	989	4.08
Not Hispanic (890)	970	4.00
Hispanic (14)	19	0.08
African, sub-Saharan:	30	0.12
African	30	0.12
Alaska Native tribes, not specified	1	0.00
Am. Ind. or Alaska Nat., not spec.	25	0.10
Albanian	21	0.09
American Indian tribes, specified:	54	0.22
Apache	1	0.00
Blackfeet	4	0.02
Cherokee (12)	15	0.06
Chippewa	1	0.00
Choctaw	4	0.02
Delaware (1)	2	0.01
Iroquois (5)	6	0.02
Latin American Indians (2)	3	0.01
Lumbee (2)	2	0.01
Navajo (1)	2	0.01
Potawatomi (1)	1	0.00
Pueblo (1)	1	0.00
Sioux	3	0.01
Ute	1	0.00
All other tribes (6)	8	0.03
American Indian tribes, not spec.	6	0.02
Arab:	88	0.36
Arab/Arabic	9	0.04
Lebanese	79	0.33
Armenian	15	0.06
Asian:	1,255	5.18
Bangladeshi (2)	2	0.01
Cambodian (3)	3	0.01
Chinese, ex. Taiwanese (179)	194	0.80
Filipino (92)	104	0.43
Hmong (1)	1	0.00
Indian (238)	260	1.07
Indonesian	2	0.01
Japanese (10)	20	0.08
Korean (504)	525	2.17
Laotian (25)	25	0.10
Malaysian (1)	5	0.02
Pakistani (13)	13	0.05
Sri Lankan (2)	2	0.01
Taiwanese (2)	4	0.02
Thai (2)	2	0.01
Vietnamese (61)	65	0.27
Other Asian, not specified (18)	28	0.12
Assyrian/Chaldean/Syriac	8	0.03
Australian	13	0.05
Austrian	109	0.45
Belgian	9	0.04
Brazilian	44	0.18
British	95	0.39
Canadian	85	0.35
Cypriot	14	0.06
Czech	65	0.27
Czechoslovakian	47	0.19
Danish	74	0.31
Dutch	340	1.40
Eastern European	43	0.18
English	2,447	10.10
Estonian	7	0.03
European	108	0.45
Finnish	7	0.03
French, except Basque	426	1.76
French Canadian	33	0.14
German	6,526	26.93
Greek	132	0.54
Guyanese	8	0.03
Hawaii Native/Pacific Islander:	21	0.09
Micronesian: (1)	1	0.00
Guamanian/Chamorro (1)	1	0.00
Polynesian: (1)	9	0.04

Notes: 1. Figures in the "Number" column do not add up to the total population due to: a) Ancestry/Race overlap — e.g. persons can report being both White and Irish, b) persons of Hispanic origin can report being any race, c) persons reporting two ancestries are counted in both categories. 2. Numbers in parentheses indicate the number of persons reporting this ancestry/race alone, not in combination with any other ancestry/race. 3. Refer to the Explanation of Data in the front of the book for more detailed information.

Native Hawaiian	4	0.02
Samoan (1)	3	0.01
Other Polynesian	2	0.01
Other Pac. Isl., not spec. (1)	11	0.05
Hispanic or Latino:	387	1.60
Central American:	12	0.05
Costa Rican	2	0.01
Guatemalan	5	0.02
Honduran	3	0.01
Salvadoran	1	0.00
Other Central American	1	0.00
Cuban	11	0.05
Dominican Republic	10	0.04
Mexican	54	0.22
Puerto Rican	194	0.80
South American:	51	0.21
Argentinean	11	0.05
Chilean	2	0.01
Colombian	12	0.05
Ecuadorian	5	0.02
Paraguayan	3	0.01
Peruvian	12	0.05
Venezuelan	5	0.02
Other South American	1	0.00
Other Hispanic or Latino	55	0.23
Hungarian	279	1.15
Irish	7,475	30.85
Israeli	15	0.06
Italian	4,083	16.85
Latvian	45	0.19
Lithuanian	102	0.42
Norwegian	152	0.63
Pennsylvania German	57	0.24
Polish	1,502	6.20
Portuguese	61	0.25
Romanian	54	0.22
Russian	467	1.93
Scotch-Irish	503	2.08
Scottish	511	2.11
Serbian	6	0.02
Slavic	25	0.10
Slovak	157	0.65
Slovene	11	0.05
Swedish	168	0.69
Swiss	92	0.38
Ukrainian	287	1.18
United States or American	845	3.49
Welsh	236	0.97
West Indian, excl. Hispanic:	65	0.27
Dutch West Indian	14	0.06
Haitian	33	0.14
Jamaican	10	0.04
Trinidadian and Tobagonian	8	0.03
White:	21,935	90.52
Not Hispanic (21,545)	21,688	89.50
Hispanic (219)	247	1.02
Yugoslavian	59	0.24

Indiana

Place Type: Borough
County: Indiana
Population: 14,895

Ancestry/Race	Number	%
African American/Black:	825	5.54
Not Hispanic (771)	821	5.51
Hispanic (2)	4	0.03
African, sub-Saharan:	73	0.49
African	11	0.07
Kenyan	40	0.27
Nigerian	22	0.15
Am. Ind. or Alaska Nat., not spec.	15	0.10
American Indian tribes, specified:	15	0.10
Cherokee (1)	9	0.06
Chippewa (1)	1	0.01
Delaware	1	0.01
Seminole	1	0.01
Sioux	1	0.01
All other tribes (1)	2	0.01
Arab:	154	1.03
Arab/Arabic	40	0.27
Egyptian	35	0.23
Iraqi	8	0.05
Lebanese	30	0.20
Palestinian	9	0.06
Syrian	32	0.21
Armenian	6	0.04
Asian:	335	2.25
Bangladeshi (12)	15	0.10
Cambodian (1)	2	0.01
Chinese, ex. Taiwanese (76)	86	0.58
Filipino (8)	12	0.08
Indian (56)	60	0.40
Indonesian (5)	7	0.05
Japanese (29)	36	0.24
Korean (33)	40	0.27
Laotian (3)	3	0.02
Malaysian (9)	9	0.06
Sri Lankan (1)	1	0.01
Taiwanese (8)	9	0.06
Thai (10)	11	0.07
Vietnamese (19)	24	0.16
Other Asian, specified	1	0.01
Other Asian, not specified (4)	19	0.13
Austrian	53	0.36
Belgian	7	0.05
British	59	0.40
Canadian	8	0.05
Celtic	7	0.05
Croatian	117	0.79
Czech	67	0.45
Czechoslovakian	148	0.99
Danish	44	0.30
Dutch	317	2.13
Eastern European	10	0.07
English	1,130	7.59
European	128	0.86
Finnish	21	0.14
French, except Basque	250	1.68
French Canadian	28	0.19
German	4,110	27.59
Greek	42	0.28
Hawaii Native/Pacific Islander:	7	0.05
Melanesian:	1	0.01
Fijian	1	0.01
Polynesian: (2)	4	0.03
Native Hawaiian (1)	2	0.01
Samoan (1)	2	0.01
Other Pac. Isl., not spec. (1)	2	0.01
Hispanic or Latino:	178	1.20
Central American:	13	0.09
Costa Rican	5	0.03
Honduran	2	0.01
Panamanian	5	0.03
Other Central American	1	0.01
Cuban	14	0.09
Mexican	53	0.36
Puerto Rican	43	0.29
South American:	20	0.13
Chilean	1	0.01
Colombian	9	0.06
Ecuadorian	2	0.01
Peruvian	3	0.02
Venezuelan	5	0.03
Other Hispanic or Latino	35	0.23
Hungarian	173	1.16
Irish	2,372	15.92
Italian	1,864	12.51
Latvian	6	0.04
Lithuanian	46	0.31
Norwegian	71	0.48
Pennsylvania German	20	0.13
Polish	1,368	9.18
Portuguese	10	0.07
Russian	145	0.97
Scandinavian	19	0.13
Scotch-Irish	482	3.24
Scottish	402	2.70
Serbian	10	0.07
Slavic	45	0.30
Slovak	445	2.99
Slovene	69	0.46
Swedish	157	1.05
Swiss	56	0.38
Ukrainian	92	0.62
United States or American	602	4.04
Welsh	187	1.26
West Indian, excl. Hispanic:	18	0.12
Jamaican	5	0.03
West Indian	13	0.09
White:	13,744	92.27
Not Hispanic (13,526)	13,629	91.50
Hispanic (104)	115	0.77

Jeannette

Place Type: City
County: Westmoreland
Population: 10,654

Ancestry/Race	Number	%
African American/Black:	676	6.35
Not Hispanic (550)	668	6.27
Hispanic (3)	8	0.08
African, sub-Saharan:	5	0.05
African	5	0.05
Am. Ind. or Alaska Nat., not spec.	19	0.18
American Indian tribes, specified:	27	0.25
Blackfeet	4	0.04
Cherokee (2)	9	0.08
Delaware (1)	1	0.01
Iroquois	4	0.04
Sioux (1)	5	0.05
Ute (1)	1	0.01
All other tribes (3)	3	0.03
American Indian tribes, not spec.	6	0.06
Arab:	109	1.02
Lebanese	6	0.06
Syrian	103	0.96
Asian:	21	0.20
Chinese, ex. Taiwanese (1)	1	0.01
Filipino (2)	6	0.06
Japanese (2)	2	0.02
Korean (5)	5	0.05
Other Asian, specified	4	0.04
Other Asian, not specified	3	0.03
Australian	7	0.07
Austrian	76	0.71
Belgian	24	0.22
British	20	0.19
Croatian	150	1.41
Czech	100	0.94
Czechoslovakian	19	0.18
Danish	7	0.07
Dutch	287	2.69
English	952	8.92
Finnish	9	0.08
French, except Basque	196	1.84
French Canadian	5	0.05
German	2,754	25.80
Greek	36	0.34
Hawaii Native/Pacific Islander:	8	0.08
Polynesian: (3)	3	0.03
Native Hawaiian (1)	1	0.01
Samoan (2)	2	0.02
Other Pac. Isl., specified	4	0.04
Other Pac. Isl., not spec. (1)	1	0.01
Hispanic or Latino:	53	0.50
Central American:	7	0.07
Guatemalan	1	0.01
Panamanian	6	0.06
Cuban	10	0.09
Mexican	15	0.14
Puerto Rican	10	0.09
South American:	5	0.05
Argentinean	3	0.03
Colombian	2	0.02
Other Hispanic or Latino	6	0.06
Hungarian	159	1.49

Notes: 1. Figures in the "Number" column do not add up to the total population due to: a) Ancestry/Race overlap — e.g. persons can report being both White and Irish, b) persons of Hispanic origin can report being any race, c) persons reporting two ancestries are counted in both categories. 2. Numbers in parentheses indicate the number of persons reporting this ancestry/race alone, not in combination with any other ancestry/race. 3. Refer to the Explanation of Data in the front of the book for more detailed information.

Ancestry/Race	Number	%
Iranian	7	0.07
Irish	1,637	15.33
Italian	2,619	24.53
Lithuanian	71	0.67
Norwegian	10	0.09
Pennsylvania German	53	0.50
Polish	895	8.38
Romanian	7	0.07
Russian	83	0.78
Scotch-Irish	147	1.38
Scottish	235	2.20
Serbian	106	0.99
Slavic	29	0.27
Slovak	202	1.89
Slovene	46	0.43
Swedish	89	0.83
Ukrainian	141	1.32
United States or American	440	4.12
Welsh	187	1.75
West Indian, excl. Hispanic:	5	0.05
Jamaican	5	0.05
White:	10,044	94.27
Not Hispanic (9,856)	10,005	93.91
Hispanic (32)	39	0.37
Yugoslavian	15	0.14

Johnstown

Place Type: City
County: Cambria
Population: 23,906

Ancestry/Race	Number	%
African American/Black:	2,921	12.22
Not Hispanic (2,520)	2,857	11.95
Hispanic (41)	64	0.27
African, sub-Saharan:	150	0.63
African	150	0.63
Am. Ind. or Alaska Nat., not spec.	46	0.19
American Indian tribes, specified:	61	0.26
Apache (3)	7	0.03
Blackfeet (2)	13	0.05
Cherokee (8)	22	0.09
Cheyenne (1)	1	0.00
Choctaw (1)	1	0.00
Delaware	2	0.01
Iroquois (3)	6	0.03
Seminole	1	0.00
Sioux (1)	4	0.02
All other tribes (1)	4	0.02
American Indian tribes, not spec.	5	0.02
Arab:	148	0.62
Lebanese	141	0.59
Syrian	4	0.02
Other Arab	3	0.01
Asian:	109	0.46
Chinese, ex. Taiwanese (9)	14	0.06
Filipino (7)	24	0.10
Indian (26)	31	0.13
Japanese	7	0.03
Korean (10)	12	0.05
Pakistani (9)	10	0.04
Thai (1)	1	0.00
Vietnamese (5)	5	0.02
Other Asian, specified	3	0.01
Other Asian, not specified	2	0.01
Austrian	91	0.38
Belgian	5	0.02
Brazilian	13	0.05
British	9	0.04
Canadian	10	0.04
Carpatho Rusyn	67	0.28
Croatian	389	1.63
Czech	109	0.46
Czechoslovakian	63	0.26
Dutch	544	2.28
Eastern European	4	0.02
English	1,362	5.70
European	25	0.10
French, except Basque	247	1.03
French Canadian	28	0.12
German	6,047	25.29
Greek	57	0.24
Hawaii Native/Pacific Islander:	21	0.09
Polynesian: (9)	12	0.05
Native Hawaiian (5)	6	0.03
Samoan (4)	6	0.03
Other Pac. Isl., specified	3	0.01
Other Pac. Isl., not spec. (3)	6	0.03
Hispanic or Latino:	380	1.59
Central American:	2	0.01
Guatemalan	1	0.00
Salvadoran	1	0.00
Cuban	27	0.11
Dominican Republic	7	0.03
Mexican	179	0.75
Puerto Rican	87	0.36
South American:	8	0.03
Colombian	3	0.01
Ecuadorian	3	0.01
Other South American	2	0.01
Other Hispanic or Latino	70	0.29
Hungarian	463	1.94
Iranian	7	0.03
Irish	3,400	14.22
Italian	2,119	8.86
Lithuanian	48	0.20
Norwegian	3	0.01
Pennsylvania German	312	1.31
Polish	1,858	7.77
Romanian	20	0.08
Russian	273	1.14
Scandinavian	46	0.19
Scotch-Irish	166	0.69
Scottish	235	0.98
Serbian	304	1.27
Slavic	125	0.52
Slovak	1,862	7.79
Slovene	167	0.70
Swedish	76	0.32
Swiss	16	0.07
Ukrainian	348	1.46
United States or American	1,082	4.53
Welsh	361	1.51
White:	21,042	88.02
Not Hispanic (20,417)	20,805	87.03
Hispanic (210)	237	0.99
Yugoslavian	6	0.03

King of Prussia

Place Type: Census Designated Place
County: Montgomery
Population: 18,511

Ancestry/Race	Number	%
Afghan	44	0.24
African American/Black:	875	4.73
Not Hispanic (777)	862	4.66
Hispanic (11)	13	0.07
African, sub-Saharan:	71	0.38
African	30	0.16
Cape Verdean	7	0.04
Ghanian	14	0.08
Nigerian	5	0.03
South African	15	0.08
Am. Ind. or Alaska Nat., not spec.	24	0.13
Albanian	27	0.15
American Indian tribes, specified:	39	0.21
Apache (2)	2	0.01
Blackfeet	1	0.01
Cherokee (3)	12	0.06
Choctaw	4	0.02
Creek (1)	1	0.01
Delaware	2	0.01
Iroquois	3	0.02
Latin American Indians	4	0.02
All other tribes (9)	10	0.05
American Indian tribes, not spec.	11	0.06
Arab:	105	0.57
Egyptian	39	0.21
Lebanese	18	0.10
Syrian	20	0.11
Other Arab	28	0.15
Armenian	66	0.36
Asian:	2,120	11.45
Cambodian (19)	23	0.12
Chinese, ex. Taiwanese (442)	482	2.60
Filipino (209)	223	1.20
Indian (913)	956	5.16
Indonesian (7)	9	0.05
Japanese (38)	41	0.22
Korean (130)	141	0.76
Laotian (17)	21	0.11
Pakistani (26)	40	0.22
Sri Lankan (2)	2	0.01
Taiwanese (12)	24	0.13
Thai (8)	11	0.06
Vietnamese (86)	90	0.49
Other Asian, specified (4)	7	0.04
Other Asian, not specified (17)	50	0.27
Austrian	91	0.49
Basque	6	0.03
Brazilian	37	0.20
British	71	0.38
Canadian	39	0.21
Carpatho Rusyn	7	0.04
Croatian	6	0.03
Czech	30	0.16
Czechoslovakian	57	0.31
Danish	59	0.32
Dutch	225	1.21
Eastern European	60	0.32
English	1,813	9.78
European	188	1.01
Finnish	9	0.05
French, except Basque	354	1.91
French Canadian	58	0.31
German	3,616	19.50
Greek	139	0.75
Guyanese	18	0.10
Hawaii Native/Pacific Islander:	17	0.09
Polynesian: (3)	3	0.02
Native Hawaiian (1)	1	0.01
Samoan (2)	2	0.01
Other Pac. Isl., not spec. (4)	14	0.08
Hispanic or Latino:	354	1.91
Central American:	14	0.08
Costa Rican	1	0.01
Guatemalan	4	0.02
Honduran	5	0.03
Panamanian	1	0.01
Salvadoran	3	0.02
Cuban	42	0.23
Dominican Republic	4	0.02
Mexican	67	0.36
Puerto Rican	100	0.54
South American:	67	0.36
Argentinean	9	0.05
Bolivian	3	0.02
Chilean	5	0.03
Colombian	19	0.10
Ecuadorian	5	0.03
Paraguayan	2	0.01
Peruvian	12	0.06
Uruguayan	2	0.01
Venezuelan	7	0.04
Other South American	3	0.02
Other Hispanic or Latino	60	0.32
Hungarian	240	1.29
Icelander	5	0.03
Iranian	51	0.28
Irish	3,765	20.31
Israeli	21	0.11
Italian	3,143	16.95
Latvian	6	0.03
Lithuanian	117	0.63
Maltese	11	0.06
Northern European	14	0.08
Norwegian	26	0.14

Notes: 1. Figures in the "Number" column do not add up to the total population due to: a) Ancestry/Race overlap — e.g. persons can report being both White and Irish, b) persons of Hispanic origin can report being any race, c) persons reporting two ancestries are counted in both categories. 2. Numbers in parentheses indicate the number of persons reporting this ancestry/race alone, not in combination with any other ancestry/race. 3. Refer to the Explanation of Data in the front of the book for more detailed information.

Pennsylvania German	124	0.67
Polish	1,519	8.19
Portuguese	47	0.25
Romanian	59	0.32
Russian	470	2.54
Scotch-Irish	308	1.66
Scottish	206	1.11
Slavic	24	0.13
Slovak	214	1.15
Swedish	164	0.88
Swiss	42	0.23
Ukrainian	213	1.15
United States or American	693	3.74
Welsh	212	1.14
West Indian, excl. Hispanic:	77	0.42
Bahamian	18	0.10
Jamaican	19	0.10
Trinidadian and Tobagonian	26	0.14
U.S. Virgin Islander	4	0.02
West Indian	10	0.05
White:	15,494	83.70
Not Hispanic (15,113)	15,282	82.56
Hispanic (195)	212	1.15
Yugoslavian	31	0.17

Kingston

Place Type: Borough
County: Luzerne
Population: 13,855

Ancestry/Race	Number	%
African American/Black:	120	0.87
Not Hispanic (103)	117	0.84
Hispanic (3)	3	0.02
Am. Ind. or Alaska Nat., not spec.	14	0.10
American Indian tribes, specified:	17	0.12
Blackfeet (2)	4	0.03
Cherokee	2	0.01
Iroquois	2	0.01
Kiowa (1)	1	0.01
Latin American Indians	2	0.01
Puget Sound Salish (4)	4	0.03
Sioux	2	0.01
Arab:	78	0.56
Arab/Arabic	6	0.04
Lebanese	56	0.40
Syrian	16	0.12
Asian:	236	1.70
Cambodian (3)	3	0.02
Chinese, ex. Taiwanese (80)	83	0.60
Filipino (20)	20	0.14
Indian (55)	59	0.43
Indonesian (1)	1	0.01
Japanese (14)	17	0.12
Korean (19)	21	0.15
Pakistani (3)	6	0.04
Taiwanese (2)	2	0.01
Thai (2)	2	0.01
Vietnamese (12)	12	0.09
Other Asian, not specified (1)	10	0.07
Australian	5	0.04
Austrian	145	1.05
Belgian	3	0.02
Brazilian	5	0.04
Bulgarian	4	0.03
Canadian	11	0.08
Carpatho Rusyn	14	0.10
Croatian	36	0.26
Czech	29	0.21
Czechoslovakian	22	0.16
Danish	5	0.04
Dutch	220	1.59
Eastern European	26	0.19
English	1,276	9.21
European	95	0.69
French, except Basque	223	1.61
French Canadian	17	0.12
German	2,058	14.85
Greek	95	0.69
Hawaii Native/Pacific Islander:	1	0.01
Micronesian: (1)	1	0.01
Guamanian/Chamorro (1)	1	0.01
Hispanic or Latino:	111	0.80
Central American:	1	0.01
Panamanian	1	0.01
Cuban	5	0.04
Dominican Republic	4	0.03
Mexican	19	0.14
Puerto Rican	48	0.35
South American:	5	0.04
Chilean	2	0.01
Colombian	1	0.01
Peruvian	2	0.01
Other Hispanic or Latino	29	0.21
Hungarian	135	0.97
Iranian	7	0.05
Irish	2,791	20.14
Italian	1,445	10.43
Latvian	11	0.08
Lithuanian	550	3.97
Norwegian	27	0.19
Pennsylvania German	107	0.77
Polish	2,583	18.64
Portuguese	7	0.05
Romanian	38	0.27
Russian	557	4.02
Scotch-Irish	94	0.68
Scottish	193	1.39
Serbian	20	0.14
Slavic	8	0.06
Slovak	676	4.88
Slovene	16	0.12
Swedish	109	0.79
Swiss	7	0.05
Ukrainian	148	1.07
United States or American	511	3.69
Welsh	914	6.60
White:	13,479	97.29
Not Hispanic (13,351)	13,406	96.76
Hispanic (66)	73	0.53
Yugoslavian	22	0.16

Lancaster

Place Type: City
County: Lancaster
Population: 56,348

Ancestry/Race	Number	%
African American/Black:	9,195	16.32
Not Hispanic (7,067)	7,882	13.99
Hispanic (872)	1,313	2.33
African, sub-Saharan:	597	1.06
African	455	0.81
Ethiopian	95	0.17
Kenyan	8	0.01
Liberian	8	0.01
Nigerian	4	0.01
South African	8	0.01
Other sub-Saharan African	19	0.03
Am. Ind. or Alaska Nat., not spec.	259	0.46
Albanian	6	0.01
American Indian tribes, specified:	259	0.46
Apache	14	0.02
Blackfeet (2)	9	0.02
Cherokee (20)	78	0.14
Cheyenne	1	0.00
Chippewa (1)	5	0.01
Comanche	4	0.01
Cree (2)	3	0.01
Crow	2	0.00
Delaware (3)	10	0.02
Iroquois (4)	8	0.01
Latin American Indians (22)	48	0.09
Lumbee (1)	1	0.00
Navajo (8)	16	0.03
Potawatomi	1	0.00
Pueblo (4)	7	0.01
Seminole	2	0.00
Shoshone (3)	4	0.01
Sioux (5)	18	0.03
All other tribes (17)	28	0.05
American Indian tribes, not spec.	48	0.09
Arab:	59	0.10
Arab/Arabic	6	0.01
Egyptian	7	0.01
Lebanese	17	0.03
Moroccan	16	0.03
Syrian	13	0.02
Armenian	28	0.05
Asian:	1,643	2.92
Cambodian (177)	218	0.39
Chinese, ex. Taiwanese (176)	222	0.39
Filipino (34)	62	0.11
Indian (127)	156	0.28
Indonesian (2)	3	0.01
Japanese (41)	51	0.09
Korean (64)	75	0.13
Laotian (1)	1	0.00
Malaysian (1)	1	0.00
Pakistani (4)	5	0.01
Sri Lankan (3)	4	0.01
Taiwanese (2)	2	0.00
Thai (5)	20	0.04
Vietnamese (678)	742	1.32
Other Asian, specified (3)	8	0.01
Other Asian, not specified (36)	73	0.13
Austrian	105	0.19
Belgian	12	0.02
British	133	0.24
Bulgarian	17	0.03
Canadian	48	0.09
Celtic	6	0.01
Croatian	24	0.04
Czech	39	0.07
Czechoslovakian	22	0.04
Danish	53	0.09
Dutch	516	0.92
Eastern European	29	0.05
English	2,504	4.44
European	113	0.20
Finnish	22	0.04
French, except Basque	847	1.50
French Canadian	148	0.26
German	11,771	20.89
German Russian	9	0.02
Greek	302	0.54
Hawaii Native/Pacific Islander:	115	0.20
Micronesian: (13)	18	0.03
Guamanian/Chamorro (13)	18	0.03
Polynesian: (16)	33	0.06
Native Hawaiian (12)	25	0.04
Samoan (4)	6	0.01
Tongan	1	0.00
Other Polynesian	1	0.00
Other Pac. Isl., specified	5	0.01
Other Pac. Isl., not spec. (18)	59	0.10
Hispanic or Latino:	17,331	30.76
Central American:	174	0.31
Costa Rican	17	0.03
Guatemalan	22	0.04
Honduran	38	0.07
Nicaraguan	2	0.00
Panamanian	11	0.02
Salvadoran	76	0.13
Other Central American	8	0.01
Cuban	299	0.53
Dominican Republic	531	0.94
Mexican	479	0.85
Puerto Rican	13,717	24.34
South American:	274	0.49
Argentinean	14	0.02
Bolivian	2	0.00
Chilean	11	0.02
Colombian	114	0.20
Ecuadorian	51	0.09
Paraguayan	1	0.00
Peruvian	50	0.09
Uruguayan	6	0.01

Notes: 1. Figures in the "Number" column do not add up to the total population due to: a) Ancestry/Race overlap — e.g. persons can report being both White and Irish, b) persons of Hispanic origin can report being any race, c) persons reporting two ancestries are counted in both categories. 2. Numbers in parentheses indicate the number of persons reporting this ancestry/race alone, not in combination with any other ancestry/race. 3. Refer to the Explanation of Data in the front of the book for more detailed information.

Ancestry/Race	Number	%
Venezuelan	17	0.03
Other South American	8	0.01
Other Hispanic or Latino	1,857	3.30
Hungarian	154	0.27
Icelander	11	0.02
Iranian	26	0.05
Irish	4,252	7.55
Italian	2,192	3.89
Latvian	6	0.01
Lithuanian	81	0.14
Macedonian	16	0.03
Maltese	9	0.02
Northern European	51	0.09
Norwegian	176	0.31
Pennsylvania German	222	0.39
Polish	845	1.50
Portuguese	29	0.05
Romanian	38	0.07
Russian	179	0.32
Scotch-Irish	533	0.95
Scottish	576	1.02
Serbian	26	0.05
Slavic	20	0.04
Slovak	137	0.24
Swedish	261	0.46
Swiss	545	0.97
Turkish	16	0.03
Ukrainian	70	0.12
United States or American	3,142	5.58
Welsh	341	0.61
West Indian, excl. Hispanic:	411	0.73
Bahamian	5	0.01
British West Indian	6	0.01
Haitian	153	0.27
Jamaican	113	0.20
Trinidadian and Tobagonian	24	0.04
West Indian	110	0.20
White:	36,347	64.50
Not Hispanic (29,196)	30,095	53.41
Hispanic (5,487)	6,252	11.10
Yugoslavian	50	0.09

Lancaster

Place Type: Township
County: Lancaster
Population: 13,944

Ancestry/Race	Number	%
African American/Black:	1,090	7.82
Not Hispanic (828)	951	6.82
Hispanic (72)	139	1.00
African, sub-Saharan:	47	0.34
African	47	0.34
Am. Ind. or Alaska Nat., not spec.	34	0.24
Albanian	26	0.19
American Indian tribes, specified:	23	0.16
Blackfeet	5	0.04
Cherokee (2)	8	0.06
Latin American Indians	3	0.02
Seminole	2	0.01
All other tribes (3)	5	0.04
Arab:	29	0.21
Lebanese	19	0.14
Syrian	10	0.07
Armenian	15	0.11
Asian:	339	2.43
Cambodian (30)	33	0.24
Chinese, ex. Taiwanese (55)	72	0.52
Filipino (23)	27	0.19
Indian (30)	32	0.23
Japanese (12)	12	0.09
Korean (22)	24	0.17
Laotian (1)	1	0.01
Sri Lankan (2)	2	0.01
Thai (5)	6	0.04
Vietnamese (94)	113	0.81
Other Asian, not specified (3)	17	0.12
Australian	9	0.06
Austrian	39	0.28
Belgian	16	0.12
British	100	0.72
Bulgarian	5	0.04
Canadian	35	0.25
Celtic	28	0.20
Croatian	74	0.53
Czech	31	0.22
Czechoslovakian	25	0.18
Danish	60	0.43
Dutch	152	1.10
English	1,469	10.60
European	151	1.09
French, except Basque	370	2.67
French Canadian	86	0.62
German	4,783	34.51
Greek	209	1.51
Hawaii Native/Pacific Islander:	8	0.06
Polynesian: (1)	4	0.03
Native Hawaiian	3	0.02
Samoan (1)	1	0.01
Other Pac. Isl., not spec.	4	0.03
Hispanic or Latino:	1,346	9.65
Central American:	13	0.09
Costa Rican	1	0.01
Guatemalan	3	0.02
Honduran	1	0.01
Nicaraguan	4	0.03
Panamanian	2	0.01
Salvadoran	2	0.01
Cuban	23	0.16
Dominican Republic	48	0.34
Mexican	57	0.41
Puerto Rican	1,011	7.25
South American:	55	0.39
Argentinean	3	0.02
Bolivian	1	0.01
Chilean	5	0.04
Colombian	32	0.23
Ecuadorian	1	0.01
Peruvian	8	0.06
Uruguayan	2	0.01
Venezuelan	2	0.01
Other South American	1	0.01
Other Hispanic or Latino	139	1.00
Hungarian	10	0.07
Irish	1,688	12.18
Italian	741	5.35
Latvian	7	0.05
Lithuanian	73	0.53
New Zealander	9	0.06
Northern European	5	0.04
Norwegian	58	0.42
Pennsylvania German	39	0.28
Polish	390	2.81
Portuguese	18	0.13
Romanian	18	0.13
Russian	84	0.61
Scandinavian	19	0.14
Scotch-Irish	221	1.59
Scottish	251	1.81
Serbian	7	0.05
Slovak	46	0.33
Slovene	11	0.08
Swedish	65	0.47
Swiss	204	1.47
Ukrainian	45	0.32
United States or American	597	4.31
Welsh	183	1.32
West Indian, excl. Hispanic:	22	0.16
Haitian	19	0.14
West Indian	3	0.02
White:	11,937	85.61
Not Hispanic (11,268)	11,412	81.84
Hispanic (456)	525	3.77
Yugoslavian	41	0.30

Lansdale

Place Type: Borough
County: Montgomery
Population: 16,071

Ancestry/Race	Number	%
African American/Black:	753	4.69
Not Hispanic (629)	736	4.58
Hispanic (5)	17	0.11
African, sub-Saharan:	59	0.37
African	30	0.19
Ethiopian	15	0.09
Liberian	8	0.05
Other sub-Saharan African	6	0.04
Am. Ind. or Alaska Nat., not spec.	38	0.24
Albanian	105	0.65
American Indian tribes, specified:	31	0.19
Apache	1	0.01
Blackfeet	4	0.02
Cherokee (2)	10	0.06
Chippewa (1)	1	0.01
Choctaw (1)	1	0.01
Iroquois	3	0.02
Latin American Indians (4)	6	0.04
Sioux (1)	2	0.01
All other tribes (1)	3	0.02
American Indian tribes, not spec.	1	0.01
Arab:	72	0.45
Arab/Arabic	52	0.32
Palestinian	20	0.12
Asian:	1,413	8.79
Bangladeshi (105)	125	0.78
Cambodian (97)	130	0.81
Chinese, ex. Taiwanese (107)	118	0.73
Filipino (61)	73	0.45
Indian (405)	440	2.74
Japanese (21)	27	0.17
Korean (234)	244	1.52
Laotian (15)	20	0.12
Malaysian (1)	1	0.01
Pakistani (8)	8	0.05
Sri Lankan	1	0.01
Taiwanese (2)	3	0.02
Thai (6)	24	0.15
Vietnamese (185)	191	1.19
Other Asian, not specified (2)	8	0.05
Austrian	36	0.22
Belgian	19	0.12
British	36	0.22
Bulgarian	9	0.06
Canadian	28	0.17
Celtic	6	0.04
Croatian	4	0.02
Czech	37	0.23
Czechoslovakian	6	0.04
Danish	27	0.17
Dutch	201	1.25
Eastern European	27	0.17
English	1,443	8.98
Estonian	25	0.16
European	122	0.76
Finnish	10	0.06
French, except Basque	230	1.43
French Canadian	110	0.68
German	4,269	26.56
Greek	26	0.16
Hawaii Native/Pacific Islander:	33	0.21
Polynesian: (24)	28	0.17
Native Hawaiian (3)	3	0.02
Samoan (21)	25	0.16
Other Pac. Isl., not spec. (1)	5	0.03
Hispanic or Latino:	466	2.90
Central American:	32	0.20
Guatemalan	7	0.04
Honduran	9	0.06
Nicaraguan	3	0.02
Panamanian	6	0.04
Salvadoran	2	0.01
Other Central American	5	0.03

Notes: 1. Figures in the "Number" column do not add up to the total population due to: a) Ancestry/Race overlap — e.g. persons can report being both White and Irish, b) persons of Hispanic origin can report being any race, c) persons reporting two ancestries are counted in both categories. 2. Numbers in parentheses indicate the number of persons reporting this ancestry/race alone, not in combination with any other ancestry/race. 3. Refer to the Explanation of Data in the front of the book for more detailed information.

Cuban	7	0.04
Dominican Republic	3	0.02
Mexican	102	0.63
Puerto Rican	194	1.21
South American:	47	0.29
Colombian	17	0.11
Ecuadorian	8	0.05
Peruvian	14	0.09
Uruguayan	4	0.02
Venezuelan	2	0.01
Other South American	2	0.01
Other Hispanic or Latino	81	0.50
Hungarian	107	0.67
Irish	3,556	22.13
Italian	2,106	13.10
Latvian	5	0.03
Lithuanian	60	0.37
Luxemburger	5	0.03
Northern European	27	0.17
Norwegian	37	0.23
Pennsylvania German	210	1.31
Polish	914	5.69
Portuguese	34	0.21
Russian	102	0.63
Scandinavian	8	0.05
Scotch-Irish	287	1.79
Scottish	249	1.55
Serbian	13	0.08
Slavic	10	0.06
Slovak	66	0.41
Slovene	17	0.11
Swedish	133	0.83
Swiss	114	0.71
Ukrainian	222	1.38
United States or American	870	5.41
Welsh	188	1.17
West Indian, excl. Hispanic:	86	0.54
British West Indian	1	0.01
Jamaican	62	0.39
Trinidadian and Tobagonian	23	0.14
White:	13,911	86.56
Not Hispanic (13,433)	13,569	84.43
Hispanic (292)	342	2.13
Yugoslavian	18	0.11

Lansdowne

Place Type: Borough
County: Delaware
Population: 11,044

Ancestry/Race	Number	%
African American/Black:	2,241	20.29
Not Hispanic (2,063)	2,198	19.90
Hispanic (33)	43	0.39
African, sub-Saharan:	110	1.00
African	61	0.55
Kenyan	3	0.03
Liberian	23	0.21
Nigerian	6	0.05
Sudanese	8	0.07
Other sub-Saharan African	9	0.08
Alaska Native tribes, specified:	1	0.01
Eskimo (1)	1	0.01
Am. Ind. or Alaska Nat., not spec.	26	0.24
American Indian tribes, specified:	56	0.51
Apache	2	0.02
Blackfeet (1)	6	0.05
Cherokee (1)	24	0.22
Chippewa	1	0.01
Creek	1	0.01
Crow	2	0.02
Iroquois	4	0.04
Kiowa	2	0.02
Latin American Indians (1)	1	0.01
Seminole	3	0.03
Sioux	3	0.03
All other tribes	7	0.06
American Indian tribes, not spec.	4	0.04
Arab:	44	0.40
Egyptian	26	0.24
Lebanese	14	0.13
Syrian	4	0.04
Armenian	31	0.28
Asian:	395	3.58
Bangladeshi (3)	3	0.03
Cambodian (15)	17	0.15
Chinese, ex. Taiwanese (60)	73	0.66
Filipino (38)	61	0.55
Indian (85)	100	0.91
Indonesian (1)	1	0.01
Japanese (6)	11	0.10
Korean (11)	16	0.14
Pakistani (17)	19	0.17
Sri Lankan (1)	1	0.01
Taiwanese (2)	2	0.02
Thai (1)	2	0.02
Vietnamese (54)	64	0.58
Other Asian, not specified (18)	25	0.23
Austrian	39	0.35
British	52	0.47
Canadian	19	0.17
Celtic	21	0.19
Croatian	9	0.08
Czech	21	0.19
Czechoslovakian	22	0.20
Danish	21	0.19
Dutch	64	0.58
Eastern European	8	0.07
English	1,020	9.27
European	69	0.63
Finnish	20	0.18
French, except Basque	195	1.77
French Canadian	12	0.11
German	1,915	17.40
Greek	127	1.15
Hawaii Native/Pacific Islander:	4	0.04
Micronesian: (1)	1	0.01
Guamanian/Chamorro (1)	1	0.01
Other Pac. Isl., not spec.	3	0.03
Hispanic or Latino:	163	1.48
Central American:	11	0.10
Costa Rican	1	0.01
Guatemalan	2	0.02
Honduran	3	0.03
Panamanian	4	0.04
Salvadoran	1	0.01
Cuban	20	0.18
Dominican Republic	2	0.02
Mexican	19	0.17
Puerto Rican	52	0.47
South American:	29	0.26
Chilean	2	0.02
Colombian	3	0.03
Ecuadorian	4	0.04
Peruvian	7	0.06
Uruguayan	5	0.05
Other South American	8	0.07
Other Hispanic or Latino	30	0.27
Hungarian	172	1.56
Iranian	14	0.13
Irish	3,378	30.69
Italian	1,566	14.23
Latvian	9	0.08
Lithuanian	82	0.74
Northern European	9	0.08
Norwegian	65	0.59
Pennsylvania German	73	0.66
Polish	410	3.72
Portuguese	56	0.51
Russian	157	1.43
Scandinavian	23	0.21
Scotch-Irish	310	2.82
Scottish	163	1.48
Serbian	22	0.20
Slavic	5	0.05
Slovak	108	0.98
Swedish	85	0.77
Swiss	41	0.37
Ukrainian	51	0.46
United States or American	402	3.65
Welsh	76	0.69
West Indian, excl. Hispanic:	242	2.20
Bermudan	15	0.14
British West Indian	22	0.20
Haitian	38	0.35
Jamaican	155	1.41
West Indian	12	0.11
White:	8,491	76.88
Not Hispanic (8,236)	8,397	76.03
Hispanic (75)	94	0.85
Yugoslavian	21	0.19

Lebanon

Place Type: City
County: Lebanon
Population: 24,461

Ancestry/Race	Number	%
African American/Black:	939	3.84
Not Hispanic (610)	699	2.86
Hispanic (180)	240	0.98
African, sub-Saharan:	110	0.45
African	95	0.39
Ugandan	15	0.06
Am. Ind. or Alaska Nat., not spec.	69	0.28
American Indian tribes, specified:	68	0.28
Blackfeet (2)	5	0.02
Cherokee (11)	26	0.11
Iroquois (1)	3	0.01
Latin American Indians (4)	17	0.07
Navajo (1)	1	0.00
Pueblo	2	0.01
Sioux (1)	5	0.02
Yaqui (1)	1	0.00
All other tribes (3)	8	0.03
American Indian tribes, not spec.	5	0.02
Arab:	34	0.14
Arab/Arabic	10	0.04
Egyptian	13	0.05
Lebanese	11	0.04
Asian:	301	1.23
Cambodian (46)	56	0.23
Chinese, ex. Taiwanese (16)	18	0.07
Filipino (25)	34	0.14
Indian (25)	34	0.14
Indonesian (1)	2	0.01
Japanese (5)	9	0.04
Korean (10)	16	0.07
Pakistani (1)	4	0.02
Thai (6)	8	0.03
Vietnamese (77)	81	0.33
Other Asian, specified	1	0.00
Other Asian, not specified (30)	38	0.16
Austrian	66	0.27
British	38	0.16
Bulgarian	7	0.03
Canadian	9	0.04
Croatian	32	0.13
Czech	9	0.04
Czechoslovakian	91	0.37
Danish	40	0.16
Dutch	726	2.97
English	747	3.05
European	41	0.17
French, except Basque	266	1.09
French Canadian	40	0.16
German	8,522	34.84
Greek	44	0.18
Hawaii Native/Pacific Islander:	42	0.17
Micronesian: (3)	9	0.04
Guamanian/Chamorro (3)	9	0.04
Polynesian: (17)	21	0.09
Native Hawaiian (7)	10	0.04
Samoan (10)	11	0.04
Other Pac. Isl., specified	1	0.00
Other Pac. Isl., not spec. (5)	11	0.04
Hispanic or Latino:	4,019	16.43
Central American:	37	0.15

Notes: 1. Figures in the "Number" column do not add up to the total population due to: a) Ancestry/Race overlap — e.g. persons can report being both White and Irish, b) persons of Hispanic origin can report being any race, c) persons reporting two ancestries are counted in both categories. 2. Numbers in parentheses indicate the number of persons reporting this ancestry/race alone, not in combination with any other ancestry/race. 3. Refer to the Explanation of Data in the front of the book for more detailed information.

Ancestry/Race	Number	%
Guatemalan	3	0.01
Honduran	8	0.03
Nicaraguan	6	0.02
Panamanian	12	0.05
Salvadoran	8	0.03
Cuban	69	0.28
Dominican Republic	94	0.38
Mexican	226	0.92
Puerto Rican	3,053	12.48
South American:	65	0.27
Argentinean	5	0.02
Chilean	5	0.02
Colombian	26	0.11
Ecuadorian	13	0.05
Peruvian	2	0.01
Uruguayan	4	0.02
Venezuelan	6	0.02
Other South American	4	0.02
Other Hispanic or Latino	475	1.94
Hungarian	261	1.07
Irish	1,836	7.51
Israeli	9	0.04
Italian	1,171	4.79
Latvian	9	0.04
Lithuanian	33	0.13
Macedonian	8	0.03
Norwegian	52	0.21
Pennsylvania German	399	1.63
Polish	349	1.43
Portuguese	21	0.09
Russian	109	0.45
Scandinavian	7	0.03
Scotch-Irish	219	0.90
Scottish	223	0.91
Serbian	35	0.14
Slavic	76	0.31
Slovak	291	1.19
Slovene	18	0.07
Swedish	102	0.42
Swiss	213	0.87
Ukrainian	76	0.31
United States or American	2,221	9.08
Welsh	78	0.32
West Indian, excl. Hispanic:	152	0.62
Jamaican	70	0.29
Trinidadian and Tobagonian	49	0.20
West Indian	33	0.13
White:	21,276	86.98
Not Hispanic (19,297)	19,473	79.61
Hispanic (1,618)	1,803	7.37
Yugoslavian	68	0.28

Levittown

Place Type: Census Designated Place
County: Bucks
Population: 53,966

Ancestry/Race	Number	%
African American/Black:	1,520	2.82
Not Hispanic (1,274)	1,454	2.69
Hispanic (47)	66	0.12
African, sub-Saharan:	142	0.26
African	142	0.26
Alaska Native tribes, specified:	6	0.01
Alaska Athabascan (2)	6	0.01
Am. Ind. or Alaska Nat., not spec.	105	0.19
Alsatian	9	0.02
American Indian tribes, specified:	113	0.21
Apache	2	0.00
Blackfeet (3)	6	0.01
Cherokee (13)	28	0.05
Chickasaw	1	0.00
Comanche (2)	5	0.01
Creek (5)	5	0.01
Delaware (1)	5	0.01
Iroquois (15)	34	0.06
Latin American Indians	1	0.00
Lumbee (4)	4	0.01
Navajo (1)	4	0.01
Seminole (1)	1	0.00
Sioux (4)	9	0.02
All other tribes	8	0.01
American Indian tribes, not spec.	19	0.04
Arab:	73	0.14
Arab/Arabic	30	0.06
Lebanese	25	0.05
Syrian	18	0.03
Armenian	25	0.05
Asian:	700	1.30
Cambodian (9)	13	0.02
Chinese, ex. Taiwanese (76)	96	0.18
Filipino (116)	164	0.30
Indian (127)	146	0.27
Indonesian (1)	2	0.00
Japanese (16)	31	0.06
Korean (113)	143	0.26
Malaysian	1	0.00
Pakistani (8)	9	0.02
Sri Lankan	1	0.00
Taiwanese (2)	2	0.00
Thai (13)	22	0.04
Vietnamese (20)	27	0.05
Other Asian, specified (3)	3	0.01
Other Asian, not specified (13)	40	0.07
Austrian	139	0.26
Basque	11	0.02
Belgian	9	0.02
British	223	0.42
Bulgarian	19	0.04
Canadian	54	0.10
Celtic	11	0.02
Croatian	79	0.15
Czech	134	0.25
Czechoslovakian	53	0.10
Danish	93	0.17
Dutch	793	1.48
English	5,880	10.95
Estonian	16	0.03
European	118	0.22
French, except Basque	1,172	2.18
French Canadian	257	0.48
German	15,351	28.59
Greek	181	0.34
Hawaii Native/Pacific Islander:	42	0.08
Micronesian: (17)	22	0.04
Guamanian/Chamorro (17)	22	0.04
Polynesian: (3)	10	0.02
Native Hawaiian (1)	5	0.01
Samoan (2)	5	0.01
Other Pac. Isl., not spec. (2)	10	0.02
Hispanic or Latino:	1,199	2.22
Central American:	14	0.03
Costa Rican	7	0.01
Guatemalan	3	0.01
Honduran	3	0.01
Salvadoran	1	0.00
Cuban	42	0.08
Dominican Republic	30	0.06
Mexican	224	0.42
Puerto Rican	590	1.09
South American:	78	0.14
Argentinean	9	0.02
Bolivian	2	0.00
Chilean	3	0.01
Colombian	42	0.08
Ecuadorian	3	0.01
Peruvian	8	0.01
Uruguayan	1	0.00
Venezuelan	1	0.00
Other South American	9	0.02
Other Hispanic or Latino	221	0.41
Hungarian	573	1.07
Iranian	25	0.05
Irish	17,123	31.89
Italian	8,700	16.20
Latvian	16	0.03
Lithuanian	559	1.04
Luxemburger	8	0.01
New Zealander	5	0.01
Norwegian	115	0.21
Pennsylvania German	279	0.52
Polish	5,121	9.54
Portuguese	32	0.06
Romanian	118	0.22
Russian	974	1.81
Scandinavian	20	0.04
Scotch-Irish	848	1.58
Scottish	1,223	2.28
Serbian	20	0.04
Slavic	83	0.15
Slovak	649	1.21
Slovene	25	0.05
Swedish	559	1.04
Swiss	81	0.15
Turkish	93	0.17
Ukrainian	856	1.59
United States or American	1,760	3.28
Welsh	756	1.41
West Indian, excl. Hispanic:	83	0.15
British West Indian	24	0.04
Haitian	11	0.02
Trinidadian and Tobagonian	16	0.03
West Indian	32	0.06
White:	51,483	95.40
Not Hispanic (50,264)	50,761	94.06
Hispanic (658)	722	1.34
Yugoslavian	21	0.04

Limerick

Place Type: Township
County: Montgomery
Population: 13,534

Ancestry/Race	Number	%
Afghan	6	0.04
African American/Black:	336	2.48
Not Hispanic (281)	325	2.40
Hispanic (4)	11	0.08
Am. Ind. or Alaska Nat., not spec.	23	0.17
American Indian tribes, specified:	40	0.30
Apache (1)	1	0.01
Cherokee (5)	22	0.16
Chickasaw (1)	1	0.01
Iroquois	1	0.01
Latin American Indians (2)	2	0.01
Osage (1)	1	0.01
Seminole	1	0.01
Sioux	1	0.01
All other tribes (7)	10	0.07
American Indian tribes, not spec.	7	0.05
Arab:	18	0.13
Arab/Arabic	13	0.10
Lebanese	5	0.04
Armenian	9	0.07
Asian:	213	1.57
Cambodian (1)	1	0.01
Chinese, ex. Taiwanese (43)	56	0.41
Filipino (9)	14	0.10
Indian (66)	72	0.53
Indonesian (2)	5	0.04
Japanese (9)	12	0.09
Korean (27)	30	0.22
Pakistani (6)	6	0.04
Vietnamese (11)	11	0.08
Other Asian, specified	2	0.01
Other Asian, not specified (1)	4	0.03
Australian	19	0.14
Austrian	76	0.56
Belgian	12	0.09
British	91	0.67
Croatian	31	0.23
Czech	31	0.23
Czechoslovakian	63	0.47
Danish	37	0.27
Dutch	412	3.04
English	1,494	11.04
European	105	0.78
French, except Basque	240	1.77

Notes: 1. Figures in the "Number" column do not add up to the total population due to: a) Ancestry/Race overlap — e.g. persons can report being both White and Irish, b) persons of Hispanic origin can report being any race, c) persons reporting two ancestries are counted in both categories. 2. Numbers in parentheses indicate the number of persons reporting this ancestry/race alone, not in combination with any other ancestry/race. 3. Refer to the Explanation of Data in the front of the book for more detailed information.

Ancestry/Race	Number	%
French Canadian	95	0.70
German	3,992	29.50
Greek	74	0.55
Hawaii Native/Pacific Islander:	9	0.07
Micronesian:	1	0.01
Guamanian/Chamorro	1	0.01
Polynesian:	1	0.01
Native Hawaiian	1	0.01
Other Pac. Isl., specified	2	0.01
Other Pac. Isl., not spec.	5	0.04
Hispanic or Latino:	179	1.32
Central American:	10	0.07
Costa Rican	1	0.01
Guatemalan	2	0.01
Panamanian	4	0.03
Salvadoran	3	0.02
Cuban	12	0.09
Mexican	39	0.29
Puerto Rican	53	0.39
South American:	21	0.16
Argentinean	1	0.01
Bolivian	5	0.04
Chilean	8	0.06
Colombian	2	0.01
Peruvian	3	0.02
Venezuelan	2	0.01
Other Hispanic or Latino	44	0.33
Hungarian	60	0.44
Irish	3,349	24.75
Italian	2,554	18.87
Latvian	16	0.12
Lithuanian	107	0.79
Norwegian	98	0.72
Pennsylvania German	229	1.69
Polish	975	7.20
Portuguese	7	0.05
Russian	105	0.78
Scotch-Irish	197	1.46
Scottish	308	2.28
Serbian	29	0.21
Slavic	7	0.05
Slovak	183	1.35
Slovene	9	0.07
Swedish	128	0.95
Swiss	145	1.07
Turkish	8	0.06
Ukrainian	115	0.85
United States or American	464	3.43
Welsh	167	1.23
West Indian, excl. Hispanic:	40	0.30
Jamaican	40	0.30
White:	12,957	95.74
Not Hispanic (12,752)	12,836	94.84
Hispanic (119)	121	0.89

Logan

Place Type: Township
County: Blair
Population: 11,925

Ancestry/Race	Number	%
African American/Black:	86	0.72
Not Hispanic (68)	84	0.70
Hispanic (2)	2	0.02
African, sub-Saharan:	17	0.14
Nigerian	17	0.14
Am. Ind. or Alaska Nat., not spec.	12	0.10
American Indian tribes, specified:	21	0.18
Cherokee (2)	3	0.03
Creek (1)	1	0.01
Delaware (2)	9	0.08
Iroquois	6	0.05
Sioux	1	0.01
All other tribes	1	0.01
Arab:	31	0.26
Arab/Arabic	5	0.04
Lebanese	26	0.22
Asian:	64	0.54
Chinese, ex. Taiwanese (8)	10	0.08
Filipino (1)	7	0.06
Indian (23)	25	0.21
Japanese (8)	8	0.07
Korean (3)	6	0.05
Taiwanese (2)	2	0.02
Thai (1)	2	0.02
Vietnamese (1)	1	0.01
Other Asian, not specified (2)	3	0.03
Australian	7	0.06
Austrian	30	0.25
British	46	0.39
Canadian	15	0.13
Croatian	19	0.16
Czech	27	0.23
Danish	26	0.22
Dutch	313	2.63
English	874	7.33
European	50	0.42
French, except Basque	406	3.41
French Canadian	63	0.53
German	4,812	40.36
Greek	41	0.34
Hawaii Native/Pacific Islander:	1	0.01
Micronesian: (1)	1	0.01
Guamanian/Chamorro (1)	1	0.01
Hispanic or Latino:	48	0.40
Cuban	3	0.03
Mexican	5	0.04
Puerto Rican	18	0.15
South American:	3	0.03
Ecuadorian	2	0.02
Other South American	1	0.01
Other Hispanic or Latino	19	0.16
Hungarian	57	0.48
Irish	2,388	20.03
Italian	1,383	11.60
Lithuanian	123	1.03
Norwegian	16	0.13
Pennsylvania German	61	0.51
Polish	615	5.16
Russian	10	0.08
Scotch-Irish	221	1.85
Scottish	253	2.12
Slavic	19	0.16
Slovak	59	0.49
Swedish	77	0.65
Swiss	59	0.49
Ukrainian	94	0.79
United States or American	1,018	8.54
Welsh	140	1.17
White:	11,789	98.86
Not Hispanic (11,699)	11,750	98.53
Hispanic (37)	39	0.33
Yugoslavian	31	0.26

Lower Allen

Place Type: Township
County: Cumberland
Population: 17,437

Ancestry/Race	Number	%
Afghan	19	0.11
African American/Black:	1,925	11.04
Not Hispanic (1,876)	1,912	10.97
Hispanic (13)	13	0.07
African, sub-Saharan:	29	0.17
African	29	0.17
Am. Ind. or Alaska Nat., not spec.	16	0.09
Albanian	8	0.05
American Indian tribes, specified:	31	0.18
Apache	1	0.01
Blackfeet	1	0.01
Cherokee (7)	12	0.07
Chippewa	1	0.01
Cree (2)	2	0.01
Creek	2	0.01
Crow	1	0.01
Iroquois	3	0.02
Kiowa	1	0.01
Lumbee	2	0.01
Navajo (1)	1	0.01
Sioux (1)	1	0.01
All other tribes	3	0.02
American Indian tribes, not spec.	4	0.02
Arab:	99	0.57
Egyptian	15	0.09
Lebanese	23	0.13
Syrian	15	0.09
Other Arab	46	0.26
Armenian	20	0.11
Asian:	370	2.12
Cambodian (7)	7	0.04
Chinese, ex. Taiwanese (39)	41	0.24
Filipino (23)	29	0.17
Indian (64)	67	0.38
Japanese (16)	17	0.10
Korean (84)	88	0.50
Laotian (1)	1	0.01
Pakistani (1)	2	0.01
Taiwanese (1)	1	0.01
Thai (1)	3	0.02
Vietnamese (81)	85	0.49
Other Asian, not specified (11)	29	0.17
Austrian	87	0.50
Belgian	6	0.03
British	18	0.10
Bulgarian	19	0.11
Canadian	26	0.15
Croatian	132	0.76
Czech	62	0.36
Czechoslovakian	59	0.34
Danish	20	0.11
Dutch	396	2.27
Eastern European	16	0.09
English	1,363	7.82
European	118	0.68
Finnish	4	0.02
French, except Basque	380	2.18
French Canadian	59	0.34
German	4,744	27.21
Greek	16	0.09
Hawaii Native/Pacific Islander:	13	0.07
Polynesian: (8)	11	0.06
Native Hawaiian (8)	11	0.06
Other Pac. Isl., not spec. (2)	2	0.01
Hispanic or Latino:	641	3.68
Central American:	15	0.09
Costa Rican	1	0.01
Honduran	10	0.06
Nicaraguan	1	0.01
Panamanian	1	0.01
Salvadoran	2	0.01
Cuban	13	0.07
Dominican Republic	1	0.01
Mexican	40	0.23
Puerto Rican	506	2.90
South American:	11	0.06
Chilean	2	0.01
Colombian	1	0.01
Ecuadorian	1	0.01
Paraguayan	1	0.01
Peruvian	6	0.03
Other Hispanic or Latino	55	0.32
Hungarian	96	0.55
Irish	2,097	12.03
Italian	923	5.29
Lithuanian	54	0.31
Northern European	11	0.06
Norwegian	91	0.52
Pennsylvania German	92	0.53
Polish	487	2.79
Portuguese	15	0.09
Romanian	26	0.15
Russian	70	0.40
Scandinavian	10	0.06
Scotch-Irish	424	2.43
Scottish	305	1.75
Serbian	33	0.19
Slovak	173	0.99

Notes: 1. Figures in the "Number" column do not add up to the total population due to: a) Ancestry/Race overlap — e.g. persons can report being both White and Irish, b) persons of Hispanic origin can report being any race, c) persons reporting two ancestries are counted in both categories. 2. Numbers in parentheses indicate the number of persons reporting this ancestry/race alone, not in combination with any other ancestry/race. 3. Refer to the Explanation of Data in the front of the book for more detailed information.

Slovene	7	0.04
Swedish	243	1.39
Swiss	116	0.67
Turkish	19	0.11
Ukrainian	62	0.36
United States or American	856	4.91
Welsh	257	1.47
White:	15,063	86.39
Not Hispanic (14,417)	14,530	83.33
Hispanic (529)	533	3.06
Yugoslavian	138	0.79

Lower Burrell

Place Type: City
County: Westmoreland
Population: 12,608

Ancestry/Race	Number	%
African American/Black:	151	1.20
Not Hispanic (117)	148	1.17
Hispanic	3	0.02
Am. Ind. or Alaska Nat., not spec.	3	0.02
American Indian tribes, specified:	26	0.21
Cherokee (3)	17	0.13
Iroquois	8	0.06
Latin American Indians (1)	1	0.01
Arab:	165	1.31
Lebanese	17	0.13
Syrian	148	1.17
Asian:	58	0.46
Chinese, ex. Taiwanese (17)	18	0.14
Filipino (4)	5	0.04
Indian (9)	10	0.08
Japanese (2)	4	0.03
Korean (6)	6	0.05
Thai (2)	2	0.02
Vietnamese (5)	6	0.05
Other Asian, not specified	7	0.06
Austrian	20	0.16
Belgian	65	0.51
British	15	0.12
Bulgarian	11	0.09
Canadian	12	0.10
Croatian	46	0.36
Czech	42	0.33
Czechoslovakian	23	0.18
Dutch	210	1.66
Eastern European	24	0.19
English	1,241	9.83
European	30	0.24
Finnish	19	0.15
French, except Basque	161	1.28
French Canadian	30	0.24
German	3,567	28.25
Greek	39	0.31
Hawaii Native/Pacific Islander:	4	0.03
Polynesian: (2)	4	0.03
Native Hawaiian (2)	2	0.02
Samoan	2	0.02
Hispanic or Latino:	56	0.44
Central American:	1	0.01
Honduran	1	0.01
Mexican	22	0.17
Puerto Rican	6	0.05
South American:	1	0.01
Venezuelan	1	0.01
Other Hispanic or Latino	26	0.21
Hungarian	96	0.76
Irish	1,752	13.88
Italian	2,394	18.96
Lithuanian	39	0.31
Norwegian	30	0.24
Pennsylvania German	7	0.06
Polish	1,989	15.75
Portuguese	13	0.10
Romanian	8	0.06
Russian	153	1.21
Scotch-Irish	422	3.34
Scottish	255	2.02
Serbian	30	0.24
Slavic	39	0.31
Slovak	1,226	9.71
Slovene	37	0.29
Swedish	224	1.77
Swiss	36	0.29
Ukrainian	298	2.36
United States or American	630	4.99
Welsh	91	0.72
West Indian, excl. Hispanic:	12	0.10
Jamaican	12	0.10
White:	12,425	98.55
Not Hispanic (12,308)	12,374	98.14
Hispanic (41)	51	0.40

Lower Gwynedd

Place Type: Township
County: Montgomery
Population: 10,422

Ancestry/Race	Number	%
African American/Black:	872	8.37
Not Hispanic (809)	861	8.26
Hispanic (2)	11	0.11
African, sub-Saharan:	45	0.43
African	24	0.23
Kenyan	21	0.20
Am. Ind. or Alaska Nat., not spec.	27	0.26
American Indian tribes, specified:	10	0.10
Blackfeet (1)	1	0.01
Cherokee	3	0.03
Choctaw	1	0.01
Iroquois (1)	1	0.01
Latin American Indians (1)	1	0.01
All other tribes (1)	3	0.03
American Indian tribes, not spec.	1	0.01
Arab:	38	0.36
Lebanese	16	0.15
Moroccan	22	0.21
Armenian	50	0.48
Asian:	467	4.48
Chinese, ex. Taiwanese (73)	83	0.80
Filipino (15)	22	0.21
Indian (103)	114	1.09
Indonesian (1)	1	0.01
Japanese (16)	23	0.22
Korean (180)	189	1.81
Malaysian (3)	4	0.04
Taiwanese (17)	17	0.16
Vietnamese (7)	10	0.10
Other Asian, specified (1)	1	0.01
Other Asian, not specified	3	0.03
Austrian	116	1.11
Belgian	4	0.04
British	67	0.64
Canadian	20	0.19
Celtic	10	0.10
Czech	23	0.22
Czechoslovakian	4	0.04
Danish	9	0.09
Dutch	94	0.90
Eastern European	97	0.93
English	1,408	13.51
European	70	0.67
Finnish	16	0.15
French, except Basque	207	1.99
French Canadian	52	0.50
German	2,228	21.38
Greek	95	0.91
Hawaii Native/Pacific Islander:	3	0.03
Other Pac. Isl., not spec. (1)	3	0.03
Hispanic or Latino:	109	1.05
Central American:	4	0.04
Costa Rican	2	0.02
Honduran	1	0.01
Nicaraguan	1	0.01
Cuban	9	0.09
Mexican	24	0.23
Puerto Rican	29	0.28
South American:	10	0.10
Colombian	4	0.04
Ecuadorian	3	0.03
Peruvian	1	0.01
Venezuelan	1	0.01
Other South American	1	0.01
Other Hispanic or Latino	33	0.32
Hungarian	91	0.87
Iranian	23	0.22
Irish	1,816	17.42
Italian	1,560	14.97
Latvian	29	0.28
Lithuanian	33	0.32
Northern European	6	0.06
Norwegian	71	0.68
Pennsylvania German	25	0.24
Polish	439	4.21
Portuguese	15	0.14
Romanian	24	0.23
Russian	559	5.36
Scandinavian	13	0.12
Scotch-Irish	200	1.92
Scottish	192	1.84
Slovak	95	0.91
Slovene	8	0.08
Swedish	85	0.82
Swiss	95	0.91
Turkish	9	0.09
Ukrainian	114	1.09
United States or American	306	2.94
Welsh	160	1.54
West Indian, excl. Hispanic:	71	0.68
Bahamian	15	0.14
Jamaican	49	0.47
West Indian	7	0.07
White:	9,130	87.60
Not Hispanic (8,970)	9,049	86.83
Hispanic (76)	81	0.78
Yugoslavian	12	0.12

Lower Macungie

Place Type: Township
County: Lehigh
Population: 19,220

Ancestry/Race	Number	%
African American/Black:	152	0.79
Not Hispanic (108)	143	0.74
Hispanic (4)	9	0.05
Am. Ind. or Alaska Nat., not spec.	19	0.10
Albanian	30	0.16
American Indian tribes, specified:	28	0.15
Apache	1	0.01
Blackfeet	2	0.01
Cherokee (11)	17	0.09
Chippewa (1)	1	0.01
Delaware (1)	4	0.02
Iroquois (1)	1	0.01
Latin American Indians	1	0.01
Seminole	1	0.01
American Indian tribes, not spec.	8	0.04
Arab:	213	1.11
Egyptian	61	0.32
Lebanese	73	0.38
Syrian	79	0.41
Armenian	26	0.14
Asian:	887	4.61
Chinese, ex. Taiwanese (314)	328	1.71
Filipino (26)	36	0.19
Indian (296)	305	1.59
Indonesian	3	0.02
Japanese (16)	27	0.14
Korean (93)	103	0.54
Pakistani (9)	9	0.05
Taiwanese (31)	34	0.18
Thai (7)	8	0.04
Vietnamese (22)	23	0.12
Other Asian, specified (3)	3	0.02
Other Asian, not specified (2)	8	0.04

Notes: 1. Figures in the "Number" column do not add up to the total population due to: a) Ancestry/Race overlap — e.g. persons can report being both White and Irish, b) persons of Hispanic origin can report being any race, c) persons reporting two ancestries are counted in both categories. 2. Numbers in parentheses indicate the number of persons reporting this ancestry/race alone, not in combination with any other ancestry/race. 3. Refer to the Explanation of Data in the front of the book for more detailed information.

Austrian	378	1.97
Brazilian	28	0.15
British	126	0.66
Canadian	26	0.14
Croatian	10	0.05
Czech	59	0.31
Czechoslovakian	33	0.17
Danish	39	0.20
Dutch	442	2.30
Eastern European	146	0.76
English	1,764	9.18
European	128	0.67
Finnish	6	0.03
French, except Basque	433	2.25
French Canadian	52	0.27
German	6,703	34.88
Greek	151	0.79
Hawaii Native/Pacific Islander:	2	0.01
Polynesian:	2	0.01
Native Hawaiian	2	0.01
Hispanic or Latino:	292	1.52
Central American:	15	0.08
Guatemalan	5	0.03
Honduran	1	0.01
Panamanian	2	0.01
Salvadoran	6	0.03
Other Central American	1	0.01
Cuban	19	0.10
Dominican Republic	6	0.03
Mexican	43	0.22
Puerto Rican	103	0.54
South American:	42	0.22
Argentinean	3	0.02
Chilean	4	0.02
Colombian	12	0.06
Ecuadorian	2	0.01
Paraguayan	1	0.01
Peruvian	12	0.06
Venezuelan	8	0.04
Other Hispanic or Latino	64	0.33
Hungarian	413	2.15
Iranian	67	0.35
Irish	2,669	13.89
Italian	2,247	11.69
Latvian	13	0.07
Lithuanian	115	0.60
Norwegian	46	0.24
Pennsylvania German	951	4.95
Polish	1,421	7.39
Portuguese	29	0.15
Romanian	30	0.16
Russian	263	1.37
Scotch-Irish	299	1.56
Scottish	496	2.58
Slavic	21	0.11
Slovak	466	2.42
Slovene	7	0.04
Swedish	134	0.70
Swiss	105	0.55
Ukrainian	480	2.50
United States or American	774	4.03
Welsh	356	1.85
West Indian, excl. Hispanic:	21	0.11
Jamaican	14	0.07
West Indian	7	0.04
White:	18,145	94.41
Not Hispanic (17,827)	17,935	93.31
Hispanic (196)	210	1.09
Yugoslavian	6	0.03

Lower Makefield

Place Type: Township
County: Bucks
Population: 32,681

Ancestry/Race	Number	%
African American/Black:	671	2.05
Not Hispanic (582)	658	2.01
Hispanic (10)	13	0.04
African, sub-Saharan:	56	0.17
African	22	0.07
Kenyan	11	0.03
South African	19	0.06
Other sub-Saharan African	4	0.01
Am. Ind. or Alaska Nat., not spec.	35	0.11
Albanian	36	0.11
American Indian tribes, specified:	42	0.13
Apache	5	0.02
Blackfeet	3	0.01
Cherokee (3)	10	0.03
Choctaw (1)	1	0.00
Creek (5)	5	0.02
Delaware (1)	2	0.01
Iroquois (1)	1	0.00
Latin American Indians (3)	4	0.01
Seminole	1	0.00
Sioux	2	0.01
All other tribes (3)	8	0.02
American Indian tribes, not spec.	4	0.01
Arab:	218	0.67
Egyptian	21	0.06
Lebanese	154	0.47
Moroccan	19	0.06
Palestinian	4	0.01
Syrian	5	0.02
Other Arab	15	0.05
Armenian	9	0.03
Asian:	1,339	4.10
Chinese, ex. Taiwanese (233)	258	0.79
Filipino (93)	112	0.34
Indian (514)	535	1.64
Indonesian (5)	5	0.02
Japanese (38)	54	0.17
Korean (194)	206	0.63
Pakistani (46)	50	0.15
Sri Lankan (7)	9	0.03
Taiwanese (26)	27	0.08
Thai (4)	7	0.02
Vietnamese (28)	30	0.09
Other Asian, specified	4	0.01
Other Asian, not specified (15)	42	0.13
Australian	19	0.06
Austrian	220	0.67
Belgian	43	0.13
Brazilian	7	0.02
British	359	1.10
Canadian	34	0.10
Celtic	19	0.06
Croatian	82	0.25
Cypriot	6	0.02
Czech	99	0.30
Czechoslovakian	61	0.19
Danish	111	0.34
Dutch	398	1.22
Eastern European	269	0.82
English	3,737	11.43
Estonian	18	0.06
European	204	0.62
Finnish	115	0.35
French, except Basque	664	2.03
French Canadian	82	0.25
German	6,822	20.87
German Russian	10	0.03
Greek	409	1.25
Hawaii Native/Pacific Islander:	16	0.05
Polynesian: (1)	6	0.02
Native Hawaiian	4	0.01
Samoan (1)	1	0.00
Tongan	1	0.00
Other Pac. Isl., specified	4	0.01
Other Pac. Isl., not spec.	6	0.02
Hispanic or Latino:	463	1.42
Central American:	22	0.07
Costa Rican	4	0.01
Guatemalan	7	0.02
Honduran	3	0.01
Nicaraguan	1	0.00
Panamanian	1	0.00
Salvadoran	2	0.01
Other Central American	4	0.01
Cuban	54	0.17
Dominican Republic	11	0.03
Mexican	88	0.27
Puerto Rican	126	0.39
South American:	76	0.23
Argentinean	4	0.01
Chilean	6	0.02
Colombian	31	0.09
Ecuadorian	4	0.01
Peruvian	20	0.06
Uruguayan	1	0.00
Venezuelan	8	0.02
Other South American	2	0.01
Other Hispanic or Latino	86	0.26
Hungarian	734	2.25
Iranian	46	0.14
Irish	7,811	23.90
Israeli	40	0.12
Italian	6,234	19.08
Latvian	30	0.09
Lithuanian	305	0.93
Maltese	9	0.03
Northern European	53	0.16
Norwegian	274	0.84
Pennsylvania German	35	0.11
Polish	2,893	8.85
Portuguese	8	0.02
Romanian	136	0.42
Russian	1,595	4.88
Scandinavian	13	0.04
Scotch-Irish	467	1.43
Scottish	837	2.56
Serbian	21	0.06
Slavic	40	0.12
Slovak	356	1.09
Slovene	21	0.06
Swedish	273	0.84
Swiss	119	0.36
Turkish	17	0.05
Ukrainian	505	1.55
United States or American	1,378	4.22
Welsh	355	1.09
West Indian, excl. Hispanic:	39	0.12
Barbadian	8	0.02
Haitian	3	0.01
Jamaican	7	0.02
Trinidadian and Tobagonian	21	0.06
White:	30,725	94.01
Not Hispanic (30,136)	30,335	92.82
Hispanic (362)	390	1.19
Yugoslavian	18	0.06

Lower Merion

Place Type: Township
County: Montgomery
Population: 59,850

Ancestry/Race	Number	%
African American/Black:	2,965	4.95
Not Hispanic (2,669)	2,912	4.87
Hispanic (25)	53	0.09
African, sub-Saharan:	327	0.55
African	181	0.30
Ethiopian	25	0.04
Nigerian	32	0.05
South African	45	0.08
Ugandan	38	0.06
Zimbabwean	6	0.01
Alaska Native tribes, specified:	2	0.00
Tlingit-Haida	1	0.00
All other tribes	1	0.00
Am. Ind. or Alaska Nat., not spec.	79	0.13
Albanian	57	0.10
Alsatian	20	0.03
American Indian tribes, specified:	85	0.14
Apache	1	0.00
Blackfeet (1)	2	0.00
Cherokee (5)	29	0.05

Notes: 1. Figures in the "Number" column do not add up to the total population due to: a) Ancestry/Race overlap — e.g. persons can report being both White and Irish, b) persons of Hispanic origin can report being any race, c) persons reporting two ancestries are counted in both categories. 2. Numbers in parentheses indicate the number of persons reporting this ancestry/race alone, not in combination with any other ancestry/race. 3. Refer to the Explanation of Data in the front of the book for more detailed information.

Ancestry/Race	Number	%
Cheyenne	1	0.00
Chippewa (1)	1	0.00
Choctaw (2)	6	0.01
Cree	3	0.01
Creek	2	0.00
Delaware (1)	2	0.00
Iroquois (2)	9	0.02
Latin American Indians (12)	14	0.02
Sioux (2)	4	0.01
All other tribes (2)	11	0.02
American Indian tribes, not spec.	4	0.01
Arab:	383	0.64
Egyptian	120	0.20
Iraqi	21	0.04
Lebanese	122	0.20
Moroccan	14	0.02
Palestinian	20	0.03
Syrian	36	0.06
Other Arab	50	0.08
Armenian	223	0.37
Asian:	2,330	3.89
Bangladeshi (1)	1	0.00
Cambodian (3)	3	0.01
Chinese, ex. Taiwanese (629)	687	1.15
Filipino (153)	195	0.33
Indian (502)	545	0.91
Indonesian (3)	3	0.01
Japanese (126)	168	0.28
Korean (340)	396	0.66
Laotian (1)	1	0.00
Malaysian (3)	5	0.01
Pakistani (29)	35	0.06
Sri Lankan (12)	13	0.02
Taiwanese (20)	21	0.04
Thai (38)	45	0.08
Vietnamese (108)	115	0.19
Other Asian, specified (8)	10	0.02
Other Asian, not specified (45)	87	0.15
Australian	30	0.05
Austrian	609	1.02
Basque	18	0.03
Belgian	69	0.12
British	557	0.93
Bulgarian	39	0.07
Canadian	116	0.19
Celtic	29	0.05
Croatian	41	0.07
Cypriot	16	0.03
Czech	206	0.34
Czechoslovakian	53	0.09
Danish	122	0.20
Dutch	610	1.02
Eastern European	1,389	2.32
English	5,573	9.31
Estonian	6	0.01
European	853	1.43
Finnish	33	0.06
French, except Basque	1,309	2.19
French Canadian	176	0.29
German	6,979	11.66
German Russian	6	0.01
Greek	506	0.85
Hawaii Native/Pacific Islander:	68	0.11
Melanesian: (1)	1	0.00
Fijian (1)	1	0.00
Micronesian: (4)	6	0.01
Guamanian/Chamorro (4)	6	0.01
Polynesian: (30)	35	0.06
Native Hawaiian (12)	15	0.03
Samoan (7)	9	0.02
Tongan (11)	11	0.02
Other Pac. Isl., not spec. (6)	26	0.04
Hispanic or Latino:	956	1.60
Central American:	58	0.10
Costa Rican	5	0.01
Guatemalan	14	0.02
Honduran	12	0.02
Nicaraguan	1	0.00
Panamanian	6	0.01
Salvadoran	15	0.03
Other Central American	5	0.01
Cuban	102	0.17
Dominican Republic	17	0.03
Mexican	170	0.28
Puerto Rican	135	0.23
South American:	220	0.37
Argentinean	41	0.07
Bolivian	4	0.01
Chilean	15	0.03
Colombian	64	0.11
Ecuadorian	13	0.02
Paraguayan	11	0.02
Peruvian	28	0.05
Uruguayan	8	0.01
Venezuelan	24	0.04
Other South American	12	0.02
Other Hispanic or Latino	254	0.42
Hungarian	802	1.34
Iranian	131	0.22
Irish	9,016	15.06
Israeli	353	0.59
Italian	5,994	10.02
Latvian	71	0.12
Lithuanian	271	0.45
New Zealander	41	0.07
Northern European	123	0.21
Norwegian	298	0.50
Pennsylvania German	43	0.07
Polish	3,258	5.44
Portuguese	58	0.10
Romanian	438	0.73
Russian	6,737	11.26
Scandinavian	39	0.07
Scotch-Irish	902	1.51
Scottish	1,203	2.01
Serbian	14	0.02
Slavic	28	0.05
Slovak	179	0.30
Slovene	4	0.01
Swedish	695	1.16
Swiss	263	0.44
Turkish	85	0.14
Ukrainian	535	0.89
United States or American	3,507	5.86
Welsh	667	1.11
West Indian, excl. Hispanic:	295	0.49
British West Indian	18	0.03
Haitian	23	0.04
Jamaican	167	0.28
Trinidadian and Tobagonian	61	0.10
West Indian	26	0.04
White:	54,587	91.21
Not Hispanic (53,423)	53,896	90.05
Hispanic (624)	691	1.15
Yugoslavian	63	0.11

Lower Moreland

Place Type: Township
County: Montgomery
Population: 11,281

Ancestry/Race	Number	%
African American/Black:	71	0.63
Not Hispanic (59)	70	0.62
Hispanic (1)	1	0.01
African, sub-Saharan:	8	0.07
African	8	0.07
Am. Ind. or Alaska Nat., not spec.	10	0.09
Albanian	41	0.36
American Indian tribes, specified:	4	0.04
Cherokee (1)	2	0.02
Delaware	1	0.01
Latin American Indians (1)	1	0.01
Armenian	115	1.02
Asian:	402	3.56
Cambodian (1)	3	0.03
Chinese, ex. Taiwanese (43)	48	0.43
Filipino (18)	21	0.19
Indian (88)	92	0.82
Japanese (2)	2	0.02
Korean (196)	202	1.79
Pakistani (10)	12	0.11
Sri Lankan (1)	1	0.01
Taiwanese (7)	7	0.06
Thai (5)	5	0.04
Vietnamese (5)	5	0.04
Other Asian, specified	2	0.02
Other Asian, not specified (2)	2	0.02
Austrian	92	0.82
Belgian	35	0.31
Brazilian	6	0.05
British	15	0.13
Canadian	24	0.21
Croatian	6	0.05
Czech	22	0.20
Czechoslovakian	10	0.09
Danish	19	0.17
Dutch	109	0.97
Eastern European	93	0.82
English	921	8.16
Estonian	5	0.04
European	63	0.56
Finnish	17	0.15
French, except Basque	126	1.12
French Canadian	9	0.08
German	2,035	18.04
Greek	158	1.40
Hawaii Native/Pacific Islander:	4	0.04
Polynesian:	1	0.01
Samoan	1	0.01
Other Pac. Isl., specified	2	0.02
Other Pac. Isl., not spec.	1	0.01
Hispanic or Latino:	103	0.91
Central American:	2	0.02
Guatemalan	2	0.02
Cuban	11	0.10
Dominican Republic	3	0.03
Mexican	22	0.20
Puerto Rican	19	0.17
South American:	23	0.20
Argentinean	10	0.09
Chilean	1	0.01
Colombian	4	0.04
Peruvian	2	0.02
Venezuelan	1	0.01
Other South American	5	0.04
Other Hispanic or Latino	23	0.20
Hungarian	161	1.43
Iranian	9	0.08
Irish	2,070	18.35
Israeli	35	0.31
Italian	1,391	12.33
Lithuanian	123	1.09
Norwegian	69	0.61
Polish	697	6.18
Portuguese	74	0.66
Romanian	115	1.02
Russian	1,648	14.61
Scotch-Irish	73	0.65
Scottish	145	1.29
Slavic	13	0.12
Swedish	178	1.58
Swiss	6	0.05
Turkish	7	0.06
Ukrainian	184	1.63
United States or American	656	5.82
Welsh	98	0.87
West Indian, excl. Hispanic:	22	0.20
Jamaican	22	0.20
White:	10,808	95.81
Not Hispanic (10,681)	10,724	95.06
Hispanic (76)	84	0.74
Yugoslavian	21	0.19

Notes: 1. Figures in the "Number" column do not add up to the total population due to: a) Ancestry/Race overlap — e.g. persons can report being both White and Irish, b) persons of Hispanic origin can report being any race, c) persons reporting two ancestries are counted in both categories. 2. Numbers in parentheses indicate the number of persons reporting this ancestry/race alone, not in combination with any other ancestry/race. 3. Refer to the Explanation of Data in the front of the book for more detailed information.

Lower Paxton

Place Type: Township
County: Dauphin
Population: 44,424

Ancestry/Race	Number	%
Acadian/Cajun	8	0.02
African American/Black:	4,022	9.05
Not Hispanic (3,597)	3,906	8.79
Hispanic (83)	116	0.26
African, sub-Saharan:	288	0.65
African	113	0.25
Nigerian	104	0.23
South African	24	0.05
Ugandan	6	0.01
Other sub-Saharan African	41	0.09
Alaska Native tribes, specified:	1	0.00
Alaska Athabascan	1	0.00
Am. Ind. or Alaska Nat., not spec.	61	0.14
American Indian tribes, specified:	92	0.21
Apache (1)	1	0.00
Blackfeet	7	0.02
Cherokee (7)	31	0.07
Chippewa	1	0.00
Choctaw	2	0.00
Comanche	2	0.00
Delaware	3	0.01
Iroquois (2)	6	0.01
Kiowa (1)	1	0.00
Latin American Indians (3)	5	0.01
Lumbee	1	0.00
Navajo (1)	2	0.00
Paiute	3	0.01
Pueblo	2	0.00
Seminole	5	0.01
Sioux (1)	6	0.01
Yakama (1)	1	0.00
All other tribes (8)	13	0.03
American Indian tribes, not spec.	10	0.02
Arab:	201	0.45
Arab/Arabic	20	0.05
Egyptian	58	0.13
Lebanese	74	0.17
Moroccan	18	0.04
Syrian	31	0.07
Armenian	16	0.04
Asian:	1,328	2.99
Bangladeshi (4)	4	0.01
Cambodian (16)	16	0.04
Chinese, ex. Taiwanese (138)	158	0.36
Filipino (67)	96	0.22
Indian (500)	519	1.17
Indonesian (8)	8	0.02
Japanese (28)	42	0.09
Korean (82)	89	0.20
Laotian (5)	6	0.01
Pakistani (41)	46	0.10
Sri Lankan (2)	2	0.00
Taiwanese (7)	10	0.02
Thai (3)	6	0.01
Vietnamese (265)	276	0.62
Other Asian, specified (3)	8	0.02
Other Asian, not specified (20)	42	0.09
Austrian	170	0.38
Belgian	9	0.02
Brazilian	9	0.02
British	134	0.30
Bulgarian	9	0.02
Canadian	26	0.06
Carpatho Rusyn	37	0.08
Croatian	328	0.74
Czech	189	0.43
Czechoslovakian	94	0.21
Danish	63	0.14
Dutch	996	2.24
Eastern European	121	0.27
English	2,845	6.40
Estonian	8	0.02
European	138	0.31
Finnish	54	0.12
French, except Basque	919	2.07
French Canadian	120	0.27
German	14,550	32.75
Greek	160	0.36
Hawaii Native/Pacific Islander:	22	0.05
Melanesian: (2)	2	0.00
Fijian (2)	2	0.00
Micronesian: (2)	3	0.01
Guamanian/Chamorro (2)	3	0.01
Polynesian: (4)	6	0.01
Native Hawaiian (4)	6	0.01
Other Pac. Isl., specified	4	0.01
Other Pac. Isl., not spec. (2)	7	0.02
Hispanic or Latino:	1,053	2.37
Central American:	32	0.07
Costa Rican	1	0.00
Guatemalan	5	0.01
Honduran	7	0.02
Nicaraguan	4	0.01
Panamanian	10	0.02
Salvadoran	5	0.01
Cuban	73	0.16
Dominican Republic	55	0.12
Mexican	177	0.40
Puerto Rican	496	1.12
South American:	77	0.17
Argentinean	1	0.00
Colombian	27	0.06
Ecuadorian	21	0.05
Paraguayan	1	0.00
Peruvian	17	0.04
Venezuelan	9	0.02
Other South American	1	0.00
Other Hispanic or Latino	143	0.32
Hungarian	344	0.77
Icelander	7	0.02
Iranian	24	0.05
Irish	6,291	14.16
Israeli	24	0.05
Italian	4,198	9.45
Latvian	10	0.02
Lithuanian	365	0.82
Macedonian	44	0.10
Northern European	60	0.14
Norwegian	276	0.62
Pennsylvania German	400	0.90
Polish	2,239	5.04
Portuguese	66	0.15
Romanian	79	0.18
Russian	608	1.37
Scandinavian	38	0.09
Scotch-Irish	778	1.75
Scottish	650	1.46
Serbian	148	0.33
Slavic	132	0.30
Slovak	410	0.92
Slovene	88	0.20
Swedish	382	0.86
Swiss	266	0.60
Turkish	19	0.04
Ukrainian	438	0.99
United States or American	2,876	6.47
Welsh	775	1.74
West Indian, excl. Hispanic:	119	0.27
Barbadian	11	0.02
British West Indian	6	0.01
Haitian	27	0.06
Jamaican	68	0.15
Trinidadian and Tobagonian	7	0.02
White:	38,931	87.64
Not Hispanic (37,965)	38,389	86.42
Hispanic (466)	542	1.22
Yugoslavian	229	0.52

Lower Pottsgrove

Place Type: Township
County: Montgomery
Population: 11,213

Ancestry/Race	Number	%
African American/Black:	992	8.85
Not Hispanic (914)	982	8.76
Hispanic (7)	10	0.09
African, sub-Saharan:	22	0.19
African	22	0.19
Am. Ind. or Alaska Nat., not spec.	18	0.16
American Indian tribes, specified:	39	0.35
Apache	2	0.02
Blackfeet	5	0.04
Cherokee (2)	14	0.12
Delaware	4	0.04
Iroquois (2)	3	0.03
Seminole	1	0.01
Sioux	1	0.01
All other tribes (5)	9	0.08
American Indian tribes, not spec.	1	0.01
Arab:	27	0.24
Egyptian	12	0.11
Moroccan	9	0.08
Other Arab	6	0.05
Asian:	125	1.11
Cambodian (6)	6	0.05
Chinese, ex. Taiwanese (15)	16	0.14
Filipino (13)	19	0.17
Indian (27)	28	0.25
Japanese (3)	7	0.06
Korean (15)	16	0.14
Pakistani (3)	3	0.03
Thai (2)	5	0.04
Vietnamese (13)	13	0.12
Other Asian, specified (1)	4	0.04
Other Asian, not specified (1)	8	0.07
Australian	8	0.07
Austrian	55	0.49
British	70	0.62
Canadian	10	0.09
Croatian	7	0.06
Czech	6	0.05
Czechoslovakian	21	0.19
Danish	18	0.16
Dutch	475	4.20
English	1,041	9.21
European	66	0.58
French, except Basque	282	2.50
French Canadian	18	0.16
German	3,345	29.60
German Russian	10	0.09
Greek	87	0.77
Hawaii Native/Pacific Islander:	8	0.07
Micronesian: (2)	2	0.02
Guamanian/Chamorro (2)	2	0.02
Polynesian: (2)	6	0.05
Native Hawaiian (2)	6	0.05
Hispanic or Latino:	137	1.22
Cuban	7	0.06
Dominican Republic	4	0.04
Mexican	23	0.21
Puerto Rican	68	0.61
South American:	4	0.04
Colombian	3	0.03
Ecuadorian	1	0.01
Other Hispanic or Latino	31	0.28
Hungarian	226	2.00
Irish	2,151	19.03
Italian	1,664	14.72
Lithuanian	74	0.65
Norwegian	66	0.58
Pennsylvania German	268	2.37
Polish	909	8.04
Portuguese	20	0.18
Romanian	20	0.18
Russian	106	0.94
Scandinavian	8	0.07

Notes: 1. Figures in the "Number" column do not add up to the total population due to: a) Ancestry/Race overlap — e.g. persons can report being both White and Irish, b) persons of Hispanic origin can report being any race, c) persons reporting two ancestries are counted in both categories. 2. Numbers in parentheses indicate the number of persons reporting this ancestry/race alone, not in combination with any other ancestry/race. 3. Refer to the Explanation of Data in the front of the book for more detailed information.

Scotch-Irish	133	1.18
Scottish	235	2.08
Slavic	15	0.13
Slovak	145	1.28
Swedish	151	1.34
Swiss	28	0.25
Ukrainian	184	1.63
United States or American	336	2.97
Welsh	106	0.94
West Indian, excl. Hispanic:	76	0.67
Barbadian	12	0.11
Jamaican	57	0.50
West Indian	7	0.06
White:	10,120	90.25
Not Hispanic (9,917)	10,021	89.37
Hispanic (87)	99	0.88
Yugoslavian	9	0.08

Lower Providence

Place Type: Township
County: Montgomery
Population: 22,390

Ancestry/Race	Number	%
African American/Black:	1,656	7.40
Not Hispanic (1,615)	1,644	7.34
Hispanic (9)	12	0.05
African, sub-Saharan:	50	0.22
African	43	0.19
Other sub-Saharan African	7	0.03
Am. Ind. or Alaska Nat., not spec.	14	0.06
Albanian	32	0.14
American Indian tribes, specified:	35	0.16
Blackfeet	1	0.00
Cherokee (6)	16	0.07
Chippewa (1)	1	0.00
Choctaw	2	0.01
Delaware (1)	3	0.01
Iroquois (2)	3	0.01
Navajo	2	0.01
Pueblo (4)	4	0.02
Sioux	1	0.00
All other tribes (2)	2	0.01
American Indian tribes, not spec.	2	0.01
Arab:	116	0.52
Egyptian	67	0.30
Lebanese	31	0.14
Palestinian	14	0.06
Other Arab	4	0.02
Armenian	6	0.03
Asian:	1,115	4.98
Cambodian (2)	3	0.01
Chinese, ex. Taiwanese (308)	326	1.46
Filipino (39)	47	0.21
Indian (436)	454	2.03
Japanese (15)	22	0.10
Korean (130)	142	0.63
Laotian (9)	10	0.04
Pakistani (13)	13	0.06
Sri Lankan	1	0.00
Taiwanese (6)	6	0.03
Thai (2)	2	0.01
Vietnamese (58)	60	0.27
Other Asian, not specified (16)	29	0.13
Australian	17	0.08
Austrian	86	0.38
Basque	12	0.05
Brazilian	41	0.18
British	91	0.41
Canadian	24	0.11
Croatian	6	0.03
Czech	43	0.19
Czechoslovakian	21	0.09
Danish	29	0.13
Dutch	339	1.51
Eastern European	58	0.26
English	2,459	10.97
European	127	0.57
Finnish	9	0.04
French, except Basque	567	2.53
French Canadian	186	0.83
German	4,552	20.31
Greek	60	0.27
Hawaii Native/Pacific Islander:	19	0.08
Micronesian: (3)	3	0.01
Guamanian/Chamorro (3)	3	0.01
Polynesian: (10)	14	0.06
Native Hawaiian (7)	10	0.04
Samoan (3)	4	0.02
Other Pac. Isl., not spec. (2)	2	0.01
Hispanic or Latino:	470	2.10
Central American:	4	0.02
Guatemalan	1	0.00
Honduran	1	0.00
Panamanian	1	0.00
Other Central American	1	0.00
Cuban	20	0.09
Dominican Republic	9	0.04
Mexican	89	0.40
Puerto Rican	142	0.63
South American:	18	0.08
Argentinean	1	0.00
Bolivian	2	0.01
Chilean	4	0.02
Colombian	5	0.02
Ecuadorian	3	0.01
Peruvian	2	0.01
Venezuelan	1	0.00
Other Hispanic or Latino	188	0.84
Hungarian	170	0.76
Irish	5,474	24.43
Italian	4,645	20.73
Lithuanian	53	0.24
Luxemburger	6	0.03
Northern European	34	0.15
Norwegian	130	0.58
Pennsylvania German	150	0.67
Polish	1,842	8.22
Portuguese	35	0.16
Romanian	9	0.04
Russian	271	1.21
Scandinavian	27	0.12
Scotch-Irish	280	1.25
Scottish	363	1.62
Slavic	5	0.02
Slovak	274	1.22
Swedish	211	0.94
Swiss	128	0.57
Ukrainian	270	1.20
United States or American	613	2.74
Welsh	347	1.55
West Indian, excl. Hispanic:	25	0.11
Trinidadian and Tobagonian	11	0.05
U.S. Virgin Islander	5	0.02
West Indian	9	0.04
White:	19,432	86.79
Not Hispanic (19,087)	19,191	85.71
Hispanic (227)	241	1.08
Yugoslavian	9	0.04

Lower Salford

Place Type: Township
County: Montgomery
Population: 12,893

Ancestry/Race	Number	%
African American/Black:	431	3.34
Not Hispanic (378)	428	3.32
Hispanic (1)	3	0.02
African, sub-Saharan:	7	0.05
Ethiopian	7	0.05
Am. Ind. or Alaska Nat., not spec.	10	0.08
Albanian	24	0.19
American Indian tribes, specified:	16	0.12
Blackfeet	3	0.02
Cherokee (2)	6	0.05
Kiowa	1	0.01
Latin American Indians (3)	5	0.04
Navajo (1)	1	0.01
American Indian tribes, not spec.	1	0.01
Arab:	45	0.35
Lebanese	17	0.13
Other Arab	28	0.22
Asian:	350	2.71
Cambodian (10)	10	0.08
Chinese, ex. Taiwanese (56)	72	0.56
Filipino (25)	35	0.27
Indian (104)	108	0.84
Japanese (9)	15	0.12
Korean (29)	33	0.26
Taiwanese (8)	8	0.06
Thai (3)	3	0.02
Vietnamese (41)	53	0.41
Other Asian, specified (4)	4	0.03
Other Asian, not specified (5)	9	0.07
Australian	16	0.12
Austrian	41	0.32
Belgian	16	0.12
Brazilian	16	0.12
British	61	0.47
Canadian	32	0.25
Czech	31	0.24
Czechoslovakian	24	0.19
Dutch	148	1.15
Eastern European	17	0.13
English	1,362	10.56
Estonian	9	0.07
European	97	0.75
Finnish	20	0.16
French, except Basque	434	3.37
French Canadian	40	0.31
German	4,407	34.18
Greek	8	0.06
Hawaii Native/Pacific Islander:	7	0.05
Other Pac. Isl., not spec. (6)	7	0.05
Hispanic or Latino:	183	1.42
Central American:	11	0.09
Guatemalan	1	0.01
Honduran	9	0.07
Panamanian	1	0.01
Cuban	6	0.05
Mexican	25	0.19
Puerto Rican	96	0.74
South American:	13	0.10
Argentinean	1	0.01
Colombian	8	0.06
Ecuadorian	1	0.01
Peruvian	3	0.02
Other Hispanic or Latino	32	0.25
Hungarian	86	0.67
Iranian	22	0.17
Irish	2,954	22.91
Israeli	7	0.05
Italian	1,785	13.84
Latvian	36	0.28
Lithuanian	182	1.41
Maltese	11	0.09
Norwegian	121	0.94
Pennsylvania German	170	1.32
Polish	1,034	8.02
Portuguese	41	0.32
Russian	103	0.80
Scotch-Irish	167	1.30
Scottish	190	1.47
Serbian	8	0.06
Slovak	87	0.67
Slovene	28	0.22
Swedish	153	1.19
Swiss	177	1.37
Ukrainian	239	1.85
United States or American	460	3.57
Welsh	118	0.92
West Indian, excl. Hispanic:	39	0.30
Jamaican	39	0.30
White:	12,146	94.21
Not Hispanic (11,918)	12,005	93.11
Hispanic (126)	141	1.09
Yugoslavian	44	0.34

Notes: 1. Figures in the "Number" column do not add up to the total population due to: a) Ancestry/Race overlap — e.g. persons can report being both White and Irish, b) persons of Hispanic origin can report being any race, c) persons reporting two ancestries are counted in both categories. 2. Numbers in parentheses indicate the number of persons reporting this ancestry/race alone, not in combination with any other ancestry/race. 3. Refer to the Explanation of Data in the front of the book for more detailed information.

Lower Southampton

Place Type: Township
County: Bucks
Population: 19,276

Ancestry/Race	Number	%
African American/Black:	243	1.26
Not Hispanic (195)	229	1.19
Hispanic (12)	14	0.07
African, sub-Saharan:	25	0.13
African	13	0.07
Liberian	12	0.06
Am. Ind. or Alaska Nat., not spec.	20	0.10
Albanian	15	0.08
American Indian tribes, specified:	28	0.15
Blackfeet	2	0.01
Cherokee	8	0.04
Crow	1	0.01
Delaware	4	0.02
Latin American Indians (1)	4	0.02
Lumbee	1	0.01
Sioux	2	0.01
All other tribes (3)	6	0.03
American Indian tribes, not spec.	4	0.02
Arab:	10	0.05
Moroccan	10	0.05
Armenian	27	0.14
Asian:	314	1.63
Chinese, ex. Taiwanese (56)	64	0.33
Filipino (21)	26	0.13
Indian (105)	113	0.59
Indonesian	1	0.01
Japanese (8)	15	0.08
Korean (45)	49	0.25
Laotian (1)	1	0.01
Taiwanese (3)	3	0.02
Thai (1)	1	0.01
Vietnamese (10)	17	0.09
Other Asian, not specified (8)	24	0.12
Australian	6	0.03
Austrian	192	1.00
Belgian	12	0.06
British	27	0.14
Canadian	18	0.09
Celtic	40	0.21
Croatian	51	0.26
Czech	28	0.15
Czechoslovakian	54	0.28
Danish	49	0.25
Dutch	219	1.14
Eastern European	69	0.36
English	2,112	10.96
Estonian	9	0.05
European	95	0.49
Finnish	7	0.04
French, except Basque	443	2.30
French Canadian	55	0.29
German	5,526	28.67
Greek	106	0.55
Hawaii Native/Pacific Islander:	11	0.06
Polynesian: (2)	4	0.02
Native Hawaiian	2	0.01
Samoan (2)	2	0.01
Other Pac. Isl., not spec.	7	0.04
Hispanic or Latino:	272	1.41
Central American:	12	0.06
Costa Rican	5	0.03
Guatemalan	1	0.01
Honduran	2	0.01
Panamanian	1	0.01
Salvadoran	3	0.02
Cuban	24	0.12
Dominican Republic	4	0.02
Mexican	34	0.18
Puerto Rican	96	0.50
South American:	42	0.22
Argentinean	9	0.05
Bolivian	2	0.01
Colombian	9	0.05
Ecuadorian	2	0.01
Paraguayan	4	0.02
Peruvian	12	0.06
Other South American	4	0.02
Other Hispanic or Latino	60	0.31
Hungarian	262	1.36
Irish	4,972	25.79
Israeli	20	0.10
Italian	3,222	16.72
Lithuanian	133	0.69
Northern European	40	0.21
Norwegian	77	0.40
Pennsylvania German	111	0.58
Polish	1,748	9.07
Portuguese	15	0.08
Romanian	39	0.20
Russian	1,051	5.45
Scotch-Irish	395	2.05
Scottish	324	1.68
Slavic	7	0.04
Slovak	53	0.27
Swedish	59	0.31
Swiss	44	0.23
Turkish	30	0.16
Ukrainian	627	3.25
United States or American	983	5.10
Welsh	333	1.73
West Indian, excl. Hispanic:	70	0.36
Barbadian	14	0.07
Jamaican	38	0.20
West Indian	18	0.09
White:	18,696	96.99
Not Hispanic (18,415)	18,521	96.08
Hispanic (156)	175	0.91

Loyalsock

Place Type: Township
County: Lycoming
Population: 10,876

Ancestry/Race	Number	%
African American/Black:	338	3.11
Not Hispanic (283)	333	3.06
Hispanic (4)	5	0.05
African, sub-Saharan:	6	0.06
African	6	0.06
Am. Ind. or Alaska Nat., not spec.	11	0.10
American Indian tribes, specified:	38	0.35
Apache (2)	4	0.04
Blackfeet	1	0.01
Cherokee	7	0.06
Chippewa (3)	6	0.06
Choctaw	1	0.01
Comanche	1	0.01
Delaware (1)	1	0.01
Latin American Indians	1	0.01
Seminole	1	0.01
Sioux	8	0.07
Yaqui	1	0.01
All other tribes (1)	6	0.06
American Indian tribes, not spec.	4	0.04
Arab:	13	0.12
Lebanese	13	0.12
Armenian	11	0.10
Asian:	138	1.27
Chinese, ex. Taiwanese (24)	31	0.29
Filipino (13)	17	0.16
Indian (46)	52	0.48
Japanese (4)	6	0.06
Korean (16)	19	0.17
Pakistani (6)	6	0.06
Thai (1)	1	0.01
Vietnamese (1)	3	0.03
Other Asian, not specified (2)	3	0.03
Australian	7	0.06
Austrian	16	0.15
Belgian	20	0.18
British	31	0.29
Canadian	18	0.17
Czech	22	0.20
Czechoslovakian	16	0.15
Danish	10	0.09
Dutch	288	2.65
English	921	8.47
European	31	0.29
Finnish	11	0.10
French, except Basque	276	2.54
French Canadian	79	0.73
German	3,746	34.44
Greek	20	0.18
Hawaii Native/Pacific Islander:	6	0.06
Micronesian: (1)	1	0.01
Guamanian/Chamorro (1)	1	0.01
Polynesian:	3	0.03
Native Hawaiian	3	0.03
Other Pac. Isl., not spec.	2	0.02
Hispanic or Latino:	93	0.86
Central American:	2	0.02
Guatemalan	1	0.01
Nicaraguan	1	0.01
Cuban	17	0.16
Dominican Republic	1	0.01
Mexican	24	0.22
Puerto Rican	26	0.24
South American:	3	0.03
Colombian	3	0.03
Other Hispanic or Latino	20	0.18
Hungarian	54	0.50
Icelander	6	0.06
Irish	1,182	10.87
Italian	688	6.33
Lithuanian	54	0.50
Northern European	27	0.25
Norwegian	41	0.38
Pennsylvania German	48	0.44
Polish	491	4.51
Portuguese	7	0.06
Romanian	28	0.26
Russian	51	0.47
Scandinavian	11	0.10
Scotch-Irish	249	2.29
Scottish	318	2.92
Slovak	97	0.89
Swedish	107	0.98
Swiss	23	0.21
Ukrainian	43	0.40
United States or American	932	8.57
Welsh	160	1.47
White:	10,417	95.78
Not Hispanic (10,261)	10,357	95.23
Hispanic (51)	60	0.55

Manchester

Place Type: Township
County: York
Population: 12,700

Ancestry/Race	Number	%
African American/Black:	314	2.47
Not Hispanic (259)	300	2.36
Hispanic (7)	14	0.11
African, sub-Saharan:	48	0.38
African	16	0.13
South African	32	0.25
Am. Ind. or Alaska Nat., not spec.	8	0.06
American Indian tribes, specified:	22	0.17
Blackfeet (1)	1	0.01
Cherokee (5)	7	0.06
Chippewa (1)	1	0.01
Latin American Indians (2)	3	0.02
Navajo (1)	3	0.02
All other tribes (3)	7	0.06
American Indian tribes, not spec.	2	0.02
Asian:	247	1.94
Bangladeshi (3)	3	0.02
Chinese, ex. Taiwanese (45)	54	0.43
Filipino (15)	23	0.18
Indian (62)	62	0.49

Notes: 1. Figures in the "Number" column do not add up to the total population due to: a) Ancestry/Race overlap — e.g. persons can report being both White and Irish, b) persons of Hispanic origin can report being any race, c) persons reporting two ancestries are counted in both categories. 2. Numbers in parentheses indicate the number of persons reporting this ancestry/race alone, not in combination with any other ancestry/race. 3. Refer to the Explanation of Data in the front of the book for more detailed information.

Indonesian (1)	1	0.01
Japanese (2)	7	0.06
Korean (27)	32	0.25
Laotian (14)	14	0.11
Taiwanese (1)	1	0.01
Thai	1	0.01
Vietnamese (43)	46	0.36
Other Asian, not specified (3)	3	0.02
Australian	6	0.05
Austrian	40	0.31
British	39	0.31
Canadian	14	0.11
Croatian	22	0.17
Czechoslovakian	10	0.08
Dutch	265	2.09
English	1,050	8.27
European	93	0.73
Finnish	40	0.31
French, except Basque	237	1.87
French Canadian	58	0.46
German	5,648	44.48
Greek	18	0.14
Hawaii Native/Pacific Islander:	7	0.06
Micronesian: (2)	3	0.02
Guamanian/Chamorro (2)	3	0.02
Polynesian: (1)	4	0.03
Native Hawaiian (1)	4	0.03
Hispanic or Latino:	211	1.66
Central American:	19	0.15
Costa Rican	1	0.01
Guatemalan	3	0.02
Nicaraguan	4	0.03
Panamanian	1	0.01
Salvadoran	5	0.04
Other Central American	5	0.04
Cuban	3	0.02
Dominican Republic	6	0.05
Mexican	18	0.14
Puerto Rican	94	0.74
South American:	21	0.17
Argentinean	2	0.02
Chilean	4	0.03
Colombian	10	0.08
Ecuadorian	4	0.03
Other South American	1	0.01
Other Hispanic or Latino	50	0.39
Hungarian	33	0.26
Irish	1,576	12.41
Italian	665	5.24
Lithuanian	12	0.09
Norwegian	126	0.99
Pennsylvania German	59	0.46
Polish	372	2.93
Romanian	36	0.28
Russian	46	0.36
Scandinavian	5	0.04
Scotch-Irish	179	1.41
Scottish	291	2.29
Slovak	40	0.31
Slovene	8	0.06
Swedish	149	1.17
Swiss	108	0.85
Ukrainian	21	0.17
United States or American	1,275	10.04
Welsh	153	1.20
West Indian, excl. Hispanic:	86	0.68
Haitian	16	0.13
Jamaican	70	0.55
White:	12,076	95.09
Not Hispanic (11,890)	11,972	94.27
Hispanic (83)	104	0.82

Manheim

Place Type: Township
County: Lancaster
Population: 33,697

Ancestry/Race	Number	%
African American/Black:	632	1.88
Not Hispanic (470)	582	1.73
Hispanic (21)	50	0.15
African, sub-Saharan:	49	0.15
African	24	0.07
Ethiopian	25	0.07
Am. Ind. or Alaska Nat., not spec.	30	0.09
Albanian	9	0.03
American Indian tribes, specified:	68	0.20
Apache	1	0.00
Blackfeet (1)	3	0.01
Cherokee (6)	25	0.07
Cheyenne	3	0.01
Chippewa (1)	1	0.00
Creek	2	0.01
Delaware (1)	3	0.01
Iroquois (3)	6	0.02
Latin American Indians (1)	1	0.00
Navajo (4)	8	0.02
Seminole	1	0.00
Sioux (1)	2	0.01
All other tribes (8)	12	0.04
American Indian tribes, not spec.	9	0.03
Arab:	90	0.27
Lebanese	24	0.07
Palestinian	40	0.12
Syrian	26	0.08
Armenian	18	0.05
Asian:	1,181	3.50
Bangladeshi (2)	2	0.01
Cambodian (59)	66	0.20
Chinese, ex. Taiwanese (206)	236	0.70
Filipino (16)	32	0.09
Indian (134)	159	0.47
Indonesian (3)	8	0.02
Japanese (34)	52	0.15
Korean (64)	72	0.21
Laotian (9)	11	0.03
Malaysian (1)	1	0.00
Pakistani (2)	9	0.03
Sri Lankan (2)	2	0.01
Taiwanese	4	0.01
Thai (6)	6	0.02
Vietnamese (467)	489	1.45
Other Asian, specified (6)	8	0.02
Other Asian, not specified (14)	24	0.07
Austrian	100	0.30
Belgian	32	0.09
Brazilian	17	0.05
British	295	0.87
Canadian	31	0.09
Celtic	6	0.02
Croatian	86	0.25
Czech	70	0.21
Czechoslovakian	42	0.12
Danish	106	0.31
Dutch	684	2.03
Eastern European	68	0.20
English	3,943	11.68
European	334	0.99
Finnish	9	0.03
French, except Basque	928	2.75
French Canadian	166	0.49
German	12,740	37.73
Greek	402	1.19
Hawaii Native/Pacific Islander:	10	0.03
Micronesian: (1)	2	0.01
Guamanian/Chamorro (1)	2	0.01
Polynesian: (1)	1	0.00
Native Hawaiian (1)	1	0.00
Other Pac. Isl., specified	2	0.01
Other Pac. Isl., not spec.	5	0.01
Hispanic or Latino:	932	2.77
Central American:	26	0.08
Costa Rican	1	0.00
Guatemalan	3	0.01
Honduran	6	0.02
Nicaraguan	2	0.01
Panamanian	2	0.01
Salvadoran	10	0.03
Other Central American	2	0.01
Cuban	18	0.05
Dominican Republic	31	0.09
Mexican	82	0.24
Puerto Rican	565	1.68
South American:	58	0.17
Argentinean	2	0.01
Colombian	27	0.08
Ecuadorian	8	0.02
Paraguayan	1	0.00
Peruvian	10	0.03
Uruguayan	1	0.00
Venezuelan	1	0.00
Other South American	8	0.02
Other Hispanic or Latino	152	0.45
Hungarian	295	0.87
Irish	3,876	11.48
Italian	2,337	6.92
Latvian	19	0.06
Lithuanian	172	0.51
Luxemburger	7	0.02
Northern European	10	0.03
Norwegian	139	0.41
Pennsylvania German	187	0.55
Polish	1,208	3.58
Portuguese	22	0.07
Romanian	63	0.19
Russian	414	1.23
Scandinavian	23	0.07
Scotch-Irish	935	2.77
Scottish	842	2.49
Serbian	66	0.20
Slavic	49	0.15
Slovak	207	0.61
Slovene	45	0.13
Swedish	273	0.81
Swiss	1,018	3.01
Turkish	15	0.04
Ukrainian	172	0.51
United States or American	2,253	6.67
Welsh	590	1.75
West Indian, excl. Hispanic:	15	0.04
Bermudan	6	0.02
Jamaican	9	0.03
White:	31,733	94.17
Not Hispanic (30,895)	31,158	92.47
Hispanic (505)	575	1.71
Yugoslavian	16	0.05

Manor

Place Type: Township
County: Lancaster
Population: 16,498

Ancestry/Race	Number	%
African American/Black:	281	1.70
Not Hispanic (208)	264	1.60
Hispanic (15)	17	0.10
African, sub-Saharan:	34	0.21
Kenyan	27	0.16
Liberian	7	0.04
Am. Ind. or Alaska Nat., not spec.	17	0.10
American Indian tribes, specified:	47	0.28
Cherokee (1)	26	0.16
Choctaw	1	0.01
Delaware	1	0.01
Iroquois	1	0.01
Latin American Indians (3)	3	0.02
Ottawa	3	0.02
Sioux	3	0.02
All other tribes (7)	9	0.05
American Indian tribes, not spec.	5	0.03
Arab:	14	0.09
Lebanese	14	0.09
Asian:	230	1.39
Cambodian (13)	14	0.08
Chinese, ex. Taiwanese (41)	47	0.28
Filipino (6)	12	0.07
Indian (29)	34	0.21
Japanese (6)	6	0.04

Notes: 1. Figures in the "Number" column do not add up to the total population due to: a) Ancestry/Race overlap — e.g. persons can report being both White and Irish, b) persons of Hispanic origin can report being any race, c) persons reporting two ancestries are counted in both categories. 2. Numbers in parentheses indicate the number of persons reporting this ancestry/race alone, not in combination with any other ancestry/race. 3. Refer to the Explanation of Data in the front of the book for more detailed information.

Korean (23)	23	0.14
Laotian (5)	5	0.03
Thai	1	0.01
Vietnamese (78)	82	0.50
Other Asian, not specified (3)	6	0.04
Australian	13	0.08
Austrian	29	0.18
Belgian	23	0.14
British	84	0.51
Canadian	4	0.02
Croatian	27	0.16
Czech	23	0.14
Czechoslovakian	39	0.24
Danish	47	0.29
Dutch	122	0.74
Eastern European	18	0.11
English	1,393	8.47
European	151	0.92
Finnish	12	0.07
French, except Basque	341	2.07
French Canadian	29	0.18
German	7,269	44.22
German Russian	14	0.09
Greek	87	0.53
Hawaii Native/Pacific Islander:	7	0.04
Micronesian: (1)	4	0.02
Guamanian/Chamorro (1)	4	0.02
Polynesian:	1	0.01
Native Hawaiian	1	0.01
Other Pac. Isl., not spec. (1)	2	0.01
Hispanic or Latino:	376	2.28
Central American:	16	0.10
Guatemalan	3	0.02
Honduran	3	0.02
Nicaraguan	1	0.01
Panamanian	4	0.02
Salvadoran	5	0.03
Cuban	5	0.03
Dominican Republic	4	0.02
Mexican	32	0.19
Puerto Rican	269	1.63
South American:	18	0.11
Chilean	2	0.01
Colombian	7	0.04
Ecuadorian	1	0.01
Paraguayan	1	0.01
Peruvian	1	0.01
Uruguayan	1	0.01
Other South American	5	0.03
Other Hispanic or Latino	32	0.19
Hungarian	146	0.89
Irish	1,795	10.92
Italian	851	5.18
Latvian	8	0.05
Lithuanian	55	0.33
New Zealander	11	0.07
Norwegian	15	0.09
Pennsylvania German	74	0.45
Polish	454	2.76
Romanian	9	0.05
Russian	104	0.63
Scotch-Irish	567	3.45
Scottish	229	1.39
Slavic	5	0.03
Slovak	43	0.26
Swedish	180	1.10
Swiss	602	3.66
Ukrainian	17	0.10
United States or American	1,068	6.50
Welsh	127	0.77
West Indian, excl. Hispanic:	14	0.09
Jamaican	7	0.04
West Indian	7	0.04
White:	15,904	96.40
Not Hispanic (15,557)	15,662	94.93
Hispanic (222)	242	1.47
Yugoslavian	24	0.15

Marple

Place Type: Township
County: Delaware
Population: 23,737

Ancestry/Race	Number	%
Afghan	32	0.13
African American/Black:	291	1.23
Not Hispanic (258)	287	1.21
Hispanic (3)	4	0.02
African, sub-Saharan:	5	0.02
Ethiopian	5	0.02
Alaska Native tribes, specified:	1	0.00
Eskimo	1	0.00
Am. Ind. or Alaska Nat., not spec.	10	0.04
Alsatian	12	0.05
American Indian tribes, specified:	30	0.13
Blackfeet	3	0.01
Cherokee (6)	14	0.06
Iroquois (1)	1	0.00
Latin American Indians (1)	1	0.00
Pueblo	1	0.00
All other tribes (5)	10	0.04
American Indian tribes, not spec.	4	0.02
Arab:	207	0.87
Lebanese	131	0.55
Palestinian	44	0.19
Syrian	32	0.13
Armenian	281	1.18
Asian:	1,383	5.83
Bangladeshi (8)	8	0.03
Chinese, ex. Taiwanese (273)	298	1.26
Filipino (17)	25	0.11
Indian (240)	246	1.04
Indonesian	4	0.02
Japanese (4)	10	0.04
Korean (634)	647	2.73
Laotian	1	0.00
Pakistani (6)	6	0.03
Sri Lankan (1)	1	0.00
Taiwanese (14)	23	0.10
Thai (5)	5	0.02
Vietnamese (75)	82	0.35
Other Asian, not specified (11)	27	0.11
Australian	6	0.03
Austrian	113	0.48
Belgian	16	0.07
Brazilian	4	0.02
British	93	0.39
Bulgarian	7	0.03
Canadian	19	0.08
Celtic	6	0.03
Croatian	29	0.12
Czech	75	0.32
Czechoslovakian	50	0.21
Danish	72	0.30
Dutch	236	0.99
Eastern European	130	0.55
English	2,144	9.03
Estonian	7	0.03
European	114	0.48
Finnish	7	0.03
French, except Basque	464	1.95
French Canadian	24	0.10
German	4,012	16.90
Greek	849	3.58
Hawaii Native/Pacific Islander:	15	0.06
Micronesian:	3	0.01
Guamanian/Chamorro	3	0.01
Other Pac. Isl., not spec.	12	0.05
Hispanic or Latino:	156	0.66
Central American:	5	0.02
Guatemalan	2	0.01
Nicaraguan	1	0.00
Salvadoran	2	0.01
Cuban	13	0.05
Mexican	22	0.09
Puerto Rican	28	0.12
South American:	36	0.15
Argentinean	7	0.03
Bolivian	2	0.01
Colombian	7	0.03
Ecuadorian	3	0.01
Peruvian	2	0.01
Uruguayan	7	0.03
Venezuelan	7	0.03
Other South American	1	0.00
Other Hispanic or Latino	52	0.22
Hungarian	179	0.75
Iranian	55	0.23
Irish	6,796	28.63
Israeli	6	0.03
Italian	6,076	25.60
Latvian	31	0.13
Lithuanian	129	0.54
Northern European	26	0.11
Norwegian	83	0.35
Pennsylvania German	50	0.21
Polish	923	3.89
Portuguese	20	0.08
Romanian	87	0.37
Russian	721	3.04
Scandinavian	7	0.03
Scotch-Irish	440	1.85
Scottish	248	1.04
Serbian	12	0.05
Slovak	92	0.39
Slovene	15	0.06
Swedish	149	0.63
Swiss	135	0.57
Turkish	11	0.05
Ukrainian	212	0.89
United States or American	705	2.97
Welsh	221	0.93
West Indian, excl. Hispanic:	3	0.01
Jamaican	3	0.01
White:	22,104	93.12
Not Hispanic (21,856)	21,971	92.56
Hispanic (124)	133	0.56
Yugoslavian	25	0.11

McCandless Township

Place Type: Census Designated Place
County: Allegheny
Population: 29,022

Ancestry/Race	Number	%
African American/Black:	425	1.46
Not Hispanic (368)	417	1.44
Hispanic (7)	8	0.03
African, sub-Saharan:	104	0.36
African	47	0.16
Ethiopian	7	0.02
South African	35	0.12
Ugandan	7	0.02
Other sub-Saharan African	8	0.03
Am. Ind. or Alaska Nat., not spec.	18	0.06
American Indian tribes, specified:	30	0.10
Cherokee (2)	13	0.04
Comanche	1	0.00
Delaware (1)	2	0.01
Iroquois (2)	5	0.02
Pueblo	2	0.01
Sioux	1	0.00
All other tribes (6)	6	0.02
American Indian tribes, not spec.	3	0.01
Arab:	191	0.66
Arab/Arabic	14	0.05
Jordanian	5	0.02
Lebanese	144	0.50
Syrian	28	0.10
Asian:	1,058	3.65
Chinese, ex. Taiwanese (283)	309	1.06
Filipino (51)	62	0.21
Indian (366)	387	1.33
Indonesian	6	0.02
Japanese (19)	31	0.11
Korean (121)	136	0.47

Notes: 1. Figures in the "Number" column do not add up to the total population due to: a) Ancestry/Race overlap — e.g. persons can report being both White and Irish, b) persons of Hispanic origin can report being any race, c) persons reporting two ancestries are counted in both categories. 2. Numbers in parentheses indicate the number of persons reporting this ancestry/race alone, not in combination with any other ancestry/race. 3. Refer to the Explanation of Data in the front of the book for more detailed information.

Pakistani (23)	23	0.08
Sri Lankan (12)	12	0.04
Taiwanese (17)	17	0.06
Thai (12)	12	0.04
Vietnamese (14)	19	0.07
Other Asian, specified (2)	4	0.01
Other Asian, not specified (4)	40	0.14
Australian	7	0.02
Austrian	307	1.06
Belgian	26	0.09
British	88	0.30
Bulgarian	7	0.02
Canadian	66	0.23
Carpatho Rusyn	13	0.04
Croatian	642	2.21
Czech	351	1.21
Czechoslovakian	186	0.64
Danish	51	0.18
Dutch	336	1.16
Eastern European	82	0.28
English	3,088	10.64
European	128	0.44
Finnish	22	0.08
French, except Basque	717	2.47
French Canadian	85	0.29
German	9,494	32.71
Greek	238	0.82
Hawaii Native/Pacific Islander:	17	0.06
Micronesian: (1)	3	0.01
Guamanian/Chamorro (1)	3	0.01
Polynesian: (1)	3	0.01
Native Hawaiian (1)	1	0.00
Tongan	2	0.01
Other Pac. Isl., not spec.	11	0.04
Hispanic or Latino:	202	0.70
Central American:	10	0.03
Costa Rican	1	0.00
Guatemalan	2	0.01
Honduran	4	0.01
Salvadoran	3	0.01
Cuban	8	0.03
Dominican Republic	3	0.01
Mexican	84	0.29
Puerto Rican	38	0.13
South American:	34	0.12
Argentinean	5	0.02
Colombian	2	0.01
Ecuadorian	8	0.03
Peruvian	10	0.03
Venezuelan	8	0.03
Other South American	1	0.00
Other Hispanic or Latino	25	0.09
Hungarian	337	1.16
Irish	5,318	18.32
Israeli	32	0.11
Italian	4,036	13.91
Latvian	22	0.08
Lithuanian	214	0.74
New Zealander	5	0.02
Norwegian	110	0.38
Pennsylvania German	48	0.17
Polish	2,127	7.33
Portuguese	23	0.08
Romanian	8	0.03
Russian	322	1.11
Scandinavian	19	0.07
Scotch-Irish	852	2.94
Scottish	674	2.32
Serbian	78	0.27
Slavic	28	0.10
Slovak	824	2.84
Slovene	106	0.37
Swedish	188	0.65
Swiss	160	0.55
Turkish	16	0.06
Ukrainian	385	1.33
United States or American	872	3.00
Welsh	281	0.97
West Indian, excl. Hispanic:	14	0.05
British West Indian	6	0.02
Jamaican	8	0.03
White:	27,638	95.23
Not Hispanic (27,303)	27,480	94.69
Hispanic (146)	158	0.54

McKeesport

Place Type: City
County: Allegheny
Population: 24,040

Ancestry/Race	Number	%
Acadian/Cajun	6	0.02
African American/Black:	6,286	26.15
Not Hispanic (5,822)	6,185	25.73
Hispanic (59)	101	0.42
African, sub-Saharan:	221	0.92
African	213	0.89
Nigerian	8	0.03
Am. Ind. or Alaska Nat., not spec.	77	0.32
Albanian	8	0.03
American Indian tribes, specified:	95	0.40
Apache	1	0.00
Blackfeet (3)	8	0.03
Cherokee (10)	45	0.19
Cheyenne (2)	2	0.01
Chippewa (2)	5	0.02
Cree (1)	1	0.00
Delaware (2)	6	0.02
Iroquois (5)	9	0.04
Latin American Indians (3)	7	0.03
Seminole	1	0.00
Sioux	5	0.02
Yaqui	1	0.00
All other tribes (2)	4	0.02
American Indian tribes, not spec.	8	0.03
Arab:	53	0.22
Iraqi	16	0.07
Lebanese	16	0.07
Syrian	21	0.09
Asian:	76	0.32
Chinese, ex. Taiwanese (3)	3	0.01
Filipino (10)	16	0.07
Indian (4)	16	0.07
Japanese (4)	9	0.04
Korean (3)	9	0.04
Pakistani	3	0.01
Thai (1)	1	0.00
Other Asian, not specified (5)	19	0.08
Austrian	33	0.14
Brazilian	6	0.02
British	39	0.16
Canadian	5	0.02
Carpatho Rusyn	34	0.14
Croatian	541	2.25
Czech	73	0.30
Czechoslovakian	72	0.30
Danish	8	0.03
Dutch	107	0.45
English	1,476	6.14
European	10	0.04
French, except Basque	175	0.73
French Canadian	28	0.12
German	3,852	16.04
Greek	104	0.43
Hawaii Native/Pacific Islander:	4	0.02
Polynesian: (1)	1	0.00
Native Hawaiian (1)	1	0.00
Other Pac. Isl., not spec. (1)	3	0.01
Hispanic or Latino:	361	1.50
Central American:	2	0.01
Costa Rican	1	0.00
Panamanian	1	0.00
Cuban	10	0.04
Mexican	143	0.59
Puerto Rican	107	0.45
South American:	9	0.04
Ecuadorian	2	0.01
Peruvian	2	0.01
Venezuelan	4	0.02
Other South American	1	0.00
Other Hispanic or Latino	90	0.37
Hungarian	945	3.93
Irish	3,020	12.57
Italian	2,280	9.49
Lithuanian	36	0.15
Norwegian	5	0.02
Pennsylvania German	14	0.06
Polish	1,839	7.66
Portuguese	17	0.07
Romanian	43	0.18
Russian	233	0.97
Scandinavian	16	0.07
Scotch-Irish	307	1.28
Scottish	315	1.31
Serbian	177	0.74
Slavic	79	0.33
Slovak	1,340	5.58
Slovene	44	0.18
Swedish	366	1.52
Swiss	16	0.07
Turkish	7	0.03
Ukrainian	102	0.42
United States or American	1,029	4.28
Welsh	289	1.20
West Indian, excl. Hispanic:	86	0.36
Haitian	54	0.22
Jamaican	14	0.06
Trinidadian and Tobagonian	18	0.07
White:	17,831	74.17
Not Hispanic (17,238)	17,628	73.33
Hispanic (168)	203	0.84

Meadville

Place Type: City
County: Crawford
Population: 13,685

Ancestry/Race	Number	%
African American/Black:	825	6.03
Not Hispanic (683)	818	5.98
Hispanic (3)	7	0.05
African, sub-Saharan:	53	0.39
African	46	0.34
Ethiopian	7	0.05
Am. Ind. or Alaska Nat., not spec.	38	0.28
American Indian tribes, specified:	38	0.28
Apache (2)	2	0.01
Blackfeet	4	0.03
Cherokee (2)	15	0.11
Creek	1	0.01
Delaware (1)	1	0.01
Iroquois (2)	7	0.05
Paiute (1)	1	0.01
Pueblo (1)	1	0.01
Sioux (1)	1	0.01
Yakama (1)	1	0.01
All other tribes (2)	4	0.03
American Indian tribes, not spec.	2	0.01
Arab:	36	0.26
Lebanese	30	0.22
Syrian	6	0.04
Asian:	119	0.87
Chinese, ex. Taiwanese (11)	19	0.14
Filipino (16)	19	0.14
Indian (16)	20	0.15
Japanese (13)	18	0.13
Korean (13)	14	0.10
Pakistani (6)	6	0.04
Thai (1)	1	0.01
Vietnamese (6)	6	0.04
Other Asian, not specified (4)	16	0.12
Austrian	34	0.25
Belgian	11	0.08
British	44	0.32
Canadian	7	0.05
Celtic	16	0.12
Croatian	23	0.17
Czech	45	0.33

Notes: 1. Figures in the "Number" column do not add up to the total population due to: a) Ancestry/Race overlap — e.g. persons can report being both White and Irish, b) persons of Hispanic origin can report being any race, c) persons reporting two ancestries are counted in both categories. 2. Numbers in parentheses indicate the number of persons reporting this ancestry/race alone, not in combination with any other ancestry/race. 3. Refer to the Explanation of Data in the front of the book for more detailed information.

Ancestry/Race	Number	%
Czechoslovakian	35	0.26
Danish	24	0.18
Dutch	277	2.03
Eastern European	8	0.06
English	1,643	12.02
European	179	1.31
Finnish	17	0.12
French, except Basque	539	3.94
French Canadian	59	0.43
German	3,539	25.89
Greek	25	0.18
Guyanese	7	0.05
Hawaii Native/Pacific Islander:	18	0.13
Micronesian: (1)	3	0.02
Guamanian/Chamorro (1)	3	0.02
Polynesian: (4)	6	0.04
Native Hawaiian (3)	4	0.03
Samoan (1)	2	0.01
Other Pac. Isl., not spec. (1)	9	0.07
Hispanic or Latino:	152	1.11
Central American:	5	0.04
Guatemalan	2	0.01
Nicaraguan	2	0.01
Panamanian	1	0.01
Cuban	6	0.04
Mexican	54	0.39
Puerto Rican	24	0.18
South American:	14	0.10
Chilean	1	0.01
Colombian	5	0.04
Peruvian	6	0.04
Other South American	2	0.01
Other Hispanic or Latino	49	0.36
Hungarian	111	0.81
Icelander	10	0.07
Irish	1,964	14.37
Italian	1,572	11.50
Lithuanian	12	0.09
Northern European	8	0.06
Norwegian	101	0.74
Pennsylvania German	99	0.72
Polish	898	6.57
Portuguese	15	0.11
Romanian	6	0.04
Russian	94	0.69
Scandinavian	23	0.17
Scotch-Irish	447	3.27
Scottish	388	2.84
Serbian	14	0.10
Slovak	82	0.60
Slovene	41	0.30
Swedish	227	1.66
Swiss	47	0.34
Turkish	7	0.05
Ukrainian	48	0.35
United States or American	666	4.87
Welsh	191	1.40
West Indian, excl. Hispanic:	7	0.05
Jamaican	7	0.05
White:	12,819	93.67
Not Hispanic (12,496)	12,705	92.84
Hispanic (91)	114	0.83

Middle Smithfield

Place Type: Township
County: Monroe
Population: 11,495

Ancestry/Race	Number	%
African American/Black:	1,012	8.80
Not Hispanic (852)	938	8.16
Hispanic (29)	74	0.64
African, sub-Saharan:	81	0.70
African	81	0.70
Am. Ind. or Alaska Nat., not spec.	35	0.30
American Indian tribes, specified:	46	0.40
Apache (2)	3	0.03
Blackfeet (1)	5	0.04
Cherokee (1)	9	0.08
Delaware (5)	9	0.08
Iroquois (1)	7	0.06
Latin American Indians (2)	7	0.06
Sioux (2)	4	0.03
All other tribes (1)	2	0.02
American Indian tribes, not spec.	4	0.03
Arab:	13	0.11
Egyptian	13	0.11
Asian:	201	1.75
Chinese, ex. Taiwanese (14)	17	0.15
Filipino (55)	64	0.56
Indian (39)	49	0.43
Indonesian (3)	3	0.03
Japanese (8)	12	0.10
Korean (24)	33	0.29
Malaysian (1)	2	0.02
Pakistani	1	0.01
Vietnamese (5)	5	0.04
Other Asian, specified (1)	3	0.03
Other Asian, not specified	12	0.10
Austrian	38	0.33
Brazilian	18	0.16
British	35	0.30
Canadian	10	0.09
Croatian	7	0.06
Czech	89	0.77
Czechoslovakian	41	0.36
Danish	21	0.18
Dutch	314	2.73
English	742	6.45
European	38	0.33
French, except Basque	346	3.01
French Canadian	57	0.50
German	2,527	21.98
Greek	89	0.77
Hawaii Native/Pacific Islander:	4	0.03
Polynesian: (1)	2	0.02
Native Hawaiian (1)	2	0.02
Other Pac. Isl., not spec.	2	0.02
Hispanic or Latino:	990	8.61
Central American:	45	0.39
Costa Rican	7	0.06
Guatemalan	1	0.01
Honduran	15	0.13
Panamanian	9	0.08
Salvadoran	13	0.11
Cuban	46	0.40
Dominican Republic	45	0.39
Mexican	40	0.35
Puerto Rican	565	4.92
South American:	100	0.87
Argentinean	6	0.05
Chilean	4	0.03
Colombian	42	0.37
Ecuadorian	16	0.14
Peruvian	26	0.23
Venezuelan	4	0.03
Other South American	2	0.02
Other Hispanic or Latino	149	1.30
Hungarian	148	1.29
Irish	2,713	23.60
Italian	1,905	16.57
Latvian	29	0.25
Lithuanian	60	0.52
Maltese	2	0.02
Norwegian	39	0.34
Pennsylvania German	100	0.87
Polish	860	7.48
Portuguese	27	0.23
Romanian	25	0.22
Russian	189	1.64
Scandinavian	23	0.20
Scotch-Irish	82	0.71
Scottish	172	1.50
Slavic	32	0.28
Slovak	50	0.43
Slovene	8	0.07
Swedish	156	1.36
Swiss	15	0.13
Ukrainian	81	0.70
United States or American	754	6.56
Welsh	120	1.04
West Indian, excl. Hispanic:	127	1.10
Barbadian	8	0.07
Belizean	10	0.09
Haitian	8	0.07
Jamaican	38	0.33
Trinidadian and Tobagonian	27	0.23
West Indian	36	0.31
White:	10,020	87.17
Not Hispanic (9,287)	9,426	82.00
Hispanic (511)	594	5.17

Middletown

Place Type: Township
County: Bucks
Population: 44,141

Ancestry/Race	Number	%
African American/Black:	1,055	2.39
Not Hispanic (905)	1,024	2.32
Hispanic (22)	31	0.07
African, sub-Saharan:	49	0.11
African	49	0.11
Alaska Native tribes, not specified	1	0.00
Am. Ind. or Alaska Nat., not spec.	84	0.19
Albanian	19	0.04
Alsatian	9	0.02
American Indian tribes, specified:	83	0.19
Apache (1)	1	0.00
Blackfeet (2)	7	0.02
Cherokee (3)	16	0.04
Choctaw (1)	1	0.00
Comanche (1)	2	0.00
Delaware (2)	7	0.02
Iroquois (9)	21	0.05
Latin American Indians (2)	3	0.01
Lumbee (7)	7	0.02
Pueblo	1	0.00
Seminole	1	0.00
Sioux (1)	4	0.01
All other tribes (4)	10	0.02
American Indian tribes, not spec.	15	0.03
Arab:	185	0.42
Arab/Arabic	30	0.07
Egyptian	48	0.11
Lebanese	27	0.06
Palestinian	41	0.09
Syrian	28	0.06
Other Arab	11	0.02
Armenian	70	0.16
Asian:	1,207	2.73
Bangladeshi (7)	7	0.02
Cambodian (8)	8	0.02
Chinese, ex. Taiwanese (184)	198	0.45
Filipino (125)	173	0.39
Indian (365)	388	0.88
Indonesian (1)	1	0.00
Japanese (21)	31	0.07
Korean (264)	278	0.63
Pakistani (17)	36	0.08
Sri Lankan	1	0.00
Taiwanese (8)	8	0.02
Thai (9)	12	0.03
Vietnamese (17)	21	0.05
Other Asian, not specified (21)	45	0.10
Assyrian/Chaldean/Syriac	19	0.04
Australian	14	0.03
Austrian	125	0.28
Basque	11	0.02
Belgian	46	0.10
British	182	0.41
Canadian	91	0.21
Croatian	103	0.23
Czech	153	0.35
Czechoslovakian	78	0.18
Danish	136	0.31
Dutch	604	1.37
Eastern European	64	0.14

Notes: 1. Figures in the "Number" column do not add up to the total population due to: a) Ancestry/Race overlap — e.g. persons can report being both White and Irish, b) persons of Hispanic origin can report being any race, c) persons reporting two ancestries are counted in both categories. 2. Numbers in parentheses indicate the number of persons reporting this ancestry/race alone, not in combination with any other ancestry/race. 3. Refer to the Explanation of Data in the front of the book for more detailed information.

English	5,049	11.44
European	281	0.64
Finnish	28	0.06
French, except Basque	1,110	2.51
French Canadian	231	0.52
German	11,598	26.27
Greek	198	0.45
Hawaii Native/Pacific Islander:	13	0.03
Micronesian:	1	0.00
Guamanian/Chamorro	1	0.00
Polynesian: (1)	4	0.01
Native Hawaiian (1)	4	0.01
Other Pac. Isl., not spec. (1)	8	0.02
Hispanic or Latino:	757	1.71
Central American:	37	0.08
Costa Rican	7	0.02
Guatemalan	8	0.02
Honduran	9	0.02
Nicaraguan	1	0.00
Panamanian	4	0.01
Salvadoran	5	0.01
Other Central American	3	0.01
Cuban	37	0.08
Dominican Republic	17	0.04
Mexican	115	0.26
Puerto Rican	350	0.79
South American:	71	0.16
Argentinean	18	0.04
Bolivian	3	0.01
Chilean	4	0.01
Colombian	26	0.06
Ecuadorian	5	0.01
Peruvian	8	0.02
Uruguayan	1	0.00
Venezuelan	1	0.00
Other South American	5	0.01
Other Hispanic or Latino	130	0.29
Hungarian	434	0.98
Icelander	7	0.02
Irish	13,406	30.37
Italian	6,923	15.68
Latvian	68	0.15
Lithuanian	573	1.30
Macedonian	7	0.02
New Zealander	5	0.01
Northern European	23	0.05
Norwegian	101	0.23
Pennsylvania German	65	0.15
Polish	3,945	8.94
Portuguese	49	0.11
Romanian	106	0.24
Russian	1,134	2.57
Scandinavian	18	0.04
Scotch-Irish	630	1.43
Scottish	917	2.08
Serbian	7	0.02
Slavic	83	0.19
Slovak	499	1.13
Slovene	11	0.02
Swedish	302	0.68
Swiss	89	0.20
Turkish	20	0.05
Ukrainian	629	1.42
United States or American	1,712	3.88
Welsh	852	1.93
West Indian, excl. Hispanic:	116	0.26
Belizean	9	0.02
Haitian	69	0.16
Jamaican	22	0.05
Trinidadian and Tobagonian	16	0.04
White:	41,787	94.67
Not Hispanic (40,963)	41,279	93.52
Hispanic (469)	508	1.15
Yugoslavian	25	0.06

Middletown

Place Type: Township
County: Delaware
Population: 16,064

Ancestry/Race	Number	%
African American/Black:	551	3.43
Not Hispanic (490)	535	3.33
Hispanic (5)	16	0.10
African, sub-Saharan:	21	0.13
African	21	0.13
Am. Ind. or Alaska Nat., not spec.	7	0.04
Alsatian	8	0.05
American Indian tribes, specified:	25	0.16
Cherokee	9	0.06
Chickasaw	1	0.01
Choctaw	2	0.01
Cree	1	0.01
Delaware	4	0.02
Iroquois (3)	4	0.02
Lumbee	1	0.01
Navajo (1)	1	0.01
Seminole (1)	2	0.01
Arab:	35	0.22
Egyptian	28	0.17
Lebanese	7	0.04
Armenian	62	0.39
Asian:	324	2.02
Chinese, ex. Taiwanese (66)	79	0.49
Filipino (14)	26	0.16
Indian (97)	97	0.60
Japanese (1)	4	0.02
Korean (76)	91	0.57
Pakistani (6)	9	0.06
Sri Lankan (3)	3	0.02
Taiwanese (2)	2	0.01
Vietnamese (1)	3	0.02
Other Asian, not specified (6)	10	0.06
Australian	11	0.07
Austrian	68	0.42
Belgian	21	0.13
British	91	0.57
Canadian	19	0.12
Celtic	13	0.08
Croatian	7	0.04
Czech	20	0.12
Czechoslovakian	17	0.11
Danish	40	0.25
Dutch	262	1.63
Eastern European	33	0.21
English	2,651	16.50
European	86	0.54
French, except Basque	360	2.24
French Canadian	66	0.41
German	3,603	22.43
Greek	118	0.73
Hawaii Native/Pacific Islander:	7	0.04
Micronesian:	1	0.01
Guamanian/Chamorro	1	0.01
Polynesian:	2	0.01
Native Hawaiian	1	0.01
Samoan	1	0.01
Other Pac. Isl., not spec. (3)	4	0.02
Hispanic or Latino:	139	0.87
Central American:	6	0.04
Guatemalan	2	0.01
Honduran	3	0.02
Salvadoran	1	0.01
Cuban	18	0.11
Mexican	46	0.29
Puerto Rican	23	0.14
South American:	5	0.03
Argentinean	1	0.01
Colombian	3	0.02
Venezuelan	1	0.01
Other Hispanic or Latino	41	0.26
Hungarian	123	0.77
Iranian	7	0.04
Irish	4,262	26.53
Italian	2,755	17.15
Latvian	6	0.04
Lithuanian	129	0.80
Maltese	22	0.14
Norwegian	84	0.52
Pennsylvania German	47	0.29
Polish	854	5.32
Portuguese	25	0.16
Romanian	6	0.04
Russian	165	1.03
Scandinavian	32	0.20
Scotch-Irish	501	3.12
Scottish	401	2.50
Serbian	20	0.12
Slavic	31	0.19
Slovak	69	0.43
Swedish	141	0.88
Swiss	91	0.57
Turkish	5	0.03
Ukrainian	216	1.34
United States or American	657	4.09
Welsh	332	2.07
White:	15,245	94.90
Not Hispanic (15,049)	15,130	94.19
Hispanic (96)	115	0.72

Millcreek

Place Type: Township
County: Erie
Population: 52,129

Ancestry/Race	Number	%
African American/Black:	685	1.31
Not Hispanic (560)	666	1.28
Hispanic (10)	19	0.04
African, sub-Saharan:	109	0.21
African	55	0.11
Ethiopian	29	0.06
South African	7	0.01
Sudanese	18	0.03
Am. Ind. or Alaska Nat., not spec.	54	0.10
Albanian	32	0.06
American Indian tribes, specified:	64	0.12
Cherokee (4)	20	0.04
Cheyenne	1	0.00
Chickasaw (1)	1	0.00
Creek	1	0.00
Delaware	1	0.00
Iroquois (10)	24	0.05
Latin American Indians (1)	1	0.00
Lumbee (1)	4	0.01
Pima (1)	1	0.00
Pueblo	1	0.00
Sioux (5)	5	0.01
All other tribes (2)	4	0.01
American Indian tribes, not spec.	6	0.01
Arab:	152	0.29
Arab/Arabic	26	0.05
Iraqi	5	0.01
Lebanese	81	0.16
Syrian	40	0.08
Armenian	53	0.10
Asian:	827	1.59
Bangladeshi (3)	6	0.01
Chinese, ex. Taiwanese (145)	161	0.31
Filipino (69)	99	0.19
Indian (276)	294	0.56
Indonesian (6)	7	0.01
Japanese (25)	41	0.08
Korean (81)	95	0.18
Malaysian (1)	1	0.00
Pakistani (7)	10	0.02
Sri Lankan (10)	12	0.02
Taiwanese (7)	8	0.02
Thai (7)	14	0.03
Vietnamese (47)	55	0.11
Other Asian, specified (2)	2	0.00
Other Asian, not specified (8)	22	0.04
Australian	4	0.01

Notes: 1. Figures in the "Number" column do not add up to the total population due to: a) Ancestry/Race overlap — e.g. persons can report being both White and Irish, b) persons of Hispanic origin can report being any race, c) persons reporting two ancestries are counted in both categories. 2. Numbers in parentheses indicate the number of persons reporting this ancestry/race alone, not in combination with any other ancestry/race. 3. Refer to the Explanation of Data in the front of the book for more detailed information.

Austrian	126	0.24
Belgian	62	0.12
Brazilian	8	0.02
British	111	0.21
Canadian	79	0.15
Celtic	41	0.08
Croatian	66	0.13
Czech	269	0.52
Czechoslovakian	266	0.51
Danish	315	0.60
Dutch	733	1.41
Eastern European	31	0.06
English	5,270	10.11
European	193	0.37
Finnish	118	0.23
French, except Basque	1,309	2.51
French Canadian	335	0.64
German	18,194	34.91
Greek	275	0.53
Hawaii Native/Pacific Islander:	29	0.06
Micronesian: (1)	6	0.01
Guamanian/Chamorro	4	0.01
Other Micronesian (1)	2	0.00
Polynesian: (4)	13	0.02
Native Hawaiian (1)	6	0.01
Samoan	4	0.01
Tongan (3)	3	0.01
Other Pac. Isl., not spec. (2)	10	0.02
Hispanic or Latino:	518	0.99
Central American:	12	0.02
Costa Rican	1	0.00
Honduran	2	0.00
Panamanian	2	0.00
Salvadoran	7	0.01
Cuban	17	0.03
Dominican Republic	4	0.01
Mexican	187	0.36
Puerto Rican	138	0.26
South American:	50	0.10
Argentinean	6	0.01
Chilean	4	0.01
Colombian	22	0.04
Ecuadorian	9	0.02
Peruvian	2	0.00
Venezuelan	3	0.01
Other South American	4	0.01
Other Hispanic or Latino	110	0.21
Hungarian	714	1.37
Irish	9,064	17.39
Italian	8,506	16.32
Latvian	21	0.04
Lithuanian	142	0.27
Macedonian	6	0.01
New Zealander	7	0.01
Norwegian	169	0.32
Pennsylvania German	169	0.32
Polish	7,000	13.43
Portuguese	276	0.53
Romanian	177	0.34
Russian	700	1.34
Scandinavian	15	0.03
Scotch-Irish	1,239	2.38
Scottish	862	1.65
Serbian	59	0.11
Slavic	184	0.35
Slovak	928	1.78
Slovene	89	0.17
Swedish	1,552	2.98
Swiss	117	0.22
Ukrainian	417	0.80
United States or American	1,657	3.18
Welsh	426	0.82
West Indian, excl. Hispanic:	32	0.06
Haitian	4	0.01
Jamaican	8	0.02
Trinidadian and Tobagonian	20	0.04
White:	50,622	97.11
Not Hispanic (49,979)	50,242	96.38
Hispanic (353)	380	0.73
Yugoslavian	167	0.32

Montgomery

Place Type: Township
County: Montgomery
Population: 22,025

Ancestry/Race	Number	%
African American/Black:	911	4.14
Not Hispanic (844)	895	4.06
Hispanic (8)	16	0.07
African, sub-Saharan:	49	0.22
African	44	0.20
Cape Verdean	5	0.02
Am. Ind. or Alaska Nat., not spec.	33	0.15
Albanian	26	0.12
American Indian tribes, specified:	36	0.16
Blackfeet	1	0.00
Cherokee (1)	8	0.04
Cheyenne	1	0.00
Creek	2	0.01
Iroquois	3	0.01
Latin American Indians (1)	5	0.02
Pima	2	0.01
Sioux	2	0.01
All other tribes (10)	12	0.05
American Indian tribes, not spec.	1	0.00
Arab:	137	0.62
Arab/Arabic	49	0.22
Egyptian	22	0.10
Jordanian	27	0.12
Lebanese	18	0.08
Palestinian	13	0.06
Syrian	8	0.04
Armenian	272	1.23
Asian:	2,154	9.78
Bangladeshi (4)	11	0.05
Cambodian (14)	14	0.06
Chinese, ex. Taiwanese (330)	360	1.63
Filipino (100)	111	0.50
Indian (600)	632	2.87
Indonesian (1)	1	0.00
Japanese (12)	24	0.11
Korean (716)	755	3.43
Malaysian (1)	2	0.01
Pakistani (25)	25	0.11
Taiwanese (44)	45	0.20
Thai (4)	4	0.02
Vietnamese (127)	135	0.61
Other Asian, specified (1)	4	0.02
Other Asian, not specified (22)	31	0.14
Australian	37	0.17
Austrian	117	0.53
Belgian	16	0.07
Brazilian	31	0.14
British	146	0.66
Bulgarian	8	0.04
Canadian	34	0.15
Croatian	6	0.03
Czech	79	0.36
Czechoslovakian	54	0.25
Danish	24	0.11
Dutch	423	1.92
Eastern European	60	0.27
English	2,465	11.19
Estonian	10	0.05
European	132	0.60
Finnish	7	0.03
French, except Basque	404	1.83
French Canadian	26	0.12
German	4,992	22.67
Greek	58	0.26
Hawaii Native/Pacific Islander:	8	0.04
Micronesian:	1	0.00
Guamanian/Chamorro	1	0.00
Polynesian: (3)	4	0.02
Samoan (3)	4	0.02
Other Pac. Isl., specified	1	0.00
Other Pac. Isl., not spec.	2	0.01
Hispanic or Latino:	279	1.27
Central American:	7	0.03
Guatemalan	1	0.00
Nicaraguan	3	0.01
Panamanian	3	0.01
Cuban	34	0.15
Dominican Republic	1	0.00
Mexican	60	0.27
Puerto Rican	88	0.40
South American:	38	0.17
Argentinean	7	0.03
Bolivian	2	0.01
Chilean	1	0.00
Colombian	18	0.08
Ecuadorian	3	0.01
Peruvian	3	0.01
Venezuelan	3	0.01
Other South American	1	0.00
Other Hispanic or Latino	51	0.23
Hungarian	355	1.61
Icelander	6	0.03
Irish	5,203	23.62
Israeli	36	0.16
Italian	3,457	15.70
Latvian	13	0.06
Lithuanian	159	0.72
Northern European	7	0.03
Norwegian	132	0.60
Pennsylvania German	90	0.41
Polish	992	4.50
Portuguese	36	0.16
Romanian	39	0.18
Russian	554	2.52
Scandinavian	11	0.05
Scotch-Irish	371	1.68
Scottish	530	2.41
Serbian	8	0.04
Slavic	45	0.20
Slovak	155	0.70
Slovene	7	0.03
Swedish	289	1.31
Swiss	75	0.34
Turkish	19	0.09
Ukrainian	252	1.14
United States or American	785	3.56
Welsh	233	1.06
West Indian, excl. Hispanic:	46	0.21
Haitian	32	0.15
Jamaican	14	0.06
White:	19,020	86.36
Not Hispanic (18,644)	18,787	85.30
Hispanic (209)	233	1.06
Yugoslavian	30	0.14

Montgomeryville

Place Type: Census Designated Place
County: Montgomery
Population: 12,031

Ancestry/Race	Number	%
African American/Black:	422	3.51
Not Hispanic (387)	410	3.41
Hispanic (5)	12	0.10
African, sub-Saharan:	9	0.08
African	9	0.08
Am. Ind. or Alaska Nat., not spec.	17	0.14
Albanian	26	0.22
American Indian tribes, specified:	22	0.18
Cherokee (1)	6	0.05
Cheyenne	1	0.01
Creek	2	0.02
Iroquois	3	0.02
Latin American Indians (1)	4	0.03
Pima	2	0.02
Sioux	2	0.02
All other tribes (2)	2	0.02
Arab:	85	0.71
Arab/Arabic	37	0.31
Jordanian	27	0.23
Palestinian	13	0.11
Syrian	8	0.07

Notes: 1. Figures in the "Number" column do not add up to the total population due to: a) Ancestry/Race overlap — e.g. persons can report being both White and Irish, b) persons of Hispanic origin can report being any race, c) persons reporting two ancestries are counted in both categories. 2. Numbers in parentheses indicate the number of persons reporting this ancestry/race alone, not in combination with any other ancestry/race. 3. Refer to the Explanation of Data in the front of the book for more detailed information.

Ancestry/Race	Number	%
Armenian	78	0.65
Asian:	1,002	8.33
Bangladeshi (4)	11	0.09
Cambodian (8)	8	0.07
Chinese, ex. Taiwanese (133)	145	1.21
Filipino (41)	51	0.42
Indian (326)	349	2.90
Indonesian (1)	1	0.01
Japanese (5)	7	0.06
Korean (293)	307	2.55
Pakistani (10)	10	0.08
Taiwanese (28)	28	0.23
Thai (3)	3	0.02
Vietnamese (65)	66	0.55
Other Asian, specified	1	0.01
Other Asian, not specified (7)	15	0.12
Australian	37	0.31
Austrian	63	0.53
Belgian	16	0.13
Brazilian	31	0.26
British	119	1.00
Bulgarian	8	0.07
Canadian	20	0.17
Croatian	6	0.05
Czech	52	0.43
Czechoslovakian	32	0.27
Danish	9	0.08
Dutch	312	2.61
Eastern European	41	0.34
English	1,230	10.29
Estonian	10	0.08
European	32	0.27
Finnish	7	0.06
French, except Basque	203	1.70
French Canadian	26	0.22
German	2,900	24.25
Greek	48	0.40
Hawaii Native/Pacific Islander:	6	0.05
Micronesian:	1	0.01
Guamanian/Chamorro	1	0.01
Polynesian: (3)	3	0.02
Samoan (3)	3	0.02
Other Pac. Isl., specified	1	0.01
Other Pac. Isl., not spec.	1	0.01
Hispanic or Latino:	165	1.37
Central American:	4	0.03
Guatemalan	1	0.01
Nicaraguan	3	0.02
Cuban	22	0.18
Dominican Republic	1	0.01
Mexican	29	0.24
Puerto Rican	64	0.53
South American:	17	0.14
Argentinean	3	0.02
Bolivian	2	0.02
Colombian	6	0.05
Ecuadorian	3	0.02
Peruvian	2	0.02
Other South American	1	0.01
Other Hispanic or Latino	28	0.23
Hungarian	186	1.56
Irish	3,165	26.47
Italian	1,678	14.03
Latvian	13	0.11
Lithuanian	90	0.75
Northern European	7	0.06
Norwegian	98	0.82
Pennsylvania German	73	0.61
Polish	618	5.17
Portuguese	20	0.17
Romanian	15	0.13
Russian	229	1.92
Scandinavian	11	0.09
Scotch-Irish	218	1.82
Scottish	309	2.58
Slavic	24	0.20
Slovak	105	0.88
Swedish	221	1.85
Swiss	35	0.29
Turkish	19	0.16
Ukrainian	108	0.90
United States or American	385	3.22
Welsh	116	0.97
West Indian, excl. Hispanic:	37	0.31
Haitian	23	0.19
Jamaican	14	0.12
White:	10,613	88.21
Not Hispanic (10,416)	10,484	87.14
Hispanic (117)	129	1.07
Yugoslavian	30	0.25

Moon

Place Type: Township
County: Allegheny
Population: 22,290

Ancestry/Race	Number	%
African American/Black:	892	4.00
Not Hispanic (794)	882	3.96
Hispanic (4)	10	0.04
African, sub-Saharan:	89	0.40
African	52	0.23
Kenyan	13	0.06
Senegalese	12	0.05
Other sub-Saharan African	12	0.05
Am. Ind. or Alaska Nat., not spec.	30	0.13
American Indian tribes, specified:	41	0.18
Apache (1)	1	0.00
Blackfeet	1	0.00
Cherokee (5)	23	0.10
Chippewa	2	0.01
Choctaw	1	0.00
Cree	1	0.00
Creek	1	0.00
Iroquois	1	0.00
Latin American Indians	5	0.02
Navajo	5	0.00
Sioux	1	0.00
Yakama (1)	1	0.00
All other tribes	2	0.01
Arab:	186	0.83
Arab/Arabic	7	0.03
Lebanese	122	0.55
Syrian	57	0.26
Asian:	499	2.24
Cambodian (6)	6	0.03
Chinese, ex. Taiwanese (69)	82	0.37
Filipino (64)	81	0.36
Indian (174)	182	0.82
Indonesian (2)	2	0.01
Japanese (4)	14	0.06
Korean (50)	57	0.26
Malaysian (1)	1	0.00
Pakistani (18)	19	0.09
Sri Lankan (1)	5	0.02
Taiwanese (15)	15	0.07
Thai (5)	6	0.03
Vietnamese (14)	21	0.09
Other Asian, not specified (5)	8	0.04
Austrian	137	0.61
Belgian	50	0.22
Brazilian	12	0.05
British	36	0.16
Canadian	37	0.17
Carpatho Rusyn	30	0.13
Croatian	404	1.81
Czech	163	0.73
Czechoslovakian	121	0.54
Danish	8	0.04
Dutch	227	1.02
Eastern European	14	0.06
English	2,130	9.56
European	144	0.65
Finnish	48	0.22
French, except Basque	527	2.36
French Canadian	51	0.23
German	6,138	27.54
Greek	198	0.89
Hawaii Native/Pacific Islander:	22	0.10
Micronesian: (1)	1	0.00
Guamanian/Chamorro (1)	1	0.00
Polynesian: (3)	19	0.09
Native Hawaiian (2)	15	0.07
Samoan (1)	4	0.02
Other Pac. Isl., not spec.	2	0.01
Hispanic or Latino:	220	0.99
Central American:	3	0.01
Guatemalan	1	0.00
Honduran	1	0.00
Salvadoran	1	0.00
Cuban	13	0.06
Dominican Republic	3	0.01
Mexican	70	0.31
Puerto Rican	44	0.20
South American:	21	0.09
Argentinean	3	0.01
Chilean	9	0.04
Colombian	3	0.01
Ecuadorian	1	0.00
Peruvian	4	0.02
Other South American	1	0.00
Other Hispanic or Latino	66	0.30
Hungarian	337	1.51
Iranian	23	0.10
Irish	3,775	16.94
Italian	4,383	19.66
Latvian	9	0.04
Lithuanian	131	0.59
Norwegian	35	0.16
Pennsylvania German	5	0.02
Polish	2,140	9.60
Portuguese	42	0.19
Romanian	26	0.12
Russian	215	0.96
Scandinavian	38	0.17
Scotch-Irish	734	3.29
Scottish	361	1.62
Serbian	86	0.39
Slavic	78	0.35
Slovak	788	3.54
Slovene	135	0.61
Swedish	210	0.94
Swiss	48	0.22
Turkish	15	0.07
Ukrainian	314	1.41
United States or American	732	3.28
Welsh	277	1.24
West Indian, excl. Hispanic:	8	0.04
Barbadian	8	0.04
White:	20,960	94.03
Not Hispanic (20,607)	20,773	93.19
Hispanic (161)	187	0.84
Yugoslavian	23	0.10

Morrisville

Place Type: Borough
County: Bucks
Population: 10,023

Ancestry/Race	Number	%
African American/Black:	1,993	19.88
Not Hispanic (1,885)	1,951	19.47
Hispanic (33)	42	0.42
African, sub-Saharan:	334	3.33
African	184	1.84
Liberian	81	0.81
Nigerian	36	0.36
South African	9	0.09
Other sub-Saharan African	24	0.24
Am. Ind. or Alaska Nat., not spec.	20	0.20
American Indian tribes, specified:	40	0.40
Blackfeet	8	0.08
Cherokee	6	0.06
Crow (2)	2	0.02
Delaware	4	0.04
Iroquois (1)	10	0.10
Latin American Indians (1)	2	0.02
Lumbee	2	0.02

Notes: 1. Figures in the "Number" column do not add up to the total population due to: a) Ancestry/Race overlap — e.g. persons can report being both White and Irish, b) persons of Hispanic origin can report being any race, c) persons reporting two ancestries are counted in both categories. 2. Numbers in parentheses indicate the number of persons reporting this ancestry/race alone, not in combination with any other ancestry/race. 3. Refer to the Explanation of Data in the front of the book for more detailed information.

Pueblo (1)	1	0.01
Seminole	2	0.02
Sioux	1	0.01
All other tribes	2	0.02
American Indian tribes, not spec.	3	0.03
Asian:	152	1.52
Chinese, ex. Taiwanese (19)	33	0.33
Filipino (21)	29	0.29
Indian (54)	56	0.56
Indonesian (1)	3	0.03
Japanese (1)	5	0.05
Korean (10)	12	0.12
Pakistani (4)	5	0.05
Taiwanese (1)	1	0.01
Vietnamese (2)	4	0.04
Other Asian, specified (1)	1	0.01
Other Asian, not specified (2)	3	0.03
Austrian	20	0.20
British	15	0.15
Canadian	38	0.38
Celtic	13	0.13
Croatian	7	0.07
Czech	26	0.26
Czechoslovakian	94	0.94
Dutch	101	1.01
Eastern European	23	0.23
English	1,291	12.89
European	72	0.72
French, except Basque	126	1.26
French Canadian	53	0.53
German	2,161	21.57
Greek	46	0.46
Hawaii Native/Pacific Islander:	2	0.02
Other Pac. Isl., not spec.	2	0.02
Hispanic or Latino:	483	4.82
Central American:	60	0.60
Costa Rican	10	0.10
Guatemalan	36	0.36
Honduran	1	0.01
Panamanian	5	0.05
Salvadoran	7	0.07
Other Central American	1	0.01
Cuban	11	0.11
Dominican Republic	7	0.07
Mexican	30	0.30
Puerto Rican	276	2.75
South American:	23	0.23
Argentinean	6	0.06
Colombian	6	0.06
Ecuadorian	3	0.03
Peruvian	2	0.02
Uruguayan	1	0.01
Other South American	5	0.05
Other Hispanic or Latino	76	0.76
Hungarian	170	1.70
Irish	2,001	19.97
Italian	1,369	13.66
Lithuanian	85	0.85
Macedonian	22	0.22
Norwegian	32	0.32
Pennsylvania German	50	0.50
Polish	949	9.47
Portuguese	21	0.21
Russian	144	1.44
Scotch-Irish	157	1.57
Scottish	246	2.46
Slavic	19	0.19
Slovak	37	0.37
Swedish	116	1.16
Swiss	7	0.07
Turkish	8	0.08
Ukrainian	92	0.92
United States or American	351	3.50
Welsh	177	1.77
West Indian, excl. Hispanic:	126	1.26
Dutch West Indian	15	0.15
Haitian	39	0.39
Jamaican	52	0.52
Trinidadian and Tobagonian	8	0.08
West Indian	12	0.12
White:	7,730	77.12
Not Hispanic (7,394)	7,486	74.69
Hispanic (221)	244	2.43

Mount Lebanon

Place Type: Census Designated Place
County: Allegheny
Population: 33,017

Ancestry/Race	Number	%
African American/Black:	253	0.77
Not Hispanic (200)	249	0.75
Hispanic (2)	4	0.01
African, sub-Saharan:	11	0.03
African	4	0.01
South African	7	0.02
Am. Ind. or Alaska Nat., not spec.	13	0.04
Alsatian	8	0.02
American Indian tribes, specified:	24	0.07
Blackfeet (7)	8	0.02
Cherokee	4	0.01
Chippewa	1	0.00
Comanche	1	0.00
Latin American Indians (5)	5	0.02
Lumbee	1	0.00
Osage (1)	1	0.00
All other tribes (2)	3	0.01
American Indian tribes, not spec.	4	0.01
Arab:	410	1.24
Arab/Arabic	20	0.06
Egyptian	9	0.03
Jordanian	10	0.03
Lebanese	191	0.58
Palestinian	3	0.01
Syrian	114	0.35
Other Arab	63	0.19
Armenian	14	0.04
Asian:	879	2.66
Chinese, ex. Taiwanese (322)	346	1.05
Filipino (46)	63	0.19
Hmong	1	0.00
Indian (167)	201	0.61
Indonesian (3)	3	0.01
Japanese (31)	41	0.12
Korean (56)	75	0.23
Pakistani (6)	11	0.03
Sri Lankan	1	0.00
Taiwanese (13)	13	0.04
Thai (9)	10	0.03
Vietnamese (81)	90	0.27
Other Asian, specified (2)	2	0.01
Other Asian, not specified (9)	22	0.07
Australian	8	0.02
Austrian	372	1.13
Belgian	54	0.16
British	334	1.01
Bulgarian	105	0.32
Canadian	66	0.20
Carpatho Rusyn	36	0.11
Celtic	7	0.02
Croatian	264	0.80
Czech	140	0.42
Czechoslovakian	102	0.31
Danish	74	0.22
Dutch	290	0.88
Eastern European	176	0.53
English	4,030	12.21
European	454	1.38
Finnish	50	0.15
French, except Basque	834	2.53
French Canadian	54	0.16
German	8,706	26.37
Greek	506	1.53
Hawaii Native/Pacific Islander:	6	0.02
Micronesian: (1)	2	0.01
Guamanian/Chamorro (1)	2	0.01
Polynesian: (1)	1	0.00
Native Hawaiian (1)	1	0.00
Other Pac. Isl., not spec. (2)	3	0.01
Hispanic or Latino:	263	0.80
Central American:	14	0.04
Costa Rican	1	0.00
Guatemalan	5	0.02
Honduran	2	0.01
Nicaraguan	5	0.02
Panamanian	1	0.00
Cuban	19	0.06
Dominican Republic	6	0.02
Mexican	89	0.27
Puerto Rican	37	0.11
South American:	46	0.14
Argentinean	5	0.02
Chilean	4	0.01
Colombian	8	0.02
Ecuadorian	5	0.02
Peruvian	2	0.01
Venezuelan	15	0.05
Other South American	7	0.02
Other Hispanic or Latino	52	0.16
Hungarian	604	1.83
Iranian	28	0.08
Irish	7,623	23.09
Italian	4,915	14.89
Latvian	29	0.09
Lithuanian	383	1.16
Northern European	64	0.19
Norwegian	214	0.65
Pennsylvania German	41	0.12
Polish	2,350	7.12
Portuguese	16	0.05
Romanian	99	0.30
Russian	942	2.85
Scandinavian	47	0.14
Scotch-Irish	1,017	3.08
Scottish	940	2.85
Serbian	146	0.44
Slavic	13	0.04
Slovak	750	2.27
Slovene	47	0.14
Swedish	419	1.27
Swiss	254	0.77
Turkish	34	0.10
Ukrainian	320	0.97
United States or American	1,018	3.08
Welsh	739	2.24
White:	31,950	96.77
Not Hispanic (31,569)	31,735	96.12
Hispanic (197)	215	0.65
Yugoslavian	56	0.17

Mount Pleasant

Place Type: Township
County: Westmoreland
Population: 11,153

Ancestry/Race	Number	%
African American/Black:	40	0.36
Not Hispanic (28)	40	0.36
Am. Ind. or Alaska Nat., not spec.	8	0.07
American Indian tribes, specified:	14	0.13
Cherokee	6	0.05
Iroquois	6	0.05
Latin American Indians (1)	1	0.01
All other tribes	1	0.01
Arab:	51	0.46
Lebanese	21	0.19
Moroccan	7	0.06
Syrian	23	0.21
Asian:	12	0.11
Chinese, ex. Taiwanese (3)	4	0.04
Filipino (1)	1	0.01
Japanese	1	0.01
Korean (1)	4	0.04
Vietnamese	1	0.01
Other Asian, not specified	1	0.01
Austrian	42	0.38
Canadian	12	0.11
Carpatho Rusyn	21	0.19

Notes: 1. Figures in the "Number" column do not add up to the total population due to: a) Ancestry/Race overlap — e.g. persons can report being both White and Irish, b) persons of Hispanic origin can report being any race, c) persons reporting two ancestries are counted in both categories. 2. Numbers in parentheses indicate the number of persons reporting this ancestry/race alone, not in combination with any other ancestry/race. 3. Refer to the Explanation of Data in the front of the book for more detailed information.

Croatian	96	0.86
Czech	161	1.44
Czechoslovakian	91	0.81
Dutch	407	3.64
English	860	7.68
European	70	0.63
French, except Basque	83	0.74
German	3,100	27.70
Greek	37	0.33
Hawaii Native/Pacific Islander:	1	0.01
Polynesian: (1)	1	0.01
Native Hawaiian (1)	1	0.01
Hispanic or Latino:	44	0.39
Cuban	4	0.04
Mexican	16	0.14
South American:	3	0.03
Colombian	1	0.01
Peruvian	1	0.01
Venezuelan	1	0.01
Other Hispanic or Latino	21	0.19
Hungarian	343	3.06
Irish	1,324	11.83
Italian	918	8.20
Lithuanian	6	0.05
Norwegian	5	0.04
Pennsylvania German	104	0.93
Polish	1,889	16.88
Russian	86	0.77
Scotch-Irish	146	1.30
Scottish	175	1.56
Serbian	38	0.34
Slavic	49	0.44
Slovak	1,270	11.35
Slovene	8	0.07
Swedish	70	0.63
Swiss	7	0.06
Ukrainian	76	0.68
United States or American	369	3.30
Welsh	78	0.70
West Indian, excl. Hispanic:	16	0.14
West Indian	16	0.14
White:	11,105	99.57
Not Hispanic (11,024)	11,065	99.21
Hispanic (40)	40	0.36

Mountain Top

Place Type: Census Designated Place
County: Luzerne
Population: 15,269

Ancestry/Race	Number	%
African American/Black:	105	0.69
Not Hispanic (74)	97	0.64
Hispanic (8)	8	0.05
African, sub-Saharan:	6	0.04
Nigerian	6	0.04
Am. Ind. or Alaska Nat., not spec.	6	0.04
American Indian tribes, specified:	17	0.11
Blackfeet	1	0.01
Cherokee	2	0.01
Chippewa (2)	7	0.05
Choctaw	1	0.01
Iroquois	1	0.01
Latin American Indians (2)	2	0.01
Pueblo	3	0.02
Arab:	137	0.90
Lebanese	52	0.34
Syrian	85	0.56
Asian:	287	1.88
Bangladeshi (3)	3	0.02
Chinese, ex. Taiwanese (44)	58	0.38
Filipino (14)	21	0.14
Indian (103)	108	0.71
Indonesian (1)	1	0.01
Japanese (11)	12	0.08
Korean (33)	37	0.24
Pakistani (9)	10	0.07
Taiwanese (13)	16	0.10
Vietnamese (7)	10	0.07
Other Asian, not specified (6)	11	0.07
Austrian	139	0.91
Canadian	35	0.23
Croatian	8	0.05
Czech	54	0.35
Czechoslovakian	71	0.47
Danish	21	0.14
Dutch	509	3.34
Eastern European	7	0.05
English	1,509	9.89
European	29	0.19
French, except Basque	233	1.53
French Canadian	39	0.26
German	3,347	21.94
Greek	72	0.47
Hawaii Native/Pacific Islander:	7	0.05
Polynesian:	6	0.04
Native Hawaiian	6	0.04
Other Pac. Isl., not spec.	1	0.01
Hispanic or Latino:	165	1.08
Central American:	11	0.07
Guatemalan	3	0.02
Honduran	1	0.01
Nicaraguan	3	0.02
Panamanian	3	0.02
Salvadoran	1	0.01
Cuban	14	0.09
Mexican	19	0.12
Puerto Rican	68	0.45
South American:	13	0.09
Bolivian	3	0.02
Colombian	3	0.02
Peruvian	2	0.01
Other South American	5	0.03
Other Hispanic or Latino	40	0.26
Hungarian	91	0.60
Irish	2,676	17.54
Israeli	6	0.04
Italian	2,178	14.28
Lithuanian	350	2.29
Norwegian	76	0.50
Pennsylvania German	396	2.60
Polish	4,047	26.53
Portuguese	3	0.02
Romanian	10	0.07
Russian	474	3.11
Scandinavian	4	0.03
Scotch-Irish	91	0.60
Scottish	181	1.19
Serbian	15	0.10
Slavic	14	0.09
Slovak	649	4.25
Slovene	6	0.04
Swedish	62	0.41
Swiss	57	0.37
Ukrainian	305	2.00
United States or American	572	3.75
Welsh	1,133	7.43
West Indian, excl. Hispanic:	7	0.05
Haitian	7	0.05
White:	14,891	97.52
Not Hispanic (14,692)	14,761	96.67
Hispanic (122)	130	0.85
Yugoslavian	8	0.05

Muhlenberg

Place Type: Township
County: Berks
Population: 16,305

Ancestry/Race	Number	%
African American/Black:	250	1.53
Not Hispanic (189)	228	1.40
Hispanic (9)	22	0.13
African, sub-Saharan:	6	0.04
Other sub-Saharan African	6	0.04
Am. Ind. or Alaska Nat., not spec.	10	0.06
American Indian tribes, specified:	32	0.20
Blackfeet	4	0.02
Cherokee (3)	20	0.12
Choctaw (1)	2	0.01
Delaware	2	0.01
Seminole	1	0.01
All other tribes	3	0.02
American Indian tribes, not spec.	7	0.04
Arab:	23	0.14
Egyptian	16	0.10
Other Arab	7	0.04
Asian:	144	0.88
Chinese, ex. Taiwanese (33)	37	0.23
Filipino (6)	7	0.04
Indian (28)	36	0.22
Japanese (4)	8	0.05
Korean (4)	4	0.02
Thai (3)	6	0.04
Vietnamese (33)	40	0.25
Other Asian, not specified (4)	6	0.04
Australian	6	0.04
Austrian	113	0.69
British	19	0.12
Canadian	7	0.04
Cypriot	9	0.06
Czech	29	0.18
Czechoslovakian	32	0.20
Danish	15	0.09
Dutch	558	3.43
Eastern European	8	0.05
English	868	5.33
European	38	0.23
Finnish	4	0.02
French, except Basque	326	2.00
French Canadian	20	0.12
German	6,849	42.06
Greek	158	0.97
Hawaii Native/Pacific Islander:	7	0.04
Polynesian:	7	0.04
Native Hawaiian	7	0.04
Hispanic or Latino:	638	3.91
Central American:	11	0.07
Costa Rican	1	0.01
Guatemalan	4	0.02
Nicaraguan	2	0.01
Panamanian	1	0.01
Salvadoran	3	0.02
Cuban	1	0.01
Dominican Republic	9	0.06
Mexican	209	1.28
Puerto Rican	337	2.07
South American:	10	0.06
Bolivian	1	0.01
Colombian	3	0.02
Ecuadorian	1	0.01
Peruvian	3	0.02
Venezuelan	1	0.01
Other South American	1	0.01
Other Hispanic or Latino	61	0.37
Hungarian	30	0.18
Irish	1,995	12.25
Italian	2,093	12.85
Lithuanian	100	0.61
Norwegian	15	0.09
Pennsylvania German	761	4.67
Polish	1,336	8.20
Portuguese	7	0.04
Romanian	29	0.18
Russian	111	0.68
Scotch-Irish	111	0.68
Scottish	192	1.18
Slavic	23	0.14
Slovak	117	0.72
Slovene	6	0.04
Swedish	107	0.66
Swiss	73	0.45
Turkish	8	0.05
Ukrainian	131	0.80
United States or American	875	5.37
Welsh	304	1.87
West Indian, excl. Hispanic:	19	0.12
Barbadian	19	0.12

Notes: 1. Figures in the "Number" column do not add up to the total population due to: a) Ancestry/Race overlap — e.g. persons can report being both White and Irish, b) persons of Hispanic origin can report being any race, c) persons reporting two ancestries are counted in both categories. 2. Numbers in parentheses indicate the number of persons reporting this ancestry/race alone, not in combination with any other ancestry/race. 3. Refer to the Explanation of Data in the front of the book for more detailed information.

White:	15,693	96.25
Not Hispanic (15,251)	15,342	94.09
Hispanic (317)	351	2.15
Yugoslavian	20	0.12

Munhall

Place Type: Borough
County: Allegheny
Population: 12,264

Ancestry/Race	Number	%
African American/Black:	482	3.93
Not Hispanic (413)	477	3.89
Hispanic (2)	5	0.04
African, sub-Saharan:	24	0.20
African	24	0.20
Am. Ind. or Alaska Nat., not spec.	20	0.16
American Indian tribes, specified:	26	0.21
Blackfeet	3	0.02
Cherokee	8	0.07
Delaware	2	0.02
Iroquois	2	0.02
Latin American Indians	4	0.03
Ottawa (1)	1	0.01
Sioux	3	0.02
Ute	3	0.02
American Indian tribes, not spec.	2	0.02
Arab:	71	0.58
Lebanese	8	0.07
Syrian	63	0.51
Armenian	8	0.07
Asian:	93	0.76
Chinese, ex. Taiwanese (10)	13	0.11
Filipino (7)	8	0.07
Hmong (3)	3	0.02
Indian (7)	7	0.06
Japanese (4)	8	0.07
Korean (5)	11	0.09
Laotian (1)	3	0.02
Pakistani (1)	1	0.01
Vietnamese (33)	36	0.29
Other Asian, specified	2	0.02
Other Asian, not specified (1)	1	0.01
Austrian	63	0.51
Belgian	7	0.06
British	24	0.20
Bulgarian	18	0.15
Canadian	9	0.07
Carpatho Rusyn	7	0.06
Celtic	5	0.04
Croatian	181	1.48
Czech	75	0.61
Czechoslovakian	103	0.84
Dutch	79	0.64
Eastern European	13	0.11
English	1,034	8.43
European	61	0.50
French, except Basque	161	1.31
French Canadian	11	0.09
German	2,609	21.27
Greek	28	0.23
Hawaii Native/Pacific Islander:	3	0.02
Micronesian:	1	0.01
Guamanian/Chamorro	1	0.01
Other Pac. Isl., specified	2	0.02
Hispanic or Latino:	98	0.80
Central American:	3	0.02
Guatemalan	3	0.02
Cuban	1	0.01
Mexican	45	0.37
Puerto Rican	20	0.16
South American:	1	0.01
Chilean	1	0.01
Other Hispanic or Latino	28	0.23
Hungarian	938	7.65
Irish	2,779	22.66
Italian	1,307	10.66
Lithuanian	156	1.27
Macedonian	40	0.33
Northern European	5	0.04
Norwegian	7	0.06
Pennsylvania German	33	0.27
Polish	927	7.56
Romanian	14	0.11
Russian	162	1.32
Scotch-Irish	277	2.26
Scottish	287	2.34
Serbian	71	0.58
Slavic	69	0.56
Slovak	2,363	19.27
Swedish	53	0.43
Ukrainian	88	0.72
United States or American	304	2.48
Welsh	243	1.98
West Indian, excl. Hispanic:	5	0.04
West Indian	5	0.04
White:	11,733	95.67
Not Hispanic (11,558)	11,659	95.07
Hispanic (66)	74	0.60

Municipality of Monroeville

Place Type: Borough
County: Allegheny
Population: 29,349

Ancestry/Race	Number	%
African American/Black:	2,639	8.99
Not Hispanic (2,425)	2,617	8.92
Hispanic (7)	22	0.07
African, sub-Saharan:	214	0.73
African	181	0.62
Nigerian	13	0.04
South African	20	0.07
Am. Ind. or Alaska Nat., not spec.	54	0.18
Albanian	9	0.03
American Indian tribes, specified:	76	0.26
Blackfeet	3	0.01
Cherokee (5)	37	0.13
Chippewa (1)	3	0.01
Creek (1)	1	0.00
Crow	2	0.01
Delaware (1)	1	0.00
Iroquois (4)	5	0.02
Latin American Indians (1)	1	0.00
Lumbee	1	0.00
Navajo (2)	3	0.01
Pueblo (1)	5	0.02
Seminole	5	0.02
Sioux (1)	2	0.01
All other tribes (2)	7	0.02
American Indian tribes, not spec.	2	0.01
Arab:	224	0.76
Arab/Arabic	24	0.08
Lebanese	81	0.28
Moroccan	21	0.07
Palestinian	7	0.02
Syrian	84	0.29
Other Arab	7	0.02
Armenian	6	0.02
Asian:	1,441	4.91
Bangladeshi (7)	7	0.02
Chinese, ex. Taiwanese (233)	262	0.89
Filipino (30)	45	0.15
Indian (730)	783	2.67
Indonesian (13)	13	0.04
Japanese (25)	34	0.12
Korean (109)	128	0.44
Malaysian (1)	1	0.00
Pakistani (57)	71	0.24
Taiwanese (19)	37	0.13
Thai (4)	4	0.01
Vietnamese (9)	12	0.04
Other Asian, not specified (26)	44	0.15
Austrian	181	0.62
Belgian	33	0.11
Brazilian	12	0.04
British	67	0.23
Bulgarian	6	0.02
Canadian	30	0.10
Carpatho Rusyn	47	0.16
Celtic	19	0.06
Croatian	419	1.43
Czech	104	0.35
Czechoslovakian	134	0.46
Danish	35	0.12
Dutch	263	0.90
Eastern European	65	0.22
English	2,679	9.13
European	143	0.49
Finnish	9	0.03
French, except Basque	527	1.80
French Canadian	63	0.21
German	6,911	23.55
Greek	312	1.06
Hawaii Native/Pacific Islander:	27	0.09
Micronesian: (2)	2	0.01
Guamanian/Chamorro (2)	2	0.01
Polynesian: (9)	18	0.06
Native Hawaiian (2)	5	0.02
Samoan (7)	12	0.04
Other Polynesian	1	0.00
Other Pac. Isl., not spec. (2)	7	0.02
Hispanic or Latino:	225	0.77
Central American:	6	0.02
Costa Rican	2	0.01
Guatemalan	2	0.01
Panamanian	2	0.01
Cuban	12	0.04
Mexican	75	0.26
Puerto Rican	55	0.19
South American:	32	0.11
Argentinean	2	0.01
Chilean	1	0.00
Colombian	7	0.02
Ecuadorian	3	0.01
Paraguayan	1	0.00
Peruvian	12	0.04
Uruguayan	5	0.02
Venezuelan	1	0.00
Other Hispanic or Latino	45	0.15
Hungarian	565	1.93
Iranian	41	0.14
Irish	4,246	14.47
Italian	4,735	16.13
Lithuanian	163	0.56
Macedonian	14	0.05
Norwegian	43	0.15
Pennsylvania German	25	0.09
Polish	2,330	7.94
Portuguese	17	0.06
Romanian	67	0.23
Russian	523	1.78
Scandinavian	5	0.02
Scotch-Irish	734	2.50
Scottish	753	2.57
Serbian	195	0.66
Slavic	140	0.48
Slovak	1,297	4.42
Slovene	105	0.36
Swedish	258	0.88
Swiss	127	0.43
Turkish	39	0.13
Ukrainian	268	0.91
United States or American	907	3.09
Welsh	308	1.05
West Indian, excl. Hispanic:	87	0.30
Barbadian	22	0.07
Haitian	10	0.03
Jamaican	51	0.17
West Indian	4	0.01
White:	25,398	86.54
Not Hispanic (24,971)	25,236	85.99
Hispanic (147)	162	0.55
Yugoslavian	72	0.25

Notes: 1. Figures in the "Number" column do not add up to the total population due to: a) Ancestry/Race overlap — e.g. persons can report being both White and Irish, b) persons of Hispanic origin can report being any race, c) persons reporting two ancestries are counted in both categories. 2. Numbers in parentheses indicate the number of persons reporting this ancestry/race alone, not in combination with any other ancestry/race. 3. Refer to the Explanation of Data in the front of the book for more detailed information.

Municipality of Murrysville

Place Type: Borough
County: Westmoreland
Population: 18,872

Ancestry/Race	Number	%
African American/Black:	148	0.78
Not Hispanic (111)	143	0.76
Hispanic (5)	5	0.03
African, sub-Saharan:	89	0.47
African	63	0.33
South African	26	0.14
Am. Ind. or Alaska Nat., not spec.	18	0.10
Albanian	40	0.21
Alsatian	9	0.05
American Indian tribes, specified:	13	0.07
Blackfeet	1	0.01
Cherokee (2)	3	0.02
Choctaw (2)	2	0.01
Iroquois	2	0.01
Sioux (5)	5	0.03
American Indian tribes, not spec.	6	0.03
Arab:	95	0.50
Lebanese	88	0.47
Syrian	7	0.04
Armenian	11	0.06
Asian:	674	3.57
Chinese, ex. Taiwanese (240)	255	1.35
Filipino (6)	17	0.09
Indian (225)	244	1.29
Japanese (31)	34	0.18
Korean (55)	58	0.31
Pakistani (22)	27	0.14
Sri Lankan (8)	8	0.04
Taiwanese (11)	11	0.06
Thai (6)	6	0.03
Vietnamese (2)	4	0.02
Other Asian, specified (1)	4	0.02
Other Asian, not specified (5)	6	0.03
Austrian	117	0.62
British	87	0.46
Canadian	15	0.08
Croatian	295	1.56
Czech	171	0.91
Czechoslovakian	160	0.85
Danish	50	0.27
Dutch	166	0.88
Eastern European	78	0.41
English	1,811	9.60
European	59	0.31
Finnish	32	0.17
French, except Basque	331	1.76
French Canadian	22	0.12
German	5,398	28.63
Greek	120	0.64
Hawaii Native/Pacific Islander:	7	0.04
Micronesian: (2)	2	0.01
Guamanian/Chamorro (2)	2	0.01
Polynesian:	1	0.01
Native Hawaiian	1	0.01
Other Pac. Isl., specified	3	0.02
Other Pac. Isl., not spec.	1	0.01
Hispanic or Latino:	106	0.56
Central American:	3	0.02
Nicaraguan	2	0.01
Panamanian	1	0.01
Cuban	6	0.03
Dominican Republic	3	0.02
Mexican	50	0.26
Puerto Rican	23	0.12
South American:	13	0.07
Argentinean	1	0.01
Colombian	4	0.02
Ecuadorian	4	0.02
Paraguayan	1	0.01
Venezuelan	3	0.02
Other Hispanic or Latino	8	0.04
Hungarian	423	2.24
Irish	3,109	16.49
Italian	3,085	16.36
Latvian	16	0.08
Lithuanian	141	0.75
Northern European	17	0.09
Norwegian	120	0.64
Pennsylvania German	55	0.29
Polish	1,912	10.14
Portuguese	14	0.07
Romanian	31	0.16
Russian	236	1.25
Scotch-Irish	558	2.96
Scottish	541	2.87
Serbian	90	0.48
Slavic	26	0.14
Slovak	876	4.65
Slovene	233	1.24
Swedish	234	1.24
Swiss	97	0.51
Turkish	48	0.25
Ukrainian	222	1.18
United States or American	669	3.55
Welsh	362	1.92
West Indian, excl. Hispanic:	47	0.25
Haitian	8	0.04
Jamaican	22	0.12
West Indian	17	0.09
White:	18,092	95.87
Not Hispanic (17,918)	18,008	95.42
Hispanic (82)	84	0.45

Nanticoke

Place Type: City
County: Luzerne
Population: 10,955

Ancestry/Race	Number	%
African American/Black:	45	0.41
Not Hispanic (29)	44	0.40
Hispanic (1)	1	0.01
Am. Ind. or Alaska Nat., not spec.	12	0.11
American Indian tribes, specified:	10	0.09
Apache (1)	1	0.01
Cherokee (1)	4	0.04
Iroquois (1)	1	0.01
All other tribes (3)	4	0.04
Arab:	72	0.66
Egyptian	7	0.06
Lebanese	29	0.26
Syrian	36	0.33
Asian:	38	0.35
Chinese, ex. Taiwanese (2)	4	0.04
Filipino (4)	4	0.04
Indian (12)	13	0.12
Japanese (4)	6	0.05
Korean (2)	5	0.05
Vietnamese (4)	4	0.04
Other Asian, not specified	2	0.02
Austrian	14	0.13
British	20	0.18
Croatian	6	0.05
Czech	26	0.24
Czechoslovakian	13	0.12
Dutch	341	3.11
English	568	5.17
European	4	0.04
Finnish	8	0.07
French, except Basque	59	0.54
German	1,419	12.92
Greek	7	0.06
Hawaii Native/Pacific Islander:	1	0.01
Polynesian: (1)	1	0.01
Native Hawaiian (1)	1	0.01
Hispanic or Latino:	49	0.45
Cuban	1	0.01
Mexican	16	0.15
Puerto Rican	19	0.17
South American:	2	0.02
Colombian	2	0.02
Other Hispanic or Latino	11	0.10
Hungarian	28	0.25
Irish	1,183	10.77
Italian	919	8.37
Lithuanian	318	2.90
Pennsylvania German	150	1.37
Polish	5,444	49.58
Portuguese	14	0.13
Russian	218	1.99
Scotch-Irish	28	0.25
Scottish	44	0.40
Slavic	45	0.41
Slovak	585	5.33
Slovene	23	0.21
Swedish	53	0.48
Ukrainian	301	2.74
United States or American	269	2.45
Welsh	702	6.39
White:	10,865	99.18
Not Hispanic (10,802)	10,833	98.89
Hispanic (26)	32	0.29
Yugoslavian	20	0.18

Nether Providence Township

Place Type: Census Designated Place
County: Delaware
Population: 13,456

Ancestry/Race	Number	%
African American/Black:	868	6.45
Not Hispanic (811)	851	6.32
Hispanic (13)	17	0.13
African, sub-Saharan:	106	0.79
African	71	0.53
Ghanian	15	0.11
Other sub-Saharan African	20	0.15
Am. Ind. or Alaska Nat., not spec.	22	0.16
Albanian	14	0.10
American Indian tribes, specified:	32	0.24
Blackfeet	4	0.03
Cherokee (1)	14	0.10
Choctaw	4	0.03
Delaware	3	0.02
Iroquois (1)	2	0.01
Latin American Indians (1)	1	0.01
Sioux	2	0.01
All other tribes	2	0.01
Arab:	107	0.80
Egyptian	13	0.10
Lebanese	80	0.59
Syrian	14	0.10
Armenian	61	0.45
Asian:	363	2.70
Bangladeshi (7)	7	0.05
Cambodian (2)	2	0.01
Chinese, ex. Taiwanese (117)	129	0.96
Filipino (19)	25	0.19
Indian (83)	91	0.68
Japanese (17)	22	0.16
Korean (48)	53	0.39
Taiwanese (1)	2	0.01
Thai (5)	9	0.07
Vietnamese (10)	11	0.08
Other Asian, not specified (2)	12	0.09
Austrian	39	0.29
Belgian	18	0.13
Brazilian	8	0.06
British	83	0.62
Bulgarian	12	0.09
Canadian	21	0.16
Croatian	32	0.24
Czech	39	0.29
Czechoslovakian	29	0.22
Danish	12	0.09
Dutch	145	1.08
Eastern European	91	0.68
English	1,908	14.18

Notes: 1. Figures in the "Number" column do not add up to the total population due to: a) Ancestry/Race overlap — e.g. persons can report being both White and Irish, b) persons of Hispanic origin can report being any race, c) persons reporting two ancestries are counted in both categories. 2. Numbers in parentheses indicate the number of persons reporting this ancestry/race alone, not in combination with any other ancestry/race. 3. Refer to the Explanation of Data in the front of the book for more detailed information.

Ancestry/Race	Number	%
European	173	1.29
Finnish	8	0.06
French, except Basque	228	1.69
French Canadian	25	0.19
German	2,525	18.76
Greek	141	1.05
Hawaii Native/Pacific Islander:	7	0.05
Polynesian: (4)	5	0.04
Native Hawaiian (4)	5	0.04
Other Pac. Isl., not spec. (1)	2	0.01
Hispanic or Latino:	152	1.13
Central American:	8	0.06
Costa Rican	2	0.01
Guatemalan	1	0.01
Honduran	4	0.03
Panamanian	1	0.01
Cuban	10	0.07
Dominican Republic	1	0.01
Mexican	30	0.22
Puerto Rican	36	0.27
South American:	31	0.23
Argentinean	8	0.06
Bolivian	3	0.02
Chilean	9	0.07
Colombian	1	0.01
Ecuadorian	2	0.01
Peruvian	3	0.02
Venezuelan	4	0.03
Other South American	1	0.01
Other Hispanic or Latino	36	0.27
Hungarian	149	1.11
Iranian	76	0.56
Irish	3,231	24.01
Israeli	31	0.23
Italian	2,228	16.56
Lithuanian	120	0.89
Northern European	84	0.62
Norwegian	146	1.09
Pennsylvania German	20	0.15
Polish	513	3.81
Portuguese	7	0.05
Romanian	13	0.10
Russian	394	2.93
Scotch-Irish	247	1.84
Scottish	393	2.92
Slavic	5	0.04
Slovak	37	0.27
Soviet Union	27	0.20
Swedish	206	1.53
Swiss	44	0.33
Turkish	22	0.16
Ukrainian	319	2.37
United States or American	521	3.87
Welsh	201	1.49
West Indian, excl. Hispanic:	28	0.21
Jamaican	22	0.16
Trinidadian and Tobagonian	6	0.04
White:	12,246	91.01
Not Hispanic (12,028)	12,142	90.23
Hispanic (93)	104	0.77

New Britain

Place Type: Township
County: Bucks
Population: 10,698

Ancestry/Race	Number	%
Acadian/Cajun	4	0.04
African American/Black:	164	1.53
Not Hispanic (143)	161	1.50
Hispanic (1)	3	0.03
African, sub-Saharan:	14	0.13
Other sub-Saharan African	14	0.13
Am. Ind. or Alaska Nat., not spec.	11	0.10
Albanian	8	0.07
American Indian tribes, specified:	17	0.16
Blackfeet (3)	3	0.03
Cherokee (3)	5	0.05
Delaware	3	0.03
Latin American Indians (1)	2	0.02
Sioux	3	0.03
All other tribes (1)	1	0.01
Arab:	25	0.23
Egyptian	6	0.06
Lebanese	19	0.18
Armenian	12	0.11
Asian:	167	1.56
Chinese, ex. Taiwanese (19)	26	0.24
Filipino (2)	9	0.08
Indian (24)	33	0.31
Indonesian (1)	1	0.01
Japanese (4)	12	0.11
Korean (40)	44	0.41
Taiwanese (1)	1	0.01
Thai (1)	1	0.01
Vietnamese (26)	27	0.25
Other Asian, not specified (4)	13	0.12
Australian	5	0.05
Austrian	96	0.90
Belgian	14	0.13
British	20	0.19
Canadian	26	0.24
Carpatho Rusyn	4	0.04
Croatian	22	0.21
Cypriot	31	0.29
Czech	83	0.78
Czechoslovakian	53	0.50
Danish	17	0.16
Dutch	194	1.81
Eastern European	14	0.13
English	1,562	14.60
European	82	0.77
French, except Basque	198	1.85
French Canadian	44	0.41
German	3,244	30.32
Greek	61	0.57
Hawaii Native/Pacific Islander:	1	0.01
Polynesian:	1	0.01
Native Hawaiian	1	0.01
Hispanic or Latino:	137	1.28
Central American:	7	0.07
Costa Rican	1	0.01
Guatemalan	3	0.03
Honduran	2	0.02
Salvadoran	1	0.01
Cuban	8	0.07
Dominican Republic	4	0.04
Mexican	28	0.26
Puerto Rican	50	0.47
South American:	12	0.11
Argentinean	3	0.03
Colombian	5	0.05
Ecuadorian	3	0.03
Other South American	1	0.01
Other Hispanic or Latino	28	0.26
Hungarian	142	1.33
Irish	3,014	28.17
Italian	1,439	13.45
Latvian	6	0.06
Lithuanian	51	0.48
Luxemburger	4	0.04
Northern European	12	0.11
Norwegian	18	0.17
Pennsylvania German	123	1.15
Polish	617	5.77
Portuguese	22	0.21
Romanian	28	0.26
Russian	195	1.82
Scandinavian	9	0.08
Scotch-Irish	196	1.83
Scottish	205	1.92
Slavic	53	0.50
Slovak	96	0.90
Slovene	5	0.05
Swedish	161	1.50
Swiss	44	0.41
Ukrainian	129	1.21
United States or American	662	6.19
Welsh	268	2.51
West Indian, excl. Hispanic:	5	0.05
Other West Indian	5	0.05
White:	10,366	96.90
Not Hispanic (10,206)	10,268	95.98
Hispanic (92)	98	0.92
Yugoslavian	28	0.26

New Castle

Place Type: City
County: Lawrence
Population: 26,309

Ancestry/Race	Number	%
African American/Black:	3,151	11.98
Not Hispanic (2,820)	3,115	11.84
Hispanic (19)	36	0.14
African, sub-Saharan:	150	0.57
African	150	0.57
Am. Ind. or Alaska Nat., not spec.	50	0.19
American Indian tribes, specified:	94	0.36
Apache	6	0.02
Blackfeet (2)	11	0.04
Cherokee (7)	54	0.21
Cheyenne	1	0.00
Chippewa	1	0.00
Choctaw (1)	1	0.00
Iroquois (4)	9	0.03
Seminole	1	0.00
Sioux (1)	5	0.02
All other tribes (1)	5	0.02
American Indian tribes, not spec.	6	0.02
Arab:	507	1.93
Arab/Arabic	13	0.05
Egyptian	14	0.05
Lebanese	235	0.89
Moroccan	5	0.02
Palestinian	17	0.06
Syrian	218	0.83
Other Arab	5	0.02
Asian:	92	0.35
Chinese, ex. Taiwanese (12)	12	0.05
Filipino (13)	23	0.09
Indian (5)	14	0.05
Japanese (2)	12	0.05
Korean (10)	18	0.07
Taiwanese	1	0.00
Vietnamese (4)	5	0.02
Other Asian, not specified	7	0.03
Austrian	29	0.11
Belgian	20	0.08
British	24	0.09
Canadian	6	0.02
Carpatho Rusyn	17	0.06
Celtic	7	0.03
Croatian	148	0.56
Czech	35	0.13
Czechoslovakian	21	0.08
Danish	11	0.04
Dutch	426	1.62
Eastern European	12	0.05
English	1,622	6.16
European	22	0.08
Finnish	66	0.25
French, except Basque	264	1.00
French Canadian	32	0.12
German	5,029	19.11
Greek	270	1.03
Hawaii Native/Pacific Islander:	7	0.03
Micronesian:	1	0.00
Guamanian/Chamorro	1	0.00
Polynesian: (2)	5	0.02
Native Hawaiian (1)	3	0.01
Other Polynesian (1)	2	0.01
Other Pac. Isl., not spec.	1	0.00
Hispanic or Latino:	199	0.76
Cuban	8	0.03
Dominican Republic	8	0.03
Mexican	71	0.27
Puerto Rican	65	0.25

Notes: 1. Figures in the "Number" column do not add up to the total population due to: a) Ancestry/Race overlap — e.g. persons can report being both White and Irish, b) persons of Hispanic origin can report being any race, c) persons reporting two ancestries are counted in both categories. 2. Numbers in parentheses indicate the number of persons reporting this ancestry/race alone, not in combination with any other ancestry/race. 3. Refer to the Explanation of Data in the front of the book for more detailed information.

South American:	4	0.02
Argentinean	1	0.00
Chilean	1	0.00
Paraguayan	1	0.00
Venezuelan	1	0.00
Other Hispanic or Latino	43	0.16
Hungarian	228	0.87
Irish	3,770	14.33
Italian	8,127	30.89
Latvian	7	0.03
Lithuanian	34	0.13
Norwegian	13	0.05
Pennsylvania German	31	0.12
Polish	1,808	6.87
Portuguese	21	0.08
Romanian	117	0.44
Russian	245	0.93
Scandinavian	4	0.02
Scotch-Irish	731	2.78
Scottish	325	1.24
Serbian	13	0.05
Slavic	113	0.43
Slovak	483	1.84
Slovene	34	0.13
Swedish	93	0.35
Swiss	10	0.04
Turkish	7	0.03
Ukrainian	79	0.30
United States or American	816	3.10
Welsh	476	1.81
West Indian, excl. Hispanic:	10	0.04
Trinidadian and Tobagonian	10	0.04
White:	23,275	88.47
Not Hispanic (22,729)	23,145	87.97
Hispanic (100)	130	0.49
Yugoslavian	11	0.04

New Kensington

Place Type: City
County: Westmoreland
Population: 14,701

Ancestry/Race	Number	%
African American/Black:	1,637	11.14
Not Hispanic (1,428)	1,616	10.99
Hispanic (19)	21	0.14
African, sub-Saharan:	79	0.54
African	64	0.43
South African	15	0.10
Am. Ind. or Alaska Nat., not spec.	25	0.17
American Indian tribes, specified:	41	0.28
Blackfeet	2	0.01
Cherokee (3)	21	0.14
Choctaw	2	0.01
Crow	1	0.01
Iroquois (1)	4	0.03
Latin American Indians (1)	1	0.01
Navajo (2)	3	0.02
Potawatomi (1)	1	0.01
Seminole	3	0.02
Sioux	1	0.01
All other tribes (1)	2	0.01
American Indian tribes, not spec.	2	0.01
Arab:	331	2.25
Arab/Arabic	12	0.08
Lebanese	65	0.44
Syrian	254	1.72
Armenian	14	0.10
Asian:	48	0.33
Chinese, ex. Taiwanese (19)	20	0.14
Filipino (2)	3	0.02
Indian (4)	7	0.05
Japanese (1)	6	0.04
Korean (2)	4	0.03
Malaysian	1	0.01
Other Asian, not specified (4)	7	0.05
Austrian	48	0.33
Belgian	151	1.03
British	34	0.23
Canadian	19	0.13
Croatian	79	0.54
Czech	56	0.38
Czechoslovakian	144	0.98
Danish	12	0.08
Dutch	175	1.19
English	1,113	7.56
European	6	0.04
Finnish	17	0.12
French, except Basque	178	1.21
French Canadian	12	0.08
German	3,377	22.93
Greek	151	1.03
Hawaii Native/Pacific Islander:	3	0.02
Polynesian: (1)	1	0.01
Tongan (1)	1	0.01
Other Pac. Isl., not spec.	2	0.01
Hispanic or Latino:	106	0.72
Central American:	3	0.02
Honduran	3	0.02
Cuban	16	0.11
Dominican Republic	4	0.03
Mexican	32	0.22
Puerto Rican	27	0.18
South American:	4	0.03
Venezuelan	4	0.03
Other Hispanic or Latino	20	0.14
Hungarian	178	1.21
Irish	2,074	14.08
Italian	2,850	19.35
Lithuanian	96	0.65
New Zealander	12	0.08
Northern European	4	0.03
Norwegian	13	0.09
Pennsylvania German	113	0.77
Polish	2,141	14.54
Russian	155	1.05
Scandinavian	19	0.13
Scotch-Irish	492	3.34
Scottish	346	2.35
Serbian	13	0.09
Slavic	49	0.33
Slovak	781	5.30
Slovene	63	0.43
Swedish	133	0.90
Swiss	16	0.11
Ukrainian	201	1.36
United States or American	302	2.05
Welsh	131	0.89
White:	13,133	89.33
Not Hispanic (12,847)	13,060	88.84
Hispanic (68)	73	0.50

Newberry

Place Type: Township
County: York
Population: 14,332

Ancestry/Race	Number	%
African American/Black:	150	1.05
Not Hispanic (111)	143	1.00
Hispanic (7)	7	0.05
African, sub-Saharan:	46	0.32
African	35	0.24
Cape Verdean	11	0.08
Alaska Native tribes, not specified	2	0.01
Am. Ind. or Alaska Nat., not spec.	19	0.13
American Indian tribes, specified:	35	0.24
Blackfeet (1)	6	0.04
Cherokee (4)	14	0.10
Iroquois	2	0.01
Kiowa	1	0.01
Latin American Indians (7)	7	0.05
Navajo	1	0.01
All other tribes (3)	4	0.03
Asian:	107	0.75
Chinese, ex. Taiwanese (8)	10	0.07
Filipino (6)	15	0.10
Indian (15)	20	0.14
Japanese (7)	9	0.06
Korean (18)	27	0.19
Laotian (3)	3	0.02
Thai (3)	3	0.02
Vietnamese (7)	12	0.08
Other Asian, specified	1	0.01
Other Asian, not specified (1)	7	0.05
Austrian	7	0.05
Belgian	8	0.06
Brazilian	5	0.03
British	28	0.20
Croatian	77	0.54
Czech	73	0.51
Czechoslovakian	11	0.08
Danish	23	0.16
Dutch	486	3.39
English	917	6.40
European	40	0.28
French, except Basque	353	2.46
French Canadian	50	0.35
German	5,766	40.25
Greek	45	0.31
Hawaii Native/Pacific Islander:	11	0.08
Micronesian: (2)	2	0.01
Guamanian/Chamorro (2)	2	0.01
Polynesian: (4)	8	0.06
Native Hawaiian (3)	7	0.05
Samoan (1)	1	0.01
Other Pac. Isl., specified	1	0.01
Hispanic or Latino:	214	1.49
Central American:	6	0.04
Panamanian	6	0.04
Cuban	10	0.07
Dominican Republic	1	0.01
Mexican	46	0.32
Puerto Rican	95	0.66
South American:	14	0.10
Bolivian	1	0.01
Colombian	5	0.03
Peruvian	5	0.03
Other South American	3	0.02
Other Hispanic or Latino	42	0.29
Hungarian	52	0.36
Irish	2,064	14.41
Italian	827	5.77
Lithuanian	83	0.58
Norwegian	47	0.33
Pennsylvania German	186	1.30
Polish	514	3.59
Romanian	9	0.06
Russian	63	0.44
Scotch-Irish	296	2.07
Scottish	78	0.54
Serbian	39	0.27
Slavic	6	0.04
Slovak	49	0.34
Slovene	26	0.18
Swedish	136	0.95
Swiss	72	0.50
Ukrainian	31	0.22
United States or American	1,292	9.02
Welsh	207	1.44
West Indian, excl. Hispanic:	19	0.13
Haitian	19	0.13
White:	14,055	98.07
Not Hispanic (13,816)	13,912	97.07
Hispanic (127)	143	1.00
Yugoslavian	43	0.30

Newtown

Place Type: Township
County: Bucks
Population: 18,206

Ancestry/Race	Number	%
African American/Black:	232	1.27
Not Hispanic (184)	223	1.22
Hispanic (7)	9	0.05
African, sub-Saharan:	19	0.10

Notes: 1. Figures in the "Number" column do not add up to the total population due to: a) Ancestry/Race overlap — e.g. persons can report being both White and Irish, b) persons of Hispanic origin can report being any race, c) persons reporting two ancestries are counted in both categories. 2. Numbers in parentheses indicate the number of persons reporting this ancestry/race alone, not in combination with any other ancestry/race. 3. Refer to the Explanation of Data in the front of the book for more detailed information.

Ancestry/Race	Number	%
African	10	0.05
South African	9	0.05
Am. Ind. or Alaska Nat., not spec.	16	0.09
Albanian	10	0.05
American Indian tribes, specified:	30	0.16
Blackfeet	1	0.01
Cherokee (1)	13	0.07
Delaware	2	0.01
Iroquois (1)	4	0.02
Latin American Indians (1)	1	0.01
Osage	3	0.02
All other tribes (2)	6	0.03
American Indian tribes, not spec.	3	0.02
Arab:	29	0.16
Egyptian	18	0.10
Lebanese	11	0.06
Armenian	44	0.24
Asian:	829	4.55
Chinese, ex. Taiwanese (232)	250	1.37
Filipino (55)	69	0.38
Indian (242)	263	1.44
Indonesian	3	0.02
Japanese (11)	29	0.16
Korean (140)	150	0.82
Pakistani (10)	10	0.05
Taiwanese (11)	11	0.06
Thai (1)	1	0.01
Vietnamese (12)	13	0.07
Other Asian, specified (1)	1	0.01
Other Asian, not specified (15)	29	0.16
Assyrian/Chaldean/Syriac	36	0.20
Austrian	122	0.67
Belgian	48	0.26
British	129	0.71
Canadian	117	0.64
Croatian	61	0.33
Czech	75	0.41
Czechoslovakian	53	0.29
Danish	41	0.22
Dutch	297	1.63
Eastern European	245	1.34
English	2,276	12.47
European	125	0.69
French, except Basque	282	1.55
French Canadian	108	0.59
German	4,166	22.83
Greek	147	0.81
Hawaii Native/Pacific Islander:	6	0.03
Polynesian:	2	0.01
Native Hawaiian	2	0.01
Other Pac. Isl., not spec.	4	0.02
Hispanic or Latino:	242	1.33
Central American:	15	0.08
Costa Rican	1	0.01
Panamanian	2	0.01
Salvadoran	12	0.07
Cuban	31	0.17
Mexican	38	0.21
Puerto Rican	78	0.43
South American:	31	0.17
Argentinean	3	0.02
Chilean	9	0.05
Colombian	10	0.05
Ecuadorian	3	0.02
Paraguayan	1	0.01
Peruvian	1	0.01
Venezuelan	1	0.01
Other South American	3	0.02
Other Hispanic or Latino	49	0.27
Hungarian	397	2.18
Irish	4,040	22.14
Israeli	25	0.14
Italian	3,126	17.13
Lithuanian	141	0.77
Northern European	42	0.23
Norwegian	146	0.80
Pennsylvania German	12	0.07
Polish	1,171	6.42
Portuguese	6	0.03
Romanian	85	0.47
Russian	1,040	5.70
Scandinavian	40	0.22
Scotch-Irish	470	2.58
Scottish	297	1.63
Slavic	23	0.13
Slovak	201	1.10
Swedish	128	0.70
Swiss	63	0.35
Ukrainian	255	1.40
United States or American	897	4.92
Welsh	256	1.40
West Indian, excl. Hispanic:	18	0.10
Haitian	18	0.10
White:	17,197	94.46
Not Hispanic (16,862)	16,995	93.35
Hispanic (190)	202	1.11
Yugoslavian	7	0.04

Newtown

Place Type: Township
County: Delaware
Population: 11,700

Ancestry/Race	Number	%
African American/Black:	102	0.87
Not Hispanic (75)	99	0.85
Hispanic (2)	3	0.03
African, sub-Saharan:	31	0.26
African	14	0.12
South African	17	0.15
Am. Ind. or Alaska Nat., not spec.	8	0.07
Albanian	6	0.05
American Indian tribes, specified:	16	0.14
Blackfeet (1)	2	0.02
Cherokee (5)	7	0.06
Creek (1)	1	0.01
Potawatomi	4	0.03
Sioux	1	0.01
All other tribes	1	0.01
American Indian tribes, not spec.	1	0.01
Arab:	82	0.70
Iraqi	53	0.45
Lebanese	21	0.18
Syrian	8	0.07
Armenian	188	1.61
Asian:	304	2.60
Bangladeshi (4)	4	0.03
Chinese, ex. Taiwanese (24)	36	0.31
Filipino (13)	18	0.15
Indian (71)	75	0.64
Japanese (3)	4	0.03
Korean (115)	127	1.09
Pakistani (13)	13	0.11
Vietnamese (22)	22	0.19
Other Asian, not specified (2)	5	0.04
Assyrian/Chaldean/Syriac	28	0.24
Australian	18	0.15
Austrian	28	0.24
Belgian	6	0.05
British	40	0.34
Canadian	36	0.31
Cypriot	20	0.17
Czech	24	0.21
Czechoslovakian	23	0.20
Danish	23	0.20
Dutch	134	1.15
Eastern European	22	0.19
English	1,980	16.92
European	9	0.08
Finnish	11	0.09
French, except Basque	252	2.15
French Canadian	37	0.32
German	2,165	18.50
Greek	91	0.78
Hawaii Native/Pacific Islander:	1	0.01
Polynesian:	1	0.01
Samoan	1	0.01
Hispanic or Latino:	81	0.69
Central American:	8	0.07
Guatemalan	5	0.04
Nicaraguan	1	0.01
Other Central American	2	0.02
Cuban	7	0.06
Mexican	21	0.18
Puerto Rican	8	0.07
South American:	15	0.13
Argentinean	1	0.01
Colombian	7	0.06
Ecuadorian	1	0.01
Peruvian	5	0.04
Venezuelan	1	0.01
Other Hispanic or Latino	22	0.19
Hungarian	84	0.72
Irish	3,833	32.76
Italian	2,411	20.61
Latvian	11	0.09
Lithuanian	122	1.04
Maltese	5	0.04
Norwegian	108	0.92
Pennsylvania German	33	0.28
Polish	435	3.72
Portuguese	7	0.06
Russian	204	1.74
Scandinavian	23	0.20
Scotch-Irish	296	2.53
Scottish	251	2.15
Serbian	8	0.07
Slovak	32	0.27
Swedish	132	1.13
Swiss	34	0.29
Ukrainian	91	0.78
United States or American	389	3.32
Welsh	192	1.64
White:	11,319	96.74
Not Hispanic (11,194)	11,258	96.22
Hispanic (57)	61	0.52
Yugoslavian	8	0.07

Norristown

Place Type: Borough
County: Montgomery
Population: 31,282

Ancestry/Race	Number	%
African American/Black:	11,490	36.73
Not Hispanic (10,738)	11,282	36.07
Hispanic (149)	208	0.66
African, sub-Saharan:	660	2.11
African	535	1.71
Cape Verdean	4	0.01
Kenyan	13	0.04
Liberian	10	0.03
Nigerian	64	0.20
South African	20	0.06
Other sub-Saharan African	14	0.04
Am. Ind. or Alaska Nat., not spec.	123	0.39
Albanian	7	0.02
American Indian tribes, specified:	145	0.46
Apache	1	0.00
Blackfeet	7	0.02
Cherokee (10)	49	0.16
Cheyenne (1)	1	0.00
Choctaw	1	0.00
Comanche	1	0.00
Creek	4	0.01
Crow (3)	3	0.01
Delaware (3)	11	0.04
Iroquois (1)	6	0.02
Latin American Indians (14)	29	0.09
Lumbee (1)	1	0.00
Navajo	3	0.01
Osage	1	0.00
Shoshone (1)	1	0.00
Sioux	8	0.03
All other tribes (6)	18	0.06
American Indian tribes, not spec.	7	0.02
Arab:	27	0.09
Arab/Arabic	4	0.01

Notes: 1. Figures in the "Number" column do not add up to the total population due to: a) Ancestry/Race overlap — e.g. persons can report being both White and Irish, b) persons of Hispanic origin can report being any race, c) persons reporting two ancestries are counted in both categories. 2. Numbers in parentheses indicate the number of persons reporting this ancestry/race alone, not in combination with any other ancestry/race. 3. Refer to the Explanation of Data in the front of the book for more detailed information.

Ancestry/Race	Number	%
Lebanese	23	0.07
Armenian	13	0.04
Asian:	1,057	3.38
Bangladeshi (4)	4	0.01
Cambodian (32)	48	0.15
Chinese, ex. Taiwanese (172)	202	0.65
Filipino (44)	72	0.23
Indian (224)	237	0.76
Indonesian (2)	2	0.01
Japanese (16)	27	0.09
Korean (124)	135	0.43
Laotian (2)	2	0.01
Pakistani (15)	26	0.08
Sri Lankan (3)	3	0.01
Taiwanese (2)	2	0.01
Thai (2)	6	0.02
Vietnamese (241)	255	0.82
Other Asian, specified (1)	3	0.01
Other Asian, not specified (20)	33	0.11
Australian	25	0.08
Austrian	12	0.04
Belgian	7	0.02
British	65	0.21
Canadian	9	0.03
Celtic	23	0.07
Croatian	22	0.07
Czech	48	0.15
Czechoslovakian	10	0.03
Danish	7	0.02
Dutch	485	1.55
English	1,479	4.73
European	71	0.23
French, except Basque	272	0.87
French Canadian	56	0.18
German	3,063	9.79
Greek	97	0.31
Hawaii Native/Pacific Islander:	23	0.07
Micronesian: (3)	3	0.01
Guamanian/Chamorro (3)	3	0.01
Polynesian: (5)	7	0.02
Native Hawaiian (2)	4	0.01
Samoan (3)	3	0.01
Other Pac. Isl., not spec. (2)	13	0.04
Hispanic or Latino:	3,282	10.49
Central American:	52	0.17
Costa Rican	8	0.03
Guatemalan	15	0.05
Nicaraguan	1	0.00
Panamanian	9	0.03
Salvadoran	19	0.06
Cuban	66	0.21
Dominican Republic	60	0.19
Mexican	1,931	6.17
Puerto Rican	868	2.77
South American:	49	0.16
Argentinean	3	0.01
Bolivian	1	0.00
Chilean	2	0.01
Colombian	30	0.10
Ecuadorian	1	0.00
Peruvian	5	0.02
Venezuelan	6	0.02
Other South American	1	0.00
Other Hispanic or Latino	256	0.82
Hungarian	120	0.38
Irish	3,812	12.19
Italian	5,198	16.62
Lithuanian	60	0.19
Northern European	17	0.05
Norwegian	56	0.18
Pennsylvania German	265	0.85
Polish	1,043	3.33
Portuguese	27	0.09
Romanian	23	0.07
Russian	179	0.57
Scandinavian	9	0.03
Scotch-Irish	185	0.59
Scottish	257	0.82
Slavic	25	0.08
Slovak	177	0.57
Slovene	41	0.13
Swedish	82	0.26
Swiss	31	0.10
Turkish	4	0.01
Ukrainian	137	0.44
United States or American	678	2.17
Welsh	169	0.54
West Indian, excl. Hispanic:	440	1.41
Bahamian	21	0.07
Barbadian	7	0.02
Haitian	63	0.20
Jamaican	294	0.94
Trinidadian and Tobagonian	7	0.02
West Indian	48	0.15
White:	17,725	56.66
Not Hispanic (15,440)	16,045	51.29
Hispanic (1,552)	1,680	5.37
Yugoslavian	30	0.10

North Fayette

Place Type: Township
County: Allegheny
Population: 12,254

Ancestry/Race	Number	%
African American/Black:	344	2.81
Not Hispanic (313)	338	2.76
Hispanic (6)	6	0.05
African, sub-Saharan:	79	0.64
African	68	0.56
Cape Verdean	11	0.09
Am. Ind. or Alaska Nat., not spec.	10	0.08
American Indian tribes, specified:	22	0.18
Blackfeet (1)	1	0.01
Cherokee (2)	8	0.07
Chippewa (3)	3	0.02
Iroquois	1	0.01
Lumbee (1)	1	0.01
Navajo (1)	1	0.01
Sioux (2)	3	0.02
All other tribes	4	0.03
American Indian tribes, not spec.	1	0.01
Arab:	74	0.60
Lebanese	22	0.18
Syrian	52	0.42
Armenian	32	0.26
Asian:	338	2.76
Chinese, ex. Taiwanese (17)	21	0.17
Filipino (25)	32	0.26
Indian (238)	241	1.97
Japanese (5)	12	0.10
Korean (10)	10	0.08
Pakistani (3)	3	0.02
Thai (1)	1	0.01
Vietnamese (2)	2	0.02
Other Asian, not specified (5)	16	0.13
Austrian	53	0.43
Belgian	148	1.21
British	39	0.32
Canadian	7	0.06
Croatian	134	1.09
Czech	62	0.51
Czechoslovakian	30	0.24
Danish	21	0.17
Dutch	95	0.78
English	1,177	9.61
European	42	0.34
Finnish	24	0.20
French, except Basque	412	3.36
French Canadian	59	0.48
German	3,498	28.56
Greek	104	0.85
Hawaii Native/Pacific Islander:	3	0.02
Polynesian: (1)	3	0.02
Native Hawaiian	1	0.01
Samoan (1)	2	0.02
Hispanic or Latino:	108	0.88
Central American:	2	0.02
Costa Rican	1	0.01
Honduran	1	0.01
Cuban	2	0.02
Dominican Republic	1	0.01
Mexican	34	0.28
Puerto Rican	27	0.22
South American:	11	0.09
Argentinean	1	0.01
Colombian	2	0.02
Ecuadorian	3	0.02
Peruvian	3	0.02
Other South American	2	0.02
Other Hispanic or Latino	31	0.25
Hungarian	262	2.14
Icelander	5	0.04
Iranian	35	0.29
Irish	2,531	20.66
Italian	1,817	14.83
Lithuanian	95	0.78
Maltese	14	0.11
Norwegian	31	0.25
Pennsylvania German	43	0.35
Polish	1,149	9.38
Portuguese	6	0.05
Russian	163	1.33
Scandinavian	7	0.06
Scotch-Irish	377	3.08
Scottish	231	1.89
Serbian	80	0.65
Slavic	11	0.09
Slovak	362	2.96
Slovene	138	1.13
Swedish	122	1.00
Swiss	21	0.17
Turkish	14	0.11
Ukrainian	159	1.30
United States or American	378	3.09
Welsh	149	1.22
White:	11,586	94.55
Not Hispanic (11,442)	11,505	93.89
Hispanic (76)	81	0.66
Yugoslavian	8	0.07

North Huntingdon

Place Type: Township
County: Westmoreland
Population: 29,123

Ancestry/Race	Number	%
African American/Black:	116	0.40
Not Hispanic (92)	115	0.39
Hispanic	1	0.00
Am. Ind. or Alaska Nat., not spec.	11	0.04
American Indian tribes, specified:	35	0.12
Blackfeet	4	0.01
Cherokee (3)	9	0.03
Chickasaw	2	0.01
Choctaw (1)	2	0.01
Colville (1)	1	0.00
Iroquois (4)	8	0.03
Latin American Indians	2	0.01
Sioux (1)	1	0.00
All other tribes	6	0.02
American Indian tribes, not spec.	1	0.00
Arab:	144	0.49
Lebanese	7	0.02
Syrian	137	0.47
Asian:	170	0.58
Cambodian (1)	7	0.02
Chinese, ex. Taiwanese (37)	43	0.15
Filipino (14)	22	0.08
Indian (21)	29	0.10
Japanese (14)	31	0.11
Korean (14)	21	0.07
Thai (1)	1	0.00
Vietnamese (4)	5	0.02
Other Asian, not specified (1)	11	0.04
Austrian	194	0.66
Belgian	18	0.06
Brazilian	5	0.02

Notes: 1. Figures in the "Number" column do not add up to the total population due to: a) Ancestry/Race overlap — e.g. persons can report being both White and Irish, b) persons of Hispanic origin can report being any race, c) persons reporting two ancestries are counted in both categories. 2. Numbers in parentheses indicate the number of persons reporting this ancestry/race alone, not in combination with any other ancestry/race. 3. Refer to the Explanation of Data in the front of the book for more detailed information.

Ancestry/Race	Number	%
British	32	0.11
Bulgarian	8	0.03
Canadian	7	0.02
Carpatho Rusyn	11	0.04
Celtic	19	0.07
Croatian	652	2.23
Czech	306	1.05
Czechoslovakian	245	0.84
Danish	7	0.02
Dutch	262	0.90
English	3,391	11.62
European	52	0.18
Finnish	7	0.02
French, except Basque	554	1.90
French Canadian	27	0.09
German	8,358	28.64
Greek	168	0.58
Hawaii Native/Pacific Islander:	6	0.02
Polynesian: (5)	5	0.02
Native Hawaiian (3)	3	0.01
Samoan (2)	2	0.01
Other Pac. Isl., not spec. (1)	1	0.00
Hispanic or Latino:	120	0.41
Cuban	11	0.04
Dominican Republic	10	0.03
Mexican	58	0.20
Puerto Rican	9	0.03
South American:	7	0.02
Colombian	5	0.02
Venezuelan	1	0.00
Other South American	1	0.00
Other Hispanic or Latino	25	0.09
Hungarian	1,031	3.53
Irish	4,848	16.61
Italian	4,826	16.54
Latvian	7	0.02
Lithuanian	168	0.58
Northern European	32	0.11
Norwegian	37	0.13
Pennsylvania German	144	0.49
Polish	3,078	10.55
Romanian	37	0.13
Russian	351	1.20
Scandinavian	69	0.24
Scotch-Irish	730	2.50
Scottish	749	2.57
Serbian	427	1.46
Slavic	103	0.35
Slovak	2,446	8.38
Slovene	256	0.88
Swedish	534	1.83
Swiss	86	0.29
Ukrainian	365	1.25
United States or American	972	3.33
Welsh	504	1.73
White:	28,882	99.17
Not Hispanic (28,675)	28,774	98.80
Hispanic (105)	108	0.37
Yugoslavian	29	0.10

North Lebanon

Place Type: Township
County: Lebanon
Population: 10,629

Ancestry/Race	Number	%
African American/Black:	147	1.38
Not Hispanic (87)	108	1.02
Hispanic (31)	39	0.37
Am. Ind. or Alaska Nat., not spec.	12	0.11
American Indian tribes, specified:	18	0.17
Blackfeet	1	0.01
Cherokee (3)	8	0.08
Chippewa	3	0.03
Sioux (1)	2	0.02
All other tribes (1)	4	0.04
American Indian tribes, not spec.	3	0.03
Arab:	15	0.14
Lebanese	15	0.14
Asian:	149	1.40
Cambodian (27)	34	0.32
Chinese, ex. Taiwanese (7)	13	0.12
Filipino (8)	9	0.08
Indian (7)	8	0.08
Japanese (1)	5	0.05
Korean (18)	20	0.19
Pakistani (5)	5	0.05
Thai	2	0.02
Vietnamese (45)	51	0.48
Other Asian, not specified (2)	2	0.02
Austrian	10	0.09
British	16	0.15
Croatian	34	0.32
Czech	48	0.45
Czechoslovakian	17	0.16
Danish	11	0.10
Dutch	248	2.33
English	392	3.69
European	14	0.13
French, except Basque	185	1.74
French Canadian	45	0.42
German	4,483	42.18
Greek	18	0.17
Hawaii Native/Pacific Islander:	1	0.01
Other Pac. Isl., not spec.	1	0.01
Hispanic or Latino:	570	5.36
Central American:	9	0.08
Costa Rican	1	0.01
Honduran	1	0.01
Panamanian	2	0.02
Salvadoran	5	0.05
Cuban	5	0.05
Dominican Republic	27	0.25
Mexican	18	0.17
Puerto Rican	415	3.90
South American:	9	0.08
Argentinean	1	0.01
Bolivian	1	0.01
Chilean	1	0.01
Colombian	3	0.03
Ecuadorian	1	0.01
Paraguayan	1	0.01
Peruvian	1	0.01
Other Hispanic or Latino	87	0.82
Hungarian	86	0.81
Irish	955	8.98
Italian	620	5.83
Lithuanian	27	0.25
Norwegian	26	0.24
Pennsylvania German	327	3.08
Polish	418	3.93
Russian	23	0.22
Scotch-Irish	96	0.90
Scottish	23	0.22
Slavic	14	0.13
Slovak	150	1.41
Slovene	7	0.07
Swedish	4	0.04
Swiss	164	1.54
Ukrainian	89	0.84
United States or American	1,027	9.66
Welsh	127	1.19
White:	10,129	95.30
Not Hispanic (9,787)	9,833	92.51
Hispanic (259)	296	2.78
Yugoslavian	11	0.10

North Middleton

Place Type: Township
County: Cumberland
Population: 10,197

Ancestry/Race	Number	%
Afghan	38	0.37
African American/Black:	397	3.89
Not Hispanic (345)	393	3.85
Hispanic (3)	4	0.04
Am. Ind. or Alaska Nat., not spec.	22	0.22
American Indian tribes, specified:	20	0.20
Cherokee (3)	8	0.08
Creek	2	0.02
Iroquois (1)	1	0.01
Lumbee (4)	5	0.05
Potawatomi (2)	2	0.02
All other tribes	2	0.02
American Indian tribes, not spec.	4	0.04
Arab:	10	0.10
Lebanese	10	0.10
Asian:	200	1.96
Cambodian (1)	2	0.02
Chinese, ex. Taiwanese (14)	16	0.16
Filipino (21)	33	0.32
Indian (33)	38	0.37
Japanese (9)	14	0.14
Korean (40)	45	0.44
Laotian (1)	5	0.05
Malaysian (1)	3	0.03
Thai (4)	4	0.04
Vietnamese (29)	33	0.32
Other Asian, not specified (2)	7	0.07
Assyrian/Chaldean/Syriac	8	0.08
Austrian	8	0.08
Belgian	11	0.11
Canadian	14	0.14
Croatian	43	0.42
Czech	57	0.56
Danish	16	0.16
Dutch	294	2.88
Eastern European	6	0.06
English	1,031	10.11
European	177	1.74
Finnish	10	0.10
French, except Basque	256	2.51
German	3,421	33.55
Greek	5	0.05
Hawaii Native/Pacific Islander:	16	0.16
Micronesian: (1)	4	0.04
Guamanian/Chamorro (1)	4	0.04
Polynesian: (10)	11	0.11
Native Hawaiian (5)	6	0.06
Samoan (5)	5	0.05
Other Pac. Isl., not spec.	1	0.01
Hispanic or Latino:	151	1.48
Central American:	12	0.12
Costa Rican	1	0.01
Honduran	6	0.06
Panamanian	5	0.05
Cuban	5	0.05
Mexican	33	0.32
Puerto Rican	71	0.70
South American:	6	0.06
Argentinean	2	0.02
Colombian	1	0.01
Venezuelan	3	0.03
Other Hispanic or Latino	24	0.24
Hungarian	27	0.26
Irish	1,193	11.70
Italian	418	4.10
Lithuanian	9	0.09
Norwegian	43	0.42
Pennsylvania German	110	1.08
Polish	292	2.86
Romanian	7	0.07
Russian	42	0.41
Scandinavian	9	0.09
Scotch-Irish	188	1.84
Scottish	159	1.56
Serbian	6	0.06
Slavic	5	0.05
Slovak	39	0.38
Swedish	43	0.42
Swiss	58	0.57
Turkish	36	0.35
Ukrainian	34	0.33
United States or American	1,528	14.98
Welsh	195	1.91
West Indian, excl. Hispanic:	7	0.07
Trinidadian and Tobagonian	7	0.07

Notes: 1. Figures in the "Number" column do not add up to the total population due to: a) Ancestry/Race overlap — e.g. persons can report being both White and Irish, b) persons of Hispanic origin can report being any race, c) persons reporting two ancestries are counted in both categories. 2. Numbers in parentheses indicate the number of persons reporting this ancestry/race alone, not in combination with any other ancestry/race. 3. Refer to the Explanation of Data in the front of the book for more detailed information.

White:	9,582	93.97
Not Hispanic (9,404)	9,495	93.12
Hispanic (84)	87	0.85
Yugoslavian	30	0.29

North Strabane

Place Type: Township
County: Washington
Population: 10,057

Ancestry/Race	Number	%
African American/Black:	233	2.32
Not Hispanic (208)	229	2.28
Hispanic (1)	4	0.04
Am. Ind. or Alaska Nat., not spec.	3	0.03
American Indian tribes, specified:	6	0.06
Cherokee	3	0.03
Cree	1	0.01
Iroquois	2	0.02
Arab:	50	0.50
Lebanese	8	0.08
Syrian	42	0.42
Asian:	88	0.88
Chinese, ex. Taiwanese (6)	6	0.06
Filipino (4)	5	0.05
Indian (42)	45	0.45
Japanese (10)	12	0.12
Korean (7)	7	0.07
Vietnamese (12)	13	0.13
Austrian	42	0.42
Belgian	8	0.08
Brazilian	13	0.13
British	15	0.15
Croatian	159	1.58
Czech	95	0.94
Czechoslovakian	86	0.86
Danish	20	0.20
Dutch	112	1.11
English	1,017	10.11
European	91	0.90
Finnish	30	0.30
French, except Basque	261	2.60
French Canadian	25	0.25
German	2,402	23.88
Greek	209	2.08
Hawaii Native/Pacific Islander:	2	0.02
Polynesian: (1)	1	0.01
Native Hawaiian (1)	1	0.01
Other Pac. Isl., not spec. (1)	1	0.01
Hispanic or Latino:	61	0.61
Central American:	1	0.01
Panamanian	1	0.01
Mexican	33	0.33
Puerto Rican	13	0.13
South American:	2	0.02
Bolivian	1	0.01
Colombian	1	0.01
Other Hispanic or Latino	12	0.12
Hungarian	221	2.20
Irish	1,673	16.64
Italian	2,117	21.05
Lithuanian	29	0.29
Norwegian	14	0.14
Polish	1,160	11.53
Russian	186	1.85
Scotch-Irish	431	4.29
Scottish	159	1.58
Serbian	9	0.09
Slavic	20	0.20
Slovak	486	4.83
Slovene	359	3.57
Swedish	74	0.74
Swiss	53	0.53
Ukrainian	84	0.84
United States or American	435	4.33
Welsh	110	1.09
White:	9,739	96.84
Not Hispanic (9,668)	9,701	96.46
Hispanic (32)	38	0.38
Yugoslavian	11	0.11

North Union

Place Type: Township
County: Fayette
Population: 14,140

Ancestry/Race	Number	%
African American/Black:	415	2.93
Not Hispanic (359)	405	2.86
Hispanic (9)	10	0.07
African, sub-Saharan:	80	0.57
African	80	0.57
Am. Ind. or Alaska Nat., not spec.	23	0.16
American Indian tribes, specified:	12	0.08
Blackfeet (1)	1	0.01
Cherokee (3)	5	0.04
Iroquois (1)	1	0.01
Latin American Indians (1)	2	0.01
All other tribes (2)	3	0.02
Arab:	130	0.92
Lebanese	120	0.85
Syrian	10	0.07
Asian:	54	0.38
Chinese, ex. Taiwanese (5)	10	0.07
Filipino (8)	9	0.06
Indian (6)	6	0.04
Japanese (6)	11	0.08
Korean (4)	4	0.03
Taiwanese (1)	2	0.01
Thai (1)	1	0.01
Vietnamese (4)	9	0.06
Other Asian, specified	1	0.01
Other Asian, not specified	1	0.01
Austrian	52	0.37
Belgian	17	0.12
British	18	0.13
Canadian	6	0.04
Carpatho Rusyn	11	0.08
Croatian	61	0.43
Czech	124	0.88
Czechoslovakian	122	0.86
Dutch	610	4.31
Eastern European	32	0.23
English	1,387	9.81
French, except Basque	174	1.23
German	2,950	20.86
Greek	57	0.40
Hawaii Native/Pacific Islander:	4	0.03
Micronesian: (1)	2	0.01
Guamanian/Chamorro (1)	1	0.01
Other Micronesian	1	0.01
Polynesian: (1)	1	0.01
Samoan (1)	1	0.01
Other Pac. Isl., specified	1	0.01
Hispanic or Latino:	60	0.42
Central American:	2	0.01
Panamanian	2	0.01
Cuban	1	0.01
Mexican	16	0.11
Puerto Rican	10	0.07
Other Hispanic or Latino	31	0.22
Hungarian	211	1.49
Irish	2,104	14.88
Italian	1,595	11.28
Pennsylvania German	102	0.72
Polish	952	6.73
Russian	157	1.11
Scotch-Irish	174	1.23
Scottish	121	0.86
Serbian	6	0.04
Slavic	18	0.13
Slovak	1,476	10.44
Slovene	21	0.15
Swedish	57	0.40
Ukrainian	32	0.23
United States or American	921	6.51
Welsh	91	0.64
West Indian, excl. Hispanic:	9	0.06
Dutch West Indian	9	0.06
White:	13,690	96.82
Not Hispanic (13,580)	13,644	96.49
Hispanic (39)	46	0.33
Yugoslavian	25	0.18

North Versailles

Place Type: Census Designated Place
County: Allegheny
Population: 11,125

Ancestry/Race	Number	%
African American/Black:	1,193	10.72
Not Hispanic (1,079)	1,177	10.58
Hispanic (8)	16	0.14
African, sub-Saharan:	53	0.48
African	53	0.48
Am. Ind. or Alaska Nat., not spec.	28	0.25
Albanian	9	0.08
American Indian tribes, specified:	20	0.18
Blackfeet (2)	7	0.06
Cherokee (1)	4	0.04
Creek	1	0.01
Iroquois	7	0.06
Seminole	1	0.01
American Indian tribes, not spec.	8	0.07
Arab:	14	0.13
Syrian	9	0.08
Other Arab	5	0.04
Asian:	109	0.98
Chinese, ex. Taiwanese (34)	36	0.32
Filipino (11)	21	0.19
Indian (21)	25	0.22
Japanese (3)	6	0.05
Korean (8)	12	0.11
Vietnamese (8)	8	0.07
Other Asian, not specified	1	0.01
Austrian	18	0.16
Belgian	7	0.06
British	15	0.13
Croatian	399	3.59
Czech	79	0.71
Czechoslovakian	37	0.33
Dutch	111	1.00
English	832	7.49
European	33	0.30
Finnish	7	0.06
French, except Basque	175	1.57
French Canadian	9	0.08
German	2,436	21.92
Greek	58	0.52
Hawaii Native/Pacific Islander:	4	0.04
Polynesian: (1)	1	0.01
Samoan (1)	1	0.01
Other Pac. Isl., not spec. (2)	3	0.03
Hispanic or Latino:	54	0.49
Central American:	1	0.01
Guatemalan	1	0.01
Cuban	5	0.04
Mexican	23	0.21
Puerto Rican	8	0.07
South American:	2	0.02
Argentinean	1	0.01
Peruvian	1	0.01
Other Hispanic or Latino	15	0.13
Hungarian	358	3.22
Irish	2,325	20.92
Italian	1,961	17.65
Lithuanian	23	0.21
Norwegian	17	0.15
Pennsylvania German	14	0.13
Polish	1,044	9.39
Portuguese	5	0.04
Romanian	6	0.05
Russian	121	1.09
Scotch-Irish	173	1.56
Scottish	239	2.15
Serbian	143	1.29
Slavic	92	0.83

Notes: 1. Figures in the "Number" column do not add up to the total population due to: a) Ancestry/Race overlap — e.g. persons can report being both White and Irish, b) persons of Hispanic origin can report being any race, c) persons reporting two ancestries are counted in both categories. 2. Numbers in parentheses indicate the number of persons reporting this ancestry/race alone, not in combination with any other ancestry/race. 3. Refer to the Explanation of Data in the front of the book for more detailed information.

Slovak	875	7.87
Slovene	46	0.41
Swedish	165	1.48
Ukrainian	89	0.80
United States or American	400	3.60
Welsh	79	0.71
White:	9,890	88.90
Not Hispanic (9,747)	9,864	88.67
Hispanic (22)	26	0.23
Yugoslavian	13	0.12

North Whitehall

Place Type: Township
County: Lehigh
Population: 14,731

Ancestry/Race	Number	%
African American/Black:	162	1.10
Not Hispanic (114)	145	0.98
Hispanic (9)	17	0.12
Am. Ind. or Alaska Nat., not spec.	10	0.07
Albanian	8	0.05
American Indian tribes, specified:	47	0.32
Blackfeet	3	0.02
Cherokee (6)	25	0.17
Delaware (1)	6	0.04
Iroquois (1)	1	0.01
Latin American Indians	3	0.02
Navajo	1	0.01
All other tribes (1)	8	0.05
American Indian tribes, not spec.	2	0.01
Arab:	115	0.78
Lebanese	65	0.44
Syrian	50	0.34
Asian:	143	0.97
Chinese, ex. Taiwanese (21)	32	0.22
Filipino (13)	23	0.16
Indian (25)	29	0.20
Japanese (3)	5	0.03
Korean (20)	24	0.16
Pakistani (8)	8	0.05
Thai (2)	3	0.02
Vietnamese (6)	8	0.05
Other Asian, specified	3	0.02
Other Asian, not specified (5)	8	0.05
Austrian	365	2.48
Belgian	10	0.07
British	18	0.12
Canadian	73	0.50
Carpatho Rusyn	6	0.04
Croatian	26	0.18
Czech	36	0.24
Czechoslovakian	6	0.04
Danish	32	0.22
Dutch	440	2.99
English	873	5.93
Estonian	9	0.06
European	38	0.26
Finnish	23	0.16
French, except Basque	301	2.04
French Canadian	43	0.29
German	5,446	36.97
Greek	38	0.26
Hawaii Native/Pacific Islander:	7	0.05
Micronesian:	1	0.01
Guamanian/Chamorro	1	0.01
Polynesian: (2)	3	0.02
Native Hawaiian (2)	3	0.02
Other Pac. Isl., not spec.	3	0.02
Hispanic or Latino:	244	1.66
Central American:	9	0.06
Costa Rican	6	0.04
Honduran	1	0.01
Other Central American	2	0.01
Cuban	7	0.05
Dominican Republic	1	0.01
Mexican	16	0.11
Puerto Rican	139	0.94
South American:	12	0.08
Argentinean	3	0.02
Chilean	3	0.02
Colombian	4	0.03
Ecuadorian	1	0.01
Paraguayan	1	0.01
Other Hispanic or Latino	60	0.41
Hungarian	374	2.54
Irish	1,412	9.59
Italian	1,530	10.39
Lithuanian	111	0.75
Northern European	5	0.03
Norwegian	62	0.42
Pennsylvania German	1,421	9.65
Polish	690	4.68
Portuguese	55	0.37
Russian	147	1.00
Scotch-Irish	95	0.64
Scottish	184	1.25
Slovak	638	4.33
Slovene	6	0.04
Swedish	50	0.34
Swiss	24	0.16
Turkish	6	0.04
Ukrainian	627	4.26
United States or American	990	6.72
Welsh	368	2.50
West Indian, excl. Hispanic:	6	0.04
Jamaican	6	0.04
White:	14,387	97.66
Not Hispanic (14,147)	14,232	96.61
Hispanic (118)	155	1.05

Northampton

Place Type: Township
County: Bucks
Population: 39,384

Ancestry/Race	Number	%
Afghan	15	0.04
African American/Black:	202	0.51
Not Hispanic (157)	194	0.49
Hispanic (6)	8	0.02
African, sub-Saharan:	10	0.03
African	10	0.03
Alaska Native tribes, specified:	1	0.00
Eskimo	1	0.00
Am. Ind. or Alaska Nat., not spec.	24	0.06
Albanian	61	0.16
American Indian tribes, specified:	26	0.07
Apache	1	0.00
Blackfeet	2	0.01
Cherokee (1)	6	0.02
Delaware	3	0.01
Iroquois (1)	1	0.00
Latin American Indians (1)	1	0.00
Lumbee (1)	1	0.00
Menominee	1	0.00
Navajo	3	0.01
Sioux (2)	2	0.01
All other tribes (2)	5	0.01
American Indian tribes, not spec.	4	0.01
Arab:	72	0.18
Arab/Arabic	6	0.02
Egyptian	8	0.02
Iraqi	9	0.02
Lebanese	18	0.05
Syrian	24	0.06
Other Arab	7	0.02
Armenian	56	0.14
Asian:	827	2.10
Bangladeshi	2	0.01
Chinese, ex. Taiwanese (188)	213	0.54
Filipino (48)	62	0.16
Hmong (1)	1	0.00
Indian (274)	305	0.77
Japanese (21)	43	0.11
Korean (126)	134	0.34
Laotian (7)	7	0.02
Pakistani (10)	10	0.03
Taiwanese (15)	19	0.05
Thai (1)	1	0.00
Vietnamese (9)	15	0.04
Other Asian, specified (2)	2	0.01
Other Asian, not specified (1)	13	0.03
Assyrian/Chaldean/Syriac	13	0.03
Austrian	203	0.52
Belgian	22	0.06
British	197	0.50
Canadian	81	0.21
Croatian	21	0.05
Czech	70	0.18
Czechoslovakian	76	0.19
Danish	51	0.13
Dutch	366	0.93
Eastern European	121	0.31
English	3,590	9.12
Estonian	24	0.06
European	279	0.71
Finnish	6	0.02
French, except Basque	544	1.38
French Canadian	124	0.32
German	9,098	23.12
Greek	271	0.69
Hawaii Native/Pacific Islander:	10	0.03
Polynesian: (1)	4	0.01
Native Hawaiian	1	0.00
Samoan (1)	3	0.01
Other Pac. Isl., not spec. (2)	6	0.02
Hispanic or Latino:	325	0.83
Central American:	11	0.03
Costa Rican	5	0.01
Guatemalan	1	0.00
Honduran	1	0.00
Panamanian	4	0.01
Cuban	50	0.13
Dominican Republic	3	0.01
Mexican	61	0.15
Puerto Rican	131	0.33
South American:	34	0.09
Argentinean	4	0.01
Bolivian	1	0.00
Chilean	1	0.00
Colombian	13	0.03
Ecuadorian	2	0.01
Paraguayan	1	0.00
Peruvian	10	0.03
Uruguayan	2	0.01
Other Hispanic or Latino	35	0.09
Hungarian	550	1.40
Iranian	11	0.03
Irish	10,604	26.95
Israeli	56	0.14
Italian	6,510	16.55
Latvian	84	0.21
Lithuanian	344	0.87
Macedonian	9	0.02
Maltese	9	0.02
Northern European	18	0.05
Norwegian	138	0.35
Pennsylvania German	80	0.20
Polish	3,001	7.63
Portuguese	107	0.27
Romanian	250	0.64
Russian	2,951	7.50
Scandinavian	21	0.05
Scotch-Irish	621	1.58
Scottish	678	1.72
Serbian	8	0.02
Slavic	9	0.02
Slovak	259	0.66
Slovene	40	0.10
Swedish	226	0.57
Swiss	157	0.40
Ukrainian	1,147	2.92
United States or American	2,034	5.17
Welsh	345	0.88
White:	38,418	97.55
Not Hispanic (37,960)	38,152	96.87
Hispanic (245)	266	0.68

Notes: 1. Figures in the "Number" column do not add up to the total population due to: a) Ancestry/Race overlap — e.g. persons can report being both White and Irish, b) persons of Hispanic origin can report being any race, c) persons reporting two ancestries are counted in both categories. 2. Numbers in parentheses indicate the number of persons reporting this ancestry/race alone, not in combination with any other ancestry/race. 3. Refer to the Explanation of Data in the front of the book for more detailed information.

Yugoslavian	14	0.04

Oil City

Place Type: City
County: Venango
Population: 11,504

Ancestry/Race	Number	%
African American/Black:	128	1.11
Not Hispanic (102)	128	1.11
African, sub-Saharan:	5	0.04
Cape Verdean	5	0.04
Alaska Native tribes, specified:	1	0.01
Eskimo (1)	1	0.01
Am. Ind. or Alaska Nat., not spec.	23	0.20
American Indian tribes, specified:	34	0.30
Apache	1	0.01
Blackfeet	1	0.01
Cherokee (1)	8	0.07
Chippewa (2)	3	0.03
Delaware (3)	3	0.03
Iroquois (6)	11	0.10
Latin American Indians	2	0.02
Sioux	4	0.03
All other tribes	1	0.01
American Indian tribes, not spec.	1	0.01
Asian:	35	0.30
Cambodian	1	0.01
Chinese, ex. Taiwanese (1)	2	0.02
Filipino (5)	5	0.04
Indian (3)	3	0.03
Japanese (11)	11	0.10
Korean (7)	7	0.06
Thai (1)	1	0.01
Vietnamese (3)	3	0.03
Other Asian, specified (1)	1	0.01
Other Asian, not specified (1)	1	0.01
Austrian	14	0.12
British	17	0.15
Bulgarian	8	0.07
Canadian	8	0.07
Celtic	7	0.06
Croatian	49	0.43
Czech	12	0.10
Czechoslovakian	15	0.13
Dutch	471	4.09
English	730	6.35
French, except Basque	164	1.43
French Canadian	31	0.27
German	3,748	32.58
Greek	26	0.23
Hawaii Native/Pacific Islander:	8	0.07
Micronesian: (1)	2	0.02
Guamanian/Chamorro (1)	2	0.02
Polynesian: (4)	6	0.05
Native Hawaiian (3)	5	0.04
Samoan (1)	1	0.01
Hispanic or Latino:	72	0.63
Central American:	3	0.03
Guatemalan	1	0.01
Honduran	2	0.02
Cuban	3	0.03
Mexican	25	0.22
Puerto Rican	6	0.05
South American:	1	0.01
Argentinean	1	0.01
Other Hispanic or Latino	34	0.30
Hungarian	72	0.63
Irish	2,411	20.96
Italian	642	5.58
Lithuanian	7	0.06
Norwegian	31	0.27
Pennsylvania German	75	0.65
Polish	1,083	9.41
Russian	24	0.21
Scandinavian	11	0.10
Scotch-Irish	307	2.67
Scottish	186	1.62
Serbian	7	0.06
Slavic	12	0.10
Slovak	57	0.50
Slovene	11	0.10
Swedish	322	2.80
Swiss	40	0.35
Ukrainian	41	0.36
United States or American	824	7.16
Welsh	193	1.68
West Indian, excl. Hispanic:	56	0.49
Haitian	45	0.39
Jamaican	11	0.10
White:	11,320	98.40
Not Hispanic (11,198)	11,257	97.85
Hispanic (58)	63	0.55

Palmer

Place Type: Township
County: Northampton
Population: 16,809

Ancestry/Race	Number	%
Acadian/Cajun	4	0.02
African American/Black:	428	2.55
Not Hispanic (344)	408	2.43
Hispanic (16)	20	0.12
African, sub-Saharan:	33	0.20
African	22	0.13
Ugandan	5	0.03
Zimbabwean	6	0.04
Am. Ind. or Alaska Nat., not spec.	11	0.07
Albanian	6	0.04
American Indian tribes, specified:	20	0.12
Apache	1	0.01
Cherokee	6	0.04
Cheyenne	3	0.02
Chippewa	1	0.01
Delaware	1	0.01
Iroquois (3)	3	0.02
Menominee (1)	1	0.01
Ottawa	1	0.01
All other tribes	3	0.02
American Indian tribes, not spec.	4	0.02
Arab:	170	1.01
Arab/Arabic	9	0.05
Egyptian	27	0.16
Lebanese	116	0.69
Syrian	18	0.11
Asian:	365	2.17
Cambodian (6)	6	0.04
Chinese, ex. Taiwanese (38)	42	0.25
Filipino (41)	60	0.36
Indian (128)	141	0.84
Indonesian (1)	1	0.01
Japanese (9)	18	0.11
Korean (21)	24	0.14
Pakistani	1	0.01
Taiwanese (4)	5	0.03
Vietnamese (49)	58	0.35
Other Asian, specified (1)	5	0.03
Other Asian, not specified (2)	4	0.02
Austrian	134	0.80
Basque	9	0.05
Belgian	10	0.06
British	34	0.20
Celtic	12	0.07
Croatian	12	0.07
Czech	28	0.17
Czechoslovakian	84	0.50
Danish	31	0.18
Dutch	708	4.21
Eastern European	47	0.28
English	1,574	9.36
European	121	0.72
Finnish	7	0.04
French, except Basque	308	1.83
French Canadian	134	0.80
German	5,092	30.29
Greek	109	0.65
Guyanese	28	0.17
Hawaii Native/Pacific Islander:	7	0.04
Polynesian: (3)	3	0.02
Samoan (3)	3	0.02
Other Pac. Isl., specified	1	0.01
Other Pac. Isl., not spec. (1)	3	0.02
Hispanic or Latino:	393	2.34
Central American:	7	0.04
Costa Rican	1	0.01
Guatemalan	4	0.02
Honduran	1	0.01
Salvadoran	1	0.01
Cuban	14	0.08
Dominican Republic	10	0.06
Mexican	44	0.26
Puerto Rican	179	1.06
South American:	65	0.39
Argentinean	5	0.03
Bolivian	1	0.01
Chilean	6	0.04
Colombian	48	0.29
Ecuadorian	1	0.01
Peruvian	2	0.01
Uruguayan	1	0.01
Venezuelan	1	0.01
Other Hispanic or Latino	74	0.44
Hungarian	469	2.79
Iranian	5	0.03
Irish	2,474	14.72
Italian	3,792	22.56
Lithuanian	87	0.52
Maltese	19	0.11
Norwegian	21	0.12
Pennsylvania German	574	3.41
Polish	1,023	6.09
Portuguese	5	0.03
Romanian	21	0.12
Russian	197	1.17
Scandinavian	13	0.08
Scotch-Irish	183	1.09
Scottish	290	1.73
Slavic	7	0.04
Slovak	263	1.56
Slovene	18	0.11
Swedish	173	1.03
Swiss	85	0.51
Ukrainian	267	1.59
United States or American	722	4.30
Welsh	347	2.06
West Indian, excl. Hispanic:	33	0.20
British West Indian	3	0.02
Jamaican	16	0.10
Trinidadian and Tobagonian	11	0.07
West Indian	3	0.02
White:	15,999	95.18
Not Hispanic (15,599)	15,723	93.54
Hispanic (255)	276	1.64
Yugoslavian	10	0.06

Patton

Place Type: Township
County: Centre
Population: 11,420

Ancestry/Race	Number	%
African American/Black:	480	4.20
Not Hispanic (395)	460	4.03
Hispanic (10)	20	0.18
African, sub-Saharan:	23	0.20
African	23	0.20
Am. Ind. or Alaska Nat., not spec.	19	0.17
American Indian tribes, specified:	38	0.33
Apache	3	0.03
Blackfeet	1	0.01
Cherokee (4)	13	0.11
Chippewa	3	0.03
Choctaw	1	0.01
Cree	1	0.01
Delaware	1	0.01
Iroquois (3)	6	0.05

Notes: 1. Figures in the "Number" column do not add up to the total population due to: a) Ancestry/Race overlap — e.g. persons can report being both White and Irish, b) persons of Hispanic origin can report being any race, c) persons reporting two ancestries are counted in both categories. 2. Numbers in parentheses indicate the number of persons reporting this ancestry/race alone, not in combination with any other ancestry/race. 3. Refer to the Explanation of Data in the front of the book for more detailed information.

Latin American Indians (1)	3	0.03
Shoshone	1	0.01
Sioux	2	0.02
All other tribes (2)	3	0.03
American Indian tribes, not spec.	2	0.02
Arab:	72	0.63
Arab/Arabic	25	0.22
Egyptian	25	0.22
Jordanian	22	0.19
Asian:	578	5.06
Bangladeshi (2)	2	0.02
Cambodian (4)	5	0.04
Chinese, ex. Taiwanese (182)	194	1.70
Filipino (20)	27	0.24
Indian (146)	158	1.38
Indonesian (1)	1	0.01
Japanese (45)	50	0.44
Korean (65)	79	0.69
Laotian (1)	1	0.01
Malaysian (2)	3	0.03
Sri Lankan (1)	2	0.02
Taiwanese (8)	11	0.10
Thai (5)	7	0.06
Vietnamese (12)	14	0.12
Other Asian, not specified (15)	24	0.21
Austrian	78	0.68
British	71	0.62
Canadian	61	0.53
Carpatho Rusyn	8	0.07
Celtic	13	0.11
Croatian	72	0.63
Cypriot	8	0.07
Czech	5	0.04
Czechoslovakian	104	0.91
Danish	43	0.38
Dutch	210	1.84
Eastern European	42	0.37
English	1,281	11.22
European	176	1.54
Finnish	7	0.06
French, except Basque	235	2.06
French Canadian	74	0.65
German	3,332	29.18
Greek	95	0.83
Hawaii Native/Pacific Islander:	9	0.08
Micronesian: (5)	5	0.04
Other Micronesian (5)	5	0.04
Polynesian: (2)	2	0.02
Native Hawaiian (2)	2	0.02
Other Pac. Isl., not spec.	2	0.02
Hispanic or Latino:	247	2.16
Central American:	22	0.19
Costa Rican	2	0.02
Guatemalan	10	0.09
Honduran	2	0.02
Nicaraguan	1	0.01
Panamanian	3	0.03
Salvadoran	1	0.01
Other Central American	3	0.03
Cuban	11	0.10
Dominican Republic	3	0.03
Mexican	45	0.39
Puerto Rican	75	0.66
South American:	42	0.37
Argentinean	5	0.04
Bolivian	2	0.02
Chilean	2	0.02
Colombian	9	0.08
Ecuadorian	7	0.06
Peruvian	10	0.09
Venezuelan	7	0.06
Other Hispanic or Latino	49	0.43
Hungarian	106	0.93
Irish	1,510	13.22
Italian	916	8.02
Latvian	12	0.11
Lithuanian	45	0.39
Macedonian	9	0.08
Norwegian	120	1.05
Pennsylvania German	34	0.30
Polish	811	7.10
Portuguese	48	0.42
Romanian	30	0.26
Russian	227	1.99
Scotch-Irish	213	1.87
Scottish	362	3.17
Serbian	11	0.10
Slavic	12	0.11
Slovak	162	1.42
Swedish	235	2.06
Swiss	41	0.36
Turkish	8	0.07
Ukrainian	70	0.61
United States or American	647	5.67
Welsh	282	2.47
West Indian, excl. Hispanic:	47	0.41
Haitian	40	0.35
Jamaican	7	0.06
White:	10,360	90.72
Not Hispanic (10,059)	10,205	89.36
Hispanic (132)	155	1.36
Yugoslavian	8	0.07

Penn Hills

Place Type: Census Designated Place
County: Allegheny
Population: 46,809

Ancestry/Race	Number	%
Acadian/Cajun	10	0.02
African American/Black:	11,745	25.09
Not Hispanic (11,294)	11,664	24.92
Hispanic (53)	81	0.17
African, sub-Saharan:	264	0.56
African	163	0.35
Ethiopian	9	0.02
Liberian	9	0.02
Nigerian	59	0.13
Sierra Leonean	15	0.03
Other sub-Saharan African	9	0.02
Alaska Native tribes, specified:	1	0.00
Aleut	1	0.00
Am. Ind. or Alaska Nat., not spec.	105	0.22
Alsatian	14	0.03
American Indian tribes, specified:	104	0.22
Apache	5	0.01
Blackfeet (3)	20	0.04
Cherokee (12)	46	0.10
Chickasaw	2	0.00
Chippewa	1	0.00
Choctaw	3	0.01
Creek	1	0.00
Delaware (3)	5	0.01
Iroquois	3	0.01
Latin American Indians (3)	3	0.01
Seminole (1)	4	0.01
Sioux (3)	6	0.01
Yakama	1	0.00
All other tribes (2)	4	0.01
American Indian tribes, not spec.	22	0.05
Arab:	92	0.20
Egyptian	47	0.10
Lebanese	28	0.06
Syrian	17	0.04
Asian:	347	0.74
Bangladeshi (2)	2	0.00
Chinese, ex. Taiwanese (36)	49	0.10
Filipino (20)	49	0.10
Indian (83)	99	0.21
Japanese (8)	22	0.05
Korean (23)	30	0.06
Laotian (4)	4	0.01
Malaysian (1)	2	0.00
Pakistani (7)	11	0.02
Taiwanese (2)	2	0.00
Thai (8)	11	0.02
Vietnamese (41)	47	0.10
Other Asian, specified (5)	6	0.01
Other Asian, not specified (8)	13	0.03
Austrian	166	0.35
Belgian	39	0.08
Brazilian	9	0.02
British	111	0.24
Bulgarian	17	0.04
Canadian	67	0.14
Carpatho Rusyn	10	0.02
Celtic	37	0.08
Croatian	350	0.75
Czech	319	0.68
Czechoslovakian	101	0.22
Danish	5	0.01
Dutch	352	0.75
English	3,509	7.50
European	38	0.08
Finnish	21	0.04
French, except Basque	913	1.95
French Canadian	59	0.13
German	10,653	22.76
Greek	326	0.70
Hawaii Native/Pacific Islander:	26	0.06
Micronesian: (1)	1	0.00
Guamanian/Chamorro (1)	1	0.00
Polynesian:	12	0.03
Native Hawaiian	8	0.02
Samoan	3	0.01
Other Polynesian	1	0.00
Other Pac. Isl., specified	1	0.00
Other Pac. Isl., not spec. (4)	12	0.03
Hispanic or Latino:	297	0.63
Central American:	13	0.03
Guatemalan	2	0.00
Honduran	1	0.00
Panamanian	5	0.01
Salvadoran	5	0.01
Cuban	17	0.04
Dominican Republic	3	0.01
Mexican	98	0.21
Puerto Rican	66	0.14
South American:	23	0.05
Argentinean	2	0.00
Colombian	12	0.03
Ecuadorian	2	0.00
Venezuelan	4	0.01
Other South American	3	0.01
Other Hispanic or Latino	77	0.16
Hungarian	541	1.16
Iranian	20	0.04
Irish	8,103	17.31
Italian	9,483	20.26
Latvian	20	0.04
Lithuanian	114	0.24
Norwegian	30	0.06
Pennsylvania German	20	0.04
Polish	2,800	5.98
Portuguese	6	0.01
Romanian	85	0.18
Russian	474	1.01
Scotch-Irish	979	2.09
Scottish	906	1.94
Serbian	78	0.17
Slavic	97	0.21
Slovak	1,473	3.15
Slovene	183	0.39
Swedish	234	0.50
Swiss	93	0.20
Turkish	26	0.06
Ukrainian	286	0.61
United States or American	1,460	3.12
Welsh	474	1.01
West Indian, excl. Hispanic:	57	0.12
Barbadian	12	0.03
Jamaican	13	0.03
U.S. Virgin Islander	11	0.02
West Indian	21	0.04
White:	34,842	74.43
Not Hispanic (34,295)	34,663	74.05
Hispanic (148)	179	0.38
Yugoslavian	61	0.13

Notes: 1. Figures in the "Number" column do not add up to the total population due to: a) Ancestry/Race overlap — e.g. persons can report being both White and Irish, b) persons of Hispanic origin can report being any race, c) persons reporting two ancestries are counted in both categories. 2. Numbers in parentheses indicate the number of persons reporting this ancestry/race alone, not in combination with any other ancestry/race. 3. Refer to the Explanation of Data in the front of the book for more detailed information.

Penn

Place Type: Township
County: Westmoreland
Population: 19,591

Ancestry/Race	Number	%
African American/Black:	90	0.46
Not Hispanic (74)	90	0.46
Am. Ind. or Alaska Nat., not spec.	22	0.11
American Indian tribes, specified:	17	0.09
Cherokee (4)	10	0.05
Choctaw	1	0.01
Navajo	4	0.02
All other tribes (1)	2	0.01
American Indian tribes, not spec.	3	0.02
Arab:	38	0.19
Lebanese	18	0.09
Syrian	20	0.10
Asian:	113	0.58
Chinese, ex. Taiwanese (11)	14	0.07
Filipino (13)	27	0.14
Indian (35)	36	0.18
Japanese (20)	22	0.11
Korean (4)	6	0.03
Taiwanese (2)	2	0.01
Thai (1)	1	0.01
Vietnamese (2)	2	0.01
Other Asian, specified	3	0.02
Austrian	111	0.57
Belgian	16	0.08
British	56	0.29
Canadian	30	0.15
Carpatho Rusyn	5	0.03
Croatian	283	1.44
Czech	204	1.04
Czechoslovakian	103	0.53
Danish	16	0.08
Dutch	239	1.22
English	2,062	10.52
European	122	0.62
French, except Basque	269	1.37
French Canadian	31	0.16
German	5,906	30.13
Greek	55	0.28
Hawaii Native/Pacific Islander:	7	0.04
Micronesian: (2)	2	0.01
Guamanian/Chamorro (2)	2	0.01
Polynesian: (2)	2	0.01
Native Hawaiian (2)	2	0.01
Other Pac. Isl., specified	3	0.02
Hispanic or Latino:	86	0.44
Cuban	14	0.07
Dominican Republic	1	0.01
Mexican	32	0.16
Puerto Rican	8	0.04
South American:	8	0.04
Colombian	1	0.01
Ecuadorian	3	0.02
Peruvian	3	0.02
Other South American	1	0.01
Other Hispanic or Latino	23	0.12
Hungarian	298	1.52
Iranian	25	0.13
Irish	2,959	15.10
Italian	4,051	20.67
Lithuanian	82	0.42
Norwegian	66	0.34
Pennsylvania German	77	0.39
Polish	2,241	11.43
Romanian	28	0.14
Russian	108	0.55
Scotch-Irish	445	2.27
Scottish	389	1.98
Serbian	236	1.20
Slavic	101	0.52
Slovak	1,194	6.09
Slovene	338	1.72
Swedish	269	1.37
Swiss	75	0.38
Ukrainian	274	1.40
United States or American	872	4.45
Welsh	268	1.37
White:	19,385	98.95
Not Hispanic (19,259)	19,317	98.60
Hispanic (51)	68	0.35
Yugoslavian	66	0.34

Penn

Place Type: Township
County: York
Population: 14,592

Ancestry/Race	Number	%
African American/Black:	99	0.68
Not Hispanic (71)	97	0.66
Hispanic (1)	2	0.01
African, sub-Saharan:	4	0.03
African	4	0.03
Am. Ind. or Alaska Nat., not spec.	14	0.10
American Indian tribes, specified:	34	0.23
Apache (1)	1	0.01
Blackfeet	5	0.03
Cherokee (3)	13	0.09
Chippewa (3)	3	0.02
Comanche	1	0.01
Creek	1	0.01
Delaware	1	0.01
Iroquois (2)	2	0.01
Latin American Indians	1	0.01
Lumbee (1)	2	0.01
Navajo (1)	1	0.01
Yaqui	2	0.01
All other tribes (1)	1	0.01
American Indian tribes, not spec.	6	0.04
Arab:	32	0.22
Lebanese	25	0.17
Syrian	7	0.05
Asian:	144	0.99
Chinese, ex. Taiwanese (22)	22	0.15
Filipino (21)	35	0.24
Indian (28)	29	0.20
Japanese (6)	12	0.08
Korean (20)	23	0.16
Pakistani	1	0.01
Taiwanese (3)	3	0.02
Thai (3)	3	0.02
Vietnamese (12)	12	0.08
Other Asian, not specified (4)	4	0.03
Australian	10	0.07
Austrian	41	0.28
British	16	0.11
Canadian	5	0.03
Croatian	11	0.08
Czech	22	0.15
Czechoslovakian	12	0.08
Dutch	86	0.59
English	902	6.18
European	155	1.06
Finnish	25	0.17
French, except Basque	302	2.07
French Canadian	22	0.15
German	6,050	41.46
Greek	50	0.34
Hawaii Native/Pacific Islander:	4	0.03
Other Pac. Isl., not spec. (3)	4	0.03
Hispanic or Latino:	153	1.05
Central American:	9	0.06
Costa Rican	3	0.02
Guatemalan	3	0.02
Salvadoran	3	0.02
Cuban	3	0.02
Mexican	67	0.46
Puerto Rican	31	0.21
South American:	8	0.05
Argentinean	2	0.01
Colombian	3	0.02
Peruvian	2	0.01
Other South American	1	0.01
Other Hispanic or Latino	35	0.24
Hungarian	77	0.53
Irish	1,841	12.62
Italian	1,013	6.94
Lithuanian	20	0.14
Macedonian	11	0.08
Norwegian	82	0.56
Pennsylvania German	54	0.37
Polish	301	2.06
Portuguese	10	0.07
Romanian	29	0.20
Russian	59	0.40
Scotch-Irish	95	0.65
Scottish	191	1.31
Serbian	39	0.27
Slovak	17	0.12
Swedish	12	0.08
Swiss	57	0.39
Ukrainian	29	0.20
United States or American	1,497	10.26
Welsh	79	0.54
West Indian, excl. Hispanic:	6	0.04
West Indian	6	0.04
White:	14,301	98.01
Not Hispanic (14,138)	14,211	97.39
Hispanic (83)	90	0.62

Peters

Place Type: Township
County: Washington
Population: 17,566

Ancestry/Race	Number	%
African American/Black:	93	0.53
Not Hispanic (82)	87	0.50
Hispanic (2)	6	0.03
African, sub-Saharan:	7	0.04
South African	7	0.04
American Indian tribes, specified:	14	0.08
Apache (1)	1	0.01
Cherokee (3)	7	0.04
Iroquois	2	0.01
Kiowa	1	0.01
Latin American Indians (1)	1	0.01
Sioux	1	0.01
All other tribes	1	0.01
Arab:	260	1.48
Arab/Arabic	16	0.09
Lebanese	143	0.81
Syrian	70	0.40
Other Arab	31	0.18
Armenian	17	0.10
Asian:	228	1.30
Chinese, ex. Taiwanese (40)	46	0.26
Filipino (24)	32	0.18
Indian (72)	78	0.44
Japanese (22)	32	0.18
Korean (22)	23	0.13
Vietnamese (4)	4	0.02
Other Asian, not specified (7)	13	0.07
Austrian	102	0.58
Belgian	23	0.13
British	62	0.35
Bulgarian	22	0.13
Canadian	42	0.24
Carpatho Rusyn	7	0.04
Croatian	230	1.31
Czech	63	0.36
Czechoslovakian	73	0.42
Danish	45	0.26
Dutch	266	1.51
Eastern European	9	0.05
English	2,424	13.80
European	142	0.81
Finnish	38	0.22
French, except Basque	400	2.28
French Canadian	46	0.26
German	5,202	29.61
Greek	230	1.31

Notes: 1. Figures in the "Number" column do not add up to the total population due to: a) Ancestry/Race overlap — e.g. persons can report being both White and Irish, b) persons of Hispanic origin can report being any race, c) persons reporting two ancestries are counted in both categories. 2. Numbers in parentheses indicate the number of persons reporting this ancestry/race alone, not in combination with any other ancestry/race. 3. Refer to the Explanation of Data in the front of the book for more detailed information.

Hawaii Native/Pacific Islander:	9	0.05
Polynesian: (3)	4	0.02
Native Hawaiian (1)	2	0.01
Samoan (2)	2	0.01
Other Pac. Isl., not spec. (2)	5	0.03
Hispanic or Latino:	127	0.72
Central American:	9	0.05
Guatemalan	6	0.03
Nicaraguan	2	0.01
Other Central American	1	0.01
Cuban	7	0.04
Dominican Republic	2	0.01
Mexican	37	0.21
Puerto Rican	24	0.14
South American:	14	0.08
Argentinean	4	0.02
Chilean	5	0.03
Colombian	3	0.02
Other South American	2	0.01
Other Hispanic or Latino	34	0.19
Hungarian	281	1.60
Irish	3,593	20.45
Israeli	9	0.05
Italian	3,498	19.91
Latvian	20	0.11
Lithuanian	193	1.10
Macedonian	7	0.04
Norwegian	44	0.25
Pennsylvania German	27	0.15
Polish	1,452	8.27
Portuguese	99	0.56
Romanian	12	0.07
Russian	219	1.25
Scandinavian	18	0.10
Scotch-Irish	453	2.58
Scottish	442	2.52
Serbian	71	0.40
Slavic	48	0.27
Slovak	497	2.83
Slovene	96	0.55
Swedish	264	1.50
Swiss	84	0.48
Turkish	20	0.11
Ukrainian	151	0.86
United States or American	915	5.21
Welsh	231	1.32
White:	17,242	98.16
Not Hispanic (17,091)	17,140	97.57
Hispanic (90)	102	0.58
Yugoslavian	30	0.17

Philadelphia

Place Type: City
County: Philadelphia
Population: 1,517,550

Ancestry/Race	Number	%
Acadian/Cajun	23	0.00
Afghan	201	0.01
African American/Black:	672,162	44.29
Not Hispanic (646,123)	659,241	43.44
Hispanic (9,701)	12,921	0.85
African, sub-Saharan:	24,682	1.63
African	19,570	1.29
Cape Verdean	304	0.02
Ethiopian	758	0.05
Ghanian	297	0.02
Kenyan	71	0.00
Liberian	863	0.06
Nigerian	1,443	0.10
Senegalese	28	0.00
Sierra Leonean	169	0.01
Somalian	28	0.00
South African	141	0.01
Sudanese	264	0.02
Ugandan	17	0.00
Zairian	26	0.00
Zimbabwean	16	0.00
Other sub-Saharan African	687	0.05
Alaska Native tribes, specified:	26	0.00
Alaska Athabascan (1)	6	0.00
Aleut (5)	6	0.00
Eskimo (3)	12	0.00
Tlingit-Haida (1)	2	0.00
Alaska Native tribes, not specified	8	0.00
Am. Ind. or Alaska Nat., not spec.	5,574	0.37
Albanian	1,715	0.11
Alsatian	58	0.00
American Indian tribes, specified:	4,717	0.31
Apache (26)	90	0.01
Blackfeet (82)	430	0.03
Cherokee (495)	1,957	0.13
Cheyenne (3)	16	0.00
Chickasaw (3)	19	0.00
Chippewa (16)	40	0.00
Choctaw (11)	54	0.00
Colville	1	0.00
Comanche (2)	7	0.00
Cree	11	0.00
Creek (12)	40	0.00
Crow (5)	34	0.00
Delaware (56)	208	0.01
Houma	2	0.00
Iroquois (61)	184	0.01
Kiowa	1	0.00
Latin American Indians (200)	512	0.03
Lumbee (46)	83	0.01
Menominee	7	0.00
Navajo (24)	52	0.00
Osage (2)	4	0.00
Ottawa (1)	4	0.00
Potawatomi (11)	14	0.00
Pueblo (18)	54	0.00
Seminole (30)	134	0.01
Shoshone (4)	11	0.00
Sioux (39)	136	0.01
Tohono O'Odham (1)	3	0.00
Ute	1	0.00
Yaqui (3)	5	0.00
Yuman (2)	2	0.00
All other tribes (248)	601	0.04
American Indian tribes, not spec.	779	0.05
Arab:	5,271	0.35
Arab/Arabic	1,002	0.07
Egyptian	893	0.06
Iraqi	264	0.02
Jordanian	115	0.01
Lebanese	1,029	0.07
Moroccan	579	0.04
Palestinian	741	0.05
Syrian	254	0.02
Other Arab	394	0.03
Armenian	842	0.06
Asian:	76,421	5.04
Bangladeshi (130)	209	0.01
Cambodian (6,570)	7,761	0.51
Chinese, ex. Taiwanese (17,390)	19,205	1.27
Filipino (4,012)	5,232	0.34
Hmong (122)	140	0.01
Indian (12,819)	14,191	0.94
Indonesian (429)	601	0.04
Japanese (1,216)	1,695	0.11
Korean (6,556)	7,059	0.47
Laotian (1,001)	1,123	0.07
Malaysian (71)	101	0.01
Pakistani (791)	1,096	0.07
Sri Lankan (57)	66	0.00
Taiwanese (393)	467	0.03
Thai (301)	401	0.03
Vietnamese (11,608)	12,968	0.85
Other Asian, specified (59)	159	0.01
Other Asian, not specified (2,488)	3,947	0.26
Assyrian/Chaldean/Syriac	18	0.00
Australian	139	0.01
Austrian	3,787	0.25
Basque	23	0.00
Belgian	466	0.03
Brazilian	1,083	0.07
British	2,599	0.17
Bulgarian	71	0.00
Canadian	1,059	0.07
Celtic	232	0.02
Croatian	637	0.04
Cypriot	25	0.00
Czech	1,466	0.10
Czechoslovakian	955	0.06
Danish	950	0.06
Dutch	5,444	0.36
Eastern European	2,551	0.17
English	44,513	2.93
Estonian	55	0.00
European	3,502	0.23
Finnish	376	0.02
French, except Basque	11,258	0.74
French Canadian	1,971	0.13
German	123,058	8.11
German Russian	24	0.00
Greek	4,414	0.29
Guyanese	331	0.02
Hawaii Native/Pacific Islander:	2,379	0.16
Melanesian: (3)	5	0.00
Fijian (1)	3	0.00
Other Melanesian (2)	2	0.00
Micronesian: (129)	187	0.01
Guamanian/Chamorro (121)	176	0.01
Other Micronesian (8)	11	0.00
Polynesian: (357)	629	0.04
Native Hawaiian (183)	384	0.03
Samoan (157)	214	0.01
Tongan	4	0.00
Other Polynesian (17)	27	0.00
Other Pac. Isl., specified	84	0.01
Other Pac. Isl., not spec. (235)	1,474	0.10
Hispanic or Latino:	128,928	8.50
Central American:	2,846	0.19
Costa Rican	501	0.03
Guatemalan	518	0.03
Honduran	466	0.03
Nicaraguan	544	0.04
Panamanian	378	0.02
Salvadoran	337	0.02
Other Central American	102	0.01
Cuban	2,730	0.18
Dominican Republic	4,337	0.29
Mexican	6,220	0.41
Puerto Rican	91,527	6.03
South American:	4,761	0.31
Argentinean	531	0.03
Bolivian	55	0.00
Chilean	182	0.01
Colombian	2,414	0.16
Ecuadorian	420	0.03
Paraguayan	38	0.00
Peruvian	471	0.03
Uruguayan	86	0.01
Venezuelan	409	0.03
Other South American	155	0.01
Other Hispanic or Latino	16,507	1.09
Hungarian	5,848	0.39
Icelander	11	0.00
Iranian	613	0.04
Irish	206,350	13.60
Israeli	931	0.06
Italian	140,139	9.23
Latvian	466	0.03
Lithuanian	5,681	0.37
Luxemburger	8	0.00
Macedonian	96	0.01
Maltese	54	0.00
New Zealander	43	0.00
Northern European	392	0.03
Norwegian	2,201	0.15
Pennsylvania German	1,857	0.12
Polish	65,508	4.32
Portuguese	2,589	0.17
Romanian	3,009	0.20
Russian	26,375	1.74
Scandinavian	305	0.02
Scotch-Irish	9,109	0.60

Notes: 1. Figures in the "Number" column do not add up to the total population due to: a) Ancestry/Race overlap — e.g. persons can report being both White and Irish, b) persons of Hispanic origin can report being any race, c) persons reporting two ancestries are counted in both categories. 2. Numbers in parentheses indicate the number of persons reporting this ancestry/race alone, not in combination with any other ancestry/race. 3. Refer to the Explanation of Data in the front of the book for more detailed information.

Ancestry/Race	Number	%
Scottish	8,323	0.55
Serbian	286	0.02
Slavic	391	0.03
Slovak	2,388	0.16
Slovene	113	0.01
Soviet Union	43	0.00
Swedish	3,597	0.24
Swiss	1,218	0.08
Turkish	595	0.04
Ukrainian	15,665	1.03
United States or American	27,843	1.83
Welsh	4,922	0.32
West Indian, excl. Hispanic:	18,376	1.21
Bahamian	175	0.01
Barbadian	568	0.04
Belizean	72	0.00
Bermudan	40	0.00
British West Indian	671	0.04
Dutch West Indian	23	0.00
Haitian	4,221	0.28
Jamaican	9,249	0.61
Trinidadian and Tobagonian	1,738	0.11
U.S. Virgin Islander	51	0.00
West Indian	1,513	0.10
Other West Indian	55	0.00
White:	703,584	46.36
Not Hispanic (644,395)	658,721	43.41
Hispanic (38,872)	44,863	2.96
Yugoslavian	701	0.05

Phoenixville

Place Type: Borough
County: Chester
Population: 14,788

Ancestry/Race	Number	%
African American/Black:	1,270	8.59
Not Hispanic (1,127)	1,243	8.41
Hispanic (6)	27	0.18
African, sub-Saharan:	60	0.40
African	51	0.34
Cape Verdean	9	0.06
Am. Ind. or Alaska Nat., not spec.	27	0.18
Albanian	17	0.11
American Indian tribes, specified:	55	0.37
Apache	1	0.01
Blackfeet (2)	6	0.04
Cherokee (3)	18	0.12
Chippewa	1	0.01
Iroquois	1	0.01
Latin American Indians (5)	9	0.06
Sioux	2	0.01
Tohono O'Odham	2	0.01
Yaqui (1)	4	0.03
All other tribes (1)	11	0.07
American Indian tribes, not spec.	7	0.05
Arab:	77	0.52
Arab/Arabic	13	0.09
Egyptian	14	0.09
Lebanese	11	0.07
Moroccan	26	0.18
Syrian	6	0.04
Other Arab	7	0.05
Armenian	6	0.04
Asian:	417	2.82
Bangladeshi (2)	2	0.01
Chinese, ex. Taiwanese (46)	58	0.39
Filipino (54)	63	0.43
Indian (105)	111	0.75
Japanese (9)	20	0.14
Korean (19)	22	0.15
Laotian (1)	1	0.01
Pakistani (1)	1	0.01
Taiwanese (1)	2	0.01
Thai	1	0.01
Vietnamese (93)	105	0.71
Other Asian, specified (1)	2	0.01
Other Asian, not specified (14)	29	0.20
Australian	27	0.18
Austrian	68	0.46
Belgian	8	0.05
British	113	0.76
Canadian	14	0.09
Czech	82	0.55
Czechoslovakian	71	0.48
Danish	6	0.04
Dutch	382	2.58
Eastern European	17	0.11
English	1,539	10.38
European	65	0.44
French, except Basque	191	1.29
French Canadian	33	0.22
German	3,409	23.00
Greek	83	0.56
Hawaii Native/Pacific Islander:	7	0.05
Micronesian: (3)	3	0.02
Guamanian/Chamorro (3)	3	0.02
Polynesian:	3	0.02
Samoan	3	0.02
Other Pac. Isl., specified	1	0.01
Hispanic or Latino:	432	2.92
Central American:	26	0.18
Guatemalan	7	0.05
Honduran	2	0.01
Panamanian	6	0.04
Salvadoran	8	0.05
Other Central American	3	0.02
Cuban	19	0.13
Dominican Republic	9	0.06
Mexican	108	0.73
Puerto Rican	154	1.04
South American:	26	0.18
Argentinean	7	0.05
Bolivian	2	0.01
Colombian	3	0.02
Ecuadorian	2	0.01
Peruvian	5	0.03
Venezuelan	6	0.04
Other South American	2	0.01
Other Hispanic or Latino	90	0.61
Hungarian	376	2.54
Icelander	6	0.04
Iranian	21	0.14
Irish	3,262	22.00
Israeli	8	0.05
Italian	2,035	13.73
Latvian	11	0.07
Lithuanian	52	0.35
Northern European	18	0.12
Norwegian	86	0.58
Pennsylvania German	177	1.19
Polish	1,292	8.72
Portuguese	8	0.05
Romanian	15	0.10
Russian	217	1.46
Scandinavian	11	0.07
Scotch-Irish	205	1.38
Scottish	257	1.73
Serbian	6	0.04
Slavic	43	0.29
Slovak	567	3.82
Swedish	78	0.53
Swiss	30	0.20
Ukrainian	406	2.74
United States or American	401	2.71
Welsh	242	1.63
West Indian, excl. Hispanic:	35	0.24
Jamaican	20	0.13
Trinidadian and Tobagonian	15	0.10
White:	13,048	88.23
Not Hispanic (12,647)	12,805	86.59
Hispanic (210)	243	1.64
Yugoslavian	5	0.03

Pittsburgh

Place Type: City
County: Allegheny
Population: 334,563

Ancestry/Race	Number	%
Acadian/Cajun	8	0.00
Afghan	12	0.00
African American/Black:	93,904	28.07
Not Hispanic (90,183)	93,132	27.84
Hispanic (567)	772	0.23
African, sub-Saharan:	4,338	1.30
African	3,736	1.12
Cape Verdean	13	0.00
Ethiopian	52	0.02
Ghanian	65	0.02
Kenyan	58	0.02
Liberian	37	0.01
Nigerian	113	0.03
Senegalese	51	0.02
Sierra Leonean	9	0.00
South African	35	0.01
Sudanese	21	0.01
Ugandan	5	0.00
Other sub-Saharan African	143	0.04
Alaska Native tribes, specified:	3	0.00
Alaska Athabascan (1)	2	0.00
Eskimo	1	0.00
Alaska Native tribes, not specified	3	0.00
Am. Ind. or Alaska Nat., not spec.	949	0.28
Albanian	17	0.01
Alsatian	72	0.02
American Indian tribes, specified:	1,149	0.34
Apache (9)	33	0.01
Blackfeet (13)	122	0.04
Cherokee (127)	542	0.16
Cheyenne (1)	1	0.00
Chickasaw (1)	2	0.00
Chippewa (7)	17	0.01
Choctaw (3)	22	0.01
Comanche (1)	3	0.00
Cree (2)	16	0.00
Creek (4)	23	0.01
Crow (1)	3	0.00
Delaware	4	0.00
Iroquois (35)	98	0.03
Kiowa (1)	1	0.00
Latin American Indians (21)	46	0.01
Lumbee (4)	11	0.00
Menominee	1	0.00
Navajo	26	0.01
Osage	4	0.00
Ottawa	1	0.00
Pima	1	0.00
Potawatomi (1)	1	0.00
Pueblo (1)	7	0.00
Seminole (2)	18	0.01
Shoshone (1)	3	0.00
Sioux (18)	51	0.02
Tohono O'Odham	3	0.00
Ute (4)	4	0.00
All other tribes (22)	85	0.03
American Indian tribes, not spec.	186	0.06
Arab:	2,374	0.71
Arab/Arabic	324	0.10
Egyptian	278	0.08
Iraqi	12	0.00
Lebanese	1,065	0.32
Moroccan	74	0.02
Palestinian	61	0.02
Syrian	447	0.13
Other Arab	113	0.03
Armenian	63	0.02
Asian:	10,474	3.13
Bangladeshi (36)	42	0.01
Cambodian (34)	48	0.01
Chinese, ex. Taiwanese (2,717)	2,953	0.88
Filipino (354)	516	0.15
Hmong (2)	4	0.00

Notes: 1. Figures in the "Number" column do not add up to the total population due to: a) Ancestry/Race overlap — e.g. persons can report being both White and Irish, b) persons of Hispanic origin can report being any race, c) persons reporting two ancestries are counted in both categories. 2. Numbers in parentheses indicate the number of persons reporting this ancestry/race alone, not in combination with any other ancestry/race. 3. Refer to the Explanation of Data in the front of the book for more detailed information.

Ancestry/Race	Number	%
Indian (2,007)	2,204	0.66
Indonesian (92)	105	0.03
Japanese (676)	813	0.24
Korean (1,013)	1,113	0.33
Laotian (20)	23	0.01
Malaysian (22)	48	0.01
Pakistani (76)	93	0.03
Sri Lankan (23)	31	0.01
Taiwanese (233)	270	0.08
Thai (202)	243	0.07
Vietnamese (724)	787	0.24
Other Asian, specified (22)	82	0.02
Other Asian, not specified (834)	1,099	0.33
Assyrian/Chaldean/Syriac	6	0.00
Australian	65	0.02
Austrian	1,517	0.45
Belgian	246	0.07
Brazilian	83	0.02
British	993	0.30
Bulgarian	59	0.02
Canadian	397	0.12
Carpatho Rusyn	116	0.03
Celtic	79	0.02
Croatian	2,981	0.89
Cypriot	16	0.00
Czech	1,141	0.34
Czechoslovakian	935	0.28
Danish	208	0.06
Dutch	1,510	0.45
Eastern European	865	0.26
English	15,352	4.59
Estonian	13	0.00
European	1,818	0.54
Finnish	142	0.04
French, except Basque	4,713	1.41
French Canadian	619	0.19
German	65,976	19.72
German Russian	47	0.01
Greek	1,833	0.55
Guyanese	49	0.01
Hawaii Native/Pacific Islander:	293	0.09
Melanesian: (1)	2	0.00
Fijian (1)	2	0.00
Micronesian: (18)	31	0.01
Guamanian/Chamorro (18)	30	0.01
Other Micronesian	1	0.00
Polynesian: (65)	118	0.04
Native Hawaiian (26)	63	0.02
Samoan (39)	53	0.02
Other Polynesian	2	0.00
Other Pac. Isl., specified	31	0.01
Other Pac. Isl., not spec. (26)	111	0.03
Hispanic or Latino:	4,425	1.32
Central American:	170	0.05
Costa Rican	11	0.00
Guatemalan	39	0.01
Honduran	18	0.01
Nicaraguan	19	0.01
Panamanian	48	0.01
Salvadoran	27	0.01
Other Central American	8	0.00
Cuban	294	0.09
Dominican Republic	53	0.02
Mexican	1,235	0.37
Puerto Rican	808	0.24
South American:	610	0.18
Argentinean	132	0.04
Bolivian	17	0.01
Chilean	80	0.02
Colombian	116	0.03
Ecuadorian	24	0.01
Paraguayan	2	0.00
Peruvian	90	0.03
Uruguayan	11	0.00
Venezuelan	121	0.04
Other South American	17	0.01
Other Hispanic or Latino	1,255	0.38
Hungarian	3,961	1.18
Icelander	15	0.00
Iranian	182	0.05
Irish	52,845	15.80
Israeli	248	0.07
Italian	39,632	11.85
Latvian	101	0.03
Lithuanian	2,413	0.72
Luxemburger	21	0.01
Macedonian	77	0.02
Maltese	8	0.00
New Zealander	53	0.02
Northern European	109	0.03
Norwegian	755	0.23
Pennsylvania German	177	0.05
Polish	28,178	8.42
Portuguese	162	0.05
Romanian	727	0.22
Russian	6,697	2.00
Scandinavian	86	0.03
Scotch-Irish	4,363	1.30
Scottish	4,189	1.25
Serbian	1,002	0.30
Slavic	517	0.15
Slovak	6,566	1.96
Slovene	624	0.19
Swedish	1,944	0.58
Swiss	595	0.18
Turkish	327	0.10
Ukrainian	3,067	0.92
United States or American	7,398	2.21
Welsh	2,816	0.84
West Indian, excl. Hispanic:	709	0.21
Barbadian	24	0.01
Bermudan	13	0.00
Dutch West Indian	30	0.01
Haitian	101	0.03
Jamaican	227	0.07
Trinidadian and Tobagonian	117	0.03
U.S. Virgin Islander	15	0.00
West Indian	182	0.05
White:	230,266	68.83
Not Hispanic (223,982)	227,669	68.05
Hispanic (2,276)	2,597	0.78
Yugoslavian	495	0.15

Plains

Place Type: Township
County: Luzerne
Population: 10,906

Ancestry/Race	Number	%
African American/Black:	58	0.53
Not Hispanic (51)	56	0.51
Hispanic (1)	2	0.02
Am. Ind. or Alaska Nat., not spec.	3	0.03
American Indian tribes, specified:	2	0.02
Cherokee (1)	1	0.01
Choctaw (1)	1	0.01
American Indian tribes, not spec.	3	0.03
Arab:	104	0.95
Lebanese	28	0.26
Syrian	76	0.70
Asian:	102	0.94
Bangladeshi (4)	4	0.04
Chinese, ex. Taiwanese (13)	13	0.12
Filipino (13)	20	0.18
Indian (37)	37	0.34
Japanese (2)	3	0.03
Korean (6)	6	0.06
Pakistani (7)	7	0.06
Vietnamese (1)	4	0.04
Other Asian, not specified (4)	8	0.07
Australian	8	0.07
Austrian	18	0.17
British	8	0.07
Croatian	15	0.14
Czech	37	0.34
Czechoslovakian	43	0.39
Danish	14	0.13
Dutch	155	1.42
English	649	5.95
European	15	0.14
Finnish	16	0.15
French, except Basque	46	0.42
French Canadian	28	0.26
German	977	8.96
Greek	55	0.50
Hawaii Native/Pacific Islander:	1	0.01
Polynesian:	1	0.01
Samoan	1	0.01
Hispanic or Latino:	56	0.51
Central American:	1	0.01
Costa Rican	1	0.01
Cuban	2	0.02
Mexican	15	0.14
Puerto Rican	30	0.28
Other Hispanic or Latino	8	0.07
Hungarian	38	0.35
Irish	1,713	15.71
Italian	2,092	19.18
Lithuanian	473	4.34
Pennsylvania German	24	0.22
Polish	3,606	33.06
Romanian	4	0.04
Russian	611	5.60
Scotch-Irish	14	0.13
Scottish	71	0.65
Slovak	725	6.65
Slovene	16	0.15
Swedish	21	0.19
Ukrainian	318	2.92
United States or American	198	1.82
Welsh	443	4.06
White:	10,752	98.59
Not Hispanic (10,683)	10,705	98.16
Hispanic (41)	47	0.43

Plum

Place Type: Borough
County: Allegheny
Population: 26,940

Ancestry/Race	Number	%
African American/Black:	809	3.00
Not Hispanic (740)	805	2.99
Hispanic (3)	4	0.01
African, sub-Saharan:	76	0.28
African	16	0.06
Nigerian	60	0.22
Am. Ind. or Alaska Nat., not spec.	22	0.08
Albanian	26	0.10
American Indian tribes, specified:	39	0.14
Blackfeet (4)	4	0.01
Cherokee (1)	17	0.06
Chickasaw (3)	3	0.01
Delaware	1	0.00
Iroquois (1)	5	0.02
Latin American Indians	1	0.00
Potawatomi	4	0.01
Sioux (1)	1	0.00
All other tribes	3	0.01
American Indian tribes, not spec.	1	0.00
Arab:	116	0.43
Lebanese	53	0.20
Syrian	63	0.23
Armenian	5	0.02
Asian:	268	0.99
Bangladeshi (1)	1	0.00
Chinese, ex. Taiwanese (51)	52	0.19
Filipino (14)	29	0.11
Indian (100)	102	0.38
Indonesian	1	0.00
Japanese (5)	10	0.04
Korean (23)	27	0.10
Pakistani (8)	8	0.03
Taiwanese (5)	5	0.02
Thai (1)	5	0.02
Vietnamese (16)	20	0.07
Other Asian, not specified (3)	8	0.03
Austrian	148	0.55

Notes: 1. Figures in the "Number" column do not add up to the total population due to: a) Ancestry/Race overlap — e.g. persons can report being both White and Irish, b) persons of Hispanic origin can report being any race, c) persons reporting two ancestries are counted in both categories. 2. Numbers in parentheses indicate the number of persons reporting this ancestry/race alone, not in combination with any other ancestry/race. 3. Refer to the Explanation of Data in the front of the book for more detailed information.

Ancestry/Race	Number	%
Belgian	19	0.07
British	88	0.33
Bulgarian	5	0.02
Canadian	20	0.07
Carpatho Rusyn	38	0.14
Croatian	313	1.16
Czech	207	0.77
Czechoslovakian	94	0.35
Danish	50	0.19
Dutch	183	0.68
Eastern European	14	0.05
English	2,741	10.17
European	111	0.41
Finnish	24	0.09
French, except Basque	521	1.93
French Canadian	42	0.16
German	7,690	28.54
Greek	126	0.47
Hawaii Native/Pacific Islander:	11	0.04
Micronesian: (6)	9	0.03
Guamanian/Chamorro (6)	9	0.03
Other Pac. Isl., not spec. (1)	2	0.01
Hispanic or Latino:	167	0.62
Central American:	16	0.06
Costa Rican	1	0.00
Guatemalan	2	0.01
Honduran	4	0.01
Nicaraguan	5	0.02
Panamanian	2	0.01
Salvadoran	2	0.01
Cuban	17	0.06
Mexican	40	0.15
Puerto Rican	26	0.10
South American:	21	0.08
Argentinean	3	0.01
Ecuadorian	1	0.00
Peruvian	1	0.00
Uruguayan	6	0.02
Venezuelan	5	0.02
Other South American	5	0.02
Other Hispanic or Latino	47	0.17
Hungarian	597	2.22
Irish	5,764	21.40
Italian	6,311	23.43
Lithuanian	83	0.31
Northern European	4	0.01
Norwegian	46	0.17
Pennsylvania German	43	0.16
Polish	2,640	9.80
Portuguese	18	0.07
Romanian	21	0.08
Russian	426	1.58
Scotch-Irish	811	3.01
Scottish	676	2.51
Serbian	132	0.49
Slavic	37	0.14
Slovak	1,294	4.80
Slovene	204	0.76
Swedish	213	0.79
Swiss	31	0.12
Turkish	9	0.03
Ukrainian	226	0.84
United States or American	850	3.16
Welsh	263	0.98
West Indian, excl. Hispanic:	51	0.19
British West Indian	13	0.05
Haitian	21	0.08
Jamaican	17	0.06
White:	25,872	96.04
Not Hispanic (25,617)	25,727	95.50
Hispanic (137)	145	0.54
Yugoslavian	74	0.27

Plumstead

Place Type: Township
County: Bucks
Population: 11,409

Ancestry/Race	Number	%
African American/Black:	108	0.95
Not Hispanic (80)	104	0.91
Hispanic (1)	4	0.04
African, sub-Saharan:	12	0.11
African	2	0.02
South African	10	0.09
Am. Ind. or Alaska Nat., not spec.	18	0.16
American Indian tribes, specified:	33	0.29
Blackfeet (4)	6	0.05
Cherokee (1)	5	0.04
Chippewa	1	0.01
Cree (1)	2	0.02
Iroquois	1	0.01
Kiowa	5	0.04
Latin American Indians (1)	10	0.09
Navajo (1)	1	0.01
Puget Sound Salish (1)	1	0.01
All other tribes	1	0.01
American Indian tribes, not spec.	9	0.08
Armenian	20	0.18
Asian:	137	1.20
Chinese, ex. Taiwanese (21)	22	0.19
Filipino (12)	18	0.16
Indian (22)	23	0.20
Japanese (7)	10	0.09
Korean (24)	33	0.29
Taiwanese (1)	1	0.01
Thai (2)	2	0.02
Vietnamese (23)	23	0.20
Other Asian, specified	2	0.02
Other Asian, not specified (3)	3	0.03
Austrian	63	0.55
British	36	0.32
Canadian	52	0.46
Croatian	8	0.07
Czech	72	0.63
Czechoslovakian	19	0.17
Danish	34	0.30
Dutch	163	1.43
Eastern European	32	0.28
English	1,430	12.53
French, except Basque	384	3.37
French Canadian	43	0.38
German	3,588	31.45
Greek	71	0.62
Guyanese	16	0.14
Hawaii Native/Pacific Islander:	3	0.03
Polynesian: (1)	1	0.01
Native Hawaiian (1)	1	0.01
Other Pac. Isl., specified	1	0.01
Other Pac. Isl., not spec.	1	0.01
Hispanic or Latino:	226	1.98
Central American:	15	0.13
Costa Rican	4	0.04
Guatemalan	9	0.08
Nicaraguan	2	0.02
Cuban	17	0.15
Dominican Republic	2	0.02
Mexican	107	0.94
Puerto Rican	41	0.36
South American:	8	0.07
Argentinean	3	0.03
Colombian	3	0.03
Ecuadorian	2	0.02
Other Hispanic or Latino	36	0.32
Hungarian	178	1.56
Irish	3,088	27.07
Italian	1,809	15.86
Latvian	14	0.12
Lithuanian	120	1.05
Northern European	8	0.07
Norwegian	58	0.51
Pennsylvania German	41	0.36
Polish	830	7.27
Portuguese	54	0.47
Russian	258	2.26
Scotch-Irish	291	2.55
Scottish	202	1.77
Serbian	8	0.07
Slavic	8	0.07
Slovak	153	1.34
Swedish	92	0.81
Swiss	66	0.58
Ukrainian	276	2.42
United States or American	353	3.09
Welsh	192	1.68
West Indian, excl. Hispanic:	38	0.33
Barbadian	17	0.15
Jamaican	21	0.18
White:	11,076	97.08
Not Hispanic (10,844)	10,925	95.76
Hispanic (150)	151	1.32
Yugoslavian	8	0.07

Plymouth

Place Type: Township
County: Montgomery
Population: 16,045

Ancestry/Race	Number	%
African American/Black:	741	4.62
Not Hispanic (663)	733	4.57
Hispanic (6)	8	0.05
African, sub-Saharan:	17	0.11
African	17	0.11
Am. Ind. or Alaska Nat., not spec.	26	0.16
Albanian	6	0.04
American Indian tribes, specified:	28	0.17
Blackfeet	6	0.04
Cherokee (4)	11	0.07
Comanche	1	0.01
Iroquois (1)	1	0.01
Latin American Indians (1)	4	0.02
All other tribes (4)	5	0.03
American Indian tribes, not spec.	1	0.01
Arab:	124	0.77
Egyptian	30	0.19
Lebanese	6	0.04
Syrian	88	0.55
Armenian	26	0.16
Asian:	890	5.55
Chinese, ex. Taiwanese (180)	185	1.15
Filipino (63)	74	0.46
Indian (199)	210	1.31
Japanese (17)	21	0.13
Korean (310)	324	2.02
Laotian (4)	4	0.02
Pakistani (17)	20	0.12
Sri Lankan (1)	1	0.01
Taiwanese (10)	10	0.06
Thai (2)	2	0.01
Vietnamese (21)	23	0.14
Other Asian, not specified (2)	16	0.10
Australian	5	0.03
Austrian	87	0.54
Belgian	11	0.07
Brazilian	15	0.09
British	36	0.22
Canadian	8	0.05
Croatian	47	0.29
Czech	10	0.06
Czechoslovakian	32	0.20
Danish	17	0.11
Dutch	250	1.56
Eastern European	115	0.72
English	1,329	8.28
European	47	0.29
French, except Basque	185	1.15
French Canadian	35	0.22
German	2,880	17.95
Greek	77	0.48
Hawaii Native/Pacific Islander:	3	0.02
Polynesian: (2)	3	0.02
Native Hawaiian (1)	1	0.01
Samoan	1	0.01
Other Polynesian (1)	1	0.01
Hispanic or Latino:	201	1.25
Central American:	6	0.04
Costa Rican	1	0.01

Notes: 1. Figures in the "Number" column do not add up to the total population due to: a) Ancestry/Race overlap — e.g. persons can report being both White and Irish, b) persons of Hispanic origin can report being any race, c) persons reporting two ancestries are counted in both categories. 2. Numbers in parentheses indicate the number of persons reporting this ancestry/race alone, not in combination with any other ancestry/race. 3. Refer to the Explanation of Data in the front of the book for more detailed information.

Ancestry/Race	Number	%
Panamanian	2	0.01
Salvadoran	3	0.02
Cuban	12	0.07
Dominican Republic	4	0.02
Mexican	59	0.37
Puerto Rican	61	0.38
South American:	19	0.12
Argentinean	3	0.02
Colombian	6	0.04
Ecuadorian	4	0.02
Peruvian	6	0.04
Other Hispanic or Latino	40	0.25
Hungarian	121	0.75
Irish	3,747	23.35
Italian	3,850	24.00
Latvian	45	0.28
Lithuanian	104	0.65
Northern European	14	0.09
Norwegian	117	0.73
Pennsylvania German	96	0.60
Polish	1,660	10.35
Portuguese	21	0.13
Romanian	21	0.13
Russian	540	3.37
Scandinavian	7	0.04
Scotch-Irish	222	1.38
Scottish	174	1.08
Slavic	43	0.27
Slovak	143	0.89
Swedish	67	0.42
Swiss	6	0.04
Ukrainian	180	1.12
United States or American	692	4.31
Welsh	187	1.17
White:	14,434	89.96
Not Hispanic (14,184)	14,287	89.04
Hispanic (137)	147	0.92

Pottstown

Place Type: Borough
County: Montgomery
Population: 21,859

Ancestry/Race	Number	%
African American/Black:	3,699	16.92
Not Hispanic (3,221)	3,563	16.30
Hispanic (70)	136	0.62
African, sub-Saharan:	127	0.58
African	127	0.58
Alaska Native tribes, not specified	1	0.00
Am. Ind. or Alaska Nat., not spec.	74	0.34
Alsatian	10	0.05
American Indian tribes, specified:	92	0.42
Apache (4)	4	0.02
Blackfeet (3)	8	0.04
Cherokee (9)	36	0.16
Cheyenne	1	0.00
Chickasaw (1)	1	0.00
Chippewa	1	0.00
Comanche	1	0.00
Delaware	3	0.01
Iroquois (1)	5	0.02
Latin American Indians (4)	6	0.03
Lumbee (1)	2	0.01
Navajo	2	0.01
Pima	1	0.00
Seminole	4	0.02
Sioux (4)	10	0.05
All other tribes (3)	7	0.03
American Indian tribes, not spec.	4	0.02
Arab:	17	0.08
Egyptian	17	0.08
Asian:	196	0.90
Cambodian (3)	3	0.01
Chinese, ex. Taiwanese (55)	58	0.27
Filipino (18)	29	0.13
Indian (18)	26	0.12
Japanese (4)	9	0.04
Korean (11)	17	0.08
Taiwanese	4	0.02
Thai (1)	3	0.01
Vietnamese (27)	31	0.14
Other Asian, specified	1	0.00
Other Asian, not specified (3)	15	0.07
Austrian	163	0.75
Basque	7	0.03
British	35	0.16
Canadian	24	0.11
Czech	42	0.19
Czechoslovakian	46	0.21
Danish	28	0.13
Dutch	1,082	4.97
Eastern European	7	0.03
English	1,310	6.02
Estonian	12	0.06
European	107	0.49
French, except Basque	327	1.50
French Canadian	40	0.18
German	5,505	25.29
Greek	116	0.53
Hawaii Native/Pacific Islander:	28	0.13
Micronesian: (1)	1	0.00
Other Micronesian (1)	1	0.00
Polynesian: (15)	19	0.09
Native Hawaiian (5)	8	0.04
Samoan (10)	11	0.05
Other Pac. Isl., specified	1	0.00
Other Pac. Isl., not spec. (3)	7	0.03
Hispanic or Latino:	990	4.53
Central American:	31	0.14
Costa Rican	11	0.05
Guatemalan	2	0.01
Honduran	2	0.01
Nicaraguan	1	0.00
Panamanian	12	0.05
Salvadoran	3	0.01
Cuban	12	0.05
Dominican Republic	4	0.02
Mexican	107	0.49
Puerto Rican	711	3.25
South American:	15	0.07
Argentinean	3	0.01
Chilean	1	0.00
Colombian	1	0.00
Ecuadorian	6	0.03
Peruvian	3	0.01
Other South American	1	0.00
Other Hispanic or Latino	110	0.50
Hungarian	413	1.90
Icelander	11	0.05
Irish	2,963	13.61
Italian	2,143	9.84
Latvian	6	0.03
Lithuanian	98	0.45
Norwegian	60	0.28
Pennsylvania German	514	2.36
Polish	1,372	6.30
Portuguese	21	0.10
Romanian	24	0.11
Russian	101	0.46
Scandinavian	10	0.05
Scotch-Irish	182	0.84
Scottish	167	0.77
Slavic	73	0.34
Slovak	431	1.98
Swedish	222	1.02
Swiss	82	0.38
Ukrainian	367	1.69
United States or American	1,030	4.73
Welsh	304	1.40
West Indian, excl. Hispanic:	48	0.22
Jamaican	18	0.08
West Indian	30	0.14
White:	17,860	81.71
Not Hispanic (16,930)	17,351	79.38
Hispanic (413)	509	2.33
Yugoslavian	5	0.02

Pottsville

Place Type: City
County: Schuylkill
Population: 15,549

Ancestry/Race	Number	%
African American/Black:	428	2.75
Not Hispanic (345)	417	2.68
Hispanic (7)	11	0.07
African, sub-Saharan:	69	0.44
African	62	0.40
Cape Verdean	7	0.05
Am. Ind. or Alaska Nat., not spec.	18	0.12
American Indian tribes, specified:	35	0.23
Apache (2)	3	0.02
Blackfeet	4	0.03
Cherokee (2)	7	0.05
Comanche	1	0.01
Delaware (2)	8	0.05
Iroquois (5)	7	0.05
Kiowa (1)	1	0.01
Latin American Indians	3	0.02
All other tribes	1	0.01
American Indian tribes, not spec.	2	0.01
Arab:	216	1.39
Arab/Arabic	10	0.06
Lebanese	182	1.17
Syrian	11	0.07
Other Arab	13	0.08
Asian:	99	0.64
Chinese, ex. Taiwanese (26)	28	0.18
Filipino (3)	7	0.05
Indian (28)	36	0.23
Japanese (1)	4	0.03
Korean (15)	17	0.11
Pakistani (5)	5	0.03
Other Asian, not specified (1)	2	0.01
Austrian	50	0.32
Brazilian	15	0.10
British	25	0.16
Canadian	5	0.03
Carpatho Rusyn	9	0.06
Croatian	19	0.12
Czech	128	0.82
Czechoslovakian	61	0.39
Danish	31	0.20
Dutch	1,282	8.25
Eastern European	8	0.05
English	709	4.56
European	36	0.23
French, except Basque	153	0.98
French Canadian	4	0.03
German	4,670	30.06
Greek	86	0.55
Hawaii Native/Pacific Islander:	3	0.02
Polynesian: (1)	3	0.02
Native Hawaiian (1)	3	0.02
Hispanic or Latino:	190	1.22
Central American:	3	0.02
Honduran	1	0.01
Panamanian	1	0.01
Salvadoran	1	0.01
Cuban	5	0.03
Dominican Republic	6	0.04
Mexican	62	0.40
Puerto Rican	81	0.52
South American:	8	0.05
Chilean	1	0.01
Peruvian	2	0.01
Uruguayan	2	0.01
Other South American	3	0.02
Other Hispanic or Latino	25	0.16
Hungarian	86	0.55
Irish	3,708	23.87
Italian	1,638	10.54
Lithuanian	649	4.18
Norwegian	87	0.56
Pennsylvania German	337	2.17
Polish	1,353	8.71

Notes: 1. Figures in the "Number" column do not add up to the total population due to: a) Ancestry/Race overlap — e.g. persons can report being both White and Irish, b) persons of Hispanic origin can report being any race, c) persons reporting two ancestries are counted in both categories. 2. Numbers in parentheses indicate the number of persons reporting this ancestry/race alone, not in combination with any other ancestry/race. 3. Refer to the Explanation of Data in the front of the book for more detailed information.

Portuguese	12	0.08
Romanian	21	0.14
Russian	105	0.68
Scotch-Irish	65	0.42
Scottish	112	0.72
Slavic	57	0.37
Slovak	528	3.40
Slovene	6	0.04
Swedish	31	0.20
Swiss	10	0.06
Ukrainian	422	2.72
United States or American	426	2.74
Welsh	711	4.58
West Indian, excl. Hispanic:	7	0.05
British West Indian	7	0.05
White:	15,012	96.55
Not Hispanic (14,794)	14,901	95.83
Hispanic (91)	111	0.71

Radnor Township

Place Type: Census Designated Place
County: Delaware
Population: 30,878

Ancestry/Race	Number	%
African American/Black:	1,067	3.46
Not Hispanic (935)	1,042	3.37
Hispanic (18)	25	0.08
African, sub-Saharan:	95	0.31
African	60	0.19
Sierra Leonean	14	0.05
South African	21	0.07
Alaska Native tribes, specified:	1	0.00
Eskimo	1	0.00
Am. Ind. or Alaska Nat., not spec.	48	0.16
Alsatian	9	0.03
American Indian tribes, specified:	46	0.15
Apache	1	0.00
Blackfeet	2	0.01
Cherokee (2)	18	0.06
Chippewa (1)	2	0.01
Iroquois (1)	2	0.01
Latin American Indians (1)	5	0.02
Pima	2	0.01
Puget Sound Salish (1)	1	0.00
Seminole	4	0.01
Sioux (1)	1	0.00
All other tribes (2)	8	0.03
American Indian tribes, not spec.	10	0.03
Arab:	197	0.64
Arab/Arabic	23	0.07
Egyptian	33	0.11
Lebanese	114	0.37
Moroccan	6	0.02
Palestinian	9	0.03
Syrian	12	0.04
Armenian	54	0.17
Asian:	1,930	6.25
Cambodian (3)	3	0.01
Chinese, ex. Taiwanese (505)	539	1.75
Filipino (75)	101	0.33
Hmong (1)	1	0.00
Indian (370)	409	1.32
Indonesian (6)	9	0.03
Japanese (214)	227	0.74
Korean (359)	388	1.26
Malaysian	1	0.00
Pakistani (39)	39	0.13
Sri Lankan (4)	4	0.01
Taiwanese (21)	26	0.08
Thai (15)	17	0.06
Vietnamese (30)	32	0.10
Other Asian, specified (6)	7	0.02
Other Asian, not specified (87)	127	0.41
Australian	34	0.11
Austrian	164	0.53
Belgian	38	0.12
Brazilian	17	0.06
British	279	0.90
Canadian	110	0.36
Carpatho Rusyn	6	0.02
Celtic	30	0.10
Croatian	62	0.20
Czech	169	0.55
Czechoslovakian	54	0.17
Danish	91	0.29
Dutch	361	1.17
Eastern European	137	0.44
English	4,279	13.86
Estonian	9	0.03
European	270	0.87
Finnish	28	0.09
French, except Basque	998	3.23
French Canadian	143	0.46
German	5,644	18.28
Greek	270	0.87
Hawaii Native/Pacific Islander:	13	0.04
Polynesian: (2)	2	0.01
Native Hawaiian (2)	2	0.01
Other Pac. Isl., specified	1	0.00
Other Pac. Isl., not spec. (3)	10	0.03
Hispanic or Latino:	628	2.03
Central American:	55	0.18
Costa Rican	6	0.02
Guatemalan	15	0.05
Honduran	3	0.01
Nicaraguan	8	0.03
Panamanian	8	0.03
Salvadoran	11	0.04
Other Central American	4	0.01
Cuban	80	0.26
Dominican Republic	14	0.05
Mexican	73	0.24
Puerto Rican	128	0.41
South American:	73	0.24
Argentinean	5	0.02
Bolivian	6	0.02
Chilean	7	0.02
Colombian	20	0.06
Ecuadorian	7	0.02
Paraguayan	2	0.01
Peruvian	13	0.04
Uruguayan	1	0.00
Venezuelan	8	0.03
Other South American	4	0.01
Other Hispanic or Latino	205	0.66
Hungarian	217	0.70
Icelander	7	0.02
Iranian	121	0.39
Irish	7,477	24.21
Israeli	52	0.17
Italian	5,299	17.16
Latvian	40	0.13
Lithuanian	229	0.74
Northern European	20	0.06
Norwegian	194	0.63
Pennsylvania German	69	0.22
Polish	1,326	4.29
Portuguese	44	0.14
Romanian	94	0.30
Russian	834	2.70
Scandinavian	31	0.10
Scotch-Irish	523	1.69
Scottish	1,111	3.60
Serbian	15	0.05
Slavic	8	0.03
Slovak	97	0.31
Slovene	6	0.02
Swedish	351	1.14
Swiss	159	0.51
Turkish	8	0.03
Ukrainian	143	0.46
United States or American	643	2.08
Welsh	423	1.37
West Indian, excl. Hispanic:	80	0.26
Haitian	32	0.10
Jamaican	32	0.10
West Indian	16	0.05
White:	27,912	90.39
Not Hispanic (27,239)	27,470	88.96
Hispanic (413)	442	1.43
Yugoslavian	54	0.17

Reading

Place Type: City
County: Berks
Population: 81,207

Ancestry/Race	Number	%
Afghan	85	0.10
African American/Black:	11,471	14.13
Not Hispanic (8,799)	9,779	12.04
Hispanic (1,148)	1,692	2.08
African, sub-Saharan:	660	0.81
African	470	0.58
Ghanian	6	0.01
Nigerian	40	0.05
Sierra Leonean	85	0.10
South African	39	0.05
Other sub-Saharan African	20	0.02
Am. Ind. or Alaska Nat., not spec.	429	0.53
Albanian	27	0.03
Alsatian	14	0.02
American Indian tribes, specified:	327	0.40
Apache (6)	9	0.01
Blackfeet (5)	27	0.03
Cherokee (26)	95	0.12
Chickasaw (1)	3	0.00
Chippewa (3)	6	0.01
Choctaw	9	0.01
Comanche	1	0.00
Creek (1)	4	0.00
Delaware (3)	19	0.02
Iroquois (2)	6	0.01
Kiowa (1)	1	0.00
Latin American Indians (39)	96	0.12
Lumbee (1)	4	0.00
Navajo (2)	5	0.01
Pueblo (4)	5	0.01
Puget Sound Salish	1	0.00
Seminole	5	0.01
Sioux (5)	13	0.02
All other tribes (5)	18	0.02
American Indian tribes, not spec.	55	0.07
Arab:	37	0.05
Arab/Arabic	4	0.00
Egyptian	21	0.03
Lebanese	12	0.01
Asian:	1,570	1.93
Cambodian (10)	10	0.01
Chinese, ex. Taiwanese (106)	130	0.16
Filipino (61)	78	0.10
Hmong (25)	32	0.04
Indian (141)	186	0.23
Indonesian (10)	11	0.01
Japanese (37)	60	0.07
Korean (48)	70	0.09
Laotian (50)	58	0.07
Malaysian	1	0.00
Pakistani (5)	14	0.02
Sri Lankan (1)	1	0.00
Thai (6)	11	0.01
Vietnamese (743)	786	0.97
Other Asian, specified (4)	19	0.02
Other Asian, not specified (30)	103	0.13
Australian	14	0.02
Austrian	112	0.14
Belgian	6	0.01
British	69	0.08
Bulgarian	6	0.01
Canadian	12	0.01
Croatian	27	0.03
Czech	63	0.08
Czechoslovakian	110	0.14
Danish	77	0.09
Dutch	2,039	2.51
Eastern European	39	0.05
English	2,112	2.60

Notes: 1. Figures in the "Number" column do not add up to the total population due to: a) Ancestry/Race overlap — e.g. persons can report being both White and Irish, b) persons of Hispanic origin can report being any race, c) persons reporting two ancestries are counted in both categories. 2. Numbers in parentheses indicate the number of persons reporting this ancestry/race alone, not in combination with any other ancestry/race. 3. Refer to the Explanation of Data in the front of the book for more detailed information.

European	159	0.20
French, except Basque	1,007	1.24
French Canadian	96	0.12
German	14,199	17.49
German Russian	17	0.02
Greek	331	0.41
Guyanese	27	0.03
Hawaii Native/Pacific Islander:	188	0.23
Micronesian: (10)	22	0.03
Guamanian/Chamorro (10)	22	0.03
Polynesian: (12)	47	0.06
Native Hawaiian (3)	26	0.03
Samoan (9)	19	0.02
Other Polynesian	2	0.00
Other Pac. Isl., specified	14	0.02
Other Pac. Isl., not spec. (9)	105	0.13
Hispanic or Latino:	30,302	37.31
Central American:	432	0.53
Costa Rican	1	0.00
Guatemalan	121	0.15
Honduran	63	0.08
Nicaraguan	33	0.04
Panamanian	25	0.03
Salvadoran	172	0.21
Other Central American	17	0.02
Cuban	217	0.27
Dominican Republic	1,696	2.09
Mexican	5,503	6.78
Puerto Rican	19,054	23.46
South American:	483	0.59
Argentinean	14	0.02
Bolivian	6	0.01
Chilean	11	0.01
Colombian	356	0.44
Ecuadorian	56	0.07
Peruvian	19	0.02
Venezuelan	13	0.02
Other South American	8	0.01
Other Hispanic or Latino	2,917	3.59
Hungarian	267	0.33
Irish	5,158	6.35
Italian	5,243	6.46
Lithuanian	259	0.32
Northern European	7	0.01
Norwegian	117	0.14
Pennsylvania German	2,472	3.04
Polish	3,904	4.81
Portuguese	84	0.10
Romanian	466	0.57
Russian	291	0.36
Scotch-Irish	289	0.36
Scottish	445	0.55
Slavic	57	0.07
Slovak	450	0.55
Slovene	23	0.03
Swedish	199	0.25
Swiss	277	0.34
Turkish	35	0.04
Ukrainian	352	0.43
United States or American	2,758	3.40
Welsh	892	1.10
West Indian, excl. Hispanic:	502	0.62
Barbadian	27	0.03
British West Indian	9	0.01
Dutch West Indian	6	0.01
Haitian	95	0.12
Jamaican	246	0.30
Trinidadian and Tobagonian	92	0.11
U.S. Virgin Islander	13	0.02
West Indian	7	0.01
Other West Indian	7	0.01
White:	50,667	62.39
Not Hispanic (39,038)	40,310	49.64
Hispanic (9,021)	10,357	12.75
Yugoslavian	34	0.04

Richland

Place Type: Township
County: Cambria
Population: 12,598

Ancestry/Race	Number	%
African American/Black:	114	0.90
Not Hispanic (93)	109	0.87
Hispanic (5)	5	0.04
African, sub-Saharan:	21	0.17
African	21	0.17
Am. Ind. or Alaska Nat., not spec.	3	0.02
American Indian tribes, specified:	20	0.16
Apache (2)	2	0.02
Cherokee (1)	7	0.06
Cheyenne	1	0.01
Iroquois	2	0.02
Latin American Indians (1)	2	0.02
Sioux (5)	6	0.05
American Indian tribes, not spec.	2	0.02
Arab:	34	0.27
Lebanese	27	0.21
Syrian	7	0.06
Asian:	218	1.73
Chinese, ex. Taiwanese (48)	62	0.49
Filipino (25)	28	0.22
Indian (61)	67	0.53
Japanese (5)	7	0.06
Korean (18)	23	0.18
Sri Lankan (1)	3	0.02
Taiwanese (1)	9	0.07
Thai (1)	1	0.01
Vietnamese (6)	11	0.09
Other Asian, not specified (2)	7	0.06
Australian	6	0.05
Austrian	56	0.44
Belgian	8	0.06
British	11	0.09
Canadian	39	0.31
Carpatho Rusyn	8	0.06
Croatian	216	1.71
Czech	28	0.22
Czechoslovakian	67	0.53
Danish	29	0.23
Dutch	190	1.51
Eastern European	15	0.12
English	945	7.50
European	89	0.71
Finnish	22	0.17
French, except Basque	170	1.35
German	4,151	32.95
Greek	36	0.29
Hawaii Native/Pacific Islander:	1	0.01
Polynesian:	1	0.01
Native Hawaiian	1	0.01
Hispanic or Latino:	65	0.52
Central American:	9	0.07
Honduran	2	0.02
Panamanian	5	0.04
Salvadoran	2	0.02
Cuban	2	0.02
Mexican	14	0.11
Puerto Rican	18	0.14
South American:	2	0.02
Colombian	1	0.01
Ecuadorian	1	0.01
Other Hispanic or Latino	20	0.16
Hungarian	281	2.23
Irish	1,536	12.19
Italian	1,004	7.97
Lithuanian	59	0.47
Northern European	7	0.06
Norwegian	7	0.06
Pennsylvania German	128	1.02
Polish	1,225	9.72
Portuguese	10	0.08
Romanian	16	0.13
Russian	162	1.29
Scotch-Irish	200	1.59
Scottish	217	1.72
Serbian	32	0.25
Slavic	28	0.22
Slovak	862	6.84
Slovene	145	1.15
Swedish	45	0.36
Swiss	49	0.39
Ukrainian	270	2.14
United States or American	624	4.95
Welsh	195	1.55
White:	12,292	97.57
Not Hispanic (12,190)	12,246	97.21
Hispanic (46)	46	0.37
Yugoslavian	14	0.11

Ridley

Place Type: Township
County: Delaware
Population: 30,791

Ancestry/Race	Number	%
African American/Black:	1,415	4.60
Not Hispanic (1,295)	1,385	4.50
Hispanic (18)	30	0.10
African, sub-Saharan:	268	0.87
African	213	0.69
Ethiopian	19	0.06
Sierra Leonean	8	0.03
Other sub-Saharan African	28	0.09
Am. Ind. or Alaska Nat., not spec.	41	0.13
American Indian tribes, specified:	33	0.11
Blackfeet	3	0.01
Cherokee (2)	10	0.03
Chickasaw	2	0.01
Choctaw	1	0.00
Comanche (1)	1	0.00
Crow	3	0.01
Delaware (1)	5	0.02
Lumbee	1	0.00
Navajo (3)	3	0.01
All other tribes	4	0.01
American Indian tribes, not spec.	6	0.02
Arab:	166	0.54
Arab/Arabic	28	0.09
Egyptian	33	0.11
Jordanian	15	0.05
Lebanese	59	0.19
Moroccan	8	0.03
Palestinian	10	0.03
Syrian	13	0.04
Armenian	53	0.17
Asian:	577	1.87
Cambodian (9)	9	0.03
Chinese, ex. Taiwanese (69)	77	0.25
Filipino (136)	161	0.52
Hmong (1)	1	0.00
Indian (155)	165	0.54
Indonesian	1	0.00
Japanese (13)	20	0.06
Korean (49)	53	0.17
Laotian (1)	1	0.00
Malaysian (5)	5	0.02
Pakistani (16)	24	0.08
Taiwanese (2)	2	0.01
Thai (3)	6	0.02
Vietnamese (36)	38	0.12
Other Asian, not specified (3)	14	0.05
Australian	10	0.03
Austrian	72	0.23
Belgian	37	0.12
British	103	0.33
Canadian	23	0.07
Celtic	16	0.05
Croatian	7	0.02
Czech	91	0.30
Czechoslovakian	37	0.12
Danish	48	0.16
Dutch	376	1.22
English	3,335	10.83

Notes: 1. Figures in the "Number" column do n[illegible] up to the total population due to: a) Ancestry/Race overlap — e.g. persons can report being both White and Irish, b) persons of Hispanic origin can report being any race, c) [illegible] reporting two ancestries are counted in both categories. 2. Numbers in parentheses indicate the number of persons reporting this ancestry/race alone, not in combin[illegible] with any other ancestry/race. 3. Refer to the Explanation of Data in the front of the book for more detailed information.

Ancestry/Race	Number	%
European	44	0.14
Finnish	34	0.11
French, except Basque	586	1.90
French Canadian	112	0.36
German	5,553	18.03
Greek	82	0.27
Hawaii Native/Pacific Islander:	25	0.08
Micronesian: (3)	3	0.01
Guamanian/Chamorro (3)	3	0.01
Polynesian: (11)	18	0.06
Native Hawaiian (8)	15	0.05
Samoan (1)	1	0.00
Other Polynesian (2)	2	0.01
Other Pac. Isl., not spec.	4	0.01
Hispanic or Latino:	282	0.92
Central American:	10	0.03
Costa Rican	2	0.01
Guatemalan	1	0.00
Nicaraguan	1	0.00
Panamanian	3	0.01
Salvadoran	1	0.00
Other Central American	2	0.01
Cuban	11	0.04
Mexican	75	0.24
Puerto Rican	107	0.35
South American:	37	0.12
Argentinean	13	0.04
Chilean	2	0.01
Colombian	6	0.02
Ecuadorian	4	0.01
Peruvian	3	0.01
Venezuelan	5	0.02
Other South American	4	0.01
Other Hispanic or Latino	42	0.14
Hungarian	203	0.66
Iranian	6	0.02
Irish	11,455	37.20
Italian	7,245	23.53
Latvian	18	0.06
Lithuanian	257	0.83
Maltese	8	0.03
Norwegian	95	0.31
Pennsylvania German	190	0.62
Polish	1,935	6.28
Portuguese	33	0.11
Romanian	6	0.02
Russian	319	1.04
Scandinavian	25	0.08
Scotch-Irish	571	1.85
Scottish	531	1.72
Slavic	78	0.25
Slovak	172	0.56
Swedish	165	0.54
Swiss	23	0.07
Turkish	40	0.13
Ukrainian	636	2.07
United States or American	779	2.53
Welsh	634	2.06
West Indian, excl. Hispanic:	44	0.14
Barbadian	10	0.03
Haitian	9	0.03
Jamaican	25	0.08
White:	28,836	93.65
Not Hispanic (28,428)	28,624	92.96
Hispanic (198)	212	0.69

Robinson Township

Place Type: Census Designated Place
County: Allegheny
Population: 12,289

Ancestry/Race	Number	%
African American/Black:	254	2.07
Not Hispanic (230)	249	2.03
Hispanic (4)	5	0.04
African, sub-Saharan:	29	0.24
African	20	0.16
Ugandan	9	0.07
Alaska Native tribes, specified:	4	0.03
Alaska Athabascan (1)	3	0.02
Eskimo (1)	1	0.01
Am. Ind. or Alaska Nat., not spec.	9	0.07
American Indian tribes, specified:	7	0.06
Cherokee (1)	2	0.02
Chickasaw (1)	1	0.01
Iroquois	1	0.01
Latin American Indians	1	0.01
Sioux (1)	1	0.01
All other tribes	1	0.01
Arab:	58	0.47
Egyptian	18	0.15
Lebanese	17	0.14
Syrian	16	0.13
Other Arab	7	0.06
Asian:	282	2.29
Chinese, ex. Taiwanese (34)	40	0.33
Filipino (10)	14	0.11
Indian (153)	160	1.30
Japanese (6)	11	0.09
Korean (18)	25	0.20
Pakistani (7)	7	0.06
Taiwanese (6)	6	0.05
Thai (2)	2	0.02
Vietnamese (14)	15	0.12
Other Asian, not specified (1)	2	0.02
Australian	34	0.28
Austrian	169	1.38
Belgian	10	0.08
British	93	0.76
Canadian	17	0.14
Carpatho Rusyn	7	0.06
Croatian	147	1.20
Czech	142	1.16
Czechoslovakian	139	1.13
Dutch	99	0.81
Eastern European	11	0.09
English	987	8.03
Estonian	10	0.08
European	44	0.36
French, except Basque	190	1.55
French Canadian	10	0.08
German	3,393	27.61
Greek	100	0.81
Hawaii Native/Pacific Islander:	5	0.04
Micronesian: (1)	1	0.01
Guamanian/Chamorro (1)	1	0.01
Polynesian: (2)	3	0.02
Native Hawaiian (2)	3	0.02
Other Pac. Isl., not spec.	1	0.01
Hispanic or Latino:	90	0.73
Central American:	1	0.01
Panamanian	1	0.01
Dominican Republic	1	0.01
Mexican	46	0.37
Puerto Rican	14	0.11
South American:	9	0.07
Peruvian	6	0.05
Venezuelan	3	0.02
Other Hispanic or Latino	19	0.15
Hungarian	225	1.83
Irish	2,513	20.45
Italian	2,625	21.36
Lithuanian	108	0.88
Northern European	9	0.07
Norwegian	27	0.22
Pennsylvania German	6	0.05
Polish	1,324	10.77
Portuguese	9	0.07
Romanian	18	0.15
Russian	270	2.20
Scandinavian	20	0.16
Scotch-Irish	324	2.64
Scottish	195	1.59
Serbian	59	0.48
Slavic	26	0.21
Slovak	587	4.78
Slovene	139	1.13
Swedish	109	0.89
Swiss	65	0.53
Turkish	6	0.05
Ukrainian	319	2.60
United States or American	385	3.13
Welsh	125	1.02
West Indian, excl. Hispanic:	8	0.07
Jamaican	8	0.07
White:	11,769	95.77
Not Hispanic (11,642)	11,701	95.22
Hispanic (63)	68	0.55

Ross Township

Place Type: Census Designated Place
County: Allegheny
Population: 32,551

Ancestry/Race	Number	%
African American/Black:	511	1.57
Not Hispanic (459)	505	1.55
Hispanic (4)	6	0.02
African, sub-Saharan:	96	0.29
African	25	0.08
Somalian	58	0.18
South African	13	0.04
Alaska Native tribes, specified:	1	0.00
Aleut (1)	1	0.00
Am. Ind. or Alaska Nat., not spec.	32	0.10
Albanian	6	0.02
American Indian tribes, specified:	38	0.12
Blackfeet (1)	3	0.01
Cherokee (10)	20	0.06
Choctaw	1	0.00
Creek (2)	2	0.01
Iroquois	4	0.01
Navajo	1	0.00
Sioux	1	0.00
All other tribes (4)	6	0.02
American Indian tribes, not spec.	4	0.01
Arab:	146	0.45
Arab/Arabic	7	0.02
Egyptian	14	0.04
Lebanese	57	0.17
Moroccan	6	0.02
Syrian	54	0.17
Other Arab	8	0.02
Armenian	39	0.12
Asian:	636	1.95
Bangladeshi (3)	4	0.01
Chinese, ex. Taiwanese (192)	205	0.63
Filipino (43)	51	0.16
Indian (193)	203	0.62
Japanese (12)	18	0.06
Korean (88)	94	0.29
Laotian (8)	8	0.02
Malaysian	1	0.00
Pakistani (13)	13	0.04
Taiwanese (4)	4	0.01
Thai (3)	3	0.01
Vietnamese (12)	15	0.05
Other Asian, specified	1	0.00
Other Asian, not specified (10)	16	0.05
Austrian	264	0.81
Basque	7	0.02
Belgian	24	0.07
Brazilian	10	0.03
British	69	0.21
Canadian	18	0.06
Carpatho Rusyn	27	0.08
Celtic	6	0.02
Croatian	568	1.74
Czech	344	1.06
Czechoslovakian	104	0.32
Danish	119	0.37
Dutch	182	0.56
Eastern European	49	0.15
English	2,285	7.01
European	273	0.84
Finnish	13	0.04
French, except Basque	707	2.17
French Canadian	73	0.22

Notes: 1. Figures in the "Number" column do not add up to the total population due to: a) Ancestry/Race overlap — e.g. persons can report being both White and Irish, b) persons of Hispanic origin can report being any race, c) persons reporting two ancestries are counted in both categories. 2. Numbers in parentheses indicate the number of persons reporting this ancestry/race alone, not in combination with any other ancestry/race. 3. Refer to the Explanation of Data in the front of the book for more detailed information.

German	12,589	38.64
Greek	316	0.97
Guyanese	8	0.02
Hawaii Native/Pacific Islander:	32	0.10
Micronesian: (3)	3	0.01
Guamanian/Chamorro (3)	3	0.01
Polynesian: (13)	17	0.05
Native Hawaiian (13)	16	0.05
Samoan	1	0.00
Other Pac. Isl., specified	1	0.00
Other Pac. Isl., not spec. (5)	11	0.03
Hispanic or Latino:	237	0.73
Central American:	15	0.05
Costa Rican	4	0.01
Guatemalan	5	0.02
Honduran	3	0.01
Salvadoran	3	0.01
Cuban	6	0.02
Dominican Republic	2	0.01
Mexican	88	0.27
Puerto Rican	43	0.13
South American:	34	0.10
Argentinean	1	0.00
Chilean	5	0.02
Colombian	8	0.02
Ecuadorian	7	0.02
Paraguayan	1	0.00
Peruvian	8	0.02
Venezuelan	3	0.01
Other South American	1	0.00
Other Hispanic or Latino	49	0.15
Hungarian	377	1.16
Iranian	30	0.09
Irish	7,143	21.92
Italian	4,411	13.54
Latvian	25	0.08
Lithuanian	245	0.75
Northern European	12	0.04
Norwegian	87	0.27
Pennsylvania German	22	0.07
Polish	2,776	8.52
Portuguese	7	0.02
Romanian	11	0.03
Russian	373	1.14
Scandinavian	8	0.02
Scotch-Irish	786	2.41
Scottish	647	1.99
Serbian	49	0.15
Slavic	32	0.10
Slovak	1,199	3.68
Slovene	122	0.37
Swedish	298	0.91
Swiss	226	0.69
Ukrainian	416	1.28
United States or American	1,044	3.20
Welsh	304	0.93
West Indian, excl. Hispanic:	9	0.03
Jamaican	9	0.03
White:	31,373	96.38
Not Hispanic (31,046)	31,184	95.80
Hispanic (179)	189	0.58
Yugoslavian	35	0.11

Rostraver

Place Type: Township
County: Westmoreland
Population: 11,634

Ancestry/Race	Number	%
African American/Black:	268	2.30
Not Hispanic (225)	265	2.28
Hispanic (1)	3	0.03
African, sub-Saharan:	50	0.43
African	50	0.43
Am. Ind. or Alaska Nat., not spec.	11	0.09
American Indian tribes, specified:	18	0.15
Cherokee (1)	6	0.05
Chickasaw	1	0.01
Chippewa (2)	2	0.02
Choctaw	3	0.03
Latin American Indians (1)	1	0.01
Lumbee (1)	1	0.01
Shoshone	1	0.01
Sioux (3)	3	0.03
Arab:	72	0.62
Lebanese	56	0.48
Syrian	16	0.14
Asian:	38	0.33
Chinese, ex. Taiwanese (7)	8	0.07
Filipino (5)	7	0.06
Indian (16)	17	0.15
Japanese	1	0.01
Korean (4)	4	0.03
Other Asian, specified	1	0.01
Austrian	94	0.81
Belgian	47	0.40
British	7	0.06
Bulgarian	8	0.07
Carpatho Rusyn	6	0.05
Croatian	197	1.69
Czech	69	0.59
Czechoslovakian	63	0.54
Danish	14	0.12
Dutch	144	1.24
English	1,353	11.63
European	18	0.15
Finnish	8	0.07
French, except Basque	189	1.62
French Canadian	24	0.21
German	2,427	20.86
Greek	124	1.07
Hawaii Native/Pacific Islander:	7	0.06
Polynesian: (2)	6	0.05
Native Hawaiian (2)	6	0.05
Other Pac. Isl., not spec. (1)	1	0.01
Hispanic or Latino:	61	0.52
Central American:	3	0.03
Panamanian	3	0.03
Cuban	3	0.03
Mexican	19	0.16
Puerto Rican	7	0.06
Other Hispanic or Latino	29	0.25
Hungarian	399	3.43
Irish	1,603	13.78
Israeli	5	0.04
Italian	2,601	22.36
Lithuanian	55	0.47
Macedonian	7	0.06
Norwegian	6	0.05
Pennsylvania German	36	0.31
Polish	1,302	11.19
Portuguese	14	0.12
Russian	447	3.84
Scotch-Irish	240	2.06
Scottish	164	1.41
Serbian	55	0.47
Slavic	26	0.22
Slovak	895	7.69
Slovene	172	1.48
Swedish	86	0.74
Swiss	26	0.22
Ukrainian	151	1.30
United States or American	475	4.08
Welsh	147	1.26
West Indian, excl. Hispanic:	16	0.14
Jamaican	16	0.14
White:	11,337	97.45
Not Hispanic (11,219)	11,281	96.97
Hispanic (54)	56	0.48
Yugoslavian	26	0.22

Saint Marys

Place Type: City
County: Elk
Population: 14,502

Ancestry/Race	Number	%
African American/Black:	39	0.27
Not Hispanic (30)	36	0.25
Hispanic (3)	3	0.02
African, sub-Saharan:	2	0.01
African	2	0.01
Am. Ind. or Alaska Nat., not spec.	16	0.11
American Indian tribes, specified:	18	0.12
Blackfeet	1	0.01
Cherokee	6	0.04
Cheyenne	1	0.01
Chippewa (2)	2	0.01
Latin American Indians (1)	1	0.01
Navajo (1)	1	0.01
Potawatomi	1	0.01
Sioux	5	0.03
American Indian tribes, not spec.	6	0.04
Arab:	16	0.11
Lebanese	16	0.11
Asian:	72	0.50
Chinese, ex. Taiwanese (14)	16	0.11
Filipino (23)	30	0.21
Indian (15)	15	0.10
Japanese (3)	3	0.02
Korean (2)	2	0.01
Taiwanese (2)	2	0.01
Thai (1)	1	0.01
Other Asian, not specified (1)	3	0.02
Australian	8	0.06
Austrian	129	0.89
British	17	0.12
Croatian	51	0.35
Czech	99	0.68
Czechoslovakian	75	0.52
Danish	21	0.14
Dutch	178	1.23
English	801	5.52
European	11	0.08
French, except Basque	280	1.93
French Canadian	23	0.16
German	8,226	56.72
Greek	10	0.07
Hawaii Native/Pacific Islander:	17	0.12
Polynesian: (13)	17	0.12
Native Hawaiian (7)	11	0.08
Samoan (6)	6	0.04
Hispanic or Latino:	44	0.30
Central American:	7	0.05
Guatemalan	2	0.01
Other Central American	5	0.03
Cuban	2	0.01
Mexican	4	0.03
Puerto Rican	8	0.06
South American:	4	0.03
Peruvian	4	0.03
Other Hispanic or Latino	19	0.13
Hungarian	62	0.43
Irish	1485	10.24
Italian	2[illegible]73	14.29
Lithuanian	53	0.37
Norwegian	35	0.24
Pennsylvania German	30	0.21
Polish	[illegible]51	4.49
Portuguese	17	0.12
Russian	12	0.08
Scotch-Irish	245	1.69
Scottish	136	0.94
Slavic	[illegible]0	0.21
Slovak	12[illegible]	0.84
Slovene	[illegible]	0.39
Swedish	54[illegible]	3.76
Swiss	2[illegible]	0.16
Ukrainian	48	0.33
United States or American	584	4.03
Welsh	35	0.24
White:	14,364	[illegible]9.05
Not Hispanic (14,299)	14,342	[illegible].90
Hispanic (22)	22	0.[illegible]
Yugoslavian	41	0.28

Notes: 1. Figures in the "Number" column do not add up to the total population due to: a) Ancestry/Race overlap — e.g. persons can report being both White and Irish, b) persons of Hispanic origin can report being any race, c) persons reporting two ancestries are counted in both categories. 2. Numbers in parentheses indicate the number of persons reporting this ancestry/race alone, not in combination with any other ancestry/race. 3. Refer to the Explanation of Data in the front of the book for more detailed information.

Salisbury

Place Type: Township
County: Lancaster
Population: 10,012

Ancestry/Race	Number	%
African American/Black:	105	1.05
Not Hispanic (76)	105	1.05
African, sub-Saharan:	6	0.06
Ethiopian	6	0.06
Am. Ind. or Alaska Nat., not spec.	15	0.15
Alsatian	6	0.06
American Indian tribes, specified:	21	0.21
Cherokee (1)	7	0.07
Chippewa	2	0.02
Crow (1)	1	0.01
Delaware (5)	5	0.05
Iroquois (1)	1	0.01
Latin American Indians	1	0.01
Navajo (1)	1	0.01
All other tribes (2)	3	0.03
Arab:	27	0.27
Jordanian	7	0.07
Lebanese	20	0.20
Asian:	55	0.55
Chinese, ex. Taiwanese (10)	11	0.11
Filipino (10)	15	0.15
Hmong (18)	18	0.18
Japanese (3)	3	0.03
Korean (3)	3	0.03
Laotian (2)	2	0.02
Vietnamese (1)	1	0.01
Other Asian, not specified (2)	2	0.02
Belgian	6	0.06
British	41	0.41
Czech	15	0.15
Czechoslovakian	15	0.15
Danish	27	0.27
Dutch	253	2.53
English	464	4.63
European	76	0.76
Finnish	7	0.07
French, except Basque	120	1.20
French Canadian	11	0.11
German	3,423	34.19
Greek	24	0.24
Hawaii Native/Pacific Islander:	12	0.12
Polynesian: (4)	10	0.10
Native Hawaiian (2)	8	0.08
Samoan (2)	2	0.02
Other Pac. Isl., not spec.	2	0.02
Hispanic or Latino:	108	1.08
Central American:	2	0.02
Costa Rican	2	0.02
Cuban	18	0.18
Mexican	11	0.11
Puerto Rican	55	0.55
South American:	4	0.04
Bolivian	1	0.01
Colombian	3	0.03
Other Hispanic or Latino	18	0.18
Hungarian	33	0.33
Irish	1,085	10.84
Italian	560	5.59
Latvian	6	0.06
Lithuanian	28	0.28
Norwegian	21	0.21
Pennsylvania German	144	1.44
Polish	285	2.85
Portuguese	7	0.07
Romanian	4	0.04
Russian	8	0.08
Scandinavian	21	0.21
Scotch-Irish	144	1.44
Scottish	99	0.99
Slovak	10	0.10
Swedish	92	0.92
Swiss	457	4.56
Ukrainian	8	0.08
United States or American	1,006	10.05
Welsh	79	0.79
White:	9,835	98.23
Not Hispanic (9,692)	9,759	97.47
Hispanic (67)	76	0.76
Yugoslavian	22	0.22

Salisbury

Place Type: Township
County: Lehigh
Population: 13,498

Ancestry/Race	Number	%
African American/Black:	232	1.72
Not Hispanic (192)	212	1.57
Hispanic (12)	20	0.15
African, sub-Saharan:	4	0.03
African	4	0.03
Am. Ind. or Alaska Nat., not spec.	8	0.06
American Indian tribes, specified:	7	0.05
Apache	1	0.01
Cherokee (1)	2	0.01
Delaware (1)	1	0.01
Iroquois (1)	1	0.01
Seminole	1	0.01
Yaqui	1	0.01
American Indian tribes, not spec.	1	0.01
Arab:	193	1.43
Arab/Arabic	3	0.02
Lebanese	73	0.54
Syrian	117	0.87
Asian:	239	1.77
Cambodian (2)	2	0.01
Chinese, ex. Taiwanese (37)	47	0.35
Filipino (10)	13	0.10
Indian (60)	63	0.47
Japanese (8)	13	0.10
Korean (28)	34	0.25
Pakistani	2	0.01
Taiwanese (1)	1	0.01
Thai (4)	4	0.03
Vietnamese (48)	51	0.38
Other Asian, not specified (1)	9	0.07
Austrian	3[illegible]6	2.64
British	40	0.30
Canadian	[illegible]	0.06
Czech	70	0.52
Czechoslovakian	42	0.31
Danish	7	0.05
Dutch	404	2.99
Eastern European	31	0.23
English	819	6.07
European	39	0.29
Finnish	6	0.04
French, except Basque	274	2.03
French Canadian	72	0.53
German	4,561	33.79
Greek	38	0.28
Guyanese	5	0.04
Hawaii Native/Pacific Islander:	5	0.04
Micronesian: (1)	1	0.01
Guamanian/Chamorro (1)	1	0.01
Polynesian: (1)	1	0.01
Native Hawaiian (1)	1	0.01
Other Pac. Isl., not spec. (3)	3	0.02
Hispanic or Latino:	289	2.14
Central American:	13	0.10
Costa Rican	1	0.01
Guatemalan	4	0.03
Honduran	3	0.02
Nicaraguan	1	0.01
Panamanian	1	0.01
Salvadoran	3	0.02
Cuban	11	0.08
Dominican Republic	4	0.03
Mexican	39	0.29
Puerto Rican	160	1.19
South American:	10	0.07
Chilean	1	0.01
Colombian	2	0.01
Ecuadorian	1	0.01
Peruvian	5	0.04
Other South American	1	0.01
Other Hispanic or Latino	52	0.39
Hungarian	725	5.37
Iranian	8	0.06
Irish	1,801	13.34
Italian	1,521	11.27
Latvian	9	0.07
Lithuanian	56	0.41
Norwegian	74	0.55
Pennsylvania German	730	5.41
Polish	848	6.28
Portuguese	52	0.39
Romanian	17	0.13
Russian	184	1.36
Scotch-Irish	143	1.06
Scottish	213	1.58
Slovak	755	5.59
Swedish	129	0.96
Swiss	95	0.70
Ukrainian	335	2.48
United States or American	605	4.48
Welsh	371	2.75
West Indian, excl. Hispanic:	12	0.09
Jamaican	12	0.09
White:	12,958	96.00
Not Hispanic (12,733)	12,798	94.81
Hispanic (146)	160	1.19
Yugoslavian	14	0.10

Sandy

Place Type: Township
County: Clearfield
Population: 11,556

Ancestry/Race	Number	%
African American/Black:	31	0.27
Not Hispanic (22)	30	0.26
Hispanic (1)	1	0.01
Am. Ind. or Alaska Nat., not spec.	19	0.16
American Indian tribes, specified:	17	0.15
Blackfeet	2	0.02
Cherokee (3)	6	0.05
Chippewa	1	0.01
Creek	1	0.01
Iroquois	5	0.04
All other tribes	2	0.02
Arab:	19	0.16
Lebanese	19	0.16
Asian:	83	0.72
Chinese, ex. Taiwanese (13)	14	0.12
Filipino (15)	17	0.15
Indian (25)	27	0.23
Japanese (2)	4	0.03
Korean (8)	14	0.12
Taiwanese (3)	3	0.03
Vietnamese (3)	3	0.03
Other Asian, not specified	1	0.01
Austrian	88	0.76
Belgian	16	0.14
British	13	0.11
Canadian	8	0.07
Croatian	32	0.28
Czech	23	0.20
Czechoslovakian	11	0.10
Danish	43	0.37
Dutch	366	3.17
English	1,305	11.29
European	59	0.51
French, except Basque	301	2.60
French Canadian	24	0.21
German	2,873	24.86
Greek	21	0.18
Hawaii Native/Pacific Islander:	3	0.03
Micronesian: (3)	3	0.03
Guamanian/Chamorro (3)	3	0.03
Hispanic or Latino:	52	0.45

Notes: 1. Figures in the "Number" column do not add up to the total population due to: a) Ancestry/Race overlap — e.g. persons can report being both White and Irish, b) persons of Hispanic origin can report being any race, c) persons reporting two ancestries are counted in both categories. 2. Numbers in parentheses indicate the number of persons reporting this ancestry/race alone, not in combination with any other ancestry/race. 3. Refer to the Explanation of Data in the front of the book for more detailed information.

Ancestry/Race	Number	%
Cuban	1	0.01
Mexican	20	0.17
Puerto Rican	8	0.07
South American:	5	0.04
Paraguayan	1	0.01
Peruvian	4	0.03
Other Hispanic or Latino	18	0.16
Hungarian	64	0.55
Irish	1,223	10.58
Italian	1,238	10.71
Lithuanian	254	2.20
Pennsylvania German	98	0.85
Polish	656	5.68
Romanian	11	0.10
Russian	34	0.29
Scandinavian	16	0.14
Scotch-Irish	238	2.06
Scottish	301	2.60
Serbian	16	0.14
Slavic	99	0.86
Slovak	236	2.04
Swedish	346	2.99
Swiss	45	0.39
Ukrainian	25	0.22
United States or American	675	5.84
Welsh	84	0.73
White:	11,443	99.02
Not Hispanic (11,353)	11,400	98.65
Hispanic (39)	43	0.37

Scott Township

Place Type: Census Designated Place
County: Allegheny
Population: 17,288

Ancestry/Race	Number	%
African American/Black:	237	1.37
Not Hispanic (198)	236	1.37
Hispanic	1	0.01
Am. Ind. or Alaska Nat., not spec.	10	0.06
American Indian tribes, specified:	17	0.10
Blackfeet	3	0.02
Cherokee (4)	7	0.04
Iroquois	1	0.01
Latin American Indians (1)	1	0.01
Seminole (2)	2	0.01
All other tribes (3)	3	0.02
American Indian tribes, not spec.	4	0.02
Arab:	294	1.70
Arab/Arabic	60	0.35
Egyptian	32	0.19
Lebanese	109	0.63
Palestinian	12	0.07
Syrian	35	0.20
Other Arab	46	0.27
Armenian	11	0.06
Asian:	1,126	6.51
Bangladeshi (5)	5	0.03
Chinese, ex. Taiwanese (79)	80	0.46
Filipino (19)	19	0.11
Indian (891)	920	5.32
Indonesian (1)	1	0.01
Japanese (14)	16	0.09
Korean (9)	16	0.09
Laotian	1	0.01
Pakistani (11)	11	0.06
Sri Lankan (4)	4	0.02
Thai (2)	3	0.02
Vietnamese (23)	23	0.13
Other Asian, specified (1)	1	0.01
Other Asian, not specified (3)	26	0.15
Austrian	162	0.94
Belgian	14	0.08
British	89	0.51
Canadian	16	0.09
Croatian	161	0.93
Czech	158	0.91
Czechoslovakian	71	0.41
Danish	6	0.03
Dutch	97	0.56
Eastern European	9	0.05
English	1,391	8.05
European	15	0.09
Finnish	7	0.04
French, except Basque	377	2.18
French Canadian	52	0.30
German	4,363	25.24
Greek	107	0.62
Hawaii Native/Pacific Islander:	7	0.04
Micronesian:	1	0.01
Guamanian/Chamorro	1	0.01
Polynesian: (2)	2	0.01
Native Hawaiian (1)	1	0.01
Samoan (1)	1	0.01
Other Pac. Isl., not spec.	4	0.02
Hispanic or Latino:	117	0.68
Central American:	11	0.06
Guatemalan	1	0.01
Honduran	1	0.01
Panamanian	3	0.02
Salvadoran	1	0.01
Other Central American	5	0.03
Cuban	5	0.03
Mexican	40	0.23
Puerto Rican	20	0.12
South American:	15	0.09
Chilean	2	0.01
Colombian	1	0.01
Ecuadorian	3	0.02
Peruvian	3	0.02
Venezuelan	6	0.03
Other Hispanic or Latino	26	0.15
Hungarian	192	1.11
Iranian	32	0.19
Irish	3,419	19.78
Israeli	44	0.25
Italian	3,484	20.15
Lithuanian	171	0.99
Northern European	8	0.05
Norwegian	32	0.19
Pennsylvania German	15	0.09
Polish	1,826	10.56
Portuguese	14	0.08
Romanian	46	0.27
Russian	304	1.76
Scotch-Irish	487	2.82
Scottish	307	1.78
Serbian	42	0.24
Slavic	41	0.24
Slovak	461	2.67
Slovene	103	0.60
Swedish	160	0.93
Swiss	46	0.27
Turkish	36	0.21
Ukrainian	298	1.72
United States or American	334	1.93
Welsh	328	1.90
White:	15,934	92.17
Not Hispanic (15,706)	15,841	91.63
Hispanic (86)	93	0.54
Yugoslavian	21	0.12

Scranton

Place Type: City
County: Lackawanna
Population: 76,415

Ancestry/Race	Number	%
African American/Black:	2,744	3.59
Not Hispanic (2,200)	2,587	3.39
Hispanic (104)	157	0.21
African, sub-Saharan:	214	0.28
African	170	0.22
Kenyan	31	0.04
Nigerian	6	0.01
Ugandan	7	0.01
Alaska Native tribes, not specified	1	0.00
Am. Ind. or Alaska Nat., not spec.	133	0.17
Alsatian	21	0.03
American Indian tribes, specified:	92	0.12
Apache (1)	1	0.00
Blackfeet	5	0.01
Cherokee (5)	34	0.04
Cheyenne	1	0.00
Chippewa (1)	2	0.00
Choctaw (1)	4	0.01
Cree	2	0.00
Creek (5)	5	0.01
Iroquois (10)	17	0.02
Latin American Indians (5)	8	0.01
Navajo (1)	1	0.00
Potawatomi (1)	1	0.00
Sioux (1)	4	0.01
All other tribes (5)	7	0.01
American Indian tribes, not spec.	10	0.01
Arab:	740	0.97
Arab/Arabic	7	0.01
Egyptian	52	0.07
Lebanese	608	0.80
Moroccan	29	0.04
Syrian	44	0.06
Armenian	13	0.02
Asian:	974	1.27
Bangladeshi (6)	7	0.01
Cambodian (1)	1	0.00
Chinese, ex. Taiwanese (113)	128	0.17
Filipino (33)	47	0.06
Indian (310)	341	0.45
Indonesian (5)	8	0.01
Japanese (17)	26	0.03
Korean (44)	66	0.09
Laotian (97)	116	0.15
Malaysian (3)	3	0.00
Pakistani (10)	17	0.02
Taiwanese (14)	17	0.02
Thai (6)	9	0.01
Vietnamese (114)	121	0.16
Other Asian, specified	1	0.00
Other Asian, not specified (38)	66	0.09
Australian	9	0.01
Austrian	241	0.32
Belgian	5	0.01
Brazilian	30	0.04
British	73	0.10
Bulgarian	13	0.02
Canadian	7	0.01
Carpatho Rusyn	36	0.05
Celtic	16	0.02
Croatian	17	0.02
Czech	102	0.13
Czechoslovakian	117	0.15
Danish	47	0.06
Dutch	703	0.92
Eastern European	22	0.03
English	4,432	5.80
European	155	0.20
French, except Basque	832	1.09
French Canadian	113	0.15
German	11,979	15.68
Greek	213	0.28
Hawaii Native/Pacific Islander:	36	0.05
Micronesian: (6)	8	0.01
Guamanian/Chamorro (4)	6	0.01
Other Micronesian (2)	2	0.00
Polynesian: (4)	11	0.01
Native Hawaiian (3)	9	0.01
Samoan (1)	2	0.00
Other Pac. Isl., not spec. (5)	17	0.02
Hispanic or Latino:	1,999	2.62
Central American:	60	0.08
Costa Rican	4	0.01
Guatemalan	6	0.01
Honduran	33	0.04
Nicaraguan	3	0.00
Salvadoran	14	0.02
Cuban	52	0.07
Dominican Republic	51	0.07
Mexican	566	0.74

Notes: 1. Figures in the "Number" column do not add up to the total population due to: a) Ancestry/Race overlap — e.g. persons can report being both White and Irish, b) persons of Hispanic origin can report being any race, c) persons reporting two ancestries are counted in both categories. 2. Numbers in parentheses indicate the number of persons reporting this ancestry/race alone, not in combination with any other ancestry/race. 3. Refer to the Explanation of Data in the front of the book for more detailed information.

Puerto Rican	892	1.17
South American:	77	0.10
Argentinean	3	0.00
Chilean	4	0.01
Colombian	23	0.03
Ecuadorian	6	0.01
Peruvian	31	0.04
Uruguayan	2	0.00
Venezuelan	4	0.01
Other South American	4	0.01
Other Hispanic or Latino	301	0.39
Hungarian	549	0.72
Icelander	7	0.01
Irish	23,171	30.32
Israeli	26	0.03
Italian	14,833	19.41
Latvian	6	0.01
Lithuanian	1,880	2.46
Maltese	6	0.01
Norwegian	113	0.15
Pennsylvania German	163	0.21
Polish	11,311	14.80
Portuguese	60	0.08
Romanian	40	0.05
Russian	2,325	3.04
Scandinavian	7	0.01
Scotch-Irish	558	0.73
Scottish	679	0.89
Serbian	4	0.01
Slavic	31	0.04
Slovak	1,458	1.91
Slovene	48	0.06
Swedish	332	0.43
Swiss	158	0.21
Ukrainian	1,373	1.80
United States or American	2,114	2.77
Welsh	5,300	6.94
West Indian, excl. Hispanic:	67	0.09
British West Indian	7	0.01
Haitian	12	0.02
Jamaican	24	0.03
Trinidadian and Tobagonian	12	0.02
West Indian	12	0.02
White:	72,200	94.48
Not Hispanic (70,512)	71,117	93.07
Hispanic (968)	1,083	1.42
Yugoslavian	8	0.01

Shaler Township

Place Type: Census Designated Place
County: Allegheny
Population: 29,757

Ancestry/Race	Number	%
African American/Black:	160	0.54
Not Hispanic (121)	159	0.53
Hispanic (1)	1	0.00
African, sub-Saharan:	14	0.05
African	6	0.02
South African	8	0.03
Am. Ind. or Alaska Nat., not spec.	40	0.13
American Indian tribes, specified:	30	0.10
Apache	1	0.00
Blackfeet	1	0.00
Cherokee	10	0.03
Iroquois (1)	6	0.02
Latin American Indians (1)	3	0.01
Navajo (4)	4	0.01
Sioux (3)	3	0.01
All other tribes (1)	2	0.01
American Indian tribes, not spec.	5	0.02
Arab:	83	0.28
Arab/Arabic	14	0.05
Lebanese	55	0.18
Syrian	14	0.05
Armenian	20	0.07
Asian:	319	1.07
Bangladeshi (3)	3	0.01
Chinese, ex. Taiwanese (54)	65	0.22
Filipino (26)	32	0.11
Indian (128)	140	0.47
Japanese (6)	15	0.05
Korean (16)	17	0.06
Pakistani (12)	14	0.05
Sri Lankan (5)	5	0.02
Taiwanese (1)	1	0.00
Thai (1)	2	0.01
Vietnamese (14)	18	0.06
Other Asian, specified	1	0.00
Other Asian, not specified (1)	6	0.02
Austrian	183	0.61
Belgian	35	0.12
British	33	0.11
Bulgarian	6	0.02
Canadian	30	0.10
Carpatho Rusyn	12	0.04
Croatian	1,338	4.50
Czech	279	0.94
Czechoslovakian	45	0.15
Danish	5	0.02
Dutch	157	0.53
Eastern European	34	0.11
English	1,798	6.04
European	130	0.44
Finnish	14	0.05
French, except Basque	417	1.40
French Canadian	40	0.13
German	11,348	38.14
Greek	191	0.64
Hawaii Native/Pacific Islander:	14	0.05
Micronesian:	1	0.00
Guamanian/Chamorro	1	0.00
Polynesian: (7)	12	0.04
Native Hawaiian (5)	9	0.03
Samoan (2)	3	0.01
Other Pac. Isl., specified	1	0.00
Hispanic or Latino:	155	0.52
Central American:	3	0.01
Nicaraguan	1	0.00
Panamanian	1	0.00
Salvadoran	1	0.00
Cuban	8	0.03
Dominican Republic	2	0.01
Mexican	70	0.24
Puerto Rican	23	0.08
South American:	26	0.09
Argentinean	10	0.03
Chilean	5	0.02
Colombian	5	0.02
Ecuadorian	1	0.00
Paraguayan	1	0.00
Peruvian	3	0.01
Venezuelan	1	0.00
Other Hispanic or Latino	23	0.08
Hungarian	274	0.92
Irish	6,937	23.31
Italian	5,169	17.37
Lithuanian	190	0.64
Northern European	7	0.02
Norwegian	28	0.09
Pennsylvania German	36	0.12
Polish	4,059	13.64
Portuguese	10	0.03
Romanian	7	0.02
Russian	251	0.84
Scotch-Irish	612	2.06
Scottish	320	1.08
Serbian	107	0.36
Slavic	73	0.25
Slovak	711	2.39
Slovene	275	0.92
Swedish	211	0.71
Swiss	147	0.49
Turkish	15	0.05
Ukrainian	288	0.97
United States or American	918	3.08
Welsh	294	0.99
West Indian, excl. Hispanic:	6	0.02
Trinidadian and Tobagonian	6	0.02
White:	29,295	98.45
Not Hispanic (29,017)	29,164	98.01
Hispanic (122)	131	0.44
Yugoslavian	118	0.40

Sharon

Place Type: City
County: Mercer
Population: 16,328

Ancestry/Race	Number	%
African American/Black:	1,992	12.20
Not Hispanic (1,764)	1,965	12.03
Hispanic (7)	27	0.17
African, sub-Saharan:	5	0.03
South African	5	0.03
Alaska Native tribes, not specified	4	0.02
Am. Ind. or Alaska Nat., not spec.	61	0.37
Alsatian	7	0.04
American Indian tribes, specified:	83	0.51
Blackfeet	12	0.07
Cherokee (7)	40	0.24
Cheyenne	4	0.02
Crow	1	0.01
Delaware (3)	4	0.02
Iroquois (3)	6	0.04
Latin American Indians	1	0.01
Navajo	1	0.01
Seminole (1)	1	0.01
Sioux	2	0.01
All other tribes (4)	11	0.07
American Indian tribes, not spec.	8	0.05
Arab:	132	0.81
Arab/Arabic	65	0.40
Lebanese	53	0.32
Syrian	14	0.09
Asian:	65	0.40
Chinese, ex. Taiwanese (14)	17	0.10
Filipino (2)	6	0.04
Indian (1)	1	0.01
Japanese (4)	10	0.06
Korean (10)	16	0.10
Laotian (2)	2	0.01
Thai (1)	1	0.01
Other Asian, specified	1	0.01
Other Asian, not specified	11	0.07
Austrian	22	0.13
British	18	0.11
Carpatho Rusyn	9	0.06
Croatian	227	1.39
Czech	50	0.31
Czechoslovakian	61	0.37
Dutch	359	2.20
English	1,421	8.70
European	21	0.13
Finnish	9	0.06
French, except Basque	325	1.99
French Canadian	50	0.31
German	3,906	23.92
Greek	89	0.55
Guyanese	3	0.02
Hawaii Native/Pacific Islander:	9	0.06
Micronesian:	2	0.01
Guamanian/Chamorro	1	0.01
Other Micronesian	1	0.01
Polynesian: (3)	6	0.04
Native Hawaiian (2)	4	0.02
Other Polynesian (1)	2	0.01
Other Pac. Isl., specified	1	0.01
Hispanic or Latino:	144	0.88
Central American:	6	0.04
Guatemalan	3	0.02
Nicaraguan	1	0.01
Panamanian	2	0.01
Cuban	17	0.10
Mexican	42	0.26
Puerto Rican	56	0.34
South American:	6	0.04
Chilean	4	0.02

Notes: 1. Figures in the "Number" column do not add up to the total population due to: a) Ancestry/Race overlap — e.g. persons can report being both White and Irish, b) persons of Hispanic origin can report being any race, c) persons reporting two ancestries are counted in both categories. 2. Numbers in parentheses indicate the number of persons reporting this ancestry/race alone, not in combination with any other ancestry/race. 3. Refer to the Explanation of Data in the front of the book for more detailed information.

Ancestry/Race	Number	%
Peruvian	1	0.01
Uruguayan	1	0.01
Other Hispanic or Latino	17	0.10
Hungarian	407	2.49
Irish	2,635	16.14
Italian	2,022	12.38
Lithuanian	64	0.39
Norwegian	10	0.06
Pennsylvania German	32	0.20
Polish	895	5.48
Portuguese	10	0.06
Romanian	85	0.52
Russian	154	0.94
Scotch-Irish	411	2.52
Scottish	207	1.27
Serbian	54	0.33
Slavic	97	0.59
Slovak	895	5.48
Slovene	60	0.37
Swedish	142	0.87
Swiss	28	0.17
Ukrainian	81	0.50
United States or American	580	3.55
Welsh	617	3.78
West Indian, excl. Hispanic:	21	0.13
Haitian	21	0.13
White:	14,422	88.33
Not Hispanic (14,028)	14,307	87.62
Hispanic (86)	115	0.70
Yugoslavian	13	0.08

Shiloh

Place Type: Census Designated Place
County: York
Population: 10,192

Ancestry/Race	Number	%
African American/Black:	214	2.10
Not Hispanic (172)	210	2.06
Hispanic (2)	4	0.04
African, sub-Saharan:	15	0.15
African	15	0.15
Am. Ind. or Alaska Nat., not spec.	11	0.11
American Indian tribes, specified:	15	0.15
Apache	1	0.01
Cherokee (1)	7	0.07
Chippewa (1)	1	0.01
Creek (5)	5	0.05
Pueblo	1	0.01
Arab:	16	0.16
Arab/Arabic	9	0.09
Lebanese	7	0.07
Armenian	17	0.17
Asian:	169	1.66
Cambodian (6)	6	0.06
Chinese, ex. Taiwanese (26)	26	0.26
Filipino (5)	5	0.05
Indian (52)	55	0.54
Japanese (9)	15	0.15
Korean (14)	20	0.20
Laotian (3)	3	0.03
Pakistani (3)	3	0.03
Vietnamese (33)	34	0.33
Other Asian, not specified	2	0.02
Austrian	26	0.25
Belgian	14	0.14
British	9	0.09
Canadian	6	0.06
Croatian	28	0.27
Czech	6	0.06
Czechoslovakian	24	0.23
Danish	40	0.39
Dutch	136	1.33
English	679	6.63
European	64	0.63
Finnish	7	0.07
French, except Basque	109	1.06
French Canadian	29	0.28
German	3,883	37.92
Greek	176	1.72
Hawaii Native/Pacific Islander:	6	0.06
Micronesian:	6	0.06
Guamanian/Chamorro	1	0.01
Other Micronesian	5	0.05
Hispanic or Latino:	108	1.06
Central American:	2	0.02
Honduran	2	0.02
Dominican Republic	2	0.02
Mexican	12	0.12
Puerto Rican	62	0.61
South American:	9	0.09
Argentinean	1	0.01
Chilean	2	0.02
Colombian	3	0.03
Peruvian	1	0.01
Other South American	2	0.02
Other Hispanic or Latino	21	0.21
Hungarian	14	0.14
Irish	1,135	11.09
Italian	522	5.10
Lithuanian	7	0.07
Norwegian	89	0.87
Pennsylvania German	60	0.59
Polish	314	3.07
Romanian	10	0.10
Russian	34	0.33
Scotch-Irish	132	1.29
Scottish	144	1.41
Slovak	44	0.43
Swedish	82	0.80
Swiss	67	0.65
Ukrainian	13	0.13
United States or American	1,140	11.13
Welsh	120	1.17
West Indian, excl. Hispanic:	22	0.21
British West Indian	7	0.07
U.S. Virgin Islander	15	0.15
White:	9,826	96.41
Not Hispanic (9,659)	9,752	95.68
Hispanic (63)	74	0.73

Silver Spring

Place Type: Township
County: Cumberland
Population: 10,592

Ancestry/Race	Number	%
African American/Black:	61	0.58
Not Hispanic (38)	58	0.55
Hispanic (1)	3	0.03
Am. Ind. or Alaska Nat., not spec.	6	0.06
American Indian tribes, specified:	26	0.25
Apache	1	0.01
Blackfeet	1	0.01
Cherokee	10	0.09
Chippewa (1)	1	0.01
Creek (1)	2	0.02
Delaware (1)	1	0.01
Iroquois (4)	9	0.08
Osage	1	0.01
American Indian tribes, not spec.	1	0.01
Arab:	43	0.41
Palestinian	29	0.27
Other Arab	14	0.13
Asian:	276	2.61
Chinese, ex. Taiwanese (9)	10	0.09
Filipino (12)	15	0.14
Indian (94)	96	0.91
Japanese (1)	3	0.03
Korean (54)	70	0.66
Laotian (10)	13	0.12
Pakistani (15)	15	0.14
Taiwanese (4)	4	0.04
Vietnamese (40)	45	0.42
Other Asian, specified	3	0.03
Other Asian, not specified	2	0.02
Austrian	31	0.29
Belgian	10	0.09
British	70	0.66
Canadian	41	0.39
Croatian	18	0.17
Czechoslovakian	54	0.51
Danish	62	0.59
Dutch	275	2.60
English	1,196	11.29
European	42	0.40
Finnish	5	0.05
French, except Basque	340	3.21
French Canadian	55	0.52
German	3,889	36.72
Greek	67	0.63
Hawaii Native/Pacific Islander:	8	0.08
Micronesian:	1	0.01
Guamanian/Chamorro	1	0.01
Polynesian: (4)	4	0.04
Native Hawaiian (4)	4	0.04
Other Pac. Isl., specified	3	0.03
Hispanic or Latino:	77	0.73
Central American:	5	0.05
Costa Rican	1	0.01
Guatemalan	3	0.03
Salvadoran	1	0.01
Cuban	6	0.06
Dominican Republic	5	0.05
Mexican	22	0.21
Puerto Rican	17	0.16
South American:	4	0.04
Argentinean	1	0.01
Colombian	1	0.01
Paraguayan	1	0.01
Other South American	1	0.01
Other Hispanic or Latino	18	0.17
Hungarian	123	1.16
Iranian	9	0.08
Irish	1,448	13.67
Italian	889	8.39
Lithuanian	51	0.48
Norwegian	75	0.71
Pennsylvania German	102	0.96
Polish	513	4.84
Portuguese	9	0.08
Romanian	41	0.39
Russian	26	0.25
Scandinavian	14	0.13
Scotch-Irish	291	2.75
Scottish	211	1.99
Serbian	8	0.08
Slovak	216	2.04
Slovene	8	0.08
Swedish	54	0.51
Swiss	87	0.82
Ukrainian	62	0.59
United States or American	611	5.77
Welsh	150	1.42
White:	10,260	96.87
Not Hispanic (10,135)	10,203	96.33
Hispanic (49)	57	0.54
Yugoslavian	20	0.19

South Fayette

Place Type: Township
County: Allegheny
Population: 12,271

Ancestry/Race	Number	%
African American/Black:	463	3.77
Not Hispanic (427)	455	3.71
Hispanic (2)	8	0.07
African, sub-Saharan:	32	0.26
African	8	0.07
South African	24	0.20
Am. Ind. or Alaska Nat., not spec.	6	0.05
American Indian tribes, specified:	20	0.16
Cherokee	15	0.12
Chippewa	1	0.01
Pueblo	2	0.02
Sioux	1	0.01

...tes: 1. Figures in the "Number" column do not add up to the total population due to: a) Ancestry/Race overlap — e.g. persons can report being both White and Irish, b) persons ...nic origin can report being any race, c) persons reporting two ancestries are counted in both categories. 2. Numbers in parentheses indicate the number of persons ...s ancestry/race alone, not in combination with any other ancestry/race. 3. Refer to the Explanation of Data in the front of the book for more detailed information.

All other tribes	1	0.01
Arab:	119	0.97
Egyptian	15	0.12
Lebanese	43	0.35
Palestinian	7	0.06
Syrian	54	0.44
Asian:	218	1.78
Bangladeshi (4)	4	0.03
Chinese, ex. Taiwanese (38)	40	0.33
Filipino (8)	16	0.13
Indian (124)	127	1.03
Indonesian (2)	2	0.02
Japanese (4)	6	0.05
Korean (5)	10	0.08
Pakistani (4)	4	0.03
Taiwanese (2)	2	0.02
Vietnamese (1)	2	0.02
Other Asian, not specified (3)	5	0.04
Austrian	91	0.74
Belgian	164	1.34
Brazilian	16	0.13
British	20	0.16
Croatian	25	0.20
Czech	164	1.34
Czechoslovakian	11	0.09
Danish	31	0.25
Dutch	15	0.12
Eastern European	38	0.31
English	1,009	8.22
European	26	0.21
Finnish	9	0.07
French, except Basque	363	2.96
French Canadian	35	0.29
German	3,257	26.54
Greek	22	0.18
Hawaii Native/Pacific Islander:	9	0.07
Micronesian: (6)	6	0.05
Guamanian/Chamorro (6)	6	0.05
Polynesian:	1	0.01
Native Hawaiian	1	0.01
Other Pac. Isl., not spec.	2	0.02
Hispanic or Latino:	88	0.72
Central American:	4	0.03
Guatemalan	1	0.01
Panamanian	3	0.02
Cuban	4	0.03
Dominican Republic	1	0.01
Mexican	34	0.28
Puerto Rican	22	0.18
South American:	4	0.03
Argentinean	1	0.01
Chilean	1	0.01
Colombian	1	0.01
Venezuelan	1	0.01
Other Hispanic or Latino	19	0.15
Hungarian	340	2.77
Iranian	13	0.11
Irish	2,143	17.46
Italian	2,442	19.90
Lithuanian	193	1.57
Norwegian	8	0.07
Pennsylvania German	8	0.07
Polish	1,510	12.31
Romanian	23	0.19
Russian	227	1.85
Scotch-Irish	360	2.93
Scottish	272	2.22
Serbian	18	0.15
Slavic	16	0.13
Slovak	354	2.88
Slovene	199	1.62
Swedish	32	0.26
Swiss	9	0.07
Ukrainian	124	1.01
United States or American	419	3.41
Welsh	95	0.77
White:	11,592	94.47
Not Hispanic (11,475)	11,537	94.02
Hispanic (51)	55	0.45
Yugoslavian	11	0.09

South Middleton

Place Type: Township
County: Cumberland
Population: 12,939

Ancestry/Race	Number	%
African American/Black:	129	1.00
Not Hispanic (85)	120	0.93
Hispanic (2)	9	0.07
African, sub-Saharan:	36	0.28
African	36	0.28
Am. Ind. or Alaska Nat., not spec.	16	0.12
Alsatian	9	0.07
American Indian tribes, specified:	16	0.12
Blackfeet	1	0.01
Cherokee	3	0.02
Iroquois (1)	7	0.05
Navajo	2	0.02
Pueblo (2)	2	0.02
Seminole	1	0.01
American Indian tribes, not spec.	3	0.02
Arab:	89	0.69
Egyptian	63	0.49
Lebanese	16	0.12
Other Arab	10	0.08
Asian:	147	1.14
Chinese, ex. Taiwanese (19)	20	0.15
Filipino (16)	19	0.15
Indian (11)	11	0.09
Indonesian (1)	1	0.01
Japanese (6)	11	0.09
Korean (23)	27	0.21
Laotian (5)	5	0.04
Thai (4)	4	0.03
Vietnamese (26)	26	0.20
Other Asian, not specified (11)	23	0.18
Austrian	32	0.25
Belgian	31	0.24
British	64	0.49
Croatian	9	0.07
Czech	45	0.35
Czechoslovakian	18	0.14
Danish	20	0.15
Dutch	430	3.32
Eastern European	7	0.05
English	1,350	10.43
European	70	0.54
French, except Basque	339	2.62
French Canadian	36	0.28
German	4,806	37.14
Greek	30	0.23
Hawaii Native/Pacific Islander:	14	0.11
Micronesian: (8)	11	0.09
Guamanian/Chamorro (8)	11	0.09
Polynesian: (3)	3	0.02
Native Hawaiian (3)	3	0.02
Hispanic or Latino:	116	0.90
Central American:	6	0.05
Guatemalan	5	0.04
Panamanian	1	0.01
Cuban	7	0.05
Dominican Republic	1	0.01
Mexican	41	0.32
Puerto Rican	34	0.26
South American:	7	0.05
Colombian	4	0.03
Venezuelan	2	0.02
Other South American	1	0.01
Other Hispanic or Latino	20	0.15
Hungarian	60	0.46
Irish	1,669	12.90
Italian	549	4.24
Lithuanian	26	0.20
Norwegian	28	0.22
Pennsylvania German	122	0.94
Polish	468	3.62
Portuguese	11	0.09
Romanian	12	0.09
Russian	64	0.49
Scotch-Irish	522	4.03
Scottish	290	2.24
Serbian	21	0.16
Slavic	10	0.08
Slovak	64	0.49
Swedish	80	0.62
Swiss	119	0.92
Ukrainian	14	0.11
United States or American	1,283	9.91
Welsh	156	1.21
White:	12,663	97.87
Not Hispanic (12,507)	12,587	97.28
Hispanic (64)	76	0.59
Yugoslavian	9	0.07

South Park Township

Place Type: Census Designated Place
County: Allegheny
Population: 14,340

Ancestry/Race	Number	%
African American/Black:	510	3.56
Not Hispanic (458)	507	3.54
Hispanic (2)	3	0.02
African, sub-Saharan:	58	0.40
African	58	0.40
Alaska Native tribes, specified:	1	0.01
Alaska Athabascan (1)	1	0.01
Am. Ind. or Alaska Nat., not spec.	15	0.10
American Indian tribes, specified:	13	0.09
Blackfeet	1	0.01
Cherokee	2	0.01
Cree (1)	1	0.01
Iroquois	1	0.01
Ottawa	2	0.01
Seminole	1	0.01
Sioux	1	0.01
All other tribes (2)	4	0.03
Arab:	82	0.57
Lebanese	69	0.48
Syrian	13	0.09
Asian:	120	0.84
Chinese, ex. Taiwanese (34)	34	0.24
Filipino (6)	11	0.08
Indian (40)	41	0.29
Japanese (3)	7	0.05
Korean (13)	13	0.09
Laotian (1)	1	0.01
Thai (1)	1	0.01
Vietnamese (11)	11	0.08
Other Asian, not specified	1	0.01
Austrian	98	0.68
Belgian	19	0.13
Brazilian	30	0.21
British	10	0.07
Croatian	171	1.19
Czech	118	0.82
Czechoslovakian	59	0.41
Dutch	123	0.86
English	1,229	8.57
European	101	0.70
Finnish	63	0.44
French, except Basque	217	1.51
French Canadian	11	0.08
German	4,976	34.70
Greek	67	0.47
Hawaii Native/Pacific Islander:	9	0.06
Micronesian: (1)	1	0.01
Other Micronesian (1)	1	0.01
Polynesian: (3)	6	0.04
Native Hawaiian (1)	4	0.03
Samoan (2)	2	0.01
Other Pac. Isl., not spec. (2)	2	0.01
Hispanic or Latino:	79	0.55
Central American:	1	0.01
Honduran	1	0.01
Dominican Republic	2	0.01
Mexican	20	0.14
Puerto Rican	20	0.14

Notes: 1. Figures in the "Number" column do not add up to the total population due to: a) Ancestry/Race overlap — e.g. persons can report being both White and Irish, b) perso[illegible] of Hispanic origin can report being any race, c) persons reporting two ancestries are counted in both categories. 2. Numbers in parentheses indicate the number of persons [illegible] reporting this ancestry/race alone, not in combination with any other ancestry/race. 3. Refer to the Explanation of Data in the front of the book for more detailed inform[illegible]

South American:	6	0.04
Colombian	1	0.01
Venezuelan	5	0.03
Other Hispanic or Latino	30	0.21
Hungarian	294	2.05
Irish	2,929	20.43
Italian	2,883	20.10
Lithuanian	102	0.71
Norwegian	41	0.29
Polish	1,593	11.11
Portuguese	23	0.16
Romanian	18	0.13
Russian	152	1.06
Scandinavian	8	0.06
Scotch-Irish	437	3.05
Scottish	191	1.33
Serbian	82	0.57
Slavic	43	0.30
Slovak	843	5.88
Slovene	122	0.85
Swedish	87	0.61
Swiss	42	0.29
Ukrainian	243	1.69
United States or American	477	3.33
Welsh	197	1.37
West Indian, excl. Hispanic:	11	0.08
Bermudan	11	0.08
White:	13,733	95.77
Not Hispanic (13,597)	13,674	95.36
Hispanic (48)	59	0.41
Yugoslavian	17	0.12

South Union

Place Type: Township
County: Fayette
Population: 11,337

Ancestry/Race	Number	%
African American/Black:	430	3.79
Not Hispanic (368)	424	3.74
Hispanic (3)	6	0.05
African, sub-Saharan:	13	0.12
African	13	0.12
Am. Ind. or Alaska Nat., not spec.	7	0.06
American Indian tribes, specified:	22	0.19
Apache	2	0.02
Blackfeet (1)	1	0.01
Cherokee (2)	13	0.11
Iroquois (1)	3	0.03
Latin American Indians (1)	1	0.01
Sioux	1	0.01
All other tribes (1)	1	0.01
Arab:	108	0.96
Lebanese	99	0.88
Syrian	9	0.08
Asian:	105	0.93
Chinese, ex. Taiwanese (15)	17	0.15
Filipino (11)	16	0.14
Indian (37)	37	0.33
Indonesian (1)	1	0.01
Japanese (1)	1	0.01
Korean (20)	21	0.19
Pakistani (1)	1	0.01
Thai (2)	3	0.03
Vietnamese (5)	5	0.04
Other Asian, not specified (2)	3	0.03
Austrian	115	1.02
Belgian	26	0.23
Croatian	117	1.04
Czech	114	1.01
Czechoslovakian	85	0.75
Danish	8	0.07
Dutch	376	3.33
Eastern European	23	0.20
English	1,123	9.95
French, except Basque	56	0.50
German	1,869	16.56
Greek	5	0.04
Hawaii Native/Pacific Islander:	11	0.10
Polynesian: (1)	5	0.04
Native Hawaiian	1	0.01
Samoan (1)	4	0.04
Other Pac. Isl., not spec.	6	0.05
Hispanic or Latino:	37	0.33
Central American:	8	0.07
Guatemalan	2	0.02
Honduran	2	0.02
Salvadoran	2	0.02
Other Central American	2	0.02
Mexican	13	0.11
Puerto Rican	1	0.01
South American:	2	0.02
Colombian	1	0.01
Paraguayan	1	0.01
Other Hispanic or Latino	13	0.11
Hungarian	200	1.77
Irish	1,524	13.50
Italian	1,722	15.26
Lithuanian	10	0.09
Macedonian	9	0.08
Pennsylvania German	44	0.39
Polish	1,274	11.29
Romanian	19	0.17
Russian	153	1.36
Scandinavian	23	0.20
Scotch-Irish	358	3.17
Scottish	225	1.99
Serbian	11	0.10
Slavic	36	0.32
Slovak	1,068	9.46
Slovene	22	0.19
Swedish	44	0.39
Swiss	36	0.32
Ukrainian	29	0.26
United States or American	704	6.24
Welsh	108	0.96
White:	10,842	95.63
Not Hispanic (10,735)	10,816	95.40
Hispanic (23)	26	0.23
Yugoslavian	11	0.10

South Whitehall

Place Type: Township
County: Lehigh
Population: 18,028

Ancestry/Race	Number	%
African American/Black:	213	1.18
Not Hispanic (172)	200	1.11
Hispanic (12)	13	0.07
Am. Ind. or Alaska Nat., not spec.	18	0.10
Alsatian	5	0.03
American Indian tribes, specified:	10	0.06
Blackfeet (1)	1	0.01
Cherokee	2	0.01
Cheyenne	1	0.01
Chippewa (1)	1	0.01
Delaware	1	0.01
Iroquois	2	0.01
Latin American Indians	2	0.01
American Indian tribes, not spec.	5	0.03
Arab:	169	0.94
Arab/Arabic	44	0.24
Lebanese	20	0.11
Palestinian	10	0.06
Syrian	95	0.53
Asian:	436	2.42
Chinese, ex. Taiwanese (80)	91	0.50
Filipino (13)	21	0.12
Indian (149)	170	0.94
Indonesian	1	0.01
Japanese (6)	11	0.06
Korean (53)	56	0.31
Pakistani (9)	11	0.06
Taiwanese (4)	7	0.04
Vietnamese (45)	46	0.26
Other Asian, specified (5)	6	0.03
Other Asian, not specified (5)	16	0.09
Australian	11	0.06
Austrian	497	2.76
British	32	0.18
Canadian	105	0.58
Carpatho Rusyn	8	0.04
Croatian	33	0.18
Czech	44	0.24
Czechoslovakian	97	0.54
Danish	30	0.17
Dutch	400	2.22
Eastern European	153	0.85
English	1,508	8.36
European	79	0.44
Finnish	21	0.12
French, except Basque	380	2.11
French Canadian	84	0.47
German	6,059	33.61
Greek	241	1.34
Hawaii Native/Pacific Islander:	1	0.01
Other Pac. Isl., specified	1	0.01
Hispanic or Latino:	272	1.51
Central American:	6	0.03
Costa Rican	1	0.01
Guatemalan	3	0.02
Nicaraguan	1	0.01
Panamanian	1	0.01
Cuban	12	0.07
Dominican Republic	18	0.10
Mexican	26	0.14
Puerto Rican	115	0.64
South American:	34	0.19
Argentinean	5	0.03
Chilean	6	0.03
Colombian	5	0.03
Ecuadorian	5	0.03
Peruvian	12	0.07
Venezuelan	1	0.01
Other Hispanic or Latino	61	0.34
Hungarian	484	2.68
Iranian	5	0.03
Irish	2,254	12.50
Israeli	34	0.19
Italian	1,565	8.68
Latvian	35	0.19
Lithuanian	170	0.94
Northern European	25	0.14
Norwegian	49	0.27
Pennsylvania German	1,036	5.75
Polish	705	3.91
Portuguese	46	0.26
Romanian	20	0.11
Russian	591	3.28
Scotch-Irish	257	1.43
Scottish	257	1.43
Slavic	22	0.12
Slovak	544	3.02
Slovene	42	0.23
Swedish	66	0.37
Swiss	83	0.46
Turkish	6	0.03
Ukrainian	373	2.07
United States or American	850	4.71
Welsh	324	1.80
White:	17,362	96.31
Not Hispanic (17,091)	17,176	95.27
Hispanic (156)	186	1.03
Yugoslavian	26	0.14

Spring Garden

Place Type: Township
County: York
Population: 11,974

Ancestry/Race	Number	%
African American/Black:	242	2.02
Not Hispanic (188)	228	1.90
Hispanic (11)	14	0.12
African, sub-Saharan:	9	0.08
Ghanian	9	0.08

Notes: 1. Figures in the "Number" column do not add up to the total population due to: a) Ancestry/Race overlap — e.g. persons can report being both White and Irish, b) persons of Hispanic origin can report being any race, c) persons reporting two ancestries are counted in both categories. 2. Numbers in parentheses indicate the number of persons reporting this ancestry/race alone, not in combination with any other ancestry/race. 3. Refer to the Explanation of Data in the front of the book for more detailed information.

Ancestry/Race	Number	%
Am. Ind. or Alaska Nat., not spec.	6	0.05
Albanian	6	0.05
Alsatian	7	0.06
American Indian tribes, specified:	16	0.13
Blackfeet	1	0.01
Cherokee (3)	6	0.05
Choctaw	4	0.03
Cree (1)	1	0.01
Latin American Indians (1)	1	0.01
All other tribes (2)	3	0.03
American Indian tribes, not spec.	1	0.01
Arab:	19	0.16
Lebanese	13	0.11
Syrian	6	0.05
Armenian	12	0.10
Asian:	129	1.08
Cambodian (3)	3	0.03
Chinese, ex. Taiwanese (25)	28	0.23
Filipino (4)	10	0.08
Indian (19)	22	0.18
Indonesian	4	0.03
Japanese (6)	10	0.08
Korean (12)	17	0.14
Pakistani (1)	1	0.01
Taiwanese (1)	1	0.01
Thai	1	0.01
Vietnamese (22)	23	0.19
Other Asian, specified (5)	5	0.04
Other Asian, not specified (3)	4	0.03
Australian	7	0.06
Austrian	65	0.54
Belgian	7	0.06
British	61	0.51
Canadian	48	0.40
Croatian	15	0.13
Czech	37	0.31
Czechoslovakian	19	0.16
Danish	12	0.10
Dutch	232	1.94
Eastern European	16	0.13
English	1,147	9.58
European	72	0.60
Finnish	24	0.20
French, except Basque	296	2.47
French Canadian	76	0.63
German	4,578	38.22
Greek	111	0.93
Hawaii Native/Pacific Islander:	8	0.07
Micronesian:	5	0.04
Guamanian/Chamorro	5	0.04
Polynesian: (2)	2	0.02
Native Hawaiian (2)	2	0.02
Other Pac. Isl., not spec.	1	0.01
Hispanic or Latino:	196	1.64
Central American:	6	0.05
Costa Rican	4	0.03
Panamanian	2	0.02
Cuban	8	0.07
Dominican Republic	6	0.05
Mexican	24	0.20
Puerto Rican	97	0.81
South American:	21	0.18
Argentinean	3	0.03
Colombian	3	0.03
Paraguayan	3	0.03
Peruvian	6	0.05
Uruguayan	2	0.02
Other South American	4	0.03
Other Hispanic or Latino	34	0.28
Hungarian	68	0.57
Irish	1,605	13.40
Italian	988	8.25
Lithuanian	12	0.10
Northern European	7	0.06
Norwegian	80	0.67
Pennsylvania German	46	0.38
Polish	354	2.96
Portuguese	15	0.13
Romanian	5	0.04
Russian	158	1.32
Scandinavian	6	0.05
Scotch-Irish	335	2.80
Scottish	300	2.50
Serbian	5	0.04
Slavic	26	0.22
Slovak	91	0.76
Swedish	93	0.78
Swiss	139	1.16
Ukrainian	86	0.72
United States or American	915	7.64
Welsh	114	0.95
West Indian, excl. Hispanic:	10	0.08
Jamaican	10	0.08
White:	11,603	96.90
Not Hispanic (11,393)	11,470	95.79
Hispanic (121)	133	1.11

Spring

Place Type: Township
County: Berks
Population: 21,805

Ancestry/Race	Number	%
African American/Black:	562	2.58
Not Hispanic (413)	508	2.33
Hispanic (45)	54	0.25
African, sub-Saharan:	24	0.11
African	24	0.11
Am. Ind. or Alaska Nat., not spec.	31	0.14
American Indian tribes, specified:	27	0.12
Blackfeet	1	0.00
Cherokee (2)	4	0.02
Delaware (2)	8	0.04
Latin American Indians	5	0.02
Lumbee	2	0.01
Potawatomi (4)	4	0.02
Sioux	1	0.00
All other tribes (2)	2	0.01
American Indian tribes, not spec.	2	0.01
Arab:	49	0.22
Lebanese	15	0.07
Syrian	34	0.16
Armenian	13	0.06
Asian:	517	2.37
Chinese, ex. Taiwanese (125)	132	0.61
Filipino (27)	33	0.15
Hmong (6)	6	0.03
Indian (200)	209	0.96
Indonesian (1)	1	0.00
Japanese (19)	21	0.10
Korean (21)	31	0.14
Laotian (4)	4	0.02
Pakistani (2)	2	0.01
Taiwanese (7)	8	0.04
Thai (1)	1	0.00
Vietnamese (34)	35	0.16
Other Asian, specified (1)	3	0.01
Other Asian, not specified (18)	31	0.14
Australian	9	0.04
Austrian	122	0.56
Belgian	7	0.03
Brazilian	7	0.03
British	41	0.19
Canadian	33	0.15
Croatian	34	0.16
Czech	38	0.17
Czechoslovakian	144	0.66
Danish	97	0.44
Dutch	604	2.77
Eastern European	9	0.04
English	1,611	7.39
European	43	0.20
French, except Basque	481	2.21
French Canadian	101	0.46
German	8,641	39.63
Greek	172	0.79
Hawaii Native/Pacific Islander:	11	0.05
Micronesian: (2)	2	0.01
Guamanian/Chamorro (2)	2	0.01
Polynesian:	1	0.00
Native Hawaiian	1	0.00
Other Pac. Isl., not spec.	8	0.04
Hispanic or Latino:	631	2.89
Central American:	14	0.06
Costa Rican	1	0.00
Guatemalan	1	0.00
Honduran	3	0.01
Nicaraguan	1	0.00
Panamanian	6	0.03
Salvadoran	2	0.01
Cuban	20	0.09
Dominican Republic	42	0.19
Mexican	46	0.21
Puerto Rican	327	1.50
South American:	60	0.28
Argentinean	2	0.01
Bolivian	2	0.01
Chilean	1	0.00
Colombian	44	0.20
Ecuadorian	5	0.02
Peruvian	1	0.00
Other South American	5	0.02
Other Hispanic or Latino	122	0.56
Hungarian	176	0.81
Icelander	11	0.05
Irish	2,755	12.63
Italian	2,663	12.21
Lithuanian	132	0.61
Northern European	7	0.03
Norwegian	34	0.16
Pennsylvania German	510	2.34
Polish	1,971	9.04
Portuguese	39	0.18
Romanian	7	0.03
Russian	133	0.61
Scotch-Irish	287	1.32
Scottish	416	1.91
Slavic	76	0.35
Slovak	376	1.72
Slovene	32	0.15
Swedish	110	0.50
Swiss	124	0.57
Ukrainian	247	1.13
United States or American	1,220	5.60
Welsh	406	1.86
White:	20,608	94.51
Not Hispanic (20,091)	20,252	92.88
Hispanic (308)	356	1.63
Yugoslavian	51	0.23

Springettsbury

Place Type: Township
County: York
Population: 23,883

Ancestry/Race	Number	%
African American/Black:	1,143	4.79
Not Hispanic (999)	1,101	4.61
Hispanic (23)	42	0.18
African, sub-Saharan:	18	0.08
African	18	0.08
Alaska Native tribes, specified:	1	0.00
Eskimo (1)	1	0.00
Am. Ind. or Alaska Nat., not spec.	24	0.10
Albanian	12	0.05
American Indian tribes, specified:	32	0.13
Cherokee (10)	17	0.07
Delaware	2	0.01
Houma (1)	1	0.00
Iroquois	3	0.01
Latin American Indians (2)	2	0.01
Navajo	1	0.00
Pueblo (1)	2	0.01
All other tribes (1)	4	0.02
American Indian tribes, not spec.	4	0.02
Arab:	70	0.29
Egyptian	34	0.14
Lebanese	18	0.08

Notes: 1. Figures in the "Number" column do not add up to the total population due to: a) Ancestry/Race overlap — e.g. persons can report being both White and Irish, b) persons of Hispanic origin can report being any race, c) persons reporting two ancestries are counted in both categories. 2. Numbers in parentheses indicate the number of persons reporting this ancestry/race alone, not in combination with any other ancestry/race. 3. Refer to the Explanation of Data in the front of the book for more detailed information.

Ancestry/Race	Number	%
Palestinian	4	0.02
Syrian	7	0.03
Other Arab	7	0.03
Asian:	624	2.61
Bangladeshi (1)	1	0.00
Cambodian (12)	12	0.05
Chinese, ex. Taiwanese (130)	138	0.58
Filipino (16)	21	0.09
Indian (159)	162	0.68
Indonesian (1)	2	0.01
Japanese (19)	20	0.08
Korean (88)	97	0.41
Laotian	1	0.00
Malaysian (1)	1	0.00
Pakistani (5)	6	0.03
Sri Lankan (11)	11	0.05
Taiwanese (7)	7	0.03
Thai (3)	6	0.03
Vietnamese (121)	123	0.52
Other Asian, specified	1	0.00
Other Asian, not specified (12)	15	0.06
Austrian	75	0.31
British	99	0.41
Canadian	13	0.05
Croatian	49	0.21
Czech	96	0.40
Czechoslovakian	15	0.06
Danish	19	0.08
Dutch	325	1.36
Eastern European	42	0.18
English	2,255	9.44
European	129	0.54
Finnish	16	0.07
French, except Basque	469	1.96
French Canadian	94	0.39
German	8,767	36.71
Greek	138	0.58
Hawaii Native/Pacific Islander:	17	0.07
Micronesian: (2)	2	0.01
Other Micronesian (2)	2	0.01
Polynesian: (5)	5	0.02
Native Hawaiian (1)	1	0.00
Samoan (4)	4	0.02
Other Pac. Isl., not spec. (1)	10	0.04
Hispanic or Latino:	661	2.77
Central American:	25	0.10
Guatemalan	5	0.02
Honduran	8	0.03
Panamanian	3	0.01
Salvadoran	9	0.04
Cuban	36	0.15
Dominican Republic	54	0.23
Mexican	65	0.27
Puerto Rican	338	1.42
South American:	45	0.19
Argentinean	8	0.03
Colombian	19	0.08
Ecuadorian	7	0.03
Peruvian	7	0.03
Uruguayan	2	0.01
Other South American	2	0.01
Other Hispanic or Latino	98	0.41
Hungarian	90	0.38
Irish	2,614	10.95
Israeli	9	0.04
Italian	1,455	6.09
Latvian	5	0.02
Lithuanian	54	0.23
Northern European	9	0.04
Norwegian	99	0.41
Pennsylvania German	130	0.54
Polish	749	3.14
Portuguese	7	0.03
Romanian	12	0.05
Russian	127	0.53
Scandinavian	50	0.21
Scotch-Irish	528	2.21
Scottish	354	1.48
Serbian	9	0.04
Slavic	9	0.04
Slovak	121	0.51
Slovene	13	0.05
Swedish	207	0.87
Swiss	157	0.66
Ukrainian	142	0.59
United States or American	1,643	6.88
Welsh	229	0.96
West Indian, excl. Hispanic:	10	0.04
Haitian	10	0.04
White:	21,984	92.05
Not Hispanic (21,397)	21,569	90.31
Hispanic (370)	415	1.74
Yugoslavian	38	0.16

Springfield

Place Type: Census Designated Place
County: Delaware
Population: 23,677

Ancestry/Race	Number	%
African American/Black:	213	0.90
Not Hispanic (166)	205	0.87
Hispanic (4)	8	0.03
African, sub-Saharan:	61	0.26
Nigerian	61	0.26
Am. Ind. or Alaska Nat., not spec.	14	0.06
Albanian	10	0.04
American Indian tribes, specified:	27	0.11
Cherokee (4)	11	0.05
Choctaw	1	0.00
Crow (1)	1	0.00
Delaware (1)	2	0.01
Iroquois	1	0.00
Latin American Indians	1	0.00
Lumbee	1	0.00
All other tribes (2)	9	0.04
Armenian	191	0.81
Asian:	522	2.20
Bangladeshi (10)	10	0.04
Cambodian	7	0.03
Chinese, ex. Taiwanese (90)	107	0.45
Filipino (34)	44	0.19
Indian (145)	154	0.65
Japanese (13)	14	0.06
Korean (104)	112	0.47
Pakistani (1)	5	0.02
Taiwanese (8)	12	0.05
Thai (5)	5	0.02
Vietnamese (43)	47	0.20
Other Asian, not specified (4)	5	0.02
Australian	8	0.03
Austrian	79	0.33
Belgian	11	0.05
British	73	0.31
Canadian	24	0.10
Celtic	8	0.03
Croatian	23	0.10
Czech	43	0.18
Czechoslovakian	50	0.21
Danish	53	0.22
Dutch	194	0.82
English	2,685	11.34
European	89	0.38
French, except Basque	340	1.44
French Canadian	53	0.22
German	4,232	17.87
Greek	202	0.85
Hawaii Native/Pacific Islander:	8	0.03
Micronesian: (3)	3	0.01
Guamanian/Chamorro (3)	3	0.01
Other Pac. Isl., not spec.	5	0.02
Hispanic or Latino:	146	0.62
Central American:	11	0.05
Honduran	3	0.01
Nicaraguan	3	0.01
Panamanian	1	0.00
Salvadoran	4	0.02
Cuban	10	0.04
Mexican	32	0.14
Puerto Rican	31	0.13
South American:	18	0.08
Argentinean	4	0.02
Bolivian	1	0.00
Chilean	1	0.00
Colombian	3	0.01
Ecuadorian	3	0.01
Peruvian	3	0.01
Venezuelan	2	0.01
Other South American	1	0.00
Other Hispanic or Latino	44	0.19
Hungarian	162	0.68
Iranian	17	0.07
Irish	9,000	38.01
Italian	6,424	27.13
Lithuanian	138	0.58
Northern European	27	0.11
Norwegian	54	0.23
Pennsylvania German	80	0.34
Polish	1,345	5.68
Portuguese	42	0.18
Romanian	28	0.12
Russian	339	1.43
Scandinavian	5	0.02
Scotch-Irish	590	2.49
Scottish	337	1.42
Serbian	7	0.03
Slovak	81	0.34
Slovene	19	0.08
Swedish	181	0.76
Swiss	108	0.46
Turkish	16	0.07
Ukrainian	258	1.09
United States or American	498	2.10
Welsh	226	0.95
West Indian, excl. Hispanic:	5	0.02
Dutch West Indian	5	0.02
White:	22,979	97.05
Not Hispanic (22,766)	22,865	96.57
Hispanic (102)	114	0.48
Yugoslavian	24	0.10

Springfield

Place Type: Township
County: Montgomery
Population: 19,533

Ancestry/Race	Number	%
Acadian/Cajun	11	0.06
African American/Black:	1,690	8.65
Not Hispanic (1,606)	1,667	8.53
Hispanic (17)	23	0.12
African, sub-Saharan:	27	0.14
African	19	0.10
South African	8	0.04
Am. Ind. or Alaska Nat., not spec.	21	0.11
Alsatian	7	0.04
American Indian tribes, specified:	27	0.14
Cherokee (4)	11	0.06
Cheyenne	1	0.01
Creek	1	0.01
Delaware	3	0.02
Iroquois (2)	2	0.01
Lumbee	3	0.02
Navajo (1)	1	0.01
All other tribes (4)	5	0.03
American Indian tribes, not spec.	4	0.02
Arab:	35	0.18
Arab/Arabic	29	0.15
Lebanese	6	0.03
Armenian	55	0.28
Asian:	438	2.24
Cambodian (1)	1	0.01
Chinese, ex. Taiwanese (63)	82	0.42
Filipino (18)	29	0.15
Indian (46)	53	0.27
Indonesian	3	0.02
Japanese (13)	16	0.08
Korean (171)	175	0.90

Notes: 1. Figures in the "Number" column do not add up to the total population due to: a) Ancestry/Race overlap — e.g. persons can report being both White and Irish, b) persons of Hispanic origin can report being any race, c) persons reporting two ancestries are counted in both categories. 2. Numbers in parentheses indicate the number of persons reporting this ancestry/race alone, not in combination with any other ancestry/race. 3. Refer to the Explanation of Data in the front of the book for more detailed information.

Taiwanese (1)	1	0.01
Thai (3)	3	0.02
Vietnamese (50)	53	0.27
Other Asian, specified	2	0.01
Other Asian, not specified (10)	20	0.10
Australian	8	0.04
Austrian	107	0.55
Belgian	19	0.10
British	65	0.33
Canadian	13	0.07
Celtic	45	0.23
Croatian	16	0.08
Czech	50	0.26
Czechoslovakian	48	0.25
Danish	47	0.24
Dutch	245	1.25
Eastern European	95	0.49
English	2,630	13.46
European	131	0.67
Finnish	2	0.01
French, except Basque	394	2.02
French Canadian	40	0.20
German	3,997	20.46
Greek	81	0.41
Hawaii Native/Pacific Islander:	3	0.02
Polynesian: (1)	1	0.01
Native Hawaiian (1)	1	0.01
Other Pac. Isl., specified	2	0.01
Hispanic or Latino:	203	1.04
Central American:	10	0.05
Costa Rican	2	0.01
Guatemalan	3	0.02
Honduran	2	0.01
Panamanian	2	0.01
Other Central American	1	0.01
Cuban	23	0.12
Dominican Republic	2	0.01
Mexican	27	0.14
Puerto Rican	72	0.37
South American:	39	0.20
Argentinean	3	0.02
Bolivian	7	0.04
Chilean	6	0.03
Colombian	8	0.04
Ecuadorian	6	0.03
Peruvian	2	0.01
Venezuelan	4	0.02
Other South American	3	0.02
Other Hispanic or Latino	30	0.15
Hungarian	134	0.69
Icelander	12	0.06
Iranian	20	0.10
Irish	4,858	24.87
Israeli	41	0.21
Italian	2,427	12.43
Lithuanian	248	1.27
Northern European	17	0.09
Norwegian	84	0.43
Pennsylvania German	28	0.14
Polish	960	4.91
Portuguese	84	0.43
Romanian	58	0.30
Russian	460	2.35
Scotch-Irish	512	2.62
Scottish	441	2.26
Slavic	32	0.16
Slovak	87	0.45
Swedish	109	0.56
Swiss	88	0.45
Ukrainian	255	1.31
United States or American	869	4.45
Welsh	261	1.34
West Indian, excl. Hispanic:	129	0.66
Barbadian	18	0.09
Bermudan	5	0.03
British West Indian	5	0.03
Jamaican	76	0.39
Trinidadian and Tobagonian	10	0.05
West Indian	15	0.08
White:	17,409	89.13
Not Hispanic (17,170)	17,275	88.44
Hispanic (124)	134	0.69
Yugoslavian	13	0.07

State College

Place Type: Borough
County: Centre
Population: 38,420

Ancestry/Race	Number	%
Afghan	13	0.03
African American/Black:	1,565	4.07
Not Hispanic (1,371)	1,494	3.89
Hispanic (46)	71	0.18
African, sub-Saharan:	198	0.52
African	103	0.27
Ethiopian	10	0.03
Nigerian	38	0.10
South African	17	0.04
Zimbabwean	14	0.04
Other sub-Saharan African	16	0.04
Alaska Native tribes, specified:	3	0.01
Eskimo (2)	2	0.01
Tlingit-Haida (1)	1	0.00
Am. Ind. or Alaska Nat., not spec.	53	0.14
Alsatian	8	0.02
American Indian tribes, specified:	81	0.21
Blackfeet	4	0.01
Cherokee (8)	27	0.07
Chickasaw	1	0.00
Choctaw (1)	2	0.01
Cree (1)	2	0.01
Creek (1)	1	0.00
Delaware (2)	2	0.01
Iroquois (5)	9	0.02
Latin American Indians (2)	9	0.02
Lumbee	1	0.00
Navajo (3)	5	0.01
Pueblo (1)	1	0.00
Seminole	2	0.01
Ute	1	0.00
All other tribes (7)	14	0.04
American Indian tribes, not spec.	3	0.01
Arab:	223	0.58
Arab/Arabic	39	0.10
Egyptian	51	0.13
Lebanese	57	0.15
Palestinian	3	0.01
Syrian	52	0.14
Other Arab	21	0.05
Armenian	10	0.03
Asian:	3,718	9.68
Bangladeshi (6)	6	0.02
Cambodian (12)	13	0.03
Chinese, ex. Taiwanese (1,209)	1,286	3.35
Filipino (91)	117	0.30
Hmong (1)	4	0.01
Indian (768)	806	2.10
Indonesian (8)	18	0.05
Japanese (170)	209	0.54
Korean (637)	667	1.74
Laotian (9)	9	0.02
Malaysian (6)	8	0.02
Pakistani (24)	28	0.07
Sri Lankan (19)	22	0.06
Taiwanese (93)	105	0.27
Thai (54)	57	0.15
Vietnamese (117)	135	0.35
Other Asian, specified (21)	25	0.07
Other Asian, not specified (79)	203	0.53
Assyrian/Chaldean/Syriac	10	0.03
Austrian	254	0.66
Belgian	40	0.10
Brazilian	46	0.12
British	311	0.81
Bulgarian	65	0.17
Canadian	99	0.26
Carpatho Rusyn	9	0.02
Croatian	152	0.40
Czech	190	0.49
Czechoslovakian	205	0.53
Danish	117	0.30
Dutch	493	1.28
Eastern European	65	0.17
English	3,354	8.73
Estonian	8	0.02
European	533	1.39
Finnish	74	0.19
French, except Basque	809	2.11
French Canadian	170	0.44
German	9,388	24.44
Greek	163	0.42
Guyanese	7	0.02
Hawaii Native/Pacific Islander:	149	0.39
Melanesian: (4)	4	0.01
Other Melanesian (4)	4	0.01
Polynesian: (10)	16	0.04
Native Hawaiian (3)	7	0.02
Samoan (7)	8	0.02
Other Polynesian	1	0.00
Other Pac. Isl., specified	3	0.01
Other Pac. Isl., not spec. (36)	126	0.33
Hispanic or Latino:	1,159	3.02
Central American:	50	0.13
Costa Rican	5	0.01
Guatemalan	12	0.03
Honduran	4	0.01
Nicaraguan	4	0.01
Panamanian	7	0.02
Salvadoran	16	0.04
Other Central American	2	0.01
Cuban	66	0.17
Dominican Republic	36	0.09
Mexican	197	0.51
Puerto Rican	345	0.90
South American:	207	0.54
Argentinean	27	0.07
Bolivian	10	0.03
Chilean	20	0.05
Colombian	57	0.15
Ecuadorian	21	0.05
Paraguayan	1	0.00
Peruvian	30	0.08
Uruguayan	7	0.02
Venezuelan	25	0.07
Other South American	9	0.02
Other Hispanic or Latino	258	0.67
Hungarian	412	1.07
Iranian	34	0.09
Irish	5,762	15.00
Israeli	30	0.08
Italian	4,659	12.13
Latvian	22	0.06
Lithuanian	247	0.64
Luxemburger	19	0.05
Northern European	19	0.05
Norwegian	206	0.54
Pennsylvania German	120	0.31
Polish	2,402	6.25
Portuguese	73	0.19
Romanian	135	0.35
Russian	1,002	2.61
Scandinavian	31	0.08
Scotch-Irish	737	1.92
Scottish	872	2.27
Serbian	57	0.15
Slavic	99	0.26
Slovak	561	1.46
Slovene	30	0.08
Swedish	615	1.60
Swiss	222	0.58
Turkish	62	0.16
Ukrainian	436	1.13
United States or American	796	2.07
Welsh	374	0.97
West Indian, excl. Hispanic:	162	0.42
Barbadian	6	0.02
Dutch West Indian	13	0.03
Haitian	7	0.02

Notes: 1. Figures in the "Number" column do not add up to the total population due to: a) Ancestry/Race overlap — e.g. persons can report being both White and Irish, b) persons of Hispanic origin can report being any race, c) persons reporting two ancestries are counted in both categories. 2. Numbers in parentheses indicate the number of persons reporting this ancestry/race alone, not in combination with any other ancestry/race. 3. Refer to the Explanation of Data in the front of the book for more detailed information.

Jamaican	118	0.31
West Indian	18	0.05
White:	32,823	85.43
Not Hispanic (31,862)	32,225	83.88
Hispanic (530)	598	1.56
Yugoslavian	40	0.10

Stroud

Place Type: Township
County: Monroe
Population: 13,978

Ancestry/Race	Number	%
African American/Black:	1,083	7.75
Not Hispanic (898)	997	7.13
Hispanic (62)	86	0.62
African, sub-Saharan:	81	0.58
African	49	0.35
Ghanian	14	0.10
South African	8	0.06
Other sub-Saharan African	10	0.07
Am. Ind. or Alaska Nat., not spec.	24	0.17
American Indian tribes, specified:	42	0.30
Apache (2)	2	0.01
Blackfeet (2)	2	0.01
Cherokee (5)	14	0.10
Delaware (3)	5	0.04
Iroquois (1)	9	0.06
Latin American Indians	5	0.04
All other tribes (2)	5	0.04
American Indian tribes, not spec.	5	0.04
Arab:	60	0.43
Egyptian	50	0.36
Lebanese	10	0.07
Asian:	284	2.03
Bangladeshi (1)	1	0.01
Chinese, ex. Taiwanese (42)	57	0.41
Filipino (39)	44	0.31
Indian (62)	74	0.53
Indonesian (8)	8	0.06
Japanese (3)	8	0.06
Korean (37)	39	0.28
Laotian (1)	1	0.01
Pakistani (16)	16	0.11
Taiwanese (4)	4	0.03
Thai (1)	1	0.01
Vietnamese (11)	13	0.09
Other Asian, not specified (4)	18	0.13
Austrian	92	0.66
Belgian	8	0.06
British	36	0.26
Canadian	78	0.56
Czech	77	0.55
Czechoslovakian	19	0.14
Danish	16	0.11
Dutch	448	3.21
Eastern European	18	0.13
English	1,161	8.31
Estonian	7	0.05
European	69	0.49
Finnish	7	0.05
French, except Basque	427	3.06
French Canadian	68	0.49
German	3,340	23.90
Greek	170	1.22
Hawaii Native/Pacific Islander:	7	0.05
Micronesian: (2)	2	0.01
Guamanian/Chamorro (2)	2	0.01
Other Pac. Isl., not spec.	5	0.04
Hispanic or Latino:	1,029	7.36
Central American:	25	0.18
Costa Rican	2	0.01
Guatemalan	1	0.01
Honduran	3	0.02
Panamanian	6	0.04
Salvadoran	10	0.07
Other Central American	3	0.02
Cuban	47	0.34
Dominican Republic	41	0.29
Mexican	42	0.30
Puerto Rican	588	4.21
South American:	114	0.82
Argentinean	7	0.05
Chilean	1	0.01
Colombian	40	0.29
Ecuadorian	28	0.20
Peruvian	32	0.23
Uruguayan	6	0.04
Other Hispanic or Latino	172	1.23
Hungarian	97	0.69
Irish	2,192	15.68
Italian	2,517	18.01
Latvian	11	0.08
Lithuanian	61	0.44
Norwegian	124	0.89
Pennsylvania German	226	1.62
Polish	1,008	7.21
Portuguese	50	0.36
Romanian	20	0.14
Russian	326	2.33
Scotch-Irish	146	1.04
Scottish	183	1.31
Serbian	22	0.16
Slovak	36	0.26
Swedish	109	0.78
Swiss	46	0.33
Ukrainian	61	0.44
United States or American	815	5.83
Welsh	258	1.85
West Indian, excl. Hispanic:	83	0.59
Haitian	39	0.28
Jamaican	12	0.09
Trinidadian and Tobagonian	11	0.08
West Indian	21	0.15
White:	12,274	87.81
Not Hispanic (11,546)	11,693	83.65
Hispanic (521)	581	4.16

Sunbury

Place Type: City
County: Northumberland
Population: 10,610

Ancestry/Race	Number	%
African American/Black:	192	1.81
Not Hispanic (122)	165	1.56
Hispanic (15)	27	0.25
African, sub-Saharan:	8	0.08
African	8	0.08
Am. Ind. or Alaska Nat., not spec.	26	0.25
American Indian tribes, specified:	32	0.30
Blackfeet	2	0.02
Cherokee (1)	13	0.12
Comanche	1	0.01
Creek (1)	1	0.01
Delaware (1)	1	0.01
Iroquois (3)	3	0.03
Latin American Indians (1)	1	0.01
Potawatomi	1	0.01
Sioux (3)	3	0.03
All other tribes (1)	6	0.06
American Indian tribes, not spec.	2	0.02
Arab:	18	0.17
Syrian	18	0.17
Asian:	41	0.39
Cambodian	2	0.02
Chinese, ex. Taiwanese (12)	15	0.14
Filipino (8)	11	0.10
Indian (2)	5	0.05
Japanese (1)	1	0.01
Korean	1	0.01
Pakistani	1	0.01
Vietnamese (1)	2	0.02
Other Asian, not specified (2)	3	0.03
Austrian	29	0.27
Belgian	6	0.06
British	8	0.08
Canadian	6	0.06
Czech	10	0.09
Czechoslovakian	17	0.16
Danish	5	0.05
Dutch	614	5.79
English	457	4.31
European	53	0.50
French, except Basque	185	1.74
French Canadian	28	0.26
German	3,533	33.30
Hawaii Native/Pacific Islander:	4	0.04
Polynesian: (2)	3	0.03
Native Hawaiian (2)	2	0.02
Samoan	1	0.01
Other Pac. Isl., not spec.	1	0.01
Hispanic or Latino:	328	3.09
Dominican Republic	1	0.01
Mexican	45	0.42
Puerto Rican	245	2.31
South American:	7	0.07
Chilean	3	0.03
Colombian	3	0.03
Ecuadorian	1	0.01
Other Hispanic or Latino	30	0.28
Hungarian	25	0.24
Irish	1,080	10.18
Italian	511	4.82
Lithuanian	47	0.44
Norwegian	43	0.41
Pennsylvania German	302	2.85
Polish	385	3.63
Russian	22	0.21
Scotch-Irish	159	1.50
Scottish	53	0.50
Slavic	4	0.04
Slovak	44	0.41
Swedish	16	0.15
Swiss	30	0.28
Turkish	5	0.05
Ukrainian	83	0.78
United States or American	1,469	13.85
Welsh	150	1.41
West Indian, excl. Hispanic:	5	0.05
Haitian	5	0.05
White:	10,209	96.22
Not Hispanic (10,014)	10,104	95.23
Hispanic (93)	105	0.99

Susquehanna

Place Type: Township
County: Dauphin
Population: 21,895

Ancestry/Race	Number	%
African American/Black:	4,516	20.63
Not Hispanic (4,157)	4,416	20.17
Hispanic (84)	100	0.46
African, sub-Saharan:	327	1.50
African	298	1.37
Cape Verdean	8	0.04
Ethiopian	13	0.06
Nigerian	8	0.04
Am. Ind. or Alaska Nat., not spec.	40	0.18
American Indian tribes, specified:	54	0.25
Blackfeet (2)	5	0.02
Cherokee (5)	19	0.09
Cheyenne	1	0.00
Delaware	1	0.00
Iroquois	1	0.00
Latin American Indians (1)	2	0.01
Navajo (1)	1	0.00
Osage	1	0.00
Seminole	1	0.00
Sioux (2)	5	0.02
All other tribes (6)	17	0.08
American Indian tribes, not spec.	2	0.01
Arab:	75	0.34
Arab/Arabic	38	0.17
Lebanese	19	0.09
Other Arab	18	0.08

Notes: 1. Figures in the "Number" column do not add up to the total population due to: a) Ancestry/Race overlap — e.g. persons can report being both White and Irish, b) persons of Hispanic origin can report being any race, c) persons reporting two ancestries are counted in both categories. 2. Numbers in parentheses indicate the number of persons reporting this ancestry/race alone, not in combination with any other ancestry/race. 3. Refer to the Explanation of Data in the front of the book for more detailed information.

Armenian	61	0.28
Asian:	571	2.61
Cambodian (5)	7	0.03
Chinese, ex. Taiwanese (63)	80	0.37
Filipino (20)	27	0.12
Indian (125)	130	0.59
Indonesian	1	0.00
Japanese (17)	35	0.16
Korean (35)	43	0.20
Laotian (1)	3	0.01
Malaysian (1)	1	0.00
Pakistani (4)	5	0.02
Taiwanese (8)	8	0.04
Thai (3)	4	0.02
Vietnamese (176)	194	0.89
Other Asian, not specified (12)	33	0.15
Australian	5	0.02
Austrian	130	0.60
Belgian	10	0.05
British	84	0.39
Canadian	22	0.10
Croatian	165	0.76
Czech	47	0.22
Czechoslovakian	100	0.46
Danish	9	0.04
Dutch	481	2.21
Eastern European	249	1.15
English	1,325	6.09
European	143	0.66
Finnish	14	0.06
French, except Basque	292	1.34
French Canadian	23	0.11
German	5,199	23.91
Greek	141	0.65
Guyanese	8	0.04
Hawaii Native/Pacific Islander:	12	0.05
Micronesian: (1)	2	0.01
Guamanian/Chamorro	1	0.00
Other Micronesian (1)	1	0.00
Polynesian: (3)	4	0.02
Native Hawaiian (2)	3	0.01
Samoan (1)	1	0.00
Other Pac. Isl., not spec.	6	0.03
Hispanic or Latino:	492	2.25
Central American:	16	0.07
Costa Rican	4	0.02
Honduran	1	0.00
Panamanian	7	0.03
Salvadoran	4	0.02
Cuban	18	0.08
Dominican Republic	6	0.03
Mexican	96	0.44
Puerto Rican	256	1.17
South American:	33	0.15
Chilean	1	0.00
Colombian	9	0.04
Ecuadorian	14	0.06
Peruvian	6	0.03
Other South American	3	0.01
Other Hispanic or Latino	67	0.31
Hungarian	358	1.65
Icelander	5	0.02
Iranian	5	0.02
Irish	2,153	9.90
Israeli	62	0.29
Italian	1,663	7.65
Latvian	38	0.17
Lithuanian	100	0.46
Macedonian	9	0.04
Northern European	8	0.04
Norwegian	115	0.53
Pennsylvania German	178	0.82
Polish	1,038	4.77
Portuguese	8	0.04
Romanian	46	0.21
Russian	476	2.19
Scotch-Irish	421	1.94
Scottish	250	1.15
Serbian	19	0.09
Slavic	37	0.17
Slovak	189	0.87
Slovene	11	0.05
Swedish	165	0.76
Swiss	62	0.29
Ukrainian	245	1.13
United States or American	1,234	5.67
Welsh	485	2.23
West Indian, excl. Hispanic:	105	0.48
Barbadian	6	0.03
Bermudan	11	0.05
Haitian	12	0.06
Jamaican	19	0.09
Trinidadian and Tobagonian	24	0.11
West Indian	33	0.15
White:	16,872	77.06
Not Hispanic (16,311)	16,652	76.05
Hispanic (176)	220	1.00
Yugoslavian	40	0.18

Swatara

Place Type: Township
County: Dauphin
Population: 22,611

Ancestry/Race	Number	%
African American/Black:	3,915	17.31
Not Hispanic (3,553)	3,791	16.77
Hispanic (60)	124	0.55
African, sub-Saharan:	248	1.09
African	138	0.61
Ghanian	5	0.02
Nigerian	34	0.15
Ugandan	64	0.28
Other sub-Saharan African	7	0.03
Alaska Native tribes, specified:	1	0.00
Alaska Athabascan	1	0.00
Am. Ind. or Alaska Nat., not spec.	34	0.15
American Indian tribes, specified:	54	0.24
Apache	1	0.00
Blackfeet	2	0.01
Cherokee (6)	26	0.11
Chippewa (1)	1	0.00
Choctaw	1	0.00
Iroquois (2)	8	0.04
Kiowa	1	0.00
Latin American Indians (1)	1	0.00
Sioux	3	0.01
All other tribes (4)	10	0.04
American Indian tribes, not spec.	14	0.06
Arab:	20	0.09
Lebanese	7	0.03
Moroccan	6	0.03
Syrian	7	0.03
Armenian	14	0.06
Asian:	462	2.04
Cambodian (13)	13	0.06
Chinese, ex. Taiwanese (51)	56	0.25
Filipino (15)	20	0.09
Indian (51)	61	0.27
Indonesian (1)	2	0.01
Japanese (5)	10	0.04
Korean (25)	28	0.12
Pakistani (1)	3	0.01
Sri Lankan (2)	2	0.01
Taiwanese (8)	8	0.04
Thai	2	0.01
Vietnamese (212)	230	1.02
Other Asian, not specified (10)	27	0.12
Austrian	64	0.28
Belgian	21	0.09
British	59	0.26
Bulgarian	17	0.08
Canadian	20	0.09
Croatian	595	2.63
Czech	26	0.11
Czechoslovakian	23	0.10
Danish	7	0.03
Dutch	462	2.04
Eastern European	7	0.03
English	898	3.96
European	151	0.67
Finnish	13	0.06
French, except Basque	251	1.11
French Canadian	61	0.27
German	6,369	28.11
Greek	68	0.30
Hawaii Native/Pacific Islander:	21	0.09
Micronesian:	1	0.00
Guamanian/Chamorro	1	0.00
Polynesian: (3)	9	0.04
Native Hawaiian (1)	3	0.01
Samoan (2)	6	0.03
Other Pac. Isl., not spec. (8)	11	0.05
Hispanic or Latino:	1,071	4.74
Central American:	10	0.04
Costa Rican	1	0.00
Guatemalan	3	0.01
Nicaraguan	1	0.00
Panamanian	5	0.02
Cuban	40	0.18
Dominican Republic	25	0.11
Mexican	265	1.17
Puerto Rican	576	2.55
South American:	21	0.09
Colombian	2	0.01
Ecuadorian	13	0.06
Peruvian	4	0.02
Venezuelan	2	0.01
Other Hispanic or Latino	134	0.59
Hungarian	308	1.36
Irish	2,474	10.92
Italian	2,070	9.14
Latvian	21	0.09
Lithuanian	145	0.64
Macedonian	43	0.19
Norwegian	12	0.05
Pennsylvania German	302	1.33
Polish	808	3.57
Romanian	11	0.05
Russian	132	0.58
Scandinavian	11	0.05
Scotch-Irish	331	1.46
Scottish	238	1.05
Serbian	155	0.68
Slavic	43	0.19
Slovak	184	0.81
Slovene	85	0.38
Swedish	95	0.42
Swiss	126	0.56
Turkish	15	0.07
Ukrainian	53	0.23
United States or American	1,041	4.60
Welsh	314	1.39
West Indian, excl. Hispanic:	55	0.24
Jamaican	47	0.21
West Indian	8	0.04
White:	18,087	79.99
Not Hispanic (17,170)	17,469	77.26
Hispanic (510)	618	2.73
Yugoslavian	135	0.60

Towamencin

Place Type: Township
County: Montgomery
Population: 17,597

Ancestry/Race	Number	%
African American/Black:	709	4.03
Not Hispanic (608)	704	4.00
Hispanic (3)	5	0.03
African, sub-Saharan:	144	0.82
African	52	0.30
Ethiopian	70	0.40
Ghanian	7	0.04
Nigerian	15	0.09
Am. Ind. or Alaska Nat., not spec.	22	0.13
Albanian	18	0.10
American Indian tribes, specified:	39	0.22

Notes: 1. Figures in the "Number" column do not add up to the total population due to: a) Ancestry/Race overlap — e.g. persons can report being both White and Irish, b) persons of Hispanic origin can report being any race, c) persons reporting two ancestries are counted in both categories. 2. Numbers in parentheses indicate the number of persons reporting this ancestry/race alone, not in combination with any other ancestry/race. 3. Refer to the Explanation of Data in the front of the book for more detailed information.

Blackfeet	1	0.01
Cherokee (1)	15	0.09
Delaware (1)	2	0.01
Iroquois (1)	1	0.01
Kiowa (3)	3	0.02
Latin American Indians	1	0.01
Lumbee (3)	6	0.03
Seminole	2	0.01
All other tribes (3)	8	0.05
American Indian tribes, not spec.	10	0.06
Arab:	34	0.19
Egyptian	18	0.10
Moroccan	8	0.05
Syrian	8	0.05
Armenian	20	0.11
Asian:	1,213	6.89
Cambodian (9)	17	0.10
Chinese, ex. Taiwanese (215)	257	1.46
Filipino (54)	63	0.36
Indian (331)	355	2.02
Indonesian	2	0.01
Japanese (27)	38	0.22
Korean (305)	326	1.85
Malaysian (1)	1	0.01
Pakistani (14)	14	0.08
Taiwanese (9)	17	0.10
Thai (3)	7	0.04
Vietnamese (94)	97	0.55
Other Asian, specified (4)	4	0.02
Other Asian, not specified (11)	15	0.09
Austrian	69	0.39
Basque	5	0.03
Belgian	10	0.06
British	158	0.90
Canadian	51	0.29
Croatian	12	0.07
Czech	120	0.68
Czechoslovakian	81	0.46
Danish	90	0.51
Dutch	218	1.24
Eastern European	51	0.29
English	2,011	11.43
Estonian	15	0.09
European	113	0.64
Finnish	21	0.12
French, except Basque	381	2.16
French Canadian	58	0.33
German	5,176	29.41
Greek	27	0.15
Hawaii Native/Pacific Islander:	19	0.11
Micronesian: (3)	5	0.03
Guamanian/Chamorro (3)	5	0.03
Polynesian: (1)	1	0.01
Native Hawaiian (1)	1	0.01
Other Pac. Isl., not spec.	13	0.07
Hispanic or Latino:	291	1.65
Central American:	28	0.16
Costa Rican	1	0.01
Guatemalan	4	0.02
Honduran	6	0.03
Panamanian	7	0.04
Salvadoran	4	0.02
Other Central American	6	0.03
Cuban	23	0.13
Dominican Republic	3	0.02
Mexican	36	0.20
Puerto Rican	92	0.52
South American:	38	0.22
Argentinean	11	0.06
Colombian	12	0.07
Ecuadorian	5	0.03
Peruvian	5	0.03
Venezuelan	2	0.01
Other South American	3	0.02
Other Hispanic or Latino	71	0.40
Hungarian	221	1.26
Irish	4,280	24.32
Israeli	6	0.03
Italian	2,748	15.61
Latvian	30	0.17
Lithuanian	148	0.84
Maltese	13	0.07
Norwegian	138	0.78
Pennsylvania German	216	1.23
Polish	1,230	6.99
Portuguese	32	0.18
Russian	320	1.82
Scandinavian	66	0.37
Scotch-Irish	245	1.39
Scottish	390	2.22
Slavic	7	0.04
Slovak	75	0.43
Slovene	35	0.20
Swedish	108	0.61
Swiss	137	0.78
Turkish	5	0.03
Ukrainian	259	1.47
United States or American	780	4.43
Welsh	321	1.82
West Indian, excl. Hispanic:	110	0.62
Barbadian	8	0.05
British West Indian	5	0.03
Haitian	12	0.07
Jamaican	79	0.45
Trinidadian and Tobagonian	6	0.03
White:	15,736	89.42
Not Hispanic (15,340)	15,526	88.23
Hispanic (198)	210	1.19
Yugoslavian	8	0.05

Tredyffrin

Place Type: Township
County: Chester
Population: 29,062

Ancestry/Race	Number	%
African American/Black:	880	3.03
Not Hispanic (806)	859	2.96
Hispanic (19)	21	0.07
African, sub-Saharan:	155	0.53
African	78	0.27
Nigerian	22	0.08
South African	27	0.09
Other sub-Saharan African	28	0.10
Am. Ind. or Alaska Nat., not spec.	29	0.10
Albanian	57	0.20
Alsatian	22	0.08
American Indian tribes, specified:	39	0.13
Cherokee (5)	14	0.05
Choctaw	1	0.00
Cree (1)	1	0.00
Delaware (4)	4	0.01
Iroquois	2	0.01
Latin American Indians (6)	7	0.02
Potawatomi	1	0.00
Seminole	1	0.00
Ute (1)	1	0.00
Yaqui (1)	1	0.00
All other tribes (2)	6	0.02
American Indian tribes, not spec.	2	0.01
Arab:	147	0.51
Arab/Arabic	20	0.07
Egyptian	43	0.15
Lebanese	43	0.15
Palestinian	4	0.01
Syrian	6	0.02
Other Arab	31	0.11
Armenian	147	0.51
Asian:	1,613	5.55
Bangladeshi	3	0.01
Cambodian (2)	2	0.01
Chinese, ex. Taiwanese (562)	593	2.04
Filipino (54)	64	0.22
Indian (473)	499	1.72
Indonesian	2	0.01
Japanese (59)	82	0.28
Korean (160)	176	0.61
Laotian (5)	6	0.02
Malaysian (1)	1	0.00
Pakistani (18)	23	0.08
Sri Lankan (7)	9	0.03
Taiwanese (32)	38	0.13
Thai (2)	6	0.02
Vietnamese (83)	86	0.30
Other Asian, specified (6)	6	0.02
Other Asian, not specified (12)	17	0.06
Australian	26	0.09
Austrian	231	0.79
Belgian	90	0.31
Brazilian	18	0.06
British	405	1.39
Bulgarian	14	0.05
Canadian	55	0.19
Croatian	60	0.21
Czech	228	0.78
Czechoslovakian	74	0.25
Danish	87	0.30
Dutch	606	2.09
Eastern European	120	0.41
English	4,683	16.11
European	157	0.54
Finnish	61	0.21
French, except Basque	878	3.02
French Canadian	127	0.44
German	6,314	21.73
Greek	260	0.89
Hawaii Native/Pacific Islander:	10	0.03
Micronesian: (1)	1	0.00
Guamanian/Chamorro (1)	1	0.00
Polynesian: (1)	4	0.01
Native Hawaiian	2	0.01
Samoan (1)	2	0.01
Other Pac. Isl., not spec. (2)	5	0.02
Hispanic or Latino:	350	1.20
Central American:	11	0.04
Guatemalan	3	0.01
Honduran	3	0.01
Panamanian	2	0.01
Salvadoran	3	0.01
Cuban	36	0.12
Dominican Republic	3	0.01
Mexican	73	0.25
Puerto Rican	80	0.28
South American:	63	0.22
Argentinean	13	0.04
Chilean	8	0.03
Colombian	8	0.03
Ecuadorian	7	0.02
Paraguayan	2	0.01
Peruvian	7	0.02
Uruguayan	1	0.00
Venezuelan	11	0.04
Other South American	6	0.02
Other Hispanic or Latino	84	0.29
Hungarian	326	1.12
Iranian	94	0.32
Irish	6,235	21.45
Italian	3,872	13.32
Latvian	9	0.03
Lithuanian	262	0.90
Macedonian	6	0.02
Maltese	8	0.03
New Zealander	6	0.02
Northern European	7	0.02
Norwegian	385	1.32
Pennsylvania German	67	0.23
Polish	1,271	4.37
Portuguese	7	0.02
Romanian	76	0.26
Russian	899	3.09
Scandinavian	49	0.17
Scotch-Irish	729	2.51
Scottish	1,099	3.78
Serbian	43	0.15
Slavic	19	0.07
Slovak	163	0.56
Slovene	20	0.07
Swedish	516	1.78
Swiss	226	0.78

Notes: 1. Figures in the "Number" column do not add up to the total population due to: a) Ancestry/Race overlap — e.g. persons can report being both White and Irish, b) persons of Hispanic origin can report being any race, c) persons reporting two ancestries are counted in both categories. 2. Numbers in parentheses indicate the number of persons reporting this ancestry/race alone, not in combination with any other ancestry/race. 3. Refer to the Explanation of Data in the front of the book for more detailed information.

Ancestry/Race	Number	%
Turkish	17	0.06
Ukrainian	203	0.70
United States or American	1,192	4.10
Welsh	514	1.77
West Indian, excl. Hispanic:	11	0.04
Jamaican	11	0.04
White:	26,591	91.50
Not Hispanic (26,170)	26,338	90.63
Hispanic (242)	253	0.87
Yugoslavian	30	0.10

Uniontown

Place Type: City
County: Fayette
Population: 12,422

Ancestry/Race	Number	%
African American/Black:	1,822	14.67
Not Hispanic (1,681)	1,811	14.58
Hispanic (5)	11	0.09
African, sub-Saharan:	24	0.19
African	24	0.19
Am. Ind. or Alaska Nat., not spec.	24	0.19
American Indian tribes, specified:	16	0.13
Apache (1)	3	0.02
Cherokee (2)	8	0.06
Chippewa (1)	1	0.01
Crow (1)	1	0.01
Latin American Indians (1)	1	0.01
Sioux (1)	1	0.01
All other tribes (1)	1	0.01
American Indian tribes, not spec.	6	0.05
Arab:	152	1.22
Lebanese	138	1.11
Syrian	14	0.11
Asian:	74	0.60
Cambodian	1	0.01
Chinese, ex. Taiwanese (12)	14	0.11
Filipino (5)	10	0.08
Indian (9)	16	0.13
Japanese (4)	6	0.05
Korean (3)	5	0.04
Pakistani	3	0.02
Vietnamese (16)	16	0.13
Other Asian, not specified (1)	3	0.02
Austrian	39	0.31
British	9	0.07
Carpatho Rusyn	54	0.43
Croatian	128	1.03
Czech	76	0.61
Czechoslovakian	117	0.94
Danish	23	0.19
Dutch	480	3.87
English	912	7.34
European	98	0.79
French, except Basque	179	1.44
French Canadian	10	0.08
German	1,720	13.85
Greek	51	0.41
Hawaii Native/Pacific Islander:	5	0.04
Polynesian: (2)	3	0.02
Native Hawaiian (1)	2	0.02
Samoan (1)	1	0.01
Other Pac. Isl., not spec. (2)	2	0.02
Hispanic or Latino:	68	0.55
Central American:	6	0.05
Guatemalan	1	0.01
Panamanian	5	0.04
Cuban	2	0.02
Dominican Republic	2	0.02
Mexican	15	0.12
Puerto Rican	18	0.14
Other Hispanic or Latino	25	0.20
Hungarian	153	1.23
Irish	1,685	13.57
Italian	1,158	9.33
Norwegian	29	0.23
Pennsylvania German	17	0.14
Polish	1,001	8.06
Russian	97	0.78
Scotch-Irish	101	0.81
Scottish	223	1.80
Serbian	58	0.47
Slavic	33	0.27
Slovak	605	4.87
Swedish	32	0.26
Swiss	21	0.17
Turkish	15	0.12
Ukrainian	6	0.05
United States or American	745	6.00
Welsh	42	0.34
White:	10,609	85.40
Not Hispanic (10,413)	10,563	85.03
Hispanic (42)	46	0.37
Yugoslavian	13	0.10

Unity

Place Type: Township
County: Westmoreland
Population: 21,137

Ancestry/Race	Number	%
African American/Black:	89	0.42
Not Hispanic (68)	87	0.41
Hispanic	2	0.01
Alaska Native tribes, specified:	1	0.00
Tlingit-Haida (1)	1	0.00
Am. Ind. or Alaska Nat., not spec.	28	0.13
American Indian tribes, specified:	29	0.14
Cherokee (2)	10	0.05
Chickasaw (2)	5	0.02
Choctaw (3)	3	0.01
Iroquois (6)	8	0.04
Navajo	1	0.00
All other tribes	2	0.01
Arab:	107	0.51
Lebanese	77	0.37
Moroccan	30	0.14
Asian:	212	1.00
Bangladeshi (3)	3	0.01
Chinese, ex. Taiwanese (34)	40	0.19
Filipino (10)	20	0.09
Indian (54)	56	0.26
Japanese (46)	56	0.26
Korean (15)	15	0.07
Pakistani	1	0.00
Sri Lankan (6)	6	0.03
Taiwanese (1)	1	0.00
Thai (2)	2	0.01
Vietnamese (4)	6	0.03
Other Asian, not specified (5)	6	0.03
Austrian	76	0.36
Belgian	72	0.34
British	110	0.52
Croatian	145	0.69
Czech	180	0.86
Czechoslovakian	114	0.54
Dutch	414	1.97
Eastern European	11	0.05
English	1,820	8.65
European	73	0.35
Finnish	29	0.14
French, except Basque	336	1.60
French Canadian	34	0.16
German	6,657	31.65
Greek	13	0.06
Hawaii Native/Pacific Islander:	7	0.03
Micronesian: (3)	4	0.02
Guamanian/Chamorro (2)	3	0.01
Other Micronesian (1)	1	0.00
Polynesian: (1)	2	0.01
Native Hawaiian (1)	1	0.00
Samoan	1	0.00
Other Pac. Isl., not spec.	1	0.00
Hispanic or Latino:	88	0.42
Central American:	1	0.00
Salvadoran	1	0.00
Cuban	2	0.01
Mexican	40	0.19
Puerto Rican	13	0.06
South American:	10	0.05
Argentinean	1	0.00
Bolivian	1	0.00
Colombian	6	0.03
Other South American	2	0.01
Other Hispanic or Latino	22	0.10
Hungarian	449	2.13
Irish	3,017	14.34
Italian	3,537	16.81
Lithuanian	85	0.40
Norwegian	33	0.16
Pennsylvania German	82	0.39
Polish	2,104	10.00
Romanian	10	0.05
Russian	149	0.71
Scotch-Irish	509	2.42
Scottish	431	2.05
Serbian	37	0.18
Slavic	81	0.39
Slovak	1,662	7.90
Slovene	113	0.54
Swedish	225	1.07
Swiss	45	0.21
Ukrainian	290	1.38
United States or American	886	4.21
Welsh	211	1.00
White:	20,821	98.50
Not Hispanic (20,681)	20,753	98.18
Hispanic (59)	68	0.32
Yugoslavian	15	0.07

Upper Allen

Place Type: Township
County: Cumberland
Population: 15,338

Ancestry/Race	Number	%
African American/Black:	238	1.55
Not Hispanic (177)	210	1.37
Hispanic (20)	28	0.18
African, sub-Saharan:	69	0.45
African	30	0.20
Kenyan	7	0.05
Nigerian	7	0.05
Other sub-Saharan African	25	0.16
Am. Ind. or Alaska Nat., not spec.	12	0.08
American Indian tribes, specified:	38	0.25
Apache	2	0.01
Blackfeet	2	0.01
Cherokee (4)	9	0.06
Chippewa	4	0.03
Choctaw	3	0.02
Cree	1	0.01
Creek	2	0.01
Crow	1	0.01
Delaware	1	0.01
Iroquois (3)	5	0.03
Ottawa	1	0.01
Paiute	1	0.01
Shoshone	1	0.01
All other tribes (2)	5	0.03
American Indian tribes, not spec.	3	0.02
Arab:	20	0.13
Arab/Arabic	6	0.04
Lebanese	14	0.09
Armenian	26	0.17
Asian:	327	2.13
Cambodian (5)	6	0.04
Chinese, ex. Taiwanese (20)	38	0.25
Filipino (18)	34	0.22
Indian (76)	83	0.54
Indonesian (2)	3	0.02
Japanese (14)	20	0.13
Korean (47)	53	0.35
Laotian (11)	16	0.10
Pakistani (18)	18	0.12
Taiwanese (2)	2	0.01

Notes: 1. Figures in the "Number" column do not add up to the total population due to: a) Ancestry/Race overlap — e.g. persons can report being both White and Irish, b) persons of Hispanic origin can report being any race, c) persons reporting two ancestries are counted in both categories. 2. Numbers in parentheses indicate the number of persons reporting this ancestry/race alone, not in combination with any other ancestry/race. 3. Refer to the Explanation of Data in the front of the book for more detailed information.

Vietnamese (35)	38	0.25
Other Asian, specified	1	0.01
Other Asian, not specified (2)	15	0.10
Austrian	96	0.63
Belgian	15	0.10
British	89	0.58
Bulgarian	14	0.09
Canadian	65	0.43
Croatian	50	0.33
Czech	52	0.34
Czechoslovakian	23	0.15
Dutch	335	2.19
Eastern European	9	0.06
English	1,825	11.94
European	295	1.93
Finnish	20	0.13
French, except Basque	485	3.17
French Canadian	87	0.57
German	5,830	38.15
Greek	69	0.45
Hawaii Native/Pacific Islander:	14	0.09
Micronesian: (1)	4	0.03
Guamanian/Chamorro (1)	4	0.03
Polynesian: (3)	6	0.04
Native Hawaiian (3)	6	0.04
Other Pac. Isl., specified	1	0.01
Other Pac. Isl., not spec. (1)	3	0.02
Hispanic or Latino:	219	1.43
Central American:	16	0.10
Guatemalan	7	0.05
Honduran	4	0.03
Nicaraguan	1	0.01
Panamanian	2	0.01
Other Central American	2	0.01
Cuban	11	0.07
Dominican Republic	8	0.05
Mexican	25	0.16
Puerto Rican	119	0.78
South American:	14	0.09
Bolivian	2	0.01
Colombian	4	0.03
Paraguayan	1	0.01
Peruvian	5	0.03
Venezuelan	2	0.01
Other Hispanic or Latino	26	0.17
Hungarian	145	0.95
Irish	1,944	12.72
Italian	1,166	7.63
Lithuanian	38	0.25
Luxemburger	8	0.05
Norwegian	67	0.44
Pennsylvania German	135	0.88
Polish	621	4.06
Romanian	19	0.12
Russian	107	0.70
Scandinavian	12	0.08
Scotch-Irish	381	2.49
Scottish	354	2.32
Serbian	66	0.43
Slavic	26	0.17
Slovak	81	0.53
Swedish	242	1.58
Swiss	237	1.55
Ukrainian	93	0.61
United States or American	712	4.66
Welsh	239	1.56
West Indian, excl. Hispanic:	10	0.07
Jamaican	10	0.07
White:	14,760	96.23
Not Hispanic (14,551)	14,652	95.53
Hispanic (95)	108	0.70
Yugoslavian	87	0.57

Upper Chichester

Place Type: Township
County: Delaware
Population: 16,842

Ancestry/Race	Number	%
Acadian/Cajun	6	0.04
African American/Black:	1,834	10.89
Not Hispanic (1,732)	1,802	10.70
Hispanic (12)	32	0.19
African, sub-Saharan:	228	1.35
African	74	0.44
Ethiopian	43	0.26
Nigerian	63	0.37
Sierra Leonean	41	0.24
Other sub-Saharan African	7	0.04
Am. Ind. or Alaska Nat., not spec.	27	0.16
American Indian tribes, specified:	63	0.37
Blackfeet (2)	6	0.04
Cherokee (1)	18	0.11
Cheyenne	1	0.01
Chippewa (2)	2	0.01
Cree	3	0.02
Delaware	6	0.04
Iroquois (4)	7	0.04
Lumbee (1)	4	0.02
Menominee (1)	1	0.01
Paiute	1	0.01
Pueblo	1	0.01
Seminole	2	0.01
Sioux	1	0.01
All other tribes (4)	10	0.06
American Indian tribes, not spec.	7	0.04
Arab:	21	0.12
Egyptian	15	0.09
Lebanese	6	0.04
Armenian	7	0.04
Asian:	383	2.27
Cambodian (6)	8	0.05
Chinese, ex. Taiwanese (71)	76	0.45
Filipino (29)	42	0.25
Indian (142)	147	0.87
Indonesian (1)	2	0.01
Japanese (5)	6	0.04
Korean (37)	45	0.27
Laotian (1)	1	0.01
Pakistani (2)	2	0.01
Thai (4)	6	0.04
Vietnamese (39)	42	0.25
Other Asian, not specified	6	0.04
Austrian	32	0.19
British	62	0.37
Canadian	27	0.16
Czech	30	0.18
Czechoslovakian	30	0.18
Danish	58	0.34
Dutch	231	1.37
Eastern European	7	0.04
English	2,110	12.53
European	16	0.10
Finnish	34	0.20
French, except Basque	368	2.19
French Canadian	67	0.40
German	3,203	19.02
Greek	74	0.44
Hawaii Native/Pacific Islander:	7	0.04
Polynesian:	3	0.02
Native Hawaiian	3	0.02
Other Pac. Isl., not spec. (1)	4	0.02
Hispanic or Latino:	196	1.16
Central American:	3	0.02
Guatemalan	1	0.01
Nicaraguan	1	0.01
Panamanian	1	0.01
Cuban	7	0.04
Dominican Republic	2	0.01
Mexican	34	0.20
Puerto Rican	92	0.55
South American:	20	0.12
Argentinean	11	0.07
Chilean	2	0.01
Colombian	4	0.02
Peruvian	1	0.01
Other South American	2	0.01
Other Hispanic or Latino	38	0.23
Hungarian	94	0.56
Iranian	20	0.12
Irish	4,280	25.41
Israeli	6	0.04
Italian	3,420	20.31
Latvian	8	0.05
Lithuanian	77	0.46
Maltese	24	0.14
Norwegian	67	0.40
Pennsylvania German	112	0.67
Polish	1,355	8.05
Portuguese	84	0.50
Romanian	36	0.21
Russian	161	0.96
Scotch-Irish	336	2.00
Scottish	205	1.22
Serbian	5	0.03
Slavic	41	0.24
Slovak	36	0.21
Slovene	9	0.05
Swedish	158	0.94
Swiss	64	0.38
Turkish	24	0.14
Ukrainian	306	1.82
United States or American	648	3.85
Welsh	405	2.40
West Indian, excl. Hispanic:	31	0.18
Barbadian	26	0.15
Jamaican	5	0.03
White:	14,624	86.83
Not Hispanic (14,383)	14,495	86.06
Hispanic (101)	129	0.77
Yugoslavian	5	0.03

Upper Darby

Place Type: Township
County: Delaware
Population: 81,821

Ancestry/Race	Number	%
Afghan	20	0.02
African American/Black:	9,911	12.11
Not Hispanic (9,124)	9,710	11.87
Hispanic (146)	201	0.25
African, sub-Saharan:	1,496	1.83
African	711	0.87
Cape Verdean	12	0.01
Ethiopian	110	0.13
Ghanian	79	0.10
Kenyan	22	0.03
Liberian	101	0.12
Nigerian	171	0.21
Senegalese	6	0.01
Sierra Leonean	27	0.03
Somalian	29	0.04
South African	52	0.06
Other sub-Saharan African	176	0.22
Am. Ind. or Alaska Nat., not spec.	172	0.21
Albanian	307	0.38
American Indian tribes, specified:	152	0.19
Apache (4)	6	0.01
Blackfeet	11	0.01
Cherokee (9)	66	0.08
Chippewa (1)	2	0.00
Choctaw (3)	4	0.00
Cree	1	0.00
Creek	2	0.00
Delaware (9)	12	0.01
Iroquois (1)	8	0.01
Latin American Indians (6)	9	0.01
Lumbee	3	0.00
Navajo (4)	4	0.00
Osage	1	0.00
Pueblo (1)	1	0.00
Seminole	2	0.00
Sioux (4)	7	0.01
All other tribes (4)	13	0.02
American Indian tribes, not spec.	24	0.03
Arab:	351	0.43
Arab/Arabic	88	0.11

Notes: 1. Figures in the "Number" column do not add up to the total population due to: a) Ancestry/Race overlap — e.g. persons can report being both White and Irish, b) persons of Hispanic origin can report being any race, c) persons reporting two ancestries are counted in both categories. 2. Numbers in parentheses indicate the number of persons reporting this ancestry/race alone, not in combination with any other ancestry/race. 3. Refer to the Explanation of Data in the front of the book for more detailed information.

Egyptian	92	0.11
Jordanian	22	0.03
Lebanese	62	0.08
Moroccan	24	0.03
Syrian	30	0.04
Other Arab	33	0.04
Armenian	632	0.77
Asian:	7,950	9.72
Bangladeshi (46)	60	0.07
Cambodian (166)	210	0.26
Chinese, ex. Taiwanese (1,429)	1,604	1.96
Filipino (296)	368	0.45
Hmong (48)	58	0.07
Indian (1,997)	2,132	2.61
Indonesian (11)	14	0.02
Japanese (115)	151	0.18
Korean (924)	968	1.18
Laotian (156)	195	0.24
Malaysian (9)	12	0.01
Pakistani (203)	255	0.31
Sri Lankan (1)	1	0.00
Taiwanese (22)	24	0.03
Thai (48)	63	0.08
Vietnamese (1,487)	1,618	1.98
Other Asian, specified (8)	9	0.01
Other Asian, not specified (87)	208	0.25
Australian	6	0.01
Austrian	252	0.31
Belgian	29	0.04
Brazilian	35	0.04
British	283	0.35
Bulgarian	37	0.05
Canadian	134	0.16
Celtic	19	0.02
Croatian	11	0.01
Cypriot	48	0.06
Czech	87	0.11
Czechoslovakian	48	0.06
Danish	65	0.08
Dutch	602	0.74
Eastern European	35	0.04
English	6,448	7.88
European	184	0.22
Finnish	126	0.15
French, except Basque	1,209	1.48
French Canadian	297	0.36
German	11,414	13.95
Greek	1,605	1.96
Guyanese	78	0.10
Hawaii Native/Pacific Islander:	83	0.10
Micronesian: (4)	11	0.01
Guamanian/Chamorro (4)	11	0.01
Polynesian: (9)	16	0.02
Native Hawaiian (5)	8	0.01
Samoan (4)	7	0.01
Other Polynesian	1	0.00
Other Pac. Isl., specified	1	0.00
Other Pac. Isl., not spec. (8)	55	0.07
Hispanic or Latino:	1,343	1.64
Central American:	73	0.09
Costa Rican	15	0.02
Guatemalan	13	0.02
Honduran	23	0.03
Panamanian	3	0.00
Salvadoran	15	0.02
Other Central American	4	0.00
Cuban	80	0.10
Dominican Republic	10	0.01
Mexican	217	0.27
Puerto Rican	398	0.49
South American:	192	0.23
Argentinean	20	0.02
Bolivian	4	0.00
Chilean	2	0.00
Colombian	20	0.02
Ecuadorian	66	0.08
Paraguayan	15	0.02
Peruvian	35	0.04
Venezuelan	22	0.03
Other South American	8	0.01
Other Hispanic or Latino	373	0.46
Hungarian	331	0.40
Iranian	16	0.02
Irish	27,905	34.10
Israeli	9	0.01
Italian	16,035	19.60
Latvian	74	0.09
Lithuanian	446	0.55
Macedonian	7	0.01
Maltese	8	0.01
New Zealander	8	0.01
Northern European	20	0.02
Norwegian	233	0.28
Pennsylvania German	235	0.29
Polish	2,911	3.56
Portuguese	119	0.15
Romanian	76	0.09
Russian	481	0.59
Scandinavian	50	0.06
Scotch-Irish	1,469	1.80
Scottish	767	0.94
Serbian	14	0.02
Slavic	68	0.08
Slovak	246	0.30
Slovene	10	0.01
Swedish	348	0.43
Swiss	128	0.16
Turkish	71	0.09
Ukrainian	449	0.55
United States or American	2,139	2.61
Welsh	516	0.63
West Indian, excl. Hispanic:	1,023	1.25
Barbadian	45	0.05
British West Indian	17	0.02
Dutch West Indian	16	0.02
Haitian	213	0.26
Jamaican	576	0.70
Trinidadian and Tobagonian	117	0.14
West Indian	39	0.05
White:	64,278	78.56
Not Hispanic (62,525)	63,486	77.59
Hispanic (697)	792	0.97
Yugoslavian	30	0.04

Upper Dublin

Place Type: Township
County: Montgomery
Population: 25,878

Ancestry/Race	Number	%
African American/Black:	1,467	5.67
Not Hispanic (1,389)	1,451	5.61
Hispanic (13)	16	0.06
African, sub-Saharan:	71	0.27
African	23	0.09
Ethiopian	27	0.10
Nigerian	21	0.08
Am. Ind. or Alaska Nat., not spec.	26	0.10
Alsatian	21	0.08
American Indian tribes, specified:	28	0.11
Apache	2	0.01
Blackfeet (1)	2	0.01
Cherokee (2)	7	0.03
Chickasaw (1)	2	0.01
Choctaw (2)	2	0.01
Creek	2	0.01
Iroquois	3	0.01
Latin American Indians (2)	2	0.01
Lumbee (1)	1	0.00
Navajo	1	0.00
Yaqui	1	0.00
All other tribes (1)	3	0.01
American Indian tribes, not spec.	5	0.02
Arab:	68	0.26
Jordanian	36	0.14
Lebanese	18	0.07
Palestinian	6	0.02
Syrian	8	0.03
Armenian	57	0.22
Asian:	1,688	6.52
Cambodian (4)	8	0.03
Chinese, ex. Taiwanese (402)	429	1.66
Filipino (35)	44	0.17
Indian (201)	209	0.81
Indonesian (2)	3	0.01
Japanese (23)	34	0.13
Korean (800)	816	3.15
Pakistani (2)	2	0.01
Sri Lankan (2)	3	0.01
Taiwanese (67)	67	0.26
Thai (13)	15	0.06
Vietnamese (30)	30	0.12
Other Asian, specified (2)	4	0.02
Other Asian, not specified (10)	24	0.09
Australian	7	0.03
Austrian	220	0.85
Belgian	23	0.09
British	220	0.85
Bulgarian	6	0.02
Canadian	49	0.19
Carpatho Rusyn	12	0.05
Croatian	39	0.15
Czech	35	0.14
Czechoslovakian	41	0.16
Danish	91	0.35
Dutch	268	1.04
Eastern European	502	1.94
English	2,639	10.20
Estonian	7	0.03
European	151	0.58
Finnish	7	0.03
French, except Basque	516	1.99
French Canadian	39	0.15
German	4,924	19.03
German Russian	10	0.04
Greek	97	0.37
Hawaii Native/Pacific Islander:	3	0.01
Micronesian: (1)	1	0.00
Guamanian/Chamorro (1)	1	0.00
Other Pac. Isl., not spec.	2	0.01
Hispanic or Latino:	233	0.90
Central American:	10	0.04
Costa Rican	1	0.00
Guatemalan	2	0.01
Nicaraguan	1	0.00
Panamanian	6	0.02
Cuban	19	0.07
Dominican Republic	4	0.02
Mexican	27	0.10
Puerto Rican	75	0.29
South American:	46	0.18
Argentinean	17	0.07
Chilean	1	0.00
Colombian	7	0.03
Ecuadorian	2	0.01
Paraguayan	1	0.00
Peruvian	4	0.02
Uruguayan	5	0.02
Venezuelan	6	0.02
Other South American	3	0.01
Other Hispanic or Latino	52	0.20
Hungarian	341	1.32
Iranian	57	0.22
Irish	5,510	21.29
Israeli	55	0.21
Italian	3,672	14.19
Lithuanian	146	0.56
New Zealander	17	0.07
Norwegian	122	0.47
Pennsylvania German	52	0.20
Polish	1,558	6.02
Portuguese	46	0.18
Romanian	147	0.57
Russian	2,243	8.67
Scandinavian	36	0.14
Scotch-Irish	336	1.30
Scottish	463	1.79
Serbian	5	0.02
Slavic	12	0.05

Notes: 1. Figures in the "Number" column do not add up to the total population due to: a) Ancestry/Race overlap — e.g. persons can report being both White and Irish, b) persons of Hispanic origin can report being any race, c) persons reporting two ancestries are counted in both categories. 2. Numbers in parentheses indicate the number of persons reporting this ancestry/race alone, not in combination with any other ancestry/race. 3. Refer to the Explanation of Data in the front of the book for more detailed information.

Slovak	133	0.51
Slovene	7	0.03
Swedish	267	1.03
Swiss	123	0.48
Turkish	7	0.03
Ukrainian	293	1.13
United States or American	1,034	4.00
Welsh	437	1.69
West Indian, excl. Hispanic:	31	0.12
Jamaican	31	0.12
White:	22,770	87.99
Not Hispanic (22,463)	22,584	87.27
Hispanic (174)	186	0.72
Yugoslavian	13	0.05

Upper Gwynedd

Place Type: Township
County: Montgomery
Population: 14,243

Ancestry/Race	Number	%
African American/Black:	610	4.28
Not Hispanic (562)	601	4.22
Hispanic (4)	9	0.06
African, sub-Saharan:	72	0.51
African	28	0.20
Ghanian	23	0.16
Nigerian	15	0.11
Sudanese	6	0.04
Am. Ind. or Alaska Nat., not spec.	20	0.14
Albanian	5	0.04
American Indian tribes, specified:	13	0.09
Cherokee (1)	6	0.04
Chippewa (1)	1	0.01
Creek (1)	1	0.01
Crow	2	0.01
Delaware	1	0.01
Latin American Indians (1)	1	0.01
All other tribes	1	0.01
American Indian tribes, not spec.	5	0.04
Arab:	39	0.27
Egyptian	7	0.05
Lebanese	25	0.18
Other Arab	7	0.05
Asian:	1,199	8.42
Cambodian (3)	8	0.06
Chinese, ex. Taiwanese (233)	244	1.71
Filipino (59)	63	0.44
Indian (358)	386	2.71
Japanese (22)	33	0.23
Korean (319)	335	2.35
Laotian (4)	4	0.03
Pakistani (6)	6	0.04
Sri Lankan (3)	3	0.02
Taiwanese (6)	11	0.08
Thai (8)	11	0.08
Vietnamese (76)	87	0.61
Other Asian, not specified (3)	8	0.06
Austrian	167	1.17
Belgian	6	0.04
Brazilian	20	0.14
British	101	0.71
Canadian	52	0.37
Croatian	6	0.04
Czech	58	0.41
Czechoslovakian	14	0.10
Danish	52	0.37
Dutch	264	1.85
Eastern European	47	0.33
English	1,654	11.61
European	99	0.70
Finnish	8	0.06
French, except Basque	381	2.67
French Canadian	66	0.46
German	3,588	25.19
Greek	28	0.20
Hawaii Native/Pacific Islander:	4	0.03
Other Pac. Isl., not spec.	4	0.03
Hispanic or Latino:	207	1.45
Central American:	10	0.07
Costa Rican	3	0.02
Guatemalan	2	0.01
Honduran	1	0.01
Panamanian	4	0.03
Cuban	4	0.03
Mexican	45	0.32
Puerto Rican	88	0.62
South American:	29	0.20
Argentinean	2	0.01
Bolivian	1	0.01
Colombian	9	0.06
Ecuadorian	7	0.05
Paraguayan	1	0.01
Peruvian	4	0.03
Venezuelan	4	0.03
Other South American	1	0.01
Other Hispanic or Latino	31	0.22
Hungarian	151	1.06
Iranian	25	0.18
Irish	3,157	22.17
Israeli	9	0.06
Italian	2,099	14.74
Lithuanian	101	0.71
Northern European	16	0.11
Norwegian	103	0.72
Pennsylvania German	56	0.39
Polish	978	6.87
Portuguese	60	0.42
Romanian	37	0.26
Russian	291	2.04
Scandinavian	22	0.15
Scotch-Irish	280	1.97
Scottish	269	1.89
Slavic	12	0.08
Slovak	166	1.17
Slovene	7	0.05
Swedish	113	0.79
Swiss	42	0.29
Ukrainian	157	1.10
United States or American	485	3.41
Welsh	241	1.69
White:	12,462	87.50
Not Hispanic (12,211)	12,305	86.39
Hispanic (147)	157	1.10
Yugoslavian	15	0.11

Upper Macungie

Place Type: Township
County: Lehigh
Population: 13,895

Ancestry/Race	Number	%
Acadian/Cajun	5	0.04
African American/Black:	203	1.46
Not Hispanic (160)	198	1.42
Hispanic (4)	5	0.04
African, sub-Saharan:	40	0.29
African	34	0.24
Other sub-Saharan African	6	0.04
Am. Ind. or Alaska Nat., not spec.	14	0.10
Albanian	8	0.06
American Indian tribes, specified:	7	0.05
Cherokee (1)	1	0.01
Cree	1	0.01
Iroquois	1	0.01
Latin American Indians (2)	2	0.01
All other tribes	2	0.01
American Indian tribes, not spec.	2	0.01
Arab:	109	0.78
Arab/Arabic	32	0.23
Egyptian	9	0.06
Lebanese	18	0.13
Syrian	50	0.36
Asian:	672	4.84
Chinese, ex. Taiwanese (185)	202	1.45
Filipino (23)	32	0.23
Indian (285)	307	2.21
Indonesian	1	0.01
Japanese (10)	22	0.16
Korean (30)	40	0.29
Malaysian	7	0.05
Pakistani (13)	14	0.10
Sri Lankan (3)	3	0.02
Taiwanese	3	0.02
Vietnamese (23)	25	0.18
Other Asian, not specified (4)	16	0.12
Austrian	134	0.96
Brazilian	6	0.04
British	121	0.87
Canadian	5	0.04
Croatian	13	0.09
Czech	17	0.12
Czechoslovakian	80	0.58
Danish	5	0.04
Dutch	265	1.91
Eastern European	45	0.32
English	926	6.66
European	67	0.48
French, except Basque	232	1.67
French Canadian	40	0.29
German	4,610	33.18
Greek	70	0.50
Hawaii Native/Pacific Islander:	4	0.03
Micronesian:	1	0.01
Guamanian/Chamorro	1	0.01
Other Pac. Isl., not spec.	3	0.02
Hispanic or Latino:	235	1.69
Central American:	8	0.06
Guatemalan	5	0.04
Panamanian	2	0.01
Salvadoran	1	0.01
Cuban	12	0.09
Dominican Republic	5	0.04
Mexican	28	0.20
Puerto Rican	92	0.66
South American:	31	0.22
Argentinean	7	0.05
Chilean	2	0.01
Colombian	3	0.02
Ecuadorian	2	0.01
Paraguayan	1	0.01
Peruvian	12	0.09
Venezuelan	4	0.03
Other Hispanic or Latino	59	0.42
Hungarian	226	1.63
Iranian	88	0.63
Irish	1,752	12.61
Israeli	14	0.10
Italian	1,436	10.33
Latvian	7	0.05
Lithuanian	114	0.82
Northern European	7	0.05
Norwegian	22	0.16
Pennsylvania German	883	6.35
Polish	1,005	7.23
Portuguese	8	0.06
Russian	201	1.45
Scotch-Irish	196	1.41
Scottish	136	0.98
Serbian	38	0.27
Slovak	557	4.01
Slovene	20	0.14
Swedish	112	0.81
Swiss	47	0.34
Turkish	30	0.22
Ukrainian	320	2.30
United States or American	701	5.04
Welsh	248	1.78
West Indian, excl. Hispanic:	60	0.43
Jamaican	48	0.35
Trinidadian and Tobagonian	12	0.09
White:	13,029	93.77
Not Hispanic (12,775)	12,870	92.62
Hispanic (142)	159	1.14
Yugoslavian	14	0.10

Notes: 1. Figures in the "Number" column do not add up to the total population due to: a) Ancestry/Race overlap — e.g. persons can report being both White and Irish, b) persons of Hispanic origin can report being any race, c) persons reporting two ancestries are counted in both categories. 2. Numbers in parentheses indicate the number of persons reporting this ancestry/race alone, not in combination with any other ancestry/race. 3. Refer to the Explanation of Data in the front of the book for more detailed information.

Upper Merion

Place Type: Township
County: Montgomery
Population: 26,863

Ancestry/Race	Number	%
Afghan	44	0.16
African American/Black:	1,361	5.07
Not Hispanic (1,233)	1,347	5.01
Hispanic (12)	14	0.05
African, sub-Saharan:	81	0.30
African	40	0.15
Cape Verdean	7	0.03
Ghanian	14	0.05
Nigerian	5	0.02
South African	15	0.06
Alaska Native tribes, specified:	1	0.00
Eskimo (1)	1	0.00
Am. Ind. or Alaska Nat., not spec.	27	0.10
Albanian	27	0.10
Alsatian	9	0.03
American Indian tribes, specified:	51	0.19
Apache (2)	2	0.01
Blackfeet	1	0.00
Cherokee (4)	15	0.06
Choctaw	4	0.01
Creek (1)	1	0.00
Delaware	2	0.01
Iroquois	3	0.01
Latin American Indians	4	0.01
Menominee	2	0.01
Pueblo	2	0.01
Sioux	1	0.00
All other tribes (10)	14	0.05
American Indian tribes, not spec.	11	0.04
Arab:	109	0.41
Egyptian	39	0.15
Lebanese	22	0.08
Syrian	20	0.07
Other Arab	28	0.10
Armenian	106	0.39
Asian:	2,482	9.24
Bangladeshi	6	0.02
Cambodian (19)	23	0.09
Chinese, ex. Taiwanese (527)	577	2.15
Filipino (219)	238	0.89
Indian (1,014)	1,073	3.99
Indonesian (7)	9	0.03
Japanese (44)	54	0.20
Korean (155)	176	0.66
Laotian (18)	22	0.08
Malaysian (1)	1	0.00
Pakistani (53)	67	0.25
Sri Lankan (2)	2	0.01
Taiwanese (12)	27	0.10
Thai (8)	12	0.04
Vietnamese (118)	130	0.48
Other Asian, specified (4)	7	0.03
Other Asian, not specified (20)	58	0.22
Austrian	122	0.45
Basque	6	0.02
Belgian	18	0.07
Brazilian	37	0.14
British	112	0.42
Canadian	50	0.19
Carpatho Rusyn	7	0.03
Croatian	6	0.02
Czech	74	0.28
Czechoslovakian	72	0.27
Danish	78	0.29
Dutch	423	1.58
Eastern European	135	0.50
English	2,515	9.37
European	223	0.83
Finnish	16	0.06
French, except Basque	486	1.81
French Canadian	115	0.43
German	5,194	19.35
Greek	172	0.64
Guyanese	18	0.07
Hawaii Native/Pacific Islander:	27	0.10
Micronesian: (6)	6	0.02
Guamanian/Chamorro (6)	6	0.02
Polynesian: (3)	3	0.01
Native Hawaiian (1)	1	0.00
Samoan (2)	2	0.01
Other Pac. Isl., not spec. (5)	18	0.07
Hispanic or Latino:	481	1.79
Central American:	21	0.08
Costa Rican	1	0.00
Guatemalan	8	0.03
Honduran	6	0.02
Panamanian	1	0.00
Salvadoran	5	0.02
Cuban	64	0.24
Dominican Republic	4	0.01
Mexican	113	0.42
Puerto Rican	117	0.44
South American:	90	0.34
Argentinean	13	0.05
Bolivian	3	0.01
Chilean	5	0.02
Colombian	25	0.09
Ecuadorian	10	0.04
Paraguayan	3	0.01
Peruvian	13	0.05
Uruguayan	2	0.01
Venezuelan	13	0.05
Other South American	3	0.01
Other Hispanic or Latino	72	0.27
Hungarian	271	1.01
Icelander	5	0.02
Iranian	58	0.22
Irish	5,611	20.90
Israeli	21	0.08
Italian	4,626	17.23
Latvian	6	0.02
Lithuanian	175	0.65
Maltese	11	0.04
Northern European	14	0.05
Norwegian	128	0.48
Pennsylvania German	135	0.50
Polish	2,278	8.49
Portuguese	47	0.18
Romanian	87	0.32
Russian	740	2.76
Scandinavian	5	0.02
Scotch-Irish	526	1.96
Scottish	374	1.39
Serbian	6	0.02
Slavic	24	0.09
Slovak	410	1.53
Swedish	276	1.03
Swiss	77	0.29
Ukrainian	363	1.35
United States or American	898	3.35
Welsh	379	1.41
West Indian, excl. Hispanic:	107	0.40
Bahamian	18	0.07
Jamaican	39	0.15
Trinidadian and Tobagonian	26	0.10
U.S. Virgin Islander	4	0.01
West Indian	20	0.07
White:	23,031	85.74
Not Hispanic (22,477)	22,713	84.55
Hispanic (290)	318	1.18
Yugoslavian	47	0.18

Upper Moreland

Place Type: Township
County: Montgomery
Population: 24,993

Ancestry/Race	Number	%
African American/Black:	1,197	4.79
Not Hispanic (1,067)	1,152	4.61
Hispanic (23)	45	0.18
African, sub-Saharan:	115	0.46
African	101	0.40
South African	14	0.06
Alaska Native tribes, not specified	1	0.00
Am. Ind. or Alaska Nat., not spec.	34	0.14
Albanian	7	0.03
American Indian tribes, specified:	59	0.24
Blackfeet	6	0.02
Cherokee (6)	17	0.07
Chippewa (1)	4	0.02
Creek	4	0.02
Delaware (1)	4	0.02
Iroquois	9	0.04
Navajo	1	0.00
Sioux (1)	4	0.02
All other tribes (6)	10	0.04
American Indian tribes, not spec.	6	0.02
Arab:	93	0.37
Arab/Arabic	19	0.08
Egyptian	16	0.06
Lebanese	25	0.10
Palestinian	6	0.02
Syrian	17	0.07
Other Arab	10	0.04
Armenian	7	0.03
Asian:	862	3.45
Cambodian (1)	2	0.01
Chinese, ex. Taiwanese (127)	132	0.53
Filipino (61)	75	0.30
Indian (227)	238	0.95
Indonesian (2)	3	0.01
Japanese (37)	50	0.20
Korean (232)	246	0.98
Laotian (18)	22	0.09
Malaysian (1)	2	0.01
Pakistani (11)	11	0.04
Sri Lankan (1)	1	0.00
Taiwanese (7)	7	0.03
Thai (11)	13	0.05
Vietnamese (41)	42	0.17
Other Asian, specified (1)	1	0.00
Other Asian, not specified (8)	17	0.07
Austrian	79	0.32
Belgian	7	0.03
Brazilian	15	0.06
British	138	0.55
Canadian	13	0.05
Croatian	19	0.08
Czech	34	0.14
Czechoslovakian	7	0.03
Danish	64	0.26
Dutch	267	1.07
Eastern European	43	0.17
English	3,145	12.58
European	140	0.56
French, except Basque	545	2.18
French Canadian	91	0.36
German	7,526	30.11
Greek	167	0.67
Hawaii Native/Pacific Islander:	15	0.06
Micronesian: (1)	4	0.02
Guamanian/Chamorro (1)	4	0.02
Polynesian: (2)	4	0.02
Native Hawaiian (1)	3	0.01
Samoan (1)	1	0.00
Other Pac. Isl., not spec. (3)	7	0.03
Hispanic or Latino:	432	1.73
Central American:	34	0.14
Costa Rican	12	0.05
Guatemalan	8	0.03
Honduran	5	0.02
Panamanian	7	0.03
Salvadoran	2	0.01
Cuban	24	0.10
Dominican Republic	6	0.02
Mexican	70	0.28
Puerto Rican	197	0.79
South American:	37	0.15
Argentinean	11	0.04
Chilean	4	0.02
Colombian	6	0.02

Notes: 1. Figures in the "Number" column do not add up to the total population due to: a) Ancestry/Race overlap — e.g. persons can report being both White and Irish, b) persons of Hispanic origin can report being any race, c) persons reporting two ancestries are counted in both categories. 2. Numbers in parentheses indicate the number of persons reporting this ancestry/race alone, not in combination with any other ancestry/race. 3. Refer to the Explanation of Data in the front of the book for more detailed information.

Ecuadorian	5	0.02
Peruvian	1	0.00
Venezuelan	8	0.03
Other South American	2	0.01
Other Hispanic or Latino	64	0.26
Hungarian	250	1.00
Irish	6,579	26.32
Italian	3,341	13.37
Latvian	27	0.11
Lithuanian	194	0.78
Northern European	30	0.12
Norwegian	105	0.42
Pennsylvania German	97	0.39
Polish	1,492	5.97
Portuguese	73	0.29
Romanian	55	0.22
Russian	759	3.04
Scandinavian	6	0.02
Scotch-Irish	432	1.73
Scottish	482	1.93
Slavic	22	0.09
Slovak	68	0.27
Swedish	242	0.97
Swiss	38	0.15
Turkish	18	0.07
Ukrainian	239	0.96
United States or American	841	3.36
Welsh	414	1.66
West Indian, excl. Hispanic:	40	0.16
Haitian	6	0.02
Jamaican	34	0.14
White:	22,895	91.61
Not Hispanic (22,453)	22,630	90.55
Hispanic (220)	265	1.06

Upper Providence Township

Place Type: Census Designated Place
County: Delaware
Population: 10,509

Ancestry/Race	Number	%
Afghan	14	0.13
African American/Black:	442	4.21
Not Hispanic (408)	432	4.11
Hispanic (2)	10	0.10
African, sub-Saharan:	29	0.28
Kenyan	4	0.04
Other sub-Saharan African	25	0.24
Am. Ind. or Alaska Nat., not spec.	4	0.04
American Indian tribes, specified:	17	0.16
Cherokee (1)	8	0.08
Chippewa (1)	1	0.01
Choctaw	1	0.01
Delaware	1	0.01
Latin American Indians (1)	1	0.01
Osage (1)	1	0.01
Sioux	1	0.01
All other tribes (2)	3	0.03
American Indian tribes, not spec.	1	0.01
Arab:	60	0.57
Lebanese	41	0.39
Palestinian	19	0.18
Armenian	68	0.65
Asian:	354	3.37
Cambodian (3)	3	0.03
Chinese, ex. Taiwanese (99)	107	1.02
Filipino (21)	26	0.25
Hmong (1)	1	0.01
Indian (95)	102	0.97
Indonesian	1	0.01
Japanese (11)	14	0.13
Korean (49)	50	0.48
Pakistani (6)	6	0.06
Taiwanese (15)	15	0.14
Vietnamese (11)	14	0.13
Other Asian, not specified (8)	15	0.14
Austrian	58	0.55
Belgian	31	0.29
British	125	1.19
Canadian	25	0.24
Celtic	15	0.14
Croatian	5	0.05
Czech	9	0.09
Czechoslovakian	103	0.98
Danish	66	0.63
Dutch	154	1.47
Eastern European	17	0.16
English	1,369	13.03
European	127	1.21
Finnish	5	0.05
French, except Basque	250	2.38
French Canadian	50	0.48
German	2,229	21.21
Greek	49	0.47
Hawaii Native/Pacific Islander:	1	0.01
Other Pac. Isl., not spec.	1	0.01
Hispanic or Latino:	112	1.07
Central American:	7	0.07
Guatemalan	7	0.07
Cuban	8	0.08
Dominican Republic	2	0.02
Mexican	16	0.15
Puerto Rican	21	0.20
South American:	19	0.18
Argentinean	2	0.02
Bolivian	2	0.02
Colombian	7	0.07
Ecuadorian	1	0.01
Peruvian	1	0.01
Venezuelan	4	0.04
Other South American	2	0.02
Other Hispanic or Latino	39	0.37
Hungarian	55	0.52
Irish	2,978	28.34
Italian	1,880	17.89
Latvian	11	0.10
Lithuanian	55	0.52
Norwegian	153	1.46
Pennsylvania German	19	0.18
Polish	583	5.55
Portuguese	17	0.16
Romanian	7	0.07
Russian	283	2.69
Scandinavian	5	0.05
Scotch-Irish	198	1.88
Scottish	171	1.63
Slavic	7	0.07
Slovak	66	0.63
Slovene	14	0.13
Swedish	86	0.82
Swiss	28	0.27
Ukrainian	217	2.06
United States or American	335	3.19
Welsh	124	1.18
West Indian, excl. Hispanic:	16	0.15
Haitian	7	0.07
West Indian	9	0.09
White:	9,727	92.56
Not Hispanic (9,574)	9,641	91.74
Hispanic (76)	86	0.82

Upper Providence

Place Type: Township
County: Montgomery
Population: 15,398

Ancestry/Race	Number	%
African American/Black:	434	2.82
Not Hispanic (391)	429	2.79
Hispanic (4)	5	0.03
African, sub-Saharan:	27	0.18
Ghanian	10	0.06
Nigerian	17	0.11
Alaska Native tribes, specified:	1	0.01
Tlingit-Haida (1)	1	0.01
Am. Ind. or Alaska Nat., not spec.	23	0.15
Albanian	18	0.12
Alsatian	5	0.03
American Indian tribes, specified:	17	0.11
Apache (1)	1	0.01
Blackfeet	2	0.01
Cherokee (1)	8	0.05
Navajo (1)	1	0.01
Ottawa	1	0.01
Potawatomi (1)	1	0.01
Seminole (1)	2	0.01
All other tribes	1	0.01
American Indian tribes, not spec.	3	0.02
Arab:	101	0.66
Egyptian	8	0.05
Jordanian	68	0.44
Lebanese	25	0.16
Armenian	13	0.08
Asian:	484	3.14
Cambodian (3)	3	0.02
Chinese, ex. Taiwanese (126)	144	0.94
Filipino (20)	27	0.18
Indian (192)	199	1.29
Japanese (2)	16	0.10
Korean (40)	43	0.28
Pakistani (2)	2	0.01
Sri Lankan (1)	1	0.01
Taiwanese (1)	1	0.01
Thai (2)	2	0.01
Vietnamese (29)	31	0.20
Other Asian, specified (2)	2	0.01
Other Asian, not specified (5)	13	0.08
Austrian	60	0.39
British	98	0.64
Bulgarian	4	0.03
Canadian	31	0.20
Carpatho Rusyn	8	0.05
Croatian	6	0.04
Czech	99	0.64
Czechoslovakian	27	0.18
Danish	55	0.36
Dutch	454	2.95
Eastern European	14	0.09
English	1,573	10.22
European	145	0.94
French, except Basque	399	2.59
French Canadian	74	0.48
German	3,908	25.38
Greek	101	0.66
Hawaii Native/Pacific Islander:	5	0.03
Polynesian: (1)	2	0.01
Native Hawaiian (1)	1	0.01
Samoan	1	0.01
Other Pac. Isl., not spec. (3)	3	0.02
Hispanic or Latino:	207	1.34
Central American:	11	0.07
Guatemalan	1	0.01
Honduran	3	0.02
Salvadoran	5	0.03
Other Central American	2	0.01
Cuban	26	0.17
Dominican Republic	2	0.01
Mexican	30	0.19
Puerto Rican	49	0.32
South American:	33	0.21
Argentinean	9	0.06
Chilean	4	0.03
Colombian	5	0.03
Ecuadorian	2	0.01
Paraguayan	1	0.01
Peruvian	6	0.04
Venezuelan	1	0.01
Other South American	5	0.03
Other Hispanic or Latino	56	0.36
Hungarian	261	1.70
Irish	3,942	25.60
Israeli	8	0.05
Italian	3,321	21.57
Lithuanian	54	0.35
Norwegian	69	0.45
Pennsylvania German	115	0.75
Polish	1,378	8.95

Notes: 1. Figures in the "Number" column do not add up to the total population due to: a) Ancestry/Race overlap — e.g. persons can report being both White and Irish, b) persons of Hispanic origin can report being any race, c) persons reporting two ancestries are counted in both categories. 2. Numbers in parentheses indicate the number of persons reporting this ancestry/race alone, not in combination with any other ancestry/race. 3. Refer to the Explanation of Data in the front of the book for more detailed information.

Ancestry/Race	Number	%
Portuguese	57	0.37
Romanian	32	0.21
Russian	214	1.39
Scandinavian	14	0.09
Scotch-Irish	213	1.38
Scottish	189	1.23
Serbian	23	0.15
Slavic	29	0.19
Slovak	303	1.97
Slovene	18	0.12
Swedish	125	0.81
Swiss	52	0.34
Ukrainian	235	1.53
United States or American	428	2.78
Welsh	231	1.50
West Indian, excl. Hispanic:	28	0.18
Jamaican	28	0.18
White:	14,500	94.17
Not Hispanic (14,248)	14,338	93.12
Hispanic (151)	162	1.05

Upper Saint Clair

Place Type: Census Designated Place
County: Allegheny
Population: 20,053

Ancestry/Race	Number	%
African American/Black:	169	0.84
Not Hispanic (132)	162	0.81
Hispanic (4)	7	0.03
African, sub-Saharan:	16	0.08
African	16	0.08
Am. Ind. or Alaska Nat., not spec.	15	0.07
Albanian	14	0.07
American Indian tribes, specified:	13	0.06
Cherokee	3	0.01
Chippewa (1)	1	0.00
Comanche (1)	2	0.01
Creek (1)	1	0.00
Delaware	2	0.01
Iroquois	1	0.00
Navajo	1	0.00
All other tribes	2	0.01
Arab:	182	0.91
Lebanese	71	0.35
Palestinian	5	0.02
Syrian	99	0.49
Other Arab	7	0.03
Asian:	879	4.38
Bangladeshi (8)	8	0.04
Chinese, ex. Taiwanese (153)	167	0.83
Filipino (47)	63	0.31
Indian (406)	425	2.12
Indonesian (3)	3	0.01
Japanese (78)	84	0.42
Korean (61)	77	0.38
Malaysian	1	0.00
Sri Lankan (3)	3	0.01
Taiwanese (10)	10	0.05
Thai (10)	10	0.05
Vietnamese (20)	20	0.10
Other Asian, not specified	8	0.04
Australian	5	0.02
Austrian	131	0.65
Belgian	48	0.24
Brazilian	34	0.17
British	85	0.42
Canadian	60	0.30
Carpatho Rusyn	10	0.05
Croatian	190	0.95
Czech	166	0.83
Czechoslovakian	135	0.67
Danish	28	0.14
Dutch	164	0.82
Eastern European	206	1.03
English	2,408	12.01
European	200	1.00
Finnish	36	0.18
French, except Basque	508	2.53
French Canadian	162	0.81
German	5,424	27.05
Greek	190	0.95
Hawaii Native/Pacific Islander:	5	0.02
Micronesian: (4)	4	0.02
Guamanian/Chamorro (4)	4	0.02
Other Pac. Isl., not spec. (1)	1	0.00
Hispanic or Latino:	157	0.78
Central American:	11	0.05
Costa Rican	1	0.00
Guatemalan	4	0.02
Nicaraguan	4	0.02
Panamanian	1	0.00
Salvadoran	1	0.00
Cuban	18	0.09
Dominican Republic	3	0.01
Mexican	50	0.25
Puerto Rican	25	0.12
South American:	10	0.05
Argentinean	2	0.01
Colombian	4	0.02
Peruvian	2	0.01
Venezuelan	2	0.01
Other Hispanic or Latino	40	0.20
Hungarian	385	1.92
Iranian	62	0.31
Irish	3,839	19.14
Italian	2,941	14.67
Latvian	26	0.13
Lithuanian	118	0.59
Norwegian	70	0.35
Pennsylvania German	8	0.04
Polish	1,561	7.78
Romanian	37	0.18
Russian	565	2.82
Scandinavian	34	0.17
Scotch-Irish	826	4.12
Scottish	566	2.82
Serbian	63	0.31
Slavic	60	0.30
Slovak	463	2.31
Slovene	95	0.47
Swedish	382	1.90
Swiss	183	0.91
Turkish	45	0.22
Ukrainian	229	1.14
United States or American	855	4.26
Welsh	425	2.12
White:	19,072	95.11
Not Hispanic (18,826)	18,928	94.39
Hispanic (136)	144	0.72
Yugoslavian	30	0.15

Upper Saucon

Place Type: Township
County: Lehigh
Population: 11,939

Ancestry/Race	Number	%
African American/Black:	95	0.80
Not Hispanic (81)	93	0.78
Hispanic (2)	2	0.02
Am. Ind. or Alaska Nat., not spec.	16	0.13
American Indian tribes, specified:	13	0.11
Blackfeet	1	0.01
Cherokee (1)	4	0.03
Chippewa (1)	1	0.01
Delaware	1	0.01
Iroquois	3	0.03
Latin American Indians (1)	1	0.01
All other tribes	2	0.02
American Indian tribes, not spec.	1	0.01
Arab:	38	0.32
Lebanese	7	0.06
Syrian	19	0.16
Other Arab	12	0.10
Asian:	157	1.32
Chinese, ex. Taiwanese (28)	32	0.27
Filipino (9)	17	0.14
Indian (33)	35	0.29
Japanese (6)	9	0.08
Korean (32)	35	0.29
Sri Lankan (2)	2	0.02
Taiwanese (1)	1	0.01
Thai (2)	2	0.02
Vietnamese (19)	21	0.18
Other Asian, not specified (2)	3	0.03
Australian	6	0.05
Austrian	303	2.54
Belgian	15	0.13
British	50	0.42
Canadian	7	0.06
Croatian	17	0.14
Czech	27	0.23
Czechoslovakian	91	0.76
Danish	21	0.18
Dutch	473	3.96
Eastern European	6	0.05
English	990	8.29
European	63	0.53
Finnish	28	0.23
French, except Basque	398	3.33
French Canadian	79	0.66
German	4,779	40.03
Greek	136	1.14
Hawaii Native/Pacific Islander:	5	0.04
Polynesian:	3	0.03
Native Hawaiian	2	0.02
Samoan	1	0.01
Other Pac. Isl., not spec. (1)	2	0.02
Hispanic or Latino:	128	1.07
Central American:	10	0.08
Honduran	2	0.02
Panamanian	5	0.04
Salvadoran	3	0.03
Cuban	13	0.11
Dominican Republic	5	0.04
Mexican	16	0.13
Puerto Rican	47	0.39
South American:	16	0.13
Colombian	4	0.03
Ecuadorian	5	0.04
Venezuelan	1	0.01
Other South American	6	0.05
Other Hispanic or Latino	21	0.18
Hungarian	362	3.03
Iranian	50	0.42
Irish	1,900	15.91
Italian	1,194	10.00
Latvian	5	0.04
Lithuanian	86	0.72
Northern European	10	0.08
Norwegian	40	0.34
Pennsylvania German	569	4.77
Polish	916	7.67
Portuguese	18	0.15
Romanian	15	0.13
Russian	146	1.22
Scandinavian	16	0.13
Scotch-Irish	198	1.66
Scottish	256	2.14
Serbian	69	0.58
Slavic	28	0.23
Slovak	261	2.19
Slovene	7	0.06
Swedish	121	1.01
Swiss	11	0.09
Ukrainian	284	2.38
United States or American	626	5.24
Welsh	215	1.80
White:	11,661	97.67
Not Hispanic (11,523)	11,578	96.98
Hispanic (71)	83	0.70
Yugoslavian	47	0.39

Notes: 1. Figures in the "Number" column do not add up to the total population due to: a) Ancestry/Race overlap — e.g. persons can report being both White and Irish, b) persons of Hispanic origin can report being any race, c) persons reporting two ancestries are counted in both categories. 2. Numbers in parentheses indicate the number of persons reporting this ancestry/race alone, not in combination with any other ancestry/race. 3. Refer to the Explanation of Data in the front of the book for more detailed information.

Upper Southampton

Place Type: Township
County: Bucks
Population: 15,764

Ancestry/Race	Number	%
African American/Black:	144	0.91
Not Hispanic (121)	142	0.90
Hispanic (1)	2	0.01
African, sub-Saharan:	15	0.10
African	15	0.10
Am. Ind. or Alaska Nat., not spec.	4	0.03
Albanian	11	0.07
American Indian tribes, specified:	25	0.16
Cherokee (1)	11	0.07
Delaware (3)	4	0.03
Latin American Indians (1)	1	0.01
Seminole	3	0.02
Sioux (1)	1	0.01
All other tribes (4)	5	0.03
Arab:	57	0.36
Egyptian	7	0.04
Moroccan	19	0.12
Other Arab	31	0.20
Armenian	14	0.09
Asian:	291	1.85
Chinese, ex. Taiwanese (42)	44	0.28
Filipino (28)	34	0.22
Indian (73)	87	0.55
Indonesian (1)	1	0.01
Japanese (9)	15	0.10
Korean (55)	62	0.39
Sri Lankan (1)	1	0.01
Taiwanese (2)	2	0.01
Thai (1)	1	0.01
Vietnamese (16)	16	0.10
Other Asian, not specified (2)	28	0.18
Austrian	113	0.72
Belgian	13	0.08
British	24	0.15
Canadian	22	0.14
Croatian	30	0.19
Czech	43	0.27
Czechoslovakian	47	0.30
Danish	10	0.06
Dutch	144	0.91
Eastern European	13	0.08
English	1,507	9.56
European	73	0.46
French, except Basque	292	1.85
French Canadian	23	0.15
German	4,588	29.10
Greek	34	0.22
Hawaii Native/Pacific Islander:	9	0.06
Micronesian: (1)	2	0.01
Guamanian/Chamorro (1)	2	0.01
Polynesian: (1)	2	0.01
Native Hawaiian (1)	2	0.01
Other Pac. Isl., not spec. (1)	5	0.03
Hispanic or Latino:	127	0.81
Central American:	4	0.03
Guatemalan	1	0.01
Honduran	1	0.01
Nicaraguan	2	0.01
Cuban	8	0.05
Dominican Republic	1	0.01
Mexican	31	0.20
Puerto Rican	37	0.23
South American:	18	0.11
Argentinean	3	0.02
Colombian	5	0.03
Peruvian	10	0.06
Other Hispanic or Latino	28	0.18
Hungarian	180	1.14
Iranian	6	0.04
Irish	4,520	28.67
Israeli	4	0.03
Italian	2,219	14.08
Latvian	5	0.03
Lithuanian	106	0.67
Northern European	8	0.05
Norwegian	60	0.38
Pennsylvania German	39	0.25
Polish	1,218	7.73
Portuguese	5	0.03
Romanian	37	0.23
Russian	727	4.61
Scandinavian	18	0.11
Scotch-Irish	328	2.08
Scottish	304	1.93
Slavic	42	0.27
Slovak	112	0.71
Slovene	10	0.06
Swedish	84	0.53
Swiss	22	0.14
Ukrainian	390	2.47
United States or American	966	6.13
Welsh	211	1.34
West Indian, excl. Hispanic:	16	0.10
West Indian	16	0.10
White:	15,348	97.36
Not Hispanic (15,178)	15,246	96.71
Hispanic (92)	102	0.65
Yugoslavian	31	0.20

Uwchlan

Place Type: Township
County: Chester
Population: 16,576

Ancestry/Race	Number	%
African American/Black:	354	2.14
Not Hispanic (301)	343	2.07
Hispanic (5)	11	0.07
Am. Ind. or Alaska Nat., not spec.	17	0.10
American Indian tribes, specified:	29	0.17
Apache (2)	2	0.01
Blackfeet	4	0.02
Cherokee (2)	11	0.07
Choctaw	1	0.01
Crow	1	0.01
Iroquois	2	0.01
Latin American Indians (2)	2	0.01
All other tribes (5)	6	0.04
Arab:	96	0.58
Egyptian	34	0.21
Lebanese	19	0.11
Syrian	43	0.26
Armenian	15	0.09
Asian:	602	3.63
Bangladeshi (4)	4	0.02
Cambodian (2)	5	0.03
Chinese, ex. Taiwanese (155)	174	1.05
Filipino (15)	17	0.10
Indian (237)	253	1.53
Indonesian (1)	2	0.01
Japanese (10)	12	0.07
Korean (47)	61	0.37
Malaysian	2	0.01
Pakistani (4)	4	0.02
Sri Lankan (2)	2	0.01
Vietnamese (38)	51	0.31
Other Asian, specified	1	0.01
Other Asian, not specified (7)	14	0.08
Assyrian/Chaldean/Syriac	7	0.04
Austrian	95	0.57
Belgian	17	0.10
Brazilian	33	0.20
British	184	1.11
Canadian	9	0.05
Celtic	6	0.04
Croatian	24	0.14
Czech	52	0.31
Czechoslovakian	30	0.18
Danish	63	0.38
Dutch	353	2.13
Eastern European	18	0.11
English	2,454	14.80
Estonian	31	0.19
European	90	0.54
Finnish	35	0.21
French, except Basque	365	2.20
French Canadian	135	0.81
German	4,358	26.29
Greek	157	0.95
Hawaii Native/Pacific Islander:	3	0.02
Polynesian: (1)	1	0.01
Native Hawaiian (1)	1	0.01
Other Pac. Isl., specified	1	0.01
Other Pac. Isl., not spec.	1	0.01
Hispanic or Latino:	205	1.24
Central American:	4	0.02
Costa Rican	1	0.01
Guatemalan	1	0.01
Honduran	1	0.01
Salvadoran	1	0.01
Cuban	18	0.11
Dominican Republic	1	0.01
Mexican	48	0.29
Puerto Rican	66	0.40
South American:	37	0.22
Argentinean	3	0.02
Bolivian	2	0.01
Chilean	1	0.01
Colombian	21	0.13
Ecuadorian	1	0.01
Peruvian	4	0.02
Venezuelan	4	0.02
Other South American	1	0.01
Other Hispanic or Latino	31	0.19
Hungarian	105	0.63
Irish	4,573	27.59
Italian	2,708	16.34
Latvian	13	0.08
Lithuanian	119	0.72
Northern European	52	0.31
Norwegian	224	1.35
Pennsylvania German	24	0.14
Polish	916	5.53
Portuguese	7	0.04
Romanian	23	0.14
Russian	213	1.28
Scandinavian	28	0.17
Scotch-Irish	332	2.00
Scottish	503	3.03
Serbian	27	0.16
Slavic	28	0.17
Slovak	108	0.65
Slovene	18	0.11
Swedish	241	1.45
Swiss	242	1.46
Ukrainian	229	1.38
United States or American	430	2.59
Welsh	272	1.64
White:	15,647	94.40
Not Hispanic (15,376)	15,488	93.44
Hispanic (150)	159	0.96
Yugoslavian	23	0.14

Warminster

Place Type: Township
County: Bucks
Population: 31,383

Ancestry/Race	Number	%
African American/Black:	1,216	3.87
Not Hispanic (1,005)	1,152	3.67
Hispanic (33)	64	0.20
African, sub-Saharan:	122	0.39
African	120	0.38
Nigerian	2	0.01
Am. Ind. or Alaska Nat., not spec.	31	0.10
Albanian	33	0.11
American Indian tribes, specified:	43	0.14
Blackfeet	3	0.01
Cherokee (4)	13	0.04
Creek (2)	5	0.02

Notes: 1. Figures in the "Number" column do not add up to the total population due to: a) Ancestry/Race overlap — e.g. persons can report being both White and Irish, b) persons of Hispanic origin can report being any race, c) persons reporting two ancestries are counted in both categories. 2. Numbers in parentheses indicate the number of persons reporting this ancestry/race alone, not in combination with any other ancestry/race. 3. Refer to the Explanation of Data in the front of the book for more detailed information.

Delaware (1)	2	0.01
Latin American Indians (6)	7	0.02
Navajo	1	0.00
Potawatomi	4	0.01
Seminole (1)	1	0.00
Shoshone (1)	1	0.00
Sioux (1)	2	0.01
Yaqui (1)	1	0.00
All other tribes (2)	3	0.01
American Indian tribes, not spec.	14	0.04
Arab:	91	0.29
Lebanese	87	0.28
Syrian	4	0.01
Asian:	765	2.44
Bangladeshi (2)	2	0.01
Cambodian (8)	9	0.03
Chinese, ex. Taiwanese (82)	102	0.33
Filipino (97)	146	0.47
Hmong (3)	7	0.02
Indian (262)	286	0.91
Japanese (17)	29	0.09
Korean (99)	104	0.33
Malaysian (2)	5	0.02
Pakistani (6)	6	0.02
Taiwanese	2	0.01
Vietnamese (31)	38	0.12
Other Asian, specified (1)	1	0.00
Other Asian, not specified (9)	28	0.09
Assyrian/Chaldean/Syriac	8	0.03
Austrian	104	0.33
Belgian	7	0.02
British	95	0.30
Canadian	31	0.10
Croatian	10	0.03
Czech	60	0.19
Czechoslovakian	60	0.19
Danish	19	0.06
Dutch	293	0.93
Eastern European	31	0.10
English	3,235	10.30
Estonian	8	0.03
European	253	0.81
Finnish	17	0.05
French, except Basque	604	1.92
French Canadian	152	0.48
German	9,092	28.95
Greek	96	0.31
Hawaii Native/Pacific Islander:	40	0.13
Micronesian:	2	0.01
Guamanian/Chamorro	1	0.00
Other Micronesian	1	0.00
Polynesian: (9)	23	0.07
Native Hawaiian (5)	13	0.04
Samoan (3)	5	0.02
Tongan (1)	4	0.01
Other Polynesian	1	0.00
Other Pac. Isl., not spec. (9)	15	0.05
Hispanic or Latino:	1,454	4.63
Central American:	90	0.29
Costa Rican	7	0.02
Guatemalan	18	0.06
Honduran	15	0.05
Nicaraguan	3	0.01
Salvadoran	43	0.14
Other Central American	4	0.01
Cuban	26	0.08
Dominican Republic	16	0.05
Mexican	386	1.23
Puerto Rican	684	2.18
South American:	50	0.16
Argentinean	4	0.01
Chilean	4	0.01
Colombian	6	0.02
Ecuadorian	4	0.01
Peruvian	18	0.06
Uruguayan	1	0.00
Venezuelan	4	0.01
Other South American	9	0.03
Other Hispanic or Latino	202	0.64
Hungarian	285	0.91
Icelander	16	0.05
Iranian	4	0.01
Irish	9,143	29.11
Italian	4,582	14.59
Latvian	46	0.15
Lithuanian	203	0.65
Northern European	23	0.07
Norwegian	151	0.48
Pennsylvania German	132	0.42
Polish	2,216	7.06
Portuguese	7	0.02
Romanian	57	0.18
Russian	545	1.74
Scandinavian	6	0.02
Scotch-Irish	497	1.58
Scottish	507	1.61
Serbian	5	0.02
Slavic	37	0.12
Slovak	308	0.98
Swedish	198	0.63
Swiss	57	0.18
Turkish	13	0.04
Ukrainian	508	1.62
United States or American	1,384	4.41
Welsh	483	1.54
West Indian, excl. Hispanic:	55	0.18
Bermudan	6	0.02
Haitian	6	0.02
Jamaican	36	0.11
Trinidadian and Tobagonian	7	0.02
White:	28,889	92.05
Not Hispanic (27,928)	28,184	89.81
Hispanic (630)	705	2.25
Yugoslavian	6	0.02

Warren

Place Type: City
County: Warren
Population: 10,259

Ancestry/Race	Number	%
Acadian/Cajun	6	0.06
African American/Black:	35	0.34
Not Hispanic (20)	34	0.33
Hispanic (1)	1	0.01
Am. Ind. or Alaska Nat., not spec.	9	0.09
Albanian	23	0.22
American Indian tribes, specified:	43	0.42
Blackfeet	1	0.01
Cherokee (1)	15	0.15
Iroquois (11)	20	0.19
Latin American Indians	1	0.01
Osage (1)	2	0.02
Sioux (1)	2	0.02
All other tribes (1)	2	0.02
American Indian tribes, not spec.	1	0.01
Arab:	29	0.28
Arab/Arabic	8	0.08
Lebanese	4	0.04
Syrian	17	0.17
Asian:	41	0.40
Chinese, ex. Taiwanese (13)	14	0.14
Filipino (2)	3	0.03
Indian (12)	12	0.12
Japanese (1)	1	0.01
Korean (7)	7	0.07
Vietnamese (2)	2	0.02
Other Asian, specified	1	0.01
Other Asian, not specified	1	0.01
Austrian	23	0.22
Canadian	17	0.17
Carpatho Rusyn	7	0.07
Croatian	5	0.05
Czech	21	0.20
Czechoslovakian	28	0.27
Danish	270	2.63
Dutch	236	2.30
English	1,042	10.16
European	129	1.26
French, except Basque	221	2.15
French Canadian	52	0.51
German	2,523	24.59
Greek	58	0.57
Hawaii Native/Pacific Islander:	3	0.03
Polynesian: (2)	3	0.03
Native Hawaiian (1)	2	0.02
Samoan (1)	1	0.01
Hispanic or Latino:	40	0.39
Cuban	6	0.06
Mexican	7	0.07
Puerto Rican	9	0.09
South American:	1	0.01
Ecuadorian	1	0.01
Other Hispanic or Latino	17	0.17
Hungarian	38	0.37
Irish	1,533	14.94
Italian	1,293	12.60
Lithuanian	27	0.26
Norwegian	20	0.19
Pennsylvania German	41	0.40
Polish	539	5.25
Portuguese	2	0.02
Romanian	13	0.13
Scandinavian	13	0.13
Scotch-Irish	314	3.06
Scottish	242	2.36
Slavic	16	0.16
Slovak	73	0.71
Slovene	22	0.21
Swedish	1,247	12.16
Swiss	91	0.89
Ukrainian	84	0.82
United States or American	523	5.10
Welsh	156	1.52
West Indian, excl. Hispanic:	4	0.04
West Indian	4	0.04
White:	10,164	99.07
Not Hispanic (10,079)	10,132	98.76
Hispanic (29)	32	0.31

Warrington

Place Type: Township
County: Bucks
Population: 17,580

Ancestry/Race	Number	%
African American/Black:	386	2.20
Not Hispanic (328)	374	2.13
Hispanic (11)	12	0.07
Am. Ind. or Alaska Nat., not spec.	16	0.09
American Indian tribes, specified:	21	0.12
Blackfeet	4	0.02
Cherokee (3)	6	0.03
Delaware	1	0.01
Iroquois	3	0.02
Latin American Indians (1)	1	0.01
Sioux (3)	3	0.02
All other tribes (1)	3	0.02
American Indian tribes, not spec.	4	0.02
Arab:	49	0.28
Arab/Arabic	24	0.14
Lebanese	5	0.03
Syrian	20	0.11
Armenian	12	0.07
Asian:	481	2.74
Bangladeshi (3)	3	0.02
Cambodian (15)	15	0.09
Chinese, ex. Taiwanese (125)	134	0.76
Filipino (50)	56	0.32
Indian (96)	106	0.60
Japanese (5)	9	0.05
Korean (75)	82	0.47
Laotian (2)	5	0.03
Taiwanese (6)	9	0.05
Thai (3)	3	0.02
Vietnamese (45)	46	0.26
Other Asian, specified	4	0.02
Other Asian, not specified (8)	9	0.05

Notes: 1. Figures in the "Number" column do not add up to the total population due to: a) Ancestry/Race overlap — e.g. persons can report being both White and Irish, b) persons of Hispanic origin can report being any race, c) persons reporting two ancestries are counted in both categories. 2. Numbers in parentheses indicate the number of persons reporting this ancestry/race alone, not in combination with any other ancestry/race. 3. Refer to the Explanation of Data in the front of the book for more detailed information.

Ancestry/Race	Number	%
Assyrian/Chaldean/Syriac	8	0.05
Austrian	119	0.68
Belgian	16	0.09
British	56	0.32
Canadian	57	0.32
Czech	51	0.29
Czechoslovakian	58	0.33
Danish	27	0.15
Dutch	266	1.51
Eastern European	109	0.62
English	1,813	10.31
European	84	0.48
Finnish	10	0.06
French, except Basque	335	1.91
French Canadian	165	0.94
German	5,331	30.32
German Russian	6	0.03
Greek	75	0.43
Guyanese	6	0.03
Hawaii Native/Pacific Islander:	21	0.12
Micronesian: (3)	5	0.03
Guamanian/Chamorro (3)	5	0.03
Polynesian: (4)	6	0.03
Native Hawaiian (3)	4	0.02
Samoan	1	0.01
Tongan (1)	1	0.01
Other Pac. Isl., specified	4	0.02
Other Pac. Isl., not spec. (6)	6	0.03
Hispanic or Latino:	275	1.56
Central American:	13	0.07
Guatemalan	5	0.03
Honduran	4	0.02
Nicaraguan	1	0.01
Salvadoran	3	0.02
Cuban	25	0.14
Mexican	59	0.34
Puerto Rican	112	0.64
South American:	29	0.16
Argentinean	8	0.05
Colombian	7	0.04
Ecuadorian	5	0.03
Peruvian	3	0.02
Venezuelan	2	0.01
Other South American	4	0.02
Other Hispanic or Latino	37	0.21
Hungarian	160	0.91
Irish	5,226	29.73
Israeli	9	0.05
Italian	3,619	20.59
Latvian	10	0.06
Lithuanian	184	1.05
Norwegian	121	0.69
Pennsylvania German	67	0.38
Polish	1,551	8.82
Portuguese	32	0.18
Romanian	35	0.20
Russian	360	2.05
Scotch-Irish	180	1.02
Scottish	375	2.13
Slovak	129	0.73
Swedish	92	0.52
Swiss	51	0.29
Ukrainian	236	1.34
United States or American	521	2.96
Welsh	242	1.38
West Indian, excl. Hispanic:	33	0.19
Barbadian	18	0.10
Trinidadian and Tobagonian	15	0.09
White:	16,671	94.83
Not Hispanic (16,398)	16,499	93.85
Hispanic (155)	172	0.98
Yugoslavian	22	0.13

Warwick

Place Type: Township
County: Bucks
Population: 11,977

Ancestry/Race	Number	%
African American/Black:	147	1.23
Not Hispanic (123)	145	1.21
Hispanic (1)	2	0.02
African, sub-Saharan:	9	0.08
African	9	0.08
Am. Ind. or Alaska Nat., not spec.	3	0.03
Albanian	11	0.09
Alsatian	42	0.35
American Indian tribes, specified:	17	0.14
Blackfeet	1	0.01
Cherokee	1	0.01
Latin American Indians (1)	1	0.01
Lumbee (2)	2	0.02
Navajo	5	0.04
All other tribes (5)	7	0.06
Arab:	6	0.05
Syrian	6	0.05
Armenian	10	0.08
Asian:	286	2.39
Cambodian (5)	5	0.04
Chinese, ex. Taiwanese (64)	66	0.55
Filipino (22)	27	0.23
Indian (80)	86	0.72
Indonesian (2)	2	0.02
Japanese (7)	9	0.08
Korean (41)	48	0.40
Sri Lankan (2)	2	0.02
Thai (1)	1	0.01
Vietnamese (31)	33	0.28
Other Asian, specified (1)	1	0.01
Other Asian, not specified	6	0.05
Austrian	95	0.79
British	67	0.56
Canadian	30	0.25
Croatian	12	0.10
Czech	21	0.18
Czechoslovakian	13	0.11
Danish	37	0.31
Dutch	145	1.21
Eastern European	58	0.48
English	1,354	11.31
European	171	1.43
French, except Basque	209	1.75
French Canadian	94	0.78
German	3,222	26.90
Greek	80	0.67
Hawaii Native/Pacific Islander:	6	0.05
Micronesian: (1)	1	0.01
Guamanian/Chamorro (1)	1	0.01
Polynesian: (4)	4	0.03
Native Hawaiian (1)	1	0.01
Samoan (3)	3	0.03
Other Pac. Isl., not spec. (1)	1	0.01
Hispanic or Latino:	123	1.03
Central American:	4	0.03
Costa Rican	1	0.01
Guatemalan	2	0.02
Salvadoran	1	0.01
Cuban	12	0.10
Mexican	16	0.13
Puerto Rican	49	0.41
South American:	14	0.12
Argentinean	3	0.03
Chilean	1	0.01
Colombian	3	0.03
Ecuadorian	1	0.01
Paraguayan	2	0.02
Peruvian	4	0.03
Other Hispanic or Latino	28	0.23
Hungarian	120	1.00
Irish	3,330	27.80
Italian	2,225	18.58
Latvian	7	0.06
Lithuanian	136	1.14
Maltese	7	0.06
Northern European	11	0.09
Norwegian	29	0.24
Pennsylvania German	25	0.21
Polish	846	7.06
Portuguese	10	0.08
Romanian	23	0.19
Russian	499	4.17
Scandinavian	7	0.06
Scotch-Irish	165	1.38
Scottish	146	1.22
Slavic	23	0.19
Slovak	122	1.02
Swedish	86	0.72
Swiss	6	0.05
Ukrainian	253	2.11
United States or American	728	6.08
Welsh	72	0.60
West Indian, excl. Hispanic:	9	0.08
Dutch West Indian	9	0.08
White:	11,558	96.50
Not Hispanic (11,391)	11,447	95.57
Hispanic (99)	111	0.93
Yugoslavian	7	0.06

Warwick

Place Type: Township
County: Lancaster
Population: 15,475

Ancestry/Race	Number	%
African American/Black:	132	0.85
Not Hispanic (72)	116	0.75
Hispanic (3)	16	0.10
Am. Ind. or Alaska Nat., not spec.	22	0.14
Alsatian	9	0.06
American Indian tribes, specified:	17	0.11
Cherokee (2)	11	0.07
Cree (1)	1	0.01
Delaware (2)	2	0.01
Latin American Indians	1	0.01
Lumbee (1)	1	0.01
All other tribes (1)	1	0.01
American Indian tribes, not spec.	1	0.01
Asian:	165	1.07
Cambodian (1)	2	0.01
Chinese, ex. Taiwanese (10)	13	0.08
Filipino (14)	17	0.11
Hmong (17)	17	0.11
Indian (10)	13	0.08
Indonesian (1)	2	0.01
Japanese (15)	22	0.14
Korean (23)	29	0.19
Laotian (3)	6	0.04
Taiwanese (2)	2	0.01
Thai	1	0.01
Vietnamese (23)	27	0.17
Other Asian, not specified (8)	14	0.09
Austrian	53	0.34
British	61	0.39
Croatian	24	0.16
Czech	58	0.37
Czechoslovakian	52	0.34
Danish	14	0.09
Dutch	160	1.03
English	1,310	8.47
European	193	1.25
Finnish	21	0.14
French, except Basque	493	3.19
French Canadian	49	0.32
German	6,845	44.23
Greek	150	0.97
Hawaii Native/Pacific Islander:	7	0.05
Micronesian: (4)	4	0.03
Guamanian/Chamorro (4)	4	0.03
Polynesian: (1)	1	0.01
Samoan (1)	1	0.01
Other Pac. Isl., not spec. (2)	2	0.01
Hispanic or Latino:	241	1.56
Central American:	9	0.06
Honduran	1	0.01
Nicaraguan	5	0.03
Salvadoran	3	0.02
Cuban	7	0.05
Dominican Republic	1	0.01

Notes: 1. Figures in the "Number" column do not add up to the total population due to: a) Ancestry/Race overlap — e.g. persons can report being both White and Irish, b) persons of Hispanic origin can report being any race, c) persons reporting two ancestries are counted in both categories. 2. Numbers in parentheses indicate the number of persons reporting this ancestry/race alone, not in combination with any other ancestry/race. 3. Refer to the Explanation of Data in the front of the book for more detailed information.

Mexican	44	0.28
Puerto Rican	123	0.79
South American:	15	0.10
Argentinean	1	0.01
Colombian	10	0.06
Ecuadorian	2	0.01
Peruvian	2	0.01
Other Hispanic or Latino	42	0.27
Hungarian	38	0.25
Irish	1,947	12.58
Italian	815	5.27
Lithuanian	39	0.25
Northern European	9	0.06
Norwegian	84	0.54
Pennsylvania German	71	0.46
Polish	463	2.99
Romanian	6	0.04
Russian	129	0.83
Scandinavian	6	0.04
Scotch-Irish	295	1.91
Scottish	253	1.63
Slavic	28	0.18
Slovak	91	0.59
Swedish	140	0.90
Swiss	472	3.05
Ukrainian	76	0.49
United States or American	1,384	8.94
Welsh	192	1.24
White:	15,174	98.05
Not Hispanic (14,920)	15,000	96.93
Hispanic (129)	174	1.12
Yugoslavian	7	0.05

Washington

Place Type: City
County: Washington
Population: 15,268

Ancestry/Race	Number	%
African American/Black:	2,506	16.41
Not Hispanic (2,214)	2,482	16.26
Hispanic (15)	24	0.16
African, sub-Saharan:	83	0.54
African	83	0.54
Alaska Native tribes, specified:	1	0.01
Eskimo (1)	1	0.01
Am. Ind. or Alaska Nat., not spec.	42	0.28
American Indian tribes, specified:	43	0.28
Blackfeet	4	0.03
Cherokee (3)	19	0.12
Chickasaw	1	0.01
Choctaw	1	0.01
Cree (1)	1	0.01
Delaware (2)	3	0.02
Navajo (1)	2	0.01
Pueblo	1	0.01
Sioux (6)	10	0.07
All other tribes (1)	1	0.01
American Indian tribes, not spec.	5	0.03
Arab:	101	0.66
Lebanese	26	0.17
Syrian	75	0.49
Asian:	99	0.65
Chinese, ex. Taiwanese (18)	22	0.14
Filipino (10)	22	0.14
Indian (14)	19	0.12
Indonesian	1	0.01
Japanese (3)	7	0.05
Korean (9)	10	0.07
Taiwanese	1	0.01
Thai (1)	2	0.01
Vietnamese (12)	13	0.09
Other Asian, not specified (2)	2	0.01
Austrian	30	0.20
Belgian	7	0.05
British	23	0.15
Canadian	34	0.22
Croatian	95	0.62
Czech	62	0.40
Czechoslovakian	73	0.48
Danish	25	0.16
Dutch	251	1.64
Eastern European	9	0.06
English	1,447	9.45
European	19	0.12
French, except Basque	246	1.61
French Canadian	10	0.07
German	3,173	20.72
Greek	67	0.44
Hawaii Native/Pacific Islander:	6	0.04
Polynesian: (3)	4	0.03
Native Hawaiian (3)	3	0.02
Samoan	1	0.01
Other Pac. Isl., not spec.	2	0.01
Hispanic or Latino:	144	0.94
Central American:	2	0.01
Honduran	1	0.01
Panamanian	1	0.01
Cuban	6	0.04
Dominican Republic	2	0.01
Mexican	36	0.24
Puerto Rican	33	0.22
South American:	7	0.05
Colombian	1	0.01
Paraguayan	2	0.01
Peruvian	3	0.02
Other South American	1	0.01
Other Hispanic or Latino	59	0.39
Hungarian	280	1.83
Irish	2,820	18.42
Italian	2,106	13.75
Lithuanian	87	0.57
Luxemburger	4	0.03
New Zealander	7	0.05
Norwegian	13	0.08
Pennsylvania German	39	0.25
Polish	977	6.38
Portuguese	8	0.05
Romanian	14	0.09
Russian	194	1.27
Scotch-Irish	844	5.51
Scottish	226	1.48
Serbian	63	0.41
Slovak	252	1.65
Slovene	18	0.12
Swedish	72	0.47
Swiss	18	0.12
Turkish	6	0.04
Ukrainian	65	0.42
United States or American	668	4.36
Welsh	264	1.72
West Indian, excl. Hispanic:	10	0.07
Jamaican	10	0.07
White:	12,815	83.93
Not Hispanic (12,439)	12,737	83.42
Hispanic (62)	78	0.51
Yugoslavian	4	0.03

Washington

Place Type: Township
County: Franklin
Population: 11,559

Ancestry/Race	Number	%
African American/Black:	136	1.18
Not Hispanic (109)	128	1.11
Hispanic (8)	8	0.07
Am. Ind. or Alaska Nat., not spec.	8	0.07
American Indian tribes, specified:	27	0.23
Blackfeet	1	0.01
Cherokee (3)	10	0.09
Chippewa (1)	2	0.02
Choctaw (2)	2	0.02
Creek (1)	1	0.01
Delaware (1)	1	0.01
Latin American Indians (1)	1	0.01
Navajo (1)	1	0.01
Osage (2)	2	0.02
Sioux	4	0.03
Ute	1	0.01
All other tribes (1)	1	0.01
American Indian tribes, not spec.	4	0.03
Arab:	5	0.04
Egyptian	5	0.04
Asian:	126	1.09
Chinese, ex. Taiwanese (5)	5	0.04
Filipino (10)	15	0.13
Indian (21)	22	0.19
Indonesian	2	0.02
Japanese (3)	9	0.08
Korean (52)	57	0.49
Pakistani (1)	1	0.01
Thai (2)	2	0.02
Vietnamese (4)	8	0.07
Other Asian, not specified (5)	5	0.04
Australian	24	0.21
Austrian	44	0.38
British	32	0.28
Canadian	56	0.48
Czech	20	0.17
Dutch	233	2.01
English	1,096	9.47
European	70	0.61
French, except Basque	441	3.81
French Canadian	51	0.44
German	4,202	36.32
Hawaii Native/Pacific Islander:	7	0.06
Micronesian: (1)	1	0.01
Guamanian/Chamorro (1)	1	0.01
Polynesian: (3)	4	0.03
Native Hawaiian (3)	4	0.03
Other Pac. Isl., not spec.	2	0.02
Hispanic or Latino:	93	0.80
Central American:	6	0.05
Guatemalan	1	0.01
Panamanian	5	0.04
Cuban	8	0.07
Dominican Republic	3	0.03
Mexican	35	0.30
Puerto Rican	25	0.22
Other Hispanic or Latino	16	0.14
Hungarian	9	0.08
Irish	1,240	10.72
Italian	283	2.45
Norwegian	47	0.41
Pennsylvania German	7	0.06
Polish	145	1.25
Portuguese	10	0.09
Romanian	9	0.08
Russian	42	0.36
Scotch-Irish	318	2.75
Scottish	142	1.23
Serbian	7	0.06
Slavic	7	0.06
Slovak	33	0.29
Swedish	62	0.54
Swiss	97	0.84
Ukrainian	29	0.25
United States or American	1,417	12.25
Welsh	155	1.34
West Indian, excl. Hispanic:	12	0.10
Jamaican	12	0.10
White:	11,275	97.54
Not Hispanic (11,169)	11,220	97.07
Hispanic (52)	55	0.48

Weigelstown

Place Type: Census Designated Place
County: York
Population: 10,117

Ancestry/Race	Number	%
African American/Black:	150	1.48
Not Hispanic (119)	146	1.44
Hispanic (4)	4	0.04
African, sub-Saharan:	30	0.30
African	30	0.30

Notes: 1. Figures in the "Number" column do not add up to the total population due to: a) Ancestry/Race overlap — e.g. persons can report being both White and Irish, b) persons of Hispanic origin can report being any race, c) persons reporting two ancestries are counted in both categories. 2. Numbers in parentheses indicate the number of persons reporting this ancestry/race alone, not in combination with any other ancestry/race. 3. Refer to the Explanation of Data in the front of the book for more detailed information.

Am. Ind. or Alaska Nat., not spec.	9	0.09
American Indian tribes, specified:	27	0.27
Cherokee (2)	11	0.11
Chippewa	1	0.01
Creek (6)	6	0.06
Iroquois (3)	4	0.04
Lumbee (1)	1	0.01
Sioux (1)	3	0.03
All other tribes (1)	1	0.01
American Indian tribes, not spec.	1	0.01
Asian:	76	0.75
Bangladeshi (2)	3	0.03
Cambodian	4	0.04
Chinese, ex. Taiwanese (2)	2	0.02
Filipino (9)	15	0.15
Indian (10)	11	0.11
Japanese (3)	7	0.07
Korean (10)	11	0.11
Vietnamese (15)	17	0.17
Other Asian, not specified (4)	6	0.06
Austrian	13	0.13
Croatian	6	0.06
Czech	13	0.13
Dutch	304	3.01
English	742	7.35
European	34	0.34
French, except Basque	207	2.05
French Canadian	49	0.49
German	4,373	43.31
Greek	84	0.83
Hawaii Native/Pacific Islander:	15	0.15
Micronesian: (1)	12	0.12
Guamanian/Chamorro (1)	12	0.12
Polynesian:	3	0.03
Native Hawaiian	3	0.03
Hispanic or Latino:	144	1.42
Central American:	4	0.04
Nicaraguan	4	0.04
Cuban	2	0.02
Mexican	22	0.22
Puerto Rican	93	0.92
South American:	4	0.04
Argentinean	1	0.01
Ecuadorian	3	0.03
Other Hispanic or Latino	19	0.19
Hungarian	25	0.25
Irish	931	9.22
Italian	497	4.92
New Zealander	9	0.09
Norwegian	33	0.33
Pennsylvania German	33	0.33
Polish	253	2.51
Russian	13	0.13
Scotch-Irish	171	1.69
Scottish	109	1.08
Slavic	19	0.19
Slovak	24	0.24
Swedish	86	0.85
Swiss	79	0.78
Ukrainian	66	0.65
United States or American	1,037	10.27
Welsh	64	0.63
White:	9,833	97.19
Not Hispanic (9,703)	9,772	96.59
Hispanic (54)	61	0.60

West Bradford

Place Type: Township
County: Chester
Population: 10,775

Ancestry/Race	Number	%
Afghan	18	0.17
African American/Black:	607	5.63
Not Hispanic (514)	576	5.35
Hispanic (18)	31	0.29
African, sub-Saharan:	6	0.06
African	6	0.06
Am. Ind. or Alaska Nat., not spec.	23	0.21
American Indian tribes, specified:	67	0.62
Apache (1)	2	0.02
Blackfeet	1	0.01
Cherokee (4)	31	0.29
Cheyenne	1	0.01
Chickasaw (2)	2	0.02
Chippewa (4)	4	0.04
Choctaw (2)	2	0.02
Creek (1)	3	0.03
Delaware (1)	2	0.02
Iroquois (2)	6	0.06
Latin American Indians (3)	4	0.04
Seminole (1)	1	0.01
Sioux	1	0.01
All other tribes (3)	7	0.06
American Indian tribes, not spec.	6	0.06
Arab:	65	0.60
Jordanian	28	0.26
Moroccan	31	0.29
Palestinian	6	0.06
Armenian	8	0.07
Asian:	94	0.87
Cambodian (1)	1	0.01
Chinese, ex. Taiwanese (13)	27	0.25
Filipino (9)	13	0.12
Indian (13)	17	0.16
Indonesian (1)	1	0.01
Japanese (1)	1	0.01
Korean (10)	11	0.10
Malaysian	1	0.01
Thai (1)	2	0.02
Vietnamese (14)	16	0.15
Other Asian, not specified	4	0.04
Belgian	43	0.40
British	31	0.29
Canadian	40	0.37
Croatian	23	0.21
Czech	14	0.13
Czechoslovakian	18	0.17
Danish	79	0.73
Dutch	208	1.93
English	1,523	14.13
European	63	0.58
French, except Basque	199	1.85
French Canadian	15	0.14
German	2,646	24.56
Greek	71	0.66
Hawaii Native/Pacific Islander:	9	0.08
Micronesian: (1)	2	0.02
Guamanian/Chamorro (1)	2	0.02
Polynesian:	4	0.04
Samoan	4	0.04
Other Pac. Isl., not spec.	3	0.03
Hispanic or Latino:	190	1.76
Central American:	1	0.01
Salvadoran	1	0.01
Cuban	7	0.06
Dominican Republic	6	0.06
Mexican	46	0.43
Puerto Rican	84	0.78
South American:	15	0.14
Argentinean	6	0.06
Bolivian	3	0.03
Colombian	2	0.02
Ecuadorian	3	0.03
Venezuelan	1	0.01
Other Hispanic or Latino	31	0.29
Hungarian	93	0.86
Irish	2,707	25.12
Italian	1,800	16.71
Lithuanian	40	0.37
Northern European	12	0.11
Norwegian	69	0.64
Pennsylvania German	35	0.32
Polish	603	5.60
Romanian	19	0.18
Russian	95	0.88
Scotch-Irish	220	2.04
Scottish	322	2.99
Slavic	22	0.20
Slovak	52	0.48
Swedish	118	1.10
Swiss	41	0.38
Ukrainian	81	0.75
United States or American	525	4.87
Welsh	156	1.45
West Indian, excl. Hispanic:	46	0.43
Jamaican	26	0.24
Trinidadian and Tobagonian	20	0.19
White:	10,051	93.28
Not Hispanic (9,836)	9,922	92.08
Hispanic (121)	129	1.20
Yugoslavian	53	0.49

West Chester

Place Type: Borough
County: Chester
Population: 17,861

Ancestry/Race	Number	%
African American/Black:	3,231	18.09
Not Hispanic (2,922)	3,056	17.11
Hispanic (128)	175	0.98
African, sub-Saharan:	189	1.06
African	168	0.94
Kenyan	21	0.12
Alaska Native tribes, specified:	1	0.01
Alaska Athabascan	1	0.01
Am. Ind. or Alaska Nat., not spec.	68	0.38
American Indian tribes, specified:	53	0.30
Apache (1)	1	0.01
Blackfeet	5	0.03
Cherokee (8)	25	0.14
Chippewa (3)	3	0.02
Delaware (3)	6	0.03
Latin American Indians (1)	2	0.01
Navajo	2	0.01
Potawatomi (1)	1	0.01
Seminole	1	0.01
Sioux (2)	3	0.02
All other tribes (3)	4	0.02
American Indian tribes, not spec.	9	0.05
Arab:	43	0.24
Arab/Arabic	14	0.08
Egyptian	8	0.04
Palestinian	13	0.07
Syrian	8	0.04
Armenian	40	0.22
Asian:	332	1.86
Cambodian (8)	8	0.04
Chinese, ex. Taiwanese (57)	71	0.40
Filipino (25)	37	0.21
Hmong (1)	1	0.01
Indian (77)	89	0.50
Indonesian (2)	4	0.02
Japanese (15)	23	0.13
Korean (26)	34	0.19
Laotian (1)	1	0.01
Malaysian (3)	5	0.03
Pakistani (3)	3	0.02
Taiwanese (1)	2	0.01
Thai (5)	5	0.03
Vietnamese (27)	32	0.18
Other Asian, specified	1	0.01
Other Asian, not specified (3)	16	0.09
Australian	12	0.07
Austrian	49	0.27
Belgian	9	0.05
British	106	0.59
Canadian	29	0.16
Celtic	7	0.04
Croatian	11	0.06
Czech	55	0.31
Czechoslovakian	30	0.17
Danish	47	0.26
Dutch	186	1.04
English	1,670	9.34
European	60	0.34
Finnish	15	0.08

Notes: 1. Figures in the "Number" column do not add up to the total population due to: a) Ancestry/Race overlap — e.g. persons can report being both White and Irish, b) persons of Hispanic origin can report being any race, c) persons reporting two ancestries are counted in both categories. 2. Numbers in parentheses indicate the number of persons reporting this ancestry/race alone, not in combination with any other ancestry/race. 3. Refer to the Explanation of Data in the front of the book for more detailed information.

Ancestry/Race	Number	%
French, except Basque	411	2.30
French Canadian	29	0.16
German	3,222	18.03
Greek	120	0.67
Hawaii Native/Pacific Islander:	28	0.16
Micronesian: (5)	6	0.03
Guamanian/Chamorro (5)	6	0.03
Polynesian: (3)	5	0.03
Native Hawaiian (2)	4	0.02
Samoan (1)	1	0.01
Other Pac. Isl., not spec. (5)	17	0.10
Hispanic or Latino:	1,596	8.94
Central American:	23	0.13
Guatemalan	1	0.01
Honduran	2	0.01
Nicaraguan	4	0.02
Panamanian	13	0.07
Salvadoran	2	0.01
Other Central American	1	0.01
Cuban	18	0.10
Dominican Republic	22	0.12
Mexican	450	2.52
Puerto Rican	855	4.79
South American:	78	0.44
Argentinean	6	0.03
Bolivian	3	0.02
Chilean	5	0.03
Colombian	36	0.20
Ecuadorian	14	0.08
Peruvian	5	0.03
Venezuelan	6	0.03
Other South American	3	0.02
Other Hispanic or Latino	150	0.84
Hungarian	81	0.45
Iranian	14	0.08
Irish	3,683	20.61
Italian	2,540	14.21
Latvian	15	0.08
Lithuanian	103	0.58
Norwegian	64	0.36
Pennsylvania German	119	0.67
Polish	936	5.24
Portuguese	16	0.09
Romanian	5	0.03
Russian	337	1.89
Scandinavian	13	0.07
Scotch-Irish	489	2.74
Scottish	353	1.98
Slavic	41	0.23
Slovak	118	0.66
Slovene	5	0.03
Swedish	177	0.99
Swiss	73	0.41
Turkish	15	0.08
Ukrainian	178	1.00
United States or American	284	1.59
Welsh	330	1.85
West Indian, excl. Hispanic:	59	0.33
Haitian	6	0.03
Jamaican	5	0.03
Trinidadian and Tobagonian	14	0.08
West Indian	34	0.19
White:	13,746	76.96
Not Hispanic (12,788)	12,959	72.55
Hispanic (687)	787	4.41
Yugoslavian	8	0.04

West Deer

Place Type: Township
County: Allegheny
Population: 11,563

Ancestry/Race	Number	%
African American/Black:	55	0.48
Not Hispanic (34)	55	0.48
Am. Ind. or Alaska Nat., not spec.	9	0.08
American Indian tribes, specified:	19	0.16
Cherokee (4)	12	0.10
Iroquois	1	0.01
Sioux (4)	6	0.05
American Indian tribes, not spec.	3	0.03
Asian:	26	0.22
Chinese, ex. Taiwanese (10)	10	0.09
Filipino (5)	5	0.04
Indian (4)	4	0.03
Korean (6)	7	0.06
Austrian	41	0.35
Belgian	34	0.29
British	9	0.08
Canadian	6	0.05
Croatian	393	3.40
Czech	78	0.67
Czechoslovakian	62	0.54
Dutch	26	0.22
Eastern European	7	0.06
English	755	6.53
European	24	0.21
Finnish	18	0.16
French, except Basque	191	1.65
French Canadian	26	0.22
German	3,958	34.23
Greek	85	0.74
Hispanic or Latino:	49	0.42
Central American:	2	0.02
Guatemalan	2	0.02
Mexican	15	0.13
Puerto Rican	19	0.16
Other Hispanic or Latino	13	0.11
Hungarian	167	1.44
Irish	2,251	19.47
Italian	2,082	18.01
Lithuanian	28	0.24
Macedonian	16	0.14
Pennsylvania German	11	0.10
Polish	1,592	13.77
Romanian	7	0.06
Russian	385	3.33
Scandinavian	7	0.06
Scotch-Irish	304	2.63
Scottish	178	1.54
Serbian	29	0.25
Slavic	18	0.16
Slovak	543	4.70
Slovene	121	1.05
Swedish	54	0.47
Swiss	53	0.46
Ukrainian	44	0.38
United States or American	346	2.99
Welsh	241	2.08
White:	11,473	99.22
Not Hispanic (11,403)	11,432	98.87
Hispanic (37)	41	0.35
Yugoslavian	13	0.11

West Goshen

Place Type: Township
County: Chester
Population: 20,495

Ancestry/Race	Number	%
African American/Black:	948	4.63
Not Hispanic (847)	914	4.46
Hispanic (24)	34	0.17
African, sub-Saharan:	80	0.39
African	55	0.27
Nigerian	16	0.08
Other sub-Saharan African	9	0.04
Am. Ind. or Alaska Nat., not spec.	6	0.03
Albanian	14	0.07
Alsatian	10	0.05
American Indian tribes, specified:	20	0.10
Cherokee (1)	7	0.03
Choctaw (1)	1	0.00
Iroquois (1)	1	0.00
Latin American Indians (2)	2	0.01
Lumbee (1)	1	0.00
Navajo	2	0.01
Potawatomi	1	0.00
All other tribes (2)	5	0.02
American Indian tribes, not spec.	3	0.01
Arab:	58	0.28
Lebanese	42	0.20
Palestinian	16	0.08
Armenian	53	0.26
Asian:	843	4.11
Bangladeshi (3)	3	0.01
Cambodian (8)	10	0.05
Chinese, ex. Taiwanese (181)	191	0.93
Filipino (43)	52	0.25
Indian (348)	364	1.78
Japanese (15)	27	0.13
Korean (55)	66	0.32
Laotian (4)	6	0.03
Pakistani (26)	26	0.13
Sri Lankan (4)	4	0.02
Taiwanese (5)	7	0.03
Thai (2)	4	0.02
Vietnamese (57)	69	0.34
Other Asian, specified (3)	3	0.01
Other Asian, not specified (7)	11	0.05
Austrian	94	0.46
Basque	9	0.04
Belgian	28	0.14
British	122	0.60
Canadian	57	0.28
Croatian	15	0.07
Czech	85	0.41
Czechoslovakian	96	0.47
Danish	113	0.55
Dutch	345	1.68
Eastern European	23	0.11
English	2,542	12.40
European	89	0.43
Finnish	4	0.02
French, except Basque	461	2.25
French Canadian	87	0.42
German	4,530	22.10
Greek	178	0.87
Hawaii Native/Pacific Islander:	6	0.03
Polynesian: (2)	3	0.01
Native Hawaiian (1)	2	0.01
Samoan (1)	1	0.00
Other Pac. Isl., not spec.	3	0.01
Hispanic or Latino:	410	2.00
Central American:	6	0.03
Costa Rican	1	0.00
Guatemalan	2	0.01
Salvadoran	2	0.01
Other Central American	1	0.00
Cuban	15	0.07
Dominican Republic	9	0.04
Mexican	83	0.40
Puerto Rican	173	0.84
South American:	45	0.22
Argentinean	4	0.02
Bolivian	4	0.02
Chilean	6	0.03
Colombian	15	0.07
Ecuadorian	2	0.01
Peruvian	3	0.01
Uruguayan	5	0.02
Venezuelan	2	0.01
Other South American	4	0.02
Other Hispanic or Latino	79	0.39
Hungarian	143	0.70
Iranian	18	0.09
Irish	6,257	30.53
Israeli	14	0.07
Italian	3,454	16.85
Lithuanian	148	0.72
Northern European	36	0.18
Norwegian	245	1.20
Pennsylvania German	93	0.45
Polish	1,145	5.59
Romanian	23	0.11
Russian	395	1.93
Scandinavian	11	0.05
Scotch-Irish	561	2.74

Notes: 1. Figures in the "Number" column do not add up to the total population due to: a) Ancestry/Race overlap — e.g. persons can report being both White and Irish, b) persons of Hispanic origin can report being any race, c) persons reporting two ancestries are counted in both categories. 2. Numbers in parentheses indicate the number of persons reporting this ancestry/race alone, not in combination with any other ancestry/race. 3. Refer to the Explanation of Data in the front of the book for more detailed information.

Ancestry/Race	Number	%
Scottish	507	2.47
Slavic	5	0.02
Slovak	121	0.59
Slovene	25	0.12
Swedish	400	1.95
Swiss	41	0.20
Ukrainian	143	0.70
United States or American	747	3.64
Welsh	432	2.11
West Indian, excl. Hispanic:	38	0.19
Barbadian	17	0.08
Jamaican	21	0.10
White:	18,682	91.15
Not Hispanic (18,306)	18,423	89.89
Hispanic (243)	259	1.26
Yugoslavian	80	0.39

West Hempfield

Place Type: Township
County: Lancaster
Population: 15,128

Ancestry/Race	Number	%
African American/Black:	372	2.46
Not Hispanic (263)	326	2.15
Hispanic (20)	46	0.30
African, sub-Saharan:	10	0.07
African	10	0.07
Am. Ind. or Alaska Nat., not spec.	12	0.08
Albanian	9	0.06
American Indian tribes, specified:	19	0.13
Apache (1)	1	0.01
Cherokee (1)	6	0.04
Chippewa (2)	2	0.01
Creek (1)	1	0.01
Iroquois	1	0.01
Latin American Indians	1	0.01
Navajo	1	0.01
Osage (1)	1	0.01
Pueblo	1	0.01
Sioux	1	0.01
All other tribes (3)	3	0.02
American Indian tribes, not spec.	1	0.01
Arab:	76	0.50
Egyptian	4	0.03
Lebanese	62	0.41
Syrian	10	0.07
Asian:	259	1.71
Cambodian (9)	9	0.06
Chinese, ex. Taiwanese (44)	46	0.30
Filipino (12)	16	0.11
Indian (36)	43	0.28
Japanese (4)	10	0.07
Korean (24)	28	0.19
Pakistani (10)	10	0.07
Sri Lankan (2)	2	0.01
Thai (4)	4	0.03
Vietnamese (82)	86	0.57
Other Asian, not specified (5)	5	0.03
Austrian	4	0.03
British	52	0.34
Canadian	14	0.09
Croatian	20	0.13
Czech	28	0.18
Czechoslovakian	62	0.41
Danish	20	0.13
Dutch	254	1.68
English	1,175	7.76
European	93	0.61
French, except Basque	227	1.50
French Canadian	9	0.06
German	6,251	41.28
Greek	81	0.53
Hawaii Native/Pacific Islander:	3	0.02
Micronesian:	1	0.01
Guamanian/Chamorro	1	0.01
Polynesian: (1)	2	0.01
Native Hawaiian	1	0.01
Samoan (1)	1	0.01
Hispanic or Latino:	690	4.56
Central American:	8	0.05
Costa Rican	1	0.01
Guatemalan	1	0.01
Honduran	1	0.01
Salvadoran	4	0.03
Other Central American	1	0.01
Cuban	11	0.07
Dominican Republic	6	0.04
Mexican	43	0.28
Puerto Rican	531	3.51
South American:	12	0.08
Chilean	2	0.01
Colombian	3	0.02
Peruvian	2	0.01
Venezuelan	2	0.01
Other South American	3	0.02
Other Hispanic or Latino	79	0.52
Hungarian	115	0.76
Irish	2,047	13.52
Italian	1,051	6.94
Lithuanian	101	0.67
Norwegian	74	0.49
Pennsylvania German	35	0.23
Polish	395	2.61
Russian	76	0.50
Scotch-Irish	297	1.96
Scottish	174	1.15
Serbian	9	0.06
Slovak	70	0.46
Swedish	68	0.45
Swiss	391	2.58
Ukrainian	69	0.46
United States or American	1,275	8.42
Welsh	201	1.33
White:	14,273	94.35
Not Hispanic (13,798)	13,912	91.96
Hispanic (307)	361	2.39
Yugoslavian	26	0.17

West Lampeter

Place Type: Township
County: Lancaster
Population: 13,145

Ancestry/Race	Number	%
African American/Black:	128	0.97
Not Hispanic (99)	116	0.88
Hispanic (5)	12	0.09
Am. Ind. or Alaska Nat., not spec.	4	0.03
Alsatian	7	0.05
American Indian tribes, specified:	15	0.11
Cherokee (2)	6	0.05
Lumbee	1	0.01
Navajo (1)	1	0.01
All other tribes (2)	7	0.05
Arab:	17	0.13
Lebanese	17	0.13
Armenian	7	0.05
Asian:	92	0.70
Chinese, ex. Taiwanese (16)	18	0.14
Filipino (22)	32	0.24
Indian (12)	12	0.09
Japanese (13)	13	0.10
Korean (9)	9	0.07
Sri Lankan (2)	2	0.02
Vietnamese (5)	5	0.04
Other Asian, not specified	1	0.01
Austrian	31	0.24
British	32	0.24
Canadian	34	0.26
Croatian	10	0.08
Czech	22	0.17
Czechoslovakian	37	0.28
Danish	58	0.44
Dutch	129	0.98
Eastern European	11	0.08
English	1,738	13.26
Estonian	12	0.09
European	117	0.89
Finnish	21	0.16
French, except Basque	299	2.28
French Canadian	48	0.37
German	5,641	43.03
Greek	107	0.82
Hawaii Native/Pacific Islander:	5	0.04
Polynesian:	4	0.03
Native Hawaiian	1	0.01
Samoan	3	0.02
Other Pac. Isl., not spec. (1)	1	0.01
Hispanic or Latino:	226	1.72
Central American:	2	0.02
Guatemalan	1	0.01
Honduran	1	0.01
Cuban	8	0.06
Dominican Republic	8	0.06
Mexican	15	0.11
Puerto Rican	173	1.32
Other Hispanic or Latino	20	0.15
Hungarian	80	0.61
Iranian	8	0.06
Irish	1,436	10.96
Italian	901	6.87
Lithuanian	54	0.41
Norwegian	54	0.41
Pennsylvania German	43	0.33
Polish	458	3.49
Portuguese	8	0.06
Romanian	17	0.13
Russian	113	0.86
Scandinavian	8	0.06
Scotch-Irish	357	2.72
Scottish	315	2.40
Slavic	34	0.26
Slovak	37	0.28
Swedish	117	0.89
Swiss	251	1.91
Ukrainian	34	0.26
United States or American	1,226	9.35
Welsh	214	1.63
White:	12,848	97.74
Not Hispanic (12,690)	12,730	96.84
Hispanic (107)	118	0.90

West Manchester

Place Type: Township
County: York
Population: 17,035

Ancestry/Race	Number	%
African American/Black:	360	2.11
Not Hispanic (283)	351	2.06
Hispanic (3)	9	0.05
African, sub-Saharan:	31	0.18
African	31	0.18
Am. Ind. or Alaska Nat., not spec.	21	0.12
American Indian tribes, specified:	25	0.15
Apache	3	0.02
Cherokee (2)	12	0.07
Chippewa (1)	1	0.01
Creek (5)	5	0.03
Iroquois (1)	1	0.01
Latin American Indians	2	0.01
Pueblo	1	0.01
Arab:	26	0.15
Arab/Arabic	9	0.05
Lebanese	7	0.04
Syrian	10	0.06
Armenian	17	0.10
Asian:	242	1.42
Cambodian (10)	10	0.06
Chinese, ex. Taiwanese (39)	40	0.23
Filipino (12)	15	0.09
Indian (59)	64	0.38
Japanese (11)	17	0.10
Korean (20)	26	0.15
Laotian (8)	8	0.05
Pakistani (3)	3	0.02

Notes: 1. Figures in the "Number" column do not add up to the total population due to: a) Ancestry/Race overlap — e.g. persons can report being both White and Irish, b) persons of Hispanic origin can report being any race, c) persons reporting two ancestries are counted in both categories. 2. Numbers in parentheses indicate the number of persons reporting this ancestry/race alone, not in combination with any other ancestry/race. 3. Refer to the Explanation of Data in the front of the book for more detailed information.

Ancestry/Race	Number	%
Taiwanese (1)	4	0.02
Vietnamese (44)	47	0.28
Other Asian, specified	4	0.02
Other Asian, not specified (1)	4	0.02
Austrian	38	0.22
Belgian	14	0.08
British	31	0.18
Canadian	6	0.04
Croatian	33	0.19
Czech	6	0.04
Czechoslovakian	24	0.14
Danish	40	0.24
Dutch	311	1.83
English	1,100	6.47
European	77	0.45
Finnish	7	0.04
French, except Basque	282	1.66
French Canadian	60	0.35
German	6,638	39.03
Greek	208	1.22
Hawaii Native/Pacific Islander:	16	0.09
Micronesian:	6	0.04
Guamanian/Chamorro	1	0.01
Other Micronesian	5	0.03
Polynesian: (2)	5	0.03
Native Hawaiian (1)	1	0.01
Samoan (1)	4	0.02
Other Pac. Isl., specified	4	0.02
Other Pac. Isl., not spec. (1)	1	0.01
Hispanic or Latino:	206	1.21
Central American:	7	0.04
Guatemalan	1	0.01
Honduran	2	0.01
Nicaraguan	4	0.02
Cuban	4	0.02
Dominican Republic	2	0.01
Mexican	28	0.16
Puerto Rican	116	0.68
South American:	12	0.07
Argentinean	1	0.01
Chilean	2	0.01
Colombian	3	0.02
Ecuadorian	1	0.01
Peruvian	3	0.02
Other South American	2	0.01
Other Hispanic or Latino	37	0.22
Hungarian	19	0.11
Irish	1,702	10.01
Italian	766	4.50
Lithuanian	7	0.04
Norwegian	96	0.56
Pennsylvania German	99	0.58
Polish	520	3.06
Portuguese	9	0.05
Romanian	16	0.09
Russian	57	0.34
Scotch-Irish	256	1.51
Scottish	201	1.18
Slavic	6	0.04
Slovak	65	0.38
Slovene	6	0.04
Swedish	112	0.66
Swiss	148	0.87
Ukrainian	30	0.18
United States or American	2,114	12.43
Welsh	169	0.99
West Indian, excl. Hispanic:	41	0.24
British West Indian	7	0.04
Jamaican	19	0.11
U.S. Virgin Islander	15	0.09
White:	16,437	96.49
Not Hispanic (16,171)	16,312	95.76
Hispanic (100)	125	0.73

West Mifflin

Place Type: Borough
County: Allegheny
Population: 22,464

Ancestry/Race	Number	%
African American/Black:	2,110	9.39
Not Hispanic (1,986)	2,102	9.36
Hispanic (1)	8	0.04
African, sub-Saharan:	93	0.41
African	93	0.41
Am. Ind. or Alaska Nat., not spec.	22	0.10
American Indian tribes, specified:	46	0.20
Blackfeet (5)	12	0.05
Cherokee (9)	20	0.09
Cheyenne	1	0.00
Choctaw	1	0.00
Cree (1)	1	0.00
Iroquois (3)	3	0.01
Latin American Indians (1)	1	0.00
Navajo	1	0.00
Seminole	3	0.01
Sioux (1)	1	0.00
All other tribes	2	0.01
American Indian tribes, not spec.	4	0.02
Arab:	117	0.52
Lebanese	97	0.43
Syrian	20	0.09
Asian:	96	0.43
Chinese, ex. Taiwanese (7)	9	0.04
Filipino (10)	14	0.06
Indian (8)	13	0.06
Indonesian (1)	7	0.03
Japanese (2)	17	0.08
Korean (5)	7	0.03
Pakistani (4)	4	0.02
Sri Lankan (1)	1	0.00
Taiwanese	1	0.00
Vietnamese (14)	14	0.06
Other Asian, specified	1	0.00
Other Asian, not specified (4)	8	0.04
Austrian	144	0.64
Bulgarian	5	0.02
Canadian	8	0.04
Carpatho Rusyn	34	0.15
Croatian	542	2.41
Czech	176	0.78
Czechoslovakian	143	0.64
Dutch	50	0.22
Eastern European	7	0.03
English	1,864	8.30
Finnish	8	0.04
French, except Basque	292	1.30
French Canadian	12	0.05
German	5,301	23.60
German Russian	5	0.02
Greek	58	0.26
Hawaii Native/Pacific Islander:	18	0.08
Micronesian: (3)	3	0.01
Guamanian/Chamorro (3)	3	0.01
Polynesian: (1)	8	0.04
Native Hawaiian	4	0.02
Samoan (1)	4	0.02
Other Pac. Isl., specified	1	0.00
Other Pac. Isl., not spec. (6)	6	0.03
Hispanic or Latino:	127	0.57
Central American:	3	0.01
Guatemalan	2	0.01
Honduran	1	0.00
Cuban	12	0.05
Mexican	25	0.11
Puerto Rican	34	0.15
South American:	3	0.01
Colombian	1	0.00
Paraguayan	1	0.00
Venezuelan	1	0.00
Other Hispanic or Latino	50	0.22
Hungarian	1,452	6.46
Iranian	6	0.03
Irish	3,406	15.16
Italian	2,651	11.80
Lithuanian	146	0.65
Macedonian	20	0.09
Norwegian	33	0.15
Polish	2,438	10.85
Portuguese	15	0.07
Romanian	28	0.12
Russian	328	1.46
Scotch-Irish	310	1.38
Scottish	465	2.07
Serbian	332	1.48
Slavic	70	0.31
Slovak	3,607	16.06
Slovene	72	0.32
Swedish	291	1.30
Swiss	37	0.16
Ukrainian	105	0.47
United States or American	782	3.48
Welsh	316	1.41
White:	20,299	90.36
Not Hispanic (20,058)	20,207	89.95
Hispanic (79)	92	0.41

West Norriton

Place Type: Census Designated Place
County: Montgomery
Population: 14,901

Ancestry/Race	Number	%
African American/Black:	1,001	6.72
Not Hispanic (900)	990	6.64
Hispanic (9)	11	0.07
African, sub-Saharan:	70	0.47
African	61	0.41
Ghanian	9	0.06
Am. Ind. or Alaska Nat., not spec.	12	0.08
American Indian tribes, specified:	26	0.17
Cherokee (1)	11	0.07
Iroquois	1	0.01
Latin American Indians (2)	2	0.01
Seminole	1	0.01
Sioux (1)	1	0.01
All other tribes (7)	10	0.07
American Indian tribes, not spec.	1	0.01
Arab:	27	0.18
Egyptian	9	0.06
Lebanese	9	0.06
Syrian	9	0.06
Armenian	21	0.14
Asian:	462	3.10
Cambodian	6	0.04
Chinese, ex. Taiwanese (105)	123	0.83
Filipino (32)	48	0.32
Indian (158)	160	1.07
Japanese (4)	6	0.04
Korean (46)	55	0.37
Pakistani (13)	13	0.09
Sri Lankan (1)	1	0.01
Taiwanese (5)	6	0.04
Thai (1)	1	0.01
Vietnamese (28)	34	0.23
Other Asian, not specified (1)	9	0.06
Austrian	98	0.66
British	134	0.90
Canadian	15	0.10
Croatian	9	0.06
Czech	31	0.21
Czechoslovakian	30	0.20
Danish	28	0.19
Dutch	328	2.20
Eastern European	19	0.13
English	1,647	11.05
European	98	0.66
French, except Basque	223	1.50
French Canadian	71	0.48
German	3,279	22.01
Greek	104	0.70
Hawaii Native/Pacific Islander:	11	0.07

Notes: 1. Figures in the "Number" column do not add up to the total population due to: a) Ancestry/Race overlap — e.g. persons can report being both White and Irish, b) persons of Hispanic origin can report being any race, c) persons reporting two ancestries are counted in both categories. 2. Numbers in parentheses indicate the number of persons reporting this ancestry/race alone, not in combination with any other ancestry/race. 3. Refer to the Explanation of Data in the front of the book for more detailed information.

Ancestry/Race	Number	%
Polynesian: (7)	8	0.05
Native Hawaiian (1)	2	0.01
Other Polynesian (6)	6	0.04
Other Pac. Isl., not spec. (1)	3	0.02
Hispanic or Latino:	236	1.58
Central American:	4	0.03
Guatemalan	1	0.01
Nicaraguan	1	0.01
Panamanian	2	0.01
Cuban	17	0.11
Dominican Republic	4	0.03
Mexican	74	0.50
Puerto Rican	83	0.56
South American:	21	0.14
Argentinean	4	0.03
Chilean	1	0.01
Colombian	7	0.05
Ecuadorian	1	0.01
Paraguayan	2	0.01
Peruvian	2	0.01
Uruguayan	2	0.01
Venezuelan	2	0.01
Other Hispanic or Latino	33	0.22
Hungarian	185	1.24
Irish	3,765	25.27
Italian	3,802	25.52
Latvian	17	0.11
Lithuanian	63	0.42
New Zealander	7	0.05
Norwegian	73	0.49
Pennsylvania German	92	0.62
Polish	1,184	7.95
Portuguese	53	0.36
Russian	213	1.43
Scandinavian	8	0.05
Scotch-Irish	218	1.46
Scottish	184	1.23
Serbian	32	0.21
Slavic	9	0.06
Slovak	179	1.20
Swedish	47	0.32
Swiss	49	0.33
Turkish	30	0.20
Ukrainian	61	0.41
United States or American	402	2.70
Welsh	228	1.53
West Indian, excl. Hispanic:	61	0.41
Bahamian	10	0.07
Jamaican	22	0.15
Trinidadian and Tobagonian	29	0.19
White:	13,468	90.38
Not Hispanic (13,185)	13,305	89.29
Hispanic (150)	163	1.09

West Whiteland

Place Type: Township
County: Chester
Population: 16,499

Ancestry/Race	Number	%
African American/Black:	959	5.81
Not Hispanic (860)	927	5.62
Hispanic (27)	32	0.19
Am. Ind. or Alaska Nat., not spec.	37	0.22
American Indian tribes, specified:	39	0.24
Apache	1	0.01
Blackfeet (1)	1	0.01
Cherokee (4)	13	0.08
Chippewa	2	0.01
Delaware (1)	1	0.01
Iroquois (3)	6	0.04
Latin American Indians (4)	4	0.02
Sioux	1	0.01
All other tribes (6)	10	0.06
American Indian tribes, not spec.	1	0.01
Arab:	42	0.25
Lebanese	42	0.25
Armenian	20	0.12
Asian:	655	3.97
Chinese, ex. Taiwanese (128)	141	0.85
Filipino (32)	42	0.25
Indian (273)	288	1.75
Japanese (19)	25	0.15
Korean (55)	57	0.35
Laotian (1)	2	0.01
Pakistani (5)	6	0.04
Sri Lankan (4)	4	0.02
Taiwanese (1)	1	0.01
Thai (2)	2	0.01
Vietnamese (62)	69	0.42
Other Asian, specified (3)	5	0.03
Other Asian, not specified (7)	13	0.08
Australian	27	0.16
Austrian	144	0.87
Belgian	10	0.06
British	26	0.16
Canadian	74	0.45
Croatian	24	0.15
Czech	44	0.27
Czechoslovakian	76	0.46
Danish	126	0.76
Dutch	269	1.63
Eastern European	17	0.10
English	2,383	14.44
European	75	0.45
Finnish	47	0.28
French, except Basque	419	2.54
French Canadian	75	0.45
German	3,795	23.00
Greek	201	1.22
Hawaii Native/Pacific Islander:	15	0.09
Micronesian:	1	0.01
Guamanian/Chamorro	1	0.01
Polynesian: (8)	8	0.05
Tongan (3)	3	0.02
Other Polynesian (5)	5	0.03
Other Pac. Isl., specified	2	0.01
Other Pac. Isl., not spec. (2)	4	0.02
Hispanic or Latino:	330	2.00
Central American:	14	0.08
Costa Rican	2	0.01
Panamanian	7	0.04
Salvadoran	3	0.02
Other Central American	2	0.01
Cuban	12	0.07
Dominican Republic	11	0.07
Mexican	74	0.45
Puerto Rican	132	0.80
South American:	51	0.31
Argentinean	3	0.02
Bolivian	3	0.02
Chilean	3	0.02
Colombian	16	0.10
Ecuadorian	9	0.05
Paraguayan	2	0.01
Peruvian	7	0.04
Uruguayan	1	0.01
Venezuelan	6	0.04
Other South American	1	0.01
Other Hispanic or Latino	36	0.22
Hungarian	258	1.56
Irish	4,031	24.43
Italian	2,700	16.36
Latvian	21	0.13
Lithuanian	56	0.34
Luxemburger	11	0.07
Macedonian	5	0.03
Northern European	32	0.19
Norwegian	51	0.31
Pennsylvania German	77	0.47
Polish	904	5.48
Portuguese	45	0.27
Romanian	56	0.34
Russian	265	1.61
Scotch-Irish	357	2.16
Scottish	530	3.21
Serbian	6	0.04
Slavic	38	0.23
Slovak	168	1.02
Slovene	20	0.12
Swedish	265	1.61
Swiss	55	0.33
Ukrainian	185	1.12
United States or American	641	3.89
Welsh	395	2.39
West Indian, excl. Hispanic:	78	0.47
Haitian	8	0.05
Jamaican	35	0.21
West Indian	35	0.21
White:	14,870	90.13
Not Hispanic (14,523)	14,640	88.73
Hispanic (219)	230	1.39

Westtown

Place Type: Township
County: Chester
Population: 10,352

Ancestry/Race	Number	%
African American/Black:	291	2.81
Not Hispanic (262)	275	2.66
Hispanic (6)	16	0.15
African, sub-Saharan:	24	0.23
African	22	0.21
Nigerian	2	0.02
Alaska Native tribes, specified:	2	0.02
Tlingit-Haida (1)	2	0.02
Am. Ind. or Alaska Nat., not spec.	6	0.06
American Indian tribes, specified:	14	0.14
Cherokee (1)	5	0.05
Chippewa (1)	1	0.01
Choctaw	1	0.01
Latin American Indians	2	0.02
Navajo	1	0.01
Ute	1	0.01
Yakama (1)	1	0.01
All other tribes (2)	2	0.02
American Indian tribes, not spec.	1	0.01
Arab:	5	0.05
Syrian	5	0.05
Armenian	27	0.26
Asian:	273	2.64
Chinese, ex. Taiwanese (73)	75	0.72
Filipino (11)	14	0.14
Indian (77)	83	0.80
Indonesian (2)	4	0.04
Japanese (18)	21	0.20
Korean (30)	36	0.35
Malaysian (2)	2	0.02
Pakistani (5)	5	0.05
Sri Lankan (3)	3	0.03
Taiwanese (4)	4	0.04
Thai (1)	3	0.03
Vietnamese (20)	20	0.19
Other Asian, not specified (1)	3	0.03
Australian	10	0.10
Austrian	83	0.81
Belgian	20	0.19
Brazilian	27	0.26
British	57	0.55
Canadian	87	0.84
Celtic	4	0.04
Croatian	18	0.17
Czech	75	0.73
Czechoslovakian	66	0.64
Danish	52	0.50
Dutch	102	0.99
Eastern European	30	0.29
English	1,538	14.93
European	112	1.09
French, except Basque	353	3.43
French Canadian	26	0.25
German	2,489	24.17
Greek	92	0.89
Hawaii Native/Pacific Islander:	3	0.03
Polynesian: (1)	2	0.02
Native Hawaiian (1)	2	0.02
Other Pac. Isl., not spec.	1	0.01

Notes: 1. Figures in the "Number" column do not add up to the total population due to: a) Ancestry/Race overlap — e.g. persons can report being both White and Irish, b) persc of Hispanic origin can report being any race, c) persons reporting two ancestries are counted in both categories. 2. Numbers in parentheses indicate the number of persons reporting this ancestry/race alone, not in combination with any other ancestry/race. 3. Refer to the Explanation of Data in the front of the book for more detailed information.

Ancestry/Race	Number	%
Hispanic or Latino:	117	1.13
Central American:	5	0.05
Guatemalan	1	0.01
Nicaraguan	1	0.01
Panamanian	2	0.02
Other Central American	1	0.01
Cuban	11	0.11
Dominican Republic	1	0.01
Mexican	20	0.19
Puerto Rican	47	0.45
South American:	16	0.15
Argentinean	1	0.01
Chilean	2	0.02
Colombian	2	0.02
Ecuadorian	2	0.02
Peruvian	1	0.01
Uruguayan	4	0.04
Venezuelan	1	0.01
Other South American	3	0.03
Other Hispanic or Latino	17	0.16
Hungarian	85	0.83
Irish	3,201	31.08
Italian	1,788	17.36
Latvian	5	0.05
Lithuanian	67	0.65
Luxemburger	5	0.05
Northern European	34	0.33
Norwegian	46	0.45
Pennsylvania German	38	0.37
Polish	594	5.77
Romanian	40	0.39
Russian	163	1.58
Scandinavian	9	0.09
Scotch-Irish	320	3.11
Scottish	356	3.46
Slavic	8	0.08
Slovak	70	0.68
Slovene	5	0.05
Swedish	83	0.81
Swiss	32	0.31
Ukrainian	107	1.04
United States or American	296	2.87
Welsh	195	1.89
White:	9,777	94.45
Not Hispanic (9,653)	9,694	93.64
Hispanic (75)	83	0.80
Yugoslavian	12	0.12

White

Place Type: Township
County: Indiana
Population: 14,034

Ancestry/Race	Number	%
African American/Black:	395	2.81
Not Hispanic (346)	393	2.80
Hispanic (2)	2	0.01
African, sub-Saharan:	52	0.37
African	21	0.15
Ghanian	20	0.14
South African	11	0.08
Alaska Native tribes, not specified	1	0.01
Am. Ind. or Alaska Nat., not spec.	15	0.11
American Indian tribes, specified:	18	0.13
Apache (1)	1	0.01
Blackfeet	3	0.02
Cherokee	2	0.01
Chippewa (1)	1	0.01
Choctaw (1)	1	0.01
Creek	1	0.01
Iroquois (4)	4	0.03
Sioux (2)	2	0.01
All other tribes	3	0.02
American Indian tribes, not spec.	4	0.03
Arab:	105	0.75
Arab/Arabic	66	0.47
...banese	20	0.14
[illegible]	19	0.14
[illegible]	24	0.17
Asian:	331	2.36
Bangladeshi (10)	11	0.08
Chinese, ex. Taiwanese (56)	58	0.41
Filipino (14)	17	0.12
Indian (98)	104	0.74
Japanese (21)	23	0.16
Korean (50)	50	0.36
Malaysian (2)	2	0.01
Pakistani (6)	6	0.04
Taiwanese (22)	24	0.17
Thai (5)	5	0.04
Vietnamese (5)	5	0.04
Other Asian, not specified (11)	26	0.19
Australian	9	0.06
Austrian	67	0.48
Belgian	22	0.16
British	71	0.51
Canadian	9	0.06
Croatian	45	0.32
Czech	18	0.13
Czechoslovakian	40	0.29
Dutch	380	2.71
Eastern European	7	0.05
English	1,456	10.37
European	87	0.62
French, except Basque	367	2.62
French Canadian	27	0.19
German	4,035	28.75
Greek	47	0.33
Hawaii Native/Pacific Islander:	2	0.01
Polynesian:	2	0.01
Native Hawaiian	2	0.01
Hispanic or Latino:	97	0.69
Central American:	10	0.07
Guatemalan	5	0.04
Panamanian	4	0.03
Salvadoran	1	0.01
Cuban	3	0.02
Mexican	28	0.20
Puerto Rican	13	0.09
South American:	18	0.13
Argentinean	2	0.01
Colombian	7	0.05
Peruvian	4	0.03
Other South American	5	0.04
Other Hispanic or Latino	25	0.18
Hungarian	136	0.97
Iranian	14	0.10
Irish	2,094	14.92
Italian	1,583	11.28
Lithuanian	51	0.36
Northern European	15	0.11
Norwegian	52	0.37
Pennsylvania German	78	0.56
Polish	807	5.75
Russian	174	1.24
Scotch-Irish	477	3.40
Scottish	335	2.39
Serbian	22	0.16
Slavic	19	0.14
Slovak	638	4.55
Slovene	55	0.39
Swedish	166	1.18
Swiss	52	0.37
Ukrainian	121	0.86
United States or American	591	4.21
Welsh	330	2.35
West Indian, excl. Hispanic:	36	0.26
Trinidadian and Tobagonian	36	0.26
White:	13,326	94.96
Not Hispanic (13,142)	13,246	94.39
Hispanic (74)	80	0.57
Yugoslavian	44	0.31

Whitehall

Place Type: Borough
County: Allegheny
Population: 14,444

Ancestry/Race	Number	%
African American/Black:	234	1.62
Not Hispanic (202)	228	1.58
Hispanic (3)	6	0.04
Am. Ind. or Alaska Nat., not spec.	7	0.05
Albanian	22	0.15
American Indian tribes, specified:	15	0.10
Blackfeet	1	0.01
Cherokee	8	0.06
Creek	1	0.01
Delaware	3	0.02
Iroquois	1	0.01
Latin American Indians (1)	1	0.01
Arab:	67	0.46
Lebanese	53	0.37
Syrian	14	0.10
Asian:	157	1.09
Chinese, ex. Taiwanese (42)	47	0.33
Filipino (6)	15	0.10
Indian (20)	21	0.15
Indonesian (1)	1	0.01
Japanese (5)	6	0.04
Korean (7)	8	0.06
Vietnamese (52)	57	0.39
Other Asian, not specified (1)	2	0.01
Austrian	73	0.51
Belgian	17	0.12
Brazilian	19	0.13
British	14	0.10
Bulgarian	24	0.17
Canadian	8	0.06
Carpatho Rusyn	7	0.05
Croatian	193	1.34
Czech	29	0.20
Czechoslovakian	58	0.40
Danish	15	0.10
Dutch	51	0.35
Eastern European	6	0.04
English	1,088	7.53
French, except Basque	237	1.64
French Canadian	8	0.06
German	5,224	36.17
Greek	157	1.09
Hawaii Native/Pacific Islander:	10	0.07
Micronesian: (2)	2	0.01
Guamanian/Chamorro (2)	2	0.01
Other Pac. Isl., not spec.	8	0.06
Hispanic or Latino:	96	0.66
Central American:	2	0.01
Guatemalan	1	0.01
Salvadoran	1	0.01
Cuban	5	0.03
Dominican Republic	2	0.01
Mexican	34	0.24
Puerto Rican	20	0.14
South American:	9	0.06
Colombian	5	0.03
Peruvian	3	0.02
Uruguayan	1	0.01
Other Hispanic or Latino	24	0.17
Hungarian	215	1.49
Iranian	26	0.18
Irish	2,918	20.20
Italian	2,505	17.34
Lithuanian	254	1.76
Macedonian	16	0.11
Norwegian	52	0.36
Pennsylvania German	18	0.12
Polish	1,519	10.52
Romanian	10	0.07
Russian	146	1.01
Scotch-Irish	340	2.35
Scottish	337	2.33
Serbian	72	0.50

... the "Number" column do not add up to the total population due to: a) Ancestry/Race overlap — e.g. persons can report being both White and Irish, b) persons ... can report being any race, c) persons reporting two ancestries are counted in both categories. 2. Numbers in parentheses indicate the number of persons ...cestry/race alone, not in combination with any other ancestry/race. 3. Refer to the Explanation of Data in the front of the book for more detailed information.

Ancestry/Race	Number	%
Slovak	586	4.06
Slovene	63	0.44
Swedish	96	0.66
Swiss	18	0.12
Ukrainian	237	1.64
United States or American	422	2.92
Welsh	216	1.50
West Indian, excl. Hispanic:	19	0.13
West Indian	13	0.09
Other West Indian	6	0.04
White:	14,050	97.27
Not Hispanic (13,895)	13,987	96.84
Hispanic (58)	63	0.44
Yugoslavian	275	1.90

Whitehall

Place Type: Township
County: Lehigh
Population: 24,896

Ancestry/Race	Number	%
African American/Black:	763	3.06
Not Hispanic (633)	696	2.80
Hispanic (49)	67	0.27
African, sub-Saharan:	23	0.09
African	23	0.09
Am. Ind. or Alaska Nat., not spec.	19	0.08
Albanian	6	0.02
American Indian tribes, specified:	42	0.17
Blackfeet	1	0.00
Cherokee (8)	14	0.06
Chippewa	1	0.00
Choctaw (4)	5	0.02
Delaware (1)	7	0.03
Iroquois (2)	3	0.01
Latin American Indians (3)	3	0.01
Lumbee	1	0.00
Navajo (1)	1	0.00
Pueblo	1	0.00
Sioux (1)	2	0.01
All other tribes (3)	3	0.01
American Indian tribes, not spec.	9	0.04
Arab:	834	3.35
Arab/Arabic	131	0.53
Egyptian	23	0.09
Lebanese	240	0.96
Moroccan	19	0.08
Syrian	421	1.69
Armenian	8	0.03
Asian:	988	3.97
Bangladeshi (9)	10	0.04
Chinese, ex. Taiwanese (140)	146	0.59
Filipino (37)	50	0.20
Hmong (1)	1	0.00
Indian (365)	393	1.58
Indonesian (4)	4	0.02
Japanese (11)	20	0.08
Korean (105)	112	0.45
Laotian (1)	1	0.00
Malaysian (7)	7	0.03
Pakistani (22)	27	0.11
Sri Lankan (3)	3	0.01
Taiwanese	2	0.01
Thai (5)	5	0.02
Vietnamese (178)	178	0.71
Other Asian, specified (2)	2	0.01
Other Asian, not specified (3)	27	0.11
Austrian	1,065	4.28
Brazilian	9	0.04
British	51	0.20
Canadian	25	0.10
Croatian	121	0.49
Czech	49	0.20
Czechoslovakian	94	0.38
Danish	34	0.14
Dutch	745	2.99
Eastern European	20	0.08
English	1,233	4.95
European	45	0.18
Finnish	5	0.02
French, except Basque	336	1.35
French Canadian	50	0.20
German	7,553	30.34
Greek	131	0.53
Guyanese	21	0.08
Hawaii Native/Pacific Islander:	24	0.10
Micronesian: (3)	3	0.01
Guamanian/Chamorro (1)	1	0.00
Other Micronesian (2)	2	0.01
Polynesian: (9)	15	0.06
Native Hawaiian (2)	3	0.01
Samoan (7)	11	0.04
Other Polynesian	1	0.00
Other Pac. Isl., not spec. (3)	6	0.02
Hispanic or Latino:	1,089	4.37
Central American:	42	0.17
Costa Rican	1	0.00
Guatemalan	16	0.06
Honduran	9	0.04
Panamanian	7	0.03
Salvadoran	8	0.03
Other Central American	1	0.00
Cuban	29	0.12
Dominican Republic	79	0.32
Mexican	85	0.34
Puerto Rican	567	2.28
South American:	97	0.39
Argentinean	4	0.02
Chilean	3	0.01
Colombian	55	0.22
Ecuadorian	11	0.04
Peruvian	20	0.08
Venezuelan	3	0.01
Other South American	1	0.00
Other Hispanic or Latino	190	0.76
Hungarian	845	3.39
Irish	2,556	10.27
Italian	2,818	11.32
Lithuanian	93	0.37
Macedonian	15	0.06
Norwegian	125	0.50
Pennsylvania German	1,311	5.27
Polish	1,374	5.52
Portuguese	51	0.20
Romanian	9	0.04
Russian	218	0.88
Scandinavian	11	0.04
Scotch-Irish	193	0.78
Scottish	175	0.70
Serbian	9	0.04
Slavic	7	0.03
Slovak	1,470	5.90
Slovene	11	0.04
Swedish	50	0.20
Swiss	46	0.18
Ukrainian	848	3.41
United States or American	1,219	4.90
Welsh	505	2.03
West Indian, excl. Hispanic:	83	0.33
Dutch West Indian	18	0.07
Jamaican	60	0.24
West Indian	5	0.02
White:	22,793	91.55
Not Hispanic (21,996)	22,180	89.09
Hispanic (549)	613	2.46
Yugoslavian	17	0.07

Whitemarsh

Place Type: Township
County: Montgomery
Population: 16,702

Ancestry/Race	Number	%
African American/Black:	403	2.41
Not Hispanic (355)	387	2.32
Hispanic (14)	16	0.10
African, sub-Saharan:	79	0.47
African	41	0.25
Cape Verdean	33	0.20
Sudanese	5	0.03
Alaska Native tribes, specified:	1	0.01
Aleut (1)	1	0.01
Am. Ind. or Alaska Nat., not spec.	7	0.04
Albanian	7	0.04
American Indian tribes, specified:	17	0.10
Blackfeet (1)	1	0.01
Cherokee (2)	12	0.07
Iroquois	1	0.01
Latin American Indians	1	0.01
Navajo	1	0.01
All other tribes	1	0.01
Arab:	176	1.05
Arab/Arabic	8	0.05
Egyptian	22	0.13
Iraqi	53	0.32
Lebanese	8	0.05
Syrian	50	0.30
Other Arab	35	0.21
Armenian	26	0.16
Asian:	672	4.02
Cambodian (1)	1	0.01
Chinese, ex. Taiwanese (125)	135	0.81
Filipino (24)	30	0.18
Indian (131)	143	0.86
Japanese (15)	21	0.13
Korean (267)	270	1.62
Laotian (2)	2	0.01
Pakistani	6	0.04
Sri Lankan (3)	3	0.02
Taiwanese (8)	8	0.05
Thai	1	0.01
Vietnamese (22)	25	0.15
Other Asian, specified (4)	4	0.02
Other Asian, not specified (9)	23	0.14
Austrian	167	1.00
Brazilian	18	0.11
British	46	0.28
Celtic	29	0.17
Czech	55	0.33
Czechoslovakian	9	0.05
Danish	22	0.13
Dutch	124	0.74
Eastern European	130	0.78
English	1,752	10.49
European	180	1.08
Finnish	8	0.05
French, except Basque	270	1.62
German	3,049	18.26
Greek	38	0.23
Hawaii Native/Pacific Islander:	2	0.01
Other Pac. Isl., not spec.	2	0.01
Hispanic or Latino:	165	0.99
Central American:	4	0.02
Guatemalan	1	0.01
Honduran	1	0.01
Panamanian	2	0.01
Cuban	21	0.13
Mexican	43	0.26
Puerto Rican	57	0.34
South American:	21	0.13
Argentinean	3	0.02
Chilean	2	0.01
Colombian	8	0.05
Ecuadorian	2	0.01
Peruvian	2	0.01
Venezuelan	2	0.01
Other South American	2	0.01
Other Hispanic or Latino	19	0.11
Hungarian	262	1.57
Iranian	60	0.36
Irish	4,301	25.75
Israeli	14	0.08
Italian	2,862	17.14
Latvian	50	0.30
Lithuanian	66	0.40
Northern European	18	0.11
Norwegian	76	0.46
Pennsylvania German	63	0.38

Notes: 1. Figures in the "Number" column do not add up to the total population due to: a) Ancestry/Race overlap — e.g. persons can report being both White and Irish, b) persons of Hispanic origin can report being any race, c) persons reporting two ancestries are counted in both categories. 2. Numbers in parentheses indicate the number of persons reporting this ancestry/race alone, not in combination with any other ancestry/race. 3. Refer to the Explanation of Data in the front of the book for more detailed information.

Polish	1,534	9.18
Portuguese	8	0.05
Romanian	149	0.89
Russian	1,386	8.30
Scandinavian	12	0.07
Scotch-Irish	234	1.40
Scottish	336	2.01
Slovak	49	0.29
Slovene	13	0.08
Swedish	196	1.17
Swiss	53	0.32
Ukrainian	80	0.48
United States or American	641	3.84
Welsh	258	1.54
White:	15,673	93.84
Not Hispanic (15,448)	15,534	93.01
Hispanic (134)	139	0.83

Whitpain

Place Type: Township
County: Montgomery
Population: 18,562

Ancestry/Race	Number	%
Acadian/Cajun	9	0.05
African American/Black:	925	4.98
Not Hispanic (861)	912	4.91
Hispanic (9)	13	0.07
African, sub-Saharan:	150	0.80
African	83	0.44
Ethiopian	42	0.22
Nigerian	25	0.13
Am. Ind. or Alaska Nat., not spec.	24	0.13
Albanian	44	0.24
American Indian tribes, specified:	35	0.19
Apache	1	0.01
Cherokee (6)	8	0.04
Delaware (1)	5	0.03
Iroquois	3	0.02
Latin American Indians (1)	1	0.01
Sioux	8	0.04
All other tribes (3)	9	0.05
Arab:	63	0.34
Egyptian	41	0.22
Lebanese	12	0.06
Other Arab	10	0.05
Armenian	59	0.32
Asian:	1,538	8.29
Cambodian (1)	5	0.03
Chinese, ex. Taiwanese (282)	307	1.65
Filipino (45)	57	0.31
Indian (317)	330	1.78
Japanese (30)	37	0.20
Korean (697)	716	3.86
Malaysian (1)	1	0.01
Pakistani (18)	18	0.10
Sri Lankan (8)	16	0.09
Taiwanese (5)	5	0.03
Thai (7)	7	0.04
Vietnamese (14)	17	0.09
Other Asian, specified (9)	9	0.05
Other Asian, not specified (8)	13	0.07
Austrian	116	0.62
Belgian	17	0.09
British	159	0.85
Canadian	139	0.74
Croatian	22	0.12
Czech	50	0.27
Czechoslovakian	21	0.11
Danish	58	0.31
Dutch	204	1.09
Eastern European	61	0.33
English	1,768	9.45
European	142	0.76
Finnish	10	0.05
French, except Basque	288	1.54
French Canadian	95	0.51
German	3,692	19.74
Greek	65	0.35
Hawaii Native/Pacific Islander:	2	0.01
Polynesian:	2	0.01
Samoan	1	0.01
Other Polynesian	1	0.01
Hispanic or Latino:	247	1.33
Central American:	9	0.05
Guatemalan	2	0.01
Honduran	1	0.01
Nicaraguan	1	0.01
Panamanian	3	0.02
Salvadoran	2	0.01
Cuban	17	0.09
Dominican Republic	1	0.01
Mexican	34	0.18
Puerto Rican	50	0.27
South American:	78	0.42
Argentinean	8	0.04
Bolivian	6	0.03
Chilean	3	0.02
Colombian	23	0.12
Ecuadorian	6	0.03
Paraguayan	5	0.03
Peruvian	11	0.06
Venezuelan	14	0.08
Other South American	2	0.01
Other Hispanic or Latino	58	0.31
Hungarian	171	0.91
Irish	4,401	23.53
Italian	3,223	17.23
Latvian	7	0.04
Lithuanian	134	0.72
Northern European	14	0.07
Norwegian	80	0.43
Pennsylvania German	97	0.52
Polish	1,461	7.81
Portuguese	25	0.13
Romanian	23	0.12
Russian	987	5.28
Scandinavian	8	0.04
Scotch-Irish	287	1.53
Scottish	350	1.87
Slavic	15	0.08
Slovak	197	1.05
Swedish	156	0.83
Swiss	110	0.59
Turkish	13	0.07
Ukrainian	182	0.97
United States or American	820	4.38
Welsh	160	0.86
West Indian, excl. Hispanic:	37	0.20
Jamaican	26	0.14
West Indian	11	0.06
White:	16,144	86.97
Not Hispanic (15,839)	15,939	85.87
Hispanic (182)	205	1.10
Yugoslavian	9	0.05

Wilkes-Barre

Place Type: City
County: Luzerne
Population: 43,123

Ancestry/Race	Number	%
African American/Black:	2,493	5.78
Not Hispanic (2,129)	2,405	5.58
Hispanic (64)	88	0.20
African, sub-Saharan:	199	0.46
African	124	0.29
Ethiopian	8	0.02
Ghanian	10	0.02
Zairian	57	0.13
Alaska Native tribes, specified:	3	0.01
Alaska Athabascan (2)	2	0.00
Eskimo (1)	1	0.00
Alaska Native tribes, not specified	1	0.00
Am. Ind. or Alaska Nat., not spec.	68	0.16
American Indian tribes, specified:	77	0.18
Apache (1)	1	0.00
Blackfeet (2)	4	0.01
Cherokee (7)	30	0.07
Cheyenne (1)	1	0.00
Chippewa (1)	1	0.00
Choctaw	1	0.00
Delaware (2)	2	0.00
Iroquois (3)	3	0.01
Latin American Indians (1)	13	0.03
Menominee	1	0.00
Pueblo (1)	1	0.00
Puget Sound Salish (1)	1	0.00
Sioux (5)	7	0.02
All other tribes	11	0.03
American Indian tribes, not spec.	12	0.03
Arab:	934	2.17
Arab/Arabic	26	0.06
Jordanian	14	0.03
Lebanese	527	1.22
Palestinian	5	0.01
Syrian	362	0.84
Asian:	428	0.99
Bangladeshi (1)	1	0.00
Chinese, ex. Taiwanese (37)	47	0.11
Filipino (37)	50	0.12
Indian (48)	56	0.13
Indonesian	1	0.00
Japanese (14)	25	0.06
Korean (26)	41	0.10
Malaysian (1)	1	0.00
Pakistani (1)	1	0.00
Taiwanese (1)	1	0.00
Thai (1)	3	0.01
Vietnamese (168)	180	0.42
Other Asian, specified	5	0.01
Other Asian, not specified (4)	16	0.04
Australian	23	0.05
Austrian	206	0.48
British	36	0.08
Canadian	45	0.10
Carpatho Rusyn	16	0.04
Croatian	13	0.03
Czech	73	0.17
Czechoslovakian	45	0.10
Danish	45	0.10
Dutch	768	1.78
Eastern European	14	0.03
English	2,458	5.70
European	69	0.16
Finnish	15	0.03
French, except Basque	326	0.76
French Canadian	30	0.07
German	7,523	17.45
Greek	177	0.41
Guyanese	9	0.02
Hawaii Native/Pacific Islander:	34	0.08
Micronesian: (3)	4	0.01
Guamanian/Chamorro (3)	4	0.01
Polynesian: (8)	10	0.02
Native Hawaiian (2)	3	0.01
Samoan (6)	7	0.02
Other Pac. Isl., specified	5	0.01
Other Pac. Isl., not spec. (3)	15	0.03
Hispanic or Latino:	683	1.58
Central American:	11	0.03
Costa Rican	1	0.00
Guatemalan	1	0.00
Honduran	2	0.00
Nicaraguan	2	0.00
Panamanian	4	0.01
Salvadoran	1	0.00
Cuban	23	0.05
Dominican Republic	13	0.03
Mexican	181	0.42
Puerto Rican	248	0.58
South American:	20	0.05
Argentinean	1	0.00
Bolivian	2	0.00
Colombian	3	0.01
Ecuadorian	1	0.00
Peruvian	11	0.03
Other South American	2	0.00

Notes: 1. Figures in the "Number" column do not add up to the total population due to: a) Ancestry/Race overlap — e.g. persons can report being both White and Irish, b) persons of Hispanic origin can report being any race, c) persons reporting two ancestries are counted in both categories. 2. Numbers in parentheses indicate the number of persons reporting this ancestry/race alone, not in combination with any other ancestry/race. 3. Refer to the Explanation of Data in the front of the book for more detailed information.

Other Hispanic or Latino	187	0.43
Hungarian	210	0.49
Iranian	21	0.05
Irish	9,417	21.84
Italian	4,767	11.05
Lithuanian	1,644	3.81
Northern European	6	0.01
Norwegian	27	0.06
Pennsylvania German	464	1.08
Polish	8,547	19.82
Portuguese	69	0.16
Romanian	54	0.13
Russian	1,571	3.64
Scotch-Irish	227	0.53
Scottish	371	0.86
Serbian	22	0.05
Slavic	51	0.12
Slovak	2,281	5.29
Slovene	56	0.13
Swedish	188	0.44
Swiss	12	0.03
Ukrainian	523	1.21
United States or American	1,057	2.45
Welsh	2,650	6.15
West Indian, excl. Hispanic:	52	0.12
Bahamian	13	0.03
Jamaican	39	0.09
White:	40,240	93.31
Not Hispanic (39,433)	39,820	92.34
Hispanic (368)	420	0.97
Yugoslavian	5	0.01

Wilkinsburg

Place Type: Borough
County: Allegheny
Population: 19,196

Ancestry/Race	Number	%
African American/Black:	13,152	68.51
Not Hispanic (12,684)	13,040	67.93
Hispanic (84)	112	0.58
African, sub-Saharan:	550	2.87
African	486	2.53
Ghanian	10	0.05
Kenyan	17	0.09
Liberian	13	0.07
Nigerian	24	0.13
Am. Ind. or Alaska Nat., not spec.	118	0.61
American Indian tribes, specified:	141	0.73
Apache (3)	4	0.02
Blackfeet (9)	18	0.09
Cherokee (9)	80	0.42
Cheyenne	4	0.02
Chickasaw	2	0.01
Creek (5)	8	0.04
Iroquois (1)	2	0.01
Kiowa	1	0.01
Latin American Indians (2)	4	0.02
Navajo	1	0.01
Pueblo	1	0.01
Seminole (1)	10	0.05
Sioux (1)	1	0.01
All other tribes	5	0.03
American Indian tribes, not spec.	10	0.05
Arab:	120	0.63
Arab/Arabic	17	0.09
Egyptian	32	0.17
Lebanese	30	0.16
Moroccan	33	0.17
Other Arab	8	0.04
Asian:	220	1.15
Chinese, ex. Taiwanese (21)	34	0.18
Filipino (8)	17	0.09
Indian (71)	84	0.44
Indonesian	5	0.03
Japanese (12)	14	0.07
Korean (30)	31	0.16
Thai (1)	4	0.02
Vietnamese (2)	4	0.02
Other Asian, specified	4	0.02
Other Asian, not specified (7)	23	0.12
Austrian	22	0.11
Belgian	9	0.05
British	23	0.12
Canadian	4	0.02
Croatian	84	0.44
Czech	28	0.15
Czechoslovakian	62	0.32
Danish	13	0.07
Dutch	56	0.29
Eastern European	40	0.21
English	670	3.49
European	33	0.17
Finnish	6	0.03
French, except Basque	126	0.66
French Canadian	13	0.07
German	1,424	7.42
Greek	69	0.36
Hawaii Native/Pacific Islander:	23	0.12
Polynesian: (6)	9	0.05
Native Hawaiian (4)	5	0.03
Samoan (2)	4	0.02
Other Pac. Isl., specified	4	0.02
Other Pac. Isl., not spec. (6)	10	0.05
Hispanic or Latino:	216	1.13
Central American:	10	0.05
Costa Rican	2	0.01
Honduran	3	0.02
Nicaraguan	1	0.01
Panamanian	3	0.02
Other Central American	1	0.01
Cuban	12	0.06
Dominican Republic	10	0.05
Mexican	36	0.19
Puerto Rican	59	0.31
South American:	21	0.11
Argentinean	4	0.02
Bolivian	2	0.01
Chilean	1	0.01
Colombian	9	0.05
Peruvian	2	0.01
Venezuelan	1	0.01
Other South American	2	0.01
Other Hispanic or Latino	68	0.35
Hungarian	133	0.69
Iranian	15	0.08
Irish	1,001	5.21
Italian	969	5.05
Latvian	14	0.07
Lithuanian	99	0.52
Norwegian	49	0.26
Pennsylvania German	11	0.06
Polish	289	1.51
Portuguese	6	0.03
Russian	103	0.54
Scotch-Irish	209	1.09
Scottish	176	0.92
Serbian	15	0.08
Slavic	34	0.18
Slovak	204	1.06
Slovene	24	0.13
Swedish	42	0.22
Swiss	7	0.04
Ukrainian	34	0.18
United States or American	345	1.80
Welsh	113	0.59
West Indian, excl. Hispanic:	127	0.66
British West Indian	5	0.03
Haitian	5	0.03
Jamaican	83	0.43
Trinidadian and Tobagonian	5	0.03
U.S. Virgin Islander	18	0.09
West Indian	11	0.06
White:	5,912	30.80
Not Hispanic (5,558)	5,838	30.41
Hispanic (57)	74	0.39

Williamsport

Place Type: City
County: Lycoming
Population: 30,706

Ancestry/Race	Number	%
African American/Black:	4,271	13.91
Not Hispanic (3,873)	4,223	13.75
Hispanic (37)	48	0.16
African, sub-Saharan:	234	0.76
African	234	0.76
Am. Ind. or Alaska Nat., not spec.	106	0.35
American Indian tribes, specified:	104	0.34
Apache (1)	5	0.02
Blackfeet (2)	5	0.02
Cherokee (16)	22	0.07
Chippewa (13)	15	0.05
Comanche (1)	1	0.00
Delaware (3)	4	0.01
Iroquois (9)	14	0.05
Latin American Indians (1)	3	0.01
Lumbee (3)	3	0.01
Navajo (1)	1	0.00
Pueblo	2	0.01
Shoshone	1	0.00
Sioux (7)	15	0.05
Yaqui	1	0.00
All other tribes (2)	12	0.04
American Indian tribes, not spec.	23	0.07
Arab:	28	0.09
Lebanese	14	0.05
Syrian	14	0.05
Armenian	6	0.02
Asian:	230	0.75
Chinese, ex. Taiwanese (31)	44	0.14
Filipino (30)	40	0.13
Hmong (1)	1	0.00
Indian (45)	51	0.17
Indonesian (4)	5	0.02
Japanese (8)	14	0.05
Korean (33)	45	0.15
Laotian	1	0.00
Thai (2)	3	0.01
Vietnamese (12)	13	0.04
Other Asian, specified (1)	2	0.01
Other Asian, not specified (8)	11	0.04
Australian	5	0.02
Austrian	70	0.23
Belgian	17	0.06
British	131	0.43
Canadian	33	0.11
Croatian	10	0.03
Czech	52	0.17
Czechoslovakian	56	0.18
Danish	58	0.19
Dutch	1,017	3.31
English	2,288	7.45
European	104	0.34
Finnish	17	0.06
French, except Basque	741	2.41
French Canadian	83	0.27
German	8,979	29.24
Greek	130	0.42
Hawaii Native/Pacific Islander:	12	0.04
Micronesian: (1)	2	0.01
Guamanian/Chamorro (1)	2	0.01
Polynesian: (3)	8	0.03
Native Hawaiian (2)	7	0.02
Samoan (1)	1	0.00
Other Pac. Isl., specified	1	0.00
Other Pac. Isl., not spec.	1	0.00
Hispanic or Latino:	340	1.11
Central American:	12	0.04
Costa Rican	8	0.03
Guatemalan	1	0.00
Panamanian	1	0.00
Salvadoran	1	0.00
Other Central American	1	0.00
Cuban	16	0.05

Notes: 1. Figures in the "Number" column do not add up to the total population due to: a) Ancestry/Race overlap — e.g. persons can report being both White and Irish, b) persons of Hispanic origin can report being any race, c) persons reporting two ancestries are counted in both categories. 2. Numbers in parentheses indicate the number of persons reporting this ancestry/race alone, not in combination with any other ancestry/race. 3. Refer to the Explanation of Data in the front of the book for more detailed information.

Ancestry/Race	Number	%
Dominican Republic	5	0.02
Mexican	86	0.28
Puerto Rican	141	0.46
South American:	8	0.03
Chilean	3	0.01
Colombian	3	0.01
Peruvian	2	0.01
Other Hispanic or Latino	72	0.23
Hungarian	37	0.12
Irish	3,653	11.90
Italian	2,684	8.74
Lithuanian	115	0.37
Northern European	10	0.03
Norwegian	108	0.35
Pennsylvania German	535	1.74
Polish	1,069	3.48
Portuguese	4	0.01
Romanian	31	0.10
Russian	179	0.58
Scandinavian	32	0.10
Scotch-Irish	391	1.27
Scottish	290	0.94
Slavic	9	0.03
Slovak	143	0.47
Swedish	221	0.72
Swiss	51	0.17
Ukrainian	67	0.22
United States or American	1,828	5.95
Welsh	447	1.46
West Indian, excl. Hispanic:	42	0.14
Jamaican	3	0.01
Trinidadian and Tobagonian	11	0.04
U.S. Virgin Islander	21	0.07
West Indian	7	0.02
White:	26,327	85.74
Not Hispanic (25,666)	26,144	85.14
Hispanic (161)	183	0.60
Yugoslavian	19	0.06

Willistown

Place Type: Township
County: Chester
Population: 10,011

Ancestry/Race	Number	%
African American/Black:	225	2.25
Not Hispanic (212)	220	2.20
Hispanic (2)	5	0.05
African, sub-Saharan:	26	0.26
African	26	0.26
Am. Ind. or Alaska Nat., not spec.	5	0.05
American Indian tribes, specified:	10	0.10
Blackfeet	1	0.01
Cherokee	3	0.03
Chippewa (1)	2	0.02
Navajo (2)	2	0.02
Seminole (2)	2	0.02
Arab:	81	0.81
Arab/Arabic	42	0.42
Iraqi	7	0.07
Lebanese	17	0.17
Syrian	15	0.15
Armenian	58	0.58
Asian:	142	1.42
Chinese, ex. Taiwanese (23)	23	0.23
Filipino (8)	9	0.09
Indian (32)	37	0.37
Japanese (3)	3	0.03
Korean (43)	44	0.44
Laotian (2)	2	0.02
Pakistani	1	0.01
Taiwanese (2)	2	0.02
Vietnamese (11)	11	0.11
Other Asian, specified (1)	1	0.01
Other Asian, not specified (2)	9	0.09
Australian	15	0.15
Austrian	72	0.72
Belgian	5	0.05
Brazilian	6	0.06
British	90	0.90
Canadian	49	0.49
Croatian	55	0.55
Czech	36	0.36
Czechoslovakian	56	0.56
Danish	52	0.52
Dutch	123	1.23
Eastern European	18	0.18
English	1,696	16.94
European	75	0.75
French, except Basque	241	2.41
French Canadian	24	0.24
German	2,309	23.06
Greek	121	1.21
Hawaii Native/Pacific Islander:	10	0.10
Polynesian: (10)	10	0.10
Native Hawaiian (10)	10	0.10
Hispanic or Latino:	81	0.81
Cuban	2	0.02
Mexican	22	0.22
Puerto Rican	13	0.13
South American:	16	0.16
Argentinean	9	0.09
Chilean	1	0.01
Paraguayan	1	0.01
Peruvian	1	0.01
Other South American	4	0.04
Other Hispanic or Latino	28	0.28
Hungarian	146	1.46
Iranian	7	0.07
Irish	2,882	28.79
Italian	1,348	13.47
Latvian	25	0.25
Lithuanian	90	0.90
Northern European	5	0.05
Norwegian	115	1.15
Pennsylvania German	53	0.53
Polish	405	4.05
Portuguese	45	0.45
Russian	112	1.12
Scandinavian	5	0.05
Scotch-Irish	346	3.46
Scottish	399	3.99
Slovak	86	0.86
Slovene	8	0.08
Swedish	164	1.64
Swiss	45	0.45
Turkish	5	0.05
Ukrainian	85	0.85
United States or American	362	3.62
Welsh	168	1.68
West Indian, excl. Hispanic:	5	0.05
Haitian	5	0.05
White:	9,618	96.07
Not Hispanic (9,541)	9,563	95.52
Hispanic (55)	55	0.55
Yugoslavian	17	0.17

Willow Grove

Place Type: Census Designated Place
County: Montgomery
Population: 16,234

Ancestry/Race	Number	%
African American/Black:	1,169	7.20
Not Hispanic (1,046)	1,131	6.97
Hispanic (22)	38	0.23
African, sub-Saharan:	59	0.37
African	38	0.24
Nigerian	7	0.04
South African	14	0.09
Am. Ind. or Alaska Nat., not spec.	27	0.17
Albanian	7	0.04
American Indian tribes, specified:	37	0.23
Apache	1	0.01
Blackfeet	5	0.03
Cherokee (4)	19	0.12
Chippewa	2	0.01
Delaware	1	0.01
Iroquois	1	0.01
Navajo	1	0.01
Sioux	2	0.01
All other tribes (2)	5	0.03
American Indian tribes, not spec.	3	0.02
Arab:	64	0.40
Arab/Arabic	13	0.08
Egyptian	16	0.10
Lebanese	19	0.12
Palestinian	6	0.04
Other Arab	10	0.06
Armenian	7	0.04
Asian:	553	3.41
Cambodian (4)	5	0.03
Chinese, ex. Taiwanese (56)	59	0.36
Filipino (42)	50	0.31
Indian (120)	128	0.79
Japanese (27)	38	0.23
Korean (146)	161	0.99
Laotian (18)	22	0.14
Malaysian (1)	2	0.01
Pakistani (11)	11	0.07
Sri Lankan (1)	1	0.01
Taiwanese (6)	6	0.04
Thai (11)	13	0.08
Vietnamese (43)	44	0.27
Other Asian, not specified (5)	13	0.08
Austrian	50	0.31
British	68	0.43
Canadian	4	0.03
Czechoslovakian	6	0.04
Danish	50	0.31
Dutch	152	0.95
Eastern European	43	0.27
English	1,757	11.03
European	118	0.74
French, except Basque	304	1.91
French Canadian	94	0.59
German	4,533	28.45
Greek	91	0.57
Hawaii Native/Pacific Islander:	13	0.08
Micronesian:	3	0.02
Guamanian/Chamorro	3	0.02
Polynesian: (1)	3	0.02
Native Hawaiian	2	0.01
Samoan (1)	1	0.01
Other Pac. Isl., not spec. (3)	7	0.04
Hispanic or Latino:	255	1.57
Central American:	19	0.12
Costa Rican	11	0.07
Guatemalan	1	0.01
Honduran	4	0.02
Panamanian	2	0.01
Salvadoran	1	0.01
Cuban	17	0.10
Dominican Republic	4	0.02
Mexican	40	0.25
Puerto Rican	110	0.68
South American:	14	0.09
Argentinean	2	0.01
Chilean	2	0.01
Colombian	3	0.02
Ecuadorian	1	0.01
Venezuelan	4	0.02
Other South American	2	0.01
Other Hispanic or Latino	51	0.31
Hungarian	221	1.39
Irish	4,289	26.92
Italian	2,268	14.24
Latvian	39	0.24
Lithuanian	170	1.07
Northern European	18	0.11
Norwegian	75	0.47
Pennsylvania German	38	0.24
Polish	883	5.54
Portuguese	67	0.42
Romanian	47	0.30
Russian	420	2.64
Scotch-Irish	265	1.66
Scottish	359	2.25

Notes: 1. Figures in the "Number" column do not add up to the total population due to: a) Ancestry/Race overlap — e.g. persons can report being both White and Irish, b) persons of Hispanic origin can report being any race, c) persons reporting two ancestries are counted in both categories. 2. Numbers in parentheses indicate the number of persons reporting this ancestry/race alone, not in combination with any other ancestry/race. 3. Refer to the Explanation of Data in the front of the book for more detailed information.

Slavic	17	0.11
Slovak	43	0.27
Swedish	129	0.81
Swiss	36	0.23
Ukrainian	122	0.77
United States or American	456	2.86
Welsh	220	1.38
West Indian, excl. Hispanic:	35	0.22
Jamaican	18	0.11
Trinidadian and Tobagonian	17	0.11
White:	14,536	89.54
Not Hispanic (14,241)	14,372	88.53
Hispanic (137)	164	1.01

Windsor

Place Type: Township
County: York
Population: 12,807

Ancestry/Race	Number	%
African American/Black:	72	0.56
Not Hispanic (48)	66	0.52
Hispanic (3)	6	0.05
African, sub-Saharan:	23	0.18
South African	23	0.18
Am. Ind. or Alaska Nat., not spec.	9	0.07
American Indian tribes, specified:	17	0.13
Apache (1)	1	0.01
Blackfeet (1)	3	0.02
Cherokee (1)	4	0.03
Choctaw (2)	3	0.02
Latin American Indians (1)	1	0.01
Sioux (1)	1	0.01
All other tribes (2)	4	0.03
Asian:	94	0.73
Cambodian (2)	2	0.02
Chinese, ex. Taiwanese (14)	14	0.11
Filipino (5)	5	0.04
Indian (8)	10	0.08
Japanese (1)	5	0.04
Korean (20)	22	0.17
Pakistani (5)	6	0.05
Taiwanese (3)	3	0.02
Vietnamese (18)	20	0.16
Other Asian, not specified (1)	7	0.05
British	6	0.05
Czech	29	0.23
Czechoslovakian	28	0.22
Dutch	155	1.21
English	925	7.22
European	144	1.12
Finnish	12	0.09
French, except Basque	452	3.53
French Canadian	8	0.06
German	5,608	43.79
Greek	77	0.60
Hawaii Native/Pacific Islander:	7	0.05
Polynesian: (1)	1	0.01
Native Hawaiian (1)	1	0.01
Other Pac. Isl., not spec. (4)	6	0.05
Hispanic or Latino:	118	0.92
Central American:	4	0.03
Guatemalan	1	0.01
Honduran	3	0.02
Cuban	1	0.01
Mexican	13	0.10
Puerto Rican	58	0.45
South American:	10	0.08
Argentinean	1	0.01
Colombian	2	0.02
Ecuadorian	1	0.01
Peruvian	6	0.05
Other Hispanic or Latino	32	0.25
Hungarian	12	0.09
Irish	1,206	9.42
Italian	723	5.65
Lithuanian	56	0.44
Norwegian	76	0.59
Pennsylvania German	119	0.93
Polish	297	2.32
Scandinavian	19	0.15
Scotch-Irish	332	2.59
Scottish	206	1.61
Slovak	38	0.30
Swedish	29	0.23
Swiss	54	0.42
Ukrainian	29	0.23
United States or American	1,243	9.71
Welsh	76	0.59
White:	12,629	98.61
Not Hispanic (12,486)	12,539	97.91
Hispanic (70)	90	0.70
Yugoslavian	23	0.18

Woodlyn

Place Type: Census Designated Place
County: Delaware
Population: 10,036

Ancestry/Race	Number	%
African American/Black:	976	9.72
Not Hispanic (903)	950	9.47
Hispanic (15)	26	0.26
African, sub-Saharan:	220	2.20
African	192	1.92
Sierra Leonean	8	0.08
Other sub-Saharan African	20	0.20
Am. Ind. or Alaska Nat., not spec.	28	0.28
American Indian tribes, specified:	17	0.17
Blackfeet	3	0.03
Cherokee (1)	4	0.04
Comanche (1)	1	0.01
Crow	3	0.03
Lumbee	1	0.01
Navajo (3)	3	0.03
All other tribes	2	0.02
American Indian tribes, not spec.	6	0.06
Arab:	75	0.75
Egyptian	33	0.33
Lebanese	42	0.42
Armenian	17	0.17
Asian:	137	1.37
Chinese, ex. Taiwanese (21)	25	0.25
Filipino (10)	12	0.12
Hmong (1)	1	0.01
Indian (37)	40	0.40
Indonesian	1	0.01
Japanese (5)	8	0.08
Korean (22)	23	0.23
Laotian (1)	1	0.01
Pakistani (12)	13	0.13
Taiwanese (2)	2	0.02
Thai	3	0.03
Vietnamese (5)	6	0.06
Other Asian, not specified	2	0.02
Austrian	18	0.18
Belgian	9	0.09
British	47	0.47
Canadian	15	0.15
Czech	17	0.17
Danish	30	0.30
Dutch	176	1.76
English	1,061	10.60
European	6	0.06
Finnish	5	0.05
French, except Basque	249	2.49
French Canadian	8	0.08
German	1,474	14.73
Greek	29	0.29
Hawaii Native/Pacific Islander:	12	0.12
Micronesian: (3)	3	0.03
Guamanian/Chamorro (3)	3	0.03
Polynesian: (4)	7	0.07
Native Hawaiian (3)	6	0.06
Samoan (1)	1	0.01
Other Pac. Isl., not spec.	2	0.02
Hispanic or Latino:	138	1.38
Central American:	3	0.03
Salvadoran	1	0.01
Other Central American	2	0.02
Cuban	5	0.05
Mexican	38	0.38
Puerto Rican	65	0.65
South American:	13	0.13
Argentinean	6	0.06
Chilean	1	0.01
Colombian	5	0.05
Peruvian	1	0.01
Other Hispanic or Latino	14	0.14
Hungarian	47	0.47
Irish	3,386	33.83
Italian	2,061	20.59
Latvian	18	0.18
Lithuanian	82	0.82
Maltese	8	0.08
Pennsylvania German	76	0.76
Polish	768	7.67
Portuguese	8	0.08
Romanian	6	0.06
Russian	143	1.43
Scandinavian	11	0.11
Scotch-Irish	195	1.95
Scottish	127	1.27
Slavic	32	0.32
Slovak	74	0.74
Swedish	74	0.74
Swiss	8	0.08
Ukrainian	197	1.97
United States or American	345	3.45
Welsh	330	3.30
West Indian, excl. Hispanic:	10	0.10
Barbadian	10	0.10
White:	8,927	88.95
Not Hispanic (8,737)	8,832	88.00
Hispanic (83)	95	0.95

Yeadon

Place Type: Borough
County: Delaware
Population: 11,762

Ancestry/Race	Number	%
African American/Black:	9,731	82.73
Not Hispanic (9,459)	9,672	82.23
Hispanic (41)	59	0.50
African, sub-Saharan:	777	6.59
African	437	3.70
Ethiopian	93	0.79
Ghanian	49	0.42
Liberian	109	0.92
Nigerian	31	0.26
Sierra Leonean	15	0.13
Other sub-Saharan African	43	0.36
Am. Ind. or Alaska Nat., not spec.	67	0.57
American Indian tribes, specified:	34	0.29
Apache (1)	1	0.01
Blackfeet	1	0.01
Cherokee (1)	14	0.12
Chippewa	1	0.01
Iroquois	1	0.01
Lumbee (1)	1	0.01
Seminole	4	0.03
Sioux	1	0.01
Yaqui	3	0.03
All other tribes (3)	7	0.06
American Indian tribes, not spec.	4	0.03
Armenian	7	0.06
Asian:	145	1.23
Bangladeshi (3)	3	0.03
Cambodian (3)	3	0.03
Chinese, ex. Taiwanese (18)	28	0.24
Filipino (10)	18	0.15
Indian (35)	46	0.39
Japanese (3)	5	0.04
Korean (4)	4	0.03
Laotian (4)	4	0.03
Thai (3)	11	0.09

Notes: 1. Figures in the "Number" column do not add up to the total population due to: a) Ancestry/Race overlap — e.g. persons can report being both White and Irish, b) persons of Hispanic origin can report being any race, c) persons reporting two ancestries are counted in both categories. 2. Numbers in parentheses indicate the number of persons reporting this ancestry/race alone, not in combination with any other ancestry/race. 3. Refer to the Explanation of Data in the front of the book for more detailed information.

Ancestry/Race	Number	%
Vietnamese (15)	17	0.14
Other Asian, not specified (4)	6	0.05
British	6	0.05
Czech	5	0.04
Czechoslovakian	8	0.07
English	274	2.32
European	9	0.08
French, except Basque	29	0.25
German	329	2.79
Hawaii Native/Pacific Islander:	16	0.14
Polynesian:	2	0.02
Native Hawaiian	2	0.02
Other Pac. Isl., not spec. (1)	14	0.12
Hispanic or Latino:	120	1.02
Central American:	11	0.09
Costa Rican	1	0.01
Honduran	6	0.05
Panamanian	4	0.03
Cuban	6	0.05
Dominican Republic	3	0.03
Mexican	9	0.08
Puerto Rican	54	0.46
South American:	3	0.03
Venezuelan	3	0.03
Other Hispanic or Latino	34	0.29
Irish	612	5.19
Italian	512	4.34
Lithuanian	14	0.12
Pennsylvania German	5	0.04
Polish	67	0.57
Russian	14	0.12
Scotch-Irish	90	0.76
Scottish	36	0.31
Swedish	31	0.26
Swiss	12	0.10
Ukrainian	9	0.08
United States or American	199	1.69
Welsh	39	0.33
West Indian, excl. Hispanic:	507	4.30
Barbadian	27	0.23
British West Indian	24	0.20
Haitian	95	0.81
Jamaican	297	2.52
Trinidadian and Tobagonian	64	0.54
White:	1,939	16.49
Not Hispanic (1,809)	1,907	16.21
Hispanic (21)	32	0.27

York

Place Type: City
County: York
Population: 40,862

Ancestry/Race	Number	%
African American/Black:	11,269	27.58
Not Hispanic (9,798)	10,612	25.97
Hispanic (472)	657	1.61
African, sub-Saharan:	601	1.47
African	529	1.29
Ghanian	22	0.05
Liberian	2	0.00
Nigerian	29	0.07
Sierra Leonean	12	0.03
Ugandan	7	0.02
Am. Ind. or Alaska Nat., not spec.	191	0.47
Albanian	5	0.01
American Indian tribes, specified:	211	0.52
Apache (2)	12	0.03
Blackfeet (2)	11	0.03
Cherokee (14)	89	0.22
Cheyenne	1	0.00
Chippewa (1)	2	0.00
Choctaw (1)	1	0.00
Cree (2)	2	0.00
Delaware (7)	11	0.03
Houma	1	0.00
Iroquois (1)	10	0.02
Latin American Indians (9)	25	0.06
Navajo (1)	2	0.00
Pueblo (1)	2	0.00
Seminole	1	0.00
Sioux (4)	7	0.02
All other tribes (17)	34	0.08
American Indian tribes, not spec.	28	0.07
Arab:	32	0.08
Arab/Arabic	11	0.03
Egyptian	4	0.01
Lebanese	5	0.01
Moroccan	12	0.03
Armenian	7	0.02
Asian:	749	1.83
Bangladeshi (9)	11	0.03
Cambodian (118)	162	0.40
Chinese, ex. Taiwanese (74)	99	0.24
Filipino (23)	40	0.10
Indian (67)	100	0.24
Indonesian (1)	2	0.00
Japanese (18)	32	0.08
Korean (18)	28	0.07
Laotian (5)	7	0.02
Malaysian (1)	1	0.00
Thai (2)	4	0.01
Vietnamese (216)	236	0.58
Other Asian, not specified (14)	27	0.07
Australian	8	0.02
Austrian	56	0.14
Brazilian	30	0.07
British	96	0.23
Canadian	17	0.04
Croatian	6	0.01
Czech	34	0.08
Czechoslovakian	15	0.04
Danish	7	0.02
Dutch	529	1.29
English	1,604	3.92
Estonian	4	0.01
European	219	0.54
Finnish	17	0.04
French, except Basque	268	0.66
French Canadian	25	0.06
German	8,641	21.13
German Russian	8	0.02
Greek	198	0.48
Hawaii Native/Pacific Islander:	73	0.18
Micronesian: (18)	21	0.05
Guamanian/Chamorro (7)	10	0.02
Other Micronesian (11)	11	0.03
Polynesian: (7)	26	0.06
Native Hawaiian (3)	18	0.04
Samoan (4)	8	0.02
Other Pac. Isl., not spec. (2)	26	0.06
Hispanic or Latino:	7,026	17.19
Central American:	94	0.23
Costa Rican	8	0.02
Guatemalan	2	0.00
Honduran	13	0.03
Nicaraguan	4	0.01
Panamanian	20	0.05
Salvadoran	42	0.10
Other Central American	5	0.01
Cuban	94	0.23
Dominican Republic	241	0.59
Mexican	738	1.81
Puerto Rican	4,977	12.18
South American:	62	0.15
Argentinean	4	0.01
Bolivian	1	0.00
Chilean	9	0.02
Colombian	24	0.06
Ecuadorian	16	0.04
Peruvian	3	0.01
Venezuelan	4	0.01
Other South American	1	0.00
Other Hispanic or Latino	820	2.01
Hungarian	35	0.09
Iranian	11	0.03
Irish	2,278	5.57
Israeli	47	0.11
Italian	1,345	3.29
Latvian	6	0.01
Lithuanian	32	0.08
Norwegian	73	0.18
Pennsylvania German	307	0.75
Polish	761	1.86
Portuguese	27	0.07
Romanian	26	0.06
Russian	64	0.16
Scandinavian	6	0.01
Scotch-Irish	436	1.07
Scottish	304	0.74
Slavic	11	0.03
Slovak	15	0.04
Swedish	128	0.31
Swiss	163	0.40
Ukrainian	37	0.09
United States or American	2,682	6.56
Welsh	226	0.55
West Indian, excl. Hispanic:	164	0.40
Barbadian	4	0.01
Jamaican	129	0.32
Trinidadian and Tobagonian	10	0.02
West Indian	21	0.05
White:	25,647	62.76
Not Hispanic (22,142)	23,029	56.36
Hispanic (2,274)	2,618	6.41
Yugoslavian	23	0.06

York

Place Type: Township
County: York
Population: 23,637

Ancestry/Race	Number	%
African American/Black:	412	1.74
Not Hispanic (349)	392	1.66
Hispanic (10)	20	0.08
African, sub-Saharan:	27	0.11
African	9	0.04
Ethiopian	5	0.02
South African	13	0.05
Am. Ind. or Alaska Nat., not spec.	31	0.13
American Indian tribes, specified:	40	0.17
Apache (1)	3	0.01
Blackfeet	2	0.01
Cherokee (1)	13	0.05
Cheyenne	1	0.00
Chippewa (1)	1	0.00
Crow	2	0.01
Delaware (6)	6	0.03
Iroquois	1	0.00
Latin American Indians	1	0.00
Potawatomi (2)	2	0.01
Pueblo (1)	1	0.00
Seminole (1)	1	0.00
Shoshone	1	0.00
Sioux (1)	1	0.00
All other tribes (1)	4	0.02
Arab:	16	0.07
Lebanese	8	0.03
Syrian	8	0.03
Asian:	349	1.48
Cambodian (1)	2	0.01
Chinese, ex. Taiwanese (41)	51	0.22
Filipino (8)	16	0.07
Indian (93)	99	0.42
Japanese (11)	21	0.09
Korean (67)	78	0.33
Laotian (2)	3	0.01
Malaysian	1	0.00
Pakistani (4)	4	0.02
Sri Lankan (9)	9	0.04
Taiwanese (1)	2	0.01
Vietnamese (42)	46	0.19
Other Asian, specified (2)	4	0.02
Other Asian, not specified (9)	13	0.05
Australian	9	0.04
Austrian	75	0.32
Belgian	9	0.04

Notes: 1. Figures in the "Number" column do not add up to the total population due to: a) Ancestry/Race overlap — e.g. persons can report being both White and Irish, b) persons of Hispanic origin can report being any race, c) persons reporting two ancestries are counted in both categories. 2. Numbers in parentheses indicate the number of persons reporting this ancestry/race alone, not in combination with any other ancestry/race. 3. Refer to the Explanation of Data in the front of the book for more detailed information.

Ancestry/Race	Number	%
British	59	0.25
Canadian	29	0.12
Croatian	8	0.03
Czech	49	0.21
Czechoslovakian	53	0.22
Danish	23	0.10
Dutch	517	2.19
English	2,246	9.50
European	191	0.81
French, except Basque	504	2.13
French Canadian	51	0.22
German	10,192	43.12
Greek	112	0.47
Hawaii Native/Pacific Islander:	18	0.08
Polynesian: (1)	6	0.03
Native Hawaiian (1)	6	0.03
Other Pac. Isl., not spec. (5)	12	0.05
Hispanic or Latino:	337	1.43
Central American:	20	0.08
Costa Rican	6	0.03
Guatemalan	2	0.01
Nicaraguan	4	0.02
Panamanian	2	0.01
Salvadoran	6	0.03
Cuban	18	0.08
Dominican Republic	3	0.01
Mexican	61	0.26
Puerto Rican	166	0.70
South American:	24	0.10
Bolivian	2	0.01
Chilean	1	0.00
Colombian	11	0.05
Peruvian	7	0.03
Uruguayan	2	0.01
Venezuelan	1	0.00
Other Hispanic or Latino	45	0.19
Hungarian	69	0.29
Irish	2,980	12.61
Italian	1,778	7.52
Lithuanian	44	0.19
Norwegian	137	0.58
Pennsylvania German	196	0.83
Polish	767	3.24
Portuguese	70	0.30
Romanian	26	0.11
Russian	129	0.55
Scandinavian	11	0.05
Scotch-Irish	553	2.34
Scottish	448	1.90
Serbian	10	0.04
Slavic	67	0.28
Slovak	167	0.71
Slovene	14	0.06
Swedish	173	0.73
Swiss	148	0.63
Ukrainian	91	0.38
United States or American	1,850	7.83
Welsh	255	1.08
West Indian, excl. Hispanic:	8	0.03
Jamaican	2	0.01
Trinidadian and Tobagonian	6	0.03
White:	22,839	96.62
Not Hispanic (22,481)	22,601	95.62
Hispanic (199)	238	1.01
Yugoslavian	56	0.24

Barrington

Place Type: Town
County: Bristol
Population: 16,819

Ancestry/Race	Number	%
Afghan	8	0.05
African American/Black:	141	0.84
Not Hispanic (111)	132	0.78
Hispanic (4)	9	0.05
African, sub-Saharan:	91	0.54
African	25	0.15
Cape Verdean	21	0.12
Kenyan	30	0.18
South African	15	0.09
Am. Ind. or Alaska Nat., not spec.	16	0.10
American Indian tribes, specified:	35	0.21
Apache	1	0.01
Blackfeet	3	0.02
Cherokee (4)	10	0.06
Chippewa (2)	2	0.01
Delaware (2)	2	0.01
Iroquois (2)	2	0.01
Osage	1	0.01
Potawatomi	1	0.01
All other tribes (3)	13	0.08
American Indian tribes, not spec.	2	0.01
Arab:	85	0.51
Egyptian	34	0.20
Lebanese	38	0.23
Syrian	13	0.08
Armenian	121	0.72
Asian:	361	2.15
Cambodian (1)	1	0.01
Chinese, ex. Taiwanese (118)	136	0.81
Filipino (23)	29	0.17
Indian (76)	83	0.49
Japanese (17)	33	0.20
Korean (38)	41	0.24
Laotian (1)	3	0.02
Sri Lankan (2)	3	0.02
Taiwanese (2)	2	0.01
Thai (7)	8	0.05
Vietnamese (6)	8	0.05
Other Asian, not specified (3)	14	0.08
Austrian	103	0.61
Belgian	15	0.09
British	132	0.78
Canadian	134	0.80
Celtic	24	0.14
Croatian	9	0.05
Czech	9	0.05
Czechoslovakian	6	0.04
Danish	129	0.77
Dutch	135	0.80
Eastern European	43	0.26
English	3,587	21.33
Estonian	23	0.14
European	95	0.56
Finnish	13	0.08
French, except Basque	1,182	7.03
French Canadian	602	3.58
German	1,687	10.03
Greek	164	0.98
Hawaii Native/Pacific Islander:	8	0.05
Polynesian:	5	0.03
Native Hawaiian	5	0.03
Other Pac. Isl., not spec.	3	0.02
Hispanic or Latino:	177	1.05
Central American:	9	0.05
Costa Rican	1	0.01
Guatemalan	1	0.01
Nicaraguan	4	0.02
Panamanian	3	0.02
Cuban	27	0.16
Dominican Republic	10	0.06
Mexican	15	0.09
Puerto Rican	35	0.21
South American:	31	0.18
Argentinean	5	0.03
Chilean	5	0.03
Colombian	11	0.07
Ecuadorian	3	0.02
Peruvian	2	0.01
Venezuelan	3	0.02
Other South American	2	0.01
Other Hispanic or Latino	50	0.30
Hungarian	96	0.57
Icelander	19	0.11
Iranian	9	0.05
Irish	4,004	23.81
Israeli	8	0.05
Italian	3,284	19.53
Latvian	7	0.04
Lithuanian	86	0.51
Maltese	18	0.11
Norwegian	176	1.05
Pennsylvania German	14	0.08
Polish	746	4.44
Portuguese	1,291	7.68
Romanian	4	0.02
Russian	432	2.57
Scandinavian	14	0.08
Scotch-Irish	467	2.78
Scottish	634	3.77
Slovak	32	0.19
Swedish	368	2.19
Swiss	46	0.27
Ukrainian	65	0.39
United States or American	561	3.34
Welsh	105	0.62
West Indian, excl. Hispanic:	40	0.24
Barbadian	8	0.05
Jamaican	32	0.19
White:	16,325	97.06
Not Hispanic (16,092)	16,195	96.29
Hispanic (117)	130	0.77

Bristol

Place Type: Census Designated Place
County: Bristol
Population: 22,469

Ancestry/Race	Number	%
African American/Black:	194	0.86
Not Hispanic (132)	179	0.80
Hispanic (8)	15	0.07
African, sub-Saharan:	38	0.17
Cape Verdean	38	0.17
Am. Ind. or Alaska Nat., not spec.	45	0.20
American Indian tribes, specified:	44	0.20
Apache	1	0.00
Cherokee (9)	17	0.08
Chickasaw	2	0.01
Iroquois	2	0.01
Latin American Indians (2)	2	0.01
Potawatomi (1)	1	0.00
Pueblo (1)	1	0.00
Yakama (1)	1	0.00
All other tribes (4)	17	0.08
American Indian tribes, not spec.	4	0.02
Arab:	33	0.15
Lebanese	17	0.08
Syrian	8	0.04
Other Arab	8	0.04
Armenian	31	0.14
Asian:	207	0.92
Cambodian (5)	6	0.03
Chinese, ex. Taiwanese (54)	64	0.28
Filipino (28)	50	0.22
Indian (15)	22	0.10
Japanese (9)	12	0.05
Korean (16)	22	0.10
Laotian (2)	2	0.01
Pakistani (1)	4	0.02
Taiwanese (1)	1	0.00
Thai (1)	2	0.01
Vietnamese (8)	8	0.04
Other Asian, specified	1	0.00
Other Asian, not specified (5)	13	0.06
Australian	64	0.28
Austrian	24	0.11
Belgian	17	0.08
British	49	0.22
Canadian	87	0.39
Croatian	10	0.04
Czech	7	0.03
Czechoslovakian	9	0.04
Danish	38	0.17
Dutch	137	0.61
Eastern European	25	0.11
English	2,365	10.53

Notes: 1. Figures in the "Number" column do not add up to the total population due to: a) Ancestry/Race overlap — e.g. persons can report being both White and Irish, b) persons of Hispanic origin can report being any race, c) persons reporting two ancestries are counted in both categories. 2. Numbers in parentheses indicate the number of persons reporting this ancestry/race alone, not in combination with any other ancestry/race. 3. Refer to the Explanation of Data in the front of the book for more detailed information.

European	35	0.16
Finnish	22	0.10
French, except Basque	1,903	8.47
French Canadian	774	3.44
German	1,074	4.78
Greek	146	0.65
Hawaii Native/Pacific Islander:	32	0.14
Micronesian: (1)	1	0.00
Guamanian/Chamorro (1)	1	0.00
Polynesian: (8)	8	0.04
Samoan (8)	8	0.04
Other Pac. Isl., not spec. (1)	23	0.10
Hispanic or Latino:	289	1.29
Central American:	10	0.04
Costa Rican	1	0.00
Guatemalan	4	0.02
Nicaraguan	1	0.00
Panamanian	3	0.01
Salvadoran	1	0.00
Cuban	12	0.05
Dominican Republic	20	0.09
Mexican	90	0.40
Puerto Rican	67	0.30
South American:	29	0.13
Argentinean	8	0.04
Colombian	8	0.04
Ecuadorian	3	0.01
Peruvian	4	0.02
Venezuelan	5	0.02
Other South American	1	0.00
Other Hispanic or Latino	61	0.27
Hungarian	59	0.26
Iranian	9	0.04
Irish	3,195	14.22
Italian	4,758	21.18
Lithuanian	48	0.21
Maltese	5	0.02
Norwegian	62	0.28
Polish	755	3.36
Portuguese	8,266	36.79
Russian	102	0.45
Scotch-Irish	178	0.79
Scottish	377	1.68
Slavic	14	0.06
Slovene	9	0.04
Swedish	298	1.33
Swiss	17	0.08
Ukrainian	45	0.20
United States or American	500	2.23
Welsh	39	0.17
West Indian, excl. Hispanic:	14	0.06
Jamaican	6	0.03
West Indian	8	0.04
White:	22,042	98.10
Not Hispanic (21,628)	21,831	97.16
Hispanic (198)	211	0.94
Yugoslavian	18	0.08

Burrillville

Place Type: Town
County: Providence
Population: 15,796

Ancestry/Race	Number	%
African American/Black:	48	0.30
Not Hispanic (28)	41	0.26
Hispanic (6)	7	0.04
African, sub-Saharan:	6	0.04
Cape Verdean	6	0.04
Am. Ind. or Alaska Nat., not spec.	22	0.14
Albanian	43	0.27
American Indian tribes, specified:	48	0.30
Apache (1)	1	0.01
Blackfeet (2)	8	0.05
Cherokee	6	0.04
Chippewa	4	0.03
Choctaw	1	0.01
Cree (4)	7	0.04
Creek	1	0.01
Iroquois (1)	3	0.02
Latin American Indians (2)	2	0.01
Sioux	1	0.01
Ute (1)	1	0.01
All other tribes (7)	13	0.08
American Indian tribes, not spec.	1	0.01
Arab:	51	0.32
Lebanese	36	0.23
Syrian	15	0.09
Armenian	68	0.43
Asian:	53	0.34
Cambodian (2)	5	0.03
Chinese, ex. Taiwanese (10)	12	0.08
Filipino (4)	5	0.03
Indian (4)	8	0.05
Japanese (9)	9	0.06
Korean (1)	2	0.01
Laotian	4	0.03
Thai (1)	1	0.01
Vietnamese (2)	4	0.03
Other Asian, not specified (1)	3	0.02
Austrian	6	0.04
Belgian	43	0.27
Brazilian	6	0.04
British	18	0.11
Bulgarian	17	0.11
Canadian	96	0.61
Czechoslovakian	22	0.14
Danish	18	0.11
Dutch	80	0.51
English	2,433	15.40
European	19	0.12
Finnish	7	0.04
French, except Basque	4,579	28.99
French Canadian	2,866	18.14
German	961	6.08
Greek	77	0.49
Hawaii Native/Pacific Islander:	6	0.04
Micronesian: (3)	3	0.02
Guamanian/Chamorro (3)	3	0.02
Polynesian: (1)	3	0.02
Native Hawaiian (1)	1	0.01
Samoan	2	0.01
Hispanic or Latino:	132	0.84
Central American:	3	0.02
Guatemalan	2	0.01
Salvadoran	1	0.01
Cuban	3	0.02
Dominican Republic	4	0.03
Mexican	42	0.27
Puerto Rican	29	0.18
South American:	12	0.08
Colombian	9	0.06
Ecuadorian	1	0.01
Paraguayan	2	0.01
Other Hispanic or Latino	39	0.25
Hungarian	27	0.17
Irish	2,935	18.58
Italian	2,064	13.07
Lithuanian	56	0.35
Northern European	6	0.04
Norwegian	37	0.23
Polish	988	6.25
Portuguese	493	3.12
Russian	21	0.13
Scotch-Irish	199	1.26
Scottish	305	1.93
Swedish	323	2.04
Swiss	18	0.11
Ukrainian	45	0.28
United States or American	541	3.42
Welsh	72	0.46
White:	15,650	99.08
Not Hispanic (15,475)	15,549	98.44
Hispanic (94)	101	0.64
Yugoslavian	16	0.10

Central Falls

Place Type: City
County: Providence
Population: 18,928

Ancestry/Race	Number	%
African American/Black:	1,477	7.80
Not Hispanic (816)	1,053	5.56
Hispanic (285)	424	2.24
African, sub-Saharan:	1,034	5.46
African	41	0.22
Cape Verdean	961	5.08
Ghanian	6	0.03
Liberian	19	0.10
Other sub-Saharan African	7	0.04
Alaska Native tribes, specified:	1	0.01
Aleut (1)	1	0.01
Am. Ind. or Alaska Nat., not spec.	107	0.57
American Indian tribes, specified:	73	0.39
Apache	5	0.03
Blackfeet	2	0.01
Cherokee	9	0.05
Choctaw	1	0.01
Cree (1)	1	0.01
Iroquois (2)	5	0.03
Latin American Indians (16)	19	0.10
Pueblo (1)	1	0.01
Seminole	1	0.01
Sioux	2	0.01
All other tribes (15)	27	0.14
American Indian tribes, not spec.	19	0.10
Arab:	172	0.91
Arab/Arabic	6	0.03
Lebanese	26	0.14
Syrian	140	0.74
Armenian	23	0.12
Asian:	182	0.96
Cambodian (30)	31	0.16
Chinese, ex. Taiwanese (35)	43	0.23
Filipino (2)	9	0.05
Indian (26)	36	0.19
Indonesian (1)	1	0.01
Japanese	1	0.01
Korean (4)	5	0.03
Vietnamese (5)	5	0.03
Other Asian, specified (2)	2	0.01
Other Asian, not specified (23)	49	0.26
Assyrian/Chaldean/Syriac	16	0.08
Bulgarian	12	0.06
Canadian	73	0.39
Carpatho Rusyn	4	0.02
Czech	7	0.04
Danish	6	0.03
Dutch	29	0.15
English	446	2.36
European	3	0.02
French, except Basque	1,310	6.92
French Canadian	1,305	6.89
German	80	0.42
Hawaii Native/Pacific Islander:	36	0.19
Micronesian: (2)	2	0.01
Guamanian/Chamorro (2)	2	0.01
Polynesian: (4)	9	0.05
Native Hawaiian	5	0.03
Samoan (4)	4	0.02
Other Pac. Isl., not spec. (2)	25	0.13
Hispanic or Latino:	9,041	47.77
Central American:	1,420	7.50
Costa Rican	1	0.01
Guatemalan	1,202	6.35
Honduran	30	0.16
Nicaraguan	3	0.02
Panamanian	5	0.03
Salvadoran	156	0.82
Other Central American	23	0.12
Cuban	38	0.20
Dominican Republic	575	3.04
Mexican	677	3.58
Puerto Rican	2,249	11.88

Notes: 1. Figures in the "Number" column do not add up to the total population due to: a) Ancestry/Race overlap — e.g. persons can report being both White and Irish, b) persons of Hispanic origin can report being any race, c) persons reporting two ancestries are counted in both categories. 2. Numbers in parentheses indicate the number of persons reporting this ancestry/race alone, not in combination with any other ancestry/race. 3. Refer to the Explanation of Data in the front of the book for more detailed information.

Ancestry/Race	Number	%
South American:	1,999	10.56
Argentinean	18	0.10
Bolivian	16	0.08
Chilean	2	0.01
Colombian	1,882	9.94
Ecuadorian	13	0.07
Peruvian	22	0.12
Venezuelan	44	0.23
Other South American	2	0.01
Other Hispanic or Latino	2,083	11.00
Irish	981	5.18
Israeli	6	0.03
Italian	458	2.42
Lithuanian	9	0.05
Polish	533	2.82
Portuguese	1,633	8.63
Russian	7	0.04
Scotch-Irish	26	0.14
Scottish	58	0.31
Slovene	12	0.06
Swedish	12	0.06
Ukrainian	48	0.25
United States or American	895	4.73
West Indian, excl. Hispanic:	22	0.12
Haitian	6	0.03
Jamaican	8	0.04
West Indian	8	0.04
White:	11,909	62.92
Not Hispanic (7,577)	8,078	42.68
Hispanic (3,243)	3,831	20.24

Coventry

Place Type: Town
County: Kent
Population: 33,668

Ancestry/Race	Number	%
African American/Black:	224	0.67
Not Hispanic (122)	213	0.63
Hispanic (9)	11	0.03
African, sub-Saharan:	41	0.12
African	9	0.03
Cape Verdean	19	0.06
Nigerian	13	0.04
Am. Ind. or Alaska Nat., not spec.	55	0.16
American Indian tribes, specified:	111	0.33
Apache	2	0.01
Blackfeet	7	0.02
Cherokee (5)	19	0.06
Chippewa	1	0.00
Creek	2	0.01
Delaware (1)	2	0.01
Iroquois (1)	4	0.01
Latin American Indians (5)	5	0.01
Lumbee	1	0.00
Navajo	1	0.00
Sioux (1)	3	0.01
Ute (2)	2	0.01
All other tribes (23)	62	0.18
American Indian tribes, not spec.	13	0.04
Arab:	78	0.23
Lebanese	6	0.02
Syrian	72	0.21
Armenian	183	0.54
Asian:	279	0.83
Cambodian (18)	21	0.06
Chinese, ex. Taiwanese (58)	81	0.24
Filipino (21)	52	0.15
Indian (23)	30	0.09
Japanese (11)	31	0.09
Korean (19)	22	0.07
Laotian (13)	17	0.05
Pakistani (1)	2	0.01
Taiwanese (2)	2	0.01
Thai (4)	5	0.01
Vietnamese (10)	12	0.04
Other Asian, not specified (3)	4	0.01
Australian	10	0.03
Austrian	107	0.32
Belgian	22	0.07
Brazilian	8	0.02
British	48	0.14
Canadian	198	0.59
Czech	23	0.07
Czechoslovakian	12	0.04
Danish	21	0.06
Dutch	246	0.73
English	5,977	17.77
European	12	0.04
Finnish	56	0.17
French, except Basque	6,548	19.47
French Canadian	2,876	8.55
German	2,488	7.40
Greek	306	0.91
Hawaii Native/Pacific Islander:	19	0.06
Micronesian: (4)	5	0.01
Guamanian/Chamorro (4)	5	0.01
Polynesian: (3)	6	0.02
Native Hawaiian (3)	6	0.02
Other Pac. Isl., not spec. (2)	8	0.02
Hispanic or Latino:	385	1.14
Central American:	32	0.10
Costa Rican	6	0.02
Guatemalan	10	0.03
Honduran	10	0.03
Nicaraguan	3	0.01
Panamanian	1	0.00
Salvadoran	2	0.01
Cuban	28	0.08
Dominican Republic	12	0.04
Mexican	80	0.24
Puerto Rican	129	0.38
South American:	25	0.07
Argentinean	6	0.02
Bolivian	4	0.01
Chilean	1	0.00
Colombian	2	0.01
Ecuadorian	2	0.01
Uruguayan	3	0.01
Venezuelan	1	0.00
Other South American	6	0.02
Other Hispanic or Latino	79	0.23
Hungarian	113	0.34
Irish	7,898	23.48
Italian	6,547	19.46
Lithuanian	204	0.61
Norwegian	101	0.30
Polish	2,013	5.98
Portuguese	2,507	7.45
Romanian	32	0.10
Russian	162	0.48
Scandinavian	46	0.14
Scotch-Irish	452	1.34
Scottish	717	2.13
Slovak	11	0.03
Swedish	1,045	3.11
Swiss	28	0.08
Turkish	6	0.02
Ukrainian	93	0.28
United States or American	1,217	3.62
Welsh	69	0.21
White:	33,156	98.48
Not Hispanic (32,605)	32,881	97.66
Hispanic (254)	275	0.82
Yugoslavian	8	0.02

Cranston

Place Type: City
County: Providence
Population: 79,269

Ancestry/Race	Number	%
African American/Black:	3,361	4.24
Not Hispanic (2,574)	2,929	3.70
Hispanic (352)	432	0.54
African, sub-Saharan:	656	0.83
African	112	0.14
Cape Verdean	400	0.50
Ethiopian	13	0.02
Ghanian	30	0.04
Liberian	9	0.01
Nigerian	73	0.09
Other sub-Saharan African	19	0.02
Alaska Native tribes, specified:	2	0.00
Alaska Athabascan (1)	1	0.00
Aleut (1)	1	0.00
Am. Ind. or Alaska Nat., not spec.	204	0.26
Albanian	40	0.05
American Indian tribes, specified:	267	0.34
Apache	1	0.00
Blackfeet (4)	9	0.01
Cherokee (6)	29	0.04
Chippewa (3)	4	0.01
Cree (2)	2	0.00
Delaware (6)	11	0.01
Iroquois (2)	8	0.01
Kiowa	2	0.00
Latin American Indians (6)	11	0.01
Lumbee (4)	4	0.01
Menominee (2)	2	0.00
Navajo (1)	1	0.00
Potawatomi (2)	2	0.00
Pueblo (2)	2	0.00
Seminole	1	0.00
Sioux (6)	6	0.01
All other tribes (100)	172	0.22
American Indian tribes, not spec.	18	0.02
Arab:	615	0.78
Arab/Arabic	55	0.07
Egyptian	59	0.07
Jordanian	28	0.04
Lebanese	249	0.31
Syrian	224	0.28
Armenian	1,555	1.96
Asian:	2,974	3.75
Bangladeshi (4)	4	0.01
Cambodian (862)	987	1.25
Chinese, ex. Taiwanese (619)	681	0.86
Filipino (247)	305	0.38
Hmong (62)	69	0.09
Indian (222)	258	0.33
Indonesian (5)	5	0.01
Japanese (46)	68	0.09
Korean (105)	121	0.15
Laotian (99)	119	0.15
Malaysian (5)	6	0.01
Pakistani (20)	22	0.03
Sri Lankan (1)	1	0.00
Taiwanese (3)	4	0.01
Thai (19)	27	0.03
Vietnamese (138)	159	0.20
Other Asian, specified (9)	10	0.01
Other Asian, not specified (74)	128	0.16
Australian	36	0.05
Austrian	195	0.25
Belgian	32	0.04
Brazilian	43	0.05
British	77	0.10
Bulgarian	39	0.05
Canadian	110	0.14
Celtic	14	0.02
Czech	40	0.05
Czechoslovakian	24	0.03
Danish	89	0.11
Dutch	275	0.35
Eastern European	78	0.10
English	8,140	10.27
Estonian	6	0.01
European	140	0.18
Finnish	59	0.07
French, except Basque	6,157	7.77
French Canadian	2,343	2.96
German	3,029	3.82
Greek	910	1.15
Hawaii Native/Pacific Islander:	78	0.10
Micronesian: (10)	11	0.01
Guamanian/Chamorro (10)	11	0.01
Polynesian: (13)	23	0.03

Notes: 1. Figures in the "Number" column do not add up to the total population due to: a) Ancestry/Race overlap — e.g. persons can report being both White and Irish, b) persons of Hispanic origin can report being any race, c) persons reporting two ancestries are counted in both categories. 2. Numbers in parentheses indicate the number of persons reporting this ancestry/race alone, not in combination with any other ancestry/race. 3. Refer to the Explanation of Data in the front of the book for more detailed information.

Native Hawaiian (12)	19	0.02
Samoan (1)	4	0.01
Other Pac. Isl., not spec. (10)	44	0.06
Hispanic or Latino:	3,613	4.56
Central American:	340	0.43
Costa Rican	5	0.01
Guatemalan	266	0.34
Honduran	10	0.01
Nicaraguan	16	0.02
Panamanian	6	0.01
Salvadoran	30	0.04
Other Central American	7	0.01
Cuban	88	0.11
Dominican Republic	734	0.93
Mexican	185	0.23
Puerto Rican	946	1.19
South American:	363	0.46
Argentinean	12	0.02
Bolivian	98	0.12
Chilean	5	0.01
Colombian	131	0.17
Ecuadorian	44	0.06
Paraguayan	1	0.00
Peruvian	39	0.05
Uruguayan	1	0.00
Venezuelan	12	0.02
Other South American	20	0.03
Other Hispanic or Latino	957	1.21
Hungarian	203	0.26
Icelander	34	0.04
Iranian	67	0.08
Irish	15,429	19.46
Israeli	10	0.01
Italian	27,359	34.51
Latvian	25	0.03
Lithuanian	269	0.34
New Zealander	7	0.01
Northern European	6	0.01
Norwegian	264	0.33
Pennsylvania German	7	0.01
Polish	2,396	3.02
Portuguese	4,282	5.40
Romanian	96	0.12
Russian	1,030	1.30
Scandinavian	16	0.02
Scotch-Irish	678	0.86
Scottish	1,171	1.48
Slavic	16	0.02
Slovak	65	0.08
Swedish	1,608	2.03
Swiss	31	0.04
Turkish	20	0.03
Ukrainian	232	0.29
United States or American	1,586	2.00
Welsh	145	0.18
West Indian, excl. Hispanic:	236	0.30
Haitian	171	0.22
Jamaican	56	0.07
Trinidadian and Tobagonian	6	0.01
West Indian	3	0.00
White:	71,635	90.37
Not Hispanic (69,104)	69,847	88.11
Hispanic (1,599)	1,788	2.26
Yugoslavian	7	0.01

Cumberland

Place Type: Town
County: Providence
Population: 31,840

Ancestry/Race	Number	%
African American/Black:	248	0.78
Not Hispanic (161)	224	0.70
Hispanic (19)	24	0.08
African, sub-Saharan:	184	0.58
Cape Verdean	184	0.58
Alaska Native tribes, specified:	2	0.01
Alaska Athabascan (2)	2	0.01
Am. Ind. or Alaska Nat., not spec.	45	0.14
Albanian	8	0.03
American Indian tribes, specified:	33	0.10
Blackfeet	1	0.00
Cherokee (1)	4	0.01
Iroquois	2	0.01
Latin American Indians (2)	4	0.01
Seminole	1	0.00
Shoshone	1	0.00
Sioux	1	0.00
All other tribes (5)	19	0.06
American Indian tribes, not spec.	2	0.01
Arab:	374	1.17
Arab/Arabic	8	0.03
Egyptian	20	0.06
Lebanese	40	0.13
Syrian	306	0.96
Armenian	126	0.40
Asian:	320	1.01
Cambodian (6)	6	0.02
Chinese, ex. Taiwanese (73)	81	0.25
Filipino (19)	29	0.09
Indian (75)	80	0.25
Indonesian (1)	1	0.00
Japanese (7)	18	0.06
Korean (27)	32	0.10
Laotian (16)	18	0.06
Pakistani (11)	18	0.06
Thai (5)	5	0.02
Vietnamese (21)	21	0.07
Other Asian, specified (3)	3	0.01
Other Asian, not specified	8	0.03
Austrian	56	0.18
Belgian	57	0.18
Brazilian	9	0.03
British	93	0.29
Canadian	111	0.35
Croatian	42	0.13
Czech	23	0.07
Danish	29	0.09
Dutch	163	0.51
Eastern European	41	0.13
English	4,307	13.53
European	52	0.16
Finnish	37	0.12
French, except Basque	5,378	16.89
French Canadian	4,612	14.48
German	1,464	4.60
Greek	227	0.71
Hawaii Native/Pacific Islander:	21	0.07
Polynesian: (8)	10	0.03
Native Hawaiian (6)	8	0.03
Samoan (2)	2	0.01
Other Pac. Isl., not spec.	11	0.03
Hispanic or Latino:	667	2.09
Central American:	50	0.16
Costa Rican	5	0.02
Guatemalan	36	0.11
Salvadoran	9	0.03
Cuban	11	0.03
Dominican Republic	31	0.10
Mexican	38	0.12
Puerto Rican	124	0.39
South American:	232	0.73
Argentinean	1	0.00
Chilean	2	0.01
Colombian	210	0.66
Ecuadorian	5	0.02
Peruvian	1	0.00
Venezuelan	5	0.02
Other South American	8	0.03
Other Hispanic or Latino	181	0.57
Hungarian	24	0.08
Icelander	14	0.04
Irish	7,481	23.50
Italian	3,816	11.98
Latvian	14	0.04
Lithuanian	89	0.28
Norwegian	52	0.16
Pennsylvania German	6	0.02
Polish	2,215	6.96
Portuguese	4,279	13.44
Romanian	21	0.07
Russian	181	0.57
Scandinavian	5	0.02
Scotch-Irish	540	1.70
Scottish	739	2.32
Slovak	45	0.14
Slovene	7	0.02
Swedish	375	1.18
Swiss	119	0.37
Turkish	51	0.16
Ukrainian	116	0.36
United States or American	831	2.61
Welsh	38	0.12
White:	31,069	97.58
Not Hispanic (30,400)	30,605	96.12
Hispanic (403)	464	1.46

East Greenwich

Place Type: Town
County: Kent
Population: 12,948

Ancestry/Race	Number	%
African American/Black:	108	0.83
Not Hispanic (84)	102	0.79
Hispanic (5)	6	0.05
African, sub-Saharan:	60	0.46
Cape Verdean	32	0.25
Nigerian	18	0.14
South African	10	0.08
Am. Ind. or Alaska Nat., not spec.	10	0.08
American Indian tribes, specified:	34	0.26
Blackfeet (1)	5	0.04
Cherokee (1)	5	0.04
Iroquois (1)	3	0.02
Latin American Indians	4	0.03
Seminole (1)	1	0.01
Ute	1	0.01
All other tribes (2)	15	0.12
American Indian tribes, not spec.	1	0.01
Arab:	114	0.88
Arab/Arabic	6	0.05
Lebanese	73	0.56
Syrian	35	0.27
Armenian	97	0.75
Asian:	367	2.83
Cambodian (2)	2	0.02
Chinese, ex. Taiwanese (116)	125	0.97
Filipino (38)	47	0.36
Indian (62)	67	0.52
Indonesian (1)	1	0.01
Japanese (23)	31	0.24
Korean (34)	39	0.30
Laotian (11)	11	0.08
Pakistani (7)	11	0.08
Sri Lankan (3)	3	0.02
Taiwanese (10)	10	0.08
Thai	1	0.01
Vietnamese (11)	11	0.08
Other Asian, not specified (5)	8	0.06
Australian	14	0.11
Austrian	41	0.32
Belgian	5	0.04
British	67	0.52
Bulgarian	17	0.13
Canadian	35	0.27
Croatian	16	0.12
Czechoslovakian	9	0.07
Danish	25	0.19
Dutch	262	2.02
Eastern European	65	0.50
English	2,484	19.18
European	168	1.30
Finnish	19	0.15
French, except Basque	812	6.27
French Canadian	471	3.64
German	1,424	11.00
Greek	165	1.27

Notes: 1. Figures in the "Number" column do not add up to the total population due to: a) Ancestry/Race overlap — e.g. persons can report being both White and Irish, b) persons of Hispanic origin can report being any race, c) persons reporting two ancestries are counted in both categories. 2. Numbers in parentheses indicate the number of persons reporting this ancestry/race alone, not in combination with any other ancestry/race. 3. Refer to the Explanation of Data in the front of the book for more detailed information.

Hawaii Native/Pacific Islander:	3	0.02
Other Pac. Isl., not spec. (1)	3	0.02
Hispanic or Latino:	117	0.90
Central American:	9	0.07
Guatemalan	2	0.02
Panamanian	4	0.03
Salvadoran	3	0.02
Cuban	13	0.10
Dominican Republic	16	0.12
Mexican	15	0.12
Puerto Rican	17	0.13
South American:	20	0.15
Argentinean	3	0.02
Chilean	3	0.02
Colombian	8	0.06
Ecuadorian	3	0.02
Uruguayan	2	0.02
Venezuelan	1	0.01
Other Hispanic or Latino	27	0.21
Hungarian	39	0.30
Irish	3,004	23.20
Italian	2,696	20.82
Latvian	18	0.14
Lithuanian	37	0.29
Norwegian	147	1.14
Pennsylvania German	13	0.10
Polish	590	4.56
Portuguese	406	3.14
Romanian	23	0.18
Russian	387	2.99
Scandinavian	34	0.26
Scotch-Irish	157	1.21
Scottish	538	4.16
Slavic	4	0.03
Swedish	635	4.90
Swiss	94	0.73
Ukrainian	55	0.42
United States or American	352	2.72
Welsh	84	0.65
West Indian, excl. Hispanic:	15	0.12
Barbadian	15	0.12
White:	12,471	96.32
Not Hispanic (12,308)	12,385	95.65
Hispanic (75)	86	0.66

East Providence

Place Type: City
County: Providence
Population: 48,688

Ancestry/Race	Number	%
Afghan	28	0.06
African American/Black:	3,382	6.95
Not Hispanic (2,391)	3,285	6.75
Hispanic (54)	97	0.20
African, sub-Saharan:	2,682	5.51
African	84	0.17
Cape Verdean	2,383	4.89
Liberian	45	0.09
Nigerian	78	0.16
Other sub-Saharan African	92	0.19
Am. Ind. or Alaska Nat., not spec.	206	0.42
American Indian tribes, specified:	434	0.89
Apache (2)	3	0.01
Blackfeet (3)	25	0.05
Cherokee (6)	51	0.10
Chickasaw (3)	3	0.01
Chippewa (1)	3	0.01
Choctaw	2	0.00
Creek (1)	1	0.00
Delaware	2	0.00
Iroquois (3)	17	0.03
Latin American Indians (3)	15	0.03
Potawatomi (2)	7	0.01
Seminole (2)	7	0.01
Sioux (2)	5	0.01
All other tribes (120)	293	0.60
American Indian tribes, not spec.	18	0.04
Arab:	561	1.15
Arab/Arabic	43	0.09
Egyptian	24	0.05
Lebanese	346	0.71
Syrian	135	0.28
Other Arab	13	0.03
Armenian	245	0.50
Asian:	695	1.43
Cambodian (5)	5	0.01
Chinese, ex. Taiwanese (204)	219	0.45
Filipino (54)	83	0.17
Hmong (9)	9	0.02
Indian (92)	114	0.23
Japanese (28)	52	0.11
Korean (77)	79	0.16
Laotian (6)	6	0.01
Malaysian (3)	3	0.01
Pakistani (17)	20	0.04
Sri Lankan (3)	12	0.02
Taiwanese (18)	18	0.04
Thai (7)	9	0.02
Vietnamese (13)	21	0.04
Other Asian, specified (1)	1	0.00
Other Asian, not specified (12)	44	0.09
Assyrian/Chaldean/Syriac	23	0.05
Australian	17	0.03
Austrian	103	0.21
Belgian	6	0.01
Brazilian	292	0.60
British	82	0.17
Canadian	89	0.18
Czech	23	0.05
Czechoslovakian	32	0.07
Danish	50	0.10
Dutch	226	0.46
Eastern European	27	0.06
English	5,289	10.86
European	80	0.16
Finnish	6	0.01
French, except Basque	3,590	7.37
French Canadian	1,648	3.38
German	1,952	4.01
Greek	195	0.40
Hawaii Native/Pacific Islander:	89	0.18
Micronesian: (5)	15	0.03
Guamanian/Chamorro (5)	15	0.03
Polynesian: (13)	16	0.03
Native Hawaiian (6)	8	0.02
Samoan (7)	7	0.01
Other Polynesian	1	0.00
Other Pac. Isl., not spec. (5)	58	0.12
Hispanic or Latino:	922	1.89
Central American:	48	0.10
Guatemalan	32	0.07
Honduran	2	0.00
Nicaraguan	5	0.01
Panamanian	5	0.01
Salvadoran	2	0.00
Other Central American	2	0.00
Cuban	25	0.05
Dominican Republic	60	0.12
Mexican	111	0.23
Puerto Rican	306	0.63
South American:	125	0.26
Argentinean	18	0.04
Bolivian	11	0.02
Chilean	1	0.00
Colombian	47	0.10
Ecuadorian	12	0.02
Peruvian	20	0.04
Venezuelan	10	0.02
Other South American	6	0.01
Other Hispanic or Latino	247	0.51
Hungarian	100	0.21
Iranian	10	0.02
Irish	8,417	17.29
Israeli	11	0.02
Italian	5,627	11.56
Lithuanian	57	0.12
Northern European	10	0.02
Norwegian	169	0.35
Polish	1,400	2.88
Portuguese	15,032	30.87
Romanian	7	0.01
Russian	264	0.54
Scandinavian	23	0.05
Scotch-Irish	446	0.92
Scottish	854	1.75
Slovak	8	0.02
Swedish	1,013	2.08
Swiss	39	0.08
Turkish	46	0.09
Ukrainian	184	0.38
United States or American	1,104	2.27
Welsh	106	0.22
West Indian, excl. Hispanic:	85	0.17
Bahamian	8	0.02
Haitian	34	0.07
Jamaican	17	0.03
West Indian	26	0.05
White:	43,417	89.17
Not Hispanic (41,630)	42,848	88.01
Hispanic (481)	569	1.17
Yugoslavian	16	0.03

Johnston

Place Type: Town
County: Providence
Population: 28,195

Ancestry/Race	Number	%
African American/Black:	244	0.87
Not Hispanic (171)	226	0.80
Hispanic (13)	18	0.06
African, sub-Saharan:	178	0.63
Cape Verdean	124	0.44
Nigerian	48	0.17
Sudanese	6	0.02
Am. Ind. or Alaska Nat., not spec.	39	0.14
American Indian tribes, specified:	56	0.20
Blackfeet	5	0.02
Cherokee (3)	8	0.03
Chippewa (1)	1	0.00
Iroquois (1)	4	0.01
Latin American Indians (3)	4	0.01
Lumbee (2)	2	0.01
Sioux (1)	3	0.01
All other tribes (12)	29	0.10
American Indian tribes, not spec.	1	0.00
Arab:	350	1.24
Arab/Arabic	6	0.02
Egyptian	10	0.04
Lebanese	157	0.56
Syrian	177	0.63
Armenian	133	0.47
Asian:	391	1.39
Cambodian (31)	31	0.11
Chinese, ex. Taiwanese (55)	60	0.21
Filipino (18)	26	0.09
Hmong (7)	7	0.02
Indian (43)	59	0.21
Japanese (3)	10	0.04
Korean (27)	28	0.10
Laotian (72)	94	0.33
Pakistani (1)	5	0.02
Thai (1)	1	0.00
Vietnamese (30)	39	0.14
Other Asian, not specified (4)	31	0.11
Assyrian/Chaldean/Syriac	7	0.02
Austrian	20	0.07
British	27	0.10
Bulgarian	29	0.10
Canadian	51	0.18
Croatian	7	0.02
Czechoslovakian	11	0.04
Danish	8	0.03
Dutch	134	0.47
English	2,118	7.51
Finnish	19	0.07
French, except Basque	2,681	9.50

Notes: 1. Figures in the "Number" column do not add up to the total population due to: a) Ancestry/Race overlap — e.g. persons can report being both White and Irish, b) persons of Hispanic origin can report being any race, c) persons reporting two ancestries are counted in both categories. 2. Numbers in parentheses indicate the number of persons reporting this ancestry/race alone, not in combination with any other ancestry/race. 3. Refer to the Explanation of Data in the front of the book for more detailed information.

French Canadian	1,317	4.67
German	755	2.68
Greek	200	0.71
Hawaii Native/Pacific Islander:	24	0.09
Micronesian: (6)	7	0.02
Guamanian/Chamorro (6)	7	0.02
Polynesian: (8)	8	0.03
Native Hawaiian (8)	8	0.03
Other Pac. Isl., not spec.	9	0.03
Hispanic or Latino:	533	1.89
Central American:	69	0.24
Guatemalan	64	0.23
Panamanian	3	0.01
Other Central American	2	0.01
Cuban	12	0.04
Dominican Republic	27	0.10
Mexican	60	0.21
Puerto Rican	96	0.34
South American:	110	0.39
Argentinean	1	0.00
Bolivian	46	0.16
Chilean	2	0.01
Colombian	35	0.12
Ecuadorian	13	0.05
Peruvian	6	0.02
Uruguayan	1	0.00
Venezuelan	1	0.00
Other South American	5	0.02
Other Hispanic or Latino	159	0.56
Hungarian	7	0.02
Iranian	41	0.15
Irish	4,342	15.39
Italian	15,114	53.56
Lithuanian	114	0.40
Norwegian	64	0.23
Polish	916	3.25
Portuguese	1,206	4.27
Russian	92	0.33
Scandinavian	33	0.12
Scotch-Irish	235	0.83
Scottish	188	0.67
Slovak	21	0.07
Swedish	209	0.74
Swiss	10	0.04
Ukrainian	79	0.28
United States or American	472	1.67
Welsh	33	0.12
White:	27,461	97.40
Not Hispanic (26,916)	27,077	96.03
Hispanic (338)	384	1.36

Lincoln

Place Type: Town
County: Providence
Population: 20,898

Ancestry/Race	Number	%
African American/Black:	226	1.08
Not Hispanic (166)	212	1.01
Hispanic (10)	14	0.07
African, sub-Saharan:	119	0.57
African	9	0.04
Cape Verdean	86	0.41
Nigerian	17	0.08
South African	7	0.03
Am. Ind. or Alaska Nat., not spec.	29	0.14
Albanian	30	0.14
American Indian tribes, specified:	58	0.28
Blackfeet (1)	6	0.03
Cherokee (1)	8	0.04
Chippewa	1	0.00
Choctaw (1)	1	0.00
Cree	11	0.05
Iroquois	1	0.00
Latin American Indians	1	0.00
Pueblo	1	0.00
Sioux (1)	6	0.03
All other tribes (6)	22	0.11
American Indian tribes, not spec.	5	0.02
Arab:	477	2.28
Arab/Arabic	48	0.23
Lebanese	96	0.46
Syrian	333	1.59
Armenian	89	0.43
Asian:	427	2.04
Cambodian (7)	9	0.04
Chinese, ex. Taiwanese (107)	120	0.57
Filipino (24)	35	0.17
Indian (134)	146	0.70
Japanese (11)	19	0.09
Korean (20)	25	0.12
Laotian (13)	15	0.07
Pakistani (21)	24	0.11
Sri Lankan (4)	4	0.02
Thai (2)	3	0.01
Vietnamese (15)	18	0.09
Other Asian, not specified (4)	9	0.04
Austrian	23	0.11
Belgian	29	0.14
Brazilian	5	0.02
British	71	0.34
Canadian	68	0.33
Celtic	16	0.08
Croatian	27	0.13
Czechoslovakian	36	0.17
Danish	16	0.08
Dutch	71	0.34
Eastern European	10	0.05
English	2,370	11.34
European	134	0.64
Finnish	31	0.15
French, except Basque	3,362	16.09
French Canadian	3,485	16.68
German	906	4.34
Greek	36	0.17
Hawaii Native/Pacific Islander:	11	0.05
Micronesian: (1)	3	0.01
Other Micronesian (1)	3	0.01
Polynesian: (1)	3	0.01
Native Hawaiian (1)	3	0.01
Other Pac. Isl., not spec.	5	0.02
Hispanic or Latino:	343	1.64
Central American:	24	0.11
Costa Rican	1	0.00
Guatemalan	15	0.07
Honduran	2	0.01
Panamanian	1	0.00
Salvadoran	5	0.02
Cuban	11	0.05
Dominican Republic	27	0.13
Mexican	21	0.10
Puerto Rican	97	0.46
South American:	79	0.38
Bolivian	6	0.03
Colombian	68	0.33
Ecuadorian	3	0.01
Paraguayan	1	0.00
Venezuelan	1	0.00
Other Hispanic or Latino	84	0.40
Hungarian	7	0.03
Iranian	36	0.17
Irish	3,545	16.96
Italian	3,779	18.08
Lithuanian	68	0.33
Northern European	24	0.11
Norwegian	59	0.28
Pennsylvania German	9	0.04
Polish	1,396	6.68
Portuguese	1,636	7.83
Romanian	9	0.04
Russian	186	0.89
Scotch-Irish	249	1.19
Scottish	509	2.44
Slovak	7	0.03
Swedish	254	1.22
Swiss	38	0.18
Turkish	117	0.56
Ukrainian	171	0.82
United States or American	614	2.94
Welsh	48	0.23
West Indian, excl. Hispanic:	6	0.03
West Indian	6	0.03
White:	20,179	96.56
Not Hispanic (19,736)	19,918	95.31
Hispanic (231)	261	1.25
Yugoslavian	7	0.03

Middletown

Place Type: Town
County: Newport
Population: 17,334

Ancestry/Race	Number	%
Acadian/Cajun	34	0.20
African American/Black:	1,010	5.83
Not Hispanic (796)	968	5.58
Hispanic (23)	42	0.24
African, sub-Saharan:	323	1.86
African	170	0.98
Cape Verdean	88	0.51
Nigerian	47	0.27
South African	18	0.10
Am. Ind. or Alaska Nat., not spec.	66	0.38
American Indian tribes, specified:	94	0.54
Blackfeet (4)	10	0.06
Cherokee (11)	28	0.16
Chippewa	3	0.02
Choctaw (2)	2	0.01
Iroquois (1)	5	0.03
Latin American Indians (4)	10	0.06
Lumbee	1	0.01
Sioux (2)	3	0.02
All other tribes (13)	32	0.18
American Indian tribes, not spec.	3	0.02
Arab:	59	0.34
Arab/Arabic	8	0.05
Iraqi	11	0.06
Lebanese	33	0.19
Syrian	7	0.04
Armenian	87	0.50
Asian:	523	3.02
Bangladeshi (4)	4	0.02
Cambodian (1)	1	0.01
Chinese, ex. Taiwanese (45)	58	0.33
Filipino (216)	294	1.70
Indian (23)	31	0.18
Japanese (35)	56	0.32
Korean (23)	40	0.23
Malaysian (2)	2	0.01
Pakistani (2)	4	0.02
Thai (7)	11	0.06
Vietnamese (14)	16	0.09
Other Asian, not specified (1)	6	0.03
Austrian	46	0.27
Belgian	15	0.09
Brazilian	22	0.13
British	148	0.85
Canadian	55	0.32
Celtic	18	0.10
Croatian	77	0.44
Czech	67	0.39
Czechoslovakian	65	0.37
Danish	58	0.33
Dutch	174	1.00
Eastern European	7	0.04
English	2,608	15.05
Estonian	9	0.05
European	164	0.95
Finnish	31	0.18
French, except Basque	1,052	6.07
French Canadian	506	2.92
German	1,783	10.29
Greek	237	1.37
Guyanese	7	0.04
Hawaii Native/Pacific Islander:	48	0.28
Micronesian: (4)	9	0.05
Guamanian/Chamorro (4)	9	0.05
Polynesian: (10)	25	0.14

Notes: 1. Figures in the "Number" column do not add up to the total population due to: a) Ancestry/Race overlap — e.g. persons can report being both White and Irish, b) persons of Hispanic origin can report being any race, c) persons reporting two ancestries are counted in both categories. 2. Numbers in parentheses indicate the number of persons reporting this ancestry/race alone, not in combination with any other ancestry/race. 3. Refer to the Explanation of Data in the front of the book for more detailed information.

Ancestry/Race	Number	%
Native Hawaiian (6)	20	0.12
Samoan (3)	4	0.02
Tongan (1)	1	0.01
Other Pac. Isl., not spec. (4)	14	0.08
Hispanic or Latino:	508	2.93
Central American:	17	0.10
Costa Rican	1	0.01
Guatemalan	5	0.03
Honduran	2	0.01
Panamanian	3	0.02
Salvadoran	1	0.01
Other Central American	5	0.03
Cuban	23	0.13
Dominican Republic	10	0.06
Mexican	125	0.72
Puerto Rican	197	1.14
South American:	29	0.17
Argentinean	6	0.03
Chilean	5	0.03
Colombian	10	0.06
Ecuadorian	3	0.02
Paraguayan	2	0.01
Peruvian	2	0.01
Other South American	1	0.01
Other Hispanic or Latino	107	0.62
Hungarian	68	0.39
Irish	4,507	26.00
Italian	2,035	11.74
Lithuanian	56	0.32
Northern European	16	0.09
Norwegian	185	1.07
Polish	576	3.32
Portuguese	2,107	12.16
Romanian	33	0.19
Russian	84	0.48
Scandinavian	7	0.04
Scotch-Irish	334	1.93
Scottish	475	2.74
Slavic	33	0.19
Slovak	34	0.20
Swedish	261	1.51
Swiss	19	0.11
Ukrainian	35	0.20
United States or American	707	4.08
Welsh	84	0.48
West Indian, excl. Hispanic:	89	0.51
British West Indian	11	0.06
Haitian	24	0.14
Jamaican	28	0.16
West Indian	26	0.15
White:	15,799	91.14
Not Hispanic (15,180)	15,485	89.33
Hispanic (268)	314	1.81
Yugoslavian	6	0.03

Narragansett

Place Type: Town
County: Washington
Population: 16,361

Ancestry/Race	Number	%
African American/Black:	219	1.34
Not Hispanic (119)	197	1.20
Hispanic (3)	22	0.13
African, sub-Saharan:	49	0.30
Cape Verdean	24	0.15
Kenyan	25	0.15
Alaska Native tribes, specified:	1	0.01
Eskimo (1)	1	0.01
Am. Ind. or Alaska Nat., not spec.	35	0.21
American Indian tribes, specified:	188	1.15
Blackfeet (2)	2	0.01
Cherokee (4)	17	0.10
Cree	2	0.01
Creek (1)	1	0.01
Delaware	2	0.01
Iroquois (2)	6	0.04
Kiowa	1	0.01
Navajo	1	0.01
All other tribes (110)	156	0.95
American Indian tribes, not spec.	8	0.05
Arab:	22	0.13
Syrian	22	0.13
Armenian	77	0.47
Asian:	182	1.11
Cambodian (1)	1	0.01
Chinese, ex. Taiwanese (42)	54	0.33
Filipino (18)	42	0.26
Indian (18)	22	0.13
Japanese (17)	27	0.17
Korean (14)	20	0.12
Sri Lankan (1)	1	0.01
Thai (1)	2	0.01
Vietnamese (5)	9	0.06
Other Asian, not specified (3)	4	0.02
Austrian	34	0.21
Belgian	76	0.46
British	52	0.32
Canadian	86	0.53
Czechoslovakian	65	0.40
Danish	18	0.11
Dutch	187	1.14
Eastern European	24	0.15
English	3,091	18.89
European	58	0.35
Finnish	51	0.31
French, except Basque	1,275	7.79
French Canadian	857	5.24
German	1,219	7.45
Greek	67	0.41
Hawaii Native/Pacific Islander:	14	0.09
Micronesian: (1)	2	0.01
Guamanian/Chamorro (1)	2	0.01
Polynesian: (2)	8	0.05
Native Hawaiian (1)	7	0.04
Samoan (1)	1	0.01
Other Pac. Isl., not spec.	4	0.02
Hispanic or Latino:	204	1.25
Central American:	17	0.10
Guatemalan	9	0.06
Honduran	1	0.01
Nicaraguan	2	0.01
Panamanian	2	0.01
Other Central American	3	0.02
Cuban	8	0.05
Dominican Republic	14	0.09
Mexican	22	0.13
Puerto Rican	46	0.28
South American:	26	0.16
Argentinean	5	0.03
Bolivian	6	0.04
Chilean	2	0.01
Colombian	8	0.05
Ecuadorian	1	0.01
Venezuelan	3	0.02
Other South American	1	0.01
Other Hispanic or Latino	71	0.43
Hungarian	46	0.28
Iranian	30	0.18
Irish	5,197	31.76
Italian	3,369	20.59
Lithuanian	86	0.53
Maltese	10	0.06
Northern European	33	0.20
Norwegian	89	0.54
Polish	696	4.25
Portuguese	516	3.15
Romanian	20	0.12
Russian	176	1.08
Scandinavian	27	0.17
Scotch-Irish	487	2.98
Scottish	424	2.59
Slovak	16	0.10
Swedish	387	2.37
Swiss	60	0.37
Turkish	24	0.15
Ukrainian	39	0.24
United States or American	499	3.05
Welsh	71	0.43
West Indian, excl. Hispanic:	38	0.23
Jamaican	11	0.07
Trinidadian and Tobagonian	6	0.04
U.S. Virgin Islander	21	0.13
White:	15,877	97.04
Not Hispanic (15,545)	15,728	96.13
Hispanic (135)	149	0.91
Yugoslavian	13	0.08

Newport East

Place Type: Census Designated Place
County: Newport
Population: 11,463

Ancestry/Race	Number	%
Acadian/Cajun	7	0.06
African American/Black:	592	5.16
Not Hispanic (456)	572	4.99
Hispanic (7)	20	0.17
African, sub-Saharan:	222	1.90
African	116	0.99
Cape Verdean	81	0.69
Nigerian	19	0.16
South African	6	0.05
Am. Ind. or Alaska Nat., not spec.	40	0.35
American Indian tribes, specified:	59	0.51
Blackfeet (4)	8	0.07
Cherokee (8)	17	0.15
Choctaw (1)	1	0.01
Iroquois	1	0.01
Latin American Indians (4)	6	0.05
Lumbee	1	0.01
Sioux (2)	3	0.03
All other tribes (10)	22	0.19
American Indian tribes, not spec.	3	0.03
Arab:	45	0.39
Arab/Arabic	8	0.07
Iraqi	11	0.09
Lebanese	26	0.22
Armenian	44	0.38
Asian:	293	2.56
Chinese, ex. Taiwanese (27)	34	0.30
Filipino (129)	176	1.54
Indian (8)	10	0.09
Japanese (22)	28	0.24
Korean (17)	29	0.25
Malaysian (2)	2	0.02
Pakistani (2)	4	0.03
Vietnamese (6)	6	0.05
Other Asian, not specified	4	0.03
Austrian	26	0.22
Belgian	15	0.13
Brazilian	22	0.19
British	119	1.02
Canadian	55	0.47
Celtic	10	0.09
Croatian	6	0.05
Czech	37	0.32
Czechoslovakian	5	0.04
Danish	33	0.28
Dutch	113	0.97
English	1,866	15.98
Estonian	9	0.08
European	103	0.88
Finnish	27	0.23
French, except Basque	785	6.72
French Canadian	412	3.53
German	987	8.45
Greek	83	0.71
Guyanese	7	0.06
Hawaii Native/Pacific Islander:	23	0.20
Micronesian: (4)	5	0.04
Guamanian/Chamorro (4)	5	0.04
Polynesian: (5)	9	0.08
Native Hawaiian (3)	7	0.06
Samoan (1)	1	0.01
Tongan (1)	1	0.01
Other Pac. Isl., not spec. (4)	9	0.08
Hispanic or Latino:	249	2.17

Notes: 1. Figures in the "Number" column do not add up to the total population due to: a) Ancestry/Race overlap — e.g. persons can report being both White and Irish, b) persons of Hispanic origin can report being any race, c) persons reporting two ancestries are counted in both categories. 2. Numbers in parentheses indicate the number of persons reporting this ancestry/race alone, not in combination with any other ancestry/race. 3. Refer to the Explanation of Data in the front of the book for more detailed information.

Ancestry/Race	Number	%
Central American:	1	0.01
Honduran	1	0.01
Cuban	10	0.09
Dominican Republic	3	0.03
Mexican	48	0.42
Puerto Rican	114	0.99
South American:	21	0.18
Argentinean	6	0.05
Chilean	3	0.03
Colombian	7	0.06
Ecuadorian	3	0.03
Peruvian	1	0.01
Other South American	1	0.01
Other Hispanic or Latino	52	0.45
Hungarian	15	0.13
Irish	3,336	28.57
Italian	1,374	11.77
Lithuanian	32	0.27
Northern European	16	0.14
Norwegian	139	1.19
Polish	412	3.53
Portuguese	1,635	14.00
Romanian	25	0.21
Russian	47	0.40
Scandinavian	7	0.06
Scotch-Irish	215	1.84
Scottish	378	3.24
Slavic	25	0.21
Slovak	18	0.15
Swedish	157	1.34
Swiss	19	0.16
Ukrainian	28	0.24
United States or American	409	3.50
Welsh	35	0.30
West Indian, excl. Hispanic:	11	0.09
British West Indian	11	0.09
White:	10,585	92.34
Not Hispanic (10,237)	10,428	90.97
Hispanic (132)	157	1.37
Yugoslavian	6	0.05

Newport

Place Type: City
County: Newport
Population: 26,475

Ancestry/Race	Number	%
African American/Black:	2,565	9.69
Not Hispanic (1,893)	2,340	8.84
Hispanic (160)	225	0.85
African, sub-Saharan:	330	1.25
African	121	0.46
Cape Verdean	182	0.69
Ethiopian	11	0.04
South African	10	0.04
Zimbabwean	6	0.02
Am. Ind. or Alaska Nat., not spec.	155	0.59
Albanian	9	0.03
Alsatian	6	0.02
American Indian tribes, specified:	328	1.24
Apache (1)	8	0.03
Blackfeet (1)	18	0.07
Cherokee (23)	75	0.28
Chippewa (1)	2	0.01
Choctaw (2)	7	0.03
Comanche	3	0.01
Cree (1)	2	0.01
Creek	3	0.01
Crow	1	0.00
Delaware (1)	1	0.00
Iroquois (4)	12	0.05
Kiowa (1)	1	0.00
Latin American Indians (10)	16	0.06
Lumbee (2)	2	0.01
Navajo (2)	2	0.01
Osage (1)	1	0.00
Pueblo (2)	3	0.01
Seminole	5	0.02
Sioux	3	0.01
Ute	1	0.00
All other tribes (104)	162	0.61
American Indian tribes, not spec.	17	0.06
Arab:	146	0.55
Arab/Arabic	14	0.05
Egyptian	15	0.06
Lebanese	74	0.28
Moroccan	20	0.08
Syrian	19	0.07
Other Arab	4	0.02
Armenian	90	0.34
Asian:	519	1.96
Cambodian (3)	5	0.02
Chinese, ex. Taiwanese (72)	83	0.31
Filipino (127)	212	0.80
Indian (35)	46	0.17
Indonesian (1)	1	0.00
Japanese (33)	54	0.20
Korean (42)	52	0.20
Laotian (3)	5	0.02
Malaysian (1)	1	0.00
Pakistani (1)	9	0.03
Sri Lankan (1)	1	0.00
Taiwanese (1)	1	0.00
Thai (6)	8	0.03
Vietnamese (12)	18	0.07
Other Asian, specified	1	0.00
Other Asian, not specified (10)	22	0.08
Assyrian/Chaldean/Syriac	6	0.02
Australian	27	0.10
Austrian	43	0.16
Basque	16	0.06
Belgian	5	0.02
Brazilian	41	0.15
British	192	0.73
Canadian	129	0.49
Croatian	4	0.02
Czech	25	0.09
Czechoslovakian	31	0.12
Danish	96	0.36
Dutch	345	1.30
Eastern European	39	0.15
English	3,424	12.93
European	169	0.64
Finnish	28	0.11
French, except Basque	1,313	4.96
French Canadian	724	2.73
German	2,835	10.71
Greek	297	1.12
Guyanese	6	0.02
Hawaii Native/Pacific Islander:	75	0.28
Melanesian:	1	0.00
Other Melanesian	1	0.00
Micronesian: (7)	11	0.04
Guamanian/Chamorro (7)	11	0.04
Polynesian: (9)	36	0.14
Native Hawaiian (9)	33	0.12
Samoan	2	0.01
Other Polynesian	1	0.00
Other Pac. Isl., specified	1	0.00
Other Pac. Isl., not spec. (7)	26	0.10
Hispanic or Latino:	1,467	5.54
Central American:	91	0.34
Guatemalan	46	0.17
Honduran	2	0.01
Nicaraguan	1	0.00
Panamanian	6	0.02
Salvadoran	33	0.12
Other Central American	3	0.01
Cuban	49	0.19
Dominican Republic	72	0.27
Mexican	227	0.86
Puerto Rican	626	2.36
South American:	86	0.32
Argentinean	7	0.03
Bolivian	14	0.05
Chilean	8	0.03
Colombian	23	0.09
Ecuadorian	16	0.06
Peruvian	10	0.04
Uruguayan	2	0.01
Venezuelan	3	0.01
Other South American	3	0.01
Other Hispanic or Latino	316	1.19
Hungarian	99	0.37
Icelander	18	0.07
Irish	7,349	27.76
Israeli	19	0.07
Italian	3,015	11.39
Latvian	8	0.03
Lithuanian	56	0.21
New Zealander	16	0.06
Northern European	10	0.04
Norwegian	187	0.71
Pennsylvania German	14	0.05
Polish	851	3.21
Portuguese	1,934	7.31
Romanian	15	0.06
Russian	361	1.36
Scandinavian	44	0.17
Scotch-Irish	420	1.59
Scottish	772	2.92
Serbian	7	0.03
Slovak	22	0.08
Slovene	6	0.02
Swedish	514	1.94
Swiss	68	0.26
Turkish	7	0.03
Ukrainian	22	0.08
United States or American	1,340	5.06
Welsh	150	0.57
West Indian, excl. Hispanic:	144	0.54
Jamaican	58	0.22
Trinidadian and Tobagonian	5	0.02
West Indian	81	0.31
White:	22,935	86.63
Not Hispanic (21,623)	22,190	83.81
Hispanic (649)	745	2.81
Yugoslavian	17	0.06

North Kingstown

Place Type: Town
County: Washington
Population: 26,326

Ancestry/Race	Number	%
African American/Black:	393	1.49
Not Hispanic (246)	363	1.38
Hispanic (10)	30	0.11
African, sub-Saharan:	73	0.28
African	13	0.05
Cape Verdean	41	0.16
Ethiopian	6	0.02
Liberian	13	0.05
Alaska Native tribes, specified:	3	0.01
Alaska Athabascan	1	0.00
Tlingit-Haida (2)	2	0.01
Am. Ind. or Alaska Nat., not spec.	67	0.25
Alsatian	6	0.02
American Indian tribes, specified:	195	0.74
Apache (2)	6	0.02
Cherokee (4)	31	0.12
Cheyenne	1	0.00
Choctaw	2	0.01
Cree (2)	2	0.01
Iroquois (2)	6	0.02
Latin American Indians (4)	8	0.03
Navajo (1)	2	0.01
Potawatomi (1)	4	0.02
Sioux (2)	7	0.03
All other tribes (78)	126	0.48
American Indian tribes, not spec.	17	0.06
Arab:	148	0.56
Arab/Arabic	16	0.06
Egyptian	4	0.02
Lebanese	62	0.24
Syrian	66	0.25
Armenian	173	0.66
Asian:	334	1.27

Notes: 1. Figures in the "Number" column do not add up to the total population due to: a) Ancestry/Race overlap — e.g. persons can report being both White and Irish, b) persons of Hispanic origin can report being any race, c) persons reporting two ancestries are counted in both categories. 2. Numbers in parentheses indicate the number of persons reporting this ancestry/race alone, not in combination with any other ancestry/race. 3. Refer to the Explanation of Data in the front of the book for more detailed information.

Cambodian (4)	4	0.02
Chinese, ex. Taiwanese (49)	60	0.23
Filipino (51)	83	0.32
Indian (54)	70	0.27
Indonesian (2)	2	0.01
Japanese (43)	61	0.23
Korean (21)	25	0.09
Laotian (7)	7	0.03
Pakistani	1	0.00
Sri Lankan (1)	2	0.01
Taiwanese (5)	5	0.02
Thai (2)	2	0.01
Vietnamese (7)	8	0.03
Other Asian, specified	1	0.00
Other Asian, not specified (1)	2	0.01
Australian	9	0.03
Austrian	83	0.32
Belgian	17	0.06
Brazilian	6	0.02
British	171	0.65
Bulgarian	6	0.02
Canadian	153	0.58
Croatian	13	0.05
Cypriot	4	0.02
Czech	98	0.37
Czechoslovakian	21	0.08
Danish	176	0.67
Dutch	234	0.89
Eastern European	17	0.06
English	5,702	21.66
Estonian	35	0.13
European	142	0.54
Finnish	47	0.18
French, except Basque	2,958	11.24
French Canadian	1,620	6.15
German	2,514	9.55
Greek	188	0.71
Hawaii Native/Pacific Islander:	21	0.08
Micronesian: (1)	3	0.01
Guamanian/Chamorro (1)	3	0.01
Polynesian: (7)	16	0.06
Native Hawaiian (6)	15	0.06
Samoan (1)	1	0.00
Other Pac. Isl., not spec. (1)	2	0.01
Hispanic or Latino:	465	1.77
Central American:	35	0.13
Costa Rican	1	0.00
Guatemalan	7	0.03
Honduran	3	0.01
Nicaraguan	1	0.00
Panamanian	17	0.06
Salvadoran	3	0.01
Other Central American	3	0.01
Cuban	23	0.09
Dominican Republic	27	0.10
Mexican	59	0.22
Puerto Rican	198	0.75
South American:	35	0.13
Argentinean	1	0.00
Bolivian	5	0.02
Chilean	1	0.00
Colombian	14	0.05
Ecuadorian	4	0.02
Paraguayan	1	0.00
Peruvian	4	0.02
Venezuelan	3	0.01
Other South American	2	0.01
Other Hispanic or Latino	88	0.33
Hungarian	68	0.26
Irish	6,796	25.81
Israeli	7	0.03
Italian	4,308	16.36
Latvian	51	0.19
Lithuanian	85	0.32
Macedonian	6	0.02
Northern European	5	0.02
Norwegian	215	0.82
Pennsylvania German	14	0.05
Polish	1,332	5.06
Portuguese	983	3.73
Russian	263	1.00
Scandinavian	23	0.09
Scotch-Irish	465	1.77
Scottish	917	3.48
Serbian	14	0.05
Slavic	8	0.03
Slovak	45	0.17
Swedish	1,132	4.30
Swiss	33	0.13
Turkish	5	0.02
Ukrainian	63	0.24
United States or American	747	2.84
Welsh	115	0.44
West Indian, excl. Hispanic:	58	0.22
Belizean	15	0.06
Jamaican	26	0.10
West Indian	17	0.06
White:	25,491	96.83
Not Hispanic (24,936)	25,186	95.67
Hispanic (260)	305	1.16
Yugoslavian	6	0.02

North Providence

Place Type: Census Designated Place
County: Providence
Population: 32,411

Ancestry/Race	Number	%
Afghan	21	0.06
African American/Black:	999	3.08
Not Hispanic (823)	944	2.91
Hispanic (36)	55	0.17
African, sub-Saharan:	521	1.61
African	69	0.21
Cape Verdean	345	1.06
Ghanian	30	0.09
Nigerian	50	0.15
Senegalese	16	0.05
Other sub-Saharan African	11	0.03
Am. Ind. or Alaska Nat., not spec.	62	0.19
Albanian	15	0.05
American Indian tribes, specified:	67	0.21
Blackfeet	4	0.01
Cherokee (3)	5	0.02
Creek	1	0.00
Iroquois	2	0.01
Latin American Indians	2	0.01
Navajo (3)	3	0.01
Paiute (1)	1	0.00
All other tribes (21)	49	0.15
American Indian tribes, not spec.	9	0.03
Arab:	275	0.85
Arab/Arabic	19	0.06
Egyptian	8	0.02
Lebanese	167	0.52
Syrian	81	0.25
Armenian	471	1.45
Asian:	725	2.24
Bangladeshi (2)	3	0.01
Cambodian (5)	5	0.02
Chinese, ex. Taiwanese (169)	196	0.60
Filipino (66)	106	0.33
Hmong (6)	6	0.02
Indian (142)	166	0.51
Indonesian (11)	11	0.03
Japanese (17)	25	0.08
Korean (75)	95	0.29
Laotian (16)	16	0.05
Pakistani (11)	12	0.04
Thai (22)	22	0.07
Vietnamese (28)	29	0.09
Other Asian, specified (3)	4	0.01
Other Asian, not specified (17)	29	0.09
Austrian	14	0.04
Belgian	35	0.11
Brazilian	32	0.10
British	57	0.18
Canadian	34	0.10
Danish	20	0.06
Dutch	100	0.31
English	2,402	7.41
European	13	0.04
Finnish	18	0.06
French, except Basque	3,616	11.16
French Canadian	1,660	5.12
German	677	2.09
Greek	278	0.86
Hawaii Native/Pacific Islander:	38	0.12
Micronesian: (2)	2	0.01
Guamanian/Chamorro (2)	2	0.01
Polynesian: (2)	6	0.02
Native Hawaiian (2)	6	0.02
Other Pac. Isl., specified	1	0.00
Other Pac. Isl., not spec. (3)	29	0.09
Hispanic or Latino:	1,247	3.85
Central American:	71	0.22
Costa Rican	2	0.01
Guatemalan	55	0.17
Honduran	4	0.01
Nicaraguan	2	0.01
Panamanian	1	0.00
Salvadoran	4	0.01
Other Central American	3	0.01
Cuban	25	0.08
Dominican Republic	92	0.28
Mexican	131	0.40
Puerto Rican	241	0.74
South American:	300	0.93
Argentinean	12	0.04
Bolivian	60	0.19
Chilean	1	0.00
Colombian	178	0.55
Ecuadorian	11	0.03
Peruvian	10	0.03
Uruguayan	3	0.01
Venezuelan	14	0.04
Other South American	11	0.03
Other Hispanic or Latino	387	1.19
Iranian	28	0.09
Irish	5,721	17.65
Italian	13,924	42.96
Lithuanian	107	0.33
Northern European	7	0.02
Norwegian	55	0.17
Polish	989	3.05
Portuguese	2,303	7.11
Russian	311	0.96
Scotch-Irish	155	0.48
Scottish	277	0.85
Slavic	9	0.03
Slovak	18	0.06
Slovene	9	0.03
Swedish	311	0.96
Swiss	22	0.07
Turkish	34	0.10
Ukrainian	95	0.29
United States or American	711	2.19
Welsh	7	0.02
West Indian, excl. Hispanic:	62	0.19
British West Indian	8	0.02
Haitian	36	0.11
West Indian	18	0.06
White:	30,271	93.40
Not Hispanic (29,103)	29,451	90.87
Hispanic (709)	820	2.53

North Smithfield

Place Type: Town
County: Providence
Population: 10,618

Ancestry/Race	Number	%
African American/Black:	61	0.57
Not Hispanic (45)	59	0.56
Hispanic	2	0.02
African, sub-Saharan:	72	0.68
Cape Verdean	44	0.41
South African	17	0.16

Notes: 1. Figures in the "Number" column do not add up to the total population due to: a) Ancestry/Race overlap — e.g. persons can report being both White and Irish, b) persons of Hispanic origin can report being any race, c) persons reporting two ancestries are counted in both categories. 2. Numbers in parentheses indicate the number of persons reporting this ancestry/race alone, not in combination with any other ancestry/race. 3. Refer to the Explanation of Data in the front of the book for more detailed information.

Other sub-Saharan African	11	0.10
Am. Ind. or Alaska Nat., not spec.	16	0.15
Albanian	8	0.08
Alsatian	6	0.06
American Indian tribes, specified:	12	0.11
Apache	1	0.01
Cherokee (1)	1	0.01
Iroquois (3)	7	0.07
Latin American Indians	1	0.01
Shoshone (2)	2	0.02
American Indian tribes, not spec.	3	0.03
Arab:	179	1.69
Lebanese	35	0.33
Syrian	144	1.36
Armenian	8	0.08
Asian:	65	0.61
Chinese, ex. Taiwanese (16)	16	0.15
Filipino (5)	8	0.08
Indian (17)	21	0.20
Japanese	1	0.01
Korean (9)	10	0.09
Laotian (3)	3	0.03
Pakistani (3)	3	0.03
Other Asian, not specified (2)	3	0.03
Belgian	18	0.17
British	15	0.14
Canadian	147	1.38
Croatian	11	0.10
Czechoslovakian	27	0.25
Danish	29	0.27
Dutch	35	0.33
English	1,061	9.99
Finnish	34	0.32
French, except Basque	2,495	23.50
French Canadian	2,821	26.57
German	314	2.96
Greek	27	0.25
Hispanic or Latino:	50	0.47
Central American:	1	0.01
Guatemalan	1	0.01
Cuban	3	0.03
Dominican Republic	1	0.01
Mexican	8	0.08
Puerto Rican	11	0.10
South American:	7	0.07
Argentinean	1	0.01
Colombian	4	0.04
Peruvian	1	0.01
Venezuelan	1	0.01
Other Hispanic or Latino	19	0.18
Irish	1,576	14.84
Italian	1,575	14.83
Lithuanian	27	0.25
Macedonian	29	0.27
Northern European	27	0.25
Norwegian	47	0.44
Polish	704	6.63
Portuguese	276	2.60
Romanian	52	0.49
Russian	25	0.24
Scotch-Irish	116	1.09
Scottish	193	1.82
Slavic	14	0.13
Slovak	11	0.10
Swedish	210	1.98
Swiss	19	0.18
Ukrainian	266	2.51
United States or American	238	2.24
Welsh	31	0.29
West Indian, excl. Hispanic:	7	0.07
Haitian	7	0.07
White:	10,483	98.73
Not Hispanic (10,402)	10,439	98.31
Hispanic (38)	44	0.41

Pawtucket

Place Type: City
County: Providence
Population: 72,958

Ancestry/Race	Number	%
Acadian/Cajun	15	0.02
African American/Black:	7,066	9.69
Not Hispanic (4,876)	6,388	8.76
Hispanic (458)	678	0.93
African, sub-Saharan:	7,691	10.54
African	493	0.68
Cape Verdean	6,243	8.56
Ghanian	150	0.21
Liberian	325	0.45
Nigerian	404	0.55
Senegalese	37	0.05
Sierra Leonean	14	0.02
Other sub-Saharan African	25	0.03
Alaska Native tribes, specified:	5	0.01
Tlingit-Haida	5	0.01
Am. Ind. or Alaska Nat., not spec.	257	0.35
Albanian	28	0.04
American Indian tribes, specified:	269	0.37
Apache (2)	2	0.00
Blackfeet (3)	19	0.03
Cherokee (21)	47	0.06
Cheyenne (1)	1	0.00
Chippewa (3)	5	0.01
Cree	1	0.00
Creek	5	0.01
Delaware	1	0.00
Iroquois (4)	13	0.02
Latin American Indians (23)	44	0.06
Lumbee	1	0.00
Navajo (1)	1	0.00
Pueblo (4)	4	0.01
Shoshone	1	0.00
Sioux (1)	7	0.01
All other tribes (51)	117	0.16
American Indian tribes, not spec.	52	0.07
Arab:	701	0.96
Arab/Arabic	103	0.14
Egyptian	8	0.01
Jordanian	7	0.01
Lebanese	181	0.25
Syrian	388	0.53
Other Arab	14	0.02
Armenian	239	0.33
Asian:	851	1.17
Cambodian (8)	18	0.02
Chinese, ex. Taiwanese (191)	238	0.33
Filipino (81)	125	0.17
Indian (172)	202	0.28
Indonesian (9)	11	0.02
Japanese (10)	21	0.03
Korean (29)	40	0.05
Laotian (22)	25	0.03
Pakistani (6)	17	0.02
Sri Lankan (11)	12	0.02
Taiwanese (3)	4	0.01
Thai (3)	7	0.01
Vietnamese (57)	59	0.08
Other Asian, specified	3	0.00
Other Asian, not specified (7)	69	0.09
Australian	15	0.02
Austrian	19	0.03
Belgian	36	0.05
Brazilian	84	0.12
British	90	0.12
Bulgarian	6	0.01
Canadian	308	0.42
Czech	39	0.05
Czechoslovakian	13	0.02
Danish	72	0.10
Dutch	173	0.24
Eastern European	45	0.06
English	5,592	7.66
European	44	0.06
Finnish	60	0.08
French, except Basque	9,574	13.12
French Canadian	5,427	7.44
German	2,108	2.89
Greek	466	0.64
Guyanese	6	0.01
Hawaii Native/Pacific Islander:	308	0.42
Melanesian:	2	0.00
Fijian	2	0.00
Micronesian: (19)	22	0.03
Guamanian/Chamorro (17)	18	0.02
Other Micronesian (2)	4	0.01
Polynesian: (18)	31	0.04
Native Hawaiian (11)	21	0.03
Samoan (7)	10	0.01
Other Pac. Isl., specified	3	0.00
Other Pac. Isl., not spec. (5)	250	0.34
Hispanic or Latino:	10,141	13.90
Central American:	749	1.03
Costa Rican	13	0.02
Guatemalan	618	0.85
Honduran	30	0.04
Nicaraguan	12	0.02
Panamanian	21	0.03
Salvadoran	51	0.07
Other Central American	4	0.01
Cuban	75	0.10
Dominican Republic	804	1.10
Mexican	581	0.80
Puerto Rican	3,298	4.52
South American:	2,397	3.29
Argentinean	6	0.01
Bolivian	29	0.04
Chilean	7	0.01
Colombian	2,143	2.94
Ecuadorian	49	0.07
Paraguayan	1	0.00
Peruvian	71	0.10
Uruguayan	4	0.01
Venezuelan	70	0.10
Other South American	17	0.02
Other Hispanic or Latino	2,237	3.07
Hungarian	45	0.06
Iranian	20	0.03
Irish	10,033	13.75
Italian	5,424	7.43
Latvian	26	0.04
Lithuanian	92	0.13
Macedonian	7	0.01
Northern European	28	0.04
Norwegian	187	0.26
Polish	3,627	4.97
Portuguese	8,463	11.60
Romanian	39	0.05
Russian	588	0.81
Scotch-Irish	640	0.88
Scottish	859	1.18
Slavic	10	0.01
Slovak	7	0.01
Swedish	624	0.86
Swiss	57	0.08
Ukrainian	147	0.20
United States or American	2,791	3.83
Welsh	71	0.10
West Indian, excl. Hispanic:	486	0.67
Barbadian	29	0.04
Belizean	25	0.03
British West Indian	48	0.07
Haitian	174	0.24
Jamaican	62	0.08
Trinidadian and Tobagonian	75	0.10
West Indian	73	0.10
White:	57,370	78.63
Not Hispanic (50,436)	52,198	71.55
Hispanic (4,568)	5,172	7.09
Yugoslavian	19	0.03

Notes: 1. Figures in the "Number" column do not add up to the total population due to: a) Ancestry/Race overlap — e.g. persons can report being both White and Irish, b) persons of Hispanic origin can report being any race, c) persons reporting two ancestries are counted in both categories. 2. Numbers in parentheses indicate the number of persons reporting this ancestry/race alone, not in combination with any other ancestry/race. 3. Refer to the Explanation of Data in the front of the book for more detailed information.

Portsmouth

Place Type: Town
County: Newport
Population: 17,149

Ancestry/Race	Number	%
African American/Black:	251	1.46
Not Hispanic (194)	242	1.41
Hispanic (7)	9	0.05
African, sub-Saharan:	27	0.16
Cape Verdean	27	0.16
Am. Ind. or Alaska Nat., not spec.	20	0.12
Albanian	10	0.06
American Indian tribes, specified:	65	0.38
Blackfeet (2)	5	0.03
Cherokee (7)	27	0.16
Chickasaw (2)	2	0.01
Chippewa (1)	4	0.02
Choctaw (1)	2	0.01
Creek (1)	1	0.01
Iroquois (1)	1	0.01
Latin American Indians (1)	1	0.01
Osage	2	0.01
Pueblo	1	0.01
Seminole	2	0.01
All other tribes (9)	17	0.10
American Indian tribes, not spec.	9	0.05
Arab:	131	0.76
Egyptian	22	0.13
Jordanian	10	0.06
Lebanese	73	0.43
Syrian	26	0.15
Armenian	102	0.59
Asian:	308	1.80
Bangladeshi (4)	4	0.02
Chinese, ex. Taiwanese (42)	55	0.32
Filipino (71)	95	0.55
Indian (32)	35	0.20
Japanese (35)	48	0.28
Korean (26)	37	0.22
Pakistani (3)	3	0.02
Thai (4)	5	0.03
Vietnamese (17)	19	0.11
Other Asian, specified	2	0.01
Other Asian, not specified	5	0.03
Austrian	67	0.39
Belgian	6	0.03
Brazilian	28	0.16
British	195	1.14
Canadian	70	0.41
Celtic	37	0.22
Croatian	30	0.17
Czech	8	0.05
Czechoslovakian	20	0.12
Danish	77	0.45
Dutch	214	1.25
English	3,173	18.50
Estonian	15	0.09
European	106	0.62
Finnish	9	0.05
French, except Basque	1,514	8.83
French Canadian	698	4.07
German	2,119	12.36
Greek	114	0.66
Hawaii Native/Pacific Islander:	17	0.10
Micronesian: (2)	4	0.02
Guamanian/Chamorro (2)	4	0.02
Polynesian: (3)	7	0.04
Native Hawaiian (3)	7	0.04
Other Pac. Isl., specified	2	0.01
Other Pac. Isl., not spec. (1)	4	0.02
Hispanic or Latino:	249	1.45
Central American:	7	0.04
Guatemalan	4	0.02
Honduran	1	0.01
Panamanian	2	0.01
Cuban	17	0.10
Dominican Republic	9	0.05
Mexican	99	0.58
Puerto Rican	56	0.33
South American:	6	0.03
Argentinean	2	0.01
Colombian	1	0.01
Ecuadorian	3	0.02
Other Hispanic or Latino	55	0.32
Hungarian	43	0.25
Iranian	19	0.11
Irish	4,240	24.72
Italian	1,866	10.88
Lithuanian	65	0.38
New Zealander	7	0.04
Norwegian	154	0.90
Pennsylvania German	15	0.09
Polish	914	5.33
Portuguese	2,452	14.30
Romanian	22	0.13
Russian	147	0.86
Scandinavian	8	0.05
Scotch-Irish	306	1.78
Scottish	442	2.58
Slovak	103	0.60
Slovene	8	0.05
Swedish	240	1.40
Swiss	59	0.34
Ukrainian	25	0.15
United States or American	463	2.70
Welsh	48	0.28
West Indian, excl. Hispanic:	16	0.09
Jamaican	5	0.03
Trinidadian and Tobagonian	4	0.02
West Indian	7	0.04
White:	16,580	96.68
Not Hispanic (16,269)	16,398	95.62
Hispanic (163)	182	1.06
Yugoslavian	16	0.09

Providence

Place Type: City
County: Providence
Population: 173,618

Ancestry/Race	Number	%
African American/Black:	29,700	17.11
Not Hispanic (22,103)	25,090	14.45
Hispanic (3,140)	4,610	2.66
African, sub-Saharan:	7,500	4.32
African	1,890	1.09
Cape Verdean	3,705	2.13
Ethiopian	18	0.01
Ghanian	270	0.16
Kenyan	34	0.02
Liberian	609	0.35
Nigerian	889	0.51
Sierra Leonean	7	0.00
South African	7	0.00
Other sub-Saharan African	71	0.04
Alaska Native tribes, specified:	10	0.01
Alaska Athabascan (3)	3	0.00
Aleut	2	0.00
Eskimo (2)	5	0.00
Alaska Native tribes, not specified	2	0.00
Am. Ind. or Alaska Nat., not spec.	1,568	0.90
Albanian	9	0.01
Alsatian	8	0.00
American Indian tribes, specified:	1,912	1.10
Apache (7)	22	0.01
Blackfeet (22)	89	0.05
Cherokee (69)	267	0.15
Cheyenne	3	0.00
Chickasaw (2)	3	0.00
Chippewa (2)	8	0.00
Choctaw (1)	5	0.00
Comanche	1	0.00
Cree	3	0.00
Creek (2)	7	0.00
Delaware (5)	7	0.00
Iroquois (10)	38	0.02
Kiowa	1	0.00
Latin American Indians (135)	310	0.18
Lumbee (1)	4	0.00
Menominee	2	0.00
Navajo (5)	9	0.01
Potawatomi (3)	9	0.01
Pueblo (7)	20	0.01
Puget Sound Salish	1	0.00
Seminole (2)	4	0.00
Sioux (4)	14	0.01
Tohono O'Odham (1)	1	0.00
Yuman (3)	3	0.00
All other tribes (697)	1,081	0.62
American Indian tribes, not spec.	325	0.19
Arab:	755	0.43
Arab/Arabic	55	0.03
Egyptian	40	0.02
Jordanian	23	0.01
Lebanese	415	0.24
Palestinian	12	0.01
Syrian	163	0.09
Other Arab	47	0.03
Armenian	1,092	0.63
Asian:	12,530	7.22
Bangladeshi (18)	24	0.01
Cambodian (3,216)	3,758	2.16
Chinese, ex. Taiwanese (1,359)	1,615	0.93
Filipino (437)	625	0.36
Hmong (847)	946	0.54
Indian (1,055)	1,318	0.76
Indonesian (24)	36	0.02
Japanese (269)	418	0.24
Korean (573)	630	0.36
Laotian (1,436)	1,718	0.99
Malaysian (33)	40	0.02
Pakistani (44)	62	0.04
Sri Lankan (18)	23	0.01
Taiwanese (120)	144	0.08
Thai (97)	156	0.09
Vietnamese (215)	270	0.16
Other Asian, specified (2)	26	0.01
Other Asian, not specified (445)	721	0.42
Assyrian/Chaldean/Syriac	71	0.04
Australian	19	0.01
Austrian	337	0.19
Belgian	87	0.05
Brazilian	77	0.04
British	536	0.31
Bulgarian	9	0.01
Canadian	388	0.22
Carpatho Rusyn	13	0.01
Celtic	17	0.01
Croatian	35	0.02
Cypriot	24	0.01
Czech	108	0.06
Czechoslovakian	82	0.05
Danish	209	0.12
Dutch	553	0.32
Eastern European	478	0.28
English	8,532	4.91
Estonian	14	0.01
European	729	0.42
Finnish	114	0.07
French, except Basque	6,551	3.77
French Canadian	2,735	1.58
German	5,911	3.40
Greek	666	0.38
Guyanese	11	0.01
Hawaii Native/Pacific Islander:	682	0.39
Melanesian: (3)	4	0.00
Fijian (3)	4	0.00
Micronesian: (157)	188	0.11
Guamanian/Chamorro (157)	187	0.11
Other Micronesian	1	0.00
Polynesian: (55)	114	0.07
Native Hawaiian (19)	74	0.04
Samoan (36)	39	0.02
Other Polynesian	1	0.00
Other Pac. Isl., specified	11	0.01
Other Pac. Isl., not spec. (55)	365	0.21
Hispanic or Latino:	52,146	30.03

Notes: 1. Figures in the "Number" column do not add up to the total population due to: a) Ancestry/Race overlap — e.g. persons can report being both White and Irish, b) persons of Hispanic origin can report being any race, c) persons reporting two ancestries are counted in both categories. 2. Numbers in parentheses indicate the number of persons reporting this ancestry/race alone, not in combination with any other ancestry/race. 3. Refer to the Explanation of Data in the front of the book for more detailed information.

Ancestry/Race	Number	%
Central American:	8,011	4.61
Costa Rican	54	0.03
Guatemalan	6,396	3.68
Honduran	355	0.20
Nicaraguan	53	0.03
Panamanian	103	0.06
Salvadoran	871	0.50
Other Central American	179	0.10
Cuban	468	0.27
Dominican Republic	14,638	8.43
Mexican	2,237	1.29
Puerto Rican	12,712	7.32
South American:	2,241	1.29
Argentinean	98	0.06
Bolivian	634	0.37
Chilean	55	0.03
Colombian	693	0.40
Ecuadorian	297	0.17
Peruvian	242	0.14
Uruguayan	7	0.00
Venezuelan	147	0.08
Other South American	68	0.04
Other Hispanic or Latino	11,839	6.82
Hungarian	370	0.21
Iranian	69	0.04
Irish	16,748	9.65
Israeli	92	0.05
Italian	23,960	13.80
Latvian	19	0.01
Lithuanian	532	0.31
Luxemburger	8	0.00
Macedonian	14	0.01
New Zealander	15	0.01
Northern European	57	0.03
Norwegian	417	0.24
Pennsylvania German	20	0.01
Polish	4,118	2.37
Portuguese	7,002	4.03
Romanian	296	0.17
Russian	2,411	1.39
Scandinavian	39	0.02
Scotch-Irish	813	0.47
Scottish	1,754	1.01
Serbian	27	0.02
Slavic	10	0.01
Slovak	87	0.05
Slovene	15	0.01
Soviet Union	34	0.02
Swedish	1,117	0.64
Swiss	150	0.09
Turkish	270	0.16
Ukrainian	448	0.26
United States or American	4,255	2.45
Welsh	457	0.26
West Indian, excl. Hispanic:	2,821	1.62
Bahamian	8	0.00
Barbadian	15	0.01
Belizean	19	0.01
Bermudan	15	0.01
British West Indian	76	0.04
Dutch West Indian	3	0.00
Haitian	1,878	1.08
Jamaican	488	0.28
Trinidadian and Tobagonian	133	0.08
U.S. Virgin Islander	24	0.01
West Indian	162	0.09
White:	100,834	58.08
Not Hispanic (79,451)	82,908	47.75
Hispanic (15,215)	17,926	10.32
Yugoslavian	65	0.04

Scituate

Place Type: Town
County: Providence
Population: 10,324

Ancestry/Race	Number	%
African American/Black:	46	0.45
Not Hispanic (29)	45	0.44
Hispanic (1)	1	0.01
African, sub-Saharan:	9	0.09
Cape Verdean	9	0.09
Am. Ind. or Alaska Nat., not spec.	8	0.08
American Indian tribes, specified:	15	0.15
Blackfeet	1	0.01
Cherokee (1)	3	0.03
Iroquois	3	0.03
All other tribes (1)	8	0.08
American Indian tribes, not spec.	4	0.04
Arab:	137	1.33
Lebanese	50	0.48
Syrian	87	0.84
Armenian	75	0.73
Asian:	69	0.67
Cambodian (1)	1	0.01
Chinese, ex. Taiwanese (27)	28	0.27
Filipino (12)	15	0.15
Indian (4)	4	0.04
Japanese (2)	6	0.06
Korean (12)	12	0.12
Laotian (1)	1	0.01
Vietnamese	1	0.01
Other Asian, not specified (1)	1	0.01
Austrian	22	0.21
Belgian	10	0.10
British	27	0.26
Canadian	31	0.30
Dutch	70	0.68
English	1,989	19.27
European	31	0.30
Finnish	31	0.30
French, except Basque	1,547	14.98
French Canadian	696	6.74
German	680	6.59
Greek	32	0.31
Hawaii Native/Pacific Islander:	4	0.04
Micronesian:	1	0.01
Guamanian/Chamorro	1	0.01
Polynesian: (1)	1	0.01
Samoan (1)	1	0.01
Other Pac. Isl., not spec. (2)	2	0.02
Hispanic or Latino:	77	0.75
Central American:	9	0.09
Guatemalan	6	0.06
Honduran	2	0.02
Salvadoran	1	0.01
Cuban	4	0.04
Dominican Republic	2	0.02
Mexican	12	0.12
Puerto Rican	11	0.11
South American:	14	0.14
Argentinean	2	0.02
Bolivian	2	0.02
Chilean	1	0.01
Colombian	5	0.05
Uruguayan	3	0.03
Venezuelan	1	0.01
Other Hispanic or Latino	25	0.24
Hungarian	16	0.15
Irish	2,096	20.30
Italian	2,814	27.26
Lithuanian	15	0.15
Norwegian	27	0.26
Polish	636	6.16
Portuguese	504	4.88
Russian	36	0.35
Scotch-Irish	176	1.70
Scottish	271	2.62
Slovak	37	0.36
Swedish	319	3.09
Ukrainian	37	0.36
United States or American	687	6.65
Welsh	40	0.39
White:	10,190	98.70
Not Hispanic (10,078)	10,134	98.16
Hispanic (53)	56	0.54
Yugoslavian	22	0.21

Smithfield

Place Type: Town
County: Providence
Population: 20,613

Ancestry/Race	Number	%
African American/Black:	204	0.99
Not Hispanic (161)	198	0.96
Hispanic (4)	6	0.03
African, sub-Saharan:	54	0.26
African	19	0.09
Cape Verdean	26	0.13
Liberian	5	0.02
Nigerian	4	0.02
Am. Ind. or Alaska Nat., not spec.	28	0.14
Albanian	14	0.07
American Indian tribes, specified:	34	0.16
Blackfeet	1	0.00
Cherokee	3	0.01
Chippewa (1)	1	0.00
Cree	1	0.00
Creek	1	0.00
Iroquois (3)	4	0.02
Latin American Indians (1)	2	0.01
Shoshone (1)	1	0.00
All other tribes (11)	20	0.10
American Indian tribes, not spec.	6	0.03
Arab:	95	0.46
Lebanese	22	0.11
Moroccan	7	0.03
Syrian	66	0.32
Armenian	143	0.69
Asian:	249	1.21
Cambodian (10)	10	0.05
Chinese, ex. Taiwanese (58)	69	0.33
Filipino (16)	19	0.09
Hmong (13)	13	0.06
Indian (30)	43	0.21
Japanese (20)	25	0.12
Korean (15)	23	0.11
Laotian (6)	11	0.05
Pakistani	3	0.01
Taiwanese (1)	1	0.00
Thai (1)	3	0.01
Vietnamese (10)	13	0.06
Other Asian, specified (1)	4	0.02
Other Asian, not specified	12	0.06
Austrian	52	0.25
Belgian	25	0.12
Brazilian	6	0.03
British	24	0.12
Canadian	85	0.41
Czech	16	0.08
Czechoslovakian	6	0.03
Danish	71	0.34
Dutch	61	0.30
English	2,828	13.74
European	11	0.05
Finnish	22	0.11
French, except Basque	2,456	11.93
French Canadian	1,904	9.25
German	1,292	6.28
Greek	248	1.20
Hawaii Native/Pacific Islander:	15	0.07
Micronesian: (2)	2	0.01
Guamanian/Chamorro (2)	2	0.01
Polynesian:	4	0.02
Native Hawaiian	2	0.01
Samoan	2	0.01
Other Pac. Isl., specified	3	0.01
Other Pac. Isl., not spec. (1)	6	0.03
Hispanic or Latino:	191	0.93
Central American:	14	0.07
Costa Rican	2	0.01
Guatemalan	10	0.05
Panamanian	2	0.01
Cuban	15	0.07
Dominican Republic	12	0.06
Mexican	35	0.17

Notes: 1. Figures in the "Number" column do not add up to the total population due to: a) Ancestry/Race overlap — e.g. persons can report being both White and Irish, b) persons of Hispanic origin can report being any race, c) persons reporting two ancestries are counted in both categories. 2. Numbers in parentheses indicate the number of persons reporting this ancestry/race alone, not in combination with any other ancestry/race. 3. Refer to the Explanation of Data in the front of the book for more detailed information.

Puerto Rican	46	0.22
South American:	31	0.15
Argentinean	5	0.02
Bolivian	5	0.02
Chilean	2	0.01
Colombian	10	0.05
Ecuadorian	8	0.04
Peruvian	1	0.00
Other Hispanic or Latino	38	0.18
Hungarian	38	0.18
Irish	4,480	21.76
Italian	6,411	31.14
Latvian	7	0.03
Lithuanian	87	0.42
Norwegian	102	0.50
Polish	1,084	5.26
Portuguese	961	4.67
Romanian	60	0.29
Russian	165	0.80
Scotch-Irish	208	1.01
Scottish	365	1.77
Slovak	50	0.24
Slovene	7	0.03
Swedish	359	1.74
Swiss	55	0.27
Turkish	28	0.14
Ukrainian	80	0.39
United States or American	569	2.76
Welsh	35	0.17
West Indian, excl. Hispanic:	105	0.51
British West Indian	48	0.23
Jamaican	24	0.12
Trinidadian and Tobagonian	26	0.13
West Indian	7	0.03
White:	20,175	97.88
Not Hispanic (19,929)	20,022	97.13
Hispanic (137)	153	0.74

South Kingstown

Place Type: Town
County: Washington
Population: 27,921

Ancestry/Race	Number	%
Acadian/Cajun	9	0.03
African American/Black:	704	2.52
Not Hispanic (408)	644	2.31
Hispanic (29)	60	0.21
African, sub-Saharan:	83	0.30
African	34	0.12
Cape Verdean	25	0.09
Liberian	8	0.03
Nigerian	8	0.03
Other sub-Saharan African	8	0.03
Alaska Native tribes, specified:	2	0.01
Eskimo	1	0.00
Tlingit-Haida (1)	1	0.00
Alaska Native tribes, not specified	2	0.01
Am. Ind. or Alaska Nat., not spec.	163	0.58
Albanian	18	0.06
American Indian tribes, specified:	496	1.78
Apache (1)	1	0.00
Cherokee (9)	28	0.10
Chippewa (1)	2	0.01
Choctaw (1)	1	0.00
Cree (1)	1	0.00
Iroquois (3)	10	0.04
Latin American Indians (1)	1	0.00
Navajo	2	0.01
Paiute (2)	2	0.01
Potawatomi (1)	2	0.01
Seminole	2	0.01
All other tribes (297)	444	1.59
American Indian tribes, not spec.	35	0.13
Arab:	198	0.71
Jordanian	11	0.04
Lebanese	113	0.40
Syrian	74	0.27
Armenian	98	0.35
Asian:	985	3.53
Cambodian (59)	71	0.25
Chinese, ex. Taiwanese (298)	324	1.16
Filipino (39)	51	0.18
Hmong (18)	18	0.06
Indian (163)	184	0.66
Indonesian (5)	5	0.02
Japanese (33)	46	0.16
Korean (137)	147	0.53
Laotian (29)	35	0.13
Malaysian (3)	3	0.01
Pakistani (2)	7	0.03
Sri Lankan (4)	6	0.02
Taiwanese (9)	14	0.05
Thai (5)	15	0.05
Vietnamese (28)	31	0.11
Other Asian, specified (1)	2	0.01
Other Asian, not specified (11)	26	0.09
Austrian	164	0.59
Belgian	12	0.04
Brazilian	18	0.06
British	111	0.40
Bulgarian	9	0.03
Canadian	125	0.45
Czech	8	0.03
Czechoslovakian	42	0.15
Danish	85	0.30
Dutch	276	0.99
Eastern European	38	0.14
English	5,206	18.65
Estonian	11	0.04
European	243	0.87
Finnish	69	0.25
French, except Basque	2,541	9.10
French Canadian	1,112	3.98
German	2,380	8.52
Greek	159	0.57
Hawaii Native/Pacific Islander:	49	0.18
Melanesian:	2	0.01
Fijian	2	0.01
Micronesian: (4)	4	0.01
Guamanian/Chamorro (2)	2	0.01
Other Micronesian (2)	2	0.01
Polynesian: (11)	20	0.07
Native Hawaiian (6)	11	0.04
Samoan (5)	7	0.03
Other Polynesian	2	0.01
Other Pac. Isl., specified	1	0.00
Other Pac. Isl., not spec.	22	0.08
Hispanic or Latino:	493	1.77
Central American:	38	0.14
Costa Rican	5	0.02
Guatemalan	18	0.06
Honduran	5	0.02
Nicaraguan	1	0.00
Panamanian	9	0.03
Cuban	6	0.02
Dominican Republic	77	0.28
Mexican	74	0.27
Puerto Rican	136	0.49
South American:	80	0.29
Argentinean	6	0.02
Bolivian	6	0.02
Chilean	5	0.02
Colombian	35	0.13
Ecuadorian	8	0.03
Paraguayan	4	0.01
Peruvian	3	0.01
Venezuelan	13	0.05
Other Hispanic or Latino	82	0.29
Hungarian	96	0.34
Iranian	63	0.23
Irish	6,670	23.89
Israeli	50	0.18
Italian	4,599	16.47
Latvian	16	0.06
Lithuanian	160	0.57
Northern European	16	0.06
Norwegian	169	0.61
Polish	1,376	4.93
Portuguese	837	3.00
Romanian	37	0.13
Russian	385	1.38
Scandinavian	85	0.30
Scotch-Irish	458	1.64
Scottish	914	3.27
Slavic	19	0.07
Slovak	57	0.20
Slovene	8	0.03
Swedish	836	2.99
Swiss	38	0.14
Turkish	54	0.19
Ukrainian	169	0.61
United States or American	977	3.50
Welsh	106	0.38
West Indian, excl. Hispanic:	40	0.14
Haitian	8	0.03
Jamaican	32	0.11
White:	25,781	92.34
Not Hispanic (25,230)	25,516	91.39
Hispanic (210)	265	0.95

Tiverton

Place Type: Town
County: Newport
Population: 15,260

Ancestry/Race	Number	%
African American/Black:	98	0.64
Not Hispanic (61)	88	0.58
Hispanic (4)	10	0.07
African, sub-Saharan:	21	0.14
Cape Verdean	21	0.14
Am. Ind. or Alaska Nat., not spec.	16	0.10
American Indian tribes, specified:	53	0.35
Blackfeet (4)	11	0.07
Cherokee (2)	4	0.03
Delaware (1)	1	0.01
Iroquois (1)	4	0.03
Latin American Indians	3	0.02
Sioux	1	0.01
All other tribes (14)	29	0.19
American Indian tribes, not spec.	2	0.01
Arab:	131	0.86
Lebanese	84	0.55
Syrian	47	0.31
Asian:	93	0.61
Chinese, ex. Taiwanese (7)	10	0.07
Filipino (23)	38	0.25
Indian (9)	11	0.07
Japanese (9)	12	0.08
Korean (5)	7	0.05
Thai (2)	2	0.01
Vietnamese (2)	3	0.02
Other Asian, not specified (2)	10	0.07
Austrian	11	0.07
Basque	7	0.05
Belgian	18	0.12
Brazilian	6	0.04
British	15	0.10
Canadian	82	0.54
Czechoslovakian	12	0.08
Danish	29	0.19
Dutch	59	0.39
English	2,186	14.33
European	8	0.05
French, except Basque	2,205	14.45
French Canadian	1,298	8.51
German	881	5.77
Greek	85	0.56
Hawaii Native/Pacific Islander:	11	0.07
Micronesian: (1)	2	0.01
Guamanian/Chamorro (1)	2	0.01
Polynesian: (3)	7	0.05
Native Hawaiian (1)	5	0.03
Samoan (2)	2	0.01
Other Pac. Isl., not spec. (1)	2	0.01
Hispanic or Latino:	104	0.68
Central American:	2	0.01

Notes: 1. Figures in the "Number" column do not add up to the total population due to: a) Ancestry/Race overlap — e.g. persons can report being both White and Irish, b) persons of Hispanic origin can report being any race, c) persons reporting two ancestries are counted in both categories. 2. Numbers in parentheses indicate the number of persons reporting this ancestry/race alone, not in combination with any other ancestry/race. 3. Refer to the Explanation of Data in the front of the book for more detailed information.

Ancestry/Race	Number	%
Honduran	1	0.01
Panamanian	1	0.01
Cuban	8	0.05
Dominican Republic	7	0.05
Mexican	16	0.10
Puerto Rican	40	0.26
South American:	11	0.07
Chilean	2	0.01
Colombian	4	0.03
Peruvian	1	0.01
Other South American	4	0.03
Other Hispanic or Latino	20	0.13
Hungarian	12	0.08
Irish	2,485	16.28
Italian	998	6.54
Latvian	6	0.04
Norwegian	31	0.20
Polish	720	4.72
Portuguese	4,783	31.34
Romanian	15	0.10
Russian	65	0.43
Scandinavian	13	0.09
Scotch-Irish	208	1.36
Scottish	229	1.50
Swedish	203	1.33
Swiss	18	0.12
Ukrainian	22	0.14
United States or American	600	3.93
Welsh	7	0.05
White:	15,058	98.68
Not Hispanic (14,896)	14,991	98.24
Hispanic (56)	67	0.44
Yugoslavian	6	0.04

Valley Falls

Place Type: Census Designated Place
County: Providence
Population: 11,599

Ancestry/Race	Number	%
African American/Black:	115	0.99
Not Hispanic (78)	95	0.82
Hispanic (18)	20	0.17
African, sub-Saharan:	46	0.40
Cape Verdean	46	0.40
Alaska Native tribes, specified:	2	0.02
Alaska Athabascan (2)	2	0.02
Am. Ind. or Alaska Nat., not spec.	22	0.19
American Indian tribes, specified:	15	0.13
Cherokee (1)	2	0.02
Iroquois	2	0.02
Sioux	1	0.01
All other tribes (2)	10	0.09
American Indian tribes, not spec.	1	0.01
Arab:	175	1.52
Arab/Arabic	8	0.07
Egyptian	20	0.17
Syrian	147	1.27
Armenian	37	0.32
Asian:	83	0.72
Cambodian (2)	2	0.02
Chinese, ex. Taiwanese (21)	21	0.18
Filipino (2)	7	0.06
Indian (15)	18	0.16
Indonesian (1)	1	0.01
Japanese	3	0.03
Korean (6)	11	0.09
Laotian (3)	3	0.03
Pakistani (5)	6	0.05
Thai (1)	1	0.01
Vietnamese (4)	4	0.03
Other Asian, not specified	6	0.05
Austrian	38	0.33
Belgian	16	0.14
Brazilian	9	0.08
British	37	0.32
Czech	23	0.20
Dutch	19	0.16
English	1,333	11.55
European	8	0.07
Finnish	8	0.07
French, except Basque	1,835	15.91
French Canadian	1,217	10.55
German	423	3.67
Greek	19	0.16
Hawaii Native/Pacific Islander:	8	0.07
Other Pac. Isl., not spec.	8	0.07
Hispanic or Latino:	457	3.94
Central American:	22	0.19
Costa Rican	1	0.01
Guatemalan	19	0.16
Salvadoran	2	0.02
Cuban	4	0.03
Dominican Republic	14	0.12
Mexican	16	0.14
Puerto Rican	77	0.66
South American:	179	1.54
Chilean	2	0.02
Colombian	165	1.42
Ecuadorian	2	0.02
Venezuelan	2	0.02
Other South American	8	0.07
Other Hispanic or Latino	145	1.25
Hungarian	24	0.21
Irish	2,575	22.32
Italian	912	7.91
Lithuanian	12	0.10
Norwegian	14	0.12
Polish	950	8.23
Portuguese	2,753	23.86
Russian	35	0.30
Scotch-Irish	105	0.91
Scottish	172	1.49
Swedish	88	0.76
Swiss	30	0.26
Turkish	20	0.17
Ukrainian	50	0.43
United States or American	267	2.31
White:	11,259	97.07
Not Hispanic (10,841)	10,939	94.31
Hispanic (280)	320	2.76

Warren

Place Type: Town
County: Bristol
Population: 11,360

Ancestry/Race	Number	%
African American/Black:	147	1.29
Not Hispanic (88)	140	1.23
Hispanic (6)	7	0.06
African, sub-Saharan:	34	0.30
African	7	0.06
Cape Verdean	27	0.24
Am. Ind. or Alaska Nat., not spec.	24	0.21
Albanian	7	0.06
Alsatian	4	0.04
American Indian tribes, specified:	42	0.37
Blackfeet (1)	1	0.01
Cherokee (2)	7	0.06
Creek	2	0.02
Iroquois (1)	4	0.04
Potawatomi (3)	3	0.03
Sioux	2	0.02
All other tribes (8)	23	0.20
American Indian tribes, not spec.	1	0.01
Arab:	103	0.91
Egyptian	13	0.11
Lebanese	78	0.69
Syrian	12	0.11
Armenian	14	0.12
Asian:	84	0.74
Chinese, ex. Taiwanese (29)	31	0.27
Filipino (10)	20	0.18
Indian (6)	7	0.06
Japanese (2)	8	0.07
Korean (2)	2	0.02
Thai (4)	6	0.05
Vietnamese (3)	3	0.03
Other Asian, not specified (1)	7	0.06
Austrian	19	0.17
Belgian	8	0.07
Brazilian	11	0.10
British	47	0.41
Canadian	36	0.32
Czech	6	0.05
Czechoslovakian	94	0.83
Danish	11	0.10
Dutch	62	0.55
English	1,371	12.07
European	40	0.35
Finnish	10	0.09
French, except Basque	1,731	15.24
French Canadian	762	6.71
German	466	4.10
Greek	32	0.28
Hawaii Native/Pacific Islander:	17	0.15
Polynesian: (1)	3	0.03
Native Hawaiian	1	0.01
Samoan (1)	2	0.02
Other Pac. Isl., not spec. (3)	14	0.12
Hispanic or Latino:	106	0.93
Central American:	2	0.02
Guatemalan	1	0.01
Honduran	1	0.01
Cuban	3	0.03
Dominican Republic	6	0.05
Mexican	16	0.14
Puerto Rican	28	0.25
South American:	16	0.14
Colombian	3	0.03
Ecuadorian	4	0.04
Venezuelan	3	0.03
Other South American	6	0.05
Other Hispanic or Latino	35	0.31
Hungarian	24	0.21
Iranian	23	0.20
Irish	1,648	14.51
Italian	1,966	17.31
Lithuanian	39	0.34
Luxemburger	21	0.18
Norwegian	39	0.34
Polish	800	7.04
Portuguese	3,537	31.14
Russian	37	0.33
Scotch-Irish	112	0.99
Scottish	228	2.01
Slovak	7	0.06
Slovene	7	0.06
Swedish	113	0.99
Swiss	6	0.05
United States or American	321	2.83
Welsh	33	0.29
West Indian, excl. Hispanic:	36	0.32
Haitian	36	0.32
White:	11,126	97.94
Not Hispanic (10,931)	11,055	97.32
Hispanic (68)	71	0.63

Warwick

Place Type: City
County: Kent
Population: 85,808

Ancestry/Race	Number	%
African American/Black:	1,351	1.57
Not Hispanic (932)	1,248	1.45
Hispanic (64)	103	0.12
African, sub-Saharan:	372	0.43
African	91	0.11
Cape Verdean	250	0.29
Liberian	21	0.02
South African	5	0.01
Other sub-Saharan African	5	0.01
Alaska Native tribes, specified:	6	0.01
Aleut	6	0.01
Am. Ind. or Alaska Nat., not spec.	177	0.21

Notes: 1. Figures in the "Number" column do not add up to the total population due to: a) Ancestry/Race overlap — e.g. persons can report being both White and Irish, b) persons of Hispanic origin can report being any race, c) persons reporting two ancestries are counted in both categories. 2. Numbers in parentheses indicate the number of persons reporting this ancestry/race alone, not in combination with any other ancestry/race. 3. Refer to the Explanation of Data in the front of the book for more detailed information.

Albanian	5	0.01
American Indian tribes, specified:	383	0.45
Apache (3)	5	0.01
Blackfeet (8)	28	0.03
Cherokee (10)	41	0.05
Cheyenne (1)	3	0.00
Chippewa (2)	3	0.00
Choctaw (1)	6	0.01
Cree	1	0.00
Creek	3	0.00
Delaware	2	0.00
Iroquois (9)	22	0.03
Latin American Indians (4)	9	0.01
Navajo (1)	1	0.00
Osage	1	0.00
Paiute (1)	1	0.00
Pima (5)	10	0.01
Potawatomi (2)	2	0.00
Pueblo (1)	1	0.00
Seminole	2	0.00
Sioux (1)	14	0.02
Yuman	1	0.00
All other tribes (107)	227	0.26
American Indian tribes, not spec.	31	0.04
Arab:	570	0.66
Egyptian	76	0.09
Lebanese	337	0.39
Syrian	143	0.17
Other Arab	14	0.02
Armenian	872	1.02
Asian:	1,550	1.81
Bangladeshi (5)	5	0.01
Cambodian (109)	127	0.15
Chinese, ex. Taiwanese (293)	323	0.38
Filipino (183)	254	0.30
Hmong (34)	37	0.04
Indian (211)	262	0.31
Indonesian (2)	4	0.00
Japanese (55)	91	0.11
Korean (109)	130	0.15
Laotian (58)	67	0.08
Malaysian	1	0.00
Pakistani (30)	37	0.04
Sri Lankan (4)	4	0.00
Taiwanese (16)	19	0.02
Thai (29)	39	0.05
Vietnamese (62)	65	0.08
Other Asian, specified (4)	6	0.01
Other Asian, not specified (53)	79	0.09
Assyrian/Chaldean/Syriac	9	0.01
Australian	6	0.01
Austrian	223	0.26
Belgian	83	0.10
Brazilian	7	0.01
British	246	0.29
Canadian	319	0.37
Croatian	14	0.02
Czech	70	0.08
Czechoslovakian	76	0.09
Danish	123	0.14
Dutch	489	0.57
Eastern European	49	0.06
English	14,450	16.84
Estonian	33	0.04
European	147	0.17
Finnish	157	0.18
French, except Basque	10,713	12.48
French Canadian	4,233	4.93
German	5,197	6.06
Greek	388	0.45
Hawaii Native/Pacific Islander:	41	0.05
Micronesian: (6)	6	0.01
Guamanian/Chamorro (6)	6	0.01
Polynesian: (6)	19	0.02
Native Hawaiian (4)	13	0.02
Samoan (1)	2	0.00
Other Polynesian (1)	4	0.00
Other Pac. Isl., not spec. (3)	16	0.02
Hispanic or Latino:	1,372	1.60
Central American:	63	0.07
Costa Rican	1	0.00
Guatemalan	42	0.05
Honduran	4	0.00
Nicaraguan	2	0.00
Panamanian	7	0.01
Salvadoran	4	0.00
Other Central American	3	0.00
Cuban	58	0.07
Dominican Republic	180	0.21
Mexican	215	0.25
Puerto Rican	374	0.44
South American:	143	0.17
Argentinean	14	0.02
Bolivian	11	0.01
Chilean	4	0.00
Colombian	53	0.06
Ecuadorian	18	0.02
Peruvian	28	0.03
Uruguayan	2	0.00
Venezuelan	6	0.01
Other South American	7	0.01
Other Hispanic or Latino	339	0.40
Hungarian	142	0.17
Iranian	51	0.06
Irish	24,403	28.44
Israeli	5	0.01
Italian	19,549	22.78
Latvian	11	0.01
Lithuanian	318	0.37
Norwegian	476	0.55
Polish	3,249	3.79
Portuguese	5,867	6.84
Romanian	24	0.03
Russian	833	0.97
Scandinavian	28	0.03
Scotch-Irish	1,588	1.85
Scottish	1,896	2.21
Slovak	21	0.02
Slovene	5	0.01
Swedish	2,759	3.22
Swiss	94	0.11
Turkish	16	0.02
Ukrainian	236	0.28
United States or American	2,433	2.84
Welsh	321	0.37
West Indian, excl. Hispanic:	116	0.14
Barbadian	17	0.02
Dutch West Indian	5	0.01
Haitian	56	0.07
Jamaican	18	0.02
Trinidadian and Tobagonian	9	0.01
West Indian	11	0.01
White:	82,636	96.30
Not Hispanic (80,920)	81,766	95.29
Hispanic (775)	870	1.01
Yugoslavian	14	0.02

West Warwick

Place Type: Census Designated Place
County: Kent
Population: 29,581

Ancestry/Race	Number	%
African American/Black:	466	1.58
Not Hispanic (306)	439	1.48
Hispanic (22)	27	0.09
African, sub-Saharan:	133	0.45
African	8	0.03
Cape Verdean	116	0.39
Other sub-Saharan African	9	0.03
Am. Ind. or Alaska Nat., not spec.	103	0.35
Albanian	7	0.02
American Indian tribes, specified:	159	0.54
Apache (1)	1	0.00
Blackfeet (1)	12	0.04
Cherokee (10)	24	0.08
Cheyenne (1)	1	0.00
Chippewa (1)	6	0.02
Choctaw	1	0.00
Cree (1)	1	0.00
Creek	2	0.01
Crow	2	0.01
Iroquois (3)	6	0.02
Latin American Indians (5)	5	0.02
Navajo	1	0.00
Ottawa (1)	2	0.01
Sioux (3)	3	0.01
All other tribes (40)	92	0.31
American Indian tribes, not spec.	5	0.02
Arab:	155	0.52
Arab/Arabic	22	0.07
Jordanian	7	0.02
Lebanese	66	0.22
Palestinian	9	0.03
Syrian	51	0.17
Armenian	175	0.59
Asian:	538	1.82
Bangladeshi (3)	3	0.01
Cambodian (16)	24	0.08
Chinese, ex. Taiwanese (147)	161	0.54
Filipino (115)	152	0.51
Hmong (5)	7	0.02
Indian (54)	70	0.24
Japanese (6)	20	0.07
Korean (18)	30	0.10
Laotian (14)	22	0.07
Pakistani (6)	6	0.02
Taiwanese (6)	7	0.02
Thai (3)	3	0.01
Vietnamese (5)	6	0.02
Other Asian, not specified (10)	27	0.09
Austrian	13	0.04
Belgian	27	0.09
Brazilian	81	0.27
British	73	0.25
Canadian	151	0.51
Croatian	8	0.03
Czech	41	0.14
Czechoslovakian	22	0.07
Danish	65	0.22
Dutch	164	0.55
English	3,515	11.88
European	50	0.17
Finnish	24	0.08
French, except Basque	5,473	18.50
French Canadian	2,779	9.39
German	1,561	5.28
Greek	55	0.19
Hawaii Native/Pacific Islander:	30	0.10
Micronesian: (3)	9	0.03
Guamanian/Chamorro (3)	9	0.03
Polynesian: (4)	8	0.03
Native Hawaiian (4)	7	0.02
Samoan	1	0.00
Other Pac. Isl., not spec.	13	0.04
Hispanic or Latino:	918	3.10
Central American:	58	0.20
Costa Rican	1	0.00
Guatemalan	35	0.12
Honduran	11	0.04
Nicaraguan	3	0.01
Salvadoran	8	0.03
Cuban	18	0.06
Dominican Republic	61	0.21
Mexican	346	1.17
Puerto Rican	220	0.74
South American:	69	0.23
Argentinean	3	0.01
Bolivian	1	0.00
Chilean	1	0.00
Colombian	26	0.09
Ecuadorian	5	0.02
Peruvian	11	0.04
Uruguayan	14	0.05
Venezuelan	7	0.02
Other South American	1	0.00
Other Hispanic or Latino	146	0.49
Hungarian	117	0.40
Icelander	7	0.02

Notes: 1. Figures in the "Number" column do not add up to the total population due to: a) Ancestry/Race overlap — e.g. persons can report being both White and Irish, b) persons of Hispanic origin can report being any race, c) persons reporting two ancestries are counted in both categories. 2. Numbers in parentheses indicate the number of persons reporting this ancestry/race alone, not in combination with any other ancestry/race. 3. Refer to the Explanation of Data in the front of the book for more detailed information.

Ancestry/Race	Number	%
Iranian	10	0.03
Irish	5,646	19.09
Israeli	6	0.02
Italian	6,703	22.66
Lithuanian	100	0.34
Norwegian	114	0.39
Pennsylvania German	10	0.03
Polish	1,591	5.38
Portuguese	2,958	10.00
Russian	126	0.43
Scotch-Irish	330	1.12
Scottish	444	1.50
Slavic	9	0.03
Slovak	89	0.30
Slovene	8	0.03
Swedish	658	2.22
Swiss	22	0.07
Ukrainian	50	0.17
United States or American	666	2.25
Welsh	77	0.26
West Indian, excl. Hispanic:	17	0.06
British West Indian	17	0.06
White:	28,221	95.40
Not Hispanic (27,306)	27,724	93.72
Hispanic (434)	497	1.68

Westerly

Place Type: Town
County: Washington
Population: 22,966

Ancestry/Race	Number	%
African American/Black:	253	1.10
Not Hispanic (160)	248	1.08
Hispanic (4)	5	0.02
African, sub-Saharan:	79	0.34
African	3	0.01
Cape Verdean	51	0.22
Liberian	14	0.06
Other sub-Saharan African	11	0.05
Am. Ind. or Alaska Nat., not spec.	33	0.14
Albanian	6	0.03
American Indian tribes, specified:	195	0.85
Apache	2	0.01
Blackfeet	8	0.03
Cherokee (5)	19	0.08
Chippewa (3)	8	0.03
Choctaw	4	0.02
Cree	1	0.00
Creek	3	0.01
Delaware (2)	3	0.01
Iroquois	4	0.02
Latin American Indians	1	0.00
Sioux	3	0.01
All other tribes (99)	139	0.61
American Indian tribes, not spec.	1	0.00
Arab:	74	0.32
Lebanese	43	0.19
Syrian	14	0.06
Other Arab	17	0.07
Armenian	34	0.15
Asian:	525	2.29
Chinese, ex. Taiwanese (357)	380	1.65
Filipino (19)	40	0.17
Indian (16)	23	0.10
Japanese (9)	10	0.04
Korean (22)	31	0.13
Laotian (9)	12	0.05
Taiwanese (2)	4	0.02
Thai (3)	5	0.02
Vietnamese (2)	5	0.02
Other Asian, not specified (8)	15	0.07
Austrian	34	0.15
Belgian	68	0.30
British	200	0.87
Canadian	68	0.30
Celtic	12	0.05
Czech	28	0.12
Czechoslovakian	38	0.17
Danish	50	0.22
Dutch	100	0.44
Eastern European	16	0.07
English	3,264	14.21
European	54	0.24
Finnish	102	0.44
French, except Basque	2,196	9.56
French Canadian	794	3.46
German	2,057	8.96
Greek	249	1.08
Hawaii Native/Pacific Islander:	7	0.03
Polynesian:	3	0.01
Native Hawaiian	2	0.01
Samoan	1	0.00
Other Pac. Isl., not spec.	4	0.02
Hispanic or Latino:	270	1.18
Central American:	6	0.03
Guatemalan	3	0.01
Honduran	1	0.00
Panamanian	1	0.00
Salvadoran	1	0.00
Cuban	5	0.02
Dominican Republic	2	0.01
Mexican	77	0.34
Puerto Rican	111	0.48
South American:	18	0.08
Argentinean	1	0.00
Bolivian	3	0.01
Colombian	12	0.05
Ecuadorian	2	0.01
Other Hispanic or Latino	51	0.22
Hungarian	40	0.17
Irish	4,089	17.80
Italian	7,863	34.24
Lithuanian	105	0.46
Northern European	14	0.06
Norwegian	131	0.57
Pennsylvania German	11	0.05
Polish	1,056	4.60
Portuguese	856	3.73
Romanian	7	0.03
Russian	203	0.88
Scandinavian	8	0.03
Scotch-Irish	315	1.37
Scottish	1,037	4.52
Slovak	16	0.07
Swedish	387	1.69
Swiss	41	0.18
Ukrainian	74	0.32
United States or American	833	3.63
Welsh	76	0.33
West Indian, excl. Hispanic:	44	0.19
Haitian	9	0.04
Jamaican	26	0.11
West Indian	9	0.04
White:	22,116	96.30
Not Hispanic (21,669)	21,920	95.45
Hispanic (188)	196	0.85

Woonsocket

Place Type: City
County: Providence
Population: 43,224

Ancestry/Race	Number	%
African American/Black:	2,448	5.66
Not Hispanic (1,692)	2,139	4.95
Hispanic (228)	309	0.71
African, sub-Saharan:	677	1.57
African	286	0.66
Cape Verdean	190	0.44
Liberian	45	0.10
Nigerian	79	0.18
Senegalese	28	0.06
Other sub-Saharan African	49	0.11
Alaska Native tribes, specified:	1	0.00
Eskimo	1	0.00
Am. Ind. or Alaska Nat., not spec.	189	0.44
Albanian	45	0.10
American Indian tribes, specified:	171	0.40
Apache	4	0.01
Blackfeet (5)	19	0.04
Cherokee (3)	33	0.08
Chickasaw	2	0.00
Chippewa	3	0.01
Comanche (2)	2	0.00
Cree	1	0.00
Crow	1	0.00
Iroquois (1)	10	0.02
Latin American Indians (5)	6	0.01
Lumbee	1	0.00
Seminole	1	0.00
Sioux (4)	15	0.03
All other tribes (28)	73	0.17
American Indian tribes, not spec.	7	0.02
Arab:	230	0.53
Arab/Arabic	41	0.09
Egyptian	5	0.01
Lebanese	7	0.02
Moroccan	7	0.02
Syrian	170	0.39
Armenian	25	0.06
Asian:	2,183	5.05
Cambodian (113)	146	0.34
Chinese, ex. Taiwanese (68)	110	0.25
Filipino (39)	75	0.17
Indian (90)	118	0.27
Japanese (1)	14	0.03
Korean (10)	14	0.03
Laotian (1,082)	1,293	2.99
Pakistani (2)	12	0.03
Thai (13)	20	0.05
Vietnamese (209)	253	0.59
Other Asian, not specified (64)	128	0.30
Austrian	7	0.02
Belgian	71	0.16
British	104	0.24
Canadian	400	0.93
Czech	21	0.05
Czechoslovakian	16	0.04
Danish	21	0.05
Dutch	153	0.35
English	2,241	5.18
European	65	0.15
Finnish	27	0.06
French, except Basque	9,902	22.91
French Canadian	10,008	23.15
German	1,356	3.14
Greek	155	0.36
Hawaii Native/Pacific Islander:	60	0.14
Micronesian: (6)	6	0.01
Guamanian/Chamorro (6)	6	0.01
Polynesian: (3)	15	0.03
Native Hawaiian (3)	14	0.03
Samoan	1	0.00
Other Pac. Isl., not spec. (5)	39	0.09
Hispanic or Latino:	4,030	9.32
Central American:	86	0.20
Costa Rican	5	0.01
Guatemalan	47	0.11
Honduran	13	0.03
Panamanian	5	0.01
Salvadoran	15	0.03
Other Central American	1	0.00
Cuban	22	0.05
Dominican Republic	343	0.79
Mexican	168	0.39
Puerto Rican	2,798	6.47
South American:	65	0.15
Colombian	37	0.09
Ecuadorian	4	0.01
Paraguayan	1	0.00
Peruvian	12	0.03
Uruguayan	1	0.00
Venezuelan	3	0.01
Other South American	7	0.02
Other Hispanic or Latino	548	1.27
Hungarian	60	0.14
Icelander	22	0.05

Notes: 1. Figures in the "Number" column do not add up to the total population due to: a) Ancestry/Race overlap — e.g. persons can report being both White and Irish, b) persons of Hispanic origin can report being any race, c) persons reporting two ancestries are counted in both categories. 2. Numbers in parentheses indicate the number of persons reporting this ancestry/race alone, not in combination with any other ancestry/race. 3. Refer to the Explanation of Data in the front of the book for more detailed information.

Ancestry/Race	Number	%
Irish	4,626	10.70
Italian	4,092	9.47
Latvian	36	0.08
Lithuanian	69	0.16
Macedonian	29	0.07
Norwegian	79	0.18
Polish	1,776	4.11
Portuguese	1,202	2.78
Romanian	118	0.27
Russian	81	0.19
Scandinavian	19	0.04
Scotch-Irish	220	0.51
Scottish	458	1.06
Slavic	13	0.03
Swedish	286	0.66
Swiss	23	0.05
Turkish	11	0.03
Ukrainian	259	0.60
United States or American	1,347	3.12
Welsh	28	0.06
West Indian, excl. Hispanic:	64	0.15
British West Indian	8	0.02
Jamaican	17	0.04
Trinidadian and Tobagonian	8	0.02
U.S. Virgin Islander	25	0.06
West Indian	6	0.01
White:	36,956	85.50
Not Hispanic (34,503)	35,303	81.67
Hispanic (1,432)	1,653	3.82
Yugoslavian	37	0.09

Aiken

Place Type: City
County: Aiken
Population: 25,337

Ancestry/Race	Number	%
Afghan	6	0.02
African American/Black:	7,802	30.79
Not Hispanic (7,623)	7,733	30.52
Hispanic (55)	69	0.27
African, sub-Saharan:	536	2.12
African	501	1.98
Nigerian	12	0.05
South African	23	0.09
Alaska Native tribes, specified:	5	0.02
Alaska Athabascan (3)	3	0.01
Eskimo (2)	2	0.01
Am. Ind. or Alaska Nat., not spec.	43	0.17
Albanian	25	0.10
American Indian tribes, specified:	112	0.44
Apache (2)	4	0.02
Blackfeet	7	0.03
Cherokee (10)	49	0.19
Chickasaw (3)	4	0.02
Chippewa (4)	9	0.04
Choctaw	3	0.01
Creek (3)	4	0.02
Iroquois	1	0.00
Latin American Indians (3)	4	0.02
Lumbee (1)	1	0.00
Shoshone (1)	1	0.00
Sioux	3	0.01
All other tribes (17)	22	0.09
American Indian tribes, not spec.	14	0.06
Arab:	68	0.27
Arab/Arabic	23	0.09
Lebanese	36	0.14
Syrian	9	0.04
Armenian	9	0.04
Asian:	398	1.57
Cambodian (2)	3	0.01
Chinese, ex. Taiwanese (71)	79	0.31
Filipino (23)	37	0.15
Hmong (3)	3	0.01
Indian (88)	96	0.38
Indonesian (1)	1	0.00
Japanese (64)	72	0.28
Korean (29)	43	0.17
Malaysian (1)	1	0.00
Pakistani (3)	3	0.01
Taiwanese (6)	6	0.02
Thai (3)	5	0.02
Vietnamese (19)	27	0.11
Other Asian, specified	2	0.01
Other Asian, not specified (10)	20	0.08
Austrian	43	0.17
Belgian	47	0.19
British	192	0.76
Bulgarian	8	0.03
Canadian	83	0.33
Croatian	15	0.06
Czech	30	0.12
Czechoslovakian	43	0.17
Danish	31	0.12
Dutch	249	0.98
Eastern European	23	0.09
English	3,493	13.78
European	195	0.77
Finnish	22	0.09
French, except Basque	581	2.29
French Canadian	42	0.17
German	2,985	11.78
Greek	41	0.16
Hawaii Native/Pacific Islander:	13	0.05
Micronesian:	2	0.01
Guamanian/Chamorro	2	0.01
Polynesian: (1)	5	0.02
Native Hawaiian (1)	5	0.02
Other Pac. Isl., specified	1	0.00
Other Pac. Isl., not spec. (2)	5	0.02
Hispanic or Latino:	378	1.49
Central American:	17	0.07
Costa Rican	5	0.02
Guatemalan	8	0.03
Panamanian	2	0.01
Salvadoran	2	0.01
Cuban	28	0.11
Dominican Republic	2	0.01
Mexican	151	0.60
Puerto Rican	99	0.39
South American:	12	0.05
Argentinean	4	0.02
Colombian	2	0.01
Ecuadorian	1	0.00
Peruvian	3	0.01
Other South American	2	0.01
Other Hispanic or Latino	69	0.27
Hungarian	108	0.43
Iranian	26	0.10
Irish	2,562	10.11
Italian	861	3.40
Latvian	7	0.03
Lithuanian	44	0.17
New Zealander	25	0.10
Northern European	29	0.11
Norwegian	101	0.40
Pennsylvania German	20	0.08
Polish	322	1.27
Portuguese	45	0.18
Romanian	7	0.03
Russian	81	0.32
Scandinavian	22	0.09
Scotch-Irish	951	3.75
Scottish	611	2.41
Serbian	7	0.03
Slovak	56	0.22
Slovene	29	0.11
Swedish	154	0.61
Swiss	58	0.23
Ukrainian	7	0.03
United States or American	2,185	8.62
Welsh	157	0.62
West Indian, excl. Hispanic:	65	0.26
Haitian	10	0.04
Jamaican	45	0.18
West Indian	10	0.04
White:	17,092	67.46
Not Hispanic (16,693)	16,887	66.65
Hispanic (188)	205	0.81

Anderson

Place Type: City
County: Anderson
Population: 25,514

Ancestry/Race	Number	%
African American/Black:	8,834	34.62
Not Hispanic (8,653)	8,792	34.46
Hispanic (25)	42	0.16
African, sub-Saharan:	321	1.27
African	296	1.17
Ghanian	12	0.05
Nigerian	7	0.03
Other sub-Saharan African	6	0.02
Alaska Native tribes, specified:	1	0.00
Eskimo (1)	1	0.00
Am. Ind. or Alaska Nat., not spec.	65	0.25
American Indian tribes, specified:	87	0.34
Blackfeet	4	0.02
Cherokee (12)	40	0.16
Chippewa	2	0.01
Choctaw (1)	2	0.01
Creek (1)	1	0.00
Crow	4	0.02
Latin American Indians (1)	2	0.01
Lumbee (5)	5	0.02
Navajo (1)	9	0.04
Seminole	5	0.02
Sioux	8	0.03
All other tribes (5)	5	0.02
American Indian tribes, not spec.	9	0.04
Arab:	53	0.21
Arab/Arabic	4	0.02
Egyptian	6	0.02
Lebanese	9	0.04
Syrian	34	0.13
Armenian	3	0.01
Asian:	265	1.04
Chinese, ex. Taiwanese (44)	55	0.22
Filipino (9)	17	0.07
Indian (63)	80	0.31
Indonesian (1)	6	0.02
Japanese (23)	28	0.11
Korean (17)	22	0.09
Laotian (1)	2	0.01
Pakistani (4)	10	0.04
Thai (1)	1	0.00
Vietnamese (23)	24	0.09
Other Asian, specified	2	0.01
Other Asian, not specified (10)	18	0.07
Austrian	37	0.15
Belgian	6	0.02
British	107	0.42
Canadian	62	0.25
Celtic	9	0.04
Czech	4	0.02
Danish	20	0.08
Dutch	181	0.72
Eastern European	13	0.05
English	2,064	8.18
European	188	0.74
Finnish	6	0.02
French, except Basque	456	1.81
French Canadian	59	0.23
German	1,789	7.09
Greek	96	0.38
Guyanese	10	0.04
Hawaii Native/Pacific Islander:	33	0.13
Micronesian: (7)	12	0.05
Guamanian/Chamorro (7)	12	0.05
Polynesian: (2)	17	0.07
Native Hawaiian (2)	17	0.07
Other Pac. Isl., specified	2	0.01
Other Pac. Isl., not spec.	2	0.01
Hispanic or Latino:	377	1.48
Central American:	16	0.06
Costa Rican	1	0.00

Notes: 1. Figures in the "Number" column do not add up to the total population due to: a) Ancestry/Race overlap — e.g. persons can report being both White and Irish, b) persons of Hispanic origin can report being any race, c) persons reporting two ancestries are counted in both categories. 2. Numbers in parentheses indicate the number of persons reporting this ancestry/race alone, not in combination with any other ancestry/race. 3. Refer to the Explanation of Data in the front of the book for more detailed information.

Guatemalan	2	0.01
Honduran	6	0.02
Nicaraguan	1	0.00
Panamanian	3	0.01
Salvadoran	3	0.01
Cuban	14	0.05
Dominican Republic	4	0.02
Mexican	199	0.78
Puerto Rican	58	0.23
South American:	15	0.06
Bolivian	2	0.01
Chilean	2	0.01
Colombian	9	0.04
Peruvian	1	0.00
Other South American	1	0.00
Other Hispanic or Latino	71	0.28
Hungarian	43	0.17
Irish	2,055	8.14
Italian	439	1.74
Lithuanian	15	0.06
Northern European	6	0.02
Norwegian	77	0.31
Polish	236	0.94
Portuguese	14	0.06
Romanian	16	0.06
Russian	11	0.04
Scandinavian	7	0.03
Scotch-Irish	1,184	4.69
Scottish	325	1.29
Swedish	244	0.97
Swiss	51	0.20
Ukrainian	30	0.12
United States or American	3,057	12.11
Welsh	101	0.40
West Indian, excl. Hispanic:	45	0.18
Barbadian	5	0.02
Jamaican	7	0.03
Trinidadian and Tobagonian	27	0.11
U.S. Virgin Islander	6	0.02
White:	16,319	63.96
Not Hispanic (15,935)	16,142	63.27
Hispanic (170)	177	0.69

Beaufort

Place Type: City
County: Beaufort
Population: 12,950

Ancestry/Race	Number	%
Acadian/Cajun	7	0.05
African American/Black:	3,369	26.02
Not Hispanic (3,218)	3,320	25.64
Hispanic (38)	49	0.38
African, sub-Saharan:	54	0.42
African	31	0.24
Ghanian	23	0.18
Alaska Native tribes, specified:	1	0.01
Tlingit-Haida (1)	1	0.01
Am. Ind. or Alaska Nat., not spec.	40	0.31
American Indian tribes, specified:	56	0.43
Apache	1	0.01
Blackfeet	2	0.02
Cherokee (7)	18	0.14
Chickasaw (1)	1	0.01
Chippewa (2)	2	0.02
Choctaw (1)	2	0.02
Colville (1)	1	0.01
Comanche	2	0.02
Cree	1	0.01
Iroquois (1)	3	0.02
Latin American Indians (3)	6	0.05
Lumbee (3)	5	0.04
Navajo (1)	2	0.02
Pueblo (1)	1	0.01
Puget Sound Salish (1)	1	0.01
Seminole (1)	1	0.01
Sioux (1)	3	0.02
Yaqui (1)	1	0.01
All other tribes (3)	3	0.02
American Indian tribes, not spec.	4	0.03
Arab:	35	0.27
Moroccan	32	0.25
Syrian	3	0.02
Asian:	212	1.64
Cambodian (2)	2	0.02
Chinese, ex. Taiwanese (18)	26	0.20
Filipino (37)	59	0.46
Indian (27)	31	0.24
Japanese (26)	44	0.34
Korean (13)	20	0.15
Malaysian	1	0.01
Pakistani (1)	1	0.01
Thai (4)	7	0.05
Vietnamese (3)	3	0.02
Other Asian, specified	6	0.05
Other Asian, not specified (5)	12	0.09
Australian	7	0.05
Austrian	29	0.23
Belgian	23	0.18
British	75	0.59
Bulgarian	5	0.04
Croatian	7	0.05
Czech	100	0.78
Czechoslovakian	27	0.21
Danish	45	0.35
Dutch	204	1.60
English	1,600	12.51
European	146	1.14
Finnish	5	0.04
French, except Basque	554	4.33
French Canadian	60	0.47
German	1,730	13.53
Greek	17	0.13
Guyanese	7	0.05
Hawaii Native/Pacific Islander:	43	0.33
Micronesian:	6	0.05
Guamanian/Chamorro	6	0.05
Polynesian: (12)	23	0.18
Native Hawaiian (8)	18	0.14
Samoan (4)	5	0.04
Other Pac. Isl., specified	5	0.04
Other Pac. Isl., not spec. (4)	9	0.07
Hispanic or Latino:	568	4.39
Central American:	38	0.29
Costa Rican	3	0.02
Guatemalan	6	0.05
Honduran	6	0.05
Nicaraguan	5	0.04
Panamanian	14	0.11
Salvadoran	4	0.03
Cuban	31	0.24
Dominican Republic	11	0.08
Mexican	241	1.86
Puerto Rican	120	0.93
South American:	27	0.21
Bolivian	2	0.02
Colombian	12	0.09
Ecuadorian	5	0.04
Paraguayan	1	0.01
Peruvian	5	0.04
Venezuelan	2	0.02
Other Hispanic or Latino	100	0.77
Hungarian	81	0.63
Iranian	5	0.04
Irish	1,488	11.63
Italian	435	3.40
Lithuanian	22	0.17
Norwegian	138	1.08
Polish	372	2.91
Portuguese	31	0.24
Russian	69	0.54
Scandinavian	38	0.30
Scotch-Irish	287	2.24
Scottish	456	3.57
Slovak	10	0.08
Swedish	69	0.54
Swiss	16	0.13
United States or American	797	6.23
Welsh	66	0.52
West Indian, excl. Hispanic:	53	0.41
Bahamian	11	0.09
British West Indian	10	0.08
Haitian	20	0.16
Jamaican	12	0.09
White:	9,181	70.90
Not Hispanic (8,762)	8,921	68.89
Hispanic (226)	260	2.01
Yugoslavian	11	0.09

Berea

Place Type: Census Designated Place
County: Greenville
Population: 14,158

Ancestry/Race	Number	%
African American/Black:	2,332	16.47
Not Hispanic (2,226)	2,281	16.11
Hispanic (31)	51	0.36
African, sub-Saharan:	185	1.31
African	185	1.31
Am. Ind. or Alaska Nat., not spec.	48	0.34
American Indian tribes, specified:	37	0.26
Blackfeet	1	0.01
Cherokee (4)	26	0.18
Chippewa (1)	1	0.01
Creek (2)	2	0.01
Latin American Indians (1)	4	0.03
Lumbee (1)	1	0.01
Navajo	1	0.01
Paiute	1	0.01
American Indian tribes, not spec.	6	0.04
Asian:	240	1.70
Cambodian (1)	1	0.01
Chinese, ex. Taiwanese (12)	14	0.10
Filipino (9)	13	0.09
Indian (19)	20	0.14
Indonesian (1)	1	0.01
Japanese (3)	5	0.04
Korean (11)	14	0.10
Malaysian (2)	2	0.01
Vietnamese (146)	154	1.09
Other Asian, specified	3	0.02
Other Asian, not specified	13	0.09
British	40	0.28
Celtic	15	0.11
Dutch	188	1.33
English	840	5.94
European	39	0.28
Finnish	6	0.04
French, except Basque	185	1.31
French Canadian	18	0.13
German	1,011	7.14
Greek	123	0.87
Hawaii Native/Pacific Islander:	8	0.06
Polynesian: (1)	5	0.04
Native Hawaiian (1)	4	0.03
Samoan	1	0.01
Other Pac. Isl., specified	3	0.02
Hispanic or Latino:	1,902	13.43
Central American:	321	2.27
Costa Rican	119	0.84
Guatemalan	41	0.29
Honduran	105	0.74
Nicaraguan	14	0.10
Panamanian	1	0.01
Salvadoran	30	0.21
Other Central American	11	0.08
Cuban	27	0.19
Dominican Republic	4	0.03
Mexican	712	5.03
Puerto Rican	74	0.52
South American:	379	2.68
Colombian	361	2.55
Ecuadorian	2	0.01
Peruvian	12	0.08
Venezuelan	1	0.01
Other South American	3	0.02
Other Hispanic or Latino	385	2.72

Notes: 1. Figures in the "Number" column do not add up to the total population due to: a) Ancestry/Race overlap — e.g. persons can report being both White and Irish, b) persons of Hispanic origin can report being any race, c) persons reporting two ancestries are counted in both categories. 2. Numbers in parentheses indicate the number of persons reporting this ancestry/race alone, not in combination with any other ancestry/race. 3. Refer to the Explanation of Data in the front of the book for more detailed information.

Irish	1,119	7.91
Italian	190	1.34
Lithuanian	9	0.06
Norwegian	42	0.30
Polish	95	0.67
Portuguese	8	0.06
Russian	6	0.04
Scotch-Irish	482	3.41
Scottish	209	1.48
Slovak	38	0.27
Swedish	21	0.15
Swiss	7	0.05
Ukrainian	4	0.03
United States or American	2,256	15.94
Welsh	34	0.24
West Indian, excl. Hispanic:	7	0.05
Belizean	7	0.05
White:	10,939	77.26
Not Hispanic (9,633)	9,750	68.87
Hispanic (1,084)	1,189	8.40

Cayce

Place Type: City
County: Lexington
Population: 12,150

Ancestry/Race	Number	%
Acadian/Cajun	16	0.13
African American/Black:	2,772	22.81
Not Hispanic (2,728)	2,764	22.75
Hispanic (6)	8	0.07
African, sub-Saharan:	80	0.67
African	40	0.33
Cape Verdean	32	0.27
Nigerian	8	0.07
Am. Ind. or Alaska Nat., not spec.	28	0.23
American Indian tribes, specified:	38	0.31
Cherokee (8)	25	0.21
Choctaw (1)	1	0.01
Creek (1)	1	0.01
Latin American Indians (1)	1	0.01
Lumbee (2)	4	0.03
Seminole	1	0.01
Yaqui (1)	1	0.01
All other tribes (4)	4	0.03
American Indian tribes, not spec.	3	0.02
Arab:	47	0.39
Egyptian	40	0.33
Lebanese	7	0.06
Armenian	7	0.06
Asian:	152	1.25
Cambodian (1)	3	0.02
Chinese, ex. Taiwanese (16)	19	0.16
Filipino (13)	14	0.12
Indian (69)	70	0.58
Japanese (4)	10	0.08
Korean (5)	10	0.08
Laotian (6)	8	0.07
Taiwanese	2	0.02
Vietnamese (8)	9	0.07
Other Asian, specified	1	0.01
Other Asian, not specified (6)	6	0.05
Australian	6	0.05
Brazilian	16	0.13
British	24	0.20
Canadian	6	0.05
Czech	33	0.28
Czechoslovakian	20	0.17
Danish	37	0.31
Dutch	131	1.09
English	1,155	9.65
European	131	1.09
Finnish	5	0.04
French, except Basque	178	1.49
French Canadian	14	0.12
German	1,505	12.57
Greek	29	0.24
Hawaii Native/Pacific Islander:	25	0.21
Micronesian: (1)	1	0.01
Guamanian/Chamorro (1)	1	0.01
Polynesian: (12)	16	0.13
Native Hawaiian (1)	5	0.04
Samoan (11)	11	0.09
Other Pac. Isl., not spec. (5)	8	0.07
Hispanic or Latino:	155	1.28
Central American:	10	0.08
Guatemalan	3	0.02
Honduran	1	0.01
Nicaraguan	2	0.02
Panamanian	4	0.03
Cuban	6	0.05
Mexican	81	0.67
Puerto Rican	31	0.26
South American:	4	0.03
Peruvian	2	0.02
Other South American	2	0.02
Other Hispanic or Latino	23	0.19
Hungarian	60	0.50
Irish	1,260	10.53
Israeli	9	0.08
Italian	370	3.09
Lithuanian	4	0.03
Northern European	10	0.08
Norwegian	40	0.33
Polish	150	1.25
Russian	40	0.33
Scandinavian	14	0.12
Scotch-Irish	466	3.89
Scottish	277	2.31
Swedish	44	0.37
Swiss	33	0.28
Ukrainian	12	0.10
United States or American	1,694	14.15
Welsh	84	0.70
West Indian, excl. Hispanic:	14	0.12
Trinidadian and Tobagonian	6	0.05
West Indian	8	0.07
White:	9,144	75.26
Not Hispanic (8,990)	9,068	74.63
Hispanic (68)	76	0.63
Yugoslavian	9	0.08

Charleston

Place Type: City
County: Charleston
Population: 96,650

Ancestry/Race	Number	%
Acadian/Cajun	8	0.01
Afghan	7	0.01
African American/Black:	33,268	34.42
Not Hispanic (32,688)	33,058	34.20
Hispanic (176)	210	0.22
African, sub-Saharan:	1,243	1.29
African	1,096	1.14
Cape Verdean	11	0.01
Nigerian	82	0.09
South African	54	0.06
Alaska Native tribes, specified:	6	0.01
Alaska Athabascan (1)	2	0.00
Aleut (1)	1	0.00
Eskimo (1)	2	0.00
Tlingit-Haida (1)	1	0.00
Alaska Native tribes, not specified	2	0.00
Am. Ind. or Alaska Nat., not spec.	161	0.17
Albanian	18	0.02
Alsatian	5	0.01
American Indian tribes, specified:	231	0.24
Blackfeet (2)	13	0.01
Cherokee (39)	124	0.13
Chickasaw (1)	4	0.00
Chippewa	3	0.00
Choctaw (2)	5	0.01
Comanche (1)	1	0.00
Cree	1	0.00
Creek (4)	6	0.01
Crow (2)	2	0.00
Delaware (1)	4	0.00
Iroquois (3)	6	0.01
Latin American Indians (2)	8	0.01
Lumbee (6)	9	0.01
Navajo (1)	2	0.00
Potawatomi (4)	5	0.01
Pueblo	1	0.00
Seminole	2	0.00
Sioux (4)	6	0.01
Ute	1	0.00
All other tribes (8)	28	0.03
American Indian tribes, not spec.	20	0.02
Arab:	364	0.38
Arab/Arabic	103	0.11
Egyptian	37	0.04
Lebanese	141	0.15
Palestinian	29	0.03
Syrian	47	0.05
Other Arab	7	0.01
Armenian	18	0.02
Asian:	1,500	1.55
Bangladeshi (4)	4	0.00
Cambodian (1)	3	0.00
Chinese, ex. Taiwanese (293)	331	0.34
Filipino (200)	265	0.27
Indian (289)	342	0.35
Indonesian (4)	8	0.01
Japanese (121)	152	0.16
Korean (105)	140	0.14
Malaysian (3)	4	0.00
Pakistani (10)	13	0.01
Sri Lankan (9)	12	0.01
Taiwanese (7)	7	0.01
Thai (20)	27	0.03
Vietnamese (87)	103	0.11
Other Asian, specified (1)	4	0.00
Other Asian, not specified (34)	85	0.09
Australian	6	0.01
Austrian	172	0.18
Basque	8	0.01
Belgian	114	0.12
Brazilian	21	0.02
British	713	0.74
Bulgarian	45	0.05
Canadian	134	0.14
Celtic	40	0.04
Croatian	92	0.10
Cypriot	6	0.01
Czech	199	0.21
Czechoslovakian	68	0.07
Danish	162	0.17
Dutch	887	0.92
Eastern European	199	0.21
English	10,481	10.91
European	818	0.85
Finnish	101	0.11
French, except Basque	2,667	2.78
French Canadian	387	0.40
German	10,279	10.70
Greek	722	0.75
Hawaii Native/Pacific Islander:	98	0.10
Melanesian:	1	0.00
Other Melanesian	1	0.00
Micronesian: (23)	25	0.03
Guamanian/Chamorro (6)	8	0.01
Other Micronesian (17)	17	0.02
Polynesian: (15)	33	0.03
Native Hawaiian (7)	21	0.02
Samoan (8)	12	0.01
Other Pac. Isl., specified	2	0.00
Other Pac. Isl., not spec. (17)	37	0.04
Hispanic or Latino:	1,462	1.51
Central American:	59	0.06
Costa Rican	8	0.01
Guatemalan	5	0.01
Honduran	14	0.01
Nicaraguan	3	0.00
Panamanian	22	0.02
Salvadoran	6	0.01
Other Central American	1	0.00
Cuban	116	0.12

Notes: 1. Figures in the "Number" column do not add up to the total population due to: a) Ancestry/Race overlap — e.g. persons can report being both White and Irish, b) persons of Hispanic origin can report being any race, c) persons reporting two ancestries are counted in both categories. 2. Numbers in parentheses indicate the number of persons reporting this ancestry/race alone, not in combination with any other ancestry/race. 3. Refer to the Explanation of Data in the front of the book for more detailed information.

Ancestry/Race	Number	%
Dominican Republic	23	0.02
Mexican	504	0.52
Puerto Rican	231	0.24
South American:	161	0.17
Argentinean	25	0.03
Bolivian	18	0.02
Chilean	6	0.01
Colombian	36	0.04
Ecuadorian	14	0.01
Paraguayan	2	0.00
Peruvian	15	0.02
Uruguayan	2	0.00
Venezuelan	27	0.03
Other South American	16	0.02
Other Hispanic or Latino	368	0.38
Hungarian	412	0.43
Icelander	7	0.01
Iranian	38	0.04
Irish	8,767	9.12
Israeli	14	0.01
Italian	3,083	3.21
Latvian	76	0.08
Lithuanian	241	0.25
Maltese	7	0.01
Northern European	44	0.05
Norwegian	494	0.51
Pennsylvania German	14	0.01
Polish	1,542	1.60
Portuguese	45	0.05
Romanian	56	0.06
Russian	805	0.84
Scandinavian	125	0.13
Scotch-Irish	3,048	3.17
Scottish	3,168	3.30
Serbian	40	0.04
Slavic	39	0.04
Slovak	62	0.06
Slovene	18	0.02
Swedish	605	0.63
Swiss	133	0.14
Turkish	21	0.02
Ukrainian	149	0.16
United States or American	5,979	6.22
Welsh	616	0.64
West Indian, excl. Hispanic:	206	0.21
Bahamian	7	0.01
Barbadian	44	0.05
British West Indian	11	0.01
Dutch West Indian	7	0.01
Haitian	9	0.01
Jamaican	95	0.10
West Indian	33	0.03
White:	61,615	63.75
Not Hispanic (60,187)	60,776	62.88
Hispanic (777)	839	0.87
Yugoslavian	52	0.05

Clemson

Place Type: City
County: Pickens
Population: 11,939

Ancestry/Race	Number	%
African American/Black:	1,389	11.63
Not Hispanic (1,349)	1,378	11.54
Hispanic (10)	11	0.09
African, sub-Saharan:	76	0.63
African	44	0.36
Cape Verdean	4	0.03
Ghanian	28	0.23
Am. Ind. or Alaska Nat., not spec.	12	0.10
American Indian tribes, specified:	20	0.17
Cherokee (4)	12	0.10
Choctaw	1	0.01
Creek	1	0.01
Iroquois (1)	3	0.03
Latin American Indians (1)	2	0.02
Seminole (1)	1	0.01
American Indian tribes, not spec.	2	0.02
Arab:	113	0.93
Egyptian	78	0.64
Lebanese	35	0.29
Asian:	736	6.16
Bangladeshi (1)	1	0.01
Cambodian (5)	5	0.04
Chinese, ex. Taiwanese (178)	185	1.55
Filipino (15)	23	0.19
Indian (330)	344	2.88
Indonesian (6)	9	0.08
Japanese (24)	32	0.27
Korean (45)	48	0.40
Malaysian (1)	1	0.01
Pakistani (5)	7	0.06
Sri Lankan (8)	8	0.07
Taiwanese (7)	9	0.08
Thai (34)	35	0.29
Vietnamese (9)	9	0.08
Other Asian, not specified (10)	20	0.17
Austrian	35	0.29
Belgian	44	0.36
Brazilian	14	0.12
British	254	2.10
Bulgarian	15	0.12
Canadian	15	0.12
Celtic	21	0.17
Croatian	11	0.09
Czech	7	0.06
Czechoslovakian	6	0.05
Danish	28	0.23
Dutch	125	1.03
Eastern European	12	0.10
English	1,814	14.98
European	144	1.19
Finnish	26	0.21
French, except Basque	256	2.11
French Canadian	17	0.14
German	1,613	13.32
Greek	49	0.40
Hawaii Native/Pacific Islander:	11	0.09
Melanesian:	1	0.01
Other Melanesian	1	0.01
Micronesian:	4	0.03
Guamanian/Chamorro	4	0.03
Polynesian: (2)	3	0.03
Native Hawaiian (2)	2	0.02
Samoan	1	0.01
Other Pac. Isl., not spec. (1)	3	0.03
Hispanic or Latino:	217	1.82
Central American:	19	0.16
Costa Rican	4	0.03
Guatemalan	1	0.01
Honduran	8	0.07
Nicaraguan	1	0.01
Panamanian	5	0.04
Cuban	17	0.14
Dominican Republic	1	0.01
Mexican	101	0.85
Puerto Rican	14	0.12
South American:	34	0.28
Chilean	1	0.01
Colombian	18	0.15
Ecuadorian	4	0.03
Peruvian	1	0.01
Venezuelan	4	0.03
Other South American	6	0.05
Other Hispanic or Latino	31	0.26
Hungarian	61	0.50
Irish	1,151	9.50
Italian	323	2.67
Latvian	8	0.07
Lithuanian	30	0.25
Northern European	39	0.32
Norwegian	60	0.50
Pennsylvania German	14	0.12
Polish	133	1.10
Portuguese	13	0.11
Romanian	27	0.22
Russian	47	0.39
Scotch-Irish	728	6.01
Scottish	374	3.09
Slavic	8	0.07
Slovak	13	0.11
Slovene	7	0.06
Swedish	139	1.15
Swiss	30	0.25
Turkish	45	0.37
Ukrainian	34	0.28
United States or American	1,044	8.62
Welsh	94	0.78
West Indian, excl. Hispanic:	10	0.08
Haitian	10	0.08
White:	9,769	81.82
Not Hispanic (9,540)	9,628	80.64
Hispanic (128)	141	1.18

Columbia

Place Type: City
County: Richland
Population: 116,278

Ancestry/Race	Number	%
African American/Black:	54,256	46.66
Not Hispanic (53,052)	53,720	46.20
Hispanic (413)	536	0.46
African, sub-Saharan:	1,564	1.35
African	1,378	1.19
Cape Verdean	7	0.01
Ghanian	18	0.02
Nigerian	103	0.09
Sierra Leonean	5	0.00
South African	5	0.00
Other sub-Saharan African	48	0.04
Alaska Native tribes, specified:	5	0.00
Alaska Athabascan (1)	1	0.00
Aleut (1)	2	0.00
Eskimo (1)	1	0.00
All other tribes (1)	1	0.00
Alaska Native tribes, not specified	3	0.00
Am. Ind. or Alaska Nat., not spec.	270	0.23
American Indian tribes, specified:	411	0.35
Apache (2)	9	0.01
Blackfeet (2)	25	0.02
Cherokee (51)	175	0.15
Cheyenne (1)	4	0.00
Chickasaw (2)	2	0.00
Chippewa (8)	13	0.01
Choctaw (9)	17	0.01
Comanche (2)	2	0.00
Creek (2)	3	0.00
Crow (1)	1	0.00
Delaware	2	0.00
Houma (1)	2	0.00
Iroquois (7)	12	0.01
Kiowa (1)	1	0.00
Latin American Indians (17)	24	0.02
Lumbee (6)	12	0.01
Navajo (18)	21	0.02
Osage (1)	1	0.00
Ottawa	1	0.00
Potawatomi (2)	2	0.00
Pueblo	2	0.00
Puget Sound Salish (1)	2	0.00
Seminole (2)	6	0.01
Shoshone (2)	2	0.00
Sioux (12)	16	0.01
Ute	1	0.00
All other tribes (31)	53	0.05
American Indian tribes, not spec.	42	0.04
Arab:	449	0.39
Arab/Arabic	70	0.06
Egyptian	31	0.03
Jordanian	6	0.01
Lebanese	242	0.21
Moroccan	23	0.02
Syrian	35	0.03
Other Arab	42	0.04
Armenian	68	0.06
Asian:	2,533	2.18

Notes: 1. Figures in the "Number" column do not add up to the total population due to: a) Ancestry/Race overlap — e.g. persons can report being both White and Irish, b) persons of Hispanic origin can report being any race, c) persons reporting two ancestries are counted in both categories. 2. Numbers in parentheses indicate the number of persons reporting this ancestry/race alone, not in combination with any other ancestry/race. 3. Refer to the Explanation of Data in the front of the book for more detailed information.

Ancestry/Race	Number	%
Bangladeshi (7)	7	0.01
Cambodian (5)	6	0.01
Chinese, ex. Taiwanese (430)	504	0.43
Filipino (216)	325	0.28
Hmong (4)	4	0.00
Indian (570)	641	0.55
Indonesian (11)	18	0.02
Japanese (109)	161	0.14
Korean (353)	447	0.38
Laotian (7)	13	0.01
Malaysian (6)	6	0.01
Pakistani (8)	9	0.01
Sri Lankan (10)	12	0.01
Taiwanese (23)	28	0.02
Thai (45)	58	0.05
Vietnamese (118)	132	0.11
Other Asian, specified (4)	16	0.01
Other Asian, not specified (58)	146	0.13
Australian	42	0.04
Austrian	143	0.12
Belgian	22	0.02
Brazilian	50	0.04
British	743	0.64
Bulgarian	27	0.02
Canadian	125	0.11
Celtic	32	0.03
Croatian	29	0.03
Czech	139	0.12
Czechoslovakian	67	0.06
Danish	79	0.07
Dutch	694	0.60
English	8,937	7.70
European	974	0.84
Finnish	78	0.07
French, except Basque	2,227	1.92
French Canadian	315	0.27
German	9,616	8.29
Greek	421	0.36
Guyanese	13	0.01
Hawaii Native/Pacific Islander:	228	0.20
Melanesian: (1)	1	0.00
Fijian (1)	1	0.00
Micronesian: (36)	51	0.04
Guamanian/Chamorro (30)	44	0.04
Other Micronesian (6)	7	0.01
Polynesian: (52)	109	0.09
Native Hawaiian (29)	69	0.06
Samoan (21)	32	0.03
Tongan (1)	3	0.00
Other Polynesian (1)	5	0.00
Other Pac. Isl., specified	12	0.01
Other Pac. Isl., not spec. (13)	55	0.05
Hispanic or Latino:	3,520	3.03
Central American:	202	0.17
Costa Rican	11	0.01
Guatemalan	44	0.04
Honduran	15	0.01
Nicaraguan	12	0.01
Panamanian	81	0.07
Salvadoran	35	0.03
Other Central American	4	0.00
Cuban	125	0.11
Dominican Republic	68	0.06
Mexican	1,387	1.19
Puerto Rican	886	0.76
South American:	225	0.19
Argentinean	17	0.01
Bolivian	5	0.00
Chilean	14	0.01
Colombian	80	0.07
Ecuadorian	39	0.03
Paraguayan	2	0.00
Peruvian	28	0.02
Uruguayan	3	0.00
Venezuelan	27	0.02
Other South American	10	0.01
Other Hispanic or Latino	627	0.54
Hungarian	98	0.08
Iranian	5	0.00
Irish	7,133	6.15
Israeli	35	0.03
Italian	2,467	2.13
Latvian	33	0.03
Lithuanian	176	0.15
Luxemburger	17	0.01
Maltese	9	0.01
Northern European	12	0.01
Norwegian	596	0.51
Polish	1,059	0.91
Portuguese	98	0.08
Romanian	42	0.04
Russian	362	0.31
Scandinavian	81	0.07
Scotch-Irish	3,824	3.30
Scottish	2,564	2.21
Serbian	10	0.01
Slavic	26	0.02
Slovak	100	0.09
Slovene	15	0.01
Swedish	409	0.35
Swiss	206	0.18
Turkish	35	0.03
Ukrainian	78	0.07
United States or American	6,060	5.22
Welsh	431	0.37
West Indian, excl. Hispanic:	512	0.44
Bahamian	8	0.01
Barbadian	11	0.01
Belizean	32	0.03
Bermudan	25	0.02
British West Indian	12	0.01
Haitian	50	0.04
Jamaican	268	0.23
Trinidadian and Tobagonian	56	0.05
U.S. Virgin Islander	10	0.01
West Indian	40	0.03
White:	58,295	50.13
Not Hispanic (55,993)	56,847	48.89
Hispanic (1,243)	1,448	1.25
Yugoslavian	23	0.02

Conway

Place Type: City
County: Horry
Population: 11,788

Ancestry/Race	Number	%
African American/Black:	4,986	42.30
Not Hispanic (4,917)	4,964	42.11
Hispanic (16)	22	0.19
African, sub-Saharan:	51	0.43
African	51	0.43
Am. Ind. or Alaska Nat., not spec.	21	0.18
American Indian tribes, specified:	27	0.23
Blackfeet	2	0.02
Cherokee (2)	10	0.08
Creek (1)	1	0.01
Iroquois	3	0.03
Latin American Indians (1)	1	0.01
Lumbee (1)	2	0.02
All other tribes (8)	8	0.07
Asian:	114	0.97
Chinese, ex. Taiwanese (22)	27	0.23
Filipino (8)	17	0.14
Indian (29)	35	0.30
Indonesian (2)	2	0.02
Japanese (4)	7	0.06
Korean (4)	5	0.04
Laotian (1)	1	0.01
Malaysian (1)	1	0.01
Thai (1)	2	0.02
Vietnamese (9)	9	0.08
Other Asian, not specified (2)	8	0.07
Austrian	22	0.19
British	23	0.19
Canadian	17	0.14
Czechoslovakian	35	0.30
Danish	7	0.06
Dutch	106	0.90
English	889	7.54
European	6	0.05
Finnish	13	0.11
French, except Basque	209	1.77
French Canadian	27	0.23
German	795	6.74
Greek	15	0.13
Hawaii Native/Pacific Islander:	6	0.05
Micronesian: (1)	1	0.01
Guamanian/Chamorro (1)	1	0.01
Polynesian: (2)	5	0.04
Native Hawaiian (2)	5	0.04
Hispanic or Latino:	221	1.87
Central American:	16	0.14
Honduran	9	0.08
Salvadoran	7	0.06
Cuban	4	0.03
Mexican	117	0.99
Puerto Rican	16	0.14
South American:	12	0.10
Bolivian	1	0.01
Peruvian	6	0.05
Other South American	5	0.04
Other Hispanic or Latino	56	0.48
Hungarian	26	0.22
Irish	775	6.57
Italian	156	1.32
Norwegian	14	0.12
Polish	125	1.06
Russian	28	0.24
Scotch-Irish	178	1.51
Scottish	161	1.36
Slavic	6	0.05
Slovak	5	0.04
Swedish	125	1.06
Swiss	10	0.08
United States or American	1,607	13.62
Welsh	39	0.33
West Indian, excl. Hispanic:	22	0.19
West Indian	22	0.19
White:	6,642	56.35
Not Hispanic (6,468)	6,522	55.33
Hispanic (112)	120	1.02

Dentsville

Place Type: Census Designated Place
County: Richland
Population: 13,009

Ancestry/Race	Number	%
African American/Black:	7,685	59.07
Not Hispanic (7,516)	7,601	58.43
Hispanic (65)	84	0.65
African, sub-Saharan:	179	1.40
African	117	0.91
Ethiopian	51	0.40
South African	11	0.09
Am. Ind. or Alaska Nat., not spec.	35	0.27
American Indian tribes, specified:	62	0.48
Apache	1	0.01
Blackfeet	5	0.04
Cherokee (17)	41	0.32
Chickasaw	1	0.01
Iroquois	1	0.01
Latin American Indians (1)	4	0.03
Lumbee (1)	2	0.02
Seminole	3	0.02
All other tribes (3)	4	0.03
American Indian tribes, not spec.	1	0.01
Arab:	8	0.06
Lebanese	8	0.06
Asian:	394	3.03
Chinese, ex. Taiwanese (28)	32	0.25
Filipino (53)	72	0.55
Indian (121)	135	1.04
Japanese (15)	27	0.21
Korean (71)	85	0.65
Pakistani (3)	3	0.02
Thai (3)	6	0.05

Notes: 1. Figures in the "Number" column do not add up to the total population due to: a) Ancestry/Race overlap — e.g. persons can report being both White and Irish, b) persons of Hispanic origin can report being any race, c) persons reporting two ancestries are counted in both categories. 2. Numbers in parentheses indicate the number of persons reporting this ancestry/race alone, not in combination with any other ancestry/race. 3. Refer to the Explanation of Data in the front of the book for more detailed information.

Vietnamese (27)	27	0.21
Other Asian, not specified (1)	7	0.05
Austrian	24	0.19
Belgian	16	0.12
British	38	0.30
Bulgarian	5	0.04
Canadian	7	0.05
Czechoslovakian	7	0.05
Danish	39	0.30
Dutch	49	0.38
English	677	5.28
European	63	0.49
French, except Basque	181	1.41
French Canadian	50	0.39
German	835	6.51
German Russian	16	0.12
Greek	44	0.34
Guyanese	19	0.15
Hawaii Native/Pacific Islander:	12	0.09
Micronesian: (4)	5	0.04
Guamanian/Chamorro (4)	5	0.04
Polynesian: (2)	5	0.04
Native Hawaiian	2	0.02
Samoan (2)	3	0.02
Other Pac. Isl., not spec.	2	0.02
Hispanic or Latino:	377	2.90
Central American:	36	0.28
Costa Rican	2	0.02
Guatemalan	2	0.02
Honduran	7	0.05
Nicaraguan	2	0.02
Panamanian	21	0.16
Salvadoran	2	0.02
Cuban	18	0.14
Dominican Republic	6	0.05
Mexican	126	0.97
Puerto Rican	120	0.92
South American:	19	0.15
Argentinean	1	0.01
Chilean	4	0.03
Colombian	3	0.02
Ecuadorian	1	0.01
Paraguayan	1	0.01
Peruvian	1	0.01
Venezuelan	8	0.06
Other Hispanic or Latino	52	0.40
Hungarian	5	0.04
Irish	608	4.74
Italian	292	2.28
Norwegian	44	0.34
Polish	72	0.56
Portuguese	13	0.10
Russian	31	0.24
Scotch-Irish	251	1.96
Scottish	144	1.12
Slavic	6	0.05
Swedish	36	0.28
Swiss	9	0.07
Ukrainian	13	0.10
United States or American	710	5.54
Welsh	29	0.23
West Indian, excl. Hispanic:	19	0.15
Jamaican	19	0.15
White:	4,842	37.22
Not Hispanic (4,564)	4,696	36.10
Hispanic (126)	146	1.12

Easley

Place Type: City
County: Pickens
Population: 17,754

Ancestry/Race	Number	%
African American/Black:	2,137	12.04
Not Hispanic (2,083)	2,122	11.95
Hispanic (13)	15	0.08
African, sub-Saharan:	64	0.36
African	64	0.36
Alaska Native tribes, specified:	1	0.01
Aleut	1	0.01
Am. Ind. or Alaska Nat., not spec.	32	0.18
Albanian	7	0.04
American Indian tribes, specified:	41	0.23
Cherokee (9)	35	0.20
Chippewa (2)	2	0.01
Latin American Indians (2)	2	0.01
Lumbee (2)	2	0.01
American Indian tribes, not spec.	6	0.03
Arab:	9	0.05
Syrian	9	0.05
Asian:	144	0.81
Chinese, ex. Taiwanese (27)	36	0.20
Filipino (16)	24	0.14
Indian (21)	32	0.18
Japanese (11)	19	0.11
Korean (6)	11	0.06
Vietnamese (5)	7	0.04
Other Asian, specified	1	0.01
Other Asian, not specified (4)	14	0.08
Austrian	30	0.17
British	54	0.30
Canadian	26	0.14
Celtic	25	0.14
Czech	36	0.20
Czechoslovakian	3	0.02
Danish	29	0.16
Dutch	214	1.19
English	1,893	10.54
European	358	1.99
French, except Basque	375	2.09
French Canadian	85	0.47
German	1,795	9.99
Greek	45	0.25
Hawaii Native/Pacific Islander:	16	0.09
Micronesian: (2)	2	0.01
Guamanian/Chamorro (2)	2	0.01
Polynesian: (3)	10	0.06
Native Hawaiian (3)	9	0.05
Samoan	1	0.01
Other Pac. Isl., specified	1	0.01
Other Pac. Isl., not spec. (1)	3	0.02
Hispanic or Latino:	501	2.82
Central American:	21	0.12
Costa Rican	3	0.02
Guatemalan	3	0.02
Nicaraguan	15	0.08
Cuban	12	0.07
Dominican Republic	8	0.05
Mexican	321	1.81
Puerto Rican	53	0.30
South American:	24	0.14
Argentinean	2	0.01
Colombian	15	0.08
Ecuadorian	1	0.01
Peruvian	6	0.03
Other Hispanic or Latino	62	0.35
Hungarian	12	0.07
Irish	1,878	10.45
Italian	180	1.00
Lithuanian	18	0.10
Northern European	6	0.03
Norwegian	74	0.41
Pennsylvania German	13	0.07
Polish	165	0.92
Portuguese	8	0.04
Russian	62	0.35
Scandinavian	19	0.11
Scotch-Irish	716	3.99
Scottish	567	3.16
Slovak	14	0.08
Swedish	53	0.30
Swiss	30	0.17
Ukrainian	16	0.09
United States or American	3,333	18.55
Welsh	45	0.25
West Indian, excl. Hispanic:	8	0.04
Jamaican	8	0.04
White:	15,286	86.10
Not Hispanic (14,910)	15,015	84.57
Hispanic (243)	271	1.53
Yugoslavian	6	0.03

Florence

Place Type: City
County: Florence
Population: 30,248

Ancestry/Race	Number	%
African American/Black:	13,621	45.03
Not Hispanic (13,481)	13,558	44.82
Hispanic (60)	63	0.21
African, sub-Saharan:	434	1.43
African	333	1.10
Ghanian	7	0.02
Nigerian	15	0.05
South African	50	0.16
Other sub-Saharan African	29	0.10
Alaska Native tribes, specified:	2	0.01
Tlingit-Haida (2)	2	0.01
Am. Ind. or Alaska Nat., not spec.	51	0.17
American Indian tribes, specified:	76	0.25
Apache	1	0.00
Blackfeet (1)	2	0.01
Cherokee (5)	26	0.09
Chippewa (9)	11	0.04
Choctaw	1	0.00
Iroquois (1)	4	0.01
Latin American Indians (6)	9	0.03
Lumbee (4)	9	0.03
Seminole (1)	1	0.00
Sioux (1)	1	0.00
All other tribes (7)	11	0.04
American Indian tribes, not spec.	4	0.01
Arab:	75	0.25
Lebanese	63	0.21
Syrian	12	0.04
Asian:	405	1.34
Chinese, ex. Taiwanese (113)	116	0.38
Filipino (51)	65	0.21
Indian (45)	50	0.17
Japanese (35)	39	0.13
Korean (26)	36	0.12
Pakistani	1	0.00
Taiwanese (49)	50	0.17
Thai (5)	11	0.04
Vietnamese (20)	21	0.07
Other Asian, specified	1	0.00
Other Asian, not specified (7)	15	0.05
Austrian	18	0.06
Belgian	34	0.11
British	117	0.39
Canadian	32	0.11
Celtic	7	0.02
Czech	12	0.04
Czechoslovakian	11	0.04
Danish	41	0.14
Dutch	184	0.61
English	2,350	7.75
European	347	1.14
Finnish	7	0.02
French, except Basque	458	1.51
French Canadian	73	0.24
German	1,728	5.70
Greek	245	0.81
Hawaii Native/Pacific Islander:	15	0.05
Polynesian: (4)	7	0.02
Native Hawaiian (4)	6	0.02
Samoan	1	0.00
Other Pac. Isl., specified	1	0.00
Other Pac. Isl., not spec.	7	0.02
Hispanic or Latino:	229	0.76
Central American:	18	0.06
Costa Rican	5	0.02
Honduran	1	0.00
Nicaraguan	1	0.00
Panamanian	6	0.02
Salvadoran	4	0.01
Other Central American	1	0.00

Notes: 1. Figures in the "Number" column do not add up to the total population due to: a) Ancestry/Race overlap — e.g. persons can report being both White and Irish, b) persons of Hispanic origin can report being any race, c) persons reporting two ancestries are counted in both categories. 2. Numbers in parentheses indicate the number of persons reporting this ancestry/race alone, not in combination with any other ancestry/race. 3. Refer to the Explanation of Data in the front of the book for more detailed information.

Ancestry/Race	Number	%
Cuban	12	0.04
Dominican Republic	7	0.02
Mexican	87	0.29
Puerto Rican	39	0.13
South American:	28	0.09
Argentinean	1	0.00
Colombian	9	0.03
Ecuadorian	4	0.01
Paraguayan	1	0.00
Uruguayan	5	0.02
Venezuelan	5	0.02
Other South American	3	0.01
Other Hispanic or Latino	38	0.13
Hungarian	60	0.20
Irish	1,609	5.31
Italian	376	1.24
Northern European	22	0.07
Norwegian	164	0.54
Polish	205	0.68
Russian	85	0.28
Scandinavian	15	0.05
Scotch-Irish	1,329	4.39
Scottish	799	2.64
Slavic	7	0.02
Slovak	16	0.05
Swedish	64	0.21
Swiss	26	0.09
Turkish	5	0.02
United States or American	2,550	8.41
Welsh	156	0.51
West Indian, excl. Hispanic:	18	0.06
Barbadian	7	0.02
Jamaican	11	0.04
White:	16,183	53.50
Not Hispanic (15,944)	16,087	53.18
Hispanic (76)	96	0.32

Forest Acres

Place Type: City
County: Richland
Population: 10,558

Ancestry/Race	Number	%
African American/Black:	1,672	15.84
Not Hispanic (1,631)	1,661	15.73
Hispanic (8)	11	0.10
African, sub-Saharan:	28	0.26
African	13	0.12
Other sub-Saharan African	15	0.14
Alaska Native tribes, specified:	1	0.01
Eskimo (1)	1	0.01
Am. Ind. or Alaska Nat., not spec.	20	0.19
American Indian tribes, specified:	20	0.19
Cherokee (5)	11	0.10
Latin American Indians	2	0.02
Seminole	1	0.01
Sioux	1	0.01
All other tribes (3)	5	0.05
American Indian tribes, not spec.	2	0.02
Arab:	44	0.41
Egyptian	9	0.08
Iraqi	6	0.06
Lebanese	17	0.16
Palestinian	7	0.07
Other Arab	5	0.05
Asian:	165	1.56
Bangladeshi (1)	1	0.01
Chinese, ex. Taiwanese (34)	40	0.38
Filipino (29)	32	0.30
Indian (22)	29	0.27
Indonesian (1)	1	0.01
Japanese (6)	17	0.16
Korean (18)	26	0.25
Laotian (1)	1	0.01
Thai (2)	2	0.02
Vietnamese (5)	7	0.07
Other Asian, specified	2	0.02
Other Asian, not specified (2)	7	0.07
Austrian	3	0.03
Belgian	6	0.06
Brazilian	29	0.27
British	61	0.57
Celtic	12	0.11
Croatian	6	0.06
Czech	22	0.21
Czechoslovakian	11	0.10
Danish	47	0.44
Dutch	127	1.19
English	1,818	17.03
European	72	0.67
French, except Basque	360	3.37
French Canadian	8	0.07
German	1,175	11.01
Greek	73	0.68
Hawaii Native/Pacific Islander:	12	0.11
Micronesian:	1	0.01
Guamanian/Chamorro	1	0.01
Polynesian: (1)	9	0.09
Native Hawaiian	8	0.08
Samoan (1)	1	0.01
Other Pac. Isl., specified	1	0.01
Other Pac. Isl., not spec.	1	0.01
Hispanic or Latino:	268	2.54
Central American:	21	0.20
Guatemalan	2	0.02
Honduran	2	0.02
Nicaraguan	1	0.01
Panamanian	15	0.14
Salvadoran	1	0.01
Cuban	26	0.25
Dominican Republic	3	0.03
Mexican	102	0.97
Puerto Rican	43	0.41
South American:	29	0.27
Argentinean	1	0.01
Chilean	1	0.01
Colombian	8	0.08
Ecuadorian	6	0.06
Peruvian	1	0.01
Venezuelan	12	0.11
Other Hispanic or Latino	44	0.42
Hungarian	12	0.11
Irish	939	8.80
Italian	143	1.34
Latvian	6	0.06
Lithuanian	45	0.42
Northern European	32	0.30
Norwegian	38	0.36
Pennsylvania German	6	0.06
Polish	157	1.47
Portuguese	31	0.29
Romanian	11	0.10
Russian	133	1.25
Scandinavian	10	0.09
Scotch-Irish	830	7.78
Scottish	517	4.84
Serbian	6	0.06
Slovak	7	0.07
Swedish	100	0.94
Swiss	64	0.60
Ukrainian	25	0.23
United States or American	1,245	11.66
Welsh	93	0.87
West Indian, excl. Hispanic:	33	0.31
Barbadian	7	0.07
Jamaican	14	0.13
West Indian	12	0.11
White:	8,647	81.90
Not Hispanic (8,410)	8,497	80.48
Hispanic (128)	150	1.42

Gaffney

Place Type: City
County: Cherokee
Population: 12,968

Ancestry/Race	Number	%
African American/Black:	5,769	44.49
Not Hispanic (5,703)	5,736	44.23
Hispanic (27)	33	0.25
African, sub-Saharan:	85	0.66
African	85	0.66
Am. Ind. or Alaska Nat., not spec.	20	0.15
American Indian tribes, specified:	22	0.17
Apache (1)	2	0.02
Cherokee (2)	15	0.12
Cheyenne (1)	1	0.01
Choctaw (1)	1	0.01
All other tribes (2)	3	0.02
American Indian tribes, not spec.	1	0.01
Asian:	86	0.66
Chinese, ex. Taiwanese (16)	24	0.19
Filipino (6)	11	0.08
Indian (19)	24	0.19
Japanese (6)	6	0.05
Korean (5)	9	0.07
Pakistani (3)	4	0.03
Other Asian, specified	2	0.02
Other Asian, not specified (4)	6	0.05
Austrian	6	0.05
British	39	0.30
Canadian	12	0.09
Croatian	10	0.08
Danish	10	0.08
Dutch	119	0.92
English	619	4.78
European	109	0.84
Finnish	6	0.05
French, except Basque	110	0.85
German	581	4.49
Greek	11	0.08
Hawaii Native/Pacific Islander:	11	0.08
Micronesian: (2)	3	0.02
Guamanian/Chamorro (2)	3	0.02
Polynesian: (1)	5	0.04
Native Hawaiian (1)	4	0.03
Samoan	1	0.01
Other Pac. Isl., specified	2	0.02
Other Pac. Isl., not spec. (1)	1	0.01
Hispanic or Latino:	257	1.98
Central American:	16	0.12
Costa Rican	1	0.01
Guatemalan	6	0.05
Honduran	2	0.02
Nicaraguan	3	0.02
Panamanian	4	0.03
Cuban	1	0.01
Dominican Republic	2	0.02
Mexican	143	1.10
Puerto Rican	45	0.35
South American:	1	0.01
Peruvian	1	0.01
Other Hispanic or Latino	49	0.38
Irish	870	6.72
Italian	77	0.59
Lithuanian	6	0.05
Polish	49	0.38
Portuguese	6	0.05
Scotch-Irish	347	2.68
Scottish	115	0.89
Slovak	35	0.27
Swedish	40	0.31
Ukrainian	11	0.08
United States or American	2,110	16.30
Welsh	47	0.36
White:	7,006	54.03
Not Hispanic (6,854)	6,917	53.34
Hispanic (81)	89	0.69

Gantt

Place Type: Census Designated Place
County: Greenville
Population: 13,962

Ancestry/Race	Number	%
African American/Black:	8,902	63.76
Not Hispanic (8,776)	8,855	63.42

Notes: 1. Figures in the "Number" column do not add up to the total population due to: a) Ancestry/Race overlap — e.g. persons can report being both White and Irish, b) persons of Hispanic origin can report being any race, c) persons reporting two ancestries are counted in both categories. 2. Numbers in parentheses indicate the number of persons reporting this ancestry/race alone, not in combination with any other ancestry/race. 3. Refer to the Explanation of Data in the front of the book for more detailed information.

Ancestry/Race	Number	%
Hispanic (34)	47	0.34
African, sub-Saharan:	165	1.18
African	108	0.77
Ethiopian	10	0.07
Nigerian	47	0.34
Am. Ind. or Alaska Nat., not spec.	29	0.21
American Indian tribes, specified:	38	0.27
Blackfeet	3	0.02
Cherokee (4)	24	0.17
Iroquois (1)	1	0.01
Latin American Indians (1)	6	0.04
Navajo	1	0.01
Pueblo	1	0.01
All other tribes	2	0.01
American Indian tribes, not spec.	7	0.05
Arab:	16	0.11
Lebanese	16	0.11
Asian:	69	0.49
Chinese, ex. Taiwanese (5)	5	0.04
Filipino (9)	19	0.14
Indian (12)	13	0.09
Japanese (5)	9	0.06
Korean (1)	4	0.03
Thai (3)	3	0.02
Vietnamese (10)	10	0.07
Other Asian, specified	1	0.01
Other Asian, not specified (2)	5	0.04
British	36	0.26
Canadian	38	0.27
Czechoslovakian	6	0.04
Dutch	50	0.36
English	511	3.65
European	61	0.44
Finnish	8	0.06
French, except Basque	133	0.95
French Canadian	14	0.10
German	472	3.37
Greek	61	0.44
Hawaii Native/Pacific Islander:	9	0.06
Micronesian: (1)	1	0.01
Guamanian/Chamorro (1)	1	0.01
Other Pac. Isl., specified	1	0.01
Other Pac. Isl., not spec. (6)	7	0.05
Hispanic or Latino:	419	3.00
Central American:	18	0.13
Costa Rican	5	0.04
Guatemalan	2	0.01
Honduran	1	0.01
Nicaraguan	3	0.02
Panamanian	1	0.01
Other Central American	6	0.04
Cuban	8	0.06
Dominican Republic	2	0.01
Mexican	271	1.94
Puerto Rican	37	0.27
South American:	21	0.15
Chilean	1	0.01
Colombian	14	0.10
Ecuadorian	2	0.01
Other South American	4	0.03
Other Hispanic or Latino	62	0.44
Irish	499	3.56
Italian	44	0.31
Lithuanian	10	0.07
Luxemburger	8	0.06
Norwegian	14	0.10
Polish	33	0.24
Russian	10	0.07
Scotch-Irish	177	1.26
Scottish	181	1.29
Swedish	15	0.11
Ukrainian	25	0.18
United States or American	1,133	8.09
Welsh	63	0.45
White:	4,840	34.67
Not Hispanic (4,564)	4,659	33.37
Hispanic (164)	181	1.30
Yugoslavian	8	0.06

Goose Creek

Place Type: City
County: Berkeley
Population: 29,208

Ancestry/Race	Number	%
Acadian/Cajun	20	0.07
African American/Black:	4,372	14.97
Not Hispanic (4,099)	4,288	14.68
Hispanic (54)	84	0.29
African, sub-Saharan:	84	0.29
African	76	0.26
Cape Verdean	4	0.01
Ghanian	4	0.01
Alaska Native tribes, specified:	1	0.00
Tlingit-Haida	1	0.00
Am. Ind. or Alaska Nat., not spec.	90	0.31
Albanian	7	0.02
Alsatian	19	0.07
American Indian tribes, specified:	247	0.85
Apache (1)	2	0.01
Blackfeet (6)	10	0.03
Cherokee (29)	105	0.36
Cheyenne	1	0.00
Chickasaw (2)	2	0.01
Chippewa (1)	2	0.01
Choctaw (9)	15	0.05
Comanche (1)	1	0.00
Creek (2)	4	0.01
Crow	1	0.00
Delaware (3)	3	0.01
Iroquois (2)	9	0.03
Kiowa	1	0.00
Latin American Indians (7)	13	0.04
Lumbee (6)	7	0.02
Menominee	1	0.00
Navajo (7)	7	0.02
Osage	4	0.01
Ottawa (1)	2	0.01
Potawatomi (1)	1	0.00
Pueblo (3)	3	0.01
Seminole	2	0.01
Shoshone (4)	4	0.01
Sioux (3)	4	0.01
Ute (1)	1	0.00
All other tribes (32)	42	0.14
American Indian tribes, not spec.	26	0.09
Arab:	100	0.34
Arab/Arabic	39	0.13
Egyptian	10	0.03
Jordanian	8	0.03
Lebanese	26	0.09
Other Arab	17	0.06
Asian:	1,088	3.73
Cambodian (2)	2	0.01
Chinese, ex. Taiwanese (78)	118	0.40
Filipino (498)	659	2.26
Hmong (1)	1	0.00
Indian (39)	47	0.16
Indonesian	1	0.00
Japanese (44)	92	0.31
Korean (42)	68	0.23
Laotian (2)	2	0.01
Malaysian	2	0.01
Pakistani (8)	8	0.03
Taiwanese (3)	4	0.01
Thai (6)	15	0.05
Vietnamese (20)	37	0.13
Other Asian, specified	2	0.01
Other Asian, not specified (15)	30	0.10
Australian	36	0.12
Austrian	19	0.07
Belgian	31	0.11
British	198	0.68
Canadian	38	0.13
Celtic	14	0.05
Czech	57	0.20
Czechoslovakian	64	0.22
Danish	93	0.32
Dutch	318	1.09
Eastern European	12	0.04
English	2,505	8.59
European	278	0.95
Finnish	7	0.02
French, except Basque	844	2.89
French Canadian	193	0.66
German	4,166	14.29
Greek	152	0.52
Hawaii Native/Pacific Islander:	83	0.28
Micronesian: (10)	19	0.07
Guamanian/Chamorro (10)	17	0.06
Other Micronesian	2	0.01
Polynesian: (19)	55	0.19
Native Hawaiian (15)	46	0.16
Samoan (4)	8	0.03
Other Polynesian	1	0.00
Other Pac. Isl., not spec. (4)	9	0.03
Hispanic or Latino:	1,182	4.05
Central American:	74	0.25
Costa Rican	1	0.00
Guatemalan	8	0.03
Honduran	3	0.01
Nicaraguan	2	0.01
Panamanian	18	0.06
Salvadoran	36	0.12
Other Central American	6	0.02
Cuban	47	0.16
Dominican Republic	19	0.07
Mexican	463	1.59
Puerto Rican	271	0.93
South American:	71	0.24
Bolivian	2	0.01
Chilean	4	0.01
Colombian	36	0.12
Ecuadorian	16	0.05
Peruvian	5	0.02
Uruguayan	1	0.00
Venezuelan	6	0.02
Other South American	1	0.00
Other Hispanic or Latino	237	0.81
Hungarian	132	0.45
Icelander	6	0.02
Iranian	9	0.03
Irish	3,401	11.66
Italian	1,477	5.06
Latvian	11	0.04
Lithuanian	17	0.06
New Zealander	8	0.03
Norwegian	360	1.23
Polish	643	2.20
Portuguese	36	0.12
Russian	142	0.49
Scandinavian	49	0.17
Scotch-Irish	670	2.30
Scottish	634	2.17
Slavic	15	0.05
Slovak	9	0.03
Slovene	18	0.06
Swedish	264	0.91
Swiss	38	0.13
Ukrainian	17	0.06
United States or American	3,110	10.66
Welsh	175	0.60
West Indian, excl. Hispanic:	94	0.32
British West Indian	9	0.03
Jamaican	43	0.15
Trinidadian and Tobagonian	35	0.12
West Indian	7	0.02
White:	23,510	80.49
Not Hispanic (22,386)	22,893	78.38
Hispanic (543)	617	2.11
Yugoslavian	48	0.16

Notes: 1. Figures in the "Number" column do not add up to the total population due to: a) Ancestry/Race overlap — e.g. persons can report being both White and Irish, b) persons of Hispanic origin can report being any race, c) persons reporting two ancestries are counted in both categories. 2. Numbers in parentheses indicate the number of persons reporting this ancestry/race alone, not in combination with any other ancestry/race. 3. Refer to the Explanation of Data in the front of the book for more detailed information.

Greenville

Place Type: City
County: Greenville
Population: 56,002

Ancestry/Race	Number	%
Acadian/Cajun	21	0.04
African American/Black:	19,273	34.41
Not Hispanic (18,866)	19,100	34.11
Hispanic (142)	173	0.31
African, sub-Saharan:	785	1.39
African	620	1.10
Liberian	5	0.01
Nigerian	11	0.02
Other sub-Saharan African	149	0.26
Alaska Native tribes, specified:	4	0.01
Aleut (1)	1	0.00
Eskimo (3)	3	0.01
Am. Ind. or Alaska Nat., not spec.	99	0.18
Albanian	16	0.03
American Indian tribes, specified:	136	0.24
Apache	2	0.00
Blackfeet (1)	5	0.01
Cherokee (24)	84	0.15
Cheyenne	1	0.00
Chickasaw (1)	1	0.00
Chippewa (2)	2	0.00
Choctaw (3)	3	0.01
Comanche	1	0.00
Creek (3)	3	0.01
Delaware	1	0.00
Iroquois	2	0.00
Latin American Indians (5)	11	0.02
Lumbee (1)	2	0.00
Navajo (1)	3	0.01
Potawatomi (2)	3	0.01
Pueblo	1	0.00
Seminole (1)	1	0.00
Sioux (1)	1	0.00
Yaqui (1)	1	0.00
All other tribes (3)	8	0.01
American Indian tribes, not spec.	8	0.01
Arab:	189	0.34
Arab/Arabic	9	0.02
Lebanese	175	0.31
Syrian	5	0.01
Armenian	14	0.02
Asian:	850	1.52
Cambodian (7)	7	0.01
Chinese, ex. Taiwanese (101)	120	0.21
Filipino (67)	100	0.18
Hmong (3)	3	0.01
Indian (166)	191	0.34
Indonesian (3)	7	0.01
Japanese (58)	83	0.15
Korean (86)	97	0.17
Malaysian	1	0.00
Pakistani (9)	12	0.02
Sri Lankan (6)	6	0.01
Taiwanese (10)	11	0.02
Thai (19)	22	0.04
Vietnamese (140)	147	0.26
Other Asian, specified (2)	6	0.01
Other Asian, not specified (18)	37	0.07
Assyrian/Chaldean/Syriac	14	0.02
Australian	15	0.03
Austrian	114	0.20
Belgian	15	0.03
Brazilian	29	0.05
British	398	0.71
Bulgarian	6	0.01
Canadian	123	0.22
Croatian	11	0.02
Czech	37	0.07
Czechoslovakian	65	0.12
Danish	108	0.19
Dutch	681	1.21
Eastern European	30	0.05
English	6,018	10.68
European	484	0.86
Finnish	14	0.02
French, except Basque	1,006	1.79
French Canadian	227	0.40
German	5,018	8.91
Greek	290	0.51
Hawaii Native/Pacific Islander:	63	0.11
Micronesian: (16)	20	0.04
Guamanian/Chamorro (1)	5	0.01
Other Micronesian (15)	15	0.03
Polynesian: (14)	19	0.03
Native Hawaiian (8)	12	0.02
Samoan (5)	6	0.01
Other Polynesian (1)	1	0.00
Other Pac. Isl., specified	4	0.01
Other Pac. Isl., not spec. (5)	20	0.04
Hispanic or Latino:	1,927	3.44
Central American:	85	0.15
Costa Rican	12	0.02
Guatemalan	33	0.06
Honduran	18	0.03
Nicaraguan	6	0.01
Panamanian	2	0.00
Salvadoran	11	0.02
Other Central American	3	0.01
Cuban	38	0.07
Dominican Republic	24	0.04
Mexican	927	1.66
Puerto Rican	189	0.34
South American:	351	0.63
Argentinean	5	0.01
Bolivian	4	0.01
Chilean	2	0.00
Colombian	288	0.51
Ecuadorian	9	0.02
Paraguayan	1	0.00
Peruvian	27	0.05
Uruguayan	2	0.00
Venezuelan	9	0.02
Other South American	4	0.01
Other Hispanic or Latino	313	0.56
Hungarian	84	0.15
Iranian	19	0.03
Irish	3,889	6.90
Italian	999	1.77
Latvian	38	0.07
Lithuanian	34	0.06
Luxemburger	5	0.01
Maltese	8	0.01
New Zealander	5	0.01
Northern European	62	0.11
Norwegian	281	0.50
Pennsylvania German	17	0.03
Polish	431	0.77
Portuguese	23	0.04
Romanian	17	0.03
Russian	122	0.22
Scandinavian	66	0.12
Scotch-Irish	2,540	4.51
Scottish	1,712	3.04
Serbian	21	0.04
Slavic	17	0.03
Slovak	13	0.02
Swedish	258	0.46
Swiss	116	0.21
Ukrainian	34	0.06
United States or American	4,870	8.64
Welsh	331	0.59
West Indian, excl. Hispanic:	80	0.14
Barbadian	14	0.02
Bermudan	4	0.01
Haitian	22	0.04
Jamaican	26	0.05
Trinidadian and Tobagonian	8	0.01
West Indian	6	0.01
White:	35,259	62.96
Not Hispanic (33,917)	34,247	61.15
Hispanic (871)	1,012	1.81
Yugoslavian	12	0.02

Greenwood

Place Type: City
County: Greenwood
Population: 22,071

Ancestry/Race	Number	%
African American/Black:	10,121	45.86
Not Hispanic (9,957)	10,027	45.43
Hispanic (87)	94	0.43
African, sub-Saharan:	134	0.61
African	116	0.53
Kenyan	12	0.05
Other sub-Saharan African	6	0.03
Alaska Native tribes, specified:	2	0.01
Alaska Athabascan (2)	2	0.01
Alaska Native tribes, not specified	3	0.01
Am. Ind. or Alaska Nat., not spec.	54	0.24
American Indian tribes, specified:	49	0.22
Apache (1)	5	0.02
Blackfeet	8	0.04
Cherokee (3)	13	0.06
Choctaw	3	0.01
Creek	1	0.00
Latin American Indians	13	0.06
Navajo (2)	2	0.01
Puget Sound Salish (1)	1	0.00
Seminole (1)	1	0.00
All other tribes (2)	2	0.01
American Indian tribes, not spec.	20	0.09
Arab:	16	0.07
Lebanese	16	0.07
Armenian	6	0.03
Asian:	230	1.04
Chinese, ex. Taiwanese (33)	37	0.17
Filipino (24)	27	0.12
Indian (23)	27	0.12
Japanese (65)	70	0.32
Korean (8)	9	0.04
Taiwanese (1)	2	0.01
Thai (1)	1	0.00
Vietnamese (33)	37	0.17
Other Asian, specified	6	0.03
Other Asian, not specified (3)	14	0.06
Austrian	18	0.08
British	91	0.42
Croatian	11	0.05
Czechoslovakian	8	0.04
Danish	11	0.05
Dutch	88	0.40
English	1,193	5.45
Estonian	10	0.05
European	205	0.94
French, except Basque	184	0.84
French Canadian	25	0.11
German	910	4.16
Greek	78	0.36
Hawaii Native/Pacific Islander:	31	0.14
Micronesian: (7)	7	0.03
Guamanian/Chamorro (7)	7	0.03
Polynesian: (6)	12	0.05
Native Hawaiian (5)	10	0.05
Samoan (1)	2	0.01
Other Pac. Isl., specified	6	0.03
Other Pac. Isl., not spec. (2)	6	0.03
Hispanic or Latino:	1,440	6.52
Central American:	34	0.15
Guatemalan	21	0.10
Honduran	9	0.04
Nicaraguan	1	0.00
Panamanian	1	0.00
Salvadoran	1	0.00
Other Central American	1	0.00
Cuban	13	0.06
Dominican Republic	7	0.03
Mexican	1,175	5.32
Puerto Rican	79	0.36
South American:	23	0.10
Argentinean	2	0.01
Chilean	5	0.02

Notes: 1. Figures in the "Number" column do not add up to the total population due to: a) Ancestry/Race overlap — e.g. persons can report being both White and Irish, b) persons of Hispanic origin can report being any race, c) persons reporting two ancestries are counted in both categories. 2. Numbers in parentheses indicate the number of persons reporting this ancestry/race alone, not in combination with any other ancestry/race. 3. Refer to the Explanation of Data in the front of the book for more detailed information.

Colombian	5	0.02
Ecuadorian	1	0.00
Venezuelan	4	0.02
Other South American	6	0.03
Other Hispanic or Latino	109	0.49
Irish	1,033	4.72
Italian	196	0.90
Lithuanian	19	0.09
Northern European	15	0.07
Norwegian	38	0.17
Pennsylvania German	12	0.05
Polish	79	0.36
Portuguese	22	0.10
Russian	27	0.12
Scandinavian	7	0.03
Scotch-Irish	516	2.36
Scottish	270	1.23
Swedish	22	0.10
Swiss	30	0.14
United States or American	2,707	12.38
Welsh	34	0.16
West Indian, excl. Hispanic:	19	0.09
Trinidadian and Tobagonian	19	0.09
White:	11,175	50.63
Not Hispanic (10,328)	10,409	47.16
Hispanic (729)	766	3.47

Greer

Place Type: City
County: Greenville
Population: 16,843

Ancestry/Race	Number	%
African American/Black:	3,371	20.01
Not Hispanic (3,269)	3,336	19.81
Hispanic (14)	35	0.21
African, sub-Saharan:	17	0.10
African	7	0.04
South African	10	0.06
Am. Ind. or Alaska Nat., not spec.	30	0.18
Albanian	24	0.15
American Indian tribes, specified:	45	0.27
Blackfeet	1	0.01
Cherokee (13)	30	0.18
Cree	1	0.01
Latin American Indians (7)	7	0.04
Lumbee (2)	3	0.02
All other tribes (3)	3	0.02
American Indian tribes, not spec.	4	0.02
Arab:	4	0.02
Lebanese	4	0.02
Armenian	17	0.10
Asian:	239	1.42
Chinese, ex. Taiwanese (42)	50	0.30
Filipino (26)	34	0.20
Indian (40)	44	0.26
Indonesian (5)	5	0.03
Japanese (11)	23	0.14
Korean (11)	14	0.08
Laotian (10)	10	0.06
Pakistani (5)	5	0.03
Taiwanese (1)	1	0.01
Thai (3)	7	0.04
Vietnamese (32)	34	0.20
Other Asian, not specified (5)	12	0.07
Belgian	5	0.03
Brazilian	8	0.05
British	87	0.53
Bulgarian	7	0.04
Canadian	22	0.13
Celtic	9	0.05
Czech	61	0.37
Czechoslovakian	41	0.25
Danish	10	0.06
Dutch	217	1.31
English	1,330	8.04
European	71	0.43
Finnish	39	0.24
French, except Basque	301	1.82
French Canadian	73	0.44
German	1,480	8.95
Greek	16	0.10
Hawaii Native/Pacific Islander:	21	0.12
Micronesian: (3)	3	0.02
Guamanian/Chamorro (3)	3	0.02
Polynesian: (2)	13	0.08
Native Hawaiian (2)	13	0.08
Other Pac. Isl., not spec. (5)	5	0.03
Hispanic or Latino:	1,377	8.18
Central American:	68	0.40
Costa Rican	5	0.03
Guatemalan	6	0.04
Honduran	50	0.30
Nicaraguan	1	0.01
Panamanian	1	0.01
Salvadoran	2	0.01
Other Central American	3	0.02
Cuban	8	0.05
Dominican Republic	3	0.02
Mexican	1,036	6.15
Puerto Rican	80	0.47
South American:	64	0.38
Argentinean	4	0.02
Bolivian	1	0.01
Chilean	8	0.05
Colombian	46	0.27
Peruvian	5	0.03
Other Hispanic or Latino	118	0.70
Hungarian	56	0.34
Iranian	76	0.46
Irish	1,696	10.26
Italian	491	2.97
Lithuanian	15	0.09
Northern European	11	0.07
Norwegian	69	0.42
Polish	134	0.81
Romanian	20	0.12
Russian	62	0.37
Scandinavian	9	0.05
Scotch-Irish	404	2.44
Scottish	342	2.07
Swedish	96	0.58
Swiss	16	0.10
Ukrainian	25	0.15
United States or American	2,701	16.33
Welsh	127	0.77
West Indian, excl. Hispanic:	9	0.05
Jamaican	9	0.05
White:	12,544	74.48
Not Hispanic (11,809)	11,935	70.86
Hispanic (552)	609	3.62

Hanahan

Place Type: City
County: Berkeley
Population: 12,937

Ancestry/Race	Number	%
African American/Black:	1,719	13.29
Not Hispanic (1,634)	1,693	13.09
Hispanic (11)	26	0.20
African, sub-Saharan:	80	0.62
African	67	0.52
South African	13	0.10
Am. Ind. or Alaska Nat., not spec.	24	0.19
American Indian tribes, specified:	76	0.59
Apache (1)	5	0.04
Blackfeet (1)	2	0.02
Cherokee (21)	39	0.30
Choctaw	2	0.02
Comanche (1)	1	0.01
Cree	1	0.01
Crow	2	0.02
Delaware (1)	1	0.01
Iroquois	4	0.03
Latin American Indians (1)	1	0.01
Lumbee (2)	2	0.02
Navajo	1	0.01
Seminole (1)	1	0.01
Sioux (1)	2	0.02
All other tribes (8)	12	0.09
American Indian tribes, not spec.	8	0.06
Arab:	26	0.20
Lebanese	26	0.20
Asian:	336	2.60
Cambodian (4)	5	0.04
Chinese, ex. Taiwanese (42)	46	0.36
Filipino (68)	87	0.67
Indian (33)	44	0.34
Indonesian	2	0.02
Japanese (10)	18	0.14
Korean (35)	38	0.29
Pakistani (8)	8	0.06
Thai (2)	4	0.03
Vietnamese (59)	61	0.47
Other Asian, specified (1)	1	0.01
Other Asian, not specified (1)	22	0.17
Austrian	36	0.28
Belgian	5	0.04
Brazilian	32	0.25
British	28	0.22
Bulgarian	11	0.09
Canadian	47	0.36
Croatian	19	0.15
Czech	43	0.33
Czechoslovakian	18	0.14
Danish	94	0.73
Dutch	202	1.57
English	1,535	11.91
European	150	1.16
French, except Basque	650	5.04
French Canadian	51	0.40
German	1,611	12.50
Greek	112	0.87
Hawaii Native/Pacific Islander:	19	0.15
Micronesian: (1)	2	0.02
Guamanian/Chamorro	1	0.01
Other Micronesian (1)	1	0.01
Polynesian: (5)	11	0.09
Native Hawaiian (1)	7	0.05
Samoan (4)	4	0.03
Other Pac. Isl., not spec.	6	0.05
Hispanic or Latino:	410	3.17
Central American:	19	0.15
Costa Rican	3	0.02
Guatemalan	7	0.05
Honduran	4	0.03
Nicaraguan	1	0.01
Panamanian	3	0.02
Salvadoran	1	0.01
Cuban	4	0.03
Dominican Republic	2	0.02
Mexican	215	1.66
Puerto Rican	60	0.46
South American:	25	0.19
Colombian	6	0.05
Ecuadorian	5	0.04
Peruvian	7	0.05
Venezuelan	6	0.05
Other South American	1	0.01
Other Hispanic or Latino	85	0.66
Hungarian	46	0.36
Irish	1,654	12.83
Italian	551	4.27
Luxemburger	6	0.05
Norwegian	67	0.52
Polish	173	1.34
Portuguese	19	0.15
Russian	9	0.07
Scotch-Irish	373	2.89
Scottish	344	2.67
Slovak	9	0.07
Swedish	32	0.25
Swiss	6	0.05
Ukrainian	28	0.22
United States or American	1,330	10.32
Welsh	76	0.59
West Indian, excl. Hispanic:	28	0.22

Notes: 1. Figures in the "Number" column do not add up to the total population due to: a) Ancestry/Race overlap — e.g. persons can report being both White and Irish, b) persons of Hispanic origin can report being any race, c) persons reporting two ancestries are counted in both categories. 2. Numbers in parentheses indicate the number of persons reporting this ancestry/race alone, not in combination with any other ancestry/race. 3. Refer to the Explanation of Data in the front of the book for more detailed information.

Bahamian	18	0.14
Jamaican	10	0.08
White:	10,755	83.13
Not Hispanic (10,362)	10,523	81.34
Hispanic (201)	232	1.79

Hilton Head Island

Place Type: Town
County: Beaufort
Population: 33,862

Ancestry/Race	Number	%
Acadian/Cajun	12	0.04
African American/Black:	2,884	8.52
Not Hispanic (2,758)	2,843	8.40
Hispanic (39)	41	0.12
African, sub-Saharan:	175	0.52
African	168	0.50
South African	7	0.02
Alaska Native tribes, specified:	3	0.01
Aleut	1	0.00
Eskimo (2)	2	0.01
Am. Ind. or Alaska Nat., not spec.	39	0.12
Albanian	44	0.13
American Indian tribes, specified:	64	0.19
Blackfeet (2)	3	0.01
Cherokee (4)	23	0.07
Chickasaw (1)	1	0.00
Chippewa	1	0.00
Choctaw (2)	2	0.01
Creek (2)	3	0.01
Delaware (1)	1	0.00
Iroquois (2)	3	0.01
Kiowa	1	0.00
Latin American Indians (6)	16	0.05
Navajo (1)	1	0.00
Osage (1)	1	0.00
Seminole (1)	1	0.00
All other tribes (2)	7	0.02
American Indian tribes, not spec.	11	0.03
Arab:	111	0.33
Arab/Arabic	14	0.04
Egyptian	13	0.04
Lebanese	27	0.08
Moroccan	7	0.02
Palestinian	7	0.02
Syrian	37	0.11
Other Arab	6	0.02
Armenian	29	0.09
Asian:	246	0.73
Cambodian (1)	1	0.00
Chinese, ex. Taiwanese (46)	60	0.18
Filipino (24)	38	0.11
Indian (20)	25	0.07
Indonesian (1)	2	0.01
Japanese (18)	31	0.09
Korean (31)	35	0.10
Laotian (3)	3	0.01
Thai (3)	3	0.01
Vietnamese (26)	31	0.09
Other Asian, specified (1)	2	0.01
Other Asian, not specified (4)	15	0.04
Australian	8	0.02
Austrian	174	0.52
Belgian	37	0.11
Brazilian	8	0.02
British	217	0.64
Bulgarian	7	0.02
Canadian	241	0.71
Croatian	51	0.15
Czech	93	0.28
Czechoslovakian	91	0.27
Danish	223	0.66
Dutch	569	1.68
Eastern European	34	0.10
English	5,647	16.72
Estonian	9	0.03
European	377	1.12
Finnish	90	0.27
French, except Basque	1,246	3.69
French Canadian	275	0.81
German	5,960	17.65
Greek	130	0.38
Guyanese	8	0.02
Hawaii Native/Pacific Islander:	15	0.04
Micronesian: (1)	1	0.00
Guamanian/Chamorro (1)	1	0.00
Polynesian:	3	0.01
Native Hawaiian	3	0.01
Other Pac. Isl., not spec. (7)	11	0.03
Hispanic or Latino:	3,886	11.48
Central American:	505	1.49
Costa Rican	140	0.41
Guatemalan	38	0.11
Honduran	239	0.71
Nicaraguan	46	0.14
Panamanian	17	0.05
Salvadoran	13	0.04
Other Central American	12	0.04
Cuban	35	0.10
Mexican	2,553	7.54
Puerto Rican	79	0.23
South American:	204	0.60
Argentinean	73	0.22
Bolivian	9	0.03
Chilean	11	0.03
Colombian	55	0.16
Peruvian	6	0.02
Uruguayan	7	0.02
Venezuelan	36	0.11
Other South American	7	0.02
Other Hispanic or Latino	510	1.51
Hungarian	254	0.75
Icelander	15	0.04
Iranian	7	0.02
Irish	4,896	14.50
Israeli	13	0.04
Italian	2,045	6.05
Lithuanian	111	0.33
Northern European	24	0.07
Norwegian	464	1.37
Pennsylvania German	19	0.06
Polish	1,066	3.16
Portuguese	60	0.18
Romanian	37	0.11
Russian	401	1.19
Scandinavian	50	0.15
Scotch-Irish	922	2.73
Scottish	1,281	3.79
Serbian	7	0.02
Slavic	60	0.18
Slovak	93	0.28
Slovene	28	0.08
Swedish	427	1.26
Swiss	201	0.60
Turkish	8	0.02
Ukrainian	146	0.43
United States or American	2,140	6.34
Welsh	383	1.13
West Indian, excl. Hispanic:	9	0.03
Jamaican	9	0.03
White:	29,246	86.37
Not Hispanic (26,752)	26,955	79.60
Hispanic (2,141)	2,291	6.77

Irmo

Place Type: Town
County: Richland
Population: 11,039

Ancestry/Race	Number	%
African American/Black:	2,269	20.55
Not Hispanic (2,220)	2,259	20.46
Hispanic (5)	10	0.09
African, sub-Saharan:	79	0.71
African	79	0.71
Am. Ind. or Alaska Nat., not spec.	14	0.13
Albanian	9	0.08
American Indian tribes, specified:	38	0.34
Cherokee (2)	14	0.13
Cheyenne (1)	1	0.01
Choctaw	3	0.03
Iroquois (1)	1	0.01
Latin American Indians (2)	2	0.02
Lumbee (5)	5	0.05
Navajo	1	0.01
Osage (1)	1	0.01
Sioux (3)	4	0.04
All other tribes (5)	6	0.05
American Indian tribes, not spec.	1	0.01
Arab:	42	0.38
Arab/Arabic	8	0.07
Iraqi	18	0.16
Lebanese	16	0.14
Asian:	182	1.65
Chinese, ex. Taiwanese (34)	35	0.32
Filipino (13)	17	0.15
Indian (75)	75	0.68
Japanese (10)	19	0.17
Korean (11)	14	0.13
Pakistani (4)	4	0.04
Thai	2	0.02
Vietnamese (9)	12	0.11
Other Asian, not specified (2)	4	0.04
Austrian	55	0.50
Belgian	7	0.06
British	103	0.93
Canadian	18	0.16
Czech	24	0.22
Czechoslovakian	8	0.07
Danish	8	0.07
Dutch	160	1.44
Eastern European	8	0.07
English	1,180	10.62
European	166	1.49
French, except Basque	270	2.43
French Canadian	43	0.39
German	1,594	14.35
Greek	55	0.50
Hawaii Native/Pacific Islander:	13	0.12
Micronesian: (1)	1	0.01
Guamanian/Chamorro (1)	1	0.01
Polynesian: (7)	8	0.07
Native Hawaiian (7)	8	0.07
Other Pac. Isl., not spec. (1)	4	0.04
Hispanic or Latino:	157	1.42
Central American:	6	0.05
Guatemalan	2	0.02
Honduran	1	0.01
Panamanian	1	0.01
Other Central American	2	0.02
Cuban	15	0.14
Dominican Republic	2	0.02
Mexican	46	0.42
Puerto Rican	57	0.52
South American:	10	0.09
Argentinean	1	0.01
Colombian	4	0.04
Peruvian	3	0.03
Venezuelan	2	0.02
Other Hispanic or Latino	21	0.19
Hungarian	31	0.28
Iranian	39	0.35
Irish	1,148	10.33
Italian	459	4.13
Norwegian	104	0.94
Pennsylvania German	7	0.06
Polish	56	0.50
Portuguese	5	0.05
Russian	50	0.45
Scandinavian	16	0.14
Scotch-Irish	511	4.60
Scottish	358	3.22
Slovene	12	0.11
Swedish	127	1.14
Swiss	14	0.13
Ukrainian	30	0.27
United States or American	965	8.69

Notes: 1. Figures in the "Number" column do not add up to the total population due to: a) Ancestry/Race overlap — e.g. persons can report being both White and Irish, b) persons of Hispanic origin can report being any race, c) persons reporting two ancestries are counted in both categories. 2. Numbers in parentheses indicate the number of persons reporting this ancestry/race alone, not in combination with any other ancestry/race. 3. Refer to the Explanation of Data in the front of the book for more detailed information.

Welsh	91	0.82
West Indian, excl. Hispanic:	6	0.05
Jamaican	6	0.05
White:	8,550	77.45
Not Hispanic (8,370)	8,443	76.48
Hispanic (103)	107	0.97
Yugoslavian	5	0.05

Ladson

Place Type: Census Designated Place
County: Berkeley
Population: 13,264

Ancestry/Race	Number	%
African American/Black:	2,990	22.54
Not Hispanic (2,907)	2,962	22.33
Hispanic (19)	28	0.21
African, sub-Saharan:	82	0.62
African	82	0.62
Alaska Native tribes, specified:	3	0.02
Aleut (3)	3	0.02
Alaska Native tribes, not specified	1	0.01
Am. Ind. or Alaska Nat., not spec.	73	0.55
American Indian tribes, specified:	154	1.16
Apache (1)	4	0.03
Blackfeet (1)	2	0.02
Cherokee (40)	78	0.59
Chickasaw	1	0.01
Chippewa (3)	6	0.05
Choctaw (1)	4	0.03
Cree (1)	1	0.01
Creek (1)	1	0.01
Delaware	1	0.01
Iroquois	5	0.04
Latin American Indians	3	0.02
Lumbee (7)	7	0.05
Osage	1	0.01
Pueblo (1)	1	0.01
Seminole	7	0.05
Sioux	4	0.03
All other tribes (18)	28	0.21
American Indian tribes, not spec.	17	0.13
Asian:	356	2.68
Chinese, ex. Taiwanese (14)	23	0.17
Filipino (178)	229	1.73
Indian (23)	27	0.20
Japanese (18)	27	0.20
Korean (14)	18	0.14
Taiwanese (2)	2	0.02
Thai (6)	8	0.06
Vietnamese (7)	11	0.08
Other Asian, specified	1	0.01
Other Asian, not specified (7)	10	0.08
Austrian	24	0.18
Belgian	17	0.13
British	41	0.31
Canadian	19	0.14
Croatian	13	0.10
Czech	19	0.14
Czechoslovakian	7	0.05
Danish	31	0.23
Dutch	153	1.15
English	1,304	9.79
European	63	0.47
French, except Basque	274	2.06
French Canadian	67	0.50
German	1,944	14.60
Greek	48	0.36
Hawaii Native/Pacific Islander:	27	0.20
Micronesian: (2)	4	0.03
Guamanian/Chamorro (2)	4	0.03
Polynesian: (6)	15	0.11
Native Hawaiian (5)	14	0.11
Samoan (1)	1	0.01
Other Pac. Isl., specified	1	0.01
Other Pac. Isl., not spec. (1)	7	0.05
Hispanic or Latino:	394	2.97
Central American:	13	0.10
Costa Rican	3	0.02
Guatemalan	3	0.02
Nicaraguan	2	0.02
Panamanian	2	0.02
Salvadoran	3	0.02
Cuban	18	0.14
Dominican Republic	20	0.15
Mexican	171	1.29
Puerto Rican	83	0.63
South American:	16	0.12
Argentinean	2	0.02
Chilean	1	0.01
Colombian	4	0.03
Peruvian	8	0.06
Venezuelan	1	0.01
Other Hispanic or Latino	73	0.55
Hungarian	39	0.29
Irish	1,321	9.92
Italian	520	3.91
Lithuanian	7	0.05
Northern European	93	0.70
Norwegian	40	0.30
Polish	126	0.95
Portuguese	31	0.23
Russian	12	0.09
Scandinavian	17	0.13
Scotch-Irish	248	1.86
Scottish	331	2.49
Slovak	38	0.29
Swedish	142	1.07
Swiss	57	0.43
Ukrainian	8	0.06
United States or American	1,494	11.22
Welsh	37	0.28
West Indian, excl. Hispanic:	27	0.20
Jamaican	20	0.15
West Indian	7	0.05
White:	9,704	73.16
Not Hispanic (9,345)	9,524	71.80
Hispanic (165)	180	1.36

Mauldin

Place Type: City
County: Greenville
Population: 15,224

Ancestry/Race	Number	%
African American/Black:	3,234	21.24
Not Hispanic (3,161)	3,222	21.16
Hispanic (8)	12	0.08
African, sub-Saharan:	139	0.92
African	133	0.88
Liberian	6	0.04
Am. Ind. or Alaska Nat., not spec.	23	0.15
American Indian tribes, specified:	67	0.44
Apache	1	0.01
Blackfeet (1)	5	0.03
Cherokee (12)	35	0.23
Choctaw	1	0.01
Comanche	1	0.01
Creek (2)	2	0.01
Latin American Indians (11)	11	0.07
Osage (1)	1	0.01
Potawatomi (1)	1	0.01
Seminole	1	0.01
Shoshone (3)	3	0.02
Sioux	2	0.01
Yaqui (1)	1	0.01
All other tribes (2)	2	0.01
Arab:	74	0.49
Lebanese	23	0.15
Other Arab	51	0.34
Armenian	22	0.15
Asian:	409	2.69
Cambodian (3)	3	0.02
Chinese, ex. Taiwanese (61)	69	0.45
Filipino (35)	59	0.39
Indian (73)	75	0.49
Indonesian (2)	2	0.01
Japanese (69)	80	0.53
Korean (30)	45	0.30
Pakistani (1)	1	0.01
Sri Lankan (9)	9	0.06
Thai (2)	3	0.02
Vietnamese (39)	44	0.29
Other Asian, specified (1)	1	0.01
Other Asian, not specified (10)	18	0.12
Australian	11	0.07
Austrian	6	0.04
Belgian	28	0.19
British	99	0.66
Canadian	21	0.14
Czech	62	0.41
Czechoslovakian	10	0.07
Danish	32	0.21
Dutch	336	2.23
English	1,656	10.98
European	143	0.95
Finnish	23	0.15
French, except Basque	364	2.41
French Canadian	87	0.58
German	1,697	11.25
Greek	7	0.05
Hawaii Native/Pacific Islander:	25	0.16
Polynesian: (17)	20	0.13
Native Hawaiian (8)	9	0.06
Samoan (8)	10	0.07
Other Polynesian (1)	1	0.01
Other Pac. Isl., not spec.	5	0.03
Hispanic or Latino:	416	2.73
Central American:	16	0.11
Costa Rican	4	0.03
Honduran	2	0.01
Nicaraguan	7	0.05
Panamanian	1	0.01
Other Central American	2	0.01
Cuban	14	0.09
Mexican	171	1.12
Puerto Rican	38	0.25
South American:	83	0.55
Argentinean	1	0.01
Chilean	6	0.04
Colombian	63	0.41
Ecuadorian	2	0.01
Peruvian	6	0.04
Venezuelan	1	0.01
Other South American	4	0.03
Other Hispanic or Latino	94	0.62
Hungarian	55	0.36
Iranian	19	0.13
Irish	1,527	10.12
Italian	476	3.16
Northern European	24	0.16
Norwegian	102	0.68
Polish	287	1.90
Portuguese	32	0.21
Romanian	27	0.18
Russian	68	0.45
Scandinavian	5	0.03
Scotch-Irish	458	3.04
Scottish	284	1.88
Slavic	8	0.05
Slovak	17	0.11
Swedish	146	0.97
Swiss	20	0.13
Ukrainian	63	0.42
United States or American	1,933	12.82
Welsh	70	0.46
West Indian, excl. Hispanic:	90	0.60
Bahamian	35	0.23
Jamaican	30	0.20
Trinidadian and Tobagonian	25	0.17
White:	11,470	75.34
Not Hispanic (11,071)	11,211	73.64
Hispanic (233)	259	1.70

Notes: 1. Figures in the "Number" column do not add up to the total population due to: a) Ancestry/Race overlap — e.g. persons can report being both White and Irish, b) persons of Hispanic origin can report being any race, c) persons reporting two ancestries are counted in both categories. 2. Numbers in parentheses indicate the number of persons reporting this ancestry/race alone, not in combination with any other ancestry/race. 3. Refer to the Explanation of Data in the front of the book for more detailed information.

Mount Pleasant

Place Type: Town
County: Charleston
Population: 47,609

Ancestry/Race	Number	%
African American/Black:	3,529	7.41
Not Hispanic (3,445)	3,521	7.40
Hispanic (8)	8	0.02
African, sub-Saharan:	275	0.58
African	258	0.54
Ethiopian	8	0.02
South African	9	0.02
Am. Ind. or Alaska Nat., not spec.	61	0.13
Alsatian	16	0.03
American Indian tribes, specified:	125	0.26
Blackfeet	2	0.00
Cherokee (36)	75	0.16
Chickasaw	2	0.00
Chippewa (3)	8	0.02
Choctaw	1	0.00
Comanche (1)	1	0.00
Delaware (1)	4	0.01
Iroquois	3	0.01
Latin American Indians (4)	7	0.01
Lumbee (2)	5	0.01
Sioux (1)	2	0.00
All other tribes (8)	15	0.03
American Indian tribes, not spec.	15	0.03
Arab:	147	0.31
Lebanese	139	0.29
Syrian	8	0.02
Armenian	33	0.07
Asian:	688	1.45
Chinese, ex. Taiwanese (152)	172	0.36
Filipino (50)	86	0.18
Indian (171)	183	0.38
Japanese (31)	57	0.12
Korean (59)	66	0.14
Malaysian	1	0.00
Pakistani (23)	23	0.05
Sri Lankan (4)	7	0.01
Taiwanese (4)	6	0.01
Thai (6)	9	0.02
Vietnamese (31)	38	0.08
Other Asian, specified (11)	12	0.03
Other Asian, not specified (8)	28	0.06
Australian	25	0.05
Austrian	174	0.37
Belgian	16	0.03
Brazilian	15	0.03
British	352	0.74
Canadian	128	0.27
Croatian	37	0.08
Czech	179	0.38
Czechoslovakian	29	0.06
Danish	119	0.25
Dutch	671	1.42
Eastern European	22	0.05
English	8,090	17.07
Estonian	9	0.02
European	886	1.87
Finnish	38	0.08
French, except Basque	1,902	4.01
French Canadian	342	0.72
German	7,849	16.56
Greek	247	0.52
Guyanese	8	0.02
Hawaii Native/Pacific Islander:	49	0.10
Micronesian: (4)	12	0.03
Guamanian/Chamorro (4)	12	0.03
Polynesian: (5)	15	0.03
Native Hawaiian (3)	9	0.02
Samoan (2)	6	0.01
Other Pac. Isl., specified	1	0.00
Other Pac. Isl., not spec. (1)	21	0.04
Hispanic or Latino:	635	1.33
Central American:	22	0.05
Costa Rican	5	0.01
Guatemalan	2	0.00
Honduran	7	0.01
Nicaraguan	2	0.00
Panamanian	4	0.01
Other Central American	2	0.00
Cuban	38	0.08
Dominican Republic	4	0.01
Mexican	236	0.50
Puerto Rican	102	0.21
South American:	87	0.18
Argentinean	16	0.03
Chilean	12	0.03
Colombian	21	0.04
Ecuadorian	10	0.02
Paraguayan	2	0.00
Peruvian	6	0.01
Venezuelan	3	0.01
Other South American	17	0.04
Other Hispanic or Latino	146	0.31
Hungarian	217	0.46
Icelander	13	0.03
Iranian	69	0.15
Irish	6,511	13.74
Israeli	13	0.03
Italian	2,544	5.37
Latvian	14	0.03
Lithuanian	207	0.44
Macedonian	6	0.01
Maltese	11	0.02
New Zealander	120	0.25
Northern European	88	0.19
Norwegian	442	0.93
Pennsylvania German	26	0.05
Polish	1,039	2.19
Portuguese	94	0.20
Romanian	20	0.04
Russian	359	0.76
Scandinavian	91	0.19
Scotch-Irish	2,107	4.45
Scottish	2,151	4.54
Slavic	33	0.07
Slovak	166	0.35
Slovene	17	0.04
Swedish	488	1.03
Swiss	185	0.39
Turkish	9	0.02
Ukrainian	94	0.20
United States or American	4,344	9.17
Welsh	649	1.37
West Indian, excl. Hispanic:	71	0.15
Barbadian	2	0.00
U.S. Virgin Islander	24	0.05
West Indian	45	0.09
White:	43,265	90.88
Not Hispanic (42,515)	42,817	89.93
Hispanic (413)	448	0.94
Yugoslavian	53	0.11

Myrtle Beach

Place Type: City
County: Horry
Population: 22,759

Ancestry/Race	Number	%
African American/Black:	3,014	13.24
Not Hispanic (2,859)	2,964	13.02
Hispanic (44)	50	0.22
African, sub-Saharan:	45	0.20
African	45	0.20
Am. Ind. or Alaska Nat., not spec.	64	0.28
Albanian	23	0.10
Alsatian	10	0.04
American Indian tribes, specified:	137	0.60
Apache (3)	4	0.02
Blackfeet (1)	2	0.01
Cherokee (28)	66	0.29
Chippewa (1)	2	0.01
Choctaw (1)	2	0.01
Cree	1	0.00
Creek (2)	3	0.01
Delaware	1	0.00
Iroquois (3)	8	0.04
Latin American Indians (2)	9	0.04
Lumbee (12)	13	0.06
Navajo (3)	6	0.03
Seminole (1)	1	0.00
Sioux (2)	4	0.02
Ute (1)	1	0.00
All other tribes (10)	14	0.06
American Indian tribes, not spec.	18	0.08
Arab:	100	0.44
Lebanese	90	0.40
Moroccan	10	0.04
Asian:	423	1.86
Cambodian (1)	1	0.00
Chinese, ex. Taiwanese (27)	35	0.15
Filipino (32)	53	0.23
Hmong	1	0.00
Indian (57)	78	0.34
Indonesian (2)	2	0.01
Japanese (24)	45	0.20
Korean (18)	25	0.11
Laotian (2)	4	0.02
Pakistani	6	0.03
Sri Lankan (2)	2	0.01
Taiwanese	3	0.01
Thai (8)	11	0.05
Vietnamese (97)	102	0.45
Other Asian, specified (1)	1	0.00
Other Asian, not specified (19)	54	0.24
Australian	11	0.05
Austrian	30	0.13
Brazilian	93	0.41
British	80	0.35
Canadian	56	0.25
Celtic	7	0.03
Croatian	27	0.12
Czech	17	0.08
Czechoslovakian	54	0.24
Danish	60	0.27
Dutch	295	1.30
English	2,920	12.92
European	41	0.18
Finnish	47	0.21
French, except Basque	562	2.49
French Canadian	100	0.44
German	2,498	11.05
Greek	220	0.97
Hawaii Native/Pacific Islander:	47	0.21
Micronesian: (23)	29	0.13
Guamanian/Chamorro (23)	24	0.11
Other Micronesian	5	0.02
Polynesian: (5)	9	0.04
Native Hawaiian (1)	5	0.02
Samoan (4)	4	0.02
Other Pac. Isl., not spec. (1)	9	0.04
Hispanic or Latino:	1,062	4.67
Central American:	93	0.41
Costa Rican	17	0.07
Guatemalan	37	0.16
Honduran	18	0.08
Nicaraguan	8	0.04
Panamanian	3	0.01
Salvadoran	6	0.03
Other Central American	4	0.02
Cuban	12	0.05
Dominican Republic	8	0.04
Mexican	682	3.00
Puerto Rican	95	0.42
South American:	38	0.17
Argentinean	9	0.04
Chilean	1	0.00
Colombian	13	0.06
Ecuadorian	4	0.02
Venezuelan	5	0.02
Other South American	6	0.03
Other Hispanic or Latino	134	0.59
Hungarian	34	0.15
Irish	2,674	11.83

Notes: 1. Figures in the "Number" column do not add up to the total population due to: a) Ancestry/Race overlap — e.g. persons can report being both White and Irish, b) persons of Hispanic origin can report being any race, c) persons reporting two ancestries are counted in both categories. 2. Numbers in parentheses indicate the number of persons reporting this ancestry/race alone, not in combination with any other ancestry/race. 3. Refer to the Explanation of Data in the front of the book for more detailed information.

Ancestry/Race	Number	%
Israeli	201	0.89
Italian	1,177	5.21
Lithuanian	62	0.27
Norwegian	97	0.43
Pennsylvania German	10	0.04
Polish	584	2.58
Portuguese	69	0.31
Romanian	36	0.16
Russian	47	0.21
Scandinavian	20	0.09
Scotch-Irish	808	3.57
Scottish	793	3.51
Serbian	8	0.04
Slavic	13	0.06
Slovak	13	0.06
Slovene	12	0.05
Swedish	213	0.94
Swiss	37	0.16
Turkish	30	0.13
Ukrainian	9	0.04
United States or American	2,267	10.03
Welsh	189	0.84
West Indian, excl. Hispanic:	38	0.17
Barbadian	9	0.04
West Indian	29	0.13
White:	18,810	82.65
Not Hispanic (18,016)	18,321	80.50
Hispanic (456)	489	2.15
Yugoslavian	7	0.03

Newberry

Place Type: Town
County: Newberry
Population: 10,580

Ancestry/Race	Number	%
African American/Black:	4,418	41.76
Not Hispanic (4,347)	4,383	41.43
Hispanic (29)	35	0.33
African, sub-Saharan:	34	0.32
African	34	0.32
Am. Ind. or Alaska Nat., not spec.	32	0.30
American Indian tribes, specified:	52	0.49
Apache	2	0.02
Cherokee (13)	27	0.26
Iroquois	1	0.01
Latin American Indians (11)	11	0.10
Ottawa (1)	1	0.01
Puget Sound Salish (1)	1	0.01
Sioux (1)	1	0.01
Tohono O'Odham (1)	3	0.03
All other tribes (1)	5	0.05
American Indian tribes, not spec.	10	0.09
Arab:	64	0.61
Lebanese	64	0.61
Asian:	85	0.80
Chinese, ex. Taiwanese (19)	19	0.18
Filipino (5)	6	0.06
Indian (6)	8	0.08
Japanese (2)	4	0.04
Korean (7)	7	0.07
Laotian (4)	4	0.04
Pakistani (3)	3	0.03
Vietnamese (15)	16	0.15
Other Asian, not specified (3)	18	0.17
British	21	0.20
Danish	74	0.71
Dutch	59	0.56
English	684	6.53
European	145	1.38
French, except Basque	110	1.05
French Canadian	22	0.21
German	971	9.27
Greek	23	0.22
Hawaii Native/Pacific Islander:	22	0.21
Micronesian: (10)	11	0.10
Guamanian/Chamorro (9)	9	0.09
Other Micronesian (1)	2	0.02
Polynesian: (2)	7	0.07
Native Hawaiian (1)	6	0.06
Samoan (1)	1	0.01
Other Pac. Isl., not spec. (1)	4	0.04
Hispanic or Latino:	1,004	9.49
Central American:	66	0.62
Guatemalan	54	0.51
Honduran	11	0.10
Panamanian	1	0.01
Cuban	15	0.14
Dominican Republic	1	0.01
Mexican	832	7.86
Puerto Rican	21	0.20
South American:	7	0.07
Colombian	6	0.06
Venezuelan	1	0.01
Other Hispanic or Latino	62	0.59
Irish	434	4.14
Italian	126	1.20
Norwegian	27	0.26
Polish	23	0.22
Scotch-Irish	154	1.47
Scottish	58	0.55
Swedish	51	0.49
United States or American	1,040	9.93
Welsh	13	0.12
West Indian, excl. Hispanic:	13	0.12
Jamaican	13	0.12
White:	5,732	54.18
Not Hispanic (5,056)	5,107	48.27
Hispanic (536)	625	5.91

North Augusta

Place Type: City
County: Aiken
Population: 17,574

Ancestry/Race	Number	%
African American/Black:	3,357	19.10
Not Hispanic (3,286)	3,342	19.02
Hispanic (13)	15	0.09
African, sub-Saharan:	82	0.48
African	82	0.48
Alaska Native tribes, specified:	1	0.01
Aleut (1)	1	0.01
Am. Ind. or Alaska Nat., not spec.	23	0.13
American Indian tribes, specified:	80	0.46
Apache (1)	1	0.01
Blackfeet (1)	2	0.01
Cherokee (17)	43	0.24
Chickasaw (3)	3	0.02
Chippewa (3)	3	0.02
Choctaw	3	0.02
Comanche (2)	3	0.02
Creek (1)	2	0.01
Delaware (1)	1	0.01
Iroquois	2	0.01
Latin American Indians (1)	5	0.03
Lumbee	1	0.01
Navajo (1)	1	0.01
Paiute (1)	1	0.01
Sioux	1	0.01
All other tribes (5)	8	0.05
American Indian tribes, not spec.	6	0.03
Arab:	55	0.32
Lebanese	14	0.08
Palestinian	22	0.13
Syrian	19	0.11
Armenian	9	0.05
Asian:	250	1.42
Chinese, ex. Taiwanese (40)	46	0.26
Filipino (19)	29	0.17
Indian (43)	47	0.27
Japanese (5)	10	0.06
Korean (17)	27	0.15
Laotian (10)	11	0.06
Malaysian (1)	1	0.01
Pakistani	3	0.02
Thai (1)	3	0.02
Vietnamese (66)	68	0.39
Other Asian, specified	1	0.01
Other Asian, not specified (1)	4	0.02
Belgian	8	0.05
British	53	0.31
Canadian	64	0.37
Croatian	20	0.12
Czech	20	0.12
Czechoslovakian	7	0.04
Danish	31	0.18
Dutch	140	0.82
English	2,180	12.69
European	254	1.48
Finnish	10	0.06
French, except Basque	535	3.11
French Canadian	111	0.65
German	2,061	12.00
Greek	4	0.02
Hawaii Native/Pacific Islander:	25	0.14
Micronesian: (1)	3	0.02
Guamanian/Chamorro (1)	3	0.02
Polynesian: (4)	13	0.07
Native Hawaiian (2)	10	0.06
Samoan (2)	3	0.02
Other Pac. Isl., specified	1	0.01
Other Pac. Isl., not spec. (4)	8	0.05
Hispanic or Latino:	424	2.41
Central American:	44	0.25
Costa Rican	27	0.15
Guatemalan	3	0.02
Honduran	7	0.04
Nicaraguan	3	0.02
Panamanian	2	0.01
Other Central American	2	0.01
Cuban	10	0.06
Dominican Republic	4	0.02
Mexican	217	1.23
Puerto Rican	57	0.32
South American:	16	0.09
Argentinean	1	0.01
Chilean	3	0.02
Colombian	6	0.03
Paraguayan	1	0.01
Peruvian	5	0.03
Other Hispanic or Latino	76	0.43
Hungarian	14	0.08
Icelander	14	0.08
Iranian	17	0.10
Irish	1,652	9.62
Italian	412	2.40
Lithuanian	8	0.05
Luxemburger	5	0.03
Northern European	7	0.04
Norwegian	39	0.23
Pennsylvania German	8	0.05
Polish	181	1.05
Portuguese	38	0.22
Romanian	6	0.03
Russian	20	0.12
Scotch-Irish	550	3.20
Scottish	517	3.01
Slovak	14	0.08
Swedish	50	0.29
Swiss	43	0.25
Ukrainian	9	0.05
United States or American	2,319	13.50
Welsh	156	0.91
West Indian, excl. Hispanic:	40	0.23
Haitian	11	0.06
Jamaican	29	0.17
White:	13,803	78.54
Not Hispanic (13,429)	13,567	77.20
Hispanic (218)	236	1.34
Yugoslavian	12	0.07

Notes: 1. Figures in the "Number" column do not add up to the total population due to: a) Ancestry/Race overlap — e.g. persons can report being both White and Irish, b) persons of Hispanic origin can report being any race, c) persons reporting two ancestries are counted in both categories. 2. Numbers in parentheses indicate the number of persons reporting this ancestry/race alone, not in combination with any other ancestry/race. 3. Refer to the Explanation of Data in the front of the book for more detailed information.

North Charleston

Place Type: City
County: Charleston
Population: 79,641

Ancestry/Race	Number	%
Acadian/Cajun	26	0.03
African American/Black:	40,093	50.34
Not Hispanic (39,096)	39,732	49.89
Hispanic (252)	361	0.45
African, sub-Saharan:	526	0.66
African	507	0.64
Kenyan	6	0.01
Sierra Leonean	13	0.02
Alaska Native tribes, specified:	1	0.00
Eskimo (1)	1	0.00
Am. Ind. or Alaska Nat., not spec.	299	0.38
Albanian	14	0.02
American Indian tribes, specified:	415	0.52
Apache (9)	14	0.02
Blackfeet (1)	10	0.01
Cherokee (62)	188	0.24
Chickasaw	6	0.01
Chippewa (2)	6	0.01
Choctaw (3)	13	0.02
Comanche (5)	6	0.01
Creek (3)	6	0.01
Crow (1)	2	0.00
Delaware	3	0.00
Iroquois (5)	11	0.01
Latin American Indians (41)	45	0.06
Lumbee (17)	20	0.03
Navajo (6)	9	0.01
Osage (2)	2	0.00
Paiute (1)	1	0.00
Potawatomi	1	0.00
Pueblo	2	0.00
Puget Sound Salish (1)	1	0.00
Seminole (4)	9	0.01
Sioux (4)	8	0.01
Tohono O'Odham (1)	1	0.00
All other tribes (25)	51	0.06
American Indian tribes, not spec.	68	0.09
Arab:	21	0.03
Arab/Arabic	7	0.01
Lebanese	8	0.01
Other Arab	6	0.01
Armenian	7	0.01
Asian:	1,722	2.16
Cambodian	1	0.00
Chinese, ex. Taiwanese (187)	233	0.29
Filipino (551)	745	0.94
Hmong (1)	1	0.00
Indian (103)	146	0.18
Indonesian	1	0.00
Japanese (59)	100	0.13
Korean (71)	110	0.14
Laotian (1)	1	0.00
Malaysian	3	0.00
Pakistani (5)	5	0.01
Taiwanese (5)	6	0.01
Thai (29)	51	0.06
Vietnamese (190)	209	0.26
Other Asian, specified	6	0.01
Other Asian, not specified (36)	104	0.13
Australian	13	0.02
Austrian	61	0.08
Basque	5	0.01
Belgian	39	0.05
Brazilian	48	0.06
British	286	0.36
Bulgarian	29	0.04
Canadian	99	0.12
Croatian	10	0.01
Czech	129	0.16
Czechoslovakian	22	0.03
Danish	163	0.21
Dutch	741	0.93
English	4,262	5.36
European	257	0.32
Finnish	53	0.07
French, except Basque	1,427	1.80
French Canadian	490	0.62
German	5,498	6.92
Greek	116	0.15
Hawaii Native/Pacific Islander:	158	0.20
Micronesian: (25)	48	0.06
Guamanian/Chamorro (25)	48	0.06
Polynesian: (38)	76	0.10
Native Hawaiian (11)	39	0.05
Samoan (18)	26	0.03
Other Polynesian (9)	11	0.01
Other Pac. Isl., specified	4	0.01
Other Pac. Isl., not spec. (11)	30	0.04
Hispanic or Latino:	3,163	3.97
Central American:	144	0.18
Costa Rican	7	0.01
Guatemalan	48	0.06
Honduran	22	0.03
Nicaraguan	2	0.00
Panamanian	54	0.07
Salvadoran	9	0.01
Other Central American	2	0.00
Cuban	68	0.09
Dominican Republic	30	0.04
Mexican	1,882	2.36
Puerto Rican	468	0.59
South American:	69	0.09
Argentinean	12	0.02
Bolivian	4	0.01
Chilean	7	0.01
Colombian	24	0.03
Ecuadorian	9	0.01
Peruvian	6	0.01
Venezuelan	4	0.01
Other South American	3	0.00
Other Hispanic or Latino	502	0.63
Hungarian	99	0.12
Icelander	8	0.01
Iranian	10	0.01
Irish	4,283	5.39
Israeli	6	0.01
Italian	1,536	1.93
Latvian	10	0.01
Lithuanian	19	0.02
Northern European	38	0.05
Norwegian	355	0.45
Pennsylvania German	19	0.02
Polish	678	0.85
Portuguese	66	0.08
Romanian	22	0.03
Russian	143	0.18
Scandinavian	26	0.03
Scotch-Irish	1,012	1.27
Scottish	779	0.98
Serbian	15	0.02
Slavic	8	0.01
Slovak	107	0.13
Swedish	170	0.21
Swiss	66	0.08
Ukrainian	45	0.06
United States or American	5,354	6.74
Welsh	246	0.31
West Indian, excl. Hispanic:	283	0.36
Bahamian	20	0.03
Barbadian	7	0.01
Haitian	14	0.02
Jamaican	95	0.12
Trinidadian and Tobagonian	60	0.08
West Indian	87	0.11
White:	36,765	46.16
Not Hispanic (34,443)	35,365	44.41
Hispanic (1,208)	1,400	1.76

North Myrtle Beach

Place Type: City
County: Horry
Population: 10,974

Ancestry/Race	Number	%
African American/Black:	281	2.56
Not Hispanic (246)	271	2.47
Hispanic (7)	10	0.09
Am. Ind. or Alaska Nat., not spec.	31	0.28
American Indian tribes, specified:	75	0.68
Blackfeet (2)	2	0.02
Cherokee (17)	43	0.39
Chippewa (1)	1	0.01
Choctaw	2	0.02
Iroquois	1	0.01
Lumbee (13)	14	0.13
Navajo (1)	1	0.01
Osage (1)	1	0.01
Pueblo	3	0.03
Sioux	2	0.02
All other tribes (1)	5	0.05
American Indian tribes, not spec.	4	0.04
Arab:	19	0.17
Lebanese	6	0.05
Moroccan	7	0.06
Other Arab	6	0.05
Armenian	16	0.15
Asian:	85	0.77
Chinese, ex. Taiwanese (15)	15	0.14
Filipino (13)	16	0.15
Indian (15)	21	0.19
Japanese (4)	4	0.04
Korean (2)	5	0.05
Pakistani (1)	1	0.01
Thai (3)	3	0.03
Vietnamese (9)	9	0.08
Other Asian, not specified (7)	11	0.10
Austrian	37	0.34
Belgian	23	0.21
British	55	0.50
Bulgarian	7	0.06
Canadian	78	0.71
Croatian	10	0.09
Czech	22	0.20
Czechoslovakian	9	0.08
Danish	13	0.12
Dutch	136	1.24
English	1,813	16.47
European	79	0.72
French, except Basque	424	3.85
French Canadian	103	0.94
German	1,840	16.72
Greek	89	0.81
Hawaii Native/Pacific Islander:	17	0.15
Micronesian: (6)	7	0.06
Guamanian/Chamorro (6)	7	0.06
Other Pac. Isl., not spec. (9)	10	0.09
Hispanic or Latino:	259	2.36
Central American:	53	0.48
Costa Rican	6	0.05
Guatemalan	38	0.35
Honduran	5	0.05
Nicaraguan	3	0.03
Salvadoran	1	0.01
Cuban	7	0.06
Dominican Republic	2	0.02
Mexican	100	0.91
Puerto Rican	47	0.43
South American:	11	0.10
Argentinean	1	0.01
Chilean	2	0.02
Ecuadorian	3	0.03
Paraguayan	3	0.03
Other South American	2	0.02
Other Hispanic or Latino	39	0.36
Hungarian	89	0.81
Irish	1,448	13.16
Italian	559	5.08

Notes: 1. Figures in the "Number" column do not add up to the total population due to: a) Ancestry/Race overlap — e.g. persons can report being both White and Irish, b) persons of Hispanic origin can report being any race, c) persons reporting two ancestries are counted in both categories. 2. Numbers in parentheses indicate the number of persons reporting this ancestry/race alone, not in combination with any other ancestry/race. 3. Refer to the Explanation of Data in the front of the book for more detailed information.

Ancestry/Race	Number	%
Latvian	6	0.05
Lithuanian	43	0.39
Macedonian	17	0.15
Norwegian	36	0.33
Polish	218	1.98
Portuguese	14	0.13
Romanian	6	0.05
Russian	104	0.94
Scandinavian	15	0.14
Scotch-Irish	609	5.53
Scottish	350	3.18
Serbian	8	0.07
Slavic	15	0.14
Slovak	5	0.05
Swedish	95	0.86
Swiss	25	0.23
Turkish	10	0.09
Ukrainian	23	0.21
United States or American	1,188	10.79
Welsh	150	1.36
West Indian, excl. Hispanic:	30	0.27
Trinidadian and Tobagonian	30	0.27
White:	10,456	95.28
Not Hispanic (10,249)	10,323	94.07
Hispanic (121)	133	1.21

Orangeburg

Place Type: City
County: Orangeburg
Population: 12,765

Ancestry/Race	Number	%
African American/Black:	8,680	68.00
Not Hispanic (8,577)	8,631	67.61
Hispanic (41)	49	0.38
African, sub-Saharan:	302	2.33
African	236	1.82
Ethiopian	8	0.06
Liberian	12	0.09
Nigerian	19	0.15
Sudanese	27	0.21
Alaska Native tribes, specified:	1	0.01
Tlingit-Haida	1	0.01
Am. Ind. or Alaska Nat., not spec.	34	0.27
American Indian tribes, specified:	21	0.16
Blackfeet	5	0.04
Cherokee (2)	13	0.10
Chippewa	1	0.01
Choctaw	1	0.01
Sioux	1	0.01
American Indian tribes, not spec.	2	0.02
Arab:	22	0.17
Lebanese	5	0.04
Palestinian	17	0.13
Asian:	167	1.31
Chinese, ex. Taiwanese (18)	18	0.14
Filipino (5)	5	0.04
Indian (81)	85	0.67
Indonesian (1)	1	0.01
Japanese (16)	23	0.18
Korean (6)	9	0.07
Laotian (1)	1	0.01
Vietnamese (13)	15	0.12
Other Asian, specified	4	0.03
Other Asian, not specified (3)	6	0.05
Austrian	11	0.08
British	15	0.12
Dutch	74	0.57
English	594	4.58
European	31	0.24
Finnish	6	0.05
French, except Basque	135	1.04
French Canadian	7	0.05
German	597	4.60
Hawaii Native/Pacific Islander:	15	0.12
Micronesian:	2	0.02
Guamanian/Chamorro	2	0.02
Polynesian: (5)	7	0.05
Samoan (5)	7	0.05
Other Pac. Isl., specified	4	0.03
Other Pac. Isl., not spec.	2	0.02
Hispanic or Latino:	165	1.29
Central American:	17	0.13
Costa Rican	2	0.02
Honduran	1	0.01
Panamanian	12	0.09
Salvadoran	1	0.01
Other Central American	1	0.01
Cuban	11	0.09
Mexican	73	0.57
Puerto Rican	21	0.16
South American:	7	0.05
Argentinean	1	0.01
Colombian	2	0.02
Paraguayan	2	0.02
Peruvian	1	0.01
Venezuelan	1	0.01
Other Hispanic or Latino	36	0.28
Hungarian	13	0.10
Irish	327	2.52
Italian	49	0.38
Norwegian	20	0.15
Polish	57	0.44
Portuguese	8	0.06
Russian	43	0.33
Scandinavian	8	0.06
Scotch-Irish	176	1.36
Scottish	105	0.81
Swedish	37	0.29
Swiss	9	0.07
Ukrainian	15	0.12
United States or American	722	5.56
Welsh	7	0.05
West Indian, excl. Hispanic:	136	1.05
Bahamian	6	0.05
Barbadian	32	0.25
Haitian	34	0.26
Jamaican	21	0.16
Trinidadian and Tobagonian	31	0.24
U.S. Virgin Islander	12	0.09
White:	3,835	30.04
Not Hispanic (3,758)	3,789	29.68
Hispanic (43)	46	0.36

Parker

Place Type: Census Designated Place
County: Greenville
Population: 10,760

Ancestry/Race	Number	%
African American/Black:	1,849	17.18
Not Hispanic (1,782)	1,836	17.06
Hispanic (6)	13	0.12
African, sub-Saharan:	58	0.54
African	21	0.20
Nigerian	37	0.35
Alaska Native tribes, specified:	1	0.01
Eskimo	1	0.01
Am. Ind. or Alaska Nat., not spec.	38	0.35
American Indian tribes, specified:	36	0.33
Cherokee (9)	23	0.21
Choctaw	2	0.02
Latin American Indians (2)	2	0.02
Navajo	1	0.01
Potawatomi (2)	2	0.02
Sioux (2)	6	0.06
American Indian tribes, not spec.	4	0.04
Arab:	14	0.13
Arab/Arabic	4	0.04
Lebanese	10	0.09
Asian:	40	0.37
Chinese, ex. Taiwanese (1)	3	0.03
Filipino (1)	3	0.03
Indian (1)	1	0.01
Japanese (1)	1	0.01
Korean (4)	5	0.05
Vietnamese (21)	21	0.20
Other Asian, specified	2	0.02
Other Asian, not specified (3)	4	0.04
British	23	0.22
Canadian	17	0.16
Czechoslovakian	7	0.07
Dutch	100	0.94
English	519	4.87
European	30	0.28
French, except Basque	103	0.97
French Canadian	18	0.17
German	358	3.36
Greek	5	0.05
Hawaii Native/Pacific Islander:	14	0.13
Polynesian: (2)	6	0.06
Native Hawaiian (1)	5	0.05
Samoan (1)	1	0.01
Other Pac. Isl., specified	2	0.02
Other Pac. Isl., not spec. (4)	6	0.06
Hispanic or Latino:	684	6.36
Central American:	65	0.60
Costa Rican	8	0.07
Guatemalan	18	0.17
Honduran	17	0.16
Salvadoran	9	0.08
Other Central American	13	0.12
Cuban	13	0.12
Dominican Republic	1	0.01
Mexican	387	3.60
Puerto Rican	44	0.41
South American:	85	0.79
Colombian	73	0.68
Other South American	12	0.11
Other Hispanic or Latino	89	0.83
Irish	901	8.46
Italian	111	1.04
Polish	4	0.04
Romanian	5	0.05
Scotch-Irish	118	1.11
Scottish	115	1.08
Swedish	11	0.10
United States or American	2,526	23.72
Welsh	34	0.32
West Indian, excl. Hispanic:	8	0.08
Jamaican	8	0.08
White:	8,630	80.20
Not Hispanic (8,108)	8,213	76.33
Hispanic (385)	417	3.88

Red Hill

Place Type: Census Designated Place
County: Horry
Population: 10,509

Ancestry/Race	Number	%
African American/Black:	822	7.82
Not Hispanic (770)	814	7.75
Hispanic (1)	8	0.08
African, sub-Saharan:	17	0.16
African	17	0.16
Am. Ind. or Alaska Nat., not spec.	33	0.31
American Indian tribes, specified:	80	0.76
Apache (2)	5	0.05
Blackfeet	1	0.01
Cherokee (14)	38	0.36
Chippewa (1)	2	0.02
Choctaw (1)	1	0.01
Cree (1)	1	0.01
Iroquois	2	0.02
Latin American Indians (12)	12	0.11
Lumbee (7)	7	0.07
All other tribes (11)	11	0.10
American Indian tribes, not spec.	5	0.05
Arab:	27	0.25
Arab/Arabic	10	0.09
Lebanese	8	0.08
Syrian	9	0.08
Asian:	110	1.05
Chinese, ex. Taiwanese (8)	8	0.08
Filipino (17)	22	0.21
Indian (25)	25	0.24

Notes: 1. Figures in the "Number" column do not add up to the total population due to: a) Ancestry/Race overlap — e.g. persons can report being both White and Irish, b) persons of Hispanic origin can report being any race, c) persons reporting two ancestries are counted in both categories. 2. Numbers in parentheses indicate the number of persons reporting this ancestry/race alone, not in combination with any other ancestry/race. 3. Refer to the Explanation of Data in the front of the book for more detailed information.

Japanese (3)	10	0.10
Korean (7)	7	0.07
Laotian (5)	5	0.05
Malaysian	1	0.01
Thai (11)	12	0.11
Vietnamese (2)	3	0.03
Other Asian, specified	6	0.06
Other Asian, not specified (4)	11	0.10
Austrian	18	0.17
British	31	0.29
Croatian	8	0.08
Czech	35	0.33
Czechoslovakian	10	0.09
Danish	8	0.08
Dutch	216	2.03
English	1,364	12.84
European	82	0.77
Finnish	9	0.08
French, except Basque	219	2.06
French Canadian	42	0.40
German	1,393	13.11
Greek	38	0.36
Hawaii Native/Pacific Islander:	17	0.16
Micronesian: (2)	2	0.02
Guamanian/Chamorro (2)	2	0.02
Polynesian: (6)	6	0.06
Native Hawaiian (6)	6	0.06
Other Pac. Isl., specified	4	0.04
Other Pac. Isl., not spec.	5	0.05
Hispanic or Latino:	327	3.11
Central American:	18	0.17
Costa Rican	1	0.01
Guatemalan	6	0.06
Honduran	11	0.10
Cuban	3	0.03
Mexican	196	1.87
Puerto Rican	47	0.45
South American:	13	0.12
Argentinean	1	0.01
Bolivian	1	0.01
Chilean	1	0.01
Colombian	8	0.08
Other South American	2	0.02
Other Hispanic or Latino	50	0.48
Hungarian	42	0.40
Irish	1,480	13.93
Italian	454	4.27
Lithuanian	14	0.13
Norwegian	60	0.56
Pennsylvania German	9	0.08
Polish	252	2.37
Portuguese	36	0.34
Russian	50	0.47
Scotch-Irish	306	2.88
Scottish	286	2.69
Slovak	71	0.67
Swedish	156	1.47
Swiss	31	0.29
Ukrainian	38	0.36
United States or American	1,654	15.57
Welsh	21	0.20
West Indian, excl. Hispanic:	32	0.30
Jamaican	32	0.30
White:	9,440	89.83
Not Hispanic (9,151)	9,257	88.09
Hispanic (170)	183	1.74

Rock Hill

Place Type: City
County: York
Population: 49,765

Ancestry/Race	Number	%
African American/Black:	18,768	37.71
Not Hispanic (18,484)	18,648	37.47
Hispanic (94)	120	0.24
African, sub-Saharan:	540	1.08
African	512	1.02
Ethiopian	28	0.06
Alaska Native tribes, specified:	1	0.00
Eskimo (1)	1	0.00
Am. Ind. or Alaska Nat., not spec.	111	0.22
American Indian tribes, specified:	289	0.58
Apache (1)	3	0.01
Blackfeet	5	0.01
Cherokee (33)	84	0.17
Chippewa (1)	3	0.01
Choctaw (1)	3	0.01
Creek (2)	7	0.01
Delaware	2	0.00
Iroquois	2	0.00
Latin American Indians (1)	2	0.00
Lumbee (3)	4	0.01
Navajo (1)	2	0.00
Pima (2)	3	0.01
Pueblo	1	0.00
Seminole (1)	6	0.01
Sioux (1)	3	0.01
All other tribes (123)	159	0.32
American Indian tribes, not spec.	15	0.03
Arab:	89	0.18
Egyptian	21	0.04
Lebanese	68	0.14
Asian:	823	1.65
Bangladeshi (5)	5	0.01
Cambodian (25)	39	0.08
Chinese, ex. Taiwanese (74)	99	0.20
Filipino (47)	63	0.13
Hmong (1)	1	0.00
Indian (161)	183	0.37
Indonesian (2)	2	0.00
Japanese (9)	21	0.04
Korean (30)	45	0.09
Laotian (2)	4	0.01
Malaysian	2	0.00
Pakistani (2)	3	0.01
Sri Lankan (4)	4	0.01
Taiwanese (1)	1	0.00
Thai (6)	7	0.01
Vietnamese (283)	303	0.61
Other Asian, specified	3	0.01
Other Asian, not specified (19)	38	0.08
Austrian	18	0.04
Belgian	10	0.02
Brazilian	6	0.01
British	194	0.39
Canadian	112	0.22
Croatian	33	0.07
Czech	50	0.10
Czechoslovakian	27	0.05
Danish	27	0.05
Dutch	494	0.98
Eastern European	6	0.01
English	3,679	7.33
European	201	0.40
Finnish	11	0.02
French, except Basque	862	1.72
French Canadian	197	0.39
German	3,276	6.52
Greek	50	0.10
Hawaii Native/Pacific Islander:	48	0.10
Micronesian: (1)	3	0.01
Guamanian/Chamorro (1)	3	0.01
Polynesian: (4)	23	0.05
Native Hawaiian (4)	16	0.03
Samoan	7	0.01
Other Pac. Isl., specified	3	0.01
Other Pac. Isl., not spec. (8)	19	0.04
Hispanic or Latino:	1,236	2.48
Central American:	71	0.14
Costa Rican	11	0.02
Guatemalan	2	0.00
Honduran	26	0.05
Nicaraguan	11	0.02
Panamanian	8	0.02
Salvadoran	12	0.02
Other Central American	1	0.00
Cuban	35	0.07
Dominican Republic	11	0.02
Mexican	669	1.34
Puerto Rican	117	0.24
South American:	126	0.25
Argentinean	3	0.01
Bolivian	1	0.00
Chilean	4	0.01
Colombian	83	0.17
Ecuadorian	8	0.02
Peruvian	7	0.01
Uruguayan	18	0.04
Venezuelan	1	0.00
Other South American	1	0.00
Other Hispanic or Latino	207	0.42
Hungarian	152	0.30
Iranian	33	0.07
Irish	3,533	7.04
Italian	1,237	2.46
Lithuanian	24	0.05
Maltese	5	0.01
Northern European	11	0.02
Norwegian	211	0.42
Pennsylvania German	49	0.10
Polish	518	1.03
Portuguese	7	0.01
Romanian	11	0.02
Russian	54	0.11
Scandinavian	61	0.12
Scotch-Irish	2,385	4.75
Scottish	1,007	2.01
Serbian	14	0.03
Slovak	84	0.17
Slovene	7	0.01
Swedish	130	0.26
Swiss	55	0.11
Turkish	10	0.02
Ukrainian	86	0.17
United States or American	4,292	8.55
Welsh	187	0.37
West Indian, excl. Hispanic:	100	0.20
British West Indian	9	0.02
Haitian	21	0.04
Jamaican	41	0.08
West Indian	29	0.06
White:	29,629	59.54
Not Hispanic (28,648)	29,000	58.27
Hispanic (582)	629	1.26
Yugoslavian	39	0.08

Saint Andrews

Place Type: Census Designated Place
County: Richland
Population: 21,814

Ancestry/Race	Number	%
African American/Black:	11,642	53.37
Not Hispanic (11,427)	11,557	52.98
Hispanic (66)	85	0.39
African, sub-Saharan:	461	2.12
African	455	2.09
Nigerian	6	0.03
Am. Ind. or Alaska Nat., not spec.	52	0.24
American Indian tribes, specified:	84	0.39
Apache	3	0.01
Blackfeet	2	0.01
Cherokee (20)	46	0.21
Chickasaw	1	0.00
Choctaw	2	0.01
Comanche (1)	1	0.00
Cree (1)	1	0.00
Creek (1)	2	0.01
Iroquois	1	0.00
Latin American Indians	5	0.02
Lumbee (6)	6	0.03
Navajo (2)	2	0.01
Seminole (1)	1	0.00
Sioux	1	0.00
All other tribes (4)	10	0.05
American Indian tribes, not spec.	2	0.01
Arab:	43	0.20

Notes: 1. Figures in the "Number" column do not add up to the total population due to: a) Ancestry/Race overlap — e.g. persons can report being both White and Irish, b) persons of Hispanic origin can report being any race, c) persons reporting two ancestries are counted in both categories. 2. Numbers in parentheses indicate the number of persons reporting this ancestry/race alone, not in combination with any other ancestry/race. 3. Refer to the Explanation of Data in the front of the book for more detailed information.

Arab/Arabic	26	0.12
Lebanese	6	0.03
Other Arab	11	0.05
Armenian	10	0.05
Asian:	480	2.20
Cambodian (2)	2	0.01
Chinese, ex. Taiwanese (65)	71	0.33
Filipino (32)	51	0.23
Indian (115)	124	0.57
Indonesian	4	0.02
Japanese (31)	43	0.20
Korean (61)	73	0.33
Laotian (4)	5	0.02
Malaysian (1)	1	0.00
Pakistani (4)	4	0.02
Sri Lankan (4)	4	0.02
Thai (6)	10	0.05
Vietnamese (62)	64	0.29
Other Asian, not specified (9)	24	0.11
Austrian	31	0.14
Belgian	6	0.03
British	72	0.33
Bulgarian	21	0.10
Canadian	37	0.17
Croatian	7	0.03
Danish	8	0.04
Dutch	120	0.55
Eastern European	9	0.04
English	1,236	5.68
European	142	0.65
French, except Basque	292	1.34
French Canadian	88	0.40
German	1,475	6.78
Greek	28	0.13
Hawaii Native/Pacific Islander:	29	0.13
Micronesian: (6)	9	0.04
Guamanian/Chamorro (1)	3	0.01
Other Micronesian (5)	6	0.03
Polynesian: (4)	7	0.03
Native Hawaiian (2)	3	0.01
Samoan (2)	4	0.02
Other Pac. Isl., not spec. (5)	13	0.06
Hispanic or Latino:	431	1.98
Central American:	22	0.10
Guatemalan	3	0.01
Honduran	5	0.02
Panamanian	9	0.04
Salvadoran	3	0.01
Other Central American	2	0.01
Cuban	21	0.10
Dominican Republic	6	0.03
Mexican	155	0.71
Puerto Rican	127	0.58
South American:	25	0.11
Colombian	9	0.04
Ecuadorian	2	0.01
Paraguayan	2	0.01
Peruvian	5	0.02
Venezuelan	7	0.03
Other Hispanic or Latino	75	0.34
Hungarian	26	0.12
Irish	1,214	5.58
Italian	362	1.66
Lithuanian	17	0.08
Northern European	17	0.08
Norwegian	57	0.26
Pennsylvania German	11	0.05
Polish	198	0.91
Portuguese	9	0.04
Russian	60	0.28
Scandinavian	7	0.03
Scotch-Irish	473	2.17
Scottish	209	0.96
Slavic	8	0.04
Slovak	27	0.12
Soviet Union	7	0.03
Swedish	26	0.12
Swiss	42	0.19
Turkish	17	0.08
Ukrainian	11	0.05
United States or American	1,136	5.22
Welsh	142	0.65
West Indian, excl. Hispanic:	53	0.24
Haitian	11	0.05
Jamaican	34	0.16
West Indian	8	0.04
White:	9,576	43.90
Not Hispanic (9,213)	9,379	43.00
Hispanic (179)	197	0.90

Seven Oaks

Place Type: Census Designated Place
County: Lexington
Population: 15,755

Ancestry/Race	Number	%
African American/Black:	3,461	21.97
Not Hispanic (3,374)	3,436	21.81
Hispanic (14)	25	0.16
African, sub-Saharan:	268	1.69
African	261	1.65
Nigerian	7	0.04
Alaska Native tribes, specified:	1	0.01
Eskimo	1	0.01
Am. Ind. or Alaska Nat., not spec.	22	0.14
American Indian tribes, specified:	62	0.39
Cherokee (16)	30	0.19
Cheyenne	1	0.01
Chickasaw	2	0.01
Choctaw (2)	2	0.01
Creek	1	0.01
Delaware	1	0.01
Latin American Indians (6)	10	0.06
Lumbee (1)	2	0.01
Pueblo (4)	4	0.03
Sioux (2)	2	0.01
All other tribes (1)	7	0.04
American Indian tribes, not spec.	7	0.04
Arab:	26	0.16
Lebanese	26	0.16
Asian:	504	3.20
Bangladeshi (5)	5	0.03
Chinese, ex. Taiwanese (89)	91	0.58
Filipino (30)	37	0.23
Indian (162)	170	1.08
Japanese (14)	26	0.17
Korean (77)	85	0.54
Laotian (6)	6	0.04
Pakistani (7)	7	0.04
Thai (4)	5	0.03
Vietnamese (39)	44	0.28
Other Asian, not specified (9)	28	0.18
Australian	15	0.09
Austrian	15	0.09
Belgian	26	0.16
British	86	0.54
Bulgarian	30	0.19
Canadian	91	0.57
Czech	7	0.04
Czechoslovakian	22	0.14
Danish	20	0.13
Dutch	228	1.44
English	1,977	12.48
European	290	1.83
Finnish	17	0.11
French, except Basque	381	2.40
French Canadian	72	0.45
German	1,746	11.02
Greek	64	0.40
Hawaii Native/Pacific Islander:	17	0.11
Micronesian: (4)	8	0.05
Guamanian/Chamorro (3)	7	0.04
Other Micronesian (1)	1	0.01
Polynesian: (3)	4	0.03
Native Hawaiian (3)	4	0.03
Other Pac. Isl., not spec. (2)	5	0.03
Hispanic or Latino:	298	1.89
Central American:	22	0.14
Costa Rican	2	0.01
Guatemalan	2	0.01
Honduran	1	0.01
Panamanian	15	0.10
Salvadoran	1	0.01
Other Central American	1	0.01
Cuban	23	0.15
Dominican Republic	2	0.01
Mexican	94	0.60
Puerto Rican	72	0.46
South American:	25	0.16
Argentinean	1	0.01
Chilean	4	0.03
Colombian	6	0.04
Ecuadorian	2	0.01
Paraguayan	1	0.01
Peruvian	10	0.06
Venezuelan	1	0.01
Other Hispanic or Latino	60	0.38
Hungarian	71	0.45
Iranian	12	0.08
Irish	1,305	8.24
Italian	498	3.14
Latvian	6	0.04
Lithuanian	9	0.06
Norwegian	101	0.64
Pennsylvania German	8	0.05
Polish	263	1.66
Portuguese	4	0.03
Romanian	6	0.04
Russian	66	0.42
Scandinavian	33	0.21
Scotch-Irish	710	4.48
Scottish	391	2.47
Slavic	7	0.04
Slovak	13	0.08
Slovene	9	0.06
Swedish	83	0.52
Swiss	8	0.05
Ukrainian	61	0.39
United States or American	1,705	10.76
Welsh	122	0.77
West Indian, excl. Hispanic:	125	0.79
Bahamian	87	0.55
Jamaican	28	0.18
West Indian	10	0.06
White:	11,728	74.44
Not Hispanic (11,412)	11,545	73.28
Hispanic (170)	183	1.16
Yugoslavian	47	0.30

Simpsonville

Place Type: City
County: Greenville
Population: 14,352

Ancestry/Race	Number	%
Acadian/Cajun	11	0.08
African American/Black:	2,032	14.16
Not Hispanic (1,964)	2,019	14.07
Hispanic (11)	13	0.09
African, sub-Saharan:	168	1.17
African	144	1.00
South African	24	0.17
Am. Ind. or Alaska Nat., not spec.	25	0.17
American Indian tribes, specified:	44	0.31
Blackfeet	3	0.02
Cherokee (12)	30	0.21
Cheyenne	1	0.01
Iroquois (1)	1	0.01
Latin American Indians (4)	4	0.03
Lumbee (1)	1	0.01
Navajo (1)	1	0.01
All other tribes (2)	3	0.02
Arab:	124	0.86
Arab/Arabic	19	0.13
Egyptian	30	0.21
Jordanian	26	0.18
Lebanese	22	0.15
Other Arab	27	0.19

Notes: 1. Figures in the "Number" column do not add up to the total population due to: a) Ancestry/Race overlap — e.g. persons can report being both White and Irish, b) persons of Hispanic origin can report being any race, c) persons reporting two ancestries are counted in both categories. 2. Numbers in parentheses indicate the number of persons reporting this ancestry/race alone, not in combination with any other ancestry/race. 3. Refer to the Explanation of Data in the front of the book for more detailed information.

Ancestry/Race	Number	%
Armenian	8	0.06
Asian:	142	0.99
Cambodian (7)	7	0.05
Chinese, ex. Taiwanese (25)	27	0.19
Filipino (25)	29	0.20
Indian (21)	25	0.17
Japanese (9)	16	0.11
Korean (5)	8	0.06
Pakistani (2)	2	0.01
Sri Lankan (1)	2	0.01
Taiwanese	1	0.01
Thai (3)	3	0.02
Vietnamese (9)	10	0.07
Other Asian, specified	1	0.01
Other Asian, not specified (5)	11	0.08
Australian	6	0.04
Austrian	9	0.06
Belgian	7	0.05
British	142	0.99
Canadian	61	0.42
Czechoslovakian	37	0.26
Dutch	221	1.54
Eastern European	13	0.09
English	1,301	9.06
European	46	0.32
Finnish	16	0.11
French, except Basque	310	2.16
French Canadian	116	0.81
German	1,602	11.15
Greek	18	0.13
Hawaii Native/Pacific Islander:	14	0.10
Micronesian: (2)	2	0.01
Guamanian/Chamorro (2)	2	0.01
Polynesian: (2)	4	0.03
Samoan	2	0.01
Tongan (2)	2	0.01
Other Pac. Isl., specified	1	0.01
Other Pac. Isl., not spec. (2)	7	0.05
Hispanic or Latino:	667	4.65
Central American:	24	0.17
Costa Rican	5	0.03
Honduran	8	0.06
Panamanian	3	0.02
Salvadoran	8	0.06
Cuban	2	0.01
Dominican Republic	1	0.01
Mexican	325	2.26
Puerto Rican	62	0.43
South American:	145	1.01
Colombian	134	0.93
Ecuadorian	1	0.01
Peruvian	1	0.01
Venezuelan	3	0.02
Other South American	6	0.04
Other Hispanic or Latino	108	0.75
Hungarian	55	0.38
Irish	1,788	12.45
Italian	602	4.19
Lithuanian	32	0.22
Norwegian	43	0.30
Polish	149	1.04
Portuguese	12	0.08
Russian	16	0.11
Scandinavian	7	0.05
Scotch-Irish	594	4.13
Scottish	224	1.56
Slovak	37	0.26
Slovene	33	0.23
Swedish	92	0.64
Swiss	22	0.15
Ukrainian	32	0.22
United States or American	2,107	14.67
Welsh	48	0.33
West Indian, excl. Hispanic:	11	0.08
Barbadian	11	0.08
White:	12,037	83.87
Not Hispanic (11,418)	11,550	80.48
Hispanic (449)	487	3.39
Yugoslavian	22	0.15

Socastee

Place Type: Census Designated Place
County: Horry
Population: 14,295

Ancestry/Race	Number	%
African American/Black:	1,089	7.62
Not Hispanic (958)	1,038	7.26
Hispanic (44)	51	0.36
African, sub-Saharan:	51	0.36
African	51	0.36
Am. Ind. or Alaska Nat., not spec.	34	0.24
Alsatian	8	0.06
American Indian tribes, specified:	61	0.43
Apache (1)	1	0.01
Blackfeet	2	0.01
Cherokee (11)	27	0.19
Cheyenne	1	0.01
Choctaw	3	0.02
Comanche	1	0.01
Iroquois (3)	4	0.03
Latin American Indians (1)	2	0.01
Lumbee (6)	7	0.05
Navajo (1)	1	0.01
Sioux (1)	2	0.01
All other tribes (6)	10	0.07
American Indian tribes, not spec.	7	0.05
Arab:	4	0.03
Lebanese	4	0.03
Asian:	380	2.66
Cambodian (4)	4	0.03
Chinese, ex. Taiwanese (27)	38	0.27
Filipino (36)	63	0.44
Indian (18)	19	0.13
Indonesian (1)	1	0.01
Japanese (15)	22	0.15
Korean (23)	28	0.20
Laotian (1)	1	0.01
Taiwanese (5)	5	0.03
Thai (28)	40	0.28
Vietnamese (132)	135	0.94
Other Asian, specified	6	0.04
Other Asian, not specified (8)	18	0.13
Australian	2	0.01
Austrian	11	0.08
British	57	0.40
Canadian	9	0.06
Carpatho Rusyn	6	0.04
Croatian	16	0.11
Czech	53	0.37
Czechoslovakian	50	0.35
Danish	6	0.04
Dutch	217	1.53
English	1,462	10.27
Estonian	10	0.07
European	110	0.77
Finnish	28	0.20
French, except Basque	336	2.36
French Canadian	77	0.54
German	1,824	12.82
Greek	51	0.36
Hawaii Native/Pacific Islander:	37	0.26
Micronesian: (9)	13	0.09
Guamanian/Chamorro (8)	12	0.08
Other Micronesian (1)	1	0.01
Polynesian: (7)	8	0.06
Native Hawaiian (3)	4	0.03
Samoan (4)	4	0.03
Other Pac. Isl., specified	5	0.03
Other Pac. Isl., not spec. (2)	11	0.08
Hispanic or Latino:	666	4.66
Central American:	22	0.15
Guatemalan	8	0.06
Honduran	1	0.01
Nicaraguan	7	0.05
Panamanian	2	0.01
Salvadoran	4	0.03
Cuban	8	0.06
Dominican Republic	5	0.03
Mexican	440	3.08
Puerto Rican	94	0.66
South American:	27	0.19
Argentinean	2	0.01
Bolivian	2	0.01
Chilean	1	0.01
Colombian	16	0.11
Ecuadorian	1	0.01
Peruvian	4	0.03
Venezuelan	1	0.01
Other Hispanic or Latino	70	0.49
Hungarian	67	0.47
Iranian	7	0.05
Irish	1,978	13.90
Israeli	7	0.05
Italian	833	5.85
Lithuanian	83	0.58
Northern European	6	0.04
Norwegian	67	0.47
Pennsylvania German	21	0.15
Polish	380	2.67
Portuguese	14	0.10
Russian	53	0.37
Scandinavian	9	0.06
Scotch-Irish	515	3.62
Scottish	356	2.50
Slavic	5	0.04
Slovak	15	0.11
Swedish	67	0.47
Swiss	71	0.50
Ukrainian	31	0.22
United States or American	2,076	14.59
Welsh	83	0.58
West Indian, excl. Hispanic:	34	0.24
Haitian	25	0.18
Trinidadian and Tobagonian	9	0.06
White:	12,602	88.16
Not Hispanic (12,096)	12,264	85.79
Hispanic (314)	338	2.36

Spartanburg

Place Type: City
County: Spartanburg
Population: 39,673

Ancestry/Race	Number	%
African American/Black:	19,863	50.07
Not Hispanic (19,559)	19,748	49.78
Hispanic (99)	115	0.29
African, sub-Saharan:	350	0.89
African	305	0.77
Liberian	10	0.03
Nigerian	4	0.01
Other sub-Saharan African	31	0.08
Alaska Native tribes, specified:	2	0.01
Eskimo	1	0.00
Tlingit-Haida (1)	1	0.00
Am. Ind. or Alaska Nat., not spec.	86	0.22
American Indian tribes, specified:	83	0.21
Apache (5)	5	0.01
Blackfeet	1	0.00
Cherokee (14)	45	0.11
Chippewa (1)	1	0.00
Choctaw (6)	6	0.02
Creek (5)	5	0.01
Delaware	1	0.00
Iroquois	1	0.00
Latin American Indians	3	0.01
Lumbee (5)	5	0.01
Seminole (1)	1	0.00
Sioux	4	0.01
All other tribes (2)	5	0.01
American Indian tribes, not spec.	7	0.02
Arab:	73	0.19
Arab/Arabic	16	0.04
Egyptian	18	0.05
Lebanese	35	0.09
Palestinian	4	0.01
Asian:	633	1.60

Notes: 1. Figures in the "Number" column do not add up to the total population due to: a) Ancestry/Race overlap — e.g. persons can report being both White and Irish, b) persons of Hispanic origin can report being any race, c) persons reporting two ancestries are counted in both categories. 2. Numbers in parentheses indicate the number of persons reporting this ancestry/race alone, not in combination with any other ancestry/race. 3. Refer to the Explanation of Data in the front of the book for more detailed information.

Cambodian (11)	21	0.05
Chinese, ex. Taiwanese (73)	82	0.21
Filipino (47)	58	0.15
Hmong (31)	38	0.10
Indian (165)	183	0.46
Indonesian	5	0.01
Japanese (20)	37	0.09
Korean (8)	11	0.03
Laotian (65)	69	0.17
Malaysian	1	0.00
Pakistani (13)	16	0.04
Thai (10)	11	0.03
Vietnamese (36)	42	0.11
Other Asian, specified	4	0.01
Other Asian, not specified (42)	55	0.14
Austrian	61	0.15
Brazilian	4	0.01
British	156	0.40
Canadian	94	0.24
Croatian	13	0.03
Cypriot	17	0.04
Czech	30	0.08
Czechoslovakian	37	0.09
Danish	63	0.16
Dutch	179	0.45
Eastern European	4	0.01
English	2,916	7.40
Estonian	11	0.03
European	240	0.61
French, except Basque	387	0.98
French Canadian	158	0.40
German	1,892	4.80
Greek	58	0.15
Hawaii Native/Pacific Islander:	49	0.12
Micronesian: (5)	10	0.03
Guamanian/Chamorro (5)	10	0.03
Polynesian: (12)	20	0.05
Native Hawaiian (8)	14	0.04
Samoan (4)	6	0.02
Other Pac. Isl., specified	4	0.01
Other Pac. Isl., not spec. (5)	15	0.04
Hispanic or Latino:	706	1.78
Central American:	45	0.11
Costa Rican	1	0.00
Guatemalan	10	0.03
Honduran	5	0.01
Nicaraguan	2	0.01
Panamanian	16	0.04
Salvadoran	7	0.02
Other Central American	4	0.01
Cuban	29	0.07
Dominican Republic	2	0.01
Mexican	356	0.90
Puerto Rican	125	0.32
South American:	53	0.13
Argentinean	9	0.02
Bolivian	1	0.00
Chilean	2	0.01
Colombian	22	0.06
Peruvian	9	0.02
Venezuelan	9	0.02
Other South American	1	0.00
Other Hispanic or Latino	96	0.24
Hungarian	71	0.18
Icelander	19	0.05
Irish	2,008	5.10
Italian	616	1.56
Lithuanian	19	0.05
Luxemburger	6	0.02
Northern European	23	0.06
Norwegian	111	0.28
Pennsylvania German	8	0.02
Polish	230	0.58
Portuguese	41	0.10
Romanian	9	0.02
Russian	106	0.27
Scandinavian	20	0.05
Scotch-Irish	1,418	3.60
Scottish	717	1.82
Slovak	18	0.05
Swedish	86	0.22
Swiss	67	0.17
Ukrainian	27	0.07
United States or American	3,393	8.61
Welsh	214	0.54
West Indian, excl. Hispanic:	50	0.13
Bahamian	14	0.04
Jamaican	10	0.03
Trinidadian and Tobagonian	10	0.03
West Indian	16	0.04
White:	18,974	47.83
Not Hispanic (18,433)	18,665	47.05
Hispanic (274)	309	0.78
Yugoslavian	8	0.02

Summerville

Place Type: Town
County: Dorchester
Population: 27,752

Ancestry/Race	Number	%
African American/Black:	5,529	19.92
Not Hispanic (5,355)	5,479	19.74
Hispanic (24)	50	0.18
African, sub-Saharan:	103	0.36
African	103	0.36
Alaska Native tribes, not specified	1	0.00
Am. Ind. or Alaska Nat., not spec.	89	0.32
Albanian	8	0.03
American Indian tribes, specified:	152	0.55
Apache (1)	2	0.01
Blackfeet (1)	1	0.00
Cherokee (33)	87	0.31
Chippewa (2)	2	0.01
Choctaw (3)	4	0.01
Comanche	3	0.01
Creek (1)	2	0.01
Iroquois (1)	1	0.00
Latin American Indians	2	0.01
Lumbee (3)	3	0.01
Navajo (1)	1	0.00
Ottawa (1)	1	0.00
Seminole (1)	3	0.01
Sioux (3)	4	0.01
All other tribes (25)	36	0.13
American Indian tribes, not spec.	17	0.06
Arab:	54	0.19
Egyptian	10	0.04
Lebanese	10	0.04
Palestinian	11	0.04
Syrian	23	0.08
Armenian	9	0.03
Asian:	359	1.29
Chinese, ex. Taiwanese (50)	60	0.22
Filipino (77)	129	0.46
Indian (24)	34	0.12
Indonesian	2	0.01
Japanese (20)	30	0.11
Korean (25)	33	0.12
Taiwanese (4)	5	0.02
Thai (4)	7	0.03
Vietnamese (30)	33	0.12
Other Asian, not specified (8)	26	0.09
Australian	8	0.03
Austrian	38	0.13
Brazilian	19	0.07
British	218	0.77
Canadian	90	0.32
Celtic	23	0.08
Croatian	34	0.12
Czech	61	0.22
Danish	12	0.04
Dutch	535	1.89
English	3,545	12.54
European	307	1.09
Finnish	68	0.24
French, except Basque	851	3.01
French Canadian	207	0.73
German	3,852	13.63
Greek	190	0.67
Guyanese	6	0.02
Hawaii Native/Pacific Islander:	41	0.15
Micronesian: (12)	20	0.07
Guamanian/Chamorro (4)	7	0.03
Other Micronesian (8)	13	0.05
Polynesian: (2)	8	0.03
Native Hawaiian (2)	7	0.03
Samoan	1	0.00
Other Pac. Isl., not spec. (2)	13	0.05
Hispanic or Latino:	547	1.97
Central American:	34	0.12
Costa Rican	1	0.00
Guatemalan	10	0.04
Honduran	11	0.04
Panamanian	11	0.04
Other Central American	1	0.00
Cuban	29	0.10
Dominican Republic	1	0.00
Mexican	214	0.77
Puerto Rican	122	0.44
South American:	24	0.09
Argentinean	5	0.02
Colombian	7	0.03
Ecuadorian	10	0.04
Peruvian	1	0.00
Venezuelan	1	0.00
Other Hispanic or Latino	123	0.44
Hungarian	179	0.63
Irish	2,975	10.52
Italian	1,071	3.79
Lithuanian	21	0.07
Norwegian	233	0.82
Pennsylvania German	7	0.02
Polish	538	1.90
Portuguese	78	0.28
Romanian	13	0.05
Russian	143	0.51
Scandinavian	21	0.07
Scotch-Irish	909	3.22
Scottish	905	3.20
Serbian	17	0.06
Slavic	9	0.03
Slovak	37	0.13
Slovene	7	0.02
Swedish	212	0.75
Swiss	89	0.31
Ukrainian	15	0.05
United States or American	3,101	10.97
Welsh	280	0.99
West Indian, excl. Hispanic:	19	0.07
Belizean	8	0.03
Haitian	11	0.04
White:	21,703	78.20
Not Hispanic (21,131)	21,376	77.03
Hispanic (290)	327	1.18
Yugoslavian	25	0.09

Sumter

Place Type: City
County: Sumter
Population: 39,643

Ancestry/Race	Number	%
African American/Black:	18,600	46.92
Not Hispanic (18,256)	18,459	46.56
Hispanic (101)	141	0.36
African, sub-Saharan:	643	1.60
African	598	1.49
Cape Verdean	16	0.04
Nigerian	8	0.02
South African	10	0.02
Other sub-Saharan African	11	0.03
Alaska Native tribes, specified:	1	0.00
Tlingit-Haida (1)	1	0.00
Am. Ind. or Alaska Nat., not spec.	74	0.19
Albanian	5	0.01
American Indian tribes, specified:	152	0.38
Apache (4)	10	0.03

Notes: 1. Figures in the "Number" column do not add up to the total population due to: a) Ancestry/Race overlap — e.g. persons can report being both White and Irish, b) persons of Hispanic origin can report being any race, c) persons reporting two ancestries are counted in both categories. 2. Numbers in parentheses indicate the number of persons reporting this ancestry/race alone, not in combination with any other ancestry/race. 3. Refer to the Explanation of Data in the front of the book for more detailed information.

Blackfeet	2	0.01
Cherokee (17)	64	0.16
Chippewa (4)	4	0.01
Choctaw (2)	6	0.02
Comanche	2	0.01
Delaware	1	0.00
Iroquois (2)	17	0.04
Latin American Indians (8)	10	0.03
Lumbee (16)	17	0.04
Navajo (3)	8	0.02
Seminole	1	0.00
Sioux (1)	4	0.01
All other tribes (2)	6	0.02
American Indian tribes, not spec.	16	0.04
Arab:	75	0.19
Arab/Arabic	10	0.02
Egyptian	8	0.02
Lebanese	39	0.10
Syrian	8	0.02
Other Arab	10	0.02
Asian:	730	1.84
Cambodian (10)	10	0.03
Chinese, ex. Taiwanese (68)	86	0.22
Filipino (124)	205	0.52
Indian (107)	112	0.28
Japanese (36)	76	0.19
Korean (67)	92	0.23
Laotian (5)	5	0.01
Malaysian (1)	2	0.01
Pakistani (20)	20	0.05
Taiwanese (2)	4	0.01
Thai (19)	35	0.09
Vietnamese (30)	36	0.09
Other Asian, specified	6	0.02
Other Asian, not specified (9)	41	0.10
Australian	8	0.02
Austrian	31	0.08
Basque	6	0.01
Belgian	5	0.01
Brazilian	21	0.05
British	182	0.45
Canadian	7	0.02
Croatian	12	0.03
Czech	31	0.08
Czechoslovakian	26	0.06
Danish	89	0.22
Dutch	352	0.88
English	3,269	8.13
European	146	0.36
Finnish	49	0.12
French, except Basque	775	1.93
French Canadian	228	0.57
German	2,833	7.04
Greek	45	0.11
Hawaii Native/Pacific Islander:	83	0.21
Micronesian: (9)	21	0.05
Guamanian/Chamorro (9)	21	0.05
Polynesian: (17)	41	0.10
Native Hawaiian (5)	25	0.06
Samoan (12)	16	0.04
Other Pac. Isl., specified	6	0.02
Other Pac. Isl., not spec. (1)	15	0.04
Hispanic or Latino:	938	2.37
Central American:	53	0.13
Costa Rican	1	0.00
Guatemalan	21	0.05
Honduran	1	0.00
Panamanian	20	0.05
Salvadoran	7	0.02
Other Central American	3	0.01
Cuban	43	0.11
Dominican Republic	8	0.02
Mexican	363	0.92
Puerto Rican	216	0.54
South American:	16	0.04
Bolivian	4	0.01
Colombian	5	0.01
Peruvian	3	0.01
Venezuelan	2	0.01
Other South American	2	0.01
Other Hispanic or Latino	239	0.60
Hungarian	114	0.28
Iranian	8	0.02
Irish	2,530	6.29
Italian	615	1.53
Lithuanian	19	0.05
Maltese	6	0.01
Norwegian	77	0.19
Pennsylvania German	9	0.02
Polish	392	0.97
Portuguese	48	0.12
Romanian	7	0.02
Russian	26	0.06
Scandinavian	51	0.13
Scotch-Irish	936	2.33
Scottish	790	1.96
Slovak	22	0.05
Slovene	10	0.02
Swedish	123	0.31
Swiss	89	0.22
Turkish	36	0.09
Ukrainian	19	0.05
United States or American	3,953	9.83
Welsh	199	0.49
West Indian, excl. Hispanic:	170	0.42
Bahamian	9	0.02
Barbadian	32	0.08
British West Indian	16	0.04
Haitian	7	0.02
Jamaican	62	0.15
West Indian	44	0.11
White:	20,023	50.51
Not Hispanic (19,300)	19,605	49.45
Hispanic (355)	418	1.05
Yugoslavian	12	0.03

Taylors

Place Type: Census Designated Place
County: Greenville
Population: 20,125

Ancestry/Race	Number	%
Acadian/Cajun	12	0.06
African American/Black:	2,950	14.66
Not Hispanic (2,830)	2,921	14.51
Hispanic (26)	29	0.14
African, sub-Saharan:	72	0.36
African	72	0.36
Am. Ind. or Alaska Nat., not spec.	24	0.12
Albanian	45	0.23
American Indian tribes, specified:	80	0.40
Apache (1)	1	0.00
Cherokee (6)	39	0.19
Cheyenne (2)	2	0.01
Chickasaw	5	0.02
Chippewa	1	0.00
Creek (1)	2	0.01
Iroquois	1	0.00
Latin American Indians (13)	14	0.07
Lumbee (2)	3	0.01
Navajo (1)	1	0.00
Potawatomi (4)	4	0.02
Seminole (1)	2	0.01
All other tribes (4)	5	0.02
American Indian tribes, not spec.	8	0.04
Arab:	73	0.37
Arab/Arabic	8	0.04
Lebanese	59	0.30
Syrian	6	0.03
Asian:	374	1.86
Cambodian (2)	2	0.01
Chinese, ex. Taiwanese (29)	40	0.20
Filipino (19)	29	0.14
Indian (46)	59	0.29
Japanese (1)	2	0.01
Korean (24)	24	0.12
Malaysian	1	0.00
Pakistani (2)	6	0.03
Taiwanese	1	0.00
Thai	4	0.02
Vietnamese (175)	182	0.90
Other Asian, not specified (5)	24	0.12
Belgian	20	0.10
British	138	0.70
Canadian	13	0.07
Celtic	36	0.18
Croatian	56	0.28
Czech	40	0.20
Czechoslovakian	13	0.07
Danish	17	0.09
Dutch	295	1.49
English	2,725	13.73
Estonian	7	0.04
European	320	1.61
Finnish	13	0.07
French, except Basque	606	3.05
French Canadian	33	0.17
German	2,543	12.81
Greek	106	0.53
Hawaii Native/Pacific Islander:	11	0.05
Polynesian: (7)	10	0.05
Native Hawaiian (7)	10	0.05
Other Pac. Isl., not spec.	1	0.00
Hispanic or Latino:	586	2.91
Central American:	75	0.37
Costa Rican	8	0.04
Guatemalan	31	0.15
Honduran	11	0.05
Nicaraguan	1	0.00
Panamanian	2	0.01
Salvadoran	17	0.08
Other Central American	5	0.02
Cuban	24	0.12
Dominican Republic	32	0.16
Mexican	193	0.96
Puerto Rican	89	0.44
South American:	73	0.36
Chilean	2	0.01
Colombian	54	0.27
Ecuadorian	1	0.00
Peruvian	2	0.01
Venezuelan	6	0.03
Other South American	8	0.04
Other Hispanic or Latino	100	0.50
Hungarian	45	0.23
Iranian	10	0.05
Irish	2,025	10.20
Italian	850	4.28
Lithuanian	36	0.18
Northern European	11	0.06
Norwegian	81	0.41
Polish	246	1.24
Portuguese	6	0.03
Russian	83	0.42
Scotch-Irish	952	4.80
Scottish	527	2.65
Serbian	9	0.05
Slovak	41	0.21
Slovene	12	0.06
Swedish	164	0.83
Swiss	82	0.41
Ukrainian	77	0.39
United States or American	2,786	14.03
Welsh	159	0.80
West Indian, excl. Hispanic:	28	0.14
British West Indian	9	0.05
Jamaican	19	0.10
White:	16,640	82.68
Not Hispanic (16,134)	16,317	81.08
Hispanic (286)	323	1.60

Wade Hampton

Place Type: Census Designated Place
County: Greenville
Population: 20,458

Ancestry/Race	Number	%
Acadian/Cajun	40	0.20

Notes: 1. Figures in the "Number" column do not add up to the total population due to: a) Ancestry/Race overlap — e.g. persons can report being both White and Irish, b) persons of Hispanic origin can report being any race, c) persons reporting two ancestries are counted in both categories. 2. Numbers in parentheses indicate the number of persons reporting this ancestry/race alone, not in combination with any other ancestry/race. 3. Refer to the Explanation of Data in the front of the book for more detailed information.

Ancestry/Race	Number	%
African American/Black:	1,721	8.41
Not Hispanic (1,638)	1,692	8.27
Hispanic (14)	29	0.14
African, sub-Saharan:	55	0.27
African	55	0.27
Am. Ind. or Alaska Nat., not spec.	26	0.13
American Indian tribes, specified:	46	0.22
Cherokee (10)	26	0.13
Chippewa	3	0.01
Choctaw (3)	4	0.02
Creek	1	0.00
Iroquois	3	0.01
Latin American Indians (1)	1	0.00
Lumbee (2)	2	0.01
Sioux (1)	1	0.00
Yaqui (1)	1	0.00
All other tribes (1)	4	0.02
American Indian tribes, not spec.	11	0.05
Arab:	225	1.11
Arab/Arabic	103	0.51
Egyptian	8	0.04
Iraqi	8	0.04
Lebanese	68	0.33
Syrian	22	0.11
Other Arab	16	0.08
Armenian	9	0.04
Asian:	731	3.57
Cambodian (1)	2	0.01
Chinese, ex. Taiwanese (55)	65	0.32
Filipino (17)	18	0.09
Indian (121)	129	0.63
Indonesian (4)	4	0.02
Japanese (26)	29	0.14
Korean (41)	43	0.21
Malaysian (1)	1	0.00
Pakistani (17)	17	0.08
Taiwanese (1)	1	0.00
Thai (3)	3	0.01
Vietnamese (376)	394	1.93
Other Asian, specified (1)	3	0.01
Other Asian, not specified (7)	22	0.11
Austrian	58	0.29
Belgian	10	0.05
Brazilian	29	0.14
British	100	0.49
Canadian	18	0.09
Croatian	36	0.18
Czech	71	0.35
Danish	35	0.17
Dutch	316	1.56
Eastern European	9	0.04
English	2,677	13.18
European	271	1.33
Finnish	6	0.03
French, except Basque	462	2.27
French Canadian	63	0.31
German	2,234	11.00
Greek	256	1.26
Hawaii Native/Pacific Islander:	23	0.11
Micronesian: (8)	8	0.04
Guamanian/Chamorro (6)	6	0.03
Other Micronesian (2)	2	0.01
Polynesian: (1)	1	0.00
Other Polynesian (1)	1	0.00
Other Pac. Isl., specified	2	0.01
Other Pac. Isl., not spec. (4)	12	0.06
Hispanic or Latino:	1,255	6.13
Central American:	100	0.49
Costa Rican	6	0.03
Guatemalan	31	0.15
Honduran	26	0.13
Nicaraguan	1	0.00
Salvadoran	25	0.12
Other Central American	11	0.05
Cuban	23	0.11
Dominican Republic	23	0.11
Mexican	699	3.42
Puerto Rican	93	0.45
South American:	154	0.75
Argentinean	7	0.03
Chilean	1	0.00
Colombian	122	0.60
Ecuadorian	2	0.01
Paraguayan	2	0.01
Peruvian	13	0.06
Other South American	7	0.03
Other Hispanic or Latino	163	0.80
Hungarian	31	0.15
Irish	2,060	10.14
Italian	683	3.36
Latvian	6	0.03
Lithuanian	12	0.06
Northern European	19	0.09
Norwegian	128	0.63
Polish	170	0.84
Portuguese	69	0.34
Russian	48	0.24
Scotch-Irish	1,046	5.15
Scottish	712	3.51
Slovak	23	0.11
Slovene	9	0.04
Swedish	90	0.44
Swiss	52	0.26
Ukrainian	59	0.29
United States or American	2,437	12.00
Welsh	144	0.71
West Indian, excl. Hispanic:	56	0.28
Bahamian	16	0.08
Jamaican	40	0.20
White:	17,557	85.82
Not Hispanic (16,674)	16,809	82.16
Hispanic (685)	748	3.66
Yugoslavian	10	0.05

West Columbia

Place Type: City
County: Lexington
Population: 13,064

Ancestry/Race	Number	%
African American/Black:	2,675	20.48
Not Hispanic (2,561)	2,624	20.09
Hispanic (27)	51	0.39
African, sub-Saharan:	322	2.43
African	253	1.91
Nigerian	47	0.35
Senegalese	22	0.17
Alaska Native tribes, specified:	3	0.02
Alaska Athabascan	3	0.02
Am. Ind. or Alaska Nat., not spec.	35	0.27
Albanian	7	0.05
American Indian tribes, specified:	57	0.44
Apache (1)	2	0.02
Cherokee (7)	28	0.21
Choctaw	1	0.01
Latin American Indians (4)	10	0.08
Sioux	1	0.01
All other tribes (8)	15	0.11
American Indian tribes, not spec.	9	0.07
Arab:	34	0.26
Arab/Arabic	14	0.11
Egyptian	6	0.05
Lebanese	14	0.11
Armenian	19	0.14
Asian:	266	2.04
Bangladeshi (3)	5	0.04
Cambodian (1)	1	0.01
Chinese, ex. Taiwanese (106)	111	0.85
Filipino (9)	15	0.11
Indian (45)	53	0.41
Japanese (10)	14	0.11
Korean (14)	19	0.15
Laotian (6)	6	0.05
Pakistani (3)	5	0.04
Taiwanese	4	0.03
Thai (5)	7	0.05
Vietnamese (11)	11	0.08
Other Asian, specified	1	0.01
Other Asian, not specified (6)	14	0.11
Belgian	8	0.06
British	48	0.36
Canadian	8	0.06
Celtic	16	0.12
Croatian	9	0.07
Danish	5	0.04
Dutch	241	1.82
English	1,209	9.13
European	135	1.02
French, except Basque	303	2.29
French Canadian	20	0.15
German	1,373	10.36
Greek	48	0.36
Hawaii Native/Pacific Islander:	9	0.07
Micronesian: (1)	1	0.01
Guamanian/Chamorro (1)	1	0.01
Polynesian: (1)	6	0.05
Native Hawaiian (1)	2	0.02
Samoan	4	0.03
Other Pac. Isl., specified	1	0.01
Other Pac. Isl., not spec.	1	0.01
Hispanic or Latino:	609	4.66
Central American:	52	0.40
Guatemalan	32	0.24
Honduran	3	0.02
Nicaraguan	7	0.05
Panamanian	8	0.06
Salvadoran	2	0.02
Cuban	16	0.12
Mexican	408	3.12
Puerto Rican	42	0.32
South American:	16	0.12
Chilean	2	0.02
Colombian	3	0.02
Ecuadorian	3	0.02
Peruvian	2	0.02
Venezuelan	4	0.03
Other South American	2	0.02
Other Hispanic or Latino	75	0.57
Hungarian	20	0.15
Irish	1,189	8.97
Italian	216	1.63
Lithuanian	6	0.05
Norwegian	70	0.53
Polish	107	0.81
Romanian	9	0.07
Russian	61	0.46
Scandinavian	15	0.11
Scotch-Irish	502	3.79
Scottish	252	1.90
Slovene	4	0.03
Swedish	36	0.27
Swiss	6	0.05
United States or American	1,722	13.00
Welsh	27	0.20
West Indian, excl. Hispanic:	24	0.18
Barbadian	9	0.07
Trinidadian and Tobagonian	6	0.05
West Indian	9	0.07
White:	9,895	75.74
Not Hispanic (9,483)	9,605	73.52
Hispanic (255)	290	2.22
Yugoslavian	6	0.05

Aberdeen

Place Type: City
County: Brown
Population: 24,658

Ancestry/Race	Number	%
African American/Black:	139	0.56
Not Hispanic (89)	133	0.54
Hispanic (3)	6	0.02
African, sub-Saharan:	7	0.03
African	7	0.03
Alaska Native tribes, specified:	2	0.01
Alaska Athabascan (1)	1	0.00
Eskimo (1)	1	0.00
Alaska Native tribes, not specified	1	0.00

Notes: 1. Figures in the "Number" column do not add up to the total population due to: a) Ancestry/Race overlap — e.g. persons can report being both White and Irish, b) persons of Hispanic origin can report being any race, c) persons reporting two ancestries are counted in both categories. 2. Numbers in parentheses indicate the number of persons reporting this ancestry/race alone, not in combination with any other ancestry/race. 3. Refer to the Explanation of Data in the front of the book for more detailed information.

Am. Ind. or Alaska Nat., not spec.	136	0.55
American Indian tribes, specified:	789	3.20
Apache (4)	8	0.03
Blackfeet (4)	4	0.02
Cherokee (6)	10	0.04
Cheyenne (11)	19	0.08
Chippewa (72)	88	0.36
Choctaw (1)	2	0.01
Creek (5)	5	0.02
Iroquois (3)	6	0.02
Menominee (1)	1	0.00
Navajo (8)	8	0.03
Paiute (1)	1	0.00
Potawatomi (1)	3	0.01
Pueblo (2)	2	0.01
Seminole (1)	1	0.00
Shoshone (3)	4	0.02
Sioux (483)	566	2.30
Yuman (3)	3	0.01
All other tribes (46)	58	0.24
American Indian tribes, not spec.	16	0.06
Arab:	8	0.03
Syrian	8	0.03
Asian:	173	0.70
Bangladeshi (1)	1	0.00
Chinese, ex. Taiwanese (41)	45	0.18
Filipino (18)	31	0.13
Indian (19)	21	0.09
Indonesian (2)	2	0.01
Japanese (14)	19	0.08
Korean (16)	19	0.08
Laotian	2	0.01
Pakistani (4)	4	0.02
Thai	1	0.00
Vietnamese (16)	25	0.10
Other Asian, not specified	3	0.01
Austrian	24	0.10
Belgian	38	0.15
British	37	0.15
Canadian	23	0.09
Celtic	6	0.02
Croatian	27	0.11
Czech	234	0.95
Czechoslovakian	26	0.11
Danish	360	1.46
Dutch	735	2.99
English	1,672	6.79
European	20	0.08
Finnish	292	1.19
French, except Basque	739	3.00
French Canadian	92	0.37
German	13,206	53.66
German Russian	27	0.11
Greek	37	0.15
Hawaii Native/Pacific Islander:	51	0.21
Micronesian: (4)	9	0.04
Guamanian/Chamorro (4)	8	0.03
Other Micronesian	1	0.00
Polynesian: (22)	40	0.16
Native Hawaiian (2)	11	0.04
Samoan (5)	10	0.04
Tongan (15)	19	0.08
Other Pac. Isl., not spec.	2	0.01
Hispanic or Latino:	196	0.79
Central American:	2	0.01
Costa Rican	1	0.00
Salvadoran	1	0.00
Cuban	2	0.01
Dominican Republic	2	0.01
Mexican	103	0.42
Puerto Rican	27	0.11
South American:	4	0.02
Bolivian	1	0.00
Colombian	3	0.01
Other Hispanic or Latino	56	0.23
Hungarian	71	0.29
Icelander	28	0.11
Irish	2,098	8.52
Italian	190	0.77
Lithuanian	5	0.02
Luxemburger	18	0.07
Northern European	21	0.09
Norwegian	3,681	14.96
Pennsylvania German	20	0.08
Polish	413	1.68
Romanian	13	0.05
Russian	1,448	5.88
Scandinavian	182	0.74
Scotch-Irish	259	1.05
Scottish	256	1.04
Swedish	895	3.64
Swiss	64	0.26
Ukrainian	5	0.02
United States or American	683	2.78
Welsh	73	0.30
West Indian, excl. Hispanic:	4	0.02
Haitian	4	0.02
White:	23,556	95.53
Not Hispanic (23,209)	23,419	94.98
Hispanic (119)	137	0.56
Yugoslavian	4	0.02

Brookings

Place Type: City
County: Brookings
Population: 18,504

Ancestry/Race	Number	%
African American/Black:	115	0.62
Not Hispanic (79)	108	0.58
Hispanic (2)	7	0.04
African, sub-Saharan:	41	0.22
Liberian	31	0.17
Other sub-Saharan African	10	0.05
Alaska Native tribes, specified:	3	0.02
Tlingit-Haida (3)	3	0.02
Am. Ind. or Alaska Nat., not spec.	56	0.30
American Indian tribes, specified:	178	0.96
Cherokee (1)	4	0.02
Cheyenne (3)	3	0.02
Chippewa (6)	10	0.05
Latin American Indians	4	0.02
Pima (3)	3	0.02
Potawatomi (3)	3	0.02
Sioux (108)	135	0.73
Yaqui (2)	2	0.01
All other tribes (10)	14	0.08
American Indian tribes, not spec.	8	0.04
Arab:	83	0.45
Egyptian	32	0.17
Lebanese	25	0.13
Syrian	13	0.07
Other Arab	13	0.07
Asian:	418	2.26
Bangladeshi (11)	14	0.08
Chinese, ex. Taiwanese (121)	135	0.73
Filipino (16)	29	0.16
Indian (69)	85	0.46
Indonesian (3)	3	0.02
Japanese (17)	24	0.13
Korean (61)	69	0.37
Laotian (1)	1	0.01
Malaysian (3)	7	0.04
Pakistani (4)	4	0.02
Taiwanese (1)	1	0.01
Thai (11)	17	0.09
Vietnamese (11)	17	0.09
Other Asian, specified (7)	7	0.04
Other Asian, not specified (2)	5	0.03
Austrian	71	0.38
Belgian	110	0.59
Brazilian	16	0.09
British	73	0.39
Canadian	11	0.06
Croatian	12	0.06
Czech	262	1.41
Czechoslovakian	144	0.78
Danish	655	3.53
Dutch	825	4.45
English	1,053	5.67
European	24	0.13
Finnish	134	0.72
French, except Basque	501	2.70
French Canadian	71	0.38
German	8,241	44.40
Greek	76	0.41
Hawaii Native/Pacific Islander:	11	0.06
Polynesian: (4)	4	0.02
Native Hawaiian (3)	3	0.02
Samoan (1)	1	0.01
Other Pac. Isl., not spec. (6)	7	0.04
Hispanic or Latino:	139	0.75
Central American:	2	0.01
Salvadoran	2	0.01
Cuban	3	0.02
Mexican	64	0.35
Puerto Rican	12	0.06
South American:	9	0.05
Chilean	3	0.02
Colombian	1	0.01
Venezuelan	5	0.03
Other Hispanic or Latino	49	0.26
Hungarian	33	0.18
Icelander	7	0.04
Iranian	70	0.38
Irish	1,814	9.77
Italian	187	1.01
Luxemburger	11	0.06
New Zealander	10	0.05
Norwegian	4,580	24.68
Polish	328	1.77
Portuguese	8	0.04
Romanian	8	0.04
Russian	117	0.63
Scandinavian	46	0.25
Scotch-Irish	97	0.52
Scottish	237	1.28
Slovak	20	0.11
Swedish	1,001	5.39
Swiss	64	0.34
Ukrainian	15	0.08
United States or American	398	2.14
Welsh	91	0.49
White:	17,819	96.30
Not Hispanic (17,598)	17,730	95.82
Hispanic (72)	89	0.48

Huron

Place Type: City
County: Beadle
Population: 11,893

Ancestry/Race	Number	%
African American/Black:	158	1.33
Not Hispanic (114)	158	1.33
African, sub-Saharan:	20	0.17
African	20	0.17
Am. Ind. or Alaska Nat., not spec.	67	0.56
American Indian tribes, specified:	141	1.19
Apache (2)	6	0.05
Blackfeet (1)	3	0.03
Cherokee (1)	11	0.09
Cheyenne (1)	1	0.01
Chippewa (4)	8	0.07
Latin American Indians (1)	2	0.02
Potawatomi (1)	1	0.01
Seminole (1)	1	0.01
Sioux (78)	99	0.83
All other tribes (7)	9	0.08
American Indian tribes, not spec.	2	0.02
Arab:	13	0.11
Arab/Arabic	3	0.03
Syrian	10	0.08
Armenian	9	0.08
Asian:	70	0.59
Chinese, ex. Taiwanese (10)	10	0.08
Filipino (7)	14	0.12
Indian (20)	25	0.21

Notes: 1. Figures in the "Number" column do not add up to the total population due to: a) Ancestry/Race overlap — e.g. persons can report being both White and Irish, b) persons of Hispanic origin can report being any race, c) persons reporting two ancestries are counted in both categories. 2. Numbers in parentheses indicate the number of persons reporting this ancestry/race alone, not in combination with any other ancestry/race. 3. Refer to the Explanation of Data in the front of the book for more detailed information.

Ancestry/Race	Number	%
Indonesian	1	0.01
Japanese (3)	5	0.04
Korean (5)	10	0.08
Vietnamese (3)	3	0.03
Other Asian, specified (2)	2	0.02
Austrian	32	0.27
Basque	9	0.08
Belgian	11	0.09
British	44	0.37
Canadian	6	0.05
Czech	124	1.03
Czechoslovakian	39	0.33
Danish	195	1.63
Dutch	487	4.06
English	993	8.29
European	59	0.49
Finnish	60	0.50
French, except Basque	490	4.09
French Canadian	71	0.59
German	5,767	48.13
Greek	8	0.07
Hawaii Native/Pacific Islander:	5	0.04
Micronesian: (1)	2	0.02
Guamanian/Chamorro (1)	2	0.02
Polynesian: (1)	2	0.02
Native Hawaiian (1)	2	0.02
Other Pac. Isl., not spec. (1)	1	0.01
Hispanic or Latino:	143	1.20
Central American:	4	0.03
Guatemalan	3	0.03
Nicaraguan	1	0.01
Mexican	81	0.68
Puerto Rican	16	0.13
South American:	4	0.03
Chilean	3	0.03
Colombian	1	0.01
Other Hispanic or Latino	38	0.32
Hungarian	7	0.06
Irish	1,421	11.86
Italian	78	0.65
Lithuanian	10	0.08
Luxemburger	4	0.03
Norwegian	1,683	14.05
Pennsylvania German	10	0.08
Polish	285	2.38
Russian	161	1.34
Scandinavian	59	0.49
Scotch-Irish	201	1.68
Scottish	218	1.82
Slavic	6	0.05
Swedish	423	3.53
Swiss	32	0.27
Ukrainian	32	0.27
United States or American	514	4.29
Welsh	31	0.26
White:	11,526	96.91
Not Hispanic (11,332)	11,433	96.13
Hispanic (76)	93	0.78

Mitchell

Place Type: City
County: Davison
Population: 14,558

Ancestry/Race	Number	%
African American/Black:	77	0.53
Not Hispanic (44)	71	0.49
Hispanic (3)	6	0.04
African, sub-Saharan:	52	0.35
Nigerian	52	0.35
Alaska Native tribes, specified:	1	0.01
Alaska Athabascan (1)	1	0.01
Am. Ind. or Alaska Nat., not spec.	147	1.01
American Indian tribes, specified:	264	1.81
Apache	4	0.03
Blackfeet (2)	2	0.01
Cherokee (2)	4	0.03
Cheyenne	1	0.01
Chippewa (12)	12	0.08
Choctaw	2	0.01
Crow (1)	1	0.01
Latin American Indians (1)	1	0.01
Navajo	2	0.01
Sioux (193)	232	1.59
All other tribes (3)	3	0.02
American Indian tribes, not spec.	6	0.04
Arab:	8	0.05
Syrian	8	0.05
Asian:	93	0.64
Cambodian (11)	16	0.11
Chinese, ex. Taiwanese (4)	12	0.08
Filipino (10)	16	0.11
Indian (8)	9	0.06
Indonesian (1)	1	0.01
Japanese (9)	12	0.08
Korean (12)	14	0.10
Pakistani (3)	3	0.02
Thai (1)	1	0.01
Vietnamese (3)	7	0.05
Other Asian, not specified	2	0.01
Austrian	20	0.14
Belgian	68	0.46
British	15	0.10
Czech	385	2.62
Czechoslovakian	62	0.42
Danish	273	1.86
Dutch	795	5.41
English	1,109	7.55
European	36	0.25
French, except Basque	494	3.36
French Canadian	124	0.84
German	6,917	47.08
German Russian	12	0.08
Greek	17	0.12
Hawaii Native/Pacific Islander:	17	0.12
Micronesian: (1)	1	0.01
Guamanian/Chamorro (1)	1	0.01
Polynesian: (1)	10	0.07
Native Hawaiian (1)	7	0.05
Samoan	3	0.02
Other Pac. Isl., not spec. (2)	6	0.04
Hispanic or Latino:	112	0.77
Central American:	1	0.01
Panamanian	1	0.01
Cuban	6	0.04
Dominican Republic	1	0.01
Mexican	68	0.47
Puerto Rican	8	0.05
South American:	3	0.02
Colombian	2	0.01
Venezuelan	1	0.01
Other Hispanic or Latino	25	0.17
Hungarian	54	0.37
Icelander	5	0.03
Irish	1,632	11.11
Italian	133	0.91
Luxemburger	69	0.47
Norwegian	1,711	11.65
Polish	147	1.00
Romanian	11	0.07
Russian	170	1.16
Scandinavian	57	0.39
Scotch-Irish	107	0.73
Scottish	91	0.62
Slavic	17	0.12
Slovak	8	0.05
Swedish	487	3.31
Swiss	86	0.59
United States or American	667	4.54
Welsh	128	0.87
West Indian, excl. Hispanic:	8	0.05
Jamaican	8	0.05
White:	14,038	96.43
Not Hispanic (13,879)	13,977	96.01
Hispanic (43)	61	0.42

Pierre

Place Type: City
County: Hughes
Population: 13,876

Ancestry/Race	Number	%
African American/Black:	49	0.35
Not Hispanic (27)	48	0.35
Hispanic (1)	1	0.01
African, sub-Saharan:	18	0.13
African	18	0.13
Alaska Native tribes, specified:	2	0.01
Tlingit-Haida (2)	2	0.01
Am. Ind. or Alaska Nat., not spec.	170	1.23
American Indian tribes, specified:	1,166	8.40
Blackfeet (5)	5	0.04
Cherokee (5)	10	0.07
Cheyenne (6)	22	0.16
Chippewa (49)	57	0.41
Choctaw (3)	3	0.02
Latin American Indians (1)	1	0.01
Navajo (1)	3	0.02
Pueblo (2)	2	0.01
Seminole (1)	1	0.01
Sioux (867)	996	7.18
Yuman (3)	3	0.02
All other tribes (47)	63	0.45
American Indian tribes, not spec.	53	0.38
Arab:	22	0.16
Lebanese	22	0.16
Asian:	94	0.68
Bangladeshi (4)	4	0.03
Chinese, ex. Taiwanese (16)	18	0.13
Filipino (11)	20	0.14
Indian (9)	15	0.11
Japanese (9)	11	0.08
Korean (11)	16	0.12
Pakistani	2	0.01
Vietnamese (1)	3	0.02
Other Asian, not specified (2)	5	0.04
Austrian	3	0.02
Belgian	54	0.39
British	6	0.04
Canadian	14	0.10
Celtic	14	0.10
Czech	417	2.99
Czechoslovakian	43	0.31
Danish	445	3.19
Dutch	357	2.56
English	1,137	8.14
European	24	0.17
Finnish	33	0.24
French, except Basque	551	3.94
French Canadian	109	0.78
German	5,666	40.56
German Russian	6	0.04
Hawaii Native/Pacific Islander:	5	0.04
Micronesian: (2)	3	0.02
Guamanian/Chamorro (2)	3	0.02
Polynesian: (1)	2	0.01
Native Hawaiian (1)	2	0.01
Hispanic or Latino:	173	1.25
Central American:	2	0.01
Honduran	1	0.01
Panamanian	1	0.01
Dominican Republic	2	0.01
Mexican	95	0.68
Puerto Rican	13	0.09
South American:	4	0.03
Bolivian	1	0.01
Colombian	3	0.02
Other Hispanic or Latino	57	0.41
Hungarian	35	0.25
Irish	1,699	12.16
Italian	88	0.63
Lithuanian	10	0.07
Luxemburger	36	0.26
Northern European	5	0.04
Norwegian	1,985	14.21

Notes: 1. Figures in the "Number" column do not add up to the total population due to: a) Ancestry/Race overlap — e.g. persons can report being both White and Irish, b) persons of Hispanic origin can report being any race, c) persons reporting two ancestries are counted in both categories. 2. Numbers in parentheses indicate the number of persons reporting this ancestry/race alone, not in combination with any other ancestry/race. 3. Refer to the Explanation of Data in the front of the book for more detailed information.

Polish	139	1.00
Portuguese	12	0.09
Russian	144	1.03
Scandinavian	79	0.57
Scotch-Irish	159	1.14
Scottish	278	1.99
Swedish	446	3.19
Swiss	108	0.77
United States or American	500	3.58
Welsh	108	0.77
White:	12,534	90.33
Not Hispanic (12,257)	12,434	89.61
Hispanic (80)	100	0.72
Yugoslavian	10	0.07

Rapid City

Place Type: City
County: Pennington
Population: 59,607

Ancestry/Race	Number	%
African American/Black:	912	1.53
Not Hispanic (550)	855	1.43
Hispanic (29)	57	0.10
African, sub-Saharan:	111	0.19
African	75	0.13
Ethiopian	24	0.04
Kenyan	7	0.01
Sudanese	5	0.01
Alaska Native tribes, specified:	21	0.04
Alaska Athabascan (3)	5	0.01
Aleut (6)	9	0.02
Eskimo (3)	3	0.01
Tlingit-Haida (3)	4	0.01
Alaska Native tribes, not specified	4	0.01
Am. Ind. or Alaska Nat., not spec.	1,012	1.70
Alsatian	7	0.01
American Indian tribes, specified:	5,837	9.79
Apache (3)	5	0.01
Blackfeet (14)	22	0.04
Cherokee (22)	65	0.11
Cheyenne (41)	76	0.13
Chickasaw	5	0.01
Chippewa (30)	47	0.08
Choctaw (9)	19	0.03
Colville (2)	2	0.00
Cree (4)	4	0.01
Creek	7	0.01
Crow (9)	11	0.02
Delaware	4	0.01
Iroquois (14)	20	0.03
Kiowa (2)	4	0.01
Latin American Indians (5)	10	0.02
Menominee	2	0.00
Navajo (45)	64	0.11
Osage	2	0.00
Ottawa (1)	1	0.00
Potawatomi (4)	4	0.01
Pueblo (12)	13	0.02
Puget Sound Salish (1)	1	0.00
Seminole (4)	8	0.01
Shoshone (9)	12	0.02
Sioux (4,570)	5,256	8.82
Ute (3)	3	0.01
Yakama (5)	6	0.01
Yuman	1	0.00
All other tribes (126)	163	0.27
American Indian tribes, not spec.	341	0.57
Arab:	129	0.22
Arab/Arabic	21	0.04
Egyptian	8	0.01
Lebanese	47	0.08
Moroccan	8	0.01
Syrian	22	0.04
Other Arab	23	0.04
Asian:	869	1.46
Bangladeshi (13)	13	0.02
Cambodian (2)	2	0.00
Chinese, ex. Taiwanese (105)	129	0.22
Filipino (85)	178	0.30
Indian (107)	122	0.20
Indonesian (1)	3	0.01
Japanese (94)	149	0.25
Korean (65)	94	0.16
Laotian (10)	10	0.02
Pakistani (2)	3	0.01
Taiwanese (2)	7	0.01
Thai (36)	47	0.08
Vietnamese (41)	64	0.11
Other Asian, specified (4)	9	0.02
Other Asian, not specified (20)	39	0.07
Australian	15	0.03
Austrian	135	0.23
Basque	4	0.01
Belgian	67	0.11
Brazilian	13	0.02
British	217	0.36
Canadian	63	0.11
Celtic	10	0.02
Croatian	36	0.06
Czech	938	1.58
Czechoslovakian	126	0.21
Danish	1,074	1.80
Dutch	1,876	3.15
English	5,876	9.87
European	226	0.38
Finnish	260	0.44
French, except Basque	1,958	3.29
French Canadian	368	0.62
German	20,088	33.76
German Russian	5	0.01
Greek	81	0.14
Hawaii Native/Pacific Islander:	86	0.14
Micronesian: (4)	13	0.02
Guamanian/Chamorro (4)	13	0.02
Polynesian: (26)	59	0.10
Native Hawaiian (17)	42	0.07
Samoan (7)	10	0.02
Tongan (2)	6	0.01
Other Polynesian	1	0.00
Other Pac. Isl., specified	1	0.00
Other Pac. Isl., not spec. (5)	13	0.02
Hispanic or Latino:	1,650	2.77
Central American:	45	0.08
Guatemalan	2	0.00
Honduran	10	0.02
Nicaraguan	4	0.01
Panamanian	19	0.03
Salvadoran	6	0.01
Other Central American	4	0.01
Cuban	20	0.03
Dominican Republic	5	0.01
Mexican	1,021	1.71
Puerto Rican	130	0.22
South American:	18	0.03
Chilean	2	0.00
Colombian	6	0.01
Ecuadorian	1	0.00
Peruvian	5	0.01
Venezuelan	1	0.00
Other South American	3	0.01
Other Hispanic or Latino	411	0.69
Hungarian	105	0.18
Icelander	15	0.03
Irish	8,185	13.75
Italian	1,369	2.30
Latvian	48	0.08
Lithuanian	29	0.05
Luxemburger	46	0.08
Maltese	6	0.01
New Zealander	29	0.05
Northern European	31	0.05
Norwegian	6,496	10.92
Pennsylvania German	61	0.10
Polish	907	1.52
Portuguese	44	0.07
Romanian	36	0.06
Russian	747	1.26
Scandinavian	370	0.62
Scotch-Irish	823	1.38
Scottish	954	1.60
Serbian	13	0.02
Slavic	28	0.05
Slovak	10	0.02
Swedish	2,251	3.78
Swiss	236	0.40
Turkish	8	0.01
Ukrainian	57	0.10
United States or American	2,701	4.54
Welsh	377	0.63
West Indian, excl. Hispanic:	6	0.01
Jamaican	6	0.01
White:	51,726	86.78
Not Hispanic (49,621)	50,863	85.33
Hispanic (645)	863	1.45
Yugoslavian	101	0.17

Sioux Falls

Place Type: City
County: Minnehaha
Population: 123,975

Ancestry/Race	Number	%
African American/Black:	2,958	2.39
Not Hispanic (2,198)	2,886	2.33
Hispanic (28)	72	0.06
African, sub-Saharan:	1,272	1.03
African	325	0.26
Ethiopian	452	0.36
Kenyan	6	0.00
Nigerian	91	0.07
Sierra Leonean	23	0.02
Somalian	61	0.05
South African	9	0.01
Sudanese	297	0.24
Other sub-Saharan African	8	0.01
Alaska Native tribes, specified:	5	0.00
Alaska Athabascan	5	0.00
Alaska Native tribes, not specified	5	0.00
Am. Ind. or Alaska Nat., not spec.	1,043	0.84
Albanian	9	0.01
American Indian tribes, specified:	2,174	1.75
Apache	3	0.00
Blackfeet (2)	8	0.01
Cherokee (37)	77	0.06
Cheyenne (12)	38	0.03
Chippewa (57)	85	0.07
Choctaw (1)	7	0.01
Comanche (2)	7	0.01
Creek	5	0.00
Crow (4)	7	0.01
Iroquois (3)	6	0.00
Kiowa (1)	2	0.00
Latin American Indians (4)	10	0.01
Lumbee (1)	3	0.00
Menominee (2)	2	0.00
Navajo (16)	18	0.01
Paiute (1)	1	0.00
Potawatomi	1	0.00
Pueblo (1)	1	0.00
Seminole (3)	7	0.01
Sioux (1,473)	1,775	1.43
Yuman (1)	1	0.00
All other tribes (65)	110	0.09
American Indian tribes, not spec.	77	0.06
Arab:	456	0.37
Arab/Arabic	84	0.07
Egyptian	39	0.03
Iraqi	47	0.04
Lebanese	187	0.15
Palestinian	25	0.02
Syrian	41	0.03
Other Arab	33	0.03
Armenian	32	0.03
Asian:	1,980	1.60
Bangladeshi	2	0.00
Cambodian (36)	49	0.04
Chinese, ex. Taiwanese (208)	278	0.22

Notes: 1. Figures in the "Number" column do not add up to the total population due to: a) Ancestry/Race overlap — e.g. persons can report being both White and Irish, b) persons of Hispanic origin can report being any race, c) persons reporting two ancestries are counted in both categories. 2. Numbers in parentheses indicate the number of persons reporting this ancestry/race alone, not in combination with any other ancestry/race. 3. Refer to the Explanation of Data in the front of the book for more detailed information.

Ancestry/Race	Number	%
Filipino (97)	175	0.14
Hmong (26)	35	0.03
Indian (158)	192	0.15
Indonesian (1)	1	0.00
Japanese (53)	100	0.08
Korean (151)	196	0.16
Laotian (204)	228	0.18
Malaysian (4)	6	0.00
Pakistani (1)	3	0.00
Sri Lankan (5)	5	0.00
Taiwanese (2)	4	0.00
Thai (26)	34	0.03
Vietnamese (413)	468	0.38
Other Asian, specified (1)	8	0.01
Other Asian, not specified (65)	196	0.16
Assyrian/Chaldean/Syriac	15	0.01
Australian	30	0.02
Austrian	170	0.14
Belgian	331	0.27
British	204	0.16
Canadian	48	0.04
Croatian	59	0.05
Czech	1,537	1.24
Czechoslovakian	232	0.19
Danish	3,800	3.06
Dutch	7,841	6.32
Eastern European	5	0.00
English	8,157	6.57
Estonian	20	0.02
European	517	0.42
Finnish	350	0.28
French, except Basque	3,991	3.22
French Canadian	694	0.56
German	50,520	40.71
Greek	226	0.18
Hawaii Native/Pacific Islander:	127	0.10
Melanesian: (5)	6	0.00
Fijian (5)	6	0.00
Micronesian: (29)	38	0.03
Guamanian/Chamorro (29)	38	0.03
Polynesian: (32)	64	0.05
Native Hawaiian (20)	50	0.04
Samoan (10)	12	0.01
Tongan (2)	2	0.00
Other Pac. Isl., not spec. (2)	19	0.02
Hispanic or Latino:	3,087	2.49
Central American:	567	0.46
Costa Rican	6	0.00
Guatemalan	387	0.31
Honduran	16	0.01
Nicaraguan	21	0.02
Panamanian	12	0.01
Salvadoran	82	0.07
Other Central American	43	0.03
Cuban	62	0.05
Dominican Republic	10	0.01
Mexican	1,557	1.26
Puerto Rican	125	0.10
South American:	74	0.06
Argentinean	7	0.01
Bolivian	4	0.00
Chilean	22	0.02
Colombian	17	0.01
Ecuadorian	7	0.01
Peruvian	9	0.01
Venezuelan	1	0.00
Other South American	7	0.01
Other Hispanic or Latino	692	0.56
Hungarian	145	0.12
Icelander	47	0.04
Iranian	65	0.05
Irish	15,004	12.09
Italian	1,268	1.02
Latvian	69	0.06
Lithuanian	47	0.04
Luxemburger	350	0.28
Macedonian	6	0.00
Northern European	110	0.09
Norwegian	23,218	18.71
Pennsylvania German	57	0.05
Polish	2,040	1.64
Portuguese	21	0.02
Romanian	43	0.03
Russian	784	0.63
Scandinavian	685	0.55
Scotch-Irish	1,267	1.02
Scottish	1,144	0.92
Serbian	42	0.03
Slavic	6	0.00
Slovak	63	0.05
Slovene	41	0.03
Swedish	5,822	4.69
Swiss	367	0.30
Turkish	31	0.02
Ukrainian	443	0.36
United States or American	4,205	3.39
Welsh	741	0.60
West Indian, excl. Hispanic:	25	0.02
Bermudan	17	0.01
West Indian	8	0.01
White:	115,744	93.36
Not Hispanic (112,703)	114,251	92.16
Hispanic (1,235)	1,493	1.20
Yugoslavian	648	0.52

Watertown

Place Type: City
County: Codington
Population: 20,237

Ancestry/Race	Number	%
African American/Black:	62	0.31
Not Hispanic (25)	56	0.28
Hispanic (3)	6	0.03
African, sub-Saharan:	8	0.04
African	4	0.02
Nigerian	4	0.02
Alaska Native tribes, specified:	2	0.01
Tlingit-Haida	2	0.01
Am. Ind. or Alaska Nat., not spec.	67	0.33
American Indian tribes, specified:	356	1.76
Apache (1)	1	0.00
Blackfeet	2	0.01
Cherokee (3)	8	0.04
Cheyenne	1	0.00
Chippewa (8)	14	0.07
Cree	1	0.00
Latin American Indians (1)	1	0.00
Potawatomi (2)	3	0.01
Pueblo (1)	4	0.02
Sioux (240)	310	1.53
All other tribes (7)	11	0.05
American Indian tribes, not spec.	22	0.11
Arab:	13	0.06
Lebanese	13	0.06
Asian:	100	0.49
Chinese, ex. Taiwanese (8)	8	0.04
Filipino (18)	31	0.15
Indian (4)	5	0.02
Japanese (5)	6	0.03
Korean (10)	15	0.07
Laotian (1)	1	0.00
Pakistani (1)	1	0.00
Thai (3)	5	0.02
Vietnamese (12)	22	0.11
Other Asian, specified (1)	1	0.00
Other Asian, not specified (3)	5	0.02
Austrian	11	0.05
Belgian	113	0.56
British	13	0.06
Canadian	47	0.23
Croatian	13	0.06
Czech	264	1.30
Czechoslovakian	20	0.10
Danish	350	1.72
Dutch	868	4.27
English	1,075	5.29
European	66	0.32
Finnish	76	0.37
French, except Basque	608	2.99
French Canadian	125	0.62
German	10,182	50.14
Greek	7	0.03
Hawaii Native/Pacific Islander:	9	0.04
Micronesian:	2	0.01
Guamanian/Chamorro	2	0.01
Polynesian: (3)	5	0.02
Native Hawaiian (2)	4	0.02
Samoan (1)	1	0.00
Other Pac. Isl., not spec. (1)	2	0.01
Hispanic or Latino:	259	1.28
Central American:	2	0.01
Panamanian	1	0.00
Other Central American	1	0.00
Cuban	1	0.00
Mexican	182	0.90
Puerto Rican	16	0.08
South American:	2	0.01
Colombian	1	0.00
Peruvian	1	0.00
Other Hispanic or Latino	56	0.28
Hungarian	10	0.05
Icelander	9	0.04
Irish	1,912	9.41
Italian	170	0.84
Latvian	10	0.05
Luxemburger	23	0.11
Norwegian	4,926	24.26
Polish	582	2.87
Russian	95	0.47
Scandinavian	152	0.75
Scotch-Irish	143	0.70
Scottish	204	1.00
Slovene	9	0.04
Swedish	727	3.58
Swiss	58	0.29
Ukrainian	10	0.05
United States or American	734	3.61
Welsh	39	0.19
White:	19,650	97.10
Not Hispanic (19,384)	19,539	96.55
Hispanic (95)	111	0.55

Yankton

Place Type: City
County: Yankton
Population: 13,528

Ancestry/Race	Number	%
African American/Black:	269	1.99
Not Hispanic (218)	264	1.95
Hispanic (4)	5	0.04
African, sub-Saharan:	48	0.36
African	42	0.31
Ethiopian	6	0.04
Alaska Native tribes, specified:	5	0.04
Eskimo (1)	5	0.04
Alaska Native tribes, not specified	1	0.01
Am. Ind. or Alaska Nat., not spec.	60	0.44
American Indian tribes, specified:	212	1.57
Blackfeet	1	0.01
Cherokee (1)	6	0.04
Cheyenne (1)	1	0.01
Chippewa (8)	9	0.07
Cree	1	0.01
Creek (1)	2	0.01
Latin American Indians (2)	5	0.04
Menominee (1)	1	0.01
Seminole (1)	2	0.01
Sioux (140)	172	1.27
All other tribes (9)	12	0.09
American Indian tribes, not spec.	9	0.07
Arab:	51	0.38
Lebanese	6	0.04
Palestinian	7	0.05
Syrian	38	0.28
Armenian	7	0.05
Asian:	97	0.72

Notes: 1. Figures in the "Number" column do not add up to the total population due to: a) Ancestry/Race overlap — e.g. persons can report being both White and Irish, b) persons of Hispanic origin can report being any race, c) persons reporting two ancestries are counted in both categories. 2. Numbers in parentheses indicate the number of persons reporting this ancestry/race alone, not in combination with any other ancestry/race. 3. Refer to the Explanation of Data in the front of the book for more detailed information.

Ancestry/Race	Number	%
Cambodian (1)	2	0.01
Chinese, ex. Taiwanese (17)	22	0.16
Filipino (13)	21	0.16
Indian (3)	3	0.02
Japanese (3)	9	0.07
Korean (12)	16	0.12
Laotian	2	0.01
Taiwanese	1	0.01
Thai (1)	1	0.01
Vietnamese (8)	9	0.07
Other Asian, not specified (8)	11	0.08
Austrian	36	0.27
Belgian	8	0.06
British	29	0.22
Canadian	6	0.04
Czech	979	7.28
Czechoslovakian	194	1.44
Danish	797	5.92
Dutch	372	2.77
English	795	5.91
European	10	0.07
Finnish	25	0.19
French, except Basque	222	1.65
French Canadian	26	0.19
German	5,681	42.23
Greek	21	0.16
Hawaii Native/Pacific Islander:	8	0.06
Micronesian: (1)	1	0.01
Other Micronesian (1)	1	0.01
Polynesian: (2)	3	0.02
Native Hawaiian (1)	2	0.01
Other Polynesian (1)	1	0.01
Other Pac. Isl., not spec. (1)	4	0.03
Hispanic or Latino:	333	2.46
Central American:	11	0.08
Guatemalan	5	0.04
Nicaraguan	1	0.01
Panamanian	5	0.04
Cuban	3	0.02
Mexican	252	1.86
Puerto Rican	7	0.05
South American:	14	0.10
Argentinean	3	0.02
Chilean	6	0.04
Colombian	5	0.04
Other Hispanic or Latino	46	0.34
Iranian	6	0.04
Irish	1,537	11.42
Italian	193	1.43
Lithuanian	17	0.13
Luxemburger	33	0.25
Norwegian	1,815	13.49
Pennsylvania German	7	0.05
Polish	169	1.26
Portuguese	21	0.16
Romanian	7	0.05
Russian	115	0.85
Scandinavian	33	0.25
Scotch-Irish	110	0.82
Scottish	102	0.76
Slovak	6	0.04
Slovene	6	0.04
Swedish	495	3.68
Swiss	38	0.28
Ukrainian	10	0.07
United States or American	597	4.44
Welsh	36	0.27
West Indian, excl. Hispanic:	10	0.07
Jamaican	5	0.04
West Indian	5	0.04
White:	12,874	95.17
Not Hispanic (12,566)	12,669	93.65
Hispanic (198)	205	1.52

Athens

Place Type: City
County: McMinn
Population: 13,220

Ancestry/Race	Number	%
African American/Black:	1,312	9.92
Not Hispanic (1,213)	1,281	9.69
Hispanic (19)	31	0.23
African, sub-Saharan:	43	0.33
African	43	0.33
Am. Ind. or Alaska Nat., not spec.	18	0.14
American Indian tribes, specified:	64	0.48
Apache (1)	1	0.01
Cherokee (15)	52	0.39
Latin American Indians (1)	1	0.01
Pueblo	3	0.02
Puget Sound Salish (1)	1	0.01
Seminole (1)	3	0.02
Shoshone (2)	2	0.02
All other tribes (1)	1	0.01
American Indian tribes, not spec.	9	0.07
Arab:	9	0.07
Syrian	9	0.07
Asian:	204	1.54
Chinese, ex. Taiwanese (7)	7	0.05
Filipino (11)	17	0.13
Indian (31)	35	0.26
Japanese (76)	82	0.62
Korean (7)	8	0.06
Laotian (36)	36	0.27
Thai (2)	2	0.02
Vietnamese (9)	9	0.07
Other Asian, not specified (2)	8	0.06
British	25	0.19
Canadian	5	0.04
Dutch	125	0.96
English	1,111	8.52
European	169	1.30
Finnish	8	0.06
French, except Basque	158	1.21
French Canadian	9	0.07
German	979	7.51
Greek	43	0.33
Hawaii Native/Pacific Islander:	16	0.12
Micronesian: (7)	7	0.05
Guamanian/Chamorro (7)	7	0.05
Polynesian: (2)	9	0.07
Native Hawaiian	7	0.05
Samoan (2)	2	0.02
Hispanic or Latino:	398	3.01
Central American:	13	0.10
Guatemalan	10	0.08
Honduran	3	0.02
Cuban	8	0.06
Dominican Republic	8	0.06
Mexican	152	1.15
Puerto Rican	30	0.23
South American:	74	0.56
Bolivian	1	0.01
Colombian	63	0.48
Ecuadorian	4	0.03
Venezuelan	6	0.05
Other Hispanic or Latino	113	0.85
Irish	1,221	9.37
Italian	55	0.42
Norwegian	67	0.51
Polish	25	0.19
Portuguese	7	0.05
Russian	7	0.05
Scotch-Irish	445	3.41
Scottish	219	1.68
Slovak	9	0.07
Swedish	105	0.81
United States or American	3,213	24.65
Welsh	26	0.20
White:	11,572	87.53
Not Hispanic (11,247)	11,383	86.10
Hispanic (166)	189	1.43
Yugoslavian	25	0.19

Bartlett

Place Type: City
County: Shelby
Population: 40,543

Ancestry/Race	Number	%
Acadian/Cajun	10	0.02
African American/Black:	2,040	5.03
Not Hispanic (1,965)	2,031	5.01
Hispanic (6)	9	0.02
African, sub-Saharan:	106	0.26
African	63	0.16
Somalian	33	0.08
South African	10	0.02
Am. Ind. or Alaska Nat., not spec.	53	0.13
American Indian tribes, specified:	153	0.38
Apache (1)	2	0.00
Blackfeet	1	0.00
Cherokee (57)	107	0.26
Chickasaw	2	0.00
Chippewa (3)	8	0.02
Choctaw (3)	7	0.02
Creek (1)	1	0.00
Iroquois (3)	3	0.01
Kiowa (1)	1	0.00
Latin American Indians (1)	2	0.00
Navajo (2)	2	0.00
Puget Sound Salish (1)	1	0.00
Sioux	6	0.01
Ute	2	0.00
All other tribes (1)	8	0.02
American Indian tribes, not spec.	17	0.04
Arab:	114	0.28
Arab/Arabic	38	0.09
Lebanese	34	0.08
Syrian	42	0.10
Asian:	626	1.54
Cambodian (5)	5	0.01
Chinese, ex. Taiwanese (128)	149	0.37
Filipino (122)	154	0.38
Hmong (6)	6	0.01
Indian (48)	59	0.15
Japanese (32)	63	0.16
Korean (58)	78	0.19
Laotian (11)	11	0.03
Malaysian	3	0.01
Pakistani (8)	8	0.02
Taiwanese (3)	4	0.01
Thai (7)	11	0.03
Vietnamese (55)	60	0.15
Other Asian, specified (1)	1	0.00
Other Asian, not specified (9)	14	0.03
Australian	22	0.05
Austrian	36	0.09
Belgian	24	0.06
Brazilian	6	0.01
British	87	0.22
Canadian	34	0.08
Czech	90	0.22
Czechoslovakian	13	0.03
Danish	89	0.22
Dutch	738	1.83
English	5,274	13.08
European	443	1.10
Finnish	36	0.09
French, except Basque	1,176	2.92
French Canadian	148	0.37
German	5,082	12.61
Greek	143	0.35
Hawaii Native/Pacific Islander:	24	0.06
Micronesian: (6)	6	0.01
Guamanian/Chamorro (6)	6	0.01
Polynesian: (9)	15	0.04
Native Hawaiian (3)	3	0.01
Samoan (5)	7	0.02
Tongan	3	0.01
Other Polynesian (1)	2	0.00

Notes: 1. Figures in the "Number" column do not add up to the total population due to: a) Ancestry/Race overlap — e.g. persons can report being both White and Irish, b) persons of Hispanic origin can report being any race, c) persons reporting two ancestries are counted in both categories. 2. Numbers in parentheses indicate the number of persons reporting this ancestry/race alone, not in combination with any other ancestry/race. 3. Refer to the Explanation of Data in the front of the book for more detailed information.

Ancestry/Race	Number	%
Other Pac. Isl., not spec. (3)	3	0.01
Hispanic or Latino:	462	1.14
Central American:	25	0.06
Costa Rican	3	0.01
Guatemalan	4	0.01
Honduran	9	0.02
Nicaraguan	3	0.01
Panamanian	1	0.00
Salvadoran	5	0.01
Cuban	24	0.06
Dominican Republic	2	0.00
Mexican	238	0.59
Puerto Rican	70	0.17
South American:	22	0.05
Argentinean	1	0.00
Bolivian	7	0.02
Chilean	2	0.00
Colombian	3	0.01
Peruvian	1	0.00
Venezuelan	8	0.02
Other Hispanic or Latino	81	0.20
Hungarian	39	0.10
Iranian	37	0.09
Irish	5,786	14.35
Italian	1,396	3.46
Latvian	8	0.02
Lithuanian	120	0.30
Northern European	22	0.05
Norwegian	257	0.64
Pennsylvania German	14	0.03
Polish	653	1.62
Portuguese	53	0.13
Romanian	8	0.02
Russian	40	0.10
Scandinavian	13	0.03
Scotch-Irish	1,805	4.48
Scottish	1,157	2.87
Serbian	8	0.02
Slovak	23	0.06
Slovene	16	0.04
Swedish	234	0.58
Swiss	35	0.09
Ukrainian	28	0.07
United States or American	5,467	13.56
Welsh	314	0.78
West Indian, excl. Hispanic:	23	0.06
British West Indian	5	0.01
Dutch West Indian	8	0.02
Haitian	5	0.01
Trinidadian and Tobagonian	5	0.01
White:	37,761	93.14
Not Hispanic (37,178)	37,438	92.34
Hispanic (298)	323	0.80

Bloomingdale

Place Type: Census Designated Place
County: Sullivan
Population: 10,350

Ancestry/Race	Number	%
African American/Black:	50	0.48
Not Hispanic (29)	49	0.47
Hispanic	1	0.01
Am. Ind. or Alaska Nat., not spec.	15	0.14
American Indian tribes, specified:	36	0.35
Apache (1)	1	0.01
Cherokee (20)	28	0.27
Creek (1)	1	0.01
All other tribes (6)	6	0.06
American Indian tribes, not spec.	1	0.01
Asian:	13	0.13
Chinese, ex. Taiwanese (1)	1	0.01
Filipino (4)	4	0.04
Indian (3)	5	0.05
Vietnamese (2)	3	0.03
British	37	0.36
Canadian	7	0.07
Dutch	254	2.45
English	1,308	12.60
European	22	0.21
French, except Basque	101	0.97
French Canadian	8	0.08
German	764	7.36
Greek	7	0.07
Hawaii Native/Pacific Islander:	2	0.02
Polynesian: (1)	2	0.02
Native Hawaiian (1)	2	0.02
Hispanic or Latino:	81	0.78
Central American:	2	0.02
Costa Rican	1	0.01
Salvadoran	1	0.01
Cuban	2	0.02
Mexican	21	0.20
Puerto Rican	5	0.05
Other Hispanic or Latino	51	0.49
Irish	1,156	11.13
Italian	108	1.04
Norwegian	7	0.07
Pennsylvania German	6	0.06
Polish	13	0.13
Scotch-Irish	125	1.20
Scottish	158	1.52
Swedish	22	0.21
United States or American	2,521	24.28
Welsh	21	0.20
White:	10,257	99.10
Not Hispanic (10,147)	10,192	98.47
Hispanic (51)	65	0.63
Yugoslavian	35	0.34

Brentwood

Place Type: City
County: Williamson
Population: 23,445

Ancestry/Race	Number	%
African American/Black:	486	2.07
Not Hispanic (442)	484	2.06
Hispanic	2	0.01
African, sub-Saharan:	98	0.41
African	24	0.10
Nigerian	31	0.13
South African	7	0.03
Zimbabwean	36	0.15
Alaska Native tribes, specified:	1	0.00
Eskimo	1	0.00
Am. Ind. or Alaska Nat., not spec.	24	0.10
Alsatian	13	0.05
American Indian tribes, specified:	38	0.16
Cherokee (9)	16	0.07
Chickasaw (2)	2	0.01
Choctaw (1)	1	0.00
Iroquois (2)	7	0.03
Latin American Indians (1)	1	0.00
Lumbee (2)	2	0.01
Osage	2	0.01
Seminole	1	0.00
All other tribes (4)	6	0.03
American Indian tribes, not spec.	2	0.01
Arab:	137	0.58
Egyptian	16	0.07
Iraqi	19	0.08
Lebanese	67	0.28
Other Arab	35	0.15
Asian:	645	2.75
Chinese, ex. Taiwanese (101)	114	0.49
Filipino (20)	25	0.11
Indian (205)	210	0.90
Japanese (118)	134	0.57
Korean (83)	88	0.38
Malaysian (4)	4	0.02
Pakistani (15)	15	0.06
Sri Lankan (1)	5	0.02
Taiwanese (6)	6	0.03
Thai (1)	2	0.01
Vietnamese (11)	12	0.05
Other Asian, specified (5)	5	0.02
Other Asian, not specified (6)	25	0.11
Australian	15	0.06
Austrian	60	0.25
British	140	0.59
Canadian	58	0.24
Czech	82	0.34
Czechoslovakian	35	0.15
Danish	83	0.35
Dutch	262	1.10
Eastern European	12	0.05
English	5,085	21.34
European	385	1.62
Finnish	57	0.24
French, except Basque	952	4.00
French Canadian	116	0.49
German	3,988	16.74
Greek	29	0.12
Hawaii Native/Pacific Islander:	2	0.01
Other Pac. Isl., not spec.	2	0.01
Hispanic or Latino:	259	1.10
Central American:	12	0.05
Guatemalan	2	0.01
Honduran	2	0.01
Nicaraguan	1	0.00
Panamanian	4	0.02
Salvadoran	1	0.00
Other Central American	2	0.01
Cuban	22	0.09
Dominican Republic	5	0.02
Mexican	90	0.38
Puerto Rican	24	0.10
South American:	34	0.15
Argentinean	2	0.01
Chilean	4	0.02
Colombian	21	0.09
Ecuadorian	5	0.02
Paraguayan	2	0.01
Other Hispanic or Latino	72	0.31
Hungarian	83	0.35
Iranian	151	0.63
Irish	2,768	11.62
Italian	692	2.90
Latvian	7	0.03
Lithuanian	17	0.07
Norwegian	280	1.18
Pennsylvania German	8	0.03
Polish	683	2.87
Portuguese	64	0.27
Romanian	26	0.11
Russian	114	0.48
Scandinavian	52	0.22
Scotch-Irish	1,293	5.43
Scottish	1,004	4.21
Slovak	34	0.14
Slovene	21	0.09
Swedish	217	0.91
Swiss	152	0.64
Ukrainian	12	0.05
United States or American	2,613	10.97
Welsh	270	1.13
White:	22,323	95.21
Not Hispanic (21,976)	22,094	94.24
Hispanic (211)	229	0.98
Yugoslavian	66	0.28

Bristol

Place Type: City
County: Sullivan
Population: 24,821

Ancestry/Race	Number	%
African American/Black:	783	3.15
Not Hispanic (728)	774	3.12
Hispanic (8)	9	0.04
African, sub-Saharan:	25	0.10
African	14	0.06
Kenyan	11	0.04
Alaska Native tribes, specified:	2	0.01
Aleut (1)	1	0.00
Eskimo (1)	1	0.00

Notes: 1. Figures in the "Number" column do not add up to the total population due to: a) Ancestry/Race overlap — e.g. persons can report being both White and Irish, b) persons of Hispanic origin can report being any race, c) persons reporting two ancestries are counted in both categories. 2. Numbers in parentheses indicate the number of persons reporting this ancestry/race alone, not in combination with any other ancestry/race. 3. Refer to the Explanation of Data in the front of the book for more detailed information.

Alaska Native tribes, not specified	1	0.00
Am. Ind. or Alaska Nat., not spec.	39	0.16
Albanian	6	0.02
American Indian tribes, specified:	123	0.50
Apache (3)	3	0.01
Blackfeet (1)	6	0.02
Cherokee (37)	90	0.36
Cheyenne	1	0.00
Choctaw	2	0.01
Iroquois (3)	3	0.01
Lumbee (3)	4	0.02
Sioux (2)	5	0.02
All other tribes (9)	9	0.04
American Indian tribes, not spec.	16	0.06
Arab:	41	0.16
Lebanese	23	0.09
Syrian	18	0.07
Asian:	177	0.71
Bangladeshi (1)	1	0.00
Chinese, ex. Taiwanese (26)	27	0.11
Filipino (18)	22	0.09
Indian (56)	57	0.23
Japanese (12)	13	0.05
Korean (12)	17	0.07
Laotian (5)	5	0.02
Malaysian (1)	1	0.00
Pakistani (2)	2	0.01
Thai (2)	2	0.01
Vietnamese (20)	21	0.08
Other Asian, specified (1)	2	0.01
Other Asian, not specified (2)	7	0.03
Assyrian/Chaldean/Syriac	6	0.02
Australian	4	0.02
Austrian	13	0.05
Belgian	6	0.02
British	57	0.23
Canadian	14	0.06
Celtic	5	0.02
Czech	6	0.02
Danish	20	0.08
Dutch	414	1.66
English	2,998	12.00
European	126	0.50
French, except Basque	326	1.30
French Canadian	39	0.16
German	2,667	10.68
Greek	29	0.12
Hawaii Native/Pacific Islander:	9	0.04
Micronesian: (2)	2	0.01
Guamanian/Chamorro (2)	2	0.01
Polynesian:	5	0.02
Native Hawaiian	5	0.02
Other Pac. Isl., specified	1	0.00
Other Pac. Isl., not spec.	1	0.00
Hispanic or Latino:	170	0.68
Central American:	8	0.03
Guatemalan	1	0.00
Honduran	4	0.02
Panamanian	2	0.01
Other Central American	1	0.00
Cuban	1	0.00
Mexican	82	0.33
Puerto Rican	24	0.10
South American:	6	0.02
Chilean	2	0.01
Colombian	2	0.01
Peruvian	1	0.00
Venezuelan	1	0.00
Other Hispanic or Latino	49	0.20
Hungarian	62	0.25
Irish	2,438	9.76
Italian	354	1.42
Northern European	9	0.04
Norwegian	54	0.22
Polish	228	0.91
Russian	6	0.02
Scandinavian	7	0.03
Scotch-Irish	962	3.85
Scottish	405	1.62
Swedish	98	0.39
Swiss	18	0.07
Ukrainian	79	0.32
United States or American	4,452	17.82
Welsh	147	0.59
West Indian, excl. Hispanic:	15	0.06
Dutch West Indian	15	0.06
White:	23,774	95.78
Not Hispanic (23,496)	23,649	95.28
Hispanic (121)	125	0.50
Yugoslavian	63	0.25

Brownsville

Place Type: City
County: Haywood
Population: 10,748

Ancestry/Race	Number	%
African American/Black:	6,554	60.98
Not Hispanic (6,496)	6,518	60.64
Hispanic (30)	36	0.33
African, sub-Saharan:	17	0.16
African	17	0.16
Am. Ind. or Alaska Nat., not spec.	11	0.10
American Indian tribes, specified:	19	0.18
Cherokee	10	0.09
Choctaw (1)	1	0.01
Creek (1)	1	0.01
Sioux	2	0.02
All other tribes	5	0.05
American Indian tribes, not spec.	8	0.07
Asian:	19	0.18
Chinese, ex. Taiwanese (4)	4	0.04
Filipino (4)	4	0.04
Indian (3)	7	0.07
Other Asian, specified	1	0.01
Other Asian, not specified	3	0.03
Belgian	20	0.19
British	10	0.09
Canadian	8	0.07
Czech	6	0.06
Danish	9	0.08
Dutch	15	0.14
English	439	4.09
European	111	1.03
French, except Basque	40	0.37
French Canadian	30	0.28
German	136	1.27
Hawaii Native/Pacific Islander:	12	0.11
Polynesian: (1)	4	0.04
Native Hawaiian (1)	1	0.01
Samoan	3	0.03
Other Pac. Isl., specified	1	0.01
Other Pac. Isl., not spec. (7)	7	0.07
Hispanic or Latino:	388	3.61
Central American:	21	0.20
Guatemalan	4	0.04
Honduran	10	0.09
Salvadoran	7	0.07
Mexican	304	2.83
Puerto Rican	5	0.05
South American:	2	0.02
Ecuadorian	2	0.02
Other Hispanic or Latino	56	0.52
Iranian	8	0.07
Irish	327	3.05
Italian	61	0.57
Polish	11	0.10
Scotch-Irish	181	1.69
Scottish	45	0.42
Swedish	36	0.34
United States or American	1,084	10.10
Welsh	30	0.28
White:	3,976	36.99
Not Hispanic (3,799)	3,831	35.64
Hispanic (126)	145	1.35

Chattanooga

Place Type: City
County: Hamilton
Population: 155,554

Ancestry/Race	Number	%
Acadian/Cajun	14	0.01
African American/Black:	57,034	36.67
Not Hispanic (55,874)	56,764	36.49
Hispanic (212)	270	0.17
African, sub-Saharan:	1,024	0.66
African	992	0.64
Ghanian	15	0.01
Nigerian	9	0.01
Zimbabwean	8	0.01
Alaska Native tribes, specified:	4	0.00
Alaska Athabascan	1	0.00
Eskimo (1)	2	0.00
Tlingit-Haida (1)	1	0.00
Am. Ind. or Alaska Nat., not spec.	307	0.20
Albanian	7	0.00
American Indian tribes, specified:	754	0.48
Apache (5)	13	0.01
Blackfeet (6)	17	0.01
Cherokee (181)	529	0.34
Cheyenne (1)	1	0.00
Chickasaw (1)	2	0.00
Chippewa (8)	8	0.01
Choctaw (6)	9	0.01
Comanche (2)	2	0.00
Cree	1	0.00
Creek (4)	14	0.01
Crow (2)	7	0.00
Delaware (1)	3	0.00
Iroquois (9)	17	0.01
Kiowa	1	0.00
Latin American Indians (39)	45	0.03
Lumbee (8)	10	0.01
Navajo (1)	2	0.00
Osage (1)	1	0.00
Ottawa (3)	4	0.00
Potawatomi (1)	3	0.00
Pueblo (1)	1	0.00
Puget Sound Salish	1	0.00
Seminole	8	0.01
Shoshone (1)	5	0.00
Sioux (7)	16	0.01
All other tribes (14)	34	0.02
American Indian tribes, not spec.	62	0.04
Arab:	352	0.23
Arab/Arabic	41	0.03
Egyptian	55	0.04
Iraqi	46	0.03
Jordanian	10	0.01
Lebanese	63	0.04
Palestinian	106	0.07
Syrian	6	0.00
Other Arab	25	0.02
Armenian	36	0.02
Asian:	2,795	1.80
Bangladeshi (3)	7	0.00
Cambodian (74)	83	0.05
Chinese, ex. Taiwanese (276)	328	0.21
Filipino (215)	288	0.19
Indian (933)	1,016	0.65
Indonesian (11)	11	0.01
Japanese (117)	142	0.09
Korean (227)	264	0.17
Laotian (28)	39	0.03
Pakistani (79)	95	0.06
Sri Lankan (4)	4	0.00
Taiwanese (40)	50	0.03
Thai (11)	16	0.01
Vietnamese (300)	323	0.21
Other Asian, specified (5)	27	0.02
Other Asian, not specified (50)	102	0.07
Australian	15	0.01
Austrian	80	0.05
Basque	10	0.01

Notes: 1. Figures in the "Number" column do not add up to the total population due to: a) Ancestry/Race overlap — e.g. persons can report being both White and Irish, b) persons of Hispanic origin can report being any race, c) persons reporting two ancestries are counted in both categories. 2. Numbers in parentheses indicate the number of persons reporting this ancestry/race alone, not in combination with any other ancestry/race. 3. Refer to the Explanation of Data in the front of the book for more detailed information.

Belgian	22	0.01
Brazilian	28	0.02
British	708	0.46
Bulgarian	28	0.02
Canadian	181	0.12
Celtic	40	0.03
Croatian	18	0.01
Czech	131	0.08
Czechoslovakian	148	0.10
Danish	119	0.08
Dutch	1,759	1.13
Eastern European	56	0.04
English	12,281	7.90
European	908	0.58
Finnish	156	0.10
French, except Basque	2,377	1.53
French Canadian	252	0.16
German	9,989	6.42
German Russian	22	0.01
Greek	360	0.23
Hawaii Native/Pacific Islander:	270	0.17
Melanesian: (1)	1	0.00
Fijian (1)	1	0.00
Micronesian: (106)	120	0.08
Guamanian/Chamorro (106)	120	0.08
Polynesian: (40)	65	0.04
Native Hawaiian (11)	20	0.01
Samoan (29)	44	0.03
Tongan	1	0.00
Other Pac. Isl., specified	16	0.01
Other Pac. Isl., not spec. (17)	68	0.04
Hispanic or Latino:	3,281	2.11
Central American:	626	0.40
Costa Rican	14	0.01
Guatemalan	556	0.36
Honduran	19	0.01
Nicaraguan	5	0.00
Panamanian	12	0.01
Salvadoran	11	0.01
Other Central American	9	0.01
Cuban	121	0.08
Dominican Republic	30	0.02
Mexican	1,637	1.05
Puerto Rican	255	0.16
South American:	90	0.06
Argentinean	5	0.00
Bolivian	2	0.00
Chilean	5	0.00
Colombian	44	0.03
Ecuadorian	5	0.00
Paraguayan	1	0.00
Peruvian	10	0.01
Venezuelan	14	0.01
Other South American	4	0.00
Other Hispanic or Latino	522	0.34
Hungarian	206	0.13
Icelander	7	0.00
Iranian	89	0.06
Irish	11,615	7.47
Italian	1,712	1.10
Latvian	18	0.01
Lithuanian	119	0.08
Luxemburger	8	0.01
New Zealander	5	0.00
Northern European	73	0.05
Norwegian	418	0.27
Pennsylvania German	16	0.01
Polish	756	0.49
Portuguese	38	0.02
Romanian	23	0.01
Russian	300	0.19
Scandinavian	64	0.04
Scotch-Irish	3,429	2.21
Scottish	2,956	1.90
Serbian	33	0.02
Slavic	35	0.02
Slovak	43	0.03
Slovene	28	0.02
Swedish	524	0.34
Swiss	263	0.17
Turkish	10	0.01
Ukrainian	93	0.06
United States or American	19,092	12.28
Welsh	713	0.46
West Indian, excl. Hispanic:	277	0.18
Bahamian	10	0.01
Barbadian	34	0.02
Bermudan	6	0.00
British West Indian	17	0.01
Dutch West Indian	11	0.01
Haitian	13	0.01
Jamaican	136	0.09
Trinidadian and Tobagonian	22	0.01
West Indian	28	0.02
White:	94,482	60.74
Not Hispanic (91,582)	93,003	59.79
Hispanic (1,292)	1,479	0.95
Yugoslavian	165	0.11

Clarksville

Place Type: City
County: Montgomery
Population: 103,455

Ancestry/Race	Number	%
Acadian/Cajun	21	0.02
Afghan	7	0.01
African American/Black:	25,536	24.68
Not Hispanic (23,692)	24,968	24.13
Hispanic (338)	568	0.55
African, sub-Saharan:	1,218	1.17
African	1,147	1.11
Cape Verdean	22	0.02
Ethiopian	4	0.00
Liberian	6	0.01
Nigerian	6	0.01
South African	33	0.03
Alaska Native tribes, specified:	13	0.01
Alaska Athabascan (5)	5	0.00
Aleut (1)	2	0.00
Eskimo (3)	6	0.01
Alaska Native tribes, not specified	6	0.01
Am. Ind. or Alaska Nat., not spec.	371	0.36
Albanian	15	0.01
American Indian tribes, specified:	894	0.86
Apache (14)	33	0.03
Blackfeet (6)	41	0.04
Cherokee (124)	423	0.41
Cheyenne (1)	2	0.00
Chickasaw (1)	18	0.02
Chippewa (18)	27	0.03
Choctaw (18)	30	0.03
Comanche (7)	12	0.01
Creek (6)	19	0.02
Crow (1)	1	0.00
Delaware (9)	12	0.01
Iroquois (15)	32	0.03
Kiowa (1)	1	0.00
Latin American Indians (14)	35	0.03
Lumbee (14)	17	0.02
Menominee	1	0.00
Navajo (19)	28	0.03
Osage (3)	3	0.00
Paiute (1)	1	0.00
Pima (2)	3	0.00
Potawatomi	1	0.00
Pueblo (4)	12	0.01
Seminole (1)	5	0.00
Shoshone (1)	2	0.00
Sioux (31)	53	0.05
Tohono O'Odham (1)	2	0.00
Ute	2	0.00
Yaqui (3)	5	0.00
All other tribes (41)	73	0.07
American Indian tribes, not spec.	66	0.06
Arab:	118	0.11
Arab/Arabic	9	0.01
Egyptian	45	0.04
Jordanian	5	0.00
Lebanese	26	0.03
Palestinian	5	0.00
Syrian	28	0.03
Armenian	31	0.03
Asian:	3,368	3.26
Bangladeshi (13)	13	0.01
Cambodian (8)	9	0.01
Chinese, ex. Taiwanese (93)	184	0.18
Filipino (348)	580	0.56
Hmong (1)	1	0.00
Indian (269)	301	0.29
Indonesian (7)	11	0.01
Japanese (169)	291	0.28
Korean (1,021)	1,538	1.49
Laotian (11)	18	0.02
Malaysian (2)	4	0.00
Pakistani (1)	3	0.00
Taiwanese (2)	4	0.00
Thai (62)	95	0.09
Vietnamese (114)	155	0.15
Other Asian, specified (6)	17	0.02
Other Asian, not specified (70)	144	0.14
Australian	8	0.01
Austrian	131	0.13
Belgian	21	0.02
British	313	0.30
Bulgarian	4	0.00
Canadian	103	0.10
Celtic	51	0.05
Croatian	75	0.07
Czech	298	0.29
Czechoslovakian	171	0.16
Danish	210	0.20
Dutch	1,573	1.52
Eastern European	24	0.02
English	7,722	7.44
Estonian	7	0.01
European	971	0.94
Finnish	139	0.13
French, except Basque	2,079	2.00
French Canadian	702	0.68
German	13,035	12.56
German Russian	9	0.01
Greek	199	0.19
Guyanese	7	0.01
Hawaii Native/Pacific Islander:	483	0.47
Melanesian: (1)	5	0.00
Fijian (1)	1	0.00
Other Melanesian	4	0.00
Micronesian: (119)	164	0.16
Guamanian/Chamorro (93)	130	0.13
Other Micronesian (26)	34	0.03
Polynesian: (124)	227	0.22
Native Hawaiian (48)	118	0.11
Samoan (75)	107	0.10
Other Polynesian (1)	2	0.00
Other Pac. Isl., specified	7	0.01
Other Pac. Isl., not spec. (13)	80	0.08
Hispanic or Latino:	6,241	6.03
Central American:	485	0.47
Costa Rican	12	0.01
Guatemalan	35	0.03
Honduran	44	0.04
Nicaraguan	15	0.01
Panamanian	333	0.32
Salvadoran	43	0.04
Other Central American	3	0.00
Cuban	144	0.14
Dominican Republic	77	0.07
Mexican	2,375	2.30
Puerto Rican	2,045	1.98
South American:	138	0.13
Argentinean	12	0.01
Bolivian	6	0.01
Chilean	5	0.00
Colombian	64	0.06
Ecuadorian	8	0.01
Peruvian	28	0.03
Uruguayan	2	0.00
Venezuelan	9	0.01

Notes: 1. Figures in the "Number" column do not add up to the total population due to: a) Ancestry/Race overlap — e.g. persons can report being both White and Irish, b) persons of Hispanic origin can report being any race, c) persons reporting two ancestries are counted in both categories. 2. Numbers in parentheses indicate the number of persons reporting this ancestry/race alone, not in combination with any other ancestry/race. 3. Refer to the Explanation of Data in the front of the book for more detailed information.

Ancestry/Race	Number	%
Other South American	4	0.00
Other Hispanic or Latino	977	0.94
Hungarian	269	0.26
Iranian	65	0.06
Irish	10,002	9.64
Italian	2,868	2.76
Latvian	15	0.01
Lithuanian	49	0.05
New Zealander	4	0.00
Northern European	41	0.04
Norwegian	547	0.53
Pennsylvania German	13	0.01
Polish	1,294	1.25
Portuguese	182	0.18
Romanian	8	0.01
Russian	239	0.23
Scandinavian	190	0.18
Scotch-Irish	2,192	2.11
Scottish	1,886	1.82
Serbian	4	0.00
Slavic	20	0.02
Slovak	55	0.05
Swedish	722	0.70
Swiss	137	0.13
Turkish	8	0.01
Ukrainian	92	0.09
United States or American	11,205	10.80
Welsh	464	0.45
West Indian, excl. Hispanic:	439	0.42
Bahamian	8	0.01
Belizean	5	0.00
Bermudan	6	0.01
British West Indian	62	0.06
Dutch West Indian	10	0.01
Haitian	26	0.03
Jamaican	267	0.26
U.S. Virgin Islander	14	0.01
West Indian	41	0.04
White:	72,960	70.52
Not Hispanic (67,562)	69,797	67.47
Hispanic (2,692)	3,163	3.06
Yugoslavian	217	0.21

Cleveland

Place Type: City
County: Bradley
Population: 37,192

Ancestry/Race	Number	%
Acadian/Cajun	9	0.02
African American/Black:	2,791	7.50
Not Hispanic (2,588)	2,751	7.40
Hispanic (20)	40	0.11
African, sub-Saharan:	128	0.34
African	108	0.29
Other sub-Saharan African	20	0.05
Am. Ind. or Alaska Nat., not spec.	99	0.27
American Indian tribes, specified:	196	0.53
Apache (3)	7	0.02
Blackfeet (1)	7	0.02
Cherokee (26)	125	0.34
Chickasaw (1)	1	0.00
Chippewa (1)	3	0.01
Choctaw (2)	6	0.02
Comanche (1)	1	0.00
Creek (4)	6	0.02
Crow (1)	1	0.00
Iroquois (4)	8	0.02
Latin American Indians (7)	14	0.04
Lumbee (1)	1	0.00
Navajo (1)	2	0.01
Potawatomi (1)	1	0.00
Pueblo	3	0.01
Sioux	5	0.01
Yaqui	1	0.00
All other tribes (1)	4	0.01
American Indian tribes, not spec.	12	0.03
Arab:	35	0.09
Egyptian	12	0.03
Palestinian	4	0.01
Other Arab	19	0.05
Armenian	23	0.06
Asian:	449	1.21
Chinese, ex. Taiwanese (27)	45	0.12
Filipino (19)	36	0.10
Indian (227)	247	0.66
Japanese (12)	20	0.05
Korean (30)	40	0.11
Laotian (15)	15	0.04
Taiwanese (1)	1	0.00
Thai (1)	4	0.01
Vietnamese (16)	18	0.05
Other Asian, specified	1	0.00
Other Asian, not specified (7)	22	0.06
Austrian	37	0.10
Belgian	15	0.04
Brazilian	37	0.10
British	231	0.62
Bulgarian	20	0.05
Canadian	38	0.10
Celtic	23	0.06
Czech	94	0.25
Czechoslovakian	20	0.05
Danish	64	0.17
Dutch	630	1.70
Eastern European	9	0.02
English	3,867	10.41
Estonian	6	0.02
European	272	0.73
Finnish	17	0.05
French, except Basque	627	1.69
French Canadian	80	0.22
German	3,383	9.11
Greek	86	0.23
Guyanese	12	0.03
Hawaii Native/Pacific Islander:	44	0.12
Micronesian: (4)	7	0.02
Guamanian/Chamorro (1)	1	0.00
Other Micronesian (3)	6	0.02
Polynesian: (5)	23	0.06
Native Hawaiian (2)	16	0.04
Samoan (3)	6	0.02
Other Polynesian	1	0.00
Other Pac. Isl., specified	1	0.00
Other Pac. Isl., not spec. (2)	13	0.03
Hispanic or Latino:	1,066	2.87
Central American:	67	0.18
Costa Rican	3	0.01
Guatemalan	27	0.07
Honduran	25	0.07
Nicaraguan	3	0.01
Panamanian	6	0.02
Salvadoran	2	0.01
Other Central American	1	0.00
Cuban	21	0.06
Dominican Republic	15	0.04
Mexican	577	1.55
Puerto Rican	171	0.46
South American:	58	0.16
Argentinean	7	0.02
Chilean	10	0.03
Colombian	16	0.04
Ecuadorian	16	0.04
Peruvian	5	0.01
Venezuelan	2	0.01
Other South American	2	0.01
Other Hispanic or Latino	157	0.42
Hungarian	76	0.20
Iranian	48	0.13
Irish	4,052	10.91
Italian	729	1.96
Lithuanian	37	0.10
Norwegian	237	0.64
Pennsylvania German	21	0.06
Polish	330	0.89
Romanian	6	0.02
Russian	72	0.19
Scotch-Irish	929	2.50
Scottish	646	1.74
Slovak	30	0.08
Swedish	278	0.75
Swiss	10	0.03
Ukrainian	112	0.30
United States or American	6,496	17.49
Welsh	167	0.45
West Indian, excl. Hispanic:	170	0.46
Bahamian	41	0.11
Belizean	8	0.02
Bermudan	9	0.02
Dutch West Indian	19	0.05
Jamaican	57	0.15
Trinidadian and Tobagonian	13	0.04
West Indian	23	0.06
White:	33,575	90.27
Not Hispanic (32,611)	33,017	88.77
Hispanic (491)	558	1.50
Yugoslavian	17	0.05

Collierville

Place Type: Town
County: Shelby
Population: 31,872

Ancestry/Race	Number	%
African American/Black:	2,382	7.47
Not Hispanic (2,332)	2,367	7.43
Hispanic (5)	15	0.05
African, sub-Saharan:	126	0.40
African	44	0.14
Ethiopian	44	0.14
Zimbabwean	38	0.12
Alaska Native tribes, specified:	1	0.00
Tlingit-Haida (1)	1	0.00
Am. Ind. or Alaska Nat., not spec.	42	0.13
American Indian tribes, specified:	87	0.27
Blackfeet (2)	2	0.01
Cherokee (19)	41	0.13
Chippewa (1)	2	0.01
Choctaw (3)	15	0.05
Creek (4)	4	0.01
Iroquois (1)	1	0.00
Latin American Indians (1)	2	0.01
Lumbee	3	0.01
Potawatomi	5	0.02
Shoshone (1)	1	0.00
Sioux (1)	1	0.00
All other tribes (7)	10	0.03
American Indian tribes, not spec.	7	0.02
Arab:	114	0.36
Egyptian	15	0.05
Lebanese	25	0.08
Palestinian	39	0.12
Syrian	35	0.11
Armenian	7	0.02
Asian:	559	1.75
Cambodian (7)	7	0.02
Chinese, ex. Taiwanese (127)	148	0.46
Filipino (22)	42	0.13
Indian (82)	94	0.29
Indonesian (3)	3	0.01
Japanese (33)	46	0.14
Korean (137)	146	0.46
Laotian (2)	2	0.01
Malaysian (1)	1	0.00
Pakistani (6)	7	0.02
Taiwanese (3)	10	0.03
Thai (3)	4	0.01
Vietnamese (35)	36	0.11
Other Asian, not specified (1)	13	0.04
Austrian	86	0.27
Belgian	5	0.02
Brazilian	11	0.03
British	245	0.77
Canadian	81	0.25
Czech	63	0.20
Czechoslovakian	54	0.17
Danish	34	0.11
Dutch	355	1.11

Notes: 1. Figures in the "Number" column do not add up to the total population due to: a) Ancestry/Race overlap — e.g. persons can report being both White and Irish, b) persons of Hispanic origin can report being any race, c) persons reporting two ancestries are counted in both categories. 2. Numbers in parentheses indicate the number of persons reporting this ancestry/race alone, not in combination with any other ancestry/race. 3. Refer to the Explanation of Data in the front of the book for more detailed information.

English	4,526	14.20
European	593	1.86
Finnish	51	0.16
French, except Basque	919	2.88
French Canadian	131	0.41
German	4,102	12.87
Greek	109	0.34
Hawaii Native/Pacific Islander:	21	0.07
Micronesian:	3	0.01
Guamanian/Chamorro	3	0.01
Polynesian: (3)	12	0.04
Native Hawaiian (3)	12	0.04
Other Pac. Isl., not spec. (1)	6	0.02
Hispanic or Latino:	481	1.51
Central American:	13	0.04
Costa Rican	2	0.01
Guatemalan	2	0.01
Panamanian	3	0.01
Salvadoran	1	0.00
Other Central American	5	0.02
Cuban	25	0.08
Mexican	244	0.77
Puerto Rican	68	0.21
South American:	31	0.10
Argentinean	5	0.02
Chilean	1	0.00
Colombian	12	0.04
Ecuadorian	2	0.01
Peruvian	2	0.01
Venezuelan	9	0.03
Other Hispanic or Latino	100	0.31
Hungarian	50	0.16
Irish	3,936	12.35
Italian	1,479	4.64
Norwegian	261	0.82
Polish	548	1.72
Romanian	7	0.02
Russian	140	0.44
Scandinavian	62	0.19
Scotch-Irish	1,106	3.47
Scottish	1,097	3.44
Serbian	57	0.18
Slavic	8	0.03
Slovak	35	0.11
Swedish	251	0.79
Swiss	67	0.21
Ukrainian	45	0.14
United States or American	4,588	14.39
Welsh	215	0.67
West Indian, excl. Hispanic:	10	0.03
Haitian	10	0.03
White:	28,868	90.57
Not Hispanic (28,337)	28,513	89.46
Hispanic (306)	355	1.11
Yugoslavian	22	0.07

Columbia

Place Type: City
County: Maury
Population: 33,055

Ancestry/Race	Number	%
African American/Black:	7,235	21.89
Not Hispanic (6,920)	7,054	21.34
Hispanic (64)	181	0.55
African, sub-Saharan:	277	0.84
African	219	0.66
Nigerian	58	0.18
Am. Ind. or Alaska Nat., not spec.	79	0.24
Albanian	9	0.03
American Indian tribes, specified:	124	0.38
Apache (2)	2	0.01
Blackfeet (1)	3	0.01
Cherokee (15)	47	0.14
Cheyenne (3)	3	0.01
Chippewa (12)	12	0.04
Creek (2)	2	0.01
Iroquois (1)	5	0.02
Latin American Indians (1)	32	0.10
Menominee (1)	1	0.00
Navajo (1)	1	0.00
Osage	1	0.00
Ottawa (1)	1	0.00
Paiute (1)	2	0.01
Shoshone	1	0.00
Sioux (1)	10	0.03
All other tribes (1)	1	0.00
American Indian tribes, not spec.	4	0.01
Arab:	68	0.21
Lebanese	45	0.14
Syrian	23	0.07
Asian:	179	0.54
Chinese, ex. Taiwanese (8)	13	0.04
Filipino (37)	43	0.13
Indian (51)	66	0.20
Japanese (10)	11	0.03
Korean (5)	7	0.02
Pakistani (9)	10	0.03
Thai (1)	1	0.00
Vietnamese (9)	10	0.03
Other Asian, not specified (5)	18	0.05
Austrian	17	0.05
Belgian	4	0.01
British	93	0.28
Canadian	71	0.21
Celtic	10	0.03
Croatian	16	0.05
Czech	7	0.02
Czechoslovakian	6	0.02
Danish	46	0.14
Dutch	388	1.17
English	2,419	7.32
European	219	0.66
Finnish	34	0.10
French, except Basque	639	1.93
French Canadian	101	0.31
German	2,335	7.06
Greek	6	0.02
Hawaii Native/Pacific Islander:	22	0.07
Micronesian: (6)	8	0.02
Guamanian/Chamorro (6)	8	0.02
Polynesian: (2)	10	0.03
Native Hawaiian (2)	9	0.03
Samoan	1	0.00
Other Pac. Isl., not spec. (1)	4	0.01
Hispanic or Latino:	1,554	4.70
Central American:	21	0.06
Guatemalan	13	0.04
Honduran	1	0.00
Nicaraguan	2	0.01
Panamanian	2	0.01
Salvadoran	2	0.01
Other Central American	1	0.00
Cuban	51	0.15
Dominican Republic	19	0.06
Mexican	1,226	3.71
Puerto Rican	42	0.13
South American:	27	0.08
Argentinean	1	0.00
Chilean	1	0.00
Colombian	13	0.04
Ecuadorian	1	0.00
Peruvian	5	0.02
Venezuelan	1	0.00
Other South American	5	0.02
Other Hispanic or Latino	168	0.51
Hungarian	46	0.14
Icelander	8	0.02
Irish	2,688	8.13
Italian	514	1.55
Lithuanian	60	0.18
Norwegian	89	0.27
Polish	342	1.03
Portuguese	15	0.05
Romanian	44	0.13
Russian	40	0.12
Scotch-Irish	821	2.48
Scottish	365	1.10
Serbian	16	0.05
Swedish	157	0.47
Swiss	39	0.12
United States or American	6,140	18.57
Welsh	88	0.27
White:	25,084	75.89
Not Hispanic (24,049)	24,288	73.48
Hispanic (620)	796	2.41

Cookeville

Place Type: City
County: Putnam
Population: 23,923

Ancestry/Race	Number	%
Acadian/Cajun	6	0.02
African American/Black:	775	3.24
Not Hispanic (692)	768	3.21
Hispanic (5)	7	0.03
African, sub-Saharan:	56	0.23
African	47	0.19
Ghanian	4	0.02
Other sub-Saharan African	5	0.02
Am. Ind. or Alaska Nat., not spec.	50	0.21
Albanian	21	0.09
American Indian tribes, specified:	68	0.28
Apache	3	0.01
Blackfeet (2)	10	0.04
Cherokee (8)	38	0.16
Chickasaw (2)	2	0.01
Chippewa (1)	1	0.00
Choctaw (1)	1	0.00
Comanche (1)	2	0.01
Creek	1	0.00
Iroquois (1)	2	0.01
Latin American Indians (1)	2	0.01
Ottawa (1)	1	0.00
Paiute	1	0.00
Pueblo	2	0.01
Sioux (1)	1	0.00
All other tribes (1)	1	0.00
American Indian tribes, not spec.	10	0.04
Arab:	46	0.19
Arab/Arabic	33	0.14
Lebanese	7	0.03
Other Arab	6	0.02
Asian:	525	2.19
Bangladeshi (2)	8	0.03
Chinese, ex. Taiwanese (99)	100	0.42
Filipino (38)	53	0.22
Indian (212)	235	0.98
Indonesian	2	0.01
Japanese (13)	25	0.10
Korean (19)	25	0.10
Laotian (7)	7	0.03
Malaysian	3	0.01
Sri Lankan (1)	1	0.00
Taiwanese (6)	6	0.03
Thai (10)	10	0.04
Vietnamese (16)	17	0.07
Other Asian, specified	2	0.01
Other Asian, not specified (17)	31	0.13
Austrian	29	0.12
Basque	18	0.07
Belgian	8	0.03
British	140	0.58
Canadian	26	0.11
Celtic	7	0.03
Croatian	8	0.03
Czech	20	0.08
Czechoslovakian	33	0.14
Danish	16	0.07
Dutch	263	1.09
Eastern European	8	0.03
English	2,718	11.25
European	262	1.08
Finnish	5	0.02
French, except Basque	450	1.86
French Canadian	111	0.46
German	2,143	8.87

Notes: 1. Figures in the "Number" column do not add up to the total population due to: a) Ancestry/Race overlap — e.g. persons can report being both White and Irish, b) persons of Hispanic origin can report being any race, c) persons reporting two ancestries are counted in both categories. 2. Numbers in parentheses indicate the number of persons reporting this ancestry/race alone, not in combination with any other ancestry/race. 3. Refer to the Explanation of Data in the front of the book for more detailed information.

Ancestry/Race	Number	%
Greek	24	0.10
Hawaii Native/Pacific Islander:	64	0.27
Micronesian: (42)	43	0.18
Guamanian/Chamorro (42)	43	0.18
Polynesian: (8)	13	0.05
Native Hawaiian (2)	6	0.03
Samoan (6)	7	0.03
Other Pac. Isl., specified	2	0.01
Other Pac. Isl., not spec.	6	0.03
Hispanic or Latino:	1,009	4.22
Central American:	305	1.27
Costa Rican	5	0.02
Guatemalan	288	1.20
Honduran	2	0.01
Nicaraguan	1	0.00
Panamanian	2	0.01
Salvadoran	1	0.00
Other Central American	6	0.03
Cuban	14	0.06
Dominican Republic	2	0.01
Mexican	525	2.19
Puerto Rican	19	0.08
South American:	15	0.06
Argentinean	3	0.01
Bolivian	1	0.00
Chilean	1	0.00
Colombian	6	0.03
Ecuadorian	1	0.00
Venezuelan	2	0.01
Other South American	1	0.00
Other Hispanic or Latino	129	0.54
Hungarian	21	0.09
Irish	2,217	9.18
Italian	330	1.37
Lithuanian	50	0.21
New Zealander	1	0.00
Norwegian	103	0.43
Polish	186	0.77
Portuguese	23	0.10
Romanian	5	0.02
Russian	42	0.17
Scandinavian	25	0.10
Scotch-Irish	950	3.93
Scottish	522	2.16
Serbian	29	0.12
Swedish	52	0.22
Swiss	10	0.04
Turkish	16	0.07
Ukrainian	19	0.08
United States or American	5,277	21.84
Welsh	183	0.76
West Indian, excl. Hispanic:	16	0.07
Jamaican	16	0.07
White:	22,034	92.10
Not Hispanic (21,439)	21,653	90.51
Hispanic (358)	381	1.59
Yugoslavian	44	0.18

Dickson

Place Type: City
County: Dickson
Population: 12,244

Ancestry/Race	Number	%
African American/Black:	1,176	9.60
Not Hispanic (1,062)	1,157	9.45
Hispanic (19)	19	0.16
African, sub-Saharan:	53	0.42
African	53	0.42
Am. Ind. or Alaska Nat., not spec.	50	0.41
American Indian tribes, specified:	79	0.65
Apache	2	0.02
Blackfeet (1)	5	0.04
Cherokee (12)	35	0.29
Cheyenne (1)	2	0.02
Chickasaw (2)	2	0.02
Choctaw (3)	5	0.04
Creek (2)	4	0.03
Iroquois (1)	4	0.03
Kiowa (1)	1	0.01
Latin American Indians (1)	1	0.01
Menominee (1)	1	0.01
Osage	1	0.01
Paiute	2	0.02
Pueblo (6)	8	0.07
Shoshone	1	0.01
All other tribes (1)	5	0.04
American Indian tribes, not spec.	2	0.02
Arab:	16	0.13
Arab/Arabic	16	0.13
Asian:	83	0.68
Chinese, ex. Taiwanese (2)	3	0.02
Filipino (5)	9	0.07
Hmong (1)	1	0.01
Indian (28)	29	0.24
Japanese (16)	21	0.17
Korean (1)	1	0.01
Laotian (4)	5	0.04
Vietnamese (11)	13	0.11
Other Asian, not specified	1	0.01
Belgian	34	0.27
British	23	0.18
Canadian	7	0.06
Czech	12	0.10
Danish	8	0.06
Dutch	55	0.44
Eastern European	16	0.13
English	842	6.73
European	55	0.44
French, except Basque	216	1.73
French Canadian	38	0.30
German	939	7.51
Greek	61	0.49
Hispanic or Latino:	238	1.94
Central American:	13	0.11
Costa Rican	1	0.01
Guatemalan	9	0.07
Salvadoran	3	0.02
Cuban	5	0.04
Mexican	164	1.34
Puerto Rican	30	0.25
South American:	2	0.02
Colombian	1	0.01
Venezuelan	1	0.01
Other Hispanic or Latino	24	0.20
Hungarian	8	0.06
Irish	1,185	9.47
Italian	200	1.60
Norwegian	15	0.12
Polish	81	0.65
Russian	8	0.06
Scandinavian	8	0.06
Scotch-Irish	260	2.08
Scottish	237	1.89
Slavic	11	0.09
Swedish	11	0.09
Swiss	22	0.18
Ukrainian	11	0.09
United States or American	2,352	18.81
Welsh	86	0.69
West Indian, excl. Hispanic:	7	0.06
Haitian	5	0.04
Jamaican	2	0.02
White:	10,940	89.35
Not Hispanic (10,644)	10,814	88.32
Hispanic (113)	126	1.03

Dyersburg

Place Type: City
County: Dyer
Population: 17,452

Ancestry/Race	Number	%
African American/Black:	3,936	22.55
Not Hispanic (3,833)	3,918	22.45
Hispanic (10)	18	0.10
African, sub-Saharan:	132	0.76
African	132	0.76
Am. Ind. or Alaska Nat., not spec.	28	0.16
American Indian tribes, specified:	70	0.40
Apache (1)	1	0.01
Blackfeet	1	0.01
Cherokee (11)	47	0.27
Chippewa (2)	2	0.01
Choctaw (1)	2	0.01
Cree (1)	1	0.01
Creek	1	0.01
Delaware (1)	1	0.01
Iroquois	4	0.02
Sioux (6)	6	0.03
Tohono O'Odham (2)	2	0.01
All other tribes (2)	2	0.01
American Indian tribes, not spec.	2	0.01
Arab:	38	0.22
Arab/Arabic	20	0.11
Lebanese	18	0.10
Asian:	123	0.70
Chinese, ex. Taiwanese (19)	23	0.13
Filipino (11)	12	0.07
Indian (32)	42	0.24
Japanese (1)	5	0.03
Korean (3)	7	0.04
Thai (3)	3	0.02
Vietnamese (24)	24	0.14
Other Asian, specified	3	0.02
Other Asian, not specified (1)	4	0.02
Austrian	9	0.05
British	97	0.56
Canadian	35	0.20
Celtic	40	0.23
Danish	10	0.06
Dutch	204	1.17
English	1,513	8.66
French, except Basque	211	1.21
French Canadian	17	0.10
German	1,083	6.20
Hawaii Native/Pacific Islander:	8	0.05
Polynesian: (4)	5	0.03
Native Hawaiian (4)	4	0.02
Samoan	1	0.01
Other Pac. Isl., specified	3	0.02
Hispanic or Latino:	237	1.36
Central American:	5	0.03
Honduran	2	0.01
Panamanian	3	0.02
Cuban	7	0.04
Mexican	182	1.04
Puerto Rican	15	0.09
South American:	2	0.01
Colombian	2	0.01
Other Hispanic or Latino	26	0.15
Hungarian	10	0.06
Irish	1,905	10.91
Italian	167	0.96
Norwegian	25	0.14
Polish	23	0.13
Russian	19	0.11
Scotch-Irish	320	1.83
Scottish	136	0.78
Slovak	8	0.05
Swedish	65	0.37
United States or American	3,031	17.36
Welsh	29	0.17
West Indian, excl. Hispanic:	9	0.05
Jamaican	9	0.05
White:	13,353	76.51
Not Hispanic (13,087)	13,223	75.77
Hispanic (121)	130	0.74

East Brainerd

Place Type: Census Designated Place
County: Hamilton
Population: 14,132

Ancestry/Race	Number	%
African American/Black:	1,137	8.05
Not Hispanic (1,099)	1,129	7.99

Notes: 1. Figures in the "Number" column do not add up to the total population due to: a) Ancestry/Race overlap — e.g. persons can report being both White and Irish, b) persons of Hispanic origin can report being any race, c) persons reporting two ancestries are counted in both categories. 2. Numbers in parentheses indicate the number of persons reporting this ancestry/race alone, not in combination with any other ancestry/race. 3. Refer to the Explanation of Data in the front of the book for more detailed information.

Ancestry/Race	Number	%
Hispanic (2)	8	0.06
African, sub-Saharan:	114	0.82
African	61	0.44
Nigerian	53	0.38
Am. Ind. or Alaska Nat., not spec.	16	0.11
American Indian tribes, specified:	39	0.28
Cherokee (12)	32	0.23
Chippewa	3	0.02
Latin American Indians	2	0.01
Sioux (1)	1	0.01
All other tribes (1)	1	0.01
American Indian tribes, not spec.	5	0.04
Arab:	22	0.16
Arab/Arabic	12	0.09
Egyptian	10	0.07
Asian:	356	2.52
Cambodian (23)	23	0.16
Chinese, ex. Taiwanese (26)	35	0.25
Filipino (29)	35	0.25
Indian (113)	116	0.82
Indonesian	1	0.01
Japanese (6)	11	0.08
Korean (80)	86	0.61
Laotian (2)	2	0.01
Pakistani (4)	7	0.05
Thai (2)	4	0.03
Vietnamese (24)	24	0.17
Other Asian, specified	1	0.01
Other Asian, not specified (5)	11	0.08
Austrian	20	0.14
Belgian	12	0.09
British	64	0.46
Bulgarian	8	0.06
Canadian	7	0.05
Celtic	20	0.14
Croatian	7	0.05
Czech	65	0.47
Czechoslovakian	10	0.07
Danish	23	0.17
Dutch	162	1.17
Eastern European	30	0.22
English	1,947	14.01
European	201	1.45
Finnish	42	0.30
French, except Basque	303	2.18
French Canadian	32	0.23
German	1,573	11.32
Greek	67	0.48
Hawaii Native/Pacific Islander:	8	0.06
Micronesian: (1)	2	0.01
Guamanian/Chamorro	1	0.01
Other Micronesian (1)	1	0.01
Polynesian:	5	0.04
Native Hawaiian	5	0.04
Other Pac. Isl., not spec.	1	0.01
Hispanic or Latino:	193	1.37
Central American:	13	0.09
Guatemalan	4	0.03
Honduran	2	0.01
Panamanian	5	0.04
Other Central American	2	0.01
Cuban	19	0.13
Dominican Republic	17	0.12
Mexican	49	0.35
Puerto Rican	27	0.19
South American:	25	0.18
Colombian	8	0.06
Peruvian	10	0.07
Venezuelan	6	0.04
Other South American	1	0.01
Other Hispanic or Latino	43	0.30
Hungarian	9	0.06
Irish	1,604	11.55
Italian	243	1.75
Lithuanian	14	0.10
Northern European	9	0.06
Norwegian	156	1.12
Pennsylvania German	10	0.07
Polish	234	1.68
Portuguese	20	0.14
Romanian	5	0.04
Russian	53	0.38
Scandinavian	56	0.40
Scotch-Irish	601	4.33
Scottish	621	4.47
Slavic	6	0.04
Slovak	6	0.04
Swedish	105	0.76
Swiss	30	0.22
Ukrainian	58	0.42
United States or American	1,773	12.76
Welsh	164	1.18
White:	12,610	89.23
Not Hispanic (12,379)	12,478	88.30
Hispanic (111)	132	0.93

East Ridge

Place Type: City
County: Hamilton
Population: 20,640

Ancestry/Race	Number	%
African American/Black:	713	3.45
Not Hispanic (660)	707	3.43
Hispanic (2)	6	0.03
African, sub-Saharan:	161	0.78
African	154	0.74
Liberian	7	0.03
Am. Ind. or Alaska Nat., not spec.	32	0.16
American Indian tribes, specified:	96	0.47
Apache (1)	1	0.00
Blackfeet (1)	3	0.01
Cherokee (28)	68	0.33
Chippewa (6)	6	0.03
Choctaw (2)	3	0.01
Iroquois (3)	4	0.02
Latin American Indians	1	0.00
Navajo	2	0.01
Sioux	2	0.01
Ute (1)	2	0.01
All other tribes (3)	4	0.02
American Indian tribes, not spec.	15	0.07
Arab:	8	0.04
Lebanese	8	0.04
Asian:	391	1.89
Cambodian (55)	56	0.27
Chinese, ex. Taiwanese (51)	53	0.26
Filipino (16)	28	0.14
Indian (72)	78	0.38
Japanese (14)	18	0.09
Korean (49)	59	0.29
Laotian (38)	41	0.20
Pakistani (3)	6	0.03
Taiwanese (14)	14	0.07
Thai (13)	15	0.07
Vietnamese (10)	10	0.05
Other Asian, specified	3	0.01
Other Asian, not specified (7)	10	0.05
Belgian	8	0.04
British	201	0.97
Bulgarian	10	0.05
Canadian	28	0.13
Danish	9	0.04
Dutch	238	1.15
English	2,347	11.30
European	99	0.48
Finnish	8	0.04
French, except Basque	327	1.57
French Canadian	10	0.05
German	2,209	10.64
Greek	15	0.07
Hawaii Native/Pacific Islander:	16	0.08
Micronesian: (1)	1	0.00
Guamanian/Chamorro (1)	1	0.00
Polynesian: (4)	6	0.03
Native Hawaiian (1)	3	0.01
Samoan (2)	2	0.01
Other Polynesian (1)	1	0.00
Other Pac. Isl., specified	3	0.01
Other Pac. Isl., not spec. (1)	6	0.03
Hispanic or Latino:	225	1.09
Central American:	25	0.12
Costa Rican	1	0.00
Guatemalan	19	0.09
Nicaraguan	1	0.00
Panamanian	4	0.02
Cuban	8	0.04
Mexican	132	0.64
Puerto Rican	21	0.10
South American:	10	0.05
Argentinean	1	0.00
Chilean	1	0.00
Colombian	4	0.02
Peruvian	2	0.01
Other South American	2	0.01
Other Hispanic or Latino	29	0.14
Hungarian	34	0.16
Iranian	8	0.04
Irish	2,230	10.74
Italian	329	1.58
Lithuanian	54	0.26
Luxemburger	18	0.09
Norwegian	27	0.13
Polish	153	0.74
Portuguese	13	0.06
Russian	114	0.55
Scandinavian	9	0.04
Scotch-Irish	889	4.28
Scottish	345	1.66
Slovak	33	0.16
Swedish	86	0.41
Swiss	48	0.23
Ukrainian	4	0.02
United States or American	4,194	20.19
Welsh	81	0.39
West Indian, excl. Hispanic:	15	0.07
Bermudan	4	0.02
Jamaican	7	0.03
Trinidadian and Tobagonian	4	0.02
White:	19,456	94.26
Not Hispanic (19,137)	19,307	93.54
Hispanic (125)	149	0.72
Yugoslavian	250	1.20

Elizabethton

Place Type: City
County: Carter
Population: 13,372

Ancestry/Race	Number	%
African American/Black:	378	2.83
Not Hispanic (329)	377	2.82
Hispanic (1)	1	0.01
Am. Ind. or Alaska Nat., not spec.	33	0.25
Alsatian	15	0.11
American Indian tribes, specified:	45	0.34
Apache	1	0.01
Blackfeet	2	0.01
Cherokee (8)	36	0.27
Comanche (1)	1	0.01
Creek	1	0.01
All other tribes (2)	4	0.03
American Indian tribes, not spec.	2	0.01
Asian:	100	0.75
Chinese, ex. Taiwanese (15)	15	0.11
Filipino (26)	31	0.23
Indian (2)	5	0.04
Japanese (3)	8	0.06
Korean (3)	4	0.03
Laotian (7)	14	0.10
Vietnamese (5)	5	0.04
Other Asian, specified	6	0.04
Other Asian, not specified (9)	12	0.09
Brazilian	8	0.06
British	87	0.65
Canadian	11	0.08
Danish	16	0.12
Dutch	227	1.69

Notes: 1. Figures in the "Number" column do not add up to the total population due to: a) Ancestry/Race overlap — e.g. persons can report being both White and Irish, b) persons of Hispanic origin can report being any race, c) persons reporting two ancestries are counted in both categories. 2. Numbers in parentheses indicate the number of persons reporting this ancestry/race alone, not in combination with any other ancestry/race. 3. Refer to the Explanation of Data in the front of the book for more detailed information.

Ancestry/Race	Number	%
Eastern European	13	0.10
English	1,385	10.31
Estonian	9	0.07
European	14	0.10
Finnish	8	0.06
French, except Basque	329	2.45
French Canadian	53	0.39
German	1,709	12.72
Greek	6	0.04
Hawaii Native/Pacific Islander:	8	0.06
Micronesian: (1)	1	0.01
Guamanian/Chamorro (1)	1	0.01
Polynesian:	1	0.01
Native Hawaiian	1	0.01
Other Pac. Isl., specified	6	0.04
Hispanic or Latino:	158	1.18
Central American:	5	0.04
Guatemalan	1	0.01
Honduran	2	0.01
Panamanian	2	0.01
Cuban	6	0.04
Dominican Republic	4	0.03
Mexican	100	0.75
Puerto Rican	7	0.05
South American:	7	0.05
Chilean	2	0.01
Colombian	3	0.02
Peruvian	1	0.01
Venezuelan	1	0.01
Other Hispanic or Latino	29	0.22
Hungarian	26	0.19
Irish	1,103	8.21
Italian	161	1.20
Latvian	8	0.06
Macedonian	9	0.07
Norwegian	76	0.57
Polish	73	0.54
Russian	30	0.22
Scandinavian	33	0.25
Scotch-Irish	499	3.71
Scottish	450	3.35
Swedish	60	0.45
Swiss	19	0.14
United States or American	2,527	18.81
Welsh	100	0.74
West Indian, excl. Hispanic:	8	0.06
Jamaican	8	0.06
White:	12,880	96.32
Not Hispanic (12,664)	12,787	95.63
Hispanic (80)	93	0.70

Farragut

Place Type: Town
County: Knox
Population: 17,720

Ancestry/Race	Number	%
African American/Black:	337	1.90
Not Hispanic (314)	329	1.86
Hispanic (5)	8	0.05
African, sub-Saharan:	10	0.06
Nigerian	10	0.06
Alaska Native tribes, specified:	4	0.02
Alaska Athabascan (1)	1	0.01
Eskimo (3)	3	0.02
Am. Ind. or Alaska Nat., not spec.	11	0.06
Albanian	33	0.18
American Indian tribes, specified:	31	0.17
Cherokee (6)	13	0.07
Choctaw	1	0.01
Comanche (4)	4	0.02
Creek (2)	2	0.01
Iroquois (1)	1	0.01
Lumbee (1)	1	0.01
Pima	1	0.01
Pueblo (1)	1	0.01
Sioux (1)	2	0.01
All other tribes (4)	5	0.03
American Indian tribes, not spec.	1	0.01
Arab:	164	0.92
Arab/Arabic	10	0.06
Egyptian	17	0.10
Lebanese	88	0.49
Other Arab	49	0.27
Asian:	630	3.56
Bangladeshi (3)	4	0.02
Chinese, ex. Taiwanese (103)	129	0.73
Filipino (30)	47	0.27
Indian (227)	231	1.30
Indonesian	3	0.02
Japanese (58)	68	0.38
Korean (53)	59	0.33
Laotian (1)	2	0.01
Malaysian (3)	3	0.02
Pakistani (13)	14	0.08
Sri Lankan (8)	8	0.05
Taiwanese (31)	39	0.22
Thai (2)	2	0.01
Vietnamese (8)	9	0.05
Other Asian, specified	1	0.01
Other Asian, not specified (10)	11	0.06
Austrian	53	0.30
Belgian	149	0.83
British	134	0.75
Canadian	17	0.10
Croatian	8	0.04
Cypriot	7	0.04
Czech	85	0.48
Danish	47	0.26
Dutch	352	1.97
English	3,605	20.16
European	328	1.83
Finnish	16	0.09
French, except Basque	467	2.61
French Canadian	112	0.63
German	3,302	18.47
Greek	143	0.80
Hawaii Native/Pacific Islander:	6	0.03
Other Pac. Isl., specified	1	0.01
Other Pac. Isl., not spec.	5	0.03
Hispanic or Latino:	189	1.07
Central American:	5	0.03
Costa Rican	1	0.01
Honduran	1	0.01
Panamanian	1	0.01
Other Central American	2	0.01
Cuban	10	0.06
Mexican	89	0.50
Puerto Rican	25	0.14
South American:	14	0.08
Argentinean	2	0.01
Bolivian	1	0.01
Chilean	1	0.01
Colombian	6	0.03
Peruvian	2	0.01
Venezuelan	2	0.01
Other Hispanic or Latino	46	0.26
Hungarian	75	0.42
Irish	2,204	12.33
Italian	693	3.88
Latvian	9	0.05
Lithuanian	70	0.39
Northern European	16	0.09
Norwegian	206	1.15
Polish	398	2.23
Portuguese	32	0.18
Romanian	167	0.93
Russian	57	0.32
Scotch-Irish	898	5.02
Scottish	739	4.13
Slovak	46	0.26
Slovene	23	0.13
Swedish	181	1.01
Swiss	163	0.91
Turkish	15	0.08
United States or American	1,740	9.73
Welsh	146	0.82
White:	16,742	94.48
Not Hispanic (16,500)	16,597	93.66
Hispanic (135)	145	0.82

Franklin

Place Type: City
County: Williamson
Population: 41,842

Ancestry/Race	Number	%
Afghan	27	0.06
African American/Black:	4,448	10.63
Not Hispanic (4,316)	4,422	10.57
Hispanic (14)	26	0.06
African, sub-Saharan:	450	1.08
African	418	1.00
Nigerian	10	0.02
South African	9	0.02
Zimbabwean	5	0.01
Other sub-Saharan African	8	0.02
Alaska Native tribes, specified:	1	0.00
Tlingit-Haida (1)	1	0.00
Am. Ind. or Alaska Nat., not spec.	65	0.16
Albanian	38	0.09
American Indian tribes, specified:	129	0.31
Apache (1)	8	0.02
Blackfeet	6	0.01
Cherokee (24)	64	0.15
Cheyenne (1)	1	0.00
Chippewa (6)	7	0.02
Choctaw (6)	9	0.02
Comanche	3	0.01
Creek (3)	3	0.01
Delaware (3)	5	0.01
Iroquois (2)	2	0.00
Kiowa	2	0.00
Latin American Indians (1)	3	0.01
Lumbee (1)	1	0.00
Navajo	1	0.00
Osage (1)	1	0.00
Ottawa (1)	1	0.00
Potawatomi (3)	3	0.01
Seminole (1)	1	0.00
Sioux (1)	2	0.00
All other tribes (5)	6	0.01
American Indian tribes, not spec.	10	0.02
Arab:	195	0.47
Arab/Arabic	5	0.01
Lebanese	9	0.02
Other Arab	181	0.43
Armenian	41	0.10
Asian:	804	1.92
Bangladeshi (4)	4	0.01
Cambodian (4)	4	0.01
Chinese, ex. Taiwanese (154)	166	0.40
Filipino (46)	65	0.16
Indian (139)	161	0.38
Indonesian (2)	2	0.00
Japanese (98)	113	0.27
Korean (165)	196	0.47
Laotian (2)	2	0.00
Malaysian	2	0.00
Pakistani (7)	9	0.02
Sri Lankan (5)	5	0.01
Taiwanese (1)	1	0.00
Thai (3)	4	0.01
Vietnamese (21)	23	0.05
Other Asian, specified (2)	3	0.01
Other Asian, not specified (14)	44	0.11
Australian	27	0.06
Austrian	91	0.22
Belgian	57	0.14
British	235	0.56
Bulgarian	23	0.06
Canadian	117	0.28
Celtic	10	0.02
Croatian	67	0.16
Czech	116	0.28
Czechoslovakian	79	0.19
Danish	120	0.29
Dutch	813	1.95

Notes: 1. Figures in the "Number" column do not add up to the total population due to: a) Ancestry/Race overlap — e.g. persons can report being both White and Irish, b) persons of Hispanic origin can report being any race, c) persons reporting two ancestries are counted in both categories. 2. Numbers in parentheses indicate the number of persons reporting this ancestry/race alone, not in combination with any other ancestry/race. 3. Refer to the Explanation of Data in the front of the book for more detailed information.

Ancestry/Race	Number	%
Eastern European	20	0.05
English	5,798	13.89
European	533	1.28
Finnish	45	0.11
French, except Basque	1,329	3.18
French Canadian	117	0.28
German	6,149	14.73
German Russian	8	0.02
Greek	158	0.38
Hawaii Native/Pacific Islander:	29	0.07
Micronesian: (13)	14	0.03
Guamanian/Chamorro (6)	7	0.02
Other Micronesian (7)	7	0.02
Polynesian: (5)	11	0.03
Native Hawaiian (4)	8	0.02
Samoan (1)	2	0.00
Other Polynesian	1	0.00
Other Pac. Isl., specified	1	0.00
Other Pac. Isl., not spec. (1)	3	0.01
Hispanic or Latino:	2,025	4.84
Central American:	52	0.12
Costa Rican	3	0.01
Guatemalan	22	0.05
Honduran	16	0.04
Nicaraguan	1	0.00
Panamanian	3	0.01
Salvadoran	5	0.01
Other Central American	2	0.00
Cuban	45	0.11
Dominican Republic	2	0.00
Mexican	1,500	3.58
Puerto Rican	81	0.19
South American:	68	0.16
Argentinean	4	0.01
Bolivian	3	0.01
Chilean	10	0.02
Colombian	22	0.05
Ecuadorian	2	0.00
Paraguayan	1	0.00
Peruvian	13	0.03
Uruguayan	3	0.01
Venezuelan	10	0.02
Other Hispanic or Latino	277	0.66
Hungarian	212	0.51
Irish	5,541	13.27
Israeli	11	0.03
Italian	1,649	3.95
Latvian	12	0.03
Lithuanian	90	0.22
Maltese	24	0.06
New Zealander	8	0.02
Northern European	26	0.06
Norwegian	527	1.26
Pennsylvania German	19	0.05
Polish	1,048	2.51
Portuguese	35	0.08
Romanian	25	0.06
Russian	199	0.48
Scandinavian	24	0.06
Scotch-Irish	1,391	3.33
Scottish	1,167	2.79
Serbian	27	0.06
Slavic	32	0.08
Slovak	47	0.11
Slovene	9	0.02
Swedish	391	0.94
Swiss	51	0.12
Turkish	22	0.05
Ukrainian	121	0.29
United States or American	4,073	9.75
Welsh	485	1.16
West Indian, excl. Hispanic:	61	0.15
Bermudan	5	0.01
British West Indian	14	0.03
Jamaican	29	0.07
West Indian	13	0.03
White:	35,766	85.48
Not Hispanic (34,377)	34,676	82.87
Hispanic (991)	1,090	2.61
Yugoslavian	47	0.11

Gallatin

Place Type: City
County: Sumner
Population: 23,230

Ancestry/Race	Number	%
African American/Black:	4,226	18.19
Not Hispanic (4,064)	4,195	18.06
Hispanic (17)	31	0.13
African, sub-Saharan:	604	2.60
African	452	1.95
South African	13	0.06
Sudanese	139	0.60
Am. Ind. or Alaska Nat., not spec.	63	0.27
American Indian tribes, specified:	104	0.45
Apache (1)	2	0.01
Cherokee (23)	78	0.34
Choctaw (3)	5	0.02
Creek	2	0.01
Iroquois (3)	3	0.01
Lumbee (2)	2	0.01
Navajo (1)	1	0.00
Potawatomi (1)	1	0.00
Sioux (3)	6	0.03
All other tribes (3)	4	0.02
American Indian tribes, not spec.	10	0.04
Arab:	12	0.05
Lebanese	12	0.05
Asian:	139	0.60
Chinese, ex. Taiwanese (17)	21	0.09
Filipino (5)	6	0.03
Indian (27)	35	0.15
Japanese (8)	9	0.04
Korean (7)	9	0.04
Thai (5)	5	0.02
Vietnamese (21)	24	0.10
Other Asian, not specified (8)	30	0.13
Austrian	7	0.03
Belgian	9	0.04
British	108	0.46
Canadian	13	0.06
Celtic	11	0.05
Croatian	7	0.03
Czech	26	0.11
Danish	49	0.21
Dutch	174	0.75
Eastern European	7	0.03
English	2,134	9.18
European	247	1.06
Finnish	7	0.03
French, except Basque	260	1.12
French Canadian	54	0.23
German	1,619	6.97
Greek	8	0.03
Hawaii Native/Pacific Islander:	31	0.13
Melanesian:	2	0.01
Fijian	2	0.01
Micronesian: (3)	4	0.02
Guamanian/Chamorro (3)	4	0.02
Polynesian: (13)	19	0.08
Native Hawaiian (3)	9	0.04
Samoan (8)	8	0.03
Other Polynesian (2)	2	0.01
Other Pac. Isl., not spec.	6	0.03
Hispanic or Latino:	801	3.45
Central American:	85	0.37
Costa Rican	12	0.05
Guatemalan	13	0.06
Honduran	3	0.01
Panamanian	9	0.04
Salvadoran	48	0.21
Cuban	9	0.04
Dominican Republic	1	0.00
Mexican	479	2.06
Puerto Rican	45	0.19
South American:	6	0.03
Argentinean	1	0.00
Colombian	1	0.00
Ecuadorian	3	0.01
Peruvian	1	0.00
Other Hispanic or Latino	176	0.76
Hungarian	12	0.05
Irish	1,873	8.06
Italian	180	0.77
Norwegian	44	0.19
Polish	100	0.43
Portuguese	7	0.03
Romanian	54	0.23
Russian	6	0.03
Scandinavian	9	0.04
Scotch-Irish	642	2.76
Scottish	282	1.21
Serbian	15	0.06
Slovak	19	0.08
Swedish	64	0.28
Swiss	23	0.10
Turkish	5	0.02
United States or American	4,305	18.53
Welsh	92	0.40
White:	18,435	79.36
Not Hispanic (17,877)	18,087	77.86
Hispanic (312)	348	1.50

Germantown

Place Type: City
County: Shelby
Population: 37,348

Ancestry/Race	Number	%
Acadian/Cajun	26	0.07
African American/Black:	916	2.45
Not Hispanic (867)	914	2.45
Hispanic (2)	2	0.01
African, sub-Saharan:	42	0.11
African	35	0.09
Cape Verdean	7	0.02
Alaska Native tribes, specified:	2	0.01
Eskimo (2)	2	0.01
Am. Ind. or Alaska Nat., not spec.	33	0.09
American Indian tribes, specified:	100	0.27
Apache (1)	1	0.00
Cherokee (12)	59	0.16
Chickasaw (3)	3	0.01
Chippewa (1)	4	0.01
Choctaw (8)	14	0.04
Iroquois	1	0.00
Latin American Indians	1	0.00
Menominee	4	0.01
Osage	1	0.00
Potawatomi (2)	2	0.01
Yaqui (2)	2	0.01
All other tribes (6)	8	0.02
American Indian tribes, not spec.	10	0.03
Arab:	169	0.45
Arab/Arabic	17	0.05
Egyptian	18	0.05
Lebanese	87	0.23
Palestinian	22	0.06
Syrian	25	0.07
Armenian	28	0.08
Asian:	1,440	3.86
Bangladeshi (11)	11	0.03
Cambodian (1)	1	0.00
Chinese, ex. Taiwanese (305)	334	0.89
Filipino (34)	53	0.14
Indian (461)	485	1.30
Indonesian (1)	1	0.00
Japanese (119)	134	0.36
Korean (230)	249	0.67
Laotian (1)	1	0.00
Pakistani (26)	40	0.11
Sri Lankan (1)	1	0.00
Taiwanese (28)	28	0.07
Thai (16)	17	0.05
Vietnamese (42)	45	0.12
Other Asian, not specified (19)	40	0.11
Australian	48	0.13
Austrian	129	0.35

Notes: 1. Figures in the "Number" column do not add up to the total population due to: a) Ancestry/Race overlap — e.g. persons can report being both White and Irish, b) persons of Hispanic origin can report being any race, c) persons reporting two ancestries are counted in both categories. 2. Numbers in parentheses indicate the number of persons reporting this ancestry/race alone, not in combination with any other ancestry/race. 3. Refer to the Explanation of Data in the front of the book for more detailed information.

Basque	16	0.04
Brazilian	7	0.02
British	272	0.73
Bulgarian	7	0.02
Canadian	118	0.32
Celtic	15	0.04
Croatian	16	0.04
Czech	127	0.34
Czechoslovakian	45	0.12
Danish	118	0.32
Dutch	550	1.48
Eastern European	47	0.13
English	7,013	18.81
European	756	2.03
Finnish	52	0.14
French, except Basque	1,104	2.96
French Canadian	62	0.17
German	5,465	14.66
Greek	208	0.56
Hawaii Native/Pacific Islander:	18	0.05
Polynesian: (9)	11	0.03
Native Hawaiian (4)	6	0.02
Samoan (5)	5	0.01
Other Pac. Isl., not spec. (4)	7	0.02
Hispanic or Latino:	407	1.09
Central American:	13	0.03
Costa Rican	2	0.01
Guatemalan	1	0.00
Honduran	3	0.01
Nicaraguan	4	0.01
Panamanian	1	0.00
Salvadoran	2	0.01
Cuban	63	0.17
Dominican Republic	7	0.02
Mexican	158	0.42
Puerto Rican	38	0.10
South American:	49	0.13
Argentinean	9	0.02
Bolivian	2	0.01
Chilean	4	0.01
Colombian	13	0.03
Ecuadorian	6	0.02
Paraguayan	3	0.01
Peruvian	2	0.01
Uruguayan	2	0.01
Venezuelan	6	0.02
Other South American	2	0.01
Other Hispanic or Latino	79	0.21
Hungarian	307	0.82
Icelander	6	0.02
Iranian	185	0.50
Irish	4,933	13.23
Italian	1,999	5.36
Latvian	30	0.08
Lithuanian	21	0.06
New Zealander	7	0.02
Northern European	17	0.05
Norwegian	274	0.73
Polish	866	2.32
Portuguese	15	0.04
Romanian	16	0.04
Russian	524	1.41
Scandinavian	15	0.04
Scotch-Irish	1,966	5.27
Scottish	1,421	3.81
Slovak	74	0.20
Swedish	461	1.24
Swiss	85	0.23
Ukrainian	69	0.19
United States or American	4,080	10.94
Welsh	417	1.12
White:	34,993	93.69
Not Hispanic (34,389)	34,647	92.77
Hispanic (323)	346	0.93

Goodlettsville

Place Type: City
County: Davidson
Population: 13,780

Ancestry/Race	Number	%
Acadian/Cajun	10	0.07
Afghan	26	0.19
African American/Black:	1,409	10.22
Not Hispanic (1,349)	1,398	10.15
Hispanic (5)	11	0.08
Am. Ind. or Alaska Nat., not spec.	29	0.21
American Indian tribes, specified:	59	0.43
Blackfeet	6	0.04
Cherokee (7)	34	0.25
Chippewa	1	0.01
Choctaw	5	0.04
Creek (1)	2	0.01
Iroquois (2)	2	0.01
Latin American Indians (3)	4	0.03
Lumbee	1	0.01
Sioux	1	0.01
Yaqui (1)	1	0.01
All other tribes (1)	2	0.01
American Indian tribes, not spec.	5	0.04
Asian:	269	1.95
Chinese, ex. Taiwanese (27)	34	0.25
Filipino (35)	43	0.31
Indian (71)	79	0.57
Japanese (13)	15	0.11
Korean (45)	54	0.39
Laotian	1	0.01
Pakistani (8)	8	0.06
Vietnamese (16)	19	0.14
Other Asian, specified (2)	10	0.07
Other Asian, not specified (2)	6	0.04
Australian	14	0.10
Belgian	7	0.05
British	186	1.34
Canadian	46	0.33
Cypriot	6	0.04
Czech	27	0.20
Czechoslovakian	18	0.13
Danish	55	0.40
Dutch	130	0.94
English	1,504	10.86
European	121	0.87
French, except Basque	181	1.31
French Canadian	51	0.37
German	1,395	10.08
Greek	19	0.14
Hawaii Native/Pacific Islander:	16	0.12
Micronesian: (1)	1	0.01
Guamanian/Chamorro (1)	1	0.01
Polynesian: (1)	5	0.04
Native Hawaiian (1)	5	0.04
Other Pac. Isl., specified	5	0.04
Other Pac. Isl., not spec.	5	0.04
Hispanic or Latino:	204	1.48
Central American:	7	0.05
Guatemalan	3	0.02
Other Central American	4	0.03
Cuban	8	0.06
Dominican Republic	1	0.01
Mexican	103	0.75
Puerto Rican	27	0.20
South American:	5	0.04
Colombian	4	0.03
Other South American	1	0.01
Other Hispanic or Latino	53	0.38
Hungarian	14	0.10
Irish	1,438	10.39
Italian	230	1.66
Lithuanian	7	0.05
Northern European	83	0.60
Norwegian	46	0.33
Polish	106	0.77
Portuguese	8	0.06
Romanian	28	0.20
Russian	22	0.16
Scotch-Irish	327	2.36
Scottish	252	1.82
Slovak	24	0.17
Swedish	93	0.67
Swiss	29	0.21
Ukrainian	8	0.06
United States or American	2,512	18.14
Welsh	102	0.74
White:	12,047	87.42
Not Hispanic (11,802)	11,926	86.55
Hispanic (107)	121	0.88
Yugoslavian	10	0.07

Greeneville

Place Type: Town
County: Greene
Population: 15,198

Ancestry/Race	Number	%
African American/Black:	913	6.01
Not Hispanic (870)	905	5.95
Hispanic (3)	8	0.05
African, sub-Saharan:	46	0.30
African	46	0.30
Am. Ind. or Alaska Nat., not spec.	27	0.18
American Indian tribes, specified:	32	0.21
Blackfeet (1)	1	0.01
Cherokee (9)	21	0.14
Comanche	1	0.01
Kiowa	1	0.01
Latin American Indians (3)	3	0.02
Navajo (3)	3	0.02
All other tribes (2)	2	0.01
American Indian tribes, not spec.	1	0.01
Arab:	18	0.12
Lebanese	12	0.08
Syrian	6	0.04
Asian:	90	0.59
Chinese, ex. Taiwanese (14)	14	0.09
Filipino (14)	14	0.09
Indian (27)	29	0.19
Japanese (18)	19	0.13
Korean (3)	3	0.02
Laotian (1)	1	0.01
Thai (1)	2	0.01
Vietnamese (1)	1	0.01
Other Asian, not specified (3)	7	0.05
Belgian	18	0.12
British	26	0.17
Canadian	30	0.20
Celtic	13	0.08
Danish	59	0.38
Dutch	243	1.58
English	1,240	8.07
European	96	0.63
French, except Basque	89	0.58
French Canadian	35	0.23
German	1,580	10.29
Greek	127	0.83
Hawaii Native/Pacific Islander:	6	0.04
Micronesian: (3)	3	0.02
Guamanian/Chamorro (3)	3	0.02
Polynesian:	3	0.02
Native Hawaiian	3	0.02
Hispanic or Latino:	226	1.49
Central American:	9	0.06
Guatemalan	4	0.03
Honduran	5	0.03
Cuban	6	0.04
Mexican	156	1.03
Puerto Rican	21	0.14
South American:	3	0.02
Argentinean	1	0.01
Colombian	2	0.01
Other Hispanic or Latino	31	0.20
Hungarian	15	0.10
Irish	1,248	8.13
Italian	316	2.06

Notes: 1. Figures in the "Number" column do not add up to the total population due to: a) Ancestry/Race overlap — e.g. persons can report being both White and Irish, b) persons of Hispanic origin can report being any race, c) persons reporting two ancestries are counted in both categories. 2. Numbers in parentheses indicate the number of persons reporting this ancestry/race alone, not in combination with any other ancestry/race. 3. Refer to the Explanation of Data in the front of the book for more detailed information.

Ancestry/Race	Number	%
Norwegian	27	0.18
Polish	103	0.67
Scotch-Irish	522	3.40
Scottish	175	1.14
Slovak	20	0.13
Swedish	103	0.67
Swiss	6	0.04
United States or American	2,390	15.56
Welsh	108	0.70
West Indian, excl. Hispanic:	36	0.23
Bahamian	16	0.10
Dutch West Indian	20	0.13
White:	14,071	92.58
Not Hispanic (13,893)	13,964	91.88
Hispanic (93)	107	0.70
Yugoslavian	37	0.24

Hendersonville

Place Type: City
County: Sumner
Population: 40,620

Ancestry/Race	Number	%
Acadian/Cajun	11	0.03
African American/Black:	1,754	4.32
Not Hispanic (1,663)	1,740	4.28
Hispanic (10)	14	0.03
African, sub-Saharan:	52	0.13
African	52	0.13
Alaska Native tribes, specified:	1	0.00
Eskimo (1)	1	0.00
Am. Ind. or Alaska Nat., not spec.	73	0.18
American Indian tribes, specified:	184	0.45
Apache	14	0.03
Blackfeet	2	0.00
Cherokee (35)	92	0.23
Chickasaw (2)	6	0.01
Chippewa (3)	4	0.01
Choctaw (6)	6	0.01
Comanche	4	0.01
Cree	3	0.01
Creek	3	0.01
Crow	1	0.00
Houma (1)	1	0.00
Iroquois (2)	6	0.01
Kiowa (1)	1	0.00
Latin American Indians (2)	3	0.01
Lumbee (1)	2	0.00
Navajo	7	0.02
Osage	4	0.01
Potawatomi	2	0.00
Pueblo (1)	1	0.00
Seminole	1	0.00
Sioux (6)	8	0.02
Yaqui	2	0.00
All other tribes (7)	11	0.03
American Indian tribes, not spec.	11	0.03
Arab:	79	0.19
Arab/Arabic	14	0.03
Jordanian	27	0.07
Lebanese	11	0.03
Palestinian	18	0.04
Syrian	9	0.02
Armenian	6	0.01
Asian:	537	1.32
Chinese, ex. Taiwanese (62)	81	0.20
Filipino (61)	84	0.21
Indian (87)	96	0.24
Japanese (76)	86	0.21
Korean (38)	45	0.11
Pakistani (22)	22	0.05
Sri Lankan (8)	8	0.02
Taiwanese (4)	5	0.01
Thai (3)	9	0.02
Vietnamese (70)	77	0.19
Other Asian, not specified (11)	24	0.06
Austrian	90	0.22
Belgian	21	0.05
Brazilian	34	0.08
British	273	0.67
Canadian	64	0.16
Czech	137	0.34
Czechoslovakian	23	0.06
Danish	65	0.16
Dutch	717	1.77
English	5,244	12.94
European	447	1.10
Finnish	65	0.16
French, except Basque	1,091	2.69
French Canadian	300	0.74
German	5,721	14.11
Greek	146	0.36
Hawaii Native/Pacific Islander:	33	0.08
Micronesian:	1	0.00
Guamanian/Chamorro	1	0.00
Polynesian: (10)	19	0.05
Native Hawaiian (2)	11	0.03
Samoan (2)	2	0.00
Other Polynesian (6)	6	0.01
Other Pac. Isl., not spec. (2)	13	0.03
Hispanic or Latino:	696	1.71
Central American:	43	0.11
Costa Rican	5	0.01
Guatemalan	8	0.02
Honduran	4	0.01
Nicaraguan	7	0.02
Panamanian	2	0.00
Salvadoran	17	0.04
Cuban	24	0.06
Mexican	343	0.84
Puerto Rican	72	0.18
South American:	44	0.11
Argentinean	1	0.00
Chilean	7	0.02
Colombian	7	0.02
Ecuadorian	1	0.00
Peruvian	15	0.04
Uruguayan	2	0.00
Venezuelan	7	0.02
Other South American	4	0.01
Other Hispanic or Latino	170	0.42
Hungarian	118	0.29
Iranian	58	0.14
Irish	5,858	14.45
Italian	1,314	3.24
Lithuanian	39	0.10
Luxemburger	33	0.08
Northern European	121	0.30
Norwegian	365	0.90
Pennsylvania German	12	0.03
Polish	623	1.54
Portuguese	65	0.16
Romanian	155	0.38
Russian	104	0.26
Scandinavian	57	0.14
Scotch-Irish	1,378	3.40
Scottish	1,175	2.90
Slavic	9	0.02
Slovak	88	0.22
Swedish	369	0.91
Swiss	26	0.06
Ukrainian	45	0.11
United States or American	6,277	15.48
Welsh	266	0.66
West Indian, excl. Hispanic:	17	0.04
British West Indian	12	0.03
Haitian	5	0.01
White:	38,091	93.77
Not Hispanic (37,364)	37,671	92.74
Hispanic (385)	420	1.03
Yugoslavian	8	0.02

Jackson

Place Type: City
County: Madison
Population: 59,643

Ancestry/Race	Number	%
African American/Black:	25,377	42.55
Not Hispanic (24,957)	25,227	42.30
Hispanic (134)	150	0.25
African, sub-Saharan:	827	1.39
African	714	1.20
Ethiopian	38	0.06
Kenyan	10	0.02
Nigerian	53	0.09
Other sub-Saharan African	12	0.02
Alaska Native tribes, specified:	2	0.00
Alaska Athabascan	2	0.00
Am. Ind. or Alaska Nat., not spec.	145	0.24
American Indian tribes, specified:	115	0.19
Apache	5	0.01
Blackfeet (5)	6	0.01
Cherokee (27)	79	0.13
Chickasaw (4)	5	0.01
Chippewa (1)	1	0.00
Choctaw (2)	3	0.01
Comanche (1)	2	0.00
Kiowa (1)	1	0.00
Latin American Indians (2)	4	0.01
Navajo	1	0.00
Potawatomi (1)	1	0.00
Seminole	1	0.00
Sioux (3)	3	0.01
Yaqui (1)	1	0.00
All other tribes (1)	2	0.00
American Indian tribes, not spec.	18	0.03
Arab:	51	0.09
Egyptian	11	0.02
Lebanese	25	0.04
Palestinian	15	0.03
Asian:	618	1.04
Bangladeshi (1)	1	0.00
Cambodian (3)	5	0.01
Chinese, ex. Taiwanese (74)	106	0.18
Filipino (91)	116	0.19
Indian (123)	138	0.23
Indonesian (4)	5	0.01
Japanese (61)	71	0.12
Korean (42)	61	0.10
Pakistani (9)	9	0.02
Taiwanese (3)	10	0.02
Thai (1)	3	0.01
Vietnamese (40)	49	0.08
Other Asian, specified	7	0.01
Other Asian, not specified (9)	37	0.06
Austrian	34	0.06
Belgian	36	0.06
British	127	0.21
Bulgarian	5	0.01
Canadian	122	0.20
Celtic	13	0.02
Croatian	31	0.05
Czech	44	0.07
Czechoslovakian	33	0.06
Danish	33	0.06
Dutch	399	0.67
Eastern European	36	0.06
English	4,260	7.14
Estonian	7	0.01
European	414	0.69
Finnish	80	0.13
French, except Basque	778	1.30
French Canadian	172	0.29
German	3,208	5.38
Greek	51	0.09
Hawaii Native/Pacific Islander:	31	0.05
Melanesian: (1)	1	0.00
Fijian (1)	1	0.00
Micronesian: (2)	3	0.01
Guamanian/Chamorro (2)	3	0.01
Polynesian: (3)	10	0.02
Native Hawaiian (1)	5	0.01
Samoan (1)	4	0.01
Other Polynesian (1)	1	0.00
Other Pac. Isl., specified	7	0.01
Other Pac. Isl., not spec.	10	0.02
Hispanic or Latino:	1,289	2.16

Notes: 1. Figures in the "Number" column do not add up to the total population due to: a) Ancestry/Race overlap — e.g. persons can report being both White and Irish, b) persons of Hispanic origin can report being any race, c) persons reporting two ancestries are counted in both categories. 2. Numbers in parentheses indicate the number of persons reporting this ancestry/race alone, not in combination with any other ancestry/race. 3. Refer to the Explanation of Data in the front of the book for more detailed information.

Ancestry/Race	Number	%
Central American:	52	0.09
Costa Rican	1	0.00
Guatemalan	4	0.01
Honduran	44	0.07
Panamanian	1	0.00
Salvadoran	2	0.00
Cuban	21	0.04
Dominican Republic	1	0.00
Mexican	879	1.47
Puerto Rican	61	0.10
South American:	42	0.07
Chilean	7	0.01
Colombian	6	0.01
Ecuadorian	5	0.01
Peruvian	13	0.02
Venezuelan	5	0.01
Other South American	6	0.01
Other Hispanic or Latino	233	0.39
Hungarian	26	0.04
Irish	4,321	7.24
Italian	697	1.17
Lithuanian	7	0.01
Norwegian	199	0.33
Polish	368	0.62
Romanian	7	0.01
Russian	77	0.13
Scandinavian	15	0.03
Scotch-Irish	1,430	2.40
Scottish	802	1.34
Slavic	6	0.01
Slovak	5	0.01
Swedish	81	0.14
Swiss	53	0.09
Ukrainian	8	0.01
United States or American	6,875	11.52
Welsh	149	0.25
West Indian, excl. Hispanic:	124	0.21
Dutch West Indian	6	0.01
Haitian	6	0.01
Jamaican	74	0.12
Trinidadian and Tobagonian	38	0.06
White:	33,315	55.86
Not Hispanic (32,317)	32,688	54.81
Hispanic (566)	627	1.05
Yugoslavian	8	0.01

Johnson City

Place Type: City
County: Washington
Population: 55,469

Ancestry/Race	Number	%
Acadian/Cajun	13	0.02
Afghan	6	0.01
African American/Black:	3,865	6.97
Not Hispanic (3,522)	3,823	6.89
Hispanic (27)	42	0.08
African, sub-Saharan:	291	0.53
African	245	0.44
Kenyan	7	0.01
Liberian	13	0.02
Nigerian	16	0.03
South African	10	0.02
Alaska Native tribes, specified:	4	0.01
Alaska Athabascan	3	0.01
Eskimo	1	0.00
Am. Ind. or Alaska Nat., not spec.	112	0.20
Albanian	11	0.02
American Indian tribes, specified:	270	0.49
Apache (4)	5	0.01
Blackfeet	3	0.01
Cherokee (59)	187	0.34
Chippewa (2)	4	0.01
Comanche	1	0.00
Creek (1)	3	0.01
Crow	1	0.00
Delaware (2)	3	0.01
Iroquois (3)	5	0.01
Latin American Indians (2)	3	0.01
Lumbee (3)	4	0.01
Navajo (1)	1	0.00
Osage (1)	1	0.00
Pima	1	0.00
Potawatomi	2	0.00
Seminole (1)	1	0.00
Sioux (3)	8	0.01
Tohono O'Odham (1)	1	0.00
Ute (2)	3	0.01
Yaqui	1	0.00
All other tribes (20)	32	0.06
American Indian tribes, not spec.	19	0.03
Arab:	107	0.19
Arab/Arabic	60	0.11
Lebanese	32	0.06
Other Arab	15	0.03
Asian:	813	1.47
Bangladeshi (3)	3	0.01
Cambodian (1)	1	0.00
Chinese, ex. Taiwanese (169)	183	0.33
Filipino (63)	98	0.18
Indian (266)	285	0.51
Indonesian (1)	2	0.00
Japanese (24)	45	0.08
Korean (46)	60	0.11
Laotian (5)	6	0.01
Malaysian (2)	3	0.01
Pakistani (21)	24	0.04
Taiwanese (8)	10	0.02
Thai (4)	8	0.01
Vietnamese (36)	47	0.08
Other Asian, specified (1)	4	0.01
Other Asian, not specified (22)	34	0.06
Austrian	99	0.18
Basque	7	0.01
Belgian	60	0.11
British	356	0.64
Canadian	86	0.16
Croatian	45	0.08
Czech	34	0.06
Czechoslovakian	27	0.05
Danish	55	0.10
Dutch	888	1.61
Eastern European	7	0.01
English	6,592	11.92
European	477	0.86
Finnish	50	0.09
French, except Basque	843	1.52
French Canadian	246	0.44
German	6,542	11.83
Greek	119	0.22
Hawaii Native/Pacific Islander:	25	0.05
Micronesian: (2)	5	0.01
Guamanian/Chamorro (2)	5	0.01
Polynesian: (8)	15	0.03
Native Hawaiian (4)	9	0.02
Samoan (4)	6	0.01
Other Pac. Isl., specified	2	0.00
Other Pac. Isl., not spec. (2)	3	0.01
Hispanic or Latino:	1,048	1.89
Central American:	46	0.08
Guatemalan	6	0.01
Honduran	15	0.03
Nicaraguan	9	0.02
Panamanian	12	0.02
Salvadoran	1	0.00
Other Central American	3	0.01
Cuban	48	0.09
Dominican Republic	11	0.02
Mexican	599	1.08
Puerto Rican	104	0.19
South American:	59	0.11
Argentinean	6	0.01
Bolivian	2	0.00
Chilean	2	0.00
Colombian	14	0.03
Ecuadorian	19	0.03
Peruvian	7	0.01
Venezuelan	5	0.01
Other South American	4	0.01
Other Hispanic or Latino	181	0.33
Hungarian	117	0.21
Icelander	12	0.02
Irish	6,294	11.38
Italian	1,048	1.89
Latvian	6	0.01
Lithuanian	72	0.13
Northern European	22	0.04
Norwegian	305	0.55
Polish	502	0.91
Portuguese	71	0.13
Romanian	17	0.03
Russian	179	0.32
Scandinavian	99	0.18
Scotch-Irish	2,313	4.18
Scottish	1,354	2.45
Slavic	9	0.02
Slovak	72	0.13
Swedish	269	0.49
Swiss	106	0.19
Turkish	10	0.02
Ukrainian	21	0.04
United States or American	8,981	16.23
Welsh	398	0.72
West Indian, excl. Hispanic:	64	0.12
Bermudan	5	0.01
Dutch West Indian	10	0.02
Haitian	3	0.01
Jamaican	19	0.03
Trinidadian and Tobagonian	12	0.02
West Indian	15	0.03
White:	50,632	91.28
Not Hispanic (49,354)	49,958	90.06
Hispanic (619)	674	1.22
Yugoslavian	5	0.01

Kingsport

Place Type: City
County: Sullivan
Population: 44,905

Ancestry/Race	Number	%
African American/Black:	2,073	4.62
Not Hispanic (1,885)	2,045	4.55
Hispanic (12)	28	0.06
African, sub-Saharan:	95	0.21
African	95	0.21
Alaska Native tribes, specified:	1	0.00
Tlingit-Haida	1	0.00
Am. Ind. or Alaska Nat., not spec.	93	0.21
Alsatian	8	0.02
American Indian tribes, specified:	191	0.43
Apache	3	0.01
Blackfeet	8	0.02
Cherokee (44)	139	0.31
Cheyenne	1	0.00
Chippewa (1)	2	0.00
Comanche (1)	1	0.00
Creek (2)	10	0.02
Delaware (1)	1	0.00
Iroquois (3)	6	0.01
Lumbee (1)	1	0.00
Navajo (3)	5	0.01
Paiute (1)	1	0.00
Sioux (1)	4	0.01
All other tribes (6)	9	0.02
American Indian tribes, not spec.	27	0.06
Arab:	103	0.23
Arab/Arabic	5	0.01
Lebanese	77	0.17
Moroccan	6	0.01
Syrian	15	0.03
Asian:	455	1.01
Chinese, ex. Taiwanese (139)	155	0.35
Filipino (23)	39	0.09
Indian (133)	148	0.33
Japanese (5)	19	0.04
Korean (30)	42	0.09
Laotian (2)	2	0.00

Notes: 1. Figures in the "Number" column do not add up to the total population due to: a) Ancestry/Race overlap — e.g. persons can report being both White and Irish, b) persons of Hispanic origin can report being any race, c) persons reporting two ancestries are counted in both categories. 2. Numbers in parentheses indicate the number of persons reporting this ancestry/race alone, not in combination with any other ancestry/race. 3. Refer to the Explanation of Data in the front of the book for more detailed information.

Sri Lankan (1)	1	0.00
Taiwanese (4)	4	0.01
Thai (2)	5	0.01
Vietnamese (13)	17	0.04
Other Asian, specified	7	0.02
Other Asian, not specified (3)	16	0.04
Australian	11	0.02
Austrian	18	0.04
Belgian	25	0.06
Brazilian	24	0.05
British	244	0.55
Canadian	84	0.19
Celtic	20	0.04
Czech	54	0.12
Czechoslovakian	6	0.01
Danish	23	0.05
Dutch	972	2.18
Eastern European	4	0.01
English	5,872	13.18
European	209	0.47
Finnish	13	0.03
French, except Basque	847	1.90
French Canadian	126	0.28
German	4,495	10.09
Greek	84	0.19
Hawaii Native/Pacific Islander:	26	0.06
Micronesian: (1)	2	0.00
Guamanian/Chamorro (1)	2	0.00
Polynesian: (9)	12	0.03
Native Hawaiian (5)	8	0.02
Samoan (4)	4	0.01
Other Pac. Isl., specified	7	0.02
Other Pac. Isl., not spec.	5	0.01
Hispanic or Latino:	471	1.05
Central American:	16	0.04
Costa Rican	1	0.00
Guatemalan	5	0.01
Honduran	2	0.00
Salvadoran	7	0.02
Other Central American	1	0.00
Cuban	20	0.04
Mexican	249	0.55
Puerto Rican	43	0.10
South American:	20	0.04
Bolivian	1	0.00
Colombian	1	0.00
Ecuadorian	2	0.00
Peruvian	9	0.02
Uruguayan	1	0.00
Venezuelan	6	0.01
Other Hispanic or Latino	123	0.27
Hungarian	71	0.16
Icelander	4	0.01
Irish	4,903	11.00
Israeli	6	0.01
Italian	512	1.15
Northern European	23	0.05
Norwegian	172	0.39
Pennsylvania German	7	0.02
Polish	233	0.52
Portuguese	8	0.02
Russian	38	0.09
Scotch-Irish	1,963	4.41
Scottish	1,025	2.30
Slovak	6	0.01
Swedish	146	0.33
Swiss	15	0.03
Turkish	14	0.03
United States or American	7,453	16.73
Welsh	175	0.39
West Indian, excl. Hispanic:	21	0.05
Dutch West Indian	5	0.01
Haitian	6	0.01
Jamaican	10	0.02
White:	42,355	94.32
Not Hispanic (41,613)	42,031	93.60
Hispanic (293)	324	0.72
Yugoslavian	39	0.09

Knoxville

Place Type: City
County: Knox
Population: 173,890

Ancestry/Race	Number	%
Acadian/Cajun	36	0.02
African American/Black:	29,286	16.84
Not Hispanic (28,015)	29,065	16.71
Hispanic (156)	221	0.13
African, sub-Saharan:	938	0.54
African	818	0.47
Cape Verdean	10	0.01
Ethiopian	29	0.02
Kenyan	13	0.01
Nigerian	33	0.02
Sierra Leonean	5	0.00
South African	10	0.01
Other sub-Saharan African	20	0.01
Alaska Native tribes, specified:	9	0.01
Aleut (2)	3	0.00
Eskimo (2)	4	0.00
Tlingit-Haida	2	0.00
Alaska Native tribes, not specified	4	0.00
Am. Ind. or Alaska Nat., not spec.	423	0.24
Alsatian	6	0.00
American Indian tribes, specified:	1,039	0.60
Apache (8)	22	0.01
Blackfeet (4)	31	0.02
Cherokee (220)	720	0.41
Cheyenne (1)	3	0.00
Chickasaw	3	0.00
Chippewa (5)	16	0.01
Choctaw (13)	23	0.01
Comanche	1	0.00
Cree	6	0.00
Creek (2)	11	0.01
Crow (2)	6	0.00
Delaware (4)	9	0.01
Iroquois (7)	15	0.01
Latin American Indians (21)	39	0.02
Lumbee (19)	22	0.01
Menominee	1	0.00
Navajo (1)	3	0.00
Osage (2)	2	0.00
Ottawa (1)	1	0.00
Potawatomi	1	0.00
Pueblo	1	0.00
Shoshone	1	0.00
Sioux (18)	34	0.02
Tohono O'Odham (1)	1	0.00
Ute (1)	1	0.00
Yaqui	2	0.00
Yuman (1)	1	0.00
All other tribes (33)	63	0.04
American Indian tribes, not spec.	75	0.04
Arab:	557	0.32
Arab/Arabic	186	0.11
Egyptian	57	0.03
Iraqi	10	0.01
Jordanian	93	0.05
Lebanese	88	0.05
Moroccan	33	0.02
Palestinian	12	0.01
Syrian	32	0.02
Other Arab	46	0.03
Armenian	7	0.00
Asian:	3,058	1.76
Bangladeshi (11)	11	0.01
Cambodian (11)	12	0.01
Chinese, ex. Taiwanese (627)	693	0.40
Filipino (183)	290	0.17
Hmong (1)	4	0.00
Indian (473)	533	0.31
Indonesian (27)	34	0.02
Japanese (209)	272	0.16
Korean (378)	437	0.25
Laotian (30)	34	0.02
Malaysian (35)	57	0.03
Pakistani (34)	44	0.03
Sri Lankan (6)	8	0.00
Taiwanese (34)	46	0.03
Thai (32)	41	0.02
Vietnamese (317)	354	0.20
Other Asian, specified (12)	19	0.01
Other Asian, not specified (60)	169	0.10
Australian	18	0.01
Austrian	270	0.16
Basque	8	0.00
Belgian	100	0.06
Brazilian	26	0.01
British	966	0.56
Canadian	200	0.12
Carpatho Rusyn	7	0.00
Celtic	85	0.05
Croatian	97	0.06
Czech	132	0.08
Czechoslovakian	57	0.03
Danish	215	0.12
Dutch	3,052	1.76
Eastern European	95	0.05
English	17,674	10.18
European	1,538	0.89
Finnish	121	0.07
French, except Basque	2,946	1.70
French Canadian	281	0.16
German	17,333	9.98
German Russian	22	0.01
Greek	380	0.22
Guyanese	12	0.01
Hawaii Native/Pacific Islander:	143	0.08
Melanesian:	1	0.00
Other Melanesian	1	0.00
Micronesian: (28)	39	0.02
Guamanian/Chamorro (19)	28	0.02
Other Micronesian (9)	11	0.01
Polynesian: (23)	53	0.03
Native Hawaiian (14)	38	0.02
Samoan (9)	14	0.01
Other Polynesian	1	0.00
Other Pac. Isl., specified	6	0.00
Other Pac. Isl., not spec. (9)	44	0.03
Hispanic or Latino:	2,751	1.58
Central American:	181	0.10
Costa Rican	16	0.01
Guatemalan	61	0.04
Honduran	40	0.02
Nicaraguan	8	0.00
Panamanian	25	0.01
Salvadoran	23	0.01
Other Central American	8	0.00
Cuban	119	0.07
Dominican Republic	12	0.01
Mexican	1,474	0.85
Puerto Rican	291	0.17
South American:	144	0.08
Argentinean	24	0.01
Bolivian	8	0.00
Chilean	10	0.01
Colombian	33	0.02
Ecuadorian	11	0.01
Paraguayan	1	0.00
Peruvian	18	0.01
Venezuelan	30	0.02
Other South American	9	0.01
Other Hispanic or Latino	530	0.30
Hungarian	325	0.19
Iranian	101	0.06
Irish	17,050	9.82
Israeli	25	0.01
Italian	3,223	1.86
Latvian	25	0.01
Lithuanian	145	0.08
Macedonian	32	0.02
Northern European	33	0.02
Norwegian	791	0.46
Pennsylvania German	13	0.01
Polish	1,606	0.92
Portuguese	161	0.09

Notes: 1. Figures in the "Number" column do not add up to the total population due to: a) Ancestry/Race overlap — e.g. persons can report being both White and Irish, b) persons of Hispanic origin can report being any race, c) persons reporting two ancestries are counted in both categories. 2. Numbers in parentheses indicate the number of persons reporting this ancestry/race alone, not in combination with any other ancestry/race. 3. Refer to the Explanation of Data in the front of the book for more detailed information.

Romanian	211	0.12
Russian	579	0.33
Scandinavian	186	0.11
Scotch-Irish	6,779	3.90
Scottish	4,360	2.51
Serbian	10	0.01
Slavic	46	0.03
Slovak	42	0.02
Slovene	27	0.02
Swedish	960	0.55
Swiss	525	0.30
Turkish	157	0.09
Ukrainian	153	0.09
United States or American	23,175	13.34
Welsh	1,248	0.72
West Indian, excl. Hispanic:	331	0.19
Bahamian	15	0.01
Barbadian	17	0.01
Bermudan	8	0.00
British West Indian	11	0.01
Dutch West Indian	140	0.08
Haitian	12	0.01
Jamaican	90	0.05
Trinidadian and Tobagonian	13	0.01
West Indian	25	0.01
White:	140,965	81.07
Not Hispanic (137,336)	139,473	80.21
Hispanic (1,275)	1,492	0.86
Yugoslavian	123	0.07

La Vergne

Place Type: City
County: Rutherford
Population: 18,687

Ancestry/Race	Number	%
African American/Black:	2,150	11.51
Not Hispanic (2,038)	2,107	11.28
Hispanic (21)	43	0.23
African, sub-Saharan:	357	1.89
African	323	1.71
Nigerian	34	0.18
Am. Ind. or Alaska Nat., not spec.	47	0.25
American Indian tribes, specified:	105	0.56
Apache (1)	1	0.01
Blackfeet	4	0.02
Cherokee (40)	76	0.41
Chickasaw	1	0.01
Chippewa (1)	3	0.02
Comanche	1	0.01
Crow (3)	3	0.02
Iroquois (3)	3	0.02
Latin American Indians	3	0.02
Osage (1)	1	0.01
Ottawa (1)	1	0.01
Seminole (1)	1	0.01
Sioux	1	0.01
All other tribes (4)	6	0.03
American Indian tribes, not spec.	7	0.04
Arab:	72	0.38
Arab/Arabic	23	0.12
Egyptian	8	0.04
Moroccan	8	0.04
Palestinian	33	0.17
Asian:	315	1.69
Cambodian (3)	4	0.02
Chinese, ex. Taiwanese (10)	18	0.10
Filipino (18)	28	0.15
Hmong (1)	1	0.01
Indian (32)	40	0.21
Japanese (9)	18	0.10
Korean (43)	50	0.27
Laotian (95)	99	0.53
Malaysian (3)	3	0.02
Taiwanese	1	0.01
Thai (4)	5	0.03
Vietnamese (2)	11	0.06
Other Asian, not specified (24)	37	0.20
Australian	28	0.15
British	52	0.27
Canadian	19	0.10
Czech	7	0.04
Dutch	352	1.86
English	1,427	7.54
European	129	0.68
Finnish	31	0.16
French, except Basque	534	2.82
French Canadian	92	0.49
German	1,849	9.78
Greek	22	0.12
Hawaii Native/Pacific Islander:	24	0.13
Micronesian: (7)	9	0.05
Guamanian/Chamorro (7)	9	0.05
Polynesian: (4)	8	0.04
Native Hawaiian (2)	3	0.02
Samoan (2)	5	0.03
Other Pac. Isl., not spec. (2)	7	0.04
Hispanic or Latino:	661	3.54
Central American:	46	0.25
Guatemalan	10	0.05
Honduran	1	0.01
Nicaraguan	2	0.01
Panamanian	1	0.01
Salvadoran	24	0.13
Other Central American	8	0.04
Cuban	13	0.07
Dominican Republic	5	0.03
Mexican	335	1.79
Puerto Rican	146	0.78
South American:	16	0.09
Argentinean	1	0.01
Bolivian	2	0.01
Chilean	1	0.01
Ecuadorian	2	0.01
Peruvian	4	0.02
Venezuelan	6	0.03
Other Hispanic or Latino	100	0.54
Hungarian	55	0.29
Irish	2,238	11.83
Israeli	7	0.04
Italian	653	3.45
Lithuanian	7	0.04
Norwegian	186	0.98
Polish	240	1.27
Portuguese	8	0.04
Romanian	21	0.11
Russian	19	0.10
Scandinavian	35	0.19
Scotch-Irish	531	2.81
Scottish	373	1.97
Slovak	62	0.33
Swedish	213	1.13
Swiss	19	0.10
Ukrainian	44	0.23
United States or American	3,599	19.03
Welsh	133	0.70
West Indian, excl. Hispanic:	34	0.18
Dutch West Indian	34	0.18
White:	16,014	85.70
Not Hispanic (15,450)	15,627	83.62
Hispanic (340)	387	2.07

Lawrenceburg

Place Type: City
County: Lawrence
Population: 10,796

Ancestry/Race	Number	%
African American/Black:	467	4.33
Not Hispanic (424)	465	4.31
Hispanic (1)	2	0.02
Alaska Native tribes, specified:	3	0.03
Alaska Athabascan (1)	1	0.01
Aleut	2	0.02
Am. Ind. or Alaska Nat., not spec.	27	0.25
American Indian tribes, specified:	54	0.50
Blackfeet (1)	1	0.01
Cherokee (27)	42	0.39
Chickasaw (3)	3	0.03
Chippewa (4)	4	0.04
Choctaw (1)	2	0.02
Osage	1	0.01
All other tribes (1)	1	0.01
American Indian tribes, not spec.	12	0.11
Asian:	51	0.47
Chinese, ex. Taiwanese (4)	4	0.04
Filipino (5)	8	0.07
Indian (11)	12	0.11
Japanese (4)	6	0.06
Korean (13)	13	0.12
Thai (1)	3	0.03
Vietnamese (2)	2	0.02
Other Asian, specified (1)	1	0.01
Other Asian, not specified (1)	2	0.02
Austrian	6	0.06
Belgian	6	0.06
British	36	0.34
Bulgarian	13	0.12
Canadian	26	0.25
Czech	10	0.10
Danish	25	0.24
Dutch	80	0.76
English	653	6.24
European	29	0.28
French, except Basque	186	1.78
French Canadian	13	0.12
German	824	7.87
Hawaii Native/Pacific Islander:	12	0.11
Polynesian: (2)	11	0.10
Native Hawaiian	8	0.07
Samoan (2)	3	0.03
Other Pac. Isl., not spec. (1)	1	0.01
Hispanic or Latino:	180	1.67
Central American:	4	0.04
Honduran	1	0.01
Salvadoran	1	0.01
Other Central American	2	0.02
Cuban	9	0.08
Mexican	123	1.14
Puerto Rican	20	0.19
Other Hispanic or Latino	24	0.22
Irish	1,216	11.61
Italian	123	1.17
Polish	73	0.70
Portuguese	12	0.11
Scotch-Irish	212	2.02
Scottish	101	0.96
Swedish	20	0.19
United States or American	2,227	21.26
White:	10,181	94.30
Not Hispanic (9,989)	10,088	93.44
Hispanic (83)	93	0.86

Lebanon

Place Type: City
County: Wilson
Population: 20,235

Ancestry/Race	Number	%
African American/Black:	2,891	14.29
Not Hispanic (2,779)	2,878	14.22
Hispanic (10)	13	0.06
African, sub-Saharan:	100	0.49
African	71	0.35
Nigerian	29	0.14
Am. Ind. or Alaska Nat., not spec.	39	0.19
Albanian	7	0.03
American Indian tribes, specified:	111	0.55
Apache	1	0.00
Blackfeet (1)	3	0.01
Cherokee (16)	57	0.28
Chickasaw	1	0.00
Chippewa (2)	4	0.02
Choctaw (4)	9	0.04
Comanche (1)	1	0.00
Creek (10)	14	0.07
Delaware	1	0.00

Notes: 1. Figures in the "Number" column do not add up to the total population due to: a) Ancestry/Race overlap — e.g. persons can report being both White and Irish, b) persons of Hispanic origin can report being any race, c) persons reporting two ancestries are counted in both categories. 2. Numbers in parentheses indicate the number of persons reporting this ancestry/race alone, not in combination with any other ancestry/race. 3. Refer to the Explanation of Data in the front of the book for more detailed information.

Ancestry/Race	Number	%
Iroquois	1	0.00
Latin American Indians (4)	4	0.02
Navajo (2)	2	0.01
Potawatomi (1)	2	0.01
Pueblo (1)	1	0.00
All other tribes (7)	10	0.05
American Indian tribes, not spec.	6	0.03
Arab:	28	0.14
Arab/Arabic	19	0.09
Lebanese	9	0.04
Asian:	191	0.94
Chinese, ex. Taiwanese (29)	34	0.17
Filipino (6)	14	0.07
Indian (75)	79	0.39
Japanese (22)	22	0.11
Korean (14)	16	0.08
Laotian (3)	4	0.02
Thai (2)	3	0.01
Vietnamese (11)	11	0.05
Other Asian, specified (1)	2	0.01
Other Asian, not specified (1)	6	0.03
Australian	9	0.04
British	79	0.39
Canadian	43	0.21
Czech	15	0.07
Czechoslovakian	22	0.11
Danish	13	0.06
Dutch	209	1.03
Eastern European	7	0.03
English	1,972	9.72
Estonian	6	0.03
European	97	0.48
French, except Basque	429	2.11
French Canadian	42	0.21
German	1,487	7.33
Greek	56	0.28
Hawaii Native/Pacific Islander:	20	0.10
Micronesian:	1	0.00
Guamanian/Chamorro	1	0.00
Polynesian: (5)	16	0.08
Native Hawaiian (4)	13	0.06
Samoan (1)	3	0.01
Other Pac. Isl., specified	1	0.00
Other Pac. Isl., not spec. (2)	2	0.01
Hispanic or Latino:	457	2.26
Central American:	22	0.11
Costa Rican	2	0.01
Guatemalan	16	0.08
Panamanian	1	0.00
Salvadoran	1	0.00
Other Central American	2	0.01
Cuban	7	0.03
Mexican	320	1.58
Puerto Rican	25	0.12
South American:	3	0.01
Colombian	1	0.00
Venezuelan	2	0.01
Other Hispanic or Latino	80	0.40
Hungarian	13	0.06
Irish	1,793	8.83
Israeli	7	0.03
Italian	293	1.44
Latvian	18	0.09
Norwegian	72	0.35
Polish	144	0.71
Portuguese	21	0.10
Russian	18	0.09
Scandinavian	12	0.06
Scotch-Irish	501	2.47
Scottish	281	1.38
Swedish	64	0.32
Swiss	13	0.06
Ukrainian	5	0.02
United States or American	5,002	24.64
Welsh	62	0.31
West Indian, excl. Hispanic:	7	0.03
Dutch West Indian	2	0.01
Jamaican	5	0.02
White:	16,990	83.96
Not Hispanic (16,553)	16,745	82.75
Hispanic (220)	245	1.21

Lewisburg

Place Type: City
County: Marshall
Population: 10,413

Ancestry/Race	Number	%
African American/Black:	1,656	15.90
Not Hispanic (1,604)	1,651	15.86
Hispanic (4)	5	0.05
African, sub-Saharan:	24	0.23
African	24	0.23
Alaska Native tribes, specified:	1	0.01
Alaska Athabascan (1)	1	0.01
Am. Ind. or Alaska Nat., not spec.	27	0.26
American Indian tribes, specified:	26	0.25
Blackfeet	1	0.01
Cherokee (2)	15	0.14
Chippewa (2)	2	0.02
Choctaw (2)	2	0.02
Lumbee	1	0.01
Osage	1	0.01
All other tribes	4	0.04
American Indian tribes, not spec.	7	0.07
Asian:	60	0.58
Chinese, ex. Taiwanese (5)	6	0.06
Filipino (19)	22	0.21
Indian (5)	8	0.08
Japanese (15)	16	0.15
Korean (3)	6	0.06
Laotian (1)	1	0.01
Other Asian, not specified	1	0.01
British	19	0.18
Canadian	11	0.11
Czech	6	0.06
Danish	6	0.06
Dutch	123	1.19
English	838	8.08
European	14	0.14
Finnish	5	0.05
French, except Basque	130	1.25
French Canadian	57	0.55
German	683	6.59
Greek	21	0.20
Hawaii Native/Pacific Islander:	4	0.04
Micronesian: (2)	2	0.02
Guamanian/Chamorro (2)	2	0.02
Polynesian: (1)	2	0.02
Native Hawaiian	1	0.01
Samoan (1)	1	0.01
Hispanic or Latino:	536	5.15
Central American:	4	0.04
Guatemalan	2	0.02
Honduran	2	0.02
Cuban	3	0.03
Mexican	438	4.21
Puerto Rican	28	0.27
Other Hispanic or Latino	63	0.61
Hungarian	13	0.13
Irish	818	7.89
Italian	64	0.62
Lithuanian	5	0.05
Norwegian	77	0.74
Pennsylvania German	4	0.04
Polish	68	0.66
Scandinavian	8	0.08
Scotch-Irish	297	2.86
Scottish	162	1.56
Slavic	6	0.06
Swedish	49	0.47
United States or American	2,365	22.81
Welsh	19	0.18
White:	8,428	80.94
Not Hispanic (8,099)	8,187	78.62
Hispanic (227)	241	2.31

Martin

Place Type: City
County: Weakley
Population: 10,515

Ancestry/Race	Number	%
African American/Black:	1,685	16.02
Not Hispanic (1,633)	1,672	15.90
Hispanic (9)	13	0.12
African, sub-Saharan:	122	1.16
African	100	0.95
Nigerian	14	0.13
Senegalese	8	0.08
Am. Ind. or Alaska Nat., not spec.	14	0.13
American Indian tribes, specified:	16	0.15
Apache	1	0.01
Cherokee (3)	8	0.08
Chickasaw	1	0.01
Choctaw (1)	3	0.03
Houma (1)	1	0.01
Latin American Indians	1	0.01
All other tribes	1	0.01
Arab:	129	1.22
Arab/Arabic	65	0.62
Egyptian	20	0.19
Jordanian	5	0.05
Lebanese	16	0.15
Palestinian	5	0.05
Syrian	9	0.09
Other Arab	9	0.09
Asian:	474	4.51
Chinese, ex. Taiwanese (83)	96	0.91
Filipino (22)	25	0.24
Indian (49)	52	0.49
Indonesian (1)	1	0.01
Japanese (76)	80	0.76
Korean (142)	145	1.38
Malaysian (1)	1	0.01
Pakistani	1	0.01
Taiwanese (26)	37	0.35
Thai (9)	10	0.10
Vietnamese (7)	9	0.09
Other Asian, not specified (6)	17	0.16
Assyrian/Chaldean/Syriac	21	0.20
Belgian	17	0.16
British	41	0.39
Canadian	18	0.17
Celtic	9	0.09
Danish	17	0.16
Dutch	74	0.70
English	778	7.38
European	303	2.87
French, except Basque	139	1.32
French Canadian	7	0.07
German	565	5.36
Greek	42	0.40
Hawaii Native/Pacific Islander:	3	0.03
Polynesian:	2	0.02
Native Hawaiian	2	0.02
Other Pac. Isl., not spec.	1	0.01
Hispanic or Latino:	191	1.82
Central American:	4	0.04
Honduran	1	0.01
Panamanian	3	0.03
Cuban	1	0.01
Mexican	140	1.33
Puerto Rican	12	0.11
South American:	11	0.10
Chilean	1	0.01
Colombian	1	0.01
Ecuadorian	1	0.01
Venezuelan	8	0.08
Other Hispanic or Latino	23	0.22
Irish	1,078	10.22
Italian	111	1.05
Lithuanian	9	0.09
Macedonian	8	0.08
Norwegian	56	0.53
Pennsylvania German	8	0.08

Notes: 1. Figures in the "Number" column do not add up to the total population due to: a) Ancestry/Race overlap — e.g. persons can report being both White and Irish, b) persons of Hispanic origin can report being any race, c) persons reporting two ancestries are counted in both categories. 2. Numbers in parentheses indicate the number of persons reporting this ancestry/race alone, not in combination with any other ancestry/race. 3. Refer to the Explanation of Data in the front of the book for more detailed information.

Ancestry/Race	Number	%
Polish	52	0.49
Romanian	24	0.23
Russian	17	0.16
Scotch-Irish	231	2.19
Scottish	164	1.56
Swedish	43	0.41
Ukrainian	12	0.11
United States or American	1,954	18.53
Welsh	58	0.55
West Indian, excl. Hispanic:	16	0.15
Dutch West Indian	16	0.15
White:	8,318	79.11
Not Hispanic (8,162)	8,240	78.36
Hispanic (73)	78	0.74

Maryville

Place Type: City
County: Blount
Population: 23,120

Ancestry/Race	Number	%
Acadian/Cajun	14	0.06
African American/Black:	768	3.32
Not Hispanic (670)	755	3.27
Hispanic (11)	13	0.06
African, sub-Saharan:	77	0.33
African	72	0.31
Kenyan	5	0.02
Alaska Native tribes, specified:	7	0.03
Eskimo	3	0.01
Tlingit-Haida (4)	4	0.02
Am. Ind. or Alaska Nat., not spec.	40	0.17
American Indian tribes, specified:	101	0.44
Blackfeet	1	0.00
Cherokee (22)	72	0.31
Chickasaw (2)	2	0.01
Choctaw (4)	4	0.02
Creek (1)	3	0.01
Iroquois	5	0.02
Latin American Indians (1)	1	0.00
Lumbee (1)	1	0.00
Pima	1	0.00
Sioux	1	0.00
All other tribes (2)	10	0.04
American Indian tribes, not spec.	6	0.03
Arab:	88	0.38
Iraqi	20	0.09
Jordanian	19	0.08
Lebanese	49	0.21
Asian:	418	1.81
Chinese, ex. Taiwanese (19)	27	0.12
Filipino (12)	20	0.09
Indian (20)	23	0.10
Indonesian (2)	3	0.01
Japanese (243)	264	1.14
Korean (20)	23	0.10
Laotian (2)	2	0.01
Malaysian (3)	5	0.02
Pakistani (2)	4	0.02
Taiwanese (5)	5	0.02
Thai (7)	8	0.03
Vietnamese (9)	9	0.04
Other Asian, not specified (9)	25	0.11
Austrian	8	0.03
Belgian	12	0.05
Brazilian	26	0.11
British	111	0.48
Canadian	11	0.05
Celtic	28	0.12
Czech	61	0.26
Czechoslovakian	18	0.08
Danish	33	0.14
Dutch	491	2.12
English	2,801	12.09
European	152	0.66
Finnish	6	0.03
French, except Basque	565	2.44
French Canadian	61	0.26
German	3,078	13.29
Greek	24	0.10
Hawaii Native/Pacific Islander:	15	0.06
Micronesian: (4)	6	0.03
Guamanian/Chamorro (4)	6	0.03
Polynesian: (4)	8	0.03
Native Hawaiian (2)	4	0.02
Samoan (2)	4	0.02
Other Pac. Isl., not spec.	1	0.00
Hispanic or Latino:	318	1.38
Central American:	18	0.08
Guatemalan	3	0.01
Honduran	7	0.03
Nicaraguan	1	0.00
Panamanian	3	0.01
Salvadoran	4	0.02
Cuban	10	0.04
Dominican Republic	8	0.03
Mexican	195	0.84
Puerto Rican	25	0.11
South American:	12	0.05
Bolivian	1	0.00
Chilean	1	0.00
Colombian	5	0.02
Ecuadorian	4	0.02
Venezuelan	1	0.00
Other Hispanic or Latino	50	0.22
Hungarian	8	0.03
Irish	2,602	11.23
Italian	280	1.21
Lithuanian	69	0.30
Luxemburger	7	0.03
Macedonian	12	0.05
Northern European	24	0.10
Norwegian	109	0.47
Polish	340	1.47
Portuguese	29	0.13
Russian	41	0.18
Scandinavian	59	0.25
Scotch-Irish	1,315	5.68
Scottish	652	2.81
Serbian	20	0.09
Slavic	14	0.06
Slovak	34	0.15
Slovene	27	0.12
Swedish	159	0.69
Swiss	47	0.20
Turkish	14	0.06
Ukrainian	21	0.09
United States or American	4,088	17.65
Welsh	217	0.94
West Indian, excl. Hispanic:	38	0.16
Dutch West Indian	23	0.10
Jamaican	9	0.04
West Indian	6	0.03
White:	21,888	94.67
Not Hispanic (21,463)	21,688	93.81
Hispanic (174)	200	0.87
Yugoslavian	44	0.19

McMinnville

Place Type: City
County: Warren
Population: 12,749

Ancestry/Race	Number	%
Acadian/Cajun	9	0.07
African American/Black:	566	4.44
Not Hispanic (525)	559	4.38
Hispanic (4)	7	0.05
African, sub-Saharan:	22	0.17
African	22	0.17
Am. Ind. or Alaska Nat., not spec.	30	0.24
American Indian tribes, specified:	35	0.27
Cherokee (9)	30	0.24
Choctaw	1	0.01
Comanche (1)	1	0.01
Lumbee (1)	1	0.01
All other tribes (1)	2	0.02
American Indian tribes, not spec.	5	0.04
Asian:	136	1.07
Chinese, ex. Taiwanese (19)	19	0.15
Filipino (10)	10	0.08
Indian (21)	31	0.24
Japanese (61)	63	0.49
Korean (1)	1	0.01
Vietnamese (7)	7	0.05
Other Asian, not specified	5	0.04
British	73	0.57
Bulgarian	9	0.07
Czechoslovakian	27	0.21
Danish	12	0.09
Dutch	146	1.15
English	890	6.98
European	87	0.68
Finnish	11	0.09
French, except Basque	111	0.87
French Canadian	94	0.74
German	825	6.47
Hawaii Native/Pacific Islander:	11	0.09
Polynesian: (6)	8	0.06
Samoan (6)	8	0.06
Other Pac. Isl., not spec. (1)	3	0.02
Hispanic or Latino:	868	6.81
Central American:	10	0.08
Guatemalan	3	0.02
Salvadoran	7	0.05
Cuban	13	0.10
Mexican	751	5.89
Puerto Rican	41	0.32
South American:	1	0.01
Colombian	1	0.01
Other Hispanic or Latino	52	0.41
Hungarian	20	0.16
Irish	1,296	10.17
Italian	118	0.93
Northern European	9	0.07
Norwegian	41	0.32
Polish	115	0.90
Scandinavian	10	0.08
Scotch-Irish	262	2.06
Scottish	136	1.07
Swedish	63	0.49
United States or American	2,910	22.84
Welsh	26	0.20
White:	11,426	89.62
Not Hispanic (11,101)	11,204	87.88
Hispanic (172)	222	1.74

Memphis

Place Type: City
County: Shelby
Population: 650,100

Ancestry/Race	Number	%
Acadian/Cajun	76	0.01
Afghan	31	0.00
African American/Black:	402,367	61.89
Not Hispanic (397,732)	400,616	61.62
Hispanic (1,476)	1,751	0.27
African, sub-Saharan:	10,794	1.66
African	9,612	1.48
Ethiopian	134	0.02
Ghanian	27	0.00
Kenyan	65	0.01
Liberian	48	0.01
Nigerian	591	0.09
Somalian	116	0.02
South African	52	0.01
Sudanese	31	0.00
Other sub-Saharan African	118	0.02
Alaska Native tribes, specified:	13	0.00
Alaska Athabascan (2)	9	0.00
Aleut (1)	2	0.00
Eskimo	2	0.00
Am. Ind. or Alaska Nat., not spec.	1,406	0.22
Albanian	23	0.00
Alsatian	8	0.00
American Indian tribes, specified:	1,642	0.25

Notes: 1. Figures in the "Number" column do not add up to the total population due to: a) Ancestry/Race overlap — e.g. persons can report being both White and Irish, b) persons of Hispanic origin can report being any race, c) persons reporting two ancestries are counted in both categories. 2. Numbers in parentheses indicate the number of persons reporting this ancestry/race alone, not in combination with any other ancestry/race. 3. Refer to the Explanation of Data in the front of the book for more detailed information.

Ancestry/Race	Number	%
Apache (20)	58	0.01
Blackfeet (8)	54	0.01
Cherokee (275)	870	0.13
Cheyenne (1)	2	0.00
Chickasaw (5)	30	0.00
Chippewa (9)	18	0.00
Choctaw (66)	171	0.03
Comanche (1)	9	0.00
Cree (1)	5	0.00
Creek (8)	34	0.01
Crow	3	0.00
Delaware (1)	7	0.00
Iroquois (23)	30	0.00
Kiowa (1)	1	0.00
Latin American Indians (80)	102	0.02
Lumbee (7)	12	0.00
Menominee (1)	1	0.00
Navajo (10)	21	0.00
Osage	1	0.00
Paiute (1)	6	0.00
Pima	3	0.00
Potawatomi (2)	4	0.00
Pueblo (5)	21	0.00
Puget Sound Salish (1)	1	0.00
Seminole (1)	7	0.00
Shoshone (8)	12	0.00
Sioux (25)	55	0.01
Tohono O'Odham	1	0.00
Ute (1)	1	0.00
Yaqui (1)	7	0.00
Yuman (1)	2	0.00
All other tribes (29)	93	0.01
American Indian tribes, not spec.	192	0.03
Arab:	1,837	0.28
Arab/Arabic	476	0.07
Egyptian	77	0.01
Iraqi	130	0.02
Jordanian	122	0.02
Lebanese	390	0.06
Moroccan	24	0.00
Palestinian	288	0.04
Syrian	128	0.02
Other Arab	202	0.03
Armenian	102	0.02
Asian:	11,193	1.72
Bangladeshi (24)	25	0.00
Cambodian (465)	533	0.08
Chinese, ex. Taiwanese (1,721)	1,919	0.30
Filipino (578)	830	0.13
Hmong (43)	47	0.01
Indian (2,216)	2,487	0.38
Indonesian (13)	24	0.00
Japanese (293)	446	0.07
Korean (659)	795	0.12
Laotian (293)	330	0.05
Malaysian (20)	30	0.00
Pakistani (147)	174	0.03
Sri Lankan (13)	15	0.00
Taiwanese (20)	33	0.01
Thai (103)	116	0.02
Vietnamese (2,529)	2,707	0.42
Other Asian, specified (12)	61	0.01
Other Asian, not specified (210)	621	0.10
Australian	20	0.00
Austrian	410	0.06
Basque	21	0.00
Belgian	66	0.01
Brazilian	81	0.01
British	1,542	0.24
Bulgarian	30	0.00
Canadian	423	0.07
Celtic	140	0.02
Croatian	114	0.02
Czech	329	0.05
Czechoslovakian	204	0.03
Danish	512	0.08
Dutch	3,655	0.56
Eastern European	279	0.04
English	34,030	5.24
Estonian	11	0.00
European	4,163	0.64
Finnish	129	0.02
French, except Basque	7,464	1.15
French Canadian	955	0.15
German	27,044	4.16
German Russian	9	0.00
Greek	830	0.13
Guyanese	106	0.02
Hawaii Native/Pacific Islander:	592	0.09
Melanesian: (1)	1	0.00
Other Melanesian (1)	1	0.00
Micronesian: (96)	137	0.02
Guamanian/Chamorro (95)	136	0.02
Other Micronesian (1)	1	0.00
Polynesian: (101)	261	0.04
Native Hawaiian (44)	144	0.02
Samoan (49)	90	0.01
Tongan (5)	10	0.00
Other Polynesian (3)	17	0.00
Other Pac. Isl., specified	43	0.01
Other Pac. Isl., not spec. (38)	150	0.02
Hispanic or Latino:	19,317	2.97
Central American:	865	0.13
Costa Rican	28	0.00
Guatemalan	155	0.02
Honduran	320	0.05
Nicaraguan	34	0.01
Panamanian	94	0.01
Salvadoran	188	0.03
Other Central American	46	0.01
Cuban	521	0.08
Dominican Republic	45	0.01
Mexican	14,087	2.17
Puerto Rican	742	0.11
South American:	413	0.06
Argentinean	33	0.01
Bolivian	16	0.00
Chilean	64	0.01
Colombian	141	0.02
Ecuadorian	16	0.00
Paraguayan	3	0.00
Peruvian	28	0.00
Uruguayan	12	0.00
Venezuelan	72	0.01
Other South American	28	0.00
Other Hispanic or Latino	2,644	0.41
Hungarian	543	0.08
Icelander	96	0.01
Iranian	262	0.04
Irish	31,924	4.91
Israeli	50	0.01
Italian	10,170	1.56
Latvian	103	0.02
Lithuanian	186	0.03
Luxemburger	14	0.00
Maltese	8	0.00
New Zealander	15	0.00
Northern European	104	0.02
Norwegian	1,281	0.20
Pennsylvania German	30	0.00
Polish	3,253	0.50
Portuguese	161	0.02
Romanian	166	0.03
Russian	1,713	0.26
Scandinavian	229	0.04
Scotch-Irish	11,311	1.74
Scottish	7,522	1.16
Serbian	49	0.01
Slavic	72	0.01
Slovak	269	0.04
Slovene	40	0.01
Swedish	1,663	0.26
Swiss	377	0.06
Turkish	46	0.01
Ukrainian	335	0.05
United States or American	29,105	4.48
Welsh	1,391	0.21
West Indian, excl. Hispanic:	545	0.08
Bahamian	15	0.00
Barbadian	7	0.00
Belizean	12	0.00
British West Indian	58	0.01
Haitian	123	0.02
Jamaican	207	0.03
Trinidadian and Tobagonian	35	0.01
U.S. Virgin Islander	14	0.00
West Indian	64	0.01
Other West Indian	10	0.00
White:	228,633	35.17
Not Hispanic (216,174)	220,230	33.88
Hispanic (7,554)	8,403	1.29
Yugoslavian	169	0.03

Middle Valley

Place Type: Census Designated Place
County: Hamilton
Population: 11,854

Ancestry/Race	Number	%
African American/Black:	234	1.97
Not Hispanic (222)	234	1.97
Am. Ind. or Alaska Nat., not spec.	6	0.05
American Indian tribes, specified:	64	0.54
Apache	3	0.03
Blackfeet	3	0.03
Cherokee (16)	36	0.30
Choctaw	1	0.01
Creek	4	0.03
Iroquois (3)	3	0.03
Latin American Indians	1	0.01
Lumbee (3)	3	0.03
Osage (2)	2	0.02
Yaqui	1	0.01
All other tribes (5)	7	0.06
Arab:	42	0.36
Iraqi	31	0.26
Jordanian	9	0.08
Other Arab	2	0.02
Asian:	135	1.14
Cambodian (6)	6	0.05
Chinese, ex. Taiwanese (34)	36	0.30
Filipino (5)	8	0.07
Indian (21)	21	0.18
Japanese (4)	4	0.03
Korean (17)	20	0.17
Laotian (5)	5	0.04
Pakistani (4)	5	0.04
Sri Lankan (1)	1	0.01
Thai (2)	2	0.02
Vietnamese (23)	24	0.20
Other Asian, not specified (1)	3	0.03
Assyrian/Chaldean/Syriac	7	0.06
Austrian	6	0.05
Belgian	5	0.04
British	88	0.75
Bulgarian	19	0.16
Canadian	15	0.13
Celtic	5	0.04
Croatian	8	0.07
Czechoslovakian	12	0.10
Danish	9	0.08
Dutch	217	1.84
English	1,330	11.29
European	63	0.53
French, except Basque	181	1.54
French Canadian	17	0.14
German	1,276	10.83
Greek	36	0.31
Hawaii Native/Pacific Islander:	7	0.06
Polynesian:	4	0.03
Samoan	4	0.03
Other Pac. Isl., not spec. (3)	3	0.03
Hispanic or Latino:	95	0.80
Cuban	3	0.03
Mexican	40	0.34
Puerto Rican	14	0.12
South American:	9	0.08
Peruvian	4	0.03
Venezuelan	1	0.01

Notes: 1. Figures in the "Number" column do not add up to the total population due to: a) Ancestry/Race overlap — e.g. persons can report being both White and Irish, b) persons of Hispanic origin can report being any race, c) persons reporting two ancestries are counted in both categories. 2. Numbers in parentheses indicate the number of persons reporting this ancestry/race alone, not in combination with any other ancestry/race. 3. Refer to the Explanation of Data in the front of the book for more detailed information.

Other South American	4	0.03
Other Hispanic or Latino	29	0.24
Hungarian	9	0.08
Irish	1,298	11.02
Italian	298	2.53
Lithuanian	44	0.37
Luxemburger	6	0.05
Norwegian	81	0.69
Polish	103	0.87
Portuguese	8	0.07
Russian	20	0.17
Scandinavian	8	0.07
Scotch-Irish	324	2.75
Scottish	191	1.62
Serbian	6	0.05
Swedish	61	0.52
Swiss	7	0.06
Ukrainian	11	0.09
United States or American	2,631	22.33
Welsh	70	0.59
White:	11,441	96.52
Not Hispanic (11,307)	11,372	95.93
Hispanic (61)	69	0.58
Yugoslavian	62	0.53

Millington

Place Type: City
County: Shelby
Population: 10,433

Ancestry/Race	Number	%
Acadian/Cajun	8	0.08
African American/Black:	2,375	22.76
Not Hispanic (2,274)	2,341	22.44
Hispanic (31)	34	0.33
African, sub-Saharan:	61	0.60
African	61	0.60
Am. Ind. or Alaska Nat., not spec.	32	0.31
American Indian tribes, specified:	108	1.04
Apache (5)	5	0.05
Blackfeet (4)	10	0.10
Cherokee (36)	63	0.60
Chippewa (1)	1	0.01
Choctaw (2)	4	0.04
Iroquois	2	0.02
Latin American Indians (4)	9	0.09
Osage (1)	1	0.01
Paiute	2	0.02
Sioux (4)	4	0.04
All other tribes (3)	7	0.07
American Indian tribes, not spec.	3	0.03
Arab:	11	0.11
Lebanese	11	0.11
Asian:	366	3.51
Chinese, ex. Taiwanese (24)	31	0.30
Filipino (186)	247	2.37
Indian (5)	8	0.08
Japanese (21)	36	0.35
Korean (10)	22	0.21
Laotian (1)	2	0.02
Taiwanese (1)	1	0.01
Thai (1)	2	0.02
Vietnamese (1)	4	0.04
Other Asian, specified (2)	2	0.02
Other Asian, not specified (9)	11	0.11
Austrian	6	0.06
British	73	0.71
Canadian	10	0.10
Czechoslovakian	11	0.11
Danish	33	0.32
Dutch	77	0.75
English	864	8.45
European	93	0.91
French, except Basque	252	2.46
French Canadian	65	0.64
German	1,067	10.44
Greek	11	0.11
Hawaii Native/Pacific Islander:	35	0.34
Melanesian: (1)	2	0.02
Other Melanesian (1)	2	0.02
Micronesian: (5)	8	0.08
Guamanian/Chamorro (5)	8	0.08
Polynesian: (10)	23	0.22
Native Hawaiian (5)	16	0.15
Samoan (5)	7	0.07
Other Pac. Isl., not spec.	2	0.02
Hispanic or Latino:	486	4.66
Central American:	6	0.06
Costa Rican	1	0.01
Honduran	3	0.03
Panamanian	2	0.02
Cuban	11	0.11
Dominican Republic	8	0.08
Mexican	289	2.77
Puerto Rican	50	0.48
South American:	2	0.02
Chilean	1	0.01
Colombian	1	0.01
Other Hispanic or Latino	120	1.15
Iranian	7	0.07
Irish	1,279	12.51
Italian	399	3.90
Norwegian	106	1.04
Polish	59	0.58
Portuguese	8	0.08
Russian	24	0.23
Scandinavian	6	0.06
Scotch-Irish	138	1.35
Scottish	113	1.11
Swedish	19	0.19
Ukrainian	26	0.25
United States or American	1,135	11.10
Welsh	11	0.11
White:	7,585	72.70
Not Hispanic (7,133)	7,297	69.94
Hispanic (250)	288	2.76

Morristown

Place Type: City
County: Hamblen
Population: 24,965

Ancestry/Race	Number	%
African American/Black:	2,033	8.14
Not Hispanic (1,843)	2,002	8.02
Hispanic (27)	31	0.12
African, sub-Saharan:	48	0.19
African	48	0.19
Am. Ind. or Alaska Nat., not spec.	62	0.25
Alsatian	9	0.04
American Indian tribes, specified:	117	0.47
Apache (1)	2	0.01
Blackfeet	2	0.01
Cherokee (25)	82	0.33
Chickasaw (1)	1	0.00
Comanche (1)	1	0.00
Creek	2	0.01
Latin American Indians (10)	22	0.09
Lumbee (2)	2	0.01
Seminole	1	0.00
All other tribes (2)	2	0.01
American Indian tribes, not spec.	12	0.05
Asian:	192	0.77
Cambodian (4)	4	0.02
Chinese, ex. Taiwanese (6)	9	0.04
Filipino (35)	38	0.15
Indian (66)	72	0.29
Japanese (28)	28	0.11
Korean (11)	12	0.05
Laotian (1)	1	0.00
Thai	1	0.00
Vietnamese (18)	21	0.08
Other Asian, specified	3	0.01
Other Asian, not specified (1)	3	0.01
Austrian	7	0.03
Brazilian	6	0.02
British	45	0.18
Canadian	30	0.12
Croatian	7	0.03
Czech	7	0.03
Czechoslovakian	7	0.03
Danish	25	0.10
Dutch	501	1.98
English	2,351	9.30
European	128	0.51
Finnish	44	0.17
French, except Basque	242	0.96
French Canadian	74	0.29
German	1,792	7.09
Greek	7	0.03
Hawaii Native/Pacific Islander:	33	0.13
Micronesian: (24)	27	0.11
Guamanian/Chamorro (17)	18	0.07
Other Micronesian (7)	9	0.04
Polynesian: (2)	3	0.01
Native Hawaiian (1)	1	0.00
Samoan (1)	2	0.01
Other Pac. Isl., specified	3	0.01
Hispanic or Latino:	2,603	10.43
Central American:	129	0.52
Guatemalan	100	0.40
Honduran	20	0.08
Nicaraguan	3	0.01
Panamanian	1	0.00
Salvadoran	5	0.02
Cuban	28	0.11
Dominican Republic	1	0.00
Mexican	2,281	9.14
Puerto Rican	47	0.19
South American:	12	0.05
Argentinean	2	0.01
Bolivian	1	0.00
Chilean	1	0.00
Colombian	5	0.02
Ecuadorian	1	0.00
Venezuelan	1	0.00
Other South American	1	0.00
Other Hispanic or Latino	105	0.42
Hungarian	21	0.08
Irish	2,166	8.57
Italian	202	0.80
Lithuanian	14	0.06
Norwegian	77	0.30
Polish	146	0.58
Scandinavian	18	0.07
Scotch-Irish	673	2.66
Scottish	302	1.19
Slovak	5	0.02
Swedish	48	0.19
Ukrainian	17	0.07
United States or American	5,225	20.67
Welsh	56	0.22
West Indian, excl. Hispanic:	18	0.07
Haitian	5	0.02
Trinidadian and Tobagonian	13	0.05
White:	21,209	84.95
Not Hispanic (19,957)	20,204	80.93
Hispanic (946)	1,005	4.03

Mount Juliet

Place Type: City
County: Wilson
Population: 12,366

Ancestry/Race	Number	%
African American/Black:	525	4.25
Not Hispanic (486)	524	4.24
Hispanic	1	0.01
African, sub-Saharan:	79	0.64
African	79	0.64
Am. Ind. or Alaska Nat., not spec.	20	0.16
American Indian tribes, specified:	79	0.64
Apache	1	0.01
Cherokee (16)	39	0.32
Chickasaw (2)	2	0.02
Chippewa (10)	17	0.14
Choctaw (2)	7	0.06

Notes: 1. Figures in the "Number" column do not add up to the total population due to: a) Ancestry/Race overlap — e.g. persons can report being both White and Irish, b) persons of Hispanic origin can report being any race, c) persons reporting two ancestries are counted in both categories. 2. Numbers in parentheses indicate the number of persons reporting this ancestry/race alone, not in combination with any other ancestry/race. 3. Refer to the Explanation of Data in the front of the book for more detailed information.

Creek (3)	6	0.05
Delaware	1	0.01
Ottawa (1)	1	0.01
Potawatomi	1	0.01
Pueblo (1)	1	0.01
All other tribes	3	0.02
American Indian tribes, not spec.	6	0.05
Arab:	83	0.68
Lebanese	13	0.11
Moroccan	20	0.16
Palestinian	50	0.41
Asian:	77	0.62
Chinese, ex. Taiwanese (19)	20	0.16
Filipino (20)	26	0.21
Indian (7)	7	0.06
Japanese (5)	7	0.06
Korean (9)	9	0.07
Taiwanese (1)	2	0.02
Thai (2)	5	0.04
Vietnamese (1)	1	0.01
Austrian	15	0.12
Belgian	22	0.18
British	68	0.55
Canadian	20	0.16
Croatian	8	0.07
Czech	15	0.12
Danish	33	0.27
Dutch	200	1.63
English	1,258	10.24
European	195	1.59
French, except Basque	288	2.34
French Canadian	45	0.37
German	1,524	12.41
Greek	66	0.54
Hawaii Native/Pacific Islander:	4	0.03
Micronesian:	1	0.01
Guamanian/Chamorro	1	0.01
Polynesian: (1)	3	0.02
Native Hawaiian (1)	2	0.02
Samoan	1	0.01
Hispanic or Latino:	145	1.17
Central American:	12	0.10
Guatemalan	8	0.06
Nicaraguan	1	0.01
Salvadoran	3	0.02
Cuban	7	0.06
Mexican	71	0.57
Puerto Rican	8	0.06
South American:	7	0.06
Argentinean	1	0.01
Chilean	1	0.01
Colombian	3	0.02
Other South American	2	0.02
Other Hispanic or Latino	40	0.32
Hungarian	59	0.48
Irish	1,539	12.53
Italian	296	2.41
Latvian	7	0.06
Northern European	27	0.22
Norwegian	78	0.63
Polish	191	1.55
Russian	20	0.16
Scotch-Irish	437	3.56
Scottish	259	2.11
Slovak	33	0.27
Swedish	48	0.39
Swiss	9	0.07
Ukrainian	6	0.05
United States or American	2,444	19.89
Welsh	112	0.91
West Indian, excl. Hispanic:	65	0.53
Jamaican	65	0.53
White:	11,725	94.82
Not Hispanic (11,505)	11,607	93.86
Hispanic (102)	118	0.95
Yugoslavian	10	0.08

Murfreesboro

Place Type: City
County: Rutherford
Population: 68,816

Ancestry/Race	Number	%
Acadian/Cajun	17	0.02
African American/Black:	9,900	14.39
Not Hispanic (9,506)	9,828	14.28
Hispanic (54)	72	0.10
African, sub-Saharan:	718	1.04
African	618	0.90
Nigerian	56	0.08
South African	30	0.04
Other sub-Saharan African	14	0.02
Alaska Native tribes, specified:	5	0.01
Aleut (1)	3	0.00
Eskimo (1)	2	0.00
Am. Ind. or Alaska Nat., not spec.	170	0.25
Albanian	33	0.05
American Indian tribes, specified:	247	0.36
Apache (5)	7	0.01
Blackfeet (3)	7	0.01
Cherokee (61)	149	0.22
Cheyenne	1	0.00
Chickasaw	1	0.00
Chippewa (2)	4	0.01
Choctaw (4)	7	0.01
Creek (4)	8	0.01
Houma (2)	2	0.00
Iroquois (1)	2	0.00
Kiowa (3)	3	0.00
Latin American Indians (5)	10	0.01
Lumbee	4	0.01
Navajo (5)	6	0.01
Osage (2)	2	0.00
Potawatomi (1)	1	0.00
Pueblo	3	0.00
Seminole (1)	3	0.00
Sioux (4)	10	0.01
All other tribes (14)	17	0.02
American Indian tribes, not spec.	34	0.05
Arab:	154	0.22
Arab/Arabic	11	0.02
Iraqi	2	0.00
Jordanian	48	0.07
Lebanese	53	0.08
Moroccan	7	0.01
Syrian	8	0.01
Other Arab	25	0.04
Asian:	2,165	3.15
Bangladeshi (5)	5	0.01
Cambodian (6)	6	0.01
Chinese, ex. Taiwanese (144)	173	0.25
Filipino (56)	92	0.13
Hmong	2	0.00
Indian (308)	336	0.49
Indonesian (9)	15	0.02
Japanese (215)	238	0.35
Korean (120)	143	0.21
Laotian (762)	884	1.28
Malaysian (1)	3	0.00
Pakistani (3)	4	0.01
Sri Lankan (4)	7	0.01
Taiwanese (2)	2	0.00
Thai (54)	60	0.09
Vietnamese (42)	54	0.08
Other Asian, specified	2	0.00
Other Asian, not specified (100)	139	0.20
Australian	7	0.01
Austrian	57	0.08
Belgian	10	0.01
Brazilian	19	0.03
British	478	0.69
Canadian	60	0.09
Celtic	45	0.07
Croatian	8	0.01
Czech	88	0.13
Czechoslovakian	23	0.03
Danish	95	0.14
Dutch	839	1.22
English	7,897	11.45
European	436	0.63
Finnish	22	0.03
French, except Basque	1,656	2.40
French Canadian	211	0.31
German	6,977	10.12
German Russian	6	0.01
Greek	137	0.20
Hawaii Native/Pacific Islander:	52	0.08
Micronesian:	2	0.00
Guamanian/Chamorro	2	0.00
Polynesian: (16)	35	0.05
Native Hawaiian (8)	23	0.03
Samoan (5)	9	0.01
Tongan (3)	3	0.00
Other Pac. Isl., not spec. (2)	15	0.02
Hispanic or Latino:	2,430	3.53
Central American:	133	0.19
Costa Rican	7	0.01
Guatemalan	45	0.07
Honduran	11	0.02
Nicaraguan	18	0.03
Panamanian	6	0.01
Salvadoran	34	0.05
Other Central American	12	0.02
Cuban	46	0.07
Dominican Republic	1	0.00
Mexican	1,779	2.59
Puerto Rican	107	0.16
South American:	68	0.10
Argentinean	2	0.00
Bolivian	2	0.00
Chilean	3	0.00
Colombian	25	0.04
Ecuadorian	3	0.00
Paraguayan	1	0.00
Peruvian	11	0.02
Venezuelan	17	0.02
Other South American	4	0.01
Other Hispanic or Latino	296	0.43
Hungarian	78	0.11
Iranian	97	0.14
Irish	6,653	9.65
Israeli	5	0.01
Italian	1,650	2.39
Lithuanian	23	0.03
Maltese	18	0.03
Northern European	49	0.07
Norwegian	433	0.63
Pennsylvania German	12	0.02
Polish	963	1.40
Portuguese	19	0.03
Romanian	69	0.10
Russian	137	0.20
Scandinavian	23	0.03
Scotch-Irish	2,206	3.20
Scottish	1,615	2.34
Slavic	9	0.01
Slovak	40	0.06
Swedish	493	0.71
Swiss	250	0.36
Ukrainian	58	0.08
United States or American	8,782	12.74
Welsh	475	0.69
West Indian, excl. Hispanic:	25	0.04
Jamaican	7	0.01
Trinidadian and Tobagonian	11	0.02
U.S. Virgin Islander	7	0.01
White:	55,695	80.93
Not Hispanic (53,963)	54,604	79.35
Hispanic (984)	1,091	1.59
Yugoslavian	57	0.08

Notes: 1. Figures in the "Number" column do not add up to the total population due to: a) Ancestry/Race overlap — e.g. persons can report being both White and Irish, b) persons of Hispanic origin can report being any race, c) persons reporting two ancestries are counted in both categories. 2. Numbers in parentheses indicate the number of persons reporting this ancestry/race alone, not in combination with any other ancestry/race. 3. Refer to the Explanation of Data in the front of the book for more detailed information.

Nashville-Davidson

Place Type: Special City
County: Davidson
Population: 545,524

Ancestry/Race	Number	%
Acadian/Cajun	185	0.03
Afghan	199	0.04
African American/Black:	149,970	27.49
Not Hispanic (145,483)	148,965	27.31
Hispanic (752)	1,005	0.18
African, sub-Saharan:	7,825	1.43
African	5,495	1.01
Cape Verdean	14	0.00
Ethiopian	431	0.08
Ghanian	118	0.02
Kenyan	5	0.00
Liberian	86	0.02
Nigerian	812	0.15
Somalian	321	0.06
South African	88	0.02
Sudanese	158	0.03
Zimbabwean	29	0.01
Other sub-Saharan African	268	0.05
Alaska Native tribes, specified:	23	0.00
Alaska Athabascan (1)	4	0.00
Aleut (4)	5	0.00
Eskimo (4)	8	0.00
Tlingit-Haida (3)	6	0.00
Alaska Native tribes, not specified	5	0.00
Am. Ind. or Alaska Nat., not spec.	1,257	0.23
Albanian	338	0.06
Alsatian	15	0.00
American Indian tribes, specified:	2,566	0.47
Apache (28)	75	0.01
Blackfeet (11)	80	0.01
Cherokee (483)	1,443	0.26
Cheyenne (7)	17	0.00
Chickasaw (18)	41	0.01
Chippewa (24)	52	0.01
Choctaw (57)	130	0.02
Colville (1)	1	0.00
Comanche (2)	10	0.00
Cree (3)	10	0.00
Creek (52)	76	0.01
Crow (3)	8	0.00
Delaware (3)	8	0.00
Houma (9)	9	0.00
Iroquois (46)	78	0.01
Kiowa (3)	4	0.00
Latin American Indians (87)	156	0.03
Lumbee (17)	20	0.00
Menominee (1)	1	0.00
Navajo (31)	53	0.01
Osage (9)	10	0.00
Ottawa (5)	8	0.00
Paiute (3)	3	0.00
Pima (5)	6	0.00
Potawatomi (6)	9	0.00
Pueblo (2)	12	0.00
Seminole (14)	31	0.01
Shoshone (3)	4	0.00
Sioux (30)	64	0.01
Ute (1)	3	0.00
Yaqui (2)	2	0.00
Yuman (1)	3	0.00
All other tribes (66)	139	0.03
American Indian tribes, not spec.	281	0.05
Arab:	4,761	0.87
Arab/Arabic	379	0.07
Egyptian	918	0.17
Iraqi	598	0.11
Jordanian	105	0.02
Lebanese	568	0.10
Moroccan	15	0.00
Palestinian	130	0.02
Syrian	123	0.02
Other Arab	1,925	0.35
Armenian	265	0.05
Asian:	15,972	2.93
Bangladeshi (65)	79	0.01
Cambodian (410)	472	0.09
Chinese, ex. Taiwanese (1,837)	2,049	0.38
Filipino (796)	1,068	0.20
Hmong (2)	2	0.00
Indian (2,607)	2,962	0.54
Indonesian (29)	53	0.01
Japanese (644)	839	0.15
Korean (1,596)	1,810	0.33
Laotian (1,791)	2,045	0.37
Malaysian (34)	43	0.01
Pakistani (124)	170	0.03
Sri Lankan (24)	27	0.00
Taiwanese (79)	96	0.02
Thai (291)	350	0.06
Vietnamese (1,972)	2,134	0.39
Other Asian, specified (21)	39	0.01
Other Asian, not specified (472)	1,734	0.32
Assyrian/Chaldean/Syriac	22	0.00
Australian	174	0.03
Austrian	593	0.11
Basque	26	0.00
Belgian	247	0.05
Brazilian	58	0.01
British	3,480	0.64
Bulgarian	18	0.00
Canadian	726	0.13
Carpatho Rusyn	6	0.00
Celtic	162	0.03
Croatian	266	0.05
Czech	881	0.16
Czechoslovakian	483	0.09
Danish	1,128	0.21
Dutch	6,005	1.10
Eastern European	264	0.05
English	49,163	9.01
Estonian	71	0.01
European	5,242	0.96
Finnish	325	0.06
French, except Basque	9,867	1.81
French Canadian	1,637	0.30
German	48,035	8.80
Greek	901	0.17
Guyanese	126	0.02
Hawaii Native/Pacific Islander:	751	0.14
Melanesian: (12)	14	0.00
Fijian (5)	7	0.00
Other Melanesian (7)	7	0.00
Micronesian: (58)	88	0.02
Guamanian/Chamorro (57)	85	0.02
Other Micronesian (1)	3	0.00
Polynesian: (267)	401	0.07
Native Hawaiian (81)	155	0.03
Samoan (181)	237	0.04
Tongan (1)	1	0.00
Other Polynesian (4)	8	0.00
Other Pac. Isl., specified	14	0.00
Other Pac. Isl., not spec. (61)	234	0.04
Hispanic or Latino:	25,774	4.72
Central American:	2,563	0.47
Costa Rican	153	0.03
Guatemalan	679	0.12
Honduran	535	0.10
Nicaraguan	81	0.01
Panamanian	92	0.02
Salvadoran	855	0.16
Other Central American	168	0.03
Cuban	799	0.15
Dominican Republic	90	0.02
Mexican	16,082	2.95
Puerto Rican	1,869	0.34
South American:	813	0.15
Argentinean	54	0.01
Bolivian	22	0.00
Chilean	80	0.01
Colombian	274	0.05
Ecuadorian	47	0.01
Paraguayan	3	0.00
Peruvian	114	0.02
Uruguayan	6	0.00
Venezuelan	165	0.03
Other South American	48	0.01
Other Hispanic or Latino	3,558	0.65
Hungarian	1,093	0.20
Icelander	50	0.01
Iranian	515	0.09
Irish	48,414	8.87
Israeli	98	0.02
Italian	10,289	1.89
Latvian	116	0.02
Lithuanian	412	0.08
Luxemburger	31	0.01
Macedonian	37	0.01
Maltese	6	0.00
New Zealander	12	0.00
Northern European	219	0.04
Norwegian	2,837	0.52
Pennsylvania German	91	0.02
Polish	5,142	0.94
Portuguese	566	0.10
Romanian	340	0.06
Russian	2,802	0.51
Scandinavian	519	0.10
Scotch-Irish	15,608	2.86
Scottish	11,108	2.04
Serbian	223	0.04
Slavic	93	0.02
Slovak	562	0.10
Slovene	104	0.02
Swedish	2,923	0.54
Swiss	979	0.18
Turkish	109	0.02
Ukrainian	641	0.12
United States or American	59,521	10.91
Welsh	2,865	0.53
West Indian, excl. Hispanic:	1,271	0.23
Bahamian	88	0.02
Barbadian	28	0.01
Belizean	27	0.00
Bermudan	10	0.00
British West Indian	32	0.01
Dutch West Indian	43	0.01
Haitian	356	0.07
Jamaican	318	0.06
Trinidadian and Tobagonian	175	0.03
U.S. Virgin Islander	34	0.01
West Indian	160	0.03
White:	368,247	67.50
Not Hispanic (349,104)	356,627	65.37
Hispanic (10,477)	11,620	2.13
Yugoslavian	570	0.10

Oak Ridge

Place Type: City
County: Anderson
Population: 27,387

Ancestry/Race	Number	%
African American/Black:	2,437	8.90
Not Hispanic (2,229)	2,424	8.85
Hispanic (10)	13	0.05
African, sub-Saharan:	75	0.27
African	75	0.27
Am. Ind. or Alaska Nat., not spec.	78	0.28
Albanian	36	0.13
American Indian tribes, specified:	172	0.63
Apache	1	0.00
Blackfeet	7	0.03
Cherokee (34)	129	0.47
Chippewa	3	0.01
Choctaw (4)	10	0.04
Comanche (1)	1	0.00
Cree	1	0.00
Crow (1)	1	0.00
Delaware (1)	1	0.00
Iroquois (1)	3	0.01
Latin American Indians (2)	3	0.01
Lumbee (1)	3	0.01

Notes: 1. Figures in the "Number" column do not add up to the total population due to: a) Ancestry/Race overlap — e.g. persons can report being both White and Irish, b) persons of Hispanic origin can report being any race, c) persons reporting two ancestries are counted in both categories. 2. Numbers in parentheses indicate the number of persons reporting this ancestry/race alone, not in combination with any other ancestry/race. 3. Refer to the Explanation of Data in the front of the book for more detailed information.

Ancestry/Race	Number	%
Navajo (2)	2	0.01
Sioux (2)	3	0.01
All other tribes (4)	4	0.01
American Indian tribes, not spec.	7	0.03
Arab:	63	0.23
Arab/Arabic	16	0.06
Lebanese	42	0.15
Palestinian	5	0.02
Asian:	676	2.47
Bangladeshi (11)	11	0.04
Chinese, ex. Taiwanese (152)	172	0.63
Filipino (42)	58	0.21
Hmong (8)	8	0.03
Indian (138)	146	0.53
Indonesian	2	0.01
Japanese (38)	61	0.22
Korean (73)	78	0.28
Malaysian	5	0.02
Pakistani (6)	13	0.05
Sri Lankan (4)	4	0.01
Taiwanese (27)	28	0.10
Thai (5)	11	0.04
Vietnamese (57)	63	0.23
Other Asian, specified (3)	3	0.01
Other Asian, not specified (5)	13	0.05
Australian	5	0.02
Austrian	109	0.40
Belgian	31	0.11
British	310	1.13
Canadian	116	0.42
Celtic	8	0.03
Croatian	31	0.11
Czech	32	0.12
Czechoslovakian	46	0.17
Danish	66	0.24
Dutch	582	2.12
Eastern European	30	0.11
English	4,375	15.96
Estonian	6	0.02
European	612	2.23
Finnish	7	0.03
French, except Basque	554	2.02
French Canadian	103	0.38
German	3,270	11.93
Greek	39	0.14
Hawaii Native/Pacific Islander:	16	0.06
Micronesian: (4)	8	0.03
Guamanian/Chamorro (4)	8	0.03
Polynesian: (1)	3	0.01
Native Hawaiian (1)	2	0.01
Other Polynesian	1	0.00
Other Pac. Isl., not spec. (1)	5	0.02
Hispanic or Latino:	529	1.93
Central American:	13	0.05
Guatemalan	2	0.01
Honduran	4	0.01
Panamanian	4	0.01
Salvadoran	2	0.01
Other Central American	1	0.00
Cuban	13	0.05
Mexican	295	1.08
Puerto Rican	50	0.18
South American:	35	0.13
Argentinean	11	0.04
Bolivian	4	0.01
Chilean	5	0.02
Colombian	4	0.01
Ecuadorian	2	0.01
Peruvian	4	0.01
Venezuelan	4	0.01
Other South American	1	0.00
Other Hispanic or Latino	123	0.45
Hungarian	132	0.48
Iranian	52	0.19
Irish	3,024	11.03
Italian	479	1.75
Latvian	12	0.04
Lithuanian	28	0.10
Maltese	7	0.03
Northern European	65	0.24
Norwegian	229	0.84
Pennsylvania German	9	0.03
Polish	400	1.46
Portuguese	4	0.01
Romanian	20	0.07
Russian	198	0.72
Scandinavian	25	0.09
Scotch-Irish	1,296	4.73
Scottish	997	3.64
Serbian	6	0.02
Slovak	29	0.11
Slovene	8	0.03
Swedish	279	1.02
Swiss	92	0.34
Turkish	33	0.12
Ukrainian	27	0.10
United States or American	3,416	12.46
Welsh	252	0.92
West Indian, excl. Hispanic:	7	0.03
Dutch West Indian	7	0.03
White:	24,236	88.49
Not Hispanic (23,517)	23,908	87.30
Hispanic (298)	328	1.20

Red Bank

Place Type: City
County: Hamilton
Population: 12,418

Ancestry/Race	Number	%
African American/Black:	1,082	8.71
Not Hispanic (1,017)	1,070	8.62
Hispanic (6)	12	0.10
African, sub-Saharan:	23	0.18
African	23	0.18
Alaska Native tribes, specified:	4	0.03
Aleut (1)	1	0.01
Tlingit-Haida	3	0.02
Am. Ind. or Alaska Nat., not spec.	40	0.32
American Indian tribes, specified:	90	0.72
Apache (2)	3	0.02
Blackfeet (2)	6	0.05
Cherokee (25)	58	0.47
Chippewa (4)	4	0.03
Choctaw (1)	2	0.02
Creek (1)	1	0.01
Crow	2	0.02
Latin American Indians (1)	3	0.02
Navajo	6	0.05
Osage	3	0.02
Sioux (1)	1	0.01
All other tribes	1	0.01
American Indian tribes, not spec.	8	0.06
Arab:	19	0.15
Lebanese	9	0.07
Other Arab	10	0.08
Asian:	148	1.19
Cambodian (3)	6	0.05
Chinese, ex. Taiwanese (16)	18	0.14
Filipino (16)	20	0.16
Indian (21)	27	0.22
Japanese (5)	10	0.08
Korean (11)	12	0.10
Laotian (9)	9	0.07
Taiwanese (1)	1	0.01
Thai (9)	10	0.08
Vietnamese (13)	20	0.16
Other Asian, not specified (4)	15	0.12
Austrian	29	0.23
Basque	7	0.06
Belgian	8	0.06
British	97	0.77
Canadian	30	0.24
Czechoslovakian	7	0.06
Dutch	303	2.42
Eastern European	7	0.06
English	1,263	10.08
European	123	0.98
French, except Basque	274	2.19
French Canadian	52	0.41
German	1,031	8.23
Greek	79	0.63
Hawaii Native/Pacific Islander:	15	0.12
Micronesian: (3)	7	0.06
Guamanian/Chamorro (3)	7	0.06
Polynesian: (4)	8	0.06
Native Hawaiian (3)	5	0.04
Samoan (1)	3	0.02
Hispanic or Latino:	352	2.83
Central American:	12	0.10
Costa Rican	4	0.03
Guatemalan	4	0.03
Honduran	4	0.03
Cuban	16	0.13
Dominican Republic	1	0.01
Mexican	240	1.93
Puerto Rican	25	0.20
South American:	8	0.06
Colombian	1	0.01
Peruvian	1	0.01
Venezuelan	3	0.02
Other South American	3	0.02
Other Hispanic or Latino	50	0.40
Hungarian	13	0.10
Irish	1,581	12.61
Italian	150	1.20
Lithuanian	6	0.05
Norwegian	34	0.27
Polish	149	1.19
Russian	33	0.26
Scotch-Irish	352	2.81
Scottish	299	2.39
Slovak	6	0.05
Swedish	28	0.22
Swiss	14	0.11
United States or American	2,053	16.38
Welsh	111	0.89
West Indian, excl. Hispanic:	9	0.07
Dutch West Indian	9	0.07
White:	11,039	88.90
Not Hispanic (10,726)	10,859	87.45
Hispanic (153)	180	1.45

Sevierville

Place Type: City
County: Sevier
Population: 11,757

Ancestry/Race	Number	%
African American/Black:	162	1.38
Not Hispanic (136)	160	1.36
Hispanic (1)	2	0.02
African, sub-Saharan:	33	0.28
South African	33	0.28
Am. Ind. or Alaska Nat., not spec.	29	0.25
American Indian tribes, specified:	85	0.72
Apache	3	0.03
Blackfeet (2)	4	0.03
Cherokee (24)	57	0.48
Chippewa	3	0.03
Comanche	1	0.01
Delaware (1)	1	0.01
Iroquois (2)	4	0.03
Latin American Indians	3	0.03
Navajo	3	0.03
Seminole	3	0.03
Sioux	1	0.01
All other tribes	2	0.02
American Indian tribes, not spec.	9	0.08
Armenian	8	0.07
Asian:	128	1.09
Bangladeshi (4)	4	0.03
Chinese, ex. Taiwanese (31)	33	0.28
Filipino (12)	14	0.12
Indian (39)	44	0.37
Japanese (4)	7	0.06
Korean (1)	4	0.03
Pakistani (1)	1	0.01

Notes: 1. Figures in the "Number" column do not add up to the total population due to: a) Ancestry/Race overlap — e.g. persons can report being both White and Irish, b) persons of Hispanic origin can report being any race, c) persons reporting two ancestries are counted in both categories. 2. Numbers in parentheses indicate the number of persons reporting this ancestry/race alone, not in combination with any other ancestry/race. 3. Refer to the Explanation of Data in the front of the book for more detailed information.

Ancestry/Race	Number	%
Taiwanese (1)	1	0.01
Thai (3)	3	0.03
Vietnamese (13)	13	0.11
Other Asian, not specified	4	0.03
British	74	0.63
Canadian	23	0.19
Czech	61	0.52
Czechoslovakian	23	0.19
Dutch	176	1.49
English	959	8.10
European	33	0.28
French, except Basque	370	3.13
French Canadian	63	0.53
German	1,490	12.59
Greek	32	0.27
Hawaii Native/Pacific Islander:	5	0.04
Micronesian:	1	0.01
Guamanian/Chamorro	1	0.01
Polynesian: (2)	4	0.03
Native Hawaiian	2	0.02
Samoan (2)	2	0.02
Hispanic or Latino:	190	1.62
Central American:	6	0.05
Costa Rican	1	0.01
Guatemalan	1	0.01
Honduran	2	0.02
Nicaraguan	2	0.02
Cuban	13	0.11
Dominican Republic	5	0.04
Mexican	107	0.91
Puerto Rican	13	0.11
South American:	4	0.03
Colombian	4	0.03
Other Hispanic or Latino	42	0.36
Hungarian	62	0.52
Irish	1,167	9.86
Italian	425	3.59
Norwegian	60	0.51
Pennsylvania German	6	0.05
Polish	115	0.97
Romanian	7	0.06
Russian	10	0.08
Scandinavian	7	0.06
Scotch-Irish	546	4.61
Scottish	109	0.92
Slavic	9	0.08
Swedish	55	0.46
Swiss	9	0.08
United States or American	2,459	20.78
Welsh	54	0.46
White:	11,367	96.68
Not Hispanic (11,163)	11,274	95.89
Hispanic (81)	93	0.79

Shelbyville

Place Type: City
County: Bedford
Population: 16,105

Ancestry/Race	Number	%
African American/Black:	2,502	15.54
Not Hispanic (2,382)	2,452	15.23
Hispanic (30)	50	0.31
African, sub-Saharan:	29	0.18
African	29	0.18
Am. Ind. or Alaska Nat., not spec.	57	0.35
American Indian tribes, specified:	75	0.47
Cherokee (8)	39	0.24
Chickasaw (2)	3	0.02
Choctaw	1	0.01
Crow	1	0.01
Iroquois	1	0.01
Latin American Indians (18)	26	0.16
Navajo (2)	2	0.01
Potawatomi (1)	1	0.01
Shoshone	1	0.01
American Indian tribes, not spec.	3	0.02
Arab:	7	0.04
Lebanese	7	0.04
Asian:	139	0.86
Chinese, ex. Taiwanese (2)	2	0.01
Filipino (13)	16	0.10
Indian (24)	36	0.22
Japanese (55)	57	0.35
Korean (4)	10	0.06
Laotian (7)	9	0.06
Vietnamese (6)	6	0.04
Other Asian, not specified (1)	3	0.02
British	53	0.33
Canadian	9	0.06
Dutch	152	0.95
English	986	6.13
European	62	0.39
French, except Basque	292	1.82
French Canadian	18	0.11
German	733	4.56
Hawaii Native/Pacific Islander:	15	0.09
Micronesian: (7)	9	0.06
Guamanian/Chamorro (7)	9	0.06
Polynesian: (1)	2	0.01
Native Hawaiian	1	0.01
Samoan (1)	1	0.01
Other Pac. Isl., not spec.	4	0.02
Hispanic or Latino:	2,343	14.55
Central American:	96	0.60
Costa Rican	1	0.01
Guatemalan	73	0.45
Honduran	12	0.07
Panamanian	1	0.01
Salvadoran	3	0.02
Other Central American	6	0.04
Cuban	7	0.04
Mexican	2,054	12.75
Puerto Rican	8	0.05
South American:	2	0.01
Venezuelan	2	0.01
Other Hispanic or Latino	176	1.09
Hungarian	7	0.04
Irish	1,004	6.25
Italian	159	0.99
Norwegian	8	0.05
Polish	60	0.37
Romanian	24	0.15
Russian	14	0.09
Scandinavian	10	0.06
Scotch-Irish	198	1.23
Scottish	155	0.96
Swedish	7	0.04
Swiss	9	0.06
United States or American	3,676	22.87
Welsh	33	0.21
White:	12,669	78.67
Not Hispanic (11,056)	11,192	69.49
Hispanic (1,367)	1,477	9.17
Yugoslavian	25	0.16

Smyrna

Place Type: Town
County: Rutherford
Population: 25,569

Ancestry/Race	Number	%
African American/Black:	2,139	8.37
Not Hispanic (1,981)	2,110	8.25
Hispanic (18)	29	0.11
African, sub-Saharan:	45	0.18
African	45	0.18
Alaska Native tribes, not specified	2	0.01
Am. Ind. or Alaska Nat., not spec.	51	0.20
American Indian tribes, specified:	127	0.50
Apache (3)	4	0.02
Blackfeet (2)	4	0.02
Cherokee (13)	65	0.25
Chickasaw	2	0.01
Chippewa (3)	3	0.01
Choctaw (8)	9	0.04
Comanche (1)	2	0.01
Creek	1	0.00
Delaware	1	0.00
Iroquois (4)	4	0.02
Kiowa (1)	1	0.00
Latin American Indians (1)	2	0.01
Lumbee (4)	4	0.02
Navajo (2)	5	0.02
Pueblo (3)	3	0.01
Seminole (3)	4	0.02
Sioux (2)	6	0.02
All other tribes (5)	7	0.03
American Indian tribes, not spec.	7	0.03
Arab:	87	0.34
Arab/Arabic	24	0.09
Egyptian	6	0.02
Iraqi	42	0.17
Lebanese	15	0.06
Asian:	376	1.47
Chinese, ex. Taiwanese (25)	28	0.11
Filipino (31)	43	0.17
Indian (23)	26	0.10
Indonesian (1)	1	0.00
Japanese (12)	19	0.07
Korean (18)	23	0.09
Laotian (143)	151	0.59
Pakistani (1)	1	0.00
Taiwanese (1)	3	0.01
Thai (9)	14	0.05
Vietnamese (24)	26	0.10
Other Asian, not specified (17)	41	0.16
Austrian	9	0.04
Belgian	9	0.04
British	66	0.26
Croatian	9	0.04
Czech	9	0.04
Czechoslovakian	27	0.11
Danish	51	0.20
Dutch	407	1.60
English	2,314	9.12
European	209	0.82
French, except Basque	380	1.50
French Canadian	45	0.18
German	2,520	9.93
Greek	7	0.03
Hawaii Native/Pacific Islander:	24	0.09
Micronesian: (10)	10	0.04
Guamanian/Chamorro (9)	9	0.04
Other Micronesian (1)	1	0.00
Polynesian: (3)	5	0.02
Native Hawaiian (1)	1	0.00
Samoan (2)	4	0.02
Other Pac. Isl., not spec. (7)	9	0.04
Hispanic or Latino:	1,101	4.31
Central American:	134	0.52
Costa Rican	1	0.00
Guatemalan	60	0.23
Honduran	5	0.02
Nicaraguan	3	0.01
Panamanian	7	0.03
Salvadoran	57	0.22
Other Central American	1	0.00
Cuban	31	0.12
Dominican Republic	3	0.01
Mexican	675	2.64
Puerto Rican	71	0.28
South American:	14	0.05
Chilean	4	0.02
Colombian	3	0.01
Ecuadorian	2	0.01
Peruvian	4	0.02
Other South American	1	0.00
Other Hispanic or Latino	173	0.68
Hungarian	10	0.04
Irish	3,208	12.64
Italian	502	1.98
Norwegian	145	0.57
Polish	388	1.53
Portuguese	8	0.03
Russian	51	0.20
Scotch-Irish	673	2.65
Scottish	387	1.52

Notes: 1. Figures in the "Number" column do not add up to the total population due to: a) Ancestry/Race overlap — e.g. persons can report being both White and Irish, b) persons of Hispanic origin can report being any race, c) persons reporting two ancestries are counted in both categories. 2. Numbers in parentheses indicate the number of persons reporting this ancestry/race alone, not in combination with any other ancestry/race. 3. Refer to the Explanation of Data in the front of the book for more detailed information.

Ancestry/Race	Number	%
Slavic	9	0.04
Slovak	15	0.06
Swedish	109	0.43
Swiss	19	0.07
Ukrainian	27	0.11
United States or American	4,739	18.67
Welsh	126	0.50
West Indian, excl. Hispanic:	22	0.09
Bahamian	15	0.06
Jamaican	7	0.03
White:	22,670	88.66
Not Hispanic (21,756)	22,065	86.30
Hispanic (547)	605	2.37
Yugoslavian	18	0.07

Soddy-Daisy

Place Type: City
County: Hamilton
Population: 11,530

Ancestry/Race	Number	%
African American/Black:	79	0.69
Not Hispanic (68)	78	0.68
Hispanic (1)	1	0.01
Am. Ind. or Alaska Nat., not spec.	27	0.23
American Indian tribes, specified:	59	0.51
Apache	4	0.03
Cherokee (12)	43	0.37
Cree	1	0.01
Creek	2	0.02
Crow	2	0.02
Latin American Indians	2	0.02
Potawatomi (1)	1	0.01
Sioux (3)	3	0.03
All other tribes	1	0.01
American Indian tribes, not spec.	1	0.01
Arab:	64	0.56
Arab/Arabic	44	0.38
Lebanese	10	0.09
Syrian	10	0.09
Asian:	35	0.30
Chinese, ex. Taiwanese (1)	1	0.01
Filipino (5)	7	0.06
Indonesian	2	0.02
Japanese (2)	3	0.03
Korean (8)	14	0.12
Vietnamese (4)	5	0.04
Other Asian, not specified (2)	3	0.03
British	51	0.44
Canadian	9	0.08
Celtic	34	0.30
Dutch	340	2.96
English	925	8.05
European	107	0.93
French, except Basque	132	1.15
German	858	7.46
Hawaii Native/Pacific Islander:	1	0.01
Polynesian: (1)	1	0.01
Samoan (1)	1	0.01
Hispanic or Latino:	92	0.80
Central American:	5	0.04
Honduran	4	0.03
Panamanian	1	0.01
Cuban	1	0.01
Mexican	49	0.42
Puerto Rican	11	0.10
South American:	1	0.01
Venezuelan	1	0.01
Other Hispanic or Latino	25	0.22
Irish	1,440	12.53
Italian	174	1.51
Norwegian	20	0.17
Polish	57	0.50
Scotch-Irish	220	1.91
Scottish	224	1.95
Slavic	8	0.07
Swedish	28	0.24
Ukrainian	7	0.06
United States or American	3,111	27.06
Welsh	126	1.10
White:	11,389	98.78
Not Hispanic (11,245)	11,314	98.13
Hispanic (72)	75	0.65
Yugoslavian	9	0.08

Springfield

Place Type: City
County: Robertson
Population: 14,329

Ancestry/Race	Number	%
African American/Black:	3,763	26.26
Not Hispanic (3,663)	3,706	25.86
Hispanic (49)	57	0.40
African, sub-Saharan:	218	1.54
African	218	1.54
Am. Ind. or Alaska Nat., not spec.	55	0.38
American Indian tribes, specified:	37	0.26
Apache	1	0.01
Blackfeet (2)	2	0.01
Cherokee (13)	27	0.19
Chickasaw	1	0.01
Chippewa (3)	3	0.02
Creek (1)	1	0.01
Latin American Indians (1)	1	0.01
All other tribes (1)	1	0.01
American Indian tribes, not spec.	6	0.04
Arab:	4	0.03
Lebanese	4	0.03
Asian:	102	0.71
Chinese, ex. Taiwanese (8)	11	0.08
Filipino (8)	10	0.07
Indian (24)	24	0.17
Japanese (14)	16	0.11
Korean (20)	26	0.18
Vietnamese	2	0.01
Other Asian, not specified (6)	13	0.09
Belgian	5	0.04
British	23	0.16
Croatian	23	0.16
Czech	5	0.04
Czechoslovakian	7	0.05
Dutch	159	1.12
English	952	6.72
European	100	0.71
Finnish	9	0.06
French, except Basque	99	0.70
French Canadian	5	0.04
German	741	5.23
Greek	5	0.04
Hawaii Native/Pacific Islander:	5	0.03
Micronesian: (3)	3	0.02
Guamanian/Chamorro (3)	3	0.02
Other Pac. Isl., not spec. (2)	2	0.01
Hispanic or Latino:	995	6.94
Central American:	51	0.36
Costa Rican	1	0.01
Guatemalan	30	0.21
Honduran	12	0.08
Salvadoran	3	0.02
Other Central American	5	0.03
Cuban	1	0.01
Mexican	853	5.95
Puerto Rican	27	0.19
South American:	3	0.02
Chilean	3	0.02
Other Hispanic or Latino	60	0.42
Hungarian	7	0.05
Irish	923	6.51
Italian	103	0.73
Lithuanian	6	0.04
Norwegian	30	0.21
Polish	5	0.04
Scotch-Irish	222	1.57
Scottish	127	0.90
Swedish	34	0.24
Swiss	14	0.10
United States or American	2,442	17.23
Welsh	40	0.28
West Indian, excl. Hispanic:	17	0.12
Dutch West Indian	9	0.06
Jamaican	8	0.06
White:	10,205	71.22
Not Hispanic (9,459)	9,534	66.54
Hispanic (652)	671	4.68

Tullahoma

Place Type: City
County: Coffee
Population: 17,994

Ancestry/Race	Number	%
African American/Black:	1,363	7.57
Not Hispanic (1,208)	1,352	7.51
Hispanic (8)	11	0.06
African, sub-Saharan:	70	0.39
African	70	0.39
Am. Ind. or Alaska Nat., not spec.	35	0.19
American Indian tribes, specified:	102	0.57
Apache (3)	3	0.02
Blackfeet (1)	4	0.02
Cherokee (26)	72	0.40
Choctaw (3)	11	0.06
Iroquois	1	0.01
Osage	1	0.01
Ottawa	1	0.01
Potawatomi	1	0.01
Puget Sound Salish (3)	3	0.02
All other tribes (1)	5	0.03
American Indian tribes, not spec.	9	0.05
Arab:	8	0.04
Lebanese	8	0.04
Asian:	211	1.17
Bangladeshi (4)	4	0.02
Chinese, ex. Taiwanese (56)	57	0.32
Filipino (20)	28	0.16
Indian (38)	38	0.21
Japanese (13)	20	0.11
Korean (19)	22	0.12
Taiwanese (4)	4	0.02
Thai (2)	2	0.01
Vietnamese (25)	28	0.16
Other Asian, not specified	8	0.04
Austrian	20	0.11
British	97	0.54
Canadian	33	0.18
Czech	21	0.12
Danish	36	0.20
Dutch	375	2.08
English	2,167	12.04
European	162	0.90
Finnish	18	0.10
French, except Basque	322	1.79
French Canadian	56	0.31
German	1,908	10.60
Greek	17	0.09
Hawaii Native/Pacific Islander:	14	0.08
Micronesian: (2)	4	0.02
Guamanian/Chamorro (2)	4	0.02
Polynesian: (4)	6	0.03
Native Hawaiian	1	0.01
Samoan (4)	4	0.02
Other Polynesian	1	0.01
Other Pac. Isl., not spec. (3)	4	0.02
Hispanic or Latino:	307	1.71
Central American:	7	0.04
Panamanian	6	0.03
Salvadoran	1	0.01
Cuban	5	0.03
Dominican Republic	1	0.01
Mexican	216	1.20
Puerto Rican	21	0.12
South American:	3	0.02
Colombian	1	0.01
Venezuelan	1	0.01
Other South American	1	0.01
Other Hispanic or Latino	54	0.30

Notes: 1. Figures in the "Number" column do not add up to the total population due to: a) Ancestry/Race overlap — e.g. persons can report being both White and Irish, b) persons of Hispanic origin can report being any race, c) persons reporting two ancestries are counted in both categories. 2. Numbers in parentheses indicate the number of persons reporting this ancestry/race alone, not in combination with any other ancestry/race. 3. Refer to the Explanation of Data in the front of the book for more detailed information.

Ancestry/Race	Number	%
Hungarian	7	0.04
Iranian	16	0.09
Irish	2,168	12.05
Italian	210	1.17
Norwegian	7	0.04
Polish	128	0.71
Russian	32	0.18
Scandinavian	13	0.07
Scotch-Irish	553	3.07
Scottish	356	1.98
Swedish	173	0.96
Swiss	26	0.14
Ukrainian	11	0.06
United States or American	2,848	15.83
Welsh	70	0.39
West Indian, excl. Hispanic:	10	0.06
Dutch West Indian	10	0.06
White:	16,405	91.17
Not Hispanic (15,971)	16,220	90.14
Hispanic (168)	185	1.03

Union City

Place Type: City
County: Obion
Population: 10,876

Ancestry/Race	Number	%
Acadian/Cajun	8	0.07
African American/Black:	2,373	21.82
Not Hispanic (2,299)	2,352	21.63
Hispanic (17)	21	0.19
Am. Ind. or Alaska Nat., not spec.	36	0.33
American Indian tribes, specified:	30	0.28
Apache (2)	4	0.04
Blackfeet	3	0.03
Cherokee	19	0.17
Choctaw	1	0.01
Iroquois (1)	1	0.01
Sioux (1)	1	0.01
All other tribes (1)	1	0.01
American Indian tribes, not spec.	7	0.06
Asian:	43	0.40
Chinese, ex. Taiwanese (2)	2	0.02
Filipino (2)	2	0.02
Indian (13)	19	0.17
Indonesian (1)	1	0.01
Korean (4)	8	0.07
Vietnamese (8)	8	0.07
Other Asian, specified	1	0.01
Other Asian, not specified (1)	2	0.02
British	36	0.34
Celtic	7	0.07
Croatian	6	0.06
Czech	6	0.06
Czechoslovakian	6	0.06
Danish	21	0.20
Dutch	68	0.64
English	897	8.38
European	63	0.59
Finnish	4	0.04
French, except Basque	97	0.91
French Canadian	12	0.11
German	861	8.04
Hawaii Native/Pacific Islander:	15	0.14
Micronesian: (13)	13	0.12
Guamanian/Chamorro (13)	13	0.12
Other Pac. Isl., specified	1	0.01
Other Pac. Isl., not spec. (1)	1	0.01
Hispanic or Latino:	371	3.41
Central American:	24	0.22
Costa Rican	2	0.02
Guatemalan	18	0.17
Honduran	4	0.04
Mexican	291	2.68
Puerto Rican	3	0.03
South American:	6	0.06
Venezuelan	5	0.05
Other South American	1	0.01
Other Hispanic or Latino	47	0.43
Hungarian	6	0.06
Irish	941	8.79
Italian	115	1.07
Norwegian	11	0.10
Polish	59	0.55
Scotch-Irish	278	2.60
Scottish	85	0.79
Swedish	11	0.10
Swiss	11	0.10
United States or American	1,834	17.13
Welsh	20	0.19
West Indian, excl. Hispanic:	5	0.05
Dutch West Indian	5	0.05
White:	8,300	76.31
Not Hispanic (8,038)	8,121	74.67
Hispanic (167)	179	1.65

Abilene

Place Type: City
County: Taylor
Population: 115,930

Ancestry/Race	Number	%
Acadian/Cajun	83	0.07
African American/Black:	10,997	9.49
Not Hispanic (9,947)	10,540	9.09
Hispanic (268)	457	0.39
African, sub-Saharan:	444	0.38
African	308	0.27
Kenyan	21	0.02
Nigerian	110	0.09
Other sub-Saharan African	5	0.00
Alaska Native tribes, specified:	13	0.01
Alaska Athabascan (2)	3	0.00
Aleut (3)	5	0.00
Eskimo (2)	4	0.00
Tlingit-Haida	1	0.00
Alaska Native tribes, not specified		0.00
Am. Ind. or Alaska Nat., not spec.	361	0.31
American Indian tribes, specified:	867	0.75
Apache (31)	67	0.06
Blackfeet (8)	28	0.02
Cherokee (109)	330	0.28
Cheyenne (1)	2	0.00
Chickasaw (19)	34	0.03
Chippewa (2)	13	0.01
Choctaw (48)	84	0.07
Comanche (9)	27	0.02
Creek (7)	13	0.01
Crow (1)	4	0.00
Delaware (1)	3	0.00
Iroquois (3)	11	0.01
Kiowa (2)	3	0.00
Latin American Indians (63)	79	0.07
Menominee	1	0.00
Navajo (23)	31	0.03
Osage (5)	9	0.01
Paiute (1)	2	0.00
Potawatomi (3)	4	0.00
Pueblo (8)	10	0.01
Seminole (2)	10	0.01
Sioux (21)	30	0.03
Tohono O'Odham (1)	1	0.00
Ute (5)	6	0.01
Yaqui (1)	3	0.00
Yuman (1)	1	0.00
All other tribes (34)	61	0.05
American Indian tribes, not spec.	71	0.06
Arab:	67	0.06
Arab/Arabic	16	0.01
Egyptian	6	0.01
Lebanese	45	0.04
Armenian	42	0.04
Asian:	2,236	1.93
Bangladeshi (1)	1	0.00
Cambodian (53)	70	0.06
Chinese, ex. Taiwanese (199)	270	0.23
Filipino (557)	798	0.69
Hmong (3)	4	0.00
Indian (158)	194	0.17
Indonesian (13)	15	0.01
Japanese (100)	191	0.16
Korean (135)	240	0.21
Laotian (10)	11	0.01
Malaysian (2)	2	0.00
Pakistani (11)	14	0.01
Taiwanese (12)	17	0.01
Thai (103)	166	0.14
Vietnamese (90)	118	0.10
Other Asian, specified (2)	7	0.01
Other Asian, not specified (51)	118	0.10
Australian	22	0.02
Austrian	110	0.09
Belgian	32	0.03
Brazilian	29	0.03
British	526	0.45
Bulgarian	13	0.01
Canadian	184	0.16
Celtic	43	0.04
Croatian	13	0.01
Cypriot	10	0.01
Czech	249	0.22
Czechoslovakian	58	0.05
Danish	324	0.28
Dutch	1,668	1.44
Eastern European	12	0.01
English	10,087	8.71
European	728	0.63
Finnish	54	0.05
French, except Basque	2,261	1.95
French Canadian	562	0.49
German	11,781	10.17
Greek	74	0.06
Hawaii Native/Pacific Islander:	162	0.14
Micronesian: (35)	54	0.05
Guamanian/Chamorro (32)	50	0.04
Other Micronesian (3)	4	0.00
Polynesian: (35)	69	0.06
Native Hawaiian (21)	52	0.04
Samoan (13)	15	0.01
Tongan (1)	1	0.00
Other Polynesian	1	0.00
Other Pac. Isl., specified	5	0.00
Other Pac. Isl., not spec. (10)	34	0.03
Hispanic or Latino:	22,548	19.45
Central American:	175	0.15
Costa Rican	8	0.01
Guatemalan	21	0.02
Honduran	14	0.01
Nicaraguan	52	0.04
Panamanian	47	0.04
Salvadoran	25	0.02
Other Central American	8	0.01
Cuban	41	0.04
Dominican Republic	26	0.02
Mexican	15,745	13.58
Puerto Rican	414	0.36
South American:	81	0.07
Argentinean	6	0.01
Bolivian	2	0.00
Chilean	1	0.00
Colombian	28	0.02
Ecuadorian	5	0.00
Peruvian	23	0.02
Uruguayan	6	0.01
Venezuelan	5	0.00
Other South American	5	0.00
Other Hispanic or Latino	6,066	5.23
Hungarian	181	0.16
Iranian	16	0.01
Irish	9,317	8.05
Italian	1,648	1.42
Latvian	18	0.02
Lithuanian	97	0.08
Maltese	8	0.01
Northern European	132	0.11
Norwegian	737	0.64
Pennsylvania German	22	0.02
Polish	1,069	0.92

Notes: 1. Figures in the "Number" column do not add up to the total population due to: a) Ancestry/Race overlap — e.g. persons can report being both White and Irish, b) persons of Hispanic origin can report being any race, c) persons reporting two ancestries are counted in both categories. 2. Numbers in parentheses indicate the number of persons reporting this ancestry/race alone, not in combination with any other ancestry/race. 3. Refer to the Explanation of Data in the front of the book for more detailed information.

Ancestry/Race	Number	%
Portuguese	69	0.06
Romanian	27	0.02
Russian	148	0.13
Scandinavian	78	0.07
Scotch-Irish	2,337	2.02
Scottish	2,349	2.03
Serbian	14	0.01
Slovak	110	0.09
Slovene	14	0.01
Swedish	821	0.71
Swiss	60	0.05
Turkish	22	0.02
Ukrainian	62	0.05
United States or American	13,965	12.06
Welsh	536	0.46
West Indian, excl. Hispanic:	321	0.28
Barbadian	9	0.01
Belizean	48	0.04
British West Indian	13	0.01
Dutch West Indian	92	0.08
Haitian	24	0.02
Jamaican	92	0.08
Trinidadian and Tobagonian	9	0.01
U.S. Virgin Islander	7	0.01
West Indian	27	0.02
White:	92,910	80.14
Not Hispanic (79,712)	81,144	69.99
Hispanic (10,790)	11,766	10.15
Yugoslavian	5	0.00

Addison

Place Type: Town
County: Dallas
Population: 14,166

Ancestry/Race	Number	%
Acadian/Cajun	9	0.07
Afghan	8	0.06
African American/Black:	1,450	10.24
Not Hispanic (1,317)	1,388	9.80
Hispanic (47)	62	0.44
African, sub-Saharan:	394	2.86
African	154	1.12
Ethiopian	115	0.83
Nigerian	86	0.62
Somalian	30	0.22
Other sub-Saharan African	9	0.07
Am. Ind. or Alaska Nat., not spec.	26	0.18
American Indian tribes, specified:	92	0.65
Apache (2)	5	0.04
Blackfeet	3	0.02
Cherokee (14)	37	0.26
Cheyenne (1)	1	0.01
Chickasaw (3)	3	0.02
Chippewa	4	0.03
Choctaw (4)	11	0.08
Comanche (4)	5	0.04
Creek (1)	1	0.01
Crow (1)	1	0.01
Iroquois (1)	1	0.01
Kiowa (1)	1	0.01
Latin American Indians (5)	11	0.08
Navajo (1)	2	0.01
Osage (1)	1	0.01
Ottawa (1)	1	0.01
Sioux (2)	2	0.01
All other tribes (2)	2	0.01
American Indian tribes, not spec.	6	0.04
Arab:	71	0.51
Arab/Arabic	28	0.20
Lebanese	43	0.31
Asian:	1,242	8.77
Bangladeshi (9)	9	0.06
Cambodian (16)	20	0.14
Chinese, ex. Taiwanese (144)	170	1.20
Filipino (52)	71	0.50
Indian (449)	465	3.28
Indonesian (5)	7	0.05
Japanese (28)	41	0.29
Korean (152)	157	1.11
Laotian (4)	6	0.04
Malaysian (2)	9	0.06
Pakistani (41)	60	0.42
Sri Lankan (2)	2	0.01
Taiwanese (14)	16	0.11
Thai (5)	5	0.04
Vietnamese (143)	148	1.04
Other Asian, specified (8)	11	0.08
Other Asian, not specified (17)	45	0.32
Australian	26	0.19
Austrian	68	0.49
Basque	8	0.06
Belgian	8	0.06
Brazilian	52	0.38
British	124	0.90
Canadian	38	0.28
Croatian	11	0.08
Czech	51	0.37
Czechoslovakian	21	0.15
Danish	69	0.50
Dutch	241	1.75
English	1,213	8.79
European	102	0.74
Finnish	24	0.17
French, except Basque	315	2.28
French Canadian	49	0.36
German	1,597	11.57
Hawaii Native/Pacific Islander:	32	0.23
Micronesian: (1)	3	0.02
Guamanian/Chamorro (1)	3	0.02
Polynesian: (8)	13	0.09
Native Hawaiian (3)	8	0.06
Samoan (5)	5	0.04
Other Pac. Isl., not spec. (6)	16	0.11
Hispanic or Latino:	3,406	24.04
Central American:	331	2.34
Costa Rican	25	0.18
Guatemalan	31	0.22
Honduran	33	0.23
Nicaraguan	10	0.07
Panamanian	5	0.04
Salvadoran	208	1.47
Other Central American	19	0.13
Cuban	22	0.16
Dominican Republic	2	0.01
Mexican	2,280	16.09
Puerto Rican	53	0.37
South American:	133	0.94
Argentinean	1	0.01
Bolivian	2	0.01
Chilean	1	0.01
Colombian	76	0.54
Ecuadorian	6	0.04
Peruvian	16	0.11
Uruguayan	7	0.05
Venezuelan	15	0.11
Other South American	9	0.06
Other Hispanic or Latino	585	4.13
Hungarian	23	0.17
Iranian	75	0.54
Irish	1,166	8.45
Italian	351	2.54
Lithuanian	75	0.54
Maltese	9	0.07
Northern European	20	0.14
Norwegian	148	1.07
Polish	360	2.61
Portuguese	21	0.15
Romanian	10	0.07
Russian	131	0.95
Scandinavian	20	0.14
Scotch-Irish	179	1.30
Scottish	361	2.62
Serbian	10	0.07
Slovak	53	0.38
Swedish	205	1.49
Ukrainian	25	0.18
United States or American	1,047	7.59
Welsh	77	0.56
West Indian, excl. Hispanic:	8	0.06
Trinidadian and Tobagonian	8	0.06
White:	9,993	70.54
Not Hispanic (7,945)	8,156	57.57
Hispanic (1,658)	1,837	12.97
Yugoslavian	17	0.12

Alamo

Place Type: City
County: Hidalgo
Population: 14,760

Ancestry/Race	Number	%
Acadian/Cajun	10	0.07
African American/Black:	47	0.32
Not Hispanic (15)	17	0.12
Hispanic (16)	30	0.20
Am. Ind. or Alaska Nat., not spec.	67	0.45
American Indian tribes, specified:	16	0.11
Cherokee	5	0.03
Chippewa (1)	1	0.01
Choctaw (1)	2	0.01
Iroquois (3)	3	0.02
Latin American Indians (1)	3	0.02
Paiute (1)	1	0.01
All other tribes	1	0.01
American Indian tribes, not spec.	10	0.07
Asian:	20	0.14
Filipino (8)	15	0.10
Indian (3)	3	0.02
Japanese	1	0.01
Korean (1)	1	0.01
Austrian	9	0.06
Canadian	24	0.16
Czech	41	0.27
Danish	56	0.37
Dutch	148	0.98
English	399	2.65
Finnish	34	0.23
French, except Basque	75	0.50
French Canadian	14	0.09
German	890	5.90
German Russian	10	0.07
Hawaii Native/Pacific Islander:	3	0.02
Other Pac. Isl., not spec.	3	0.02
Hispanic or Latino:	11,528	78.10
Central American:	20	0.14
Costa Rican	8	0.05
Guatemalan	4	0.03
Honduran	1	0.01
Nicaraguan	2	0.01
Salvadoran	1	0.01
Other Central American	4	0.03
Cuban	2	0.01
Dominican Republic	2	0.01
Mexican	10,067	68.20
Puerto Rican	18	0.12
South American:	2	0.01
Colombian	2	0.01
Other Hispanic or Latino	1,417	9.60
Irish	378	2.51
Italian	45	0.30
Norwegian	102	0.68
Pennsylvania German	22	0.15
Polish	76	0.50
Russian	17	0.11
Scotch-Irish	83	0.55
Scottish	76	0.50
Slovene	10	0.07
Swedish	142	0.94
Swiss	21	0.14
Ukrainian	10	0.07
United States or American	611	4.05
White:	12,600	85.37
Not Hispanic (3,154)	3,188	21.60
Hispanic (9,187)	9,412	63.77

Notes: 1. Figures in the "Number" column do not add up to the total population due to: a) Ancestry/Race overlap — e.g. persons can report being both White and Irish, b) persons of Hispanic origin can report being any race, c) persons reporting two ancestries are counted in both categories. 2. Numbers in parentheses indicate the number of persons reporting this ancestry/race alone, not in combination with any other ancestry/race. 3. Refer to the Explanation of Data in the front of the book for more detailed information.

Aldine

Place Type: Census Designated Place
County: Harris
Population: 13,979

Ancestry/Race	Number	%
African American/Black:	847	6.06
Not Hispanic (798)	811	5.80
Hispanic (18)	36	0.26
African, sub-Saharan:	3	0.02
African	3	0.02
Am. Ind. or Alaska Nat., not spec.	80	0.57
American Indian tribes, specified:	45	0.32
Cherokee (13)	18	0.13
Kiowa	1	0.01
Latin American Indians (14)	18	0.13
Navajo (2)	2	0.01
Shoshone	1	0.01
Sioux (1)	1	0.01
Ute	1	0.01
All other tribes (1)	3	0.02
American Indian tribes, not spec.	14	0.10
Asian:	515	3.68
Chinese, ex. Taiwanese (19)	26	0.19
Filipino (23)	28	0.20
Indian (62)	72	0.52
Japanese (5)	8	0.06
Korean (9)	9	0.06
Laotian (103)	113	0.81
Pakistani	1	0.01
Vietnamese (217)	218	1.56
Other Asian, specified (1)	1	0.01
Other Asian, not specified (32)	39	0.28
Czech	72	0.51
Czechoslovakian	41	0.29
Dutch	45	0.32
English	265	1.89
European	21	0.15
French, except Basque	143	1.02
German	646	4.61
Hawaii Native/Pacific Islander:	11	0.08
Polynesian: (5)	6	0.04
Native Hawaiian (3)	4	0.03
Samoan (2)	2	0.01
Other Pac. Isl., not spec. (5)	5	0.04
Hispanic or Latino:	7,875	56.33
Central American:	363	2.60
Costa Rican	6	0.04
Guatemalan	35	0.25
Honduran	70	0.50
Nicaraguan	12	0.09
Salvadoran	218	1.56
Other Central American	22	0.16
Cuban	23	0.16
Mexican	6,266	44.82
Puerto Rican	48	0.34
South American:	37	0.26
Argentinean	8	0.06
Chilean	4	0.03
Colombian	6	0.04
Ecuadorian	1	0.01
Peruvian	6	0.04
Uruguayan	1	0.01
Venezuelan	5	0.04
Other South American	6	0.04
Other Hispanic or Latino	1,138	8.14
Hungarian	19	0.14
Irish	548	3.91
Italian	204	1.46
Norwegian	25	0.18
Polish	226	1.61
Romanian	18	0.13
Russian	17	0.12
Scotch-Irish	84	0.60
Scottish	39	0.28
Swedish	16	0.11
United States or American	1,222	8.73
West Indian, excl. Hispanic:	9	0.06
Trinidadian and Tobagonian	9	0.06
White:	8,686	62.14
Not Hispanic (4,731)	4,802	34.35
Hispanic (3,558)	3,884	27.78

Alice

Place Type: City
County: Jim Wells
Population: 19,010

Ancestry/Race	Number	%
African American/Black:	180	0.95
Not Hispanic (131)	141	0.74
Hispanic (33)	39	0.21
Am. Ind. or Alaska Nat., not spec.	68	0.36
American Indian tribes, specified:	50	0.26
Apache (1)	1	0.01
Blackfeet	1	0.01
Cherokee (1)	6	0.03
Chickasaw (1)	1	0.01
Chippewa	1	0.01
Comanche	1	0.01
Creek	2	0.01
Iroquois	1	0.01
Latin American Indians (13)	14	0.07
Navajo (8)	8	0.04
Seminole	6	0.03
Shoshone (1)	1	0.01
Sioux	7	0.04
American Indian tribes, not spec.	23	0.12
Asian:	169	0.89
Chinese, ex. Taiwanese (18)	18	0.09
Filipino (43)	48	0.25
Indian (46)	55	0.29
Korean (10)	13	0.07
Pakistani (4)	6	0.03
Thai	1	0.01
Vietnamese (11)	11	0.06
Other Asian, not specified (7)	17	0.09
British	25	0.13
Croatian	10	0.05
Czech	26	0.14
Danish	6	0.03
Dutch	55	0.29
English	374	1.98
European	15	0.08
Finnish	11	0.06
French, except Basque	121	0.64
French Canadian	13	0.07
German	698	3.69
Hawaii Native/Pacific Islander:	21	0.11
Micronesian: (5)	6	0.03
Guamanian/Chamorro	1	0.01
Other Micronesian (5)	5	0.03
Polynesian: (4)	5	0.03
Native Hawaiian (3)	4	0.02
Samoan (1)	1	0.01
Other Pac. Isl., not spec. (7)	10	0.05
Hispanic or Latino:	14,837	78.05
Central American:	23	0.12
Guatemalan	8	0.04
Honduran	1	0.01
Panamanian	3	0.02
Salvadoran	6	0.03
Other Central American	4	0.02
Cuban	19	0.10
Mexican	8,296	43.64
Puerto Rican	16	0.08
South American:	11	0.06
Argentinean	1	0.01
Colombian	6	0.03
Venezuelan	4	0.02
Other Hispanic or Latino	6,472	34.05
Hungarian	5	0.03
Irish	474	2.51
Italian	37	0.20
Polish	79	0.42
Scotch-Irish	74	0.39
Scottish	48	0.25
Swedish	27	0.14
Swiss	12	0.06
United States or American	657	3.47
Welsh	7	0.04
White:	15,156	79.73
Not Hispanic (3,824)	3,866	20.34
Hispanic (10,898)	11,290	59.39

Allen

Place Type: City
County: Collin
Population: 43,554

Ancestry/Race	Number	%
Acadian/Cajun	27	0.06
Afghan	25	0.06
African American/Black:	2,071	4.76
Not Hispanic (1,889)	2,029	4.66
Hispanic (26)	42	0.10
African, sub-Saharan:	266	0.61
African	90	0.21
Ethiopian	29	0.07
Ghanian	18	0.04
Kenyan	9	0.02
Nigerian	53	0.12
South African	17	0.04
Other sub-Saharan African	50	0.12
Alaska Native tribes, specified:	1	0.00
Tlingit-Haida (1)	1	0.00
Am. Ind. or Alaska Nat., not spec.	62	0.14
American Indian tribes, specified:	352	0.81
Apache (5)	8	0.02
Blackfeet (2)	11	0.03
Cherokee (57)	131	0.30
Chickasaw (18)	23	0.05
Chippewa (3)	4	0.01
Choctaw (46)	76	0.17
Comanche (2)	6	0.01
Creek (17)	24	0.06
Delaware (5)	5	0.01
Iroquois	1	0.00
Kiowa (2)	3	0.01
Latin American Indians (3)	7	0.02
Lumbee (9)	9	0.02
Navajo (8)	10	0.02
Osage (5)	6	0.01
Ottawa (1)	1	0.00
Potawatomi (6)	7	0.02
Pueblo (2)	4	0.01
Sioux (2)	3	0.01
Yakama (1)	1	0.00
Yaqui (1)	1	0.00
All other tribes (9)	11	0.03
American Indian tribes, not spec.	7	0.02
Arab:	249	0.57
Arab/Arabic	10	0.02
Egyptian	50	0.12
Jordanian	28	0.06
Lebanese	95	0.22
Moroccan	8	0.02
Syrian	36	0.08
Other Arab	22	0.05
Armenian	46	0.11
Asian:	1,866	4.28
Bangladeshi (1)	3	0.01
Cambodian (7)	8	0.02
Chinese, ex. Taiwanese (265)	302	0.69
Filipino (129)	181	0.42
Indian (458)	498	1.14
Indonesian (4)	5	0.01
Japanese (50)	88	0.20
Korean (162)	185	0.42
Laotian (5)	8	0.02
Malaysian (1)	2	0.00
Pakistani (76)	84	0.19
Sri Lankan (4)	4	0.01
Taiwanese (10)	11	0.03
Thai (26)	38	0.09
Vietnamese (362)	379	0.87
Other Asian, specified (3)	5	0.01

Notes: 1. Figures in the "Number" column do not add up to the total population due to: a) Ancestry/Race overlap — e.g. persons can report being both White and Irish, b) persons of Hispanic origin can report being any race, c) persons reporting two ancestries are counted in both categories. 2. Numbers in parentheses indicate the number of persons reporting this ancestry/race alone, not in combination with any other ancestry/race. 3. Refer to the Explanation of Data in the front of the book for more detailed information.

Ancestry/Race	Number	%
Other Asian, not specified (31)	65	0.15
Australian	14	0.03
Austrian	60	0.14
Belgian	85	0.20
Brazilian	31	0.07
British	290	0.67
Canadian	341	0.78
Croatian	74	0.17
Czech	225	0.52
Czechoslovakian	76	0.17
Danish	253	0.58
Dutch	739	1.70
Eastern European	8	0.02
English	5,516	12.69
European	684	1.57
Finnish	45	0.10
French, except Basque	1,588	3.65
French Canadian	278	0.64
German	7,853	18.07
Greek	272	0.63
Hawaii Native/Pacific Islander:	40	0.09
Micronesian: (5)	9	0.02
Guamanian/Chamorro (5)	9	0.02
Polynesian: (4)	13	0.03
Native Hawaiian (3)	9	0.02
Samoan	3	0.01
Tongan (1)	1	0.00
Other Pac. Isl., not spec. (11)	18	0.04
Hispanic or Latino:	3,038	6.98
Central American:	123	0.28
Costa Rican	11	0.03
Guatemalan	14	0.03
Honduran	20	0.05
Nicaraguan	15	0.03
Panamanian	30	0.07
Salvadoran	31	0.07
Other Central American	2	0.00
Cuban	68	0.16
Dominican Republic	1	0.00
Mexican	1,945	4.47
Puerto Rican	131	0.30
South American:	130	0.30
Argentinean	4	0.01
Bolivian	5	0.01
Chilean	10	0.02
Colombian	51	0.12
Ecuadorian	7	0.02
Paraguayan	3	0.01
Peruvian	28	0.06
Venezuelan	20	0.05
Other South American	2	0.00
Other Hispanic or Latino	640	1.47
Hungarian	199	0.46
Icelander	9	0.02
Iranian	54	0.12
Irish	6,207	14.28
Italian	2,012	4.63
Lithuanian	54	0.12
Luxemburger	11	0.03
New Zealander	7	0.02
Northern European	38	0.09
Norwegian	660	1.52
Pennsylvania German	18	0.04
Polish	914	2.10
Portuguese	58	0.13
Romanian	43	0.10
Russian	198	0.46
Scandinavian	112	0.26
Scotch-Irish	843	1.94
Scottish	1,319	3.04
Serbian	6	0.01
Slavic	37	0.09
Slovak	28	0.06
Slovene	9	0.02
Swedish	682	1.57
Swiss	147	0.34
Turkish	17	0.04
Ukrainian	62	0.14
United States or American	4,449	10.24
Welsh	376	0.87
West Indian, excl. Hispanic:	46	0.11
Dutch West Indian	9	0.02
Jamaican	37	0.09
White:	38,652	88.75
Not Hispanic (36,239)	36,719	84.31
Hispanic (1,714)	1,933	4.44
Yugoslavian	9	0.02

Alvin

Place Type: City
County: Brazoria
Population: 21,413

Ancestry/Race	Number	%
Acadian/Cajun	54	0.25
African American/Black:	510	2.38
Not Hispanic (437)	488	2.28
Hispanic (15)	22	0.10
African, sub-Saharan:	6	0.03
African	6	0.03
Alaska Native tribes, specified:	1	0.00
Eskimo	1	0.00
Am. Ind. or Alaska Nat., not spec.	77	0.36
Albanian	13	0.06
American Indian tribes, specified:	170	0.79
Apache (1)	9	0.04
Blackfeet (1)	7	0.03
Cherokee (26)	83	0.39
Chickasaw (2)	5	0.02
Chippewa (4)	6	0.03
Choctaw (4)	19	0.09
Comanche	1	0.00
Creek	1	0.00
Houma (3)	3	0.01
Iroquois (1)	1	0.00
Latin American Indians (2)	4	0.02
Navajo	3	0.01
Osage (1)	1	0.00
Potawatomi (1)	2	0.01
Seminole (1)	1	0.00
Shoshone (1)	2	0.01
Sioux	2	0.01
Yaqui (4)	4	0.02
All other tribes (8)	16	0.07
American Indian tribes, not spec.	12	0.06
Arab:	36	0.17
Lebanese	15	0.07
Syrian	21	0.10
Asian:	231	1.08
Cambodian (4)	4	0.02
Chinese, ex. Taiwanese (9)	17	0.08
Filipino (5)	21	0.10
Indian (57)	60	0.28
Japanese (5)	17	0.08
Korean (9)	14	0.07
Malaysian (1)	3	0.01
Pakistani (61)	69	0.32
Sri Lankan (3)	3	0.01
Thai (2)	3	0.01
Vietnamese (6)	9	0.04
Other Asian, specified (2)	2	0.01
Other Asian, not specified (6)	9	0.04
Australian	29	0.13
Austrian	5	0.02
Brazilian	7	0.03
British	65	0.30
Canadian	2	0.01
Celtic	10	0.05
Czech	317	1.46
Czechoslovakian	17	0.08
Danish	53	0.24
Dutch	251	1.16
English	1,707	7.87
European	154	0.71
Finnish	51	0.24
French, except Basque	804	3.71
French Canadian	44	0.20
German	2,457	11.33
Greek	35	0.16
Hawaii Native/Pacific Islander:	16	0.07
Micronesian:	1	0.00
Guamanian/Chamorro	1	0.00
Polynesian: (12)	15	0.07
Native Hawaiian (9)	10	0.05
Samoan (3)	5	0.02
Hispanic or Latino:	6,014	28.09
Central American:	113	0.53
Costa Rican	4	0.02
Guatemalan	9	0.04
Honduran	21	0.10
Nicaraguan	6	0.03
Panamanian	7	0.03
Salvadoran	66	0.31
Cuban	30	0.14
Dominican Republic	1	0.00
Mexican	4,631	21.63
Puerto Rican	52	0.24
South American:	24	0.11
Chilean	6	0.03
Colombian	7	0.03
Peruvian	7	0.03
Venezuelan	3	0.01
Other South American	1	0.00
Other Hispanic or Latino	1,163	5.43
Hungarian	23	0.11
Irish	1,864	8.60
Italian	421	1.94
Lithuanian	14	0.06
Norwegian	97	0.45
Polish	277	1.28
Portuguese	5	0.02
Russian	72	0.33
Scandinavian	25	0.12
Scotch-Irish	396	1.83
Scottish	358	1.65
Slavic	10	0.05
Slovak	24	0.11
Swedish	127	0.59
Swiss	58	0.27
Ukrainian	19	0.09
United States or American	1,800	8.30
Welsh	82	0.38
West Indian, excl. Hispanic:	25	0.12
Dutch West Indian	25	0.12
White:	18,320	85.56
Not Hispanic (14,402)	14,685	68.58
Hispanic (3,216)	3,635	16.98

Amarillo

Place Type: City
County: Potter
Population: 173,627

Ancestry/Race	Number	%
Acadian/Cajun	16	0.01
African American/Black:	11,178	6.44
Not Hispanic (10,067)	10,697	6.16
Hispanic (291)	481	0.28
African, sub-Saharan:	582	0.34
African	558	0.32
Cape Verdean	4	0.00
Nigerian	20	0.01
Alaska Native tribes, specified:	12	0.01
Tlingit-Haida (9)	10	0.01
All other tribes (2)	2	0.00
Alaska Native tribes, not specified	7	0.00
Am. Ind. or Alaska Nat., not spec.	729	0.42
Albanian	48	0.03
American Indian tribes, specified:	1,674	0.96
Apache (52)	108	0.06
Blackfeet (13)	37	0.02
Cherokee (198)	557	0.32
Cheyenne (5)	11	0.01
Chickasaw (35)	61	0.04
Chippewa (9)	13	0.01
Choctaw (139)	283	0.16
Comanche (28)	64	0.04
Cree (1)	1	0.00

Notes: 1. Figures in the "Number" column do not add up to the total population due to: a) Ancestry/Race overlap — e.g. persons can report being both White and Irish, b) persons of Hispanic origin can report being any race, c) persons reporting two ancestries are counted in both categories. 2. Numbers in parentheses indicate the number of persons reporting this ancestry/race alone, not in combination with any other ancestry/race. 3. Refer to the Explanation of Data in the front of the book for more detailed information.

Creek (31)	55	0.03
Crow (1)	2	0.00
Delaware (5)	14	0.01
Iroquois (9)	15	0.01
Kiowa (6)	14	0.01
Latin American Indians (101)	137	0.08
Menominee	2	0.00
Navajo (46)	70	0.04
Osage (5)	10	0.01
Ottawa (4)	5	0.00
Paiute (1)	2	0.00
Pima (4)	4	0.00
Potawatomi (8)	18	0.01
Pueblo (27)	36	0.02
Seminole (7)	17	0.01
Shoshone	3	0.00
Sioux (23)	42	0.02
Tohono O'Odham	1	0.00
Ute (3)	3	0.00
Yaqui (1)	2	0.00
All other tribes (43)	87	0.05
American Indian tribes, not spec.	176	0.10
Arab:	368	0.21
Arab/Arabic	124	0.07
Iraqi	46	0.03
Jordanian	21	0.01
Lebanese	111	0.06
Palestinian	8	0.00
Syrian	13	0.01
Other Arab	45	0.03
Armenian	11	0.01
Asian:	4,140	2.38
Bangladeshi (3)	3	0.00
Cambodian (9)	12	0.01
Chinese, ex. Taiwanese (219)	254	0.15
Filipino (153)	228	0.13
Indian (422)	513	0.30
Indonesian (3)	7	0.00
Japanese (54)	125	0.07
Korean (53)	83	0.05
Laotian (1,030)	1,137	0.65
Malaysian (4)	5	0.00
Pakistani (36)	42	0.02
Sri Lankan	1	0.00
Taiwanese (2)	4	0.00
Thai (62)	81	0.05
Vietnamese (1,376)	1,459	0.84
Other Asian, specified (1)	18	0.01
Other Asian, not specified (83)	168	0.10
Australian	47	0.03
Austrian	189	0.11
Basque	14	0.01
Belgian	30	0.02
British	524	0.30
Bulgarian	19	0.01
Canadian	220	0.13
Celtic	62	0.04
Croatian	58	0.03
Czech	464	0.27
Czechoslovakian	141	0.08
Danish	423	0.24
Dutch	2,655	1.53
Eastern European	34	0.02
English	15,309	8.82
European	949	0.55
Finnish	33	0.02
French, except Basque	3,758	2.17
French Canadian	426	0.25
German	19,672	11.34
Greek	184	0.11
Hawaii Native/Pacific Islander:	153	0.09
Micronesian: (6)	11	0.01
Guamanian/Chamorro (6)	11	0.01
Polynesian: (41)	79	0.05
Native Hawaiian (26)	61	0.04
Samoan (15)	18	0.01
Other Pac. Isl., specified	8	0.00
Other Pac. Isl., not spec. (17)	55	0.03
Hispanic or Latino:	37,947	21.86
Central American:	224	0.13
Costa Rican	5	0.00
Guatemalan	48	0.03
Honduran	66	0.04
Nicaraguan	11	0.01
Panamanian	25	0.01
Salvadoran	65	0.04
Other Central American	4	0.00
Cuban	111	0.06
Dominican Republic	14	0.01
Mexican	26,760	15.41
Puerto Rican	220	0.13
South American:	93	0.05
Argentinean	4	0.00
Bolivian	3	0.00
Chilean	21	0.01
Colombian	24	0.01
Ecuadorian	5	0.00
Paraguayan	1	0.00
Peruvian	15	0.01
Uruguayan	2	0.00
Venezuelan	17	0.01
Other South American	1	0.00
Other Hispanic or Latino	10,525	6.06
Hungarian	121	0.07
Icelander	11	0.01
Iranian	80	0.05
Irish	14,961	8.62
Italian	2,187	1.26
Latvian	5	0.00
Lithuanian	64	0.04
Northern European	32	0.02
Norwegian	1,130	0.65
Pennsylvania German	48	0.03
Polish	984	0.57
Portuguese	114	0.07
Romanian	31	0.02
Russian	217	0.13
Scandinavian	68	0.04
Scotch-Irish	3,643	2.10
Scottish	2,931	1.69
Serbian	11	0.01
Slavic	50	0.03
Slovak	40	0.02
Swedish	993	0.57
Swiss	196	0.11
Turkish	4	0.00
Ukrainian	55	0.03
United States or American	18,352	10.58
Welsh	829	0.48
West Indian, excl. Hispanic:	267	0.15
Dutch West Indian	259	0.15
Jamaican	8	0.00
White:	138,120	79.55
Not Hispanic (118,821)	120,784	69.57
Hispanic (15,742)	17,336	9.98
Yugoslavian	286	0.16

Angleton

Place Type: City
County: Brazoria
Population: 18,130

Ancestry/Race	Number	%
Acadian/Cajun	52	0.28
African American/Black:	2,154	11.88
Not Hispanic (2,032)	2,098	11.57
Hispanic (31)	56	0.31
African, sub-Saharan:	80	0.44
African	50	0.27
Ugandan	23	0.13
Other sub-Saharan African	7	0.04
Am. Ind. or Alaska Nat., not spec.	60	0.33
Albanian	9	0.05
American Indian tribes, specified:	100	0.55
Apache (2)	7	0.04
Blackfeet (2)	4	0.02
Cherokee (12)	25	0.14
Chickasaw	2	0.01
Chippewa (1)	1	0.01
Choctaw (10)	16	0.09
Comanche (1)	2	0.01
Creek (1)	1	0.01
Delaware	1	0.01
Latin American Indians (14)	15	0.08
Ottawa	6	0.03
Potawatomi (5)	6	0.03
Sioux (1)	3	0.02
Yaqui (3)	3	0.02
All other tribes (3)	8	0.04
American Indian tribes, not spec.	7	0.04
Arab:	17	0.09
Lebanese	17	0.09
Asian:	256	1.41
Cambodian	4	0.02
Chinese, ex. Taiwanese (15)	16	0.09
Filipino (22)	34	0.19
Indian (42)	50	0.28
Japanese (9)	15	0.08
Korean (5)	14	0.08
Laotian	2	0.01
Pakistani (2)	2	0.01
Taiwanese (2)	2	0.01
Thai (5)	10	0.06
Vietnamese (96)	104	0.57
Other Asian, specified	1	0.01
Other Asian, not specified	2	0.01
Austrian	7	0.04
British	24	0.13
Canadian	11	0.06
Croatian	21	0.11
Czech	226	1.24
Czechoslovakian	77	0.42
Danish	24	0.13
Dutch	212	1.16
English	1,189	6.51
European	94	0.51
Finnish	7	0.04
French, except Basque	616	3.37
French Canadian	106	0.58
German	2,091	11.44
Greek	12	0.07
Hawaii Native/Pacific Islander:	11	0.06
Micronesian: (5)	6	0.03
Guamanian/Chamorro (5)	6	0.03
Polynesian: (2)	4	0.02
Native Hawaiian (1)	2	0.01
Samoan (1)	2	0.01
Other Pac. Isl., not spec.	1	0.01
Hispanic or Latino:	4,205	23.19
Central American:	52	0.29
Costa Rican	1	0.01
Guatemalan	18	0.10
Honduran	2	0.01
Nicaraguan	1	0.01
Panamanian	6	0.03
Salvadoran	17	0.09
Other Central American	7	0.04
Cuban	10	0.06
Mexican	3,198	17.64
Puerto Rican	39	0.22
South American:	20	0.11
Argentinean	1	0.01
Chilean	7	0.04
Colombian	9	0.05
Peruvian	1	0.01
Venezuelan	1	0.01
Other South American	1	0.01
Other Hispanic or Latino	886	4.89
Hungarian	20	0.11
Iranian	30	0.16
Irish	1,343	7.35
Italian	234	1.28
Norwegian	112	0.61
Pennsylvania German	5	0.03
Polish	100	0.55
Portuguese	5	0.03
Russian	29	0.16
Scandinavian	7	0.04
Scotch-Irish	419	2.29

Notes: 1. Figures in the "Number" column do not add up to the total population due to: a) Ancestry/Race overlap — e.g. persons can report being both White and Irish, b) persons of Hispanic origin can report being any race, c) persons reporting two ancestries are counted in both categories. 2. Numbers in parentheses indicate the number of persons reporting this ancestry/race alone, not in combination with any other ancestry/race. 3. Refer to the Explanation of Data in the front of the book for more detailed information.

Ancestry/Race	Number	%
Scottish	180	0.98
Slovak	14	0.08
Slovene	30	0.16
Swedish	148	0.81
United States or American	2,120	11.60
Welsh	24	0.13
West Indian, excl. Hispanic:	54	0.30
Jamaican	45	0.25
Trinidadian and Tobagonian	9	0.05
White:	13,995	77.19
Not Hispanic (11,452)	11,621	64.10
Hispanic (2,184)	2,374	13.09
Yugoslavian	10	0.05

Arlington

Place Type: City
County: Tarrant
Population: 332,969

Ancestry/Race	Number	%
Acadian/Cajun	74	0.02
Afghan	38	0.01
African American/Black:	48,196	14.47
Not Hispanic (45,061)	47,116	14.15
Hispanic (666)	1,080	0.32
African, sub-Saharan:	5,245	1.58
African	2,568	0.77
Ethiopian	107	0.03
Ghanian	244	0.07
Kenyan	408	0.12
Liberian	70	0.02
Nigerian	1,302	0.39
Senegalese	28	0.01
Sierra Leonean	18	0.01
Somalian	211	0.06
South African	31	0.01
Sudanese	51	0.02
Ugandan	12	0.00
Other sub-Saharan African	195	0.06
Alaska Native tribes, specified:	20	0.01
Alaska Athabascan	3	0.00
Aleut (3)	3	0.00
Eskimo (4)	5	0.00
Tlingit-Haida (7)	9	0.00
Alaska Native tribes, not specified	3	0.00
Am. Ind. or Alaska Nat., not spec.	1,116	0.34
Albanian	8	0.00
Alsatian	21	0.01
American Indian tribes, specified:	2,641	0.79
Apache (67)	134	0.04
Blackfeet (21)	74	0.02
Cherokee (334)	1,042	0.31
Cheyenne (4)	9	0.00
Chickasaw (48)	83	0.02
Chippewa (19)	37	0.01
Choctaw (211)	390	0.12
Colville	1	0.00
Comanche (35)	84	0.03
Cree	3	0.00
Creek (38)	98	0.03
Crow (2)	6	0.00
Delaware (7)	17	0.01
Houma (2)	2	0.00
Iroquois (30)	46	0.01
Kiowa (22)	28	0.01
Latin American Indians (86)	150	0.05
Lumbee (5)	5	0.00
Menominee	3	0.00
Navajo (33)	64	0.02
Osage (9)	24	0.01
Ottawa (1)	5	0.00
Potawatomi (16)	25	0.01
Pueblo (8)	19	0.01
Puget Sound Salish (1)	1	0.00
Seminole (12)	30	0.01
Shoshone	6	0.00
Sioux (29)	66	0.02
Tohono O'Odham	1	0.00
Ute	1	0.00
Yakama (2)	2	0.00
Yaqui (3)	4	0.00
All other tribes (87)	177	0.05
American Indian tribes, not spec.	244	0.07
Arab:	2,741	0.82
Arab/Arabic	645	0.19
Egyptian	173	0.05
Iraqi	187	0.06
Jordanian	169	0.05
Lebanese	489	0.15
Moroccan	46	0.01
Palestinian	622	0.19
Syrian	197	0.06
Other Arab	213	0.06
Armenian	72	0.02
Asian:	22,456	6.74
Bangladeshi (139)	197	0.06
Cambodian (96)	113	0.03
Chinese, ex. Taiwanese (2,720)	3,008	0.90
Filipino (948)	1,305	0.39
Hmong (33)	40	0.01
Indian (3,120)	3,439	1.03
Indonesian (101)	135	0.04
Japanese (329)	538	0.16
Korean (888)	1,050	0.32
Laotian (82)	103	0.03
Malaysian (41)	70	0.02
Pakistani (576)	788	0.24
Sri Lankan (40)	46	0.01
Taiwanese (317)	365	0.11
Thai (258)	306	0.09
Vietnamese (9,606)	9,954	2.99
Other Asian, specified (65)	88	0.03
Other Asian, not specified (377)	911	0.27
Assyrian/Chaldean/Syriac	11	0.00
Australian	146	0.04
Austrian	624	0.19
Basque	18	0.01
Belgian	208	0.06
Brazilian	102	0.03
British	1,568	0.47
Bulgarian	125	0.04
Canadian	415	0.12
Celtic	106	0.03
Croatian	78	0.02
Czech	2,008	0.60
Czechoslovakian	568	0.17
Danish	848	0.25
Dutch	4,586	1.38
Eastern European	69	0.02
English	28,838	8.67
European	2,084	0.63
Finnish	355	0.11
French, except Basque	8,434	2.54
French Canadian	1,233	0.37
German	37,847	11.38
Greek	705	0.21
Guyanese	66	0.02
Hawaii Native/Pacific Islander:	835	0.25
Melanesian: (1)	4	0.00
Fijian (1)	1	0.00
Other Melanesian	3	0.00
Micronesian: (98)	150	0.05
Guamanian/Chamorro (75)	117	0.04
Other Micronesian (23)	33	0.01
Polynesian: (300)	456	0.14
Native Hawaiian (95)	208	0.06
Samoan (133)	157	0.05
Tongan (66)	79	0.02
Other Polynesian (6)	12	0.00
Other Pac. Isl., specified	18	0.01
Other Pac. Isl., not spec. (72)	207	0.06
Hispanic or Latino:	60,817	18.27
Central American:	1,495	0.45
Costa Rican	95	0.03
Guatemalan	218	0.07
Honduran	166	0.05
Nicaraguan	75	0.02
Panamanian	122	0.04
Salvadoran	755	0.23
Other Central American	64	0.02
Cuban	339	0.10
Dominican Republic	87	0.03
Mexican	46,766	14.05
Puerto Rican	2,081	0.62
South American:	901	0.27
Argentinean	58	0.02
Bolivian	33	0.01
Chilean	38	0.01
Colombian	396	0.12
Ecuadorian	72	0.02
Paraguayan	2	0.00
Peruvian	174	0.05
Uruguayan	12	0.00
Venezuelan	85	0.03
Other South American	31	0.01
Other Hispanic or Latino	9,148	2.75
Hungarian	655	0.20
Icelander	18	0.01
Iranian	1,000	0.30
Irish	28,487	8.56
Israeli	11	0.00
Italian	7,571	2.28
Latvian	32	0.01
Lithuanian	289	0.09
Luxemburger	43	0.01
Macedonian	36	0.01
Maltese	24	0.01
New Zealander	56	0.02
Northern European	53	0.02
Norwegian	2,569	0.77
Pennsylvania German	58	0.02
Polish	4,250	1.28
Portuguese	340	0.10
Romanian	127	0.04
Russian	1,057	0.32
Scandinavian	416	0.13
Scotch-Irish	6,023	1.81
Scottish	6,042	1.82
Serbian	23	0.01
Slavic	103	0.03
Slovak	302	0.09
Slovene	92	0.03
Swedish	2,917	0.88
Swiss	559	0.17
Turkish	223	0.07
Ukrainian	351	0.11
United States or American	25,940	7.80
Welsh	1,879	0.56
West Indian, excl. Hispanic:	833	0.25
Bahamian	8	0.00
Barbadian	34	0.01
Belizean	73	0.02
Bermudan	5	0.00
British West Indian	51	0.02
Dutch West Indian	98	0.03
Haitian	45	0.01
Jamaican	301	0.09
Trinidadian and Tobagonian	52	0.02
U.S. Virgin Islander	12	0.00
West Indian	154	0.05
White:	233,461	70.11
Not Hispanic (198,591)	203,832	61.22
Hispanic (26,788)	29,629	8.90
Yugoslavian	266	0.08

Atascocita

Place Type: Census Designated Place
County: Harris
Population: 35,757

Ancestry/Race	Number	%
Acadian/Cajun	49	0.14
African American/Black:	4,819	13.48
Not Hispanic (4,611)	4,758	13.31
Hispanic (37)	61	0.17
African, sub-Saharan:	392	1.09
African	353	0.98
South African	26	0.07

Notes: 1. Figures in the "Number" column do not add up to the total population due to: a) Ancestry/Race overlap — e.g. persons can report being both White and Irish, b) persons of Hispanic origin can report being any race, c) persons reporting two ancestries are counted in both categories. 2. Numbers in parentheses indicate the number of persons reporting this ancestry/race alone, not in combination with any other ancestry/race. 3. Refer to the Explanation of Data in the front of the book for more detailed information.

Ugandan	13	0.04
Alaska Native tribes, specified:	1	0.00
Eskimo (1)	1	0.00
Am. Ind. or Alaska Nat., not spec.	94	0.26
American Indian tribes, specified:	183	0.51
Apache (2)	6	0.02
Blackfeet	4	0.01
Cherokee (21)	86	0.24
Cheyenne	2	0.01
Chickasaw (2)	3	0.01
Chippewa (1)	1	0.00
Choctaw (10)	18	0.05
Creek (6)	14	0.04
Delaware	1	0.00
Iroquois	3	0.01
Latin American Indians (3)	6	0.02
Navajo	2	0.01
Ottawa (4)	4	0.01
Potawatomi	2	0.01
Seminole	2	0.01
Shoshone (5)	8	0.02
Sioux (5)	6	0.02
All other tribes (12)	15	0.04
American Indian tribes, not spec.	7	0.02
Arab:	96	0.27
Arab/Arabic	15	0.04
Egyptian	32	0.09
Lebanese	15	0.04
Palestinian	34	0.09
Armenian	15	0.04
Asian:	1,057	2.96
Bangladeshi (4)	4	0.01
Cambodian (17)	24	0.07
Chinese, ex. Taiwanese (152)	174	0.49
Filipino (102)	142	0.40
Indian (230)	259	0.72
Indonesian (4)	6	0.02
Japanese (29)	60	0.17
Korean (62)	75	0.21
Laotian (12)	13	0.04
Malaysian (1)	1	0.00
Pakistani (40)	52	0.15
Sri Lankan (4)	4	0.01
Taiwanese (11)	11	0.03
Thai (26)	30	0.08
Vietnamese (155)	158	0.44
Other Asian, specified	1	0.00
Other Asian, not specified (13)	43	0.12
Australian	41	0.11
Austrian	22	0.06
Belgian	23	0.06
Brazilian	11	0.03
British	233	0.65
Canadian	118	0.33
Czech	282	0.78
Czechoslovakian	153	0.43
Danish	78	0.22
Dutch	362	1.01
English	3,559	9.89
European	281	0.78
Finnish	53	0.15
French, except Basque	1,493	4.15
French Canadian	299	0.83
German	5,418	15.06
Greek	151	0.42
Guyanese	21	0.06
Hawaii Native/Pacific Islander:	41	0.11
Micronesian: (10)	20	0.06
Guamanian/Chamorro (10)	18	0.05
Other Micronesian	2	0.01
Polynesian: (2)	12	0.03
Native Hawaiian (2)	12	0.03
Other Pac. Isl., specified	1	0.00
Other Pac. Isl., not spec. (3)	8	0.02
Hispanic or Latino:	4,297	12.02
Central American:	127	0.36
Costa Rican	4	0.01
Guatemalan	15	0.04
Honduran	11	0.03
Nicaraguan	17	0.05
Panamanian	19	0.05
Salvadoran	58	0.16
Other Central American	3	0.01
Cuban	62	0.17
Dominican Republic	11	0.03
Mexican	3,002	8.40
Puerto Rican	135	0.38
South American:	147	0.41
Argentinean	15	0.04
Bolivian	2	0.01
Chilean	2	0.01
Colombian	54	0.15
Ecuadorian	16	0.04
Peruvian	6	0.02
Venezuelan	43	0.12
Other South American	9	0.03
Other Hispanic or Latino	813	2.27
Hungarian	113	0.31
Iranian	13	0.04
Irish	4,440	12.34
Israeli	13	0.04
Italian	1,051	2.92
Lithuanian	46	0.13
Norwegian	243	0.68
Pennsylvania German	6	0.02
Polish	809	2.25
Portuguese	41	0.11
Romanian	30	0.08
Russian	66	0.18
Scandinavian	61	0.17
Scotch-Irish	558	1.55
Scottish	652	1.81
Serbian	19	0.05
Slavic	8	0.02
Slovak	29	0.08
Swedish	396	1.10
Swiss	110	0.31
Turkish	12	0.03
Ukrainian	40	0.11
United States or American	2,709	7.53
Welsh	315	0.88
West Indian, excl. Hispanic:	127	0.35
Jamaican	121	0.34
Trinidadian and Tobagonian	6	0.02
White:	28,541	79.82
Not Hispanic (25,377)	25,772	72.08
Hispanic (2,499)	2,769	7.74
Yugoslavian	31	0.09

Athens

Place Type: City
County: Henderson
Population: 11,297

Ancestry/Race	Number	%
African American/Black:	2,218	19.63
Not Hispanic (2,154)	2,191	19.39
Hispanic (18)	27	0.24
African, sub-Saharan:	26	0.23
African	26	0.23
Am. Ind. or Alaska Nat., not spec.	15	0.13
American Indian tribes, specified:	51	0.45
Apache (2)	2	0.02
Blackfeet	2	0.02
Cherokee (13)	23	0.20
Chickasaw (3)	8	0.07
Choctaw (2)	4	0.04
Creek (3)	3	0.03
Iroquois	1	0.01
Latin American Indians (2)	6	0.05
Potawatomi	1	0.01
All other tribes	1	0.01
American Indian tribes, not spec.	6	0.05
Arab:	23	0.20
Jordanian	23	0.20
Asian:	88	0.78
Chinese, ex. Taiwanese (12)	13	0.12
Filipino (11)	14	0.12
Indian (17)	19	0.17
Japanese (12)	15	0.13
Korean (2)	4	0.04
Pakistani (5)	5	0.04
Vietnamese (8)	10	0.09
Other Asian, specified	1	0.01
Other Asian, not specified (4)	7	0.06
Canadian	19	0.17
Celtic	17	0.15
Czech	11	0.10
Dutch	41	0.36
English	912	8.06
European	54	0.48
French, except Basque	99	0.87
French Canadian	10	0.09
German	713	6.30
Hawaii Native/Pacific Islander:	17	0.15
Polynesian: (7)	13	0.12
Native Hawaiian (4)	10	0.09
Tongan (3)	3	0.03
Other Pac. Isl., specified	1	0.01
Other Pac. Isl., not spec.	3	0.03
Hispanic or Latino:	1,962	17.37
Central American:	45	0.40
Honduran	39	0.35
Nicaraguan	1	0.01
Panamanian	1	0.01
Salvadoran	3	0.03
Other Central American	1	0.01
Cuban	6	0.05
Mexican	1,739	15.39
Puerto Rican	3	0.03
South American:	6	0.05
Argentinean	5	0.04
Colombian	1	0.01
Other Hispanic or Latino	163	1.44
Hungarian	23	0.20
Irish	889	7.86
Italian	99	0.87
Norwegian	38	0.34
Polish	11	0.10
Russian	13	0.11
Scotch-Irish	204	1.80
Scottish	111	0.98
Swedish	24	0.21
Swiss	10	0.09
United States or American	1,509	13.34
Welsh	31	0.27
White:	8,298	73.45
Not Hispanic (6,986)	7,056	62.46
Hispanic (1,164)	1,242	10.99

Austin

Place Type: City
County: Travis
Population: 656,562

Ancestry/Race	Number	%
Acadian/Cajun	601	0.09
Afghan	21	0.00
African American/Black:	69,943	10.65
Not Hispanic (64,259)	67,117	10.22
Hispanic (1,697)	2,826	0.43
African, sub-Saharan:	4,683	0.71
African	2,935	0.45
Cape Verdean	19	0.00
Ethiopian	254	0.04
Ghanian	42	0.01
Kenyan	58	0.01
Liberian	17	0.00
Nigerian	713	0.11
Sierra Leonean	12	0.00
Somalian	94	0.01
South African	320	0.05
Sudanese	8	0.00
Ugandan	8	0.00
Zimbabwean	31	0.00
Other sub-Saharan African	172	0.03
Alaska Native tribes, specified:	38	0.01
Alaska Athabascan (3)	4	0.00

Notes: 1. Figures in the "Number" column do not add up to the total population due to: a) Ancestry/Race overlap — e.g. persons can report being both White and Irish, b) persons of Hispanic origin can report being any race, c) persons reporting two ancestries are counted in both categories. 2. Numbers in parentheses indicate the number of persons reporting this ancestry/race alone, not in combination with any other ancestry/race. 3. Refer to the Explanation of Data in the front of the book for more detailed information.

Aleut (1)	3	0.00
Eskimo (13)	22	0.00
Tlingit-Haida (3)	6	0.00
All other tribes (3)	3	0.00
Alaska Native tribes, not specified	13	0.00
Am. Ind. or Alaska Nat., not spec.	2,871	0.44
Albanian	92	0.01
Alsatian	87	0.01
American Indian tribes, specified:	4,148	0.63
Apache (119)	219	0.03
Blackfeet (24)	108	0.02
Cherokee (465)	1,429	0.22
Cheyenne (7)	15	0.00
Chickasaw (33)	75	0.01
Chippewa (31)	63	0.01
Choctaw (170)	366	0.06
Colville (1)	2	0.00
Comanche (37)	112	0.02
Cree (8)	16	0.00
Creek (31)	89	0.01
Crow (2)	11	0.00
Delaware (16)	30	0.00
Houma (1)	1	0.00
Iroquois (27)	79	0.01
Kiowa (6)	14	0.00
Latin American Indians (537)	776	0.12
Lumbee (11)	16	0.00
Menominee (8)	9	0.00
Navajo (53)	88	0.01
Osage (13)	38	0.01
Ottawa (5)	12	0.00
Paiute (5)	11	0.00
Pima (4)	5	0.00
Potawatomi (25)	41	0.01
Pueblo (23)	46	0.01
Puget Sound Salish (2)	2	0.00
Seminole (10)	30	0.00
Shoshone (4)	10	0.00
Sioux (52)	107	0.02
Tohono O'Odham (3)	3	0.00
Ute (4)	12	0.00
Yakama (1)	2	0.00
Yaqui (12)	26	0.00
All other tribes (152)	285	0.04
American Indian tribes, not spec.	548	0.08
Arab:	3,177	0.48
Arab/Arabic	496	0.08
Egyptian	136	0.02
Iraqi	40	0.01
Jordanian	101	0.02
Lebanese	1,748	0.27
Moroccan	65	0.01
Palestinian	72	0.01
Syrian	270	0.04
Other Arab	249	0.04
Armenian	252	0.04
Asian:	35,922	5.47
Bangladeshi (135)	157	0.02
Cambodian (164)	214	0.03
Chinese, ex. Taiwanese (7,490)	8,470	1.29
Filipino (1,582)	2,269	0.35
Hmong (2)	2	0.00
Indian (7,749)	8,330	1.27
Indonesian (147)	229	0.03
Japanese (1,164)	1,807	0.28
Korean (3,441)	4,006	0.61
Laotian (100)	129	0.02
Malaysian (46)	70	0.01
Pakistani (599)	818	0.12
Sri Lankan (133)	156	0.02
Taiwanese (603)	760	0.12
Thai (456)	666	0.10
Vietnamese (5,942)	6,426	0.98
Other Asian, specified (96)	147	0.02
Other Asian, not specified (540)	1,266	0.19
Assyrian/Chaldean/Syriac	20	0.00
Australian	306	0.05
Austrian	1,198	0.18
Basque	94	0.01
Belgian	524	0.08
Brazilian	440	0.07
British	4,753	0.72
Bulgarian	149	0.02
Canadian	1,170	0.18
Celtic	383	0.06
Croatian	421	0.06
Cypriot	46	0.01
Czech	6,299	0.96
Czechoslovakian	1,604	0.24
Danish	2,590	0.39
Dutch	6,591	1.00
Eastern European	571	0.09
English	57,443	8.75
Estonian	27	0.00
European	6,347	0.97
Finnish	798	0.12
French, except Basque	17,520	2.67
French Canadian	2,821	0.43
German	84,350	12.85
German Russian	15	0.00
Greek	1,437	0.22
Guyanese	38	0.01
Hawaii Native/Pacific Islander:	1,082	0.16
Melanesian: (1)	4	0.00
Fijian	3	0.00
Other Melanesian (1)	1	0.00
Micronesian: (107)	180	0.03
Guamanian/Chamorro (95)	159	0.02
Other Micronesian (12)	21	0.00
Polynesian: (258)	475	0.07
Native Hawaiian (182)	345	0.05
Samoan (69)	106	0.02
Tongan (4)	10	0.00
Other Polynesian (3)	14	0.00
Other Pac. Isl., specified	30	0.00
Other Pac. Isl., not spec. (95)	393	0.06
Hispanic or Latino:	200,579	30.55
Central American:	4,290	0.65
Costa Rican	134	0.02
Guatemalan	748	0.11
Honduran	1,065	0.16
Nicaraguan	456	0.07
Panamanian	345	0.05
Salvadoran	1,331	0.20
Other Central American	211	0.03
Cuban	1,425	0.22
Dominican Republic	129	0.02
Mexican	153,868	23.44
Puerto Rican	2,529	0.39
South American:	2,161	0.33
Argentinean	242	0.04
Bolivian	109	0.02
Chilean	168	0.03
Colombian	596	0.09
Ecuadorian	143	0.02
Paraguayan	20	0.00
Peruvian	359	0.05
Uruguayan	32	0.00
Venezuelan	390	0.06
Other South American	102	0.02
Other Hispanic or Latino	36,177	5.51
Hungarian	1,741	0.27
Icelander	30	0.00
Iranian	1,369	0.21
Irish	55,063	8.39
Israeli	226	0.03
Italian	16,185	2.47
Latvian	153	0.02
Lithuanian	791	0.12
Luxemburger	50	0.01
Macedonian	43	0.01
Maltese	23	0.00
New Zealander	73	0.01
Northern European	823	0.13
Norwegian	5,544	0.84
Pennsylvania German	112	0.02
Polish	9,466	1.44
Portuguese	872	0.13
Romanian	490	0.07
Russian	4,168	0.64
Scandinavian	935	0.14
Scotch-Irish	16,024	2.44
Scottish	15,382	2.34
Serbian	237	0.04
Slavic	255	0.04
Slovak	645	0.10
Slovene	348	0.05
Swedish	7,553	1.15
Swiss	1,633	0.25
Turkish	355	0.05
Ukrainian	854	0.13
United States or American	28,052	4.27
Welsh	4,261	0.65
West Indian, excl. Hispanic:	1,241	0.19
Barbadian	39	0.01
Belizean	15	0.00
British West Indian	86	0.01
Dutch West Indian	109	0.02
Haitian	191	0.03
Jamaican	547	0.08
Trinidadian and Tobagonian	128	0.02
U.S. Virgin Islander	28	0.00
West Indian	90	0.01
Other West Indian	8	0.00
White:	445,388	67.84
Not Hispanic (347,554)	355,695	54.18
Hispanic (81,546)	89,693	13.66
Yugoslavian	603	0.09

Balch Springs

Place Type: City
County: Dallas
Population: 19,375

Ancestry/Race	Number	%
Acadian/Cajun	7	0.04
African American/Black:	3,698	19.09
Not Hispanic (3,518)	3,614	18.65
Hispanic (71)	84	0.43
African, sub-Saharan:	266	1.37
African	224	1.15
Ethiopian	12	0.06
Nigerian	30	0.15
Alaska Native tribes, specified:	1	0.01
Eskimo (1)	1	0.01
Am. Ind. or Alaska Nat., not spec.	119	0.61
American Indian tribes, specified:	232	1.20
Apache (1)	11	0.06
Blackfeet (1)	6	0.03
Cherokee (20)	67	0.35
Cheyenne	1	0.01
Chickasaw (3)	9	0.05
Chippewa (1)	1	0.01
Choctaw (40)	68	0.35
Comanche (9)	9	0.05
Creek (9)	10	0.05
Delaware	4	0.02
Iroquois	5	0.03
Latin American Indians (10)	13	0.07
Menominee (4)	4	0.02
Navajo (2)	4	0.02
Osage	1	0.01
Potawatomi (4)	5	0.03
Seminole (1)	1	0.01
Sioux (1)	1	0.01
All other tribes (4)	12	0.06
American Indian tribes, not spec.	14	0.07
Arab:	15	0.08
Jordanian	15	0.08
Asian:	178	0.92
Bangladeshi (2)	2	0.01
Cambodian (10)	10	0.05
Chinese, ex. Taiwanese (12)	21	0.11
Filipino (20)	35	0.18
Indian (12)	12	0.06
Indonesian (1)	2	0.01
Japanese (3)	7	0.04
Korean (5)	5	0.03
Laotian (5)	5	0.03

Notes: 1. Figures in the "Number" column do not add up to the total population due to: a) Ancestry/Race overlap — e.g. persons can report being both White and Irish, b) persons of Hispanic origin can report being any race, c) persons reporting two ancestries are counted in both categories. 2. Numbers in parentheses indicate the number of persons reporting this ancestry/race alone, not in combination with any other ancestry/race. 3. Refer to the Explanation of Data in the front of the book for more detailed information.

Pakistani (11)	12	0.06
Thai (2)	2	0.01
Vietnamese (29)	35	0.18
Other Asian, specified (2)	11	0.06
Other Asian, not specified (5)	19	0.10
Austrian	6	0.03
Belgian	6	0.03
Brazilian	8	0.04
British	62	0.32
Canadian	24	0.12
Czech	30	0.15
Czechoslovakian	7	0.04
Danish	12	0.06
Dutch	201	1.03
English	973	5.01
European	14	0.07
French, except Basque	331	1.70
French Canadian	24	0.12
German	1,220	6.28
Greek	41	0.21
Hawaii Native/Pacific Islander:	20	0.10
Micronesian: (1)	3	0.02
Guamanian/Chamorro (1)	3	0.02
Polynesian: (2)	5	0.03
Native Hawaiian	2	0.01
Samoan (2)	3	0.02
Other Pac. Isl., not spec. (2)	12	0.06
Hispanic or Latino:	4,983	25.72
Central American:	130	0.67
Costa Rican	5	0.03
Guatemalan	19	0.10
Honduran	17	0.09
Panamanian	8	0.04
Salvadoran	79	0.41
Other Central American	2	0.01
Cuban	27	0.14
Dominican Republic	2	0.01
Mexican	3,964	20.46
Puerto Rican	24	0.12
South American:	20	0.10
Colombian	5	0.03
Peruvian	12	0.06
Venezuelan	3	0.02
Other Hispanic or Latino	816	4.21
Hungarian	21	0.11
Iranian	42	0.22
Irish	1,666	8.57
Italian	341	1.75
Norwegian	45	0.23
Pennsylvania German	9	0.05
Polish	72	0.37
Romanian	35	0.18
Russian	11	0.06
Scandinavian	6	0.03
Scotch-Irish	181	0.93
Scottish	129	0.66
Swedish	86	0.44
Swiss	6	0.03
Ukrainian	7	0.04
United States or American	1,937	9.97
Welsh	64	0.33
West Indian, excl. Hispanic:	63	0.32
Dutch West Indian	45	0.23
Jamaican	18	0.09
White:	12,672	65.40
Not Hispanic (10,249)	10,531	54.35
Hispanic (1,937)	2,141	11.05
Yugoslavian	6	0.03

Bay City

Place Type: City
County: Matagorda
Population: 18,667

Ancestry/Race	Number	%
Acadian/Cajun	32	0.17
African American/Black:	3,346	17.92
Not Hispanic (3,191)	3,269	17.51
Hispanic (30)	77	0.41
African, sub-Saharan:	129	0.69
African	111	0.60
Nigerian	9	0.05
Other sub-Saharan African	9	0.05
Alaska Native tribes, specified:	4	0.02
Aleut	4	0.02
Am. Ind. or Alaska Nat., not spec.	90	0.48
Alsatian	14	0.08
American Indian tribes, specified:	71	0.38
Apache (2)	7	0.04
Blackfeet (3)	5	0.03
Cherokee (4)	16	0.09
Cheyenne (1)	1	0.01
Chippewa	1	0.01
Choctaw (10)	14	0.07
Comanche	1	0.01
Houma (1)	1	0.01
Latin American Indians (16)	20	0.11
Osage (2)	2	0.01
Potawatomi	1	0.01
Pueblo	1	0.01
Sioux (1)	1	0.01
American Indian tribes, not spec.	46	0.25
Asian:	216	1.16
Cambodian (1)	5	0.03
Chinese, ex. Taiwanese (8)	9	0.05
Filipino (38)	58	0.31
Indian (70)	73	0.39
Japanese	13	0.07
Korean	4	0.02
Laotian (1)	4	0.02
Pakistani (2)	2	0.01
Thai (1)	1	0.01
Vietnamese (31)	33	0.18
Other Asian, not specified (4)	14	0.07
Austrian	20	0.11
Belgian	42	0.23
British	24	0.13
Canadian	10	0.05
Czech	438	2.35
Czechoslovakian	83	0.45
Danish	60	0.32
Dutch	119	0.64
English	1,172	6.29
European	101	0.54
French, except Basque	353	1.89
French Canadian	56	0.30
German	1,905	10.22
Greek	5	0.03
Hawaii Native/Pacific Islander:	20	0.11
Micronesian: (7)	8	0.04
Guamanian/Chamorro (7)	8	0.04
Polynesian: (1)	1	0.01
Native Hawaiian (1)	1	0.01
Other Pac. Isl., not spec. (5)	11	0.06
Hispanic or Latino:	6,484	34.74
Central American:	36	0.19
Costa Rican	1	0.01
Guatemalan	19	0.10
Honduran	4	0.02
Panamanian	1	0.01
Salvadoran	10	0.05
Other Central American	1	0.01
Cuban	5	0.03
Mexican	4,785	25.63
Puerto Rican	10	0.05
South American:	8	0.04
Bolivian	2	0.01
Colombian	5	0.03
Peruvian	1	0.01
Other Hispanic or Latino	1,640	8.79
Hungarian	29	0.16
Iranian	13	0.07
Irish	1,195	6.41
Italian	213	1.14
Norwegian	40	0.21
Pennsylvania German	14	0.08
Polish	127	0.68
Portuguese	42	0.23
Romanian	18	0.10
Russian	108	0.58
Scotch-Irish	291	1.56
Scottish	193	1.04
Swedish	52	0.28
Swiss	26	0.14
Ukrainian	17	0.09
United States or American	953	5.11
Welsh	61	0.33
West Indian, excl. Hispanic:	62	0.33
Jamaican	34	0.18
West Indian	28	0.15
White:	11,907	63.79
Not Hispanic (8,612)	8,757	46.91
Hispanic (2,890)	3,150	16.87

Baytown

Place Type: City
County: Harris
Population: 66,430

Ancestry/Race	Number	%
Acadian/Cajun	144	0.22
African American/Black:	9,287	13.98
Not Hispanic (8,726)	9,044	13.61
Hispanic (162)	243	0.37
African, sub-Saharan:	419	0.63
African	405	0.60
Kenyan	9	0.01
Nigerian	5	0.01
Alaska Native tribes, specified:	1	0.00
Eskimo	1	0.00
Am. Ind. or Alaska Nat., not spec.	247	0.37
American Indian tribes, specified:	353	0.53
Apache (1)	9	0.01
Blackfeet (7)	13	0.02
Cherokee (41)	130	0.20
Cheyenne (1)	1	0.00
Chickasaw (3)	10	0.02
Chippewa (1)	7	0.01
Choctaw (18)	35	0.05
Comanche (5)	10	0.02
Cree	1	0.00
Creek (5)	13	0.02
Delaware (3)	3	0.00
Iroquois (4)	6	0.01
Kiowa (1)	2	0.00
Latin American Indians (45)	60	0.09
Lumbee (1)	1	0.00
Navajo (5)	11	0.02
Ottawa (2)	3	0.00
Potawatomi (2)	2	0.00
Pueblo (1)	3	0.00
Seminole	1	0.00
Shoshone (2)	4	0.01
Sioux	6	0.01
Yaqui (3)	5	0.01
All other tribes (5)	17	0.03
American Indian tribes, not spec.	50	0.08
Arab:	73	0.11
Egyptian	12	0.02
Lebanese	40	0.06
Moroccan	13	0.02
Syrian	8	0.01
Asian:	842	1.27
Bangladeshi (4)	5	0.01
Cambodian (2)	2	0.00
Chinese, ex. Taiwanese (62)	78	0.12
Filipino (113)	144	0.22
Indian (220)	260	0.39
Indonesian (2)	2	0.00
Japanese (23)	38	0.06
Korean (49)	67	0.10
Malaysian (1)	1	0.00
Pakistani (42)	60	0.09
Sri Lankan (1)	1	0.00
Taiwanese (5)	10	0.02
Thai (10)	14	0.02
Vietnamese (88)	100	0.15
Other Asian, specified (1)	5	0.01

Notes: 1. Figures in the "Number" column do not add up to the total population due to: a) Ancestry/Race overlap — e.g. persons can report being both White and Irish, b) persons of Hispanic origin can report being any race, c) persons reporting two ancestries are counted in both categories. 2. Numbers in parentheses indicate the number of persons reporting this ancestry/race alone, not in combination with any other ancestry/race. 3. Refer to the Explanation of Data in the front of the book for more detailed information.

Ancestry/Race	Number	%
Other Asian, not specified (27)	55	0.08
Austrian	65	0.10
Belgian	24	0.04
Brazilian	24	0.04
British	144	0.22
Canadian	69	0.10
Czech	454	0.68
Czechoslovakian	160	0.24
Danish	151	0.23
Dutch	524	0.78
Eastern European	17	0.03
English	4,170	6.23
European	267	0.40
Finnish	9	0.01
French, except Basque	2,149	3.21
French Canadian	297	0.44
German	4,764	7.12
Greek	68	0.10
Guyanese	11	0.02
Hawaii Native/Pacific Islander:	132	0.20
Micronesian: (2)	2	0.00
Guamanian/Chamorro (2)	2	0.00
Polynesian: (31)	44	0.07
Native Hawaiian (17)	19	0.03
Samoan (6)	13	0.02
Tongan (1)	4	0.01
Other Polynesian (7)	8	0.01
Other Pac. Isl., specified	4	0.01
Other Pac. Isl., not spec. (18)	82	0.12
Hispanic or Latino:	22,748	34.24
Central American:	194	0.29
Costa Rican	1	0.00
Guatemalan	12	0.02
Honduran	54	0.08
Nicaraguan	15	0.02
Panamanian	9	0.01
Salvadoran	92	0.14
Other Central American	11	0.02
Cuban	43	0.06
Dominican Republic	31	0.05
Mexican	19,123	28.79
Puerto Rican	163	0.25
South American:	58	0.09
Argentinean	1	0.00
Chilean	20	0.03
Colombian	18	0.03
Ecuadorian	2	0.00
Peruvian	8	0.01
Uruguayan	1	0.00
Venezuelan	7	0.01
Other South American	1	0.00
Other Hispanic or Latino	3,136	4.72
Hungarian	27	0.04
Iranian	65	0.10
Irish	4,114	6.15
Italian	921	1.38
Lithuanian	5	0.01
New Zealander	7	0.01
Northern European	19	0.03
Norwegian	175	0.26
Pennsylvania German	8	0.01
Polish	545	0.81
Portuguese	12	0.02
Romanian	6	0.01
Russian	73	0.11
Scandinavian	32	0.05
Scotch-Irish	951	1.42
Scottish	780	1.17
Serbian	26	0.04
Slovak	23	0.03
Slovene	23	0.03
Swedish	265	0.40
Swiss	58	0.09
Ukrainian	30	0.04
United States or American	5,535	8.27
Welsh	209	0.31
West Indian, excl. Hispanic:	823	1.23
British West Indian	224	0.33
Dutch West Indian	7	0.01
Jamaican	33	0.05
Trinidadian and Tobagonian	267	0.40
U.S. Virgin Islander	71	0.11
West Indian	221	0.33
White:	46,617	70.17
Not Hispanic (33,328)	33,849	50.95
Hispanic (11,760)	12,768	19.22

Beaumont

Place Type: City
County: Jefferson
Population: 113,866

Ancestry/Race	Number	%
Acadian/Cajun	501	0.44
African American/Black:	52,829	46.40
Not Hispanic (51,928)	52,461	46.07
Hispanic (278)	368	0.32
African, sub-Saharan:	1,483	1.30
African	1,353	1.19
Ethiopian	11	0.01
Ghanian	51	0.04
Nigerian	60	0.05
Other sub-Saharan African	8	0.01
Alaska Native tribes, specified:	1	0.00
Aleut	1	0.00
Am. Ind. or Alaska Nat., not spec.	247	0.22
Albanian	26	0.02
Alsatian	7	0.01
American Indian tribes, specified:	444	0.39
Apache (9)	22	0.02
Blackfeet (1)	12	0.01
Cherokee (64)	184	0.16
Cheyenne	2	0.00
Chickasaw (5)	7	0.01
Chippewa (2)	5	0.00
Choctaw (13)	48	0.04
Comanche	11	0.01
Creek (5)	11	0.01
Delaware	1	0.00
Houma	1	0.00
Iroquois (6)	7	0.01
Latin American Indians (16)	35	0.03
Navajo (5)	9	0.01
Osage (4)	4	0.00
Ottawa (1)	1	0.00
Potawatomi (2)	5	0.00
Pueblo (1)	1	0.00
Seminole	2	0.00
Sioux (6)	21	0.02
Yuman (5)	7	0.01
All other tribes (29)	48	0.04
American Indian tribes, not spec.	39	0.03
Arab:	448	0.39
Arab/Arabic	63	0.06
Egyptian	9	0.01
Lebanese	304	0.27
Moroccan	8	0.01
Syrian	38	0.03
Other Arab	26	0.02
Armenian	9	0.01
Asian:	3,226	2.83
Bangladeshi (43)	47	0.04
Cambodian (10)	14	0.01
Chinese, ex. Taiwanese (297)	361	0.32
Filipino (599)	675	0.59
Indian (571)	640	0.56
Indonesian (1)	1	0.00
Japanese (30)	62	0.05
Korean (64)	80	0.07
Laotian	1	0.00
Malaysian (4)	7	0.01
Pakistani (96)	139	0.12
Sri Lankan (8)	9	0.01
Taiwanese (9)	10	0.01
Thai (51)	67	0.06
Vietnamese (938)	999	0.88
Other Asian, specified (3)	17	0.01
Other Asian, not specified (46)	97	0.09
Australian	7	0.01
Austrian	83	0.07
Belgian	78	0.07
British	446	0.39
Canadian	93	0.08
Celtic	97	0.09
Croatian	43	0.04
Czech	316	0.28
Czechoslovakian	112	0.10
Danish	185	0.16
Dutch	808	0.71
Eastern European	41	0.04
English	6,986	6.13
European	492	0.43
Finnish	40	0.04
French, except Basque	4,891	4.29
French Canadian	1,099	0.96
German	6,828	6.00
Greek	169	0.15
Hawaii Native/Pacific Islander:	109	0.10
Micronesian: (14)	24	0.02
Guamanian/Chamorro (13)	23	0.02
Other Micronesian (1)	1	0.00
Polynesian: (24)	37	0.03
Native Hawaiian (12)	23	0.02
Samoan (12)	14	0.01
Other Pac. Isl., specified	13	0.01
Other Pac. Isl., not spec. (8)	35	0.03
Hispanic or Latino:	9,028	7.93
Central American:	174	0.15
Costa Rican	2	0.00
Guatemalan	49	0.04
Honduran	19	0.02
Nicaraguan	29	0.03
Panamanian	21	0.02
Salvadoran	42	0.04
Other Central American	12	0.01
Cuban	146	0.13
Dominican Republic	10	0.01
Mexican	7,117	6.25
Puerto Rican	238	0.21
South American:	109	0.10
Argentinean	14	0.01
Bolivian	2	0.00
Chilean	8	0.01
Colombian	26	0.02
Ecuadorian	4	0.00
Peruvian	25	0.02
Venezuelan	21	0.02
Other South American	9	0.01
Other Hispanic or Latino	1,234	1.08
Hungarian	131	0.12
Iranian	123	0.11
Irish	6,535	5.74
Italian	3,112	2.73
Lithuanian	28	0.02
Northern European	3	0.00
Norwegian	226	0.20
Pennsylvania German	10	0.01
Polish	591	0.52
Portuguese	86	0.08
Romanian	13	0.01
Russian	174	0.15
Scandinavian	57	0.05
Scotch-Irish	1,817	1.60
Scottish	1,064	0.93
Serbian	10	0.01
Slavic	5	0.00
Slovak	22	0.02
Swedish	535	0.47
Swiss	102	0.09
Turkish	30	0.03
Ukrainian	72	0.06
United States or American	5,370	4.72
Welsh	230	0.20
West Indian, excl. Hispanic:	93	0.08
British West Indian	13	0.01
Dutch West Indian	10	0.01
Jamaican	62	0.05
U.S. Virgin Islander	8	0.01
White:	54,074	47.49

Notes: 1. Figures in the "Number" column do not add up to the total population due to: a) Ancestry/Race overlap — e.g. persons can report being both White and Irish, b) persons of Hispanic origin can report being any race, c) persons reporting two ancestries are counted in both categories. 2. Numbers in parentheses indicate the number of persons reporting this ancestry/race alone, not in combination with any other ancestry/race. 3. Refer to the Explanation of Data in the front of the book for more detailed information.

Not Hispanic (48,595)	49,427	43.41
Hispanic (4,231)	4,647	4.08
Yugoslavian	6	0.01

Bedford

Place Type: City
County: Tarrant
Population: 47,152

Ancestry/Race	Number	%
Acadian/Cajun	28	0.06
African American/Black:	1,887	4.00
Not Hispanic (1,698)	1,847	3.92
Hispanic (24)	40	0.08
African, sub-Saharan:	402	0.85
African	161	0.34
Ghanian	18	0.04
Kenyan	28	0.06
Nigerian	63	0.13
Sudanese	43	0.09
Zairian	85	0.18
Other sub-Saharan African	4	0.01
Alaska Native tribes, specified:	5	0.01
Alaska Athabascan (1)	1	0.00
Eskimo	2	0.00
Tlingit-Haida (1)	1	0.00
All other tribes (1)	1	0.00
Am. Ind. or Alaska Nat., not spec.	84	0.18
Albanian	165	0.35
American Indian tribes, specified:	389	0.82
Apache (12)	18	0.04
Blackfeet (3)	6	0.01
Cherokee (62)	153	0.32
Chickasaw (12)	21	0.04
Chippewa	2	0.00
Choctaw (38)	62	0.13
Comanche (18)	22	0.05
Creek (7)	15	0.03
Delaware (3)	3	0.01
Houma (1)	1	0.00
Iroquois (5)	12	0.03
Kiowa (1)	5	0.01
Latin American Indians (2)	7	0.01
Lumbee (2)	6	0.01
Navajo (1)	2	0.00
Osage (2)	13	0.03
Potawatomi (3)	4	0.01
Seminole (2)	3	0.01
Sioux (1)	9	0.02
Tohono O'Odham (1)	1	0.00
Yakama	1	0.00
Yaqui (4)	4	0.01
All other tribes (11)	19	0.04
American Indian tribes, not spec.	38	0.08
Arab:	183	0.39
Arab/Arabic	7	0.01
Egyptian	43	0.09
Iraqi	11	0.02
Jordanian	63	0.13
Lebanese	52	0.11
Moroccan	7	0.01
Armenian	19	0.04
Asian:	2,009	4.26
Bangladeshi (7)	9	0.02
Cambodian (6)	6	0.01
Chinese, ex. Taiwanese (240)	309	0.66
Filipino (120)	165	0.35
Hmong (3)	3	0.01
Indian (514)	580	1.23
Indonesian (4)	4	0.01
Japanese (52)	88	0.19
Korean (248)	275	0.58
Laotian (34)	45	0.10
Malaysian (1)	2	0.00
Pakistani (63)	74	0.16
Sri Lankan (11)	11	0.02
Taiwanese (27)	35	0.07
Thai (21)	30	0.06
Vietnamese (271)	293	0.62
Other Asian, specified (8)	14	0.03
Other Asian, not specified (38)	66	0.14
Australian	49	0.10
Austrian	116	0.25
Basque	10	0.02
Belgian	161	0.34
Brazilian	9	0.02
British	341	0.72
Canadian	99	0.21
Celtic	59	0.13
Croatian	50	0.11
Czech	392	0.83
Czechoslovakian	54	0.11
Danish	216	0.46
Dutch	806	1.71
Eastern European	11	0.02
English	6,665	14.16
European	430	0.91
Finnish	60	0.13
French, except Basque	1,473	3.13
French Canadian	217	0.46
German	8,033	17.07
Greek	129	0.27
Hawaii Native/Pacific Islander:	184	0.39
Melanesian: (1)	1	0.00
Fijian (1)	1	0.00
Micronesian: (9)	10	0.02
Guamanian/Chamorro (7)	8	0.02
Other Micronesian (2)	2	0.00
Polynesian: (88)	159	0.34
Native Hawaiian (13)	46	0.10
Samoan (14)	21	0.04
Tongan (52)	65	0.14
Other Polynesian (9)	27	0.06
Other Pac. Isl., not spec. (10)	14	0.03
Hispanic or Latino:	3,403	7.22
Central American:	112	0.24
Costa Rican	14	0.03
Guatemalan	17	0.04
Honduran	16	0.03
Nicaraguan	13	0.03
Panamanian	18	0.04
Salvadoran	34	0.07
Cuban	48	0.10
Dominican Republic	16	0.03
Mexican	2,124	4.50
Puerto Rican	339	0.72
South American:	112	0.24
Argentinean	14	0.03
Bolivian	4	0.01
Chilean	3	0.01
Colombian	34	0.07
Ecuadorian	2	0.00
Peruvian	39	0.08
Uruguayan	4	0.01
Venezuelan	6	0.01
Other South American	6	0.01
Other Hispanic or Latino	652	1.38
Hungarian	197	0.42
Iranian	51	0.11
Irish	6,279	13.34
Italian	1,488	3.16
Latvian	14	0.03
Lithuanian	103	0.22
Macedonian	5	0.01
Northern European	24	0.05
Norwegian	708	1.50
Pennsylvania German	44	0.09
Polish	961	2.04
Portuguese	56	0.12
Romanian	3	0.01
Russian	231	0.49
Scandinavian	94	0.20
Scotch-Irish	1,221	2.59
Scottish	1,197	2.54
Serbian	28	0.06
Slovak	56	0.12
Slovene	11	0.02
Swedish	541	1.15
Swiss	101	0.21
Ukrainian	95	0.20
United States or American	4,235	9.00
Welsh	283	0.60
West Indian, excl. Hispanic:	189	0.40
Dutch West Indian	17	0.04
Jamaican	156	0.33
West Indian	16	0.03
White:	42,113	89.31
Not Hispanic (39,338)	39,921	84.66
Hispanic (1,982)	2,192	4.65
Yugoslavian	25	0.05

Beeville

Place Type: City
County: Bee
Population: 13,129

Ancestry/Race	Number	%
Acadian/Cajun	9	0.07
African American/Black:	417	3.18
Not Hispanic (354)	370	2.82
Hispanic (23)	47	0.36
Am. Ind. or Alaska Nat., not spec.	69	0.53
American Indian tribes, specified:	53	0.40
Apache (3)	6	0.05
Cherokee (7)	19	0.14
Chickasaw (1)	3	0.02
Choctaw (1)	3	0.02
Creek (1)	1	0.01
Iroquois (1)	1	0.01
Latin American Indians (11)	16	0.12
Potawatomi (1)	1	0.01
Tohono O'Odham	1	0.01
All other tribes (2)	2	0.02
American Indian tribes, not spec.	5	0.04
Arab:	8	0.06
Lebanese	8	0.06
Asian:	124	0.94
Chinese, ex. Taiwanese (3)	3	0.02
Filipino (43)	63	0.48
Indian (2)	3	0.02
Japanese (13)	20	0.15
Korean (3)	7	0.05
Malaysian	1	0.01
Pakistani (14)	14	0.11
Vietnamese (10)	10	0.08
Other Asian, not specified (1)	3	0.02
Australian	7	0.05
British	12	0.09
Canadian	27	0.21
Croatian	8	0.06
Czech	148	1.13
Czechoslovakian	43	0.33
Danish	11	0.08
Dutch	42	0.32
English	577	4.40
European	9	0.07
French, except Basque	154	1.17
French Canadian	33	0.25
German	767	5.85
Hawaii Native/Pacific Islander:	16	0.12
Micronesian: (3)	8	0.06
Guamanian/Chamorro (3)	8	0.06
Polynesian: (3)	5	0.04
Native Hawaiian (3)	5	0.04
Other Pac. Isl., not spec.	3	0.02
Hispanic or Latino:	8,884	67.67
Central American:	16	0.12
Guatemalan	1	0.01
Honduran	1	0.01
Panamanian	6	0.05
Salvadoran	7	0.05
Other Central American	1	0.01
Cuban	4	0.03
Mexican	5,175	39.42
Puerto Rican	18	0.14
South American:	2	0.02
Colombian	2	0.02
Other Hispanic or Latino	3,669	27.95

Notes: 1. Figures in the "Number" column do not add up to the total population due to: a) Ancestry/Race overlap — e.g. persons can report being both White and Irish, b) persons of Hispanic origin can report being any race, c) persons reporting two ancestries are counted in both categories. 2. Numbers in parentheses indicate the number of persons reporting this ancestry/race alone, not in combination with any other ancestry/race. 3. Refer to the Explanation of Data in the front of the book for more detailed information.

Ancestry/Race	Number	%
Iranian	8	0.06
Irish	660	5.03
Italian	28	0.21
Norwegian	25	0.19
Pennsylvania German	9	0.07
Polish	81	0.62
Portuguese	7	0.05
Scotch-Irish	129	0.98
Scottish	107	0.82
Slovene	10	0.08
Swedish	17	0.13
United States or American	351	2.68
Welsh	9	0.07
West Indian, excl. Hispanic:	15	0.11
Dutch West Indian	9	0.07
Haitian	6	0.05
White:	9,830	74.87
Not Hispanic (3,667)	3,758	28.62
Hispanic (5,797)	6,072	46.25
Yugoslavian	11	0.08

Bellaire

Place Type: City
County: Harris
Population: 15,642

Ancestry/Race	Number	%
African American/Black:	164	1.05
Not Hispanic (130)	155	0.99
Hispanic (1)	9	0.06
African, sub-Saharan:	25	0.16
African	8	0.05
South African	17	0.11
Alaska Native tribes, specified:	1	0.01
Aleut	1	0.01
Am. Ind. or Alaska Nat., not spec.	16	0.10
Alsatian	5	0.03
American Indian tribes, specified:	74	0.47
Cherokee (25)	35	0.22
Cheyenne	1	0.01
Chickasaw (4)	13	0.08
Chippewa	1	0.01
Choctaw (2)	7	0.04
Cree	1	0.01
Creek (1)	2	0.01
Iroquois	2	0.01
Latin American Indians (2)	3	0.02
Ottawa	2	0.01
Potawatomi	1	0.01
Sioux (1)	2	0.01
All other tribes (2)	4	0.03
Arab:	122	0.78
Egyptian	6	0.04
Lebanese	76	0.49
Moroccan	5	0.03
Palestinian	35	0.22
Armenian	4	0.03
Asian:	1,112	7.11
Chinese, ex. Taiwanese (454)	486	3.11
Filipino (26)	41	0.26
Indian (219)	235	1.50
Indonesian (4)	4	0.03
Japanese (29)	56	0.36
Korean (37)	43	0.27
Malaysian (3)	3	0.02
Pakistani (2)	5	0.03
Taiwanese (93)	96	0.61
Thai (19)	21	0.13
Vietnamese (82)	87	0.56
Other Asian, not specified (18)	35	0.22
Australian	20	0.13
Austrian	74	0.47
Brazilian	29	0.19
British	189	1.21
Canadian	60	0.39
Croatian	7	0.04
Czech	334	2.14
Czechoslovakian	20	0.13
Danish	71	0.46
Dutch	186	1.19
Eastern European	94	0.60
English	2,104	13.50
European	207	1.33
Finnish	18	0.12
French, except Basque	625	4.01
French Canadian	55	0.35
German	2,711	17.40
Greek	53	0.34
Hawaii Native/Pacific Islander:	17	0.11
Micronesian: (2)	2	0.01
Guamanian/Chamorro (2)	2	0.01
Polynesian: (6)	6	0.04
Native Hawaiian (3)	3	0.02
Samoan (3)	3	0.02
Other Pac. Isl., not spec. (2)	9	0.06
Hispanic or Latino:	1,221	7.81
Central American:	51	0.33
Costa Rican	10	0.06
Guatemalan	1	0.01
Honduran	5	0.03
Nicaraguan	9	0.06
Panamanian	6	0.04
Salvadoran	17	0.11
Other Central American	3	0.02
Cuban	81	0.52
Dominican Republic	1	0.01
Mexican	745	4.76
Puerto Rican	52	0.33
South American:	119	0.76
Argentinean	21	0.13
Bolivian	3	0.02
Chilean	8	0.05
Colombian	50	0.32
Ecuadorian	8	0.05
Paraguayan	1	0.01
Peruvian	5	0.03
Uruguayan	1	0.01
Venezuelan	13	0.08
Other South American	9	0.06
Other Hispanic or Latino	172	1.10
Hungarian	87	0.56
Icelander	8	0.05
Iranian	24	0.15
Irish	2,069	13.28
Israeli	42	0.27
Italian	805	5.17
Lithuanian	44	0.28
Luxemburger	6	0.04
Northern European	13	0.08
Norwegian	172	1.10
Polish	404	2.59
Portuguese	27	0.17
Romanian	23	0.15
Russian	283	1.82
Scandinavian	9	0.06
Scotch-Irish	536	3.44
Scottish	426	2.73
Serbian	8	0.05
Slavic	16	0.10
Slovene	34	0.22
Swedish	99	0.64
Swiss	102	0.65
Turkish	9	0.06
Ukrainian	47	0.30
United States or American	1,234	7.92
Welsh	86	0.55
White:	14,157	90.51
Not Hispanic (13,041)	13,221	84.52
Hispanic (898)	936	5.98
Yugoslavian	5	0.03

Belton

Place Type: City
County: Bell
Population: 14,623

Ancestry/Race	Number	%
African American/Black:	1,264	8.64
Not Hispanic (1,156)	1,207	8.25
Hispanic (28)	57	0.39
African, sub-Saharan:	33	0.22
African	33	0.22
Am. Ind. or Alaska Nat., not spec.	72	0.49
American Indian tribes, specified:	103	0.70
Apache (6)	7	0.05
Cherokee (22)	49	0.34
Chippewa (2)	2	0.01
Choctaw (8)	17	0.12
Comanche	2	0.01
Creek (4)	4	0.03
Delaware	4	0.03
Iroquois	1	0.01
Latin American Indians (1)	3	0.02
Navajo (2)	2	0.01
Sioux (2)	2	0.01
Ute (1)	2	0.01
Yaqui (1)	1	0.01
All other tribes (2)	7	0.05
American Indian tribes, not spec.	21	0.14
Arab:	11	0.07
Syrian	11	0.07
Asian:	188	1.29
Chinese, ex. Taiwanese (12)	14	0.10
Filipino (23)	30	0.21
Indian (35)	39	0.27
Indonesian (2)	2	0.01
Japanese (30)	41	0.28
Korean (26)	45	0.31
Malaysian (1)	1	0.01
Pakistani (4)	4	0.03
Vietnamese (6)	7	0.05
Other Asian, specified	3	0.02
Other Asian, not specified	2	0.01
Belgian	16	0.11
British	36	0.24
Canadian	10	0.07
Celtic	22	0.15
Czech	209	1.42
Czechoslovakian	5	0.03
Danish	14	0.10
Dutch	236	1.60
Eastern European	8	0.05
English	919	6.25
European	162	1.10
French, except Basque	216	1.47
French Canadian	42	0.29
German	1,671	11.36
Greek	11	0.07
Hawaii Native/Pacific Islander:	22	0.15
Melanesian: (1)	1	0.01
Other Melanesian (1)	1	0.01
Micronesian: (1)	2	0.01
Guamanian/Chamorro (1)	2	0.01
Polynesian: (2)	4	0.03
Native Hawaiian (1)	3	0.02
Samoan (1)	1	0.01
Other Pac. Isl., not spec. (11)	15	0.10
Hispanic or Latino:	3,675	25.13
Central American:	20	0.14
Guatemalan	6	0.04
Honduran	2	0.01
Panamanian	8	0.05
Salvadoran	4	0.03
Cuban	2	0.01
Dominican Republic	2	0.01
Mexican	2,778	19.00
Puerto Rican	69	0.47
South American:	7	0.05
Colombian	4	0.03
Peruvian	3	0.02
Other Hispanic or Latino	797	5.45
Iranian	6	0.04
Irish	1,263	8.58
Italian	307	2.09
Norwegian	81	0.55
Polish	80	0.54
Russian	13	0.09
Scandinavian	34	0.23

Notes: 1. Figures in the "Number" column do not add up to the total population due to: a) Ancestry/Race overlap — e.g. persons can report being both White and Irish, b) persons of Hispanic origin can report being any race, c) persons reporting two ancestries are counted in both categories. 2. Numbers in parentheses indicate the number of persons reporting this ancestry/race alone, not in combination with any other ancestry/race. 3. Refer to the Explanation of Data in the front of the book for more detailed information.

Scotch-Irish	537	3.65
Scottish	185	1.26
Slovak	17	0.12
Swedish	54	0.37
Ukrainian	19	0.13
United States or American	1,177	8.00
Welsh	89	0.60
West Indian, excl. Hispanic:	6	0.04
Dutch West Indian	6	0.04
White:	10,967	75.00
Not Hispanic (9,386)	9,562	65.39
Hispanic (1,241)	1,405	9.61
Yugoslavian	16	0.11

Benbrook

Place Type: City
County: Tarrant
Population: 20,208

Ancestry/Race	Number	%
African American/Black:	972	4.81
Not Hispanic (886)	947	4.69
Hispanic (8)	25	0.12
African, sub-Saharan:	24	0.12
African	24	0.12
Am. Ind. or Alaska Nat., not spec.	45	0.22
Alsatian	10	0.05
American Indian tribes, specified:	167	0.83
Apache (1)	2	0.01
Blackfeet (1)	1	0.00
Cherokee (24)	60	0.30
Chickasaw (3)	8	0.04
Chippewa (2)	2	0.01
Choctaw (27)	40	0.20
Comanche (3)	4	0.02
Creek (6)	9	0.04
Iroquois (2)	3	0.01
Kiowa (2)	2	0.01
Latin American Indians	5	0.02
Navajo (5)	5	0.02
Osage (1)	1	0.00
Potawatomi	4	0.02
Pueblo (1)	1	0.00
Shoshone (1)	1	0.00
Sioux (2)	6	0.03
All other tribes (5)	13	0.06
American Indian tribes, not spec.	5	0.02
Arab:	70	0.35
Arab/Arabic	10	0.05
Egyptian	9	0.05
Lebanese	34	0.17
Syrian	17	0.09
Asian:	535	2.65
Bangladeshi	1	0.00
Cambodian (4)	9	0.04
Chinese, ex. Taiwanese (67)	83	0.41
Filipino (58)	79	0.39
Indian (85)	94	0.47
Indonesian	1	0.00
Japanese (25)	44	0.22
Korean (105)	117	0.58
Laotian (1)	1	0.00
Malaysian (1)	1	0.00
Pakistani (16)	18	0.09
Taiwanese (7)	7	0.03
Thai (34)	37	0.18
Vietnamese (18)	21	0.10
Other Asian, specified (1)	4	0.02
Other Asian, not specified (10)	18	0.09
Austrian	16	0.08
Belgian	21	0.11
British	172	0.87
Canadian	34	0.17
Czech	182	0.92
Czechoslovakian	95	0.48
Danish	69	0.35
Dutch	226	1.14
English	2,827	14.23
European	139	0.70
Finnish	42	0.21
French, except Basque	717	3.61
French Canadian	52	0.26
German	3,332	16.78
Greek	134	0.67
Guyanese	13	0.07
Hawaii Native/Pacific Islander:	29	0.14
Micronesian: (2)	11	0.05
Guamanian/Chamorro (2)	11	0.05
Polynesian: (4)	11	0.05
Native Hawaiian (4)	11	0.05
Other Pac. Isl., specified	2	0.01
Other Pac. Isl., not spec. (3)	5	0.02
Hispanic or Latino:	1,406	6.96
Central American:	14	0.07
Costa Rican	4	0.02
Guatemalan	2	0.01
Honduran	2	0.01
Nicaraguan	2	0.01
Panamanian	2	0.01
Salvadoran	2	0.01
Cuban	15	0.07
Dominican Republic	4	0.02
Mexican	1,016	5.03
Puerto Rican	36	0.18
South American:	23	0.11
Argentinean	8	0.04
Colombian	7	0.03
Ecuadorian	1	0.00
Peruvian	6	0.03
Venezuelan	1	0.00
Other Hispanic or Latino	298	1.47
Hungarian	29	0.15
Icelander	20	0.10
Irish	2,607	13.13
Italian	538	2.71
Lithuanian	4	0.02
Northern European	3	0.02
Norwegian	218	1.10
Polish	236	1.19
Portuguese	16	0.08
Russian	65	0.33
Scandinavian	18	0.09
Scotch-Irish	692	3.48
Scottish	405	2.04
Slavic	20	0.10
Slovak	13	0.07
Slovene	23	0.12
Swedish	152	0.77
Swiss	32	0.16
Turkish	12	0.06
Ukrainian	30	0.15
United States or American	1,997	10.05
Welsh	100	0.50
West Indian, excl. Hispanic:	52	0.26
Bermudan	8	0.04
Dutch West Indian	12	0.06
Jamaican	32	0.16
White:	18,179	89.96
Not Hispanic (17,092)	17,334	85.78
Hispanic (752)	845	4.18

Big Spring

Place Type: City
County: Howard
Population: 25,233

Ancestry/Race	Number	%
Acadian/Cajun	4	0.02
African American/Black:	1,429	5.66
Not Hispanic (1,258)	1,318	5.22
Hispanic (81)	111	0.44
African, sub-Saharan:	71	0.28
African	60	0.24
Ghanian	6	0.02
Nigerian	5	0.02
Alaska Native tribes, specified:	2	0.01
Alaska Athabascan (2)	2	0.01
Alaska Native tribes, not specified	1	0.00
Am. Ind. or Alaska Nat., not spec.	80	0.32
American Indian tribes, specified:	191	0.76
Apache (5)	13	0.05
Blackfeet (2)	6	0.02
Cherokee (24)	58	0.23
Chickasaw (9)	11	0.04
Chippewa (1)	1	0.00
Choctaw (13)	20	0.08
Comanche (2)	13	0.05
Creek	2	0.01
Crow (1)	1	0.00
Latin American Indians (18)	30	0.12
Navajo (11)	15	0.06
Potawatomi (1)	1	0.00
Pueblo	1	0.00
Seminole (1)	1	0.00
Sioux (1)	9	0.04
Ute	1	0.00
Yakama	1	0.00
All other tribes (3)	7	0.03
American Indian tribes, not spec.	24	0.10
Arab:	16	0.06
Arab/Arabic	9	0.04
Lebanese	7	0.03
Asian:	219	0.87
Chinese, ex. Taiwanese (25)	30	0.12
Filipino (31)	39	0.15
Indian (37)	42	0.17
Japanese (6)	12	0.05
Korean (13)	18	0.07
Pakistani (16)	17	0.07
Taiwanese (2)	2	0.01
Thai (6)	13	0.05
Vietnamese (15)	27	0.11
Other Asian, specified (4)	8	0.03
Other Asian, not specified (4)	11	0.04
Australian	8	0.03
Austrian	13	0.05
Belgian	16	0.06
British	49	0.19
Canadian	11	0.04
Czech	18	0.07
Danish	21	0.08
Dutch	146	0.58
English	1,387	5.47
European	100	0.39
French, except Basque	286	1.13
French Canadian	30	0.12
German	1,471	5.80
Greek	7	0.03
Hawaii Native/Pacific Islander:	23	0.09
Micronesian:	1	0.00
Guamanian/Chamorro	1	0.00
Polynesian: (4)	12	0.05
Native Hawaiian (3)	10	0.04
Samoan (1)	2	0.01
Other Pac. Isl., specified	4	0.02
Other Pac. Isl., not spec.	6	0.02
Hispanic or Latino:	11,265	44.64
Central American:	117	0.46
Guatemalan	29	0.11
Honduran	20	0.08
Nicaraguan	26	0.10
Panamanian	7	0.03
Salvadoran	35	0.14
Cuban	36	0.14
Dominican Republic	42	0.17
Mexican	8,377	33.20
Puerto Rican	46	0.18
South American:	145	0.57
Argentinean	6	0.02
Bolivian	1	0.00
Chilean	3	0.01
Colombian	98	0.39
Ecuadorian	8	0.03
Peruvian	10	0.04
Venezuelan	19	0.08
Other Hispanic or Latino	2,502	9.92
Irish	1,506	5.94
Italian	214	0.84

Notes: 1. Figures in the "Number" column do not add up to the total population due to: a) Ancestry/Race overlap — e.g. persons can report being both White and Irish, b) persons of Hispanic origin can report being any race, c) persons reporting two ancestries are counted in both categories. 2. Numbers in parentheses indicate the number of persons reporting this ancestry/race alone, not in combination with any other ancestry/race. 3. Refer to the Explanation of Data in the front of the book for more detailed information.

New Zealander	29	0.11
Norwegian	74	0.29
Polish	74	0.29
Portuguese	7	0.03
Russian	29	0.11
Scotch-Irish	343	1.35
Scottish	224	0.88
Swedish	46	0.18
Ukrainian	15	0.06
United States or American	2,414	9.52
Welsh	7	0.03
West Indian, excl. Hispanic:	66	0.26
Dutch West Indian	45	0.18
Haitian	21	0.08
White:	19,876	78.77
Not Hispanic (12,210)	12,445	49.32
Hispanic (7,142)	7,431	29.45

Borger

Place Type: City
County: Hutchinson
Population: 14,302

Ancestry/Race	Number	%
African American/Black:	561	3.92
Not Hispanic (516)	540	3.78
Hispanic (7)	21	0.15
African, sub-Saharan:	60	0.42
African	60	0.42
Alaska Native tribes, specified:	1	0.01
Aleut (1)	1	0.01
Am. Ind. or Alaska Nat., not spec.	54	0.38
American Indian tribes, specified:	273	1.91
Apache (4)	7	0.05
Blackfeet (4)	6	0.04
Cherokee (69)	125	0.87
Chickasaw (9)	13	0.09
Chippewa	2	0.01
Choctaw (27)	47	0.33
Comanche (5)	7	0.05
Creek	5	0.03
Delaware (3)	10	0.07
Latin American Indians (2)	7	0.05
Navajo (6)	6	0.04
Osage (6)	6	0.04
Potawatomi (4)	9	0.06
Pueblo (2)	4	0.03
Seminole (2)	3	0.02
Sioux (1)	6	0.04
All other tribes (8)	10	0.07
American Indian tribes, not spec.	12	0.08
Arab:	13	0.09
Lebanese	13	0.09
Asian:	90	0.63
Chinese, ex. Taiwanese (8)	13	0.09
Filipino (26)	31	0.22
Indian (13)	13	0.09
Japanese (3)	14	0.10
Korean (6)	7	0.05
Laotian	2	0.01
Thai (2)	2	0.01
Vietnamese (3)	3	0.02
Other Asian, specified	1	0.01
Other Asian, not specified	4	0.03
Austrian	10	0.07
Belgian	6	0.04
British	47	0.33
Celtic	3	0.02
Croatian	9	0.06
Czech	67	0.47
Czechoslovakian	47	0.33
Danish	35	0.25
Dutch	419	2.93
English	1,372	9.61
European	77	0.54
Finnish	8	0.06
French, except Basque	255	1.79
French Canadian	25	0.18
German	1,161	8.13
Greek	23	0.16
Hawaii Native/Pacific Islander:	11	0.08
Melanesian:	1	0.01
Fijian	1	0.01
Micronesian:	1	0.01
Guamanian/Chamorro	1	0.01
Polynesian: (4)	7	0.05
Native Hawaiian	2	0.01
Samoan (3)	3	0.02
Tongan (1)	2	0.01
Other Pac. Isl., specified	1	0.01
Other Pac. Isl., not spec.	1	0.01
Hispanic or Latino:	2,817	19.70
Central American:	12	0.08
Costa Rican	1	0.01
Honduran	10	0.07
Salvadoran	1	0.01
Cuban	1	0.01
Mexican	2,343	16.38
Puerto Rican	18	0.13
South American:	2	0.01
Colombian	1	0.01
Venezuelan	1	0.01
Other Hispanic or Latino	441	3.08
Hungarian	6	0.04
Iranian	7	0.05
Irish	1,505	10.54
Italian	91	0.64
Norwegian	96	0.67
Polish	85	0.60
Scotch-Irish	253	1.77
Scottish	134	0.94
Slavic	19	0.13
Swedish	87	0.61
Swiss	16	0.11
United States or American	1,894	13.27
Welsh	64	0.45
West Indian, excl. Hispanic:	27	0.19
Dutch West Indian	27	0.19
White:	12,161	85.03
Not Hispanic (10,559)	10,729	75.02
Hispanic (1,276)	1,432	10.01

Brenham

Place Type: City
County: Washington
Population: 13,507

Ancestry/Race	Number	%
African American/Black:	3,008	22.27
Not Hispanic (2,922)	2,962	21.93
Hispanic (38)	46	0.34
African, sub-Saharan:	213	1.59
African	213	1.59
Am. Ind. or Alaska Nat., not spec.	15	0.11
American Indian tribes, specified:	44	0.33
Apache	1	0.01
Blackfeet	1	0.01
Cherokee (4)	13	0.10
Cheyenne	1	0.01
Chickasaw (3)	3	0.02
Choctaw (3)	6	0.04
Comanche	1	0.01
Creek (1)	1	0.01
Latin American Indians (11)	11	0.08
Potawatomi (1)	1	0.01
All other tribes	5	0.04
American Indian tribes, not spec.	2	0.01
Arab:	26	0.19
Syrian	26	0.19
Asian:	285	2.11
Bangladeshi (6)	6	0.04
Cambodian (1)	3	0.02
Chinese, ex. Taiwanese (9)	16	0.12
Filipino (15)	19	0.14
Indian (14)	17	0.13
Korean (1)	4	0.03
Pakistani (5)	5	0.04
Thai (1)	2	0.01
Vietnamese (179)	196	1.45
Other Asian, not specified (11)	17	0.13
Austrian	26	0.19
British	41	0.31
Canadian	43	0.32
Czech	402	2.99
Czechoslovakian	49	0.36
Danish	9	0.07
Dutch	192	1.43
English	949	7.06
European	49	0.36
Finnish	6	0.04
French, except Basque	271	2.02
French Canadian	29	0.22
German	3,451	25.69
Greek	42	0.31
Hawaii Native/Pacific Islander:	5	0.04
Polynesian: (1)	2	0.01
Native Hawaiian (1)	2	0.01
Other Pac. Isl., not spec.	3	0.02
Hispanic or Latino:	1,384	10.25
Central American:	41	0.30
Costa Rican	2	0.01
Guatemalan	1	0.01
Honduran	4	0.03
Nicaraguan	1	0.01
Panamanian	1	0.01
Salvadoran	29	0.21
Other Central American	3	0.02
Cuban	2	0.01
Dominican Republic	3	0.02
Mexican	1,062	7.86
Puerto Rican	16	0.12
South American:	10	0.07
Argentinean	4	0.03
Chilean	3	0.02
Peruvian	1	0.01
Venezuelan	2	0.01
Other Hispanic or Latino	250	1.85
Irish	967	7.20
Italian	107	0.80
Northern European	15	0.11
Norwegian	44	0.33
Polish	552	4.11
Russian	20	0.15
Scotch-Irish	266	1.98
Scottish	172	1.28
Swedish	114	0.85
Swiss	19	0.14
United States or American	501	3.73
Welsh	32	0.24
White:	9,598	71.06
Not Hispanic (8,842)	8,915	66.00
Hispanic (612)	683	5.06
Yugoslavian	59	0.44

Brownsville

Place Type: City
County: Cameron
Population: 139,722

Ancestry/Race	Number	%
Acadian/Cajun	36	0.03
African American/Black:	731	0.52
Not Hispanic (276)	316	0.23
Hispanic (299)	415	0.30
African, sub-Saharan:	90	0.06
African	90	0.06
Alaska Native tribes, specified:	1	0.00
All other tribes (1)	1	0.00
Am. Ind. or Alaska Nat., not spec.	424	0.30
American Indian tribes, specified:	293	0.21
Apache (2)	11	0.01
Blackfeet	6	0.00
Cherokee (11)	30	0.02
Chickasaw (1)	1	0.00
Chippewa (1)	1	0.00
Choctaw	5	0.00
Comanche (2)	4	0.00

Notes: 1. Figures in the "Number" column do not add up to the total population due to: a) Ancestry/Race overlap — e.g. persons can report being both White and Irish, b) persons of Hispanic origin can report being any race, c) persons reporting two ancestries are counted in both categories. 2. Numbers in parentheses indicate the number of persons reporting this ancestry/race alone, not in combination with any other ancestry/race. 3. Refer to the Explanation of Data in the front of the book for more detailed information.

Ancestry/Race	Number	%
Cree	1	0.00
Creek (1)	5	0.00
Iroquois (1)	3	0.00
Latin American Indians (150)	196	0.14
Navajo (3)	3	0.00
Osage (2)	2	0.00
Pueblo (2)	6	0.00
Seminole	1	0.00
Sioux (5)	10	0.01
All other tribes (4)	8	0.01
American Indian tribes, not spec.	93	0.07
Arab:	118	0.08
Arab/Arabic	37	0.03
Lebanese	35	0.02
Syrian	5	0.00
Other Arab	41	0.03
Asian:	946	0.68
Bangladeshi (6)	6	0.00
Chinese, ex. Taiwanese (61)	108	0.08
Filipino (384)	423	0.30
Indian (128)	170	0.12
Japanese (29)	42	0.03
Korean (68)	73	0.05
Pakistani (12)	16	0.01
Sri Lankan (4)	4	0.00
Thai (1)	1	0.00
Vietnamese (35)	42	0.03
Other Asian, not specified (17)	61	0.04
Austrian	55	0.04
Basque	18	0.01
Belgian	45	0.03
British	155	0.11
Canadian	169	0.12
Czech	45	0.03
Czechoslovakian	33	0.02
Danish	55	0.04
Dutch	205	0.15
Eastern European	18	0.01
English	1,315	0.94
European	75	0.05
French, except Basque	598	0.43
French Canadian	70	0.05
German	1,993	1.42
Greek	38	0.03
Guyanese	5	0.00
Hawaii Native/Pacific Islander:	79	0.06
Micronesian: (3)	6	0.00
Guamanian/Chamorro (3)	6	0.00
Polynesian: (26)	37	0.03
Native Hawaiian (16)	23	0.02
Samoan (8)	12	0.01
Other Polynesian (2)	2	0.00
Other Pac. Isl., not spec. (17)	36	0.03
Hispanic or Latino:	127,535	91.28
Central American:	388	0.28
Costa Rican	12	0.01
Guatemalan	54	0.04
Honduran	122	0.09
Nicaraguan	55	0.04
Panamanian	8	0.01
Salvadoran	91	0.07
Other Central American	46	0.03
Cuban	159	0.11
Dominican Republic	18	0.01
Mexican	103,297	73.93
Puerto Rican	215	0.15
South American:	162	0.12
Argentinean	23	0.02
Bolivian	8	0.01
Chilean	13	0.01
Colombian	46	0.03
Ecuadorian	9	0.01
Paraguayan	6	0.00
Peruvian	24	0.02
Uruguayan	2	0.00
Venezuelan	7	0.01
Other South American	24	0.02
Other Hispanic or Latino	23,296	16.67
Hungarian	25	0.02
Icelander	12	0.01
Iranian	12	0.01
Irish	1,201	0.86
Italian	602	0.43
Lithuanian	9	0.01
Luxemburger	9	0.01
Norwegian	351	0.25
Polish	322	0.23
Portuguese	56	0.04
Romanian	22	0.02
Russian	83	0.06
Scandinavian	14	0.01
Scotch-Irish	577	0.41
Scottish	184	0.13
Slovak	19	0.01
Swedish	141	0.10
Swiss	43	0.03
Ukrainian	83	0.06
United States or American	3,837	2.74
Welsh	74	0.05
West Indian, excl. Hispanic:	14	0.01
Haitian	8	0.01
Jamaican	6	0.00
White:	117,048	83.77
Not Hispanic (10,826)	11,036	7.90
Hispanic (103,257)	106,012	75.87

Brownwood

Place Type: City
County: Brown
Population: 18,813

Ancestry/Race	Number	%
Acadian/Cajun	9	0.05
African American/Black:	1,113	5.92
Not Hispanic (1,008)	1,078	5.73
Hispanic (29)	35	0.19
African, sub-Saharan:	12	0.06
African	12	0.06
Am. Ind. or Alaska Nat., not spec.	80	0.43
American Indian tribes, specified:	125	0.66
Apache (9)	14	0.07
Blackfeet (1)	1	0.01
Cherokee (25)	60	0.32
Chickasaw (2)	3	0.02
Choctaw (5)	10	0.05
Comanche (3)	5	0.03
Creek (2)	4	0.02
Latin American Indians (4)	13	0.07
Lumbee (2)	2	0.01
Osage (1)	4	0.02
Potawatomi (1)	1	0.01
Sioux (1)	3	0.02
All other tribes (5)	5	0.03
American Indian tribes, not spec.	7	0.04
Arab:	26	0.14
Arab/Arabic	10	0.05
Egyptian	7	0.04
Jordanian	9	0.05
Asian:	147	0.78
Cambodian (5)	5	0.03
Chinese, ex. Taiwanese (38)	41	0.22
Filipino (8)	9	0.05
Indian (11)	19	0.10
Japanese (6)	7	0.04
Korean (11)	14	0.07
Laotian (1)	1	0.01
Pakistani (1)	1	0.01
Taiwanese (4)	7	0.04
Thai (3)	3	0.02
Vietnamese (18)	20	0.11
Other Asian, not specified (5)	20	0.11
Austrian	18	0.10
Belgian	5	0.03
British	54	0.29
Canadian	26	0.14
Celtic	8	0.04
Croatian	4	0.02
Czech	11	0.06
Czechoslovakian	23	0.12
Danish	62	0.33
Dutch	292	1.56
English	1,450	7.73
European	100	0.53
French, except Basque	254	1.35
French Canadian	76	0.40
German	1,692	9.01
Greek	29	0.15
Hawaii Native/Pacific Islander:	16	0.09
Micronesian:	2	0.01
Guamanian/Chamorro	2	0.01
Polynesian:	6	0.03
Native Hawaiian	4	0.02
Samoan	2	0.01
Other Pac. Isl., not spec.	8	0.04
Hispanic or Latino:	4,014	21.34
Central American:	11	0.06
Guatemalan	1	0.01
Honduran	5	0.03
Nicaraguan	1	0.01
Panamanian	1	0.01
Salvadoran	3	0.02
Cuban	2	0.01
Mexican	3,232	17.18
Puerto Rican	45	0.24
South American:	5	0.03
Argentinean	1	0.01
Colombian	2	0.01
Ecuadorian	2	0.01
Other Hispanic or Latino	719	3.82
Hungarian	26	0.14
Icelander	6	0.03
Irish	1,641	8.74
Italian	185	0.99
Norwegian	38	0.20
Polish	143	0.76
Russian	29	0.15
Scandinavian	6	0.03
Scotch-Irish	321	1.71
Scottish	273	1.45
Swedish	69	0.37
Swiss	12	0.06
United States or American	2,365	12.60
Welsh	33	0.18
West Indian, excl. Hispanic:	23	0.12
Dutch West Indian	23	0.12
White:	15,921	84.63
Not Hispanic (13,406)	13,591	72.24
Hispanic (2,159)	2,330	12.39

Brushy Creek

Place Type: Census Designated Place
County: Williamson
Population: 15,371

Ancestry/Race	Number	%
Acadian/Cajun	20	0.13
African American/Black:	678	4.41
Not Hispanic (618)	667	4.34
Hispanic (9)	11	0.07
African, sub-Saharan:	185	1.16
African	68	0.43
Kenyan	41	0.26
Nigerian	76	0.48
Alaska Native tribes, specified:	2	0.01
Aleut (1)	1	0.01
Eskimo	1	0.01
Am. Ind. or Alaska Nat., not spec.	20	0.13
Alsatian	25	0.16
American Indian tribes, specified:	97	0.63
Apache (1)	4	0.03
Cherokee (13)	39	0.25
Chickasaw (6)	7	0.05
Choctaw (1)	6	0.04
Comanche	3	0.02
Creek	4	0.03
Delaware (1)	3	0.02
Latin American Indians (1)	2	0.01
Potawatomi	3	0.02

Notes: 1. Figures in the "Number" column do not add up to the total population due to: a) Ancestry/Race overlap — e.g. persons can report being both White and Irish, b) persons of Hispanic origin can report being any race, c) persons reporting two ancestries are counted in both categories. 2. Numbers in parentheses indicate the number of persons reporting this ancestry/race alone, not in combination with any other ancestry/race. 3. Refer to the Explanation of Data in the front of the book for more detailed information.

Pueblo (2)	2	0.01
Seminole (3)	3	0.02
Shoshone (2)	2	0.01
Sioux	4	0.03
Ute (1)	3	0.02
Yaqui (1)	1	0.01
All other tribes (5)	11	0.07
American Indian tribes, not spec.	1	0.01
Arab:	101	0.64
Lebanese	84	0.53
Palestinian	17	0.11
Armenian	23	0.14
Asian:	1,169	7.61
Bangladeshi (9)	9	0.06
Cambodian (1)	1	0.01
Chinese, ex. Taiwanese (228)	259	1.68
Filipino (61)	83	0.54
Indian (379)	397	2.58
Indonesian (9)	9	0.06
Japanese (23)	44	0.29
Korean (85)	94	0.61
Laotian (5)	5	0.03
Pakistani (24)	27	0.18
Sri Lankan (7)	7	0.05
Taiwanese (26)	26	0.17
Thai (7)	9	0.06
Vietnamese (144)	155	1.01
Other Asian, not specified (30)	44	0.29
Austrian	59	0.37
Belgian	14	0.09
British	96	0.60
Canadian	67	0.42
Celtic	10	0.06
Croatian	17	0.11
Czech	235	1.48
Czechoslovakian	69	0.43
Danish	88	0.55
Dutch	217	1.36
English	2,185	13.74
European	228	1.43
Finnish	38	0.24
French, except Basque	582	3.66
French Canadian	94	0.59
German	3,308	20.81
Greek	32	0.20
Guyanese	16	0.10
Hawaii Native/Pacific Islander:	28	0.18
Micronesian:	4	0.03
Guamanian/Chamorro	4	0.03
Polynesian: (13)	22	0.14
Native Hawaiian (6)	15	0.10
Samoan (7)	7	0.05
Other Pac. Isl., not spec.	2	0.01
Hispanic or Latino:	1,572	10.23
Central American:	31	0.20
Costa Rican	5	0.03
Guatemalan	3	0.02
Honduran	8	0.05
Panamanian	7	0.05
Salvadoran	7	0.05
Other Central American	1	0.01
Cuban	15	0.10
Dominican Republic	6	0.04
Mexican	1,132	7.36
Puerto Rican	70	0.46
South American:	54	0.35
Argentinean	5	0.03
Bolivian	4	0.03
Chilean	4	0.03
Colombian	27	0.18
Ecuadorian	2	0.01
Peruvian	2	0.01
Uruguayan	2	0.01
Venezuelan	3	0.02
Other South American	5	0.03
Other Hispanic or Latino	264	1.72
Hungarian	77	0.48
Iranian	55	0.35
Irish	2,021	12.71
Italian	765	4.81
Lithuanian	50	0.31
Norwegian	253	1.59
Polish	335	2.11
Portuguese	8	0.05
Russian	57	0.36
Scandinavian	87	0.55
Scotch-Irish	440	2.77
Scottish	401	2.52
Slavic	15	0.09
Slovak	10	0.06
Slovene	15	0.09
Swedish	278	1.75
Swiss	54	0.34
Ukrainian	34	0.21
United States or American	1,002	6.30
Welsh	152	0.96
West Indian, excl. Hispanic:	10	0.06
Dutch West Indian	10	0.06
White:	13,046	84.87
Not Hispanic (11,847)	12,065	78.49
Hispanic (904)	981	6.38

Bryan

Place Type: City
County: Brazos
Population: 65,660

Ancestry/Race	Number	%
Acadian/Cajun	14	0.02
African American/Black:	11,918	18.15
Not Hispanic (11,520)	11,720	17.85
Hispanic (115)	198	0.30
African, sub-Saharan:	496	0.75
African	447	0.68
Nigerian	32	0.05
Other sub-Saharan African	17	0.03
Alaska Native tribes, specified:	2	0.00
Aleut (2)	2	0.00
Am. Ind. or Alaska Nat., not spec.	181	0.28
Alsatian	20	0.03
American Indian tribes, specified:	299	0.46
Apache (4)	21	0.03
Blackfeet (2)	7	0.01
Cherokee (44)	119	0.18
Chickasaw (2)	3	0.00
Chippewa (1)	3	0.00
Choctaw (12)	26	0.04
Comanche (1)	4	0.01
Creek (7)	8	0.01
Delaware (1)	1	0.00
Iroquois	4	0.01
Kiowa (1)	1	0.00
Latin American Indians (21)	44	0.07
Lumbee (1)	1	0.00
Navajo (1)	1	0.00
Osage (1)	2	0.00
Ottawa (2)	2	0.00
Potawatomi (2)	7	0.01
Pueblo	1	0.00
Seminole (1)	2	0.00
Sioux (4)	11	0.02
Tohono O'Odham (5)	5	0.01
Yaqui (1)	1	0.00
All other tribes (11)	25	0.04
American Indian tribes, not spec.	59	0.09
Arab:	199	0.30
Arab/Arabic	16	0.02
Egyptian	40	0.06
Lebanese	52	0.08
Syrian	15	0.02
Other Arab	76	0.12
Asian:	1,284	1.96
Bangladeshi (15)	15	0.02
Cambodian (1)	1	0.00
Chinese, ex. Taiwanese (277)	303	0.46
Filipino (53)	74	0.11
Hmong	1	0.00
Indian (280)	321	0.49
Indonesian (17)	25	0.04
Japanese (52)	76	0.12
Korean (153)	182	0.28
Laotian (2)	2	0.00
Malaysian (4)	4	0.01
Pakistani (29)	30	0.05
Sri Lankan (4)	4	0.01
Taiwanese (12)	13	0.02
Thai (21)	31	0.05
Vietnamese (123)	137	0.21
Other Asian, specified	5	0.01
Other Asian, not specified (22)	60	0.09
Australian	14	0.02
Austrian	44	0.07
Belgian	49	0.07
British	220	0.33
Bulgarian	10	0.02
Canadian	87	0.13
Croatian	23	0.03
Czech	1,330	2.01
Czechoslovakian	192	0.29
Danish	148	0.22
Dutch	620	0.94
Eastern European	6	0.01
English	4,739	7.17
Estonian	6	0.01
European	450	0.68
Finnish	25	0.04
French, except Basque	1,184	1.79
French Canadian	206	0.31
German	7,563	11.45
Greek	57	0.09
Hawaii Native/Pacific Islander:	87	0.13
Micronesian: (17)	24	0.04
Guamanian/Chamorro (17)	24	0.04
Polynesian: (23)	31	0.05
Native Hawaiian (13)	19	0.03
Samoan (10)	12	0.02
Other Pac. Isl., specified	4	0.01
Other Pac. Isl., not spec. (12)	28	0.04
Hispanic or Latino:	18,271	27.83
Central American:	155	0.24
Costa Rican	5	0.01
Guatemalan	49	0.07
Honduran	28	0.04
Nicaraguan	5	0.01
Panamanian	12	0.02
Salvadoran	46	0.07
Other Central American	10	0.02
Cuban	59	0.09
Dominican Republic	9	0.01
Mexican	14,755	22.47
Puerto Rican	110	0.17
South American:	94	0.14
Argentinean	12	0.02
Bolivian	2	0.00
Chilean	5	0.01
Colombian	23	0.04
Ecuadorian	11	0.02
Paraguayan	1	0.00
Peruvian	17	0.03
Uruguayan	3	0.00
Venezuelan	18	0.03
Other South American	2	0.00
Other Hispanic or Latino	3,089	4.70
Hungarian	88	0.13
Iranian	78	0.12
Irish	4,813	7.28
Israeli	12	0.02
Italian	1,918	2.90
Latvian	13	0.02
Lithuanian	14	0.02
Macedonian	11	0.02
Norwegian	390	0.59
Polish	1,096	1.66
Portuguese	96	0.15
Russian	93	0.14
Scandinavian	24	0.04
Scotch-Irish	1,459	2.21
Scottish	1,020	1.54
Serbian	7	0.01

Notes: 1. Figures in the "Number" column do not add up to the total population due to: a) Ancestry/Race overlap — e.g. persons can report being both White and Irish, b) persons of Hispanic origin can report being any race, c) persons reporting two ancestries are counted in both categories. 2. Numbers in parentheses indicate the number of persons reporting this ancestry/race alone, not in combination with any other ancestry/race. 3. Refer to the Explanation of Data in the front of the book for more detailed information.

Ancestry/Race	Number	%
Slavic	15	0.02
Slovene	9	0.01
Swedish	382	0.58
Swiss	64	0.10
Turkish	7	0.01
Ukrainian	14	0.02
United States or American	2,843	4.30
Welsh	292	0.44
West Indian, excl. Hispanic:	31	0.05
Dutch West Indian	16	0.02
Haitian	15	0.02
White:	43,671	66.51
Not Hispanic (33,943)	34,475	52.51
Hispanic (8,509)	9,196	14.01
Yugoslavian	58	0.09

Burkburnett

Place Type: City
County: Wichita
Population: 10,927

Ancestry/Race	Number	%
Acadian/Cajun	12	0.11
African American/Black:	345	3.16
Not Hispanic (312)	339	3.10
Hispanic (3)	6	0.05
Am. Ind. or Alaska Nat., not spec.	30	0.27
American Indian tribes, specified:	179	1.64
Apache (3)	7	0.06
Blackfeet	1	0.01
Cherokee (28)	55	0.50
Chickasaw (17)	32	0.29
Chippewa	1	0.01
Choctaw (31)	49	0.45
Comanche (2)	5	0.05
Creek (1)	2	0.02
Kiowa (9)	10	0.09
Latin American Indians (2)	5	0.05
Navajo	5	0.05
Paiute (1)	1	0.01
Seminole (3)	3	0.03
All other tribes (2)	3	0.03
American Indian tribes, not spec.	6	0.05
Asian:	118	1.08
Chinese, ex. Taiwanese (7)	12	0.11
Filipino (19)	31	0.28
Indian (9)	13	0.12
Japanese (16)	31	0.28
Korean (8)	13	0.12
Thai (4)	7	0.06
Vietnamese (4)	7	0.06
Other Asian, not specified (1)	4	0.04
Australian	7	0.06
Austrian	48	0.44
Belgian	23	0.21
British	30	0.28
Canadian	17	0.16
Celtic	10	0.09
Czech	27	0.25
Danish	26	0.24
Dutch	272	2.50
English	1,280	11.78
European	56	0.52
French, except Basque	404	3.72
French Canadian	6	0.06
German	1,261	11.61
Hawaii Native/Pacific Islander:	18	0.16
Micronesian: (2)	3	0.03
Guamanian/Chamorro (2)	3	0.03
Polynesian: (6)	12	0.11
Native Hawaiian (4)	9	0.08
Samoan (2)	3	0.03
Other Pac. Isl., not spec.	3	0.03
Hispanic or Latino:	677	6.20
Central American:	2	0.02
Costa Rican	1	0.01
Salvadoran	1	0.01
Cuban	1	0.01
Dominican Republic	4	0.04
Mexican	440	4.03
Puerto Rican	29	0.27
South American:	7	0.06
Chilean	1	0.01
Colombian	6	0.05
Other Hispanic or Latino	194	1.78
Irish	1,196	11.01
Italian	305	2.81
Northern European	45	0.41
Norwegian	117	1.08
Pennsylvania German	32	0.29
Polish	135	1.24
Russian	14	0.13
Scotch-Irish	228	2.10
Scottish	140	1.29
Slavic	8	0.07
Swedish	48	0.44
Swiss	10	0.09
Ukrainian	12	0.11
United States or American	1,507	13.87
Welsh	37	0.34
West Indian, excl. Hispanic:	20	0.18
Belizean	7	0.06
Dutch West Indian	13	0.12
White:	10,112	92.54
Not Hispanic (9,606)	9,754	89.27
Hispanic (302)	358	3.28

Burleson

Place Type: City
County: Johnson
Population: 20,976

Ancestry/Race	Number	%
Acadian/Cajun	50	0.24
African American/Black:	113	0.54
Not Hispanic (78)	99	0.47
Hispanic (6)	14	0.07
African, sub-Saharan:	30	0.14
African	20	0.09
Sudanese	10	0.05
Alaska Native tribes, specified:	7	0.03
Aleut	4	0.02
Eskimo (3)	3	0.01
Am. Ind. or Alaska Nat., not spec.	53	0.25
American Indian tribes, specified:	195	0.93
Apache (1)	7	0.03
Blackfeet (1)	6	0.03
Cherokee (23)	84	0.40
Chickasaw (3)	15	0.07
Chippewa (1)	1	0.00
Choctaw (11)	27	0.13
Cree (2)	2	0.01
Creek (3)	9	0.04
Iroquois	3	0.01
Kiowa (1)	1	0.00
Latin American Indians (4)	5	0.02
Navajo	1	0.00
Potawatomi (4)	6	0.03
Pueblo (1)	5	0.02
Seminole (1)	4	0.02
Sioux (5)	6	0.03
Yaqui	1	0.00
All other tribes (4)	12	0.06
American Indian tribes, not spec.	2	0.01
Arab:	53	0.25
Arab/Arabic	7	0.03
Egyptian	9	0.04
Lebanese	37	0.17
Armenian	34	0.16
Asian:	170	0.81
Bangladeshi (1)	1	0.00
Cambodian	3	0.01
Chinese, ex. Taiwanese (9)	15	0.07
Filipino (15)	29	0.14
Indian (14)	20	0.10
Japanese (10)	20	0.10
Korean (12)	16	0.08
Laotian (13)	13	0.06
Malaysian (1)	1	0.00
Pakistani (15)	20	0.10
Thai (9)	10	0.05
Vietnamese (5)	9	0.04
Other Asian, not specified (7)	13	0.06
Australian	25	0.12
Austrian	9	0.04
British	86	0.40
Canadian	26	0.12
Czech	99	0.47
Czechoslovakian	51	0.24
Danish	38	0.18
Dutch	459	2.16
English	2,303	10.83
European	182	0.86
French, except Basque	619	2.91
French Canadian	17	0.08
German	3,321	15.62
Greek	61	0.29
Hawaii Native/Pacific Islander:	25	0.12
Micronesian: (5)	11	0.05
Guamanian/Chamorro (5)	11	0.05
Polynesian: (4)	12	0.06
Native Hawaiian (3)	11	0.05
Samoan (1)	1	0.00
Other Pac. Isl., not spec. (1)	2	0.01
Hispanic or Latino:	1,135	5.41
Central American:	12	0.06
Costa Rican	1	0.00
Guatemalan	5	0.02
Honduran	1	0.00
Panamanian	3	0.01
Salvadoran	2	0.01
Cuban	19	0.09
Mexican	773	3.69
Puerto Rican	51	0.24
South American:	26	0.12
Argentinean	6	0.03
Colombian	8	0.04
Peruvian	8	0.04
Other South American	4	0.02
Other Hispanic or Latino	254	1.21
Hungarian	40	0.19
Irish	2,534	11.92
Italian	340	1.60
Latvian	48	0.23
Lithuanian	93	0.44
Northern European	16	0.08
Norwegian	58	0.27
Pennsylvania German	5	0.02
Polish	206	0.97
Portuguese	12	0.06
Romanian	6	0.03
Russian	38	0.18
Scotch-Irish	428	2.01
Scottish	518	2.44
Swedish	134	0.63
Swiss	49	0.23
Turkish	20	0.09
Ukrainian	11	0.05
United States or American	3,402	16.00
Welsh	77	0.36
West Indian, excl. Hispanic:	46	0.22
Dutch West Indian	46	0.22
White:	20,337	96.95
Not Hispanic (19,332)	19,534	93.13
Hispanic (726)	803	3.83

Canyon Lake

Place Type: Census Designated Place
County: Comal
Population: 16,870

Ancestry/Race	Number	%
Acadian/Cajun	33	0.20
African American/Black:	83	0.49
Not Hispanic (52)	80	0.47
Hispanic (1)	3	0.02
African, sub-Saharan:	38	0.23

Notes: 1. Figures in the "Number" column do not add up to the total population due to: a) Ancestry/Race overlap — e.g. persons can report being both White and Irish, b) persons of Hispanic origin can report being any race, c) persons reporting two ancestries are counted in both categories. 2. Numbers in parentheses indicate the number of persons reporting this ancestry/race alone, not in combination with any other ancestry/race. 3. Refer to the Explanation of Data in the front of the book for more detailed information.

Ancestry/Race	Number	%
African	11	0.07
South African	27	0.16
Alaska Native tribes, specified:	1	0.01
Eskimo	1	0.01
Am. Ind. or Alaska Nat., not spec.	42	0.25
Alsatian	7	0.04
American Indian tribes, specified:	151	0.90
Apache (5)	9	0.05
Blackfeet (3)	8	0.05
Cherokee (21)	63	0.37
Chickasaw (3)	7	0.04
Chippewa (1)	1	0.01
Choctaw (4)	18	0.11
Comanche (2)	6	0.04
Creek	1	0.01
Kiowa (2)	2	0.01
Latin American Indians	2	0.01
Menominee	2	0.01
Navajo	3	0.02
Osage (1)	5	0.03
Ottawa (4)	4	0.02
Potawatomi (2)	2	0.01
Seminole	1	0.01
Shoshone (1)	1	0.01
Sioux (4)	8	0.05
All other tribes (5)	8	0.05
American Indian tribes, not spec.	17	0.10
Asian:	51	0.30
Chinese, ex. Taiwanese (4)	6	0.04
Filipino (11)	17	0.10
Indian (1)	2	0.01
Indonesian (1)	1	0.01
Japanese (6)	14	0.08
Korean	1	0.01
Taiwanese (2)	2	0.01
Thai (2)	2	0.01
Vietnamese (4)	6	0.04
Austrian	19	0.11
Belgian	16	0.09
British	49	0.29
Canadian	29	0.17
Celtic	16	0.09
Czech	204	1.21
Czechoslovakian	48	0.28
Danish	35	0.21
Dutch	312	1.85
English	1,776	10.52
European	131	0.78
Finnish	16	0.09
French, except Basque	618	3.66
French Canadian	58	0.34
German	4,023	23.82
Greek	48	0.28
Hawaii Native/Pacific Islander:	11	0.07
Micronesian: (4)	4	0.02
Guamanian/Chamorro (1)	1	0.01
Other Micronesian (3)	3	0.02
Polynesian: (1)	4	0.02
Native Hawaiian (1)	3	0.02
Other Polynesian	1	0.01
Other Pac. Isl., not spec.	3	0.02
Hispanic or Latino:	1,648	9.77
Central American:	14	0.08
Guatemalan	2	0.01
Honduran	6	0.04
Nicaraguan	1	0.01
Panamanian	2	0.01
Salvadoran	3	0.02
Cuban	7	0.04
Mexican	1,164	6.90
Puerto Rican	24	0.14
South American:	12	0.07
Argentinean	1	0.01
Chilean	2	0.01
Colombian	2	0.01
Ecuadorian	1	0.01
Paraguayan	4	0.02
Peruvian	1	0.01
Other South American	1	0.01
Other Hispanic or Latino	427	2.53
Hungarian	149	0.88
Irish	2,413	14.29
Italian	421	2.49
Lithuanian	11	0.07
Northern European	13	0.08
Norwegian	248	1.47
Pennsylvania German	12	0.07
Polish	302	1.79
Portuguese	25	0.15
Russian	28	0.17
Scandinavian	20	0.12
Scotch-Irish	630	3.73
Scottish	453	2.68
Slovak	11	0.07
Swedish	292	1.73
Swiss	39	0.23
United States or American	1,651	9.78
Welsh	97	0.57
West Indian, excl. Hispanic:	7	0.04
Dutch West Indian	7	0.04
White:	16,259	96.38
Not Hispanic (14,866)	15,040	89.15
Hispanic (1,137)	1,219	7.23

Canyon

Place Type: City
County: Randall
Population: 12,875

Ancestry/Race	Number	%
African American/Black:	280	2.17
Not Hispanic (240)	260	2.02
Hispanic (7)	20	0.16
African, sub-Saharan:	13	0.10
Kenyan	13	0.10
Alaska Native tribes, specified:	1	0.01
Aleut (1)	1	0.01
Alaska Native tribes, not specified	3	0.02
Am. Ind. or Alaska Nat., not spec.	50	0.39
American Indian tribes, specified:	72	0.56
Apache (1)	6	0.05
Blackfeet	1	0.01
Cherokee (6)	19	0.15
Cheyenne	1	0.01
Chickasaw (1)	2	0.02
Choctaw (5)	10	0.08
Comanche	2	0.02
Creek	2	0.02
Delaware (1)	3	0.02
Kiowa	3	0.02
Navajo (6)	6	0.05
Osage (1)	1	0.01
Pueblo	1	0.01
Seminole	2	0.02
Sioux (8)	9	0.07
Ute	1	0.01
Yakama	1	0.01
All other tribes (2)	2	0.02
American Indian tribes, not spec.	3	0.02
Asian:	297	2.31
Bangladeshi (3)	3	0.02
Cambodian (2)	2	0.02
Chinese, ex. Taiwanese (43)	44	0.34
Filipino (3)	6	0.05
Indian (36)	37	0.29
Indonesian (2)	2	0.02
Japanese (7)	19	0.15
Korean (118)	121	0.94
Laotian (19)	20	0.16
Pakistani (2)	3	0.02
Taiwanese (8)	9	0.07
Thai (11)	13	0.10
Other Asian, not specified (9)	18	0.14
Austrian	23	0.18
Basque	9	0.07
Brazilian	5	0.04
British	100	0.77
Canadian	27	0.21
Celtic	5	0.04
Czech	48	0.37
Czechoslovakian	9	0.07
Danish	59	0.46
Dutch	160	1.23
English	1,340	10.34
European	78	0.60
French, except Basque	308	2.38
French Canadian	59	0.46
German	1,801	13.90
Greek	22	0.17
Hawaii Native/Pacific Islander:	7	0.05
Polynesian: (1)	3	0.02
Native Hawaiian	2	0.02
Samoan (1)	1	0.01
Other Pac. Isl., not spec. (4)	4	0.03
Hispanic or Latino:	1,382	10.73
Central American:	5	0.04
Guatemalan	1	0.01
Panamanian	3	0.02
Salvadoran	1	0.01
Dominican Republic	1	0.01
Mexican	950	7.38
Puerto Rican	8	0.06
South American:	3	0.02
Argentinean	1	0.01
Bolivian	1	0.01
Other South American	1	0.01
Other Hispanic or Latino	415	3.22
Hungarian	19	0.15
Irish	1,380	10.65
Italian	132	1.02
Northern European	8	0.06
Norwegian	140	1.08
Polish	49	0.38
Romanian	5	0.04
Russian	6	0.05
Scandinavian	13	0.10
Scotch-Irish	270	2.08
Scottish	340	2.62
Slovene	17	0.13
Swedish	100	0.77
Swiss	19	0.15
Ukrainian	8	0.06
United States or American	1,832	14.14
Welsh	14	0.11
White:	11,541	89.64
Not Hispanic (10,837)	10,935	84.93
Hispanic (535)	606	4.71

Carrollton

Place Type: City
County: Denton
Population: 109,576

Ancestry/Race	Number	%
Acadian/Cajun	38	0.03
African American/Black:	7,375	6.73
Not Hispanic (6,713)	7,146	6.52
Hispanic (149)	229	0.21
African, sub-Saharan:	492	0.45
African	197	0.18
Cape Verdean	22	0.02
Ethiopian	8	0.01
Ghanian	36	0.03
Nigerian	182	0.17
South African	35	0.03
Other sub-Saharan African	12	0.01
Alaska Native tribes, specified:	6	0.01
Alaska Athabascan (4)	5	0.00
Tlingit-Haida (1)	1	0.00
Alaska Native tribes, not specified	1	0.00
Am. Ind. or Alaska Nat., not spec.	289	0.26
Albanian	16	0.01
American Indian tribes, specified:	659	0.60
Apache (4)	12	0.01
Blackfeet (3)	8	0.01
Cherokee (104)	250	0.23
Cheyenne	1	0.00
Chickasaw (18)	35	0.03

Notes: 1. Figures in the "Number" column do not add up to the total population due to: a) Ancestry/Race overlap — e.g. persons can report being both White and Irish, b) persons of Hispanic origin can report being any race, c) persons reporting two ancestries are counted in both categories. 2. Numbers in parentheses indicate the number of persons reporting this ancestry/race alone, not in combination with any other ancestry/race. 3. Refer to the Explanation of Data in the front of the book for more detailed information.

Ancestry/Race	Number	%
Chippewa (5)	7	0.01
Choctaw (61)	112	0.10
Comanche (11)	18	0.02
Cree	1	0.00
Creek (17)	24	0.02
Crow (3)	3	0.00
Delaware (2)	3	0.00
Iroquois (4)	12	0.01
Kiowa (2)	8	0.01
Latin American Indians (40)	48	0.04
Lumbee (1)	1	0.00
Navajo (12)	15	0.01
Osage (1)	4	0.00
Ottawa	1	0.00
Paiute (2)	5	0.00
Potawatomi (3)	8	0.01
Pueblo (7)	7	0.01
Seminole (2)	5	0.00
Shoshone	1	0.00
Sioux (19)	31	0.03
Yaqui (2)	2	0.00
All other tribes (22)	37	0.03
American Indian tribes, not spec.	64	0.06
Arab:	688	0.63
Arab/Arabic	100	0.09
Iraqi	21	0.02
Lebanese	478	0.44
Moroccan	7	0.01
Syrian	25	0.02
Other Arab	57	0.05
Armenian	124	0.11
Asian:	13,140	11.99
Bangladeshi (43)	49	0.04
Cambodian (729)	848	0.77
Chinese, ex. Taiwanese (969)	1,145	1.04
Filipino (411)	528	0.48
Hmong (1)	1	0.00
Indian (4,385)	4,625	4.22
Indonesian (16)	19	0.02
Japanese (224)	308	0.28
Korean (1,428)	1,504	1.37
Laotian (24)	33	0.03
Malaysian (7)	11	0.01
Pakistani (864)	1,083	0.99
Sri Lankan (1)	1	0.00
Taiwanese (41)	53	0.05
Thai (78)	97	0.09
Vietnamese (2,338)	2,442	2.23
Other Asian, specified (5)	14	0.01
Other Asian, not specified (164)	379	0.35
Assyrian/Chaldean/Syriac	32	0.03
Australian	26	0.02
Austrian	163	0.15
Belgian	73	0.07
Brazilian	91	0.08
British	490	0.45
Bulgarian	2	0.00
Canadian	181	0.17
Celtic	10	0.01
Croatian	49	0.04
Czech	528	0.48
Czechoslovakian	166	0.15
Danish	577	0.53
Dutch	1,279	1.17
English	11,477	10.51
European	1,107	1.01
Finnish	132	0.12
French, except Basque	2,918	2.67
French Canadian	426	0.39
German	13,902	12.73
Greek	236	0.22
Guyanese	22	0.02
Hawaii Native/Pacific Islander:	160	0.15
Melanesian: (1)	1	0.00
Fijian (1)	1	0.00
Micronesian: (13)	27	0.02
Guamanian/Chamorro (12)	25	0.02
Other Micronesian (1)	2	0.00
Polynesian: (53)	86	0.08
Native Hawaiian (23)	53	0.05
Samoan (26)	27	0.02
Tongan (2)	4	0.00
Other Polynesian (2)	2	0.00
Other Pac. Isl., specified	7	0.01
Other Pac. Isl., not spec. (8)	39	0.04
Hispanic or Latino:	21,400	19.53
Central American:	1,429	1.30
Costa Rican	44	0.04
Guatemalan	127	0.12
Honduran	137	0.13
Nicaraguan	130	0.12
Panamanian	55	0.05
Salvadoran	885	0.81
Other Central American	51	0.05
Cuban	321	0.29
Dominican Republic	50	0.05
Mexican	15,749	14.37
Puerto Rican	380	0.35
South American:	639	0.58
Argentinean	40	0.04
Bolivian	13	0.01
Chilean	29	0.03
Colombian	233	0.21
Ecuadorian	76	0.07
Paraguayan	9	0.01
Peruvian	164	0.15
Uruguayan	6	0.01
Venezuelan	30	0.03
Other South American	39	0.04
Other Hispanic or Latino	2,832	2.58
Hungarian	257	0.24
Icelander	17	0.02
Iranian	519	0.48
Irish	10,433	9.55
Israeli	7	0.01
Italian	3,247	2.97
Latvian	10	0.01
Lithuanian	111	0.10
New Zealander	19	0.02
Northern European	16	0.01
Norwegian	855	0.78
Pennsylvania German	17	0.02
Polish	1,658	1.52
Portuguese	185	0.17
Romanian	169	0.15
Russian	549	0.50
Scandinavian	92	0.08
Scotch-Irish	2,227	2.04
Scottish	2,049	1.88
Slavic	24	0.02
Slovak	71	0.07
Slovene	28	0.03
Swedish	1,305	1.19
Swiss	159	0.15
Turkish	17	0.02
Ukrainian	158	0.14
United States or American	8,317	7.62
Welsh	747	0.68
West Indian, excl. Hispanic:	242	0.22
Barbadian	27	0.02
Belizean	2	0.00
Bermudan	4	0.00
British West Indian	23	0.02
Dutch West Indian	65	0.06
Jamaican	67	0.06
Trinidadian and Tobagonian	22	0.02
Other West Indian	32	0.03
White:	81,160	74.07
Not Hispanic (67,078)	68,485	62.50
Hispanic (11,680)	12,675	11.57
Yugoslavian	130	0.12

Cedar Hill

Place Type: City
County: Dallas
Population: 32,093

Ancestry/Race	Number	%
African American/Black:	11,039	34.40
Not Hispanic (10,727)	10,918	34.02
Hispanic (61)	121	0.38
African, sub-Saharan:	794	2.47
African	703	2.19
Cape Verdean	5	0.02
Nigerian	36	0.11
South African	8	0.02
Other sub-Saharan African	42	0.13
Alaska Native tribes, specified:	4	0.01
Alaska Athabascan	1	0.00
Eskimo (3)	3	0.01
Am. Ind. or Alaska Nat., not spec.	77	0.24
American Indian tribes, specified:	238	0.74
Apache (9)	20	0.06
Cherokee (21)	70	0.22
Cheyenne	1	0.00
Chickasaw (2)	4	0.01
Chippewa (7)	13	0.04
Choctaw (14)	26	0.08
Comanche (5)	9	0.03
Creek (7)	15	0.05
Crow	3	0.01
Delaware (1)	1	0.00
Houma (2)	2	0.01
Iroquois	2	0.01
Kiowa (1)	1	0.00
Latin American Indians (17)	21	0.07
Navajo	2	0.01
Osage	2	0.01
Potawatomi (2)	5	0.02
Pueblo (1)	2	0.01
Seminole (1)	3	0.01
Sioux (4)	12	0.04
Ute (1)	1	0.00
Yaqui (1)	1	0.00
All other tribes (11)	22	0.07
American Indian tribes, not spec.	25	0.08
Arab:	76	0.24
Arab/Arabic	76	0.24
Asian:	798	2.49
Cambodian (3)	3	0.01
Chinese, ex. Taiwanese (36)	56	0.17
Filipino (224)	286	0.89
Hmong (19)	27	0.08
Indian (91)	111	0.35
Indonesian (6)	6	0.02
Japanese (28)	46	0.14
Korean (33)	49	0.15
Laotian (27)	32	0.10
Pakistani (18)	22	0.07
Taiwanese (2)	2	0.01
Thai (5)	6	0.02
Vietnamese (118)	121	0.38
Other Asian, specified (1)	2	0.01
Other Asian, not specified (14)	29	0.09
Austrian	17	0.05
Basque	26	0.08
Belgian	15	0.05
Brazilian	8	0.02
British	197	0.61
Canadian	75	0.23
Croatian	9	0.03
Czech	87	0.27
Czechoslovakian	20	0.06
Danish	100	0.31
Dutch	291	0.91
English	2,312	7.19
European	226	0.70
Finnish	6	0.02
French, except Basque	580	1.80
French Canadian	129	0.40
German	3,276	10.19
Greek	28	0.09
Hawaii Native/Pacific Islander:	42	0.13
Micronesian: (4)	9	0.03
Guamanian/Chamorro (4)	9	0.03
Polynesian: (8)	17	0.05
Native Hawaiian (5)	14	0.04
Samoan (2)	2	0.01
Tongan (1)	1	0.00

Notes: 1. Figures in the "Number" column do not add up to the total population due to: a) Ancestry/Race overlap — e.g. persons can report being both White and Irish, b) persons of Hispanic origin can report being any race, c) persons reporting two ancestries are counted in both categories. 2. Numbers in parentheses indicate the number of persons reporting this ancestry/race alone, not in combination with any other ancestry/race. 3. Refer to the Explanation of Data in the front of the book for more detailed information.

Other Pac. Isl., not spec. (3)	16	0.05
Hispanic or Latino:	3,822	11.91
Central American:	63	0.20
Costa Rican	5	0.02
Guatemalan	3	0.01
Honduran	8	0.02
Nicaraguan	4	0.01
Panamanian	14	0.04
Salvadoran	23	0.07
Other Central American	6	0.02
Cuban	20	0.06
Dominican Republic	4	0.01
Mexican	2,867	8.93
Puerto Rican	107	0.33
South American:	52	0.16
Argentinean	2	0.01
Bolivian	4	0.01
Chilean	2	0.01
Colombian	24	0.07
Ecuadorian	7	0.02
Peruvian	8	0.02
Venezuelan	4	0.01
Other South American	1	0.00
Other Hispanic or Latino	709	2.21
Hungarian	80	0.25
Icelander	6	0.02
Iranian	36	0.11
Irish	2,723	8.47
Italian	547	1.70
Lithuanian	28	0.09
Northern European	6	0.02
Norwegian	162	0.50
Polish	192	0.60
Portuguese	19	0.06
Romanian	7	0.02
Russian	32	0.10
Scandinavian	12	0.04
Scotch-Irish	347	1.08
Scottish	477	1.48
Slovak	22	0.07
Swedish	172	0.54
Swiss	37	0.12
Turkish	5	0.02
Ukrainian	13	0.04
United States or American	2,370	7.37
Welsh	115	0.36
West Indian, excl. Hispanic:	60	0.19
Barbadian	4	0.01
Dutch West Indian	40	0.12
Jamaican	7	0.02
West Indian	9	0.03
White:	18,751	58.43
Not Hispanic (16,317)	16,650	51.88
Hispanic (1,869)	2,101	6.55
Yugoslavian	6	0.02

Cedar Park

Place Type: City
County: Williamson
Population: 26,049

Ancestry/Race	Number	%
Acadian/Cajun	51	0.20
African American/Black:	947	3.64
Not Hispanic (822)	891	3.42
Hispanic (43)	56	0.21
African, sub-Saharan:	113	0.44
African	74	0.29
Ethiopian	12	0.05
South African	14	0.05
Zimbabwean	6	0.02
Other sub-Saharan African	7	0.03
Alaska Native tribes, specified:	3	0.01
Eskimo	3	0.01
Am. Ind. or Alaska Nat., not spec.	63	0.24
Albanian	15	0.06
Alsatian	16	0.06
American Indian tribes, specified:	157	0.60
Apache (6)	11	0.04
Cherokee (15)	50	0.19
Cheyenne (5)	6	0.02
Chickasaw (1)	2	0.01
Chippewa	2	0.01
Choctaw (10)	26	0.10
Comanche (2)	2	0.01
Creek	4	0.02
Delaware (1)	4	0.02
Houma (1)	1	0.00
Iroquois (1)	5	0.02
Kiowa (1)	5	0.02
Latin American Indians (3)	5	0.02
Lumbee (1)	1	0.00
Navajo (1)	1	0.00
Osage (2)	4	0.02
Puget Sound Salish	2	0.01
Seminole (1)	7	0.03
Sioux	2	0.01
Yaqui	2	0.01
All other tribes (7)	15	0.06
American Indian tribes, not spec.	6	0.02
Arab:	81	0.31
Arab/Arabic	21	0.08
Lebanese	38	0.15
Palestinian	17	0.07
Syrian	5	0.02
Asian:	838	3.22
Bangladeshi (6)	6	0.02
Cambodian (36)	37	0.14
Chinese, ex. Taiwanese (127)	154	0.59
Filipino (50)	78	0.30
Indian (173)	179	0.69
Indonesian (5)	10	0.04
Japanese (21)	50	0.19
Korean (80)	102	0.39
Laotian (4)	4	0.02
Malaysian (1)	2	0.01
Pakistani (11)	12	0.05
Sri Lankan (4)	10	0.04
Taiwanese (7)	11	0.04
Thai (15)	18	0.07
Vietnamese (114)	137	0.53
Other Asian, not specified (13)	28	0.11
Austrian	69	0.27
Belgian	19	0.07
British	114	0.44
Canadian	15	0.06
Celtic	11	0.04
Croatian	16	0.06
Czech	317	1.23
Czechoslovakian	64	0.25
Danish	216	0.84
Dutch	462	1.79
Eastern European	7	0.03
English	2,910	11.29
European	230	0.89
Finnish	63	0.24
French, except Basque	1,013	3.93
French Canadian	258	1.00
German	5,260	20.41
Greek	93	0.36
Hawaii Native/Pacific Islander:	34	0.13
Micronesian: (2)	5	0.02
Guamanian/Chamorro (2)	5	0.02
Polynesian: (13)	22	0.08
Native Hawaiian (12)	19	0.07
Samoan (1)	3	0.01
Other Pac. Isl., not spec.	7	0.03
Hispanic or Latino:	3,516	13.50
Central American:	76	0.29
Costa Rican	6	0.02
Guatemalan	15	0.06
Honduran	12	0.05
Nicaraguan	7	0.03
Panamanian	18	0.07
Salvadoran	18	0.07
Cuban	28	0.11
Dominican Republic	5	0.02
Mexican	2,454	9.42
Puerto Rican	110	0.42
South American:	54	0.21
Argentinean	2	0.01
Chilean	3	0.01
Colombian	26	0.10
Ecuadorian	1	0.00
Peruvian	12	0.05
Venezuelan	7	0.03
Other South American	3	0.01
Other Hispanic or Latino	789	3.03
Hungarian	115	0.45
Iranian	50	0.19
Irish	2,932	11.37
Italian	1,194	4.63
Lithuanian	40	0.16
Luxemburger	28	0.11
Northern European	13	0.05
Norwegian	464	1.80
Polish	596	2.31
Portuguese	45	0.17
Romanian	30	0.12
Russian	159	0.62
Scandinavian	51	0.20
Scotch-Irish	471	1.83
Scottish	750	2.91
Serbian	7	0.03
Slavic	29	0.11
Slovak	65	0.25
Slovene	22	0.09
Swedish	390	1.51
Swiss	113	0.44
Ukrainian	29	0.11
United States or American	1,893	7.34
Welsh	196	0.76
West Indian, excl. Hispanic:	80	0.31
Jamaican	73	0.28
Trinidadian and Tobagonian	7	0.03
White:	23,034	88.43
Not Hispanic (20,584)	20,903	80.24
Hispanic (1,926)	2,131	8.18
Yugoslavian	9	0.03

Channelview

Place Type: Census Designated Place
County: Harris
Population: 29,685

Ancestry/Race	Number	%
Acadian/Cajun	80	0.27
African American/Black:	3,993	13.45
Not Hispanic (3,798)	3,880	13.07
Hispanic (69)	113	0.38
African, sub-Saharan:	152	0.51
African	152	0.51
Am. Ind. or Alaska Nat., not spec.	107	0.36
American Indian tribes, specified:	191	0.64
Apache (3)	11	0.04
Blackfeet (2)	3	0.01
Cherokee (22)	78	0.26
Chickasaw (1)	2	0.01
Choctaw (7)	19	0.06
Comanche (5)	8	0.03
Creek (1)	2	0.01
Crow (1)	1	0.00
Delaware (2)	2	0.01
Iroquois (6)	8	0.03
Kiowa (2)	2	0.01
Latin American Indians (16)	20	0.07
Lumbee	4	0.01
Navajo (1)	5	0.02
Osage	1	0.00
Potawatomi (1)	1	0.00
Pueblo (2)	5	0.02
Sioux	2	0.01
Yaqui	4	0.01
Yuman (1)	1	0.00
All other tribes (6)	12	0.04
American Indian tribes, not spec.	31	0.10
Arab:	39	0.13
Arab/Arabic	11	0.04

Notes: 1. Figures in the "Number" column do not add up to the total population due to: a) Ancestry/Race overlap — e.g. persons can report being both White and Irish, b) persons of Hispanic origin can report being any race, c) persons reporting two ancestries are counted in both categories. 2. Numbers in parentheses indicate the number of persons reporting this ancestry/race alone, not in combination with any other ancestry/race. 3. Refer to the Explanation of Data in the front of the book for more detailed information.

Ancestry/Race	Number	%
Egyptian	7	0.02
Palestinian	21	0.07
Armenian	19	0.06
Asian:	684	2.30
Cambodian (2)	3	0.01
Chinese, ex. Taiwanese (74)	99	0.33
Filipino (128)	145	0.49
Indian (40)	56	0.19
Japanese (9)	14	0.05
Korean (13)	16	0.05
Malaysian (1)	1	0.00
Pakistani (11)	11	0.04
Taiwanese (1)	1	0.00
Thai (5)	7	0.02
Vietnamese (274)	300	1.01
Other Asian, specified	1	0.00
Other Asian, not specified (19)	30	0.10
Austrian	33	0.11
Canadian	6	0.02
Celtic	10	0.03
Czech	107	0.36
Czechoslovakian	9	0.03
Dutch	151	0.51
English	1,215	4.08
European	152	0.51
French, except Basque	618	2.07
French Canadian	154	0.52
German	1,530	5.14
Greek	74	0.25
Guyanese	68	0.23
Hawaii Native/Pacific Islander:	63	0.21
Micronesian: (6)	13	0.04
Guamanian/Chamorro (6)	12	0.04
Other Micronesian	1	0.00
Polynesian: (5)	23	0.08
Native Hawaiian (2)	13	0.04
Samoan	1	0.00
Tongan (3)	6	0.02
Other Polynesian	3	0.01
Other Pac. Isl., specified	1	0.00
Other Pac. Isl., not spec. (6)	26	0.09
Hispanic or Latino:	11,017	37.11
Central American:	303	1.02
Costa Rican	9	0.03
Guatemalan	56	0.19
Honduran	44	0.15
Nicaraguan	13	0.04
Panamanian	3	0.01
Salvadoran	167	0.56
Other Central American	11	0.04
Cuban	33	0.11
Dominican Republic	18	0.06
Mexican	8,770	29.54
Puerto Rican	100	0.34
South American:	97	0.33
Argentinean	9	0.03
Bolivian	1	0.00
Chilean	8	0.03
Colombian	40	0.13
Ecuadorian	12	0.04
Peruvian	9	0.03
Venezuelan	7	0.02
Other South American	11	0.04
Other Hispanic or Latino	1,696	5.71
Hungarian	6	0.02
Irish	1,862	6.25
Israeli	6	0.02
Italian	290	0.97
Norwegian	34	0.11
Pennsylvania German	9	0.03
Polish	102	0.34
Romanian	39	0.13
Russian	14	0.05
Scotch-Irish	205	0.69
Scottish	85	0.29
Slovak	5	0.02
Slovene	17	0.06
Swedish	87	0.29
Swiss	7	0.02
United States or American	3,050	10.24
Welsh	44	0.15
West Indian, excl. Hispanic:	148	0.50
Dutch West Indian	9	0.03
Jamaican	95	0.32
Trinidadian and Tobagonian	34	0.11
West Indian	10	0.03
White:	19,492	65.66
Not Hispanic (13,841)	14,089	47.46
Hispanic (4,905)	5,403	18.20

Cinco Ranch

Place Type: Census Designated Place
County: Fort Bend
Population: 11,196

Ancestry/Race	Number	%
African American/Black:	334	2.98
Not Hispanic (315)	326	2.91
Hispanic (4)	8	0.07
African, sub-Saharan:	148	1.32
African	59	0.53
Nigerian	61	0.54
South African	28	0.25
Am. Ind. or Alaska Nat., not spec.	11	0.10
American Indian tribes, specified:	36	0.32
Apache	1	0.01
Cherokee	8	0.07
Chickasaw (3)	3	0.03
Choctaw (9)	13	0.12
Comanche	2	0.02
Creek (4)	4	0.04
Latin American Indians	2	0.02
Osage (1)	1	0.01
Sioux	1	0.01
All other tribes (1)	1	0.01
American Indian tribes, not spec.	6	0.05
Arab:	33	0.29
Lebanese	33	0.29
Armenian	36	0.32
Asian:	809	7.23
Bangladeshi (5)	5	0.04
Chinese, ex. Taiwanese (231)	248	2.22
Filipino (58)	64	0.57
Indian (239)	252	2.25
Indonesian (6)	6	0.05
Japanese (18)	34	0.30
Korean (60)	62	0.55
Malaysian (4)	4	0.04
Pakistani (14)	14	0.13
Sri Lankan (1)	1	0.01
Taiwanese (8)	8	0.07
Thai (3)	5	0.04
Vietnamese (67)	75	0.67
Other Asian, specified (3)	3	0.03
Other Asian, not specified (15)	28	0.25
Australian	22	0.20
Austrian	42	0.37
Belgian	14	0.12
British	290	2.58
Canadian	32	0.28
Croatian	19	0.17
Cypriot	39	0.35
Czech	239	2.13
Czechoslovakian	44	0.39
Danish	58	0.52
Dutch	168	1.50
English	1,722	15.32
European	166	1.48
French, except Basque	616	5.48
French Canadian	126	1.12
German	1,783	15.87
Greek	110	0.98
Guyanese	13	0.12
Hawaii Native/Pacific Islander:	2	0.02
Polynesian: (2)	2	0.02
Native Hawaiian (1)	1	0.01
Samoan (1)	1	0.01
Hispanic or Latino:	654	5.84
Central American:	14	0.13
Costa Rican	1	0.01
Guatemalan	7	0.06
Honduran	1	0.01
Nicaraguan	3	0.03
Panamanian	1	0.01
Salvadoran	1	0.01
Cuban	28	0.25
Dominican Republic	7	0.06
Mexican	311	2.78
Puerto Rican	32	0.29
South American:	139	1.24
Argentinean	14	0.13
Bolivian	6	0.05
Colombian	46	0.41
Ecuadorian	6	0.05
Peruvian	10	0.09
Uruguayan	5	0.04
Venezuelan	38	0.34
Other South American	14	0.13
Other Hispanic or Latino	123	1.10
Hungarian	108	0.96
Irish	1,240	11.03
Israeli	7	0.06
Italian	602	5.36
Norwegian	152	1.35
Polish	358	3.19
Portuguese	38	0.34
Russian	99	0.88
Scandinavian	55	0.49
Scotch-Irish	307	2.73
Scottish	432	3.84
Serbian	9	0.08
Slovak	8	0.07
Swedish	112	1.00
Swiss	91	0.81
United States or American	1,030	9.17
Welsh	153	1.36
White:	9,976	89.10
Not Hispanic (9,325)	9,418	84.12
Hispanic (518)	558	4.98

Cleburne

Place Type: City
County: Johnson
Population: 26,005

Ancestry/Race	Number	%
African American/Black:	1,242	4.78
Not Hispanic (1,130)	1,195	4.60
Hispanic (24)	47	0.18
African, sub-Saharan:	20	0.08
African	5	0.02
South African	15	0.06
Am. Ind. or Alaska Nat., not spec.	79	0.30
American Indian tribes, specified:	179	0.69
Apache (6)	10	0.04
Blackfeet (4)	8	0.03
Cherokee (17)	66	0.25
Chickasaw (1)	3	0.01
Choctaw (14)	23	0.09
Comanche (2)	5	0.02
Cree (1)	1	0.00
Creek (2)	4	0.02
Iroquois (3)	3	0.01
Latin American Indians (14)	19	0.07
Navajo (4)	6	0.02
Osage	1	0.00
Seminole (4)	7	0.03
Shoshone	2	0.01
Sioux	2	0.01
Yaqui	1	0.00
All other tribes (9)	18	0.07
American Indian tribes, not spec.	14	0.05
Arab:	8	0.03
Syrian	8	0.03
Asian:	147	0.57
Bangladeshi (3)	3	0.01
Chinese, ex. Taiwanese (19)	26	0.10
Filipino (15)	22	0.08

Notes: 1. Figures in the "Number" column do not add up to the total population due to: a) Ancestry/Race overlap — e.g. persons can report being both White and Irish, b) persons of Hispanic origin can report being any race, c) persons reporting two ancestries are counted in both categories. 2. Numbers in parentheses indicate the number of persons reporting this ancestry/race alone, not in combination with any other ancestry/race. 3. Refer to the Explanation of Data in the front of the book for more detailed information.

Ancestry/Race	Number	%
Indian (37)	40	0.15
Indonesian (1)	1	0.00
Japanese (3)	12	0.05
Korean (18)	23	0.09
Laotian (1)	1	0.00
Malaysian (1)	1	0.00
Thai (1)	1	0.00
Vietnamese (5)	5	0.02
Other Asian, specified	4	0.02
Other Asian, not specified (2)	8	0.03
Australian	10	0.04
Austrian	8	0.03
Basque	13	0.05
British	32	0.12
Canadian	26	0.10
Czech	33	0.13
Czechoslovakian	47	0.18
Danish	35	0.13
Dutch	469	1.79
Eastern European	4	0.02
English	2,419	9.23
European	96	0.37
French, except Basque	413	1.58
French Canadian	93	0.35
German	2,319	8.85
Greek	17	0.06
Hawaii Native/Pacific Islander:	72	0.28
Micronesian: (34)	37	0.14
Guamanian/Chamorro	1	0.00
Other Micronesian (34)	36	0.14
Polynesian: (2)	7	0.03
Native Hawaiian (2)	3	0.01
Samoan	4	0.02
Other Pac. Isl., specified	4	0.02
Other Pac. Isl., not spec. (19)	24	0.09
Hispanic or Latino:	5,175	19.90
Central American:	61	0.23
Costa Rican	5	0.02
Guatemalan	25	0.10
Honduran	8	0.03
Panamanian	6	0.02
Salvadoran	15	0.06
Other Central American	2	0.01
Cuban	10	0.04
Dominican Republic	3	0.01
Mexican	4,345	16.71
Puerto Rican	42	0.16
South American:	21	0.08
Chilean	1	0.00
Colombian	2	0.01
Venezuelan	16	0.06
Other South American	2	0.01
Other Hispanic or Latino	693	2.66
Hungarian	17	0.06
Icelander	32	0.12
Irish	2,538	9.69
Italian	260	0.99
Lithuanian	9	0.03
Northern European	10	0.04
Norwegian	126	0.48
Polish	73	0.28
Portuguese	38	0.15
Romanian	12	0.05
Russian	14	0.05
Scandinavian	26	0.10
Scotch-Irish	585	2.23
Scottish	610	2.33
Slovene	6	0.02
Swedish	95	0.36
Swiss	46	0.18
Ukrainian	14	0.05
United States or American	3,485	13.30
Welsh	98	0.37
West Indian, excl. Hispanic:	24	0.09
Dutch West Indian	13	0.05
U.S. Virgin Islander	11	0.04
White:	22,858	87.90
Not Hispanic (19,220)	19,420	74.68
Hispanic (3,228)	3,438	13.22
Yugoslavian	11	0.04

Cloverleaf

Place Type: Census Designated Place
County: Harris
Population: 23,508

Ancestry/Race	Number	%
Acadian/Cajun	8	0.03
African American/Black:	3,897	16.58
Not Hispanic (3,726)	3,811	16.21
Hispanic (61)	86	0.37
African, sub-Saharan:	59	0.25
African	59	0.25
Am. Ind. or Alaska Nat., not spec.	102	0.43
American Indian tribes, specified:	131	0.56
Apache (8)	9	0.04
Blackfeet	9	0.04
Cherokee (11)	42	0.18
Cheyenne	1	0.00
Chickasaw (1)	1	0.00
Choctaw (6)	13	0.06
Comanche (6)	8	0.03
Creek (1)	3	0.01
Houma (1)	1	0.00
Latin American Indians (24)	30	0.13
Navajo	1	0.00
Osage	1	0.00
Sioux (2)	5	0.02
All other tribes (4)	7	0.03
American Indian tribes, not spec.	3	0.01
Arab:	16	0.07
Egyptian	6	0.03
Syrian	10	0.04
Asian:	389	1.65
Chinese, ex. Taiwanese (42)	45	0.19
Filipino (71)	81	0.34
Indian (77)	78	0.33
Japanese (5)	7	0.03
Korean (9)	14	0.06
Pakistani (18)	18	0.08
Thai (5)	5	0.02
Vietnamese (118)	128	0.54
Other Asian, specified	2	0.01
Other Asian, not specified (6)	11	0.05
Austrian	13	0.06
British	69	0.29
Canadian	7	0.03
Celtic	11	0.05
Croatian	7	0.03
Czech	105	0.45
Czechoslovakian	24	0.10
Danish	8	0.03
Dutch	167	0.71
English	1,123	4.78
European	197	0.84
Finnish	9	0.04
French, except Basque	402	1.71
French Canadian	99	0.42
German	1,289	5.48
Greek	41	0.17
Hawaii Native/Pacific Islander:	24	0.10
Micronesian: (9)	10	0.04
Guamanian/Chamorro (9)	10	0.04
Polynesian:	2	0.01
Native Hawaiian	2	0.01
Other Pac. Isl., specified	2	0.01
Other Pac. Isl., not spec. (2)	10	0.04
Hispanic or Latino:	10,423	44.34
Central American:	450	1.91
Costa Rican	13	0.06
Guatemalan	40	0.17
Honduran	104	0.44
Nicaraguan	15	0.06
Panamanian	4	0.02
Salvadoran	253	1.08
Other Central American	21	0.09
Cuban	23	0.10
Dominican Republic	3	0.01
Mexican	8,278	35.21
Puerto Rican	48	0.20
South American:	74	0.31
Argentinean	1	0.00
Chilean	13	0.06
Colombian	56	0.24
Ecuadorian	2	0.01
Peruvian	2	0.01
Other Hispanic or Latino	1,547	6.58
Irish	1,315	5.59
Italian	156	0.66
Lithuanian	14	0.06
Norwegian	74	0.31
Polish	101	0.43
Portuguese	21	0.09
Romanian	49	0.21
Russian	31	0.13
Scandinavian	10	0.04
Scotch-Irish	162	0.69
Scottish	159	0.68
Slovak	40	0.17
Swedish	59	0.25
Ukrainian	8	0.03
United States or American	1,502	6.39
Welsh	31	0.13
White:	14,381	61.17
Not Hispanic (8,737)	8,921	37.95
Hispanic (5,079)	5,460	23.23

Clute

Place Type: City
County: Brazoria
Population: 10,424

Ancestry/Race	Number	%
Acadian/Cajun	42	0.41
African American/Black:	855	8.20
Not Hispanic (766)	799	7.67
Hispanic (32)	56	0.54
African, sub-Saharan:	43	0.42
African	43	0.42
Am. Ind. or Alaska Nat., not spec.	54	0.52
American Indian tribes, specified:	56	0.54
Apache (6)	7	0.07
Cherokee (10)	13	0.12
Cheyenne (1)	1	0.01
Choctaw (5)	8	0.08
Latin American Indians (12)	15	0.14
Ottawa (3)	4	0.04
Potawatomi (1)	2	0.02
Pueblo (1)	1	0.01
Sioux	2	0.02
All other tribes	3	0.03
American Indian tribes, not spec.	6	0.06
Arab:	7	0.07
Arab/Arabic	7	0.07
Asian:	134	1.29
Chinese, ex. Taiwanese (2)	9	0.09
Filipino (8)	13	0.12
Indian (28)	39	0.37
Japanese (7)	7	0.07
Korean (8)	10	0.10
Malaysian (8)	8	0.08
Pakistani (5)	13	0.12
Thai (1)	1	0.01
Vietnamese (20)	20	0.19
Other Asian, specified	1	0.01
Other Asian, not specified (10)	13	0.12
Austrian	8	0.08
British	4	0.04
Celtic	8	0.08
Croatian	7	0.07
Czech	132	1.28
Czechoslovakian	14	0.14
Dutch	109	1.06
English	506	4.91
European	6	0.06
Finnish	32	0.31
French, except Basque	245	2.38
French Canadian	58	0.56
German	820	7.96

Notes: 1. Figures in the "Number" column do not add up to the total population due to: a) Ancestry/Race overlap — e.g. persons can report being both White and Irish, b) persons of Hispanic origin can report being any race, c) persons reporting two ancestries are counted in both categories. 2. Numbers in parentheses indicate the number of persons reporting this ancestry/race alone, not in combination with any other ancestry/race. 3. Refer to the Explanation of Data in the front of the book for more detailed information.

Greek	14	0.14
Hawaii Native/Pacific Islander:	17	0.16
Micronesian:	1	0.01
Guamanian/Chamorro	1	0.01
Polynesian: (1)	13	0.12
Native Hawaiian (1)	7	0.07
Samoan	6	0.06
Other Pac. Isl., not spec.	3	0.03
Hispanic or Latino:	5,013	48.09
Central American:	32	0.31
Costa Rican	3	0.03
Guatemalan	11	0.11
Honduran	2	0.02
Nicaraguan	4	0.04
Salvadoran	4	0.04
Other Central American	8	0.08
Cuban	5	0.05
Dominican Republic	1	0.01
Mexican	4,092	39.26
Puerto Rican	34	0.33
South American:	16	0.15
Chilean	1	0.01
Colombian	4	0.04
Ecuadorian	8	0.08
Venezuelan	3	0.03
Other Hispanic or Latino	833	7.99
Hungarian	13	0.13
Irish	612	5.94
Italian	117	1.14
Norwegian	45	0.44
Polish	78	0.76
Romanian	25	0.24
Russian	20	0.19
Scandinavian	8	0.08
Scotch-Irish	162	1.57
Scottish	165	1.60
Swedish	43	0.42
Ukrainian	8	0.08
United States or American	564	5.47
Welsh	49	0.48
White:	7,000	67.15
Not Hispanic (4,415)	4,497	43.14
Hispanic (2,279)	2,503	24.01

College Station

Place Type: City
County: Brazos
Population: 67,890

Ancestry/Race	Number	%
Acadian/Cajun	78	0.11
African American/Black:	3,852	5.67
Not Hispanic (3,647)	3,776	5.56
Hispanic (51)	76	0.11
African, sub-Saharan:	504	0.74
African	247	0.36
Kenyan	6	0.01
Nigerian	186	0.27
Sierra Leonean	11	0.02
South African	18	0.03
Other sub-Saharan African	36	0.05
Alaska Native tribes, specified:	2	0.00
Aleut	1	0.00
Tlingit-Haida (1)	1	0.00
Am. Ind. or Alaska Nat., not spec.	127	0.19
Alsatian	8	0.01
American Indian tribes, specified:	301	0.44
Apache (6)	17	0.03
Blackfeet	4	0.01
Cherokee (41)	113	0.17
Cheyenne	1	0.00
Chickasaw (7)	14	0.02
Chippewa (3)	3	0.00
Choctaw (26)	48	0.07
Comanche (3)	11	0.02
Cree	1	0.00
Creek (4)	10	0.01
Crow	1	0.00
Delaware (2)	3	0.00
Houma (1)	1	0.00
Iroquois	4	0.01
Kiowa (4)	5	0.01
Latin American Indians (7)	23	0.03
Lumbee (2)	2	0.00
Navajo	3	0.00
Osage (2)	3	0.00
Paiute	2	0.00
Potawatomi	1	0.00
Pueblo (3)	3	0.00
Puget Sound Salish (1)	1	0.00
Seminole (1)	3	0.00
Sioux (1)	6	0.01
Yaqui	1	0.00
All other tribes (8)	17	0.03
American Indian tribes, not spec.	51	0.08
Arab:	297	0.44
Arab/Arabic	69	0.10
Egyptian	43	0.06
Jordanian	25	0.04
Lebanese	28	0.04
Palestinian	10	0.01
Other Arab	122	0.18
Armenian	24	0.04
Asian:	5,457	8.04
Bangladeshi (56)	64	0.09
Cambodian (4)	5	0.01
Chinese, ex. Taiwanese (1,414)	1,512	2.23
Filipino (149)	199	0.29
Hmong (1)	1	0.00
Indian (1,291)	1,370	2.02
Indonesian (109)	123	0.18
Japanese (106)	157	0.23
Korean (1,026)	1,078	1.59
Laotian (7)	7	0.01
Malaysian (6)	10	0.01
Pakistani (109)	139	0.20
Sri Lankan (22)	25	0.04
Taiwanese (152)	181	0.27
Thai (85)	99	0.15
Vietnamese (274)	297	0.44
Other Asian, specified (6)	19	0.03
Other Asian, not specified (69)	171	0.25
Australian	33	0.05
Austrian	192	0.28
Belgian	125	0.18
Brazilian	84	0.12
British	529	0.78
Bulgarian	38	0.06
Canadian	150	0.22
Carpatho Rusyn	6	0.01
Celtic	8	0.01
Cypriot	18	0.03
Czech	1,398	2.06
Czechoslovakian	264	0.39
Danish	360	0.53
Dutch	722	1.06
English	7,430	10.94
Estonian	34	0.05
European	782	1.15
Finnish	110	0.16
French, except Basque	2,029	2.99
French Canadian	176	0.26
German	12,741	18.76
Greek	226	0.33
Hawaii Native/Pacific Islander:	109	0.16
Melanesian: (1)	1	0.00
Fijian (1)	1	0.00
Micronesian: (14)	20	0.03
Guamanian/Chamorro (14)	16	0.02
Other Micronesian	4	0.01
Polynesian: (28)	42	0.06
Native Hawaiian (18)	27	0.04
Samoan (8)	9	0.01
Tongan	3	0.00
Other Polynesian (2)	3	0.00
Other Pac. Isl., specified	1	0.00
Other Pac. Isl., not spec. (1)	45	0.07
Hispanic or Latino:	6,759	9.96
Central American:	310	0.46
Costa Rican	33	0.05
Guatemalan	73	0.11
Honduran	47	0.07
Nicaraguan	56	0.08
Panamanian	58	0.09
Salvadoran	24	0.04
Other Central American	19	0.03
Cuban	84	0.12
Dominican Republic	8	0.01
Mexican	4,437	6.54
Puerto Rican	163	0.24
South American:	412	0.61
Argentinean	35	0.05
Bolivian	29	0.04
Chilean	15	0.02
Colombian	116	0.17
Ecuadorian	39	0.06
Paraguayan	1	0.00
Peruvian	56	0.08
Uruguayan	3	0.00
Venezuelan	90	0.13
Other South American	28	0.04
Other Hispanic or Latino	1,345	1.98
Hungarian	154	0.23
Icelander	19	0.03
Iranian	136	0.20
Irish	6,804	10.02
Israeli	12	0.02
Italian	2,198	3.24
Latvian	17	0.03
Lithuanian	95	0.14
Norwegian	630	0.93
Polish	1,785	2.63
Portuguese	20	0.03
Romanian	58	0.09
Russian	261	0.38
Scandinavian	56	0.08
Scotch-Irish	1,944	2.86
Scottish	1,843	2.71
Serbian	55	0.08
Slavic	6	0.01
Slovak	23	0.03
Slovene	19	0.03
Swedish	762	1.12
Swiss	200	0.29
Turkish	187	0.28
Ukrainian	92	0.14
United States or American	3,694	5.44
Welsh	393	0.58
West Indian, excl. Hispanic:	76	0.11
Dutch West Indian	8	0.01
Haitian	19	0.03
Jamaican	23	0.03
Trinidadian and Tobagonian	26	0.04
White:	55,773	82.15
Not Hispanic (51,362)	52,110	76.76
Hispanic (3,311)	3,663	5.40
Yugoslavian	86	0.13

Colleyville

Place Type: City
County: Tarrant
Population: 19,636

Ancestry/Race	Number	%
Acadian/Cajun	44	0.22
African American/Black:	291	1.48
Not Hispanic (257)	286	1.46
Hispanic	5	0.03
African, sub-Saharan:	29	0.15
African	17	0.09
Sierra Leonean	12	0.06
Am. Ind. or Alaska Nat., not spec.	24	0.12
American Indian tribes, specified:	144	0.73
Apache (1)	1	0.01
Blackfeet (1)	2	0.01
Cherokee (27)	74	0.38
Cheyenne	1	0.01
Chickasaw (2)	8	0.04

Notes: 1. Figures in the "Number" column do not add up to the total population due to: a) Ancestry/Race overlap — e.g. persons can report being both White and Irish, b) persons of Hispanic origin can report being any race, c) persons reporting two ancestries are counted in both categories. 2. Numbers in parentheses indicate the number of persons reporting this ancestry/race alone, not in combination with any other ancestry/race. 3. Refer to the Explanation of Data in the front of the book for more detailed information.

Ancestry/Race	Number	%
Chippewa	1	0.01
Choctaw (19)	25	0.13
Comanche (4)	6	0.03
Creek (2)	6	0.03
Houma (3)	3	0.02
Latin American Indians (3)	3	0.02
Osage (4)	4	0.02
Ottawa	1	0.01
Potawatomi	2	0.01
Seminole (1)	2	0.01
Sioux	1	0.01
All other tribes (3)	4	0.02
American Indian tribes, not spec.	9	0.05
Arab:	120	0.61
Egyptian	66	0.34
Lebanese	13	0.07
Other Arab	41	0.21
Armenian	34	0.17
Asian:	720	3.67
Cambodian (2)	2	0.01
Chinese, ex. Taiwanese (107)	126	0.64
Filipino (58)	66	0.34
Indian (227)	252	1.28
Indonesian (4)	7	0.04
Japanese (35)	53	0.27
Korean (69)	72	0.37
Laotian (1)	6	0.03
Pakistani (43)	58	0.30
Taiwanese (6)	6	0.03
Thai (3)	3	0.02
Vietnamese (40)	46	0.23
Other Asian, specified (1)	6	0.03
Other Asian, not specified (6)	17	0.09
Assyrian/Chaldean/Syriac	8	0.04
Australian	9	0.05
Austrian	54	0.28
Basque	15	0.08
Belgian	30	0.15
British	223	1.14
Canadian	163	0.83
Croatian	42	0.21
Czech	134	0.68
Czechoslovakian	26	0.13
Danish	83	0.42
Dutch	306	1.56
Eastern European	14	0.07
English	3,205	16.37
European	395	2.02
Finnish	24	0.12
French, except Basque	818	4.18
French Canadian	137	0.70
German	4,796	24.50
Greek	37	0.19
Hawaii Native/Pacific Islander:	14	0.07
Micronesian: (4)	4	0.02
Guamanian/Chamorro (4)	4	0.02
Polynesian: (2)	2	0.01
Native Hawaiian (2)	2	0.01
Other Pac. Isl., specified	5	0.03
Other Pac. Isl., not spec.	3	0.02
Hispanic or Latino:	634	3.23
Central American:	17	0.09
Costa Rican	2	0.01
Guatemalan	1	0.01
Honduran	1	0.01
Nicaraguan	7	0.04
Panamanian	5	0.03
Salvadoran	1	0.01
Cuban	34	0.17
Dominican Republic	1	0.01
Mexican	364	1.85
Puerto Rican	45	0.23
South American:	41	0.21
Argentinean	5	0.03
Bolivian	9	0.05
Chilean	1	0.01
Colombian	16	0.08
Ecuadorian	1	0.01
Paraguayan	2	0.01
Peruvian	6	0.03
Venezuelan	1	0.01
Other Hispanic or Latino	132	0.67
Hungarian	148	0.76
Iranian	29	0.15
Irish	2,872	14.67
Israeli	7	0.04
Italian	883	4.51
Latvian	13	0.07
Lithuanian	50	0.26
Northern European	40	0.20
Norwegian	545	2.78
Pennsylvania German	8	0.04
Polish	458	2.34
Portuguese	8	0.04
Russian	70	0.36
Scandinavian	28	0.14
Scotch-Irish	536	2.74
Scottish	550	2.81
Serbian	15	0.08
Slavic	14	0.07
Slovak	48	0.25
Slovene	11	0.06
Swedish	455	2.32
Swiss	105	0.54
Ukrainian	24	0.12
United States or American	1,610	8.23
Welsh	199	1.02
White:	18,537	94.40
Not Hispanic (17,814)	18,016	91.75
Hispanic (475)	521	2.65

Conroe

Place Type: City
County: Montgomery
Population: 36,811

Ancestry/Race	Number	%
Acadian/Cajun	69	0.19
African American/Black:	4,229	11.49
Not Hispanic (4,015)	4,101	11.14
Hispanic (82)	128	0.35
African, sub-Saharan:	216	0.59
African	157	0.43
Nigerian	59	0.16
Am. Ind. or Alaska Nat., not spec.	78	0.21
American Indian tribes, specified:	193	0.52
Apache (3)	11	0.03
Blackfeet (4)	7	0.02
Cherokee (21)	60	0.16
Cheyenne (2)	5	0.01
Chickasaw (5)	9	0.02
Chippewa (1)	1	0.00
Choctaw (8)	17	0.05
Comanche (3)	11	0.03
Creek (4)	5	0.01
Delaware (3)	3	0.01
Iroquois (1)	2	0.01
Latin American Indians (31)	42	0.11
Lumbee (1)	1	0.00
Navajo (1)	3	0.01
Osage (2)	2	0.01
Potawatomi	2	0.01
Pueblo	2	0.01
Seminole (1)	1	0.00
Sioux	3	0.01
All other tribes (4)	6	0.02
American Indian tribes, not spec.	21	0.06
Arab:	55	0.15
Arab/Arabic	8	0.02
Palestinian	6	0.02
Syrian	6	0.02
Other Arab	35	0.10
Asian:	486	1.32
Cambodian (31)	47	0.13
Chinese, ex. Taiwanese (56)	68	0.18
Filipino (50)	61	0.17
Indian (84)	112	0.30
Indonesian (1)	3	0.01
Japanese (12)	21	0.06
Korean (15)	26	0.07
Malaysian	2	0.01
Pakistani (28)	47	0.13
Thai (1)	2	0.01
Vietnamese (45)	53	0.14
Other Asian, specified (4)	11	0.03
Other Asian, not specified (9)	33	0.09
Austrian	40	0.11
Brazilian	23	0.06
British	72	0.20
Canadian	27	0.07
Celtic	7	0.02
Croatian	7	0.02
Czech	162	0.44
Czechoslovakian	50	0.14
Danish	93	0.25
Dutch	386	1.05
English	2,439	6.65
European	264	0.72
French, except Basque	1,008	2.75
French Canadian	132	0.36
German	3,661	9.99
Greek	79	0.22
Hawaii Native/Pacific Islander:	35	0.10
Micronesian: (11)	15	0.04
Guamanian/Chamorro (11)	15	0.04
Polynesian: (3)	11	0.03
Native Hawaiian (2)	10	0.03
Samoan (1)	1	0.00
Other Pac. Isl., specified	1	0.00
Other Pac. Isl., not spec. (4)	8	0.02
Hispanic or Latino:	12,006	32.62
Central American:	882	2.40
Costa Rican	2	0.01
Guatemalan	64	0.17
Honduran	426	1.16
Nicaraguan	7	0.02
Panamanian	1	0.00
Salvadoran	358	0.97
Other Central American	24	0.07
Cuban	28	0.08
Dominican Republic	8	0.02
Mexican	9,437	25.64
Puerto Rican	67	0.18
South American:	48	0.13
Argentinean	4	0.01
Bolivian	1	0.00
Chilean	3	0.01
Colombian	13	0.04
Ecuadorian	6	0.02
Peruvian	9	0.02
Venezuelan	7	0.02
Other South American	5	0.01
Other Hispanic or Latino	1,536	4.17
Hungarian	87	0.24
Iranian	13	0.04
Irish	2,902	7.92
Italian	579	1.58
Latvian	25	0.07
Norwegian	151	0.41
Pennsylvania German	8	0.02
Polish	428	1.17
Portuguese	20	0.05
Russian	23	0.06
Scandinavian	10	0.03
Scotch-Irish	674	1.84
Scottish	446	1.22
Slovak	36	0.10
Swedish	226	0.62
Swiss	56	0.15
United States or American	2,777	7.58
Welsh	123	0.34
West Indian, excl. Hispanic:	41	0.11
Belizean	22	0.06
British West Indian	6	0.02
Jamaican	13	0.04
White:	27,149	73.75
Not Hispanic (20,060)	20,280	55.09
Hispanic (6,133)	6,869	18.66

Notes: 1. Figures in the "Number" column do not add up to the total population due to: a) Ancestry/Race overlap — e.g. persons can report being both White and Irish, b) persons of Hispanic origin can report being any race, c) persons reporting two ancestries are counted in both categories. 2. Numbers in parentheses indicate the number of persons reporting this ancestry/race alone, not in combination with any other ancestry/race. 3. Refer to the Explanation of Data in the front of the book for more detailed information.

Converse

Place Type: City
County: Bexar
Population: 11,508

Ancestry/Race	Number	%
Acadian/Cajun	8	0.07
African American/Black:	1,607	13.96
Not Hispanic (1,471)	1,553	13.49
Hispanic (28)	54	0.47
African, sub-Saharan:	30	0.26
African	30	0.26
Alaska Native tribes, specified:	2	0.02
Alaska Athabascan	2	0.02
Am. Ind. or Alaska Nat., not spec.	57	0.50
American Indian tribes, specified:	98	0.85
Apache	3	0.03
Blackfeet (1)	4	0.03
Cherokee (4)	29	0.25
Cheyenne (1)	1	0.01
Chippewa (2)	5	0.04
Choctaw (1)	3	0.03
Comanche (2)	8	0.07
Creek	2	0.02
Iroquois (3)	3	0.03
Latin American Indians (7)	7	0.06
Lumbee (2)	2	0.02
Navajo (1)	4	0.03
Osage	1	0.01
Pueblo (1)	1	0.01
Seminole	1	0.01
Sioux (3)	11	0.10
All other tribes (11)	13	0.11
American Indian tribes, not spec.	9	0.08
Asian:	377	3.28
Chinese, ex. Taiwanese (6)	17	0.15
Filipino (87)	121	1.05
Indian (27)	32	0.28
Indonesian	3	0.03
Japanese (27)	53	0.46
Korean (38)	55	0.48
Pakistani (3)	5	0.04
Taiwanese	4	0.03
Thai (24)	39	0.34
Vietnamese (31)	38	0.33
Other Asian, specified (1)	2	0.02
Other Asian, not specified (5)	8	0.07
Australian	17	0.15
Austrian	29	0.25
Belgian	6	0.05
British	60	0.52
Canadian	28	0.24
Czech	62	0.54
Czechoslovakian	25	0.22
Danish	56	0.49
Dutch	111	0.96
English	616	5.35
European	97	0.84
French, except Basque	381	3.31
French Canadian	112	0.97
German	1,961	17.04
Greek	35	0.30
Hawaii Native/Pacific Islander:	28	0.24
Micronesian: (8)	9	0.08
Guamanian/Chamorro (8)	9	0.08
Polynesian: (6)	14	0.12
Native Hawaiian (5)	13	0.11
Samoan (1)	1	0.01
Other Pac. Isl., not spec.	5	0.04
Hispanic or Latino:	3,388	29.44
Central American:	33	0.29
Costa Rican	1	0.01
Guatemalan	2	0.02
Panamanian	22	0.19
Salvadoran	6	0.05
Other Central American	2	0.02
Cuban	7	0.06
Mexican	2,378	20.66
Puerto Rican	128	1.11
South American:	16	0.14
Argentinean	1	0.01
Bolivian	6	0.05
Chilean	1	0.01
Colombian	5	0.04
Ecuadorian	1	0.01
Peruvian	2	0.02
Other Hispanic or Latino	826	7.18
Hungarian	13	0.11
Irish	976	8.48
Israeli	7	0.06
Italian	444	3.86
Northern European	9	0.08
Norwegian	61	0.53
Polish	296	2.57
Russian	26	0.23
Scotch-Irish	108	0.94
Scottish	238	2.07
Slavic	11	0.10
Slovak	22	0.19
Swedish	34	0.30
Ukrainian	13	0.11
United States or American	793	6.89
Welsh	44	0.38
West Indian, excl. Hispanic:	23	0.20
Dutch West Indian	7	0.06
Trinidadian and Tobagonian	16	0.14
White:	8,368	72.71
Not Hispanic (6,089)	6,290	54.66
Hispanic (1,896)	2,078	18.06

Coppell

Place Type: City
County: Dallas
Population: 35,958

Ancestry/Race	Number	%
Acadian/Cajun	9	0.03
African American/Black:	1,278	3.55
Not Hispanic (1,161)	1,241	3.45
Hispanic (13)	37	0.10
African, sub-Saharan:	179	0.50
African	29	0.08
Nigerian	144	0.40
South African	6	0.02
Alaska Native tribes, specified:	1	0.00
Eskimo	1	0.00
Am. Ind. or Alaska Nat., not spec.	75	0.21
Albanian	4	0.01
American Indian tribes, specified:	164	0.46
Apache	1	0.00
Blackfeet (2)	3	0.01
Cherokee (27)	59	0.16
Cheyenne (1)	1	0.00
Chickasaw (3)	10	0.03
Chippewa (1)	2	0.01
Choctaw (20)	34	0.09
Comanche (4)	6	0.02
Creek (2)	6	0.02
Delaware (1)	1	0.00
Iroquois	6	0.02
Kiowa	2	0.01
Latin American Indians (1)	7	0.02
Navajo (4)	4	0.01
Osage (3)	8	0.02
Pueblo (1)	2	0.01
Seminole	3	0.01
Sioux	1	0.00
All other tribes (4)	8	0.02
American Indian tribes, not spec.	13	0.04
Arab:	233	0.65
Arab/Arabic	15	0.04
Egyptian	34	0.09
Jordanian	8	0.02
Lebanese	151	0.42
Syrian	17	0.05
Other Arab	8	0.02
Armenian	14	0.04
Asian:	3,754	10.44
Bangladeshi (9)	13	0.04
Cambodian (52)	62	0.17
Chinese, ex. Taiwanese (529)	603	1.68
Filipino (82)	146	0.41
Indian (1,213)	1,281	3.56
Indonesian (16)	20	0.06
Japanese (214)	274	0.76
Korean (776)	802	2.23
Laotian (3)	3	0.01
Malaysian (1)	2	0.01
Pakistani (70)	106	0.29
Sri Lankan (26)	33	0.09
Taiwanese (19)	24	0.07
Thai (33)	37	0.10
Vietnamese (237)	255	0.71
Other Asian, specified	7	0.02
Other Asian, not specified (21)	86	0.24
Australian	38	0.11
Austrian	70	0.19
Belgian	19	0.05
Brazilian	23	0.06
British	223	0.62
Canadian	133	0.37
Celtic	4	0.01
Croatian	15	0.04
Czech	224	0.62
Czechoslovakian	77	0.21
Danish	115	0.32
Dutch	542	1.51
Eastern European	29	0.08
English	4,503	12.52
Estonian	10	0.03
European	356	0.99
Finnish	276	0.77
French, except Basque	944	2.63
French Canadian	164	0.46
German	5,983	16.64
Greek	127	0.35
Hawaii Native/Pacific Islander:	44	0.12
Micronesian: (6)	6	0.02
Guamanian/Chamorro (4)	4	0.01
Other Micronesian (2)	2	0.01
Polynesian: (2)	12	0.03
Native Hawaiian (2)	11	0.03
Tongan	1	0.00
Other Pac. Isl., not spec.	26	0.07
Hispanic or Latino:	2,490	6.92
Central American:	96	0.27
Costa Rican	17	0.05
Guatemalan	21	0.06
Honduran	4	0.01
Nicaraguan	10	0.03
Panamanian	9	0.03
Salvadoran	32	0.09
Other Central American	3	0.01
Cuban	110	0.31
Dominican Republic	12	0.03
Mexican	1,605	4.46
Puerto Rican	101	0.28
South American:	114	0.32
Argentinean	8	0.02
Bolivian	1	0.00
Chilean	13	0.04
Colombian	36	0.10
Ecuadorian	7	0.02
Paraguayan	1	0.00
Peruvian	22	0.06
Uruguayan	1	0.00
Venezuelan	21	0.06
Other South American	4	0.01
Other Hispanic or Latino	452	1.26
Hungarian	97	0.27
Iranian	137	0.38
Irish	4,359	12.12
Israeli	8	0.02
Italian	1,588	4.42
Latvian	20	0.06
Lithuanian	19	0.05
Northern European	147	0.41
Norwegian	695	1.93

Notes: 1. Figures in the "Number" column do not add up to the total population due to: a) Ancestry/Race overlap — e.g. persons can report being both White and Irish, b) persons of Hispanic origin can report being any race, c) persons reporting two ancestries are counted in both categories. 2. Numbers in parentheses indicate the number of persons reporting this ancestry/race alone, not in combination with any other ancestry/race. 3. Refer to the Explanation of Data in the front of the book for more detailed information.

Pennsylvania German	17	0.05
Polish	800	2.23
Portuguese	82	0.23
Romanian	43	0.12
Russian	221	0.61
Scandinavian	80	0.22
Scotch-Irish	990	2.75
Scottish	1,122	3.12
Slavic	9	0.03
Slovak	25	0.07
Slovene	23	0.06
Swedish	555	1.54
Swiss	139	0.39
Turkish	10	0.03
Ukrainian	55	0.15
United States or American	2,855	7.94
Welsh	262	0.73
West Indian, excl. Hispanic:	15	0.04
British West Indian	15	0.04
White:	30,464	84.72
Not Hispanic (28,285)	28,691	79.79
Hispanic (1,644)	1,773	4.93
Yugoslavian	8	0.02

Copperas Cove

Place Type: City
County: Coryell
Population: 29,592

Ancestry/Race	Number	%
Acadian/Cajun	18	0.06
African American/Black:	6,613	22.35
Not Hispanic (5,875)	6,348	21.45
Hispanic (172)	265	0.90
African, sub-Saharan:	215	0.72
African	200	0.67
Ethiopian	15	0.05
Alaska Native tribes, specified:	3	0.01
Alaska Athabascan	1	0.00
Eskimo (1)	1	0.00
Tlingit-Haida (1)	1	0.00
Am. Ind. or Alaska Nat., not spec.	129	0.44
American Indian tribes, specified:	385	1.30
Apache (5)	9	0.03
Blackfeet (3)	21	0.07
Cherokee (60)	153	0.52
Cheyenne (1)	1	0.00
Chickasaw (6)	6	0.02
Chippewa (1)	1	0.00
Choctaw (6)	26	0.09
Comanche (4)	6	0.02
Cree	3	0.01
Creek (7)	7	0.02
Crow	1	0.00
Houma (1)	1	0.00
Iroquois (8)	12	0.04
Kiowa (8)	8	0.03
Latin American Indians (23)	35	0.12
Lumbee (5)	10	0.03
Menominee (3)	5	0.02
Navajo (5)	14	0.05
Osage	2	0.01
Ottawa (3)	3	0.01
Potawatomi (6)	7	0.02
Pueblo (5)	13	0.04
Puget Sound Salish (1)	3	0.01
Seminole (1)	4	0.01
Sioux (9)	14	0.05
Yaqui	2	0.01
All other tribes (7)	18	0.06
American Indian tribes, not spec.	28	0.09
Arab:	61	0.20
Arab/Arabic	47	0.16
Lebanese	9	0.03
Palestinian	5	0.02
Asian:	1,312	4.43
Cambodian (7)	7	0.02
Chinese, ex. Taiwanese (43)	92	0.31
Filipino (170)	290	0.98
Hmong (1)	1	0.00
Indian (29)	49	0.17
Indonesian (2)	2	0.01
Japanese (76)	154	0.52
Korean (339)	521	1.76
Laotian (2)	2	0.01
Pakistani (4)	4	0.01
Sri Lankan	1	0.00
Taiwanese	1	0.00
Thai (37)	66	0.22
Vietnamese (46)	73	0.25
Other Asian, specified (1)	2	0.01
Other Asian, not specified (21)	47	0.16
Austrian	38	0.13
Basque	5	0.02
Belgian	54	0.18
Brazilian	8	0.03
British	89	0.30
Bulgarian	12	0.04
Canadian	39	0.13
Croatian	13	0.04
Czech	97	0.32
Czechoslovakian	32	0.11
Danish	96	0.32
Dutch	358	1.19
English	1,932	6.44
European	321	1.07
Finnish	25	0.08
French, except Basque	762	2.54
French Canadian	300	1.00
German	5,459	18.20
German Russian	17	0.06
Greek	51	0.17
Guyanese	14	0.05
Hawaii Native/Pacific Islander:	286	0.97
Micronesian: (46)	76	0.26
Guamanian/Chamorro (44)	72	0.24
Other Micronesian (2)	4	0.01
Polynesian: (117)	177	0.60
Native Hawaiian (27)	70	0.24
Samoan (88)	103	0.35
Tongan (2)	4	0.01
Other Pac. Isl., not spec. (7)	33	0.11
Hispanic or Latino:	3,460	11.69
Central American:	197	0.67
Costa Rican	4	0.01
Guatemalan	2	0.01
Honduran	22	0.07
Nicaraguan	8	0.03
Panamanian	131	0.44
Salvadoran	26	0.09
Other Central American	4	0.01
Cuban	53	0.18
Dominican Republic	32	0.11
Mexican	1,737	5.87
Puerto Rican	809	2.73
South American:	52	0.18
Argentinean	5	0.02
Chilean	2	0.01
Colombian	18	0.06
Ecuadorian	8	0.03
Peruvian	13	0.04
Venezuelan	6	0.02
Other Hispanic or Latino	580	1.96
Hungarian	129	0.43
Icelander	30	0.10
Iranian	9	0.03
Irish	3,048	10.16
Israeli	10	0.03
Italian	943	3.14
Lithuanian	7	0.02
Norwegian	584	1.95
Pennsylvania German	5	0.02
Polish	469	1.56
Portuguese	10	0.03
Russian	71	0.24
Scotch-Irish	448	1.49
Scottish	494	1.65
Slovak	15	0.05
Slovene	16	0.05
Swedish	244	0.81
Swiss	94	0.31
Turkish	26	0.09
Ukrainian	21	0.07
United States or American	2,485	8.28
Welsh	136	0.45
West Indian, excl. Hispanic:	192	0.64
Belizean	11	0.04
British West Indian	42	0.14
Dutch West Indian	10	0.03
Jamaican	71	0.24
Trinidadian and Tobagonian	13	0.04
West Indian	45	0.15
White:	20,546	69.43
Not Hispanic (17,946)	18,847	63.69
Hispanic (1,394)	1,699	5.74
Yugoslavian	36	0.12

Corinth

Place Type: City
County: Denton
Population: 11,325

Ancestry/Race	Number	%
African American/Black:	523	4.62
Not Hispanic (472)	514	4.54
Hispanic (3)	9	0.08
African, sub-Saharan:	13	0.11
African	13	0.11
Am. Ind. or Alaska Nat., not spec.	19	0.17
Albanian	2	0.02
American Indian tribes, specified:	116	1.02
Apache	1	0.01
Blackfeet (3)	3	0.03
Cherokee (19)	42	0.37
Chickasaw (2)	5	0.04
Chippewa (1)	2	0.02
Choctaw (20)	31	0.27
Comanche (2)	3	0.03
Creek (4)	7	0.06
Crow	2	0.02
Pueblo (3)	3	0.03
Seminole (1)	6	0.05
Sioux (1)	1	0.01
All other tribes (6)	10	0.09
American Indian tribes, not spec.	10	0.09
Asian:	331	2.92
Cambodian (9)	9	0.08
Chinese, ex. Taiwanese (42)	45	0.40
Filipino (35)	50	0.44
Indian (65)	71	0.63
Japanese (12)	25	0.22
Korean (30)	35	0.31
Laotian (5)	5	0.04
Pakistani (48)	60	0.53
Taiwanese (2)	2	0.02
Thai (9)	10	0.09
Vietnamese (10)	10	0.09
Other Asian, specified	4	0.04
Other Asian, not specified (2)	5	0.04
Assyrian/Chaldean/Syriac	10	0.09
Austrian	21	0.18
British	38	0.33
Canadian	23	0.20
Celtic	5	0.04
Croatian	41	0.36
Czech	45	0.39
Czechoslovakian	27	0.24
Danish	90	0.79
Dutch	159	1.39
English	1,356	11.87
European	155	1.36
Finnish	63	0.55
French, except Basque	263	2.30
French Canadian	124	1.09
German	1,738	15.21
Greek	49	0.43
Guyanese	8	0.07
Hawaii Native/Pacific Islander:	22	0.19

Notes: 1. Figures in the "Number" column do not add up to the total population due to: a) Ancestry/Race overlap — e.g. persons can report being both White and Irish, b) persons of Hispanic origin can report being any race, c) persons reporting two ancestries are counted in both categories. 2. Numbers in parentheses indicate the number of persons reporting this ancestry/race alone, not in combination with any other ancestry/race. 3. Refer to the Explanation of Data in the front of the book for more detailed information.

Ancestry/Race	Number	%
Micronesian: (1)	3	0.03
Guamanian/Chamorro (1)	3	0.03
Polynesian: (5)	11	0.10
Native Hawaiian (2)	4	0.04
Samoan (3)	7	0.06
Other Pac. Isl., not spec.	8	0.07
Hispanic or Latino:	690	6.09
Central American:	25	0.22
Costa Rican	3	0.03
Guatemalan	1	0.01
Honduran	1	0.01
Nicaraguan	3	0.03
Panamanian	1	0.01
Salvadoran	16	0.14
Cuban	21	0.19
Dominican Republic	1	0.01
Mexican	452	3.99
Puerto Rican	46	0.41
South American:	17	0.15
Argentinean	2	0.02
Chilean	1	0.01
Colombian	4	0.04
Peruvian	1	0.01
Uruguayan	1	0.01
Venezuelan	7	0.06
Other South American	1	0.01
Other Hispanic or Latino	128	1.13
Hungarian	70	0.61
Icelander	14	0.12
Irish	1,511	13.23
Italian	509	4.46
Lithuanian	12	0.11
Northern European	12	0.11
Norwegian	199	1.74
Polish	193	1.69
Portuguese	28	0.25
Russian	37	0.32
Scandinavian	8	0.07
Scotch-Irish	158	1.38
Scottish	302	2.64
Slovak	16	0.14
Swedish	229	2.00
Swiss	37	0.32
Ukrainian	13	0.11
United States or American	1,330	11.64
Welsh	100	0.88
West Indian, excl. Hispanic:	30	0.26
Dutch West Indian	8	0.07
West Indian	11	0.10
Other West Indian	11	0.10
White:	10,223	90.27
Not Hispanic (9,649)	9,800	86.53
Hispanic (382)	423	3.74

Corpus Christi

Place Type: City
County: Nueces
Population: 277,454

Ancestry/Race	Number	%
Acadian/Cajun	107	0.04
African American/Black:	14,095	5.08
Not Hispanic (12,404)	13,056	4.71
Hispanic (565)	1,039	0.37
African, sub-Saharan:	510	0.18
African	429	0.15
Nigerian	81	0.03
Alaska Native tribes, specified:	15	0.01
Alaska Athabascan	2	0.00
Aleut	2	0.00
Eskimo (2)	3	0.00
Tlingit-Haida (7)	8	0.00
Alaska Native tribes, not specified	5	0.00
Am. Ind. or Alaska Nat., not spec.	1,229	0.44
Alsatian	8	0.00
American Indian tribes, specified:	1,749	0.63
Apache (58)	162	0.06
Blackfeet (13)	40	0.01
Cherokee (190)	578	0.21
Cheyenne (4)	8	0.00
Chickasaw (12)	28	0.01
Chippewa (32)	44	0.02
Choctaw (56)	122	0.04
Comanche (28)	51	0.02
Creek (29)	63	0.02
Crow (2)	3	0.00
Delaware (7)	12	0.00
Houma (3)	4	0.00
Iroquois (13)	27	0.01
Kiowa (3)	6	0.00
Latin American Indians (183)	282	0.10
Lumbee (5)	7	0.00
Navajo (32)	48	0.02
Osage (9)	14	0.01
Ottawa (1)	2	0.00
Paiute (2)	3	0.00
Pima (4)	9	0.00
Potawatomi (13)	18	0.01
Pueblo (4)	12	0.00
Puget Sound Salish (2)	11	0.00
Seminole (6)	24	0.01
Shoshone	5	0.00
Sioux (46)	73	0.03
Tohono O'Odham	1	0.00
Ute	1	0.00
Yaqui (6)	12	0.00
All other tribes (39)	79	0.03
American Indian tribes, not spec.	215	0.08
Arab:	507	0.18
Arab/Arabic	77	0.03
Egyptian	41	0.01
Lebanese	283	0.10
Moroccan	7	0.00
Palestinian	6	0.00
Syrian	53	0.02
Other Arab	40	0.01
Armenian	19	0.01
Asian:	4,705	1.70
Bangladeshi (2)	2	0.00
Cambodian (4)	9	0.00
Chinese, ex. Taiwanese (330)	447	0.16
Filipino (1,477)	1,931	0.70
Hmong (4)	5	0.00
Indian (628)	707	0.25
Indonesian (6)	23	0.01
Japanese (164)	332	0.12
Korean (329)	418	0.15
Laotian (46)	52	0.02
Malaysian (1)	3	0.00
Pakistani (44)	64	0.02
Sri Lankan (5)	5	0.00
Taiwanese (8)	14	0.01
Thai (84)	117	0.04
Vietnamese (278)	341	0.12
Other Asian, specified (6)	27	0.01
Other Asian, not specified (81)	208	0.07
Australian	81	0.03
Austrian	352	0.13
Basque	26	0.01
Belgian	91	0.03
Brazilian	93	0.03
British	574	0.21
Bulgarian	78	0.03
Canadian	426	0.15
Celtic	77	0.03
Croatian	118	0.04
Czech	2,337	0.84
Czechoslovakian	660	0.24
Danish	498	0.18
Dutch	2,120	0.76
Eastern European	40	0.01
English	15,884	5.72
Estonian	8	0.00
European	1,287	0.46
Finnish	144	0.05
French, except Basque	5,327	1.92
French Canadian	976	0.35
German	24,611	8.87
Greek	507	0.18
Hawaii Native/Pacific Islander:	450	0.16
Micronesian: (62)	84	0.03
Guamanian/Chamorro (51)	69	0.02
Other Micronesian (11)	15	0.01
Polynesian: (81)	185	0.07
Native Hawaiian (53)	145	0.05
Samoan (28)	39	0.01
Other Polynesian	1	0.00
Other Pac. Isl., specified	17	0.01
Other Pac. Isl., not spec. (66)	164	0.06
Hispanic or Latino:	150,737	54.33
Central American:	427	0.15
Costa Rican	20	0.01
Guatemalan	69	0.02
Honduran	96	0.03
Nicaraguan	36	0.01
Panamanian	79	0.03
Salvadoran	98	0.04
Other Central American	29	0.01
Cuban	334	0.12
Dominican Republic	42	0.02
Mexican	98,146	35.37
Puerto Rican	745	0.27
South American:	410	0.15
Argentinean	41	0.01
Bolivian	13	0.00
Chilean	51	0.02
Colombian	144	0.05
Ecuadorian	10	0.00
Paraguayan	1	0.00
Peruvian	52	0.02
Uruguayan	5	0.00
Venezuelan	74	0.03
Other South American	19	0.01
Other Hispanic or Latino	50,633	18.25
Hungarian	325	0.12
Iranian	100	0.04
Irish	17,977	6.48
Israeli	17	0.01
Italian	3,932	1.42
Latvian	11	0.00
Lithuanian	85	0.03
Luxemburger	9	0.00
Maltese	11	0.00
New Zealander	20	0.01
Northern European	80	0.03
Norwegian	1,394	0.50
Pennsylvania German	26	0.01
Polish	2,522	0.91
Portuguese	130	0.05
Romanian	77	0.03
Russian	397	0.14
Scandinavian	135	0.05
Scotch-Irish	4,365	1.57
Scottish	3,072	1.11
Serbian	16	0.01
Slavic	61	0.02
Slovak	81	0.03
Slovene	69	0.02
Swedish	1,309	0.47
Swiss	300	0.11
Turkish	26	0.01
Ukrainian	152	0.05
United States or American	11,641	4.19
Welsh	845	0.30
West Indian, excl. Hispanic:	393	0.14
Bahamian	13	0.00
Barbadian	20	0.01
Belizean	23	0.01
Bermudan	31	0.01
British West Indian	7	0.00
Dutch West Indian	107	0.04
Haitian	7	0.00
Jamaican	163	0.06
Trinidadian and Tobagonian	11	0.00
West Indian	11	0.00
White:	206,308	74.36
Not Hispanic (106,901)	109,251	39.38
Hispanic (91,813)	97,057	34.98
Yugoslavian	39	0.01

Notes: 1. Figures in the "Number" column do not add up to the total population due to: a) Ancestry/Race overlap — e.g. persons can report being both White and Irish, b) persons of Hispanic origin can report being any race, c) persons reporting two ancestries are counted in both categories. 2. Numbers in parentheses indicate the number of persons reporting this ancestry/race alone, not in combination with any other ancestry/race. 3. Refer to the Explanation of Data in the front of the book for more detailed information.

Corsicana

Place Type: City
County: Navarro
Population: 24,485

Ancestry/Race	Number	%
African American/Black:	5,913	24.15
Not Hispanic (5,727)	5,823	23.78
Hispanic (48)	90	0.37
African, sub-Saharan:	501	2.05
African	465	1.90
Other sub-Saharan African	36	0.15
Am. Ind. or Alaska Nat., not spec.	78	0.32
American Indian tribes, specified:	110	0.45
Apache (4)	5	0.02
Blackfeet (1)	3	0.01
Cherokee (15)	43	0.18
Cheyenne	1	0.00
Choctaw (6)	11	0.04
Comanche (2)	4	0.02
Creek (1)	1	0.00
Kiowa (1)	1	0.00
Latin American Indians (31)	32	0.13
Osage	1	0.00
Potawatomi	1	0.00
Seminole	2	0.01
Tohono O'Odham	2	0.01
All other tribes (3)	3	0.01
American Indian tribes, not spec.	18	0.07
Arab:	74	0.30
Egyptian	48	0.20
Lebanese	23	0.09
Moroccan	3	0.01
Asian:	204	0.83
Chinese, ex. Taiwanese (25)	27	0.11
Filipino (44)	52	0.21
Indian (49)	54	0.22
Indonesian (1)	1	0.00
Japanese (14)	20	0.08
Korean (5)	10	0.04
Pakistani (1)	2	0.01
Thai	1	0.00
Vietnamese (10)	12	0.05
Other Asian, specified (2)	3	0.01
Other Asian, not specified (2)	22	0.09
Austrian	13	0.05
British	24	0.10
Canadian	11	0.05
Celtic	4	0.02
Czech	105	0.43
Czechoslovakian	22	0.09
Danish	46	0.19
Dutch	169	0.69
English	1,497	6.13
European	22	0.09
French, except Basque	320	1.31
French Canadian	23	0.09
German	952	3.90
Greek	6	0.02
Hawaii Native/Pacific Islander:	143	0.58
Micronesian: (67)	75	0.31
Other Micronesian (67)	75	0.31
Polynesian: (12)	22	0.09
Native Hawaiian (11)	20	0.08
Samoan (1)	2	0.01
Other Pac. Isl., specified	1	0.00
Other Pac. Isl., not spec. (34)	45	0.18
Hispanic or Latino:	5,502	22.47
Central American:	38	0.16
Guatemalan	3	0.01
Honduran	1	0.00
Panamanian	8	0.03
Salvadoran	19	0.08
Other Central American	7	0.03
Cuban	14	0.06
Mexican	4,810	19.64
Puerto Rican	28	0.11
South American:	9	0.04
Argentinean	1	0.00
Colombian	3	0.01
Peruvian	3	0.01
Venezuelan	2	0.01
Other Hispanic or Latino	603	2.46
Hungarian	17	0.07
Iranian	5	0.02
Irish	1,614	6.61
Italian	260	1.06
Lithuanian	13	0.05
Northern European	8	0.03
Norwegian	43	0.18
Polish	114	0.47
Portuguese	8	0.03
Romanian	3	0.01
Russian	14	0.06
Scandinavian	36	0.15
Scotch-Irish	381	1.56
Scottish	213	0.87
Slovak	15	0.06
Swedish	39	0.16
Swiss	23	0.09
Ukrainian	7	0.03
United States or American	3,086	12.64
Welsh	41	0.17
West Indian, excl. Hispanic:	77	0.32
British West Indian	25	0.10
Dutch West Indian	2	0.01
Haitian	16	0.07
Trinidadian and Tobagonian	34	0.14
White:	14,872	60.74
Not Hispanic (12,687)	12,865	52.54
Hispanic (1,828)	2,007	8.20

Dallas

Place Type: City
County: Dallas
Population: 1,188,580

Ancestry/Race	Number	%
Acadian/Cajun	221	0.02
Afghan	83	0.01
African American/Black:	314,678	26.48
Not Hispanic (304,824)	310,185	26.10
Hispanic (3,133)	4,493	0.38
African, sub-Saharan:	18,242	1.54
African	10,470	0.88
Cape Verdean	71	0.01
Ethiopian	3,006	0.25
Ghanian	172	0.01
Kenyan	361	0.03
Liberian	14	0.00
Nigerian	2,365	0.20
Sierra Leonean	264	0.02
Somalian	167	0.01
South African	680	0.06
Sudanese	116	0.01
Ugandan	34	0.00
Zairian	52	0.00
Zimbabwean	222	0.02
Other sub-Saharan African	248	0.02
Alaska Native tribes, specified:	48	0.00
Alaska Athabascan (5)	6	0.00
Aleut (5)	7	0.00
Eskimo (10)	16	0.00
Tlingit-Haida (6)	16	0.00
All other tribes	3	0.00
Alaska Native tribes, not specified	14	0.00
Am. Ind. or Alaska Nat., not spec.	4,171	0.35
Albanian	202	0.02
Alsatian	125	0.01
American Indian tribes, specified:	6,578	0.55
Apache (90)	192	0.02
Blackfeet (35)	127	0.01
Cherokee (658)	1,889	0.16
Cheyenne (18)	43	0.00
Chickasaw (131)	236	0.02
Chippewa (34)	55	0.00
Choctaw (700)	1,112	0.09
Colville (2)	2	0.00
Comanche (73)	144	0.01
Cree (2)	5	0.00
Creek (134)	248	0.02
Crow (4)	11	0.00
Delaware (21)	35	0.00
Houma (6)	9	0.00
Iroquois (23)	54	0.00
Kiowa (53)	95	0.01
Latin American Indians (851)	1,219	0.10
Lumbee (8)	9	0.00
Navajo (136)	189	0.02
Osage (27)	53	0.00
Ottawa (6)	8	0.00
Paiute (2)	2	0.00
Potawatomi (47)	81	0.01
Pueblo (49)	73	0.01
Puget Sound Salish	3	0.00
Seminole (37)	79	0.01
Shoshone (7)	13	0.00
Sioux (108)	168	0.01
Tohono O'Odham (16)	17	0.00
Ute (1)	3	0.00
Yakama (4)	5	0.00
Yaqui	6	0.00
Yuman (10)	10	0.00
All other tribes (232)	383	0.03
American Indian tribes, not spec.	797	0.07
Arab:	4,137	0.35
Arab/Arabic	824	0.07
Egyptian	218	0.02
Iraqi	168	0.01
Jordanian	379	0.03
Lebanese	1,341	0.11
Moroccan	239	0.02
Palestinian	149	0.01
Syrian	382	0.03
Other Arab	437	0.04
Armenian	311	0.03
Asian:	37,458	3.15
Bangladeshi (236)	325	0.03
Cambodian (853)	968	0.08
Chinese, ex. Taiwanese (5,459)	6,114	0.51
Filipino (2,037)	2,680	0.23
Hmong (13)	14	0.00
Indian (7,675)	8,625	0.73
Indonesian (154)	176	0.01
Japanese (835)	1,307	0.11
Korean (3,209)	3,578	0.30
Laotian (986)	1,169	0.10
Malaysian (68)	96	0.01
Pakistani (841)	1,062	0.09
Sri Lankan (47)	59	0.00
Taiwanese (303)	407	0.03
Thai (522)	656	0.06
Vietnamese (7,584)	8,084	0.68
Other Asian, specified (104)	219	0.02
Other Asian, not specified (618)	1,919	0.16
Australian	312	0.03
Austrian	1,599	0.13
Basque	102	0.01
Belgian	528	0.04
Brazilian	451	0.04
British	4,278	0.36
Bulgarian	219	0.02
Canadian	1,377	0.12
Carpatho Rusyn	27	0.00
Celtic	267	0.02
Croatian	479	0.04
Czech	3,598	0.30
Czechoslovakian	1,285	0.11
Danish	2,205	0.19
Dutch	7,159	0.60
Eastern European	879	0.07
English	68,355	5.75
Estonian	36	0.00
European	5,739	0.48
Finnish	527	0.04
French, except Basque	18,072	1.52
French Canadian	2,527	0.21
German	73,062	6.15

Notes: 1. Figures in the "Number" column do not add up to the total population due to: a) Ancestry/Race overlap — e.g. persons can report being both White and Irish, b) persons of Hispanic origin can report being any race, c) persons reporting two ancestries are counted in both categories. 2. Numbers in parentheses indicate the number of persons reporting this ancestry/race alone, not in combination with any other ancestry/race. 3. Refer to the Explanation of Data in the front of the book for more detailed information.

Ancestry/Race	Number	%
German Russian	27	0.00
Greek	2,119	0.18
Guyanese	64	0.01
Hawaii Native/Pacific Islander:	1,483	0.12
Melanesian: (13)	17	0.00
Fijian (13)	16	0.00
Other Melanesian	1	0.00
Micronesian: (166)	217	0.02
Guamanian/Chamorro (156)	201	0.02
Other Micronesian (10)	16	0.00
Polynesian: (265)	511	0.04
Native Hawaiian (123)	295	0.02
Samoan (134)	192	0.02
Tongan (2)	5	0.00
Other Polynesian (6)	19	0.00
Other Pac. Isl., specified	95	0.01
Other Pac. Isl., not spec. (143)	643	0.05
Hispanic or Latino:	422,587	35.55
Central American:	14,972	1.26
Costa Rican	418	0.04
Guatemalan	1,950	0.16
Honduran	2,637	0.22
Nicaraguan	407	0.03
Panamanian	319	0.03
Salvadoran	8,582	0.72
Other Central American	659	0.06
Cuban	2,283	0.19
Dominican Republic	219	0.02
Mexican	350,491	29.49
Puerto Rican	2,369	0.20
South American:	2,895	0.24
Argentinean	222	0.02
Bolivian	119	0.01
Chilean	170	0.01
Colombian	862	0.07
Ecuadorian	229	0.02
Paraguayan	15	0.00
Peruvian	853	0.07
Uruguayan	22	0.00
Venezuelan	275	0.02
Other South American	128	0.01
Other Hispanic or Latino	49,358	4.15
Hungarian	1,703	0.14
Icelander	71	0.01
Iranian	1,994	0.17
Irish	58,746	4.94
Israeli	736	0.06
Italian	16,058	1.35
Latvian	111	0.01
Lithuanian	867	0.07
Luxemburger	12	0.00
Macedonian	6	0.00
Maltese	57	0.00
New Zealander	57	0.00
Northern European	559	0.05
Norwegian	5,596	0.47
Pennsylvania German	124	0.01
Polish	9,642	0.81
Portuguese	600	0.05
Romanian	954	0.08
Russian	6,152	0.52
Scandinavian	662	0.06
Scotch-Irish	16,308	1.37
Scottish	14,482	1.22
Serbian	216	0.02
Slavic	211	0.02
Slovak	437	0.04
Slovene	129	0.01
Swedish	6,748	0.57
Swiss	1,803	0.15
Turkish	300	0.03
Ukrainian	923	0.08
United States or American	48,183	4.06
Welsh	4,060	0.34
West Indian, excl. Hispanic:	1,837	0.15
Barbadian	49	0.00
Belizean	152	0.01
British West Indian	73	0.01
Dutch West Indian	234	0.02
Haitian	73	0.01
Jamaican	865	0.07
Trinidadian and Tobagonian	95	0.01
U.S. Virgin Islander	20	0.00
West Indian	270	0.02
Other West Indian	6	0.00
White:	630,419	53.04
Not Hispanic (410,777)	420,044	35.34
Hispanic (193,432)	210,375	17.70
Yugoslavian	1,618	0.14

De Soto

Place Type: City
County: Dallas
Population: 37,646

Ancestry/Race	Number	%
Acadian/Cajun	5	0.01
African American/Black:	17,350	46.09
Not Hispanic (17,067)	17,242	45.80
Hispanic (75)	108	0.29
African, sub-Saharan:	641	1.70
African	548	1.46
Cape Verdean	21	0.06
Nigerian	72	0.19
Am. Ind. or Alaska Nat., not spec.	76	0.20
American Indian tribes, specified:	179	0.48
Apache (1)	3	0.01
Blackfeet	4	0.01
Cherokee (27)	74	0.20
Chickasaw (4)	6	0.02
Chippewa (1)	2	0.01
Choctaw (20)	37	0.10
Comanche (1)	3	0.01
Creek (1)	3	0.01
Delaware (1)	4	0.01
Iroquois (1)	1	0.00
Kiowa (7)	7	0.02
Latin American Indians (2)	5	0.01
Navajo (2)	4	0.01
Osage (1)	1	0.00
Pima (1)	1	0.00
Potawatomi (2)	2	0.01
Seminole (1)	1	0.00
Sioux (4)	5	0.01
Yaqui	1	0.00
All other tribes (5)	15	0.04
American Indian tribes, not spec.	18	0.05
Arab:	92	0.24
Egyptian	44	0.12
Moroccan	8	0.02
Palestinian	40	0.11
Armenian	11	0.03
Asian:	594	1.58
Bangladeshi (5)	5	0.01
Chinese, ex. Taiwanese (62)	79	0.21
Filipino (77)	92	0.24
Indian (121)	134	0.36
Indonesian (2)	9	0.02
Japanese (24)	49	0.13
Korean (103)	114	0.30
Laotian (11)	12	0.03
Pakistani (1)	1	0.00
Taiwanese (1)	1	0.00
Thai (3)	5	0.01
Vietnamese (53)	62	0.16
Other Asian, specified (1)	3	0.01
Other Asian, not specified (8)	28	0.07
Australian	18	0.05
Austrian	17	0.05
Belgian	15	0.04
British	132	0.35
Canadian	23	0.06
Croatian	8	0.02
Czech	142	0.38
Czechoslovakian	64	0.17
Danish	74	0.20
Dutch	294	0.78
Eastern European	8	0.02
English	2,757	7.33
European	290	0.77
Finnish	3	0.01
French, except Basque	502	1.33
French Canadian	34	0.09
German	2,898	7.70
Greek	32	0.09
Hawaii Native/Pacific Islander:	38	0.10
Micronesian: (1)	1	0.00
Guamanian/Chamorro (1)	1	0.00
Polynesian: (5)	20	0.05
Native Hawaiian (4)	15	0.04
Tongan (1)	5	0.01
Other Pac. Isl., specified	1	0.00
Other Pac. Isl., not spec. (7)	16	0.04
Hispanic or Latino:	2,750	7.30
Central American:	81	0.22
Costa Rican	5	0.01
Guatemalan	20	0.05
Honduran	13	0.03
Panamanian	19	0.05
Salvadoran	23	0.06
Other Central American	1	0.00
Cuban	27	0.07
Dominican Republic	3	0.01
Mexican	2,052	5.45
Puerto Rican	65	0.17
South American:	28	0.07
Argentinean	3	0.01
Chilean	1	0.00
Colombian	9	0.02
Ecuadorian	2	0.01
Paraguayan	1	0.00
Peruvian	3	0.01
Venezuelan	3	0.01
Other South American	6	0.02
Other Hispanic or Latino	494	1.31
Hungarian	88	0.23
Irish	2,268	6.03
Italian	457	1.21
Latvian	6	0.02
Lithuanian	30	0.08
Luxemburger	9	0.02
Maltese	7	0.02
Northern European	41	0.11
Norwegian	285	0.76
Pennsylvania German	22	0.06
Polish	210	0.56
Portuguese	11	0.03
Romanian	19	0.05
Russian	39	0.10
Scandinavian	70	0.19
Scotch-Irish	598	1.59
Scottish	507	1.35
Serbian	8	0.02
Slovak	65	0.17
Slovene	6	0.02
Swedish	194	0.52
Swiss	34	0.09
Ukrainian	26	0.07
United States or American	2,271	6.04
Welsh	122	0.32
West Indian, excl. Hispanic:	57	0.15
Jamaican	50	0.13
Trinidadian and Tobagonian	7	0.02
White:	18,791	49.91
Not Hispanic (16,818)	17,103	45.43
Hispanic (1,564)	1,688	4.48
Yugoslavian	39	0.10

Deer Park

Place Type: City
County: Harris
Population: 28,520

Ancestry/Race	Number	%
Acadian/Cajun	26	0.09
African American/Black:	412	1.44
Not Hispanic (360)	386	1.35
Hispanic (14)	26	0.09

Notes: 1. Figures in the "Number" column do not add up to the total population due to: a) Ancestry/Race overlap — e.g. persons can report being both White and Irish, b) persons of Hispanic origin can report being any race, c) persons reporting two ancestries are counted in both categories. 2. Numbers in parentheses indicate the number of persons reporting this ancestry/race alone, not in combination with any other ancestry/race. 3. Refer to the Explanation of Data in the front of the book for more detailed information.

Ancestry/Race	Number	%
African, sub-Saharan:	32	0.11
African	12	0.04
Nigerian	11	0.04
South African	9	0.03
Am. Ind. or Alaska Nat., not spec.	62	0.22
American Indian tribes, specified:	196	0.69
Apache	6	0.02
Blackfeet (1)	11	0.04
Cherokee (20)	68	0.24
Chickasaw (7)	11	0.04
Chippewa	2	0.01
Choctaw (21)	40	0.14
Comanche	1	0.00
Creek (1)	3	0.01
Crow	1	0.00
Delaware	3	0.01
Iroquois (7)	9	0.03
Latin American Indians (5)	5	0.02
Lumbee (2)	2	0.01
Navajo	1	0.00
Osage (2)	3	0.01
Potawatomi (6)	6	0.02
Sioux (8)	12	0.04
Yuman (2)	2	0.01
All other tribes (4)	10	0.04
American Indian tribes, not spec.	9	0.03
Arab:	80	0.28
Egyptian	45	0.16
Lebanese	35	0.12
Asian:	455	1.60
Bangladeshi (1)	1	0.00
Chinese, ex. Taiwanese (15)	36	0.13
Filipino (53)	76	0.27
Indian (61)	80	0.28
Indonesian (1)	2	0.01
Japanese (16)	36	0.13
Korean (64)	77	0.27
Laotian	6	0.02
Pakistani (20)	33	0.12
Thai (5)	5	0.02
Vietnamese (68)	75	0.26
Other Asian, specified	1	0.00
Other Asian, not specified (11)	27	0.09
Australian	10	0.04
Austrian	33	0.12
Basque	15	0.05
Belgian	54	0.19
British	68	0.24
Canadian	15	0.05
Czech	261	0.92
Czechoslovakian	44	0.15
Danish	82	0.29
Dutch	415	1.46
English	2,435	8.58
European	213	0.75
French, except Basque	1,208	4.25
French Canadian	240	0.85
German	4,065	14.32
Greek	53	0.19
Hawaii Native/Pacific Islander:	62	0.22
Micronesian: (9)	16	0.06
Guamanian/Chamorro (9)	16	0.06
Polynesian: (21)	27	0.09
Native Hawaiian (16)	21	0.07
Samoan (5)	6	0.02
Other Pac. Isl., specified	1	0.00
Other Pac. Isl., not spec. (7)	18	0.06
Hispanic or Latino:	4,341	15.22
Central American:	84	0.29
Costa Rican	12	0.04
Guatemalan	4	0.01
Honduran	8	0.03
Nicaraguan	5	0.02
Panamanian	6	0.02
Salvadoran	48	0.17
Other Central American	1	0.00
Cuban	60	0.21
Dominican Republic	1	0.00
Mexican	3,083	10.81
Puerto Rican	89	0.31
South American:	52	0.18
Argentinean	6	0.02
Chilean	3	0.01
Colombian	5	0.02
Ecuadorian	5	0.02
Peruvian	8	0.03
Venezuelan	11	0.04
Other South American	14	0.05
Other Hispanic or Latino	972	3.41
Hungarian	65	0.23
Iranian	12	0.04
Irish	2,943	10.37
Italian	839	2.96
Lithuanian	9	0.03
Northern European	20	0.07
Norwegian	146	0.51
Polish	436	1.54
Portuguese	13	0.05
Russian	22	0.08
Scotch-Irish	731	2.57
Scottish	419	1.48
Serbian	8	0.03
Slovene	23	0.08
Swedish	173	0.61
Swiss	25	0.09
Turkish	5	0.02
Ukrainian	13	0.05
United States or American	3,757	13.23
Welsh	97	0.34
West Indian, excl. Hispanic:	35	0.12
Barbadian	13	0.05
Dutch West Indian	22	0.08
White:	26,127	91.61
Not Hispanic (23,048)	23,321	81.77
Hispanic (2,624)	2,806	9.84

Del Rio

Place Type: City
County: Val Verde
Population: 33,867

Ancestry/Race	Number	%
African American/Black:	470	1.39
Not Hispanic (339)	379	1.12
Hispanic (70)	91	0.27
African, sub-Saharan:	56	0.16
African	13	0.04
Nigerian	43	0.13
Am. Ind. or Alaska Nat., not spec.	142	0.42
American Indian tribes, specified:	176	0.52
Apache (4)	10	0.03
Cherokee (26)	42	0.12
Cheyenne	2	0.01
Chickasaw	1	0.00
Chippewa (4)	4	0.01
Choctaw (3)	14	0.04
Comanche	4	0.01
Creek	1	0.00
Latin American Indians (42)	50	0.15
Navajo (6)	10	0.03
Pueblo	2	0.01
Puget Sound Salish	1	0.00
Seminole (4)	14	0.04
Sioux (2)	6	0.02
All other tribes (12)	15	0.04
American Indian tribes, not spec.	54	0.16
Arab:	34	0.10
Arab/Arabic	7	0.02
Lebanese	27	0.08
Asian:	230	0.68
Chinese, ex. Taiwanese (13)	27	0.08
Filipino (63)	83	0.25
Indian (8)	10	0.03
Japanese (11)	24	0.07
Korean (42)	49	0.14
Thai (8)	10	0.03
Vietnamese (8)	13	0.04
Other Asian, not specified (4)	14	0.04
Australian	11	0.03
British	58	0.17
Canadian	45	0.13
Czech	55	0.16
Danish	17	0.05
Dutch	133	0.39
English	865	2.54
European	15	0.04
Finnish	23	0.07
French, except Basque	193	0.57
French Canadian	176	0.52
German	1,264	3.71
Hawaii Native/Pacific Islander:	34	0.10
Micronesian: (2)	4	0.01
Guamanian/Chamorro (2)	4	0.01
Polynesian: (4)	14	0.04
Native Hawaiian (4)	13	0.04
Other Polynesian	1	0.00
Other Pac. Isl., not spec. (11)	16	0.05
Hispanic or Latino:	27,446	81.04
Central American:	39	0.12
Costa Rican	3	0.01
Guatemalan	9	0.03
Honduran	11	0.03
Nicaraguan	2	0.01
Panamanian	7	0.02
Salvadoran	6	0.02
Other Central American	1	0.00
Cuban	26	0.08
Dominican Republic	2	0.01
Mexican	23,474	69.31
Puerto Rican	76	0.22
South American:	14	0.04
Argentinean	1	0.00
Colombian	2	0.01
Ecuadorian	3	0.01
Peruvian	8	0.02
Other Hispanic or Latino	3,815	11.26
Hungarian	10	0.03
Irish	876	2.57
Italian	268	0.79
Northern European	10	0.03
Norwegian	50	0.15
Polish	76	0.22
Portuguese	12	0.04
Russian	14	0.04
Scotch-Irish	138	0.40
Scottish	115	0.34
Serbian	7	0.02
Swedish	88	0.26
Swiss	19	0.06
United States or American	841	2.47
Welsh	82	0.24
West Indian, excl. Hispanic:	11	0.03
Haitian	11	0.03
White:	26,936	79.53
Not Hispanic (5,648)	5,782	17.07
Hispanic (20,457)	21,154	62.46

Denison

Place Type: City
County: Grayson
Population: 22,773

Ancestry/Race	Number	%
African American/Black:	2,154	9.46
Not Hispanic (1,938)	2,116	9.29
Hispanic (26)	38	0.17
African, sub-Saharan:	80	0.35
African	80	0.35
Alaska Native tribes, specified:	2	0.01
Aleut (1)	1	0.00
Eskimo (1)	1	0.00
Am. Ind. or Alaska Nat., not spec.	153	0.67
American Indian tribes, specified:	623	2.74
Apache (2)	10	0.04
Blackfeet (4)	8	0.04
Cherokee (55)	185	0.81
Cheyenne	2	0.01
Chickasaw (38)	71	0.31

Notes: 1. Figures in the "Number" column do not add up to the total population due to: a) Ancestry/Race overlap — e.g. persons can report being both White and Irish, b) persons of Hispanic origin can report being any race, c) persons reporting two ancestries are counted in both categories. 2. Numbers in parentheses indicate the number of persons reporting this ancestry/race alone, not in combination with any other ancestry/race. 3. Refer to the Explanation of Data in the front of the book for more detailed information.

Chippewa (2)	2	0.01
Choctaw (140)	275	1.21
Comanche (9)	15	0.07
Creek (5)	12	0.05
Crow	1	0.00
Delaware (2)	4	0.02
Iroquois (1)	4	0.02
Kiowa (1)	1	0.00
Latin American Indians	5	0.02
Lumbee (1)	1	0.00
Navajo	1	0.00
Osage (1)	1	0.00
Potawatomi (1)	3	0.01
Pueblo (1)	2	0.01
Seminole (1)	1	0.00
Shoshone	2	0.01
Sioux	1	0.00
All other tribes (7)	16	0.07
American Indian tribes, not spec.	35	0.15
Asian:	142	0.62
Cambodian (2)	2	0.01
Chinese, ex. Taiwanese (11)	14	0.06
Filipino (11)	12	0.05
Indian (38)	46	0.20
Indonesian (4)	4	0.02
Japanese (5)	11	0.05
Korean (11)	14	0.06
Laotian (3)	3	0.01
Pakistani (7)	7	0.03
Thai (5)	6	0.03
Vietnamese (4)	13	0.06
Other Asian, specified	1	0.00
Other Asian, not specified (3)	9	0.04
Austrian	41	0.18
British	44	0.19
Canadian	6	0.03
Croatian	4	0.02
Czech	48	0.21
Czechoslovakian	14	0.06
Danish	23	0.10
Dutch	338	1.49
English	1,817	7.99
European	132	0.58
Finnish	26	0.11
French, except Basque	546	2.40
French Canadian	22	0.10
German	2,352	10.35
Greek	7	0.03
Hawaii Native/Pacific Islander:	31	0.14
Micronesian: (2)	5	0.02
Guamanian/Chamorro	3	0.01
Other Micronesian (2)	2	0.01
Polynesian: (5)	15	0.07
Native Hawaiian (5)	14	0.06
Samoan	1	0.00
Other Pac. Isl., specified	1	0.00
Other Pac. Isl., not spec. (7)	10	0.04
Hispanic or Latino:	1,190	5.23
Central American:	15	0.07
Guatemalan	2	0.01
Honduran	1	0.00
Panamanian	7	0.03
Salvadoran	5	0.02
Cuban	4	0.02
Mexican	870	3.82
Puerto Rican	36	0.16
South American:	9	0.04
Bolivian	1	0.00
Chilean	3	0.01
Colombian	3	0.01
Venezuelan	1	0.00
Other South American	1	0.00
Other Hispanic or Latino	256	1.12
Icelander	6	0.03
Irish	2,564	11.28
Italian	321	1.41
Lithuanian	29	0.13
Norwegian	155	0.68
Polish	59	0.26
Portuguese	28	0.12
Romanian	19	0.08
Russian	38	0.17
Scandinavian	12	0.05
Scotch-Irish	464	2.04
Scottish	145	0.64
Slovak	4	0.02
Swedish	146	0.64
Ukrainian	8	0.04
United States or American	2,973	13.08
Welsh	97	0.43
West Indian, excl. Hispanic:	49	0.22
Dutch West Indian	41	0.18
Haitian	8	0.04
White:	19,744	86.70
Not Hispanic (18,602)	19,138	84.04
Hispanic (532)	606	2.66

Denton

Place Type: City
County: Denton
Population: 80,537

Ancestry/Race	Number	%
Acadian/Cajun	38	0.05
Afghan	15	0.02
African American/Black:	7,758	9.63
Not Hispanic (7,255)	7,593	9.43
Hispanic (89)	165	0.20
African, sub-Saharan:	379	0.47
African	241	0.30
Kenyan	39	0.05
Nigerian	80	0.10
Sierra Leonean	12	0.01
South African	7	0.01
Alaska Native tribes, specified:	11	0.01
Alaska Athabascan (1)	6	0.01
Eskimo (2)	3	0.00
Tlingit-Haida (2)	2	0.00
Alaska Native tribes, not specified	1	0.00
Am. Ind. or Alaska Nat., not spec.	222	0.28
American Indian tribes, specified:	681	0.85
Apache (9)	21	0.03
Blackfeet (7)	13	0.02
Cherokee (94)	254	0.32
Cheyenne	1	0.00
Chickasaw (30)	48	0.06
Chippewa (5)	8	0.01
Choctaw (64)	103	0.13
Comanche (6)	17	0.02
Cree (3)	4	0.00
Creek (11)	17	0.02
Delaware	3	0.00
Iroquois (3)	7	0.01
Kiowa (15)	17	0.02
Latin American Indians (23)	41	0.05
Menominee	2	0.00
Navajo (14)	24	0.03
Osage (5)	7	0.01
Paiute (1)	1	0.00
Potawatomi (4)	5	0.01
Pueblo (6)	11	0.01
Seminole (3)	11	0.01
Shoshone (1)	1	0.00
Sioux (7)	17	0.02
Ute (1)	1	0.00
Yakama	1	0.00
Yaqui (1)	3	0.00
All other tribes (15)	43	0.05
American Indian tribes, not spec.	74	0.09
Arab:	336	0.42
Arab/Arabic	77	0.10
Egyptian	20	0.02
Lebanese	139	0.17
Palestinian	5	0.01
Syrian	30	0.04
Other Arab	65	0.08
Armenian	16	0.02
Asian:	3,196	3.97
Bangladeshi (21)	30	0.04
Cambodian (4)	5	0.01
Chinese, ex. Taiwanese (628)	699	0.87
Filipino (138)	216	0.27
Indian (620)	667	0.83
Indonesian (35)	40	0.05
Japanese (241)	309	0.38
Korean (501)	550	0.68
Laotian (6)	8	0.01
Malaysian (8)	10	0.01
Pakistani (38)	62	0.08
Sri Lankan (4)	4	0.00
Taiwanese (106)	125	0.16
Thai (123)	148	0.18
Vietnamese (152)	169	0.21
Other Asian, specified (18)	32	0.04
Other Asian, not specified (52)	122	0.15
Australian	21	0.03
Austrian	106	0.13
Belgian	16	0.02
Brazilian	22	0.03
British	597	0.74
Canadian	162	0.20
Celtic	88	0.11
Croatian	34	0.04
Czech	578	0.72
Czechoslovakian	160	0.20
Danish	231	0.29
Dutch	984	1.22
Eastern European	8	0.01
English	7,520	9.33
Estonian	27	0.03
European	743	0.92
Finnish	99	0.12
French, except Basque	2,489	3.09
French Canadian	278	0.35
German	10,283	12.76
Greek	109	0.14
Guyanese	8	0.01
Hawaii Native/Pacific Islander:	95	0.12
Micronesian: (16)	21	0.03
Guamanian/Chamorro (16)	21	0.03
Polynesian: (23)	40	0.05
Native Hawaiian (13)	28	0.03
Samoan (3)	5	0.01
Tongan (7)	7	0.01
Other Pac. Isl., specified	12	0.01
Other Pac. Isl., not spec. (4)	22	0.03
Hispanic or Latino:	13,188	16.38
Central American:	436	0.54
Costa Rican	8	0.01
Guatemalan	217	0.27
Honduran	34	0.04
Nicaraguan	20	0.02
Panamanian	11	0.01
Salvadoran	113	0.14
Other Central American	33	0.04
Cuban	74	0.09
Dominican Republic	3	0.00
Mexican	10,331	12.83
Puerto Rican	188	0.23
South American:	226	0.28
Argentinean	15	0.02
Bolivian	11	0.01
Chilean	15	0.02
Colombian	85	0.11
Ecuadorian	20	0.02
Paraguayan	4	0.00
Peruvian	53	0.07
Venezuelan	17	0.02
Other South American	6	0.01
Other Hispanic or Latino	1,930	2.40
Hungarian	116	0.14
Icelander	29	0.04
Iranian	162	0.20
Irish	7,751	9.62
Israeli	44	0.05
Italian	2,090	2.59
Latvian	7	0.01
Lithuanian	38	0.05
Maltese	26	0.03

Notes: 1. Figures in the "Number" column do not add up to the total population due to: a) Ancestry/Race overlap — e.g. persons can report being both White and Irish, b) persons of Hispanic origin can report being any race, c) persons reporting two ancestries are counted in both categories. 2. Numbers in parentheses indicate the number of persons reporting this ancestry/race alone, not in combination with any other ancestry/race. 3. Refer to the Explanation of Data in the front of the book for more detailed information.

New Zealander	5	0.01
Northern European	43	0.05
Norwegian	822	1.02
Pennsylvania German	9	0.01
Polish	1,019	1.26
Portuguese	155	0.19
Romanian	58	0.07
Russian	185	0.23
Scandinavian	73	0.09
Scotch-Irish	1,955	2.43
Scottish	2,130	2.64
Serbian	31	0.04
Slavic	15	0.02
Slovak	124	0.15
Swedish	707	0.88
Swiss	202	0.25
Turkish	50	0.06
Ukrainian	59	0.07
United States or American	6,744	8.37
Welsh	512	0.64
West Indian, excl. Hispanic:	144	0.18
British West Indian	8	0.01
Dutch West Indian	71	0.09
Jamaican	29	0.04
Trinidadian and Tobagonian	36	0.04
White:	62,570	77.69
Not Hispanic (55,585)	56,645	70.33
Hispanic (5,315)	5,925	7.36
Yugoslavian	11	0.01

Dickinson

Place Type: City
County: Galveston
Population: 17,093

Ancestry/Race	Number	%
Acadian/Cajun	11	0.06
African American/Black:	1,883	11.02
Not Hispanic (1,776)	1,844	10.79
Hispanic (22)	39	0.23
African, sub-Saharan:	46	0.27
African	27	0.16
Nigerian	19	0.11
Alaska Native tribes, specified:	3	0.02
Aleut (3)	3	0.02
Am. Ind. or Alaska Nat., not spec.	39	0.23
Albanian	36	0.21
Alsatian	5	0.03
American Indian tribes, specified:	127	0.74
Apache (2)	3	0.02
Blackfeet (1)	1	0.01
Cherokee (27)	43	0.25
Cheyenne (1)	1	0.01
Chickasaw	2	0.01
Choctaw (9)	20	0.12
Creek (2)	2	0.01
Crow	1	0.01
Delaware	7	0.04
Iroquois (1)	1	0.01
Latin American Indians (22)	28	0.16
Lumbee	1	0.01
Navajo	1	0.01
Osage (1)	2	0.01
Potawatomi (1)	1	0.01
Yuman (1)	4	0.02
All other tribes (3)	9	0.05
American Indian tribes, not spec.	13	0.08
Arab:	13	0.08
Arab/Arabic	5	0.03
Syrian	8	0.05
Asian:	263	1.54
Chinese, ex. Taiwanese (31)	37	0.22
Filipino (23)	36	0.21
Indian (25)	31	0.18
Indonesian	3	0.02
Japanese (12)	16	0.09
Korean (7)	10	0.06
Malaysian	3	0.02
Pakistani (11)	12	0.07
Taiwanese	2	0.01
Thai	1	0.01
Vietnamese (92)	99	0.58
Other Asian, not specified (2)	13	0.08
Australian	8	0.05
Austrian	31	0.18
British	57	0.34
Canadian	48	0.28
Celtic	6	0.04
Croatian	7	0.04
Czech	171	1.01
Czechoslovakian	17	0.10
Danish	54	0.32
Dutch	96	0.57
English	1,246	7.35
European	48	0.28
French, except Basque	576	3.40
French Canadian	42	0.25
German	1,901	11.22
Greek	41	0.24
Hawaii Native/Pacific Islander:	15	0.09
Melanesian:	1	0.01
Fijian	1	0.01
Micronesian:	1	0.01
Guamanian/Chamorro	1	0.01
Polynesian:	4	0.02
Native Hawaiian	3	0.02
Samoan	1	0.01
Other Pac. Isl., not spec. (6)	9	0.05
Hispanic or Latino:	4,256	24.90
Central American:	50	0.29
Guatemalan	9	0.05
Honduran	13	0.08
Panamanian	3	0.02
Salvadoran	25	0.15
Cuban	10	0.06
Mexican	3,395	19.86
Puerto Rican	51	0.30
South American:	22	0.13
Argentinean	1	0.01
Chilean	4	0.02
Colombian	5	0.03
Ecuadorian	1	0.01
Peruvian	1	0.01
Venezuelan	10	0.06
Other Hispanic or Latino	728	4.26
Hungarian	6	0.04
Iranian	13	0.08
Irish	1,481	8.74
Italian	699	4.12
Latvian	14	0.08
Lithuanian	10	0.06
Northern European	7	0.04
Norwegian	100	0.59
Polish	143	0.84
Portuguese	32	0.19
Russian	14	0.08
Scandinavian	20	0.12
Scotch-Irish	225	1.33
Scottish	150	0.89
Slavic	17	0.10
Slovak	10	0.06
Swedish	96	0.57
Swiss	11	0.06
United States or American	1,245	7.35
Welsh	60	0.35
West Indian, excl. Hispanic:	65	0.38
Bahamian	8	0.05
Belizean	25	0.15
British West Indian	6	0.04
Dutch West Indian	21	0.12
Jamaican	5	0.03
White:	12,729	74.47
Not Hispanic (10,569)	10,739	62.83
Hispanic (1,798)	1,990	11.64

Donna

Place Type: City
County: Hidalgo
Population: 14,768

Ancestry/Race	Number	%
African American/Black:	58	0.39
Not Hispanic (24)	24	0.16
Hispanic (30)	34	0.23
Am. Ind. or Alaska Nat., not spec.	68	0.46
American Indian tribes, specified:	18	0.12
Apache	3	0.02
Choctaw	1	0.01
Latin American Indians (10)	10	0.07
Navajo (2)	2	0.01
Sioux (2)	2	0.01
American Indian tribes, not spec.	12	0.08
Asian:	29	0.20
Chinese, ex. Taiwanese (1)	1	0.01
Filipino (26)	26	0.18
Indian	1	0.01
Other Asian, not specified	1	0.01
Austrian	17	0.12
British	8	0.05
Czech	16	0.11
Czechoslovakian	32	0.22
Danish	22	0.15
Dutch	44	0.30
English	301	2.06
European	7	0.05
French, except Basque	32	0.22
German	441	3.03
Greek	14	0.10
Hispanic or Latino:	12,886	87.26
Central American:	18	0.12
Costa Rican	1	0.01
Guatemalan	4	0.03
Honduran	8	0.05
Nicaraguan	1	0.01
Salvadoran	1	0.01
Other Central American	3	0.02
Cuban	1	0.01
Mexican	10,596	71.75
Puerto Rican	13	0.09
South American:	7	0.05
Bolivian	5	0.03
Venezuelan	2	0.01
Other Hispanic or Latino	2,251	15.24
Hungarian	8	0.05
Irish	115	0.79
Italian	39	0.27
Luxemburger	8	0.05
Norwegian	88	0.60
Polish	29	0.20
Scotch-Irish	69	0.47
Scottish	57	0.39
Slovene	10	0.07
Swedish	79	0.54
United States or American	228	1.56
Welsh	62	0.43
White:	11,581	78.42
Not Hispanic (1,801)	1,821	12.33
Hispanic (9,432)	9,760	66.09

Dumas

Place Type: City
County: Moore
Population: 13,747

Ancestry/Race	Number	%
African American/Black:	111	0.81
Not Hispanic (75)	81	0.59
Hispanic (24)	30	0.22
Am. Ind. or Alaska Nat., not spec.	50	0.36
American Indian tribes, specified:	116	0.84
Apache (4)	9	0.07
Cherokee (12)	31	0.23
Cheyenne (1)	3	0.02

Notes: 1. Figures in the "Number" column do not add up to the total population due to: a) Ancestry/Race overlap — e.g. persons can report being both White and Irish, b) persons of Hispanic origin can report being any race, c) persons reporting two ancestries are counted in both categories. 2. Numbers in parentheses indicate the number of persons reporting this ancestry/race alone, not in combination with any other ancestry/race. 3. Refer to the Explanation of Data in the front of the book for more detailed information.

Chickasaw (1)	1	0.01
Choctaw (19)	35	0.25
Creek (2)	5	0.04
Delaware (2)	3	0.02
Iroquois	1	0.01
Latin American Indians (2)	3	0.02
Navajo (4)	6	0.04
Osage	3	0.02
Pueblo (3)	3	0.02
Sioux (6)	8	0.06
All other tribes (2)	5	0.04
American Indian tribes, not spec.	12	0.09
Asian:	194	1.41
Filipino (11)	19	0.14
Indian (27)	35	0.25
Japanese (1)	2	0.01
Korean (1)	4	0.03
Laotian (88)	100	0.73
Thai	4	0.03
Vietnamese (19)	21	0.15
Other Asian, not specified (7)	9	0.07
Austrian	8	0.06
British	43	0.31
Celtic	20	0.15
Czech	38	0.28
Czechoslovakian	7	0.05
Danish	16	0.12
Dutch	78	0.57
English	660	4.83
European	12	0.09
Finnish	8	0.06
French, except Basque	136	0.99
German	1,265	9.25
German Russian	10	0.07
Hawaii Native/Pacific Islander:	6	0.04
Micronesian:	2	0.01
Guamanian/Chamorro	2	0.01
Polynesian: (3)	3	0.02
Native Hawaiian (1)	1	0.01
Samoan (2)	2	0.01
Other Pac. Isl., not spec.	1	0.01
Hispanic or Latino:	5,876	42.74
Central American:	15	0.11
Guatemalan	11	0.08
Salvadoran	4	0.03
Cuban	8	0.06
Mexican	4,485	32.63
Puerto Rican	14	0.10
South American:	32	0.23
Chilean	31	0.23
Peruvian	1	0.01
Other Hispanic or Latino	1,322	9.62
Hungarian	13	0.10
Irish	1,014	7.41
Italian	31	0.23
Norwegian	51	0.37
Polish	40	0.29
Scotch-Irish	105	0.77
Scottish	154	1.13
Slovak	25	0.18
Swedish	9	0.07
Swiss	19	0.14
United States or American	1,295	9.47
Welsh	53	0.39
White:	9,689	70.48
Not Hispanic (7,462)	7,544	54.88
Hispanic (1,899)	2,145	15.60

Duncanville

Place Type: City
County: Dallas
Population: 36,081

Ancestry/Race	Number	%
Acadian/Cajun	6	0.02
African American/Black:	9,178	25.44
Not Hispanic (8,837)	9,026	25.02
Hispanic (97)	152	0.42
African, sub-Saharan:	532	1.48
African	468	1.30
Nigerian	64	0.18
Am. Ind. or Alaska Nat., not spec.	61	0.17
Alsatian	13	0.04
American Indian tribes, specified:	228	0.63
Apache (2)	4	0.01
Blackfeet	1	0.00
Cherokee (25)	86	0.24
Chickasaw (2)	10	0.03
Chippewa (2)	4	0.01
Choctaw (28)	59	0.16
Colville	1	0.00
Comanche (1)	2	0.01
Creek (3)	7	0.02
Crow (1)	1	0.00
Iroquois	3	0.01
Kiowa	1	0.00
Latin American Indians (2)	11	0.03
Navajo (11)	11	0.03
Osage (1)	3	0.01
Ottawa (2)	2	0.01
Potawatomi (1)	6	0.02
Seminole	2	0.01
Sioux (4)	6	0.02
All other tribes (4)	8	0.02
American Indian tribes, not spec.	16	0.04
Arab:	242	0.67
Arab/Arabic	152	0.42
Lebanese	15	0.04
Palestinian	75	0.21
Armenian	34	0.09
Asian:	888	2.46
Bangladeshi (9)	11	0.03
Cambodian (4)	4	0.01
Chinese, ex. Taiwanese (73)	103	0.29
Filipino (118)	152	0.42
Hmong (35)	41	0.11
Indian (73)	95	0.26
Japanese (41)	73	0.20
Korean (117)	137	0.38
Laotian (92)	104	0.29
Pakistani (14)	23	0.06
Taiwanese (7)	7	0.02
Thai (13)	15	0.04
Vietnamese (82)	91	0.25
Other Asian, specified (3)	3	0.01
Other Asian, not specified (18)	29	0.08
Australian	42	0.12
Austrian	33	0.09
Belgian	29	0.08
British	259	0.72
Canadian	28	0.08
Celtic	8	0.02
Croatian	24	0.07
Czech	102	0.28
Czechoslovakian	86	0.24
Danish	51	0.14
Dutch	483	1.34
English	3,449	9.58
Estonian	9	0.03
European	199	0.55
Finnish	55	0.15
French, except Basque	558	1.55
French Canadian	129	0.36
German	3,192	8.87
Greek	71	0.20
Hawaii Native/Pacific Islander:	49	0.14
Melanesian: (1)	1	0.00
Other Melanesian (1)	1	0.00
Micronesian: (9)	9	0.02
Guamanian/Chamorro (9)	9	0.02
Polynesian: (11)	17	0.05
Native Hawaiian (7)	11	0.03
Samoan (4)	6	0.02
Other Pac. Isl., not spec. (10)	22	0.06
Hispanic or Latino:	5,522	15.30
Central American:	130	0.36
Guatemalan	36	0.10
Honduran	20	0.06
Nicaraguan	13	0.04
Panamanian	3	0.01
Salvadoran	46	0.13
Other Central American	12	0.03
Cuban	29	0.08
Dominican Republic	10	0.03
Mexican	4,227	11.72
Puerto Rican	80	0.22
South American:	83	0.23
Argentinean	2	0.01
Chilean	5	0.01
Colombian	33	0.09
Ecuadorian	9	0.02
Peruvian	16	0.04
Venezuelan	7	0.02
Other South American	11	0.03
Other Hispanic or Latino	963	2.67
Hungarian	92	0.26
Iranian	74	0.21
Irish	2,632	7.31
Italian	403	1.12
Latvian	7	0.02
Lithuanian	31	0.09
Luxemburger	26	0.07
Northern European	25	0.07
Norwegian	385	1.07
Polish	308	0.86
Portuguese	37	0.10
Romanian	14	0.04
Russian	64	0.18
Scandinavian	26	0.07
Scotch-Irish	613	1.70
Scottish	520	1.44
Serbian	6	0.02
Slovak	36	0.10
Swedish	284	0.79
Swiss	44	0.12
Turkish	22	0.06
Ukrainian	47	0.13
United States or American	3,536	9.83
Welsh	253	0.70
West Indian, excl. Hispanic:	79	0.22
Dutch West Indian	31	0.09
Jamaican	41	0.11
West Indian	7	0.02
White:	23,665	65.59
Not Hispanic (20,388)	20,741	57.48
Hispanic (2,667)	2,924	8.10
Yugoslavian	18	0.05

Eagle Pass

Place Type: City
County: Maverick
Population: 22,413

Ancestry/Race	Number	%
African American/Black:	86	0.38
Not Hispanic (27)	32	0.14
Hispanic (33)	54	0.24
Am. Ind. or Alaska Nat., not spec.	54	0.24
American Indian tribes, specified:	46	0.21
Apache	3	0.01
Cherokee	2	0.01
Choctaw (4)	4	0.02
Latin American Indians (6)	14	0.06
All other tribes (19)	23	0.10
American Indian tribes, not spec.	28	0.12
Asian:	208	0.93
Chinese, ex. Taiwanese (6)	15	0.07
Filipino (88)	95	0.42
Indian (37)	41	0.18
Japanese (3)	11	0.05
Korean (20)	23	0.10
Other Asian, specified	1	0.00
Other Asian, not specified (12)	22	0.10
British	26	0.11
Bulgarian	5	0.02
Canadian	15	0.07
Czech	11	0.05
Czechoslovakian	9	0.04

Notes: 1. Figures in the "Number" column do not add up to the total population due to: a) Ancestry/Race overlap — e.g. persons can report being both White and Irish, b) persons of Hispanic origin can report being any race, c) persons reporting two ancestries are counted in both categories. 2. Numbers in parentheses indicate the number of persons reporting this ancestry/race alone, not in combination with any other ancestry/race. 3. Refer to the Explanation of Data in the front of the book for more detailed information.

Ancestry/Race	Number	%
Dutch	17	0.07
English	77	0.34
European	28	0.12
French, except Basque	98	0.43
French Canadian	11	0.05
German	209	0.92
Greek	7	0.03
Hawaii Native/Pacific Islander:	24	0.11
Polynesian: (1)	17	0.08
Native Hawaiian	7	0.03
Samoan (1)	10	0.04
Other Pac. Isl., specified	1	0.00
Other Pac. Isl., not spec.	6	0.03
Hispanic or Latino:	21,269	94.90
Central American:	11	0.05
Honduran	2	0.01
Nicaraguan	3	0.01
Panamanian	4	0.02
Salvadoran	1	0.00
Other Central American	1	0.00
Cuban	8	0.04
Dominican Republic	11	0.05
Mexican	17,965	80.15
Puerto Rican	63	0.28
South American:	44	0.20
Argentinean	3	0.01
Bolivian	1	0.00
Chilean	4	0.02
Colombian	18	0.08
Ecuadorian	1	0.00
Peruvian	6	0.03
Venezuelan	11	0.05
Other Hispanic or Latino	3,167	14.13
Irish	160	0.70
Italian	53	0.23
Lithuanian	12	0.05
Norwegian	37	0.16
Polish	59	0.26
Portuguese	18	0.08
Scotch-Irish	54	0.24
Scottish	59	0.26
Swedish	8	0.04
United States or American	299	1.31
Welsh	8	0.04
White:	16,946	75.61
Not Hispanic (884)	921	4.11
Hispanic (15,418)	16,025	71.50

Edinburg

Place Type: City
County: Hidalgo
Population: 48,465

Ancestry/Race	Number	%
African American/Black:	342	0.71
Not Hispanic (196)	221	0.46
Hispanic (85)	121	0.25
African, sub-Saharan:	41	0.08
African	41	0.08
Alaska Native tribes, specified:	2	0.00
Eskimo (1)	2	0.00
Alaska Native tribes, not specified	3	0.01
Am. Ind. or Alaska Nat., not spec.	149	0.31
Alsatian	13	0.03
American Indian tribes, specified:	135	0.28
Apache (3)	4	0.01
Cherokee (7)	17	0.04
Chickasaw (1)	2	0.00
Choctaw (6)	6	0.01
Comanche (1)	1	0.00
Cree	1	0.00
Latin American Indians (53)	82	0.17
Navajo (3)	4	0.01
Pueblo (1)	1	0.00
Sioux (1)	1	0.00
Tohono O'Odham (1)	1	0.00
Ute	1	0.00
All other tribes (6)	14	0.03
American Indian tribes, not spec.	37	0.08
Arab:	20	0.04
Arab/Arabic	5	0.01
Lebanese	6	0.01
Syrian	9	0.02
Asian:	401	0.83
Bangladeshi (1)	1	0.00
Chinese, ex. Taiwanese (32)	43	0.09
Filipino (159)	189	0.39
Indian (60)	70	0.14
Indonesian	1	0.00
Japanese (20)	31	0.06
Korean (9)	12	0.02
Malaysian	1	0.00
Pakistani (1)	1	0.00
Thai (7)	8	0.02
Vietnamese (17)	18	0.04
Other Asian, not specified (8)	26	0.05
Belgian	28	0.06
British	40	0.08
Canadian	36	0.07
Croatian	15	0.03
Czech	33	0.07
Czechoslovakian	21	0.04
Danish	56	0.11
Dutch	44	0.09
English	749	1.53
European	148	0.30
French, except Basque	205	0.42
French Canadian	108	0.22
German	1,097	2.25
Greek	12	0.02
Hawaii Native/Pacific Islander:	30	0.06
Micronesian:	1	0.00
Guamanian/Chamorro	1	0.00
Polynesian: (17)	19	0.04
Native Hawaiian (12)	13	0.03
Samoan (5)	6	0.01
Other Pac. Isl., not spec. (2)	10	0.02
Hispanic or Latino:	42,981	88.68
Central American:	84	0.17
Costa Rican	1	0.00
Guatemalan	22	0.05
Honduran	11	0.02
Nicaraguan	12	0.02
Panamanian	6	0.01
Salvadoran	15	0.03
Other Central American	17	0.04
Cuban	15	0.03
Dominican Republic	9	0.02
Mexican	34,655	71.51
Puerto Rican	94	0.19
South American:	88	0.18
Argentinean	12	0.02
Bolivian	4	0.01
Chilean	14	0.03
Colombian	35	0.07
Ecuadorian	4	0.01
Peruvian	6	0.01
Venezuelan	10	0.02
Other South American	3	0.01
Other Hispanic or Latino	8,036	16.58
Hungarian	19	0.04
Iranian	26	0.05
Irish	684	1.40
Italian	268	0.55
Luxemburger	11	0.02
Norwegian	46	0.09
Polish	201	0.41
Russian	35	0.07
Scandinavian	26	0.05
Scotch-Irish	259	0.53
Scottish	168	0.34
Slovene	13	0.03
Swedish	49	0.10
Swiss	12	0.02
Turkish	22	0.05
Ukrainian	8	0.02
United States or American	1,285	2.63
Welsh	22	0.05
White:	36,521	75.36
Not Hispanic (4,772)	4,887	10.08
Hispanic (30,761)	31,634	65.27
Yugoslavian	13	0.03

El Campo

Place Type: City
County: Wharton
Population: 10,945

Ancestry/Race	Number	%
Acadian/Cajun	22	0.20
African American/Black:	1,336	12.21
Not Hispanic (1,268)	1,285	11.74
Hispanic (32)	51	0.47
African, sub-Saharan:	175	1.62
African	175	1.62
Am. Ind. or Alaska Nat., not spec.	23	0.21
American Indian tribes, specified:	31	0.28
Apache (1)	2	0.02
Cherokee (2)	8	0.07
Choctaw	5	0.05
Latin American Indians (11)	13	0.12
Osage (1)	1	0.01
All other tribes (2)	2	0.02
American Indian tribes, not spec.	6	0.05
Arab:	11	0.10
Lebanese	11	0.10
Asian:	47	0.43
Chinese, ex. Taiwanese (9)	9	0.08
Filipino (1)	1	0.01
Indian (8)	11	0.10
Japanese (1)	1	0.01
Korean (2)	2	0.02
Sri Lankan (1)	1	0.01
Thai (1)	1	0.01
Vietnamese (6)	7	0.06
Other Asian, specified	6	0.05
Other Asian, not specified (2)	8	0.07
Austrian	11	0.10
Czech	1,176	10.87
Czechoslovakian	125	1.16
Danish	224	2.07
Dutch	38	0.35
English	490	4.53
French, except Basque	183	1.69
French Canadian	39	0.36
German	1,271	11.75
Hawaii Native/Pacific Islander:	10	0.09
Micronesian: (1)	3	0.03
Other Micronesian (1)	3	0.03
Other Pac. Isl., specified	6	0.05
Other Pac. Isl., not spec.	1	0.01
Hispanic or Latino:	4,234	38.68
Central American:	14	0.13
Guatemalan	3	0.03
Honduran	2	0.02
Panamanian	2	0.02
Salvadoran	7	0.06
Mexican	2,890	26.40
Puerto Rican	9	0.08
South American:	2	0.02
Peruvian	1	0.01
Uruguayan	1	0.01
Other Hispanic or Latino	1,319	12.05
Irish	773	7.14
Italian	60	0.55
Norwegian	17	0.16
Polish	88	0.81
Russian	27	0.25
Scotch-Irish	127	1.17
Scottish	38	0.35
Swedish	118	1.09
United States or American	502	4.64
Welsh	15	0.14
White:	7,726	70.59
Not Hispanic (5,352)	5,389	49.24
Hispanic (2,208)	2,337	21.35

Notes: 1. Figures in the "Number" column do not add up to the total population due to: a) Ancestry/Race overlap — e.g. persons can report being both White and Irish, b) persons of Hispanic origin can report being any race, c) persons reporting two ancestries are counted in both categories. 2. Numbers in parentheses indicate the number of persons reporting this ancestry/race alone, not in combination with any other ancestry/race. 3. Refer to the Explanation of Data in the front of the book for more detailed information.

El Paso

Place Type: City
County: El Paso
Population: 563,662

Ancestry/Race	Number	%
Acadian/Cajun	71	0.01
African American/Black:	19,998	3.55
Not Hispanic (15,768)	17,070	3.03
Hispanic (1,818)	2,928	0.52
African, sub-Saharan:	1,202	0.21
African	887	0.16
Cape Verdean	11	0.00
Ethiopian	9	0.00
Ghanian	15	0.00
Kenyan	33	0.01
Liberian	14	0.00
Nigerian	145	0.03
South African	30	0.01
Other sub-Saharan African	58	0.01
Alaska Native tribes, specified:	11	0.00
Alaska Athabascan (1)	1	0.00
Eskimo (3)	3	0.00
Tlingit-Haida (5)	5	0.00
All other tribes (2)	2	0.00
Alaska Native tribes, not specified	14	0.00
Am. Ind. or Alaska Nat., not spec.	2,810	0.50
Alsatian	56	0.01
American Indian tribes, specified:	3,279	0.58
Apache (159)	285	0.05
Blackfeet (21)	48	0.01
Cherokee (177)	464	0.08
Cheyenne (21)	35	0.01
Chickasaw (5)	15	0.00
Chippewa (18)	26	0.00
Choctaw (63)	111	0.02
Colville (2)	2	0.00
Comanche (23)	49	0.01
Cree	1	0.00
Creek (25)	42	0.01
Crow	1	0.00
Delaware (4)	6	0.00
Houma (2)	3	0.00
Iroquois (26)	33	0.01
Kiowa (4)	7	0.00
Latin American Indians (503)	670	0.12
Lumbee (9)	12	0.00
Menominee	1	0.00
Navajo (101)	131	0.02
Osage (4)	12	0.00
Ottawa (5)	7	0.00
Paiute (4)	4	0.00
Pima (2)	2	0.00
Potawatomi (12)	18	0.00
Pueblo (784)	910	0.16
Puget Sound Salish (4)	4	0.00
Seminole (3)	14	0.00
Sioux (57)	90	0.02
Tohono O'Odham (5)	25	0.00
Ute (1)	5	0.00
Yakama	2	0.00
Yaqui (30)	48	0.01
Yuman (2)	2	0.00
All other tribes (103)	194	0.03
American Indian tribes, not spec.	462	0.08
Arab:	2,105	0.37
Arab/Arabic	257	0.05
Egyptian	63	0.01
Jordanian	89	0.02
Lebanese	1,142	0.20
Moroccan	8	0.00
Palestinian	115	0.02
Syrian	352	0.06
Other Arab	79	0.01
Armenian	129	0.02
Asian:	8,726	1.55
Bangladeshi (8)	11	0.00
Cambodian (4)	9	0.00
Chinese, ex. Taiwanese (926)	1,238	0.22
Filipino (1,294)	1,741	0.31
Hmong	1	0.00
Indian (887)	1,083	0.19
Indonesian (27)	42	0.01
Japanese (945)	1,436	0.25
Korean (1,611)	2,108	0.37
Laotian (12)	17	0.00
Malaysian	6	0.00
Pakistani (25)	48	0.01
Sri Lankan (9)	9	0.00
Taiwanese (54)	69	0.01
Thai (79)	113	0.02
Vietnamese (229)	317	0.06
Other Asian, specified (8)	28	0.00
Other Asian, not specified (132)	450	0.08
Australian	61	0.01
Austrian	591	0.10
Basque	74	0.01
Belgian	188	0.03
Brazilian	122	0.02
British	1,018	0.18
Canadian	415	0.07
Carpatho Rusyn	38	0.01
Celtic	127	0.02
Croatian	92	0.02
Czech	477	0.08
Czechoslovakian	246	0.04
Danish	733	0.13
Dutch	2,075	0.37
Eastern European	102	0.02
English	15,719	2.79
European	1,776	0.31
Finnish	194	0.03
French, except Basque	5,608	0.99
French Canadian	956	0.17
German	25,770	4.57
German Russian	37	0.01
Greek	456	0.08
Guyanese	9	0.00
Hawaii Native/Pacific Islander:	1,064	0.19
Micronesian: (208)	328	0.06
Guamanian/Chamorro (201)	310	0.05
Other Micronesian (7)	18	0.00
Polynesian: (296)	520	0.09
Native Hawaiian (148)	313	0.06
Samoan (140)	187	0.03
Tongan (6)	8	0.00
Other Polynesian (2)	12	0.00
Other Pac. Isl., specified	13	0.00
Other Pac. Isl., not spec. (71)	203	0.04
Hispanic or Latino:	431,875	76.62
Central American:	1,228	0.22
Costa Rican	54	0.01
Guatemalan	239	0.04
Honduran	149	0.03
Nicaraguan	113	0.02
Panamanian	369	0.07
Salvadoran	250	0.04
Other Central American	54	0.01
Cuban	476	0.08
Dominican Republic	126	0.02
Mexican	359,699	63.81
Puerto Rican	3,660	0.65
South American:	747	0.13
Argentinean	134	0.02
Bolivian	36	0.01
Chilean	65	0.01
Colombian	225	0.04
Ecuadorian	57	0.01
Paraguayan	6	0.00
Peruvian	111	0.02
Uruguayan	3	0.00
Venezuelan	67	0.01
Other South American	43	0.01
Other Hispanic or Latino	65,939	11.70
Hungarian	575	0.10
Icelander	53	0.01
Iranian	255	0.05
Irish	16,469	2.92
Israeli	26	0.00
Italian	6,800	1.21
Latvian	33	0.01
Lithuanian	236	0.04
Luxemburger	11	0.00
Macedonian	26	0.00
New Zealander	11	0.00
Northern European	112	0.02
Norwegian	1,887	0.33
Pennsylvania German	53	0.01
Polish	2,964	0.53
Portuguese	292	0.05
Romanian	201	0.04
Russian	1,350	0.24
Scandinavian	158	0.03
Scotch-Irish	3,933	0.70
Scottish	3,492	0.62
Serbian	58	0.01
Slavic	86	0.02
Slovak	218	0.04
Slovene	38	0.01
Swedish	1,502	0.27
Swiss	268	0.05
Turkish	15	0.00
Ukrainian	199	0.04
United States or American	15,060	2.67
Welsh	1,157	0.21
West Indian, excl. Hispanic:	505	0.09
Barbadian	21	0.00
Belizean	11	0.00
British West Indian	9	0.00
Dutch West Indian	32	0.01
Haitian	171	0.03
Jamaican	143	0.03
Trinidadian and Tobagonian	21	0.00
U.S. Virgin Islander	8	0.00
West Indian	89	0.02
White:	430,142	76.31
Not Hispanic (103,422)	106,960	18.98
Hispanic (309,639)	323,182	57.34
Yugoslavian	115	0.02

Ennis

Place Type: City
County: Ellis
Population: 16,045

Ancestry/Race	Number	%
Acadian/Cajun	10	0.06
African American/Black:	2,405	14.99
Not Hispanic (2,336)	2,371	14.78
Hispanic (24)	34	0.21
African, sub-Saharan:	214	1.33
African	214	1.33
Alaska Native tribes, specified:	1	0.01
Tlingit-Haida (1)	1	0.01
Am. Ind. or Alaska Nat., not spec.	57	0.36
Albanian	11	0.07
American Indian tribes, specified:	55	0.34
Apache	1	0.01
Blackfeet (1)	2	0.01
Cherokee (4)	17	0.11
Chickasaw (4)	4	0.02
Choctaw (4)	10	0.06
Cree	2	0.01
Houma (1)	2	0.01
Latin American Indians (6)	10	0.06
Navajo (1)	2	0.01
Potawatomi (1)	1	0.01
Yuman	1	0.01
All other tribes (3)	3	0.02
American Indian tribes, not spec.	5	0.03
Arab:	36	0.22
Palestinian	16	0.10
Other Arab	20	0.12
Asian:	81	0.50
Bangladeshi (2)	2	0.01
Chinese, ex. Taiwanese (6)	10	0.06
Filipino (13)	19	0.12
Indian (14)	22	0.14

Notes: 1. Figures in the "Number" column do not add up to the total population due to: a) Ancestry/Race overlap — e.g. persons can report being both White and Irish, b) persons of Hispanic origin can report being any race, c) persons reporting two ancestries are counted in both categories. 2. Numbers in parentheses indicate the number of persons reporting this ancestry/race alone, not in combination with any other ancestry/race. 3. Refer to the Explanation of Data in the front of the book for more detailed information.

Japanese (1)	8	0.05
Korean	1	0.01
Laotian	1	0.01
Pakistani (5)	9	0.06
Taiwanese (1)	1	0.01
Vietnamese (4)	5	0.03
Other Asian, not specified	3	0.02
British	10	0.06
Canadian	9	0.06
Celtic	5	0.03
Croatian	14	0.09
Czech	942	5.88
Czechoslovakian	205	1.28
Dutch	42	0.26
English	855	5.33
European	29	0.18
French, except Basque	214	1.33
French Canadian	35	0.22
German	927	5.78
Greek	18	0.11
Hawaii Native/Pacific Islander:	6	0.04
Polynesian: (1)	4	0.02
Native Hawaiian	1	0.01
Samoan (1)	3	0.02
Other Pac. Isl., not spec.	2	0.01
Hispanic or Latino:	5,325	33.19
Central American:	19	0.12
Honduran	1	0.01
Nicaraguan	1	0.01
Panamanian	1	0.01
Salvadoran	16	0.10
Cuban	9	0.06
Mexican	4,569	28.48
Puerto Rican	7	0.04
South American:	6	0.04
Chilean	3	0.02
Colombian	2	0.01
Venezuelan	1	0.01
Other Hispanic or Latino	715	4.46
Hungarian	30	0.19
Irish	963	6.01
Italian	127	0.79
Norwegian	90	0.56
Polish	93	0.58
Portuguese	23	0.14
Russian	29	0.18
Scotch-Irish	246	1.53
Scottish	174	1.09
Slovak	15	0.09
Swedish	50	0.31
Swiss	7	0.04
United States or American	1,406	8.77
Welsh	29	0.18
West Indian, excl. Hispanic:	10	0.06
Bahamian	4	0.02
Dutch West Indian	6	0.04
White:	10,966	68.35
Not Hispanic (8,193)	8,281	51.61
Hispanic (2,488)	2,685	16.73

Euless

Place Type: City
County: Tarrant
Population: 46,005

Ancestry/Race	Number	%
Acadian/Cajun	66	0.14
African American/Black:	3,249	7.06
Not Hispanic (2,943)	3,185	6.92
Hispanic (44)	64	0.14
African, sub-Saharan:	776	1.68
African	343	0.74
Ethiopian	16	0.03
Liberian	100	0.22
Nigerian	70	0.15
Sierra Leonean	28	0.06
Somalian	55	0.12
Sudanese	15	0.03
Ugandan	15	0.03
Other sub-Saharan African	134	0.29
Alaska Native tribes, specified:	3	0.01
Aleut	1	0.00
Eskimo (2)	2	0.00
Alaska Native tribes, not specified	1	0.00
Am. Ind. or Alaska Nat., not spec.	156	0.34
Albanian	18	0.04
American Indian tribes, specified:	389	0.85
Apache (6)	14	0.03
Blackfeet (1)	6	0.01
Cherokee (63)	149	0.32
Cheyenne	2	0.00
Chickasaw (7)	10	0.02
Chippewa (2)	4	0.01
Choctaw (31)	43	0.09
Comanche (12)	20	0.04
Creek (11)	26	0.06
Delaware (4)	5	0.01
Iroquois (3)	6	0.01
Kiowa (3)	4	0.01
Latin American Indians (16)	25	0.05
Lumbee (4)	4	0.01
Menominee	1	0.00
Navajo (6)	9	0.02
Osage (5)	10	0.02
Paiute (2)	2	0.00
Pima	3	0.01
Potawatomi (4)	6	0.01
Pueblo (4)	7	0.02
Puget Sound Salish (2)	3	0.01
Seminole (1)	5	0.01
Shoshone	1	0.00
Sioux	3	0.01
All other tribes (12)	21	0.05
American Indian tribes, not spec.	46	0.10
Arab:	339	0.74
Arab/Arabic	65	0.14
Jordanian	8	0.02
Lebanese	84	0.18
Palestinian	104	0.23
Syrian	39	0.08
Other Arab	39	0.08
Armenian	46	0.10
Asian:	3,814	8.29
Bangladeshi (14)	14	0.03
Cambodian (8)	13	0.03
Chinese, ex. Taiwanese (166)	230	0.50
Filipino (151)	216	0.47
Indian (1,283)	1,400	3.04
Indonesian (2)	6	0.01
Japanese (57)	91	0.20
Korean (170)	199	0.43
Laotian (380)	407	0.88
Malaysian (13)	14	0.03
Pakistani (411)	562	1.22
Sri Lankan (17)	21	0.05
Taiwanese (7)	10	0.02
Thai (77)	91	0.20
Vietnamese (320)	337	0.73
Other Asian, specified (15)	21	0.05
Other Asian, not specified (123)	182	0.40
Austrian	42	0.09
Basque	23	0.05
Belgian	7	0.02
Brazilian	45	0.10
British	373	0.81
Bulgarian	91	0.20
Canadian	76	0.16
Celtic	10	0.02
Croatian	45	0.10
Czech	298	0.65
Czechoslovakian	52	0.11
Danish	151	0.33
Dutch	721	1.56
Eastern European	9	0.02
English	4,084	8.86
European	441	0.96
Finnish	128	0.28
French, except Basque	1,500	3.25
French Canadian	159	0.34
German	6,548	14.21
Greek	126	0.27
Guyanese	26	0.06
Hawaii Native/Pacific Islander:	1,010	2.20
Melanesian: (2)	2	0.00
Fijian (2)	2	0.00
Micronesian: (11)	16	0.03
Guamanian/Chamorro (7)	12	0.03
Other Micronesian (4)	4	0.01
Polynesian: (789)	925	2.01
Native Hawaiian (53)	87	0.19
Samoan (57)	70	0.15
Tongan (642)	710	1.54
Other Polynesian (37)	58	0.13
Other Pac. Isl., not spec. (31)	67	0.15
Hispanic or Latino:	6,125	13.31
Central American:	180	0.39
Costa Rican	13	0.03
Guatemalan	26	0.06
Honduran	19	0.04
Nicaraguan	6	0.01
Panamanian	19	0.04
Salvadoran	88	0.19
Other Central American	9	0.02
Cuban	58	0.13
Dominican Republic	17	0.04
Mexican	4,103	8.92
Puerto Rican	645	1.40
South American:	162	0.35
Argentinean	9	0.02
Bolivian	4	0.01
Chilean	20	0.04
Colombian	54	0.12
Ecuadorian	23	0.05
Peruvian	22	0.05
Uruguayan	3	0.01
Venezuelan	14	0.03
Other South American	13	0.03
Other Hispanic or Latino	960	2.09
Hungarian	112	0.24
Irish	4,834	10.49
Italian	1,277	2.77
Latvian	11	0.02
Lithuanian	8	0.02
Luxemburger	13	0.03
Macedonian	9	0.02
Northern European	46	0.10
Norwegian	355	0.77
Pennsylvania German	26	0.06
Polish	691	1.50
Portuguese	44	0.10
Romanian	28	0.06
Russian	137	0.30
Scandinavian	43	0.09
Scotch-Irish	896	1.94
Scottish	977	2.12
Slavic	17	0.04
Slovak	21	0.05
Swedish	384	0.83
Swiss	53	0.11
Turkish	16	0.03
Ukrainian	79	0.17
United States or American	3,744	8.12
Welsh	330	0.72
West Indian, excl. Hispanic:	221	0.48
Belizean	11	0.02
Dutch West Indian	58	0.13
Haitian	8	0.02
Jamaican	144	0.31
White:	35,741	77.69
Not Hispanic (31,468)	32,127	69.83
Hispanic (3,275)	3,614	7.86
Yugoslavian	27	0.06

Notes: 1. Figures in the "Number" column do not add up to the total population due to: a) Ancestry/Race overlap — e.g. persons can report being both White and Irish, b) persons of Hispanic origin can report being any race, c) persons reporting two ancestries are counted in both categories. 2. Numbers in parentheses indicate the number of persons reporting this ancestry/race alone, not in combination with any other ancestry/race. 3. Refer to the Explanation of Data in the front of the book for more detailed information.

Farmers Branch

Place Type: City
County: Dallas
Population: 27,508

Ancestry/Race	Number	%
African American/Black:	745	2.71
Not Hispanic (639)	691	2.51
Hispanic (22)	54	0.20
African, sub-Saharan:	114	0.40
African	38	0.13
Nigerian	33	0.12
South African	10	0.04
Other sub-Saharan African	33	0.12
Am. Ind. or Alaska Nat., not spec.	95	0.35
American Indian tribes, specified:	196	0.71
Apache (3)	10	0.04
Blackfeet	1	0.00
Cherokee (20)	71	0.26
Cheyenne (4)	4	0.01
Chickasaw (12)	19	0.07
Chippewa (1)	1	0.00
Choctaw (16)	41	0.15
Creek (2)	7	0.03
Delaware (1)	1	0.00
Kiowa (3)	5	0.02
Latin American Indians (7)	10	0.04
Potawatomi	1	0.00
Pueblo (2)	2	0.01
Seminole (1)	1	0.00
Sioux (2)	8	0.03
All other tribes (5)	14	0.05
American Indian tribes, not spec.	11	0.04
Arab:	115	0.41
Arab/Arabic	21	0.07
Iraqi	42	0.15
Lebanese	52	0.18
Asian:	963	3.50
Bangladeshi (3)	3	0.01
Cambodian (14)	32	0.12
Chinese, ex. Taiwanese (85)	110	0.40
Filipino (50)	59	0.21
Indian (183)	213	0.77
Indonesian (3)	3	0.01
Japanese (21)	30	0.11
Korean (119)	137	0.50
Laotian (2)	2	0.01
Malaysian (1)	1	0.00
Pakistani (18)	22	0.08
Sri Lankan (1)	1	0.00
Taiwanese (4)	9	0.03
Thai (15)	19	0.07
Vietnamese (255)	287	1.04
Other Asian, specified	3	0.01
Other Asian, not specified (7)	32	0.12
Assyrian/Chaldean/Syriac	14	0.05
Australian	7	0.02
Austrian	41	0.14
Belgian	29	0.10
British	60	0.21
Bulgarian	16	0.06
Canadian	15	0.05
Celtic	20	0.07
Croatian	35	0.12
Czech	125	0.44
Czechoslovakian	79	0.28
Danish	59	0.21
Dutch	389	1.37
English	2,458	8.68
European	221	0.78
Finnish	10	0.04
French, except Basque	641	2.26
French Canadian	174	0.61
German	2,550	9.00
Greek	50	0.18
Hawaii Native/Pacific Islander:	11	0.04
Micronesian: (5)	6	0.02
Guamanian/Chamorro (4)	5	0.02
Other Micronesian (1)	1	0.00
Polynesian: (4)	5	0.02
Native Hawaiian (3)	4	0.01
Samoan (1)	1	0.00
Hispanic or Latino:	10,241	37.23
Central American:	909	3.30
Costa Rican	10	0.04
Guatemalan	70	0.25
Honduran	63	0.23
Nicaraguan	30	0.11
Panamanian	7	0.03
Salvadoran	692	2.52
Other Central American	37	0.13
Cuban	74	0.27
Dominican Republic	3	0.01
Mexican	7,859	28.57
Puerto Rican	66	0.24
South American:	133	0.48
Argentinean	8	0.03
Bolivian	6	0.02
Chilean	14	0.05
Colombian	51	0.19
Ecuadorian	7	0.03
Paraguayan	1	0.00
Peruvian	22	0.08
Venezuelan	16	0.06
Other South American	8	0.03
Other Hispanic or Latino	1,197	4.35
Hungarian	58	0.20
Icelander	11	0.04
Iranian	28	0.10
Irish	2,311	8.16
Israeli	9	0.03
Italian	500	1.77
Lithuanian	37	0.13
Norwegian	246	0.87
Polish	344	1.21
Portuguese	17	0.06
Russian	119	0.42
Scandinavian	6	0.02
Scotch-Irish	693	2.45
Scottish	560	1.98
Serbian	11	0.04
Slovak	15	0.05
Slovene	6	0.02
Swedish	223	0.79
Swiss	78	0.28
Ukrainian	20	0.07
United States or American	1,985	7.01
Welsh	114	0.40
West Indian, excl. Hispanic:	12	0.04
Barbadian	12	0.04
White:	22,223	80.79
Not Hispanic (15,360)	15,631	56.82
Hispanic (6,200)	6,592	23.96

Flower Mound

Place Type: Town
County: Denton
Population: 50,702

Ancestry/Race	Number	%
Acadian/Cajun	19	0.04
Afghan	31	0.06
African American/Black:	1,630	3.21
Not Hispanic (1,461)	1,583	3.12
Hispanic (21)	47	0.09
African, sub-Saharan:	173	0.34
African	55	0.11
Cape Verdean	29	0.06
Ghanian	6	0.01
Nigerian	43	0.08
Somalian	37	0.07
South African	3	0.01
Alaska Native tribes, specified:	1	0.00
Eskimo (1)	1	0.00
Alaska Native tribes, not specified	1	0.00
Am. Ind. or Alaska Nat., not spec.	111	0.22
Albanian	63	0.12
Alsatian	6	0.01
American Indian tribes, specified:	323	0.64
Apache (2)	11	0.02
Blackfeet (1)	9	0.02
Cherokee (45)	111	0.22
Cheyenne	1	0.00
Chickasaw (9)	17	0.03
Chippewa (4)	7	0.01
Choctaw (17)	44	0.09
Comanche (3)	3	0.01
Creek (8)	14	0.03
Delaware	2	0.00
Iroquois (6)	7	0.01
Latin American Indians (2)	11	0.02
Lumbee (2)	2	0.00
Navajo (1)	9	0.02
Osage (8)	10	0.02
Pima	2	0.00
Potawatomi (3)	6	0.01
Seminole (5)	5	0.01
Sioux (3)	5	0.01
Yakama (1)	4	0.01
Yaqui	1	0.00
Yuman (2)	2	0.00
All other tribes (19)	40	0.08
American Indian tribes, not spec.	11	0.02
Arab:	231	0.45
Arab/Arabic	99	0.19
Egyptian	71	0.14
Lebanese	33	0.06
Syrian	28	0.05
Armenian	7	0.01
Asian:	1,835	3.62
Cambodian (3)	3	0.01
Chinese, ex. Taiwanese (282)	329	0.65
Filipino (144)	213	0.42
Indian (557)	601	1.19
Indonesian (2)	3	0.01
Japanese (70)	142	0.28
Korean (245)	272	0.54
Pakistani (36)	44	0.09
Sri Lankan (6)	6	0.01
Taiwanese (15)	17	0.03
Thai (14)	17	0.03
Vietnamese (139)	146	0.29
Other Asian, specified (4)	5	0.01
Other Asian, not specified (12)	37	0.07
Austrian	118	0.23
Belgian	54	0.11
Brazilian	8	0.02
British	309	0.60
Bulgarian	23	0.04
Canadian	165	0.32
Croatian	60	0.12
Czech	495	0.97
Czechoslovakian	191	0.37
Danish	273	0.53
Dutch	882	1.72
Eastern European	17	0.03
English	7,723	15.08
European	655	1.28
Finnish	82	0.16
French, except Basque	1,674	3.27
French Canadian	285	0.56
German	10,595	20.69
Greek	239	0.47
Hawaii Native/Pacific Islander:	72	0.14
Micronesian: (2)	12	0.02
Guamanian/Chamorro (2)	12	0.02
Polynesian: (22)	51	0.10
Native Hawaiian (10)	33	0.07
Samoan (7)	9	0.02
Tongan	1	0.00
Other Polynesian (5)	8	0.02
Other Pac. Isl., not spec. (3)	9	0.02
Hispanic or Latino:	2,855	5.63
Central American:	93	0.18
Costa Rican	19	0.04
Guatemalan	10	0.02
Honduran	4	0.01
Nicaraguan	11	0.02

Notes: 1. Figures in the "Number" column do not add up to the total population due to: a) Ancestry/Race overlap — e.g. persons can report being both White and Irish, b) persons of Hispanic origin can report being any race, c) persons reporting two ancestries are counted in both categories. 2. Numbers in parentheses indicate the number of persons reporting this ancestry/race alone, not in combination with any other ancestry/race. 3. Refer to the Explanation of Data in the front of the book for more detailed information.

Panamanian	20	0.04
Salvadoran	24	0.05
Other Central American	5	0.01
Cuban	85	0.17
Dominican Republic	11	0.02
Mexican	1,703	3.36
Puerto Rican	217	0.43
South American:	147	0.29
Argentinean	3	0.01
Bolivian	6	0.01
Chilean	9	0.02
Colombian	66	0.13
Ecuadorian	8	0.02
Paraguayan	1	0.00
Peruvian	38	0.07
Uruguayan	1	0.00
Venezuelan	12	0.02
Other South American	3	0.01
Other Hispanic or Latino	599	1.18
Hungarian	190	0.37
Iranian	137	0.27
Irish	7,774	15.18
Italian	2,248	4.39
Lithuanian	54	0.11
Maltese	3	0.01
New Zealander	6	0.01
Northern European	18	0.04
Norwegian	966	1.89
Pennsylvania German	11	0.02
Polish	1,583	3.09
Portuguese	72	0.14
Romanian	9	0.02
Russian	359	0.70
Scandinavian	44	0.09
Scotch-Irish	1,118	2.18
Scottish	1,764	3.45
Serbian	36	0.07
Slavic	34	0.07
Slovak	60	0.12
Swedish	1,024	2.00
Swiss	105	0.21
Turkish	29	0.06
Ukrainian	151	0.29
United States or American	4,473	8.74
Welsh	564	1.10
West Indian, excl. Hispanic:	162	0.32
Bahamian	24	0.05
Dutch West Indian	8	0.02
Haitian	10	0.02
Jamaican	58	0.11
Trinidadian and Tobagonian	54	0.11
West Indian	8	0.02
White:	46,486	91.68
Not Hispanic (44,055)	44,585	87.94
Hispanic (1,698)	1,901	3.75
Yugoslavian	208	0.41

Forest Hill

Place Type: City
County: Tarrant
Population: 12,949

Ancestry/Race	Number	%
African American/Black:	7,463	57.63
Not Hispanic (7,355)	7,414	57.26
Hispanic (34)	49	0.38
African, sub-Saharan:	148	1.14
African	148	1.14
Am. Ind. or Alaska Nat., not spec.	35	0.27
American Indian tribes, specified:	69	0.53
Apache	2	0.02
Blackfeet	1	0.01
Cherokee (10)	26	0.20
Chippewa (2)	2	0.02
Choctaw (3)	8	0.06
Comanche	5	0.04
Creek (1)	5	0.04
Iroquois	5	0.04
Latin American Indians (1)	6	0.05
Seminole	5	0.04
Sioux (1)	1	0.01
All other tribes (1)	3	0.02
American Indian tribes, not spec.	4	0.03
Asian:	156	1.20
Cambodian (1)	1	0.01
Chinese, ex. Taiwanese (7)	8	0.06
Filipino (14)	16	0.12
Indian (24)	25	0.19
Japanese (8)	8	0.06
Korean (3)	4	0.03
Laotian (1)	2	0.02
Taiwanese	1	0.01
Thai (1)	2	0.02
Vietnamese (82)	83	0.64
Other Asian, not specified (5)	6	0.05
British	20	0.15
Croatian	7	0.05
Czechoslovakian	7	0.05
Dutch	10	0.08
English	152	1.18
Estonian	8	0.06
European	10	0.08
French, except Basque	36	0.28
German	251	1.94
Hawaii Native/Pacific Islander:	2	0.02
Polynesian: (1)	1	0.01
Native Hawaiian (1)	1	0.01
Other Pac. Isl., not spec.	1	0.01
Hispanic or Latino:	2,349	18.14
Central American:	25	0.19
Costa Rican	1	0.01
Guatemalan	6	0.05
Honduran	7	0.05
Panamanian	3	0.02
Salvadoran	8	0.06
Cuban	24	0.19
Dominican Republic	6	0.05
Mexican	1,987	15.34
Puerto Rican	22	0.17
South American:	22	0.17
Argentinean	2	0.02
Colombian	17	0.13
Ecuadorian	1	0.01
Peruvian	1	0.01
Venezuelan	1	0.01
Other Hispanic or Latino	263	2.03
Irish	309	2.39
Italian	45	0.35
Norwegian	19	0.15
Polish	49	0.38
Portuguese	19	0.15
Romanian	6	0.05
Scotch-Irish	34	0.26
Scottish	53	0.41
Swiss	6	0.05
United States or American	548	4.24
West Indian, excl. Hispanic:	14	0.11
Dutch West Indian	9	0.07
Jamaican	5	0.04
White:	4,498	34.74
Not Hispanic (2,967)	3,024	23.35
Hispanic (1,387)	1,474	11.38

Fort Hood

Place Type: Census Designated Place
County: Coryell
Population: 33,711

Ancestry/Race	Number	%
Acadian/Cajun	28	0.08
African American/Black:	11,390	33.79
Not Hispanic (10,346)	10,924	32.40
Hispanic (305)	466	1.38
African, sub-Saharan:	444	1.32
African	416	1.24
Ethiopian	12	0.04
Nigerian	16	0.05
Alaska Native tribes, specified:	25	0.07
Alaska Athabascan (10)	10	0.03
Aleut	3	0.01
Eskimo (4)	10	0.03
Tlingit-Haida (2)	2	0.01
Am. Ind. or Alaska Nat., not spec.	182	0.54
American Indian tribes, specified:	471	1.40
Apache (22)	40	0.12
Blackfeet (14)	24	0.07
Cherokee (43)	125	0.37
Cheyenne (1)	2	0.01
Chickasaw (9)	11	0.03
Chippewa (2)	7	0.02
Choctaw (22)	30	0.09
Comanche (5)	9	0.03
Cree	2	0.01
Creek (6)	11	0.03
Crow	1	0.00
Iroquois (12)	23	0.07
Kiowa	2	0.01
Latin American Indians (18)	25	0.07
Lumbee (9)	13	0.04
Menominee (2)	2	0.01
Navajo (34)	42	0.12
Ottawa	1	0.00
Paiute (1)	2	0.01
Potawatomi (4)	5	0.01
Pueblo (6)	6	0.02
Puget Sound Salish	3	0.01
Seminole (2)	6	0.02
Sioux (22)	29	0.09
Tohono O'Odham (2)	3	0.01
Ute (1)	3	0.01
Yakama (1)	1	0.00
Yaqui (2)	2	0.01
All other tribes (20)	41	0.12
American Indian tribes, not spec.	59	0.18
Arab:	76	0.23
Egyptian	8	0.02
Lebanese	25	0.07
Palestinian	8	0.02
Syrian	35	0.10
Armenian	24	0.07
Asian:	1,189	3.53
Bangladeshi (1)	1	0.00
Cambodian (13)	22	0.07
Chinese, ex. Taiwanese (40)	81	0.24
Filipino (315)	484	1.44
Hmong (15)	16	0.05
Indian (26)	54	0.16
Indonesian (1)	1	0.00
Japanese (20)	73	0.22
Korean (187)	292	0.87
Laotian (11)	16	0.05
Malaysian (2)	2	0.01
Pakistani	1	0.00
Thai (14)	27	0.08
Vietnamese (39)	50	0.15
Other Asian, specified (1)	3	0.01
Other Asian, not specified (19)	66	0.20
Austrian	16	0.05
Belgian	9	0.03
Brazilian	39	0.12
British	85	0.25
Canadian	87	0.26
Celtic	7	0.02
Croatian	27	0.08
Czech	64	0.19
Czechoslovakian	47	0.14
Danish	34	0.10
Dutch	305	0.91
English	1,413	4.21
European	388	1.15
Finnish	7	0.02
French, except Basque	684	2.04
French Canadian	215	0.64
German	3,894	11.59
Greek	63	0.19
Guyanese	6	0.02
Hawaii Native/Pacific Islander:	480	1.42
Melanesian: (3)	5	0.01

Notes: 1. Figures in the "Number" column do not add up to the total population due to: a) Ancestry/Race overlap — e.g. persons can report being both White and Irish, b) persons of Hispanic origin can report being any race, c) persons reporting two ancestries are counted in both categories. 2. Numbers in parentheses indicate the number of persons reporting this ancestry/race alone, not in combination with any other ancestry/race. 3. Refer to the Explanation of Data in the front of the book for more detailed information.

Ancestry/Race	Number	%
Fijian (2)	2	0.01
Other Melanesian (1)	3	0.01
Micronesian: (125)	170	0.50
Guamanian/Chamorro (85)	126	0.37
Other Micronesian (40)	44	0.13
Polynesian: (139)	245	0.73
Native Hawaiian (55)	127	0.38
Samoan (80)	107	0.32
Tongan (4)	6	0.02
Other Polynesian	5	0.01
Other Pac. Isl., specified	1	0.00
Other Pac. Isl., not spec. (12)	59	0.18
Hispanic or Latino:	5,630	16.70
Central American:	260	0.77
Costa Rican	8	0.02
Guatemalan	13	0.04
Honduran	27	0.08
Nicaraguan	19	0.06
Panamanian	148	0.44
Salvadoran	43	0.13
Other Central American	2	0.01
Cuban	52	0.15
Dominican Republic	104	0.31
Mexican	2,726	8.09
Puerto Rican	1,540	4.57
South American:	169	0.50
Argentinean	3	0.01
Bolivian	5	0.01
Chilean	12	0.04
Colombian	59	0.18
Ecuadorian	21	0.06
Paraguayan	2	0.00
Peruvian	50	0.15
Venezuelan	14	0.04
Other South American	4	0.01
Other Hispanic or Latino	779	2.31
Hungarian	84	0.25
Icelander	8	0.02
Iranian	6	0.02
Irish	2,753	8.19
Italian	1,055	3.14
Latvian	7	0.02
Lithuanian	48	0.14
Northern European	9	0.03
Norwegian	367	1.09
Polish	451	1.34
Portuguese	62	0.18
Russian	148	0.44
Scandinavian	24	0.07
Scotch-Irish	348	1.04
Scottish	376	1.12
Serbian	28	0.08
Slavic	7	0.02
Slovak	24	0.07
Slovene	9	0.03
Swedish	255	0.76
Swiss	37	0.11
Turkish	14	0.04
Ukrainian	55	0.16
United States or American	1,564	4.66
Welsh	102	0.30
West Indian, excl. Hispanic:	253	0.75
British West Indian	27	0.08
Haitian	27	0.08
Jamaican	137	0.41
Trinidadian and Tobagonian	20	0.06
U.S. Virgin Islander	8	0.02
West Indian	34	0.10
White:	18,225	54.06
Not Hispanic (15,274)	16,080	47.70
Hispanic (1,829)	2,145	6.36

Fort Worth

Place Type: City
County: Tarrant
Population: 534,694

Ancestry/Race	Number	%
Acadian/Cajun	191	0.04
Afghan	52	0.01
African American/Black:	111,298	20.82
Not Hispanic (106,988)	109,379	20.46
Hispanic (1,322)	1,919	0.36
African, sub-Saharan:	4,417	0.82
African	3,840	0.72
Ethiopian	7	0.00
Ghanian	36	0.01
Kenyan	55	0.01
Liberian	29	0.01
Nigerian	266	0.05
Senegalese	10	0.00
South African	45	0.01
Sudanese	60	0.01
Zairian	14	0.00
Other sub-Saharan African	55	0.01
Alaska Native tribes, specified:	21	0.00
Alaska Athabascan (1)	3	0.00
Eskimo (8)	12	0.00
Tlingit-Haida (6)	6	0.00
Alaska Native tribes, not specified	19	0.00
Am. Ind. or Alaska Nat., not spec.	2,082	0.39
Albanian	279	0.05
American Indian tribes, specified:	3,553	0.66
Apache (63)	162	0.03
Blackfeet (16)	77	0.01
Cherokee (385)	1,214	0.23
Cheyenne (4)	17	0.00
Chickasaw (50)	123	0.02
Chippewa (38)	61	0.01
Choctaw (224)	470	0.09
Comanche (69)	150	0.03
Cree (1)	4	0.00
Creek (44)	78	0.01
Crow (9)	11	0.00
Delaware (7)	14	0.00
Houma (12)	18	0.00
Iroquois (25)	40	0.01
Kiowa (26)	42	0.01
Latin American Indians (415)	545	0.10
Lumbee	3	0.00
Menominee (2)	2	0.00
Navajo (48)	64	0.01
Osage (6)	16	0.00
Ottawa (2)	4	0.00
Paiute (1)	1	0.00
Pima	3	0.00
Potawatomi (35)	50	0.01
Pueblo (25)	39	0.01
Puget Sound Salish (3)	3	0.00
Seminole (8)	44	0.01
Shoshone (6)	10	0.00
Sioux (45)	84	0.02
Tohono O'Odham (6)	7	0.00
Ute (2)	6	0.00
Yakama (1)	1	0.00
Yaqui (1)	3	0.00
Yuman	1	0.00
All other tribes (97)	186	0.03
American Indian tribes, not spec.	331	0.06
Arab:	1,475	0.28
Arab/Arabic	431	0.08
Egyptian	128	0.02
Iraqi	79	0.01
Jordanian	121	0.02
Lebanese	338	0.06
Moroccan	9	0.00
Palestinian	60	0.01
Syrian	100	0.02
Other Arab	209	0.04
Armenian	114	0.02
Asian:	16,613	3.11
Bangladeshi (53)	64	0.01
Cambodian (388)	467	0.09
Chinese, ex. Taiwanese (1,152)	1,403	0.26
Filipino (978)	1,359	0.25
Hmong (37)	39	0.01
Indian (2,590)	2,922	0.55
Indonesian (27)	50	0.01
Japanese (413)	742	0.14
Korean (1,064)	1,253	0.23
Laotian (840)	984	0.18
Malaysian (35)	45	0.01
Pakistani (214)	301	0.06
Sri Lankan (32)	36	0.01
Taiwanese (27)	49	0.01
Thai (240)	349	0.07
Vietnamese (5,415)	5,666	1.06
Other Asian, specified (53)	111	0.02
Other Asian, not specified (327)	773	0.14
Assyrian/Chaldean/Syriac	27	0.01
Australian	83	0.02
Austrian	565	0.11
Basque	6	0.00
Belgian	195	0.04
Brazilian	130	0.02
British	1,938	0.36
Bulgarian	5	0.00
Canadian	606	0.11
Carpatho Rusyn	37	0.01
Celtic	109	0.02
Croatian	175	0.03
Czech	1,513	0.28
Czechoslovakian	690	0.13
Danish	984	0.18
Dutch	5,231	0.98
Eastern European	81	0.02
English	34,747	6.49
Estonian	9	0.00
European	2,871	0.54
Finnish	371	0.07
French, except Basque	9,741	1.82
French Canadian	1,255	0.23
German	39,403	7.36
German Russian	14	0.00
Greek	590	0.11
Guyanese	23	0.00
Hawaii Native/Pacific Islander:	772	0.14
Melanesian: (2)	2	0.00
Fijian (2)	2	0.00
Micronesian: (109)	156	0.03
Guamanian/Chamorro (105)	150	0.03
Other Micronesian (4)	6	0.00
Polynesian: (178)	355	0.07
Native Hawaiian (79)	186	0.03
Samoan (37)	77	0.01
Tongan (58)	80	0.01
Other Polynesian (4)	12	0.00
Other Pac. Isl., specified	46	0.01
Other Pac. Isl., not spec. (42)	213	0.04
Hispanic or Latino:	159,368	29.81
Central American:	1,581	0.30
Costa Rican	53	0.01
Guatemalan	304	0.06
Honduran	350	0.07
Nicaraguan	84	0.02
Panamanian	143	0.03
Salvadoran	575	0.11
Other Central American	72	0.01
Cuban	608	0.11
Dominican Republic	104	0.02
Mexican	132,894	24.85
Puerto Rican	1,892	0.35
South American:	904	0.17
Argentinean	65	0.01
Bolivian	27	0.01
Chilean	82	0.02
Colombian	359	0.07
Ecuadorian	56	0.01
Paraguayan	3	0.00
Peruvian	115	0.02
Uruguayan	11	0.00
Venezuelan	147	0.03
Other South American	39	0.01
Other Hispanic or Latino	21,385	4.00
Hungarian	459	0.09
Icelander	25	0.00
Iranian	122	0.02
Irish	33,209	6.20
Israeli	26	0.00

Notes: 1. Figures in the "Number" column do not add up to the total population due to: a) Ancestry/Race overlap — e.g. persons can report being both White and Irish, b) persons of Hispanic origin can report being any race, c) persons reporting two ancestries are counted in both categories. 2. Numbers in parentheses indicate the number of persons reporting this ancestry/race alone, not in combination with any other ancestry/race. 3. Refer to the Explanation of Data in the front of the book for more detailed information.

Ancestry/Race	Number	%
Italian	7,607	1.42
Latvian	22	0.00
Lithuanian	400	0.07
Luxemburger	40	0.01
Macedonian	17	0.00
Maltese	17	0.00
New Zealander	52	0.01
Northern European	223	0.04
Norwegian	3,050	0.57
Pennsylvania German	87	0.02
Polish	4,368	0.82
Portuguese	481	0.09
Romanian	179	0.03
Russian	1,374	0.26
Scandinavian	458	0.09
Scotch-Irish	8,654	1.62
Scottish	7,923	1.48
Serbian	130	0.02
Slavic	49	0.01
Slovak	170	0.03
Slovene	47	0.01
Swedish	2,971	0.55
Swiss	528	0.10
Turkish	55	0.01
Ukrainian	317	0.06
United States or American	34,680	6.48
Welsh	2,061	0.38
West Indian, excl. Hispanic:	1,080	0.20
Belizean	34	0.01
British West Indian	47	0.01
Dutch West Indian	195	0.04
Haitian	30	0.01
Jamaican	641	0.12
Trinidadian and Tobagonian	49	0.01
U.S. Virgin Islander	45	0.01
West Indian	39	0.01
White:	331,448	61.99
Not Hispanic (244,966)	250,412	46.83
Hispanic (74,193)	81,036	15.16
Yugoslavian	1,005	0.19

Freeport

Place Type: City
County: Brazoria
Population: 12,708

Ancestry/Race	Number	%
Acadian/Cajun	45	0.35
African American/Black:	1,764	13.88
Not Hispanic (1,664)	1,702	13.39
Hispanic (36)	62	0.49
African, sub-Saharan:	48	0.38
African	48	0.38
Alaska Native tribes, specified:	5	0.04
Eskimo (1)	5	0.04
Am. Ind. or Alaska Nat., not spec.	59	0.46
American Indian tribes, specified:	46	0.36
Apache	3	0.02
Cherokee (11)	18	0.14
Chickasaw (1)	1	0.01
Chippewa (1)	1	0.01
Choctaw (4)	4	0.03
Creek (1)	1	0.01
Latin American Indians (12)	13	0.10
Ottawa (1)	1	0.01
Seminole	1	0.01
All other tribes (2)	3	0.02
American Indian tribes, not spec.	14	0.11
Asian:	90	0.71
Filipino (17)	26	0.20
Indian (16)	32	0.25
Japanese	12	0.09
Pakistani (2)	5	0.04
Vietnamese (10)	13	0.10
Other Asian, not specified	2	0.02
British	6	0.05
Canadian	7	0.06
Croatian	63	0.50
Czech	170	1.34
Czechoslovakian	13	0.10
Danish	14	0.11
Dutch	143	1.12
English	385	3.03
European	7	0.06
French, except Basque	201	1.58
French Canadian	19	0.15
German	568	4.47
Hawaii Native/Pacific Islander:	25	0.20
Micronesian:	2	0.02
Guamanian/Chamorro	2	0.02
Polynesian:	19	0.15
Native Hawaiian	8	0.06
Samoan	10	0.08
Other Polynesian	1	0.01
Other Pac. Isl., not spec. (1)	4	0.03
Hispanic or Latino:	6,614	52.05
Central American:	99	0.78
Costa Rican	1	0.01
Guatemalan	3	0.02
Honduran	4	0.03
Nicaraguan	52	0.41
Salvadoran	31	0.24
Other Central American	8	0.06
Cuban	3	0.02
Mexican	5,202	40.93
Puerto Rican	16	0.13
South American:	2	0.02
Colombian	1	0.01
Peruvian	1	0.01
Other Hispanic or Latino	1,292	10.17
Hungarian	7	0.06
Irish	498	3.92
Italian	46	0.36
Lithuanian	6	0.05
Norwegian	16	0.13
Polish	84	0.66
Portuguese	4	0.03
Scandinavian	10	0.08
Scotch-Irish	145	1.14
Scottish	90	0.71
Swedish	9	0.07
United States or American	696	5.47
Welsh	38	0.30
West Indian, excl. Hispanic:	19	0.15
Dutch West Indian	8	0.06
Jamaican	3	0.02
Trinidadian and Tobagonian	8	0.06
White:	8,182	64.38
Not Hispanic (4,224)	4,328	34.06
Hispanic (3,598)	3,854	30.33
Yugoslavian	38	0.30

Friendswood

Place Type: City
County: Galveston
Population: 29,037

Ancestry/Race	Number	%
Acadian/Cajun	20	0.07
African American/Black:	864	2.98
Not Hispanic (774)	837	2.88
Hispanic (9)	27	0.09
African, sub-Saharan:	131	0.46
African	106	0.37
South African	25	0.09
Alaska Native tribes, specified:	2	0.01
Alaska Athabascan	2	0.01
Am. Ind. or Alaska Nat., not spec.	52	0.18
Albanian	11	0.04
Alsatian	9	0.03
American Indian tribes, specified:	194	0.67
Apache (2)	8	0.03
Blackfeet (1)	8	0.03
Cherokee (26)	68	0.23
Cheyenne (1)	2	0.01
Chickasaw (10)	11	0.04
Chippewa	1	0.00
Choctaw (14)	25	0.09
Comanche	6	0.02
Cree	1	0.00
Creek (8)	9	0.03
Delaware (1)	5	0.02
Houma (3)	3	0.01
Iroquois (2)	4	0.01
Kiowa	1	0.00
Latin American Indians (9)	11	0.04
Lumbee (1)	3	0.01
Navajo (4)	4	0.01
Osage	1	0.00
Potawatomi (1)	4	0.01
Seminole (2)	4	0.01
Sioux	3	0.01
All other tribes (2)	12	0.04
American Indian tribes, not spec.	11	0.04
Arab:	74	0.26
Iraqi	10	0.03
Lebanese	64	0.22
Armenian	40	0.14
Asian:	859	2.96
Bangladeshi (5)	8	0.03
Cambodian (9)	9	0.03
Chinese, ex. Taiwanese (104)	132	0.45
Filipino (79)	108	0.37
Indian (137)	166	0.57
Indonesian (2)	2	0.01
Japanese (25)	58	0.20
Korean (27)	34	0.12
Laotian (2)	2	0.01
Pakistani (21)	30	0.10
Sri Lankan (12)	14	0.05
Taiwanese (20)	20	0.07
Thai (12)	16	0.06
Vietnamese (207)	225	0.77
Other Asian, specified (2)	3	0.01
Other Asian, not specified (16)	32	0.11
Australian	9	0.03
Austrian	36	0.13
Belgian	43	0.15
British	135	0.47
Canadian	25	0.09
Celtic	10	0.03
Croatian	28	0.10
Czech	398	1.39
Czechoslovakian	98	0.34
Danish	153	0.53
Dutch	381	1.33
English	4,111	14.31
European	341	1.19
Finnish	36	0.13
French, except Basque	1,570	5.46
French Canadian	261	0.91
German	5,112	17.79
Greek	129	0.45
Hawaii Native/Pacific Islander:	13	0.04
Melanesian: (2)	2	0.01
Fijian (2)	2	0.01
Micronesian:	2	0.01
Guamanian/Chamorro	2	0.01
Polynesian: (1)	5	0.02
Native Hawaiian	3	0.01
Samoan (1)	2	0.01
Other Pac. Isl., not spec. (1)	4	0.01
Hispanic or Latino:	2,553	8.79
Central American:	78	0.27
Costa Rican	2	0.01
Honduran	16	0.06
Nicaraguan	1	0.00
Panamanian	11	0.04
Salvadoran	46	0.16
Other Central American	2	0.01
Cuban	64	0.22
Dominican Republic	5	0.02
Mexican	1,728	5.95
Puerto Rican	101	0.35
South American:	99	0.34
Argentinean	17	0.06
Bolivian	10	0.03
Chilean	3	0.01

Notes: 1. Figures in the "Number" column do not add up to the total population due to: a) Ancestry/Race overlap — e.g. persons can report being both White and Irish, b) persons of Hispanic origin can report being any race, c) persons reporting two ancestries are counted in both categories. 2. Numbers in parentheses indicate the number of persons reporting this ancestry/race alone, not in combination with any other ancestry/race. 3. Refer to the Explanation of Data in the front of the book for more detailed information.

Colombian	17	0.06
Ecuadorian	5	0.02
Peruvian	23	0.08
Uruguayan	5	0.02
Venezuelan	16	0.06
Other South American	3	0.01
Other Hispanic or Latino	478	1.65
Hungarian	78	0.27
Iranian	59	0.21
Irish	3,485	12.13
Israeli	34	0.12
Italian	1,172	4.08
Lithuanian	51	0.18
Norwegian	325	1.13
Pennsylvania German	7	0.02
Polish	721	2.51
Romanian	8	0.03
Russian	165	0.57
Scandinavian	35	0.12
Scotch-Irish	862	3.00
Scottish	816	2.84
Slavic	41	0.14
Slovak	31	0.11
Slovene	20	0.07
Swedish	209	0.73
Swiss	46	0.16
Ukrainian	27	0.09
United States or American	2,606	9.07
Welsh	233	0.81
West Indian, excl. Hispanic:	49	0.17
Belizean	49	0.17
White:	26,577	91.53
Not Hispanic (24,548)	24,839	85.54
Hispanic (1,610)	1,738	5.99

Frisco

Place Type: City
County: Collin
Population: 33,714

Ancestry/Race	Number	%
Acadian/Cajun	50	0.15
Afghan	30	0.09
African American/Black:	1,368	4.06
Not Hispanic (1,229)	1,311	3.89
Hispanic (39)	57	0.17
African, sub-Saharan:	208	0.62
African	136	0.41
Ghanian	18	0.05
Kenyan	23	0.07
Nigerian	31	0.09
Alaska Native tribes, specified:	1	0.00
Eskimo	1	0.00
Am. Ind. or Alaska Nat., not spec.	72	0.21
American Indian tribes, specified:	207	0.61
Apache (3)	5	0.01
Blackfeet (4)	9	0.03
Cherokee (30)	79	0.23
Chickasaw (18)	22	0.07
Chippewa	1	0.00
Choctaw (23)	44	0.13
Comanche (1)	1	0.00
Creek (3)	5	0.01
Delaware (2)	2	0.01
Iroquois (2)	4	0.01
Latin American Indians (1)	2	0.01
Lumbee (3)	3	0.01
Navajo (1)	3	0.01
Osage	2	0.01
Potawatomi	1	0.00
Pueblo	1	0.00
Seminole (2)	3	0.01
Sioux (5)	8	0.02
Yakama	1	0.00
All other tribes (6)	11	0.03
American Indian tribes, not spec.	3	0.01
Arab:	78	0.23
Lebanese	31	0.09
Syrian	47	0.14
Armenian	37	0.11
Asian:	1,014	3.01
Bangladeshi (3)	3	0.01
Cambodian (2)	5	0.01
Chinese, ex. Taiwanese (162)	199	0.59
Filipino (77)	139	0.41
Indian (193)	225	0.67
Indonesian (6)	6	0.02
Japanese (26)	42	0.12
Korean (123)	148	0.44
Laotian (5)	5	0.01
Malaysian (3)	7	0.02
Pakistani (23)	30	0.09
Sri Lankan (1)	3	0.01
Taiwanese (6)	6	0.02
Thai (11)	18	0.05
Vietnamese (106)	123	0.36
Other Asian, specified (9)	13	0.04
Other Asian, not specified (18)	42	0.12
Austrian	119	0.36
Belgian	16	0.05
British	70	0.21
Canadian	193	0.58
Celtic	9	0.03
Croatian	53	0.16
Czech	249	0.74
Czechoslovakian	68	0.20
Danish	192	0.57
Dutch	540	1.61
English	3,926	11.72
Estonian	12	0.04
European	389	1.16
Finnish	37	0.11
French, except Basque	1,004	3.00
French Canadian	238	0.71
German	6,213	18.55
Greek	86	0.26
Guyanese	32	0.10
Hawaii Native/Pacific Islander:	48	0.14
Micronesian: (6)	17	0.05
Guamanian/Chamorro (5)	16	0.05
Other Micronesian (1)	1	0.00
Polynesian: (3)	11	0.03
Native Hawaiian (1)	6	0.02
Samoan (2)	4	0.01
Other Polynesian	1	0.00
Other Pac. Isl., specified	1	0.00
Other Pac. Isl., not spec. (1)	19	0.06
Hispanic or Latino:	3,716	11.02
Central American:	76	0.23
Costa Rican	5	0.01
Guatemalan	8	0.02
Honduran	9	0.03
Nicaraguan	13	0.04
Panamanian	19	0.06
Salvadoran	18	0.05
Other Central American	4	0.01
Cuban	83	0.25
Dominican Republic	5	0.01
Mexican	2,781	8.25
Puerto Rican	81	0.24
South American:	89	0.26
Argentinean	1	0.00
Bolivian	2	0.01
Chilean	7	0.02
Colombian	28	0.08
Ecuadorian	7	0.02
Peruvian	13	0.04
Uruguayan	2	0.01
Venezuelan	23	0.07
Other South American	6	0.02
Other Hispanic or Latino	601	1.78
Hungarian	152	0.45
Icelander	8	0.02
Iranian	108	0.32
Irish	3,888	11.61
Israeli	6	0.02
Italian	1,497	4.47
Lithuanian	97	0.29
Northern European	67	0.20
Norwegian	327	0.98
Pennsylvania German	10	0.03
Polish	817	2.44
Portuguese	112	0.33
Romanian	44	0.13
Russian	177	0.53
Scandinavian	34	0.10
Scotch-Irish	715	2.13
Scottish	832	2.48
Serbian	6	0.02
Slavic	2	0.01
Slovak	27	0.08
Slovene	8	0.02
Swedish	611	1.82
Swiss	96	0.29
Turkish	8	0.02
Ukrainian	181	0.54
United States or American	2,917	8.71
Welsh	307	0.92
West Indian, excl. Hispanic:	54	0.16
Belizean	8	0.02
Dutch West Indian	7	0.02
Jamaican	20	0.06
Other West Indian	19	0.06
White:	29,997	88.97
Not Hispanic (27,433)	27,790	82.43
Hispanic (1,984)	2,207	6.55

Gainesville

Place Type: City
County: Cooke
Population: 15,538

Ancestry/Race	Number	%
African American/Black:	1,007	6.48
Not Hispanic (913)	978	6.29
Hispanic (20)	29	0.19
Alaska Native tribes, specified:	6	0.04
Alaska Athabascan (3)	3	0.02
Aleut	3	0.02
Am. Ind. or Alaska Nat., not spec.	106	0.68
American Indian tribes, specified:	207	1.33
Apache (4)	7	0.05
Cherokee (31)	71	0.46
Chickasaw (28)	39	0.25
Chippewa (2)	2	0.01
Choctaw (24)	37	0.24
Comanche	1	0.01
Creek (5)	9	0.06
Crow (1)	1	0.01
Delaware	1	0.01
Iroquois (2)	2	0.01
Kiowa (1)	1	0.01
Latin American Indians (11)	12	0.08
Navajo (3)	3	0.02
Osage (1)	1	0.01
Paiute	1	0.01
Potawatomi (4)	4	0.03
Seminole (2)	2	0.01
Sioux (3)	7	0.05
All other tribes (3)	6	0.04
American Indian tribes, not spec.	10	0.06
Arab:	17	0.11
Syrian	17	0.11
Asian:	123	0.79
Chinese, ex. Taiwanese (8)	9	0.06
Filipino (12)	21	0.14
Indian (30)	32	0.21
Indonesian (1)	1	0.01
Japanese (4)	11	0.07
Korean (4)	8	0.05
Pakistani (19)	22	0.14
Thai	1	0.01
Vietnamese (5)	5	0.03
Other Asian, not specified (1)	13	0.08
Australian	7	0.05
Austrian	8	0.05
Belgian	20	0.13
British	7	0.05

Notes: 1. Figures in the "Number" column do not add up to the total population due to: a) Ancestry/Race overlap — e.g. persons can report being both White and Irish, b) persons of Hispanic origin can report being any race, c) persons reporting two ancestries are counted in both categories. 2. Numbers in parentheses indicate the number of persons reporting this ancestry/race alone, not in combination with any other ancestry/race. 3. Refer to the Explanation of Data in the front of the book for more detailed information.

Ancestry/Race	Number	%
Bulgarian	12	0.08
Canadian	31	0.20
Czech	41	0.26
Czechoslovakian	13	0.08
Danish	18	0.12
Dutch	294	1.90
English	1,173	7.58
European	57	0.37
Finnish	9	0.06
French, except Basque	271	1.75
French Canadian	6	0.04
German	1,777	11.49
Greek	12	0.08
Hawaii Native/Pacific Islander:	17	0.11
Micronesian: (1)	3	0.02
Guamanian/Chamorro (1)	3	0.02
Polynesian:	4	0.03
Native Hawaiian	1	0.01
Samoan	3	0.02
Other Pac. Isl., not spec.	10	0.06
Hispanic or Latino:	2,714	17.47
Central American:	25	0.16
Honduran	2	0.01
Panamanian	2	0.01
Salvadoran	21	0.14
Cuban	2	0.01
Mexican	2,349	15.12
Puerto Rican	16	0.10
South American:	8	0.05
Chilean	2	0.01
Colombian	1	0.01
Peruvian	4	0.03
Other South American	1	0.01
Other Hispanic or Latino	314	2.02
Hungarian	15	0.10
Irish	1,312	8.48
Italian	142	0.92
Norwegian	48	0.31
Polish	145	0.94
Portuguese	8	0.05
Russian	6	0.04
Scotch-Irish	257	1.66
Scottish	277	1.79
Swedish	70	0.45
United States or American	1,900	12.28
Welsh	28	0.18
West Indian, excl. Hispanic:	39	0.25
Dutch West Indian	39	0.25
White:	12,867	82.81
Not Hispanic (11,449)	11,651	74.98
Hispanic (1,101)	1,216	7.83
Yugoslavian	43	0.28

Galena Park

Place Type: City
County: Harris
Population: 10,592

Ancestry/Race	Number	%
African American/Black:	828	7.82
Not Hispanic (803)	814	7.69
Hispanic (7)	14	0.13
African, sub-Saharan:	135	1.28
African	135	1.28
Am. Ind. or Alaska Nat., not spec.	96	0.91
American Indian tribes, specified:	42	0.40
Apache (1)	1	0.01
Cherokee (5)	8	0.08
Chickasaw (1)	4	0.04
Choctaw (2)	9	0.08
Latin American Indians (13)	15	0.14
Navajo	1	0.01
Potawatomi	2	0.02
Pueblo (1)	1	0.01
All other tribes (1)	1	0.01
American Indian tribes, not spec.	8	0.08
Arab:	22	0.21
Arab/Arabic	22	0.21
Asian:	55	0.52
Chinese, ex. Taiwanese (3)	7	0.07
Filipino (27)	30	0.28
Indian (5)	6	0.06
Japanese	3	0.03
Korean (1)	2	0.02
Laotian (2)	2	0.02
Pakistani (1)	1	0.01
Thai (1)	1	0.01
Other Asian, not specified (2)	3	0.03
Czech	51	0.48
English	276	2.61
French, except Basque	110	1.04
French Canadian	7	0.07
German	365	3.45
Greek	43	0.41
Hawaii Native/Pacific Islander:	3	0.03
Polynesian: (1)	3	0.03
Native Hawaiian (1)	3	0.03
Hispanic or Latino:	7,343	69.33
Central American:	97	0.92
Costa Rican	5	0.05
Guatemalan	2	0.02
Honduran	5	0.05
Nicaraguan	8	0.08
Salvadoran	63	0.59
Other Central American	14	0.13
Cuban	3	0.03
Mexican	6,334	59.80
Puerto Rican	16	0.15
South American:	13	0.12
Chilean	6	0.06
Colombian	5	0.05
Peruvian	1	0.01
Uruguayan	1	0.01
Other Hispanic or Latino	880	8.31
Irish	339	3.20
Italian	41	0.39
Norwegian	6	0.06
Polish	35	0.33
Portuguese	8	0.08
Scotch-Irish	99	0.94
Scottish	19	0.18
Swiss	6	0.06
Ukrainian	18	0.17
United States or American	430	4.06
Welsh	9	0.09
White:	7,083	66.87
Not Hispanic (2,347)	2,386	22.53
Hispanic (4,363)	4,697	44.34

Galveston

Place Type: City
County: Galveston
Population: 57,247

Ancestry/Race	Number	%
Acadian/Cajun	26	0.05
African American/Black:	14,888	26.01
Not Hispanic (14,422)	14,637	25.57
Hispanic (170)	251	0.44
African, sub-Saharan:	410	0.72
African	363	0.63
Ghanian	15	0.03
Nigerian	12	0.02
Other sub-Saharan African	20	0.03
Alaska Native tribes, specified:	3	0.01
Alaska Athabascan	1	0.00
Aleut (1)	1	0.00
Eskimo	1	0.00
Alaska Native tribes, not specified	1	0.00
Am. Ind. or Alaska Nat., not spec.	161	0.28
American Indian tribes, specified:	298	0.52
Apache (15)	20	0.03
Blackfeet (3)	8	0.01
Cherokee (46)	116	0.20
Cheyenne (1)	1	0.00
Chickasaw (2)	2	0.00
Chippewa (4)	6	0.01
Choctaw (10)	20	0.03
Comanche (2)	8	0.01
Creek (2)	3	0.01
Delaware (1)	1	0.00
Houma (1)	1	0.00
Iroquois (2)	8	0.01
Kiowa (1)	2	0.00
Latin American Indians (22)	42	0.07
Navajo (2)	2	0.00
Osage (4)	6	0.01
Paiute (6)	6	0.01
Potawatomi (1)	4	0.01
Seminole	1	0.00
Sioux (3)	7	0.01
Yaqui	3	0.01
All other tribes (18)	31	0.05
American Indian tribes, not spec.	41	0.07
Arab:	154	0.27
Arab/Arabic	14	0.02
Egyptian	33	0.06
Lebanese	77	0.13
Moroccan	10	0.02
Syrian	9	0.02
Other Arab	11	0.02
Armenian	20	0.03
Asian:	2,069	3.61
Bangladeshi (2)	2	0.00
Cambodian (18)	18	0.03
Chinese, ex. Taiwanese (460)	490	0.86
Filipino (319)	384	0.67
Indian (505)	537	0.94
Indonesian (2)	9	0.02
Japanese (65)	81	0.14
Korean (143)	162	0.28
Laotian (1)	2	0.00
Malaysian	2	0.00
Pakistani (48)	56	0.10
Sri Lankan (4)	4	0.01
Taiwanese (24)	28	0.05
Thai (6)	8	0.01
Vietnamese (211)	218	0.38
Other Asian, specified	2	0.00
Other Asian, not specified (16)	66	0.12
Assyrian/Chaldean/Syriac	7	0.01
Australian	25	0.04
Austrian	155	0.27
Belgian	17	0.03
Brazilian	27	0.05
British	204	0.36
Canadian	96	0.17
Croatian	56	0.10
Czech	246	0.43
Czechoslovakian	109	0.19
Danish	80	0.14
Dutch	430	0.75
Eastern European	36	0.06
English	3,165	5.53
European	432	0.76
Finnish	21	0.04
French, except Basque	1,455	2.54
French Canadian	172	0.30
German	4,841	8.47
Greek	197	0.34
Guyanese	20	0.03
Hawaii Native/Pacific Islander:	92	0.16
Micronesian: (9)	11	0.02
Guamanian/Chamorro (7)	9	0.02
Other Micronesian (2)	2	0.00
Polynesian: (23)	43	0.08
Native Hawaiian (21)	41	0.07
Samoan (2)	2	0.00
Other Pac. Isl., specified	1	0.00
Other Pac. Isl., not spec. (10)	37	0.06
Hispanic or Latino:	14,753	25.77
Central American:	651	1.14
Costa Rican	13	0.02
Guatemalan	94	0.16
Honduran	165	0.29
Nicaraguan	14	0.02
Panamanian	14	0.02
Salvadoran	312	0.55

Notes: 1. Figures in the "Number" column do not add up to the total population due to: a) Ancestry/Race overlap — e.g. persons can report being both White and Irish, b) persons of Hispanic origin can report being any race, c) persons reporting two ancestries are counted in both categories. 2. Numbers in parentheses indicate the number of persons reporting this ancestry/race alone, not in combination with any other ancestry/race. 3. Refer to the Explanation of Data in the front of the book for more detailed information.

Other Central American	39	0.07
Cuban	66	0.12
Dominican Republic	10	0.02
Mexican	11,430	19.97
Puerto Rican	147	0.26
South American:	149	0.26
Argentinean	12	0.02
Bolivian	9	0.02
Chilean	14	0.02
Colombian	48	0.08
Ecuadorian	11	0.02
Paraguayan	5	0.01
Peruvian	20	0.03
Uruguayan	1	0.00
Venezuelan	14	0.02
Other South American	15	0.03
Other Hispanic or Latino	2,300	4.02
Hungarian	85	0.15
Iranian	50	0.09
Irish	4,073	7.12
Israeli	40	0.07
Italian	2,072	3.62
Latvian	8	0.01
Lithuanian	13	0.02
Northern European	5	0.01
Norwegian	305	0.53
Polish	614	1.07
Portuguese	16	0.03
Romanian	9	0.02
Russian	163	0.29
Scandinavian	36	0.06
Scotch-Irish	837	1.46
Scottish	547	0.96
Serbian	23	0.04
Slavic	14	0.02
Slovak	40	0.07
Slovene	11	0.02
Swedish	387	0.68
Swiss	85	0.15
Ukrainian	122	0.21
United States or American	2,353	4.11
Welsh	231	0.40
West Indian, excl. Hispanic:	58	0.10
Barbadian	14	0.02
Belizean	18	0.03
Haitian	7	0.01
Jamaican	5	0.01
Trinidadian and Tobagonian	9	0.02
Other West Indian	5	0.01
White:	34,731	60.67
Not Hispanic (25,277)	25,824	45.11
Hispanic (8,305)	8,907	15.56
Yugoslavian	117	0.20

Garland

Place Type: City
County: Dallas
Population: 215,768

Ancestry/Race	Number	%
Acadian/Cajun	46	0.02
African American/Black:	26,810	12.43
Not Hispanic (25,326)	26,293	12.19
Hispanic (283)	517	0.24
African, sub-Saharan:	2,497	1.16
African	1,127	0.52
Ethiopian	316	0.15
Ghanian	41	0.02
Kenyan	37	0.02
Liberian	11	0.01
Nigerian	820	0.38
Sierra Leonean	25	0.01
South African	48	0.02
Other sub-Saharan African	72	0.03
Alaska Native tribes, specified:	6	0.00
Alaska Athabascan	2	0.00
Eskimo (1)	3	0.00
Tlingit-Haida	1	0.00
Alaska Native tribes, not specified	2	0.00
Am. Ind. or Alaska Nat., not spec.	745	0.35
Albanian	77	0.04
American Indian tribes, specified:	1,653	0.77
Apache (24)	63	0.03
Blackfeet (8)	26	0.01
Cherokee (199)	557	0.26
Cheyenne (7)	10	0.00
Chickasaw (41)	85	0.04
Chippewa (9)	19	0.01
Choctaw (180)	324	0.15
Colville (2)	2	0.00
Comanche (19)	40	0.02
Cree (2)	4	0.00
Creek (43)	63	0.03
Crow (2)	3	0.00
Delaware (4)	11	0.01
Houma (1)	3	0.00
Iroquois (14)	20	0.01
Kiowa (5)	5	0.00
Latin American Indians (99)	171	0.08
Lumbee (2)	2	0.00
Navajo (32)	42	0.02
Osage (5)	20	0.01
Paiute	2	0.00
Potawatomi (12)	16	0.01
Pueblo (11)	20	0.01
Puget Sound Salish (1)	1	0.00
Seminole (8)	23	0.01
Shoshone (3)	7	0.00
Sioux (11)	20	0.01
Tohono O'Odham	1	0.00
All other tribes (46)	93	0.04
American Indian tribes, not spec.	122	0.06
Arab:	658	0.30
Arab/Arabic	140	0.06
Egyptian	44	0.02
Iraqi	33	0.02
Jordanian	107	0.05
Lebanese	217	0.10
Palestinian	97	0.04
Other Arab	20	0.01
Armenian	7	0.00
Asian:	17,401	8.06
Bangladeshi (56)	65	0.03
Cambodian (411)	471	0.22
Chinese, ex. Taiwanese (1,727)	1,984	0.92
Filipino (1,120)	1,338	0.62
Hmong (3)	3	0.00
Indian (3,056)	3,321	1.54
Indonesian (7)	19	0.01
Japanese (137)	257	0.12
Korean (1,024)	1,115	0.52
Laotian (537)	629	0.29
Malaysian (2)	10	0.00
Pakistani (330)	424	0.20
Sri Lankan (12)	16	0.01
Taiwanese (49)	80	0.04
Thai (151)	177	0.08
Vietnamese (6,736)	7,023	3.25
Other Asian, specified (11)	20	0.01
Other Asian, not specified (200)	449	0.21
Australian	58	0.03
Austrian	262	0.12
Basque	34	0.02
Belgian	143	0.07
Brazilian	87	0.04
British	666	0.31
Bulgarian	6	0.00
Canadian	272	0.13
Celtic	94	0.04
Croatian	96	0.04
Cypriot	35	0.02
Czech	945	0.44
Czechoslovakian	286	0.13
Danish	302	0.14
Dutch	2,014	0.93
Eastern European	7	0.00
English	15,829	7.33
Estonian	21	0.01
European	1,626	0.75
Finnish	133	0.06
French, except Basque	4,342	2.01
French Canadian	622	0.29
German	19,666	9.11
German Russian	9	0.00
Greek	281	0.13
Guyanese	90	0.04
Hawaii Native/Pacific Islander:	320	0.15
Micronesian: (40)	63	0.03
Guamanian/Chamorro (39)	61	0.03
Other Micronesian (1)	2	0.00
Polynesian: (84)	141	0.07
Native Hawaiian (54)	91	0.04
Samoan (29)	49	0.02
Other Polynesian (1)	1	0.00
Other Pac. Isl., specified	2	0.00
Other Pac. Isl., not spec. (17)	114	0.05
Hispanic or Latino:	55,192	25.58
Central American:	3,212	1.49
Costa Rican	79	0.04
Guatemalan	813	0.38
Honduran	306	0.14
Nicaraguan	50	0.02
Panamanian	59	0.03
Salvadoran	1,737	0.81
Other Central American	168	0.08
Cuban	282	0.13
Dominican Republic	31	0.01
Mexican	42,452	19.67
Puerto Rican	640	0.30
South American:	705	0.33
Argentinean	27	0.01
Bolivian	41	0.02
Chilean	29	0.01
Colombian	320	0.15
Ecuadorian	62	0.03
Paraguayan	1	0.00
Peruvian	139	0.06
Uruguayan	3	0.00
Venezuelan	47	0.02
Other South American	36	0.02
Other Hispanic or Latino	7,870	3.65
Hungarian	290	0.13
Icelander	37	0.02
Iranian	214	0.10
Irish	16,092	7.45
Israeli	101	0.05
Italian	3,609	1.67
Latvian	22	0.01
Lithuanian	88	0.04
Northern European	73	0.03
Norwegian	1,258	0.58
Pennsylvania German	52	0.02
Polish	1,772	0.82
Portuguese	190	0.09
Romanian	136	0.06
Russian	533	0.25
Scandinavian	194	0.09
Scotch-Irish	3,455	1.60
Scottish	3,460	1.60
Serbian	30	0.01
Slavic	24	0.01
Slovak	127	0.06
Slovene	74	0.03
Soviet Union	15	0.01
Swedish	1,119	0.52
Swiss	263	0.12
Turkish	7	0.00
Ukrainian	152	0.07
United States or American	17,564	8.13
Welsh	959	0.44
West Indian, excl. Hispanic:	546	0.25
Barbadian	21	0.01
Belizean	188	0.09
British West Indian	22	0.01
Dutch West Indian	102	0.05
Jamaican	73	0.03
Trinidadian and Tobagonian	102	0.05
U.S. Virgin Islander	7	0.00
West Indian	31	0.01

Notes: 1. Figures in the "Number" column do not add up to the total population due to: a) Ancestry/Race overlap — e.g. persons can report being both White and Irish, b) persons of Hispanic origin can report being any race, c) persons reporting two ancestries are counted in both categories. 2. Numbers in parentheses indicate the number of persons reporting this ancestry/race alone, not in combination with any other ancestry/race. 3. Refer to the Explanation of Data in the front of the book for more detailed information.

White:	146,000	67.67
Not Hispanic (114,985)	117,531	54.47
Hispanic (25,850)	28,469	13.19
Yugoslavian	74	0.03

Gatesville

Place Type: City
County: Coryell
Population: 15,591

Ancestry/Race	Number	%
African American/Black:	4,224	27.09
Not Hispanic (4,206)	4,217	27.05
Hispanic (4)	7	0.04
Am. Ind. or Alaska Nat., not spec.	30	0.19
American Indian tribes, specified:	62	0.40
Apache (1)	2	0.01
Blackfeet	2	0.01
Cherokee (11)	25	0.16
Chickasaw	2	0.01
Chippewa (4)	4	0.03
Choctaw (5)	9	0.06
Crow (1)	1	0.01
Delaware (3)	3	0.02
Navajo (3)	4	0.03
Pueblo	1	0.01
Seminole (2)	2	0.01
Sioux	2	0.01
All other tribes (2)	5	0.03
American Indian tribes, not spec.	2	0.01
Asian:	66	0.42
Cambodian (1)	1	0.01
Chinese, ex. Taiwanese (2)	2	0.01
Filipino (11)	18	0.12
Indian (14)	14	0.09
Japanese (13)	13	0.08
Korean (2)	5	0.03
Thai (5)	5	0.03
Vietnamese (2)	2	0.01
Other Asian, specified	2	0.01
Other Asian, not specified (4)	4	0.03
Belgian	5	0.03
Czech	42	0.28
Dutch	75	0.49
English	424	2.78
European	81	0.53
French, except Basque	153	1.00
French Canadian	30	0.20
German	660	4.33
Hawaii Native/Pacific Islander:	16	0.10
Polynesian: (4)	6	0.04
Native Hawaiian (4)	5	0.03
Samoan	1	0.01
Other Pac. Isl., specified	2	0.01
Other Pac. Isl., not spec. (4)	8	0.05
Hispanic or Latino:	2,297	14.73
Central American:	10	0.06
Honduran	2	0.01
Panamanian	6	0.04
Salvadoran	2	0.01
Cuban	1	0.01
Dominican Republic	1	0.01
Mexican	1,923	12.33
Puerto Rican	35	0.22
South American:	6	0.04
Colombian	4	0.03
Venezuelan	2	0.01
Other Hispanic or Latino	321	2.06
Hungarian	5	0.03
Irish	536	3.52
Italian	59	0.39
Norwegian	39	0.26
Polish	36	0.24
Russian	13	0.09
Scotch-Irish	176	1.15
Scottish	105	0.69
Swedish	14	0.09
United States or American	1,101	7.22
Welsh	35	0.23
White:	9,932	63.70
Not Hispanic (8,932)	8,984	57.62
Hispanic (922)	948	6.08

Georgetown

Place Type: City
County: Williamson
Population: 28,339

Ancestry/Race	Number	%
Acadian/Cajun	32	0.11
African American/Black:	1,048	3.70
Not Hispanic (932)	999	3.53
Hispanic (28)	49	0.17
African, sub-Saharan:	76	0.27
African	61	0.22
Nigerian	15	0.05
Am. Ind. or Alaska Nat., not spec.	82	0.29
Albanian	9	0.03
Alsatian	9	0.03
American Indian tribes, specified:	110	0.39
Apache (6)	7	0.02
Blackfeet	1	0.00
Cherokee (11)	38	0.13
Cheyenne (2)	2	0.01
Chickasaw (1)	1	0.00
Chippewa	3	0.01
Choctaw (8)	14	0.05
Creek	2	0.01
Crow	1	0.00
Delaware	1	0.00
Kiowa	3	0.01
Latin American Indians (12)	17	0.06
Navajo (2)	3	0.01
Pima	1	0.00
Potawatomi (1)	1	0.00
Pueblo (1)	2	0.01
Sioux	4	0.01
Yaqui	2	0.01
All other tribes (3)	7	0.02
American Indian tribes, not spec.	15	0.05
Arab:	120	0.43
Egyptian	10	0.04
Lebanese	68	0.24
Palestinian	13	0.05
Syrian	29	0.10
Armenian	7	0.02
Asian:	298	1.05
Cambodian (10)	11	0.04
Chinese, ex. Taiwanese (55)	68	0.24
Filipino (12)	25	0.09
Indian (47)	61	0.22
Japanese (15)	37	0.13
Korean (22)	37	0.13
Laotian (1)	1	0.00
Pakistani (3)	8	0.03
Taiwanese (1)	1	0.00
Thai (4)	8	0.03
Vietnamese (12)	24	0.08
Other Asian, specified	4	0.01
Other Asian, not specified (5)	13	0.05
Australian	15	0.05
Austrian	53	0.19
Basque	5	0.02
Belgian	13	0.05
British	278	0.98
Bulgarian	14	0.05
Canadian	70	0.25
Celtic	7	0.02
Croatian	12	0.04
Czech	561	1.99
Czechoslovakian	61	0.22
Danish	178	0.63
Dutch	503	1.78
English	4,398	15.58
European	311	1.10
Finnish	29	0.10
French, except Basque	978	3.46
French Canadian	172	0.61
German	5,265	18.65
Greek	69	0.24
Hawaii Native/Pacific Islander:	37	0.13
Micronesian: (4)	9	0.03
Guamanian/Chamorro (4)	9	0.03
Polynesian: (8)	19	0.07
Native Hawaiian (5)	11	0.04
Samoan (3)	3	0.01
Other Polynesian	5	0.02
Other Pac. Isl., specified	3	0.01
Other Pac. Isl., not spec. (3)	6	0.02
Hispanic or Latino:	5,121	18.07
Central American:	40	0.14
Guatemalan	6	0.02
Honduran	10	0.04
Nicaraguan	4	0.01
Panamanian	2	0.01
Salvadoran	17	0.06
Other Central American	1	0.00
Cuban	15	0.05
Mexican	3,925	13.85
Puerto Rican	126	0.44
South American:	21	0.07
Argentinean	1	0.00
Bolivian	2	0.01
Chilean	4	0.01
Colombian	6	0.02
Ecuadorian	1	0.00
Peruvian	3	0.01
Venezuelan	3	0.01
Other South American	1	0.00
Other Hispanic or Latino	994	3.51
Hungarian	46	0.16
Iranian	6	0.02
Irish	3,145	11.14
Italian	673	2.38
Latvian	13	0.05
Lithuanian	22	0.08
Luxemburger	8	0.03
New Zealander	6	0.02
Northern European	6	0.02
Norwegian	302	1.07
Pennsylvania German	29	0.10
Polish	366	1.30
Portuguese	66	0.23
Romanian	13	0.05
Russian	136	0.48
Scandinavian	45	0.16
Scotch-Irish	914	3.24
Scottish	703	2.49
Slavic	28	0.10
Slovak	17	0.06
Swedish	586	2.08
Swiss	116	0.41
Ukrainian	23	0.08
United States or American	1,919	6.80
Welsh	194	0.69
West Indian, excl. Hispanic:	27	0.10
Belizean	13	0.05
Dutch West Indian	8	0.03
Jamaican	6	0.02
White:	24,662	87.02
Not Hispanic (21,763)	21,993	77.61
Hispanic (2,437)	2,669	9.42

Grand Prairie

Place Type: City
County: Dallas
Population: 127,427

Ancestry/Race	Number	%
Acadian/Cajun	75	0.06
Afghan	21	0.02
African American/Black:	17,996	14.12
Not Hispanic (16,948)	17,518	13.75
Hispanic (294)	478	0.38
African, sub-Saharan:	1,262	0.99
African	578	0.45
Cape Verdean	8	0.01

Notes: 1. Figures in the "Number" column do not add up to the total population due to: a) Ancestry/Race overlap — e.g. persons can report being both White and Irish, b) persons of Hispanic origin can report being any race, c) persons reporting two ancestries are counted in both categories. 2. Numbers in parentheses indicate the number of persons reporting this ancestry/race alone, not in combination with any other ancestry/race. 3. Refer to the Explanation of Data in the front of the book for more detailed information.

Ancestry/Race	Number	%
Ghanian	152	0.12
Kenyan	7	0.01
Nigerian	462	0.36
South African	5	0.00
Ugandan	16	0.01
Zairian	7	0.01
Other sub-Saharan African	27	0.02
Alaska Native tribes, not specified	2	0.00
Am. Ind. or Alaska Nat., not spec.	459	0.36
American Indian tribes, specified:	1,205	0.95
Apache (37)	62	0.05
Blackfeet (7)	22	0.02
Cherokee (145)	374	0.29
Cheyenne (3)	7	0.01
Chickasaw (40)	53	0.04
Chippewa (6)	12	0.01
Choctaw (111)	212	0.17
Comanche (26)	38	0.03
Creek (20)	29	0.02
Crow	2	0.00
Delaware (2)	5	0.00
Iroquois (7)	20	0.02
Kiowa (25)	27	0.02
Latin American Indians (62)	111	0.09
Lumbee (2)	5	0.00
Navajo (30)	42	0.03
Osage (5)	11	0.01
Pima	1	0.00
Potawatomi (7)	15	0.01
Pueblo (11)	16	0.01
Seminole (10)	12	0.01
Sioux (23)	38	0.03
Yaqui	6	0.00
All other tribes (48)	85	0.07
American Indian tribes, not spec.	128	0.10
Arab:	344	0.27
Arab/Arabic	84	0.07
Jordanian	26	0.02
Lebanese	160	0.13
Palestinian	74	0.06
Armenian	16	0.01
Asian:	6,460	5.07
Bangladeshi (17)	20	0.02
Cambodian (24)	36	0.03
Chinese, ex. Taiwanese (396)	486	0.38
Filipino (774)	985	0.77
Hmong (28)	37	0.03
Indian (730)	816	0.64
Indonesian (7)	14	0.01
Japanese (74)	170	0.13
Korean (305)	370	0.29
Laotian (432)	499	0.39
Malaysian (3)	4	0.00
Pakistani (91)	112	0.09
Taiwanese (24)	34	0.03
Thai (65)	76	0.06
Vietnamese (2,442)	2,589	2.03
Other Asian, specified (3)	12	0.01
Other Asian, not specified (98)	200	0.16
Australian	7	0.01
Austrian	72	0.06
Belgian	32	0.03
Brazilian	195	0.15
British	331	0.26
Canadian	200	0.16
Celtic	5	0.00
Croatian	32	0.03
Czech	402	0.32
Czechoslovakian	191	0.15
Danish	263	0.21
Dutch	1,176	0.93
English	7,610	5.99
European	629	0.50
Finnish	54	0.04
French, except Basque	2,185	1.72
French Canadian	370	0.29
German	10,726	8.44
Greek	101	0.08
Guyanese	7	0.01
Hawaii Native/Pacific Islander:	172	0.13
Melanesian:	1	0.00
Other Melanesian	1	0.00
Micronesian: (20)	32	0.03
Guamanian/Chamorro (18)	30	0.02
Other Micronesian (2)	2	0.00
Polynesian: (42)	89	0.07
Native Hawaiian (19)	56	0.04
Samoan (9)	15	0.01
Tongan (14)	17	0.01
Other Polynesian	1	0.00
Other Pac. Isl., specified	4	0.00
Other Pac. Isl., not spec. (12)	46	0.04
Hispanic or Latino:	42,038	32.99
Central American:	911	0.71
Costa Rican	25	0.02
Guatemalan	73	0.06
Honduran	67	0.05
Nicaraguan	97	0.08
Panamanian	38	0.03
Salvadoran	554	0.43
Other Central American	57	0.04
Cuban	176	0.14
Dominican Republic	41	0.03
Mexican	32,209	25.28
Puerto Rican	812	0.64
South American:	277	0.22
Argentinean	32	0.03
Bolivian	5	0.00
Chilean	10	0.01
Colombian	95	0.07
Ecuadorian	27	0.02
Paraguayan	1	0.00
Peruvian	66	0.05
Uruguayan	4	0.00
Venezuelan	23	0.02
Other South American	14	0.01
Other Hispanic or Latino	7,612	5.97
Hungarian	207	0.16
Icelander	7	0.01
Iranian	218	0.17
Irish	9,035	7.11
Italian	1,901	1.50
Latvian	7	0.01
Lithuanian	117	0.09
New Zealander	9	0.01
Northern European	29	0.02
Norwegian	930	0.73
Pennsylvania German	18	0.01
Polish	1,291	1.02
Portuguese	211	0.17
Romanian	83	0.07
Russian	227	0.18
Scandinavian	40	0.03
Scotch-Irish	1,771	1.39
Scottish	1,852	1.46
Serbian	56	0.04
Slavic	6	0.00
Slovak	52	0.04
Slovene	14	0.01
Swedish	510	0.40
Swiss	131	0.10
Ukrainian	31	0.02
United States or American	8,528	6.71
Welsh	473	0.37
West Indian, excl. Hispanic:	415	0.33
Bahamian	13	0.01
Belizean	7	0.01
British West Indian	55	0.04
Dutch West Indian	66	0.05
Haitian	27	0.02
Jamaican	165	0.13
Trinidadian and Tobagonian	47	0.04
U.S. Virgin Islander	8	0.01
West Indian	27	0.02
White:	82,613	64.83
Not Hispanic (60,118)	61,578	48.32
Hispanic (18,852)	21,035	16.51
Yugoslavian	29	0.02

Grapevine

Place Type: City
County: Tarrant
Population: 42,059

Ancestry/Race	Number	%
Afghan	18	0.04
African American/Black:	1,107	2.63
Not Hispanic (952)	1,041	2.48
Hispanic (49)	66	0.16
African, sub-Saharan:	134	0.32
African	57	0.14
South African	77	0.18
Alaska Native tribes, specified:	5	0.01
Eskimo (1)	1	0.00
Tlingit-Haida (4)	4	0.01
Am. Ind. or Alaska Nat., not spec.	93	0.22
Albanian	52	0.12
American Indian tribes, specified:	361	0.86
Apache (3)	7	0.02
Blackfeet (1)	8	0.02
Cherokee (71)	158	0.38
Cheyenne	2	0.00
Chickasaw (11)	24	0.06
Chippewa (2)	3	0.01
Choctaw (32)	57	0.14
Comanche (1)	3	0.01
Creek (13)	23	0.05
Crow	2	0.00
Delaware (1)	2	0.00
Kiowa	2	0.00
Latin American Indians (6)	12	0.03
Navajo (1)	6	0.01
Osage (4)	7	0.02
Potawatomi (6)	10	0.02
Pueblo (2)	2	0.00
Seminole (1)	1	0.00
Sioux (5)	15	0.04
Yaqui (1)	1	0.00
All other tribes (5)	16	0.04
American Indian tribes, not spec.	39	0.09
Arab:	143	0.34
Arab/Arabic	11	0.03
Egyptian	6	0.01
Lebanese	69	0.16
Palestinian	15	0.04
Syrian	42	0.10
Asian:	1,273	3.03
Bangladeshi (8)	10	0.02
Cambodian (6)	6	0.01
Chinese, ex. Taiwanese (168)	200	0.48
Filipino (71)	101	0.24
Indian (392)	432	1.03
Indonesian (11)	15	0.04
Japanese (53)	94	0.22
Korean (123)	134	0.32
Laotian (5)	5	0.01
Malaysian (1)	2	0.00
Pakistani (48)	59	0.14
Sri Lankan (6)	6	0.01
Taiwanese (17)	18	0.04
Thai (24)	25	0.06
Vietnamese (89)	100	0.24
Other Asian, specified (4)	4	0.01
Other Asian, not specified (37)	62	0.15
Austrian	175	0.42
Belgian	57	0.14
Brazilian	54	0.13
British	304	0.72
Bulgarian	40	0.09
Canadian	148	0.35
Celtic	8	0.02
Croatian	29	0.07
Czech	345	0.82
Czechoslovakian	60	0.14
Danish	146	0.35
Dutch	777	1.84
English	5,653	13.42
European	348	0.83

Notes: 1. Figures in the "Number" column do not add up to the total population due to: a) Ancestry/Race overlap — e.g. persons can report being both White and Irish, b) persons of Hispanic origin can report being any race, c) persons reporting two ancestries are counted in both categories. 2. Numbers in parentheses indicate the number of persons reporting this ancestry/race alone, not in combination with any other ancestry/race. 3. Refer to the Explanation of Data in the front of the book for more detailed information.

Ancestry/Race	Number	%
Finnish	61	0.14
French, except Basque	1,231	2.92
French Canadian	220	0.52
German	8,582	20.37
Greek	185	0.44
Hawaii Native/Pacific Islander:	72	0.17
Micronesian: (10)	13	0.03
Guamanian/Chamorro (8)	11	0.03
Other Micronesian (2)	2	0.00
Polynesian: (16)	39	0.09
Native Hawaiian (3)	18	0.04
Samoan	1	0.00
Tongan (12)	17	0.04
Other Polynesian (1)	3	0.01
Other Pac. Isl., not spec. (5)	20	0.05
Hispanic or Latino:	4,860	11.56
Central American:	112	0.27
Costa Rican	5	0.01
Guatemalan	23	0.05
Honduran	13	0.03
Nicaraguan	2	0.00
Panamanian	9	0.02
Salvadoran	54	0.13
Other Central American	6	0.01
Cuban	55	0.13
Dominican Republic	13	0.03
Mexican	3,786	9.00
Puerto Rican	203	0.48
South American:	79	0.19
Argentinean	2	0.00
Bolivian	2	0.00
Chilean	1	0.00
Colombian	31	0.07
Ecuadorian	3	0.01
Peruvian	11	0.03
Venezuelan	22	0.05
Other South American	7	0.02
Other Hispanic or Latino	612	1.46
Hungarian	142	0.34
Iranian	80	0.19
Irish	5,532	13.13
Italian	1,589	3.77
Lithuanian	79	0.19
Northern European	26	0.06
Norwegian	683	1.62
Pennsylvania German	15	0.04
Polish	1,078	2.56
Portuguese	23	0.05
Romanian	55	0.13
Russian	268	0.64
Scandinavian	74	0.18
Scotch-Irish	971	2.30
Scottish	1,366	3.24
Slavic	35	0.08
Slovak	139	0.33
Slovene	6	0.01
Swedish	819	1.94
Swiss	100	0.24
Turkish	11	0.03
Ukrainian	9	0.02
United States or American	3,456	8.20
Welsh	396	0.94
West Indian, excl. Hispanic:	76	0.18
British West Indian	9	0.02
Jamaican	21	0.05
Trinidadian and Tobagonian	16	0.04
West Indian	30	0.07
White:	37,703	89.64
Not Hispanic (34,425)	34,857	82.88
Hispanic (2,656)	2,846	6.77
Yugoslavian	60	0.14

Greenville

Place Type: City
County: Hunt
Population: 23,960

Ancestry/Race	Number	%
Acadian/Cajun	5	0.02
African American/Black:	4,673	19.50
Not Hispanic (4,490)	4,607	19.23
Hispanic (28)	66	0.28
African, sub-Saharan:	92	0.38
African	85	0.35
Nigerian	7	0.03
Alaska Native tribes, not specified	1	0.00
Am. Ind. or Alaska Nat., not spec.	93	0.39
American Indian tribes, specified:	158	0.66
Apache	3	0.01
Blackfeet (2)	3	0.01
Cherokee (22)	72	0.30
Cheyenne (1)	3	0.01
Chickasaw (1)	4	0.02
Chippewa (1)	1	0.00
Choctaw (22)	29	0.12
Comanche (1)	4	0.02
Creek (3)	8	0.03
Crow (1)	1	0.00
Iroquois (2)	3	0.01
Latin American Indians (9)	13	0.05
Osage	1	0.00
Potawatomi (1)	1	0.00
Puget Sound Salish (1)	1	0.00
Seminole	3	0.01
Sioux (1)	3	0.01
All other tribes (3)	5	0.02
American Indian tribes, not spec.	6	0.03
Arab:	14	0.06
Lebanese	4	0.02
Other Arab	10	0.04
Asian:	220	0.92
Chinese, ex. Taiwanese (31)	35	0.15
Filipino (28)	39	0.16
Hmong	1	0.00
Indian (15)	38	0.16
Japanese (8)	18	0.08
Korean (19)	25	0.10
Pakistani (3)	5	0.02
Thai (13)	13	0.05
Vietnamese (16)	18	0.08
Other Asian, specified (1)	7	0.03
Other Asian, not specified (9)	21	0.09
Belgian	9	0.04
British	44	0.18
Canadian	3	0.01
Czech	7	0.03
Czechoslovakian	13	0.05
Danish	37	0.15
Dutch	277	1.15
English	1,841	7.64
European	122	0.51
Finnish	4	0.02
French, except Basque	366	1.52
French Canadian	27	0.11
German	1,551	6.43
Hawaii Native/Pacific Islander:	24	0.10
Polynesian: (9)	14	0.06
Native Hawaiian (4)	9	0.04
Samoan (4)	4	0.02
Other Polynesian (1)	1	0.00
Other Pac. Isl., specified	6	0.03
Other Pac. Isl., not spec.	4	0.02
Hispanic or Latino:	3,511	14.65
Central American:	41	0.17
Guatemalan	20	0.08
Honduran	10	0.04
Panamanian	4	0.02
Salvadoran	7	0.03
Cuban	11	0.05
Dominican Republic	1	0.00
Mexican	2,990	12.48
Puerto Rican	75	0.31
South American:	18	0.08
Argentinean	1	0.00
Colombian	15	0.06
Ecuadorian	1	0.00
Other South American	1	0.00
Other Hispanic or Latino	375	1.57
Hungarian	60	0.25
Irish	2,106	8.73
Italian	276	1.14
Northern European	50	0.21
Norwegian	111	0.46
Polish	83	0.34
Portuguese	17	0.07
Romanian	10	0.04
Russian	7	0.03
Scandinavian	39	0.16
Scotch-Irish	494	2.05
Scottish	244	1.01
Slavic	9	0.04
Slovak	7	0.03
Swedish	88	0.36
Swiss	33	0.14
Ukrainian	23	0.10
United States or American	2,786	11.55
Welsh	275	1.14
West Indian, excl. Hispanic:	22	0.09
Bahamian	11	0.05
Dutch West Indian	11	0.05
White:	17,127	71.48
Not Hispanic (15,397)	15,650	65.32
Hispanic (1,305)	1,477	6.16
Yugoslavian	18	0.07

Groves

Place Type: City
County: Jefferson
Population: 15,733

Ancestry/Race	Number	%
Acadian/Cajun	187	1.18
African American/Black:	235	1.49
Not Hispanic (206)	230	1.46
Hispanic (2)	5	0.03
Am. Ind. or Alaska Nat., not spec.	31	0.20
American Indian tribes, specified:	78	0.50
Apache (1)	3	0.02
Blackfeet (1)	1	0.01
Cherokee (13)	29	0.18
Choctaw (4)	8	0.05
Comanche	2	0.01
Creek (2)	2	0.01
Houma (1)	1	0.01
Iroquois (1)	2	0.01
Latin American Indians	17	0.11
Lumbee (1)	1	0.01
Navajo (1)	3	0.02
Osage	1	0.01
Potawatomi (3)	3	0.02
Sioux	3	0.02
All other tribes (1)	2	0.01
American Indian tribes, not spec.	9	0.06
Arab:	51	0.32
Lebanese	43	0.27
Palestinian	8	0.05
Armenian	6	0.04
Asian:	289	1.84
Chinese, ex. Taiwanese (8)	18	0.11
Filipino (20)	24	0.15
Indian (24)	25	0.16
Japanese (4)	8	0.05
Korean (5)	8	0.05
Laotian (3)	3	0.02
Pakistani (10)	12	0.08
Taiwanese	2	0.01
Thai (2)	2	0.01
Vietnamese (182)	185	1.18
Other Asian, not specified (1)	2	0.01
Belgian	4	0.03
British	78	0.49
Czech	11	0.07
Czechoslovakian	16	0.10
Danish	6	0.04
Dutch	266	1.68
English	1,357	8.56
European	178	1.12
French, except Basque	2,864	18.08

Notes: 1. Figures in the "Number" column do not add up to the total population due to: a) Ancestry/Race overlap — e.g. persons can report being both White and Irish, b) persons of Hispanic origin can report being any race, c) persons reporting two ancestries are counted in both categories. 2. Numbers in parentheses indicate the number of persons reporting this ancestry/race alone, not in combination with any other ancestry/race. 3. Refer to the Explanation of Data in the front of the book for more detailed information.

Ancestry/Race	Number	%
French Canadian	806	5.09
German	1,569	9.90
Greek	4	0.03
Hawaii Native/Pacific Islander:	5	0.03
Polynesian: (5)	5	0.03
Native Hawaiian (5)	5	0.03
Hispanic or Latino:	1,231	7.82
Central American:	56	0.36
Guatemalan	10	0.06
Honduran	23	0.15
Nicaraguan	17	0.11
Panamanian	3	0.02
Salvadoran	1	0.01
Other Central American	2	0.01
Cuban	18	0.11
Mexican	935	5.94
Puerto Rican	18	0.11
South American:	7	0.04
Chilean	2	0.01
Uruguayan	5	0.03
Other Hispanic or Latino	197	1.25
Iranian	28	0.18
Irish	1,755	11.08
Italian	724	4.57
Norwegian	49	0.31
Pennsylvania German	7	0.04
Polish	77	0.49
Portuguese	6	0.04
Russian	8	0.05
Scotch-Irish	398	2.51
Scottish	185	1.17
Slovene	13	0.08
Swedish	75	0.47
United States or American	1,483	9.36
Welsh	59	0.37
White:	14,888	94.63
Not Hispanic (13,877)	13,990	88.92
Hispanic (827)	898	5.71

Haltom City

Place Type: City
County: Tarrant
Population: 39,018

Ancestry/Race	Number	%
Acadian/Cajun	10	0.03
African American/Black:	1,215	3.11
Not Hispanic (1,054)	1,150	2.95
Hispanic (34)	65	0.17
African, sub-Saharan:	142	0.36
African	90	0.23
Ethiopian	12	0.03
Kenyan	29	0.07
Zairian	11	0.03
Alaska Native tribes, specified:	5	0.01
Aleut (1)	1	0.00
Eskimo	1	0.00
Tlingit-Haida (3)	3	0.01
Am. Ind. or Alaska Nat., not spec.	163	0.42
American Indian tribes, specified:	355	0.91
Apache (7)	10	0.03
Blackfeet	11	0.03
Cherokee (35)	111	0.28
Cheyenne	2	0.01
Chickasaw (8)	20	0.05
Chippewa (4)	4	0.01
Choctaw (30)	66	0.17
Comanche (6)	14	0.04
Cree (1)	1	0.00
Creek (20)	27	0.07
Houma (2)	2	0.01
Iroquois (6)	7	0.02
Kiowa (5)	7	0.02
Latin American Indians (9)	21	0.05
Lumbee	2	0.01
Menominee (1)	4	0.01
Navajo (5)	6	0.02
Osage (1)	1	0.00
Ottawa (4)	4	0.01
Paiute (1)	1	0.00
Potawatomi (1)	2	0.01
Pueblo (9)	10	0.03
Puget Sound Salish (2)	2	0.01
Sioux (1)	5	0.01
All other tribes (9)	15	0.04
American Indian tribes, not spec.	27	0.07
Arab:	91	0.23
Arab/Arabic	42	0.11
Egyptian	9	0.02
Lebanese	26	0.07
Syrian	6	0.02
Other Arab	8	0.02
Armenian	54	0.14
Asian:	3,332	8.54
Bangladeshi (8)	8	0.02
Cambodian (11)	22	0.06
Chinese, ex. Taiwanese (82)	99	0.25
Filipino (68)	101	0.26
Hmong (25)	26	0.07
Indian (250)	302	0.77
Indonesian (1)	3	0.01
Japanese (18)	31	0.08
Korean (54)	62	0.16
Laotian (904)	1,017	2.61
Malaysian (2)	2	0.01
Pakistani (46)	48	0.12
Sri Lankan (7)	8	0.02
Taiwanese (1)	2	0.01
Thai (58)	86	0.22
Vietnamese (1,348)	1,386	3.55
Other Asian, specified (9)	18	0.05
Other Asian, not specified (68)	111	0.28
Australian	15	0.04
Austrian	5	0.01
Brazilian	51	0.13
British	68	0.17
Bulgarian	6	0.02
Canadian	26	0.07
Celtic	46	0.12
Croatian	11	0.03
Czech	132	0.34
Czechoslovakian	54	0.14
Danish	25	0.06
Dutch	688	1.75
English	3,245	8.27
European	105	0.27
French, except Basque	766	1.95
French Canadian	164	0.42
German	3,920	9.99
Greek	50	0.13
Hawaii Native/Pacific Islander:	101	0.26
Micronesian: (8)	17	0.04
Guamanian/Chamorro (5)	9	0.02
Other Micronesian (3)	8	0.02
Polynesian: (23)	50	0.13
Native Hawaiian (7)	22	0.06
Samoan (3)	7	0.02
Tongan (13)	21	0.05
Other Pac. Isl., specified	2	0.01
Other Pac. Isl., not spec. (13)	32	0.08
Hispanic or Latino:	7,771	19.92
Central American:	162	0.42
Costa Rican	10	0.03
Guatemalan	20	0.05
Honduran	15	0.04
Nicaraguan	3	0.01
Panamanian	9	0.02
Salvadoran	96	0.25
Other Central American	9	0.02
Cuban	96	0.25
Dominican Republic	3	0.01
Mexican	6,087	15.60
Puerto Rican	164	0.42
South American:	43	0.11
Argentinean	9	0.02
Chilean	6	0.02
Colombian	20	0.05
Ecuadorian	1	0.00
Peruvian	4	0.01
Other South American	3	0.01
Other Hispanic or Latino	1,216	3.12
Hungarian	7	0.02
Icelander	7	0.02
Iranian	15	0.04
Irish	3,559	9.07
Italian	409	1.04
Latvian	10	0.03
Lithuanian	19	0.05
Norwegian	227	0.58
Polish	411	1.05
Portuguese	30	0.08
Romanian	19	0.05
Russian	32	0.08
Scandinavian	42	0.11
Scotch-Irish	627	1.60
Scottish	488	1.24
Slavic	9	0.02
Slovak	31	0.08
Slovene	8	0.02
Swedish	224	0.57
Swiss	13	0.03
Ukrainian	10	0.03
United States or American	4,940	12.59
Welsh	187	0.48
West Indian, excl. Hispanic:	137	0.35
Dutch West Indian	58	0.15
Jamaican	79	0.20
White:	30,782	78.89
Not Hispanic (26,306)	26,753	68.57
Hispanic (3,667)	4,029	10.33
Yugoslavian	24	0.06

Harker Heights

Place Type: City
County: Bell
Population: 17,308

Ancestry/Race	Number	%
Acadian/Cajun	49	0.28
Afghan	10	0.06
African American/Black:	2,807	16.22
Not Hispanic (2,535)	2,722	15.73
Hispanic (50)	85	0.49
African, sub-Saharan:	100	0.58
African	100	0.58
Alaska Native tribes, specified:	5	0.03
Alaska Athabascan (5)	5	0.03
Am. Ind. or Alaska Nat., not spec.	72	0.42
American Indian tribes, specified:	175	1.01
Apache (9)	16	0.09
Blackfeet (1)	13	0.08
Cherokee (23)	57	0.33
Chickasaw	2	0.01
Chippewa (5)	8	0.05
Choctaw (7)	11	0.06
Comanche (1)	3	0.02
Creek (2)	3	0.02
Delaware (4)	4	0.02
Iroquois (5)	5	0.03
Kiowa (1)	1	0.01
Latin American Indians (5)	6	0.03
Lumbee (1)	1	0.01
Menominee	1	0.01
Navajo (2)	3	0.02
Ottawa (1)	1	0.01
Paiute	3	0.02
Potawatomi (3)	3	0.02
Pueblo	1	0.01
Seminole	1	0.01
Sioux (11)	15	0.09
Yaqui (4)	4	0.02
All other tribes (5)	13	0.08
American Indian tribes, not spec.	21	0.12
Arab:	90	0.52
Lebanese	15	0.09
Moroccan	10	0.06
Syrian	38	0.22
Other Arab	27	0.16

Notes: 1. Figures in the "Number" column do not add up to the total population due to: a) Ancestry/Race overlap — e.g. persons can report being both White and Irish, b) persons of Hispanic origin can report being any race, c) persons reporting two ancestries are counted in both categories. 2. Numbers in parentheses indicate the number of persons reporting this ancestry/race alone, not in combination with any other ancestry/race. 3. Refer to the Explanation of Data in the front of the book for more detailed information.

Ancestry/Race	Number	%
Asian:	846	4.89
Chinese, ex. Taiwanese (23)	49	0.28
Filipino (114)	154	0.89
Indian (49)	55	0.32
Indonesian (1)	1	0.01
Japanese (52)	91	0.53
Korean (307)	391	2.26
Pakistani (7)	9	0.05
Sri Lankan (1)	1	0.01
Thai (15)	29	0.17
Vietnamese (21)	32	0.18
Other Asian, specified (1)	5	0.03
Other Asian, not specified (20)	29	0.17
Austrian	16	0.09
Belgian	7	0.04
British	22	0.13
Canadian	29	0.17
Czech	230	1.33
Czechoslovakian	50	0.29
Danish	74	0.43
Dutch	318	1.84
English	1,416	8.18
European	194	1.12
French, except Basque	507	2.93
French Canadian	91	0.53
German	2,648	15.30
Greek	53	0.31
Hawaii Native/Pacific Islander:	125	0.72
Micronesian: (30)	44	0.25
Guamanian/Chamorro (29)	42	0.24
Other Micronesian (1)	2	0.01
Polynesian: (38)	61	0.35
Native Hawaiian (21)	41	0.24
Samoan (17)	20	0.12
Other Pac. Isl., not spec. (2)	20	0.12
Hispanic or Latino:	2,153	12.44
Central American:	87	0.50
Costa Rican	1	0.01
Guatemalan	14	0.08
Honduran	4	0.02
Nicaraguan	5	0.03
Panamanian	51	0.29
Salvadoran	1	0.01
Other Central American	11	0.06
Cuban	34	0.20
Dominican Republic	17	0.10
Mexican	1,277	7.38
Puerto Rican	362	2.09
South American:	25	0.14
Colombian	17	0.10
Ecuadorian	5	0.03
Peruvian	1	0.01
Uruguayan	1	0.01
Other South American	1	0.01
Other Hispanic or Latino	351	2.03
Hungarian	77	0.44
Iranian	10	0.06
Irish	1,866	10.78
Italian	467	2.70
Lithuanian	8	0.05
New Zealander	5	0.03
Northern European	6	0.03
Norwegian	283	1.63
Polish	314	1.81
Portuguese	62	0.36
Romanian	6	0.03
Russian	36	0.21
Scandinavian	22	0.13
Scotch-Irish	327	1.89
Scottish	262	1.51
Serbian	23	0.13
Slovak	6	0.03
Swedish	296	1.71
Swiss	51	0.29
Turkish	10	0.06
Ukrainian	5	0.03
United States or American	1,631	9.42
Welsh	55	0.32
West Indian, excl. Hispanic:	51	0.29
Dutch West Indian	11	0.06
Jamaican	40	0.23
White:	12,774	73.80
Not Hispanic (11,343)	11,720	67.71
Hispanic (926)	1,054	6.09
Yugoslavian	14	0.08

Harlingen

Place Type: City
County: Cameron
Population: 57,564

Ancestry/Race	Number	%
Acadian/Cajun	9	0.02
African American/Black:	619	1.08
Not Hispanic (425)	457	0.79
Hispanic (103)	162	0.28
African, sub-Saharan:	101	0.18
African	21	0.04
Nigerian	74	0.13
South African	6	0.01
Am. Ind. or Alaska Nat., not spec.	211	0.37
Alsatian	5	0.01
American Indian tribes, specified:	192	0.33
Apache	5	0.01
Blackfeet (1)	4	0.01
Cherokee (15)	40	0.07
Cheyenne (2)	5	0.01
Chickasaw (4)	6	0.01
Chippewa (1)	5	0.01
Choctaw (3)	5	0.01
Comanche (7)	8	0.01
Creek	3	0.01
Delaware (1)	1	0.00
Iroquois	1	0.00
Kiowa (1)	1	0.00
Latin American Indians (58)	69	0.12
Osage (1)	2	0.00
Potawatomi (1)	1	0.00
Pueblo (3)	3	0.01
Seminole (1)	2	0.00
Sioux (1)	3	0.01
Ute (1)	1	0.00
Yaqui (1)	1	0.00
Yuman (1)	1	0.00
All other tribes (12)	25	0.04
American Indian tribes, not spec.	51	0.09
Arab:	87	0.15
Arab/Arabic	49	0.09
Lebanese	38	0.07
Armenian	25	0.04
Asian:	598	1.04
Bangladeshi (4)	5	0.01
Chinese, ex. Taiwanese (70)	98	0.17
Filipino (251)	273	0.47
Indian (78)	83	0.14
Japanese (29)	43	0.07
Korean (10)	12	0.02
Malaysian (3)	3	0.01
Pakistani (9)	23	0.04
Sri Lankan (5)	5	0.01
Taiwanese (10)	10	0.02
Thai (3)	4	0.01
Vietnamese (23)	26	0.05
Other Asian, specified (1)	1	0.00
Other Asian, not specified (2)	12	0.02
Austrian	40	0.07
Basque	20	0.03
Belgian	27	0.05
British	190	0.33
Canadian	114	0.20
Croatian	19	0.03
Czech	148	0.26
Czechoslovakian	57	0.10
Danish	52	0.09
Dutch	267	0.46
Eastern European	7	0.01
English	2,563	4.45
European	156	0.27
Finnish	17	0.03
French, except Basque	593	1.03
French Canadian	75	0.13
German	2,983	5.18
Greek	5	0.01
Guyanese	13	0.02
Hawaii Native/Pacific Islander:	40	0.07
Micronesian: (10)	11	0.02
Guamanian/Chamorro (10)	11	0.02
Polynesian: (4)	15	0.03
Native Hawaiian (2)	12	0.02
Samoan (2)	2	0.00
Other Polynesian	1	0.00
Other Pac. Isl., not spec. (2)	14	0.02
Hispanic or Latino:	41,881	72.76
Central American:	158	0.27
Costa Rican	3	0.01
Guatemalan	15	0.03
Honduran	36	0.06
Nicaraguan	35	0.06
Panamanian	10	0.02
Salvadoran	53	0.09
Other Central American	6	0.01
Cuban	57	0.10
Dominican Republic	4	0.01
Mexican	31,922	55.45
Puerto Rican	241	0.42
South American:	54	0.09
Argentinean	19	0.03
Bolivian	2	0.00
Chilean	1	0.00
Colombian	13	0.02
Ecuadorian	3	0.01
Paraguayan	3	0.01
Peruvian	4	0.01
Venezuelan	6	0.01
Other South American	3	0.01
Other Hispanic or Latino	9,445	16.41
Hungarian	42	0.07
Icelander	4	0.01
Iranian	24	0.04
Irish	1,962	3.40
Italian	467	0.81
Lithuanian	20	0.03
Luxemburger	15	0.03
Norwegian	349	0.61
Polish	211	0.37
Portuguese	22	0.04
Russian	28	0.05
Scandinavian	22	0.04
Scotch-Irish	578	1.00
Scottish	444	0.77
Serbian	18	0.03
Slovak	7	0.01
Slovene	5	0.01
Swedish	266	0.46
Swiss	85	0.15
Turkish	5	0.01
Ukrainian	20	0.03
United States or American	2,318	4.02
Welsh	153	0.27
West Indian, excl. Hispanic:	50	0.09
Barbadian	13	0.02
Haitian	14	0.02
Jamaican	18	0.03
Other West Indian	5	0.01
White:	46,677	81.09
Not Hispanic (14,410)	14,601	25.36
Hispanic (30,880)	32,076	55.72
Yugoslavian	10	0.02

Henderson

Place Type: City
County: Rusk
Population: 11,273

Ancestry/Race	Number	%
Acadian/Cajun	11	0.10
African American/Black:	2,543	22.56
Not Hispanic (2,506)	2,529	22.43

Notes: 1. Figures in the "Number" column do not add up to the total population due to: a) Ancestry/Race overlap — e.g. persons can report being both White and Irish, b) persons of Hispanic origin can report being any race, c) persons reporting two ancestries are counted in both categories. 2. Numbers in parentheses indicate the number of persons reporting this ancestry/race alone, not in combination with any other ancestry/race. 3. Refer to the Explanation of Data in the front of the book for more detailed information.

Ancestry/Race	Number	%
Hispanic (12)	14	0.12
African, sub-Saharan:	9	0.08
African	9	0.08
Am. Ind. or Alaska Nat., not spec.	9	0.08
American Indian tribes, specified:	43	0.38
Blackfeet	1	0.01
Cherokee (5)	21	0.19
Cheyenne (1)	1	0.01
Chickasaw (1)	1	0.01
Chippewa (3)	4	0.04
Choctaw (2)	4	0.04
Creek (1)	1	0.01
Iroquois	1	0.01
Latin American Indians (1)	1	0.01
Osage (3)	3	0.03
Sioux (1)	1	0.01
All other tribes (4)	4	0.04
American Indian tribes, not spec.	9	0.08
Asian:	62	0.55
Chinese, ex. Taiwanese (5)	6	0.05
Filipino (16)	20	0.18
Indian (13)	15	0.13
Japanese (4)	4	0.04
Korean (5)	5	0.04
Pakistani (7)	7	0.06
Sri Lankan (1)	1	0.01
Thai (1)	1	0.01
Vietnamese (1)	1	0.01
Other Asian, specified	1	0.01
Other Asian, not specified	1	0.01
Belgian	4	0.04
British	48	0.42
Canadian	6	0.05
Czech	9	0.08
Czechoslovakian	6	0.05
Dutch	25	0.22
English	874	7.72
European	3	0.03
French, except Basque	83	0.73
French Canadian	39	0.34
German	666	5.88
Hawaii Native/Pacific Islander:	7	0.06
Polynesian: (1)	3	0.03
Native Hawaiian	2	0.02
Tongan (1)	1	0.01
Other Pac. Isl., specified	1	0.01
Other Pac. Isl., not spec.	3	0.03
Hispanic or Latino:	1,330	11.80
Central American:	53	0.47
Guatemalan	1	0.01
Panamanian	1	0.01
Salvadoran	51	0.45
Cuban	4	0.04
Mexican	1,063	9.43
Puerto Rican	11	0.10
South American:	4	0.04
Peruvian	4	0.04
Other Hispanic or Latino	195	1.73
Irish	806	7.12
Italian	127	1.12
Norwegian	13	0.11
Polish	35	0.31
Scotch-Irish	242	2.14
Scottish	142	1.25
Swedish	17	0.15
Swiss	7	0.06
United States or American	1,389	12.26
Welsh	35	0.31
West Indian, excl. Hispanic:	8	0.07
Dutch West Indian	8	0.07
White:	7,895	70.03
Not Hispanic (7,295)	7,348	65.18
Hispanic (481)	547	4.85

Hereford

Place Type: City
County: Deaf Smith
Population: 14,597

Ancestry/Race	Number	%
African American/Black:	287	1.97
Not Hispanic (229)	242	1.66
Hispanic (28)	45	0.31
Alaska Native tribes, not specified	1	0.01
Am. Ind. or Alaska Nat., not spec.	73	0.50
American Indian tribes, specified:	80	0.55
Apache (4)	10	0.07
Blackfeet	1	0.01
Cherokee (12)	18	0.12
Choctaw (4)	13	0.09
Comanche	1	0.01
Crow	1	0.01
Kiowa	2	0.01
Latin American Indians (8)	10	0.07
Navajo (3)	3	0.02
Osage (1)	1	0.01
Ottawa (6)	6	0.04
Pueblo (1)	1	0.01
Sioux	5	0.03
All other tribes (5)	8	0.05
American Indian tribes, not spec.	23	0.16
Arab:	15	0.10
Lebanese	15	0.10
Asian:	63	0.43
Chinese, ex. Taiwanese (1)	2	0.01
Filipino (3)	4	0.03
Indian (13)	20	0.14
Korean (2)	2	0.01
Pakistani	4	0.03
Thai (4)	6	0.04
Vietnamese (7)	10	0.07
Other Asian, specified	4	0.03
Other Asian, not specified (4)	11	0.08
Austrian	25	0.17
British	17	0.12
Canadian	21	0.14
Czech	17	0.12
Dutch	115	0.79
English	702	4.82
European	19	0.13
French, except Basque	125	0.86
French Canadian	49	0.34
German	923	6.34
Greek	24	0.16
Hawaii Native/Pacific Islander:	27	0.18
Micronesian: (6)	6	0.04
Guamanian/Chamorro (6)	6	0.04
Polynesian: (9)	14	0.10
Native Hawaiian (5)	9	0.06
Samoan (4)	5	0.03
Other Pac. Isl., specified	4	0.03
Other Pac. Isl., not spec.	3	0.02
Hispanic or Latino:	8,958	61.37
Central American:	8	0.05
Salvadoran	8	0.05
Cuban	1	0.01
Mexican	6,317	43.28
Puerto Rican	8	0.05
South American:	3	0.02
Colombian	3	0.02
Other Hispanic or Latino	2,621	17.96
Irish	699	4.80
Italian	73	0.50
Norwegian	35	0.24
Polish	89	0.61
Russian	12	0.08
Scandinavian	5	0.03
Scotch-Irish	135	0.93
Scottish	108	0.74
Slavic	7	0.05
Swedish	21	0.14
Swiss	12	0.08
Ukrainian	18	0.12
United States or American	1,040	7.14
Welsh	15	0.10
West Indian, excl. Hispanic:	6	0.04
Dutch West Indian	6	0.04
White:	10,508	71.99
Not Hispanic (5,278)	5,323	36.47
Hispanic (4,920)	5,185	35.52

Hewitt

Place Type: City
County: McLennan
Population: 11,085

Ancestry/Race	Number	%
African American/Black:	885	7.98
Not Hispanic (840)	869	7.84
Hispanic (13)	16	0.14
African, sub-Saharan:	21	0.20
African	21	0.20
Am. Ind. or Alaska Nat., not spec.	13	0.12
American Indian tribes, specified:	64	0.58
Apache (6)	7	0.06
Cherokee (23)	34	0.31
Cheyenne	1	0.01
Chickasaw	1	0.01
Choctaw (3)	3	0.03
Creek (2)	2	0.02
Latin American Indians (5)	5	0.05
Lumbee	1	0.01
Navajo (1)	5	0.05
Ottawa	3	0.03
All other tribes	2	0.02
American Indian tribes, not spec.	1	0.01
Arab:	11	0.10
Palestinian	11	0.10
Asian:	324	2.92
Chinese, ex. Taiwanese (29)	45	0.41
Filipino (49)	71	0.64
Indian (38)	38	0.34
Japanese (8)	11	0.10
Korean (26)	30	0.27
Pakistani (18)	21	0.19
Sri Lankan (4)	4	0.04
Taiwanese (1)	2	0.02
Thai (3)	5	0.05
Vietnamese (77)	85	0.77
Other Asian, specified	1	0.01
Other Asian, not specified	11	0.10
Austrian	8	0.07
Belgian	19	0.18
British	8	0.07
Canadian	25	0.23
Czech	208	1.94
Czechoslovakian	42	0.39
Danish	35	0.33
Dutch	103	0.96
English	1,304	12.16
European	54	0.50
French, except Basque	259	2.41
German	1,766	16.46
Greek	22	0.21
Hawaii Native/Pacific Islander:	11	0.10
Micronesian: (4)	7	0.06
Guamanian/Chamorro (3)	6	0.05
Other Micronesian (1)	1	0.01
Polynesian: (3)	3	0.03
Native Hawaiian (3)	3	0.03
Other Pac. Isl., specified	1	0.01
Hispanic or Latino:	1,029	9.28
Central American:	16	0.14
Honduran	1	0.01
Panamanian	7	0.06
Salvadoran	7	0.06
Other Central American	1	0.01
Cuban	8	0.07
Mexican	680	6.13
Puerto Rican	48	0.43
South American:	15	0.14
Argentinean	2	0.02

Notes: 1. Figures in the "Number" column do not add up to the total population due to: a) Ancestry/Race overlap — e.g. persons can report being both White and Irish, b) persons of Hispanic origin can report being any race, c) persons reporting two ancestries are counted in both categories. 2. Numbers in parentheses indicate the number of persons reporting this ancestry/race alone, not in combination with any other ancestry/race. 3. Refer to the Explanation of Data in the front of the book for more detailed information.

Ancestry/Race	Number	%
Chilean	1	0.01
Colombian	6	0.05
Ecuadorian	1	0.01
Venezuelan	3	0.03
Other South American	2	0.02
Other Hispanic or Latino	262	2.36
Hungarian	18	0.17
Icelander	26	0.24
Irish	1,170	10.91
Italian	175	1.63
Northern European	40	0.37
Norwegian	158	1.47
Polish	166	1.55
Romanian	6	0.06
Russian	11	0.10
Scandinavian	8	0.07
Scotch-Irish	273	2.55
Scottish	287	2.68
Serbian	10	0.09
Slavic	6	0.06
Swedish	56	0.52
Swiss	13	0.12
Ukrainian	10	0.09
United States or American	873	8.14
Welsh	26	0.24
West Indian, excl. Hispanic:	19	0.18
Dutch West Indian	19	0.18
White:	9,453	85.28
Not Hispanic (8,800)	8,893	80.23
Hispanic (520)	560	5.05

Highland Village

Place Type: City
County: Denton
Population: 12,173

Ancestry/Race	Number	%
African American/Black:	207	1.70
Not Hispanic (176)	203	1.67
Hispanic (3)	4	0.03
African, sub-Saharan:	16	0.13
African	9	0.07
South African	7	0.06
Am. Ind. or Alaska Nat., not spec.	20	0.16
American Indian tribes, specified:	73	0.60
Apache	1	0.01
Blackfeet (1)	1	0.01
Cherokee (12)	18	0.15
Chickasaw (1)	4	0.03
Chippewa (2)	2	0.02
Choctaw (8)	16	0.13
Creek (7)	8	0.07
Delaware (5)	5	0.04
Iroquois	1	0.01
Latin American Indians	3	0.02
Osage	1	0.01
Potawatomi	1	0.01
Sioux (2)	8	0.07
Ute (1)	1	0.01
All other tribes (3)	3	0.02
Arab:	53	0.44
Egyptian	9	0.07
Lebanese	44	0.36
Armenian	20	0.16
Asian:	272	2.23
Chinese, ex. Taiwanese (46)	56	0.46
Filipino (14)	17	0.14
Indian (86)	93	0.76
Japanese (29)	41	0.34
Korean (26)	28	0.23
Taiwanese (3)	8	0.07
Thai (1)	3	0.02
Vietnamese (20)	20	0.16
Other Asian, specified (1)	1	0.01
Other Asian, not specified (3)	5	0.04
Assyrian/Chaldean/Syriac	14	0.12
Australian	6	0.05
Austrian	59	0.49
Belgian	13	0.11
Brazilian	26	0.21
British	237	1.95
Canadian	52	0.43
Cypriot	7	0.06
Czech	192	1.58
Czechoslovakian	31	0.25
Danish	65	0.53
Dutch	229	1.88
English	2,070	17.02
European	90	0.74
Finnish	26	0.21
French, except Basque	514	4.23
French Canadian	101	0.83
German	2,642	21.72
Greek	90	0.74
Hawaii Native/Pacific Islander:	8	0.07
Polynesian: (1)	5	0.04
Native Hawaiian (1)	4	0.03
Samoan	1	0.01
Other Pac. Isl., not spec. (1)	3	0.02
Hispanic or Latino:	421	3.46
Central American:	20	0.16
Guatemalan	6	0.05
Honduran	3	0.02
Panamanian	1	0.01
Salvadoran	10	0.08
Cuban	18	0.15
Dominican Republic	7	0.06
Mexican	221	1.82
Puerto Rican	22	0.18
South American:	29	0.24
Argentinean	6	0.05
Colombian	12	0.10
Peruvian	9	0.07
Venezuelan	2	0.02
Other Hispanic or Latino	104	0.85
Hungarian	81	0.67
Icelander	5	0.04
Iranian	25	0.21
Irish	1,732	14.24
Italian	652	5.36
Lithuanian	65	0.53
Northern European	7	0.06
Norwegian	175	1.44
Pennsylvania German	7	0.06
Polish	414	3.40
Portuguese	36	0.30
Romanian	11	0.09
Russian	121	0.99
Scandinavian	22	0.18
Scotch-Irish	457	3.76
Scottish	367	3.02
Slovak	12	0.10
Slovene	8	0.07
Swedish	306	2.52
Swiss	5	0.04
Ukrainian	21	0.17
United States or American	1,113	9.15
Welsh	94	0.77
West Indian, excl. Hispanic:	37	0.30
Bahamian	7	0.06
Dutch West Indian	21	0.17
Jamaican	9	0.07
White:	11,603	95.32
Not Hispanic (11,165)	11,276	92.63
Hispanic (303)	327	2.69
Yugoslavian	27	0.22

Houston

Place Type: City
County: Harris
Population: 1,953,631

Ancestry/Race	Number	%
Acadian/Cajun	882	0.05
Afghan	44	0.00
African American/Black:	505,101	25.85
Not Hispanic (487,851)	495,338	25.35
Hispanic (6,645)	9,763	0.50
African, sub-Saharan:	27,841	1.42
African	15,009	0.77
Cape Verdean	26	0.00
Ethiopian	848	0.04
Ghanian	532	0.03
Kenyan	457	0.02
Liberian	251	0.01
Nigerian	8,726	0.45
Senegalese	31	0.00
Sierra Leonean	84	0.00
Somalian	300	0.02
South African	764	0.04
Sudanese	99	0.01
Ugandan	46	0.00
Zimbabwean	3	0.00
Other sub-Saharan African	665	0.03
Alaska Native tribes, specified:	40	0.00
Alaska Athabascan (3)	7	0.00
Aleut (4)	8	0.00
Eskimo (10)	18	0.00
Tlingit-Haida (2)	6	0.00
All other tribes	1	0.00
Alaska Native tribes, not specified	15	0.00
Am. Ind. or Alaska Nat., not spec.	7,193	0.37
Albanian	301	0.02
Alsatian	193	0.01
American Indian tribes, specified:	7,618	0.39
Apache (114)	297	0.02
Blackfeet (40)	170	0.01
Cherokee (728)	2,159	0.11
Cheyenne (5)	22	0.00
Chickasaw (79)	134	0.01
Chippewa (48)	88	0.00
Choctaw (256)	662	0.03
Colville	1	0.00
Comanche (55)	120	0.01
Cree (3)	20	0.00
Creek (88)	175	0.01
Crow (5)	12	0.00
Delaware (12)	21	0.00
Houma (4)	10	0.00
Iroquois (53)	97	0.00
Kiowa (9)	17	0.00
Latin American Indians (1,642)	2,425	0.12
Lumbee (16)	20	0.00
Menominee	1	0.00
Navajo (51)	103	0.01
Osage (20)	51	0.00
Ottawa (7)	15	0.00
Paiute (2)	7	0.00
Pima (4)	7	0.00
Potawatomi (20)	45	0.00
Pueblo (39)	83	0.00
Puget Sound Salish (2)	4	0.00
Seminole (17)	61	0.00
Shoshone (2)	13	0.00
Sioux (68)	169	0.01
Tohono O'Odham (3)	3	0.00
Ute (4)	6	0.00
Yakama (1)	4	0.00
Yaqui (9)	31	0.00
Yuman (6)	10	0.00
All other tribes (253)	555	0.03
American Indian tribes, not spec.	1,141	0.06
Arab:	11,322	0.58
Arab/Arabic	2,728	0.14
Egyptian	1,286	0.07
Iraqi	227	0.01
Jordanian	567	0.03
Lebanese	3,052	0.16
Moroccan	284	0.01
Palestinian	1,135	0.06
Syrian	849	0.04
Other Arab	1,194	0.06
Armenian	761	0.04
Asian:	116,608	5.97
Bangladeshi (341)	464	0.02
Cambodian (758)	907	0.05
Chinese, ex. Taiwanese (22,462)	24,695	1.26
Filipino (7,890)	9,276	0.47

Notes: 1. Figures in the "Number" column do not add up to the total population due to: a) Ancestry/Race overlap — e.g. persons can report being both White and Irish, b) persons of Hispanic origin can report being any race, c) persons reporting two ancestries are counted in both categories. 2. Numbers in parentheses indicate the number of persons reporting this ancestry/race alone, not in combination with any other ancestry/race. 3. Refer to the Explanation of Data in the front of the book for more detailed information.

Ancestry/Race	Number	%
Hmong (4)	6	0.00
Indian (20,149)	22,549	1.15
Indonesian (524)	709	0.04
Japanese (2,519)	3,277	0.17
Korean (5,544)	6,172	0.32
Laotian (284)	346	0.02
Malaysian (127)	182	0.01
Pakistani (4,756)	6,490	0.33
Sri Lankan (200)	220	0.01
Taiwanese (1,539)	1,846	0.09
Thai (748)	928	0.05
Vietnamese (32,261)	33,922	1.74
Other Asian, specified (141)	357	0.02
Other Asian, not specified (1,439)	4,262	0.22
Assyrian/Chaldean/Syriac	42	0.00
Australian	614	0.03
Austrian	2,041	0.10
Basque	138	0.01
Belgian	967	0.05
Brazilian	980	0.05
British	7,483	0.38
Bulgarian	295	0.02
Canadian	2,420	0.12
Carpatho Rusyn	9	0.00
Celtic	255	0.01
Croatian	648	0.03
Cypriot	33	0.00
Czech	9,545	0.49
Czechoslovakian	2,148	0.11
Danish	2,804	0.14
Dutch	9,822	0.50
Eastern European	833	0.04
English	98,067	5.02
Estonian	56	0.00
European	8,720	0.45
Finnish	844	0.04
French, except Basque	36,790	1.88
French Canadian	5,419	0.28
German	118,564	6.07
German Russian	17	0.00
Greek	3,980	0.20
Guyanese	202	0.01
Hawaii Native/Pacific Islander:	2,899	0.15
Melanesian: (26)	37	0.00
Fijian (26)	33	0.00
Other Melanesian	4	0.00
Micronesian: (333)	475	0.02
Guamanian/Chamorro (309)	442	0.02
Other Micronesian (24)	33	0.00
Polynesian: (478)	877	0.04
Native Hawaiian (227)	511	0.03
Samoan (220)	319	0.02
Tongan (28)	31	0.00
Other Polynesian (3)	16	0.00
Other Pac. Isl., specified	172	0.01
Other Pac. Isl., not spec. (333)	1,338	0.07
Hispanic or Latino:	730,865	37.41
Central American:	60,642	3.10
Costa Rican	567	0.03
Guatemalan	7,220	0.37
Honduran	10,284	0.53
Nicaraguan	2,196	0.11
Panamanian	792	0.04
Salvadoran	36,799	1.88
Other Central American	2,784	0.14
Cuban	4,970	0.25
Dominican Republic	990	0.05
Mexican	527,442	27.00
Puerto Rican	6,906	0.35
South American:	13,214	0.68
Argentinean	1,256	0.06
Bolivian	480	0.02
Chilean	591	0.03
Colombian	5,821	0.30
Ecuadorian	864	0.04
Paraguayan	48	0.00
Peruvian	1,656	0.08
Uruguayan	230	0.01
Venezuelan	1,592	0.08
Other South American	676	0.03
Other Hispanic or Latino	116,701	5.97
Hungarian	3,161	0.16
Icelander	87	0.00
Iranian	4,436	0.23
Irish	83,633	4.28
Israeli	661	0.03
Italian	31,899	1.63
Latvian	255	0.01
Lithuanian	1,202	0.06
Luxemburger	46	0.00
Macedonian	52	0.00
Maltese	81	0.00
New Zealander	102	0.01
Northern European	582	0.03
Norwegian	7,367	0.38
Pennsylvania German	174	0.01
Polish	19,297	0.99
Portuguese	1,466	0.07
Romanian	1,448	0.07
Russian	8,423	0.43
Scandinavian	1,092	0.06
Scotch-Irish	21,553	1.10
Scottish	20,171	1.03
Serbian	264	0.01
Slavic	306	0.02
Slovak	922	0.05
Slovene	297	0.02
Swedish	8,798	0.45
Swiss	2,226	0.11
Turkish	764	0.04
Ukrainian	1,693	0.09
United States or American	71,531	3.66
Welsh	5,325	0.27
West Indian, excl. Hispanic:	6,543	0.33
Bahamian	154	0.01
Barbadian	102	0.01
Belizean	379	0.02
Bermudan	17	0.00
British West Indian	450	0.02
Dutch West Indian	117	0.01
Haitian	592	0.03
Jamaican	2,344	0.12
Trinidadian and Tobagonian	1,097	0.06
U.S. Virgin Islander	272	0.01
West Indian	975	0.05
Other West Indian	44	0.00
White:	1,012,413	51.82
Not Hispanic (601,851)	618,504	31.66
Hispanic (360,759)	393,909	20.16
Yugoslavian	1,789	0.09

Humble

Place Type: City
County: Harris
Population: 14,579

Ancestry/Race	Number	%
African American/Black:	2,206	15.13
Not Hispanic (2,075)	2,143	14.70
Hispanic (38)	63	0.43
African, sub-Saharan:	130	0.89
African	93	0.63
Nigerian	37	0.25
Alaska Native tribes, specified:	3	0.02
Eskimo (2)	3	0.02
Am. Ind. or Alaska Nat., not spec.	77	0.53
American Indian tribes, specified:	124	0.85
Apache (2)	7	0.05
Blackfeet	7	0.05
Cherokee (24)	52	0.36
Chickasaw (2)	2	0.01
Chippewa (1)	1	0.01
Choctaw (4)	10	0.07
Comanche	1	0.01
Creek (1)	2	0.01
Houma (2)	2	0.01
Latin American Indians (20)	34	0.23
Shoshone (1)	1	0.01
Yaqui	2	0.01
All other tribes (3)	3	0.02
American Indian tribes, not spec.	9	0.06
Arab:	28	0.19
Arab/Arabic	6	0.04
Lebanese	5	0.03
Palestinian	17	0.12
Armenian	8	0.05
Asian:	558	3.83
Cambodian (7)	7	0.05
Chinese, ex. Taiwanese (39)	47	0.32
Filipino (59)	79	0.54
Indian (85)	104	0.71
Japanese (10)	18	0.12
Korean (32)	42	0.29
Malaysian (3)	3	0.02
Pakistani (49)	68	0.47
Sri Lankan (1)	1	0.01
Thai (6)	8	0.05
Vietnamese (151)	153	1.05
Other Asian, specified (12)	12	0.08
Other Asian, not specified (10)	16	0.11
Australian	10	0.07
Austrian	14	0.10
British	21	0.14
Canadian	5	0.03
Croatian	6	0.04
Czech	39	0.27
Czechoslovakian	7	0.05
Danish	8	0.05
Dutch	186	1.27
English	928	6.32
European	64	0.44
French, except Basque	467	3.18
French Canadian	55	0.37
German	1,312	8.94
Greek	27	0.18
Hawaii Native/Pacific Islander:	52	0.36
Micronesian: (16)	23	0.16
Guamanian/Chamorro (16)	21	0.14
Other Micronesian	2	0.01
Polynesian: (5)	11	0.08
Native Hawaiian (1)	7	0.05
Samoan (4)	4	0.03
Other Pac. Isl., not spec. (17)	18	0.12
Hispanic or Latino:	3,406	23.36
Central American:	241	1.65
Costa Rican	5	0.03
Guatemalan	56	0.38
Honduran	52	0.36
Nicaraguan	23	0.16
Panamanian	9	0.06
Salvadoran	72	0.49
Other Central American	24	0.16
Cuban	22	0.15
Dominican Republic	2	0.01
Mexican	2,331	15.99
Puerto Rican	70	0.48
South American:	68	0.47
Argentinean	3	0.02
Colombian	25	0.17
Ecuadorian	8	0.05
Peruvian	13	0.09
Venezuelan	8	0.05
Other South American	11	0.08
Other Hispanic or Latino	672	4.61
Hungarian	7	0.05
Iranian	11	0.07
Irish	1,167	7.95
Italian	383	2.61
Latvian	7	0.05
Norwegian	65	0.44
Polish	171	1.16
Portuguese	21	0.14
Russian	7	0.05
Scotch-Irish	232	1.58
Scottish	168	1.14
Slavic	10	0.07
Swedish	30	0.20
Swiss	22	0.15
Ukrainian	9	0.06

Notes: 1. Figures in the "Number" column do not add up to the total population due to: a) Ancestry/Race overlap — e.g. persons can report being both White and Irish, b) persons of Hispanic origin can report being any race, c) persons reporting two ancestries are counted in both categories. 2. Numbers in parentheses indicate the number of persons reporting this ancestry/race alone, not in combination with any other ancestry/race. 3. Refer to the Explanation of Data in the front of the book for more detailed information.

United States or American	1,672	11.39
Welsh	9	0.06
West Indian, excl. Hispanic:	81	0.55
British West Indian	10	0.07
Haitian	5	0.03
Jamaican	6	0.04
Trinidadian and Tobagonian	31	0.21
West Indian	29	0.20
White:	10,455	71.71
Not Hispanic (8,295)	8,468	58.08
Hispanic (1,799)	1,987	13.63

Huntsville

Place Type: City
County: Walker
Population: 35,078

Ancestry/Race	Number	%
Acadian/Cajun	19	0.05
African American/Black:	9,329	26.60
Not Hispanic (9,114)	9,246	26.36
Hispanic (55)	83	0.24
African, sub-Saharan:	160	0.46
African	118	0.34
Ghanian	10	0.03
Kenyan	10	0.03
Liberian	12	0.03
Nigerian	10	0.03
Alaska Native tribes, specified:	1	0.00
Tlingit-Haida (1)	1	0.00
Am. Ind. or Alaska Nat., not spec.	78	0.22
American Indian tribes, specified:	148	0.42
Apache	1	0.00
Blackfeet (3)	7	0.02
Cherokee (21)	55	0.16
Cheyenne (1)	1	0.00
Chickasaw (2)	2	0.01
Chippewa (4)	4	0.01
Choctaw (18)	31	0.09
Comanche (2)	5	0.01
Cree	1	0.00
Creek (2)	3	0.01
Kiowa (1)	1	0.00
Latin American Indians (10)	16	0.05
Navajo (2)	3	0.01
Osage	2	0.01
Potawatomi (1)	1	0.00
Pueblo (1)	1	0.00
Seminole (1)	1	0.00
Sioux	2	0.01
All other tribes (8)	11	0.03
American Indian tribes, not spec.	19	0.05
Arab:	28	0.08
Lebanese	22	0.06
Moroccan	6	0.02
Asian:	484	1.38
Bangladeshi (2)	6	0.02
Cambodian (18)	19	0.05
Chinese, ex. Taiwanese (51)	59	0.17
Filipino (55)	65	0.19
Indian (105)	122	0.35
Indonesian (5)	6	0.02
Japanese (35)	43	0.12
Korean (17)	21	0.06
Laotian (6)	9	0.03
Malaysian (1)	1	0.00
Pakistani (10)	17	0.05
Sri Lankan (2)	2	0.01
Taiwanese (3)	4	0.01
Thai	4	0.01
Vietnamese (39)	45	0.13
Other Asian, specified	3	0.01
Other Asian, not specified (36)	58	0.17
Australian	18	0.05
Austrian	3	0.01
Belgian	7	0.02
British	160	0.46
Bulgarian	9	0.03
Canadian	41	0.12
Czech	243	0.69
Czechoslovakian	92	0.26
Danish	63	0.18
Dutch	223	0.64
English	1,835	5.25
European	216	0.62
Finnish	11	0.03
French, except Basque	732	2.09
French Canadian	146	0.42
German	2,805	8.02
Greek	33	0.09
Hawaii Native/Pacific Islander:	75	0.21
Micronesian: (1)	4	0.01
Guamanian/Chamorro (1)	4	0.01
Polynesian: (12)	17	0.05
Native Hawaiian (2)	4	0.01
Samoan (10)	13	0.04
Other Pac. Isl., specified	3	0.01
Other Pac. Isl., not spec. (11)	51	0.15
Hispanic or Latino:	5,689	16.22
Central American:	258	0.74
Costa Rican	5	0.01
Guatemalan	5	0.01
Honduran	14	0.04
Nicaraguan	19	0.05
Panamanian	4	0.01
Salvadoran	203	0.58
Other Central American	8	0.02
Cuban	15	0.04
Dominican Republic	6	0.02
Mexican	4,753	13.55
Puerto Rican	58	0.17
South American:	29	0.08
Argentinean	3	0.01
Chilean	1	0.00
Colombian	7	0.02
Ecuadorian	2	0.01
Peruvian	3	0.01
Venezuelan	13	0.04
Other Hispanic or Latino	570	1.62
Hungarian	36	0.10
Iranian	17	0.05
Irish	2,150	6.15
Italian	449	1.28
Lithuanian	18	0.05
Macedonian	13	0.04
Northern European	8	0.02
Norwegian	84	0.24
Pennsylvania German	26	0.07
Polish	390	1.11
Portuguese	28	0.08
Romanian	24	0.07
Russian	39	0.11
Scandinavian	14	0.04
Scotch-Irish	649	1.86
Scottish	412	1.18
Slovak	11	0.03
Swedish	181	0.52
Swiss	25	0.07
Ukrainian	14	0.04
United States or American	1,925	5.50
Welsh	86	0.25
West Indian, excl. Hispanic:	108	0.31
Dutch West Indian	21	0.06
Haitian	11	0.03
Jamaican	76	0.22
White:	23,535	67.09
Not Hispanic (19,384)	19,651	56.02
Hispanic (3,691)	3,884	11.07

Hurst

Place Type: City
County: Tarrant
Population: 36,273

Ancestry/Race	Number	%
Acadian/Cajun	38	0.10
African American/Black:	1,617	4.46
Not Hispanic (1,447)	1,537	4.24
Hispanic (52)	80	0.22
African, sub-Saharan:	458	1.26
African	316	0.87
Liberian	106	0.29
Sierra Leonean	12	0.03
Sudanese	24	0.07
Alaska Native tribes, specified:	3	0.01
Eskimo	1	0.00
Tlingit-Haida (2)	2	0.01
Am. Ind. or Alaska Nat., not spec.	78	0.22
American Indian tribes, specified:	376	1.04
Apache (8)	19	0.05
Blackfeet (2)	5	0.01
Cherokee (39)	136	0.37
Chickasaw (9)	20	0.06
Chippewa (4)	4	0.01
Choctaw (37)	76	0.21
Comanche (9)	21	0.06
Cree (2)	2	0.01
Creek (3)	10	0.03
Crow (1)	1	0.00
Delaware (1)	4	0.01
Houma	1	0.00
Iroquois	5	0.01
Kiowa (1)	5	0.01
Latin American Indians (8)	10	0.03
Navajo (1)	1	0.00
Osage (2)	2	0.01
Paiute (1)	1	0.00
Potawatomi (3)	3	0.01
Pueblo (2)	2	0.01
Seminole (1)	1	0.00
Sioux (5)	10	0.03
Yuman (1)	1	0.00
All other tribes (26)	36	0.10
American Indian tribes, not spec.	35	0.10
Arab:	64	0.18
Arab/Arabic	33	0.09
Egyptian	23	0.06
Lebanese	8	0.02
Armenian	28	0.08
Asian:	821	2.26
Bangladeshi (22)	22	0.06
Cambodian (20)	31	0.09
Chinese, ex. Taiwanese (64)	80	0.22
Filipino (60)	102	0.28
Indian (199)	216	0.60
Indonesian (3)	4	0.01
Japanese (30)	47	0.13
Korean (40)	53	0.15
Laotian (10)	17	0.05
Pakistani (24)	36	0.10
Sri Lankan (1)	3	0.01
Taiwanese (11)	11	0.03
Thai (22)	29	0.08
Vietnamese (116)	132	0.36
Other Asian, specified	3	0.01
Other Asian, not specified (19)	35	0.10
Australian	4	0.01
Austrian	56	0.15
Basque	28	0.08
Belgian	14	0.04
Brazilian	13	0.04
British	175	0.48
Canadian	61	0.17
Celtic	14	0.04
Croatian	13	0.04
Czech	237	0.65
Czechoslovakian	50	0.14
Danish	136	0.37
Dutch	555	1.53
English	4,367	12.03
European	267	0.74
Finnish	25	0.07
French, except Basque	1,275	3.51
French Canadian	107	0.29
German	5,025	13.84
Greek	123	0.34
Hawaii Native/Pacific Islander:	167	0.46
Micronesian: (8)	9	0.02

Notes: 1. Figures in the "Number" column do not add up to the total population due to: a) Ancestry/Race overlap — e.g. persons can report being both White and Irish, b) persons of Hispanic origin can report being any race, c) persons reporting two ancestries are counted in both categories. 2. Numbers in parentheses indicate the number of persons reporting this ancestry/race alone, not in combination with any other ancestry/race. 3. Refer to the Explanation of Data in the front of the book for more detailed information.

Ancestry/Race	Number	%
Guamanian/Chamorro (1)	2	0.01
Other Micronesian (7)	7	0.02
Polynesian: (87)	142	0.39
Native Hawaiian (18)	33	0.09
Samoan (12)	28	0.08
Tongan (44)	60	0.17
Other Polynesian (13)	21	0.06
Other Pac. Isl., not spec. (1)	16	0.04
Hispanic or Latino:	3,999	11.02
Central American:	123	0.34
Guatemalan	10	0.03
Honduran	11	0.03
Nicaraguan	4	0.01
Panamanian	10	0.03
Salvadoran	80	0.22
Other Central American	8	0.02
Cuban	20	0.06
Dominican Republic	22	0.06
Mexican	2,912	8.03
Puerto Rican	143	0.39
South American:	47	0.13
Argentinean	7	0.02
Chilean	4	0.01
Colombian	14	0.04
Ecuadorian	11	0.03
Peruvian	6	0.02
Venezuelan	1	0.00
Other South American	4	0.01
Other Hispanic or Latino	732	2.02
Hungarian	51	0.14
Irish	4,347	11.97
Israeli	9	0.02
Italian	913	2.51
Latvian	13	0.04
Lithuanian	41	0.11
Northern European	6	0.02
Norwegian	440	1.21
Pennsylvania German	10	0.03
Polish	642	1.77
Portuguese	43	0.12
Romanian	30	0.08
Russian	121	0.33
Scandinavian	30	0.08
Scotch-Irish	1,044	2.88
Scottish	774	2.13
Serbian	8	0.02
Slavic	7	0.02
Slovak	29	0.08
Swedish	364	1.00
Swiss	83	0.23
Turkish	26	0.07
Ukrainian	63	0.17
United States or American	4,079	11.24
Welsh	459	1.26
West Indian, excl. Hispanic:	47	0.13
Dutch West Indian	47	0.13
White:	31,815	87.71
Not Hispanic (29,320)	29,775	82.09
Hispanic (1,869)	2,040	5.62
Yugoslavian	70	0.19

Irving

Place Type: City
County: Dallas
Population: 191,615

Ancestry/Race	Number	%
Acadian/Cajun	25	0.01
Afghan	98	0.05
African American/Black:	20,747	10.83
Not Hispanic (19,254)	20,144	10.51
Hispanic (329)	603	0.31
African, sub-Saharan:	2,903	1.52
African	1,212	0.63
Ethiopian	286	0.15
Ghanian	237	0.12
Kenyan	102	0.05
Liberian	15	0.01
Nigerian	679	0.35
Senegalese	33	0.02
Somalian	54	0.03
South African	67	0.03
Sudanese	31	0.02
Ugandan	15	0.01
Zairian	40	0.02
Zimbabwean	43	0.02
Other sub-Saharan African	89	0.05
Alaska Native tribes, specified:	11	0.01
Alaska Athabascan (3)	4	0.00
Eskimo (2)	6	0.00
All other tribes	1	0.00
Alaska Native tribes, not specified	2	0.00
Am. Ind. or Alaska Nat., not spec.	689	0.36
Albanian	42	0.02
American Indian tribes, specified:	1,480	0.77
Apache (19)	42	0.02
Blackfeet (12)	35	0.02
Cherokee (177)	461	0.24
Cheyenne (7)	11	0.01
Chickasaw (42)	79	0.04
Chippewa (12)	20	0.01
Choctaw (168)	265	0.14
Comanche (16)	49	0.03
Cree	2	0.00
Creek (23)	52	0.03
Crow	1	0.00
Delaware (8)	8	0.00
Iroquois (8)	20	0.01
Kiowa (17)	23	0.01
Latin American Indians (87)	149	0.08
Lumbee (1)	2	0.00
Navajo (45)	55	0.03
Osage (10)	16	0.01
Ottawa (1)	1	0.00
Pima (8)	8	0.00
Potawatomi (10)	12	0.01
Pueblo (3)	7	0.00
Puget Sound Salish (1)	1	0.00
Seminole (8)	21	0.01
Shoshone (1)	1	0.00
Sioux (21)	37	0.02
Tohono O'Odham (3)	3	0.00
Ute	2	0.00
Yaqui (2)	2	0.00
Yuman	1	0.00
All other tribes (69)	94	0.05
American Indian tribes, not spec.	137	0.07
Arab:	977	0.51
Arab/Arabic	229	0.12
Egyptian	104	0.05
Iraqi	64	0.03
Jordanian	63	0.03
Lebanese	211	0.11
Moroccan	26	0.01
Palestinian	160	0.08
Syrian	27	0.01
Other Arab	93	0.05
Armenian	22	0.01
Asian:	17,357	9.06
Bangladeshi (230)	270	0.14
Cambodian (90)	125	0.07
Chinese, ex. Taiwanese (1,512)	1,680	0.88
Filipino (705)	842	0.44
Hmong (27)	32	0.02
Indian (6,268)	6,594	3.44
Indonesian (98)	111	0.06
Japanese (598)	718	0.37
Korean (2,554)	2,688	1.40
Laotian (434)	480	0.25
Malaysian (13)	22	0.01
Pakistani (536)	681	0.36
Sri Lankan (31)	36	0.02
Taiwanese (79)	114	0.06
Thai (266)	297	0.15
Vietnamese (1,771)	1,880	0.98
Other Asian, specified (184)	222	0.12
Other Asian, not specified (218)	565	0.29
Assyrian/Chaldean/Syriac	6	0.00
Australian	105	0.05
Austrian	210	0.11
Belgian	86	0.04
Brazilian	168	0.09
British	785	0.41
Bulgarian	16	0.01
Canadian	421	0.22
Celtic	64	0.03
Croatian	77	0.04
Czech	856	0.45
Czechoslovakian	306	0.16
Danish	467	0.24
Dutch	1,712	0.89
Eastern European	58	0.03
English	12,800	6.68
Estonian	25	0.01
European	806	0.42
Finnish	302	0.16
French, except Basque	3,490	1.82
French Canadian	520	0.27
German	16,542	8.63
Greek	358	0.19
Guyanese	30	0.02
Hawaii Native/Pacific Islander:	438	0.23
Melanesian:	1	0.00
Fijian	1	0.00
Micronesian: (59)	77	0.04
Guamanian/Chamorro (30)	46	0.02
Other Micronesian (29)	31	0.02
Polynesian: (115)	175	0.09
Native Hawaiian (48)	89	0.05
Samoan (34)	45	0.02
Tongan (22)	24	0.01
Other Polynesian (11)	17	0.01
Other Pac. Isl., specified	8	0.00
Other Pac. Isl., not spec. (71)	177	0.09
Hispanic or Latino:	59,838	31.23
Central American:	6,225	3.25
Costa Rican	55	0.03
Guatemalan	221	0.12
Honduran	470	0.25
Nicaraguan	79	0.04
Panamanian	91	0.05
Salvadoran	5,102	2.66
Other Central American	207	0.11
Cuban	272	0.14
Dominican Republic	65	0.03
Mexican	42,318	22.08
Puerto Rican	679	0.35
South American:	1,028	0.54
Argentinean	240	0.13
Bolivian	22	0.01
Chilean	61	0.03
Colombian	258	0.13
Ecuadorian	91	0.05
Paraguayan	5	0.00
Peruvian	181	0.09
Uruguayan	9	0.00
Venezuelan	118	0.06
Other South American	43	0.02
Other Hispanic or Latino	9,251	4.83
Hungarian	293	0.15
Iranian	361	0.19
Irish	13,528	7.06
Israeli	28	0.01
Italian	3,519	1.84
Latvian	23	0.01
Lithuanian	93	0.05
Luxemburger	26	0.01
New Zealander	13	0.01
Northern European	120	0.06
Norwegian	1,284	0.67
Pennsylvania German	50	0.03
Polish	1,928	1.01
Portuguese	224	0.12
Romanian	53	0.03
Russian	565	0.29
Scandinavian	119	0.06
Scotch-Irish	2,768	1.44
Scottish	2,751	1.44
Serbian	24	0.01

Notes: 1. Figures in the "Number" column do not add up to the total population due to: a) Ancestry/Race overlap — e.g. persons can report being both White and Irish, b) persons of Hispanic origin can report being any race, c) persons reporting two ancestries are counted in both categories. 2. Numbers in parentheses indicate the number of persons reporting this ancestry/race alone, not in combination with any other ancestry/race. 3. Refer to the Explanation of Data in the front of the book for more detailed information.

Slavic	29	0.02
Slovak	128	0.07
Slovene	27	0.01
Swedish	1,297	0.68
Swiss	288	0.15
Turkish	46	0.02
Ukrainian	357	0.19
United States or American	13,091	6.83
Welsh	881	0.46
West Indian, excl. Hispanic:	592	0.31
Bahamian	30	0.02
Barbadian	11	0.01
Belizean	83	0.04
British West Indian	8	0.00
Dutch West Indian	58	0.03
Haitian	42	0.02
Jamaican	169	0.09
Trinidadian and Tobagonian	60	0.03
U.S. Virgin Islander	12	0.01
West Indian	119	0.06
White:	127,950	66.77
Not Hispanic (92,445)	94,634	49.39
Hispanic (30,574)	33,316	17.39
Yugoslavian	88	0.05

Jacinto City

Place Type: City
County: Harris
Population: 10,302

Ancestry/Race	Number	%
African American/Black:	133	1.29
Not Hispanic (104)	107	1.04
Hispanic (23)	26	0.25
African, sub-Saharan:	14	0.14
African	14	0.14
Am. Ind. or Alaska Nat., not spec.	69	0.67
American Indian tribes, specified:	50	0.49
Apache (5)	6	0.06
Cherokee (5)	12	0.12
Comanche	1	0.01
Kiowa (2)	2	0.02
Latin American Indians (19)	21	0.20
Pueblo	1	0.01
Shoshone (1)	1	0.01
All other tribes (1)	6	0.06
American Indian tribes, not spec.	15	0.15
Arab:	8	0.08
Lebanese	8	0.08
Asian:	48	0.47
Chinese, ex. Taiwanese (1)	3	0.03
Filipino (1)	3	0.03
Indian (11)	15	0.15
Indonesian (5)	5	0.05
Japanese (3)	5	0.05
Korean (2)	2	0.02
Pakistani	3	0.03
Vietnamese (1)	5	0.05
Other Asian, not specified	7	0.07
British	10	0.10
Czech	62	0.61
Danish	7	0.07
Dutch	33	0.32
English	194	1.91
European	38	0.37
French, except Basque	93	0.91
French Canadian	21	0.21
German	312	3.07
Hawaii Native/Pacific Islander:	1	0.01
Other Pac. Isl., not spec. (1)	1	0.01
Hispanic or Latino:	7,767	75.39
Central American:	148	1.44
Costa Rican	3	0.03
Guatemalan	1	0.01
Honduran	19	0.18
Nicaraguan	8	0.08
Salvadoran	113	1.10
Other Central American	4	0.04
Cuban	14	0.14
Dominican Republic	1	0.01
Mexican	6,584	63.91
Puerto Rican	15	0.15
South American:	16	0.16
Colombian	14	0.14
Peruvian	2	0.02
Other Hispanic or Latino	989	9.60
Hungarian	5	0.05
Icelander	9	0.09
Irish	334	3.28
Italian	53	0.52
Norwegian	29	0.29
Polish	31	0.30
Scotch-Irish	28	0.28
Scottish	30	0.30
Swedish	23	0.23
United States or American	491	4.83
West Indian, excl. Hispanic:	8	0.08
Other West Indian	8	0.08
White:	7,397	71.80
Not Hispanic (2,341)	2,385	23.15
Hispanic (4,683)	5,012	48.65

Jacksonville

Place Type: City
County: Cherokee
Population: 13,868

Ancestry/Race	Number	%
African American/Black:	3,089	22.27
Not Hispanic (2,988)	3,058	22.05
Hispanic (21)	31	0.22
African, sub-Saharan:	128	0.92
African	128	0.92
Alaska Native tribes, not specified	2	0.01
Am. Ind. or Alaska Nat., not spec.	42	0.30
American Indian tribes, specified:	59	0.43
Apache	1	0.01
Blackfeet (1)	3	0.02
Cherokee (17)	30	0.22
Chippewa (3)	3	0.02
Choctaw (1)	4	0.03
Creek	1	0.01
Latin American Indians (8)	9	0.06
Pueblo	1	0.01
All other tribes (4)	7	0.05
American Indian tribes, not spec.	5	0.04
Asian:	125	0.90
Cambodian (4)	5	0.04
Chinese, ex. Taiwanese (25)	29	0.21
Filipino (21)	29	0.21
Indian (20)	22	0.16
Indonesian (2)	2	0.01
Japanese (3)	4	0.03
Korean (8)	8	0.06
Vietnamese (3)	4	0.03
Other Asian, specified (2)	2	0.01
Other Asian, not specified (6)	20	0.14
Belgian	8	0.06
British	9	0.06
Czech	54	0.39
Czechoslovakian	17	0.12
Danish	8	0.06
Dutch	90	0.65
English	917	6.60
European	15	0.11
Finnish	11	0.08
French, except Basque	175	1.26
French Canadian	39	0.28
German	703	5.06
Hawaii Native/Pacific Islander:	33	0.24
Micronesian: (1)	3	0.02
Guamanian/Chamorro (1)	3	0.02
Polynesian: (13)	16	0.12
Native Hawaiian (2)	5	0.04
Samoan (11)	11	0.08
Other Pac. Isl., not spec. (4)	14	0.10
Hispanic or Latino:	3,195	23.04
Central American:	36	0.26
Guatemalan	7	0.05
Honduran	14	0.10
Nicaraguan	8	0.06
Salvadoran	7	0.05
Cuban	14	0.10
Mexican	2,836	20.45
Puerto Rican	25	0.18
South American:	5	0.04
Ecuadorian	2	0.01
Peruvian	2	0.01
Other South American	1	0.01
Other Hispanic or Latino	279	2.01
Irish	1,051	7.57
Italian	107	0.77
Northern European	18	0.13
Norwegian	47	0.34
Polish	15	0.11
Portuguese	7	0.05
Scandinavian	5	0.04
Scotch-Irish	227	1.63
Scottish	94	0.68
Swedish	30	0.22
Swiss	5	0.04
Ukrainian	7	0.05
United States or American	1,255	9.03
Welsh	10	0.07
West Indian, excl. Hispanic:	12	0.09
Bahamian	9	0.06
Jamaican	3	0.02
White:	8,879	64.03
Not Hispanic (7,424)	7,529	54.29
Hispanic (1,258)	1,350	9.73

Jollyville

Place Type: Census Designated Place
County: Williamson
Population: 15,813

Ancestry/Race	Number	%
Acadian/Cajun	58	0.38
African American/Black:	803	5.08
Not Hispanic (735)	778	4.92
Hispanic (7)	25	0.16
African, sub-Saharan:	122	0.79
African	87	0.56
Nigerian	26	0.17
South African	9	0.06
Alaska Native tribes, specified:	2	0.01
Alaska Athabascan (1)	2	0.01
Alaska Native tribes, not specified	1	0.01
Am. Ind. or Alaska Nat., not spec.	34	0.22
American Indian tribes, specified:	84	0.53
Apache (3)	4	0.03
Blackfeet	2	0.01
Cherokee (9)	37	0.23
Chickasaw (1)	2	0.01
Choctaw (7)	12	0.08
Comanche (2)	4	0.03
Creek (1)	4	0.03
Houma	1	0.01
Iroquois (2)	2	0.01
Kiowa (1)	1	0.01
Latin American Indians (2)	4	0.03
Navajo (1)	1	0.01
Osage	2	0.01
Potawatomi	2	0.01
Sioux (2)	3	0.02
Yuman (1)	1	0.01
All other tribes (2)	2	0.01
American Indian tribes, not spec.	4	0.03
Arab:	121	0.78
Egyptian	38	0.25
Lebanese	38	0.25
Palestinian	10	0.06
Other Arab	35	0.23
Asian:	1,502	9.50
Cambodian (8)	8	0.05
Chinese, ex. Taiwanese (475)	519	3.28
Filipino (68)	86	0.54

Notes: 1. Figures in the "Number" column do not add up to the total population due to: a) Ancestry/Race overlap — e.g. persons can report being both White and Irish, b) persons of Hispanic origin can report being any race, c) persons reporting two ancestries are counted in both categories. 2. Numbers in parentheses indicate the number of persons reporting this ancestry/race alone, not in combination with any other ancestry/race. 3. Refer to the Explanation of Data in the front of the book for more detailed information.

Ancestry/Race	Number	%
Indian (297)	319	2.02
Indonesian (7)	7	0.04
Japanese (35)	71	0.45
Korean (102)	110	0.70
Laotian (1)	1	0.01
Malaysian (2)	2	0.01
Pakistani (7)	7	0.04
Sri Lankan (7)	7	0.04
Taiwanese (34)	48	0.30
Thai (28)	30	0.19
Vietnamese (230)	246	1.56
Other Asian, specified (2)	3	0.02
Other Asian, not specified (15)	38	0.24
Assyrian/Chaldean/Syriac	9	0.06
Austrian	26	0.17
Basque	7	0.05
Belgian	31	0.20
British	182	1.18
Canadian	66	0.43
Croatian	34	0.22
Czech	172	1.11
Czechoslovakian	18	0.12
Danish	45	0.29
Dutch	154	1.00
English	1,613	10.43
European	123	0.80
Finnish	43	0.28
French, except Basque	551	3.56
French Canadian	128	0.83
German	2,910	18.82
Greek	90	0.58
Hawaii Native/Pacific Islander:	19	0.12
Polynesian: (3)	12	0.08
Native Hawaiian (3)	11	0.07
Samoan	1	0.01
Other Pac. Isl., not spec.	7	0.04
Hispanic or Latino:	1,808	11.43
Central American:	55	0.35
Guatemalan	2	0.01
Honduran	3	0.02
Nicaraguan	17	0.11
Panamanian	12	0.08
Salvadoran	21	0.13
Cuban	17	0.11
Dominican Republic	1	0.01
Mexican	1,239	7.84
Puerto Rican	46	0.29
South American:	38	0.24
Argentinean	9	0.06
Chilean	1	0.01
Colombian	11	0.07
Ecuadorian	1	0.01
Peruvian	1	0.01
Venezuelan	11	0.07
Other South American	4	0.03
Other Hispanic or Latino	412	2.61
Hungarian	36	0.23
Iranian	64	0.41
Irish	2,062	13.33
Italian	422	2.73
Latvian	13	0.08
Lithuanian	24	0.16
Northern European	31	0.20
Norwegian	75	0.48
Polish	386	2.50
Portuguese	93	0.60
Russian	173	1.12
Scotch-Irish	327	2.11
Scottish	322	2.08
Serbian	24	0.16
Slavic	21	0.14
Slovak	10	0.06
Slovene	11	0.07
Swedish	237	1.53
Swiss	63	0.41
Ukrainian	9	0.06
United States or American	1,194	7.72
Welsh	99	0.64
West Indian, excl. Hispanic:	56	0.36
Jamaican	27	0.17
Trinidadian and Tobagonian	29	0.19
White:	12,936	81.81
Not Hispanic (11,640)	11,845	74.91
Hispanic (981)	1,091	6.90
Yugoslavian	25	0.16

Katy

Place Type: City
County: Harris
Population: 11,775

Ancestry/Race	Number	%
Acadian/Cajun	21	0.18
African American/Black:	528	4.48
Not Hispanic (488)	514	4.37
Hispanic (11)	14	0.12
African, sub-Saharan:	4	0.03
African	4	0.03
Am. Ind. or Alaska Nat., not spec.	30	0.25
American Indian tribes, specified:	76	0.65
Blackfeet	8	0.07
Cherokee (8)	22	0.19
Choctaw (4)	7	0.06
Comanche	1	0.01
Cree	1	0.01
Creek (5)	5	0.04
Delaware (1)	1	0.01
Latin American Indians (8)	11	0.09
Navajo (2)	2	0.02
Osage (3)	5	0.04
Potawatomi (7)	7	0.06
Seminole (1)	1	0.01
Sioux	1	0.01
All other tribes (4)	4	0.03
American Indian tribes, not spec.	16	0.14
Arab:	7	0.06
Lebanese	7	0.06
Armenian	8	0.07
Asian:	88	0.75
Chinese, ex. Taiwanese (5)	6	0.05
Filipino (25)	32	0.27
Indian (6)	6	0.05
Japanese (4)	8	0.07
Korean (5)	9	0.08
Pakistani (5)	15	0.13
Thai (2)	2	0.02
Vietnamese (6)	6	0.05
Other Asian, specified (1)	3	0.03
Other Asian, not specified	1	0.01
Austrian	38	0.32
Belgian	9	0.08
British	16	0.14
Canadian	10	0.09
Czech	151	1.29
Czechoslovakian	59	0.50
Danish	7	0.06
Dutch	281	2.40
English	1,241	10.58
European	57	0.49
Finnish	9	0.08
French, except Basque	371	3.16
French Canadian	82	0.70
German	1,897	16.17
Greek	31	0.26
Hawaii Native/Pacific Islander:	7	0.06
Micronesian: (3)	3	0.03
Guamanian/Chamorro (3)	3	0.03
Polynesian: (2)	4	0.03
Native Hawaiian (2)	4	0.03
Hispanic or Latino:	2,797	23.75
Central American:	73	0.62
Costa Rican	3	0.03
Guatemalan	9	0.08
Honduran	4	0.03
Nicaraguan	1	0.01
Panamanian	1	0.01
Salvadoran	54	0.46
Other Central American	1	0.01
Cuban	30	0.25
Mexican	2,233	18.96
Puerto Rican	30	0.25
South American:	52	0.44
Argentinean	4	0.03
Bolivian	5	0.04
Chilean	1	0.01
Colombian	15	0.13
Ecuadorian	2	0.02
Peruvian	3	0.03
Uruguayan	4	0.03
Venezuelan	14	0.12
Other South American	4	0.03
Other Hispanic or Latino	379	3.22
Hungarian	26	0.22
Irish	1,071	9.13
Italian	198	1.69
Norwegian	94	0.80
Pennsylvania German	28	0.24
Polish	198	1.69
Portuguese	5	0.04
Russian	48	0.41
Scandinavian	8	0.07
Scotch-Irish	349	2.98
Scottish	192	1.64
Slavic	9	0.08
Slovene	13	0.11
Swedish	126	1.07
Swiss	7	0.06
Ukrainian	44	0.38
United States or American	1,284	10.95
Welsh	88	0.75
West Indian, excl. Hispanic:	9	0.08
Dutch West Indian	9	0.08
White:	10,114	85.89
Not Hispanic (8,275)	8,371	71.09
Hispanic (1,614)	1,743	14.80
Yugoslavian	7	0.06

Keller

Place Type: City
County: Tarrant
Population: 27,345

Ancestry/Race	Number	%
Afghan	35	0.13
African American/Black:	456	1.67
Not Hispanic (384)	440	1.61
Hispanic (8)	16	0.06
African, sub-Saharan:	71	0.26
African	37	0.14
Ghanian	27	0.10
South African	7	0.03
Alaska Native tribes, specified:	1	0.00
Aleut	1	0.00
Am. Ind. or Alaska Nat., not spec.	30	0.11
Albanian	47	0.17
Alsatian	6	0.02
American Indian tribes, specified:	203	0.74
Apache (2)	3	0.01
Blackfeet (1)	1	0.00
Cherokee (38)	105	0.38
Chickasaw (8)	14	0.05
Choctaw (16)	25	0.09
Comanche (1)	5	0.02
Creek (14)	21	0.08
Iroquois	2	0.01
Latin American Indians (3)	6	0.02
Navajo (2)	2	0.01
Potawatomi	4	0.01
Seminole (2)	3	0.01
All other tribes (7)	12	0.04
American Indian tribes, not spec.	4	0.01
Arab:	62	0.23
Arab/Arabic	2	0.01
Egyptian	8	0.03
Lebanese	39	0.14
Palestinian	13	0.05
Armenian	26	0.10
Asian:	626	2.29

Notes: 1. Figures in the "Number" column do not add up to the total population due to: a) Ancestry/Race overlap — e.g. persons can report being both White and Irish, b) persons of Hispanic origin can report being any race, c) persons reporting two ancestries are counted in both categories. 2. Numbers in parentheses indicate the number of persons reporting this ancestry/race alone, not in combination with any other ancestry/race. 3. Refer to the Explanation of Data in the front of the book for more detailed information.

Ancestry/Race	Number	%
Bangladeshi (10)	10	0.04
Cambodian (10)	21	0.08
Chinese, ex. Taiwanese (73)	101	0.37
Filipino (40)	61	0.22
Indian (120)	150	0.55
Indonesian (3)	3	0.01
Japanese (24)	52	0.19
Korean (29)	38	0.14
Laotian (18)	20	0.07
Malaysian (1)	2	0.01
Pakistani (18)	19	0.07
Taiwanese (4)	4	0.01
Thai (18)	22	0.08
Vietnamese (75)	94	0.34
Other Asian, specified (4)	7	0.03
Other Asian, not specified (8)	22	0.08
Austrian	47	0.17
Belgian	29	0.11
British	237	0.87
Bulgarian	35	0.13
Canadian	121	0.44
Celtic	35	0.13
Croatian	101	0.37
Czech	281	1.03
Czechoslovakian	38	0.14
Danish	183	0.67
Dutch	534	1.96
Eastern European	27	0.10
English	4,178	15.30
European	293	1.07
Finnish	38	0.14
French, except Basque	799	2.93
French Canadian	124	0.45
German	5,055	18.51
Greek	79	0.29
Hawaii Native/Pacific Islander:	31	0.11
Micronesian: (5)	6	0.02
Guamanian/Chamorro (2)	3	0.01
Other Micronesian (3)	3	0.01
Polynesian: (3)	15	0.05
Native Hawaiian (2)	11	0.04
Samoan	3	0.01
Tongan (1)	1	0.00
Other Pac. Isl., not spec. (2)	10	0.04
Hispanic or Latino:	1,234	4.51
Central American:	17	0.06
Costa Rican	4	0.01
Guatemalan	3	0.01
Honduran	4	0.01
Nicaraguan	1	0.00
Panamanian	3	0.01
Salvadoran	2	0.01
Cuban	45	0.16
Dominican Republic	7	0.03
Mexican	769	2.81
Puerto Rican	97	0.35
South American:	35	0.13
Argentinean	1	0.00
Bolivian	1	0.00
Chilean	2	0.01
Colombian	10	0.04
Ecuadorian	2	0.01
Paraguayan	3	0.01
Peruvian	3	0.01
Venezuelan	10	0.04
Other South American	3	0.01
Other Hispanic or Latino	264	0.97
Hungarian	149	0.55
Iranian	40	0.15
Irish	4,082	14.95
Italian	1,099	4.02
Lithuanian	31	0.11
Macedonian	8	0.03
Norwegian	432	1.58
Pennsylvania German	9	0.03
Polish	574	2.10
Portuguese	14	0.05
Russian	37	0.14
Scandinavian	93	0.34
Scotch-Irish	724	2.65
Scottish	815	2.98
Serbian	10	0.04
Slavic	12	0.04
Slovak	79	0.29
Slovene	2	0.01
Swedish	417	1.53
Swiss	77	0.28
Turkish	35	0.13
Ukrainian	49	0.18
United States or American	2,854	10.45
Welsh	170	0.62
West Indian, excl. Hispanic:	46	0.17
Dutch West Indian	20	0.07
Trinidadian and Tobagonian	17	0.06
West Indian	9	0.03
White:	25,987	95.03
Not Hispanic (24,809)	25,083	91.73
Hispanic (825)	904	3.31
Yugoslavian	4	0.01

Kerrville

Place Type: City
County: Kerr
Population: 20,425

Ancestry/Race	Number	%
Acadian/Cajun	13	0.06
African American/Black:	646	3.16
Not Hispanic (579)	599	2.93
Hispanic (31)	47	0.23
African, sub-Saharan:	6	0.03
African	6	0.03
Am. Ind. or Alaska Nat., not spec.	68	0.33
Alsatian	39	0.19
American Indian tribes, specified:	178	0.87
Apache (3)	16	0.08
Blackfeet (1)	1	0.00
Cherokee (14)	62	0.30
Cheyenne	4	0.02
Chickasaw (2)	5	0.02
Chippewa (1)	1	0.00
Choctaw (5)	14	0.07
Comanche (5)	10	0.05
Cree (4)	4	0.02
Iroquois	1	0.00
Latin American Indians (10)	11	0.05
Lumbee (3)	3	0.01
Navajo (2)	5	0.02
Osage	2	0.01
Pueblo	1	0.00
Seminole (10)	19	0.09
Shoshone (1)	1	0.00
Sioux (2)	2	0.01
Yaqui (1)	2	0.01
All other tribes (8)	14	0.07
American Indian tribes, not spec.	12	0.06
Arab:	33	0.16
Arab/Arabic	6	0.03
Lebanese	20	0.10
Palestinian	7	0.03
Asian:	183	0.90
Cambodian (4)	5	0.02
Chinese, ex. Taiwanese (18)	24	0.12
Filipino (25)	43	0.21
Indian (29)	40	0.20
Japanese (3)	14	0.07
Korean (7)	10	0.05
Laotian (2)	2	0.01
Pakistani (5)	6	0.03
Thai (1)	2	0.01
Vietnamese (16)	20	0.10
Other Asian, not specified (2)	17	0.08
Austrian	9	0.04
Belgian	5	0.02
British	73	0.35
Canadian	54	0.26
Celtic	6	0.03
Czech	253	1.22
Czechoslovakian	27	0.13
Danish	99	0.48
Dutch	287	1.38
English	2,734	13.16
European	84	0.40
Finnish	33	0.16
French, except Basque	730	3.52
French Canadian	73	0.35
German	3,414	16.44
Greek	47	0.23
Hawaii Native/Pacific Islander:	22	0.11
Micronesian: (4)	6	0.03
Guamanian/Chamorro (4)	6	0.03
Polynesian: (12)	16	0.08
Native Hawaiian (9)	12	0.06
Samoan (3)	4	0.02
Hispanic or Latino:	4,643	22.73
Central American:	26	0.13
Costa Rican	2	0.01
Guatemalan	7	0.03
Honduran	4	0.02
Panamanian	4	0.02
Salvadoran	8	0.04
Other Central American	1	0.00
Cuban	11	0.05
Mexican	3,509	17.18
Puerto Rican	8	0.04
South American:	12	0.06
Argentinean	1	0.00
Colombian	5	0.02
Ecuadorian	3	0.01
Peruvian	2	0.01
Venezuelan	1	0.00
Other Hispanic or Latino	1,077	5.27
Hungarian	21	0.10
Iranian	12	0.06
Irish	1,815	8.74
Italian	364	1.75
Lithuanian	8	0.04
Norwegian	273	1.31
Polish	215	1.04
Russian	27	0.13
Scandinavian	7	0.03
Scotch-Irish	823	3.96
Scottish	494	2.38
Slavic	9	0.04
Slovak	16	0.08
Slovene	8	0.04
Swedish	167	0.80
Swiss	17	0.08
Ukrainian	8	0.04
United States or American	1,825	8.79
Welsh	86	0.41
White:	17,855	87.42
Not Hispanic (14,854)	15,007	73.47
Hispanic (2,689)	2,848	13.94

Kilgore

Place Type: City
County: Gregg
Population: 11,301

Ancestry/Race	Number	%
Acadian/Cajun	2	0.02
African American/Black:	1,430	12.65
Not Hispanic (1,381)	1,414	12.51
Hispanic (13)	16	0.14
African, sub-Saharan:	179	1.60
African	163	1.46
Nigerian	6	0.05
Other sub-Saharan African	10	0.09
Am. Ind. or Alaska Nat., not spec.	26	0.23
American Indian tribes, specified:	98	0.87
Apache	3	0.03
Blackfeet	2	0.02
Cherokee (17)	51	0.45
Chickasaw (1)	4	0.04
Choctaw (4)	20	0.18
Latin American Indians (2)	10	0.09
Navajo (1)	1	0.01

Notes: 1. Figures in the "Number" column do not add up to the total population due to: a) Ancestry/Race overlap — e.g. persons can report being both White and Irish, b) persons of Hispanic origin can report being any race, c) persons reporting two ancestries are counted in both categories. 2. Numbers in parentheses indicate the number of persons reporting this ancestry/race alone, not in combination with any other ancestry/race. 3. Refer to the Explanation of Data in the front of the book for more detailed information.

Pueblo	1	0.01
Seminole	1	0.01
All other tribes (4)	5	0.04
American Indian tribes, not spec.	4	0.04
Arab:	6	0.05
Syrian	6	0.05
Asian:	87	0.77
Chinese, ex. Taiwanese (11)	11	0.10
Filipino (3)	7	0.06
Indian (19)	21	0.19
Indonesian (4)	4	0.04
Japanese (16)	19	0.17
Korean (8)	8	0.07
Pakistani (4)	4	0.04
Sri Lankan (1)	1	0.01
Vietnamese (4)	4	0.04
Other Asian, specified (4)	4	0.04
Other Asian, not specified (3)	4	0.04
Belgian	8	0.07
British	19	0.17
Celtic	11	0.10
Czech	33	0.30
Czechoslovakian	5	0.04
Dutch	120	1.07
English	995	8.91
Finnish	26	0.23
French, except Basque	232	2.08
French Canadian	29	0.26
German	960	8.59
Hawaii Native/Pacific Islander:	7	0.06
Micronesian: (2)	2	0.02
Guamanian/Chamorro (2)	2	0.02
Polynesian: (1)	4	0.04
Native Hawaiian (1)	4	0.04
Other Pac. Isl., not spec.	1	0.01
Hispanic or Latino:	1,256	11.11
Central American:	2	0.02
Honduran	1	0.01
Salvadoran	1	0.01
Cuban	6	0.05
Mexican	1,059	9.37
Puerto Rican	6	0.05
South American:	3	0.03
Venezuelan	3	0.03
Other Hispanic or Latino	180	1.59
Hungarian	56	0.50
Irish	1,095	9.80
Italian	161	1.44
Norwegian	5	0.04
Polish	21	0.19
Russian	17	0.15
Scandinavian	6	0.05
Scotch-Irish	211	1.89
Scottish	274	2.45
Swedish	111	0.99
United States or American	1,814	16.24
Welsh	24	0.21
West Indian, excl. Hispanic:	9	0.08
Dutch West Indian	9	0.08
White:	8,973	79.40
Not Hispanic (8,456)	8,537	75.54
Hispanic (384)	436	3.86

Killeen

Place Type: City
County: Bell
Population: 86,911

Ancestry/Race	Number	%
Acadian/Cajun	51	0.06
African American/Black:	31,408	36.14
Not Hispanic (28,267)	30,013	34.53
Hispanic (842)	1,395	1.61
African, sub-Saharan:	1,151	1.33
African	1,061	1.22
Cape Verdean	7	0.01
Ghanian	35	0.04
Nigerian	33	0.04
Ugandan	10	0.01
Other sub-Saharan African	5	0.01
Alaska Native tribes, specified:	8	0.01
Alaska Athabascan (3)	3	0.00
Eskimo (3)	4	0.00
Tlingit-Haida	1	0.00
Am. Ind. or Alaska Nat., not spec.	460	0.53
Alsatian	24	0.03
American Indian tribes, specified:	962	1.11
Apache (22)	62	0.07
Blackfeet (20)	47	0.05
Cherokee (96)	327	0.38
Cheyenne (1)	1	0.00
Chickasaw (4)	14	0.02
Chippewa (21)	30	0.03
Choctaw (27)	63	0.07
Colville	1	0.00
Comanche (2)	9	0.01
Cree	1	0.00
Creek (18)	29	0.03
Delaware	6	0.01
Iroquois (11)	21	0.02
Kiowa (4)	8	0.01
Latin American Indians (30)	69	0.08
Lumbee (9)	16	0.02
Navajo (57)	72	0.08
Osage	5	0.01
Ottawa (4)	5	0.01
Paiute	1	0.00
Pima (1)	1	0.00
Potawatomi (5)	7	0.01
Pueblo (6)	12	0.01
Seminole (4)	4	0.00
Sioux (19)	34	0.04
Tohono O'Odham (1)	1	0.00
Ute (2)	2	0.00
Yaqui (1)	4	0.00
All other tribes (64)	110	0.13
American Indian tribes, not spec.	103	0.12
Arab:	114	0.13
Arab/Arabic	42	0.05
Egyptian	7	0.01
Lebanese	15	0.02
Palestinian	12	0.01
Syrian	38	0.04
Armenian	47	0.05
Asian:	5,445	6.27
Bangladeshi (4)	5	0.01
Cambodian (8)	9	0.01
Chinese, ex. Taiwanese (126)	227	0.26
Filipino (923)	1,284	1.48
Hmong (3)	4	0.00
Indian (123)	186	0.21
Indonesian (2)	10	0.01
Japanese (212)	430	0.49
Korean (1,869)	2,587	2.98
Laotian (21)	29	0.03
Malaysian (1)	2	0.00
Pakistani (17)	22	0.03
Sri Lankan (3)	3	0.00
Taiwanese (8)	11	0.01
Thai (115)	189	0.22
Vietnamese (164)	245	0.28
Other Asian, specified (4)	18	0.02
Other Asian, not specified (90)	184	0.21
Australian	6	0.01
Austrian	119	0.14
Belgian	48	0.06
Brazilian	24	0.03
British	177	0.20
Canadian	158	0.18
Celtic	18	0.02
Croatian	49	0.06
Czech	155	0.18
Czechoslovakian	88	0.10
Danish	161	0.19
Dutch	856	0.99
Eastern European	20	0.02
English	3,435	3.96
European	427	0.49
Finnish	115	0.13
French, except Basque	1,610	1.85
French Canadian	454	0.52
German	10,331	11.90
German Russian	30	0.03
Greek	150	0.17
Guyanese	21	0.02
Hawaii Native/Pacific Islander:	1,260	1.45
Micronesian: (426)	541	0.62
Guamanian/Chamorro (407)	516	0.59
Other Micronesian (19)	25	0.03
Polynesian: (274)	565	0.65
Native Hawaiian (109)	302	0.35
Samoan (161)	245	0.28
Tongan (1)	2	0.00
Other Polynesian (3)	16	0.02
Other Pac. Isl., specified	4	0.00
Other Pac. Isl., not spec. (61)	150	0.17
Hispanic or Latino:	15,469	17.80
Central American:	765	0.88
Costa Rican	23	0.03
Guatemalan	30	0.03
Honduran	49	0.06
Nicaraguan	22	0.03
Panamanian	596	0.69
Salvadoran	36	0.04
Other Central American	9	0.01
Cuban	116	0.13
Dominican Republic	162	0.19
Mexican	7,409	8.52
Puerto Rican	4,499	5.18
South American:	262	0.30
Argentinean	5	0.01
Bolivian	7	0.01
Chilean	4	0.00
Colombian	113	0.13
Ecuadorian	50	0.06
Paraguayan	1	0.00
Peruvian	55	0.06
Venezuelan	17	0.02
Other South American	10	0.01
Other Hispanic or Latino	2,256	2.60
Hungarian	104	0.12
Icelander	16	0.02
Iranian	19	0.02
Irish	5,480	6.31
Italian	1,616	1.86
Latvian	23	0.03
Lithuanian	30	0.03
Northern European	8	0.01
Norwegian	439	0.51
Pennsylvania German	19	0.02
Polish	848	0.98
Portuguese	90	0.10
Romanian	62	0.07
Russian	119	0.14
Scandinavian	56	0.06
Scotch-Irish	767	0.88
Scottish	1,192	1.37
Serbian	8	0.01
Slavic	67	0.08
Slovak	15	0.02
Slovene	14	0.02
Swedish	507	0.58
Swiss	66	0.08
Turkish	16	0.02
Ukrainian	100	0.12
United States or American	4,460	5.14
Welsh	204	0.23
West Indian, excl. Hispanic:	851	0.98
Bahamian	56	0.06
Barbadian	27	0.03
Belizean	18	0.02
British West Indian	29	0.03
Dutch West Indian	17	0.02
Haitian	103	0.12
Jamaican	393	0.45
Trinidadian and Tobagonian	44	0.05
U.S. Virgin Islander	50	0.06
West Indian	114	0.13
White:	43,222	49.73

Notes: 1. Figures in the "Number" column do not add up to the total population due to: a) Ancestry/Race overlap — e.g. persons can report being both White and Irish, b) persons of Hispanic origin can report being any race, c) persons reporting two ancestries are counted in both categories. 2. Numbers in parentheses indicate the number of persons reporting this ancestry/race alone, not in combination with any other ancestry/race. 3. Refer to the Explanation of Data in the front of the book for more detailed information.

Not Hispanic (34,570)	36,968	42.54
Hispanic (5,218)	6,254	7.20
Yugoslavian	42	0.05

Kingsville

Place Type: City
County: Kleberg
Population: 25,575

Ancestry/Race	Number	%
Acadian/Cajun	8	0.03
African American/Black:	1,191	4.66
Not Hispanic (1,045)	1,082	4.23
Hispanic (66)	109	0.43
African, sub-Saharan:	52	0.20
African	52	0.20
Alaska Native tribes, specified:	2	0.01
Tlingit-Haida (2)	2	0.01
Am. Ind. or Alaska Nat., not spec.	120	0.47
American Indian tribes, specified:	143	0.56
Apache (11)	16	0.06
Cherokee (18)	50	0.20
Chickasaw (1)	1	0.00
Chippewa (5)	7	0.03
Choctaw (4)	10	0.04
Comanche (2)	7	0.03
Creek (1)	3	0.01
Iroquois	4	0.02
Kiowa (3)	3	0.01
Latin American Indians (18)	23	0.09
Lumbee	1	0.00
Navajo (1)	1	0.00
Osage (4)	4	0.02
Pueblo (1)	2	0.01
Sioux	2	0.01
Yaqui	1	0.00
All other tribes (2)	8	0.03
American Indian tribes, not spec.	25	0.10
Arab:	43	0.17
Arab/Arabic	14	0.05
Moroccan	29	0.11
Asian:	542	2.12
Bangladeshi (1)	1	0.00
Chinese, ex. Taiwanese (69)	81	0.32
Filipino (129)	161	0.63
Indian (145)	152	0.59
Indonesian	2	0.01
Japanese (19)	34	0.13
Korean (26)	30	0.12
Laotian (1)	1	0.00
Pakistani	1	0.00
Sri Lankan (1)	1	0.00
Taiwanese (2)	2	0.01
Thai (4)	5	0.02
Vietnamese (25)	30	0.12
Other Asian, specified (5)	5	0.02
Other Asian, not specified (13)	36	0.14
Australian	10	0.04
Austrian	38	0.15
Brazilian	4	0.02
Canadian	86	0.34
Croatian	7	0.03
Czech	155	0.61
Czechoslovakian	6	0.02
Danish	32	0.13
Dutch	116	0.45
Eastern European	9	0.04
English	1,126	4.41
European	72	0.28
Finnish	9	0.04
French, except Basque	282	1.10
French Canadian	21	0.08
German	1,847	7.23
Greek	24	0.09
Hawaii Native/Pacific Islander:	29	0.11
Micronesian: (2)	2	0.01
Guamanian/Chamorro (2)	2	0.01
Polynesian: (4)	13	0.05
Native Hawaiian (2)	8	0.03
Samoan (2)	2	0.01
Other Polynesian	3	0.01
Other Pac. Isl., not spec. (11)	14	0.05
Hispanic or Latino:	17,151	67.06
Central American:	39	0.15
Guatemalan	5	0.02
Honduran	13	0.05
Panamanian	11	0.04
Salvadoran	7	0.03
Other Central American	3	0.01
Cuban	41	0.16
Dominican Republic	3	0.01
Mexican	11,838	46.29
Puerto Rican	61	0.24
South American:	28	0.11
Argentinean	5	0.02
Chilean	1	0.00
Colombian	9	0.04
Ecuadorian	2	0.01
Venezuelan	11	0.04
Other Hispanic or Latino	5,141	20.10
Irish	854	3.34
Israeli	17	0.07
Italian	270	1.06
Lithuanian	5	0.02
Norwegian	97	0.38
Pennsylvania German	7	0.03
Polish	262	1.03
Portuguese	21	0.08
Russian	26	0.10
Scandinavian	6	0.02
Scotch-Irish	239	0.94
Scottish	287	1.12
Slovak	29	0.11
Slovene	5	0.02
Swedish	77	0.30
Swiss	16	0.06
United States or American	1,016	3.98
Welsh	26	0.10
West Indian, excl. Hispanic:	14	0.05
Dutch West Indian	6	0.02
West Indian	8	0.03
White:	18,945	74.08
Not Hispanic (6,666)	6,829	26.70
Hispanic (11,519)	12,116	47.37

La Homa

Place Type: Census Designated Place
County: Hidalgo
Population: 10,433

Ancestry/Race	Number	%
African American/Black:	14	0.13
Not Hispanic (4)	4	0.04
Hispanic (8)	10	0.10
Am. Ind. or Alaska Nat., not spec.	1	0.01
American Indian tribes, specified:	14	0.13
Choctaw (1)	1	0.01
Latin American Indians	13	0.12
American Indian tribes, not spec.	5	0.05
Asian:	9	0.09
Chinese, ex. Taiwanese (1)	2	0.02
Filipino (1)	1	0.01
Japanese (1)	1	0.01
Vietnamese (1)	1	0.01
Other Asian, not specified (3)	4	0.04
Canadian	34	0.32
English	32	0.30
German	56	0.53
Hispanic or Latino:	10,196	97.73
Central American:	17	0.16
Honduran	3	0.03
Nicaraguan	8	0.08
Salvadoran	6	0.06
Cuban	13	0.12
Mexican	9,666	92.65
Puerto Rican	2	0.02
South American:	2	0.02
Ecuadorian	2	0.02
Other Hispanic or Latino	496	4.75
Swedish	19	0.18
United States or American	259	2.47
White:	9,198	88.16
Not Hispanic (222)	224	2.15
Hispanic (8,948)	8,974	86.02

La Marque

Place Type: City
County: Galveston
Population: 13,682

Ancestry/Race	Number	%
African American/Black:	4,835	35.34
Not Hispanic (4,692)	4,767	34.84
Hispanic (54)	68	0.50
African, sub-Saharan:	127	0.92
African	127	0.92
Alaska Native tribes, specified:	1	0.01
Alaska Athabascan (1)	1	0.01
Am. Ind. or Alaska Nat., not spec.	40	0.29
American Indian tribes, specified:	87	0.64
Apache (2)	7	0.05
Blackfeet	1	0.01
Cherokee (8)	29	0.21
Chickasaw	1	0.01
Chippewa (1)	2	0.01
Choctaw (12)	23	0.17
Comanche (1)	4	0.03
Creek	3	0.02
Crow	1	0.01
Houma (2)	2	0.01
Latin American Indians (1)	3	0.02
Navajo (3)	3	0.02
Potawatomi (1)	1	0.01
Seminole (1)	2	0.01
Sioux	1	0.01
All other tribes (3)	4	0.03
American Indian tribes, not spec.	6	0.04
Asian:	111	0.81
Chinese, ex. Taiwanese (8)	13	0.10
Filipino (27)	42	0.31
Indian (12)	20	0.15
Japanese (3)	9	0.07
Korean (5)	8	0.06
Pakistani (1)	2	0.01
Vietnamese (7)	11	0.08
Other Asian, specified (1)	1	0.01
Other Asian, not specified	5	0.04
Austrian	42	0.30
Belgian	12	0.09
British	35	0.25
Canadian	7	0.05
Croatian	5	0.04
Czech	54	0.39
Czechoslovakian	49	0.35
Danish	19	0.14
Dutch	156	1.12
English	802	5.78
European	72	0.52
French, except Basque	438	3.16
French Canadian	43	0.31
German	1,262	9.10
Greek	52	0.37
Hawaii Native/Pacific Islander:	7	0.05
Micronesian: (4)	4	0.03
Guamanian/Chamorro (4)	4	0.03
Polynesian:	1	0.01
Native Hawaiian	1	0.01
Other Pac. Isl., not spec.	2	0.01
Hispanic or Latino:	2,111	15.43
Central American:	17	0.12
Costa Rican	4	0.03
Guatemalan	2	0.01
Honduran	3	0.02
Panamanian	1	0.01
Salvadoran	6	0.04
Other Central American	1	0.01
Cuban	5	0.04

Notes: 1. Figures in the "Number" column do not add up to the total population due to: a) Ancestry/Race overlap — e.g. persons can report being both White and Irish, b) persons of Hispanic origin can report being any race, c) persons reporting two ancestries are counted in both categories. 2. Numbers in parentheses indicate the number of persons reporting this ancestry/race alone, not in combination with any other ancestry/race. 3. Refer to the Explanation of Data in the front of the book for more detailed information.

Ancestry/Race	Number	%
Mexican	1,701	12.43
Puerto Rican	33	0.24
South American:	6	0.04
Argentinean	2	0.01
Chilean	1	0.01
Colombian	1	0.01
Peruvian	2	0.01
Other Hispanic or Latino	349	2.55
Hungarian	34	0.25
Irish	872	6.29
Italian	264	1.90
Norwegian	81	0.58
Pennsylvania German	7	0.05
Polish	125	0.90
Romanian	6	0.04
Scotch-Irish	182	1.31
Scottish	107	0.77
Slavic	8	0.06
Slovak	8	0.06
Swedish	101	0.73
Swiss	22	0.16
Ukrainian	11	0.08
United States or American	1,054	7.60
Welsh	67	0.48
West Indian, excl. Hispanic:	42	0.30
Barbadian	13	0.09
Haitian	6	0.04
Trinidadian and Tobagonian	16	0.12
West Indian	7	0.05
White:	7,904	57.77
Not Hispanic (6,583)	6,723	49.14
Hispanic (1,057)	1,181	8.63
Yugoslavian	20	0.14

La Porte

Place Type: City
County: Harris
Population: 31,880

Ancestry/Race	Number	%
Acadian/Cajun	75	0.24
African American/Black:	2,108	6.61
Not Hispanic (1,941)	2,030	6.37
Hispanic (52)	78	0.24
African, sub-Saharan:	207	0.65
African	184	0.58
Nigerian	23	0.07
Alaska Native tribes, specified:	1	0.00
Alaska Athabascan	1	0.00
Am. Ind. or Alaska Nat., not spec.	88	0.28
American Indian tribes, specified:	184	0.58
Apache (5)	6	0.02
Blackfeet	1	0.00
Cherokee (43)	83	0.26
Chickasaw	2	0.01
Chippewa (5)	6	0.02
Choctaw (9)	32	0.10
Comanche (5)	6	0.02
Creek (3)	7	0.02
Latin American Indians (5)	10	0.03
Osage	2	0.01
Ottawa (1)	1	0.00
Potawatomi (2)	3	0.01
Pueblo (1)	1	0.00
Seminole	1	0.00
Sioux (1)	6	0.02
Ute (3)	3	0.01
All other tribes (11)	14	0.04
American Indian tribes, not spec.	46	0.14
Arab:	76	0.24
Arab/Arabic	72	0.23
Lebanese	4	0.01
Asian:	455	1.43
Cambodian (1)	1	0.00
Chinese, ex. Taiwanese (22)	30	0.09
Filipino (69)	85	0.27
Indian (61)	80	0.25
Japanese (17)	24	0.08
Korean (39)	65	0.20
Laotian (3)	4	0.01
Pakistani (7)	13	0.04
Taiwanese	1	0.00
Thai (2)	4	0.01
Vietnamese (110)	118	0.37
Other Asian, specified (3)	3	0.01
Other Asian, not specified (17)	27	0.08
Australian	8	0.03
Austrian	31	0.10
Basque	6	0.02
Brazilian	2	0.01
British	107	0.34
Canadian	38	0.12
Celtic	9	0.03
Croatian	9	0.03
Czech	214	0.67
Czechoslovakian	30	0.09
Danish	40	0.13
Dutch	386	1.21
English	2,497	7.83
European	223	0.70
French, except Basque	1,487	4.66
French Canadian	286	0.90
German	4,172	13.08
Greek	44	0.14
Hawaii Native/Pacific Islander:	43	0.13
Micronesian: (12)	14	0.04
Guamanian/Chamorro (12)	14	0.04
Polynesian: (9)	19	0.06
Native Hawaiian (7)	15	0.05
Samoan (2)	4	0.01
Other Pac. Isl., not spec. (4)	10	0.03
Hispanic or Latino:	6,520	20.45
Central American:	111	0.35
Costa Rican	8	0.03
Guatemalan	24	0.08
Honduran	21	0.07
Nicaraguan	14	0.04
Panamanian	11	0.03
Salvadoran	27	0.08
Other Central American	6	0.02
Cuban	74	0.23
Dominican Republic	10	0.03
Mexican	4,601	14.43
Puerto Rican	149	0.47
South American:	84	0.26
Argentinean	1	0.00
Chilean	2	0.01
Colombian	37	0.12
Peruvian	24	0.08
Uruguayan	1	0.00
Venezuelan	18	0.06
Other South American	1	0.00
Other Hispanic or Latino	1,491	4.68
Hungarian	53	0.17
Iranian	13	0.04
Irish	2,827	8.86
Italian	700	2.19
Latvian	9	0.03
Lithuanian	7	0.02
Macedonian	8	0.03
Norwegian	230	0.72
Pennsylvania German	6	0.02
Polish	491	1.54
Portuguese	49	0.15
Romanian	16	0.05
Russian	67	0.21
Scotch-Irish	519	1.63
Scottish	426	1.34
Serbian	7	0.02
Slovak	54	0.17
Swedish	210	0.66
Swiss	14	0.04
Ukrainian	29	0.09
United States or American	2,783	8.72
Welsh	105	0.33
West Indian, excl. Hispanic:	41	0.13
Dutch West Indian	17	0.05
West Indian	24	0.08
White:	26,518	83.18
Not Hispanic (22,529)	22,810	71.55
Hispanic (3,417)	3,708	11.63

Lake Jackson

Place Type: City
County: Brazoria
Population: 26,386

Ancestry/Race	Number	%
Acadian/Cajun	46	0.17
African American/Black:	1,106	4.19
Not Hispanic (998)	1,067	4.04
Hispanic (25)	39	0.15
African, sub-Saharan:	47	0.18
African	41	0.15
Zimbabwean	6	0.02
Alaska Native tribes, specified:	1	0.00
Alaska Athabascan (1)	1	0.00
Am. Ind. or Alaska Nat., not spec.	62	0.23
American Indian tribes, specified:	158	0.60
Apache (3)	4	0.02
Blackfeet	8	0.03
Cherokee (18)	50	0.19
Chickasaw (1)	6	0.02
Chippewa (3)	3	0.01
Choctaw (18)	28	0.11
Colville (1)	3	0.01
Comanche (1)	4	0.02
Creek (5)	8	0.03
Delaware (3)	6	0.02
Latin American Indians (4)	5	0.02
Osage	3	0.01
Potawatomi	2	0.01
Seminole	3	0.01
Sioux	2	0.01
Yaqui (1)	1	0.00
All other tribes (13)	22	0.08
American Indian tribes, not spec.	10	0.04
Arab:	103	0.39
Iraqi	7	0.03
Lebanese	69	0.26
Syrian	22	0.08
Other Arab	5	0.02
Armenian	9	0.03
Asian:	744	2.82
Bangladeshi (7)	7	0.03
Cambodian (10)	11	0.04
Chinese, ex. Taiwanese (152)	173	0.66
Filipino (63)	86	0.33
Indian (163)	172	0.65
Indonesian (4)	5	0.02
Japanese (45)	52	0.20
Korean (47)	57	0.22
Pakistani (4)	6	0.02
Taiwanese (12)	15	0.06
Thai	2	0.01
Vietnamese (137)	151	0.57
Other Asian, specified (1)	1	0.00
Other Asian, not specified (2)	6	0.02
Australian	9	0.03
Austrian	57	0.21
Basque	25	0.09
Belgian	8	0.03
Brazilian	19	0.07
British	158	0.60
Canadian	88	0.33
Celtic	6	0.02
Croatian	6	0.02
Czech	618	2.33
Czechoslovakian	207	0.78
Danish	88	0.33
Dutch	395	1.49
English	3,259	12.29
European	268	1.01
French, except Basque	1,284	4.84
French Canadian	185	0.70
German	4,769	17.99
Greek	55	0.21
Hawaii Native/Pacific Islander:	10	0.04

Notes: 1. Figures in the "Number" column do not add up to the total population due to: a) Ancestry/Race overlap — e.g. persons can report being both White and Irish, b) persons of Hispanic origin can report being any race, c) persons reporting two ancestries are counted in both categories. 2. Numbers in parentheses indicate the number of persons reporting this ancestry/race alone, not in combination with any other ancestry/race. 3. Refer to the Explanation of Data in the front of the book for more detailed information.

Micronesian: (1)	2	0.01
Guamanian/Chamorro (1)	2	0.01
Polynesian: (1)	3	0.01
Native Hawaiian (1)	3	0.01
Other Pac. Isl., not spec. (3)	5	0.02
Hispanic or Latino:	3,879	14.70
Central American:	52	0.20
Costa Rican	2	0.01
Guatemalan	12	0.05
Honduran	6	0.02
Nicaraguan	2	0.01
Panamanian	2	0.01
Salvadoran	11	0.04
Other Central American	17	0.06
Cuban	17	0.06
Mexican	2,799	10.61
Puerto Rican	59	0.22
South American:	66	0.25
Argentinean	11	0.04
Bolivian	18	0.07
Chilean	7	0.03
Colombian	18	0.07
Ecuadorian	6	0.02
Peruvian	2	0.01
Venezuelan	3	0.01
Other South American	1	0.00
Other Hispanic or Latino	886	3.36
Hungarian	73	0.28
Iranian	6	0.02
Irish	2,855	10.77
Israeli	5	0.02
Italian	638	2.41
Lithuanian	43	0.16
Northern European	21	0.08
Norwegian	172	0.65
Polish	364	1.37
Portuguese	65	0.25
Romanian	9	0.03
Russian	87	0.33
Scandinavian	36	0.14
Scotch-Irish	703	2.65
Scottish	586	2.21
Serbian	26	0.10
Slavic	16	0.06
Slovene	4	0.02
Swedish	398	1.50
Swiss	124	0.47
Turkish	8	0.03
Ukrainian	29	0.11
United States or American	2,479	9.35
Welsh	168	0.63
West Indian, excl. Hispanic:	17	0.06
Dutch West Indian	6	0.02
Jamaican	8	0.03
West Indian	3	0.01
White:	23,189	87.88
Not Hispanic (20,476)	20,729	78.56
Hispanic (2,278)	2,460	9.32
Yugoslavian	6	0.02

Lancaster

Place Type: City
County: Dallas
Population: 25,894

Ancestry/Race	Number	%
African American/Black:	13,920	53.76
Not Hispanic (13,654)	13,814	53.35
Hispanic (71)	106	0.41
African, sub-Saharan:	445	1.72
African	426	1.65
Nigerian	6	0.02
Other sub-Saharan African	13	0.05
Alaska Native tribes, specified:	1	0.00
Eskimo	1	0.00
Am. Ind. or Alaska Nat., not spec.	98	0.38
American Indian tribes, specified:	149	0.58
Apache	7	0.03
Blackfeet	1	0.00
Cherokee (18)	57	0.22
Cheyenne	1	0.00
Chickasaw (2)	5	0.02
Chippewa	1	0.00
Choctaw (24)	36	0.14
Comanche (1)	5	0.02
Creek (2)	4	0.02
Iroquois	1	0.00
Latin American Indians (1)	3	0.01
Potawatomi (1)	1	0.00
Pueblo (8)	8	0.03
Seminole (1)	3	0.01
Ute	1	0.00
Yakama (1)	1	0.00
All other tribes (8)	14	0.05
American Indian tribes, not spec.	19	0.07
Arab:	91	0.35
Arab/Arabic	69	0.27
Iraqi	10	0.04
Jordanian	12	0.05
Asian:	153	0.59
Cambodian (2)	7	0.03
Chinese, ex. Taiwanese (14)	17	0.07
Filipino (31)	40	0.15
Indian (19)	26	0.10
Japanese (6)	10	0.04
Korean (11)	19	0.07
Malaysian (1)	1	0.00
Pakistani	2	0.01
Thai (1)	2	0.01
Vietnamese (13)	14	0.05
Other Asian, specified	2	0.01
Other Asian, not specified (1)	13	0.05
British	26	0.10
Canadian	8	0.03
Czech	138	0.53
Czechoslovakian	47	0.18
Danish	8	0.03
Dutch	289	1.12
English	1,201	4.64
European	147	0.57
French, except Basque	369	1.43
French Canadian	36	0.14
German	1,302	5.03
Guyanese	49	0.19
Hawaii Native/Pacific Islander:	29	0.11
Micronesian: (3)	6	0.02
Guamanian/Chamorro (3)	6	0.02
Polynesian: (4)	11	0.04
Native Hawaiian (3)	7	0.03
Samoan (1)	3	0.01
Tongan	1	0.00
Other Pac. Isl., specified	2	0.01
Other Pac. Isl., not spec. (7)	10	0.04
Hispanic or Latino:	3,001	11.59
Central American:	39	0.15
Costa Rican	5	0.02
Guatemalan	5	0.02
Honduran	12	0.05
Nicaraguan	1	0.00
Panamanian	5	0.02
Salvadoran	10	0.04
Other Central American	1	0.00
Cuban	6	0.02
Dominican Republic	4	0.02
Mexican	2,259	8.72
Puerto Rican	69	0.27
South American:	9	0.03
Argentinean	2	0.01
Colombian	5	0.02
Peruvian	2	0.01
Other Hispanic or Latino	615	2.38
Hungarian	6	0.02
Iranian	20	0.08
Irish	1,200	4.63
Italian	147	0.57
Norwegian	43	0.17
Polish	104	0.40
Portuguese	25	0.10
Russian	18	0.07
Scandinavian	15	0.06
Scotch-Irish	262	1.01
Scottish	247	0.95
Slovak	24	0.09
Swedish	49	0.19
Swiss	18	0.07
United States or American	1,313	5.07
Welsh	84	0.32
West Indian, excl. Hispanic:	12	0.05
Belizean	6	0.02
Haitian	6	0.02
White:	10,130	39.12
Not Hispanic (8,703)	8,955	34.58
Hispanic (1,041)	1,175	4.54

Laredo

Place Type: City
County: Webb
Population: 176,576

Ancestry/Race	Number	%
African American/Black:	825	0.47
Not Hispanic (276)	312	0.18
Hispanic (376)	513	0.29
African, sub-Saharan:	147	0.08
African	147	0.08
Am. Ind. or Alaska Nat., not spec.	577	0.33
American Indian tribes, specified:	291	0.16
Apache (5)	15	0.01
Blackfeet (6)	8	0.00
Cherokee (14)	35	0.02
Chippewa (2)	2	0.00
Choctaw (2)	7	0.00
Creek (1)	5	0.00
Iroquois (1)	1	0.00
Latin American Indians (138)	176	0.10
Navajo (4)	4	0.00
Ottawa (1)	1	0.00
Pueblo	5	0.00
Seminole	1	0.00
Shoshone (1)	4	0.00
Sioux (8)	12	0.01
Yaqui (2)	2	0.00
All other tribes (4)	13	0.01
American Indian tribes, not spec.	169	0.10
Arab:	290	0.16
Arab/Arabic	78	0.04
Lebanese	175	0.10
Syrian	28	0.02
Other Arab	9	0.01
Armenian	6	0.00
Asian:	1,068	0.60
Bangladeshi (5)	5	0.00
Chinese, ex. Taiwanese (97)	137	0.08
Filipino (201)	246	0.14
Indian (214)	275	0.16
Indonesian (2)	2	0.00
Japanese (70)	92	0.05
Korean (133)	147	0.08
Pakistani (1)	5	0.00
Sri Lankan (3)	3	0.00
Taiwanese (11)	17	0.01
Thai (4)	6	0.00
Vietnamese (49)	62	0.04
Other Asian, specified (5)	7	0.00
Other Asian, not specified (12)	64	0.04
Australian	6	0.00
Austrian	5	0.00
Basque	33	0.02
Belgian	25	0.01
British	44	0.02
Bulgarian	54	0.03
Canadian	103	0.06
Celtic	28	0.02
Czech	35	0.02
Czechoslovakian	12	0.01
Dutch	156	0.09
English	1,094	0.62
European	111	0.06

Notes: 1. Figures in the "Number" column do not add up to the total population due to: a) Ancestry/Race overlap — e.g. persons can report being both White and Irish, b) persons of Hispanic origin can report being any race, c) persons reporting two ancestries are counted in both categories. 2. Numbers in parentheses indicate the number of persons reporting this ancestry/race alone, not in combination with any other ancestry/race. 3. Refer to the Explanation of Data in the front of the book for more detailed information.

Ancestry/Race	Number	%
Finnish	5	0.00
French, except Basque	420	0.24
French Canadian	36	0.02
German	1,614	0.91
Greek	41	0.02
Hawaii Native/Pacific Islander:	80	0.05
Micronesian: (9)	11	0.01
Guamanian/Chamorro (9)	11	0.01
Polynesian: (22)	34	0.02
Native Hawaiian (4)	13	0.01
Samoan (17)	20	0.01
Tongan (1)	1	0.00
Other Pac. Isl., specified	1	0.00
Other Pac. Isl., not spec. (16)	34	0.02
Hispanic or Latino:	166,216	94.13
Central American:	349	0.20
Costa Rican	11	0.01
Guatemalan	56	0.03
Honduran	106	0.06
Nicaraguan	27	0.02
Panamanian	13	0.01
Salvadoran	102	0.06
Other Central American	34	0.02
Cuban	110	0.06
Dominican Republic	13	0.01
Mexican	133,185	75.43
Puerto Rican	294	0.17
South American:	128	0.07
Argentinean	11	0.01
Bolivian	5	0.00
Chilean	8	0.00
Colombian	53	0.03
Ecuadorian	4	0.00
Paraguayan	1	0.00
Peruvian	30	0.02
Uruguayan	1	0.00
Venezuelan	9	0.01
Other South American	6	0.00
Other Hispanic or Latino	32,137	18.20
Hungarian	15	0.01
Irish	890	0.50
Israeli	16	0.01
Italian	774	0.44
Lithuanian	21	0.01
Northern European	9	0.01
Norwegian	87	0.05
Pennsylvania German	6	0.00
Polish	266	0.15
Portuguese	16	0.01
Romanian	8	0.00
Russian	111	0.06
Scandinavian	22	0.01
Scotch-Irish	384	0.22
Scottish	274	0.15
Slovak	24	0.01
Slovene	7	0.00
Swedish	64	0.04
Swiss	45	0.03
Ukrainian	8	0.00
United States or American	3,563	2.02
Welsh	39	0.02
West Indian, excl. Hispanic:	17	0.01
British West Indian	4	0.00
Haitian	4	0.00
Trinidadian and Tobagonian	9	0.01
White:	149,389	84.60
Not Hispanic (8,891)	9,110	5.16
Hispanic (136,376)	140,279	79.44
Yugoslavian	7	0.00

League City

Place Type: City
County: Galveston
Population: 45,444

Ancestry/Race	Number	%
Acadian/Cajun	118	0.26
African American/Black:	2,481	5.46
Not Hispanic (2,297)	2,450	5.39
Hispanic (14)	31	0.07
African, sub-Saharan:	164	0.36
African	143	0.32
Ghanian	10	0.02
Nigerian	11	0.02
Alaska Native tribes, specified:	10	0.02
Aleut (5)	5	0.01
Eskimo (4)	5	0.01
Am. Ind. or Alaska Nat., not spec.	74	0.16
Albanian	10	0.02
American Indian tribes, specified:	261	0.57
Apache (4)	14	0.03
Blackfeet (4)	8	0.02
Cherokee (37)	100	0.22
Cheyenne (2)	2	0.00
Chickasaw (5)	6	0.01
Chippewa (3)	5	0.01
Choctaw (19)	39	0.09
Comanche (3)	4	0.01
Creek (5)	6	0.01
Houma (1)	1	0.00
Iroquois	2	0.00
Latin American Indians (24)	34	0.07
Navajo (2)	4	0.01
Osage	6	0.01
Ottawa	1	0.00
Pima (1)	1	0.00
Potawatomi (1)	2	0.00
Pueblo (4)	5	0.01
Seminole (1)	2	0.00
Sioux (1)	5	0.01
Ute (1)	1	0.00
All other tribes (8)	13	0.03
American Indian tribes, not spec.	17	0.04
Arab:	301	0.66
Arab/Arabic	19	0.04
Egyptian	4	0.01
Lebanese	190	0.42
Palestinian	16	0.04
Syrian	8	0.02
Other Arab	64	0.14
Armenian	32	0.07
Asian:	1,715	3.77
Bangladeshi (7)	12	0.03
Cambodian (11)	11	0.02
Chinese, ex. Taiwanese (264)	326	0.72
Filipino (227)	291	0.64
Indian (336)	367	0.81
Indonesian	1	0.00
Japanese (53)	91	0.20
Korean (54)	75	0.17
Laotian	1	0.00
Pakistani (39)	57	0.13
Sri Lankan (4)	4	0.01
Taiwanese (12)	17	0.04
Thai (18)	23	0.05
Vietnamese (372)	386	0.85
Other Asian, specified (1)	3	0.01
Other Asian, not specified (13)	50	0.11
Australian	32	0.07
Austrian	129	0.28
Belgian	20	0.04
Brazilian	34	0.08
British	496	1.10
Canadian	275	0.61
Celtic	20	0.04
Croatian	33	0.07
Czech	333	0.74
Czechoslovakian	63	0.14
Danish	236	0.52
Dutch	679	1.50
Eastern European	5	0.01
English	4,886	10.79
European	226	0.50
Finnish	56	0.12
French, except Basque	1,882	4.16
French Canadian	433	0.96
German	8,080	17.84
Greek	137	0.30
Hawaii Native/Pacific Islander:	59	0.13
Melanesian: (1)	1	0.00
Fijian (1)	1	0.00
Micronesian: (5)	9	0.02
Guamanian/Chamorro (5)	8	0.02
Other Micronesian	1	0.00
Polynesian: (9)	31	0.07
Native Hawaiian (5)	25	0.06
Samoan (3)	5	0.01
Tongan (1)	1	0.00
Other Pac. Isl., specified	2	0.00
Other Pac. Isl., not spec. (9)	16	0.04
Hispanic or Latino:	6,130	13.49
Central American:	177	0.39
Costa Rican	18	0.04
Guatemalan	13	0.03
Honduran	35	0.08
Nicaraguan	17	0.04
Panamanian	15	0.03
Salvadoran	69	0.15
Other Central American	10	0.02
Cuban	76	0.17
Dominican Republic	36	0.08
Mexican	4,327	9.52
Puerto Rican	253	0.56
South American:	204	0.45
Argentinean	9	0.02
Bolivian	37	0.08
Chilean	7	0.02
Colombian	68	0.15
Ecuadorian	5	0.01
Paraguayan	2	0.00
Peruvian	33	0.07
Venezuelan	37	0.08
Other South American	6	0.01
Other Hispanic or Latino	1,057	2.33
Hungarian	193	0.43
Icelander	11	0.02
Iranian	121	0.27
Irish	5,112	11.29
Italian	2,028	4.48
Lithuanian	51	0.11
Macedonian	13	0.03
Northern European	8	0.02
Norwegian	772	1.70
Polish	969	2.14
Portuguese	76	0.17
Romanian	24	0.05
Russian	141	0.31
Scandinavian	78	0.17
Scotch-Irish	884	1.95
Scottish	983	2.17
Slavic	21	0.05
Slovak	9	0.02
Slovene	35	0.08
Swedish	663	1.46
Swiss	116	0.26
Turkish	59	0.13
Ukrainian	76	0.17
United States or American	4,062	8.97
Welsh	303	0.67
West Indian, excl. Hispanic:	76	0.17
Bahamian	6	0.01
British West Indian	13	0.03
Dutch West Indian	7	0.02
Haitian	8	0.02
Jamaican	33	0.07
Trinidadian and Tobagonian	2	0.00
West Indian	7	0.02
White:	38,968	85.75
Not Hispanic (34,807)	35,296	77.67
Hispanic (3,363)	3,672	8.08
Yugoslavian	53	0.12

Levelland

Place Type: City
County: Hockley
Population: 12,866

Ancestry/Race	Number	%

Notes: 1. Figures in the "Number" column do not add up to the total population due to: a) Ancestry/Race overlap — e.g. persons can report being both White and Irish, b) persons of Hispanic origin can report being any race, c) persons reporting two ancestries are counted in both categories. 2. Numbers in parentheses indicate the number of persons reporting this ancestry/race alone, not in combination with any other ancestry/race. 3. Refer to the Explanation of Data in the front of the book for more detailed information.

Ancestry/Race	Number	%
African American/Black:	718	5.58
Not Hispanic (671)	695	5.40
Hispanic (19)	23	0.18
African, sub-Saharan:	34	0.26
African	34	0.26
Am. Ind. or Alaska Nat., not spec.	78	0.61
American Indian tribes, specified:	78	0.61
Apache	3	0.02
Blackfeet	1	0.01
Cherokee (10)	22	0.17
Chickasaw (10)	10	0.08
Chippewa (2)	2	0.02
Choctaw (3)	16	0.12
Creek (4)	6	0.05
Iroquois (1)	1	0.01
Latin American Indians (3)	6	0.05
Pima (1)	1	0.01
Potawatomi (1)	1	0.01
Seminole (1)	1	0.01
Shoshone (1)	1	0.01
All other tribes (5)	7	0.05
American Indian tribes, not spec.	30	0.23
Arab:	5	0.04
Lebanese	5	0.04
Asian:	41	0.32
Chinese, ex. Taiwanese (3)	8	0.06
Filipino (1)	1	0.01
Indian (8)	9	0.07
Indonesian	1	0.01
Korean (5)	5	0.04
Thai (5)	5	0.04
Other Asian, not specified	12	0.09
Australian	32	0.25
Austrian	6	0.05
Belgian	12	0.09
Brazilian	14	0.11
British	24	0.19
Czech	17	0.13
Czechoslovakian	18	0.14
Danish	58	0.45
Dutch	125	0.97
English	786	6.12
European	24	0.19
French, except Basque	117	0.91
French Canadian	18	0.14
German	804	6.26
Hawaii Native/Pacific Islander:	11	0.09
Micronesian: (4)	4	0.03
Guamanian/Chamorro (4)	4	0.03
Polynesian: (2)	7	0.05
Native Hawaiian (1)	1	0.01
Samoan (1)	6	0.05
Hispanic or Latino:	5,045	39.21
Central American:	8	0.06
Honduran	3	0.02
Nicaraguan	5	0.04
Cuban	5	0.04
Dominican Republic	1	0.01
Mexican	2,918	22.68
Puerto Rican	4	0.03
South American:	3	0.02
Argentinean	1	0.01
Bolivian	1	0.01
Other South American	1	0.01
Other Hispanic or Latino	2,106	16.37
Irish	925	7.21
Italian	82	0.64
Norwegian	18	0.14
Polish	57	0.44
Romanian	36	0.28
Russian	10	0.08
Scotch-Irish	197	1.53
Scottish	169	1.32
Swedish	52	0.41
Swiss	24	0.19
Turkish	8	0.06
Ukrainian	5	0.04
United States or American	1,428	11.12
Welsh	30	0.23
West Indian, excl. Hispanic:	36	0.28
Dutch West Indian	36	0.28
White:	9,304	72.31
Not Hispanic (6,976)	7,060	54.87
Hispanic (2,074)	2,244	17.44

Lewisville

Place Type: City
County: Denton
Population: 77,737

Ancestry/Race	Number	%
Acadian/Cajun	70	0.09
African American/Black:	6,165	7.93
Not Hispanic (5,628)	5,963	7.67
Hispanic (119)	202	0.26
African, sub-Saharan:	623	0.80
African	366	0.47
Kenyan	8	0.01
Nigerian	185	0.24
Somalian	12	0.02
South African	33	0.04
Zimbabwean	19	0.02
Alaska Native tribes, specified:	13	0.02
Alaska Athabascan (1)	1	0.00
Aleut (3)	4	0.01
Eskimo (1)	6	0.01
All other tribes (2)	2	0.00
Alaska Native tribes, not specified	6	0.01
Am. Ind. or Alaska Nat., not spec.	272	0.35
Alsatian	6	0.01
American Indian tribes, specified:	672	0.86
Apache (6)	17	0.02
Blackfeet (1)	8	0.01
Cherokee (95)	218	0.28
Cheyenne (2)	2	0.00
Chickasaw (26)	46	0.06
Chippewa (5)	10	0.01
Choctaw (71)	112	0.14
Comanche (8)	15	0.02
Cree (1)	3	0.00
Creek (4)	28	0.04
Crow (1)	2	0.00
Delaware (4)	5	0.01
Houma (1)	1	0.00
Iroquois (2)	14	0.02
Kiowa (10)	15	0.02
Latin American Indians (32)	90	0.12
Lumbee (1)	2	0.00
Navajo (8)	14	0.02
Osage (1)	2	0.00
Potawatomi (6)	6	0.01
Pueblo (7)	7	0.01
Seminole (2)	3	0.00
Sioux (13)	21	0.03
Yaqui (5)	5	0.01
All other tribes (14)	26	0.03
American Indian tribes, not spec.	64	0.08
Arab:	255	0.33
Arab/Arabic	66	0.09
Egyptian	22	0.03
Jordanian	48	0.06
Lebanese	74	0.10
Syrian	33	0.04
Other Arab	12	0.02
Armenian	14	0.02
Asian:	3,472	4.47
Bangladeshi (21)	22	0.03
Cambodian (54)	60	0.08
Chinese, ex. Taiwanese (380)	429	0.55
Filipino (240)	333	0.43
Indian (991)	1,045	1.34
Indonesian (6)	12	0.02
Japanese (75)	151	0.19
Korean (375)	423	0.54
Laotian (19)	22	0.03
Malaysian (4)	12	0.02
Pakistani (70)	83	0.11
Sri Lankan (5)	15	0.02
Taiwanese (7)	16	0.02
Thai (30)	38	0.05
Vietnamese (663)	701	0.90
Other Asian, specified (3)	5	0.01
Other Asian, not specified (42)	105	0.14
Australian	35	0.05
Austrian	75	0.10
Basque	7	0.01
Belgian	24	0.03
Brazilian	106	0.14
British	364	0.47
Bulgarian	7	0.01
Canadian	234	0.30
Celtic	8	0.01
Croatian	39	0.05
Cypriot	12	0.02
Czech	390	0.50
Czechoslovakian	185	0.24
Danish	345	0.45
Dutch	1,477	1.91
English	7,091	9.15
European	486	0.63
Finnish	9	0.01
French, except Basque	2,429	3.13
French Canadian	333	0.43
German	11,524	14.87
Greek	160	0.21
Guyanese	13	0.02
Hawaii Native/Pacific Islander:	95	0.12
Micronesian: (7)	13	0.02
Guamanian/Chamorro (7)	13	0.02
Polynesian: (10)	35	0.05
Native Hawaiian (5)	24	0.03
Samoan (4)	10	0.01
Other Polynesian (1)	1	0.00
Other Pac. Isl., specified	1	0.00
Other Pac. Isl., not spec. (8)	46	0.06
Hispanic or Latino:	13,799	17.75
Central American:	460	0.59
Costa Rican	9	0.01
Guatemalan	34	0.04
Honduran	52	0.07
Nicaraguan	24	0.03
Panamanian	30	0.04
Salvadoran	284	0.37
Other Central American	27	0.03
Cuban	134	0.17
Dominican Republic	20	0.03
Mexican	10,534	13.55
Puerto Rican	401	0.52
South American:	260	0.33
Argentinean	23	0.03
Bolivian	6	0.01
Chilean	23	0.03
Colombian	79	0.10
Ecuadorian	23	0.03
Paraguayan	4	0.01
Peruvian	57	0.07
Uruguayan	2	0.00
Venezuelan	30	0.04
Other South American	13	0.02
Other Hispanic or Latino	1,990	2.56
Hungarian	193	0.25
Iranian	189	0.24
Irish	9,283	11.98
Italian	2,444	3.15
Lithuanian	36	0.05
Luxemburger	9	0.01
Macedonian	9	0.01
New Zealander	8	0.01
Northern European	65	0.08
Norwegian	866	1.12
Pennsylvania German	5	0.01
Polish	1,157	1.49
Portuguese	61	0.08
Romanian	86	0.11
Russian	289	0.37
Scandinavian	97	0.13
Scotch-Irish	1,624	2.10
Scottish	1,577	2.03
Serbian	32	0.04

Notes: 1. Figures in the "Number" column do not add up to the total population due to: a) Ancestry/Race overlap — e.g. persons can report being both White and Irish, b) persons of Hispanic origin can report being any race, c) persons reporting two ancestries are counted in both categories. 2. Numbers in parentheses indicate the number of persons reporting this ancestry/race alone, not in combination with any other ancestry/race. 3. Refer to the Explanation of Data in the front of the book for more detailed information.

Slovak	31	0.04
Swedish	642	0.83
Swiss	135	0.17
Turkish	40	0.05
Ukrainian	48	0.06
United States or American	7,155	9.23
Welsh	532	0.69
West Indian, excl. Hispanic:	197	0.25
Bahamian	14	0.02
Dutch West Indian	59	0.08
Haitian	36	0.05
Jamaican	88	0.11
White:	61,621	79.27
Not Hispanic (53,706)	54,641	70.29
Hispanic (6,309)	6,980	8.98
Yugoslavian	68	0.09

Lockhart

Place Type: City
County: Caldwell
Population: 11,615

Ancestry/Race	Number	%
African American/Black:	1,540	13.26
Not Hispanic (1,448)	1,485	12.79
Hispanic (25)	55	0.47
African, sub-Saharan:	80	0.70
African	71	0.62
Nigerian	9	0.08
Alaska Native tribes, specified:	4	0.03
Eskimo	4	0.03
Am. Ind. or Alaska Nat., not spec.	34	0.29
American Indian tribes, specified:	83	0.71
Apache (1)	2	0.02
Blackfeet (1)	3	0.03
Cherokee (7)	25	0.22
Choctaw (2)	15	0.13
Comanche (1)	1	0.01
Cree	1	0.01
Iroquois	1	0.01
Kiowa (1)	1	0.01
Latin American Indians (14)	17	0.15
Navajo (4)	4	0.03
Osage	2	0.02
Pueblo (1)	1	0.01
Sioux (3)	6	0.05
All other tribes (3)	4	0.03
American Indian tribes, not spec.	16	0.14
Arab:	7	0.06
Lebanese	7	0.06
Asian:	66	0.57
Cambodian	3	0.03
Chinese, ex. Taiwanese (13)	13	0.11
Filipino (13)	20	0.17
Indian (2)	6	0.05
Japanese (2)	4	0.03
Korean (1)	2	0.02
Malaysian	1	0.01
Vietnamese (5)	6	0.05
Other Asian, specified	1	0.01
Other Asian, not specified	10	0.09
Austrian	7	0.06
British	23	0.20
Canadian	37	0.32
Croatian	6	0.05
Czech	48	0.42
Czechoslovakian	15	0.13
Dutch	26	0.23
English	586	5.13
European	25	0.22
Finnish	6	0.05
French, except Basque	110	0.96
French Canadian	10	0.09
German	1,153	10.10
Greek	11	0.10
Hawaii Native/Pacific Islander:	9	0.08
Polynesian: (2)	3	0.03
Native Hawaiian (2)	2	0.02
Samoan	1	0.01
Other Pac. Isl., specified	1	0.01
Other Pac. Isl., not spec. (5)	5	0.04
Hispanic or Latino:	5,507	47.41
Central American:	7	0.06
Costa Rican	2	0.02
Guatemalan	1	0.01
Honduran	1	0.01
Salvadoran	3	0.03
Cuban	12	0.10
Mexican	3,963	34.12
Puerto Rican	44	0.38
South American:	1	0.01
Colombian	1	0.01
Other Hispanic or Latino	1,480	12.74
Iranian	8	0.07
Irish	730	6.40
Italian	76	0.67
Northern European	6	0.05
Norwegian	71	0.62
Pennsylvania German	7	0.06
Polish	88	0.77
Portuguese	17	0.15
Russian	12	0.11
Scandinavian	7	0.06
Scotch-Irish	236	2.07
Scottish	113	0.99
Serbian	6	0.05
Swedish	104	0.91
United States or American	312	2.73
Welsh	67	0.59
West Indian, excl. Hispanic:	5	0.04
Dutch West Indian	5	0.04
White:	7,887	67.90
Not Hispanic (4,492)	4,572	39.36
Hispanic (3,106)	3,315	28.54
Yugoslavian	6	0.05

Longview

Place Type: City
County: Gregg
Population: 73,344

Ancestry/Race	Number	%
Acadian/Cajun	59	0.08
African American/Black:	16,516	22.52
Not Hispanic (16,126)	16,390	22.35
Hispanic (88)	126	0.17
African, sub-Saharan:	545	0.74
African	502	0.69
Kenyan	29	0.04
Nigerian	14	0.02
Alaska Native tribes, specified:	1	0.00
Eskimo (1)	1	0.00
Am. Ind. or Alaska Nat., not spec.	215	0.29
American Indian tribes, specified:	484	0.66
Apache (2)	10	0.01
Blackfeet (2)	9	0.01
Cherokee (65)	194	0.26
Cheyenne (1)	2	0.00
Chickasaw (8)	27	0.04
Chippewa (3)	4	0.01
Choctaw (45)	83	0.11
Comanche (2)	4	0.01
Creek (10)	15	0.02
Delaware (7)	9	0.01
Kiowa (2)	4	0.01
Latin American Indians (26)	32	0.04
Navajo (4)	7	0.01
Osage	2	0.00
Potawatomi (5)	6	0.01
Pueblo (4)	6	0.01
Puget Sound Salish	2	0.00
Seminole	1	0.00
Sioux (14)	17	0.02
Ute (2)	2	0.00
Yakama	1	0.00
Yaqui	1	0.00
All other tribes (27)	46	0.06
American Indian tribes, not spec.	45	0.06
Arab:	120	0.16
Arab/Arabic	7	0.01
Lebanese	92	0.13
Palestinian	16	0.02
Syrian	5	0.01
Armenian	6	0.01
Asian:	757	1.03
Cambodian (1)	1	0.00
Chinese, ex. Taiwanese (116)	141	0.19
Filipino (61)	102	0.14
Hmong	1	0.00
Indian (151)	161	0.22
Indonesian (4)	4	0.01
Japanese (14)	31	0.04
Korean (53)	76	0.10
Laotian (1)	1	0.00
Malaysian (12)	13	0.02
Pakistani (23)	30	0.04
Taiwanese (13)	13	0.02
Thai (8)	12	0.02
Vietnamese (129)	140	0.19
Other Asian, specified (7)	16	0.02
Other Asian, not specified (5)	15	0.02
Austrian	78	0.11
Basque	7	0.01
Belgian	7	0.01
Brazilian	10	0.01
British	303	0.41
Canadian	80	0.11
Celtic	15	0.02
Croatian	36	0.05
Czech	177	0.24
Czechoslovakian	61	0.08
Danish	54	0.07
Dutch	918	1.25
Eastern European	6	0.01
English	6,157	8.42
European	466	0.64
Finnish	27	0.04
French, except Basque	1,720	2.35
French Canadian	387	0.53
German	5,855	8.00
Greek	31	0.04
Guyanese	11	0.02
Hawaii Native/Pacific Islander:	47	0.06
Micronesian: (5)	6	0.01
Guamanian/Chamorro (5)	6	0.01
Polynesian: (7)	28	0.04
Native Hawaiian (7)	25	0.03
Samoan	1	0.00
Tongan	2	0.00
Other Pac. Isl., specified	4	0.01
Other Pac. Isl., not spec. (3)	9	0.01
Hispanic or Latino:	7,564	10.31
Central American:	125	0.17
Costa Rican	1	0.00
Guatemalan	38	0.05
Honduran	25	0.03
Nicaraguan	1	0.00
Panamanian	3	0.00
Salvadoran	46	0.06
Other Central American	11	0.01
Cuban	31	0.04
Dominican Republic	4	0.01
Mexican	6,440	8.78
Puerto Rican	72	0.10
South American:	38	0.05
Argentinean	3	0.00
Bolivian	4	0.01
Chilean	7	0.01
Colombian	5	0.01
Ecuadorian	5	0.01
Peruvian	9	0.01
Venezuelan	4	0.01
Other South American	1	0.00
Other Hispanic or Latino	854	1.16
Hungarian	61	0.08
Iranian	23	0.03
Irish	6,075	8.30
Italian	1,054	1.44

Notes: 1. Figures in the "Number" column do not add up to the total population due to: a) Ancestry/Race overlap — e.g. persons can report being both White and Irish, b) persons of Hispanic origin can report being any race, c) persons reporting two ancestries are counted in both categories. 2. Numbers in parentheses indicate the number of persons reporting this ancestry/race alone, not in combination with any other ancestry/race. 3. Refer to the Explanation of Data in the front of the book for more detailed information.

Lithuanian	13	0.02
Macedonian	4	0.01
Norwegian	437	0.60
Pennsylvania German	17	0.02
Polish	374	0.51
Portuguese	64	0.09
Romanian	5	0.01
Russian	119	0.16
Scandinavian	15	0.02
Scotch-Irish	1,263	1.73
Scottish	1,104	1.51
Serbian	18	0.02
Slovak	17	0.02
Swedish	397	0.54
Swiss	81	0.11
Turkish	9	0.01
Ukrainian	6	0.01
United States or American	7,442	10.17
Welsh	282	0.39
West Indian, excl. Hispanic:	69	0.09
Dutch West Indian	56	0.08
Jamaican	13	0.02
White:	52,393	71.43
Not Hispanic (48,028)	48,645	66.32
Hispanic (3,389)	3,748	5.11
Yugoslavian	26	0.04

Lubbock

Place Type: City
County: Lubbock
Population: 199,564

Ancestry/Race	Number	%
Acadian/Cajun	34	0.02
African American/Black:	18,110	9.07
Not Hispanic (16,907)	17,440	8.74
Hispanic (385)	670	0.34
African, sub-Saharan:	1,097	0.55
African	914	0.46
Ethiopian	4	0.00
Ghanian	6	0.00
Nigerian	90	0.05
Senegalese	9	0.00
Sierra Leonean	17	0.01
South African	13	0.01
Other sub-Saharan African	44	0.02
Alaska Native tribes, specified:	1	0.00
Eskimo	1	0.00
Alaska Native tribes, not specified	1	0.00
Am. Ind. or Alaska Nat., not spec.	679	0.34
Albanian	27	0.01
Alsatian	7	0.00
American Indian tribes, specified:	1,084	0.54
Apache (68)	107	0.05
Blackfeet (4)	13	0.01
Cherokee (132)	310	0.16
Cheyenne (7)	11	0.01
Chickasaw (40)	51	0.03
Chippewa (16)	28	0.01
Choctaw (80)	179	0.09
Comanche (8)	30	0.02
Creek (15)	26	0.01
Crow	1	0.00
Delaware (4)	5	0.00
Houma	1	0.00
Iroquois (8)	15	0.01
Kiowa (8)	8	0.00
Latin American Indians (72)	90	0.05
Lumbee (2)	2	0.00
Navajo (35)	45	0.02
Osage (2)	8	0.00
Ottawa	1	0.00
Pima (1)	1	0.00
Potawatomi (14)	23	0.01
Pueblo (3)	7	0.00
Seminole (7)	17	0.01
Shoshone	3	0.00
Sioux (22)	33	0.02
Tohono O'Odham (1)	1	0.00
Ute (1)	1	0.00
Yaqui (17)	22	0.01
Yuman (1)	1	0.00
All other tribes (16)	44	0.02
American Indian tribes, not spec.	179	0.09
Arab:	525	0.26
Arab/Arabic	67	0.03
Egyptian	89	0.04
Iraqi	9	0.00
Jordanian	21	0.01
Lebanese	254	0.13
Palestinian	51	0.03
Syrian	17	0.01
Other Arab	17	0.01
Armenian	17	0.01
Asian:	3,720	1.86
Bangladeshi (27)	35	0.02
Cambodian (3)	4	0.00
Chinese, ex. Taiwanese (672)	756	0.38
Filipino (427)	571	0.29
Indian (910)	979	0.49
Indonesian (21)	23	0.01
Japanese (98)	203	0.10
Korean (263)	327	0.16
Laotian (19)	25	0.01
Malaysian (15)	25	0.01
Pakistani (21)	40	0.02
Sri Lankan (38)	40	0.02
Taiwanese (42)	51	0.03
Thai (93)	121	0.06
Vietnamese (295)	332	0.17
Other Asian, specified (15)	35	0.02
Other Asian, not specified (55)	153	0.08
Australian	22	0.01
Austrian	253	0.13
Belgian	69	0.03
Brazilian	42	0.02
British	853	0.43
Canadian	216	0.11
Celtic	47	0.02
Croatian	33	0.02
Czech	599	0.30
Czechoslovakian	168	0.08
Danish	310	0.16
Dutch	2,363	1.18
Eastern European	28	0.01
English	18,417	9.23
European	1,164	0.58
Finnish	120	0.06
French, except Basque	3,437	1.72
French Canadian	399	0.20
German	18,622	9.33
Greek	181	0.09
Hawaii Native/Pacific Islander:	197	0.10
Melanesian: (2)	2	0.00
Other Melanesian (2)	2	0.00
Micronesian: (11)	30	0.02
Guamanian/Chamorro (8)	27	0.01
Other Micronesian (3)	3	0.00
Polynesian: (33)	77	0.04
Native Hawaiian (19)	42	0.02
Samoan (11)	22	0.01
Tongan (2)	2	0.00
Other Polynesian (1)	11	0.01
Other Pac. Isl., specified	16	0.01
Other Pac. Isl., not spec. (19)	72	0.04
Hispanic or Latino:	54,786	27.45
Central American:	145	0.07
Costa Rican	13	0.01
Guatemalan	21	0.01
Honduran	31	0.02
Nicaraguan	21	0.01
Panamanian	27	0.01
Salvadoran	21	0.01
Other Central American	11	0.01
Cuban	79	0.04
Dominican Republic	7	0.00
Mexican	32,404	16.24
Puerto Rican	350	0.18
South American:	211	0.11
Argentinean	15	0.01
Bolivian	15	0.01
Chilean	25	0.01
Colombian	73	0.04
Ecuadorian	17	0.01
Paraguayan	2	0.00
Peruvian	40	0.02
Venezuelan	11	0.01
Other South American	13	0.01
Other Hispanic or Latino	21,590	10.82
Hungarian	179	0.09
Iranian	103	0.05
Irish	15,569	7.80
Israeli	5	0.00
Italian	2,314	1.16
Latvian	15	0.01
Lithuanian	47	0.02
Luxemburger	5	0.00
New Zealander	28	0.01
Northern European	77	0.04
Norwegian	1,097	0.55
Pennsylvania German	11	0.01
Polish	1,266	0.63
Portuguese	127	0.06
Romanian	63	0.03
Russian	478	0.24
Scandinavian	114	0.06
Scotch-Irish	4,693	2.35
Scottish	3,238	1.62
Serbian	12	0.01
Slavic	36	0.02
Slovak	61	0.03
Slovene	7	0.00
Swedish	1,021	0.51
Swiss	211	0.11
Turkish	94	0.05
Ukrainian	75	0.04
United States or American	18,232	9.14
Welsh	1,099	0.55
West Indian, excl. Hispanic:	285	0.14
Dutch West Indian	142	0.07
Jamaican	132	0.07
Trinidadian and Tobagonian	6	0.00
West Indian	5	0.00
White:	148,853	74.59
Not Hispanic (122,330)	123,822	62.05
Hispanic (23,096)	25,031	12.54
Yugoslavian	30	0.02

Lufkin

Place Type: City
County: Angelina
Population: 32,709

Ancestry/Race	Number	%
Acadian/Cajun	6	0.02
African American/Black:	8,851	27.06
Not Hispanic (8,603)	8,735	26.71
Hispanic (90)	116	0.35
African, sub-Saharan:	126	0.39
African	126	0.39
Am. Ind. or Alaska Nat., not spec.	66	0.20
American Indian tribes, specified:	124	0.38
Apache (4)	9	0.03
Blackfeet	7	0.02
Cherokee (14)	41	0.13
Chickasaw	2	0.01
Choctaw (7)	18	0.06
Comanche (1)	1	0.00
Creek	3	0.01
Iroquois (1)	1	0.00
Latin American Indians (15)	17	0.05
Lumbee (4)	4	0.01
Osage (3)	6	0.02
Pueblo (1)	1	0.00
Shoshone	1	0.00
Sioux (2)	4	0.01
All other tribes (6)	9	0.03
American Indian tribes, not spec.	12	0.04

Notes: 1. Figures in the "Number" column do not add up to the total population due to: a) Ancestry/Race overlap — e.g. persons can report being both White and Irish, b) persons of Hispanic origin can report being any race, c) persons reporting two ancestries are counted in both categories. 2. Numbers in parentheses indicate the number of persons reporting this ancestry/race alone, not in combination with any other ancestry/race. 3. Refer to the Explanation of Data in the front of the book for more detailed information.

Ancestry/Race	Number	%
Arab:	45	0.14
Lebanese	45	0.14
Armenian	17	0.05
Asian:	520	1.59
Cambodian (18)	20	0.06
Chinese, ex. Taiwanese (70)	77	0.24
Filipino (96)	107	0.33
Indian (183)	204	0.62
Japanese (6)	16	0.05
Korean (28)	36	0.11
Malaysian (1)	1	0.00
Pakistani (23)	25	0.08
Vietnamese (13)	14	0.04
Other Asian, specified	1	0.00
Other Asian, not specified (8)	19	0.06
Austrian	16	0.05
Brazilian	7	0.02
British	54	0.17
Canadian	31	0.10
Croatian	25	0.08
Czech	79	0.24
Czechoslovakian	67	0.21
Danish	7	0.02
Dutch	381	1.17
English	2,574	7.89
European	81	0.25
Finnish	5	0.02
French, except Basque	696	2.13
French Canadian	107	0.33
German	1,427	4.37
Greek	25	0.08
Hawaii Native/Pacific Islander:	15	0.05
Micronesian: (2)	4	0.01
Guamanian/Chamorro (2)	4	0.01
Polynesian: (4)	7	0.02
Native Hawaiian (4)	6	0.02
Samoan	1	0.00
Other Pac. Isl., specified	1	0.00
Other Pac. Isl., not spec.	3	0.01
Hispanic or Latino:	5,754	17.59
Central American:	90	0.28
Costa Rican	1	0.00
Guatemalan	8	0.02
Honduran	2	0.01
Panamanian	1	0.00
Salvadoran	71	0.22
Other Central American	7	0.02
Cuban	12	0.04
Dominican Republic	1	0.00
Mexican	4,771	14.59
Puerto Rican	24	0.07
South American:	34	0.10
Bolivian	2	0.01
Chilean	1	0.00
Colombian	5	0.02
Peruvian	21	0.06
Venezuelan	5	0.02
Other Hispanic or Latino	822	2.51
Hungarian	17	0.05
Irish	2,105	6.45
Italian	284	0.87
Lithuanian	31	0.10
Norwegian	84	0.26
Polish	193	0.59
Portuguese	6	0.02
Russian	31	0.10
Scandinavian	36	0.11
Scotch-Irish	613	1.88
Scottish	360	1.10
Slavic	5	0.02
Swedish	41	0.13
Swiss	26	0.08
United States or American	3,206	9.83
Welsh	49	0.15
West Indian, excl. Hispanic:	44	0.13
Belizean	12	0.04
Jamaican	26	0.08
West Indian	6	0.02
White:	20,018	61.20
Not Hispanic (17,567)	17,776	54.35
Hispanic (2,032)	2,242	6.85
Yugoslavian	21	0.06

Mansfield

Place Type: City
County: Tarrant
Population: 28,031

Ancestry/Race	Number	%
African American/Black:	1,339	4.78
Not Hispanic (1,214)	1,298	4.63
Hispanic (18)	41	0.15
African, sub-Saharan:	105	0.36
African	74	0.26
Nigerian	31	0.11
Alaska Native tribes, specified:	2	0.01
Eskimo	2	0.01
Am. Ind. or Alaska Nat., not spec.	81	0.29
Albanian	21	0.07
American Indian tribes, specified:	199	0.71
Apache (1)	11	0.04
Cherokee (42)	89	0.32
Cheyenne (1)	1	0.00
Chickasaw (8)	8	0.03
Chippewa	1	0.00
Choctaw (16)	33	0.12
Comanche	6	0.02
Creek (3)	3	0.01
Delaware (1)	1	0.00
Latin American Indians (8)	11	0.04
Navajo (5)	6	0.02
Osage (1)	4	0.01
Potawatomi (1)	4	0.01
Seminole	2	0.01
All other tribes (13)	19	0.07
American Indian tribes, not spec.	10	0.04
Arab:	32	0.11
Arab/Arabic	19	0.07
Lebanese	7	0.02
Palestinian	6	0.02
Armenian	7	0.02
Asian:	425	1.52
Cambodian (7)	9	0.03
Chinese, ex. Taiwanese (29)	42	0.15
Filipino (53)	72	0.26
Hmong (3)	3	0.01
Indian (52)	64	0.23
Japanese (9)	27	0.10
Korean (23)	27	0.10
Laotian (17)	19	0.07
Malaysian (3)	6	0.02
Pakistani (5)	8	0.03
Taiwanese (1)	1	0.00
Thai (5)	7	0.02
Vietnamese (121)	129	0.46
Other Asian, not specified (8)	11	0.04
Australian	18	0.06
Austrian	24	0.08
Basque	6	0.02
Belgian	16	0.06
British	134	0.46
Canadian	79	0.27
Celtic	41	0.14
Czech	185	0.64
Czechoslovakian	60	0.21
Danish	78	0.27
Dutch	360	1.24
Eastern European	11	0.04
English	2,813	9.70
European	241	0.83
Finnish	24	0.08
French, except Basque	478	1.65
French Canadian	193	0.67
German	4,263	14.71
Greek	24	0.08
Hawaii Native/Pacific Islander:	16	0.06
Micronesian:	2	0.01
Guamanian/Chamorro	2	0.01
Polynesian: (4)	7	0.02
Native Hawaiian (4)	7	0.02
Other Pac. Isl., not spec. (1)	7	0.02
Hispanic or Latino:	3,574	12.75
Central American:	26	0.09
Costa Rican	4	0.01
Guatemalan	9	0.03
Honduran	2	0.01
Panamanian	3	0.01
Salvadoran	8	0.03
Cuban	81	0.29
Dominican Republic	2	0.01
Mexican	2,861	10.21
Puerto Rican	75	0.27
South American:	25	0.09
Argentinean	3	0.01
Bolivian	4	0.01
Chilean	1	0.00
Colombian	10	0.04
Ecuadorian	1	0.00
Paraguayan	1	0.00
Venezuelan	4	0.01
Other South American	1	0.00
Other Hispanic or Latino	504	1.80
Hungarian	35	0.12
Irish	3,065	10.57
Italian	997	3.44
Latvian	9	0.03
Macedonian	17	0.06
Northern European	63	0.22
Norwegian	269	0.93
Polish	385	1.33
Portuguese	7	0.02
Romanian	26	0.09
Russian	69	0.24
Scandinavian	15	0.05
Scotch-Irish	498	1.72
Scottish	618	2.13
Slavic	22	0.08
Slovak	31	0.11
Swedish	245	0.85
Swiss	51	0.18
Turkish	5	0.02
Ukrainian	67	0.23
United States or American	3,820	13.18
Welsh	364	1.26
West Indian, excl. Hispanic:	64	0.22
Bahamian	10	0.03
Dutch West Indian	25	0.09
Haitian	20	0.07
Jamaican	9	0.03
White:	24,648	87.93
Not Hispanic (22,513)	22,753	81.17
Hispanic (1,708)	1,895	6.76
Yugoslavian	35	0.12

Marshall

Place Type: City
County: Harrison
Population: 23,935

Ancestry/Race	Number	%
Acadian/Cajun	42	0.18
Afghan	13	0.05
African American/Black:	9,309	38.89
Not Hispanic (9,194)	9,263	38.70
Hispanic (43)	46	0.19
African, sub-Saharan:	254	1.06
African	238	1.00
Kenyan	7	0.03
Zimbabwean	9	0.04
Alaska Native tribes, specified:	1	0.00
Eskimo	1	0.00
Am. Ind. or Alaska Nat., not spec.	63	0.26
American Indian tribes, specified:	96	0.40
Apache (2)	2	0.01
Blackfeet	2	0.01
Cherokee (21)	46	0.19
Cheyenne	1	0.00
Chickasaw (3)	4	0.02

Notes: 1. Figures in the "Number" column do not add up to the total population due to: a) Ancestry/Race overlap — e.g. persons can report being both White and Irish, b) persons of Hispanic origin can report being any race, c) persons reporting two ancestries are counted in both categories. 2. Numbers in parentheses indicate the number of persons reporting this ancestry/race alone, not in combination with any other ancestry/race. 3. Refer to the Explanation of Data in the front of the book for more detailed information.

Choctaw (7)	12	0.05
Comanche (1)	1	0.00
Creek (1)	2	0.01
Houma (1)	1	0.00
Latin American Indians (3)	7	0.03
Lumbee (1)	1	0.00
Navajo	1	0.00
Osage	1	0.00
Sioux (1)	2	0.01
All other tribes (12)	13	0.05
American Indian tribes, not spec.	5	0.02
Arab:	71	0.30
Lebanese	71	0.30
Asian:	176	0.74
Bangladeshi (1)	1	0.00
Cambodian (7)	7	0.03
Chinese, ex. Taiwanese (23)	28	0.12
Filipino (6)	13	0.05
Indian (58)	79	0.33
Indonesian (1)	1	0.00
Japanese (8)	8	0.03
Korean (6)	7	0.03
Malaysian (1)	2	0.01
Pakistani (2)	2	0.01
Taiwanese (3)	3	0.01
Thai (7)	7	0.03
Vietnamese (4)	5	0.02
Other Asian, specified	4	0.02
Other Asian, not specified (1)	9	0.04
Austrian	25	0.10
Belgian	8	0.03
British	37	0.15
Canadian	17	0.07
Croatian	16	0.07
Czech	13	0.05
Danish	28	0.12
Dutch	179	0.75
English	1,418	5.93
European	98	0.41
Finnish	21	0.09
French, except Basque	412	1.72
French Canadian	59	0.25
German	1,137	4.76
Greek	16	0.07
Hawaii Native/Pacific Islander:	19	0.08
Micronesian: (2)	2	0.01
Guamanian/Chamorro (2)	2	0.01
Polynesian: (3)	5	0.02
Native Hawaiian (3)	4	0.02
Samoan	1	0.00
Other Pac. Isl., specified	4	0.02
Other Pac. Isl., not spec. (5)	8	0.03
Hispanic or Latino:	2,069	8.64
Central American:	12	0.05
Guatemalan	1	0.00
Honduran	6	0.03
Nicaraguan	2	0.01
Salvadoran	3	0.01
Cuban	8	0.03
Mexican	1,841	7.69
Puerto Rican	17	0.07
South American:	6	0.03
Colombian	1	0.00
Ecuadorian	5	0.02
Other Hispanic or Latino	185	0.77
Hungarian	17	0.07
Irish	1,447	6.05
Italian	116	0.49
Northern European	7	0.03
Norwegian	88	0.37
Polish	23	0.10
Portuguese	14	0.06
Romanian	7	0.03
Russian	7	0.03
Scandinavian	23	0.10
Scotch-Irish	355	1.49
Scottish	316	1.32
Slovak	10	0.04
Swedish	37	0.15
Swiss	21	0.09
Ukrainian	18	0.08
United States or American	2,409	10.08
Welsh	76	0.32
West Indian, excl. Hispanic:	25	0.10
Dutch West Indian	14	0.06
Jamaican	11	0.05
White:	13,257	55.39
Not Hispanic (12,304)	12,415	51.87
Hispanic (778)	842	3.52

McAllen

Place Type: City
County: Hidalgo
Population: 106,414

Ancestry/Race	Number	%
African American/Black:	773	0.73
Not Hispanic (487)	534	0.50
Hispanic (160)	239	0.22
African, sub-Saharan:	210	0.20
African	167	0.16
Cape Verdean	6	0.01
Ghanian	25	0.02
Zairian	6	0.01
Other sub-Saharan African	6	0.01
Alaska Native tribes, specified:	1	0.00
Aleut	1	0.00
Am. Ind. or Alaska Nat., not spec.	281	0.26
American Indian tribes, specified:	263	0.25
Apache (16)	23	0.02
Blackfeet (1)	6	0.01
Cherokee (23)	70	0.07
Chippewa (2)	6	0.01
Choctaw (6)	8	0.01
Comanche	1	0.00
Creek	1	0.00
Delaware	1	0.00
Houma (3)	3	0.00
Iroquois (1)	4	0.00
Latin American Indians (71)	94	0.09
Navajo (1)	6	0.01
Osage (2)	4	0.00
Pueblo (2)	5	0.00
Seminole (1)	5	0.00
Sioux (4)	5	0.00
Ute (1)	1	0.00
All other tribes (9)	20	0.02
American Indian tribes, not spec.	94	0.09
Arab:	323	0.30
Arab/Arabic	27	0.03
Lebanese	205	0.19
Palestinian	65	0.06
Syrian	14	0.01
Other Arab	12	0.01
Armenian	29	0.03
Asian:	2,365	2.22
Bangladeshi (3)	3	0.00
Chinese, ex. Taiwanese (166)	235	0.22
Filipino (987)	1,067	1.00
Hmong (3)	3	0.00
Indian (357)	398	0.37
Indonesian (3)	5	0.00
Japanese (173)	206	0.19
Korean (172)	189	0.18
Malaysian (1)	2	0.00
Pakistani (20)	25	0.02
Sri Lankan (2)	3	0.00
Taiwanese (26)	41	0.04
Thai (11)	12	0.01
Vietnamese (54)	66	0.06
Other Asian, specified (1)	4	0.00
Other Asian, not specified (46)	106	0.10
Australian	15	0.01
Austrian	121	0.11
Belgian	24	0.02
Brazilian	28	0.03
British	96	0.09
Canadian	240	0.23
Carpatho Rusyn	10	0.01
Celtic	63	0.06
Croatian	16	0.02
Czech	158	0.15
Czechoslovakian	45	0.04
Danish	128	0.12
Dutch	533	0.50
Eastern European	27	0.03
English	2,984	2.81
European	112	0.11
Finnish	97	0.09
French, except Basque	857	0.81
French Canadian	88	0.08
German	4,042	3.81
Greek	77	0.07
Guyanese	12	0.01
Hawaii Native/Pacific Islander:	85	0.08
Micronesian: (5)	20	0.02
Guamanian/Chamorro (5)	20	0.02
Polynesian: (21)	32	0.03
Native Hawaiian (13)	23	0.02
Samoan (5)	6	0.01
Tongan (3)	3	0.00
Other Pac. Isl., specified	1	0.00
Other Pac. Isl., not spec. (15)	32	0.03
Hispanic or Latino:	85,427	80.28
Central American:	263	0.25
Costa Rican	6	0.01
Guatemalan	33	0.03
Honduran	68	0.06
Nicaraguan	48	0.05
Panamanian	20	0.02
Salvadoran	77	0.07
Other Central American	11	0.01
Cuban	198	0.19
Dominican Republic	64	0.06
Mexican	69,931	65.72
Puerto Rican	366	0.34
South American:	352	0.33
Argentinean	77	0.07
Bolivian	7	0.01
Chilean	34	0.03
Colombian	106	0.10
Ecuadorian	14	0.01
Paraguayan	2	0.00
Peruvian	69	0.06
Uruguayan	1	0.00
Venezuelan	31	0.03
Other South American	11	0.01
Other Hispanic or Latino	14,253	13.39
Hungarian	114	0.11
Iranian	66	0.06
Irish	2,536	2.39
Italian	902	0.85
Lithuanian	35	0.03
Norwegian	471	0.44
Pennsylvania German	15	0.01
Polish	456	0.43
Portuguese	54	0.05
Romanian	104	0.10
Russian	174	0.16
Scandinavian	73	0.07
Scotch-Irish	493	0.46
Scottish	470	0.44
Slavic	20	0.02
Slovak	9	0.01
Swedish	504	0.47
Swiss	71	0.07
Turkish	33	0.03
Ukrainian	89	0.08
United States or American	3,018	2.84
Welsh	174	0.16
West Indian, excl. Hispanic:	77	0.07
Barbadian	5	0.00
Dutch West Indian	8	0.01
Jamaican	64	0.06
White:	86,168	80.97
Not Hispanic (17,924)	18,256	17.16
Hispanic (65,567)	67,912	63.82
Yugoslavian	62	0.06

Notes: 1. Figures in the "Number" column do not add up to the total population due to: a) Ancestry/Race overlap — e.g. persons can report being both White and Irish, b) persons of Hispanic origin can report being any race, c) persons reporting two ancestries are counted in both categories. 2. Numbers in parentheses indicate the number of persons reporting this ancestry/race alone, not in combination with any other ancestry/race. 3. Refer to the Explanation of Data in the front of the book for more detailed information.

McKinney

Place Type: City
County: Collin
Population: 54,369

Ancestry/Race	Number	%
Acadian/Cajun	18	0.03
African American/Black:	4,160	7.65
Not Hispanic (3,876)	4,066	7.48
Hispanic (37)	94	0.17
African, sub-Saharan:	168	0.31
African	127	0.23
Ethiopian	21	0.04
Ghanian	7	0.01
South African	13	0.02
Alaska Native tribes, specified:	1	0.00
Aleut (1)	1	0.00
Am. Ind. or Alaska Nat., not spec.	169	0.31
Albanian	42	0.08
American Indian tribes, specified:	424	0.78
Apache (2)	6	0.01
Blackfeet (2)	8	0.01
Cherokee (69)	175	0.32
Chickasaw (14)	29	0.05
Chippewa (2)	4	0.01
Choctaw (48)	79	0.15
Comanche (1)	3	0.01
Cree	5	0.01
Creek (5)	22	0.04
Crow	2	0.00
Delaware (1)	3	0.01
Kiowa (3)	3	0.01
Latin American Indians (18)	27	0.05
Navajo	1	0.00
Osage (1)	2	0.00
Potawatomi (4)	12	0.02
Pueblo (1)	1	0.00
Seminole (1)	2	0.00
Sioux (5)	10	0.02
Ute (1)	1	0.00
All other tribes (18)	29	0.05
American Indian tribes, not spec.	23	0.04
Arab:	282	0.52
Arab/Arabic	12	0.02
Iraqi	62	0.11
Lebanese	146	0.27
Syrian	62	0.11
Armenian	42	0.08
Asian:	1,016	1.87
Cambodian (5)	5	0.01
Chinese, ex. Taiwanese (147)	190	0.35
Filipino (105)	146	0.27
Indian (232)	259	0.48
Indonesian (7)	10	0.02
Japanese (48)	77	0.14
Korean (81)	103	0.19
Laotian (4)	4	0.01
Malaysian (1)	1	0.00
Pakistani (30)	34	0.06
Taiwanese (4)	6	0.01
Thai (16)	20	0.04
Vietnamese (85)	92	0.17
Other Asian, specified (8)	19	0.03
Other Asian, not specified (21)	50	0.09
Australian	37	0.07
Austrian	74	0.14
Basque	11	0.02
Belgian	49	0.09
British	323	0.59
Canadian	336	0.62
Croatian	31	0.06
Czech	214	0.39
Czechoslovakian	70	0.13
Danish	181	0.33
Dutch	769	1.41
Eastern European	29	0.05
English	5,838	10.73
European	539	0.99
Finnish	72	0.13
French, except Basque	1,535	2.82
French Canadian	384	0.71
German	8,309	15.28
Greek	76	0.14
Guyanese	8	0.01
Hawaii Native/Pacific Islander:	73	0.13
Micronesian: (4)	8	0.01
Guamanian/Chamorro (4)	6	0.01
Other Micronesian	2	0.00
Polynesian: (17)	29	0.05
Native Hawaiian (2)	14	0.03
Samoan (14)	14	0.03
Tongan (1)	1	0.00
Other Pac. Isl., specified	9	0.02
Other Pac. Isl., not spec. (14)	27	0.05
Hispanic or Latino:	9,876	18.16
Central American:	202	0.37
Costa Rican	7	0.01
Guatemalan	22	0.04
Honduran	58	0.11
Nicaraguan	3	0.01
Panamanian	14	0.03
Salvadoran	78	0.14
Other Central American	20	0.04
Cuban	65	0.12
Dominican Republic	5	0.01
Mexican	7,789	14.33
Puerto Rican	148	0.27
South American:	102	0.19
Argentinean	3	0.01
Bolivian	8	0.01
Chilean	6	0.01
Colombian	24	0.04
Ecuadorian	8	0.01
Paraguayan	1	0.00
Peruvian	25	0.05
Uruguayan	1	0.00
Venezuelan	24	0.04
Other South American	2	0.00
Other Hispanic or Latino	1,565	2.88
Hungarian	151	0.28
Icelander	24	0.04
Iranian	50	0.09
Irish	5,767	10.60
Italian	1,652	3.04
Latvian	12	0.02
Lithuanian	94	0.17
Northern European	35	0.06
Norwegian	544	1.00
Pennsylvania German	10	0.02
Polish	728	1.34
Portuguese	99	0.18
Romanian	21	0.04
Russian	202	0.37
Scandinavian	75	0.14
Scotch-Irish	1,312	2.41
Scottish	1,163	2.14
Slavic	39	0.07
Slovak	10	0.02
Slovene	48	0.09
Swedish	639	1.17
Swiss	116	0.21
Turkish	31	0.06
Ukrainian	78	0.14
United States or American	5,610	10.32
Welsh	419	0.77
West Indian, excl. Hispanic:	52	0.10
British West Indian	5	0.01
Dutch West Indian	18	0.03
Jamaican	22	0.04
West Indian	7	0.01
White:	43,635	80.26
Not Hispanic (38,854)	39,427	72.52
Hispanic (3,774)	4,208	7.74
Yugoslavian	33	0.06

Mercedes

Place Type: City
County: Hidalgo
Population: 13,649

Ancestry/Race	Number	%
African American/Black:	60	0.44
Not Hispanic (14)	16	0.12
Hispanic (35)	44	0.32
African, sub-Saharan:	7	0.05
African	7	0.05
Am. Ind. or Alaska Nat., not spec.	103	0.75
American Indian tribes, specified:	30	0.22
Apache (1)	1	0.01
Cherokee	2	0.01
Choctaw	1	0.01
Latin American Indians (16)	22	0.16
Shoshone (1)	1	0.01
All other tribes (2)	3	0.02
American Indian tribes, not spec.	15	0.11
Asian:	16	0.12
Chinese, ex. Taiwanese	1	0.01
Indian (1)	5	0.04
Vietnamese (5)	5	0.04
Other Asian, not specified (3)	5	0.04
British	8	0.06
Canadian	8	0.06
Czech	26	0.19
Czechoslovakian	10	0.07
Danish	6	0.04
Dutch	18	0.13
Eastern European	7	0.05
English	203	1.46
European	9	0.06
Finnish	19	0.14
French, except Basque	32	0.23
French Canadian	26	0.19
German	336	2.42
Hawaii Native/Pacific Islander:	3	0.02
Micronesian: (1)	1	0.01
Guamanian/Chamorro (1)	1	0.01
Polynesian:	1	0.01
Native Hawaiian	1	0.01
Other Pac. Isl., not spec.	1	0.01
Hispanic or Latino:	12,286	90.01
Central American:	19	0.14
Costa Rican	1	0.01
Guatemalan	13	0.10
Nicaraguan	1	0.01
Salvadoran	2	0.01
Other Central American	2	0.01
Cuban	2	0.01
Mexican	9,325	68.32
Puerto Rican	16	0.12
Other Hispanic or Latino	2,924	21.42
Hungarian	6	0.04
Irish	121	0.87
Italian	14	0.10
Norwegian	92	0.66
Polish	53	0.38
Scotch-Irish	66	0.48
Scottish	28	0.20
Swedish	47	0.34
United States or American	310	2.24
White:	11,134	81.57
Not Hispanic (1,328)	1,337	9.80
Hispanic (9,512)	9,797	71.78

Mesquite

Place Type: City
County: Dallas
Population: 124,523

Ancestry/Race	Number	%
Acadian/Cajun	4	0.00
African American/Black:	17,145	13.77
Not Hispanic (16,422)	16,870	13.55
Hispanic (163)	275	0.22

Notes: 1. Figures in the "Number" column do not add up to the total population due to: a) Ancestry/Race overlap — e.g. persons can report being both White and Irish, b) persons of Hispanic origin can report being any race, c) persons reporting two ancestries are counted in both categories. 2. Numbers in parentheses indicate the number of persons reporting this ancestry/race alone, not in combination with any other ancestry/race. 3. Refer to the Explanation of Data in the front of the book for more detailed information.

Ancestry/Race	Number	%
African, sub-Saharan:	1,141	0.92
African	559	0.45
Ethiopian	49	0.04
Ghanian	67	0.05
Nigerian	383	0.31
Sierra Leonean	63	0.05
South African	15	0.01
Other sub-Saharan African	5	0.00
Alaska Native tribes, specified:	10	0.01
Aleut (4)	9	0.01
Tlingit-Haida (1)	1	0.00
Am. Ind. or Alaska Nat., not spec.	362	0.29
Alsatian	8	0.01
American Indian tribes, specified:	1,059	0.85
Apache (6)	26	0.02
Blackfeet (5)	16	0.01
Cherokee (152)	386	0.31
Cheyenne (1)	4	0.00
Chickasaw (35)	53	0.04
Chippewa (9)	10	0.01
Choctaw (161)	257	0.21
Comanche (24)	36	0.03
Cree	2	0.00
Creek (18)	35	0.03
Crow	1	0.00
Delaware (1)	3	0.00
Houma (2)	2	0.00
Iroquois (11)	15	0.01
Kiowa (6)	12	0.01
Latin American Indians (26)	63	0.05
Lumbee (1)	1	0.00
Menominee	1	0.00
Navajo (4)	11	0.01
Osage	2	0.00
Ottawa (1)	3	0.00
Pima	1	0.00
Potawatomi (23)	25	0.02
Pueblo (3)	5	0.00
Puget Sound Salish (1)	1	0.00
Seminole (1)	3	0.00
Shoshone	4	0.00
Sioux (10)	29	0.02
Tohono O'Odham (1)	1	0.00
All other tribes (28)	51	0.04
American Indian tribes, not spec.	84	0.07
Arab:	610	0.49
Arab/Arabic	185	0.15
Egyptian	23	0.02
Iraqi	8	0.01
Jordanian	102	0.08
Lebanese	112	0.09
Palestinian	143	0.11
Syrian	37	0.03
Armenian	17	0.01
Asian:	5,225	4.20
Bangladeshi (25)	27	0.02
Cambodian (104)	108	0.09
Chinese, ex. Taiwanese (158)	244	0.20
Filipino (1,022)	1,150	0.92
Indian (2,282)	2,378	1.91
Indonesian (3)	13	0.01
Japanese (54)	105	0.08
Korean (111)	143	0.11
Laotian (30)	37	0.03
Malaysian (2)	2	0.00
Pakistani (57)	74	0.06
Sri Lankan (8)	10	0.01
Taiwanese (11)	13	0.01
Thai (30)	40	0.03
Vietnamese (629)	672	0.54
Other Asian, specified (3)	6	0.00
Other Asian, not specified (84)	203	0.16
Assyrian/Chaldean/Syriac	28	0.02
Austrian	56	0.04
Belgian	9	0.01
Brazilian	20	0.02
British	216	0.17
Canadian	77	0.06
Celtic	35	0.03
Croatian	17	0.01
Czech	470	0.38
Czechoslovakian	215	0.17
Danish	106	0.09
Dutch	1,921	1.54
Eastern European	10	0.01
English	9,627	7.73
European	1,053	0.85
Finnish	54	0.04
French, except Basque	2,997	2.41
French Canadian	295	0.24
German	11,976	9.61
Greek	198	0.16
Hawaii Native/Pacific Islander:	136	0.11
Melanesian: (3)	3	0.00
Fijian (3)	3	0.00
Micronesian: (17)	36	0.03
Guamanian/Chamorro (16)	35	0.03
Other Micronesian (1)	1	0.00
Polynesian: (36)	62	0.05
Native Hawaiian (25)	47	0.04
Samoan (11)	15	0.01
Other Pac. Isl., specified	2	0.00
Other Pac. Isl., not spec. (9)	33	0.03
Hispanic or Latino:	19,500	15.66
Central American:	383	0.31
Costa Rican	35	0.03
Guatemalan	63	0.05
Honduran	58	0.05
Nicaraguan	20	0.02
Panamanian	30	0.02
Salvadoran	165	0.13
Other Central American	12	0.01
Cuban	128	0.10
Dominican Republic	52	0.04
Mexican	14,893	11.96
Puerto Rican	339	0.27
South American:	236	0.19
Argentinean	10	0.01
Bolivian	12	0.01
Chilean	13	0.01
Colombian	50	0.04
Ecuadorian	12	0.01
Paraguayan	3	0.00
Peruvian	97	0.08
Uruguayan	3	0.00
Venezuelan	18	0.01
Other South American	18	0.01
Other Hispanic or Latino	3,469	2.79
Hungarian	143	0.11
Iranian	121	0.10
Irish	11,155	8.95
Israeli	8	0.01
Italian	2,469	1.98
Latvian	11	0.01
Lithuanian	89	0.07
Luxemburger	24	0.02
New Zealander	18	0.01
Northern European	22	0.02
Norwegian	526	0.42
Pennsylvania German	9	0.01
Polish	972	0.78
Portuguese	80	0.06
Romanian	57	0.05
Russian	243	0.20
Scandinavian	83	0.07
Scotch-Irish	1,799	1.44
Scottish	1,485	1.19
Serbian	55	0.04
Slovak	66	0.05
Slovene	6	0.00
Swedish	674	0.54
Swiss	84	0.07
Turkish	5	0.00
Ukrainian	57	0.05
United States or American	15,311	12.29
Welsh	575	0.46
West Indian, excl. Hispanic:	240	0.19
Dutch West Indian	77	0.06
Jamaican	116	0.09
Trinidadian and Tobagonian	47	0.04
White:	94,080	75.55
Not Hispanic (81,388)	82,909	66.58
Hispanic (10,184)	11,171	8.97
Yugoslavian	10	0.01

Midland

Place Type: City
County: Midland
Population: 94,996

Ancestry/Race	Number	%
Acadian/Cajun	46	0.05
African American/Black:	8,305	8.74
Not Hispanic (7,811)	8,064	8.49
Hispanic (137)	241	0.25
African, sub-Saharan:	307	0.32
African	280	0.29
Nigerian	27	0.03
Alaska Native tribes, specified:	1	0.00
Aleut (1)	1	0.00
Am. Ind. or Alaska Nat., not spec.	348	0.37
Albanian	21	0.02
Alsatian	24	0.03
American Indian tribes, specified:	554	0.58
Apache (22)	39	0.04
Blackfeet (4)	6	0.01
Cherokee (63)	174	0.18
Chickasaw (17)	28	0.03
Chippewa (2)	4	0.00
Choctaw (66)	95	0.10
Colville (1)	1	0.00
Comanche (10)	21	0.02
Creek (10)	15	0.02
Delaware (3)	10	0.01
Iroquois (2)	3	0.00
Kiowa (5)	6	0.01
Latin American Indians (45)	52	0.05
Lumbee (5)	5	0.01
Navajo (12)	15	0.02
Osage (5)	11	0.01
Ottawa	1	0.00
Pima (1)	1	0.00
Potawatomi (6)	10	0.01
Pueblo (1)	2	0.00
Seminole (2)	2	0.00
Sioux (4)	10	0.01
Tohono O'Odham (2)	6	0.01
Ute	7	0.01
Yaqui	1	0.00
All other tribes (19)	29	0.03
American Indian tribes, not spec.	74	0.08
Arab:	147	0.15
Arab/Arabic	8	0.01
Egyptian	24	0.03
Iraqi	17	0.02
Jordanian	5	0.01
Lebanese	87	0.09
Syrian	6	0.01
Armenian	10	0.01
Asian:	1,192	1.25
Bangladeshi (5)	6	0.01
Cambodian (21)	26	0.03
Chinese, ex. Taiwanese (175)	212	0.22
Filipino (161)	209	0.22
Indian (295)	320	0.34
Indonesian (8)	22	0.02
Japanese (26)	54	0.06
Korean (81)	102	0.11
Laotian (11)	13	0.01
Pakistani (45)	54	0.06
Taiwanese (1)	2	0.00
Thai (12)	19	0.02
Vietnamese (75)	92	0.10
Other Asian, specified (2)	8	0.01
Other Asian, not specified (23)	53	0.06
Assyrian/Chaldean/Syriac	16	0.02
Australian	35	0.04
Austrian	112	0.12
Basque	13	0.01

Notes: 1. Figures in the "Number" column do not add up to the total population due to: a) Ancestry/Race overlap — e.g. persons can report being both White and Irish, b) persons of Hispanic origin can report being any race, c) persons reporting two ancestries are counted in both categories. 2. Numbers in parentheses indicate the number of persons reporting this ancestry/race alone, not in combination with any other ancestry/race. 3. Refer to the Explanation of Data in the front of the book for more detailed information.

Belgian	33	0.03
British	296	0.31
Canadian	85	0.09
Celtic	28	0.03
Croatian	39	0.04
Czech	257	0.27
Czechoslovakian	107	0.11
Danish	293	0.31
Dutch	1,114	1.17
English	8,310	8.73
European	687	0.72
Finnish	36	0.04
French, except Basque	2,068	2.17
French Canadian	239	0.25
German	9,765	10.26
Greek	69	0.07
Guyanese	16	0.02
Hawaii Native/Pacific Islander:	57	0.06
Micronesian: (9)	11	0.01
Guamanian/Chamorro (9)	11	0.01
Polynesian: (9)	19	0.02
Native Hawaiian (7)	13	0.01
Samoan (2)	5	0.01
Other Polynesian	1	0.00
Other Pac. Isl., specified	2	0.00
Other Pac. Isl., not spec. (11)	25	0.03
Hispanic or Latino:	27,543	28.99
Central American:	77	0.08
Costa Rican	2	0.00
Guatemalan	10	0.01
Honduran	7	0.01
Nicaraguan	16	0.02
Panamanian	5	0.01
Salvadoran	34	0.04
Other Central American	3	0.00
Cuban	17	0.02
Dominican Republic	9	0.01
Mexican	20,726	21.82
Puerto Rican	65	0.07
South American:	84	0.09
Argentinean	16	0.02
Bolivian	1	0.00
Chilean	2	0.00
Colombian	24	0.03
Ecuadorian	5	0.01
Peruvian	23	0.02
Venezuelan	12	0.01
Other South American	1	0.00
Other Hispanic or Latino	6,565	6.91
Hungarian	109	0.11
Iranian	41	0.04
Irish	7,116	7.48
Italian	1,350	1.42
Latvian	40	0.04
Lithuanian	71	0.07
Luxemburger	7	0.01
Northern European	100	0.11
Norwegian	639	0.67
Pennsylvania German	16	0.02
Polish	590	0.62
Portuguese	8	0.01
Romanian	68	0.07
Russian	125	0.13
Scandinavian	37	0.04
Scotch-Irish	1,882	1.98
Scottish	1,818	1.91
Serbian	8	0.01
Slavic	6	0.01
Slovak	14	0.01
Slovene	22	0.02
Swedish	579	0.61
Swiss	101	0.11
Turkish	21	0.02
Ukrainian	102	0.11
United States or American	7,445	7.82
Welsh	479	0.50
West Indian, excl. Hispanic:	150	0.16
Dutch West Indian	95	0.10
Haitian	34	0.04
Trinidadian and Tobagonian	21	0.02
White:	73,357	77.22
Not Hispanic (57,603)	58,225	61.29
Hispanic (14,132)	15,132	15.93
Yugoslavian	32	0.03

Mineral Wells

Place Type: City
County: Palo Pinto
Population: 16,946

Ancestry/Race	Number	%
African American/Black:	1,563	9.22
Not Hispanic (1,478)	1,537	9.07
Hispanic (9)	26	0.15
African, sub-Saharan:	11	0.06
African	11	0.06
Alaska Native tribes, specified:	1	0.01
Alaska Athabascan	1	0.01
Am. Ind. or Alaska Nat., not spec.	40	0.24
American Indian tribes, specified:	125	0.74
Apache (1)	6	0.04
Cherokee (16)	46	0.27
Cheyenne (1)	3	0.02
Chickasaw (14)	16	0.09
Choctaw (13)	21	0.12
Comanche (3)	11	0.06
Creek (4)	4	0.02
Latin American Indians (3)	3	0.02
Navajo (2)	2	0.01
Potawatomi	1	0.01
Pueblo (1)	1	0.01
Sioux (1)	4	0.02
All other tribes (2)	7	0.04
American Indian tribes, not spec.	17	0.10
Arab:	10	0.06
Syrian	10	0.06
Asian:	141	0.83
Chinese, ex. Taiwanese (9)	10	0.06
Filipino (26)	40	0.24
Indian (40)	41	0.24
Japanese (12)	15	0.09
Korean (5)	8	0.05
Laotian (3)	3	0.02
Pakistani (4)	9	0.05
Thai (1)	2	0.01
Vietnamese (7)	8	0.05
Other Asian, specified (3)	3	0.02
Other Asian, not specified	2	0.01
Australian	6	0.04
Belgian	7	0.04
British	13	0.08
Canadian	7	0.04
Czech	46	0.27
Czechoslovakian	7	0.04
Danish	15	0.09
Dutch	254	1.50
English	1,070	6.32
European	167	0.99
French, except Basque	295	1.74
French Canadian	39	0.23
German	1,464	8.65
Greek	36	0.21
Hawaii Native/Pacific Islander:	3	0.02
Polynesian: (1)	1	0.01
Samoan (1)	1	0.01
Other Pac. Isl., not spec.	2	0.01
Hispanic or Latino:	3,265	19.27
Central American:	18	0.11
Guatemalan	7	0.04
Panamanian	2	0.01
Salvadoran	9	0.05
Dominican Republic	1	0.01
Mexican	2,741	16.17
Puerto Rican	25	0.15
South American:	1	0.01
Ecuadorian	1	0.01
Other Hispanic or Latino	479	2.83
Hungarian	5	0.03
Irish	1,472	8.70
Italian	138	0.82
Norwegian	82	0.48
Polish	20	0.12
Russian	10	0.06
Scandinavian	6	0.04
Scotch-Irish	203	1.20
Scottish	132	0.78
Swedish	49	0.29
Swiss	50	0.30
Ukrainian	5	0.03
United States or American	2,061	12.17
Welsh	20	0.12
West Indian, excl. Hispanic:	37	0.22
Dutch West Indian	10	0.06
Jamaican	16	0.09
Trinidadian and Tobagonian	11	0.06
White:	13,448	79.36
Not Hispanic (11,835)	11,987	70.74
Hispanic (1,330)	1,461	8.62
Yugoslavian	10	0.06

Mission Bend

Place Type: Census Designated Place
County: Fort Bend
Population: 30,831

Ancestry/Race	Number	%
Acadian/Cajun	15	0.05
African American/Black:	6,902	22.39
Not Hispanic (6,546)	6,770	21.96
Hispanic (82)	132	0.43
African, sub-Saharan:	954	3.09
African	336	1.09
Kenyan	60	0.19
Liberian	22	0.07
Nigerian	496	1.61
South African	23	0.07
Other sub-Saharan African	17	0.06
Alaska Native tribes, specified:	1	0.00
Eskimo (1)	1	0.00
Alaska Native tribes, not specified	1	0.00
Am. Ind. or Alaska Nat., not spec.	86	0.28
American Indian tribes, specified:	108	0.35
Apache (1)	5	0.02
Blackfeet	5	0.02
Cherokee (12)	42	0.14
Chickasaw	2	0.01
Chippewa (1)	1	0.00
Choctaw (7)	9	0.03
Comanche (1)	2	0.01
Iroquois (1)	1	0.00
Kiowa (1)	1	0.00
Latin American Indians (16)	26	0.08
Pueblo (2)	2	0.01
Puget Sound Salish (1)	1	0.00
All other tribes (7)	11	0.04
American Indian tribes, not spec.	11	0.04
Arab:	316	1.02
Arab/Arabic	39	0.13
Egyptian	40	0.13
Lebanese	119	0.39
Palestinian	6	0.02
Other Arab	112	0.36
Armenian	15	0.05
Asian:	5,793	18.79
Bangladeshi (13)	14	0.05
Cambodian (45)	48	0.16
Chinese, ex. Taiwanese (702)	770	2.50
Filipino (915)	1,006	3.26
Hmong	1	0.00
Indian (1,418)	1,537	4.99
Indonesian (6)	12	0.04
Japanese (23)	45	0.15
Korean (104)	109	0.35
Laotian (10)	11	0.04
Malaysian (1)	2	0.01
Pakistani (338)	481	1.56
Sri Lankan (4)	4	0.01
Taiwanese (37)	50	0.16

Notes: 1. Figures in the "Number" column do not add up to the total population due to: a) Ancestry/Race overlap — e.g. persons can report being both White and Irish, b) persons of Hispanic origin can report being any race, c) persons reporting two ancestries are counted in both categories. 2. Numbers in parentheses indicate the number of persons reporting this ancestry/race alone, not in combination with any other ancestry/race. 3. Refer to the Explanation of Data in the front of the book for more detailed information.

Ancestry/Race	Number	%
Thai (29)	34	0.11
Vietnamese (1,401)	1,468	4.76
Other Asian, specified (2)	5	0.02
Other Asian, not specified (93)	196	0.64
Austrian	63	0.20
Brazilian	23	0.07
British	80	0.26
Bulgarian	34	0.11
Canadian	26	0.08
Croatian	31	0.10
Czech	184	0.60
Czechoslovakian	65	0.21
Danish	22	0.07
Dutch	132	0.43
English	1,241	4.02
European	173	0.56
French, except Basque	840	2.72
French Canadian	106	0.34
German	2,412	7.81
Hawaii Native/Pacific Islander:	85	0.28
Micronesian: (4)	9	0.03
Guamanian/Chamorro (4)	9	0.03
Polynesian: (19)	24	0.08
Native Hawaiian (1)	4	0.01
Samoan (18)	19	0.06
Other Polynesian	1	0.00
Other Pac. Isl., specified	2	0.01
Other Pac. Isl., not spec. (2)	50	0.16
Hispanic or Latino:	8,343	27.06
Central American:	935	3.03
Costa Rican	47	0.15
Guatemalan	114	0.37
Honduran	97	0.31
Nicaraguan	77	0.25
Panamanian	39	0.13
Salvadoran	489	1.59
Other Central American	72	0.23
Cuban	221	0.72
Dominican Republic	52	0.17
Mexican	4,080	13.23
Puerto Rican	283	0.92
South American:	790	2.56
Argentinean	62	0.20
Bolivian	15	0.05
Chilean	35	0.11
Colombian	458	1.49
Ecuadorian	61	0.20
Peruvian	70	0.23
Uruguayan	16	0.05
Venezuelan	46	0.15
Other South American	27	0.09
Other Hispanic or Latino	1,982	6.43
Hungarian	20	0.06
Iranian	132	0.43
Irish	1,576	5.10
Italian	589	1.91
Lithuanian	18	0.06
Norwegian	239	0.77
Pennsylvania German	12	0.04
Polish	295	0.95
Portuguese	25	0.08
Romanian	34	0.11
Russian	110	0.36
Scandinavian	28	0.09
Scotch-Irish	311	1.01
Scottish	412	1.33
Slovak	34	0.11
Swedish	77	0.25
Swiss	56	0.18
Turkish	10	0.03
Ukrainian	27	0.09
United States or American	2,121	6.86
Welsh	69	0.22
West Indian, excl. Hispanic:	478	1.55
Belizean	35	0.11
Haitian	10	0.03
Jamaican	371	1.20
West Indian	62	0.20
White:	15,168	49.20
Not Hispanic (9,806)	10,222	33.15
Hispanic (4,475)	4,946	16.04
Yugoslavian	6	0.02

Mission

Place Type: City
County: Hidalgo
Population: 45,408

Ancestry/Race	Number	%
African American/Black:	226	0.50
Not Hispanic (115)	138	0.30
Hispanic (53)	88	0.19
African, sub-Saharan:	17	0.04
African	17	0.04
Am. Ind. or Alaska Nat., not spec.	99	0.22
American Indian tribes, specified:	85	0.19
Apache (4)	8	0.02
Cherokee (4)	15	0.03
Chickasaw	1	0.00
Chippewa (3)	4	0.01
Choctaw (2)	10	0.02
Comanche	1	0.00
Cree	1	0.00
Creek (3)	3	0.01
Iroquois	1	0.00
Latin American Indians (25)	31	0.07
Potawatomi (1)	1	0.00
Pueblo	1	0.00
Seminole	2	0.00
Sioux	1	0.00
All other tribes (5)	5	0.01
American Indian tribes, not spec.	69	0.15
Arab:	82	0.18
Egyptian	21	0.05
Iraqi	10	0.02
Lebanese	42	0.09
Palestinian	9	0.02
Armenian	8	0.02
Asian:	376	0.83
Cambodian (3)	3	0.01
Chinese, ex. Taiwanese (24)	32	0.07
Filipino (161)	188	0.41
Indian (17)	29	0.06
Indonesian (1)	1	0.00
Japanese (20)	34	0.07
Korean (35)	37	0.08
Pakistani (3)	3	0.01
Taiwanese (4)	4	0.01
Thai (3)	5	0.01
Vietnamese (7)	7	0.02
Other Asian, not specified (1)	33	0.07
Austrian	42	0.09
Belgian	23	0.05
Canadian	29	0.06
Celtic	9	0.02
Croatian	9	0.02
Czech	81	0.18
Czechoslovakian	53	0.12
Danish	141	0.31
Dutch	187	0.41
English	1,115	2.43
European	34	0.07
Finnish	56	0.12
French, except Basque	314	0.68
French Canadian	84	0.18
German	2,099	4.57
Hawaii Native/Pacific Islander:	6	0.01
Micronesian: (1)	2	0.00
Guamanian/Chamorro (1)	2	0.00
Polynesian: (2)	2	0.00
Native Hawaiian (2)	2	0.00
Other Pac. Isl., not spec.	2	0.00
Hispanic or Latino:	36,794	81.03
Central American:	61	0.13
Costa Rican	2	0.00
Guatemalan	5	0.01
Honduran	6	0.01
Nicaraguan	16	0.04
Panamanian	1	0.00
Salvadoran	29	0.06
Other Central American	2	0.00
Cuban	26	0.06
Dominican Republic	16	0.04
Mexican	30,495	67.16
Puerto Rican	121	0.27
South American:	62	0.14
Argentinean	15	0.03
Chilean	9	0.02
Colombian	18	0.04
Paraguayan	4	0.01
Peruvian	4	0.01
Venezuelan	5	0.01
Other South American	7	0.02
Other Hispanic or Latino	6,013	13.24
Hungarian	22	0.05
Irish	1,139	2.48
Italian	159	0.35
Lithuanian	8	0.02
Norwegian	273	0.59
Pennsylvania German	8	0.02
Polish	221	0.48
Romanian	9	0.02
Russian	99	0.22
Scandinavian	19	0.04
Scotch-Irish	198	0.43
Scottish	320	0.70
Slovak	8	0.02
Swedish	156	0.34
Swiss	53	0.12
Ukrainian	7	0.02
United States or American	1,032	2.25
Welsh	110	0.24
White:	36,219	79.76
Not Hispanic (8,033)	8,156	17.96
Hispanic (27,216)	28,063	61.80

Missouri City

Place Type: City
County: Fort Bend
Population: 52,913

Ancestry/Race	Number	%
Acadian/Cajun	29	0.06
Afghan	7	0.01
African American/Black:	20,683	39.09
Not Hispanic (20,149)	20,486	38.72
Hispanic (141)	197	0.37
African, sub-Saharan:	1,323	2.52
African	652	1.24
Ghanian	62	0.12
Kenyan	11	0.02
Nigerian	578	1.10
South African	20	0.04
Am. Ind. or Alaska Nat., not spec.	108	0.20
American Indian tribes, specified:	160	0.30
Apache (2)	2	0.00
Blackfeet	8	0.02
Cherokee (15)	61	0.12
Chickasaw (5)	9	0.02
Chippewa	1	0.00
Choctaw (13)	19	0.04
Comanche	2	0.00
Creek (6)	13	0.02
Iroquois	4	0.01
Latin American Indians (5)	13	0.02
Menominee (2)	2	0.00
Potawatomi	2	0.00
Pueblo (1)	2	0.00
Sioux (3)	4	0.01
Ute	1	0.00
All other tribes (9)	17	0.03
American Indian tribes, not spec.	10	0.02
Arab:	570	1.09
Arab/Arabic	81	0.15
Egyptian	38	0.07
Jordanian	55	0.10
Lebanese	130	0.25
Palestinian	171	0.33

Notes: 1. Figures in the "Number" column do not add up to the total population due to: a) Ancestry/Race overlap — e.g. persons can report being both White and Irish, b) persons of Hispanic origin can report being any race, c) persons reporting two ancestries are counted in both categories. 2. Numbers in parentheses indicate the number of persons reporting this ancestry/race alone, not in combination with any other ancestry/race. 3. Refer to the Explanation of Data in the front of the book for more detailed information.

Ancestry/Race	Number	%
Syrian	52	0.10
Other Arab	43	0.08
Armenian	13	0.02
Asian:	6,034	11.40
Bangladeshi (11)	12	0.02
Cambodian (10)	13	0.02
Chinese, ex. Taiwanese (1,424)	1,522	2.88
Filipino (929)	1,006	1.90
Indian (1,946)	2,042	3.86
Indonesian (19)	21	0.04
Japanese (45)	81	0.15
Korean (81)	94	0.18
Malaysian (2)	3	0.01
Pakistani (253)	294	0.56
Sri Lankan (4)	4	0.01
Taiwanese (81)	109	0.21
Thai (53)	65	0.12
Vietnamese (610)	639	1.21
Other Asian, specified (7)	7	0.01
Other Asian, not specified (58)	122	0.23
Australian	37	0.07
Austrian	112	0.21
Basque	32	0.06
British	286	0.55
Canadian	120	0.23
Celtic	22	0.04
Croatian	28	0.05
Czech	335	0.64
Czechoslovakian	186	0.35
Danish	104	0.20
Dutch	358	0.68
Eastern European	62	0.12
English	3,486	6.64
European	149	0.28
French, except Basque	1,089	2.08
French Canadian	363	0.69
German	4,335	8.26
Greek	121	0.23
Guyanese	134	0.26
Hawaii Native/Pacific Islander:	66	0.12
Micronesian: (3)	5	0.01
Guamanian/Chamorro (3)	5	0.01
Polynesian: (7)	18	0.03
Native Hawaiian (3)	7	0.01
Samoan (3)	7	0.01
Other Polynesian (1)	4	0.01
Other Pac. Isl., not spec. (11)	43	0.08
Hispanic or Latino:	5,755	10.88
Central American:	419	0.79
Costa Rican	4	0.01
Guatemalan	43	0.08
Honduran	40	0.08
Nicaraguan	12	0.02
Panamanian	40	0.08
Salvadoran	247	0.47
Other Central American	33	0.06
Cuban	115	0.22
Dominican Republic	8	0.02
Mexican	3,695	6.98
Puerto Rican	134	0.25
South American:	283	0.53
Argentinean	40	0.08
Bolivian	6	0.01
Chilean	12	0.02
Colombian	113	0.21
Ecuadorian	13	0.02
Peruvian	37	0.07
Venezuelan	47	0.09
Other South American	15	0.03
Other Hispanic or Latino	1,101	2.08
Hungarian	107	0.20
Iranian	210	0.40
Irish	2,864	5.46
Italian	1,314	2.50
Latvian	9	0.02
Lithuanian	70	0.13
Luxemburger	26	0.05
Northern European	38	0.07
Norwegian	245	0.47
Pennsylvania German	5	0.01
Polish	732	1.39
Portuguese	6	0.01
Romanian	12	0.02
Russian	156	0.30
Scandinavian	15	0.03
Scotch-Irish	582	1.11
Scottish	696	1.33
Serbian	7	0.01
Slavic	42	0.08
Slovak	69	0.13
Swedish	382	0.73
Swiss	66	0.13
Turkish	42	0.08
Ukrainian	35	0.07
United States or American	2,445	4.66
Welsh	194	0.37
West Indian, excl. Hispanic:	806	1.54
Bahamian	8	0.02
Barbadian	21	0.04
British West Indian	55	0.10
Dutch West Indian	9	0.02
Haitian	66	0.13
Jamaican	514	0.98
Trinidadian and Tobagonian	58	0.11
West Indian	75	0.14
White:	24,198	45.73
Not Hispanic (20,448)	20,943	39.58
Hispanic (2,987)	3,255	6.15

Mount Pleasant

Place Type: City
County: Titus
Population: 13,935

Ancestry/Race	Number	%
African American/Black:	2,281	16.37
Not Hispanic (2,208)	2,245	16.11
Hispanic (22)	36	0.26
African, sub-Saharan:	57	0.41
African	57	0.41
Alaska Native tribes, specified:	3	0.02
Alaska Athabascan	3	0.02
Am. Ind. or Alaska Nat., not spec.	47	0.34
Albanian	5	0.04
American Indian tribes, specified:	81	0.58
Cherokee (6)	16	0.11
Chickasaw	1	0.01
Choctaw (16)	35	0.25
Comanche (2)	3	0.02
Creek (4)	4	0.03
Latin American Indians (14)	14	0.10
Shoshone	3	0.02
Yaqui	1	0.01
All other tribes	4	0.03
American Indian tribes, not spec.	6	0.04
Asian:	146	1.05
Chinese, ex. Taiwanese (11)	13	0.09
Filipino (42)	43	0.31
Indian (43)	54	0.39
Japanese (2)	9	0.06
Korean (8)	8	0.06
Pakistani (8)	15	0.11
Vietnamese (1)	1	0.01
Other Asian, not specified (1)	3	0.02
Australian	7	0.05
British	27	0.19
Canadian	11	0.08
Celtic	18	0.13
Czech	29	0.21
Czechoslovakian	15	0.11
Danish	9	0.06
Dutch	131	0.93
English	565	4.02
European	72	0.51
French, except Basque	156	1.11
German	465	3.31
Hawaii Native/Pacific Islander:	8	0.06
Polynesian:	5	0.04
Native Hawaiian	1	0.01
Samoan	4	0.03
Other Pac. Isl., not spec. (1)	3	0.02
Hispanic or Latino:	5,664	40.65
Central American:	81	0.58
Guatemalan	1	0.01
Honduran	29	0.21
Nicaraguan	4	0.03
Salvadoran	44	0.32
Other Central American	3	0.02
Cuban	8	0.06
Mexican	5,115	36.71
Puerto Rican	16	0.11
South American:	7	0.05
Colombian	2	0.01
Venezuelan	5	0.04
Other Hispanic or Latino	437	3.14
Irish	609	4.33
Italian	54	0.38
Norwegian	8	0.06
Polish	27	0.19
Scotch-Irish	124	0.88
Scottish	126	0.90
Swedish	15	0.11
Swiss	11	0.08
United States or American	1,327	9.44
Welsh	33	0.23
West Indian, excl. Hispanic:	10	0.07
Dutch West Indian	10	0.07
White:	8,176	58.67
Not Hispanic (5,802)	5,873	42.15
Hispanic (2,099)	2,303	16.53

Nacogdoches

Place Type: City
County: Nacogdoches
Population: 29,914

Ancestry/Race	Number	%
African American/Black:	7,610	25.44
Not Hispanic (7,442)	7,549	25.24
Hispanic (53)	61	0.20
African, sub-Saharan:	188	0.62
African	183	0.60
Nigerian	5	0.02
Am. Ind. or Alaska Nat., not spec.	81	0.27
American Indian tribes, specified:	130	0.43
Apache	1	0.00
Cherokee (11)	57	0.19
Chickasaw (1)	4	0.01
Choctaw (14)	19	0.06
Creek	2	0.01
Delaware	2	0.01
Houma	2	0.01
Iroquois (2)	4	0.01
Latin American Indians (13)	14	0.05
Navajo (3)	8	0.03
Osage (1)	1	0.00
Potawatomi (1)	1	0.00
Seminole	2	0.01
Sioux (2)	2	0.01
All other tribes (8)	11	0.04
American Indian tribes, not spec.	12	0.04
Arab:	22	0.07
Jordanian	9	0.03
Lebanese	13	0.04
Asian:	435	1.45
Bangladeshi	3	0.01
Cambodian (13)	14	0.05
Chinese, ex. Taiwanese (62)	76	0.25
Filipino (99)	117	0.39
Indian (54)	61	0.20
Indonesian (2)	2	0.01
Japanese (18)	32	0.11
Korean (16)	31	0.10
Laotian (5)	5	0.02
Pakistani (4)	9	0.03
Taiwanese (2)	5	0.02
Thai (5)	6	0.02
Vietnamese (44)	49	0.16

Notes: 1. Figures in the "Number" column do not add up to the total population due to: a) Ancestry/Race overlap — e.g. persons can report being both White and Irish, b) persons of Hispanic origin can report being any race, c) persons reporting two ancestries are counted in both categories. 2. Numbers in parentheses indicate the number of persons reporting this ancestry/race alone, not in combination with any other ancestry/race. 3. Refer to the Explanation of Data in the front of the book for more detailed information.

Ancestry/Race	Number	%
Other Asian, specified	6	0.02
Other Asian, not specified (5)	19	0.06
Austrian	31	0.10
Belgian	7	0.02
Brazilian	15	0.05
British	132	0.44
Canadian	22	0.07
Czech	117	0.39
Czechoslovakian	95	0.31
Danish	69	0.23
Dutch	218	0.72
English	2,914	9.61
European	233	0.77
Finnish	7	0.02
French, except Basque	745	2.46
French Canadian	74	0.24
German	2,310	7.62
Greek	16	0.05
Hawaii Native/Pacific Islander:	51	0.17
Micronesian: (4)	4	0.01
Guamanian/Chamorro (4)	4	0.01
Polynesian: (24)	34	0.11
Native Hawaiian (14)	21	0.07
Samoan (10)	12	0.04
Tongan	1	0.00
Other Pac. Isl., specified	5	0.02
Other Pac. Isl., not spec. (4)	8	0.03
Hispanic or Latino:	3,236	10.82
Central American:	90	0.30
Costa Rican	5	0.02
Guatemalan	2	0.01
Honduran	14	0.05
Nicaraguan	4	0.01
Panamanian	8	0.03
Salvadoran	55	0.18
Other Central American	2	0.01
Cuban	15	0.05
Dominican Republic	3	0.01
Mexican	2,560	8.56
Puerto Rican	36	0.12
South American:	26	0.09
Argentinean	2	0.01
Bolivian	3	0.01
Chilean	2	0.01
Colombian	9	0.03
Ecuadorian	2	0.01
Peruvian	4	0.01
Venezuelan	1	0.00
Other South American	3	0.01
Other Hispanic or Latino	506	1.69
Hungarian	16	0.05
Iranian	17	0.06
Irish	2,387	7.87
Italian	476	1.57
Northern European	11	0.04
Norwegian	179	0.59
Polish	244	0.80
Portuguese	9	0.03
Russian	55	0.18
Scandinavian	33	0.11
Scotch-Irish	692	2.28
Scottish	407	1.34
Slovak	19	0.06
Swedish	194	0.64
Swiss	54	0.18
Turkish	18	0.06
Ukrainian	5	0.02
United States or American	2,248	7.42
Welsh	125	0.41
West Indian, excl. Hispanic:	53	0.17
Dutch West Indian	27	0.09
Jamaican	7	0.02
West Indian	19	0.06
White:	20,142	67.33
Not Hispanic (18,524)	18,755	62.70
Hispanic (1,212)	1,387	4.64
Yugoslavian	23	0.08

Nederland

Place Type: City
County: Jefferson
Population: 17,422

Ancestry/Race	Number	%
Acadian/Cajun	286	1.65
African American/Black:	168	0.96
Not Hispanic (151)	163	0.94
Hispanic (4)	5	0.03
Am. Ind. or Alaska Nat., not spec.	26	0.15
American Indian tribes, specified:	95	0.55
Apache (5)	5	0.03
Blackfeet	1	0.01
Cherokee (17)	40	0.23
Cheyenne	1	0.01
Chickasaw (3)	3	0.02
Choctaw (6)	10	0.06
Creek (6)	7	0.04
Latin American Indians (2)	5	0.03
Lumbee (1)	1	0.01
Navajo	5	0.03
Potawatomi (2)	3	0.02
Seminole	1	0.01
Sioux (2)	2	0.01
All other tribes (5)	11	0.06
American Indian tribes, not spec.	1	0.01
Arab:	74	0.43
Lebanese	29	0.17
Syrian	45	0.26
Armenian	7	0.04
Asian:	390	2.24
Chinese, ex. Taiwanese (19)	25	0.14
Filipino (57)	65	0.37
Indian (59)	62	0.36
Japanese (7)	14	0.08
Korean (1)	4	0.02
Pakistani (30)	31	0.18
Thai (2)	4	0.02
Vietnamese (169)	175	1.00
Other Asian, specified (1)	2	0.01
Other Asian, not specified (6)	8	0.05
Assyrian/Chaldean/Syriac	24	0.14
Austrian	22	0.13
Basque	8	0.05
Belgian	7	0.04
British	44	0.25
Canadian	15	0.09
Czech	31	0.18
Czechoslovakian	4	0.02
Danish	26	0.15
Dutch	524	3.03
Eastern European	28	0.16
English	1,797	10.38
European	84	0.49
Finnish	6	0.03
French, except Basque	2,252	13.01
French Canadian	707	4.09
German	2,003	11.57
Hawaii Native/Pacific Islander:	14	0.08
Micronesian: (4)	4	0.02
Guamanian/Chamorro (4)	4	0.02
Polynesian:	6	0.03
Native Hawaiian	6	0.03
Other Pac. Isl., not spec. (3)	4	0.02
Hispanic or Latino:	1,089	6.25
Central American:	30	0.17
Costa Rican	2	0.01
Honduran	20	0.11
Nicaraguan	2	0.01
Panamanian	3	0.02
Salvadoran	2	0.01
Other Central American	1	0.01
Cuban	9	0.05
Mexican	789	4.53
Puerto Rican	23	0.13
South American:	10	0.06
Argentinean	2	0.01
Chilean	3	0.02
Colombian	2	0.01
Ecuadorian	2	0.01
Venezuelan	1	0.01
Other Hispanic or Latino	228	1.31
Irish	2,159	12.48
Italian	751	4.34
Norwegian	103	0.60
Polish	147	0.85
Portuguese	6	0.03
Russian	15	0.09
Scandinavian	14	0.08
Scotch-Irish	471	2.72
Scottish	255	1.47
Slovak	6	0.03
Swedish	66	0.38
Swiss	25	0.14
Ukrainian	27	0.16
United States or American	2,066	11.94
Welsh	58	0.34
West Indian, excl. Hispanic:	31	0.18
Other West Indian	31	0.18
White:	16,487	94.63
Not Hispanic (15,642)	15,760	90.46
Hispanic (649)	727	4.17
Yugoslavian	6	0.03

New Braunfels

Place Type: City
County: Comal
Population: 36,494

Ancestry/Race	Number	%
Acadian/Cajun	18	0.05
African American/Black:	601	1.65
Not Hispanic (468)	522	1.43
Hispanic (33)	79	0.22
African, sub-Saharan:	24	0.07
African	24	0.07
Alaska Native tribes, specified:	3	0.01
Aleut (1)	2	0.01
Eskimo (1)	1	0.00
Am. Ind. or Alaska Nat., not spec.	139	0.38
American Indian tribes, specified:	196	0.54
Apache (7)	11	0.03
Blackfeet (1)	3	0.01
Cherokee (20)	58	0.16
Cheyenne	1	0.00
Chickasaw (2)	8	0.02
Chippewa (4)	5	0.01
Choctaw (8)	18	0.05
Comanche (1)	8	0.02
Creek (3)	11	0.03
Iroquois (3)	3	0.01
Latin American Indians (17)	20	0.05
Navajo (7)	10	0.03
Osage (3)	4	0.01
Ottawa	1	0.00
Potawatomi (1)	1	0.00
Puget Sound Salish (1)	1	0.00
Seminole (2)	2	0.01
Shoshone (3)	3	0.01
Sioux (1)	2	0.01
Yaqui	1	0.00
All other tribes (18)	25	0.07
American Indian tribes, not spec.	19	0.05
Arab:	101	0.27
Arab/Arabic	14	0.04
Lebanese	79	0.21
Syrian	8	0.02
Asian:	311	0.85
Cambodian (2)	2	0.01
Chinese, ex. Taiwanese (35)	43	0.12
Filipino (28)	50	0.14
Indian (61)	70	0.19
Indonesian (1)	3	0.01
Japanese (20)	43	0.12
Korean (17)	32	0.09
Pakistani (7)	7	0.02
Taiwanese (1)	1	0.00

Notes: 1. Figures in the "Number" column do not add up to the total population due to: a) Ancestry/Race overlap — e.g. persons can report being both White and Irish, b) persons of Hispanic origin can report being any race, c) persons reporting two ancestries are counted in both categories. 2. Numbers in parentheses indicate the number of persons reporting this ancestry/race alone, not in combination with any other ancestry/race. 3. Refer to the Explanation of Data in the front of the book for more detailed information.

Thai (5)	9	0.02
Vietnamese (29)	33	0.09
Other Asian, specified (1)	3	0.01
Other Asian, not specified (2)	15	0.04
Austrian	62	0.17
Belgian	9	0.02
British	155	0.42
Canadian	18	0.05
Celtic	7	0.02
Croatian	7	0.02
Czech	423	1.15
Czechoslovakian	36	0.10
Danish	52	0.14
Dutch	329	0.89
Eastern European	24	0.07
English	2,706	7.34
European	84	0.23
Finnish	11	0.03
French, except Basque	1,035	2.81
French Canadian	121	0.33
German	8,417	22.82
Greek	8	0.02
Hawaii Native/Pacific Islander:	26	0.07
Micronesian: (5)	5	0.01
Guamanian/Chamorro (5)	5	0.01
Polynesian: (4)	15	0.04
Native Hawaiian (3)	13	0.04
Samoan (1)	2	0.01
Other Pac. Isl., specified	1	0.00
Other Pac. Isl., not spec. (2)	5	0.01
Hispanic or Latino:	12,599	34.52
Central American:	31	0.08
Costa Rican	2	0.01
Guatemalan	8	0.02
Honduran	4	0.01
Panamanian	5	0.01
Salvadoran	12	0.03
Cuban	7	0.02
Dominican Republic	6	0.02
Mexican	9,308	25.51
Puerto Rican	65	0.18
South American:	26	0.07
Argentinean	4	0.01
Bolivian	2	0.01
Colombian	7	0.02
Ecuadorian	2	0.01
Peruvian	8	0.02
Venezuelan	2	0.01
Other South American	1	0.00
Other Hispanic or Latino	3,156	8.65
Hungarian	94	0.25
Iranian	6	0.02
Irish	2,895	7.85
Italian	491	1.33
Lithuanian	20	0.05
Macedonian	5	0.01
New Zealander	5	0.01
Norwegian	231	0.63
Polish	683	1.85
Portuguese	13	0.04
Romanian	16	0.04
Russian	19	0.05
Scandinavian	5	0.01
Scotch-Irish	868	2.35
Scottish	534	1.45
Serbian	4	0.01
Slovak	16	0.04
Slovene	17	0.05
Swedish	236	0.64
Swiss	48	0.13
Turkish	9	0.02
Ukrainian	31	0.08
United States or American	2,144	5.81
Welsh	127	0.34
West Indian, excl. Hispanic:	40	0.11
Dutch West Indian	27	0.07
Trinidadian and Tobagonian	13	0.04
White:	31,500	86.32
Not Hispanic (22,793)	23,043	63.14
Hispanic (7,970)	8,457	23.17

New Territory

Place Type: Census Designated Place
County: Fort Bend
Population: 13,861

Ancestry/Race	Number	%
Acadian/Cajun	13	0.09
Afghan	31	0.22
African American/Black:	1,464	10.56
Not Hispanic (1,385)	1,456	10.50
Hispanic (4)	8	0.06
African, sub-Saharan:	300	2.16
African	137	0.99
Kenyan	47	0.34
Liberian	6	0.04
Nigerian	110	0.79
Alaska Native tribes, specified:	1	0.01
Eskimo	1	0.01
Am. Ind. or Alaska Nat., not spec.	25	0.18
American Indian tribes, specified:	42	0.30
Blackfeet	3	0.02
Cherokee (7)	13	0.09
Choctaw (3)	8	0.06
Comanche (2)	3	0.02
Creek (1)	1	0.01
Kiowa (1)	1	0.01
Latin American Indians (4)	5	0.04
Pueblo (1)	1	0.01
All other tribes (4)	7	0.05
American Indian tribes, not spec.	2	0.01
Arab:	216	1.56
Arab/Arabic	82	0.59
Egyptian	25	0.18
Iraqi	9	0.06
Jordanian	17	0.12
Lebanese	77	0.55
Syrian	6	0.04
Asian:	3,900	28.14
Bangladeshi (16)	17	0.12
Cambodian (3)	3	0.02
Chinese, ex. Taiwanese (798)	873	6.30
Filipino (334)	385	2.78
Indian (1,690)	1,725	12.44
Indonesian (1)	2	0.01
Japanese (11)	22	0.16
Korean (34)	51	0.37
Laotian (2)	2	0.01
Malaysian	2	0.01
Pakistani (255)	316	2.28
Sri Lankan (3)	3	0.02
Taiwanese (59)	74	0.53
Thai (12)	12	0.09
Vietnamese (299)	318	2.29
Other Asian, specified (4)	11	0.08
Other Asian, not specified (31)	84	0.61
Austrian	13	0.09
British	135	0.97
Canadian	112	0.81
Czech	256	1.84
Czechoslovakian	50	0.36
Danish	70	0.50
Dutch	51	0.37
Eastern European	32	0.23
English	1,262	9.09
European	227	1.63
Finnish	32	0.23
French, except Basque	492	3.54
French Canadian	107	0.77
German	1,567	11.28
Greek	54	0.39
Hawaii Native/Pacific Islander:	33	0.24
Micronesian:	1	0.01
Guamanian/Chamorro	1	0.01
Polynesian: (1)	4	0.03
Native Hawaiian (1)	4	0.03
Other Pac. Isl., specified	7	0.05
Other Pac. Isl., not spec. (5)	21	0.15
Hispanic or Latino:	1,157	8.35
Central American:	46	0.33
Costa Rican	2	0.01
Guatemalan	3	0.02
Honduran	8	0.06
Nicaraguan	17	0.12
Panamanian	1	0.01
Salvadoran	10	0.07
Other Central American	5	0.04
Cuban	61	0.44
Dominican Republic	8	0.06
Mexican	667	4.81
Puerto Rican	42	0.30
South American:	101	0.73
Argentinean	20	0.14
Bolivian	1	0.01
Chilean	1	0.01
Colombian	29	0.21
Ecuadorian	1	0.01
Peruvian	10	0.07
Venezuelan	32	0.23
Other South American	7	0.05
Other Hispanic or Latino	232	1.67
Hungarian	15	0.11
Icelander	7	0.05
Iranian	7	0.05
Irish	1,405	10.12
Italian	469	3.38
Norwegian	135	0.97
Polish	352	2.53
Portuguese	30	0.22
Romanian	60	0.43
Russian	44	0.32
Scandinavian	19	0.14
Scotch-Irish	139	1.00
Scottish	250	1.80
Slovak	9	0.06
Swedish	173	1.25
Swiss	7	0.05
Turkish	11	0.08
Ukrainian	6	0.04
United States or American	865	6.23
Welsh	129	0.93
West Indian, excl. Hispanic:	123	0.89
Dutch West Indian	7	0.05
Jamaican	22	0.16
Trinidadian and Tobagonian	74	0.53
West Indian	20	0.14
White:	8,282	59.75
Not Hispanic (7,328)	7,569	54.61
Hispanic (651)	713	5.14
Yugoslavian	10	0.07

North Richland Hills

Place Type: City
County: Tarrant
Population: 55,635

Ancestry/Race	Number	%
Acadian/Cajun	8	0.01
African American/Black:	1,636	2.94
Not Hispanic (1,472)	1,596	2.87
Hispanic (29)	40	0.07
African, sub-Saharan:	269	0.48
African	117	0.21
Ethiopian	7	0.01
Ghanian	51	0.09
Ugandan	17	0.03
Zairian	36	0.06
Other sub-Saharan African	41	0.07
Alaska Native tribes, specified:	3	0.01
Eskimo (2)	2	0.00
Tlingit-Haida (1)	1	0.00
Am. Ind. or Alaska Nat., not spec.	160	0.29
Albanian	84	0.15
American Indian tribes, specified:	485	0.87
Apache (10)	20	0.04
Blackfeet (1)	3	0.01
Cherokee (55)	170	0.31
Cheyenne (1)	1	0.00
Chickasaw (13)	37	0.07

Notes: 1. Figures in the "Number" column do not add up to the total population due to: a) Ancestry/Race overlap — e.g. persons can report being both White and Irish, b) persons of Hispanic origin can report being any race, c) persons reporting two ancestries are counted in both categories. 2. Numbers in parentheses indicate the number of persons reporting this ancestry/race alone, not in combination with any other ancestry/race. 3. Refer to the Explanation of Data in the front of the book for more detailed information.

Chippewa (3)	3	0.01
Choctaw (48)	97	0.17
Colville (1)	2	0.00
Comanche (4)	17	0.03
Cree (1)	2	0.00
Creek (9)	13	0.02
Crow	2	0.00
Delaware (3)	4	0.01
Iroquois (9)	9	0.02
Kiowa (2)	7	0.01
Latin American Indians (10)	19	0.03
Lumbee	1	0.00
Navajo (11)	15	0.03
Osage (1)	5	0.01
Paiute	1	0.00
Pueblo	3	0.01
Seminole (3)	4	0.01
Shoshone (2)	2	0.00
Sioux (5)	11	0.02
All other tribes (20)	37	0.07
American Indian tribes, not spec.	31	0.06
Arab:	135	0.24
Arab/Arabic	16	0.03
Egyptian	34	0.06
Iraqi	9	0.02
Lebanese	65	0.12
Syrian	11	0.02
Armenian	14	0.03
Asian:	1,780	3.20
Bangladeshi (3)	3	0.01
Cambodian (10)	13	0.02
Chinese, ex. Taiwanese (135)	197	0.35
Filipino (109)	163	0.29
Hmong (8)	8	0.01
Indian (319)	337	0.61
Indonesian (3)	6	0.01
Japanese (39)	91	0.16
Korean (71)	88	0.16
Laotian (193)	206	0.37
Malaysian	4	0.01
Pakistani (77)	106	0.19
Sri Lankan (5)	5	0.01
Taiwanese (7)	7	0.01
Thai (38)	50	0.09
Vietnamese (399)	415	0.75
Other Asian, specified (3)	15	0.03
Other Asian, not specified (38)	66	0.12
Australian	52	0.09
Austrian	98	0.18
Basque	9	0.02
Belgian	17	0.03
British	243	0.44
Canadian	108	0.19
Croatian	18	0.03
Czech	228	0.41
Czechoslovakian	56	0.10
Danish	220	0.40
Dutch	829	1.49
English	6,971	12.56
European	599	1.08
Finnish	54	0.10
French, except Basque	1,360	2.45
French Canadian	425	0.77
German	8,789	15.84
Greek	148	0.27
Hawaii Native/Pacific Islander:	136	0.24
Micronesian: (11)	16	0.03
Guamanian/Chamorro (5)	10	0.02
Other Micronesian (6)	6	0.01
Polynesian: (70)	96	0.17
Native Hawaiian (11)	27	0.05
Samoan (2)	5	0.01
Tongan (57)	64	0.12
Other Pac. Isl., not spec. (10)	24	0.04
Hispanic or Latino:	5,276	9.48
Central American:	136	0.24
Costa Rican	2	0.00
Guatemalan	21	0.04
Honduran	23	0.04
Nicaraguan	17	0.03
Panamanian	10	0.02
Salvadoran	62	0.11
Other Central American	1	0.00
Cuban	69	0.12
Dominican Republic	7	0.01
Mexican	3,568	6.41
Puerto Rican	311	0.56
South American:	91	0.16
Argentinean	13	0.02
Chilean	5	0.01
Colombian	27	0.05
Ecuadorian	6	0.01
Paraguayan	2	0.00
Peruvian	14	0.03
Uruguayan	2	0.00
Venezuelan	18	0.03
Other South American	4	0.01
Other Hispanic or Latino	1,094	1.97
Hungarian	78	0.14
Iranian	85	0.15
Irish	6,686	12.05
Italian	1,474	2.66
Lithuanian	29	0.05
Luxemburger	9	0.02
Northern European	40	0.07
Norwegian	687	1.24
Polish	958	1.73
Portuguese	76	0.14
Romanian	10	0.02
Russian	136	0.25
Scandinavian	93	0.17
Scotch-Irish	1,179	2.12
Scottish	1,292	2.33
Slavic	5	0.01
Slovak	28	0.05
Slovene	10	0.02
Swedish	609	1.10
Swiss	101	0.18
Ukrainian	87	0.16
United States or American	7,107	12.81
Welsh	416	0.75
West Indian, excl. Hispanic:	133	0.24
Dutch West Indian	105	0.19
Jamaican	28	0.05
White:	50,253	90.33
Not Hispanic (46,255)	46,926	84.35
Hispanic (2,969)	3,327	5.98
Yugoslavian	85	0.15

Odessa

Place Type: City
County: Ector
Population: 90,943

Ancestry/Race	Number	%
Acadian/Cajun	24	0.03
African American/Black:	5,683	6.25
Not Hispanic (5,165)	5,370	5.90
Hispanic (182)	313	0.34
African, sub-Saharan:	237	0.26
African	229	0.25
Other sub-Saharan African	8	0.01
Alaska Native tribes, specified:	2	0.00
Alaska Athabascan (1)	1	0.00
Eskimo	1	0.00
Am. Ind. or Alaska Nat., not spec.	446	0.49
American Indian tribes, specified:	696	0.77
Apache (27)	56	0.06
Blackfeet (2)	6	0.01
Cherokee (99)	235	0.26
Cheyenne	1	0.00
Chickasaw (25)	34	0.04
Chippewa (2)	12	0.01
Choctaw (44)	72	0.08
Comanche (7)	29	0.03
Cree (1)	1	0.00
Creek (5)	19	0.02
Crow (2)	3	0.00
Delaware	2	0.00
Iroquois (5)	5	0.01
Latin American Indians (90)	103	0.11
Lumbee (1)	1	0.00
Navajo (22)	34	0.04
Osage (7)	7	0.01
Pima (2)	2	0.00
Potawatomi (16)	22	0.02
Pueblo (5)	6	0.01
Seminole (3)	9	0.01
Shoshone (2)	2	0.00
Sioux (7)	11	0.01
Ute (1)	1	0.00
Yakama (2)	2	0.00
Yaqui (2)	3	0.00
All other tribes (11)	18	0.02
American Indian tribes, not spec.	60	0.07
Arab:	69	0.08
Arab/Arabic	4	0.00
Lebanese	33	0.04
Syrian	7	0.01
Other Arab	25	0.03
Asian:	997	1.10
Cambodian (6)	6	0.01
Chinese, ex. Taiwanese (80)	101	0.11
Filipino (297)	368	0.40
Indian (234)	258	0.28
Indonesian (1)	1	0.00
Japanese (31)	71	0.08
Korean (24)	43	0.05
Malaysian (1)	1	0.00
Pakistani (8)	8	0.01
Taiwanese (7)	8	0.01
Thai (14)	16	0.02
Vietnamese (74)	75	0.08
Other Asian, specified (5)	11	0.01
Other Asian, not specified (7)	30	0.03
Australian	6	0.01
Austrian	72	0.08
Belgian	15	0.02
British	217	0.24
Bulgarian	5	0.01
Canadian	48	0.05
Czech	126	0.14
Czechoslovakian	41	0.05
Danish	92	0.10
Dutch	943	1.04
Eastern European	9	0.01
English	6,566	7.21
European	384	0.42
Finnish	33	0.04
French, except Basque	1,650	1.81
French Canadian	83	0.09
German	6,046	6.64
German Russian	13	0.01
Greek	56	0.06
Hawaii Native/Pacific Islander:	74	0.08
Micronesian: (3)	8	0.01
Guamanian/Chamorro (3)	8	0.01
Polynesian: (32)	41	0.05
Native Hawaiian (28)	35	0.04
Samoan (4)	6	0.01
Other Pac. Isl., specified	4	0.00
Other Pac. Isl., not spec. (2)	21	0.02
Hispanic or Latino:	37,671	41.42
Central American:	34	0.04
Costa Rican	1	0.00
Guatemalan	5	0.01
Nicaraguan	5	0.01
Panamanian	12	0.01
Salvadoran	11	0.01
Cuban	28	0.03
Dominican Republic	11	0.01
Mexican	28,753	31.62
Puerto Rican	98	0.11
South American:	44	0.05
Argentinean	7	0.01
Bolivian	3	0.00
Chilean	2	0.00
Colombian	5	0.01
Ecuadorian	6	0.01

Notes: 1. Figures in the "Number" column do not add up to the total population due to: a) Ancestry/Race overlap — e.g. persons can report being both White and Irish, b) persons of Hispanic origin can report being any race, c) persons reporting two ancestries are counted in both categories. 2. Numbers in parentheses indicate the number of persons reporting this ancestry/race alone, not in combination with any other ancestry/race. 3. Refer to the Explanation of Data in the front of the book for more detailed information.

Ancestry/Race	Number	%
Peruvian	14	0.02
Uruguayan	1	0.00
Venezuelan	5	0.01
Other South American	1	0.00
Other Hispanic or Latino	8,703	9.57
Hungarian	66	0.07
Irish	5,966	6.55
Israeli	10	0.01
Italian	730	0.80
Lithuanian	11	0.01
Luxemburger	7	0.01
Northern European	13	0.01
Norwegian	382	0.42
Pennsylvania German	8	0.01
Polish	292	0.32
Portuguese	38	0.04
Romanian	33	0.04
Russian	43	0.05
Scandinavian	30	0.03
Scotch-Irish	1,373	1.51
Scottish	1,066	1.17
Slavic	4	0.00
Swedish	336	0.37
Swiss	127	0.14
Ukrainian	34	0.04
United States or American	6,581	7.23
Welsh	377	0.41
West Indian, excl. Hispanic:	238	0.26
Barbadian	6	0.01
Dutch West Indian	196	0.22
Jamaican	27	0.03
Trinidadian and Tobagonian	9	0.01
White:	69,200	76.09
Not Hispanic (46,179)	46,827	51.49
Hispanic (20,602)	22,373	24.60
Yugoslavian	15	0.02

Orange

Place Type: City
County: Orange
Population: 18,643

Ancestry/Race	Number	%
Acadian/Cajun	235	1.27
African American/Black:	6,700	35.94
Not Hispanic (6,556)	6,655	35.70
Hispanic (37)	45	0.24
African, sub-Saharan:	286	1.54
African	286	1.54
Am. Ind. or Alaska Nat., not spec.	47	0.25
Albanian	14	0.08
American Indian tribes, specified:	111	0.60
Apache (2)	3	0.02
Blackfeet	1	0.01
Cherokee (21)	56	0.30
Cheyenne	2	0.01
Choctaw (2)	8	0.04
Comanche	2	0.01
Creek (2)	3	0.02
Latin American Indians (2)	3	0.02
Paiute (4)	4	0.02
Pueblo	2	0.01
Seminole (2)	6	0.03
Sioux (6)	6	0.03
All other tribes (4)	15	0.08
American Indian tribes, not spec.	10	0.05
Arab:	8	0.04
Lebanese	8	0.04
Asian:	253	1.36
Bangladeshi	1	0.01
Chinese, ex. Taiwanese (12)	16	0.09
Filipino (9)	15	0.08
Indian (31)	38	0.20
Japanese (9)	14	0.08
Korean (20)	25	0.13
Laotian (6)	6	0.03
Malaysian	1	0.01
Pakistani (3)	3	0.02
Thai (2)	2	0.01
Vietnamese (110)	112	0.60
Other Asian, specified	2	0.01
Other Asian, not specified (13)	18	0.10
Austrian	17	0.09
Belgian	10	0.05
British	34	0.18
Canadian	67	0.36
Czech	37	0.20
Dutch	122	0.66
English	1,117	6.03
European	21	0.11
French, except Basque	1,013	5.47
French Canadian	379	2.05
German	1,170	6.31
Greek	26	0.14
Hawaii Native/Pacific Islander:	19	0.10
Micronesian: (12)	12	0.06
Guamanian/Chamorro (11)	11	0.06
Other Micronesian (1)	1	0.01
Polynesian: (3)	5	0.03
Native Hawaiian	1	0.01
Samoan (3)	4	0.02
Other Pac. Isl., specified	1	0.01
Other Pac. Isl., not spec.	1	0.01
Hispanic or Latino:	675	3.62
Central American:	13	0.07
Costa Rican	1	0.01
Honduran	1	0.01
Nicaraguan	1	0.01
Salvadoran	6	0.03
Other Central American	4	0.02
Cuban	11	0.06
Mexican	451	2.42
Puerto Rican	18	0.10
South American:	8	0.04
Colombian	6	0.03
Ecuadorian	1	0.01
Peruvian	1	0.01
Other Hispanic or Latino	174	0.93
Hungarian	11	0.06
Irish	1,288	6.95
Italian	428	2.31
Lithuanian	7	0.04
Norwegian	53	0.29
Polish	68	0.37
Portuguese	29	0.16
Russian	6	0.03
Scandinavian	4	0.02
Scotch-Irish	246	1.33
Scottish	133	0.72
Slavic	10	0.05
Slovak	6	0.03
Slovene	7	0.04
Swedish	34	0.18
Swiss	6	0.03
Turkish	6	0.03
United States or American	1,737	9.37
Welsh	49	0.26
White:	11,502	61.70
Not Hispanic (10,909)	11,081	59.44
Hispanic (386)	421	2.26
Yugoslavian	17	0.09

Palestine

Place Type: City
County: Anderson
Population: 17,598

Ancestry/Race	Number	%
Acadian/Cajun	27	0.15
African American/Black:	4,442	25.24
Not Hispanic (4,330)	4,404	25.03
Hispanic (29)	38	0.22
African, sub-Saharan:	256	1.44
African	256	1.44
Alaska Native tribes, specified:	1	0.01
Eskimo (1)	1	0.01
Am. Ind. or Alaska Nat., not spec.	63	0.36
American Indian tribes, specified:	86	0.49
Apache	1	0.01
Blackfeet	4	0.02
Cherokee (8)	41	0.23
Choctaw (6)	9	0.05
Comanche	1	0.01
Creek	2	0.01
Latin American Indians (7)	8	0.05
Lumbee (11)	11	0.06
Navajo (1)	1	0.01
Potawatomi (1)	1	0.01
Pueblo	1	0.01
Seminole	1	0.01
Sioux (2)	2	0.01
All other tribes (2)	3	0.02
American Indian tribes, not spec.	4	0.02
Arab:	16	0.09
Lebanese	16	0.09
Asian:	169	0.96
Cambodian (6)	6	0.03
Chinese, ex. Taiwanese (6)	6	0.03
Filipino (58)	64	0.36
Indian (30)	32	0.18
Japanese (14)	24	0.14
Korean (4)	9	0.05
Pakistani	1	0.01
Taiwanese (4)	4	0.02
Thai (2)	4	0.02
Vietnamese (13)	14	0.08
Other Asian, specified	1	0.01
Other Asian, not specified (2)	4	0.02
Austrian	24	0.13
British	11	0.06
Canadian	13	0.07
Czech	6	0.03
Danish	33	0.19
Dutch	136	0.76
English	1,198	6.74
European	132	0.74
Finnish	11	0.06
French, except Basque	263	1.48
French Canadian	95	0.53
German	1,115	6.27
Greek	56	0.31
Hawaii Native/Pacific Islander:	23	0.13
Micronesian: (3)	4	0.02
Guamanian/Chamorro (3)	4	0.02
Polynesian: (8)	10	0.06
Native Hawaiian (5)	7	0.04
Samoan (3)	3	0.02
Other Pac. Isl., specified	1	0.01
Other Pac. Isl., not spec. (2)	8	0.05
Hispanic or Latino:	2,619	14.88
Central American:	114	0.65
Guatemalan	38	0.22
Honduran	11	0.06
Panamanian	3	0.02
Salvadoran	55	0.31
Other Central American	7	0.04
Cuban	7	0.04
Dominican Republic	2	0.01
Mexican	2,142	12.17
Puerto Rican	58	0.33
South American:	8	0.05
Argentinean	2	0.01
Chilean	1	0.01
Colombian	5	0.03
Other Hispanic or Latino	288	1.64
Hungarian	24	0.13
Irish	1,102	6.20
Italian	85	0.48
New Zealander	9	0.05
Norwegian	50	0.28
Polish	101	0.57
Portuguese	14	0.08
Romanian	9	0.05
Russian	10	0.06
Scotch-Irish	370	2.08
Scottish	252	1.42
Swedish	15	0.08
Turkish	10	0.06

Notes: 1. Figures in the "Number" column do not add up to the total population due to: a) Ancestry/Race overlap — e.g. persons can report being both White and Irish, b) persons of Hispanic origin can report being any race, c) persons reporting two ancestries are counted in both categories. 2. Numbers in parentheses indicate the number of persons reporting this ancestry/race alone, not in combination with any other ancestry/race. 3. Refer to the Explanation of Data in the front of the book for more detailed information.

United States or American	2,388	13.43
Welsh	44	0.25
West Indian, excl. Hispanic:	33	0.19
Dutch West Indian	6	0.03
Jamaican	16	0.09
Other West Indian	11	0.06
White:	11,590	65.86
Not Hispanic (10,292)	10,436	59.30
Hispanic (1,077)	1,154	6.56

Pampa

Place Type: City
County: Gray
Population: 17,887

Ancestry/Race	Number	%
African American/Black:	772	4.32
Not Hispanic (669)	738	4.13
Hispanic (20)	34	0.19
African, sub-Saharan:	20	0.11
African	20	0.11
Alaska Native tribes, specified:	11	0.06
Alaska Athabascan (6)	6	0.03
Aleut (2)	3	0.02
Tlingit-Haida	2	0.01
Am. Ind. or Alaska Nat., not spec.	116	0.65
American Indian tribes, specified:	352	1.97
Apache (5)	21	0.12
Blackfeet	18	0.10
Cherokee (49)	160	0.89
Cheyenne (2)	4	0.02
Chickasaw (6)	16	0.09
Chippewa	3	0.02
Choctaw (14)	46	0.26
Comanche (3)	11	0.06
Cree (5)	5	0.03
Creek (3)	7	0.04
Crow	2	0.01
Delaware (1)	2	0.01
Kiowa (4)	4	0.02
Latin American Indians (3)	4	0.02
Navajo (7)	10	0.06
Osage	2	0.01
Paiute (4)	4	0.02
Potawatomi (3)	4	0.02
Seminole (1)	4	0.02
Shoshone	1	0.01
Sioux (13)	14	0.08
All other tribes (9)	10	0.06
American Indian tribes, not spec.	23	0.13
Arab:	9	0.05
Egyptian	9	0.05
Asian:	103	0.58
Chinese, ex. Taiwanese (13)	18	0.10
Filipino (24)	37	0.21
Indian (26)	31	0.17
Japanese (1)	1	0.01
Korean (6)	10	0.06
Vietnamese (2)	2	0.01
Other Asian, not specified	4	0.02
British	31	0.17
Canadian	15	0.08
Czech	19	0.11
Danish	42	0.23
Dutch	334	1.87
English	1,545	8.64
European	83	0.46
Finnish	6	0.03
French, except Basque	284	1.59
French Canadian	16	0.09
German	1,761	9.84
Hawaii Native/Pacific Islander:	13	0.07
Micronesian: (1)	1	0.01
Guamanian/Chamorro (1)	1	0.01
Polynesian: (3)	7	0.04
Native Hawaiian (1)	5	0.03
Samoan (2)	2	0.01
Other Pac. Isl., not spec. (1)	5	0.03
Hispanic or Latino:	2,454	13.72
Central American:	2	0.01
Costa Rican	1	0.01
Panamanian	1	0.01
Mexican	1,939	10.84
Puerto Rican	3	0.02
South American:	5	0.03
Chilean	1	0.01
Colombian	4	0.02
Other Hispanic or Latino	505	2.82
Hungarian	17	0.10
Irish	1,674	9.36
Italian	122	0.68
Northern European	8	0.04
Norwegian	73	0.41
Pennsylvania German	13	0.07
Polish	125	0.70
Portuguese	11	0.06
Russian	7	0.04
Scotch-Irish	407	2.27
Scottish	263	1.47
Swedish	60	0.34
Turkish	10	0.06
Ukrainian	5	0.03
United States or American	2,880	16.10
Welsh	42	0.23
West Indian, excl. Hispanic:	70	0.39
Dutch West Indian	59	0.33
Jamaican	11	0.06
White:	15,409	86.15
Not Hispanic (14,170)	14,481	80.96
Hispanic (799)	928	5.19

Paris

Place Type: City
County: Lamar
Population: 25,898

Ancestry/Race	Number	%
Acadian/Cajun	5	0.02
African American/Black:	5,921	22.86
Not Hispanic (5,729)	5,872	22.67
Hispanic (37)	49	0.19
African, sub-Saharan:	111	0.43
African	111	0.43
Alaska Native tribes, specified:	1	0.00
Eskimo (1)	1	0.00
Am. Ind. or Alaska Nat., not spec.	110	0.42
American Indian tribes, specified:	355	1.37
Apache (2)	2	0.01
Blackfeet	2	0.01
Cherokee (28)	83	0.32
Cheyenne (2)	2	0.01
Chickasaw (4)	5	0.02
Choctaw (127)	212	0.82
Comanche (3)	6	0.02
Creek (1)	3	0.01
Delaware (2)	3	0.01
Iroquois	1	0.00
Latin American Indians (1)	13	0.05
Navajo (1)	1	0.00
Osage	1	0.00
Ottawa (3)	3	0.01
Pima	1	0.00
Potawatomi (1)	1	0.00
Seminole (1)	1	0.00
Sioux (4)	5	0.02
All other tribes (1)	10	0.04
American Indian tribes, not spec.	3	0.01
Arab:	7	0.03
Arab/Arabic	7	0.03
Asian:	217	0.84
Chinese, ex. Taiwanese (20)	23	0.09
Filipino (54)	66	0.25
Indian (41)	53	0.20
Japanese (11)	14	0.05
Korean (10)	11	0.04
Laotian	1	0.00
Pakistani (9)	13	0.05
Sri Lankan	1	0.00
Thai (2)	3	0.01
Vietnamese (21)	22	0.08
Other Asian, specified	2	0.01
Other Asian, not specified (4)	8	0.03
Austrian	17	0.07
Belgian	18	0.07
British	58	0.22
Czech	20	0.08
Czechoslovakian	28	0.11
Dutch	510	1.97
English	1,778	6.87
European	44	0.17
French, except Basque	305	1.18
French Canadian	21	0.08
German	1,847	7.14
Greek	16	0.06
Hawaii Native/Pacific Islander:	13	0.05
Micronesian: (5)	5	0.02
Guamanian/Chamorro (1)	1	0.00
Other Micronesian (4)	4	0.02
Polynesian: (1)	5	0.02
Native Hawaiian (1)	4	0.02
Samoan	1	0.00
Other Pac. Isl., not spec. (1)	3	0.01
Hispanic or Latino:	1,068	4.12
Central American:	12	0.05
Costa Rican	5	0.02
Guatemalan	1	0.00
Panamanian	6	0.02
Cuban	15	0.06
Dominican Republic	3	0.01
Mexican	829	3.20
Puerto Rican	19	0.07
South American:	6	0.02
Chilean	2	0.01
Ecuadorian	1	0.00
Venezuelan	3	0.01
Other Hispanic or Latino	184	0.71
Hungarian	28	0.11
Irish	2,360	9.12
Italian	360	1.39
Lithuanian	13	0.05
Norwegian	135	0.52
Pennsylvania German	6	0.02
Polish	115	0.44
Portuguese	24	0.09
Scandinavian	19	0.07
Scotch-Irish	369	1.43
Scottish	263	1.02
Slovak	5	0.02
Slovene	5	0.02
Swedish	101	0.39
Swiss	16	0.06
Turkish	51	0.20
United States or American	3,574	13.81
Welsh	107	0.41
West Indian, excl. Hispanic:	56	0.22
Dutch West Indian	56	0.22
White:	19,246	74.31
Not Hispanic (18,332)	18,629	71.93
Hispanic (552)	617	2.38
Yugoslavian	9	0.03

Pasadena

Place Type: City
County: Harris
Population: 141,674

Ancestry/Race	Number	%
Acadian/Cajun	102	0.07
African American/Black:	2,679	1.89
Not Hispanic (2,068)	2,269	1.60
Hispanic (248)	410	0.29
African, sub-Saharan:	207	0.15
African	148	0.10
Ghanian	15	0.01
Nigerian	44	0.03
Alaska Native tribes, specified:	6	0.00
Aleut (1)	2	0.00

Notes: 1. Figures in the "Number" column do not add up to the total population due to: a) Ancestry/Race overlap — e.g. persons can report being both White and Irish, b) persons of Hispanic origin can report being any race, c) persons reporting two ancestries are counted in both categories. 2. Numbers in parentheses indicate the number of persons reporting this ancestry/race alone, not in combination with any other ancestry/race. 3. Refer to the Explanation of Data in the front of the book for more detailed information.

Ancestry/Race	Number	%
Eskimo (4)	4	0.00
Alaska Native tribes, not specified	2	0.00
Am. Ind. or Alaska Nat., not spec.	593	0.42
Albanian	8	0.01
Alsatian	11	0.01
American Indian tribes, specified:	911	0.64
Apache (20)	51	0.04
Blackfeet (3)	15	0.01
Cherokee (111)	301	0.21
Cheyenne (1)	3	0.00
Chickasaw (9)	15	0.01
Chippewa (7)	9	0.01
Choctaw (37)	94	0.07
Comanche (10)	19	0.01
Cree (3)	4	0.00
Creek (13)	32	0.02
Crow	2	0.00
Delaware (3)	9	0.01
Iroquois (4)	7	0.00
Kiowa (3)	5	0.00
Latin American Indians (161)	220	0.16
Lumbee (1)	1	0.00
Navajo (5)	11	0.01
Osage (12)	13	0.01
Ottawa (5)	5	0.00
Paiute	1	0.00
Potawatomi (1)	2	0.00
Pueblo (9)	13	0.01
Seminole (7)	11	0.01
Shoshone (1)	3	0.00
Sioux (7)	11	0.01
Tohono O'Odham (3)	3	0.00
Ute (2)	2	0.00
Yaqui (3)	6	0.00
All other tribes (24)	43	0.03
American Indian tribes, not spec.	104	0.07
Arab:	615	0.43
Arab/Arabic	131	0.09
Egyptian	77	0.05
Iraqi	17	0.01
Lebanese	66	0.05
Palestinian	200	0.14
Syrian	106	0.07
Other Arab	18	0.01
Armenian	9	0.01
Asian:	3,013	2.13
Bangladeshi (5)	6	0.00
Cambodian (48)	54	0.04
Chinese, ex. Taiwanese (268)	328	0.23
Filipino (177)	260	0.18
Indian (949)	1,015	0.72
Indonesian (5)	7	0.00
Japanese (87)	147	0.10
Korean (187)	213	0.15
Laotian	1	0.00
Pakistani (59)	93	0.07
Sri Lankan (1)	5	0.00
Taiwanese (26)	33	0.02
Thai (15)	25	0.02
Vietnamese (686)	724	0.51
Other Asian, specified (2)	9	0.01
Other Asian, not specified (43)	93	0.07
Australian	23	0.02
Austrian	128	0.09
Basque	13	0.01
Belgian	73	0.05
British	464	0.33
Canadian	118	0.08
Celtic	40	0.03
Croatian	16	0.01
Czech	922	0.65
Czechoslovakian	113	0.08
Danish	131	0.09
Dutch	1,428	1.01
Eastern European	7	0.00
English	8,328	5.88
European	572	0.40
Finnish	71	0.05
French, except Basque	3,271	2.31
French Canadian	540	0.38
German	11,055	7.80
Greek	240	0.17
Hawaii Native/Pacific Islander:	130	0.09
Micronesian: (24)	35	0.02
Guamanian/Chamorro (24)	35	0.02
Polynesian: (24)	49	0.03
Native Hawaiian (16)	33	0.02
Samoan (8)	16	0.01
Other Pac. Isl., specified	4	0.00
Other Pac. Isl., not spec. (10)	42	0.03
Hispanic or Latino:	68,348	48.24
Central American:	1,900	1.34
Costa Rican	36	0.03
Guatemalan	193	0.14
Honduran	354	0.25
Nicaraguan	61	0.04
Panamanian	46	0.03
Salvadoran	1,109	0.78
Other Central American	101	0.07
Cuban	303	0.21
Dominican Republic	61	0.04
Mexican	54,725	38.63
Puerto Rican	530	0.37
South American:	434	0.31
Argentinean	20	0.01
Bolivian	12	0.01
Chilean	4	0.00
Colombian	243	0.17
Ecuadorian	30	0.02
Paraguayan	9	0.01
Peruvian	66	0.05
Uruguayan	11	0.01
Venezuelan	36	0.03
Other South American	3	0.00
Other Hispanic or Latino	10,395	7.34
Hungarian	216	0.15
Iranian	63	0.04
Irish	9,434	6.66
Israeli	17	0.01
Italian	1,988	1.40
Latvian	17	0.01
Lithuanian	40	0.03
Northern European	28	0.02
Norwegian	558	0.39
Pennsylvania German	6	0.00
Polish	1,265	0.89
Portuguese	98	0.07
Romanian	137	0.10
Russian	180	0.13
Scandinavian	147	0.10
Scotch-Irish	2,281	1.61
Scottish	1,318	0.93
Serbian	13	0.01
Slavic	4	0.00
Slovak	94	0.07
Slovene	16	0.01
Swedish	580	0.41
Swiss	194	0.14
Ukrainian	50	0.04
United States or American	10,965	7.74
Welsh	425	0.30
West Indian, excl. Hispanic:	152	0.11
British West Indian	8	0.01
Dutch West Indian	25	0.02
Jamaican	11	0.01
Trinidadian and Tobagonian	108	0.08
White:	105,171	74.23
Not Hispanic (66,923)	68,014	48.01
Hispanic (34,296)	37,157	26.23
Yugoslavian	24	0.02

Pearland

Place Type: City
County: Brazoria
Population: 37,640

Ancestry/Race	Number	%
Acadian/Cajun	32	0.09
African American/Black:	2,105	5.59
Not Hispanic (1,968)	2,049	5.44
Hispanic (38)	56	0.15
African, sub-Saharan:	116	0.31
African	73	0.19
Nigerian	43	0.11
Alaska Native tribes, specified:	1	0.00
Alaska Athabascan (1)	1	0.00
Am. Ind. or Alaska Nat., not spec.	69	0.18
Albanian	9	0.02
American Indian tribes, specified:	233	0.62
Apache (7)	13	0.03
Blackfeet	6	0.02
Cherokee (30)	69	0.18
Chickasaw (2)	4	0.01
Chippewa (4)	8	0.02
Choctaw (21)	35	0.09
Comanche (1)	5	0.01
Creek (4)	11	0.03
Delaware (1)	2	0.01
Iroquois (2)	10	0.03
Kiowa	4	0.01
Latin American Indians (9)	13	0.03
Navajo (1)	1	0.00
Osage (1)	5	0.01
Ottawa (8)	9	0.02
Potawatomi (1)	4	0.01
Seminole	8	0.02
Sioux	2	0.01
Tohono O'Odham (1)	4	0.01
Yaqui	2	0.01
All other tribes (7)	18	0.05
American Indian tribes, not spec.	22	0.06
Arab:	163	0.43
Lebanese	51	0.14
Palestinian	104	0.28
Syrian	8	0.02
Asian:	1,553	4.13
Bangladeshi (10)	10	0.03
Cambodian (32)	42	0.11
Chinese, ex. Taiwanese (132)	170	0.45
Filipino (176)	217	0.58
Indian (153)	168	0.45
Indonesian (4)	5	0.01
Japanese (20)	33	0.09
Korean (77)	91	0.24
Laotian (1)	2	0.01
Pakistani (40)	43	0.11
Sri Lankan (14)	14	0.04
Taiwanese (5)	5	0.01
Thai (2)	4	0.01
Vietnamese (665)	697	1.85
Other Asian, specified (1)	1	0.00
Other Asian, not specified (27)	51	0.14
Austrian	57	0.15
Belgian	29	0.08
British	168	0.45
Canadian	80	0.21
Croatian	27	0.07
Czech	598	1.59
Czechoslovakian	196	0.52
Danish	129	0.34
Dutch	667	1.77
Eastern European	7	0.02
English	3,758	10.00
European	245	0.65
Finnish	17	0.05
French, except Basque	1,544	4.11
French Canadian	332	0.88
German	5,761	15.32
Greek	91	0.24
Hawaii Native/Pacific Islander:	21	0.06
Melanesian: (2)	2	0.01
Fijian (2)	2	0.01
Micronesian: (6)	6	0.02
Guamanian/Chamorro (6)	6	0.02
Polynesian: (3)	4	0.01
Native Hawaiian	1	0.00
Samoan (3)	3	0.01
Other Pac. Isl., not spec. (3)	9	0.02
Hispanic or Latino:	6,107	16.22

Notes: 1. Figures in the "Number" column do not add up to the total population due to: a) Ancestry/Race overlap — e.g. persons can report being both White and Irish, b) persons of Hispanic origin can report being any race, c) persons reporting two ancestries are counted in both categories. 2. Numbers in parentheses indicate the number of persons reporting this ancestry/race alone, not in combination with any other ancestry/race. 3. Refer to the Explanation of Data in the front of the book for more detailed information.

Ancestry/Race	Number	%
Central American:	84	0.22
Costa Rican	3	0.01
Guatemalan	11	0.03
Honduran	13	0.03
Nicaraguan	3	0.01
Panamanian	7	0.02
Salvadoran	37	0.10
Other Central American	10	0.03
Cuban	73	0.19
Dominican Republic	12	0.03
Mexican	4,525	12.02
Puerto Rican	89	0.24
South American:	70	0.19
Argentinean	3	0.01
Bolivian	2	0.01
Chilean	3	0.01
Colombian	39	0.10
Ecuadorian	5	0.01
Peruvian	8	0.02
Venezuelan	3	0.01
Other South American	7	0.02
Other Hispanic or Latino	1,254	3.33
Hungarian	207	0.55
Irish	3,776	10.04
Italian	1,250	3.32
Lithuanian	6	0.02
Luxemburger	50	0.13
New Zealander	13	0.03
Northern European	51	0.14
Norwegian	404	1.07
Polish	608	1.62
Portuguese	44	0.12
Romanian	31	0.08
Russian	124	0.33
Scotch-Irish	776	2.06
Scottish	664	1.77
Slovene	7	0.02
Swedish	361	0.96
Swiss	98	0.26
Turkish	17	0.05
Ukrainian	43	0.11
United States or American	2,790	7.42
Welsh	272	0.72
West Indian, excl. Hispanic:	70	0.19
Dutch West Indian	16	0.04
Jamaican	35	0.09
Trinidadian and Tobagonian	1	0.00
West Indian	18	0.05
White:	31,726	84.29
Not Hispanic (27,629)	28,002	74.39
Hispanic (3,471)	3,724	9.89

Pecan Grove

Place Type: Census Designated Place
County: Fort Bend
Population: 13,551

Ancestry/Race	Number	%
Acadian/Cajun	16	0.12
African American/Black:	470	3.47
Not Hispanic (444)	468	3.45
Hispanic (2)	2	0.01
African, sub-Saharan:	22	0.16
African	14	0.10
Nigerian	8	0.06
Am. Ind. or Alaska Nat., not spec.	8	0.06
American Indian tribes, specified:	59	0.44
Apache (3)	3	0.02
Cherokee (12)	32	0.24
Chickasaw (1)	3	0.02
Choctaw (4)	6	0.04
Comanche	5	0.04
Delaware	1	0.01
Latin American Indians	2	0.01
Osage (2)	2	0.01
Seminole	2	0.01
Tohono O'Odham (1)	1	0.01
Ute	1	0.01
All other tribes (1)	1	0.01
American Indian tribes, not spec.	1	0.01
Arab:	30	0.22
Lebanese	30	0.22
Asian:	236	1.74
Cambodian (2)	2	0.01
Chinese, ex. Taiwanese (44)	53	0.39
Filipino (37)	56	0.41
Indian (33)	33	0.24
Indonesian (4)	5	0.04
Japanese (13)	24	0.18
Korean (6)	10	0.07
Pakistani (4)	4	0.03
Taiwanese (4)	4	0.03
Thai (5)	10	0.07
Vietnamese (17)	19	0.14
Other Asian, specified (3)	4	0.03
Other Asian, not specified (7)	12	0.09
Austrian	18	0.13
Belgian	28	0.21
British	199	1.48
Canadian	48	0.36
Czech	608	4.52
Czechoslovakian	53	0.39
Danish	88	0.65
Dutch	123	0.91
English	1,965	14.60
European	207	1.54
Finnish	12	0.09
French, except Basque	710	5.28
French Canadian	113	0.84
German	2,964	22.02
Greek	9	0.07
Hawaii Native/Pacific Islander:	2	0.01
Other Pac. Isl., not spec.	2	0.01
Hispanic or Latino:	1,230	9.08
Central American:	26	0.19
Costa Rican	1	0.01
Guatemalan	1	0.01
Honduran	8	0.06
Nicaraguan	1	0.01
Panamanian	9	0.07
Salvadoran	6	0.04
Cuban	28	0.21
Dominican Republic	1	0.01
Mexican	833	6.15
Puerto Rican	41	0.30
South American:	60	0.44
Argentinean	3	0.02
Bolivian	1	0.01
Chilean	7	0.05
Colombian	27	0.20
Ecuadorian	7	0.05
Venezuelan	11	0.08
Other South American	4	0.03
Other Hispanic or Latino	241	1.78
Hungarian	78	0.58
Iranian	10	0.07
Irish	1,817	13.50
Italian	742	5.51
Northern European	27	0.20
Norwegian	193	1.43
Pennsylvania German	7	0.05
Polish	451	3.35
Portuguese	74	0.55
Romanian	19	0.14
Russian	72	0.53
Scandinavian	26	0.19
Scotch-Irish	343	2.55
Scottish	403	2.99
Slavic	25	0.19
Slovak	7	0.05
Swedish	142	1.06
Swiss	101	0.75
Ukrainian	5	0.04
United States or American	771	5.73
Welsh	90	0.67
West Indian, excl. Hispanic:	15	0.11
Jamaican	15	0.11
White:	12,550	92.61
Not Hispanic (11,548)	11,661	86.05
Hispanic (823)	889	6.56

Pflugerville

Place Type: City
County: Travis
Population: 16,335

Ancestry/Race	Number	%
African American/Black:	1,648	10.09
Not Hispanic (1,509)	1,599	9.79
Hispanic (36)	49	0.30
African, sub-Saharan:	235	1.44
African	113	0.69
Ghanian	60	0.37
Nigerian	50	0.31
South African	12	0.07
Am. Ind. or Alaska Nat., not spec.	37	0.23
Albanian	14	0.09
American Indian tribes, specified:	70	0.43
Apache (2)	2	0.01
Blackfeet	8	0.05
Cherokee (8)	29	0.18
Chickasaw (1)	3	0.02
Chippewa	1	0.01
Choctaw (4)	8	0.05
Comanche (1)	3	0.02
Iroquois (1)	2	0.01
Latin American Indians (4)	4	0.02
Navajo	1	0.01
Osage (1)	1	0.01
Potawatomi	1	0.01
Sioux (2)	2	0.01
Yaqui (1)	4	0.02
All other tribes	1	0.01
American Indian tribes, not spec.	1	0.01
Arab:	121	0.74
Arab/Arabic	31	0.19
Lebanese	56	0.34
Other Arab	34	0.21
Asian:	827	5.06
Bangladeshi	4	0.02
Cambodian (34)	37	0.23
Chinese, ex. Taiwanese (61)	83	0.51
Filipino (43)	77	0.47
Indian (93)	103	0.63
Japanese (23)	43	0.26
Korean (49)	61	0.37
Laotian (2)	2	0.01
Malaysian (3)	3	0.02
Pakistani (15)	15	0.09
Thai (2)	5	0.03
Vietnamese (343)	362	2.22
Other Asian, specified (1)	5	0.03
Other Asian, not specified (18)	27	0.17
Austrian	20	0.12
Belgian	6	0.04
British	63	0.38
Czech	200	1.22
Czechoslovakian	20	0.12
Danish	83	0.51
Dutch	186	1.14
Eastern European	6	0.04
English	1,629	9.95
European	122	0.75
Finnish	22	0.13
French, except Basque	649	3.97
French Canadian	131	0.80
German	3,555	21.72
Greek	51	0.31
Hawaii Native/Pacific Islander:	27	0.17
Micronesian: (2)	4	0.02
Guamanian/Chamorro (1)	3	0.02
Other Micronesian (1)	1	0.01
Polynesian: (12)	19	0.12
Native Hawaiian (6)	13	0.08
Samoan (6)	6	0.04
Other Pac. Isl., specified	3	0.02
Other Pac. Isl., not spec.	1	0.01
Hispanic or Latino:	2,727	16.69

Notes: 1. Figures in the "Number" column do not add up to the total population due to: a) Ancestry/Race overlap — e.g. persons can report being both White and Irish, b) persons of Hispanic origin can report being any race, c) persons reporting two ancestries are counted in both categories. 2. Numbers in parentheses indicate the number of persons reporting this ancestry/race alone, not in combination with any other ancestry/race. 3. Refer to the Explanation of Data in the front of the book for more detailed information.

Ancestry/Race	Number	%
Central American:	33	0.20
Costa Rican	7	0.04
Guatemalan	7	0.04
Honduran	5	0.03
Nicaraguan	1	0.01
Panamanian	5	0.03
Salvadoran	8	0.05
Cuban	17	0.10
Dominican Republic	1	0.01
Mexican	1,970	12.06
Puerto Rican	82	0.50
South American:	24	0.15
Argentinean	3	0.02
Chilean	6	0.04
Colombian	12	0.07
Venezuelan	2	0.01
Other South American	1	0.01
Other Hispanic or Latino	600	3.67
Hungarian	10	0.06
Irish	1,920	11.73
Italian	518	3.17
Northern European	8	0.05
Norwegian	183	1.12
Pennsylvania German	10	0.06
Polish	283	1.73
Portuguese	52	0.32
Romanian	21	0.13
Russian	54	0.33
Scandinavian	31	0.19
Scotch-Irish	425	2.60
Scottish	402	2.46
Serbian	64	0.39
Slovene	36	0.22
Swedish	263	1.61
Swiss	91	0.56
Ukrainian	9	0.05
United States or American	892	5.45
Welsh	116	0.71
White:	13,014	79.67
Not Hispanic (11,092)	11,327	69.34
Hispanic (1,515)	1,687	10.33
Yugoslavian	12	0.07

Pharr

Place Type: City
County: Hidalgo
Population: 46,660

Ancestry/Race	Number	%
African American/Black:	142	0.30
Not Hispanic (33)	47	0.10
Hispanic (77)	95	0.20
African, sub-Saharan:	30	0.06
African	30	0.06
Am. Ind. or Alaska Nat., not spec.	257	0.55
American Indian tribes, specified:	102	0.22
Apache (1)	2	0.00
Blackfeet	2	0.00
Cherokee (9)	17	0.04
Chippewa (1)	4	0.01
Choctaw (3)	4	0.01
Comanche	1	0.00
Cree (4)	4	0.01
Creek	1	0.00
Iroquois (1)	1	0.00
Latin American Indians (52)	59	0.13
Ottawa	1	0.00
Seminole	1	0.00
Sioux (1)	1	0.00
All other tribes (2)	4	0.01
American Indian tribes, not spec.	38	0.08
Asian:	134	0.29
Chinese, ex. Taiwanese (26)	32	0.07
Filipino (31)	33	0.07
Indian (29)	36	0.08
Japanese (10)	13	0.03
Korean (6)	8	0.02
Laotian (1)	1	0.00
Vietnamese (5)	5	0.01
Other Asian, specified	1	0.00
Other Asian, not specified	5	0.01
Austrian	34	0.07
Belgian	7	0.02
Brazilian	20	0.04
British	10	0.02
Canadian	75	0.16
Czech	35	0.08
Czechoslovakian	16	0.03
Danish	50	0.11
Dutch	58	0.12
English	827	1.77
European	18	0.04
French, except Basque	201	0.43
French Canadian	22	0.05
German	1,004	2.15
Greek	16	0.03
Hawaii Native/Pacific Islander:	15	0.03
Micronesian: (1)	1	0.00
Guamanian/Chamorro (1)	1	0.00
Polynesian: (12)	12	0.03
Native Hawaiian (12)	12	0.03
Other Pac. Isl., specified	1	0.00
Other Pac. Isl., not spec.	1	0.00
Hispanic or Latino:	42,282	90.62
Central American:	67	0.14
Guatemalan	18	0.04
Honduran	13	0.03
Nicaraguan	8	0.02
Salvadoran	23	0.05
Other Central American	5	0.01
Cuban	11	0.02
Dominican Republic	1	0.00
Mexican	36,574	78.38
Puerto Rican	66	0.14
South American:	16	0.03
Chilean	1	0.00
Colombian	8	0.02
Paraguayan	1	0.00
Peruvian	3	0.01
Venezuelan	1	0.00
Other South American	2	0.00
Other Hispanic or Latino	5,547	11.89
Irish	405	0.87
Italian	133	0.29
Luxemburger	8	0.02
Norwegian	113	0.24
Polish	79	0.17
Scotch-Irish	275	0.59
Scottish	132	0.28
Swedish	94	0.20
Swiss	24	0.05
Ukrainian	23	0.05
United States or American	917	1.97
Welsh	36	0.08
West Indian, excl. Hispanic:	8	0.02
West Indian	8	0.02
White:	37,986	81.41
Not Hispanic (4,136)	4,192	8.98
Hispanic (32,939)	33,794	72.43

Plainview

Place Type: City
County: Hale
Population: 22,336

Ancestry/Race	Number	%
African American/Black:	1,374	6.15
Not Hispanic (1,262)	1,309	5.86
Hispanic (50)	65	0.29
African, sub-Saharan:	32	0.14
African	28	0.13
Nigerian	4	0.02
Am. Ind. or Alaska Nat., not spec.	169	0.76
American Indian tribes, specified:	167	0.75
Apache (17)	24	0.11
Blackfeet (2)	3	0.01
Cherokee (23)	52	0.23
Cheyenne	3	0.01
Chickasaw (7)	9	0.04
Choctaw (8)	13	0.06
Comanche (4)	7	0.03
Creek (5)	6	0.03
Delaware (1)	1	0.00
Kiowa (1)	3	0.01
Latin American Indians (18)	21	0.09
Navajo (13)	13	0.06
Osage	2	0.01
Pueblo	3	0.01
Sioux (1)	1	0.00
All other tribes (3)	6	0.03
American Indian tribes, not spec.	35	0.16
Arab:	6	0.03
Lebanese	6	0.03
Asian:	135	0.60
Chinese, ex. Taiwanese (13)	20	0.09
Filipino (23)	29	0.13
Indian (26)	28	0.13
Japanese (13)	24	0.11
Korean (8)	10	0.04
Thai (1)	2	0.01
Vietnamese (7)	8	0.04
Other Asian, specified	1	0.00
Other Asian, not specified (3)	13	0.06
Basque	6	0.03
British	23	0.10
Canadian	35	0.16
Croatian	6	0.03
Czech	62	0.28
Czechoslovakian	12	0.05
Danish	52	0.23
Dutch	124	0.56
English	1,127	5.06
European	41	0.18
French, except Basque	255	1.15
French Canadian	35	0.16
German	1,200	5.39
Greek	6	0.03
Hawaii Native/Pacific Islander:	23	0.10
Micronesian: (11)	12	0.05
Guamanian/Chamorro (11)	12	0.05
Polynesian: (3)	8	0.04
Native Hawaiian (2)	7	0.03
Samoan (1)	1	0.00
Other Pac. Isl., not spec.	3	0.01
Hispanic or Latino:	11,131	49.83
Central American:	13	0.06
Guatemalan	3	0.01
Honduran	1	0.00
Nicaraguan	1	0.00
Panamanian	4	0.02
Salvadoran	4	0.02
Cuban	8	0.04
Dominican Republic	3	0.01
Mexican	7,252	32.47
Puerto Rican	16	0.07
South American:	1	0.00
Bolivian	1	0.00
Other Hispanic or Latino	3,838	17.18
Irish	1,019	4.58
Italian	183	0.82
Norwegian	38	0.17
Polish	43	0.19
Romanian	6	0.03
Russian	73	0.33
Scandinavian	7	0.03
Scotch-Irish	277	1.24
Scottish	215	0.97
Serbian	6	0.03
Swedish	64	0.29
Swiss	3	0.01
United States or American	1,729	7.77
Welsh	74	0.33
West Indian, excl. Hispanic:	29	0.13
Barbadian	9	0.04
Dutch West Indian	14	0.06
Jamaican	6	0.03
White:	14,663	65.65
Not Hispanic (9,580)	9,714	43.49

Notes: 1. Figures in the "Number" column do not add up to the total population due to: a) Ancestry/Race overlap — e.g. persons can report being both White and Irish, b) persons of Hispanic origin can report being any race, c) persons reporting two ancestries are counted in both categories. 2. Numbers in parentheses indicate the number of persons reporting this ancestry/race alone, not in combination with any other ancestry/race. 3. Refer to the Explanation of Data in the front of the book for more detailed information.

Hispanic (4,538)	4,949	22.16
Yugoslavian	11	0.05

Plano

Place Type: City
County: Collin
Population: 222,030

Ancestry/Race	Number	%
Acadian/Cajun	139	0.06
Afghan	132	0.06
African American/Black:	11,985	5.40
Not Hispanic (10,989)	11,665	5.25
Hispanic (166)	320	0.14
African, sub-Saharan:	1,421	0.64
African	503	0.23
Ethiopian	375	0.17
Ghanian	11	0.00
Nigerian	215	0.10
South African	167	0.08
Sudanese	24	0.01
Other sub-Saharan African	126	0.06
Alaska Native tribes, specified:	23	0.01
Alaska Athabascan (5)	6	0.00
Aleut (3)	3	0.00
Eskimo	1	0.00
Tlingit-Haida (1)	13	0.01
Alaska Native tribes, not specified	3	0.00
Am. Ind. or Alaska Nat., not spec.	428	0.19
Albanian	240	0.11
Alsatian	7	0.00
American Indian tribes, specified:	1,238	0.56
Apache (12)	32	0.01
Blackfeet (5)	19	0.01
Cherokee (138)	442	0.20
Cheyenne	2	0.00
Chickasaw (29)	60	0.03
Chippewa (22)	31	0.01
Choctaw (121)	222	0.10
Colville (1)	2	0.00
Comanche (10)	22	0.01
Cree (4)	8	0.00
Creek (23)	49	0.02
Delaware (4)	9	0.00
Houma (5)	5	0.00
Iroquois (15)	25	0.01
Kiowa (1)	4	0.00
Latin American Indians (43)	107	0.05
Menominee (1)	1	0.00
Navajo (4)	12	0.01
Osage (5)	23	0.01
Ottawa	1	0.00
Paiute	4	0.00
Pima (3)	5	0.00
Potawatomi (15)	28	0.01
Pueblo (8)	10	0.00
Seminole (2)	9	0.00
Sioux (12)	16	0.01
Tohono O'Odham	5	0.00
Yaqui (1)	1	0.00
Yuman (2)	2	0.00
All other tribes (44)	82	0.04
American Indian tribes, not spec.	91	0.04
Arab:	1,777	0.80
Arab/Arabic	167	0.08
Egyptian	257	0.12
Jordanian	136	0.06
Lebanese	652	0.29
Moroccan	51	0.02
Palestinian	47	0.02
Syrian	160	0.07
Other Arab	307	0.14
Armenian	220	0.10
Asian:	24,816	11.18
Bangladeshi (129)	154	0.07
Cambodian (73)	89	0.04
Chinese, ex. Taiwanese (8,974)	9,477	4.27
Filipino (994)	1,248	0.56
Hmong (6)	8	0.00
Indian (6,321)	6,644	2.99
Indonesian (63)	94	0.04
Japanese (586)	804	0.36
Korean (1,760)	1,916	0.86
Laotian (50)	63	0.03
Malaysian (28)	34	0.02
Pakistani (465)	578	0.26
Sri Lankan (73)	84	0.04
Taiwanese (550)	702	0.32
Thai (190)	249	0.11
Vietnamese (1,745)	1,900	0.86
Other Asian, specified (37)	63	0.03
Other Asian, not specified (223)	709	0.32
Australian	151	0.07
Austrian	663	0.30
Basque	37	0.02
Belgian	376	0.17
Brazilian	209	0.09
British	1,802	0.81
Bulgarian	68	0.03
Canadian	1,014	0.46
Celtic	95	0.04
Croatian	301	0.14
Czech	1,380	0.62
Czechoslovakian	436	0.20
Danish	1,157	0.52
Dutch	2,671	1.20
Eastern European	319	0.14
English	26,546	11.94
Estonian	13	0.01
European	2,884	1.30
Finnish	444	0.20
French, except Basque	6,617	2.98
French Canadian	1,181	0.53
German	36,276	16.32
Greek	926	0.42
Hawaii Native/Pacific Islander:	231	0.10
Melanesian: (7)	7	0.00
Fijian (7)	7	0.00
Micronesian: (22)	28	0.01
Guamanian/Chamorro (22)	28	0.01
Polynesian: (43)	87	0.04
Native Hawaiian (30)	72	0.03
Samoan (10)	12	0.01
Tongan (1)	1	0.00
Other Polynesian (2)	2	0.00
Other Pac. Isl., specified	3	0.00
Other Pac. Isl., not spec. (24)	106	0.05
Hispanic or Latino:	22,357	10.07
Central American:	1,269	0.57
Costa Rican	68	0.03
Guatemalan	234	0.11
Honduran	216	0.10
Nicaraguan	70	0.03
Panamanian	68	0.03
Salvadoran	546	0.25
Other Central American	67	0.03
Cuban	334	0.15
Dominican Republic	32	0.01
Mexican	15,541	7.00
Puerto Rican	751	0.34
South American:	901	0.41
Argentinean	90	0.04
Bolivian	20	0.01
Chilean	70	0.03
Colombian	267	0.12
Ecuadorian	46	0.02
Paraguayan	9	0.00
Peruvian	250	0.11
Uruguayan	2	0.00
Venezuelan	85	0.04
Other South American	62	0.03
Other Hispanic or Latino	3,529	1.59
Hungarian	893	0.40
Icelander	8	0.00
Iranian	2,152	0.97
Irish	23,979	10.79
Israeli	104	0.05
Italian	9,042	4.07
Latvian	86	0.04
Lithuanian	525	0.24
Luxemburger	57	0.03
Macedonian	36	0.02
Maltese	111	0.05
New Zealander	55	0.02
Northern European	68	0.03
Norwegian	3,034	1.36
Pennsylvania German	44	0.02
Polish	5,490	2.47
Portuguese	316	0.14
Romanian	240	0.11
Russian	2,722	1.22
Scandinavian	356	0.16
Scotch-Irish	5,027	2.26
Scottish	5,888	2.65
Serbian	60	0.03
Slavic	10	0.00
Slovak	367	0.17
Slovene	86	0.04
Swedish	3,201	1.44
Swiss	804	0.36
Turkish	196	0.09
Ukrainian	575	0.26
United States or American	15,200	6.84
Welsh	1,643	0.74
West Indian, excl. Hispanic:	515	0.23
Barbadian	18	0.01
Belizean	66	0.03
Bermudan	10	0.00
British West Indian	38	0.02
Dutch West Indian	38	0.02
Haitian	56	0.03
Jamaican	164	0.07
Trinidadian and Tobagonian	65	0.03
U.S. Virgin Islander	25	0.01
West Indian	35	0.02
White:	178,070	80.20
Not Hispanic (161,543)	164,535	74.10
Hispanic (12,218)	13,535	6.10
Yugoslavian	233	0.10

Port Arthur

Place Type: City
County: Jefferson
Population: 57,755

Ancestry/Race	Number	%
Acadian/Cajun	409	0.71
African American/Black:	25,564	44.26
Not Hispanic (25,118)	25,360	43.91
Hispanic (122)	204	0.35
African, sub-Saharan:	339	0.59
African	324	0.56
Ethiopian	10	0.02
Nigerian	5	0.01
Am. Ind. or Alaska Nat., not spec.	197	0.34
American Indian tribes, specified:	269	0.47
Apache (1)	6	0.01
Blackfeet (2)	5	0.01
Cherokee (28)	85	0.15
Cheyenne	1	0.00
Chickasaw	1	0.00
Chippewa (1)	2	0.00
Choctaw (11)	20	0.03
Comanche	1	0.00
Cree (3)	3	0.01
Creek (3)	7	0.01
Houma (1)	1	0.00
Iroquois	1	0.00
Latin American Indians (64)	91	0.16
Navajo (5)	6	0.01
Osage	3	0.01
Potawatomi (1)	1	0.00
Pueblo (1)	1	0.00
Seminole	3	0.01
Sioux (2)	5	0.01
All other tribes (8)	26	0.05
American Indian tribes, not spec.	33	0.06
Arab:	49	0.08

Notes: 1. Figures in the "Number" column do not add up to the total population due to: a) Ancestry/Race overlap — e.g. persons can report being both White and Irish, b) persons of Hispanic origin can report being any race, c) persons reporting two ancestries are counted in both categories. 2. Numbers in parentheses indicate the number of persons reporting this ancestry/race alone, not in combination with any other ancestry/race. 3. Refer to the Explanation of Data in the front of the book for more detailed information.

Ancestry/Race	Number	%
Arab/Arabic	4	0.01
Lebanese	30	0.05
Syrian	15	0.03
Asian:	3,632	6.29
Cambodian (5)	5	0.01
Chinese, ex. Taiwanese (22)	32	0.06
Filipino (76)	107	0.19
Hmong	1	0.00
Indian (297)	332	0.57
Japanese (9)	15	0.03
Korean (35)	45	0.08
Laotian (22)	27	0.05
Pakistani (82)	97	0.17
Taiwanese (6)	9	0.02
Thai (10)	13	0.02
Vietnamese (2,781)	2,869	4.97
Other Asian, specified	14	0.02
Other Asian, not specified (33)	66	0.11
Austrian	18	0.03
British	71	0.12
Canadian	112	0.19
Cypriot	4	0.01
Czech	45	0.08
Czechoslovakian	23	0.04
Danish	19	0.03
Dutch	246	0.43
English	1,833	3.17
European	58	0.10
French, except Basque	3,416	5.91
French Canadian	1,064	1.84
German	2,432	4.21
Greek	83	0.14
Hawaii Native/Pacific Islander:	49	0.08
Micronesian:	8	0.01
Guamanian/Chamorro	8	0.01
Polynesian: (6)	15	0.03
Native Hawaiian (1)	9	0.02
Samoan (5)	6	0.01
Other Pac. Isl., specified	14	0.02
Other Pac. Isl., not spec. (3)	12	0.02
Hispanic or Latino:	10,081	17.45
Central American:	658	1.14
Costa Rican	1	0.00
Guatemalan	26	0.05
Honduran	95	0.16
Nicaraguan	432	0.75
Panamanian	8	0.01
Salvadoran	77	0.13
Other Central American	19	0.03
Cuban	31	0.05
Dominican Republic	6	0.01
Mexican	7,830	13.56
Puerto Rican	48	0.08
South American:	65	0.11
Argentinean	3	0.01
Chilean	11	0.02
Colombian	11	0.02
Ecuadorian	3	0.01
Peruvian	7	0.01
Uruguayan	1	0.00
Venezuelan	14	0.02
Other South American	15	0.03
Other Hispanic or Latino	1,443	2.50
Hungarian	10	0.02
Iranian	20	0.03
Irish	2,325	4.03
Italian	1,032	1.79
Lithuanian	13	0.02
Luxemburger	13	0.02
Norwegian	112	0.19
Polish	163	0.28
Portuguese	35	0.06
Russian	28	0.05
Scotch-Irish	528	0.91
Scottish	304	0.53
Slovak	4	0.01
Swedish	146	0.25
Swiss	2	0.00
Ukrainian	4	0.01
United States or American	2,275	3.94
Welsh	92	0.16
West Indian, excl. Hispanic:	109	0.19
Barbadian	33	0.06
Jamaican	11	0.02
Trinidadian and Tobagonian	7	0.01
U.S. Virgin Islander	8	0.01
West Indian	16	0.03
Other West Indian	34	0.06
White:	23,445	40.59
Not Hispanic (18,387)	18,801	32.55
Hispanic (4,141)	4,644	8.04

Port Lavaca

Place Type: City
County: Calhoun
Population: 12,035

Ancestry/Race	Number	%
African American/Black:	525	4.36
Not Hispanic (472)	495	4.11
Hispanic (16)	30	0.25
African, sub-Saharan:	13	0.11
African	13	0.11
Alaska Native tribes, specified:	2	0.02
Eskimo (1)	1	0.01
Tlingit-Haida (1)	1	0.01
Am. Ind. or Alaska Nat., not spec.	37	0.31
American Indian tribes, specified:	41	0.34
Apache (5)	11	0.09
Cherokee (3)	7	0.06
Cheyenne	4	0.03
Chippewa (1)	1	0.01
Choctaw (2)	3	0.02
Creek	3	0.02
Houma	1	0.01
Kiowa	1	0.01
Latin American Indians (5)	5	0.04
Navajo	1	0.01
Seminole (1)	1	0.01
All other tribes (2)	3	0.02
American Indian tribes, not spec.	5	0.04
Arab:	16	0.13
Lebanese	5	0.04
Syrian	11	0.09
Asian:	536	4.45
Cambodian	6	0.05
Chinese, ex. Taiwanese (226)	250	2.08
Filipino (22)	29	0.24
Indian (18)	20	0.17
Japanese (4)	12	0.10
Korean (6)	6	0.05
Pakistani	4	0.03
Taiwanese (118)	142	1.18
Thai (3)	3	0.02
Vietnamese (58)	58	0.48
Other Asian, not specified	6	0.05
Austrian	15	0.12
British	7	0.06
Canadian	14	0.12
Czech	269	2.24
Czechoslovakian	18	0.15
Danish	12	0.10
Dutch	33	0.27
English	526	4.38
European	7	0.06
Finnish	7	0.06
French, except Basque	144	1.20
French Canadian	13	0.11
German	1,048	8.72
Hawaii Native/Pacific Islander:	21	0.17
Polynesian: (4)	9	0.07
Native Hawaiian	3	0.02
Samoan (4)	6	0.05
Other Pac. Isl., not spec. (6)	12	0.10
Hispanic or Latino:	6,272	52.11
Central American:	18	0.15
Guatemalan	3	0.02
Honduran	1	0.01
Salvadoran	13	0.11
Other Central American	1	0.01
Cuban	7	0.06
Mexican	4,736	39.35
Puerto Rican	44	0.37
South American:	5	0.04
Chilean	2	0.02
Venezuelan	3	0.02
Other Hispanic or Latino	1,462	12.15
Irish	591	4.92
Italian	95	0.79
Norwegian	44	0.37
Polish	101	0.84
Portuguese	19	0.16
Russian	5	0.04
Scotch-Irish	119	0.99
Scottish	87	0.72
Swedish	52	0.43
United States or American	664	5.53
West Indian, excl. Hispanic:	8	0.07
Dutch West Indian	8	0.07
White:	8,928	74.18
Not Hispanic (4,697)	4,750	39.47
Hispanic (3,962)	4,178	34.72

Port Neches

Place Type: City
County: Jefferson
Population: 13,601

Ancestry/Race	Number	%
Acadian/Cajun	244	1.80
African American/Black:	147	1.08
Not Hispanic (122)	143	1.05
Hispanic (4)	4	0.03
African, sub-Saharan:	11	0.08
African	11	0.08
Alaska Native tribes, specified:	3	0.02
Aleut (1)	1	0.01
Eskimo (2)	2	0.01
Am. Ind. or Alaska Nat., not spec.	32	0.24
American Indian tribes, specified:	73	0.54
Apache (1)	3	0.02
Cherokee (18)	33	0.24
Cheyenne (1)	1	0.01
Choctaw (6)	9	0.07
Comanche (1)	4	0.03
Creek (3)	3	0.02
Iroquois (1)	2	0.01
Lumbee (2)	2	0.01
Navajo (2)	4	0.03
Osage (2)	2	0.01
Ottawa (1)	1	0.01
Potawatomi (1)	2	0.01
Seminole	1	0.01
All other tribes (4)	6	0.04
American Indian tribes, not spec.	11	0.08
Arab:	29	0.21
Lebanese	19	0.14
Syrian	10	0.07
Asian:	235	1.73
Chinese, ex. Taiwanese (15)	19	0.14
Filipino (46)	48	0.35
Indian (19)	22	0.16
Japanese (12)	17	0.12
Korean (16)	18	0.13
Pakistani (9)	13	0.10
Vietnamese (83)	87	0.64
Other Asian, not specified (11)	11	0.08
Austrian	11	0.08
British	183	1.35
Canadian	24	0.18
Carpatho Rusyn	10	0.07
Czech	7	0.05
Czechoslovakian	10	0.07
Danish	7	0.05
Dutch	263	1.94
English	1,505	11.11
European	19	0.14
French, except Basque	2,281	16.84

Notes: 1. Figures in the "Number" column do not add up to the total population due to: a) Ancestry/Race overlap — e.g. persons can report being both White and Irish, b) persons of Hispanic origin can report being any race, c) persons reporting two ancestries are counted in both categories. 2. Numbers in parentheses indicate the number of persons reporting this ancestry/race alone, not in combination with any other ancestry/race. 3. Refer to the Explanation of Data in the front of the book for more detailed information.

Ancestry/Race	Number	%
French Canadian	729	5.38
German	1,394	10.29
Greek	27	0.20
Hawaii Native/Pacific Islander:	1	0.01
Polynesian: (1)	1	0.01
Native Hawaiian (1)	1	0.01
Hispanic or Latino:	690	5.07
Central American:	17	0.12
Guatemalan	2	0.01
Honduran	7	0.05
Nicaraguan	2	0.01
Panamanian	1	0.01
Salvadoran	5	0.04
Cuban	12	0.09
Mexican	494	3.63
Puerto Rican	10	0.07
South American:	18	0.13
Argentinean	5	0.04
Colombian	2	0.01
Peruvian	11	0.08
Other Hispanic or Latino	139	1.02
Irish	1,429	10.55
Italian	581	4.29
Lithuanian	15	0.11
Norwegian	35	0.26
Polish	69	0.51
Portuguese	64	0.47
Russian	17	0.13
Scandinavian	26	0.19
Scotch-Irish	339	2.50
Scottish	145	1.07
Slavic	8	0.06
Slovak	14	0.10
Slovene	5	0.04
Swedish	51	0.38
Ukrainian	56	0.41
United States or American	1,288	9.51
Welsh	58	0.43
West Indian, excl. Hispanic:	12	0.09
British West Indian	12	0.09
White:	13,030	95.80
Not Hispanic (12,410)	12,507	91.96
Hispanic (477)	523	3.85

Portland

Place Type: City
County: San Patricio
Population: 14,827

Ancestry/Race	Number	%
Acadian/Cajun	16	0.11
African American/Black:	676	4.56
Not Hispanic (583)	628	4.24
Hispanic (27)	48	0.32
African, sub-Saharan:	3	0.02
African	3	0.02
Am. Ind. or Alaska Nat., not spec.	43	0.29
American Indian tribes, specified:	122	0.82
Blackfeet	7	0.05
Cherokee (11)	31	0.21
Chickasaw (5)	10	0.07
Chippewa	1	0.01
Choctaw (11)	20	0.13
Comanche (3)	8	0.05
Creek (3)	9	0.06
Delaware (1)	1	0.01
Iroquois (6)	8	0.05
Latin American Indians (9)	10	0.07
Navajo	6	0.04
Osage (1)	1	0.01
Sioux (2)	4	0.03
All other tribes (3)	6	0.04
American Indian tribes, not spec.	16	0.11
Arab:	44	0.29
Lebanese	37	0.25
Syrian	7	0.05
Asian:	247	1.67
Chinese, ex. Taiwanese (19)	27	0.18
Filipino (89)	141	0.95
Indian (25)	30	0.20
Japanese (5)	16	0.11
Korean (11)	17	0.11
Taiwanese (1)	1	0.01
Vietnamese (2)	7	0.05
Other Asian, not specified (3)	8	0.05
Austrian	5	0.03
British	65	0.43
Canadian	19	0.13
Celtic	23	0.15
Czech	211	1.41
Czechoslovakian	28	0.19
Danish	74	0.50
Dutch	118	0.79
English	1,482	9.92
European	134	0.90
Finnish	30	0.20
French, except Basque	572	3.83
French Canadian	51	0.34
German	2,494	16.69
Greek	58	0.39
Guyanese	12	0.08
Hawaii Native/Pacific Islander:	51	0.34
Melanesian:	1	0.01
Other Melanesian	1	0.01
Micronesian: (19)	32	0.22
Guamanian/Chamorro (19)	30	0.20
Other Micronesian	2	0.01
Polynesian: (7)	11	0.07
Native Hawaiian (3)	6	0.04
Samoan (4)	4	0.03
Other Polynesian	1	0.01
Other Pac. Isl., not spec. (4)	7	0.05
Hispanic or Latino:	3,870	26.10
Central American:	22	0.15
Costa Rican	5	0.03
Guatemalan	3	0.02
Honduran	4	0.03
Nicaraguan	2	0.01
Panamanian	7	0.05
Salvadoran	1	0.01
Cuban	10	0.07
Dominican Republic	1	0.01
Mexican	2,614	17.63
Puerto Rican	62	0.42
South American:	27	0.18
Bolivian	2	0.01
Colombian	9	0.06
Ecuadorian	4	0.03
Peruvian	4	0.03
Venezuelan	5	0.03
Other South American	3	0.02
Other Hispanic or Latino	1,134	7.65
Hungarian	27	0.18
Irish	1,560	10.44
Italian	354	2.37
Latvian	7	0.05
Lithuanian	10	0.07
Norwegian	100	0.67
Polish	200	1.34
Portuguese	23	0.15
Russian	23	0.15
Scandinavian	21	0.14
Scotch-Irish	296	1.98
Scottish	226	1.51
Slovene	5	0.03
Swedish	200	1.34
Swiss	22	0.15
Turkish	11	0.07
Ukrainian	76	0.51
United States or American	938	6.28
Welsh	126	0.84
West Indian, excl. Hispanic:	110	0.74
Dutch West Indian	8	0.05
Trinidadian and Tobagonian	14	0.09
West Indian	88	0.59
White:	12,796	86.30
Not Hispanic (9,914)	10,094	68.08
Hispanic (2,510)	2,702	18.22
Yugoslavian	7	0.05

Richardson

Place Type: City
County: Dallas
Population: 91,802

Ancestry/Race	Number	%
Acadian/Cajun	31	0.03
Afghan	146	0.16
African American/Black:	6,095	6.64
Not Hispanic (5,586)	5,954	6.49
Hispanic (89)	141	0.15
African, sub-Saharan:	1,013	1.11
African	371	0.40
Ethiopian	266	0.29
Kenyan	6	0.01
Liberian	38	0.04
Nigerian	262	0.29
Somalian	4	0.00
South African	12	0.01
Sudanese	24	0.03
Zairian	13	0.01
Other sub-Saharan African	17	0.02
Alaska Native tribes, specified:	2	0.00
Tlingit-Haida	2	0.00
Am. Ind. or Alaska Nat., not spec.	244	0.27
Albanian	10	0.01
American Indian tribes, specified:	678	0.74
Apache (10)	20	0.02
Blackfeet	8	0.01
Cherokee (87)	222	0.24
Cheyenne (2)	5	0.01
Chickasaw (13)	28	0.03
Chippewa (2)	5	0.01
Choctaw (56)	108	0.12
Comanche (12)	20	0.02
Cree	1	0.00
Creek (14)	27	0.03
Crow	1	0.00
Delaware (1)	3	0.00
Iroquois	1	0.00
Kiowa (1)	4	0.00
Latin American Indians (43)	105	0.11
Lumbee (2)	2	0.00
Navajo (6)	11	0.01
Osage (3)	19	0.02
Ottawa (2)	4	0.00
Paiute	1	0.00
Potawatomi (10)	15	0.02
Pueblo (9)	18	0.02
Seminole (7)	10	0.01
Shoshone (5)	6	0.01
Sioux	5	0.01
Tohono O'Odham (2)	2	0.00
All other tribes (12)	27	0.03
American Indian tribes, not spec.	27	0.03
Arab:	1,506	1.64
Arab/Arabic	447	0.49
Egyptian	73	0.08
Iraqi	38	0.04
Jordanian	72	0.08
Lebanese	336	0.37
Moroccan	13	0.01
Palestinian	79	0.09
Syrian	162	0.18
Other Arab	286	0.31
Armenian	111	0.12
Asian:	11,800	12.85
Bangladeshi (90)	111	0.12
Cambodian (95)	106	0.12
Chinese, ex. Taiwanese (3,320)	3,548	3.86
Filipino (401)	487	0.53
Hmong (2)	2	0.00
Indian (2,448)	2,640	2.88
Indonesian (24)	28	0.03
Japanese (213)	288	0.31
Korean (1,082)	1,133	1.23
Laotian (43)	56	0.06
Malaysian (13)	24	0.03
Pakistani (525)	627	0.68

Notes: 1. Figures in the "Number" column do not add up to the total population due to: a) Ancestry/Race overlap — e.g. persons can report being both White and Irish, b) persons of Hispanic origin can report being any race, c) persons reporting two ancestries are counted in both categories. 2. Numbers in parentheses indicate the number of persons reporting this ancestry/race alone, not in combination with any other ancestry/race. 3. Refer to the Explanation of Data in the front of the book for more detailed information.

Sri Lankan (23)	23	0.03
Taiwanese (207)	285	0.31
Thai (95)	128	0.14
Vietnamese (1,790)	1,903	2.07
Other Asian, specified (13)	26	0.03
Other Asian, not specified (125)	385	0.42
Australian	95	0.10
Austrian	181	0.20
Basque	8	0.01
Belgian	104	0.11
Brazilian	17	0.02
British	551	0.60
Bulgarian	9	0.01
Canadian	91	0.10
Celtic	43	0.05
Croatian	99	0.11
Cypriot	25	0.03
Czech	471	0.51
Czechoslovakian	165	0.18
Danish	426	0.46
Dutch	1,131	1.23
Eastern European	45	0.05
English	11,497	12.55
European	1,152	1.26
Finnish	44	0.05
French, except Basque	2,889	3.15
French Canadian	486	0.53
German	12,962	14.15
German Russian	5	0.01
Greek	265	0.29
Guyanese	8	0.01
Hawaii Native/Pacific Islander:	167	0.18
Melanesian: (1)	1	0.00
Fijian (1)	1	0.00
Micronesian: (10)	13	0.01
Guamanian/Chamorro (10)	12	0.01
Other Micronesian	1	0.00
Polynesian: (20)	68	0.07
Native Hawaiian (13)	42	0.05
Samoan (3)	15	0.02
Tongan (4)	10	0.01
Other Polynesian	1	0.00
Other Pac. Isl., specified	9	0.01
Other Pac. Isl., not spec. (24)	76	0.08
Hispanic or Latino:	9,420	10.26
Central American:	639	0.70
Costa Rican	57	0.06
Guatemalan	93	0.10
Honduran	214	0.23
Nicaraguan	16	0.02
Panamanian	48	0.05
Salvadoran	177	0.19
Other Central American	34	0.04
Cuban	120	0.13
Dominican Republic	23	0.03
Mexican	6,765	7.37
Puerto Rican	248	0.27
South American:	300	0.33
Argentinean	27	0.03
Bolivian	26	0.03
Chilean	29	0.03
Colombian	76	0.08
Ecuadorian	27	0.03
Paraguayan	13	0.01
Peruvian	61	0.07
Uruguayan	4	0.00
Venezuelan	20	0.02
Other South American	17	0.02
Other Hispanic or Latino	1,325	1.44
Hungarian	313	0.34
Icelander	10	0.01
Iranian	369	0.40
Irish	9,364	10.22
Italian	2,651	2.89
Latvian	43	0.05
Lithuanian	88	0.10
Luxemburger	6	0.01
New Zealander	7	0.01
Northern European	85	0.09
Norwegian	1,171	1.28
Pennsylvania German	11	0.01
Polish	1,806	1.97
Portuguese	178	0.19
Romanian	85	0.09
Russian	893	0.97
Scandinavian	65	0.07
Scotch-Irish	2,906	3.17
Scottish	2,734	2.98
Slavic	33	0.04
Slovak	114	0.12
Slovene	59	0.06
Swedish	1,124	1.23
Swiss	318	0.35
Turkish	65	0.07
Ukrainian	139	0.15
United States or American	7,008	7.65
Welsh	928	1.01
West Indian, excl. Hispanic:	310	0.34
Barbadian	8	0.01
Dutch West Indian	38	0.04
Haitian	33	0.04
Jamaican	144	0.16
Trinidadian and Tobagonian	52	0.06
West Indian	35	0.04
White:	71,117	77.47
Not Hispanic (63,850)	65,302	71.13
Hispanic (5,359)	5,815	6.33
Yugoslavian	79	0.09

Richmond

Place Type: City
County: Fort Bend
Population: 11,081

Ancestry/Race	Number	%
African American/Black:	1,552	14.01
Not Hispanic (1,482)	1,510	13.63
Hispanic (19)	42	0.38
African, sub-Saharan:	43	0.39
African	43	0.39
Am. Ind. or Alaska Nat., not spec.	51	0.46
American Indian tribes, specified:	39	0.35
Blackfeet	1	0.01
Cherokee (2)	10	0.09
Chickasaw	1	0.01
Creek (3)	3	0.03
Iroquois (1)	1	0.01
Latin American Indians (17)	22	0.20
All other tribes	1	0.01
American Indian tribes, not spec.	16	0.14
Asian:	75	0.68
Chinese, ex. Taiwanese (7)	9	0.08
Filipino (11)	14	0.13
Indian (21)	23	0.21
Japanese	2	0.02
Korean (3)	3	0.03
Pakistani (6)	10	0.09
Vietnamese (5)	5	0.05
Other Asian, not specified (3)	9	0.08
Austrian	6	0.05
British	20	0.18
Czech	241	2.18
Czechoslovakian	66	0.60
Danish	16	0.14
Dutch	46	0.42
English	483	4.36
European	16	0.14
French, except Basque	124	1.12
German	621	5.61
Hawaii Native/Pacific Islander:	12	0.11
Micronesian: (2)	2	0.02
Guamanian/Chamorro (2)	2	0.02
Polynesian: (2)	3	0.03
Native Hawaiian (2)	2	0.02
Samoan	1	0.01
Other Pac. Isl., not spec. (4)	7	0.06
Hispanic or Latino:	6,506	58.71
Central American:	200	1.80
Guatemalan	1	0.01
Honduran	25	0.23
Nicaraguan	1	0.01
Salvadoran	160	1.44
Other Central American	13	0.12
Cuban	3	0.03
Mexican	4,853	43.80
Puerto Rican	10	0.09
South American:	1	0.01
Colombian	1	0.01
Other Hispanic or Latino	1,439	12.99
Hungarian	15	0.14
Irish	422	3.81
Italian	82	0.74
Lithuanian	5	0.05
Norwegian	21	0.19
Polish	95	0.86
Russian	10	0.09
Scotch-Irish	192	1.73
Scottish	56	0.51
Swedish	18	0.16
Ukrainian	6	0.05
United States or American	365	3.30
West Indian, excl. Hispanic:	36	0.33
Jamaican	27	0.24
West Indian	9	0.08
White:	5,958	53.77
Not Hispanic (2,964)	2,997	27.05
Hispanic (2,710)	2,961	26.72

Rio Grande City

Place Type: City
County: Starr
Population: 11,923

Ancestry/Race	Number	%
African American/Black:	49	0.41
Not Hispanic (4)	4	0.03
Hispanic (32)	45	0.38
African, sub-Saharan:	23	0.19
African	23	0.19
Am. Ind. or Alaska Nat., not spec.	43	0.36
American Indian tribes, specified:	23	0.19
Apache	2	0.02
Cherokee (1)	1	0.01
Chickasaw	1	0.01
Iroquois	1	0.01
Latin American Indians (14)	14	0.12
All other tribes (3)	4	0.03
Asian:	141	1.18
Chinese, ex. Taiwanese (1)	2	0.02
Filipino (98)	99	0.83
Indian (3)	5	0.04
Indonesian (1)	1	0.01
Korean (1)	2	0.02
Malaysian (1)	1	0.01
Pakistani (6)	10	0.08
Vietnamese (16)	16	0.13
Other Asian, not specified (3)	5	0.04
Dutch	9	0.07
English	31	0.25
European	12	0.10
French, except Basque	41	0.34
German	3	0.02
Hawaii Native/Pacific Islander:	10	0.08
Micronesian:	6	0.05
Guamanian/Chamorro	6	0.05
Other Pac. Isl., not spec. (1)	4	0.03
Hispanic or Latino:	11,433	95.89
Central American:	26	0.22
Guatemalan	13	0.11
Honduran	6	0.05
Nicaraguan	6	0.05
Salvadoran	1	0.01
Cuban	1	0.01
Mexican	9,241	77.51
Puerto Rican	9	0.08
South American:	2	0.02
Colombian	2	0.02
Other Hispanic or Latino	2,154	18.07

Notes: 1. Figures in the "Number" column do not add up to the total population due to: a) Ancestry/Race overlap — e.g. persons can report being both White and Irish, b) persons of Hispanic origin can report being any race, c) persons reporting two ancestries are counted in both categories. 2. Numbers in parentheses indicate the number of persons reporting this ancestry/race alone, not in combination with any other ancestry/race. 3. Refer to the Explanation of Data in the front of the book for more detailed information.

Irish	45	0.37
Norwegian	16	0.13
Scotch-Irish	12	0.10
Scottish	11	0.09
United States or American	223	1.83
White:	10,194	85.50
Not Hispanic (317)	334	2.80
Hispanic (9,576)	9,860	82.70

Robstown

Place Type: City
County: Nueces
Population: 12,727

Ancestry/Race	Number	%
African American/Black:	194	1.52
Not Hispanic (175)	179	1.41
Hispanic (5)	15	0.12
Am. Ind. or Alaska Nat., not spec.	75	0.59
American Indian tribes, specified:	25	0.20
Apache (9)	9	0.07
Cherokee (2)	3	0.02
Chippewa (2)	2	0.02
Choctaw	4	0.03
Comanche (1)	1	0.01
Creek	1	0.01
Latin American Indians (4)	5	0.04
American Indian tribes, not spec.	6	0.05
Asian:	32	0.25
Filipino (1)	8	0.06
Indian (17)	22	0.17
Japanese	1	0.01
Vietnamese (1)	1	0.01
British	7	0.05
Celtic	14	0.11
Czech	52	0.41
Czechoslovakian	57	0.45
Dutch	11	0.09
English	30	0.23
European	20	0.16
French, except Basque	7	0.05
French Canadian	29	0.23
German	147	1.15
Hawaii Native/Pacific Islander:	14	0.11
Micronesian: (2)	5	0.04
Guamanian/Chamorro (2)	5	0.04
Polynesian: (2)	5	0.04
Native Hawaiian (2)	5	0.04
Other Pac. Isl., not spec. (4)	4	0.03
Hispanic or Latino:	11,848	93.09
Central American:	12	0.09
Guatemalan	3	0.02
Honduran	4	0.03
Panamanian	1	0.01
Other Central American	4	0.03
Cuban	2	0.02
Mexican	7,334	57.63
Puerto Rican	7	0.06
South American:	3	0.02
Chilean	2	0.02
Ecuadorian	1	0.01
Other Hispanic or Latino	4,490	35.28
Iranian	10	0.08
Irish	33	0.26
Luxemburger	6	0.05
Norwegian	6	0.05
Polish	3	0.02
Scotch-Irish	10	0.08
Swedish	6	0.05
United States or American	290	2.27
Welsh	6	0.05
White:	8,967	70.46
Not Hispanic (617)	658	5.17
Hispanic (7,906)	8,309	65.29

Rockwall

Place Type: City
County: Rockwall
Population: 17,976

Ancestry/Race	Number	%
Acadian/Cajun	77	0.42
African American/Black:	565	3.14
Not Hispanic (533)	558	3.10
Hispanic (6)	7	0.04
African, sub-Saharan:	98	0.53
African	62	0.34
Kenyan	27	0.15
South African	9	0.05
Alaska Native tribes, specified:	2	0.01
Aleut (2)	2	0.01
Am. Ind. or Alaska Nat., not spec.	33	0.18
American Indian tribes, specified:	98	0.55
Apache	1	0.01
Blackfeet	1	0.01
Cherokee (21)	42	0.23
Chickasaw (5)	7	0.04
Choctaw (10)	23	0.13
Iroquois	2	0.01
Kiowa	1	0.01
Latin American Indians (4)	4	0.02
Navajo (4)	4	0.02
Osage	1	0.01
Seminole	1	0.01
Sioux (2)	2	0.01
All other tribes (4)	9	0.05
American Indian tribes, not spec.	12	0.07
Arab:	54	0.29
Arab/Arabic	5	0.03
Lebanese	37	0.20
Syrian	12	0.07
Asian:	314	1.75
Cambodian (4)	4	0.02
Chinese, ex. Taiwanese (32)	40	0.22
Filipino (47)	67	0.37
Indian (58)	70	0.39
Indonesian (1)	4	0.02
Japanese (25)	29	0.16
Korean (37)	44	0.24
Laotian (1)	1	0.01
Pakistani (7)	9	0.05
Thai (6)	6	0.03
Vietnamese (20)	24	0.13
Other Asian, not specified (5)	16	0.09
Australian	19	0.10
Austrian	28	0.15
Belgian	55	0.30
British	196	1.07
Canadian	17	0.09
Croatian	27	0.15
Czech	114	0.62
Czechoslovakian	27	0.15
Danish	106	0.58
Dutch	492	2.69
Eastern European	43	0.23
English	2,284	12.47
European	403	2.20
Finnish	21	0.11
French, except Basque	425	2.32
French Canadian	157	0.86
German	2,385	13.02
Greek	53	0.29
Hawaii Native/Pacific Islander:	13	0.07
Micronesian: (2)	4	0.02
Guamanian/Chamorro (1)	3	0.02
Other Micronesian (1)	1	0.01
Polynesian: (3)	4	0.02
Native Hawaiian (1)	2	0.01
Samoan (2)	2	0.01
Other Pac. Isl., not spec. (1)	5	0.03
Hispanic or Latino:	1,157	6.44
Central American:	54	0.30
Costa Rican	2	0.01
Guatemalan	4	0.02
Honduran	1	0.01
Panamanian	3	0.02
Salvadoran	27	0.15
Other Central American	17	0.09
Cuban	14	0.08
Dominican Republic	1	0.01
Mexican	859	4.78
Puerto Rican	44	0.24
South American:	16	0.09
Argentinean	1	0.01
Chilean	1	0.01
Colombian	4	0.02
Peruvian	3	0.02
Venezuelan	3	0.02
Other South American	4	0.02
Other Hispanic or Latino	169	0.94
Hungarian	53	0.29
Iranian	29	0.16
Irish	2,036	11.11
Italian	465	2.54
Latvian	16	0.09
Lithuanian	5	0.03
Northern European	53	0.29
Norwegian	163	0.89
Polish	171	0.93
Portuguese	9	0.05
Russian	68	0.37
Scandinavian	34	0.19
Scotch-Irish	301	1.64
Scottish	467	2.55
Slovak	18	0.10
Swedish	188	1.03
Swiss	96	0.52
Turkish	18	0.10
Ukrainian	36	0.20
United States or American	2,457	13.41
Welsh	60	0.33
West Indian, excl. Hispanic:	44	0.24
Dutch West Indian	26	0.14
Jamaican	6	0.03
West Indian	12	0.07
White:	16,625	92.48
Not Hispanic (15,814)	15,945	88.70
Hispanic (607)	680	3.78

Rosenberg

Place Type: City
County: Fort Bend
Population: 24,043

Ancestry/Race	Number	%
Acadian/Cajun	5	0.02
African American/Black:	2,137	8.89
Not Hispanic (1,981)	2,049	8.52
Hispanic (71)	88	0.37
African, sub-Saharan:	108	0.45
African	54	0.22
Nigerian	54	0.22
Am. Ind. or Alaska Nat., not spec.	102	0.42
American Indian tribes, specified:	90	0.37
Apache (3)	7	0.03
Blackfeet (1)	3	0.01
Cherokee (3)	25	0.10
Chickasaw (1)	3	0.01
Choctaw (7)	17	0.07
Iroquois	2	0.01
Latin American Indians (14)	21	0.09
Navajo (1)	1	0.00
Sioux (1)	1	0.00
All other tribes (4)	10	0.04
American Indian tribes, not spec.	3	0.01
Arab:	28	0.12
Lebanese	28	0.12
Asian:	159	0.66
Chinese, ex. Taiwanese (15)	25	0.10
Filipino (19)	34	0.14
Indian (15)	25	0.10
Indonesian	1	0.00
Japanese (4)	6	0.02

Notes: 1. Figures in the "Number" column do not add up to the total population due to: a) Ancestry/Race overlap — e.g. persons can report being both White and Irish, b) persons of Hispanic origin can report being any race, c) persons reporting two ancestries are counted in both categories. 2. Numbers in parentheses indicate the number of persons reporting this ancestry/race alone, not in combination with any other ancestry/race. 3. Refer to the Explanation of Data in the front of the book for more detailed information.

Ancestry/Race	Number	%
Korean (13)	16	0.07
Pakistani (6)	9	0.04
Thai (2)	4	0.02
Vietnamese (14)	19	0.08
Other Asian, not specified (3)	20	0.08
Austrian	18	0.07
Basque	8	0.03
British	19	0.08
Celtic	9	0.04
Croatian	9	0.04
Czech	1,202	4.97
Czechoslovakian	98	0.41
Danish	48	0.20
Dutch	116	0.48
English	819	3.39
European	6	0.02
Finnish	12	0.05
French, except Basque	273	1.13
French Canadian	47	0.19
German	2,243	9.28
Greek	7	0.03
Hawaii Native/Pacific Islander:	22	0.09
Micronesian: (2)	6	0.02
Guamanian/Chamorro (2)	6	0.02
Polynesian: (7)	10	0.04
Native Hawaiian (6)	9	0.04
Samoan (1)	1	0.00
Other Pac. Isl., not spec. (1)	6	0.02
Hispanic or Latino:	13,215	54.96
Central American:	372	1.55
Guatemalan	13	0.05
Honduran	13	0.05
Nicaraguan	2	0.01
Panamanian	1	0.00
Salvadoran	338	1.41
Other Central American	5	0.02
Cuban	21	0.09
Mexican	9,930	41.30
Puerto Rican	52	0.22
South American:	20	0.08
Argentinean	1	0.00
Bolivian	2	0.01
Colombian	5	0.02
Peruvian	5	0.02
Venezuelan	7	0.03
Other Hispanic or Latino	2,820	11.73
Hungarian	25	0.10
Irish	1,237	5.12
Italian	165	0.68
Lithuanian	9	0.04
Norwegian	45	0.19
Polish	545	2.25
Romanian	5	0.02
Russian	33	0.14
Scandinavian	19	0.08
Scotch-Irish	196	0.81
Scottish	101	0.42
Swedish	66	0.27
Swiss	15	0.06
Ukrainian	24	0.10
United States or American	952	3.94
Welsh	30	0.12
West Indian, excl. Hispanic:	18	0.07
Dutch West Indian	18	0.07
White:	16,398	68.20
Not Hispanic (8,515)	8,690	36.14
Hispanic (7,278)	7,708	32.06

Round Rock

Place Type: City
County: Williamson
Population: 61,136

Ancestry/Race	Number	%
Acadian/Cajun	14	0.02
African American/Black:	5,132	8.39
Not Hispanic (4,560)	4,884	7.99
Hispanic (158)	248	0.41
African, sub-Saharan:	438	0.73
African	195	0.32
Ethiopian	33	0.05
Ghanian	11	0.02
Liberian	23	0.04
Nigerian	123	0.20
Somalian	23	0.04
South African	23	0.04
Other sub-Saharan African	7	0.01
Alaska Native tribes, specified:	2	0.00
Alaska Athabascan (1)	1	0.00
Aleut (1)	1	0.00
Am. Ind. or Alaska Nat., not spec.	176	0.29
American Indian tribes, specified:	378	0.62
Apache (15)	21	0.03
Blackfeet (1)	16	0.03
Cherokee (50)	129	0.21
Cheyenne (1)	1	0.00
Chickasaw (7)	11	0.02
Chippewa (4)	7	0.01
Choctaw (30)	42	0.07
Comanche (2)	10	0.02
Cree	1	0.00
Creek (5)	10	0.02
Crow (1)	1	0.00
Delaware	2	0.00
Houma	1	0.00
Iroquois (3)	5	0.01
Kiowa (3)	3	0.00
Latin American Indians (37)	45	0.07
Lumbee (3)	4	0.01
Menominee	1	0.00
Navajo (16)	18	0.03
Osage (2)	3	0.00
Ottawa	1	0.00
Potawatomi (4)	7	0.01
Pueblo	3	0.00
Seminole (3)	3	0.00
Sioux (3)	6	0.01
Yuman (3)	3	0.00
All other tribes (14)	24	0.04
American Indian tribes, not spec.	24	0.04
Arab:	179	0.30
Lebanese	84	0.14
Palestinian	55	0.09
Syrian	40	0.07
Armenian	19	0.03
Asian:	2,266	3.71
Cambodian (20)	31	0.05
Chinese, ex. Taiwanese (257)	348	0.57
Filipino (203)	333	0.54
Indian (346)	376	0.62
Indonesian (6)	6	0.01
Japanese (64)	142	0.23
Korean (204)	275	0.45
Laotian (5)	9	0.01
Malaysian (2)	4	0.01
Pakistani (104)	127	0.21
Sri Lankan (4)	4	0.01
Taiwanese (18)	20	0.03
Thai (21)	26	0.04
Vietnamese (414)	462	0.76
Other Asian, specified	2	0.00
Other Asian, not specified (49)	101	0.17
Australian	11	0.02
Austrian	111	0.18
Basque	6	0.01
Belgian	111	0.18
Brazilian	17	0.03
British	251	0.42
Canadian	178	0.29
Celtic	9	0.01
Croatian	13	0.02
Czech	753	1.25
Czechoslovakian	138	0.23
Danish	211	0.35
Dutch	755	1.25
Eastern European	15	0.02
English	5,895	9.76
European	745	1.23
Finnish	90	0.15
French, except Basque	2,011	3.33
French Canadian	277	0.46
German	10,889	18.03
Greek	169	0.28
Hawaii Native/Pacific Islander:	140	0.23
Micronesian: (21)	33	0.05
Guamanian/Chamorro (19)	31	0.05
Other Micronesian (2)	2	0.00
Polynesian: (24)	71	0.12
Native Hawaiian (9)	39	0.06
Samoan (15)	27	0.04
Tongan	1	0.00
Other Polynesian	4	0.01
Other Pac. Isl., specified	2	0.00
Other Pac. Isl., not spec. (14)	34	0.06
Hispanic or Latino:	13,511	22.10
Central American:	192	0.31
Costa Rican	2	0.00
Guatemalan	18	0.03
Honduran	46	0.08
Nicaraguan	22	0.04
Panamanian	34	0.06
Salvadoran	59	0.10
Other Central American	11	0.02
Cuban	83	0.14
Dominican Republic	11	0.02
Mexican	9,919	16.22
Puerto Rican	374	0.61
South American:	127	0.21
Argentinean	7	0.01
Bolivian	8	0.01
Chilean	18	0.03
Colombian	48	0.08
Ecuadorian	10	0.02
Paraguayan	1	0.00
Peruvian	8	0.01
Venezuelan	20	0.03
Other South American	7	0.01
Other Hispanic or Latino	2,805	4.59
Hungarian	134	0.22
Iranian	62	0.10
Irish	6,528	10.81
Italian	2,110	3.49
Latvian	14	0.02
Lithuanian	22	0.04
Luxemburger	17	0.03
Macedonian	7	0.01
Northern European	70	0.12
Norwegian	739	1.22
Pennsylvania German	10	0.02
Polish	950	1.57
Portuguese	118	0.20
Romanian	20	0.03
Russian	130	0.22
Scandinavian	121	0.20
Scotch-Irish	1,318	2.18
Scottish	1,436	2.38
Serbian	22	0.04
Slavic	14	0.02
Slovak	51	0.08
Slovene	6	0.01
Swedish	960	1.59
Swiss	125	0.21
Turkish	14	0.02
Ukrainian	23	0.04
United States or American	3,221	5.33
Welsh	394	0.65
West Indian, excl. Hispanic:	94	0.16
Barbadian	13	0.02
Belizean	6	0.01
Dutch West Indian	7	0.01
Haitian	7	0.01
Jamaican	61	0.10
White:	48,261	78.94
Not Hispanic (40,113)	40,869	66.85
Hispanic (6,814)	7,392	12.09
Yugoslavian	7	0.01

Notes: 1. Figures in the "Number" column do not add up to the total population due to: a) Ancestry/Race overlap — e.g. persons can report being both White and Irish, b) persons of Hispanic origin can report being any race, c) persons reporting two ancestries are counted in both categories. 2. Numbers in parentheses indicate the number of persons reporting this ancestry/race alone, not in combination with any other ancestry/race. 3. Refer to the Explanation of Data in the front of the book for more detailed information.

Rowlett

Place Type: City
County: Dallas
Population: 44,503

Ancestry/Race	Number	%
Acadian/Cajun	71	0.16
Afghan	24	0.05
African American/Black:	4,162	9.35
Not Hispanic (3,959)	4,093	9.20
Hispanic (51)	69	0.16
African, sub-Saharan:	669	1.51
African	390	0.88
Ethiopian	35	0.08
Nigerian	221	0.50
South African	23	0.05
Am. Ind. or Alaska Nat., not spec.	81	0.18
Alsatian	5	0.01
American Indian tribes, specified:	292	0.66
Apache (3)	4	0.01
Blackfeet (2)	7	0.02
Cherokee (38)	80	0.18
Chickasaw (8)	10	0.02
Choctaw (56)	82	0.18
Comanche (2)	4	0.01
Cree	1	0.00
Creek (3)	15	0.03
Delaware (5)	6	0.01
Kiowa (1)	1	0.00
Latin American Indians (19)	22	0.05
Lumbee (5)	5	0.01
Navajo (4)	6	0.01
Osage (1)	5	0.01
Ottawa (1)	1	0.00
Potawatomi	2	0.00
Seminole	4	0.01
Sioux (3)	12	0.03
Ute	2	0.00
All other tribes (10)	23	0.05
American Indian tribes, not spec.	13	0.03
Arab:	223	0.50
Arab/Arabic	17	0.04
Egyptian	7	0.02
Jordanian	8	0.02
Lebanese	139	0.31
Palestinian	22	0.05
Other Arab	30	0.07
Armenian	21	0.05
Asian:	1,703	3.83
Bangladeshi	1	0.00
Cambodian (38)	49	0.11
Chinese, ex. Taiwanese (139)	178	0.40
Filipino (271)	320	0.72
Indian (370)	390	0.88
Indonesian (1)	10	0.02
Japanese (24)	41	0.09
Korean (85)	103	0.23
Laotian (27)	34	0.08
Malaysian (1)	1	0.00
Pakistani (15)	24	0.05
Thai (28)	42	0.09
Vietnamese (437)	458	1.03
Other Asian, not specified (25)	52	0.12
Australian	9	0.02
Austrian	50	0.11
Basque	6	0.01
Belgian	42	0.09
Brazilian	28	0.06
British	183	0.41
Canadian	108	0.24
Croatian	17	0.04
Czech	333	0.75
Czechoslovakian	109	0.25
Danish	154	0.35
Dutch	645	1.46
English	4,425	9.98
European	236	0.53
Finnish	50	0.11
French, except Basque	1,330	3.00
French Canadian	234	0.53
German	5,916	13.35
Greek	72	0.16
Guyanese	10	0.02
Hawaii Native/Pacific Islander:	60	0.13
Micronesian: (10)	11	0.02
Guamanian/Chamorro (5)	6	0.01
Other Micronesian (5)	5	0.01
Polynesian: (14)	35	0.08
Native Hawaiian (5)	18	0.04
Samoan (9)	16	0.04
Other Polynesian	1	0.00
Other Pac. Isl., not spec. (1)	14	0.03
Hispanic or Latino:	3,899	8.76
Central American:	132	0.30
Costa Rican	16	0.04
Guatemalan	32	0.07
Honduran	19	0.04
Nicaraguan	7	0.02
Panamanian	4	0.01
Salvadoran	53	0.12
Other Central American	1	0.00
Cuban	62	0.14
Dominican Republic	10	0.02
Mexican	2,656	5.97
Puerto Rican	135	0.30
South American:	123	0.28
Argentinean	1	0.00
Bolivian	1	0.00
Chilean	1	0.00
Colombian	66	0.15
Ecuadorian	7	0.02
Peruvian	18	0.04
Uruguayan	2	0.00
Venezuelan	16	0.04
Other South American	11	0.02
Other Hispanic or Latino	781	1.75
Hungarian	73	0.16
Irish	5,138	11.59
Italian	1,128	2.54
Lithuanian	27	0.06
Macedonian	6	0.01
Northern European	25	0.06
Norwegian	269	0.61
Polish	810	1.83
Portuguese	19	0.04
Romanian	33	0.07
Russian	143	0.32
Scandinavian	51	0.12
Scotch-Irish	935	2.11
Scottish	922	2.08
Slavic	30	0.07
Slovak	17	0.04
Swedish	434	0.98
Swiss	73	0.16
Turkish	13	0.03
Ukrainian	58	0.13
United States or American	4,410	9.95
Welsh	183	0.41
West Indian, excl. Hispanic:	54	0.12
Bahamian	6	0.01
Dutch West Indian	7	0.02
Jamaican	30	0.07
West Indian	11	0.02
White:	37,111	83.39
Not Hispanic (34,417)	34,862	78.34
Hispanic (1,989)	2,249	5.05
Yugoslavian	29	0.07

Saginaw

Place Type: City
County: Tarrant
Population: 12,374

Ancestry/Race	Number	%
African American/Black:	256	2.07
Not Hispanic (226)	242	1.96
Hispanic (13)	14	0.11
African, sub-Saharan:	14	0.11
African	8	0.06
Sudanese	6	0.05
Am. Ind. or Alaska Nat., not spec.	35	0.28
American Indian tribes, specified:	145	1.17
Blackfeet	1	0.01
Cherokee (27)	58	0.47
Chickasaw (2)	4	0.03
Chippewa (3)	3	0.02
Choctaw (10)	17	0.14
Comanche	6	0.05
Creek (5)	5	0.04
Crow (1)	1	0.01
Kiowa (6)	9	0.07
Latin American Indians (9)	10	0.08
Navajo (4)	5	0.04
Osage (2)	2	0.02
Potawatomi (1)	1	0.01
Pueblo (1)	3	0.02
Seminole (1)	1	0.01
Sioux (4)	6	0.05
All other tribes (10)	13	0.11
American Indian tribes, not spec.	5	0.04
Arab:	8	0.06
Lebanese	8	0.06
Asian:	237	1.92
Chinese, ex. Taiwanese (10)	13	0.11
Filipino (36)	55	0.44
Indian (7)	15	0.12
Japanese (16)	29	0.23
Korean (21)	32	0.26
Laotian (5)	6	0.05
Thai (12)	19	0.15
Vietnamese (36)	50	0.40
Other Asian, specified	1	0.01
Other Asian, not specified (7)	17	0.14
Austrian	9	0.07
Brazilian	11	0.09
British	35	0.28
Canadian	11	0.09
Czech	88	0.71
Czechoslovakian	25	0.20
Danish	46	0.37
Dutch	176	1.42
English	891	7.19
European	50	0.40
Finnish	23	0.19
French, except Basque	263	2.12
French Canadian	42	0.34
German	1,679	13.54
Hawaii Native/Pacific Islander:	5	0.04
Micronesian:	1	0.01
Guamanian/Chamorro	1	0.01
Polynesian:	3	0.02
Native Hawaiian	3	0.02
Other Pac. Isl., not spec.	1	0.01
Hispanic or Latino:	1,823	14.73
Central American:	4	0.03
Panamanian	4	0.03
Dominican Republic	1	0.01
Mexican	1,367	11.05
Puerto Rican	47	0.38
South American:	22	0.18
Argentinean	2	0.02
Colombian	7	0.06
Ecuadorian	4	0.03
Peruvian	7	0.06
Venezuelan	2	0.02
Other Hispanic or Latino	382	3.09
Hungarian	39	0.31
Irish	1,472	11.87
Italian	328	2.65
Lithuanian	7	0.06
Norwegian	77	0.62
Polish	73	0.59
Portuguese	69	0.56
Russian	9	0.07
Scandinavian	12	0.10
Scotch-Irish	201	1.62
Scottish	146	1.18
Slavic	11	0.09

Notes: 1. Figures in the "Number" column do not add up to the total population due to: a) Ancestry/Race overlap — e.g. persons can report being both White and Irish, b) persons of Hispanic origin can report being any race, c) persons reporting two ancestries are counted in both categories. 2. Numbers in parentheses indicate the number of persons reporting this ancestry/race alone, not in combination with any other ancestry/race. 3. Refer to the Explanation of Data in the front of the book for more detailed information.

Slovak	11	0.09
Slovene	12	0.10
Swedish	56	0.45
Swiss	8	0.06
Turkish	19	0.15
United States or American	1,277	10.30
Welsh	71	0.57
West Indian, excl. Hispanic:	11	0.09
Dutch West Indian	11	0.09
White:	11,100	89.70
Not Hispanic (9,928)	10,069	81.37
Hispanic (916)	1,031	8.33

San Angelo

Place Type: City
County: Tom Green
Population: 88,439

Ancestry/Race	Number	%
Acadian/Cajun	29	0.03
African American/Black:	4,629	5.23
Not Hispanic (4,013)	4,295	4.86
Hispanic (172)	334	0.38
African, sub-Saharan:	154	0.17
African	134	0.15
Nigerian	20	0.02
Alaska Native tribes, specified:	7	0.01
Alaska Athabascan	1	0.00
Aleut (2)	2	0.00
Eskimo	3	0.00
Tlingit-Haida (1)	1	0.00
Alaska Native tribes, not specified	2	0.00
Am. Ind. or Alaska Nat., not spec.	384	0.43
Alsatian	6	0.01
American Indian tribes, specified:	624	0.71
Apache (30)	49	0.06
Blackfeet (4)	17	0.02
Cherokee (68)	195	0.22
Cheyenne (1)	2	0.00
Chickasaw (14)	21	0.02
Chippewa (9)	15	0.02
Choctaw (46)	87	0.10
Colville	1	0.00
Comanche (2)	20	0.02
Creek (5)	11	0.01
Crow	1	0.00
Iroquois (3)	4	0.00
Latin American Indians (43)	57	0.06
Lumbee (6)	6	0.01
Menominee (1)	1	0.00
Navajo (7)	8	0.01
Osage	2	0.00
Pima (1)	4	0.00
Potawatomi (12)	23	0.03
Pueblo (5)	12	0.01
Puget Sound Salish (1)	1	0.00
Seminole (2)	10	0.01
Shoshone (2)	5	0.01
Sioux (14)	23	0.03
Tohono O'Odham (4)	4	0.00
Ute (1)	7	0.01
Yakama (1)	1	0.00
All other tribes (19)	37	0.04
American Indian tribes, not spec.	64	0.07
Arab:	65	0.07
Arab/Arabic	9	0.01
Lebanese	35	0.04
Palestinian	21	0.02
Asian:	1,216	1.37
Bangladeshi (6)	6	0.01
Cambodian (1)	1	0.00
Chinese, ex. Taiwanese (84)	114	0.13
Filipino (186)	303	0.34
Hmong (1)	2	0.00
Indian (111)	127	0.14
Indonesian (1)	1	0.00
Japanese (44)	94	0.11
Korean (105)	181	0.20
Laotian (66)	78	0.09
Malaysian	1	0.00
Pakistani (9)	11	0.01
Sri Lankan (1)	1	0.00
Taiwanese (1)	2	0.00
Thai (37)	55	0.06
Vietnamese (156)	180	0.20
Other Asian, specified (2)	4	0.00
Other Asian, not specified (17)	55	0.06
Australian	17	0.02
Austrian	58	0.07
Basque	9	0.01
Belgian	59	0.07
Brazilian	14	0.02
British	270	0.30
Bulgarian	9	0.01
Canadian	96	0.11
Croatian	66	0.07
Czech	627	0.71
Czechoslovakian	255	0.29
Danish	181	0.20
Dutch	934	1.05
English	7,141	8.06
European	611	0.69
Finnish	56	0.06
French, except Basque	1,807	2.04
French Canadian	201	0.23
German	11,083	12.51
Greek	201	0.23
Hawaii Native/Pacific Islander:	137	0.15
Micronesian: (30)	37	0.04
Guamanian/Chamorro (29)	36	0.04
Other Micronesian (1)	1	0.00
Polynesian: (34)	75	0.08
Native Hawaiian (25)	60	0.07
Samoan (8)	12	0.01
Other Polynesian (1)	3	0.00
Other Pac. Isl., specified	1	0.00
Other Pac. Isl., not spec. (5)	24	0.03
Hispanic or Latino:	29,321	33.15
Central American:	65	0.07
Costa Rican	2	0.00
Guatemalan	6	0.01
Honduran	13	0.01
Nicaraguan	4	0.00
Panamanian	28	0.03
Salvadoran	10	0.01
Other Central American	2	0.00
Cuban	43	0.05
Dominican Republic	3	0.00
Mexican	22,337	25.26
Puerto Rican	278	0.31
South American:	42	0.05
Argentinean	1	0.00
Bolivian	2	0.00
Chilean	1	0.00
Colombian	15	0.02
Ecuadorian	6	0.01
Paraguayan	1	0.00
Peruvian	13	0.01
Other South American	3	0.00
Other Hispanic or Latino	6,553	7.41
Hungarian	99	0.11
Iranian	29	0.03
Irish	7,369	8.32
Italian	1,111	1.25
Lithuanian	62	0.07
Luxemburger	14	0.02
New Zealander	6	0.01
Northern European	132	0.15
Norwegian	660	0.74
Pennsylvania German	48	0.05
Polish	758	0.86
Portuguese	45	0.05
Romanian	28	0.03
Russian	142	0.16
Scandinavian	67	0.08
Scotch-Irish	2,236	2.52
Scottish	1,410	1.59
Serbian	37	0.04
Slavic	61	0.07
Slovak	37	0.04
Slovene	8	0.01
Swedish	506	0.57
Swiss	89	0.10
Turkish	42	0.05
Ukrainian	60	0.07
United States or American	6,986	7.88
Welsh	362	0.41
West Indian, excl. Hispanic:	162	0.18
Belizean	8	0.01
Dutch West Indian	113	0.13
Haitian	3	0.00
Jamaican	3	0.00
Trinidadian and Tobagonian	24	0.03
West Indian	11	0.01
White:	70,087	79.25
Not Hispanic (52,934)	53,715	60.74
Hispanic (15,249)	16,372	18.51
Yugoslavian	32	0.04

San Antonio

Place Type: City
County: Bexar
Population: 1,144,646

Ancestry/Race	Number	%
Acadian/Cajun	337	0.03
Afghan	49	0.00
African American/Black:	84,250	7.36
Not Hispanic (74,778)	78,542	6.86
Hispanic (3,342)	5,708	0.50
African, sub-Saharan:	4,192	0.37
African	3,508	0.31
Cape Verdean	34	0.00
Ethiopian	48	0.00
Ghanian	8	0.00
Liberian	6	0.00
Nigerian	303	0.03
Senegalese	56	0.00
South African	83	0.01
Sudanese	83	0.01
Zairian	9	0.00
Zimbabwean	18	0.00
Other sub-Saharan African	36	0.00
Alaska Native tribes, specified:	52	0.00
Alaska Athabascan (4)	10	0.00
Aleut (6)	12	0.00
Eskimo (12)	17	0.00
Tlingit-Haida (8)	13	0.00
Alaska Native tribes, not specified	23	0.00
Am. Ind. or Alaska Nat., not spec.	6,958	0.61
Albanian	52	0.00
Alsatian	482	0.04
American Indian tribes, specified:	6,814	0.60
Apache (340)	590	0.05
Blackfeet (29)	148	0.01
Cherokee (640)	1,963	0.17
Cheyenne (8)	32	0.00
Chickasaw (38)	102	0.01
Chippewa (59)	111	0.01
Choctaw (164)	411	0.04
Colville	1	0.00
Comanche (52)	140	0.01
Cree	14	0.00
Creek (46)	116	0.01
Crow (8)	22	0.00
Delaware (13)	22	0.00
Houma (1)	3	0.00
Iroquois (51)	102	0.01
Kiowa (7)	9	0.00
Latin American Indians (1,107)	1,624	0.14
Lumbee (13)	23	0.00
Menominee (2)	4	0.00
Navajo (113)	191	0.02
Osage (13)	28	0.00
Ottawa (5)	10	0.00
Paiute (18)	22	0.00
Pima (9)	11	0.00
Potawatomi (26)	42	0.00

Notes: 1. Figures in the "Number" column do not add up to the total population due to: a) Ancestry/Race overlap — e.g. persons can report being both White and Irish, b) persons of Hispanic origin can report being any race, c) persons reporting two ancestries are counted in both categories. 2. Numbers in parentheses indicate the number of persons reporting this ancestry/race alone, not in combination with any other ancestry/race. 3. Refer to the Explanation of Data in the front of the book for more detailed information.

Ancestry/Race	Number	%
Pueblo (62)	115	0.01
Puget Sound Salish (4)	8	0.00
Seminole (37)	104	0.01
Shoshone (2)	12	0.00
Sioux (106)	203	0.02
Tohono O'Odham (12)	15	0.00
Ute (2)	7	0.00
Yaqui (31)	61	0.01
Yuman (2)	5	0.00
All other tribes (309)	543	0.05
American Indian tribes, not spec.	1,664	0.15
Arab:	3,787	0.33
Arab/Arabic	1,011	0.09
Egyptian	203	0.02
Iraqi	5	0.00
Jordanian	236	0.02
Lebanese	1,389	0.12
Moroccan	96	0.01
Palestinian	184	0.02
Syrian	256	0.02
Other Arab	407	0.04
Armenian	314	0.03
Asian:	24,633	2.15
Bangladeshi (35)	44	0.00
Cambodian (121)	143	0.01
Chinese, ex. Taiwanese (3,108)	3,972	0.35
Filipino (3,815)	5,580	0.49
Hmong (4)	7	0.00
Indian (3,378)	3,927	0.34
Indonesian (41)	73	0.01
Japanese (1,267)	2,414	0.21
Korean (2,102)	2,957	0.26
Laotian (131)	156	0.01
Malaysian (10)	28	0.00
Pakistani (334)	456	0.04
Sri Lankan (39)	47	0.00
Taiwanese (163)	223	0.02
Thai (481)	725	0.06
Vietnamese (2,168)	2,453	0.21
Other Asian, specified (26)	101	0.01
Other Asian, not specified (380)	1,327	0.12
Assyrian/Chaldean/Syriac	11	0.00
Australian	156	0.01
Austrian	1,199	0.10
Basque	189	0.02
Belgian	726	0.06
Brazilian	110	0.01
British	2,833	0.25
Bulgarian	33	0.00
Canadian	1,379	0.12
Celtic	314	0.03
Croatian	409	0.04
Czech	4,622	0.40
Czechoslovakian	1,141	0.10
Danish	2,166	0.19
Dutch	7,096	0.62
Eastern European	336	0.03
English	57,099	4.99
Estonian	14	0.00
European	4,343	0.38
Finnish	447	0.04
French, except Basque	19,624	1.71
French Canadian	3,493	0.31
German	103,366	9.03
German Russian	23	0.00
Greek	2,060	0.18
Guyanese	118	0.01
Hawaii Native/Pacific Islander:	2,093	0.18
Melanesian: (2)	4	0.00
Fijian	2	0.00
Other Melanesian (2)	2	0.00
Micronesian: (385)	573	0.05
Guamanian/Chamorro (363)	540	0.05
Other Micronesian (22)	33	0.00
Polynesian: (447)	896	0.08
Native Hawaiian (306)	663	0.06
Samoan (133)	214	0.02
Tongan (3)	5	0.00
Other Polynesian (5)	14	0.00
Other Pac. Isl., specified	41	0.00
Other Pac. Isl., not spec. (221)	579	0.05
Hispanic or Latino:	671,394	58.66
Central American:	3,492	0.31
Costa Rican	143	0.01
Guatemalan	584	0.05
Honduran	641	0.06
Nicaraguan	395	0.03
Panamanian	853	0.07
Salvadoran	665	0.06
Other Central American	211	0.02
Cuban	1,491	0.13
Dominican Republic	267	0.02
Mexican	473,420	41.36
Puerto Rican	7,774	0.68
South American:	2,288	0.20
Argentinean	223	0.02
Bolivian	73	0.01
Chilean	150	0.01
Colombian	888	0.08
Ecuadorian	113	0.01
Paraguayan	19	0.00
Peruvian	470	0.04
Uruguayan	26	0.00
Venezuelan	169	0.01
Other South American	157	0.01
Other Hispanic or Latino	182,662	15.96
Hungarian	1,272	0.11
Icelander	95	0.01
Iranian	954	0.08
Irish	59,637	5.21
Israeli	188	0.02
Italian	21,697	1.90
Latvian	158	0.01
Lithuanian	938	0.08
Luxemburger	30	0.00
Macedonian	7	0.00
Maltese	47	0.00
New Zealander	39	0.00
Northern European	492	0.04
Norwegian	4,914	0.43
Pennsylvania German	124	0.01
Polish	14,475	1.26
Portuguese	1,341	0.12
Romanian	449	0.04
Russian	3,126	0.27
Scandinavian	691	0.06
Scotch-Irish	14,938	1.31
Scottish	11,915	1.04
Serbian	66	0.01
Slavic	224	0.02
Slovak	549	0.05
Slovene	204	0.02
Swedish	5,322	0.46
Swiss	1,359	0.12
Turkish	247	0.02
Ukrainian	761	0.07
United States or American	36,123	3.16
Welsh	3,598	0.31
West Indian, excl. Hispanic:	1,486	0.13
Bahamian	33	0.00
Barbadian	63	0.01
Belizean	96	0.01
Bermudan	28	0.00
British West Indian	51	0.00
Dutch West Indian	230	0.02
Haitian	152	0.01
Jamaican	444	0.04
Trinidadian and Tobagonian	199	0.02
U.S. Virgin Islander	24	0.00
West Indian	166	0.01
White:	810,913	70.84
Not Hispanic (364,357)	374,557	32.72
Hispanic (410,351)	436,356	38.12
Yugoslavian	368	0.03

San Benito

Place Type: City
County: Cameron
Population: 23,444

Ancestry/Race	Number	%
African American/Black:	100	0.43
Not Hispanic (27)	34	0.15
Hispanic (47)	66	0.28
African, sub-Saharan:	37	0.16
African	32	0.14
Nigerian	5	0.02
Am. Ind. or Alaska Nat., not spec.	60	0.26
American Indian tribes, specified:	50	0.21
Apache (1)	1	0.00
Cherokee (5)	9	0.04
Chickasaw	1	0.00
Choctaw (1)	2	0.01
Creek (2)	2	0.01
Latin American Indians (20)	21	0.09
Potawatomi	4	0.02
All other tribes (6)	10	0.04
American Indian tribes, not spec.	37	0.16
Arab:	13	0.06
Lebanese	13	0.06
Asian:	75	0.32
Filipino (19)	19	0.08
Indian (26)	28	0.12
Japanese (4)	10	0.04
Korean (5)	5	0.02
Thai (1)	1	0.00
Other Asian, not specified (3)	12	0.05
Canadian	8	0.03
Czechoslovakian	6	0.03
Danish	40	0.17
Dutch	44	0.19
Eastern European	6	0.03
English	509	2.16
European	5	0.02
French, except Basque	157	0.66
French Canadian	36	0.15
German	645	2.73
Hawaii Native/Pacific Islander:	7	0.03
Micronesian: (1)	6	0.03
Guamanian/Chamorro (1)	6	0.03
Other Pac. Isl., not spec.	1	0.00
Hispanic or Latino:	20,380	86.93
Central American:	36	0.15
Guatemalan	2	0.01
Honduran	12	0.05
Nicaraguan	2	0.01
Panamanian	1	0.00
Salvadoran	19	0.08
Cuban	10	0.04
Dominican Republic	2	0.01
Mexican	14,893	63.53
Puerto Rican	37	0.16
South American:	8	0.03
Argentinean	1	0.00
Chilean	2	0.01
Colombian	5	0.02
Other Hispanic or Latino	5,394	23.01
Irish	367	1.55
Italian	66	0.28
Northern European	24	0.10
Norwegian	53	0.22
Pennsylvania German	6	0.03
Polish	73	0.31
Portuguese	8	0.03
Scandinavian	12	0.05
Scotch-Irish	88	0.37
Scottish	107	0.45
Swedish	103	0.44
Swiss	11	0.05
Ukrainian	10	0.04
United States or American	510	2.16
Welsh	38	0.16
West Indian, excl. Hispanic:	32	0.14
Jamaican	32	0.14

Notes: 1. Figures in the "Number" column do not add up to the total population due to: a) Ancestry/Race overlap — e.g. persons can report being both White and Irish, b) persons of Hispanic origin can report being any race, c) persons reporting two ancestries are counted in both categories. 2. Numbers in parentheses indicate the number of persons reporting this ancestry/race alone, not in combination with any other ancestry/race. 3. Refer to the Explanation of Data in the front of the book for more detailed information.

	Number	%
White:	18,382	78.41
Not Hispanic (2,919)	2,962	12.63
Hispanic (14,935)	15,420	65.77

San Elizario

Place Type: Census Designated Place
County: El Paso
Population: 11,046

Ancestry/Race	Number	%
African American/Black:	29	0.26
Not Hispanic (5)	6	0.05
Hispanic (12)	23	0.21
African, sub-Saharan:	9	0.08
African	9	0.08
Am. Ind. or Alaska Nat., not spec.	9	0.08
American Indian tribes, specified:	71	0.64
Apache (3)	22	0.20
Latin American Indians (1)	1	0.01
Pueblo (25)	28	0.25
Sioux (1)	20	0.18
American Indian tribes, not spec.	7	0.06
Asian:	4	0.04
Chinese, ex. Taiwanese (1)	2	0.02
Japanese	2	0.02
Hawaii Native/Pacific Islander:	1	0.01
Polynesian: (1)	1	0.01
Native Hawaiian (1)	1	0.01
Hispanic or Latino:	10,812	97.88
Central American:	8	0.07
Guatemalan	2	0.02
Honduran	1	0.01
Nicaraguan	1	0.01
Salvadoran	4	0.04
Cuban	1	0.01
Mexican	10,496	95.02
Puerto Rican	17	0.15
South American:	1	0.01
Ecuadorian	1	0.01
Other Hispanic or Latino	289	2.62
Irish	14	0.13
United States or American	135	1.24
White:	10,500	95.06
Not Hispanic (169)	177	1.60
Hispanic (10,251)	10,323	93.45

San Juan

Place Type: City
County: Hidalgo
Population: 26,229

Ancestry/Race	Number	%
Afghan	10	0.04
African American/Black:	121	0.46
Not Hispanic (29)	36	0.14
Hispanic (59)	85	0.32
Am. Ind. or Alaska Nat., not spec.	94	0.36
American Indian tribes, specified:	87	0.33
Apache (7)	8	0.03
Cherokee	11	0.04
Choctaw (1)	2	0.01
Iroquois	1	0.00
Latin American Indians (39)	47	0.18
Navajo	5	0.02
Potawatomi	1	0.00
Yaqui (1)	1	0.00
All other tribes (6)	11	0.04
American Indian tribes, not spec.	27	0.10
Asian:	30	0.11
Chinese, ex. Taiwanese (1)	2	0.01
Filipino (17)	18	0.07
Indian (4)	6	0.02
Japanese (1)	1	0.00
Korean	2	0.01
Taiwanese	1	0.00
Austrian	8	0.03
British	11	0.04
Canadian	11	0.04
Czech	21	0.08
Danish	19	0.07
Dutch	43	0.16
English	194	0.74
French, except Basque	53	0.20
French Canadian	21	0.08
German	225	0.86
Hawaii Native/Pacific Islander:	14	0.05
Micronesian: (7)	7	0.03
Guamanian/Chamorro (7)	7	0.03
Polynesian: (1)	3	0.01
Native Hawaiian	2	0.01
Samoan (1)	1	0.00
Other Pac. Isl., not spec. (1)	4	0.02
Hispanic or Latino:	24,950	95.12
Central American:	72	0.27
Costa Rican	7	0.03
Guatemalan	21	0.08
Honduran	29	0.11
Nicaraguan	1	0.00
Panamanian	1	0.00
Salvadoran	11	0.04
Other Central American	2	0.01
Cuban	21	0.08
Dominican Republic	5	0.02
Mexican	22,175	84.54
Puerto Rican	41	0.16
South American:	2	0.01
Chilean	1	0.00
Peruvian	1	0.00
Other Hispanic or Latino	2,634	10.04
Irish	203	0.78
Italian	60	0.23
Maltese	13	0.05
Norwegian	25	0.10
Polish	28	0.11
Scotch-Irish	11	0.04
Scottish	61	0.23
Swedish	25	0.10
Swiss	13	0.05
United States or American	356	1.36
Welsh	13	0.05
White:	21,753	82.93
Not Hispanic (1,166)	1,202	4.58
Hispanic (20,127)	20,551	78.35

San Marcos

Place Type: City
County: Hays
Population: 34,733

Ancestry/Race	Number	%
Acadian/Cajun	7	0.02
African American/Black:	2,101	6.05
Not Hispanic (1,860)	1,974	5.68
Hispanic (61)	127	0.37
African, sub-Saharan:	226	0.66
African	197	0.58
Ethiopian	13	0.04
Nigerian	8	0.02
Other sub-Saharan African	8	0.02
Alaska Native tribes, specified:	3	0.01
Eskimo (2)	2	0.01
Tlingit-Haida	1	0.00
Alaska Native tribes, not specified	9	0.03
Am. Ind. or Alaska Nat., not spec.	169	0.49
Alsatian	24	0.07
American Indian tribes, specified:	229	0.66
Apache (2)	14	0.04
Blackfeet (2)	9	0.03
Cherokee (31)	73	0.21
Cheyenne	1	0.00
Chickasaw (3)	7	0.02
Chippewa (1)	1	0.00
Choctaw (12)	23	0.07
Comanche (2)	4	0.01
Creek (1)	3	0.01
Crow	1	0.00
Houma (2)	2	0.01
Iroquois	3	0.01
Latin American Indians (30)	42	0.12
Navajo (1)	3	0.01
Osage (2)	4	0.01
Potawatomi	3	0.01
Pueblo	2	0.01
Seminole	4	0.01
Shoshone	1	0.00
Sioux (7)	12	0.03
Ute (3)	3	0.01
Yakama	1	0.00
Yuman	2	0.01
All other tribes (7)	11	0.03
American Indian tribes, not spec.	30	0.09
Arab:	52	0.15
Arab/Arabic	11	0.03
Lebanese	41	0.12
Asian:	596	1.72
Bangladeshi (1)	1	0.00
Cambodian (1)	2	0.01
Chinese, ex. Taiwanese (85)	108	0.31
Filipino (50)	73	0.21
Indian (102)	126	0.36
Indonesian (1)	1	0.00
Japanese (76)	102	0.29
Korean (28)	49	0.14
Laotian (7)	10	0.03
Pakistani (6)	16	0.05
Sri Lankan (6)	6	0.02
Taiwanese (2)	2	0.01
Thai (10)	15	0.04
Vietnamese (38)	45	0.13
Other Asian, specified	1	0.00
Other Asian, not specified (6)	39	0.11
Austrian	38	0.11
Basque	9	0.03
Belgian	16	0.05
British	148	0.44
Canadian	58	0.17
Celtic	5	0.01
Czech	498	1.46
Czechoslovakian	126	0.37
Danish	75	0.22
Dutch	361	1.06
English	2,245	6.60
European	329	0.97
Finnish	19	0.06
French, except Basque	995	2.93
French Canadian	69	0.20
German	5,209	15.32
Greek	39	0.11
Hawaii Native/Pacific Islander:	82	0.24
Micronesian: (11)	18	0.05
Guamanian/Chamorro (8)	15	0.04
Other Micronesian (3)	3	0.01
Polynesian: (22)	36	0.10
Native Hawaiian (16)	25	0.07
Samoan (6)	11	0.03
Other Pac. Isl., specified	1	0.00
Other Pac. Isl., not spec. (5)	27	0.08
Hispanic or Latino:	12,676	36.50
Central American:	62	0.18
Costa Rican	3	0.01
Guatemalan	18	0.05
Honduran	3	0.01
Nicaraguan	7	0.02
Panamanian	16	0.05
Salvadoran	12	0.03
Other Central American	3	0.01
Cuban	24	0.07
Dominican Republic	5	0.01
Mexican	9,058	26.08
Puerto Rican	126	0.36
South American:	56	0.16
Argentinean	2	0.01
Bolivian	8	0.02
Chilean	6	0.02
Colombian	16	0.05
Ecuadorian	7	0.02
Peruvian	6	0.02

Notes: 1. Figures in the "Number" column do not add up to the total population due to: a) Ancestry/Race overlap — e.g. persons can report being both White and Irish, b) persons of Hispanic origin can report being any race, c) persons reporting two ancestries are counted in both categories. 2. Numbers in parentheses indicate the number of persons reporting this ancestry/race alone, not in combination with any other ancestry/race. 3. Refer to the Explanation of Data in the front of the book for more detailed information.

Ancestry/Race	Number	%
Venezuelan	4	0.01
Other South American	7	0.02
Other Hispanic or Latino	3,345	9.63
Hungarian	103	0.30
Iranian	33	0.10
Irish	2,824	8.30
Italian	994	2.92
Lithuanian	46	0.14
Macedonian	10	0.03
Northern European	76	0.22
Norwegian	339	1.00
Pennsylvania German	8	0.02
Polish	565	1.66
Portuguese	21	0.06
Romanian	5	0.01
Russian	124	0.36
Scandinavian	45	0.13
Scotch-Irish	652	1.92
Scottish	826	2.43
Serbian	10	0.03
Slavic	8	0.02
Slovak	30	0.09
Swedish	251	0.74
Swiss	62	0.18
Turkish	8	0.02
Ukrainian	47	0.14
United States or American	1,303	3.83
Welsh	251	0.74
West Indian, excl. Hispanic:	44	0.13
Haitian	14	0.04
Jamaican	30	0.09
White:	26,066	75.05
Not Hispanic (19,165)	19,516	56.19
Hispanic (6,035)	6,550	18.86
Yugoslavian	12	0.04

Schertz

Place Type: City
County: Guadalupe
Population: 18,694

Ancestry/Race	Number	%
Acadian/Cajun	8	0.04
African American/Black:	1,379	7.38
Not Hispanic (1,193)	1,308	7.00
Hispanic (35)	71	0.38
African, sub-Saharan:	17	0.09
African	17	0.09
Am. Ind. or Alaska Nat., not spec.	61	0.33
Alsatian	3	0.02
American Indian tribes, specified:	160	0.86
Apache (7)	12	0.06
Blackfeet (3)	7	0.04
Cherokee (27)	68	0.36
Chickasaw (4)	5	0.03
Choctaw (4)	10	0.05
Comanche	1	0.01
Creek (1)	1	0.01
Iroquois (1)	3	0.02
Latin American Indians (11)	23	0.12
Lumbee (4)	4	0.02
Navajo (9)	16	0.09
Pueblo	2	0.01
Sioux (1)	1	0.01
All other tribes (3)	7	0.04
American Indian tribes, not spec.	6	0.03
Arab:	39	0.21
Arab/Arabic	21	0.11
Lebanese	18	0.10
Asian:	518	2.77
Chinese, ex. Taiwanese (18)	35	0.19
Filipino (98)	149	0.80
Indian (25)	28	0.15
Japanese (50)	111	0.59
Korean (82)	113	0.60
Laotian (2)	2	0.01
Pakistani (1)	1	0.01
Taiwanese (2)	2	0.01
Thai (14)	24	0.13
Vietnamese (14)	21	0.11
Other Asian, specified (2)	9	0.05
Other Asian, not specified (16)	23	0.12
Australian	9	0.05
Belgian	13	0.07
British	90	0.49
Canadian	33	0.18
Celtic	24	0.13
Croatian	20	0.11
Czech	199	1.08
Czechoslovakian	34	0.18
Danish	48	0.26
Dutch	203	1.10
English	1,752	9.49
European	44	0.24
Finnish	39	0.21
French, except Basque	687	3.72
French Canadian	174	0.94
German	3,789	20.53
Greek	48	0.26
Guyanese	8	0.04
Hawaii Native/Pacific Islander:	60	0.32
Melanesian: (2)	2	0.01
Fijian (2)	2	0.01
Micronesian: (14)	14	0.07
Guamanian/Chamorro (14)	14	0.07
Polynesian: (15)	32	0.17
Native Hawaiian (7)	23	0.12
Samoan (4)	5	0.03
Other Polynesian (4)	4	0.02
Other Pac. Isl., specified	5	0.03
Other Pac. Isl., not spec. (3)	7	0.04
Hispanic or Latino:	3,640	19.47
Central American:	32	0.17
Costa Rican	2	0.01
Guatemalan	4	0.02
Nicaraguan	6	0.03
Panamanian	16	0.09
Salvadoran	2	0.01
Other Central American	2	0.01
Cuban	24	0.13
Dominican Republic	6	0.03
Mexican	2,452	13.12
Puerto Rican	176	0.94
South American:	21	0.11
Argentinean	8	0.04
Chilean	4	0.02
Colombian	9	0.05
Other Hispanic or Latino	929	4.97
Hungarian	68	0.37
Irish	2,296	12.44
Italian	558	3.02
Lithuanian	2	0.01
Norwegian	146	0.79
Polish	490	2.65
Portuguese	30	0.16
Russian	82	0.44
Scotch-Irish	539	2.92
Scottish	623	3.38
Slavic	12	0.07
Slovene	1	0.01
Swedish	164	0.89
Swiss	19	0.10
Turkish	9	0.05
Ukrainian	25	0.14
United States or American	1,293	7.01
Welsh	91	0.49
West Indian, excl. Hispanic:	4	0.02
Dutch West Indian	4	0.02
White:	15,899	85.05
Not Hispanic (13,026)	13,364	71.49
Hispanic (2,310)	2,535	13.56
Yugoslavian	8	0.04

Seagoville

Place Type: City
County: Dallas
Population: 10,823

Ancestry/Race	Number	%
Acadian/Cajun	2	0.02
African American/Black:	1,086	10.03
Not Hispanic (1,028)	1,062	9.81
Hispanic (13)	24	0.22
African, sub-Saharan:	63	0.59
African	50	0.47
Nigerian	8	0.08
South African	5	0.05
Alaska Native tribes, specified:	1	0.01
Alaska Athabascan (1)	1	0.01
Am. Ind. or Alaska Nat., not spec.	57	0.53
American Indian tribes, specified:	93	0.86
Apache (1)	3	0.03
Blackfeet	3	0.03
Cherokee (28)	49	0.45
Chickasaw (3)	4	0.04
Choctaw (9)	16	0.15
Comanche (1)	2	0.02
Creek (1)	2	0.02
Iroquois (1)	1	0.01
Latin American Indians (2)	7	0.06
Sioux (4)	5	0.05
All other tribes	1	0.01
American Indian tribes, not spec.	5	0.05
Arab:	5	0.05
Moroccan	5	0.05
Asian:	80	0.74
Cambodian (1)	1	0.01
Chinese, ex. Taiwanese (5)	6	0.06
Filipino (15)	15	0.14
Indian (23)	31	0.29
Indonesian (1)	1	0.01
Japanese (3)	7	0.06
Korean (7)	7	0.06
Pakistani (1)	1	0.01
Thai (2)	2	0.02
Vietnamese (2)	2	0.02
Other Asian, specified	1	0.01
Other Asian, not specified (1)	6	0.06
Canadian	23	0.22
Celtic	8	0.08
Czech	52	0.49
Czechoslovakian	19	0.18
Danish	10	0.09
Dutch	87	0.82
English	283	2.67
European	41	0.39
French, except Basque	93	0.88
French Canadian	19	0.18
German	965	9.10
Greek	8	0.08
Hawaii Native/Pacific Islander:	11	0.10
Micronesian: (2)	2	0.02
Guamanian/Chamorro (2)	2	0.02
Polynesian: (1)	3	0.03
Native Hawaiian (1)	3	0.03
Other Pac. Isl., not spec. (5)	6	0.06
Hispanic or Latino:	1,905	17.60
Central American:	24	0.22
Costa Rican	4	0.04
Guatemalan	3	0.03
Honduran	4	0.04
Panamanian	1	0.01
Salvadoran	12	0.11
Cuban	16	0.15
Dominican Republic	3	0.03
Mexican	1,465	13.54
Puerto Rican	27	0.25
South American:	40	0.37
Bolivian	2	0.02
Colombian	36	0.33
Other South American	2	0.02
Other Hispanic or Latino	330	3.05

Notes: 1. Figures in the "Number" column do not add up to the total population due to: a) Ancestry/Race overlap — e.g. persons can report being both White and Irish, b) persons of Hispanic origin can report being any race, c) persons reporting two ancestries are counted in both categories. 2. Numbers in parentheses indicate the number of persons reporting this ancestry/race alone, not in combination with any other ancestry/race. 3. Refer to the Explanation of Data in the front of the book for more detailed information.

Ancestry/Race	Number	%
Hungarian	7	0.07
Irish	972	9.16
Italian	121	1.14
Lithuanian	16	0.15
Norwegian	63	0.59
Polish	42	0.40
Portuguese	2	0.02
Russian	6	0.06
Scandinavian	6	0.06
Scotch-Irish	108	1.02
Scottish	112	1.06
Swedish	34	0.32
Ukrainian	6	0.06
United States or American	971	9.15
Welsh	32	0.30
West Indian, excl. Hispanic:	6	0.06
Bahamian	6	0.06
White:	8,761	80.95
Not Hispanic (7,618)	7,725	71.38
Hispanic (906)	1,036	9.57

Seguin

Place Type: City
County: Guadalupe
Population: 22,011

Ancestry/Race	Number	%
Acadian/Cajun	5	0.02
African American/Black:	2,103	9.55
Not Hispanic (1,946)	2,009	9.13
Hispanic (56)	94	0.43
African, sub-Saharan:	114	0.52
African	101	0.46
Nigerian	7	0.03
Somalian	6	0.03
Am. Ind. or Alaska Nat., not spec.	122	0.55
Alsatian	5	0.02
American Indian tribes, specified:	68	0.31
Apache (3)	6	0.03
Blackfeet	4	0.02
Cherokee (10)	25	0.11
Cheyenne (1)	1	0.00
Chickasaw	2	0.01
Choctaw (2)	3	0.01
Creek (1)	1	0.00
Delaware	1	0.00
Kiowa	1	0.00
Latin American Indians (10)	13	0.06
Potawatomi (3)	5	0.02
Pueblo (1)	1	0.00
Sioux (1)	2	0.01
All other tribes (1)	3	0.01
American Indian tribes, not spec.	25	0.11
Arab:	45	0.21
Other Arab	45	0.21
Asian:	254	1.15
Cambodian	5	0.02
Chinese, ex. Taiwanese (18)	25	0.11
Filipino (14)	28	0.13
Indian (30)	43	0.20
Japanese (37)	46	0.21
Korean (7)	10	0.05
Malaysian (1)	1	0.00
Pakistani (5)	9	0.04
Sri Lankan	1	0.00
Taiwanese	1	0.00
Vietnamese (59)	66	0.30
Other Asian, not specified (12)	19	0.09
Austrian	13	0.06
Belgian	10	0.05
British	23	0.11
Canadian	10	0.05
Croatian	12	0.05
Czech	97	0.44
Czechoslovakian	11	0.05
Danish	39	0.18
Dutch	57	0.26
English	954	4.37
European	36	0.16
Finnish	6	0.03
French, except Basque	241	1.10
French Canadian	89	0.41
German	3,118	14.29
Greek	18	0.08
Hawaii Native/Pacific Islander:	26	0.12
Micronesian: (7)	7	0.03
Guamanian/Chamorro (7)	7	0.03
Polynesian: (3)	13	0.06
Native Hawaiian (3)	12	0.05
Samoan	1	0.00
Other Pac. Isl., not spec. (2)	6	0.03
Hispanic or Latino:	11,669	53.01
Central American:	35	0.16
Guatemalan	7	0.03
Honduran	3	0.01
Nicaraguan	1	0.00
Panamanian	1	0.00
Salvadoran	21	0.10
Other Central American	2	0.01
Cuban	12	0.05
Mexican	8,158	37.06
Puerto Rican	38	0.17
South American:	30	0.14
Argentinean	4	0.02
Bolivian	5	0.02
Chilean	2	0.01
Colombian	9	0.04
Ecuadorian	2	0.01
Peruvian	5	0.02
Venezuelan	3	0.01
Other Hispanic or Latino	3,396	15.43
Hungarian	12	0.05
Irish	791	3.62
Italian	116	0.53
Lithuanian	11	0.05
Norwegian	254	1.16
Pennsylvania German	6	0.03
Polish	118	0.54
Portuguese	27	0.12
Russian	38	0.17
Scandinavian	10	0.05
Scotch-Irish	258	1.18
Scottish	172	0.79
Slavic	28	0.13
Slovene	12	0.05
Swedish	129	0.59
Ukrainian	24	0.11
United States or American	674	3.09
Welsh	40	0.18
West Indian, excl. Hispanic:	18	0.08
Jamaican	11	0.05
Other West Indian	7	0.03
White:	15,114	68.67
Not Hispanic (7,967)	8,102	36.81
Hispanic (6,430)	7,012	31.86

Sherman

Place Type: City
County: Grayson
Population: 35,082

Ancestry/Race	Number	%
Acadian/Cajun	76	0.22
African American/Black:	4,164	11.87
Not Hispanic (3,884)	4,092	11.66
Hispanic (54)	72	0.21
African, sub-Saharan:	112	0.32
African	87	0.25
Nigerian	7	0.02
Other sub-Saharan African	18	0.05
Alaska Native tribes, specified:	3	0.01
Aleut (2)	3	0.01
Alaska Native tribes, not specified	4	0.01
Am. Ind. or Alaska Nat., not spec.	208	0.59
American Indian tribes, specified:	625	1.78
Apache (6)	15	0.04
Blackfeet	7	0.02
Cherokee (57)	172	0.49
Cheyenne (1)	1	0.00
Chickasaw (26)	57	0.16
Chippewa (1)	2	0.01
Choctaw (164)	255	0.73
Comanche (8)	10	0.03
Creek (7)	19	0.05
Crow	1	0.00
Delaware (6)	6	0.02
Houma (1)	1	0.00
Iroquois (1)	2	0.01
Kiowa (2)	2	0.01
Latin American Indians (19)	23	0.07
Navajo (2)	4	0.01
Osage (5)	5	0.01
Potawatomi (4)	10	0.03
Seminole (3)	3	0.01
Sioux (2)	7	0.02
All other tribes (14)	23	0.07
American Indian tribes, not spec.	45	0.13
Arab:	64	0.18
Arab/Arabic	18	0.05
Jordanian	10	0.03
Lebanese	30	0.09
Syrian	6	0.02
Asian:	495	1.41
Bangladeshi (11)	11	0.03
Cambodian (5)	7	0.02
Chinese, ex. Taiwanese (43)	55	0.16
Filipino (47)	68	0.19
Indian (139)	155	0.44
Indonesian (2)	2	0.01
Japanese (12)	24	0.07
Korean (29)	41	0.12
Laotian (1)	2	0.01
Malaysian (1)	1	0.00
Pakistani (23)	27	0.08
Sri Lankan (1)	3	0.01
Taiwanese (6)	7	0.02
Thai (4)	8	0.02
Vietnamese (31)	36	0.10
Other Asian, specified (1)	4	0.01
Other Asian, not specified (6)	44	0.13
Australian	8	0.02
Austrian	22	0.06
Belgian	6	0.02
British	73	0.21
Canadian	50	0.14
Czech	146	0.42
Czechoslovakian	33	0.09
Danish	49	0.14
Dutch	497	1.42
English	3,231	9.24
European	292	0.84
Finnish	41	0.12
French, except Basque	718	2.05
French Canadian	41	0.12
German	3,284	9.39
Greek	19	0.05
Hawaii Native/Pacific Islander:	54	0.15
Micronesian: (2)	3	0.01
Guamanian/Chamorro (1)	2	0.01
Other Micronesian (1)	1	0.00
Polynesian: (5)	11	0.03
Native Hawaiian (4)	9	0.03
Samoan (1)	2	0.01
Other Pac. Isl., specified	3	0.01
Other Pac. Isl., not spec. (5)	37	0.11
Hispanic or Latino:	4,260	12.14
Central American:	162	0.46
Costa Rican	4	0.01
Guatemalan	5	0.01
Honduran	2	0.01
Nicaraguan	3	0.01
Panamanian	11	0.03
Salvadoran	134	0.38
Other Central American	3	0.01
Cuban	12	0.03
Dominican Republic	1	0.00
Mexican	3,512	10.01
Puerto Rican	34	0.10

Notes: 1. Figures in the "Number" column do not add up to the total population due to: a) Ancestry/Race overlap — e.g. persons can report being both White and Irish, b) persons of Hispanic origin can report being any race, c) persons reporting two ancestries are counted in both categories. 2. Numbers in parentheses indicate the number of persons reporting this ancestry/race alone, not in combination with any other ancestry/race. 3. Refer to the Explanation of Data in the front of the book for more detailed information.

Ancestry/Race	Number	%
South American:	14	0.04
Argentinean	5	0.01
Chilean	1	0.00
Colombian	1	0.00
Peruvian	2	0.01
Venezuelan	1	0.00
Other South American	4	0.01
Other Hispanic or Latino	525	1.50
Hungarian	46	0.13
Iranian	7	0.02
Irish	2,942	8.42
Italian	581	1.66
Lithuanian	7	0.02
Northern European	7	0.02
Norwegian	204	0.58
Pennsylvania German	39	0.11
Polish	194	0.55
Portuguese	15	0.04
Russian	101	0.29
Scandinavian	40	0.11
Scotch-Irish	709	2.03
Scottish	516	1.48
Serbian	8	0.02
Slovak	7	0.02
Swedish	176	0.50
Swiss	52	0.15
Ukrainian	9	0.03
United States or American	3,832	10.96
Welsh	207	0.59
West Indian, excl. Hispanic:	39	0.11
Dutch West Indian	35	0.10
Jamaican	4	0.01
White:	28,339	80.78
Not Hispanic (25,485)	26,052	74.26
Hispanic (2,041)	2,287	6.52
Yugoslavian	8	0.02

Snyder

Place Type: City
County: Scurry
Population: 10,783

Ancestry/Race	Number	%
African American/Black:	538	4.99
Not Hispanic (500)	518	4.80
Hispanic (6)	20	0.19
African, sub-Saharan:	13	0.12
African	13	0.12
Am. Ind. or Alaska Nat., not spec.	49	0.45
American Indian tribes, specified:	49	0.45
Apache (3)	4	0.04
Cherokee (6)	14	0.13
Chickasaw (3)	8	0.07
Choctaw (2)	5	0.05
Comanche (2)	2	0.02
Creek (1)	1	0.01
Kiowa (1)	1	0.01
Latin American Indians (7)	7	0.06
Navajo (1)	1	0.01
Osage (1)	1	0.01
Ottawa	1	0.01
Potawatomi	1	0.01
Sioux (1)	2	0.02
All other tribes (1)	1	0.01
American Indian tribes, not spec.	6	0.06
Asian:	34	0.32
Chinese, ex. Taiwanese (8)	8	0.07
Filipino (1)	5	0.05
Indian (4)	4	0.04
Japanese (5)	7	0.06
Korean (4)	5	0.05
Laotian (1)	1	0.01
Vietnamese (4)	4	0.04
Australian	8	0.07
British	6	0.06
Canadian	7	0.06
Czech	11	0.10
Czechoslovakian	6	0.06
Danish	14	0.13
Dutch	50	0.46
English	796	7.37
European	26	0.24
French, except Basque	119	1.10
German	746	6.91
Greek	3	0.03
Hawaii Native/Pacific Islander:	2	0.02
Polynesian:	1	0.01
Native Hawaiian	1	0.01
Other Pac. Isl., not spec.	1	0.01
Hispanic or Latino:	3,427	31.78
Central American:	1	0.01
Salvadoran	1	0.01
Cuban	2	0.02
Mexican	2,216	20.55
Puerto Rican	4	0.04
South American:	7	0.06
Argentinean	1	0.01
Chilean	2	0.02
Colombian	4	0.04
Other Hispanic or Latino	1,197	11.10
Irish	897	8.31
Norwegian	25	0.23
Pennsylvania German	9	0.08
Polish	20	0.19
Portuguese	6	0.06
Scotch-Irish	162	1.50
Scottish	114	1.06
Swedish	13	0.12
United States or American	1,282	11.87
Welsh	50	0.46
West Indian, excl. Hispanic:	27	0.25
Dutch West Indian	27	0.25
White:	8,698	80.66
Not Hispanic (6,732)	6,795	63.02
Hispanic (1,787)	1,903	17.65

Socorro

Place Type: City
County: El Paso
Population: 27,152

Ancestry/Race	Number	%
African American/Black:	125	0.46
Not Hispanic (30)	36	0.13
Hispanic (66)	89	0.33
African, sub-Saharan:	9	0.03
African	9	0.03
Am. Ind. or Alaska Nat., not spec.	157	0.58
American Indian tribes, specified:	219	0.81
Apache (11)	12	0.04
Cherokee (2)	7	0.03
Choctaw	2	0.01
Latin American Indians (19)	26	0.10
Lumbee	1	0.00
Navajo (4)	4	0.01
Pueblo (160)	165	0.61
Yaqui (2)	2	0.01
American Indian tribes, not spec.	35	0.13
Asian:	40	0.15
Chinese, ex. Taiwanese (8)	14	0.05
Filipino (8)	9	0.03
Indian (2)	7	0.03
Japanese	4	0.01
Vietnamese (2)	2	0.01
Other Asian, specified	1	0.00
Other Asian, not specified	3	0.01
Canadian	3	0.01
English	52	0.19
French, except Basque	49	0.18
French Canadian	7	0.03
German	120	0.43
Hawaii Native/Pacific Islander:	8	0.03
Other Pac. Isl., specified	1	0.00
Other Pac. Isl., not spec. (4)	7	0.03
Hispanic or Latino:	26,183	96.43
Central American:	10	0.04
Costa Rican	2	0.01
Guatemalan	3	0.01
Honduran	1	0.00
Salvadoran	4	0.01
Cuban	5	0.02
Mexican	22,438	82.64
Puerto Rican	29	0.11
South American:	5	0.02
Chilean	2	0.01
Colombian	2	0.01
Venezuelan	1	0.00
Other Hispanic or Latino	3,696	13.61
Icelander	6	0.02
Iranian	18	0.06
Irish	87	0.31
Italian	75	0.27
Lithuanian	7	0.03
Polish	7	0.03
Scottish	10	0.04
United States or American	618	2.22
Welsh	18	0.06
West Indian, excl. Hispanic:	16	0.06
West Indian	16	0.06
White:	20,651	76.06
Not Hispanic (729)	749	2.76
Hispanic (19,203)	19,902	73.30

South Houston

Place Type: City
County: Harris
Population: 15,833

Ancestry/Race	Number	%
Acadian/Cajun	22	0.14
African American/Black:	229	1.45
Not Hispanic (139)	159	1.00
Hispanic (26)	70	0.44
African, sub-Saharan:	6	0.04
African	6	0.04
Alaska Native tribes, specified:	1	0.01
Alaska Athabascan (1)	1	0.01
Am. Ind. or Alaska Nat., not spec.	80	0.51
American Indian tribes, specified:	79	0.50
Apache (1)	1	0.01
Blackfeet (2)	2	0.01
Cherokee (7)	19	0.12
Choctaw (5)	11	0.07
Comanche (1)	1	0.01
Creek	1	0.01
Latin American Indians (19)	35	0.22
Navajo	3	0.02
Ottawa (2)	2	0.01
Seminole	1	0.01
Yaqui (1)	1	0.01
All other tribes (2)	2	0.01
American Indian tribes, not spec.	8	0.05
Arab:	66	0.42
Arab/Arabic	66	0.42
Asian:	192	1.21
Bangladeshi (6)	6	0.04
Cambodian (6)	10	0.06
Chinese, ex. Taiwanese (9)	31	0.20
Filipino (12)	23	0.15
Indian (20)	46	0.29
Japanese (3)	5	0.03
Korean (5)	5	0.03
Pakistani (1)	6	0.04
Vietnamese (36)	40	0.25
Other Asian, not specified (5)	20	0.13
Canadian	10	0.06
Czech	39	0.25
Danish	15	0.10
Dutch	54	0.34
Eastern European	12	0.08
English	340	2.16
European	18	0.11
French, except Basque	108	0.69
French Canadian	13	0.08
German	546	3.47
Greek	6	0.04
Hawaii Native/Pacific Islander:	12	0.08

Notes: 1. Figures in the "Number" column do not add up to the total population due to: a) Ancestry/Race overlap — e.g. persons can report being both White and Irish, b) persons of Hispanic origin can report being any race, c) persons reporting two ancestries are counted in both categories. 2. Numbers in parentheses indicate the number of persons reporting this ancestry/race alone, not in combination with any other ancestry/race. 3. Refer to the Explanation of Data in the front of the book for more detailed information.

Ancestry/Race	Number	%
Polynesian: (5)	6	0.04
Native Hawaiian (4)	4	0.03
Samoan (1)	2	0.01
Other Pac. Isl., not spec. (3)	6	0.04
Hispanic or Latino:	12,338	77.93
Central American:	364	2.30
Costa Rican	4	0.03
Guatemalan	26	0.16
Honduran	66	0.42
Nicaraguan	5	0.03
Panamanian	2	0.01
Salvadoran	255	1.61
Other Central American	6	0.04
Cuban	22	0.14
Dominican Republic	1	0.01
Mexican	10,190	64.36
Puerto Rican	49	0.31
South American:	39	0.25
Argentinean	1	0.01
Chilean	1	0.01
Colombian	15	0.09
Paraguayan	1	0.01
Peruvian	14	0.09
Venezuelan	3	0.02
Other South American	4	0.03
Other Hispanic or Latino	1,673	10.57
Irish	396	2.52
Italian	136	0.87
Norwegian	6	0.04
Pennsylvania German	5	0.03
Polish	22	0.14
Romanian	9	0.06
Scotch-Irish	82	0.52
Scottish	76	0.48
Swedish	30	0.19
United States or American	303	1.93
Welsh	23	0.15
West Indian, excl. Hispanic:	15	0.10
Dutch West Indian	6	0.04
Trinidadian and Tobagonian	9	0.06
White:	10,997	69.46
Not Hispanic (3,103)	3,192	20.16
Hispanic (7,241)	7,805	49.30

Southlake

Place Type: City
County: Tarrant
Population: 21,519

Ancestry/Race	Number	%
Acadian/Cajun	51	0.24
African American/Black:	331	1.54
Not Hispanic (296)	327	1.52
Hispanic (3)	4	0.02
African, sub-Saharan:	21	0.10
African	12	0.06
South African	9	0.04
Am. Ind. or Alaska Nat., not spec.	28	0.13
Albanian	24	0.11
American Indian tribes, specified:	105	0.49
Blackfeet	1	0.00
Cherokee (15)	40	0.19
Chickasaw (1)	10	0.05
Choctaw (10)	20	0.09
Comanche (1)	1	0.00
Creek	4	0.02
Crow	1	0.00
Delaware	2	0.01
Kiowa	2	0.01
Latin American Indians (1)	1	0.00
Navajo (1)	1	0.00
Osage	2	0.01
Potawatomi (1)	2	0.01
Pueblo (3)	3	0.01
Shoshone	1	0.00
Sioux	1	0.00
All other tribes (5)	13	0.06
American Indian tribes, not spec.	3	0.01
Arab:	188	0.87
Arab/Arabic	21	0.10
Lebanese	124	0.58
Syrian	43	0.20
Armenian	15	0.07
Asian:	493	2.29
Bangladeshi	4	0.02
Cambodian (3)	3	0.01
Chinese, ex. Taiwanese (113)	133	0.62
Filipino (36)	55	0.26
Hmong (3)	3	0.01
Indian (125)	131	0.61
Indonesian (6)	6	0.03
Japanese (30)	53	0.25
Korean (31)	38	0.18
Laotian	1	0.00
Pakistani (8)	11	0.05
Sri Lankan (3)	4	0.02
Thai (3)	6	0.03
Vietnamese (14)	23	0.11
Other Asian, specified	1	0.00
Other Asian, not specified (2)	21	0.10
Australian	2	0.01
Austrian	68	0.32
Belgian	31	0.14
British	200	0.93
Bulgarian	9	0.04
Canadian	99	0.46
Croatian	76	0.35
Czech	137	0.64
Czechoslovakian	8	0.04
Danish	214	1.00
Dutch	331	1.54
English	3,763	17.50
Estonian	12	0.06
European	191	0.89
Finnish	106	0.49
French, except Basque	643	2.99
French Canadian	169	0.79
German	4,616	21.47
Greek	73	0.34
Hawaii Native/Pacific Islander:	8	0.04
Polynesian:	4	0.02
Native Hawaiian	4	0.02
Other Pac. Isl., specified	1	0.00
Other Pac. Isl., not spec. (2)	3	0.01
Hispanic or Latino:	789	3.67
Central American:	16	0.07
Costa Rican	4	0.02
Honduran	1	0.00
Nicaraguan	2	0.01
Panamanian	5	0.02
Salvadoran	1	0.00
Other Central American	3	0.01
Cuban	74	0.34
Dominican Republic	7	0.03
Mexican	425	1.97
Puerto Rican	62	0.29
South American:	51	0.24
Argentinean	4	0.02
Chilean	2	0.01
Colombian	13	0.06
Paraguayan	2	0.01
Peruvian	13	0.06
Uruguayan	7	0.03
Venezuelan	2	0.01
Other South American	8	0.04
Other Hispanic or Latino	154	0.72
Hungarian	111	0.52
Iranian	42	0.20
Irish	2,992	13.92
Italian	1,103	5.13
Latvian	17	0.08
Lithuanian	84	0.39
Northern European	55	0.26
Norwegian	393	1.83
Polish	553	2.57
Portuguese	54	0.25
Romanian	7	0.03
Russian	203	0.94
Scandinavian	27	0.13
Scotch-Irish	548	2.55
Scottish	835	3.88
Slavic	32	0.15
Slovak	58	0.27
Slovene	9	0.04
Swedish	515	2.40
Swiss	79	0.37
Turkish	7	0.03
Ukrainian	5	0.02
United States or American	1,899	8.83
Welsh	277	1.29
West Indian, excl. Hispanic:	4	0.02
Haitian	4	0.02
White:	20,572	95.60
Not Hispanic (19,789)	19,944	92.68
Hispanic (556)	628	2.92
Yugoslavian	80	0.37

Spring

Place Type: Census Designated Place
County: Harris
Population: 36,385

Ancestry/Race	Number	%
Acadian/Cajun	58	0.16
African American/Black:	2,691	7.40
Not Hispanic (2,500)	2,606	7.16
Hispanic (44)	85	0.23
African, sub-Saharan:	189	0.52
African	94	0.26
Nigerian	95	0.26
Alaska Native tribes, specified:	5	0.01
Aleut (2)	2	0.01
Eskimo	1	0.00
Tlingit-Haida (2)	2	0.01
Alaska Native tribes, not specified	1	0.00
Am. Ind. or Alaska Nat., not spec.	131	0.36
American Indian tribes, specified:	259	0.71
Apache (3)	9	0.02
Blackfeet (2)	5	0.01
Cherokee (22)	103	0.28
Cheyenne (3)	3	0.01
Chickasaw	3	0.01
Chippewa (1)	1	0.00
Choctaw (24)	34	0.09
Comanche (1)	4	0.01
Creek (5)	7	0.02
Delaware (2)	2	0.01
Houma (2)	3	0.01
Iroquois (1)	2	0.01
Kiowa (1)	1	0.00
Latin American Indians (10)	16	0.04
Lumbee (4)	4	0.01
Navajo	3	0.01
Osage (3)	4	0.01
Ottawa (5)	6	0.02
Potawatomi (3)	7	0.02
Pueblo (1)	7	0.02
Seminole	1	0.00
Sioux (6)	11	0.03
Yaqui	3	0.01
All other tribes (13)	20	0.05
American Indian tribes, not spec.	24	0.07
Arab:	167	0.46
Arab/Arabic	58	0.16
Jordanian	76	0.21
Lebanese	18	0.05
Syrian	9	0.02
Other Arab	6	0.02
Armenian	7	0.02
Asian:	694	1.91
Bangladeshi (8)	9	0.02
Cambodian (6)	6	0.02
Chinese, ex. Taiwanese (34)	55	0.15
Filipino (113)	171	0.47
Indian (91)	103	0.28
Indonesian (1)	1	0.00
Japanese (30)	56	0.15
Korean (31)	44	0.12

Notes: 1. Figures in the "Number" column do not add up to the total population due to: a) Ancestry/Race overlap — e.g. persons can report being both White and Irish, b) persons of Hispanic origin can report being any race, c) persons reporting two ancestries are counted in both categories. 2. Numbers in parentheses indicate the number of persons reporting this ancestry/race alone, not in combination with any other ancestry/race. 3. Refer to the Explanation of Data in the front of the book for more detailed information.

Laotian (3)	3	0.01
Pakistani (58)	74	0.20
Taiwanese (4)	4	0.01
Thai (8)	9	0.02
Vietnamese (109)	123	0.34
Other Asian, specified (1)	3	0.01
Other Asian, not specified (9)	33	0.09
Austrian	28	0.08
Belgian	63	0.17
Brazilian	18	0.05
British	109	0.30
Canadian	69	0.19
Celtic	19	0.05
Croatian	24	0.07
Czech	388	1.06
Czechoslovakian	178	0.49
Danish	160	0.44
Dutch	508	1.39
English	2,824	7.75
European	283	0.78
Finnish	90	0.25
French, except Basque	1,518	4.17
French Canadian	189	0.52
German	6,209	17.04
Greek	139	0.38
Hawaii Native/Pacific Islander:	95	0.26
Micronesian: (8)	10	0.03
Guamanian/Chamorro (8)	10	0.03
Polynesian: (35)	71	0.20
Native Hawaiian (11)	39	0.11
Samoan (5)	10	0.03
Tongan (19)	22	0.06
Other Pac. Isl., not spec. (2)	14	0.04
Hispanic or Latino:	5,844	16.06
Central American:	294	0.81
Costa Rican	16	0.04
Guatemalan	71	0.20
Honduran	57	0.16
Nicaraguan	14	0.04
Panamanian	8	0.02
Salvadoran	112	0.31
Other Central American	16	0.04
Cuban	58	0.16
Dominican Republic	20	0.05
Mexican	3,752	10.31
Puerto Rican	257	0.71
South American:	221	0.61
Argentinean	38	0.10
Bolivian	2	0.01
Chilean	12	0.03
Colombian	75	0.21
Ecuadorian	17	0.05
Peruvian	49	0.13
Uruguayan	5	0.01
Venezuelan	22	0.06
Other South American	1	0.00
Other Hispanic or Latino	1,242	3.41
Hungarian	57	0.16
Irish	4,629	12.71
Italian	1,308	3.59
Latvian	33	0.09
Lithuanian	10	0.03
Luxemburger	8	0.02
Norwegian	334	0.92
Polish	1,090	2.99
Portuguese	21	0.06
Romanian	51	0.14
Russian	145	0.40
Scandinavian	32	0.09
Scotch-Irish	800	2.20
Scottish	755	2.07
Serbian	26	0.07
Slavic	32	0.09
Slovak	43	0.12
Swedish	262	0.72
Swiss	73	0.20
Turkish	10	0.03
Ukrainian	81	0.22
United States or American	3,441	9.44
Welsh	211	0.58
West Indian, excl. Hispanic:	158	0.43
Barbadian	7	0.02
Belizean	10	0.03
Dutch West Indian	24	0.07
Jamaican	54	0.15
Trinidadian and Tobagonian	53	0.15
West Indian	10	0.03
White:	30,967	85.11
Not Hispanic (26,808)	27,255	74.91
Hispanic (3,395)	3,712	10.20
Yugoslavian	6	0.02

Stafford

Place Type: City
County: Fort Bend
Population: 15,681

Ancestry/Race	Number	%
Acadian/Cajun	5	0.03
African American/Black:	3,055	19.48
Not Hispanic (2,905)	2,977	18.98
Hispanic (51)	78	0.50
African, sub-Saharan:	386	2.47
African	208	1.33
Nigerian	158	1.01
South African	7	0.04
Other sub-Saharan African	13	0.08
Am. Ind. or Alaska Nat., not spec.	49	0.31
American Indian tribes, specified:	66	0.42
Apache (2)	2	0.01
Blackfeet (1)	8	0.05
Cherokee (12)	23	0.15
Chippewa (1)	1	0.01
Choctaw	9	0.06
Creek (2)	3	0.02
Delaware (2)	3	0.02
Houma (1)	1	0.01
Latin American Indians (3)	4	0.03
Navajo (2)	2	0.01
Osage	1	0.01
Sioux (5)	5	0.03
All other tribes (3)	4	0.03
American Indian tribes, not spec.	16	0.10
Arab:	160	1.02
Arab/Arabic	55	0.35
Lebanese	69	0.44
Syrian	12	0.08
Other Arab	24	0.15
Asian:	3,376	21.53
Bangladeshi (4)	4	0.03
Cambodian (5)	5	0.03
Chinese, ex. Taiwanese (498)	552	3.52
Filipino (500)	533	3.40
Indian (1,149)	1,219	7.77
Indonesian (11)	14	0.09
Japanese (8)	8	0.05
Korean (40)	44	0.28
Laotian (3)	4	0.03
Malaysian (4)	4	0.03
Pakistani (245)	348	2.22
Sri Lankan	3	0.02
Taiwanese (23)	24	0.15
Thai (21)	26	0.17
Vietnamese (458)	506	3.23
Other Asian, specified	1	0.01
Other Asian, not specified (61)	81	0.52
Australian	7	0.04
Austrian	26	0.17
Belgian	7	0.04
British	39	0.25
Czech	145	0.93
Czechoslovakian	7	0.04
Danish	32	0.20
Dutch	125	0.80
English	709	4.54
European	56	0.36
French, except Basque	420	2.69
French Canadian	96	0.61
German	1,169	7.48
Greek	64	0.41
Guyanese	18	0.12
Hawaii Native/Pacific Islander:	33	0.21
Micronesian: (3)	4	0.03
Guamanian/Chamorro (3)	4	0.03
Polynesian: (3)	3	0.02
Samoan (3)	3	0.02
Other Pac. Isl., specified	1	0.01
Other Pac. Isl., not spec. (3)	25	0.16
Hispanic or Latino:	3,653	23.30
Central American:	99	0.63
Costa Rican	4	0.03
Guatemalan	25	0.16
Honduran	3	0.02
Nicaraguan	5	0.03
Panamanian	13	0.08
Salvadoran	48	0.31
Other Central American	1	0.01
Cuban	26	0.17
Mexican	2,588	16.50
Puerto Rican	65	0.41
South American:	145	0.92
Argentinean	14	0.09
Bolivian	2	0.01
Colombian	42	0.27
Ecuadorian	3	0.02
Paraguayan	24	0.15
Peruvian	18	0.11
Venezuelan	30	0.19
Other South American	12	0.08
Other Hispanic or Latino	730	4.66
Hungarian	35	0.22
Iranian	75	0.48
Irish	777	4.97
Israeli	10	0.06
Italian	445	2.85
Latvian	15	0.10
Lithuanian	9	0.06
Norwegian	31	0.20
Polish	138	0.88
Portuguese	18	0.12
Romanian	7	0.04
Russian	19	0.12
Scotch-Irish	115	0.74
Scottish	212	1.36
Slovak	19	0.12
Swedish	47	0.30
Swiss	19	0.12
Turkish	6	0.04
Ukrainian	22	0.14
United States or American	541	3.46
Welsh	20	0.13
West Indian, excl. Hispanic:	244	1.56
Bahamian	17	0.11
Bermudan	12	0.08
British West Indian	28	0.18
Jamaican	98	0.63
Trinidadian and Tobagonian	30	0.19
West Indian	59	0.38
White:	7,709	49.16
Not Hispanic (5,590)	5,792	36.94
Hispanic (1,772)	1,917	12.22

Stephenville

Place Type: City
County: Erath
Population: 14,921

Ancestry/Race	Number	%
Acadian/Cajun	10	0.07
African American/Black:	259	1.74
Not Hispanic (217)	250	1.68
Hispanic (2)	9	0.06
African, sub-Saharan:	29	0.19
African	29	0.19
Alaska Native tribes, specified:	1	0.01
Aleut (1)	1	0.01
Am. Ind. or Alaska Nat., not spec.	58	0.39
American Indian tribes, specified:	111	0.74

Notes: 1. Figures in the "Number" column do not add up to the total population due to: a) Ancestry/Race overlap — e.g. persons can report being both White and Irish, b) persons of Hispanic origin can report being any race, c) persons reporting two ancestries are counted in both categories. 2. Numbers in parentheses indicate the number of persons reporting this ancestry/race alone, not in combination with any other ancestry/race. 3. Refer to the Explanation of Data in the front of the book for more detailed information.

Blackfeet (1)	3	0.02
Cherokee (13)	36	0.24
Chickasaw (1)	2	0.01
Chippewa	1	0.01
Choctaw (2)	9	0.06
Comanche (2)	5	0.03
Creek (3)	4	0.03
Delaware	1	0.01
Latin American Indians (21)	27	0.18
Pueblo	7	0.05
Seminole (1)	3	0.02
Shoshone	1	0.01
Sioux (4)	4	0.03
Yaqui (1)	1	0.01
All other tribes (4)	7	0.05
American Indian tribes, not spec.	11	0.07
Armenian	10	0.07
Asian:	142	0.95
Chinese, ex. Taiwanese (14)	22	0.15
Filipino (13)	20	0.13
Indian (35)	40	0.27
Japanese (6)	7	0.05
Korean (8)	13	0.09
Malaysian (3)	3	0.02
Taiwanese (5)	7	0.05
Thai (5)	5	0.03
Vietnamese (4)	7	0.05
Other Asian, not specified	18	0.12
Austrian	7	0.05
Basque	11	0.07
British	22	0.15
Canadian	5	0.03
Czech	106	0.70
Czechoslovakian	62	0.41
Danish	32	0.21
Dutch	268	1.78
English	1,521	10.11
European	97	0.64
French, except Basque	345	2.29
French Canadian	55	0.37
German	1,780	11.83
Greek	24	0.16
Hawaii Native/Pacific Islander:	18	0.12
Micronesian: (2)	2	0.01
Guamanian/Chamorro (2)	2	0.01
Polynesian: (2)	9	0.06
Native Hawaiian (1)	6	0.04
Samoan (1)	3	0.02
Other Pac. Isl., not spec. (4)	7	0.05
Hispanic or Latino:	1,725	11.56
Central American:	3	0.02
Costa Rican	3	0.02
Cuban	6	0.04
Dominican Republic	2	0.01
Mexican	1,342	8.99
Puerto Rican	27	0.18
South American:	8	0.05
Chilean	3	0.02
Colombian	4	0.03
Venezuelan	1	0.01
Other Hispanic or Latino	337	2.26
Hungarian	6	0.04
Irish	1,658	11.02
Italian	183	1.22
Northern European	70	0.47
Norwegian	41	0.27
Polish	85	0.56
Portuguese	16	0.11
Russian	5	0.03
Scotch-Irish	331	2.20
Scottish	265	1.76
Serbian	11	0.07
Swedish	118	0.78
Swiss	10	0.07
Ukrainian	7	0.05
United States or American	1,870	12.43
Welsh	41	0.27
West Indian, excl. Hispanic:	30	0.20
Dutch West Indian	30	0.20
White:	13,803	92.51
Not Hispanic (12,686)	12,807	85.83
Hispanic (868)	996	6.68

Sugar Land

Place Type: City
County: Fort Bend
Population: 63,328

Ancestry/Race	Number	%
Acadian/Cajun	35	0.06
Afghan	29	0.05
African American/Black:	3,473	5.48
Not Hispanic (3,242)	3,400	5.37
Hispanic (52)	73	0.12
African, sub-Saharan:	569	0.90
African	112	0.18
Ethiopian	5	0.01
Ghanian	26	0.04
Liberian	9	0.01
Nigerian	363	0.57
South African	54	0.09
Alaska Native tribes, specified:	1	0.00
Eskimo	1	0.00
Am. Ind. or Alaska Nat., not spec.	124	0.20
Albanian	8	0.01
American Indian tribes, specified:	199	0.31
Apache (4)	4	0.01
Blackfeet	2	0.00
Cherokee (31)	76	0.12
Chickasaw	1	0.00
Choctaw (19)	38	0.06
Comanche (1)	7	0.01
Creek (11)	16	0.03
Delaware (2)	6	0.01
Houma (1)	1	0.00
Iroquois	2	0.00
Latin American Indians (11)	15	0.02
Lumbee (2)	2	0.00
Osage (3)	4	0.01
Ottawa (5)	5	0.01
Potawatomi	2	0.00
Seminole	2	0.00
Sioux (1)	3	0.00
All other tribes (5)	13	0.02
American Indian tribes, not spec.	26	0.04
Arab:	994	1.57
Arab/Arabic	78	0.12
Egyptian	190	0.30
Jordanian	83	0.13
Lebanese	271	0.43
Moroccan	19	0.03
Palestinian	153	0.24
Syrian	155	0.24
Other Arab	45	0.07
Armenian	22	0.03
Asian:	16,206	25.59
Bangladeshi (20)	24	0.04
Cambodian (13)	16	0.03
Chinese, ex. Taiwanese (5,712)	5,997	9.47
Filipino (1,193)	1,299	2.05
Indian (4,326)	4,573	7.22
Indonesian (49)	59	0.09
Japanese (72)	140	0.22
Korean (373)	397	0.63
Malaysian (19)	23	0.04
Pakistani (856)	1,032	1.63
Sri Lankan (15)	15	0.02
Taiwanese (703)	836	1.32
Thai (44)	63	0.10
Vietnamese (1,241)	1,341	2.12
Other Asian, specified (14)	16	0.03
Other Asian, not specified (138)	375	0.59
Australian	35	0.06
Austrian	118	0.19
Basque	7	0.01
Belgian	22	0.03
Brazilian	27	0.04
British	602	0.95
Bulgarian	16	0.03
Canadian	185	0.29
Croatian	58	0.09
Czech	993	1.56
Czechoslovakian	208	0.33
Danish	361	0.57
Dutch	714	1.12
Eastern European	47	0.07
English	6,947	10.94
European	443	0.70
Finnish	76	0.12
French, except Basque	2,247	3.54
French Canadian	269	0.42
German	9,282	14.62
Greek	293	0.46
Guyanese	35	0.06
Hawaii Native/Pacific Islander:	60	0.09
Micronesian: (5)	6	0.01
Guamanian/Chamorro (5)	5	0.01
Other Micronesian	1	0.00
Polynesian: (7)	20	0.03
Native Hawaiian (4)	16	0.03
Samoan (3)	3	0.00
Other Polynesian	1	0.00
Other Pac. Isl., not spec. (6)	34	0.05
Hispanic or Latino:	5,053	7.98
Central American:	200	0.32
Costa Rican	14	0.02
Guatemalan	31	0.05
Honduran	27	0.04
Nicaraguan	23	0.04
Panamanian	11	0.02
Salvadoran	78	0.12
Other Central American	16	0.03
Cuban	254	0.40
Dominican Republic	27	0.04
Mexican	2,881	4.55
Puerto Rican	206	0.33
South American:	440	0.69
Argentinean	58	0.09
Bolivian	28	0.04
Chilean	24	0.04
Colombian	157	0.25
Ecuadorian	43	0.07
Paraguayan	4	0.01
Peruvian	42	0.07
Uruguayan	4	0.01
Venezuelan	47	0.07
Other South American	33	0.05
Other Hispanic or Latino	1,045	1.65
Hungarian	162	0.26
Iranian	423	0.67
Irish	5,896	9.28
Italian	1,959	3.08
Latvian	11	0.02
Lithuanian	63	0.10
Macedonian	18	0.03
Northern European	58	0.09
Norwegian	645	1.02
Pennsylvania German	30	0.05
Polish	1,419	2.23
Portuguese	134	0.21
Romanian	60	0.09
Russian	608	0.96
Scandinavian	63	0.10
Scotch-Irish	1,243	1.96
Scottish	1,274	2.01
Serbian	8	0.01
Slavic	15	0.02
Slovak	16	0.03
Slovene	25	0.04
Swedish	485	0.76
Swiss	117	0.18
Turkish	32	0.05
Ukrainian	56	0.09
United States or American	3,377	5.32
Welsh	238	0.37
West Indian, excl. Hispanic:	151	0.24
Barbadian	45	0.07
Jamaican	92	0.14
Trinidadian and Tobagonian	10	0.02

Notes: 1. Figures in the "Number" column do not add up to the total population due to: a) Ancestry/Race overlap — e.g. persons can report being both White and Irish, b) persons of Hispanic origin can report being any race, c) persons reporting two ancestries are counted in both categories. 2. Numbers in parentheses indicate the number of persons reporting this ancestry/race alone, not in combination with any other ancestry/race. 3. Refer to the Explanation of Data in the front of the book for more detailed information.

Ancestry/Race	Number	%
West Indian	4	0.01
White:	42,908	67.76
Not Hispanic (38,526)	39,388	62.20
Hispanic (3,272)	3,520	5.56
Yugoslavian	21	0.03

Sulphur Springs

Place Type: City
County: Hopkins
Population: 14,551

Ancestry/Race	Number	%
African American/Black:	2,120	14.57
Not Hispanic (2,055)	2,096	14.40
Hispanic (21)	24	0.16
African, sub-Saharan:	16	0.11
African	16	0.11
Am. Ind. or Alaska Nat., not spec.	67	0.46
American Indian tribes, specified:	118	0.81
Apache	4	0.03
Blackfeet (2)	3	0.02
Cherokee (14)	40	0.27
Cheyenne (3)	3	0.02
Chickasaw (1)	4	0.03
Chippewa (3)	3	0.02
Choctaw (19)	27	0.19
Creek (4)	4	0.03
Latin American Indians (2)	9	0.06
Lumbee (4)	4	0.03
Seminole (1)	1	0.01
Sioux (2)	3	0.02
Ute (8)	8	0.05
All other tribes (2)	5	0.03
American Indian tribes, not spec.	7	0.05
Asian:	71	0.49
Chinese, ex. Taiwanese (15)	15	0.10
Filipino (9)	12	0.08
Indian (6)	7	0.05
Japanese (2)	7	0.05
Korean (4)	5	0.03
Sri Lankan (1)	1	0.01
Thai (4)	4	0.03
Vietnamese (14)	15	0.10
Other Asian, not specified (3)	5	0.03
Belgian	8	0.05
British	27	0.19
Celtic	7	0.05
Czech	7	0.05
Czechoslovakian	11	0.08
Danish	2	0.01
Dutch	306	2.10
English	1,269	8.71
European	60	0.41
Finnish	8	0.05
French, except Basque	226	1.55
French Canadian	7	0.05
German	721	4.95
Hawaii Native/Pacific Islander:	24	0.16
Micronesian: (6)	7	0.05
Guamanian/Chamorro (5)	5	0.03
Other Micronesian (1)	2	0.01
Polynesian: (2)	14	0.10
Native Hawaiian (2)	8	0.05
Samoan	6	0.04
Other Pac. Isl., not spec. (1)	3	0.02
Hispanic or Latino:	1,191	8.19
Central American:	38	0.26
Costa Rican	2	0.01
Guatemalan	7	0.05
Honduran	9	0.06
Panamanian	1	0.01
Salvadoran	19	0.13
Cuban	2	0.01
Mexican	985	6.77
Puerto Rican	13	0.09
South American:	5	0.03
Chilean	4	0.03
Colombian	1	0.01
Other Hispanic or Latino	148	1.02
Irish	1,345	9.23
Italian	97	0.67
Norwegian	97	0.67
Pennsylvania German	5	0.03
Polish	71	0.49
Russian	22	0.15
Scotch-Irish	236	1.62
Scottish	151	1.04
Slovak	22	0.15
Swedish	65	0.45
United States or American	2,543	17.45
Welsh	6	0.04
White:	11,743	80.70
Not Hispanic (11,031)	11,139	76.55
Hispanic (539)	604	4.15

Sweetwater

Place Type: City
County: Nolan
Population: 11,415

Ancestry/Race	Number	%
African American/Black:	732	6.41
Not Hispanic (640)	692	6.06
Hispanic (26)	40	0.35
African, sub-Saharan:	6	0.05
African	6	0.05
Am. Ind. or Alaska Nat., not spec.	35	0.31
American Indian tribes, specified:	47	0.41
Apache (4)	7	0.06
Cherokee (5)	14	0.12
Chickasaw	1	0.01
Choctaw (3)	8	0.07
Comanche	1	0.01
Latin American Indians (4)	4	0.04
Navajo (4)	4	0.04
Sioux	3	0.03
All other tribes (3)	5	0.04
American Indian tribes, not spec.	18	0.16
Asian:	45	0.39
Chinese, ex. Taiwanese (3)	3	0.03
Filipino (11)	15	0.13
Indian (11)	17	0.15
Japanese (3)	3	0.03
Korean (1)	1	0.01
Pakistani (1)	1	0.01
Thai (2)	2	0.02
Vietnamese (3)	3	0.03
British	34	0.30
Czech	13	0.11
Czechoslovakian	16	0.14
Dutch	93	0.81
English	641	5.60
European	31	0.27
Finnish	8	0.07
French, except Basque	199	1.74
French Canadian	15	0.13
German	726	6.35
Hawaii Native/Pacific Islander:	9	0.08
Micronesian: (3)	3	0.03
Guamanian/Chamorro (3)	3	0.03
Polynesian: (5)	6	0.05
Native Hawaiian	1	0.01
Samoan (5)	5	0.04
Hispanic or Latino:	3,618	31.70
Central American:	1	0.01
Honduran	1	0.01
Cuban	3	0.03
Mexican	2,562	22.44
Puerto Rican	2	0.02
South American:	1	0.01
Colombian	1	0.01
Other Hispanic or Latino	1,049	9.19
Irish	804	7.03
Italian	12	0.10
Norwegian	4	0.03
Polish	14	0.12
Portuguese	11	0.10
Romanian	4	0.03
Russian	18	0.16
Scotch-Irish	209	1.83
Scottish	118	1.03
Swedish	81	0.71
United States or American	1,763	15.41
Welsh	18	0.16
West Indian, excl. Hispanic:	6	0.05
Dutch West Indian	6	0.05
White:	8,825	77.31
Not Hispanic (7,015)	7,103	62.23
Hispanic (1,579)	1,722	15.09

Taylor

Place Type: City
County: Williamson
Population: 13,575

Ancestry/Race	Number	%
Acadian/Cajun	5	0.04
African American/Black:	1,979	14.58
Not Hispanic (1,902)	1,936	14.26
Hispanic (27)	43	0.32
African, sub-Saharan:	37	0.27
African	37	0.27
Am. Ind. or Alaska Nat., not spec.	56	0.41
American Indian tribes, specified:	73	0.54
Apache (1)	5	0.04
Cherokee (10)	25	0.18
Chickasaw (1)	3	0.02
Choctaw (1)	4	0.03
Comanche	2	0.01
Creek	1	0.01
Houma (1)	1	0.01
Kiowa (1)	1	0.01
Latin American Indians (10)	14	0.10
Lumbee	1	0.01
Navajo	1	0.01
Osage (1)	1	0.01
Pueblo	1	0.01
Seminole (4)	7	0.05
All other tribes (2)	6	0.04
American Indian tribes, not spec.	1	0.01
Arab:	27	0.20
Syrian	27	0.20
Asian:	66	0.49
Filipino (14)	20	0.15
Indian (19)	28	0.21
Indonesian (1)	1	0.01
Japanese (2)	4	0.03
Korean (5)	6	0.04
Laotian	1	0.01
Thai (3)	3	0.02
Vietnamese (2)	2	0.01
Other Asian, not specified	1	0.01
Belgian	3	0.02
British	32	0.24
Czech	1,175	8.67
Czechoslovakian	148	1.09
Danish	44	0.32
Dutch	72	0.53
English	652	4.81
European	26	0.19
Finnish	6	0.04
French, except Basque	140	1.03
French Canadian	4	0.03
German	2,053	15.15
Greek	4	0.03
Hawaii Native/Pacific Islander:	7	0.05
Polynesian: (7)	7	0.05
Native Hawaiian (7)	7	0.05
Hispanic or Latino:	4,626	34.08
Central American:	12	0.09
Honduran	1	0.01
Nicaraguan	1	0.01
Salvadoran	8	0.06
Other Central American	2	0.01
Cuban	1	0.01
Dominican Republic	2	0.01
Mexican	3,620	26.67

Notes: 1. Figures in the "Number" column do not add up to the total population due to: a) Ancestry/Race overlap — e.g. persons can report being both White and Irish, b) persons of Hispanic origin can report being any race, c) persons reporting two ancestries are counted in both categories. 2. Numbers in parentheses indicate the number of persons reporting this ancestry/race alone, not in combination with any other ancestry/race. 3. Refer to the Explanation of Data in the front of the book for more detailed information.

Ancestry/Race	Number	%
Puerto Rican	11	0.08
South American:	6	0.04
Chilean	1	0.01
Ecuadorian	4	0.03
Peruvian	1	0.01
Other Hispanic or Latino	974	7.17
Hungarian	8	0.06
Irish	815	6.01
Italian	114	0.84
Lithuanian	11	0.08
Norwegian	131	0.97
Polish	89	0.66
Russian	11	0.08
Scotch-Irish	203	1.50
Scottish	142	1.05
Slovene	6	0.04
Swedish	213	1.57
Swiss	17	0.13
United States or American	355	2.62
Welsh	35	0.26
West Indian, excl. Hispanic:	7	0.05
Belizean	7	0.05
White:	9,460	69.69
Not Hispanic (6,862)	6,951	51.20
Hispanic (2,350)	2,509	18.48
Yugoslavian	6	0.04

Temple

Place Type: City
County: Bell
Population: 54,514

Ancestry/Race	Number	%
Acadian/Cajun	14	0.03
African American/Black:	9,414	17.27
Not Hispanic (8,818)	9,131	16.75
Hispanic (170)	283	0.52
African, sub-Saharan:	306	0.56
African	244	0.45
Ethiopian	9	0.02
Kenyan	11	0.02
Nigerian	35	0.06
South African	7	0.01
Am. Ind. or Alaska Nat., not spec.	182	0.33
Albanian	7	0.01
American Indian tribes, specified:	339	0.62
Apache (17)	26	0.05
Blackfeet (5)	14	0.03
Cherokee (46)	138	0.25
Cheyenne	2	0.00
Chickasaw (8)	9	0.02
Chippewa (4)	4	0.01
Choctaw (34)	53	0.10
Comanche (12)	17	0.03
Creek (5)	7	0.01
Crow (1)	1	0.00
Delaware	1	0.00
Houma (4)	4	0.01
Iroquois (4)	5	0.01
Latin American Indians (6)	11	0.02
Navajo (5)	10	0.02
Osage	2	0.00
Ottawa (1)	1	0.00
Potawatomi (1)	2	0.00
Seminole	2	0.00
Shoshone (1)	1	0.00
Sioux (9)	10	0.02
All other tribes (12)	19	0.03
American Indian tribes, not spec.	29	0.05
Arab:	52	0.10
Egyptian	18	0.03
Lebanese	34	0.06
Asian:	1,093	2.00
Chinese, ex. Taiwanese (157)	195	0.36
Filipino (97)	168	0.31
Hmong (5)	5	0.01
Indian (343)	361	0.66
Indonesian (1)	1	0.00
Japanese (40)	85	0.16
Korean (81)	139	0.25
Pakistani (12)	14	0.03
Sri Lankan (1)	1	0.00
Taiwanese	1	0.00
Thai (9)	10	0.02
Vietnamese (48)	54	0.10
Other Asian, specified (2)	12	0.02
Other Asian, not specified (19)	47	0.09
Austrian	78	0.14
Brazilian	22	0.04
British	214	0.39
Canadian	112	0.21
Celtic	22	0.04
Croatian	8	0.01
Czech	1,342	2.47
Czechoslovakian	290	0.53
Danish	104	0.19
Dutch	661	1.21
English	4,697	8.63
European	365	0.67
French, except Basque	1,389	2.55
French Canadian	382	0.70
German	7,460	13.70
Greek	34	0.06
Hawaii Native/Pacific Islander:	98	0.18
Micronesian: (19)	28	0.05
Guamanian/Chamorro (18)	27	0.05
Other Micronesian (1)	1	0.00
Polynesian: (27)	47	0.09
Native Hawaiian (21)	41	0.08
Samoan (5)	5	0.01
Tongan (1)	1	0.00
Other Pac. Isl., specified	3	0.01
Other Pac. Isl., not spec. (4)	20	0.04
Hispanic or Latino:	9,716	17.82
Central American:	91	0.17
Costa Rican	2	0.00
Guatemalan	11	0.02
Honduran	30	0.06
Nicaraguan	1	0.00
Panamanian	15	0.03
Salvadoran	28	0.05
Other Central American	4	0.01
Cuban	36	0.07
Dominican Republic	7	0.01
Mexican	7,273	13.34
Puerto Rican	378	0.69
South American:	37	0.07
Argentinean	3	0.01
Colombian	13	0.02
Ecuadorian	1	0.00
Peruvian	7	0.01
Venezuelan	8	0.01
Other South American	5	0.01
Other Hispanic or Latino	1,894	3.47
Hungarian	46	0.08
Iranian	42	0.08
Irish	4,814	8.84
Italian	998	1.83
Latvian	31	0.06
Lithuanian	36	0.07
Northern European	7	0.01
Norwegian	491	0.90
Polish	430	0.79
Portuguese	14	0.03
Romanian	36	0.07
Russian	34	0.06
Scandinavian	34	0.06
Scotch-Irish	1,200	2.20
Scottish	1,032	1.90
Slavic	8	0.01
Slovak	24	0.04
Slovene	37	0.07
Swedish	291	0.53
Swiss	121	0.22
Ukrainian	52	0.10
United States or American	4,574	8.40
Welsh	261	0.48
West Indian, excl. Hispanic:	149	0.27
Bahamian	9	0.02
Dutch West Indian	23	0.04
Jamaican	33	0.06
Trinidadian and Tobagonian	12	0.02
West Indian	72	0.13
White:	39,117	71.76
Not Hispanic (34,176)	34,782	63.80
Hispanic (3,854)	4,335	7.95

Terrell

Place Type: City
County: Kaufman
Population: 13,606

Ancestry/Race	Number	%
African American/Black:	4,452	32.72
Not Hispanic (4,367)	4,429	32.55
Hispanic (19)	23	0.17
African, sub-Saharan:	102	0.75
African	102	0.75
Am. Ind. or Alaska Nat., not spec.	32	0.24
Albanian	28	0.21
American Indian tribes, specified:	83	0.61
Apache (3)	10	0.07
Blackfeet	4	0.03
Cherokee (14)	32	0.24
Cheyenne (1)	2	0.01
Choctaw (5)	8	0.06
Comanche	1	0.01
Creek	2	0.01
Iroquois	2	0.01
Latin American Indians (2)	4	0.03
Lumbee (1)	1	0.01
Navajo (1)	1	0.01
Osage	1	0.01
Potawatomi	1	0.01
Seminole (2)	2	0.01
Sioux	2	0.01
Yakama	1	0.01
Yaqui	2	0.01
All other tribes (4)	7	0.05
American Indian tribes, not spec.	7	0.05
Arab:	6	0.04
Lebanese	6	0.04
Asian:	101	0.74
Cambodian	6	0.04
Chinese, ex. Taiwanese (3)	7	0.05
Filipino (2)	5	0.04
Indian (33)	36	0.26
Japanese (7)	9	0.07
Korean (5)	6	0.04
Laotian (16)	16	0.12
Thai (1)	1	0.01
Vietnamese (1)	1	0.01
Other Asian, not specified (5)	14	0.10
Austrian	9	0.07
Belgian	14	0.10
British	21	0.15
Canadian	13	0.10
Czech	17	0.12
Czechoslovakian	22	0.16
Dutch	204	1.50
English	834	6.13
European	38	0.28
French, except Basque	215	1.58
French Canadian	10	0.07
German	776	5.70
Greek	4	0.03
Hawaii Native/Pacific Islander:	7	0.05
Polynesian: (3)	5	0.04
Native Hawaiian (3)	3	0.02
Samoan	2	0.01
Other Pac. Isl., not spec.	2	0.01
Hispanic or Latino:	2,390	17.57
Central American:	3	0.02
Honduran	1	0.01
Salvadoran	2	0.01
Cuban	9	0.07
Mexican	2,162	15.89
Puerto Rican	8	0.06

Notes: 1. Figures in the "Number" column do not add up to the total population due to: a) Ancestry/Race overlap — e.g. persons can report being both White and Irish, b) persons of Hispanic origin can report being any race, c) persons reporting two ancestries are counted in both categories. 2. Numbers in parentheses indicate the number of persons reporting this ancestry/race alone, not in combination with any other ancestry/race. 3. Refer to the Explanation of Data in the front of the book for more detailed information.

South American:	2	0.01
Chilean	1	0.01
Colombian	1	0.01
Other Hispanic or Latino	206	1.51
Hungarian	16	0.12
Irish	899	6.60
Italian	100	0.73
Norwegian	31	0.23
Polish	39	0.29
Russian	7	0.05
Scandinavian	8	0.06
Scotch-Irish	295	2.17
Scottish	102	0.75
Slavic	6	0.04
Swedish	42	0.31
United States or American	993	7.29
Welsh	12	0.09
West Indian, excl. Hispanic:	20	0.15
Jamaican	20	0.15
White:	7,732	56.83
Not Hispanic (6,591)	6,683	49.12
Hispanic (941)	1,049	7.71
Yugoslavian	4	0.03

Texarkana

Place Type: City
County: Bowie
Population: 34,782

Ancestry/Race	Number	%
Acadian/Cajun	20	0.06
African American/Black:	13,063	37.56
Not Hispanic (12,816)	12,974	37.30
Hispanic (69)	89	0.26
African, sub-Saharan:	284	0.81
African	284	0.81
Alaska Native tribes, specified:	3	0.01
Alaska Athabascan (1)	1	0.00
Aleut (1)	2	0.01
Am. Ind. or Alaska Nat., not spec.	76	0.22
American Indian tribes, specified:	202	0.58
Apache	4	0.01
Blackfeet (1)	1	0.00
Cherokee (38)	102	0.29
Chickasaw (1)	2	0.01
Chippewa (1)	2	0.01
Choctaw (24)	39	0.11
Comanche (1)	3	0.01
Creek (9)	10	0.03
Crow	2	0.01
Delaware (2)	2	0.01
Iroquois	1	0.00
Latin American Indians (1)	2	0.01
Navajo (1)	4	0.01
Osage (1)	1	0.00
Pueblo (1)	7	0.02
Sioux	5	0.01
Tohono O'Odham (4)	4	0.01
All other tribes (2)	11	0.03
American Indian tribes, not spec.	15	0.04
Arab:	22	0.06
Syrian	13	0.04
Other Arab	9	0.03
Asian:	356	1.02
Cambodian (1)	1	0.00
Chinese, ex. Taiwanese (29)	42	0.12
Filipino (58)	73	0.21
Indian (43)	64	0.18
Indonesian (1)	2	0.01
Japanese (9)	14	0.04
Korean (55)	68	0.20
Pakistani (1)	1	0.00
Thai (1)	1	0.00
Vietnamese (45)	46	0.13
Other Asian, specified	4	0.01
Other Asian, not specified (8)	40	0.12
Belgian	6	0.02
British	109	0.31
Canadian	121	0.35
Czech	117	0.34
Czechoslovakian	22	0.06
Danish	62	0.18
Dutch	357	1.02
Eastern European	12	0.03
English	2,224	6.37
European	95	0.27
Finnish	30	0.09
French, except Basque	684	1.96
French Canadian	61	0.17
German	2,121	6.08
Greek	85	0.24
Hawaii Native/Pacific Islander:	30	0.09
Micronesian: (7)	8	0.02
Guamanian/Chamorro (2)	2	0.01
Other Micronesian (5)	6	0.02
Polynesian: (7)	14	0.04
Native Hawaiian	4	0.01
Samoan (7)	10	0.03
Other Pac. Isl., specified	4	0.01
Other Pac. Isl., not spec. (3)	4	0.01
Hispanic or Latino:	1,012	2.91
Central American:	2	0.01
Guatemalan	2	0.01
Cuban	5	0.01
Mexican	774	2.23
Puerto Rican	34	0.10
South American:	18	0.05
Argentinean	6	0.02
Chilean	4	0.01
Colombian	2	0.01
Paraguayan	4	0.01
Venezuelan	2	0.01
Other Hispanic or Latino	179	0.51
Hungarian	19	0.05
Iranian	6	0.02
Irish	2,733	7.83
Italian	432	1.24
Norwegian	78	0.22
Pennsylvania German	10	0.03
Polish	196	0.56
Portuguese	18	0.05
Russian	32	0.09
Scotch-Irish	761	2.18
Scottish	407	1.17
Slovak	24	0.07
Swedish	142	0.41
Swiss	43	0.12
United States or American	3,495	10.01
Welsh	163	0.47
West Indian, excl. Hispanic:	66	0.19
Dutch West Indian	48	0.14
Haitian	10	0.03
West Indian	8	0.02
White:	20,904	60.10
Not Hispanic (20,220)	20,497	58.93
Hispanic (363)	407	1.17
Yugoslavian	31	0.09

Texas City

Place Type: City
County: Galveston
Population: 41,521

Ancestry/Race	Number	%
Acadian/Cajun	31	0.07
African American/Black:	11,629	28.01
Not Hispanic (11,268)	11,427	27.52
Hispanic (139)	202	0.49
African, sub-Saharan:	861	2.08
African	838	2.02
Ghanian	23	0.06
Alaska Native tribes, specified:	7	0.02
Aleut (1)	4	0.01
Eskimo	3	0.01
Am. Ind. or Alaska Nat., not spec.	111	0.27
American Indian tribes, specified:	206	0.50
Apache (7)	18	0.04
Blackfeet (1)	2	0.00
Cherokee (39)	85	0.20
Chickasaw (5)	7	0.02
Chippewa (4)	5	0.01
Choctaw (8)	20	0.05
Comanche (1)	6	0.01
Cree	1	0.00
Creek (1)	1	0.00
Houma (3)	3	0.01
Iroquois (2)	2	0.00
Latin American Indians (13)	17	0.04
Navajo	1	0.00
Osage (1)	3	0.01
Ottawa (6)	6	0.01
Potawatomi (3)	4	0.01
Seminole	1	0.00
Sioux (4)	6	0.01
Ute (1)	1	0.00
All other tribes (9)	17	0.04
American Indian tribes, not spec.	24	0.06
Arab:	16	0.04
Arab/Arabic	8	0.02
Other Arab	8	0.02
Asian:	488	1.18
Bangladeshi (1)	1	0.00
Cambodian (8)	9	0.02
Chinese, ex. Taiwanese (27)	42	0.10
Filipino (54)	94	0.23
Indian (74)	93	0.22
Japanese (16)	27	0.07
Korean (20)	29	0.07
Laotian (6)	12	0.03
Malaysian	1	0.00
Pakistani (5)	8	0.02
Taiwanese (2)	2	0.00
Thai (4)	4	0.01
Vietnamese (130)	145	0.35
Other Asian, specified (1)	3	0.01
Other Asian, not specified (3)	18	0.04
Australian	10	0.02
Austrian	13	0.03
Belgian	6	0.01
British	110	0.27
Canadian	34	0.08
Celtic	13	0.03
Croatian	26	0.06
Czech	215	0.52
Czechoslovakian	47	0.11
Danish	90	0.22
Dutch	391	0.94
Eastern European	6	0.01
English	2,564	6.19
European	168	0.41
Finnish	9	0.02
French, except Basque	1,173	2.83
French Canadian	156	0.38
German	3,924	9.48
Greek	60	0.14
Hawaii Native/Pacific Islander:	50	0.12
Melanesian: (3)	3	0.01
Fijian (3)	3	0.01
Micronesian: (6)	11	0.03
Guamanian/Chamorro (5)	8	0.02
Other Micronesian (1)	3	0.01
Polynesian: (9)	18	0.04
Native Hawaiian (4)	13	0.03
Samoan (5)	5	0.01
Other Pac. Isl., specified	2	0.00
Other Pac. Isl., not spec. (2)	16	0.04
Hispanic or Latino:	8,520	20.52
Central American:	138	0.33
Costa Rican	1	0.00
Guatemalan	10	0.02
Honduran	34	0.08
Nicaraguan	3	0.01
Panamanian	12	0.03
Salvadoran	73	0.18
Other Central American	5	0.01
Cuban	59	0.14
Dominican Republic	2	0.00
Mexican	6,777	16.32

Notes: 1. Figures in the "Number" column do not add up to the total population due to: a) Ancestry/Race overlap — e.g. persons can report being both White and Irish, b) persons of Hispanic origin can report being any race, c) persons reporting two ancestries are counted in both categories. 2. Numbers in parentheses indicate the number of persons reporting this ancestry/race alone, not in combination with any other ancestry/race. 3. Refer to the Explanation of Data in the front of the book for more detailed information.

Puerto Rican	172	0.41
South American:	34	0.08
Argentinean	2	0.00
Bolivian	2	0.00
Chilean	3	0.01
Colombian	3	0.01
Ecuadorian	9	0.02
Peruvian	1	0.00
Venezuelan	12	0.03
Other South American	2	0.00
Other Hispanic or Latino	1,338	3.22
Hungarian	19	0.05
Iranian	101	0.24
Irish	3,068	7.41
Italian	987	2.38
Lithuanian	17	0.04
Maltese	23	0.06
Northern European	8	0.02
Norwegian	245	0.59
Polish	270	0.65
Portuguese	46	0.11
Romanian	10	0.02
Russian	13	0.03
Scandinavian	18	0.04
Scotch-Irish	539	1.30
Scottish	471	1.14
Serbian	15	0.04
Swedish	250	0.60
Swiss	24	0.06
Ukrainian	39	0.09
United States or American	3,090	7.47
Welsh	50	0.12
West Indian, excl. Hispanic:	42	0.10
Haitian	10	0.02
Jamaican	18	0.04
U.S. Virgin Islander	7	0.02
West Indian	7	0.02
White:	25,964	62.53
Not Hispanic (20,804)	21,112	50.85
Hispanic (4,420)	4,852	11.69
Yugoslavian	37	0.09

The Colony

Place Type: City
County: Denton
Population: 26,531

Ancestry/Race	Number	%
Acadian/Cajun	21	0.08
African American/Black:	1,520	5.73
Not Hispanic (1,358)	1,478	5.57
Hispanic (17)	42	0.16
African, sub-Saharan:	113	0.42
African	102	0.38
Ghanian	11	0.04
Alaska Native tribes, specified:	1	0.00
Eskimo (1)	1	0.00
Am. Ind. or Alaska Nat., not spec.	68	0.26
Alsatian	10	0.04
American Indian tribes, specified:	276	1.04
Apache (2)	5	0.02
Blackfeet (1)	4	0.02
Cherokee (25)	73	0.28
Cheyenne	4	0.02
Chickasaw (10)	20	0.08
Chippewa (2)	3	0.01
Choctaw (62)	81	0.31
Comanche	1	0.00
Creek (5)	10	0.04
Delaware (2)	2	0.01
Iroquois (3)	7	0.03
Kiowa (4)	4	0.02
Latin American Indians (3)	5	0.02
Navajo (5)	7	0.03
Osage (3)	9	0.03
Pima (1)	1	0.00
Potawatomi (3)	6	0.02
Pueblo (4)	4	0.02
Seminole (1)	2	0.01
Sioux (4)	6	0.02
Ute (2)	2	0.01
All other tribes (9)	20	0.08
American Indian tribes, not spec.	17	0.06
Arab:	122	0.46
Arab/Arabic	8	0.03
Egyptian	71	0.27
Syrian	7	0.03
Other Arab	36	0.14
Armenian	8	0.03
Asian:	609	2.30
Cambodian (22)	28	0.11
Chinese, ex. Taiwanese (53)	68	0.26
Filipino (76)	119	0.45
Indian (73)	91	0.34
Indonesian	1	0.00
Japanese (20)	54	0.20
Korean (54)	66	0.25
Laotian (3)	3	0.01
Malaysian (1)	1	0.00
Pakistani (5)	6	0.02
Taiwanese (1)	1	0.00
Thai (11)	18	0.07
Vietnamese (112)	128	0.48
Other Asian, specified	5	0.02
Other Asian, not specified (6)	20	0.08
Australian	9	0.03
Austrian	46	0.17
Belgian	8	0.03
British	165	0.62
Canadian	71	0.27
Croatian	17	0.06
Czech	186	0.70
Czechoslovakian	37	0.14
Danish	204	0.77
Dutch	567	2.13
English	2,742	10.28
European	213	0.80
Finnish	16	0.06
French, except Basque	755	2.83
French Canadian	124	0.47
German	5,082	19.06
German Russian	30	0.11
Greek	105	0.39
Hawaii Native/Pacific Islander:	34	0.13
Micronesian: (1)	2	0.01
Guamanian/Chamorro (1)	2	0.01
Polynesian: (8)	19	0.07
Native Hawaiian (4)	14	0.05
Samoan (4)	4	0.02
Other Polynesian	1	0.00
Other Pac. Isl., specified	4	0.02
Other Pac. Isl., not spec. (3)	9	0.03
Hispanic or Latino:	3,519	13.26
Central American:	156	0.59
Costa Rican	1	0.00
Guatemalan	16	0.06
Honduran	8	0.03
Nicaraguan	11	0.04
Panamanian	23	0.09
Salvadoran	85	0.32
Other Central American	12	0.05
Cuban	64	0.24
Dominican Republic	3	0.01
Mexican	2,343	8.83
Puerto Rican	118	0.44
South American:	79	0.30
Argentinean	10	0.04
Chilean	8	0.03
Colombian	33	0.12
Ecuadorian	2	0.01
Peruvian	5	0.02
Uruguayan	2	0.01
Venezuelan	15	0.06
Other South American	4	0.02
Other Hispanic or Latino	756	2.85
Hungarian	36	0.14
Iranian	45	0.17
Irish	3,012	11.30
Italian	900	3.38
Norwegian	243	0.91
Pennsylvania German	11	0.04
Polish	503	1.89
Portuguese	10	0.04
Romanian	68	0.26
Russian	155	0.58
Scandinavian	9	0.03
Scotch-Irish	626	2.35
Scottish	567	2.13
Slovak	55	0.21
Slovene	7	0.03
Swedish	179	0.67
Swiss	51	0.19
Turkish	22	0.08
Ukrainian	102	0.38
United States or American	2,231	8.37
Welsh	238	0.89
West Indian, excl. Hispanic:	43	0.16
Jamaican	43	0.16
White:	23,058	86.91
Not Hispanic (20,552)	20,979	79.07
Hispanic (1,857)	2,079	7.84
Yugoslavian	32	0.12

The Woodlands

Place Type: Census Designated Place
County: Montgomery
Population: 55,649

Ancestry/Race	Number	%
Acadian/Cajun	49	0.09
African American/Black:	1,086	1.95
Not Hispanic (952)	1,049	1.89
Hispanic (21)	37	0.07
African, sub-Saharan:	95	0.17
African	24	0.04
Nigerian	35	0.06
South African	36	0.06
Alaska Native tribes, specified:	5	0.01
Aleut (3)	4	0.01
Eskimo (1)	1	0.00
Am. Ind. or Alaska Nat., not spec.	68	0.12
American Indian tribes, specified:	269	0.48
Apache (2)	8	0.01
Blackfeet (1)	6	0.01
Cherokee (42)	112	0.20
Cheyenne	2	0.00
Chickasaw (12)	14	0.03
Chippewa (2)	8	0.01
Choctaw (10)	27	0.05
Comanche (1)	8	0.01
Creek (2)	8	0.01
Crow (1)	1	0.00
Houma (1)	1	0.00
Iroquois (4)	9	0.02
Kiowa	1	0.00
Latin American Indians (5)	9	0.02
Lumbee (4)	4	0.01
Navajo (2)	2	0.00
Osage (9)	9	0.02
Potawatomi (1)	2	0.00
Pueblo (1)	4	0.01
Puget Sound Salish (1)	1	0.00
Seminole (1)	6	0.01
Sioux (1)	4	0.01
Yakama (1)	1	0.00
All other tribes (11)	22	0.04
American Indian tribes, not spec.	10	0.02
Arab:	151	0.27
Egyptian	39	0.07
Lebanese	112	0.20
Armenian	80	0.14
Asian:	1,893	3.40
Cambodian (1)	1	0.00
Chinese, ex. Taiwanese (321)	385	0.69
Filipino (186)	242	0.43
Hmong	1	0.00
Indian (643)	692	1.24
Indonesian (14)	19	0.03

Notes: 1. Figures in the "Number" column do not add up to the total population due to: a) Ancestry/Race overlap — e.g. persons can report being both White and Irish, b) persons of Hispanic origin can report being any race, c) persons reporting two ancestries are counted in both categories. 2. Numbers in parentheses indicate the number of persons reporting this ancestry/race alone, not in combination with any other ancestry/race. 3. Refer to the Explanation of Data in the front of the book for more detailed information.

Ancestry/Race	Number	%
Japanese (81)	158	0.28
Korean (62)	99	0.18
Laotian (1)	1	0.00
Malaysian (9)	13	0.02
Pakistani (25)	39	0.07
Sri Lankan (20)	21	0.04
Taiwanese (31)	35	0.06
Thai (10)	13	0.02
Vietnamese (93)	106	0.19
Other Asian, specified	1	0.00
Other Asian, not specified (32)	67	0.12
Assyrian/Chaldean/Syriac	27	0.05
Australian	43	0.08
Austrian	201	0.36
Basque	21	0.04
Belgian	41	0.07
Brazilian	80	0.14
British	857	1.54
Canadian	324	0.58
Celtic	16	0.03
Croatian	73	0.13
Cypriot	6	0.01
Czech	507	0.91
Czechoslovakian	115	0.21
Danish	303	0.54
Dutch	1,153	2.07
Eastern European	25	0.04
English	8,896	15.94
European	1,073	1.92
Finnish	60	0.11
French, except Basque	2,610	4.68
French Canadian	427	0.76
German	11,653	20.87
Greek	310	0.56
Guyanese	25	0.04
Hawaii Native/Pacific Islander:	54	0.10
Micronesian: (3)	5	0.01
Guamanian/Chamorro (2)	4	0.01
Other Micronesian (1)	1	0.00
Polynesian: (16)	28	0.05
Native Hawaiian (13)	24	0.04
Samoan (3)	4	0.01
Other Pac. Isl., not spec. (11)	21	0.04
Hispanic or Latino:	3,697	6.64
Central American:	221	0.40
Costa Rican	19	0.03
Guatemalan	72	0.13
Honduran	32	0.06
Nicaraguan	19	0.03
Panamanian	12	0.02
Salvadoran	62	0.11
Other Central American	5	0.01
Cuban	106	0.19
Dominican Republic	3	0.01
Mexican	2,118	3.81
Puerto Rican	202	0.36
South American:	390	0.70
Argentinean	81	0.15
Bolivian	4	0.01
Chilean	27	0.05
Colombian	121	0.22
Ecuadorian	18	0.03
Paraguayan	1	0.00
Peruvian	32	0.06
Uruguayan	8	0.01
Venezuelan	78	0.14
Other South American	20	0.04
Other Hispanic or Latino	657	1.18
Hungarian	239	0.43
Icelander	67	0.12
Iranian	95	0.17
Irish	7,288	13.06
Israeli	17	0.03
Italian	3,128	5.60
Latvian	8	0.01
Lithuanian	68	0.12
Luxemburger	33	0.06
Macedonian	8	0.01
Maltese	7	0.01
Northern European	101	0.18
Norwegian	1,099	1.97
Polish	1,623	2.91
Portuguese	159	0.28
Romanian	15	0.03
Russian	479	0.86
Scandinavian	52	0.09
Scotch-Irish	1,541	2.76
Scottish	1,991	3.57
Serbian	64	0.11
Slovak	188	0.34
Slovene	76	0.14
Swedish	734	1.31
Swiss	197	0.35
Turkish	32	0.06
Ukrainian	186	0.33
United States or American	4,473	8.01
Welsh	557	1.00
West Indian, excl. Hispanic:	221	0.40
Dutch West Indian	10	0.02
Jamaican	167	0.30
Trinidadian and Tobagonian	37	0.07
West Indian	7	0.01
White:	52,076	93.58
Not Hispanic (48,674)	49,151	88.32
Hispanic (2,725)	2,925	5.26
Yugoslavian	113	0.20

Tyler

Place Type: City
County: Smith
Population: 83,650

Ancestry/Race	Number	%
Acadian/Cajun	70	0.08
African American/Black:	22,625	27.05
Not Hispanic (22,155)	22,461	26.85
Hispanic (120)	164	0.20
African, sub-Saharan:	941	1.12
African	804	0.96
Ethiopian	6	0.01
Nigerian	103	0.12
South African	28	0.03
Am. Ind. or Alaska Nat., not spec.	189	0.23
American Indian tribes, specified:	379	0.45
Apache (9)	23	0.03
Blackfeet (3)	6	0.01
Cherokee (39)	118	0.14
Chickasaw (8)	14	0.02
Chippewa (2)	4	0.00
Choctaw (21)	61	0.07
Comanche	3	0.00
Creek (2)	9	0.01
Crow	4	0.00
Iroquois	3	0.00
Latin American Indians (53)	61	0.07
Lumbee (2)	3	0.00
Menominee	1	0.00
Navajo (6)	9	0.01
Osage (1)	3	0.00
Ottawa (4)	5	0.01
Potawatomi	3	0.00
Pueblo (2)	2	0.00
Seminole (5)	7	0.01
Sioux (5)	17	0.02
All other tribes (20)	23	0.03
American Indian tribes, not spec.	45	0.05
Arab:	169	0.20
Arab/Arabic	14	0.02
Egyptian	39	0.05
Lebanese	116	0.14
Asian:	1,002	1.20
Bangladeshi (4)	9	0.01
Cambodian (3)	3	0.00
Chinese, ex. Taiwanese (125)	147	0.18
Filipino (211)	253	0.30
Indian (169)	196	0.23
Indonesian (1)	1	0.00
Japanese (46)	64	0.08
Korean (58)	73	0.09
Laotian (2)	2	0.00
Malaysian	3	0.00
Pakistani (54)	84	0.10
Taiwanese (1)	2	0.00
Thai (13)	13	0.02
Vietnamese (66)	77	0.09
Other Asian, specified (2)	16	0.02
Other Asian, not specified (36)	59	0.07
Australian	6	0.01
Austrian	51	0.06
Basque	22	0.03
Belgian	24	0.03
Brazilian	34	0.04
British	423	0.50
Canadian	123	0.15
Celtic	102	0.12
Croatian	6	0.01
Cypriot	6	0.01
Czech	200	0.24
Czechoslovakian	51	0.06
Danish	104	0.12
Dutch	791	0.94
Eastern European	7	0.01
English	6,829	8.14
European	534	0.64
Finnish	14	0.02
French, except Basque	1,444	1.72
French Canadian	135	0.16
German	6,144	7.33
Greek	56	0.07
Hawaii Native/Pacific Islander:	81	0.10
Melanesian: (1)	1	0.00
Fijian (1)	1	0.00
Micronesian: (6)	13	0.02
Guamanian/Chamorro (4)	4	0.00
Other Micronesian (2)	9	0.01
Polynesian: (10)	31	0.04
Native Hawaiian (9)	19	0.02
Samoan (1)	12	0.01
Other Pac. Isl., specified	14	0.02
Other Pac. Isl., not spec. (15)	22	0.03
Hispanic or Latino:	13,234	15.82
Central American:	189	0.23
Costa Rican	1	0.00
Guatemalan	14	0.02
Honduran	30	0.04
Nicaraguan	28	0.03
Panamanian	13	0.02
Salvadoran	87	0.10
Other Central American	16	0.02
Cuban	21	0.03
Dominican Republic	9	0.01
Mexican	11,407	13.64
Puerto Rican	113	0.14
South American:	42	0.05
Argentinean	1	0.00
Bolivian	3	0.00
Colombian	17	0.02
Ecuadorian	6	0.01
Peruvian	9	0.01
Venezuelan	4	0.00
Other South American	2	0.00
Other Hispanic or Latino	1,453	1.74
Hungarian	51	0.06
Iranian	33	0.04
Irish	6,036	7.20
Italian	937	1.12
Lithuanian	29	0.03
Luxemburger	9	0.01
Northern European	7	0.01
Norwegian	440	0.52
Pennsylvania German	11	0.01
Polish	458	0.55
Portuguese	59	0.07
Romanian	10	0.01
Russian	109	0.13
Scandinavian	53	0.06
Scotch-Irish	1,604	1.91
Scottish	1,458	1.74
Serbian	10	0.01

Notes: 1. Figures in the "Number" column do not add up to the total population due to: a) Ancestry/Race overlap — e.g. persons can report being both White and Irish, b) persons of Hispanic origin can report being any race, c) persons reporting two ancestries are counted in both categories. 2. Numbers in parentheses indicate the number of persons reporting this ancestry/race alone, not in combination with any other ancestry/race. 3. Refer to the Explanation of Data in the front of the book for more detailed information.

Slavic	10	0.01
Swedish	428	0.51
Swiss	101	0.12
Turkish	9	0.01
Ukrainian	60	0.07
United States or American	7,687	9.17
Welsh	433	0.52
West Indian, excl. Hispanic:	49	0.06
Bahamian	8	0.01
Dutch West Indian	16	0.02
Haitian	6	0.01
Jamaican	19	0.02
White:	52,974	63.33
Not Hispanic (46,486)	47,049	56.25
Hispanic (5,309)	5,925	7.08
Yugoslavian	37	0.04

Universal City

Place Type: City
County: Bexar
Population: 14,849

Ancestry/Race	Number	%
African American/Black:	1,073	7.23
Not Hispanic (922)	1,022	6.88
Hispanic (32)	51	0.34
African, sub-Saharan:	46	0.31
African	46	0.31
Alaska Native tribes, specified:	3	0.02
Aleut (1)	1	0.01
Eskimo	1	0.01
Tlingit-Haida	1	0.01
Alaska Native tribes, not specified	1	0.01
Am. Ind. or Alaska Nat., not spec.	71	0.48
Alsatian	8	0.05
American Indian tribes, specified:	130	0.88
Apache (5)	6	0.04
Blackfeet	1	0.01
Cherokee (16)	40	0.27
Cheyenne	1	0.01
Chickasaw (1)	4	0.03
Chippewa (13)	13	0.09
Choctaw (4)	8	0.05
Cree	1	0.01
Creek (2)	2	0.01
Delaware	2	0.01
Iroquois	1	0.01
Latin American Indians (8)	13	0.09
Lumbee	1	0.01
Navajo	3	0.02
Osage (1)	1	0.01
Potawatomi	2	0.01
Pueblo (2)	5	0.03
Seminole	7	0.05
Shoshone (1)	1	0.01
Sioux (2)	3	0.02
Yaqui (1)	1	0.01
All other tribes (12)	14	0.09
American Indian tribes, not spec.	10	0.07
Arab:	8	0.05
Lebanese	8	0.05
Asian:	602	4.05
Chinese, ex. Taiwanese (44)	64	0.43
Filipino (117)	159	1.07
Indian (67)	73	0.49
Indonesian	1	0.01
Japanese (45)	92	0.62
Korean (64)	90	0.61
Pakistani	1	0.01
Taiwanese	1	0.01
Thai (21)	32	0.22
Vietnamese (61)	74	0.50
Other Asian, specified	3	0.02
Other Asian, not specified (5)	12	0.08
Australian	7	0.05
Austrian	19	0.13
Basque	10	0.07
Belgian	8	0.05
Brazilian	17	0.11
British	94	0.63
Canadian	32	0.22
Celtic	13	0.09
Croatian	23	0.15
Czech	163	1.10
Czechoslovakian	27	0.18
Danish	40	0.27
Dutch	123	0.83
English	1,862	12.52
European	201	1.35
Finnish	26	0.17
French, except Basque	607	4.08
French Canadian	65	0.44
German	2,738	18.41
Greek	32	0.22
Hawaii Native/Pacific Islander:	63	0.42
Melanesian: (1)	1	0.01
Other Melanesian (1)	1	0.01
Micronesian: (21)	22	0.15
Guamanian/Chamorro (19)	19	0.13
Other Micronesian (2)	3	0.02
Polynesian: (11)	25	0.17
Native Hawaiian (10)	23	0.15
Samoan	1	0.01
Other Polynesian (1)	1	0.01
Other Pac. Isl., specified	2	0.01
Other Pac. Isl., not spec. (7)	13	0.09
Hispanic or Latino:	3,206	21.59
Central American:	41	0.28
Costa Rican	1	0.01
Guatemalan	14	0.09
Honduran	5	0.03
Nicaraguan	2	0.01
Panamanian	15	0.10
Salvadoran	4	0.03
Cuban	7	0.05
Dominican Republic	1	0.01
Mexican	2,163	14.57
Puerto Rican	139	0.94
South American:	29	0.20
Chilean	2	0.01
Colombian	11	0.07
Ecuadorian	1	0.01
Paraguayan	1	0.01
Peruvian	1	0.01
Venezuelan	8	0.05
Other South American	5	0.03
Other Hispanic or Latino	826	5.56
Hungarian	69	0.46
Icelander	5	0.03
Irish	2,056	13.83
Italian	529	3.56
Lithuanian	5	0.03
Luxemburger	18	0.12
Norwegian	175	1.18
Polish	203	1.37
Portuguese	67	0.45
Romanian	8	0.05
Russian	11	0.07
Scotch-Irish	415	2.79
Scottish	317	2.13
Slavic	7	0.05
Slovak	19	0.13
Slovene	7	0.05
Swedish	147	0.99
Swiss	97	0.65
Ukrainian	37	0.25
United States or American	974	6.55
Welsh	69	0.46
West Indian, excl. Hispanic:	19	0.13
British West Indian	14	0.09
West Indian	5	0.03
White:	12,425	83.68
Not Hispanic (9,878)	10,156	68.40
Hispanic (2,082)	2,269	15.28
Yugoslavian	23	0.15

University Park

Place Type: City
County: Dallas
Population: 23,324

Ancestry/Race	Number	%
Acadian/Cajun	6	0.03
African American/Black:	351	1.50
Not Hispanic (324)	340	1.46
Hispanic (9)	11	0.05
African, sub-Saharan:	125	0.54
Ghanian	32	0.14
Nigerian	41	0.18
South African	52	0.22
Alaska Native tribes, specified:	1	0.00
Aleut (1)	1	0.00
Am. Ind. or Alaska Nat., not spec.	23	0.10
American Indian tribes, specified:	74	0.32
Apache	3	0.01
Cherokee (22)	39	0.17
Chickasaw (1)	1	0.00
Chippewa (1)	1	0.00
Choctaw (4)	9	0.04
Comanche (1)	2	0.01
Cree	1	0.00
Creek (1)	4	0.02
Kiowa	1	0.00
Latin American Indians	1	0.00
Lumbee (5)	5	0.02
Navajo (1)	1	0.00
Potawatomi (3)	3	0.01
Sioux	1	0.00
All other tribes (2)	2	0.01
American Indian tribes, not spec.	7	0.03
Arab:	143	0.61
Arab/Arabic	8	0.03
Egyptian	31	0.13
Lebanese	84	0.36
Palestinian	20	0.09
Armenian	18	0.08
Asian:	627	2.69
Bangladeshi (1)	2	0.01
Cambodian (1)	1	0.00
Chinese, ex. Taiwanese (208)	249	1.07
Filipino (18)	35	0.15
Indian (132)	136	0.58
Japanese (46)	61	0.26
Korean (57)	63	0.27
Laotian (3)	3	0.01
Malaysian	1	0.00
Pakistani (9)	10	0.04
Sri Lankan (1)	1	0.00
Taiwanese (6)	9	0.04
Thai (4)	4	0.02
Vietnamese (22)	30	0.13
Other Asian, not specified (3)	22	0.09
Assyrian/Chaldean/Syriac	8	0.03
Australian	67	0.29
Austrian	50	0.21
Belgian	63	0.27
British	412	1.76
Bulgarian	28	0.12
Canadian	63	0.27
Celtic	8	0.03
Croatian	15	0.06
Czech	190	0.81
Czechoslovakian	43	0.18
Danish	137	0.59
Dutch	350	1.50
Eastern European	10	0.04
English	4,954	21.22
European	498	2.13
Finnish	13	0.06
French, except Basque	1,041	4.46
French Canadian	85	0.36
German	3,699	15.85
Greek	142	0.61
Hawaii Native/Pacific Islander:	17	0.07
Polynesian: (2)	8	0.03

Notes: 1. Figures in the "Number" column do not add up to the total population due to: a) Ancestry/Race overlap — e.g. persons can report being both White and Irish, b) persons of Hispanic origin can report being any race, c) persons reporting two ancestries are counted in both categories. 2. Numbers in parentheses indicate the number of persons reporting this ancestry/race alone, not in combination with any other ancestry/race. 3. Refer to the Explanation of Data in the front of the book for more detailed information.

Ancestry/Race	Number	%
Native Hawaiian	5	0.02
Samoan (1)	2	0.01
Tongan (1)	1	0.00
Other Pac. Isl., not spec. (2)	9	0.04
Hispanic or Latino:	723	3.10
Central American:	26	0.11
Costa Rican	3	0.01
Guatemalan	9	0.04
Honduran	5	0.02
Nicaraguan	1	0.00
Panamanian	2	0.01
Salvadoran	3	0.01
Other Central American	3	0.01
Cuban	23	0.10
Dominican Republic	4	0.02
Mexican	487	2.09
Puerto Rican	23	0.10
South American:	47	0.20
Argentinean	4	0.02
Bolivian	4	0.02
Chilean	5	0.02
Colombian	14	0.06
Ecuadorian	3	0.01
Peruvian	7	0.03
Uruguayan	4	0.02
Venezuelan	5	0.02
Other South American	1	0.00
Other Hispanic or Latino	113	0.48
Hungarian	84	0.36
Icelander	9	0.04
Iranian	11	0.05
Irish	2,660	11.40
Italian	654	2.80
Lithuanian	18	0.08
Maltese	19	0.08
Northern European	88	0.38
Norwegian	368	1.58
Pennsylvania German	12	0.05
Polish	437	1.87
Portuguese	13	0.06
Romanian	54	0.23
Russian	226	0.97
Scandinavian	72	0.31
Scotch-Irish	1,000	4.28
Scottish	1,072	4.59
Serbian	24	0.10
Slavic	13	0.06
Slovene	32	0.14
Swedish	319	1.37
Swiss	211	0.90
Turkish	13	0.06
Ukrainian	40	0.17
United States or American	1,977	8.47
Welsh	242	1.04
West Indian, excl. Hispanic:	64	0.27
Jamaican	38	0.16
Trinidadian and Tobagonian	26	0.11
White:	22,175	95.07
Not Hispanic (21,523)	21,668	92.90
Hispanic (479)	507	2.17
Yugoslavian	17	0.07

Uvalde

Place Type: City
County: Uvalde
Population: 14,929

Ancestry/Race	Number	%
Acadian/Cajun	8	0.05
African American/Black:	92	0.62
Not Hispanic (45)	58	0.39
Hispanic (25)	34	0.23
Am. Ind. or Alaska Nat., not spec.	71	0.48
Alsatian	6	0.04
American Indian tribes, specified:	56	0.38
Apache (2)	5	0.03
Cherokee (6)	23	0.15
Chickasaw (2)	2	0.01
Choctaw	3	0.02
Comanche	1	0.01
Creek	2	0.01
Latin American Indians (6)	9	0.06
Navajo (1)	1	0.01
Sioux	3	0.02
All other tribes (7)	7	0.05
American Indian tribes, not spec.	17	0.11
Asian:	98	0.66
Cambodian (2)	2	0.01
Chinese, ex. Taiwanese (4)	4	0.03
Filipino (40)	52	0.35
Indian (10)	19	0.13
Indonesian	1	0.01
Japanese (6)	7	0.05
Korean (2)	3	0.02
Vietnamese (3)	3	0.02
Other Asian, not specified (5)	7	0.05
Austrian	19	0.13
British	23	0.15
Canadian	6	0.04
Czech	15	0.10
Danish	13	0.09
Dutch	47	0.31
English	524	3.48
European	34	0.23
Finnish	7	0.05
French, except Basque	121	0.80
French Canadian	23	0.15
German	692	4.59
Greek	26	0.17
Hawaii Native/Pacific Islander:	16	0.11
Micronesian: (1)	1	0.01
Guamanian/Chamorro (1)	1	0.01
Polynesian: (5)	7	0.05
Native Hawaiian (1)	3	0.02
Samoan (4)	4	0.03
Other Pac. Isl., not spec. (4)	8	0.05
Hispanic or Latino:	11,268	75.48
Central American:	6	0.04
Guatemalan	1	0.01
Nicaraguan	3	0.02
Salvadoran	2	0.01
Cuban	4	0.03
Mexican	7,818	52.37
Puerto Rican	18	0.12
South American:	9	0.06
Argentinean	3	0.02
Chilean	3	0.02
Venezuelan	3	0.02
Other Hispanic or Latino	3,413	22.86
Irish	472	3.13
Italian	41	0.27
Lithuanian	19	0.13
Norwegian	91	0.60
Polish	31	0.21
Scotch-Irish	167	1.11
Scottish	106	0.70
Slovene	10	0.07
Swedish	7	0.05
Swiss	8	0.05
United States or American	512	3.40
Welsh	17	0.11
West Indian, excl. Hispanic:	3	0.02
Dutch West Indian	3	0.02
White:	11,341	75.97
Not Hispanic (3,470)	3,515	23.54
Hispanic (7,468)	7,826	52.42

Vernon

Place Type: City
County: Wilbarger
Population: 11,660

Ancestry/Race	Number	%
African American/Black:	1,173	10.06
Not Hispanic (1,107)	1,151	9.87
Hispanic (18)	22	0.19
African, sub-Saharan:	49	0.42
African	49	0.42
Am. Ind. or Alaska Nat., not spec.	36	0.31
American Indian tribes, specified:	90	0.77
Apache (2)	3	0.03
Cherokee (10)	37	0.32
Chickasaw	3	0.03
Choctaw (18)	25	0.21
Comanche (2)	2	0.02
Creek (6)	7	0.06
Iroquois (1)	1	0.01
Latin American Indians (3)	5	0.04
Sioux (1)	1	0.01
All other tribes (4)	6	0.05
American Indian tribes, not spec.	10	0.09
Arab:	7	0.06
Arab/Arabic	7	0.06
Asian:	114	0.98
Chinese, ex. Taiwanese (20)	24	0.21
Filipino (30)	33	0.28
Indian (9)	18	0.15
Japanese (7)	12	0.10
Korean (3)	6	0.05
Pakistani	1	0.01
Taiwanese (1)	1	0.01
Thai	1	0.01
Vietnamese (4)	6	0.05
Other Asian, specified (5)	7	0.06
Other Asian, not specified	5	0.04
British	36	0.31
Celtic	10	0.09
Czech	29	0.25
Czechoslovakian	24	0.21
Danish	17	0.15
Dutch	296	2.53
Eastern European	5	0.04
English	790	6.76
European	29	0.25
French, except Basque	94	0.80
French Canadian	13	0.11
German	935	8.00
Greek	6	0.05
Hawaii Native/Pacific Islander:	7	0.06
Micronesian:	1	0.01
Guamanian/Chamorro	1	0.01
Polynesian: (2)	3	0.03
Native Hawaiian (2)	3	0.03
Other Pac. Isl., specified	2	0.02
Other Pac. Isl., not spec.	1	0.01
Hispanic or Latino:	2,611	22.39
Central American:	5	0.04
Honduran	5	0.04
Cuban	2	0.02
Mexican	2,015	17.28
Puerto Rican	24	0.21
South American:	3	0.03
Colombian	3	0.03
Other Hispanic or Latino	562	4.82
Irish	1,350	11.56
Italian	23	0.20
Lithuanian	8	0.07
Norwegian	16	0.14
Polish	34	0.29
Portuguese	7	0.06
Scotch-Irish	212	1.81
Scottish	62	0.53
Swedish	6	0.05
Swiss	49	0.42
Ukrainian	8	0.07
United States or American	1,248	10.68
Welsh	40	0.34
West Indian, excl. Hispanic:	38	0.33
Dutch West Indian	38	0.33
White:	9,101	78.05
Not Hispanic (7,691)	7,779	66.72
Hispanic (1,209)	1,322	11.34

Notes: 1. Figures in the "Number" column do not add up to the total population due to: a) Ancestry/Race overlap — e.g. persons can report being both White and Irish, b) persons of Hispanic origin can report being any race, c) persons reporting two ancestries are counted in both categories. 2. Numbers in parentheses indicate the number of persons reporting this ancestry/race alone, not in combination with any other ancestry/race. 3. Refer to the Explanation of Data in the front of the book for more detailed information.

Victoria

Place Type: City
County: Victoria
Population: 60,603

Ancestry/Race	Number	%
Acadian/Cajun	15	0.02
African American/Black:	4,845	7.99
Not Hispanic (4,453)	4,603	7.60
Hispanic (146)	242	0.40
African, sub-Saharan:	151	0.25
African	151	0.25
Alaska Native tribes, specified:	4	0.01
Tlingit-Haida (4)	4	0.01
Am. Ind. or Alaska Nat., not spec.	196	0.32
Alsatian	24	0.04
American Indian tribes, specified:	269	0.44
Apache (8)	16	0.03
Blackfeet	2	0.00
Cherokee (27)	73	0.12
Chickasaw (7)	9	0.01
Chippewa (2)	2	0.00
Choctaw (14)	30	0.05
Comanche (3)	11	0.02
Creek (2)	9	0.01
Crow	1	0.00
Delaware (2)	4	0.01
Iroquois (4)	5	0.01
Latin American Indians (29)	42	0.07
Navajo (12)	12	0.02
Osage (3)	6	0.01
Ottawa	1	0.00
Paiute (4)	4	0.01
Potawatomi (1)	1	0.00
Pueblo (7)	8	0.01
Sioux (2)	7	0.01
Tohono O'Odham	1	0.00
Yaqui (7)	8	0.01
All other tribes (12)	18	0.03
American Indian tribes, not spec.	55	0.09
Arab:	256	0.42
Arab/Arabic	21	0.03
Egyptian	6	0.01
Lebanese	150	0.25
Syrian	79	0.13
Armenian	12	0.02
Asian:	742	1.22
Cambodian (7)	7	0.01
Chinese, ex. Taiwanese (155)	182	0.30
Filipino (95)	122	0.20
Indian (135)	163	0.27
Indonesian (4)	6	0.01
Japanese (10)	26	0.04
Korean (23)	28	0.05
Pakistani (21)	23	0.04
Taiwanese (25)	39	0.06
Thai (5)	6	0.01
Vietnamese (101)	104	0.17
Other Asian, specified	1	0.00
Other Asian, not specified (14)	35	0.06
Australian	24	0.04
Austrian	50	0.08
Belgian	38	0.06
British	184	0.30
Canadian	119	0.20
Czech	2,089	3.46
Czechoslovakian	266	0.44
Danish	96	0.16
Dutch	457	0.76
English	4,018	6.65
European	171	0.28
French, except Basque	1,456	2.41
French Canadian	88	0.15
German	8,970	14.84
Greek	126	0.21
Hawaii Native/Pacific Islander:	45	0.07
Micronesian: (7)	10	0.02
Guamanian/Chamorro (7)	10	0.02
Polynesian: (16)	27	0.04
Native Hawaiian (8)	15	0.02
Samoan (8)	11	0.02
Other Polynesian	1	0.00
Other Pac. Isl., specified	1	0.00
Other Pac. Isl., not spec. (1)	7	0.01
Hispanic or Latino:	26,012	42.92
Central American:	74	0.12
Costa Rican	5	0.01
Guatemalan	6	0.01
Honduran	12	0.02
Nicaraguan	13	0.02
Panamanian	9	0.01
Salvadoran	26	0.04
Other Central American	3	0.00
Cuban	40	0.07
Dominican Republic	1	0.00
Mexican	17,812	29.39
Puerto Rican	135	0.22
South American:	42	0.07
Argentinean	2	0.00
Chilean	2	0.00
Colombian	11	0.02
Ecuadorian	5	0.01
Peruvian	8	0.01
Uruguayan	1	0.00
Venezuelan	12	0.02
Other South American	1	0.00
Other Hispanic or Latino	7,908	13.05
Hungarian	63	0.10
Icelander	21	0.03
Iranian	37	0.06
Irish	4,004	6.62
Israeli	13	0.02
Italian	971	1.61
Latvian	11	0.02
Lithuanian	12	0.02
Maltese	9	0.01
Northern European	6	0.01
Norwegian	193	0.32
Pennsylvania German	28	0.05
Polish	829	1.37
Portuguese	16	0.03
Romanian	8	0.01
Russian	38	0.06
Scandinavian	22	0.04
Scotch-Irish	939	1.55
Scottish	677	1.12
Slavic	13	0.02
Slovak	5	0.01
Slovene	8	0.01
Swedish	327	0.54
Swiss	56	0.09
Ukrainian	52	0.09
United States or American	2,575	4.26
Welsh	178	0.29
West Indian, excl. Hispanic:	19	0.03
Dutch West Indian	12	0.02
West Indian	7	0.01
White:	44,390	73.25
Not Hispanic (28,917)	29,308	48.36
Hispanic (14,223)	15,082	24.89
Yugoslavian	6	0.01

Vidor

Place Type: City
County: Orange
Population: 11,440

Ancestry/Race	Number	%
Acadian/Cajun	152	1.34
African American/Black:	8	0.07
Not Hispanic (8)	8	0.07
Am. Ind. or Alaska Nat., not spec.	54	0.47
American Indian tribes, specified:	87	0.76
Apache (3)	3	0.03
Blackfeet	5	0.04
Cherokee (15)	48	0.42
Cheyenne	2	0.02
Chickasaw	1	0.01
Chippewa	1	0.01
Choctaw (8)	11	0.10
Comanche	1	0.01
Creek (2)	2	0.02
Latin American Indians	5	0.04
Lumbee	1	0.01
Menominee	2	0.02
Sioux	1	0.01
Tohono O'Odham	1	0.01
Yaqui	1	0.01
All other tribes (1)	2	0.02
American Indian tribes, not spec.	7	0.06
Arab:	7	0.06
Lebanese	7	0.06
Armenian	21	0.18
Asian:	41	0.36
Chinese, ex. Taiwanese (5)	6	0.05
Filipino (7)	11	0.10
Indian (6)	6	0.05
Japanese (1)	8	0.07
Korean (1)	1	0.01
Pakistani	2	0.02
Vietnamese (2)	5	0.04
Other Asian, specified	1	0.01
Other Asian, not specified	1	0.01
British	20	0.18
Canadian	37	0.33
Celtic	2	0.02
Czechoslovakian	28	0.25
Danish	23	0.20
Dutch	79	0.69
English	934	8.21
European	8	0.07
French, except Basque	1,017	8.94
French Canadian	371	3.26
German	1,065	9.36
Greek	10	0.09
Hawaii Native/Pacific Islander:	8	0.07
Micronesian: (1)	1	0.01
Other Micronesian (1)	1	0.01
Polynesian: (2)	2	0.02
Native Hawaiian (2)	2	0.02
Other Pac. Isl., specified	1	0.01
Other Pac. Isl., not spec.	4	0.03
Hispanic or Latino:	399	3.49
Central American:	3	0.03
Honduran	1	0.01
Salvadoran	1	0.01
Other Central American	1	0.01
Cuban	2	0.02
Mexican	320	2.80
Puerto Rican	3	0.03
South American:	4	0.03
Colombian	4	0.03
Other Hispanic or Latino	67	0.59
Hungarian	8	0.07
Icelander	4	0.04
Irish	1,282	11.27
Israeli	31	0.27
Italian	297	2.61
Lithuanian	9	0.08
Norwegian	25	0.22
Polish	34	0.30
Romanian	22	0.19
Scandinavian	7	0.06
Scotch-Irish	220	1.93
Scottish	109	0.96
Swedish	29	0.25
Swiss	15	0.13
Turkish	13	0.11
Ukrainian	4	0.04
United States or American	2,008	17.65
Welsh	39	0.34
White:	11,264	98.46
Not Hispanic (10,844)	10,951	95.73
Hispanic (291)	313	2.74
Yugoslavian	11	0.10

Notes: 1. Figures in the "Number" column do not add up to the total population due to: a) Ancestry/Race overlap — e.g. persons can report being both White and Irish, b) persons of Hispanic origin can report being any race, c) persons reporting two ancestries are counted in both categories. 2. Numbers in parentheses indicate the number of persons reporting this ancestry/race alone, not in combination with any other ancestry/race. 3. Refer to the Explanation of Data in the front of the book for more detailed information.

Waco

Place Type: City
County: McLennan
Population: 113,726

Ancestry/Race	Number	%
Acadian/Cajun	13	0.01
African American/Black:	26,461	23.27
Not Hispanic (25,477)	26,028	22.89
Hispanic (277)	433	0.38
African, sub-Saharan:	512	0.45
African	390	0.34
Cape Verdean	8	0.01
Liberian	5	0.00
Nigerian	70	0.06
South African	19	0.02
Sudanese	13	0.01
Other sub-Saharan African	7	0.01
Alaska Native tribes, specified:	8	0.01
Alaska Athabascan (4)	5	0.00
Eskimo (2)	2	0.00
Tlingit-Haida (1)	1	0.00
Am. Ind. or Alaska Nat., not spec.	452	0.40
American Indian tribes, specified:	545	0.48
Apache (24)	46	0.04
Blackfeet (1)	9	0.01
Cherokee (78)	212	0.19
Cheyenne (1)	2	0.00
Chickasaw (8)	11	0.01
Chippewa (3)	7	0.01
Choctaw (30)	66	0.06
Colville (3)	3	0.00
Comanche (8)	19	0.02
Cree (1)	2	0.00
Creek (5)	12	0.01
Delaware (1)	1	0.00
Iroquois	6	0.01
Kiowa (1)	3	0.00
Latin American Indians (60)	89	0.08
Navajo (4)	4	0.00
Osage	7	0.01
Ottawa	1	0.00
Pima	1	0.00
Potawatomi (1)	5	0.00
Pueblo (1)	2	0.00
Seminole (1)	2	0.00
Shoshone (1)	1	0.00
Sioux (5)	8	0.01
Tohono O'Odham (3)	3	0.00
Yaqui (1)	2	0.00
All other tribes (11)	21	0.02
American Indian tribes, not spec.	120	0.11
Arab:	339	0.30
Arab/Arabic	64	0.06
Jordanian	20	0.02
Lebanese	188	0.16
Syrian	67	0.06
Armenian	18	0.02
Asian:	2,002	1.76
Bangladeshi (4)	5	0.00
Cambodian (6)	9	0.01
Chinese, ex. Taiwanese (388)	462	0.41
Filipino (154)	241	0.21
Indian (332)	377	0.33
Indonesian (4)	6	0.01
Japanese (50)	79	0.07
Korean (210)	258	0.23
Laotian (3)	6	0.01
Malaysian (1)	2	0.00
Pakistani (33)	56	0.05
Sri Lankan (2)	2	0.00
Taiwanese (35)	43	0.04
Thai (25)	39	0.03
Vietnamese (248)	283	0.25
Other Asian, specified (2)	24	0.02
Other Asian, not specified (33)	110	0.10
Australian	21	0.02
Austrian	42	0.04
Belgian	23	0.02
Brazilian	7	0.01
British	383	0.34
Bulgarian	14	0.01
Canadian	50	0.04
Carpatho Rusyn	2	0.00
Celtic	11	0.01
Croatian	32	0.03
Czech	1,030	0.90
Czechoslovakian	340	0.30
Danish	105	0.09
Dutch	640	0.56
Eastern European	6	0.01
English	7,288	6.39
European	471	0.41
Finnish	17	0.01
French, except Basque	1,709	1.50
French Canadian	170	0.15
German	10,500	9.21
Greek	124	0.11
Guyanese	8	0.01
Hawaii Native/Pacific Islander:	146	0.13
Micronesian: (12)	18	0.02
Guamanian/Chamorro (12)	18	0.02
Polynesian: (34)	44	0.04
Native Hawaiian (25)	31	0.03
Samoan (9)	13	0.01
Other Pac. Isl., specified	18	0.02
Other Pac. Isl., not spec. (15)	66	0.06
Hispanic or Latino:	26,885	23.64
Central American:	202	0.18
Costa Rican	8	0.01
Guatemalan	26	0.02
Honduran	43	0.04
Nicaraguan	5	0.00
Panamanian	24	0.02
Salvadoran	75	0.07
Other Central American	21	0.02
Cuban	72	0.06
Dominican Republic	5	0.00
Mexican	21,450	18.86
Puerto Rican	265	0.23
South American:	101	0.09
Argentinean	11	0.01
Bolivian	1	0.00
Chilean	9	0.01
Colombian	41	0.04
Ecuadorian	4	0.00
Peruvian	9	0.01
Uruguayan	1	0.00
Venezuelan	20	0.02
Other South American	5	0.00
Other Hispanic or Latino	4,790	4.21
Hungarian	72	0.06
Iranian	54	0.05
Irish	6,860	6.02
Italian	1,486	1.30
Latvian	8	0.01
Lithuanian	51	0.04
Macedonian	9	0.01
Maltese	7	0.01
New Zealander	7	0.01
Northern European	30	0.03
Norwegian	721	0.63
Pennsylvania German	41	0.04
Polish	759	0.67
Portuguese	18	0.02
Romanian	77	0.07
Russian	150	0.13
Scandinavian	21	0.02
Scotch-Irish	2,173	1.91
Scottish	1,503	1.32
Slavic	6	0.01
Slovak	15	0.01
Slovene	28	0.02
Swedish	507	0.44
Swiss	163	0.14
Turkish	8	0.01
Ukrainian	27	0.02
United States or American	6,694	5.87
Welsh	326	0.29
West Indian, excl. Hispanic:	83	0.07
Dutch West Indian	55	0.05
Jamaican	21	0.02
U.S. Virgin Islander	7	0.01
White:	71,217	62.62
Not Hispanic (58,096)	59,133	52.00
Hispanic (11,023)	12,084	10.63
Yugoslavian	35	0.03

Watauga

Place Type: City
County: Tarrant
Population: 21,908

Ancestry/Race	Number	%
Acadian/Cajun	16	0.07
African American/Black:	568	2.59
Not Hispanic (483)	544	2.48
Hispanic (15)	24	0.11
African, sub-Saharan:	61	0.28
African	61	0.28
Alaska Native tribes, specified:	1	0.00
Aleut (1)	1	0.00
Am. Ind. or Alaska Nat., not spec.	72	0.33
American Indian tribes, specified:	216	0.99
Apache (7)	7	0.03
Blackfeet (4)	6	0.03
Cherokee (37)	91	0.42
Cheyenne	1	0.00
Chickasaw (6)	10	0.05
Chippewa (1)	1	0.00
Choctaw (20)	42	0.19
Comanche (2)	3	0.01
Creek (5)	9	0.04
Delaware (4)	5	0.02
Iroquois (1)	4	0.02
Latin American Indians (2)	6	0.03
Lumbee	1	0.00
Navajo (9)	10	0.05
Osage (1)	2	0.01
Potawatomi (1)	1	0.00
Pueblo (4)	5	0.02
Sioux (2)	6	0.03
All other tribes (2)	6	0.03
American Indian tribes, not spec.	10	0.05
Arab:	14	0.06
Lebanese	14	0.06
Armenian	15	0.07
Asian:	979	4.47
Chinese, ex. Taiwanese (18)	43	0.20
Filipino (66)	91	0.42
Hmong (2)	2	0.01
Indian (80)	90	0.41
Indonesian	2	0.01
Japanese (14)	32	0.15
Korean (23)	34	0.16
Laotian (166)	192	0.88
Pakistani (1)	3	0.01
Taiwanese (2)	3	0.01
Thai (25)	39	0.18
Vietnamese (373)	407	1.86
Other Asian, specified (1)	2	0.01
Other Asian, not specified (18)	39	0.18
Austrian	15	0.07
Belgian	7	0.03
British	112	0.51
Bulgarian	21	0.10
Canadian	76	0.35
Celtic	38	0.17
Croatian	7	0.03
Czech	131	0.60
Czechoslovakian	28	0.13
Danish	57	0.26
Dutch	484	2.22
English	1,867	8.55
European	136	0.62
Finnish	53	0.24
French, except Basque	811	3.71
French Canadian	32	0.15

Notes: 1. Figures in the "Number" column do not add up to the total population due to: a) Ancestry/Race overlap — e.g. persons can report being both White and Irish, b) persons of Hispanic origin can report being any race, c) persons reporting two ancestries are counted in both categories. 2. Numbers in parentheses indicate the number of persons reporting this ancestry/race alone, not in combination with any other ancestry/race. 3. Refer to the Explanation of Data in the front of the book for more detailed information.

Ancestry/Race	Number	%
German	3,096	14.17
Greek	16	0.07
Hawaii Native/Pacific Islander:	73	0.33
Micronesian: (2)	4	0.02
Guamanian/Chamorro (2)	4	0.02
Polynesian: (30)	49	0.22
Native Hawaiian (5)	18	0.08
Samoan (3)	3	0.01
Tongan (18)	24	0.11
Other Polynesian (4)	4	0.02
Other Pac. Isl., not spec. (11)	20	0.09
Hispanic or Latino:	2,335	10.66
Central American:	32	0.15
Costa Rican	5	0.02
Guatemalan	6	0.03
Honduran	1	0.00
Panamanian	8	0.04
Salvadoran	12	0.05
Cuban	19	0.09
Mexican	1,649	7.53
Puerto Rican	153	0.70
South American:	45	0.21
Argentinean	2	0.01
Chilean	4	0.02
Colombian	23	0.10
Ecuadorian	4	0.02
Peruvian	5	0.02
Venezuelan	3	0.01
Other South American	4	0.02
Other Hispanic or Latino	437	1.99
Hungarian	47	0.22
Irish	2,618	11.98
Israeli	22	0.10
Italian	516	2.36
Lithuanian	28	0.13
Norwegian	224	1.03
Polish	344	1.57
Portuguese	6	0.03
Romanian	5	0.02
Russian	22	0.10
Scandinavian	27	0.12
Scotch-Irish	494	2.26
Scottish	428	1.96
Slavic	29	0.13
Slovak	16	0.07
Slovene	6	0.03
Swedish	207	0.95
Swiss	51	0.23
Ukrainian	63	0.29
United States or American	3,270	14.97
Welsh	60	0.27
West Indian, excl. Hispanic:	10	0.05
Dutch West Indian	10	0.05
White:	19,483	88.93
Not Hispanic (17,752)	18,027	82.29
Hispanic (1,320)	1,456	6.65

Waxahachie

Place Type: City
County: Ellis
Population: 21,426

Ancestry/Race	Number	%
African American/Black:	3,739	17.45
Not Hispanic (3,624)	3,689	17.22
Hispanic (39)	50	0.23
African, sub-Saharan:	149	0.70
African	117	0.55
Sierra Leonean	20	0.09
South African	12	0.06
Am. Ind. or Alaska Nat., not spec.	68	0.32
Albanian	32	0.15
American Indian tribes, specified:	176	0.82
Apache	5	0.02
Blackfeet (1)	1	0.00
Cherokee (41)	81	0.38
Chickasaw (8)	8	0.04
Chippewa (9)	9	0.04
Choctaw (8)	15	0.07
Comanche (1)	4	0.02
Cree	1	0.00
Creek (5)	6	0.03
Crow (1)	1	0.00
Iroquois	3	0.01
Kiowa (1)	1	0.00
Latin American Indians (5)	12	0.06
Navajo (10)	11	0.05
Potawatomi (2)	2	0.01
Pueblo (1)	3	0.01
Seminole (1)	2	0.01
Sioux (1)	2	0.01
Tohono O'Odham	1	0.00
Ute (3)	3	0.01
All other tribes (5)	5	0.02
American Indian tribes, not spec.	19	0.09
Arab:	24	0.11
Arab/Arabic	13	0.06
Syrian	11	0.05
Asian:	120	0.56
Chinese, ex. Taiwanese (13)	16	0.07
Filipino (8)	10	0.05
Indian (29)	32	0.15
Japanese (1)	7	0.03
Korean (19)	22	0.10
Pakistani	1	0.00
Sri Lankan (1)	1	0.00
Thai (9)	9	0.04
Other Asian, specified	3	0.01
Other Asian, not specified (5)	19	0.09
Austrian	23	0.11
Belgian	4	0.02
British	36	0.17
Canadian	22	0.10
Celtic	26	0.12
Croatian	8	0.04
Czech	125	0.58
Czechoslovakian	41	0.19
Danish	57	0.27
Dutch	200	0.94
English	1,589	7.44
European	39	0.18
Finnish	6	0.03
French, except Basque	419	1.96
French Canadian	84	0.39
German	1,988	9.30
Hawaii Native/Pacific Islander:	12	0.06
Polynesian:	4	0.02
Native Hawaiian	3	0.01
Samoan	1	0.00
Other Pac. Isl., specified	3	0.01
Other Pac. Isl., not spec. (1)	5	0.02
Hispanic or Latino:	4,229	19.74
Central American:	24	0.11
Guatemalan	7	0.03
Honduran	7	0.03
Nicaraguan	3	0.01
Panamanian	2	0.01
Salvadoran	3	0.01
Other Central American	2	0.01
Cuban	9	0.04
Mexican	3,338	15.58
Puerto Rican	32	0.15
South American:	18	0.08
Argentinean	2	0.01
Bolivian	2	0.01
Colombian	5	0.02
Ecuadorian	2	0.01
Peruvian	1	0.00
Venezuelan	6	0.03
Other Hispanic or Latino	808	3.77
Irish	1,885	8.82
Italian	377	1.76
Lithuanian	5	0.02
Norwegian	90	0.42
Polish	130	0.61
Portuguese	5	0.02
Russian	8	0.04
Scandinavian	9	0.04
Scotch-Irish	501	2.34
Scottish	268	1.25
Swedish	168	0.79
Swiss	56	0.26
United States or American	1,911	8.94
Welsh	104	0.49
West Indian, excl. Hispanic:	10	0.05
Dutch West Indian	10	0.05
White:	15,479	72.24
Not Hispanic (13,159)	13,352	62.32
Hispanic (1,935)	2,127	9.93

Weatherford

Place Type: City
County: Parker
Population: 19,000

Ancestry/Race	Number	%
Acadian/Cajun	21	0.11
African American/Black:	439	2.31
Not Hispanic (384)	415	2.18
Hispanic (10)	24	0.13
African, sub-Saharan:	44	0.23
African	36	0.19
Ugandan	8	0.04
Alaska Native tribes, specified:	1	0.01
Eskimo (1)	1	0.01
Am. Ind. or Alaska Nat., not spec.	63	0.33
Alsatian	2	0.01
American Indian tribes, specified:	164	0.86
Apache (2)	6	0.03
Blackfeet	1	0.01
Cherokee (49)	80	0.42
Chickasaw (4)	5	0.03
Choctaw (22)	33	0.17
Comanche (2)	4	0.02
Creek (4)	4	0.02
Houma (1)	1	0.01
Latin American Indians (5)	6	0.03
Navajo (3)	4	0.02
Pima (1)	2	0.01
Potawatomi (8)	11	0.06
Sioux (3)	3	0.02
All other tribes (1)	4	0.02
American Indian tribes, not spec.	19	0.10
Arab:	50	0.26
Arab/Arabic	6	0.03
Lebanese	11	0.06
Other Arab	33	0.17
Asian:	154	0.81
Cambodian (19)	24	0.13
Chinese, ex. Taiwanese (8)	8	0.04
Filipino (22)	25	0.13
Indian (22)	27	0.14
Indonesian (4)	4	0.02
Japanese (4)	6	0.03
Korean (13)	16	0.08
Laotian	2	0.01
Pakistani (1)	1	0.01
Sri Lankan (6)	6	0.03
Thai (12)	12	0.06
Vietnamese (2)	5	0.03
Other Asian, not specified (10)	18	0.09
Austrian	29	0.15
Basque	5	0.03
Belgian	7	0.04
British	20	0.10
Canadian	24	0.13
Czech	35	0.18
Czechoslovakian	32	0.17
Danish	44	0.23
Dutch	202	1.05
English	2,543	13.28
European	136	0.71
Finnish	63	0.33
French, except Basque	443	2.31
French Canadian	76	0.40
German	2,246	11.73
Greek	25	0.13
Hawaii Native/Pacific Islander:	8	0.04

Notes: 1. Figures in the "Number" column do not add up to the total population due to: a) Ancestry/Race overlap — e.g. persons can report being both White and Irish, b) persons of Hispanic origin can report being any race, c) persons reporting two ancestries are counted in both categories. 2. Numbers in parentheses indicate the number of persons reporting this ancestry/race alone, not in combination with any other ancestry/race. 3. Refer to the Explanation of Data in the front of the book for more detailed information.

Micronesian: (4)	6	0.03
Guamanian/Chamorro (2)	4	0.02
Other Micronesian (2)	2	0.01
Other Pac. Isl., not spec. (1)	2	0.01
Hispanic or Latino:	1,943	10.23
Central American:	11	0.06
Costa Rican	1	0.01
Guatemalan	5	0.03
Honduran	2	0.01
Panamanian	1	0.01
Salvadoran	2	0.01
Cuban	3	0.02
Mexican	1,554	8.18
Puerto Rican	14	0.07
South American:	3	0.02
Colombian	1	0.01
Ecuadorian	1	0.01
Other South American	1	0.01
Other Hispanic or Latino	358	1.88
Hungarian	22	0.11
Irish	2,184	11.40
Italian	197	1.03
Lithuanian	70	0.37
Northern European	8	0.04
Norwegian	61	0.32
Pennsylvania German	10	0.05
Polish	71	0.37
Portuguese	4	0.02
Russian	23	0.12
Scandinavian	30	0.16
Scotch-Irish	359	1.87
Scottish	440	2.30
Slovak	53	0.28
Swedish	27	0.14
Swiss	57	0.30
Turkish	7	0.04
Ukrainian	2	0.01
United States or American	2,321	12.12
Welsh	100	0.52
West Indian, excl. Hispanic:	22	0.11
Dutch West Indian	22	0.11
White:	17,516	92.19
Not Hispanic (16,241)	16,390	86.26
Hispanic (1,030)	1,126	5.93

Wells Branch

Place Type: Census Designated Place
County: Travis
Population: 11,271

Ancestry/Race	Number	%
Acadian/Cajun	16	0.14
African American/Black:	1,165	10.34
Not Hispanic (1,062)	1,129	10.02
Hispanic (26)	36	0.32
African, sub-Saharan:	44	0.39
African	34	0.30
Ghanian	10	0.09
Am. Ind. or Alaska Nat., not spec.	32	0.28
Alsatian	10	0.09
American Indian tribes, specified:	59	0.52
Apache (1)	5	0.04
Blackfeet (2)	2	0.02
Cherokee (11)	22	0.20
Chickasaw	3	0.03
Chippewa	1	0.01
Choctaw (2)	4	0.04
Comanche	3	0.03
Creek	1	0.01
Iroquois	1	0.01
Latin American Indians (4)	5	0.04
Navajo (2)	2	0.02
Osage	3	0.03
Seminole (1)	1	0.01
Sioux (1)	1	0.01
All other tribes (4)	5	0.04
American Indian tribes, not spec.	16	0.14
Arab:	80	0.71
Arab/Arabic	9	0.08
Lebanese	29	0.26
Palestinian	12	0.11
Other Arab	30	0.27
Asian:	1,194	10.59
Bangladeshi (5)	5	0.04
Cambodian (7)	8	0.07
Chinese, ex. Taiwanese (138)	153	1.36
Filipino (31)	48	0.43
Hmong (2)	2	0.02
Indian (449)	467	4.14
Indonesian (4)	8	0.07
Japanese (22)	33	0.29
Korean (139)	148	1.31
Laotian (1)	1	0.01
Malaysian	1	0.01
Pakistani (43)	56	0.50
Sri Lankan (1)	1	0.01
Taiwanese (7)	9	0.08
Thai (9)	18	0.16
Vietnamese (181)	194	1.72
Other Asian, specified	2	0.02
Other Asian, not specified (22)	40	0.35
Austrian	41	0.36
Brazilian	16	0.14
British	74	0.66
Canadian	30	0.27
Celtic	5	0.04
Czech	165	1.47
Czechoslovakian	75	0.67
Danish	29	0.26
Dutch	61	0.54
English	1,147	10.20
European	49	0.44
French, except Basque	341	3.03
French Canadian	96	0.85
German	2,101	18.68
Greek	23	0.20
Hawaii Native/Pacific Islander:	29	0.26
Micronesian: (4)	5	0.04
Guamanian/Chamorro (3)	4	0.04
Other Micronesian (1)	1	0.01
Polynesian: (8)	8	0.07
Native Hawaiian (8)	8	0.07
Other Pac. Isl., specified	1	0.01
Other Pac. Isl., not spec. (7)	15	0.13
Hispanic or Latino:	1,880	16.68
Central American:	49	0.43
Costa Rican	4	0.04
Guatemalan	3	0.03
Honduran	8	0.07
Nicaraguan	12	0.11
Panamanian	15	0.13
Salvadoran	6	0.05
Other Central American	1	0.01
Cuban	15	0.13
Dominican Republic	4	0.04
Mexican	1,277	11.33
Puerto Rican	59	0.52
South American:	57	0.51
Argentinean	1	0.01
Bolivian	8	0.07
Colombian	19	0.17
Ecuadorian	2	0.02
Peruvian	10	0.09
Venezuelan	10	0.09
Other South American	7	0.06
Other Hispanic or Latino	419	3.72
Iranian	38	0.34
Irish	1,244	11.06
Italian	372	3.31
Lithuanian	15	0.13
Norwegian	120	1.07
Polish	299	2.66
Portuguese	67	0.60
Russian	40	0.36
Scotch-Irish	243	2.16
Scottish	325	2.89
Slavic	11	0.10
Slovak	10	0.09
Swedish	221	1.96
Swiss	34	0.30
United States or American	569	5.06
Welsh	85	0.76
West Indian, excl. Hispanic:	32	0.28
British West Indian	11	0.10
Jamaican	21	0.19
White:	8,319	73.81
Not Hispanic (6,966)	7,153	63.46
Hispanic (1,070)	1,166	10.35

Weslaco

Place Type: City
County: Hidalgo
Population: 26,935

Ancestry/Race	Number	%
African American/Black:	99	0.37
Not Hispanic (32)	32	0.12
Hispanic (40)	67	0.25
African, sub-Saharan:	8	0.03
African	8	0.03
Alaska Native tribes, specified:	2	0.01
Aleut (1)	1	0.00
Eskimo (1)	1	0.00
Am. Ind. or Alaska Nat., not spec.	119	0.44
American Indian tribes, specified:	54	0.20
Apache (5)	7	0.03
Blackfeet (1)	1	0.00
Cherokee (6)	13	0.05
Cheyenne	1	0.00
Chippewa (2)	2	0.01
Choctaw (1)	1	0.00
Latin American Indians (16)	19	0.07
Lumbee	1	0.00
Navajo	1	0.00
Osage	1	0.00
Ottawa (1)	1	0.00
Shoshone	1	0.00
Sioux	1	0.00
All other tribes (2)	4	0.01
American Indian tribes, not spec.	16	0.06
Asian:	329	1.22
Chinese, ex. Taiwanese (30)	32	0.12
Filipino (183)	188	0.70
Indian (49)	49	0.18
Indonesian	3	0.01
Japanese (5)	6	0.02
Korean (9)	10	0.04
Malaysian	2	0.01
Pakistani (11)	13	0.05
Vietnamese (14)	14	0.05
Other Asian, not specified (5)	12	0.04
Austrian	10	0.04
Basque	7	0.03
Belgian	5	0.02
British	54	0.20
Canadian	96	0.36
Croatian	8	0.03
Czech	12	0.04
Danish	74	0.28
Dutch	193	0.72
English	745	2.78
Estonian	9	0.03
European	12	0.04
French, except Basque	228	0.85
French Canadian	27	0.10
German	1,055	3.94
Hawaii Native/Pacific Islander:	19	0.07
Polynesian: (15)	16	0.06
Native Hawaiian (13)	14	0.05
Samoan (2)	2	0.01
Other Pac. Isl., not spec.	3	0.01
Hispanic or Latino:	22,560	83.76
Central American:	32	0.12
Costa Rican	1	0.00
Guatemalan	4	0.01
Honduran	16	0.06
Nicaraguan	4	0.01
Panamanian	1	0.00

Notes: 1. Figures in the "Number" column do not add up to the total population due to: a) Ancestry/Race overlap — e.g. persons can report being both White and Irish, b) persons of Hispanic origin can report being any race, c) persons reporting two ancestries are counted in both categories. 2. Numbers in parentheses indicate the number of persons reporting this ancestry/race alone, not in combination with any other ancestry/race. 3. Refer to the Explanation of Data in the front of the book for more detailed information.

Ancestry/Race	Number	%
Salvadoran	6	0.02
Cuban	4	0.01
Dominican Republic	6	0.02
Mexican	18,157	67.41
Puerto Rican	47	0.17
South American:	28	0.10
Argentinean	1	0.00
Chilean	2	0.01
Colombian	6	0.02
Ecuadorian	3	0.01
Peruvian	6	0.02
Uruguayan	1	0.00
Venezuelan	7	0.03
Other South American	2	0.01
Other Hispanic or Latino	4,286	15.91
Hungarian	4	0.01
Iranian	11	0.04
Irish	598	2.23
Italian	111	0.41
Northern European	23	0.09
Norwegian	185	0.69
Polish	91	0.34
Portuguese	21	0.08
Russian	7	0.03
Scandinavian	6	0.02
Scotch-Irish	134	0.50
Scottish	151	0.56
Swedish	64	0.24
Swiss	28	0.10
Ukrainian	19	0.07
United States or American	463	1.73
Welsh	26	0.10
White:	20,723	76.94
Not Hispanic (3,961)	3,999	14.85
Hispanic (16,218)	16,724	62.09

West Odessa

Place Type: Census Designated Place
County: Ector
Population: 17,799

Ancestry/Race	Number	%
African American/Black:	166	0.93
Not Hispanic (109)	132	0.74
Hispanic (22)	34	0.19
Alaska Native tribes, specified:	2	0.01
Aleut (2)	2	0.01
Am. Ind. or Alaska Nat., not spec.	95	0.53
American Indian tribes, specified:	188	1.06
Apache (3)	13	0.07
Blackfeet (7)	7	0.04
Cherokee (20)	60	0.34
Chickasaw (7)	13	0.07
Choctaw (10)	19	0.11
Comanche (5)	6	0.03
Cree (1)	1	0.01
Creek	1	0.01
Latin American Indians (33)	36	0.20
Navajo (11)	12	0.07
Osage	1	0.01
Potawatomi (2)	2	0.01
Pueblo (1)	2	0.01
Seminole (1)	4	0.02
Sioux (4)	8	0.04
All other tribes (1)	3	0.02
American Indian tribes, not spec.	27	0.15
Asian:	54	0.30
Chinese, ex. Taiwanese (2)	6	0.03
Filipino (7)	8	0.04
Indian (1)	4	0.02
Indonesian (1)	1	0.01
Japanese	13	0.07
Korean (5)	7	0.04
Thai	1	0.01
Other Asian, specified	4	0.02
Other Asian, not specified	10	0.06
Canadian	7	0.04
Celtic	40	0.22
Czech	49	0.28
Dutch	218	1.22
English	827	4.65
European	8	0.04
French, except Basque	226	1.27
French Canadian	8	0.04
German	977	5.49
Greek	8	0.04
Hawaii Native/Pacific Islander:	18	0.10
Micronesian:	1	0.01
Guamanian/Chamorro	1	0.01
Polynesian: (10)	11	0.06
Native Hawaiian (8)	9	0.05
Samoan (2)	2	0.01
Other Pac. Isl., specified	4	0.02
Other Pac. Isl., not spec. (1)	2	0.01
Hispanic or Latino:	8,552	48.05
Central American:	5	0.03
Guatemalan	1	0.01
Panamanian	3	0.02
Salvadoran	1	0.01
Cuban	12	0.07
Mexican	6,600	37.08
Puerto Rican	4	0.02
South American:	1	0.01
Chilean	1	0.01
Other Hispanic or Latino	1,930	10.84
Hungarian	17	0.10
Irish	1,001	5.62
Italian	50	0.28
Maltese	6	0.03
Northern European	56	0.31
Norwegian	36	0.20
Polish	45	0.25
Portuguese	19	0.11
Romanian	6	0.03
Russian	20	0.11
Scotch-Irish	161	0.90
Scottish	123	0.69
Serbian	15	0.08
Swedish	26	0.15
Swiss	7	0.04
Ukrainian	8	0.04
United States or American	1,842	10.35
Welsh	16	0.09
West Indian, excl. Hispanic:	40	0.22
Dutch West Indian	40	0.22
White:	13,158	73.93
Not Hispanic (8,892)	9,017	50.66
Hispanic (3,859)	4,141	23.27

West University Place

Place Type: City
County: Harris
Population: 14,211

Ancestry/Race	Number	%
Acadian/Cajun	16	0.11
African American/Black:	85	0.60
Not Hispanic (64)	75	0.53
Hispanic (7)	10	0.07
African, sub-Saharan:	50	0.35
South African	43	0.30
Zimbabwean	7	0.05
Alaska Native tribes, specified:	1	0.01
Alaska Athabascan	1	0.01
Am. Ind. or Alaska Nat., not spec.	9	0.06
Alsatian	8	0.06
American Indian tribes, specified:	29	0.20
Apache (1)	2	0.01
Cherokee (4)	16	0.11
Cheyenne	1	0.01
Choctaw	3	0.02
Comanche	1	0.01
Creek	1	0.01
Delaware	3	0.02
Potawatomi (1)	1	0.01
Sioux	1	0.01
American Indian tribes, not spec.	4	0.03
Arab:	94	0.66
Arab/Arabic	19	0.13
Lebanese	70	0.49
Other Arab	5	0.04
Armenian	54	0.38
Asian:	763	5.37
Bangladeshi (2)	2	0.01
Chinese, ex. Taiwanese (232)	271	1.91
Filipino (38)	43	0.30
Indian (229)	250	1.76
Indonesian	5	0.04
Japanese (9)	20	0.14
Korean (31)	33	0.23
Malaysian (4)	4	0.03
Pakistani (9)	9	0.06
Taiwanese (22)	23	0.16
Thai (12)	12	0.08
Vietnamese (69)	73	0.51
Other Asian, specified (2)	3	0.02
Other Asian, not specified (7)	15	0.11
Australian	51	0.36
Austrian	91	0.64
Basque	14	0.10
Belgian	11	0.08
British	214	1.51
Canadian	45	0.32
Celtic	21	0.15
Croatian	8	0.06
Czech	78	0.55
Czechoslovakian	46	0.32
Danish	49	0.34
Dutch	265	1.86
Eastern European	28	0.20
English	2,686	18.90
European	380	2.67
Finnish	36	0.25
French, except Basque	754	5.31
French Canadian	96	0.68
German	2,330	16.40
Greek	113	0.80
Hawaii Native/Pacific Islander:	15	0.11
Micronesian:	1	0.01
Guamanian/Chamorro	1	0.01
Polynesian:	2	0.01
Native Hawaiian	2	0.01
Other Pac. Isl., specified	1	0.01
Other Pac. Isl., not spec. (3)	11	0.08
Hispanic or Latino:	671	4.72
Central American:	63	0.44
Costa Rican	3	0.02
Guatemalan	13	0.09
Honduran	6	0.04
Nicaraguan	2	0.01
Panamanian	14	0.10
Salvadoran	20	0.14
Other Central American	5	0.04
Cuban	35	0.25
Mexican	332	2.34
Puerto Rican	28	0.20
South American:	79	0.56
Argentinean	12	0.08
Bolivian	1	0.01
Chilean	1	0.01
Colombian	20	0.14
Ecuadorian	3	0.02
Peruvian	15	0.11
Venezuelan	23	0.16
Other South American	4	0.03
Other Hispanic or Latino	134	0.94
Hungarian	136	0.96
Iranian	29	0.20
Irish	1,575	11.08
Israeli	32	0.23
Italian	660	4.64
Latvian	5	0.04
Lithuanian	82	0.58
Maltese	7	0.05
Northern European	24	0.17
Norwegian	250	1.76
Polish	381	2.68
Portuguese	12	0.08

Notes: 1. Figures in the "Number" column do not add up to the total population due to: a) Ancestry/Race overlap — e.g. persons can report being both White and Irish, b) persons of Hispanic origin can report being any race, c) persons reporting two ancestries are counted in both categories. 2. Numbers in parentheses indicate the number of persons reporting this ancestry/race alone, not in combination with any other ancestry/race. 3. Refer to the Explanation of Data in the front of the book for more detailed information.

Ancestry/Race	Number	%
Russian	255	1.79
Scandinavian	68	0.48
Scotch-Irish	445	3.13
Scottish	582	4.10
Slavic	7	0.05
Slovak	35	0.25
Slovene	18	0.13
Swedish	258	1.82
Swiss	89	0.63
Turkish	9	0.06
Ukrainian	86	0.61
United States or American	1,037	7.30
Welsh	85	0.60
West Indian, excl. Hispanic:	2	0.01
Jamaican	2	0.01
White:	13,312	93.67
Not Hispanic (12,602)	12,758	89.78
Hispanic (524)	554	3.90
Yugoslavian	36	0.25

White Settlement

Place Type: City
County: Tarrant
Population: 14,831

Ancestry/Race	Number	%
Acadian/Cajun	11	0.07
African American/Black:	707	4.77
Not Hispanic (590)	684	4.61
Hispanic (10)	23	0.16
African, sub-Saharan:	33	0.22
African	12	0.08
Cape Verdean	8	0.05
Nigerian	13	0.09
Am. Ind. or Alaska Nat., not spec.	70	0.47
American Indian tribes, specified:	206	1.39
Apache (5)	10	0.07
Blackfeet	7	0.05
Cherokee (15)	87	0.59
Chickasaw (1)	5	0.03
Chippewa (1)	2	0.01
Choctaw (22)	43	0.29
Comanche (1)	9	0.06
Creek (5)	6	0.04
Delaware	2	0.01
Kiowa (3)	4	0.03
Latin American Indians (9)	11	0.07
Navajo (2)	3	0.02
Ottawa (3)	3	0.02
Potawatomi (1)	1	0.01
Sioux (3)	9	0.06
All other tribes (2)	4	0.03
American Indian tribes, not spec.	10	0.07
Asian:	299	2.02
Cambodian (1)	2	0.01
Chinese, ex. Taiwanese (12)	14	0.09
Filipino (107)	136	0.92
Indian (15)	16	0.11
Indonesian (1)	1	0.01
Japanese (20)	33	0.22
Korean (22)	36	0.24
Pakistani (7)	12	0.08
Thai (10)	20	0.13
Vietnamese (10)	10	0.07
Other Asian, specified	3	0.02
Other Asian, not specified (11)	16	0.11
Australian	7	0.05
British	25	0.17
Canadian	28	0.19
Czech	63	0.42
Danish	20	0.13
Dutch	295	1.99
English	1,331	8.97
European	164	1.11
Finnish	16	0.11
French, except Basque	259	1.75
French Canadian	6	0.04
German	1,689	11.38
Greek	21	0.14
Hawaii Native/Pacific Islander:	22	0.15
Micronesian: (2)	3	0.02
Guamanian/Chamorro (2)	3	0.02
Polynesian: (8)	14	0.09
Native Hawaiian (6)	10	0.07
Samoan (2)	4	0.03
Other Pac. Isl., specified	3	0.02
Other Pac. Isl., not spec. (1)	2	0.01
Hispanic or Latino:	2,017	13.60
Central American:	46	0.31
Guatemalan	4	0.03
Honduran	11	0.07
Nicaraguan	13	0.09
Salvadoran	16	0.11
Other Central American	2	0.01
Cuban	4	0.03
Mexican	1,522	10.26
Puerto Rican	26	0.18
South American:	4	0.03
Colombian	1	0.01
Peruvian	1	0.01
Other South American	2	0.01
Other Hispanic or Latino	415	2.80
Hungarian	39	0.26
Icelander	8	0.05
Irish	1,529	10.30
Italian	245	1.65
Lithuanian	18	0.12
Norwegian	161	1.09
Polish	75	0.51
Portuguese	23	0.16
Romanian	6	0.04
Russian	33	0.22
Scandinavian	16	0.11
Scotch-Irish	330	2.22
Scottish	237	1.60
Swedish	133	0.90
Swiss	6	0.04
United States or American	1,815	12.23
Welsh	29	0.20
West Indian, excl. Hispanic:	23	0.16
Dutch West Indian	23	0.16
White:	13,193	88.96
Not Hispanic (11,579)	11,896	80.21
Hispanic (1,151)	1,297	8.75

Wichita Falls

Place Type: City
County: Wichita
Population: 104,197

Ancestry/Race	Number	%
Acadian/Cajun	50	0.05
African American/Black:	13,750	13.20
Not Hispanic (12,705)	13,371	12.83
Hispanic (215)	379	0.36
African, sub-Saharan:	360	0.35
African	322	0.31
Ethiopian	7	0.01
Nigerian	16	0.02
Other sub-Saharan African	15	0.01
Alaska Native tribes, specified:	13	0.01
Alaska Athabascan	2	0.00
Aleut (3)	3	0.00
Eskimo (1)	4	0.00
Tlingit-Haida (4)	4	0.00
Alaska Native tribes, not specified	2	0.00
Am. Ind. or Alaska Nat., not spec.	383	0.37
Albanian	7	0.01
American Indian tribes, specified:	1,320	1.27
Apache (12)	48	0.05
Blackfeet (9)	35	0.03
Cherokee (184)	462	0.44
Cheyenne (2)	4	0.00
Chickasaw (45)	81	0.08
Chippewa (20)	27	0.03
Choctaw (163)	281	0.27
Colville	1	0.00
Comanche (35)	61	0.06
Cree	4	0.00
Creek (11)	31	0.03
Delaware (1)	6	0.01
Iroquois	15	0.01
Kiowa (17)	23	0.02
Latin American Indians (43)	61	0.06
Lumbee (11)	14	0.01
Menominee (2)	2	0.00
Navajo (13)	32	0.03
Osage (4)	8	0.01
Ottawa (1)	1	0.00
Pima	1	0.00
Potawatomi (4)	9	0.01
Pueblo (9)	12	0.01
Seminole (1)	11	0.01
Shoshone (1)	1	0.00
Sioux (13)	36	0.03
Ute	1	0.00
Yaqui (1)	5	0.00
All other tribes (23)	47	0.05
American Indian tribes, not spec.	89	0.09
Arab:	230	0.22
Arab/Arabic	18	0.02
Lebanese	177	0.17
Moroccan	5	0.00
Syrian	5	0.00
Other Arab	25	0.02
Armenian	47	0.05
Asian:	3,043	2.92
Bangladeshi (9)	10	0.01
Cambodian (11)	13	0.01
Chinese, ex. Taiwanese (143)	226	0.22
Filipino (510)	786	0.75
Hmong (2)	3	0.00
Indian (282)	353	0.34
Indonesian (6)	8	0.01
Japanese (200)	303	0.29
Korean (181)	277	0.27
Laotian (10)	14	0.01
Malaysian	4	0.00
Pakistani (32)	37	0.04
Taiwanese (2)	7	0.01
Thai (52)	81	0.08
Vietnamese (782)	829	0.80
Other Asian, specified (3)	8	0.01
Other Asian, not specified (21)	84	0.08
Australian	12	0.01
Austrian	107	0.10
Basque	10	0.01
Belgian	51	0.05
Brazilian	30	0.03
British	369	0.36
Canadian	120	0.12
Celtic	26	0.03
Croatian	19	0.02
Czech	450	0.43
Czechoslovakian	157	0.15
Danish	268	0.26
Dutch	1,554	1.50
Eastern European	11	0.01
English	7,992	7.69
European	582	0.56
Finnish	265	0.26
French, except Basque	2,532	2.44
French Canadian	351	0.34
German	13,074	12.58
German Russian	14	0.01
Greek	174	0.17
Hawaii Native/Pacific Islander:	266	0.26
Melanesian: (1)	1	0.00
Fijian (1)	1	0.00
Micronesian: (38)	67	0.06
Guamanian/Chamorro (31)	57	0.05
Other Micronesian (7)	10	0.01
Polynesian: (58)	143	0.14
Native Hawaiian (42)	115	0.11
Samoan (14)	23	0.02
Tongan (2)	2	0.00
Other Polynesian	3	0.00
Other Pac. Isl., specified	4	0.00

Notes: 1. Figures in the "Number" column do not add up to the total population due to: a) Ancestry/Race overlap — e.g. persons can report being both White and Irish, b) persons of Hispanic origin can report being any race, c) persons reporting two ancestries are counted in both categories. 2. Numbers in parentheses indicate the number of persons reporting this ancestry/race alone, not in combination with any other ancestry/race. 3. Refer to the Explanation of Data in the front of the book for more detailed information.

Ancestry/Race	Number	%
Other Pac. Isl., not spec. (6)	51	0.05
Hispanic or Latino:	14,570	13.98
Central American:	150	0.14
Costa Rican	4	0.00
Guatemalan	20	0.02
Honduran	18	0.02
Nicaraguan	25	0.02
Panamanian	54	0.05
Salvadoran	24	0.02
Other Central American	5	0.00
Cuban	78	0.07
Dominican Republic	15	0.01
Mexican	11,034	10.59
Puerto Rican	453	0.43
South American:	138	0.13
Argentinean	3	0.00
Bolivian	1	0.00
Chilean	7	0.01
Colombian	48	0.05
Ecuadorian	14	0.01
Peruvian	42	0.04
Uruguayan	1	0.00
Venezuelan	12	0.01
Other South American	10	0.01
Other Hispanic or Latino	2,702	2.59
Hungarian	281	0.27
Icelander	7	0.01
Iranian	6	0.01
Irish	9,805	9.44
Italian	2,118	2.04
Latvian	8	0.01
Lithuanian	27	0.03
Northern European	23	0.02
Norwegian	873	0.84
Pennsylvania German	5	0.00
Polish	1,091	1.05
Portuguese	131	0.13
Romanian	39	0.04
Russian	265	0.26
Scandinavian	118	0.11
Scotch-Irish	2,010	1.93
Scottish	1,658	1.60
Serbian	19	0.02
Slavic	50	0.05
Slovak	42	0.04
Slovene	20	0.02
Swedish	647	0.62
Swiss	178	0.17
Turkish	64	0.06
Ukrainian	47	0.05
United States or American	9,844	9.47
Welsh	400	0.38
West Indian, excl. Hispanic:	482	0.46
Bahamian	23	0.02
British West Indian	67	0.06
Dutch West Indian	152	0.15
Haitian	27	0.03
Jamaican	121	0.12
Trinidadian and Tobagonian	8	0.01
U.S. Virgin Islander	9	0.01
West Indian	68	0.07
Other West Indian	7	0.01
White:	80,805	77.55
Not Hispanic (71,782)	73,425	70.47
Hispanic (6,476)	7,380	7.08

Wylie

Place Type: City
County: Collin
Population: 15,132

Ancestry/Race	Number	%
African American/Black:	353	2.33
Not Hispanic (305)	340	2.25
Hispanic (8)	13	0.09
African, sub-Saharan:	56	0.37
African	51	0.34
Nigerian	5	0.03
Alaska Native tribes, not specified	2	0.01
Am. Ind. or Alaska Nat., not spec.	43	0.28
American Indian tribes, specified:	184	1.22
Apache	4	0.03
Blackfeet	1	0.01
Cherokee (19)	68	0.45
Chickasaw (10)	16	0.11
Chippewa (2)	2	0.01
Choctaw (19)	43	0.28
Comanche (1)	1	0.01
Creek (5)	6	0.04
Delaware (1)	1	0.01
Latin American Indians (5)	11	0.07
Lumbee	2	0.01
Navajo (1)	1	0.01
Potawatomi (3)	3	0.02
Pueblo (1)	1	0.01
Puget Sound Salish (1)	1	0.01
Seminole	1	0.01
Sioux (6)	6	0.04
Yaqui (1)	2	0.01
All other tribes (6)	14	0.09
American Indian tribes, not spec.	4	0.03
Arab:	18	0.12
Jordanian	9	0.06
Lebanese	9	0.06
Asian:	129	0.85
Bangladeshi (2)	2	0.01
Chinese, ex. Taiwanese (5)	13	0.09
Filipino (15)	24	0.16
Indian (2)	5	0.03
Japanese (7)	14	0.09
Korean (23)	31	0.20
Laotian (2)	2	0.01
Pakistani (5)	6	0.04
Thai (1)	2	0.01
Vietnamese (23)	23	0.15
Other Asian, not specified (6)	7	0.05
Australian	5	0.03
Austrian	1	0.01
Basque	5	0.03
Brazilian	3	0.02
British	76	0.51
Canadian	19	0.13
Celtic	52	0.35
Croatian	8	0.05
Czech	46	0.31
Czechoslovakian	59	0.39
Danish	21	0.14
Dutch	199	1.33
English	1,446	9.66
European	156	1.04
Finnish	10	0.07
French, except Basque	443	2.96
French Canadian	45	0.30
German	2,158	14.42
Greek	30	0.20
Hawaii Native/Pacific Islander:	15	0.10
Micronesian: (2)	3	0.02
Guamanian/Chamorro (2)	3	0.02
Polynesian: (1)	11	0.07
Native Hawaiian (1)	10	0.07
Samoan	1	0.01
Other Pac. Isl., not spec. (1)	1	0.01
Hispanic or Latino:	1,580	10.44
Central American:	22	0.15
Costa Rican	1	0.01
Guatemalan	9	0.06
Honduran	2	0.01
Nicaraguan	2	0.01
Panamanian	2	0.01
Salvadoran	6	0.04
Cuban	7	0.05
Mexican	1,171	7.74
Puerto Rican	31	0.20
South American:	10	0.07
Argentinean	5	0.03
Bolivian	1	0.01
Colombian	3	0.02
Peruvian	1	0.01
Other Hispanic or Latino	339	2.24
Hungarian	64	0.43
Irish	1,803	12.05
Italian	300	2.00
New Zealander	8	0.05
Norwegian	100	0.67
Polish	228	1.52
Portuguese	4	0.03
Romanian	13	0.09
Russian	57	0.38
Scandinavian	88	0.59
Scotch-Irish	176	1.18
Scottish	222	1.48
Slovak	2	0.01
Swedish	164	1.10
Swiss	48	0.32
United States or American	2,558	17.09
Welsh	93	0.62
West Indian, excl. Hispanic:	24	0.16
Dutch West Indian	24	0.16
White:	13,954	92.22
Not Hispanic (12,877)	13,050	86.24
Hispanic (810)	904	5.97
Yugoslavian	6	0.04

American Fork

Place Type: City
County: Utah
Population: 21,941

Ancestry/Race	Number	%
African American/Black:	68	0.31
Not Hispanic (31)	63	0.29
Hispanic (4)	5	0.02
Alaska Native tribes, specified:	1	0.00
Eskimo (1)	1	0.00
Am. Ind. or Alaska Nat., not spec.	45	0.21
American Indian tribes, specified:	110	0.50
Apache	7	0.03
Cherokee (4)	17	0.08
Cheyenne (2)	2	0.01
Chickasaw (2)	2	0.01
Chippewa	5	0.02
Choctaw	1	0.00
Delaware	4	0.02
Iroquois (1)	1	0.00
Latin American Indians (2)	2	0.01
Navajo (20)	26	0.12
Potawatomi (2)	2	0.01
Pueblo (4)	6	0.03
Seminole	1	0.00
Shoshone	4	0.02
Sioux (7)	14	0.06
Ute (1)	7	0.03
All other tribes (4)	9	0.04
American Indian tribes, not spec.	11	0.05
Arab:	54	0.25
Arab/Arabic	46	0.21
Palestinian	8	0.04
Asian:	219	1.00
Cambodian (4)	4	0.02
Chinese, ex. Taiwanese (41)	60	0.27
Filipino (17)	39	0.18
Indian (7)	12	0.05
Japanese (27)	47	0.21
Korean (15)	18	0.08
Laotian (2)	6	0.03
Thai (1)	3	0.01
Vietnamese (22)	23	0.10
Other Asian, not specified (6)	7	0.03
Australian	16	0.07
Austrian	47	0.21
Basque	25	0.11
Brazilian	11	0.05
British	445	2.03
Canadian	170	0.78
Czech	26	0.12
Danish	1,672	7.63
Dutch	339	1.55
English	7,753	35.36

Notes: 1. Figures in the "Number" column do not add up to the total population due to: a) Ancestry/Race overlap — e.g. persons can report being both White and Irish, b) persons of Hispanic origin can report being any race, c) persons reporting two ancestries are counted in both categories. 2. Numbers in parentheses indicate the number of persons reporting this ancestry/race alone, not in combination with any other ancestry/race. 3. Refer to the Explanation of Data in the front of the book for more detailed information.

Ancestry/Race	Number	%
European	578	2.64
Finnish	18	0.08
French, except Basque	371	1.69
French Canadian	47	0.21
German	2,105	9.60
Greek	66	0.30
Hawaii Native/Pacific Islander:	143	0.65
Micronesian: (6)	7	0.03
Guamanian/Chamorro (3)	3	0.01
Other Micronesian (3)	4	0.02
Polynesian: (41)	121	0.55
Native Hawaiian (17)	56	0.26
Samoan (7)	38	0.17
Tongan (16)	25	0.11
Other Polynesian (1)	2	0.01
Other Pac. Isl., not spec. (2)	15	0.07
Hispanic or Latino:	1,011	4.61
Central American:	30	0.14
Guatemalan	4	0.02
Honduran	6	0.03
Nicaraguan	4	0.02
Panamanian	2	0.01
Salvadoran	14	0.06
Dominican Republic	8	0.04
Mexican	703	3.20
Puerto Rican	20	0.09
South American:	51	0.23
Argentinean	14	0.06
Bolivian	8	0.04
Chilean	11	0.05
Colombian		0.00
Ecuadorian	12	0.05
Peruvian	2	0.01
Uruguayan		0.00
Venezuelan	2	0.01
Other Hispanic or Latino	199	0.91
Icelander	15	0.07
Irish	872	3.98
Italian	447	2.04
Lithuanian	9	0.04
Norwegian	623	2.84
Pennsylvania German	7	0.03
Polish	57	0.26
Portuguese	18	0.08
Romanian	121	0.55
Russian	7	0.03
Scandinavian	190	0.87
Scotch-Irish	161	0.73
Scottish	1,112	5.07
Swedish	846	3.86
Swiss	249	1.14
Ukrainian	9	0.04
United States or American	2,334	10.65
Welsh	540	2.46
White:	21,176	96.51
Not Hispanic (20,413)	20,601	93.89
Hispanic (483)	575	2.62

Bountiful

Place Type: City
County: Davis
Population: 41,301

Ancestry/Race	Number	%
African American/Black:	168	0.41
Not Hispanic (96)	160	0.39
Hispanic (2)	8	0.02
African, sub-Saharan:	21	0.05
South African	5	0.01
Zimbabwean	7	0.02
Other sub-Saharan African	9	0.02
Am. Ind. or Alaska Nat., not spec.	54	0.13
Albanian	8	0.02
American Indian tribes, specified:	143	0.35
Apache (2)	3	0.01
Blackfeet	1	0.00
Cherokee (12)	35	0.08
Chickasaw (2)	2	0.00
Chippewa (2)	4	0.01
Choctaw (3)	6	0.01
Comanche	1	0.00
Delaware	1	0.00
Iroquois	1	0.00
Latin American Indians (6)	7	0.02
Navajo (23)	26	0.06
Paiute (1)	2	0.00
Pueblo (1)	2	0.00
Puget Sound Salish (1)	1	0.00
Shoshone (4)	5	0.01
Sioux (5)	13	0.03
Ute (2)	6	0.01
All other tribes (18)	27	0.07
American Indian tribes, not spec.	2	0.00
Arab:	52	0.13
Lebanese	9	0.02
Palestinian	15	0.04
Syrian	28	0.07
Armenian	39	0.09
Asian:	726	1.76
Cambodian (5)	5	0.01
Chinese, ex. Taiwanese (162)	205	0.50
Filipino (22)	68	0.16
Indian (15)	29	0.07
Indonesian	1	0.00
Japanese (133)	243	0.59
Korean (58)	81	0.20
Laotian (3)	5	0.01
Malaysian (1)	10	0.02
Pakistani (1)	1	0.00
Taiwanese (3)	3	0.01
Thai (9)	15	0.04
Vietnamese (21)	30	0.07
Other Asian, not specified (17)	30	0.07
Australian	14	0.03
Austrian	35	0.08
Basque	33	0.08
Brazilian	14	0.03
British	953	2.30
Bulgarian	5	0.01
Canadian	43	0.10
Celtic	13	0.03
Croatian	29	0.07
Czech	36	0.09
Czechoslovakian	31	0.07
Danish	3,842	9.28
Dutch	961	2.32
Eastern European	6	0.01
English	14,764	35.67
Estonian	13	0.03
European	1,233	2.98
Finnish	128	0.31
French, except Basque	1,032	2.49
French Canadian	108	0.26
German	4,857	11.73
Greek	361	0.87
Hawaii Native/Pacific Islander:	262	0.63
Melanesian: (3)	5	0.01
Fijian (3)	5	0.01
Micronesian: (5)	7	0.02
Other Micronesian (5)	7	0.02
Polynesian: (112)	226	0.55
Native Hawaiian (13)	62	0.15
Samoan (58)	91	0.22
Tongan (39)	61	0.15
Other Polynesian (2)	12	0.03
Other Pac. Isl., not spec. (13)	24	0.06
Hispanic or Latino:	1,197	2.90
Central American:	56	0.14
Costa Rican	1	0.00
Guatemalan	19	0.05
Honduran	3	0.01
Nicaraguan	3	0.01
Panamanian	1	0.00
Salvadoran	27	0.07
Other Central American	2	0.00
Cuban	10	0.02
Dominican Republic	2	0.00
Mexican	575	1.39
Puerto Rican	48	0.12
South American:	207	0.50
Argentinean	33	0.08
Bolivian	4	0.01
Chilean	35	0.08
Colombian	28	0.07
Ecuadorian	17	0.04
Peruvian	76	0.18
Uruguayan	1	0.00
Venezuelan	5	0.01
Other South American	8	0.02
Other Hispanic or Latino	299	0.72
Hungarian	58	0.14
Icelander	44	0.11
Iranian	32	0.08
Irish	1,992	4.81
Italian	1,137	2.75
Lithuanian	64	0.15
Maltese	6	0.01
Northern European	117	0.28
Norwegian	1,234	2.98
Pennsylvania German	29	0.07
Polish	214	0.52
Portuguese	67	0.16
Romanian	31	0.07
Russian	67	0.16
Scandinavian	508	1.23
Scotch-Irish	605	1.46
Scottish	2,235	5.40
Serbian	8	0.02
Slovak	43	0.10
Swedish	2,170	5.24
Swiss	1,181	2.85
Ukrainian	79	0.19
United States or American	2,692	6.50
Welsh	1,302	3.15
White:	39,987	96.82
Not Hispanic (38,846)	39,239	95.01
Hispanic (623)	748	1.81
Yugoslavian	72	0.17

Brigham City

Place Type: City
County: Box Elder
Population: 17,411

Ancestry/Race	Number	%
African American/Black:	66	0.38
Not Hispanic (36)	57	0.33
Hispanic (5)	9	0.05
African, sub-Saharan:	15	0.09
African	5	0.03
Nigerian	8	0.05
South African	2	0.01
Alaska Native tribes, specified:	4	0.02
Aleut (4)	4	0.02
Am. Ind. or Alaska Nat., not spec.	43	0.25
Albanian	5	0.03
American Indian tribes, specified:	373	2.14
Apache (4)	5	0.03
Blackfeet (1)	2	0.01
Cherokee (7)	24	0.14
Chippewa (3)	5	0.03
Choctaw (3)	5	0.03
Creek	1	0.01
Crow (1)	3	0.02
Delaware	4	0.02
Iroquois	1	0.01
Latin American Indians	3	0.02
Navajo (107)	149	0.86
Pima	2	0.01
Pueblo (18)	32	0.18
Seminole	1	0.01
Shoshone (43)	54	0.31
Sioux (17)	36	0.21
Tohono O'Odham (2)	3	0.02
Ute (6)	10	0.06
Yaqui	1	0.01
All other tribes (24)	32	0.18
American Indian tribes, not spec.	7	0.04

Notes: 1. Figures in the "Number" column do not add up to the total population due to: a) Ancestry/Race overlap — e.g. persons can report being both White and Irish, b) persons of Hispanic origin can report being any race, c) persons reporting two ancestries are counted in both categories. 2. Numbers in parentheses indicate the number of persons reporting this ancestry/race alone, not in combination with any other ancestry/race. 3. Refer to the Explanation of Data in the front of the book for more detailed information.

Ancestry/Race	Number	%
Asian:	205	1.18
Cambodian (2)	3	0.02
Chinese, ex. Taiwanese (14)	18	0.10
Filipino (22)	32	0.18
Indian (5)	12	0.07
Indonesian (2)	2	0.01
Japanese (52)	86	0.49
Korean (13)	15	0.09
Laotian (1)	1	0.01
Pakistani (1)	1	0.01
Thai	2	0.01
Vietnamese (16)	24	0.14
Other Asian, not specified (4)	9	0.05
Australian	32	0.18
Austrian	31	0.18
Basque	5	0.03
Brazilian	5	0.03
British	124	0.71
Canadian	13	0.07
Czech	18	0.10
Czechoslovakian	7	0.04
Danish	2,076	11.93
Dutch	254	1.46
English	5,576	32.04
European	409	2.35
Finnish	14	0.08
French, except Basque	429	2.47
French Canadian	49	0.28
German	1,978	11.37
Greek	26	0.15
Hawaii Native/Pacific Islander:	31	0.18
Micronesian: (1)	1	0.01
Other Micronesian (1)	1	0.01
Polynesian: (13)	19	0.11
Native Hawaiian (8)	11	0.06
Samoan (1)	4	0.02
Tongan (4)	4	0.02
Other Pac. Isl., not spec. (4)	11	0.06
Hispanic or Latino:	1,335	7.67
Central American:	30	0.17
Guatemalan	5	0.03
Honduran	3	0.02
Nicaraguan	3	0.02
Panamanian	1	0.01
Salvadoran	17	0.10
Other Central American	1	0.01
Cuban	8	0.05
Dominican Republic	1	0.01
Mexican	1,015	5.83
Puerto Rican	4	0.02
South American:	26	0.15
Chilean	11	0.06
Colombian	1	0.01
Peruvian	10	0.06
Venezuelan	4	0.02
Other Hispanic or Latino	251	1.44
Hungarian	24	0.14
Irish	853	4.90
Italian	238	1.37
Lithuanian	38	0.22
Northern European	47	0.27
Norwegian	530	3.05
Polish	190	1.09
Portuguese	14	0.08
Romanian	14	0.08
Russian	10	0.06
Scandinavian	126	0.72
Scotch-Irish	220	1.26
Scottish	673	3.87
Slovak	9	0.05
Swedish	930	5.34
Swiss	420	2.41
Ukrainian	16	0.09
United States or American	1,142	6.56
Welsh	421	2.42
White:	16,195	93.02
Not Hispanic (15,452)	15,627	89.75
Hispanic (438)	568	3.26
Yugoslavian	8	0.05

Canyon Rim

Place Type: Census Designated Place
County: Salt Lake
Population: 10,428

Ancestry/Race	Number	%
African American/Black:	75	0.72
Not Hispanic (53)	70	0.67
Hispanic (3)	5	0.05
African, sub-Saharan:	14	0.13
African	14	0.13
Am. Ind. or Alaska Nat., not spec.	21	0.20
American Indian tribes, specified:	40	0.38
Apache	1	0.01
Blackfeet (1)	1	0.01
Cherokee (2)	5	0.05
Choctaw (1)	2	0.02
Creek (1)	1	0.01
Iroquois	5	0.05
Latin American Indians (3)	3	0.03
Navajo (8)	13	0.12
Potawatomi (1)	2	0.02
Pueblo (2)	2	0.02
Seminole (1)	3	0.03
Ute (1)	1	0.01
All other tribes	1	0.01
American Indian tribes, not spec.	1	0.01
Arab:	87	0.82
Arab/Arabic	52	0.49
Lebanese	35	0.33
Asian:	209	2.00
Cambodian (1)	1	0.01
Chinese, ex. Taiwanese (45)	53	0.51
Filipino (7)	11	0.11
Indian (5)	12	0.12
Indonesian (3)	5	0.05
Japanese (58)	73	0.70
Korean (16)	27	0.26
Sri Lankan (1)	1	0.01
Vietnamese (6)	6	0.06
Other Asian, specified (7)	7	0.07
Other Asian, not specified (10)	13	0.12
Austrian	47	0.44
Basque	9	0.09
Belgian	41	0.39
Brazilian	22	0.21
British	237	2.24
Canadian	43	0.41
Croatian	6	0.06
Czech	5	0.05
Danish	812	7.68
Dutch	444	4.20
Eastern European	7	0.07
English	3,844	36.37
European	400	3.78
Finnish	7	0.07
French, except Basque	339	3.21
French Canadian	17	0.16
German	1,287	12.18
Greek	92	0.87
Hawaii Native/Pacific Islander:	45	0.43
Polynesian: (24)	36	0.35
Native Hawaiian (3)	11	0.11
Samoan	1	0.01
Tongan (21)	24	0.23
Other Pac. Isl., not spec. (9)	9	0.09
Hispanic or Latino:	250	2.40
Central American:	6	0.06
Guatemalan	2	0.02
Honduran	3	0.03
Salvadoran	1	0.01
Cuban	1	0.01
Mexican	145	1.39
Puerto Rican	4	0.04
South American:	26	0.25
Argentinean	6	0.06
Bolivian	6	0.06
Chilean	3	0.03
Colombian	1	0.01
Peruvian	9	0.09
Venezuelan	1	0.01
Other Hispanic or Latino	68	0.65
Icelander	9	0.09
Iranian	10	0.09
Irish	652	6.17
Italian	292	2.76
Latvian	10	0.09
Lithuanian	11	0.10
New Zealander	20	0.19
Northern European	20	0.19
Norwegian	437	4.13
Polish	106	1.00
Romanian	9	0.09
Russian	40	0.38
Scandinavian	343	3.25
Scotch-Irish	169	1.60
Scottish	561	5.31
Slavic	26	0.25
Slovak	7	0.07
Swedish	542	5.13
Swiss	155	1.47
United States or American	480	4.54
Welsh	191	1.81
West Indian, excl. Hispanic:	4	0.04
Jamaican	4	0.04
White:	10,063	96.50
Not Hispanic (9,801)	9,892	94.86
Hispanic (145)	171	1.64
Yugoslavian	30	0.28

Cedar City

Place Type: City
County: Iron
Population: 20,527

Ancestry/Race	Number	%
African American/Black:	146	0.71
Not Hispanic (91)	139	0.68
Hispanic (6)	7	0.03
African, sub-Saharan:	8	0.04
Other sub-Saharan African	8	0.04
Alaska Native tribes, specified:	1	0.00
Eskimo (1)	1	0.00
Alaska Native tribes, not specified	1	0.00
Am. Ind. or Alaska Nat., not spec.	66	0.32
American Indian tribes, specified:	600	2.92
Apache (5)	7	0.03
Blackfeet (3)	6	0.03
Cherokee (2)	19	0.09
Cheyenne	7	0.03
Chickasaw	1	0.00
Chippewa (1)	1	0.00
Choctaw	3	0.01
Iroquois (2)	3	0.01
Latin American Indians (4)	14	0.07
Navajo (215)	260	1.27
Paiute (181)	208	1.01
Pueblo (10)	15	0.07
Shoshone (7)	9	0.04
Sioux (2)	5	0.02
Ute (13)	23	0.11
Yakama	1	0.00
Yuman	1	0.00
All other tribes (4)	17	0.08
American Indian tribes, not spec.	23	0.11
Arab:	32	0.16
Iraqi	5	0.02
Lebanese	6	0.03
Other Arab	21	0.10
Armenian	11	0.05
Asian:	306	1.49
Cambodian (1)	2	0.01
Chinese, ex. Taiwanese (28)	39	0.19
Filipino (16)	37	0.18
Indian (19)	21	0.10
Indonesian	2	0.01
Japanese (109)	132	0.64
Korean (40)	44	0.21

Notes: 1. Figures in the "Number" column do not add up to the total population due to: a) Ancestry/Race overlap — e.g. persons can report being both White and Irish, b) persons of Hispanic origin can report being any race, c) persons reporting two ancestries are counted in both categories. 2. Numbers in parentheses indicate the number of persons reporting this ancestry/race alone, not in combination with any other ancestry/race. 3. Refer to the Explanation of Data in the front of the book for more detailed information.

Laotian (4)	4	0.02
Pakistani (2)	2	0.01
Taiwanese (2)	3	0.01
Thai (2)	3	0.01
Vietnamese (1)	6	0.03
Other Asian, not specified (1)	11	0.05
Australian	30	0.15
Austrian	13	0.06
Basque	5	0.02
Belgian	7	0.03
British	244	1.19
Canadian	44	0.21
Celtic	17	0.08
Czech	23	0.11
Danish	1,140	5.54
Dutch	567	2.76
English	6,290	30.57
European	553	2.69
Finnish	11	0.05
French, except Basque	461	2.24
French Canadian	52	0.25
German	1,977	9.61
Greek	27	0.13
Hawaii Native/Pacific Islander:	113	0.55
Micronesian: (6)	9	0.04
Guamanian/Chamorro (6)	9	0.04
Polynesian: (52)	98	0.48
Native Hawaiian (14)	33	0.16
Samoan (14)	31	0.15
Tongan (20)	29	0.14
Other Polynesian (4)	5	0.02
Other Pac. Isl., not spec. (2)	6	0.03
Hispanic or Latino:	850	4.14
Central American:	8	0.04
Costa Rican	1	0.00
Guatemalan	4	0.02
Salvadoran	3	0.01
Cuban	3	0.01
Dominican Republic	1	0.00
Mexican	615	3.00
Puerto Rican	30	0.15
South American:	23	0.11
Bolivian	2	0.01
Chilean	3	0.01
Colombian	4	0.02
Ecuadorian	1	0.00
Peruvian	9	0.04
Uruguayan	1	0.00
Other South American	3	0.01
Other Hispanic or Latino	170	0.83
Hungarian	46	0.22
Icelander	28	0.14
Irish	1,330	6.46
Italian	488	2.37
Lithuanian	30	0.15
New Zealander	7	0.03
Northern European	13	0.06
Norwegian	407	1.98
Pennsylvania German	5	0.02
Polish	102	0.50
Portuguese	76	0.37
Romanian	6	0.03
Scandinavian	266	1.29
Scotch-Irish	281	1.37
Scottish	1,196	5.81
Slovak	7	0.03
Swedish	776	3.77
Swiss	344	1.67
Ukrainian	43	0.21
United States or American	1,756	8.53
Welsh	680	3.30
White:	19,231	93.69
Not Hispanic (18,509)	18,752	91.35
Hispanic (388)	479	2.33
Yugoslavian	7	0.03

Centerville

Place Type: City
County: Davis
Population: 14,585

Ancestry/Race	Number	%
African American/Black:	66	0.45
Not Hispanic (33)	63	0.43
Hispanic	3	0.02
African, sub-Saharan:	8	0.06
Other sub-Saharan African	8	0.06
Am. Ind. or Alaska Nat., not spec.	11	0.08
American Indian tribes, specified:	41	0.28
Blackfeet	1	0.01
Cherokee (4)	6	0.04
Chippewa (2)	6	0.04
Choctaw	1	0.01
Creek (1)	1	0.01
Iroquois	1	0.01
Latin American Indians	5	0.03
Navajo (13)	13	0.09
Sioux (1)	1	0.01
Tohono O'Odham	1	0.01
Ute	1	0.01
Yaqui	2	0.01
All other tribes (2)	2	0.01
American Indian tribes, not spec.	4	0.03
Arab:	11	0.08
Lebanese	11	0.08
Armenian	16	0.11
Asian:	169	1.16
Chinese, ex. Taiwanese (14)	27	0.19
Filipino (1)	4	0.03
Indian (17)	23	0.16
Japanese (39)	66	0.45
Korean (15)	23	0.16
Thai (5)	11	0.08
Vietnamese (2)	5	0.03
Other Asian, not specified (9)	10	0.07
Australian	9	0.06
Austrian	7	0.05
Basque	7	0.05
Belgian	15	0.10
British	292	2.03
Bulgarian	16	0.11
Canadian	28	0.19
Czech	8	0.06
Danish	1,373	9.55
Dutch	337	2.35
English	6,138	42.71
European	401	2.79
French, except Basque	193	1.34
French Canadian	75	0.52
German	1,915	13.33
Greek	16	0.11
Hawaii Native/Pacific Islander:	64	0.44
Polynesian: (29)	64	0.44
Native Hawaiian (13)	31	0.21
Samoan (8)	12	0.08
Tongan (8)	15	0.10
Other Polynesian	6	0.04
Hispanic or Latino:	285	1.95
Central American:	10	0.07
Guatemalan	4	0.03
Honduran	2	0.01
Salvadoran	2	0.01
Other Central American	2	0.01
Dominican Republic	1	0.01
Mexican	138	0.95
Puerto Rican	6	0.04
South American:	50	0.34
Argentinean	1	0.01
Chilean	16	0.11
Colombian	9	0.06
Ecuadorian	6	0.04
Paraguayan	4	0.03
Peruvian	12	0.08
Venezuelan	2	0.01
Other Hispanic or Latino	80	0.55
Hungarian	7	0.05
Irish	878	6.11
Israeli	19	0.13
Italian	342	2.38
Luxemburger	15	0.10
Norwegian	614	4.27
Pennsylvania German	7	0.05
Polish	112	0.78
Russian	51	0.35
Scandinavian	155	1.08
Scotch-Irish	156	1.09
Scottish	1,014	7.06
Slovene	16	0.11
Swedish	787	5.48
Swiss	306	2.13
United States or American	940	6.54
Welsh	311	2.16
West Indian, excl. Hispanic:	9	0.06
Haitian	9	0.06
White:	14,282	97.92
Not Hispanic (13,988)	14,094	96.63
Hispanic (168)	188	1.29
Yugoslavian	68	0.47

Clearfield

Place Type: City
County: Davis
Population: 25,974

Ancestry/Race	Number	%
African American/Black:	1,158	4.46
Not Hispanic (903)	1,100	4.24
Hispanic (35)	58	0.22
African, sub-Saharan:	55	0.21
African	45	0.17
South African	10	0.04
Alaska Native tribes, specified:	3	0.01
Eskimo	3	0.01
Am. Ind. or Alaska Nat., not spec.	196	0.75
Albanian	9	0.03
American Indian tribes, specified:	425	1.64
Apache (8)	19	0.07
Blackfeet (5)	9	0.03
Cherokee (27)	71	0.27
Cheyenne (1)	6	0.02
Chickasaw (2)	2	0.01
Chippewa (5)	10	0.04
Choctaw (5)	11	0.04
Colville (4)	5	0.02
Comanche (1)	1	0.00
Cree	1	0.00
Creek (2)	5	0.02
Iroquois (2)	5	0.02
Kiowa (1)	4	0.02
Latin American Indians (10)	12	0.05
Navajo (99)	117	0.45
Paiute	1	0.00
Pima (1)	6	0.02
Potawatomi	3	0.01
Pueblo (12)	13	0.05
Puget Sound Salish (1)	2	0.01
Shoshone (9)	17	0.07
Sioux (22)	32	0.12
Ute (10)	21	0.08
Yaqui	3	0.01
All other tribes (32)	49	0.19
American Indian tribes, not spec.	22	0.08
Arab:	148	0.57
Arab/Arabic	61	0.24
Lebanese	53	0.20
Moroccan	26	0.10
Syrian	8	0.03
Asian:	1,095	4.22
Bangladeshi	1	0.00
Cambodian (6)	6	0.02
Chinese, ex. Taiwanese (48)	72	0.28
Filipino (244)	360	1.39
Hmong (2)	10	0.04
Indian (15)	36	0.14

Notes: 1. Figures in the "Number" column do not add up to the total population due to: a) Ancestry/Race overlap — e.g. persons can report being both White and Irish, b) persons of Hispanic origin can report being any race, c) persons reporting two ancestries are counted in both categories. 2. Numbers in parentheses indicate the number of persons reporting this ancestry/race alone, not in combination with any other ancestry/race. 3. Refer to the Explanation of Data in the front of the book for more detailed information.

Indonesian (5)	8	0.03
Japanese (82)	141	0.54
Korean (85)	121	0.47
Laotian (58)	77	0.30
Sri Lankan	1	0.00
Taiwanese	1	0.00
Thai (81)	126	0.49
Vietnamese (35)	37	0.14
Other Asian, specified	1	0.00
Other Asian, not specified (55)	97	0.37
Basque	15	0.06
Belgian	34	0.13
British	175	0.68
Bulgarian	12	0.05
Canadian	51	0.20
Croatian	6	0.02
Czech	45	0.17
Czechoslovakian	57	0.22
Danish	898	3.46
Dutch	647	2.50
English	5,787	22.33
European	566	2.18
Finnish	13	0.05
French, except Basque	719	2.77
French Canadian	100	0.39
German	3,345	12.91
Greek	100	0.39
Hawaii Native/Pacific Islander:	177	0.68
Micronesian: (25)	48	0.18
Guamanian/Chamorro (15)	26	0.10
Other Micronesian (10)	22	0.08
Polynesian: (41)	92	0.35
Native Hawaiian (16)	40	0.15
Samoan (4)	25	0.10
Tongan (13)	16	0.06
Other Polynesian (8)	11	0.04
Other Pac. Isl., not spec. (6)	37	0.14
Hispanic or Latino:	2,747	10.58
Central American:	78	0.30
Costa Rican	2	0.01
Guatemalan	24	0.09
Honduran	15	0.06
Nicaraguan	2	0.01
Panamanian	14	0.05
Salvadoran	21	0.08
Cuban	17	0.07
Mexican	1,654	6.37
Puerto Rican	101	0.39
South American:	69	0.27
Argentinean	16	0.06
Bolivian	4	0.02
Chilean	17	0.07
Colombian	7	0.03
Ecuadorian	6	0.02
Paraguayan	1	0.00
Peruvian	15	0.06
Venezuelan	3	0.01
Other Hispanic or Latino	828	3.19
Hungarian	36	0.14
Irish	2,055	7.93
Israeli	12	0.05
Italian	780	3.01
Lithuanian	7	0.03
Northern European	111	0.43
Norwegian	642	2.48
Polish	223	0.86
Portuguese	75	0.29
Romanian	19	0.07
Russian	14	0.05
Scandinavian	89	0.34
Scotch-Irish	276	1.06
Scottish	625	2.41
Slavic	8	0.03
Swedish	655	2.53
Swiss	243	0.94
Turkish	8	0.03
United States or American	1,950	7.52
Welsh	413	1.59
West Indian, excl. Hispanic:	11	0.04
Jamaican	5	0.02
West Indian	6	0.02
White:	22,378	86.16
Not Hispanic (20,515)	21,035	80.98
Hispanic (1,090)	1,343	5.17
Yugoslavian	40	0.15

Clinton

Place Type: City
County: Davis
Population: 12,585

Ancestry/Race	Number	%
African American/Black:	170	1.35
Not Hispanic (116)	152	1.21
Hispanic (11)	18	0.14
African, sub-Saharan:	17	0.13
African	17	0.13
Am. Ind. or Alaska Nat., not spec.	27	0.21
American Indian tribes, specified:	82	0.65
Apache	3	0.02
Cherokee (7)	15	0.12
Cheyenne (1)	4	0.03
Choctaw (3)	3	0.02
Cree (1)	1	0.01
Creek (3)	4	0.03
Latin American Indians (2)	3	0.02
Navajo (34)	38	0.30
Pueblo (1)	4	0.03
Sioux (3)	3	0.02
All other tribes (2)	4	0.03
American Indian tribes, not spec.	5	0.04
Arab:	11	0.09
Lebanese	11	0.09
Armenian	21	0.17
Asian:	328	2.61
Chinese, ex. Taiwanese (10)	24	0.19
Filipino (47)	78	0.62
Hmong (11)	11	0.09
Indian (6)	8	0.06
Japanese (40)	66	0.52
Korean (30)	39	0.31
Laotian (26)	28	0.22
Thai (20)	25	0.20
Vietnamese (27)	32	0.25
Other Asian, not specified (7)	17	0.14
Australian	26	0.21
Austrian	25	0.20
Brazilian	18	0.14
British	57	0.45
Canadian	19	0.15
Croatian	9	0.07
Czech	7	0.06
Czechoslovakian	7	0.06
Danish	935	7.39
Dutch	608	4.80
English	3,324	26.26
European	255	2.01
French, except Basque	427	3.37
French Canadian	54	0.43
German	1,519	12.00
Greek	74	0.58
Hawaii Native/Pacific Islander:	70	0.56
Micronesian: (10)	10	0.08
Other Micronesian (10)	10	0.08
Polynesian: (20)	46	0.37
Native Hawaiian (3)	19	0.15
Samoan (9)	15	0.12
Tongan (4)	4	0.03
Other Polynesian (4)	8	0.06
Other Pac. Isl., not spec. (6)	14	0.11
Hispanic or Latino:	1,011	8.03
Central American:	14	0.11
Guatemalan	7	0.06
Nicaraguan	2	0.02
Panamanian	3	0.02
Salvadoran	1	0.01
Other Central American	1	0.01
Cuban	2	0.02
Mexican	562	4.47
Puerto Rican	34	0.27
South American:	13	0.10
Bolivian	3	0.02
Colombian	2	0.02
Ecuadorian	4	0.03
Peruvian	1	0.01
Venezuelan	2	0.02
Other South American	1	0.01
Other Hispanic or Latino	386	3.07
Hungarian	11	0.09
Icelander	11	0.09
Irish	922	7.29
Italian	276	2.18
Lithuanian	47	0.37
Northern European	54	0.43
Norwegian	270	2.13
Polish	11	0.09
Portuguese	21	0.17
Russian	9	0.07
Scandinavian	71	0.56
Scotch-Irish	234	1.85
Scottish	580	4.58
Slavic	6	0.05
Swedish	446	3.52
Swiss	77	0.61
Ukrainian	13	0.10
United States or American	955	7.55
Welsh	221	1.75
West Indian, excl. Hispanic:	11	0.09
Jamaican	11	0.09
White:	11,630	92.41
Not Hispanic (10,960)	11,118	88.34
Hispanic (410)	512	4.07

Cottonwood Heights

Place Type: Census Designated Place
County: Salt Lake
Population: 27,569

Ancestry/Race	Number	%
Acadian/Cajun	4	0.01
Afghan	76	0.28
African American/Black:	254	0.92
Not Hispanic (174)	229	0.83
Hispanic (19)	25	0.09
African, sub-Saharan:	23	0.08
African	23	0.08
Alaska Native tribes, specified:	3	0.01
Aleut	1	0.00
Eskimo (1)	1	0.00
Tlingit-Haida	1	0.00
Am. Ind. or Alaska Nat., not spec.	39	0.14
American Indian tribes, specified:	93	0.34
Apache (2)	6	0.02
Blackfeet (2)	2	0.01
Cherokee (3)	6	0.02
Cheyenne	2	0.01
Chickasaw (1)	1	0.00
Chippewa	4	0.01
Choctaw (5)	5	0.02
Delaware (1)	1	0.00
Iroquois (1)	1	0.00
Latin American Indians	3	0.01
Navajo (33)	41	0.15
Ottawa	2	0.01
Paiute (3)	3	0.01
Potawatomi	1	0.00
Pueblo	2	0.01
Seminole (1)	1	0.00
Shoshone (1)	1	0.00
Sioux	3	0.01
Tohono O'Odham (1)	1	0.00
Ute (1)	4	0.01
All other tribes (2)	3	0.01
American Indian tribes, not spec.	4	0.01
Arab:	183	0.67
Arab/Arabic	26	0.09
Egyptian	21	0.08
Iraqi	31	0.11

Notes: 1. Figures in the "Number" column do not add up to the total population due to: a) Ancestry/Race overlap — e.g. persons can report being both White and Irish, b) persons of Hispanic origin can report being any race, c) persons reporting two ancestries are counted in both categories. 2. Numbers in parentheses indicate the number of persons reporting this ancestry/race alone, not in combination with any other ancestry/race. 3. Refer to the Explanation of Data in the front of the book for more detailed information.

Ancestry/Race	Number	%
Jordanian	12	0.04
Lebanese	45	0.16
Palestinian	7	0.03
Other Arab	41	0.15
Armenian	228	0.83
Asian:	881	3.20
Cambodian (3)	6	0.02
Chinese, ex. Taiwanese (201)	263	0.95
Filipino (25)	61	0.22
Indian (81)	96	0.35
Indonesian (1)	5	0.02
Japanese (130)	211	0.77
Korean (90)	105	0.38
Laotian (2)	3	0.01
Pakistani (8)	8	0.03
Taiwanese (29)	40	0.15
Thai (14)	16	0.06
Vietnamese (16)	18	0.07
Other Asian, specified	6	0.02
Other Asian, not specified (5)	43	0.16
Australian	16	0.06
Austrian	80	0.29
Basque	16	0.06
Belgian	20	0.07
Brazilian	9	0.03
British	674	2.46
Canadian	70	0.26
Celtic	17	0.06
Croatian	27	0.10
Czech	135	0.49
Czechoslovakian	34	0.12
Danish	1,624	5.93
Dutch	732	2.67
English	8,428	30.79
European	347	1.27
Finnish	117	0.43
French, except Basque	653	2.39
French Canadian	203	0.74
German	3,926	14.34
Greek	252	0.92
Hawaii Native/Pacific Islander:	166	0.60
Melanesian: (6)	6	0.02
Fijian (6)	6	0.02
Micronesian: (4)	4	0.01
Guamanian/Chamorro (1)	1	0.00
Other Micronesian (3)	3	0.01
Polynesian: (73)	141	0.51
Native Hawaiian (26)	69	0.25
Samoan (21)	35	0.13
Tongan (25)	35	0.13
Other Polynesian (1)	2	0.01
Other Pac. Isl., specified	5	0.02
Other Pac. Isl., not spec. (5)	10	0.04
Hispanic or Latino:	846	3.07
Central American:	31	0.11
Guatemalan	10	0.04
Honduran	1	0.00
Panamanian	4	0.01
Salvadoran	15	0.05
Other Central American	1	0.00
Cuban	15	0.05
Dominican Republic	6	0.02
Mexican	441	1.60
Puerto Rican	36	0.13
South American:	56	0.20
Argentinean	3	0.01
Bolivian	3	0.01
Chilean	11	0.04
Colombian	16	0.06
Ecuadorian	8	0.03
Paraguayan	1	0.00
Peruvian	11	0.04
Uruguayan	1	0.00
Venezuelan	1	0.00
Other South American	1	0.00
Other Hispanic or Latino	261	0.95
Hungarian	68	0.25
Icelander	27	0.10
Iranian	109	0.40
Irish	2,128	7.77
Italian	954	3.49
Latvian	34	0.12
Lithuanian	11	0.04
New Zealander	6	0.02
Norwegian	1,097	4.01
Polish	379	1.38
Portuguese	59	0.22
Russian	161	0.59
Scandinavian	329	1.20
Scotch-Irish	480	1.75
Scottish	1,496	5.47
Slavic	5	0.02
Slovak	34	0.12
Swedish	1,754	6.41
Swiss	475	1.74
Ukrainian	37	0.14
United States or American	1,525	5.57
Welsh	651	2.38
West Indian, excl. Hispanic:	6	0.02
Haitian	6	0.02
White:	26,243	95.19
Not Hispanic (25,322)	25,698	93.21
Hispanic (475)	545	1.98
Yugoslavian	27	0.10

Cottonwood West

Place Type: Census Designated Place
County: Salt Lake
Population: 18,727

Ancestry/Race	Number	%
Afghan	7	0.04
African American/Black:	210	1.12
Not Hispanic (130)	189	1.01
Hispanic (16)	21	0.11
African, sub-Saharan:	32	0.17
African	24	0.13
South African	8	0.04
Alaska Native tribes, specified:	3	0.02
Alaska Athabascan	1	0.01
Aleut (1)	1	0.01
Tlingit-Haida (1)	1	0.01
Am. Ind. or Alaska Nat., not spec.	37	0.20
American Indian tribes, specified:	110	0.59
Apache (1)	1	0.01
Blackfeet (1)	1	0.01
Cherokee (6)	27	0.14
Chippewa (1)	1	0.01
Choctaw	3	0.02
Cree	1	0.01
Creek (1)	1	0.01
Crow	3	0.02
Iroquois	3	0.02
Latin American Indians (8)	9	0.05
Lumbee (1)	1	0.01
Navajo (26)	34	0.18
Ottawa	1	0.01
Paiute	3	0.02
Pueblo	2	0.01
Sioux (1)	2	0.01
Ute (5)	6	0.03
Yakama (1)	1	0.01
All other tribes (9)	10	0.05
American Indian tribes, not spec.	5	0.03
Arab:	31	0.17
Lebanese	19	0.10
Palestinian	12	0.06
Armenian	39	0.21
Asian:	570	3.04
Chinese, ex. Taiwanese (98)	128	0.68
Filipino (28)	44	0.23
Indian (91)	102	0.54
Indonesian	2	0.01
Japanese (114)	165	0.88
Korean (55)	61	0.33
Malaysian	1	0.01
Taiwanese (12)	12	0.06
Thai (7)	7	0.04
Vietnamese (14)	21	0.11
Other Asian, specified (4)	6	0.03
Other Asian, not specified (9)	21	0.11
Australian	59	0.32
Austrian	69	0.37
Basque	16	0.09
Belgian	11	0.06
British	248	1.33
Bulgarian	8	0.04
Canadian	34	0.18
Celtic	11	0.06
Czech	16	0.09
Czechoslovakian	41	0.22
Danish	1,175	6.31
Dutch	411	2.21
Eastern European	28	0.15
English	5,867	31.53
European	242	1.30
Finnish	74	0.40
French, except Basque	394	2.12
French Canadian	71	0.38
German	2,303	12.38
Greek	287	1.54
Hawaii Native/Pacific Islander:	78	0.42
Micronesian: (3)	3	0.02
Guamanian/Chamorro (2)	2	0.01
Other Micronesian (1)	1	0.01
Polynesian: (26)	63	0.34
Native Hawaiian (6)	34	0.18
Samoan (6)	9	0.05
Tongan (9)	12	0.06
Other Polynesian (5)	8	0.04
Other Pac. Isl., specified	1	0.01
Other Pac. Isl., not spec. (3)	11	0.06
Hispanic or Latino:	787	4.20
Central American:	23	0.12
Costa Rican	1	0.01
Guatemalan	3	0.02
Panamanian	1	0.01
Salvadoran	15	0.08
Other Central American	3	0.02
Cuban	7	0.04
Dominican Republic	3	0.02
Mexican	482	2.57
Puerto Rican	31	0.17
South American:	69	0.37
Argentinean	15	0.08
Chilean	5	0.03
Colombian	5	0.03
Ecuadorian	10	0.05
Peruvian	17	0.09
Uruguayan	5	0.03
Venezuelan	3	0.02
Other South American	9	0.05
Other Hispanic or Latino	172	0.92
Hungarian	87	0.47
Icelander	28	0.15
Iranian	63	0.34
Irish	1,367	7.35
Italian	672	3.61
New Zealander	30	0.16
Northern European	15	0.08
Norwegian	719	3.86
Pennsylvania German	18	0.10
Polish	243	1.31
Portuguese	36	0.19
Romanian	18	0.10
Russian	129	0.69
Scandinavian	108	0.58
Scotch-Irish	327	1.76
Scottish	1,456	7.82
Slovak	10	0.05
Slovene	7	0.04
Swedish	1,127	6.06
Swiss	328	1.76
Ukrainian	39	0.21
United States or American	1,067	5.73
Welsh	619	3.33
West Indian, excl. Hispanic:	15	0.08
Barbadian	15	0.08
White:	17,751	94.79

Notes: 1. Figures in the "Number" column do not add up to the total population due to: a) Ancestry/Race overlap — e.g. persons can report being both White and Irish, b) persons of Hispanic origin can report being any race, c) persons reporting two ancestries are counted in both categories. 2. Numbers in parentheses indicate the number of persons reporting this ancestry/race alone, not in combination with any other ancestry/race. 3. Refer to the Explanation of Data in the front of the book for more detailed information.

Not Hispanic (16,989)	17,238	92.05
Hispanic (442)	513	2.74
Yugoslavian	187	1.00

Draper

Place Type: City
County: Salt Lake
Population: 25,220

Ancestry/Race	Number	%
African American/Black:	453	1.80
Not Hispanic (363)	422	1.67
Hispanic (21)	31	0.12
African, sub-Saharan:	103	0.40
African	97	0.38
South African	6	0.02
Alaska Native tribes, specified:	2	0.01
Aleut	2	0.01
Am. Ind. or Alaska Nat., not spec.	72	0.29
American Indian tribes, specified:	258	1.02
Apache (9)	17	0.07
Blackfeet (2)	10	0.04
Cherokee (5)	32	0.13
Cheyenne (2)	3	0.01
Chickasaw	1	0.00
Chippewa (3)	5	0.02
Choctaw (4)	9	0.04
Comanche (1)	1	0.00
Cree (2)	2	0.01
Crow	1	0.00
Iroquois	6	0.02
Latin American Indians (11)	21	0.08
Navajo (51)	59	0.23
Paiute (4)	8	0.03
Potawatomi	1	0.00
Pueblo (6)	8	0.03
Shoshone (6)	7	0.03
Sioux (11)	18	0.07
Ute (15)	21	0.08
Yaqui (2)	2	0.01
All other tribes (12)	26	0.10
American Indian tribes, not spec.	15	0.06
Arab:	59	0.23
Iraqi	16	0.06
Lebanese	37	0.15
Other Arab	6	0.02
Armenian	6	0.02
Asian:	499	1.98
Cambodian (9)	9	0.04
Chinese, ex. Taiwanese (109)	132	0.52
Filipino (23)	49	0.19
Indian (28)	35	0.14
Indonesian (1)	3	0.01
Japanese (56)	122	0.48
Korean (40)	52	0.21
Laotian (8)	15	0.06
Malaysian	1	0.00
Pakistani (1)	1	0.00
Taiwanese (2)	3	0.01
Thai (5)	10	0.04
Vietnamese (36)	45	0.18
Other Asian, specified (1)	2	0.01
Other Asian, not specified (8)	20	0.08
Austrian	73	0.29
Basque	7	0.03
Belgian	23	0.09
Brazilian	15	0.06
British	453	1.78
Canadian	143	0.56
Celtic	21	0.08
Croatian	7	0.03
Czech	6	0.02
Czechoslovakian	13	0.05
Danish	1,693	6.66
Dutch	734	2.89
Eastern European	8	0.03
English	7,200	28.31
Estonian	9	0.04
European	562	2.21
Finnish	79	0.31
French, except Basque	852	3.35
French Canadian	120	0.47
German	3,165	12.44
Greek	130	0.51
Hawaii Native/Pacific Islander:	181	0.72
Micronesian: (2)	4	0.02
Guamanian/Chamorro (2)	4	0.02
Polynesian: (78)	159	0.63
Native Hawaiian (14)	46	0.18
Samoan (31)	55	0.22
Tongan (31)	46	0.18
Other Polynesian (2)	12	0.05
Other Pac. Isl., not spec. (9)	18	0.07
Hispanic or Latino:	1,469	5.82
Central American:	16	0.06
Costa Rican	1	0.00
Guatemalan	5	0.02
Honduran	2	0.01
Nicaraguan	1	0.00
Salvadoran	6	0.02
Other Central American	1	0.00
Cuban	29	0.11
Dominican Republic	3	0.01
Mexican	927	3.68
Puerto Rican	63	0.25
South American:	80	0.32
Argentinean	24	0.10
Bolivian	2	0.01
Chilean	6	0.02
Colombian	25	0.10
Ecuadorian	4	0.02
Peruvian	10	0.04
Uruguayan	2	0.01
Venezuelan	3	0.01
Other South American	4	0.02
Other Hispanic or Latino	351	1.39
Hungarian	17	0.07
Icelander	62	0.24
Iranian	32	0.13
Irish	1,631	6.41
Italian	833	3.27
Norwegian	793	3.12
Polish	226	0.89
Portuguese	82	0.32
Romanian	36	0.14
Russian	214	0.84
Scandinavian	436	1.71
Scotch-Irish	239	0.94
Scottish	1,077	4.23
Serbian	18	0.07
Slavic	6	0.02
Slovak	7	0.03
Swedish	1,187	4.67
Swiss	283	1.11
Ukrainian	21	0.08
United States or American	1,611	6.33
Welsh	642	2.52
West Indian, excl. Hispanic:	11	0.04
Jamaican	6	0.02
U.S. Virgin Islander	5	0.02
White:	23,462	93.03
Not Hispanic (22,429)	22,756	90.23
Hispanic (584)	706	2.80

East Millcreek

Place Type: Census Designated Place
County: Salt Lake
Population: 21,385

Ancestry/Race	Number	%
African American/Black:	147	0.69
Not Hispanic (89)	141	0.66
Hispanic (2)	6	0.03
African, sub-Saharan:	42	0.20
African	35	0.16
South African	7	0.03
Am. Ind. or Alaska Nat., not spec.	34	0.16
American Indian tribes, specified:	48	0.22
Apache	1	0.00
Blackfeet	1	0.00
Cherokee	11	0.05
Chippewa	1	0.00
Choctaw (1)	1	0.00
Creek (2)	3	0.01
Crow (1)	1	0.00
Latin American Indians (3)	5	0.02
Navajo (4)	7	0.03
Pueblo (1)	2	0.01
Puget Sound Salish	2	0.01
Sioux (3)	6	0.03
Ute	2	0.01
Yaqui	3	0.01
All other tribes (1)	2	0.01
American Indian tribes, not spec.	5	0.02
Arab:	41	0.19
Egyptian	6	0.03
Lebanese	35	0.16
Armenian	68	0.32
Asian:	443	2.07
Cambodian (1)	1	0.00
Chinese, ex. Taiwanese (120)	164	0.77
Filipino (9)	23	0.11
Indian (20)	29	0.14
Indonesian	2	0.01
Japanese (73)	119	0.56
Korean (37)	41	0.19
Pakistani (4)	4	0.02
Sri Lankan (3)	4	0.02
Taiwanese (4)	7	0.03
Thai (6)	8	0.04
Vietnamese (8)	14	0.07
Other Asian, not specified (14)	27	0.13
Australian	30	0.14
Austrian	181	0.85
Basque	18	0.08
Belgian	19	0.09
Brazilian	6	0.03
British	423	1.98
Canadian	71	0.33
Celtic	9	0.04
Croatian	6	0.03
Czech	34	0.16
Czechoslovakian	16	0.07
Danish	2,078	9.71
Dutch	485	2.27
English	8,210	38.36
European	327	1.53
Finnish	73	0.34
French, except Basque	592	2.77
French Canadian	38	0.18
German	3,135	14.65
Greek	279	1.30
Hawaii Native/Pacific Islander:	113	0.53
Micronesian: (2)	2	0.01
Other Micronesian (2)	2	0.01
Polynesian: (41)	95	0.44
Native Hawaiian (4)	25	0.12
Samoan (8)	20	0.09
Tongan (28)	43	0.20
Other Polynesian (1)	7	0.03
Other Pac. Isl., not spec. (7)	16	0.07
Hispanic or Latino:	586	2.74
Central American:	10	0.05
Guatemalan	6	0.03
Honduran	1	0.00
Nicaraguan	1	0.00
Panamanian	1	0.00
Salvadoran	1	0.00
Cuban	13	0.06
Dominican Republic	5	0.02
Mexican	281	1.31
Puerto Rican	16	0.07
South American:	85	0.40
Argentinean	5	0.02
Bolivian	1	0.00
Chilean	11	0.05
Colombian	25	0.12
Ecuadorian	4	0.02

Notes: 1. Figures in the "Number" column do not add up to the total population due to: a) Ancestry/Race overlap — e.g. persons can report being both White and Irish, b) persons of Hispanic origin can report being any race, c) persons reporting two ancestries are counted in both categories. 2. Numbers in parentheses indicate the number of persons reporting this ancestry/race alone, not in combination with any other ancestry/race. 3. Refer to the Explanation of Data in the front of the book for more detailed information.

Peruvian	29	0.14
Venezuelan	8	0.04
Other South American	2	0.01
Other Hispanic or Latino	176	0.82
Hungarian	16	0.07
Iranian	28	0.13
Irish	1,300	6.07
Italian	572	2.67
Latvian	7	0.03
Lithuanian	19	0.09
Luxemburger	6	0.03
Northern European	46	0.21
Norwegian	869	4.06
Polish	162	0.76
Portuguese	11	0.05
Romanian	42	0.20
Russian	128	0.60
Scandinavian	322	1.50
Scotch-Irish	312	1.46
Scottish	1,023	4.78
Slovak	44	0.21
Swedish	1,599	7.47
Swiss	506	2.36
Ukrainian	33	0.15
United States or American	942	4.40
Welsh	638	2.98
White:	20,644	96.53
Not Hispanic (20,008)	20,288	94.87
Hispanic (316)	356	1.66
Yugoslavian	35	0.16

Farmington

Place Type: City
County: Davis
Population: 12,081

Ancestry/Race	Number	%
African American/Black:	71	0.59
Not Hispanic (43)	60	0.50
Hispanic (1)	11	0.09
Alaska Native tribes, not specified	1	0.01
Am. Ind. or Alaska Nat., not spec.	27	0.22
American Indian tribes, specified:	67	0.55
Apache (2)	3	0.02
Blackfeet (2)	2	0.02
Cherokee (8)	15	0.12
Iroquois (4)	5	0.04
Latin American Indians (6)	8	0.07
Navajo (17)	19	0.16
Paiute (1)	1	0.01
Potawatomi	1	0.01
Pueblo (1)	1	0.01
Shoshone (1)	1	0.01
Tohono O'Odham (1)	1	0.01
Ute	1	0.01
All other tribes (6)	9	0.07
American Indian tribes, not spec.	5	0.04
Armenian	16	0.13
Asian:	169	1.40
Cambodian (4)	4	0.03
Chinese, ex. Taiwanese (17)	41	0.34
Filipino (6)	19	0.16
Indian (5)	5	0.04
Japanese (50)	65	0.54
Korean (8)	19	0.16
Laotian (2)	2	0.02
Thai (1)	5	0.04
Vietnamese (3)	4	0.03
Other Asian, not specified (2)	5	0.04
Australian	7	0.06
Austrian	23	0.19
Belgian	4	0.03
British	383	3.14
Canadian	58	0.48
Danish	889	7.28
Dutch	195	1.60
English	5,217	42.74
European	256	2.10
French, except Basque	125	1.02
French Canadian	50	0.41
German	1,412	11.57
Greek	79	0.65
Hawaii Native/Pacific Islander:	32	0.26
Micronesian:	1	0.01
Guamanian/Chamorro	1	0.01
Polynesian: (15)	25	0.21
Native Hawaiian (2)	8	0.07
Samoan (7)	7	0.06
Tongan (4)	7	0.06
Other Polynesian (2)	3	0.02
Other Pac. Isl., not spec. (5)	6	0.05
Hispanic or Latino:	360	2.98
Central American:	14	0.12
Guatemalan	8	0.07
Salvadoran	6	0.05
Cuban	4	0.03
Dominican Republic	1	0.01
Mexican	262	2.17
Puerto Rican	7	0.06
South American:	18	0.15
Argentinean	2	0.02
Bolivian	1	0.01
Chilean	3	0.02
Colombian	5	0.04
Ecuadorian	2	0.02
Peruvian	2	0.02
Venezuelan	3	0.02
Other Hispanic or Latino	54	0.45
Hungarian	65	0.53
Icelander	28	0.23
Irish	486	3.98
Italian	294	2.41
Northern European	11	0.09
Norwegian	418	3.42
Polish	54	0.44
Portuguese	48	0.39
Romanian	12	0.10
Russian	37	0.30
Scandinavian	346	2.83
Scotch-Irish	109	0.89
Scottish	604	4.95
Slovak	31	0.25
Swedish	579	4.74
Swiss	240	1.97
United States or American	710	5.82
Welsh	286	2.34
White:	11,656	96.48
Not Hispanic (11,389)	11,463	94.88
Hispanic (168)	193	1.60
Yugoslavian	6	0.05

Holladay

Place Type: City
County: Salt Lake
Population: 14,561

Ancestry/Race	Number	%
African American/Black:	91	0.62
Not Hispanic (57)	75	0.52
Hispanic (10)	16	0.11
African, sub-Saharan:	20	0.14
African	20	0.14
Am. Ind. or Alaska Nat., not spec.	7	0.05
American Indian tribes, specified:	60	0.41
Cherokee (2)	10	0.07
Creek	4	0.03
Crow	1	0.01
Iroquois (1)	2	0.01
Latin American Indians (3)	4	0.03
Navajo (9)	17	0.12
Potawatomi (1)	1	0.01
Pueblo	1	0.01
Seminole (2)	2	0.01
Shoshone	1	0.01
Sioux (1)	4	0.03
Ute	2	0.01
All other tribes (1)	11	0.08
American Indian tribes, not spec.	5	0.03
Arab:	79	0.54
Arab/Arabic	29	0.20
Egyptian	26	0.18
Lebanese	24	0.16
Armenian	6	0.04
Asian:	333	2.29
Chinese, ex. Taiwanese (82)	95	0.65
Filipino (13)	30	0.21
Indian (27)	32	0.22
Indonesian (2)	5	0.03
Japanese (67)	99	0.68
Korean (14)	19	0.13
Laotian	1	0.01
Malaysian	1	0.01
Pakistani	1	0.01
Sri Lankan (7)	7	0.05
Taiwanese (7)	12	0.08
Thai (2)	4	0.03
Vietnamese (14)	14	0.10
Other Asian, not specified (1)	13	0.09
Australian	18	0.12
Austrian	62	0.43
Belgian	40	0.27
British	422	2.90
Bulgarian	25	0.17
Canadian	26	0.18
Celtic	16	0.11
Croatian	10	0.07
Czech	16	0.11
Czechoslovakian	13	0.09
Danish	1,107	7.61
Dutch	375	2.58
Eastern European	10	0.07
English	5,285	36.32
European	396	2.72
Finnish	23	0.16
French, except Basque	262	1.80
French Canadian	23	0.16
German	1,842	12.66
Greek	130	0.89
Hawaii Native/Pacific Islander:	61	0.42
Polynesian: (27)	51	0.35
Native Hawaiian (9)	18	0.12
Samoan (4)	9	0.06
Tongan (13)	19	0.13
Other Polynesian (1)	5	0.03
Other Pac. Isl., not spec. (2)	10	0.07
Hispanic or Latino:	272	1.87
Central American:	11	0.08
Guatemalan	6	0.04
Nicaraguan	1	0.01
Panamanian	1	0.01
Salvadoran	3	0.02
Cuban	4	0.03
Dominican Republic	3	0.02
Mexican	122	0.84
Puerto Rican	22	0.15
South American:	23	0.16
Argentinean	1	0.01
Bolivian	2	0.01
Chilean	9	0.06
Colombian	4	0.03
Peruvian	6	0.04
Uruguayan	1	0.01
Other Hispanic or Latino	87	0.60
Hungarian	20	0.14
Iranian	43	0.30
Irish	927	6.37
Israeli	6	0.04
Italian	406	2.79
Latvian	13	0.09
Lithuanian	17	0.12
Luxemburger	7	0.05
Northern European	91	0.63
Norwegian	519	3.57
Polish	137	0.94
Portuguese	11	0.08
Romanian	38	0.26
Russian	142	0.98
Scandinavian	194	1.33

Notes: 1. Figures in the "Number" column do not add up to the total population due to: a) Ancestry/Race overlap — e.g. persons can report being both White and Irish, b) persons of Hispanic origin can report being any race, c) persons reporting two ancestries are counted in both categories. 2. Numbers in parentheses indicate the number of persons reporting this ancestry/race alone, not in combination with any other ancestry/race. 3. Refer to the Explanation of Data in the front of the book for more detailed information.

Scotch-Irish	167	1.15
Scottish	963	6.62
Slovak	6	0.04
Swedish	1,263	8.68
Swiss	287	1.97
Ukrainian	44	0.30
United States or American	556	3.82
Welsh	428	2.94
White:	14,105	96.87
Not Hispanic (13,744)	13,919	95.59
Hispanic (157)	186	1.28
Yugoslavian	34	0.23

Kaysville

Place Type: City
County: Davis
Population: 20,351

Ancestry/Race	Number	%
African American/Black:	100	0.49
Not Hispanic (59)	91	0.45
Hispanic (4)	9	0.04
Alaska Native tribes, specified:	1	0.00
Tlingit-Haida	1	0.00
Am. Ind. or Alaska Nat., not spec.	17	0.08
American Indian tribes, specified:	75	0.37
Apache (1)	8	0.04
Cherokee (1)	10	0.05
Chickasaw (1)	1	0.00
Choctaw	2	0.01
Comanche	3	0.01
Iroquois	2	0.01
Latin American Indians (1)	1	0.00
Navajo (26)	31	0.15
Pueblo	1	0.00
Sioux (3)	3	0.01
Ute (3)	6	0.03
All other tribes (5)	7	0.03
American Indian tribes, not spec.	5	0.02
Arab:	46	0.22
Arab/Arabic	5	0.02
Palestinian	4	0.02
Other Arab	37	0.18
Armenian	10	0.05
Asian:	224	1.10
Chinese, ex. Taiwanese (15)	27	0.13
Filipino (9)	28	0.14
Indian (13)	20	0.10
Japanese (34)	71	0.35
Korean (24)	40	0.20
Laotian (4)	4	0.02
Pakistani (11)	11	0.05
Taiwanese (2)	4	0.02
Thai (6)	7	0.03
Vietnamese (5)	8	0.04
Other Asian, not specified (4)	4	0.02
Australian	13	0.06
Austrian	26	0.13
Basque	16	0.08
Belgian	25	0.12
Brazilian	38	0.18
British	625	3.02
Canadian	39	0.19
Croatian	6	0.03
Czech	22	0.11
Czechoslovakian	16	0.08
Danish	1,839	8.88
Dutch	439	2.12
English	8,488	40.99
European	630	3.04
Finnish	80	0.39
French, except Basque	673	3.25
French Canadian	54	0.26
German	2,622	12.66
Greek	127	0.61
Hawaii Native/Pacific Islander:	68	0.33
Micronesian: (5)	5	0.02
Other Micronesian (5)	5	0.02
Polynesian: (31)	62	0.30
Native Hawaiian (7)	23	0.11
Samoan (24)	37	0.18
Tongan	1	0.00
Other Polynesian	1	0.00
Other Pac. Isl., not spec. (1)	1	0.00
Hispanic or Latino:	606	2.98
Central American:	35	0.17
Costa Rican	1	0.00
Guatemalan	24	0.12
Honduran	2	0.01
Nicaraguan	6	0.03
Panamanian	1	0.00
Other Central American	1	0.00
Cuban	1	0.00
Mexican	340	1.67
Puerto Rican	17	0.08
South American:	42	0.21
Argentinean	11	0.05
Bolivian	5	0.02
Chilean	1	0.00
Colombian	10	0.05
Peruvian	8	0.04
Venezuelan	7	0.03
Other Hispanic or Latino	171	0.84
Hungarian	41	0.20
Icelander	25	0.12
Irish	1,029	4.97
Italian	313	1.51
Lithuanian	26	0.13
Northern European	64	0.31
Norwegian	683	3.30
Polish	117	0.56
Portuguese	30	0.14
Romanian	8	0.04
Russian	7	0.03
Scandinavian	421	2.03
Scotch-Irish	171	0.83
Scottish	1,143	5.52
Slovak	11	0.05
Swedish	925	4.47
Swiss	454	2.19
Ukrainian	29	0.14
United States or American	1,500	7.24
Welsh	575	2.78
White:	19,865	97.61
Not Hispanic (19,299)	19,448	95.56
Hispanic (354)	417	2.05
Yugoslavian	13	0.06

Kearns

Place Type: Census Designated Place
County: Salt Lake
Population: 33,659

Ancestry/Race	Number	%
Afghan	9	0.03
African American/Black:	321	0.95
Not Hispanic (179)	264	0.78
Hispanic (42)	57	0.17
African, sub-Saharan:	10	0.03
African	10	0.03
Alaska Native tribes, specified:	7	0.02
Alaska Athabascan (1)	1	0.00
Eskimo	5	0.01
Tlingit-Haida	1	0.00
Am. Ind. or Alaska Nat., not spec.	151	0.45
American Indian tribes, specified:	422	1.25
Apache (9)	25	0.07
Blackfeet (2)	5	0.01
Cherokee (9)	50	0.15
Cheyenne (1)	1	0.00
Chippewa (10)	10	0.03
Choctaw (2)	6	0.02
Cree	1	0.00
Creek (2)	2	0.01
Crow (7)	7	0.02
Delaware	1	0.00
Iroquois (6)	11	0.03
Latin American Indians (17)	40	0.12
Navajo (84)	123	0.37
Paiute (5)	5	0.01
Pima (1)	7	0.02
Potawatomi (3)	3	0.01
Pueblo (4)	10	0.03
Seminole	2	0.01
Shoshone (1)	12	0.04
Sioux (8)	24	0.07
Ute (10)	26	0.08
Yaqui (1)	1	0.00
Yuman	3	0.01
All other tribes (35)	47	0.14
American Indian tribes, not spec.	29	0.09
Arab:	40	0.12
Arab/Arabic	16	0.05
Lebanese	17	0.05
Palestinian	7	0.02
Asian:	763	2.27
Cambodian (36)	44	0.13
Chinese, ex. Taiwanese (44)	75	0.22
Filipino (39)	72	0.21
Indian (47)	62	0.18
Indonesian (7)	14	0.04
Japanese (34)	82	0.24
Korean (14)	21	0.06
Laotian (120)	153	0.45
Malaysian (5)	5	0.01
Pakistani (7)	7	0.02
Thai (11)	12	0.04
Vietnamese (177)	191	0.57
Other Asian, specified (4)	4	0.01
Other Asian, not specified (17)	21	0.06
Australian	24	0.07
Austrian	70	0.21
Basque	12	0.04
Belgian	48	0.14
Brazilian	60	0.18
British	264	0.79
Canadian	24	0.07
Croatian	13	0.04
Czech	48	0.14
Czechoslovakian	4	0.01
Danish	1,204	3.58
Dutch	545	1.62
English	6,630	19.72
Estonian	7	0.02
European	850	2.53
Finnish	57	0.17
French, except Basque	564	1.68
French Canadian	90	0.27
German	3,489	10.38
Greek	61	0.18
Hawaii Native/Pacific Islander:	908	2.70
Melanesian: (1)	1	0.00
Fijian (1)	1	0.00
Polynesian: (731)	867	2.58
Native Hawaiian (7)	35	0.10
Samoan (385)	421	1.25
Tongan (313)	377	1.12
Other Polynesian (26)	34	0.10
Other Pac. Isl., not spec. (33)	40	0.12
Hispanic or Latino:	6,604	19.62
Central American:	276	0.82
Costa Rican	16	0.05
Guatemalan	68	0.20
Honduran	21	0.06
Nicaraguan	10	0.03
Panamanian	11	0.03
Salvadoran	128	0.38
Other Central American	22	0.07
Cuban	20	0.06
Dominican Republic	6	0.02
Mexican	4,555	13.53
Puerto Rican	99	0.29
South American:	202	0.60
Argentinean	23	0.07
Bolivian	8	0.02
Chilean	13	0.04
Colombian	6	0.02
Ecuadorian	8	0.02

Notes: 1. Figures in the "Number" column do not add up to the total population due to: a) Ancestry/Race overlap — e.g. persons can report being both White and Irish, b) persons of Hispanic origin can report being any race, c) persons reporting two ancestries are counted in both categories. 2. Numbers in parentheses indicate the number of persons reporting this ancestry/race alone, not in combination with any other ancestry/race. 3. Refer to the Explanation of Data in the front of the book for more detailed information.

Ancestry/Race	Number	%
Peruvian	54	0.16
Uruguayan	8	0.02
Venezuelan	66	0.20
Other South American	16	0.05
Other Hispanic or Latino	1,446	4.30
Hungarian	45	0.13
Icelander	46	0.14
Irish	1,803	5.36
Italian	670	1.99
Lithuanian	13	0.04
Luxemburger	8	0.02
Northern European	41	0.12
Norwegian	646	1.92
Pennsylvania German	6	0.02
Polish	223	0.66
Portuguese	13	0.04
Romanian	9	0.03
Russian	63	0.19
Scandinavian	84	0.25
Scotch-Irish	251	0.75
Scottish	1,146	3.41
Slovak	18	0.05
Swedish	899	2.67
Swiss	257	0.76
United States or American	3,116	9.27
Welsh	647	1.92
West Indian, excl. Hispanic:	9	0.03
British West Indian	4	0.01
Jamaican	5	0.01
White:	28,287	84.04
Not Hispanic (24,707)	25,142	74.70
Hispanic (2,818)	3,145	9.34
Yugoslavian	151	0.45

Layton

Place Type: City
County: Davis
Population: 58,474

Ancestry/Race	Number	%
Acadian/Cajun	5	0.01
African American/Black:	1,219	2.08
Not Hispanic (907)	1,149	1.96
Hispanic (36)	70	0.12
African, sub-Saharan:	152	0.26
African	152	0.26
Alaska Native tribes, specified:	12	0.02
Aleut	3	0.01
Eskimo (2)	6	0.01
Tlingit-Haida	2	0.00
All other tribes	1	0.00
Am. Ind. or Alaska Nat., not spec.	163	0.28
Albanian	7	0.01
American Indian tribes, specified:	433	0.74
Apache	11	0.02
Blackfeet	4	0.01
Cherokee (30)	81	0.14
Cheyenne	2	0.00
Chickasaw	2	0.00
Chippewa (5)	15	0.03
Choctaw (7)	15	0.03
Colville	2	0.00
Comanche (1)	1	0.00
Cree (1)	2	0.00
Creek (1)	3	0.01
Crow	2	0.00
Iroquois	2	0.00
Kiowa (1)	4	0.01
Latin American Indians (22)	27	0.05
Lumbee	1	0.00
Navajo (117)	142	0.24
Paiute (1)	4	0.01
Potawatomi	3	0.01
Pueblo (5)	10	0.02
Seminole (1)	1	0.00
Shoshone (2)	4	0.01
Sioux (10)	21	0.04
Ute (5)	9	0.02
Yaqui (1)	5	0.01
All other tribes (30)	60	0.10
American Indian tribes, not spec.	26	0.04
Arab:	149	0.25
Egyptian	9	0.02
Jordanian	5	0.01
Lebanese	86	0.15
Moroccan	9	0.02
Palestinian	24	0.04
Syrian	5	0.01
Other Arab	11	0.02
Armenian	28	0.05
Asian:	1,843	3.15
Cambodian	1	0.00
Chinese, ex. Taiwanese (112)	167	0.29
Filipino (311)	477	0.82
Hmong (2)	2	0.00
Indian (53)	91	0.16
Indonesian (3)	6	0.01
Japanese (260)	442	0.76
Korean (163)	226	0.39
Laotian (59)	88	0.15
Pakistani (9)	17	0.03
Sri Lankan (1)	1	0.00
Taiwanese (2)	4	0.01
Thai (107)	145	0.25
Vietnamese (76)	96	0.16
Other Asian, specified (1)	6	0.01
Other Asian, not specified (30)	74	0.13
Australian	46	0.08
Austrian	75	0.13
Basque	37	0.06
Belgian	5	0.01
Brazilian	97	0.17
British	576	0.98
Bulgarian	52	0.09
Canadian	193	0.33
Celtic	11	0.02
Croatian	21	0.04
Czech	100	0.17
Czechoslovakian	34	0.06
Danish	3,019	5.15
Dutch	1,620	2.76
Eastern European	8	0.01
English	17,067	29.09
Estonian	5	0.01
European	1,462	2.49
Finnish	110	0.19
French, except Basque	1,685	2.87
French Canadian	193	0.33
German	7,239	12.34
German Russian	7	0.01
Greek	209	0.36
Hawaii Native/Pacific Islander:	301	0.51
Micronesian: (36)	47	0.08
Guamanian/Chamorro (32)	43	0.07
Other Micronesian (4)	4	0.01
Polynesian: (102)	229	0.39
Native Hawaiian (31)	103	0.18
Samoan (47)	76	0.13
Tongan (23)	32	0.05
Other Polynesian (1)	18	0.03
Other Pac. Isl., not spec. (9)	25	0.04
Hispanic or Latino:	4,068	6.96
Central American:	73	0.12
Costa Rican	5	0.01
Guatemalan	18	0.03
Honduran	3	0.01
Nicaraguan	7	0.01
Panamanian	12	0.02
Salvadoran	26	0.04
Other Central American	2	0.00
Cuban	25	0.04
Dominican Republic	22	0.04
Mexican	2,486	4.25
Puerto Rican	121	0.21
South American:	160	0.27
Argentinean	19	0.03
Bolivian	6	0.01
Chilean	26	0.04
Colombian	26	0.04
Ecuadorian	14	0.02
Peruvian	26	0.04
Uruguayan	2	0.00
Venezuelan	35	0.06
Other South American	6	0.01
Other Hispanic or Latino	1,181	2.02
Hungarian	105	0.18
Icelander	48	0.08
Iranian	53	0.09
Irish	3,702	6.31
Israeli	4	0.01
Italian	1,657	2.82
Lithuanian	65	0.11
Maltese	17	0.03
New Zealander	39	0.07
Northern European	152	0.26
Norwegian	1,373	2.34
Pennsylvania German	6	0.01
Polish	549	0.94
Portuguese	147	0.25
Romanian	66	0.11
Russian	172	0.29
Scandinavian	487	0.83
Scotch-Irish	712	1.21
Scottish	2,472	4.21
Slavic	7	0.01
Slovak	66	0.11
Slovene	87	0.15
Swedish	2,084	3.55
Swiss	520	0.89
Turkish	9	0.02
Ukrainian	105	0.18
United States or American	4,775	8.14
Welsh	1,223	2.08
West Indian, excl. Hispanic:	18	0.03
Barbadian	7	0.01
Trinidadian and Tobagonian	11	0.02
White:	53,869	92.12
Not Hispanic (50,820)	51,737	88.48
Hispanic (1,753)	2,132	3.65
Yugoslavian	46	0.08

Lehi

Place Type: City
County: Utah
Population: 19,028

Ancestry/Race	Number	%
African American/Black:	89	0.47
Not Hispanic (47)	81	0.43
Hispanic	8	0.04
African, sub-Saharan:	18	0.09
African	18	0.09
Am. Ind. or Alaska Nat., not spec.	39	0.20
American Indian tribes, specified:	122	0.64
Apache	2	0.01
Blackfeet (1)	1	0.01
Cherokee (3)	9	0.05
Cheyenne	1	0.01
Chickasaw (1)	2	0.01
Chippewa	1	0.01
Colville (1)	1	0.01
Iroquois	1	0.01
Latin American Indians (7)	8	0.04
Navajo (49)	61	0.32
Osage	1	0.01
Paiute (3)	3	0.02
Pima (1)	1	0.01
Pueblo	2	0.01
Sioux (1)	2	0.01
Tohono O'Odham (2)	2	0.01
Ute (1)	2	0.01
All other tribes (15)	22	0.12
American Indian tribes, not spec.	4	0.02
Asian:	159	0.84
Chinese, ex. Taiwanese (12)	19	0.10
Filipino (16)	25	0.13
Hmong (5)	7	0.04
Indian (8)	21	0.11

Notes: 1. Figures in the "Number" column do not add up to the total population due to: a) Ancestry/Race overlap — e.g. persons can report being both White and Irish, b) persons of Hispanic origin can report being any race, c) persons reporting two ancestries are counted in both categories. 2. Numbers in parentheses indicate the number of persons reporting this ancestry/race alone, not in combination with any other ancestry/race. 3. Refer to the Explanation of Data in the front of the book for more detailed information.

Indonesian (1)	1	0.01
Japanese (19)	41	0.22
Korean (8)	23	0.12
Laotian (7)	7	0.04
Vietnamese (5)	11	0.06
Other Asian, not specified (1)	4	0.02
Australian	27	0.14
Austrian	19	0.10
Basque	13	0.07
Brazilian	31	0.16
British	201	1.05
Canadian	93	0.49
Czech	9	0.05
Czechoslovakian	10	0.05
Danish	1,516	7.92
Dutch	434	2.27
English	6,596	34.44
European	487	2.54
Finnish	53	0.28
French, except Basque	536	2.80
French Canadian	16	0.08
German	1,823	9.52
Greek	25	0.13
Hawaii Native/Pacific Islander:	140	0.74
Micronesian: (1)	1	0.01
Guamanian/Chamorro (1)	1	0.01
Polynesian: (69)	131	0.69
Native Hawaiian (11)	29	0.15
Samoan (43)	64	0.34
Tongan (14)	31	0.16
Other Polynesian (1)	7	0.04
Other Pac. Isl., not spec. (3)	8	0.04
Hispanic or Latino:	569	2.99
Central American:	29	0.15
Costa Rican	3	0.02
Guatemalan	1	0.01
Nicaraguan	2	0.01
Panamanian	1	0.01
Salvadoran	17	0.09
Other Central American	5	0.03
Cuban	5	0.03
Dominican Republic	3	0.02
Mexican	341	1.79
Puerto Rican	17	0.09
South American:	26	0.14
Argentinean	4	0.02
Bolivian	5	0.03
Chilean	4	0.02
Colombian	5	0.03
Peruvian	5	0.03
Venezuelan	3	0.02
Other Hispanic or Latino	148	0.78
Hungarian	7	0.04
Irish	809	4.22
Italian	229	1.20
Northern European	81	0.42
Norwegian	496	2.59
Polish	40	0.21
Portuguese	22	0.11
Romanian	9	0.05
Russian	28	0.15
Scandinavian	207	1.08
Scotch-Irish	99	0.52
Scottish	891	4.65
Slovak	7	0.04
Slovene	7	0.04
Swedish	1,076	5.62
Swiss	251	1.31
United States or American	1,718	8.97
Welsh	485	2.53
White:	18,437	96.89
Not Hispanic (17,950)	18,126	95.26
Hispanic (256)	311	1.63
Yugoslavian	7	0.04

Logan

Place Type: City
County: Cache
Population: 42,670

Ancestry/Race	Number	%
African American/Black:	398	0.93
Not Hispanic (253)	353	0.83
Hispanic (19)	45	0.11
African, sub-Saharan:	86	0.20
African	34	0.08
Ethiopian	28	0.07
South African	24	0.06
Alaska Native tribes, specified:	5	0.01
Alaska Athabascan	1	0.00
Eskimo (3)	3	0.01
Tlingit-Haida (1)	1	0.00
Alaska Native tribes, not specified	1	0.00
Am. Ind. or Alaska Nat., not spec.	107	0.25
Albanian	9	0.02
American Indian tribes, specified:	360	0.84
Apache (5)	7	0.02
Blackfeet (2)	5	0.01
Cherokee (4)	22	0.05
Cheyenne	1	0.00
Chippewa	2	0.00
Choctaw (1)	2	0.00
Comanche (1)	1	0.00
Creek	4	0.01
Iroquois (1)	2	0.00
Latin American Indians (11)	22	0.05
Menominee (1)	1	0.00
Navajo (198)	221	0.52
Paiute (2)	2	0.00
Pima	1	0.00
Potawatomi (4)	4	0.01
Pueblo (8)	8	0.02
Puget Sound Salish (1)	1	0.00
Seminole	4	0.01
Shoshone (4)	6	0.01
Sioux (5)	11	0.03
Ute (5)	11	0.03
All other tribes (15)	22	0.05
American Indian tribes, not spec.	18	0.04
Arab:	184	0.43
Arab/Arabic	36	0.08
Jordanian	17	0.04
Lebanese	79	0.18
Syrian	8	0.02
Other Arab	44	0.10
Armenian	37	0.09
Asian:	1,788	4.19
Cambodian (147)	174	0.41
Chinese, ex. Taiwanese (443)	493	1.16
Filipino (39)	59	0.14
Indian (191)	208	0.49
Indonesian (7)	14	0.03
Japanese (166)	230	0.54
Korean (180)	194	0.45
Laotian (38)	46	0.11
Malaysian (12)	18	0.04
Pakistani (9)	9	0.02
Taiwanese (37)	41	0.10
Thai (37)	49	0.11
Vietnamese (160)	183	0.43
Other Asian, specified (5)	6	0.01
Other Asian, not specified (36)	64	0.15
Australian	51	0.12
Austrian	40	0.09
Basque	30	0.07
Belgian	52	0.12
Brazilian	9	0.02
British	603	1.41
Bulgarian	9	0.02
Canadian	138	0.32
Celtic	8	0.02
Croatian	8	0.02
Czech	44	0.10
Czechoslovakian	20	0.05
Danish	2,985	6.99
Dutch	779	1.82
English	12,176	28.50
European	985	2.31
Finnish	113	0.26
French, except Basque	745	1.74
French Canadian	59	0.14
German	4,735	11.08
Greek	29	0.07
Hawaii Native/Pacific Islander:	190	0.45
Melanesian: (4)	6	0.01
Fijian (4)	6	0.01
Micronesian: (3)	4	0.01
Guamanian/Chamorro (2)	3	0.01
Other Micronesian (1)	1	0.00
Polynesian: (107)	161	0.38
Native Hawaiian (29)	51	0.12
Samoan (25)	36	0.08
Tongan (49)	64	0.15
Other Polynesian (4)	10	0.02
Other Pac. Isl., specified	1	0.00
Other Pac. Isl., not spec. (3)	18	0.04
Hispanic or Latino:	3,509	8.22
Central American:	321	0.75
Costa Rican	7	0.02
Guatemalan	120	0.28
Honduran	23	0.05
Nicaraguan	1	0.00
Panamanian	11	0.03
Salvadoran	152	0.36
Other Central American	7	0.02
Cuban	13	0.03
Dominican Republic	3	0.01
Mexican	2,407	5.64
Puerto Rican	47	0.11
South American:	173	0.41
Argentinean	37	0.09
Bolivian	19	0.04
Chilean	23	0.05
Colombian	15	0.04
Ecuadorian	8	0.02
Peruvian	38	0.09
Uruguayan	5	0.01
Venezuelan	23	0.05
Other South American	5	0.01
Other Hispanic or Latino	545	1.28
Hungarian	95	0.22
Icelander	15	0.04
Iranian	30	0.07
Irish	1,995	4.67
Italian	684	1.60
Lithuanian	19	0.04
Northern European	27	0.06
Norwegian	1,272	2.98
Pennsylvania German	7	0.02
Polish	277	0.65
Portuguese	16	0.04
Romanian	52	0.12
Russian	125	0.29
Scandinavian	832	1.95
Scotch-Irish	307	0.72
Scottish	2,196	5.14
Slavic	45	0.11
Slovak	25	0.06
Slovene	37	0.09
Swedish	2,095	4.90
Swiss	1,132	2.65
Ukrainian	27	0.06
United States or American	2,398	5.61
Welsh	1,008	2.36
White:	38,534	90.31
Not Hispanic (36,458)	36,830	86.31
Hispanic (1,489)	1,704	3.99
Yugoslavian	41	0.10

Notes: 1. Figures in the "Number" column do not add up to the total population due to: a) Ancestry/Race overlap — e.g. persons can report being both White and Irish, b) persons of Hispanic origin can report being any race, c) persons reporting two ancestries are counted in both categories. 2. Numbers in parentheses indicate the number of persons reporting this ancestry/race alone, not in combination with any other ancestry/race. 3. Refer to the Explanation of Data in the front of the book for more detailed information.

Magna

Place Type: Census Designated Place
County: Salt Lake
Population: 22,770

Ancestry/Race	Number	%
African American/Black:	210	0.92
Not Hispanic (106)	147	0.65
Hispanic (39)	63	0.28
African, sub-Saharan:	16	0.07
African	16	0.07
Alaska Native tribes, specified:	1	0.00
Alaska Athabascan (1)	1	0.00
Am. Ind. or Alaska Nat., not spec.	54	0.24
American Indian tribes, specified:	262	1.15
Apache (1)	4	0.02
Blackfeet (2)	12	0.05
Cherokee (5)	37	0.16
Cheyenne (5)	5	0.02
Chippewa (2)	2	0.01
Choctaw (1)	4	0.02
Iroquois (2)	3	0.01
Latin American Indians (26)	27	0.12
Lumbee (3)	3	0.01
Menominee (1)	1	0.00
Navajo (94)	103	0.45
Paiute (8)	8	0.04
Pueblo	11	0.05
Seminole	1	0.00
Shoshone (1)	2	0.01
Sioux (6)	9	0.04
Tohono O'Odham	1	0.00
Ute (12)	25	0.11
Yuman	1	0.00
All other tribes (1)	3	0.01
American Indian tribes, not spec.	22	0.10
Asian:	252	1.11
Cambodian (1)	1	0.00
Chinese, ex. Taiwanese (17)	40	0.18
Filipino (21)	40	0.18
Indian (6)	11	0.05
Indonesian	1	0.00
Japanese (28)	49	0.22
Korean (15)	31	0.14
Laotian (21)	28	0.12
Pakistani	4	0.02
Vietnamese (22)	30	0.13
Other Asian, not specified (4)	17	0.07
Austrian	128	0.56
Basque	57	0.25
Belgian	3	0.01
British	211	0.93
Canadian	21	0.09
Croatian	5	0.02
Czech	26	0.11
Czechoslovakian	10	0.04
Danish	696	3.06
Dutch	535	2.35
English	5,145	22.59
European	406	1.78
Finnish	7	0.03
French, except Basque	270	1.19
French Canadian	112	0.49
German	2,760	12.12
Greek	161	0.71
Hawaii Native/Pacific Islander:	420	1.84
Micronesian: (17)	17	0.07
Guamanian/Chamorro (6)	6	0.03
Other Micronesian (11)	11	0.05
Polynesian: (285)	373	1.64
Native Hawaiian (7)	20	0.09
Samoan (102)	133	0.58
Tongan (174)	214	0.94
Other Polynesian (2)	6	0.03
Other Pac. Isl., not spec. (7)	30	0.13
Hispanic or Latino:	3,416	15.00
Central American:	96	0.42
Costa Rican	3	0.01
Guatemalan	27	0.12
Honduran	9	0.04
Nicaraguan	8	0.04
Panamanian	7	0.03
Salvadoran	40	0.18
Other Central American	2	0.01
Cuban	14	0.06
Mexican	2,208	9.70
Puerto Rican	49	0.22
South American:	163	0.72
Argentinean	17	0.07
Bolivian	6	0.03
Chilean	41	0.18
Colombian	16	0.07
Ecuadorian	22	0.10
Peruvian	14	0.06
Uruguayan	4	0.02
Venezuelan	35	0.15
Other South American	8	0.04
Other Hispanic or Latino	886	3.89
Hungarian	3	0.01
Icelander	6	0.03
Irish	1,411	6.20
Italian	658	2.89
Lithuanian	2	0.01
New Zealander	22	0.10
Norwegian	454	1.99
Polish	228	1.00
Portuguese	18	0.08
Russian	10	0.04
Scandinavian	232	1.02
Scotch-Irish	107	0.47
Scottish	658	2.89
Slavic	7	0.03
Slovak	27	0.12
Swedish	675	2.96
Swiss	204	0.90
Ukrainian	10	0.04
United States or American	1,836	8.06
Welsh	551	2.42
West Indian, excl. Hispanic:	10	0.04
Belizean	10	0.04
White:	20,111	88.32
Not Hispanic (18,348)	18,626	81.80
Hispanic (1,294)	1,485	6.52
Yugoslavian	45	0.20

Midvale

Place Type: City
County: Salt Lake
Population: 27,029

Ancestry/Race	Number	%
African American/Black:	419	1.55
Not Hispanic (215)	283	1.05
Hispanic (104)	136	0.50
African, sub-Saharan:	37	0.14
African	12	0.04
Ghanian	12	0.04
Other sub-Saharan African	13	0.05
Alaska Native tribes, specified:	5	0.02
Alaska Athabascan (2)	2	0.01
Aleut (1)	2	0.01
Tlingit-Haida (1)	1	0.00
Am. Ind. or Alaska Nat., not spec.	121	0.45
American Indian tribes, specified:	338	1.25
Apache (11)	15	0.06
Blackfeet (1)	3	0.01
Cherokee (5)	22	0.08
Cheyenne (2)	2	0.01
Choctaw (2)	3	0.01
Comanche (1)	2	0.01
Creek	2	0.01
Iroquois (2)	2	0.01
Latin American Indians (30)	43	0.16
Lumbee	1	0.00
Navajo (131)	156	0.58
Paiute (2)	4	0.01
Pima (1)	2	0.01
Potawatomi	1	0.00
Pueblo (3)	3	0.01
Puget Sound Salish (6)	6	0.02
Seminole	4	0.01
Shoshone (4)	9	0.03
Sioux (10)	21	0.08
Ute (4)	6	0.02
Yakama	1	0.00
All other tribes (16)	30	0.11
American Indian tribes, not spec.	26	0.10
Arab:	99	0.37
Arab/Arabic	15	0.06
Egyptian	10	0.04
Lebanese	74	0.27
Armenian	49	0.18
Asian:	673	2.49
Cambodian (8)	12	0.04
Chinese, ex. Taiwanese (147)	170	0.63
Filipino (46)	85	0.31
Hmong (1)	1	0.00
Indian (52)	60	0.22
Indonesian	2	0.01
Japanese (63)	102	0.38
Korean (64)	81	0.30
Laotian (35)	44	0.16
Pakistani (3)	4	0.01
Taiwanese (11)	11	0.04
Thai (3)	6	0.02
Vietnamese (27)	42	0.16
Other Asian, specified (7)	14	0.05
Other Asian, not specified (21)	39	0.14
Austrian	15	0.06
Basque	13	0.05
Belgian	15	0.06
Brazilian	23	0.09
British	212	0.78
Canadian	76	0.28
Croatian	9	0.03
Czechoslovakian	40	0.15
Danish	1,038	3.84
Dutch	577	2.13
English	6,102	22.57
European	377	1.39
Finnish	37	0.14
French, except Basque	596	2.20
French Canadian	125	0.46
German	2,989	11.05
Greek	182	0.67
Hawaii Native/Pacific Islander:	239	0.88
Melanesian: (1)	2	0.01
Fijian (1)	2	0.01
Micronesian: (1)	2	0.01
Guamanian/Chamorro	1	0.00
Other Micronesian (1)	1	0.00
Polynesian: (141)	198	0.73
Native Hawaiian (22)	41	0.15
Samoan (78)	94	0.35
Tongan (38)	59	0.22
Other Polynesian (3)	4	0.01
Other Pac. Isl., not spec. (8)	37	0.14
Hispanic or Latino:	5,613	20.77
Central American:	90	0.33
Costa Rican	3	0.01
Guatemalan	28	0.10
Honduran	5	0.02
Nicaraguan	10	0.04
Panamanian	3	0.01
Salvadoran	39	0.14
Other Central American	2	0.01
Cuban	18	0.07
Dominican Republic	8	0.03
Mexican	4,400	16.28
Puerto Rican	134	0.50
South American:	134	0.50
Argentinean	15	0.06
Bolivian	4	0.01
Chilean	16	0.06
Colombian	26	0.10
Ecuadorian	5	0.02
Paraguayan	1	0.00
Peruvian	35	0.13

Notes: 1. Figures in the "Number" column do not add up to the total population due to: a) Ancestry/Race overlap — e.g. persons can report being both White and Irish, b) persons of Hispanic origin can report being any race, c) persons reporting two ancestries are counted in both categories. 2. Numbers in parentheses indicate the number of persons reporting this ancestry/race alone, not in combination with any other ancestry/race. 3. Refer to the Explanation of Data in the front of the book for more detailed information.

Uruguayan	8	0.03
Venezuelan	15	0.06
Other South American	9	0.03
Other Hispanic or Latino	829	3.07
Hungarian	71	0.26
Icelander	30	0.11
Iranian	20	0.07
Irish	1,677	6.20
Italian	876	3.24
Lithuanian	21	0.08
Northern European	27	0.10
Norwegian	756	2.80
Polish	220	0.81
Portuguese	89	0.33
Romanian	7	0.03
Russian	89	0.33
Scandinavian	224	0.83
Scotch-Irish	217	0.80
Scottish	935	3.46
Slovene	25	0.09
Swedish	979	3.62
Swiss	222	0.82
Ukrainian	15	0.06
United States or American	1,444	5.34
Welsh	351	1.30
White:	22,934	84.85
Not Hispanic (19,847)	20,185	74.68
Hispanic (2,436)	2,749	10.17
Yugoslavian	117	0.43

Millcreek

Place Type: Census Designated Place
County: Salt Lake
Population: 30,377

Ancestry/Race	Number	%
African American/Black:	648	2.13
Not Hispanic (440)	592	1.95
Hispanic (36)	56	0.18
African, sub-Saharan:	44	0.14
Ethiopian	21	0.07
South African	23	0.08
Alaska Native tribes, specified:	2	0.01
Eskimo (1)	2	0.01
Alaska Native tribes, not specified	1	0.00
Am. Ind. or Alaska Nat., not spec.	162	0.53
Albanian	33	0.11
American Indian tribes, specified:	393	1.29
Apache	10	0.03
Blackfeet (2)	3	0.01
Cherokee (10)	42	0.14
Cheyenne (1)	4	0.01
Chippewa (4)	6	0.02
Choctaw (2)	4	0.01
Creek (1)	1	0.00
Crow (2)	3	0.01
Iroquois (6)	7	0.02
Latin American Indians (11)	22	0.07
Navajo (159)	191	0.63
Paiute (4)	6	0.02
Pima (1)	1	0.00
Potawatomi (2)	3	0.01
Pueblo (1)	7	0.02
Seminole	2	0.01
Shoshone (3)	6	0.02
Sioux (9)	18	0.06
Ute (17)	28	0.09
Yaqui (1)	1	0.00
Yuman (2)	2	0.01
All other tribes (20)	26	0.09
American Indian tribes, not spec.	19	0.06
Arab:	220	0.72
Egyptian	5	0.02
Iraqi	77	0.25
Jordanian	24	0.08
Lebanese	78	0.26
Other Arab	36	0.12
Armenian	224	0.73
Asian:	1,176	3.87
Bangladeshi (1)	1	0.00
Cambodian (3)	4	0.01
Chinese, ex. Taiwanese (321)	355	1.17
Filipino (50)	86	0.28
Indian (100)	109	0.36
Indonesian (5)	6	0.02
Japanese (190)	268	0.88
Korean (162)	178	0.59
Laotian (2)	8	0.03
Pakistani (10)	17	0.06
Sri Lankan (3)	4	0.01
Taiwanese (8)	8	0.03
Thai (14)	16	0.05
Vietnamese (43)	56	0.18
Other Asian, specified (2)	2	0.01
Other Asian, not specified (13)	58	0.19
Assyrian/Chaldean/Syriac	10	0.03
Australian	32	0.10
Austrian	125	0.41
Basque	39	0.13
Belgian	38	0.12
Brazilian	83	0.27
British	238	0.78
Bulgarian	11	0.04
Canadian	88	0.29
Carpatho Rusyn	13	0.04
Croatian	9	0.03
Czech	117	0.38
Czechoslovakian	26	0.09
Danish	1,532	5.02
Dutch	681	2.23
Eastern European	8	0.03
English	7,657	25.08
European	434	1.42
Finnish	59	0.19
French, except Basque	790	2.59
French Canadian	163	0.53
German	3,510	11.50
Greek	388	1.27
Hawaii Native/Pacific Islander:	319	1.05
Micronesian: (18)	24	0.08
Guamanian/Chamorro	5	0.02
Other Micronesian (18)	19	0.06
Polynesian: (156)	282	0.93
Native Hawaiian (33)	57	0.19
Samoan (45)	107	0.35
Tongan (70)	103	0.34
Other Polynesian (8)	15	0.05
Other Pac. Isl., not spec. (5)	13	0.04
Hispanic or Latino:	2,780	9.15
Central American:	82	0.27
Costa Rican	5	0.02
Guatemalan	18	0.06
Honduran	21	0.07
Nicaraguan	4	0.01
Panamanian	3	0.01
Salvadoran	31	0.10
Cuban	16	0.05
Dominican Republic	7	0.02
Mexican	1,569	5.17
Puerto Rican	81	0.27
South American:	302	0.99
Argentinean	41	0.13
Bolivian	3	0.01
Chilean	57	0.19
Colombian	46	0.15
Ecuadorian	15	0.05
Peruvian	56	0.18
Uruguayan	1	0.00
Venezuelan	75	0.25
Other South American	8	0.03
Other Hispanic or Latino	723	2.38
Hungarian	51	0.17
Icelander	32	0.10
Irish	1,827	5.99
Italian	824	2.70
Latvian	29	0.10
Lithuanian	25	0.08
Northern European	47	0.15
Norwegian	658	2.16
Polish	250	0.82
Portuguese	55	0.18
Romanian	36	0.12
Russian	261	0.86
Scandinavian	368	1.21
Scotch-Irish	339	1.11
Scottish	1,225	4.01
Serbian	32	0.10
Slovak	45	0.15
Swedish	1,504	4.93
Swiss	629	2.06
Turkish	10	0.03
Ukrainian	103	0.34
United States or American	1,438	4.71
Welsh	704	2.31
West Indian, excl. Hispanic:	29	0.10
Belizean	17	0.06
Jamaican	12	0.04
White:	27,252	89.71
Not Hispanic (24,985)	25,593	84.25
Hispanic (1,463)	1,659	5.46
Yugoslavian	609	2.00

Murray

Place Type: City
County: Salt Lake
Population: 34,024

Ancestry/Race	Number	%
African American/Black:	467	1.37
Not Hispanic (303)	414	1.22
Hispanic (33)	53	0.16
African, sub-Saharan:	84	0.25
African	43	0.13
Kenyan	10	0.03
Nigerian	16	0.05
South African	15	0.04
Alaska Native tribes, specified:	1	0.00
Eskimo (1)	1	0.00
Alaska Native tribes, not specified		0.00
Am. Ind. or Alaska Nat., not spec.	84	0.25
American Indian tribes, specified:	229	0.67
Apache (2)	3	0.01
Blackfeet (4)	8	0.02
Cherokee (13)	41	0.12
Choctaw (4)	6	0.02
Creek (1)	1	0.00
Crow (1)	1	0.00
Iroquois	1	0.00
Latin American Indians (1)	3	0.01
Navajo (95)	117	0.34
Paiute (1)	2	0.01
Potawatomi (1)	1	0.00
Pueblo (3)	4	0.01
Seminole (4)	4	0.01
Shoshone	4	0.01
Sioux (2)	2	0.01
Ute (5)	5	0.01
All other tribes (8)	26	0.08
American Indian tribes, not spec.	13	0.04
Arab:	35	0.10
Arab/Arabic	5	0.01
Iraqi	8	0.02
Lebanese	11	0.03
Palestinian	8	0.02
Other Arab	3	0.01
Armenian	20	0.06
Asian:	808	2.37
Cambodian (13)	13	0.04
Chinese, ex. Taiwanese (123)	172	0.51
Filipino (37)	66	0.19
Hmong (1)	1	0.00
Indian (56)	70	0.21
Indonesian (1)	6	0.02
Japanese (163)	224	0.66
Korean (58)	71	0.21
Laotian (7)	7	0.02
Malaysian (1)	2	0.01
Pakistani (41)	43	0.13

Notes: 1. Figures in the "Number" column do not add up to the total population due to: a) Ancestry/Race overlap — e.g. persons can report being both White and Irish, b) persons of Hispanic origin can report being any race, c) persons reporting two ancestries are counted in both categories. 2. Numbers in parentheses indicate the number of persons reporting this ancestry/race alone, not in combination with any other ancestry/race. 3. Refer to the Explanation of Data in the front of the book for more detailed information.

Thai (4)	10	0.03
Vietnamese (90)	103	0.30
Other Asian, specified (5)	7	0.02
Other Asian, not specified (4)	13	0.04
Australian	17	0.05
Austrian	62	0.18
Basque	15	0.04
Belgian	13	0.04
Brazilian	29	0.09
British	568	1.67
Bulgarian	10	0.03
Canadian	108	0.32
Celtic	32	0.09
Croatian	14	0.04
Czech	23	0.07
Czechoslovakian	7	0.02
Danish	2,380	7.02
Dutch	885	2.61
Eastern European	7	0.02
English	10,768	31.75
European	677	2.00
Finnish	156	0.46
French, except Basque	702	2.07
French Canadian	112	0.33
German	4,507	13.29
Greek	343	1.01
Hawaii Native/Pacific Islander:	218	0.64
Micronesian: (1)	5	0.01
Guamanian/Chamorro (1)	5	0.01
Polynesian: (97)	193	0.57
Native Hawaiian (10)	39	0.11
Samoan (48)	82	0.24
Tongan (33)	58	0.17
Other Polynesian (6)	14	0.04
Other Pac. Isl., specified	2	0.01
Other Pac. Isl., not spec. (11)	18	0.05
Hispanic or Latino:	2,549	7.49
Central American:	97	0.29
Costa Rican	6	0.02
Guatemalan	39	0.11
Honduran	15	0.04
Nicaraguan	8	0.02
Panamanian	2	0.01
Salvadoran	21	0.06
Other Central American	6	0.02
Cuban	12	0.04
Dominican Republic	11	0.03
Mexican	1,599	4.70
Puerto Rican	58	0.17
South American:	99	0.29
Argentinean	22	0.06
Bolivian	1	0.00
Chilean	14	0.04
Colombian	10	0.03
Ecuadorian	3	0.01
Peruvian	28	0.08
Uruguayan	1	0.00
Venezuelan	16	0.05
Other South American	4	0.01
Other Hispanic or Latino	673	1.98
Hungarian	47	0.14
Icelander	13	0.04
Iranian	89	0.26
Irish	2,347	6.92
Israeli	4	0.01
Italian	1,143	3.37
Lithuanian	30	0.09
Luxemburger	7	0.02
Northern European	48	0.14
Norwegian	945	2.79
Pennsylvania German	10	0.03
Polish	235	0.69
Portuguese	7	0.02
Russian	127	0.37
Scandinavian	490	1.44
Scotch-Irish	312	0.92
Scottish	1,470	4.33
Slavic	16	0.05
Slovak	9	0.03
Slovene	19	0.06
Swedish	2,192	6.46
Swiss	494	1.46
Ukrainian	30	0.09
United States or American	1,920	5.66
Welsh	844	2.49
West Indian, excl. Hispanic:	20	0.06
Jamaican	20	0.06
White:	31,747	93.31
Not Hispanic (29,805)	30,213	88.80
Hispanic (1,348)	1,534	4.51
Yugoslavian	37	0.11

North Ogden

Place Type: City
County: Weber
Population: 15,026

Ancestry/Race	Number	%
Acadian/Cajun	12	0.08
African American/Black:	67	0.45
Not Hispanic (54)	66	0.44
Hispanic (1)	1	0.01
African, sub-Saharan:	5	0.03
African	5	0.03
Alaska Native tribes, specified:	1	0.01
Eskimo (1)	1	0.01
Am. Ind. or Alaska Nat., not spec.	17	0.11
American Indian tribes, specified:	63	0.42
Apache (1)	2	0.01
Cherokee (2)	10	0.07
Cheyenne	1	0.01
Chippewa (2)	2	0.01
Comanche (3)	3	0.02
Crow	1	0.01
Iroquois (1)	1	0.01
Latin American Indians (1)	1	0.01
Navajo (15)	18	0.12
Paiute (2)	3	0.02
Potawatomi (2)	2	0.01
Pueblo	6	0.04
Shoshone (3)	4	0.03
Sioux (1)	2	0.01
Ute (1)	1	0.01
All other tribes (2)	6	0.04
American Indian tribes, not spec.	1	0.01
Arab:	98	0.66
Egyptian	84	0.56
Other Arab	14	0.09
Armenian	4	0.03
Asian:	172	1.14
Cambodian (6)	6	0.04
Chinese, ex. Taiwanese (6)	8	0.05
Filipino (13)	23	0.15
Indonesian	1	0.01
Japanese (37)	71	0.47
Korean (22)	26	0.17
Laotian (14)	15	0.10
Taiwanese (4)	4	0.03
Thai	1	0.01
Vietnamese (7)	7	0.05
Other Asian, not specified (9)	10	0.07
Australian	34	0.23
Austrian	55	0.37
Belgian	7	0.05
Brazilian	21	0.14
British	216	1.45
Canadian	42	0.28
Czech	24	0.16
Czechoslovakian	14	0.09
Danish	1,042	6.98
Dutch	503	3.37
English	5,344	35.79
European	405	2.71
Finnish	39	0.26
French, except Basque	194	1.30
French Canadian	55	0.37
German	1,590	10.65
Greek	67	0.45
Hawaii Native/Pacific Islander:	18	0.12
Micronesian: (5)	5	0.03
Other Micronesian (5)	5	0.03
Polynesian: (3)	10	0.07
Native Hawaiian (2)	6	0.04
Samoan (1)	1	0.01
Tongan	2	0.01
Other Polynesian	1	0.01
Other Pac. Isl., not spec. (2)	3	0.02
Hispanic or Latino:	577	3.84
Central American:	33	0.22
Costa Rican	6	0.04
Guatemalan	1	0.01
Honduran	2	0.01
Nicaraguan	1	0.01
Salvadoran	22	0.15
Other Central American	1	0.01
Cuban	1	0.01
Mexican	330	2.20
Puerto Rican	6	0.04
South American:	21	0.14
Argentinean	8	0.05
Ecuadorian	7	0.05
Peruvian	4	0.03
Uruguayan	1	0.01
Venezuelan	1	0.01
Other Hispanic or Latino	186	1.24
Hungarian	5	0.03
Iranian	5	0.03
Irish	753	5.04
Italian	467	3.13
Lithuanian	6	0.04
Luxemburger	8	0.05
Northern European	45	0.30
Norwegian	290	1.94
Pennsylvania German	5	0.03
Polish	86	0.58
Portuguese	47	0.31
Russian	20	0.13
Scandinavian	110	0.74
Scotch-Irish	170	1.14
Scottish	753	5.04
Slovene	14	0.09
Swedish	682	4.57
Swiss	184	1.23
Turkish	5	0.03
Ukrainian	14	0.09
United States or American	1,170	7.84
Welsh	395	2.65
West Indian, excl. Hispanic:	7	0.05
Haitian	7	0.05
White:	14,544	96.79
Not Hispanic (14,124)	14,221	94.64
Hispanic (288)	323	2.15
Yugoslavian	16	0.11

Ogden

Place Type: City
County: Weber
Population: 77,226

Ancestry/Race	Number	%
African American/Black:	2,273	2.94
Not Hispanic (1,630)	2,015	2.61
Hispanic (155)	258	0.33
African, sub-Saharan:	250	0.32
African	200	0.26
Ethiopian	3	0.00
Nigerian	13	0.02
South African	31	0.04
Other sub-Saharan African	3	0.00
Alaska Native tribes, specified:	14	0.02
Alaska Athabascan	1	0.00
Aleut	1	0.00
Eskimo (9)	12	0.02
Alaska Native tribes, not specified	1	0.00
Am. Ind. or Alaska Nat., not spec.	378	0.49
Alsatian	5	0.01
American Indian tribes, specified:	1,072	1.39
Apache (23)	46	0.06

Notes: 1. Figures in the "Number" column do not add up to the total population due to: a) Ancestry/Race overlap — e.g. persons can report being both White and Irish, b) persons of Hispanic origin can report being any race, c) persons reporting two ancestries are counted in both categories. 2. Numbers in parentheses indicate the number of persons reporting this ancestry/race alone, not in combination with any other ancestry/race. 3. Refer to the Explanation of Data in the front of the book for more detailed information.

Ancestry/Race	Number	%
Blackfeet (10)	22	0.03
Cherokee (40)	139	0.18
Cheyenne (3)	5	0.01
Chickasaw (1)	6	0.01
Chippewa (13)	21	0.03
Choctaw (4)	12	0.02
Colville (1)	1	0.00
Comanche (7)	8	0.01
Cree (3)	3	0.00
Creek (1)	2	0.00
Crow (1)	4	0.01
Delaware	5	0.01
Houma (1)	1	0.00
Iroquois (3)	9	0.01
Latin American Indians (39)	97	0.13
Lumbee (2)	5	0.01
Menominee	1	0.00
Navajo (274)	360	0.47
Paiute (2)	3	0.00
Pima (2)	2	0.00
Potawatomi (1)	2	0.00
Pueblo (16)	22	0.03
Puget Sound Salish	1	0.00
Seminole (2)	6	0.01
Shoshone (47)	68	0.09
Sioux (25)	59	0.08
Tohono O'Odham	1	0.00
Ute (29)	58	0.08
Yakama (4)	4	0.01
Yaqui	4	0.01
Yuman (1)	1	0.00
All other tribes (62)	94	0.12
American Indian tribes, not spec.	84	0.11
Arab:	115	0.15
Arab/Arabic	18	0.02
Egyptian	26	0.03
Lebanese	49	0.06
Other Arab	22	0.03
Armenian	20	0.03
Asian:	1,586	2.05
Bangladeshi (2)	2	0.00
Cambodian (5)	8	0.01
Chinese, ex. Taiwanese (142)	219	0.28
Filipino (174)	285	0.37
Hmong (47)	55	0.07
Indian (52)	85	0.11
Indonesian (5)	15	0.02
Japanese (288)	407	0.53
Korean (66)	104	0.13
Laotian (63)	79	0.10
Malaysian (2)	2	0.00
Pakistani (3)	5	0.01
Sri Lankan (2)	2	0.00
Taiwanese (13)	21	0.03
Thai (33)	55	0.07
Vietnamese (136)	154	0.20
Other Asian, not specified (41)	88	0.11
Australian	42	0.05
Austrian	108	0.14
Basque	18	0.02
Belgian	32	0.04
British	622	0.81
Bulgarian	3	0.00
Canadian	141	0.18
Croatian	5	0.01
Czech	145	0.19
Czechoslovakian	47	0.06
Danish	2,533	3.28
Dutch	1,919	2.48
English	16,190	20.96
European	1,073	1.39
Finnish	98	0.13
French, except Basque	1,344	1.74
French Canadian	382	0.49
German	7,317	9.47
German Russian	5	0.01
Greek	140	0.18
Hawaii Native/Pacific Islander:	266	0.34
Melanesian: (3)	3	0.00
Fijian (3)	3	0.00
Micronesian: (13)	23	0.03
Guamanian/Chamorro (5)	11	0.01
Other Micronesian (8)	12	0.02
Polynesian: (91)	180	0.23
Native Hawaiian (42)	90	0.12
Samoan (32)	61	0.08
Tongan (14)	20	0.03
Other Polynesian (3)	9	0.01
Other Pac. Isl., not spec. (22)	60	0.08
Hispanic or Latino:	18,253	23.64
Central American:	310	0.40
Costa Rican	9	0.01
Guatemalan	75	0.10
Honduran	16	0.02
Nicaraguan	18	0.02
Panamanian	2	0.00
Salvadoran	178	0.23
Other Central American	12	0.02
Cuban	35	0.05
Dominican Republic	3	0.00
Mexican	13,524	17.51
Puerto Rican	194	0.25
South American:	192	0.25
Argentinean	31	0.04
Bolivian	10	0.01
Chilean	45	0.06
Colombian	21	0.03
Ecuadorian	12	0.02
Paraguayan	3	0.00
Peruvian	40	0.05
Uruguayan	12	0.02
Venezuelan	8	0.01
Other South American	10	0.01
Other Hispanic or Latino	3,995	5.17
Hungarian	117	0.15
Icelander	68	0.09
Iranian	49	0.06
Irish	4,823	6.24
Italian	1,955	2.53
Latvian	5	0.01
Lithuanian	39	0.05
Luxemburger	8	0.01
New Zealander	34	0.04
Northern European	58	0.08
Norwegian	1,427	1.85
Pennsylvania German	25	0.03
Polish	621	0.80
Portuguese	76	0.10
Romanian	30	0.04
Russian	343	0.44
Scandinavian	513	0.66
Scotch-Irish	878	1.14
Scottish	3,016	3.90
Serbian	31	0.04
Slavic	8	0.01
Slovak	60	0.08
Slovene	11	0.01
Swedish	2,180	2.82
Swiss	589	0.76
Turkish	29	0.04
Ukrainian	46	0.06
United States or American	4,373	5.66
Welsh	1,333	1.73
West Indian, excl. Hispanic:	34	0.04
Haitian	16	0.02
Jamaican	14	0.02
Trinidadian and Tobagonian	4	0.01
White:	62,965	81.53
Not Hispanic (54,216)	55,307	71.62
Hispanic (6,800)	7,658	9.92
Yugoslavian	38	0.05

Oquirrh

Place Type: Census Designated Place
County: Salt Lake
Population: 10,390

Ancestry/Race	Number	%
African American/Black:	88	0.85
Not Hispanic (63)	79	0.76
Hispanic (9)	9	0.09
Am. Ind. or Alaska Nat., not spec.	19	0.18
American Indian tribes, specified:	74	0.71
Apache (1)	5	0.05
Blackfeet	1	0.01
Cherokee (3)	11	0.11
Choctaw (1)	7	0.07
Crow	1	0.01
Latin American Indians (2)	9	0.09
Navajo (16)	29	0.28
Paiute	2	0.02
Pueblo (1)	2	0.02
Sioux (2)	4	0.04
Ute (2)	3	0.03
American Indian tribes, not spec.	3	0.03
Arab:	32	0.31
Lebanese	32	0.31
Asian:	194	1.87
Cambodian (8)	8	0.08
Chinese, ex. Taiwanese (11)	19	0.18
Filipino (11)	17	0.16
Indian (16)	19	0.18
Japanese (7)	19	0.18
Korean (4)	7	0.07
Laotian (37)	50	0.48
Pakistani (4)	12	0.12
Taiwanese (4)	4	0.04
Thai (4)	5	0.05
Vietnamese (28)	30	0.29
Other Asian, not specified	4	0.04
Austrian	13	0.13
Basque	16	0.15
Belgian	45	0.43
Brazilian	48	0.46
British	83	0.80
Canadian	59	0.57
Czech	6	0.06
Danish	582	5.62
Dutch	491	4.74
English	2,411	23.27
European	197	1.90
French, except Basque	183	1.77
German	1,228	11.85
Greek	75	0.72
Hawaii Native/Pacific Islander:	221	2.13
Melanesian: (5)	5	0.05
Fijian (5)	5	0.05
Micronesian: (2)	2	0.02
Other Micronesian (2)	2	0.02
Polynesian: (138)	198	1.91
Native Hawaiian (3)	5	0.05
Samoan (82)	120	1.15
Tongan (36)	51	0.49
Other Polynesian (17)	22	0.21
Other Pac. Isl., not spec. (2)	16	0.15
Hispanic or Latino:	1,307	12.58
Central American:	59	0.57
Guatemalan	19	0.18
Honduran	4	0.04
Panamanian	2	0.02
Salvadoran	30	0.29
Other Central American	4	0.04
Cuban	3	0.03
Dominican Republic	3	0.03
Mexican	751	7.23
Puerto Rican	20	0.19
South American:	102	0.98
Argentinean	1	0.01
Bolivian	3	0.03
Chilean	13	0.13
Colombian	24	0.23
Ecuadorian	2	0.02
Peruvian	33	0.32
Venezuelan	14	0.13
Other South American	12	0.12
Other Hispanic or Latino	369	3.55
Irish	498	4.81
Italian	283	2.73
New Zealander	6	0.06

Notes: 1. Figures in the "Number" column do not add up to the total population due to: a) Ancestry/Race overlap — e.g. persons can report being both White and Irish, b) persons of Hispanic origin can report being any race, c) persons reporting two ancestries are counted in both categories. 2. Numbers in parentheses indicate the number of persons reporting this ancestry/race alone, not in combination with any other ancestry/race. 3. Refer to the Explanation of Data in the front of the book for more detailed information.

Ancestry/Race	Number	%
Norwegian	201	1.94
Polish	48	0.46
Scandinavian	92	0.89
Scotch-Irish	133	1.28
Scottish	320	3.09
Swedish	701	6.77
Swiss	139	1.34
United States or American	1,214	11.72
Welsh	156	1.51
White:	9,305	89.56
Not Hispanic (8,508)	8,654	83.29
Hispanic (594)	651	6.27
Yugoslavian	11	0.11

Orem

Place Type: City
County: Utah
Population: 84,324

Ancestry/Race	Number	%
African American/Black:	488	0.58
Not Hispanic (267)	450	0.53
Hispanic (13)	38	0.05
African, sub-Saharan:	109	0.13
African	69	0.08
Nigerian	14	0.02
South African	16	0.02
Zimbabwean	10	0.01
Alaska Native tribes, specified:	9	0.01
Alaska Athabascan	1	0.00
Aleut	1	0.00
Eskimo	1	0.00
Tlingit-Haida (1)	2	0.00
All other tribes	4	0.00
Am. Ind. or Alaska Nat., not spec.	174	0.21
American Indian tribes, specified:	831	0.99
Apache (9)	22	0.03
Blackfeet (4)	11	0.01
Cherokee (27)	90	0.11
Cheyenne (5)	10	0.01
Chickasaw (1)	2	0.00
Chippewa (2)	9	0.01
Choctaw (8)	16	0.02
Comanche (1)	11	0.01
Cree	1	0.00
Creek	2	0.00
Crow (1)	1	0.00
Delaware (4)	5	0.01
Houma	1	0.00
Iroquois (14)	20	0.02
Kiowa (1)	2	0.00
Latin American Indians (18)	40	0.05
Navajo (269)	369	0.44
Osage	1	0.00
Ottawa	5	0.01
Paiute (2)	2	0.00
Pima	2	0.00
Potawatomi	1	0.00
Pueblo (21)	47	0.06
Puget Sound Salish	1	0.00
Seminole	2	0.00
Shoshone (9)	16	0.02
Sioux (22)	38	0.05
Ute (20)	22	0.03
All other tribes (49)	82	0.10
American Indian tribes, not spec.	20	0.02
Arab:	158	0.19
Arab/Arabic	53	0.06
Egyptian	46	0.05
Iraqi	5	0.01
Lebanese	43	0.05
Palestinian	11	0.01
Armenian	36	0.04
Asian:	1,824	2.16
Bangladeshi (5)	5	0.01
Cambodian (5)	5	0.01
Chinese, ex. Taiwanese (383)	549	0.65
Filipino (75)	160	0.19
Hmong (5)	5	0.01
Indian (105)	118	0.14
Indonesian (1)	5	0.01
Japanese (226)	418	0.50
Korean (169)	237	0.28
Laotian (63)	92	0.11
Pakistani (1)	5	0.01
Taiwanese (9)	13	0.02
Thai (25)	41	0.05
Vietnamese (40)	51	0.06
Other Asian, specified	1	0.00
Other Asian, not specified (81)	119	0.14
Australian	121	0.14
Austrian	50	0.06
Basque	25	0.03
Belgian	31	0.04
Brazilian	154	0.18
British	1,730	2.05
Bulgarian	15	0.02
Canadian	475	0.56
Celtic	10	0.01
Croatian	17	0.02
Czech	157	0.19
Czechoslovakian	13	0.02
Danish	6,324	7.50
Dutch	1,438	1.71
Eastern European	12	0.01
English	28,796	34.15
European	3,017	3.58
Finnish	154	0.18
French, except Basque	1,973	2.34
French Canadian	334	0.40
German	9,096	10.79
Greek	165	0.20
Hawaii Native/Pacific Islander:	1,207	1.43
Melanesian: (5)	14	0.02
Fijian (5)	14	0.02
Micronesian: (15)	33	0.04
Guamanian/Chamorro (1)	7	0.01
Other Micronesian (14)	26	0.03
Polynesian: (625)	1,090	1.29
Native Hawaiian (122)	322	0.38
Samoan (229)	347	0.41
Tongan (242)	341	0.40
Other Polynesian (32)	80	0.09
Other Pac. Isl., not spec. (35)	70	0.08
Hispanic or Latino:	7,217	8.56
Central American:	321	0.38
Costa Rican	29	0.03
Guatemalan	80	0.09
Honduran	38	0.05
Nicaraguan	18	0.02
Panamanian	3	0.00
Salvadoran	146	0.17
Other Central American	7	0.01
Cuban	37	0.04
Dominican Republic	35	0.04
Mexican	4,565	5.41
Puerto Rican	125	0.15
South American:	1,057	1.25
Argentinean	344	0.41
Bolivian	31	0.04
Chilean	177	0.21
Colombian	81	0.10
Ecuadorian	89	0.11
Paraguayan	4	0.00
Peruvian	185	0.22
Uruguayan	17	0.02
Venezuelan	106	0.13
Other South American	23	0.03
Other Hispanic or Latino	1,077	1.28
Hungarian	56	0.07
Icelander	299	0.35
Iranian	87	0.10
Irish	4,008	4.75
Italian	1,742	2.07
Lithuanian	12	0.01
Maltese	35	0.04
New Zealander	51	0.06
Northern European	119	0.14
Norwegian	2,334	2.77
Polish	670	0.79
Portuguese	312	0.37
Romanian	46	0.05
Russian	190	0.23
Scandinavian	757	0.90
Scotch-Irish	1,075	1.27
Scottish	4,230	5.02
Serbian	7	0.01
Slavic	14	0.02
Slovak	23	0.03
Slovene	8	0.01
Swedish	3,672	4.35
Swiss	1,663	1.97
Turkish	11	0.01
Ukrainian	53	0.06
United States or American	5,243	6.22
Welsh	2,216	2.63
West Indian, excl. Hispanic:	13	0.02
Jamaican	8	0.01
West Indian	5	0.01
White:	78,210	92.75
Not Hispanic (73,076)	74,157	87.94
Hispanic (3,491)	4,053	4.81
Yugoslavian	79	0.09

Payson

Place Type: City
County: Utah
Population: 12,716

Ancestry/Race	Number	%
African American/Black:	32	0.25
Not Hispanic (13)	24	0.19
Hispanic (3)	8	0.06
Alaska Native tribes, specified:	2	0.02
Eskimo (2)	2	0.02
Am. Ind. or Alaska Nat., not spec.	13	0.10
American Indian tribes, specified:	73	0.57
Apache (1)	2	0.02
Cherokee (6)	21	0.17
Chickasaw	1	0.01
Chippewa (4)	4	0.03
Choctaw (2)	2	0.02
Iroquois	4	0.03
Lumbee	1	0.01
Navajo (11)	17	0.13
Pueblo (2)	2	0.02
Puget Sound Salish (1)	1	0.01
Shoshone (1)	2	0.02
Sioux (1)	2	0.02
Ute (2)	5	0.04
All other tribes (8)	9	0.07
American Indian tribes, not spec.	2	0.02
Asian:	75	0.59
Chinese, ex. Taiwanese (5)	9	0.07
Filipino (15)	20	0.16
Indian (13)	18	0.14
Japanese (9)	17	0.13
Taiwanese	1	0.01
Thai (1)	2	0.02
Vietnamese (1)	1	0.01
Other Asian, not specified (4)	7	0.06
Australian	27	0.21
British	78	0.61
Canadian	35	0.27
Czech	10	0.08
Danish	843	6.57
Dutch	243	1.89
English	3,804	29.66
European	148	1.15
Finnish	9	0.07
French, except Basque	106	0.83
French Canadian	22	0.17
German	1,223	9.54
Greek	9	0.07
Hawaii Native/Pacific Islander:	45	0.35
Micronesian: (1)	1	0.01
Guamanian/Chamorro (1)	1	0.01
Polynesian: (28)	43	0.34

Notes: 1. Figures in the "Number" column do not add up to the total population due to: a) Ancestry/Race overlap — e.g. persons can report being both White and Irish, b) persons of Hispanic origin can report being any race, c) persons reporting two ancestries are counted in both categories. 2. Numbers in parentheses indicate the number of persons reporting this ancestry/race alone, not in combination with any other ancestry/race. 3. Refer to the Explanation of Data in the front of the book for more detailed information.

Native Hawaiian (1)	2	0.02
Samoan (11)	14	0.11
Tongan (10)	16	0.13
Other Polynesian (6)	11	0.09
Other Pac. Isl., not spec. (1)	1	0.01
Hispanic or Latino:	864	6.79
Central American:	21	0.17
Guatemalan	1	0.01
Panamanian	1	0.01
Salvadoran	18	0.14
Other Central American	1	0.01
Cuban	2	0.02
Dominican Republic	1	0.01
Mexican	622	4.89
Puerto Rican	10	0.08
South American:	13	0.10
Argentinean	1	0.01
Chilean	2	0.02
Colombian	2	0.02
Ecuadorian	1	0.01
Peruvian	7	0.06
Other Hispanic or Latino	195	1.53
Hungarian	15	0.12
Icelander	37	0.29
Irish	598	4.66
Italian	136	1.06
Norwegian	355	2.77
Polish	121	0.94
Russian	21	0.16
Scandinavian	96	0.75
Scotch-Irish	127	0.99
Scottish	523	4.08
Swedish	554	4.32
Swiss	61	0.48
United States or American	1,444	11.26
Welsh	302	2.35
White:	12,117	95.29
Not Hispanic (11,628)	11,716	92.14
Hispanic (328)	401	3.15

Pleasant Grove

Place Type: City
County: Utah
Population: 23,468

Ancestry/Race	Number	%
African American/Black:	127	0.54
Not Hispanic (64)	119	0.51
Hispanic (4)	8	0.03
African, sub-Saharan:	20	0.08
African	20	0.08
Alaska Native tribes, specified:	1	0.00
Aleut (1)	1	0.00
Alaska Native tribes, not specified	1	0.00
Am. Ind. or Alaska Nat., not spec.	32	0.14
American Indian tribes, specified:	136	0.58
Apache (4)	5	0.02
Blackfeet (4)	9	0.04
Cherokee (7)	23	0.10
Cheyenne	3	0.01
Chippewa	1	0.00
Colville (1)	1	0.00
Comanche (1)	1	0.00
Delaware (1)	1	0.00
Iroquois (3)	5	0.02
Latin American Indians (2)	8	0.03
Navajo (24)	32	0.14
Pueblo (5)	9	0.04
Seminole (1)	1	0.00
Shoshone (2)	5	0.02
Sioux (1)	3	0.01
Tohono O'Odham (1)	3	0.01
Ute (1)	3	0.01
All other tribes (10)	23	0.10
American Indian tribes, not spec.	5	0.02
Asian:	220	0.94
Cambodian (4)	4	0.02
Chinese, ex. Taiwanese (46)	60	0.26
Filipino (4)	32	0.14
Indian (15)	15	0.06
Indonesian (1)	3	0.01
Japanese (16)	44	0.19
Korean (30)	37	0.16
Laotian (1)	2	0.01
Pakistani	2	0.01
Taiwanese (1)	2	0.01
Thai (3)	6	0.03
Vietnamese (4)	7	0.03
Other Asian, not specified	6	0.03
Assyrian/Chaldean/Syriac	8	0.03
Australian	28	0.12
Austrian	52	0.22
Brazilian	47	0.20
British	356	1.51
Canadian	91	0.39
Celtic	7	0.03
Czech	8	0.03
Danish	1,614	6.86
Dutch	314	1.33
English	8,406	35.71
European	908	3.86
Finnish	45	0.19
French, except Basque	667	2.83
French Canadian	56	0.24
German	2,579	10.96
Greek	38	0.16
Hawaii Native/Pacific Islander:	207	0.88
Melanesian: (1)	4	0.02
Fijian (1)	4	0.02
Micronesian: (8)	9	0.04
Guamanian/Chamorro (1)	2	0.01
Other Micronesian (7)	7	0.03
Polynesian: (73)	178	0.76
Native Hawaiian (24)	66	0.28
Samoan (23)	47	0.20
Tongan (15)	41	0.17
Other Polynesian (11)	24	0.10
Other Pac. Isl., not spec. (2)	16	0.07
Hispanic or Latino:	1,069	4.56
Central American:	57	0.24
Costa Rican	11	0.05
Guatemalan	23	0.10
Honduran	1	0.00
Nicaraguan	9	0.04
Panamanian	1	0.00
Salvadoran	9	0.04
Other Central American	3	0.01
Cuban	3	0.01
Dominican Republic	5	0.02
Mexican	715	3.05
Puerto Rican	11	0.05
South American:	129	0.55
Argentinean	37	0.16
Chilean	32	0.14
Colombian	10	0.04
Ecuadorian	5	0.02
Peruvian	28	0.12
Uruguayan	2	0.01
Venezuelan	14	0.06
Other South American	1	0.00
Other Hispanic or Latino	149	0.63
Hungarian	6	0.03
Irish	1,037	4.41
Italian	545	2.32
Lithuanian	10	0.04
New Zealander	11	0.05
Northern European	28	0.12
Norwegian	725	3.08
Polish	59	0.25
Portuguese	55	0.23
Romanian	22	0.09
Russian	86	0.37
Scandinavian	324	1.38
Scotch-Irish	230	0.98
Scottish	1,213	5.15
Serbian	5	0.02
Slavic	16	0.07
Slovak	9	0.04
Slovene	17	0.07
Swedish	952	4.04
Swiss	356	1.51
Turkish	7	0.03
Ukrainian	18	0.08
United States or American	1,917	8.14
Welsh	680	2.89
West Indian, excl. Hispanic:	8	0.03
Jamaican	8	0.03
White:	22,662	96.57
Not Hispanic (21,745)	22,017	93.82
Hispanic (585)	645	2.75
Yugoslavian	8	0.03

Provo

Place Type: City
County: Utah
Population: 105,166

Ancestry/Race	Number	%
Acadian/Cajun	16	0.02
African American/Black:	743	0.71
Not Hispanic (432)	638	0.61
Hispanic (54)	105	0.10
African, sub-Saharan:	179	0.17
African	49	0.05
Ghanian	9	0.01
South African	117	0.11
Other sub-Saharan African	4	0.00
Alaska Native tribes, specified:	25	0.02
Alaska Athabascan (2)	3	0.00
Aleut (3)	5	0.00
Eskimo (1)	3	0.00
Tlingit-Haida (9)	11	0.01
All other tribes (3)	3	0.00
Alaska Native tribes, not specified	2	0.00
Am. Ind. or Alaska Nat., not spec.	287	0.27
Albanian	29	0.03
Alsatian	7	0.01
American Indian tribes, specified:	1,057	1.01
Apache (10)	23	0.02
Blackfeet (12)	31	0.03
Cherokee (24)	121	0.12
Chickasaw (2)	4	0.00
Chippewa (6)	20	0.02
Choctaw (6)	15	0.01
Colville (1)	4	0.00
Comanche	4	0.00
Cree	4	0.00
Creek	3	0.00
Crow	1	0.00
Iroquois (22)	42	0.04
Kiowa	3	0.00
Latin American Indians (31)	62	0.06
Lumbee (1)	4	0.00
Menominee	2	0.00
Navajo (351)	434	0.41
Osage (1)	6	0.01
Paiute (6)	11	0.01
Potawatomi (2)	2	0.00
Pueblo (22)	41	0.04
Puget Sound Salish (1)	1	0.00
Seminole (1)	2	0.00
Shoshone (2)	5	0.00
Sioux (57)	72	0.07
Tohono O'Odham (3)	3	0.00
Ute (11)	16	0.02
Yakama (1)	1	0.00
Yaqui (2)	6	0.01
Yuman	4	0.00
All other tribes (64)	110	0.10
American Indian tribes, not spec.	31	0.03
Arab:	184	0.17
Arab/Arabic	18	0.02
Jordanian	9	0.01
Lebanese	115	0.11
Moroccan	2	0.00
Palestinian	18	0.02
Syrian	20	0.02
Other Arab	2	0.00

Notes: 1. Figures in the "Number" column do not add up to the total population due to: a) Ancestry/Race overlap — e.g. persons can report being both White and Irish, b) persons of Hispanic origin can report being any race, c) persons reporting two ancestries are counted in both categories. 2. Numbers in parentheses indicate the number of persons reporting this ancestry/race alone, not in combination with any other ancestry/race. 3. Refer to the Explanation of Data in the front of the book for more detailed information.

Ancestry/Race	Number	%
Armenian	75	0.07
Asian:	2,853	2.71
Cambodian (35)	49	0.05
Chinese, ex. Taiwanese (627)	901	0.86
Filipino (92)	255	0.24
Hmong (5)	5	0.00
Indian (135)	172	0.16
Indonesian (4)	21	0.02
Japanese (389)	675	0.64
Korean (327)	397	0.38
Laotian (49)	60	0.06
Malaysian (4)	4	0.00
Pakistani (11)	16	0.02
Sri Lankan (8)	8	0.01
Taiwanese (34)	40	0.04
Thai (27)	42	0.04
Vietnamese (76)	105	0.10
Other Asian, specified (3)	10	0.01
Other Asian, not specified (53)	93	0.09
Australian	230	0.22
Austrian	191	0.18
Basque	35	0.03
Belgian	132	0.13
Brazilian	154	0.15
British	2,487	2.36
Bulgarian	67	0.06
Canadian	473	0.45
Celtic	13	0.01
Croatian	82	0.08
Czech	73	0.07
Czechoslovakian	110	0.10
Danish	7,627	7.25
Dutch	1,868	1.77
Eastern European	20	0.02
English	32,044	30.44
Estonian	30	0.03
European	2,803	2.66
Finnish	213	0.20
French, except Basque	2,451	2.33
French Canadian	334	0.32
German	12,148	11.54
Greek	221	0.21
Guyanese	9	0.01
Hawaii Native/Pacific Islander:	1,646	1.57
Melanesian: (10)	12	0.01
Fijian (10)	12	0.01
Micronesian: (16)	36	0.03
Guamanian/Chamorro (6)	15	0.01
Other Micronesian (10)	21	0.02
Polynesian: (753)	1,488	1.41
Native Hawaiian (144)	466	0.44
Samoan (253)	425	0.40
Tongan (276)	439	0.42
Other Polynesian (80)	158	0.15
Other Pac. Isl., specified	1	0.00
Other Pac. Isl., not spec. (35)	109	0.10
Hispanic or Latino:	11,013	10.47
Central American:	677	0.64
Costa Rican	33	0.03
Guatemalan	221	0.21
Honduran	64	0.06
Nicaraguan	30	0.03
Panamanian	38	0.04
Salvadoran	274	0.26
Other Central American	17	0.02
Cuban	62	0.06
Dominican Republic	54	0.05
Mexican	7,048	6.70
Puerto Rican	310	0.29
South American:	1,273	1.21
Argentinean	308	0.29
Bolivian	71	0.07
Chilean	206	0.20
Colombian	102	0.10
Ecuadorian	107	0.10
Peruvian	283	0.27
Uruguayan	22	0.02
Venezuelan	126	0.12
Other South American	48	0.05
Other Hispanic or Latino	1,589	1.51
Hungarian	172	0.16
Icelander	116	0.11
Iranian	23	0.02
Irish	4,932	4.69
Italian	2,560	2.43
Latvian	9	0.01
Lithuanian	57	0.05
New Zealander	4	0.00
Northern European	243	0.23
Norwegian	3,030	2.88
Pennsylvania German	6	0.01
Polish	604	0.57
Portuguese	348	0.33
Romanian	113	0.11
Russian	403	0.38
Scandinavian	1,723	1.64
Scotch-Irish	1,068	1.01
Scottish	5,151	4.89
Slavic	24	0.02
Slovak	44	0.04
Slovene	8	0.01
Swedish	4,316	4.10
Swiss	1,718	1.63
Turkish	30	0.03
Ukrainian	130	0.12
United States or American	4,806	4.57
Welsh	2,495	2.37
West Indian, excl. Hispanic:	5	0.00
West Indian	5	0.00
White:	95,335	90.65
Not Hispanic (88,311)	89,851	85.44
Hispanic (4,783)	5,484	5.21
Yugoslavian	27	0.03

Riverton

Place Type: City
County: Salt Lake
Population: 25,011

Ancestry/Race	Number	%
African American/Black:	94	0.38
Not Hispanic (54)	88	0.35
Hispanic	6	0.02
African, sub-Saharan:	8	0.03
African	8	0.03
Am. Ind. or Alaska Nat., not spec.	27	0.11
American Indian tribes, specified:	89	0.36
Apache (4)	5	0.02
Blackfeet (2)	3	0.01
Cherokee (3)	9	0.04
Chickasaw	1	0.00
Chippewa	2	0.01
Choctaw (6)	12	0.05
Iroquois (1)	7	0.03
Latin American Indians (1)	7	0.03
Navajo (4)	16	0.06
Paiute (1)	4	0.02
Pueblo (6)	6	0.02
Sioux (1)	3	0.01
Ute (2)	2	0.01
Yaqui (1)	1	0.00
All other tribes (7)	11	0.04
American Indian tribes, not spec.	9	0.04
Armenian	55	0.22
Asian:	257	1.03
Bangladeshi (1)	1	0.00
Cambodian (1)	1	0.00
Chinese, ex. Taiwanese (26)	31	0.12
Filipino (17)	31	0.12
Indian (17)	21	0.08
Indonesian (1)	1	0.00
Japanese (46)	96	0.38
Korean (16)	23	0.09
Laotian (13)	13	0.05
Pakistani (2)	4	0.02
Taiwanese (1)	1	0.00
Thai (9)	9	0.04
Vietnamese (8)	13	0.05
Other Asian, not specified (4)	12	0.05
Australian	32	0.13
Austrian	61	0.24
Basque	48	0.19
Belgian	41	0.16
British	418	1.66
Canadian	93	0.37
Croatian	15	0.06
Czech	77	0.31
Czechoslovakian	8	0.03
Danish	1,559	6.20
Dutch	754	3.00
English	7,846	31.21
European	894	3.56
Finnish	92	0.37
French, except Basque	401	1.60
French Canadian	51	0.20
German	3,495	13.90
Greek	140	0.56
Hawaii Native/Pacific Islander:	94	0.38
Melanesian:	3	0.01
Fijian	3	0.01
Micronesian: (6)	11	0.04
Other Micronesian (6)	11	0.04
Polynesian: (40)	70	0.28
Native Hawaiian (1)	5	0.02
Samoan (5)	17	0.07
Tongan (31)	38	0.15
Other Polynesian (3)	10	0.04
Other Pac. Isl., not spec. (8)	10	0.04
Hispanic or Latino:	793	3.17
Central American:	38	0.15
Costa Rican	3	0.01
Guatemalan	11	0.04
Honduran	7	0.03
Nicaraguan	2	0.01
Salvadoran	15	0.06
Cuban	5	0.02
Mexican	425	1.70
Puerto Rican	35	0.14
South American:	35	0.14
Argentinean	2	0.01
Chilean	15	0.06
Colombian	7	0.03
Peruvian	3	0.01
Venezuelan	8	0.03
Other Hispanic or Latino	255	1.02
Hungarian	5	0.02
Icelander	21	0.08
Irish	1,532	6.09
Italian	617	2.45
Lithuanian	16	0.06
Maltese	27	0.11
New Zealander	11	0.04
Northern European	10	0.04
Norwegian	1,039	4.13
Polish	212	0.84
Portuguese	35	0.14
Russian	53	0.21
Scandinavian	548	2.18
Scotch-Irish	131	0.52
Scottish	949	3.77
Swedish	1,535	6.11
Swiss	415	1.65
Ukrainian	2	0.01
United States or American	1,714	6.82
Welsh	551	2.19
West Indian, excl. Hispanic:	8	0.03
Jamaican	8	0.03
White:	24,390	97.52
Not Hispanic (23,695)	23,878	95.47
Hispanic (428)	512	2.05
Yugoslavian	59	0.23

Roy

Place Type: City
County: Weber
Population: 32,885

Ancestry/Race	Number	%

Notes: 1. Figures in the "Number" column do not add up to the total population due to: a) Ancestry/Race overlap — e.g. persons can report being both White and Irish, b) persons of Hispanic origin can report being any race, c) persons reporting two ancestries are counted in both categories. 2. Numbers in parentheses indicate the number of persons reporting this ancestry/race alone, not in combination with any other ancestry/race. 3. Refer to the Explanation of Data in the front of the book for more detailed information.

African American/Black:	500	1.52
Not Hispanic (375)	477	1.45
Hispanic (8)	23	0.07
African, sub-Saharan:	19	0.06
African	19	0.06
Alaska Native tribes, specified:	11	0.03
Alaska Athabascan	1	0.00
Eskimo (6)	8	0.02
Tlingit-Haida (2)	2	0.01
Alaska Native tribes, not specified	1	0.00
Am. Ind. or Alaska Nat., not spec.	66	0.20
American Indian tribes, specified:	234	0.71
Apache (5)	16	0.05
Blackfeet (1)	3	0.01
Cherokee (8)	26	0.08
Chickasaw (6)	7	0.02
Chippewa (5)	6	0.02
Choctaw	7	0.02
Comanche (2)	3	0.01
Creek (2)	3	0.01
Crow (1)	2	0.01
Delaware	3	0.01
Iroquois (2)	5	0.02
Kiowa	1	0.00
Latin American Indians (9)	10	0.03
Navajo (50)	63	0.19
Osage (1)	2	0.01
Potawatomi (1)	1	0.00
Pueblo (5)	5	0.02
Puget Sound Salish (1)	4	0.01
Seminole (3)	4	0.01
Shoshone (2)	10	0.03
Sioux (15)	17	0.05
Tohono O'Odham (1)	1	0.00
Ute (7)	10	0.03
Yaqui	1	0.00
All other tribes (13)	24	0.07
American Indian tribes, not spec.	8	0.02
Arab:	90	0.27
Arab/Arabic	8	0.02
Lebanese	61	0.19
Syrian	21	0.06
Asian:	789	2.40
Chinese, ex. Taiwanese (49)	61	0.19
Filipino (92)	154	0.47
Hmong (8)	9	0.03
Indian (18)	19	0.06
Indonesian	2	0.01
Japanese (142)	209	0.64
Korean (70)	94	0.29
Laotian (50)	52	0.16
Malaysian (1)	1	0.00
Taiwanese (12)	12	0.04
Thai (31)	38	0.12
Vietnamese (100)	112	0.34
Other Asian, not specified (15)	26	0.08
Australian	6	0.02
Austrian	56	0.17
Belgian	44	0.13
Brazilian	39	0.12
British	279	0.85
Canadian	111	0.34
Croatian	41	0.13
Czech	65	0.20
Czechoslovakian	7	0.02
Danish	1,764	5.39
Dutch	1,054	3.22
English	8,817	26.93
European	769	2.35
Finnish	70	0.21
French, except Basque	847	2.59
French Canadian	110	0.34
German	4,100	12.52
Greek	114	0.35
Hawaii Native/Pacific Islander:	70	0.21
Micronesian: (5)	7	0.02
Guamanian/Chamorro (5)	7	0.02
Polynesian: (25)	49	0.15
Native Hawaiian (11)	24	0.07
Samoan (10)	12	0.04
Tongan (3)	8	0.02
Other Polynesian (1)	5	0.02
Other Pac. Isl., not spec. (6)	14	0.04
Hispanic or Latino:	2,526	7.68
Central American:	42	0.13
Costa Rican	1	0.00
Guatemalan	5	0.02
Honduran	2	0.01
Nicaraguan	2	0.01
Panamanian	4	0.01
Salvadoran	26	0.08
Other Central American	2	0.01
Cuban	7	0.02
Dominican Republic	9	0.03
Mexican	1,546	4.70
Puerto Rican	36	0.11
South American:	59	0.18
Bolivian	1	0.00
Chilean	25	0.08
Colombian	8	0.02
Ecuadorian	2	0.01
Paraguayan	1	0.00
Peruvian	14	0.04
Uruguayan	1	0.00
Venezuelan	5	0.02
Other South American	2	0.01
Other Hispanic or Latino	827	2.51
Hungarian	32	0.10
Irish	2,012	6.14
Italian	1,364	4.17
Lithuanian	46	0.14
Northern European	7	0.02
Norwegian	874	2.67
Polish	289	0.88
Portuguese	86	0.26
Romanian	9	0.03
Russian	37	0.11
Scandinavian	118	0.36
Scotch-Irish	338	1.03
Scottish	1,725	5.27
Slavic	11	0.03
Slovak	17	0.05
Slovene	11	0.03
Swedish	1,324	4.04
Swiss	378	1.15
United States or American	2,187	6.68
Welsh	629	1.92
West Indian, excl. Hispanic:	27	0.08
Jamaican	27	0.08
White:	30,436	92.55
Not Hispanic (28,770)	29,157	88.66
Hispanic (1,072)	1,279	3.89
Yugoslavian	10	0.03

Saint George

Place Type: City
County: Washington
Population: 49,663

Ancestry/Race	Number	%
African American/Black:	247	0.50
Not Hispanic (110)	227	0.46
Hispanic (10)	20	0.04
African, sub-Saharan:	26	0.05
African	21	0.04
South African	5	0.01
Alaska Native tribes, specified:	4	0.01
Alaska Athabascan (1)	1	0.00
Eskimo (1)	2	0.00
All other tribes	1	0.00
Alaska Native tribes, not specified	4	0.01
Am. Ind. or Alaska Nat., not spec.	152	0.31
American Indian tribes, specified:	910	1.83
Apache (20)	28	0.06
Blackfeet	8	0.02
Cherokee (16)	62	0.12
Cheyenne (1)	1	0.00
Chickasaw (3)	10	0.02
Chippewa (2)	2	0.00
Choctaw (2)	12	0.02
Comanche (2)	2	0.00
Cree (3)	9	0.02
Creek (2)	2	0.00
Crow (1)	3	0.01
Iroquois (2)	2	0.00
Latin American Indians (11)	22	0.04
Lumbee (1)	1	0.00
Navajo (461)	533	1.07
Osage	1	0.00
Paiute (66)	90	0.18
Pima (6)	6	0.01
Pueblo (7)	9	0.02
Seminole	1	0.00
Shoshone (3)	4	0.01
Sioux (6)	18	0.04
Ute (19)	32	0.06
Yakama (1)	3	0.01
Yuman	2	0.00
All other tribes (36)	47	0.09
American Indian tribes, not spec.	52	0.10
Arab:	10	0.02
Lebanese	10	0.02
Armenian	45	0.09
Asian:	471	0.95
Cambodian (1)	1	0.00
Chinese, ex. Taiwanese (45)	82	0.17
Filipino (48)	85	0.17
Hmong (1)	1	0.00
Indian (37)	45	0.09
Indonesian (3)	4	0.01
Japanese (58)	116	0.23
Korean (40)	59	0.12
Laotian (4)	7	0.01
Malaysian (2)	2	0.00
Pakistani (1)	1	0.00
Taiwanese (4)	6	0.01
Thai (3)	16	0.03
Vietnamese (15)	22	0.04
Other Asian, specified (3)	9	0.02
Other Asian, not specified (8)	15	0.03
Australian	4	0.01
Austrian	73	0.15
Basque	23	0.05
Brazilian	80	0.16
British	383	0.77
Canadian	64	0.13
Celtic	28	0.06
Croatian	2	0.00
Czech	158	0.32
Czechoslovakian	60	0.12
Danish	2,644	5.33
Dutch	1,169	2.36
Eastern European	11	0.02
English	15,290	30.81
European	950	1.91
Finnish	122	0.25
French, except Basque	1,260	2.54
French Canadian	188	0.38
German	5,900	11.89
Greek	88	0.18
Hawaii Native/Pacific Islander:	542	1.09
Melanesian: (1)	2	0.00
Fijian (1)	2	0.00
Micronesian: (3)	8	0.02
Guamanian/Chamorro (2)	6	0.01
Other Micronesian (1)	2	0.00
Polynesian: (240)	494	0.99
Native Hawaiian (59)	165	0.33
Samoan (145)	234	0.47
Tongan (35)	71	0.14
Other Polynesian (1)	24	0.05
Other Pac. Isl., specified	4	0.01
Other Pac. Isl., not spec. (8)	34	0.07
Hispanic or Latino:	3,337	6.72
Central American:	246	0.50
Costa Rican	26	0.05
Guatemalan	47	0.09
Honduran	10	0.02
Nicaraguan	9	0.02

Notes: 1. Figures in the "Number" column do not add up to the total population due to: a) Ancestry/Race overlap — e.g. persons can report being both White and Irish, b) persons of Hispanic origin can report being any race, c) persons reporting two ancestries are counted in both categories. 2. Numbers in parentheses indicate the number of persons reporting this ancestry/race alone, not in combination with any other ancestry/race. 3. Refer to the Explanation of Data in the front of the book for more detailed information.

Panamanian	1	0.00
Salvadoran	144	0.29
Other Central American	9	0.02
Cuban	12	0.02
Dominican Republic	5	0.01
Mexican	2,382	4.80
Puerto Rican	55	0.11
South American:	103	0.21
Argentinean	25	0.05
Bolivian	3	0.01
Chilean	15	0.03
Colombian	18	0.04
Ecuadorian	1	0.00
Paraguayan	7	0.01
Peruvian	11	0.02
Uruguayan	4	0.01
Venezuelan	11	0.02
Other South American	8	0.02
Other Hispanic or Latino	534	1.08
Hungarian	111	0.22
Icelander	95	0.19
Iranian	20	0.04
Irish	3,006	6.06
Italian	1,272	2.56
Lithuanian	64	0.13
Northern European	51	0.10
Norwegian	1,394	2.81
Pennsylvania German	15	0.03
Polish	471	0.95
Portuguese	123	0.25
Romanian	5	0.01
Russian	92	0.19
Scandinavian	272	0.55
Scotch-Irish	717	1.44
Scottish	2,423	4.88
Slavic	16	0.03
Swedish	1,755	3.54
Swiss	1,043	2.10
Ukrainian	97	0.20
United States or American	4,147	8.36
Welsh	848	1.71
White:	46,634	93.90
Not Hispanic (44,215)	44,791	90.19
Hispanic (1,608)	1,843	3.71
Yugoslavian	112	0.23

Salt Lake City

Place Type: City
County: Salt Lake
Population: 181,743

Ancestry/Race	Number	%
Acadian/Cajun	25	0.01
Afghan	67	0.04
African American/Black:	4,472	2.46
Not Hispanic (3,108)	3,928	2.16
Hispanic (325)	544	0.30
African, sub-Saharan:	1,263	0.70
African	337	0.19
Cape Verdean	4	0.00
Ethiopian	23	0.01
Ghanian	73	0.04
Kenyan	53	0.03
Liberian	11	0.01
Nigerian	24	0.01
Somalian	341	0.19
South African	90	0.05
Sudanese	293	0.16
Zimbabwean	10	0.01
Other sub-Saharan African	4	0.00
Alaska Native tribes, specified:	23	0.01
Alaska Athabascan (1)	3	0.00
Aleut (1)	1	0.00
Eskimo (6)	9	0.00
Tlingit-Haida (6)	9	0.00
All other tribes (1)	1	0.00
Alaska Native tribes, not specified	3	0.00
Am. Ind. or Alaska Nat., not spec.	846	0.47
Albanian	62	0.03
American Indian tribes, specified:	2,508	1.38
Apache (43)	77	0.04
Blackfeet (7)	29	0.02
Cherokee (62)	198	0.11
Cheyenne (20)	30	0.02
Chickasaw (1)	7	0.00
Chippewa (27)	48	0.03
Choctaw (15)	37	0.02
Colville (1)	1	0.00
Comanche	3	0.00
Cree (2)	11	0.01
Creek (8)	13	0.01
Crow (4)	7	0.00
Delaware (2)	2	0.00
Houma	1	0.00
Iroquois (14)	26	0.01
Kiowa (8)	8	0.00
Latin American Indians (81)	181	0.10
Lumbee (1)	1	0.00
Menominee (1)	1	0.00
Navajo (1,032)	1,178	0.65
Osage (1)	8	0.00
Ottawa (2)	2	0.00
Paiute (34)	49	0.03
Pima (3)	8	0.00
Potawatomi (1)	4	0.00
Pueblo (20)	40	0.02
Puget Sound Salish (1)	10	0.01
Seminole	10	0.01
Shoshone (35)	55	0.03
Sioux (78)	104	0.06
Tohono O'Odham (1)	1	0.00
Ute (104)	159	0.09
Yaqui (1)	2	0.00
Yuman	1	0.00
All other tribes (131)	196	0.11
American Indian tribes, not spec.	207	0.11
Arab:	800	0.44
Arab/Arabic	46	0.03
Egyptian	24	0.01
Iraqi	67	0.04
Jordanian	31	0.02
Lebanese	304	0.17
Moroccan	9	0.00
Palestinian	41	0.02
Syrian	19	0.01
Other Arab	259	0.14
Armenian	240	0.13
Asian:	7,949	4.37
Bangladeshi (16)	16	0.01
Cambodian (85)	112	0.06
Chinese, ex. Taiwanese (1,569)	1,868	1.03
Filipino (327)	470	0.26
Hmong (3)	7	0.00
Indian (654)	759	0.42
Indonesian (18)	44	0.02
Japanese (959)	1,293	0.71
Korean (559)	643	0.35
Laotian (91)	119	0.07
Malaysian (6)	15	0.01
Pakistani (103)	137	0.08
Sri Lankan (12)	13	0.01
Taiwanese (102)	122	0.07
Thai (102)	135	0.07
Vietnamese (1,685)	1,811	1.00
Other Asian, specified (14)	34	0.02
Other Asian, not specified (142)	351	0.19
Assyrian/Chaldean/Syriac	11	0.01
Australian	110	0.06
Austrian	353	0.19
Basque	175	0.10
Belgian	73	0.04
Brazilian	125	0.07
British	2,956	1.63
Bulgarian	28	0.02
Canadian	594	0.33
Celtic	144	0.08
Croatian	557	0.31
Czech	417	0.23
Czechoslovakian	182	0.10
Danish	7,874	4.34
Dutch	3,421	1.89
Eastern European	154	0.08
English	37,879	20.88
Estonian	5	0.00
European	3,363	1.85
Finnish	419	0.23
French, except Basque	4,379	2.41
French Canadian	542	0.30
German	19,672	10.84
Greek	1,630	0.90
Guyanese	10	0.01
Hawaii Native/Pacific Islander:	4,433	2.44
Melanesian: (15)	16	0.01
Fijian (14)	15	0.01
Other Melanesian (1)	1	0.00
Micronesian: (36)	61	0.03
Guamanian/Chamorro (14)	33	0.02
Other Micronesian (22)	28	0.02
Polynesian: (2,989)	4,005	2.20
Native Hawaiian (124)	303	0.17
Samoan (523)	722	0.40
Tongan (2,245)	2,745	1.51
Other Polynesian (97)	235	0.13
Other Pac. Isl., specified	13	0.01
Other Pac. Isl., not spec. (226)	338	0.19
Hispanic or Latino:	34,254	18.85
Central American:	1,041	0.57
Costa Rican	60	0.03
Guatemalan	439	0.24
Honduran	105	0.06
Nicaraguan	43	0.02
Panamanian	16	0.01
Salvadoran	335	0.18
Other Central American	43	0.02
Cuban	201	0.11
Dominican Republic	42	0.02
Mexican	25,430	13.99
Puerto Rican	483	0.27
South American:	1,203	0.66
Argentinean	200	0.11
Bolivian	45	0.02
Chilean	188	0.10
Colombian	158	0.09
Ecuadorian	37	0.02
Paraguayan	2	0.00
Peruvian	356	0.20
Uruguayan	45	0.02
Venezuelan	132	0.07
Other South American	40	0.02
Other Hispanic or Latino	5,854	3.22
Hungarian	355	0.20
Icelander	174	0.10
Iranian	237	0.13
Irish	12,102	6.67
Israeli	98	0.05
Italian	5,135	2.83
Latvian	46	0.03
Lithuanian	234	0.13
Luxemburger	22	0.01
Macedonian	5	0.00
New Zealander	35	0.02
Northern European	457	0.25
Norwegian	4,770	2.63
Pennsylvania German	20	0.01
Polish	1,774	0.98
Portuguese	363	0.20
Romanian	244	0.13
Russian	1,041	0.57
Scandinavian	2,089	1.15
Scotch-Irish	2,312	1.27
Scottish	7,838	4.32
Serbian	87	0.05
Slavic	130	0.07
Slovak	101	0.06
Slovene	131	0.07
Swedish	6,424	3.54
Swiss	2,105	1.16
Turkish	95	0.05
Ukrainian	403	0.22

Notes: 1. Figures in the "Number" column do not add up to the total population due to: a) Ancestry/Race overlap — e.g. persons can report being both White and Irish, b) persons of Hispanic origin can report being any race, c) persons reporting two ancestries are counted in both categories. 2. Numbers in parentheses indicate the number of persons reporting this ancestry/race alone, not in combination with any other ancestry/race. 3. Refer to the Explanation of Data in the front of the book for more detailed information.

United States or American	7,825	4.31
Welsh	3,598	1.98
West Indian, excl. Hispanic:	81	0.04
Bahamian	6	0.00
Belizean	15	0.01
Haitian	44	0.02
Jamaican	12	0.01
Trinidadian and Tobagonian	4	0.00
White:	149,310	82.15
Not Hispanic (128,377)	131,523	72.37
Hispanic (15,556)	17,787	9.79
Yugoslavian	1,535	0.85

Sandy

Place Type: City
County: Salt Lake
Population: 88,418

Ancestry/Race	Number	%
Acadian/Cajun	5	0.01
African American/Black:	634	0.72
Not Hispanic (404)	569	0.64
Hispanic (41)	65	0.07
African, sub-Saharan:	80	0.09
African	35	0.04
South African	39	0.04
Ugandan	6	0.01
Alaska Native tribes, specified:	11	0.01
Alaska Athabascan (2)	2	0.00
Aleut	1	0.00
Eskimo (2)	3	0.00
Tlingit-Haida (1)	5	0.01
Am. Ind. or Alaska Nat., not spec.	127	0.14
Albanian	10	0.01
American Indian tribes, specified:	407	0.46
Apache (4)	13	0.01
Blackfeet	6	0.01
Cherokee (20)	80	0.09
Chickasaw	6	0.01
Chippewa (8)	15	0.02
Choctaw (2)	4	0.00
Comanche	5	0.01
Cree	1	0.00
Creek (2)	7	0.01
Crow (2)	2	0.00
Iroquois (4)	9	0.01
Latin American Indians (6)	12	0.01
Menominee (3)	3	0.00
Navajo (78)	107	0.12
Osage (5)	9	0.01
Paiute (5)	6	0.01
Pima (1)	2	0.00
Potawatomi (3)	5	0.01
Pueblo (8)	13	0.01
Puget Sound Salish (1)	1	0.00
Seminole	7	0.01
Shoshone (14)	15	0.02
Sioux (12)	18	0.02
Ute (6)	12	0.01
Yaqui (1)	1	0.00
All other tribes (27)	48	0.05
American Indian tribes, not spec.	29	0.03
Arab:	269	0.30
Arab/Arabic	76	0.09
Jordanian	14	0.02
Lebanese	46	0.05
Palestinian	31	0.04
Syrian	63	0.07
Other Arab	39	0.04
Armenian	177	0.20
Asian:	2,560	2.90
Bangladeshi (4)	4	0.00
Cambodian (33)	40	0.05
Chinese, ex. Taiwanese (618)	770	0.87
Filipino (115)	213	0.24
Hmong (6)	6	0.01
Indian (244)	261	0.30
Indonesian (9)	15	0.02
Japanese (329)	546	0.62
Korean (171)	236	0.27
Laotian (152)	155	0.18
Malaysian (1)	6	0.01
Pakistani (20)	31	0.04
Sri Lankan (1)	1	0.00
Taiwanese (26)	36	0.04
Thai (18)	42	0.05
Vietnamese (69)	91	0.10
Other Asian, specified (2)	3	0.00
Other Asian, not specified (52)	104	0.12
Australian	57	0.06
Austrian	290	0.33
Basque	15	0.02
Belgian	98	0.11
Brazilian	153	0.17
British	1,326	1.50
Canadian	287	0.33
Celtic	14	0.02
Croatian	44	0.05
Czech	234	0.27
Czechoslovakian	91	0.10
Danish	6,065	6.87
Dutch	1,990	2.25
Eastern European	28	0.03
English	27,315	30.95
European	1,627	1.84
Finnish	160	0.18
French, except Basque	2,322	2.63
French Canadian	270	0.31
German	13,149	14.90
German Russian	14	0.02
Greek	889	1.01
Hawaii Native/Pacific Islander:	552	0.62
Melanesian: (1)	1	0.00
Fijian (1)	1	0.00
Micronesian: (17)	21	0.02
Guamanian/Chamorro (12)	14	0.02
Other Micronesian (5)	7	0.01
Polynesian: (218)	495	0.56
Native Hawaiian (43)	149	0.17
Samoan (71)	154	0.17
Tongan (76)	153	0.17
Other Polynesian (28)	39	0.04
Other Pac. Isl., not spec. (22)	35	0.04
Hispanic or Latino:	3,875	4.38
Central American:	132	0.15
Costa Rican	7	0.01
Guatemalan	28	0.03
Honduran	16	0.02
Nicaraguan	14	0.02
Panamanian	9	0.01
Salvadoran	49	0.06
Other Central American	9	0.01
Cuban	44	0.05
Dominican Republic	11	0.01
Mexican	2,165	2.45
Puerto Rican	146	0.17
South American:	305	0.34
Argentinean	34	0.04
Bolivian	6	0.01
Chilean	26	0.03
Colombian	81	0.09
Ecuadorian	9	0.01
Peruvian	87	0.10
Uruguayan	25	0.03
Venezuelan	20	0.02
Other South American	17	0.02
Other Hispanic or Latino	1,072	1.21
Hungarian	196	0.22
Icelander	125	0.14
Iranian	231	0.26
Irish	6,167	6.99
Italian	2,832	3.21
Latvian	38	0.04
Lithuanian	49	0.06
New Zealander	37	0.04
Northern European	115	0.13
Norwegian	3,363	3.81
Pennsylvania German	13	0.01
Polish	901	1.02
Portuguese	84	0.10
Romanian	50	0.06
Russian	389	0.44
Scandinavian	1,362	1.54
Scotch-Irish	1,033	1.17
Scottish	4,198	4.76
Serbian	7	0.01
Slavic	42	0.05
Slovak	90	0.10
Swedish	4,773	5.41
Swiss	1,512	1.71
Turkish	70	0.08
Ukrainian	87	0.10
United States or American	5,680	6.44
Welsh	2,200	2.49
West Indian, excl. Hispanic:	9	0.01
U.S. Virgin Islander	9	0.01
White:	84,016	95.02
Not Hispanic (80,523)	81,563	92.25
Hispanic (2,162)	2,453	2.77
Yugoslavian	170	0.19

South Jordan

Place Type: City
County: Salt Lake
Population: 29,437

Ancestry/Race	Number	%
African American/Black:	123	0.42
Not Hispanic (80)	114	0.39
Hispanic (8)	9	0.03
African, sub-Saharan:	14	0.05
African	7	0.02
Nigerian	7	0.02
Am. Ind. or Alaska Nat., not spec.	33	0.11
American Indian tribes, specified:	71	0.24
Apache (2)	16	0.05
Blackfeet	6	0.02
Cherokee (1)	12	0.04
Choctaw	1	0.00
Colville	1	0.00
Delaware	2	0.01
Iroquois (1)	1	0.00
Latin American Indians (4)	8	0.03
Navajo (4)	5	0.02
Osage	1	0.00
Potawatomi (1)	1	0.00
Seminole	4	0.01
Sioux (2)	5	0.02
Ute	3	0.01
Yakama (1)	2	0.01
All other tribes (2)	3	0.01
American Indian tribes, not spec.	8	0.03
Arab:	10	0.03
Lebanese	10	0.03
Armenian	57	0.19
Asian:	458	1.56
Cambodian (3)	3	0.01
Chinese, ex. Taiwanese (51)	89	0.30
Filipino (48)	63	0.21
Indian (31)	35	0.12
Indonesian	1	0.00
Japanese (40)	97	0.33
Korean (32)	43	0.15
Laotian (18)	19	0.06
Pakistani (11)	29	0.10
Taiwanese (5)	5	0.02
Thai (2)	3	0.01
Vietnamese (36)	45	0.15
Other Asian, not specified (15)	26	0.09
Australian	25	0.08
Austrian	56	0.19
Basque	23	0.08
Belgian	15	0.05
Brazilian	47	0.16
British	354	1.20
Canadian	141	0.48
Croatian	8	0.03
Czech	8	0.03

Notes: 1. Figures in the "Number" column do not add up to the total population due to: a) Ancestry/Race overlap — e.g. persons can report being both White and Irish, b) persons of Hispanic origin can report being any race, c) persons reporting two ancestries are counted in both categories. 2. Numbers in parentheses indicate the number of persons reporting this ancestry/race alone, not in combination with any other ancestry/race. 3. Refer to the Explanation of Data in the front of the book for more detailed information.

Danish	2,002	6.80
Dutch	899	3.05
English	10,774	36.57
European	619	2.10
Finnish	36	0.12
French, except Basque	797	2.71
French Canadian	25	0.08
German	3,646	12.38
Greek	134	0.45
Hawaii Native/Pacific Islander:	233	0.79
Melanesian: (2)	2	0.01
Fijian (2)	2	0.01
Micronesian: (2)	6	0.02
Guamanian/Chamorro (2)	6	0.02
Polynesian: (121)	206	0.70
Native Hawaiian (5)	46	0.16
Samoan (55)	77	0.26
Tongan (59)	80	0.27
Other Polynesian (2)	3	0.01
Other Pac. Isl., not spec. (12)	19	0.06
Hispanic or Latino:	962	3.27
Central American:	40	0.14
Costa Rican	5	0.02
Guatemalan	16	0.05
Panamanian	1	0.00
Salvadoran	18	0.06
Cuban	23	0.08
Dominican Republic	1	0.00
Mexican	478	1.62
Puerto Rican	41	0.14
South American:	68	0.23
Argentinean	4	0.01
Bolivian	3	0.01
Chilean	3	0.01
Colombian	22	0.07
Ecuadorian	11	0.04
Peruvian	18	0.06
Venezuelan	2	0.01
Other South American	5	0.02
Other Hispanic or Latino	311	1.06
Hungarian	26	0.09
Icelander	6	0.02
Iranian	15	0.05
Irish	1,759	5.97
Italian	539	1.83
Northern European	19	0.06
Norwegian	790	2.68
Polish	145	0.49
Portuguese	26	0.09
Romanian	52	0.18
Russian	107	0.36
Scandinavian	428	1.45
Scotch-Irish	208	0.71
Scottish	1,602	5.44
Slavic	8	0.03
Slovak	6	0.02
Swedish	1,839	6.24
Swiss	502	1.70
Turkish	44	0.15
Ukrainian	20	0.07
United States or American	1,878	6.37
Welsh	812	2.76
West Indian, excl. Hispanic:	15	0.05
Bahamian	15	0.05
White:	28,466	96.70
Not Hispanic (27,606)	27,881	94.71
Hispanic (509)	585	1.99
Yugoslavian	59	0.20

South Ogden

Place Type: City
County: Weber
Population: 14,377

Ancestry/Race	Number	%
African American/Black:	153	1.06
Not Hispanic (99)	138	0.96
Hispanic (7)	15	0.10
African, sub-Saharan:	3	0.02
African	3	0.02
Alaska Native tribes, specified:	2	0.01
Eskimo (2)	2	0.01
Am. Ind. or Alaska Nat., not spec.	41	0.29
Alsatian	4	0.03
American Indian tribes, specified:	120	0.83
Apache	1	0.01
Cherokee (4)	15	0.10
Cheyenne (4)	4	0.03
Chippewa	1	0.01
Choctaw (3)	3	0.02
Creek (1)	1	0.01
Iroquois (2)	4	0.03
Latin American Indians	2	0.01
Navajo (37)	53	0.37
Ottawa	1	0.01
Pueblo (1)	10	0.07
Shoshone (5)	5	0.03
Ute (3)	5	0.03
All other tribes (9)	15	0.10
American Indian tribes, not spec.	6	0.04
Arab:	28	0.19
Arab/Arabic	16	0.11
Lebanese	12	0.08
Asian:	298	2.07
Bangladeshi (1)	1	0.01
Cambodian (2)	2	0.01
Chinese, ex. Taiwanese (31)	49	0.34
Filipino (8)	18	0.13
Indian (28)	34	0.24
Indonesian (1)	1	0.01
Japanese (79)	114	0.79
Korean (16)	22	0.15
Laotian (5)	10	0.07
Pakistani (4)	6	0.04
Taiwanese (1)	1	0.01
Thai (6)	10	0.07
Vietnamese (17)	17	0.12
Other Asian, specified (1)	1	0.01
Other Asian, not specified (2)	12	0.08
Austrian	28	0.19
Basque	4	0.03
Brazilian	9	0.06
British	198	1.37
Canadian	33	0.23
Celtic	4	0.03
Czech	37	0.26
Czechoslovakian	7	0.05
Danish	897	6.22
Dutch	469	3.25
English	4,657	32.30
European	225	1.56
Finnish	23	0.16
French, except Basque	339	2.35
French Canadian	41	0.28
German	1,642	11.39
Greek	51	0.35
Hawaii Native/Pacific Islander:	80	0.56
Melanesian: (1)	4	0.03
Fijian (1)	4	0.03
Micronesian: (3)	4	0.03
Guamanian/Chamorro (1)	2	0.01
Other Micronesian (2)	2	0.01
Polynesian: (31)	62	0.43
Native Hawaiian (11)	26	0.18
Samoan (18)	30	0.21
Tongan (2)	6	0.04
Other Pac. Isl., not spec. (4)	10	0.07
Hispanic or Latino:	1,056	7.35
Central American:	30	0.21
Costa Rican	2	0.01
Guatemalan	12	0.08
Honduran	4	0.03
Nicaraguan	1	0.01
Panamanian	2	0.01
Salvadoran	9	0.06
Cuban	1	0.01
Mexican	671	4.67
Puerto Rican	23	0.16
South American:	31	0.22
Argentinean	3	0.02
Bolivian	3	0.02
Chilean	11	0.08
Colombian	1	0.01
Ecuadorian	3	0.02
Peruvian	8	0.06
Venezuelan	2	0.01
Other Hispanic or Latino	300	2.09
Hungarian	32	0.22
Icelander	6	0.04
Iranian	14	0.10
Irish	939	6.51
Italian	594	4.12
Lithuanian	44	0.31
Norwegian	259	1.80
Polish	208	1.44
Portuguese	21	0.15
Romanian	13	0.09
Russian	36	0.25
Scandinavian	168	1.17
Scotch-Irish	227	1.57
Scottish	790	5.48
Slovak	4	0.03
Slovene	10	0.07
Swedish	541	3.75
Swiss	136	0.94
Turkish	17	0.12
Ukrainian	14	0.10
United States or American	897	6.22
Welsh	417	2.89
West Indian, excl. Hispanic:	6	0.04
Bermudan	6	0.04
White:	13,448	93.54
Not Hispanic (12,699)	12,883	89.61
Hispanic (458)	565	3.93
Yugoslavian	5	0.03

South Salt Lake

Place Type: City
County: Salt Lake
Population: 22,038

Ancestry/Race	Number	%
African American/Black:	802	3.64
Not Hispanic (603)	735	3.34
Hispanic (39)	67	0.30
African, sub-Saharan:	143	0.65
African	90	0.41
Somalian	47	0.21
Ugandan	6	0.03
Alaska Native tribes, specified:	6	0.03
Eskimo (2)	4	0.02
Tlingit-Haida (1)	1	0.00
All other tribes (1)	1	0.00
Alaska Native tribes, not specified	1	0.00
Am. Ind. or Alaska Nat., not spec.	245	1.11
American Indian tribes, specified:	591	2.68
Apache (4)	8	0.04
Blackfeet (3)	10	0.05
Cherokee (15)	45	0.20
Cheyenne (2)	3	0.01
Chickasaw	2	0.01
Chippewa (6)	6	0.03
Choctaw (6)	8	0.04
Comanche (1)	4	0.02
Cree (1)	2	0.01
Creek (1)	2	0.01
Delaware	3	0.01
Iroquois (1)	5	0.02
Latin American Indians (24)	33	0.15
Menominee (1)	1	0.00
Navajo (286)	314	1.42
Osage	1	0.00
Paiute (6)	9	0.04
Pima	2	0.01
Pueblo (8)	10	0.05
Seminole (1)	2	0.01
Shoshone (12)	17	0.08
Sioux (25)	30	0.14

Notes: 1. Figures in the "Number" column do not add up to the total population due to: a) Ancestry/Race overlap — e.g. persons can report being both White and Irish, b) persons of Hispanic origin can report being any race, c) persons reporting two ancestries are counted in both categories. 2. Numbers in parentheses indicate the number of persons reporting this ancestry/race alone, not in combination with any other ancestry/race. 3. Refer to the Explanation of Data in the front of the book for more detailed information.

Ancestry/Race	Number	%
Tohono O'Odham (1)	1	0.00
Ute (15)	20	0.09
Yuman (2)	2	0.01
All other tribes (19)	51	0.23
American Indian tribes, not spec.	48	0.22
Arab:	156	0.70
Arab/Arabic	19	0.09
Egyptian	7	0.03
Iraqi	27	0.12
Jordanian	32	0.14
Lebanese	27	0.12
Palestinian	31	0.14
Other Arab	13	0.06
Armenian	114	0.51
Asian:	773	3.51
Bangladeshi (1)	1	0.00
Cambodian (5)	8	0.04
Chinese, ex. Taiwanese (142)	158	0.72
Filipino (31)	47	0.21
Hmong (1)	1	0.00
Indian (55)	82	0.37
Indonesian (1)	1	0.00
Japanese (77)	114	0.52
Korean (55)	64	0.29
Laotian (32)	48	0.22
Malaysian (2)	2	0.01
Pakistani (2)	13	0.06
Taiwanese (17)	17	0.08
Thai (9)	12	0.05
Vietnamese (122)	129	0.59
Other Asian, specified (16)	18	0.08
Other Asian, not specified (8)	58	0.26
Austrian	19	0.09
Basque	5	0.02
Belgian	23	0.10
Brazilian	17	0.08
British	221	1.00
Bulgarian	13	0.06
Canadian	49	0.22
Celtic	41	0.19
Croatian	44	0.20
Czechoslovakian	12	0.05
Danish	720	3.25
Dutch	465	2.10
English	3,350	15.12
European	164	0.74
Finnish	27	0.12
French, except Basque	407	1.84
French Canadian	55	0.25
German	1,918	8.66
Greek	155	0.70
Guyanese	6	0.03
Hawaii Native/Pacific Islander:	355	1.61
Melanesian: (1)	1	0.00
Fijian (1)	1	0.00
Micronesian: (13)	15	0.07
Guamanian/Chamorro (1)	1	0.00
Other Micronesian (12)	14	0.06
Polynesian: (220)	310	1.41
Native Hawaiian (15)	31	0.14
Samoan (82)	108	0.49
Tongan (100)	136	0.62
Other Polynesian (23)	35	0.16
Other Pac. Isl., specified	2	0.01
Other Pac. Isl., not spec. (18)	27	0.12
Hispanic or Latino:	4,932	22.38
Central American:	117	0.53
Costa Rican	8	0.04
Guatemalan	29	0.13
Honduran	29	0.13
Nicaraguan	2	0.01
Panamanian	5	0.02
Salvadoran	40	0.18
Other Central American	4	0.02
Cuban	13	0.06
Dominican Republic	6	0.03
Mexican	3,581	16.25
Puerto Rican	69	0.31
South American:	189	0.86
Argentinean	31	0.14
Bolivian	6	0.03
Chilean	10	0.05
Colombian	23	0.10
Ecuadorian	10	0.05
Peruvian	37	0.17
Uruguayan	6	0.03
Venezuelan	60	0.27
Other South American	6	0.03
Other Hispanic or Latino	957	4.34
Hungarian	15	0.07
Icelander	39	0.18
Iranian	14	0.06
Irish	1,200	5.42
Italian	738	3.33
New Zealander	14	0.06
Norwegian	442	2.00
Pennsylvania German	12	0.05
Polish	200	0.90
Portuguese	32	0.14
Romanian	38	0.17
Russian	40	0.18
Scandinavian	173	0.78
Scotch-Irish	321	1.45
Scottish	707	3.19
Serbian	58	0.26
Slavic	12	0.05
Slovak	12	0.05
Slovene	16	0.07
Swedish	754	3.40
Swiss	49	0.22
Ukrainian	9	0.04
United States or American	974	4.40
Welsh	377	1.70
West Indian, excl. Hispanic:	5	0.02
West Indian	5	0.02
White:	17,375	78.84
Not Hispanic (14,476)	14,970	67.93
Hispanic (2,106)	2,405	10.91
Yugoslavian	80	0.36

Spanish Fork

Place Type: City
County: Utah
Population: 20,246

Ancestry/Race	Number	%
Acadian/Cajun	10	0.05
African American/Black:	75	0.37
Not Hispanic (38)	63	0.31
Hispanic (3)	12	0.06
African, sub-Saharan:	38	0.19
African	21	0.10
South African	17	0.08
Alaska Native tribes, specified:	5	0.02
Eskimo (1)	1	0.00
Tlingit-Haida (1)	4	0.02
Am. Ind. or Alaska Nat., not spec.	40	0.20
American Indian tribes, specified:	142	0.70
Apache (2)	3	0.01
Blackfeet (1)	1	0.00
Cherokee (2)	20	0.10
Choctaw (1)	1	0.00
Comanche (2)	2	0.01
Iroquois (1)	1	0.00
Latin American Indians	6	0.03
Navajo (58)	70	0.35
Potawatomi (4)	7	0.03
Pueblo	2	0.01
Shoshone	1	0.00
Sioux (3)	8	0.04
Ute (4)	5	0.02
All other tribes (2)	15	0.07
American Indian tribes, not spec.	3	0.01
Armenian	9	0.04
Asian:	157	0.78
Cambodian (2)	7	0.03
Chinese, ex. Taiwanese (9)	20	0.10
Filipino (7)	30	0.15
Indian (9)	23	0.11
Japanese (17)	43	0.21
Korean (10)	20	0.10
Laotian (2)	5	0.02
Thai (1)	1	0.00
Vietnamese (2)	5	0.02
Other Asian, specified	3	0.01
Australian	10	0.05
Austrian	48	0.24
Belgian	19	0.09
British	240	1.18
Canadian	48	0.24
Celtic	8	0.04
Czech	44	0.22
Danish	1,872	9.23
Dutch	465	2.29
English	6,623	32.67
European	642	3.17
Finnish	31	0.15
French, except Basque	486	2.40
French Canadian	13	0.06
German	1,976	9.75
Greek	69	0.34
Hawaii Native/Pacific Islander:	113	0.56
Polynesian: (56)	103	0.51
Native Hawaiian (20)	39	0.19
Samoan (2)	6	0.03
Tongan (34)	57	0.28
Other Polynesian	1	0.00
Other Pac. Isl., specified	3	0.01
Other Pac. Isl., not spec. (1)	7	0.03
Hispanic or Latino:	861	4.25
Central American:	32	0.16
Costa Rican	5	0.02
Honduran	3	0.01
Salvadoran	23	0.11
Other Central American	1	0.00
Dominican Republic	1	0.00
Mexican	508	2.51
Puerto Rican	32	0.16
South American:	101	0.50
Argentinean	31	0.15
Bolivian	2	0.01
Chilean	22	0.11
Colombian	13	0.06
Ecuadorian	6	0.03
Peruvian	21	0.10
Venezuelan	3	0.01
Other South American	3	0.01
Other Hispanic or Latino	187	0.92
Icelander	548	2.70
Irish	946	4.67
Italian	308	1.52
New Zealander	8	0.04
Northern European	8	0.04
Norwegian	523	2.58
Polish	106	0.52
Portuguese	6	0.03
Scandinavian	259	1.28
Scotch-Irish	181	0.89
Scottish	874	4.31
Serbian	9	0.04
Swedish	854	4.21
Swiss	177	0.87
Ukrainian	38	0.19
United States or American	1,751	8.64
Welsh	739	3.65
White:	19,554	96.58
Not Hispanic (18,925)	19,117	94.42
Hispanic (370)	437	2.16
Yugoslavian	14	0.07

Springville

Place Type: City
County: Utah
Population: 20,424

Ancestry/Race	Number	%
African American/Black:	60	0.29
Not Hispanic (20)	54	0.26

Notes: 1. Figures in the "Number" column do not add up to the total population due to: a) Ancestry/Race overlap — e.g. persons can report being both White and Irish, b) persons of Hispanic origin can report being any race, c) persons reporting two ancestries are counted in both categories. 2. Numbers in parentheses indicate the number of persons reporting this ancestry/race alone, not in combination with any other ancestry/race. 3. Refer to the Explanation of Data in the front of the book for more detailed information.

Ancestry/Race	Number	%
Hispanic (2)	6	0.03
African, sub-Saharan:	15	0.07
African	15	0.07
Alaska Native tribes, specified:	3	0.01
Eskimo (2)	3	0.01
Alaska Native tribes, not specified	1	0.00
Am. Ind. or Alaska Nat., not spec.	55	0.27
American Indian tribes, specified:	196	0.96
Apache	3	0.01
Blackfeet (3)	3	0.01
Cherokee (7)	37	0.18
Chickasaw (1)	1	0.00
Chippewa (1)	1	0.00
Choctaw (1)	2	0.01
Cree (1)	1	0.00
Crow	3	0.01
Iroquois (3)	3	0.01
Latin American Indians (9)	20	0.10
Navajo (29)	49	0.24
Paiute	2	0.01
Pueblo (2)	6	0.03
Puget Sound Salish (4)	4	0.02
Shoshone	3	0.01
Sioux (16)	22	0.11
Ute (3)	5	0.02
Yaqui	3	0.01
All other tribes (21)	28	0.14
Arab:	44	0.21
Arab/Arabic	7	0.03
Lebanese	32	0.16
Palestinian	5	0.02
Armenian	5	0.02
Asian:	168	0.82
Chinese, ex. Taiwanese (14)	33	0.16
Filipino (17)	41	0.20
Indian (7)	15	0.07
Indonesian	6	0.03
Japanese (5)	28	0.14
Korean (14)	21	0.10
Laotian (1)	1	0.00
Taiwanese	1	0.00
Thai (1)	5	0.02
Vietnamese (3)	10	0.05
Other Asian, not specified (6)	7	0.03
Australian	8	0.04
Austrian	49	0.24
Basque	5	0.02
Belgian	13	0.06
Brazilian	21	0.10
British	341	1.66
Canadian	16	0.08
Celtic	12	0.06
Croatian	7	0.03
Czech	24	0.12
Czechoslovakian	9	0.04
Danish	1,629	7.94
Dutch	419	2.04
Eastern European	8	0.04
English	6,915	33.70
European	739	3.60
Finnish	16	0.08
French, except Basque	513	2.50
French Canadian	46	0.22
German	2,278	11.10
Greek	105	0.51
Hawaii Native/Pacific Islander:	107	0.52
Micronesian: (1)	4	0.02
Guamanian/Chamorro	3	0.01
Other Micronesian (1)	1	0.00
Polynesian: (52)	96	0.47
Native Hawaiian (4)	24	0.12
Samoan (19)	23	0.11
Tongan (29)	45	0.22
Other Polynesian	4	0.02
Other Pac. Isl., not spec. (5)	7	0.03
Hispanic or Latino:	975	4.77
Central American:	58	0.28
Costa Rican	3	0.01
Guatemalan	18	0.09
Honduran	12	0.06
Salvadoran	25	0.12
Cuban	1	0.00
Dominican Republic	4	0.02
Mexican	639	3.13
Puerto Rican	31	0.15
South American:	64	0.31
Argentinean	14	0.07
Chilean	9	0.04
Colombian	3	0.01
Ecuadorian	4	0.02
Peruvian	22	0.11
Uruguayan	2	0.01
Venezuelan	10	0.05
Other Hispanic or Latino	178	0.87
Hungarian	4	0.02
Icelander	226	1.10
Iranian	21	0.10
Irish	1,144	5.58
Italian	487	2.37
Latvian	12	0.06
Northern European	104	0.51
Norwegian	558	2.72
Polish	102	0.50
Portuguese	76	0.37
Romanian	15	0.07
Scandinavian	257	1.25
Scotch-Irish	244	1.19
Scottish	985	4.80
Serbian	21	0.10
Swedish	729	3.55
Swiss	393	1.92
Ukrainian	23	0.11
United States or American	1,350	6.58
Welsh	601	2.93
West Indian, excl. Hispanic:	44	0.21
Jamaican	44	0.21
White:	19,660	96.26
Not Hispanic (18,932)	19,171	93.87
Hispanic (385)	489	2.39
Yugoslavian	48	0.23

Taylorsville

Place Type: City
County: Salt Lake
Population: 57,439

Ancestry/Race	Number	%
African American/Black:	768	1.34
Not Hispanic (463)	665	1.16
Hispanic (45)	103	0.18
African, sub-Saharan:	109	0.19
African	31	0.05
Nigerian	15	0.03
South African	41	0.07
Ugandan	22	0.04
Alaska Native tribes, specified:	10	0.02
Aleut (1)	1	0.00
Eskimo (1)	5	0.01
Tlingit-Haida (1)	3	0.01
All other tribes (1)	1	0.00
Am. Ind. or Alaska Nat., not spec.	158	0.28
American Indian tribes, specified:	623	1.08
Apache (5)	24	0.04
Blackfeet (10)	13	0.02
Cherokee (15)	42	0.07
Cheyenne (5)	5	0.01
Chickasaw	1	0.00
Chippewa (5)	7	0.01
Choctaw	11	0.02
Comanche (5)	5	0.01
Creek (4)	7	0.01
Delaware	1	0.00
Iroquois (2)	9	0.02
Kiowa	1	0.00
Latin American Indians (33)	45	0.08
Navajo (268)	300	0.52
Osage	1	0.00
Paiute	1	0.00
Potawatomi (5)	8	0.01
Pueblo (8)	17	0.03
Seminole (1)	1	0.00
Shoshone (8)	19	0.03
Sioux (17)	27	0.05
Ute (14)	24	0.04
Yaqui (1)	1	0.00
Yuman (1)	1	0.00
All other tribes (41)	52	0.09
American Indian tribes, not spec.	25	0.04
Arab:	164	0.28
Arab/Arabic	8	0.01
Iraqi	15	0.03
Lebanese	92	0.16
Other Arab	49	0.08
Armenian	71	0.12
Asian:	2,148	3.74
Bangladeshi (1)	2	0.00
Cambodian (86)	96	0.17
Chinese, ex. Taiwanese (284)	386	0.67
Filipino (96)	151	0.26
Indian (122)	135	0.24
Indonesian (9)	15	0.03
Japanese (170)	280	0.49
Korean (101)	122	0.21
Laotian (150)	190	0.33
Malaysian	1	0.00
Pakistani (14)	25	0.04
Taiwanese (6)	10	0.02
Thai (25)	39	0.07
Vietnamese (583)	622	1.08
Other Asian, specified (6)	12	0.02
Other Asian, not specified (30)	62	0.11
Australian	16	0.03
Austrian	88	0.15
Basque	120	0.21
Belgian	15	0.03
Brazilian	72	0.12
British	944	1.63
Bulgarian	49	0.08
Canadian	114	0.20
Celtic	30	0.05
Croatian	45	0.08
Czech	39	0.07
Czechoslovakian	36	0.06
Danish	3,263	5.64
Dutch	1,495	2.58
Eastern European	9	0.02
English	14,950	25.83
European	1,461	2.52
Finnish	78	0.13
French, except Basque	1,121	1.94
French Canadian	181	0.31
German	6,798	11.75
German Russian	7	0.01
Greek	359	0.62
Guyanese	19	0.03
Hawaii Native/Pacific Islander:	1,235	2.15
Melanesian: (4)	12	0.02
Fijian (4)	12	0.02
Micronesian: (13)	30	0.05
Guamanian/Chamorro (5)	18	0.03
Other Micronesian (8)	12	0.02
Polynesian: (773)	1,084	1.89
Native Hawaiian (32)	85	0.15
Samoan (424)	497	0.87
Tongan (293)	436	0.76
Other Polynesian (24)	66	0.11
Other Pac. Isl., specified	4	0.01
Other Pac. Isl., not spec. (53)	105	0.18
Hispanic or Latino:	7,022	12.23
Central American:	217	0.38
Costa Rican	14	0.02
Guatemalan	64	0.11
Honduran	29	0.05
Nicaraguan	3	0.01
Panamanian	14	0.02
Salvadoran	82	0.14
Other Central American	11	0.02
Cuban	19	0.03
Dominican Republic	25	0.04

Notes: 1. Figures in the "Number" column do not add up to the total population due to: a) Ancestry/Race overlap — e.g. persons can report being both White and Irish, b) persons of Hispanic origin can report being any race, c) persons reporting two ancestries are counted in both categories. 2. Numbers in parentheses indicate the number of persons reporting this ancestry/race alone, not in combination with any other ancestry/race. 3. Refer to the Explanation of Data in the front of the book for more detailed information.

Mexican	4,415	7.69
Puerto Rican	170	0.30
South American:	505	0.88
Argentinean	34	0.06
Bolivian	20	0.03
Chilean	47	0.08
Colombian	113	0.20
Ecuadorian	46	0.08
Paraguayan	2	0.00
Peruvian	99	0.17
Uruguayan	19	0.03
Venezuelan	89	0.15
Other South American	36	0.06
Other Hispanic or Latino	1,671	2.91
Hungarian	179	0.31
Icelander	23	0.04
Iranian	10	0.02
Irish	3,806	6.58
Italian	1,522	2.63
Lithuanian	66	0.11
Luxemburger	5	0.01
Northern European	56	0.10
Norwegian	1,137	1.96
Pennsylvania German	27	0.05
Polish	414	0.72
Portuguese	249	0.43
Romanian	36	0.06
Russian	109	0.19
Scandinavian	614	1.06
Scotch-Irish	673	1.16
Scottish	1,890	3.27
Serbian	17	0.03
Slavic	20	0.03
Swedish	2,321	4.01
Swiss	454	0.78
Ukrainian	56	0.10
United States or American	3,872	6.69
Welsh	1,146	1.98
West Indian, excl. Hispanic:	42	0.07
Bahamian	20	0.03
Haitian	4	0.01
Trinidadian and Tobagonian	18	0.03
White:	50,380	87.71
Not Hispanic (45,902)	46,637	81.19
Hispanic (3,237)	3,743	6.52
Yugoslavian	48	0.08

Tooele

Place Type: City
County: Tooele
Population: 22,502

Ancestry/Race	Number	%
African American/Black:	238	1.06
Not Hispanic (148)	207	0.92
Hispanic (18)	31	0.14
African, sub-Saharan:	12	0.05
African	7	0.03
South African	5	0.02
Alaska Native tribes, specified:	7	0.03
Alaska Athabascan (4)	4	0.02
Eskimo (3)	3	0.01
Am. Ind. or Alaska Nat., not spec.	81	0.36
American Indian tribes, specified:	359	1.60
Apache (9)	17	0.08
Blackfeet (5)	7	0.03
Cherokee (9)	50	0.22
Cheyenne (1)	5	0.02
Chickasaw	5	0.02
Chippewa (3)	10	0.04
Choctaw (8)	9	0.04
Cree (4)	5	0.02
Creek	1	0.00
Crow (2)	2	0.01
Delaware	6	0.03
Iroquois (2)	2	0.01
Latin American Indians (5)	7	0.03
Navajo (99)	120	0.53
Ottawa (3)	3	0.01
Paiute (4)	10	0.04
Potawatomi (1)	2	0.01
Pueblo (8)	16	0.07
Shoshone (12)	18	0.08
Sioux (9)	16	0.07
Tohono O'Odham	3	0.01
Ute (6)	23	0.10
Yakama (1)	3	0.01
Yuman	1	0.00
All other tribes (15)	18	0.08
American Indian tribes, not spec.	39	0.17
Arab:	4	0.02
Lebanese	4	0.02
Armenian	38	0.17
Asian:	264	1.17
Chinese, ex. Taiwanese (18)	46	0.20
Filipino (35)	79	0.35
Hmong	1	0.00
Indian (10)	15	0.07
Japanese (21)	58	0.26
Korean (26)	45	0.20
Laotian (4)	5	0.02
Vietnamese (2)	4	0.02
Other Asian, not specified (3)	11	0.05
Australian	3	0.01
Austrian	41	0.18
Belgian	53	0.24
British	280	1.24
Canadian	35	0.16
Czech	7	0.03
Czechoslovakian	22	0.10
Danish	1,127	5.01
Dutch	719	3.19
English	5,786	25.71
European	292	1.30
Finnish	100	0.44
French, except Basque	450	2.00
French Canadian	157	0.70
German	2,699	11.99
Greek	81	0.36
Hawaii Native/Pacific Islander:	92	0.41
Micronesian: (3)	11	0.05
Guamanian/Chamorro (3)	11	0.05
Polynesian: (19)	77	0.34
Native Hawaiian (4)	35	0.16
Samoan (7)	21	0.09
Tongan (8)	16	0.07
Other Polynesian	5	0.02
Other Pac. Isl., not spec. (2)	4	0.02
Hispanic or Latino:	2,271	10.09
Central American:	45	0.20
Costa Rican	2	0.01
Guatemalan	17	0.08
Honduran	2	0.01
Nicaraguan	5	0.02
Salvadoran	19	0.08
Cuban	3	0.01
Dominican Republic	4	0.02
Mexican	1,007	4.48
Puerto Rican	39	0.17
South American:	48	0.21
Argentinean	2	0.01
Chilean	11	0.05
Colombian	12	0.05
Ecuadorian	6	0.03
Peruvian	9	0.04
Uruguayan	2	0.01
Venezuelan	4	0.02
Other South American	2	0.01
Other Hispanic or Latino	1,125	5.00
Hungarian	4	0.02
Icelander	29	0.13
Irish	1,624	7.22
Italian	808	3.59
Lithuanian	7	0.03
Northern European	43	0.19
Norwegian	446	1.98
Polish	168	0.75
Portuguese	65	0.29
Romanian	16	0.07
Russian	34	0.15
Scandinavian	238	1.06
Scotch-Irish	229	1.02
Scottish	1,245	5.53
Serbian	15	0.07
Slavic	9	0.04
Slovak	15	0.07
Slovene	32	0.14
Swedish	916	4.07
Swiss	137	0.61
Ukrainian	14	0.06
United States or American	1,838	8.17
Welsh	462	2.05
West Indian, excl. Hispanic:	7	0.03
British West Indian	7	0.03
White:	20,983	93.25
Not Hispanic (19,340)	19,669	87.41
Hispanic (1,128)	1,314	5.84
Yugoslavian	137	0.61

West Jordan

Place Type: City
County: Salt Lake
Population: 68,336

Ancestry/Race	Number	%
Acadian/Cajun	9	0.01
African American/Black:	620	0.91
Not Hispanic (396)	557	0.82
Hispanic (38)	63	0.09
African, sub-Saharan:	34	0.05
African	34	0.05
Alaska Native tribes, specified:	3	0.00
Aleut (1)	1	0.00
Eskimo	2	0.00
Am. Ind. or Alaska Nat., not spec.	161	0.24
Albanian	10	0.01
American Indian tribes, specified:	497	0.73
Apache (11)	24	0.04
Blackfeet (1)	9	0.01
Cherokee (18)	47	0.07
Cheyenne (1)	1	0.00
Chickasaw	2	0.00
Chippewa (4)	6	0.01
Choctaw (2)	7	0.01
Cree (1)	3	0.00
Creek (5)	5	0.01
Crow (4)	4	0.01
Delaware	3	0.00
Iroquois (2)	7	0.01
Latin American Indians (8)	17	0.02
Lumbee (1)	1	0.00
Navajo (168)	217	0.32
Osage	3	0.00
Ottawa	1	0.00
Paiute (1)	1	0.00
Pima (3)	3	0.00
Potawatomi (2)	8	0.01
Pueblo (8)	18	0.03
Shoshone (12)	17	0.02
Sioux (17)	33	0.05
Ute (7)	18	0.03
All other tribes (17)	42	0.06
American Indian tribes, not spec.	21	0.03
Arab:	85	0.12
Lebanese	81	0.12
Other Arab	4	0.01
Armenian	36	0.05
Asian:	1,851	2.71
Cambodian (43)	54	0.08
Chinese, ex. Taiwanese (219)	299	0.44
Filipino (152)	228	0.33
Hmong (1)	4	0.01
Indian (101)	123	0.18
Indonesian (11)	12	0.02
Japanese (112)	241	0.35
Korean (79)	119	0.17
Laotian (272)	306	0.45
Malaysian (2)	2	0.00

Notes: 1. Figures in the "Number" column do not add up to the total population due to: a) Ancestry/Race overlap — e.g. persons can report being both White and Irish, b) persons of Hispanic origin can report being any race, c) persons reporting two ancestries are counted in both categories. 2. Numbers in parentheses indicate the number of persons reporting this ancestry/race alone, not in combination with any other ancestry/race. 3. Refer to the Explanation of Data in the front of the book for more detailed information.

Ancestry/Race	Number	%
Pakistani (34)	44	0.06
Sri Lankan (2)	4	0.01
Taiwanese (3)	5	0.01
Thai (31)	40	0.06
Vietnamese (237)	277	0.41
Other Asian, specified	2	0.00
Other Asian, not specified (48)	91	0.13
Australian	39	0.06
Austrian	126	0.18
Basque	43	0.06
Belgian	31	0.05
Brazilian	70	0.10
British	749	1.10
Canadian	201	0.29
Croatian	19	0.03
Czech	135	0.20
Czechoslovakian	61	0.09
Danish	4,415	6.47
Dutch	1,563	2.29
Eastern European	19	0.03
English	18,772	27.52
European	1,539	2.26
Finnish	100	0.15
French, except Basque	1,467	2.15
French Canadian	226	0.33
German	9,026	13.23
Greek	468	0.69
Hawaii Native/Pacific Islander:	921	1.35
Melanesian: (4)	4	0.01
Fijian (4)	4	0.01
Micronesian: (16)	24	0.04
Guamanian/Chamorro (9)	15	0.02
Other Micronesian (7)	9	0.01
Polynesian: (580)	843	1.23
Native Hawaiian (35)	116	0.17
Samoan (209)	277	0.41
Tongan (314)	396	0.58
Other Polynesian (22)	54	0.08
Other Pac. Isl., specified	2	0.00
Other Pac. Isl., not spec. (19)	48	0.07
Hispanic or Latino:	6,882	10.07
Central American:	198	0.29
Costa Rican	16	0.02
Guatemalan	67	0.10
Honduran	9	0.01
Nicaraguan	17	0.02
Panamanian	8	0.01
Salvadoran	78	0.11
Other Central American	3	0.00
Cuban	20	0.03
Dominican Republic	2	0.00
Mexican	4,087	5.98
Puerto Rican	186	0.27
South American:	334	0.49
Argentinean	23	0.03
Bolivian	13	0.02
Chilean	37	0.05
Colombian	66	0.10
Ecuadorian	33	0.05
Peruvian	76	0.11
Uruguayan	24	0.04
Venezuelan	43	0.06
Other South American	19	0.03
Other Hispanic or Latino	2,055	3.01
Hungarian	108	0.16
Icelander	32	0.05
Iranian	53	0.08
Irish	4,048	5.93
Italian	2,318	3.40
Lithuanian	11	0.02
Northern European	56	0.08
Norwegian	1,419	2.08
Pennsylvania German	22	0.03
Polish	481	0.71
Portuguese	178	0.26
Romanian	8	0.01
Russian	179	0.26
Scandinavian	837	1.23
Scotch-Irish	639	0.94
Scottish	3,046	4.47
Slavic	27	0.04
Slovene	6	0.01
Swedish	3,153	4.62
Swiss	723	1.06
Ukrainian	45	0.07
United States or American	4,775	7.00
Welsh	1,379	2.02
West Indian, excl. Hispanic:	53	0.08
Haitian	38	0.06
Jamaican	15	0.02
White:	62,064	90.82
Not Hispanic (57,688)	58,549	85.68
Hispanic (2,965)	3,515	5.14
Yugoslavian	235	0.34

West Valley City

Place Type: City
County: Salt Lake
Population: 108,896

Ancestry/Race	Number	%
Acadian/Cajun	6	0.01
Afghan	6	0.01
African American/Black:	1,772	1.63
Not Hispanic (1,090)	1,485	1.36
Hispanic (157)	287	0.26
African, sub-Saharan:	130	0.12
African	120	0.11
Other sub-Saharan African	10	0.01
Alaska Native tribes, specified:	15	0.01
Alaska Athabascan (1)	4	0.00
Aleut (2)	2	0.00
Eskimo (2)	9	0.01
Alaska Native tribes, not specified	2	0.00
Am. Ind. or Alaska Nat., not spec.	446	0.41
Alsatian	4	0.00
American Indian tribes, specified:	1,391	1.28
Apache (14)	35	0.03
Blackfeet (4)	16	0.01
Cherokee (46)	135	0.12
Cheyenne (8)	21	0.02
Chippewa (17)	40	0.04
Choctaw (9)	20	0.02
Colville (2)	2	0.00
Comanche (3)	8	0.01
Cree (7)	7	0.01
Creek (5)	8	0.01
Crow (1)	1	0.00
Delaware (1)	1	0.00
Iroquois (3)	4	0.00
Kiowa	1	0.00
Latin American Indians (46)	75	0.07
Menominee (3)	3	0.00
Navajo (557)	685	0.63
Osage	1	0.00
Ottawa (1)	1	0.00
Paiute (13)	15	0.01
Pima (1)	1	0.00
Potawatomi	1	0.00
Pueblo (27)	43	0.04
Puget Sound Salish	1	0.00
Seminole (1)	5	0.00
Shoshone (20)	30	0.03
Sioux (29)	67	0.06
Tohono O'Odham (2)	2	0.00
Ute (43)	63	0.06
Yaqui (1)	1	0.00
Yuman (5)	5	0.00
All other tribes (59)	93	0.09
American Indian tribes, not spec.	85	0.08
Arab:	122	0.11
Arab/Arabic	12	0.01
Iraqi	15	0.01
Lebanese	82	0.08
Syrian	13	0.01
Armenian	12	0.01
Asian:	5,761	5.29
Bangladeshi (3)	5	0.00
Cambodian (639)	805	0.74
Chinese, ex. Taiwanese (449)	691	0.63
Filipino (192)	324	0.30
Hmong (13)	13	0.01
Indian (264)	346	0.32
Indonesian (8)	13	0.01
Japanese (189)	333	0.31
Korean (81)	125	0.11
Laotian (643)	794	0.73
Pakistani (36)	52	0.05
Taiwanese (4)	7	0.01
Thai (58)	84	0.08
Vietnamese (1,734)	1,933	1.78
Other Asian, specified (2)	5	0.00
Other Asian, not specified (125)	231	0.21
Australian	52	0.05
Austrian	105	0.10
Basque	99	0.09
Belgian	38	0.03
Brazilian	73	0.07
British	900	0.83
Bulgarian	26	0.02
Canadian	306	0.28
Celtic	18	0.02
Croatian	69	0.06
Cypriot	14	0.01
Czech	91	0.08
Czechoslovakian	76	0.07
Danish	4,813	4.42
Dutch	2,508	2.30
English	22,692	20.85
European	1,697	1.56
Finnish	150	0.14
French, except Basque	2,291	2.11
French Canadian	225	0.21
German	11,165	10.26
German Russian	7	0.01
Greek	612	0.56
Hawaii Native/Pacific Islander:	4,017	3.69
Melanesian: (4)	25	0.02
Fijian (4)	25	0.02
Micronesian: (110)	132	0.12
Guamanian/Chamorro (14)	15	0.01
Other Micronesian (96)	117	0.11
Polynesian: (2,770)	3,645	3.35
Native Hawaiian (94)	265	0.24
Samoan (1,034)	1,343	1.23
Tongan (1,584)	1,880	1.73
Other Polynesian (58)	157	0.14
Other Pac. Isl., specified	1	0.00
Other Pac. Isl., not spec. (132)	214	0.20
Hispanic or Latino:	20,126	18.48
Central American:	821	0.75
Costa Rican	35	0.03
Guatemalan	275	0.25
Honduran	71	0.07
Nicaraguan	54	0.05
Panamanian	27	0.02
Salvadoran	327	0.30
Other Central American	32	0.03
Cuban	55	0.05
Dominican Republic	16	0.01
Mexican	13,534	12.43
Puerto Rican	342	0.31
South American:	873	0.80
Argentinean	65	0.06
Bolivian	38	0.03
Chilean	85	0.08
Colombian	117	0.11
Ecuadorian	76	0.07
Paraguayan	1	0.00
Peruvian	236	0.22
Uruguayan	22	0.02
Venezuelan	203	0.19
Other South American	30	0.03
Other Hispanic or Latino	4,485	4.12
Hungarian	118	0.11
Icelander	43	0.04
Iranian	23	0.02
Irish	5,666	5.21
Italian	2,388	2.19

Notes: 1. Figures in the "Number" column do not add up to the total population due to: a) Ancestry/Race overlap — e.g. persons can report being both White and Irish, b) persons of Hispanic origin can report being any race, c) persons reporting two ancestries are counted in both categories. 2. Numbers in parentheses indicate the number of persons reporting this ancestry/race alone, not in combination with any other ancestry/race. 3. Refer to the Explanation of Data in the front of the book for more detailed information.

Lithuanian	68	0.06
New Zealander	26	0.02
Northern European	75	0.07
Norwegian	1,931	1.77
Polish	749	0.69
Portuguese	167	0.15
Romanian	16	0.01
Russian	285	0.26
Scandinavian	789	0.73
Scotch-Irish	1,079	0.99
Scottish	3,205	2.95
Serbian	74	0.07
Slavic	23	0.02
Slovak	23	0.02
Slovene	12	0.01
Swedish	3,192	2.93
Swiss	669	0.61
Turkish	5	0.00
Ukrainian	171	0.16
United States or American	8,182	7.52
Welsh	1,718	1.58
West Indian, excl. Hispanic:	59	0.05
Dutch West Indian	4	0.00
Haitian	35	0.03
Trinidadian and Tobagonian	9	0.01
West Indian	11	0.01
White:	88,314	81.10
Not Hispanic (76,545)	78,351	71.95
Hispanic (8,627)	9,963	9.15
Yugoslavian	540	0.50

Bennington

Place Type: Town
County: Bennington
Population: 15,737

Ancestry/Race	Number	%
African American/Black:	137	0.87
Not Hispanic (98)	127	0.81
Hispanic (1)	10	0.06
African, sub-Saharan:	27	0.17
African	22	0.14
Ethiopian	3	0.02
South African	2	0.01
Am. Ind. or Alaska Nat., not spec.	52	0.33
American Indian tribes, specified:	53	0.34
Apache (1)	1	0.01
Blackfeet (5)	10	0.06
Cherokee (4)	8	0.05
Chickasaw (2)	2	0.01
Chippewa	1	0.01
Delaware	1	0.01
Iroquois (3)	8	0.05
Lumbee	1	0.01
Navajo	1	0.01
Shoshone	2	0.01
Sioux (1)	6	0.04
All other tribes (8)	12	0.08
American Indian tribes, not spec.	12	0.08
Arab:	56	0.35
Lebanese	49	0.31
Syrian	7	0.04
Armenian	76	0.48
Asian:	182	1.16
Cambodian (1)	1	0.01
Chinese, ex. Taiwanese (33)	36	0.23
Filipino (11)	16	0.10
Indian (38)	40	0.25
Japanese (33)	43	0.27
Korean (13)	17	0.11
Pakistani (10)	10	0.06
Thai (1)	4	0.03
Vietnamese (3)	4	0.03
Other Asian, specified (5)	5	0.03
Other Asian, not specified (2)	6	0.04
Australian	7	0.04
Austrian	31	0.20
Brazilian	11	0.07
British	79	0.50
Canadian	60	0.38
Celtic	2	0.01
Czech	38	0.24
Czechoslovakian	12	0.08
Danish	48	0.30
Dutch	382	2.41
Eastern European	30	0.19
English	2,528	15.97
European	19	0.12
Finnish	24	0.15
French, except Basque	2,339	14.78
French Canadian	1,053	6.65
German	1,679	10.61
Greek	24	0.15
Hawaii Native/Pacific Islander:	4	0.03
Micronesian: (1)	2	0.01
Guamanian/Chamorro (1)	2	0.01
Polynesian: (2)	2	0.01
Native Hawaiian (1)	1	0.01
Samoan (1)	1	0.01
Hispanic or Latino:	156	0.99
Central American:	1	0.01
Honduran	1	0.01
Cuban	4	0.03
Dominican Republic	1	0.01
Mexican	28	0.18
Puerto Rican	72	0.46
South American:	11	0.07
Argentinean	1	0.01
Colombian	4	0.03
Ecuadorian	1	0.01
Peruvian	3	0.02
Other South American	2	0.01
Other Hispanic or Latino	39	0.25
Hungarian	36	0.23
Iranian	2	0.01
Irish	2,995	18.92
Italian	1,140	7.20
Latvian	16	0.10
Lithuanian	59	0.37
Northern European	30	0.19
Norwegian	50	0.32
Pennsylvania German	4	0.03
Polish	582	3.68
Portuguese	32	0.20
Romanian	17	0.11
Russian	83	0.52
Scandinavian	11	0.07
Scotch-Irish	222	1.40
Scottish	586	3.70
Serbian	4	0.03
Slavic	5	0.03
Swedish	131	0.83
Swiss	22	0.14
Ukrainian	21	0.13
United States or American	1,088	6.87
Welsh	120	0.76
West Indian, excl. Hispanic:	8	0.05
Jamaican	8	0.05
White:	15,397	97.84
Not Hispanic (15,153)	15,272	97.05
Hispanic (105)	125	0.79
Yugoslavian	13	0.08

Brattleboro

Place Type: Town
County: Windham
Population: 12,005

Ancestry/Race	Number	%
African American/Black:	208	1.73
Not Hispanic (127)	184	1.53
Hispanic (9)	24	0.20
African, sub-Saharan:	43	0.36
African	10	0.08
Cape Verdean	26	0.22
Kenyan	7	0.06
Alaska Native tribes, specified:	2	0.02
Eskimo (2)	2	0.02
Am. Ind. or Alaska Nat., not spec.	47	0.39
Alsatian	8	0.07
American Indian tribes, specified:	98	0.82
Apache (1)	2	0.02
Blackfeet (1)	9	0.07
Cherokee (2)	20	0.17
Crow	3	0.02
Iroquois (3)	9	0.07
Latin American Indians (1)	2	0.02
Navajo	1	0.01
Osage	2	0.02
Sioux (1)	9	0.07
Tohono O'Odham (1)	1	0.01
All other tribes (10)	40	0.33
American Indian tribes, not spec.	3	0.02
Arab:	112	0.93
Egyptian	8	0.07
Lebanese	87	0.72
Syrian	17	0.14
Armenian	25	0.21
Asian:	270	2.25
Bangladeshi (2)	2	0.02
Chinese, ex. Taiwanese (61)	72	0.60
Filipino (14)	22	0.18
Indian (26)	33	0.27
Indonesian (2)	4	0.03
Japanese (21)	33	0.27
Korean (17)	23	0.19
Laotian (19)	20	0.17
Pakistani (5)	5	0.04
Taiwanese (9)	15	0.12
Thai (12)	15	0.12
Vietnamese (4)	10	0.08
Other Asian, specified (2)	4	0.03
Other Asian, not specified	12	0.10
Austrian	39	0.32
Basque	7	0.06
British	140	1.17
Canadian	49	0.41
Celtic	18	0.15
Croatian	7	0.06
Czech	37	0.31
Czechoslovakian	16	0.13
Danish	10	0.08
Dutch	234	1.95
Eastern European	45	0.37
English	2,567	21.38
European	151	1.26
Finnish	7	0.06
French, except Basque	1,465	12.20
French Canadian	591	4.92
German	1,219	10.15
Greek	66	0.55
Hawaii Native/Pacific Islander:	21	0.17
Micronesian: (3)	8	0.07
Guamanian/Chamorro (1)	6	0.05
Other Micronesian (2)	2	0.02
Polynesian: (1)	2	0.02
Native Hawaiian	1	0.01
Samoan (1)	1	0.01
Other Pac. Isl., not spec. (1)	11	0.09
Hispanic or Latino:	201	1.67
Central American:	5	0.04
Honduran	1	0.01
Nicaraguan	2	0.02
Panamanian	2	0.02
Cuban	11	0.09
Mexican	35	0.29
Puerto Rican	65	0.54
South American:	30	0.25
Argentinean	6	0.05
Bolivian	3	0.02
Chilean	4	0.03
Colombian	7	0.06
Ecuadorian	2	0.02
Peruvian	3	0.02
Uruguayan	2	0.02
Venezuelan	1	0.01
Other South American	2	0.02
Other Hispanic or Latino	55	0.46

Notes: 1. Figures in the "Number" column do not add up to the total population due to: a) Ancestry/Race overlap — e.g. persons can report being both White and Irish, b) persons of Hispanic origin can report being any race, c) persons reporting two ancestries are counted in both categories. 2. Numbers in parentheses indicate the number of persons reporting this ancestry/race alone, not in combination with any other ancestry/race. 3. Refer to the Explanation of Data in the front of the book for more detailed information.

Hungarian	82	0.68
Irish	2,264	18.86
Italian	477	3.97
Lithuanian	98	0.82
Northern European	36	0.30
Norwegian	100	0.83
Pennsylvania German	7	0.06
Polish	682	5.68
Portuguese	38	0.32
Romanian	21	0.17
Russian	214	1.78
Scandinavian	6	0.05
Scotch-Irish	203	1.69
Scottish	448	3.73
Slovak	7	0.06
Swedish	302	2.52
Swiss	80	0.67
Turkish	6	0.05
Ukrainian	103	0.86
United States or American	901	7.51
Welsh	170	1.42
White:	11,542	96.14
Not Hispanic (11,189)	11,404	94.99
Hispanic (103)	138	1.15
Yugoslavian	15	0.12

Burlington

Place Type: City
County: Chittenden
Population: 38,889

Ancestry/Race	Number	%
African American/Black:	939	2.41
Not Hispanic (673)	902	2.32
Hispanic (20)	37	0.10
African, sub-Saharan:	140	0.36
African	68	0.17
Cape Verdean	11	0.03
Ghanian	21	0.05
Nigerian	13	0.03
Somalian	15	0.04
South African	6	0.02
Other sub-Saharan African	6	0.02
Alaska Native tribes, specified:	2	0.01
Alaska Athabascan	1	0.00
Tlingit-Haida (1)	1	0.00
Am. Ind. or Alaska Nat., not spec.	180	0.46
Albanian	8	0.02
Alsatian	6	0.02
American Indian tribes, specified:	319	0.82
Apache (1)	5	0.01
Blackfeet (8)	24	0.06
Cherokee (11)	52	0.13
Cheyenne (2)	2	0.01
Chippewa (2)	3	0.01
Choctaw (7)	13	0.03
Comanche (1)	2	0.01
Cree (3)	4	0.01
Creek (1)	3	0.01
Crow	1	0.00
Delaware	5	0.01
Iroquois (11)	38	0.10
Latin American Indians (5)	16	0.04
Lumbee (1)	1	0.00
Navajo (1)	1	0.00
Ottawa	1	0.00
Potawatomi	2	0.01
Pueblo (1)	1	0.00
Seminole	1	0.00
Shoshone	1	0.00
Sioux (2)	6	0.02
All other tribes (60)	137	0.35
American Indian tribes, not spec.	13	0.03
Arab:	343	0.88
Arab/Arabic	30	0.08
Lebanese	260	0.67
Palestinian	10	0.03
Syrian	23	0.06
Other Arab	20	0.05
Armenian	184	0.47
Asian:	1,294	3.33
Bangladeshi	1	0.00
Cambodian (25)	40	0.10
Chinese, ex. Taiwanese (187)	272	0.70
Filipino (32)	51	0.13
Indian (106)	146	0.38
Indonesian (2)	5	0.01
Japanese (53)	74	0.19
Korean (73)	101	0.26
Laotian (11)	13	0.03
Malaysian (1)	1	0.00
Pakistani (6)	6	0.02
Sri Lankan (3)	3	0.01
Taiwanese (4)	5	0.01
Thai (14)	20	0.05
Vietnamese (457)	502	1.29
Other Asian, specified (2)	3	0.01
Other Asian, not specified (26)	51	0.13
Assyrian/Chaldean/Syriac	8	0.02
Australian	11	0.03
Austrian	159	0.41
Belgian	27	0.07
Brazilian	8	0.02
British	311	0.80
Canadian	262	0.67
Celtic	8	0.02
Croatian	52	0.13
Czech	142	0.37
Czechoslovakian	76	0.20
Danish	147	0.38
Dutch	570	1.47
Eastern European	94	0.24
English	5,308	13.65
Estonian	16	0.04
European	348	0.89
Finnish	58	0.15
French, except Basque	4,945	12.72
French Canadian	3,419	8.79
German	3,974	10.22
Greek	234	0.60
Guyanese	7	0.02
Hawaii Native/Pacific Islander:	31	0.08
Micronesian: (1)	4	0.01
Guamanian/Chamorro (1)	4	0.01
Polynesian: (4)	9	0.02
Native Hawaiian (1)	3	0.01
Samoan (3)	6	0.02
Other Pac. Isl., specified	1	0.00
Other Pac. Isl., not spec. (3)	17	0.04
Hispanic or Latino:	546	1.40
Central American:	33	0.08
Costa Rican	9	0.02
Guatemalan	7	0.02
Honduran	5	0.01
Nicaraguan	2	0.01
Panamanian	5	0.01
Salvadoran	5	0.01
Cuban	25	0.06
Dominican Republic	16	0.04
Mexican	119	0.31
Puerto Rican	140	0.36
South American:	66	0.17
Argentinean	10	0.03
Bolivian	1	0.00
Chilean	8	0.02
Colombian	23	0.06
Ecuadorian	7	0.02
Peruvian	6	0.02
Uruguayan	2	0.01
Venezuelan	5	0.01
Other South American	4	0.01
Other Hispanic or Latino	147	0.38
Hungarian	273	0.70
Iranian	26	0.07
Irish	6,923	17.80
Israeli	14	0.04
Italian	2,772	7.13
Latvian	37	0.10
Lithuanian	65	0.17
Northern European	63	0.16
Norwegian	323	0.83
Pennsylvania German	16	0.04
Polish	1,405	3.61
Portuguese	135	0.35
Romanian	55	0.14
Russian	765	1.97
Scandinavian	40	0.10
Scotch-Irish	719	1.85
Scottish	1,438	3.70
Serbian	97	0.25
Slavic	22	0.06
Slovak	101	0.26
Slovene	5	0.01
Swedish	634	1.63
Swiss	105	0.27
Ukrainian	227	0.58
United States or American	1,819	4.68
Welsh	365	0.94
West Indian, excl. Hispanic:	101	0.26
British West Indian	13	0.03
Haitian	21	0.05
Jamaican	13	0.03
Trinidadian and Tobagonian	21	0.05
U.S. Virgin Islander	9	0.02
West Indian	24	0.06
White:	36,637	94.21
Not Hispanic (35,570)	36,259	93.24
Hispanic (313)	378	0.97
Yugoslavian	694	1.78

Colchester

Place Type: Town
County: Chittenden
Population: 16,986

Ancestry/Race	Number	%
African American/Black:	133	0.78
Not Hispanic (105)	129	0.76
Hispanic (2)	4	0.02
African, sub-Saharan:	36	0.21
Cape Verdean	9	0.05
Ghanian	27	0.16
Am. Ind. or Alaska Nat., not spec.	18	0.11
American Indian tribes, specified:	64	0.38
Blackfeet (1)	6	0.04
Cherokee (4)	8	0.05
Cree	1	0.01
Delaware	4	0.02
Iroquois (4)	10	0.06
Navajo (2)	5	0.03
Pueblo	1	0.01
Puget Sound Salish	2	0.01
Sioux	3	0.02
All other tribes (6)	24	0.14
American Indian tribes, not spec.	2	0.01
Arab:	143	0.84
Jordanian	10	0.06
Lebanese	133	0.78
Armenian	9	0.05
Asian:	313	1.84
Bangladeshi (1)	1	0.01
Cambodian (7)	9	0.05
Chinese, ex. Taiwanese (100)	112	0.66
Filipino (12)	29	0.17
Indian (13)	16	0.09
Indonesian (4)	4	0.02
Japanese (11)	13	0.08
Korean (39)	47	0.28
Laotian (6)	6	0.04
Taiwanese (1)	1	0.01
Thai (3)	5	0.03
Vietnamese (41)	45	0.26
Other Asian, not specified (23)	25	0.15
Austrian	17	0.10
Belgian	48	0.28
Brazilian	26	0.15
British	53	0.31
Canadian	220	1.30

Notes: 1. Figures in the "Number" column do not add up to the total population due to: a) Ancestry/Race overlap — e.g. persons can report being both White and Irish, b) persons of Hispanic origin can report being any race, c) persons reporting two ancestries are counted in both categories. 2. Numbers in parentheses indicate the number of persons reporting this ancestry/race alone, not in combination with any other ancestry/race. 3. Refer to the Explanation of Data in the front of the book for more detailed information.

Celtic	8	0.05
Croatian	28	0.16
Czech	33	0.19
Czechoslovakian	35	0.21
Danish	83	0.49
Dutch	201	1.18
Eastern European	25	0.15
English	2,364	13.92
European	98	0.58
Finnish	36	0.21
French, except Basque	2,745	16.16
French Canadian	2,700	15.90
German	1,462	8.61
Greek	100	0.59
Hawaii Native/Pacific Islander:	14	0.08
Polynesian: (4)	9	0.05
Native Hawaiian	4	0.02
Samoan (4)	5	0.03
Other Pac. Isl., not spec. (2)	5	0.03
Hispanic or Latino:	189	1.11
Central American:	6	0.04
Guatemalan	1	0.01
Panamanian	4	0.02
Salvadoran	1	0.01
Cuban	10	0.06
Dominican Republic	7	0.04
Mexican	54	0.32
Puerto Rican	44	0.26
South American:	26	0.15
Argentinean	4	0.02
Chilean	1	0.01
Colombian	6	0.04
Ecuadorian	3	0.02
Peruvian	7	0.04
Venezuelan	5	0.03
Other Hispanic or Latino	42	0.25
Hungarian	18	0.11
Irish	3,354	19.75
Italian	1,310	7.71
Latvian	8	0.05
Lithuanian	32	0.19
Maltese	9	0.05
Northern European	13	0.08
Norwegian	136	0.80
Pennsylvania German	6	0.04
Polish	576	3.39
Portuguese	49	0.29
Russian	88	0.52
Scandinavian	8	0.05
Scotch-Irish	295	1.74
Scottish	690	4.06
Serbian	23	0.14
Slovak	43	0.25
Swedish	156	0.92
Swiss	7	0.04
Ukrainian	28	0.16
United States or American	991	5.83
Welsh	84	0.49
White:	16,531	97.32
Not Hispanic (16,255)	16,377	96.41
Hispanic (142)	154	0.91
Yugoslavian	62	0.37

Essex

Place Type: Town
County: Chittenden
Population: 18,626

Ancestry/Race	Number	%
Acadian/Cajun	29	0.16
African American/Black:	218	1.17
Not Hispanic (163)	213	1.14
Hispanic (1)	5	0.03
African, sub-Saharan:	10	0.05
African	10	0.05
Alaska Native tribes, specified:	2	0.01
Eskimo (2)	2	0.01
Am. Ind. or Alaska Nat., not spec.	35	0.19
Albanian	36	0.19
American Indian tribes, specified:	60	0.32
Apache (1)	1	0.01
Blackfeet (1)	3	0.02
Cherokee (3)	9	0.05
Chippewa (2)	2	0.01
Cree (1)	2	0.01
Iroquois (1)	6	0.03
Latin American Indians	2	0.01
Lumbee	3	0.02
Potawatomi (1)	1	0.01
Sioux (1)	5	0.03
All other tribes (9)	26	0.14
American Indian tribes, not spec.	8	0.04
Arab:	171	0.92
Arab/Arabic	43	0.23
Iraqi	9	0.05
Lebanese	85	0.46
Palestinian	24	0.13
Other Arab	10	0.05
Armenian	28	0.15
Asian:	514	2.76
Bangladeshi (4)	4	0.02
Cambodian (4)	14	0.08
Chinese, ex. Taiwanese (120)	134	0.72
Filipino (13)	19	0.10
Indian (115)	140	0.75
Japanese (19)	39	0.21
Korean (54)	69	0.37
Laotian (5)	5	0.03
Malaysian	1	0.01
Pakistani (4)	4	0.02
Sri Lankan (3)	3	0.02
Taiwanese (1)	1	0.01
Thai (4)	4	0.02
Vietnamese (51)	61	0.33
Other Asian, specified (1)	1	0.01
Other Asian, not specified (10)	15	0.08
Australian	4	0.02
Austrian	74	0.40
British	125	0.67
Bulgarian	5	0.03
Canadian	177	0.95
Celtic	23	0.12
Croatian	16	0.09
Czech	72	0.39
Czechoslovakian	5	0.03
Danish	66	0.35
Dutch	381	2.05
Eastern European	53	0.28
English	3,310	17.77
Estonian	5	0.03
European	301	1.62
Finnish	20	0.11
French, except Basque	2,282	12.25
French Canadian	1,967	10.56
German	2,270	12.19
Greek	27	0.14
Hawaii Native/Pacific Islander:	7	0.04
Micronesian: (1)	3	0.02
Guamanian/Chamorro (1)	3	0.02
Polynesian: (2)	3	0.02
Native Hawaiian (1)	2	0.01
Samoan (1)	1	0.01
Other Pac. Isl., not spec. (1)	1	0.01
Hispanic or Latino:	158	0.85
Central American:	7	0.04
Guatemalan	2	0.01
Honduran	4	0.02
Nicaraguan	1	0.01
Cuban	13	0.07
Dominican Republic	4	0.02
Mexican	33	0.18
Puerto Rican	38	0.20
South American:	15	0.08
Argentinean	2	0.01
Colombian	7	0.04
Ecuadorian	4	0.02
Peruvian	1	0.01
Other South American	1	0.01
Other Hispanic or Latino	48	0.26
Hungarian	108	0.58
Irish	3,770	20.24
Israeli	21	0.11
Italian	1,488	7.99
Lithuanian	56	0.30
Northern European	13	0.07
Norwegian	150	0.81
Polish	922	4.95
Portuguese	37	0.20
Romanian	17	0.09
Russian	144	0.77
Scandinavian	31	0.17
Scotch-Irish	441	2.37
Scottish	885	4.75
Serbian	6	0.03
Slovak	86	0.46
Slovene	7	0.04
Swedish	337	1.81
Swiss	40	0.21
Turkish	10	0.05
Ukrainian	50	0.27
United States or American	1,042	5.59
Welsh	188	1.01
West Indian, excl. Hispanic:	19	0.10
Bahamian	5	0.03
Jamaican	14	0.08
White:	17,951	96.38
Not Hispanic (17,651)	17,820	95.67
Hispanic (112)	131	0.70
Yugoslavian	79	0.42

Hartford

Place Type: Town
County: Windsor
Population: 10,367

Ancestry/Race	Number	%
African American/Black:	76	0.73
Not Hispanic (54)	69	0.67
Hispanic (3)	7	0.07
African, sub-Saharan:	12	0.12
African	5	0.05
Other sub-Saharan African	7	0.07
Alaska Native tribes, specified:	6	0.06
Alaska Athabascan	1	0.01
Eskimo (1)	5	0.05
Am. Ind. or Alaska Nat., not spec.	34	0.33
American Indian tribes, specified:	53	0.51
Apache	2	0.02
Cherokee (3)	11	0.11
Chippewa (1)	3	0.03
Comanche	1	0.01
Houma (1)	3	0.03
Iroquois	1	0.01
Navajo	1	0.01
Sioux	3	0.03
All other tribes (13)	28	0.27
American Indian tribes, not spec.	6	0.06
Arab:	7	0.07
Lebanese	7	0.07
Armenian	7	0.07
Asian:	116	1.12
Chinese, ex. Taiwanese (27)	34	0.33
Filipino (5)	9	0.09
Indian (15)	18	0.17
Indonesian (1)	1	0.01
Japanese (9)	14	0.14
Korean (22)	22	0.21
Laotian	2	0.02
Malaysian (6)	6	0.06
Pakistani	1	0.01
Sri Lankan (1)	1	0.01
Taiwanese (1)	3	0.03
Vietnamese	1	0.01
Other Asian, not specified (2)	4	0.04
Austrian	24	0.23
Belgian	6	0.06
British	34	0.33
Canadian	112	1.08

Notes: 1. Figures in the "Number" column do not add up to the total population due to: a) Ancestry/Race overlap — e.g. persons can report being both White and Irish, b) persons of Hispanic origin can report being any race, c) persons reporting two ancestries are counted in both categories. 2. Numbers in parentheses indicate the number of persons reporting this ancestry/race alone, not in combination with any other ancestry/race. 3. Refer to the Explanation of Data in the front of the book for more detailed information.

Celtic	5	0.05
Cypriot	5	0.05
Czech	14	0.14
Danish	56	0.54
Dutch	132	1.27
Eastern European	6	0.06
English	2,007	19.36
European	28	0.27
Finnish	28	0.27
French, except Basque	1,185	11.43
French Canadian	632	6.10
German	893	8.61
Greek	56	0.54
Hawaii Native/Pacific Islander:	6	0.06
Polynesian: (3)	6	0.06
Native Hawaiian (2)	3	0.03
Samoan (1)	3	0.03
Hispanic or Latino:	88	0.85
Central American:	1	0.01
Honduran	1	0.01
Cuban	7	0.07
Mexican	31	0.30
Puerto Rican	21	0.20
South American:	9	0.09
Bolivian	2	0.02
Chilean	1	0.01
Colombian	2	0.02
Paraguayan	1	0.01
Venezuelan	3	0.03
Other Hispanic or Latino	19	0.18
Hungarian	52	0.50
Irish	1,650	15.92
Italian	732	7.06
Latvian	11	0.11
Norwegian	90	0.87
Polish	224	2.16
Portuguese	63	0.61
Romanian	4	0.04
Russian	145	1.40
Scandinavian	29	0.28
Scotch-Irish	297	2.86
Scottish	448	4.32
Swedish	134	1.29
Swiss	10	0.10
Ukrainian	17	0.16
United States or American	714	6.89
Welsh	117	1.13
West Indian, excl. Hispanic:	12	0.12
Barbadian	4	0.04
Jamaican	8	0.08
White:	10,163	98.03
Not Hispanic (9,997)	10,091	97.34
Hispanic (61)	72	0.69

Rutland

Place Type: City
County: Rutland
Population: 17,292

Ancestry/Race	Number	%
African American/Black:	116	0.67
Not Hispanic (71)	110	0.64
Hispanic (5)	6	0.03
African, sub-Saharan:	37	0.21
African	37	0.21
Am. Ind. or Alaska Nat., not spec.	44	0.25
American Indian tribes, specified:	76	0.44
Apache (1)	2	0.01
Blackfeet	3	0.02
Cherokee (4)	16	0.09
Cheyenne (4)	4	0.02
Chippewa (1)	5	0.03
Creek	1	0.01
Iroquois (1)	5	0.03
Latin American Indians (2)	3	0.02
Paiute (3)	3	0.02
Shoshone (3)	3	0.02
Sioux (3)	7	0.04
All other tribes (4)	24	0.14
American Indian tribes, not spec.	9	0.05
Arab:	53	0.31
Lebanese	53	0.31
Asian:	103	0.60
Chinese, ex. Taiwanese (23)	26	0.15
Filipino (6)	15	0.09
Indian (21)	22	0.13
Japanese (4)	11	0.06
Korean (12)	15	0.09
Pakistani	1	0.01
Thai (4)	4	0.02
Vietnamese (2)	2	0.01
Other Asian, not specified (2)	7	0.04
Austrian	24	0.14
Brazilian	10	0.06
British	147	0.85
Canadian	70	0.40
Czech	40	0.23
Czechoslovakian	9	0.05
Danish	93	0.54
Dutch	120	0.69
Eastern European	5	0.03
English	2,311	13.36
Estonian	9	0.05
European	37	0.21
Finnish	137	0.79
French, except Basque	3,121	18.05
French Canadian	974	5.63
German	1,156	6.69
Greek	88	0.51
Hawaii Native/Pacific Islander:	14	0.08
Micronesian: (6)	7	0.04
Guamanian/Chamorro (5)	6	0.03
Other Micronesian (1)	1	0.01
Polynesian: (3)	7	0.04
Native Hawaiian (1)	5	0.03
Samoan (2)	2	0.01
Hispanic or Latino:	156	0.90
Central American:	5	0.03
Guatemalan	1	0.01
Nicaraguan	2	0.01
Panamanian	1	0.01
Salvadoran	1	0.01
Cuban	12	0.07
Dominican Republic	2	0.01
Mexican	26	0.15
Puerto Rican	33	0.19
South American:	14	0.08
Bolivian	2	0.01
Colombian	6	0.03
Ecuadorian	1	0.01
Peruvian	1	0.01
Venezuelan	4	0.02
Other Hispanic or Latino	64	0.37
Hungarian	144	0.83
Irish	4,064	23.50
Italian	2,183	12.62
Northern European	9	0.05
Norwegian	70	0.40
Pennsylvania German	20	0.12
Polish	968	5.60
Portuguese	55	0.32
Russian	83	0.48
Scotch-Irish	243	1.41
Scottish	492	2.85
Slovak	28	0.16
Swedish	415	2.40
Swiss	24	0.14
Ukrainian	33	0.19
United States or American	1,210	7.00
Welsh	273	1.58
White:	17,055	98.63
Not Hispanic (16,796)	16,931	97.91
Hispanic (116)	124	0.72

South Burlington

Place Type: City
County: Chittenden
Population: 15,814

Ancestry/Race	Number	%
African American/Black:	182	1.15
Not Hispanic (120)	165	1.04
Hispanic (12)	17	0.11
African, sub-Saharan:	14	0.09
African	4	0.03
Ethiopian	6	0.04
Senegalese	4	0.03
Am. Ind. or Alaska Nat., not spec.	23	0.15
Albanian	6	0.04
American Indian tribes, specified:	88	0.56
Blackfeet	1	0.01
Cherokee (2)	10	0.06
Chippewa (1)	1	0.01
Iroquois (5)	15	0.09
Latin American Indians (2)	11	0.07
Navajo	4	0.03
Pueblo (1)	1	0.01
Sioux (1)	1	0.01
Yaqui	1	0.01
All other tribes (11)	43	0.27
American Indian tribes, not spec.	6	0.04
Arab:	119	0.75
Egyptian	52	0.33
Lebanese	41	0.26
Other Arab	26	0.16
Armenian	47	0.30
Asian:	605	3.83
Bangladeshi	4	0.03
Cambodian (5)	5	0.03
Chinese, ex. Taiwanese (196)	213	1.35
Filipino (12)	16	0.10
Indian (176)	198	1.25
Indonesian (2)	4	0.03
Japanese (34)	44	0.28
Korean (45)	50	0.32
Laotian	1	0.01
Pakistani (5)	5	0.03
Thai (3)	3	0.02
Vietnamese (39)	45	0.28
Other Asian, specified (1)	1	0.01
Other Asian, not specified (7)	16	0.10
Assyrian/Chaldean/Syriac	11	0.07
Austrian	63	0.40
Belgian	24	0.15
Brazilian	31	0.20
British	133	0.84
Canadian	248	1.57
Celtic	12	0.08
Czech	72	0.46
Czechoslovakian	42	0.27
Danish	104	0.66
Dutch	246	1.56
Eastern European	31	0.20
English	2,906	18.38
Estonian	13	0.08
European	90	0.57
Finnish	81	0.51
French, except Basque	1,861	11.77
French Canadian	1,765	11.16
German	1,868	11.81
Greek	124	0.78
Hawaii Native/Pacific Islander:	12	0.08
Polynesian: (1)	4	0.03
Native Hawaiian (1)	3	0.02
Samoan	1	0.01
Other Pac. Isl., not spec. (1)	8	0.05
Hispanic or Latino:	192	1.21
Central American:	6	0.04
Guatemalan	2	0.01
Honduran	1	0.01
Panamanian	1	0.01
Salvadoran	2	0.01
Cuban	6	0.04

Notes: 1. Figures in the "Number" column do not add up to the total population due to: a) Ancestry/Race overlap — e.g. persons can report being both White and Irish, b) persons of Hispanic origin can report being any race, c) persons reporting two ancestries are counted in both categories. 2. Numbers in parentheses indicate the number of persons reporting this ancestry/race alone, not in combination with any other ancestry/race. 3. Refer to the Explanation of Data in the front of the book for more detailed information.

Ancestry/Race	Number	%
Dominican Republic	3	0.02
Mexican	44	0.28
Puerto Rican	44	0.28
South American:	29	0.18
Argentinean	2	0.01
Colombian	10	0.06
Ecuadorian	4	0.03
Peruvian	12	0.08
Venezuelan	1	0.01
Other Hispanic or Latino	60	0.38
Hungarian	145	0.92
Iranian	25	0.16
Irish	3,163	20.00
Israeli	22	0.14
Italian	1,268	8.02
Lithuanian	87	0.55
Norwegian	127	0.80
Polish	828	5.24
Portuguese	53	0.34
Romanian	38	0.24
Russian	356	2.25
Scandinavian	41	0.26
Scotch-Irish	321	2.03
Scottish	460	2.91
Slovak	34	0.21
Swedish	224	1.42
Swiss	78	0.49
Ukrainian	44	0.28
United States or American	628	3.97
Welsh	172	1.09
White:	15,023	95.00
Not Hispanic (14,704)	14,873	94.05
Hispanic (127)	150	0.95
Yugoslavian	22	0.14

Alexandria

Place Type: Independent City
County: Alexandria Independent City
Population: 128,283

Ancestry/Race	Number	%
Acadian/Cajun	23	0.02
Afghan	718	0.56
African American/Black:	30,769	23.99
Not Hispanic (28,463)	30,078	23.45
Hispanic (452)	691	0.54
African, sub-Saharan:	8,500	6.63
African	2,313	1.80
Ethiopian	2,721	2.12
Ghanian	1,152	0.90
Kenyan	22	0.02
Liberian	24	0.02
Nigerian	232	0.18
Sierra Leonean	493	0.38
Somalian	529	0.41
South African	4	0.00
Sudanese	435	0.34
Ugandan	84	0.07
Zairian	17	0.01
Zimbabwean	45	0.04
Other sub-Saharan African	429	0.33
Alaska Native tribes, specified:	9	0.01
Alaska Athabascan (1)	2	0.00
Aleut (1)	2	0.00
Eskimo (1)	1	0.00
Tlingit-Haida (1)	3	0.00
All other tribes	1	0.00
Alaska Native tribes, not specified	1	0.00
Am. Ind. or Alaska Nat., not spec.	339	0.26
Albanian	20	0.02
Alsatian	44	0.03
American Indian tribes, specified:	560	0.44
Apache (4)	8	0.01
Blackfeet (6)	25	0.02
Cherokee (46)	200	0.16
Cheyenne (4)	5	0.00
Chickasaw (4)	8	0.01
Chippewa (8)	24	0.02
Choctaw (5)	15	0.01
Colville (1)	1	0.00
Comanche (1)	2	0.00
Cree (1)	6	0.00
Creek (4)	10	0.01
Crow (1)	1	0.00
Delaware (1)	3	0.00
Houma (3)	3	0.00
Iroquois (15)	28	0.02
Kiowa (1)	1	0.00
Latin American Indians (30)	87	0.07
Lumbee (2)	3	0.00
Menominee (1)	1	0.00
Navajo (9)	10	0.01
Osage (2)	6	0.00
Ottawa (1)	2	0.00
Paiute	1	0.00
Pima (1)	2	0.00
Potawatomi (3)	6	0.00
Pueblo (3)	5	0.00
Seminole (1)	4	0.00
Shoshone (1)	3	0.00
Sioux (9)	31	0.02
All other tribes (26)	59	0.05
American Indian tribes, not spec.	52	0.04
Arab:	1,979	1.54
Arab/Arabic	553	0.43
Egyptian	273	0.21
Iraqi	24	0.02
Jordanian	21	0.02
Lebanese	465	0.36
Moroccan	304	0.24
Palestinian	56	0.04
Syrian	133	0.10
Other Arab	150	0.12
Armenian	139	0.11
Asian:	8,802	6.86
Bangladeshi (170)	228	0.18
Cambodian (24)	44	0.03
Chinese, ex. Taiwanese (889)	1,010	0.79
Filipino (1,107)	1,290	1.01
Hmong (2)	2	0.00
Indian (1,629)	1,872	1.46
Indonesian (44)	60	0.05
Japanese (296)	433	0.34
Korean (1,335)	1,454	1.13
Laotian (71)	95	0.07
Malaysian (13)	19	0.01
Pakistani (509)	658	0.51
Sri Lankan (15)	22	0.02
Taiwanese (23)	29	0.02
Thai (194)	226	0.18
Vietnamese (510)	571	0.45
Other Asian, specified (33)	54	0.04
Other Asian, not specified (250)	735	0.57
Assyrian/Chaldean/Syriac	17	0.01
Australian	59	0.05
Austrian	486	0.38
Basque	4	0.00
Belgian	159	0.12
Brazilian	102	0.08
British	1,134	0.88
Bulgarian	85	0.07
Canadian	212	0.17
Celtic	44	0.03
Croatian	243	0.19
Czech	612	0.48
Czechoslovakian	201	0.16
Danish	514	0.40
Dutch	1,327	1.03
Eastern European	286	0.22
English	13,465	10.50
Estonian	41	0.03
European	1,434	1.12
Finnish	173	0.13
French, except Basque	2,718	2.12
French Canadian	665	0.52
German	14,355	11.19
German Russian	13	0.01
Greek	629	0.49
Guyanese	96	0.07
Hawaii Native/Pacific Islander:	286	0.22
Melanesian: (2)	2	0.00
Fijian (2)	2	0.00
Micronesian: (37)	61	0.05
Guamanian/Chamorro (25)	45	0.04
Other Micronesian (12)	16	0.01
Polynesian: (47)	86	0.07
Native Hawaiian (24)	49	0.04
Samoan (22)	33	0.03
Other Polynesian (1)	4	0.00
Other Pac. Isl., specified	15	0.01
Other Pac. Isl., not spec. (23)	122	0.10
Hispanic or Latino:	18,882	14.72
Central American:	7,241	5.64
Costa Rican	42	0.03
Guatemalan	644	0.50
Honduran	1,326	1.03
Nicaraguan	240	0.19
Panamanian	110	0.09
Salvadoran	4,477	3.49
Other Central American	402	0.31
Cuban	280	0.22
Dominican Republic	166	0.13
Mexican	1,829	1.43
Puerto Rican	1,116	0.87
South American:	2,325	1.81
Argentinean	92	0.07
Bolivian	609	0.47
Chilean	199	0.16
Colombian	326	0.25
Ecuadorian	151	0.12
Paraguayan	9	0.01
Peruvian	646	0.50
Uruguayan	27	0.02
Venezuelan	129	0.10
Other South American	137	0.11
Other Hispanic or Latino	5,925	4.62
Hungarian	729	0.57
Icelander	38	0.03
Iranian	550	0.43
Irish	14,594	11.38
Israeli	18	0.01
Italian	5,885	4.59
Latvian	60	0.05
Lithuanian	453	0.35
Luxemburger	20	0.02
Macedonian	8	0.01
New Zealander	14	0.01
Northern European	217	0.17
Norwegian	1,256	0.98
Pennsylvania German	34	0.03
Polish	3,048	2.38
Portuguese	292	0.23
Romanian	182	0.14
Russian	1,665	1.30
Scandinavian	198	0.15
Scotch-Irish	2,581	2.01
Scottish	3,255	2.54
Serbian	91	0.07
Slavic	126	0.10
Slovak	479	0.37
Slovene	54	0.04
Swedish	1,323	1.03
Swiss	462	0.36
Turkish	229	0.18
Ukrainian	405	0.32
United States or American	3,904	3.04
Welsh	967	0.75
West Indian, excl. Hispanic:	729	0.57
Bahamian	39	0.03
Barbadian	32	0.02
Belizean	8	0.01
British West Indian	16	0.01
Haitian	88	0.07
Jamaican	380	0.30
Trinidadian and Tobagonian	103	0.08
West Indian	51	0.04
Other West Indian	12	0.01
White:	80,473	62.73
Not Hispanic (68,889)	71,390	55.65

Notes: 1. Figures in the "Number" column do not add up to the total population due to: a) Ancestry/Race overlap — e.g. persons can report being both White and Irish, b) persons of Hispanic origin can report being any race, c) persons reporting two ancestries are counted in both categories. 2. Numbers in parentheses indicate the number of persons reporting this ancestry/race alone, not in combination with any other ancestry/race. 3. Refer to the Explanation of Data in the front of the book for more detailed information.

Hispanic (7,813)	9,083	7.08
Yugoslavian	121	0.09

Annandale

Place Type: Census Designated Place
County: Fairfax
Population: 54,994

Ancestry/Race	Number	%
Afghan	294	0.53
African American/Black:	3,634	6.61
Not Hispanic (3,128)	3,455	6.28
Hispanic (96)	179	0.33
African, sub-Saharan:	1,117	2.03
African	293	0.53
Ethiopian	345	0.63
Ghanian	27	0.05
Kenyan	21	0.04
Liberian	19	0.03
Nigerian	48	0.09
Somalian	143	0.26
South African	15	0.03
Sudanese	66	0.12
Zimbabwean	48	0.09
Other sub-Saharan African	92	0.17
Alaska Native tribes, specified:	5	0.01
Eskimo (1)	4	0.01
Tlingit-Haida (1)	1	0.00
Am. Ind. or Alaska Nat., not spec.	139	0.25
Alsatian	8	0.01
American Indian tribes, specified:	256	0.47
Apache	2	0.00
Blackfeet (1)	3	0.01
Cherokee (24)	80	0.15
Cheyenne (1)	2	0.00
Chickasaw (1)	5	0.01
Chippewa	5	0.01
Choctaw (3)	11	0.02
Colville (1)	1	0.00
Comanche	2	0.00
Creek (2)	2	0.00
Delaware (3)	3	0.01
Iroquois (11)	22	0.04
Latin American Indians (31)	61	0.11
Lumbee (3)	3	0.01
Navajo (8)	8	0.01
Osage	1	0.00
Ottawa (1)	1	0.00
Potawatomi (1)	2	0.00
Pueblo (3)	3	0.01
Sioux (6)	8	0.01
Yakama	1	0.00
Yaqui	2	0.00
All other tribes (11)	28	0.05
American Indian tribes, not spec.	17	0.03
Arab:	1,418	2.58
Arab/Arabic	271	0.49
Egyptian	173	0.31
Iraqi	138	0.25
Jordanian	26	0.05
Lebanese	301	0.55
Moroccan	83	0.15
Palestinian	194	0.35
Syrian	6	0.01
Other Arab	226	0.41
Armenian	112	0.20
Asian:	11,590	21.08
Bangladeshi (21)	27	0.05
Cambodian (178)	205	0.37
Chinese, ex. Taiwanese (891)	1,005	1.83
Filipino (649)	776	1.41
Indian (1,235)	1,355	2.46
Indonesian (12)	30	0.05
Japanese (110)	182	0.33
Korean (3,651)	3,752	6.82
Laotian (59)	61	0.11
Malaysian (12)	18	0.03
Pakistani (266)	366	0.67
Sri Lankan (20)	23	0.04
Taiwanese (17)	23	0.04
Thai (94)	101	0.18
Vietnamese (3,173)	3,308	6.02
Other Asian, specified (32)	40	0.07
Other Asian, not specified (128)	318	0.58
Assyrian/Chaldean/Syriac	7	0.01
Australian	97	0.18
Austrian	222	0.40
Belgian	44	0.08
Brazilian	81	0.15
British	460	0.84
Bulgarian	20	0.04
Canadian	159	0.29
Carpatho Rusyn	4	0.01
Celtic	8	0.01
Croatian	114	0.21
Czech	88	0.16
Czechoslovakian	63	0.11
Danish	217	0.39
Dutch	573	1.04
Eastern European	155	0.28
English	6,281	11.41
Estonian	15	0.03
European	703	1.28
Finnish	74	0.13
French, except Basque	1,156	2.10
French Canadian	364	0.66
German	6,466	11.75
Greek	198	0.36
Guyanese	17	0.03
Hawaii Native/Pacific Islander:	126	0.23
Micronesian: (12)	20	0.04
Guamanian/Chamorro (9)	14	0.03
Other Micronesian (3)	6	0.01
Polynesian: (18)	57	0.10
Native Hawaiian (10)	39	0.07
Samoan (4)	11	0.02
Tongan	3	0.01
Other Polynesian (4)	4	0.01
Other Pac. Isl., specified	4	0.01
Other Pac. Isl., not spec. (11)	45	0.08
Hispanic or Latino:	7,966	14.49
Central American:	2,049	3.73
Costa Rican	22	0.04
Guatemalan	197	0.36
Honduran	132	0.24
Nicaraguan	117	0.21
Panamanian	23	0.04
Salvadoran	1,407	2.56
Other Central American	151	0.27
Cuban	199	0.36
Dominican Republic	62	0.11
Mexican	586	1.07
Puerto Rican	350	0.64
South American:	2,149	3.91
Argentinean	74	0.13
Bolivian	962	1.75
Chilean	99	0.18
Colombian	143	0.26
Ecuadorian	66	0.12
Paraguayan	11	0.02
Peruvian	545	0.99
Uruguayan	14	0.03
Venezuelan	59	0.11
Other South American	176	0.32
Other Hispanic or Latino	2,571	4.68
Hungarian	248	0.45
Iranian	300	0.55
Irish	5,650	10.27
Israeli	20	0.04
Italian	2,686	4.88
Latvian	18	0.03
Lithuanian	124	0.23
Macedonian	9	0.02
New Zealander	5	0.01
Northern European	172	0.31
Norwegian	478	0.87
Pennsylvania German	28	0.05
Polish	1,581	2.87
Portuguese	149	0.27
Romanian	37	0.07
Russian	623	1.13
Scandinavian	136	0.25
Scotch-Irish	1,215	2.21
Scottish	1,351	2.45
Serbian	97	0.18
Slavic	58	0.11
Slovak	144	0.26
Slovene	35	0.06
Swedish	463	0.84
Swiss	174	0.32
Turkish	118	0.21
Ukrainian	217	0.39
United States or American	2,375	4.31
Welsh	390	0.71
West Indian, excl. Hispanic:	126	0.23
Bermudan	13	0.02
British West Indian	28	0.05
Haitian	23	0.04
Jamaican	46	0.08
Trinidadian and Tobagonian	16	0.03
White:	37,194	67.63
Not Hispanic (31,453)	32,623	59.32
Hispanic (4,020)	4,571	8.31
Yugoslavian	74	0.13

Arlington

Place Type: Census Designated Place
County: Arlington
Population: 189,453

Ancestry/Race	Number	%
Acadian/Cajun	51	0.03
Afghan	165	0.09
African American/Black:	19,425	10.25
Not Hispanic (17,244)	18,652	9.85
Hispanic (461)	773	0.41
African, sub-Saharan:	4,376	2.31
African	1,239	0.65
Cape Verdean	17	0.01
Ethiopian	2,171	1.15
Ghanian	113	0.06
Kenyan	42	0.02
Liberian	35	0.02
Nigerian	100	0.05
Senegalese	55	0.03
Sierra Leonean	19	0.01
Somalian	136	0.07
South African	56	0.03
Sudanese	73	0.04
Ugandan	19	0.01
Zairian	7	0.00
Other sub-Saharan African	294	0.16
Alaska Native tribes, specified:	9	0.00
Alaska Athabascan (1)	2	0.00
Aleut (1)	1	0.00
Eskimo (2)	3	0.00
Tlingit-Haida (1)	3	0.00
Alaska Native tribes, not specified	1	0.00
Am. Ind. or Alaska Nat., not spec.	554	0.29
Albanian	107	0.06
Alsatian	44	0.02
American Indian tribes, specified:	935	0.49
Apache (2)	17	0.01
Blackfeet (6)	27	0.01
Cherokee (77)	262	0.14
Cheyenne	2	0.00
Chickasaw (7)	10	0.01
Chippewa (18)	23	0.01
Choctaw (20)	31	0.02
Colville (1)	1	0.00
Comanche (2)	6	0.00
Cree	5	0.00
Creek (15)	29	0.02
Crow (2)	7	0.00
Delaware	6	0.00
Houma (2)	2	0.00
Iroquois (15)	36	0.02
Kiowa (1)	4	0.00

Notes: 1. Figures in the "Number" column do not add up to the total population due to: a) Ancestry/Race overlap — e.g. persons can report being both White and Irish, b) persons of Hispanic origin can report being any race, c) persons reporting two ancestries are counted in both categories. 2. Numbers in parentheses indicate the number of persons reporting this ancestry/race alone, not in combination with any other ancestry/race. 3. Refer to the Explanation of Data in the front of the book for more detailed information.

Latin American Indians (106)	239	0.13
Lumbee (5)	7	0.00
Menominee (1)	1	0.00
Navajo (18)	22	0.01
Osage (1)	7	0.00
Paiute (1)	1	0.00
Potawatomi (4)	13	0.01
Pueblo (15)	23	0.01
Seminole (1)	3	0.00
Shoshone	2	0.00
Sioux (18)	37	0.02
Tohono O'Odham (6)	8	0.00
Ute (1)	1	0.00
Yaqui (2)	2	0.00
Yuman (1)	1	0.00
All other tribes (53)	100	0.05
American Indian tribes, not spec.	66	0.03
Arab:	3,433	1.81
Arab/Arabic	573	0.30
Egyptian	336	0.18
Iraqi	7	0.00
Jordanian	66	0.03
Lebanese	731	0.39
Moroccan	762	0.40
Palestinian	178	0.09
Syrian	254	0.13
Other Arab	526	0.28
Armenian	286	0.15
Asian:	19,135	10.10
Bangladeshi (400)	527	0.28
Cambodian (373)	434	0.23
Chinese, ex. Taiwanese (2,635)	3,053	1.61
Filipino (2,039)	2,388	1.26
Indian (3,334)	3,845	2.03
Indonesian (170)	207	0.11
Japanese (1,011)	1,284	0.68
Korean (1,572)	1,758	0.93
Laotian (171)	204	0.11
Malaysian (45)	60	0.03
Pakistani (689)	959	0.51
Sri Lankan (116)	132	0.07
Taiwanese (141)	191	0.10
Thai (446)	523	0.28
Vietnamese (2,066)	2,255	1.19
Other Asian, specified (169)	221	0.12
Other Asian, not specified (560)	1,094	0.58
Assyrian/Chaldean/Syriac	27	0.01
Australian	97	0.05
Austrian	810	0.43
Basque	123	0.06
Belgian	187	0.10
Brazilian	236	0.12
British	2,288	1.21
Bulgarian	71	0.04
Canadian	541	0.29
Celtic	70	0.04
Croatian	376	0.20
Cypriot	7	0.00
Czech	906	0.48
Czechoslovakian	343	0.18
Danish	959	0.51
Dutch	1,932	1.02
Eastern European	686	0.36
English	21,855	11.54
Estonian	133	0.07
European	3,036	1.60
Finnish	404	0.21
French, except Basque	4,469	2.36
French Canadian	1,451	0.77
German	23,893	12.61
Greek	1,310	0.69
Guyanese	53	0.03
Hawaii Native/Pacific Islander:	380	0.20
Melanesian: (1)	1	0.00
Fijian (1)	1	0.00
Micronesian: (44)	56	0.03
Guamanian/Chamorro (33)	43	0.02
Other Micronesian (11)	13	0.01
Polynesian: (69)	153	0.08
Native Hawaiian (39)	96	0.05
Samoan (28)	49	0.03
Other Polynesian (2)	8	0.00
Other Pac. Isl., specified	14	0.01
Other Pac. Isl., not spec. (29)	156	0.08
Hispanic or Latino:	35,268	18.62
Central American:	11,323	5.98
Costa Rican	119	0.06
Guatemalan	1,703	0.90
Honduran	686	0.36
Nicaraguan	481	0.25
Panamanian	159	0.08
Salvadoran	7,630	4.03
Other Central American	545	0.29
Cuban	506	0.27
Dominican Republic	230	0.12
Mexican	2,973	1.57
Puerto Rican	1,103	0.58
South American:	7,083	3.74
Argentinean	382	0.20
Bolivian	3,532	1.86
Chilean	204	0.11
Colombian	630	0.33
Ecuadorian	305	0.16
Paraguayan	82	0.04
Peruvian	1,171	0.62
Uruguayan	68	0.04
Venezuelan	247	0.13
Other South American	462	0.24
Other Hispanic or Latino	12,050	6.36
Hungarian	1,269	0.67
Icelander	57	0.03
Iranian	608	0.32
Irish	24,102	12.72
Israeli	56	0.03
Italian	9,703	5.12
Latvian	235	0.12
Lithuanian	782	0.41
Luxemburger	50	0.03
Macedonian	27	0.01
Maltese	19	0.01
New Zealander	71	0.04
Northern European	431	0.23
Norwegian	2,307	1.22
Pennsylvania German	50	0.03
Polish	5,302	2.80
Portuguese	634	0.33
Romanian	479	0.25
Russian	3,685	1.95
Scandinavian	394	0.21
Scotch-Irish	4,435	2.34
Scottish	5,336	2.82
Serbian	136	0.07
Slavic	174	0.09
Slovak	707	0.37
Slovene	101	0.05
Soviet Union	6	0.00
Swedish	2,615	1.38
Swiss	934	0.49
Turkish	430	0.23
Ukrainian	1,002	0.53
United States or American	6,346	3.35
Welsh	1,862	0.98
West Indian, excl. Hispanic:	719	0.38
Bahamian	34	0.02
Barbadian	63	0.03
British West Indian	55	0.03
Haitian	107	0.06
Jamaican	259	0.14
Trinidadian and Tobagonian	101	0.05
U.S. Virgin Islander	10	0.01
West Indian	90	0.05
White:	137,049	72.34
Not Hispanic (114,489)	118,148	62.36
Hispanic (16,112)	18,901	9.98
Yugoslavian	157	0.08

Bailey's Crossroads

Place Type: Census Designated Place
County: Fairfax
Population: 23,166

Ancestry/Race	Number	%
Acadian/Cajun	4	0.02
Afghan	129	0.56
African American/Black:	2,867	12.38
Not Hispanic (2,391)	2,602	11.23
Hispanic (123)	265	1.14
African, sub-Saharan:	886	3.88
African	255	1.12
Cape Verdean	34	0.15
Ethiopian	157	0.69
Ghanian	89	0.39
Nigerian	18	0.08
Sierra Leonean	32	0.14
Somalian	153	0.67
South African	11	0.05
Sudanese	58	0.25
Other sub-Saharan African	79	0.35
Am. Ind. or Alaska Nat., not spec.	93	0.40
Alsatian	20	0.09
American Indian tribes, specified:	155	0.67
Apache (1)	1	0.00
Blackfeet (2)	2	0.01
Cherokee (9)	20	0.09
Chickasaw	1	0.00
Chippewa (2)	3	0.01
Choctaw	6	0.03
Cree	1	0.00
Creek (1)	1	0.00
Iroquois (1)	1	0.00
Latin American Indians (40)	88	0.38
Navajo (1)	1	0.00
Osage (1)	1	0.00
Pueblo (2)	2	0.01
Puget Sound Salish	1	0.00
Seminole	1	0.00
Sioux (2)	4	0.02
Ute	1	0.00
Yuman	2	0.01
All other tribes (8)	18	0.08
American Indian tribes, not spec.	18	0.08
Arab:	2,443	10.69
Arab/Arabic	817	3.57
Egyptian	202	0.88
Iraqi	36	0.16
Jordanian	50	0.22
Lebanese	186	0.81
Moroccan	90	0.39
Palestinian	275	1.20
Syrian	143	0.63
Other Arab	644	2.82
Armenian	15	0.07
Asian:	3,395	14.66
Bangladeshi (48)	54	0.23
Cambodian (91)	119	0.51
Chinese, ex. Taiwanese (251)	299	1.29
Filipino (257)	295	1.27
Indian (372)	447	1.93
Indonesian (23)	30	0.13
Japanese (47)	66	0.28
Korean (287)	300	1.30
Laotian (26)	29	0.13
Malaysian (3)	4	0.02
Pakistani (325)	406	1.75
Sri Lankan (6)	7	0.03
Taiwanese (10)	11	0.05
Thai (44)	52	0.22
Vietnamese (902)	954	4.12
Other Asian, specified (12)	13	0.06
Other Asian, not specified (84)	309	1.33
Austrian	55	0.24
Belgian	5	0.02
Brazilian	102	0.45
British	62	0.27
Canadian	44	0.19

Notes: 1. Figures in the "Number" column do not add up to the total population due to: a) Ancestry/Race overlap — e.g. persons can report being both White and Irish, b) persons of Hispanic origin can report being any race, c) persons reporting two ancestries are counted in both categories. 2. Numbers in parentheses indicate the number of persons reporting this ancestry/race alone, not in combination with any other ancestry/race. 3. Refer to the Explanation of Data in the front of the book for more detailed information.

Croatian	6	0.03
Czech	49	0.21
Czechoslovakian	10	0.04
Danish	49	0.21
Dutch	92	0.40
Eastern European	44	0.19
English	1,146	5.01
European	123	0.54
Finnish	20	0.09
French, except Basque	192	0.84
French Canadian	55	0.24
German	966	4.23
Greek	114	0.50
Guyanese	15	0.07
Hawaii Native/Pacific Islander:	47	0.20
Micronesian: (6)	6	0.03
Guamanian/Chamorro (3)	3	0.01
Other Micronesian (3)	3	0.01
Polynesian: (4)	10	0.04
Native Hawaiian	5	0.02
Samoan (4)	5	0.02
Other Pac. Isl., not spec. (11)	31	0.13
Hispanic or Latino:	8,596	37.11
Central American:	3,567	15.40
Costa Rican	7	0.03
Guatemalan	660	2.85
Honduran	244	1.05
Nicaraguan	218	0.94
Panamanian	32	0.14
Salvadoran	2,243	9.68
Other Central American	163	0.70
Cuban	96	0.41
Dominican Republic	61	0.26
Mexican	774	3.34
Puerto Rican	160	0.69
South American:	961	4.15
Argentinean	47	0.20
Bolivian	474	2.05
Chilean	35	0.15
Colombian	86	0.37
Ecuadorian	43	0.19
Peruvian	206	0.89
Uruguayan	3	0.01
Venezuelan	21	0.09
Other South American	46	0.20
Other Hispanic or Latino	2,977	12.85
Hungarian	41	0.18
Iranian	183	0.80
Irish	1,074	4.70
Italian	432	1.89
Lithuanian	77	0.34
Luxemburger	20	0.09
Northern European	32	0.14
Norwegian	39	0.17
Polish	283	1.24
Portuguese	89	0.39
Romanian	74	0.32
Russian	199	0.87
Scandinavian	12	0.05
Scotch-Irish	212	0.93
Scottish	235	1.03
Serbian	11	0.05
Slavic	19	0.08
Slovak	46	0.20
Slovene	7	0.03
Swedish	137	0.60
Swiss	25	0.11
Turkish	17	0.07
Ukrainian	34	0.15
United States or American	399	1.75
Welsh	84	0.37
West Indian, excl. Hispanic:	98	0.43
Dutch West Indian	7	0.03
Haitian	17	0.07
Jamaican	28	0.12
Trinidadian and Tobagonian	10	0.04
West Indian	36	0.16
White:	12,885	55.62
Not Hispanic (7,741)	8,904	38.44
Hispanic (3,355)	3,981	17.18
Yugoslavian	16	0.07

Blacksburg

Place Type: Town
County: Montgomery
Population: 39,573

Ancestry/Race	Number	%
Afghan	7	0.02
African American/Black:	1,934	4.89
Not Hispanic (1,700)	1,883	4.76
Hispanic (38)	51	0.13
African, sub-Saharan:	292	0.74
African	142	0.36
Cape Verdean	19	0.05
Ethiopian	23	0.06
Ghanian	7	0.02
Kenyan	23	0.06
Nigerian	28	0.07
South African	38	0.10
Sudanese	12	0.03
Am. Ind. or Alaska Nat., not spec.	82	0.21
Albanian	74	0.19
American Indian tribes, specified:	98	0.25
Apache (1)	1	0.00
Blackfeet	5	0.01
Cherokee (16)	58	0.15
Chippewa	3	0.01
Choctaw (2)	5	0.01
Cree (1)	1	0.00
Creek	2	0.01
Iroquois (2)	5	0.01
Latin American Indians (1)	1	0.00
Potawatomi (1)	2	0.01
Shoshone	1	0.00
Sioux (1)	4	0.01
All other tribes (2)	10	0.03
American Indian tribes, not spec.	10	0.03
Arab:	448	1.14
Arab/Arabic	8	0.02
Egyptian	124	0.31
Iraqi	26	0.07
Jordanian	8	0.02
Lebanese	130	0.33
Moroccan	5	0.01
Palestinian	125	0.32
Syrian	9	0.02
Other Arab	13	0.03
Armenian	54	0.14
Asian:	3,561	9.00
Bangladeshi (23)	26	0.07
Cambodian (10)	13	0.03
Chinese, ex. Taiwanese (906)	992	2.51
Filipino (246)	312	0.79
Hmong	1	0.00
Indian (674)	732	1.85
Indonesian (21)	35	0.09
Japanese (84)	128	0.32
Korean (649)	702	1.77
Laotian (8)	14	0.04
Malaysian (17)	25	0.06
Pakistani (26)	36	0.09
Sri Lankan (21)	22	0.06
Taiwanese (38)	49	0.12
Thai (81)	114	0.29
Vietnamese (146)	175	0.44
Other Asian, specified (19)	22	0.06
Other Asian, not specified (64)	163	0.41
Australian	20	0.05
Austrian	156	0.40
Belgian	36	0.09
Brazilian	41	0.10
British	540	1.37
Bulgarian	7	0.02
Canadian	178	0.45
Carpatho Rusyn	9	0.02
Croatian	154	0.39
Czech	171	0.43
Czechoslovakian	100	0.25
Danish	161	0.41
Dutch	537	1.36
Eastern European	63	0.16
English	5,052	12.82
European	652	1.66
Finnish	98	0.25
French, except Basque	937	2.38
French Canadian	234	0.59
German	7,744	19.66
Greek	217	0.55
Hawaii Native/Pacific Islander:	66	0.17
Melanesian: (1)	1	0.00
Fijian (1)	1	0.00
Micronesian: (2)	9	0.02
Guamanian/Chamorro (2)	9	0.02
Polynesian: (12)	26	0.07
Native Hawaiian (9)	17	0.04
Samoan (3)	7	0.02
Tongan	1	0.00
Other Polynesian	1	0.00
Other Pac. Isl., not spec. (7)	30	0.08
Hispanic or Latino:	920	2.32
Central American:	90	0.23
Costa Rican	7	0.02
Guatemalan	6	0.02
Honduran	6	0.02
Nicaraguan	17	0.04
Panamanian	24	0.06
Salvadoran	26	0.07
Other Central American	4	0.01
Cuban	59	0.15
Dominican Republic	7	0.02
Mexican	197	0.50
Puerto Rican	166	0.42
South American:	201	0.51
Argentinean	32	0.08
Bolivian	28	0.07
Chilean	20	0.05
Colombian	32	0.08
Ecuadorian	18	0.05
Paraguayan	7	0.02
Peruvian	22	0.06
Uruguayan	4	0.01
Venezuelan	28	0.07
Other South American	10	0.03
Other Hispanic or Latino	200	0.51
Hungarian	265	0.67
Icelander	10	0.03
Iranian	75	0.19
Irish	5,344	13.57
Israeli	58	0.15
Italian	2,700	6.85
Latvian	6	0.02
Lithuanian	123	0.31
Luxemburger	29	0.07
Macedonian	7	0.02
New Zealander	17	0.04
Northern European	18	0.05
Norwegian	466	1.18
Pennsylvania German	10	0.03
Polish	1,186	3.01
Portuguese	58	0.15
Romanian	65	0.17
Russian	453	1.15
Scandinavian	84	0.21
Scotch-Irish	1,522	3.86
Scottish	1,649	4.19
Serbian	24	0.06
Slavic	54	0.14
Slovak	144	0.37
Swedish	540	1.37
Swiss	123	0.31
Turkish	137	0.35
Ukrainian	186	0.47
United States or American	2,134	5.42
Welsh	422	1.07
West Indian, excl. Hispanic:	80	0.20
Bahamian	21	0.05
Barbadian	8	0.02
British West Indian	12	0.03

Notes: 1. Figures in the "Number" column do not add up to the total population due to: a) Ancestry/Race overlap — e.g. persons can report being both White and Irish, b) persons of Hispanic origin can report being any race, c) persons reporting two ancestries are counted in both categories. 2. Numbers in parentheses indicate the number of persons reporting this ancestry/race alone, not in combination with any other ancestry/race. 3. Refer to the Explanation of Data in the front of the book for more detailed information.

Dutch West Indian	9	0.02
Jamaican	11	0.03
Trinidadian and Tobagonian	7	0.02
U.S. Virgin Islander	12	0.03
White:	34,131	86.25
Not Hispanic (32,869)	33,551	84.78
Hispanic (525)	580	1.47
Yugoslavian	17	0.04

Bon Air

Place Type: Census Designated Place
County: Chesterfield
Population: 16,213

Ancestry/Race	Number	%
African American/Black:	1,429	8.81
Not Hispanic (1,349)	1,406	8.67
Hispanic (17)	23	0.14
African, sub-Saharan:	162	1.00
African	151	0.93
South African	11	0.07
Am. Ind. or Alaska Nat., not spec.	23	0.14
Albanian	8	0.05
American Indian tribes, specified:	42	0.26
Apache	1	0.01
Blackfeet (2)	2	0.01
Cherokee (7)	22	0.14
Chickasaw	1	0.01
Chippewa (1)	1	0.01
Creek	1	0.01
Houma (1)	1	0.01
Navajo	1	0.01
Pueblo (1)	1	0.01
Sioux (2)	2	0.01
All other tribes (4)	9	0.06
American Indian tribes, not spec.	3	0.02
Arab:	148	0.91
Iraqi	6	0.04
Jordanian	33	0.20
Lebanese	102	0.63
Syrian	7	0.04
Asian:	475	2.93
Cambodian (40)	47	0.29
Chinese, ex. Taiwanese (77)	85	0.52
Filipino (48)	60	0.37
Indian (69)	77	0.47
Indonesian (2)	2	0.01
Japanese (12)	20	0.12
Korean (51)	54	0.33
Malaysian (1)	1	0.01
Pakistani (7)	9	0.06
Taiwanese	1	0.01
Thai	1	0.01
Vietnamese (70)	78	0.48
Other Asian, specified	2	0.01
Other Asian, not specified (24)	38	0.23
Austrian	57	0.35
Belgian	6	0.04
Brazilian	10	0.06
British	139	0.86
Canadian	37	0.23
Croatian	23	0.14
Czech	42	0.26
Czechoslovakian	35	0.22
Danish	58	0.36
Dutch	281	1.73
Eastern European	13	0.08
English	3,569	22.04
European	314	1.94
Finnish	17	0.10
French, except Basque	583	3.60
French Canadian	95	0.59
German	2,237	13.81
Greek	57	0.35
Guyanese	5	0.03
Hawaii Native/Pacific Islander:	9	0.06
Polynesian: (6)	8	0.05
Native Hawaiian (5)	7	0.04
Samoan (1)	1	0.01
Other Pac. Isl., not spec.	1	0.01
Hispanic or Latino:	281	1.73
Central American:	19	0.12
Honduran	7	0.04
Panamanian	1	0.01
Salvadoran	11	0.07
Cuban	22	0.14
Dominican Republic	4	0.02
Mexican	90	0.56
Puerto Rican	59	0.36
South American:	27	0.17
Chilean	1	0.01
Colombian	18	0.11
Peruvian	7	0.04
Other South American	1	0.01
Other Hispanic or Latino	60	0.37
Hungarian	26	0.16
Icelander	9	0.06
Iranian	55	0.34
Irish	2,104	12.99
Italian	607	3.75
Lithuanian	10	0.06
New Zealander	6	0.04
Northern European	38	0.23
Norwegian	89	0.55
Polish	246	1.52
Portuguese	8	0.05
Russian	71	0.44
Scandinavian	46	0.28
Scotch-Irish	793	4.90
Scottish	515	3.18
Serbian	14	0.09
Slovak	23	0.14
Swedish	58	0.36
Swiss	51	0.31
Turkish	18	0.11
Ukrainian	44	0.27
United States or American	1,835	11.33
Welsh	250	1.54
West Indian, excl. Hispanic:	23	0.14
Barbadian	4	0.02
British West Indian	4	0.02
Jamaican	3	0.02
West Indian	12	0.07
White:	14,237	87.81
Not Hispanic (13,965)	14,090	86.91
Hispanic (125)	147	0.91
Yugoslavian	13	0.08

Bristol

Place Type: Independent City
County: Bristol Independent City
Population: 17,367

Ancestry/Race	Number	%
African American/Black:	1,050	6.05
Not Hispanic (952)	1,025	5.90
Hispanic (15)	25	0.14
African, sub-Saharan:	52	0.30
African	52	0.30
Am. Ind. or Alaska Nat., not spec.	52	0.30
American Indian tribes, specified:	61	0.35
Apache (1)	1	0.01
Blackfeet	1	0.01
Cherokee (13)	41	0.24
Chippewa (2)	2	0.01
Choctaw	1	0.01
Cree	1	0.01
Iroquois (1)	1	0.01
Latin American Indians (1)	1	0.01
Lumbee (4)	4	0.02
Menominee	1	0.01
Navajo	1	0.01
Seminole (2)	2	0.01
Sioux	2	0.01
All other tribes (1)	2	0.01
American Indian tribes, not spec.	9	0.05
Asian:	85	0.49
Chinese, ex. Taiwanese (13)	14	0.08
Filipino (4)	11	0.06
Indian (7)	10	0.06
Japanese (15)	15	0.09
Korean (10)	14	0.08
Taiwanese (1)	1	0.01
Thai (2)	3	0.02
Vietnamese (9)	9	0.05
Other Asian, specified	2	0.01
Other Asian, not specified (3)	6	0.03
British	51	0.29
Bulgarian	8	0.05
Czech	23	0.13
Danish	9	0.05
Dutch	306	1.76
English	1,777	10.23
European	166	0.96
French, except Basque	217	1.25
French Canadian	19	0.11
German	1,733	9.98
Greek	9	0.05
Hawaii Native/Pacific Islander:	8	0.05
Polynesian: (2)	4	0.02
Native Hawaiian	1	0.01
Samoan (2)	2	0.01
Other Polynesian	1	0.01
Other Pac. Isl., specified	2	0.01
Other Pac. Isl., not spec.	2	0.01
Hispanic or Latino:	169	0.97
Central American:	1	0.01
Guatemalan	1	0.01
Cuban	7	0.04
Mexican	57	0.33
Puerto Rican	36	0.21
South American:	14	0.08
Chilean	1	0.01
Colombian	3	0.02
Ecuadorian	8	0.05
Venezuelan	2	0.01
Other Hispanic or Latino	54	0.31
Hungarian	8	0.05
Irish	1,921	11.06
Italian	255	1.47
Lithuanian	24	0.14
Norwegian	39	0.22
Polish	121	0.70
Russian	40	0.23
Scotch-Irish	582	3.35
Scottish	290	1.67
Slovak	5	0.03
Swedish	96	0.55
Swiss	6	0.03
Ukrainian	34	0.20
United States or American	3,147	18.12
Welsh	75	0.43
White:	16,248	93.56
Not Hispanic (15,964)	16,124	92.84
Hispanic (108)	124	0.71
Yugoslavian	10	0.06

Bull Run

Place Type: Census Designated Place
County: Prince William
Population: 11,337

Ancestry/Race	Number	%
Afghan	12	0.11
African American/Black:	2,306	20.34
Not Hispanic (2,126)	2,268	20.01
Hispanic (25)	38	0.34
African, sub-Saharan:	210	1.84
African	91	0.80
Ethiopian	43	0.38
Nigerian	39	0.34
Other sub-Saharan African	37	0.32
Am. Ind. or Alaska Nat., not spec.	23	0.20
American Indian tribes, specified:	64	0.56
Apache (1)	2	0.02
Blackfeet (1)	6	0.05
Cherokee (8)	31	0.27

Notes: 1. Figures in the "Number" column do not add up to the total population due to: a) Ancestry/Race overlap — e.g. persons can report being both White and Irish, b) persons of Hispanic origin can report being any race, c) persons reporting two ancestries are counted in both categories. 2. Numbers in parentheses indicate the number of persons reporting this ancestry/race alone, not in combination with any other ancestry/race. 3. Refer to the Explanation of Data in the front of the book for more detailed information.

Ancestry/Race	Number	%
Chippewa	1	0.01
Choctaw	1	0.01
Creek (1)	1	0.01
Iroquois (1)	3	0.03
Latin American Indians (2)	4	0.04
Lumbee (2)	3	0.03
Seminole (1)	1	0.01
Sioux	3	0.03
All other tribes (4)	8	0.07
American Indian tribes, not spec.	6	0.05
Asian:	722	6.37
Bangladeshi (5)	5	0.04
Cambodian (2)	2	0.02
Chinese, ex. Taiwanese (58)	67	0.59
Filipino (87)	105	0.93
Indian (194)	204	1.80
Indonesian (2)	5	0.04
Japanese (24)	39	0.34
Korean (71)	81	0.71
Laotian (23)	29	0.26
Pakistani (42)	49	0.43
Sri Lankan (2)	2	0.02
Thai (2)	8	0.07
Vietnamese (52)	62	0.55
Other Asian, specified (4)	7	0.06
Other Asian, not specified (41)	57	0.50
Austrian	6	0.05
Belgian	18	0.16
British	39	0.34
Canadian	16	0.14
Croatian	13	0.11
Czech	37	0.32
Czechoslovakian	11	0.10
Danish	25	0.22
Dutch	101	0.89
English	693	6.08
European	119	1.04
Finnish	8	0.07
French, except Basque	293	2.57
French Canadian	123	1.08
German	1,480	12.98
Greek	53	0.46
Hawaii Native/Pacific Islander:	31	0.27
Micronesian:	3	0.03
Guamanian/Chamorro	3	0.03
Polynesian: (4)	14	0.12
Native Hawaiian (4)	12	0.11
Samoan	2	0.02
Other Pac. Isl., not spec. (5)	14	0.12
Hispanic or Latino:	1,817	16.03
Central American:	657	5.80
Guatemalan	175	1.54
Honduran	44	0.39
Nicaraguan	19	0.17
Panamanian	11	0.10
Salvadoran	398	3.51
Other Central American	10	0.09
Cuban	10	0.09
Dominican Republic	18	0.16
Mexican	522	4.60
Puerto Rican	74	0.65
South American:	93	0.82
Bolivian	20	0.18
Chilean	2	0.02
Colombian	12	0.11
Ecuadorian	3	0.03
Peruvian	40	0.35
Uruguayan	2	0.02
Venezuelan	4	0.04
Other South American	10	0.09
Other Hispanic or Latino	443	3.91
Hungarian	59	0.52
Iranian	71	0.62
Irish	1,177	10.33
Italian	709	6.22
Latvian	9	0.08
Lithuanian	59	0.52
Norwegian	32	0.28
Polish	274	2.40
Portuguese	25	0.22
Romanian	5	0.04
Russian	25	0.22
Scotch-Irish	183	1.61
Scottish	165	1.45
Slovak	3	0.03
Slovene	18	0.16
Swedish	54	0.47
Swiss	17	0.15
Ukrainian	49	0.43
United States or American	886	7.77
Welsh	80	0.70
West Indian, excl. Hispanic:	99	0.87
British West Indian	8	0.07
Haitian	29	0.25
Jamaican	62	0.54
White:	7,540	66.51
Not Hispanic (6,444)	6,650	58.66
Hispanic (749)	890	7.85

Burke

Place Type: Census Designated Place
County: Fairfax
Population: 57,737

Ancestry/Race	Number	%
Acadian/Cajun	7	0.01
Afghan	562	0.97
African American/Black:	3,256	5.64
Not Hispanic (2,856)	3,153	5.46
Hispanic (54)	103	0.18
African, sub-Saharan:	598	1.04
African	102	0.18
Ethiopian	130	0.23
Ghanian	167	0.29
Liberian	24	0.04
Nigerian	52	0.09
Senegalese	10	0.02
Somalian	63	0.11
South African	5	0.01
Ugandan	38	0.07
Other sub-Saharan African	7	0.01
Am. Ind. or Alaska Nat., not spec.	110	0.19
Alsatian	11	0.02
American Indian tribes, specified:	192	0.33
Apache (1)	4	0.01
Blackfeet	3	0.01
Cherokee (19)	65	0.11
Chickasaw (2)	3	0.01
Chippewa (1)	6	0.01
Choctaw (4)	8	0.01
Comanche (6)	6	0.01
Cree (1)	3	0.01
Creek (4)	7	0.01
Iroquois (1)	4	0.01
Latin American Indians (7)	33	0.06
Lumbee	1	0.00
Navajo (2)	3	0.01
Osage (1)	2	0.00
Pueblo (1)	2	0.00
Seminole (1)	2	0.00
Sioux (6)	9	0.02
Yuman (3)	3	0.01
All other tribes (17)	28	0.05
American Indian tribes, not spec.	17	0.03
Arab:	974	1.69
Arab/Arabic	113	0.20
Egyptian	162	0.28
Iraqi	51	0.09
Jordanian	17	0.03
Lebanese	298	0.52
Moroccan	24	0.04
Palestinian	169	0.29
Syrian	36	0.06
Other Arab	104	0.18
Armenian	48	0.08
Asian:	9,501	16.46
Bangladeshi (30)	32	0.06
Cambodian (30)	42	0.07
Chinese, ex. Taiwanese (932)	1,071	1.85
Filipino (864)	1,021	1.77
Hmong	4	0.01
Indian (1,448)	1,582	2.74
Indonesian (55)	56	0.10
Japanese (102)	187	0.32
Korean (3,229)	3,383	5.86
Laotian (25)	28	0.05
Malaysian	5	0.01
Pakistani (272)	338	0.59
Taiwanese (28)	37	0.06
Thai (69)	85	0.15
Vietnamese (1,138)	1,213	2.10
Other Asian, specified (22)	24	0.04
Other Asian, not specified (125)	393	0.68
Assyrian/Chaldean/Syriac	54	0.09
Australian	146	0.25
Austrian	257	0.45
Basque	8	0.01
Belgian	65	0.11
Brazilian	37	0.06
British	584	1.01
Canadian	131	0.23
Celtic	80	0.14
Croatian	158	0.27
Cypriot	9	0.02
Czech	236	0.41
Czechoslovakian	114	0.20
Danish	405	0.70
Dutch	572	0.99
Eastern European	115	0.20
English	7,072	12.27
Estonian	8	0.01
European	1,059	1.84
Finnish	135	0.23
French, except Basque	1,573	2.73
French Canadian	355	0.62
German	9,255	16.05
Greek	396	0.69
Guyanese	6	0.01
Hawaii Native/Pacific Islander:	126	0.22
Melanesian: (1)	1	0.00
Fijian (1)	1	0.00
Micronesian: (11)	22	0.04
Guamanian/Chamorro (10)	19	0.03
Other Micronesian (1)	3	0.01
Polynesian: (29)	68	0.12
Native Hawaiian (19)	52	0.09
Samoan (8)	8	0.01
Tongan (1)	1	0.00
Other Polynesian (1)	7	0.01
Other Pac. Isl., not spec. (3)	35	0.06
Hispanic or Latino:	4,291	7.43
Central American:	705	1.22
Costa Rican	15	0.03
Guatemalan	112	0.19
Honduran	48	0.08
Nicaraguan	49	0.08
Panamanian	45	0.08
Salvadoran	402	0.70
Other Central American	34	0.06
Cuban	138	0.24
Dominican Republic	21	0.04
Mexican	429	0.74
Puerto Rican	358	0.62
South American:	1,264	2.19
Argentinean	63	0.11
Bolivian	283	0.49
Chilean	71	0.12
Colombian	151	0.26
Ecuadorian	59	0.10
Paraguayan	6	0.01
Peruvian	468	0.81
Uruguayan	13	0.02
Venezuelan	51	0.09
Other South American	99	0.17
Other Hispanic or Latino	1,376	2.38
Hungarian	339	0.59
Icelander	26	0.05
Iranian	378	0.66
Irish	7,637	13.25

Notes: 1. Figures in the "Number" column do not add up to the total population due to: a) Ancestry/Race overlap — e.g. persons can report being both White and Irish, b) persons of Hispanic origin can report being any race, c) persons reporting two ancestries are counted in both categories. 2. Numbers in parentheses indicate the number of persons reporting this ancestry/race alone, not in combination with any other ancestry/race. 3. Refer to the Explanation of Data in the front of the book for more detailed information.

Italian	3,814	6.62
Latvian	36	0.06
Lithuanian	252	0.44
Luxemburger	6	0.01
Northern European	82	0.14
Norwegian	693	1.20
Pennsylvania German	17	0.03
Polish	2,083	3.61
Portuguese	235	0.41
Romanian	19	0.03
Russian	845	1.47
Scandinavian	83	0.14
Scotch-Irish	1,347	2.34
Scottish	1,862	3.23
Serbian	25	0.04
Slavic	23	0.04
Slovak	404	0.70
Slovene	30	0.05
Soviet Union	10	0.02
Swedish	873	1.51
Swiss	215	0.37
Turkish	73	0.13
Ukrainian	255	0.44
United States or American	2,627	4.56
Welsh	582	1.01
West Indian, excl. Hispanic:	83	0.14
Bermudan	27	0.05
Haitian	6	0.01
Jamaican	25	0.04
Trinidadian and Tobagonian	8	0.01
West Indian	17	0.03
White:	44,553	77.17
Not Hispanic (40,354)	41,636	72.11
Hispanic (2,582)	2,917	5.05
Yugoslavian	13	0.02

Cave Spring

Place Type: Census Designated Place
County: Roanoke
Population: 24,941

Ancestry/Race	Number	%
African American/Black:	669	2.68
Not Hispanic (597)	660	2.65
Hispanic (8)	9	0.04
African, sub-Saharan:	150	0.60
Nigerian	11	0.04
South African	139	0.56
Am. Ind. or Alaska Nat., not spec.	40	0.16
Albanian	26	0.10
American Indian tribes, specified:	54	0.22
Blackfeet (2)	2	0.01
Cherokee (4)	26	0.10
Cheyenne (1)	1	0.00
Chippewa	1	0.00
Creek	1	0.00
Delaware	1	0.00
Iroquois (2)	2	0.01
Latin American Indians	8	0.03
Navajo	1	0.00
Seminole	2	0.01
Shoshone	1	0.00
Sioux	1	0.00
All other tribes (5)	7	0.03
American Indian tribes, not spec.	6	0.02
Arab:	259	1.04
Arab/Arabic	15	0.06
Egyptian	29	0.12
Jordanian	9	0.04
Lebanese	169	0.68
Palestinian	9	0.04
Syrian	9	0.04
Other Arab	19	0.08
Armenian	21	0.08
Asian:	822	3.30
Cambodian (1)	1	0.00
Chinese, ex. Taiwanese (137)	149	0.60
Filipino (68)	84	0.34
Indian (287)	298	1.19
Indonesian (2)	2	0.01
Japanese (47)	58	0.23
Korean (106)	120	0.48
Sri Lankan (1)	1	0.00
Taiwanese	5	0.02
Thai (3)	5	0.02
Vietnamese (68)	74	0.30
Other Asian, specified	3	0.01
Other Asian, not specified (7)	22	0.09
Austrian	106	0.43
Basque	9	0.04
Belgian	26	0.10
Brazilian	44	0.18
British	226	0.91
Canadian	55	0.22
Celtic	20	0.08
Czech	117	0.47
Czechoslovakian	67	0.27
Danish	45	0.18
Dutch	287	1.15
Eastern European	16	0.06
English	4,552	18.25
European	416	1.67
Finnish	40	0.16
French, except Basque	619	2.48
French Canadian	80	0.32
German	4,286	17.19
Greek	55	0.22
Hawaii Native/Pacific Islander:	9	0.04
Micronesian: (3)	3	0.01
Guamanian/Chamorro (3)	3	0.01
Polynesian: (2)	2	0.01
Native Hawaiian (1)	1	0.00
Samoan (1)	1	0.00
Other Pac. Isl., specified	2	0.01
Other Pac. Isl., not spec. (1)	2	0.01
Hispanic or Latino:	376	1.51
Central American:	21	0.08
Costa Rican	4	0.02
Guatemalan	5	0.02
Honduran	9	0.04
Panamanian	1	0.00
Salvadoran	2	0.01
Cuban	25	0.10
Dominican Republic	5	0.02
Mexican	134	0.54
Puerto Rican	63	0.25
South American:	38	0.15
Argentinean	5	0.02
Bolivian	2	0.01
Colombian	17	0.07
Ecuadorian	1	0.00
Peruvian	4	0.02
Venezuelan	8	0.03
Other South American	1	0.00
Other Hispanic or Latino	90	0.36
Hungarian	91	0.36
Iranian	79	0.32
Irish	3,119	12.51
Italian	1,092	4.38
Lithuanian	23	0.09
New Zealander	10	0.04
Northern European	20	0.08
Norwegian	142	0.57
Pennsylvania German	18	0.07
Polish	404	1.62
Portuguese	6	0.02
Russian	127	0.51
Scandinavian	33	0.13
Scotch-Irish	965	3.87
Scottish	1,138	4.56
Slavic	8	0.03
Slovak	31	0.12
Swedish	186	0.75
Swiss	61	0.24
Ukrainian	57	0.23
United States or American	3,481	13.96
Welsh	221	0.89
West Indian, excl. Hispanic:	92	0.37
Bahamian	11	0.04
Jamaican	35	0.14
Trinidadian and Tobagonian	46	0.18
White:	23,435	93.96
Not Hispanic (22,957)	23,180	92.94
Hispanic (229)	255	1.02
Yugoslavian	32	0.13

Centreville

Place Type: Census Designated Place
County: Fairfax
Population: 48,661

Ancestry/Race	Number	%
Afghan	366	0.75
African American/Black:	4,711	9.68
Not Hispanic (4,231)	4,582	9.42
Hispanic (91)	129	0.27
African, sub-Saharan:	539	1.11
African	210	0.43
Ethiopian	77	0.16
Ghanian	82	0.17
Liberian	6	0.01
Nigerian	62	0.13
Sierra Leonean	9	0.02
Somalian	29	0.06
South African	8	0.02
Sudanese	48	0.10
Ugandan	8	0.02
Alaska Native tribes, specified:	5	0.01
Alaska Athabascan (1)	1	0.00
Tlingit-Haida	4	0.01
Am. Ind. or Alaska Nat., not spec.	111	0.23
Albanian	26	0.05
American Indian tribes, specified:	206	0.42
Apache	5	0.01
Blackfeet	3	0.01
Cherokee (20)	74	0.15
Chickasaw (4)	7	0.01
Chippewa (6)	7	0.01
Choctaw (8)	11	0.02
Comanche (3)	3	0.01
Cree	2	0.00
Creek (2)	2	0.00
Delaware (1)	1	0.00
Iroquois (5)	12	0.02
Kiowa (4)	4	0.01
Latin American Indians (18)	24	0.05
Lumbee (1)	9	0.02
Menominee	1	0.00
Navajo (1)	1	0.00
Osage	1	0.00
Paiute (1)	1	0.00
Pueblo (2)	3	0.01
Puget Sound Salish	4	0.01
Seminole (2)	2	0.00
Sioux (3)	5	0.01
Tohono O'Odham (2)	2	0.00
All other tribes (12)	22	0.05
American Indian tribes, not spec.	13	0.03
Arab:	789	1.63
Arab/Arabic	192	0.40
Egyptian	107	0.22
Iraqi	42	0.09
Jordanian	45	0.09
Lebanese	146	0.30
Moroccan	83	0.17
Palestinian	99	0.20
Syrian	42	0.09
Other Arab	33	0.07
Armenian	61	0.13
Asian:	7,735	15.90
Bangladeshi (34)	36	0.07
Cambodian (70)	74	0.15
Chinese, ex. Taiwanese (956)	1,047	2.15
Filipino (652)	778	1.60
Indian (1,707)	1,837	3.78
Indonesian (7)	9	0.02
Japanese (94)	156	0.32
Korean (2,028)	2,152	4.42

Notes: 1. Figures in the "Number" column do not add up to the total population due to: a) Ancestry/Race overlap — e.g. persons can report being both White and Irish, b) persons of Hispanic origin can report being any race, c) persons reporting two ancestries are counted in both categories. 2. Numbers in parentheses indicate the number of persons reporting this ancestry/race alone, not in combination with any other ancestry/race. 3. Refer to the Explanation of Data in the front of the book for more detailed information.

Laotian (19)	21	0.04
Malaysian (2)	8	0.02
Pakistani (262)	324	0.67
Sri Lankan (6)	10	0.02
Taiwanese (23)	33	0.07
Thai (68)	80	0.16
Vietnamese (820)	888	1.82
Other Asian, specified (14)	21	0.04
Other Asian, not specified (87)	261	0.54
Australian	50	0.10
Austrian	230	0.47
Basque	12	0.02
Belgian	48	0.10
Brazilian	54	0.11
British	444	0.91
Canadian	114	0.23
Croatian	37	0.08
Czech	97	0.20
Czechoslovakian	110	0.23
Danish	103	0.21
Dutch	585	1.21
Eastern European	68	0.14
English	5,012	10.33
Estonian	6	0.01
European	559	1.15
Finnish	49	0.10
French, except Basque	1,197	2.47
French Canadian	230	0.47
German	7,454	15.36
German Russian	9	0.02
Greek	266	0.55
Guyanese	19	0.04
Hawaii Native/Pacific Islander:	89	0.18
Micronesian: (12)	16	0.03
Guamanian/Chamorro (11)	15	0.03
Other Micronesian (1)	1	0.00
Polynesian: (3)	22	0.05
Native Hawaiian (2)	17	0.03
Samoan	4	0.01
Other Polynesian (1)	1	0.00
Other Pac. Isl., specified	1	0.00
Other Pac. Isl., not spec. (10)	50	0.10
Hispanic or Latino:	4,461	9.17
Central American:	1,069	2.20
Costa Rican	16	0.03
Guatemalan	372	0.76
Honduran	64	0.13
Nicaraguan	60	0.12
Panamanian	27	0.06
Salvadoran	479	0.98
Other Central American	51	0.10
Cuban	119	0.24
Dominican Republic	63	0.13
Mexican	446	0.92
Puerto Rican	411	0.84
South American:	986	2.03
Argentinean	22	0.05
Bolivian	164	0.34
Chilean	36	0.07
Colombian	174	0.36
Ecuadorian	56	0.12
Paraguayan	4	0.01
Peruvian	419	0.86
Uruguayan	5	0.01
Venezuelan	47	0.10
Other South American	59	0.12
Other Hispanic or Latino	1,367	2.81
Hungarian	176	0.36
Icelander	43	0.09
Iranian	259	0.53
Irish	6,999	14.42
Israeli	6	0.01
Italian	3,306	6.81
Lithuanian	144	0.30
Northern European	18	0.04
Norwegian	385	0.79
Pennsylvania German	11	0.02
Polish	1,322	2.72
Portuguese	165	0.34
Romanian	32	0.07
Russian	399	0.82
Scandinavian	79	0.16
Scotch-Irish	888	1.83
Scottish	1,092	2.25
Serbian	24	0.05
Slavic	29	0.06
Slovak	160	0.33
Slovene	41	0.08
Swedish	461	0.95
Swiss	161	0.33
Turkish	55	0.11
Ukrainian	117	0.24
United States or American	2,351	4.84
Welsh	407	0.84
West Indian, excl. Hispanic:	208	0.43
Dutch West Indian	6	0.01
Haitian	38	0.08
Jamaican	71	0.15
Trinidadian and Tobagonian	14	0.03
West Indian	79	0.16
White:	35,181	72.30
Not Hispanic (31,539)	32,578	66.95
Hispanic (2,277)	2,603	5.35
Yugoslavian	17	0.04

Chantilly

Place Type: Census Designated Place
County: Fairfax
Population: 41,041

Ancestry/Race	Number	%
Afghan	188	0.46
African American/Black:	2,270	5.53
Not Hispanic (2,008)	2,213	5.39
Hispanic (38)	57	0.14
African, sub-Saharan:	231	0.56
African	143	0.35
Ethiopian	16	0.04
Ghanian	16	0.04
Nigerian	7	0.02
South African	26	0.06
Sudanese	12	0.03
Ugandan	11	0.03
Alaska Native tribes, specified:	1	0.00
Aleut (1)	1	0.00
Am. Ind. or Alaska Nat., not spec.	102	0.25
Alsatian	13	0.03
American Indian tribes, specified:	155	0.38
Apache (1)	4	0.01
Blackfeet	2	0.00
Cherokee (11)	45	0.11
Cheyenne	1	0.00
Chickasaw (1)	2	0.00
Chippewa (1)	1	0.00
Choctaw (5)	14	0.03
Creek (1)	1	0.00
Delaware (2)	2	0.00
Iroquois (4)	11	0.03
Latin American Indians (4)	10	0.02
Lumbee	1	0.00
Menominee	1	0.00
Navajo	4	0.01
Osage (2)	2	0.00
Ottawa (1)	1	0.00
Potawatomi (2)	3	0.01
Puget Sound Salish (1)	1	0.00
Seminole (1)	3	0.01
Shoshone (1)	1	0.00
Sioux (7)	7	0.02
All other tribes (24)	38	0.09
American Indian tribes, not spec.	8	0.02
Arab:	614	1.49
Arab/Arabic	168	0.41
Egyptian	39	0.09
Iraqi	44	0.11
Jordanian	82	0.20
Lebanese	170	0.41
Moroccan	7	0.02
Palestinian	89	0.22
Syrian	8	0.02
Other Arab	7	0.02
Armenian	69	0.17
Asian:	7,410	18.06
Bangladeshi (33)	33	0.08
Cambodian (83)	90	0.22
Chinese, ex. Taiwanese (1,070)	1,182	2.88
Filipino (581)	674	1.64
Indian (1,705)	1,806	4.40
Indonesian (10)	15	0.04
Japanese (117)	190	0.46
Korean (1,289)	1,348	3.28
Laotian (74)	80	0.19
Malaysian	5	0.01
Pakistani (198)	237	0.58
Sri Lankan (16)	20	0.05
Taiwanese (67)	84	0.20
Thai (52)	60	0.15
Vietnamese (1,243)	1,325	3.23
Other Asian, specified (17)	18	0.04
Other Asian, not specified (59)	243	0.59
Australian	76	0.18
Austrian	266	0.65
Basque	6	0.01
Belgian	172	0.42
Brazilian	24	0.06
British	299	0.73
Bulgarian	51	0.12
Canadian	156	0.38
Celtic	22	0.05
Croatian	95	0.23
Czech	130	0.32
Czechoslovakian	111	0.27
Danish	134	0.33
Dutch	644	1.57
Eastern European	73	0.18
English	4,429	10.78
European	558	1.36
Finnish	95	0.23
French, except Basque	960	2.34
French Canadian	335	0.82
German	5,786	14.08
Greek	366	0.89
Hawaii Native/Pacific Islander:	64	0.16
Micronesian: (13)	15	0.04
Guamanian/Chamorro (13)	15	0.04
Polynesian: (8)	22	0.05
Native Hawaiian (3)	13	0.03
Samoan (5)	9	0.02
Other Pac. Isl., not spec. (3)	27	0.07
Hispanic or Latino:	2,818	6.87
Central American:	801	1.95
Costa Rican	19	0.05
Guatemalan	252	0.61
Honduran	38	0.09
Nicaraguan	49	0.12
Panamanian	26	0.06
Salvadoran	373	0.91
Other Central American	44	0.11
Cuban	117	0.29
Dominican Republic	28	0.07
Mexican	385	0.94
Puerto Rican	235	0.57
South American:	476	1.16
Argentinean	23	0.06
Bolivian	88	0.21
Chilean	19	0.05
Colombian	91	0.22
Ecuadorian	31	0.08
Paraguayan	4	0.01
Peruvian	158	0.38
Uruguayan	4	0.01
Venezuelan	36	0.09
Other South American	22	0.05
Other Hispanic or Latino	776	1.89
Hungarian	345	0.84
Iranian	574	1.40
Irish	5,750	13.99
Italian	2,773	6.75
Latvian	43	0.10

Notes: 1. Figures in the "Number" column do not add up to the total population due to: a) Ancestry/Race overlap — e.g. persons can report being both White and Irish, b) persons of Hispanic origin can report being any race, c) persons reporting two ancestries are counted in both categories. 2. Numbers in parentheses indicate the number of persons reporting this ancestry/race alone, not in combination with any other ancestry/race. 3. Refer to the Explanation of Data in the front of the book for more detailed information.

Lithuanian	186	0.45
Luxemburger	14	0.03
Maltese	25	0.06
New Zealander	8	0.02
Northern European	24	0.06
Norwegian	474	1.15
Pennsylvania German	9	0.02
Polish	1,341	3.26
Portuguese	139	0.34
Romanian	85	0.21
Russian	550	1.34
Scandinavian	86	0.21
Scotch-Irish	920	2.24
Scottish	917	2.23
Serbian	35	0.09
Slavic	21	0.05
Slovak	246	0.60
Slovene	34	0.08
Swedish	518	1.26
Swiss	206	0.50
Turkish	37	0.09
Ukrainian	187	0.46
United States or American	2,231	5.43
Welsh	454	1.10
West Indian, excl. Hispanic:	187	0.46
Barbadian	30	0.07
British West Indian	5	0.01
Haitian	8	0.02
Jamaican	84	0.20
Trinidadian and Tobagonian	35	0.09
West Indian	25	0.06
White:	31,132	75.86
Not Hispanic (28,372)	29,195	71.14
Hispanic (1,726)	1,937	4.72
Yugoslavian	31	0.08

Charlottesville

Place Type: Independent City
County: Charlottesville Independent City
Population: 45,049

Ancestry/Race	Number	%
Afghan	19	0.04
African American/Black:	10,441	23.18
Not Hispanic (9,916)	10,314	22.90
Hispanic (93)	127	0.28
African, sub-Saharan:	504	1.12
African	270	0.60
Ethiopian	21	0.05
Ghanian	53	0.12
Kenyan	14	0.03
Liberian	10	0.02
Nigerian	12	0.03
Sierra Leonean	10	0.02
Somalian	21	0.05
South African	35	0.08
Sudanese	11	0.02
Ugandan	11	0.02
Other sub-Saharan African	36	0.08
Alaska Native tribes, specified:	4	0.01
Eskimo	4	0.01
Am. Ind. or Alaska Nat., not spec.	95	0.21
Albanian	75	0.17
Alsatian	7	0.02
American Indian tribes, specified:	124	0.28
Apache	1	0.00
Blackfeet	4	0.01
Cherokee (7)	56	0.12
Cheyenne (2)	2	0.00
Chippewa (1)	1	0.00
Choctaw (7)	9	0.02
Iroquois (4)	5	0.01
Latin American Indians (1)	4	0.01
Lumbee	1	0.00
Navajo	1	0.00
Potawatomi (1)	2	0.00
Seminole (1)	3	0.01
Shoshone (1)	2	0.00
Sioux (1)	5	0.01
Yaqui (1)	1	0.00
All other tribes (7)	27	0.06
American Indian tribes, not spec.	11	0.02
Arab:	191	0.42
Arab/Arabic	30	0.07
Egyptian	15	0.03
Lebanese	72	0.16
Moroccan	40	0.09
Palestinian	19	0.04
Syrian	15	0.03
Armenian	11	0.02
Asian:	2,637	5.85
Bangladeshi (6)	6	0.01
Cambodian (19)	22	0.05
Chinese, ex. Taiwanese (631)	716	1.59
Filipino (223)	275	0.61
Indian (561)	614	1.36
Indonesian (5)	6	0.01
Japanese (76)	130	0.29
Korean (332)	398	0.88
Laotian (4)	5	0.01
Malaysian (4)	6	0.01
Pakistani (32)	46	0.10
Sri Lankan (12)	13	0.03
Taiwanese (38)	50	0.11
Thai (31)	47	0.10
Vietnamese (178)	209	0.46
Other Asian, specified (12)	18	0.04
Other Asian, not specified (31)	76	0.17
Australian	33	0.07
Austrian	145	0.32
Belgian	12	0.03
Brazilian	20	0.04
British	503	1.12
Canadian	89	0.20
Celtic	26	0.06
Croatian	118	0.26
Cypriot	26	0.06
Czech	102	0.23
Czechoslovakian	66	0.15
Danish	124	0.28
Dutch	587	1.30
Eastern European	130	0.29
English	5,412	12.01
Estonian	20	0.04
European	867	1.92
Finnish	49	0.11
French, except Basque	1,003	2.23
French Canadian	283	0.63
German	5,408	12.00
Greek	241	0.53
Guyanese	11	0.02
Hawaii Native/Pacific Islander:	72	0.16
Micronesian: (4)	11	0.02
Guamanian/Chamorro (3)	10	0.02
Other Micronesian (1)	1	0.00
Polynesian: (9)	23	0.05
Native Hawaiian (6)	15	0.03
Samoan (3)	8	0.02
Other Pac. Isl., specified	5	0.01
Other Pac. Isl., not spec. (2)	33	0.07
Hispanic or Latino:	1,102	2.45
Central American:	126	0.28
Costa Rican	11	0.02
Guatemalan	6	0.01
Honduran	22	0.05
Nicaraguan	12	0.03
Panamanian	16	0.04
Salvadoran	58	0.13
Other Central American	1	0.00
Cuban	68	0.15
Dominican Republic	17	0.04
Mexican	383	0.85
Puerto Rican	144	0.32
South American:	149	0.33
Argentinean	9	0.02
Bolivian	17	0.04
Chilean	9	0.02
Colombian	43	0.10
Ecuadorian	20	0.04
Paraguayan	3	0.01
Peruvian	28	0.06
Uruguayan	3	0.01
Venezuelan	12	0.03
Other South American	5	0.01
Other Hispanic or Latino	215	0.48
Hungarian	229	0.51
Icelander	10	0.02
Iranian	35	0.08
Irish	4,353	9.66
Israeli	42	0.09
Italian	1,797	3.99
Latvian	22	0.05
Lithuanian	57	0.13
Luxemburger	5	0.01
New Zealander	11	0.02
Northern European	90	0.20
Norwegian	345	0.77
Polish	1,002	2.22
Portuguese	76	0.17
Russian	557	1.24
Scandinavian	54	0.12
Scotch-Irish	1,209	2.68
Scottish	1,579	3.51
Serbian	44	0.10
Slavic	21	0.05
Slovak	90	0.20
Slovene	5	0.01
Swedish	435	0.97
Swiss	173	0.38
Turkish	77	0.17
Ukrainian	91	0.20
United States or American	3,316	7.36
Welsh	498	1.11
West Indian, excl. Hispanic:	136	0.30
Bahamian	5	0.01
Barbadian	15	0.03
Bermudan	10	0.02
Haitian	19	0.04
Jamaican	49	0.11
Trinidadian and Tobagonian	27	0.06
West Indian	11	0.02
White:	32,096	71.25
Not Hispanic (30,825)	31,489	69.90
Hispanic (512)	607	1.35
Yugoslavian	50	0.11

Chesapeake

Place Type: Independent City
County: Chesapeake Independent City
Population: 199,184

Ancestry/Race	Number	%
Acadian/Cajun	29	0.01
African American/Black:	58,183	29.21
Not Hispanic (56,442)	57,649	28.94
Hispanic (381)	534	0.27
African, sub-Saharan:	944	0.47
African	854	0.43
Cape Verdean	7	0.00
Ethiopian	14	0.01
Ghanian	22	0.01
Nigerian	23	0.01
Other sub-Saharan African	24	0.01
Alaska Native tribes, specified:	8	0.00
Aleut (4)	4	0.00
Tlingit-Haida (3)	3	0.00
All other tribes (1)	1	0.00
Alaska Native tribes, not specified	5	0.00
Am. Ind. or Alaska Nat., not spec.	537	0.27
Albanian	39	0.02
American Indian tribes, specified:	1,125	0.56
Apache (12)	28	0.01
Blackfeet (19)	48	0.02
Cherokee (176)	533	0.27
Cheyenne (2)	4	0.00
Chickasaw (1)	3	0.00
Chippewa (23)	36	0.02
Choctaw (18)	36	0.02

Notes: 1. Figures in the "Number" column do not add up to the total population due to: a) Ancestry/Race overlap — e.g. persons can report being both White and Irish, b) persons of Hispanic origin can report being any race, c) persons reporting two ancestries are counted in both categories. 2. Numbers in parentheses indicate the number of persons reporting this ancestry/race alone, not in combination with any other ancestry/race. 3. Refer to the Explanation of Data in the front of the book for more detailed information.

Ancestry/Race	Number	%
Comanche (2)	9	0.00
Cree (1)	1	0.00
Creek (4)	12	0.01
Crow	4	0.00
Delaware (10)	18	0.01
Iroquois (20)	37	0.02
Kiowa (5)	6	0.00
Latin American Indians (22)	41	0.02
Lumbee (42)	57	0.03
Menominee (3)	3	0.00
Navajo (8)	10	0.01
Osage (5)	8	0.00
Ottawa (1)	1	0.00
Potawatomi (5)	5	0.00
Pueblo (5)	8	0.00
Seminole	11	0.01
Shoshone (3)	3	0.00
Sioux (26)	41	0.02
Ute	3	0.00
All other tribes (97)	159	0.08
American Indian tribes, not spec.	85	0.04
Arab:	364	0.18
Arab/Arabic	34	0.02
Egyptian	3	0.00
Lebanese	232	0.12
Palestinian	10	0.01
Syrian	60	0.03
Other Arab	25	0.01
Armenian	83	0.04
Asian:	4,813	2.42
Bangladeshi (2)	2	0.00
Cambodian (9)	9	0.00
Chinese, ex. Taiwanese (359)	445	0.22
Filipino (2,029)	2,637	1.32
Indian (374)	456	0.23
Indonesian (4)	8	0.00
Japanese (167)	305	0.15
Korean (258)	339	0.17
Laotian (16)	16	0.01
Malaysian	10	0.01
Pakistani (22)	28	0.01
Sri Lankan (2)	2	0.00
Taiwanese (21)	25	0.01
Thai (35)	49	0.02
Vietnamese (240)	271	0.14
Other Asian, specified (5)	25	0.01
Other Asian, not specified (79)	186	0.09
Australian	14	0.01
Austrian	348	0.17
Basque	11	0.01
Belgian	110	0.06
Brazilian	35	0.02
British	1,186	0.60
Bulgarian	11	0.01
Canadian	500	0.25
Carpatho Rusyn	30	0.02
Celtic	77	0.04
Croatian	69	0.03
Czech	396	0.20
Czechoslovakian	207	0.10
Danish	488	0.24
Dutch	2,283	1.15
Eastern European	96	0.05
English	20,988	10.54
Estonian	18	0.01
European	1,274	0.64
Finnish	128	0.06
French, except Basque	4,598	2.31
French Canadian	1,471	0.74
German	20,453	10.27
Greek	504	0.25
Guyanese	33	0.02
Hawaii Native/Pacific Islander:	296	0.15
Melanesian:	1	0.00
Fijian	1	0.00
Micronesian: (35)	63	0.03
Guamanian/Chamorro (34)	60	0.03
Other Micronesian (1)	3	0.00
Polynesian: (46)	123	0.06
Native Hawaiian (29)	94	0.05
Samoan (16)	28	0.01
Other Polynesian (1)	1	0.00
Other Pac. Isl., specified	13	0.01
Other Pac. Isl., not spec. (18)	96	0.05
Hispanic or Latino:	4,076	2.05
Central American:	222	0.11
Costa Rican	12	0.01
Guatemalan	37	0.02
Honduran	25	0.01
Nicaraguan	9	0.00
Panamanian	105	0.05
Salvadoran	14	0.01
Other Central American	20	0.01
Cuban	203	0.10
Dominican Republic	60	0.03
Mexican	1,202	0.60
Puerto Rican	1,276	0.64
South American:	180	0.09
Argentinean	11	0.01
Bolivian	7	0.00
Chilean	13	0.01
Colombian	70	0.04
Ecuadorian	13	0.01
Paraguayan	1	0.00
Peruvian	37	0.02
Uruguayan	2	0.00
Venezuelan	10	0.01
Other South American	16	0.01
Other Hispanic or Latino	933	0.47
Hungarian	599	0.30
Icelander	61	0.03
Iranian	100	0.05
Irish	18,765	9.42
Israeli	6	0.00
Italian	8,231	4.13
Latvian	43	0.02
Lithuanian	238	0.12
Luxemburger	15	0.01
New Zealander	9	0.00
Northern European	104	0.05
Norwegian	1,443	0.72
Pennsylvania German	48	0.02
Polish	3,988	2.00
Portuguese	189	0.09
Romanian	31	0.02
Russian	588	0.30
Scandinavian	125	0.06
Scotch-Irish	3,781	1.90
Scottish	4,133	2.07
Serbian	26	0.01
Slavic	54	0.03
Slovak	411	0.21
Slovene	90	0.05
Swedish	1,720	0.86
Swiss	223	0.11
Turkish	82	0.04
Ukrainian	302	0.15
United States or American	19,360	9.72
Welsh	1,277	0.64
West Indian, excl. Hispanic:	741	0.37
Bahamian	13	0.01
Barbadian	59	0.03
Belizean	7	0.00
Bermudan	19	0.01
British West Indian	21	0.01
Dutch West Indian	31	0.02
Haitian	64	0.03
Jamaican	300	0.15
Trinidadian and Tobagonian	62	0.03
U.S. Virgin Islander	9	0.00
West Indian	156	0.08
White:	135,730	68.14
Not Hispanic (131,200)	133,421	66.98
Hispanic (1,993)	2,309	1.16
Yugoslavian	49	0.02

Chester

Place Type: Census Designated Place
County: Chesterfield
Population: 17,890

Ancestry/Race	Number	%
Acadian/Cajun	16	0.09
African American/Black:	2,511	14.04
Not Hispanic (2,368)	2,461	13.76
Hispanic (35)	50	0.28
African, sub-Saharan:	126	0.71
African	70	0.39
Liberian	7	0.04
Nigerian	44	0.25
Sierra Leonean	5	0.03
Alaska Native tribes, not specified	1	0.01
Am. Ind. or Alaska Nat., not spec.	54	0.30
American Indian tribes, specified:	101	0.56
Apache (1)	2	0.01
Blackfeet	4	0.02
Cherokee (23)	57	0.32
Cheyenne	2	0.01
Chickasaw	3	0.02
Choctaw	5	0.03
Creek	2	0.01
Latin American Indians (1)	1	0.01
Lumbee (3)	3	0.02
Navajo (1)	1	0.01
Seminole	1	0.01
Sioux (1)	1	0.01
All other tribes (17)	19	0.11
American Indian tribes, not spec.	6	0.03
Arab:	21	0.12
Arab/Arabic	9	0.05
Lebanese	6	0.03
Palestinian	6	0.03
Armenian	12	0.07
Asian:	459	2.57
Bangladeshi (5)	5	0.03
Cambodian (17)	17	0.10
Chinese, ex. Taiwanese (37)	47	0.26
Filipino (44)	49	0.27
Indian (80)	87	0.49
Indonesian (1)	1	0.01
Japanese (15)	38	0.21
Korean (150)	164	0.92
Laotian (2)	2	0.01
Pakistani (9)	10	0.06
Taiwanese (4)	4	0.02
Thai (3)	5	0.03
Vietnamese (10)	13	0.07
Other Asian, not specified (9)	17	0.10
Austrian	26	0.15
British	108	0.60
Canadian	17	0.10
Czech	24	0.13
Czechoslovakian	32	0.18
Danish	30	0.17
Dutch	131	0.73
Eastern European	16	0.09
English	2,473	13.84
European	227	1.27
Finnish	17	0.10
French, except Basque	381	2.13
French Canadian	113	0.63
German	2,189	12.25
Greek	81	0.45
Guyanese	8	0.04
Hawaii Native/Pacific Islander:	34	0.19
Micronesian: (6)	8	0.04
Guamanian/Chamorro (6)	8	0.04
Polynesian: (10)	21	0.12
Native Hawaiian (7)	17	0.10
Samoan (3)	4	0.02
Other Pac. Isl., not spec. (3)	5	0.03
Hispanic or Latino:	547	3.06
Central American:	48	0.27
Costa Rican	1	0.01
Guatemalan	2	0.01

Notes: 1. Figures in the "Number" column do not add up to the total population due to: a) Ancestry/Race overlap — e.g. persons can report being both White and Irish, b) persons of Hispanic origin can report being any race, c) persons reporting two ancestries are counted in both categories. 2. Numbers in parentheses indicate the number of persons reporting this ancestry/race alone, not in combination with any other ancestry/race. 3. Refer to the Explanation of Data in the front of the book for more detailed information.

Honduran	6	0.03
Nicaraguan	2	0.01
Panamanian	8	0.04
Salvadoran	22	0.12
Other Central American	7	0.04
Cuban	18	0.10
Mexican	194	1.08
Puerto Rican	129	0.72
South American:	28	0.16
Colombian	14	0.08
Ecuadorian	9	0.05
Paraguayan	3	0.02
Peruvian	1	0.01
Other South American	1	0.01
Other Hispanic or Latino	130	0.73
Hungarian	31	0.17
Irish	1,801	10.08
Italian	607	3.40
Lithuanian	35	0.20
Norwegian	150	0.84
Pennsylvania German	6	0.03
Polish	340	1.90
Portuguese	18	0.10
Russian	56	0.31
Scandinavian	11	0.06
Scotch-Irish	350	1.96
Scottish	393	2.20
Slovak	41	0.23
Slovene	11	0.06
Swedish	30	0.17
Swiss	21	0.12
Ukrainian	9	0.05
United States or American	2,569	14.38
Welsh	153	0.86
West Indian, excl. Hispanic:	23	0.13
Jamaican	15	0.08
West Indian	8	0.04
White:	14,772	82.57
Not Hispanic (14,242)	14,452	80.78
Hispanic (299)	320	1.79
Yugoslavian	16	0.09

Christiansburg

Place Type: Town
County: Montgomery
Population: 16,947

Ancestry/Race	Number	%
African American/Black:	890	5.25
Not Hispanic (810)	877	5.17
Hispanic (9)	13	0.08
African, sub-Saharan:	90	0.53
African	90	0.53
Alaska Native tribes, specified:	1	0.01
Eskimo (1)	1	0.01
Am. Ind. or Alaska Nat., not spec.	30	0.18
American Indian tribes, specified:	65	0.38
Apache (4)	4	0.02
Blackfeet (2)	6	0.04
Cherokee (14)	44	0.26
Comanche (1)	3	0.02
Iroquois (2)	2	0.01
Navajo	1	0.01
Shoshone	1	0.01
Sioux	2	0.01
All other tribes (2)	2	0.01
American Indian tribes, not spec.	6	0.04
Arab:	25	0.15
Lebanese	25	0.15
Asian:	93	0.55
Chinese, ex. Taiwanese (18)	20	0.12
Filipino (10)	15	0.09
Indian (3)	5	0.03
Japanese (5)	6	0.04
Korean (16)	21	0.12
Malaysian (1)	2	0.01
Pakistani (3)	3	0.02
Taiwanese (1)	2	0.01
Thai	2	0.01
Vietnamese (5)	5	0.03
Other Asian, not specified (8)	12	0.07
Austrian	32	0.19
Belgian	30	0.18
British	58	0.34
Celtic	23	0.14
Croatian	8	0.05
Czech	19	0.11
Danish	24	0.14
Dutch	251	1.48
English	2,363	13.92
European	67	0.39
French, except Basque	225	1.33
French Canadian	47	0.28
German	2,369	13.95
Greek	42	0.25
Hawaii Native/Pacific Islander:	8	0.05
Melanesian: (1)	1	0.01
Other Melanesian (1)	1	0.01
Micronesian: (1)	1	0.01
Guamanian/Chamorro (1)	1	0.01
Polynesian: (1)	6	0.04
Native Hawaiian (1)	5	0.03
Other Polynesian	1	0.01
Hispanic or Latino:	168	0.99
Central American:	6	0.04
Guatemalan	1	0.01
Panamanian	3	0.02
Salvadoran	2	0.01
Cuban	6	0.04
Dominican Republic	1	0.01
Mexican	71	0.42
Puerto Rican	21	0.12
South American:	15	0.09
Bolivian	2	0.01
Chilean	6	0.04
Peruvian	7	0.04
Other Hispanic or Latino	48	0.28
Hungarian	48	0.28
Iranian	17	0.10
Irish	1,769	10.42
Italian	298	1.76
Lithuanian	6	0.04
Norwegian	67	0.39
Polish	214	1.26
Romanian	18	0.11
Russian	7	0.04
Scotch-Irish	600	3.53
Scottish	404	2.38
Slovak	33	0.19
Slovene	9	0.05
Swedish	84	0.49
Swiss	6	0.04
Ukrainian	11	0.06
United States or American	2,768	16.31
Welsh	110	0.65
West Indian, excl. Hispanic:	19	0.11
Barbadian	9	0.05
British West Indian	10	0.06
White:	15,925	93.97
Not Hispanic (15,696)	15,835	93.44
Hispanic (87)	90	0.53

Colonial Heights

Place Type: Independent City
County: Colonial Heights Independent City
Population: 16,897

Ancestry/Race	Number	%
African American/Black:	1,113	6.59
Not Hispanic (1,043)	1,090	6.45
Hispanic (16)	23	0.14
African, sub-Saharan:	100	0.59
African	12	0.07
Ghanian	27	0.16
Sierra Leonean	48	0.28
Other sub-Saharan African	13	0.08
Am. Ind. or Alaska Nat., not spec.	29	0.17
American Indian tribes, specified:	43	0.25
Apache (2)	2	0.01
Blackfeet	3	0.02
Cherokee (12)	23	0.14
Chickasaw	2	0.01
Chippewa (1)	1	0.01
Choctaw	1	0.01
Creek (1)	1	0.01
Iroquois (1)	1	0.01
Latin American Indians (1)	1	0.01
Lumbee (5)	5	0.03
Sioux	1	0.01
All other tribes (1)	2	0.01
American Indian tribes, not spec.	1	0.01
Arab:	86	0.51
Arab/Arabic	4	0.02
Jordanian	5	0.03
Lebanese	44	0.26
Syrian	5	0.03
Other Arab	28	0.17
Asian:	538	3.18
Cambodian (1)	4	0.02
Chinese, ex. Taiwanese (55)	60	0.36
Filipino (29)	34	0.20
Indian (91)	102	0.60
Indonesian (2)	2	0.01
Japanese (21)	39	0.23
Korean (174)	206	1.22
Pakistani (5)	9	0.05
Thai (4)	8	0.05
Vietnamese (60)	60	0.36
Other Asian, specified	1	0.01
Other Asian, not specified (7)	13	0.08
Australian	22	0.13
Austrian	50	0.30
British	93	0.55
Bulgarian	7	0.04
Czech	137	0.81
Czechoslovakian	43	0.25
Danish	19	0.11
Dutch	306	1.81
English	2,974	17.60
Estonian	24	0.14
European	161	0.95
Finnish	14	0.08
French, except Basque	387	2.29
French Canadian	76	0.45
German	2,024	11.98
Greek	13	0.08
Hawaii Native/Pacific Islander:	20	0.12
Micronesian: (7)	8	0.05
Guamanian/Chamorro (7)	8	0.05
Polynesian: (5)	8	0.05
Native Hawaiian (1)	3	0.02
Samoan (4)	4	0.02
Other Polynesian	1	0.01
Other Pac. Isl., specified	1	0.01
Other Pac. Isl., not spec. (2)	3	0.02
Hispanic or Latino:	274	1.62
Central American:	12	0.07
Costa Rican	2	0.01
Guatemalan	3	0.02
Panamanian	4	0.02
Salvadoran	2	0.01
Other Central American	1	0.01
Cuban	8	0.05
Dominican Republic	7	0.04
Mexican	113	0.67
Puerto Rican	67	0.40
South American:	10	0.06
Argentinean	2	0.01
Bolivian	1	0.01
Colombian	4	0.02
Peruvian	1	0.01
Venezuelan	1	0.01
Other South American	1	0.01
Other Hispanic or Latino	57	0.34
Hungarian	79	0.47
Irish	1,705	10.09
Italian	567	3.36
Latvian	17	0.10

Notes: 1. Figures in the "Number" column do not add up to the total population due to: a) Ancestry/Race overlap — e.g. persons can report being both White and Irish, b) persons of Hispanic origin can report being any race, c) persons reporting two ancestries are counted in both categories. 2. Numbers in parentheses indicate the number of persons reporting this ancestry/race alone, not in combination with any other ancestry/race. 3. Refer to the Explanation of Data in the front of the book for more detailed information.

Lithuanian	5	0.03
Macedonian	8	0.05
Norwegian	42	0.25
Polish	207	1.23
Portuguese	26	0.15
Romanian	6	0.04
Russian	43	0.25
Scotch-Irish	408	2.41
Scottish	430	2.54
Slovak	31	0.18
Swedish	42	0.25
Swiss	8	0.05
Ukrainian	34	0.20
United States or American	2,448	14.49
Welsh	169	1.00
West Indian, excl. Hispanic:	45	0.27
British West Indian	7	0.04
Haitian	4	0.02
Jamaican	23	0.14
Trinidadian and Tobagonian	11	0.07
White:	15,201	89.96
Not Hispanic (14,920)	15,054	89.09
Hispanic (132)	147	0.87

Dale City

Place Type: Census Designated Place
County: Prince William
Population: 55,971

Ancestry/Race	Number	%
Afghan	104	0.19
African American/Black:	17,095	30.54
Not Hispanic (15,845)	16,698	29.83
Hispanic (254)	397	0.71
African, sub-Saharan:	1,622	2.89
African	965	1.72
Cape Verdean	18	0.03
Ethiopian	78	0.14
Ghanian	264	0.47
Liberian	66	0.12
Nigerian	22	0.04
Sierra Leonean	37	0.07
Somalian	12	0.02
Sudanese	77	0.14
Other sub-Saharan African	83	0.15
Alaska Native tribes, specified:	5	0.01
Eskimo	4	0.01
Tlingit-Haida (1)	1	0.00
Alaska Native tribes, not specified	3	0.01
Am. Ind. or Alaska Nat., not spec.	218	0.39
American Indian tribes, specified:	434	0.78
Apache (7)	18	0.03
Blackfeet (3)	26	0.05
Cherokee (50)	194	0.35
Chickasaw (1)	1	0.00
Chippewa (1)	3	0.01
Choctaw (8)	19	0.03
Comanche	1	0.00
Cree	5	0.01
Creek (2)	15	0.03
Crow (2)	3	0.01
Iroquois (5)	16	0.03
Latin American Indians (27)	42	0.08
Lumbee (5)	10	0.02
Navajo (4)	7	0.01
Pima (1)	2	0.00
Potawatomi (1)	1	0.00
Pueblo (3)	6	0.01
Seminole (3)	5	0.01
Sioux (6)	18	0.03
Yaqui (1)	4	0.01
All other tribes (24)	38	0.07
American Indian tribes, not spec.	32	0.06
Arab:	260	0.46
Arab/Arabic	67	0.12
Egyptian	16	0.03
Jordanian	5	0.01
Lebanese	31	0.06
Moroccan	63	0.11
Palestinian	64	0.11
Syrian	7	0.01
Other Arab	7	0.01
Armenian	12	0.02
Asian:	3,709	6.63
Bangladeshi (15)	16	0.03
Cambodian (49)	50	0.09
Chinese, ex. Taiwanese (185)	244	0.44
Filipino (638)	864	1.54
Indian (535)	604	1.08
Indonesian (7)	14	0.03
Japanese (113)	211	0.38
Korean (372)	498	0.89
Laotian (82)	88	0.16
Malaysian (1)	2	0.00
Pakistani (318)	422	0.75
Sri Lankan (7)	7	0.01
Taiwanese (4)	4	0.01
Thai (71)	83	0.15
Vietnamese (286)	344	0.61
Other Asian, specified (7)	9	0.02
Other Asian, not specified (96)	249	0.44
Austrian	67	0.12
Belgian	47	0.08
Brazilian	14	0.02
British	366	0.65
Canadian	119	0.21
Celtic	87	0.16
Croatian	15	0.03
Czech	102	0.18
Czechoslovakian	53	0.09
Danish	184	0.33
Dutch	569	1.02
English	4,439	7.92
Estonian	7	0.01
European	701	1.25
Finnish	67	0.12
French, except Basque	847	1.51
French Canadian	389	0.69
German	6,923	12.35
German Russian	8	0.01
Greek	127	0.23
Guyanese	27	0.05
Hawaii Native/Pacific Islander:	192	0.34
Micronesian: (43)	62	0.11
Guamanian/Chamorro (42)	55	0.10
Other Micronesian (1)	7	0.01
Polynesian: (59)	97	0.17
Native Hawaiian (37)	65	0.12
Samoan (22)	32	0.06
Other Pac. Isl., not spec. (5)	33	0.06
Hispanic or Latino:	5,534	9.89
Central American:	1,257	2.25
Costa Rican	16	0.03
Guatemalan	142	0.25
Honduran	46	0.08
Nicaraguan	54	0.10
Panamanian	104	0.19
Salvadoran	836	1.49
Other Central American	59	0.11
Cuban	71	0.13
Dominican Republic	65	0.12
Mexican	1,116	1.99
Puerto Rican	961	1.72
South American:	535	0.96
Argentinean	12	0.02
Bolivian	75	0.13
Chilean	23	0.04
Colombian	90	0.16
Ecuadorian	57	0.10
Peruvian	211	0.38
Uruguayan	7	0.01
Venezuelan	34	0.06
Other South American	26	0.05
Other Hispanic or Latino	1,529	2.73
Hungarian	393	0.70
Iranian	107	0.19
Irish	5,735	10.23
Israeli	14	0.02
Italian	2,461	4.39
Latvian	6	0.01
Lithuanian	112	0.20
Northern European	8	0.01
Norwegian	428	0.76
Polish	1,315	2.35
Portuguese	250	0.45
Romanian	59	0.11
Russian	155	0.28
Scandinavian	14	0.02
Scotch-Irish	856	1.53
Scottish	874	1.56
Serbian	19	0.03
Slavic	15	0.03
Slovak	137	0.24
Slovene	28	0.05
Swedish	405	0.72
Swiss	122	0.22
Ukrainian	156	0.28
United States or American	4,185	7.47
Welsh	355	0.63
West Indian, excl. Hispanic:	511	0.91
Bahamian	7	0.01
Barbadian	14	0.02
British West Indian	30	0.05
Haitian	65	0.12
Jamaican	162	0.29
Trinidadian and Tobagonian	54	0.10
U.S. Virgin Islander	12	0.02
West Indian	167	0.30
White:	33,729	60.26
Not Hispanic (29,436)	30,878	55.17
Hispanic (2,382)	2,851	5.09
Yugoslavian	7	0.01

Danville

Place Type: Independent City
County: Danville Independent City
Population: 48,411

Ancestry/Race	Number	%
African American/Black:	21,535	44.48
Not Hispanic (21,267)	21,439	44.29
Hispanic (85)	96	0.20
African, sub-Saharan:	634	1.31
African	620	1.28
Sudanese	6	0.01
Other sub-Saharan African	8	0.02
Am. Ind. or Alaska Nat., not spec.	90	0.19
Albanian	17	0.04
American Indian tribes, specified:	108	0.22
Apache (4)	5	0.01
Blackfeet (3)	10	0.02
Cherokee (15)	56	0.12
Choctaw (3)	3	0.01
Creek	2	0.00
Delaware (7)	7	0.01
Iroquois	2	0.00
Kiowa (1)	1	0.00
Osage (3)	3	0.01
Sioux (3)	5	0.01
All other tribes (11)	14	0.03
American Indian tribes, not spec.	9	0.02
Arab:	83	0.17
Egyptian	55	0.11
Lebanese	13	0.03
Syrian	15	0.03
Asian:	363	0.75
Cambodian	1	0.00
Chinese, ex. Taiwanese (46)	62	0.13
Filipino (80)	89	0.18
Indian (71)	87	0.18
Indonesian (2)	2	0.00
Japanese (19)	29	0.06
Korean (21)	30	0.06
Pakistani (20)	21	0.04
Taiwanese (1)	2	0.00
Thai	1	0.00
Vietnamese (24)	29	0.06
Other Asian, specified (1)	3	0.01

Notes: 1. Figures in the "Number" column do not add up to the total population due to: a) Ancestry/Race overlap — e.g. persons can report being both White and Irish, b) persons of Hispanic origin can report being any race, c) persons reporting two ancestries are counted in both categories. 2. Numbers in parentheses indicate the number of persons reporting this ancestry/race alone, not in combination with any other ancestry/race. 3. Refer to the Explanation of Data in the front of the book for more detailed information.

Ancestry/Race	Number	%
Other Asian, not specified	7	0.01
Austrian	4	0.01
Belgian	10	0.02
British	187	0.39
Bulgarian	7	0.01
Canadian	38	0.08
Celtic	12	0.02
Czech	21	0.04
Czechoslovakian	11	0.02
Danish	15	0.03
Dutch	289	0.60
English	3,696	7.63
European	203	0.42
Finnish	18	0.04
French, except Basque	424	0.88
French Canadian	86	0.18
German	1,680	3.47
Greek	185	0.38
Hawaii Native/Pacific Islander:	41	0.08
Micronesian: (5)	11	0.02
Guamanian/Chamorro (5)	11	0.02
Polynesian: (6)	19	0.04
Native Hawaiian (5)	14	0.03
Samoan (1)	5	0.01
Other Pac. Isl., specified	2	0.00
Other Pac. Isl., not spec. (1)	9	0.02
Hispanic or Latino:	612	1.26
Central American:	20	0.04
Costa Rican	1	0.00
Guatemalan	5	0.01
Honduran	3	0.01
Panamanian	1	0.00
Salvadoran	10	0.02
Cuban	28	0.06
Dominican Republic	8	0.02
Mexican	360	0.74
Puerto Rican	57	0.12
South American:	27	0.06
Chilean	1	0.00
Colombian	17	0.04
Ecuadorian	1	0.00
Peruvian	4	0.01
Venezuelan	4	0.01
Other Hispanic or Latino	112	0.23
Hungarian	5	0.01
Irish	2,220	4.59
Italian	321	0.66
Luxemburger	6	0.01
Northern European	11	0.02
Norwegian	66	0.14
Pennsylvania German	7	0.01
Polish	99	0.20
Portuguese	21	0.04
Romanian	6	0.01
Russian	77	0.16
Scandinavian	5	0.01
Scotch-Irish	620	1.28
Scottish	594	1.23
Slovak	8	0.02
Swedish	106	0.22
Swiss	52	0.11
Ukrainian	17	0.04
United States or American	6,433	13.29
Welsh	75	0.15
West Indian, excl. Hispanic:	11	0.02
Jamaican	6	0.01
West Indian	5	0.01
White:	26,390	54.51
Not Hispanic (25,813)	26,064	53.84
Hispanic (262)	326	0.67

East Highland Park

Place Type: Census Designated Place
County: Henrico
Population: 12,488

Ancestry/Race	Number	%
African American/Black:	10,021	80.25
Not Hispanic (9,879)	9,974	79.87
Hispanic (31)	47	0.38
African, sub-Saharan:	141	1.13
African	136	1.09
Sierra Leonean	5	0.04
Am. Ind. or Alaska Nat., not spec.	46	0.37
American Indian tribes, specified:	40	0.32
Blackfeet	2	0.02
Cherokee (2)	16	0.13
Choctaw	1	0.01
Iroquois	1	0.01
Latin American Indians	1	0.01
Lumbee	1	0.01
All other tribes (13)	18	0.14
American Indian tribes, not spec.	9	0.07
Arab:	32	0.26
Arab/Arabic	9	0.07
Lebanese	23	0.18
Asian:	67	0.54
Cambodian (8)	9	0.07
Chinese, ex. Taiwanese (11)	14	0.11
Filipino (7)	10	0.08
Indian (4)	7	0.06
Japanese (1)	5	0.04
Korean (1)	2	0.02
Laotian (4)	4	0.03
Vietnamese (11)	11	0.09
Other Asian, specified	4	0.03
Other Asian, not specified (1)	1	0.01
British	7	0.06
Canadian	6	0.05
Danish	8	0.06
Dutch	19	0.15
English	529	4.24
European	19	0.15
French, except Basque	51	0.41
French Canadian	16	0.13
German	288	2.31
Greek	18	0.14
Hawaii Native/Pacific Islander:	10	0.08
Polynesian: (1)	3	0.02
Native Hawaiian (1)	1	0.01
Samoan	2	0.02
Other Pac. Isl., specified	4	0.03
Other Pac. Isl., not spec.	3	0.02
Hispanic or Latino:	125	1.00
Central American:	13	0.10
Costa Rican	1	0.01
Honduran	4	0.03
Panamanian	3	0.02
Salvadoran	5	0.04
Cuban	5	0.04
Dominican Republic	6	0.05
Mexican	39	0.31
Puerto Rican	28	0.22
South American:	5	0.04
Colombian	1	0.01
Venezuelan	4	0.03
Other Hispanic or Latino	29	0.23
Irish	302	2.42
Italian	56	0.45
Latvian	7	0.06
Northern European	16	0.13
Norwegian	6	0.05
Polish	40	0.32
Scotch-Irish	72	0.58
Scottish	31	0.25
Slavic	13	0.10
Swiss	5	0.04
Ukrainian	5	0.04
United States or American	403	3.23
Welsh	6	0.05
West Indian, excl. Hispanic:	86	0.69
Belizean	7	0.06
Jamaican	72	0.58
Trinidadian and Tobagonian	7	0.06
White:	2,392	19.15
Not Hispanic (2,261)	2,339	18.73
Hispanic (46)	53	0.42

Fairfax

Place Type: Independent City
County: Fairfax Independent City
Population: 21,498

Ancestry/Race	Number	%
Acadian/Cajun	5	0.02
Afghan	57	0.27
African American/Black:	1,240	5.77
Not Hispanic (1,035)	1,166	5.42
Hispanic (55)	74	0.34
African, sub-Saharan:	123	0.57
African	66	0.31
Ethiopian	36	0.17
Ghanian	15	0.07
South African	6	0.03
Alaska Native tribes, specified:	2	0.01
Tlingit-Haida (2)	2	0.01
Am. Ind. or Alaska Nat., not spec.	45	0.21
Albanian	13	0.06
American Indian tribes, specified:	130	0.60
Apache	3	0.01
Blackfeet	5	0.02
Cherokee (16)	49	0.23
Cheyenne	1	0.00
Chickasaw (1)	1	0.00
Chippewa (4)	5	0.02
Choctaw (3)	5	0.02
Delaware	1	0.00
Iroquois (6)	15	0.07
Latin American Indians (11)	16	0.07
Osage (1)	1	0.00
Potawatomi (2)	5	0.02
Seminole	3	0.01
Sioux	1	0.00
Tohono O'Odham (1)	1	0.00
All other tribes	18	0.08
American Indian tribes, not spec.	7	0.03
Arab:	260	1.21
Arab/Arabic	14	0.07
Egyptian	4	0.02
Lebanese	90	0.42
Moroccan	5	0.02
Syrian	37	0.17
Other Arab	110	0.51
Armenian	24	0.11
Asian:	2,913	13.55
Bangladeshi (4)	4	0.02
Cambodian (63)	74	0.34
Chinese, ex. Taiwanese (423)	476	2.21
Filipino (228)	276	1.28
Indian (555)	595	2.77
Indonesian (11)	11	0.05
Japanese (43)	61	0.28
Korean (615)	644	3.00
Laotian (22)	23	0.11
Malaysian (5)	6	0.03
Pakistani (85)	104	0.48
Sri Lankan (5)	5	0.02
Taiwanese (6)	9	0.04
Thai (43)	47	0.22
Vietnamese (415)	433	2.01
Other Asian, specified (29)	37	0.17
Other Asian, not specified (30)	108	0.50
Australian	18	0.08
Austrian	43	0.20
Belgian	33	0.15
Brazilian	16	0.07
British	190	0.88
Canadian	34	0.16
Celtic	12	0.06
Croatian	29	0.13
Cypriot	7	0.03
Czech	90	0.42
Czechoslovakian	40	0.19
Danish	37	0.17
Dutch	275	1.28
Eastern European	57	0.27
English	2,415	11.23

Notes: 1. Figures in the "Number" column do not add up to the total population due to: a) Ancestry/Race overlap — e.g. persons can report being both White and Irish, b) persons of Hispanic origin can report being any race, c) persons reporting two ancestries are counted in both categories. 2. Numbers in parentheses indicate the number of persons reporting this ancestry/race alone, not in combination with any other ancestry/race. 3. Refer to the Explanation of Data in the front of the book for more detailed information.

Estonian	8	0.04
European	300	1.40
Finnish	69	0.32
French, except Basque	544	2.53
French Canadian	127	0.59
German	2,794	13.00
Greek	229	1.07
Hawaii Native/Pacific Islander:	32	0.15
Melanesian: (1)	1	0.00
Other Melanesian (1)	1	0.00
Micronesian: (6)	7	0.03
Guamanian/Chamorro (6)	7	0.03
Polynesian: (9)	15	0.07
Native Hawaiian (8)	10	0.05
Samoan (1)	4	0.02
Other Polynesian	1	0.00
Other Pac. Isl., not spec.	9	0.04
Hispanic or Latino:	2,932	13.64
Central American:	927	4.31
Costa Rican	16	0.07
Guatemalan	145	0.67
Honduran	54	0.25
Nicaraguan	51	0.24
Panamanian	15	0.07
Salvadoran	594	2.76
Other Central American	52	0.24
Cuban	69	0.32
Dominican Republic	36	0.17
Mexican	301	1.40
Puerto Rican	112	0.52
South American:	514	2.39
Argentinean	30	0.14
Bolivian	170	0.79
Chilean	38	0.18
Colombian	35	0.16
Ecuadorian	26	0.12
Paraguayan	3	0.01
Peruvian	160	0.74
Uruguayan	1	0.00
Venezuelan	28	0.13
Other South American	23	0.11
Other Hispanic or Latino	973	4.53
Hungarian	89	0.41
Iranian	43	0.20
Irish	2,626	12.22
Israeli	8	0.04
Italian	855	3.98
Latvian	34	0.16
Lithuanian	86	0.40
Maltese	7	0.03
New Zealander	5	0.02
Northern European	57	0.27
Norwegian	267	1.24
Pennsylvania German	7	0.03
Polish	485	2.26
Portuguese	60	0.28
Romanian	50	0.23
Russian	230	1.07
Scandinavian	25	0.12
Scotch-Irish	634	2.95
Scottish	747	3.47
Serbian	14	0.07
Slovak	80	0.37
Slovene	7	0.03
Swedish	284	1.32
Swiss	100	0.47
Turkish	111	0.52
Ukrainian	102	0.47
United States or American	1,209	5.62
Welsh	178	0.83
West Indian, excl. Hispanic:	83	0.39
Bahamian	49	0.23
Haitian	10	0.05
West Indian	24	0.11
White:	16,250	75.59
Not Hispanic (14,333)	14,717	68.46
Hispanic (1,342)	1,533	7.13
Yugoslavian	16	0.07

Falls Church

Place Type: Independent City
County: Falls Church Independent City
Population: 10,377

Ancestry/Race	Number	%
Afghan	11	0.11
African American/Black:	391	3.77
Not Hispanic (321)	366	3.53
Hispanic (19)	25	0.24
African, sub-Saharan:	74	0.71
African	27	0.26
Somalian	11	0.11
Ugandan	7	0.07
Other sub-Saharan African	29	0.28
Alaska Native tribes, specified:	1	0.01
Tlingit-Haida	1	0.01
Am. Ind. or Alaska Nat., not spec.	24	0.23
American Indian tribes, specified:	53	0.51
Blackfeet	1	0.01
Cherokee (5)	21	0.20
Choctaw	2	0.02
Comanche (1)	1	0.01
Creek (1)	1	0.01
Iroquois (1)	1	0.01
Latin American Indians (2)	6	0.06
Navajo (3)	3	0.03
Osage	2	0.02
Ottawa (1)	1	0.01
Pueblo (3)	4	0.04
Sioux (2)	3	0.03
All other tribes (2)	7	0.07
American Indian tribes, not spec.	2	0.02
Arab:	67	0.65
Arab/Arabic	12	0.12
Egyptian	24	0.23
Lebanese	9	0.09
Syrian	6	0.06
Other Arab	16	0.15
Armenian	20	0.19
Asian:	805	7.76
Bangladeshi (3)	3	0.03
Cambodian (9)	9	0.09
Chinese, ex. Taiwanese (116)	150	1.45
Filipino (75)	99	0.95
Indian (186)	205	1.98
Indonesian (1)	6	0.06
Japanese (26)	37	0.36
Korean (105)	118	1.14
Malaysian (1)	1	0.01
Pakistani (9)	11	0.11
Sri Lankan (3)	3	0.03
Taiwanese (2)	7	0.07
Thai (17)	17	0.16
Vietnamese (82)	87	0.84
Other Asian, specified (8)	8	0.08
Other Asian, not specified (15)	44	0.42
Australian	21	0.20
Austrian	20	0.19
Belgian	7	0.07
British	196	1.89
Bulgarian	27	0.26
Canadian	25	0.24
Croatian	32	0.31
Czech	59	0.57
Czechoslovakian	11	0.11
Danish	57	0.55
Dutch	154	1.48
Eastern European	17	0.16
English	1,825	17.59
Estonian	5	0.05
European	196	1.89
Finnish	12	0.12
French, except Basque	375	3.61
French Canadian	80	0.77
German	1,874	18.06
Greek	109	1.05
Hawaii Native/Pacific Islander:	20	0.19
Melanesian: (4)	4	0.04
Other Melanesian (4)	4	0.04
Micronesian: (2)	3	0.03
Guamanian/Chamorro (1)	2	0.02
Other Micronesian (1)	1	0.01
Polynesian: (1)	6	0.06
Native Hawaiian	2	0.02
Samoan (1)	3	0.03
Other Polynesian	1	0.01
Other Pac. Isl., not spec.	7	0.07
Hispanic or Latino:	876	8.44
Central American:	202	1.95
Costa Rican	7	0.07
Guatemalan	15	0.14
Honduran	16	0.15
Nicaraguan	8	0.08
Panamanian	9	0.09
Salvadoran	142	1.37
Other Central American	5	0.05
Cuban	22	0.21
Dominican Republic	8	0.08
Mexican	117	1.13
Puerto Rican	59	0.57
South American:	229	2.21
Argentinean	17	0.16
Bolivian	99	0.95
Chilean	15	0.14
Colombian	23	0.22
Ecuadorian	6	0.06
Paraguayan	1	0.01
Peruvian	39	0.38
Uruguayan	1	0.01
Venezuelan	5	0.05
Other South American	23	0.22
Other Hispanic or Latino	239	2.30
Hungarian	70	0.67
Iranian	31	0.30
Irish	1,999	19.26
Italian	763	7.35
Latvian	19	0.18
Lithuanian	50	0.48
Macedonian	6	0.06
Northern European	27	0.26
Norwegian	166	1.60
Polish	392	3.78
Portuguese	38	0.37
Romanian	22	0.21
Russian	243	2.34
Scandinavian	19	0.18
Scotch-Irish	360	3.47
Scottish	595	5.73
Serbian	17	0.16
Slavic	30	0.29
Slovak	57	0.55
Slovene	23	0.22
Swedish	141	1.36
Swiss	48	0.46
Turkish	3	0.03
Ukrainian	55	0.53
United States or American	395	3.81
Welsh	164	1.58
White:	9,044	87.15
Not Hispanic (8,255)	8,441	81.34
Hispanic (562)	603	5.81

Fort Hunt

Place Type: Census Designated Place
County: Fairfax
Population: 12,923

Ancestry/Race	Number	%
African American/Black:	333	2.58
Not Hispanic (304)	329	2.55
Hispanic (2)	4	0.03
African, sub-Saharan:	22	0.17
African	18	0.14
Ethiopian	4	0.03
Alaska Native tribes, specified:	1	0.01
Tlingit-Haida (1)	1	0.01
Am. Ind. or Alaska Nat., not spec.	11	0.09

Notes: 1. Figures in the "Number" column do not add up to the total population due to: a) Ancestry/Race overlap — e.g. persons can report being both White and Irish, b) persons of Hispanic origin can report being any race, c) persons reporting two ancestries are counted in both categories. 2. Numbers in parentheses indicate the number of persons reporting this ancestry/race alone, not in combination with any other ancestry/race. 3. Refer to the Explanation of Data in the front of the book for more detailed information.

American Indian tribes, specified:	47	0.36
Apache (1)	1	0.01
Blackfeet	1	0.01
Cherokee (2)	8	0.06
Chickasaw (2)	2	0.02
Choctaw	10	0.08
Comanche (1)	1	0.01
Cree	1	0.01
Iroquois	2	0.02
Latin American Indians (1)	8	0.06
Navajo	2	0.02
Osage	1	0.01
Seminole (4)	4	0.03
Sioux (2)	2	0.02
Ute	1	0.01
Yaqui	1	0.01
All other tribes (1)	2	0.02
American Indian tribes, not spec.	6	0.05
Arab:	22	0.17
Lebanese	9	0.07
Palestinian	7	0.05
Syrian	6	0.05
Armenian	6	0.05
Asian:	424	3.28
Chinese, ex. Taiwanese (55)	65	0.50
Filipino (41)	55	0.43
Indian (53)	71	0.55
Indonesian (4)	5	0.04
Japanese (39)	53	0.41
Korean (92)	105	0.81
Pakistani (17)	17	0.13
Taiwanese (2)	2	0.02
Thai (7)	9	0.07
Vietnamese (16)	19	0.15
Other Asian, not specified (5)	23	0.18
Australian	4	0.03
Austrian	102	0.80
Basque	6	0.05
Belgian	38	0.30
Brazilian	20	0.16
British	242	1.89
Canadian	57	0.44
Celtic	6	0.05
Croatian	23	0.18
Cypriot	20	0.16
Czech	40	0.31
Czechoslovakian	32	0.25
Danish	85	0.66
Dutch	122	0.95
Eastern European	36	0.28
English	2,523	19.67
European	138	1.08
Finnish	34	0.27
French, except Basque	548	4.27
French Canadian	140	1.09
German	2,788	21.74
Greek	106	0.83
Hawaii Native/Pacific Islander:	24	0.19
Micronesian: (2)	4	0.03
Guamanian/Chamorro (2)	4	0.03
Polynesian: (2)	7	0.05
Native Hawaiian (2)	5	0.04
Samoan	2	0.02
Other Pac. Isl., not spec. (2)	13	0.10
Hispanic or Latino:	342	2.65
Central American:	38	0.29
Costa Rican	2	0.02
Guatemalan	4	0.03
Honduran	5	0.04
Nicaraguan	1	0.01
Panamanian	9	0.07
Salvadoran	15	0.12
Other Central American	2	0.02
Cuban	27	0.21
Dominican Republic	2	0.02
Mexican	74	0.57
Puerto Rican	37	0.29
South American:	87	0.67
Argentinean	3	0.02
Bolivian	13	0.10
Chilean	6	0.05
Colombian	21	0.16
Ecuadorian	16	0.12
Paraguayan	2	0.02
Peruvian	11	0.09
Uruguayan	6	0.05
Venezuelan	2	0.02
Other South American	7	0.05
Other Hispanic or Latino	77	0.60
Hungarian	109	0.85
Iranian	4	0.03
Irish	2,775	21.63
Italian	789	6.15
Lithuanian	84	0.65
Macedonian	16	0.12
Northern European	55	0.43
Norwegian	209	1.63
Polish	449	3.50
Portuguese	15	0.12
Romanian	17	0.13
Russian	291	2.27
Scandinavian	33	0.26
Scotch-Irish	505	3.94
Scottish	649	5.06
Serbian	37	0.29
Slovak	123	0.96
Slovene	19	0.15
Swedish	226	1.76
Swiss	60	0.47
Turkish	7	0.05
Ukrainian	43	0.34
United States or American	882	6.88
Welsh	227	1.77
West Indian, excl. Hispanic:	9	0.07
Jamaican	9	0.07
White:	12,170	94.17
Not Hispanic (11,739)	11,881	91.94
Hispanic (258)	289	2.24
Yugoslavian	11	0.09

Franconia

Place Type: Census Designated Place
County: Fairfax
Population: 31,907

Ancestry/Race	Number	%
Afghan	194	0.61
African American/Black:	4,611	14.45
Not Hispanic (4,263)	4,494	14.08
Hispanic (66)	117	0.37
African, sub-Saharan:	830	2.60
African	336	1.05
Ethiopian	384	1.20
Ghanian	35	0.11
Nigerian	35	0.11
Sierra Leonean	20	0.06
South African	20	0.06
Am. Ind. or Alaska Nat., not spec.	55	0.17
Albanian	59	0.18
American Indian tribes, specified:	151	0.47
Apache (1)	3	0.01
Blackfeet	4	0.01
Cherokee (20)	49	0.15
Chickasaw (1)	2	0.01
Chippewa (2)	4	0.01
Choctaw (6)	10	0.03
Comanche (2)	4	0.01
Cree (1)	1	0.00
Creek (5)	5	0.02
Iroquois	4	0.01
Latin American Indians (11)	16	0.05
Lumbee (6)	7	0.02
Navajo (5)	5	0.02
Osage	1	0.00
Paiute (2)	2	0.01
Pueblo (1)	1	0.00
Seminole	2	0.01
Sioux (9)	12	0.04
All other tribes (10)	19	0.06
American Indian tribes, not spec.	8	0.03
Arab:	561	1.75
Arab/Arabic	144	0.45
Egyptian	136	0.43
Iraqi	34	0.11
Jordanian	25	0.08
Lebanese	95	0.30
Moroccan	41	0.13
Palestinian	48	0.15
Other Arab	38	0.12
Armenian	76	0.24
Asian:	4,102	12.86
Bangladeshi (37)	50	0.16
Cambodian (15)	22	0.07
Chinese, ex. Taiwanese (439)	528	1.65
Filipino (528)	633	1.98
Indian (531)	604	1.89
Indonesian (18)	25	0.08
Japanese (84)	141	0.44
Korean (734)	824	2.58
Laotian (46)	47	0.15
Malaysian	1	0.00
Pakistani (161)	221	0.69
Sri Lankan (7)	10	0.03
Taiwanese (10)	11	0.03
Thai (114)	127	0.40
Vietnamese (553)	600	1.88
Other Asian, specified (16)	20	0.06
Other Asian, not specified (48)	238	0.75
Austrian	95	0.30
Belgian	47	0.15
Brazilian	68	0.21
British	311	0.97
Canadian	84	0.26
Croatian	50	0.16
Czech	140	0.44
Czechoslovakian	32	0.10
Danish	139	0.43
Dutch	335	1.05
Eastern European	44	0.14
English	3,568	11.16
Estonian	7	0.02
European	294	0.92
Finnish	33	0.10
French, except Basque	869	2.72
French Canadian	348	1.09
German	4,979	15.57
Greek	485	1.52
Hawaii Native/Pacific Islander:	109	0.34
Melanesian: (2)	2	0.01
Other Melanesian (2)	2	0.01
Micronesian: (10)	21	0.07
Guamanian/Chamorro (8)	16	0.05
Other Micronesian (2)	5	0.02
Polynesian: (11)	46	0.14
Native Hawaiian (4)	32	0.10
Samoan (2)	6	0.02
Other Polynesian (5)	8	0.03
Other Pac. Isl., specified	2	0.01
Other Pac. Isl., not spec. (11)	38	0.12
Hispanic or Latino:	2,337	7.32
Central American:	385	1.21
Costa Rican	8	0.03
Guatemalan	45	0.14
Honduran	32	0.10
Nicaraguan	20	0.06
Panamanian	45	0.14
Salvadoran	229	0.72
Other Central American	6	0.02
Cuban	67	0.21
Dominican Republic	36	0.11
Mexican	288	0.90
Puerto Rican	330	1.03
South American:	566	1.77
Argentinean	15	0.05
Bolivian	149	0.47
Chilean	25	0.08
Colombian	100	0.31
Ecuadorian	42	0.13
Paraguayan	1	0.00

Notes: 1. Figures in the "Number" column do not add up to the total population due to: a) Ancestry/Race overlap — e.g. persons can report being both White and Irish, b) persons of Hispanic origin can report being any race, c) persons reporting two ancestries are counted in both categories. 2. Numbers in parentheses indicate the number of persons reporting this ancestry/race alone, not in combination with any other ancestry/race. 3. Refer to the Explanation of Data in the front of the book for more detailed information.

Ancestry/Race	Number	%
Peruvian	163	0.51
Uruguayan	9	0.03
Venezuelan	33	0.10
Other South American	29	0.09
Other Hispanic or Latino	665	2.08
Hungarian	89	0.28
Iranian	123	0.38
Irish	4,208	13.16
Italian	2,518	7.88
Latvian	7	0.02
Lithuanian	137	0.43
Northern European	16	0.05
Norwegian	291	0.91
Pennsylvania German	15	0.05
Polish	1,026	3.21
Portuguese	115	0.36
Romanian	20	0.06
Russian	454	1.42
Scandinavian	98	0.31
Scotch-Irish	564	1.76
Scottish	940	2.94
Serbian	8	0.03
Slovak	79	0.25
Slovene	7	0.02
Swedish	434	1.36
Swiss	121	0.38
Turkish	102	0.32
Ukrainian	113	0.35
United States or American	1,324	4.14
Welsh	265	0.83
West Indian, excl. Hispanic:	148	0.46
Bahamian	61	0.19
Jamaican	22	0.07
Trinidadian and Tobagonian	38	0.12
West Indian	27	0.08
White:	23,074	72.32
Not Hispanic (20,744)	21,516	67.43
Hispanic (1,355)	1,558	4.88
Yugoslavian	39	0.12

Fredericksburg

Place Type: Independent City
County: Fredericksburg Independent City
Population: 19,279

Ancestry/Race	Number	%
Acadian/Cajun	17	0.09
Afghan	25	0.13
African American/Black:	4,115	21.34
Not Hispanic (3,884)	4,042	20.97
Hispanic (51)	73	0.38
African, sub-Saharan:	421	2.18
African	395	2.05
Ethiopian	17	0.09
Other sub-Saharan African	9	0.05
Alaska Native tribes, specified:	5	0.03
Eskimo (2)	5	0.03
Am. Ind. or Alaska Nat., not spec.	48	0.25
American Indian tribes, specified:	96	0.50
Apache	1	0.01
Blackfeet (1)	2	0.01
Cherokee (13)	41	0.21
Chickasaw	1	0.01
Chippewa (3)	3	0.02
Choctaw	3	0.02
Creek (2)	2	0.01
Delaware	2	0.01
Iroquois (3)	6	0.03
Kiowa (1)	1	0.01
Latin American Indians	1	0.01
Lumbee (3)	4	0.02
Navajo	2	0.01
Potawatomi (4)	9	0.05
Pueblo (3)	3	0.02
Sioux (1)	1	0.01
All other tribes (4)	14	0.07
American Indian tribes, not spec.	7	0.04
Arab:	29	0.15
Lebanese	16	0.08
Syrian	5	0.03
Other Arab	8	0.04
Armenian	14	0.07
Asian:	380	1.97
Cambodian (1)	1	0.01
Chinese, ex. Taiwanese (75)	88	0.46
Filipino (57)	80	0.41
Hmong (1)	1	0.01
Indian (35)	42	0.22
Indonesian (1)	1	0.01
Japanese (7)	17	0.09
Korean (52)	64	0.33
Laotian (9)	11	0.06
Pakistani (11)	13	0.07
Thai (6)	6	0.03
Vietnamese (28)	30	0.16
Other Asian, specified	1	0.01
Other Asian, not specified (5)	25	0.13
Austrian	86	0.45
Belgian	11	0.06
British	125	0.65
Canadian	36	0.19
Croatian	16	0.08
Czech	77	0.40
Danish	90	0.47
Dutch	258	1.34
Eastern European	13	0.07
English	2,611	13.54
European	198	1.03
Finnish	31	0.16
French, except Basque	595	3.09
French Canadian	54	0.28
German	2,482	12.87
Greek	75	0.39
Hawaii Native/Pacific Islander:	21	0.11
Micronesian: (1)	1	0.01
Guamanian/Chamorro (1)	1	0.01
Polynesian: (9)	12	0.06
Native Hawaiian (8)	10	0.05
Samoan (1)	2	0.01
Other Pac. Isl., specified	1	0.01
Other Pac. Isl., not spec. (1)	7	0.04
Hispanic or Latino:	945	4.90
Central American:	169	0.88
Costa Rican	1	0.01
Guatemalan	45	0.23
Honduran	31	0.16
Nicaraguan	4	0.02
Panamanian	5	0.03
Salvadoran	79	0.41
Other Central American	4	0.02
Cuban	23	0.12
Dominican Republic	3	0.02
Mexican	422	2.19
Puerto Rican	90	0.47
South American:	35	0.18
Argentinean	3	0.02
Chilean	1	0.01
Colombian	15	0.08
Ecuadorian	1	0.01
Peruvian	11	0.06
Uruguayan	2	0.01
Other South American	2	0.01
Other Hispanic or Latino	203	1.05
Hungarian	66	0.34
Iranian	13	0.07
Irish	2,305	11.96
Italian	863	4.48
Latvian	5	0.03
Lithuanian	63	0.33
Norwegian	159	0.82
Pennsylvania German	10	0.05
Polish	404	2.10
Portuguese	45	0.23
Romanian	17	0.09
Russian	117	0.61
Scandinavian	13	0.07
Scotch-Irish	448	2.32
Scottish	597	3.10
Slavic	19	0.10
Slovak	57	0.30
Slovene	7	0.04
Swedish	210	1.09
Swiss	31	0.16
Turkish	15	0.08
Ukrainian	66	0.34
United States or American	1,145	5.94
Welsh	237	1.23
West Indian, excl. Hispanic:	35	0.18
Haitian	20	0.10
Jamaican	8	0.04
Trinidadian and Tobagonian	7	0.04
White:	14,418	74.79
Not Hispanic (13,759)	14,015	72.70
Hispanic (349)	403	2.09

Front Royal

Place Type: Town
County: Warren
Population: 13,589

Ancestry/Race	Number	%
African American/Black:	1,267	9.32
Not Hispanic (1,170)	1,253	9.22
Hispanic (10)	14	0.10
African, sub-Saharan:	12	0.09
African	12	0.09
Alaska Native tribes, specified:	4	0.03
Aleut (3)	3	0.02
Eskimo	1	0.01
Alaska Native tribes, not specified	1	0.01
Am. Ind. or Alaska Nat., not spec.	47	0.35
American Indian tribes, specified:	55	0.40
Blackfeet (2)	3	0.02
Cherokee (10)	33	0.24
Cheyenne (3)	4	0.03
Creek (1)	1	0.01
Iroquois (1)	1	0.01
Lumbee	2	0.01
Navajo (2)	3	0.02
Potawatomi (1)	1	0.01
Sioux (1)	1	0.01
All other tribes (1)	6	0.04
American Indian tribes, not spec.	2	0.01
Asian:	107	0.79
Chinese, ex. Taiwanese (24)	27	0.20
Filipino (7)	14	0.10
Indian (28)	30	0.22
Indonesian (1)	1	0.01
Japanese (2)	4	0.03
Korean (8)	11	0.08
Pakistani (2)	3	0.02
Sri Lankan (1)	2	0.01
Taiwanese (3)	3	0.02
Thai (3)	3	0.02
Vietnamese (4)	4	0.03
Other Asian, not specified (2)	5	0.04
Austrian	19	0.14
Belgian	29	0.21
British	32	0.23
Canadian	14	0.10
Croatian	6	0.04
Czech	28	0.20
Czechoslovakian	5	0.04
Danish	13	0.09
Dutch	224	1.63
English	1,282	9.30
European	156	1.13
Finnish	4	0.03
French, except Basque	186	1.35
French Canadian	23	0.17
German	1,795	13.02
Greek	30	0.22
Guyanese	9	0.07
Hawaii Native/Pacific Islander:	12	0.09
Micronesian: (2)	3	0.02
Guamanian/Chamorro (2)	3	0.02
Polynesian: (2)	6	0.04
Native Hawaiian (1)	4	0.03

Notes: 1. Figures in the "Number" column do not add up to the total population due to: a) Ancestry/Race overlap — e.g. persons can report being both White and Irish, b) persons of Hispanic origin can report being any race, c) persons reporting two ancestries are counted in both categories. 2. Numbers in parentheses indicate the number of persons reporting this ancestry/race alone, not in combination with any other ancestry/race. 3. Refer to the Explanation of Data in the front of the book for more detailed information.

Samoan (1)	2	0.01
Other Pac. Isl., not spec. (2)	3	0.02
Hispanic or Latino:	290	2.13
Central American:	12	0.09
Guatemalan	2	0.01
Honduran	2	0.01
Nicaraguan	1	0.01
Panamanian	2	0.01
Salvadoran	5	0.04
Cuban	7	0.05
Dominican Republic	9	0.07
Mexican	145	1.07
Puerto Rican	51	0.38
South American:	24	0.18
Chilean	1	0.01
Colombian	12	0.09
Ecuadorian	1	0.01
Peruvian	6	0.04
Uruguayan	4	0.03
Other Hispanic or Latino	42	0.31
Hungarian	44	0.32
Irish	1,591	11.54
Italian	409	2.97
Latvian	8	0.06
Lithuanian	7	0.05
Norwegian	41	0.30
Pennsylvania German	26	0.19
Polish	152	1.10
Portuguese	34	0.25
Russian	45	0.33
Scandinavian	15	0.11
Scotch-Irish	394	2.86
Scottish	297	2.15
Serbian	6	0.04
Slovak	8	0.06
Swedish	16	0.12
Swiss	20	0.15
United States or American	2,985	21.66
Welsh	90	0.65
West Indian, excl. Hispanic:	7	0.05
Jamaican	7	0.05
White:	12,160	89.48
Not Hispanic (11,818)	11,961	88.02
Hispanic (182)	199	1.46

Glen Allen

Place Type: Census Designated Place
County: Henrico
Population: 12,562

Ancestry/Race	Number	%
African American/Black:	2,535	20.18
Not Hispanic (2,437)	2,513	20.00
Hispanic (17)	22	0.18
African, sub-Saharan:	109	0.85
African	98	0.77
Nigerian	11	0.09
Am. Ind. or Alaska Nat., not spec.	26	0.21
American Indian tribes, specified:	51	0.41
Apache (2)	2	0.02
Cherokee (10)	19	0.15
Chippewa (1)	1	0.01
Choctaw	1	0.01
Creek (1)	1	0.01
Iroquois (1)	1	0.01
Latin American Indians (2)	2	0.02
Sioux (2)	3	0.02
All other tribes (15)	21	0.17
American Indian tribes, not spec.	7	0.06
Arab:	18	0.14
Lebanese	18	0.14
Asian:	441	3.51
Cambodian (21)	21	0.17
Chinese, ex. Taiwanese (61)	90	0.72
Filipino (29)	32	0.25
Indian (97)	99	0.79
Japanese (10)	18	0.14
Korean (19)	26	0.21
Laotian (4)	4	0.03
Pakistani (17)	18	0.14
Thai (7)	8	0.06
Vietnamese (103)	117	0.93
Other Asian, not specified (2)	8	0.06
Austrian	11	0.09
Brazilian	8	0.06
British	56	0.44
Bulgarian	7	0.05
Canadian	30	0.23
Czech	55	0.43
Czechoslovakian	17	0.13
Danish	46	0.36
Dutch	129	1.01
English	1,932	15.13
European	194	1.52
French, except Basque	189	1.48
French Canadian	64	0.50
German	1,547	12.11
Greek	75	0.59
Hawaii Native/Pacific Islander:	10	0.08
Melanesian: (4)	4	0.03
Fijian (4)	4	0.03
Polynesian: (4)	6	0.05
Native Hawaiian (2)	4	0.03
Samoan (1)	1	0.01
Tongan (1)	1	0.01
Hispanic or Latino:	217	1.73
Central American:	16	0.13
Costa Rican	4	0.03
Honduran	1	0.01
Panamanian	9	0.07
Salvadoran	2	0.02
Cuban	8	0.06
Dominican Republic	1	0.01
Mexican	32	0.25
Puerto Rican	63	0.50
South American:	32	0.25
Bolivian	6	0.05
Chilean	3	0.02
Colombian	7	0.06
Ecuadorian	1	0.01
Paraguayan	2	0.02
Peruvian	7	0.06
Uruguayan	1	0.01
Venezuelan	5	0.04
Other Hispanic or Latino	65	0.52
Hungarian	39	0.31
Irish	1,310	10.26
Israeli	7	0.05
Italian	534	4.18
Latvian	7	0.05
Lithuanian	19	0.15
Northern European	19	0.15
Norwegian	109	0.85
Polish	139	1.09
Portuguese	24	0.19
Russian	96	0.75
Scandinavian	17	0.13
Scotch-Irish	294	2.30
Scottish	354	2.77
Slavic	16	0.13
Slovak	8	0.06
Swedish	132	1.03
Swiss	36	0.28
Ukrainian	20	0.16
United States or American	1,613	12.63
Welsh	85	0.67
West Indian, excl. Hispanic:	61	0.48
Bahamian	10	0.08
Haitian	19	0.15
Jamaican	20	0.16
U.S. Virgin Islander	12	0.09
White:	9,539	75.94
Not Hispanic (9,314)	9,437	75.12
Hispanic (98)	102	0.81

Groveton

Place Type: Census Designated Place
County: Fairfax
Population: 21,296

Ancestry/Race	Number	%
African American/Black:	4,405	20.68
Not Hispanic (4,038)	4,245	19.93
Hispanic (87)	160	0.75
African, sub-Saharan:	862	4.05
African	370	1.74
Cape Verdean	18	0.08
Ethiopian	69	0.32
Ghanian	265	1.25
Kenyan	7	0.03
Nigerian	30	0.14
Senegalese	22	0.10
Sierra Leonean	75	0.35
Other sub-Saharan African	6	0.03
Alaska Native tribes, specified:	3	0.01
Aleut	1	0.00
Tlingit-Haida (2)	2	0.01
Am. Ind. or Alaska Nat., not spec.	53	0.25
Albanian	8	0.04
American Indian tribes, specified:	104	0.49
Apache (1)	2	0.01
Blackfeet (1)	4	0.02
Cherokee (10)	33	0.15
Chippewa	1	0.00
Choctaw	4	0.02
Comanche	5	0.02
Delaware (3)	3	0.01
Iroquois (3)	6	0.03
Latin American Indians (6)	14	0.07
Lumbee (1)	1	0.00
Navajo (1)	2	0.01
Potawatomi (1)	1	0.00
Pueblo (5)	7	0.03
Seminole	3	0.01
Sioux (1)	5	0.02
All other tribes (5)	13	0.06
American Indian tribes, not spec.	7	0.03
Arab:	212	1.00
Arab/Arabic	8	0.04
Egyptian	3	0.01
Jordanian	7	0.03
Lebanese	32	0.15
Moroccan	15	0.07
Palestinian	35	0.16
Other Arab	112	0.53
Armenian	22	0.10
Asian:	1,974	9.27
Bangladeshi (15)	15	0.07
Cambodian (77)	85	0.40
Chinese, ex. Taiwanese (173)	203	0.95
Filipino (237)	273	1.28
Indian (272)	338	1.59
Indonesian (4)	5	0.02
Japanese (51)	85	0.40
Korean (187)	209	0.98
Laotian (17)	23	0.11
Malaysian (1)	1	0.00
Pakistani (275)	341	1.60
Sri Lankan (4)	4	0.02
Taiwanese (9)	10	0.05
Thai (32)	49	0.23
Vietnamese (150)	161	0.76
Other Asian, specified (8)	9	0.04
Other Asian, not specified (99)	163	0.77
Australian	16	0.08
Austrian	37	0.17
Brazilian	29	0.14
British	112	0.53
Bulgarian	6	0.03
Canadian	11	0.05
Celtic	4	0.02
Croatian	5	0.02
Czech	98	0.46
Czechoslovakian	36	0.17

Notes: 1. Figures in the "Number" column do not add up to the total population due to: a) Ancestry/Race overlap — e.g. persons can report being both White and Irish, b) persons of Hispanic origin can report being any race, c) persons reporting two ancestries are counted in both categories. 2. Numbers in parentheses indicate the number of persons reporting this ancestry/race alone, not in combination with any other ancestry/race. 3. Refer to the Explanation of Data in the front of the book for more detailed information.

Ancestry/Race	Number	%
Danish	61	0.29
Dutch	218	1.03
Eastern European	61	0.29
English	2,099	9.87
Estonian	9	0.04
European	237	1.11
Finnish	24	0.11
French, except Basque	337	1.58
French Canadian	96	0.45
German	2,448	11.51
Greek	60	0.28
Guyanese	18	0.08
Hawaii Native/Pacific Islander:	42	0.20
Melanesian: (1)	1	0.00
Fijian (1)	1	0.00
Micronesian: (3)	3	0.01
Guamanian/Chamorro (3)	3	0.01
Polynesian: (11)	13	0.06
Native Hawaiian (10)	12	0.06
Samoan (1)	1	0.00
Other Pac. Isl., not spec. (6)	25	0.12
Hispanic or Latino:	3,955	18.57
Central American:	1,520	7.14
Costa Rican	7	0.03
Guatemalan	99	0.46
Honduran	157	0.74
Nicaraguan	40	0.19
Panamanian	21	0.10
Salvadoran	1,107	5.20
Other Central American	89	0.42
Cuban	42	0.20
Dominican Republic	30	0.14
Mexican	474	2.23
Puerto Rican	233	1.09
South American:	339	1.59
Argentinean	14	0.07
Bolivian	129	0.61
Chilean	18	0.08
Colombian	40	0.19
Ecuadorian	14	0.07
Paraguayan	1	0.00
Peruvian	96	0.45
Venezuelan	11	0.05
Other South American	16	0.08
Other Hispanic or Latino	1,317	6.18
Hungarian	46	0.22
Iranian	17	0.08
Irish	2,128	10.01
Israeli	31	0.15
Italian	758	3.56
Latvian	6	0.03
Lithuanian	41	0.19
Northern European	32	0.15
Norwegian	149	0.70
Pennsylvania German	17	0.08
Polish	475	2.23
Portuguese	12	0.06
Romanian	39	0.18
Russian	136	0.64
Scandinavian	18	0.08
Scotch-Irish	455	2.14
Scottish	509	2.39
Serbian	20	0.09
Slavic	19	0.09
Slovak	57	0.27
Slovene	6	0.03
Swedish	161	0.76
Swiss	38	0.18
Turkish	26	0.12
Ukrainian	8	0.04
United States or American	948	4.46
Welsh	139	0.65
West Indian, excl. Hispanic:	181	0.85
Jamaican	111	0.52
Trinidadian and Tobagonian	40	0.19
West Indian	22	0.10
Other West Indian	8	0.04
White:	13,224	62.10
Not Hispanic (10,976)	11,387	53.47
Hispanic (1,515)	1,837	8.63
Yugoslavian	12	0.06

Hampton

Place Type: Independent City
County: Hampton Independent City
Population: 146,437

Ancestry/Race	Number	%
Acadian/Cajun	29	0.02
African American/Black:	67,446	46.06
Not Hispanic (64,795)	66,506	45.42
Hispanic (633)	940	0.64
African, sub-Saharan:	1,804	1.23
African	1,619	1.11
Cape Verdean	20	0.01
Ethiopian	39	0.03
Ghanian	59	0.04
Liberian	16	0.01
Nigerian	15	0.01
Sierra Leonean	7	0.00
South African	22	0.02
Zimbabwean	7	0.00
Alaska Native tribes, specified:	9	0.01
Alaska Athabascan (2)	6	0.00
Eskimo (2)	2	0.00
Tlingit-Haida (1)	1	0.00
Alaska Native tribes, not specified	4	0.00
Am. Ind. or Alaska Nat., not spec.	598	0.41
American Indian tribes, specified:	1,038	0.71
Apache (6)	20	0.01
Blackfeet (18)	77	0.05
Cherokee (99)	451	0.31
Cheyenne	12	0.01
Chickasaw (3)	6	0.00
Chippewa (8)	15	0.01
Choctaw (6)	22	0.02
Colville (1)	2	0.00
Comanche (1)	1	0.00
Cree	4	0.00
Creek (11)	20	0.01
Crow	1	0.00
Delaware (3)	5	0.00
Houma (1)	1	0.00
Iroquois (13)	30	0.02
Kiowa	1	0.00
Latin American Indians (11)	24	0.02
Lumbee (23)	37	0.03
Navajo (16)	20	0.01
Osage (2)	3	0.00
Ottawa (3)	5	0.00
Potawatomi (1)	1	0.00
Pueblo (2)	5	0.00
Seminole (5)	23	0.02
Shoshone	1	0.00
Sioux (12)	42	0.03
Tohono O'Odham	3	0.00
Ute (1)	1	0.00
Yuman	4	0.00
All other tribes (117)	201	0.14
American Indian tribes, not spec.	91	0.06
Arab:	286	0.20
Arab/Arabic	31	0.02
Egyptian	75	0.05
Lebanese	169	0.12
Syrian	11	0.01
Armenian	26	0.02
Asian:	3,778	2.58
Bangladeshi (4)	12	0.01
Cambodian (77)	99	0.07
Chinese, ex. Taiwanese (237)	342	0.23
Filipino (657)	981	0.67
Indian (248)	333	0.23
Indonesian (8)	13	0.01
Japanese (161)	314	0.21
Korean (377)	523	0.36
Laotian (31)	36	0.02
Malaysian (1)	3	0.00
Pakistani (27)	33	0.02
Sri Lankan (3)	6	0.00
Taiwanese (8)	25	0.02
Thai (99)	155	0.11
Vietnamese (607)	694	0.47
Other Asian, specified (4)	21	0.01
Other Asian, not specified (84)	188	0.13
Australian	30	0.02
Austrian	234	0.16
Basque	8	0.01
Belgian	82	0.06
Brazilian	8	0.01
British	707	0.48
Canadian	263	0.18
Celtic	35	0.02
Croatian	36	0.02
Czech	144	0.10
Czechoslovakian	138	0.09
Danish	216	0.15
Dutch	1,055	0.72
Eastern European	26	0.02
English	11,470	7.83
European	842	0.57
Finnish	180	0.12
French, except Basque	2,748	1.88
French Canadian	989	0.68
German	13,156	8.98
German Russian	6	0.00
Greek	438	0.30
Guyanese	20	0.01
Hawaii Native/Pacific Islander:	342	0.23
Micronesian: (63)	87	0.06
Guamanian/Chamorro (56)	75	0.05
Other Micronesian (7)	12	0.01
Polynesian: (53)	138	0.09
Native Hawaiian (44)	111	0.08
Samoan (9)	24	0.02
Other Polynesian	3	0.00
Other Pac. Isl., specified	9	0.01
Other Pac. Isl., not spec. (18)	108	0.07
Hispanic or Latino:	4,153	2.84
Central American:	315	0.22
Costa Rican	19	0.01
Guatemalan	11	0.01
Honduran	33	0.02
Nicaraguan	5	0.00
Panamanian	198	0.14
Salvadoran	45	0.03
Other Central American	4	0.00
Cuban	149	0.10
Dominican Republic	81	0.06
Mexican	1,130	0.77
Puerto Rican	1,469	1.00
South American:	128	0.09
Argentinean	6	0.00
Bolivian	7	0.00
Chilean	5	0.00
Colombian	41	0.03
Ecuadorian	15	0.01
Peruvian	35	0.02
Uruguayan	1	0.00
Venezuelan	6	0.00
Other South American	12	0.01
Other Hispanic or Latino	881	0.60
Hungarian	322	0.22
Icelander	26	0.02
Iranian	8	0.01
Irish	10,378	7.09
Italian	3,932	2.69
Latvian	14	0.01
Lithuanian	131	0.09
Luxemburger	26	0.02
Macedonian	9	0.01
Northern European	8	0.01
Norwegian	1,004	0.69
Pennsylvania German	32	0.02
Polish	2,161	1.48
Portuguese	335	0.23
Romanian	97	0.07
Russian	288	0.20
Scandinavian	115	0.08
Scotch-Irish	2,123	1.45

Notes: 1. Figures in the "Number" column do not add up to the total population due to: a) Ancestry/Race overlap — e.g. persons can report being both White and Irish, b) persons of Hispanic origin can report being any race, c) persons reporting two ancestries are counted in both categories. 2. Numbers in parentheses indicate the number of persons reporting this ancestry/race alone, not in combination with any other ancestry/race. 3. Refer to the Explanation of Data in the front of the book for more detailed information.

Scottish	2,449	1.67
Serbian	19	0.01
Slavic	24	0.02
Slovak	204	0.14
Slovene	6	0.00
Swedish	719	0.49
Swiss	218	0.15
Turkish	58	0.04
Ukrainian	239	0.16
United States or American	10,614	7.25
Welsh	738	0.50
West Indian, excl. Hispanic:	1,364	0.93
Bahamian	45	0.03
Barbadian	58	0.04
Belizean	13	0.01
Bermudan	134	0.09
British West Indian	62	0.04
Haitian	58	0.04
Jamaican	584	0.40
Trinidadian and Tobagonian	236	0.16
U.S. Virgin Islander	7	0.00
West Indian	160	0.11
Other West Indian	7	0.00
White:	74,880	51.13
Not Hispanic (70,963)	72,967	49.83
Hispanic (1,593)	1,913	1.31
Yugoslavian	90	0.06

Harrisonburg

Place Type: Independent City
County: Harrisonburg Independent City
Population: 40,468

Ancestry/Race	Number	%
Afghan	97	0.24
African American/Black:	2,726	6.74
Not Hispanic (2,266)	2,546	6.29
Hispanic (128)	180	0.44
African, sub-Saharan:	230	0.57
African	50	0.12
Ethiopian	63	0.16
Ghanian	7	0.02
Ugandan	12	0.03
Other sub-Saharan African	98	0.24
Am. Ind. or Alaska Nat., not spec.	84	0.21
Albanian	34	0.08
Alsatian	7	0.02
American Indian tribes, specified:	95	0.23
Apache (2)	2	0.00
Blackfeet	3	0.01
Cherokee (14)	49	0.12
Cheyenne	2	0.00
Chickasaw (1)	2	0.00
Chippewa	2	0.00
Choctaw (1)	1	0.00
Iroquois (3)	4	0.01
Latin American Indians (7)	10	0.02
Lumbee (2)	3	0.01
Navajo (2)	2	0.00
Osage (1)	1	0.00
Seminole	1	0.00
Sioux	2	0.00
All other tribes (7)	11	0.03
American Indian tribes, not spec.	12	0.03
Arab:	164	0.41
Egyptian	9	0.02
Iraqi	30	0.07
Lebanese	27	0.07
Moroccan	12	0.03
Syrian	25	0.06
Other Arab	61	0.15
Armenian	28	0.07
Asian:	1,712	4.23
Bangladeshi (2)	2	0.00
Cambodian (12)	16	0.04
Chinese, ex. Taiwanese (201)	253	0.63
Filipino (103)	147	0.36
Indian (176)	240	0.59
Indonesian	3	0.01
Japanese (45)	79	0.20
Korean (324)	363	0.90
Laotian (88)	115	0.28
Malaysian	2	0.00
Pakistani (70)	97	0.24
Sri Lankan (5)	7	0.02
Taiwanese (11)	13	0.03
Thai (33)	50	0.12
Vietnamese (117)	158	0.39
Other Asian, specified (4)	6	0.01
Other Asian, not specified (27)	161	0.40
Australian	8	0.02
Austrian	174	0.43
Basque	36	0.09
Belgian	24	0.06
Brazilian	62	0.15
British	252	0.62
Bulgarian	6	0.01
Canadian	90	0.22
Celtic	8	0.02
Czech	88	0.22
Czechoslovakian	21	0.05
Danish	75	0.19
Dutch	478	1.18
Eastern European	32	0.08
English	3,886	9.60
European	509	1.26
Finnish	34	0.08
French, except Basque	875	2.16
French Canadian	136	0.34
German	8,088	19.99
Greek	165	0.41
Guyanese	6	0.01
Hawaii Native/Pacific Islander:	44	0.11
Micronesian: (3)	4	0.01
Guamanian/Chamorro (3)	4	0.01
Polynesian: (4)	15	0.04
Native Hawaiian (4)	14	0.03
Samoan	1	0.00
Other Pac. Isl., not spec. (3)	25	0.06
Hispanic or Latino:	3,580	8.85
Central American:	695	1.72
Costa Rican	3	0.01
Guatemalan	89	0.22
Honduran	213	0.53
Nicaraguan	15	0.04
Panamanian	8	0.02
Salvadoran	343	0.85
Other Central American	24	0.06
Cuban	113	0.28
Dominican Republic	151	0.37
Mexican	1,623	4.01
Puerto Rican	433	1.07
South American:	98	0.24
Argentinean	4	0.01
Bolivian	10	0.02
Chilean	5	0.01
Colombian	31	0.08
Ecuadorian	12	0.03
Peruvian	16	0.04
Uruguayan	8	0.02
Venezuelan	5	0.01
Other South American	7	0.02
Other Hispanic or Latino	467	1.15
Hungarian	112	0.28
Iranian	77	0.19
Irish	4,147	10.25
Israeli	8	0.02
Italian	1,951	4.82
Latvian	7	0.02
Lithuanian	87	0.21
Luxemburger	6	0.01
Northern European	17	0.04
Norwegian	293	0.72
Pennsylvania German	35	0.09
Polish	856	2.12
Portuguese	36	0.09
Romanian	8	0.02
Russian	509	1.26
Scandinavian	149	0.37
Scotch-Irish	1,055	2.61
Scottish	872	2.15
Serbian	18	0.04
Slovak	113	0.28
Slovene	3	0.01
Swedish	456	1.13
Swiss	873	2.16
Ukrainian	118	0.29
United States or American	3,708	9.16
Welsh	278	0.69
West Indian, excl. Hispanic:	49	0.12
Haitian	15	0.04
Jamaican	11	0.03
Trinidadian and Tobagonian	23	0.06
White:	35,241	87.08
Not Hispanic (32,416)	33,155	81.93
Hispanic (1,918)	2,086	5.15
Yugoslavian	12	0.03

Herndon

Place Type: Town
County: Fairfax
Population: 21,655

Ancestry/Race	Number	%
Afghan	177	0.82
African American/Black:	2,270	10.48
Not Hispanic (2,000)	2,165	10.00
Hispanic (60)	105	0.48
African, sub-Saharan:	258	1.19
African	109	0.50
Ethiopian	41	0.19
Kenyan	9	0.04
Sudanese	38	0.18
Other sub-Saharan African	61	0.28
Am. Ind. or Alaska Nat., not spec.	72	0.33
Alsatian	15	0.07
American Indian tribes, specified:	117	0.54
Apache (1)	1	0.00
Blackfeet	2	0.01
Cherokee (8)	48	0.22
Chippewa (1)	3	0.01
Choctaw	1	0.00
Creek	1	0.00
Crow	1	0.00
Iroquois (2)	6	0.03
Latin American Indians (10)	28	0.13
Navajo	4	0.02
Osage (2)	2	0.01
Seminole (1)	5	0.02
Sioux	2	0.01
All other tribes (8)	13	0.06
American Indian tribes, not spec.	27	0.12
Arab:	375	1.73
Arab/Arabic	127	0.59
Egyptian	90	0.42
Lebanese	50	0.23
Moroccan	13	0.06
Palestinian	5	0.02
Syrian	71	0.33
Other Arab	19	0.09
Armenian	22	0.10
Asian:	3,487	16.10
Bangladeshi (46)	62	0.29
Cambodian (124)	133	0.61
Chinese, ex. Taiwanese (271)	316	1.46
Filipino (262)	302	1.39
Indian (1,126)	1,276	5.89
Indonesian (18)	28	0.13
Japanese (40)	58	0.27
Korean (146)	161	0.74
Laotian (28)	37	0.17
Malaysian (1)	5	0.02
Pakistani (276)	383	1.77
Sri Lankan (3)	8	0.04
Taiwanese (2)	8	0.04
Thai (70)	82	0.38
Vietnamese (395)	417	1.93
Other Asian, specified (21)	32	0.15

Notes: 1. Figures in the "Number" column do not add up to the total population due to: a) Ancestry/Race overlap — e.g. persons can report being both White and Irish, b) persons of Hispanic origin can report being any race, c) persons reporting two ancestries are counted in both categories. 2. Numbers in parentheses indicate the number of persons reporting this ancestry/race alone, not in combination with any other ancestry/race. 3. Refer to the Explanation of Data in the front of the book for more detailed information.

Other Asian, not specified (96)	179	0.83
Austrian	21	0.10
Brazilian	5	0.02
British	109	0.50
Canadian	43	0.20
Croatian	40	0.18
Czech	83	0.38
Danish	65	0.30
Dutch	130	0.60
Eastern European	46	0.21
English	1,865	8.61
European	260	1.20
Finnish	11	0.05
French, except Basque	532	2.46
French Canadian	67	0.31
German	2,110	9.74
German Russian	10	0.05
Greek	110	0.51
Guyanese	8	0.04
Hawaii Native/Pacific Islander:	46	0.21
Micronesian: (5)	10	0.05
Guamanian/Chamorro (5)	10	0.05
Polynesian: (5)	15	0.07
Native Hawaiian (2)	9	0.04
Samoan (3)	6	0.03
Other Pac. Isl., specified	5	0.02
Other Pac. Isl., not spec.	16	0.07
Hispanic or Latino:	5,633	26.01
Central American:	2,687	12.41
Costa Rican	10	0.05
Guatemalan	162	0.75
Honduran	424	1.96
Nicaraguan	68	0.31
Panamanian	14	0.06
Salvadoran	1,853	8.56
Other Central American	156	0.72
Cuban	28	0.13
Dominican Republic	19	0.09
Mexican	500	2.31
Puerto Rican	148	0.68
South American:	553	2.55
Argentinean	10	0.05
Bolivian	85	0.39
Chilean	21	0.10
Colombian	72	0.33
Ecuadorian	17	0.08
Paraguayan	2	0.01
Peruvian	303	1.40
Uruguayan	1	0.00
Venezuelan	20	0.09
Other South American	22	0.10
Other Hispanic or Latino	1,698	7.84
Hungarian	85	0.39
Iranian	65	0.30
Irish	2,055	9.49
Italian	792	3.66
Lithuanian	34	0.16
Northern European	15	0.07
Norwegian	273	1.26
Polish	420	1.94
Portuguese	27	0.12
Romanian	27	0.12
Russian	215	0.99
Scandinavian	32	0.15
Scotch-Irish	483	2.23
Scottish	356	1.64
Serbian	88	0.41
Slavic	21	0.10
Slovak	68	0.31
Swedish	135	0.62
Swiss	148	0.68
Turkish	62	0.29
Ukrainian	71	0.33
United States or American	905	4.18
Welsh	107	0.49
West Indian, excl. Hispanic:	134	0.62
Jamaican	79	0.36
Trinidadian and Tobagonian	55	0.25
White:	13,419	61.97
Not Hispanic (10,171)	10,673	49.29
Hispanic (2,364)	2,746	12.68
Yugoslavian	8	0.04

Highland Springs

Place Type: Census Designated Place
County: Henrico
Population: 15,137

Ancestry/Race	Number	%
African American/Black:	7,977	52.70
Not Hispanic (7,799)	7,923	52.34
Hispanic (46)	54	0.36
African, sub-Saharan:	88	0.58
African	88	0.58
Am. Ind. or Alaska Nat., not spec.	53	0.35
American Indian tribes, specified:	173	1.14
Apache	2	0.01
Blackfeet (5)	11	0.07
Cherokee (33)	77	0.51
Creek	1	0.01
Delaware (1)	1	0.01
Kiowa	2	0.01
Latin American Indians	3	0.02
Lumbee (2)	3	0.02
Osage	1	0.01
Seminole (1)	3	0.02
Sioux (1)	7	0.05
All other tribes (31)	62	0.41
American Indian tribes, not spec.	6	0.04
Arab:	24	0.16
Lebanese	24	0.16
Asian:	122	0.81
Cambodian (2)	2	0.01
Chinese, ex. Taiwanese (11)	12	0.08
Filipino (23)	29	0.19
Indian (14)	23	0.15
Japanese (3)	4	0.03
Korean (1)	2	0.01
Laotian (15)	15	0.10
Pakistani (2)	3	0.02
Taiwanese	1	0.01
Thai (1)	1	0.01
Vietnamese (20)	23	0.15
Other Asian, not specified (4)	7	0.05
Australian	5	0.03
British	24	0.16
Canadian	8	0.05
Czech	24	0.16
Czechoslovakian	18	0.12
Dutch	137	0.90
English	1,046	6.85
European	151	0.99
French, except Basque	127	0.83
French Canadian	21	0.14
German	904	5.92
Hawaii Native/Pacific Islander:	6	0.04
Micronesian:	2	0.01
Guamanian/Chamorro	2	0.01
Polynesian: (1)	3	0.02
Native Hawaiian (1)	3	0.02
Other Pac. Isl., not spec.	1	0.01
Hispanic or Latino:	235	1.55
Central American:	25	0.17
Costa Rican	1	0.01
Guatemalan	9	0.06
Honduran	1	0.01
Panamanian	2	0.01
Salvadoran	12	0.08
Cuban	8	0.05
Dominican Republic	1	0.01
Mexican	60	0.40
Puerto Rican	91	0.60
South American:	5	0.03
Colombian	4	0.03
Other South American	1	0.01
Other Hispanic or Latino	45	0.30
Hungarian	9	0.06
Irish	878	5.75
Italian	276	1.81
Norwegian	31	0.20
Pennsylvania German	6	0.04
Polish	99	0.65
Portuguese	13	0.09
Scotch-Irish	159	1.04
Scottish	238	1.56
Slovak	6	0.04
Swiss	5	0.03
United States or American	1,766	11.57
Welsh	109	0.71
West Indian, excl. Hispanic:	92	0.60
Jamaican	53	0.35
West Indian	39	0.26
White:	6,913	45.67
Not Hispanic (6,659)	6,829	45.11
Hispanic (74)	84	0.55

Hollins

Place Type: Census Designated Place
County: Roanoke
Population: 14,309

Ancestry/Race	Number	%
Acadian/Cajun	20	0.14
African American/Black:	911	6.37
Not Hispanic (849)	905	6.32
Hispanic (6)	6	0.04
African, sub-Saharan:	12	0.08
African	12	0.08
Am. Ind. or Alaska Nat., not spec.	15	0.10
American Indian tribes, specified:	42	0.29
Apache	1	0.01
Blackfeet	2	0.01
Cherokee (8)	21	0.15
Cheyenne (1)	1	0.01
Chippewa (1)	1	0.01
Latin American Indians	1	0.01
Navajo (1)	1	0.01
Pima	1	0.01
Sioux (1)	1	0.01
All other tribes (6)	12	0.08
American Indian tribes, not spec.	4	0.03
Arab:	120	0.84
Arab/Arabic	25	0.17
Lebanese	95	0.66
Armenian	6	0.04
Asian:	299	2.09
Chinese, ex. Taiwanese (42)	44	0.31
Filipino (10)	15	0.10
Indian (40)	41	0.29
Japanese (10)	14	0.10
Korean (21)	27	0.19
Laotian (3)	4	0.03
Pakistani (1)	1	0.01
Taiwanese (1)	2	0.01
Thai (5)	5	0.03
Vietnamese (121)	133	0.93
Other Asian, specified	1	0.01
Other Asian, not specified (10)	12	0.08
British	63	0.44
Canadian	8	0.06
Croatian	19	0.13
Czech	6	0.04
Danish	11	0.08
Dutch	251	1.75
English	1,756	12.26
European	183	1.28
French, except Basque	354	2.47
French Canadian	54	0.38
German	1,825	12.74
Greek	42	0.29
Hawaii Native/Pacific Islander:	4	0.03
Polynesian:	2	0.01
Native Hawaiian	2	0.01
Other Pac. Isl., not spec. (1)	2	0.01
Hispanic or Latino:	147	1.03
Central American:	11	0.08
Costa Rican	1	0.01
Guatemalan	3	0.02

Notes: 1. Figures in the "Number" column do not add up to the total population due to: a) Ancestry/Race overlap — e.g. persons can report being both White and Irish, b) persons of Hispanic origin can report being any race, c) persons reporting two ancestries are counted in both categories. 2. Numbers in parentheses indicate the number of persons reporting this ancestry/race alone, not in combination with any other ancestry/race. 3. Refer to the Explanation of Data in the front of the book for more detailed information.

Ancestry/Race	Number	%
Honduran	2	0.01
Nicaraguan	1	0.01
Other Central American	4	0.03
Cuban	6	0.04
Dominican Republic	7	0.05
Mexican	61	0.43
Puerto Rican	21	0.15
South American:	15	0.10
Chilean	2	0.01
Colombian	1	0.01
Ecuadorian	2	0.01
Peruvian	1	0.01
Venezuelan	8	0.06
Other South American	1	0.01
Other Hispanic or Latino	26	0.18
Hungarian	58	0.40
Iranian	6	0.04
Irish	1,495	10.43
Italian	178	1.24
Lithuanian	11	0.08
Norwegian	34	0.24
Polish	141	0.98
Portuguese	24	0.17
Russian	74	0.52
Scandinavian	9	0.06
Scotch-Irish	435	3.04
Scottish	322	2.25
Slovak	40	0.28
Swedish	98	0.68
Swiss	13	0.09
Turkish	7	0.05
Ukrainian	6	0.04
United States or American	2,274	15.87
Welsh	71	0.50
West Indian, excl. Hispanic:	39	0.27
Haitian	27	0.19
West Indian	12	0.08
White:	13,090	91.48
Not Hispanic (12,885)	12,994	90.81
Hispanic (90)	96	0.67

Hopewell

Place Type: Independent City
County: Hopewell Independent City
Population: 22,354

Ancestry/Race	Number	%
African American/Black:	7,663	34.28
Not Hispanic (7,414)	7,582	33.92
Hispanic (70)	81	0.36
African, sub-Saharan:	100	0.45
African	82	0.37
Other sub-Saharan African	18	0.08
Am. Ind. or Alaska Nat., not spec.	88	0.39
American Indian tribes, specified:	106	0.47
Apache (1)	1	0.00
Blackfeet	3	0.01
Cherokee (20)	48	0.21
Chickasaw	3	0.01
Choctaw (3)	12	0.05
Comanche	2	0.01
Delaware (1)	1	0.00
Iroquois (4)	6	0.03
Latin American Indians (4)	9	0.04
Lumbee (1)	2	0.01
Potawatomi	1	0.00
Sioux	2	0.01
Yuman	1	0.00
All other tribes (10)	15	0.07
American Indian tribes, not spec.	13	0.06
Arab:	6	0.03
Lebanese	6	0.03
Armenian	59	0.26
Asian:	302	1.35
Cambodian (1)	1	0.00
Chinese, ex. Taiwanese (11)	19	0.08
Filipino (23)	45	0.20
Indian (14)	22	0.10
Indonesian (3)	4	0.02
Japanese (18)	27	0.12
Korean (63)	93	0.42
Laotian	1	0.00
Malaysian	1	0.00
Pakistani (7)	9	0.04
Thai (16)	23	0.10
Vietnamese (8)	12	0.05
Other Asian, specified	3	0.01
Other Asian, not specified (12)	42	0.19
Belgian	11	0.05
Brazilian	6	0.03
British	47	0.21
Canadian	26	0.12
Celtic	15	0.07
Croatian	16	0.07
Cypriot	20	0.09
Czech	96	0.43
Czechoslovakian	67	0.30
Danish	10	0.04
Dutch	203	0.91
English	1,967	8.80
European	150	0.67
Finnish	10	0.04
French, except Basque	443	1.98
French Canadian	138	0.62
German	1,896	8.48
Greek	102	0.46
Hawaii Native/Pacific Islander:	37	0.17
Micronesian: (11)	16	0.07
Guamanian/Chamorro (10)	13	0.06
Other Micronesian (1)	3	0.01
Polynesian: (5)	16	0.07
Native Hawaiian (5)	14	0.06
Samoan	2	0.01
Other Pac. Isl., specified	2	0.01
Other Pac. Isl., not spec.	3	0.01
Hispanic or Latino:	651	2.91
Central American:	66	0.30
Guatemalan	3	0.01
Honduran	16	0.07
Nicaraguan	3	0.01
Panamanian	26	0.12
Salvadoran	18	0.08
Cuban	9	0.04
Dominican Republic	3	0.01
Mexican	196	0.88
Puerto Rican	224	1.00
South American:	9	0.04
Colombian	1	0.00
Peruvian	2	0.01
Venezuelan	5	0.02
Other South American	1	0.00
Other Hispanic or Latino	144	0.64
Hungarian	33	0.15
Iranian	7	0.03
Irish	1,418	6.34
Italian	440	1.97
Lithuanian	10	0.04
Norwegian	32	0.14
Pennsylvania German	11	0.05
Polish	174	0.78
Romanian	17	0.08
Russian	25	0.11
Scotch-Irish	431	1.93
Scottish	303	1.36
Slovak	32	0.14
Swedish	43	0.19
Swiss	47	0.21
Ukrainian	11	0.05
United States or American	2,529	11.31
Welsh	79	0.35
West Indian, excl. Hispanic:	30	0.13
Jamaican	30	0.13
White:	14,241	63.71
Not Hispanic (13,655)	13,929	62.31
Hispanic (269)	312	1.40

Hybla Valley

Place Type: Census Designated Place
County: Fairfax
Population: 16,721

Ancestry/Race	Number	%
Afghan	34	0.20
African American/Black:	4,962	29.68
Not Hispanic (4,675)	4,827	28.87
Hispanic (95)	135	0.81
African, sub-Saharan:	476	2.83
African	157	0.93
Cape Verdean	21	0.12
Ethiopian	34	0.20
Ghanian	144	0.86
Liberian	36	0.21
Nigerian	8	0.05
Sierra Leonean	18	0.11
Sudanese	15	0.09
Other sub-Saharan African	43	0.26
Alaska Native tribes, specified:	4	0.02
Aleut (4)	4	0.02
Am. Ind. or Alaska Nat., not spec.	79	0.47
Alsatian	6	0.04
American Indian tribes, specified:	99	0.59
Apache	1	0.01
Blackfeet (1)	5	0.03
Cherokee (3)	27	0.16
Chickasaw	2	0.01
Chippewa (3)	3	0.02
Choctaw (2)	2	0.01
Cree	2	0.01
Creek	2	0.01
Iroquois (4)	10	0.06
Kiowa (1)	2	0.01
Latin American Indians (8)	16	0.10
Navajo (1)	1	0.01
Paiute (1)	1	0.01
Pima (1)	1	0.01
Potawatomi (3)	4	0.02
Pueblo (1)	3	0.02
Seminole (3)	7	0.04
Sioux	3	0.02
All other tribes (4)	7	0.04
American Indian tribes, not spec.	14	0.08
Arab:	177	1.05
Arab/Arabic	50	0.30
Lebanese	8	0.05
Moroccan	6	0.04
Palestinian	75	0.45
Syrian	7	0.04
Other Arab	31	0.18
Asian:	1,612	9.64
Bangladeshi (38)	60	0.36
Cambodian (38)	41	0.25
Chinese, ex. Taiwanese (65)	79	0.47
Filipino (156)	205	1.23
Indian (232)	296	1.77
Indonesian (7)	7	0.04
Japanese (27)	44	0.26
Korean (200)	212	1.27
Laotian (35)	38	0.23
Pakistani (179)	223	1.33
Sri Lankan	1	0.01
Taiwanese (3)	3	0.02
Thai (90)	129	0.77
Vietnamese (156)	168	1.00
Other Asian, specified (2)	6	0.04
Other Asian, not specified (44)	100	0.60
Austrian	8	0.05
Belgian	18	0.11
British	63	0.37
Bulgarian	5	0.03
Canadian	38	0.23
Celtic	16	0.10
Czech	48	0.29
Czechoslovakian	10	0.06
Danish	59	0.35
Dutch	137	0.81

Notes: 1. Figures in the "Number" column do not add up to the total population due to: a) Ancestry/Race overlap — e.g. persons can report being both White and Irish, b) persons of Hispanic origin can report being any race, c) persons reporting two ancestries are counted in both categories. 2. Numbers in parentheses indicate the number of persons reporting this ancestry/race alone, not in combination with any other ancestry/race. 3. Refer to the Explanation of Data in the front of the book for more detailed information.

English	1,314	7.81
European	104	0.62
Finnish	15	0.09
French, except Basque	246	1.46
French Canadian	31	0.18
German	1,482	8.81
German Russian	6	0.04
Greek	69	0.41
Hawaii Native/Pacific Islander:	27	0.16
Polynesian: (7)	12	0.07
Native Hawaiian (3)	8	0.05
Samoan (3)	3	0.02
Tongan (1)	1	0.01
Other Pac. Isl., specified	3	0.02
Other Pac. Isl., not spec. (3)	12	0.07
Hispanic or Latino:	3,213	19.22
Central American:	1,038	6.21
Costa Rican	1	0.01
Guatemalan	68	0.41
Honduran	215	1.29
Nicaraguan	45	0.27
Panamanian	25	0.15
Salvadoran	636	3.80
Other Central American	48	0.29
Cuban	16	0.10
Dominican Republic	18	0.11
Mexican	935	5.59
Puerto Rican	153	0.92
South American:	172	1.03
Argentinean	8	0.05
Bolivian	36	0.22
Chilean	13	0.08
Colombian	26	0.16
Ecuadorian	3	0.02
Paraguayan	2	0.01
Peruvian	72	0.43
Uruguayan	2	0.01
Venezuelan	1	0.01
Other South American	9	0.05
Other Hispanic or Latino	881	5.27
Hungarian	108	0.64
Iranian	41	0.24
Irish	1,313	7.81
Italian	331	1.97
Lithuanian	6	0.04
Luxemburger	8	0.05
Maltese	7	0.04
Norwegian	99	0.59
Pennsylvania German	8	0.05
Polish	378	2.25
Portuguese	15	0.09
Russian	135	0.80
Scandinavian	52	0.31
Scotch-Irish	301	1.79
Scottish	379	2.25
Slavic	16	0.10
Slovene	11	0.07
Swedish	89	0.53
Swiss	18	0.11
Turkish	72	0.43
Ukrainian	12	0.07
United States or American	900	5.35
Welsh	94	0.56
West Indian, excl. Hispanic:	59	0.35
British West Indian	8	0.05
Haitian	10	0.06
Jamaican	5	0.03
Trinidadian and Tobagonian	17	0.10
West Indian	19	0.11
White:	8,825	52.78
Not Hispanic (6,985)	7,285	43.57
Hispanic (1,372)	1,540	9.21
Yugoslavian	64	0.38

Idylwood

Place Type: Census Designated Place
County: Fairfax
Population: 16,005

Ancestry/Race	Number	%
Afghan	118	0.73
African American/Black:	1,195	7.47
Not Hispanic (1,058)	1,132	7.07
Hispanic (51)	63	0.39
African, sub-Saharan:	222	1.38
African	106	0.66
Ethiopian	27	0.17
Senegalese	21	0.13
Somalian	17	0.11
Other sub-Saharan African	51	0.32
Alaska Native tribes, specified:	2	0.01
Aleut	1	0.01
Eskimo	1	0.01
Am. Ind. or Alaska Nat., not spec.	46	0.29
American Indian tribes, specified:	54	0.34
Blackfeet (1)	4	0.02
Cherokee (1)	9	0.06
Choctaw (2)	3	0.02
Crow (1)	2	0.01
Delaware (2)	2	0.01
Iroquois (2)	4	0.02
Latin American Indians (11)	17	0.11
Lumbee	1	0.01
Navajo (2)	2	0.01
All other tribes (6)	10	0.06
Arab:	475	2.96
Arab/Arabic	112	0.70
Egyptian	8	0.05
Iraqi	19	0.12
Jordanian	57	0.36
Lebanese	144	0.90
Moroccan	8	0.05
Palestinian	54	0.34
Syrian	47	0.29
Other Arab	26	0.16
Armenian	85	0.53
Asian:	3,364	21.02
Bangladeshi (14)	14	0.09
Cambodian (11)	15	0.09
Chinese, ex. Taiwanese (521)	564	3.52
Filipino (256)	291	1.82
Indian (983)	1,051	6.57
Indonesian (21)	26	0.16
Japanese (64)	80	0.50
Korean (352)	366	2.29
Laotian (20)	23	0.14
Pakistani (40)	66	0.41
Sri Lankan (5)	7	0.04
Taiwanese (8)	9	0.06
Thai (18)	24	0.15
Vietnamese (601)	627	3.92
Other Asian, specified (61)	78	0.49
Other Asian, not specified (35)	123	0.77
Austrian	69	0.43
Belgian	15	0.09
British	204	1.27
Bulgarian	11	0.07
Canadian	85	0.53
Carpatho Rusyn	13	0.08
Celtic	10	0.06
Croatian	9	0.06
Cypriot	11	0.07
Czech	63	0.39
Czechoslovakian	52	0.32
Danish	84	0.52
Dutch	148	0.92
English	1,561	9.72
Estonian	20	0.12
European	169	1.05
Finnish	59	0.37
French, except Basque	252	1.57
French Canadian	72	0.45
German	1,888	11.76
Greek	120	0.75
Hawaii Native/Pacific Islander:	30	0.19
Micronesian: (3)	3	0.02
Guamanian/Chamorro (3)	3	0.02
Polynesian: (3)	9	0.06
Native Hawaiian	3	0.02
Samoan (3)	5	0.03
Other Polynesian	1	0.01
Other Pac. Isl., specified	5	0.03
Other Pac. Isl., not spec. (3)	13	0.08
Hispanic or Latino:	2,621	16.38
Central American:	820	5.12
Costa Rican	19	0.12
Guatemalan	106	0.66
Honduran	28	0.17
Nicaraguan	41	0.26
Panamanian	18	0.11
Salvadoran	549	3.43
Other Central American	59	0.37
Cuban	42	0.26
Dominican Republic	20	0.12
Mexican	244	1.52
Puerto Rican	63	0.39
South American:	519	3.24
Argentinean	17	0.11
Bolivian	238	1.49
Chilean	18	0.11
Colombian	39	0.24
Ecuadorian	37	0.23
Paraguayan	1	0.01
Peruvian	119	0.74
Uruguayan	5	0.03
Venezuelan	12	0.07
Other South American	33	0.21
Other Hispanic or Latino	913	5.70
Hungarian	129	0.80
Icelander	8	0.05
Iranian	307	1.91
Irish	1,610	10.03
Israeli	10	0.06
Italian	531	3.31
Latvian	25	0.16
Lithuanian	13	0.08
Northern European	13	0.08
Norwegian	97	0.60
Polish	401	2.50
Portuguese	43	0.27
Romanian	40	0.25
Russian	232	1.45
Scandinavian	8	0.05
Scotch-Irish	270	1.68
Scottish	267	1.66
Slovak	28	0.17
Swedish	199	1.24
Swiss	57	0.36
Turkish	19	0.12
Ukrainian	32	0.20
United States or American	637	3.97
Welsh	152	0.95
West Indian, excl. Hispanic:	41	0.26
British West Indian	14	0.09
Jamaican	17	0.11
Trinidadian and Tobagonian	10	0.06
White:	10,563	66.00
Not Hispanic (8,775)	9,119	56.98
Hispanic (1,259)	1,444	9.02
Yugoslavian	46	0.29

Jefferson

Place Type: Census Designated Place
County: Fairfax
Population: 27,422

Ancestry/Race	Number	%
Afghan	38	0.14
African American/Black:	1,382	5.04
Not Hispanic (1,180)	1,288	4.70
Hispanic (65)	94	0.34
African, sub-Saharan:	182	0.67

Notes: 1. Figures in the "Number" column do not add up to the total population due to: a) Ancestry/Race overlap — e.g. persons can report being both White and Irish, b) persons of Hispanic origin can report being any race, c) persons reporting two ancestries are counted in both categories. 2. Numbers in parentheses indicate the number of persons reporting this ancestry/race alone, not in combination with any other ancestry/race. 3. Refer to the Explanation of Data in the front of the book for more detailed information.

Ancestry/Race	Number	%
African	55	0.20
Ethiopian	46	0.17
Ghanian	36	0.13
Nigerian	27	0.10
Sudanese	6	0.02
Other sub-Saharan African	12	0.04
Alaska Native tribes, specified:	1	0.00
Tlingit-Haida	1	0.00
Am. Ind. or Alaska Nat., not spec.	83	0.30
Albanian	22	0.08
Alsatian	8	0.03
American Indian tribes, specified:	117	0.43
Apache (1)	4	0.01
Blackfeet (2)	4	0.01
Cherokee (7)	24	0.09
Chippewa (7)	12	0.04
Creek (4)	4	0.01
Iroquois (2)	3	0.01
Latin American Indians (14)	30	0.11
Lumbee (2)	2	0.01
Navajo (1)	1	0.00
Ottawa	3	0.01
Pueblo (5)	5	0.02
Puget Sound Salish	1	0.00
Seminole (2)	2	0.01
Sioux (4)	5	0.02
Yaqui (3)	3	0.01
All other tribes (8)	14	0.05
American Indian tribes, not spec.	13	0.05
Arab:	451	1.65
Arab/Arabic	55	0.20
Egyptian	52	0.19
Iraqi	37	0.14
Lebanese	43	0.16
Moroccan	54	0.20
Palestinian	21	0.08
Syrian	68	0.25
Other Arab	121	0.44
Armenian	35	0.13
Asian:	5,669	20.67
Bangladeshi (34)	37	0.13
Cambodian (113)	138	0.50
Chinese, ex. Taiwanese (533)	611	2.23
Filipino (526)	601	2.19
Indian (833)	882	3.22
Indonesian (38)	42	0.15
Japanese (49)	80	0.29
Korean (289)	309	1.13
Laotian (41)	44	0.16
Malaysian (13)	23	0.08
Pakistani (128)	168	0.61
Sri Lankan (21)	23	0.08
Taiwanese (8)	15	0.05
Thai (51)	61	0.22
Vietnamese (2,375)	2,469	9.00
Other Asian, specified (23)	27	0.10
Other Asian, not specified (74)	139	0.51
Austrian	53	0.19
Belgian	16	0.06
Brazilian	14	0.05
British	178	0.65
Canadian	63	0.23
Celtic	15	0.05
Croatian	20	0.07
Czech	58	0.21
Czechoslovakian	38	0.14
Danish	82	0.30
Dutch	272	0.99
Eastern European	50	0.18
English	2,431	8.89
Estonian	8	0.03
European	402	1.47
Finnish	13	0.05
French, except Basque	568	2.08
French Canadian	182	0.67
German	2,991	10.94
Greek	155	0.57
Guyanese	47	0.17
Hawaii Native/Pacific Islander:	33	0.12
Melanesian:	1	0.00
Fijian	1	0.00
Micronesian: (3)	3	0.01
Guamanian/Chamorro (3)	3	0.01
Polynesian: (4)	12	0.04
Native Hawaiian (1)	4	0.01
Samoan (3)	8	0.03
Other Pac. Isl., not spec. (1)	17	0.06
Hispanic or Latino:	6,351	23.16
Central American:	2,054	7.49
Costa Rican	25	0.09
Guatemalan	258	0.94
Honduran	122	0.44
Nicaraguan	131	0.48
Panamanian	8	0.03
Salvadoran	1,428	5.21
Other Central American	82	0.30
Cuban	76	0.28
Dominican Republic	75	0.27
Mexican	422	1.54
Puerto Rican	131	0.48
South American:	1,269	4.63
Argentinean	69	0.25
Bolivian	703	2.56
Chilean	49	0.18
Colombian	62	0.23
Ecuadorian	56	0.20
Paraguayan	11	0.04
Peruvian	218	0.79
Uruguayan	7	0.03
Venezuelan	23	0.08
Other South American	71	0.26
Other Hispanic or Latino	2,324	8.47
Hungarian	163	0.60
Iranian	111	0.41
Irish	2,552	9.33
Israeli	7	0.03
Italian	1,044	3.82
Latvian	17	0.06
Lithuanian	44	0.16
Northern European	72	0.26
Norwegian	233	0.85
Polish	622	2.28
Portuguese	99	0.36
Romanian	41	0.15
Russian	337	1.23
Scandinavian	30	0.11
Scotch-Irish	385	1.41
Scottish	648	2.37
Serbian	32	0.12
Slavic	32	0.12
Slovak	62	0.23
Slovene	13	0.05
Swedish	246	0.90
Swiss	52	0.19
Turkish	19	0.07
Ukrainian	116	0.42
United States or American	1,292	4.73
Welsh	216	0.79
West Indian, excl. Hispanic:	84	0.31
British West Indian	34	0.12
Jamaican	8	0.03
Trinidadian and Tobagonian	23	0.08
West Indian	14	0.05
Other West Indian	5	0.02
White:	17,757	64.75
Not Hispanic (13,981)	14,420	52.59
Hispanic (2,842)	3,337	12.17
Yugoslavian	56	0.20

Lake Ridge

Place Type: Census Designated Place
County: Prince William
Population: 30,404

Ancestry/Race	Number	%
Acadian/Cajun	12	0.04
African American/Black:	5,266	17.32
Not Hispanic (4,781)	5,132	16.88
Hispanic (91)	134	0.44
African, sub-Saharan:	450	1.47
African	227	0.74
Ethiopian	100	0.33
Ghanian	4	0.01
Nigerian	78	0.26
Sierra Leonean	41	0.13
Am. Ind. or Alaska Nat., not spec.	87	0.29
American Indian tribes, specified:	122	0.40
Apache (1)	2	0.01
Blackfeet	6	0.02
Cherokee (12)	52	0.17
Cheyenne	1	0.00
Chickasaw	3	0.01
Chippewa (2)	5	0.02
Choctaw (1)	3	0.01
Comanche (1)	1	0.00
Creek (2)	3	0.01
Delaware (1)	1	0.00
Iroquois (4)	6	0.02
Latin American Indians (6)	9	0.03
Lumbee (1)	1	0.00
Navajo	1	0.00
Pima (1)	1	0.00
Potawatomi (2)	2	0.01
Seminole	3	0.01
Sioux (6)	12	0.04
All other tribes (3)	10	0.03
American Indian tribes, not spec.	8	0.03
Arab:	126	0.41
Arab/Arabic	40	0.13
Egyptian	25	0.08
Lebanese	9	0.03
Moroccan	19	0.06
Palestinian	26	0.09
Other Arab	7	0.02
Asian:	1,584	5.21
Bangladeshi (6)	8	0.03
Cambodian (12)	18	0.06
Chinese, ex. Taiwanese (111)	152	0.50
Filipino (214)	350	1.15
Indian (164)	193	0.63
Indonesian (5)	7	0.02
Japanese (68)	158	0.52
Korean (213)	288	0.95
Laotian (14)	14	0.05
Pakistani (100)	140	0.46
Sri Lankan (1)	1	0.00
Taiwanese (1)	1	0.00
Thai (32)	43	0.14
Vietnamese (62)	89	0.29
Other Asian, specified (4)	12	0.04
Other Asian, not specified (39)	110	0.36
Australian	12	0.04
Austrian	85	0.28
Basque	5	0.02
Belgian	56	0.18
Brazilian	65	0.21
British	220	0.72
Canadian	63	0.21
Celtic	7	0.02
Croatian	11	0.04
Czech	85	0.28
Czechoslovakian	100	0.33
Danish	225	0.74
Dutch	475	1.55
Eastern European	14	0.05
English	4,054	13.26
Estonian	15	0.05
European	346	1.13
Finnish	66	0.22
French, except Basque	863	2.82
French Canadian	189	0.62
German	5,100	16.68
Greek	244	0.80
Hawaii Native/Pacific Islander:	94	0.31
Micronesian: (15)	35	0.12
Guamanian/Chamorro (12)	29	0.10
Other Micronesian (3)	6	0.02
Polynesian: (11)	29	0.10
Native Hawaiian (5)	22	0.07

Notes: 1. Figures in the "Number" column do not add up to the total population due to: a) Ancestry/Race overlap — e.g. persons can report being both White and Irish, b) persons of Hispanic origin can report being any race, c) persons reporting two ancestries are counted in both categories. 2. Numbers in parentheses indicate the number of persons reporting this ancestry/race alone, not in combination with any other ancestry/race. 3. Refer to the Explanation of Data in the front of the book for more detailed information.

Ancestry/Race	Number	%
Samoan (6)	7	0.02
Other Pac. Isl., specified	2	0.01
Other Pac. Isl., not spec. (9)	28	0.09
Hispanic or Latino:	2,161	7.11
Central American:	277	0.91
Costa Rican	1	0.00
Guatemalan	42	0.14
Honduran	3	0.01
Nicaraguan	14	0.05
Panamanian	32	0.11
Salvadoran	160	0.53
Other Central American	25	0.08
Cuban	52	0.17
Dominican Republic	20	0.07
Mexican	404	1.33
Puerto Rican	444	1.46
South American:	432	1.42
Argentinean	7	0.02
Bolivian	77	0.25
Chilean	30	0.10
Colombian	40	0.13
Ecuadorian	38	0.12
Paraguayan	2	0.01
Peruvian	167	0.55
Uruguayan	8	0.03
Venezuelan	36	0.12
Other South American	27	0.09
Other Hispanic or Latino	532	1.75
Hungarian	220	0.72
Iranian	96	0.31
Irish	4,438	14.51
Israeli	9	0.03
Italian	2,065	6.75
Latvian	12	0.04
Lithuanian	115	0.38
Luxemburger	9	0.03
Maltese	14	0.05
Northern European	64	0.21
Norwegian	281	0.92
Pennsylvania German	17	0.06
Polish	964	3.15
Portuguese	134	0.44
Romanian	24	0.08
Russian	419	1.37
Scandinavian	43	0.14
Scotch-Irish	612	2.00
Scottish	879	2.87
Serbian	15	0.05
Slavic	9	0.03
Slovak	122	0.40
Slovene	19	0.06
Swedish	378	1.24
Swiss	124	0.41
Turkish	10	0.03
Ukrainian	45	0.15
United States or American	1,623	5.31
Welsh	231	0.76
West Indian, excl. Hispanic:	215	0.70
Haitian	98	0.32
Jamaican	59	0.19
Trinidadian and Tobagonian	26	0.09
West Indian	32	0.10
White:	23,458	77.15
Not Hispanic (21,363)	22,045	72.51
Hispanic (1,252)	1,413	4.65
Yugoslavian	43	0.14

Lakeside

Place Type: Census Designated Place
County: Henrico
Population: 11,157

Ancestry/Race	Number	%
African American/Black:	1,059	9.49
Not Hispanic (962)	1,038	9.30
Hispanic (14)	21	0.19
African, sub-Saharan:	148	1.33
African	72	0.65
Ethiopian	9	0.08
Kenyan	17	0.15
Sierra Leonean	50	0.45
Am. Ind. or Alaska Nat., not spec.	38	0.34
American Indian tribes, specified:	94	0.84
Apache	1	0.01
Blackfeet (1)	3	0.03
Cherokee (13)	36	0.32
Choctaw (2)	6	0.05
Latin American Indians (1)	2	0.02
Lumbee	2	0.02
Ottawa (2)	2	0.02
Potawatomi	1	0.01
Pueblo (1)	1	0.01
Shoshone	1	0.01
Sioux	1	0.01
All other tribes (31)	38	0.34
American Indian tribes, not spec.	2	0.02
Arab:	107	0.96
Arab/Arabic	24	0.22
Egyptian	15	0.13
Lebanese	41	0.37
Other Arab	27	0.24
Armenian	7	0.06
Asian:	202	1.81
Cambodian (27)	32	0.29
Chinese, ex. Taiwanese (23)	30	0.27
Filipino (26)	33	0.30
Indian (21)	25	0.22
Japanese (2)	4	0.04
Korean (6)	6	0.05
Pakistani (3)	3	0.03
Vietnamese (38)	47	0.42
Other Asian, not specified (7)	22	0.20
Austrian	33	0.30
British	65	0.58
Canadian	8	0.07
Celtic	10	0.09
Croatian	7	0.06
Czech	41	0.37
Czechoslovakian	23	0.21
Danish	24	0.22
Dutch	147	1.32
Eastern European	15	0.13
English	1,526	13.69
European	59	0.53
French, except Basque	308	2.76
French Canadian	31	0.28
German	1,297	11.64
Greek	24	0.22
Guyanese	8	0.07
Hawaii Native/Pacific Islander:	15	0.13
Micronesian: (6)	10	0.09
Guamanian/Chamorro (6)	10	0.09
Polynesian: (1)	4	0.04
Native Hawaiian	1	0.01
Other Polynesian (1)	3	0.03
Other Pac. Isl., not spec. (1)	1	0.01
Hispanic or Latino:	273	2.45
Central American:	35	0.31
Guatemalan	2	0.02
Honduran	5	0.04
Panamanian	1	0.01
Salvadoran	27	0.24
Cuban	26	0.23
Dominican Republic	2	0.02
Mexican	109	0.98
Puerto Rican	55	0.49
South American:	10	0.09
Colombian	1	0.01
Ecuadorian	1	0.01
Peruvian	8	0.07
Other Hispanic or Latino	36	0.32
Hungarian	24	0.22
Iranian	12	0.11
Irish	1,220	10.95
Italian	343	3.08
Lithuanian	12	0.11
Luxemburger	6	0.05
Northern European	6	0.05
Norwegian	73	0.66
Pennsylvania German	7	0.06
Polish	171	1.53
Portuguese	7	0.06
Russian	16	0.14
Scandinavian	23	0.21
Scotch-Irish	386	3.46
Scottish	251	2.25
Serbian	21	0.19
Slavic	18	0.16
Slovak	32	0.29
Swedish	66	0.59
Swiss	32	0.29
Ukrainian	30	0.27
United States or American	1,744	15.65
Welsh	160	1.44
West Indian, excl. Hispanic:	89	0.80
Haitian	49	0.44
Jamaican	31	0.28
Other West Indian	9	0.08
White:	9,767	87.54
Not Hispanic (9,493)	9,638	86.39
Hispanic (120)	129	1.16
Yugoslavian	109	0.98

Laurel

Place Type: Census Designated Place
County: Henrico
Population: 14,875

Ancestry/Race	Number	%
African American/Black:	3,767	25.32
Not Hispanic (3,567)	3,700	24.87
Hispanic (48)	67	0.45
African, sub-Saharan:	128	0.88
African	74	0.51
Liberian	26	0.18
Nigerian	9	0.06
Sudanese	19	0.13
Am. Ind. or Alaska Nat., not spec.	48	0.32
American Indian tribes, specified:	73	0.49
Apache (1)	1	0.01
Blackfeet	3	0.02
Cherokee (6)	24	0.16
Cree (1)	1	0.01
Creek (1)	1	0.01
Iroquois (6)	6	0.04
Latin American Indians (5)	12	0.08
Lumbee (1)	1	0.01
Seminole	3	0.02
Yakama (1)	1	0.01
All other tribes (8)	20	0.13
American Indian tribes, not spec.	11	0.07
Arab:	185	1.27
Arab/Arabic	30	0.21
Egyptian	31	0.21
Lebanese	50	0.34
Moroccan	15	0.10
Palestinian	44	0.30
Syrian	15	0.10
Armenian	34	0.23
Asian:	1,019	6.85
Bangladeshi (11)	11	0.07
Cambodian (14)	20	0.13
Chinese, ex. Taiwanese (131)	145	0.97
Filipino (61)	74	0.50
Indian (335)	361	2.43
Indonesian (5)	6	0.04
Japanese (2)	7	0.05
Korean (40)	45	0.30
Laotian (6)	6	0.04
Malaysian (1)	1	0.01
Pakistani (31)	35	0.24
Sri Lankan (5)	6	0.04
Taiwanese (2)	6	0.04
Thai (3)	8	0.05
Vietnamese (234)	241	1.62
Other Asian, specified (2)	2	0.01
Other Asian, not specified (24)	45	0.30
Austrian	14	0.10

Notes: 1. Figures in the "Number" column do not add up to the total population due to: a) Ancestry/Race overlap — e.g. persons can report being both White and Irish, b) persons of Hispanic origin can report being any race, c) persons reporting two ancestries are counted in both categories. 2. Numbers in parentheses indicate the number of persons reporting this ancestry/race alone, not in combination with any other ancestry/race. 3. Refer to the Explanation of Data in the front of the book for more detailed information.

Belgian	11	0.08
Brazilian	9	0.06
British	50	0.34
Bulgarian	20	0.14
Canadian	17	0.12
Croatian	8	0.05
Czech	90	0.62
Czechoslovakian	52	0.36
Danish	38	0.26
Dutch	115	0.79
Eastern European	8	0.05
English	1,861	12.74
European	89	0.61
Finnish	21	0.14
French, except Basque	465	3.18
French Canadian	79	0.54
German	1,531	10.48
Greek	47	0.32
Hawaii Native/Pacific Islander:	18	0.12
Micronesian: (4)	4	0.03
Guamanian/Chamorro (4)	4	0.03
Polynesian: (3)	4	0.03
Native Hawaiian (2)	3	0.02
Samoan (1)	1	0.01
Other Pac. Isl., not spec. (1)	10	0.07
Hispanic or Latino:	618	4.15
Central American:	72	0.48
Costa Rican	20	0.13
Guatemalan	7	0.05
Honduran	5	0.03
Nicaraguan	1	0.01
Panamanian	6	0.04
Salvadoran	22	0.15
Other Central American	11	0.07
Cuban	22	0.15
Dominican Republic	2	0.01
Mexican	285	1.92
Puerto Rican	101	0.68
South American:	37	0.25
Argentinean	1	0.01
Chilean	1	0.01
Colombian	14	0.09
Ecuadorian	6	0.04
Peruvian	12	0.08
Venezuelan	3	0.02
Other Hispanic or Latino	99	0.67
Hungarian	78	0.53
Iranian	6	0.04
Irish	1,576	10.79
Italian	510	3.49
Latvian	8	0.05
Lithuanian	6	0.04
Norwegian	13	0.09
Polish	171	1.17
Portuguese	29	0.20
Russian	52	0.36
Scandinavian	9	0.06
Scotch-Irish	206	1.41
Scottish	314	2.15
Serbian	5	0.03
Slovak	34	0.23
Swedish	98	0.67
Swiss	26	0.18
Turkish	10	0.07
Ukrainian	67	0.46
United States or American	1,292	8.85
Welsh	107	0.73
West Indian, excl. Hispanic:	159	1.09
British West Indian	12	0.08
Haitian	13	0.09
Jamaican	12	0.08
Trinidadian and Tobagonian	38	0.26
West Indian	84	0.58
White:	9,865	66.32
Not Hispanic (9,435)	9,613	64.63
Hispanic (231)	252	1.69
Yugoslavian	44	0.30

Leesburg

Place Type: Town
County: Loudoun
Population: 28,311

Ancestry/Race	Number	%
Afghan	47	0.17
African American/Black:	2,842	10.04
Not Hispanic (2,573)	2,792	9.86
Hispanic (31)	50	0.18
African, sub-Saharan:	132	0.47
African	88	0.31
Ethiopian	14	0.05
Ghanian	30	0.11
Alaska Native tribes, specified:	3	0.01
Alaska Athabascan (1)	1	0.00
Eskimo (2)	2	0.01
Am. Ind. or Alaska Nat., not spec.	54	0.19
Albanian	28	0.10
American Indian tribes, specified:	82	0.29
Blackfeet	3	0.01
Cherokee (7)	35	0.12
Cheyenne	1	0.00
Choctaw (4)	4	0.01
Delaware (1)	2	0.01
Iroquois	2	0.01
Latin American Indians (1)	9	0.03
Lumbee (1)	1	0.00
Navajo	2	0.01
Seminole	3	0.01
Sioux (1)	3	0.01
All other tribes (11)	17	0.06
American Indian tribes, not spec.	3	0.01
Arab:	162	0.57
Egyptian	15	0.05
Lebanese	58	0.21
Palestinian	49	0.17
Syrian	40	0.14
Armenian	14	0.05
Asian:	934	3.30
Cambodian (9)	9	0.03
Chinese, ex. Taiwanese (99)	121	0.43
Filipino (121)	168	0.59
Hmong (1)	1	0.00
Indian (199)	214	0.76
Japanese (32)	60	0.21
Korean (58)	77	0.27
Laotian (2)	2	0.01
Pakistani (83)	94	0.33
Sri Lankan (1)	3	0.01
Taiwanese (1)	2	0.01
Thai (14)	15	0.05
Vietnamese (79)	96	0.34
Other Asian, specified (1)	12	0.04
Other Asian, not specified (25)	60	0.21
Austrian	25	0.09
Belgian	32	0.11
Brazilian	9	0.03
British	268	0.95
Bulgarian	14	0.05
Canadian	69	0.24
Celtic	27	0.10
Croatian	25	0.09
Czech	151	0.53
Czechoslovakian	60	0.21
Danish	153	0.54
Dutch	256	0.91
English	3,824	13.54
Estonian	20	0.07
European	357	1.26
Finnish	31	0.11
French, except Basque	633	2.24
French Canadian	217	0.77
German	6,057	21.45
Greek	121	0.43
Hawaii Native/Pacific Islander:	38	0.13
Micronesian: (1)	3	0.01
Guamanian/Chamorro (1)	3	0.01
Polynesian: (8)	18	0.06
Native Hawaiian (4)	13	0.05
Samoan (4)	5	0.02
Other Pac. Isl., specified	7	0.02
Other Pac. Isl., not spec.	10	0.04
Hispanic or Latino:	1,667	5.89
Central American:	501	1.77
Costa Rican	5	0.02
Guatemalan	65	0.23
Honduran	16	0.06
Nicaraguan	13	0.05
Panamanian	8	0.03
Salvadoran	371	1.31
Other Central American	23	0.08
Cuban	37	0.13
Dominican Republic	11	0.04
Mexican	456	1.61
Puerto Rican	129	0.46
South American:	114	0.40
Argentinean	2	0.01
Bolivian	7	0.02
Chilean	9	0.03
Colombian	32	0.11
Peruvian	48	0.17
Venezuelan	12	0.04
Other South American	4	0.01
Other Hispanic or Latino	419	1.48
Hungarian	211	0.75
Icelander	13	0.05
Iranian	138	0.49
Irish	4,392	15.55
Italian	1,777	6.29
Latvian	20	0.07
Lithuanian	124	0.44
New Zealander	52	0.18
Northern European	29	0.10
Norwegian	339	1.20
Polish	1,016	3.60
Portuguese	55	0.19
Romanian	30	0.11
Russian	364	1.29
Scandinavian	88	0.31
Scotch-Irish	587	2.08
Scottish	1,024	3.63
Slavic	28	0.10
Slovak	140	0.50
Slovene	26	0.09
Swedish	365	1.29
Swiss	101	0.36
Ukrainian	135	0.48
United States or American	2,091	7.41
Welsh	344	1.22
West Indian, excl. Hispanic:	117	0.41
Barbadian	11	0.04
Haitian	20	0.07
Jamaican	34	0.12
Trinidadian and Tobagonian	18	0.06
U.S. Virgin Islander	18	0.06
West Indian	16	0.06
White:	24,115	85.18
Not Hispanic (22,761)	23,167	81.83
Hispanic (819)	948	3.35
Yugoslavian	60	0.21

Lincolnia

Place Type: Census Designated Place
County: Fairfax
Population: 15,788

Ancestry/Race	Number	%
Afghan	161	1.01
African American/Black:	3,235	20.49
Not Hispanic (2,933)	3,171	20.08
Hispanic (38)	64	0.41
African, sub-Saharan:	1,951	12.30
African	244	1.54
Ethiopian	571	3.60
Ghanian	117	0.74
Nigerian	14	0.09
Senegalese	8	0.05

Notes: 1. Figures in the "Number" column do not add up to the total population due to: a) Ancestry/Race overlap — e.g. persons can report being both White and Irish, b) persons of Hispanic origin can report being any race, c) persons reporting two ancestries are counted in both categories. 2. Numbers in parentheses indicate the number of persons reporting this ancestry/race alone, not in combination with any other ancestry/race. 3. Refer to the Explanation of Data in the front of the book for more detailed information.

Sierra Leonean	168	1.06
Somalian	584	3.68
Sudanese	211	1.33
Other sub-Saharan African	34	0.21
Alaska Native tribes, specified:	3	0.02
Aleut (1)	2	0.01
Tlingit-Haida	1	0.01
Am. Ind. or Alaska Nat., not spec.	24	0.15
American Indian tribes, specified:	76	0.48
Apache	2	0.01
Blackfeet	6	0.04
Cherokee (3)	16	0.10
Chippewa (3)	4	0.03
Iroquois	4	0.03
Latin American Indians (2)	13	0.08
Navajo (2)	2	0.01
Potawatomi (1)	1	0.01
Pueblo (6)	6	0.04
Seminole	1	0.01
Shoshone (1)	1	0.01
Sioux (3)	4	0.03
All other tribes (1)	16	0.10
American Indian tribes, not spec.	5	0.03
Arab:	518	3.26
Arab/Arabic	58	0.37
Egyptian	140	0.88
Iraqi	30	0.19
Lebanese	42	0.26
Moroccan	68	0.43
Palestinian	152	0.96
Other Arab	28	0.18
Armenian	33	0.21
Asian:	2,768	17.53
Bangladeshi (49)	54	0.34
Cambodian (73)	92	0.58
Chinese, ex. Taiwanese (173)	207	1.31
Filipino (190)	230	1.46
Indian (319)	350	2.22
Indonesian (4)	6	0.04
Japanese (19)	34	0.22
Korean (398)	419	2.65
Laotian (28)	28	0.18
Pakistani (352)	427	2.70
Taiwanese (1)	1	0.01
Thai (47)	50	0.32
Vietnamese (615)	654	4.14
Other Asian, specified (1)	5	0.03
Other Asian, not specified (52)	211	1.34
Austrian	49	0.31
Basque	14	0.09
Brazilian	18	0.11
British	129	0.81
Bulgarian	5	0.03
Canadian	27	0.17
Carpatho Rusyn	5	0.03
Czech	56	0.35
Czechoslovakian	10	0.06
Danish	22	0.14
Dutch	39	0.25
Eastern European	92	0.58
English	1,037	6.54
European	96	0.61
Finnish	11	0.07
French, except Basque	255	1.61
French Canadian	17	0.11
German	1,213	7.64
Greek	57	0.36
Hawaii Native/Pacific Islander:	24	0.15
Micronesian: (2)	2	0.01
Guamanian/Chamorro (1)	1	0.01
Other Micronesian (1)	1	0.01
Polynesian:	1	0.01
Native Hawaiian	1	0.01
Other Pac. Isl., specified	3	0.02
Other Pac. Isl., not spec. (1)	18	0.11
Hispanic or Latino:	3,532	22.37
Central American:	1,192	7.55
Costa Rican	6	0.04
Guatemalan	220	1.39
Honduran	94	0.60
Nicaraguan	83	0.53
Panamanian	4	0.03
Salvadoran	722	4.57
Other Central American	63	0.40
Cuban	33	0.21
Dominican Republic	9	0.06
Mexican	505	3.20
Puerto Rican	95	0.60
South American:	663	4.20
Argentinean	8	0.05
Bolivian	245	1.55
Chilean	18	0.11
Colombian	65	0.41
Ecuadorian	11	0.07
Paraguayan	7	0.04
Peruvian	209	1.32
Uruguayan	11	0.07
Venezuelan	27	0.17
Other South American	62	0.39
Other Hispanic or Latino	1,035	6.56
Hungarian	86	0.54
Iranian	66	0.42
Irish	963	6.07
Israeli	8	0.05
Italian	340	2.14
Lithuanian	15	0.09
Luxemburger	7	0.04
Northern European	16	0.10
Norwegian	115	0.72
Polish	233	1.47
Portuguese	8	0.05
Romanian	16	0.10
Russian	145	0.91
Scandinavian	98	0.62
Scotch-Irish	250	1.58
Scottish	234	1.47
Slavic	16	0.10
Slovak	81	0.51
Slovene	29	0.18
Swedish	56	0.35
Swiss	40	0.25
Turkish	106	0.67
Ukrainian	81	0.51
United States or American	498	3.14
Welsh	76	0.48
West Indian, excl. Hispanic:	79	0.50
British West Indian	7	0.04
Jamaican	50	0.32
Trinidadian and Tobagonian	11	0.07
West Indian	11	0.07
White:	8,290	52.51
Not Hispanic (6,060)	6,578	41.66
Hispanic (1,459)	1,712	10.84
Yugoslavian	42	0.26

Lorton

Place Type: Census Designated Place
County: Fairfax
Population: 17,786

Ancestry/Race	Number	%
Afghan	51	0.29
African American/Black:	6,464	36.34
Not Hispanic (6,049)	6,304	35.44
Hispanic (116)	160	0.90
African, sub-Saharan:	473	2.66
African	218	1.23
Cape Verdean	24	0.14
Ethiopian	45	0.25
Ghanian	23	0.13
Sierra Leonean	24	0.14
Somalian	111	0.63
South African	22	0.12
Other sub-Saharan African	6	0.03
Am. Ind. or Alaska Nat., not spec.	72	0.40
American Indian tribes, specified:	102	0.57
Apache	4	0.02
Blackfeet	4	0.02
Cherokee (12)	46	0.26
Chickasaw (1)	1	0.01
Chippewa	3	0.02
Choctaw (1)	4	0.02
Creek (1)	1	0.01
Houma	1	0.01
Iroquois	2	0.01
Latin American Indians (1)	5	0.03
Lumbee (3)	6	0.03
Navajo	1	0.01
Pima (2)	2	0.01
Pueblo (1)	1	0.01
Seminole (4)	4	0.02
Shoshone	1	0.01
Ute	3	0.02
All other tribes (3)	13	0.07
American Indian tribes, not spec.	5	0.03
Arab:	229	1.29
Egyptian	8	0.05
Iraqi	48	0.27
Jordanian	10	0.06
Lebanese	25	0.14
Moroccan	133	0.75
Other Arab	5	0.03
Asian:	1,630	9.16
Cambodian (16)	18	0.10
Chinese, ex. Taiwanese (81)	100	0.56
Filipino (233)	280	1.57
Indian (278)	318	1.79
Indonesian (8)	10	0.06
Japanese (21)	45	0.25
Korean (310)	337	1.89
Laotian (25)	29	0.16
Malaysian	1	0.01
Pakistani (98)	133	0.75
Sri Lankan (4)	4	0.02
Thai (42)	50	0.28
Vietnamese (163)	182	1.02
Other Asian, specified (10)	10	0.06
Other Asian, not specified (48)	113	0.64
Austrian	66	0.37
Brazilian	29	0.16
British	128	0.72
Celtic	19	0.11
Croatian	13	0.07
Czech	98	0.55
Czechoslovakian	55	0.31
Danish	24	0.14
Dutch	144	0.81
English	1,233	6.94
European	84	0.47
Finnish	29	0.16
French, except Basque	384	2.16
French Canadian	93	0.52
German	1,616	9.10
Greek	14	0.08
Guyanese	33	0.19
Hawaii Native/Pacific Islander:	54	0.30
Micronesian: (10)	15	0.08
Guamanian/Chamorro (10)	15	0.08
Polynesian: (12)	18	0.10
Native Hawaiian (9)	14	0.08
Samoan (3)	4	0.02
Other Pac. Isl., not spec.	21	0.12
Hispanic or Latino:	1,732	9.74
Central American:	367	2.06
Costa Rican	3	0.02
Guatemalan	40	0.22
Honduran	27	0.15
Nicaraguan	25	0.14
Panamanian	27	0.15
Salvadoran	233	1.31
Other Central American	12	0.07
Cuban	35	0.20
Dominican Republic	5	0.03
Mexican	199	1.12
Puerto Rican	242	1.36
South American:	280	1.57
Argentinean	7	0.04
Bolivian	43	0.24
Chilean	26	0.15

Notes: 1. Figures in the "Number" column do not add up to the total population due to: a) Ancestry/Race overlap — e.g. persons can report being both White and Irish, b) persons of Hispanic origin can report being any race, c) persons reporting two ancestries are counted in both categories. 2. Numbers in parentheses indicate the number of persons reporting this ancestry/race alone, not in combination with any other ancestry/race. 3. Refer to the Explanation of Data in the front of the book for more detailed information.

Ancestry/Race	Number	%
Colombian	40	0.22
Ecuadorian	3	0.02
Peruvian	131	0.74
Venezuelan	18	0.10
Other South American	12	0.07
Other Hispanic or Latino	604	3.40
Hungarian	84	0.47
Icelander	18	0.10
Iranian	39	0.22
Irish	1,577	8.88
Italian	773	4.35
Lithuanian	27	0.15
New Zealander	10	0.06
Northern European	9	0.05
Norwegian	68	0.38
Pennsylvania German	10	0.06
Polish	264	1.49
Portuguese	42	0.24
Russian	63	0.35
Scandinavian	21	0.12
Scotch-Irish	197	1.11
Scottish	205	1.15
Serbian	6	0.03
Slovak	24	0.14
Slovene	8	0.05
Swedish	71	0.40
Turkish	27	0.15
Ukrainian	91	0.51
United States or American	881	4.96
Welsh	85	0.48
West Indian, excl. Hispanic:	153	0.86
British West Indian	90	0.51
Haitian	5	0.03
Jamaican	45	0.25
West Indian	13	0.07
White:	9,276	52.15
Not Hispanic (7,960)	8,390	47.17
Hispanic (746)	886	4.98

Lynchburg

Place Type: Independent City
County: Lynchburg Independent City
Population: 65,269

Ancestry/Race	Number	%
African American/Black:	19,962	30.58
Not Hispanic (19,288)	19,836	30.39
Hispanic (94)	126	0.19
African, sub-Saharan:	537	0.82
African	407	0.62
Cape Verdean	14	0.02
Ethiopian	17	0.03
Kenyan	17	0.03
Nigerian	13	0.02
Sudanese	40	0.06
Other sub-Saharan African	29	0.04
Alaska Native tribes, specified:	3	0.00
Eskimo (1)	1	0.00
All other tribes	2	0.00
Am. Ind. or Alaska Nat., not spec.	202	0.31
Albanian	27	0.04
Alsatian	6	0.01
American Indian tribes, specified:	261	0.40
Apache	1	0.00
Blackfeet (4)	12	0.02
Cherokee (32)	122	0.19
Choctaw (1)	2	0.00
Comanche (6)	6	0.01
Cree	4	0.01
Delaware	1	0.00
Iroquois (6)	16	0.02
Latin American Indians	1	0.00
Lumbee (3)	6	0.01
Navajo (2)	3	0.00
Osage	1	0.00
Ottawa (1)	2	0.00
Paiute (1)	1	0.00
Potawatomi (1)	1	0.00
Seminole	1	0.00
Sioux (5)	10	0.02
All other tribes (36)	71	0.11
American Indian tribes, not spec.	21	0.03
Arab:	75	0.11
Arab/Arabic	13	0.02
Lebanese	24	0.04
Moroccan	30	0.05
Other Arab	8	0.01
Asian:	1,006	1.54
Bangladeshi (2)	3	0.00
Cambodian (6)	7	0.01
Chinese, ex. Taiwanese (148)	167	0.26
Filipino (88)	117	0.18
Indian (220)	242	0.37
Indonesian (1)	4	0.01
Japanese (42)	57	0.09
Korean (183)	209	0.32
Laotian (4)	4	0.01
Malaysian (4)	4	0.01
Pakistani (10)	16	0.02
Sri Lankan (2)	2	0.00
Taiwanese (11)	13	0.02
Thai (11)	15	0.02
Vietnamese (68)	84	0.13
Other Asian, specified (5)	11	0.02
Other Asian, not specified (27)	51	0.08
Australian	30	0.05
Austrian	39	0.06
Basque	6	0.01
Belgian	18	0.03
Brazilian	5	0.01
British	277	0.42
Canadian	40	0.06
Celtic	13	0.02
Croatian	28	0.04
Czech	97	0.15
Czechoslovakian	71	0.11
Danish	88	0.13
Dutch	708	1.08
Eastern European	8	0.01
English	7,781	11.92
European	367	0.56
Finnish	37	0.06
French, except Basque	1,245	1.91
French Canadian	247	0.38
German	5,759	8.82
Greek	78	0.12
Hawaii Native/Pacific Islander:	73	0.11
Micronesian: (5)	9	0.01
Guamanian/Chamorro (5)	8	0.01
Other Micronesian	1	0.00
Polynesian: (14)	27	0.04
Native Hawaiian (3)	10	0.02
Samoan (10)	16	0.02
Other Polynesian (1)	1	0.00
Other Pac. Isl., specified	6	0.01
Other Pac. Isl., not spec. (8)	31	0.05
Hispanic or Latino:	878	1.35
Central American:	49	0.08
Costa Rican	1	0.00
Guatemalan	6	0.01
Honduran	11	0.02
Nicaraguan	3	0.00
Panamanian	6	0.01
Salvadoran	22	0.03
Cuban	49	0.08
Dominican Republic	13	0.02
Mexican	291	0.45
Puerto Rican	189	0.29
South American:	59	0.09
Argentinean	3	0.00
Bolivian	6	0.01
Chilean	7	0.01
Colombian	16	0.02
Ecuadorian	5	0.01
Paraguayan	2	0.00
Peruvian	10	0.02
Venezuelan	8	0.01
Other South American	2	0.00
Other Hispanic or Latino	228	0.35
Hungarian	194	0.30
Iranian	19	0.03
Irish	5,283	8.09
Italian	1,286	1.97
Lithuanian	36	0.06
Maltese	16	0.02
Northern European	7	0.01
Norwegian	322	0.49
Pennsylvania German	42	0.06
Polish	638	0.98
Portuguese	51	0.08
Romanian	49	0.08
Russian	193	0.30
Scandinavian	37	0.06
Scotch-Irish	1,650	2.53
Scottish	1,513	2.32
Serbian	28	0.04
Slavic	39	0.06
Slovak	75	0.11
Slovene	14	0.02
Swedish	396	0.61
Swiss	134	0.21
Turkish	17	0.03
Ukrainian	84	0.13
United States or American	8,070	12.36
Welsh	427	0.65
West Indian, excl. Hispanic:	227	0.35
Bahamian	17	0.03
Haitian	42	0.06
Jamaican	44	0.07
Trinidadian and Tobagonian	11	0.02
U.S. Virgin Islander	6	0.01
West Indian	107	0.16
White:	44,236	67.77
Not Hispanic (43,108)	43,783	67.08
Hispanic (379)	453	0.69
Yugoslavian	28	0.04

Madison Heights

Place Type: Census Designated Place
County: Amherst
Population: 11,584

Ancestry/Race	Number	%
African American/Black:	2,335	20.16
Not Hispanic (2,252)	2,311	19.95
Hispanic (15)	24	0.21
African, sub-Saharan:	26	0.23
African	26	0.23
Am. Ind. or Alaska Nat., not spec.	39	0.34
American Indian tribes, specified:	91	0.79
Blackfeet	1	0.01
Cherokee (13)	30	0.26
Iroquois (1)	1	0.01
Latin American Indians	1	0.01
Navajo (1)	1	0.01
All other tribes (45)	57	0.49
American Indian tribes, not spec.	5	0.04
Asian:	61	0.53
Chinese, ex. Taiwanese (11)	11	0.09
Filipino (8)	11	0.09
Indian (9)	9	0.08
Japanese (6)	10	0.09
Korean (3)	3	0.03
Vietnamese (12)	12	0.10
Other Asian, specified	2	0.02
Other Asian, not specified (3)	3	0.03
British	30	0.26
Czech	27	0.24
Czechoslovakian	9	0.08
Dutch	53	0.47
English	886	7.81
Estonian	8	0.07
European	152	1.34
French, except Basque	158	1.39
French Canadian	16	0.14
German	389	3.43
Greek	40	0.35
Hawaii Native/Pacific Islander:	4	0.03

Notes: 1. Figures in the "Number" column do not add up to the total population due to: a) Ancestry/Race overlap — e.g. persons can report being both White and Irish, b) persons of Hispanic origin can report being any race, c) persons reporting two ancestries are counted in both categories. 2. Numbers in parentheses indicate the number of persons reporting this ancestry/race alone, not in combination with any other ancestry/race. 3. Refer to the Explanation of Data in the front of the book for more detailed information.

Ancestry/Race	Number	%
Polynesian:	1	0.01
Native Hawaiian	1	0.01
Other Pac. Isl., specified	2	0.02
Other Pac. Isl., not spec.	1	0.01
Hispanic or Latino:	103	0.89
Central American:	3	0.03
Guatemalan	1	0.01
Salvadoran	2	0.02
Cuban	1	0.01
Dominican Republic	1	0.01
Mexican	34	0.29
Puerto Rican	16	0.14
South American:	1	0.01
Ecuadorian	1	0.01
Other Hispanic or Latino	47	0.41
Irish	566	4.99
Italian	68	0.60
Lithuanian	23	0.20
Norwegian	9	0.08
Polish	84	0.74
Russian	21	0.19
Scotch-Irish	143	1.26
Scottish	137	1.21
Slavic	13	0.11
Swedish	66	0.58
Swiss	16	0.14
Ukrainian	21	0.19
United States or American	2,988	26.32
Welsh	48	0.42
White:	9,081	78.39
Not Hispanic (8,981)	9,046	78.09
Hispanic (31)	35	0.30

Manassas Park

Place Type: Independent City
County: Manassas Park Independent City
Population: 10,290

Ancestry/Race	Number	%
African American/Black:	1,231	11.96
Not Hispanic (1,115)	1,190	11.56
Hispanic (34)	41	0.40
African, sub-Saharan:	59	0.57
African	8	0.08
Ghanian	35	0.34
Nigerian	16	0.16
Am. Ind. or Alaska Nat., not spec.	36	0.35
American Indian tribes, specified:	58	0.56
Blackfeet	1	0.01
Cherokee (5)	30	0.29
Chickasaw (1)	1	0.01
Chippewa	1	0.01
Comanche (1)	1	0.01
Cree	1	0.01
Iroquois (4)	6	0.06
Latin American Indians (2)	3	0.03
Navajo (4)	4	0.04
Potawatomi	1	0.01
Sioux (1)	1	0.01
All other tribes (5)	8	0.08
American Indian tribes, not spec.	2	0.02
Arab:	77	0.75
Arab/Arabic	36	0.35
Iraqi	41	0.40
Armenian	6	0.06
Asian:	525	5.10
Bangladeshi	2	0.02
Cambodian (25)	29	0.28
Chinese, ex. Taiwanese (39)	56	0.54
Filipino (122)	139	1.35
Indian (61)	72	0.70
Indonesian	1	0.01
Japanese (5)	11	0.11
Korean (19)	28	0.27
Laotian (15)	26	0.25
Pakistani (2)	12	0.12
Thai (6)	7	0.07
Vietnamese (76)	97	0.94
Other Asian, not specified (27)	45	0.44
Austrian	8	0.08
Belgian	17	0.17
Brazilian	16	0.16
British	64	0.62
Bulgarian	5	0.05
Canadian	29	0.28
Czech	79	0.77
Czechoslovakian	16	0.16
Danish	9	0.09
Dutch	121	1.18
Eastern European	8	0.08
English	863	8.39
European	60	0.58
French, except Basque	216	2.10
French Canadian	51	0.50
German	1,320	12.83
Greek	76	0.74
Hawaii Native/Pacific Islander:	17	0.17
Micronesian: (5)	5	0.05
Guamanian/Chamorro (5)	5	0.05
Polynesian:	4	0.04
Native Hawaiian	3	0.03
Samoan	1	0.01
Other Pac. Isl., not spec. (2)	8	0.08
Hispanic or Latino:	1,544	15.00
Central American:	485	4.71
Costa Rican	1	0.01
Guatemalan	69	0.67
Honduran	31	0.30
Nicaraguan	18	0.17
Panamanian	2	0.02
Salvadoran	329	3.20
Other Central American	35	0.34
Cuban	11	0.11
Dominican Republic	5	0.05
Mexican	451	4.38
Puerto Rican	86	0.84
South American:	113	1.10
Argentinean	3	0.03
Bolivian	11	0.11
Chilean	5	0.05
Colombian	9	0.09
Ecuadorian	6	0.06
Peruvian	59	0.57
Uruguayan	2	0.02
Other South American	18	0.17
Other Hispanic or Latino	393	3.82
Hungarian	40	0.39
Iranian	6	0.06
Irish	1,177	11.44
Italian	437	4.25
Norwegian	62	0.60
Pennsylvania German	5	0.05
Polish	269	2.61
Portuguese	21	0.20
Russian	91	0.88
Scotch-Irish	197	1.91
Scottish	188	1.83
Slovak	9	0.09
Slovene	19	0.18
Swedish	50	0.49
Swiss	103	1.00
Turkish	23	0.22
United States or American	1,395	13.56
Welsh	29	0.28
West Indian, excl. Hispanic:	62	0.60
Haitian	4	0.04
Jamaican	44	0.43
Trinidadian and Tobagonian	6	0.06
West Indian	8	0.08
White:	7,794	75.74
Not Hispanic (6,919)	7,118	69.17
Hispanic (571)	676	6.57

Manassas

Place Type: Independent City
County: Manassas Independent City
Population: 35,135

Ancestry/Race	Number	%
Acadian/Cajun	7	0.02
Afghan	23	0.07
African American/Black:	4,893	13.93
Not Hispanic (4,430)	4,738	13.49
Hispanic (105)	155	0.44
African, sub-Saharan:	240	0.68
African	151	0.43
Ghanian	53	0.15
Liberian	29	0.08
Nigerian	7	0.02
Alaska Native tribes, specified:	1	0.00
Tlingit-Haida (1)	1	0.00
Am. Ind. or Alaska Nat., not spec.	87	0.25
Albanian	10	0.03
American Indian tribes, specified:	196	0.56
Apache (1)	2	0.01
Blackfeet	4	0.01
Cherokee (30)	70	0.20
Chickasaw	1	0.00
Chippewa (2)	8	0.02
Choctaw (4)	9	0.03
Cree (1)	2	0.01
Creek	1	0.00
Crow	1	0.00
Delaware (2)	3	0.01
Iroquois (3)	9	0.03
Latin American Indians (18)	30	0.09
Lumbee (4)	4	0.01
Menominee (2)	2	0.01
Pueblo	10	0.03
Seminole (1)	1	0.00
Sioux (4)	8	0.02
Ute	1	0.00
Yaqui	1	0.00
All other tribes (18)	29	0.08
American Indian tribes, not spec.	16	0.05
Arab:	179	0.51
Arab/Arabic	42	0.12
Lebanese	55	0.16
Palestinian	19	0.05
Syrian	49	0.14
Other Arab	14	0.04
Armenian	15	0.04
Asian:	1,447	4.12
Cambodian (46)	56	0.16
Chinese, ex. Taiwanese (139)	156	0.44
Filipino (226)	288	0.82
Indian (237)	263	0.75
Indonesian (2)	2	0.01
Japanese (36)	58	0.17
Korean (105)	129	0.37
Laotian (84)	87	0.25
Pakistani (57)	70	0.20
Sri Lankan (1)	1	0.00
Taiwanese (2)	2	0.01
Thai (21)	32	0.09
Vietnamese (174)	200	0.57
Other Asian, specified (13)	17	0.05
Other Asian, not specified (38)	86	0.24
Australian	7	0.02
Austrian	50	0.14
Belgian	27	0.08
Brazilian	16	0.05
British	369	1.05
Bulgarian	25	0.07
Canadian	33	0.09
Czech	75	0.21
Czechoslovakian	45	0.13
Danish	194	0.55
Dutch	378	1.08
Eastern European	28	0.08
English	4,006	11.40
European	273	0.78

Notes: 1. Figures in the "Number" column do not add up to the total population due to: a) Ancestry/Race overlap — e.g. persons can report being both White and Irish, b) persons of Hispanic origin can report being any race, c) persons reporting two ancestries are counted in both categories. 2. Numbers in parentheses indicate the number of persons reporting this ancestry/race alone, not in combination with any other ancestry/race. 3. Refer to the Explanation of Data in the front of the book for more detailed information.

Ancestry/Race	Number	%
Finnish	31	0.09
French, except Basque	836	2.38
French Canadian	221	0.63
German	4,976	14.16
Greek	86	0.24
Guyanese	20	0.06
Hawaii Native/Pacific Islander:	61	0.17
Micronesian: (18)	18	0.05
Guamanian/Chamorro (12)	12	0.03
Other Micronesian (6)	6	0.02
Polynesian: (9)	13	0.04
Native Hawaiian (4)	8	0.02
Samoan (3)	3	0.01
Tongan (1)	1	0.00
Other Polynesian (1)	1	0.00
Other Pac. Isl., specified	4	0.01
Other Pac. Isl., not spec. (4)	26	0.07
Hispanic or Latino:	5,316	15.13
Central American:	1,410	4.01
Costa Rican	5	0.01
Guatemalan	139	0.40
Honduran	195	0.56
Nicaraguan	44	0.13
Panamanian	36	0.10
Salvadoran	963	2.74
Other Central American	28	0.08
Cuban	46	0.13
Dominican Republic	17	0.05
Mexican	2,381	6.78
Puerto Rican	264	0.75
South American:	180	0.51
Argentinean	6	0.02
Bolivian	20	0.06
Chilean	2	0.01
Colombian	40	0.11
Ecuadorian	17	0.05
Paraguayan	2	0.01
Peruvian	62	0.18
Venezuelan	13	0.04
Other South American	18	0.05
Other Hispanic or Latino	1,018	2.90
Hungarian	164	0.47
Icelander	40	0.11
Irish	4,816	13.71
Italian	1,640	4.67
Lithuanian	47	0.13
Norwegian	208	0.59
Pennsylvania German	44	0.13
Polish	916	2.61
Portuguese	232	0.66
Romanian	5	0.01
Russian	310	0.88
Scandinavian	45	0.13
Scotch-Irish	673	1.92
Scottish	837	2.38
Serbian	11	0.03
Slovak	66	0.19
Slovene	7	0.02
Swedish	204	0.58
Swiss	69	0.20
Turkish	8	0.02
Ukrainian	122	0.35
United States or American	2,656	7.56
Welsh	332	0.94
West Indian, excl. Hispanic:	101	0.29
Jamaican	41	0.12
Trinidadian and Tobagonian	43	0.12
West Indian	17	0.05
White:	26,292	74.83
Not Hispanic (23,304)	23,858	67.90
Hispanic (2,012)	2,434	6.93
Yugoslavian	6	0.02

Martinsville

Place Type: Independent City
County: Martinsville Independent City
Population: 15,416

Ancestry/Race	Number	%
African American/Black:	6,627	42.99
Not Hispanic (6,501)	6,568	42.61
Hispanic (58)	59	0.38
African, sub-Saharan:	278	1.80
African	263	1.71
South African	15	0.10
Alaska Native tribes, specified:	1	0.01
Alaska Athabascan	1	0.01
Am. Ind. or Alaska Nat., not spec.	26	0.17
American Indian tribes, specified:	27	0.18
Cherokee (1)	17	0.11
Latin American Indians	1	0.01
Navajo (4)	4	0.03
All other tribes (4)	5	0.03
American Indian tribes, not spec.	6	0.04
Arab:	6	0.04
Lebanese	6	0.04
Asian:	85	0.55
Chinese, ex. Taiwanese (4)	8	0.05
Filipino (3)	7	0.05
Indian (17)	19	0.12
Japanese (4)	6	0.04
Korean (12)	13	0.08
Pakistani (4)	4	0.03
Vietnamese (28)	28	0.18
British	54	0.35
Croatian	6	0.04
Czech	20	0.13
Danish	25	0.16
Dutch	102	0.66
English	1,490	9.67
European	95	0.62
French, except Basque	143	0.93
French Canadian	65	0.42
German	771	5.00
Greek	14	0.09
Hawaii Native/Pacific Islander:	5	0.03
Polynesian:	1	0.01
Native Hawaiian	1	0.01
Other Pac. Isl., not spec.	4	0.03
Hispanic or Latino:	358	2.32
Central American:	26	0.17
Guatemalan	1	0.01
Honduran	2	0.01
Salvadoran	23	0.15
Cuban	2	0.01
Mexican	245	1.59
Puerto Rican	14	0.09
South American:	4	0.03
Peruvian	4	0.03
Other Hispanic or Latino	67	0.43
Hungarian	20	0.13
Irish	745	4.83
Italian	235	1.52
Lithuanian	14	0.09
Northern European	25	0.16
Norwegian	4	0.03
Polish	56	0.36
Portuguese	7	0.05
Russian	38	0.25
Scandinavian	5	0.03
Scotch-Irish	486	3.15
Scottish	207	1.34
Swedish	48	0.31
Swiss	12	0.08
United States or American	1,632	10.59
Welsh	104	0.67
West Indian, excl. Hispanic:	23	0.15
Jamaican	23	0.15
White:	8,640	56.05
Not Hispanic (8,336)	8,431	54.69
Hispanic (201)	209	1.36

McLean

Place Type: Census Designated Place
County: Fairfax
Population: 38,929

Ancestry/Race	Number	%
Acadian/Cajun	5	0.01
African American/Black:	703	1.81
Not Hispanic (602)	677	1.74
Hispanic (14)	26	0.07
African, sub-Saharan:	307	0.79
African	112	0.29
Ethiopian	23	0.06
Ghanian	25	0.06
Kenyan	5	0.01
Sierra Leonean	10	0.03
South African	19	0.05
Sudanese	49	0.13
Other sub-Saharan African	64	0.16
Alaska Native tribes, specified:	3	0.01
Tlingit-Haida (3)	3	0.01
Am. Ind. or Alaska Nat., not spec.	36	0.09
Alsatian	29	0.07
American Indian tribes, specified:	88	0.23
Apache (1)	2	0.01
Blackfeet (1)	2	0.01
Cherokee (7)	33	0.08
Chickasaw	5	0.01
Chippewa	2	0.01
Choctaw	1	0.00
Creek (1)	4	0.01
Crow (1)	1	0.00
Iroquois (2)	5	0.01
Latin American Indians (8)	24	0.06
Sioux (1)	1	0.00
Yuman (1)	1	0.00
All other tribes (2)	7	0.02
Arab:	1,233	3.16
Arab/Arabic	201	0.52
Egyptian	119	0.31
Iraqi	56	0.14
Jordanian	57	0.15
Lebanese	465	1.19
Moroccan	10	0.03
Palestinian	83	0.21
Syrian	109	0.28
Other Arab	133	0.34
Armenian	136	0.35
Asian:	4,698	12.07
Bangladeshi (15)	17	0.04
Cambodian (33)	41	0.11
Chinese, ex. Taiwanese (966)	1,081	2.78
Filipino (387)	440	1.13
Indian (658)	744	1.91
Indonesian (31)	49	0.13
Japanese (514)	584	1.50
Korean (912)	962	2.47
Malaysian (34)	42	0.11
Pakistani (25)	37	0.10
Sri Lankan (28)	31	0.08
Taiwanese (106)	122	0.31
Thai (47)	63	0.16
Vietnamese (213)	237	0.61
Other Asian, specified (32)	39	0.10
Other Asian, not specified (67)	209	0.54
Assyrian/Chaldean/Syriac	9	0.02
Australian	82	0.21
Austrian	381	0.98
Basque	8	0.02
Belgian	142	0.36
Brazilian	54	0.14
British	643	1.65
Bulgarian	18	0.05
Canadian	134	0.34
Carpatho Rusyn	20	0.05
Croatian	132	0.34
Czech	223	0.57
Czechoslovakian	54	0.14
Danish	316	0.81
Dutch	744	1.91
Eastern European	247	0.63
English	6,607	16.94
Estonian	38	0.10
European	700	1.79
Finnish	228	0.58
French, except Basque	1,197	3.07

Notes: 1. Figures in the "Number" column do not add up to the total population due to: a) Ancestry/Race overlap — e.g. persons can report being both White and Irish, b) persons of Hispanic origin can report being any race, c) persons reporting two ancestries are counted in both categories. 2. Numbers in parentheses indicate the number of persons reporting this ancestry/race alone, not in combination with any other ancestry/race. 3. Refer to the Explanation of Data in the front of the book for more detailed information.

French Canadian	243	0.62
German	6,830	17.51
Greek	422	1.08
Guyanese	13	0.03
Hawaii Native/Pacific Islander:	36	0.09
Micronesian: (4)	7	0.02
Guamanian/Chamorro (4)	7	0.02
Polynesian: (5)	10	0.03
Native Hawaiian (4)	9	0.02
Samoan (1)	1	0.00
Other Pac. Isl., not spec.	19	0.05
Hispanic or Latino:	1,564	4.02
Central American:	151	0.39
Costa Rican	8	0.02
Guatemalan	25	0.06
Honduran	14	0.04
Nicaraguan	29	0.07
Panamanian	7	0.02
Salvadoran	45	0.12
Other Central American	23	0.06
Cuban	75	0.19
Dominican Republic	34	0.09
Mexican	208	0.53
Puerto Rican	104	0.27
South American:	517	1.33
Argentinean	82	0.21
Bolivian	74	0.19
Chilean	55	0.14
Colombian	83	0.21
Ecuadorian	29	0.07
Paraguayan	4	0.01
Peruvian	118	0.30
Uruguayan	19	0.05
Venezuelan	28	0.07
Other South American	25	0.06
Other Hispanic or Latino	475	1.22
Hungarian	298	0.76
Iranian	580	1.49
Irish	6,110	15.67
Israeli	12	0.03
Italian	2,014	5.16
Latvian	56	0.14
Lithuanian	249	0.64
Luxemburger	35	0.09
Maltese	11	0.03
New Zealander	31	0.08
Northern European	141	0.36
Norwegian	446	1.14
Pennsylvania German	54	0.14
Polish	1,438	3.69
Portuguese	162	0.42
Romanian	60	0.15
Russian	1,162	2.98
Scandinavian	99	0.25
Scotch-Irish	877	2.25
Scottish	1,582	4.06
Serbian	37	0.09
Slavic	93	0.24
Slovak	93	0.24
Slovene	42	0.11
Swedish	498	1.28
Swiss	284	0.73
Turkish	132	0.34
Ukrainian	72	0.18
United States or American	1,852	4.75
Welsh	365	0.94
West Indian, excl. Hispanic:	43	0.11
Haitian	5	0.01
Jamaican	27	0.07
U.S. Virgin Islander	6	0.02
West Indian	5	0.01
White:	33,806	86.84
Not Hispanic (31,667)	32,458	83.38
Hispanic (1,251)	1,348	3.46
Yugoslavian	30	0.08

Mechanicsville

Place Type: Census Designated Place
County: Hanover
Population: 30,464

Ancestry/Race	Number	%
African American/Black:	2,048	6.72
Not Hispanic (1,939)	2,034	6.68
Hispanic (12)	14	0.05
African, sub-Saharan:	158	0.52
African	152	0.50
South African	6	0.02
Am. Ind. or Alaska Nat., not spec.	84	0.28
American Indian tribes, specified:	160	0.53
Blackfeet	4	0.01
Cherokee (30)	61	0.20
Chippewa (1)	2	0.01
Choctaw (1)	2	0.01
Comanche	1	0.00
Iroquois (2)	2	0.01
Lumbee (6)	10	0.03
Potawatomi (2)	5	0.02
Shoshone	1	0.00
Sioux	2	0.01
All other tribes (57)	70	0.23
American Indian tribes, not spec.	3	0.01
Arab:	78	0.26
Lebanese	73	0.24
Syrian	5	0.02
Armenian	15	0.05
Asian:	363	1.19
Cambodian (13)	14	0.05
Chinese, ex. Taiwanese (44)	49	0.16
Filipino (50)	80	0.26
Indian (58)	63	0.21
Japanese (17)	38	0.12
Korean (33)	41	0.13
Laotian (9)	9	0.03
Pakistani (6)	6	0.02
Taiwanese (1)	1	0.00
Thai (1)	2	0.01
Vietnamese (34)	42	0.14
Other Asian, specified	5	0.02
Other Asian, not specified (6)	13	0.04
Assyrian/Chaldean/Syriac	6	0.02
Australian	18	0.06
Austrian	35	0.11
Belgian	7	0.02
British	212	0.70
Canadian	47	0.15
Celtic	5	0.02
Croatian	7	0.02
Czech	63	0.21
Czechoslovakian	21	0.07
Danish	101	0.33
Dutch	340	1.12
English	5,001	16.42
European	448	1.47
French, except Basque	862	2.83
French Canadian	155	0.51
German	4,102	13.47
Greek	90	0.30
Hawaii Native/Pacific Islander:	13	0.04
Micronesian: (3)	3	0.01
Guamanian/Chamorro (3)	3	0.01
Polynesian:	6	0.02
Native Hawaiian	3	0.01
Samoan	1	0.00
Other Polynesian	2	0.01
Other Pac. Isl., specified	4	0.01
Hispanic or Latino:	359	1.18
Central American:	41	0.13
Costa Rican	7	0.02
Guatemalan	1	0.00
Honduran	5	0.02
Panamanian	2	0.01
Salvadoran	20	0.07
Other Central American	6	0.02
Cuban	16	0.05
Dominican Republic	3	0.01
Mexican	120	0.39
Puerto Rican	59	0.19
South American:	29	0.10
Argentinean	1	0.00
Bolivian	4	0.01
Colombian	12	0.04
Ecuadorian	3	0.01
Peruvian	5	0.02
Uruguayan	3	0.01
Venezuelan	1	0.00
Other Hispanic or Latino	91	0.30
Hungarian	85	0.28
Irish	3,815	12.53
Italian	1,343	4.41
Latvian	33	0.11
Lithuanian	49	0.16
Northern European	44	0.14
Norwegian	197	0.65
Pennsylvania German	19	0.06
Polish	472	1.55
Portuguese	26	0.09
Romanian	22	0.07
Russian	89	0.29
Scandinavian	55	0.18
Scotch-Irish	1,045	3.43
Scottish	739	2.43
Serbian	8	0.03
Slavic	13	0.04
Slovak	50	0.16
Slovene	9	0.03
Swedish	149	0.49
Swiss	40	0.13
Ukrainian	7	0.02
United States or American	4,868	15.98
Welsh	236	0.77
West Indian, excl. Hispanic:	34	0.11
Trinidadian and Tobagonian	34	0.11
White:	27,913	91.63
Not Hispanic (27,468)	27,693	90.90
Hispanic (192)	220	0.72
Yugoslavian	10	0.03

Merrifield

Place Type: Census Designated Place
County: Fairfax
Population: 11,170

Ancestry/Race	Number	%
Afghan	49	0.44
African American/Black:	722	6.46
Not Hispanic (648)	697	6.24
Hispanic (15)	25	0.22
African, sub-Saharan:	140	1.26
African	51	0.46
Ethiopian	25	0.23
Nigerian	28	0.25
Somalian	20	0.18
Other sub-Saharan African	16	0.14
Am. Ind. or Alaska Nat., not spec.	29	0.26
American Indian tribes, specified:	35	0.31
Blackfeet	1	0.01
Cherokee (2)	12	0.11
Chippewa (1)	1	0.01
Choctaw (3)	6	0.05
Iroquois (1)	1	0.01
Latin American Indians (3)	6	0.05
Lumbee (1)	1	0.01
Navajo (1)	1	0.01
Paiute (1)	1	0.01
Sioux (2)	2	0.02
Yaqui (1)	1	0.01
All other tribes (1)	2	0.02
American Indian tribes, not spec.	1	0.01
Arab:	237	2.14
Arab/Arabic	77	0.69
Egyptian	30	0.27
Iraqi	8	0.07
Jordanian	7	0.06

Notes: 1. Figures in the "Number" column do not add up to the total population due to: a) Ancestry/Race overlap — e.g. persons can report being both White and Irish, b) persons of Hispanic origin can report being any race, c) persons reporting two ancestries are counted in both categories. 2. Numbers in parentheses indicate the number of persons reporting this ancestry/race alone, not in combination with any other ancestry/race. 3. Refer to the Explanation of Data in the front of the book for more detailed information.

Ancestry/Race	Number	%
Lebanese	26	0.23
Moroccan	18	0.16
Palestinian	25	0.23
Syrian	46	0.42
Armenian	29	0.26
Asian:	3,610	32.32
Bangladeshi (13)	22	0.20
Cambodian (11)	13	0.12
Chinese, ex. Taiwanese (449)	492	4.40
Filipino (170)	200	1.79
Indian (871)	917	8.21
Indonesian (17)	29	0.26
Japanese (34)	57	0.51
Korean (869)	879	7.87
Laotian (12)	12	0.11
Malaysian (2)	2	0.02
Pakistani (74)	86	0.77
Sri Lankan (6)	6	0.05
Taiwanese (8)	10	0.09
Thai (39)	39	0.35
Vietnamese (641)	676	6.05
Other Asian, specified (42)	47	0.42
Other Asian, not specified (31)	123	1.10
Austrian	35	0.32
Belgian	10	0.09
Brazilian	31	0.28
British	127	1.15
Bulgarian	40	0.36
Czech	75	0.68
Czechoslovakian	7	0.06
Dutch	31	0.28
Eastern European	33	0.30
English	1,058	9.55
European	84	0.76
Finnish	31	0.28
French, except Basque	170	1.53
French Canadian	23	0.21
German	1,228	11.08
Greek	57	0.51
Hawaii Native/Pacific Islander:	22	0.20
Melanesian: (5)	5	0.04
Fijian (5)	5	0.04
Polynesian: (6)	7	0.06
Native Hawaiian (4)	5	0.04
Samoan (2)	2	0.02
Other Pac. Isl., not spec.	10	0.09
Hispanic or Latino:	1,442	12.91
Central American:	400	3.58
Costa Rican	5	0.04
Guatemalan	28	0.25
Honduran	31	0.28
Nicaraguan	26	0.23
Panamanian	6	0.05
Salvadoran	244	2.18
Other Central American	60	0.54
Cuban	30	0.27
Dominican Republic	24	0.21
Mexican	98	0.88
Puerto Rican	67	0.60
South American:	301	2.69
Argentinean	14	0.13
Bolivian	105	0.94
Chilean	5	0.04
Colombian	42	0.38
Ecuadorian	20	0.18
Paraguayan	5	0.04
Peruvian	77	0.69
Uruguayan	2	0.02
Venezuelan	14	0.13
Other South American	17	0.15
Other Hispanic or Latino	522	4.67
Hungarian	42	0.38
Iranian	110	0.99
Irish	941	8.49
Israeli	10	0.09
Italian	395	3.56
Latvian	7	0.06
Lithuanian	40	0.36
Northern European	6	0.05
Norwegian	49	0.44
Pennsylvania German	30	0.27
Polish	305	2.75
Portuguese	13	0.12
Romanian	24	0.22
Russian	232	2.09
Scandinavian	26	0.23
Scotch-Irish	161	1.45
Scottish	178	1.61
Serbian	8	0.07
Slovak	45	0.41
Slovene	33	0.30
Swedish	97	0.88
Swiss	15	0.14
Turkish	27	0.24
Ukrainian	58	0.52
United States or American	480	4.33
Welsh	57	0.51
West Indian, excl. Hispanic:	36	0.32
Belizean	21	0.19
Jamaican	9	0.08
Trinidadian and Tobagonian	6	0.05
White:	6,501	58.20
Not Hispanic (5,340)	5,643	50.52
Hispanic (767)	858	7.68
Yugoslavian	12	0.11

Montclair

Place Type: Census Designated Place
County: Prince William
Population: 15,728

Ancestry/Race	Number	%
African American/Black:	2,483	15.79
Not Hispanic (2,239)	2,387	15.18
Hispanic (75)	96	0.61
African, sub-Saharan:	204	1.29
African	148	0.93
Nigerian	46	0.29
Somalian	10	0.06
Alaska Native tribes, specified:	3	0.02
Alaska Athabascan (1)	1	0.01
Tlingit-Haida	2	0.01
Am. Ind. or Alaska Nat., not spec.	29	0.18
American Indian tribes, specified:	126	0.80
Apache (2)	6	0.04
Blackfeet	7	0.04
Cherokee (9)	39	0.25
Cheyenne	1	0.01
Chippewa (2)	2	0.01
Choctaw (2)	5	0.03
Comanche (2)	2	0.01
Cree (1)	3	0.02
Creek (4)	6	0.04
Delaware (1)	1	0.01
Iroquois	2	0.01
Kiowa (1)	1	0.01
Latin American Indians	1	0.01
Lumbee (7)	15	0.10
Navajo (7)	8	0.05
Paiute	1	0.01
Pima	1	0.01
Potawatomi	1	0.01
Seminole	5	0.03
Shoshone	1	0.01
Sioux (3)	7	0.04
All other tribes (10)	11	0.07
American Indian tribes, not spec.	9	0.06
Arab:	77	0.49
Arab/Arabic	9	0.06
Moroccan	5	0.03
Other Arab	63	0.40
Asian:	673	4.28
Cambodian (8)	8	0.05
Chinese, ex. Taiwanese (36)	57	0.36
Filipino (167)	224	1.42
Indian (37)	52	0.33
Japanese (29)	59	0.38
Korean (92)	125	0.79
Malaysian (1)	1	0.01
Pakistani (22)	40	0.25
Taiwanese (4)	5	0.03
Thai (14)	18	0.11
Vietnamese (35)	50	0.32
Other Asian, specified (4)	7	0.04
Other Asian, not specified (14)	27	0.17
Australian	13	0.08
Austrian	25	0.16
Belgian	34	0.21
British	225	1.42
Canadian	7	0.04
Croatian	23	0.14
Czech	47	0.30
Czechoslovakian	20	0.13
Danish	136	0.86
Dutch	249	1.57
Eastern European	10	0.06
English	2,152	13.56
European	209	1.32
Finnish	67	0.42
French, except Basque	470	2.96
French Canadian	104	0.66
German	3,144	19.81
Greek	45	0.28
Guyanese	10	0.06
Hawaii Native/Pacific Islander:	51	0.32
Micronesian: (13)	19	0.12
Guamanian/Chamorro (8)	9	0.06
Other Micronesian (5)	10	0.06
Polynesian: (13)	21	0.13
Native Hawaiian (3)	11	0.07
Samoan (10)	10	0.06
Other Pac. Isl., not spec. (6)	11	0.07
Hispanic or Latino:	709	4.51
Central American:	93	0.59
Costa Rican	7	0.04
Guatemalan	12	0.08
Honduran	4	0.03
Nicaraguan	2	0.01
Panamanian	35	0.22
Salvadoran	32	0.20
Other Central American	1	0.01
Cuban	19	0.12
Dominican Republic	14	0.09
Mexican	151	0.96
Puerto Rican	163	1.04
South American:	62	0.39
Argentinean	7	0.04
Bolivian	10	0.06
Chilean	13	0.08
Colombian	15	0.10
Ecuadorian	2	0.01
Paraguayan	1	0.01
Peruvian	9	0.06
Uruguayan	2	0.01
Other South American	3	0.02
Other Hispanic or Latino	207	1.32
Hungarian	138	0.87
Icelander	24	0.15
Irish	2,941	18.53
Italian	968	6.10
Lithuanian	49	0.31
Northern European	8	0.05
Norwegian	146	0.92
Pennsylvania German	31	0.20
Polish	583	3.67
Portuguese	52	0.33
Romanian	34	0.21
Russian	113	0.71
Scandinavian	45	0.28
Scotch-Irish	433	2.73
Scottish	517	3.26
Slavic	8	0.05
Slovak	47	0.30
Swedish	218	1.37
Swiss	7	0.04
Ukrainian	35	0.22
United States or American	929	5.85
Welsh	239	1.51
West Indian, excl. Hispanic:	52	0.33

Notes: 1. Figures in the "Number" column do not add up to the total population due to: a) Ancestry/Race overlap — e.g. persons can report being both White and Irish, b) persons of Hispanic origin can report being any race, c) persons reporting two ancestries are counted in both categories. 2. Numbers in parentheses indicate the number of persons reporting this ancestry/race alone, not in combination with any other ancestry/race. 3. Refer to the Explanation of Data in the front of the book for more detailed information.

Ancestry/Race	Number	%
Jamaican	52	0.33
White:	12,596	80.09
Not Hispanic (11,778)	12,105	76.96
Hispanic (432)	491	3.12

Mount Vernon

Place Type: Census Designated Place
County: Fairfax
Population: 28,582

Ancestry/Race	Number	%
African American/Black:	8,273	28.94
Not Hispanic (7,791)	8,097	28.33
Hispanic (113)	176	0.62
African, sub-Saharan:	1,177	4.12
African	542	1.90
Cape Verdean	18	0.06
Ethiopian	85	0.30
Ghanian	325	1.14
Liberian	57	0.20
Nigerian	11	0.04
Sierra Leonean	14	0.05
Sudanese	91	0.32
Other sub-Saharan African	34	0.12
Am. Ind. or Alaska Nat., not spec.	127	0.44
American Indian tribes, specified:	138	0.48
Apache (4)	6	0.02
Blackfeet	9	0.03
Cherokee (16)	67	0.23
Chickasaw	1	0.00
Chippewa	1	0.00
Choctaw	3	0.01
Creek	1	0.00
Iroquois (9)	10	0.03
Kiowa (1)	1	0.00
Latin American Indians (14)	17	0.06
Lumbee	1	0.00
Pueblo	1	0.00
Shoshone	2	0.01
Sioux (2)	3	0.01
All other tribes (6)	15	0.05
American Indian tribes, not spec.	14	0.05
Arab:	213	0.75
Arab/Arabic	6	0.02
Egyptian	20	0.07
Lebanese	64	0.22
Moroccan	48	0.17
Palestinian	8	0.03
Syrian	31	0.11
Other Arab	36	0.13
Armenian	30	0.10
Asian:	2,281	7.98
Bangladeshi (24)	33	0.12
Cambodian (27)	31	0.11
Chinese, ex. Taiwanese (84)	107	0.37
Filipino (223)	311	1.09
Indian (326)	418	1.46
Indonesian (6)	6	0.02
Japanese (57)	82	0.29
Korean (312)	353	1.24
Laotian (65)	81	0.28
Malaysian (7)	7	0.02
Pakistani (306)	358	1.25
Sri Lankan (3)	8	0.03
Taiwanese (8)	8	0.03
Thai (52)	68	0.24
Vietnamese (219)	245	0.86
Other Asian, specified (4)	4	0.01
Other Asian, not specified (48)	161	0.56
Austrian	75	0.26
Basque	6	0.02
Belgian	5	0.02
British	185	0.65
Canadian	55	0.19
Celtic	28	0.10
Croatian	57	0.20
Czech	109	0.38
Czechoslovakian	50	0.17
Danish	108	0.38
Dutch	377	1.32
Eastern European	17	0.06
English	3,007	10.52
European	213	0.75
Finnish	41	0.14
French, except Basque	543	1.90
French Canadian	163	0.57
German	2,909	10.18
Greek	55	0.19
Hawaii Native/Pacific Islander:	75	0.26
Micronesian: (13)	14	0.05
Guamanian/Chamorro (13)	14	0.05
Polynesian: (20)	35	0.12
Native Hawaiian (6)	20	0.07
Samoan (14)	15	0.05
Other Pac. Isl., not spec. (3)	26	0.09
Hispanic or Latino:	4,145	14.50
Central American:	1,612	5.64
Costa Rican	8	0.03
Guatemalan	86	0.30
Honduran	155	0.54
Nicaraguan	63	0.22
Panamanian	36	0.13
Salvadoran	1,133	3.96
Other Central American	131	0.46
Cuban	33	0.12
Dominican Republic	18	0.06
Mexican	490	1.71
Puerto Rican	276	0.97
South American:	235	0.82
Argentinean	6	0.02
Bolivian	56	0.20
Chilean	26	0.09
Colombian	30	0.10
Ecuadorian	15	0.05
Paraguayan	1	0.00
Peruvian	82	0.29
Uruguayan	1	0.00
Venezuelan	5	0.02
Other South American	13	0.05
Other Hispanic or Latino	1,481	5.18
Hungarian	108	0.38
Icelander	7	0.02
Iranian	75	0.26
Irish	2,490	8.71
Italian	884	3.09
Latvian	6	0.02
Lithuanian	68	0.24
Luxemburger	6	0.02
Northern European	14	0.05
Norwegian	204	0.71
Polish	483	1.69
Portuguese	65	0.23
Romanian	44	0.15
Russian	199	0.70
Scandinavian	30	0.10
Scotch-Irish	422	1.48
Scottish	616	2.16
Serbian	13	0.05
Slavic	24	0.08
Slovak	133	0.47
Slovene	21	0.07
Swedish	260	0.91
Swiss	100	0.35
Turkish	10	0.03
Ukrainian	144	0.50
United States or American	1,714	6.00
Welsh	215	0.75
West Indian, excl. Hispanic:	199	0.70
Bahamian	5	0.02
British West Indian	24	0.08
Haitian	10	0.03
Jamaican	84	0.29
Trinidadian and Tobagonian	8	0.03
U.S. Virgin Islander	23	0.08
West Indian	45	0.16
White:	16,434	57.50
Not Hispanic (13,861)	14,426	50.47
Hispanic (1,693)	2,008	7.03
Yugoslavian	39	0.14

Newington

Place Type: Census Designated Place
County: Fairfax
Population: 19,784

Ancestry/Race	Number	%
Afghan	216	1.10
African American/Black:	2,764	13.97
Not Hispanic (2,510)	2,700	13.65
Hispanic (28)	64	0.32
African, sub-Saharan:	735	3.73
African	387	1.96
Ethiopian	251	1.27
Ghanian	75	0.38
Sierra Leonean	15	0.08
Other sub-Saharan African	7	0.04
Alaska Native tribes, specified:	1	0.01
Eskimo	1	0.01
Am. Ind. or Alaska Nat., not spec.	73	0.37
Albanian	16	0.08
American Indian tribes, specified:	73	0.37
Blackfeet	2	0.01
Cherokee (8)	38	0.19
Chickasaw	1	0.01
Chippewa	1	0.01
Choctaw (1)	2	0.01
Delaware (1)	1	0.01
Latin American Indians (6)	13	0.07
Lumbee (2)	2	0.01
Puget Sound Salish	1	0.01
Sioux (5)	5	0.03
Tohono O'Odham	2	0.01
Yaqui (1)	1	0.01
All other tribes (1)	4	0.02
American Indian tribes, not spec.	13	0.07
Arab:	297	1.51
Arab/Arabic	63	0.32
Egyptian	41	0.21
Lebanese	99	0.50
Moroccan	34	0.17
Syrian	25	0.13
Other Arab	35	0.18
Armenian	69	0.35
Asian:	2,834	14.32
Bangladeshi (10)	14	0.07
Cambodian (9)	9	0.05
Chinese, ex. Taiwanese (220)	280	1.42
Filipino (329)	402	2.03
Indian (447)	513	2.59
Indonesian (15)	23	0.12
Japanese (35)	76	0.38
Korean (554)	618	3.12
Laotian (29)	32	0.16
Malaysian (1)	3	0.02
Pakistani (168)	246	1.24
Taiwanese (4)	6	0.03
Thai (49)	53	0.27
Vietnamese (333)	366	1.85
Other Asian, specified (1)	1	0.01
Other Asian, not specified (45)	192	0.97
Austrian	135	0.69
Belgian	12	0.06
Brazilian	17	0.09
British	166	0.84
Bulgarian	24	0.12
Canadian	45	0.23
Croatian	35	0.18
Cypriot	10	0.05
Czech	66	0.33
Czechoslovakian	30	0.15
Danish	49	0.25
Dutch	179	0.91
Eastern European	37	0.19
English	2,252	11.43
European	238	1.21
Finnish	30	0.15
French, except Basque	462	2.34
French Canadian	180	0.91
German	2,946	14.95

Notes: 1. Figures in the "Number" column do not add up to the total population due to: a) Ancestry/Race overlap — e.g. persons can report being both White and Irish, b) persons of Hispanic origin can report being any race, c) persons reporting two ancestries are counted in both categories. 2. Numbers in parentheses indicate the number of persons reporting this ancestry/race alone, not in combination with any other ancestry/race. 3. Refer to the Explanation of Data in the front of the book for more detailed information.

German Russian	5	0.03
Greek	106	0.54
Hawaii Native/Pacific Islander:	48	0.24
Micronesian: (9)	14	0.07
Guamanian/Chamorro (9)	14	0.07
Polynesian: (3)	12	0.06
Native Hawaiian (3)	12	0.06
Other Pac. Isl., not spec. (4)	22	0.11
Hispanic or Latino:	1,578	7.98
Central American:	298	1.51
Costa Rican	2	0.01
Guatemalan	39	0.20
Honduran	23	0.12
Nicaraguan	12	0.06
Panamanian	24	0.12
Salvadoran	181	0.91
Other Central American	17	0.09
Cuban	56	0.28
Dominican Republic	22	0.11
Mexican	187	0.95
Puerto Rican	155	0.78
South American:	411	2.08
Argentinean	8	0.04
Bolivian	108	0.55
Chilean	17	0.09
Colombian	39	0.20
Ecuadorian	15	0.08
Paraguayan	6	0.03
Peruvian	154	0.78
Uruguayan	8	0.04
Venezuelan	21	0.11
Other South American	35	0.18
Other Hispanic or Latino	449	2.27
Hungarian	71	0.36
Iranian	103	0.52
Irish	2,175	11.04
Italian	1,081	5.49
Latvian	7	0.04
Lithuanian	98	0.50
Luxemburger	6	0.03
Northern European	58	0.29
Norwegian	150	0.76
Polish	563	2.86
Portuguese	56	0.28
Romanian	42	0.21
Russian	158	0.80
Scandinavian	21	0.11
Scotch-Irish	366	1.86
Scottish	537	2.73
Serbian	3	0.02
Slavic	28	0.14
Slovak	139	0.71
Slovene	22	0.11
Swedish	270	1.37
Swiss	34	0.17
Turkish	17	0.09
Ukrainian	73	0.37
United States or American	1,241	6.30
Welsh	181	0.92
West Indian, excl. Hispanic:	60	0.30
Haitian	20	0.10
Trinidadian and Tobagonian	4	0.02
West Indian	36	0.18
White:	14,139	71.47
Not Hispanic (12,528)	13,119	66.31
Hispanic (885)	1,020	5.16
Yugoslavian	35	0.18

Newport News

Place Type: Independent City
County: Newport News Independent City
Population: 180,150

Ancestry/Race	Number	%
African American/Black:	73,111	40.58
Not Hispanic (69,538)	71,851	39.88
Hispanic (850)	1,260	0.70
African, sub-Saharan:	1,955	1.09
African	1,718	0.95
Cape Verdean	25	0.01
Ethiopian	27	0.01
Ghanian	6	0.00
Nigerian	26	0.01
Senegalese	13	0.01
Sudanese	77	0.04
Other sub-Saharan African	63	0.03
Alaska Native tribes, specified:	19	0.01
Alaska Athabascan (3)	3	0.00
Aleut (5)	5	0.00
Eskimo (4)	8	0.00
Tlingit-Haida (3)	3	0.00
Alaska Native tribes, not specified	2	0.00
Am. Ind. or Alaska Nat., not spec.	693	0.38
Albanian	6	0.00
American Indian tribes, specified:	1,300	0.72
Apache (14)	31	0.02
Blackfeet (21)	86	0.05
Cherokee (162)	611	0.34
Cheyenne	6	0.00
Chickasaw (3)	11	0.01
Chippewa (12)	19	0.01
Choctaw (17)	54	0.03
Colville (1)	1	0.00
Comanche (2)	5	0.00
Cree (3)	12	0.01
Creek (10)	24	0.01
Crow (1)	6	0.00
Delaware (5)	6	0.00
Houma (3)	3	0.00
Iroquois (17)	42	0.02
Kiowa	1	0.00
Latin American Indians (15)	28	0.02
Lumbee (24)	33	0.02
Navajo (11)	17	0.01
Osage (4)	7	0.00
Ottawa (10)	11	0.01
Pima	2	0.00
Potawatomi (3)	4	0.00
Pueblo (5)	6	0.00
Seminole (5)	14	0.01
Shoshone (1)	1	0.00
Sioux (29)	61	0.03
Yaqui	1	0.00
Yuman (1)	1	0.00
All other tribes (97)	196	0.11
American Indian tribes, not spec.	102	0.06
Arab:	404	0.22
Arab/Arabic	88	0.05
Egyptian	16	0.01
Jordanian	31	0.02
Lebanese	158	0.09
Moroccan	34	0.02
Palestinian	7	0.00
Syrian	47	0.03
Other Arab	23	0.01
Armenian	32	0.02
Asian:	5,728	3.18
Bangladeshi (13)	16	0.01
Cambodian (141)	169	0.09
Chinese, ex. Taiwanese (343)	498	0.28
Filipino (1,083)	1,526	0.85
Hmong (1)	2	0.00
Indian (223)	302	0.17
Indonesian (3)	11	0.01
Japanese (319)	557	0.31
Korean (1,210)	1,554	0.86
Laotian (42)	58	0.03
Malaysian (3)	4	0.00
Pakistani (17)	19	0.01
Sri Lankan (15)	20	0.01
Taiwanese (21)	22	0.01
Thai (89)	143	0.08
Vietnamese (501)	570	0.32
Other Asian, specified (5)	17	0.01
Other Asian, not specified (102)	240	0.13
Assyrian/Chaldean/Syriac	8	0.00
Australian	24	0.01
Austrian	203	0.11
Belgian	178	0.10
British	802	0.45
Canadian	212	0.12
Celtic	61	0.03
Croatian	101	0.06
Czech	332	0.18
Czechoslovakian	172	0.10
Danish	381	0.21
Dutch	1,958	1.09
Eastern European	58	0.03
English	14,950	8.30
European	1,703	0.95
Finnish	37	0.02
French, except Basque	3,662	2.03
French Canadian	929	0.52
German	17,243	9.57
German Russian	42	0.02
Greek	669	0.37
Guyanese	27	0.01
Hawaii Native/Pacific Islander:	490	0.27
Melanesian: (3)	3	0.00
Fijian (3)	3	0.00
Micronesian: (85)	119	0.07
Guamanian/Chamorro (60)	90	0.05
Other Micronesian (25)	29	0.02
Polynesian: (98)	244	0.14
Native Hawaiian (58)	172	0.10
Samoan (36)	61	0.03
Tongan (1)	2	0.00
Other Polynesian (3)	9	0.00
Other Pac. Isl., specified	9	0.00
Other Pac. Isl., not spec. (24)	115	0.06
Hispanic or Latino:	7,595	4.22
Central American:	546	0.30
Costa Rican	12	0.01
Guatemalan	37	0.02
Honduran	37	0.02
Nicaraguan	15	0.01
Panamanian	381	0.21
Salvadoran	56	0.03
Other Central American	8	0.00
Cuban	204	0.11
Dominican Republic	180	0.10
Mexican	1,956	1.09
Puerto Rican	3,144	1.75
South American:	295	0.16
Argentinean	14	0.01
Bolivian	9	0.00
Chilean	11	0.01
Colombian	108	0.06
Ecuadorian	42	0.02
Paraguayan	3	0.00
Peruvian	63	0.03
Uruguayan	1	0.00
Venezuelan	26	0.01
Other South American	18	0.01
Other Hispanic or Latino	1,270	0.70
Hungarian	403	0.22
Icelander	47	0.03
Iranian	55	0.03
Irish	13,350	7.41
Israeli	26	0.01
Italian	5,740	3.19
Latvian	35	0.02
Lithuanian	108	0.06
Macedonian	6	0.00
New Zealander	21	0.01
Northern European	84	0.05
Norwegian	1,105	0.61
Pennsylvania German	106	0.06
Polish	2,542	1.41
Portuguese	421	0.23
Romanian	118	0.07
Russian	592	0.33
Scandinavian	151	0.08
Scotch-Irish	2,994	1.66
Scottish	2,830	1.57
Serbian	124	0.07
Slavic	66	0.04
Slovak	237	0.13
Slovene	19	0.01

Notes: 1. Figures in the "Number" column do not add up to the total population due to: a) Ancestry/Race overlap — e.g. persons can report being both White and Irish, b) persons of Hispanic origin can report being any race, c) persons reporting two ancestries are counted in both categories. 2. Numbers in parentheses indicate the number of persons reporting this ancestry/race alone, not in combination with any other ancestry/race. 3. Refer to the Explanation of Data in the front of the book for more detailed information.

Ancestry/Race	Number	%
Swedish	913	0.51
Swiss	218	0.12
Turkish	127	0.07
Ukrainian	398	0.22
United States or American	14,113	7.83
Welsh	912	0.51
West Indian, excl. Hispanic:	1,180	0.66
Bahamian	35	0.02
Barbadian	36	0.02
Belizean	17	0.01
Bermudan	8	0.00
British West Indian	33	0.02
Dutch West Indian	5	0.00
Haitian	126	0.07
Jamaican	589	0.33
Trinidadian and Tobagonian	89	0.05
U.S. Virgin Islander	72	0.04
West Indian	157	0.09
Other West Indian	13	0.01
White:	99,800	55.40
Not Hispanic (93,624)	96,441	53.53
Hispanic (2,759)	3,359	1.86
Yugoslavian	177	0.10

Norfolk

Place Type: Independent City
County: Norfolk Independent City
Population: 234,403

Ancestry/Race	Number	%
Acadian/Cajun	88	0.04
African American/Black:	106,219	45.31
Not Hispanic (102,268)	104,688	44.66
Hispanic (1,119)	1,531	0.65
African, sub-Saharan:	2,932	1.25
African	2,478	1.06
Cape Verdean	95	0.04
Ethiopian	84	0.04
Ghanian	41	0.02
Kenyan	28	0.01
Liberian	7	0.00
Nigerian	89	0.04
Sierra Leonean	8	0.00
Somalian	7	0.00
South African	39	0.02
Other sub-Saharan African	56	0.02
Alaska Native tribes, specified:	28	0.01
Alaska Athabascan (1)	1	0.00
Aleut (4)	6	0.00
Eskimo (3)	12	0.01
Tlingit-Haida (2)	6	0.00
All other tribes (1)	3	0.00
Alaska Native tribes, not specified	2	0.00
Am. Ind. or Alaska Nat., not spec.	887	0.38
Albanian	5	0.00
American Indian tribes, specified:	1,633	0.70
Apache (13)	36	0.02
Blackfeet (23)	109	0.05
Cherokee (235)	772	0.33
Cheyenne (7)	8	0.00
Chickasaw (3)	7	0.00
Chippewa (22)	32	0.01
Choctaw (19)	40	0.02
Colville	1	0.00
Comanche (1)	11	0.00
Cree (3)	8	0.00
Creek (8)	19	0.01
Crow	1	0.00
Delaware (1)	5	0.00
Houma (1)	1	0.00
Iroquois (36)	70	0.03
Kiowa (7)	9	0.00
Latin American Indians (34)	65	0.03
Lumbee (45)	51	0.02
Menominee (2)	4	0.00
Navajo (45)	60	0.03
Osage (4)	12	0.01
Ottawa (4)	7	0.00
Paiute (1)	1	0.00
Pima (2)	3	0.00
Potawatomi (10)	12	0.01
Pueblo (10)	15	0.01
Puget Sound Salish	1	0.00
Seminole (8)	14	0.01
Shoshone (1)	2	0.00
Sioux (29)	69	0.03
Ute	1	0.00
Yaqui (3)	8	0.00
Yuman (1)	1	0.00
All other tribes (81)	178	0.08
American Indian tribes, not spec.	157	0.07
Arab:	836	0.36
Arab/Arabic	110	0.05
Egyptian	110	0.05
Jordanian	11	0.00
Lebanese	275	0.12
Moroccan	86	0.04
Palestinian	85	0.04
Syrian	36	0.02
Other Arab	123	0.05
Armenian	112	0.05
Asian:	8,510	3.63
Bangladeshi (10)	11	0.00
Cambodian (21)	33	0.01
Chinese, ex. Taiwanese (529)	694	0.30
Filipino (4,125)	5,182	2.21
Hmong (9)	10	0.00
Indian (491)	600	0.26
Indonesian (9)	12	0.01
Japanese (266)	412	0.18
Korean (297)	416	0.18
Laotian (13)	15	0.01
Malaysian (4)	31	0.01
Pakistani (32)	49	0.02
Sri Lankan (13)	14	0.01
Taiwanese (48)	63	0.03
Thai (115)	147	0.06
Vietnamese (373)	420	0.18
Other Asian, specified (7)	18	0.01
Other Asian, not specified (138)	383	0.16
Australian	34	0.01
Austrian	405	0.17
Basque	11	0.00
Belgian	154	0.07
Brazilian	27	0.01
British	1,051	0.45
Bulgarian	12	0.01
Canadian	450	0.19
Celtic	109	0.05
Croatian	114	0.05
Cypriot	69	0.03
Czech	400	0.17
Czechoslovakian	276	0.12
Danish	360	0.15
Dutch	2,136	0.91
Eastern European	144	0.06
English	16,152	6.89
European	1,414	0.60
Finnish	158	0.07
French, except Basque	4,640	1.98
French Canadian	1,413	0.60
German	20,167	8.60
German Russian	6	0.00
Greek	1,028	0.44
Guyanese	48	0.02
Hawaii Native/Pacific Islander:	613	0.26
Micronesian: (84)	144	0.06
Guamanian/Chamorro (76)	132	0.06
Other Micronesian (8)	12	0.01
Polynesian: (91)	216	0.09
Native Hawaiian (40)	140	0.06
Samoan (43)	61	0.03
Tongan (8)	11	0.00
Other Polynesian	4	0.00
Other Pac. Isl., specified	11	0.00
Other Pac. Isl., not spec. (75)	242	0.10
Hispanic or Latino:	8,915	3.80
Central American:	490	0.21
Costa Rican	21	0.01
Guatemalan	61	0.03
Honduran	94	0.04
Nicaraguan	29	0.01
Panamanian	148	0.06
Salvadoran	94	0.04
Other Central American	43	0.02
Cuban	294	0.13
Dominican Republic	219	0.09
Mexican	2,624	1.12
Puerto Rican	2,916	1.24
South American:	438	0.19
Argentinean	21	0.01
Bolivian	10	0.00
Chilean	24	0.01
Colombian	150	0.06
Ecuadorian	85	0.04
Paraguayan	5	0.00
Peruvian	92	0.04
Uruguayan	2	0.00
Venezuelan	26	0.01
Other South American	23	0.01
Other Hispanic or Latino	1,934	0.83
Hungarian	504	0.22
Icelander	87	0.04
Iranian	136	0.06
Irish	18,925	8.07
Israeli	13	0.01
Italian	8,151	3.48
Latvian	73	0.03
Lithuanian	391	0.17
Macedonian	9	0.00
Maltese	13	0.01
Northern European	78	0.03
Norwegian	1,231	0.53
Pennsylvania German	40	0.02
Polish	3,639	1.55
Portuguese	493	0.21
Romanian	200	0.09
Russian	1,113	0.47
Scandinavian	209	0.09
Scotch-Irish	3,438	1.47
Scottish	3,881	1.66
Serbian	38	0.02
Slavic	38	0.02
Slovak	219	0.09
Slovene	61	0.03
Swedish	1,246	0.53
Swiss	290	0.12
Turkish	67	0.03
Ukrainian	338	0.14
United States or American	12,290	5.24
Welsh	1,119	0.48
West Indian, excl. Hispanic:	1,723	0.74
Bahamian	36	0.02
Barbadian	40	0.02
Belizean	15	0.01
Bermudan	9	0.00
British West Indian	76	0.03
Dutch West Indian	7	0.00
Haitian	227	0.10
Jamaican	933	0.40
Trinidadian and Tobagonian	191	0.08
U.S. Virgin Islander	48	0.02
West Indian	141	0.06
White:	117,511	50.13
Not Hispanic (110,221)	113,769	48.54
Hispanic (3,137)	3,742	1.60
Yugoslavian	51	0.02

Oakton

Place Type: Census Designated Place
County: Fairfax
Population: 29,348

Ancestry/Race	Number	%
Afghan	121	0.41
African American/Black:	1,590	5.42
Not Hispanic (1,365)	1,521	5.18
Hispanic (42)	69	0.24

Notes: 1. Figures in the "Number" column do not add up to the total population due to: a) Ancestry/Race overlap — e.g. persons can report being both White and Irish, b) persons of Hispanic origin can report being any race, c) persons reporting two ancestries are counted in both categories. 2. Numbers in parentheses indicate the number of persons reporting this ancestry/race alone, not in combination with any other ancestry/race. 3. Refer to the Explanation of Data in the front of the book for more detailed information.

African, sub-Saharan:	381	1.30
African	31	0.11
Cape Verdean	18	0.06
Ethiopian	46	0.16
Ghanian	23	0.08
Kenyan	6	0.02
Nigerian	63	0.21
Somalian	118	0.40
South African	57	0.19
Other sub-Saharan African	19	0.06
Alaska Native tribes, specified:	1	0.00
Tlingit-Haida (1)	1	0.00
Am. Ind. or Alaska Nat., not spec.	74	0.25
Albanian	21	0.07
American Indian tribes, specified:	97	0.33
Blackfeet	1	0.00
Cherokee (6)	27	0.09
Chickasaw (1)	1	0.00
Chippewa (1)	1	0.00
Choctaw (3)	5	0.02
Comanche	2	0.01
Cree	3	0.01
Creek (2)	2	0.01
Iroquois (3)	4	0.01
Kiowa (1)	1	0.00
Latin American Indians (8)	19	0.06
Lumbee	1	0.00
Potawatomi (3)	3	0.01
Sioux (1)	7	0.02
Yaqui (3)	3	0.01
All other tribes (4)	17	0.06
American Indian tribes, not spec.	5	0.02
Arab:	692	2.35
Arab/Arabic	66	0.22
Egyptian	276	0.94
Iraqi	30	0.10
Jordanian	36	0.12
Lebanese	123	0.42
Moroccan	22	0.07
Palestinian	20	0.07
Syrian	24	0.08
Other Arab	95	0.32
Armenian	112	0.38
Asian:	4,549	15.50
Bangladeshi (10)	10	0.03
Cambodian (26)	30	0.10
Chinese, ex. Taiwanese (890)	975	3.32
Filipino (226)	274	0.93
Indian (885)	963	3.28
Indonesian (10)	14	0.05
Japanese (126)	178	0.61
Korean (1,108)	1,167	3.98
Laotian (3)	3	0.01
Malaysian (16)	17	0.06
Pakistani (93)	106	0.36
Sri Lankan (9)	11	0.04
Taiwanese (29)	36	0.12
Thai (61)	73	0.25
Vietnamese (411)	431	1.47
Other Asian, specified (60)	75	0.26
Other Asian, not specified (44)	186	0.63
Assyrian/Chaldean/Syriac	36	0.12
Australian	25	0.09
Austrian	140	0.48
Belgian	50	0.17
British	365	1.24
Canadian	113	0.38
Croatian	53	0.18
Czech	111	0.38
Czechoslovakian	64	0.22
Danish	80	0.27
Dutch	400	1.36
Eastern European	92	0.31
English	3,495	11.89
European	469	1.60
Finnish	32	0.11
French, except Basque	722	2.46
French Canadian	292	0.99
German	4,265	14.51
Greek	274	0.93
Guyanese	20	0.07
Hawaii Native/Pacific Islander:	62	0.21
Micronesian: (14)	16	0.05
Guamanian/Chamorro (14)	16	0.05
Polynesian: (4)	15	0.05
Native Hawaiian (4)	14	0.05
Samoan	1	0.00
Other Pac. Isl., specified	5	0.02
Other Pac. Isl., not spec. (5)	26	0.09
Hispanic or Latino:	2,831	9.65
Central American:	820	2.79
Costa Rican	9	0.03
Guatemalan	109	0.37
Honduran	91	0.31
Nicaraguan	40	0.14
Panamanian	13	0.04
Salvadoran	473	1.61
Other Central American	85	0.29
Cuban	81	0.28
Dominican Republic	32	0.11
Mexican	294	1.00
Puerto Rican	145	0.49
South American:	726	2.47
Argentinean	17	0.06
Bolivian	177	0.60
Chilean	40	0.14
Colombian	80	0.27
Ecuadorian	57	0.19
Paraguayan	5	0.02
Peruvian	257	0.88
Uruguayan	16	0.05
Venezuelan	39	0.13
Other South American	38	0.13
Other Hispanic or Latino	733	2.50
Hungarian	337	1.15
Icelander	21	0.07
Iranian	324	1.10
Irish	3,637	12.38
Israeli	29	0.10
Italian	1,939	6.60
Latvian	42	0.14
Lithuanian	177	0.60
Luxemburger	9	0.03
Maltese	9	0.03
New Zealander	30	0.10
Northern European	19	0.06
Norwegian	521	1.77
Polish	691	2.35
Portuguese	74	0.25
Romanian	63	0.21
Russian	605	2.06
Scandinavian	71	0.24
Scotch-Irish	721	2.45
Scottish	908	3.09
Serbian	13	0.04
Slovak	157	0.53
Slovene	9	0.03
Swedish	502	1.71
Swiss	154	0.52
Turkish	137	0.47
Ukrainian	141	0.48
United States or American	1,330	4.53
Welsh	307	1.04
West Indian, excl. Hispanic:	75	0.26
British West Indian	11	0.04
Jamaican	18	0.06
Trinidadian and Tobagonian	9	0.03
West Indian	37	0.13
White:	22,755	77.54
Not Hispanic (20,101)	20,844	71.02
Hispanic (1,752)	1,911	6.51
Yugoslavian	17	0.06

Petersburg

Place Type: Independent City
County: Petersburg Independent City
Population: 33,740

Ancestry/Race	Number	%
African American/Black:	26,870	79.64
Not Hispanic (26,511)	26,717	79.18
Hispanic (132)	153	0.45
African, sub-Saharan:	481	1.43
African	449	1.33
Cape Verdean	14	0.04
Kenyan	5	0.01
Other sub-Saharan African	13	0.04
Am. Ind. or Alaska Nat., not spec.	66	0.20
American Indian tribes, specified:	90	0.27
Apache	1	0.00
Blackfeet (1)	11	0.03
Cherokee (19)	47	0.14
Chippewa (1)	2	0.01
Choctaw	2	0.01
Creek	4	0.01
Iroquois	2	0.01
Latin American Indians	1	0.00
Lumbee (2)	2	0.01
Menominee (1)	1	0.00
Navajo	1	0.00
Potawatomi	1	0.00
Pueblo (1)	1	0.00
Seminole	1	0.00
Sioux (1)	3	0.01
All other tribes (3)	10	0.03
American Indian tribes, not spec.	17	0.05
Arab:	22	0.07
Lebanese	11	0.03
Palestinian	11	0.03
Asian:	321	0.95
Cambodian (1)	1	0.00
Chinese, ex. Taiwanese (17)	22	0.07
Filipino (53)	81	0.24
Indian (38)	47	0.14
Japanese (37)	45	0.13
Korean (59)	67	0.20
Laotian (1)	1	0.00
Pakistani (3)	8	0.02
Taiwanese	3	0.01
Thai (5)	11	0.03
Vietnamese (4)	10	0.03
Other Asian, specified (2)	2	0.01
Other Asian, not specified (11)	23	0.07
Austrian	36	0.11
British	101	0.30
Canadian	8	0.02
Celtic	31	0.09
Croatian	5	0.01
Czech	57	0.17
Czechoslovakian	6	0.02
Danish	30	0.09
Dutch	93	0.28
English	1,024	3.03
European	100	0.30
French, except Basque	168	0.50
French Canadian	30	0.09
German	664	1.97
Greek	56	0.17
Hawaii Native/Pacific Islander:	35	0.10
Micronesian: (1)	1	0.00
Guamanian/Chamorro (1)	1	0.00
Polynesian: (5)	21	0.06
Native Hawaiian (2)	11	0.03
Samoan (3)	10	0.03
Other Pac. Isl., not spec. (3)	13	0.04
Hispanic or Latino:	463	1.37
Central American:	18	0.05
Costa Rican	2	0.01
Honduran	4	0.01
Nicaraguan	1	0.00
Panamanian	11	0.03
Cuban	9	0.03
Dominican Republic	4	0.01
Mexican	197	0.58
Puerto Rican	138	0.41
South American:	8	0.02
Colombian	5	0.01
Ecuadorian	1	0.00
Peruvian	2	0.01

Notes: 1. Figures in the "Number" column do not add up to the total population due to: a) Ancestry/Race overlap — e.g. persons can report being both White and Irish, b) persons of Hispanic origin can report being any race, c) persons reporting two ancestries are counted in both categories. 2. Numbers in parentheses indicate the number of persons reporting this ancestry/race alone, not in combination with any other ancestry/race. 3. Refer to the Explanation of Data in the front of the book for more detailed information.

Other Hispanic or Latino	89	0.26
Hungarian	44	0.13
Icelander	12	0.04
Irish	629	1.86
Italian	191	0.57
Norwegian	13	0.04
Pennsylvania German	6	0.02
Polish	68	0.20
Portuguese	38	0.11
Romanian	18	0.05
Russian	18	0.05
Scandinavian	9	0.03
Scotch-Irish	97	0.29
Scottish	192	0.57
Swedish	40	0.12
Swiss	21	0.06
Ukrainian	18	0.05
United States or American	955	2.83
Welsh	83	0.25
West Indian, excl. Hispanic:	41	0.12
Haitian	7	0.02
Jamaican	8	0.02
West Indian	26	0.08
White:	6,447	19.11
Not Hispanic (6,131)	6,319	18.73
Hispanic (118)	128	0.38

Poquoson

Place Type: Independent City
County: Poquoson Independent City
Population: 11,566

Ancestry/Race	Number	%
Acadian/Cajun	19	0.16
African American/Black:	96	0.83
Not Hispanic (78)	93	0.80
Hispanic	3	0.03
Am. Ind. or Alaska Nat., not spec.	16	0.14
American Indian tribes, specified:	49	0.42
Blackfeet	4	0.03
Cherokee (5)	23	0.20
Choctaw (4)	5	0.04
Iroquois	1	0.01
Latin American Indians (1)	1	0.01
Lumbee (1)	1	0.01
Osage	1	0.01
Sioux	5	0.04
All other tribes (7)	8	0.07
American Indian tribes, not spec.	6	0.05
Arab:	35	0.30
Lebanese	35	0.30
Asian:	223	1.93
Chinese, ex. Taiwanese (41)	43	0.37
Filipino (28)	43	0.37
Indian (30)	36	0.31
Indonesian	1	0.01
Japanese (16)	21	0.18
Korean (49)	61	0.53
Taiwanese (4)	5	0.04
Thai (5)	5	0.04
Vietnamese	1	0.01
Other Asian, not specified (7)	7	0.06
Austrian	8	0.07
British	81	0.70
Canadian	34	0.29
Celtic	6	0.05
Croatian	50	0.43
Czech	45	0.39
Czechoslovakian	17	0.15
Danish	21	0.18
Dutch	173	1.50
Eastern European	17	0.15
English	2,786	24.09
European	204	1.76
Finnish	12	0.10
French, except Basque	269	2.33
French Canadian	85	0.73
German	1,644	14.21
Greek	123	1.06
Hawaii Native/Pacific Islander:	9	0.08
Micronesian: (2)	2	0.02
Guamanian/Chamorro (2)	2	0.02
Polynesian: (1)	5	0.04
Native Hawaiian (1)	4	0.03
Samoan	1	0.01
Other Pac. Isl., not spec. (1)	2	0.02
Hispanic or Latino:	122	1.05
Central American:	3	0.03
Nicaraguan	1	0.01
Panamanian	2	0.02
Cuban	11	0.10
Dominican Republic	1	0.01
Mexican	38	0.33
Puerto Rican	33	0.29
South American:	19	0.16
Chilean	2	0.02
Colombian	11	0.10
Ecuadorian	2	0.02
Peruvian	3	0.03
Other South American	1	0.01
Other Hispanic or Latino	17	0.15
Hungarian	40	0.35
Irish	1,274	11.02
Italian	549	4.75
Lithuanian	3	0.03
Maltese	13	0.11
Northern European	67	0.58
Norwegian	63	0.54
Pennsylvania German	7	0.06
Polish	239	2.07
Portuguese	13	0.11
Russian	37	0.32
Scandinavian	14	0.12
Scotch-Irish	369	3.19
Scottish	342	2.96
Slavic	6	0.05
Slovak	61	0.53
Swedish	79	0.68
Swiss	11	0.10
Turkish	4	0.03
Ukrainian	34	0.29
United States or American	1,474	12.74
Welsh	95	0.82
West Indian, excl. Hispanic:	17	0.15
Jamaican	5	0.04
U.S. Virgin Islander	12	0.10
White:	11,237	97.16
Not Hispanic (11,048)	11,142	96.33
Hispanic (86)	95	0.82

Portsmouth

Place Type: Independent City
County: Portsmouth Independent City
Population: 100,565

Ancestry/Race	Number	%
Acadian/Cajun	16	0.02
African American/Black:	51,767	51.48
Not Hispanic (50,569)	51,370	51.08
Hispanic (330)	397	0.39
African, sub-Saharan:	1,206	1.20
African	1,073	1.07
Cape Verdean	11	0.01
Kenyan	22	0.02
Liberian	9	0.01
Nigerian	59	0.06
Zimbabwean	6	0.01
Other sub-Saharan African	26	0.03
Alaska Native tribes, specified:	2	0.00
Alaska Athabascan	1	0.00
Eskimo (1)	1	0.00
Am. Ind. or Alaska Nat., not spec.	351	0.35
American Indian tribes, specified:	646	0.64
Apache (6)	14	0.01
Blackfeet (5)	20	0.02
Cherokee (106)	311	0.31
Cheyenne (4)	6	0.01
Chickasaw (4)	7	0.01
Chippewa	4	0.00
Choctaw (12)	19	0.02
Comanche (4)	10	0.01
Creek (6)	10	0.01
Crow (1)	1	0.00
Delaware (1)	2	0.00
Houma (1)	1	0.00
Iroquois (4)	18	0.02
Kiowa (4)	5	0.00
Latin American Indians (6)	9	0.01
Lumbee (22)	30	0.03
Navajo (3)	7	0.01
Osage (1)	1	0.00
Potawatomi (1)	1	0.00
Puget Sound Salish (1)	1	0.00
Seminole (4)	10	0.01
Sioux (15)	22	0.02
Ute (1)	3	0.00
All other tribes (79)	134	0.13
American Indian tribes, not spec.	110	0.11
Arab:	172	0.17
Arab/Arabic	19	0.02
Lebanese	21	0.02
Moroccan	49	0.05
Palestinian	62	0.06
Syrian	21	0.02
Armenian	29	0.03
Asian:	1,169	1.16
Cambodian (1)	1	0.00
Chinese, ex. Taiwanese (83)	112	0.11
Filipino (424)	612	0.61
Hmong	1	0.00
Indian (55)	92	0.09
Indonesian	1	0.00
Japanese (35)	76	0.08
Korean (70)	106	0.11
Malaysian (1)	4	0.00
Pakistani (1)	1	0.00
Sri Lankan (8)	9	0.01
Taiwanese (10)	12	0.01
Thai (15)	19	0.02
Vietnamese (46)	68	0.07
Other Asian, specified (3)	9	0.01
Other Asian, not specified (9)	46	0.05
Australian	14	0.01
Austrian	120	0.12
Belgian	37	0.04
Brazilian	20	0.02
British	314	0.31
Canadian	43	0.04
Celtic	19	0.02
Croatian	53	0.05
Czech	49	0.05
Czechoslovakian	24	0.02
Danish	162	0.16
Dutch	673	0.67
Eastern European	15	0.01
English	8,002	7.96
Estonian	4	0.00
European	495	0.49
Finnish	46	0.05
French, except Basque	1,337	1.33
French Canadian	400	0.40
German	6,034	6.00
Greek	324	0.32
Guyanese	41	0.04
Hawaii Native/Pacific Islander:	163	0.16
Melanesian:	2	0.00
Fijian	2	0.00
Micronesian: (24)	41	0.04
Guamanian/Chamorro (23)	36	0.04
Other Micronesian (1)	5	0.00
Polynesian: (19)	62	0.06
Native Hawaiian (9)	49	0.05
Samoan (10)	13	0.01
Other Pac. Isl., not spec. (23)	58	0.06
Hispanic or Latino:	1,748	1.74
Central American:	107	0.11
Costa Rican	5	0.00
Guatemalan	6	0.01

Notes: 1. Figures in the "Number" column do not add up to the total population due to: a) Ancestry/Race overlap — e.g. persons can report being both White and Irish, b) persons of Hispanic origin can report being any race, c) persons reporting two ancestries are counted in both categories. 2. Numbers in parentheses indicate the number of persons reporting this ancestry/race alone, not in combination with any other ancestry/race. 3. Refer to the Explanation of Data in the front of the book for more detailed information.

Honduran	14	0.01
Nicaraguan	8	0.01
Panamanian	66	0.07
Salvadoran	6	0.01
Other Central American	2	0.00
Cuban	87	0.09
Dominican Republic	29	0.03
Mexican	530	0.53
Puerto Rican	535	0.53
South American:	57	0.06
Argentinean	1	0.00
Bolivian	6	0.01
Chilean	5	0.00
Colombian	23	0.02
Ecuadorian	5	0.00
Peruvian	8	0.01
Venezuelan	5	0.00
Other South American	4	0.00
Other Hispanic or Latino	403	0.40
Hungarian	180	0.18
Iranian	6	0.01
Irish	6,313	6.28
Israeli	18	0.02
Italian	2,289	2.28
Lithuanian	77	0.08
Maltese	7	0.01
Northern European	28	0.03
Norwegian	508	0.51
Pennsylvania German	33	0.03
Polish	894	0.89
Portuguese	159	0.16
Romanian	43	0.04
Russian	273	0.27
Scandinavian	55	0.05
Scotch-Irish	1,549	1.54
Scottish	1,231	1.22
Serbian	5	0.00
Slavic	39	0.04
Slovak	32	0.03
Swedish	422	0.42
Swiss	135	0.13
Turkish	31	0.03
Ukrainian	83	0.08
United States or American	7,107	7.07
Welsh	342	0.34
West Indian, excl. Hispanic:	255	0.25
Barbadian	6	0.01
British West Indian	37	0.04
Haitian	18	0.02
Jamaican	164	0.16
Trinidadian and Tobagonian	6	0.01
West Indian	24	0.02
White:	47,264	47.00
Not Hispanic (45,403)	46,454	46.19
Hispanic (693)	810	0.81
Yugoslavian	13	0.01

Radford

Place Type: Independent City
County: Radford Independent City
Population: 15,859

Ancestry/Race	Number	%
African American/Black:	1,383	8.72
Not Hispanic (1,274)	1,362	8.59
Hispanic (10)	21	0.13
African, sub-Saharan:	59	0.37
African	46	0.29
Nigerian	6	0.04
South African	7	0.04
Alaska Native tribes, specified:	3	0.02
Aleut	1	0.01
Tlingit-Haida (2)	2	0.01
Am. Ind. or Alaska Nat., not spec.	29	0.18
American Indian tribes, specified:	64	0.40
Blackfeet	2	0.01
Cherokee (10)	36	0.23
Chippewa (1)	1	0.01
Choctaw (2)	2	0.01
Creek (3)	3	0.02
Iroquois	1	0.01
Latin American Indians (2)	3	0.02
Ottawa	1	0.01
Paiute	1	0.01
Seminole (1)	1	0.01
Sioux (1)	2	0.01
Yakama	2	0.01
Yaqui (1)	1	0.01
All other tribes (3)	8	0.05
American Indian tribes, not spec.	3	0.02
Asian:	303	1.91
Bangladeshi (1)	1	0.01
Cambodian (2)	3	0.02
Chinese, ex. Taiwanese (33)	41	0.26
Filipino (24)	41	0.26
Indian (58)	64	0.40
Japanese (28)	36	0.23
Korean (32)	44	0.28
Malaysian (1)	1	0.01
Pakistani (1)	1	0.01
Sri Lankan (1)	1	0.01
Taiwanese (7)	15	0.09
Thai (7)	8	0.05
Vietnamese (17)	19	0.12
Other Asian, specified (1)	1	0.01
Other Asian, not specified (12)	27	0.17
Austrian	25	0.16
British	116	0.73
Canadian	20	0.13
Czech	23	0.15
Czechoslovakian	49	0.31
Danish	38	0.24
Dutch	212	1.34
English	1,769	11.15
Estonian	6	0.04
European	196	1.24
Finnish	13	0.08
French, except Basque	248	1.56
French Canadian	128	0.81
German	2,278	14.36
Greek	45	0.28
Hawaii Native/Pacific Islander:	15	0.09
Micronesian: (1)	2	0.01
Guamanian/Chamorro (1)	2	0.01
Polynesian: (1)	4	0.03
Native Hawaiian	1	0.01
Samoan (1)	3	0.02
Other Pac. Isl., not spec. (2)	9	0.06
Hispanic or Latino:	184	1.16
Central American:	19	0.12
Guatemalan	1	0.01
Honduran	7	0.04
Nicaraguan	2	0.01
Panamanian	1	0.01
Salvadoran	7	0.04
Other Central American	1	0.01
Cuban	11	0.07
Dominican Republic	2	0.01
Mexican	45	0.28
Puerto Rican	42	0.26
South American:	23	0.15
Argentinean	3	0.02
Chilean	6	0.04
Colombian	1	0.01
Ecuadorian	1	0.01
Paraguayan	1	0.01
Peruvian	5	0.03
Uruguayan	4	0.03
Venezuelan	2	0.01
Other Hispanic or Latino	42	0.26
Hungarian	55	0.35
Iranian	24	0.15
Irish	1,855	11.70
Italian	632	3.99
Lithuanian	8	0.05
Norwegian	59	0.37
Polish	347	2.19
Portuguese	38	0.24
Romanian	6	0.04
Russian	78	0.49
Scandinavian	37	0.23
Scotch-Irish	612	3.86
Scottish	553	3.49
Serbian	6	0.04
Slavic	19	0.12
Slovak	47	0.30
Slovene	17	0.11
Swedish	129	0.81
Swiss	42	0.26
Turkish	8	0.05
Ukrainian	7	0.04
United States or American	2,096	13.22
Welsh	106	0.67
West Indian, excl. Hispanic:	30	0.19
Haitian	5	0.03
Jamaican	20	0.13
West Indian	5	0.03
White:	14,177	89.39
Not Hispanic (13,900)	14,075	88.75
Hispanic (90)	102	0.64

Reston

Place Type: Census Designated Place
County: Fairfax
Population: 56,407

Ancestry/Race	Number	%
Acadian/Cajun	7	0.01
Afghan	283	0.50
African American/Black:	5,724	10.15
Not Hispanic (5,017)	5,545	9.83
Hispanic (128)	179	0.32
African, sub-Saharan:	1,246	2.21
African	663	1.17
Cape Verdean	7	0.01
Ethiopian	32	0.06
Ghanian	157	0.28
Liberian	148	0.26
Nigerian	64	0.11
Sierra Leonean	35	0.06
South African	10	0.02
Ugandan	7	0.01
Other sub-Saharan African	123	0.22
Alaska Native tribes, specified:	4	0.01
Tlingit-Haida (4)	4	0.01
Am. Ind. or Alaska Nat., not spec.	158	0.28
Alsatian	23	0.04
American Indian tribes, specified:	224	0.40
Apache	4	0.01
Blackfeet	18	0.03
Cherokee (12)	61	0.11
Chickasaw	1	0.00
Chippewa (2)	6	0.01
Choctaw (2)	4	0.01
Comanche (1)	1	0.00
Cree (1)	6	0.01
Creek (3)	6	0.01
Crow	1	0.00
Iroquois (4)	19	0.03
Latin American Indians (25)	49	0.09
Lumbee (4)	6	0.01
Navajo (2)	2	0.00
Ottawa (1)	1	0.00
Potawatomi (1)	1	0.00
Pueblo (1)	1	0.00
Seminole	2	0.00
Sioux (5)	9	0.02
All other tribes (12)	26	0.05
American Indian tribes, not spec.	15	0.03
Arab:	740	1.31
Arab/Arabic	69	0.12
Egyptian	153	0.27
Iraqi	6	0.01
Jordanian	90	0.16
Lebanese	219	0.39
Moroccan	24	0.04
Palestinian	37	0.07
Syrian	56	0.10

Notes: 1. Figures in the "Number" column do not add up to the total population due to: a) Ancestry/Race overlap — e.g. persons can report being both White and Irish, b) persons of Hispanic origin can report being any race, c) persons reporting two ancestries are counted in both categories. 2. Numbers in parentheses indicate the number of persons reporting this ancestry/race alone, not in combination with any other ancestry/race. 3. Refer to the Explanation of Data in the front of the book for more detailed information.

Other Arab	86	0.15
Armenian	76	0.13
Asian:	6,194	10.98
Bangladeshi (66)	95	0.17
Cambodian (31)	36	0.06
Chinese, ex. Taiwanese (825)	923	1.64
Filipino (389)	511	0.91
Indian (2,071)	2,197	3.89
Indonesian (41)	44	0.08
Japanese (124)	199	0.35
Korean (549)	605	1.07
Laotian (146)	176	0.31
Malaysian (3)	8	0.01
Pakistani (285)	350	0.62
Sri Lankan (27)	27	0.05
Taiwanese (42)	44	0.08
Thai (59)	81	0.14
Vietnamese (566)	603	1.07
Other Asian, specified (40)	45	0.08
Other Asian, not specified (89)	250	0.44
Australian	88	0.16
Austrian	346	0.61
Basque	17	0.03
Belgian	75	0.13
British	713	1.26
Bulgarian	22	0.04
Canadian	249	0.44
Croatian	103	0.18
Czech	173	0.31
Czechoslovakian	121	0.21
Danish	266	0.47
Dutch	753	1.33
Eastern European	195	0.35
English	7,410	13.13
Estonian	15	0.03
European	818	1.45
Finnish	133	0.24
French, except Basque	1,646	2.92
French Canadian	522	0.92
German	8,802	15.59
Greek	306	0.54
Guyanese	18	0.03
Hawaii Native/Pacific Islander:	67	0.12
Melanesian:	2	0.00
Other Melanesian	2	0.00
Micronesian: (10)	15	0.03
Guamanian/Chamorro (10)	14	0.02
Other Micronesian	1	0.00
Polynesian: (8)	29	0.05
Native Hawaiian (4)	19	0.03
Samoan (3)	9	0.02
Other Polynesian (1)	1	0.00
Other Pac. Isl., not spec. (4)	21	0.04
Hispanic or Latino:	5,699	10.10
Central American:	1,810	3.21
Costa Rican	34	0.06
Guatemalan	115	0.20
Honduran	195	0.35
Nicaraguan	95	0.17
Panamanian	24	0.04
Salvadoran	1,260	2.23
Other Central American	87	0.15
Cuban	113	0.20
Dominican Republic	33	0.06
Mexican	767	1.36
Puerto Rican	394	0.70
South American:	858	1.52
Argentinean	57	0.10
Bolivian	215	0.38
Chilean	32	0.06
Colombian	138	0.24
Ecuadorian	39	0.07
Paraguayan	5	0.01
Peruvian	256	0.45
Uruguayan	4	0.01
Venezuelan	45	0.08
Other South American	67	0.12
Other Hispanic or Latino	1,724	3.06
Hungarian	281	0.50
Icelander	9	0.02
Iranian	600	1.06
Irish	7,127	12.63
Israeli	23	0.04
Italian	2,942	5.21
Latvian	115	0.20
Lithuanian	265	0.47
Luxemburger	13	0.02
Maltese	13	0.02
Northern European	131	0.23
Norwegian	669	1.19
Pennsylvania German	8	0.01
Polish	1,856	3.29
Portuguese	115	0.20
Romanian	120	0.21
Russian	1,088	1.93
Scandinavian	117	0.21
Scotch-Irish	1,171	2.07
Scottish	2,004	3.55
Serbian	20	0.04
Slavic	31	0.05
Slovak	148	0.26
Slovene	64	0.11
Swedish	746	1.32
Swiss	191	0.34
Turkish	52	0.09
Ukrainian	271	0.48
United States or American	2,603	4.61
Welsh	641	1.14
West Indian, excl. Hispanic:	319	0.57
Barbadian	11	0.02
Belizean	18	0.03
Haitian	78	0.14
Jamaican	109	0.19
Trinidadian and Tobagonian	85	0.15
West Indian	18	0.03
White:	43,019	76.27
Not Hispanic (38,563)	39,691	70.37
Hispanic (2,965)	3,328	5.90
Yugoslavian	51	0.09

Richmond

Place Type: Independent City
County: Richmond Independent City
Population: 197,790

Ancestry/Race	Number	%
Acadian/Cajun	17	0.01
Afghan	69	0.03
African American/Black:	114,860	58.07
Not Hispanic (112,455)	113,997	57.64
Hispanic (653)	863	0.44
African, sub-Saharan:	2,833	1.43
African	2,296	1.16
Cape Verdean	5	0.00
Ethiopian	34	0.02
Ghanian	15	0.01
Kenyan	11	0.01
Liberian	122	0.06
Nigerian	193	0.10
Sierra Leonean	20	0.01
South African	25	0.01
Zairian	40	0.02
Other sub-Saharan African	72	0.04
Alaska Native tribes, specified:	6	0.00
Alaska Athabascan	2	0.00
Aleut	1	0.00
Tlingit-Haida (2)	3	0.00
Am. Ind. or Alaska Nat., not spec.	597	0.30
Albanian	8	0.00
Alsatian	8	0.00
American Indian tribes, specified:	685	0.35
Apache (7)	15	0.01
Blackfeet (8)	69	0.03
Cherokee (91)	302	0.15
Chickasaw (1)	2	0.00
Chippewa (2)	6	0.00
Choctaw (2)	9	0.00
Comanche (1)	2	0.00
Creek (5)	11	0.01
Crow	4	0.00
Delaware	2	0.00
Iroquois (3)	15	0.01
Latin American Indians (7)	24	0.01
Lumbee (8)	15	0.01
Navajo (2)	4	0.00
Osage (1)	1	0.00
Ottawa (1)	2	0.00
Potawatomi (1)	6	0.00
Pueblo (1)	5	0.00
Puget Sound Salish	2	0.00
Seminole (2)	9	0.00
Sioux (12)	17	0.01
Ute (1)	2	0.00
Yakama	1	0.00
Yaqui	1	0.00
All other tribes (91)	159	0.08
American Indian tribes, not spec.	65	0.03
Arab:	639	0.32
Arab/Arabic	41	0.02
Egyptian	13	0.01
Iraqi	8	0.00
Jordanian	53	0.03
Lebanese	305	0.15
Moroccan	69	0.03
Palestinian	30	0.02
Syrian	58	0.03
Other Arab	62	0.03
Armenian	88	0.04
Asian:	3,108	1.57
Bangladeshi (10)	19	0.01
Cambodian (168)	211	0.11
Chinese, ex. Taiwanese (418)	496	0.25
Filipino (246)	341	0.17
Indian (481)	565	0.29
Indonesian (10)	10	0.01
Japanese (85)	144	0.07
Korean (439)	510	0.26
Laotian (14)	14	0.01
Malaysian (2)	3	0.00
Pakistani (46)	60	0.03
Sri Lankan (8)	9	0.00
Taiwanese (10)	18	0.01
Thai (30)	38	0.02
Vietnamese (275)	310	0.16
Other Asian, specified (1)	16	0.01
Other Asian, not specified (196)	344	0.17
Australian	42	0.02
Austrian	336	0.17
Basque	28	0.01
Belgian	116	0.06
Brazilian	50	0.03
British	1,115	0.56
Bulgarian	39	0.02
Canadian	124	0.06
Celtic	72	0.04
Croatian	60	0.03
Czech	337	0.17
Czechoslovakian	67	0.03
Danish	248	0.13
Dutch	1,156	0.58
Eastern European	115	0.06
English	16,881	8.53
Estonian	46	0.02
European	1,591	0.80
Finnish	60	0.03
French, except Basque	2,572	1.30
French Canadian	608	0.31
German	12,006	6.07
Greek	409	0.21
Guyanese	62	0.03
Hawaii Native/Pacific Islander:	372	0.19
Micronesian: (99)	115	0.06
Guamanian/Chamorro (99)	115	0.06
Polynesian: (41)	73	0.04
Native Hawaiian (19)	41	0.02
Samoan (22)	32	0.02
Other Pac. Isl., specified	10	0.01
Other Pac. Isl., not spec. (16)	174	0.09
Hispanic or Latino:	5,074	2.57

Notes: 1. Figures in the "Number" column do not add up to the total population due to: a) Ancestry/Race overlap — e.g. persons can report being both White and Irish, b) persons of Hispanic origin can report being any race, c) persons reporting two ancestries are counted in both categories. 2. Numbers in parentheses indicate the number of persons reporting this ancestry/race alone, not in combination with any other ancestry/race. 3. Refer to the Explanation of Data in the front of the book for more detailed information.

Ancestry/Race	Number	%
Central American:	969	0.49
Costa Rican	26	0.01
Guatemalan	425	0.21
Honduran	73	0.04
Nicaraguan	16	0.01
Panamanian	55	0.03
Salvadoran	335	0.17
Other Central American	39	0.02
Cuban	201	0.10
Dominican Republic	85	0.04
Mexican	1,457	0.74
Puerto Rican	815	0.41
South American:	202	0.10
Argentinean	37	0.02
Bolivian	21	0.01
Chilean	7	0.00
Colombian	65	0.03
Ecuadorian	18	0.01
Paraguayan	7	0.00
Peruvian	19	0.01
Uruguayan	2	0.00
Venezuelan	18	0.01
Other South American	8	0.00
Other Hispanic or Latino	1,345	0.68
Hungarian	482	0.24
Iranian	151	0.08
Irish	10,697	5.41
Israeli	60	0.03
Italian	3,838	1.94
Latvian	65	0.03
Lithuanian	211	0.11
Luxemburger	13	0.01
Maltese	6	0.00
Northern European	149	0.08
Norwegian	619	0.31
Pennsylvania German	36	0.02
Polish	1,841	0.93
Portuguese	157	0.08
Romanian	45	0.02
Russian	937	0.47
Scandinavian	127	0.06
Scotch-Irish	3,371	1.70
Scottish	3,861	1.95
Serbian	77	0.04
Slavic	67	0.03
Slovak	196	0.10
Slovene	17	0.01
Swedish	823	0.42
Swiss	226	0.11
Turkish	14	0.01
Ukrainian	277	0.14
United States or American	7,575	3.83
Welsh	1,131	0.57
West Indian, excl. Hispanic:	933	0.47
Bahamian	26	0.01
Barbadian	14	0.01
Belizean	13	0.01
Bermudan	13	0.01
British West Indian	36	0.02
Haitian	159	0.08
Jamaican	319	0.16
Trinidadian and Tobagonian	183	0.09
U.S. Virgin Islander	25	0.01
West Indian	134	0.07
Other West Indian	11	0.01
White:	77,496	39.18
Not Hispanic (74,506)	76,075	38.46
Hispanic (1,238)	1,421	0.72
Yugoslavian	79	0.04

Roanoke

Place Type: Independent City
County: Roanoke Independent City
Population: 94,911

Ancestry/Race	Number	%
Acadian/Cajun	8	0.01
African American/Black:	26,294	27.70
Not Hispanic (25,220)	26,095	27.49
Hispanic (160)	199	0.21
African, sub-Saharan:	688	0.72
African	600	0.63
Cape Verdean	4	0.00
Ghanian	9	0.01
Nigerian	15	0.02
Sierra Leonean	5	0.01
South African	55	0.06
Alaska Native tribes, specified:	1	0.00
Eskimo	1	0.00
Alaska Native tribes, not specified	3	0.00
Am. Ind. or Alaska Nat., not spec.	262	0.28
Albanian	15	0.02
Alsatian	8	0.01
American Indian tribes, specified:	346	0.36
Apache (2)	7	0.01
Blackfeet (2)	16	0.02
Cherokee (45)	209	0.22
Cheyenne (2)	2	0.00
Chickasaw	1	0.00
Chippewa (1)	3	0.00
Choctaw (5)	7	0.01
Comanche	2	0.00
Cree (1)	2	0.00
Creek (1)	2	0.00
Crow	1	0.00
Delaware	2	0.00
Iroquois (12)	19	0.02
Latin American Indians (4)	14	0.01
Lumbee (7)	8	0.01
Navajo	1	0.00
Osage	1	0.00
Potawatomi (1)	1	0.00
Pueblo	1	0.00
Seminole (3)	3	0.00
Shoshone (1)	1	0.00
Sioux	7	0.01
Yuman (3)	3	0.00
All other tribes (16)	33	0.03
American Indian tribes, not spec.	42	0.04
Arab:	553	0.58
Arab/Arabic	79	0.08
Egyptian	41	0.04
Iraqi	68	0.07
Jordanian	18	0.02
Lebanese	308	0.32
Moroccan	8	0.01
Palestinian	13	0.01
Syrian	12	0.01
Other Arab	6	0.01
Armenian	9	0.01
Asian:	1,328	1.40
Bangladeshi (2)	2	0.00
Cambodian (33)	39	0.04
Chinese, ex. Taiwanese (110)	144	0.15
Filipino (140)	180	0.19
Indian (106)	126	0.13
Indonesian	1	0.00
Japanese (44)	63	0.07
Korean (46)	59	0.06
Laotian (49)	61	0.06
Malaysian (1)	1	0.00
Pakistani (2)	3	0.00
Sri Lankan (1)	1	0.00
Taiwanese (5)	6	0.01
Thai (6)	11	0.01
Vietnamese (480)	507	0.53
Other Asian, specified (7)	14	0.01
Other Asian, not specified (58)	110	0.12
Australian	5	0.01
Austrian	110	0.12
Basque	14	0.01
Belgian	20	0.02
Brazilian	7	0.01
British	418	0.44
Canadian	109	0.11
Croatian	63	0.07
Czech	14	0.01
Czechoslovakian	33	0.03
Danish	42	0.04
Dutch	879	0.93
Eastern European	30	0.03
English	8,644	9.11
European	1,033	1.09
Finnish	6	0.01
French, except Basque	1,146	1.21
French Canadian	321	0.34
German	9,055	9.54
Greek	148	0.16
Guyanese	6	0.01
Hawaii Native/Pacific Islander:	69	0.07
Microncsian: (1)	3	0.00
Guamanian/Chamorro (1)	3	0.00
Polynesian: (18)	30	0.03
Native Hawaiian (7)	14	0.01
Samoan (11)	16	0.02
Other Pac. Isl., specified	7	0.01
Other Pac. Isl., not spec. (4)	29	0.03
Hispanic or Latino:	1,405	1.48
Central American:	167	0.18
Costa Rican	4	0.00
Guatemalan	4	0.00
Honduran	128	0.13
Nicaraguan	1	0.00
Panamanian	14	0.01
Salvadoran	14	0.01
Other Central American	2	0.00
Cuban	118	0.12
Dominican Republic	27	0.03
Mexican	486	0.51
Puerto Rican	252	0.27
South American:	45	0.05
Argentinean	2	0.00
Bolivian	1	0.00
Chilean	4	0.00
Colombian	23	0.02
Peruvian	4	0.00
Venezuelan	6	0.01
Other South American	5	0.01
Other Hispanic or Latino	310	0.33
Hungarian	220	0.23
Icelander	6	0.01
Irish	7,506	7.91
Italian	1,676	1.77
Lithuanian	26	0.03
Luxemburger	1	0.00
Macedonian	9	0.01
Maltese	7	0.01
New Zealander	10	0.01
Northern European	21	0.02
Norwegian	253	0.27
Polish	829	0.87
Portuguese	58	0.06
Romanian	58	0.06
Russian	165	0.17
Scandinavian	34	0.04
Scotch-Irish	2,586	2.72
Scottish	1,448	1.53
Serbian	7	0.01
Slavic	44	0.05
Slovak	92	0.10
Swedish	390	0.41
Swiss	70	0.07
Turkish	28	0.03
Ukrainian	50	0.05
United States or American	11,855	12.49
Welsh	538	0.57
West Indian, excl. Hispanic:	407	0.43
Haitian	169	0.18
Jamaican	115	0.12
Trinidadian and Tobagonian	5	0.01
West Indian	118	0.12
White:	67,170	70.77
Not Hispanic (65,256)	66,492	70.06
Hispanic (592)	678	0.71
Yugoslavian	358	0.38

Notes: 1. Figures in the "Number" column do not add up to the total population due to: a) Ancestry/Race overlap — e.g. persons can report being both White and Irish, b) persons of Hispanic origin can report being any race, c) persons reporting two ancestries are counted in both categories. 2. Numbers in parentheses indicate the number of persons reporting this ancestry/race alone, not in combination with any other ancestry/race. 3. Refer to the Explanation of Data in the front of the book for more detailed information.

Rose Hill

Place Type: Census Designated Place
County: Fairfax
Population: 15,058

Ancestry/Race	Number	%
Acadian/Cajun	11	0.07
Afghan	131	0.88
African American/Black:	1,547	10.27
Not Hispanic (1,396)	1,496	9.93
Hispanic (38)	51	0.34
African, sub-Saharan:	353	2.36
African	88	0.59
Ethiopian	114	0.76
Ghanian	87	0.58
Zairian	41	0.27
Other sub-Saharan African	23	0.15
Am. Ind. or Alaska Nat., not spec.	47	0.31
Albanian	6	0.04
American Indian tribes, specified:	67	0.44
Apache	1	0.01
Blackfeet (1)	1	0.01
Cherokee (11)	26	0.17
Chippewa (1)	2	0.01
Choctaw	2	0.01
Comanche (1)	1	0.01
Cree (1)	2	0.01
Creek (4)	5	0.03
Delaware (1)	1	0.01
Iroquois (3)	3	0.02
Kiowa (2)	2	0.01
Pueblo	3	0.02
Shoshone (1)	1	0.01
Sioux (1)	2	0.01
All other tribes (7)	15	0.10
American Indian tribes, not spec.	2	0.01
Arab:	216	1.45
Arab/Arabic	21	0.14
Lebanese	73	0.49
Palestinian	5	0.03
Other Arab	117	0.78
Armenian	24	0.16
Asian:	1,551	10.30
Cambodian (25)	25	0.17
Chinese, ex. Taiwanese (196)	227	1.51
Filipino (177)	227	1.51
Indian (171)	202	1.34
Indonesian (3)	7	0.05
Japanese (36)	66	0.44
Korean (208)	239	1.59
Laotian (20)	20	0.13
Pakistani (106)	134	0.89
Sri Lankan (2)	2	0.01
Taiwanese (3)	3	0.02
Thai (40)	51	0.34
Vietnamese (237)	253	1.68
Other Asian, specified (3)	3	0.02
Other Asian, not specified (20)	92	0.61
Australian	9	0.06
Austrian	29	0.19
Basque	27	0.18
Belgian	18	0.12
British	84	0.56
Canadian	6	0.04
Croatian	5	0.03
Czech	106	0.71
Czechoslovakian	8	0.05
Danish	64	0.43
Dutch	190	1.27
English	1,679	11.23
European	136	0.91
Finnish	25	0.17
French, except Basque	503	3.36
French Canadian	137	0.92
German	2,373	15.88
Greek	135	0.90
Hawaii Native/Pacific Islander:	19	0.13
Micronesian: (2)	3	0.02
Guamanian/Chamorro (1)	2	0.01
Other Micronesian (1)	1	0.01
Polynesian: (5)	13	0.09
Native Hawaiian (4)	11	0.07
Samoan (1)	2	0.01
Other Pac. Isl., not spec. (1)	3	0.02
Hispanic or Latino:	1,604	10.65
Central American:	454	3.02
Costa Rican	1	0.01
Guatemalan	29	0.19
Honduran	49	0.33
Nicaraguan	14	0.09
Panamanian	9	0.06
Salvadoran	316	2.10
Other Central American	36	0.24
Cuban	26	0.17
Dominican Republic	13	0.09
Mexican	214	1.42
Puerto Rican	109	0.72
South American:	259	1.72
Argentinean	11	0.07
Bolivian	48	0.32
Chilean	13	0.09
Colombian	36	0.24
Ecuadorian	38	0.25
Peruvian	82	0.54
Uruguayan	6	0.04
Venezuelan	8	0.05
Other South American	17	0.11
Other Hispanic or Latino	529	3.51
Hungarian	26	0.17
Icelander	22	0.15
Iranian	90	0.60
Irish	2,085	13.95
Italian	762	5.10
Latvian	6	0.04
Lithuanian	63	0.42
Northern European	30	0.20
Norwegian	108	0.72
Pennsylvania German	5	0.03
Polish	484	3.24
Portuguese	22	0.15
Romanian	33	0.22
Russian	222	1.49
Scotch-Irish	348	2.33
Scottish	406	2.72
Slavic	8	0.05
Slovak	62	0.41
Slovene	4	0.03
Swedish	159	1.06
Swiss	64	0.43
Ukrainian	56	0.37
United States or American	761	5.09
Welsh	228	1.53
West Indian, excl. Hispanic:	16	0.11
Jamaican	8	0.05
West Indian	8	0.05
White:	11,552	76.72
Not Hispanic (10,301)	10,640	70.66
Hispanic (769)	912	6.06
Yugoslavian	48	0.32

Salem

Place Type: Independent City
County: Salem Independent City
Population: 24,747

Ancestry/Race	Number	%
African American/Black:	1,540	6.22
Not Hispanic (1,444)	1,527	6.17
Hispanic (11)	13	0.05
African, sub-Saharan:	72	0.29
African	65	0.26
Ethiopian	7	0.03
Am. Ind. or Alaska Nat., not spec.	41	0.17
Albanian	18	0.07
American Indian tribes, specified:	61	0.25
Apache (1)	2	0.01
Blackfeet (2)	2	0.01
Cherokee (15)	45	0.18
Cree	1	0.00
Creek (1)	1	0.00
Crow	1	0.00
Lumbee (1)	1	0.00
Potawatomi	1	0.00
All other tribes (2)	7	0.03
American Indian tribes, not spec.	5	0.02
Arab:	86	0.35
Arab/Arabic	26	0.11
Lebanese	53	0.21
Syrian	7	0.03
Armenian	6	0.02
Asian:	277	1.12
Bangladeshi (1)	1	0.00
Cambodian (13)	14	0.06
Chinese, ex. Taiwanese (40)	44	0.18
Filipino (29)	36	0.15
Indian (60)	65	0.26
Japanese (11)	15	0.06
Korean (31)	32	0.13
Laotian (1)	5	0.02
Pakistani (1)	3	0.01
Taiwanese	1	0.00
Thai (2)	2	0.01
Vietnamese (48)	51	0.21
Other Asian, specified	3	0.01
Other Asian, not specified (1)	5	0.02
Austrian	29	0.12
Basque	8	0.03
Belgian	28	0.11
British	55	0.22
Celtic	11	0.04
Czech	9	0.04
Czechoslovakian	12	0.05
Danish	66	0.27
Dutch	379	1.53
English	3,260	13.17
European	200	0.81
Finnish	15	0.06
French, except Basque	648	2.62
French Canadian	122	0.49
German	3,801	15.36
Greek	14	0.06
Hawaii Native/Pacific Islander:	16	0.06
Polynesian: (6)	7	0.03
Native Hawaiian (5)	6	0.02
Samoan (1)	1	0.00
Other Pac. Isl., specified	3	0.01
Other Pac. Isl., not spec.	6	0.02
Hispanic or Latino:	205	0.83
Central American:	11	0.04
Costa Rican	3	0.01
Guatemalan	3	0.01
Honduran	3	0.01
Panamanian	1	0.00
Salvadoran	1	0.00
Cuban	31	0.13
Dominican Republic	1	0.00
Mexican	74	0.30
Puerto Rican	22	0.09
South American:	25	0.10
Argentinean	5	0.02
Chilean	1	0.00
Colombian	9	0.04
Ecuadorian	4	0.02
Peruvian	2	0.01
Venezuelan	4	0.02
Other Hispanic or Latino	41	0.17
Hungarian	64	0.26
Irish	2,720	10.99
Italian	620	2.51
Latvian	8	0.03
Lithuanian	44	0.18
Northern European	41	0.17
Norwegian	79	0.32
Pennsylvania German	20	0.08
Polish	293	1.18
Russian	47	0.19
Scandinavian	12	0.05
Scotch-Irish	686	2.77

Notes: 1. Figures in the "Number" column do not add up to the total population due to: a) Ancestry/Race overlap — e.g. persons can report being both White and Irish, b) persons of Hispanic origin can report being any race, c) persons reporting two ancestries are counted in both categories. 2. Numbers in parentheses indicate the number of persons reporting this ancestry/race alone, not in combination with any other ancestry/race. 3. Refer to the Explanation of Data in the front of the book for more detailed information.

Scottish	550	2.22
Slovak	13	0.05
Slovene	48	0.19
Swedish	137	0.55
Swiss	127	0.51
Ukrainian	23	0.09
United States or American	4,474	18.08
Welsh	139	0.56
West Indian, excl. Hispanic:	6	0.02
Jamaican	6	0.02
White:	22,925	92.64
Not Hispanic (22,594)	22,771	92.02
Hispanic (144)	154	0.62
Yugoslavian	116	0.47

Springfield

Place Type: Census Designated Place
County: Fairfax
Population: 30,417

Ancestry/Race	Number	%
Afghan	708	2.34
African American/Black:	2,953	9.71
Not Hispanic (2,650)	2,832	9.31
Hispanic (72)	121	0.40
African, sub-Saharan:	788	2.60
African	156	0.52
Ethiopian	376	1.24
Ghanian	108	0.36
Nigerian	6	0.02
Sierra Leonean	46	0.15
Somalian	13	0.04
Other sub-Saharan African	83	0.27
Am. Ind. or Alaska Nat., not spec.	81	0.27
Albanian	16	0.05
American Indian tribes, specified:	112	0.37
Blackfeet	1	0.00
Cherokee (5)	28	0.09
Chippewa (1)	2	0.01
Choctaw (4)	5	0.02
Comanche (1)	2	0.01
Iroquois (2)	5	0.02
Kiowa	2	0.01
Latin American Indians (28)	49	0.16
Navajo (1)	4	0.01
Potawatomi (1)	1	0.00
Pueblo (1)	1	0.00
Seminole (1)	1	0.00
Sioux	2	0.01
All other tribes (6)	9	0.03
American Indian tribes, not spec.	5	0.02
Arab:	577	1.91
Arab/Arabic	163	0.54
Egyptian	49	0.16
Jordanian	45	0.15
Lebanese	129	0.43
Palestinian	86	0.28
Syrian	39	0.13
Other Arab	66	0.22
Armenian	24	0.08
Asian:	6,979	22.94
Bangladeshi (53)	61	0.20
Cambodian (147)	156	0.51
Chinese, ex. Taiwanese (466)	545	1.79
Filipino (791)	868	2.85
Indian (906)	1,021	3.36
Indonesian (8)	10	0.03
Japanese (57)	97	0.32
Korean (815)	867	2.85
Laotian (249)	261	0.86
Malaysian (6)	7	0.02
Pakistani (354)	438	1.44
Taiwanese (12)	15	0.05
Thai (245)	283	0.93
Vietnamese (1,884)	1,960	6.44
Other Asian, specified (13)	14	0.05
Other Asian, not specified (142)	376	1.24
Austrian	112	0.37
Belgian	8	0.03
British	155	0.51
Canadian	35	0.12
Croatian	45	0.15
Czech	64	0.21
Czechoslovakian	37	0.12
Danish	89	0.29
Dutch	368	1.22
Eastern European	11	0.04
English	2,380	7.86
Estonian	3	0.01
European	271	0.90
Finnish	47	0.16
French, except Basque	499	1.65
French Canadian	205	0.68
German	3,303	10.91
Greek	138	0.46
Hawaii Native/Pacific Islander:	57	0.19
Micronesian: (6)	8	0.03
Guamanian/Chamorro (6)	7	0.02
Other Micronesian	1	0.00
Polynesian: (7)	21	0.07
Native Hawaiian (5)	12	0.04
Samoan (2)	5	0.02
Other Polynesian	4	0.01
Other Pac. Isl., not spec. (4)	28	0.09
Hispanic or Latino:	5,373	17.66
Central American:	2,039	6.70
Costa Rican	12	0.04
Guatemalan	108	0.36
Honduran	713	2.34
Nicaraguan	48	0.16
Panamanian	26	0.09
Salvadoran	990	3.25
Other Central American	142	0.47
Cuban	75	0.25
Dominican Republic	12	0.04
Mexican	405	1.33
Puerto Rican	221	0.73
South American:	776	2.55
Argentinean	37	0.12
Bolivian	260	0.85
Chilean	41	0.13
Colombian	84	0.28
Ecuadorian	28	0.09
Paraguayan	13	0.04
Peruvian	236	0.78
Uruguayan	7	0.02
Venezuelan	25	0.08
Other South American	45	0.15
Other Hispanic or Latino	1,845	6.07
Hungarian	165	0.55
Iranian	133	0.44
Irish	2,611	8.63
Italian	1,066	3.52
Lithuanian	72	0.24
Northern European	14	0.05
Norwegian	185	0.61
Polish	428	1.41
Portuguese	60	0.20
Romanian	23	0.08
Russian	223	0.74
Scandinavian	30	0.10
Scotch-Irish	515	1.70
Scottish	547	1.81
Serbian	25	0.08
Slavic	8	0.03
Slovak	119	0.39
Slovene	8	0.03
Swedish	228	0.75
Swiss	78	0.26
Turkish	59	0.19
Ukrainian	77	0.25
United States or American	1,222	4.04
Welsh	220	0.73
West Indian, excl. Hispanic:	111	0.37
Bahamian	8	0.03
British West Indian	10	0.03
Haitian	28	0.09
Jamaican	55	0.18
Trinidadian and Tobagonian	3	0.01
West Indian	7	0.02
White:	18,696	61.47
Not Hispanic (15,097)	15,825	52.03
Hispanic (2,475)	2,871	9.44
Yugoslavian	15	0.05

Staunton

Place Type: Independent City
County: Staunton Independent City
Population: 23,853

Ancestry/Race	Number	%
African American/Black:	3,520	14.76
Not Hispanic (3,305)	3,487	14.62
Hispanic (23)	33	0.14
African, sub-Saharan:	104	0.44
African	74	0.31
Cape Verdean	9	0.04
Ethiopian	14	0.06
South African	7	0.03
Alaska Native tribes, specified:	2	0.01
Tlingit-Haida (2)	2	0.01
Am. Ind. or Alaska Nat., not spec.	47	0.20
Alsatian	8	0.03
American Indian tribes, specified:	101	0.42
Apache	5	0.02
Blackfeet (2)	9	0.04
Cherokee (18)	48	0.20
Chickasaw	1	0.00
Chippewa (1)	5	0.02
Choctaw (1)	3	0.01
Comanche (1)	1	0.00
Creek	1	0.00
Delaware (1)	1	0.00
Iroquois (2)	5	0.02
Lumbee (1)	1	0.00
Navajo (2)	3	0.01
Potawatomi	1	0.00
Seminole	2	0.01
Sioux (1)	2	0.01
Tohono O'Odham	3	0.01
Yaqui	2	0.01
All other tribes (2)	8	0.03
American Indian tribes, not spec.	10	0.04
Arab:	56	0.23
Egyptian	10	0.04
Lebanese	36	0.15
Other Arab	10	0.04
Asian:	193	0.81
Bangladeshi (1)	1	0.00
Chinese, ex. Taiwanese (31)	36	0.15
Filipino (12)	27	0.11
Indian (20)	24	0.10
Japanese (13)	29	0.12
Korean (18)	29	0.12
Laotian (1)	1	0.00
Taiwanese (1)	1	0.00
Thai (5)	12	0.05
Vietnamese (5)	8	0.03
Other Asian, specified (1)	4	0.02
Other Asian, not specified (2)	21	0.09
Austrian	18	0.08
Belgian	39	0.16
Brazilian	16	0.07
British	121	0.51
Bulgarian	32	0.13
Canadian	21	0.09
Celtic	12	0.05
Croatian	9	0.04
Czech	28	0.12
Czechoslovakian	25	0.10
Danish	55	0.23
Dutch	338	1.42
Eastern European	36	0.15
English	2,377	9.97
European	175	0.73
French, except Basque	462	1.94
French Canadian	108	0.45
German	3,323	13.93

Notes: 1. Figures in the "Number" column do not add up to the total population due to: a) Ancestry/Race overlap — e.g. persons can report being both White and Irish, b) persons of Hispanic origin can report being any race, c) persons reporting two ancestries are counted in both categories. 2. Numbers in parentheses indicate the number of persons reporting this ancestry/race alone, not in combination with any other ancestry/race. 3. Refer to the Explanation of Data in the front of the book for more detailed information.

Greek	52	0.22
Hawaii Native/Pacific Islander:	26	0.11
Micronesian: (1)	5	0.02
Guamanian/Chamorro (1)	5	0.02
Polynesian:	3	0.01
Native Hawaiian	2	0.01
Samoan	1	0.00
Other Pac. Isl., specified	3	0.01
Other Pac. Isl., not spec. (1)	15	0.06
Hispanic or Latino:	265	1.11
Central American:	8	0.03
Guatemalan	1	0.00
Panamanian	3	0.01
Salvadoran	4	0.02
Cuban	18	0.08
Dominican Republic	1	0.00
Mexican	105	0.44
Puerto Rican	53	0.22
South American:	10	0.04
Chilean	1	0.00
Colombian	3	0.01
Peruvian	3	0.01
Venezuelan	3	0.01
Other Hispanic or Latino	70	0.29
Hungarian	48	0.20
Irish	2,136	8.95
Italian	689	2.89
Lithuanian	24	0.10
Norwegian	178	0.75
Pennsylvania German	21	0.09
Polish	208	0.87
Portuguese	15	0.06
Romanian	5	0.02
Russian	53	0.22
Scandinavian	56	0.23
Scotch-Irish	1,366	5.73
Scottish	517	2.17
Slovak	5	0.02
Swedish	291	1.22
Swiss	103	0.43
Ukrainian	52	0.22
United States or American	4,350	18.24
Welsh	133	0.56
West Indian, excl. Hispanic:	27	0.11
Jamaican	23	0.10
Trinidadian and Tobagonian	4	0.02
White:	20,170	84.56
Not Hispanic (19,728)	20,009	83.88
Hispanic (138)	161	0.67

Suffolk

Place Type: Independent City
County: Suffolk Independent City
Population: 63,677

Ancestry/Race	Number	%
Acadian/Cajun	7	0.01
African American/Black:	28,106	44.14
Not Hispanic (27,524)	27,860	43.75
Hispanic (194)	246	0.39
African, sub-Saharan:	619	0.97
African	581	0.91
Cape Verdean	29	0.05
Liberian	9	0.01
Alaska Native tribes, specified:	3	0.00
Aleut	1	0.00
Eskimo	1	0.00
Tlingit-Haida (1)	1	0.00
Am. Ind. or Alaska Nat., not spec.	166	0.26
Alsatian	11	0.02
American Indian tribes, specified:	318	0.50
Apache (2)	2	0.00
Blackfeet (1)	6	0.01
Cherokee (45)	154	0.24
Cheyenne (1)	1	0.00
Chickasaw (4)	7	0.01
Chippewa (6)	6	0.01
Choctaw (5)	8	0.01
Comanche (1)	1	0.00
Creek	4	0.01
Iroquois (2)	13	0.02
Latin American Indians (2)	2	0.00
Lumbee (12)	14	0.02
Menominee (1)	3	0.00
Navajo	1	0.00
Osage	3	0.00
Ottawa (2)	3	0.00
Potawatomi (1)	4	0.01
Pueblo	1	0.00
Seminole (1)	6	0.01
Sioux (5)	10	0.02
All other tribes (30)	69	0.11
American Indian tribes, not spec.	23	0.04
Arab:	66	0.10
Arab/Arabic	10	0.02
Egyptian	10	0.02
Lebanese	36	0.06
Moroccan	10	0.02
Asian:	696	1.09
Bangladeshi (8)	8	0.01
Cambodian (7)	7	0.01
Chinese, ex. Taiwanese (48)	71	0.11
Filipino (185)	250	0.39
Indian (113)	133	0.21
Indonesian (1)	3	0.00
Japanese (24)	54	0.08
Korean (50)	69	0.11
Laotian (7)	7	0.01
Sri Lankan (2)	2	0.00
Thai (7)	17	0.03
Vietnamese (24)	34	0.05
Other Asian, specified	8	0.01
Other Asian, not specified (12)	33	0.05
Australian	5	0.01
Austrian	5	0.01
Belgian	7	0.01
British	236	0.37
Canadian	66	0.10
Croatian	30	0.05
Czech	5	0.01
Czechoslovakian	17	0.03
Danish	115	0.18
Dutch	443	0.70
Eastern European	8	0.01
English	6,527	10.25
European	420	0.66
Finnish	49	0.08
French, except Basque	1,245	1.96
French Canadian	246	0.39
German	4,236	6.65
Greek	82	0.13
Hawaii Native/Pacific Islander:	57	0.09
Micronesian: (6)	12	0.02
Guamanian/Chamorro (4)	4	0.01
Other Micronesian (2)	8	0.01
Polynesian: (5)	22	0.03
Native Hawaiian (1)	9	0.01
Samoan (4)	13	0.02
Other Pac. Isl., specified	8	0.01
Other Pac. Isl., not spec. (4)	15	0.02
Hispanic or Latino:	809	1.27
Central American:	41	0.06
Guatemalan	3	0.00
Nicaraguan	5	0.01
Panamanian	28	0.04
Salvadoran	5	0.01
Cuban	45	0.07
Dominican Republic	11	0.02
Mexican	238	0.37
Puerto Rican	297	0.47
South American:	14	0.02
Argentinean	1	0.00
Colombian	6	0.01
Ecuadorian	1	0.00
Peruvian	3	0.00
Venezuelan	2	0.00
Other South American	1	0.00
Other Hispanic or Latino	163	0.26
Hungarian	169	0.27
Irish	3,936	6.18
Israeli	6	0.01
Italian	1,335	2.10
Lithuanian	51	0.08
Maltese	5	0.01
Northern European	6	0.01
Norwegian	323	0.51
Pennsylvania German	2	0.00
Polish	897	1.41
Portuguese	63	0.10
Romanian	16	0.03
Russian	220	0.35
Scandinavian	79	0.12
Scotch-Irish	1,061	1.67
Scottish	985	1.55
Slavic	8	0.01
Slovak	15	0.02
Slovene	5	0.01
Swedish	280	0.44
Swiss	20	0.03
Ukrainian	48	0.08
United States or American	7,238	11.37
Welsh	299	0.47
West Indian, excl. Hispanic:	129	0.20
Barbadian	30	0.05
British West Indian	8	0.01
Haitian	29	0.05
Jamaican	14	0.02
Trinidadian and Tobagonian	16	0.03
West Indian	32	0.05
White:	34,811	54.67
Not Hispanic (33,940)	34,420	54.05
Hispanic (331)	391	0.61
Yugoslavian	9	0.01

Timberlake

Place Type: Census Designated Place
County: Campbell
Population: 10,683

Ancestry/Race	Number	%
African American/Black:	639	5.98
Not Hispanic (569)	628	5.88
Hispanic (10)	11	0.10
African, sub-Saharan:	10	0.09
African	10	0.09
Am. Ind. or Alaska Nat., not spec.	18	0.17
American Indian tribes, specified:	38	0.36
Apache (1)	1	0.01
Blackfeet	1	0.01
Cherokee (12)	22	0.21
Chippewa (1)	2	0.02
Creek (2)	2	0.02
Delaware (1)	1	0.01
Navajo (2)	2	0.02
Sioux (3)	3	0.03
All other tribes (3)	4	0.04
American Indian tribes, not spec.	1	0.01
Asian:	211	1.98
Chinese, ex. Taiwanese (40)	47	0.44
Filipino (16)	20	0.19
Indian (17)	26	0.24
Indonesian	2	0.02
Japanese (9)	9	0.08
Korean (59)	63	0.59
Malaysian (1)	1	0.01
Thai (2)	2	0.02
Vietnamese (36)	36	0.34
Other Asian, specified	3	0.03
Other Asian, not specified (1)	2	0.02
Australian	9	0.08
British	61	0.56
Canadian	8	0.07
Croatian	26	0.24
Czechoslovakian	24	0.22
Danish	17	0.16
Dutch	169	1.55
Eastern European	9	0.08
English	1,569	14.41

Notes: 1. Figures in the "Number" column do not add up to the total population due to: a) Ancestry/Race overlap — e.g. persons can report being both White and Irish, b) persons of Hispanic origin can report being any race, c) persons reporting two ancestries are counted in both categories. 2. Numbers in parentheses indicate the number of persons reporting this ancestry/race alone, not in combination with any other ancestry/race. 3. Refer to the Explanation of Data in the front of the book for more detailed information.

European	92	0.85
Finnish	6	0.06
French, except Basque	97	0.89
French Canadian	25	0.23
German	1,206	11.08
Greek	23	0.21
Hawaii Native/Pacific Islander:	5	0.05
Micronesian: (1)	1	0.01
Other Micronesian (1)	1	0.01
Polynesian: (1)	1	0.01
Native Hawaiian (1)	1	0.01
Other Pac. Isl., specified	3	0.03
Hispanic or Latino:	108	1.01
Central American:	7	0.07
Honduran	4	0.04
Other Central American	3	0.03
Cuban	2	0.02
Dominican Republic	3	0.03
Mexican	41	0.38
Puerto Rican	11	0.10
South American:	18	0.17
Argentinean	4	0.04
Colombian	4	0.04
Ecuadorian	4	0.04
Venezuelan	1	0.01
Other South American	5	0.05
Other Hispanic or Latino	26	0.24
Hungarian	13	0.12
Irish	1,066	9.79
Italian	249	2.29
Lithuanian	9	0.08
Norwegian	91	0.84
Pennsylvania German	6	0.06
Polish	99	0.91
Scandinavian	14	0.13
Scotch-Irish	170	1.56
Scottish	281	2.58
Slovak	9	0.08
Swedish	101	0.93
Swiss	20	0.18
Ukrainian	56	0.51
United States or American	2,107	19.35
Welsh	121	1.11
West Indian, excl. Hispanic:	5	0.05
Bermudan	5	0.05
White:	9,831	92.02
Not Hispanic (9,687)	9,783	91.58
Hispanic (48)	48	0.45

Tuckahoe

Place Type: Census Designated Place
County: Henrico
Population: 43,242

Ancestry/Race	Number	%
Acadian/Cajun	15	0.03
African American/Black:	2,675	6.19
Not Hispanic (2,450)	2,598	6.01
Hispanic (49)	77	0.18
African, sub-Saharan:	237	0.55
African	88	0.20
Ghanian	76	0.18
Kenyan	12	0.03
South African	18	0.04
Sudanese	12	0.03
Other sub-Saharan African	31	0.07
Alaska Native tribes, specified:	1	0.00
Eskimo	1	0.00
Am. Ind. or Alaska Nat., not spec.	65	0.15
American Indian tribes, specified:	119	0.28
Blackfeet (4)	9	0.02
Cherokee (10)	48	0.11
Choctaw (1)	4	0.01
Creek	2	0.00
Iroquois (1)	8	0.02
Latin American Indians (4)	7	0.02
Lumbee (8)	8	0.02
Navajo (1)	2	0.00
Osage	1	0.00
Paiute (1)	1	0.00
Potawatomi	2	0.00
Pueblo (1)	1	0.00
Sioux (2)	7	0.02
All other tribes (14)	19	0.04
American Indian tribes, not spec.	8	0.02
Arab:	368	0.85
Arab/Arabic	71	0.16
Egyptian	42	0.10
Jordanian	17	0.04
Lebanese	196	0.45
Syrian	11	0.03
Other Arab	31	0.07
Armenian	62	0.14
Asian:	1,654	3.82
Bangladeshi (4)	4	0.01
Cambodian (89)	99	0.23
Chinese, ex. Taiwanese (430)	463	1.07
Filipino (97)	118	0.27
Indian (327)	349	0.81
Indonesian (3)	4	0.01
Japanese (36)	55	0.13
Korean (235)	256	0.59
Laotian (2)	2	0.00
Malaysian (4)	4	0.01
Pakistani (22)	22	0.05
Sri Lankan (8)	8	0.02
Taiwanese (9)	13	0.03
Thai (12)	18	0.04
Vietnamese (171)	177	0.41
Other Asian, specified (1)	3	0.01
Other Asian, not specified (14)	59	0.14
Australian	13	0.03
Austrian	155	0.36
Belgian	14	0.03
Brazilian	44	0.10
British	492	1.14
Canadian	186	0.43
Celtic	8	0.02
Croatian	94	0.22
Czech	122	0.28
Czechoslovakian	87	0.20
Danish	90	0.21
Dutch	638	1.48
Eastern European	82	0.19
English	9,532	22.07
European	809	1.87
Finnish	6	0.01
French, except Basque	1,153	2.67
French Canadian	230	0.53
German	5,557	12.86
Greek	230	0.53
Hawaii Native/Pacific Islander:	27	0.06
Melanesian: (3)	3	0.01
Fijian (3)	3	0.01
Micronesian: (1)	2	0.00
Guamanian/Chamorro (1)	2	0.00
Polynesian: (10)	17	0.04
Native Hawaiian (5)	12	0.03
Samoan (5)	5	0.01
Other Pac. Isl., specified	2	0.00
Other Pac. Isl., not spec.	3	0.01
Hispanic or Latino:	923	2.13
Central American:	77	0.18
Costa Rican	9	0.02
Guatemalan	16	0.04
Honduran	8	0.02
Nicaraguan	1	0.00
Panamanian	10	0.02
Salvadoran	32	0.07
Other Central American	1	0.00
Cuban	88	0.20
Dominican Republic	22	0.05
Mexican	300	0.69
Puerto Rican	189	0.44
South American:	82	0.19
Argentinean	8	0.02
Bolivian	1	0.00
Chilean	2	0.00
Colombian	30	0.07
Ecuadorian	12	0.03
Paraguayan	3	0.01
Peruvian	11	0.03
Venezuelan	13	0.03
Other South American	2	0.00
Other Hispanic or Latino	165	0.38
Hungarian	160	0.37
Iranian	89	0.21
Irish	4,958	11.48
Israeli	38	0.09
Italian	1,715	3.97
Latvian	11	0.03
Lithuanian	120	0.28
Northern European	9	0.02
Norwegian	343	0.79
Pennsylvania German	14	0.03
Polish	726	1.68
Portuguese	35	0.08
Romanian	72	0.17
Russian	695	1.61
Scandinavian	30	0.07
Scotch-Irish	1,729	4.00
Scottish	1,596	3.69
Serbian	63	0.15
Slovak	36	0.08
Slovene	47	0.11
Swedish	349	0.81
Swiss	146	0.34
Turkish	24	0.06
Ukrainian	224	0.52
United States or American	5,041	11.67
Welsh	457	1.06
West Indian, excl. Hispanic:	143	0.33
Bahamian	31	0.07
British West Indian	19	0.04
Haitian	32	0.07
U.S. Virgin Islander	5	0.01
West Indian	56	0.13
White:	38,793	89.71
Not Hispanic (37,856)	38,205	88.35
Hispanic (537)	588	1.36
Yugoslavian	206	0.48

Tysons Corner

Place Type: Census Designated Place
County: Fairfax
Population: 18,540

Ancestry/Race	Number	%
Afghan	24	0.13
African American/Black:	818	4.41
Not Hispanic (703)	786	4.24
Hispanic (13)	32	0.17
African, sub-Saharan:	322	1.74
African	55	0.30
Ethiopian	32	0.17
Kenyan	93	0.50
Liberian	7	0.04
Somalian	107	0.58
South African	28	0.15
Am. Ind. or Alaska Nat., not spec.	46	0.25
American Indian tribes, specified:	49	0.26
Blackfeet (1)	3	0.02
Cherokee (3)	25	0.13
Choctaw (1)	2	0.01
Comanche	1	0.01
Iroquois (2)	4	0.02
Latin American Indians (1)	2	0.01
Lumbee (2)	2	0.01
Navajo (1)	1	0.01
Osage	1	0.01
Pueblo (2)	2	0.01
Sioux	1	0.01
All other tribes (2)	5	0.03
American Indian tribes, not spec.	4	0.02
Arab:	1,208	6.53
Arab/Arabic	581	3.14
Egyptian	60	0.32
Lebanese	165	0.89

Notes: 1. Figures in the "Number" column do not add up to the total population due to: a) Ancestry/Race overlap — e.g. persons can report being both White and Irish, b) persons of Hispanic origin can report being any race, c) persons reporting two ancestries are counted in both categories. 2. Numbers in parentheses indicate the number of persons reporting this ancestry/race alone, not in combination with any other ancestry/race. 3. Refer to the Explanation of Data in the front of the book for more detailed information.

Palestinian	75	0.41
Syrian	59	0.32
Other Arab	268	1.45
Armenian	26	0.14
Asian:	3,834	20.68
Bangladeshi (4)	4	0.02
Cambodian (8)	8	0.04
Chinese, ex. Taiwanese (678)	747	4.03
Filipino (244)	284	1.53
Indian (869)	919	4.96
Indonesian (35)	46	0.25
Japanese (144)	170	0.92
Korean (788)	848	4.57
Laotian (6)	8	0.04
Malaysian (18)	23	0.12
Pakistani (76)	87	0.47
Sri Lankan (11)	14	0.08
Taiwanese (38)	47	0.25
Thai (31)	41	0.22
Vietnamese (222)	237	1.28
Other Asian, specified (17)	22	0.12
Other Asian, not specified (45)	329	1.77
Australian	20	0.11
Austrian	60	0.32
Basque	10	0.05
Belgian	46	0.25
British	204	1.10
Bulgarian	33	0.18
Canadian	89	0.48
Croatian	17	0.09
Czech	73	0.39
Czechoslovakian	18	0.10
Danish	49	0.26
Dutch	118	0.64
Eastern European	74	0.40
English	1,911	10.33
European	212	1.15
Finnish	107	0.58
French, except Basque	337	1.82
French Canadian	57	0.31
German	2,186	11.82
Greek	287	1.55
Guyanese	9	0.05
Hawaii Native/Pacific Islander:	54	0.29
Melanesian: (3)	3	0.02
Other Melanesian (3)	3	0.02
Micronesian: (2)	5	0.03
Guamanian/Chamorro (2)	5	0.03
Polynesian: (3)	8	0.04
Native Hawaiian (2)	6	0.03
Samoan	1	0.01
Other Polynesian (1)	1	0.01
Other Pac. Isl., not spec. (5)	38	0.20
Hispanic or Latino:	1,140	6.15
Central American:	150	0.81
Costa Rican	8	0.04
Guatemalan	17	0.09
Honduran	2	0.01
Nicaraguan	23	0.12
Panamanian	5	0.03
Salvadoran	84	0.45
Other Central American	11	0.06
Cuban	41	0.22
Dominican Republic	11	0.06
Mexican	140	0.76
Puerto Rican	84	0.45
South American:	413	2.23
Argentinean	41	0.22
Bolivian	80	0.43
Chilean	18	0.10
Colombian	121	0.65
Ecuadorian	13	0.07
Paraguayan	2	0.01
Peruvian	95	0.51
Uruguayan	14	0.08
Venezuelan	10	0.05
Other South American	19	0.10
Other Hispanic or Latino	301	1.62
Hungarian	74	0.40
Icelander	46	0.25
Iranian	879	4.75
Irish	1,973	10.66
Italian	965	5.22
Latvian	25	0.14
Lithuanian	26	0.14
New Zealander	8	0.04
Northern European	16	0.09
Norwegian	169	0.91
Pennsylvania German	11	0.06
Polish	485	2.62
Portuguese	54	0.29
Romanian	97	0.52
Russian	215	1.16
Scandinavian	39	0.21
Scotch-Irish	377	2.04
Scottish	458	2.48
Serbian	10	0.05
Slavic	6	0.03
Slovak	100	0.54
Slovene	28	0.15
Swedish	200	1.08
Swiss	76	0.41
Turkish	183	0.99
Ukrainian	29	0.16
United States or American	1,022	5.52
Welsh	172	0.93
West Indian, excl. Hispanic:	24	0.13
Haitian	24	0.13
White:	14,147	76.31
Not Hispanic (12,368)	13,234	71.38
Hispanic (833)	913	4.92
Yugoslavian	58	0.31

Vienna

Place Type: Town
County: Fairfax
Population: 14,453

Ancestry/Race	Number	%
Afghan	46	0.32
African American/Black:	550	3.81
Not Hispanic (486)	530	3.67
Hispanic (11)	20	0.14
African, sub-Saharan:	69	0.47
African	62	0.43
Ethiopian	7	0.05
Am. Ind. or Alaska Nat., not spec.	46	0.32
Alsatian	3	0.02
American Indian tribes, specified:	42	0.29
Blackfeet	1	0.01
Cherokee (1)	14	0.10
Cheyenne	2	0.01
Comanche	1	0.01
Creek (2)	2	0.01
Delaware	1	0.01
Iroquois (1)	2	0.01
Latin American Indians (2)	3	0.02
Lumbee (3)	3	0.02
Navajo (1)	4	0.03
Potawatomi	1	0.01
Sioux	1	0.01
All other tribes (1)	7	0.05
American Indian tribes, not spec.	5	0.03
Arab:	152	1.04
Egyptian	75	0.52
Lebanese	34	0.23
Syrian	11	0.08
Other Arab	32	0.22
Armenian	46	0.32
Asian:	1,598	11.06
Cambodian (12)	15	0.10
Chinese, ex. Taiwanese (316)	348	2.41
Filipino (100)	137	0.95
Indian (245)	277	1.92
Indonesian (5)	10	0.07
Japanese (46)	73	0.51
Korean (250)	276	1.91
Laotian (26)	29	0.20
Malaysian (7)	7	0.05
Pakistani (49)	51	0.35
Sri Lankan (1)	1	0.01
Taiwanese (15)	18	0.12
Thai (65)	73	0.51
Vietnamese (169)	191	1.32
Other Asian, specified (16)	20	0.14
Other Asian, not specified (19)	72	0.50
Australian	21	0.14
Austrian	55	0.38
Belgian	25	0.17
Brazilian	5	0.03
British	143	0.98
Canadian	41	0.28
Croatian	21	0.14
Cypriot	22	0.15
Czech	128	0.88
Czechoslovakian	42	0.29
Danish	56	0.38
Dutch	177	1.22
Eastern European	44	0.30
English	2,656	18.26
European	284	1.95
Finnish	32	0.22
French, except Basque	436	3.00
French Canadian	131	0.90
German	2,300	15.81
Greek	241	1.66
Hawaii Native/Pacific Islander:	17	0.12
Micronesian:	1	0.01
Guamanian/Chamorro	1	0.01
Polynesian:	2	0.01
Native Hawaiian	2	0.01
Other Pac. Isl., specified	1	0.01
Other Pac. Isl., not spec.	13	0.09
Hispanic or Latino:	1,068	7.39
Central American:	333	2.30
Costa Rican	8	0.06
Guatemalan	14	0.10
Honduran	60	0.42
Nicaraguan	18	0.12
Panamanian	1	0.01
Salvadoran	209	1.45
Other Central American	23	0.16
Cuban	19	0.13
Dominican Republic	11	0.08
Mexican	107	0.74
Puerto Rican	70	0.48
South American:	216	1.49
Argentinean	23	0.16
Bolivian	40	0.28
Chilean	7	0.05
Colombian	42	0.29
Ecuadorian	20	0.14
Paraguayan	1	0.01
Peruvian	46	0.32
Uruguayan	4	0.03
Venezuelan	17	0.12
Other South American	16	0.11
Other Hispanic or Latino	312	2.16
Hungarian	96	0.66
Icelander	6	0.04
Iranian	300	2.06
Irish	1,927	13.24
Italian	996	6.85
Latvian	14	0.10
Lithuanian	14	0.10
Northern European	8	0.05
Norwegian	207	1.42
Polish	631	4.34
Portuguese	33	0.23
Romanian	27	0.19
Russian	346	2.38
Scandinavian	31	0.21
Scotch-Irish	412	2.83
Scottish	394	2.71
Slovak	155	1.07
Slovene	21	0.14
Swedish	206	1.42
Swiss	91	0.63
Turkish	41	0.28

Notes: 1. Figures in the "Number" column do not add up to the total population due to: a) Ancestry/Race overlap — e.g. persons can report being both White and Irish, b) persons of Hispanic origin can report being any race, c) persons reporting two ancestries are counted in both categories. 2. Numbers in parentheses indicate the number of persons reporting this ancestry/race alone, not in combination with any other ancestry/race. 3. Refer to the Explanation of Data in the front of the book for more detailed information.

Ancestry/Race	Number	%
Ukrainian	88	0.60
United States or American	876	6.02
Welsh	163	1.12
White:	12,127	83.91
Not Hispanic (11,124)	11,451	79.23
Hispanic (598)	676	4.68
Yugoslavian	5	0.03

Virginia Beach

Place Type: Independent City
County: Virginia Beach Independent City
Population: 425,257

Ancestry/Race	Number	%
Acadian/Cajun	121	0.03
Afghan	28	0.01
African American/Black:	85,216	20.04
Not Hispanic (79,092)	82,978	19.51
Hispanic (1,501)	2,238	0.53
African, sub-Saharan:	2,713	0.64
African	2,358	0.55
Cape Verdean	68	0.02
Ethiopian	62	0.01
Ghanian	6	0.00
Liberian	8	0.00
Nigerian	71	0.02
Sierra Leonean	7	0.00
Somalian	5	0.00
South African	57	0.01
Sudanese	56	0.01
Other sub-Saharan African	15	0.00
Alaska Native tribes, specified:	32	0.01
Alaska Athabascan (1)	1	0.00
Aleut (2)	7	0.00
Eskimo (5)	10	0.00
Tlingit-Haida (10)	13	0.00
All other tribes	1	0.00
Alaska Native tribes, not specified	12	0.00
Am. Ind. or Alaska Nat., not spec.	1,430	0.34
Albanian	20	0.00
Alsatian	14	0.00
American Indian tribes, specified:	2,766	0.65
Apache (43)	102	0.02
Blackfeet (27)	174	0.04
Cherokee (274)	1,175	0.28
Cheyenne (8)	22	0.01
Chickasaw (5)	18	0.00
Chippewa (62)	104	0.02
Choctaw (52)	91	0.02
Colville (2)	2	0.00
Comanche (7)	15	0.00
Cree (1)	5	0.00
Creek (21)	52	0.01
Crow (2)	10	0.00
Delaware (7)	25	0.01
Houma (3)	4	0.00
Iroquois (52)	122	0.03
Kiowa (5)	16	0.00
Latin American Indians (44)	74	0.02
Lumbee (69)	98	0.02
Menominee (1)	1	0.00
Navajo (52)	76	0.02
Osage (4)	9	0.00
Ottawa (2)	3	0.00
Paiute (1)	3	0.00
Pima (1)	6	0.00
Potawatomi (6)	14	0.00
Pueblo (21)	29	0.01
Puget Sound Salish (2)	3	0.00
Seminole (7)	48	0.01
Shoshone (1)	7	0.00
Sioux (39)	85	0.02
Tohono O'Odham (2)	3	0.00
Ute (2)	8	0.00
Yakama	3	0.00
Yuman (1)	3	0.00
All other tribes (189)	356	0.08
American Indian tribes, not spec.	246	0.06
Arab:	1,876	0.44
Arab/Arabic	225	0.05
Egyptian	306	0.07
Iraqi	89	0.02
Jordanian	9	0.00
Lebanese	845	0.20
Moroccan	142	0.03
Palestinian	57	0.01
Syrian	194	0.05
Other Arab	9	0.00
Armenian	126	0.03
Asian:	25,796	6.07
Bangladeshi (21)	30	0.01
Cambodian (83)	99	0.02
Chinese, ex. Taiwanese (1,503)	1,973	0.46
Filipino (14,553)	17,429	4.10
Hmong (5)	5	0.00
Indian (1,068)	1,280	0.30
Indonesian (26)	50	0.01
Japanese (695)	1,275	0.30
Korean (924)	1,237	0.29
Laotian (33)	36	0.01
Malaysian (4)	47	0.01
Pakistani (92)	115	0.03
Sri Lankan (27)	39	0.01
Taiwanese (54)	90	0.02
Thai (132)	188	0.04
Vietnamese (1,089)	1,268	0.30
Other Asian, specified (19)	62	0.01
Other Asian, not specified (272)	573	0.13
Australian	265	0.06
Austrian	976	0.23
Basque	29	0.01
Belgian	332	0.08
Brazilian	122	0.03
British	3,127	0.74
Bulgarian	162	0.04
Canadian	1,383	0.33
Celtic	144	0.03
Croatian	343	0.08
Cypriot	84	0.02
Czech	1,344	0.32
Czechoslovakian	623	0.15
Danish	1,106	0.26
Dutch	5,860	1.38
Eastern European	314	0.07
English	50,343	11.84
Estonian	24	0.01
European	3,454	0.81
Finnish	445	0.10
French, except Basque	12,388	2.91
French Canadian	4,063	0.96
German	58,303	13.71
German Russian	22	0.01
Greek	2,463	0.58
Guyanese	216	0.05
Hawaii Native/Pacific Islander:	1,140	0.27
Melanesian: (1)	7	0.00
Fijian (1)	7	0.00
Micronesian: (184)	313	0.07
Guamanian/Chamorro (165)	285	0.07
Other Micronesian (19)	28	0.01
Polynesian: (167)	431	0.10
Native Hawaiian (94)	321	0.08
Samoan (70)	99	0.02
Other Polynesian (3)	11	0.00
Other Pac. Isl., specified	30	0.01
Other Pac. Isl., not spec. (60)	359	0.08
Hispanic or Latino:	17,770	4.18
Central American:	869	0.20
Costa Rican	67	0.02
Guatemalan	90	0.02
Honduran	86	0.02
Nicaraguan	53	0.01
Panamanian	422	0.10
Salvadoran	124	0.03
Other Central American	27	0.01
Cuban	601	0.14
Dominican Republic	397	0.09
Mexican	4,854	1.14
Puerto Rican	6,273	1.48
South American:	998	0.23
Argentinean	50	0.01
Bolivian	22	0.01
Chilean	77	0.02
Colombian	393	0.09
Ecuadorian	151	0.04
Paraguayan	8	0.00
Peruvian	174	0.04
Uruguayan	8	0.00
Venezuelan	49	0.01
Other South American	66	0.02
Other Hispanic or Latino	3,778	0.89
Hungarian	2,316	0.54
Icelander	147	0.03
Iranian	388	0.09
Irish	52,692	12.39
Israeli	91	0.02
Italian	23,949	5.63
Latvian	101	0.02
Lithuanian	917	0.22
Luxemburger	12	0.00
Macedonian	35	0.01
Maltese	99	0.02
New Zealander	7	0.00
Northern European	130	0.03
Norwegian	4,192	0.99
Pennsylvania German	222	0.05
Polish	10,781	2.54
Portuguese	1,296	0.30
Romanian	252	0.06
Russian	3,132	0.74
Scandinavian	638	0.15
Scotch-Irish	9,362	2.20
Scottish	11,175	2.63
Serbian	134	0.03
Slavic	180	0.04
Slovak	989	0.23
Slovene	144	0.03
Swedish	3,987	0.94
Swiss	667	0.16
Turkish	198	0.05
Ukrainian	1,262	0.30
United States or American	31,137	7.32
Welsh	3,144	0.74
West Indian, excl. Hispanic:	2,445	0.57
Bahamian	63	0.01
Barbadian	111	0.03
Belizean	20	0.00
Bermudan	30	0.01
British West Indian	304	0.07
Dutch West Indian	28	0.01
Haitian	166	0.04
Jamaican	1,062	0.25
Trinidadian and Tobagonian	238	0.06
U.S. Virgin Islander	96	0.02
West Indian	303	0.07
Other West Indian	24	0.01
White:	312,913	73.58
Not Hispanic (295,402)	303,258	71.31
Hispanic (8,279)	9,655	2.27
Yugoslavian	267	0.06

Waynesboro

Place Type: Independent City
County: Waynesboro Independent City
Population: 19,520

Ancestry/Race	Number	%
African American/Black:	2,103	10.77
Not Hispanic (1,935)	2,089	10.70
Hispanic (10)	14	0.07
African, sub-Saharan:	74	0.38
African	51	0.26
Other sub-Saharan African	23	0.12
Alaska Native tribes, specified:	1	0.01
Eskimo (1)	1	0.01
Am. Ind. or Alaska Nat., not spec.	54	0.28
American Indian tribes, specified:	107	0.55
Apache (1)	1	0.01

Notes: 1. Figures in the "Number" column do not add up to the total population due to: a) Ancestry/Race overlap — e.g. persons can report being both White and Irish, b) persons of Hispanic origin can report being any race, c) persons reporting two ancestries are counted in both categories. 2. Numbers in parentheses indicate the number of persons reporting this ancestry/race alone, not in combination with any other ancestry/race. 3. Refer to the Explanation of Data in the front of the book for more detailed information.

Ancestry/Race	Number	%
Blackfeet (1)	3	0.02
Cherokee (16)	64	0.33
Chickasaw (1)	1	0.01
Chippewa	1	0.01
Choctaw (3)	4	0.02
Creek (3)	3	0.02
Crow (2)	2	0.01
Delaware	3	0.02
Iroquois (1)	1	0.01
Latin American Indians (8)	8	0.04
Navajo (2)	4	0.02
Sioux (1)	2	0.01
All other tribes (6)	10	0.05
American Indian tribes, not spec.	5	0.03
Asian:	167	0.86
Chinese, ex. Taiwanese (28)	34	0.17
Filipino (8)	19	0.10
Indian (36)	55	0.28
Japanese (4)	13	0.07
Korean (8)	10	0.05
Pakistani (4)	10	0.05
Thai (1)	1	0.01
Vietnamese (16)	17	0.09
Other Asian, specified	5	0.03
Other Asian, not specified (1)	3	0.02
Austrian	7	0.04
Belgian	14	0.07
Brazilian	7	0.04
British	78	0.40
Canadian	13	0.07
Czech	39	0.20
Czechoslovakian	20	0.10
Dutch	209	1.07
English	2,105	10.78
Estonian	38	0.19
European	94	0.48
French, except Basque	299	1.53
French Canadian	39	0.20
German	2,641	13.53
German Russian	7	0.04
Greek	63	0.32
Hawaii Native/Pacific Islander:	21	0.11
Micronesian: (1)	1	0.01
Other Micronesian (1)	1	0.01
Polynesian: (3)	10	0.05
Native Hawaiian (3)	10	0.05
Other Pac. Isl., specified	4	0.02
Other Pac. Isl., not spec. (2)	6	0.03
Hispanic or Latino:	643	3.29
Central American:	9	0.05
Guatemalan	3	0.02
Honduran	4	0.02
Salvadoran	2	0.01
Cuban	9	0.05
Dominican Republic	1	0.01
Mexican	456	2.34
Puerto Rican	53	0.27
South American:	23	0.12
Argentinean	8	0.04
Chilean	3	0.02
Colombian	12	0.06
Other Hispanic or Latino	92	0.47
Hungarian	95	0.49
Iranian	23	0.12
Irish	1,883	9.65
Italian	462	2.37
Lithuanian	19	0.10
Norwegian	74	0.38
Polish	275	1.41
Portuguese	18	0.09
Romanian	7	0.04
Russian	49	0.25
Scandinavian	9	0.05
Scotch-Irish	785	4.02
Scottish	407	2.09
Serbian	9	0.05
Slovak	9	0.05
Swedish	113	0.58
Swiss	87	0.45
Ukrainian	14	0.07
United States or American	3,890	19.93
Welsh	133	0.68
White:	17,157	87.89
Not Hispanic (16,492)	16,732	85.72
Hispanic (385)	425	2.18
Yugoslavian	11	0.06

West Springfield

Place Type: Census Designated Place
County: Fairfax
Population: 28,378

Ancestry/Race	Number	%
Acadian/Cajun	9	0.03
Afghan	456	1.59
African American/Black:	1,565	5.51
Not Hispanic (1,369)	1,532	5.40
Hispanic (18)	33	0.12
African, sub-Saharan:	243	0.85
African	80	0.28
Ethiopian	66	0.23
Nigerian	23	0.08
Sierra Leonean	12	0.04
Sudanese	33	0.12
Other sub-Saharan African	29	0.10
Alaska Native tribes, specified:	2	0.01
Alaska Athabascan	1	0.00
Eskimo	1	0.00
Am. Ind. or Alaska Nat., not spec.	56	0.20
American Indian tribes, specified:	139	0.49
Apache	1	0.00
Blackfeet (8)	19	0.07
Cherokee (17)	50	0.18
Chickasaw (1)	3	0.01
Chippewa (2)	7	0.02
Choctaw (1)	4	0.01
Creek	2	0.01
Delaware	1	0.00
Iroquois (2)	5	0.02
Latin American Indians (4)	7	0.02
Navajo (3)	4	0.01
Osage	4	0.01
Potawatomi (1)	1	0.00
Pueblo (17)	17	0.06
Seminole	1	0.00
Sioux (2)	2	0.01
All other tribes (5)	11	0.04
American Indian tribes, not spec.	5	0.02
Arab:	363	1.27
Arab/Arabic	34	0.12
Egyptian	47	0.16
Jordanian	34	0.12
Lebanese	35	0.12
Palestinian	113	0.40
Other Arab	100	0.35
Armenian	57	0.20
Asian:	4,472	15.76
Bangladeshi (29)	29	0.10
Cambodian (68)	70	0.25
Chinese, ex. Taiwanese (399)	481	1.69
Filipino (360)	416	1.47
Indian (492)	573	2.02
Indonesian (7)	10	0.04
Japanese (72)	142	0.50
Korean (1,508)	1,570	5.53
Laotian (26)	26	0.09
Malaysian (5)	5	0.02
Pakistani (115)	136	0.48
Sri Lankan (8)	8	0.03
Taiwanese (25)	28	0.10
Thai (45)	57	0.20
Vietnamese (642)	697	2.46
Other Asian, specified	4	0.01
Other Asian, not specified (56)	220	0.78
Australian	9	0.03
Austrian	96	0.34
Belgian	40	0.14
Brazilian	7	0.02
British	214	0.75
Canadian	21	0.07
Carpatho Rusyn	8	0.03
Croatian	78	0.27
Czech	188	0.66
Czechoslovakian	73	0.26
Danish	166	0.58
Dutch	439	1.53
Eastern European	46	0.16
English	3,814	13.33
Estonian	12	0.04
European	480	1.68
Finnish	36	0.13
French, except Basque	584	2.04
French Canadian	209	0.73
German	4,526	15.82
Greek	163	0.57
Guyanese	60	0.21
Hawaii Native/Pacific Islander:	49	0.17
Micronesian: (8)	15	0.05
Guamanian/Chamorro (7)	14	0.05
Other Micronesian (1)	1	0.00
Polynesian: (6)	8	0.03
Native Hawaiian (5)	6	0.02
Samoan (1)	2	0.01
Other Pac. Isl., specified	2	0.01
Other Pac. Isl., not spec. (3)	24	0.08
Hispanic or Latino:	2,081	7.33
Central American:	323	1.14
Costa Rican	12	0.04
Guatemalan	34	0.12
Honduran	43	0.15
Nicaraguan	20	0.07
Panamanian	20	0.07
Salvadoran	184	0.65
Other Central American	10	0.04
Cuban	57	0.20
Dominican Republic	11	0.04
Mexican	218	0.77
Puerto Rican	180	0.63
South American:	622	2.19
Argentinean	23	0.08
Bolivian	135	0.48
Chilean	26	0.09
Colombian	88	0.31
Ecuadorian	25	0.09
Paraguayan	1	0.00
Peruvian	230	0.81
Uruguayan	18	0.06
Venezuelan	19	0.07
Other South American	57	0.20
Other Hispanic or Latino	670	2.36
Hungarian	148	0.52
Iranian	168	0.59
Irish	4,206	14.70
Italian	1,935	6.76
Latvian	31	0.11
Lithuanian	182	0.64
Northern European	36	0.13
Norwegian	343	1.20
Pennsylvania German	21	0.07
Polish	781	2.73
Portuguese	134	0.47
Romanian	44	0.15
Russian	432	1.51
Scandinavian	29	0.10
Scotch-Irish	690	2.41
Scottish	980	3.43
Slavic	21	0.07
Slovak	118	0.41
Slovene	61	0.21
Swedish	353	1.23
Swiss	122	0.43
Turkish	20	0.07
Ukrainian	49	0.17
United States or American	1,196	4.18
Welsh	361	1.26
West Indian, excl. Hispanic:	67	0.23
Barbadian	6	0.02
Haitian	39	0.14
Jamaican	6	0.02

Notes: 1. Figures in the "Number" column do not add up to the total population due to: a) Ancestry/Race overlap — e.g. persons can report being both White and Irish, b) persons of Hispanic origin can report being any race, c) persons reporting two ancestries are counted in both categories. 2. Numbers in parentheses indicate the number of persons reporting this ancestry/race alone, not in combination with any other ancestry/race. 3. Refer to the Explanation of Data in the front of the book for more detailed information.

West Indian	16	0.06
White:	22,116	77.93
Not Hispanic (20,151)	20,761	73.16
Hispanic (1,220)	1,355	4.77

Williamsburg

Place Type: Independent City
County: Williamsburg Independent City
Population: 11,998

Ancestry/Race	Number	%
African American/Black:	1,659	13.83
Not Hispanic (1,593)	1,649	13.74
Hispanic (8)	10	0.08
African, sub-Saharan:	59	0.49
African	36	0.30
Nigerian	7	0.06
South African	16	0.13
Alaska Native tribes, specified:	1	0.01
Eskimo (1)	1	0.01
Am. Ind. or Alaska Nat., not spec.	21	0.18
Albanian	14	0.12
American Indian tribes, specified:	47	0.39
Blackfeet	1	0.01
Cherokee (6)	17	0.14
Delaware (3)	3	0.03
Iroquois (1)	5	0.04
Latin American Indians (1)	1	0.01
Lumbee (1)	1	0.01
Navajo	1	0.01
Potawatomi (1)	1	0.01
Pueblo (1)	1	0.01
Seminole	1	0.01
All other tribes (8)	15	0.13
American Indian tribes, not spec.	3	0.03
Arab:	32	0.27
Lebanese	7	0.06
Moroccan	6	0.05
Palestinian	11	0.09
Syrian	8	0.07
Armenian	28	0.23
Asian:	633	5.28
Cambodian (1)	1	0.01
Chinese, ex. Taiwanese (115)	130	1.08
Filipino (67)	80	0.67
Indian (140)	156	1.30
Indonesian (2)	2	0.02
Japanese (24)	33	0.28
Korean (58)	68	0.57
Pakistani (4)	4	0.03
Sri Lankan (1)	1	0.01
Taiwanese (7)	9	0.08
Thai (4)	8	0.07
Vietnamese (35)	39	0.33
Other Asian, specified	1	0.01
Other Asian, not specified (89)	101	0.84
Assyrian/Chaldean/Syriac	6	0.05
Australian	4	0.03
Austrian	50	0.42
British	138	1.15
Canadian	24	0.20
Celtic	8	0.07
Croatian	12	0.10
Czech	20	0.17
Czechoslovakian	21	0.18
Danish	41	0.34
Dutch	153	1.28
English	1,805	15.04
Estonian	4	0.03
European	113	0.94
Finnish	9	0.08
French, except Basque	244	2.03
French Canadian	38	0.32
German	1,491	12.43
Greek	77	0.64
Hawaii Native/Pacific Islander:	16	0.13
Micronesian: (1)	2	0.02
Guamanian/Chamorro (1)	2	0.02
Polynesian: (6)	10	0.08
Native Hawaiian (6)	10	0.08
Other Pac. Isl., not spec.	4	0.03
Hispanic or Latino:	302	2.52
Central American:	19	0.16
Costa Rican	2	0.02
Guatemalan	2	0.02
Nicaraguan	2	0.02
Panamanian	2	0.02
Salvadoran	10	0.08
Other Central American	1	0.01
Cuban	15	0.13
Dominican Republic	3	0.03
Mexican	113	0.94
Puerto Rican	71	0.59
South American:	18	0.15
Argentinean	3	0.03
Bolivian	6	0.05
Colombian	2	0.02
Peruvian	3	0.03
Venezuelan	2	0.02
Other South American	2	0.02
Other Hispanic or Latino	63	0.53
Hungarian	155	1.29
Iranian	8	0.07
Irish	1,186	9.88
Israeli	6	0.05
Italian	402	3.35
Latvian	6	0.05
Lithuanian	35	0.29
Norwegian	107	0.89
Polish	298	2.48
Portuguese	33	0.28
Romanian	28	0.23
Russian	95	0.79
Scandinavian	6	0.05
Scotch-Irish	316	2.63
Scottish	390	3.25
Serbian	12	0.10
Slavic	8	0.07
Slovak	61	0.51
Swedish	158	1.32
Swiss	68	0.57
Turkish	4	0.03
Ukrainian	45	0.38
United States or American	444	3.70
Welsh	146	1.22
West Indian, excl. Hispanic:	16	0.13
British West Indian	10	0.08
Jamaican	6	0.05
White:	9,694	80.80
Not Hispanic (9,352)	9,481	79.02
Hispanic (191)	213	1.78
Yugoslavian	14	0.12

Winchester

Place Type: Independent City
County: Winchester Independent City
Population: 23,585

Ancestry/Race	Number	%
Afghan	11	0.05
African American/Black:	2,721	11.54
Not Hispanic (2,454)	2,691	11.41
Hispanic (16)	30	0.13
African, sub-Saharan:	219	0.93
African	198	0.84
Ghanian	13	0.06
Other sub-Saharan African	8	0.03
Alaska Native tribes, specified:	1	0.00
Eskimo	1	0.00
Alaska Native tribes, not specified	1	0.00
Am. Ind. or Alaska Nat., not spec.	57	0.24
American Indian tribes, specified:	144	0.61
Apache (2)	6	0.03
Blackfeet	8	0.03
Cherokee (19)	65	0.28
Choctaw	7	0.03
Cree (1)	2	0.01
Creek (1)	2	0.01
Delaware	3	0.01
Iroquois (2)	5	0.02
Latin American Indians (6)	20	0.08
Lumbee	1	0.00
Seminole	3	0.01
Sioux (1)	5	0.02
Ute (1)	1	0.00
All other tribes (5)	16	0.07
American Indian tribes, not spec.	7	0.03
Arab:	7	0.03
Lebanese	7	0.03
Asian:	439	1.86
Cambodian (2)	4	0.02
Chinese, ex. Taiwanese (78)	87	0.37
Filipino (30)	47	0.20
Indian (85)	86	0.36
Japanese (56)	62	0.26
Korean (32)	35	0.15
Laotian (1)	3	0.01
Malaysian (1)	1	0.00
Pakistani (1)	4	0.02
Sri Lankan (5)	5	0.02
Taiwanese (1)	3	0.01
Thai (6)	7	0.03
Vietnamese (69)	77	0.33
Other Asian, specified	3	0.01
Other Asian, not specified (6)	15	0.06
Austrian	66	0.28
Brazilian	8	0.03
British	104	0.44
Canadian	93	0.39
Croatian	8	0.03
Czech	62	0.26
Danish	22	0.09
Dutch	293	1.24
Eastern European	9	0.04
English	3,039	12.89
European	216	0.92
Finnish	18	0.08
French, except Basque	419	1.78
French Canadian	76	0.32
German	3,937	16.69
Greek	69	0.29
Guyanese	34	0.14
Hawaii Native/Pacific Islander:	29	0.12
Micronesian:	3	0.01
Guamanian/Chamorro	3	0.01
Polynesian: (5)	11	0.05
Native Hawaiian (5)	8	0.03
Samoan	2	0.01
Tongan	1	0.00
Other Pac. Isl., specified	3	0.01
Other Pac. Isl., not spec. (3)	12	0.05
Hispanic or Latino:	1,527	6.47
Central American:	289	1.23
Costa Rican	3	0.01
Guatemalan	41	0.17
Honduran	16	0.07
Nicaraguan	4	0.02
Panamanian	3	0.01
Salvadoran	217	0.92
Other Central American	5	0.02
Cuban	18	0.08
Dominican Republic	2	0.01
Mexican	892	3.78
Puerto Rican	97	0.41
South American:	38	0.16
Argentinean	7	0.03
Bolivian	3	0.01
Colombian	9	0.04
Paraguayan	5	0.02
Peruvian	11	0.05
Venezuelan	2	0.01
Other South American	1	0.00
Other Hispanic or Latino	191	0.81
Hungarian	18	0.08
Iranian	10	0.04
Irish	2,791	11.83
Italian	730	3.10
Latvian	7	0.03

Notes: 1. Figures in the "Number" column do not add up to the total population due to: a) Ancestry/Race overlap — e.g. persons can report being both White and Irish, b) persons of Hispanic origin can report being any race, c) persons reporting two ancestries are counted in both categories. 2. Numbers in parentheses indicate the number of persons reporting this ancestry/race alone, not in combination with any other ancestry/race. 3. Refer to the Explanation of Data in the front of the book for more detailed information.

Ancestry/Race	Number	%
Lithuanian	14	0.06
Norwegian	101	0.43
Pennsylvania German	6	0.03
Polish	380	1.61
Portuguese	82	0.35
Romanian	4	0.02
Russian	120	0.51
Scandinavian	26	0.11
Scotch-Irish	585	2.48
Scottish	676	2.87
Slovak	12	0.05
Slovene	41	0.17
Swedish	171	0.73
Swiss	35	0.15
Ukrainian	67	0.28
United States or American	2,697	11.44
Welsh	206	0.87
West Indian, excl. Hispanic:	75	0.32
Jamaican	75	0.32
White:	19,784	83.88
Not Hispanic (18,724)	19,087	80.93
Hispanic (631)	697	2.96
Yugoslavian	9	0.04

Wolf Trap

Place Type: Census Designated Place
County: Fairfax
Population: 14,001

Ancestry/Race	Number	%
Acadian/Cajun	6	0.04
Afghan	36	0.26
African American/Black:	278	1.99
Not Hispanic (245)	270	1.93
Hispanic (5)	8	0.06
African, sub-Saharan:	125	0.90
African	47	0.34
Ethiopian	24	0.17
Ghanian	8	0.06
Kenyan	25	0.18
South African	11	0.08
Other sub-Saharan African	10	0.07
Alaska Native tribes, not specified	1	0.01
Am. Ind. or Alaska Nat., not spec.	14	0.10
American Indian tribes, specified:	34	0.24
Blackfeet	2	0.01
Cherokee (3)	16	0.11
Chippewa	1	0.01
Choctaw	1	0.01
Creek (1)	1	0.01
Delaware (3)	4	0.03
Lumbee (2)	2	0.01
Osage	3	0.02
Ottawa	1	0.01
All other tribes (1)	3	0.02
Arab:	434	3.13
Arab/Arabic	90	0.65
Egyptian	113	0.81
Lebanese	114	0.82
Palestinian	33	0.24
Syrian	49	0.35
Other Arab	35	0.25
Armenian	18	0.13
Asian:	1,351	9.65
Cambodian	3	0.02
Chinese, ex. Taiwanese (275)	310	2.21
Filipino (78)	95	0.68
Indian (314)	351	2.51
Indonesian (5)	6	0.04
Japanese (56)	68	0.49
Korean (201)	214	1.53
Laotian (5)	5	0.04
Malaysian (7)	7	0.05
Pakistani (28)	33	0.24
Sri Lankan (5)	5	0.04
Taiwanese (43)	56	0.40
Thai (26)	28	0.20
Vietnamese (97)	105	0.75
Other Asian, specified (3)	4	0.03
Other Asian, not specified (16)	61	0.44
Australian	23	0.17
Austrian	91	0.66
Belgian	47	0.34
Brazilian	27	0.19
British	193	1.39
Canadian	152	1.10
Celtic	10	0.07
Croatian	27	0.19
Czech	97	0.70
Czechoslovakian	28	0.20
Danish	66	0.48
Dutch	159	1.15
Eastern European	60	0.43
English	2,741	19.75
European	144	1.04
Finnish	10	0.07
French, except Basque	579	4.17
French Canadian	38	0.27
German	2,713	19.55
Greek	81	0.58
Guyanese	6	0.04
Hawaii Native/Pacific Islander:	7	0.05
Micronesian:	1	0.01
Guamanian/Chamorro	1	0.01
Other Pac. Isl., not spec.	6	0.04
Hispanic or Latino:	368	2.63
Central American:	15	0.11
Costa Rican	3	0.02
Guatemalan	4	0.03
Honduran	1	0.01
Nicaraguan	3	0.02
Salvadoran	4	0.03
Cuban	34	0.24
Dominican Republic	6	0.04
Mexican	62	0.44
Puerto Rican	43	0.31
South American:	110	0.79
Argentinean	6	0.04
Bolivian	7	0.05
Chilean	16	0.11
Colombian	22	0.16
Ecuadorian	8	0.06
Paraguayan	4	0.03
Peruvian	26	0.19
Uruguayan	7	0.05
Venezuelan	10	0.07
Other South American	4	0.03
Other Hispanic or Latino	98	0.70
Hungarian	185	1.33
Icelander	24	0.17
Iranian	385	2.77
Irish	2,309	16.64
Israeli	8	0.06
Italian	911	6.56
Lithuanian	63	0.45
New Zealander	28	0.20
Northern European	28	0.20
Norwegian	170	1.22
Polish	517	3.73
Portuguese	51	0.37
Romanian	48	0.35
Russian	315	2.27
Scandinavian	5	0.04
Scotch-Irish	456	3.29
Scottish	326	2.35
Serbian	61	0.44
Slavic	6	0.04
Slovak	21	0.15
Slovene	4	0.03
Swedish	267	1.92
Swiss	84	0.61
Turkish	66	0.48
Ukrainian	51	0.37
United States or American	733	5.28
Welsh	169	1.22
White:	12,439	88.84
Not Hispanic (11,822)	12,138	86.69
Hispanic (282)	301	2.15

Woodbridge

Place Type: Census Designated Place
County: Prince William
Population: 31,941

Ancestry/Race	Number	%
Acadian/Cajun	6	0.02
Afghan	83	0.26
African American/Black:	8,102	25.37
Not Hispanic (7,336)	7,819	24.48
Hispanic (154)	283	0.89
African, sub-Saharan:	701	2.20
African	461	1.45
Ghanian	124	0.39
Liberian	40	0.13
Nigerian	50	0.16
South African	8	0.03
Other sub-Saharan African	18	0.06
Alaska Native tribes, specified:	3	0.01
Alaska Athabascan	1	0.00
Eskimo	2	0.01
Am. Ind. or Alaska Nat., not spec.	182	0.57
Albanian	20	0.06
American Indian tribes, specified:	256	0.80
Blackfeet (1)	10	0.03
Cherokee (20)	107	0.33
Cheyenne (2)	6	0.02
Chickasaw (3)	3	0.01
Chippewa (4)	8	0.03
Choctaw (2)	7	0.02
Comanche	2	0.01
Cree	1	0.00
Creek (5)	6	0.02
Crow	4	0.01
Delaware	2	0.01
Iroquois (2)	8	0.03
Latin American Indians (9)	36	0.11
Lumbee (3)	3	0.01
Navajo (1)	6	0.02
Pima (1)	1	0.00
Pueblo (1)	2	0.01
Puget Sound Salish	1	0.00
Seminole	5	0.02
Shoshone (2)	4	0.01
Sioux (4)	10	0.03
Tohono O'Odham	1	0.00
All other tribes (13)	23	0.07
American Indian tribes, not spec.	24	0.08
Arab:	144	0.45
Egyptian	49	0.15
Lebanese	12	0.04
Moroccan	13	0.04
Syrian	70	0.22
Armenian	6	0.02
Asian:	1,993	6.24
Bangladeshi (22)	22	0.07
Cambodian (16)	16	0.05
Chinese, ex. Taiwanese (86)	124	0.39
Filipino (308)	381	1.19
Indian (234)	271	0.85
Indonesian	1	0.00
Japanese (49)	106	0.33
Korean (255)	319	1.00
Laotian (84)	90	0.28
Malaysian	1	0.00
Pakistani (204)	231	0.72
Taiwanese (3)	3	0.01
Thai (58)	77	0.24
Vietnamese (170)	195	0.61
Other Asian, specified (5)	9	0.03
Other Asian, not specified (53)	147	0.46
Austrian	39	0.12
Belgian	21	0.07
Brazilian	7	0.02
British	154	0.48
Canadian	12	0.04
Croatian	31	0.10
Czech	136	0.43
Danish	23	0.07

Notes: 1. Figures in the "Number" column do not add up to the total population due to: a) Ancestry/Race overlap — e.g. persons can report being both White and Irish, b) persons of Hispanic origin can report being any race, c) persons reporting two ancestries are counted in both categories. 2. Numbers in parentheses indicate the number of persons reporting this ancestry/race alone, not in combination with any other ancestry/race. 3. Refer to the Explanation of Data in the front of the book for more detailed information.

Dutch	201	0.63
English	2,064	6.48
Estonian	5	0.02
European	236	0.74
Finnish	18	0.06
French, except Basque	492	1.54
French Canadian	262	0.82
German	3,403	10.68
Greek	71	0.22
Guyanese	31	0.10
Hawaii Native/Pacific Islander:	121	0.38
Micronesian: (17)	17	0.05
Guamanian/Chamorro (13)	13	0.04
Other Micronesian (4)	4	0.01
Polynesian: (24)	54	0.17
Native Hawaiian (15)	37	0.12
Samoan (9)	17	0.05
Other Pac. Isl., not spec. (9)	50	0.16
Hispanic or Latino:	6,091	19.07
Central American:	1,646	5.15
Costa Rican	3	0.01
Guatemalan	176	0.55
Honduran	74	0.23
Nicaraguan	102	0.32
Panamanian	64	0.20
Salvadoran	1,123	3.52
Other Central American	104	0.33
Cuban	21	0.07
Dominican Republic	70	0.22
Mexican	1,724	5.40
Puerto Rican	589	1.84
South American:	373	1.17
Argentinean	9	0.03
Bolivian	57	0.18
Chilean	10	0.03
Colombian	43	0.13
Ecuadorian	37	0.12
Paraguayan	1	0.00
Peruvian	161	0.50
Venezuelan	12	0.04
Other South American	43	0.13
Other Hispanic or Latino	1,668	5.22
Hungarian	165	0.52
Icelander	25	0.08
Iranian	9	0.03
Irish	2,942	9.23
Italian	936	2.94
Lithuanian	63	0.20
Norwegian	107	0.34
Pennsylvania German	7	0.02
Polish	629	1.97
Portuguese	59	0.19
Russian	90	0.28
Scandinavian	41	0.13
Scotch-Irish	344	1.08
Scottish	514	1.61
Slavic	24	0.08
Slovak	5	0.02
Slovene	7	0.02
Swedish	278	0.87
Swiss	39	0.12
Ukrainian	38	0.12
United States or American	2,663	8.36
Welsh	223	0.70
West Indian, excl. Hispanic:	355	1.11
Bahamian	5	0.02
Barbadian	10	0.03
British West Indian	9	0.03
Haitian	22	0.07
Jamaican	112	0.35
Trinidadian and Tobagonian	165	0.52
West Indian	32	0.10
White:	19,172	60.02
Not Hispanic (15,726)	16,426	51.43
Hispanic (2,270)	2,746	8.60
Yugoslavian	8	0.03

Aberdeen

Place Type: City
County: Grays Harbor
Population: 16,461

Ancestry/Race	Number	%
African American/Black:	168	1.02
Not Hispanic (62)	135	0.82
Hispanic (15)	33	0.20
African, sub-Saharan:	28	0.17
African	20	0.12
Nigerian	8	0.05
Alaska Native tribes, specified:	33	0.20
Alaska Athabascan (1)	1	0.01
Aleut (1)	3	0.02
Eskimo (5)	5	0.03
Tlingit-Haida (6)	19	0.12
All other tribes (5)	5	0.03
Alaska Native tribes, not specified	2	0.01
Am. Ind. or Alaska Nat., not spec.	180	1.09
American Indian tribes, specified:	681	4.14
Apache (1)	5	0.03
Blackfeet (4)	11	0.07
Cherokee (16)	65	0.39
Cheyenne (2)	2	0.01
Chickasaw (1)	6	0.04
Chippewa (31)	41	0.25
Choctaw (4)	14	0.09
Colville (7)	8	0.05
Comanche	1	0.01
Creek	1	0.01
Crow	2	0.01
Iroquois	1	0.01
Latin American Indians (7)	15	0.09
Navajo (1)	1	0.01
Osage (1)	2	0.01
Pima (1)	1	0.01
Potawatomi (1)	1	0.01
Pueblo (2)	3	0.02
Puget Sound Salish (36)	39	0.24
Seminole	4	0.02
Shoshone (3)	3	0.02
Sioux (7)	14	0.09
Ute (1)	1	0.01
Yakama (8)	14	0.09
All other tribes (323)	426	2.59
American Indian tribes, not spec.	22	0.13
Arab:	11	0.07
Syrian	11	0.07
Asian:	460	2.79
Cambodian (81)	92	0.56
Chinese, ex. Taiwanese (37)	50	0.30
Filipino (81)	129	0.78
Indian (15)	24	0.15
Indonesian (1)	1	0.01
Japanese (21)	36	0.22
Korean (51)	56	0.34
Laotian (6)	12	0.07
Pakistani (4)	4	0.02
Taiwanese (1)	3	0.02
Thai (10)	11	0.07
Vietnamese (15)	19	0.12
Other Asian, specified (1)	4	0.02
Other Asian, not specified (9)	19	0.12
Austrian	10	0.06
British	19	0.12
Canadian	16	0.10
Celtic	6	0.04
Croatian	171	1.04
Czech	83	0.50
Czechoslovakian	19	0.12
Danish	102	0.62
Dutch	300	1.82
English	1,654	10.03
European	101	0.61
Finnish	344	2.09
French, except Basque	633	3.84
French Canadian	153	0.93
German	3,115	18.89
Greek	142	0.86
Hawaii Native/Pacific Islander:	59	0.36
Micronesian: (7)	18	0.11
Guamanian/Chamorro	3	0.02
Other Micronesian (7)	15	0.09
Polynesian: (13)	30	0.18
Native Hawaiian (11)	27	0.16
Samoan (2)	3	0.02
Other Pac. Isl., not spec. (3)	11	0.07
Hispanic or Latino:	1,518	9.22
Central American:	109	0.66
Guatemalan	17	0.10
Honduran	2	0.01
Panamanian	2	0.01
Salvadoran	88	0.53
Cuban	4	0.02
Mexican	1,177	7.15
Puerto Rican	12	0.07
South American:	10	0.06
Colombian	8	0.05
Ecuadorian	1	0.01
Peruvian	1	0.01
Other Hispanic or Latino	206	1.25
Hungarian	30	0.18
Iranian	16	0.10
Irish	1,879	11.39
Italian	256	1.55
Lithuanian	20	0.12
Northern European	36	0.22
Norwegian	898	5.44
Pennsylvania German	17	0.10
Polish	381	2.31
Portuguese	53	0.32
Romanian	29	0.18
Russian	85	0.52
Scandinavian	78	0.47
Scotch-Irish	296	1.79
Scottish	506	3.07
Slavic	8	0.05
Swedish	757	4.59
Swiss	86	0.52
Ukrainian	25	0.15
United States or American	1,144	6.94
Welsh	148	0.90
West Indian, excl. Hispanic:	12	0.07
Dutch West Indian	6	0.04
Haitian	6	0.04
White:	14,505	88.12
Not Hispanic (13,530)	13,929	84.62
Hispanic (441)	576	3.50
Yugoslavian	29	0.18

Alderwood Manor

Place Type: Census Designated Place
County: Snohomish
Population: 15,329

Ancestry/Race	Number	%
African American/Black:	346	2.26
Not Hispanic (241)	325	2.12
Hispanic (8)	21	0.14
African, sub-Saharan:	59	0.39
African	59	0.39
Alaska Native tribes, specified:	49	0.32
Alaska Athabascan (1)	1	0.01
Aleut (7)	20	0.13
Eskimo (4)	7	0.05
Tlingit-Haida (14)	21	0.14
Alaska Native tribes, not specified	5	0.03
Am. Ind. or Alaska Nat., not spec.	72	0.47
American Indian tribes, specified:	136	0.89
Apache (1)	1	0.01
Blackfeet (4)	21	0.14
Cherokee (9)	27	0.18
Chickasaw (1)	2	0.01
Chippewa (2)	5	0.03
Choctaw	4	0.03
Colville (7)	10	0.07
Cree	3	0.02

Notes: 1. Figures in the "Number" column do not add up to the total population due to: a) Ancestry/Race overlap — e.g. persons can report being both White and Irish, b) persons of Hispanic origin can report being any race, c) persons reporting two ancestries are counted in both categories. 2. Numbers in parentheses indicate the number of persons reporting this ancestry/race alone, not in combination with any other ancestry/race. 3. Refer to the Explanation of Data in the front of the book for more detailed information.

Creek (1)	1	0.01
Iroquois (3)	8	0.05
Kiowa	3	0.02
Latin American Indians	1	0.01
Pueblo	3	0.02
Puget Sound Salish (5)	6	0.04
Shoshone	2	0.01
Sioux (9)	12	0.08
Yakama	1	0.01
All other tribes (16)	26	0.17
American Indian tribes, not spec.	15	0.10
Arab:	65	0.43
Lebanese	36	0.24
Other Arab	29	0.19
Asian:	1,814	11.83
Cambodian (76)	85	0.55
Chinese, ex. Taiwanese (251)	336	2.19
Filipino (297)	386	2.52
Indian (149)	162	1.06
Indonesian (3)	8	0.05
Japanese (100)	167	1.09
Korean (261)	292	1.90
Laotian (12)	12	0.08
Malaysian	5	0.03
Pakistani (15)	41	0.27
Taiwanese (13)	15	0.10
Thai (6)	6	0.04
Vietnamese (242)	267	1.74
Other Asian, specified	2	0.01
Other Asian, not specified (21)	30	0.20
Australian	11	0.07
Austrian	85	0.56
Belgian	73	0.48
British	136	0.89
Canadian	44	0.29
Celtic	7	0.05
Czech	68	0.45
Czechoslovakian	52	0.34
Danish	436	2.86
Dutch	219	1.44
English	1,932	12.67
European	171	1.12
Finnish	139	0.91
French, except Basque	723	4.74
French Canadian	223	1.46
German	2,992	19.61
Greek	77	0.50
Hawaii Native/Pacific Islander:	140	0.91
Melanesian: (21)	24	0.16
Fijian (21)	23	0.15
Other Melanesian	1	0.01
Micronesian: (7)	10	0.07
Guamanian/Chamorro (4)	7	0.05
Other Micronesian (3)	3	0.02
Polynesian: (21)	74	0.48
Native Hawaiian (18)	62	0.40
Samoan (2)	10	0.07
Tongan (1)	2	0.01
Other Pac. Isl., not spec. (22)	32	0.21
Hispanic or Latino:	609	3.97
Central American:	43	0.28
Costa Rican	2	0.01
Guatemalan	7	0.05
Nicaraguan	8	0.05
Panamanian	15	0.10
Salvadoran	2	0.01
Other Central American	9	0.06
Cuban	13	0.08
Dominican Republic	2	0.01
Mexican	382	2.49
Puerto Rican	34	0.22
South American:	37	0.24
Argentinean	1	0.01
Chilean	13	0.08
Colombian	4	0.03
Peruvian	9	0.06
Venezuelan	5	0.03
Other South American	5	0.03
Other Hispanic or Latino	98	0.64
Hungarian	46	0.30
Icelander	22	0.14
Iranian	26	0.17
Irish	1,579	10.35
Italian	689	4.52
Lithuanian	11	0.07
Luxemburger	9	0.06
Northern European	77	0.50
Norwegian	1,207	7.91
Pennsylvania German	7	0.05
Polish	297	1.95
Portuguese	21	0.14
Romanian	20	0.13
Russian	312	2.05
Scandinavian	164	1.08
Scotch-Irish	389	2.55
Scottish	372	2.44
Slavic	22	0.14
Slovene	15	0.10
Swedish	832	5.45
Swiss	91	0.60
Ukrainian	139	0.91
United States or American	982	6.44
Welsh	126	0.83
West Indian, excl. Hispanic:	6	0.04
Belizean	6	0.04
White:	13,048	85.12
Not Hispanic (12,334)	12,728	83.03
Hispanic (254)	320	2.09
Yugoslavian	31	0.20

Anacortes

Place Type: City
County: Skagit
Population: 14,557

Ancestry/Race	Number	%
African American/Black:	100	0.69
Not Hispanic (40)	90	0.62
Hispanic (6)	10	0.07
African, sub-Saharan:	5	0.03
African	5	0.03
Alaska Native tribes, specified:	68	0.47
Alaska Athabascan (2)	3	0.02
Aleut (8)	27	0.19
Eskimo (6)	8	0.05
Tlingit-Haida (16)	29	0.20
All other tribes	1	0.01
Alaska Native tribes, not specified	11	0.08
Am. Ind. or Alaska Nat., not spec.	50	0.34
American Indian tribes, specified:	225	1.55
Apache (4)	5	0.03
Blackfeet (13)	18	0.12
Cherokee (6)	29	0.20
Chippewa (3)	10	0.07
Choctaw (1)	6	0.04
Colville (1)	1	0.01
Comanche	2	0.01
Cree	1	0.01
Creek	4	0.03
Iroquois	1	0.01
Latin American Indians (2)	7	0.05
Navajo (1)	2	0.01
Osage	3	0.02
Potawatomi (11)	17	0.12
Puget Sound Salish (28)	63	0.43
Sioux (10)	17	0.12
Yakama (3)	4	0.03
All other tribes (20)	35	0.24
American Indian tribes, not spec.	11	0.08
Asian:	345	2.37
Cambodian (1)	1	0.01
Chinese, ex. Taiwanese (33)	52	0.36
Filipino (72)	123	0.84
Indian (17)	17	0.12
Indonesian (7)	9	0.06
Japanese (40)	63	0.43
Korean (27)	33	0.23
Malaysian	2	0.01
Pakistani (5)	5	0.03
Taiwanese (12)	12	0.08
Thai (7)	7	0.05
Vietnamese (8)	8	0.05
Other Asian, specified (2)	3	0.02
Other Asian, not specified (6)	10	0.07
Austrian	26	0.18
Basque	14	0.10
Belgian	16	0.11
British	82	0.56
Canadian	86	0.58
Celtic	13	0.09
Croatian	176	1.20
Czech	92	0.63
Czechoslovakian	40	0.27
Danish	344	2.34
Dutch	491	3.34
English	2,624	17.84
European	220	1.50
Finnish	95	0.65
French, except Basque	584	3.97
French Canadian	122	0.83
German	2,694	18.32
Greek	48	0.33
Hawaii Native/Pacific Islander:	52	0.36
Melanesian: (1)	1	0.01
Fijian (1)	1	0.01
Micronesian: (5)	11	0.08
Guamanian/Chamorro (5)	11	0.08
Polynesian: (11)	33	0.23
Native Hawaiian (8)	27	0.19
Samoan (3)	6	0.04
Other Pac. Isl., not spec. (2)	7	0.05
Hispanic or Latino:	459	3.15
Central American:	5	0.03
Guatemalan	3	0.02
Salvadoran	2	0.01
Cuban	3	0.02
Mexican	335	2.30
Puerto Rican	17	0.12
South American:	15	0.10
Chilean	5	0.03
Colombian	6	0.04
Ecuadorian	3	0.02
Other South American	1	0.01
Other Hispanic or Latino	84	0.58
Hungarian	53	0.36
Icelander	9	0.06
Iranian	7	0.05
Irish	1,964	13.35
Israeli	7	0.05
Italian	559	3.80
Lithuanian	7	0.05
New Zealander	5	0.03
Northern European	30	0.20
Norwegian	1,770	12.04
Polish	209	1.42
Portuguese	52	0.35
Romanian	25	0.17
Russian	144	0.98
Scandinavian	43	0.29
Scotch-Irish	434	2.95
Scottish	667	4.54
Slavic	22	0.15
Slovak	40	0.27
Slovene	12	0.08
Swedish	895	6.09
Swiss	78	0.53
Ukrainian	18	0.12
United States or American	582	3.96
Welsh	176	1.20
White:	13,853	95.16
Not Hispanic (13,279)	13,608	93.48
Hispanic (210)	245	1.68
Yugoslavian	34	0.23

Notes: 1. Figures in the "Number" column do not add up to the total population due to: a) Ancestry/Race overlap — e.g. persons can report being both White and Irish, b) persons of Hispanic origin can report being any race, c) persons reporting two ancestries are counted in both categories. 2. Numbers in parentheses indicate the number of persons reporting this ancestry/race alone, not in combination with any other ancestry/race. 3. Refer to the Explanation of Data in the front of the book for more detailed information.

Arlington

Place Type: City
County: Snohomish
Population: 11,713

Ancestry/Race	Number	%
African American/Black:	193	1.65
Not Hispanic (126)	179	1.53
Hispanic (6)	14	0.12
African, sub-Saharan:	34	0.29
African	34	0.29
Alaska Native tribes, specified:	13	0.11
Alaska Athabascan (1)	1	0.01
Aleut (4)	4	0.03
Tlingit-Haida (4)	8	0.07
Alaska Native tribes, not specified	1	0.01
Am. Ind. or Alaska Nat., not spec.	58	0.50
American Indian tribes, specified:	109	0.93
Apache	4	0.03
Blackfeet (2)	4	0.03
Cherokee (16)	28	0.24
Cheyenne	1	0.01
Chickasaw (2)	4	0.03
Chippewa (3)	4	0.03
Choctaw (3)	6	0.05
Comanche (2)	3	0.03
Cree (1)	1	0.01
Delaware (1)	1	0.01
Iroquois	4	0.03
Latin American Indians (2)	4	0.03
Puget Sound Salish (13)	16	0.14
Sioux (1)	1	0.01
Ute	1	0.01
Yakama (1)	1	0.01
All other tribes (17)	26	0.22
American Indian tribes, not spec.	23	0.20
Arab:	35	0.29
Lebanese	25	0.21
Syrian	10	0.08
Asian:	402	3.43
Chinese, ex. Taiwanese (13)	23	0.20
Filipino (153)	209	1.78
Indian (10)	16	0.14
Indonesian (3)	4	0.03
Japanese (24)	56	0.48
Korean (30)	46	0.39
Pakistani (3)	3	0.03
Thai (7)	21	0.18
Vietnamese (7)	11	0.09
Other Asian, not specified (3)	13	0.11
Australian	24	0.20
Austrian	55	0.46
Basque	12	0.10
Belgian	27	0.23
Brazilian	16	0.13
British	68	0.57
Bulgarian	8	0.07
Canadian	32	0.27
Celtic	13	0.11
Croatian	47	0.40
Czech	46	0.39
Czechoslovakian	30	0.25
Danish	103	0.87
Dutch	318	2.68
English	1,461	12.29
European	183	1.54
Finnish	113	0.95
French, except Basque	434	3.65
French Canadian	167	1.41
German	2,404	20.23
Greek	31	0.26
Hawaii Native/Pacific Islander:	75	0.64
Melanesian:	1	0.01
Fijian	1	0.01
Micronesian: (19)	23	0.20
Guamanian/Chamorro (17)	18	0.15
Other Micronesian (2)	5	0.04
Polynesian: (15)	33	0.28
Native Hawaiian (7)	20	0.17
Samoan (5)	9	0.08
Tongan (2)	2	0.02
Other Polynesian (1)	2	0.02
Other Pac. Isl., not spec. (4)	18	0.15
Hispanic or Latino:	683	5.83
Central American:	8	0.07
Guatemalan	7	0.06
Salvadoran	1	0.01
Cuban	19	0.16
Mexican	458	3.91
Puerto Rican	44	0.38
South American:	12	0.10
Argentinean	3	0.03
Colombian	5	0.04
Ecuadorian	4	0.03
Other Hispanic or Latino	142	1.21
Hungarian	47	0.40
Icelander	35	0.29
Iranian	40	0.34
Irish	1,593	13.40
Italian	399	3.36
Luxemburger	9	0.08
Northern European	34	0.29
Norwegian	1,294	10.89
Pennsylvania German	13	0.11
Polish	110	0.93
Portuguese	52	0.44
Romanian	21	0.18
Russian	95	0.80
Scandinavian	79	0.66
Scotch-Irish	308	2.59
Scottish	304	2.56
Slovene	13	0.11
Swedish	692	5.82
Swiss	74	0.62
Ukrainian	27	0.23
United States or American	574	4.83
Welsh	67	0.56
West Indian, excl. Hispanic:	19	0.16
Jamaican	19	0.16
White:	10,822	92.39
Not Hispanic (10,240)	10,465	89.35
Hispanic (303)	357	3.05
Yugoslavian	9	0.08

Auburn

Place Type: City
County: King
Population: 40,314

Ancestry/Race	Number	%
Acadian/Cajun	3	0.01
African American/Black:	1,413	3.50
Not Hispanic (956)	1,340	3.32
Hispanic (21)	73	0.18
African, sub-Saharan:	208	0.52
African	95	0.24
Ethiopian	47	0.12
Nigerian	9	0.02
Somalian	39	0.10
Sudanese	5	0.01
Other sub-Saharan African	13	0.03
Alaska Native tribes, specified:	114	0.28
Alaska Athabascan (8)	12	0.03
Aleut (8)	22	0.05
Eskimo (9)	22	0.05
Tlingit-Haida (34)	46	0.11
All other tribes (9)	12	0.03
Alaska Native tribes, not specified	6	0.01
Am. Ind. or Alaska Nat., not spec.	337	0.84
American Indian tribes, specified:	1,093	2.71
Apache (4)	17	0.04
Blackfeet (13)	62	0.15
Cherokee (47)	153	0.38
Cheyenne (3)	3	0.01
Chickasaw (6)	10	0.02
Chippewa (36)	59	0.15
Choctaw (9)	27	0.07
Colville (33)	40	0.10
Comanche (2)	6	0.01
Cree (2)	5	0.01
Creek	4	0.01
Crow (1)	3	0.01
Delaware (4)	7	0.02
Iroquois (1)	8	0.02
Kiowa (1)	1	0.00
Latin American Indians (5)	11	0.03
Lumbee	1	0.00
Menominee (5)	5	0.01
Navajo (23)	29	0.07
Osage	2	0.00
Ottawa (3)	3	0.01
Paiute (2)	2	0.00
Pima (1)	1	0.00
Potawatomi (1)	4	0.01
Pueblo (2)	3	0.01
Puget Sound Salish (344)	381	0.95
Seminole	3	0.01
Shoshone (3)	5	0.01
Sioux (36)	61	0.15
Yakama (26)	32	0.08
All other tribes (94)	145	0.36
American Indian tribes, not spec.	83	0.21
Arab:	289	0.72
Arab/Arabic	9	0.02
Egyptian	25	0.06
Jordanian	32	0.08
Lebanese	35	0.09
Syrian	12	0.03
Other Arab	176	0.44
Armenian	39	0.10
Asian:	2,027	5.03
Cambodian (38)	46	0.11
Chinese, ex. Taiwanese (100)	174	0.43
Filipino (363)	598	1.48
Hmong (2)	2	0.00
Indian (103)	142	0.35
Indonesian (3)	8	0.02
Japanese (160)	282	0.70
Korean (159)	204	0.51
Laotian (63)	76	0.19
Malaysian	2	0.00
Pakistani (4)	5	0.01
Taiwanese (7)	9	0.02
Thai (50)	71	0.18
Vietnamese (299)	323	0.80
Other Asian, specified (1)	6	0.01
Other Asian, not specified (29)	79	0.20
Australian	23	0.06
Austrian	102	0.25
Belgian	91	0.23
Brazilian	9	0.02
British	85	0.21
Canadian	132	0.33
Celtic	14	0.03
Croatian	23	0.06
Czech	188	0.47
Czechoslovakian	34	0.08
Danish	361	0.90
Dutch	695	1.73
Eastern European	19	0.05
English	4,270	10.60
Estonian	20	0.05
European	842	2.09
Finnish	265	0.66
French, except Basque	1,261	3.13
French Canadian	338	0.84
German	7,304	18.13
German Russian	10	0.02
Greek	106	0.26
Hawaii Native/Pacific Islander:	413	1.02
Melanesian: (1)	2	0.00
Fijian (1)	2	0.00
Micronesian: (56)	74	0.18
Guamanian/Chamorro (20)	27	0.07
Other Micronesian (36)	47	0.12
Polynesian: (108)	254	0.63
Native Hawaiian (41)	116	0.29
Samoan (64)	124	0.31

Notes: 1. Figures in the "Number" column do not add up to the total population due to: a) Ancestry/Race overlap — e.g. persons can report being both White and Irish, b) persons of Hispanic origin can report being any race, c) persons reporting two ancestries are counted in both categories. 2. Numbers in parentheses indicate the number of persons reporting this ancestry/race alone, not in combination with any other ancestry/race. 3. Refer to the Explanation of Data in the front of the book for more detailed information.

Tongan (2)	9	0.02
Other Polynesian (1)	5	0.01
Other Pac. Isl., specified	4	0.01
Other Pac. Isl., not spec. (29)	79	0.20
Hispanic or Latino:	3,019	7.49
Central American:	54	0.13
Guatemalan	11	0.03
Honduran	5	0.01
Nicaraguan	1	0.00
Panamanian	8	0.02
Salvadoran	21	0.05
Other Central American	8	0.02
Cuban	24	0.06
Mexican	2,279	5.65
Puerto Rican	111	0.28
South American:	52	0.13
Argentinean	3	0.01
Bolivian	4	0.01
Chilean	1	0.00
Colombian	14	0.03
Ecuadorian	9	0.02
Peruvian	15	0.04
Uruguayan	1	0.00
Venezuelan	1	0.00
Other South American	4	0.01
Other Hispanic or Latino	499	1.24
Hungarian	110	0.27
Icelander	28	0.07
Iranian	28	0.07
Irish	4,523	11.23
Italian	1,169	2.90
Lithuanian	64	0.16
Luxemburger	2	0.00
Northern European	106	0.26
Norwegian	2,351	5.84
Pennsylvania German	22	0.05
Polish	799	1.98
Portuguese	137	0.34
Romanian	14	0.03
Russian	560	1.39
Scandinavian	207	0.51
Scotch-Irish	875	2.17
Scottish	908	2.25
Slavic	11	0.03
Slovak	44	0.11
Swedish	1,241	3.08
Swiss	156	0.39
Turkish	6	0.01
Ukrainian	809	2.01
United States or American	2,047	5.08
Welsh	400	0.99
West Indian, excl. Hispanic:	47	0.12
Dutch West Indian	7	0.02
Jamaican	40	0.10
White:	34,980	86.77
Not Hispanic (32,220)	33,556	83.24
Hispanic (1,162)	1,424	3.53
Yugoslavian	82	0.20

Bainbridge Island

Place Type: City
County: Kitsap
Population: 20,308

Ancestry/Race	Number	%
African American/Black:	124	0.61
Not Hispanic (55)	117	0.58
Hispanic (2)	7	0.03
African, sub-Saharan:	18	0.09
African	18	0.09
Alaska Native tribes, specified:	20	0.10
Alaska Athabascan (1)	2	0.01
Aleut (1)	2	0.01
Eskimo (1)	2	0.01
Tlingit-Haida (7)	11	0.05
All other tribes (1)	3	0.01
Am. Ind. or Alaska Nat., not spec.	72	0.35
Albanian	16	0.08
Alsatian	6	0.03
American Indian tribes, specified:	253	1.25
Apache (2)	4	0.02
Blackfeet (1)	11	0.05
Cherokee (7)	35	0.17
Cheyenne	3	0.01
Chickasaw	1	0.00
Chippewa (4)	5	0.02
Choctaw (5)	8	0.04
Colville (4)	4	0.02
Iroquois	11	0.05
Latin American Indians (2)	8	0.04
Lumbee (1)	1	0.00
Menominee (1)	1	0.00
Navajo (5)	5	0.02
Paiute	1	0.00
Pima (1)	1	0.00
Puget Sound Salish (7)	60	0.30
Seminole (3)	4	0.02
Sioux (3)	15	0.07
Yaqui	1	0.00
All other tribes (27)	74	0.36
American Indian tribes, not spec.	35	0.17
Arab:	30	0.15
Lebanese	24	0.12
Other Arab	6	0.03
Asian:	808	3.98
Cambodian (1)	1	0.00
Chinese, ex. Taiwanese (93)	144	0.71
Filipino (119)	251	1.24
Indian (9)	15	0.07
Indonesian	4	0.02
Japanese (178)	277	1.36
Korean (45)	62	0.31
Laotian (1)	1	0.00
Thai (6)	15	0.07
Vietnamese (24)	27	0.13
Other Asian, specified (1)	1	0.00
Other Asian, not specified (5)	10	0.05
Australian	27	0.13
Austrian	97	0.48
Belgian	30	0.15
Brazilian	7	0.03
British	312	1.54
Canadian	206	1.01
Celtic	54	0.27
Croatian	58	0.29
Czech	107	0.53
Czechoslovakian	82	0.40
Danish	360	1.77
Dutch	363	1.79
Eastern European	61	0.30
English	4,548	22.40
Estonian	11	0.05
European	605	2.98
Finnish	122	0.60
French, except Basque	813	4.00
French Canadian	137	0.67
German	3,902	19.21
Greek	92	0.45
Hawaii Native/Pacific Islander:	70	0.34
Micronesian: (2)	7	0.03
Guamanian/Chamorro	5	0.02
Other Micronesian (2)	2	0.01
Polynesian: (20)	57	0.28
Native Hawaiian (11)	40	0.20
Samoan (8)	11	0.05
Other Polynesian (1)	6	0.03
Other Pac. Isl., not spec.	6	0.03
Hispanic or Latino:	440	2.17
Central American:	19	0.09
Costa Rican	3	0.01
Guatemalan	1	0.00
Panamanian	1	0.00
Salvadoran	11	0.05
Other Central American	3	0.01
Cuban	15	0.07
Dominican Republic	1	0.00
Mexican	223	1.10
Puerto Rican	35	0.17
South American:	34	0.17
Argentinean	6	0.03
Bolivian	1	0.00
Chilean	7	0.03
Colombian	9	0.04
Paraguayan	1	0.00
Peruvian	7	0.03
Venezuelan	2	0.01
Other South American	1	0.00
Other Hispanic or Latino	113	0.56
Hungarian	130	0.64
Icelander	39	0.19
Iranian	9	0.04
Irish	3,106	15.29
Italian	799	3.93
Latvian	29	0.14
Lithuanian	85	0.42
Northern European	140	0.69
Norwegian	1,521	7.49
Pennsylvania German	6	0.03
Polish	494	2.43
Portuguese	137	0.67
Romanian	16	0.08
Russian	517	2.55
Scandinavian	171	0.84
Scotch-Irish	754	3.71
Scottish	1,372	6.76
Serbian	8	0.04
Slavic	63	0.31
Slovak	72	0.35
Slovene	20	0.10
Swedish	968	4.77
Swiss	122	0.60
Turkish	19	0.09
Ukrainian	66	0.32
United States or American	535	2.63
Welsh	345	1.70
White:	19,364	95.35
Not Hispanic (18,624)	19,068	93.89
Hispanic (239)	296	1.46
Yugoslavian	74	0.36

Bellevue

Place Type: City
County: King
Population: 109,569

Ancestry/Race	Number	%
Acadian/Cajun	21	0.02
Afghan	67	0.06
African American/Black:	2,860	2.61
Not Hispanic (2,100)	2,730	2.49
Hispanic (83)	130	0.12
African, sub-Saharan:	574	0.53
African	239	0.22
Ethiopian	134	0.12
Ghanian	18	0.02
Kenyan	79	0.07
Sierra Leonean	8	0.01
South African	40	0.04
Sudanese	19	0.02
Ugandan	7	0.01
Other sub-Saharan African	30	0.03
Alaska Native tribes, specified:	72	0.07
Alaska Athabascan	7	0.01
Aleut (8)	14	0.01
Eskimo (9)	18	0.02
Tlingit-Haida (16)	28	0.03
All other tribes (3)	5	0.00
Alaska Native tribes, not specified	6	0.01
Am. Ind. or Alaska Nat., not spec.	285	0.26
Albanian	7	0.01
American Indian tribes, specified:	500	0.46
Apache (6)	12	0.01
Blackfeet (6)	24	0.02
Cherokee (37)	135	0.12
Cheyenne (2)	3	0.00
Chickasaw	3	0.00
Chippewa (25)	44	0.04
Choctaw (1)	9	0.01

Notes: 1. Figures in the "Number" column do not add up to the total population due to: a) Ancestry/Race overlap — e.g. persons can report being both White and Irish, b) persons of Hispanic origin can report being any race, c) persons reporting two ancestries are counted in both categories. 2. Numbers in parentheses indicate the number of persons reporting this ancestry/race alone, not in combination with any other ancestry/race. 3. Refer to the Explanation of Data in the front of the book for more detailed information.

Ancestry/Race	Number	%
Colville (5)	7	0.01
Comanche (2)	2	0.00
Creek	2	0.00
Crow	1	0.00
Delaware (1)	2	0.00
Iroquois (3)	13	0.01
Latin American Indians (18)	45	0.04
Lumbee (2)	3	0.00
Menominee	3	0.00
Navajo (6)	11	0.01
Osage	3	0.00
Ottawa	1	0.00
Paiute (2)	2	0.00
Potawatomi (2)	2	0.00
Pueblo (2)	6	0.01
Puget Sound Salish (8)	20	0.02
Seminole	5	0.00
Shoshone (1)	1	0.00
Sioux (17)	29	0.03
Yakama (4)	8	0.01
All other tribes (51)	104	0.09
American Indian tribes, not spec.	78	0.07
Arab:	827	0.76
Arab/Arabic	170	0.16
Egyptian	96	0.09
Iraqi	17	0.02
Jordanian	33	0.03
Lebanese	279	0.26
Moroccan	7	0.01
Palestinian	89	0.08
Syrian	18	0.02
Other Arab	118	0.11
Armenian	650	0.60
Asian:	21,547	19.67
Bangladeshi (8)	10	0.01
Cambodian (282)	358	0.33
Chinese, ex. Taiwanese (5,860)	6,696	6.11
Filipino (1,071)	1,443	1.32
Hmong (62)	69	0.06
Indian (2,881)	3,069	2.80
Indonesian (110)	153	0.14
Japanese (2,838)	3,538	3.23
Korean (2,141)	2,351	2.15
Laotian (244)	272	0.25
Malaysian (12)	28	0.03
Pakistani (137)	185	0.17
Sri Lankan (16)	20	0.02
Taiwanese (885)	1,056	0.96
Thai (208)	277	0.25
Vietnamese (1,497)	1,627	1.48
Other Asian, specified (41)	50	0.05
Other Asian, not specified (192)	345	0.31
Australian	121	0.11
Austrian	549	0.50
Basque	29	0.03
Belgian	108	0.10
Brazilian	41	0.04
British	1,227	1.12
Bulgarian	187	0.17
Canadian	936	0.86
Celtic	15	0.01
Croatian	173	0.16
Czech	668	0.61
Czechoslovakian	221	0.20
Danish	1,159	1.06
Dutch	1,763	1.61
Eastern European	170	0.16
English	13,993	12.82
Estonian	93	0.09
European	2,019	1.85
Finnish	660	0.60
French, except Basque	3,804	3.48
French Canadian	834	0.76
German	17,214	15.77
German Russian	10	0.01
Greek	410	0.38
Hawaii Native/Pacific Islander:	608	0.55
Melanesian: (15)	18	0.02
Fijian (15)	18	0.02
Micronesian: (52)	74	0.07
Guamanian/Chamorro (42)	60	0.05
Other Micronesian (10)	14	0.01
Polynesian: (158)	358	0.33
Native Hawaiian (92)	254	0.23
Samoan (42)	65	0.06
Tongan (17)	21	0.02
Other Polynesian (7)	18	0.02
Other Pac. Isl., specified	1	0.00
Other Pac. Isl., not spec. (24)	157	0.14
Hispanic or Latino:	5,827	5.32
Central American:	316	0.29
Costa Rican	25	0.02
Guatemalan	84	0.08
Honduran	59	0.05
Nicaraguan	16	0.01
Panamanian	19	0.02
Salvadoran	76	0.07
Other Central American	37	0.03
Cuban	105	0.10
Dominican Republic	26	0.02
Mexican	3,826	3.49
Puerto Rican	193	0.18
South American:	339	0.31
Argentinean	44	0.04
Bolivian	10	0.01
Chilean	36	0.03
Colombian	92	0.08
Ecuadorian	27	0.02
Peruvian	89	0.08
Uruguayan	3	0.00
Venezuelan	25	0.02
Other South American	13	0.01
Other Hispanic or Latino	1,022	0.93
Hungarian	539	0.49
Icelander	192	0.18
Iranian	897	0.82
Irish	11,256	10.31
Israeli	121	0.11
Italian	3,557	3.26
Latvian	155	0.14
Lithuanian	218	0.20
Luxemburger	10	0.01
Macedonian	7	0.01
Maltese	14	0.01
New Zealander	31	0.03
Northern European	412	0.38
Norwegian	5,149	4.72
Pennsylvania German	50	0.05
Polish	2,283	2.09
Portuguese	271	0.25
Romanian	559	0.51
Russian	2,547	2.33
Scandinavian	758	0.69
Scotch-Irish	1,904	1.74
Scottish	3,372	3.09
Serbian	67	0.06
Slavic	34	0.03
Slovak	96	0.09
Slovene	38	0.03
Swedish	3,874	3.55
Swiss	592	0.54
Turkish	137	0.13
Ukrainian	634	0.58
United States or American	3,677	3.37
Welsh	950	0.87
West Indian, excl. Hispanic:	145	0.13
British West Indian	7	0.01
Haitian	7	0.01
Jamaican	86	0.08
Trinidadian and Tobagonian	29	0.03
West Indian	16	0.01
White:	84,329	76.96
Not Hispanic (78,698)	81,288	74.19
Hispanic (2,743)	3,041	2.78
Yugoslavian	421	0.39

Bellingham

Place Type: City
County: Whatcom
Population: 67,171

Ancestry/Race	Number	%
Acadian/Cajun	7	0.01
African American/Black:	1,092	1.63
Not Hispanic (622)	1,011	1.51
Hispanic (33)	81	0.12
African, sub-Saharan:	150	0.22
African	106	0.16
South African	21	0.03
Other sub-Saharan African	23	0.03
Alaska Native tribes, specified:	189	0.28
Alaska Athabascan (11)	16	0.02
Aleut (30)	56	0.08
Eskimo (19)	32	0.05
Tlingit-Haida (35)	65	0.10
All other tribes (12)	20	0.03
Alaska Native tribes, not specified	19	0.03
Am. Ind. or Alaska Nat., not spec.	432	0.64
Albanian	15	0.02
Alsatian	8	0.01
American Indian tribes, specified:	1,007	1.50
Apache (3)	11	0.02
Blackfeet (15)	38	0.06
Cherokee (22)	107	0.16
Cheyenne (2)	2	0.00
Chickasaw (3)	4	0.01
Chippewa (19)	39	0.06
Choctaw (11)	32	0.05
Colville (5)	10	0.01
Comanche (1)	2	0.00
Cree (4)	10	0.01
Creek (6)	11	0.02
Crow (1)	7	0.01
Delaware	1	0.00
Iroquois (15)	23	0.03
Latin American Indians (9)	26	0.04
Lumbee (2)	5	0.01
Menominee (1)	1	0.00
Navajo (14)	18	0.03
Osage	2	0.00
Ottawa	1	0.00
Paiute (1)	1	0.00
Potawatomi (3)	4	0.01
Pueblo (4)	6	0.01
Puget Sound Salish (84)	135	0.20
Seminole	1	0.00
Shoshone (2)	2	0.00
Sioux (12)	31	0.05
Yakama (5)	15	0.02
Yaqui	1	0.00
All other tribes (323)	461	0.69
American Indian tribes, not spec.	79	0.12
Arab:	245	0.37
Arab/Arabic	24	0.04
Lebanese	121	0.18
Syrian	61	0.09
Other Arab	39	0.06
Armenian	16	0.02
Asian:	3,771	5.61
Cambodian (81)	90	0.13
Chinese, ex. Taiwanese (430)	595	0.89
Filipino (329)	552	0.82
Hmong (1)	1	0.00
Indian (401)	463	0.69
Indonesian (9)	20	0.03
Japanese (330)	559	0.83
Korean (394)	510	0.76
Laotian (19)	23	0.03
Malaysian (4)	6	0.01
Pakistani (16)	27	0.04
Taiwanese (66)	79	0.12
Thai (34)	49	0.07
Vietnamese (608)	669	1.00
Other Asian, specified (7)	20	0.03
Other Asian, not specified (50)	108	0.16

Notes: 1. Figures in the "Number" column do not add up to the total population due to: a) Ancestry/Race overlap — e.g. persons can report being both White and Irish, b) persons of Hispanic origin can report being any race, c) persons reporting two ancestries are counted in both categories. 2. Numbers in parentheses indicate the number of persons reporting this ancestry/race alone, not in combination with any other ancestry/race. 3. Refer to the Explanation of Data in the front of the book for more detailed information.

Assyrian/Chaldean/Syriac	7	0.01
Australian	52	0.08
Austrian	245	0.37
Basque	35	0.05
Belgian	72	0.11
Brazilian	14	0.02
British	635	0.95
Bulgarian	26	0.04
Canadian	625	0.94
Celtic	50	0.07
Croatian	167	0.25
Czech	189	0.28
Czechoslovakian	148	0.22
Danish	833	1.25
Dutch	2,328	3.48
Eastern European	89	0.13
English	8,761	13.11
Estonian	18	0.03
European	1,416	2.12
Finnish	292	0.44
French, except Basque	2,349	3.52
French Canadian	618	0.92
German	12,880	19.28
Greek	258	0.39
Hawaii Native/Pacific Islander:	272	0.40
Melanesian: (9)	10	0.01
Fijian (9)	10	0.01
Micronesian: (31)	46	0.07
Guamanian/Chamorro (31)	43	0.06
Other Micronesian	3	0.00
Polynesian: (67)	161	0.24
Native Hawaiian (33)	105	0.16
Samoan (32)	49	0.07
Tongan (1)	1	0.00
Other Polynesian (1)	6	0.01
Other Pac. Isl., specified	12	0.02
Other Pac. Isl., not spec. (6)	43	0.06
Hispanic or Latino:	3,111	4.63
Central American:	171	0.25
Costa Rican	16	0.02
Guatemalan	48	0.07
Honduran	18	0.03
Nicaraguan	11	0.02
Panamanian	14	0.02
Salvadoran	56	0.08
Other Central American	8	0.01
Cuban	43	0.06
Dominican Republic	9	0.01
Mexican	2,066	3.08
Puerto Rican	138	0.21
South American:	99	0.15
Argentinean	7	0.01
Bolivian	7	0.01
Chilean	12	0.02
Colombian	32	0.05
Ecuadorian	7	0.01
Peruvian	19	0.03
Venezuelan	12	0.02
Other South American	3	0.00
Other Hispanic or Latino	585	0.87
Hungarian	282	0.42
Icelander	238	0.36
Iranian	48	0.07
Irish	8,186	12.25
Italian	2,233	3.34
Latvian	19	0.03
Lithuanian	124	0.19
Luxemburger	19	0.03
Macedonian	19	0.03
New Zealander	39	0.06
Northern European	206	0.31
Norwegian	5,024	7.52
Pennsylvania German	27	0.04
Polish	1,224	1.83
Portuguese	169	0.25
Romanian	94	0.14
Russian	694	1.04
Scandinavian	574	0.86
Scotch-Irish	1,858	2.78
Scottish	3,086	4.62
Slavic	50	0.07
Slovak	48	0.07
Slovene	51	0.08
Swedish	2,913	4.36
Swiss	342	0.51
Turkish	43	0.06
Ukrainian	499	0.75
United States or American	2,938	4.40
Welsh	1,001	1.50
West Indian, excl. Hispanic:	89	0.13
Haitian	7	0.01
Jamaican	66	0.10
West Indian	16	0.02
White:	60,832	90.56
Not Hispanic (57,684)	59,221	88.16
Hispanic (1,347)	1,611	2.40
Yugoslavian	132	0.20

Bothell

Place Type: City
County: King
Population: 30,150

Ancestry/Race	Number	%
Afghan	21	0.07
African American/Black:	511	1.69
Not Hispanic (341)	490	1.63
Hispanic (9)	21	0.07
African, sub-Saharan:	77	0.26
African	34	0.11
Ethiopian	14	0.05
South African	22	0.07
Other sub-Saharan African	7	0.02
Alaska Native tribes, specified:	58	0.19
Alaska Athabascan (4)	8	0.03
Aleut (9)	22	0.07
Eskimo (6)	8	0.03
Tlingit-Haida (10)	16	0.05
All other tribes	4	0.01
Alaska Native tribes, not specified	3	0.01
Am. Ind. or Alaska Nat., not spec.	96	0.32
American Indian tribes, specified:	211	0.70
Apache (2)	2	0.01
Blackfeet (4)	11	0.04
Cherokee (10)	41	0.14
Chickasaw	2	0.01
Chippewa (9)	18	0.06
Choctaw (7)	7	0.02
Colville (1)	3	0.01
Cree (1)	5	0.02
Creek (1)	9	0.03
Crow	2	0.01
Iroquois (2)	8	0.03
Kiowa (1)	2	0.01
Latin American Indians	1	0.00
Navajo (10)	11	0.04
Paiute (1)	1	0.00
Potawatomi (1)	3	0.01
Pueblo (3)	3	0.01
Puget Sound Salish (6)	16	0.05
Seminole	6	0.02
Sioux (9)	12	0.04
Yakama (2)	3	0.01
All other tribes (32)	45	0.15
American Indian tribes, not spec.	23	0.08
Arab:	171	0.57
Arab/Arabic	30	0.10
Lebanese	76	0.25
Palestinian	37	0.12
Syrian	28	0.09
Armenian	55	0.18
Asian:	2,294	7.61
Cambodian (39)	48	0.16
Chinese, ex. Taiwanese (452)	552	1.83
Filipino (265)	408	1.35
Hmong (1)	1	0.00
Indian (180)	220	0.73
Indonesian (11)	17	0.06
Japanese (206)	347	1.15
Korean (253)	277	0.92
Laotian (13)	15	0.05
Malaysian	1	0.00
Pakistani (10)	12	0.04
Taiwanese (23)	29	0.10
Thai (25)	34	0.11
Vietnamese (224)	256	0.85
Other Asian, specified (9)	10	0.03
Other Asian, not specified (39)	67	0.22
Australian	36	0.12
Austrian	233	0.78
Basque	6	0.02
Belgian	34	0.11
Brazilian	13	0.04
British	268	0.90
Canadian	92	0.31
Celtic	14	0.05
Croatian	14	0.05
Czech	161	0.54
Czechoslovakian	46	0.15
Danish	423	1.42
Dutch	904	3.03
Eastern European	9	0.03
English	4,317	14.45
Estonian	7	0.02
European	564	1.89
Finnish	167	0.56
French, except Basque	1,231	4.12
French Canadian	224	0.75
German	5,771	19.32
Greek	94	0.31
Hawaii Native/Pacific Islander:	181	0.60
Melanesian: (15)	15	0.05
Fijian (15)	15	0.05
Micronesian: (11)	23	0.08
Guamanian/Chamorro (11)	23	0.08
Polynesian: (33)	93	0.31
Native Hawaiian (18)	67	0.22
Samoan (12)	21	0.07
Tongan (3)	4	0.01
Other Polynesian	1	0.00
Other Pac. Isl., not spec. (3)	50	0.17
Hispanic or Latino:	1,338	4.44
Central American:	38	0.13
Costa Rican	2	0.01
Guatemalan	9	0.03
Honduran	3	0.01
Nicaraguan	9	0.03
Panamanian	7	0.02
Salvadoran	5	0.02
Other Central American	3	0.01
Cuban	25	0.08
Mexican	888	2.95
Puerto Rican	58	0.19
South American:	88	0.29
Argentinean	5	0.02
Bolivian	1	0.00
Chilean	14	0.05
Colombian	24	0.08
Ecuadorian	10	0.03
Peruvian	18	0.06
Uruguayan	6	0.02
Venezuelan	7	0.02
Other South American	3	0.01
Other Hispanic or Latino	241	0.80
Hungarian	150	0.50
Icelander	21	0.07
Iranian	57	0.19
Irish	3,802	12.73
Italian	1,239	4.15
Lithuanian	66	0.22
Luxemburger	11	0.04
New Zealander	27	0.09
Northern European	162	0.54
Norwegian	2,555	8.55
Pennsylvania German	38	0.13
Polish	495	1.66
Portuguese	86	0.29
Romanian	70	0.23
Russian	340	1.14

Notes: 1. Figures in the "Number" column do not add up to the total population due to: a) Ancestry/Race overlap — e.g. persons can report being both White and Irish, b) persons of Hispanic origin can report being any race, c) persons reporting two ancestries are counted in both categories. 2. Numbers in parentheses indicate the number of persons reporting this ancestry/race alone, not in combination with any other ancestry/race. 3. Refer to the Explanation of Data in the front of the book for more detailed information.

Scandinavian	177	0.59
Scotch-Irish	807	2.70
Scottish	1,033	3.46
Serbian	13	0.04
Slavic	35	0.12
Slovak	22	0.07
Slovene	11	0.04
Swedish	1,463	4.90
Swiss	157	0.53
Turkish	8	0.03
Ukrainian	233	0.78
United States or American	1,192	3.99
Welsh	666	2.23
West Indian, excl. Hispanic:	16	0.05
Jamaican	9	0.03
West Indian	7	0.02
White:	27,117	89.94
Not Hispanic (25,581)	26,288	87.19
Hispanic (735)	829	2.75
Yugoslavian	83	0.28

Bremerton

Place Type: City
County: Kitsap
Population: 37,259

Ancestry/Race	Number	%
Acadian/Cajun	12	0.03
African American/Black:	3,509	9.42
Not Hispanic (2,723)	3,329	8.93
Hispanic (70)	180	0.48
African, sub-Saharan:	202	0.55
African	200	0.54
Nigerian	2	0.01
Alaska Native tribes, specified:	70	0.19
Alaska Athabascan (5)	6	0.02
Aleut (7)	12	0.03
Eskimo (9)	14	0.04
Tlingit-Haida (20)	33	0.09
All other tribes (1)	5	0.01
Alaska Native tribes, not specified	8	0.02
Am. Ind. or Alaska Nat., not spec.	409	1.10
American Indian tribes, specified:	1,047	2.81
Apache (15)	42	0.11
Blackfeet (22)	57	0.15
Cherokee (63)	273	0.73
Cheyenne (3)	12	0.03
Chickasaw (2)	10	0.03
Chippewa (25)	49	0.13
Choctaw (9)	32	0.09
Colville (11)	12	0.03
Comanche	1	0.00
Cree (2)	8	0.02
Creek (1)	4	0.01
Crow (2)	6	0.02
Delaware (3)	4	0.01
Iroquois (3)	11	0.03
Latin American Indians (17)	31	0.08
Navajo (21)	33	0.09
Osage	3	0.01
Ottawa (1)	5	0.01
Paiute	4	0.01
Potawatomi (1)	12	0.03
Pueblo (4)	7	0.02
Puget Sound Salish (52)	64	0.17
Seminole	8	0.02
Shoshone (1)	12	0.03
Sioux (45)	84	0.23
Tohono O'Odham	1	0.00
Ute	1	0.00
Yakama (3)	8	0.02
Yaqui	1	0.00
All other tribes (154)	252	0.68
American Indian tribes, not spec.	66	0.18
Arab:	197	0.53
Arab/Arabic	34	0.09
Lebanese	58	0.16
Syrian	6	0.02
Other Arab	99	0.27
Asian:	3,037	8.15
Cambodian (2)	2	0.01
Chinese, ex. Taiwanese (83)	147	0.39
Filipino (1,454)	2,086	5.60
Indian (44)	64	0.17
Indonesian (12)	18	0.05
Japanese (124)	270	0.72
Korean (88)	150	0.40
Laotian (3)	6	0.02
Malaysian (10)	14	0.04
Sri Lankan	1	0.00
Taiwanese (2)	3	0.01
Thai (20)	35	0.09
Vietnamese (150)	177	0.48
Other Asian, specified (2)	5	0.01
Other Asian, not specified (22)	59	0.16
Australian	36	0.10
Austrian	100	0.27
Basque	35	0.09
Belgian	5	0.01
Brazilian	10	0.03
British	172	0.46
Bulgarian	34	0.09
Canadian	121	0.33
Celtic	92	0.25
Croatian	48	0.13
Czech	116	0.31
Czechoslovakian	45	0.12
Danish	375	1.01
Dutch	888	2.40
Eastern European	11	0.03
English	3,883	10.48
European	367	0.99
Finnish	165	0.45
French, except Basque	1,511	4.08
French Canadian	290	0.78
German	6,627	17.88
Greek	51	0.14
Hawaii Native/Pacific Islander:	630	1.69
Micronesian: (208)	317	0.85
Guamanian/Chamorro (185)	285	0.76
Other Micronesian (23)	32	0.09
Polynesian: (107)	228	0.61
Native Hawaiian (71)	150	0.40
Samoan (32)	70	0.19
Tongan (4)	6	0.02
Other Polynesian	2	0.01
Other Pac. Isl., specified	2	0.01
Other Pac. Isl., not spec. (25)	83	0.22
Hispanic or Latino:	2,457	6.59
Central American:	125	0.34
Costa Rican	6	0.02
Guatemalan	72	0.19
Honduran	14	0.04
Nicaraguan	3	0.01
Panamanian	16	0.04
Salvadoran	9	0.02
Other Central American	5	0.01
Cuban	44	0.12
Dominican Republic	7	0.02
Mexican	1,415	3.80
Puerto Rican	296	0.79
South American:	44	0.12
Argentinean	1	0.00
Bolivian	1	0.00
Chilean	7	0.02
Colombian	15	0.04
Ecuadorian	6	0.02
Peruvian	5	0.01
Venezuelan	7	0.02
Other South American	2	0.01
Other Hispanic or Latino	526	1.41
Hungarian	48	0.13
Icelander	21	0.06
Irish	4,476	12.08
Italian	1,500	4.05
Latvian	5	0.01
Lithuanian	60	0.16
Luxemburger	19	0.05
Northern European	63	0.17
Norwegian	2,058	5.55
Pennsylvania German	10	0.03
Polish	509	1.37
Portuguese	82	0.22
Romanian	9	0.02
Russian	122	0.33
Scandinavian	178	0.48
Scotch-Irish	797	2.15
Scottish	915	2.47
Slovak	57	0.15
Slovene	15	0.04
Swedish	1,050	2.83
Swiss	33	0.09
Turkish	5	0.01
Ukrainian	78	0.21
United States or American	2,049	5.53
Welsh	386	1.04
West Indian, excl. Hispanic:	105	0.28
Belizean	6	0.02
Bermudan	21	0.06
British West Indian	12	0.03
Dutch West Indian	12	0.03
Haitian	8	0.02
Jamaican	29	0.08
Trinidadian and Tobagonian	6	0.02
West Indian	11	0.03
White:	29,951	80.39
Not Hispanic (26,950)	28,681	76.98
Hispanic (982)	1,270	3.41
Yugoslavian	12	0.03

Bryn Mawr-Skyway

Place Type: Census Designated Place
County: King
Population: 13,977

Ancestry/Race	Number	%
African American/Black:	3,860	27.62
Not Hispanic (3,501)	3,788	27.10
Hispanic (40)	72	0.52
African, sub-Saharan:	249	1.77
African	130	0.93
Ethiopian	68	0.48
Ghanian	22	0.16
Nigerian	29	0.21
Alaska Native tribes, specified:	24	0.17
Alaska Athabascan (2)	2	0.01
Aleut	2	0.01
Eskimo	3	0.02
Tlingit-Haida (8)	13	0.09
All other tribes (1)	4	0.03
Am. Ind. or Alaska Nat., not spec.	94	0.67
Albanian	9	0.06
American Indian tribes, specified:	141	1.01
Apache (2)	8	0.06
Blackfeet (3)	9	0.06
Cherokee (11)	23	0.16
Chippewa (5)	10	0.07
Choctaw	9	0.06
Colville (1)	1	0.01
Cree	1	0.01
Creek	1	0.01
Delaware	1	0.01
Iroquois (3)	4	0.03
Kiowa	3	0.02
Latin American Indians (4)	9	0.06
Potawatomi (4)	4	0.03
Puget Sound Salish (6)	12	0.09
Seminole	4	0.03
Sioux (4)	15	0.11
All other tribes (17)	27	0.19
American Indian tribes, not spec.	19	0.14
Arab:	7	0.05
Other Arab	7	0.05
Asian:	3,523	25.21
Cambodian (78)	88	0.63
Chinese, ex. Taiwanese (523)	626	4.48
Filipino (1,012)	1,203	8.61
Hmong (27)	28	0.20

Notes: 1. Figures in the "Number" column do not add up to the total population due to: a) Ancestry/Race overlap — e.g. persons can report being both White and Irish, b) persons of Hispanic origin can report being any race, c) persons reporting two ancestries are counted in both categories. 2. Numbers in parentheses indicate the number of persons reporting this ancestry/race alone, not in combination with any other ancestry/race. 3. Refer to the Explanation of Data in the front of the book for more detailed information.

Indian (34)	64	0.46
Indonesian	1	0.01
Japanese (402)	490	3.51
Korean (47)	58	0.41
Laotian (269)	319	2.28
Malaysian	1	0.01
Taiwanese (2)	2	0.01
Thai (9)	12	0.09
Vietnamese (511)	586	4.19
Other Asian, specified (2)	3	0.02
Other Asian, not specified (23)	42	0.30
Austrian	74	0.53
Belgian	16	0.11
British	62	0.44
Canadian	21	0.15
Celtic	19	0.14
Croatian	22	0.16
Czech	26	0.19
Czechoslovakian	9	0.06
Danish	69	0.49
Dutch	117	0.83
Eastern European	8	0.06
English	842	5.99
Estonian	6	0.04
European	112	0.80
Finnish	42	0.30
French, except Basque	388	2.76
French Canadian	36	0.26
German	1,377	9.80
Greek	8	0.06
Hawaii Native/Pacific Islander:	164	1.17
Melanesian: (1)	8	0.06
Fijian (1)	8	0.06
Micronesian: (1)	6	0.04
Guamanian/Chamorro	2	0.01
Other Micronesian (1)	4	0.03
Polynesian: (61)	119	0.85
Native Hawaiian (10)	31	0.22
Samoan (44)	70	0.50
Tongan (6)	17	0.12
Other Polynesian (1)	1	0.01
Other Pac. Isl., not spec. (7)	31	0.22
Hispanic or Latino:	635	4.54
Central American:	41	0.29
Costa Rican	1	0.01
Guatemalan	2	0.01
Honduran	4	0.03
Nicaraguan	10	0.07
Panamanian	4	0.03
Salvadoran	20	0.14
Cuban	9	0.06
Mexican	407	2.91
Puerto Rican	33	0.24
South American:	20	0.14
Chilean	15	0.11
Colombian	3	0.02
Uruguayan	1	0.01
Venezuelan	1	0.01
Other Hispanic or Latino	125	0.89
Hungarian	53	0.38
Icelander	14	0.10
Iranian	33	0.23
Irish	869	6.19
Italian	326	2.32
Northern European	26	0.19
Norwegian	492	3.50
Polish	169	1.20
Portuguese	97	0.69
Russian	48	0.34
Scandinavian	42	0.30
Scotch-Irish	235	1.67
Scottish	208	1.48
Slovene	8	0.06
Swedish	377	2.68
Swiss	49	0.35
Turkish	6	0.04
Ukrainian	31	0.22
United States or American	276	1.96
Welsh	82	0.58
West Indian, excl. Hispanic:	17	0.12
Trinidadian and Tobagonian	8	0.06
West Indian	9	0.06
White:	6,650	47.58
Not Hispanic (5,963)	6,384	45.68
Hispanic (220)	266	1.90
Yugoslavian	38	0.27

Burien

Place Type: City
County: King
Population: 31,881

Ancestry/Race	Number	%
African American/Black:	1,980	6.21
Not Hispanic (1,587)	1,893	5.94
Hispanic (51)	87	0.27
African, sub-Saharan:	239	0.75
African	149	0.47
Ethiopian	50	0.16
Nigerian	4	0.01
Senegalese	8	0.03
Somalian	20	0.06
Other sub-Saharan African	8	0.03
Alaska Native tribes, specified:	96	0.30
Alaska Athabascan (6)	8	0.03
Aleut (19)	23	0.07
Eskimo (4)	8	0.03
Tlingit-Haida (27)	45	0.14
All other tribes (8)	12	0.04
Alaska Native tribes, not specified	12	0.04
Am. Ind. or Alaska Nat., not spec.	241	0.76
Alsatian	8	0.03
American Indian tribes, specified:	458	1.44
Apache (1)	7	0.02
Blackfeet (22)	70	0.22
Cherokee (15)	76	0.24
Cheyenne (3)	3	0.01
Chickasaw	5	0.02
Chippewa (17)	34	0.11
Choctaw (5)	9	0.03
Colville (1)	3	0.01
Cree (3)	6	0.02
Creek (1)	1	0.00
Crow	3	0.01
Delaware (3)	4	0.01
Iroquois (1)	8	0.03
Kiowa	1	0.00
Latin American Indians (6)	11	0.03
Lumbee (2)	3	0.01
Navajo (6)	14	0.04
Osage	2	0.01
Potawatomi (1)	3	0.01
Pueblo (1)	1	0.00
Puget Sound Salish (17)	32	0.10
Seminole (1)	1	0.00
Shoshone	6	0.02
Sioux (16)	26	0.08
Tohono O'Odham	5	0.02
Ute	1	0.00
Yakama (4)	17	0.05
Yaqui	2	0.01
All other tribes (54)	104	0.33
American Indian tribes, not spec.	32	0.10
Arab:	78	0.25
Arab/Arabic	19	0.06
Iraqi	29	0.09
Lebanese	20	0.06
Other Arab	10	0.03
Armenian	13	0.04
Asian:	2,823	8.85
Bangladeshi (2)	2	0.01
Cambodian (178)	217	0.68
Chinese, ex. Taiwanese (171)	273	0.86
Filipino (496)	691	2.17
Hmong (12)	18	0.06
Indian (169)	192	0.60
Indonesian (2)	7	0.02
Japanese (178)	271	0.85
Korean (220)	260	0.82
Laotian (55)	63	0.20
Pakistani (12)	12	0.04
Taiwanese (1)	1	0.00
Thai (18)	26	0.08
Vietnamese (621)	669	2.10
Other Asian, specified (3)	6	0.02
Other Asian, not specified (33)	115	0.36
Australian	5	0.02
Austrian	98	0.31
Belgian	31	0.10
Brazilian	14	0.04
British	234	0.74
Bulgarian	8	0.03
Canadian	101	0.32
Celtic	15	0.05
Croatian	79	0.25
Czech	135	0.43
Czechoslovakian	45	0.14
Danish	362	1.14
Dutch	636	2.00
English	3,600	11.34
Estonian	6	0.02
European	334	1.05
Finnish	149	0.47
French, except Basque	1,122	3.53
French Canadian	284	0.89
German	4,928	15.52
Greek	109	0.34
Hawaii Native/Pacific Islander:	551	1.73
Melanesian: (10)	10	0.03
Fijian (10)	10	0.03
Micronesian: (29)	40	0.13
Guamanian/Chamorro (20)	30	0.09
Other Micronesian (9)	10	0.03
Polynesian: (294)	430	1.35
Native Hawaiian (20)	92	0.29
Samoan (241)	296	0.93
Tongan (27)	32	0.10
Other Polynesian (6)	10	0.03
Other Pac. Isl., specified	2	0.01
Other Pac. Isl., not spec. (26)	69	0.22
Hispanic or Latino:	3,397	10.66
Central American:	200	0.63
Costa Rican	17	0.05
Guatemalan	52	0.16
Honduran	57	0.18
Nicaraguan	10	0.03
Panamanian	20	0.06
Salvadoran	31	0.10
Other Central American	13	0.04
Cuban	38	0.12
Dominican Republic	2	0.01
Mexican	2,459	7.71
Puerto Rican	90	0.28
South American:	108	0.34
Argentinean	8	0.03
Bolivian	3	0.01
Chilean	21	0.07
Colombian	26	0.08
Ecuadorian	5	0.02
Peruvian	23	0.07
Uruguayan	1	0.00
Venezuelan	8	0.03
Other South American	13	0.04
Other Hispanic or Latino	500	1.57
Hungarian	83	0.26
Icelander	17	0.05
Iranian	132	0.42
Irish	3,489	10.99
Israeli	6	0.02
Italian	1,045	3.29
Latvian	23	0.07
Lithuanian	47	0.15
Luxemburger	7	0.02
Macedonian	10	0.03
Northern European	128	0.40
Norwegian	2,021	6.37
Pennsylvania German	17	0.05
Polish	456	1.44
Portuguese	31	0.10

Notes: 1. Figures in the "Number" column do not add up to the total population due to: a) Ancestry/Race overlap — e.g. persons can report being both White and Irish, b) persons of Hispanic origin can report being any race, c) persons reporting two ancestries are counted in both categories. 2. Numbers in parentheses indicate the number of persons reporting this ancestry/race alone, not in combination with any other ancestry/race. 3. Refer to the Explanation of Data in the front of the book for more detailed information.

Ancestry/Race	Number	%
Romanian	106	0.33
Russian	252	0.79
Scandinavian	154	0.49
Scotch-Irish	692	2.18
Scottish	756	2.38
Slavic	9	0.03
Slovak	15	0.05
Swedish	1,249	3.93
Swiss	187	0.59
Turkish	22	0.07
Ukrainian	298	0.94
United States or American	1,199	3.78
Welsh	434	1.37
West Indian, excl. Hispanic:	31	0.10
Dutch West Indian	15	0.05
Jamaican	8	0.03
Trinidadian and Tobagonian	8	0.03
White:	25,241	79.17
Not Hispanic (22,799)	23,682	74.28
Hispanic (1,347)	1,559	4.89
Yugoslavian	228	0.72

Camano

Place Type: Census Designated Place
County: Island
Population: 13,347

Ancestry/Race	Number	%
African American/Black:	60	0.45
Not Hispanic (29)	54	0.40
Hispanic (4)	6	0.04
Alaska Native tribes, specified:	19	0.14
Alaska Athabascan (1)	1	0.01
Aleut (2)	3	0.02
Eskimo (1)	3	0.02
Tlingit-Haida (7)	11	0.08
All other tribes (1)	1	0.01
Alaska Native tribes, not specified	4	0.03
Am. Ind. or Alaska Nat., not spec.	63	0.47
American Indian tribes, specified:	135	1.01
Apache	2	0.01
Blackfeet (3)	13	0.10
Cherokee (12)	38	0.28
Cheyenne	1	0.01
Chickasaw (1)	1	0.01
Chippewa (2)	5	0.04
Choctaw (3)	16	0.12
Colville (1)	2	0.01
Comanche (2)	3	0.02
Delaware	1	0.01
Iroquois (3)	4	0.03
Latin American Indians (2)	5	0.04
Lumbee (1)	1	0.01
Potawatomi (1)	1	0.01
Pueblo (1)	1	0.01
Puget Sound Salish (10)	10	0.07
Seminole (1)	1	0.01
Sioux (9)	10	0.07
Yakama	2	0.01
Yuman	1	0.01
All other tribes (10)	17	0.13
American Indian tribes, not spec.	31	0.23
Armenian	6	0.04
Asian:	152	1.14
Cambodian (5)	8	0.06
Chinese, ex. Taiwanese (12)	17	0.13
Filipino (29)	50	0.37
Indian (4)	8	0.06
Japanese (17)	35	0.26
Korean (17)	25	0.19
Sri Lankan	1	0.01
Vietnamese (3)	3	0.02
Other Asian, specified	2	0.01
Other Asian, not specified	3	0.02
Australian	8	0.06
Austrian	40	0.30
Belgian	49	0.36
British	75	0.55
Canadian	77	0.57
Celtic	12	0.09
Croatian	14	0.10
Czech	86	0.64
Czechoslovakian	30	0.22
Danish	234	1.73
Dutch	424	3.13
English	2,303	17.02
European	216	1.60
Finnish	127	0.94
French, except Basque	637	4.71
French Canadian	185	1.37
German	2,915	21.55
Greek	111	0.82
Hawaii Native/Pacific Islander:	63	0.47
Micronesian: (10)	14	0.10
Guamanian/Chamorro (10)	14	0.10
Polynesian: (15)	27	0.20
Native Hawaiian (6)	17	0.13
Samoan (8)	9	0.07
Other Polynesian (1)	1	0.01
Other Pac. Isl., specified	2	0.01
Other Pac. Isl., not spec. (9)	20	0.15
Hispanic or Latino:	275	2.06
Central American:	10	0.07
Costa Rican	2	0.01
Guatemalan	1	0.01
Salvadoran	7	0.05
Cuban	22	0.16
Mexican	165	1.24
Puerto Rican	9	0.07
South American:	7	0.05
Argentinean	1	0.01
Colombian	3	0.02
Peruvian	3	0.02
Other Hispanic or Latino	62	0.46
Hungarian	22	0.16
Icelander	21	0.16
Irish	1,677	12.40
Italian	414	3.06
Lithuanian	62	0.46
Maltese	3	0.02
Northern European	84	0.62
Norwegian	1,548	11.44
Pennsylvania German	12	0.09
Polish	205	1.52
Portuguese	38	0.28
Russian	76	0.56
Scandinavian	149	1.10
Scotch-Irish	412	3.05
Scottish	692	5.11
Slavic	6	0.04
Slovak	13	0.10
Slovene	4	0.03
Swedish	956	7.07
Swiss	91	0.67
Turkish	9	0.07
Ukrainian	53	0.39
United States or American	606	4.48
Welsh	181	1.34
White:	12,988	97.31
Not Hispanic (12,576)	12,786	95.80
Hispanic (185)	202	1.51
Yugoslavian	33	0.24

Camas

Place Type: City
County: Clark
Population: 12,534

Ancestry/Race	Number	%
African American/Black:	118	0.94
Not Hispanic (82)	108	0.86
Hispanic (4)	10	0.08
African, sub-Saharan:	45	0.35
African	17	0.13
Kenyan	5	0.04
Nigerian	7	0.06
South African	16	0.13
Alaska Native tribes, specified:	7	0.06
Alaska Athabascan (1)	2	0.02
Aleut	3	0.02
Eskimo (1)	1	0.01
Tlingit-Haida (1)	1	0.01
Alaska Native tribes, not specified	1	0.01
Am. Ind. or Alaska Nat., not spec.	55	0.44
American Indian tribes, specified:	105	0.84
Apache	6	0.05
Blackfeet	4	0.03
Cherokee (17)	36	0.29
Cheyenne	1	0.01
Chickasaw	1	0.01
Chippewa (4)	9	0.07
Choctaw (4)	4	0.03
Creek	1	0.01
Iroquois (1)	8	0.06
Latin American Indians (2)	2	0.02
Navajo (1)	2	0.02
Pueblo (1)	1	0.01
Puget Sound Salish (5)	5	0.04
Sioux (3)	6	0.05
Yakama	1	0.01
All other tribes (14)	18	0.14
American Indian tribes, not spec.	10	0.08
Arab:	62	0.49
Iraqi	34	0.27
Palestinian	10	0.08
Other Arab	18	0.14
Armenian	7	0.06
Asian:	574	4.58
Cambodian (3)	8	0.06
Chinese, ex. Taiwanese (129)	161	1.28
Filipino (52)	93	0.74
Indian (37)	45	0.36
Indonesian	4	0.03
Japanese (62)	104	0.83
Korean (60)	75	0.60
Laotian (5)	5	0.04
Malaysian	1	0.01
Pakistani	1	0.01
Taiwanese (11)	12	0.10
Thai (2)	2	0.02
Vietnamese (44)	44	0.35
Other Asian, specified (4)	5	0.04
Other Asian, not specified (8)	14	0.11
Australian	12	0.09
Austrian	70	0.55
Basque	7	0.06
Belgian	5	0.04
British	69	0.54
Canadian	60	0.47
Celtic	16	0.13
Croatian	11	0.09
Czech	63	0.50
Czechoslovakian	66	0.52
Danish	313	2.47
Dutch	255	2.01
English	1,672	13.18
European	227	1.79
Finnish	60	0.47
French, except Basque	544	4.29
French Canadian	100	0.79
German	2,693	21.23
Greek	6	0.05
Hawaii Native/Pacific Islander:	45	0.36
Micronesian: (3)	3	0.02
Guamanian/Chamorro (2)	2	0.02
Other Micronesian (1)	1	0.01
Polynesian: (7)	24	0.19
Native Hawaiian (3)	18	0.14
Samoan (3)	5	0.04
Other Polynesian (1)	1	0.01
Other Pac. Isl., not spec. (8)	18	0.14
Hispanic or Latino:	359	2.86
Central American:	11	0.09
Guatemalan	3	0.02
Panamanian	1	0.01
Salvadoran	7	0.06
Cuban	11	0.09
Mexican	216	1.72

Notes: 1. Figures in the "Number" column do not add up to the total population due to: a) Ancestry/Race overlap — e.g. persons can report being both White and Irish, b) persons of Hispanic origin can report being any race, c) persons reporting two ancestries are counted in both categories. 2. Numbers in parentheses indicate the number of persons reporting this ancestry/race alone, not in combination with any other ancestry/race. 3. Refer to the Explanation of Data in the front of the book for more detailed information.

Ancestry/Race	Number	%
Puerto Rican	15	0.12
South American:	13	0.10
Argentinean	6	0.05
Chilean	1	0.01
Colombian	1	0.01
Ecuadorian	1	0.01
Peruvian	4	0.03
Other Hispanic or Latino	93	0.74
Iranian	17	0.13
Irish	1,441	11.36
Italian	368	2.90
Latvian	12	0.09
Northern European	31	0.24
Norwegian	621	4.90
Polish	301	2.37
Portuguese	33	0.26
Romanian	5	0.04
Russian	71	0.56
Scandinavian	46	0.36
Scotch-Irish	384	3.03
Scottish	484	3.82
Slavic	8	0.06
Slovak	10	0.08
Slovene	12	0.09
Swedish	373	2.94
Swiss	62	0.49
Ukrainian	31	0.24
United States or American	958	7.55
Welsh	192	1.51
White:	11,782	94.00
Not Hispanic (11,318)	11,537	92.05
Hispanic (214)	245	1.95
Yugoslavian	7	0.06

Cascade-Fairwood

Place Type: Census Designated Place
County: King
Population: 34,580

Ancestry/Race	Number	%
African American/Black:	2,522	7.29
Not Hispanic (2,088)	2,456	7.10
Hispanic (19)	66	0.19
African, sub-Saharan:	379	1.10
African	193	0.56
Ethiopian	37	0.11
Kenyan	5	0.01
Nigerian	58	0.17
Somalian	41	0.12
Other sub-Saharan African	45	0.13
Alaska Native tribes, specified:	47	0.14
Alaska Athabascan (5)	5	0.01
Aleut (2)	3	0.01
Eskimo (3)	4	0.01
Tlingit-Haida (12)	33	0.10
All other tribes (1)	2	0.01
Alaska Native tribes, not specified	1	0.00
Am. Ind. or Alaska Nat., not spec.	164	0.47
Albanian	8	0.02
American Indian tribes, specified:	285	0.82
Apache (1)	4	0.01
Blackfeet (2)	18	0.05
Cherokee (16)	79	0.23
Chickasaw (1)	2	0.01
Chippewa (21)	31	0.09
Choctaw (6)	14	0.04
Colville (1)	1	0.00
Comanche	2	0.01
Cree (1)	1	0.00
Creek (1)	5	0.01
Crow	3	0.01
Delaware (2)	3	0.01
Iroquois (1)	5	0.01
Latin American Indians (2)	9	0.03
Lumbee (2)	3	0.01
Navajo (3)	3	0.01
Paiute (1)	2	0.01
Potawatomi	5	0.01
Pueblo (1)	1	0.00
Puget Sound Salish (11)	24	0.07
Seminole (1)	1	0.00
Sioux (8)	18	0.05
Ute	1	0.00
Yakama	1	0.00
All other tribes (21)	49	0.14
American Indian tribes, not spec.	52	0.15
Arab:	72	0.21
Arab/Arabic	31	0.09
Egyptian	9	0.03
Lebanese	18	0.05
Other Arab	14	0.04
Asian:	5,592	16.17
Cambodian (103)	116	0.34
Chinese, ex. Taiwanese (907)	1,112	3.22
Filipino (1,179)	1,511	4.37
Hmong (7)	9	0.03
Indian (517)	585	1.69
Indonesian (9)	11	0.03
Japanese (484)	724	2.09
Korean (373)	455	1.32
Laotian (101)	110	0.32
Malaysian (2)	4	0.01
Pakistani (6)	11	0.03
Sri Lankan (5)	5	0.01
Taiwanese (36)	44	0.13
Thai (26)	33	0.10
Vietnamese (700)	765	2.21
Other Asian, specified (16)	25	0.07
Other Asian, not specified (49)	72	0.21
Australian	52	0.15
Austrian	80	0.23
Basque	9	0.03
Belgian	34	0.10
British	185	0.54
Bulgarian	10	0.03
Canadian	261	0.76
Croatian	6	0.02
Czech	131	0.38
Czechoslovakian	37	0.11
Danish	477	1.39
Dutch	544	1.58
Eastern European	12	0.03
English	4,158	12.08
Estonian	27	0.08
European	624	1.81
Finnish	137	0.40
French, except Basque	1,335	3.88
French Canadian	282	0.82
German	5,954	17.29
German Russian	8	0.02
Greek	199	0.58
Hawaii Native/Pacific Islander:	313	0.91
Melanesian: (12)	17	0.05
Fijian (12)	17	0.05
Micronesian: (30)	37	0.11
Guamanian/Chamorro (21)	28	0.08
Other Micronesian (9)	9	0.03
Polynesian: (98)	198	0.57
Native Hawaiian (42)	115	0.33
Samoan (47)	64	0.19
Tongan (8)	15	0.04
Other Polynesian (1)	4	0.01
Other Pac. Isl., not spec. (11)	61	0.18
Hispanic or Latino:	1,420	4.11
Central American:	52	0.15
Costa Rican	8	0.02
Guatemalan	11	0.03
Honduran	4	0.01
Nicaraguan	1	0.00
Panamanian	8	0.02
Salvadoran	20	0.06
Cuban	27	0.08
Dominican Republic	4	0.01
Mexican	848	2.45
Puerto Rican	99	0.29
South American:	69	0.20
Argentinean	3	0.01
Bolivian	3	0.01
Chilean	7	0.02
Colombian	18	0.05
Ecuadorian	5	0.01
Peruvian	12	0.03
Uruguayan	4	0.01
Venezuelan	9	0.03
Other South American	8	0.02
Other Hispanic or Latino	321	0.93
Hungarian	146	0.42
Icelander	41	0.12
Iranian	8	0.02
Irish	3,368	9.78
Israeli	7	0.02
Italian	1,079	3.13
Latvian	11	0.03
Lithuanian	25	0.07
Luxemburger	39	0.11
New Zealander	12	0.03
Northern European	107	0.31
Norwegian	2,155	6.26
Pennsylvania German	7	0.02
Polish	538	1.56
Portuguese	14	0.04
Romanian	26	0.08
Russian	297	0.86
Scandinavian	330	0.96
Scotch-Irish	600	1.74
Scottish	1,013	2.94
Serbian	19	0.06
Slovak	21	0.06
Slovene	38	0.11
Swedish	1,226	3.56
Swiss	115	0.33
Turkish	25	0.07
Ukrainian	339	0.98
United States or American	1,498	4.35
Welsh	354	1.03
West Indian, excl. Hispanic:	43	0.12
Trinidadian and Tobagonian	10	0.03
West Indian	33	0.10
White:	26,515	76.68
Not Hispanic (24,624)	25,749	74.46
Hispanic (603)	766	2.22
Yugoslavian	57	0.17

Centralia

Place Type: City
County: Lewis
Population: 14,742

Ancestry/Race	Number	%
African American/Black:	101	0.69
Not Hispanic (50)	76	0.52
Hispanic (15)	25	0.17
African, sub-Saharan:	17	0.12
African	17	0.12
Alaska Native tribes, specified:	18	0.12
Alaska Athabascan	3	0.02
Aleut (4)	5	0.03
Eskimo (4)	4	0.03
Tlingit-Haida (2)	5	0.03
All other tribes	1	0.01
Alaska Native tribes, not specified	2	0.01
Am. Ind. or Alaska Nat., not spec.	91	0.62
American Indian tribes, specified:	215	1.46
Apache (1)	1	0.01
Blackfeet (4)	12	0.08
Cherokee (24)	54	0.37
Cheyenne	3	0.02
Chickasaw	2	0.01
Chippewa (2)	3	0.02
Choctaw	1	0.01
Colville (3)	4	0.03
Cree	1	0.01
Creek (1)	1	0.01
Crow (2)	2	0.01
Iroquois (2)	3	0.02
Latin American Indians (4)	6	0.04
Menominee (2)	2	0.01
Navajo	1	0.01

Notes: 1. Figures in the "Number" column do not add up to the total population due to: a) Ancestry/Race overlap — e.g. persons can report being both White and Irish, b) persons of Hispanic origin can report being any race, c) persons reporting two ancestries are counted in both categories. 2. Numbers in parentheses indicate the number of persons reporting this ancestry/race alone, not in combination with any other ancestry/race. 3. Refer to the Explanation of Data in the front of the book for more detailed information.

Ottawa (1)	1	0.01
Pueblo (3)	5	0.03
Puget Sound Salish (8)	14	0.09
Shoshone (1)	1	0.01
Sioux (1)	8	0.05
Ute	1	0.01
Yakama (3)	6	0.04
All other tribes (59)	83	0.56
American Indian tribes, not spec.	9	0.06
Armenian	7	0.05
Asian:	190	1.29
Cambodian (1)	1	0.01
Chinese, ex. Taiwanese (28)	33	0.22
Filipino (20)	42	0.28
Indian (16)	18	0.12
Japanese (5)	15	0.10
Korean (38)	48	0.33
Laotian (8)	8	0.05
Malaysian (1)	1	0.01
Thai (2)	2	0.01
Vietnamese (8)	10	0.07
Other Asian, not specified (10)	12	0.08
Australian	17	0.12
Austrian	46	0.31
Belgian	54	0.37
British	52	0.35
Bulgarian	4	0.03
Canadian	80	0.54
Croatian	25	0.17
Czech	64	0.43
Czechoslovakian	12	0.08
Danish	190	1.29
Dutch	282	1.92
English	1,677	11.39
European	179	1.22
Finnish	210	1.43
French, except Basque	575	3.91
French Canadian	154	1.05
German	2,568	17.45
Greek	58	0.39
Hawaii Native/Pacific Islander:	85	0.58
Melanesian:	2	0.01
Fijian	2	0.01
Micronesian: (8)	17	0.12
Guamanian/Chamorro (8)	17	0.12
Polynesian: (36)	59	0.40
Native Hawaiian (10)	31	0.21
Samoan (26)	27	0.18
Other Polynesian	1	0.01
Other Pac. Isl., not spec.	7	0.05
Hispanic or Latino:	1,506	10.22
Central American:	65	0.44
Guatemalan	3	0.02
Honduran	9	0.06
Panamanian	4	0.03
Salvadoran	49	0.33
Cuban	4	0.03
Mexican	1,235	8.38
Puerto Rican	18	0.12
South American:	9	0.06
Argentinean	4	0.03
Bolivian	2	0.01
Colombian	2	0.01
Ecuadorian	1	0.01
Other Hispanic or Latino	175	1.19
Hungarian	6	0.04
Irish	1,669	11.34
Italian	390	2.65
Latvian	23	0.16
Lithuanian	28	0.19
Northern European	41	0.28
Norwegian	600	4.08
Pennsylvania German	15	0.10
Polish	287	1.95
Portuguese	25	0.17
Russian	90	0.61
Scandinavian	60	0.41
Scotch-Irish	367	2.49
Scottish	420	2.85
Slavic	6	0.04
Swedish	616	4.18
Swiss	76	0.52
Ukrainian	27	0.18
United States or American	770	5.23
Welsh	107	0.73
West Indian, excl. Hispanic:	7	0.05
Dutch West Indian	7	0.05
White:	13,553	91.93
Not Hispanic (12,577)	12,806	86.87
Hispanic (655)	747	5.07

Cottage Lake

Place Type: Census Designated Place
County: King
Population: 24,330

Ancestry/Race	Number	%
African American/Black:	242	0.99
Not Hispanic (152)	236	0.97
Hispanic (2)	6	0.02
African, sub-Saharan:	84	0.35
African	79	0.33
Ethiopian	5	0.02
Alaska Native tribes, specified:	28	0.12
Alaska Athabascan (1)	3	0.01
Aleut (2)	2	0.01
Eskimo (2)	6	0.02
Tlingit-Haida (3)	11	0.05
All other tribes (2)	6	0.02
Alaska Native tribes, not specified	10	0.04
Am. Ind. or Alaska Nat., not spec.	47	0.19
American Indian tribes, specified:	102	0.42
Apache	1	0.00
Blackfeet	5	0.02
Cherokee (5)	25	0.10
Cheyenne	1	0.00
Chippewa (3)	5	0.02
Choctaw	2	0.01
Colville (3)	3	0.01
Cree (3)	4	0.02
Creek	1	0.00
Iroquois (2)	5	0.02
Latin American Indians (1)	5	0.02
Lumbee	1	0.00
Navajo (1)	3	0.01
Osage (3)	4	0.02
Paiute	1	0.00
Potawatomi	1	0.00
Puget Sound Salish (5)	10	0.04
Seminole (1)	1	0.00
Shoshone	1	0.00
Sioux (3)	3	0.01
Yakama (1)	1	0.00
All other tribes (11)	19	0.08
American Indian tribes, not spec.	17	0.07
Arab:	69	0.28
Lebanese	69	0.28
Armenian	33	0.14
Asian:	1,337	5.50
Cambodian (4)	4	0.02
Chinese, ex. Taiwanese (226)	314	1.29
Filipino (75)	180	0.74
Hmong (3)	3	0.01
Indian (110)	122	0.50
Indonesian (3)	6	0.02
Japanese (191)	331	1.36
Korean (151)	195	0.80
Laotian (10)	12	0.05
Malaysian (2)	2	0.01
Sri Lankan (7)	7	0.03
Taiwanese (38)	45	0.18
Thai (15)	24	0.10
Vietnamese (41)	48	0.20
Other Asian, specified (3)	8	0.03
Other Asian, not specified (12)	36	0.15
Austrian	65	0.27
Basque	13	0.05
Belgian	15	0.06
British	211	0.87
Bulgarian	35	0.14
Canadian	167	0.69
Celtic	10	0.04
Croatian	87	0.36
Cypriot	19	0.08
Czech	180	0.74
Czechoslovakian	20	0.08
Danish	354	1.46
Dutch	779	3.21
Eastern European	50	0.21
English	4,713	19.40
Estonian	8	0.03
European	465	1.91
Finnish	211	0.87
French, except Basque	1,045	4.30
French Canadian	161	0.66
German	5,462	22.48
Greek	97	0.40
Hawaii Native/Pacific Islander:	105	0.43
Melanesian: (3)	3	0.01
Fijian (3)	3	0.01
Micronesian: (10)	14	0.06
Guamanian/Chamorro (9)	12	0.05
Other Micronesian (1)	2	0.01
Polynesian: (26)	81	0.33
Native Hawaiian (21)	76	0.31
Samoan (3)	3	0.01
Other Polynesian (2)	2	0.01
Other Pac. Isl., not spec. (5)	7	0.03
Hispanic or Latino:	721	2.96
Central American:	22	0.09
Guatemalan	5	0.02
Honduran	2	0.01
Nicaraguan	7	0.03
Panamanian	1	0.00
Salvadoran	6	0.02
Other Central American	1	0.00
Cuban	31	0.13
Mexican	422	1.73
Puerto Rican	47	0.19
South American:	42	0.17
Argentinean	8	0.03
Chilean	9	0.04
Colombian	14	0.06
Ecuadorian	2	0.01
Peruvian	6	0.02
Venezuelan	1	0.00
Other South American	2	0.01
Other Hispanic or Latino	157	0.65
Hungarian	265	1.09
Icelander	20	0.08
Iranian	38	0.16
Irish	3,094	12.73
Italian	1,449	5.96
Latvian	15	0.06
Lithuanian	90	0.37
Northern European	160	0.66
Norwegian	1,903	7.83
Pennsylvania German	38	0.16
Polish	625	2.57
Portuguese	21	0.09
Romanian	43	0.18
Russian	249	1.02
Scandinavian	186	0.77
Scotch-Irish	673	2.77
Scottish	1,108	4.56
Serbian	26	0.11
Slavic	27	0.11
Slovak	52	0.21
Slovene	7	0.03
Swedish	1,122	4.62
Swiss	119	0.49
Turkish	8	0.03
Ukrainian	66	0.27
United States or American	965	3.97
Welsh	279	1.15
West Indian, excl. Hispanic:	34	0.14
Jamaican	34	0.14
White:	22,753	93.52
Not Hispanic (21,792)	22,301	91.66

Notes: 1. Figures in the "Number" column do not add up to the total population due to: a) Ancestry/Race overlap — e.g. persons can report being both White and Irish, b) persons of Hispanic origin can report being any race, c) persons reporting two ancestries are counted in both categories. 2. Numbers in parentheses indicate the number of persons reporting this ancestry/race alone, not in combination with any other ancestry/race. 3. Refer to the Explanation of Data in the front of the book for more detailed information.

Hispanic (366)	452	1.86
Yugoslavian	53	0.22

Covington

Place Type: City
County: King
Population: 13,783

Ancestry/Race	Number	%
African American/Black:	462	3.35
Not Hispanic (325)	431	3.13
Hispanic (11)	31	0.22
African, sub-Saharan:	5	0.04
African	5	0.04
Alaska Native tribes, specified:	28	0.20
Alaska Athabascan (1)	2	0.01
Aleut (3)	8	0.06
Eskimo (5)	5	0.04
Tlingit-Haida (5)	7	0.05
All other tribes (4)	6	0.04
Alaska Native tribes, not specified	2	0.01
Am. Ind. or Alaska Nat., not spec.	72	0.52
American Indian tribes, specified:	177	1.28
Blackfeet (1)	2	0.01
Cherokee (13)	49	0.36
Chickasaw	2	0.01
Chippewa (16)	28	0.20
Choctaw (2)	8	0.06
Colville (3)	4	0.03
Cree (1)	1	0.01
Crow	2	0.01
Iroquois	3	0.02
Latin American Indians	5	0.04
Menominee (1)	1	0.01
Navajo	1	0.01
Ottawa	1	0.01
Pima (1)	1	0.01
Potawatomi (3)	3	0.02
Puget Sound Salish (15)	20	0.15
Sioux (4)	13	0.09
Yakama (1)	1	0.01
All other tribes (15)	32	0.23
American Indian tribes, not spec.	26	0.19
Asian:	603	4.37
Cambodian (20)	20	0.15
Chinese, ex. Taiwanese (48)	73	0.53
Filipino (146)	213	1.55
Indian (22)	22	0.16
Indonesian (3)	7	0.05
Japanese (50)	103	0.75
Korean (48)	66	0.48
Pakistani (3)	7	0.05
Taiwanese (2)	3	0.02
Thai (7)	10	0.07
Vietnamese (50)	58	0.42
Other Asian, specified (3)	6	0.04
Other Asian, not specified (12)	15	0.11
Austrian	67	0.49
Belgian	26	0.19
British	77	0.56
Canadian	85	0.62
Croatian	5	0.04
Czech	69	0.50
Czechoslovakian	9	0.07
Danish	135	0.98
Dutch	251	1.82
Eastern European	7	0.05
English	1,971	14.32
European	443	3.22
Finnish	114	0.83
French, except Basque	591	4.29
French Canadian	185	1.34
German	2,815	20.45
Greek	10	0.07
Hawaii Native/Pacific Islander:	72	0.52
Micronesian: (1)	2	0.01
Guamanian/Chamorro (1)	2	0.01
Polynesian: (26)	57	0.41
Native Hawaiian (15)	35	0.25
Samoan (11)	20	0.15
Tongan	2	0.01
Other Pac. Isl., specified	2	0.01
Other Pac. Isl., not spec. (4)	11	0.08
Hispanic or Latino:	617	4.48
Central American:	11	0.08
Costa Rican	4	0.03
Nicaraguan	2	0.01
Panamanian	2	0.01
Salvadoran	3	0.02
Cuban	10	0.07
Mexican	392	2.84
Puerto Rican	52	0.38
South American:	23	0.17
Bolivian	2	0.01
Chilean	4	0.03
Colombian	13	0.09
Ecuadorian	1	0.01
Peruvian	2	0.01
Other South American	1	0.01
Other Hispanic or Latino	129	0.94
Hungarian	52	0.38
Iranian	29	0.21
Irish	1,538	11.17
Italian	653	4.74
Latvian	8	0.06
Lithuanian	32	0.23
Northern European	40	0.29
Norwegian	944	6.86
Pennsylvania German	16	0.12
Polish	280	2.03
Portuguese	72	0.52
Romanian	13	0.09
Russian	164	1.19
Scandinavian	54	0.39
Scotch-Irish	292	2.12
Scottish	446	3.24
Slovak	5	0.04
Swedish	499	3.62
Swiss	4	0.03
Ukrainian	44	0.32
United States or American	874	6.35
Welsh	224	1.63
White:	12,547	91.03
Not Hispanic (11,841)	12,184	88.40
Hispanic (271)	363	2.63
Yugoslavian	47	0.34

Des Moines

Place Type: City
County: King
Population: 29,267

Ancestry/Race	Number	%
African American/Black:	2,536	8.67
Not Hispanic (2,069)	2,473	8.45
Hispanic (37)	63	0.22
African, sub-Saharan:	412	1.40
African	222	0.75
Ethiopian	84	0.29
Kenyan	14	0.05
Somalian	54	0.18
South African	16	0.05
Other sub-Saharan African	22	0.07
Alaska Native tribes, specified:	84	0.29
Alaska Athabascan (9)	10	0.03
Aleut (10)	17	0.06
Eskimo (1)	4	0.01
Tlingit-Haida (19)	40	0.14
All other tribes (5)	13	0.04
Alaska Native tribes, not specified	1	0.00
Am. Ind. or Alaska Nat., not spec.	182	0.62
Alsatian	10	0.03
American Indian tribes, specified:	354	1.21
Apache (2)	9	0.03
Blackfeet (13)	36	0.12
Cherokee (23)	94	0.32
Cheyenne (1)	1	0.00
Chickasaw (1)	2	0.01
Chippewa (11)	25	0.09
Choctaw (1)	4	0.01
Colville (6)	8	0.03
Cree (1)	3	0.01
Creek	2	0.01
Crow (1)	5	0.02
Iroquois (2)	5	0.02
Latin American Indians (3)	3	0.01
Lumbee (1)	1	0.00
Navajo (1)	7	0.02
Osage (2)	4	0.01
Potawatomi (1)	1	0.00
Puget Sound Salish (20)	27	0.09
Shoshone (2)	3	0.01
Sioux (12)	25	0.09
Yakama (4)	8	0.03
All other tribes (46)	81	0.28
American Indian tribes, not spec.	22	0.08
Arab:	115	0.39
Arab/Arabic	81	0.28
Lebanese	15	0.05
Syrian	8	0.03
Other Arab	11	0.04
Armenian	123	0.42
Asian:	3,058	10.45
Cambodian (156)	198	0.68
Chinese, ex. Taiwanese (165)	239	0.82
Filipino (655)	872	2.98
Hmong (32)	35	0.12
Indian (193)	244	0.83
Indonesian (4)	5	0.02
Japanese (237)	361	1.23
Korean (159)	207	0.71
Laotian (155)	206	0.70
Malaysian (2)	3	0.01
Pakistani (2)	3	0.01
Sri Lankan (3)	6	0.02
Taiwanese (4)	5	0.02
Thai (36)	51	0.17
Vietnamese (498)	538	1.84
Other Asian, specified	5	0.02
Other Asian, not specified (32)	80	0.27
Australian	50	0.17
Austrian	52	0.18
Basque	37	0.13
Belgian	14	0.05
British	105	0.36
Bulgarian	7	0.02
Canadian	133	0.45
Celtic	24	0.08
Croatian	88	0.30
Czech	88	0.30
Czechoslovakian	32	0.11
Danish	497	1.69
Dutch	610	2.07
Eastern European	55	0.19
English	2,940	10.00
European	377	1.28
Finnish	214	0.73
French, except Basque	1,131	3.85
French Canadian	197	0.67
German	4,649	15.81
German Russian	11	0.04
Greek	95	0.32
Hawaii Native/Pacific Islander:	533	1.82
Micronesian: (78)	89	0.30
Guamanian/Chamorro (39)	50	0.17
Other Micronesian (39)	39	0.13
Polynesian: (297)	392	1.34
Native Hawaiian (29)	88	0.30
Samoan (248)	283	0.97
Tongan (12)	12	0.04
Other Polynesian (8)	9	0.03
Other Pac. Isl., specified	1	0.00
Other Pac. Isl., not spec. (14)	51	0.17
Hispanic or Latino:	1,936	6.61
Central American:	114	0.39
Costa Rican	5	0.02
Guatemalan	31	0.11
Honduran	25	0.09

Notes: 1. Figures in the "Number" column do not add up to the total population due to: a) Ancestry/Race overlap — e.g. persons can report being both White and Irish, b) persons of Hispanic origin can report being any race, c) persons reporting two ancestries are counted in both categories. 2. Numbers in parentheses indicate the number of persons reporting this ancestry/race alone, not in combination with any other ancestry/race. 3. Refer to the Explanation of Data in the front of the book for more detailed information.

Nicaraguan	6	0.02
Panamanian	8	0.03
Salvadoran	35	0.12
Other Central American	4	0.01
Cuban	15	0.05
Dominican Republic	1	0.00
Mexican	1,265	4.32
Puerto Rican	93	0.32
South American:	35	0.12
Argentinean	2	0.01
Bolivian	8	0.03
Chilean	4	0.01
Colombian	4	0.01
Ecuadorian	3	0.01
Peruvian	3	0.01
Venezuelan	2	0.01
Other South American	9	0.03
Other Hispanic or Latino	413	1.41
Hungarian	67	0.23
Icelander	15	0.05
Iranian	6	0.02
Irish	2,843	9.67
Italian	721	2.45
Latvian	15	0.05
Lithuanian	67	0.23
Luxemburger	9	0.03
Maltese	13	0.04
Northern European	40	0.14
Norwegian	1,727	5.87
Pennsylvania German	28	0.10
Polish	491	1.67
Portuguese	51	0.17
Romanian	14	0.05
Russian	215	0.73
Scandinavian	186	0.63
Scotch-Irish	529	1.80
Scottish	767	2.61
Serbian	16	0.05
Slavic	7	0.02
Slovak	60	0.20
Swedish	1,038	3.53
Swiss	167	0.57
Ukrainian	34	0.12
United States or American	1,473	5.01
Welsh	270	0.92
West Indian, excl. Hispanic:	16	0.05
Haitian	16	0.05
White:	22,831	78.01
Not Hispanic (20,986)	21,948	74.99
Hispanic (716)	883	3.02
Yugoslavian	80	0.27

Dishman

Place Type: Census Designated Place
County: Spokane
Population: 10,031

Ancestry/Race	Number	%
African American/Black:	128	1.28
Not Hispanic (81)	124	1.24
Hispanic	4	0.04
Alaska Native tribes, specified:	10	0.10
Alaska Athabascan	2	0.02
Aleut	1	0.01
Eskimo (4)	5	0.05
Tlingit-Haida	1	0.01
All other tribes	1	0.01
Alaska Native tribes, not specified	1	0.01
Am. Ind. or Alaska Nat., not spec.	50	0.50
American Indian tribes, specified:	218	2.17
Apache (1)	1	0.01
Blackfeet (6)	14	0.14
Cherokee (21)	36	0.36
Chickasaw (7)	7	0.07
Chippewa (31)	37	0.37
Choctaw	1	0.01
Colville (22)	26	0.26
Crow (1)	1	0.01
Iroquois	1	0.01
Latin American Indians (3)	9	0.09
Navajo	2	0.02
Osage (3)	3	0.03
Ottawa (1)	1	0.01
Puget Sound Salish (7)	7	0.07
Seminole	2	0.02
Sioux (10)	13	0.13
Yakama (1)	1	0.01
Yaqui	2	0.02
All other tribes (32)	54	0.54
American Indian tribes, not spec.	4	0.04
Arab:	36	0.36
Arab/Arabic	18	0.18
Lebanese	18	0.18
Asian:	180	1.79
Chinese, ex. Taiwanese (25)	32	0.32
Filipino (26)	48	0.48
Hmong (10)	10	0.10
Indian (4)	6	0.06
Japanese (24)	32	0.32
Korean (8)	15	0.15
Laotian (5)	5	0.05
Pakistani	1	0.01
Thai	2	0.02
Vietnamese (26)	27	0.27
Other Asian, not specified (2)	2	0.02
Australian	4	0.04
Austrian	25	0.25
Basque	8	0.08
British	56	0.56
Bulgarian	15	0.15
Canadian	36	0.36
Celtic	10	0.10
Czech	51	0.51
Czechoslovakian	8	0.08
Danish	168	1.68
Dutch	225	2.25
English	1,105	11.06
Estonian	10	0.10
European	133	1.33
Finnish	37	0.37
French, except Basque	358	3.58
French Canadian	92	0.92
German	2,532	25.34
Greek	39	0.39
Hawaii Native/Pacific Islander:	15	0.15
Micronesian: (1)	1	0.01
Guamanian/Chamorro (1)	1	0.01
Polynesian: (1)	10	0.10
Native Hawaiian (1)	9	0.09
Samoan	1	0.01
Other Pac. Isl., not spec.	4	0.04
Hispanic or Latino:	290	2.89
Central American:	5	0.05
Guatemalan	1	0.01
Panamanian	4	0.04
Mexican	190	1.89
Puerto Rican	29	0.29
South American:	7	0.07
Argentinean	5	0.05
Colombian	2	0.02
Other Hispanic or Latino	59	0.59
Hungarian	7	0.07
Iranian	4	0.04
Irish	1,263	12.64
Italian	297	2.97
Lithuanian	6	0.06
Norwegian	753	7.54
Polish	119	1.19
Portuguese	45	0.45
Romanian	64	0.64
Russian	20	0.20
Scandinavian	80	0.80
Scotch-Irish	185	1.85
Scottish	207	2.07
Serbian	5	0.05
Slavic	11	0.11
Slovak	5	0.05
Swedish	275	2.75
Swiss	38	0.38
Ukrainian	7	0.07
United States or American	406	4.06
Welsh	115	1.15
White:	9,506	94.77
Not Hispanic (9,176)	9,317	92.88
Hispanic (146)	189	1.88
Yugoslavian	21	0.21

East Hill-Meridian

Place Type: Census Designated Place
County: King
Population: 29,308

Ancestry/Race	Number	%
Acadian/Cajun	4	0.01
African American/Black:	1,661	5.67
Not Hispanic (1,342)	1,625	5.54
Hispanic (22)	36	0.12
African, sub-Saharan:	338	1.14
African	159	0.54
Ethiopian	32	0.11
Nigerian	80	0.27
Somalian	62	0.21
South African	5	0.02
Alaska Native tribes, specified:	44	0.15
Alaska Athabascan (2)	2	0.01
Aleut (3)	5	0.02
Eskimo (2)	2	0.01
Tlingit-Haida (11)	28	0.10
All other tribes (4)	7	0.02
Alaska Native tribes, not specified	3	0.01
Am. Ind. or Alaska Nat., not spec.	118	0.40
American Indian tribes, specified:	257	0.88
Apache (1)	2	0.01
Blackfeet (2)	19	0.06
Cherokee (13)	63	0.21
Cheyenne (1)	3	0.01
Chickasaw	2	0.01
Chippewa (15)	41	0.14
Choctaw	9	0.03
Colville (3)	4	0.01
Comanche (1)	1	0.00
Creek	2	0.01
Iroquois (7)	10	0.03
Kiowa (2)	2	0.01
Latin American Indians (1)	3	0.01
Navajo (1)	1	0.00
Pima	1	0.00
Potawatomi (2)	9	0.03
Puget Sound Salish (14)	22	0.08
Seminole	2	0.01
Shoshone	1	0.00
Sioux (7)	17	0.06
Yakama (1)	2	0.01
All other tribes (22)	41	0.14
American Indian tribes, not spec.	31	0.11
Arab:	64	0.22
Lebanese	17	0.06
Other Arab	47	0.16
Armenian	17	0.06
Asian:	5,023	17.14
Bangladeshi (1)	3	0.01
Cambodian (179)	193	0.66
Chinese, ex. Taiwanese (644)	796	2.72
Filipino (977)	1,180	4.03
Hmong (18)	18	0.06
Indian (753)	856	2.92
Indonesian (9)	14	0.05
Japanese (336)	521	1.78
Korean (334)	370	1.26
Laotian (65)	85	0.29
Malaysian (4)	7	0.02
Pakistani (8)	13	0.04
Taiwanese (8)	13	0.04
Thai (32)	45	0.15
Vietnamese (769)	812	2.77
Other Asian, specified (25)	30	0.10
Other Asian, not specified (21)	67	0.23
Australian	7	0.02

Notes: 1. Figures in the "Number" column do not add up to the total population due to: a) Ancestry/Race overlap — e.g. persons can report being both White and Irish, b) persons of Hispanic origin can report being any race, c) persons reporting two ancestries are counted in both categories. 2. Numbers in parentheses indicate the number of persons reporting this ancestry/race alone, not in combination with any other ancestry/race. 3. Refer to the Explanation of Data in the front of the book for more detailed information.

Austrian	71	0.24
Basque	18	0.06
Belgian	57	0.19
British	225	0.76
Bulgarian	50	0.17
Canadian	71	0.24
Celtic	20	0.07
Croatian	72	0.24
Czech	135	0.46
Czechoslovakian	33	0.11
Danish	381	1.29
Dutch	491	1.66
English	3,216	10.86
Estonian	11	0.04
European	436	1.47
Finnish	211	0.71
French, except Basque	910	3.07
French Canadian	274	0.93
German	5,731	19.35
Greek	70	0.24
Hawaii Native/Pacific Islander:	396	1.35
Melanesian: (32)	56	0.19
Fijian (32)	56	0.19
Micronesian: (17)	28	0.10
Guamanian/Chamorro (16)	26	0.09
Other Micronesian (1)	2	0.01
Polynesian: (131)	231	0.79
Native Hawaiian (53)	122	0.42
Samoan (69)	89	0.30
Tongan (9)	20	0.07
Other Pac. Isl., not spec. (6)	81	0.28
Hispanic or Latino:	1,116	3.81
Central American:	31	0.11
Costa Rican	6	0.02
Guatemalan	11	0.04
Honduran	5	0.02
Panamanian	3	0.01
Salvadoran	6	0.02
Cuban	20	0.07
Dominican Republic	1	0.00
Mexican	743	2.54
Puerto Rican	49	0.17
South American:	42	0.14
Argentinean	7	0.02
Bolivian	2	0.01
Chilean	8	0.03
Colombian	7	0.02
Ecuadorian	5	0.02
Peruvian	7	0.02
Venezuelan	6	0.02
Other Hispanic or Latino	230	0.78
Hungarian	83	0.28
Iranian	20	0.07
Irish	2,746	9.27
Italian	1,099	3.71
Latvian	15	0.05
Lithuanian	25	0.08
Luxemburger	7	0.02
Northern European	88	0.30
Norwegian	2,207	7.45
Pennsylvania German	22	0.07
Polish	470	1.59
Portuguese	61	0.21
Romanian	140	0.47
Russian	422	1.42
Scandinavian	169	0.57
Scotch-Irish	572	1.93
Scottish	775	2.62
Serbian	18	0.06
Slavic	19	0.06
Slovak	8	0.03
Slovene	7	0.02
Swedish	961	3.24
Swiss	146	0.49
Ukrainian	454	1.53
United States or American	1,334	4.50
Welsh	220	0.74
West Indian, excl. Hispanic:	7	0.02
British West Indian	7	0.02
White:	22,529	76.87
Not Hispanic (21,028)	21,890	74.69
Hispanic (488)	639	2.18
Yugoslavian	54	0.18

East Renton Highlands

Place Type: Census Designated Place
County: King
Population: 13,264

Ancestry/Race	Number	%
Acadian/Cajun	9	0.07
African American/Black:	260	1.96
Not Hispanic (185)	244	1.84
Hispanic (8)	16	0.12
African, sub-Saharan:	62	0.47
African	57	0.43
Kenyan	5	0.04
Alaska Native tribes, specified:	19	0.14
Alaska Athabascan (3)	3	0.02
Aleut (6)	10	0.08
Eskimo (2)	3	0.02
Tlingit-Haida (2)	3	0.02
Am. Ind. or Alaska Nat., not spec.	59	0.44
American Indian tribes, specified:	129	0.97
Apache (3)	5	0.04
Blackfeet (2)	8	0.06
Cherokee (4)	18	0.14
Cheyenne (1)	1	0.01
Chickasaw	1	0.01
Chippewa (10)	16	0.12
Choctaw (3)	5	0.04
Colville (1)	3	0.02
Comanche	1	0.01
Cree (1)	1	0.01
Creek (6)	6	0.05
Latin American Indians	2	0.02
Lumbee (1)	2	0.02
Navajo (1)	2	0.02
Osage	2	0.02
Pueblo (1)	1	0.01
Puget Sound Salish (7)	9	0.07
Shoshone (8)	9	0.07
Sioux (3)	7	0.05
Yakama (1)	2	0.02
All other tribes (15)	28	0.21
American Indian tribes, not spec.	17	0.13
Arab:	87	0.66
Lebanese	87	0.66
Asian:	596	4.49
Cambodian (10)	15	0.11
Chinese, ex. Taiwanese (53)	79	0.60
Filipino (64)	123	0.93
Hmong (23)	23	0.17
Indian (11)	18	0.14
Indonesian (1)	1	0.01
Japanese (127)	198	1.49
Korean (35)	53	0.40
Laotian (11)	11	0.08
Pakistani (1)	4	0.03
Taiwanese (6)	6	0.05
Thai (3)	6	0.05
Vietnamese (45)	49	0.37
Other Asian, not specified (7)	10	0.08
Austrian	62	0.47
Belgian	10	0.08
British	105	0.80
Canadian	24	0.18
Croatian	33	0.25
Czech	15	0.11
Danish	236	1.80
Dutch	250	1.91
Eastern European	42	0.32
English	1,700	12.97
European	267	2.04
Finnish	72	0.55
French, except Basque	560	4.27
French Canadian	104	0.79
German	2,915	22.24
Greek	34	0.26
Hawaii Native/Pacific Islander:	58	0.44
Micronesian: (3)	3	0.02
Guamanian/Chamorro (3)	3	0.02
Polynesian: (9)	48	0.36
Native Hawaiian (6)	30	0.23
Samoan (3)	18	0.14
Other Pac. Isl., not spec. (2)	7	0.05
Hispanic or Latino:	455	3.43
Central American:	15	0.11
Guatemalan	4	0.03
Panamanian	2	0.02
Salvadoran	8	0.06
Other Central American	1	0.01
Cuban	7	0.05
Mexican	293	2.21
Puerto Rican	19	0.14
South American:	15	0.11
Argentinean	1	0.01
Chilean	4	0.03
Colombian	3	0.02
Ecuadorian	3	0.02
Peruvian	2	0.02
Uruguayan	1	0.01
Other South American	1	0.01
Other Hispanic or Latino	106	0.80
Hungarian	48	0.37
Irish	1,807	13.79
Israeli	15	0.11
Italian	620	4.73
Latvian	11	0.08
Lithuanian	13	0.10
Northern European	35	0.27
Norwegian	1,171	8.93
Pennsylvania German	15	0.11
Polish	206	1.57
Portuguese	44	0.34
Russian	127	0.97
Scandinavian	118	0.90
Scotch-Irish	291	2.22
Scottish	363	2.77
Slavic	15	0.11
Swedish	743	5.67
Swiss	93	0.71
Ukrainian	9	0.07
United States or American	1,206	9.20
Welsh	97	0.74
White:	12,360	93.18
Not Hispanic (11,773)	12,053	90.87
Hispanic (265)	307	2.31
Yugoslavian	70	0.53

East Wenatchee Bench

Place Type: Census Designated Place
County: Douglas
Population: 13,658

Ancestry/Race	Number	%
African American/Black:	56	0.41
Not Hispanic (19)	37	0.27
Hispanic (10)	19	0.14
Alaska Native tribes, specified:	5	0.04
Eskimo (1)	1	0.01
Tlingit-Haida (3)	4	0.03
Am. Ind. or Alaska Nat., not spec.	40	0.29
American Indian tribes, specified:	178	1.30
Apache (1)	3	0.02
Blackfeet (2)	3	0.02
Cherokee (31)	53	0.39
Chippewa (1)	5	0.04
Choctaw (3)	10	0.07
Colville (12)	23	0.17
Latin American Indians (7)	12	0.09
Navajo (2)	4	0.03
Puget Sound Salish (6)	6	0.04
Sioux (10)	12	0.09
Yakama (1)	4	0.03
All other tribes (24)	43	0.31
American Indian tribes, not spec.	8	0.06
Arab:	8	0.06

Notes: 1. Figures in the "Number" column do not add up to the total population due to: a) Ancestry/Race overlap — e.g. persons can report being both White and Irish, b) persons of Hispanic origin can report being any race, c) persons reporting two ancestries are counted in both categories. 2. Numbers in parentheses indicate the number of persons reporting this ancestry/race alone, not in combination with any other ancestry/race. 3. Refer to the Explanation of Data in the front of the book for more detailed information.

Ancestry/Race	Number	%
Jordanian	8	0.06
Asian:	128	0.94
Cambodian (6)	7	0.05
Chinese, ex. Taiwanese (17)	26	0.19
Filipino (23)	36	0.26
Indian (2)	4	0.03
Japanese (12)	23	0.17
Korean (8)	13	0.10
Laotian (2)	5	0.04
Taiwanese (1)	2	0.01
Thai (3)	4	0.03
Vietnamese (7)	7	0.05
Other Asian, not specified (1)	1	0.01
Austrian	61	0.45
Belgian	21	0.15
British	43	0.32
Canadian	81	0.60
Croatian	14	0.10
Czech	98	0.72
Czechoslovakian	7	0.05
Danish	124	0.91
Dutch	367	2.70
English	1,839	13.53
European	76	0.56
Finnish	50	0.37
French, except Basque	425	3.13
French Canadian	174	1.28
German	2,670	19.64
Greek	30	0.22
Hawaii Native/Pacific Islander:	13	0.10
Micronesian: (3)	4	0.03
Guamanian/Chamorro (3)	4	0.03
Polynesian: (5)	9	0.07
Native Hawaiian (4)	7	0.05
Samoan	1	0.01
Other Polynesian (1)	1	0.01
Hispanic or Latino:	1,727	12.64
Central American:	33	0.24
Guatemalan	17	0.12
Panamanian	8	0.06
Salvadoran	6	0.04
Other Central American	2	0.01
Cuban	9	0.07
Mexican	1,447	10.59
Puerto Rican	22	0.16
South American:	23	0.17
Bolivian	4	0.03
Colombian	4	0.03
Ecuadorian	10	0.07
Peruvian	2	0.01
Venezuelan	3	0.02
Other Hispanic or Latino	193	1.41
Hungarian	43	0.32
Icelander	6	0.04
Irish	1,597	11.75
Italian	225	1.66
Northern European	21	0.15
Norwegian	798	5.87
Polish	128	0.94
Portuguese	14	0.10
Romanian	25	0.18
Russian	20	0.15
Scandinavian	70	0.51
Scotch-Irish	291	2.14
Scottish	325	2.39
Serbian	6	0.04
Swedish	404	2.97
Swiss	27	0.20
Turkish	12	0.09
Ukrainian	134	0.99
United States or American	1,007	7.41
Welsh	210	1.54
White:	12,488	91.43
Not Hispanic (11,539)	11,712	85.75
Hispanic (717)	776	5.68
Yugoslavian	24	0.18

Edmonds

Place Type: City
County: Snohomish
Population: 39,515

Ancestry/Race	Number	%
African American/Black:	754	1.91
Not Hispanic (523)	731	1.85
Hispanic (7)	23	0.06
African, sub-Saharan:	222	0.56
African	78	0.20
Ethiopian	93	0.23
Liberian	5	0.01
Somalian	27	0.07
South African	17	0.04
Other sub-Saharan African	2	0.01
Alaska Native tribes, specified:	166	0.42
Alaska Athabascan (28)	36	0.09
Aleut (36)	48	0.12
Eskimo (6)	6	0.02
Tlingit-Haida (39)	68	0.17
All other tribes (4)	8	0.02
Alaska Native tribes, not specified	13	0.03
Am. Ind. or Alaska Nat., not spec.	131	0.33
Alsatian	14	0.04
American Indian tribes, specified:	361	0.91
Apache	7	0.02
Blackfeet (7)	23	0.06
Cherokee (21)	95	0.24
Chickasaw (3)	5	0.01
Chippewa (7)	31	0.08
Choctaw (2)	9	0.02
Colville (3)	3	0.01
Cree	2	0.01
Creek	5	0.01
Crow	1	0.00
Delaware	1	0.00
Houma (1)	1	0.00
Iroquois (7)	14	0.04
Kiowa	1	0.00
Latin American Indians (6)	16	0.04
Navajo (2)	2	0.01
Osage	2	0.01
Ottawa	2	0.01
Potawatomi	2	0.01
Pueblo	2	0.01
Puget Sound Salish (11)	22	0.06
Seminole	1	0.00
Shoshone (1)	5	0.01
Sioux (18)	28	0.07
Tohono O'Odham	1	0.00
Yakama	1	0.00
Yaqui	1	0.00
Yuman	1	0.00
All other tribes (48)	77	0.19
American Indian tribes, not spec.	42	0.11
Arab:	165	0.42
Arab/Arabic	51	0.13
Egyptian	44	0.11
Lebanese	38	0.10
Syrian	25	0.06
Other Arab	7	0.02
Armenian	63	0.16
Asian:	2,816	7.13
Bangladeshi (5)	6	0.02
Cambodian (20)	26	0.07
Chinese, ex. Taiwanese (380)	514	1.30
Filipino (331)	499	1.26
Hmong (3)	4	0.01
Indian (109)	146	0.37
Indonesian (15)	24	0.06
Japanese (297)	456	1.15
Korean (694)	773	1.96
Laotian (3)	7	0.02
Malaysian (3)	6	0.02
Pakistani (33)	38	0.10
Sri Lankan (6)	7	0.02
Taiwanese (16)	23	0.06
Thai (30)	35	0.09

Ancestry/Race	Number	%
Vietnamese (156)	193	0.49
Other Asian, specified (4)	8	0.02
Other Asian, not specified (21)	51	0.13
Australian	7	0.02
Austrian	172	0.43
Basque	54	0.14
Belgian	62	0.16
Brazilian	7	0.02
British	350	0.88
Bulgarian	52	0.13
Canadian	459	1.16
Celtic	33	0.08
Croatian	88	0.22
Czech	142	0.36
Czechoslovakian	43	0.11
Danish	649	1.64
Dutch	1,027	2.59
Eastern European	21	0.05
English	6,733	17.00
Estonian	8	0.02
European	799	2.02
Finnish	361	0.91
French, except Basque	2,018	5.09
French Canadian	292	0.74
German	7,638	19.28
Greek	168	0.42
Hawaii Native/Pacific Islander:	218	0.55
Melanesian: (31)	42	0.11
Fijian (31)	42	0.11
Micronesian: (31)	43	0.11
Guamanian/Chamorro (18)	27	0.07
Other Micronesian (13)	16	0.04
Polynesian: (28)	98	0.25
Native Hawaiian (21)	78	0.20
Samoan (7)	17	0.04
Tongan	1	0.00
Other Polynesian	2	0.01
Other Pac. Isl., specified	1	0.00
Other Pac. Isl., not spec. (10)	34	0.09
Hispanic or Latino:	1,312	3.32
Central American:	52	0.13
Guatemalan	4	0.01
Honduran	9	0.02
Nicaraguan	13	0.03
Panamanian	11	0.03
Salvadoran	15	0.04
Cuban	31	0.08
Mexican	810	2.05
Puerto Rican	50	0.13
South American:	116	0.29
Argentinean	18	0.05
Bolivian	7	0.02
Chilean	20	0.05
Colombian	13	0.03
Ecuadorian	4	0.01
Peruvian	38	0.10
Uruguayan	4	0.01
Venezuelan	5	0.01
Other South American	7	0.02
Other Hispanic or Latino	253	0.64
Hungarian	202	0.51
Icelander	107	0.27
Iranian	55	0.14
Irish	5,389	13.61
Italian	1,495	3.77
Latvian	19	0.05
Lithuanian	46	0.12
Luxemburger	13	0.03
Maltese	13	0.03
New Zealander	16	0.04
Northern European	168	0.42
Norwegian	3,900	9.85
Pennsylvania German	4	0.01
Polish	668	1.69
Portuguese	72	0.18
Romanian	167	0.42
Russian	512	1.29
Scandinavian	279	0.70
Scotch-Irish	960	2.42
Scottish	1,560	3.94

Notes: 1. Figures in the "Number" column do not add up to the total population due to: a) Ancestry/Race overlap — e.g. persons can report being both White and Irish, b) persons of Hispanic origin can report being any race, c) persons reporting two ancestries are counted in both categories. 2. Numbers in parentheses indicate the number of persons reporting this ancestry/race alone, not in combination with any other ancestry/race. 3. Refer to the Explanation of Data in the front of the book for more detailed information.

Ancestry/Race	Number	%
Serbian	22	0.06
Slavic	53	0.13
Slovak	44	0.11
Swedish	2,076	5.24
Swiss	226	0.57
Turkish	7	0.02
Ukrainian	48	0.12
United States or American	1,717	4.33
Welsh	654	1.65
West Indian, excl. Hispanic:	29	0.07
Dutch West Indian	3	0.01
Jamaican	10	0.03
Trinidadian and Tobagonian	5	0.01
West Indian	11	0.03
White:	35,724	90.41
Not Hispanic (34,012)	34,934	88.41
Hispanic (654)	790	2.00
Yugoslavian	118	0.30

Elk Plain

Place Type: Census Designated Place
County: Pierce
Population: 15,697

Ancestry/Race	Number	%
African American/Black:	1,081	6.89
Not Hispanic (825)	1,021	6.50
Hispanic (23)	60	0.38
African, sub-Saharan:	141	0.90
African	122	0.78
South African	19	0.12
Alaska Native tribes, specified:	24	0.15
Alaska Athabascan	8	0.05
Aleut (2)	6	0.04
Eskimo	1	0.01
Tlingit-Haida (5)	9	0.06
Alaska Native tribes, not specified	4	0.03
Am. Ind. or Alaska Nat., not spec.	120	0.76
American Indian tribes, specified:	289	1.84
Apache (2)	8	0.05
Blackfeet (7)	28	0.18
Cherokee (25)	77	0.49
Cheyenne (1)	1	0.01
Chickasaw (1)	5	0.03
Chippewa (22)	33	0.21
Choctaw	7	0.04
Colville (3)	3	0.02
Comanche	2	0.01
Cree	2	0.01
Creek	1	0.01
Crow (1)	1	0.01
Delaware	4	0.03
Iroquois (4)	6	0.04
Kiowa (3)	3	0.02
Latin American Indians	9	0.06
Navajo	2	0.01
Ottawa	2	0.01
Pima (1)	1	0.01
Pueblo (9)	11	0.07
Puget Sound Salish (6)	10	0.06
Seminole	1	0.01
Shoshone	1	0.01
Sioux (4)	13	0.08
Yakama (4)	8	0.05
All other tribes (29)	50	0.32
American Indian tribes, not spec.	18	0.11
Arab:	16	0.10
Lebanese	16	0.10
Asian:	1,103	7.03
Cambodian (4)	4	0.03
Chinese, ex. Taiwanese (20)	70	0.45
Filipino (277)	435	2.77
Indian (17)	26	0.17
Indonesian (1)	6	0.04
Japanese (66)	181	1.15
Korean (195)	297	1.89
Laotian (2)	4	0.03
Pakistani (2)	12	0.08
Thai (14)	21	0.13
Vietnamese (2)	7	0.04
Other Asian, specified (1)	6	0.04
Other Asian, not specified (18)	34	0.22
Austrian	24	0.15
Belgian	8	0.05
British	70	0.45
Canadian	61	0.39
Celtic	23	0.15
Croatian	19	0.12
Czech	69	0.44
Czechoslovakian	11	0.07
Danish	229	1.46
Dutch	438	2.79
Eastern European	9	0.06
English	1,685	10.74
European	246	1.57
Finnish	125	0.80
French, except Basque	501	3.19
French Canadian	161	1.03
German	3,117	19.87
Greek	10	0.06
Hawaii Native/Pacific Islander:	336	2.14
Micronesian: (123)	160	1.02
Guamanian/Chamorro (123)	160	1.02
Polynesian: (81)	157	1.00
Native Hawaiian (32)	86	0.55
Samoan (49)	70	0.45
Other Polynesian	1	0.01
Other Pac. Isl., not spec. (11)	19	0.12
Hispanic or Latino:	743	4.73
Central American:	26	0.17
Costa Rican	5	0.03
Guatemalan	6	0.04
Honduran	3	0.02
Panamanian	11	0.07
Other Central American	1	0.01
Cuban	19	0.12
Dominican Republic	11	0.07
Mexican	379	2.41
Puerto Rican	132	0.84
South American:	5	0.03
Colombian	3	0.02
Ecuadorian	1	0.01
Peruvian	1	0.01
Other Hispanic or Latino	171	1.09
Hungarian	7	0.04
Icelander	69	0.44
Irish	1,763	11.24
Italian	433	2.76
Lithuanian	14	0.09
Northern European	20	0.13
Norwegian	1,094	6.97
Polish	354	2.26
Portuguese	60	0.38
Russian	171	1.09
Scandinavian	146	0.93
Scotch-Irish	227	1.45
Scottish	344	2.19
Swedish	303	1.93
Swiss	38	0.24
Ukrainian	19	0.12
United States or American	1,027	6.55
Welsh	97	0.62
West Indian, excl. Hispanic:	26	0.17
Jamaican	26	0.17
White:	13,430	85.56
Not Hispanic (12,283)	12,977	82.67
Hispanic (364)	453	2.89
Yugoslavian	40	0.25

Ellensburg

Place Type: City
County: Kittitas
Population: 15,414

Ancestry/Race	Number	%
Acadian/Cajun	9	0.06
African American/Black:	266	1.73
Not Hispanic (175)	252	1.63
Hispanic (6)	14	0.09
African, sub-Saharan:	34	0.22
African	6	0.04
Kenyan	9	0.06
Other sub-Saharan African	19	0.12
Alaska Native tribes, specified:	37	0.24
Alaska Athabascan (5)	8	0.05
Aleut (9)	11	0.07
Eskimo (2)	5	0.03
Tlingit-Haida (6)	12	0.08
All other tribes	1	0.01
Alaska Native tribes, not specified	5	0.03
Am. Ind. or Alaska Nat., not spec.	104	0.67
American Indian tribes, specified:	142	0.92
Apache (1)	4	0.03
Blackfeet	6	0.04
Cherokee (9)	34	0.22
Cheyenne	1	0.01
Chickasaw (3)	4	0.03
Chippewa (4)	6	0.04
Choctaw (5)	6	0.04
Colville (9)	11	0.07
Creek (1)	2	0.01
Crow (2)	4	0.03
Iroquois (4)	4	0.03
Latin American Indians (2)	2	0.01
Navajo	1	0.01
Osage	1	0.01
Pueblo (1)	1	0.01
Puget Sound Salish (1)	6	0.04
Shoshone	1	0.01
Sioux (13)	17	0.11
Ute	1	0.01
Yakama (7)	12	0.08
All other tribes (12)	18	0.12
American Indian tribes, not spec.	13	0.08
Arab:	8	0.05
Lebanese	8	0.05
Armenian	22	0.14
Asian:	795	5.16
Cambodian (20)	24	0.16
Chinese, ex. Taiwanese (106)	123	0.80
Filipino (38)	90	0.58
Hmong (1)	1	0.01
Indian (30)	44	0.29
Indonesian (2)	3	0.02
Japanese (302)	338	2.19
Korean (65)	78	0.51
Laotian (2)	4	0.03
Pakistani	2	0.01
Taiwanese (24)	26	0.17
Thai (8)	11	0.07
Vietnamese (18)	24	0.16
Other Asian, specified	1	0.01
Other Asian, not specified (8)	26	0.17
Australian	17	0.11
Austrian	58	0.38
Basque	14	0.09
British	140	0.91
Canadian	72	0.47
Celtic	7	0.05
Croatian	28	0.18
Czech	43	0.28
Czechoslovakian	41	0.27
Danish	145	0.94
Dutch	436	2.84
English	1,771	11.52
European	301	1.96
Finnish	102	0.66
French, except Basque	457	2.97
French Canadian	170	1.11
German	3,400	22.12
Greek	34	0.22
Hawaii Native/Pacific Islander:	56	0.36
Melanesian: (1)	2	0.01
Fijian	1	0.01
Other Melanesian (1)	1	0.01
Micronesian: (3)	9	0.06
Guamanian/Chamorro (3)	6	0.04
Other Micronesian	3	0.02

Notes: 1. Figures in the "Number" column do not add up to the total population due to: a) Ancestry/Race overlap — e.g. persons can report being both White and Irish, b) persons of Hispanic origin can report being any race, c) persons reporting two ancestries are counted in both categories. 2. Numbers in parentheses indicate the number of persons reporting this ancestry/race alone, not in combination with any other ancestry/race. 3. Refer to the Explanation of Data in the front of the book for more detailed information.

Ancestry/Race	Number	%
Polynesian: (11)	25	0.16
Native Hawaiian (1)	10	0.06
Samoan (10)	15	0.10
Other Pac. Isl., specified	1	0.01
Other Pac. Isl., not spec. (10)	19	0.12
Hispanic or Latino:	976	6.33
Central American:	20	0.13
Costa Rican	1	0.01
Guatemalan	2	0.01
Honduran	1	0.01
Nicaraguan	1	0.01
Panamanian	9	0.06
Salvadoran	6	0.04
Cuban	11	0.07
Dominican Republic	2	0.01
Mexican	788	5.11
Puerto Rican	38	0.25
South American:	12	0.08
Argentinean	2	0.01
Bolivian	1	0.01
Chilean	1	0.01
Colombian	5	0.03
Peruvian	2	0.01
Venezuelan	1	0.01
Other Hispanic or Latino	105	0.68
Hungarian	5	0.03
Icelander	12	0.08
Iranian	8	0.05
Irish	1,689	10.99
Italian	685	4.46
Latvian	6	0.04
Lithuanian	16	0.10
Luxemburger	9	0.06
Northern European	8	0.05
Norwegian	1,121	7.29
Pennsylvania German	13	0.08
Polish	257	1.67
Portuguese	7	0.05
Russian	100	0.65
Scandinavian	129	0.84
Scotch-Irish	380	2.47
Scottish	409	2.66
Serbian	12	0.08
Slavic	5	0.03
Slovak	15	0.10
Slovene	9	0.06
Swedish	590	3.84
Swiss	61	0.40
Ukrainian	21	0.14
United States or American	745	4.85
Welsh	154	1.00
White:	13,940	90.44
Not Hispanic (13,123)	13,436	87.17
Hispanic (452)	504	3.27
Yugoslavian	34	0.22

Enumclaw

Place Type: City
County: King
Population: 11,116

Ancestry/Race	Number	%
African American/Black:	62	0.56
Not Hispanic (31)	58	0.52
Hispanic (2)	4	0.04
Alaska Native tribes, specified:	17	0.15
Aleut (3)	3	0.03
Eskimo (1)	5	0.04
Tlingit-Haida (4)	9	0.08
Alaska Native tribes, not specified	3	0.03
Am. Ind. or Alaska Nat., not spec.	46	0.41
American Indian tribes, specified:	144	1.30
Apache (2)	2	0.02
Blackfeet (4)	10	0.09
Cherokee (8)	30	0.27
Cheyenne (1)	1	0.01
Chippewa (10)	17	0.15
Choctaw (1)	8	0.07
Colville (1)	1	0.01
Comanche	2	0.02
Delaware	1	0.01
Navajo (1)	1	0.01
Ottawa	2	0.02
Pima	2	0.02
Potawatomi (5)	5	0.04
Pueblo (6)	8	0.07
Puget Sound Salish (10)	17	0.15
Shoshone (1)	4	0.04
Sioux (1)	4	0.04
Yakama (3)	6	0.05
All other tribes (5)	23	0.21
American Indian tribes, not spec.	8	0.07
Asian:	155	1.39
Chinese, ex. Taiwanese (6)	14	0.13
Filipino (23)	42	0.38
Indian (12)	14	0.13
Japanese (16)	36	0.32
Korean (10)	20	0.18
Thai (2)	5	0.04
Vietnamese (18)	23	0.21
Other Asian, not specified	1	0.01
Austrian	123	1.10
Basque	15	0.13
Belgian	31	0.28
British	51	0.46
Canadian	38	0.34
Croatian	7	0.06
Czech	27	0.24
Czechoslovakian	14	0.13
Danish	137	1.23
Dutch	293	2.62
English	1,360	12.16
Estonian	9	0.08
European	216	1.93
Finnish	26	0.23
French, except Basque	622	5.56
French Canadian	146	1.31
German	2,182	19.51
Greek	54	0.48
Hawaii Native/Pacific Islander:	41	0.37
Micronesian:	2	0.02
Guamanian/Chamorro	2	0.02
Polynesian: (12)	36	0.32
Native Hawaiian (3)	21	0.19
Samoan (9)	12	0.11
Other Polynesian	3	0.03
Other Pac. Isl., not spec.	3	0.03
Hispanic or Latino:	380	3.42
Central American:	2	0.02
Panamanian	2	0.02
Cuban	7	0.06
Mexican	274	2.46
Puerto Rican	24	0.22
South American:	2	0.02
Chilean	2	0.02
Other Hispanic or Latino	71	0.64
Hungarian	21	0.19
Icelander	15	0.13
Irish	1,541	13.78
Italian	609	5.45
Latvian	9	0.08
Lithuanian	6	0.05
Maltese	9	0.08
Northern European	11	0.10
Norwegian	990	8.85
Pennsylvania German	8	0.07
Polish	139	1.24
Portuguese	21	0.19
Romanian	32	0.29
Russian	52	0.46
Scandinavian	91	0.81
Scotch-Irish	174	1.56
Scottish	362	3.24
Slovak	26	0.23
Slovene	45	0.40
Swedish	454	4.06
Swiss	78	0.70
Turkish	32	0.29
Ukrainian	44	0.39
United States or American	752	6.72
Welsh	136	1.22
White:	10,757	96.77
Not Hispanic (10,276)	10,499	94.45
Hispanic (201)	258	2.32
Yugoslavian	24	0.21

Everett

Place Type: City
County: Snohomish
Population: 91,488

Ancestry/Race	Number	%
Acadian/Cajun	8	0.01
African American/Black:	3,909	4.27
Not Hispanic (2,966)	3,722	4.07
Hispanic (95)	187	0.20
African, sub-Saharan:	401	0.44
African	276	0.30
Ethiopian	28	0.03
Ghanian	37	0.04
Nigerian	45	0.05
Sierra Leonean	5	0.01
Ugandan	10	0.01
Alaska Native tribes, specified:	278	0.30
Alaska Athabascan (17)	24	0.03
Aleut (33)	44	0.05
Eskimo (23)	57	0.06
Tlingit-Haida (93)	130	0.14
All other tribes (12)	23	0.03
Alaska Native tribes, not specified	19	0.02
Am. Ind. or Alaska Nat., not spec.	675	0.74
American Indian tribes, specified:	1,558	1.70
Apache (19)	43	0.05
Blackfeet (26)	88	0.10
Cherokee (89)	328	0.36
Cheyenne (9)	19	0.02
Chickasaw (2)	16	0.02
Chippewa (120)	162	0.18
Choctaw (8)	33	0.04
Colville (20)	20	0.02
Comanche (2)	12	0.01
Cree (8)	10	0.01
Creek (7)	8	0.01
Crow (3)	4	0.00
Delaware (1)	2	0.00
Iroquois (11)	21	0.02
Latin American Indians (20)	45	0.05
Lumbee	4	0.00
Menominee	1	0.00
Navajo (18)	37	0.04
Osage (1)	12	0.01
Ottawa (1)	1	0.00
Paiute (3)	4	0.00
Pima (1)	2	0.00
Potawatomi (4)	7	0.01
Pueblo (10)	14	0.02
Puget Sound Salish (184)	245	0.27
Seminole (3)	14	0.02
Shoshone (2)	3	0.00
Sioux (55)	106	0.12
Ute (1)	3	0.00
Yakama (22)	38	0.04
Yaqui	6	0.01
Yuman (1)	1	0.00
All other tribes (148)	249	0.27
American Indian tribes, not spec.	115	0.13
Arab:	553	0.61
Arab/Arabic	212	0.23
Egyptian	79	0.09
Iraqi	158	0.17
Lebanese	93	0.10
Syrian	5	0.01
Other Arab	6	0.01
Armenian	34	0.04
Asian:	7,165	7.83
Bangladeshi (4)	4	0.00
Cambodian (440)	507	0.55
Chinese, ex. Taiwanese (356)	503	0.55

Notes: 1. Figures in the "Number" column do not add up to the total population due to: a) Ancestry/Race overlap — e.g. persons can report being both White and Irish, b) persons of Hispanic origin can report being any race, c) persons reporting two ancestries are counted in both categories. 2. Numbers in parentheses indicate the number of persons reporting this ancestry/race alone, not in combination with any other ancestry/race. 3. Refer to the Explanation of Data in the front of the book for more detailed information.

Ancestry/Race	Number	%
Filipino (1,432)	1,840	2.01
Hmong (33)	47	0.05
Indian (521)	611	0.67
Indonesian (162)	236	0.26
Japanese (237)	456	0.50
Korean (617)	749	0.82
Laotian (267)	327	0.36
Malaysian (15)	26	0.03
Pakistani (30)	47	0.05
Sri Lankan (10)	11	0.01
Taiwanese (14)	20	0.02
Thai (83)	103	0.11
Vietnamese (1,333)	1,432	1.57
Other Asian, specified (3)	12	0.01
Other Asian, not specified (93)	234	0.26
Assyrian/Chaldean/Syriac	9	0.01
Australian	42	0.05
Austrian	210	0.23
Basque	19	0.02
Belgian	167	0.18
Brazilian	8	0.01
British	554	0.61
Bulgarian	35	0.04
Canadian	400	0.44
Celtic	25	0.03
Croatian	220	0.24
Czech	319	0.35
Czechoslovakian	119	0.13
Danish	994	1.09
Dutch	2,174	2.38
Eastern European	8	0.01
English	9,313	10.20
Estonian	70	0.08
European	1,180	1.29
Finnish	614	0.67
French, except Basque	3,354	3.67
French Canadian	773	0.85
German	15,778	17.28
Greek	251	0.27
Hawaii Native/Pacific Islander:	689	0.75
Melanesian: (35)	38	0.04
Fijian (35)	38	0.04
Micronesian: (84)	140	0.15
Guamanian/Chamorro (51)	81	0.09
Other Micronesian (33)	59	0.06
Polynesian: (166)	331	0.36
Native Hawaiian (120)	238	0.26
Samoan (42)	83	0.09
Tongan (3)	5	0.01
Other Polynesian (1)	5	0.01
Other Pac. Isl., specified	7	0.01
Other Pac. Isl., not spec. (42)	173	0.19
Hispanic or Latino:	6,539	7.15
Central American:	170	0.19
Costa Rican	14	0.02
Guatemalan	20	0.02
Honduran	19	0.02
Nicaraguan	25	0.03
Panamanian	23	0.03
Salvadoran	64	0.07
Other Central American	5	0.01
Cuban	40	0.04
Dominican Republic	10	0.01
Mexican	4,834	5.28
Puerto Rican	251	0.27
South American:	151	0.17
Argentinean	19	0.02
Bolivian	9	0.01
Chilean	21	0.02
Colombian	44	0.05
Ecuadorian	11	0.01
Peruvian	27	0.03
Venezuelan	10	0.01
Other South American	10	0.01
Other Hispanic or Latino	1,083	1.18
Hungarian	240	0.26
Icelander	149	0.16
Iranian	14	0.02
Irish	10,364	11.35
Israeli	10	0.01
Italian	2,928	3.21
Latvian	14	0.02
Lithuanian	49	0.05
Luxemburger	16	0.02
New Zealander	23	0.03
Northern European	206	0.23
Norwegian	7,203	7.89
Pennsylvania German	67	0.07
Polish	1,185	1.30
Portuguese	256	0.28
Romanian	131	0.14
Russian	1,435	1.57
Scandinavian	861	0.94
Scotch-Irish	1,764	1.93
Scottish	2,533	2.77
Serbian	15	0.02
Slavic	17	0.02
Slovak	98	0.11
Slovene	22	0.02
Swedish	3,370	3.69
Swiss	208	0.23
Ukrainian	965	1.06
United States or American	4,648	5.09
Welsh	1,028	1.13
West Indian, excl. Hispanic:	158	0.17
Belizean	17	0.02
British West Indian	8	0.01
Dutch West Indian	17	0.02
Haitian	26	0.03
Jamaican	41	0.04
U.S. Virgin Islander	7	0.01
West Indian	42	0.05
White:	77,476	84.68
Not Hispanic (71,276)	74,039	80.93
Hispanic (2,876)	3,437	3.76
Yugoslavian	191	0.21

Federal Way

Place Type: City
County: King
Population: 83,259

Ancestry/Race	Number	%
Acadian/Cajun	13	0.02
Afghan	37	0.04
African American/Black:	8,012	9.62
Not Hispanic (6,439)	7,683	9.23
Hispanic (170)	329	0.40
African, sub-Saharan:	1,033	1.24
African	713	0.86
Cape Verdean	21	0.03
Ethiopian	70	0.08
Kenyan	87	0.10
Somalian	28	0.03
Other sub-Saharan African	114	0.14
Alaska Native tribes, specified:	155	0.19
Alaska Athabascan (5)	13	0.02
Aleut (12)	20	0.02
Eskimo (6)	13	0.02
Tlingit-Haida (56)	95	0.11
All other tribes (11)	14	0.02
Alaska Native tribes, not specified	8	0.01
Am. Ind. or Alaska Nat., not spec.	568	0.68
American Indian tribes, specified:	1,016	1.22
Apache (4)	23	0.03
Blackfeet (15)	79	0.09
Cherokee (56)	276	0.33
Cheyenne (9)	12	0.01
Chickasaw (1)	10	0.01
Chippewa (47)	76	0.09
Choctaw (6)	34	0.04
Colville (6)	10	0.01
Comanche (1)	4	0.00
Cree (1)	6	0.01
Creek (2)	16	0.02
Crow (1)	3	0.00
Delaware (1)	1	0.00
Iroquois (3)	12	0.01
Kiowa (2)	2	0.00
Latin American Indians (12)	42	0.05
Lumbee (1)	1	0.00
Menominee	1	0.00
Navajo (20)	28	0.03
Osage (1)	6	0.01
Ottawa (1)	3	0.00
Potawatomi (3)	5	0.01
Pueblo (15)	24	0.03
Puget Sound Salish (35)	62	0.07
Seminole (2)	8	0.01
Shoshone	5	0.01
Sioux (34)	65	0.08
Tohono O'Odham	1	0.00
Yakama (11)	14	0.02
Yuman	1	0.00
All other tribes (106)	186	0.22
American Indian tribes, not spec.	66	0.08
Arab:	376	0.45
Arab/Arabic	17	0.02
Egyptian	8	0.01
Iraqi	27	0.03
Jordanian	26	0.03
Lebanese	41	0.05
Palestinian	66	0.08
Syrian	32	0.04
Other Arab	159	0.19
Armenian	34	0.04
Asian:	12,293	14.76
Cambodian (218)	296	0.36
Chinese, ex. Taiwanese (892)	1,261	1.51
Filipino (1,703)	2,386	2.87
Hmong (17)	27	0.03
Indian (673)	757	0.91
Indonesian (19)	39	0.05
Japanese (545)	911	1.09
Korean (4,417)	4,740	5.69
Laotian (70)	104	0.12
Malaysian (10)	19	0.02
Pakistani (47)	58	0.07
Sri Lankan (46)	55	0.07
Taiwanese (109)	133	0.16
Thai (67)	99	0.12
Vietnamese (1,032)	1,111	1.33
Other Asian, specified (6)	15	0.02
Other Asian, not specified (136)	282	0.34
Australian	22	0.03
Austrian	154	0.19
Basque	74	0.09
Belgian	106	0.13
Brazilian	40	0.05
British	376	0.45
Bulgarian	23	0.03
Canadian	355	0.43
Celtic	47	0.06
Croatian	101	0.12
Czech	267	0.32
Czechoslovakian	164	0.20
Danish	795	0.96
Dutch	1,376	1.65
Eastern European	23	0.03
English	8,608	10.34
European	1,034	1.24
Finnish	352	0.42
French, except Basque	2,234	2.68
French Canadian	594	0.71
German	13,269	15.94
German Russian	6	0.01
Greek	355	0.43
Hawaii Native/Pacific Islander:	1,408	1.69
Melanesian: (15)	30	0.04
Fijian (15)	30	0.04
Micronesian: (189)	258	0.31
Guamanian/Chamorro (122)	189	0.23
Other Micronesian (67)	69	0.08
Polynesian: (580)	934	1.12
Native Hawaiian (135)	372	0.45
Samoan (392)	486	0.58
Tongan (42)	55	0.07
Other Polynesian (11)	21	0.03
Other Pac. Isl., specified	6	0.01

Notes: 1. Figures in the "Number" column do not add up to the total population due to: a) Ancestry/Race overlap — e.g. persons can report being both White and Irish, b) persons of Hispanic origin can report being any race, c) persons reporting two ancestries are counted in both categories. 2. Numbers in parentheses indicate the number of persons reporting this ancestry/race alone, not in combination with any other ancestry/race. 3. Refer to the Explanation of Data in the front of the book for more detailed information.

Other Pac. Isl., not spec. (41)	180	0.22
Hispanic or Latino:	6,266	7.53
Central American:	271	0.33
Costa Rican	22	0.03
Guatemalan	41	0.05
Honduran	28	0.03
Nicaraguan	22	0.03
Panamanian	49	0.06
Salvadoran	95	0.11
Other Central American	14	0.02
Cuban	84	0.10
Dominican Republic	12	0.01
Mexican	4,317	5.19
Puerto Rican	364	0.44
South American:	139	0.17
Argentinean	19	0.02
Bolivian	7	0.01
Chilean	6	0.01
Colombian	47	0.06
Ecuadorian	8	0.01
Paraguayan	4	0.00
Peruvian	30	0.04
Venezuelan	6	0.01
Other South American	12	0.01
Other Hispanic or Latino	1,079	1.30
Hungarian	227	0.27
Icelander	82	0.10
Iranian	136	0.16
Irish	8,057	9.68
Italian	2,373	2.85
Latvian	56	0.07
Lithuanian	71	0.09
Luxemburger	15	0.02
Macedonian	7	0.01
Northern European	150	0.18
Norwegian	4,404	5.29
Pennsylvania German	98	0.12
Polish	1,663	2.00
Portuguese	195	0.23
Romanian	240	0.29
Russian	1,026	1.23
Scandinavian	739	0.89
Scotch-Irish	1,357	1.63
Scottish	2,082	2.50
Serbian	53	0.06
Slavic	43	0.05
Slovak	28	0.03
Slovene	36	0.04
Swedish	2,220	2.67
Swiss	442	0.53
Turkish	45	0.05
Ukrainian	1,328	1.60
United States or American	3,732	4.48
Welsh	825	0.99
West Indian, excl. Hispanic:	178	0.21
Dutch West Indian	6	0.01
Haitian	56	0.07
Jamaican	93	0.11
Trinidadian and Tobagonian	6	0.01
West Indian	17	0.02
White:	60,930	73.18
Not Hispanic (55,050)	58,060	69.73
Hispanic (2,268)	2,870	3.45
Yugoslavian	118	0.14

Five Corners

Place Type: Census Designated Place
County: Clark
Population: 12,207

Ancestry/Race	Number	%
African American/Black:	264	2.16
Not Hispanic (195)	254	2.08
Hispanic (6)	10	0.08
African, sub-Saharan:	70	0.58
African	43	0.35
Nigerian	21	0.17
Other sub-Saharan African	6	0.05
Alaska Native tribes, specified:	10	0.08
Aleut (2)	3	0.02
Tlingit-Haida (5)	7	0.06
Am. Ind. or Alaska Nat., not spec.	51	0.42
American Indian tribes, specified:	148	1.21
Apache (2)	5	0.04
Blackfeet (4)	7	0.06
Cherokee (5)	38	0.31
Chickasaw (3)	4	0.03
Chippewa (6)	9	0.07
Choctaw (2)	6	0.05
Colville (4)	5	0.04
Comanche	1	0.01
Cree (1)	6	0.05
Crow	1	0.01
Iroquois (1)	3	0.02
Latin American Indians (9)	13	0.11
Menominee (2)	2	0.02
Navajo (3)	3	0.02
Osage	1	0.01
Puget Sound Salish (3)	4	0.03
Sioux (7)	8	0.07
Yakama (1)	1	0.01
Yaqui (1)	2	0.02
All other tribes (17)	29	0.24
American Indian tribes, not spec.	4	0.03
Arab:	20	0.17
Iraqi	20	0.17
Asian:	612	5.01
Cambodian (75)	76	0.62
Chinese, ex. Taiwanese (25)	38	0.31
Filipino (93)	153	1.25
Hmong (1)	2	0.02
Indian (33)	37	0.30
Indonesian (4)	7	0.06
Japanese (14)	45	0.37
Korean (35)	50	0.41
Laotian (23)	23	0.19
Thai (3)	3	0.02
Vietnamese (165)	168	1.38
Other Asian, not specified (8)	10	0.08
Austrian	35	0.29
Belgian	28	0.23
Brazilian	3	0.02
British	68	0.56
Bulgarian	11	0.09
Canadian	93	0.77
Celtic	9	0.07
Czech	28	0.23
Danish	152	1.25
Dutch	372	3.07
Eastern European	6	0.05
English	1,467	12.10
European	98	0.81
Finnish	168	1.39
French, except Basque	477	3.94
French Canadian	144	1.19
German	2,645	21.83
Greek	96	0.79
Hawaii Native/Pacific Islander:	115	0.94
Micronesian: (32)	43	0.35
Guamanian/Chamorro (32)	43	0.35
Polynesian: (42)	60	0.49
Native Hawaiian (14)	27	0.22
Samoan (28)	31	0.25
Tongan	2	0.02
Other Pac. Isl., not spec. (2)	12	0.10
Hispanic or Latino:	505	4.14
Central American:	14	0.11
Costa Rican	1	0.01
Guatemalan	1	0.01
Nicaraguan	4	0.03
Panamanian	2	0.02
Salvadoran	4	0.03
Other Central American	2	0.02
Cuban	6	0.05
Mexican	374	3.06
Puerto Rican	11	0.09
South American:	13	0.11
Argentinean	7	0.06
Bolivian	1	0.01
Chilean	1	0.01
Other South American	4	0.03
Other Hispanic or Latino	87	0.71
Hungarian	31	0.26
Irish	1,409	11.63
Italian	461	3.80
Lithuanian	39	0.32
Macedonian	3	0.02
New Zealander	22	0.18
Northern European	48	0.40
Norwegian	673	5.55
Polish	203	1.68
Portuguese	10	0.08
Russian	133	1.10
Scandinavian	7	0.06
Scotch-Irish	161	1.33
Scottish	377	3.11
Slovene	7	0.06
Swedish	361	2.98
Swiss	45	0.37
Ukrainian	34	0.28
United States or American	942	7.77
Welsh	61	0.50
White:	11,115	91.05
Not Hispanic (10,575)	10,814	88.59
Hispanic (246)	301	2.47
Yugoslavian	39	0.32

Fort Lewis

Place Type: Census Designated Place
County: Pierce
Population: 19,089

Ancestry/Race	Number	%
Acadian/Cajun	4	0.02
African American/Black:	4,359	22.84
Not Hispanic (3,758)	4,146	21.72
Hispanic (124)	213	1.12
African, sub-Saharan:	176	0.93
African	161	0.85
Nigerian	8	0.04
Other sub-Saharan African	7	0.04
Alaska Native tribes, specified:	18	0.09
Alaska Athabascan (1)	2	0.01
Aleut (1)	2	0.01
Eskimo (7)	12	0.06
Tlingit-Haida (1)	2	0.01
Alaska Native tribes, not specified	10	0.05
Am. Ind. or Alaska Nat., not spec.	107	0.56
American Indian tribes, specified:	368	1.93
Apache (6)	21	0.11
Blackfeet (6)	25	0.13
Cherokee (27)	99	0.52
Cheyenne (1)	2	0.01
Chickasaw (1)	1	0.01
Chippewa (8)	14	0.07
Choctaw (10)	14	0.07
Comanche (3)	5	0.03
Crow (3)	3	0.02
Delaware (1)	2	0.01
Houma	3	0.02
Iroquois (5)	17	0.09
Kiowa (5)	6	0.03
Latin American Indians (8)	13	0.07
Lumbee (8)	10	0.05
Menominee (1)	1	0.01
Navajo (21)	30	0.16
Osage (3)	3	0.02
Paiute	1	0.01
Pueblo (4)	8	0.04
Puget Sound Salish	2	0.01
Seminole (4)	4	0.02
Sioux (11)	17	0.09
Ute (1)	1	0.01
Yaqui (4)	6	0.03
All other tribes (42)	60	0.31
American Indian tribes, not spec.	21	0.11
Arab:	47	0.25
Egyptian	8	0.04

Notes: 1. Figures in the "Number" column do not add up to the total population due to: a) Ancestry/Race overlap — e.g. persons can report being both White and Irish, b) persons of Hispanic origin can report being any race, c) persons reporting two ancestries are counted in both categories. 2. Numbers in parentheses indicate the number of persons reporting this ancestry/race alone, not in combination with any other ancestry/race. 3. Refer to the Explanation of Data in the front of the book for more detailed information.

Jordanian	8	0.04
Lebanese	17	0.09
Other Arab	14	0.07
Asian:	1,103	5.78
Cambodian (10)	17	0.09
Chinese, ex. Taiwanese (12)	64	0.34
Filipino (297)	469	2.46
Hmong (2)	2	0.01
Indian (21)	34	0.18
Indonesian (3)	13	0.07
Japanese (31)	95	0.50
Korean (175)	260	1.36
Laotian (13)	15	0.08
Pakistani	3	0.02
Taiwanese (4)	8	0.04
Thai (14)	27	0.14
Vietnamese (16)	26	0.14
Other Asian, specified	2	0.01
Other Asian, not specified (30)	68	0.36
Australian	8	0.04
Austrian	42	0.22
Belgian	32	0.17
Brazilian	8	0.04
British	146	0.77
Canadian	9	0.05
Celtic	13	0.07
Croatian	15	0.08
Czech	7	0.04
Czechoslovakian	7	0.04
Danish	47	0.25
Dutch	276	1.45
English	1,135	5.97
European	231	1.21
Finnish	80	0.42
French, except Basque	668	3.51
French Canadian	153	0.80
German	3,307	17.38
Greek	17	0.09
Guyanese	4	0.02
Hawaii Native/Pacific Islander:	536	2.81
Melanesian:	3	0.02
Fijian	3	0.02
Micronesian: (140)	194	1.02
Guamanian/Chamorro (101)	142	0.74
Other Micronesian (39)	52	0.27
Polynesian: (188)	281	1.47
Native Hawaiian (30)	91	0.48
Samoan (154)	183	0.96
Tongan (1)	2	0.01
Other Polynesian (3)	5	0.03
Other Pac. Isl., specified	1	0.01
Other Pac. Isl., not spec. (6)	57	0.30
Hispanic or Latino:	2,507	13.13
Central American:	200	1.05
Costa Rican	9	0.05
Guatemalan	15	0.08
Honduran	26	0.14
Nicaraguan	11	0.06
Panamanian	94	0.49
Salvadoran	33	0.17
Other Central American	12	0.06
Cuban	18	0.09
Dominican Republic	36	0.19
Mexican	1,220	6.39
Puerto Rican	604	3.16
South American:	43	0.23
Argentinean	3	0.02
Bolivian	3	0.02
Colombian	12	0.06
Ecuadorian	10	0.05
Peruvian	12	0.06
Uruguayan	1	0.01
Venezuelan	1	0.01
Other South American	1	0.01
Other Hispanic or Latino	386	2.02
Hungarian	16	0.08
Iranian	18	0.09
Irish	2,321	12.20
Italian	612	3.22
Lithuanian	53	0.28
Norwegian	348	1.83
Polish	398	2.09
Portuguese	100	0.53
Romanian	7	0.04
Russian	65	0.34
Scandinavian	48	0.25
Scotch-Irish	213	1.12
Scottish	409	2.15
Slavic	16	0.08
Slovak	16	0.08
Slovene	8	0.04
Swedish	261	1.37
Swiss	46	0.24
Turkish	6	0.03
Ukrainian	17	0.09
United States or American	595	3.13
Welsh	98	0.52
West Indian, excl. Hispanic:	239	1.26
Barbadian	2	0.01
British West Indian	7	0.04
Haitian	111	0.58
Jamaican	112	0.59
Trinidadian and Tobagonian	7	0.04
White:	12,460	65.27
Not Hispanic (10,685)	11,354	59.48
Hispanic (852)	1,106	5.79
Yugoslavian	8	0.04

Inglewood-Finn Hill

Place Type: Census Designated Place
County: King
Population: 22,661

Ancestry/Race	Number	%
Acadian/Cajun	7	0.03
Afghan	10	0.04
African American/Black:	471	2.08
Not Hispanic (307)	445	1.96
Hispanic (9)	26	0.11
African, sub-Saharan:	20	0.09
African	20	0.09
Alaska Native tribes, specified:	28	0.12
Alaska Athabascan	3	0.01
Aleut (1)	2	0.01
Tlingit-Haida (11)	16	0.07
All other tribes (7)	7	0.03
Alaska Native tribes, not specified	1	0.00
Am. Ind. or Alaska Nat., not spec.	77	0.34
American Indian tribes, specified:	188	0.83
Apache (1)	5	0.02
Blackfeet (9)	15	0.07
Cherokee (6)	43	0.19
Cheyenne	1	0.00
Chippewa (6)	14	0.06
Choctaw (2)	8	0.04
Colville (5)	8	0.04
Comanche (1)	3	0.01
Cree	1	0.00
Creek	1	0.00
Iroquois	8	0.04
Latin American Indians (10)	18	0.08
Menominee	1	0.00
Navajo (3)	8	0.04
Paiute	1	0.00
Potawatomi (1)	2	0.01
Pueblo (2)	2	0.01
Puget Sound Salish (6)	10	0.04
Seminole	1	0.00
Shoshone (2)	3	0.01
Sioux (4)	11	0.05
Yakama	3	0.01
All other tribes (6)	21	0.09
American Indian tribes, not spec.	11	0.05
Arab:	146	0.64
Egyptian	6	0.03
Lebanese	82	0.36
Syrian	17	0.08
Other Arab	41	0.18
Armenian	4	0.02
Asian:	1,870	8.25
Cambodian (54)	69	0.30
Chinese, ex. Taiwanese (311)	414	1.83
Filipino (180)	296	1.31
Indian (150)	170	0.75
Indonesian (4)	8	0.04
Japanese (194)	312	1.38
Korean (183)	230	1.01
Laotian (27)	29	0.13
Malaysian (1)	1	0.00
Pakistani (29)	29	0.13
Sri Lankan (8)	12	0.05
Taiwanese (13)	20	0.09
Thai (21)	27	0.12
Vietnamese (187)	205	0.90
Other Asian, specified (10)	13	0.06
Other Asian, not specified (12)	35	0.15
Australian	35	0.15
Austrian	97	0.43
Basque	14	0.06
Belgian	41	0.18
Brazilian	32	0.14
British	297	1.31
Bulgarian	5	0.02
Canadian	151	0.67
Celtic	21	0.09
Croatian	21	0.09
Cypriot	26	0.11
Czech	209	0.92
Czechoslovakian	50	0.22
Danish	258	1.14
Dutch	460	2.03
Eastern European	34	0.15
English	3,212	14.18
European	459	2.03
Finnish	235	1.04
French, except Basque	970	4.28
French Canadian	163	0.72
German	4,794	21.16
Greek	149	0.66
Hawaii Native/Pacific Islander:	113	0.50
Melanesian: (4)	4	0.02
Fijian (4)	4	0.02
Micronesian: (6)	8	0.04
Guamanian/Chamorro (5)	7	0.03
Other Micronesian (1)	1	0.00
Polynesian: (21)	74	0.33
Native Hawaiian (16)	62	0.27
Samoan (5)	10	0.04
Other Polynesian	2	0.01
Other Pac. Isl., specified	2	0.01
Other Pac. Isl., not spec. (11)	25	0.11
Hispanic or Latino:	860	3.80
Central American:	40	0.18
Guatemalan	11	0.05
Honduran	5	0.02
Nicaraguan	4	0.02
Panamanian	8	0.04
Salvadoran	9	0.04
Other Central American	3	0.01
Cuban	23	0.10
Mexican	552	2.44
Puerto Rican	36	0.16
South American:	61	0.27
Argentinean	1	0.00
Chilean	4	0.02
Colombian	33	0.15
Peruvian	22	0.10
Venezuelan	1	0.00
Other Hispanic or Latino	148	0.65
Hungarian	68	0.30
Icelander	68	0.30
Iranian	145	0.64
Irish	2,844	12.56
Israeli	5	0.02
Italian	681	3.01
Lithuanian	7	0.03
Northern European	41	0.18
Norwegian	1,792	7.91
Polish	514	2.27

Notes: 1. Figures in the "Number" column do not add up to the total population due to: a) Ancestry/Race overlap — e.g. persons can report being both White and Irish, b) persons of Hispanic origin can report being any race, c) persons reporting two ancestries are counted in both categories. 2. Numbers in parentheses indicate the number of persons reporting this ancestry/race alone, not in combination with any other ancestry/race. 3. Refer to the Explanation of Data in the front of the book for more detailed information.

Ancestry/Race	Number	%
Portuguese	91	0.40
Romanian	55	0.24
Russian	296	1.31
Scandinavian	165	0.73
Scotch-Irish	508	2.24
Scottish	959	4.23
Serbian	19	0.08
Slavic	4	0.02
Slovak	7	0.03
Slovene	9	0.04
Swedish	1,099	4.85
Swiss	158	0.70
Turkish	7	0.03
Ukrainian	90	0.40
United States or American	718	3.17
Welsh	399	1.76
West Indian, excl. Hispanic:	5	0.02
U.S. Virgin Islander	5	0.02
White:	20,367	89.88
Not Hispanic (19,186)	19,793	87.34
Hispanic (480)	574	2.53
Yugoslavian	14	0.06

Issaquah

Place Type: City
County: King
Population: 11,212

Ancestry/Race	Number	%
African American/Black:	157	1.40
Not Hispanic (95)	150	1.34
Hispanic (4)	7	0.06
African, sub-Saharan:	8	0.07
African	1	0.01
Ugandan	7	0.06
Alaska Native tribes, specified:	9	0.08
Aleut (1)	1	0.01
Tlingit-Haida (5)	8	0.07
Alaska Native tribes, not specified	4	0.04
Am. Ind. or Alaska Nat., not spec.	33	0.29
American Indian tribes, specified:	89	0.79
Blackfeet (2)	4	0.04
Cherokee (7)	25	0.22
Chippewa (1)	4	0.04
Choctaw (4)	8	0.07
Comanche	3	0.03
Creek	1	0.01
Crow (1)	2	0.02
Delaware	1	0.01
Iroquois	1	0.01
Latin American Indians (5)	14	0.12
Navajo (3)	3	0.03
Paiute	1	0.01
Potawatomi (1)	1	0.01
Pueblo (2)	2	0.02
Puget Sound Salish	2	0.02
Seminole (3)	3	0.03
Sioux (2)	2	0.02
Yakama (1)	3	0.03
All other tribes (4)	9	0.08
American Indian tribes, not spec.	24	0.21
Arab:	48	0.43
Lebanese	17	0.15
Palestinian	31	0.28
Armenian	7	0.06
Asian:	878	7.83
Chinese, ex. Taiwanese (254)	315	2.81
Filipino (68)	116	1.03
Indian (71)	81	0.72
Indonesian (2)	2	0.02
Japanese (98)	166	1.48
Korean (80)	92	0.82
Laotian (1)	1	0.01
Malaysian (4)	4	0.04
Taiwanese (32)	39	0.35
Thai (5)	6	0.05
Vietnamese (29)	29	0.26
Other Asian, specified	4	0.04
Other Asian, not specified (12)	23	0.21
Australian	20	0.18
Austrian	12	0.11
Basque	17	0.15
Belgian	10	0.09
British	62	0.55
Canadian	52	0.46
Carpatho Rusyn	8	0.07
Croatian	10	0.09
Czech	57	0.51
Czechoslovakian	17	0.15
Danish	264	2.36
Dutch	284	2.53
Eastern European	8	0.07
English	1,690	15.08
European	183	1.63
Finnish	90	0.80
French, except Basque	431	3.85
French Canadian	53	0.47
German	2,181	19.46
Greek	39	0.35
Hawaii Native/Pacific Islander:	46	0.41
Micronesian: (2)	3	0.03
Guamanian/Chamorro (2)	3	0.03
Polynesian: (9)	31	0.28
Native Hawaiian (7)	27	0.24
Samoan (1)	3	0.03
Tongan (1)	1	0.01
Other Pac. Isl., not spec. (1)	12	0.11
Hispanic or Latino:	555	4.95
Central American:	13	0.12
Costa Rican	4	0.04
Nicaraguan	4	0.04
Panamanian	5	0.04
Cuban	16	0.14
Dominican Republic	3	0.03
Mexican	381	3.40
Puerto Rican	24	0.21
South American:	27	0.24
Argentinean	1	0.01
Bolivian	3	0.03
Chilean	2	0.02
Colombian	7	0.06
Ecuadorian	4	0.04
Peruvian	6	0.05
Venezuelan	3	0.03
Other South American	1	0.01
Other Hispanic or Latino	91	0.81
Hungarian	96	0.86
Iranian	45	0.40
Irish	1,297	11.58
Israeli	9	0.08
Italian	342	3.05
Lithuanian	53	0.47
Northern European	32	0.29
Norwegian	685	6.11
Polish	236	2.11
Portuguese	27	0.24
Romanian	7	0.06
Russian	248	2.21
Scandinavian	142	1.27
Scotch-Irish	236	2.11
Scottish	538	4.80
Slovak	39	0.35
Slovene	11	0.10
Swedish	596	5.32
Swiss	84	0.75
Turkish	57	0.51
Ukrainian	7	0.06
United States or American	313	2.79
Welsh	166	1.48
White:	10,150	90.53
Not Hispanic (9,523)	9,770	87.14
Hispanic (338)	380	3.39
Yugoslavian	19	0.17

Kelso

Place Type: City
County: Cowlitz
Population: 11,895

Ancestry/Race	Number	%
African American/Black:	123	1.03
Not Hispanic (97)	121	1.02
Hispanic (1)	2	0.02
African, sub-Saharan:	7	0.06
African	7	0.06
Alaska Native tribes, specified:	18	0.15
Aleut (4)	7	0.06
Eskimo (7)	7	0.06
Tlingit-Haida (2)	4	0.03
Alaska Native tribes, not specified	3	0.03
Am. Ind. or Alaska Nat., not spec.	77	0.65
American Indian tribes, specified:	331	2.78
Apache (3)	9	0.08
Blackfeet (12)	32	0.27
Cherokee (32)	74	0.62
Cheyenne (1)	4	0.03
Chippewa (24)	34	0.29
Choctaw (10)	21	0.18
Colville (3)	4	0.03
Cree	1	0.01
Creek (2)	4	0.03
Iroquois (1)	2	0.02
Latin American Indians (1)	9	0.08
Lumbee (11)	11	0.09
Navajo (9)	14	0.12
Osage (1)	4	0.03
Pueblo (1)	1	0.01
Puget Sound Salish (8)	10	0.08
Sioux (16)	27	0.23
Yakama (5)	5	0.04
Yaqui (1)	1	0.01
All other tribes (34)	64	0.54
American Indian tribes, not spec.	24	0.20
Arab:	5	0.04
Lebanese	5	0.04
Asian:	171	1.44
Cambodian (15)	18	0.15
Chinese, ex. Taiwanese (12)	15	0.13
Filipino (20)	46	0.39
Indian (5)	9	0.08
Japanese (15)	26	0.22
Korean (11)	13	0.11
Laotian (5)	6	0.05
Taiwanese (1)	1	0.01
Thai (2)	2	0.02
Vietnamese (9)	17	0.14
Other Asian, not specified (13)	18	0.15
Australian	14	0.12
Austrian	36	0.30
Basque	21	0.17
Belgian	6	0.05
British	40	0.33
Canadian	27	0.22
Celtic	6	0.05
Czech	49	0.41
Czechoslovakian	15	0.12
Danish	117	0.97
Dutch	229	1.90
English	1,246	10.35
Estonian	12	0.10
European	155	1.29
Finnish	239	1.99
French, except Basque	492	4.09
French Canadian	164	1.36
German	2,132	17.72
Greek	57	0.47
Hawaii Native/Pacific Islander:	47	0.40
Micronesian: (3)	8	0.07
Guamanian/Chamorro (2)	7	0.06
Other Micronesian (1)	1	0.01
Polynesian: (8)	22	0.18
Native Hawaiian (8)	22	0.18
Other Pac. Isl., not spec. (14)	17	0.14

Notes: 1. Figures in the "Number" column do not add up to the total population due to: a) Ancestry/Race overlap — e.g. persons can report being both White and Irish, b) persons of Hispanic origin can report being any race, c) persons reporting two ancestries are counted in both categories. 2. Numbers in parentheses indicate the number of persons reporting this ancestry/race alone, not in combination with any other ancestry/race. 3. Refer to the Explanation of Data in the front of the book for more detailed information.

Ancestry/Race	Number	%
Hispanic or Latino:	824	6.93
Central American:	29	0.24
Guatemalan	12	0.10
Honduran	4	0.03
Salvadoran	12	0.10
Other Central American	1	0.01
Cuban	6	0.05
Mexican	625	5.25
Puerto Rican	13	0.11
South American:	3	0.03
Argentinean	1	0.01
Colombian	2	0.02
Other Hispanic or Latino	148	1.24
Hungarian	9	0.07
Irish	1,518	12.61
Italian	285	2.37
Norwegian	697	5.79
Polish	112	0.93
Portuguese	7	0.06
Romanian	8	0.07
Russian	91	0.76
Scandinavian	24	0.20
Scotch-Irish	178	1.48
Scottish	299	2.48
Swedish	367	3.05
Swiss	48	0.40
Ukrainian	9	0.07
United States or American	652	5.42
Welsh	101	0.84
White:	11,026	92.69
Not Hispanic (10,374)	10,612	89.21
Hispanic (348)	414	3.48
Yugoslavian	7	0.06

Kenmore

Place Type: City
County: King
Population: 18,678

Ancestry/Race	Number	%
African American/Black:	361	1.93
Not Hispanic (253)	346	1.85
Hispanic (6)	15	0.08
African, sub-Saharan:	58	0.31
African	35	0.19
Ethiopian	23	0.12
Alaska Native tribes, specified:	12	0.06
Alaska Athabascan (1)	1	0.01
Aleut (1)	3	0.02
Eskimo (2)	4	0.02
Tlingit-Haida (1)	2	0.01
All other tribes (1)	2	0.01
Alaska Native tribes, not specified	3	0.02
Am. Ind. or Alaska Nat., not spec.	63	0.34
American Indian tribes, specified:	117	0.63
Apache	6	0.03
Blackfeet (4)	8	0.04
Cherokee (6)	33	0.18
Cheyenne	1	0.01
Chickasaw	1	0.01
Chippewa (2)	9	0.05
Choctaw (2)	3	0.02
Colville (4)	4	0.02
Comanche	1	0.01
Creek	1	0.01
Iroquois	1	0.01
Kiowa (1)	1	0.01
Latin American Indians (1)	2	0.01
Navajo (1)	2	0.01
Paiute (1)	1	0.01
Potawatomi (1)	1	0.01
Puget Sound Salish (1)	7	0.04
Seminole	3	0.02
Sioux (2)	7	0.04
Yakama	4	0.02
Yuman	1	0.01
All other tribes (6)	20	0.11
American Indian tribes, not spec.	15	0.08
Arab:	91	0.49
Egyptian	31	0.17
Lebanese	24	0.13
Other Arab	36	0.19
Armenian	73	0.39
Asian:	1,618	8.66
Cambodian (5)	7	0.04
Chinese, ex. Taiwanese (347)	414	2.22
Filipino (301)	376	2.01
Indian (103)	115	0.62
Indonesian (16)	17	0.09
Japanese (167)	237	1.27
Korean (194)	216	1.16
Laotian (10)	10	0.05
Malaysian	4	0.02
Pakistani (13)	13	0.07
Sri Lankan (4)	4	0.02
Taiwanese (42)	45	0.24
Thai (24)	24	0.13
Vietnamese (74)	93	0.50
Other Asian, specified (2)	8	0.04
Other Asian, not specified (15)	35	0.19
Australian	12	0.06
Austrian	15	0.08
Belgian	47	0.25
Brazilian	18	0.10
British	82	0.44
Bulgarian	21	0.11
Canadian	58	0.31
Celtic	32	0.17
Croatian	92	0.50
Czech	72	0.39
Czechoslovakian	63	0.34
Danish	262	1.41
Dutch	428	2.31
Eastern European	49	0.26
English	2,844	15.34
Estonian	11	0.06
European	438	2.36
Finnish	130	0.70
French, except Basque	581	3.13
French Canadian	209	1.13
German	3,339	18.01
Greek	47	0.25
Hawaii Native/Pacific Islander:	77	0.41
Micronesian: (11)	12	0.06
Guamanian/Chamorro (11)	11	0.06
Other Micronesian	1	0.01
Polynesian: (17)	38	0.20
Native Hawaiian (6)	21	0.11
Samoan (10)	12	0.06
Tongan (1)	4	0.02
Other Polynesian	1	0.01
Other Pac. Isl., specified	6	0.03
Other Pac. Isl., not spec. (6)	21	0.11
Hispanic or Latino:	655	3.51
Central American:	25	0.13
Costa Rican	4	0.02
Guatemalan	6	0.03
Nicaraguan	1	0.01
Panamanian	5	0.03
Salvadoran	9	0.05
Cuban	21	0.11
Mexican	380	2.03
Puerto Rican	35	0.19
South American:	39	0.21
Argentinean	4	0.02
Bolivian	2	0.01
Chilean	4	0.02
Colombian	7	0.04
Ecuadorian	2	0.01
Peruvian	15	0.08
Venezuelan	4	0.02
Other South American	1	0.01
Other Hispanic or Latino	155	0.83
Hungarian	69	0.37
Icelander	69	0.37
Iranian	102	0.55
Irish	2,571	13.87
Israeli	19	0.10
Italian	691	3.73
Latvian	98	0.53
Lithuanian	47	0.25
Luxemburger	5	0.03
New Zealander	10	0.05
Northern European	76	0.41
Norwegian	1,572	8.48
Pennsylvania German	20	0.11
Polish	270	1.46
Portuguese	62	0.33
Romanian	49	0.26
Russian	203	1.09
Scandinavian	176	0.95
Scotch-Irish	394	2.13
Scottish	669	3.61
Slavic	15	0.08
Slovak	15	0.08
Slovene	8	0.04
Swedish	1,058	5.71
Swiss	85	0.46
Ukrainian	110	0.59
United States or American	688	3.71
Welsh	191	1.03
White:	16,696	89.39
Not Hispanic (15,822)	16,264	87.08
Hispanic (372)	432	2.31
Yugoslavian	15	0.08

Kennewick

Place Type: City
County: Benton
Population: 54,693

Ancestry/Race	Number	%
African American/Black:	943	1.72
Not Hispanic (579)	848	1.55
Hispanic (45)	95	0.17
African, sub-Saharan:	133	0.24
African	101	0.18
South African	32	0.06
Alaska Native tribes, specified:	40	0.07
Alaska Athabascan (3)	4	0.01
Aleut (7)	10	0.02
Eskimo (4)	5	0.01
Tlingit-Haida (11)	19	0.03
All other tribes	2	0.00
Alaska Native tribes, not specified	2	0.00
Am. Ind. or Alaska Nat., not spec.	274	0.50
Albanian	54	0.10
Alsatian	16	0.03
American Indian tribes, specified:	581	1.06
Apache (8)	20	0.04
Blackfeet (6)	22	0.04
Cherokee (53)	138	0.25
Cheyenne (9)	11	0.02
Chickasaw (2)	5	0.01
Chippewa (22)	33	0.06
Choctaw (16)	33	0.06
Colville (5)	7	0.01
Comanche	2	0.00
Cree (2)	10	0.02
Creek (7)	11	0.02
Crow	2	0.00
Delaware	3	0.01
Iroquois (9)	12	0.02
Latin American Indians (17)	27	0.05
Lumbee (1)	1	0.00
Navajo (5)	8	0.01
Osage (2)	2	0.00
Paiute (2)	2	0.00
Pima (5)	5	0.01
Potawatomi (5)	5	0.01
Pueblo (13)	17	0.03
Puget Sound Salish (15)	22	0.04
Seminole (4)	10	0.02
Sioux (20)	35	0.06
Yakama (16)	23	0.04
All other tribes (71)	115	0.21
American Indian tribes, not spec.	58	0.11
Arab:	28	0.05

Notes: 1. Figures in the "Number" column do not add up to the total population due to: a) Ancestry/Race overlap — e.g. persons can report being both White and Irish, b) persons of Hispanic origin can report being any race, c) persons reporting two ancestries are counted in both categories. 2. Numbers in parentheses indicate the number of persons reporting this ancestry/race alone, not in combination with any other ancestry/race. 3. Refer to the Explanation of Data in the front of the book for more detailed information.

Iraqi	9	0.02
Moroccan	6	0.01
Syrian	13	0.02
Armenian	31	0.06
Asian:	1,581	2.89
Bangladeshi	1	0.00
Cambodian (4)	8	0.01
Chinese, ex. Taiwanese (119)	203	0.37
Filipino (198)	317	0.58
Indian (134)	141	0.26
Indonesian (2)	2	0.00
Japanese (83)	158	0.29
Korean (148)	196	0.36
Laotian (115)	145	0.27
Malaysian (2)	4	0.01
Pakistani (3)	4	0.01
Sri Lankan (5)	5	0.01
Taiwanese (3)	4	0.01
Thai (30)	41	0.07
Vietnamese (248)	280	0.51
Other Asian, specified	3	0.01
Other Asian, not specified (27)	69	0.13
Assyrian/Chaldean/Syriac	6	0.01
Australian	6	0.01
Austrian	94	0.17
Basque	18	0.03
Belgian	24	0.04
British	326	0.59
Canadian	349	0.63
Celtic	51	0.09
Croatian	49	0.09
Czech	124	0.23
Czechoslovakian	39	0.07
Danish	823	1.49
Dutch	1,429	2.59
Eastern European	23	0.04
English	6,466	11.74
Estonian	8	0.01
European	686	1.25
Finnish	112	0.20
French, except Basque	2,069	3.76
French Canadian	476	0.86
German	10,764	19.54
Greek	117	0.21
Hawaii Native/Pacific Islander:	147	0.27
Micronesian: (9)	16	0.03
Guamanian/Chamorro (9)	16	0.03
Polynesian: (36)	109	0.20
Native Hawaiian (27)	83	0.15
Samoan (6)	21	0.04
Other Polynesian (3)	5	0.01
Other Pac. Isl., specified	3	0.01
Other Pac. Isl., not spec. (10)	19	0.03
Hispanic or Latino:	8,503	15.55
Central American:	119	0.22
Costa Rican	4	0.01
Guatemalan	17	0.03
Honduran	4	0.01
Nicaraguan	6	0.01
Panamanian	5	0.01
Salvadoran	77	0.14
Other Central American	6	0.01
Cuban	9	0.02
Dominican Republic	4	0.01
Mexican	6,988	12.78
Puerto Rican	68	0.12
South American:	63	0.12
Argentinean	10	0.02
Bolivian	5	0.01
Chilean	4	0.01
Colombian	10	0.02
Ecuadorian	12	0.02
Peruvian	12	0.02
Uruguayan	1	0.00
Venezuelan	3	0.01
Other South American	6	0.01
Other Hispanic or Latino	1,252	2.29
Hungarian	120	0.22
Icelander	11	0.02
Irish	6,240	11.33
Italian	1,120	2.03
Latvian	16	0.03
Lithuanian	51	0.09
Northern European	90	0.16
Norwegian	2,645	4.80
Pennsylvania German	8	0.01
Polish	736	1.34
Portuguese	134	0.24
Romanian	41	0.07
Russian	407	0.74
Scandinavian	316	0.57
Scotch-Irish	1,103	2.00
Scottish	1,331	2.42
Serbian	98	0.18
Slavic	27	0.05
Swedish	1,307	2.37
Swiss	164	0.30
Turkish	23	0.04
Ukrainian	255	0.46
United States or American	3,721	6.75
Welsh	480	0.87
West Indian, excl. Hispanic:	40	0.07
Belizean	11	0.02
Dutch West Indian	7	0.01
Jamaican	22	0.04
White:	47,072	86.07
Not Hispanic (42,720)	43,882	80.23
Hispanic (2,635)	3,190	5.83
Yugoslavian	249	0.45

Kent

Place Type: City
County: King
Population: 79,524

Ancestry/Race	Number	%
Afghan	20	0.03
African American/Black:	7,869	9.90
Not Hispanic (6,444)	7,650	9.62
Hispanic (103)	219	0.28
African, sub-Saharan:	1,013	1.28
African	466	0.59
Cape Verdean	16	0.02
Ethiopian	6	0.01
Nigerian	73	0.09
Somalian	444	0.56
Sudanese	8	0.01
Alaska Native tribes, specified:	175	0.22
Alaska Athabascan (7)	16	0.02
Aleut (17)	22	0.03
Eskimo (19)	35	0.04
Tlingit-Haida (52)	86	0.11
All other tribes (7)	16	0.02
Alaska Native tribes, not specified	21	0.03
Am. Ind. or Alaska Nat., not spec.	539	0.68
Albanian	9	0.01
American Indian tribes, specified:	960	1.21
Apache (20)	35	0.04
Blackfeet (21)	76	0.10
Cherokee (50)	250	0.31
Cheyenne (7)	13	0.02
Chickasaw	2	0.00
Chippewa (33)	59	0.07
Choctaw (7)	29	0.04
Colville (18)	30	0.04
Comanche (1)	6	0.01
Cree (5)	11	0.01
Creek (3)	8	0.01
Crow (5)	9	0.01
Delaware	2	0.00
Iroquois (2)	6	0.01
Latin American Indians (31)	42	0.05
Navajo (5)	20	0.03
Osage	4	0.01
Ottawa (2)	3	0.00
Paiute (2)	8	0.01
Pima	3	0.00
Potawatomi (2)	7	0.01
Pueblo (7)	12	0.02
Puget Sound Salish (48)	80	0.10
Seminole	1	0.00
Shoshone (2)	10	0.01
Sioux (30)	63	0.08
Tohono O'Odham (1)	1	0.00
Yakama (6)	11	0.01
Yaqui	6	0.01
All other tribes (79)	153	0.19
American Indian tribes, not spec.	93	0.12
Arab:	330	0.42
Arab/Arabic	80	0.10
Egyptian	43	0.05
Iraqi	77	0.10
Lebanese	37	0.05
Palestinian	24	0.03
Other Arab	69	0.09
Armenian	45	0.06
Asian:	9,397	11.82
Bangladeshi (5)	5	0.01
Cambodian (229)	318	0.40
Chinese, ex. Taiwanese (911)	1,259	1.58
Filipino (1,586)	2,224	2.80
Hmong (25)	26	0.03
Indian (1,380)	1,534	1.93
Indonesian (39)	64	0.08
Japanese (579)	956	1.20
Korean (836)	969	1.22
Laotian (173)	185	0.23
Malaysian (1)	4	0.01
Pakistani (38)	53	0.07
Sri Lankan (4)	4	0.01
Taiwanese (40)	55	0.07
Thai (56)	81	0.10
Vietnamese (1,309)	1,407	1.77
Other Asian, specified (12)	30	0.04
Other Asian, not specified (88)	223	0.28
Australian	10	0.01
Austrian	195	0.25
Basque	19	0.02
Belgian	114	0.14
British	484	0.61
Bulgarian	72	0.09
Canadian	393	0.50
Celtic	60	0.08
Croatian	144	0.18
Czech	216	0.27
Czechoslovakian	152	0.19
Danish	812	1.02
Dutch	1,237	1.56
Eastern European	23	0.03
English	7,178	9.05
Estonian	45	0.06
European	1,222	1.54
Finnish	457	0.58
French, except Basque	2,150	2.71
French Canadian	539	0.68
German	12,916	16.28
German Russian	23	0.03
Greek	203	0.26
Hawaii Native/Pacific Islander:	1,073	1.35
Melanesian: (56)	73	0.09
Fijian (56)	73	0.09
Micronesian: (108)	146	0.18
Guamanian/Chamorro (82)	111	0.14
Other Micronesian (26)	35	0.04
Polynesian: (382)	680	0.86
Native Hawaiian (112)	320	0.40
Samoan (245)	321	0.40
Tongan (22)	33	0.04
Other Polynesian (3)	6	0.01
Other Pac. Isl., specified	12	0.02
Other Pac. Isl., not spec. (59)	162	0.20
Hispanic or Latino:	6,466	8.13
Central American:	251	0.32
Costa Rican	19	0.02
Guatemalan	71	0.09
Honduran	51	0.06
Nicaraguan	19	0.02
Panamanian	16	0.02
Salvadoran	70	0.09

Notes: 1. Figures in the "Number" column do not add up to the total population due to: a) Ancestry/Race overlap — e.g. persons can report being both White and Irish, b) persons of Hispanic origin can report being any race, c) persons reporting two ancestries are counted in both categories. 2. Numbers in parentheses indicate the number of persons reporting this ancestry/race alone, not in combination with any other ancestry/race. 3. Refer to the Explanation of Data in the front of the book for more detailed information.

Other Central American	5	0.01
Cuban	75	0.09
Dominican Republic	15	0.02
Mexican	4,584	5.76
Puerto Rican	307	0.39
South American:	172	0.22
Argentinean	21	0.03
Bolivian	11	0.01
Chilean	10	0.01
Colombian	49	0.06
Ecuadorian	19	0.02
Paraguayan	1	0.00
Peruvian	36	0.05
Uruguayan	2	0.00
Venezuelan	13	0.02
Other South American	10	0.01
Other Hispanic or Latino	1,062	1.34
Hungarian	193	0.24
Icelander	83	0.10
Irish	7,160	9.03
Israeli	32	0.04
Italian	2,524	3.18
Latvian	7	0.01
Lithuanian	85	0.11
Luxemburger	8	0.01
Macedonian	19	0.02
Maltese	6	0.01
Northern European	139	0.18
Norwegian	4,100	5.17
Pennsylvania German	15	0.02
Polish	1,084	1.37
Portuguese	214	0.27
Romanian	330	0.42
Russian	1,061	1.34
Scandinavian	528	0.67
Scotch-Irish	1,100	1.39
Scottish	1,568	1.98
Serbian	7	0.01
Slavic	47	0.06
Slovak	120	0.15
Slovene	20	0.03
Swedish	2,264	2.85
Swiss	432	0.54
Turkish	9	0.01
Ukrainian	1,477	1.86
United States or American	3,282	4.14
Welsh	417	0.53
West Indian, excl. Hispanic:	95	0.12
Jamaican	58	0.07
West Indian	37	0.05
White:	59,617	74.97
Not Hispanic (53,964)	56,692	71.29
Hispanic (2,343)	2,925	3.68
Yugoslavian	144	0.18

Kingsgate

Place Type: Census Designated Place
County: King
Population: 12,222

Ancestry/Race	Number	%
African American/Black:	297	2.43
Not Hispanic (194)	285	2.33
Hispanic (5)	12	0.10
African, sub-Saharan:	7	0.06
Nigerian	7	0.06
Alaska Native tribes, specified:	37	0.30
Alaska Athabascan (1)	1	0.01
Aleut (4)	12	0.10
Eskimo	2	0.02
Tlingit-Haida (12)	20	0.16
All other tribes (1)	2	0.02
Alaska Native tribes, not specified	3	0.02
Am. Ind. or Alaska Nat., not spec.	68	0.56
American Indian tribes, specified:	82	0.67
Apache (1)	1	0.01
Blackfeet (1)	4	0.03
Cherokee (2)	14	0.11
Chippewa (6)	7	0.06
Choctaw (3)	4	0.03
Cree (2)	10	0.08
Iroquois (1)	3	0.02
Latin American Indians (1)	3	0.02
Navajo (1)	3	0.02
Osage	1	0.01
Puget Sound Salish (2)	6	0.05
Seminole	1	0.01
Shoshone	7	0.06
Sioux (4)	4	0.03
Tohono O'Odham	1	0.01
Yakama (1)	2	0.02
All other tribes (6)	11	0.09
American Indian tribes, not spec.	3	0.02
Arab:	16	0.13
Other Arab	16	0.13
Asian:	1,734	14.19
Cambodian (148)	175	1.43
Chinese, ex. Taiwanese (265)	307	2.51
Filipino (205)	294	2.41
Hmong (71)	77	0.63
Indian (97)	122	1.00
Indonesian (3)	5	0.04
Japanese (113)	177	1.45
Korean (110)	131	1.07
Laotian (93)	107	0.88
Malaysian (1)	1	0.01
Pakistani (24)	32	0.26
Taiwanese (6)	12	0.10
Thai (21)	34	0.28
Vietnamese (198)	213	1.74
Other Asian, specified (3)	3	0.02
Other Asian, not specified (17)	44	0.36
Australian	24	0.20
Austrian	69	0.57
Basque	11	0.09
Belgian	22	0.18
British	194	1.61
Canadian	61	0.51
Celtic	11	0.09
Croatian	5	0.04
Czech	71	0.59
Czechoslovakian	27	0.22
Danish	215	1.79
Dutch	195	1.62
Eastern European	7	0.06
English	1,704	14.17
European	165	1.37
Finnish	39	0.32
French, except Basque	352	2.93
French Canadian	160	1.33
German	2,136	17.76
Greek	49	0.41
Hawaii Native/Pacific Islander:	61	0.50
Micronesian: (11)	19	0.16
Guamanian/Chamorro (11)	19	0.16
Polynesian: (14)	32	0.26
Native Hawaiian (12)	28	0.23
Samoan (1)	1	0.01
Other Polynesian (1)	3	0.02
Other Pac. Isl., not spec. (4)	10	0.08
Hispanic or Latino:	690	5.65
Central American:	24	0.20
Costa Rican	1	0.01
Guatemalan	15	0.12
Nicaraguan	1	0.01
Panamanian	2	0.02
Salvadoran	5	0.04
Cuban	2	0.02
Mexican	503	4.12
Puerto Rican	30	0.25
South American:	48	0.39
Argentinean	2	0.02
Chilean	5	0.04
Colombian	13	0.11
Ecuadorian	3	0.02
Peruvian	18	0.15
Uruguayan	4	0.03
Venezuelan	2	0.02
Other South American	1	0.01
Other Hispanic or Latino	83	0.68
Hungarian	66	0.55
Icelander	17	0.14
Iranian	66	0.55
Irish	1,498	12.45
Italian	382	3.18
Northern European	56	0.47
Norwegian	874	7.27
Polish	398	3.31
Portuguese	17	0.14
Romanian	126	1.05
Russian	153	1.27
Scandinavian	96	0.80
Scotch-Irish	152	1.26
Scottish	588	4.89
Serbian	22	0.18
Swedish	561	4.66
Swiss	131	1.09
Ukrainian	36	0.30
United States or American	485	4.03
Welsh	343	2.85
White:	10,203	83.48
Not Hispanic (9,381)	9,758	79.84
Hispanic (390)	445	3.64
Yugoslavian	43	0.36

Kirkland

Place Type: City
County: King
Population: 45,054

Ancestry/Race	Number	%
Acadian/Cajun	9	0.02
African American/Black:	964	2.14
Not Hispanic (688)	907	2.01
Hispanic (29)	57	0.13
African, sub-Saharan:	62	0.14
African	30	0.07
Ethiopian	9	0.02
Kenyan	10	0.02
Zimbabwean	7	0.02
Other sub-Saharan African	6	0.01
Alaska Native tribes, specified:	45	0.10
Alaska Athabascan (4)	4	0.01
Aleut (10)	10	0.02
Eskimo (1)	6	0.01
Tlingit-Haida (6)	15	0.03
All other tribes (3)	10	0.02
Alaska Native tribes, not specified	12	0.03
Am. Ind. or Alaska Nat., not spec.	144	0.32
Albanian	7	0.02
Alsatian	10	0.02
American Indian tribes, specified:	265	0.59
Apache (2)	6	0.01
Blackfeet (2)	10	0.02
Cherokee (15)	54	0.12
Cheyenne	1	0.00
Chickasaw (1)	1	0.00
Chippewa (5)	12	0.03
Choctaw (3)	12	0.03
Colville (7)	10	0.02
Comanche	1	0.00
Cree (4)	5	0.01
Delaware	1	0.00
Iroquois (4)	17	0.04
Kiowa (3)	3	0.01
Latin American Indians (9)	10	0.02
Navajo (2)	6	0.01
Osage (1)	2	0.00
Ottawa (2)	2	0.00
Paiute (1)	2	0.00
Potawatomi (2)	5	0.01
Pueblo (4)	8	0.02
Puget Sound Salish (5)	13	0.03
Seminole	1	0.00
Sioux (4)	13	0.03
Yakama (2)	2	0.00
Yaqui	2	0.00
All other tribes (44)	66	0.15

Notes: 1. Figures in the "Number" column do not add up to the total population due to: a) Ancestry/Race overlap — e.g. persons can report being both White and Irish, b) persons of Hispanic origin can report being any race, c) persons reporting two ancestries are counted in both categories. 2. Numbers in parentheses indicate the number of persons reporting this ancestry/race alone, not in combination with any other ancestry/race. 3. Refer to the Explanation of Data in the front of the book for more detailed information.

American Indian tribes, not spec.	43	0.10
Arab:	98	0.22
Arab/Arabic	7	0.02
Lebanese	55	0.12
Syrian	27	0.06
Other Arab	9	0.02
Armenian	118	0.26
Asian:	4,283	9.51
Bangladeshi (2)	2	0.00
Cambodian (108)	132	0.29
Chinese, ex. Taiwanese (864)	1,025	2.28
Filipino (458)	648	1.44
Indian (506)	560	1.24
Indonesian (11)	15	0.03
Japanese (483)	706	1.57
Korean (383)	448	0.99
Laotian (66)	76	0.17
Malaysian (3)	3	0.01
Pakistani (8)	9	0.02
Sri Lankan (2)	3	0.01
Taiwanese (69)	82	0.18
Thai (32)	44	0.10
Vietnamese (369)	403	0.89
Other Asian, specified (5)	19	0.04
Other Asian, not specified (41)	108	0.24
Assyrian/Chaldean/Syriac	40	0.09
Australian	44	0.10
Austrian	113	0.25
Basque	33	0.07
Belgian	154	0.34
Brazilian	138	0.31
British	663	1.47
Bulgarian	8	0.02
Canadian	358	0.80
Celtic	33	0.07
Croatian	87	0.19
Cypriot	28	0.06
Czech	372	0.83
Czechoslovakian	53	0.12
Danish	661	1.47
Dutch	1,190	2.65
Eastern European	96	0.21
English	6,352	14.12
Estonian	43	0.10
European	810	1.80
Finnish	287	0.64
French, except Basque	1,970	4.38
French Canadian	434	0.96
German	8,699	19.34
German Russian	4	0.01
Greek	151	0.34
Hawaii Native/Pacific Islander:	203	0.45
Micronesian: (20)	29	0.06
Guamanian/Chamorro (20)	29	0.06
Polynesian: (58)	137	0.30
Native Hawaiian (40)	110	0.24
Samoan (12)	19	0.04
Tongan (6)	7	0.02
Other Polynesian	1	0.00
Other Pac. Isl., specified	1	0.00
Other Pac. Isl., not spec. (11)	36	0.08
Hispanic or Latino:	1,852	4.11
Central American:	67	0.15
Costa Rican	9	0.02
Guatemalan	9	0.02
Honduran	11	0.02
Nicaraguan	5	0.01
Panamanian	6	0.01
Salvadoran	14	0.03
Other Central American	13	0.03
Cuban	39	0.09
Dominican Republic	5	0.01
Mexican	1,159	2.57
Puerto Rican	90	0.20
South American:	114	0.25
Argentinean	9	0.02
Bolivian	2	0.00
Chilean	8	0.02
Colombian	30	0.07
Ecuadorian	6	0.01
Paraguayan	1	0.00
Peruvian	48	0.11
Venezuelan	4	0.01
Other South American	6	0.01
Other Hispanic or Latino	378	0.84
Hungarian	159	0.35
Icelander	14	0.03
Iranian	372	0.83
Irish	5,331	11.85
Israeli	50	0.11
Italian	2,046	4.55
Latvian	12	0.03
Lithuanian	134	0.30
Luxemburger	17	0.04
New Zealander	39	0.09
Northern European	176	0.39
Norwegian	3,082	6.85
Polish	992	2.21
Portuguese	100	0.22
Romanian	171	0.38
Russian	715	1.59
Scandinavian	393	0.87
Scotch-Irish	903	2.01
Scottish	1,887	4.19
Serbian	48	0.11
Slavic	13	0.03
Slovak	109	0.24
Slovene	42	0.09
Swedish	2,093	4.65
Swiss	274	0.61
Turkish	25	0.06
Ukrainian	244	0.54
United States or American	1,923	4.27
Welsh	506	1.12
West Indian, excl. Hispanic:	40	0.09
British West Indian	24	0.05
Jamaican	7	0.02
Trinidadian and Tobagonian	9	0.02
White:	39,578	87.85
Not Hispanic (37,438)	38,477	85.40
Hispanic (982)	1,101	2.44
Yugoslavian	73	0.16

Lacey

Place Type: City
County: Thurston
Population: 31,226

Ancestry/Race	Number	%
African American/Black:	1,860	5.96
Not Hispanic (1,449)	1,776	5.69
Hispanic (41)	84	0.27
African, sub-Saharan:	83	0.27
African	83	0.27
Alaska Native tribes, specified:	55	0.18
Alaska Athabascan (11)	13	0.04
Aleut (6)	12	0.04
Eskimo (4)	9	0.03
Tlingit-Haida (13)	18	0.06
All other tribes	3	0.01
Alaska Native tribes, not specified	2	0.01
Am. Ind. or Alaska Nat., not spec.	160	0.51
Alsatian	7	0.02
American Indian tribes, specified:	546	1.75
Apache (5)	12	0.04
Blackfeet (14)	47	0.15
Cherokee (33)	121	0.39
Cheyenne (4)	6	0.02
Chickasaw (2)	3	0.01
Chippewa (20)	27	0.09
Choctaw (7)	16	0.05
Colville (3)	6	0.02
Cree	5	0.02
Creek (3)	5	0.02
Crow	1	0.00
Delaware	1	0.00
Iroquois (3)	5	0.02
Kiowa	2	0.01
Latin American Indians (8)	17	0.05
Lumbee (3)	3	0.01
Menominee (3)	5	0.02
Navajo (6)	11	0.04
Osage	1	0.00
Ottawa (4)	5	0.02
Pima	1	0.00
Potawatomi	1	0.00
Pueblo (2)	2	0.01
Puget Sound Salish (47)	63	0.20
Seminole	6	0.02
Sioux (15)	25	0.08
Yakama (5)	7	0.02
All other tribes (103)	142	0.45
American Indian tribes, not spec.	49	0.16
Arab:	26	0.08
Lebanese	19	0.06
Syrian	7	0.02
Armenian	9	0.03
Asian:	3,157	10.11
Bangladeshi	5	0.02
Cambodian (246)	283	0.91
Chinese, ex. Taiwanese (152)	234	0.75
Filipino (486)	702	2.25
Indian (83)	110	0.35
Indonesian (10)	17	0.05
Japanese (149)	271	0.87
Korean (588)	771	2.47
Laotian (30)	39	0.12
Malaysian (7)	8	0.03
Pakistani (6)	10	0.03
Sri Lankan (5)	6	0.02
Taiwanese (5)	5	0.02
Thai (24)	36	0.12
Vietnamese (507)	551	1.76
Other Asian, specified (2)	7	0.02
Other Asian, not specified (64)	102	0.33
Assyrian/Chaldean/Syriac	12	0.04
Austrian	51	0.16
Belgian	10	0.03
British	298	0.96
Bulgarian	8	0.03
Canadian	139	0.45
Celtic	30	0.10
Croatian	42	0.14
Czech	68	0.22
Czechoslovakian	44	0.14
Danish	319	1.03
Dutch	508	1.63
English	3,470	11.16
European	828	2.66
Finnish	180	0.58
French, except Basque	1,134	3.65
French Canadian	310	1.00
German	6,245	20.08
Greek	110	0.35
Hawaii Native/Pacific Islander:	488	1.56
Melanesian: (1)	4	0.01
Other Melanesian (1)	4	0.01
Micronesian: (164)	190	0.61
Guamanian/Chamorro (144)	169	0.54
Other Micronesian (20)	21	0.07
Polynesian: (143)	253	0.81
Native Hawaiian (86)	178	0.57
Samoan (55)	70	0.22
Other Polynesian (2)	5	0.02
Other Pac. Isl., specified	2	0.01
Other Pac. Isl., not spec. (17)	39	0.12
Hispanic or Latino:	1,843	5.90
Central American:	114	0.37
Costa Rican	13	0.04
Guatemalan	22	0.07
Honduran	7	0.02
Nicaraguan	1	0.00
Panamanian	35	0.11
Salvadoran	32	0.10
Other Central American	4	0.01
Cuban	35	0.11
Dominican Republic	9	0.03
Mexican	988	3.16
Puerto Rican	309	0.99

Notes: 1. Figures in the "Number" column do not add up to the total population due to: a) Ancestry/Race overlap — e.g. persons can report being both White and Irish, b) persons of Hispanic origin can report being any race, c) persons reporting two ancestries are counted in both categories. 2. Numbers in parentheses indicate the number of persons reporting this ancestry/race alone, not in combination with any other ancestry/race. 3. Refer to the Explanation of Data in the front of the book for more detailed information.

Ancestry/Race	Number	%
South American:	33	0.11
Argentinean	1	0.00
Bolivian	5	0.02
Chilean	4	0.01
Colombian	5	0.02
Ecuadorian	1	0.00
Peruvian	3	0.01
Uruguayan	2	0.01
Venezuelan	1	0.00
Other South American	11	0.04
Other Hispanic or Latino	355	1.14
Hungarian	72	0.23
Icelander	33	0.11
Irish	3,347	10.76
Italian	1,005	3.23
Latvian	14	0.05
Lithuanian	14	0.05
Luxemburger	5	0.02
Macedonian	8	0.03
Northern European	63	0.20
Norwegian	1,624	5.22
Pennsylvania German	37	0.12
Polish	578	1.86
Portuguese	154	0.50
Romanian	69	0.22
Russian	230	0.74
Scandinavian	282	0.91
Scotch-Irish	845	2.72
Scottish	1,045	3.36
Slavic	12	0.04
Slovak	61	0.20
Swedish	772	2.48
Swiss	70	0.23
Ukrainian	43	0.14
United States or American	1,289	4.14
Welsh	316	1.02
West Indian, excl. Hispanic:	73	0.23
British West Indian	7	0.02
Jamaican	44	0.14
West Indian	22	0.07
White:	25,674	82.22
Not Hispanic (23,560)	24,586	78.74
Hispanic (857)	1,088	3.48
Yugoslavian	23	0.07

Lake Forest Park

Place Type: City
County: King
Population: 13,142

Ancestry/Race	Number	%
African American/Black:	299	2.28
Not Hispanic (205)	286	2.18
Hispanic (11)	13	0.10
African, sub-Saharan:	57	0.42
African	8	0.06
Somalian	28	0.21
Other sub-Saharan African	21	0.16
Alaska Native tribes, specified:	25	0.19
Alaska Athabascan	4	0.03
Aleut (3)	4	0.03
Eskimo (1)	3	0.02
Tlingit-Haida (2)	13	0.10
All other tribes (1)	1	0.01
Alaska Native tribes, not specified	3	0.02
Am. Ind. or Alaska Nat., not spec.	48	0.37
Alsatian	7	0.05
American Indian tribes, specified:	78	0.59
Blackfeet (2)	5	0.04
Cherokee (3)	16	0.12
Chippewa (2)	4	0.03
Choctaw	3	0.02
Colville (3)	3	0.02
Comanche (1)	2	0.02
Iroquois	2	0.02
Latin American Indians (2)	11	0.08
Osage	1	0.01
Potawatomi (1)	1	0.01
Pueblo (1)	2	0.02
Puget Sound Salish (2)	3	0.02
Shoshone (1)	1	0.01
Sioux	2	0.02
Yakama	1	0.01
All other tribes (13)	21	0.16
American Indian tribes, not spec.	14	0.11
Arab:	32	0.24
Lebanese	32	0.24
Asian:	1,285	9.78
Cambodian (25)	30	0.23
Chinese, ex. Taiwanese (279)	332	2.53
Filipino (160)	216	1.64
Indian (105)	116	0.88
Indonesian (4)	7	0.05
Japanese (134)	207	1.58
Korean (172)	189	1.44
Laotian (14)	14	0.11
Pakistani (6)	9	0.07
Taiwanese (42)	42	0.32
Thai (10)	14	0.11
Vietnamese (59)	62	0.47
Other Asian, specified (9)	10	0.08
Other Asian, not specified (9)	37	0.28
Australian	6	0.04
Austrian	57	0.42
Basque	5	0.04
Belgian	21	0.16
British	126	0.94
Canadian	96	0.71
Celtic	6	0.04
Croatian	5	0.04
Czech	87	0.65
Czechoslovakian	20	0.15
Danish	99	0.74
Dutch	453	3.37
Eastern European	13	0.10
English	2,170	16.14
European	335	2.49
Finnish	106	0.79
French, except Basque	349	2.60
French Canadian	111	0.83
German	2,255	16.77
Greek	28	0.21
Hawaii Native/Pacific Islander:	33	0.25
Melanesian:	1	0.01
Fijian	1	0.01
Micronesian: (4)	8	0.06
Guamanian/Chamorro (4)	6	0.05
Other Micronesian	2	0.02
Polynesian: (11)	22	0.17
Native Hawaiian (9)	18	0.14
Samoan (2)	4	0.03
Other Pac. Isl., not spec.	2	0.02
Hispanic or Latino:	294	2.24
Central American:	9	0.07
Costa Rican	2	0.02
Guatemalan	5	0.04
Honduran	1	0.01
Salvadoran	1	0.01
Cuban	13	0.10
Dominican Republic	5	0.04
Mexican	142	1.08
Puerto Rican	22	0.17
South American:	32	0.24
Argentinean	5	0.04
Bolivian	3	0.02
Chilean	7	0.05
Colombian	4	0.03
Ecuadorian	3	0.02
Peruvian	10	0.08
Other Hispanic or Latino	71	0.54
Hungarian	40	0.30
Icelander	63	0.47
Iranian	26	0.19
Irish	1,531	11.39
Italian	418	3.11
Latvian	18	0.13
Lithuanian	33	0.25
Luxemburger	6	0.04
Northern European	34	0.25
Norwegian	1,171	8.71
Polish	243	1.81
Portuguese	17	0.13
Romanian	17	0.13
Russian	161	1.20
Scandinavian	108	0.80
Scotch-Irish	482	3.59
Scottish	607	4.52
Slavic	15	0.11
Slovak	15	0.11
Slovene	21	0.16
Swedish	729	5.42
Swiss	115	0.86
Turkish	28	0.21
Ukrainian	68	0.51
United States or American	588	4.37
Welsh	148	1.10
West Indian, excl. Hispanic:	5	0.04
Haitian	5	0.04
White:	11,624	88.45
Not Hispanic (11,071)	11,445	87.09
Hispanic (142)	179	1.36
Yugoslavian	47	0.35

Lakeland North

Place Type: Census Designated Place
County: King
Population: 15,085

Ancestry/Race	Number	%
African American/Black:	617	4.09
Not Hispanic (497)	590	3.91
Hispanic (17)	27	0.18
African, sub-Saharan:	31	0.20
African	19	0.13
Ethiopian	12	0.08
Alaska Native tribes, specified:	46	0.30
Alaska Athabascan (6)	7	0.05
Aleut (1)	3	0.02
Eskimo (12)	20	0.13
Tlingit-Haida (4)	11	0.07
All other tribes (2)	5	0.03
Alaska Native tribes, not specified	5	0.03
Am. Ind. or Alaska Nat., not spec.	101	0.67
American Indian tribes, specified:	161	1.07
Blackfeet (7)	17	0.11
Cherokee (13)	39	0.26
Cheyenne (1)	1	0.01
Chickasaw (1)	1	0.01
Chippewa (17)	24	0.16
Choctaw	2	0.01
Colville	2	0.01
Delaware (3)	4	0.03
Iroquois (1)	1	0.01
Latin American Indians (1)	2	0.01
Menominee	2	0.01
Navajo	1	0.01
Paiute (2)	2	0.01
Pima (4)	4	0.03
Potawatomi	1	0.01
Pueblo	1	0.01
Puget Sound Salish (5)	8	0.05
Seminole	1	0.01
Shoshone (1)	6	0.04
Sioux (10)	11	0.07
All other tribes (20)	31	0.21
American Indian tribes, not spec.	9	0.06
Arab:	42	0.28
Egyptian	11	0.07
Lebanese	18	0.12
Other Arab	13	0.09
Armenian	10	0.07
Asian:	1,341	8.89
Cambodian (33)	40	0.27
Chinese, ex. Taiwanese (81)	131	0.87
Filipino (238)	326	2.16
Indian (119)	130	0.86
Indonesian (3)	3	0.02
Japanese (107)	167	1.11

Notes: 1. Figures in the "Number" column do not add up to the total population due to: a) Ancestry/Race overlap — e.g. persons can report being both White and Irish, b) persons of Hispanic origin can report being any race, c) persons reporting two ancestries are counted in both categories. 2. Numbers in parentheses indicate the number of persons reporting this ancestry/race alone, not in combination with any other ancestry/race. 3. Refer to the Explanation of Data in the front of the book for more detailed information.

Korean (282)	323	2.14
Laotian (6)	20	0.13
Malaysian	8	0.05
Pakistani (6)	8	0.05
Taiwanese (2)	2	0.01
Thai (10)	19	0.13
Vietnamese (98)	117	0.78
Other Asian, specified (3)	3	0.02
Other Asian, not specified (19)	44	0.29
Austrian	39	0.26
Belgian	65	0.43
Brazilian	18	0.12
British	51	0.34
Canadian	88	0.58
Celtic	12	0.08
Croatian	8	0.05
Czech	56	0.37
Danish	262	1.73
Dutch	321	2.12
English	1,505	9.94
European	258	1.70
Finnish	95	0.63
French, except Basque	585	3.86
French Canadian	154	1.02
German	2,427	16.02
German Russian	9	0.06
Greek	31	0.20
Guyanese	8	0.05
Hawaii Native/Pacific Islander:	140	0.93
Melanesian: (8)	8	0.05
Fijian (8)	8	0.05
Micronesian: (18)	29	0.19
Guamanian/Chamorro (15)	25	0.17
Other Micronesian (3)	4	0.03
Polynesian: (36)	84	0.56
Native Hawaiian (5)	44	0.29
Samoan (20)	29	0.19
Tongan (11)	11	0.07
Other Pac. Isl., not spec. (8)	19	0.13
Hispanic or Latino:	537	3.56
Central American:	24	0.16
Costa Rican	3	0.02
Guatemalan	1	0.01
Panamanian	9	0.06
Salvadoran	8	0.05
Other Central American	3	0.02
Cuban	11	0.07
Mexican	312	2.07
Puerto Rican	29	0.19
South American:	15	0.10
Argentinean	3	0.02
Bolivian	1	0.01
Chilean	2	0.01
Colombian	3	0.02
Ecuadorian	1	0.01
Peruvian	4	0.03
Venezuelan	1	0.01
Other Hispanic or Latino	146	0.97
Hungarian	61	0.40
Iranian	11	0.07
Irish	1,713	11.31
Israeli	6	0.04
Italian	548	3.62
Latvian	9	0.06
Lithuanian	26	0.17
Northern European	7	0.05
Norwegian	848	5.60
Pennsylvania German	19	0.13
Polish	484	3.20
Portuguese	63	0.42
Romanian	117	0.77
Russian	228	1.51
Scandinavian	81	0.53
Scotch-Irish	270	1.78
Scottish	356	2.35
Slovak	17	0.11
Swedish	401	2.65
Swiss	93	0.61
Turkish	28	0.18
Ukrainian	436	2.88
United States or American	1,193	7.88
Welsh	91	0.60
White:	12,972	85.99
Not Hispanic (12,224)	12,705	84.22
Hispanic (214)	267	1.77
Yugoslavian	56	0.37

Lakeland South

Place Type: Census Designated Place
County: King
Population: 11,436

Ancestry/Race	Number	%
African American/Black:	528	4.62
Not Hispanic (401)	497	4.35
Hispanic (21)	31	0.27
African, sub-Saharan:	52	0.45
African	38	0.33
Ethiopian	14	0.12
Alaska Native tribes, specified:	16	0.14
Alaska Athabascan (1)	2	0.02
Aleut (1)	3	0.03
Eskimo (1)	1	0.01
Tlingit-Haida (8)	8	0.07
All other tribes	2	0.02
Am. Ind. or Alaska Nat., not spec.	49	0.43
American Indian tribes, specified:	129	1.13
Apache	2	0.02
Blackfeet (3)	12	0.10
Cherokee (7)	35	0.31
Cheyenne	1	0.01
Chickasaw (1)	1	0.01
Chippewa (5)	5	0.04
Choctaw (1)	3	0.03
Colville (2)	3	0.03
Cree	3	0.03
Delaware (2)	2	0.02
Iroquois (4)	4	0.03
Navajo (4)	5	0.04
Osage (3)	3	0.03
Ottawa (1)	1	0.01
Pueblo (3)	3	0.03
Puget Sound Salish (2)	8	0.07
Seminole (1)	1	0.01
Sioux (12)	16	0.14
Yaqui	3	0.03
All other tribes (7)	18	0.16
American Indian tribes, not spec.	11	0.10
Asian:	908	7.94
Cambodian (6)	13	0.11
Chinese, ex. Taiwanese (46)	67	0.59
Filipino (169)	249	2.18
Indian (59)	63	0.55
Indonesian (1)	3	0.03
Japanese (66)	116	1.01
Korean (209)	242	2.12
Laotian (7)	9	0.08
Malaysian (1)	3	0.03
Pakistani	2	0.02
Taiwanese (2)	2	0.02
Thai (23)	25	0.22
Vietnamese (71)	81	0.71
Other Asian, not specified (28)	33	0.29
Austrian	8	0.07
Basque	15	0.13
Belgian	25	0.22
British	99	0.86
Canadian	64	0.56
Czech	30	0.26
Czechoslovakian	42	0.37
Danish	105	0.91
Dutch	327	2.84
Eastern European	7	0.06
English	1,243	10.81
European	159	1.38
Finnish	73	0.63
French, except Basque	388	3.37
French Canadian	56	0.49
German	2,259	19.65
Greek	47	0.41
Guyanese	24	0.21
Hawaii Native/Pacific Islander:	80	0.70
Micronesian: (8)	12	0.10
Guamanian/Chamorro (8)	12	0.10
Polynesian: (27)	50	0.44
Native Hawaiian (12)	32	0.28
Samoan (15)	18	0.16
Other Pac. Isl., not spec. (13)	18	0.16
Hispanic or Latino:	381	3.33
Central American:	16	0.14
Guatemalan	2	0.02
Nicaraguan	6	0.05
Panamanian	1	0.01
Salvadoran	7	0.06
Cuban	6	0.05
Mexican	238	2.08
Puerto Rican	39	0.34
South American:	7	0.06
Argentinean	2	0.02
Colombian	2	0.02
Peruvian	3	0.03
Other Hispanic or Latino	75	0.66
Hungarian	48	0.42
Icelander	13	0.11
Iranian	13	0.11
Irish	1,232	10.71
Italian	515	4.48
Latvian	5	0.04
New Zealander	10	0.09
Northern European	14	0.12
Norwegian	847	7.37
Polish	287	2.50
Portuguese	87	0.76
Russian	92	0.80
Scandinavian	82	0.71
Scotch-Irish	297	2.58
Scottish	358	3.11
Slovak	9	0.08
Swedish	387	3.37
Swiss	98	0.85
Ukrainian	69	0.60
United States or American	803	6.98
Welsh	132	1.15
West Indian, excl. Hispanic:	8	0.07
Haitian	8	0.07
White:	9,987	87.33
Not Hispanic (9,409)	9,762	85.36
Hispanic (190)	225	1.97
Yugoslavian	6	0.05

Lakewood

Place Type: City
County: Pierce
Population: 58,211

Ancestry/Race	Number	%
Acadian/Cajun	10	0.02
African American/Black:	8,719	14.98
Not Hispanic (6,890)	8,289	14.24
Hispanic (242)	430	0.74
African, sub-Saharan:	302	0.52
African	240	0.41
Ethiopian	8	0.01
Kenyan	17	0.03
Nigerian	23	0.04
Other sub-Saharan African	14	0.02
Alaska Native tribes, specified:	97	0.17
Alaska Athabascan (7)	9	0.02
Aleut (8)	12	0.02
Eskimo (18)	25	0.04
Tlingit-Haida (27)	50	0.09
All other tribes	1	0.00
Alaska Native tribes, not specified	4	0.01
Am. Ind. or Alaska Nat., not spec.	532	0.91
American Indian tribes, specified:	1,171	2.01
Apache (15)	35	0.06
Blackfeet (27)	124	0.21
Cherokee (60)	265	0.46

Notes: 1. Figures in the "Number" column do not add up to the total population due to: a) Ancestry/Race overlap — e.g. persons can report being both White and Irish, b) persons of Hispanic origin can report being any race, c) persons reporting two ancestries are counted in both categories. 2. Numbers in parentheses indicate the number of persons reporting this ancestry/race alone, not in combination with any other ancestry/race. 3. Refer to the Explanation of Data in the front of the book for more detailed information.

Ancestry/Race	Number	%
Cheyenne (4)	9	0.02
Chickasaw (3)	6	0.01
Chippewa (46)	81	0.14
Choctaw (8)	38	0.07
Colville (16)	18	0.03
Comanche (3)	4	0.01
Cree	8	0.01
Creek (3)	6	0.01
Crow (9)	10	0.02
Delaware (2)	7	0.01
Houma (1)	4	0.01
Iroquois (3)	12	0.02
Latin American Indians (19)	36	0.06
Navajo (27)	36	0.06
Osage	3	0.01
Ottawa (2)	4	0.01
Paiute (4)	9	0.02
Potawatomi	1	0.00
Pueblo (5)	6	0.01
Puget Sound Salish (90)	112	0.19
Seminole (3)	13	0.02
Shoshone (8)	12	0.02
Sioux (38)	67	0.12
Tohono O'Odham	2	0.00
Ute	2	0.00
Yakama (19)	24	0.04
Yaqui (1)	3	0.01
All other tribes (146)	214	0.37
American Indian tribes, not spec.	105	0.18
Arab:	43	0.07
Arab/Arabic	16	0.03
Lebanese	27	0.05
Armenian	9	0.02
Asian:	7,064	12.14
Cambodian (81)	102	0.18
Chinese, ex. Taiwanese (191)	371	0.64
Filipino (1,384)	1,873	3.22
Indian (105)	159	0.27
Indonesian (6)	13	0.02
Japanese (566)	1,011	1.74
Korean (2,244)	2,777	4.77
Laotian (13)	14	0.02
Pakistani (6)	6	0.01
Sri Lankan (11)	11	0.02
Taiwanese (9)	16	0.03
Thai (87)	152	0.26
Vietnamese (327)	391	0.67
Other Asian, specified (3)	15	0.03
Other Asian, not specified (69)	153	0.26
Australian	15	0.03
Austrian	166	0.28
Basque	12	0.02
Belgian	11	0.02
British	248	0.43
Bulgarian	8	0.01
Canadian	160	0.27
Celtic	63	0.11
Croatian	17	0.03
Czech	241	0.41
Czechoslovakian	142	0.24
Danish	455	0.78
Dutch	936	1.61
Eastern European	5	0.01
English	4,652	7.98
European	888	1.52
Finnish	164	0.28
French, except Basque	1,587	2.72
French Canadian	441	0.76
German	9,020	15.47
German Russian	28	0.05
Greek	142	0.24
Guyanese	27	0.05
Hawaii Native/Pacific Islander:	1,627	2.80
Melanesian:	1	0.00
Fijian	1	0.00
Micronesian: (276)	370	0.64
Guamanian/Chamorro (243)	331	0.57
Other Micronesian (33)	39	0.07
Polynesian: (762)	1,154	1.98
Native Hawaiian (196)	449	0.77
Samoan (545)	672	1.15
Tongan (15)	23	0.04
Other Polynesian (6)	10	0.02
Other Pac. Isl., specified	2	0.00
Other Pac. Isl., not spec. (17)	100	0.17
Hispanic or Latino:	4,941	8.49
Central American:	230	0.40
Costa Rican	5	0.01
Guatemalan	12	0.02
Honduran	11	0.02
Nicaraguan	17	0.03
Panamanian	124	0.21
Salvadoran	44	0.08
Other Central American	17	0.03
Cuban	80	0.14
Dominican Republic	32	0.05
Mexican	2,945	5.06
Puerto Rican	779	1.34
South American:	103	0.18
Argentinean	8	0.01
Bolivian	5	0.01
Chilean	10	0.02
Colombian	30	0.05
Ecuadorian	14	0.02
Paraguayan	2	0.00
Peruvian	26	0.04
Venezuelan	6	0.01
Other South American	3	0.01
Other Hispanic or Latino	772	1.33
Hungarian	113	0.19
Icelander	12	0.02
Iranian	7	0.01
Irish	5,127	8.79
Israeli	14	0.02
Italian	1,918	3.29
Lithuanian	84	0.14
Luxemburger	20	0.03
Maltese	10	0.02
Northern European	21	0.04
Norwegian	2,263	3.88
Pennsylvania German	38	0.07
Polish	993	1.70
Portuguese	247	0.42
Romanian	63	0.11
Russian	231	0.40
Scandinavian	303	0.52
Scotch-Irish	1,073	1.84
Scottish	1,067	1.83
Serbian	18	0.03
Slavic	48	0.08
Slovak	65	0.11
Slovene	12	0.02
Swedish	987	1.69
Swiss	268	0.46
Turkish	7	0.01
Ukrainian	107	0.18
United States or American	2,612	4.48
Welsh	560	0.96
West Indian, excl. Hispanic:	225	0.39
Haitian	70	0.12
Jamaican	127	0.22
West Indian	28	0.05
White:	41,011	70.45
Not Hispanic (35,829)	38,586	66.29
Hispanic (1,905)	2,425	4.17
Yugoslavian	65	0.11

Lea Hill

Place Type: Census Designated Place
County: King
Population: 10,871

Ancestry/Race	Number	%
African American/Black:	336	3.09
Not Hispanic (233)	306	2.81
Hispanic (9)	30	0.28
African, sub-Saharan:	11	0.10
African	11	0.10
Alaska Native tribes, specified:	24	0.22
Alaska Athabascan (2)	2	0.02
Aleut (4)	11	0.10
Eskimo (7)	7	0.06
Tlingit-Haida	2	0.02
All other tribes (2)	2	0.02
Am. Ind. or Alaska Nat., not spec.	51	0.47
American Indian tribes, specified:	120	1.10
Apache (1)	2	0.02
Blackfeet (6)	8	0.07
Cherokee (19)	30	0.28
Cheyenne (3)	4	0.04
Chickasaw (1)	1	0.01
Chippewa (10)	15	0.14
Choctaw (5)	5	0.05
Colville	2	0.02
Creek (9)	9	0.08
Crow	1	0.01
Delaware (2)	2	0.02
Iroquois	1	0.01
Latin American Indians (2)	2	0.02
Menominee	1	0.01
Osage	3	0.03
Puget Sound Salish (1)	6	0.06
Sioux	4	0.04
Ute	3	0.03
Yakama (1)	2	0.02
All other tribes (7)	19	0.17
American Indian tribes, not spec.	6	0.06
Arab:	30	0.28
Iraqi	16	0.15
Other Arab	14	0.13
Asian:	670	6.16
Cambodian (24)	28	0.26
Chinese, ex. Taiwanese (40)	67	0.62
Filipino (128)	191	1.76
Hmong (6)	6	0.06
Indian (53)	62	0.57
Indonesian (11)	14	0.13
Japanese (64)	111	1.02
Korean (40)	57	0.52
Laotian (4)	6	0.06
Taiwanese (3)	4	0.04
Thai (5)	7	0.06
Vietnamese (89)	95	0.87
Other Asian, specified	3	0.03
Other Asian, not specified (9)	19	0.17
Austrian	12	0.11
Belgian	13	0.12
British	43	0.40
Bulgarian	26	0.24
Canadian	69	0.65
Croatian	41	0.38
Czechoslovakian	8	0.07
Danish	41	0.38
Dutch	170	1.59
English	1,340	12.56
European	490	4.59
French, except Basque	466	4.37
French Canadian	46	0.43
German	2,396	22.46
Greek	45	0.42
Hawaii Native/Pacific Islander:	72	0.66
Melanesian: (3)	6	0.06
Fijian (3)	6	0.06
Micronesian: (4)	16	0.15
Guamanian/Chamorro (3)	7	0.06
Other Micronesian (1)	9	0.08
Polynesian: (8)	37	0.34
Native Hawaiian (5)	27	0.25
Samoan (3)	10	0.09
Other Pac. Isl., not spec. (4)	13	0.12
Hispanic or Latino:	536	4.93
Central American:	15	0.14
Costa Rican	4	0.04
Panamanian	3	0.03
Salvadoran	2	0.02
Other Central American	6	0.06
Cuban	11	0.10
Dominican Republic	2	0.02
Mexican	370	3.40

Notes: 1. Figures in the "Number" column do not add up to the total population due to: a) Ancestry/Race overlap — e.g. persons can report being both White and Irish, b) persons of Hispanic origin can report being any race, c) persons reporting two ancestries are counted in both categories. 2. Numbers in parentheses indicate the number of persons reporting this ancestry/race alone, not in combination with any other ancestry/race. 3. Refer to the Explanation of Data in the front of the book for more detailed information.

Ancestry/Race	Number	%
Puerto Rican	23	0.21
South American:	20	0.18
Bolivian	9	0.08
Chilean	4	0.04
Colombian	4	0.04
Peruvian	1	0.01
Venezuelan	2	0.02
Other Hispanic or Latino	95	0.87
Hungarian	38	0.36
Irish	937	8.78
Italian	408	3.82
Latvian	24	0.22
Lithuanian	12	0.11
Northern European	46	0.43
Norwegian	646	6.05
Polish	255	2.39
Portuguese	22	0.21
Romanian	47	0.44
Russian	26	0.24
Scandinavian	122	1.14
Scotch-Irish	161	1.51
Scottish	209	1.96
Serbian	4	0.04
Slovak	15	0.14
Swedish	198	1.86
Swiss	61	0.57
Turkish	25	0.23
Ukrainian	100	0.94
United States or American	711	6.66
Welsh	141	1.32
West Indian, excl. Hispanic:	22	0.21
Jamaican	22	0.21
White:	9,762	89.80
Not Hispanic (9,100)	9,438	86.82
Hispanic (266)	324	2.98
Yugoslavian	41	0.38

Longview

Place Type: City
County: Cowlitz
Population: 34,660

Ancestry/Race	Number	%
Acadian/Cajun	15	0.04
African American/Black:	409	1.18
Not Hispanic (227)	378	1.09
Hispanic (21)	31	0.09
African, sub-Saharan:	38	0.11
African	34	0.10
Other sub-Saharan African	4	0.01
Alaska Native tribes, specified:	30	0.09
Alaska Athabascan (4)	4	0.01
Aleut (6)	11	0.03
Eskimo (6)	9	0.03
Tlingit-Haida (6)	6	0.02
Alaska Native tribes, not specified	6	0.02
Am. Ind. or Alaska Nat., not spec.	267	0.77
American Indian tribes, specified:	796	2.30
Apache (4)	11	0.03
Blackfeet (21)	38	0.11
Cherokee (94)	211	0.61
Cheyenne (2)	2	0.01
Chickasaw (1)	8	0.02
Chippewa (39)	65	0.19
Choctaw (13)	38	0.11
Colville (1)	3	0.01
Comanche (1)	7	0.02
Creek (9)	12	0.03
Crow	1	0.00
Delaware (3)	4	0.01
Houma (1)	1	0.00
Iroquois (9)	16	0.05
Kiowa	1	0.00
Latin American Indians (14)	16	0.05
Lumbee (20)	22	0.06
Menominee	1	0.00
Navajo (2)	3	0.01
Osage	3	0.01
Paiute (2)	3	0.01
Pima (5)	5	0.01
Potawatomi (2)	6	0.02
Pueblo (5)	10	0.03
Puget Sound Salish (9)	10	0.03
Seminole (1)	1	0.00
Sioux (29)	63	0.18
Ute	2	0.01
Yakama (13)	21	0.06
Yaqui	2	0.01
Yuman (2)	8	0.02
All other tribes (114)	202	0.58
American Indian tribes, not spec.	40	0.12
Arab:	55	0.16
Arab/Arabic	8	0.02
Lebanese	47	0.14
Asian:	998	2.88
Cambodian (157)	189	0.55
Chinese, ex. Taiwanese (99)	141	0.41
Filipino (64)	119	0.34
Indian (59)	84	0.24
Indonesian (3)	5	0.01
Japanese (61)	97	0.28
Korean (61)	78	0.23
Laotian (9)	12	0.03
Pakistani (7)	9	0.03
Thai (6)	11	0.03
Vietnamese (202)	225	0.65
Other Asian, specified	2	0.01
Other Asian, not specified (11)	26	0.08
Australian	15	0.04
Austrian	45	0.13
Basque	11	0.03
Belgian	36	0.10
British	111	0.32
Bulgarian	15	0.04
Canadian	102	0.29
Celtic	15	0.04
Croatian	46	0.13
Czech	86	0.25
Czechoslovakian	32	0.09
Danish	418	1.20
Dutch	905	2.60
English	4,279	12.29
European	316	0.91
Finnish	805	2.31
French, except Basque	1,190	3.42
French Canadian	389	1.12
German	6,379	18.33
Greek	63	0.18
Hawaii Native/Pacific Islander:	126	0.36
Micronesian: (8)	16	0.05
Guamanian/Chamorro (8)	15	0.04
Other Micronesian	1	0.00
Polynesian: (29)	86	0.25
Native Hawaiian (22)	69	0.20
Samoan (7)	17	0.05
Other Pac. Isl., specified	1	0.00
Other Pac. Isl., not spec. (7)	23	0.07
Hispanic or Latino:	2,017	5.82
Central American:	35	0.10
Guatemalan	15	0.04
Honduran	9	0.03
Panamanian	2	0.01
Salvadoran	8	0.02
Other Central American	1	0.00
Cuban	17	0.05
Mexican	1,616	4.66
Puerto Rican	47	0.14
South American:	17	0.05
Argentinean	5	0.01
Chilean	2	0.01
Colombian	5	0.01
Ecuadorian	1	0.00
Peruvian	4	0.01
Other Hispanic or Latino	285	0.82
Hungarian	64	0.18
Icelander	9	0.03
Irish	3,793	10.90
Italian	914	2.63
Latvian	32	0.09
Lithuanian	19	0.05
Northern European	76	0.22
Norwegian	2,298	6.60
Pennsylvania German	64	0.18
Polish	429	1.23
Portuguese	111	0.32
Romanian	26	0.07
Russian	198	0.57
Scandinavian	147	0.42
Scotch-Irish	743	2.13
Scottish	901	2.59
Serbian	14	0.04
Slavic	8	0.02
Slovene	8	0.02
Swedish	909	2.61
Swiss	223	0.64
Ukrainian	98	0.28
United States or American	2,671	7.67
Welsh	352	1.01
West Indian, excl. Hispanic:	29	0.08
Belizean	4	0.01
Dutch West Indian	12	0.03
Jamaican	13	0.04
White:	31,896	92.03
Not Hispanic (30,229)	30,977	89.37
Hispanic (738)	919	2.65
Yugoslavian	49	0.14

Lynnwood

Place Type: City
County: Snohomish
Population: 33,847

Ancestry/Race	Number	%
Afghan	13	0.04
African American/Black:	1,413	4.17
Not Hispanic (1,070)	1,351	3.99
Hispanic (40)	62	0.18
African, sub-Saharan:	384	1.14
African	207	0.61
Ethiopian	59	0.17
Ghanian	39	0.12
Nigerian	50	0.15
Senegalese	20	0.06
Other sub-Saharan African	9	0.03
Alaska Native tribes, specified:	125	0.37
Alaska Athabascan (4)	11	0.03
Aleut (16)	23	0.07
Eskimo (4)	20	0.06
Tlingit-Haida (39)	55	0.16
All other tribes (16)	16	0.05
Alaska Native tribes, not specified	14	0.04
Am. Ind. or Alaska Nat., not spec.	144	0.43
Albanian	6	0.02
Alsatian	7	0.02
American Indian tribes, specified:	383	1.13
Apache (5)	14	0.04
Blackfeet (19)	38	0.11
Cherokee (21)	81	0.24
Cheyenne (1)	3	0.01
Chippewa (15)	26	0.08
Choctaw (5)	12	0.04
Colville (5)	8	0.02
Comanche (1)	3	0.01
Cree (1)	2	0.01
Iroquois	15	0.04
Latin American Indians (12)	24	0.07
Lumbee (1)	1	0.00
Menominee (1)	1	0.00
Navajo (4)	11	0.03
Osage (1)	1	0.00
Pima (1)	1	0.00
Pueblo (3)	3	0.01
Puget Sound Salish (4)	11	0.03
Seminole	3	0.01
Sioux (21)	36	0.11
Yakama (1)	8	0.02
Yuman (1)	1	0.00
All other tribes (45)	80	0.24

Notes: 1. Figures in the "Number" column do not add up to the total population due to: a) Ancestry/Race overlap — e.g. persons can report being both White and Irish, b) persons of Hispanic origin can report being any race, c) persons reporting two ancestries are counted in both categories. 2. Numbers in parentheses indicate the number of persons reporting this ancestry/race alone, not in combination with any other ancestry/race. 3. Refer to the Explanation of Data in the front of the book for more detailed information.

American Indian tribes, not spec.	28	0.08
Arab:	155	0.46
Arab/Arabic	37	0.11
Egyptian	57	0.17
Lebanese	36	0.11
Palestinian	8	0.02
Other Arab	17	0.05
Armenian	61	0.18
Asian:	5,370	15.87
Cambodian (190)	215	0.64
Chinese, ex. Taiwanese (714)	849	2.51
Filipino (895)	1,100	3.25
Hmong (3)	3	0.01
Indian (243)	284	0.84
Indonesian (41)	49	0.14
Japanese (240)	372	1.10
Korean (1,036)	1,103	3.26
Laotian (38)	56	0.17
Malaysian (1)	7	0.02
Pakistani (55)	69	0.20
Sri Lankan (9)	9	0.03
Taiwanese (27)	35	0.10
Thai (48)	66	0.19
Vietnamese (979)	1,028	3.04
Other Asian, specified (3)	9	0.03
Other Asian, not specified (63)	116	0.34
Assyrian/Chaldean/Syriac	12	0.04
Australian	15	0.04
Austrian	47	0.14
Belgian	18	0.05
Brazilian	18	0.05
British	197	0.58
Bulgarian	145	0.43
Canadian	120	0.36
Celtic	10	0.03
Croatian	24	0.07
Czech	104	0.31
Czechoslovakian	20	0.06
Danish	375	1.11
Dutch	694	2.06
Eastern European	10	0.03
English	3,471	10.29
Estonian	19	0.06
European	544	1.61
Finnish	201	0.60
French, except Basque	1,261	3.74
French Canadian	187	0.55
German	5,504	16.32
German Russian	11	0.03
Greek	257	0.76
Hawaii Native/Pacific Islander:	284	0.84
Melanesian: (57)	64	0.19
Fijian (57)	64	0.19
Micronesian: (21)	33	0.10
Guamanian/Chamorro (19)	31	0.09
Other Micronesian (2)	2	0.01
Polynesian: (45)	110	0.32
Native Hawaiian (32)	90	0.27
Samoan (10)	15	0.04
Tongan	1	0.00
Other Polynesian (3)	4	0.01
Other Pac. Isl., specified	1	0.00
Other Pac. Isl., not spec. (8)	76	0.22
Hispanic or Latino:	2,356	6.96
Central American:	92	0.27
Costa Rican	8	0.02
Guatemalan	11	0.03
Honduran	7	0.02
Nicaraguan	21	0.06
Panamanian	6	0.02
Salvadoran	37	0.11
Other Central American	2	0.01
Cuban	26	0.08
Dominican Republic	1	0.00
Mexican	1,633	4.82
Puerto Rican	87	0.26
South American:	109	0.32
Argentinean	8	0.02
Chilean	18	0.05
Colombian	15	0.04
Paraguayan	2	0.01
Peruvian	52	0.15
Uruguayan	6	0.02
Venezuelan	3	0.01
Other South American	5	0.01
Other Hispanic or Latino	408	1.21
Hungarian	200	0.59
Icelander	115	0.34
Iranian	133	0.39
Irish	3,366	9.98
Italian	777	2.30
Latvian	19	0.06
Lithuanian	33	0.10
New Zealander	2	0.01
Northern European	77	0.23
Norwegian	2,289	6.79
Pennsylvania German	37	0.11
Polish	839	2.49
Portuguese	44	0.13
Romanian	215	0.64
Russian	285	0.84
Scandinavian	276	0.82
Scotch-Irish	701	2.08
Scottish	1,062	3.15
Serbian	68	0.20
Slavic	28	0.08
Soviet Union	25	0.07
Swedish	1,168	3.46
Swiss	123	0.36
Turkish	43	0.13
Ukrainian	517	1.53
United States or American	1,458	4.32
Welsh	180	0.53
West Indian, excl. Hispanic:	41	0.12
Haitian	18	0.05
Jamaican	11	0.03
West Indian	12	0.04
White:	26,403	78.01
Not Hispanic (24,009)	25,054	74.02
Hispanic (1,129)	1,349	3.99
Yugoslavian	214	0.63

Maple Valley

Place Type: City
County: King
Population: 14,209

Ancestry/Race	Number	%
African American/Black:	239	1.68
Not Hispanic (143)	210	1.48
Hispanic (15)	29	0.20
African, sub-Saharan:	18	0.13
African	6	0.04
Cape Verdean	6	0.04
Somalian	6	0.04
Alaska Native tribes, specified:	17	0.12
Alaska Athabascan	2	0.01
Aleut (1)	2	0.01
Tlingit-Haida (3)	10	0.07
All other tribes	3	0.02
Am. Ind. or Alaska Nat., not spec.	53	0.37
American Indian tribes, specified:	174	1.22
Apache	6	0.04
Blackfeet (1)	8	0.06
Cherokee (17)	50	0.35
Chickasaw	1	0.01
Chippewa (15)	19	0.13
Choctaw (1)	3	0.02
Colville (2)	3	0.02
Cree (1)	1	0.01
Creek	1	0.01
Iroquois	5	0.04
Latin American Indians (4)	10	0.07
Navajo (2)	8	0.06
Osage (2)	2	0.01
Paiute (3)	5	0.04
Potawatomi	3	0.02
Puget Sound Salish (4)	19	0.13
Sioux (2)	9	0.06
Yakama (1)	1	0.01
Yaqui	3	0.02
All other tribes (12)	17	0.12
American Indian tribes, not spec.	19	0.13
Arab:	40	0.28
Lebanese	33	0.23
Syrian	7	0.05
Armenian	58	0.40
Asian:	609	4.29
Cambodian (14)	20	0.14
Chinese, ex. Taiwanese (42)	78	0.55
Filipino (112)	200	1.41
Indian (35)	46	0.32
Indonesian (1)	9	0.06
Japanese (49)	119	0.84
Korean (59)	80	0.56
Malaysian (1)	1	0.01
Thai	3	0.02
Vietnamese (22)	23	0.16
Other Asian, specified	1	0.01
Other Asian, not specified (2)	29	0.20
Australian	6	0.04
Austrian	76	0.53
British	32	0.22
Bulgarian	13	0.09
Canadian	71	0.50
Celtic	4	0.03
Czech	22	0.15
Czechoslovakian	32	0.22
Danish	191	1.33
Dutch	257	1.79
Eastern European	19	0.13
English	1,872	13.05
European	333	2.32
Finnish	97	0.68
French, except Basque	632	4.41
French Canadian	201	1.40
German	3,030	21.13
Greek	21	0.15
Hawaii Native/Pacific Islander:	57	0.40
Micronesian: (3)	8	0.06
Guamanian/Chamorro (3)	8	0.06
Polynesian: (17)	37	0.26
Native Hawaiian (13)	31	0.22
Samoan (1)	3	0.02
Tongan (3)	3	0.02
Other Pac. Isl., specified	1	0.01
Other Pac. Isl., not spec. (2)	11	0.08
Hispanic or Latino:	506	3.56
Central American:	15	0.11
Costa Rican	6	0.04
Guatemalan	1	0.01
Nicaraguan	2	0.01
Panamanian	2	0.01
Salvadoran	3	0.02
Other Central American	1	0.01
Cuban	21	0.15
Dominican Republic	1	0.01
Mexican	305	2.15
Puerto Rican	36	0.25
South American:	17	0.12
Argentinean	1	0.01
Chilean	2	0.01
Colombian	2	0.01
Ecuadorian	2	0.01
Peruvian	5	0.04
Uruguayan	1	0.01
Venezuelan	1	0.01
Other South American	3	0.02
Other Hispanic or Latino	111	0.78
Hungarian	59	0.41
Irish	1,793	12.50
Italian	793	5.53
Lithuanian	17	0.12
Norwegian	1,334	9.30
Polish	459	3.20
Portuguese	33	0.23
Romanian	49	0.34
Russian	150	1.05
Scandinavian	76	0.53

Notes: 1. Figures in the "Number" column do not add up to the total population due to: a) Ancestry/Race overlap — e.g. persons can report being both White and Irish, b) persons of Hispanic origin can report being any race, c) persons reporting two ancestries are counted in both categories. 2. Numbers in parentheses indicate the number of persons reporting this ancestry/race alone, not in combination with any other ancestry/race. 3. Refer to the Explanation of Data in the front of the book for more detailed information.

Ancestry/Race	Number	%
Scotch-Irish	272	1.90
Scottish	402	2.80
Slavic	28	0.20
Slovak	25	0.17
Swedish	529	3.69
Swiss	61	0.43
Ukrainian	126	0.88
United States or American	837	5.84
Welsh	158	1.10
White:	13,347	93.93
Not Hispanic (12,625)	13,045	91.81
Hispanic (251)	302	2.13
Yugoslavian	62	0.43

Martha Lake

Place Type: Census Designated Place
County: Snohomish
Population: 12,633

Ancestry/Race	Number	%
Afghan	16	0.13
African American/Black:	285	2.26
Not Hispanic (184)	270	2.14
Hispanic (8)	15	0.12
African, sub-Saharan:	4	0.03
Cape Verdean	4	0.03
Alaska Native tribes, specified:	28	0.22
Aleut (2)	3	0.02
Eskimo (2)	5	0.04
Tlingit-Haida (4)	13	0.10
All other tribes (2)	7	0.06
Alaska Native tribes, not specified	3	0.02
Am. Ind. or Alaska Nat., not spec.	68	0.54
American Indian tribes, specified:	123	0.97
Blackfeet (1)	4	0.03
Cherokee (8)	41	0.32
Cheyenne	1	0.01
Chickasaw	3	0.02
Chippewa (4)	10	0.08
Choctaw (1)	1	0.01
Colville (2)	2	0.02
Comanche	1	0.01
Cree (1)	3	0.02
Delaware	1	0.01
Iroquois	1	0.01
Latin American Indians (1)	5	0.04
Navajo (4)	5	0.04
Pueblo (2)	2	0.02
Puget Sound Salish (1)	2	0.02
Sioux (2)	5	0.04
Yakama	3	0.02
All other tribes (11)	32	0.25
American Indian tribes, not spec.	16	0.13
Arab:	48	0.38
Egyptian	10	0.08
Lebanese	7	0.06
Moroccan	4	0.03
Other Arab	27	0.21
Armenian	137	1.08
Asian:	1,328	10.51
Bangladeshi (3)	4	0.03
Cambodian (125)	143	1.13
Chinese, ex. Taiwanese (141)	189	1.50
Filipino (179)	247	1.96
Indian (117)	132	1.04
Indonesian (2)	3	0.02
Japanese (71)	125	0.99
Korean (147)	167	1.32
Laotian (11)	16	0.13
Pakistani (27)	28	0.22
Taiwanese (5)	7	0.06
Thai (2)	9	0.07
Vietnamese (211)	233	1.84
Other Asian, specified (4)	8	0.06
Other Asian, not specified (3)	17	0.13
Austrian	29	0.23
British	37	0.29
Canadian	64	0.51
Croatian	18	0.14
Czech	44	0.35
Czechoslovakian	17	0.13
Danish	93	0.74
Dutch	236	1.87
English	1,517	12.00
European	208	1.65
Finnish	77	0.61
French, except Basque	385	3.05
French Canadian	100	0.79
German	2,092	16.55
Greek	107	0.85
Hawaii Native/Pacific Islander:	85	0.67
Melanesian: (9)	9	0.07
Fijian (9)	9	0.07
Micronesian: (2)	10	0.08
Guamanian/Chamorro (2)	7	0.06
Other Micronesian	3	0.02
Polynesian: (16)	59	0.47
Native Hawaiian (7)	38	0.30
Samoan (8)	20	0.16
Other Polynesian (1)	1	0.01
Other Pac. Isl., not spec. (2)	7	0.06
Hispanic or Latino:	467	3.70
Central American:	19	0.15
Costa Rican	7	0.06
Guatemalan	1	0.01
Honduran	3	0.02
Nicaraguan	1	0.01
Panamanian	1	0.01
Salvadoran	5	0.04
Other Central American	1	0.01
Cuban	11	0.09
Dominican Republic	1	0.01
Mexican	288	2.28
Puerto Rican	34	0.27
South American:	23	0.18
Argentinean	2	0.02
Bolivian	2	0.02
Chilean	5	0.04
Colombian	2	0.02
Ecuadorian	2	0.02
Peruvian	8	0.06
Other South American	2	0.02
Other Hispanic or Latino	91	0.72
Irish	1,598	12.64
Italian	360	2.85
Northern European	31	0.25
Norwegian	762	6.03
Polish	177	1.40
Portuguese	73	0.58
Romanian	50	0.40
Russian	116	0.92
Scandinavian	139	1.10
Scotch-Irish	239	1.89
Scottish	456	3.61
Slavic	8	0.06
Swedish	698	5.52
Swiss	60	0.47
Ukrainian	86	0.68
United States or American	760	6.01
Welsh	188	1.49
West Indian, excl. Hispanic:	27	0.21
Jamaican	27	0.21
White:	10,994	87.03
Not Hispanic (10,349)	10,713	84.80
Hispanic (237)	281	2.22
Yugoslavian	56	0.44

Marysville

Place Type: City
County: Snohomish
Population: 25,315

Ancestry/Race	Number	%
Acadian/Cajun	6	0.02
African American/Black:	373	1.47
Not Hispanic (246)	353	1.39
Hispanic (11)	20	0.08
African, sub-Saharan:	43	0.17
African	23	0.09
South African	11	0.04
Other sub-Saharan African	9	0.04
Alaska Native tribes, specified:	79	0.31
Alaska Athabascan (3)	7	0.03
Aleut (14)	27	0.11
Eskimo (4)	13	0.05
Tlingit-Haida (19)	29	0.11
All other tribes (2)	3	0.01
Alaska Native tribes, not specified	5	0.02
Am. Ind. or Alaska Nat., not spec.	121	0.48
American Indian tribes, specified:	369	1.46
Apache (6)	6	0.02
Blackfeet (7)	17	0.07
Cherokee (27)	47	0.19
Cheyenne (2)	3	0.01
Chickasaw	1	0.00
Chippewa (27)	28	0.11
Choctaw (3)	5	0.02
Colville (7)	9	0.04
Crow	1	0.00
Delaware (2)	2	0.01
Iroquois (1)	1	0.00
Latin American Indians (7)	7	0.03
Menominee	2	0.01
Navajo (7)	8	0.03
Ottawa (1)	1	0.00
Paiute (2)	3	0.01
Potawatomi (2)	2	0.01
Pueblo (7)	8	0.03
Puget Sound Salish (84)	116	0.46
Seminole (3)	3	0.01
Shoshone	1	0.00
Sioux (14)	20	0.08
Ute (1)	2	0.01
Yakama (2)	7	0.03
Yaqui (1)	6	0.02
All other tribes (45)	63	0.25
American Indian tribes, not spec.	34	0.13
Arab:	19	0.08
Lebanese	6	0.02
Palestinian	13	0.05
Asian:	1,326	5.24
Cambodian (40)	42	0.17
Chinese, ex. Taiwanese (41)	93	0.37
Filipino (377)	521	2.06
Indian (95)	106	0.42
Indonesian (1)	13	0.05
Japanese (66)	129	0.51
Korean (110)	149	0.59
Laotian (65)	82	0.32
Malaysian	1	0.00
Pakistani (1)	3	0.01
Taiwanese (13)	13	0.05
Thai (13)	17	0.07
Vietnamese (97)	110	0.43
Other Asian, specified (3)	3	0.01
Other Asian, not specified (24)	44	0.17
Austrian	53	0.21
Basque	6	0.02
Belgian	15	0.06
British	156	0.62
Canadian	150	0.59
Celtic	14	0.06
Czech	100	0.40
Czechoslovakian	21	0.08
Danish	428	1.70
Dutch	634	2.51
Eastern European	7	0.03
English	3,066	12.16
European	321	1.27
Finnish	185	0.73
French, except Basque	1,120	4.44
French Canadian	216	0.86
German	4,885	19.37
Greek	191	0.76
Guyanese	24	0.10
Hawaii Native/Pacific Islander:	186	0.73
Micronesian: (28)	31	0.12
Guamanian/Chamorro (25)	28	0.11

Notes: 1. Figures in the "Number" column do not add up to the total population due to: a) Ancestry/Race overlap — e.g. persons can report being both White and Irish, b) persons of Hispanic origin can report being any race, c) persons reporting two ancestries are counted in both categories. 2. Numbers in parentheses indicate the number of persons reporting this ancestry/race alone, not in combination with any other ancestry/race. 3. Refer to the Explanation of Data in the front of the book for more detailed information.

Ancestry/Race	Number	%
Other Micronesian (3)	3	0.01
Polynesian: (44)	108	0.43
Native Hawaiian (35)	93	0.37
Samoan (8)	14	0.06
Other Polynesian (1)	1	0.00
Other Pac. Isl., not spec. (18)	47	0.19
Hispanic or Latino:	1,222	4.83
Central American:	22	0.09
Guatemalan	9	0.04
Panamanian	5	0.02
Salvadoran	6	0.02
Other Central American	2	0.01
Cuban	11	0.04
Dominican Republic	3	0.01
Mexican	887	3.50
Puerto Rican	64	0.25
South American:	30	0.12
Argentinean	3	0.01
Bolivian	2	0.01
Chilean	6	0.02
Colombian	16	0.06
Ecuadorian	2	0.01
Other South American	1	0.00
Other Hispanic or Latino	205	0.81
Hungarian	78	0.31
Icelander	38	0.15
Iranian	6	0.02
Irish	2,838	11.25
Italian	925	3.67
Latvian	21	0.08
Lithuanian	16	0.06
Northern European	24	0.10
Norwegian	2,454	9.73
Pennsylvania German	27	0.11
Polish	284	1.13
Portuguese	156	0.62
Romanian	20	0.08
Russian	159	0.63
Scandinavian	267	1.06
Scotch-Irish	487	1.93
Scottish	678	2.69
Slovak	6	0.02
Swedish	1,167	4.63
Swiss	177	0.70
Ukrainian	29	0.11
United States or American	1,756	6.96
Welsh	246	0.98
White:	23,021	90.94
Not Hispanic (21,762)	22,326	88.19
Hispanic (569)	695	2.75
Yugoslavian	37	0.15

Mercer Island

Place Type: City
County: King
Population: 22,036

Ancestry/Race	Number	%
African American/Black:	341	1.55
Not Hispanic (250)	330	1.50
Hispanic (1)	11	0.05
African, sub-Saharan:	97	0.44
African	40	0.18
Kenyan	8	0.04
Senegalese	9	0.04
South African	40	0.18
Alaska Native tribes, specified:	14	0.06
Aleut (1)	3	0.01
Eskimo (1)	1	0.00
Tlingit-Haida (1)	5	0.02
All other tribes (4)	5	0.02
Am. Ind. or Alaska Nat., not spec.	38	0.17
American Indian tribes, specified:	37	0.17
Apache (1)	1	0.00
Cherokee (4)	9	0.04
Chippewa (2)	6	0.03
Colville	1	0.00
Cree	1	0.00
Iroquois	2	0.01
Latin American Indians (1)	1	0.00
Potawatomi	1	0.00
Puget Sound Salish	1	0.00
Sioux (2)	4	0.02
Ute	1	0.00
All other tribes (4)	9	0.04
American Indian tribes, not spec.	10	0.05
Arab:	69	0.31
Lebanese	15	0.07
Moroccan	22	0.10
Palestinian	8	0.04
Other Arab	24	0.11
Asian:	3,040	13.80
Cambodian (1)	1	0.00
Chinese, ex. Taiwanese (1,086)	1,229	5.58
Filipino (93)	133	0.60
Indian (187)	209	0.95
Indonesian (15)	17	0.08
Japanese (582)	762	3.46
Korean (320)	365	1.66
Malaysian (1)	1	0.00
Pakistani (5)	5	0.02
Sri Lankan (1)	1	0.00
Taiwanese (163)	182	0.83
Thai (15)	20	0.09
Vietnamese (44)	58	0.26
Other Asian, specified (10)	16	0.07
Other Asian, not specified (19)	41	0.19
Austrian	192	0.87
Basque	17	0.08
Belgian	17	0.08
British	250	1.13
Bulgarian	11	0.05
Canadian	235	1.07
Celtic	15	0.07
Croatian	83	0.38
Czech	178	0.81
Czechoslovakian	23	0.10
Danish	296	1.34
Dutch	542	2.46
Eastern European	100	0.45
English	3,834	17.40
European	549	2.49
Finnish	82	0.37
French, except Basque	693	3.14
French Canadian	147	0.67
German	3,463	15.72
Greek	110	0.50
Hawaii Native/Pacific Islander:	45	0.20
Micronesian: (2)	2	0.01
Guamanian/Chamorro (2)	2	0.01
Polynesian: (9)	19	0.09
Native Hawaiian (7)	14	0.06
Samoan (2)	5	0.02
Other Pac. Isl., specified	4	0.02
Other Pac. Isl., not spec. (5)	20	0.09
Hispanic or Latino:	410	1.86
Central American:	27	0.12
Costa Rican	2	0.01
Guatemalan	10	0.05
Nicaraguan	7	0.03
Panamanian	3	0.01
Salvadoran	5	0.02
Cuban	12	0.05
Mexican	172	0.78
Puerto Rican	22	0.10
South American:	63	0.29
Argentinean	10	0.05
Bolivian	4	0.02
Chilean	5	0.02
Colombian	12	0.05
Ecuadorian	6	0.03
Peruvian	19	0.09
Venezuelan	4	0.02
Other South American	3	0.01
Other Hispanic or Latino	114	0.52
Hungarian	148	0.67
Icelander	20	0.09
Iranian	32	0.15
Irish	2,396	10.87
Israeli	12	0.05
Italian	1,133	5.14
Latvian	68	0.31
Lithuanian	63	0.29
New Zealander	9	0.04
Northern European	178	0.81
Norwegian	1,030	4.67
Polish	881	4.00
Portuguese	121	0.55
Romanian	64	0.29
Russian	939	4.26
Scandinavian	160	0.73
Scotch-Irish	519	2.36
Scottish	904	4.10
Serbian	15	0.07
Slavic	6	0.03
Slovak	65	0.29
Swedish	994	4.51
Swiss	186	0.84
Turkish	51	0.23
Ukrainian	73	0.33
United States or American	927	4.21
Welsh	194	0.88
West Indian, excl. Hispanic:	24	0.11
Jamaican	7	0.03
Trinidadian and Tobagonian	10	0.05
West Indian	7	0.03
White:	18,967	86.07
Not Hispanic (18,249)	18,637	84.58
Hispanic (281)	330	1.50
Yugoslavian	82	0.37

Mill Creek

Place Type: City
County: Snohomish
Population: 11,525

Ancestry/Race	Number	%
African American/Black:	204	1.77
Not Hispanic (161)	193	1.67
Hispanic (2)	11	0.10
African, sub-Saharan:	35	0.31
African	35	0.31
Alaska Native tribes, specified:	9	0.08
Alaska Athabascan (1)	1	0.01
Aleut (2)	2	0.02
Eskimo	1	0.01
Tlingit-Haida (3)	5	0.04
Am. Ind. or Alaska Nat., not spec.	23	0.20
American Indian tribes, specified:	53	0.46
Blackfeet (1)	4	0.03
Cherokee (5)	17	0.15
Chippewa (4)	6	0.05
Comanche	1	0.01
Cree	1	0.01
Creek (1)	1	0.01
Latin American Indians (4)	4	0.03
Navajo (3)	5	0.04
Puget Sound Salish	1	0.01
Sioux	2	0.02
All other tribes (6)	11	0.10
American Indian tribes, not spec.	6	0.05
Arab:	33	0.29
Egyptian	33	0.29
Armenian	6	0.05
Asian:	1,666	14.46
Cambodian	1	0.01
Chinese, ex. Taiwanese (245)	280	2.43
Filipino (214)	268	2.33
Indian (93)	104	0.90
Indonesian	2	0.02
Japanese (136)	193	1.67
Korean (538)	565	4.90
Laotian (5)	9	0.08
Malaysian (1)	4	0.03
Pakistani (14)	35	0.30
Taiwanese (63)	66	0.57
Thai (5)	5	0.04
Vietnamese (97)	105	0.91

Notes: 1. Figures in the "Number" column do not add up to the total population due to: a) Ancestry/Race overlap — e.g. persons can report being both White and Irish, b) persons of Hispanic origin can report being any race, c) persons reporting two ancestries are counted in both categories. 2. Numbers in parentheses indicate the number of persons reporting this ancestry/race alone, not in combination with any other ancestry/race. 3. Refer to the Explanation of Data in the front of the book for more detailed information.

Ancestry/Race	Number	%
Other Asian, specified (1)	4	0.03
Other Asian, not specified (15)	25	0.22
Austrian	9	0.08
Belgian	12	0.10
British	91	0.80
Canadian	156	1.36
Celtic	6	0.05
Croatian	34	0.30
Czech	114	1.00
Czechoslovakian	46	0.40
Danish	194	1.70
Dutch	206	1.80
Eastern European	28	0.24
English	1,684	14.72
European	229	2.00
Finnish	132	1.15
French, except Basque	559	4.88
French Canadian	59	0.52
German	2,026	17.70
German Russian	9	0.08
Greek	63	0.55
Hawaii Native/Pacific Islander:	65	0.56
Melanesian: (5)	5	0.04
Fijian (5)	5	0.04
Micronesian: (7)	19	0.16
Guamanian/Chamorro (6)	18	0.16
Other Micronesian (1)	1	0.01
Polynesian: (8)	26	0.23
Native Hawaiian (7)	23	0.20
Samoan (1)	3	0.03
Other Pac. Isl., not spec. (7)	15	0.13
Hispanic or Latino:	375	3.25
Central American:	19	0.16
Costa Rican	3	0.03
Guatemalan	1	0.01
Honduran	2	0.02
Nicaraguan	2	0.02
Panamanian	3	0.03
Salvadoran	8	0.07
Cuban	7	0.06
Dominican Republic	3	0.03
Mexican	210	1.82
Puerto Rican	22	0.19
South American:	29	0.25
Argentinean	12	0.10
Chilean	4	0.03
Colombian	3	0.03
Ecuadorian	2	0.02
Peruvian	5	0.04
Venezuelan	3	0.03
Other Hispanic or Latino	85	0.74
Hungarian	64	0.56
Iranian	146	1.28
Irish	1,330	11.62
Italian	484	4.23
Lithuanian	15	0.13
Luxemburger	6	0.05
Northern European	33	0.29
Norwegian	755	6.60
Polish	180	1.57
Portuguese	71	0.62
Romanian	9	0.08
Russian	246	2.15
Scandinavian	87	0.76
Scotch-Irish	239	2.09
Scottish	397	3.47
Serbian	15	0.13
Slovak	13	0.11
Slovene	20	0.17
Swedish	473	4.13
Swiss	60	0.52
Ukrainian	18	0.16
United States or American	227	1.98
Welsh	169	1.48
White:	9,643	83.67
Not Hispanic (9,184)	9,398	81.54
Hispanic (208)	245	2.13
Yugoslavian	44	0.38

Monroe

Place Type: City
County: Snohomish
Population: 13,795

Ancestry/Race	Number	%
African American/Black:	485	3.52
Not Hispanic (416)	465	3.37
Hispanic (18)	20	0.14
African, sub-Saharan:	21	0.16
African	11	0.08
Nigerian	10	0.07
Alaska Native tribes, specified:	19	0.14
Eskimo (4)	6	0.04
Tlingit-Haida (8)	13	0.09
Alaska Native tribes, not specified	5	0.04
Am. Ind. or Alaska Nat., not spec.	133	0.96
American Indian tribes, specified:	151	1.09
Apache	1	0.01
Blackfeet (2)	8	0.06
Cherokee (12)	28	0.20
Cheyenne	1	0.01
Chickasaw (1)	2	0.01
Chippewa (10)	22	0.16
Choctaw (4)	11	0.08
Colville (5)	5	0.04
Creek (1)	1	0.01
Iroquois	3	0.02
Latin American Indians (1)	5	0.04
Navajo (1)	1	0.01
Puget Sound Salish (9)	17	0.12
Seminole	3	0.02
Sioux (4)	11	0.08
Yakama (1)	2	0.01
All other tribes (20)	30	0.22
American Indian tribes, not spec.	17	0.12
Arab:	8	0.06
Egyptian	8	0.06
Asian:	477	3.46
Cambodian (23)	28	0.20
Chinese, ex. Taiwanese (52)	89	0.65
Filipino (53)	99	0.72
Indian (30)	36	0.26
Japanese (14)	45	0.33
Korean (39)	46	0.33
Laotian (22)	24	0.17
Pakistani (6)	6	0.04
Sri Lankan (1)	1	0.01
Taiwanese	1	0.01
Thai (2)	4	0.03
Vietnamese (61)	71	0.51
Other Asian, not specified (17)	27	0.20
Austrian	78	0.58
Belgian	9	0.07
Brazilian	7	0.05
British	68	0.51
Canadian	67	0.50
Celtic	12	0.09
Croatian	7	0.05
Czech	64	0.48
Czechoslovakian	9	0.07
Danish	135	1.00
Dutch	374	2.78
English	1,346	10.00
European	139	1.03
Finnish	57	0.42
French, except Basque	378	2.81
French Canadian	93	0.69
German	2,634	19.57
Greek	49	0.36
Hawaii Native/Pacific Islander:	76	0.55
Melanesian: (3)	3	0.02
Fijian (3)	3	0.02
Micronesian: (9)	13	0.09
Guamanian/Chamorro (8)	12	0.09
Other Micronesian (1)	1	0.01
Polynesian: (17)	35	0.25
Native Hawaiian (11)	26	0.19
Samoan (6)	9	0.07
Other Pac. Isl., not spec. (14)	25	0.18
Hispanic or Latino:	1,332	9.66
Central American:	26	0.19
Guatemalan	8	0.06
Honduran	8	0.06
Panamanian	3	0.02
Salvadoran	7	0.05
Cuban	28	0.20
Dominican Republic	1	0.01
Mexican	1,119	8.11
Puerto Rican	20	0.14
South American:	18	0.13
Argentinean	3	0.02
Bolivian	1	0.01
Chilean	3	0.02
Colombian	8	0.06
Peruvian	3	0.02
Other Hispanic or Latino	120	0.87
Hungarian	24	0.18
Icelander	7	0.05
Irish	1,303	9.68
Italian	312	2.32
Latvian	8	0.06
Lithuanian	40	0.30
Northern European	119	0.88
Norwegian	677	5.03
Polish	202	1.50
Portuguese	7	0.05
Russian	113	0.84
Scandinavian	100	0.74
Scotch-Irish	244	1.81
Scottish	392	2.91
Slovak	19	0.14
Swedish	460	3.42
Swiss	80	0.59
Ukrainian	79	0.59
United States or American	424	3.15
Welsh	231	1.72
White:	12,213	88.53
Not Hispanic (11,167)	11,445	82.96
Hispanic (715)	768	5.57
Yugoslavian	32	0.24

Moses Lake

Place Type: City
County: Grant
Population: 14,953

Ancestry/Race	Number	%
African American/Black:	313	2.09
Not Hispanic (238)	283	1.89
Hispanic (15)	30	0.20
African, sub-Saharan:	65	0.43
African	65	0.43
Alaska Native tribes, specified:	16	0.11
Alaska Athabascan (2)	2	0.01
Aleut (1)	2	0.01
Eskimo	4	0.03
Tlingit-Haida (6)	8	0.05
Am. Ind. or Alaska Nat., not spec.	69	0.46
American Indian tribes, specified:	166	1.11
Apache (1)	4	0.03
Blackfeet (5)	8	0.05
Cherokee (11)	32	0.21
Cheyenne (1)	3	0.02
Chickasaw	3	0.02
Chippewa (7)	10	0.07
Choctaw	9	0.06
Colville (8)	10	0.07
Comanche (4)	4	0.03
Iroquois (5)	7	0.05
Latin American Indians (4)	6	0.04
Navajo (2)	2	0.01
Pima (1)	1	0.01
Pueblo	1	0.01
Puget Sound Salish (1)	2	0.01
Seminole (1)	1	0.01
Sioux (7)	8	0.05
Yakama (3)	4	0.03

Notes: 1. Figures in the "Number" column do not add up to the total population due to: a) Ancestry/Race overlap — e.g. persons can report being both White and Irish, b) persons of Hispanic origin can report being any race, c) persons reporting two ancestries are counted in both categories. 2. Numbers in parentheses indicate the number of persons reporting this ancestry/race alone, not in combination with any other ancestry/race. 3. Refer to the Explanation of Data in the front of the book for more detailed information.

Ancestry/Race	Number	%
Yaqui (8)	9	0.06
All other tribes (22)	42	0.28
American Indian tribes, not spec.	11	0.07
Arab:	43	0.29
Arab/Arabic	14	0.09
Lebanese	29	0.19
Asian:	290	1.94
Chinese, ex. Taiwanese (18)	24	0.16
Filipino (29)	51	0.34
Indian (21)	25	0.17
Japanese (107)	132	0.88
Korean (22)	31	0.21
Taiwanese (2)	2	0.01
Thai (7)	8	0.05
Vietnamese (5)	7	0.05
Other Asian, specified	3	0.02
Other Asian, not specified	7	0.05
British	74	0.49
Canadian	86	0.58
Croatian	50	0.33
Czech	7	0.05
Czechoslovakian	15	0.10
Danish	66	0.44
Dutch	318	2.13
English	1,625	10.87
European	176	1.18
Finnish	55	0.37
French, except Basque	505	3.38
French Canadian	100	0.67
German	2,494	16.68
Greek	35	0.23
Hawaii Native/Pacific Islander:	23	0.15
Micronesian: (5)	6	0.04
Guamanian/Chamorro (3)	4	0.03
Other Micronesian (2)	2	0.01
Polynesian: (5)	11	0.07
Native Hawaiian (4)	8	0.05
Samoan (1)	1	0.01
Tongan	2	0.01
Other Pac. Isl., not spec.	6	0.04
Hispanic or Latino:	3,800	25.41
Central American:	50	0.33
Guatemalan	24	0.16
Honduran	1	0.01
Nicaraguan	1	0.01
Panamanian	6	0.04
Salvadoran	18	0.12
Cuban	7	0.05
Mexican	3,068	20.52
Puerto Rican	33	0.22
South American:	7	0.05
Bolivian	1	0.01
Colombian	1	0.01
Peruvian	1	0.01
Venezuelan	4	0.03
Other Hispanic or Latino	635	4.25
Hungarian	56	0.37
Icelander	10	0.07
Iranian	12	0.08
Irish	1,220	8.16
Italian	343	2.29
Northern European	54	0.36
Norwegian	593	3.97
Pennsylvania German	36	0.24
Polish	94	0.63
Portuguese	9	0.06
Russian	182	1.22
Scandinavian	118	0.79
Scotch-Irish	150	1.00
Scottish	201	1.34
Slavic	33	0.22
Swedish	489	3.27
Swiss	69	0.46
Ukrainian	108	0.72
United States or American	932	6.23
Welsh	161	1.08
West Indian, excl. Hispanic:	71	0.47
Dutch West Indian	17	0.11
Haitian	8	0.05
Jamaican	46	0.31
White:	11,968	80.04
Not Hispanic (10,314)	10,538	70.47
Hispanic (1,223)	1,430	9.56

Mount Vernon

Place Type: City
County: Skagit
Population: 26,232

Ancestry/Race	Number	%
Acadian/Cajun	11	0.04
African American/Black:	301	1.15
Not Hispanic (185)	268	1.02
Hispanic (7)	33	0.13
African, sub-Saharan:	19	0.07
African	12	0.05
Other sub-Saharan African	7	0.03
Alaska Native tribes, specified:	58	0.22
Alaska Athabascan (1)	4	0.02
Aleut (8)	10	0.04
Eskimo (4)	7	0.03
Tlingit-Haida (29)	37	0.14
Alaska Native tribes, not specified	9	0.03
Am. Ind. or Alaska Nat., not spec.	97	0.37
American Indian tribes, specified:	274	1.04
Apache (1)	1	0.00
Blackfeet (9)	18	0.07
Cherokee (11)	32	0.12
Cheyenne (1)	4	0.02
Chippewa (3)	15	0.06
Choctaw (1)	3	0.01
Colville (4)	9	0.03
Cree (1)	1	0.00
Creek (1)	1	0.00
Delaware	1	0.00
Iroquois	6	0.02
Latin American Indians (22)	29	0.11
Lumbee (6)	6	0.02
Navajo (1)	4	0.02
Puget Sound Salish (35)	52	0.20
Seminole	2	0.01
Shoshone	1	0.00
Sioux (7)	17	0.06
Tohono O'Odham (5)	5	0.02
Yakama (2)	4	0.02
Yaqui (2)	3	0.01
All other tribes (27)	60	0.23
American Indian tribes, not spec.	20	0.08
Arab:	74	0.28
Arab/Arabic	11	0.04
Lebanese	22	0.08
Syrian	41	0.16
Asian:	881	3.36
Cambodian	1	0.00
Chinese, ex. Taiwanese (134)	166	0.63
Filipino (159)	231	0.88
Indian (44)	50	0.19
Indonesian (3)	8	0.03
Japanese (187)	222	0.85
Korean (97)	107	0.41
Laotian (1)	2	0.01
Pakistani	5	0.02
Taiwanese (6)	10	0.04
Thai (14)	28	0.11
Vietnamese (10)	22	0.08
Other Asian, specified	2	0.01
Other Asian, not specified (5)	27	0.10
Australian	10	0.04
Austrian	102	0.39
Basque	4	0.02
Belgian	18	0.07
British	149	0.57
Canadian	137	0.52
Celtic	24	0.09
Croatian	62	0.24
Czech	94	0.36
Czechoslovakian	48	0.18
Danish	214	0.81
Dutch	1,068	4.06
English	2,554	9.71
Estonian	6	0.02
European	251	0.95
Finnish	62	0.24
French, except Basque	804	3.06
French Canadian	368	1.40
German	3,687	14.02
Greek	62	0.24
Hawaii Native/Pacific Islander:	74	0.28
Melanesian: (2)	2	0.01
Fijian (2)	2	0.01
Micronesian: (14)	15	0.06
Guamanian/Chamorro (14)	15	0.06
Polynesian: (15)	34	0.13
Native Hawaiian (11)	28	0.11
Samoan (3)	4	0.02
Other Polynesian (1)	2	0.01
Other Pac. Isl., not spec. (9)	23	0.09
Hispanic or Latino:	6,589	25.12
Central American:	70	0.27
Costa Rican	10	0.04
Guatemalan	23	0.09
Honduran	3	0.01
Nicaraguan	4	0.02
Panamanian	9	0.03
Salvadoran	21	0.08
Cuban	17	0.06
Dominican Republic	1	0.00
Mexican	5,501	20.97
Puerto Rican	59	0.22
South American:	37	0.14
Colombian	10	0.04
Ecuadorian	2	0.01
Peruvian	19	0.07
Venezuelan	4	0.02
Other South American	2	0.01
Other Hispanic or Latino	904	3.45
Hungarian	47	0.18
Icelander	22	0.08
Irish	2,349	8.93
Italian	732	2.78
Lithuanian	31	0.12
Luxemburger	7	0.03
Maltese	8	0.03
Northern European	32	0.12
Norwegian	1,710	6.50
Pennsylvania German	18	0.07
Polish	256	0.97
Portuguese	35	0.13
Romanian	28	0.11
Russian	154	0.59
Scandinavian	170	0.65
Scotch-Irish	595	2.26
Scottish	714	2.72
Slovak	76	0.29
Swedish	1,046	3.98
Swiss	101	0.38
Ukrainian	228	0.87
United States or American	868	3.30
Welsh	257	0.98
West Indian, excl. Hispanic:	8	0.03
Jamaican	8	0.03
White:	20,482	78.08
Not Hispanic (17,950)	18,422	70.23
Hispanic (1,839)	2,060	7.85
Yugoslavian	23	0.09

Mountlake Terrace

Place Type: City
County: Snohomish
Population: 20,362

Ancestry/Race	Number	%
Acadian/Cajun	27	0.13
African American/Black:	731	3.59
Not Hispanic (510)	700	3.44
Hispanic (4)	31	0.15
African, sub-Saharan:	125	0.62
African	104	0.51

Notes: 1. Figures in the "Number" column do not add up to the total population due to: a) Ancestry/Race overlap — e.g. persons can report being both White and Irish, b) persons of Hispanic origin can report being any race, c) persons reporting two ancestries are counted in both categories. 2. Numbers in parentheses indicate the number of persons reporting this ancestry/race alone, not in combination with any other ancestry/race. 3. Refer to the Explanation of Data in the front of the book for more detailed information.

Ancestry/Race	Number	%
Nigerian	8	0.04
South African	13	0.06
Alaska Native tribes, specified:	89	0.44
Alaska Athabascan (3)	4	0.02
Aleut (5)	9	0.04
Eskimo (8)	10	0.05
Tlingit-Haida (33)	58	0.28
All other tribes (6)	8	0.04
Alaska Native tribes, not specified	2	0.01
Am. Ind. or Alaska Nat., not spec.	91	0.45
American Indian tribes, specified:	264	1.30
Apache (6)	11	0.05
Blackfeet (4)	13	0.06
Cherokee (7)	55	0.27
Cheyenne (2)	3	0.01
Chippewa (19)	30	0.15
Choctaw (2)	7	0.03
Colville (4)	8	0.04
Comanche (2)	8	0.04
Cree (1)	1	0.00
Crow (2)	2	0.01
Iroquois (1)	9	0.04
Latin American Indians (2)	6	0.03
Navajo (6)	8	0.04
Osage (2)	3	0.01
Paiute (2)	2	0.01
Pueblo (2)	4	0.02
Puget Sound Salish (3)	9	0.04
Sioux (9)	20	0.10
Ute	1	0.00
Yakama (5)	6	0.03
Yaqui (3)	4	0.02
All other tribes (33)	54	0.27
American Indian tribes, not spec.	23	0.11
Arab:	165	0.81
Arab/Arabic	36	0.18
Egyptian	21	0.10
Lebanese	46	0.23
Palestinian	42	0.21
Syrian	12	0.06
Other Arab	8	0.04
Asian:	2,648	13.00
Bangladeshi (1)	2	0.01
Cambodian (84)	90	0.44
Chinese, ex. Taiwanese (264)	337	1.66
Filipino (570)	741	3.64
Hmong (6)	11	0.05
Indian (157)	203	1.00
Indonesian (8)	9	0.04
Japanese (105)	196	0.96
Korean (525)	562	2.76
Laotian (28)	37	0.18
Malaysian (1)	4	0.02
Pakistani (46)	51	0.25
Sri Lankan (6)	6	0.03
Taiwanese (16)	20	0.10
Thai (26)	35	0.17
Vietnamese (262)	281	1.38
Other Asian, specified (5)	15	0.07
Other Asian, not specified (14)	48	0.24
Austrian	133	0.66
Belgian	21	0.10
Brazilian	6	0.03
British	214	1.05
Bulgarian	29	0.14
Canadian	113	0.56
Croatian	48	0.24
Czech	60	0.30
Czechoslovakian	88	0.43
Danish	266	1.31
Dutch	473	2.33
English	2,357	11.61
Estonian	5	0.02
European	312	1.54
Finnish	119	0.59
French, except Basque	653	3.22
French Canadian	136	0.67
German	3,319	16.35
Greek	86	0.42
Hawaii Native/Pacific Islander:	236	1.16
Melanesian: (41)	47	0.23
Fijian (41)	47	0.23
Micronesian: (31)	47	0.23
Guamanian/Chamorro (19)	31	0.15
Other Micronesian (12)	16	0.08
Polynesian: (32)	83	0.41
Native Hawaiian (20)	60	0.29
Samoan (3)	9	0.04
Tongan (4)	8	0.04
Other Polynesian (5)	6	0.03
Other Pac. Isl., not spec. (15)	59	0.29
Hispanic or Latino:	1,151	5.65
Central American:	57	0.28
Costa Rican	7	0.03
Guatemalan	5	0.02
Honduran	3	0.01
Nicaraguan	14	0.07
Panamanian	11	0.05
Salvadoran	17	0.08
Cuban	13	0.06
Dominican Republic	1	0.00
Mexican	729	3.58
Puerto Rican	62	0.30
South American:	73	0.36
Argentinean	6	0.03
Bolivian	2	0.01
Chilean	10	0.05
Colombian	24	0.12
Ecuadorian	5	0.02
Paraguayan	1	0.00
Peruvian	14	0.07
Uruguayan	3	0.01
Venezuelan	5	0.02
Other South American	3	0.01
Other Hispanic or Latino	216	1.06
Hungarian	66	0.33
Icelander	31	0.15
Iranian	58	0.29
Irish	2,310	11.38
Italian	745	3.67
Latvian	50	0.25
Lithuanian	10	0.05
Luxemburger	8	0.04
Northern European	6	0.03
Norwegian	1,442	7.10
Pennsylvania German	27	0.13
Polish	270	1.33
Portuguese	58	0.29
Romanian	45	0.22
Russian	340	1.67
Scandinavian	155	0.76
Scotch-Irish	358	1.76
Scottish	675	3.33
Serbian	7	0.03
Slovak	9	0.04
Swedish	849	4.18
Swiss	59	0.29
Turkish	55	0.27
Ukrainian	127	0.63
United States or American	822	4.05
Welsh	200	0.99
West Indian, excl. Hispanic:	7	0.03
West Indian	7	0.03
White:	16,677	81.90
Not Hispanic (15,316)	16,050	78.82
Hispanic (505)	627	3.08
Yugoslavian	98	0.48

Mukilteo

Place Type: City
County: Snohomish
Population: 18,019

Ancestry/Race	Number	%
African American/Black:	379	2.10
Not Hispanic (262)	369	2.05
Hispanic (4)	10	0.06
African, sub-Saharan:	89	0.49
African	51	0.28
Other sub-Saharan African	38	0.21
Alaska Native tribes, specified:	48	0.27
Alaska Athabascan (3)	5	0.03
Aleut (4)	11	0.06
Eskimo (3)	5	0.03
Tlingit-Haida (13)	22	0.12
All other tribes	5	0.03
Alaska Native tribes, not specified	1	0.01
Am. Ind. or Alaska Nat., not spec.	63	0.35
American Indian tribes, specified:	161	0.89
Apache (2)	4	0.02
Blackfeet (3)	15	0.08
Cherokee (9)	42	0.23
Cheyenne	1	0.01
Chickasaw	3	0.02
Chippewa (1)	3	0.02
Choctaw (2)	8	0.04
Comanche (5)	5	0.03
Delaware (2)	3	0.02
Iroquois (2)	2	0.01
Kiowa (1)	1	0.01
Navajo (1)	3	0.02
Paiute (1)	1	0.01
Potawatomi	2	0.01
Puget Sound Salish (12)	20	0.11
Seminole	1	0.01
Sioux (4)	8	0.04
Yuman (5)	6	0.03
All other tribes (21)	33	0.18
American Indian tribes, not spec.	16	0.09
Arab:	42	0.23
Arab/Arabic	8	0.04
Lebanese	16	0.09
Other Arab	18	0.10
Asian:	2,342	13.00
Cambodian (20)	21	0.12
Chinese, ex. Taiwanese (277)	338	1.88
Filipino (238)	327	1.81
Indian (92)	120	0.67
Indonesian (6)	8	0.04
Japanese (146)	257	1.43
Korean (937)	985	5.47
Laotian (4)	14	0.08
Pakistani (15)	35	0.19
Taiwanese (21)	23	0.13
Thai (18)	20	0.11
Vietnamese (123)	137	0.76
Other Asian, specified (2)	4	0.02
Other Asian, not specified (20)	53	0.29
Australian	7	0.04
Austrian	74	0.41
Basque	13	0.07
Belgian	30	0.17
British	119	0.66
Bulgarian	17	0.09
Canadian	114	0.63
Celtic	18	0.10
Croatian	16	0.09
Czech	143	0.79
Czechoslovakian	40	0.22
Danish	176	0.98
Dutch	425	2.36
Eastern European	39	0.22
English	2,558	14.18
European	350	1.94
Finnish	86	0.48
French, except Basque	665	3.69
French Canadian	196	1.09
German	3,403	18.86
German Russian	9	0.05
Greek	58	0.32
Hawaii Native/Pacific Islander:	95	0.53
Melanesian: (10)	11	0.06
Fijian (10)	11	0.06
Micronesian: (3)	6	0.03
Guamanian/Chamorro (3)	6	0.03
Polynesian: (31)	67	0.37
Native Hawaiian (21)	56	0.31
Samoan (10)	10	0.06
Other Polynesian	1	0.01

Notes: 1. Figures in the "Number" column do not add up to the total population due to: a) Ancestry/Race overlap — e.g. persons can report being both White and Irish, b) persons of Hispanic origin can report being any race, c) persons reporting two ancestries are counted in both categories. 2. Numbers in parentheses indicate the number of persons reporting this ancestry/race alone, not in combination with any other ancestry/race. 3. Refer to the Explanation of Data in the front of the book for more detailed information.

Other Pac. Isl., specified	1	0.01
Other Pac. Isl., not spec. (1)	10	0.06
Hispanic or Latino:	522	2.90
Central American:	8	0.04
Costa Rican	6	0.03
Honduran	1	0.01
Nicaraguan	1	0.01
Cuban	12	0.07
Mexican	287	1.59
Puerto Rican	45	0.25
South American:	50	0.28
Argentinean	6	0.03
Chilean	5	0.03
Colombian	24	0.13
Ecuadorian	3	0.02
Peruvian	9	0.05
Venezuelan	1	0.01
Other South American	2	0.01
Other Hispanic or Latino	120	0.67
Hungarian	44	0.24
Icelander	14	0.08
Iranian	183	1.01
Irish	2,264	12.55
Italian	736	4.08
Latvian	31	0.17
Lithuanian	39	0.22
Northern European	89	0.49
Norwegian	1,874	10.39
Pennsylvania German	16	0.09
Polish	502	2.78
Portuguese	76	0.42
Romanian	13	0.07
Russian	136	0.75
Scandinavian	131	0.73
Scotch-Irish	340	1.88
Scottish	555	3.08
Slavic	13	0.07
Swedish	1,028	5.70
Swiss	40	0.22
Turkish	66	0.37
Ukrainian	42	0.23
United States or American	811	4.50
Welsh	149	0.83
White:	15,328	85.07
Not Hispanic (14,523)	14,992	83.20
Hispanic (264)	336	1.86
Yugoslavian	35	0.19

North Creek

Place Type: Census Designated Place
County: Snohomish
Population: 25,742

Ancestry/Race	Number	%
Afghan	12	0.05
African American/Black:	423	1.64
Not Hispanic (252)	391	1.52
Hispanic (8)	32	0.12
African, sub-Saharan:	28	0.11
African	3	0.01
Nigerian	12	0.05
South African	13	0.05
Alaska Native tribes, specified:	46	0.18
Alaska Athabascan	4	0.02
Aleut (2)	4	0.02
Tlingit-Haida (16)	35	0.14
All other tribes	3	0.01
Alaska Native tribes, not specified	3	0.01
Am. Ind. or Alaska Nat., not spec.	105	0.41
American Indian tribes, specified:	237	0.92
Apache (2)	2	0.01
Blackfeet (3)	16	0.06
Cherokee (17)	47	0.18
Cheyenne (3)	4	0.02
Chippewa (11)	18	0.07
Choctaw (2)	5	0.02
Colville (5)	10	0.04
Cree (1)	3	0.01
Creek (1)	1	0.00
Delaware (1)	1	0.00
Iroquois (4)	5	0.02
Latin American Indians (3)	8	0.03
Navajo (1)	2	0.01
Osage	4	0.02
Potawatomi (1)	1	0.00
Pueblo (3)	3	0.01
Puget Sound Salish (13)	27	0.10
Seminole (1)	2	0.01
Sioux (3)	9	0.03
Yakama (2)	3	0.01
All other tribes (36)	66	0.26
American Indian tribes, not spec.	22	0.09
Arab:	94	0.36
Lebanese	38	0.15
Moroccan	11	0.04
Syrian	23	0.09
Other Arab	22	0.08
Armenian	22	0.08
Asian:	1,850	7.19
Cambodian (93)	101	0.39
Chinese, ex. Taiwanese (237)	336	1.31
Filipino (249)	373	1.45
Hmong (1)	1	0.00
Indian (154)	174	0.68
Indonesian (6)	10	0.04
Japanese (102)	215	0.84
Korean (241)	275	1.07
Laotian (24)	33	0.13
Malaysian (1)	2	0.01
Pakistani (19)	23	0.09
Taiwanese (13)	13	0.05
Thai (27)	32	0.12
Vietnamese (201)	226	0.88
Other Asian, not specified (21)	36	0.14
Australian	10	0.04
Austrian	141	0.54
Belgian	18	0.07
British	119	0.46
Canadian	95	0.37
Celtic	39	0.15
Croatian	32	0.12
Czech	102	0.39
Czechoslovakian	38	0.15
Danish	390	1.50
Dutch	677	2.61
Eastern European	12	0.05
English	3,860	14.86
Estonian	10	0.04
European	427	1.64
Finnish	168	0.65
French, except Basque	1,064	4.10
French Canadian	275	1.06
German	5,668	21.82
Greek	77	0.30
Hawaii Native/Pacific Islander:	156	0.61
Melanesian: (14)	21	0.08
Fijian (14)	21	0.08
Micronesian: (16)	20	0.08
Guamanian/Chamorro (16)	20	0.08
Polynesian: (23)	81	0.31
Native Hawaiian (18)	69	0.27
Samoan (5)	12	0.05
Other Pac. Isl., not spec. (19)	34	0.13
Hispanic or Latino:	1,137	4.42
Central American:	46	0.18
Costa Rican	4	0.02
Guatemalan	3	0.01
Honduran	3	0.01
Nicaraguan	5	0.02
Panamanian	5	0.02
Salvadoran	25	0.10
Other Central American	1	0.00
Cuban	9	0.03
Dominican Republic	1	0.00
Mexican	752	2.92
Puerto Rican	68	0.26
South American:	61	0.24
Argentinean	7	0.03
Bolivian	9	0.03
Chilean	13	0.05
Colombian	10	0.04
Ecuadorian	1	0.00
Peruvian	12	0.05
Venezuelan	3	0.01
Other South American	6	0.02
Other Hispanic or Latino	200	0.78
Hungarian	74	0.28
Icelander	28	0.11
Iranian	113	0.43
Irish	3,260	12.55
Israeli	23	0.09
Italian	1,153	4.44
Latvian	9	0.03
Lithuanian	64	0.25
Northern European	15	0.06
Norwegian	2,079	8.00
Pennsylvania German	16	0.06
Polish	527	2.03
Portuguese	187	0.72
Romanian	22	0.08
Russian	371	1.43
Scandinavian	250	0.96
Scotch-Irish	531	2.04
Scottish	1,033	3.98
Slavic	8	0.03
Slovak	19	0.07
Swedish	1,029	3.96
Swiss	161	0.62
Ukrainian	100	0.38
United States or American	1,057	4.07
Welsh	249	0.96
West Indian, excl. Hispanic:	57	0.22
British West Indian	7	0.03
Jamaican	50	0.19
White:	23,352	90.72
Not Hispanic (21,952)	22,571	87.68
Hispanic (707)	781	3.03
Yugoslavian	50	0.19

North Marysville

Place Type: Census Designated Place
County: Snohomish
Population: 21,161

Ancestry/Race	Number	%
African American/Black:	267	1.26
Not Hispanic (143)	247	1.17
Hispanic (7)	20	0.09
African, sub-Saharan:	12	0.06
Zimbabwean	12	0.06
Alaska Native tribes, specified:	55	0.26
Alaska Athabascan (1)	1	0.00
Aleut (4)	13	0.06
Eskimo	5	0.02
Tlingit-Haida (15)	30	0.14
All other tribes (1)	6	0.03
Alaska Native tribes, not specified	10	0.05
Am. Ind. or Alaska Nat., not spec.	125	0.59
American Indian tribes, specified:	277	1.31
Blackfeet (15)	20	0.09
Cherokee (10)	40	0.19
Chippewa (18)	19	0.09
Choctaw (3)	13	0.06
Colville (7)	9	0.04
Comanche (1)	1	0.00
Cree (2)	5	0.02
Creek (1)	1	0.00
Crow (1)	1	0.00
Iroquois	1	0.00
Kiowa (1)	2	0.01
Latin American Indians (3)	4	0.02
Menominee (1)	1	0.00
Navajo (1)	3	0.01
Paiute	1	0.00
Potawatomi	1	0.00
Pueblo	2	0.01
Puget Sound Salish (69)	89	0.42
Seminole	1	0.00

Notes: 1. Figures in the "Number" column do not add up to the total population due to: a) Ancestry/Race overlap — e.g. persons can report being both White and Irish, b) persons of Hispanic origin can report being any race, c) persons reporting two ancestries are counted in both categories. 2. Numbers in parentheses indicate the number of persons reporting this ancestry/race alone, not in combination with any other ancestry/race. 3. Refer to the Explanation of Data in the front of the book for more detailed information.

Ancestry/Race	Number	%
Sioux (11)	15	0.07
Ute (1)	1	0.00
Yakama	1	0.00
Yaqui	2	0.01
All other tribes (27)	44	0.21
American Indian tribes, not spec.	36	0.17
Arab:	21	0.10
Arab/Arabic	16	0.08
Lebanese	5	0.02
Armenian	10	0.05
Asian:	964	4.56
Cambodian (1)	5	0.02
Chinese, ex. Taiwanese (16)	50	0.24
Filipino (331)	447	2.11
Indian (114)	124	0.59
Indonesian (4)	8	0.04
Japanese (65)	117	0.55
Korean (58)	74	0.35
Laotian (16)	26	0.12
Malaysian (1)	1	0.00
Taiwanese (3)	3	0.01
Thai (6)	9	0.04
Vietnamese (54)	61	0.29
Other Asian, not specified (18)	39	0.18
Australian	19	0.09
Austrian	95	0.45
Belgian	49	0.23
British	117	0.55
Canadian	104	0.49
Croatian	11	0.05
Czech	118	0.55
Czechoslovakian	25	0.12
Danish	241	1.13
Dutch	904	4.24
English	2,919	13.69
Estonian	17	0.08
European	242	1.14
Finnish	145	0.68
French, except Basque	840	3.94
French Canadian	151	0.71
German	3,756	17.62
Greek	38	0.18
Hawaii Native/Pacific Islander:	96	0.45
Melanesian: (2)	2	0.01
Fijian (2)	2	0.01
Micronesian: (6)	13	0.06
Guamanian/Chamorro (4)	10	0.05
Other Micronesian (2)	3	0.01
Polynesian: (25)	62	0.29
Native Hawaiian (16)	53	0.25
Samoan (8)	8	0.04
Other Polynesian (1)	1	0.00
Other Pac. Isl., not spec. (3)	19	0.09
Hispanic or Latino:	973	4.60
Central American:	39	0.18
Guatemalan	13	0.06
Honduran	1	0.00
Nicaraguan	2	0.01
Panamanian	10	0.05
Salvadoran	5	0.02
Other Central American	8	0.04
Cuban	12	0.06
Dominican Republic	1	0.00
Mexican	644	3.04
Puerto Rican	52	0.25
South American:	20	0.09
Chilean	2	0.01
Colombian	5	0.02
Ecuadorian	2	0.01
Peruvian	10	0.05
Other South American	1	0.00
Other Hispanic or Latino	205	0.97
Hungarian	153	0.72
Icelander	46	0.22
Iranian	35	0.16
Irish	2,675	12.55
Italian	833	3.91
Lithuanian	18	0.08
Luxemburger	7	0.03
Northern European	65	0.30
Norwegian	2,049	9.61
Pennsylvania German	9	0.04
Polish	347	1.63
Portuguese	35	0.16
Romanian	15	0.07
Russian	142	0.67
Scandinavian	183	0.86
Scotch-Irish	510	2.39
Scottish	776	3.64
Serbian	6	0.03
Slovak	7	0.03
Swedish	1,074	5.04
Swiss	112	0.53
Ukrainian	83	0.39
United States or American	1,354	6.35
Welsh	404	1.90
West Indian, excl. Hispanic:	45	0.21
Bermudan	21	0.10
Trinidadian and Tobagonian	24	0.11
White:	19,534	92.31
Not Hispanic (18,540)	18,975	89.67
Hispanic (471)	559	2.64
Yugoslavian	58	0.27

Oak Harbor

Place Type: City
County: Island
Population: 19,795

Ancestry/Race	Number	%
Acadian/Cajun	9	0.05
Afghan	7	0.04
African American/Black:	1,317	6.65
Not Hispanic (1,036)	1,255	6.34
Hispanic (42)	62	0.31
African, sub-Saharan:	130	0.65
African	130	0.65
Alaska Native tribes, specified:	29	0.15
Alaska Athabascan (2)	2	0.01
Aleut (7)	8	0.04
Eskimo (2)	6	0.03
Tlingit-Haida (10)	13	0.07
Alaska Native tribes, not specified	1	0.01
Am. Ind. or Alaska Nat., not spec.	80	0.40
American Indian tribes, specified:	350	1.77
Apache (4)	13	0.07
Blackfeet (5)	25	0.13
Cherokee (22)	94	0.47
Cheyenne (5)	9	0.05
Chickasaw (3)	6	0.03
Chippewa (7)	8	0.04
Choctaw (5)	6	0.03
Colville	1	0.01
Cree (4)	4	0.02
Iroquois (2)	7	0.04
Latin American Indians (1)	7	0.04
Lumbee (1)	1	0.01
Navajo (22)	28	0.14
Osage (2)	2	0.01
Potawatomi (3)	3	0.02
Pueblo (1)	3	0.02
Puget Sound Salish (8)	11	0.06
Seminole (2)	4	0.02
Shoshone	6	0.03
Sioux (7)	18	0.09
Tohono O'Odham (1)	1	0.01
Ute (1)	1	0.01
Yakama (2)	5	0.03
Yaqui (2)	3	0.02
All other tribes (59)	84	0.42
American Indian tribes, not spec.	25	0.13
Arab:	28	0.14
Arab/Arabic	5	0.03
Moroccan	8	0.04
Syrian	15	0.08
Armenian	24	0.12
Asian:	2,542	12.84
Cambodian (5)	5	0.03
Chinese, ex. Taiwanese (41)	75	0.38
Filipino (1,552)	1,976	9.98
Indian (21)	29	0.15
Indonesian (3)	5	0.03
Japanese (142)	266	1.34
Korean (50)	73	0.37
Laotian (4)	4	0.02
Malaysian (3)	8	0.04
Taiwanese (1)	1	0.01
Thai (11)	15	0.08
Vietnamese (24)	44	0.22
Other Asian, not specified (25)	41	0.21
Australian	38	0.19
Austrian	57	0.29
Basque	38	0.19
Belgian	86	0.43
British	220	1.11
Canadian	59	0.30
Celtic	18	0.09
Croatian	9	0.05
Czech	69	0.35
Czechoslovakian	48	0.24
Danish	179	0.90
Dutch	630	3.17
English	2,220	11.15
European	141	0.71
Finnish	69	0.35
French, except Basque	962	4.83
French Canadian	151	0.76
German	3,423	17.20
Greek	78	0.39
Guyanese	6	0.03
Hawaii Native/Pacific Islander:	300	1.52
Melanesian: (2)	3	0.02
Fijian (2)	3	0.02
Micronesian: (93)	133	0.67
Guamanian/Chamorro (85)	123	0.62
Other Micronesian (8)	10	0.05
Polynesian: (48)	119	0.60
Native Hawaiian (27)	73	0.37
Samoan (20)	41	0.21
Tongan (1)	3	0.02
Other Polynesian	2	0.01
Other Pac. Isl., not spec. (8)	45	0.23
Hispanic or Latino:	1,309	6.61
Central American:	54	0.27
Costa Rican	9	0.05
Guatemalan	8	0.04
Honduran	3	0.02
Nicaraguan	6	0.03
Panamanian	15	0.08
Salvadoran	13	0.07
Cuban	19	0.10
Dominican Republic	13	0.07
Mexican	748	3.78
Puerto Rican	163	0.82
South American:	30	0.15
Argentinean	2	0.01
Bolivian	2	0.01
Chilean	3	0.02
Colombian	12	0.06
Ecuadorian	4	0.02
Peruvian	5	0.03
Venezuelan	1	0.01
Other South American	1	0.01
Other Hispanic or Latino	282	1.42
Hungarian	72	0.36
Irish	2,729	13.71
Italian	733	3.68
Lithuanian	21	0.11
New Zealander	11	0.06
Norwegian	605	3.04
Polish	436	2.19
Portuguese	71	0.36
Russian	117	0.59
Scandinavian	64	0.32
Scotch-Irish	408	2.05
Scottish	567	2.85
Serbian	7	0.04
Slavic	6	0.03
Slovak	37	0.19

Notes: 1. Figures in the "Number" column do not add up to the total population due to: a) Ancestry/Race overlap — e.g. persons can report being both White and Irish, b) persons of Hispanic origin can report being any race, c) persons reporting two ancestries are counted in both categories. 2. Numbers in parentheses indicate the number of persons reporting this ancestry/race alone, not in combination with any other ancestry/race. 3. Refer to the Explanation of Data in the front of the book for more detailed information.

Swedish	286	1.44
Swiss	70	0.35
Turkish	12	0.06
Ukrainian	55	0.28
United States or American	1,433	7.20
Welsh	119	0.60
West Indian, excl. Hispanic:	40	0.20
Belizean	7	0.04
Haitian	21	0.11
Jamaican	12	0.06
White:	15,723	79.43
Not Hispanic (14,263)	15,014	75.85
Hispanic (570)	709	3.58
Yugoslavian	9	0.05

Olympia

Place Type: City
County: Thurston
Population: 42,514

Ancestry/Race	Number	%
African American/Black:	1,145	2.69
Not Hispanic (772)	1,082	2.55
Hispanic (33)	63	0.15
African, sub-Saharan:	95	0.22
African	71	0.17
Liberian	15	0.04
Other sub-Saharan African	9	0.02
Alaska Native tribes, specified:	71	0.17
Alaska Athabascan (3)	10	0.02
Aleut (16)	25	0.06
Eskimo (5)	8	0.02
Tlingit-Haida (12)	22	0.05
All other tribes (4)	6	0.01
Alaska Native tribes, not specified	4	0.01
Am. Ind. or Alaska Nat., not spec.	239	0.56
Albanian	6	0.01
American Indian tribes, specified:	729	1.71
Apache (8)	19	0.04
Blackfeet (13)	35	0.08
Cherokee (51)	155	0.36
Cheyenne (3)	3	0.01
Chickasaw (3)	12	0.03
Chippewa (15)	29	0.07
Choctaw (8)	19	0.04
Colville (15)	21	0.05
Comanche (1)	4	0.01
Cree (5)	13	0.03
Creek (5)	9	0.02
Crow	1	0.00
Delaware (5)	7	0.02
Iroquois (5)	15	0.04
Latin American Indians (19)	35	0.08
Lumbee	3	0.01
Menominee (2)	3	0.01
Navajo (10)	18	0.04
Osage (1)	1	0.00
Paiute (2)	2	0.00
Potawatomi (4)	7	0.02
Pueblo	5	0.01
Puget Sound Salish (38)	61	0.14
Seminole	5	0.01
Sioux (20)	37	0.09
Yakama (12)	19	0.04
Yaqui (4)	5	0.01
Yuman (1)	2	0.00
All other tribes (113)	183	0.43
American Indian tribes, not spec.	75	0.18
Arab:	116	0.27
Arab/Arabic	8	0.02
Egyptian	9	0.02
Lebanese	77	0.18
Palestinian	7	0.02
Other Arab	15	0.04
Armenian	23	0.05
Asian:	3,180	7.48
Bangladeshi (3)	3	0.01
Cambodian (98)	125	0.29
Chinese, ex. Taiwanese (308)	444	1.04
Filipino (240)	367	0.86
Indian (133)	173	0.41
Indonesian (1)	8	0.02
Japanese (207)	389	0.91
Korean (297)	395	0.93
Laotian (28)	40	0.09
Malaysian (1)	2	0.00
Pakistani (4)	5	0.01
Sri Lankan (2)	6	0.01
Taiwanese (15)	25	0.06
Thai (16)	31	0.07
Vietnamese (978)	1,074	2.53
Other Asian, specified (2)	9	0.02
Other Asian, not specified (47)	84	0.20
Assyrian/Chaldean/Syriac	6	0.01
Australian	12	0.03
Austrian	206	0.49
Basque	38	0.09
Belgian	16	0.04
Brazilian	33	0.08
British	317	0.75
Bulgarian	6	0.01
Canadian	229	0.54
Celtic	17	0.04
Croatian	95	0.22
Czech	239	0.56
Czechoslovakian	72	0.17
Danish	517	1.22
Dutch	863	2.04
Eastern European	59	0.14
English	5,825	13.76
Estonian	8	0.02
European	873	2.06
Finnish	322	0.76
French, except Basque	1,489	3.52
French Canadian	498	1.18
German	8,253	19.49
Greek	178	0.42
Hawaii Native/Pacific Islander:	286	0.67
Micronesian: (39)	63	0.15
Guamanian/Chamorro (36)	59	0.14
Other Micronesian (3)	4	0.01
Polynesian: (63)	155	0.36
Native Hawaiian (37)	117	0.28
Samoan (25)	35	0.08
Other Polynesian (1)	3	0.01
Other Pac. Isl., specified	4	0.01
Other Pac. Isl., not spec. (20)	64	0.15
Hispanic or Latino:	1,863	4.38
Central American:	64	0.15
Costa Rican	3	0.01
Guatemalan	16	0.04
Honduran	14	0.03
Panamanian	16	0.04
Salvadoran	14	0.03
Other Central American	1	0.00
Cuban	62	0.15
Dominican Republic	3	0.01
Mexican	1,100	2.59
Puerto Rican	219	0.52
South American:	86	0.20
Argentinean	5	0.01
Bolivian	7	0.02
Chilean	5	0.01
Colombian	30	0.07
Ecuadorian	10	0.02
Paraguayan	1	0.00
Peruvian	21	0.05
Venezuelan	4	0.01
Other South American	3	0.01
Other Hispanic or Latino	329	0.77
Hungarian	129	0.30
Icelander	34	0.08
Iranian	30	0.07
Irish	6,106	14.42
Israeli	6	0.01
Italian	1,407	3.32
Latvian	9	0.02
Lithuanian	100	0.24
Luxemburger	5	0.01
Northern European	96	0.23
Norwegian	2,676	6.32
Pennsylvania German	6	0.01
Polish	889	2.10
Portuguese	95	0.22
Romanian	75	0.18
Russian	425	1.00
Scandinavian	420	0.99
Scotch-Irish	1,181	2.79
Scottish	1,734	4.09
Slavic	83	0.20
Slovak	44	0.10
Slovene	20	0.05
Swedish	1,691	3.99
Swiss	240	0.57
Turkish	8	0.02
Ukrainian	95	0.22
United States or American	1,814	4.28
Welsh	408	0.96
West Indian, excl. Hispanic:	45	0.11
Jamaican	22	0.05
West Indian	23	0.05
White:	37,661	88.58
Not Hispanic (35,343)	36,530	85.92
Hispanic (903)	1,131	2.66
Yugoslavian	70	0.17

Opportunity

Place Type: Census Designated Place
County: Spokane
Population: 25,065

Ancestry/Race	Number	%
African American/Black:	374	1.49
Not Hispanic (245)	361	1.44
Hispanic (7)	13	0.05
African, sub-Saharan:	48	0.19
African	34	0.14
Senegalese	6	0.02
Other sub-Saharan African	8	0.03
Alaska Native tribes, specified:	17	0.07
Aleut (2)	3	0.01
Eskimo (4)	6	0.02
Tlingit-Haida (3)	8	0.03
Am. Ind. or Alaska Nat., not spec.	115	0.46
American Indian tribes, specified:	341	1.36
Apache (2)	4	0.02
Blackfeet (19)	44	0.18
Cherokee (19)	54	0.22
Cheyenne (1)	3	0.01
Chickasaw	1	0.00
Chippewa (13)	38	0.15
Choctaw (3)	9	0.04
Colville (27)	36	0.14
Cree	2	0.01
Creek (2)	2	0.01
Crow (1)	2	0.01
Iroquois	1	0.00
Latin American Indians (2)	6	0.02
Lumbee	1	0.00
Navajo (14)	16	0.06
Osage (2)	2	0.01
Pueblo (1)	1	0.00
Puget Sound Salish (1)	1	0.00
Seminole (1)	2	0.01
Shoshone	3	0.01
Sioux (18)	24	0.10
Ute (1)	1	0.00
Yakama (4)	7	0.03
All other tribes (43)	81	0.32
American Indian tribes, not spec.	26	0.10
Arab:	84	0.34
Arab/Arabic	16	0.06
Jordanian	22	0.09
Lebanese	24	0.10
Moroccan	12	0.05
Syrian	10	0.04
Armenian	26	0.10
Asian:	518	2.07

Notes: 1. Figures in the "Number" column do not add up to the total population due to: a) Ancestry/Race overlap — e.g. persons can report being both White and Irish, b) persons of Hispanic origin can report being any race, c) persons reporting two ancestries are counted in both categories. 2. Numbers in parentheses indicate the number of persons reporting this ancestry/race alone, not in combination with any other ancestry/race. 3. Refer to the Explanation of Data in the front of the book for more detailed information.

Cambodian (5)	5	0.02
Chinese, ex. Taiwanese (43)	67	0.27
Filipino (57)	120	0.48
Hmong (2)	2	0.01
Indian (27)	33	0.13
Indonesian (1)	4	0.02
Japanese (64)	120	0.48
Korean (26)	44	0.18
Taiwanese (1)	2	0.01
Thai (14)	17	0.07
Vietnamese (66)	81	0.32
Other Asian, not specified (10)	23	0.09
Australian	38	0.15
Austrian	63	0.25
Belgian	36	0.14
British	125	0.50
Canadian	159	0.63
Czech	72	0.29
Czechoslovakian	62	0.25
Danish	344	1.37
Dutch	600	2.40
English	2,877	11.49
European	208	0.83
Finnish	138	0.55
French, except Basque	1,222	4.88
French Canadian	320	1.28
German	6,346	25.34
Greek	88	0.35
Hawaii Native/Pacific Islander:	76	0.30
Melanesian: (3)	3	0.01
Fijian (3)	3	0.01
Micronesian: (4)	5	0.02
Guamanian/Chamorro (4)	4	0.02
Other Micronesian	1	0.00
Polynesian: (18)	52	0.21
Native Hawaiian (13)	39	0.16
Samoan (5)	12	0.05
Other Polynesian	1	0.00
Other Pac. Isl., not spec. (1)	16	0.06
Hispanic or Latino:	670	2.67
Central American:	20	0.08
Guatemalan	8	0.03
Honduran	1	0.00
Nicaraguan	2	0.01
Panamanian	4	0.02
Salvadoran	4	0.02
Other Central American	1	0.00
Cuban	9	0.04
Mexican	443	1.77
Puerto Rican	41	0.16
South American:	6	0.02
Argentinean	2	0.01
Venezuelan	3	0.01
Other South American	1	0.00
Other Hispanic or Latino	151	0.60
Hungarian	85	0.34
Icelander	7	0.03
Irish	3,549	14.17
Italian	1,000	3.99
Latvian	2	0.01
Lithuanian	26	0.10
Luxemburger	4	0.02
Northern European	6	0.02
Norwegian	1,857	7.41
Pennsylvania German	31	0.12
Polish	498	1.99
Portuguese	10	0.04
Romanian	30	0.12
Russian	214	0.85
Scandinavian	136	0.54
Scotch-Irish	582	2.32
Scottish	643	2.57
Slavic	9	0.04
Slovene	16	0.06
Swedish	899	3.59
Swiss	138	0.55
Turkish	4	0.02
Ukrainian	62	0.25
United States or American	1,676	6.69
Welsh	395	1.58
West Indian, excl. Hispanic:	8	0.03
Jamaican	8	0.03
White:	24,022	95.84
Not Hispanic (23,021)	23,525	93.86
Hispanic (419)	497	1.98
Yugoslavian	61	0.24

Orchards

Place Type: Census Designated Place
County: Clark
Population: 17,852

Ancestry/Race	Number	%
African American/Black:	402	2.25
Not Hispanic (304)	384	2.15
Hispanic (8)	18	0.10
African, sub-Saharan:	48	0.27
African	48	0.27
Alaska Native tribes, specified:	24	0.13
Alaska Athabascan (2)	3	0.02
Aleut (4)	5	0.03
Eskimo (1)	2	0.01
Tlingit-Haida (7)	11	0.06
All other tribes	3	0.02
Am. Ind. or Alaska Nat., not spec.	91	0.51
American Indian tribes, specified:	217	1.22
Apache (4)	10	0.06
Blackfeet (3)	20	0.11
Cherokee (15)	64	0.36
Cheyenne	2	0.01
Chickasaw (1)	2	0.01
Chippewa (12)	12	0.07
Choctaw (2)	5	0.03
Colville (5)	7	0.04
Comanche (1)	2	0.01
Cree	3	0.02
Creek (1)	2	0.01
Iroquois (2)	3	0.02
Latin American Indians (6)	7	0.04
Lumbee (1)	1	0.01
Menominee	1	0.01
Navajo	1	0.01
Osage	1	0.01
Pima (3)	3	0.02
Pueblo (4)	5	0.03
Puget Sound Salish (1)	1	0.01
Seminole	1	0.01
Shoshone (1)	1	0.01
Sioux (8)	13	0.07
Yakama (7)	7	0.04
Yaqui	3	0.02
All other tribes (29)	40	0.22
American Indian tribes, not spec.	6	0.03
Arab:	58	0.32
Arab/Arabic	8	0.04
Lebanese	25	0.14
Syrian	25	0.14
Asian:	997	5.58
Cambodian (99)	113	0.63
Chinese, ex. Taiwanese (87)	109	0.61
Filipino (157)	258	1.45
Hmong (8)	8	0.04
Indian (25)	37	0.21
Indonesian (4)	6	0.03
Japanese (38)	95	0.53
Korean (43)	59	0.33
Laotian (86)	92	0.52
Thai (7)	14	0.08
Vietnamese (156)	174	0.97
Other Asian, not specified (11)	32	0.18
Austrian	68	0.38
Basque	6	0.03
Belgian	12	0.07
British	36	0.20
Canadian	69	0.38
Czech	76	0.42
Czechoslovakian	16	0.09
Danish	175	0.98
Dutch	320	1.79
English	1,598	8.92
European	250	1.39
Finnish	346	1.93
French, except Basque	626	3.49
French Canadian	157	0.88
German	3,727	20.79
Greek	74	0.41
Hawaii Native/Pacific Islander:	182	1.02
Melanesian: (1)	1	0.01
Fijian (1)	1	0.01
Micronesian: (72)	85	0.48
Guamanian/Chamorro (71)	84	0.47
Other Micronesian (1)	1	0.01
Polynesian: (31)	85	0.48
Native Hawaiian (9)	53	0.30
Samoan (15)	25	0.14
Tongan (6)	6	0.03
Other Polynesian (1)	1	0.01
Other Pac. Isl., not spec.	11	0.06
Hispanic or Latino:	809	4.53
Central American:	28	0.16
Costa Rican	3	0.02
Guatemalan	10	0.06
Honduran	1	0.01
Nicaraguan	1	0.01
Panamanian	9	0.05
Salvadoran	3	0.02
Other Central American	1	0.01
Cuban	13	0.07
Dominican Republic	3	0.02
Mexican	550	3.08
Puerto Rican	39	0.22
South American:	15	0.08
Argentinean	3	0.02
Chilean	8	0.04
Colombian	1	0.01
Peruvian	3	0.02
Other Hispanic or Latino	161	0.90
Hungarian	21	0.12
Icelander	8	0.04
Irish	1,984	11.07
Italian	598	3.34
Latvian	15	0.08
Northern European	34	0.19
Norwegian	803	4.48
Pennsylvania German	24	0.13
Polish	276	1.54
Portuguese	47	0.26
Romanian	134	0.75
Russian	440	2.45
Scandinavian	116	0.65
Scotch-Irish	334	1.86
Scottish	351	1.96
Slavic	6	0.03
Slovene	8	0.04
Swedish	542	3.02
Swiss	49	0.27
Turkish	10	0.06
Ukrainian	227	1.27
United States or American	1,169	6.52
Welsh	107	0.60
West Indian, excl. Hispanic:	9	0.05
Haitian	9	0.05
White:	16,135	90.38
Not Hispanic (15,186)	15,664	87.74
Hispanic (415)	471	2.64
Yugoslavian	54	0.30

Paine Field-Lake Stickney

Place Type: Census Designated Place
County: Snohomish
Population: 24,383

Ancestry/Race	Number	%
African American/Black:	1,241	5.09
Not Hispanic (916)	1,183	4.85
Hispanic (39)	58	0.24
African, sub-Saharan:	185	0.76

Notes: 1. Figures in the "Number" column do not add up to the total population due to: a) Ancestry/Race overlap — e.g. persons can report being both White and Irish, b) persons of Hispanic origin can report being any race, c) persons reporting two ancestries are counted in both categories. 2. Numbers in parentheses indicate the number of persons reporting this ancestry/race alone, not in combination with any other ancestry/race. 3. Refer to the Explanation of Data in the front of the book for more detailed information.

African	110	0.45
Ethiopian	64	0.26
Ghanian	11	0.05
Alaska Native tribes, specified:	59	0.24
Alaska Athabascan (7)	7	0.03
Aleut (3)	7	0.03
Eskimo (9)	9	0.04
Tlingit-Haida (19)	32	0.13
All other tribes (4)	4	0.02
Am. Ind. or Alaska Nat., not spec.	204	0.84
American Indian tribes, specified:	311	1.28
Apache (2)	7	0.03
Blackfeet (6)	23	0.09
Cherokee (17)	74	0.30
Cheyenne	1	0.00
Chickasaw	1	0.00
Chippewa (20)	34	0.14
Choctaw (5)	5	0.02
Colville (4)	5	0.02
Cree (3)	6	0.02
Creek (2)	5	0.02
Delaware (3)	3	0.01
Iroquois (3)	7	0.03
Kiowa (1)	1	0.00
Latin American Indians (2)	17	0.07
Navajo (10)	10	0.04
Osage (2)	4	0.02
Potawatomi	2	0.01
Pueblo (2)	3	0.01
Puget Sound Salish (25)	28	0.11
Seminole	2	0.01
Shoshone (3)	4	0.02
Sioux (3)	19	0.08
Yakama (1)	2	0.01
Yaqui	3	0.01
All other tribes (22)	45	0.18
American Indian tribes, not spec.	47	0.19
Arab:	16	0.07
Arab/Arabic	10	0.04
Lebanese	6	0.02
Asian:	2,208	9.06
Bangladeshi (3)	3	0.01
Cambodian (131)	135	0.55
Chinese, ex. Taiwanese (95)	126	0.52
Filipino (381)	522	2.14
Indian (198)	235	0.96
Indonesian (90)	110	0.45
Japanese (82)	150	0.62
Korean (395)	457	1.87
Laotian (21)	29	0.12
Malaysian (2)	7	0.03
Pakistani (6)	28	0.11
Sri Lankan	1	0.00
Taiwanese (3)	7	0.03
Thai (22)	30	0.12
Vietnamese (289)	307	1.26
Other Asian, specified (1)	3	0.01
Other Asian, not specified (30)	58	0.24
Austrian	32	0.13
Belgian	31	0.13
Brazilian	59	0.24
British	157	0.65
Canadian	139	0.57
Czech	49	0.20
Czechoslovakian	7	0.03
Danish	359	1.48
Dutch	532	2.19
English	2,271	9.37
Estonian	4	0.02
European	151	0.62
Finnish	120	0.49
French, except Basque	729	3.01
French Canadian	208	0.86
German	4,078	16.82
Greek	68	0.28
Hawaii Native/Pacific Islander:	214	0.88
Melanesian: (28)	32	0.13
Fijian (28)	32	0.13
Micronesian: (35)	46	0.19
Guamanian/Chamorro (33)	42	0.17
Other Micronesian (2)	4	0.02
Polynesian: (45)	94	0.39
Native Hawaiian (32)	69	0.28
Samoan (13)	25	0.10
Other Pac. Isl., not spec. (13)	42	0.17
Hispanic or Latino:	2,065	8.47
Central American:	46	0.19
Guatemalan	23	0.09
Honduran	3	0.01
Nicaraguan	3	0.01
Panamanian	9	0.04
Salvadoran	8	0.03
Cuban	17	0.07
Dominican Republic	1	0.00
Mexican	1,467	6.02
Puerto Rican	89	0.37
South American:	58	0.24
Argentinean	9	0.04
Bolivian	7	0.03
Chilean	4	0.02
Colombian	18	0.07
Ecuadorian	4	0.02
Peruvian	8	0.03
Venezuelan	6	0.02
Other South American	2	0.01
Other Hispanic or Latino	387	1.59
Hungarian	133	0.55
Icelander	29	0.12
Iranian	68	0.28
Irish	2,399	9.89
Italian	812	3.35
Latvian	10	0.04
Lithuanian	17	0.07
Northern European	39	0.16
Norwegian	1,328	5.48
Pennsylvania German	17	0.07
Polish	373	1.54
Portuguese	213	0.88
Romanian	58	0.24
Russian	300	1.24
Scandinavian	104	0.43
Scotch-Irish	403	1.66
Scottish	666	2.75
Slavic	18	0.07
Slovak	12	0.05
Swedish	654	2.70
Swiss	42	0.17
Ukrainian	444	1.83
United States or American	1,293	5.33
Welsh	278	1.15
West Indian, excl. Hispanic:	77	0.32
Jamaican	64	0.26
West Indian	13	0.05
White:	19,985	81.96
Not Hispanic (18,255)	19,016	77.99
Hispanic (822)	969	3.97
Yugoslavian	25	0.10

Parkland

Place Type: Census Designated Place
County: Pierce
Population: 24,053

Ancestry/Race	Number	%
Afghan	7	0.03
African American/Black:	2,472	10.28
Not Hispanic (1,893)	2,373	9.87
Hispanic (47)	99	0.41
African, sub-Saharan:	140	0.59
African	140	0.59
Alaska Native tribes, specified:	33	0.14
Alaska Athabascan	4	0.02
Aleut (8)	10	0.04
Eskimo (10)	12	0.05
Tlingit-Haida (7)	7	0.03
Alaska Native tribes, not specified	2	0.01
Am. Ind. or Alaska Nat., not spec.	211	0.88
American Indian tribes, specified:	360	1.50
Apache (3)	9	0.04
Blackfeet (6)	38	0.16
Cherokee (29)	101	0.42
Cheyenne	1	0.00
Chickasaw	1	0.00
Chippewa (15)	25	0.10
Choctaw (2)	11	0.05
Colville (1)	3	0.01
Comanche	1	0.00
Cree	3	0.01
Crow (4)	5	0.02
Delaware	1	0.00
Iroquois (8)	9	0.04
Kiowa	3	0.01
Latin American Indians (7)	16	0.07
Navajo (1)	3	0.01
Osage (2)	4	0.02
Ottawa	1	0.00
Potawatomi	4	0.02
Pueblo (2)	3	0.01
Puget Sound Salish (15)	25	0.10
Seminole (1)	2	0.01
Sioux (3)	20	0.08
Yakama (1)	4	0.02
All other tribes (36)	67	0.28
American Indian tribes, not spec.	28	0.12
Arab:	34	0.14
Egyptian	20	0.08
Lebanese	7	0.03
Syrian	7	0.03
Armenian	7	0.03
Asian:	2,333	9.70
Cambodian (41)	66	0.27
Chinese, ex. Taiwanese (62)	150	0.62
Filipino (361)	548	2.28
Indian (25)	39	0.16
Indonesian (2)	8	0.03
Japanese (245)	402	1.67
Korean (676)	893	3.71
Laotian (2)	3	0.01
Malaysian (1)	3	0.01
Taiwanese (4)	5	0.02
Thai (32)	46	0.19
Vietnamese (64)	84	0.35
Other Asian, specified (1)	8	0.03
Other Asian, not specified (30)	78	0.32
Assyrian/Chaldean/Syriac	5	0.02
Austrian	50	0.21
Basque	12	0.05
Belgian	18	0.08
Brazilian	4	0.02
British	63	0.26
Bulgarian	20	0.08
Canadian	48	0.20
Celtic	31	0.13
Croatian	23	0.10
Czech	75	0.31
Czechoslovakian	33	0.14
Danish	271	1.13
Dutch	451	1.89
English	1,781	7.45
Estonian	9	0.04
European	405	1.69
Finnish	109	0.46
French, except Basque	786	3.29
French Canadian	262	1.10
German	4,820	20.16
German Russian	12	0.05
Greek	67	0.28
Hawaii Native/Pacific Islander:	620	2.58
Micronesian: (239)	283	1.18
Guamanian/Chamorro (232)	269	1.12
Other Micronesian (7)	14	0.06
Polynesian: (163)	288	1.20
Native Hawaiian (44)	119	0.49
Samoan (116)	155	0.64
Tongan (1)	2	0.01
Other Polynesian (2)	12	0.05
Other Pac. Isl., not spec. (19)	49	0.20
Hispanic or Latino:	1,281	5.33
Central American:	49	0.20

Notes: 1. Figures in the "Number" column do not add up to the total population due to: a) Ancestry/Race overlap — e.g. persons can report being both White and Irish, b) persons of Hispanic origin can report being any race, c) persons reporting two ancestries are counted in both categories. 2. Numbers in parentheses indicate the number of persons reporting this ancestry/race alone, not in combination with any other ancestry/race. 3. Refer to the Explanation of Data in the front of the book for more detailed information.

Ancestry/Race	Number	%
Costa Rican	3	0.01
Guatemalan	3	0.01
Honduran	4	0.02
Nicaraguan	3	0.01
Panamanian	23	0.10
Salvadoran	10	0.04
Other Central American	3	0.01
Cuban	23	0.10
Dominican Republic	17	0.07
Mexican	675	2.81
Puerto Rican	234	0.97
South American:	22	0.09
Argentinean	3	0.01
Bolivian	3	0.01
Colombian	6	0.02
Ecuadorian	2	0.01
Peruvian	4	0.02
Other South American	4	0.02
Other Hispanic or Latino	261	1.09
Hungarian	45	0.19
Icelander	19	0.08
Irish	2,725	11.40
Italian	717	3.00
Lithuanian	59	0.25
Luxemburger	6	0.03
Macedonian	10	0.04
Northern European	10	0.04
Norwegian	1,723	7.21
Polish	341	1.43
Portuguese	128	0.54
Romanian	13	0.05
Russian	122	0.51
Scandinavian	175	0.73
Scotch-Irish	394	1.65
Scottish	389	1.63
Serbian	10	0.04
Slavic	8	0.03
Slovak	16	0.07
Swedish	659	2.76
Swiss	123	0.51
Ukrainian	50	0.21
United States or American	1,326	5.55
Welsh	157	0.66
West Indian, excl. Hispanic:	118	0.49
Bahamian	4	0.02
Barbadian	7	0.03
Haitian	66	0.28
Jamaican	34	0.14
Trinidadian and Tobagonian	7	0.03
White:	19,045	79.18
Not Hispanic (17,223)	18,342	76.26
Hispanic (555)	703	2.92
Yugoslavian	5	0.02

Pasco

Place Type: City
County: Franklin
Population: 32,066

Ancestry/Race	Number	%
African American/Black:	1,194	3.72
Not Hispanic (940)	1,041	3.25
Hispanic (93)	153	0.48
African, sub-Saharan:	82	0.26
African	77	0.24
South African	5	0.02
Alaska Native tribes, specified:	17	0.05
Alaska Athabascan (5)	9	0.03
Eskimo (1)	2	0.01
Tlingit-Haida (4)	4	0.01
All other tribes (2)	2	0.01
Alaska Native tribes, not specified	3	0.01
Am. Ind. or Alaska Nat., not spec.	164	0.51
American Indian tribes, specified:	260	0.81
Apache (15)	23	0.07
Blackfeet (5)	15	0.05
Cherokee (12)	44	0.14
Cheyenne (2)	3	0.01
Chickasaw (4)	4	0.01
Chippewa (3)	6	0.02
Choctaw (9)	17	0.05
Colville (4)	8	0.02
Comanche	1	0.00
Cree	2	0.01
Creek	2	0.01
Iroquois (3)	4	0.01
Latin American Indians (23)	38	0.12
Navajo	3	0.01
Ottawa	1	0.00
Paiute (1)	1	0.00
Pima	5	0.02
Pueblo (3)	5	0.02
Puget Sound Salish (2)	4	0.01
Shoshone (4)	4	0.01
Sioux (6)	12	0.04
Tohono O'Odham	3	0.01
Yakama (2)	2	0.01
Yaqui (1)	2	0.01
All other tribes (36)	51	0.16
American Indian tribes, not spec.	14	0.04
Arab:	69	0.22
Iraqi	8	0.03
Lebanese	17	0.05
Palestinian	26	0.08
Syrian	18	0.06
Armenian	63	0.20
Asian:	750	2.34
Cambodian (20)	23	0.07
Chinese, ex. Taiwanese (43)	65	0.20
Filipino (56)	111	0.35
Hmong	1	0.00
Indian (43)	52	0.16
Indonesian	2	0.01
Japanese (21)	50	0.16
Korean (50)	56	0.17
Laotian (102)	133	0.41
Thai (1)	1	0.00
Vietnamese (209)	230	0.72
Other Asian, not specified (7)	26	0.08
Assyrian/Chaldean/Syriac	6	0.02
Australian	12	0.04
Austrian	5	0.02
Brazilian	27	0.08
British	34	0.11
Canadian	75	0.23
Croatian	30	0.09
Czech	35	0.11
Czechoslovakian	14	0.04
Danish	205	0.64
Dutch	186	0.58
English	1,534	4.80
European	348	1.09
Finnish	12	0.04
French, except Basque	379	1.19
French Canadian	82	0.26
German	2,456	7.68
German Russian	30	0.09
Greek	13	0.04
Hawaii Native/Pacific Islander:	83	0.26
Melanesian:	1	0.00
Other Melanesian	1	0.00
Micronesian: (20)	23	0.07
Guamanian/Chamorro (20)	23	0.07
Polynesian: (14)	35	0.11
Native Hawaiian (9)	23	0.07
Samoan (2)	3	0.01
Tongan (3)	9	0.03
Other Pac. Isl., not spec. (12)	24	0.07
Hispanic or Latino:	18,041	56.26
Central American:	310	0.97
Guatemalan	54	0.17
Honduran	18	0.06
Nicaraguan	16	0.05
Panamanian	1	0.00
Salvadoran	211	0.66
Other Central American	10	0.03
Cuban	42	0.13
Dominican Republic	8	0.02
Mexican	15,256	47.58
Puerto Rican	31	0.10
South American:	17	0.05
Argentinean	1	0.00
Chilean	5	0.02
Colombian	6	0.02
Peruvian	5	0.02
Other Hispanic or Latino	2,377	7.41
Hungarian	20	0.06
Icelander	19	0.06
Iranian	22	0.07
Irish	1,159	3.62
Italian	442	1.38
Lithuanian	15	0.05
Northern European	51	0.16
Norwegian	685	2.14
Pennsylvania German	4	0.01
Polish	203	0.63
Portuguese	68	0.21
Romanian	7	0.02
Russian	30	0.09
Scandinavian	72	0.23
Scotch-Irish	184	0.58
Scottish	249	0.78
Serbian	7	0.02
Slavic	9	0.03
Swedish	245	0.77
Swiss	29	0.09
Turkish	4	0.01
Ukrainian	147	0.46
United States or American	1,645	5.14
Welsh	50	0.16
White:	18,006	56.15
Not Hispanic (11,865)	12,263	38.24
Hispanic (5,054)	5,743	17.91
Yugoslavian	31	0.10

Picnic Point-North Lynnwood

Place Type: Census Designated Place
County: Snohomish
Population: 22,953

Ancestry/Race	Number	%
Acadian/Cajun	12	0.05
African American/Black:	736	3.21
Not Hispanic (495)	714	3.11
Hispanic (9)	22	0.10
African, sub-Saharan:	147	0.64
African	64	0.28
Ethiopian	51	0.22
Ghanian	16	0.07
Nigerian	7	0.03
South African	9	0.04
Alaska Native tribes, specified:	80	0.35
Alaska Athabascan (3)	11	0.05
Aleut (16)	26	0.11
Eskimo (3)	11	0.05
Tlingit-Haida (12)	28	0.12
All other tribes (2)	4	0.02
Alaska Native tribes, not specified	11	0.05
Am. Ind. or Alaska Nat., not spec.	108	0.47
American Indian tribes, specified:	214	0.93
Apache (5)	6	0.03
Blackfeet (8)	21	0.09
Cherokee (13)	43	0.19
Chippewa (6)	21	0.09
Choctaw (3)	6	0.03
Colville (4)	6	0.03
Cree (1)	5	0.02
Creek (1)	5	0.02
Crow	2	0.01
Delaware	2	0.01
Iroquois (1)	4	0.02
Latin American Indians (10)	19	0.08
Navajo	1	0.00
Osage (2)	2	0.01
Ottawa	1	0.00
Potawatomi (2)	3	0.01
Pueblo	2	0.01

Notes: 1. Figures in the "Number" column do not add up to the total population due to: a) Ancestry/Race overlap — e.g. persons can report being both White and Irish, b) persons of Hispanic origin can report being any race, c) persons reporting two ancestries are counted in both categories. 2. Numbers in parentheses indicate the number of persons reporting this ancestry/race alone, not in combination with any other ancestry/race. 3. Refer to the Explanation of Data in the front of the book for more detailed information.

Puget Sound Salish (18)	20	0.09
Shoshone (1)	1	0.00
Sioux (4)	5	0.02
Yakama (1)	3	0.01
All other tribes (23)	36	0.16
American Indian tribes, not spec.	34	0.15
Arab:	174	0.76
Arab/Arabic	47	0.21
Egyptian	85	0.37
Lebanese	22	0.10
Moroccan	9	0.04
Other Arab	11	0.05
Armenian	73	0.32
Asian:	2,955	12.87
Cambodian (91)	107	0.47
Chinese, ex. Taiwanese (303)	382	1.66
Filipino (424)	528	2.30
Indian (115)	148	0.64
Indonesian (8)	23	0.10
Japanese (143)	236	1.03
Korean (918)	973	4.24
Laotian (11)	11	0.05
Malaysian (1)	1	0.00
Pakistani (14)	21	0.09
Taiwanese (45)	54	0.24
Thai (15)	24	0.10
Vietnamese (377)	400	1.74
Other Asian, not specified (36)	47	0.20
Australian	13	0.06
Austrian	22	0.10
Basque	16	0.07
Belgian	85	0.37
British	140	0.61
Bulgarian	32	0.14
Canadian	109	0.48
Celtic	7	0.03
Croatian	34	0.15
Czech	71	0.31
Czechoslovakian	66	0.29
Danish	212	0.93
Dutch	377	1.65
English	3,083	13.51
European	314	1.38
Finnish	71	0.31
French, except Basque	679	2.97
French Canadian	143	0.63
German	4,186	18.34
Greek	109	0.48
Guyanese	7	0.03
Hawaii Native/Pacific Islander:	180	0.78
Melanesian: (12)	12	0.05
Fijian (12)	12	0.05
Micronesian: (20)	38	0.17
Guamanian/Chamorro (19)	30	0.13
Other Micronesian (1)	8	0.03
Polynesian: (34)	91	0.40
Native Hawaiian (28)	79	0.34
Samoan (1)	5	0.02
Tongan (2)	2	0.01
Other Polynesian (3)	5	0.02
Other Pac. Isl., not spec. (5)	39	0.17
Hispanic or Latino:	1,097	4.78
Central American:	34	0.15
Costa Rican	3	0.01
Guatemalan	3	0.01
Honduran	1	0.00
Nicaraguan	2	0.01
Panamanian	2	0.01
Salvadoran	22	0.10
Other Central American	1	0.00
Cuban	20	0.09
Dominican Republic	1	0.00
Mexican	697	3.04
Puerto Rican	48	0.21
South American:	50	0.22
Argentinean	5	0.02
Bolivian	5	0.02
Chilean	10	0.04
Colombian	8	0.03
Ecuadorian	3	0.01
Peruvian	14	0.06
Uruguayan	2	0.01
Venezuelan	3	0.01
Other Hispanic or Latino	247	1.08
Hungarian	105	0.46
Icelander	49	0.21
Iranian	64	0.28
Irish	2,748	12.04
Italian	783	3.43
Lithuanian	31	0.14
Luxemburger	30	0.13
New Zealander	8	0.04
Northern European	61	0.27
Norwegian	1,956	8.57
Pennsylvania German	25	0.11
Polish	356	1.56
Portuguese	68	0.30
Romanian	15	0.07
Russian	293	1.28
Scandinavian	167	0.73
Scotch-Irish	433	1.90
Scottish	632	2.77
Serbian	7	0.03
Slavic	14	0.06
Slovak	54	0.24
Swedish	1,037	4.54
Swiss	132	0.58
Ukrainian	183	0.80
United States or American	1,332	5.84
Welsh	298	1.31
White:	19,022	82.87
Not Hispanic (17,675)	18,408	80.20
Hispanic (507)	614	2.68
Yugoslavian	30	0.13

Port Angeles

Place Type: City
County: Clallam
Population: 18,397

Ancestry/Race	Number	%
Acadian/Cajun	6	0.03
African American/Black:	216	1.17
Not Hispanic (123)	203	1.10
Hispanic (4)	13	0.07
African, sub-Saharan:	12	0.06
African	7	0.04
Liberian	5	0.03
Alaska Native tribes, specified:	75	0.41
Alaska Athabascan (4)	4	0.02
Aleut (10)	16	0.09
Eskimo (12)	15	0.08
Tlingit-Haida (25)	32	0.17
All other tribes (3)	8	0.04
Alaska Native tribes, not specified	1	0.01
Am. Ind. or Alaska Nat., not spec.	159	0.86
Albanian	4	0.02
American Indian tribes, specified:	624	3.39
Apache (6)	13	0.07
Blackfeet (4)	13	0.07
Cherokee (16)	67	0.36
Cheyenne	2	0.01
Chickasaw (2)	2	0.01
Chippewa (13)	19	0.10
Choctaw (1)	6	0.03
Colville (5)	6	0.03
Comanche	2	0.01
Cree (1)	7	0.04
Creek (3)	7	0.04
Crow (1)	1	0.01
Delaware (1)	1	0.01
Iroquois	2	0.01
Latin American Indians (2)	6	0.03
Navajo (7)	15	0.08
Paiute (1)	1	0.01
Pueblo	1	0.01
Puget Sound Salish (31)	40	0.22
Seminole (1)	8	0.04
Sioux (8)	17	0.09
Yakama (6)	6	0.03
Yaqui (4)	4	0.02
Yuman	1	0.01
All other tribes (309)	377	2.05
American Indian tribes, not spec.	20	0.11
Arab:	20	0.11
Lebanese	20	0.11
Armenian	7	0.04
Asian:	374	2.03
Bangladeshi	2	0.01
Cambodian	1	0.01
Chinese, ex. Taiwanese (46)	74	0.40
Filipino (53)	101	0.55
Indian (2)	18	0.10
Indonesian (2)	3	0.02
Japanese (49)	73	0.40
Korean (56)	62	0.34
Laotian (3)	3	0.02
Taiwanese (7)	7	0.04
Thai (3)	9	0.05
Vietnamese (13)	14	0.08
Other Asian, not specified (1)	7	0.04
Australian	7	0.04
Austrian	55	0.30
Basque	4	0.02
Belgian	37	0.20
British	93	0.50
Canadian	93	0.50
Celtic	5	0.03
Croatian	6	0.03
Czech	56	0.30
Czechoslovakian	12	0.06
Danish	145	0.78
Dutch	525	2.84
Eastern European	6	0.03
English	2,605	14.10
European	192	1.04
Finnish	105	0.57
French, except Basque	928	5.02
French Canadian	314	1.70
German	3,964	21.46
Greek	26	0.14
Hawaii Native/Pacific Islander:	78	0.42
Micronesian: (17)	24	0.13
Guamanian/Chamorro (4)	8	0.04
Other Micronesian (13)	16	0.09
Polynesian: (7)	29	0.16
Native Hawaiian (4)	25	0.14
Samoan (2)	2	0.01
Tongan (1)	2	0.01
Other Pac. Isl., not spec. (8)	25	0.14
Hispanic or Latino:	430	2.34
Central American:	16	0.09
Costa Rican	1	0.01
Guatemalan	4	0.02
Honduran	4	0.02
Nicaraguan	5	0.03
Salvadoran	1	0.01
Other Central American	1	0.01
Cuban	9	0.05
Mexican	262	1.42
Puerto Rican	24	0.13
South American:	16	0.09
Argentinean	2	0.01
Bolivian	2	0.01
Chilean	6	0.03
Colombian	1	0.01
Ecuadorian	3	0.02
Peruvian	1	0.01
Venezuelan	1	0.01
Other Hispanic or Latino	103	0.56
Hungarian	99	0.54
Icelander	35	0.19
Irish	2,660	14.40
Italian	583	3.16
Latvian	8	0.04
Lithuanian	14	0.08
Luxemburger	8	0.04
Northern European	19	0.10
Norwegian	1,200	6.50

Notes: 1. Figures in the "Number" column do not add up to the total population due to: a) Ancestry/Race overlap — e.g. persons can report being both White and Irish, b) persons of Hispanic origin can report being any race, c) persons reporting two ancestries are counted in both categories. 2. Numbers in parentheses indicate the number of persons reporting this ancestry/race alone, not in combination with any other ancestry/race. 3. Refer to the Explanation of Data in the front of the book for more detailed information.

	Number	%
Pennsylvania German	7	0.04
Polish	421	2.28
Portuguese	24	0.13
Romanian	12	0.06
Russian	89	0.48
Scandinavian	138	0.75
Scotch-Irish	557	3.02
Scottish	803	4.35
Serbian	5	0.03
Slovak	12	0.06
Slovene	13	0.07
Swedish	617	3.34
Swiss	79	0.43
Turkish	6	0.03
Ukrainian	5	0.03
United States or American	1,345	7.28
Welsh	162	0.88
White:	17,294	94.00
Not Hispanic (16,572)	16,972	92.25
Hispanic (234)	322	1.75
Yugoslavian	19	0.10

Prairie Ridge

Place Type: Census Designated Place
County: Pierce
Population: 11,688

Ancestry/Race	Number	%
African American/Black:	98	0.84
Not Hispanic (61)	92	0.79
Hispanic (2)	6	0.05
African, sub-Saharan:	35	0.30
African	35	0.30
Alaska Native tribes, specified:	12	0.10
Aleut (3)	4	0.03
Eskimo (1)	2	0.02
Tlingit-Haida (2)	6	0.05
Am. Ind. or Alaska Nat., not spec.	51	0.44
American Indian tribes, specified:	207	1.77
Blackfeet (4)	12	0.10
Cherokee (12)	60	0.51
Cheyenne	2	0.02
Chickasaw (5)	7	0.06
Chippewa (7)	8	0.07
Choctaw (7)	13	0.11
Colville (6)	10	0.09
Comanche (1)	1	0.01
Creek (5)	5	0.04
Delaware	2	0.02
Iroquois	3	0.03
Latin American Indians (2)	2	0.02
Lumbee (4)	4	0.03
Navajo (1)	1	0.01
Osage	3	0.03
Pima (1)	1	0.01
Potawatomi	1	0.01
Pueblo (3)	3	0.03
Puget Sound Salish (10)	11	0.09
Seminole (1)	1	0.01
Shoshone	2	0.02
Sioux (1)	8	0.07
Yakama (5)	9	0.08
All other tribes (21)	38	0.33
American Indian tribes, not spec.	19	0.16
Asian:	241	2.06
Chinese, ex. Taiwanese (8)	28	0.24
Filipino (45)	97	0.83
Indian (2)	2	0.02
Indonesian (1)	1	0.01
Japanese (13)	50	0.43
Korean (22)	38	0.33
Thai (3)	6	0.05
Vietnamese (3)	3	0.03
Other Asian, specified (3)	6	0.05
Other Asian, not specified (2)	10	0.09
Austrian	50	0.43
Belgian	7	0.06
British	22	0.19
Canadian	17	0.15
Celtic	9	0.08
Croatian	36	0.31
Czech	9	0.08
Czechoslovakian	52	0.45
Danish	156	1.36
Dutch	366	3.18
English	1,216	10.57
Estonian	1	0.01
European	74	0.64
Finnish	131	1.14
French, except Basque	567	4.93
French Canadian	37	0.32
German	2,290	19.90
Greek	25	0.22
Hawaii Native/Pacific Islander:	72	0.62
Melanesian: (1)	1	0.01
Other Melanesian (1)	1	0.01
Micronesian: (20)	25	0.21
Guamanian/Chamorro (20)	25	0.21
Polynesian: (21)	43	0.37
Native Hawaiian (13)	33	0.28
Samoan (8)	10	0.09
Other Pac. Isl., not spec. (2)	3	0.03
Hispanic or Latino:	393	3.36
Central American:	13	0.11
Guatemalan	1	0.01
Honduran	2	0.02
Nicaraguan	5	0.04
Salvadoran	5	0.04
Cuban	4	0.03
Mexican	257	2.20
Puerto Rican	16	0.14
South American:	1	0.01
Chilean	1	0.01
Other Hispanic or Latino	102	0.87
Hungarian	16	0.14
Irish	1,529	13.29
Italian	426	3.70
Lithuanian	8	0.07
Northern European	14	0.12
Norwegian	1,097	9.53
Polish	201	1.75
Portuguese	23	0.20
Russian	86	0.75
Scandinavian	43	0.37
Scotch-Irish	231	2.01
Scottish	201	1.75
Swedish	405	3.52
Swiss	71	0.62
United States or American	583	5.07
Welsh	74	0.64
West Indian, excl. Hispanic:	48	0.42
Jamaican	48	0.42
White:	11,232	96.10
Not Hispanic (10,658)	10,934	93.55
Hispanic (256)	298	2.55
Yugoslavian	11	0.10

Pullman

Place Type: City
County: Whitman
Population: 24,675

Ancestry/Race	Number	%
Afghan	49	0.20
African American/Black:	744	3.02
Not Hispanic (581)	718	2.91
Hispanic (10)	26	0.11
African, sub-Saharan:	155	0.63
African	70	0.28
Ghanian	12	0.05
Kenyan	43	0.17
Nigerian	13	0.05
Ugandan	5	0.02
Other sub-Saharan African	12	0.05
Alaska Native tribes, specified:	30	0.12
Alaska Athabascan	4	0.02
Aleut (5)	7	0.03
Eskimo (4)	5	0.02
Tlingit-Haida (6)	12	0.05
All other tribes (1)	2	0.01
Alaska Native tribes, not specified	1	0.00
Am. Ind. or Alaska Nat., not spec.	57	0.23
American Indian tribes, specified:	269	1.09
Apache (1)	3	0.01
Blackfeet (5)	13	0.05
Cherokee (4)	52	0.21
Cheyenne (2)	2	0.01
Chickasaw	1	0.00
Chippewa (3)	7	0.03
Choctaw (3)	17	0.07
Colville (10)	17	0.07
Cree	1	0.00
Delaware (1)	1	0.00
Iroquois (3)	10	0.04
Latin American Indians (9)	15	0.06
Lumbee (1)	1	0.00
Navajo (4)	6	0.02
Osage	2	0.01
Ottawa (2)	4	0.02
Potawatomi	1	0.00
Pueblo	1	0.00
Puget Sound Salish (13)	19	0.08
Seminole (2)	2	0.01
Shoshone	1	0.00
Sioux (12)	18	0.07
Ute	1	0.00
Yakama (10)	11	0.04
Yaqui (1)	1	0.00
All other tribes (37)	62	0.25
American Indian tribes, not spec.	12	0.05
Arab:	87	0.35
Arab/Arabic	46	0.19
Jordanian	9	0.04
Lebanese	15	0.06
Moroccan	6	0.02
Other Arab	11	0.04
Armenian	37	0.15
Asian:	2,568	10.41
Bangladeshi (7)	8	0.03
Cambodian (9)	15	0.06
Chinese, ex. Taiwanese (699)	814	3.30
Filipino (114)	193	0.78
Hmong (10)	10	0.04
Indian (186)	203	0.82
Indonesian (6)	11	0.04
Japanese (342)	461	1.87
Korean (366)	418	1.69
Laotian (7)	9	0.04
Malaysian (6)	8	0.03
Pakistani (6)	11	0.04
Sri Lankan (12)	15	0.06
Taiwanese (43)	45	0.18
Thai (41)	56	0.23
Vietnamese (129)	162	0.66
Other Asian, specified (11)	16	0.06
Other Asian, not specified (33)	113	0.46
Australian	33	0.13
Austrian	64	0.26
Basque	33	0.13
Belgian	23	0.09
British	260	1.05
Canadian	99	0.40
Celtic	20	0.08
Croatian	37	0.15
Czech	144	0.58
Czechoslovakian	133	0.54
Danish	375	1.52
Dutch	588	2.38
English	2,882	11.65
Estonian	17	0.07
European	669	2.70
Finnish	120	0.49
French, except Basque	776	3.14
French Canadian	248	1.00
German	5,504	22.25
German Russian	6	0.02
Greek	83	0.34
Hawaii Native/Pacific Islander:	187	0.76

Notes: 1. Figures in the "Number" column do not add up to the total population due to: a) Ancestry/Race overlap — e.g. persons can report being both White and Irish, b) persons of Hispanic origin can report being any race, c) persons reporting two ancestries are counted in both categories. 2. Numbers in parentheses indicate the number of persons reporting this ancestry/race alone, not in combination with any other ancestry/race. 3. Refer to the Explanation of Data in the front of the book for more detailed information.

Melanesian: (1)	1	0.00
Fijian (1)	1	0.00
Micronesian: (24)	35	0.14
Guamanian/Chamorro (18)	26	0.11
Other Micronesian (6)	9	0.04
Polynesian: (59)	117	0.47
Native Hawaiian (34)	85	0.34
Samoan (23)	28	0.11
Tongan (1)	1	0.00
Other Polynesian (1)	3	0.01
Other Pac. Isl., not spec. (7)	34	0.14
Hispanic or Latino:	953	3.86
Central American:	34	0.14
Costa Rican	1	0.00
Guatemalan	7	0.03
Honduran	2	0.01
Nicaraguan	2	0.01
Panamanian	9	0.04
Salvadoran	12	0.05
Other Central American	1	0.00
Cuban	31	0.13
Mexican	543	2.20
Puerto Rican	58	0.24
South American:	109	0.44
Argentinean	15	0.06
Bolivian	5	0.02
Chilean	36	0.15
Colombian	20	0.08
Ecuadorian	14	0.06
Peruvian	7	0.03
Uruguayan	8	0.03
Venezuelan	4	0.02
Other Hispanic or Latino	178	0.72
Hungarian	44	0.18
Icelander	6	0.02
Iranian	39	0.16
Irish	2,626	10.61
Italian	858	3.47
Latvian	19	0.08
Lithuanian	46	0.19
Maltese	5	0.02
New Zealander	16	0.06
Northern European	80	0.32
Norwegian	1,869	7.55
Pennsylvania German	18	0.07
Polish	459	1.86
Portuguese	45	0.18
Romanian	53	0.21
Russian	177	0.72
Scandinavian	195	0.79
Scotch-Irish	522	2.11
Scottish	812	3.28
Serbian	33	0.13
Slavic	16	0.06
Slovak	23	0.09
Slovene	6	0.02
Swedish	910	3.68
Swiss	139	0.56
Turkish	65	0.26
Ukrainian	113	0.46
United States or American	1,253	5.06
Welsh	183	0.74
West Indian, excl. Hispanic:	16	0.06
Dutch West Indian	9	0.04
West Indian	7	0.03
White:	21,220	86.00
Not Hispanic (20,070)	20,690	83.85
Hispanic (435)	530	2.15
Yugoslavian	96	0.39

Puyallup

Place Type: City
County: Pierce
Population: 33,011

Ancestry/Race	Number	%
Acadian/Cajun	6	0.02
Afghan	8	0.02
African American/Black:	756	2.29
Not Hispanic (473)	709	2.15
Hispanic (23)	47	0.14
African, sub-Saharan:	45	0.14
African	45	0.14
Alaska Native tribes, specified:	59	0.18
Alaska Athabascan (4)	4	0.01
Aleut (5)	12	0.04
Eskimo (5)	8	0.02
Tlingit-Haida (15)	32	0.10
All other tribes (3)	3	0.01
Alaska Native tribes, not specified	6	0.02
Am. Ind. or Alaska Nat., not spec.	154	0.47
Albanian	10	0.03
American Indian tribes, specified:	448	1.36
Apache (3)	11	0.03
Blackfeet (9)	18	0.05
Cherokee (24)	86	0.26
Cheyenne (7)	8	0.02
Chickasaw (5)	6	0.02
Chippewa (16)	38	0.12
Choctaw (15)	27	0.08
Colville (9)	17	0.05
Comanche	1	0.00
Cree	1	0.00
Creek (2)	7	0.02
Delaware	2	0.01
Iroquois (3)	8	0.02
Kiowa (1)	3	0.01
Latin American Indians (3)	5	0.02
Navajo (8)	15	0.05
Osage (1)	5	0.02
Potawatomi (1)	1	0.00
Pueblo	5	0.02
Puget Sound Salish (31)	55	0.17
Seminole (1)	1	0.00
Sioux (17)	28	0.08
Yakama (2)	6	0.02
Yuman	2	0.01
All other tribes (55)	92	0.28
American Indian tribes, not spec.	50	0.15
Arab:	51	0.16
Lebanese	20	0.06
Syrian	20	0.06
Other Arab	11	0.03
Armenian	8	0.02
Asian:	1,688	5.11
Cambodian (28)	29	0.09
Chinese, ex. Taiwanese (72)	142	0.43
Filipino (237)	402	1.22
Indian (132)	164	0.50
Indonesian (1)	6	0.02
Japanese (139)	316	0.96
Korean (252)	361	1.09
Laotian (14)	14	0.04
Pakistani (2)	8	0.02
Sri Lankan (1)	3	0.01
Taiwanese (11)	13	0.04
Thai (13)	21	0.06
Vietnamese (129)	145	0.44
Other Asian, specified (1)	15	0.05
Other Asian, not specified (20)	49	0.15
Australian	13	0.04
Austrian	138	0.42
Basque	5	0.02
Belgian	33	0.10
British	239	0.73
Canadian	57	0.17
Celtic	22	0.07
Croatian	66	0.20
Czech	136	0.42
Czechoslovakian	60	0.18
Danish	435	1.33
Dutch	674	2.06
Eastern European	8	0.02
English	3,871	11.84
Estonian	13	0.04
European	468	1.43
Finnish	193	0.59
French, except Basque	1,430	4.38
French Canadian	388	1.19
German	7,638	23.37
German Russian	6	0.02
Greek	100	0.31
Hawaii Native/Pacific Islander:	252	0.76
Melanesian: (4)	4	0.01
Fijian (4)	4	0.01
Micronesian: (26)	45	0.14
Guamanian/Chamorro (26)	44	0.13
Other Micronesian	1	0.00
Polynesian: (69)	145	0.44
Native Hawaiian (36)	101	0.31
Samoan (33)	44	0.13
Other Pac. Isl., specified	4	0.01
Other Pac. Isl., not spec. (12)	54	0.16
Hispanic or Latino:	1,542	4.67
Central American:	59	0.18
Costa Rican	5	0.02
Guatemalan	8	0.02
Honduran	7	0.02
Nicaraguan	2	0.01
Panamanian	9	0.03
Salvadoran	23	0.07
Other Central American	5	0.02
Cuban	22	0.07
Dominican Republic	4	0.01
Mexican	1,065	3.23
Puerto Rican	107	0.32
South American:	17	0.05
Argentinean	1	0.00
Bolivian	1	0.00
Colombian	12	0.04
Ecuadorian	1	0.00
Other South American	2	0.01
Other Hispanic or Latino	268	0.81
Hungarian	77	0.24
Icelander	66	0.20
Iranian	14	0.04
Irish	3,892	11.91
Italian	1,418	4.34
Latvian	4	0.01
Lithuanian	37	0.11
Luxemburger	9	0.03
Northern European	95	0.29
Norwegian	2,653	8.12
Polish	800	2.45
Portuguese	128	0.39
Romanian	52	0.16
Russian	169	0.52
Scandinavian	220	0.67
Scotch-Irish	700	2.14
Scottish	909	2.78
Slavic	13	0.04
Slovak	48	0.15
Slovene	8	0.02
Swedish	1,065	3.26
Swiss	384	1.17
Ukrainian	57	0.17
United States or American	1,290	3.95
Welsh	387	1.18
West Indian, excl. Hispanic:	21	0.06
Haitian	13	0.04
Jamaican	8	0.02
White:	30,196	91.47
Not Hispanic (28,337)	29,331	88.85
Hispanic (673)	865	2.62
Yugoslavian	57	0.17

Redmond

Place Type: City
County: King
Population: 45,256

Ancestry/Race	Number	%
African American/Black:	957	2.11
Not Hispanic (659)	911	2.01
Hispanic (28)	46	0.10
African, sub-Saharan:	111	0.24
African	36	0.08
Ethiopian	34	0.07

Notes: 1. Figures in the "Number" column do not add up to the total population due to: a) Ancestry/Race overlap — e.g. persons can report being both White and Irish, b) persons of Hispanic origin can report being any race, c) persons reporting two ancestries are counted in both categories. 2. Numbers in parentheses indicate the number of persons reporting this ancestry/race alone, not in combination with any other ancestry/race. 3. Refer to the Explanation of Data in the front of the book for more detailed information.

South African	28	0.06
Other sub-Saharan African	13	0.03
Alaska Native tribes, specified:	39	0.09
Alaska Athabascan (2)	5	0.01
Aleut (7)	9	0.02
Eskimo (1)	2	0.00
Tlingit-Haida (14)	21	0.05
All other tribes (1)	2	0.00
Alaska Native tribes, not specified	3	0.01
Am. Ind. or Alaska Nat., not spec.	146	0.32
Albanian	8	0.02
American Indian tribes, specified:	247	0.55
Apache	1	0.00
Blackfeet (2)	9	0.02
Cherokee (9)	55	0.12
Chickasaw (2)	7	0.02
Chippewa (10)	20	0.04
Choctaw (3)	7	0.02
Colville (1)	1	0.00
Creek (2)	6	0.01
Crow (2)	2	0.00
Delaware (3)	4	0.01
Iroquois (3)	5	0.01
Latin American Indians (5)	9	0.02
Menominee	1	0.00
Navajo (2)	3	0.01
Potawatomi	5	0.01
Pueblo (1)	4	0.01
Puget Sound Salish (7)	8	0.02
Seminole	3	0.01
Shoshone (3)	3	0.01
Sioux (6)	12	0.03
Yakama	4	0.01
Yaqui	4	0.01
All other tribes (34)	74	0.16
American Indian tribes, not spec.	47	0.10
Arab:	286	0.63
Arab/Arabic	38	0.08
Egyptian	30	0.07
Lebanese	120	0.26
Syrian	43	0.09
Other Arab	55	0.12
Armenian	42	0.09
Asian:	6,786	14.99
Bangladeshi (5)	5	0.01
Cambodian (113)	144	0.32
Chinese, ex. Taiwanese (1,671)	1,904	4.21
Filipino (402)	583	1.29
Hmong (12)	15	0.03
Indian (1,377)	1,486	3.28
Indonesian (29)	36	0.08
Japanese (769)	989	2.19
Korean (456)	512	1.13
Laotian (74)	76	0.17
Malaysian (5)	11	0.02
Pakistani (46)	70	0.15
Sri Lankan (3)	5	0.01
Taiwanese (251)	298	0.66
Thai (76)	98	0.22
Vietnamese (353)	405	0.89
Other Asian, specified (24)	29	0.06
Other Asian, not specified (68)	120	0.27
Assyrian/Chaldean/Syriac	13	0.03
Australian	71	0.16
Austrian	170	0.37
Basque	15	0.03
Belgian	79	0.17
Brazilian	42	0.09
British	710	1.56
Bulgarian	56	0.12
Canadian	473	1.04
Celtic	15	0.03
Croatian	75	0.17
Czech	289	0.64
Czechoslovakian	111	0.24
Danish	531	1.17
Dutch	840	1.85
Eastern European	28	0.06
English	6,378	14.05
European	1,018	2.24
Finnish	266	0.59
French, except Basque	1,925	4.24
French Canadian	461	1.02
German	7,886	17.37
Greek	184	0.41
Hawaii Native/Pacific Islander:	207	0.46
Micronesian: (18)	31	0.07
Guamanian/Chamorro (15)	27	0.06
Other Micronesian (3)	4	0.01
Polynesian: (56)	121	0.27
Native Hawaiian (36)	90	0.20
Samoan (16)	23	0.05
Other Polynesian (4)	8	0.02
Other Pac. Isl., specified	4	0.01
Other Pac. Isl., not spec. (8)	51	0.11
Hispanic or Latino:	2,538	5.61
Central American:	74	0.16
Costa Rican	15	0.03
Guatemalan	19	0.04
Honduran	11	0.02
Nicaraguan	8	0.02
Panamanian	10	0.02
Salvadoran	11	0.02
Cuban	35	0.08
Dominican Republic	6	0.01
Mexican	1,783	3.94
Puerto Rican	88	0.19
South American:	182	0.40
Argentinean	23	0.05
Bolivian	3	0.01
Chilean	24	0.05
Colombian	61	0.13
Ecuadorian	21	0.05
Peruvian	24	0.05
Uruguayan	6	0.01
Venezuelan	12	0.03
Other South American	8	0.02
Other Hispanic or Latino	370	0.82
Hungarian	237	0.52
Icelander	8	0.02
Iranian	304	0.67
Irish	4,625	10.19
Israeli	137	0.30
Italian	1,765	3.89
Latvian	27	0.06
Lithuanian	25	0.06
New Zealander	8	0.02
Northern European	138	0.30
Norwegian	2,141	4.72
Pennsylvania German	16	0.04
Polish	983	2.17
Portuguese	200	0.44
Romanian	496	1.09
Russian	681	1.50
Scandinavian	406	0.89
Scotch-Irish	908	2.00
Scottish	1,719	3.79
Slavic	39	0.09
Slovak	21	0.05
Slovene	50	0.11
Swedish	1,755	3.87
Swiss	361	0.80
Turkish	9	0.02
Ukrainian	245	0.54
United States or American	1,931	4.25
Welsh	359	0.79
West Indian, excl. Hispanic:	70	0.15
Barbadian	8	0.02
Trinidadian and Tobagonian	25	0.06
U.S. Virgin Islander	37	0.08
White:	37,036	81.84
Not Hispanic (34,593)	35,577	78.61
Hispanic (1,275)	1,459	3.22
Yugoslavian	139	0.31

Renton

Place Type: City
County: King
Population: 50,052

Ancestry/Race	Number	%
Acadian/Cajun	23	0.05
Afghan	28	0.06
African American/Black:	5,001	9.99
Not Hispanic (4,142)	4,842	9.67
Hispanic (96)	159	0.32
African, sub-Saharan:	749	1.50
African	279	0.56
Ethiopian	98	0.20
Ghanian	60	0.12
Kenyan	22	0.04
Nigerian	33	0.07
Somalian	184	0.37
South African	8	0.02
Ugandan	8	0.02
Other sub-Saharan African	57	0.11
Alaska Native tribes, specified:	111	0.22
Alaska Athabascan (5)	6	0.01
Aleut (11)	26	0.05
Eskimo	6	0.01
Tlingit-Haida (20)	55	0.11
All other tribes (11)	18	0.04
Alaska Native tribes, not specified	9	0.02
Am. Ind. or Alaska Nat., not spec.	274	0.55
American Indian tribes, specified:	498	0.99
Apache (2)	9	0.02
Blackfeet (12)	49	0.10
Cherokee (15)	93	0.19
Cheyenne	4	0.01
Chickasaw	3	0.01
Chippewa (18)	51	0.10
Choctaw (4)	16	0.03
Colville (5)	10	0.02
Comanche	2	0.00
Cree (2)	6	0.01
Creek (1)	9	0.02
Delaware (1)	3	0.01
Iroquois (4)	12	0.02
Kiowa (5)	8	0.02
Latin American Indians (8)	27	0.05
Navajo (4)	10	0.02
Potawatomi	3	0.01
Pueblo (6)	7	0.01
Puget Sound Salish (13)	17	0.03
Seminole (2)	8	0.02
Shoshone	4	0.01
Sioux (11)	37	0.07
Ute	1	0.00
Yakama (15)	17	0.03
All other tribes (49)	92	0.18
American Indian tribes, not spec.	44	0.09
Arab:	107	0.21
Arab/Arabic	50	0.10
Egyptian	20	0.04
Lebanese	37	0.07
Armenian	33	0.07
Asian:	7,773	15.53
Cambodian (167)	207	0.41
Chinese, ex. Taiwanese (1,363)	1,595	3.19
Filipino (1,467)	1,805	3.61
Hmong (18)	22	0.04
Indian (494)	596	1.19
Indonesian (17)	25	0.05
Japanese (593)	815	1.63
Korean (325)	393	0.79
Laotian (216)	250	0.50
Malaysian (2)	3	0.01
Pakistani (16)	20	0.04
Sri Lankan (1)	1	0.00
Taiwanese (59)	70	0.14
Thai (54)	74	0.15
Vietnamese (1,572)	1,688	3.37
Other Asian, specified (7)	14	0.03
Other Asian, not specified (119)	195	0.39

Notes: 1. Figures in the "Number" column do not add up to the total population due to: a) Ancestry/Race overlap — e.g. persons can report being both White and Irish, b) persons of Hispanic origin can report being any race, c) persons reporting two ancestries are counted in both categories. 2. Numbers in parentheses indicate the number of persons reporting this ancestry/race alone, not in combination with any other ancestry/race. 3. Refer to the Explanation of Data in the front of the book for more detailed information.

Australian	47	0.09
Austrian	284	0.57
Basque	10	0.02
Belgian	71	0.14
British	220	0.44
Bulgarian	59	0.12
Canadian	143	0.29
Celtic	19	0.04
Croatian	81	0.16
Czech	121	0.24
Czechoslovakian	79	0.16
Danish	543	1.09
Dutch	615	1.23
English	4,400	8.82
Estonian	55	0.11
European	800	1.60
Finnish	213	0.43
French, except Basque	1,228	2.46
French Canadian	431	0.86
German	7,515	15.06
Greek	146	0.29
Hawaii Native/Pacific Islander:	473	0.95
Melanesian: (31)	32	0.06
Fijian (31)	32	0.06
Micronesian: (50)	79	0.16
Guamanian/Chamorro (41)	66	0.13
Other Micronesian (9)	13	0.03
Polynesian: (151)	267	0.53
Native Hawaiian (46)	115	0.23
Samoan (94)	129	0.26
Tongan (7)	14	0.03
Other Polynesian (4)	9	0.02
Other Pac. Isl., specified	1	0.00
Other Pac. Isl., not spec. (13)	94	0.19
Hispanic or Latino:	3,818	7.63
Central American:	215	0.43
Costa Rican	11	0.02
Guatemalan	77	0.15
Honduran	25	0.05
Nicaraguan	22	0.04
Panamanian	9	0.02
Salvadoran	64	0.13
Other Central American	7	0.01
Cuban	48	0.10
Dominican Republic	13	0.03
Mexican	2,700	5.39
Puerto Rican	98	0.20
South American:	122	0.24
Argentinean	23	0.05
Bolivian	9	0.02
Chilean	12	0.02
Colombian	38	0.08
Ecuadorian	9	0.02
Peruvian	15	0.03
Venezuelan	6	0.01
Other South American	10	0.02
Other Hispanic or Latino	622	1.24
Hungarian	241	0.48
Icelander	25	0.05
Iranian	60	0.12
Irish	4,699	9.42
Italian	1,826	3.66
Latvian	32	0.06
Lithuanian	56	0.11
Northern European	66	0.13
Norwegian	2,836	5.68
Pennsylvania German	17	0.03
Polish	668	1.34
Portuguese	149	0.30
Romanian	211	0.42
Russian	515	1.03
Scandinavian	241	0.48
Scotch-Irish	804	1.61
Scottish	1,181	2.37
Serbian	23	0.05
Slavic	5	0.01
Slovak	24	0.05
Slovene	48	0.10
Swedish	1,478	2.96
Swiss	256	0.51
Turkish	17	0.03
Ukrainian	710	1.42
United States or American	2,414	4.84
Welsh	487	0.98
West Indian, excl. Hispanic:	84	0.17
Dutch West Indian	6	0.01
Haitian	19	0.04
Jamaican	30	0.06
Trinidadian and Tobagonian	8	0.02
West Indian	21	0.04
White:	35,873	71.67
Not Hispanic (32,759)	34,253	68.43
Hispanic (1,346)	1,620	3.24
Yugoslavian	129	0.26

Richland

Place Type: City
County: Benton
Population: 38,708

Ancestry/Race	Number	%
African American/Black:	703	1.82
Not Hispanic (505)	655	1.69
Hispanic (25)	48	0.12
African, sub-Saharan:	45	0.12
African	29	0.08
Ghanian	16	0.04
Alaska Native tribes, specified:	24	0.06
Alaska Athabascan (3)	4	0.01
Aleut (2)	3	0.01
Eskimo	7	0.02
Tlingit-Haida (6)	10	0.03
Alaska Native tribes, not specified	2	0.01
Am. Ind. or Alaska Nat., not spec.	143	0.37
American Indian tribes, specified:	396	1.02
Apache (4)	14	0.04
Blackfeet (23)	27	0.07
Cherokee (45)	114	0.29
Chickasaw (1)	2	0.01
Chippewa (21)	29	0.07
Choctaw (4)	14	0.04
Colville (3)	5	0.01
Comanche (1)	2	0.01
Cree (1)	5	0.01
Creek (7)	12	0.03
Delaware (4)	4	0.01
Iroquois (6)	10	0.03
Latin American Indians (4)	9	0.02
Navajo (5)	7	0.02
Osage	2	0.01
Paiute	1	0.00
Potawatomi (5)	9	0.02
Pueblo (9)	9	0.02
Puget Sound Salish (9)	17	0.04
Sioux (13)	28	0.07
Ute	1	0.00
Yakama (9)	10	0.03
Yaqui (5)	6	0.02
All other tribes (37)	59	0.15
American Indian tribes, not spec.	15	0.04
Arab:	76	0.20
Egyptian	37	0.10
Lebanese	11	0.03
Syrian	28	0.07
Armenian	26	0.07
Asian:	1,880	4.86
Bangladeshi (8)	12	0.03
Cambodian (6)	9	0.02
Chinese, ex. Taiwanese (435)	477	1.23
Filipino (163)	233	0.60
Indian (278)	323	0.83
Indonesian (3)	8	0.02
Japanese (93)	170	0.44
Korean (150)	168	0.43
Laotian (72)	87	0.22
Pakistani (17)	18	0.05
Sri Lankan (8)	8	0.02
Taiwanese (31)	40	0.10
Thai (27)	35	0.09
Vietnamese (228)	247	0.64
Other Asian, specified (1)	7	0.02
Other Asian, not specified (13)	38	0.10
Australian	40	0.10
Austrian	161	0.42
Basque	30	0.08
Belgian	20	0.05
Brazilian	24	0.06
British	305	0.79
Bulgarian	5	0.01
Canadian	177	0.46
Croatian	127	0.33
Czech	142	0.37
Czechoslovakian	98	0.25
Danish	548	1.42
Dutch	895	2.32
Eastern European	88	0.23
English	6,002	15.53
European	1,110	2.87
Finnish	244	0.63
French, except Basque	1,414	3.66
French Canadian	417	1.08
German	7,586	19.63
German Russian	5	0.01
Greek	70	0.18
Hawaii Native/Pacific Islander:	98	0.25
Micronesian: (8)	13	0.03
Guamanian/Chamorro (5)	8	0.02
Other Micronesian (3)	5	0.01
Polynesian: (32)	67	0.17
Native Hawaiian (24)	54	0.14
Samoan (8)	12	0.03
Other Polynesian	1	0.00
Other Pac. Isl., specified	2	0.01
Other Pac. Isl., not spec. (1)	16	0.04
Hispanic or Latino:	1,826	4.72
Central American:	37	0.10
Guatemalan	9	0.02
Honduran	4	0.01
Nicaraguan	5	0.01
Panamanian	4	0.01
Salvadoran	13	0.03
Other Central American	2	0.01
Cuban	29	0.07
Dominican Republic	2	0.01
Mexican	1,262	3.26
Puerto Rican	61	0.16
South American:	45	0.12
Argentinean	3	0.01
Bolivian	1	0.00
Chilean	7	0.02
Colombian	17	0.04
Ecuadorian	6	0.02
Paraguayan	3	0.01
Peruvian	5	0.01
Venezuelan	1	0.00
Other South American	2	0.01
Other Hispanic or Latino	390	1.01
Hungarian	165	0.43
Irish	4,199	10.86
Israeli	39	0.10
Italian	1,343	3.47
Latvian	5	0.01
Lithuanian	18	0.05
Northern European	47	0.12
Norwegian	1,946	5.03
Polish	736	1.90
Portuguese	144	0.37
Romanian	91	0.24
Russian	353	0.91
Scandinavian	339	0.88
Scotch-Irish	963	2.49
Scottish	1,351	3.50
Serbian	40	0.10
Slavic	9	0.02
Slovak	85	0.22
Slovene	14	0.04
Swedish	1,298	3.36
Swiss	195	0.50
Ukrainian	276	0.71

Notes: 1. Figures in the "Number" column do not add up to the total population due to: a) Ancestry/Race overlap — e.g. persons can report being both White and Irish, b) persons of Hispanic origin can report being any race, c) persons reporting two ancestries are counted in both categories. 2. Numbers in parentheses indicate the number of persons reporting this ancestry/race alone, not in combination with any other ancestry/race. 3. Refer to the Explanation of Data in the front of the book for more detailed information.

United States or American	2,680	6.93
Welsh	563	1.46
West Indian, excl. Hispanic:	33	0.09
Dutch West Indian	8	0.02
Jamaican	25	0.06
White:	35,474	91.65
Not Hispanic (33,746)	34,382	88.82
Hispanic (916)	1,092	2.82
Yugoslavian	197	0.51

Riverton-Boulevard Park

Place Type: Census Designated Place
County: King
Population: 11,188

Ancestry/Race	Number	%
African American/Black:	1,156	10.33
Not Hispanic (904)	1,108	9.90
Hispanic (25)	48	0.43
African, sub-Saharan:	186	1.63
African	55	0.48
Ethiopian	35	0.31
Nigerian	6	0.05
Somalian	90	0.79
Alaska Native tribes, specified:	38	0.34
Alaska Athabascan	2	0.02
Aleut (2)	5	0.04
Eskimo (4)	6	0.05
Tlingit-Haida (10)	25	0.22
Alaska Native tribes, not specified	1	0.01
Am. Ind. or Alaska Nat., not spec.	100	0.89
American Indian tribes, specified:	192	1.72
Apache (2)	5	0.04
Blackfeet (9)	25	0.22
Cherokee (10)	46	0.41
Cheyenne (1)	1	0.01
Chippewa (20)	25	0.22
Choctaw (1)	2	0.02
Colville (1)	2	0.02
Comanche	1	0.01
Cree (5)	5	0.04
Creek (1)	1	0.01
Iroquois	3	0.03
Latin American Indians (7)	8	0.07
Navajo (1)	1	0.01
Osage (1)	2	0.02
Ottawa (1)	1	0.01
Paiute	1	0.01
Pima (2)	2	0.02
Pueblo (2)	3	0.03
Puget Sound Salish (2)	9	0.08
Sioux (4)	12	0.11
Tohono O'Odham (3)	3	0.03
Yakama	1	0.01
All other tribes (17)	33	0.29
American Indian tribes, not spec.	14	0.13
Arab:	18	0.16
Egyptian	5	0.04
Iraqi	12	0.11
Other Arab	1	0.01
Armenian	6	0.05
Asian:	1,567	14.01
Cambodian (199)	236	2.11
Chinese, ex. Taiwanese (71)	91	0.81
Filipino (276)	361	3.23
Hmong (109)	121	1.08
Indian (61)	65	0.58
Indonesian (3)	5	0.04
Japanese (75)	97	0.87
Korean (57)	63	0.56
Laotian (86)	102	0.91
Pakistani	1	0.01
Sri Lankan	1	0.01
Taiwanese	1	0.01
Thai (15)	22	0.20
Vietnamese (326)	344	3.07
Other Asian, specified (4)	6	0.05
Other Asian, not specified (38)	51	0.46
Austrian	37	0.32
Belgian	17	0.15
British	19	0.17
Canadian	44	0.39
Croatian	8	0.07
Czech	32	0.28
Czechoslovakian	16	0.14
Danish	54	0.47
Dutch	209	1.84
Eastern European	10	0.09
English	744	6.53
European	119	1.04
Finnish	26	0.23
French, except Basque	398	3.49
French Canadian	76	0.67
German	1,458	12.80
Greek	66	0.58
Hawaii Native/Pacific Islander:	299	2.67
Micronesian: (38)	48	0.43
Guamanian/Chamorro (11)	19	0.17
Other Micronesian (27)	29	0.26
Polynesian: (151)	204	1.82
Native Hawaiian (24)	40	0.36
Samoan (100)	114	1.02
Tongan (27)	50	0.45
Other Pac. Isl., specified	1	0.01
Other Pac. Isl., not spec. (2)	46	0.41
Hispanic or Latino:	1,755	15.69
Central American:	116	1.04
Guatemalan	17	0.15
Honduran	12	0.11
Nicaraguan	8	0.07
Panamanian	10	0.09
Salvadoran	62	0.55
Other Central American	7	0.06
Cuban	8	0.07
Dominican Republic	8	0.07
Mexican	1,277	11.41
Puerto Rican	38	0.34
South American:	24	0.21
Argentinean	4	0.04
Bolivian	1	0.01
Chilean	3	0.03
Colombian	5	0.04
Ecuadorian	3	0.03
Peruvian	4	0.04
Venezuelan	2	0.02
Other South American	2	0.02
Other Hispanic or Latino	284	2.54
Hungarian	6	0.05
Irish	936	8.22
Italian	369	3.24
Lithuanian	119	1.04
Northern European	51	0.45
Norwegian	485	4.26
Polish	91	0.80
Romanian	96	0.84
Russian	46	0.40
Scandinavian	155	1.36
Scotch-Irish	158	1.39
Scottish	212	1.86
Serbian	8	0.07
Slovene	15	0.13
Swedish	223	1.96
Swiss	22	0.19
Ukrainian	14	0.12
United States or American	652	5.72
Welsh	93	0.82
West Indian, excl. Hispanic:	41	0.36
Bahamian	10	0.09
Jamaican	20	0.18
Trinidadian and Tobagonian	11	0.10
White:	7,274	65.02
Not Hispanic (6,293)	6,648	59.42
Hispanic (549)	626	5.60
Yugoslavian	24	0.21

Salmon Creek

Place Type: Census Designated Place
County: Clark
Population: 16,767

Ancestry/Race	Number	%
African American/Black:	277	1.65
Not Hispanic (206)	269	1.60
Hispanic (5)	8	0.05
African, sub-Saharan:	29	0.17
African	29	0.17
Alaska Native tribes, specified:	22	0.13
Alaska Athabascan	6	0.04
Aleut (3)	7	0.04
Eskimo	1	0.01
Tlingit-Haida (4)	4	0.02
All other tribes (1)	4	0.02
Am. Ind. or Alaska Nat., not spec.	67	0.40
American Indian tribes, specified:	190	1.13
Apache (5)	8	0.05
Blackfeet	12	0.07
Cherokee (12)	55	0.33
Chippewa (6)	22	0.13
Choctaw	5	0.03
Colville (1)	1	0.01
Creek	1	0.01
Crow	1	0.01
Iroquois (5)	8	0.05
Kiowa (3)	3	0.02
Latin American Indians (6)	12	0.07
Navajo (3)	10	0.06
Osage	2	0.01
Potawatomi	1	0.01
Pueblo (1)	11	0.07
Sioux (3)	12	0.07
Ute (1)	1	0.01
Yakama (4)	4	0.02
All other tribes (10)	21	0.13
American Indian tribes, not spec.	9	0.05
Arab:	37	0.22
Arab/Arabic	16	0.10
Lebanese	9	0.05
Syrian	12	0.07
Asian:	585	3.49
Cambodian (7)	7	0.04
Chinese, ex. Taiwanese (90)	122	0.73
Filipino (70)	110	0.66
Indian (49)	63	0.38
Indonesian (1)	2	0.01
Japanese (44)	91	0.54
Korean (88)	102	0.61
Laotian (3)	3	0.02
Pakistani (8)	14	0.08
Taiwanese (4)	6	0.04
Thai (5)	6	0.04
Vietnamese (32)	40	0.24
Other Asian, specified (1)	3	0.02
Other Asian, not specified (8)	16	0.10
Australian	7	0.04
Austrian	15	0.09
British	147	0.88
Canadian	74	0.44
Celtic	13	0.08
Czech	61	0.36
Czechoslovakian	55	0.33
Danish	129	0.77
Dutch	401	2.40
English	2,452	14.66
Estonian	9	0.05
European	217	1.30
Finnish	63	0.38
French, except Basque	659	3.94
French Canadian	252	1.51
German	3,779	22.59
German Russian	14	0.08
Greek	102	0.61
Hawaii Native/Pacific Islander:	96	0.57
Melanesian:	3	0.02
Fijian	3	0.02

Notes: 1. Figures in the "Number" column do not add up to the total population due to: a) Ancestry/Race overlap — e.g. persons can report being both White and Irish, b) persons of Hispanic origin can report being any race, c) persons reporting two ancestries are counted in both categories. 2. Numbers in parentheses indicate the number of persons reporting this ancestry/race alone, not in combination with any other ancestry/race. 3. Refer to the Explanation of Data in the front of the book for more detailed information.

Ancestry/Race	Number	%
Micronesian: (2)	4	0.02
Guamanian/Chamorro (1)	3	0.02
Other Micronesian (1)	1	0.01
Polynesian: (18)	77	0.46
Native Hawaiian (17)	64	0.38
Samoan (1)	13	0.08
Other Pac. Isl., specified	1	0.01
Other Pac. Isl., not spec. (3)	11	0.07
Hispanic or Latino:	806	4.81
Central American:	25	0.15
Costa Rican	1	0.01
Guatemalan	11	0.07
Honduran	3	0.02
Nicaraguan	2	0.01
Panamanian	4	0.02
Salvadoran	3	0.02
Other Central American	1	0.01
Cuban	18	0.11
Mexican	593	3.54
Puerto Rican	28	0.17
South American:	7	0.04
Chilean	3	0.02
Ecuadorian	1	0.01
Peruvian	3	0.02
Other Hispanic or Latino	135	0.81
Hungarian	87	0.52
Icelander	41	0.25
Iranian	6	0.04
Irish	2,362	14.12
Italian	679	4.06
Lithuanian	15	0.09
Luxemburger	6	0.04
Macedonian	10	0.06
Northern European	37	0.22
Norwegian	1,186	7.09
Pennsylvania German	56	0.33
Polish	367	2.19
Portuguese	32	0.19
Romanian	84	0.50
Russian	103	0.62
Scandinavian	96	0.57
Scotch-Irish	415	2.48
Scottish	510	3.05
Serbian	15	0.09
Slavic	23	0.14
Slovak	6	0.04
Swedish	558	3.34
Swiss	140	0.84
Turkish	8	0.05
Ukrainian	15	0.09
United States or American	1,360	8.13
Welsh	198	1.18
White:	15,771	94.06
Not Hispanic (14,798)	15,204	90.68
Hispanic (514)	567	3.38
Yugoslavian	40	0.24

Sammamish

Place Type: City
County: King
Population: 34,104

Ancestry/Race	Number	%
African American/Black:	414	1.21
Not Hispanic (273)	385	1.13
Hispanic (16)	29	0.09
African, sub-Saharan:	71	0.21
African	19	0.06
Cape Verdean	3	0.01
Ethiopian	10	0.03
South African	39	0.11
Alaska Native tribes, specified:	39	0.11
Aleut (3)	4	0.01
Eskimo (2)	2	0.01
Tlingit-Haida (15)	29	0.09
All other tribes (4)	4	0.01
Alaska Native tribes, not specified	5	0.01
Am. Ind. or Alaska Nat., not spec.	56	0.16
American Indian tribes, specified:	134	0.39
Apache (5)	8	0.02
Blackfeet (1)	8	0.02
Cherokee (6)	33	0.10
Chickasaw	4	0.01
Chippewa (8)	10	0.03
Choctaw (2)	3	0.01
Colville (1)	1	0.00
Comanche (4)	4	0.01
Cree	3	0.01
Crow	4	0.01
Latin American Indians (2)	10	0.03
Lumbee (1)	1	0.00
Navajo	1	0.00
Osage	1	0.00
Ottawa	2	0.01
Pueblo	1	0.00
Puget Sound Salish (5)	12	0.04
Sioux (1)	11	0.03
Ute (2)	2	0.01
All other tribes (4)	15	0.04
American Indian tribes, not spec.	23	0.07
Arab:	266	0.78
Arab/Arabic	50	0.15
Egyptian	57	0.17
Lebanese	97	0.28
Moroccan	9	0.03
Syrian	16	0.05
Other Arab	37	0.11
Armenian	30	0.09
Asian:	3,330	9.76
Bangladeshi (1)	1	0.00
Cambodian (4)	6	0.02
Chinese, ex. Taiwanese (992)	1,185	3.47
Filipino (133)	232	0.68
Hmong (2)	7	0.02
Indian (448)	484	1.42
Indonesian (12)	25	0.07
Japanese (347)	602	1.77
Korean (338)	376	1.10
Laotian (6)	13	0.04
Malaysian (8)	19	0.06
Pakistani (7)	10	0.03
Sri Lankan (6)	6	0.02
Taiwanese (133)	152	0.45
Thai (14)	19	0.06
Vietnamese (109)	128	0.38
Other Asian, specified (2)	9	0.03
Other Asian, not specified (17)	56	0.16
Australian	61	0.18
Austrian	120	0.35
Basque	34	0.10
Belgian	55	0.16
Brazilian	10	0.03
British	275	0.81
Bulgarian	8	0.02
Canadian	413	1.21
Croatian	70	0.21
Czech	191	0.56
Czechoslovakian	72	0.21
Danish	736	2.16
Dutch	766	2.25
Eastern European	87	0.25
English	5,981	17.53
Estonian	20	0.06
European	765	2.24
Finnish	228	0.67
French, except Basque	1,325	3.88
French Canadian	304	0.89
German	7,693	22.55
Greek	211	0.62
Hawaii Native/Pacific Islander:	80	0.23
Melanesian: (2)	2	0.01
Fijian (2)	2	0.01
Micronesian: (11)	12	0.04
Guamanian/Chamorro (9)	10	0.03
Other Micronesian (2)	2	0.01
Polynesian: (15)	47	0.14
Native Hawaiian (11)	38	0.11
Samoan (4)	8	0.02
Other Polynesian	1	0.00
Other Pac. Isl., specified	4	0.01
Other Pac. Isl., not spec. (2)	15	0.04
Hispanic or Latino:	853	2.50
Central American:	21	0.06
Costa Rican	2	0.01
Guatemalan	5	0.01
Honduran	4	0.01
Nicaraguan	1	0.00
Panamanian	5	0.01
Salvadoran	3	0.01
Other Central American	1	0.00
Cuban	33	0.10
Dominican Republic	1	0.00
Mexican	445	1.30
Puerto Rican	63	0.18
South American:	74	0.22
Argentinean	5	0.01
Chilean	6	0.02
Colombian	26	0.08
Ecuadorian	4	0.01
Peruvian	10	0.03
Uruguayan	1	0.00
Venezuelan	15	0.04
Other South American	7	0.02
Other Hispanic or Latino	216	0.63
Hungarian	167	0.49
Icelander	17	0.05
Iranian	187	0.55
Irish	4,481	13.13
Italian	1,700	4.98
Latvian	43	0.13
Lithuanian	58	0.17
Luxemburger	50	0.15
Maltese	7	0.02
Northern European	45	0.13
Norwegian	1,880	5.51
Pennsylvania German	22	0.06
Polish	881	2.58
Portuguese	58	0.17
Romanian	97	0.28
Russian	764	2.24
Scandinavian	105	0.31
Scotch-Irish	634	1.86
Scottish	1,382	4.05
Serbian	24	0.07
Slavic	37	0.11
Slovak	82	0.24
Slovene	43	0.13
Swedish	1,384	4.06
Swiss	247	0.72
Turkish	32	0.09
Ukrainian	117	0.34
United States or American	1,408	4.13
Welsh	541	1.59
West Indian, excl. Hispanic:	48	0.14
Trinidadian and Tobagonian	38	0.11
West Indian	10	0.03
White:	30,712	90.05
Not Hispanic (29,361)	30,046	88.10
Hispanic (589)	666	1.95
Yugoslavian	31	0.09

SeaTac

Place Type: City
County: King
Population: 25,496

Ancestry/Race	Number	%
African American/Black:	2,893	11.35
Not Hispanic (2,266)	2,787	10.93
Hispanic (68)	106	0.42
African, sub-Saharan:	838	3.28
African	294	1.15
Ethiopian	105	0.41
Ghanian	5	0.02
Kenyan	24	0.09
Nigerian	19	0.07
Somalian	301	1.18
South African	6	0.02

Notes: 1. Figures in the "Number" column do not add up to the total population due to: a) Ancestry/Race overlap — e.g. persons can report being both White and Irish, b) persons of Hispanic origin can report being any race, c) persons reporting two ancestries are counted in both categories. 2. Numbers in parentheses indicate the number of persons reporting this ancestry/race alone, not in combination with any other ancestry/race. 3. Refer to the Explanation of Data in the front of the book for more detailed information.

Other sub-Saharan African	84	0.33
Alaska Native tribes, specified:	114	0.45
Alaska Athabascan (13)	14	0.05
Aleut (9)	13	0.05
Eskimo	6	0.02
Tlingit-Haida (41)	60	0.24
All other tribes (14)	21	0.08
Alaska Native tribes, not specified	2	0.01
Am. Ind. or Alaska Nat., not spec.	215	0.84
Albanian	7	0.03
American Indian tribes, specified:	445	1.75
Apache (6)	13	0.05
Blackfeet (7)	22	0.09
Cherokee (19)	97	0.38
Cheyenne (1)	2	0.01
Chickasaw (1)	2	0.01
Chippewa (23)	38	0.15
Choctaw (2)	17	0.07
Colville (7)	7	0.03
Comanche	4	0.02
Cree (6)	9	0.04
Creek (1)	2	0.01
Crow	1	0.00
Delaware	2	0.01
Iroquois (1)	3	0.01
Latin American Indians (7)	17	0.07
Menominee	1	0.00
Navajo (13)	16	0.06
Osage	4	0.02
Potawatomi (2)	2	0.01
Puget Sound Salish (15)	33	0.13
Shoshone (2)	4	0.02
Sioux (24)	39	0.15
Ute (6)	7	0.03
Yakama (2)	3	0.01
Yaqui (1)	1	0.00
All other tribes (54)	99	0.39
American Indian tribes, not spec.	37	0.15
Arab:	48	0.19
Iraqi	11	0.04
Jordanian	32	0.13
Other Arab	5	0.02
Armenian	36	0.14
Asian:	3,482	13.66
Bangladeshi (10)	13	0.05
Cambodian (249)	284	1.11
Chinese, ex. Taiwanese (180)	269	1.06
Filipino (632)	851	3.34
Hmong (104)	106	0.42
Indian (557)	629	2.47
Indonesian (9)	13	0.05
Japanese (145)	242	0.95
Korean (129)	157	0.62
Laotian (87)	101	0.40
Malaysian	4	0.02
Pakistani (12)	37	0.15
Sri Lankan	2	0.01
Taiwanese (8)	9	0.04
Thai (74)	91	0.36
Vietnamese (513)	553	2.17
Other Asian, specified (2)	6	0.02
Other Asian, not specified (40)	115	0.45
Austrian	39	0.15
Basque	5	0.02
Belgian	23	0.09
British	122	0.48
Bulgarian	15	0.06
Canadian	95	0.37
Celtic	25	0.10
Croatian	82	0.32
Czech	35	0.14
Czechoslovakian	62	0.24
Danish	165	0.65
Dutch	409	1.60
English	2,090	8.19
European	357	1.40
Finnish	98	0.38
French, except Basque	822	3.22
French Canadian	237	0.93
German	3,220	12.62
Greek	89	0.35
Hawaii Native/Pacific Islander:	882	3.46
Melanesian: (19)	22	0.09
Fijian (19)	22	0.09
Micronesian: (72)	109	0.43
Guamanian/Chamorro (45)	71	0.28
Other Micronesian (27)	38	0.15
Polynesian: (560)	705	2.77
Native Hawaiian (43)	101	0.40
Samoan (409)	493	1.93
Tongan (94)	96	0.38
Other Polynesian (14)	15	0.06
Other Pac. Isl., not spec. (11)	46	0.18
Hispanic or Latino:	3,302	12.95
Central American:	199	0.78
Costa Rican	3	0.01
Guatemalan	40	0.16
Honduran	38	0.15
Nicaraguan	5	0.02
Panamanian	4	0.02
Salvadoran	93	0.36
Other Central American	16	0.06
Cuban	60	0.24
Dominican Republic	2	0.01
Mexican	2,405	9.43
Puerto Rican	91	0.36
South American:	56	0.22
Argentinean	1	0.00
Chilean	8	0.03
Colombian	19	0.07
Ecuadorian	6	0.02
Paraguayan	1	0.00
Peruvian	10	0.04
Uruguayan	1	0.00
Venezuelan	4	0.02
Other South American	6	0.02
Other Hispanic or Latino	489	1.92
Hungarian	143	0.56
Icelander	53	0.21
Iranian	21	0.08
Irish	2,105	8.25
Italian	534	2.09
Latvian	46	0.18
Lithuanian	32	0.13
Luxemburger	7	0.03
Northern European	63	0.25
Norwegian	1,230	4.82
Pennsylvania German	7	0.03
Polish	265	1.04
Portuguese	46	0.18
Romanian	21	0.08
Russian	161	0.63
Scandinavian	103	0.40
Scotch-Irish	499	1.96
Scottish	595	2.33
Slovak	47	0.18
Swedish	685	2.68
Swiss	226	0.89
Ukrainian	106	0.42
United States or American	1,037	4.06
Welsh	158	0.62
West Indian, excl. Hispanic:	89	0.35
Dutch West Indian	12	0.05
Haitian	70	0.27
West Indian	7	0.03
White:	17,133	67.20
Not Hispanic (14,666)	15,581	61.11
Hispanic (1,361)	1,552	6.09
Yugoslavian	211	0.83

Seattle Hill-Silver Firs

Place Type: Census Designated Place
County: Snohomish
Population: 35,311

Ancestry/Race	Number	%
African American/Black:	597	1.69
Not Hispanic (394)	569	1.61
Hispanic (14)	28	0.08
African, sub-Saharan:	149	0.42
African	76	0.21
Ethiopian	43	0.12
Nigerian	22	0.06
Sudanese	8	0.02
Alaska Native tribes, specified:	65	0.18
Alaska Athabascan (5)	9	0.03
Aleut (13)	19	0.05
Eskimo (2)	4	0.01
Tlingit-Haida (18)	30	0.08
All other tribes (3)	3	0.01
Alaska Native tribes, not specified	8	0.02
Am. Ind. or Alaska Nat., not spec.	114	0.32
Albanian	18	0.05
American Indian tribes, specified:	269	0.76
Apache	5	0.01
Blackfeet (8)	22	0.06
Cherokee (7)	61	0.17
Chickasaw (2)	2	0.01
Chippewa (3)	13	0.04
Choctaw (2)	14	0.04
Colville (2)	5	0.01
Comanche	2	0.01
Cree (2)	3	0.01
Creek (2)	2	0.01
Crow	2	0.01
Delaware (1)	2	0.01
Iroquois	2	0.01
Kiowa	1	0.00
Latin American Indians (5)	8	0.02
Navajo (2)	4	0.01
Osage (1)	1	0.00
Pima (1)	1	0.00
Potawatomi	3	0.01
Pueblo (1)	1	0.00
Puget Sound Salish (15)	28	0.08
Shoshone (1)	2	0.01
Sioux (10)	27	0.08
Yakama (5)	6	0.02
Yaqui (4)	4	0.01
All other tribes (31)	48	0.14
American Indian tribes, not spec.	33	0.09
Arab:	192	0.54
Arab/Arabic	27	0.08
Egyptian	7	0.02
Lebanese	90	0.25
Palestinian	58	0.16
Other Arab	10	0.03
Armenian	20	0.06
Asian:	3,327	9.42
Cambodian (266)	291	0.82
Chinese, ex. Taiwanese (353)	462	1.31
Filipino (491)	689	1.95
Hmong (1)	1	0.00
Indian (211)	236	0.67
Indonesian (5)	7	0.02
Japanese (192)	383	1.08
Korean (479)	559	1.58
Laotian (59)	69	0.20
Pakistani (3)	4	0.01
Sri Lankan (3)	3	0.01
Taiwanese (1)	6	0.02
Thai (13)	14	0.04
Vietnamese (459)	509	1.44
Other Asian, specified	5	0.01
Other Asian, not specified (48)	89	0.25
Australian	25	0.07
Austrian	91	0.26
Belgian	14	0.04
British	271	0.76
Bulgarian	18	0.05
Canadian	150	0.42
Carpatho Rusyn	3	0.01
Croatian	8	0.02
Czech	102	0.29
Czechoslovakian	50	0.14
Danish	684	1.92
Dutch	967	2.72
Eastern European	26	0.07
English	5,058	14.23

Notes: 1. Figures in the "Number" column do not add up to the total population due to: a) Ancestry/Race overlap — e.g. persons can report being both White and Irish, b) persons of Hispanic origin can report being any race, c) persons reporting two ancestries are counted in both categories. 2. Numbers in parentheses indicate the number of persons reporting this ancestry/race alone, not in combination with any other ancestry/race. 3. Refer to the Explanation of Data in the front of the book for more detailed information.

European	551	1.55
Finnish	199	0.56
French, except Basque	1,363	3.83
French Canadian	266	0.75
German	7,564	21.28
Greek	106	0.30
Guyanese	11	0.03
Hawaii Native/Pacific Islander:	155	0.44
Melanesian: (4)	4	0.01
Fijian (4)	4	0.01
Micronesian: (24)	39	0.11
Guamanian/Chamorro (21)	36	0.10
Other Micronesian (3)	3	0.01
Polynesian: (35)	86	0.24
Native Hawaiian (28)	72	0.20
Samoan (5)	12	0.03
Tongan (2)	2	0.01
Other Pac. Isl., not spec. (8)	26	0.07
Hispanic or Latino:	1,065	3.02
Central American:	37	0.10
Costa Rican	10	0.03
Guatemalan	7	0.02
Honduran	2	0.01
Nicaraguan	8	0.02
Panamanian	6	0.02
Salvadoran	3	0.01
Other Central American	1	0.00
Cuban	33	0.09
Dominican Republic	1	0.00
Mexican	612	1.73
Puerto Rican	53	0.15
South American:	45	0.13
Argentinean	2	0.01
Bolivian	1	0.00
Chilean	4	0.01
Colombian	16	0.05
Ecuadorian	8	0.02
Peruvian	10	0.03
Other South American	4	0.01
Other Hispanic or Latino	284	0.80
Hungarian	99	0.28
Icelander	82	0.23
Iranian	6	0.02
Irish	4,519	12.71
Israeli	8	0.02
Italian	1,116	3.14
Latvian	8	0.02
Lithuanian	69	0.19
New Zealander	18	0.05
Northern European	48	0.14
Norwegian	3,075	8.65
Pennsylvania German	7	0.02
Polish	729	2.05
Portuguese	64	0.18
Romanian	70	0.20
Russian	482	1.36
Scandinavian	364	1.02
Scotch-Irish	715	2.01
Scottish	1,275	3.59
Slavic	13	0.04
Slovak	43	0.12
Slovene	9	0.03
Swedish	1,655	4.66
Swiss	136	0.38
Turkish	14	0.04
Ukrainian	228	0.64
United States or American	1,791	5.04
Welsh	461	1.30
West Indian, excl. Hispanic:	5	0.01
Barbadian	5	0.01
White:	31,385	88.88
Not Hispanic (29,854)	30,754	87.09
Hispanic (531)	631	1.79
Yugoslavian	86	0.24

Seattle

Place Type: City
County: King
Population: 563,374

Ancestry/Race	Number	%
Acadian/Cajun	84	0.01
Afghan	52	0.01
African American/Black:	55,611	9.87
Not Hispanic (46,545)	53,869	9.56
Hispanic (996)	1,742	0.31
African, sub-Saharan:	9,987	1.77
African	3,585	0.64
Cape Verdean	16	0.00
Ethiopian	4,110	0.73
Ghanian	24	0.00
Kenyan	121	0.02
Liberian	62	0.01
Nigerian	297	0.05
Senegalese	19	0.00
Sierra Leonean	25	0.00
Somalian	786	0.14
South African	221	0.04
Sudanese	171	0.03
Ugandan	85	0.02
Zairian	7	0.00
Zimbabwean	56	0.01
Other sub-Saharan African	402	0.07
Alaska Native tribes, specified:	1,426	0.25
Alaska Athabascan (48)	80	0.01
Aleut (159)	269	0.05
Eskimo (142)	216	0.04
Tlingit-Haida (393)	692	0.12
All other tribes (106)	169	0.03
Alaska Native tribes, not specified	133	0.02
Am. Ind. or Alaska Nat., not spec.	3,673	0.65
Albanian	170	0.03
Alsatian	97	0.02
American Indian tribes, specified:	6,462	1.15
Apache (64)	147	0.03
Blackfeet (208)	548	0.10
Cherokee (254)	1,320	0.23
Cheyenne (30)	57	0.01
Chickasaw (13)	30	0.01
Chippewa (165)	347	0.06
Choctaw (55)	190	0.03
Colville (80)	126	0.02
Comanche (13)	30	0.01
Cree (22)	77	0.01
Creek (24)	75	0.01
Crow (22)	50	0.01
Delaware (14)	33	0.01
Iroquois (29)	103	0.02
Kiowa (12)	15	0.00
Latin American Indians (177)	355	0.06
Lumbee (8)	20	0.00
Menominee (7)	9	0.00
Navajo (88)	148	0.03
Osage (8)	43	0.01
Ottawa (8)	14	0.00
Paiute (14)	24	0.00
Pima (7)	12	0.00
Potawatomi (17)	43	0.01
Pueblo (28)	56	0.01
Puget Sound Salish (191)	315	0.06
Seminole (11)	67	0.01
Shoshone (28)	52	0.01
Sioux (257)	511	0.09
Tohono O'Odham (5)	9	0.00
Ute (3)	12	0.00
Yakama (84)	146	0.03
Yaqui (7)	22	0.00
Yuman (3)	3	0.00
All other tribes (804)	1,453	0.26
American Indian tribes, not spec.	524	0.09
Arab:	2,321	0.41
Arab/Arabic	409	0.07
Egyptian	215	0.04
Iraqi	52	0.01
Jordanian	46	0.01
Lebanese	740	0.13
Moroccan	209	0.04
Palestinian	91	0.02
Syrian	183	0.03
Other Arab	376	0.07
Armenian	597	0.11
Asian:	87,550	15.54
Bangladeshi (19)	34	0.01
Cambodian (2,387)	2,866	0.51
Chinese, ex. Taiwanese (18,624)	21,886	3.88
Filipino (15,867)	19,567	3.47
Hmong (99)	132	0.02
Indian (2,843)	3,680	0.65
Indonesian (347)	554	0.10
Japanese (8,979)	12,113	2.15
Korean (4,863)	5,808	1.03
Laotian (2,889)	3,267	0.58
Malaysian (46)	94	0.02
Pakistani (114)	174	0.03
Sri Lankan (49)	65	0.01
Taiwanese (791)	974	0.17
Thai (839)	1,139	0.20
Vietnamese (11,943)	13,032	2.31
Other Asian, specified (122)	261	0.05
Other Asian, not specified (982)	1,904	0.34
Assyrian/Chaldean/Syriac	16	0.00
Australian	507	0.09
Austrian	2,705	0.48
Basque	319	0.06
Belgian	994	0.18
Brazilian	364	0.06
British	5,408	0.96
Bulgarian	354	0.06
Canadian	2,761	0.49
Carpatho Rusyn	11	0.00
Celtic	500	0.09
Croatian	1,432	0.25
Czech	2,812	0.50
Czechoslovakian	957	0.17
Danish	7,100	1.26
Dutch	10,415	1.85
Eastern European	1,173	0.21
English	63,869	11.34
Estonian	228	0.04
European	11,656	2.07
Finnish	3,320	0.59
French, except Basque	18,743	3.33
French Canadian	3,891	0.69
German	85,484	15.17
German Russian	72	0.01
Greek	2,812	0.50
Guyanese	31	0.01
Hawaii Native/Pacific Islander:	5,096	0.90
Melanesian: (111)	155	0.03
Fijian (110)	154	0.03
Other Melanesian (1)	1	0.00
Micronesian: (428)	806	0.14
Guamanian/Chamorro (364)	721	0.13
Other Micronesian (64)	85	0.02
Polynesian: (1,964)	3,110	0.55
Native Hawaiian (409)	1,162	0.21
Samoan (1,391)	1,685	0.30
Tongan (126)	165	0.03
Other Polynesian (38)	98	0.02
Other Pac. Isl., specified	68	0.01
Other Pac. Isl., not spec. (228)	957	0.17
Hispanic or Latino:	29,719	5.28
Central American:	1,987	0.35
Costa Rican	97	0.02
Guatemalan	439	0.08
Honduran	332	0.06
Nicaraguan	141	0.03
Panamanian	156	0.03
Salvadoran	690	0.12
Other Central American	132	0.02
Cuban	759	0.13
Dominican Republic	119	0.02
Mexican	17,886	3.17
Puerto Rican	1,466	0.26

Notes: 1. Figures in the "Number" column do not add up to the total population due to: a) Ancestry/Race overlap — e.g. persons can report being both White and Irish, b) persons of Hispanic origin can report being any race, c) persons reporting two ancestries are counted in both categories. 2. Numbers in parentheses indicate the number of persons reporting this ancestry/race alone, not in combination with any other ancestry/race. 3. Refer to the Explanation of Data in the front of the book for more detailed information.

Ancestry/Race	Number	%
South American:	1,668	0.30
Argentinean	204	0.04
Bolivian	63	0.01
Chilean	263	0.05
Colombian	357	0.06
Ecuadorian	111	0.02
Paraguayan	9	0.00
Peruvian	423	0.08
Uruguayan	26	0.00
Venezuelan	106	0.02
Other South American	106	0.02
Other Hispanic or Latino	5,834	1.04
Hungarian	2,547	0.45
Icelander	906	0.16
Iranian	719	0.13
Irish	66,326	11.77
Israeli	249	0.04
Italian	21,754	3.86
Latvian	624	0.11
Lithuanian	1,469	0.26
Luxemburger	125	0.02
Macedonian	58	0.01
Maltese	85	0.02
New Zealander	142	0.03
Northern European	2,597	0.46
Norwegian	32,018	5.68
Pennsylvania German	236	0.04
Polish	12,622	2.24
Portuguese	1,652	0.29
Romanian	1,076	0.19
Russian	9,717	1.72
Scandinavian	3,524	0.63
Scotch-Irish	12,206	2.17
Scottish	19,880	3.53
Serbian	325	0.06
Slavic	340	0.06
Slovak	647	0.11
Slovene	329	0.06
Swedish	19,413	3.45
Swiss	3,446	0.61
Turkish	710	0.13
Ukrainian	2,091	0.37
United States or American	14,343	2.55
Welsh	6,671	1.18
West Indian, excl. Hispanic:	950	0.17
Barbadian	45	0.01
Belizean	12	0.00
Bermudan	13	0.00
British West Indian	20	0.00
Haitian	111	0.02
Jamaican	598	0.11
Trinidadian and Tobagonian	41	0.01
U.S. Virgin Islander	6	0.00
West Indian	98	0.02
Other West Indian	6	0.00
White:	413,396	73.38
Not Hispanic (382,532)	398,409	70.72
Hispanic (12,357)	14,987	2.66
Yugoslavian	1,348	0.24

Shoreline

Place Type: City
County: King
Population: 53,025

Ancestry/Race	Number	%
Acadian/Cajun	27	0.05
Afghan	100	0.19
African American/Black:	1,932	3.64
Not Hispanic (1,435)	1,869	3.52
Hispanic (32)	63	0.12
African, sub-Saharan:	500	0.94
African	191	0.36
Cape Verdean	9	0.02
Ethiopian	67	0.13
Ghanian	38	0.07
Kenyan	5	0.01
Nigerian	56	0.11
Somalian	54	0.10
South African	59	0.11
Other sub-Saharan African	21	0.04
Alaska Native tribes, specified:	187	0.35
Alaska Athabascan (1)	5	0.01
Aleut (19)	33	0.06
Eskimo (15)	26	0.05
Tlingit-Haida (72)	108	0.20
All other tribes (8)	15	0.03
Alaska Native tribes, not specified	14	0.03
Am. Ind. or Alaska Nat., not spec.	273	0.51
Albanian	4	0.01
American Indian tribes, specified:	556	1.05
Apache (7)	15	0.03
Blackfeet (13)	20	0.04
Cherokee (32)	123	0.23
Cheyenne (1)	12	0.02
Chickasaw	3	0.01
Chippewa (22)	40	0.08
Choctaw (4)	13	0.02
Colville (11)	13	0.02
Comanche (2)	6	0.01
Cree (4)	7	0.01
Creek (1)	4	0.01
Crow	8	0.02
Delaware	3	0.01
Iroquois (3)	13	0.02
Kiowa	3	0.01
Latin American Indians (16)	31	0.06
Lumbee	1	0.00
Navajo (3)	3	0.01
Osage (1)	4	0.01
Ottawa (2)	3	0.01
Pima (1)	1	0.00
Pueblo (5)	7	0.01
Puget Sound Salish (14)	23	0.04
Seminole	3	0.01
Shoshone	1	0.00
Sioux (19)	30	0.06
Tohono O'Odham (1)	1	0.00
Ute	1	0.00
Yakama (4)	18	0.03
Yaqui (1)	1	0.00
All other tribes (72)	145	0.27
American Indian tribes, not spec.	44	0.08
Arab:	335	0.63
Arab/Arabic	56	0.11
Egyptian	14	0.03
Iraqi	5	0.01
Jordanian	35	0.07
Lebanese	97	0.18
Moroccan	20	0.04
Palestinian	41	0.08
Syrian	16	0.03
Other Arab	51	0.10
Armenian	19	0.04
Asian:	8,346	15.74
Cambodian (107)	124	0.23
Chinese, ex. Taiwanese (1,675)	1,974	3.72
Filipino (1,465)	1,871	3.53
Hmong (8)	8	0.02
Indian (415)	536	1.01
Indonesian (54)	76	0.14
Japanese (463)	755	1.42
Korean (1,390)	1,475	2.78
Laotian (102)	118	0.22
Malaysian (5)	7	0.01
Pakistani (54)	79	0.15
Sri Lankan (19)	22	0.04
Taiwanese (93)	126	0.24
Thai (98)	130	0.25
Vietnamese (794)	861	1.62
Other Asian, specified (5)	18	0.03
Other Asian, not specified (67)	166	0.31
Assyrian/Chaldean/Syriac	13	0.02
Australian	37	0.07
Austrian	247	0.47
Belgian	176	0.33
British	515	0.97
Canadian	368	0.69
Celtic	74	0.14
Croatian	120	0.23
Czech	251	0.47
Czechoslovakian	112	0.21
Danish	625	1.18
Dutch	1,150	2.17
Eastern European	44	0.08
English	6,604	12.47
Estonian	14	0.03
European	1,073	2.03
Finnish	320	0.60
French, except Basque	1,635	3.09
French Canadian	450	0.85
German	8,879	16.77
German Russian	9	0.02
Greek	312	0.59
Guyanese	3	0.01
Hawaii Native/Pacific Islander:	406	0.77
Melanesian: (41)	55	0.10
Fijian (41)	55	0.10
Micronesian: (26)	52	0.10
Guamanian/Chamorro (6)	26	0.05
Other Micronesian (20)	26	0.05
Polynesian: (81)	192	0.36
Native Hawaiian (40)	132	0.25
Samoan (27)	38	0.07
Tongan (10)	11	0.02
Other Polynesian (4)	11	0.02
Other Pac. Isl., specified	5	0.01
Other Pac. Isl., not spec. (20)	102	0.19
Hispanic or Latino:	2,054	3.87
Central American:	120	0.23
Costa Rican	15	0.03
Guatemalan	23	0.04
Honduran	4	0.01
Nicaraguan	26	0.05
Panamanian	9	0.02
Salvadoran	41	0.08
Other Central American	2	0.00
Cuban	27	0.05
Dominican Republic	7	0.01
Mexican	1,115	2.10
Puerto Rican	110	0.21
South American:	199	0.38
Argentinean	26	0.05
Bolivian	6	0.01
Chilean	34	0.06
Colombian	27	0.05
Ecuadorian	17	0.03
Peruvian	72	0.14
Uruguayan	1	0.00
Venezuelan	9	0.02
Other South American	7	0.01
Other Hispanic or Latino	476	0.90
Hungarian	213	0.40
Icelander	117	0.22
Iranian	177	0.33
Irish	6,411	12.11
Italian	1,379	2.60
Latvian	25	0.05
Lithuanian	44	0.08
Luxemburger	8	0.02
New Zealander	22	0.04
Northern European	152	0.29
Norwegian	4,364	8.24
Pennsylvania German	35	0.07
Polish	851	1.61
Portuguese	143	0.27
Romanian	81	0.15
Russian	616	1.16
Scandinavian	257	0.49
Scotch-Irish	1,526	2.88
Scottish	1,889	3.57
Slavic	24	0.05
Slovak	85	0.16
Slovene	19	0.04
Swedish	2,266	4.28
Swiss	261	0.49
Ukrainian	256	0.48
United States or American	1,400	2.64
Welsh	615	1.16

Notes: 1. Figures in the "Number" column do not add up to the total population due to: a) Ancestry/Race overlap — e.g. persons can report being both White and Irish, b) persons of Hispanic origin can report being any race, c) persons reporting two ancestries are counted in both categories. 2. Numbers in parentheses indicate the number of persons reporting this ancestry/race alone, not in combination with any other ancestry/race. 3. Refer to the Explanation of Data in the front of the book for more detailed information.

West Indian, excl. Hispanic:	57	0.11
Jamaican	16	0.03
Trinidadian and Tobagonian	25	0.05
West Indian	16	0.03
White:	42,681	80.49
Not Hispanic (39,878)	41,518	78.30
Hispanic (946)	1,163	2.19
Yugoslavian	233	0.44

Silverdale

Place Type: Census Designated Place
County: Kitsap
Population: 15,816

Ancestry/Race	Number	%
African American/Black:	694	4.39
Not Hispanic (538)	669	4.23
Hispanic (12)	25	0.16
African, sub-Saharan:	37	0.23
Ghanian	7	0.04
Liberian	22	0.14
South African	8	0.05
Alaska Native tribes, specified:	18	0.11
Aleut (2)	3	0.02
Eskimo (2)	3	0.02
Tlingit-Haida (10)	11	0.07
All other tribes	1	0.01
Am. Ind. or Alaska Nat., not spec.	71	0.45
American Indian tribes, specified:	205	1.30
Apache (1)	7	0.04
Blackfeet (8)	13	0.08
Cherokee (13)	62	0.39
Cheyenne	1	0.01
Chickasaw (1)	1	0.01
Chippewa (4)	7	0.04
Choctaw	5	0.03
Colville (2)	2	0.01
Comanche (1)	3	0.02
Creek	2	0.01
Iroquois (2)	5	0.03
Latin American Indians (2)	3	0.02
Lumbee (2)	3	0.02
Navajo (5)	12	0.08
Osage (2)	5	0.03
Pueblo (4)	4	0.03
Puget Sound Salish (5)	8	0.05
Seminole	2	0.01
Shoshone (3)	3	0.02
Sioux (10)	16	0.10
All other tribes (22)	41	0.26
American Indian tribes, not spec.	10	0.06
Arab:	16	0.10
Lebanese	16	0.10
Asian:	2,224	14.06
Bangladeshi	2	0.01
Cambodian (1)	1	0.01
Chinese, ex. Taiwanese (76)	128	0.81
Filipino (1,353)	1,628	10.29
Indian (44)	59	0.37
Indonesian (1)	5	0.03
Japanese (102)	202	1.28
Korean (90)	131	0.83
Laotian (1)	1	0.01
Pakistani	1	0.01
Taiwanese (1)	2	0.01
Thai (6)	11	0.07
Vietnamese (20)	25	0.16
Other Asian, specified (1)	7	0.04
Other Asian, not specified (8)	21	0.13
Austrian	22	0.14
Belgian	71	0.45
British	132	0.84
Canadian	32	0.20
Celtic	14	0.09
Croatian	63	0.40
Czech	73	0.46
Czechoslovakian	33	0.21
Danish	215	1.36
Dutch	204	1.29
English	1,977	12.54
European	212	1.34
Finnish	76	0.48
French, except Basque	616	3.91
French Canadian	76	0.48
German	2,870	18.20
Greek	53	0.34
Hawaii Native/Pacific Islander:	304	1.92
Micronesian: (61)	107	0.68
Guamanian/Chamorro (58)	103	0.65
Other Micronesian (3)	4	0.03
Polynesian: (84)	150	0.95
Native Hawaiian (48)	100	0.63
Samoan (35)	45	0.28
Other Polynesian (1)	5	0.03
Other Pac. Isl., specified	4	0.03
Other Pac. Isl., not spec. (17)	43	0.27
Hispanic or Latino:	690	4.36
Central American:	20	0.13
Costa Rican	1	0.01
Guatemalan	1	0.01
Honduran	7	0.04
Nicaraguan	3	0.02
Panamanian	1	0.01
Salvadoran	7	0.04
Cuban	9	0.06
Dominican Republic	3	0.02
Mexican	402	2.54
Puerto Rican	74	0.47
South American:	21	0.13
Argentinean	1	0.01
Chilean	4	0.03
Colombian	9	0.06
Ecuadorian	3	0.02
Peruvian	2	0.01
Venezuelan	1	0.01
Other South American	1	0.01
Other Hispanic or Latino	161	1.02
Hungarian	32	0.20
Irish	1,950	12.37
Italian	508	3.22
Lithuanian	25	0.16
Northern European	9	0.06
Norwegian	1,017	6.45
Polish	396	2.51
Portuguese	77	0.49
Romanian	8	0.05
Russian	98	0.62
Scandinavian	61	0.39
Scotch-Irish	336	2.13
Scottish	416	2.64
Serbian	11	0.07
Slovak	8	0.05
Slovene	5	0.03
Swedish	422	2.68
Swiss	105	0.67
Turkish	15	0.10
Ukrainian	30	0.19
United States or American	803	5.09
Welsh	190	1.20
West Indian, excl. Hispanic:	34	0.22
Jamaican	30	0.19
U.S. Virgin Islander	4	0.03
White:	12,892	81.51
Not Hispanic (11,854)	12,458	78.77
Hispanic (352)	434	2.74
Yugoslavian	23	0.15

South Hill

Place Type: Census Designated Place
County: Pierce
Population: 31,623

Ancestry/Race	Number	%
African American/Black:	1,007	3.18
Not Hispanic (742)	970	3.07
Hispanic (24)	37	0.12
African, sub-Saharan:	82	0.26
African	75	0.24
Nigerian	7	0.02
Alaska Native tribes, specified:	51	0.16
Alaska Athabascan	2	0.01
Aleut (7)	17	0.05
Eskimo (3)	6	0.02
Tlingit-Haida (20)	26	0.08
Alaska Native tribes, not specified	7	0.02
Am. Ind. or Alaska Nat., not spec.	125	0.40
American Indian tribes, specified:	404	1.28
Apache (5)	7	0.02
Blackfeet (3)	17	0.05
Cherokee (36)	118	0.37
Chickasaw (2)	3	0.01
Chippewa (15)	28	0.09
Choctaw (3)	22	0.07
Colville (7)	7	0.02
Cree (1)	2	0.01
Creek (4)	6	0.02
Crow	1	0.00
Delaware	1	0.00
Iroquois (3)	7	0.02
Kiowa (1)	2	0.01
Latin American Indians (2)	3	0.01
Navajo (5)	16	0.05
Ottawa	1	0.00
Potawatomi (1)	2	0.01
Pueblo (6)	7	0.02
Puget Sound Salish (26)	50	0.16
Seminole	4	0.01
Shoshone	1	0.00
Sioux (6)	14	0.04
Yakama (4)	11	0.03
All other tribes (45)	74	0.23
American Indian tribes, not spec.	52	0.16
Arab:	63	0.20
Egyptian	9	0.03
Lebanese	43	0.14
Other Arab	11	0.03
Asian:	1,670	5.28
Cambodian (14)	14	0.04
Chinese, ex. Taiwanese (86)	153	0.48
Filipino (262)	428	1.35
Indian (56)	74	0.23
Indonesian (1)	4	0.01
Japanese (134)	336	1.06
Korean (371)	494	1.56
Laotian	10	0.03
Pakistani (2)	3	0.01
Taiwanese (6)	7	0.02
Thai (19)	35	0.11
Vietnamese (47)	60	0.19
Other Asian, specified (2)	5	0.02
Other Asian, not specified (30)	47	0.15
Australian	6	0.02
Austrian	48	0.15
Basque	7	0.02
Belgian	26	0.08
British	382	1.20
Canadian	85	0.27
Celtic	23	0.07
Croatian	57	0.18
Czech	59	0.19
Czechoslovakian	102	0.32
Danish	446	1.40
Dutch	889	2.79
English	3,853	12.10
European	528	1.66
Finnish	141	0.44
French, except Basque	1,284	4.03
French Canadian	326	1.02
German	6,653	20.90
Greek	61	0.19
Hawaii Native/Pacific Islander:	271	0.86
Micronesian: (55)	93	0.29
Guamanian/Chamorro (55)	93	0.29
Polynesian: (91)	164	0.52
Native Hawaiian (42)	98	0.31
Samoan (42)	56	0.18
Tongan (1)	3	0.01
Other Polynesian (6)	7	0.02

Notes: 1. Figures in the "Number" column do not add up to the total population due to: a) Ancestry/Race overlap — e.g. persons can report being both White and Irish, b) persons of Hispanic origin can report being any race, c) persons reporting two ancestries are counted in both categories. 2. Numbers in parentheses indicate the number of persons reporting this ancestry/race alone, not in combination with any other ancestry/race. 3. Refer to the Explanation of Data in the front of the book for more detailed information.

Other Pac. Isl., specified	1	0.00
Other Pac. Isl., not spec. (6)	13	0.04
Hispanic or Latino:	1,307	4.13
Central American:	50	0.16
Costa Rican	4	0.01
Guatemalan	7	0.02
Nicaraguan	4	0.01
Panamanian	17	0.05
Salvadoran	18	0.06
Cuban	15	0.05
Dominican Republic	12	0.04
Mexican	845	2.67
Puerto Rican	92	0.29
South American:	21	0.07
Bolivian	5	0.02
Chilean	1	0.00
Colombian	7	0.02
Ecuadorian	1	0.00
Paraguayan	1	0.00
Peruvian	4	0.01
Venezuelan	2	0.01
Other Hispanic or Latino	272	0.86
Hungarian	70	0.22
Icelander	26	0.08
Irish	3,680	11.56
Israeli	18	0.06
Italian	1,522	4.78
Latvian	7	0.02
Lithuanian	18	0.06
New Zealander	26	0.08
Northern European	59	0.19
Norwegian	2,602	8.17
Pennsylvania German	26	0.08
Polish	901	2.83
Portuguese	194	0.61
Russian	172	0.54
Scandinavian	409	1.28
Scotch-Irish	525	1.65
Scottish	775	2.43
Slavic	42	0.13
Slovak	78	0.25
Slovene	27	0.08
Swedish	1,192	3.74
Swiss	160	0.50
Ukrainian	97	0.30
United States or American	2,001	6.29
Welsh	204	0.64
West Indian, excl. Hispanic:	29	0.09
Jamaican	29	0.09
White:	28,771	90.98
Not Hispanic (26,989)	27,968	88.44
Hispanic (652)	803	2.54
Yugoslavian	73	0.23

Spanaway

Place Type: Census Designated Place
County: Pierce
Population: 21,588

Ancestry/Race	Number	%
African American/Black:	2,425	11.23
Not Hispanic (1,931)	2,346	10.87
Hispanic (35)	79	0.37
African, sub-Saharan:	163	0.76
African	151	0.70
Nigerian	7	0.03
South African	5	0.02
Alaska Native tribes, specified:	31	0.14
Alaska Athabascan (1)	4	0.02
Aleut (3)	3	0.01
Eskimo (5)	9	0.04
Tlingit-Haida (8)	15	0.07
Am. Ind. or Alaska Nat., not spec.	185	0.86
American Indian tribes, specified:	529	2.45
Apache (12)	25	0.12
Blackfeet (14)	43	0.20
Cherokee (51)	130	0.60
Cheyenne (1)	6	0.03
Chickasaw (1)	2	0.01
Chippewa (9)	36	0.17
Choctaw (11)	19	0.09
Colville (13)	19	0.09
Comanche (1)	1	0.00
Cree	3	0.01
Creek (1)	2	0.01
Crow (1)	2	0.01
Houma (4)	4	0.02
Iroquois (1)	12	0.06
Latin American Indians (2)	4	0.02
Lumbee (1)	2	0.01
Navajo (4)	11	0.05
Osage (1)	7	0.03
Ottawa (13)	13	0.06
Paiute (3)	3	0.01
Potawatomi (5)	6	0.03
Pueblo (10)	10	0.05
Puget Sound Salish (28)	56	0.26
Seminole	1	0.00
Shoshone	3	0.01
Sioux (13)	28	0.13
Yakama (3)	13	0.06
All other tribes (29)	68	0.31
American Indian tribes, not spec.	23	0.11
Asian:	2,222	10.29
Cambodian (14)	39	0.18
Chinese, ex. Taiwanese (46)	117	0.54
Filipino (457)	707	3.27
Indian (25)	39	0.18
Indonesian (2)	3	0.01
Japanese (126)	324	1.50
Korean (553)	804	3.72
Laotian	1	0.00
Taiwanese (3)	3	0.01
Thai (40)	57	0.26
Vietnamese (40)	52	0.24
Other Asian, specified (6)	21	0.10
Other Asian, not specified (28)	55	0.25
Austrian	41	0.19
Belgian	23	0.11
British	6	0.03
Canadian	53	0.25
Croatian	9	0.04
Czech	45	0.21
Czechoslovakian	43	0.20
Danish	90	0.42
Dutch	448	2.09
English	1,760	8.21
Estonian	24	0.11
European	178	0.83
Finnish	36	0.17
French, except Basque	662	3.09
French Canadian	157	0.73
German	3,538	16.50
Greek	20	0.09
Hawaii Native/Pacific Islander:	658	3.05
Micronesian: (258)	316	1.46
Guamanian/Chamorro (248)	304	1.41
Other Micronesian (10)	12	0.06
Polynesian: (145)	247	1.14
Native Hawaiian (61)	143	0.66
Samoan (84)	102	0.47
Other Polynesian	2	0.01
Other Pac. Isl., specified	12	0.06
Other Pac. Isl., not spec. (49)	83	0.38
Hispanic or Latino:	1,185	5.49
Central American:	48	0.22
Costa Rican	1	0.00
Guatemalan	19	0.09
Honduran	4	0.02
Nicaraguan	1	0.00
Panamanian	22	0.10
Other Central American	1	0.00
Cuban	27	0.13
Dominican Republic	6	0.03
Mexican	634	2.94
Puerto Rican	216	1.00
South American:	20	0.09
Argentinean	1	0.00
Chilean	9	0.04
Colombian	6	0.03
Ecuadorian	1	0.00
Venezuelan	3	0.01
Other Hispanic or Latino	234	1.08
Hungarian	47	0.22
Iranian	8	0.04
Irish	2,111	9.84
Italian	886	4.13
Lithuanian	35	0.16
Luxemburger	11	0.05
Northern European	8	0.04
Norwegian	1,167	5.44
Polish	360	1.68
Portuguese	144	0.67
Russian	153	0.71
Scandinavian	93	0.43
Scotch-Irish	345	1.61
Scottish	375	1.75
Slovak	5	0.02
Swedish	360	1.68
Swiss	63	0.29
Ukrainian	48	0.22
United States or American	1,385	6.46
Welsh	141	0.66
West Indian, excl. Hispanic:	9	0.04
Jamaican	9	0.04
White:	16,706	77.39
Not Hispanic (14,867)	16,056	74.37
Hispanic (488)	650	3.01
Yugoslavian	16	0.07

Spokane

Place Type: City
County: Spokane
Population: 195,629

Ancestry/Race	Number	%
Acadian/Cajun	34	0.02
Afghan	7	0.00
African American/Black:	5,834	2.98
Not Hispanic (3,898)	5,526	2.82
Hispanic (154)	308	0.16
African, sub-Saharan:	353	0.18
African	239	0.12
Ethiopian	51	0.03
Kenyan	5	0.00
Liberian	3	0.00
Nigerian	45	0.02
South African	10	0.01
Alaska Native tribes, specified:	121	0.06
Alaska Athabascan (13)	18	0.01
Aleut (17)	29	0.01
Eskimo (19)	30	0.02
Tlingit-Haida (29)	40	0.02
All other tribes (2)	4	0.00
Alaska Native tribes, not specified	11	0.01
Am. Ind. or Alaska Nat., not spec.	1,599	0.82
Albanian	29	0.01
Alsatian	16	0.01
American Indian tribes, specified:	4,155	2.12
Apache (24)	81	0.04
Blackfeet (161)	293	0.15
Cherokee (167)	569	0.29
Cheyenne (58)	90	0.05
Chickasaw (10)	33	0.02
Chippewa (252)	444	0.23
Choctaw (33)	87	0.04
Colville (297)	394	0.20
Comanche (16)	26	0.01
Cree (23)	56	0.03
Creek (9)	34	0.02
Crow (26)	33	0.02
Delaware (6)	10	0.01
Iroquois (12)	47	0.02
Kiowa (11)	16	0.01
Latin American Indians (27)	43	0.02
Lumbee (4)	5	0.00
Menominee (1)	1	0.00
Navajo (24)	47	0.02

Notes: 1. Figures in the "Number" column do not add up to the total population due to: a) Ancestry/Race overlap — e.g. persons can report being both White and Irish, b) persons of Hispanic origin can report being any race, c) persons reporting two ancestries are counted in both categories. 2. Numbers in parentheses indicate the number of persons reporting this ancestry/race alone, not in combination with any other ancestry/race. 3. Refer to the Explanation of Data in the front of the book for more detailed information.

Osage (4)	13	0.01
Ottawa (3)	3	0.00
Paiute (8)	9	0.00
Pima (2)	2	0.00
Potawatomi (9)	12	0.01
Pueblo (8)	16	0.01
Puget Sound Salish (39)	52	0.03
Seminole (1)	10	0.01
Shoshone (11)	21	0.01
Sioux (145)	243	0.12
Tohono O'Odham (1)	3	0.00
Ute (1)	3	0.00
Yakama (35)	50	0.03
Yaqui (2)	3	0.00
All other tribes (986)	1,406	0.72
American Indian tribes, not spec.	177	0.09
Arab:	491	0.25
Arab/Arabic	264	0.13
Egyptian	28	0.01
Jordanian	8	0.00
Lebanese	119	0.06
Moroccan	7	0.00
Palestinian	15	0.01
Syrian	20	0.01
Other Arab	30	0.02
Armenian	56	0.03
Asian:	6,174	3.16
Bangladeshi (2)	2	0.00
Cambodian (32)	35	0.02
Chinese, ex. Taiwanese (516)	754	0.39
Filipino (489)	932	0.48
Hmong (267)	318	0.16
Indian (159)	236	0.12
Indonesian (7)	25	0.01
Japanese (932)	1,365	0.70
Korean (489)	714	0.36
Laotian (147)	173	0.09
Malaysian (3)	3	0.00
Pakistani (14)	26	0.01
Sri Lankan (1)	2	0.00
Taiwanese (39)	55	0.03
Thai (78)	113	0.06
Vietnamese (978)	1,076	0.55
Other Asian, specified (5)	20	0.01
Other Asian, not specified (112)	325	0.17
Assyrian/Chaldean/Syriac	16	0.01
Australian	70	0.04
Austrian	520	0.27
Basque	101	0.05
Belgian	256	0.13
British	928	0.47
Bulgarian	156	0.08
Canadian	894	0.46
Celtic	97	0.05
Croatian	200	0.10
Czech	789	0.40
Czechoslovakian	348	0.18
Danish	2,121	1.08
Dutch	4,047	2.06
Eastern European	45	0.02
English	23,755	12.11
Estonian	7	0.00
European	2,218	1.13
Finnish	754	0.38
French, except Basque	8,384	4.27
French Canadian	2,230	1.14
German	44,829	22.86
Greek	808	0.41
Hawaii Native/Pacific Islander:	754	0.39
Melanesian: (1)	2	0.00
Fijian (1)	2	0.00
Micronesian: (171)	236	0.12
Guamanian/Chamorro (109)	166	0.08
Other Micronesian (62)	70	0.04
Polynesian: (150)	381	0.19
Native Hawaiian (114)	306	0.16
Samoan (32)	61	0.03
Other Polynesian (4)	14	0.01
Other Pac. Isl., specified	5	0.00
Other Pac. Isl., not spec. (47)	130	0.07
Hispanic or Latino:	5,857	2.99
Central American:	205	0.10
Costa Rican	23	0.01
Guatemalan	37	0.02
Honduran	15	0.01
Nicaraguan	20	0.01
Panamanian	44	0.02
Salvadoran	55	0.03
Other Central American	11	0.01
Cuban	142	0.07
Dominican Republic	5	0.00
Mexican	3,553	1.82
Puerto Rican	461	0.24
South American:	134	0.07
Argentinean	29	0.01
Chilean	20	0.01
Colombian	36	0.02
Ecuadorian	17	0.01
Paraguayan	1	0.00
Peruvian	15	0.01
Uruguayan	1	0.00
Venezuelan	4	0.00
Other South American	11	0.01
Other Hispanic or Latino	1,357	0.69
Hungarian	660	0.34
Icelander	85	0.04
Iranian	97	0.05
Irish	26,966	13.75
Israeli	11	0.01
Italian	8,079	4.12
Latvian	122	0.06
Lithuanian	156	0.08
Luxemburger	30	0.02
Macedonian	5	0.00
New Zealander	28	0.01
Northern European	287	0.15
Norwegian	12,013	6.12
Pennsylvania German	32	0.02
Polish	3,259	1.66
Portuguese	479	0.24
Romanian	130	0.07
Russian	3,244	1.65
Scandinavian	1,378	0.70
Scotch-Irish	5,223	2.66
Scottish	5,691	2.90
Serbian	27	0.01
Slavic	127	0.06
Slovak	143	0.07
Slovene	99	0.05
Soviet Union	14	0.01
Swedish	7,294	3.72
Swiss	1,077	0.55
Turkish	80	0.04
Ukrainian	1,661	0.85
United States or American	10,331	5.27
Welsh	2,195	1.12
West Indian, excl. Hispanic:	63	0.03
Dutch West Indian	7	0.00
Haitian	6	0.00
Jamaican	24	0.01
Trinidadian and Tobagonian	26	0.01
White:	181,072	92.56
Not Hispanic (171,918)	177,219	90.59
Hispanic (3,100)	3,853	1.97
Yugoslavian	744	0.38

Sunnyside

Place Type: City
County: Yakima
Population: 13,905

Ancestry/Race	Number	%
African American/Black:	70	0.50
Not Hispanic (24)	30	0.22
Hispanic (31)	40	0.29
African, sub-Saharan:	8	0.06
Ethiopian	8	0.06
Am. Ind. or Alaska Nat., not spec.	70	0.50
American Indian tribes, specified:	88	0.63
Blackfeet	3	0.02
Cherokee (2)	5	0.04
Chippewa (5)	6	0.04
Choctaw (4)	4	0.03
Colville (1)	1	0.01
Comanche	1	0.01
Iroquois	1	0.01
Latin American Indians (17)	22	0.16
Shoshone	5	0.04
Sioux	2	0.01
Ute	1	0.01
Yakama (4)	16	0.12
Yuman (1)	1	0.01
All other tribes (14)	20	0.14
American Indian tribes, not spec.	9	0.06
Arab:	37	0.26
Palestinian	37	0.26
Asian:	131	0.94
Chinese, ex. Taiwanese (29)	29	0.21
Filipino (16)	26	0.19
Indian (4)	4	0.03
Japanese (10)	15	0.11
Korean (24)	24	0.17
Laotian (10)	10	0.07
Vietnamese (3)	3	0.02
Other Asian, specified	6	0.04
Other Asian, not specified	14	0.10
Canadian	22	0.16
Czech	10	0.07
Czechoslovakian	9	0.06
Danish	79	0.56
Dutch	180	1.28
English	589	4.19
European	29	0.21
Finnish	7	0.05
French, except Basque	157	1.12
French Canadian	23	0.16
German	896	6.37
Hawaii Native/Pacific Islander:	43	0.31
Micronesian:	12	0.09
Guamanian/Chamorro	12	0.09
Polynesian: (5)	9	0.06
Native Hawaiian (4)	8	0.06
Other Polynesian (1)	1	0.01
Other Pac. Isl., specified	6	0.04
Other Pac. Isl., not spec. (3)	16	0.12
Hispanic or Latino:	10,158	73.05
Central American:	57	0.41
Guatemalan	12	0.09
Honduran	11	0.08
Nicaraguan	5	0.04
Salvadoran	23	0.17
Other Central American	6	0.04
Cuban	11	0.08
Mexican	8,539	61.41
Puerto Rican	33	0.24
South American:	3	0.02
Colombian	2	0.01
Peruvian	1	0.01
Other Hispanic or Latino	1,515	10.90
Irish	398	2.83
Italian	44	0.31
Norwegian	211	1.50
Polish	8	0.06
Portuguese	13	0.09
Russian	75	0.53
Scandinavian	72	0.51
Scotch-Irish	85	0.60
Scottish	186	1.32
Swedish	119	0.85
Ukrainian	15	0.11
United States or American	293	2.08
Welsh	45	0.32
White:	6,307	45.36
Not Hispanic (3,454)	3,556	25.57
Hispanic (2,471)	2,751	19.78
Yugoslavian	12	0.09

Notes: 1. Figures in the "Number" column do not add up to the total population due to: a) Ancestry/Race overlap — e.g. persons can report being both White and Irish, b) persons of Hispanic origin can report being any race, c) persons reporting two ancestries are counted in both categories. 2. Numbers in parentheses indicate the number of persons reporting this ancestry/race alone, not in combination with any other ancestry/race. 3. Refer to the Explanation of Data in the front of the book for more detailed information.

Tacoma

Place Type: City
County: Pierce
Population: 193,556

Ancestry/Race	Number	%
Acadian/Cajun	44	0.02
Afghan	40	0.02
African American/Black:	26,461	13.67
Not Hispanic (21,187)	25,360	13.10
Hispanic (570)	1,101	0.57
African, sub-Saharan:	1,802	0.93
African	1,548	0.80
Ethiopian	41	0.02
Ghanian	57	0.03
Kenyan	77	0.04
Nigerian	67	0.03
South African	12	0.01
Alaska Native tribes, specified:	468	0.24
Alaska Athabascan (27)	43	0.02
Aleut (38)	82	0.04
Eskimo (61)	117	0.06
Tlingit-Haida (125)	192	0.10
All other tribes (20)	34	0.02
Alaska Native tribes, not specified	42	0.02
Am. Ind. or Alaska Nat., not spec.	1,779	0.92
Albanian	11	0.01
Alsatian	6	0.00
American Indian tribes, specified:	4,699	2.43
Apache (26)	90	0.05
Blackfeet (149)	396	0.20
Cherokee (158)	762	0.39
Cheyenne (48)	60	0.03
Chickasaw (4)	18	0.01
Chippewa (179)	351	0.18
Choctaw (49)	134	0.07
Colville (62)	93	0.05
Comanche (12)	22	0.01
Cree (2)	11	0.01
Creek (10)	34	0.02
Crow (8)	21	0.01
Delaware (12)	19	0.01
Houma (2)	2	0.00
Iroquois (21)	55	0.03
Kiowa (11)	13	0.01
Latin American Indians (36)	103	0.05
Lumbee	8	0.00
Navajo (45)	65	0.03
Osage (2)	13	0.01
Ottawa (5)	7	0.00
Paiute (7)	14	0.01
Pima (3)	3	0.00
Potawatomi (19)	29	0.01
Pueblo (22)	37	0.02
Puget Sound Salish (774)	956	0.49
Seminole (5)	21	0.01
Shoshone (11)	19	0.01
Sioux (128)	251	0.13
Ute (3)	6	0.00
Yakama (98)	143	0.07
Yaqui (7)	9	0.00
Yuman	3	0.00
All other tribes (649)	931	0.48
American Indian tribes, not spec.	276	0.14
Arab:	519	0.27
Arab/Arabic	76	0.04
Egyptian	77	0.04
Jordanian	21	0.01
Lebanese	178	0.09
Moroccan	24	0.01
Palestinian	5	0.00
Syrian	22	0.01
Other Arab	116	0.06
Armenian	109	0.06
Asian:	19,459	10.05
Bangladeshi (2)	2	0.00
Cambodian (3,031)	3,569	1.84
Chinese, ex. Taiwanese (684)	1,260	0.65
Filipino (2,016)	3,158	1.63
Hmong (2)	3	0.00
Indian (372)	541	0.28
Indonesian (15)	38	0.02
Japanese (996)	2,054	1.06
Korean (2,748)	3,552	1.84
Laotian (290)	371	0.19
Malaysian (7)	15	0.01
Pakistani (32)	48	0.02
Taiwanese (29)	48	0.02
Thai (153)	305	0.16
Vietnamese (3,600)	3,911	2.02
Other Asian, specified (16)	56	0.03
Other Asian, not specified (252)	528	0.27
Australian	70	0.04
Austrian	667	0.35
Basque	45	0.02
Belgian	194	0.10
Brazilian	39	0.02
British	973	0.50
Bulgarian	80	0.04
Canadian	599	0.31
Celtic	141	0.07
Croatian	430	0.22
Cypriot	11	0.01
Czech	673	0.35
Czechoslovakian	419	0.22
Danish	1,571	0.81
Dutch	3,136	1.62
Eastern European	9	0.00
English	17,406	9.01
Estonian	39	0.02
European	2,891	1.50
Finnish	658	0.34
French, except Basque	6,181	3.20
French Canadian	1,822	0.94
German	30,433	15.75
German Russian	2	0.00
Greek	836	0.43
Guyanese	8	0.00
Hawaii Native/Pacific Islander:	2,980	1.54
Melanesian: (17)	27	0.01
Fijian (17)	26	0.01
Other Melanesian	1	0.00
Micronesian: (389)	563	0.29
Guamanian/Chamorro (368)	536	0.28
Other Micronesian (21)	27	0.01
Polynesian: (1,249)	2,024	1.05
Native Hawaiian (250)	812	0.42
Samoan (958)	1,155	0.60
Tongan (27)	40	0.02
Other Polynesian (14)	17	0.01
Other Pac. Isl., specified	14	0.01
Other Pac. Isl., not spec. (107)	352	0.18
Hispanic or Latino:	13,262	6.85
Central American:	524	0.27
Costa Rican	16	0.01
Guatemalan	53	0.03
Honduran	49	0.03
Nicaraguan	13	0.01
Panamanian	183	0.09
Salvadoran	178	0.09
Other Central American	32	0.02
Cuban	181	0.09
Dominican Republic	57	0.03
Mexican	8,599	4.44
Puerto Rican	1,447	0.75
South American:	304	0.16
Argentinean	21	0.01
Bolivian	13	0.01
Chilean	37	0.02
Colombian	76	0.04
Ecuadorian	9	0.00
Paraguayan	2	0.00
Peruvian	120	0.06
Venezuelan	17	0.01
Other South American	9	0.00
Other Hispanic or Latino	2,150	1.11
Hungarian	512	0.27
Icelander	61	0.03
Iranian	90	0.05
Irish	19,843	10.27
Israeli	17	0.01
Italian	6,783	3.51
Latvian	197	0.10
Lithuanian	272	0.14
Luxemburger	19	0.01
Macedonian	12	0.01
New Zealander	13	0.01
Northern European	331	0.17
Norwegian	11,169	5.78
Pennsylvania German	162	0.08
Polish	2,947	1.53
Portuguese	660	0.34
Romanian	386	0.20
Russian	1,975	1.02
Scandinavian	1,211	0.63
Scotch-Irish	3,433	1.78
Scottish	4,126	2.14
Serbian	31	0.02
Slavic	254	0.13
Slovak	198	0.10
Slovene	48	0.02
Swedish	5,930	3.07
Swiss	877	0.45
Turkish	46	0.02
Ukrainian	1,681	0.87
United States or American	8,544	4.42
Welsh	1,575	0.82
West Indian, excl. Hispanic:	565	0.29
Bahamian	8	0.00
Bermudan	10	0.01
British West Indian	36	0.02
Dutch West Indian	9	0.00
Haitian	22	0.01
Jamaican	197	0.10
Trinidadian and Tobagonian	38	0.02
U.S. Virgin Islander	135	0.07
West Indian	99	0.05
Other West Indian	11	0.01
White:	143,426	74.10
Not Hispanic (128,696)	136,970	70.77
Hispanic (5,008)	6,456	3.34
Yugoslavian	454	0.24

Tukwila

Place Type: City
County: King
Population: 17,181

Ancestry/Race	Number	%
Afghan	12	0.07
African American/Black:	2,520	14.67
Not Hispanic (2,174)	2,465	14.35
Hispanic (24)	55	0.32
African, sub-Saharan:	474	2.76
African	181	1.05
Ethiopian	131	0.76
Nigerian	7	0.04
Senegalese	12	0.07
Somalian	137	0.80
Other sub-Saharan African	6	0.03
Alaska Native tribes, specified:	44	0.26
Alaska Athabascan (2)	3	0.02
Aleut (3)	4	0.02
Eskimo (4)	7	0.04
Tlingit-Haida (13)	23	0.13
All other tribes (2)	7	0.04
Alaska Native tribes, not specified	7	0.04
Am. Ind. or Alaska Nat., not spec.	152	0.88
American Indian tribes, specified:	248	1.44
Apache (1)	6	0.03
Blackfeet (15)	35	0.20
Cherokee (10)	52	0.30
Chickasaw	3	0.02
Chippewa (7)	16	0.09
Choctaw (1)	8	0.05
Colville (5)	6	0.03
Comanche (1)	6	0.03
Creek (1)	1	0.01

Notes: 1. Figures in the "Number" column do not add up to the total population due to: a) Ancestry/Race overlap — e.g. persons can report being both White and Irish, b) persons of Hispanic origin can report being any race, c) persons reporting two ancestries are counted in both categories. 2. Numbers in parentheses indicate the number of persons reporting this ancestry/race alone, not in combination with any other ancestry/race. 3. Refer to the Explanation of Data in the front of the book for more detailed information.

Crow	1	0.01
Iroquois (1)	6	0.03
Kiowa (1)	1	0.01
Latin American Indians (8)	15	0.09
Navajo (3)	8	0.05
Potawatomi	3	0.02
Pueblo (1)	1	0.01
Puget Sound Salish (10)	15	0.09
Seminole	3	0.02
Sioux (6)	14	0.08
Yakama (4)	5	0.03
Yaqui	1	0.01
All other tribes (28)	42	0.24
American Indian tribes, not spec.	29	0.17
Arab:	45	0.26
Egyptian	16	0.09
Lebanese	7	0.04
Other Arab	22	0.13
Armenian	63	0.37
Asian:	2,364	13.76
Bangladeshi (4)	4	0.02
Cambodian (202)	287	1.67
Chinese, ex. Taiwanese (205)	275	1.60
Filipino (394)	545	3.17
Hmong (11)	11	0.06
Indian (156)	204	1.19
Indonesian	2	0.01
Japanese (168)	232	1.35
Korean (101)	127	0.74
Laotian (111)	118	0.69
Pakistani (7)	8	0.05
Sri Lankan (1)	1	0.01
Taiwanese (8)	12	0.07
Thai (59)	76	0.44
Vietnamese (354)	374	2.18
Other Asian, specified (3)	4	0.02
Other Asian, not specified (28)	84	0.49
Austrian	34	0.20
Basque	6	0.03
Belgian	26	0.15
British	53	0.31
Bulgarian	27	0.16
Canadian	43	0.25
Croatian	30	0.17
Czech	7	0.04
Czechoslovakian	23	0.13
Danish	46	0.27
Dutch	173	1.01
Eastern European	7	0.04
English	1,052	6.11
European	187	1.09
Finnish	111	0.65
French, except Basque	339	1.97
French Canadian	116	0.67
German	1,705	9.91
Greek	117	0.68
Hawaii Native/Pacific Islander:	457	2.66
Melanesian: (22)	24	0.14
Fijian (22)	24	0.14
Micronesian: (29)	40	0.23
Guamanian/Chamorro (23)	33	0.19
Other Micronesian (6)	7	0.04
Polynesian: (223)	309	1.80
Native Hawaiian (24)	71	0.41
Samoan (176)	203	1.18
Tongan (23)	26	0.15
Other Polynesian	9	0.05
Other Pac. Isl., not spec. (31)	84	0.49
Hispanic or Latino:	2,329	13.56
Central American:	112	0.65
Costa Rican	2	0.01
Guatemalan	12	0.07
Honduran	6	0.03
Nicaraguan	8	0.05
Panamanian	6	0.03
Salvadoran	67	0.39
Other Central American	11	0.06
Cuban	17	0.10
Dominican Republic	1	0.01
Mexican	1,829	10.65
Puerto Rican	29	0.17
South American:	39	0.23
Argentinean	15	0.09
Chilean	14	0.08
Colombian	5	0.03
Ecuadorian	1	0.01
Peruvian	3	0.02
Venezuelan	1	0.01
Other Hispanic or Latino	302	1.76
Hungarian	14	0.08
Icelander	7	0.04
Iranian	14	0.08
Irish	962	5.59
Italian	437	2.54
Northern European	26	0.15
Norwegian	666	3.87
Pennsylvania German	22	0.13
Polish	209	1.21
Portuguese	18	0.10
Romanian	45	0.26
Russian	230	1.34
Scandinavian	77	0.45
Scotch-Irish	161	0.94
Scottish	330	1.92
Serbian	32	0.19
Slavic	4	0.02
Slovene	8	0.05
Swedish	455	2.64
Swiss	45	0.26
Ukrainian	49	0.28
United States or American	824	4.79
Welsh	107	0.62
West Indian, excl. Hispanic:	12	0.07
Belizean	7	0.04
Jamaican	5	0.03
White:	10,844	63.12
Not Hispanic (9,297)	9,949	57.91
Hispanic (777)	895	5.21
Yugoslavian	541	3.14

Tumwater

Place Type: City
County: Thurston
Population: 12,698

Ancestry/Race	Number	%
Acadian/Cajun	13	0.10
African American/Black:	251	1.98
Not Hispanic (173)	239	1.88
Hispanic (3)	12	0.09
African, sub-Saharan:	16	0.13
African	16	0.13
Alaska Native tribes, specified:	31	0.24
Alaska Athabascan	2	0.02
Aleut (9)	10	0.08
Eskimo (4)	7	0.06
Tlingit-Haida (9)	10	0.08
All other tribes (2)	2	0.02
Alaska Native tribes, not specified	2	0.02
Am. Ind. or Alaska Nat., not spec.	74	0.58
American Indian tribes, specified:	186	1.46
Apache (4)	4	0.03
Blackfeet (5)	8	0.06
Cherokee (27)	45	0.35
Chickasaw (1)	3	0.02
Chippewa (1)	4	0.03
Choctaw (3)	8	0.06
Colville (3)	4	0.03
Cree	2	0.02
Creek (1)	1	0.01
Delaware (4)	4	0.03
Houma (2)	2	0.02
Iroquois	5	0.04
Latin American Indians	1	0.01
Navajo (4)	4	0.03
Puget Sound Salish (10)	21	0.17
Seminole	3	0.02
Shoshone	2	0.02
Sioux (4)	8	0.06
Yakama (1)	3	0.02
All other tribes (33)	54	0.43
American Indian tribes, not spec.	10	0.08
Arab:	66	0.52
Lebanese	36	0.28
Syrian	30	0.24
Armenian	20	0.16
Asian:	652	5.13
Cambodian (9)	11	0.09
Chinese, ex. Taiwanese (54)	81	0.64
Filipino (74)	109	0.86
Indian (78)	81	0.64
Indonesian (1)	1	0.01
Japanese (40)	83	0.65
Korean (93)	125	0.98
Laotian (5)	7	0.06
Pakistani	1	0.01
Taiwanese (4)	9	0.07
Thai (5)	5	0.04
Vietnamese (121)	129	1.02
Other Asian, specified	3	0.02
Other Asian, not specified (1)	7	0.06
Austrian	46	0.36
Basque	7	0.06
Belgian	38	0.30
Brazilian	5	0.04
British	113	0.89
Canadian	112	0.89
Croatian	18	0.14
Czech	134	1.06
Danish	162	1.28
Dutch	228	1.80
Eastern European	8	0.06
English	1,610	12.73
Estonian	8	0.06
European	218	1.72
Finnish	87	0.69
French, except Basque	512	4.05
French Canadian	94	0.74
German	2,655	20.99
Hawaii Native/Pacific Islander:	87	0.69
Micronesian: (17)	23	0.18
Guamanian/Chamorro (17)	23	0.18
Polynesian: (24)	50	0.39
Native Hawaiian (15)	39	0.31
Samoan (9)	11	0.09
Other Pac. Isl., specified	2	0.02
Other Pac. Isl., not spec. (4)	12	0.09
Hispanic or Latino:	518	4.08
Central American:	20	0.16
Costa Rican	4	0.03
Guatemalan	6	0.05
Honduran	2	0.02
Panamanian	3	0.02
Salvadoran	5	0.04
Cuban	8	0.06
Dominican Republic	1	0.01
Mexican	309	2.43
Puerto Rican	49	0.39
South American:	20	0.16
Chilean	2	0.02
Colombian	12	0.09
Ecuadorian	1	0.01
Uruguayan	5	0.04
Other Hispanic or Latino	111	0.87
Hungarian	37	0.29
Icelander	41	0.32
Irish	1,748	13.82
Italian	526	4.16
Lithuanian	22	0.17
Northern European	36	0.28
Norwegian	655	5.18
Pennsylvania German	12	0.09
Polish	236	1.87
Portuguese	105	0.83
Russian	102	0.81
Scandinavian	115	0.91
Scotch-Irish	326	2.58
Scottish	325	2.57
Slavic	9	0.07

Notes: 1. Figures in the "Number" column do not add up to the total population due to: a) Ancestry/Race overlap — e.g. persons can report being both White and Irish, b) persons of Hispanic origin can report being any race, c) persons reporting two ancestries are counted in both categories. 2. Numbers in parentheses indicate the number of persons reporting this ancestry/race alone, not in combination with any other ancestry/race. 3. Refer to the Explanation of Data in the front of the book for more detailed information.

Slovak	26	0.21
Slovene	15	0.12
Swedish	549	4.34
Swiss	63	0.50
Ukrainian	13	0.10
United States or American	515	4.07
Welsh	268	2.12
West Indian, excl. Hispanic:	9	0.07
Trinidadian and Tobagonian	9	0.07
White:	11,600	91.35
Not Hispanic (10,954)	11,273	88.78
Hispanic (272)	327	2.58
Yugoslavian	8	0.06

Union Hill-Novelty Hill

Place Type: Census Designated Place
County: King
Population: 11,265

Ancestry/Race	Number	%
African American/Black:	121	1.07
Not Hispanic (88)	117	1.04
Hispanic	4	0.04
African, sub-Saharan:	14	0.13
African	7	0.06
South African	7	0.06
Alaska Native tribes, specified:	7	0.06
Alaska Athabascan	5	0.04
Tlingit-Haida (2)	2	0.02
Am. Ind. or Alaska Nat., not spec.	23	0.20
American Indian tribes, specified:	61	0.54
Apache (1)	1	0.01
Blackfeet	1	0.01
Cherokee (2)	16	0.14
Chippewa (2)	3	0.03
Choctaw (1)	1	0.01
Colville (1)	1	0.01
Comanche (1)	2	0.02
Delaware	1	0.01
Iroquois (1)	4	0.04
Latin American Indians	1	0.01
Potawatomi	1	0.01
Puget Sound Salish (9)	10	0.09
Sioux	5	0.04
Ute (1)	1	0.01
All other tribes (6)	13	0.12
American Indian tribes, not spec.	12	0.11
Arab:	39	0.35
Arab/Arabic	28	0.25
Egyptian	11	0.10
Armenian	6	0.05
Asian:	654	5.81
Chinese, ex. Taiwanese (141)	190	1.69
Filipino (20)	60	0.53
Hmong (6)	6	0.05
Indian (81)	95	0.84
Indonesian (3)	7	0.06
Japanese (107)	169	1.50
Korean (46)	60	0.53
Malaysian	1	0.01
Taiwanese (20)	20	0.18
Thai (3)	3	0.03
Vietnamese (33)	34	0.30
Other Asian, specified (2)	4	0.04
Other Asian, not specified (2)	5	0.04
Assyrian/Chaldean/Syriac	8	0.07
Australian	8	0.07
Austrian	99	0.89
Belgian	17	0.15
British	248	2.22
Canadian	118	1.06
Croatian	44	0.39
Czech	100	0.89
Czechoslovakian	13	0.12
Danish	189	1.69
Dutch	295	2.64
Eastern European	19	0.17
English	1,670	14.94
European	189	1.69
Finnish	108	0.97
French, except Basque	331	2.96
French Canadian	119	1.06
German	2,535	22.68
Greek	94	0.84
Hawaii Native/Pacific Islander:	22	0.20
Micronesian:	2	0.02
Guamanian/Chamorro	2	0.02
Polynesian: (7)	15	0.13
Native Hawaiian (5)	11	0.10
Samoan (2)	4	0.04
Other Pac. Isl., not spec.	5	0.04
Hispanic or Latino:	389	3.45
Central American:	8	0.07
Costa Rican	1	0.01
Honduran	4	0.04
Salvadoran	3	0.03
Cuban	3	0.03
Mexican	271	2.41
Puerto Rican	9	0.08
South American:	28	0.25
Argentinean	5	0.04
Bolivian	4	0.04
Chilean	1	0.01
Colombian	10	0.09
Peruvian	7	0.06
Other South American	1	0.01
Other Hispanic or Latino	70	0.62
Hungarian	109	0.98
Iranian	46	0.41
Irish	1,387	12.41
Italian	513	4.59
Lithuanian	50	0.45
Northern European	14	0.13
Norwegian	600	5.37
Pennsylvania German	4	0.04
Polish	189	1.69
Portuguese	36	0.32
Romanian	31	0.28
Russian	195	1.74
Scandinavian	118	1.06
Scotch-Irish	312	2.79
Scottish	382	3.42
Slovak	10	0.09
Swedish	539	4.82
Swiss	62	0.55
Turkish	45	0.40
Ukrainian	30	0.27
United States or American	485	4.34
Welsh	119	1.06
White:	10,485	93.08
Not Hispanic (9,979)	10,224	90.76
Hispanic (246)	261	2.32
Yugoslavian	7	0.06

University Place

Place Type: City
County: Pierce
Population: 29,933

Ancestry/Race	Number	%
Acadian/Cajun	23	0.08
African American/Black:	3,200	10.69
Not Hispanic (2,555)	3,073	10.27
Hispanic (62)	127	0.42
African, sub-Saharan:	245	0.81
African	237	0.79
Ghanian	8	0.03
Alaska Native tribes, specified:	25	0.08
Aleut (3)	7	0.02
Eskimo (5)	6	0.02
Tlingit-Haida (6)	11	0.04
All other tribes	1	0.00
Alaska Native tribes, not specified	2	0.01
Am. Ind. or Alaska Nat., not spec.	162	0.54
American Indian tribes, specified:	362	1.21
Apache (5)	19	0.06
Blackfeet (9)	24	0.08
Cherokee (28)	112	0.37
Cheyenne (2)	6	0.02
Chickasaw (6)	6	0.02
Chippewa (11)	26	0.09
Choctaw (5)	17	0.06
Colville (2)	2	0.01
Cree	1	0.00
Creek	4	0.01
Crow	4	0.01
Iroquois (1)	5	0.02
Latin American Indians (2)	14	0.05
Lumbee (2)	2	0.01
Navajo (2)	5	0.02
Osage	3	0.01
Paiute (5)	5	0.02
Potawatomi (1)	4	0.01
Pueblo (1)	4	0.01
Puget Sound Salish (11)	23	0.08
Seminole	1	0.00
Sioux (7)	13	0.04
Yakama	2	0.01
All other tribes (26)	60	0.20
American Indian tribes, not spec.	37	0.12
Arab:	132	0.44
Arab/Arabic	11	0.04
Egyptian	6	0.02
Iraqi	33	0.11
Lebanese	60	0.20
Palestinian	8	0.03
Syrian	6	0.02
Other Arab	8	0.03
Asian:	2,954	9.87
Cambodian (33)	46	0.15
Chinese, ex. Taiwanese (179)	274	0.92
Filipino (288)	480	1.60
Indian (90)	108	0.36
Indonesian (2)	8	0.03
Japanese (195)	405	1.35
Korean (1,136)	1,286	4.30
Laotian (1)	4	0.01
Malaysian (2)	2	0.01
Pakistani (1)	9	0.03
Taiwanese (16)	18	0.06
Thai (14)	23	0.08
Vietnamese (215)	222	0.74
Other Asian, specified (4)	5	0.02
Other Asian, not specified (29)	64	0.21
Austrian	120	0.40
Basque	10	0.03
Belgian	21	0.07
British	219	0.73
Bulgarian	32	0.11
Canadian	56	0.19
Croatian	63	0.21
Czech	82	0.27
Danish	329	1.09
Dutch	575	1.91
Eastern European	7	0.02
English	3,873	12.86
European	545	1.81
Finnish	169	0.56
French, except Basque	1,142	3.79
French Canadian	208	0.69
German	5,726	19.01
Greek	133	0.44
Hawaii Native/Pacific Islander:	358	1.20
Melanesian: (3)	3	0.01
Fijian (3)	3	0.01
Micronesian: (52)	86	0.29
Guamanian/Chamorro (36)	67	0.22
Other Micronesian (16)	19	0.06
Polynesian: (91)	224	0.75
Native Hawaiian (50)	152	0.51
Samoan (32)	62	0.21
Tongan (8)	9	0.03
Other Polynesian (1)	1	0.00
Other Pac. Isl., not spec. (13)	45	0.15
Hispanic or Latino:	1,150	3.84
Central American:	50	0.17
Costa Rican	5	0.02
Guatemalan	8	0.03

Notes: 1. Figures in the "Number" column do not add up to the total population due to: a) Ancestry/Race overlap — e.g. persons can report being both White and Irish, b) persons of Hispanic origin can report being any race, c) persons reporting two ancestries are counted in both categories. 2. Numbers in parentheses indicate the number of persons reporting this ancestry/race alone, not in combination with any other ancestry/race. 3. Refer to the Explanation of Data in the front of the book for more detailed information.

Ancestry/Race	Number	%
Honduran	4	0.01
Nicaraguan	2	0.01
Panamanian	24	0.08
Salvadoran	7	0.02
Cuban	27	0.09
Dominican Republic	8	0.03
Mexican	643	2.15
Puerto Rican	181	0.60
South American:	27	0.09
Argentinean	1	0.00
Colombian	12	0.04
Ecuadorian	7	0.02
Peruvian	4	0.01
Venezuelan	2	0.01
Other South American	1	0.00
Other Hispanic or Latino	214	0.71
Hungarian	48	0.16
Icelander	39	0.13
Iranian	38	0.13
Irish	3,455	11.47
Italian	1,449	4.81
Latvian	19	0.06
Lithuanian	31	0.10
New Zealander	15	0.05
Northern European	214	0.71
Norwegian	2,067	6.86
Pennsylvania German	13	0.04
Polish	681	2.26
Portuguese	97	0.32
Romanian	51	0.17
Russian	298	0.99
Scandinavian	259	0.86
Scotch-Irish	573	1.90
Scottish	1,084	3.60
Slavic	18	0.06
Slovak	24	0.08
Slovene	23	0.08
Swedish	1,509	5.01
Swiss	208	0.69
Turkish	8	0.03
Ukrainian	123	0.41
United States or American	1,324	4.40
Welsh	239	0.79
West Indian, excl. Hispanic:	47	0.16
Jamaican	47	0.16
White:	24,026	80.27
Not Hispanic (22,207)	23,360	78.04
Hispanic (504)	666	2.22
Yugoslavian	68	0.23

Vancouver

Place Type: City
County: Clark
Population: 143,560

Ancestry/Race	Number	%
Acadian/Cajun	49	0.03
African American/Black:	4,727	3.29
Not Hispanic (3,482)	4,503	3.14
Hispanic (111)	224	0.16
African, sub-Saharan:	464	0.32
African	271	0.19
Ethiopian	45	0.03
Kenyan	14	0.01
Nigerian	52	0.04
South African	35	0.02
Ugandan	29	0.02
Other sub-Saharan African	18	0.01
Alaska Native tribes, specified:	156	0.11
Alaska Athabascan (13)	14	0.01
Aleut (30)	52	0.04
Eskimo (18)	28	0.02
Tlingit-Haida (38)	50	0.03
All other tribes (10)	12	0.01
Alaska Native tribes, not specified	15	0.01
Am. Ind. or Alaska Nat., not spec.	875	0.61
Alsatian	24	0.02
American Indian tribes, specified:	1,909	1.33
Apache (20)	51	0.04
Blackfeet (25)	92	0.06
Cherokee (145)	521	0.36
Cheyenne (16)	26	0.02
Chickasaw (5)	10	0.01
Chippewa (64)	120	0.08
Choctaw (29)	80	0.06
Colville (17)	21	0.01
Comanche (1)	6	0.00
Cree (2)	13	0.01
Creek (4)	15	0.01
Crow (2)	5	0.00
Delaware (2)	6	0.00
Iroquois (8)	23	0.02
Kiowa (3)	6	0.00
Latin American Indians (43)	83	0.06
Lumbee (3)	4	0.00
Menominee (2)	6	0.00
Navajo (34)	55	0.04
Osage (4)	15	0.01
Ottawa (2)	5	0.00
Paiute (3)	11	0.01
Pima	4	0.00
Potawatomi (7)	12	0.01
Pueblo (11)	20	0.01
Puget Sound Salish (14)	28	0.02
Seminole (2)	11	0.01
Shoshone (8)	16	0.01
Sioux (79)	165	0.11
Ute (1)	5	0.00
Yakama (20)	27	0.02
Yaqui (7)	9	0.01
All other tribes (257)	438	0.31
American Indian tribes, not spec.	102	0.07
Arab:	436	0.30
Arab/Arabic	63	0.04
Egyptian	37	0.03
Lebanese	135	0.09
Moroccan	99	0.07
Palestinian	59	0.04
Syrian	6	0.00
Other Arab	37	0.03
Armenian	132	0.09
Asian:	8,287	5.77
Cambodian (373)	429	0.30
Chinese, ex. Taiwanese (1,141)	1,434	1.00
Filipino (1,003)	1,531	1.07
Hmong (7)	10	0.01
Indian (423)	540	0.38
Indonesian (14)	37	0.03
Japanese (650)	1,015	0.71
Korean (849)	1,033	0.72
Laotian (166)	193	0.13
Malaysian (9)	11	0.01
Pakistani (26)	31	0.02
Sri Lankan (30)	37	0.03
Taiwanese (88)	113	0.08
Thai (86)	117	0.08
Vietnamese (1,358)	1,460	1.02
Other Asian, specified (7)	13	0.01
Other Asian, not specified (108)	283	0.20
Australian	78	0.05
Austrian	355	0.25
Basque	78	0.05
Belgian	165	0.12
Brazilian	120	0.08
British	842	0.59
Bulgarian	34	0.02
Canadian	567	0.40
Celtic	144	0.10
Croatian	137	0.10
Czech	573	0.40
Czechoslovakian	219	0.15
Danish	1,658	1.16
Dutch	2,870	2.00
Eastern European	20	0.01
English	16,374	11.43
Estonian	38	0.03
European	1,831	1.28
Finnish	1,180	0.82
French, except Basque	5,446	3.80
French Canadian	1,455	1.02
German	26,975	18.83
Greek	388	0.27
Hawaii Native/Pacific Islander:	1,363	0.95
Melanesian: (31)	47	0.03
Fijian (31)	47	0.03
Micronesian: (220)	334	0.23
Guamanian/Chamorro (205)	306	0.21
Other Micronesian (15)	28	0.02
Polynesian: (452)	768	0.53
Native Hawaiian (167)	398	0.28
Samoan (222)	285	0.20
Tongan (56)	62	0.04
Other Polynesian (7)	23	0.02
Other Pac. Isl., specified	5	0.00
Other Pac. Isl., not spec. (57)	209	0.15
Hispanic or Latino:	9,035	6.29
Central American:	281	0.20
Costa Rican	25	0.02
Guatemalan	78	0.05
Honduran	41	0.03
Nicaraguan	24	0.02
Panamanian	50	0.03
Salvadoran	46	0.03
Other Central American	17	0.01
Cuban	128	0.09
Dominican Republic	6	0.00
Mexican	6,557	4.57
Puerto Rican	298	0.21
South American:	156	0.11
Argentinean	21	0.01
Chilean	56	0.04
Colombian	26	0.02
Ecuadorian	9	0.01
Paraguayan	1	0.00
Peruvian	24	0.02
Uruguayan	3	0.00
Venezuelan	9	0.01
Other South American	7	0.00
Other Hispanic or Latino	1,609	1.12
Hungarian	477	0.33
Icelander	58	0.04
Iranian	312	0.22
Irish	15,998	11.17
Israeli	7	0.00
Italian	4,242	2.96
Latvian	77	0.05
Lithuanian	74	0.05
Luxemburger	42	0.03
Maltese	7	0.00
New Zealander	32	0.02
Northern European	359	0.25
Norwegian	7,413	5.18
Pennsylvania German	105	0.07
Polish	2,239	1.56
Portuguese	474	0.33
Romanian	670	0.47
Russian	3,611	2.52
Scandinavian	608	0.42
Scotch-Irish	2,678	1.87
Scottish	3,888	2.71
Serbian	23	0.02
Slavic	49	0.03
Slovak	126	0.09
Slovene	72	0.05
Soviet Union	7	0.00
Swedish	4,355	3.04
Swiss	767	0.54
Turkish	36	0.03
Ukrainian	2,873	2.01
United States or American	8,934	6.24
Welsh	1,252	0.87
West Indian, excl. Hispanic:	60	0.04
Bahamian	7	0.00
British West Indian	8	0.01
Haitian	8	0.01
Jamaican	20	0.01
Trinidadian and Tobagonian	17	0.01
White:	126,605	88.19
Not Hispanic (117,958)	121,989	84.97

Notes: 1. Figures in the "Number" column do not add up to the total population due to: a) Ancestry/Race overlap — e.g. persons can report being both White and Irish, b) persons of Hispanic origin can report being any race, c) persons reporting two ancestries are counted in both categories. 2. Numbers in parentheses indicate the number of persons reporting this ancestry/race alone, not in combination with any other ancestry/race. 3. Refer to the Explanation of Data in the front of the book for more detailed information.

Ancestry/Race	Number	%
Hispanic (3,794)	4,616	3.22
Yugoslavian	423	0.30

Vashon

Place Type: Census Designated Place
County: King
Population: 10,123

Ancestry/Race	Number	%
African American/Black:	102	1.01
Not Hispanic (38)	94	0.93
Hispanic (8)	8	0.08
African, sub-Saharan:	11	0.11
African	11	0.11
Alaska Native tribes, specified:	9	0.09
Alaska Athabascan (1)	1	0.01
Aleut (1)	1	0.01
Eskimo (2)	3	0.03
Tlingit-Haida (3)	4	0.04
Alaska Native tribes, not specified	3	0.03
Am. Ind. or Alaska Nat., not spec.	59	0.58
American Indian tribes, specified:	111	1.10
Apache (1)	2	0.02
Blackfeet (2)	3	0.03
Cherokee (6)	35	0.35
Chippewa (2)	7	0.07
Choctaw (1)	3	0.03
Colville	2	0.02
Cree	1	0.01
Creek	1	0.01
Crow (1)	4	0.04
Delaware	2	0.02
Iroquois	1	0.01
Latin American Indians (3)	6	0.06
Navajo	3	0.03
Osage	1	0.01
Ottawa (1)	1	0.01
Potawatomi (1)	1	0.01
Pueblo	3	0.03
Puget Sound Salish (4)	9	0.09
Sioux (9)	12	0.12
All other tribes (8)	14	0.14
American Indian tribes, not spec.	17	0.17
Arab:	120	1.19
Arab/Arabic	6	0.06
Lebanese	101	1.00
Other Arab	13	0.13
Asian:	252	2.49
Chinese, ex. Taiwanese (33)	43	0.42
Filipino (26)	66	0.65
Indian (3)	9	0.09
Indonesian	1	0.01
Japanese (40)	61	0.60
Korean (21)	28	0.28
Laotian (2)	2	0.02
Malaysian	1	0.01
Taiwanese	1	0.01
Thai (5)	5	0.05
Vietnamese (18)	21	0.21
Other Asian, specified	1	0.01
Other Asian, not specified (8)	13	0.13
Australian	6	0.06
Austrian	74	0.73
Belgian	12	0.12
British	145	1.43
Bulgarian	18	0.18
Canadian	22	0.22
Celtic	14	0.14
Croatian	18	0.18
Czech	132	1.30
Czechoslovakian	34	0.34
Danish	172	1.70
Dutch	159	1.57
Eastern European	75	0.74
English	1,901	18.78
Estonian	23	0.23
European	295	2.91
Finnish	61	0.60
French, except Basque	556	5.49
French Canadian	91	0.90
German	1,995	19.71
Hawaii Native/Pacific Islander:	19	0.19
Micronesian: (2)	5	0.05
Guamanian/Chamorro (2)	5	0.05
Polynesian: (4)	13	0.13
Native Hawaiian (2)	11	0.11
Samoan (1)	1	0.01
Other Polynesian (1)	1	0.01
Other Pac. Isl., not spec.	1	0.01
Hispanic or Latino:	259	2.56
Central American:	11	0.11
Costa Rican	1	0.01
Guatemalan	2	0.02
Honduran	6	0.06
Nicaraguan	1	0.01
Salvadoran	1	0.01
Cuban	11	0.11
Mexican	160	1.58
Puerto Rican	17	0.17
South American:	17	0.17
Argentinean	1	0.01
Chilean	4	0.04
Colombian	6	0.06
Peruvian	5	0.05
Venezuelan	1	0.01
Other Hispanic or Latino	43	0.42
Hungarian	63	0.62
Icelander	20	0.20
Irish	1,327	13.11
Italian	345	3.41
Latvian	22	0.22
Lithuanian	41	0.41
Luxemburger	10	0.10
Northern European	99	0.98
Norwegian	750	7.41
Polish	146	1.44
Portuguese	11	0.11
Romanian	36	0.36
Russian	187	1.85
Scandinavian	73	0.72
Scotch-Irish	381	3.76
Scottish	565	5.58
Serbian	17	0.17
Slavic	14	0.14
Slovak	18	0.18
Swedish	448	4.43
Swiss	94	0.93
Ukrainian	9	0.09
United States or American	380	3.75
Welsh	261	2.58
West Indian, excl. Hispanic:	8	0.08
Jamaican	8	0.08
White:	9,729	96.11
Not Hispanic (9,308)	9,551	94.35
Hispanic (168)	178	1.76
Yugoslavian	29	0.29

Walla Walla

Place Type: City
County: Walla Walla
Population: 29,686

Ancestry/Race	Number	%
African American/Black:	894	3.01
Not Hispanic (727)	833	2.81
Hispanic (38)	61	0.21
African, sub-Saharan:	43	0.14
African	35	0.12
Ethiopian	8	0.03
Alaska Native tribes, specified:	25	0.08
Alaska Athabascan	1	0.00
Aleut (2)	3	0.01
Eskimo (2)	2	0.01
Tlingit-Haida (5)	14	0.05
All other tribes (1)	5	0.02
Alaska Native tribes, not specified	6	0.02
Am. Ind. or Alaska Nat., not spec.	230	0.77
Albanian	10	0.03
American Indian tribes, specified:	317	1.07
Apache (2)	11	0.04
Blackfeet (5)	7	0.02
Cherokee (20)	84	0.28
Cheyenne	5	0.02
Chickasaw (4)	7	0.02
Chippewa (16)	32	0.11
Choctaw (2)	6	0.02
Colville (3)	7	0.02
Comanche	2	0.01
Creek	2	0.01
Crow	1	0.00
Delaware	2	0.01
Iroquois (1)	4	0.01
Latin American Indians (12)	35	0.12
Menominee (1)	2	0.01
Navajo (5)	12	0.04
Osage	2	0.01
Paiute	2	0.01
Potawatomi	5	0.02
Pueblo (1)	3	0.01
Puget Sound Salish (1)	5	0.02
Seminole	2	0.01
Sioux (6)	15	0.05
Yakama (2)	2	0.01
Yuman (1)	2	0.01
All other tribes (49)	60	0.20
American Indian tribes, not spec.	34	0.11
Arab:	28	0.09
Arab/Arabic	12	0.04
Egyptian	9	0.03
Other Arab	7	0.02
Asian:	589	1.98
Cambodian (12)	16	0.05
Chinese, ex. Taiwanese (82)	111	0.37
Filipino (49)	102	0.34
Indian (22)	34	0.11
Indonesian	7	0.02
Japanese (42)	97	0.33
Korean (41)	67	0.23
Laotian (40)	48	0.16
Malaysian (1)	1	0.00
Pakistani (1)	1	0.00
Taiwanese (1)	2	0.01
Thai (5)	14	0.05
Vietnamese (37)	42	0.14
Other Asian, specified (2)	6	0.02
Other Asian, not specified (26)	41	0.14
Austrian	108	0.36
Basque	8	0.03
British	68	0.23
Bulgarian	27	0.09
Canadian	25	0.08
Croatian	60	0.20
Czech	31	0.10
Czechoslovakian	144	0.48
Danish	419	1.41
Dutch	539	1.81
English	3,556	11.94
European	296	0.99
Finnish	129	0.43
French, except Basque	1,106	3.71
French Canadian	284	0.95
German	5,710	19.17
German Russian	7	0.02
Greek	89	0.30
Hawaii Native/Pacific Islander:	125	0.42
Melanesian: (1)	1	0.00
Fijian (1)	1	0.00
Micronesian: (6)	10	0.03
Other Micronesian (6)	10	0.03
Polynesian: (31)	64	0.22
Native Hawaiian (10)	35	0.12
Samoan (21)	29	0.10
Other Pac. Isl., not spec. (30)	50	0.17
Hispanic or Latino:	5,170	17.42
Central American:	95	0.32
Guatemalan	10	0.03
Honduran	4	0.01
Nicaraguan	8	0.03

Notes: 1. Figures in the "Number" column do not add up to the total population due to: a) Ancestry/Race overlap — e.g. persons can report being both White and Irish, b) persons of Hispanic origin can report being any race, c) persons reporting two ancestries are counted in both categories. 2. Numbers in parentheses indicate the number of persons reporting this ancestry/race alone, not in combination with any other ancestry/race. 3. Refer to the Explanation of Data in the front of the book for more detailed information.

Panamanian	3	0.01
Salvadoran	67	0.23
Other Central American	3	0.01
Cuban	28	0.09
Dominican Republic	2	0.01
Mexican	4,240	14.28
Puerto Rican	67	0.23
South American:	28	0.09
Argentinean	4	0.01
Bolivian	3	0.01
Chilean	3	0.01
Colombian	4	0.01
Ecuadorian	1	0.00
Peruvian	13	0.04
Other Hispanic or Latino	710	2.39
Hungarian	55	0.18
Iranian	7	0.02
Irish	3,076	10.32
Israeli	9	0.03
Italian	1,198	4.02
Latvian	10	0.03
Lithuanian	19	0.06
Luxemburger	19	0.06
Northern European	50	0.17
Norwegian	1,058	3.55
Pennsylvania German	23	0.08
Polish	323	1.08
Portuguese	106	0.36
Romanian	28	0.09
Russian	139	0.47
Scandinavian	120	0.40
Scotch-Irish	646	2.17
Scottish	758	2.54
Slavic	11	0.04
Swedish	674	2.26
Swiss	131	0.44
Ukrainian	41	0.14
United States or American	1,314	4.41
Welsh	261	0.88
West Indian, excl. Hispanic:	10	0.03
West Indian	10	0.03
White:	25,622	86.31
Not Hispanic (22,458)	22,963	77.35
Hispanic (2,417)	2,659	8.96
Yugoslavian	15	0.05

Wenatchee

Place Type: City
County: Chelan
Population: 27,856

Ancestry/Race	Number	%
African American/Black:	169	0.61
Not Hispanic (73)	123	0.44
Hispanic (36)	46	0.17
African, sub-Saharan:	27	0.10
African	27	0.10
Alaska Native tribes, specified:	15	0.05
Alaska Athabascan	1	0.00
Aleut (1)	3	0.01
Eskimo (5)	5	0.02
Tlingit-Haida (2)	5	0.02
All other tribes	1	0.00
Am. Ind. or Alaska Nat., not spec.	152	0.55
American Indian tribes, specified:	345	1.24
Apache (4)	6	0.02
Blackfeet (6)	10	0.04
Cherokee (24)	71	0.25
Cheyenne (1)	2	0.01
Chippewa (23)	28	0.10
Choctaw (3)	6	0.02
Colville (35)	46	0.17
Cree (2)	2	0.01
Creek (1)	1	0.00
Delaware (1)	2	0.01
Iroquois (1)	2	0.01
Latin American Indians (29)	44	0.16
Navajo (6)	6	0.02
Ottawa	1	0.00
Paiute (4)	4	0.01
Pima (1)	1	0.00
Potawatomi	1	0.00
Pueblo (1)	2	0.01
Puget Sound Salish (8)	14	0.05
Seminole	4	0.01
Sioux (12)	22	0.08
Ute (2)	2	0.01
Yakama (5)	8	0.03
Yuman (1)	1	0.00
All other tribes (30)	59	0.21
American Indian tribes, not spec.	28	0.10
Arab:	44	0.16
Arab/Arabic	12	0.04
Lebanese	32	0.11
Armenian	7	0.02
Asian:	432	1.55
Cambodian (18)	30	0.11
Chinese, ex. Taiwanese (38)	56	0.20
Filipino (26)	66	0.24
Indian (24)	35	0.13
Japanese (48)	99	0.36
Korean (51)	63	0.23
Laotian (1)	1	0.00
Pakistani (2)	3	0.01
Taiwanese	5	0.02
Thai (15)	18	0.06
Vietnamese (32)	38	0.14
Other Asian, specified	2	0.01
Other Asian, not specified (2)	16	0.06
Australian	25	0.09
Austrian	51	0.18
Basque	2	0.01
Belgian	32	0.11
British	104	0.37
Bulgarian	5	0.02
Canadian	95	0.34
Celtic	5	0.02
Croatian	37	0.13
Czech	76	0.27
Czechoslovakian	43	0.15
Danish	419	1.49
Dutch	593	2.11
Eastern European	38	0.14
English	3,265	11.62
European	424	1.51
Finnish	16	0.06
French, except Basque	801	2.85
French Canadian	213	0.76
German	4,831	17.19
German Russian	10	0.04
Greek	29	0.10
Hawaii Native/Pacific Islander:	67	0.24
Melanesian:	2	0.01
Fijian	2	0.01
Micronesian: (20)	23	0.08
Guamanian/Chamorro (16)	19	0.07
Other Micronesian (4)	4	0.01
Polynesian: (11)	31	0.11
Native Hawaiian (9)	27	0.10
Samoan (2)	4	0.01
Other Pac. Isl., specified	1	0.00
Other Pac. Isl., not spec. (5)	10	0.04
Hispanic or Latino:	5,996	21.52
Central American:	150	0.54
Costa Rican	7	0.03
Guatemalan	33	0.12
Honduran	6	0.02
Nicaraguan	1	0.00
Panamanian	7	0.03
Salvadoran	96	0.34
Cuban	16	0.06
Mexican	5,071	18.20
Puerto Rican	33	0.12
South American:	28	0.10
Argentinean	2	0.01
Chilean	2	0.01
Colombian	1	0.00
Ecuadorian	1	0.00
Peruvian	13	0.05
Venezuelan	8	0.03
Other South American	1	0.00
Other Hispanic or Latino	698	2.51
Hungarian	103	0.37
Icelander	9	0.03
Irish	2,638	9.39
Italian	667	2.37
Lithuanian	8	0.03
Northern European	68	0.24
Norwegian	1,175	4.18
Pennsylvania German	30	0.11
Polish	229	0.82
Portuguese	8	0.03
Romanian	11	0.04
Russian	49	0.17
Scandinavian	151	0.54
Scotch-Irish	629	2.24
Scottish	810	2.88
Slovene	7	0.02
Swedish	886	3.15
Swiss	122	0.43
Ukrainian	41	0.15
United States or American	2,091	7.44
Welsh	259	0.92
West Indian, excl. Hispanic:	9	0.03
Dutch West Indian	9	0.03
White:	23,181	83.22
Not Hispanic (20,815)	21,204	76.12
Hispanic (1,728)	1,977	7.10
Yugoslavian	45	0.16

West Lake Stevens

Place Type: Census Designated Place
County: Snohomish
Population: 18,071

Ancestry/Race	Number	%
African American/Black:	279	1.54
Not Hispanic (178)	261	1.44
Hispanic (9)	18	0.10
African, sub-Saharan:	12	0.07
Nigerian	12	0.07
Alaska Native tribes, specified:	34	0.19
Alaska Athabascan	4	0.02
Aleut (3)	7	0.04
Eskimo (5)	5	0.03
Tlingit-Haida (11)	16	0.09
All other tribes (2)	2	0.01
Alaska Native tribes, not specified	1	0.01
Am. Ind. or Alaska Nat., not spec.	91	0.50
American Indian tribes, specified:	188	1.04
Apache (5)	7	0.04
Blackfeet (2)	6	0.03
Cherokee (13)	48	0.27
Chippewa (10)	17	0.09
Choctaw (1)	2	0.01
Colville (4)	4	0.02
Cree (1)	4	0.02
Creek (8)	9	0.05
Iroquois	2	0.01
Kiowa	1	0.01
Latin American Indians (1)	4	0.02
Lumbee	3	0.02
Paiute (3)	4	0.02
Potawatomi	1	0.01
Puget Sound Salish (20)	32	0.18
Seminole	2	0.01
Sioux (3)	9	0.05
Yaqui (1)	1	0.01
All other tribes (10)	32	0.18
American Indian tribes, not spec.	23	0.13
Arab:	56	0.31
Arab/Arabic	28	0.16
Egyptian	8	0.04
Lebanese	20	0.11
Asian:	576	3.19
Cambodian (20)	23	0.13
Chinese, ex. Taiwanese (39)	73	0.40
Filipino (89)	163	0.90

Notes: 1. Figures in the "Number" column do not add up to the total population due to: a) Ancestry/Race overlap — e.g. persons can report being both White and Irish, b) persons of Hispanic origin can report being any race, c) persons reporting two ancestries are counted in both categories. 2. Numbers in parentheses indicate the number of persons reporting this ancestry/race alone, not in combination with any other ancestry/race. 3. Refer to the Explanation of Data in the front of the book for more detailed information.

Ancestry/Race	Number	%
Indian (8)	8	0.04
Indonesian (1)	5	0.03
Japanese (46)	93	0.51
Korean (27)	43	0.24
Laotian (29)	38	0.21
Malaysian (1)	1	0.01
Pakistani (3)	3	0.02
Taiwanese (1)	1	0.01
Thai (3)	7	0.04
Vietnamese (58)	79	0.44
Other Asian, specified (5)	8	0.04
Other Asian, not specified (13)	31	0.17
Austrian	47	0.26
Belgian	103	0.58
British	30	0.17
Canadian	25	0.14
Celtic	17	0.10
Croatian	22	0.12
Czech	116	0.65
Czechoslovakian	31	0.17
Danish	301	1.68
Dutch	478	2.67
English	1,944	10.88
European	345	1.93
Finnish	107	0.60
French, except Basque	600	3.36
French Canadian	263	1.47
German	3,947	22.08
Greek	147	0.82
Hawaii Native/Pacific Islander:	97	0.54
Micronesian: (3)	13	0.07
Guamanian/Chamorro (2)	7	0.04
Other Micronesian (1)	6	0.03
Polynesian: (27)	71	0.39
Native Hawaiian (12)	45	0.25
Samoan (15)	24	0.13
Tongan	1	0.01
Other Polynesian	1	0.01
Other Pac. Isl., specified	1	0.01
Other Pac. Isl., not spec.	12	0.07
Hispanic or Latino:	794	4.39
Central American:	25	0.14
Costa Rican	3	0.02
Honduran	6	0.03
Nicaraguan	3	0.02
Panamanian	7	0.04
Salvadoran	6	0.03
Cuban	15	0.08
Mexican	537	2.97
Puerto Rican	53	0.29
South American:	7	0.04
Argentinean	4	0.02
Bolivian	1	0.01
Peruvian	2	0.01
Other Hispanic or Latino	157	0.87
Hungarian	52	0.29
Icelander	65	0.36
Irish	2,266	12.68
Italian	835	4.67
Lithuanian	8	0.04
Northern European	15	0.08
Norwegian	1,932	10.81
Pennsylvania German	32	0.18
Polish	518	2.90
Portuguese	89	0.50
Romanian	6	0.03
Russian	148	0.83
Scandinavian	139	0.78
Scotch-Irish	331	1.85
Scottish	450	2.52
Slovak	25	0.14
Swedish	775	4.34
Swiss	50	0.28
Ukrainian	85	0.48
United States or American	1,388	7.77
Welsh	169	0.95
West Indian, excl. Hispanic:	13	0.07
Jamaican	13	0.07
White:	16,964	93.87
Not Hispanic (16,053)	16,479	91.19
Hispanic (394)	485	2.68
Yugoslavian	28	0.16

West Valley

Place Type: Census Designated Place
County: Yakima
Population: 10,433

Ancestry/Race	Number	%
African American/Black:	139	1.33
Not Hispanic (80)	120	1.15
Hispanic (6)	19	0.18
African, sub-Saharan:	4	0.04
African	4	0.04
Alaska Native tribes, specified:	13	0.12
Aleut	2	0.02
Eskimo (1)	1	0.01
Tlingit-Haida (3)	7	0.07
All other tribes	3	0.03
Alaska Native tribes, not specified	2	0.02
Am. Ind. or Alaska Nat., not spec.	37	0.35
American Indian tribes, specified:	124	1.19
Apache	2	0.02
Blackfeet (1)	1	0.01
Cherokee (4)	26	0.25
Chickasaw (2)	2	0.02
Chippewa (3)	4	0.04
Colville (2)	2	0.02
Creek (6)	6	0.06
Iroquois (5)	7	0.07
Latin American Indians	1	0.01
Navajo (2)	3	0.03
Osage	1	0.01
Puget Sound Salish (3)	5	0.05
Sioux (5)	6	0.06
Yakama (20)	36	0.35
All other tribes (18)	22	0.21
American Indian tribes, not spec.	17	0.16
Arab:	21	0.21
Syrian	21	0.21
Armenian	11	0.11
Asian:	298	2.86
Chinese, ex. Taiwanese (27)	33	0.32
Filipino (34)	65	0.62
Indian (18)	31	0.30
Indonesian (1)	1	0.01
Japanese (14)	35	0.34
Korean (92)	98	0.94
Malaysian	2	0.02
Pakistani (7)	8	0.08
Thai (2)	3	0.03
Vietnamese (15)	18	0.17
Other Asian, specified	1	0.01
Other Asian, not specified (2)	3	0.03
British	11	0.11
Canadian	92	0.91
Croatian	9	0.09
Czech	10	0.10
Czechoslovakian	7	0.07
Danish	111	1.10
Dutch	296	2.94
English	1,156	11.49
European	262	2.60
Finnish	33	0.33
French, except Basque	522	5.19
French Canadian	92	0.91
German	2,559	25.44
Greek	23	0.23
Hawaii Native/Pacific Islander:	18	0.17
Micronesian: (3)	3	0.03
Guamanian/Chamorro (3)	3	0.03
Polynesian: (11)	15	0.14
Native Hawaiian (11)	15	0.14
Hispanic or Latino:	910	8.72
Central American:	9	0.09
Costa Rican	3	0.03
Guatemalan	1	0.01
Panamanian	2	0.02
Salvadoran	3	0.03
Cuban	3	0.03
Mexican	693	6.64
Puerto Rican	28	0.27
South American:	17	0.16
Bolivian	2	0.02
Chilean	1	0.01
Colombian	4	0.04
Peruvian	6	0.06
Other South American	4	0.04
Other Hispanic or Latino	160	1.53
Hungarian	26	0.26
Irish	1,080	10.74
Italian	132	1.31
Northern European	20	0.20
Norwegian	628	6.24
Pennsylvania German	9	0.09
Polish	154	1.53
Portuguese	8	0.08
Romanian	25	0.25
Russian	63	0.63
Scandinavian	77	0.77
Scotch-Irish	326	3.24
Scottish	433	4.30
Slovak	10	0.10
Swedish	429	4.26
Swiss	39	0.39
Ukrainian	37	0.37
United States or American	739	7.35
Welsh	92	0.91
White:	9,587	91.89
Not Hispanic (8,935)	9,113	87.35
Hispanic (413)	474	4.54

White Center

Place Type: Census Designated Place
County: King
Population: 20,975

Ancestry/Race	Number	%
Acadian/Cajun	20	0.10
African American/Black:	1,707	8.14
Not Hispanic (1,304)	1,615	7.70
Hispanic (40)	92	0.44
African, sub-Saharan:	461	2.21
African	86	0.41
Ethiopian	190	0.91
Somalian	185	0.89
Alaska Native tribes, specified:	81	0.39
Alaska Athabascan (3)	5	0.02
Aleut (13)	22	0.10
Eskimo (1)	7	0.03
Tlingit-Haida (25)	42	0.20
All other tribes (1)	5	0.02
Alaska Native tribes, not specified	7	0.03
Am. Ind. or Alaska Nat., not spec.	226	1.08
American Indian tribes, specified:	440	2.10
Apache (2)	8	0.04
Blackfeet (39)	66	0.31
Cherokee (19)	48	0.23
Cheyenne (2)	2	0.01
Chippewa (15)	34	0.16
Choctaw (2)	8	0.04
Colville	4	0.02
Comanche (2)	4	0.02
Cree	1	0.00
Creek (1)	14	0.07
Crow	5	0.02
Delaware (1)	4	0.02
Iroquois	1	0.00
Latin American Indians (15)	21	0.10
Lumbee (2)	2	0.01
Navajo (12)	18	0.09
Paiute	2	0.01
Pima (4)	5	0.02
Potawatomi	1	0.00
Pueblo (1)	1	0.00
Puget Sound Salish (27)	34	0.16
Seminole (3)	5	0.02
Shoshone (4)	8	0.04

Notes: 1. Figures in the "Number" column do not add up to the total population due to: a) Ancestry/Race overlap — e.g. persons can report being both White and Irish, b) persons of Hispanic origin can report being any race, c) persons reporting two ancestries are counted in both categories. 2. Numbers in parentheses indicate the number of persons reporting this ancestry/race alone, not in combination with any other ancestry/race. 3. Refer to the Explanation of Data in the front of the book for more detailed information.

Sioux (11)	21	0.10
Ute	1	0.00
Yakama (2)	3	0.01
All other tribes (72)	119	0.57
American Indian tribes, not spec.	21	0.10
Arab:	72	0.35
Arab/Arabic	47	0.23
Iraqi	6	0.03
Palestinian	7	0.03
Syrian	5	0.02
Other Arab	7	0.03
Asian:	5,009	23.88
Bangladeshi (4)	4	0.02
Cambodian (832)	967	4.61
Chinese, ex. Taiwanese (234)	322	1.54
Filipino (478)	622	2.97
Hmong (22)	27	0.13
Indian (84)	109	0.52
Indonesian (2)	3	0.01
Japanese (87)	134	0.64
Korean (189)	212	1.01
Laotian (110)	135	0.64
Malaysian	3	0.01
Pakistani (2)	6	0.03
Taiwanese (4)	7	0.03
Thai (26)	44	0.21
Vietnamese (2,176)	2,294	10.94
Other Asian, not specified (54)	120	0.57
Australian	37	0.18
Austrian	76	0.36
Belgian	10	0.05
British	53	0.25
Canadian	62	0.30
Croatian	35	0.17
Czech	105	0.50
Czechoslovakian	11	0.05
Danish	143	0.69
Dutch	379	1.82
Eastern European	14	0.07
English	1,691	8.11
European	292	1.40
Finnish	20	0.10
French, except Basque	764	3.66
French Canadian	126	0.60
German	2,142	10.27
Greek	45	0.22
Guyanese	8	0.04
Hawaii Native/Pacific Islander:	668	3.18
Melanesian: (6)	6	0.03
Fijian (6)	6	0.03
Micronesian: (13)	28	0.13
Guamanian/Chamorro (8)	22	0.10
Other Micronesian (5)	6	0.03
Polynesian: (494)	592	2.82
Native Hawaiian (33)	57	0.27
Samoan (380)	438	2.09
Tongan (71)	85	0.41
Other Polynesian (10)	12	0.06
Other Pac. Isl., not spec. (26)	42	0.20
Hispanic or Latino:	2,513	11.98
Central American:	169	0.81
Guatemalan	32	0.15
Honduran	29	0.14
Nicaraguan	9	0.04
Panamanian	1	0.00
Salvadoran	88	0.42
Other Central American	10	0.05
Cuban	4	0.02
Dominican Republic	4	0.02
Mexican	1,811	8.63
Puerto Rican	60	0.29
South American:	59	0.28
Bolivian	1	0.00
Chilean	14	0.07
Colombian	17	0.08
Ecuadorian	1	0.00
Peruvian	24	0.11
Other South American	2	0.01
Other Hispanic or Latino	406	1.94
Hungarian	64	0.31
Iranian	96	0.46
Irish	1,458	6.99
Italian	660	3.17
Latvian	25	0.12
Lithuanian	22	0.11
Norwegian	973	4.67
Pennsylvania German	7	0.03
Polish	344	1.65
Portuguese	30	0.14
Romanian	5	0.02
Russian	79	0.38
Scandinavian	46	0.22
Scotch-Irish	339	1.63
Scottish	412	1.98
Serbian	26	0.12
Slavic	8	0.04
Slovak	7	0.03
Swedish	411	1.97
Swiss	37	0.18
Ukrainian	147	0.71
United States or American	876	4.20
Welsh	132	0.63
West Indian, excl. Hispanic:	27	0.13
Jamaican	27	0.13
White:	12,398	59.11
Not Hispanic (10,785)	11,466	54.67
Hispanic (742)	932	4.44
Yugoslavian	101	0.48

Yakima

Place Type: City
County: Yakima
Population: 71,845

Ancestry/Race	Number	%
African American/Black:	1,916	2.67
Not Hispanic (1,308)	1,660	2.31
Hispanic (125)	256	0.36
African, sub-Saharan:	77	0.11
African	72	0.10
Senegalese	5	0.01
Alaska Native tribes, specified:	47	0.07
Alaska Athabascan (6)	9	0.01
Aleut (1)	4	0.01
Eskimo (6)	11	0.02
Tlingit-Haida (10)	15	0.02
All other tribes (2)	8	0.01
Alaska Native tribes, not specified	12	0.02
Am. Ind. or Alaska Nat., not spec.	617	0.86
Albanian	11	0.02
American Indian tribes, specified:	1,515	2.11
Apache (10)	27	0.04
Blackfeet (93)	149	0.21
Cherokee (62)	184	0.26
Cheyenne (5)	8	0.01
Chickasaw (13)	20	0.03
Chippewa (27)	48	0.07
Choctaw (10)	29	0.04
Colville (35)	48	0.07
Comanche (1)	4	0.01
Cree (2)	6	0.01
Creek (12)	18	0.03
Crow (3)	8	0.01
Delaware	4	0.01
Iroquois (9)	14	0.02
Latin American Indians (85)	129	0.18
Lumbee	4	0.01
Navajo (13)	23	0.03
Osage	5	0.01
Ottawa	1	0.00
Paiute (1)	1	0.00
Pima (14)	15	0.02
Potawatomi (5)	9	0.01
Pueblo (7)	8	0.01
Puget Sound Salish (35)	53	0.07
Seminole (2)	2	0.00
Shoshone (5)	8	0.01
Sioux (31)	52	0.07
Tohono O'Odham (1)	1	0.00
Yakama (314)	390	0.54
Yaqui (2)	6	0.01
All other tribes (149)	241	0.34
American Indian tribes, not spec.	91	0.13
Arab:	75	0.10
Arab/Arabic	30	0.04
Egyptian	21	0.03
Iraqi	5	0.01
Lebanese	13	0.02
Other Arab	6	0.01
Armenian	53	0.07
Asian:	1,297	1.81
Cambodian (1)	1	0.00
Chinese, ex. Taiwanese (172)	228	0.32
Filipino (215)	395	0.55
Indian (91)	131	0.18
Indonesian (1)	1	0.00
Japanese (95)	176	0.24
Korean (132)	160	0.22
Laotian (28)	37	0.05
Malaysian	1	0.00
Pakistani	2	0.00
Sri Lankan (5)	5	0.01
Taiwanese (3)	4	0.01
Thai (10)	17	0.02
Vietnamese (44)	52	0.07
Other Asian, specified	3	0.00
Other Asian, not specified (41)	84	0.12
Australian	6	0.01
Austrian	143	0.20
Basque	76	0.11
Belgian	72	0.10
Brazilian	9	0.01
British	267	0.37
Bulgarian	21	0.03
Canadian	282	0.39
Celtic	35	0.05
Croatian	66	0.09
Czech	176	0.24
Czechoslovakian	71	0.10
Danish	565	0.78
Dutch	1,132	1.57
English	5,673	7.85
European	476	0.66
Finnish	158	0.22
French, except Basque	2,835	3.92
French Canadian	877	1.21
German	11,193	15.48
German Russian	22	0.03
Greek	98	0.14
Hawaii Native/Pacific Islander:	211	0.29
Micronesian: (13)	26	0.04
Guamanian/Chamorro (13)	26	0.04
Polynesian: (63)	121	0.17
Native Hawaiian (33)	63	0.09
Samoan (28)	49	0.07
Tongan (1)	4	0.01
Other Polynesian (1)	5	0.01
Other Pac. Isl., specified	2	0.00
Other Pac. Isl., not spec. (24)	62	0.09
Hispanic or Latino:	24,213	33.70
Central American:	140	0.19
Costa Rican	3	0.00
Guatemalan	16	0.02
Honduran	13	0.02
Nicaraguan	34	0.05
Panamanian	1	0.00
Salvadoran	66	0.09
Other Central American	7	0.01
Cuban	30	0.04
Dominican Republic	9	0.01
Mexican	20,825	28.99
Puerto Rican	116	0.16
South American:	47	0.07
Argentinean	7	0.01
Bolivian	1	0.00
Chilean	4	0.01
Colombian	4	0.01
Ecuadorian	2	0.00
Peruvian	21	0.03

Notes: 1. Figures in the "Number" column do not add up to the total population due to: a) Ancestry/Race overlap — e.g. persons can report being both White and Irish, b) persons of Hispanic origin can report being any race, c) persons reporting two ancestries are counted in both categories. 2. Numbers in parentheses indicate the number of persons reporting this ancestry/race alone, not in combination with any other ancestry/race. 3. Refer to the Explanation of Data in the front of the book for more detailed information.

Venezuelan	5	0.01
Other South American	3	0.00
Other Hispanic or Latino	3,046	4.24
Hungarian	123	0.17
Icelander	28	0.04
Irish	6,177	8.54
Israeli	8	0.01
Italian	1,098	1.52
Latvian	20	0.03
Lithuanian	16	0.02
Luxemburger	17	0.02
Northern European	73	0.10
Norwegian	2,176	3.01
Pennsylvania German	20	0.03
Polish	405	0.56
Portuguese	136	0.19
Romanian	16	0.02
Russian	329	0.46
Scandinavian	195	0.27
Scotch-Irish	1,154	1.60
Scottish	1,396	1.93
Slavic	26	0.04
Slovak	32	0.04
Slovene	6	0.01
Swedish	1,370	1.90
Swiss	210	0.29
Ukrainian	156	0.22
United States or American	3,671	5.08
Welsh	458	0.63
West Indian, excl. Hispanic:	47	0.07
Dutch West Indian	17	0.02
Jamaican	23	0.03
West Indian	7	0.01
White:	51,854	72.17
Not Hispanic (42,928)	44,147	61.45
Hispanic (6,481)	7,707	10.73
Yugoslavian	77	0.11

Beckley

Place Type: City
County: Raleigh
Population: 17,254

Ancestry/Race	Number	%
Afghan	50	0.29
African American/Black:	4,066	23.57
Not Hispanic (3,932)	4,044	23.44
Hispanic (17)	22	0.13
African, sub-Saharan:	74	0.42
African	67	0.38
Zimbabwean	7	0.04
Am. Ind. or Alaska Nat., not spec.	43	0.25
American Indian tribes, specified:	63	0.37
Apache (1)	1	0.01
Blackfeet (2)	10	0.06
Cherokee (2)	27	0.16
Chippewa (2)	3	0.02
Comanche	1	0.01
Creek	1	0.01
Iroquois	3	0.02
Lumbee (1)	2	0.01
Navajo (1)	3	0.02
Sioux (5)	8	0.05
All other tribes	4	0.02
American Indian tribes, not spec.	9	0.05
Arab:	135	0.77
Arab/Arabic	5	0.03
Lebanese	130	0.75
Asian:	381	2.21
Bangladeshi (7)	7	0.04
Chinese, ex. Taiwanese (32)	33	0.19
Filipino (74)	87	0.50
Indian (127)	138	0.80
Indonesian	2	0.01
Japanese (9)	16	0.09
Korean (16)	23	0.13
Laotian (1)	1	0.01
Pakistani (21)	25	0.14
Sri Lankan (4)	4	0.02
Taiwanese (2)	2	0.01
Thai (1)	2	0.01
Vietnamese (17)	17	0.10
Other Asian, specified (3)	3	0.02
Other Asian, not specified (12)	21	0.12
Austrian	28	0.16
Belgian	13	0.07
British	59	0.34
Canadian	24	0.14
Croatian	7	0.04
Czech	42	0.24
Czechoslovakian	13	0.07
Danish	11	0.06
Dutch	297	1.70
English	1,478	8.48
European	151	0.87
Finnish	13	0.07
French, except Basque	158	0.91
French Canadian	16	0.09
German	1,568	9.00
Greek	15	0.09
Hawaii Native/Pacific Islander:	10	0.06
Melanesian:	1	0.01
Fijian	1	0.01
Polynesian: (1)	6	0.03
Native Hawaiian	3	0.02
Samoan (1)	2	0.01
Tongan	1	0.01
Other Pac. Isl., not spec. (2)	3	0.02
Hispanic or Latino:	128	0.74
Central American:	3	0.02
Honduran	1	0.01
Panamanian	1	0.01
Salvadoran	1	0.01
Cuban	5	0.03
Mexican	37	0.21
Puerto Rican	28	0.16
South American:	8	0.05
Argentinean	1	0.01
Colombian	4	0.02
Ecuadorian	1	0.01
Venezuelan	2	0.01
Other Hispanic or Latino	47	0.27
Hungarian	86	0.49
Irish	1,427	8.19
Italian	655	3.76
Norwegian	20	0.11
Polish	232	1.33
Russian	26	0.15
Scandinavian	16	0.09
Scotch-Irish	301	1.73
Scottish	235	1.35
Serbian	5	0.03
Slavic	1	0.01
Slovak	20	0.11
Swedish	69	0.40
Swiss	5	0.03
Ukrainian	6	0.03
United States or American	2,643	15.17
Welsh	132	0.76
White:	12,872	74.60
Not Hispanic (12,635)	12,793	74.15
Hispanic (70)	79	0.46

Bluefield

Place Type: City
County: Mercer
Population: 11,451

Ancestry/Race	Number	%
African American/Black:	2,594	22.65
Not Hispanic (2,529)	2,587	22.59
Hispanic (6)	7	0.06
African, sub-Saharan:	130	1.12
African	123	1.06
Nigerian	7	0.06
Am. Ind. or Alaska Nat., not spec.	28	0.24
American Indian tribes, specified:	33	0.29
Blackfeet	2	0.02
Cherokee (4)	17	0.15
Creek	1	0.01
Delaware	3	0.03
Iroquois	5	0.04
Pueblo (3)	3	0.03
Sioux	1	0.01
All other tribes (1)	1	0.01
American Indian tribes, not spec.	3	0.03
Arab:	20	0.17
Arab/Arabic	13	0.11
Egyptian	7	0.06
Asian:	93	0.81
Chinese, ex. Taiwanese (5)	6	0.05
Filipino (4)	10	0.09
Indian (30)	34	0.30
Japanese (3)	4	0.03
Korean (2)	2	0.02
Pakistani (3)	3	0.03
Vietnamese (11)	11	0.10
Other Asian, not specified (6)	23	0.20
Austrian	11	0.09
Belgian	9	0.08
British	40	0.35
Canadian	23	0.20
Celtic	6	0.05
Croatian	11	0.09
Czech	7	0.06
Dutch	222	1.92
English	1,259	10.87
European	50	0.43
French, except Basque	239	2.06
German	1,272	10.98
Greek	16	0.14
Hawaii Native/Pacific Islander:	1	0.01
Other Pac. Isl., not spec. (1)	1	0.01
Hispanic or Latino:	60	0.52
Cuban	10	0.09
Mexican	22	0.19
Puerto Rican	10	0.09
Other Hispanic or Latino	18	0.16
Hungarian	75	0.65
Iranian	8	0.07
Irish	1,140	9.84
Italian	317	2.74
Lithuanian	23	0.20
Norwegian	20	0.17
Polish	78	0.67
Portuguese	11	0.09
Russian	28	0.24
Scotch-Irish	253	2.18
Scottish	258	2.23
Slovak	28	0.24
Swedish	16	0.14
Swiss	5	0.04
United States or American	1,842	15.90
Welsh	29	0.25
White:	8,800	76.85
Not Hispanic (8,645)	8,758	76.48
Hispanic (39)	42	0.37

Charleston

Place Type: City
County: Kanawha
Population: 53,421

Ancestry/Race	Number	%
African American/Black:	8,656	16.20
Not Hispanic (7,998)	8,593	16.09
Hispanic (50)	63	0.12
African, sub-Saharan:	578	1.09
African	533	1.00
Ethiopian	19	0.04
Ghanian	4	0.01
Nigerian	17	0.03
Other sub-Saharan African	5	0.01
Am. Ind. or Alaska Nat., not spec.	178	0.33
American Indian tribes, specified:	264	0.49
Apache (4)	11	0.02
Blackfeet (4)	20	0.04

Notes: 1. Figures in the "Number" column do not add up to the total population due to: a) Ancestry/Race overlap — e.g. persons can report being both White and Irish, b) persons of Hispanic origin can report being any race, c) persons reporting two ancestries are counted in both categories. 2. Numbers in parentheses indicate the number of persons reporting this ancestry/race alone, not in combination with any other ancestry/race. 3. Refer to the Explanation of Data in the front of the book for more detailed information.

Cherokee (48)	172	0.32
Cheyenne (1)	1	0.00
Chippewa (1)	10	0.02
Choctaw (1)	6	0.01
Comanche	1	0.00
Creek (1)	1	0.00
Crow (1)	3	0.01
Iroquois (1)	5	0.01
Latin American Indians (1)	3	0.01
Menominee (1)	1	0.00
Navajo	2	0.00
Osage	3	0.01
Ottawa (2)	2	0.00
Paiute	1	0.00
Potawatomi	1	0.00
Seminole	1	0.00
Sioux	7	0.01
All other tribes (5)	13	0.02
American Indian tribes, not spec.	33	0.06
Arab:	1,104	2.08
Arab/Arabic	43	0.08
Egyptian	32	0.06
Lebanese	805	1.51
Palestinian	7	0.01
Syrian	158	0.30
Other Arab	59	0.11
Armenian	40	0.08
Asian:	1,164	2.18
Bangladeshi (10)	12	0.02
Chinese, ex. Taiwanese (146)	172	0.32
Filipino (139)	177	0.33
Indian (393)	432	0.81
Indonesian (3)	6	0.01
Japanese (32)	58	0.11
Korean (66)	76	0.14
Laotian (6)	10	0.02
Malaysian	4	0.01
Pakistani (64)	65	0.12
Sri Lankan (4)	4	0.01
Taiwanese (11)	12	0.02
Thai (22)	29	0.05
Vietnamese (62)	67	0.13
Other Asian, specified	1	0.00
Other Asian, not specified (10)	39	0.07
Austrian	64	0.12
Belgian	78	0.15
British	286	0.54
Bulgarian	5	0.01
Canadian	54	0.10
Celtic	34	0.06
Croatian	58	0.11
Cypriot	21	0.04
Czech	62	0.12
Czechoslovakian	88	0.17
Danish	99	0.19
Dutch	626	1.18
Eastern European	33	0.06
English	6,208	11.67
Estonian	8	0.02
European	580	1.09
Finnish	14	0.03
French, except Basque	958	1.80
French Canadian	126	0.24
German	6,603	12.41
Greek	100	0.19
Hawaii Native/Pacific Islander:	32	0.06
Melanesian: (1)	1	0.00
Other Melanesian (1)	1	0.00
Micronesian: (2)	2	0.00
Guamanian/Chamorro (2)	2	0.00
Polynesian: (7)	14	0.03
Native Hawaiian (4)	9	0.02
Samoan (2)	3	0.01
Other Polynesian (1)	2	0.00
Other Pac. Isl., specified	1	0.00
Other Pac. Isl., not spec. (6)	14	0.03
Hispanic or Latino:	432	0.81
Central American:	15	0.03
Guatemalan	4	0.01
Honduran	2	0.00
Nicaraguan	5	0.01
Panamanian	3	0.01
Salvadoran	1	0.00
Cuban	37	0.07
Dominican Republic	9	0.02
Mexican	137	0.26
Puerto Rican	83	0.16
South American:	38	0.07
Argentinean	9	0.02
Colombian	14	0.03
Ecuadorian	3	0.01
Peruvian	10	0.02
Venezuelan	2	0.00
Other Hispanic or Latino	113	0.21
Hungarian	185	0.35
Iranian	80	0.15
Irish	5,650	10.62
Israeli	7	0.01
Italian	2,094	3.94
Lithuanian	115	0.22
Luxemburger	11	0.02
Northern European	6	0.01
Norwegian	184	0.35
Pennsylvania German	21	0.04
Polish	570	1.07
Portuguese	15	0.03
Romanian	33	0.06
Russian	133	0.25
Scandinavian	67	0.13
Scotch-Irish	1,581	2.97
Scottish	1,119	2.10
Serbian	17	0.03
Slavic	25	0.05
Slovak	74	0.14
Slovene	14	0.03
Swedish	159	0.30
Swiss	146	0.27
Turkish	51	0.10
Ukrainian	87	0.16
United States or American	6,105	11.48
Welsh	612	1.15
West Indian, excl. Hispanic:	63	0.12
Haitian	5	0.01
Jamaican	32	0.06
Trinidadian and Tobagonian	5	0.01
West Indian	21	0.04
White:	43,958	82.29
Not Hispanic (42,810)	43,669	81.75
Hispanic (262)	289	0.54
Yugoslavian	27	0.05

Clarksburg

Place Type: City
County: Harrison
Population: 16,743

Ancestry/Race	Number	%
African American/Black:	735	4.39
Not Hispanic (641)	733	4.38
Hispanic	2	0.01
African, sub-Saharan:	24	0.15
African	24	0.15
Alaska Native tribes, specified:	2	0.01
Alaska Athabascan (1)	1	0.01
Tlingit-Haida	1	0.01
Am. Ind. or Alaska Nat., not spec.	48	0.29
American Indian tribes, specified:	40	0.24
Apache	1	0.01
Cherokee (4)	17	0.10
Chickasaw	1	0.01
Chippewa	2	0.01
Choctaw	1	0.01
Creek	3	0.02
Crow	1	0.01
Iroquois (1)	1	0.01
Latin American Indians (1)	1	0.01
Lumbee (1)	1	0.01
Ottawa	2	0.01
Potawatomi	1	0.01
Seminole	1	0.01
Sioux (1)	1	0.01
Yuman (1)	1	0.01
All other tribes (1)	5	0.03
American Indian tribes, not spec.	6	0.04
Arab:	69	0.42
Lebanese	52	0.31
Syrian	17	0.10
Asian:	90	0.54
Chinese, ex. Taiwanese (8)	8	0.05
Filipino (11)	16	0.10
Indian (15)	23	0.14
Japanese (3)	6	0.04
Korean (12)	19	0.11
Taiwanese	1	0.01
Thai (5)	6	0.04
Vietnamese (2)	4	0.02
Other Asian, not specified (2)	7	0.04
Belgian	59	0.36
British	56	0.34
Canadian	4	0.02
Celtic	9	0.05
Croatian	23	0.14
Czechoslovakian	51	0.31
Danish	2	0.01
Dutch	320	1.93
English	1,808	10.93
European	35	0.21
Finnish	27	0.16
French, except Basque	270	1.63
French Canadian	28	0.17
German	2,593	15.68
Greek	23	0.14
Hawaii Native/Pacific Islander:	14	0.08
Micronesian: (1)	3	0.02
Guamanian/Chamorro	2	0.01
Other Micronesian (1)	1	0.01
Polynesian: (7)	8	0.05
Samoan (7)	8	0.05
Other Pac. Isl., not spec.	3	0.02
Hispanic or Latino:	177	1.06
Central American:	3	0.02
Guatemalan	3	0.02
Cuban	6	0.04
Mexican	32	0.19
Puerto Rican	23	0.14
South American:	2	0.01
Paraguayan	1	0.01
Venezuelan	1	0.01
Other Hispanic or Latino	111	0.66
Hungarian	61	0.37
Irish	2,359	14.26
Italian	2,394	14.47
Northern European	11	0.07
Norwegian	8	0.05
Pennsylvania German	6	0.04
Polish	321	1.94
Russian	36	0.22
Scotch-Irish	452	2.73
Scottish	172	1.04
Serbian	6	0.04
Slavic	7	0.04
Slovak	120	0.73
Slovene	22	0.13
Swedish	21	0.13
Swiss	64	0.39
Ukrainian	2	0.01
United States or American	3,079	18.61
Welsh	157	0.95
White:	15,930	95.14
Not Hispanic (15,584)	15,778	94.24
Hispanic (131)	152	0.91

Cross Lanes

Place Type: Census Designated Place
County: Kanawha
Population: 10,353

Ancestry/Race	Number	%

Notes: 1. Figures in the "Number" column do not add up to the total population due to: a) Ancestry/Race overlap — e.g. persons can report being both White and Irish, b) persons of Hispanic origin can report being any race, c) persons reporting two ancestries are counted in both categories. 2. Numbers in parentheses indicate the number of persons reporting this ancestry/race alone, not in combination with any other ancestry/race. 3. Refer to the Explanation of Data in the front of the book for more detailed information.

Ancestry/Race	Number	%
African American/Black:	444	4.29
Not Hispanic (397)	443	4.28
Hispanic (1)	1	0.01
African, sub-Saharan:	30	0.30
African	30	0.30
Am. Ind. or Alaska Nat., not spec.	18	0.17
American Indian tribes, specified:	41	0.40
Apache	1	0.01
Blackfeet (1)	2	0.02
Cherokee (5)	19	0.18
Choctaw	1	0.01
Potawatomi (1)	1	0.01
Seminole	1	0.01
Shoshone	1	0.01
Sioux	2	0.02
All other tribes (11)	13	0.13
Arab:	46	0.46
Lebanese	46	0.46
Asian:	143	1.38
Chinese, ex. Taiwanese (28)	28	0.27
Filipino (20)	23	0.22
Indian (45)	47	0.45
Japanese (4)	6	0.06
Korean (6)	7	0.07
Laotian (2)	2	0.02
Pakistani (6)	6	0.06
Sri Lankan (4)	4	0.04
Taiwanese	2	0.02
Thai (3)	3	0.03
Vietnamese (10)	10	0.10
Other Asian, not specified	5	0.05
Austrian	12	0.12
Belgian	8	0.08
British	35	0.35
Czech	76	0.75
Czechoslovakian	12	0.12
Danish	14	0.14
Dutch	355	3.52
English	1,506	14.92
European	25	0.25
Finnish	11	0.11
French, except Basque	118	1.17
French Canadian	21	0.21
German	1,527	15.13
Greek	53	0.53
Hawaii Native/Pacific Islander:	2	0.02
Polynesian: (2)	2	0.02
Samoan (1)	1	0.01
Other Polynesian (1)	1	0.01
Hispanic or Latino:	59	0.57
Central American:	4	0.04
Salvadoran	4	0.04
Cuban	4	0.04
Mexican	25	0.24
Puerto Rican	10	0.10
South American:	4	0.04
Peruvian	3	0.03
Venezuelan	1	0.01
Other Hispanic or Latino	12	0.12
Hungarian	16	0.16
Irish	1,347	13.35
Italian	352	3.49
Lithuanian	35	0.35
Norwegian	95	0.94
Polish	165	1.64
Russian	14	0.14
Scotch-Irish	309	3.06
Scottish	278	2.75
Slovak	8	0.08
Swedish	13	0.13
Swiss	25	0.25
United States or American	1,263	12.52
Welsh	73	0.72
White:	9,778	94.45
Not Hispanic (9,653)	9,731	93.99
Hispanic (41)	47	0.45

Fairmont

Place Type: City
County: Marion
Population: 19,097

Ancestry/Race	Number	%
African American/Black:	1,534	8.03
Not Hispanic (1,381)	1,528	8.00
Hispanic (5)	6	0.03
African, sub-Saharan:	57	0.30
African	57	0.30
Am. Ind. or Alaska Nat., not spec.	56	0.29
American Indian tribes, specified:	74	0.39
Blackfeet (1)	5	0.03
Cherokee (14)	47	0.25
Cheyenne	1	0.01
Chippewa (2)	2	0.01
Osage (2)	2	0.01
Potawatomi (1)	1	0.01
Sioux (7)	10	0.05
All other tribes (1)	6	0.03
American Indian tribes, not spec.	17	0.09
Arab:	83	0.43
Egyptian	32	0.17
Lebanese	18	0.09
Syrian	33	0.17
Asian:	159	0.83
Chinese, ex. Taiwanese (14)	20	0.10
Filipino (8)	13	0.07
Indian (23)	31	0.16
Japanese (59)	66	0.35
Korean (5)	10	0.05
Malaysian (1)	1	0.01
Vietnamese	1	0.01
Other Asian, specified (6)	11	0.06
Other Asian, not specified (1)	6	0.03
Austrian	17	0.09
Belgian	17	0.09
British	39	0.20
Canadian	5	0.03
Croatian	41	0.21
Czech	34	0.18
Czechoslovakian	23	0.12
Danish	5	0.03
Dutch	599	3.13
Eastern European	26	0.14
English	1,951	10.18
European	126	0.66
French, except Basque	250	1.30
French Canadian	8	0.04
German	3,131	16.34
Greek	44	0.23
Hawaii Native/Pacific Islander:	9	0.05
Polynesian: (3)	3	0.02
Native Hawaiian (1)	1	0.01
Samoan (2)	2	0.01
Other Pac. Isl., specified	3	0.02
Other Pac. Isl., not spec. (1)	3	0.02
Hispanic or Latino:	157	0.82
Central American:	2	0.01
Costa Rican	1	0.01
Salvadoran	1	0.01
Cuban	5	0.03
Mexican	59	0.31
Puerto Rican	21	0.11
South American:	10	0.05
Colombian	1	0.01
Paraguayan	1	0.01
Peruvian	1	0.01
Venezuelan	4	0.02
Other South American	3	0.02
Other Hispanic or Latino	60	0.31
Hungarian	165	0.86
Irish	2,606	13.60
Italian	2,554	13.33
Lithuanian	18	0.09
Norwegian	21	0.11
Pennsylvania German	16	0.08
Polish	533	2.78
Portuguese	16	0.08
Romanian	7	0.04
Russian	95	0.50
Scotch-Irish	431	2.25
Scottish	349	1.82
Slavic	19	0.10
Slovak	53	0.28
Slovene	7	0.04
Swedish	44	0.23
Swiss	14	0.07
Ukrainian	14	0.07
United States or American	1,839	9.60
Welsh	202	1.05
West Indian, excl. Hispanic:	32	0.17
Jamaican	32	0.17
White:	17,478	91.52
Not Hispanic (17,090)	17,346	90.83
Hispanic (127)	132	0.69
Yugoslavian	26	0.14

Huntington

Place Type: City
County: Cabell
Population: 51,475

Ancestry/Race	Number	%
African American/Black:	4,230	8.22
Not Hispanic (3,829)	4,191	8.14
Hispanic (29)	39	0.08
African, sub-Saharan:	70	0.14
African	64	0.12
Kenyan	6	0.01
Am. Ind. or Alaska Nat., not spec.	146	0.28
American Indian tribes, specified:	211	0.41
Apache (2)	6	0.01
Blackfeet	7	0.01
Cherokee (28)	141	0.27
Cheyenne	1	0.00
Chickasaw	3	0.01
Choctaw (2)	7	0.01
Comanche (1)	1	0.00
Cree (1)	1	0.00
Creek (1)	1	0.00
Iroquois (2)	6	0.01
Latin American Indians (1)	7	0.01
Lumbee	2	0.00
Paiute	1	0.00
Pima (1)	1	0.00
Pueblo (1)	2	0.00
Seminole (1)	1	0.00
Sioux (3)	6	0.01
All other tribes (9)	17	0.03
American Indian tribes, not spec.	39	0.08
Arab:	245	0.48
Egyptian	5	0.01
Lebanese	197	0.38
Moroccan	6	0.01
Syrian	30	0.06
Other Arab	7	0.01
Armenian	6	0.01
Asian:	558	1.08
Chinese, ex. Taiwanese (123)	129	0.25
Filipino (53)	88	0.17
Indian (108)	132	0.26
Indonesian (1)	3	0.01
Japanese (36)	52	0.10
Korean (36)	58	0.11
Malaysian (2)	2	0.00
Pakistani (16)	17	0.03
Taiwanese (4)	5	0.01
Thai (14)	18	0.03
Vietnamese (17)	17	0.03
Other Asian, specified	1	0.00
Other Asian, not specified (12)	36	0.07
Austrian	17	0.03
British	200	0.39
Bulgarian	11	0.02
Canadian	26	0.05
Croatian	13	0.03

Notes: 1. Figures in the "Number" column do not add up to the total population due to: a) Ancestry/Race overlap — e.g. persons can report being both White and Irish, b) persons of Hispanic origin can report being any race, c) persons reporting two ancestries are counted in both categories. 2. Numbers in parentheses indicate the number of persons reporting this ancestry/race alone, not in combination with any other ancestry/race. 3. Refer to the Explanation of Data in the front of the book for more detailed information.

Ancestry/Race	Number	%
Czech	37	0.07
Czechoslovakian	44	0.09
Danish	60	0.12
Dutch	950	1.84
Eastern European	9	0.02
English	5,628	10.92
European	427	0.83
Finnish	5	0.01
French, except Basque	825	1.60
French Canadian	70	0.14
German	5,670	11.00
Greek	270	0.52
Hawaii Native/Pacific Islander:	50	0.10
Micronesian: (11)	15	0.03
Guamanian/Chamorro (6)	9	0.02
Other Micronesian (5)	6	0.01
Polynesian: (10)	21	0.04
Native Hawaiian (4)	8	0.02
Samoan (3)	7	0.01
Tongan (3)	6	0.01
Other Pac. Isl., specified	1	0.00
Other Pac. Isl., not spec. (3)	13	0.03
Hispanic or Latino:	437	0.85
Central American:	17	0.03
Costa Rican	1	0.00
Guatemalan	7	0.01
Nicaraguan	1	0.00
Panamanian	3	0.01
Salvadoran	2	0.00
Other Central American	3	0.01
Cuban	17	0.03
Dominican Republic	4	0.01
Mexican	187	0.36
Puerto Rican	37	0.07
South American:	43	0.08
Argentinean	4	0.01
Bolivian	5	0.01
Chilean	1	0.00
Colombian	20	0.04
Ecuadorian	1	0.00
Peruvian	3	0.01
Uruguayan	6	0.01
Venezuelan	1	0.00
Other South American	2	0.00
Other Hispanic or Latino	132	0.26
Hungarian	229	0.44
Iranian	38	0.07
Irish	6,063	11.77
Israeli	13	0.03
Italian	1,238	2.40
Latvian	6	0.01
Lithuanian	12	0.02
Luxemburger	11	0.02
Northern European	7	0.01
Norwegian	258	0.50
Pennsylvania German	6	0.01
Polish	530	1.03
Romanian	5	0.01
Russian	139	0.27
Scotch-Irish	1,543	2.99
Scottish	1,190	2.31
Serbian	6	0.01
Slavic	9	0.02
Slovak	8	0.02
Slovene	6	0.01
Swedish	123	0.24
Swiss	70	0.14
Turkish	29	0.06
Ukrainian	19	0.04
United States or American	7,194	13.96
Welsh	402	0.78
West Indian, excl. Hispanic:	54	0.10
Haitian	9	0.02
Jamaican	45	0.09
White:	46,843	91.00
Not Hispanic (45,868)	46,555	90.44
Hispanic (259)	288	0.56
Yugoslavian	19	0.04

Martinsburg

Place Type: City
County: Berkeley
Population: 14,972

Ancestry/Race	Number	%
African American/Black:	1,947	13.00
Not Hispanic (1,729)	1,929	12.88
Hispanic (12)	18	0.12
African, sub-Saharan:	104	0.70
African	104	0.70
Am. Ind. or Alaska Nat., not spec.	54	0.36
American Indian tribes, specified:	88	0.59
Apache (1)	1	0.01
Blackfeet (6)	7	0.05
Cherokee (10)	44	0.29
Choctaw (2)	2	0.01
Crow	2	0.01
Iroquois (5)	7	0.05
Navajo (6)	6	0.04
Sioux (3)	13	0.09
Yuman	1	0.01
All other tribes (2)	5	0.03
American Indian tribes, not spec.	7	0.05
Asian:	131	0.87
Cambodian (5)	6	0.04
Chinese, ex. Taiwanese (21)	24	0.16
Filipino (13)	21	0.14
Indian (30)	37	0.25
Japanese (4)	10	0.07
Korean (9)	10	0.07
Laotian	1	0.01
Thai (2)	4	0.03
Vietnamese (8)	10	0.07
Other Asian, not specified (1)	8	0.05
Austrian	13	0.09
Belgian	9	0.06
British	26	0.17
Canadian	5	0.03
Celtic	8	0.05
Czechoslovakian	18	0.12
Danish	58	0.39
Dutch	237	1.59
English	1,487	9.95
European	163	1.09
French, except Basque	328	2.19
French Canadian	9	0.06
German	2,875	19.24
Greek	5	0.03
Hawaii Native/Pacific Islander:	7	0.05
Micronesian: (1)	4	0.03
Guamanian/Chamorro (1)	4	0.03
Polynesian: (1)	1	0.01
Native Hawaiian (1)	1	0.01
Other Pac. Isl., not spec. (1)	2	0.01
Hispanic or Latino:	436	2.91
Central American:	16	0.11
Guatemalan	1	0.01
Nicaraguan	1	0.01
Salvadoran	10	0.07
Other Central American	4	0.03
Cuban	5	0.03
Dominican Republic	1	0.01
Mexican	290	1.94
Puerto Rican	66	0.44
South American:	4	0.03
Peruvian	2	0.01
Uruguayan	1	0.01
Venezuelan	1	0.01
Other Hispanic or Latino	54	0.36
Hungarian	52	0.35
Irish	1,687	11.29
Italian	595	3.98
Latvian	10	0.07
Lithuanian	49	0.33
Norwegian	35	0.23
Pennsylvania German	11	0.07
Polish	249	1.67
Portuguese	36	0.24
Russian	42	0.28
Scandinavian	7	0.05
Scotch-Irish	200	1.34
Scottish	276	1.85
Slavic	18	0.12
Slovak	7	0.05
Slovene	5	0.03
Swedish	76	0.51
Swiss	7	0.05
Ukrainian	23	0.15
United States or American	2,023	13.54
Welsh	148	0.99
West Indian, excl. Hispanic:	136	0.91
Barbadian	13	0.09
Bermudan	18	0.12
Jamaican	105	0.70
White:	12,838	85.75
Not Hispanic (12,341)	12,591	84.10
Hispanic (220)	247	1.65

Morgantown

Place Type: City
County: Monongalia
Population: 26,809

Ancestry/Race	Number	%
Afghan	16	0.06
African American/Black:	1,267	4.73
Not Hispanic (1,098)	1,249	4.66
Hispanic (15)	18	0.07
African, sub-Saharan:	100	0.37
African	64	0.24
Kenyan	8	0.03
Nigerian	15	0.06
South African	8	0.03
Other sub-Saharan African	5	0.02
Alaska Native tribes, not specified	1	0.00
Am. Ind. or Alaska Nat., not spec.	34	0.13
Albanian	15	0.06
American Indian tribes, specified:	90	0.34
Apache (4)	5	0.02
Blackfeet (1)	6	0.02
Cherokee (14)	55	0.21
Chippewa (2)	2	0.01
Choctaw	1	0.00
Creek (1)	2	0.01
Crow (1)	1	0.00
Delaware	1	0.00
Iroquois	2	0.01
Kiowa (2)	2	0.01
Latin American Indians (2)	2	0.01
Navajo	1	0.00
Paiute (1)	1	0.00
Sioux (1)	1	0.00
All other tribes (5)	8	0.03
American Indian tribes, not spec.	12	0.04
Arab:	185	0.68
Arab/Arabic	10	0.04
Egyptian	24	0.09
Jordanian	15	0.06
Lebanese	68	0.25
Moroccan	9	0.03
Syrian	50	0.18
Other Arab	9	0.03
Armenian	9	0.03
Asian:	1,276	4.76
Bangladeshi (9)	10	0.04
Chinese, ex. Taiwanese (385)	405	1.51
Filipino (43)	76	0.28
Indian (397)	433	1.62
Indonesian (3)	4	0.01
Japanese (61)	81	0.30
Korean (72)	81	0.30
Malaysian (8)	10	0.04
Pakistani (28)	34	0.13
Sri Lankan (8)	8	0.03
Taiwanese (27)	28	0.10
Thai (23)	29	0.11
Vietnamese (11)	28	0.10

Notes: 1. Figures in the "Number" column do not add up to the total population due to: a) Ancestry/Race overlap — e.g. persons can report being both White and Irish, b) persons of Hispanic origin can report being any race, c) persons reporting two ancestries are counted in both categories. 2. Numbers in parentheses indicate the number of persons reporting this ancestry/race alone, not in combination with any other ancestry/race. 3. Refer to the Explanation of Data in the front of the book for more detailed information.

Ancestry/Race	Number	%
Other Asian, specified (3)	6	0.02
Other Asian, not specified (20)	43	0.16
Austrian	162	0.60
Belgian	31	0.11
British	205	0.75
Canadian	8	0.03
Celtic	16	0.06
Croatian	63	0.23
Czech	123	0.45
Czechoslovakian	21	0.08
Danish	40	0.15
Dutch	423	1.56
Eastern European	47	0.17
English	3,201	11.79
European	327	1.20
Finnish	42	0.15
French, except Basque	619	2.28
French Canadian	94	0.35
German	5,619	20.69
Greek	148	0.54
Guyanese	10	0.04
Hawaii Native/Pacific Islander:	48	0.18
Micronesian: (6)	9	0.03
Guamanian/Chamorro (1)	3	0.01
Other Micronesian (5)	6	0.02
Polynesian: (3)	14	0.05
Native Hawaiian (2)	11	0.04
Samoan (1)	3	0.01
Other Pac. Isl., specified	2	0.01
Other Pac. Isl., not spec. (4)	23	0.09
Hispanic or Latino:	412	1.54
Central American:	20	0.07
Costa Rican	3	0.01
Guatemalan	5	0.02
Honduran	2	0.01
Nicaraguan	7	0.03
Panamanian	2	0.01
Salvadoran	1	0.00
Cuban	13	0.05
Dominican Republic	3	0.01
Mexican	113	0.42
Puerto Rican	61	0.23
South American:	90	0.34
Bolivian	3	0.01
Chilean	3	0.01
Colombian	51	0.19
Ecuadorian	6	0.02
Paraguayan	1	0.00
Peruvian	9	0.03
Venezuelan	12	0.04
Other South American	5	0.02
Other Hispanic or Latino	112	0.42
Hungarian	213	0.78
Icelander	26	0.10
Iranian	35	0.13
Irish	4,205	15.48
Israeli	9	0.03
Italian	3,119	11.48
Latvian	20	0.07
Lithuanian	83	0.31
New Zealander	15	0.06
Northern European	27	0.10
Norwegian	202	0.74
Pennsylvania German	9	0.03
Polish	1,305	4.80
Portuguese	26	0.10
Romanian	46	0.17
Russian	280	1.03
Scandinavian	30	0.11
Scotch-Irish	847	3.12
Scottish	813	2.99
Serbian	78	0.29
Slavic	29	0.11
Slovak	278	1.02
Swedish	266	0.98
Swiss	135	0.50
Turkish	27	0.10
Ukrainian	126	0.46
United States or American	1,499	5.52
Welsh	384	1.41
West Indian, excl. Hispanic:	101	0.37
Barbadian	16	0.06
Haitian	7	0.03
Jamaican	64	0.24
Trinidadian and Tobagonian	4	0.01
West Indian	10	0.04
White:	24,331	90.76
Not Hispanic (23,740)	24,061	89.75
Hispanic (250)	270	1.01
Yugoslavian	30	0.11

Parkersburg

Place Type: City
County: Wood
Population: 33,099

Ancestry/Race	Number	%
African American/Black:	737	2.23
Not Hispanic (556)	711	2.15
Hispanic (23)	26	0.08
African, sub-Saharan:	61	0.18
African	29	0.09
Nigerian	7	0.02
South African	25	0.08
Alaska Native tribes, specified:	1	0.00
Eskimo (1)	1	0.00
Am. Ind. or Alaska Nat., not spec.	82	0.25
American Indian tribes, specified:	115	0.35
Apache (4)	9	0.03
Blackfeet (1)	7	0.02
Cherokee (19)	69	0.21
Chickasaw	1	0.00
Chippewa (1)	2	0.01
Choctaw (2)	2	0.01
Comanche	2	0.01
Delaware	2	0.01
Iroquois (1)	3	0.01
Osage (1)	1	0.00
Pueblo (1)	1	0.00
Sioux	1	0.00
All other tribes (12)	15	0.05
American Indian tribes, not spec.	10	0.03
Arab:	128	0.39
Lebanese	75	0.23
Syrian	53	0.16
Asian:	173	0.52
Cambodian	1	0.00
Chinese, ex. Taiwanese (29)	34	0.10
Filipino (39)	50	0.15
Indian (19)	25	0.08
Indonesian	1	0.00
Japanese (21)	27	0.08
Korean (16)	19	0.06
Malaysian (1)	1	0.00
Sri Lankan (2)	2	0.01
Taiwanese	2	0.01
Thai (1)	3	0.01
Vietnamese (3)	3	0.01
Other Asian, not specified (3)	5	0.02
Australian	7	0.02
Austrian	6	0.02
Belgian	21	0.06
British	99	0.30
Canadian	15	0.05
Croatian	6	0.02
Czech	13	0.04
Czechoslovakian	26	0.08
Danish	31	0.09
Dutch	709	2.14
Eastern European	6	0.02
English	3,496	10.54
European	157	0.47
Finnish	9	0.03
French, except Basque	433	1.31
French Canadian	57	0.17
German	5,042	15.21
Greek	80	0.24
Hawaii Native/Pacific Islander:	26	0.08
Micronesian: (5)	5	0.02
Guamanian/Chamorro (5)	5	0.02
Polynesian: (7)	10	0.03
Native Hawaiian (1)	4	0.01
Samoan (5)	5	0.02
Other Polynesian (1)	1	0.00
Other Pac. Isl., not spec. (6)	11	0.03
Hispanic or Latino:	269	0.81
Central American:	16	0.05
Costa Rican	1	0.00
Panamanian	14	0.04
Other Central American	1	0.00
Cuban	8	0.02
Mexican	104	0.31
Puerto Rican	52	0.16
South American:	7	0.02
Colombian	4	0.01
Paraguayan	1	0.00
Other South American	2	0.01
Other Hispanic or Latino	82	0.25
Hungarian	82	0.25
Irish	3,732	11.26
Italian	693	2.09
Lithuanian	25	0.08
Northern European	25	0.08
Norwegian	48	0.14
Pennsylvania German	12	0.04
Polish	253	0.76
Portuguese	13	0.04
Romanian	13	0.04
Russian	37	0.11
Scotch-Irish	865	2.61
Scottish	601	1.81
Slavic	5	0.02
Slovak	12	0.04
Slovene	8	0.02
Swedish	135	0.41
Swiss	46	0.14
Ukrainian	8	0.02
United States or American	5,752	17.35
Welsh	258	0.78
West Indian, excl. Hispanic:	8	0.02
West Indian	8	0.02
White:	32,209	97.31
Not Hispanic (31,710)	32,014	96.72
Hispanic (184)	195	0.59

Saint Albans

Place Type: City
County: Kanawha
Population: 11,567

Ancestry/Race	Number	%
African American/Black:	378	3.27
Not Hispanic (325)	374	3.23
Hispanic (4)	4	0.03
African, sub-Saharan:	40	0.34
African	40	0.34
Alaska Native tribes, specified:	2	0.02
Eskimo (2)	2	0.02
Am. Ind. or Alaska Nat., not spec.	22	0.19
American Indian tribes, specified:	38	0.33
Apache	2	0.02
Blackfeet (1)	2	0.02
Cherokee (8)	26	0.22
Iroquois	5	0.04
Osage	1	0.01
Pueblo (1)	1	0.01
Sioux	1	0.01
American Indian tribes, not spec.	1	0.01
Arab:	33	0.28
Lebanese	7	0.06
Syrian	26	0.22
Asian:	71	0.61
Chinese, ex. Taiwanese (14)	14	0.12
Filipino (16)	22	0.19
Indian (2)	9	0.08
Japanese (7)	9	0.08
Korean (2)	2	0.02
Malaysian (1)	4	0.03

Notes: 1. Figures in the "Number" column do not add up to the total population due to: a) Ancestry/Race overlap — e.g. persons can report being both White and Irish, b) persons of Hispanic origin can report being any race, c) persons reporting two ancestries are counted in both categories. 2. Numbers in parentheses indicate the number of persons reporting this ancestry/race alone, not in combination with any other ancestry/race. 3. Refer to the Explanation of Data in the front of the book for more detailed information.

Ancestry/Race	Number	%
Pakistani (1)	2	0.02
Thai (1)	2	0.02
Vietnamese (3)	3	0.03
Other Asian, not specified	4	0.03
Belgian	30	0.26
British	29	0.25
Canadian	6	0.05
Celtic	5	0.04
Czech	18	0.15
Czechoslovakian	7	0.06
Danish	25	0.21
Dutch	201	1.73
Eastern European	8	0.07
English	1,863	16.01
European	89	0.77
French, except Basque	245	2.11
French Canadian	42	0.36
German	1,646	14.15
Greek	65	0.56
Hispanic or Latino:	73	0.63
Central American:	7	0.06
Honduran	1	0.01
Panamanian	2	0.02
Other Central American	4	0.03
Cuban	8	0.07
Mexican	26	0.22
Puerto Rican	9	0.08
South American:	9	0.08
Ecuadorian	1	0.01
Venezuelan	6	0.05
Other South American	2	0.02
Other Hispanic or Latino	14	0.12
Hungarian	24	0.21
Irish	1,692	14.54
Italian	521	4.48
Lithuanian	14	0.12
Norwegian	2	0.02
Pennsylvania German	15	0.13
Polish	111	0.95
Portuguese	20	0.17
Scandinavian	14	0.12
Scotch-Irish	346	2.97
Scottish	289	2.48
Slovak	28	0.24
Swedish	79	0.68
Ukrainian	15	0.13
United States or American	1,616	13.89
Welsh	75	0.64
West Indian, excl. Hispanic:	5	0.04
West Indian	5	0.04
White:	11,145	96.35
Not Hispanic (10,979)	11,092	95.89
Hispanic (52)	53	0.46

South Charleston

Place Type: City
County: Kanawha
Population: 13,390

Ancestry/Race	Number	%
African American/Black:	982	7.33
Not Hispanic (888)	974	7.27
Hispanic (5)	8	0.06
African, sub-Saharan:	99	0.72
African	99	0.72
Alaska Native tribes, specified:	1	0.01
Alaska Athabascan (1)	1	0.01
Am. Ind. or Alaska Nat., not spec.	26	0.19
American Indian tribes, specified:	35	0.26
Blackfeet	1	0.01
Cherokee (5)	22	0.16
Iroquois (1)	2	0.01
Latin American Indians (1)	1	0.01
Lumbee (1)	1	0.01
Seminole (1)	1	0.01
Sioux	1	0.01
All other tribes (1)	6	0.04
American Indian tribes, not spec.	14	0.10
Arab:	191	1.40
Arab/Arabic	17	0.12
Lebanese	158	1.16
Syrian	9	0.07
Other Arab	7	0.05
Asian:	133	0.99
Chinese, ex. Taiwanese (10)	10	0.07
Filipino (46)	51	0.38
Indian (16)	17	0.13
Japanese (7)	12	0.09
Korean (11)	16	0.12
Pakistani (6)	9	0.07
Thai (5)	6	0.04
Vietnamese (5)	6	0.04
Other Asian, specified	1	0.01
Other Asian, not specified (2)	5	0.04
Austrian	43	0.31
Belgian	40	0.29
British	81	0.59
Canadian	14	0.10
Celtic	11	0.08
Czech	16	0.12
Dutch	290	2.12
Eastern European	9	0.07
English	2,020	14.77
European	101	0.74
French, except Basque	311	2.27
French Canadian	40	0.29
German	2,096	15.33
Greek	76	0.56
Hawaii Native/Pacific Islander:	1	0.01
Other Pac. Isl., specified	1	0.01
Hispanic or Latino:	75	0.56
Cuban	5	0.04
Mexican	30	0.22
Puerto Rican	12	0.09
South American:	1	0.01
Colombian	1	0.01
Other Hispanic or Latino	27	0.20
Hungarian	61	0.45
Iranian	9	0.07
Irish	1,561	11.41
Italian	546	3.99
Latvian	6	0.04
Lithuanian	12	0.09
Macedonian	7	0.05
Norwegian	35	0.26
Polish	171	1.25
Russian	47	0.34
Scandinavian	8	0.06
Scotch-Irish	423	3.09
Scottish	312	2.28
Serbian	7	0.05
Slovak	24	0.18
Swedish	103	0.75
Swiss	5	0.04
Ukrainian	10	0.07
United States or American	1,429	10.45
Welsh	173	1.26
West Indian, excl. Hispanic:	6	0.04
West Indian	6	0.04
White:	12,322	92.02
Not Hispanic (12,113)	12,261	91.57
Hispanic (52)	61	0.46
Yugoslavian	9	0.07

Teays Valley

Place Type: Census Designated Place
County: Putnam
Population: 12,704

Ancestry/Race	Number	%
African American/Black:	142	1.12
Not Hispanic (119)	139	1.09
Hispanic	3	0.02
African, sub-Saharan:	62	0.49
African	50	0.39
Cape Verdean	12	0.09
Alaska Native tribes, specified:	2	0.02
Eskimo	1	0.01
Tlingit-Haida	1	0.01
Am. Ind. or Alaska Nat., not spec.	4	0.03
American Indian tribes, specified:	31	0.24
Apache	1	0.01
Blackfeet (1)	4	0.03
Cherokee (6)	20	0.16
Chickasaw (1)	1	0.01
Creek (1)	1	0.01
Latin American Indians	1	0.01
Sioux (3)	3	0.02
American Indian tribes, not spec.	2	0.02
Arab:	98	0.77
Arab/Arabic	66	0.52
Lebanese	32	0.25
Asian:	236	1.86
Cambodian (2)	2	0.02
Chinese, ex. Taiwanese (22)	23	0.18
Filipino (13)	17	0.13
Indian (40)	46	0.36
Japanese (74)	81	0.64
Korean (14)	17	0.13
Laotian (7)	13	0.10
Pakistani (9)	11	0.09
Sri Lankan (3)	3	0.02
Thai (6)	6	0.05
Vietnamese (7)	7	0.06
Other Asian, not specified (5)	10	0.08
Austrian	13	0.10
Belgian	11	0.09
British	31	0.24
Canadian	5	0.04
Croatian	17	0.13
Czechoslovakian	8	0.06
Danish	42	0.33
Dutch	221	1.74
English	1,642	12.95
Estonian	6	0.05
European	96	0.76
Finnish	6	0.05
French, except Basque	197	1.55
French Canadian	19	0.15
German	1,830	14.43
Greek	41	0.32
Hawaii Native/Pacific Islander:	4	0.03
Polynesian: (2)	3	0.02
Native Hawaiian (1)	1	0.01
Samoan (1)	1	0.01
Other Polynesian	1	0.01
Other Pac. Isl., not spec.	1	0.01
Hispanic or Latino:	98	0.77
Central American:	5	0.04
Costa Rican	1	0.01
Guatemalan	1	0.01
Panamanian	3	0.02
Cuban	9	0.07
Dominican Republic	3	0.02
Mexican	34	0.27
Puerto Rican	26	0.20
South American:	3	0.02
Argentinean	2	0.02
Other South American	1	0.01
Other Hispanic or Latino	18	0.14
Hungarian	26	0.21
Irish	1,542	12.16
Italian	564	4.45
Macedonian	11	0.09
Norwegian	48	0.38
Polish	229	1.81
Portuguese	33	0.26
Russian	7	0.06
Scotch-Irish	193	1.52
Scottish	221	1.74
Slovak	62	0.49
Slovene	14	0.11
Swedish	116	0.91
Swiss	81	0.64
Ukrainian	6	0.05
United States or American	2,396	18.90
Welsh	153	1.21
White:	12,313	96.92

Notes: 1. Figures in the "Number" column do not add up to the total population due to: a) Ancestry/Race overlap — e.g. persons can report being both White and Irish, b) persons of Hispanic origin can report being any race, c) persons reporting two ancestries are counted in both categories. 2. Numbers in parentheses indicate the number of persons reporting this ancestry/race alone, not in combination with any other ancestry/race. 3. Refer to the Explanation of Data in the front of the book for more detailed information.

Ancestry/Race	Number	%
Not Hispanic (12,186)	12,242	96.36
Hispanic (60)	71	0.56
Yugoslavian	22	0.17

Vienna

Place Type: City
County: Wood
Population: 10,861

Ancestry/Race	Number	%
African American/Black:	130	1.20
Not Hispanic (102)	129	1.19
Hispanic (1)	1	0.01
Alaska Native tribes, specified:	1	0.01
Aleut	1	0.01
Am. Ind. or Alaska Nat., not spec.	22	0.20
American Indian tribes, specified:	28	0.26
Apache	1	0.01
Blackfeet	5	0.05
Cherokee (3)	14	0.13
Iroquois (1)	1	0.01
Lumbee (3)	3	0.03
All other tribes (4)	4	0.04
American Indian tribes, not spec.	1	0.01
Arab:	55	0.51
Lebanese	25	0.23
Syrian	30	0.28
Asian:	159	1.46
Chinese, ex. Taiwanese (26)	26	0.24
Filipino (16)	23	0.21
Indian (74)	74	0.68
Japanese (4)	6	0.06
Korean (7)	9	0.08
Taiwanese (4)	4	0.04
Vietnamese (11)	12	0.11
Other Asian, not specified (4)	5	0.05
Austrian	6	0.06
British	108	1.01
Canadian	54	0.50
Croatian	12	0.11
Czech	12	0.11
Danish	12	0.11
Dutch	214	1.99
Eastern European	15	0.14
English	1,891	17.60
European	15	0.14
French, except Basque	237	2.21
French Canadian	11	0.10
German	2,156	20.07
Greek	27	0.25
Hawaii Native/Pacific Islander:	2	0.02
Polynesian: (2)	2	0.02
Samoan (2)	2	0.02
Hispanic or Latino:	54	0.50
Cuban	3	0.03
Mexican	28	0.26
Puerto Rican	8	0.07
South American:	7	0.06
Chilean	1	0.01
Colombian	2	0.02
Peruvian	2	0.02
Other South American	2	0.02
Other Hispanic or Latino	8	0.07
Hungarian	19	0.18
Irish	1,302	12.12
Italian	347	3.23
Northern European	13	0.12
Norwegian	25	0.23
Pennsylvania German	6	0.06
Polish	105	0.98
Scandinavian	6	0.06
Scotch-Irish	336	3.13
Scottish	475	4.42
Slovak	24	0.22
Swedish	81	0.75
Swiss	12	0.11
Ukrainian	5	0.05
United States or American	1,532	14.26
Welsh	72	0.67
West Indian, excl. Hispanic:	10	0.09
Jamaican	10	0.09
White:	10,574	97.36
Not Hispanic (10,459)	10,527	96.92
Hispanic (44)	47	0.43

Weirton

Place Type: City
County: Hancock
Population: 20,411

Ancestry/Race	Number	%
African American/Black:	847	4.15
Not Hispanic (782)	840	4.12
Hispanic (5)	7	0.03
African, sub-Saharan:	30	0.15
African	30	0.15
Alaska Native tribes, not specified	6	0.03
Am. Ind. or Alaska Nat., not spec.	21	0.10
Albanian	8	0.04
American Indian tribes, specified:	37	0.18
Blackfeet (1)	2	0.01
Cherokee (18)	27	0.13
Choctaw	1	0.00
Crow	2	0.01
Navajo	1	0.00
Sioux (1)	3	0.01
All other tribes	1	0.00
American Indian tribes, not spec.	4	0.02
Arab:	88	0.43
Jordanian	31	0.15
Lebanese	13	0.06
Moroccan	9	0.04
Syrian	35	0.17
Asian:	164	0.80
Chinese, ex. Taiwanese (14)	16	0.08
Filipino (22)	37	0.18
Indian (56)	58	0.28
Japanese (8)	11	0.05
Korean (9)	18	0.09
Taiwanese (3)	3	0.01
Vietnamese (5)	9	0.04
Other Asian, not specified	12	0.06
Austrian	87	0.43
Basque	6	0.03
Belgian	60	0.29
British	24	0.12
Croatian	219	1.07
Czech	156	0.77
Czechoslovakian	152	0.75
Danish	25	0.12
Dutch	401	1.97
Eastern European	4	0.02
English	1,882	9.24
European	78	0.38
Finnish	42	0.21
French, except Basque	304	1.49
French Canadian	22	0.11
German	3,278	16.09
Greek	592	2.91
Hawaii Native/Pacific Islander:	13	0.06
Micronesian:	3	0.01
Guamanian/Chamorro	3	0.01
Polynesian: (3)	7	0.03
Native Hawaiian (3)	4	0.02
Samoan	3	0.01
Other Pac. Isl., not spec.	3	0.01
Hispanic or Latino:	138	0.68
Central American:	5	0.02
Costa Rican	1	0.00
Nicaraguan	3	0.01
Salvadoran	1	0.00
Cuban	5	0.02
Dominican Republic	9	0.04
Mexican	57	0.28
Puerto Rican	9	0.04
South American:	2	0.01
Ecuadorian	1	0.00
Paraguayan	1	0.00
Other Hispanic or Latino	51	0.25
Hungarian	410	2.01
Irish	3,016	14.80
Italian	3,733	18.32
Lithuanian	17	0.08
Norwegian	22	0.11
Pennsylvania German	11	0.05
Polish	1,913	9.39
Portuguese	12	0.06
Romanian	111	0.54
Russian	273	1.34
Scotch-Irish	698	3.43
Scottish	517	2.54
Serbian	489	2.40
Slavic	35	0.17
Slovak	629	3.09
Slovene	53	0.26
Swedish	44	0.22
Swiss	50	0.25
Turkish	18	0.09
Ukrainian	114	0.56
United States or American	1,233	6.05
Welsh	251	1.23
White:	19,432	95.20
Not Hispanic (19,199)	19,326	94.68
Hispanic (94)	106	0.52
Yugoslavian	25	0.12

Wheeling

Place Type: City
County: Ohio
Population: 31,419

Ancestry/Race	Number	%
African American/Black:	1,769	5.63
Not Hispanic (1,556)	1,755	5.59
Hispanic (11)	14	0.04
African, sub-Saharan:	48	0.15
African	48	0.15
Alaska Native tribes, not specified	1	0.00
Am. Ind. or Alaska Nat., not spec.	42	0.13
American Indian tribes, specified:	56	0.18
Apache (1)	1	0.00
Blackfeet (1)	6	0.02
Cherokee (5)	38	0.12
Iroquois	3	0.01
Kiowa	1	0.00
Latin American Indians (2)	3	0.01
Navajo (1)	1	0.00
Sioux (1)	1	0.00
All other tribes (1)	2	0.01
American Indian tribes, not spec.	6	0.02
Arab:	529	1.69
Egyptian	20	0.06
Iraqi	27	0.09
Jordanian	12	0.04
Lebanese	447	1.43
Syrian	23	0.07
Asian:	366	1.16
Cambodian (2)	2	0.01
Chinese, ex. Taiwanese (46)	59	0.19
Filipino (46)	60	0.19
Indian (117)	144	0.46
Japanese (25)	28	0.09
Korean (17)	18	0.06
Laotian (1)	1	0.00
Malaysian (1)	1	0.00
Pakistani (1)	6	0.02
Sri Lankan (4)	7	0.02
Thai	4	0.01
Vietnamese (10)	15	0.05
Other Asian, specified (1)	2	0.01
Other Asian, not specified (6)	19	0.06
Australian	5	0.02
Austrian	86	0.27
Belgian	34	0.11
British	156	0.50
Canadian	8	0.03
Celtic	21	0.07

Notes: 1. Figures in the "Number" column do not add up to the total population due to: a) Ancestry/Race overlap — e.g. persons can report being both White and Irish, b) persons of Hispanic origin can report being any race, c) persons reporting two ancestries are counted in both categories. 2. Numbers in parentheses indicate the number of persons reporting this ancestry/race alone, not in combination with any other ancestry/race. 3. Refer to the Explanation of Data in the front of the book for more detailed information.

Croatian	143	0.46
Czech	150	0.48
Czechoslovakian	65	0.21
Danish	44	0.14
Dutch	614	1.96
Eastern European	5	0.02
English	3,744	11.96
European	214	0.68
French, except Basque	524	1.67
French Canadian	16	0.05
German	8,941	28.56
Greek	596	1.90
Hawaii Native/Pacific Islander:	22	0.07
Micronesian: (2)	2	0.01
Guamanian/Chamorro (1)	1	0.00
Other Micronesian (1)	1	0.00
Polynesian: (4)	12	0.04
Native Hawaiian (1)	8	0.03
Samoan (3)	4	0.01
Other Pac. Isl., specified	1	0.00
Other Pac. Isl., not spec. (2)	7	0.02
Hispanic or Latino:	181	0.58
Central American:	4	0.01
Costa Rican	2	0.01
Guatemalan	1	0.00
Salvadoran	1	0.00
Cuban	11	0.04
Dominican Republic	1	0.00
Mexican	56	0.18
Puerto Rican	30	0.10
South American:	18	0.06
Argentinean	4	0.01
Chilean	2	0.01
Colombian	9	0.03
Ecuadorian	1	0.00
Peruvian	1	0.00
Venezuelan	1	0.00
Other Hispanic or Latino	61	0.19
Hungarian	510	1.63
Iranian	23	0.07
Irish	5,967	19.06
Italian	2,372	7.58
Lithuanian	90	0.29
Maltese	6	0.02
Northern European	100	0.32
Norwegian	16	0.05
Pennsylvania German	7	0.02
Polish	2,047	6.54
Portuguese	9	0.03
Romanian	34	0.11
Russian	209	0.67
Scandinavian	6	0.02
Scotch-Irish	916	2.93
Scottish	617	1.97
Serbian	27	0.09
Slavic	83	0.27
Slovak	239	0.76
Slovene	76	0.24
Swedish	64	0.20
Swiss	160	0.51
Ukrainian	210	0.67
United States or American	1,981	6.33
Welsh	444	1.42
West Indian, excl. Hispanic:	21	0.07
Barbadian	10	0.03
Dutch West Indian	5	0.02
Trinidadian and Tobagonian	6	0.02
White:	29,445	93.72
Not Hispanic (28,988)	29,289	93.22
Hispanic (145)	156	0.50
Yugoslavian	58	0.19

Allouez

Place Type: Village
County: Brown
Population: 15,443

Ancestry/Race	Number	%
African American/Black:	767	4.97
Not Hispanic (708)	755	4.89
Hispanic (9)	12	0.08
Am. Ind. or Alaska Nat., not spec.	127	0.82
American Indian tribes, specified:	75	0.49
Apache	1	0.01
Cherokee	3	0.02
Chippewa (2)	5	0.03
Iroquois (33)	45	0.29
Menominee (3)	9	0.06
Osage	1	0.01
Potawatomi (1)	1	0.01
Pueblo (1)	1	0.01
Sioux (2)	2	0.01
All other tribes (3)	7	0.05
American Indian tribes, not spec.	10	0.06
Arab:	11	0.07
Lebanese	11	0.07
Asian:	154	1.00
Chinese, ex. Taiwanese (12)	16	0.10
Filipino (19)	21	0.14
Hmong (24)	25	0.16
Indian (36)	47	0.30
Japanese (8)	8	0.05
Korean (15)	19	0.12
Laotian (8)	9	0.06
Malaysian	1	0.01
Thai (1)	1	0.01
Vietnamese (5)	6	0.04
Other Asian, not specified (1)	1	0.01
Austrian	19	0.12
Belgian	1,652	10.70
Brazilian	17	0.11
British	46	0.30
Canadian	6	0.04
Celtic	7	0.05
Croatian	18	0.12
Czech	431	2.79
Czechoslovakian	7	0.05
Danish	184	1.19
Dutch	936	6.06
English	868	5.62
European	158	1.02
Finnish	176	1.14
French, except Basque	981	6.35
French Canadian	293	1.90
German	5,243	33.95
Greek	31	0.20
Hawaii Native/Pacific Islander:	1	0.01
Other Pac. Isl., not spec. (1)	1	0.01
Hispanic or Latino:	199	1.29
Cuban	7	0.05
Dominican Republic	3	0.02
Mexican	128	0.83
Puerto Rican	5	0.03
South American:	14	0.09
Bolivian	4	0.03
Chilean	1	0.01
Colombian	5	0.03
Paraguayan	3	0.02
Peruvian	1	0.01
Other Hispanic or Latino	42	0.27
Hungarian	46	0.30
Irish	1,865	12.08
Italian	441	2.86
Latvian	14	0.09
Lithuanian	19	0.12
Luxemburger	21	0.14
Northern European	23	0.15
Norwegian	655	4.24
Polish	1,121	7.26
Romanian	6	0.04
Russian	61	0.40
Scandinavian	29	0.19
Scotch-Irish	116	0.75
Scottish	228	1.48
Serbian	7	0.05
Slovak	6	0.04
Swedish	285	1.85
Swiss	40	0.26
Ukrainian	41	0.27
United States or American	415	2.69
Welsh	38	0.25
White:	14,319	92.72
Not Hispanic (14,139)	14,223	92.10
Hispanic (79)	96	0.62

Appleton

Place Type: City
County: Outagamie
Population: 70,087

Ancestry/Race	Number	%
African American/Black:	906	1.29
Not Hispanic (677)	875	1.25
Hispanic (18)	31	0.04
African, sub-Saharan:	103	0.15
African	44	0.06
Nigerian	23	0.03
South African	17	0.02
Other sub-Saharan African	19	0.03
Alaska Native tribes, specified:	9	0.01
Alaska Athabascan (2)	2	0.00
Eskimo (2)	7	0.01
Alaska Native tribes, not specified	1	0.00
Am. Ind. or Alaska Nat., not spec.	182	0.26
American Indian tribes, specified:	492	0.70
Apache (2)	8	0.01
Blackfeet (4)	8	0.01
Cherokee (15)	40	0.06
Chippewa (46)	71	0.10
Choctaw (1)	3	0.00
Comanche (2)	5	0.01
Cree (2)	4	0.01
Creek	1	0.00
Iroquois (88)	145	0.21
Kiowa (1)	3	0.00
Latin American Indians (10)	21	0.03
Menominee (66)	81	0.12
Navajo (1)	1	0.00
Potawatomi (15)	16	0.02
Pueblo	1	0.00
Puget Sound Salish (2)	6	0.01
Sioux (4)	9	0.01
Ute	2	0.00
Yakama	4	0.01
Yuman (6)	6	0.01
All other tribes (28)	57	0.08
American Indian tribes, not spec.	19	0.03
Arab:	74	0.11
Arab/Arabic	22	0.03
Iraqi	10	0.01
Lebanese	15	0.02
Moroccan	6	0.01
Palestinian	14	0.02
Other Arab	7	0.01
Armenian	39	0.06
Asian:	3,630	5.18
Bangladeshi (2)	2	0.00
Cambodian (2)	2	0.00
Chinese, ex. Taiwanese (122)	145	0.21
Filipino (58)	95	0.14
Hmong (2,451)	2,645	3.77
Indian (181)	222	0.32
Indonesian (1)	1	0.00
Japanese (35)	68	0.10
Korean (125)	163	0.23
Laotian (81)	120	0.17
Malaysian (1)	2	0.00
Taiwanese (16)	19	0.03
Thai (6)	15	0.02
Vietnamese (29)	33	0.05
Other Asian, specified (1)	1	0.00
Other Asian, not specified (71)	97	0.14
Assyrian/Chaldean/Syriac	23	0.03
Austrian	351	0.50
Belgian	967	1.38
British	199	0.28
Bulgarian	6	0.01
Canadian	172	0.25

Notes: 1. Figures in the "Number" column do not add up to the total population due to: a) Ancestry/Race overlap — e.g. persons can report being both White and Irish, b) persons of Hispanic origin can report being any race, c) persons reporting two ancestries are counted in both categories. 2. Numbers in parentheses indicate the number of persons reporting this ancestry/race alone, not in combination with any other ancestry/race. 3. Refer to the Explanation of Data in the front of the book for more detailed information.

Croatian	167	0.24
Czech	908	1.29
Czechoslovakian	173	0.25
Danish	637	0.91
Dutch	4,977	7.10
Eastern European	8	0.01
English	4,452	6.35
Estonian	6	0.01
European	433	0.62
Finnish	375	0.53
French, except Basque	3,433	4.90
French Canadian	1,360	1.94
German	34,776	49.59
German Russian	18	0.03
Greek	192	0.27
Hawaii Native/Pacific Islander:	108	0.15
Micronesian: (15)	16	0.02
Guamanian/Chamorro (5)	6	0.01
Other Micronesian (10)	10	0.01
Polynesian: (3)	17	0.02
Native Hawaiian (1)	9	0.01
Samoan (2)	8	0.01
Other Pac. Isl., not spec. (3)	75	0.11
Hispanic or Latino:	1,775	2.53
Central American:	38	0.05
Costa Rican	2	0.00
Guatemalan	4	0.01
Honduran	12	0.02
Nicaraguan	8	0.01
Panamanian	5	0.01
Salvadoran	5	0.01
Other Central American	1	0.00
Cuban	25	0.04
Dominican Republic	2	0.00
Mexican	1,313	1.87
Puerto Rican	81	0.12
South American:	50	0.07
Argentinean	2	0.00
Bolivian	1	0.00
Chilean	11	0.02
Colombian	13	0.02
Ecuadorian	3	0.00
Paraguayan	1	0.00
Peruvian	10	0.01
Venezuelan	8	0.01
Other South American	1	0.00
Other Hispanic or Latino	266	0.38
Hungarian	182	0.26
Icelander	45	0.06
Irish	8,353	11.91
Italian	1,960	2.80
Latvian	76	0.11
Lithuanian	176	0.25
Luxemburger	35	0.05
Northern European	22	0.03
Norwegian	3,889	5.55
Pennsylvania German	7	0.01
Polish	4,194	5.98
Portuguese	13	0.02
Romanian	56	0.08
Russian	478	0.68
Scandinavian	163	0.23
Scotch-Irish	423	0.60
Scottish	998	1.42
Serbian	13	0.02
Slavic	4	0.01
Slovak	56	0.08
Slovene	11	0.02
Swedish	1,753	2.50
Swiss	526	0.75
Ukrainian	91	0.13
United States or American	2,794	3.98
Welsh	282	0.40
West Indian, excl. Hispanic:	14	0.02
Jamaican	7	0.01
Trinidadian and Tobagonian	7	0.01
White:	64,797	92.45
Not Hispanic (63,249)	63,799	91.03
Hispanic (867)	998	1.42
Yugoslavian	65	0.09

Ashwaubenon

Place Type: Village
County: Brown
Population: 17,634

Ancestry/Race	Number	%
African American/Black:	160	0.91
Not Hispanic (113)	154	0.87
Hispanic (1)	6	0.03
African, sub-Saharan:	14	0.08
African	14	0.08
Alaska Native tribes, specified:	3	0.02
Eskimo (3)	3	0.02
Am. Ind. or Alaska Nat., not spec.	56	0.32
American Indian tribes, specified:	226	1.28
Apache (2)	2	0.01
Cherokee (8)	13	0.07
Chickasaw (1)	1	0.01
Chippewa (14)	26	0.15
Choctaw	1	0.01
Iroquois (87)	112	0.64
Menominee (22)	33	0.19
Navajo (1)	1	0.01
Osage (4)	8	0.05
Ottawa (1)	2	0.01
Sioux (1)	1	0.01
All other tribes (20)	26	0.15
American Indian tribes, not spec.	11	0.06
Arab:	59	0.33
Arab/Arabic	8	0.05
Egyptian	4	0.02
Lebanese	47	0.27
Armenian	27	0.15
Asian:	352	2.00
Chinese, ex. Taiwanese (42)	48	0.27
Filipino (16)	24	0.14
Hmong (72)	72	0.41
Indian (117)	126	0.71
Indonesian (2)	2	0.01
Japanese (5)	6	0.03
Korean (12)	16	0.09
Laotian (5)	5	0.03
Malaysian (1)	1	0.01
Pakistani (2)	2	0.01
Sri Lankan (1)	2	0.01
Vietnamese (29)	30	0.17
Other Asian, not specified (15)	18	0.10
Australian	7	0.04
Austrian	52	0.29
Belgian	1,384	7.83
British	42	0.24
Canadian	40	0.23
Celtic	7	0.04
Croatian	81	0.46
Czech	575	3.25
Czechoslovakian	25	0.14
Danish	242	1.37
Dutch	1,168	6.61
English	979	5.54
European	98	0.55
Finnish	293	1.66
French, except Basque	1,266	7.16
French Canadian	424	2.40
German	7,008	39.66
Greek	5	0.03
Hawaii Native/Pacific Islander:	7	0.04
Micronesian:	1	0.01
Guamanian/Chamorro	1	0.01
Polynesian: (4)	6	0.03
Native Hawaiian (1)	2	0.01
Samoan (3)	4	0.02
Hispanic or Latino:	202	1.15
Central American:	13	0.07
Guatemalan	5	0.03
Panamanian	6	0.03
Salvadoran	2	0.01
Cuban	7	0.04
Mexican	109	0.62
Puerto Rican	32	0.18
South American:	20	0.11
Bolivian	2	0.01
Chilean	1	0.01
Colombian	6	0.03
Ecuadorian	2	0.01
Peruvian	7	0.04
Venezuelan	1	0.01
Other South American	1	0.01
Other Hispanic or Latino	21	0.12
Hungarian	94	0.53
Icelander	7	0.04
Iranian	29	0.16
Irish	2,059	11.65
Italian	701	3.97
Lithuanian	45	0.25
Luxemburger	14	0.08
Northern European	23	0.13
Norwegian	845	4.78
Pennsylvania German	5	0.03
Polish	1,912	10.82
Portuguese	31	0.18
Russian	35	0.20
Scandinavian	19	0.11
Scotch-Irish	169	0.96
Scottish	131	0.74
Slovak	23	0.13
Swedish	627	3.55
Swiss	74	0.42
Ukrainian	22	0.12
United States or American	652	3.69
Welsh	153	0.87
White:	16,878	95.71
Not Hispanic (16,669)	16,763	95.06
Hispanic (95)	115	0.65
Yugoslavian	26	0.15

Baraboo

Place Type: City
County: Sauk
Population: 10,711

Ancestry/Race	Number	%
African American/Black:	78	0.73
Not Hispanic (55)	78	0.73
African, sub-Saharan:	9	0.08
African	9	0.08
Alaska Native tribes, specified:	2	0.02
Alaska Athabascan (2)	2	0.02
Am. Ind. or Alaska Nat., not spec.	16	0.15
American Indian tribes, specified:	93	0.87
Blackfeet (3)	5	0.05
Cherokee (2)	7	0.07
Chippewa (6)	8	0.07
Colville (1)	1	0.01
Comanche (1)	1	0.01
Cree	1	0.01
Iroquois	2	0.02
Menominee (1)	1	0.01
Navajo (1)	1	0.01
Potawatomi (3)	3	0.03
Pueblo (3)	3	0.03
Sioux (3)	4	0.04
Ute (1)	1	0.01
All other tribes (44)	55	0.51
American Indian tribes, not spec.	5	0.05
Arab:	9	0.08
Lebanese	9	0.08
Asian:	70	0.65
Chinese, ex. Taiwanese (9)	10	0.09
Filipino (8)	9	0.08
Indian (7)	11	0.10
Japanese (3)	8	0.07
Korean (17)	18	0.17
Taiwanese	1	0.01
Thai (2)	2	0.02
Vietnamese (10)	10	0.09
Other Asian, not specified	1	0.01
Austrian	18	0.17
Belgian	39	0.36

Notes: 1. Figures in the "Number" column do not add up to the total population due to: a) Ancestry/Race overlap — e.g. persons can report being both White and Irish, b) persons of Hispanic origin can report being any race, c) persons reporting two ancestries are counted in both categories. 2. Numbers in parentheses indicate the number of persons reporting this ancestry/race alone, not in combination with any other ancestry/race. 3. Refer to the Explanation of Data in the front of the book for more detailed information.

Brazilian	14	0.13
British	21	0.20
Celtic	7	0.07
Czech	228	2.12
Czechoslovakian	43	0.40
Danish	145	1.35
Dutch	271	2.52
English	1,032	9.61
European	50	0.47
Finnish	17	0.16
French, except Basque	347	3.23
French Canadian	114	1.06
German	4,940	46.00
Greek	16	0.15
Hawaii Native/Pacific Islander:	6	0.06
Other Pac. Isl., not spec.	6	0.06
Hispanic or Latino:	168	1.57
Central American:	7	0.07
Honduran	7	0.07
Cuban	10	0.09
Mexican	101	0.94
Puerto Rican	15	0.14
South American:	2	0.02
Bolivian	2	0.02
Other Hispanic or Latino	33	0.31
Hungarian	29	0.27
Irish	1,440	13.41
Italian	224	2.09
Lithuanian	32	0.30
Norwegian	821	7.64
Pennsylvania German	7	0.07
Polish	644	6.00
Portuguese	6	0.06
Romanian	10	0.09
Russian	39	0.36
Scandinavian	43	0.40
Scotch-Irish	163	1.52
Scottish	197	1.83
Serbian	15	0.14
Slavic	12	0.11
Slovak	29	0.27
Slovene	9	0.08
Swedish	249	2.32
Swiss	130	1.21
United States or American	521	4.85
Welsh	109	1.01
White:	10,467	97.72
Not Hispanic (10,300)	10,355	96.68
Hispanic (102)	112	1.05

Beaver Dam

Place Type: City
County: Dodge
Population: 15,169

Ancestry/Race	Number	%
African American/Black:	106	0.70
Not Hispanic (43)	79	0.52
Hispanic (23)	27	0.18
African, sub-Saharan:	7	0.05
Nigerian	7	0.05
Am. Ind. or Alaska Nat., not spec.	28	0.18
American Indian tribes, specified:	62	0.41
Cherokee (3)	10	0.07
Chippewa (11)	16	0.11
Comanche	1	0.01
Delaware (1)	1	0.01
Iroquois (2)	3	0.02
Latin American Indians (1)	1	0.01
Ottawa (4)	8	0.05
Sioux (1)	1	0.01
All other tribes (13)	21	0.14
American Indian tribes, not spec.	3	0.02
Arab:	22	0.15
Arab/Arabic	8	0.05
Lebanese	11	0.07
Other Arab	3	0.02
Asian:	128	0.84
Chinese, ex. Taiwanese (9)	14	0.09
Filipino (11)	24	0.16
Indian (33)	36	0.24
Japanese (5)	9	0.06
Korean (17)	25	0.16
Laotian (2)	2	0.01
Pakistani (3)	3	0.02
Vietnamese (7)	9	0.06
Other Asian, not specified (2)	6	0.04
Australian	6	0.04
Belgian	72	0.48
British	6	0.04
Canadian	6	0.04
Croatian	10	0.07
Czech	168	1.12
Czechoslovakian	6	0.04
Danish	73	0.49
Dutch	514	3.42
English	899	5.98
European	28	0.19
Finnish	67	0.45
French, except Basque	728	4.84
French Canadian	76	0.51
German	8,278	55.03
Greek	38	0.25
Hawaii Native/Pacific Islander:	10	0.07
Polynesian: (7)	9	0.06
Native Hawaiian	2	0.01
Samoan (6)	6	0.04
Other Polynesian (1)	1	0.01
Other Pac. Isl., not spec.	1	0.01
Hispanic or Latino:	640	4.22
Central American:	6	0.04
Guatemalan	2	0.01
Panamanian	1	0.01
Salvadoran	3	0.02
Cuban	4	0.03
Dominican Republic	1	0.01
Mexican	531	3.50
Puerto Rican	17	0.11
South American:	3	0.02
Chilean	1	0.01
Peruvian	2	0.01
Other Hispanic or Latino	78	0.51
Hungarian	151	1.00
Irish	1,706	11.34
Italian	188	1.25
Luxemburger	17	0.11
Norwegian	700	4.65
Polish	1,239	8.24
Romanian	7	0.05
Russian	47	0.31
Scandinavian	4	0.03
Scotch-Irish	105	0.70
Scottish	168	1.12
Serbian	5	0.03
Slavic	5	0.03
Slovak	33	0.22
Swedish	193	1.28
Swiss	228	1.52
Ukrainian	30	0.20
United States or American	616	4.10
Welsh	110	0.73
West Indian, excl. Hispanic:	14	0.09
British West Indian	14	0.09
White:	14,703	96.93
Not Hispanic (14,237)	14,333	94.49
Hispanic (318)	370	2.44
Yugoslavian	5	0.03

Bellevue Town

Place Type: Census Designated Place
County: Brown
Population: 11,828

Ancestry/Race	Number	%
African American/Black:	86	0.73
Not Hispanic (56)	77	0.65
Hispanic (4)	9	0.08
African, sub-Saharan:	27	0.23
African	27	0.23
Am. Ind. or Alaska Nat., not spec.	32	0.27
American Indian tribes, specified:	97	0.82
Cherokee	1	0.01
Chippewa (6)	8	0.07
Iroquois (41)	51	0.43
Latin American Indians (1)	1	0.01
Menominee (11)	13	0.11
Potawatomi (2)	2	0.02
Sioux (4)	4	0.03
Tohono O'Odham	1	0.01
All other tribes (11)	16	0.14
American Indian tribes, not spec.	3	0.03
Arab:	67	0.56
Lebanese	67	0.56
Asian:	187	1.58
Chinese, ex. Taiwanese (23)	32	0.27
Filipino (6)	9	0.08
Hmong (87)	91	0.77
Indian (5)	5	0.04
Indonesian	1	0.01
Japanese (6)	8	0.07
Korean (6)	10	0.08
Laotian (8)	10	0.08
Thai (1)	1	0.01
Vietnamese (1)	10	0.08
Other Asian, not specified (9)	10	0.08
Austrian	53	0.45
Belgian	2,053	17.24
British	11	0.09
Croatian	17	0.14
Czech	442	3.71
Czechoslovakian	49	0.41
Danish	216	1.81
Dutch	897	7.53
English	517	4.34
European	6	0.05
Finnish	142	1.19
French, except Basque	930	7.81
French Canadian	446	3.75
German	4,621	38.80
Hawaii Native/Pacific Islander:	6	0.05
Polynesian:	4	0.03
Native Hawaiian	3	0.03
Samoan	1	0.01
Other Pac. Isl., not spec. (1)	2	0.02
Hispanic or Latino:	310	2.62
Central American:	12	0.10
Guatemalan	3	0.03
Honduran	2	0.02
Panamanian	4	0.03
Salvadoran	3	0.03
Cuban	2	0.02
Mexican	240	2.03
Puerto Rican	9	0.08
South American:	17	0.14
Bolivian	1	0.01
Chilean	1	0.01
Colombian	11	0.09
Ecuadorian	1	0.01
Peruvian	3	0.03
Other Hispanic or Latino	30	0.25
Hungarian	8	0.07
Icelander	8	0.07
Irish	975	8.19
Italian	225	1.89
Lithuanian	8	0.07
Norwegian	530	4.45
Polish	1,410	11.84
Romanian	9	0.08
Russian	25	0.21
Scotch-Irish	57	0.48
Scottish	117	0.98
Slovak	7	0.06
Swedish	239	2.01
Swiss	102	0.86
United States or American	535	4.49
Welsh	13	0.11
West Indian, excl. Hispanic:	6	0.05
Haitian	6	0.05

Notes: 1. Figures in the "Number" column do not add up to the total population due to: a) Ancestry/Race overlap — e.g. persons can report being both White and Irish, b) persons of Hispanic origin can report being any race, c) persons reporting two ancestries are counted in both categories. 2. Numbers in parentheses indicate the number of persons reporting this ancestry/race alone, not in combination with any other ancestry/race. 3. Refer to the Explanation of Data in the front of the book for more detailed information.

White:	11,368	96.11
Not Hispanic (11,144)	11,202	94.71
Hispanic (140)	166	1.40
Yugoslavian	9	0.08

Beloit

Place Type: City
County: Rock
Population: 35,775

Ancestry/Race	Number	%
Acadian/Cajun	31	0.09
African American/Black:	6,002	16.78
Not Hispanic (5,428)	5,894	16.48
Hispanic (69)	108	0.30
African, sub-Saharan:	151	0.42
African	151	0.42
Alaska Native tribes, specified:	6	0.02
Eskimo (1)	1	0.00
Tlingit-Haida (3)	5	0.01
Am. Ind. or Alaska Nat., not spec.	127	0.35
American Indian tribes, specified:	217	0.61
Apache (4)	9	0.03
Blackfeet	10	0.03
Cherokee (13)	71	0.20
Chickasaw	1	0.00
Chippewa (16)	24	0.07
Choctaw	6	0.02
Comanche (1)	1	0.00
Cree	1	0.00
Creek (2)	2	0.01
Crow	1	0.00
Iroquois (2)	5	0.01
Latin American Indians (7)	13	0.04
Menominee (9)	11	0.03
Navajo	1	0.00
Pima (2)	2	0.01
Potawatomi (2)	3	0.01
Shoshone (1)	1	0.00
Sioux (6)	26	0.07
Tohono O'Odham (1)	1	0.00
All other tribes (19)	28	0.08
American Indian tribes, not spec.	3	0.01
Arab:	34	0.10
Arab/Arabic	27	0.08
Palestinian	7	0.02
Armenian	5	0.01
Asian:	559	1.56
Bangladeshi (1)	1	0.00
Cambodian (3)	4	0.01
Chinese, ex. Taiwanese (50)	89	0.25
Filipino (43)	62	0.17
Hmong (17)	17	0.05
Indian (41)	52	0.15
Indonesian (6)	7	0.02
Japanese (34)	54	0.15
Korean (33)	45	0.13
Laotian (1)	2	0.01
Malaysian (4)	4	0.01
Pakistani (5)	13	0.04
Sri Lankan (1)	1	0.00
Taiwanese (1)	1	0.00
Thai (5)	9	0.03
Vietnamese (144)	155	0.43
Other Asian, specified (5)	9	0.03
Other Asian, not specified (8)	34	0.10
Australian	5	0.01
Austrian	25	0.07
Belgian	116	0.33
Brazilian	5	0.01
British	42	0.12
Canadian	19	0.05
Croatian	29	0.08
Czech	347	0.97
Czechoslovakian	53	0.15
Danish	320	0.90
Dutch	586	1.64
Eastern European	7	0.02
English	3,332	9.35
Estonian	12	0.03
European	16	0.04
Finnish	99	0.28
French, except Basque	1,137	3.19
French Canadian	249	0.70
German	8,960	25.13
German Russian	10	0.03
Greek	124	0.35
Hawaii Native/Pacific Islander:	58	0.16
Micronesian: (7)	12	0.03
Guamanian/Chamorro (3)	6	0.02
Other Micronesian (4)	6	0.02
Polynesian: (3)	23	0.06
Native Hawaiian (2)	15	0.04
Samoan (1)	8	0.02
Other Pac. Isl., specified	3	0.01
Other Pac. Isl., not spec. (12)	20	0.06
Hispanic or Latino:	3,257	9.10
Central American:	27	0.08
Costa Rican	4	0.01
Guatemalan	3	0.01
Honduran	9	0.03
Nicaraguan	1	0.00
Panamanian	5	0.01
Salvadoran	4	0.01
Other Central American	1	0.00
Cuban	21	0.06
Dominican Republic	45	0.13
Mexican	2,790	7.80
Puerto Rican	70	0.20
South American:	23	0.06
Argentinean	1	0.00
Bolivian	1	0.00
Colombian	9	0.03
Ecuadorian	3	0.01
Peruvian	3	0.01
Venezuelan	6	0.02
Other Hispanic or Latino	281	0.79
Hungarian	87	0.24
Iranian	5	0.01
Irish	4,477	12.56
Israeli	5	0.01
Italian	1,196	3.35
Latvian	8	0.02
Lithuanian	90	0.25
Luxemburger	35	0.10
Norwegian	3,071	8.61
Pennsylvania German	26	0.07
Polish	687	1.93
Portuguese	21	0.06
Romanian	6	0.02
Russian	109	0.31
Scandinavian	57	0.16
Scotch-Irish	341	0.96
Scottish	373	1.05
Serbian	14	0.04
Slovak	21	0.06
Slovene	11	0.03
Swedish	813	2.28
Swiss	346	0.97
Ukrainian	12	0.03
United States or American	1,658	4.65
Welsh	122	0.34
West Indian, excl. Hispanic:	50	0.14
Bahamian	16	0.04
Jamaican	23	0.06
West Indian	11	0.03
White:	27,956	78.14
Not Hispanic (25,732)	26,407	73.81
Hispanic (1,302)	1,549	4.33
Yugoslavian	58	0.16

Brookfield

Place Type: City
County: Waukesha
Population: 38,649

Ancestry/Race	Number	%
Acadian/Cajun	17	0.04
African American/Black:	402	1.04
Not Hispanic (316)	391	1.01
Hispanic (5)	11	0.03
African, sub-Saharan:	26	0.07
Nigerian	26	0.07
Am. Ind. or Alaska Nat., not spec.	19	0.05
Albanian	18	0.05
Alsatian	7	0.02
American Indian tribes, specified:	63	0.16
Blackfeet	1	0.00
Cherokee (1)	5	0.01
Chippewa (6)	17	0.04
Choctaw (1)	1	0.00
Iroquois (3)	7	0.02
Latin American Indians	2	0.01
Menominee (2)	6	0.02
Ottawa (1)	3	0.01
Potawatomi (1)	1	0.00
Pueblo (1)	1	0.00
Sioux (2)	4	0.01
All other tribes (12)	15	0.04
American Indian tribes, not spec.	4	0.01
Arab:	52	0.13
Egyptian	16	0.04
Lebanese	31	0.08
Syrian	5	0.01
Armenian	135	0.35
Asian:	1,673	4.33
Bangladeshi (6)	7	0.02
Chinese, ex. Taiwanese (360)	404	1.05
Filipino (123)	159	0.41
Hmong (30)	30	0.08
Indian (552)	588	1.52
Indonesian (1)	3	0.01
Japanese (52)	72	0.19
Korean (189)	210	0.54
Laotian (7)	7	0.02
Malaysian (1)	4	0.01
Pakistani (44)	63	0.16
Sri Lankan (3)	3	0.01
Taiwanese (13)	17	0.04
Thai (9)	12	0.03
Vietnamese (54)	61	0.16
Other Asian, specified (3)	3	0.01
Other Asian, not specified (13)	30	0.08
Australian	19	0.05
Austrian	407	1.05
Belgian	120	0.31
Brazilian	21	0.05
British	134	0.35
Canadian	93	0.24
Croatian	215	0.55
Czech	490	1.26
Czechoslovakian	112	0.29
Danish	295	0.76
Dutch	687	1.77
English	2,821	7.27
Estonian	11	0.03
European	189	0.49
Finnish	267	0.69
French, except Basque	1,288	3.32
French Canadian	333	0.86
German	17,899	46.12
Greek	370	0.95
Hawaii Native/Pacific Islander:	24	0.06
Micronesian: (1)	5	0.01
Guamanian/Chamorro (1)	4	0.01
Other Micronesian	1	0.00
Polynesian: (6)	13	0.03
Native Hawaiian (5)	12	0.03
Samoan (1)	1	0.00
Other Pac. Isl., not spec.	6	0.02
Hispanic or Latino:	453	1.17
Central American:	14	0.04
Costa Rican	2	0.01
Guatemalan	4	0.01
Honduran	1	0.00
Nicaraguan	1	0.00
Panamanian	1	0.00
Salvadoran	5	0.01

Notes: 1. Figures in the "Number" column do not add up to the total population due to: a) Ancestry/Race overlap — e.g. persons can report being both White and Irish, b) persons of Hispanic origin can report being any race, c) persons reporting two ancestries are counted in both categories. 2. Numbers in parentheses indicate the number of persons reporting this ancestry/race alone, not in combination with any other ancestry/race. 3. Refer to the Explanation of Data in the front of the book for more detailed information.

Ancestry/Race	Number	%
Cuban	14	0.04
Mexican	270	0.70
Puerto Rican	60	0.16
South American:	27	0.07
Argentinean	1	0.00
Bolivian	1	0.00
Chilean	1	0.00
Colombian	7	0.02
Ecuadorian	3	0.01
Paraguayan	3	0.01
Peruvian	5	0.01
Venezuelan	3	0.01
Other South American	3	0.01
Other Hispanic or Latino	68	0.18
Hungarian	515	1.33
Icelander	5	0.01
Iranian	92	0.24
Irish	5,708	14.71
Italian	2,997	7.72
Latvian	35	0.09
Lithuanian	20	0.05
Luxemburger	61	0.16
New Zealander	23	0.06
Northern European	10	0.03
Norwegian	2,052	5.29
Polish	4,370	11.26
Portuguese	12	0.03
Romanian	32	0.08
Russian	309	0.80
Scandinavian	79	0.20
Scotch-Irish	434	1.12
Scottish	566	1.46
Serbian	139	0.36
Slavic	26	0.07
Slovak	309	0.80
Slovene	148	0.38
Swedish	1,012	2.61
Swiss	417	1.07
Ukrainian	77	0.20
United States or American	1,335	3.44
Welsh	307	0.79
West Indian, excl. Hispanic:	9	0.02
West Indian	9	0.02
White:	36,670	94.88
Not Hispanic (36,051)	36,283	93.88
Hispanic (356)	387	1.00
Yugoslavian	88	0.23

Brown Deer

Place Type: Village
County: Milwaukee
Population: 12,170

Ancestry/Race	Number	%
African American/Black:	1,658	13.62
Not Hispanic (1,516)	1,641	13.48
Hispanic (6)	17	0.14
African, sub-Saharan:	98	0.81
African	66	0.54
Nigerian	9	0.07
South African	23	0.19
Am. Ind. or Alaska Nat., not spec.	31	0.25
American Indian tribes, specified:	45	0.37
Apache (2)	2	0.02
Cherokee	4	0.03
Chippewa (6)	10	0.08
Comanche (1)	1	0.01
Delaware (1)	1	0.01
Iroquois (7)	13	0.11
Latin American Indians (1)	1	0.01
Menominee (2)	2	0.02
Shoshone	2	0.02
Sioux (1)	4	0.03
All other tribes (3)	5	0.04
American Indian tribes, not spec.	1	0.01
Arab:	56	0.46
Arab/Arabic	38	0.31
Lebanese	6	0.05
Palestinian	12	0.10
Armenian	60	0.49
Asian:	367	3.02
Chinese, ex. Taiwanese (76)	78	0.64
Filipino (21)	39	0.32
Hmong (21)	22	0.18
Indian (109)	111	0.91
Indonesian (6)	6	0.05
Japanese (15)	22	0.18
Korean (22)	25	0.21
Pakistani (11)	16	0.13
Taiwanese (4)	4	0.03
Thai (1)	4	0.03
Vietnamese (21)	21	0.17
Other Asian, not specified (12)	19	0.16
Austrian	130	1.07
Belgian	60	0.49
British	10	0.08
Bulgarian	23	0.19
Canadian	57	0.47
Croatian	47	0.39
Czech	226	1.86
Czechoslovakian	31	0.25
Danish	105	0.86
Dutch	200	1.64
English	547	4.49
European	57	0.47
Finnish	62	0.51
French, except Basque	389	3.20
French Canadian	191	1.57
German	4,828	39.67
German Russian	9	0.07
Greek	34	0.28
Hawaii Native/Pacific Islander:	8	0.07
Micronesian: (1)	2	0.02
Guamanian/Chamorro (1)	2	0.02
Polynesian: (4)	5	0.04
Native Hawaiian (2)	3	0.02
Other Polynesian (2)	2	0.02
Other Pac. Isl., not spec.	1	0.01
Hispanic or Latino:	260	2.14
Central American:	10	0.08
Costa Rican	2	0.02
Guatemalan	2	0.02
Nicaraguan	2	0.02
Panamanian	2	0.02
Other Central American	2	0.02
Cuban	24	0.20
Dominican Republic	1	0.01
Mexican	115	0.94
Puerto Rican	44	0.36
South American:	17	0.14
Argentinean	2	0.02
Bolivian	2	0.02
Colombian	3	0.02
Paraguayan	1	0.01
Venezuelan	7	0.06
Other South American	2	0.02
Other Hispanic or Latino	49	0.40
Hungarian	99	0.81
Iranian	7	0.06
Irish	1,085	8.92
Italian	590	4.85
Latvian	34	0.28
Lithuanian	8	0.07
Luxemburger	46	0.38
Northern European	2	0.02
Norwegian	391	3.21
Polish	1,332	10.94
Russian	200	1.64
Scandinavian	9	0.07
Scotch-Irish	130	1.07
Scottish	123	1.01
Serbian	8	0.07
Slovak	55	0.45
Slovene	37	0.30
Swedish	163	1.34
Swiss	45	0.37
Ukrainian	17	0.14
United States or American	486	3.99
Welsh	87	0.71
West Indian, excl. Hispanic:	27	0.22
British West Indian	18	0.15
Jamaican	9	0.07
White:	10,168	83.55
Not Hispanic (9,822)	9,986	82.05
Hispanic (162)	182	1.50

Caledonia

Place Type: Town
County: Racine
Population: 23,614

Ancestry/Race	Number	%
African American/Black:	538	2.28
Not Hispanic (469)	531	2.25
Hispanic (1)	7	0.03
Am. Ind. or Alaska Nat., not spec.	76	0.32
Albanian	11	0.05
American Indian tribes, specified:	105	0.44
Blackfeet	3	0.01
Cherokee (8)	16	0.07
Chippewa (32)	46	0.19
Choctaw	1	0.00
Creek	2	0.01
Delaware	1	0.00
Iroquois (4)	12	0.05
Latin American Indians (4)	4	0.02
Lumbee (5)	5	0.02
Menominee (2)	3	0.01
Navajo	2	0.01
Ottawa (1)	3	0.01
Potawatomi (1)	2	0.01
All other tribes (1)	5	0.02
American Indian tribes, not spec.	13	0.06
Arab:	36	0.15
Lebanese	8	0.03
Syrian	28	0.12
Armenian	168	0.71
Asian:	349	1.48
Chinese, ex. Taiwanese (38)	45	0.19
Filipino (26)	32	0.14
Hmong (6)	6	0.03
Indian (157)	165	0.70
Indonesian (1)	4	0.02
Japanese (3)	10	0.04
Korean (39)	46	0.19
Laotian (1)	1	0.00
Pakistani (5)	5	0.02
Taiwanese (4)	6	0.03
Thai (1)	1	0.00
Vietnamese (8)	15	0.06
Other Asian, specified (1)	2	0.01
Other Asian, not specified (10)	11	0.05
Australian	10	0.04
Austrian	122	0.52
Belgian	51	0.22
British	33	0.14
Croatian	120	0.51
Czech	787	3.33
Czechoslovakian	116	0.49
Danish	1,711	7.23
Dutch	645	2.73
English	1,603	6.78
European	47	0.20
Finnish	85	0.36
French, except Basque	1,011	4.28
French Canadian	370	1.56
German	9,995	42.26
German Russian	6	0.03
Greek	84	0.36
Hawaii Native/Pacific Islander:	29	0.12
Micronesian: (3)	3	0.01
Guamanian/Chamorro (3)	3	0.01
Polynesian: (2)	19	0.08
Native Hawaiian (1)	15	0.06
Samoan (1)	4	0.02
Other Pac. Isl., not spec. (6)	7	0.03
Hispanic or Latino:	736	3.12
Central American:	9	0.04

Notes: 1. Figures in the "Number" column do not add up to the total population due to: a) Ancestry/Race overlap — e.g. persons can report being both White and Irish, b) persons of Hispanic origin can report being any race, c) persons reporting two ancestries are counted in both categories. 2. Numbers in parentheses indicate the number of persons reporting this ancestry/race alone, not in combination with any other ancestry/race. 3. Refer to the Explanation of Data in the front of the book for more detailed information.

Costa Rican	3	0.01
Guatemalan	3	0.01
Salvadoran	3	0.01
Cuban	12	0.05
Dominican Republic	7	0.03
Mexican	495	2.10
Puerto Rican	64	0.27
South American:	19	0.08
Argentinean	9	0.04
Colombian	8	0.03
Peruvian	2	0.01
Other Hispanic or Latino	130	0.55
Hungarian	321	1.36
Irish	2,582	10.92
Israeli	20	0.08
Italian	1,449	6.13
Latvian	18	0.08
Lithuanian	120	0.51
Luxemburger	13	0.05
Norwegian	1,378	5.83
Pennsylvania German	25	0.11
Polish	3,073	12.99
Russian	141	0.60
Scandinavian	139	0.59
Scotch-Irish	245	1.04
Scottish	291	1.23
Serbian	91	0.38
Slavic	18	0.08
Slovak	132	0.56
Slovene	100	0.42
Swedish	506	2.14
Swiss	66	0.28
Turkish	58	0.25
Ukrainian	35	0.15
United States or American	842	3.56
Welsh	180	0.76
West Indian, excl. Hispanic:	16	0.07
Jamaican	8	0.03
West Indian	8	0.03
White:	22,501	95.29
Not Hispanic (21,792)	21,991	93.13
Hispanic (448)	510	2.16
Yugoslavian	118	0.50

Cedarburg

Place Type: City
County: Ozaukee
Population: 10,908

Ancestry/Race	Number	%
African American/Black:	39	0.36
Not Hispanic (25)	37	0.34
Hispanic (2)	2	0.02
African, sub-Saharan:	16	0.15
South African	16	0.15
Am. Ind. or Alaska Nat., not spec.	11	0.10
American Indian tribes, specified:	29	0.27
Blackfeet	3	0.03
Cherokee	5	0.05
Chippewa (6)	9	0.08
Iroquois (5)	6	0.06
Latin American Indians (2)	2	0.02
Menominee	1	0.01
Sioux	2	0.02
All other tribes	1	0.01
Arab:	7	0.06
Lebanese	7	0.06
Asian:	104	0.95
Chinese, ex. Taiwanese (14)	17	0.16
Filipino (2)	5	0.05
Indian (36)	42	0.39
Japanese (7)	17	0.16
Korean (15)	17	0.16
Taiwanese (4)	4	0.04
Thai (1)	1	0.01
Vietnamese (1)	1	0.01
Austrian	107	0.99
Belgian	13	0.12
British	75	0.70
Bulgarian	6	0.06
Canadian	43	0.40
Croatian	58	0.54
Czech	171	1.59
Czechoslovakian	39	0.36
Danish	134	1.24
Dutch	346	3.21
English	931	8.64
European	61	0.57
Finnish	43	0.40
French, except Basque	404	3.75
French Canadian	100	0.93
German	5,678	52.70
Greek	27	0.25
Hawaii Native/Pacific Islander:	5	0.05
Polynesian: (2)	4	0.04
Native Hawaiian (2)	4	0.04
Other Pac. Isl., not spec.	1	0.01
Hispanic or Latino:	94	0.86
Cuban	6	0.06
Mexican	49	0.45
Puerto Rican	14	0.13
South American:	8	0.07
Chilean	1	0.01
Colombian	4	0.04
Other South American	3	0.03
Other Hispanic or Latino	17	0.16
Hungarian	60	0.56
Irish	1,340	12.44
Italian	801	7.43
Latvian	52	0.48
Lithuanian	13	0.12
Luxemburger	78	0.72
Northern European	10	0.09
Norwegian	573	5.32
Polish	905	8.40
Portuguese	27	0.25
Romanian	16	0.15
Russian	195	1.81
Scandinavian	25	0.23
Scotch-Irish	118	1.10
Scottish	146	1.35
Slavic	13	0.12
Slovak	90	0.84
Slovene	20	0.19
Swedish	283	2.63
Swiss	98	0.91
United States or American	370	3.43
Welsh	6	0.06
White:	10,770	98.73
Not Hispanic (10,629)	10,689	97.99
Hispanic (79)	81	0.74
Yugoslavian	9	0.08

Chippewa Falls

Place Type: City
County: Chippewa
Population: 12,925

Ancestry/Race	Number	%
African American/Black:	66	0.51
Not Hispanic (36)	53	0.41
Hispanic (3)	13	0.10
Alaska Native tribes, specified:	1	0.01
Tlingit-Haida (1)	1	0.01
Alaska Native tribes, not specified	1	0.01
Am. Ind. or Alaska Nat., not spec.	25	0.19
American Indian tribes, specified:	66	0.51
Apache (2)	2	0.02
Cherokee (6)	10	0.08
Chippewa (24)	35	0.27
Iroquois (1)	1	0.01
Latin American Indians (2)	2	0.02
Menominee (1)	1	0.01
Sioux (2)	3	0.02
All other tribes (7)	12	0.09
American Indian tribes, not spec.	1	0.01
Arab:	18	0.14
Egyptian	18	0.14
Asian:	128	0.99
Chinese, ex. Taiwanese (7)	12	0.09
Filipino (27)	35	0.27
Hmong (26)	29	0.22
Indian (1)	4	0.03
Japanese (2)	14	0.11
Korean (7)	10	0.08
Taiwanese (1)	2	0.02
Thai	2	0.02
Vietnamese (10)	12	0.09
Other Asian, specified	2	0.02
Other Asian, not specified (3)	6	0.05
Australian	4	0.03
Austrian	106	0.82
Belgian	11	0.08
British	9	0.07
Canadian	20	0.15
Czech	230	1.77
Czechoslovakian	11	0.08
Danish	172	1.33
Dutch	183	1.41
English	701	5.40
European	64	0.49
Finnish	64	0.49
French, except Basque	1,069	8.24
French Canadian	447	3.44
German	5,988	46.15
Greek	15	0.12
Hawaii Native/Pacific Islander:	5	0.04
Polynesian: (1)	5	0.04
Native Hawaiian (1)	5	0.04
Hispanic or Latino:	82	0.63
Central American:	3	0.02
Guatemalan	1	0.01
Nicaraguan	1	0.01
Salvadoran	1	0.01
Cuban	5	0.04
Mexican	40	0.31
Puerto Rican	15	0.12
South American:	1	0.01
Colombian	1	0.01
Other Hispanic or Latino	18	0.14
Hungarian	8	0.06
Icelander	1	0.01
Irish	1,665	12.83
Italian	207	1.60
Lithuanian	12	0.09
Norwegian	2,471	19.04
Polish	762	5.87
Portuguese	25	0.19
Russian	48	0.37
Scandinavian	87	0.67
Scotch-Irish	168	1.29
Scottish	166	1.28
Serbian	42	0.32
Slovene	21	0.16
Swedish	507	3.91
Swiss	125	0.96
United States or American	357	2.75
Welsh	46	0.35
White:	12,713	98.36
Not Hispanic (12,579)	12,663	97.97
Hispanic (39)	50	0.39

Cudahy

Place Type: City
County: Milwaukee
Population: 18,429

Ancestry/Race	Number	%
African American/Black:	267	1.45
Not Hispanic (150)	225	1.22
Hispanic (25)	42	0.23
Alaska Native tribes, specified:	3	0.02
Alaska Athabascan (2)	3	0.02
Am. Ind. or Alaska Nat., not spec.	49	0.27
Albanian	206	1.12
American Indian tribes, specified:	205	1.11
Apache (6)	6	0.03

Notes: 1. Figures in the "Number" column do not add up to the total population due to: a) Ancestry/Race overlap — e.g. persons can report being both White and Irish, b) persons of Hispanic origin can report being any race, c) persons reporting two ancestries are counted in both categories. 2. Numbers in parentheses indicate the number of persons reporting this ancestry/race alone, not in combination with any other ancestry/race. 3. Refer to the Explanation of Data in the front of the book for more detailed information.

Blackfeet (1)	2	0.01
Cherokee (7)	19	0.10
Cheyenne (1)	1	0.01
Chippewa (52)	78	0.42
Comanche	1	0.01
Iroquois (18)	34	0.18
Latin American Indians	2	0.01
Menominee (9)	12	0.07
Ottawa (3)	4	0.02
Pima	2	0.01
Potawatomi (1)	2	0.01
Sioux (4)	12	0.07
All other tribes (20)	30	0.16
American Indian tribes, not spec.	5	0.03
Arab:	42	0.23
Egyptian	7	0.04
Lebanese	12	0.07
Syrian	23	0.12
Armenian	53	0.29
Asian:	207	1.12
Chinese, ex. Taiwanese (4)	9	0.05
Filipino (57)	78	0.42
Hmong (1)	1	0.01
Indian (30)	33	0.18
Japanese (8)	14	0.08
Korean (19)	27	0.15
Laotian (8)	10	0.05
Malaysian (1)	1	0.01
Pakistani (2)	2	0.01
Thai (1)	1	0.01
Vietnamese (13)	13	0.07
Other Asian, specified	5	0.03
Other Asian, not specified (10)	13	0.07
Australian	7	0.04
Austrian	207	1.12
Belgian	72	0.39
British	9	0.05
Celtic	9	0.05
Croatian	140	0.76
Czech	250	1.36
Czechoslovakian	175	0.95
Danish	194	1.05
Dutch	299	1.62
Eastern European	6	0.03
English	714	3.87
European	54	0.29
Finnish	114	0.62
French, except Basque	781	4.24
French Canadian	324	1.76
German	7,397	40.14
Greek	80	0.43
Hawaii Native/Pacific Islander:	23	0.12
Micronesian: (1)	2	0.01
Guamanian/Chamorro (1)	2	0.01
Polynesian: (3)	8	0.04
Native Hawaiian (1)	5	0.03
Samoan (2)	2	0.01
Other Polynesian	1	0.01
Other Pac. Isl., specified	5	0.03
Other Pac. Isl., not spec. (2)	8	0.04
Hispanic or Latino:	872	4.73
Central American:	12	0.07
Guatemalan	4	0.02
Nicaraguan	4	0.02
Salvadoran	4	0.02
Cuban	10	0.05
Mexican	453	2.46
Puerto Rican	295	1.60
South American:	10	0.05
Chilean	1	0.01
Colombian	3	0.02
Peruvian	3	0.02
Other South American	3	0.02
Other Hispanic or Latino	92	0.50
Hungarian	186	1.01
Irish	2,071	11.24
Italian	1,011	5.49
Lithuanian	82	0.44
Luxemburger	5	0.03
Macedonian	16	0.09
Norwegian	614	3.33
Pennsylvania German	5	0.03
Polish	4,889	26.53
Romanian	11	0.06
Russian	140	0.76
Scandinavian	48	0.26
Scotch-Irish	55	0.30
Scottish	215	1.17
Serbian	85	0.46
Slavic	18	0.10
Slovak	370	2.01
Slovene	48	0.26
Swedish	275	1.49
Swiss	51	0.28
Ukrainian	22	0.12
United States or American	391	2.12
Welsh	25	0.14
West Indian, excl. Hispanic:	10	0.05
Jamaican	10	0.05
White:	17,653	95.79
Not Hispanic (16,814)	17,069	92.62
Hispanic (489)	584	3.17
Yugoslavian	62	0.34

De Pere

Place Type: City
County: Brown
Population: 20,559

Ancestry/Race	Number	%
African American/Black:	165	0.80
Not Hispanic (103)	155	0.75
Hispanic (7)	10	0.05
African, sub-Saharan:	8	0.04
African	8	0.04
Alaska Native tribes, not specified	1	0.00
Am. Ind. or Alaska Nat., not spec.	22	0.11
American Indian tribes, specified:	248	1.21
Blackfeet	6	0.03
Cherokee (1)	10	0.05
Chippewa (21)	30	0.15
Choctaw (1)	2	0.01
Iroquois (111)	148	0.72
Menominee (15)	20	0.10
Navajo (1)	2	0.01
Pima	1	0.00
Potawatomi (4)	4	0.02
Sioux (1)	2	0.01
All other tribes (16)	23	0.11
American Indian tribes, not spec.	5	0.02
Arab:	17	0.08
Lebanese	17	0.08
Asian:	205	1.00
Chinese, ex. Taiwanese (25)	28	0.14
Filipino (16)	28	0.14
Hmong (21)	26	0.13
Indian (40)	43	0.21
Indonesian (2)	2	0.01
Japanese (23)	32	0.16
Korean (16)	26	0.13
Laotian (2)	2	0.01
Pakistani (5)	5	0.02
Thai	5	0.02
Vietnamese	1	0.00
Other Asian, specified	2	0.01
Other Asian, not specified (4)	5	0.02
Austrian	131	0.64
Belgian	1,756	8.55
British	33	0.16
Bulgarian	11	0.05
Canadian	20	0.10
Croatian	34	0.17
Czech	496	2.41
Czechoslovakian	17	0.08
Danish	286	1.39
Dutch	2,309	11.24
Eastern European	12	0.06
English	1,091	5.31
European	93	0.45
Finnish	152	0.74
French, except Basque	1,360	6.62
French Canadian	476	2.32
German	8,781	42.74
Greek	34	0.17
Hawaii Native/Pacific Islander:	12	0.06
Micronesian: (2)	3	0.01
Guamanian/Chamorro (1)	2	0.01
Other Micronesian (1)	1	0.00
Polynesian: (5)	5	0.02
Native Hawaiian (2)	2	0.01
Samoan (3)	3	0.01
Other Pac. Isl., specified	2	0.01
Other Pac. Isl., not spec.	2	0.01
Hispanic or Latino:	202	0.98
Central American:	7	0.03
Costa Rican	4	0.02
Guatemalan	3	0.01
Cuban	9	0.04
Dominican Republic	3	0.01
Mexican	111	0.54
Puerto Rican	15	0.07
South American:	10	0.05
Bolivian	2	0.01
Colombian	1	0.00
Ecuadorian	3	0.01
Paraguayan	1	0.00
Peruvian	3	0.01
Other Hispanic or Latino	47	0.23
Hungarian	60	0.29
Irish	2,817	13.71
Italian	610	2.97
Lithuanian	48	0.23
Luxemburger	6	0.03
Northern European	10	0.05
Norwegian	1,007	4.90
Pennsylvania German	7	0.03
Polish	2,131	10.37
Russian	77	0.37
Scandinavian	48	0.23
Scotch-Irish	177	0.86
Scottish	207	1.01
Serbian	20	0.10
Slavic	27	0.13
Slovak	16	0.08
Slovene	18	0.09
Swedish	571	2.78
Swiss	94	0.46
Ukrainian	31	0.15
United States or American	693	3.37
Welsh	37	0.18
West Indian, excl. Hispanic:	1	0.00
Jamaican	1	0.00
White:	20,050	97.52
Not Hispanic (19,738)	19,894	96.77
Hispanic (145)	156	0.76
Yugoslavian	43	0.21

Eau Claire

Place Type: City
County: Eau Claire
Population: 61,704

Ancestry/Race	Number	%
African American/Black:	628	1.02
Not Hispanic (420)	610	0.99
Hispanic (9)	18	0.03
African, sub-Saharan:	66	0.11
African	58	0.09
Nigerian	8	0.01
Alaska Native tribes, specified:	7	0.01
Alaska Athabascan (2)	5	0.01
Aleut	1	0.00
Tlingit-Haida	1	0.00
Alaska Native tribes, not specified	2	0.00
Am. Ind. or Alaska Nat., not spec.	182	0.29
Albanian	19	0.03
American Indian tribes, specified:	389	0.63
Apache (2)	7	0.01

Notes: 1. Figures in the "Number" column do not add up to the total population due to: a) Ancestry/Race overlap — e.g. persons can report being both White and Irish, b) persons of Hispanic origin can report being any race, c) persons reporting two ancestries are counted in both categories. 2. Numbers in parentheses indicate the number of persons reporting this ancestry/race alone, not in combination with any other ancestry/race. 3. Refer to the Explanation of Data in the front of the book for more detailed information.

Ancestry/Race	Number	%
Blackfeet	5	0.01
Cherokee (4)	30	0.05
Cheyenne	1	0.00
Chickasaw (1)	2	0.00
Chippewa (153)	199	0.32
Choctaw (5)	7	0.01
Cree	1	0.00
Creek (1)	1	0.00
Iroquois (7)	9	0.01
Kiowa	1	0.00
Latin American Indians (1)	2	0.00
Lumbee (1)	1	0.00
Menominee (6)	13	0.02
Ottawa (1)	1	0.00
Potawatomi	4	0.01
Pueblo	1	0.00
Seminole (1)	1	0.00
Sioux (9)	21	0.03
Tohono O'Odham (1)	1	0.00
Ute (1)	2	0.00
All other tribes (49)	79	0.13
American Indian tribes, not spec.	25	0.04
Arab:	94	0.15
Arab/Arabic	10	0.02
Egyptian	52	0.08
Lebanese	26	0.04
Syrian	6	0.01
Asian:	2,595	4.21
Cambodian (1)	2	0.00
Chinese, ex. Taiwanese (137)	166	0.27
Filipino (65)	100	0.16
Hmong (1,616)	1,776	2.88
Indian (84)	107	0.17
Indonesian (2)	8	0.01
Japanese (44)	81	0.13
Korean (103)	139	0.23
Laotian (30)	52	0.08
Malaysian (1)	1	0.00
Pakistani (1)	1	0.00
Taiwanese (4)	4	0.01
Thai (11)	13	0.02
Vietnamese (57)	64	0.10
Other Asian, specified (2)	2	0.00
Other Asian, not specified (59)	79	0.13
Australian	53	0.09
Austrian	510	0.83
Belgian	242	0.39
British	174	0.28
Bulgarian	11	0.02
Canadian	76	0.12
Celtic	22	0.04
Croatian	102	0.17
Czech	1,163	1.89
Czechoslovakian	180	0.29
Danish	788	1.28
Dutch	935	1.52
English	4,190	6.81
European	353	0.57
Finnish	426	0.69
French, except Basque	2,434	3.96
French Canadian	810	1.32
German	25,659	41.71
Greek	193	0.31
Hawaii Native/Pacific Islander:	127	0.21
Micronesian: (11)	16	0.03
Guamanian/Chamorro (8)	13	0.02
Other Micronesian (3)	3	0.00
Polynesian: (8)	27	0.04
Native Hawaiian (2)	15	0.02
Samoan (6)	12	0.02
Other Pac. Isl., not spec. (4)	84	0.14
Hispanic or Latino:	619	1.00
Central American:	17	0.03
Costa Rican	3	0.00
Guatemalan	2	0.00
Honduran	5	0.01
Nicaraguan	5	0.01
Panamanian	1	0.00
Salvadoran	1	0.00
Cuban	26	0.04
Dominican Republic	6	0.01
Mexican	266	0.43
Puerto Rican	77	0.12
South American:	62	0.10
Argentinean	11	0.02
Chilean	3	0.00
Colombian	11	0.02
Ecuadorian	5	0.01
Paraguayan	3	0.00
Peruvian	16	0.03
Venezuelan	9	0.01
Other South American	4	0.01
Other Hispanic or Latino	165	0.27
Hungarian	137	0.22
Icelander	8	0.01
Iranian	19	0.03
Irish	7,349	11.95
Israeli	8	0.01
Italian	1,549	2.52
Latvian	31	0.05
Lithuanian	103	0.17
Luxemburger	7	0.01
Macedonian	9	0.01
Northern European	39	0.06
Norwegian	15,377	25.00
Pennsylvania German	26	0.04
Polish	3,555	5.78
Portuguese	20	0.03
Romanian	12	0.02
Russian	219	0.36
Scandinavian	289	0.47
Scotch-Irish	516	0.84
Scottish	803	1.31
Serbian	5	0.01
Slavic	33	0.05
Slovak	127	0.21
Slovene	51	0.08
Swedish	2,449	3.98
Swiss	603	0.98
Ukrainian	60	0.10
United States or American	1,667	2.71
Welsh	304	0.49
White:	58,287	94.46
Not Hispanic (57,308)	57,872	93.79
Hispanic (349)	415	0.67
Yugoslavian	72	0.12

Fitchburg

Place Type: City
County: Dane
Population: 20,501

Ancestry/Race	Number	%
African American/Black:	1,985	9.68
Not Hispanic (1,745)	1,926	9.39
Hispanic (26)	59	0.29
African, sub-Saharan:	271	1.33
African	101	0.49
Ethiopian	9	0.04
Liberian	73	0.36
Nigerian	64	0.31
Senegalese	17	0.08
South African	7	0.03
Alaska Native tribes, not specified	1	0.00
Am. Ind. or Alaska Nat., not spec.	79	0.39
Albanian	93	0.45
American Indian tribes, specified:	102	0.50
Apache (2)	4	0.02
Blackfeet	4	0.02
Cherokee (2)	17	0.08
Cheyenne	1	0.00
Chippewa (10)	14	0.07
Choctaw (1)	1	0.00
Creek (1)	1	0.00
Iroquois (2)	4	0.02
Latin American Indians (2)	12	0.06
Lumbee	1	0.00
Menominee (7)	7	0.03
Navajo (1)	5	0.02
Osage (1)	1	0.00
Potawatomi (1)	2	0.01
Sioux (6)	7	0.03
Yaqui (2)	2	0.01
All other tribes (8)	19	0.09
American Indian tribes, not spec.	8	0.04
Arab:	103	0.50
Arab/Arabic	21	0.10
Iraqi	7	0.03
Lebanese	41	0.20
Moroccan	11	0.05
Palestinian	23	0.11
Asian:	766	3.74
Cambodian (10)	11	0.05
Chinese, ex. Taiwanese (145)	160	0.78
Filipino (34)	47	0.23
Hmong (127)	127	0.62
Indian (152)	162	0.79
Japanese (15)	36	0.18
Korean (75)	93	0.45
Laotian (24)	29	0.14
Malaysian (1)	4	0.02
Pakistani (28)	37	0.18
Taiwanese (2)	2	0.01
Thai (6)	9	0.04
Vietnamese (17)	26	0.13
Other Asian, specified	1	0.00
Other Asian, not specified (11)	22	0.11
Austrian	25	0.12
Belgian	91	0.45
British	100	0.49
Canadian	27	0.13
Czech	240	1.17
Czechoslovakian	8	0.04
Danish	241	1.18
Dutch	287	1.40
Eastern European	11	0.05
English	1,772	8.67
European	172	0.84
Finnish	134	0.66
French, except Basque	576	2.82
French Canadian	113	0.55
German	7,321	35.82
Greek	53	0.26
Hawaii Native/Pacific Islander:	23	0.11
Melanesian: (1)	2	0.01
Other Melanesian (1)	2	0.01
Micronesian:	1	0.00
Guamanian/Chamorro	1	0.00
Polynesian: (2)	5	0.02
Native Hawaiian (2)	5	0.02
Other Pac. Isl., specified	1	0.00
Other Pac. Isl., not spec. (5)	14	0.07
Hispanic or Latino:	1,329	6.48
Central American:	65	0.32
Costa Rican	4	0.02
Guatemalan	9	0.04
Honduran	19	0.09
Nicaraguan	9	0.04
Panamanian	12	0.06
Salvadoran	12	0.06
Cuban	7	0.03
Dominican Republic	4	0.02
Mexican	854	4.17
Puerto Rican	97	0.47
South American:	90	0.44
Argentinean	9	0.04
Chilean	5	0.02
Colombian	39	0.19
Ecuadorian	7	0.03
Paraguayan	1	0.00
Peruvian	18	0.09
Venezuelan	5	0.02
Other South American	6	0.03
Other Hispanic or Latino	212	1.03
Hungarian	79	0.39
Iranian	41	0.20
Irish	2,666	13.04
Italian	940	4.60
Lithuanian	66	0.32

Notes: 1. Figures in the "Number" column do not add up to the total population due to: a) Ancestry/Race overlap — e.g. persons can report being both White and Irish, b) persons of Hispanic origin can report being any race, c) persons reporting two ancestries are counted in both categories. 2. Numbers in parentheses indicate the number of persons reporting this ancestry/race alone, not in combination with any other ancestry/race. 3. Refer to the Explanation of Data in the front of the book for more detailed information.

Ancestry/Race	Number	%
Northern European	59	0.29
Norwegian	2,285	11.18
Polish	997	4.88
Portuguese	9	0.04
Russian	58	0.28
Scandinavian	65	0.32
Scotch-Irish	160	0.78
Scottish	322	1.58
Serbian	7	0.03
Slavic	12	0.06
Slovak	21	0.10
Slovene	7	0.03
Swedish	342	1.67
Swiss	380	1.86
Turkish	3	0.01
Ukrainian	39	0.19
United States or American	631	3.09
Welsh	122	0.60
West Indian, excl. Hispanic:	22	0.11
Haitian	9	0.04
Jamaican	13	0.06
White:	17,297	84.37
Not Hispanic (16,309)	16,643	81.18
Hispanic (540)	654	3.19
Yugoslavian	7	0.03

Fond du Lac

Place Type: City
County: Fond du Lac
Population: 42,203

Ancestry/Race	Number	%
Afghan	2	0.00
African American/Black:	937	2.22
Not Hispanic (767)	897	2.13
Hispanic (16)	40	0.09
African, sub-Saharan:	30	0.07
African	10	0.02
South African	20	0.05
Am. Ind. or Alaska Nat., not spec.	140	0.33
American Indian tribes, specified:	256	0.61
Apache (1)	2	0.00
Blackfeet	1	0.00
Cherokee (4)	16	0.04
Chippewa (55)	84	0.20
Iroquois (14)	19	0.05
Latin American Indians	2	0.00
Menominee (7)	14	0.03
Potawatomi (2)	3	0.01
Seminole	2	0.00
Sioux (3)	8	0.02
All other tribes (51)	105	0.25
American Indian tribes, not spec.	18	0.04
Arab:	236	0.56
Arab/Arabic	11	0.03
Egyptian	40	0.09
Lebanese	176	0.42
Syrian	9	0.02
Armenian	14	0.03
Asian:	778	1.84
Chinese, ex. Taiwanese (33)	40	0.09
Filipino (36)	54	0.13
Hmong (354)	408	0.97
Indian (76)	87	0.21
Indonesian	1	0.00
Japanese (23)	49	0.12
Korean (36)	50	0.12
Laotian (6)	23	0.05
Pakistani (4)	5	0.01
Taiwanese (3)	3	0.01
Thai (5)	9	0.02
Vietnamese (12)	17	0.04
Other Asian, not specified (20)	32	0.08
Australian	18	0.04
Austrian	146	0.35
Belgian	187	0.44
British	44	0.10
Canadian	75	0.18
Croatian	60	0.14
Czech	261	0.62
Czechoslovakian	36	0.09
Danish	326	0.77
Dutch	1,059	2.50
English	2,419	5.72
European	139	0.33
Finnish	145	0.34
French, except Basque	2,216	5.24
French Canadian	604	1.43
German	22,946	54.25
German Russian	5	0.01
Greek	283	0.67
Hawaii Native/Pacific Islander:	16	0.04
Micronesian: (2)	2	0.00
Guamanian/Chamorro (2)	2	0.00
Polynesian: (3)	6	0.01
Native Hawaiian (3)	6	0.01
Other Pac. Isl., not spec. (1)	8	0.02
Hispanic or Latino:	1,232	2.92
Central American:	27	0.06
Guatemalan	7	0.02
Honduran	10	0.02
Nicaraguan	2	0.00
Salvadoran	2	0.00
Other Central American	6	0.01
Cuban	15	0.04
Dominican Republic	2	0.00
Mexican	886	2.10
Puerto Rican	107	0.25
South American:	18	0.04
Chilean	1	0.00
Colombian	10	0.02
Ecuadorian	1	0.00
Paraguayan	1	0.00
Peruvian	2	0.00
Venezuelan	3	0.01
Other Hispanic or Latino	177	0.42
Hungarian	275	0.65
Irish	4,732	11.19
Italian	830	1.96
Latvian	27	0.06
Lithuanian	127	0.30
Luxemburger	56	0.13
New Zealander	21	0.05
Northern European	54	0.13
Norwegian	1,535	3.63
Pennsylvania German	24	0.06
Polish	2,564	6.06
Russian	255	0.60
Scandinavian	45	0.11
Scotch-Irish	161	0.38
Scottish	357	0.84
Slavic	16	0.04
Slovak	37	0.09
Slovene	12	0.03
Swedish	722	1.71
Swiss	301	0.71
Turkish	58	0.14
United States or American	1,887	4.46
Welsh	181	0.43
White:	39,963	94.69
Not Hispanic (38,906)	39,304	93.13
Hispanic (590)	659	1.56
Yugoslavian	50	0.12

Fort Atkinson

Place Type: City
County: Jefferson
Population: 11,621

Ancestry/Race	Number	%
African American/Black:	57	0.49
Not Hispanic (32)	47	0.40
Hispanic (8)	10	0.09
Am. Ind. or Alaska Nat., not spec.	17	0.15
Albanian	86	0.73
American Indian tribes, specified:	40	0.34
Blackfeet (1)	1	0.01
Cherokee (4)	9	0.08
Chippewa (2)	2	0.02
Iroquois (7)	7	0.06
Latin American Indians (2)	2	0.02
Menominee (3)	3	0.03
Ottawa (6)	11	0.09
Potawatomi (1)	1	0.01
Sioux	2	0.02
All other tribes (2)	2	0.02
American Indian tribes, not spec.	1	0.01
Arab:	35	0.30
Lebanese	35	0.30
Asian:	93	0.80
Chinese, ex. Taiwanese (14)	15	0.13
Filipino (19)	30	0.26
Hmong (6)	7	0.06
Indian (19)	22	0.19
Japanese (1)	1	0.01
Korean (8)	11	0.09
Taiwanese (2)	2	0.02
Other Asian, specified	1	0.01
Other Asian, not specified	4	0.03
Austrian	14	0.12
Belgian	52	0.44
British	6	0.05
Canadian	33	0.28
Croatian	28	0.24
Czech	128	1.09
Czechoslovakian	20	0.17
Danish	45	0.38
Dutch	209	1.79
English	1,169	9.98
European	87	0.74
Finnish	43	0.37
French, except Basque	358	3.06
French Canadian	68	0.58
German	5,850	49.97
German Russian	9	0.08
Greek	48	0.41
Hawaii Native/Pacific Islander:	13	0.11
Polynesian: (1)	6	0.05
Native Hawaiian	1	0.01
Samoan (1)	5	0.04
Other Pac. Isl., specified	1	0.01
Other Pac. Isl., not spec.	6	0.05
Hispanic or Latino:	508	4.37
Central American:	9	0.08
Costa Rican	2	0.02
Guatemalan	1	0.01
Panamanian	6	0.05
Cuban	5	0.04
Mexican	395	3.40
Puerto Rican	19	0.16
South American:	1	0.01
Ecuadorian	1	0.01
Other Hispanic or Latino	79	0.68
Hungarian	28	0.24
Iranian	34	0.29
Irish	1,300	11.10
Italian	325	2.78
Lithuanian	23	0.20
Luxemburger	14	0.12
Northern European	20	0.17
Norwegian	963	8.23
Pennsylvania German	8	0.07
Polish	619	5.29
Portuguese	4	0.03
Russian	6	0.05
Scandinavian	7	0.06
Scotch-Irish	64	0.55
Scottish	118	1.01
Slavic	7	0.06
Slovak	29	0.25
Slovene	13	0.11
Swedish	336	2.87
Swiss	155	1.32
Ukrainian	14	0.12
United States or American	493	4.21
Welsh	75	0.64
White:	11,252	96.82
Not Hispanic (10,904)	10,968	94.38

Notes: 1. Figures in the "Number" column do not add up to the total population due to: a) Ancestry/Race overlap — e.g. persons can report being both White and Irish, b) persons of Hispanic origin can report being any race, c) persons reporting two ancestries are counted in both categories. 2. Numbers in parentheses indicate the number of persons reporting this ancestry/race alone, not in combination with any other ancestry/race. 3. Refer to the Explanation of Data in the front of the book for more detailed information.

Hispanic (263)	284	2.44
Yugoslavian	45	0.38

Franklin

Place Type: City
County: Milwaukee
Population: 29,494

Ancestry/Race	Number	%
Acadian/Cajun	33	0.11
African American/Black:	1,584	5.37
Not Hispanic (1,489)	1,545	5.24
Hispanic (31)	39	0.13
African, sub-Saharan:	38	0.13
African	38	0.13
Alaska Native tribes, specified:	3	0.01
Alaska Athabascan (2)	2	0.01
Eskimo (1)	1	0.00
Am. Ind. or Alaska Nat., not spec.	35	0.12
American Indian tribes, specified:	119	0.40
Apache (1)	2	0.01
Cherokee (4)	10	0.03
Chippewa (19)	21	0.07
Creek	3	0.01
Iroquois (22)	35	0.12
Latin American Indians (5)	5	0.02
Menominee (9)	9	0.03
Potawatomi (3)	3	0.01
Sioux	4	0.01
All other tribes (19)	27	0.09
American Indian tribes, not spec.	8	0.03
Arab:	248	0.84
Arab/Arabic	152	0.51
Egyptian	72	0.24
Lebanese	24	0.08
Armenian	26	0.09
Asian:	690	2.34
Chinese, ex. Taiwanese (46)	53	0.18
Filipino (49)	62	0.21
Hmong (38)	38	0.13
Indian (197)	200	0.68
Indonesian (1)	4	0.01
Japanese (21)	34	0.12
Korean (85)	104	0.35
Laotian (34)	36	0.12
Pakistani (29)	31	0.11
Taiwanese (3)	3	0.01
Thai (21)	22	0.07
Vietnamese (82)	83	0.28
Other Asian, not specified (9)	20	0.07
Australian	16	0.05
Austrian	328	1.11
Belgian	48	0.16
British	12	0.04
Bulgarian	6	0.02
Canadian	46	0.16
Croatian	323	1.09
Czech	408	1.38
Czechoslovakian	131	0.44
Danish	190	0.64
Dutch	475	1.61
Eastern European	7	0.02
English	1,853	6.27
European	121	0.41
Finnish	207	0.70
French, except Basque	1,080	3.65
French Canadian	207	0.70
German	12,640	42.77
Greek	235	0.80
Hawaii Native/Pacific Islander:	21	0.07
Micronesian: (8)	9	0.03
Guamanian/Chamorro (8)	8	0.03
Other Micronesian	1	0.00
Polynesian: (2)	5	0.02
Native Hawaiian (1)	4	0.01
Samoan (1)	1	0.00
Other Pac. Isl., not spec.	7	0.02
Hispanic or Latino:	780	2.64
Central American:	12	0.04
Costa Rican	2	0.01
Guatemalan	6	0.02
Salvadoran	4	0.01
Cuban	20	0.07
Dominican Republic	2	0.01
Mexican	466	1.58
Puerto Rican	184	0.62
South American:	22	0.07
Argentinean	1	0.00
Chilean	1	0.00
Colombian	5	0.02
Peruvian	12	0.04
Venezuelan	1	0.00
Other South American	2	0.01
Other Hispanic or Latino	74	0.25
Hungarian	307	1.04
Iranian	33	0.11
Irish	3,427	11.59
Israeli	8	0.03
Italian	1,794	6.07
Latvian	16	0.05
Lithuanian	54	0.18
Luxemburger	57	0.19
Northern European	8	0.03
Norwegian	1,310	4.43
Polish	7,480	25.31
Romanian	33	0.11
Russian	169	0.57
Scandinavian	43	0.15
Scotch-Irish	177	0.60
Scottish	180	0.61
Serbian	143	0.48
Slavic	12	0.04
Slovak	203	0.69
Slovene	266	0.90
Swedish	513	1.74
Swiss	176	0.60
Ukrainian	83	0.28
United States or American	814	2.75
Welsh	206	0.70
White:	27,015	91.59
Not Hispanic (26,287)	26,473	89.76
Hispanic (488)	542	1.84
Yugoslavian	11	0.04

Germantown

Place Type: Village
County: Washington
Population: 18,260

Ancestry/Race	Number	%
African American/Black:	291	1.59
Not Hispanic (245)	284	1.56
Hispanic (2)	7	0.04
Alaska Native tribes, specified:	4	0.02
Aleut (3)	4	0.02
Am. Ind. or Alaska Nat., not spec.	17	0.09
Albanian	10	0.05
American Indian tribes, specified:	50	0.27
Apache (1)	1	0.01
Cherokee	2	0.01
Chippewa (8)	9	0.05
Iroquois (10)	16	0.09
Latin American Indians (1)	3	0.02
Menominee (4)	4	0.02
All other tribes (11)	15	0.08
American Indian tribes, not spec.	2	0.01
Arab:	68	0.37
Lebanese	58	0.32
Syrian	10	0.05
Armenian	6	0.03
Asian:	337	1.85
Chinese, ex. Taiwanese (46)	48	0.26
Filipino (22)	34	0.19
Hmong (5)	11	0.06
Indian (147)	158	0.87
Japanese (12)	16	0.09
Korean (17)	19	0.10
Laotian (1)	10	0.05
Pakistani (16)	21	0.12
Thai (2)	3	0.02
Vietnamese (6)	8	0.04
Other Asian, specified (2)	6	0.03
Other Asian, not specified (3)	3	0.02
Australian	12	0.07
Austrian	188	1.03
Belgian	125	0.69
British	11	0.06
Canadian	40	0.22
Croatian	56	0.31
Czech	301	1.65
Czechoslovakian	51	0.28
Danish	274	1.50
Dutch	411	2.25
Eastern European	6	0.03
English	945	5.18
European	145	0.80
Finnish	115	0.63
French, except Basque	556	3.05
French Canadian	229	1.26
German	10,413	57.11
Greek	93	0.51
Hawaii Native/Pacific Islander:	15	0.08
Micronesian: (6)	6	0.03
Guamanian/Chamorro (6)	6	0.03
Polynesian: (1)	1	0.01
Native Hawaiian (1)	1	0.01
Other Pac. Isl., specified	4	0.02
Other Pac. Isl., not spec.	4	0.02
Hispanic or Latino:	205	1.12
Central American:	4	0.02
Guatemalan	3	0.02
Panamanian	1	0.01
Cuban	3	0.02
Dominican Republic	1	0.01
Mexican	128	0.70
Puerto Rican	32	0.18
South American:	13	0.07
Argentinean	5	0.03
Colombian	4	0.02
Peruvian	4	0.02
Other Hispanic or Latino	24	0.13
Hungarian	152	0.83
Iranian	7	0.04
Irish	2,072	11.36
Italian	1,090	5.98
Latvian	24	0.13
Lithuanian	48	0.26
Luxemburger	53	0.29
Northern European	7	0.04
Norwegian	817	4.48
Polish	2,050	11.24
Portuguese	2	0.01
Russian	175	0.96
Scandinavian	48	0.26
Scotch-Irish	111	0.61
Scottish	117	0.64
Serbian	19	0.10
Slavic	41	0.22
Slovak	127	0.70
Slovene	10	0.05
Swedish	377	2.07
Swiss	163	0.89
Turkish	17	0.09
Ukrainian	15	0.08
United States or American	574	3.15
Welsh	42	0.23
West Indian, excl. Hispanic:	8	0.04
Haitian	8	0.04
White:	17,601	96.39
Not Hispanic (17,375)	17,451	95.57
Hispanic (123)	150	0.82

Notes: 1. Figures in the "Number" column do not add up to the total population due to: a) Ancestry/Race overlap — e.g. persons can report being both White and Irish, b) persons of Hispanic origin can report being any race, c) persons reporting two ancestries are counted in both categories. 2. Numbers in parentheses indicate the number of persons reporting this ancestry/race alone, not in combination with any other ancestry/race. 3. Refer to the Explanation of Data in the front of the book for more detailed information.

Glendale

Place Type: City
County: Milwaukee
Population: 13,367

Ancestry/Race	Number	%
African American/Black:	1,163	8.70
Not Hispanic (1,077)	1,140	8.53
Hispanic (10)	23	0.17
African, sub-Saharan:	67	0.50
African	41	0.31
Somalian	14	0.10
South African	12	0.09
Alaska Native tribes, specified:	2	0.01
Eskimo (1)	1	0.01
Tlingit-Haida (1)	1	0.01
Am. Ind. or Alaska Nat., not spec.	16	0.12
American Indian tribes, specified:	47	0.35
Blackfeet	4	0.03
Cherokee (2)	8	0.06
Chickasaw (1)	1	0.01
Chippewa (5)	9	0.07
Iroquois (1)	6	0.04
Lumbee (1)	1	0.01
Menominee (3)	3	0.02
Potawatomi (1)	1	0.01
Pueblo	1	0.01
Seminole (2)	2	0.01
All other tribes (8)	11	0.08
American Indian tribes, not spec.	1	0.01
Arab:	44	0.33
Lebanese	3	0.02
Palestinian	3	0.02
Other Arab	38	0.28
Armenian	50	0.37
Asian:	455	3.40
Bangladeshi (5)	5	0.04
Chinese, ex. Taiwanese (90)	110	0.82
Filipino (16)	38	0.28
Hmong (26)	27	0.20
Indian (130)	141	1.05
Indonesian (4)	4	0.03
Japanese (17)	23	0.17
Korean (59)	65	0.49
Pakistani (8)	12	0.09
Taiwanese (1)	1	0.01
Thai (3)	3	0.02
Vietnamese (15)	15	0.11
Other Asian, not specified (9)	11	0.08
Australian	35	0.26
Austrian	175	1.31
Belgian	33	0.25
British	124	0.93
Croatian	27	0.20
Czech	204	1.53
Czechoslovakian	63	0.47
Danish	131	0.98
Dutch	275	2.06
Eastern European	119	0.89
English	843	6.31
European	136	1.02
Finnish	43	0.32
French, except Basque	408	3.05
French Canadian	46	0.34
German	4,284	32.06
Greek	11	0.08
Hawaii Native/Pacific Islander:	16	0.12
Micronesian: (1)	1	0.01
Guamanian/Chamorro (1)	1	0.01
Polynesian: (1)	2	0.01
Native Hawaiian (1)	2	0.01
Other Pac. Isl., not spec. (11)	13	0.10
Hispanic or Latino:	236	1.77
Central American:	10	0.07
Nicaraguan	5	0.04
Panamanian	2	0.01
Salvadoran	1	0.01
Other Central American	2	0.01
Cuban	10	0.07
Dominican Republic	1	0.01
Mexican	95	0.71
Puerto Rican	60	0.45
South American:	29	0.22
Chilean	1	0.01
Colombian	16	0.12
Ecuadorian	1	0.01
Peruvian	7	0.05
Venezuelan	2	0.01
Other South American	2	0.01
Other Hispanic or Latino	31	0.23
Hungarian	211	1.58
Iranian	33	0.25
Irish	1,277	9.56
Israeli	54	0.40
Italian	717	5.37
Latvian	34	0.25
Lithuanian	83	0.62
Luxemburger	8	0.06
Norwegian	415	3.11
Polish	1,341	10.04
Romanian	89	0.67
Russian	653	4.89
Scandinavian	22	0.16
Scotch-Irish	85	0.64
Scottish	214	1.60
Slavic	17	0.13
Slovak	45	0.34
Slovene	22	0.16
Swedish	241	1.80
Swiss	66	0.49
Ukrainian	125	0.94
United States or American	431	3.23
Welsh	72	0.54
West Indian, excl. Hispanic:	34	0.25
Haitian	22	0.16
Jamaican	12	0.09
White:	11,753	87.93
Not Hispanic (11,459)	11,594	86.74
Hispanic (138)	159	1.19
Yugoslavian	22	0.16

Grafton

Place Type: Village
County: Ozaukee
Population: 10,312

Ancestry/Race	Number	%
African American/Black:	48	0.47
Not Hispanic (29)	48	0.47
African, sub-Saharan:	6	0.06
African	6	0.06
Am. Ind. or Alaska Nat., not spec.	8	0.08
American Indian tribes, specified:	30	0.29
Cherokee (2)	2	0.02
Chippewa (8)	13	0.13
Iroquois (9)	10	0.10
Ottawa (3)	3	0.03
All other tribes (2)	2	0.02
American Indian tribes, not spec.	1	0.01
Arab:	31	0.30
Syrian	31	0.30
Asian:	98	0.95
Chinese, ex. Taiwanese (39)	42	0.41
Filipino (5)	10	0.10
Hmong (4)	4	0.04
Indian (16)	23	0.22
Indonesian	1	0.01
Japanese (3)	4	0.04
Korean (8)	11	0.11
Thai (1)	1	0.01
Vietnamese (1)	2	0.02
Austrian	134	1.30
Belgian	11	0.11
British	24	0.23
Croatian	21	0.20
Czech	152	1.47
Czechoslovakian	17	0.16
Danish	49	0.47
Dutch	287	2.78
English	847	8.21
European	31	0.30
Finnish	15	0.15
French, except Basque	342	3.31
French Canadian	125	1.21
German	5,532	53.61
Greek	49	0.47
Hawaii Native/Pacific Islander:	2	0.02
Other Pac. Isl., not spec. (1)	2	0.02
Hispanic or Latino:	165	1.60
Central American:	5	0.05
Costa Rican	1	0.01
Guatemalan	1	0.01
Nicaraguan	1	0.01
Panamanian	2	0.02
Cuban	7	0.07
Mexican	107	1.04
Puerto Rican	16	0.16
South American:	1	0.01
Ecuadorian	1	0.01
Other Hispanic or Latino	29	0.28
Hungarian	96	0.93
Irish	1,485	14.39
Italian	595	5.77
Lithuanian	13	0.13
Luxemburger	65	0.63
Norwegian	317	3.07
Pennsylvania German	7	0.07
Polish	1,267	12.28
Russian	56	0.54
Scandinavian	15	0.15
Scotch-Irish	107	1.04
Scottish	54	0.52
Serbian	10	0.10
Slovak	34	0.33
Slovene	34	0.33
Swedish	161	1.56
Swiss	61	0.59
Ukrainian	13	0.13
United States or American	280	2.71
Welsh	89	0.86
White:	10,141	98.34
Not Hispanic (9,954)	10,003	97.00
Hispanic (123)	138	1.34
Yugoslavian	16	0.16

Grand Chute

Place Type: Town
County: Outagamie
Population: 18,392

Ancestry/Race	Number	%
African American/Black:	193	1.05
Not Hispanic (141)	189	1.03
Hispanic (1)	4	0.02
African, sub-Saharan:	24	0.13
African	24	0.13
Alaska Native tribes, specified:	2	0.01
Eskimo	1	0.01
Tlingit-Haida (1)	1	0.01
Am. Ind. or Alaska Nat., not spec.	35	0.19
American Indian tribes, specified:	91	0.49
Blackfeet (1)	1	0.01
Cherokee (3)	10	0.05
Chippewa (7)	9	0.05
Choctaw	1	0.01
Creek	1	0.01
Iroquois (13)	20	0.11
Latin American Indians (3)	4	0.02
Menominee (13)	18	0.10
Navajo (1)	2	0.01
Osage (1)	1	0.01
Paiute (1)	1	0.01
Pima	1	0.01
Potawatomi (1)	3	0.02
Puget Sound Salish (1)	1	0.01
Sioux (1)	4	0.02
All other tribes (5)	14	0.08

Notes: 1. Figures in the "Number" column do not add up to the total population due to: a) Ancestry/Race overlap — e.g. persons can report being both White and Irish, b) persons of Hispanic origin can report being any race, c) persons reporting two ancestries are counted in both categories. 2. Numbers in parentheses indicate the number of persons reporting this ancestry/race alone, not in combination with any other ancestry/race. 3. Refer to the Explanation of Data in the front of the book for more detailed information.

American Indian tribes, not spec.	10	0.05
Asian:	323	1.76
Chinese, ex. Taiwanese (50)	54	0.29
Filipino (14)	19	0.10
Hmong (76)	81	0.44
Indian (62)	65	0.35
Indonesian (1)	1	0.01
Japanese (7)	10	0.05
Korean (33)	37	0.20
Laotian (5)	5	0.03
Pakistani (6)	6	0.03
Sri Lankan (2)	2	0.01
Taiwanese (5)	7	0.04
Thai	2	0.01
Vietnamese (16)	20	0.11
Other Asian, not specified (2)	14	0.08
Austrian	46	0.25
Belgian	287	1.57
British	37	0.20
Bulgarian	7	0.04
Canadian	8	0.04
Celtic	33	0.18
Croatian	22	0.12
Czech	323	1.77
Czechoslovakian	68	0.37
Danish	227	1.24
Dutch	1,421	7.79
English	1,256	6.89
European	88	0.48
Finnish	222	1.22
French, except Basque	768	4.21
French Canadian	340	1.86
German	9,747	53.44
Hawaii Native/Pacific Islander:	30	0.16
Micronesian: (7)	10	0.05
Guamanian/Chamorro (2)	2	0.01
Other Micronesian (5)	8	0.04
Polynesian: (6)	7	0.04
Native Hawaiian (5)	6	0.03
Tongan (1)	1	0.01
Other Pac. Isl., not spec. (2)	13	0.07
Hispanic or Latino:	649	3.53
Central American:	11	0.06
Guatemalan	2	0.01
Honduran	2	0.01
Nicaraguan	2	0.01
Panamanian	1	0.01
Salvadoran	4	0.02
Cuban	10	0.05
Dominican Republic	3	0.02
Mexican	500	2.72
Puerto Rican	26	0.14
South American:	18	0.10
Argentinean	1	0.01
Colombian	11	0.06
Ecuadorian	1	0.01
Paraguayan	2	0.01
Peruvian	1	0.01
Venezuelan	2	0.01
Other Hispanic or Latino	81	0.44
Hungarian	63	0.35
Irish	1,866	10.23
Italian	514	2.82
Lithuanian	7	0.04
Luxemburger	17	0.09
Northern European	13	0.07
Norwegian	914	5.01
Polish	1,128	6.18
Portuguese	11	0.06
Romanian	15	0.08
Russian	24	0.13
Scandinavian	32	0.18
Scotch-Irish	87	0.48
Scottish	157	0.86
Serbian	38	0.21
Slovak	7	0.04
Slovene	6	0.03
Swedish	340	1.86
Swiss	117	0.64
Ukrainian	15	0.08
United States or American	549	3.01
Welsh	85	0.47
West Indian, excl. Hispanic:	53	0.29
Haitian	34	0.19
West Indian	19	0.10
White:	17,505	95.18
Not Hispanic (17,104)	17,215	93.60
Hispanic (236)	290	1.58

Green Bay

Place Type: City
County: Brown
Population: 102,313

Ancestry/Race	Number	%
African American/Black:	1,978	1.93
Not Hispanic (1,358)	1,883	1.84
Hispanic (49)	95	0.09
African, sub-Saharan:	94	0.09
African	72	0.07
Ethiopian	8	0.01
Nigerian	14	0.01
Alaska Native tribes, specified:	2	0.00
Alaska Athabascan (1)	1	0.00
Eskimo (1)	1	0.00
Alaska Native tribes, not specified	1	0.00
Am. Ind. or Alaska Nat., not spec.	601	0.59
Alsatian	8	0.01
American Indian tribes, specified:	3,661	3.58
Apache (3)	9	0.01
Blackfeet (4)	11	0.01
Cherokee (16)	58	0.06
Cheyenne (1)	2	0.00
Chippewa (196)	293	0.29
Choctaw (7)	7	0.01
Comanche (1)	3	0.00
Cree	3	0.00
Creek (1)	4	0.00
Crow (1)	1	0.00
Delaware (1)	1	0.00
Iroquois (1,751)	2,120	2.07
Latin American Indians (15)	41	0.04
Menominee (488)	581	0.57
Navajo (6)	7	0.01
Osage (6)	10	0.01
Ottawa (11)	18	0.02
Pima (8)	8	0.01
Potawatomi (32)	49	0.05
Pueblo (6)	10	0.01
Seminole (2)	2	0.00
Sioux (32)	54	0.05
All other tribes (301)	369	0.36
American Indian tribes, not spec.	44	0.04
Arab:	174	0.17
Arab/Arabic	13	0.01
Egyptian	6	0.01
Lebanese	112	0.11
Syrian	37	0.04
Other Arab	6	0.01
Armenian	30	0.03
Asian:	4,372	4.27
Cambodian (18)	23	0.02
Chinese, ex. Taiwanese (120)	179	0.17
Filipino (58)	94	0.09
Hmong (2,629)	2,858	2.79
Indian (174)	261	0.26
Indonesian (1)	1	0.00
Japanese (45)	83	0.08
Korean (75)	111	0.11
Laotian (355)	413	0.40
Pakistani (2)	2	0.00
Sri Lankan (9)	9	0.01
Taiwanese (2)	3	0.00
Thai (21)	23	0.02
Vietnamese (82)	93	0.09
Other Asian, specified (1)	3	0.00
Other Asian, not specified (144)	216	0.21
Australian	11	0.01
Austrian	333	0.33
Belgian	10,101	9.87
British	186	0.18
Bulgarian	16	0.02
Canadian	122	0.12
Croatian	177	0.17
Czech	2,520	2.46
Czechoslovakian	191	0.19
Danish	1,031	1.01
Dutch	4,812	4.70
English	4,692	4.58
European	520	0.51
Finnish	1,010	0.99
French, except Basque	6,130	5.99
French Canadian	3,154	3.08
German	35,842	35.01
Greek	190	0.19
Hawaii Native/Pacific Islander:	133	0.13
Micronesian: (10)	22	0.02
Guamanian/Chamorro (5)	17	0.02
Other Micronesian (5)	5	0.00
Polynesian: (22)	38	0.04
Native Hawaiian (13)	22	0.02
Samoan (7)	8	0.01
Tongan (2)	3	0.00
Other Polynesian	5	0.00
Other Pac. Isl., specified	1	0.00
Other Pac. Isl., not spec. (4)	72	0.07
Hispanic or Latino:	7,294	7.13
Central American:	281	0.27
Costa Rican	4	0.00
Guatemalan	23	0.02
Honduran	134	0.13
Nicaraguan	42	0.04
Panamanian	6	0.01
Salvadoran	49	0.05
Other Central American	23	0.02
Cuban	26	0.03
Dominican Republic	5	0.00
Mexican	5,648	5.52
Puerto Rican	387	0.38
South American:	79	0.08
Argentinean	1	0.00
Bolivian	4	0.00
Chilean	13	0.01
Colombian	19	0.02
Ecuadorian	6	0.01
Paraguayan	2	0.00
Peruvian	24	0.02
Uruguayan	3	0.00
Venezuelan	2	0.00
Other South American	5	0.00
Other Hispanic or Latino	868	0.85
Hungarian	216	0.21
Icelander	6	0.01
Irish	9,584	9.36
Italian	1,757	1.72
Latvian	26	0.03
Lithuanian	108	0.11
Luxemburger	15	0.01
Northern European	20	0.02
Norwegian	3,682	3.60
Pennsylvania German	6	0.01
Polish	10,058	9.83
Portuguese	30	0.03
Romanian	53	0.05
Russian	352	0.34
Scandinavian	101	0.10
Scotch-Irish	574	0.56
Scottish	704	0.69
Serbian	20	0.02
Slavic	33	0.03
Slovak	63	0.06
Slovene	71	0.07
Swedish	2,431	2.37
Swiss	231	0.23
Turkish	10	0.01
Ukrainian	51	0.05
United States or American	3,697	3.61
Welsh	295	0.29
West Indian, excl. Hispanic:	44	0.04

Notes: 1. Figures in the "Number" column do not add up to the total population due to: a) Ancestry/Race overlap — e.g. persons can report being both White and Irish, b) persons of Hispanic origin can report being any race, c) persons reporting two ancestries are counted in both categories. 2. Numbers in parentheses indicate the number of persons reporting this ancestry/race alone, not in combination with any other ancestry/race. 3. Refer to the Explanation of Data in the front of the book for more detailed information.

Belizean	4	0.00
Dutch West Indian	7	0.01
Jamaican	26	0.03
West Indian	7	0.01
White:	89,477	87.45
Not Hispanic (85,134)	86,379	84.43
Hispanic (2,707)	3,098	3.03
Yugoslavian	78	0.08

Greendale

Place Type: Village
County: Milwaukee
Population: 14,405

Ancestry/Race	Number	%
African American/Black:	69	0.48
Not Hispanic (38)	61	0.42
Hispanic (3)	8	0.06
African, sub-Saharan:	44	0.31
African	27	0.19
South African	17	0.12
Alaska Native tribes, specified:	1	0.01
All other tribes (1)	1	0.01
Am. Ind. or Alaska Nat., not spec.	10	0.07
Albanian	13	0.09
American Indian tribes, specified:	41	0.28
Blackfeet (1)	1	0.01
Cherokee (1)	8	0.06
Chippewa (2)	7	0.05
Iroquois (5)	8	0.06
Latin American Indians	2	0.01
Menominee (2)	3	0.02
Navajo (1)	1	0.01
Pima (1)	1	0.01
Sioux (2)	2	0.01
All other tribes (6)	8	0.06
American Indian tribes, not spec.	2	0.01
Arab:	71	0.49
Arab/Arabic	44	0.31
Lebanese	8	0.06
Palestinian	19	0.13
Armenian	9	0.06
Asian:	350	2.43
Chinese, ex. Taiwanese (32)	38	0.26
Filipino (82)	92	0.64
Hmong	1	0.01
Indian (64)	76	0.53
Indonesian	5	0.03
Japanese (13)	24	0.17
Korean (37)	38	0.26
Laotian (1)	1	0.01
Pakistani (29)	30	0.21
Thai (2)	2	0.01
Vietnamese (23)	29	0.20
Other Asian, specified (1)	1	0.01
Other Asian, not specified (3)	13	0.09
Assyrian/Chaldean/Syriac	6	0.04
Austrian	123	0.85
Belgian	54	0.37
Brazilian	8	0.06
British	28	0.19
Canadian	21	0.15
Croatian	177	1.23
Czech	264	1.83
Czechoslovakian	69	0.48
Danish	214	1.49
Dutch	213	1.48
Eastern European	7	0.05
English	1,031	7.16
Estonian	8	0.06
European	41	0.28
Finnish	38	0.26
French, except Basque	513	3.56
French Canadian	102	0.71
German	6,683	46.39
Greek	93	0.65
Hawaii Native/Pacific Islander:	10	0.07
Micronesian: (1)	2	0.01
Guamanian/Chamorro (1)	2	0.01
Polynesian:	2	0.01
Native Hawaiian	1	0.01
Samoan	1	0.01
Other Pac. Isl., not spec.	6	0.04
Hispanic or Latino:	340	2.36
Central American:	9	0.06
Guatemalan	6	0.04
Honduran	2	0.01
Panamanian	1	0.01
Cuban	3	0.02
Dominican Republic	7	0.05
Mexican	197	1.37
Puerto Rican	56	0.39
South American:	19	0.13
Bolivian	3	0.02
Chilean	2	0.01
Colombian	9	0.06
Ecuadorian	1	0.01
Paraguayan	1	0.01
Peruvian	3	0.02
Other Hispanic or Latino	49	0.34
Hungarian	145	1.01
Iranian	8	0.06
Irish	1,683	11.68
Italian	869	6.03
Latvian	22	0.15
Lithuanian	70	0.49
Luxemburger	58	0.40
Maltese	4	0.03
Northern European	10	0.07
Norwegian	646	4.48
Polish	3,260	22.63
Romanian	17	0.12
Russian	130	0.90
Scandinavian	42	0.29
Scotch-Irish	126	0.87
Scottish	201	1.40
Serbian	53	0.37
Slavic	45	0.31
Slovak	48	0.33
Slovene	67	0.47
Swedish	271	1.88
Swiss	106	0.74
Ukrainian	30	0.21
United States or American	287	1.99
Welsh	48	0.33
White:	13,948	96.83
Not Hispanic (13,607)	13,679	94.96
Hispanic (248)	269	1.87
Yugoslavian	83	0.58

Greenfield

Place Type: City
County: Milwaukee
Population: 35,476

Ancestry/Race	Number	%
African American/Black:	450	1.27
Not Hispanic (342)	437	1.23
Hispanic (6)	13	0.04
African, sub-Saharan:	45	0.13
African	16	0.05
Other sub-Saharan African	29	0.08
Alaska Native tribes, specified:	4	0.01
Alaska Athabascan (1)	1	0.00
Eskimo	3	0.01
Am. Ind. or Alaska Nat., not spec.	67	0.19
Albanian	7	0.02
American Indian tribes, specified:	185	0.52
Apache (5)	10	0.03
Blackfeet (1)	4	0.01
Cherokee (3)	8	0.02
Chippewa (31)	47	0.13
Choctaw	3	0.01
Cree	1	0.00
Creek	2	0.01
Iroquois (36)	55	0.16
Latin American Indians (1)	4	0.01
Lumbee (1)	1	0.00
Menominee (9)	13	0.04
Navajo (1)	1	0.00
Ottawa (4)	4	0.01
Pima (1)	1	0.00
Potawatomi (1)	1	0.00
Sioux (1)	5	0.01
All other tribes (17)	25	0.07
American Indian tribes, not spec.	8	0.02
Arab:	134	0.38
Arab/Arabic	7	0.02
Egyptian	44	0.12
Jordanian	8	0.02
Lebanese	17	0.05
Palestinian	49	0.14
Syrian	9	0.03
Armenian	23	0.06
Asian:	921	2.60
Chinese, ex. Taiwanese (87)	101	0.28
Filipino (110)	130	0.37
Hmong (13)	13	0.04
Indian (292)	313	0.88
Indonesian	3	0.01
Japanese (23)	31	0.09
Korean (82)	85	0.24
Laotian (28)	34	0.10
Pakistani (32)	42	0.12
Taiwanese (2)	2	0.01
Thai (5)	15	0.04
Vietnamese (107)	123	0.35
Other Asian, specified	3	0.01
Other Asian, not specified (8)	26	0.07
Assyrian/Chaldean/Syriac	14	0.04
Australian	7	0.02
Austrian	234	0.66
Belgian	118	0.33
British	75	0.21
Bulgarian	16	0.05
Canadian	7	0.02
Celtic	8	0.02
Croatian	349	0.98
Czech	542	1.53
Czechoslovakian	144	0.41
Danish	272	0.77
Dutch	431	1.21
English	1,620	4.57
Estonian	17	0.05
European	158	0.45
Finnish	351	0.99
French, except Basque	1,536	4.33
French Canadian	307	0.87
German	15,390	43.38
Greek	279	0.79
Hawaii Native/Pacific Islander:	25	0.07
Micronesian: (2)	3	0.01
Guamanian/Chamorro (2)	3	0.01
Polynesian: (4)	17	0.05
Native Hawaiian (2)	14	0.04
Samoan (2)	3	0.01
Other Pac. Isl., specified	2	0.01
Other Pac. Isl., not spec. (1)	3	0.01
Hispanic or Latino:	1,376	3.88
Central American:	28	0.08
Costa Rican	8	0.02
Guatemalan	5	0.01
Honduran	1	0.00
Nicaraguan	7	0.02
Salvadoran	5	0.01
Other Central American	2	0.01
Cuban	25	0.07
Dominican Republic	7	0.02
Mexican	819	2.31
Puerto Rican	287	0.81
South American:	29	0.08
Bolivian	3	0.01
Chilean	3	0.01
Colombian	12	0.03
Paraguayan	1	0.00
Peruvian	7	0.02
Other South American	3	0.01
Other Hispanic or Latino	181	0.51

Notes: 1. Figures in the "Number" column do not add up to the total population due to: a) Ancestry/Race overlap — e.g. persons can report being both White and Irish, b) persons of Hispanic origin can report being any race, c) persons reporting two ancestries are counted in both categories. 2. Numbers in parentheses indicate the number of persons reporting this ancestry/race alone, not in combination with any other ancestry/race. 3. Refer to the Explanation of Data in the front of the book for more detailed information.

Hungarian	246	0.69
Icelander	32	0.09
Irish	3,760	10.60
Italian	1,489	4.20
Latvian	72	0.20
Lithuanian	60	0.17
Luxemburger	52	0.15
Northern European	15	0.04
Norwegian	1,461	4.12
Pennsylvania German	8	0.02
Polish	9,310	26.24
Romanian	30	0.08
Russian	308	0.87
Scandinavian	58	0.16
Scotch-Irish	143	0.40
Scottish	240	0.68
Serbian	281	0.79
Slavic	83	0.23
Slovak	124	0.35
Slovene	242	0.68
Swedish	644	1.82
Swiss	207	0.58
Turkish	8	0.02
Ukrainian	86	0.24
United States or American	549	1.55
Welsh	136	0.38
West Indian, excl. Hispanic:	10	0.03
Jamaican	10	0.03
White:	33,661	94.88
Not Hispanic (32,512)	32,783	92.41
Hispanic (735)	878	2.47
Yugoslavian	116	0.33

Hartford

Place Type: City
County: Washington
Population: 10,905

Ancestry/Race	Number	%
African American/Black:	57	0.52
Not Hispanic (21)	46	0.42
Hispanic (8)	11	0.10
Am. Ind. or Alaska Nat., not spec.	20	0.18
American Indian tribes, specified:	45	0.41
Cherokee (3)	7	0.06
Chippewa (12)	15	0.14
Iroquois (3)	3	0.03
Latin American Indians (2)	2	0.02
Menominee (2)	3	0.03
Potawatomi	5	0.05
Seminole	1	0.01
Sioux (1)	1	0.01
All other tribes (2)	8	0.07
Asian:	74	0.68
Chinese, ex. Taiwanese (4)	8	0.07
Filipino (3)	4	0.04
Hmong (1)	3	0.03
Indian (28)	30	0.28
Indonesian	1	0.01
Japanese (3)	5	0.05
Korean (7)	14	0.13
Pakistani (1)	2	0.02
Thai (1)	2	0.02
Vietnamese (1)	3	0.03
Other Asian, not specified	2	0.02
Austrian	8	0.07
Belgian	56	0.51
Brazilian	24	0.22
British	14	0.13
Canadian	16	0.15
Czech	56	0.51
Czechoslovakian	7	0.06
Danish	66	0.60
Dutch	127	1.16
English	568	5.17
Finnish	90	0.82
French, except Basque	440	4.01
French Canadian	83	0.76
German	5,890	53.65
Greek	8	0.07
Hawaii Native/Pacific Islander:	5	0.05
Micronesian: (5)	5	0.05
Guamanian/Chamorro (5)	5	0.05
Hispanic or Latino:	326	2.99
Cuban	2	0.02
Mexican	240	2.20
Puerto Rican	47	0.43
South American:	5	0.05
Argentinean	1	0.01
Colombian	4	0.04
Other Hispanic or Latino	32	0.29
Hungarian	27	0.25
Irish	1,351	12.31
Italian	408	3.72
Lithuanian	23	0.21
Luxemburger	10	0.09
Norwegian	531	4.84
Pennsylvania German	5	0.05
Polish	1,103	10.05
Portuguese	8	0.07
Russian	90	0.82
Scandinavian	29	0.26
Scotch-Irish	74	0.67
Scottish	85	0.77
Slovak	39	0.36
Swedish	132	1.20
Swiss	108	0.98
United States or American	443	4.04
Welsh	24	0.22
White:	10,644	97.61
Not Hispanic (10,391)	10,459	95.91
Hispanic (154)	185	1.70
Yugoslavian	9	0.08

Howard

Place Type: Village
County: Brown
Population: 13,546

Ancestry/Race	Number	%
African American/Black:	153	1.13
Not Hispanic (98)	152	1.12
Hispanic (1)	1	0.01
African, sub-Saharan:	22	0.16
African	22	0.16
Am. Ind. or Alaska Nat., not spec.	35	0.26
Albanian	34	0.25
American Indian tribes, specified:	156	1.15
Blackfeet (1)	1	0.01
Cherokee (1)	2	0.01
Chippewa (26)	31	0.23
Choctaw	2	0.01
Cree	4	0.03
Iroquois (39)	74	0.55
Menominee (17)	22	0.16
Ottawa (4)	4	0.03
Pima (1)	1	0.01
Potawatomi (2)	2	0.01
Sioux	1	0.01
All other tribes (8)	12	0.09
American Indian tribes, not spec.	3	0.02
Arab:	21	0.16
Lebanese	21	0.16
Asian:	136	1.00
Chinese, ex. Taiwanese (12)	21	0.16
Filipino (5)	12	0.09
Hmong (47)	47	0.35
Indian (10)	11	0.08
Indonesian	1	0.01
Japanese (4)	9	0.07
Korean (10)	11	0.08
Laotian (2)	8	0.06
Vietnamese (7)	7	0.05
Other Asian, not specified (8)	9	0.07
Austrian	42	0.31
Belgian	1,388	10.25
British	16	0.12
Canadian	8	0.06
Croatian	59	0.44
Czech	359	2.65
Czechoslovakian	41	0.30
Danish	172	1.27
Dutch	683	5.04
Eastern European	10	0.07
English	532	3.93
European	89	0.66
Finnish	216	1.60
French, except Basque	1,073	7.93
French Canadian	486	3.59
German	6,061	44.77
Greek	33	0.24
Hawaii Native/Pacific Islander:	13	0.10
Polynesian: (1)	2	0.01
Native Hawaiian (1)	1	0.01
Samoan	1	0.01
Other Pac. Isl., not spec.	11	0.08
Hispanic or Latino:	147	1.09
Central American:	8	0.06
Costa Rican	1	0.01
Guatemalan	4	0.03
Panamanian	2	0.01
Salvadoran	1	0.01
Cuban	5	0.04
Mexican	74	0.55
Puerto Rican	12	0.09
South American:	6	0.04
Bolivian	1	0.01
Chilean	1	0.01
Colombian	2	0.01
Ecuadorian	1	0.01
Paraguayan	1	0.01
Other Hispanic or Latino	42	0.31
Hungarian	11	0.08
Irish	1,595	11.78
Italian	322	2.38
Northern European	6	0.04
Norwegian	569	4.20
Pennsylvania German	9	0.07
Polish	2,051	15.15
Portuguese	11	0.08
Russian	84	0.62
Scandinavian	98	0.72
Scotch-Irish	71	0.52
Scottish	80	0.59
Slovak	12	0.09
Slovene	8	0.06
Swedish	448	3.31
Swiss	24	0.18
Ukrainian	43	0.32
United States or American	589	4.35
Welsh	44	0.32
West Indian, excl. Hispanic:	8	0.06
Jamaican	8	0.06
White:	13,154	97.11
Not Hispanic (12,938)	13,054	96.37
Hispanic (88)	100	0.74
Yugoslavian	25	0.18

Janesville

Place Type: City
County: Rock
Population: 59,498

Ancestry/Race	Number	%
African American/Black:	1,037	1.74
Not Hispanic (726)	1,000	1.68
Hispanic (22)	37	0.06
African, sub-Saharan:	20	0.03
African	20	0.03
Alaska Native tribes, specified:	2	0.00
Eskimo (2)	2	0.00
Alaska Native tribes, not specified	2	0.00
Am. Ind. or Alaska Nat., not spec.	109	0.18
Alsatian	6	0.01
American Indian tribes, specified:	239	0.40
Apache	4	0.01
Blackfeet (1)	15	0.03

Notes: 1. Figures in the "Number" column do not add up to the total population due to: a) Ancestry/Race overlap — e.g. persons can report being both White and Irish, b) persons of Hispanic origin can report being any race, c) persons reporting two ancestries are counted in both categories. 2. Numbers in parentheses indicate the number of persons reporting this ancestry/race alone, not in combination with any other ancestry/race. 3. Refer to the Explanation of Data in the front of the book for more detailed information.

Cherokee (14)	55	0.09
Cheyenne	1	0.00
Chippewa (28)	52	0.09
Choctaw (1)	4	0.01
Colville (1)	1	0.00
Comanche	4	0.01
Cree (1)	3	0.01
Crow	1	0.00
Delaware (1)	1	0.00
Iroquois (6)	13	0.02
Latin American Indians (6)	9	0.02
Menominee (2)	4	0.01
Navajo (1)	1	0.00
Osage	1	0.00
Ottawa (2)	4	0.01
Potawatomi (2)	5	0.01
Sioux (7)	16	0.03
Tohono O'Odham (1)	1	0.00
Ute (2)	4	0.01
All other tribes (24)	40	0.07
American Indian tribes, not spec.	13	0.02
Arab:	59	0.10
Lebanese	24	0.04
Palestinian	30	0.05
Syrian	5	0.01
Armenian	6	0.01
Asian:	752	1.26
Bangladeshi (3)	3	0.01
Cambodian (168)	209	0.35
Chinese, ex. Taiwanese (78)	90	0.15
Filipino (46)	90	0.15
Indian (47)	76	0.13
Indonesian (2)	2	0.00
Japanese (34)	46	0.08
Korean (37)	64	0.11
Laotian (60)	76	0.13
Pakistani (6)	6	0.01
Sri Lankan (1)	2	0.00
Taiwanese (3)	3	0.01
Thai (7)	8	0.01
Vietnamese (48)	51	0.09
Other Asian, not specified (14)	26	0.04
Assyrian/Chaldean/Syriac	5	0.01
Australian	3	0.01
Austrian	211	0.36
Belgian	156	0.26
British	125	0.21
Bulgarian	12	0.02
Canadian	53	0.09
Croatian	56	0.09
Czech	922	1.55
Czechoslovakian	154	0.26
Danish	833	1.40
Dutch	1,237	2.08
English	6,994	11.78
European	152	0.26
Finnish	87	0.15
French, except Basque	2,182	3.68
French Canadian	471	0.79
German	24,329	40.98
Greek	62	0.10
Hawaii Native/Pacific Islander:	38	0.06
Micronesian: (8)	8	0.01
Guamanian/Chamorro (8)	8	0.01
Polynesian: (8)	15	0.03
Native Hawaiian (3)	6	0.01
Samoan (5)	9	0.02
Other Pac. Isl., not spec. (3)	15	0.03
Hispanic or Latino:	1,569	2.64
Central American:	28	0.05
Guatemalan	1	0.00
Honduran	8	0.01
Nicaraguan	1	0.00
Panamanian	1	0.00
Salvadoran	11	0.02
Other Central American	6	0.01
Cuban	11	0.02
Dominican Republic	7	0.01
Mexican	1,219	2.05
Puerto Rican	98	0.16
South American:	16	0.03
Argentinean	4	0.01
Chilean	1	0.00
Colombian	7	0.01
Ecuadorian	1	0.00
Paraguayan	1	0.00
Peruvian	1	0.00
Venezuelan	1	0.00
Other Hispanic or Latino	190	0.32
Hungarian	274	0.46
Icelander	13	0.02
Iranian	40	0.07
Irish	9,604	16.18
Italian	1,769	2.98
Latvian	77	0.13
Lithuanian	122	0.21
Luxemburger	20	0.03
Northern European	31	0.05
Norwegian	9,106	15.34
Pennsylvania German	28	0.05
Polish	2,069	3.49
Portuguese	46	0.08
Romanian	11	0.02
Russian	101	0.17
Scandinavian	121	0.20
Scotch-Irish	787	1.33
Scottish	855	1.44
Serbian	18	0.03
Slavic	33	0.06
Slovak	99	0.17
Slovene	6	0.01
Swedish	1,565	2.64
Swiss	1,219	2.05
Ukrainian	31	0.05
United States or American	2,589	4.36
Welsh	486	0.82
White:	57,348	96.39
Not Hispanic (55,840)	56,386	94.77
Hispanic (842)	962	1.62
Yugoslavian	43	0.07

Kaukauna

Place Type: City
County: Outagamie
Population: 12,983

Ancestry/Race	Number	%
African American/Black:	59	0.45
Not Hispanic (35)	57	0.44
Hispanic	2	0.02
Am. Ind. or Alaska Nat., not spec.	20	0.15
American Indian tribes, specified:	147	1.13
Apache	1	0.01
Cherokee	7	0.05
Chippewa (6)	10	0.08
Iroquois (64)	98	0.75
Latin American Indians (1)	1	0.01
Menominee (7)	9	0.07
Ottawa (1)	2	0.02
All other tribes (6)	19	0.15
American Indian tribes, not spec.	2	0.02
Arab:	30	0.23
Lebanese	10	0.08
Syrian	20	0.15
Asian:	307	2.36
Cambodian (1)	2	0.02
Chinese, ex. Taiwanese (13)	14	0.11
Filipino	3	0.02
Hmong (245)	256	1.97
Indian (12)	12	0.09
Japanese (3)	3	0.02
Korean (3)	5	0.04
Laotian (8)	8	0.06
Thai (1)	1	0.01
Other Asian, not specified	3	0.02
Austrian	37	0.28
Belgian	270	2.08
British	13	0.10
Celtic	3	0.02
Czech	137	1.05
Danish	123	0.95
Dutch	2,735	21.05
English	434	3.34
European	35	0.27
Finnish	19	0.15
French, except Basque	653	5.03
French Canadian	269	2.07
German	6,424	49.44
Greek	20	0.15
Hawaii Native/Pacific Islander:	17	0.13
Micronesian: (6)	6	0.05
Other Micronesian (6)	6	0.05
Polynesian: (1)	2	0.02
Native Hawaiian (1)	2	0.02
Other Pac. Isl., not spec. (2)	9	0.07
Hispanic or Latino:	103	0.79
Central American:	2	0.02
Salvadoran	2	0.02
Cuban	3	0.02
Dominican Republic	1	0.01
Mexican	67	0.52
Puerto Rican	4	0.03
South American:	4	0.03
Chilean	1	0.01
Colombian	1	0.01
Peruvian	2	0.02
Other Hispanic or Latino	22	0.17
Hungarian	34	0.26
Icelander	5	0.04
Irish	1,465	11.28
Italian	202	1.55
Latvian	5	0.04
Lithuanian	37	0.28
Norwegian	392	3.02
Polish	706	5.43
Russian	8	0.06
Scandinavian	17	0.13
Scotch-Irish	68	0.52
Scottish	98	0.75
Slavic	6	0.05
Slovene	22	0.17
Swedish	136	1.05
Swiss	64	0.49
Ukrainian	21	0.16
United States or American	687	5.29
Welsh	134	1.03
White:	12,504	96.31
Not Hispanic (12,343)	12,437	95.79
Hispanic (53)	67	0.52
Yugoslavian	9	0.07

Kenosha

Place Type: City
County: Kenosha
Population: 90,352

Ancestry/Race	Number	%
African American/Black:	7,804	8.64
Not Hispanic (6,810)	7,540	8.35
Hispanic (133)	264	0.29
African, sub-Saharan:	517	0.57
African	469	0.52
Nigerian	6	0.01
Somalian	25	0.03
South African	9	0.01
Other sub-Saharan African	8	0.01
Alaska Native tribes, specified:	8	0.01
Aleut (3)	6	0.01
Eskimo (1)	2	0.00
Alaska Native tribes, not specified	1	0.00
Am. Ind. or Alaska Nat., not spec.	239	0.26
Albanian	249	0.27
American Indian tribes, specified:	593	0.66
Apache (4)	18	0.02
Blackfeet (4)	26	0.03
Cherokee (58)	153	0.17
Chickasaw (1)	5	0.01
Chippewa (69)	150	0.17

Notes: 1. Figures in the "Number" column do not add up to the total population due to: a) Ancestry/Race overlap — e.g. persons can report being both White and Irish, b) persons of Hispanic origin can report being any race, c) persons reporting two ancestries are counted in both categories. 2. Numbers in parentheses indicate the number of persons reporting this ancestry/race alone, not in combination with any other ancestry/race. 3. Refer to the Explanation of Data in the front of the book for more detailed information.

Choctaw (4)	15	0.02
Comanche (1)	3	0.00
Creek (5)	7	0.01
Iroquois (26)	44	0.05
Latin American Indians (7)	22	0.02
Lumbee (4)	4	0.00
Menominee (35)	47	0.05
Navajo	5	0.01
Osage	3	0.00
Ottawa (2)	3	0.00
Pima	1	0.00
Potawatomi (4)	9	0.01
Pueblo (3)	6	0.01
Puget Sound Salish	1	0.00
Seminole	4	0.00
Sioux (12)	26	0.03
Ute	1	0.00
All other tribes (25)	40	0.04
American Indian tribes, not spec.	64	0.07
Arab:	341	0.38
Arab/Arabic	143	0.16
Egyptian	5	0.01
Lebanese	104	0.11
Palestinian	59	0.07
Syrian	22	0.02
Other Arab	8	0.01
Armenian	130	0.14
Asian:	1,193	1.32
Bangladeshi (2)	2	0.00
Cambodian (4)	4	0.00
Chinese, ex. Taiwanese (85)	117	0.13
Filipino (241)	332	0.37
Indian (252)	287	0.32
Indonesian (1)	2	0.00
Japanese (65)	119	0.13
Korean (136)	175	0.19
Laotian (2)	2	0.00
Pakistani (40)	45	0.05
Sri Lankan (11)	12	0.01
Taiwanese (3)	7	0.01
Thai (7)	16	0.02
Vietnamese (22)	30	0.03
Other Asian, not specified (14)	43	0.05
Assyrian/Chaldean/Syriac	6	0.01
Australian	14	0.02
Austrian	240	0.26
Belgian	254	0.28
Brazilian	16	0.02
British	196	0.22
Bulgarian	10	0.01
Canadian	114	0.13
Celtic	35	0.04
Croatian	367	0.40
Czech	756	0.83
Czechoslovakian	251	0.28
Danish	2,189	2.41
Dutch	1,924	2.12
English	6,518	7.19
European	507	0.56
Finnish	897	0.99
French, except Basque	3,830	4.22
French Canadian	666	0.73
German	28,533	31.47
Greek	401	0.44
Guyanese	5	0.01
Hawaii Native/Pacific Islander:	87	0.10
Micronesian: (9)	29	0.03
Guamanian/Chamorro (9)	29	0.03
Polynesian: (23)	41	0.05
Native Hawaiian (7)	20	0.02
Samoan (16)	17	0.02
Other Polynesian	4	0.00
Other Pac. Isl., not spec. (6)	17	0.02
Hispanic or Latino:	9,003	9.96
Central American:	203	0.22
Costa Rican	9	0.01
Guatemalan	72	0.08
Honduran	34	0.04
Nicaraguan	51	0.06
Panamanian	8	0.01
Salvadoran	23	0.03
Other Central American	6	0.01
Cuban	61	0.07
Dominican Republic	18	0.02
Mexican	6,149	6.81
Puerto Rican	930	1.03
South American:	101	0.11
Argentinean	24	0.03
Bolivian	1	0.00
Chilean	2	0.00
Colombian	32	0.04
Ecuadorian	8	0.01
Paraguayan	7	0.01
Peruvian	13	0.01
Venezuelan	6	0.01
Other South American	8	0.01
Other Hispanic or Latino	1,541	1.71
Hungarian	442	0.49
Icelander	11	0.01
Iranian	14	0.02
Irish	10,396	11.47
Israeli	5	0.01
Italian	10,790	11.90
Latvian	20	0.02
Lithuanian	890	0.98
Luxemburger	51	0.06
Macedonian	12	0.01
Northern European	47	0.05
Norwegian	3,787	4.18
Pennsylvania German	65	0.07
Polish	7,663	8.45
Portuguese	92	0.10
Romanian	56	0.06
Russian	569	0.63
Scandinavian	206	0.23
Scotch-Irish	763	0.84
Scottish	1,145	1.26
Serbian	238	0.26
Slavic	67	0.07
Slovak	612	0.67
Slovene	105	0.12
Swedish	2,677	2.95
Swiss	317	0.35
Turkish	32	0.04
Ukrainian	140	0.15
United States or American	3,142	3.47
Welsh	539	0.59
West Indian, excl. Hispanic:	109	0.12
Bermudan	16	0.02
Haitian	30	0.03
Jamaican	42	0.05
West Indian	21	0.02
White:	77,457	85.73
Not Hispanic (71,686)	73,034	80.83
Hispanic (3,880)	4,423	4.90
Yugoslavian	197	0.22

La Crosse

Place Type: City
County: La Crosse
Population: 51,818

Ancestry/Race	Number	%
Afghan	12	0.02
African American/Black:	1,040	2.01
Not Hispanic (775)	987	1.90
Hispanic (31)	53	0.10
African, sub-Saharan:	58	0.11
African	41	0.08
Kenyan	17	0.03
Alaska Native tribes, specified:	2	0.00
Alaska Athabascan (1)	1	0.00
Eskimo	1	0.00
Am. Ind. or Alaska Nat., not spec.	117	0.23
American Indian tribes, specified:	351	0.68
Apache (1)	3	0.01
Blackfeet	6	0.01
Cherokee (17)	52	0.10
Chippewa (45)	57	0.11
Choctaw	3	0.01
Cree	2	0.00
Creek (3)	3	0.01
Iroquois (2)	6	0.01
Latin American Indians (3)	9	0.02
Menominee (5)	14	0.03
Navajo (2)	3	0.01
Osage	1	0.00
Potawatomi (9)	13	0.03
Pueblo (6)	6	0.01
Sioux (12)	24	0.05
All other tribes (98)	149	0.29
American Indian tribes, not spec.	18	0.03
Arab:	294	0.57
Arab/Arabic	6	0.01
Egyptian	6	0.01
Jordanian	60	0.12
Lebanese	151	0.29
Syrian	71	0.14
Armenian	7	0.01
Asian:	2,739	5.29
Bangladeshi (1)	1	0.00
Cambodian (9)	9	0.02
Chinese, ex. Taiwanese (104)	141	0.27
Filipino (34)	58	0.11
Hmong (1,729)	1,893	3.65
Indian (97)	154	0.30
Indonesian (4)	4	0.01
Japanese (33)	62	0.12
Korean (108)	128	0.25
Laotian (111)	140	0.27
Sri Lankan (2)	2	0.00
Taiwanese (6)	6	0.01
Thai (8)	18	0.03
Vietnamese (44)	55	0.11
Other Asian, specified	1	0.00
Other Asian, not specified (47)	67	0.13
Australian	35	0.07
Austrian	254	0.49
Belgian	120	0.23
British	203	0.39
Bulgarian	19	0.04
Canadian	25	0.05
Celtic	9	0.02
Croatian	61	0.12
Czech	1,318	2.55
Czechoslovakian	183	0.35
Danish	519	1.01
Dutch	786	1.52
Eastern European	19	0.04
English	2,901	5.62
European	150	0.29
Finnish	147	0.28
French, except Basque	1,812	3.51
French Canadian	413	0.80
German	21,617	41.86
German Russian	12	0.02
Greek	90	0.17
Hawaii Native/Pacific Islander:	107	0.21
Melanesian: (1)	1	0.00
Other Melanesian (1)	1	0.00
Micronesian: (4)	4	0.01
Guamanian/Chamorro (4)	4	0.01
Polynesian: (8)	19	0.04
Native Hawaiian (4)	15	0.03
Samoan (4)	4	0.01
Other Pac. Isl., not spec. (5)	83	0.16
Hispanic or Latino:	592	1.14
Central American:	19	0.04
Guatemalan	9	0.02
Honduran	2	0.00
Nicaraguan	3	0.01
Panamanian	2	0.00
Salvadoran	2	0.00
Other Central American	1	0.00
Cuban	50	0.10
Dominican Republic	6	0.01
Mexican	302	0.58
Puerto Rican	69	0.13
South American:	31	0.06

Notes: 1. Figures in the "Number" column do not add up to the total population due to: a) Ancestry/Race overlap — e.g. persons can report being both White and Irish, b) persons of Hispanic origin can report being any race, c) persons reporting two ancestries are counted in both categories. 2. Numbers in parentheses indicate the number of persons reporting this ancestry/race alone, not in combination with any other ancestry/race. 3. Refer to the Explanation of Data in the front of the book for more detailed information.

Ancestry/Race	Number	%
Argentinean	1	0.00
Bolivian	1	0.00
Chilean	3	0.01
Colombian	17	0.03
Ecuadorian	2	0.00
Paraguayan	1	0.00
Peruvian	1	0.00
Uruguayan	1	0.00
Venezuelan	3	0.01
Other South American	1	0.00
Other Hispanic or Latino	115	0.22
Hungarian	145	0.28
Icelander	34	0.07
Iranian	9	0.02
Irish	7,339	14.21
Israeli	8	0.02
Italian	1,338	2.59
Latvian	15	0.03
Lithuanian	61	0.12
Luxemburger	54	0.10
Northern European	48	0.09
Norwegian	10,570	20.47
Pennsylvania German	18	0.03
Polish	2,693	5.22
Portuguese	49	0.09
Romanian	24	0.05
Russian	244	0.47
Scandinavian	205	0.40
Scotch-Irish	436	0.84
Scottish	666	1.29
Serbian	33	0.06
Slavic	7	0.01
Slovak	40	0.08
Slovene	84	0.16
Swedish	1,164	2.25
Swiss	536	1.04
Ukrainian	35	0.07
United States or American	1,531	2.96
Welsh	245	0.47
West Indian, excl. Hispanic:	53	0.10
Jamaican	29	0.06
Trinidadian and Tobagonian	12	0.02
West Indian	12	0.02
White:	47,983	92.60
Not Hispanic (47,158)	47,625	91.91
Hispanic (296)	358	0.69
Yugoslavian	22	0.04

Little Chute

Place Type: Village
County: Outagamie
Population: 10,476

Ancestry/Race	Number	%
African American/Black:	21	0.20
Not Hispanic (10)	21	0.20
Am. Ind. or Alaska Nat., not spec.	13	0.12
American Indian tribes, specified:	78	0.74
Apache	1	0.01
Blackfeet	3	0.03
Chippewa (9)	14	0.13
Creek	3	0.03
Iroquois (28)	41	0.39
Latin American Indians (1)	2	0.02
Menominee (2)	4	0.04
Potawatomi (2)	2	0.02
Sioux	1	0.01
All other tribes (4)	7	0.07
American Indian tribes, not spec.	5	0.05
Arab:	9	0.09
Lebanese	9	0.09
Asian:	107	1.02
Cambodian (1)	1	0.01
Chinese, ex. Taiwanese (3)	3	0.03
Filipino (3)	9	0.09
Hmong (37)	46	0.44
Indian (14)	15	0.14
Korean (6)	8	0.08
Laotian (2)	12	0.11
Thai (2)	4	0.04
Vietnamese (1)	2	0.02
Other Asian, not specified (3)	7	0.07
Austrian	95	0.91
Belgian	192	1.84
Croatian	9	0.09
Czech	140	1.34
Czechoslovakian	17	0.16
Danish	100	0.96
Dutch	3,277	31.36
English	333	3.19
European	88	0.84
Finnish	53	0.51
French, except Basque	397	3.80
French Canadian	122	1.17
German	4,470	42.78
Greek	12	0.11
Hawaii Native/Pacific Islander:	5	0.05
Micronesian: (2)	3	0.03
Guamanian/Chamorro (2)	3	0.03
Polynesian: (1)	1	0.01
Tongan (1)	1	0.01
Other Pac. Isl., not spec.	1	0.01
Hispanic or Latino:	175	1.67
Central American:	5	0.05
Honduran	5	0.05
Cuban	1	0.01
Mexican	140	1.34
Puerto Rican	6	0.06
South American:	3	0.03
Chilean	2	0.02
Other South American	1	0.01
Other Hispanic or Latino	20	0.19
Irish	949	9.08
Italian	196	1.88
Latvian	11	0.11
Norwegian	378	3.62
Pennsylvania German	7	0.07
Polish	484	4.63
Portuguese	38	0.36
Russian	10	0.10
Scandinavian	6	0.06
Scotch-Irish	18	0.17
Scottish	70	0.67
Serbian	12	0.11
Slavic	6	0.06
Swedish	149	1.43
Swiss	20	0.19
United States or American	801	7.67
Welsh	13	0.12
White:	10,229	97.64
Not Hispanic (10,098)	10,152	96.91
Hispanic (60)	77	0.74

Madison

Place Type: City
County: Dane
Population: 208,054

Ancestry/Race	Number	%
Acadian/Cajun	32	0.02
Afghan	6	0.00
African American/Black:	14,234	6.84
Not Hispanic (11,987)	13,891	6.68
Hispanic (168)	343	0.16
African, sub-Saharan:	1,319	0.64
African	808	0.39
Ethiopian	72	0.03
Ghanian	23	0.01
Liberian	44	0.02
Nigerian	169	0.08
Senegalese	8	0.00
Sierra Leonean	28	0.01
Somalian	10	0.00
South African	59	0.03
Ugandan	6	0.00
Other sub-Saharan African	92	0.04
Alaska Native tribes, specified:	18	0.01
Aleut (3)	5	0.00
Eskimo (7)	8	0.00
Tlingit-Haida (1)	4	0.00
All other tribes (1)	1	0.00
Alaska Native tribes, not specified	1	0.00
Am. Ind. or Alaska Nat., not spec.	598	0.29
Albanian	96	0.05
Alsatian	9	0.00
American Indian tribes, specified:	1,225	0.59
Apache (7)	16	0.01
Blackfeet (4)	21	0.01
Cherokee (42)	227	0.11
Cheyenne (3)	6	0.00
Chickasaw (4)	6	0.00
Chippewa (102)	192	0.09
Choctaw (16)	35	0.02
Colville (1)	1	0.00
Comanche (4)	7	0.00
Cree	6	0.00
Creek	9	0.00
Crow (1)	5	0.00
Delaware (2)	5	0.00
Houma	1	0.00
Iroquois (57)	123	0.06
Kiowa (1)	2	0.00
Latin American Indians (32)	80	0.04
Lumbee (5)	9	0.00
Menominee (35)	52	0.02
Navajo (15)	25	0.01
Osage	1	0.00
Ottawa (2)	3	0.00
Pima (1)	1	0.00
Potawatomi (9)	26	0.01
Pueblo (3)	9	0.00
Seminole	5	0.00
Shoshone (2)	5	0.00
Sioux (29)	76	0.04
Yaqui (3)	3	0.00
All other tribes (164)	268	0.13
American Indian tribes, not spec.	93	0.04
Arab:	941	0.45
Arab/Arabic	122	0.06
Egyptian	248	0.12
Iraqi	13	0.01
Jordanian	18	0.01
Lebanese	228	0.11
Moroccan	74	0.04
Palestinian	44	0.02
Syrian	102	0.05
Other Arab	92	0.04
Armenian	191	0.09
Asian:	13,804	6.63
Bangladeshi (11)	12	0.01
Cambodian (303)	331	0.16
Chinese, ex. Taiwanese (3,199)	3,566	1.71
Filipino (342)	555	0.27
Hmong (1,842)	2,053	0.99
Indian (1,763)	1,984	0.95
Indonesian (198)	243	0.12
Japanese (597)	873	0.42
Korean (1,603)	1,740	0.84
Laotian (407)	476	0.23
Malaysian (58)	66	0.03
Pakistani (68)	98	0.05
Sri Lankan (31)	44	0.02
Taiwanese (332)	389	0.19
Thai (273)	316	0.15
Vietnamese (466)	538	0.26
Other Asian, specified (65)	103	0.05
Other Asian, not specified (247)	417	0.20
Australian	70	0.03
Austrian	933	0.45
Basque	32	0.02
Belgian	1,023	0.49
Brazilian	104	0.05
British	1,095	0.53
Bulgarian	59	0.03
Canadian	518	0.25
Carpatho Rusyn	7	0.00
Celtic	91	0.04
Croatian	441	0.21

Notes: 1. Figures in the "Number" column do not add up to the total population due to: a) Ancestry/Race overlap — e.g. persons can report being both White and Irish, b) persons of Hispanic origin can report being any race, c) persons reporting two ancestries are counted in both categories. 2. Numbers in parentheses indicate the number of persons reporting this ancestry/race alone, not in combination with any other ancestry/race. 3. Refer to the Explanation of Data in the front of the book for more detailed information.

Cypriot	7	0.00
Czech	2,821	1.36
Czechoslovakian	667	0.32
Danish	2,688	1.30
Dutch	4,352	2.10
Eastern European	408	0.20
English	20,330	9.80
Estonian	29	0.01
European	2,358	1.14
Finnish	911	0.44
French, except Basque	6,509	3.14
French Canadian	1,445	0.70
German	74,418	35.86
Greek	922	0.44
Hawaii Native/Pacific Islander:	270	0.13
Melanesian: (1)	2	0.00
Fijian (1)	1	0.00
Other Melanesian	1	0.00
Micronesian: (17)	29	0.01
Guamanian/Chamorro (14)	26	0.01
Other Micronesian (3)	3	0.00
Polynesian: (46)	112	0.05
Native Hawaiian (30)	87	0.04
Samoan (15)	22	0.01
Other Polynesian (1)	3	0.00
Other Pac. Isl., specified	11	0.01
Other Pac. Isl., not spec. (12)	116	0.06
Hispanic or Latino:	8,512	4.09
Central American:	452	0.22
Costa Rican	47	0.02
Guatemalan	70	0.03
Honduran	128	0.06
Nicaraguan	98	0.05
Panamanian	43	0.02
Salvadoran	46	0.02
Other Central American	20	0.01
Cuban	189	0.09
Dominican Republic	47	0.02
Mexican	5,164	2.48
Puerto Rican	711	0.34
South American:	779	0.37
Argentinean	85	0.04
Bolivian	37	0.02
Chilean	101	0.05
Colombian	235	0.11
Ecuadorian	38	0.02
Paraguayan	22	0.01
Peruvian	116	0.06
Uruguayan	17	0.01
Venezuelan	95	0.05
Other South American	33	0.02
Other Hispanic or Latino	1,170	0.56
Hungarian	954	0.46
Icelander	96	0.05
Iranian	206	0.10
Irish	30,141	14.52
Israeli	152	0.07
Italian	7,986	3.85
Latvian	129	0.06
Lithuanian	684	0.33
Luxemburger	93	0.04
Macedonian	23	0.01
Maltese	9	0.00
New Zealander	26	0.01
Northern European	367	0.18
Norwegian	21,487	10.35
Pennsylvania German	65	0.03
Polish	11,144	5.37
Portuguese	173	0.08
Romanian	144	0.07
Russian	3,164	1.52
Scandinavian	908	0.44
Scotch-Irish	2,292	1.10
Scottish	3,780	1.82
Serbian	160	0.08
Slavic	171	0.08
Slovak	354	0.17
Slovene	141	0.07
Soviet Union	11	0.01
Swedish	5,603	2.70
Swiss	3,898	1.88
Turkish	245	0.12
Ukrainian	552	0.27
United States or American	5,545	2.67
Welsh	1,790	0.86
West Indian, excl. Hispanic:	351	0.17
Bahamian	36	0.02
Barbadian	20	0.01
British West Indian	16	0.01
Haitian	41	0.02
Jamaican	121	0.06
Trinidadian and Tobagonian	86	0.04
West Indian	31	0.01
White:	178,831	85.95
Not Hispanic (170,509)	173,934	83.60
Hispanic (4,180)	4,897	2.35
Yugoslavian	282	0.14

Manitowoc

Place Type: City
County: Manitowoc
Population: 34,053

Ancestry/Race	Number	%
African American/Black:	275	0.81
Not Hispanic (191)	257	0.75
Hispanic (11)	18	0.05
Alaska Native tribes, specified:	2	0.01
Alaska Athabascan (2)	2	0.01
Am. Ind. or Alaska Nat., not spec.	79	0.23
American Indian tribes, specified:	222	0.65
Apache (2)	3	0.01
Cherokee (2)	7	0.02
Chippewa (41)	55	0.16
Iroquois (61)	95	0.28
Latin American Indians (4)	8	0.02
Menominee (17)	23	0.07
Potawatomi (4)	5	0.01
Sioux (3)	3	0.01
All other tribes (8)	23	0.07
American Indian tribes, not spec.	15	0.04
Arab:	45	0.13
Lebanese	45	0.13
Armenian	11	0.03
Asian:	1,413	4.15
Bangladeshi (3)	3	0.01
Chinese, ex. Taiwanese (31)	37	0.11
Filipino (21)	38	0.11
Hmong (976)	1,042	3.06
Indian (40)	67	0.20
Indonesian (1)	1	0.00
Japanese (7)	14	0.04
Korean (13)	20	0.06
Laotian (68)	85	0.25
Pakistani (12)	12	0.04
Sri Lankan (2)	2	0.01
Thai (18)	22	0.06
Vietnamese (36)	39	0.11
Other Asian, specified	4	0.01
Other Asian, not specified (26)	27	0.08
Australian	3	0.01
Austrian	55	0.16
Belgian	456	1.34
British	48	0.14
Canadian	44	0.13
Croatian	77	0.23
Czech	3,004	8.84
Czechoslovakian	151	0.44
Danish	320	0.94
Dutch	492	1.45
English	1,677	4.93
European	103	0.30
Finnish	74	0.22
French, except Basque	1,845	5.43
French Canadian	704	2.07
German	16,910	49.74
Greek	85	0.25
Hawaii Native/Pacific Islander:	39	0.11
Micronesian: (5)	8	0.02
Guamanian/Chamorro (5)	8	0.02
Polynesian: (17)	21	0.06
Native Hawaiian (14)	18	0.05
Samoan (3)	3	0.01
Other Pac. Isl., specified	4	0.01
Other Pac. Isl., not spec. (3)	6	0.02
Hispanic or Latino:	859	2.52
Central American:	6	0.02
Guatemalan	2	0.01
Honduran	1	0.00
Salvadoran	2	0.01
Other Central American	1	0.00
Cuban	9	0.03
Mexican	639	1.88
Puerto Rican	35	0.10
South American:	25	0.07
Argentinean	5	0.01
Chilean	1	0.00
Colombian	6	0.02
Ecuadorian	2	0.01
Peruvian	8	0.02
Other South American	3	0.01
Other Hispanic or Latino	145	0.43
Hungarian	91	0.27
Iranian	11	0.03
Irish	3,033	8.92
Italian	495	1.46
Lithuanian	38	0.11
Luxemburger	19	0.06
Northern European	29	0.09
Norwegian	1,947	5.73
Polish	4,473	13.16
Portuguese	41	0.12
Romanian	18	0.05
Russian	113	0.33
Scandinavian	32	0.09
Scotch-Irish	139	0.41
Scottish	264	0.78
Serbian	20	0.06
Slavic	34	0.10
Slovak	46	0.14
Slovene	21	0.06
Swedish	590	1.74
Swiss	108	0.32
Ukrainian	25	0.07
United States or American	1,469	4.32
Welsh	74	0.22
West Indian, excl. Hispanic:	19	0.06
Bahamian	7	0.02
Haitian	12	0.04
White:	32,004	93.98
Not Hispanic (31,253)	31,482	92.45
Hispanic (460)	522	1.53
Yugoslavian	60	0.18

Marinette

Place Type: City
County: Marinette
Population: 11,749

Ancestry/Race	Number	%
African American/Black:	61	0.52
Not Hispanic (42)	58	0.49
Hispanic (2)	3	0.03
African, sub-Saharan:	9	0.08
African	9	0.08
Am. Ind. or Alaska Nat., not spec.	39	0.33
American Indian tribes, specified:	94	0.80
Cherokee (3)	6	0.05
Chippewa (28)	43	0.37
Cree	1	0.01
Iroquois (7)	10	0.09
Latin American Indians (7)	9	0.08
Menominee (3)	7	0.06
Navajo (1)	1	0.01
Ottawa (3)	3	0.03
Potawatomi (6)	9	0.08
Sioux (1)	3	0.03
All other tribes	2	0.02

Notes: 1. Figures in the "Number" column do not add up to the total population due to: a) Ancestry/Race overlap — e.g. persons can report being both White and Irish, b) persons of Hispanic origin can report being any race, c) persons reporting two ancestries are counted in both categories. 2. Numbers in parentheses indicate the number of persons reporting this ancestry/race alone, not in combination with any other ancestry/race. 3. Refer to the Explanation of Data in the front of the book for more detailed information.

Ancestry/Race	Number	%
Armenian	13	0.11
Asian:	58	0.49
Chinese, ex. Taiwanese (3)	3	0.03
Filipino (2)	7	0.06
Indian (1)	1	0.01
Japanese (8)	10	0.09
Korean (11)	11	0.09
Pakistani	6	0.05
Taiwanese (7)	8	0.07
Thai (5)	8	0.07
Vietnamese (4)	4	0.03
Australian	6	0.05
Austrian	90	0.77
Belgian	302	2.58
British	28	0.24
Canadian	13	0.11
Croatian	8	0.07
Czech	293	2.50
Czechoslovakian	25	0.21
Danish	207	1.77
Dutch	307	2.62
English	540	4.61
European	20	0.17
Finnish	143	1.22
French, except Basque	1,261	10.76
French Canadian	797	6.80
German	4,734	40.40
Hawaii Native/Pacific Islander:	11	0.09
Polynesian: (1)	5	0.04
Native Hawaiian (1)	5	0.04
Other Pac. Isl., not spec.	6	0.05
Hispanic or Latino:	123	1.05
Central American:	5	0.04
Costa Rican	2	0.02
Guatemalan	3	0.03
Cuban	4	0.03
Dominican Republic	3	0.03
Mexican	43	0.37
Puerto Rican	24	0.20
South American:	10	0.09
Bolivian	1	0.01
Colombian	4	0.03
Ecuadorian	2	0.02
Peruvian	3	0.03
Other Hispanic or Latino	34	0.29
Hungarian	6	0.05
Irish	1,014	8.65
Italian	272	2.32
Latvian	20	0.17
Lithuanian	6	0.05
Maltese	4	0.03
Northern European	15	0.13
Norwegian	593	5.06
Polish	1,101	9.40
Portuguese	9	0.08
Russian	45	0.38
Scandinavian	54	0.46
Scotch-Irish	84	0.72
Scottish	95	0.81
Slavic	10	0.09
Slovak	27	0.23
Slovene	23	0.20
Swedish	798	6.81
Swiss	23	0.20
Ukrainian	38	0.32
United States or American	488	4.16
Welsh	15	0.13
White:	11,545	98.26
Not Hispanic (11,374)	11,462	97.56
Hispanic (73)	83	0.71
Yugoslavian	7	0.06

Marshfield

Place Type: City
County: Wood
Population: 18,800

Ancestry/Race	Number	%
African American/Black:	100	0.53
Not Hispanic (74)	99	0.53
Hispanic	1	0.01
African, sub-Saharan:	130	0.69
Nigerian	130	0.69
Alaska Native tribes, specified:	3	0.02
Alaska Athabascan (3)	3	0.02
Am. Ind. or Alaska Nat., not spec.	26	0.14
American Indian tribes, specified:	54	0.29
Cherokee (1)	10	0.05
Chippewa (8)	12	0.06
Iroquois	5	0.03
Kiowa (1)	1	0.01
Latin American Indians (1)	1	0.01
Ottawa (1)	2	0.01
Potawatomi (11)	15	0.08
Pueblo (1)	1	0.01
Sioux (3)	3	0.02
All other tribes (2)	4	0.02
American Indian tribes, not spec.	11	0.06
Arab:	14	0.07
Egyptian	7	0.04
Syrian	7	0.04
Armenian	11	0.06
Asian:	293	1.56
Bangladeshi (2)	2	0.01
Chinese, ex. Taiwanese (61)	65	0.35
Filipino (27)	37	0.20
Hmong (29)	29	0.15
Indian (63)	64	0.34
Japanese (14)	15	0.08
Korean (18)	31	0.16
Laotian (13)	13	0.07
Pakistani (9)	9	0.05
Sri Lankan	1	0.01
Taiwanese (2)	5	0.03
Thai (1)	1	0.01
Vietnamese (18)	18	0.10
Other Asian, not specified (2)	3	0.02
Austrian	110	0.58
Belgian	21	0.11
British	29	0.15
Canadian	9	0.05
Croatian	45	0.24
Czech	237	1.26
Czechoslovakian	30	0.16
Danish	315	1.67
Dutch	354	1.88
English	1,407	7.48
European	33	0.18
Finnish	187	0.99
French, except Basque	679	3.61
French Canadian	205	1.09
German	10,510	55.88
Greek	27	0.14
Hawaii Native/Pacific Islander:	2	0.01
Micronesian: (1)	1	0.01
Guamanian/Chamorro (1)	1	0.01
Polynesian:	1	0.01
Native Hawaiian	1	0.01
Hispanic or Latino:	146	0.78
Central American:	1	0.01
Guatemalan	1	0.01
Cuban	3	0.02
Mexican	81	0.43
Puerto Rican	17	0.09
South American:	7	0.04
Argentinean	1	0.01
Colombian	3	0.02
Paraguayan	1	0.01
Peruvian	1	0.01
Uruguayan	1	0.01
Other Hispanic or Latino	37	0.20
Hungarian	25	0.13
Iranian	6	0.03
Irish	1,649	8.77
Italian	346	1.84
Latvian	9	0.05
Lithuanian	26	0.14
Luxemburger	16	0.09
Norwegian	1,487	7.91
Pennsylvania German	24	0.13
Polish	1,210	6.43
Russian	33	0.18
Scandinavian	23	0.12
Scotch-Irish	77	0.41
Scottish	204	1.08
Slavic	2	0.01
Slovak	54	0.29
Slovene	66	0.35
Swedish	434	2.31
Swiss	217	1.15
Ukrainian	23	0.12
United States or American	772	4.10
Welsh	38	0.20
White:	18,376	97.74
Not Hispanic (18,158)	18,264	97.15
Hispanic (101)	112	0.60
Yugoslavian	31	0.16

Menasha

Place Type: City
County: Winnebago
Population: 16,331

Ancestry/Race	Number	%
African American/Black:	138	0.85
Not Hispanic (81)	128	0.78
Hispanic (7)	10	0.06
African, sub-Saharan:	13	0.08
African	13	0.08
Am. Ind. or Alaska Nat., not spec.	29	0.18
American Indian tribes, specified:	119	0.73
Apache	1	0.01
Cherokee (3)	10	0.06
Chippewa (9)	12	0.07
Comanche (3)	3	0.02
Iroquois (36)	47	0.29
Latin American Indians	2	0.01
Menominee (10)	14	0.09
Paiute (2)	2	0.01
Potawatomi (6)	6	0.04
Sioux	3	0.02
All other tribes (15)	19	0.12
American Indian tribes, not spec.	2	0.01
Armenian	3	0.02
Asian:	314	1.92
Cambodian (4)	4	0.02
Chinese, ex. Taiwanese (12)	17	0.10
Filipino (9)	18	0.11
Hmong (175)	189	1.16
Indian (23)	38	0.23
Japanese (4)	9	0.06
Korean (13)	15	0.09
Laotian	1	0.01
Pakistani (1)	3	0.02
Thai (2)	3	0.02
Vietnamese (12)	12	0.07
Other Asian, not specified (2)	5	0.03
Austrian	62	0.38
Belgian	164	1.00
British	40	0.24
Bulgarian	6	0.04
Canadian	75	0.46
Croatian	46	0.28
Czech	250	1.53
Czechoslovakian	15	0.09
Danish	265	1.62
Dutch	875	5.34
English	762	4.65
European	57	0.35
Finnish	118	0.72
French, except Basque	897	5.47
French Canadian	417	2.55
German	8,718	53.21
Greek	17	0.10
Hawaii Native/Pacific Islander:	11	0.07
Polynesian: (1)	2	0.01
Native Hawaiian (1)	2	0.01
Other Pac. Isl., not spec. (3)	9	0.06

Notes: 1. Figures in the "Number" column do not add up to the total population due to: a) Ancestry/Race overlap — e.g. persons can report being both White and Irish, b) persons of Hispanic origin can report being any race, c) persons reporting two ancestries are counted in both categories. 2. Numbers in parentheses indicate the number of persons reporting this ancestry/race alone, not in combination with any other ancestry/race. 3. Refer to the Explanation of Data in the front of the book for more detailed information.

Hispanic or Latino:	590	3.61
Central American:	9	0.06
Costa Rican	1	0.01
Guatemalan	6	0.04
Honduran	1	0.01
Salvadoran	1	0.01
Cuban	7	0.04
Dominican Republic	1	0.01
Mexican	463	2.84
Puerto Rican	16	0.10
South American:	5	0.03
Chilean	1	0.01
Colombian	1	0.01
Peruvian	1	0.01
Venezuelan	2	0.01
Other Hispanic or Latino	89	0.54
Hungarian	37	0.23
Irish	1,727	10.54
Italian	403	2.46
Latvian	12	0.07
Lithuanian	16	0.10
Norwegian	987	6.02
Polish	1,899	11.59
Portuguese	29	0.18
Russian	114	0.70
Scandinavian	41	0.25
Scotch-Irish	103	0.63
Scottish	138	0.84
Serbian	36	0.22
Slavic	10	0.06
Slovak	23	0.14
Swedish	422	2.58
Swiss	72	0.44
United States or American	554	3.38
Welsh	82	0.50
White:	15,639	95.76
Not Hispanic (15,171)	15,293	93.64
Hispanic (310)	346	2.12
Yugoslavian	60	0.37

Menasha

Place Type: Town
County: Winnebago
Population: 15,858

Ancestry/Race	Number	%
African American/Black:	88	0.55
Not Hispanic (56)	77	0.49
Hispanic (6)	11	0.07
African, sub-Saharan:	44	0.28
Liberian	10	0.06
South African	34	0.21
Alaska Native tribes, specified:	2	0.01
Eskimo	2	0.01
Am. Ind. or Alaska Nat., not spec.	23	0.15
American Indian tribes, specified:	86	0.54
Cherokee	3	0.02
Chippewa (11)	13	0.08
Choctaw (1)	1	0.01
Comanche	3	0.02
Delaware (1)	2	0.01
Iroquois (22)	31	0.20
Kiowa (1)	1	0.01
Latin American Indians (5)	6	0.04
Menominee (4)	10	0.06
Ottawa	1	0.01
Potawatomi (2)	2	0.01
All other tribes (8)	13	0.08
American Indian tribes, not spec.	5	0.03
Arab:	44	0.28
Lebanese	44	0.28
Asian:	298	1.88
Chinese, ex. Taiwanese (15)	19	0.12
Filipino (5)	9	0.06
Hmong (150)	152	0.96
Indian (53)	54	0.34
Japanese (5)	10	0.06
Korean (9)	15	0.09
Laotian (11)	12	0.08
Pakistani (3)	3	0.02
Sri Lankan (2)	2	0.01
Taiwanese (1)	1	0.01
Thai (4)	5	0.03
Vietnamese (4)	6	0.04
Other Asian, not specified (1)	10	0.06
Australian	27	0.17
Austrian	11	0.07
Belgian	231	1.45
British	88	0.55
Canadian	21	0.13
Croatian	39	0.24
Czech	147	0.92
Czechoslovakian	17	0.11
Danish	226	1.42
Dutch	1,111	6.97
English	809	5.08
European	27	0.17
Finnish	102	0.64
French, except Basque	1,007	6.32
French Canadian	266	1.67
German	8,699	54.57
Greek	18	0.11
Hawaii Native/Pacific Islander:	8	0.05
Micronesian: (2)	2	0.01
Guamanian/Chamorro (2)	2	0.01
Polynesian: (4)	4	0.03
Native Hawaiian (2)	2	0.01
Samoan (2)	2	0.01
Other Pac. Isl., not spec.	2	0.01
Hispanic or Latino:	493	3.11
Central American:	4	0.03
Guatemalan	1	0.01
Honduran	1	0.01
Salvadoran	2	0.01
Cuban	8	0.05
Mexican	388	2.45
Puerto Rican	14	0.09
South American:	12	0.08
Chilean	7	0.04
Colombian	3	0.02
Other South American	2	0.01
Other Hispanic or Latino	67	0.42
Hungarian	38	0.24
Iranian	30	0.19
Irish	1,679	10.53
Italian	471	2.95
Lithuanian	22	0.14
Luxemburger	7	0.04
Norwegian	880	5.52
Pennsylvania German	9	0.06
Polish	1,579	9.91
Russian	57	0.36
Scandinavian	22	0.14
Scotch-Irish	185	1.16
Scottish	147	0.92
Slovak	8	0.05
Slovene	8	0.05
Swedish	470	2.95
Swiss	133	0.83
Ukrainian	19	0.12
United States or American	360	2.26
Welsh	16	0.10
White:	15,258	96.22
Not Hispanic (14,887)	14,974	94.43
Hispanic (248)	284	1.79
Yugoslavian	43	0.27

Menomonee Falls

Place Type: Village
County: Waukesha
Population: 32,647

Ancestry/Race	Number	%
African American/Black:	571	1.75
Not Hispanic (474)	557	1.71
Hispanic (5)	14	0.04
African, sub-Saharan:	69	0.21
African	30	0.09
Ghanian	19	0.06
Zimbabwean	20	0.06
Am. Ind. or Alaska Nat., not spec.	29	0.09
Albanian	7	0.02
Alsatian	6	0.02
American Indian tribes, specified:	100	0.31
Apache (2)	3	0.01
Blackfeet (1)	2	0.01
Cherokee (1)	12	0.04
Cheyenne	2	0.01
Chickasaw	1	0.00
Chippewa (13)	25	0.08
Iroquois (15)	24	0.07
Latin American Indians	1	0.00
Menominee (7)	9	0.03
Ottawa	2	0.01
Puget Sound Salish (1)	1	0.00
Shoshone	1	0.00
Sioux	1	0.00
All other tribes (7)	16	0.05
American Indian tribes, not spec.	2	0.01
Arab:	68	0.21
Lebanese	5	0.02
Palestinian	24	0.07
Syrian	39	0.12
Armenian	19	0.06
Asian:	345	1.06
Chinese, ex. Taiwanese (65)	72	0.22
Filipino (43)	61	0.19
Hmong (8)	8	0.02
Indian (72)	74	0.23
Indonesian (1)	1	0.00
Japanese (21)	37	0.11
Korean (39)	46	0.14
Laotian (2)	3	0.01
Pakistani (6)	6	0.02
Taiwanese (2)	3	0.01
Thai (11)	11	0.03
Vietnamese (16)	18	0.06
Other Asian, specified	4	0.01
Other Asian, not specified	1	0.00
Austrian	266	0.81
Belgian	151	0.46
British	113	0.35
Canadian	60	0.18
Croatian	251	0.77
Cypriot	12	0.04
Czech	415	1.27
Czechoslovakian	167	0.51
Danish	349	1.07
Dutch	661	2.02
Eastern European	10	0.03
English	2,299	7.04
Estonian	11	0.03
European	220	0.67
Finnish	230	0.70
French, except Basque	1,557	4.77
French Canadian	331	1.01
German	18,204	55.76
Greek	191	0.59
Hawaii Native/Pacific Islander:	17	0.05
Micronesian: (1)	1	0.00
Guamanian/Chamorro (1)	1	0.00
Polynesian: (5)	10	0.03
Native Hawaiian (4)	9	0.03
Samoan (1)	1	0.00
Other Pac. Isl., specified	4	0.01
Other Pac. Isl., not spec.	2	0.01
Hispanic or Latino:	377	1.15
Central American:	12	0.04
Guatemalan	8	0.02
Honduran	2	0.01
Salvadoran	2	0.01
Cuban	9	0.03
Dominican Republic	2	0.01
Mexican	203	0.62
Puerto Rican	60	0.18
South American:	23	0.07
Argentinean	2	0.01
Colombian	12	0.04

Notes: 1. Figures in the "Number" column do not add up to the total population due to: a) Ancestry/Race overlap — e.g. persons can report being both White and Irish, b) persons of Hispanic origin can report being any race, c) persons reporting two ancestries are counted in both categories. 2. Numbers in parentheses indicate the number of persons reporting this ancestry/race alone, not in combination with any other ancestry/race. 3. Refer to the Explanation of Data in the front of the book for more detailed information.

Ancestry/Race	Number	%
Ecuadorian	1	0.00
Paraguayan	2	0.01
Peruvian	4	0.01
Venezuelan	1	0.00
Other South American	1	0.00
Other Hispanic or Latino	68	0.21
Hungarian	295	0.90
Iranian	16	0.05
Irish	3,776	11.57
Italian	1,967	6.03
Latvian	32	0.10
Lithuanian	92	0.28
Luxemburger	27	0.08
New Zealander	5	0.02
Northern European	8	0.02
Norwegian	1,678	5.14
Pennsylvania German	6	0.02
Polish	3,768	11.54
Portuguese	6	0.02
Romanian	23	0.07
Russian	222	0.68
Scandinavian	63	0.19
Scotch-Irish	214	0.66
Scottish	379	1.16
Serbian	38	0.12
Slavic	8	0.02
Slovak	181	0.55
Slovene	87	0.27
Swedish	759	2.32
Swiss	294	0.90
Ukrainian	14	0.04
United States or American	1,074	3.29
Welsh	166	0.51
West Indian, excl. Hispanic:	48	0.15
Dutch West Indian	12	0.04
Jamaican	36	0.11
White:	31,739	97.22
Not Hispanic (31,225)	31,433	96.28
Hispanic (279)	306	0.94
Yugoslavian	45	0.14

Menomonie

Place Type: City
County: Dunn
Population: 14,937

Ancestry/Race	Number	%
African American/Black:	145	0.97
Not Hispanic (114)	145	0.97
African, sub-Saharan:	6	0.04
Nigerian	6	0.04
Alaska Native tribes, specified:	1	0.01
Eskimo	1	0.01
Am. Ind. or Alaska Nat., not spec.	34	0.23
American Indian tribes, specified:	79	0.53
Cherokee (7)	22	0.15
Chippewa (25)	31	0.21
Comanche (1)	1	0.01
Cree	5	0.03
Delaware	1	0.01
Iroquois (2)	3	0.02
Navajo	2	0.01
Ottawa (1)	1	0.01
Potawatomi (1)	1	0.01
Sioux (1)	5	0.03
All other tribes (5)	7	0.05
American Indian tribes, not spec.	7	0.05
Arab:	17	0.11
Lebanese	17	0.11
Asian:	567	3.80
Cambodian (1)	1	0.01
Chinese, ex. Taiwanese (47)	55	0.37
Filipino (8)	19	0.13
Hmong (274)	293	1.96
Indian (38)	53	0.35
Indonesian (3)	3	0.02
Japanese (18)	22	0.15
Korean (35)	48	0.32
Laotian (13)	13	0.09
Malaysian (2)	3	0.02
Taiwanese (7)	7	0.05
Thai (8)	8	0.05
Vietnamese (5)	7	0.05
Other Asian, specified (1)	1	0.01
Other Asian, not specified (18)	34	0.23
Assyrian/Chaldean/Syriac	15	0.10
Austrian	181	1.21
Belgian	129	0.86
British	74	0.49
Canadian	13	0.09
Celtic	10	0.07
Czech	263	1.75
Czechoslovakian	77	0.51
Danish	205	1.37
Dutch	248	1.65
English	776	5.18
European	57	0.38
Finnish	45	0.30
French, except Basque	582	3.88
French Canadian	130	0.87
German	6,140	40.95
Greek	37	0.25
Hawaii Native/Pacific Islander:	19	0.13
Micronesian:	1	0.01
Guamanian/Chamorro	1	0.01
Polynesian: (1)	3	0.02
Native Hawaiian (1)	2	0.01
Samoan	1	0.01
Other Pac. Isl., not spec. (1)	15	0.10
Hispanic or Latino:	170	1.14
Central American:	1	0.01
Other Central American	1	0.01
Cuban	1	0.01
Dominican Republic	3	0.02
Mexican	90	0.60
Puerto Rican	8	0.05
South American:	37	0.25
Chilean	5	0.03
Colombian	7	0.05
Venezuelan	25	0.17
Other Hispanic or Latino	30	0.20
Hungarian	8	0.05
Irish	1,326	8.84
Italian	348	2.32
Latvian	31	0.21
Lithuanian	17	0.11
New Zealander	95	0.63
Northern European	25	0.17
Norwegian	2,899	19.33
Polish	670	4.47
Portuguese	12	0.08
Romanian	1	0.01
Russian	55	0.37
Scandinavian	64	0.43
Scotch-Irish	135	0.90
Scottish	270	1.80
Serbian	2	0.01
Slavic	7	0.05
Slovak	27	0.18
Slovene	7	0.05
Swedish	707	4.71
Swiss	98	0.65
Ukrainian	7	0.05
United States or American	274	1.83
Welsh	14	0.09
White:	14,155	94.76
Not Hispanic (13,939)	14,074	94.22
Hispanic (70)	81	0.54
Yugoslavian	7	0.05

Mequon

Place Type: City
County: Ozaukee
Population: 21,823

Ancestry/Race	Number	%
African American/Black:	544	2.49
Not Hispanic (490)	540	2.47
Hispanic (2)	4	0.02
African, sub-Saharan:	67	0.31
African	23	0.11
Ghanian	18	0.08
Nigerian	9	0.04
South African	17	0.08
Alaska Native tribes, specified:	2	0.01
Aleut (1)	1	0.00
Eskimo	1	0.00
Am. Ind. or Alaska Nat., not spec.	11	0.05
American Indian tribes, specified:	36	0.16
Cherokee	5	0.02
Chippewa (1)	2	0.01
Choctaw	1	0.00
Delaware (1)	1	0.00
Iroquois (7)	10	0.05
Latin American Indians	1	0.00
Sioux (2)	5	0.02
Yuman	2	0.01
All other tribes (5)	9	0.04
American Indian tribes, not spec.	5	0.02
Arab:	36	0.16
Egyptian	36	0.16
Armenian	6	0.03
Asian:	597	2.74
Chinese, ex. Taiwanese (103)	115	0.53
Filipino (14)	24	0.11
Hmong (12)	12	0.05
Indian (227)	243	1.11
Indonesian (1)	2	0.01
Japanese (12)	37	0.17
Korean (82)	85	0.39
Laotian (6)	6	0.03
Pakistani (27)	28	0.13
Taiwanese (10)	10	0.05
Thai (5)	5	0.02
Vietnamese (13)	13	0.06
Other Asian, not specified (10)	17	0.08
Australian	7	0.03
Austrian	180	0.82
Belgian	93	0.43
British	98	0.45
Bulgarian	25	0.11
Canadian	27	0.12
Croatian	82	0.38
Czech	265	1.21
Czechoslovakian	37	0.17
Danish	257	1.18
Dutch	634	2.90
Eastern European	102	0.47
English	2,001	9.16
European	108	0.49
Finnish	102	0.47
French, except Basque	549	2.51
French Canadian	76	0.35
German	9,130	41.79
Greek	162	0.74
Hawaii Native/Pacific Islander:	12	0.05
Micronesian: (3)	3	0.01
Guamanian/Chamorro (3)	3	0.01
Polynesian: (1)	5	0.02
Native Hawaiian (1)	5	0.02
Other Pac. Isl., not spec. (2)	4	0.02
Hispanic or Latino:	261	1.20
Central American:	13	0.06
Costa Rican	2	0.01
Guatemalan	2	0.01
Nicaraguan	3	0.01
Salvadoran	4	0.02
Other Central American	2	0.01
Cuban	10	0.05
Mexican	88	0.40
Puerto Rican	51	0.23
South American:	52	0.24
Argentinean	6	0.03
Bolivian	3	0.01
Chilean	3	0.01
Colombian	13	0.06
Ecuadorian	1	0.00
Paraguayan	2	0.01

Notes: 1. Figures in the "Number" column do not add up to the total population due to: a) Ancestry/Race overlap — e.g. persons can report being both White and Irish, b) persons of Hispanic origin can report being any race, c) persons reporting two ancestries are counted in both categories. 2. Numbers in parentheses indicate the number of persons reporting this ancestry/race alone, not in combination with any other ancestry/race. 3. Refer to the Explanation of Data in the front of the book for more detailed information.

Peruvian	13	0.06
Uruguayan	2	0.01
Venezuelan	4	0.02
Other South American	5	0.02
Other Hispanic or Latino	47	0.22
Hungarian	151	0.69
Iranian	38	0.17
Irish	3,043	13.93
Israeli	8	0.04
Italian	1,210	5.54
Latvian	7	0.03
Lithuanian	65	0.30
Luxemburger	56	0.26
Macedonian	16	0.07
Northern European	43	0.20
Norwegian	989	4.53
Polish	1,906	8.72
Portuguese	37	0.17
Romanian	53	0.24
Russian	809	3.70
Scandinavian	76	0.35
Scotch-Irish	237	1.08
Scottish	267	1.22
Serbian	43	0.20
Slavic	9	0.04
Slovak	105	0.48
Slovene	77	0.35
Swedish	522	2.39
Swiss	232	1.06
Turkish	33	0.15
Ukrainian	133	0.61
United States or American	1,080	4.94
Welsh	164	0.75
West Indian, excl. Hispanic:	8	0.04
West Indian	8	0.04
White:	20,723	94.96
Not Hispanic (20,360)	20,512	93.99
Hispanic (189)	211	0.97
Yugoslavian	4	0.02

Merrill

Place Type: City
County: Lincoln
Population: 10,146

Ancestry/Race	Number	%
African American/Black:	40	0.39
Not Hispanic (19)	39	0.38
Hispanic (1)	1	0.01
Alaska Native tribes, specified:	2	0.02
Tlingit-Haida (1)	2	0.02
Am. Ind. or Alaska Nat., not spec.	35	0.34
American Indian tribes, specified:	51	0.50
Apache (2)	6	0.06
Blackfeet	4	0.04
Cherokee (1)	5	0.05
Chippewa (14)	18	0.18
Iroquois (4)	4	0.04
Menominee (5)	5	0.05
Potawatomi (2)	2	0.02
Sioux	1	0.01
All other tribes (2)	6	0.06
American Indian tribes, not spec.	1	0.01
Armenian	8	0.08
Asian:	57	0.56
Chinese, ex. Taiwanese (11)	16	0.16
Filipino (6)	11	0.11
Hmong (6)	6	0.06
Indian	1	0.01
Japanese	1	0.01
Korean (2)	3	0.03
Laotian (4)	4	0.04
Thai (8)	12	0.12
Vietnamese	1	0.01
Other Asian, not specified (2)	2	0.02
Austrian	23	0.23
Belgian	6	0.06
British	4	0.04
Croatian	7	0.07
Czech	122	1.20
Czechoslovakian	12	0.12
Danish	93	0.92
Dutch	155	1.53
English	357	3.52
Estonian	12	0.12
European	2	0.02
Finnish	48	0.47
French, except Basque	617	6.08
French Canadian	176	1.74
German	5,567	54.89
Greek	21	0.21
Hawaii Native/Pacific Islander:	6	0.06
Micronesian: (3)	5	0.05
Guamanian/Chamorro (3)	5	0.05
Polynesian: (1)	1	0.01
Native Hawaiian (1)	1	0.01
Hispanic or Latino:	104	1.03
Central American:	3	0.03
Guatemalan	2	0.02
Nicaraguan	1	0.01
Mexican	65	0.64
Puerto Rican	5	0.05
Other Hispanic or Latino	31	0.31
Hungarian	16	0.16
Irish	880	8.68
Italian	178	1.76
Latvian	18	0.18
Lithuanian	10	0.10
New Zealander	4	0.04
Northern European	16	0.16
Norwegian	632	6.23
Polish	826	8.14
Romanian	8	0.08
Russian	36	0.35
Scandinavian	22	0.22
Scotch-Irish	35	0.35
Scottish	87	0.86
Slavic	18	0.18
Slovak	21	0.21
Slovene	10	0.10
Swedish	559	5.51
Swiss	84	0.83
Ukrainian	25	0.25
United States or American	334	3.29
Welsh	18	0.18
White:	9,983	98.39
Not Hispanic (9,869)	9,922	97.79
Hispanic (51)	61	0.60
Yugoslavian	5	0.05

Middleton

Place Type: City
County: Dane
Population: 15,770

Ancestry/Race	Number	%
African American/Black:	412	2.61
Not Hispanic (308)	404	2.56
Hispanic (3)	8	0.05
African, sub-Saharan:	21	0.13
African	17	0.11
Nigerian	4	0.03
Am. Ind. or Alaska Nat., not spec.	16	0.10
Albanian	10	0.06
American Indian tribes, specified:	98	0.62
Apache	1	0.01
Blackfeet (1)	6	0.04
Cherokee (2)	15	0.10
Chippewa (12)	16	0.10
Choctaw	1	0.01
Colville (3)	3	0.02
Iroquois (5)	5	0.03
Latin American Indians (7)	9	0.06
Menominee (3)	4	0.03
Navajo (2)	3	0.02
Osage (1)	1	0.01
Ottawa	1	0.01
Potawatomi (1)	1	0.01
Puget Sound Salish (1)	1	0.01
Sioux (5)	5	0.03
All other tribes (18)	26	0.16
American Indian tribes, not spec.	9	0.06
Arab:	99	0.64
Egyptian	33	0.21
Lebanese	66	0.42
Asian:	500	3.17
Chinese, ex. Taiwanese (121)	148	0.94
Filipino (29)	41	0.26
Indian (154)	162	1.03
Indonesian (1)	1	0.01
Japanese (10)	18	0.11
Korean (64)	75	0.48
Laotian (6)	6	0.04
Malaysian (1)	6	0.04
Taiwanese (2)	3	0.02
Thai (2)	5	0.03
Vietnamese (12)	13	0.08
Other Asian, specified	6	0.04
Other Asian, not specified (8)	16	0.10
Austrian	81	0.52
Belgian	71	0.46
British	92	0.59
Canadian	27	0.17
Croatian	37	0.24
Czech	320	2.06
Czechoslovakian	30	0.19
Danish	240	1.54
Dutch	281	1.81
English	1,798	11.55
European	179	1.15
Finnish	82	0.53
French, except Basque	462	2.97
French Canadian	108	0.69
German	7,007	45.01
Greek	67	0.43
Hawaii Native/Pacific Islander:	7	0.04
Polynesian: (4)	5	0.03
Native Hawaiian (4)	4	0.03
Other Polynesian	1	0.01
Other Pac. Isl., not spec.	2	0.01
Hispanic or Latino:	444	2.82
Central American:	13	0.08
Costa Rican	2	0.01
Guatemalan	2	0.01
Honduran	3	0.02
Nicaraguan	2	0.01
Salvadoran	4	0.03
Cuban	14	0.09
Dominican Republic	5	0.03
Mexican	191	1.21
Puerto Rican	45	0.29
South American:	84	0.53
Bolivian	35	0.22
Chilean	6	0.04
Colombian	31	0.20
Ecuadorian	8	0.05
Venezuelan	3	0.02
Other South American	1	0.01
Other Hispanic or Latino	92	0.58
Hungarian	62	0.40
Iranian	7	0.04
Irish	2,235	14.36
Italian	434	2.79
Latvian	14	0.09
Lithuanian	60	0.39
Luxemburger	19	0.12
Northern European	67	0.43
Norwegian	1,655	10.63
Polish	917	5.89
Portuguese	7	0.04
Romanian	8	0.05
Russian	154	0.99
Scandinavian	13	0.08
Scotch-Irish	134	0.86
Scottish	251	1.61
Serbian	18	0.12
Slovak	17	0.11
Slovene	8	0.05

Notes: 1. Figures in the "Number" column do not add up to the total population due to: a) Ancestry/Race overlap — e.g. persons can report being both White and Irish, b) persons of Hispanic origin can report being any race, c) persons reporting two ancestries are counted in both categories. 2. Numbers in parentheses indicate the number of persons reporting this ancestry/race alone, not in combination with any other ancestry/race. 3. Refer to the Explanation of Data in the front of the book for more detailed information.

Swedish	480	3.08
Swiss	341	2.19
Ukrainian	44	0.28
United States or American	469	3.01
Welsh	119	0.76
White:	14,744	93.49
Not Hispanic (14,308)	14,501	91.95
Hispanic (213)	243	1.54
Yugoslavian	9	0.06

Milwaukee

Place Type: City
County: Milwaukee
Population: 596,974

Ancestry/Race	Number	%
Acadian/Cajun	69	0.01
Afghan	8	0.00
African American/Black:	230,503	38.61
Not Hispanic (220,432)	226,742	37.98
Hispanic (2,501)	3,761	0.63
African, sub-Saharan:	7,627	1.28
African	6,662	1.12
Ethiopian	145	0.02
Ghanian	23	0.00
Kenyan	43	0.01
Liberian	19	0.00
Nigerian	321	0.05
Senegalese	14	0.00
Sierra Leonean	63	0.01
Somalian	48	0.01
South African	71	0.01
Sudanese	25	0.00
Ugandan	132	0.02
Other sub-Saharan African	61	0.01
Alaska Native tribes, specified:	22	0.00
Alaska Athabascan (2)	7	0.00
Aleut (2)	2	0.00
Eskimo (4)	10	0.00
Tlingit-Haida	1	0.00
All other tribes (2)	2	0.00
Alaska Native tribes, not specified	3	0.00
Am. Ind. or Alaska Nat., not spec.	3,074	0.51
Albanian	230	0.04
Alsatian	34	0.01
American Indian tribes, specified:	5,869	0.98
Apache (36)	86	0.01
Blackfeet (20)	183	0.03
Cherokee (153)	688	0.12
Cheyenne (15)	27	0.00
Chickasaw (4)	15	0.00
Chippewa (1,030)	1,493	0.25
Choctaw (18)	85	0.01
Colville (3)	3	0.00
Comanche (3)	11	0.00
Cree (3)	15	0.00
Creek (13)	44	0.01
Crow (8)	17	0.00
Delaware (1)	6	0.00
Houma (1)	2	0.00
Iroquois (884)	1,209	0.20
Kiowa (2)	4	0.00
Latin American Indians (146)	275	0.05
Lumbee (9)	12	0.00
Menominee (366)	509	0.09
Navajo (7)	22	0.00
Osage	2	0.00
Ottawa (43)	69	0.01
Paiute	3	0.00
Pima (6)	7	0.00
Potawatomi (101)	131	0.02
Pueblo (2)	16	0.00
Puget Sound Salish (1)	3	0.00
Seminole (6)	19	0.00
Shoshone (1)	3	0.00
Sioux (89)	190	0.03
Ute (4)	6	0.00
Yaqui (3)	5	0.00
All other tribes (469)	709	0.12
American Indian tribes, not spec.	378	0.06
Arab:	1,879	0.31
Arab/Arabic	893	0.15
Egyptian	103	0.02
Iraqi	15	0.00
Jordanian	140	0.02
Lebanese	198	0.03
Moroccan	33	0.01
Palestinian	257	0.04
Syrian	88	0.01
Other Arab	152	0.03
Armenian	302	0.05
Asian:	20,659	3.46
Bangladeshi (7)	11	0.00
Cambodian (72)	94	0.02
Chinese, ex. Taiwanese (1,197)	1,503	0.25
Filipino (826)	1,250	0.21
Hmong (7,682)	8,418	1.41
Indian (2,313)	2,779	0.47
Indonesian (61)	112	0.02
Japanese (328)	557	0.09
Korean (505)	689	0.12
Laotian (1,921)	2,236	0.37
Malaysian (40)	45	0.01
Pakistani (224)	299	0.05
Sri Lankan (25)	36	0.01
Taiwanese (35)	45	0.01
Thai (146)	194	0.03
Vietnamese (1,224)	1,357	0.23
Other Asian, specified (17)	51	0.01
Other Asian, not specified (548)	983	0.16
Assyrian/Chaldean/Syriac	16	0.00
Australian	66	0.01
Austrian	2,477	0.41
Basque	7	0.00
Belgian	1,100	0.18
Brazilian	42	0.01
British	575	0.10
Bulgarian	107	0.02
Canadian	401	0.07
Celtic	52	0.01
Croatian	2,272	0.38
Czech	3,940	0.66
Czechoslovakian	964	0.16
Danish	2,596	0.43
Dutch	4,097	0.69
Eastern European	98	0.02
English	15,742	2.64
Estonian	31	0.01
European	1,935	0.32
Finnish	1,506	0.25
French, except Basque	11,751	1.97
French Canadian	3,161	0.53
German	124,484	20.85
German Russian	112	0.02
Greek	1,576	0.26
Guyanese	38	0.01
Hawaii Native/Pacific Islander:	813	0.14
Melanesian: (6)	9	0.00
Fijian (4)	4	0.00
Other Melanesian (2)	5	0.00
Micronesian: (67)	108	0.02
Guamanian/Chamorro (65)	106	0.02
Other Micronesian (2)	2	0.00
Polynesian: (150)	289	0.05
Native Hawaiian (64)	173	0.03
Samoan (83)	110	0.02
Tongan (2)	3	0.00
Other Polynesian (1)	3	0.00
Other Pac. Isl., specified	22	0.00
Other Pac. Isl., not spec. (76)	385	0.06
Hispanic or Latino:	71,646	12.00
Central American:	1,212	0.20
Costa Rican	161	0.03
Guatemalan	171	0.03
Honduran	151	0.03
Nicaraguan	318	0.05
Panamanian	87	0.01
Salvadoran	271	0.05
Other Central American	53	0.01
Cuban	637	0.11
Dominican Republic	305	0.05
Mexican	43,300	7.25
Puerto Rican	19,613	3.29
South American:	647	0.11
Argentinean	41	0.01
Bolivian	23	0.00
Chilean	84	0.01
Colombian	239	0.04
Ecuadorian	52	0.01
Paraguayan	11	0.00
Peruvian	111	0.02
Uruguayan	4	0.00
Venezuelan	61	0.01
Other South American	21	0.00
Other Hispanic or Latino	5,932	0.99
Hungarian	2,798	0.47
Icelander	42	0.01
Iranian	247	0.04
Irish	37,726	6.32
Israeli	42	0.01
Italian	17,499	2.93
Latvian	285	0.05
Lithuanian	821	0.14
Luxemburger	328	0.05
Macedonian	6	0.00
New Zealander	15	0.00
Northern European	88	0.01
Norwegian	12,144	2.03
Pennsylvania German	61	0.01
Polish	57,485	9.63
Portuguese	143	0.02
Romanian	315	0.05
Russian	3,374	0.57
Scandinavian	476	0.08
Scotch-Irish	2,457	0.41
Scottish	2,889	0.48
Serbian	1,750	0.29
Slavic	303	0.05
Slovak	1,577	0.26
Slovene	1,145	0.19
Soviet Union	16	0.00
Swedish	5,693	0.95
Swiss	1,649	0.28
Turkish	163	0.03
Ukrainian	948	0.16
United States or American	11,106	1.86
Welsh	1,577	0.26
West Indian, excl. Hispanic:	1,600	0.27
Bahamian	16	0.00
Barbadian	35	0.01
Belizean	49	0.01
Bermudan	9	0.00
British West Indian	91	0.02
Haitian	98	0.02
Jamaican	1,152	0.19
Trinidadian and Tobagonian	42	0.01
West Indian	104	0.02
Other West Indian	4	0.00
White:	310,734	52.05
Not Hispanic (270,989)	279,184	46.77
Hispanic (27,390)	31,550	5.28
Yugoslavian	616	0.10

Monroe

Place Type: City
County: Green
Population: 10,843

Ancestry/Race	Number	%
African American/Black:	63	0.58
Not Hispanic (36)	61	0.56
Hispanic (2)	2	0.02
Alaska Native tribes, specified:	1	0.01
Aleut	1	0.01
Am. Ind. or Alaska Nat., not spec.	12	0.11
Albanian	9	0.08
American Indian tribes, specified:	51	0.47
Apache	1	0.01

Notes: 1. Figures in the "Number" column do not add up to the total population due to: a) Ancestry/Race overlap — e.g. persons can report being both White and Irish, b) persons of Hispanic origin can report being any race, c) persons reporting two ancestries are counted in both categories. 2. Numbers in parentheses indicate the number of persons reporting this ancestry/race alone, not in combination with any other ancestry/race. 3. Refer to the Explanation of Data in the front of the book for more detailed information.

Ancestry/Race	Number	%
Blackfeet	1	0.01
Cherokee (9)	15	0.14
Chippewa (5)	6	0.06
Choctaw (1)	1	0.01
Iroquois (1)	3	0.03
Latin American Indians	1	0.01
Menominee (2)	5	0.05
Navajo	1	0.01
Potawatomi (1)	1	0.01
Sioux (3)	4	0.04
Yuman (2)	2	0.02
All other tribes (5)	10	0.09
American Indian tribes, not spec.	2	0.02
Asian:	57	0.53
Chinese, ex. Taiwanese (3)	10	0.09
Filipino (4)	7	0.06
Indian (11)	13	0.12
Japanese (1)	6	0.06
Korean (6)	6	0.06
Laotian	2	0.02
Malaysian	4	0.04
Taiwanese	2	0.02
Thai (3)	3	0.03
Vietnamese (3)	3	0.03
Other Asian, not specified	1	0.01
Austrian	46	0.43
Belgian	7	0.06
British	40	0.37
Croatian	2	0.02
Czech	103	0.95
Czechoslovakian	14	0.13
Danish	71	0.66
Dutch	265	2.45
English	972	8.99
European	5	0.05
Finnish	40	0.37
French, except Basque	241	2.23
French Canadian	69	0.64
German	4,398	40.68
Hawaii Native/Pacific Islander:	1	0.01
Micronesian:	1	0.01
Guamanian/Chamorro	1	0.01
Hispanic or Latino:	158	1.46
Central American:	3	0.03
Panamanian	1	0.01
Salvadoran	2	0.02
Cuban	4	0.04
Mexican	109	1.01
Puerto Rican	8	0.07
South American:	1	0.01
Other South American	1	0.01
Other Hispanic or Latino	33	0.30
Hungarian	27	0.25
Irish	1,200	11.10
Italian	233	2.16
Lithuanian	10	0.09
Luxemburger	8	0.07
New Zealander	5	0.05
Norwegian	1,642	15.19
Pennsylvania German	30	0.28
Polish	249	2.30
Russian	4	0.04
Scotch-Irish	101	0.93
Scottish	67	0.62
Swedish	158	1.46
Swiss	2,582	23.88
Ukrainian	6	0.06
United States or American	525	4.86
Welsh	45	0.42
White:	10,669	98.40
Not Hispanic (10,517)	10,576	97.54
Hispanic (79)	93	0.86

Mount Pleasant

Place Type: Town
County: Racine
Population: 23,142

Ancestry/Race	Number	%
African American/Black:	1,595	6.89
Not Hispanic (1,451)	1,549	6.69
Hispanic (28)	46	0.20
Am. Ind. or Alaska Nat., not spec.	42	0.18
Albanian	54	0.23
American Indian tribes, specified:	75	0.32
Apache	2	0.01
Blackfeet	2	0.01
Cherokee (2)	4	0.02
Cheyenne (1)	1	0.00
Chippewa (11)	31	0.13
Iroquois (2)	8	0.03
Latin American Indians (6)	6	0.03
Menominee (2)	8	0.03
Navajo (1)	1	0.00
Ottawa (4)	4	0.02
Sioux	3	0.01
All other tribes (3)	5	0.02
American Indian tribes, not spec.	9	0.04
Arab:	11	0.05
Arab/Arabic	11	0.05
Armenian	109	0.47
Asian:	335	1.45
Chinese, ex. Taiwanese (53)	58	0.25
Filipino (36)	52	0.22
Indian (114)	128	0.55
Indonesian (4)	6	0.03
Japanese (13)	18	0.08
Korean (25)	29	0.13
Laotian (8)	9	0.04
Pakistani (5)	5	0.02
Sri Lankan (7)	7	0.03
Taiwanese (2)	2	0.01
Thai (1)	3	0.01
Vietnamese (9)	9	0.04
Other Asian, specified	2	0.01
Other Asian, not specified (1)	7	0.03
Austrian	118	0.51
Belgian	164	0.71
British	60	0.26
Bulgarian	13	0.06
Canadian	37	0.16
Celtic	16	0.07
Croatian	83	0.36
Czech	443	1.92
Czechoslovakian	125	0.54
Danish	2,117	9.16
Dutch	775	3.35
English	1,994	8.63
European	61	0.26
Finnish	146	0.63
French, except Basque	803	3.47
French Canadian	219	0.95
German	8,788	38.02
Greek	99	0.43
Hawaii Native/Pacific Islander:	16	0.07
Micronesian:	2	0.01
Guamanian/Chamorro	2	0.01
Polynesian: (3)	7	0.03
Native Hawaiian	2	0.01
Samoan (1)	3	0.01
Tongan (2)	2	0.01
Other Pac. Isl., specified	1	0.00
Other Pac. Isl., not spec. (4)	6	0.03
Hispanic or Latino:	1,149	4.96
Central American:	11	0.05
Costa Rican	4	0.02
Guatemalan	4	0.02
Honduran	1	0.00
Nicaraguan	2	0.01
Cuban	4	0.02
Dominican Republic	1	0.00
Mexican	864	3.73
Puerto Rican	61	0.26
South American:	13	0.06
Argentinean	1	0.00
Bolivian	1	0.00
Colombian	4	0.02
Peruvian	1	0.00
Venezuelan	6	0.03
Other Hispanic or Latino	195	0.84
Hungarian	271	1.17
Irish	2,335	10.10
Italian	1,487	6.43
Lithuanian	151	0.65
Luxemburger	12	0.05
Macedonian	14	0.06
Northern European	49	0.21
Norwegian	1,388	6.00
Pennsylvania German	10	0.04
Polish	1,875	8.11
Portuguese	10	0.04
Romanian	20	0.09
Russian	102	0.44
Scandinavian	57	0.25
Scotch-Irish	181	0.78
Scottish	256	1.11
Serbian	128	0.55
Slavic	8	0.03
Slovak	243	1.05
Slovene	71	0.31
Swedish	655	2.83
Swiss	149	0.64
Ukrainian	9	0.04
United States or American	738	3.19
Welsh	100	0.43
West Indian, excl. Hispanic:	31	0.13
Jamaican	31	0.13
White:	20,863	90.15
Not Hispanic (20,004)	20,170	87.16
Hispanic (631)	693	2.99
Yugoslavian	106	0.46

Muskego

Place Type: City
County: Waukesha
Population: 21,397

Ancestry/Race	Number	%
African American/Black:	82	0.38
Not Hispanic (34)	79	0.37
Hispanic	3	0.01
Alaska Native tribes, specified:	3	0.01
Eskimo (3)	3	0.01
Am. Ind. or Alaska Nat., not spec.	22	0.10
Albanian	6	0.03
American Indian tribes, specified:	63	0.29
Cherokee	10	0.05
Chippewa (14)	19	0.09
Cree	1	0.00
Iroquois (12)	12	0.06
Menominee (2)	3	0.01
Potawatomi (2)	6	0.03
Sioux	2	0.01
All other tribes (9)	10	0.05
American Indian tribes, not spec.	1	0.00
Arab:	46	0.22
Lebanese	46	0.22
Armenian	30	0.14
Asian:	147	0.69
Chinese, ex. Taiwanese (22)	24	0.11
Filipino (9)	15	0.07
Indian (8)	20	0.09
Japanese (14)	31	0.14
Korean (19)	20	0.09
Laotian	2	0.01
Malaysian (1)	1	0.00
Pakistani (1)	1	0.00
Taiwanese (3)	3	0.01
Thai (3)	3	0.01
Vietnamese (17)	18	0.08
Other Asian, specified	7	0.03
Other Asian, not specified	2	0.01
Austrian	132	0.62
Belgian	99	0.46
British	30	0.14
Canadian	35	0.16
Croatian	179	0.84
Czech	272	1.27

Notes: 1. Figures in the "Number" column do not add up to the total population due to: a) Ancestry/Race overlap — e.g. persons can report being both White and Irish, b) persons of Hispanic origin can report being any race, c) persons reporting two ancestries are counted in both categories. 2. Numbers in parentheses indicate the number of persons reporting this ancestry/race alone, not in combination with any other ancestry/race. 3. Refer to the Explanation of Data in the front of the book for more detailed information.

Czechoslovakian	77	0.36
Danish	194	0.91
Dutch	300	1.40
English	1,253	5.86
European	52	0.24
Finnish	129	0.60
French, except Basque	905	4.23
French Canadian	150	0.70
German	10,874	50.83
Greek	126	0.59
Hawaii Native/Pacific Islander:	13	0.06
Micronesian: (1)	1	0.00
Guamanian/Chamorro (1)	1	0.00
Polynesian: (4)	4	0.02
Samoan (4)	4	0.02
Other Pac. Isl., specified	6	0.03
Other Pac. Isl., not spec.	2	0.01
Hispanic or Latino:	281	1.31
Central American:	2	0.01
Costa Rican	2	0.01
Cuban	12	0.06
Mexican	192	0.90
Puerto Rican	33	0.15
South American:	6	0.03
Bolivian	1	0.00
Colombian	2	0.01
Paraguayan	2	0.01
Peruvian	1	0.00
Other Hispanic or Latino	36	0.17
Hungarian	135	0.63
Irish	2,621	12.25
Italian	1,279	5.98
Latvian	45	0.21
Lithuanian	87	0.41
Norwegian	1,197	5.60
Pennsylvania German	20	0.09
Polish	5,106	23.87
Portuguese	21	0.10
Romanian	7	0.03
Russian	122	0.57
Scandinavian	24	0.11
Scotch-Irish	130	0.61
Scottish	167	0.78
Serbian	180	0.84
Slavic	39	0.18
Slovak	51	0.24
Slovene	75	0.35
Swedish	557	2.60
Swiss	121	0.57
Ukrainian	42	0.20
United States or American	780	3.65
Welsh	57	0.27
White:	21,127	98.74
Not Hispanic (20,810)	20,921	97.78
Hispanic (182)	206	0.96
Yugoslavian	27	0.13

Neenah

Place Type: City
County: Winnebago
Population: 24,507

Ancestry/Race	Number	%
African American/Black:	170	0.69
Not Hispanic (79)	163	0.67
Hispanic (5)	7	0.03
Am. Ind. or Alaska Nat., not spec.	41	0.17
American Indian tribes, specified:	218	0.89
Apache (1)	1	0.00
Blackfeet	2	0.01
Cherokee	8	0.03
Cheyenne (1)	1	0.00
Chippewa (22)	26	0.11
Choctaw	2	0.01
Cree (1)	1	0.00
Creek	1	0.00
Delaware	1	0.00
Iroquois (26)	58	0.24
Latin American Indians (5)	9	0.04
Menominee (12)	24	0.10
Ottawa (1)	4	0.02
Pima (1)	1	0.00
Potawatomi (21)	37	0.15
Pueblo	1	0.00
Seminole	2	0.01
Sioux	6	0.02
All other tribes (18)	33	0.13
American Indian tribes, not spec.	9	0.04
Arab:	17	0.07
Egyptian	12	0.05
Syrian	5	0.02
Armenian	26	0.11
Asian:	313	1.28
Chinese, ex. Taiwanese (36)	43	0.18
Filipino (10)	26	0.11
Hmong (92)	105	0.43
Indian (29)	31	0.13
Japanese (11)	20	0.08
Korean (25)	37	0.15
Laotian (3)	3	0.01
Pakistani (1)	2	0.01
Sri Lankan	2	0.01
Taiwanese (2)	2	0.01
Thai (6)	6	0.02
Vietnamese (10)	23	0.09
Other Asian, specified (1)	1	0.00
Other Asian, not specified (5)	12	0.05
Australian	5	0.02
Austrian	25	0.10
Belgian	211	0.87
British	113	0.46
Canadian	43	0.18
Croatian	35	0.14
Czech	383	1.57
Czechoslovakian	56	0.23
Danish	588	2.42
Dutch	1,300	5.34
English	1,458	5.99
European	126	0.52
Finnish	229	0.94
French, except Basque	1,254	5.15
French Canadian	465	1.91
German	13,179	54.15
Greek	67	0.28
Hawaii Native/Pacific Islander:	16	0.07
Micronesian:	1	0.00
Guamanian/Chamorro	1	0.00
Polynesian: (1)	8	0.03
Native Hawaiian	7	0.03
Other Polynesian (1)	1	0.00
Other Pac. Isl., not spec.	7	0.03
Hispanic or Latino:	495	2.02
Central American:	17	0.07
Costa Rican	2	0.01
Guatemalan	3	0.01
Honduran	1	0.00
Nicaraguan	5	0.02
Panamanian	3	0.01
Salvadoran	1	0.00
Other Central American	2	0.01
Cuban	4	0.02
Mexican	347	1.42
Puerto Rican	30	0.12
South American:	7	0.03
Argentinean	3	0.01
Chilean	2	0.01
Ecuadorian	1	0.00
Venezuelan	1	0.00
Other Hispanic or Latino	90	0.37
Hungarian	25	0.10
Icelander	52	0.21
Irish	2,882	11.84
Italian	652	2.68
Lithuanian	6	0.02
Northern European	20	0.08
Norwegian	1,377	5.66
Polish	2,243	9.22
Russian	131	0.54
Scandinavian	78	0.32
Scotch-Irish	105	0.43
Scottish	257	1.06
Slovak	23	0.09
Swedish	569	2.34
Swiss	138	0.57
Ukrainian	34	0.14
United States or American	786	3.23
Welsh	225	0.92
West Indian, excl. Hispanic:	14	0.06
West Indian	14	0.06
White:	23,822	97.20
Not Hispanic (23,295)	23,545	96.07
Hispanic (252)	277	1.13
Yugoslavian	19	0.08

New Berlin

Place Type: City
County: Waukesha
Population: 38,220

Ancestry/Race	Number	%
Acadian/Cajun	10	0.03
African American/Black:	246	0.64
Not Hispanic (167)	238	0.62
Hispanic (2)	8	0.02
African, sub-Saharan:	65	0.17
African	20	0.05
South African	45	0.12
Alaska Native tribes, specified:	1	0.00
Tlingit-Haida (1)	1	0.00
Am. Ind. or Alaska Nat., not spec.	27	0.07
Albanian	10	0.03
American Indian tribes, specified:	101	0.26
Cherokee (1)	9	0.02
Cheyenne	2	0.01
Chippewa (25)	31	0.08
Creek (1)	1	0.00
Iroquois (11)	15	0.04
Latin American Indians (3)	5	0.01
Lumbee	1	0.00
Menominee (5)	5	0.01
Ottawa (3)	4	0.01
Potawatomi (4)	5	0.01
Seminole (2)	2	0.01
Sioux	1	0.00
All other tribes (11)	20	0.05
American Indian tribes, not spec.	10	0.03
Arab:	38	0.10
Arab/Arabic	6	0.02
Lebanese	19	0.05
Palestinian	13	0.03
Armenian	83	0.22
Asian:	989	2.59
Chinese, ex. Taiwanese (208)	239	0.63
Filipino (68)	92	0.24
Indian (312)	320	0.84
Indonesian (1)	4	0.01
Japanese (51)	69	0.18
Korean (100)	115	0.30
Laotian (4)	7	0.02
Malaysian (1)	1	0.00
Pakistani (24)	24	0.06
Sri Lankan (9)	9	0.02
Taiwanese (11)	12	0.03
Thai (6)	8	0.02
Vietnamese (56)	66	0.17
Other Asian, specified (13)	14	0.04
Other Asian, not specified (5)	9	0.02
Austrian	506	1.32
Belgian	99	0.26
Brazilian	31	0.08
British	50	0.13
Bulgarian	8	0.02
Canadian	87	0.23
Carpatho Rusyn	8	0.02
Celtic	9	0.02
Croatian	475	1.24
Czech	672	1.75
Czechoslovakian	114	0.30

Notes: 1. Figures in the "Number" column do not add up to the total population due to: a) Ancestry/Race overlap — e.g. persons can report being both White and Irish, b) persons of Hispanic origin can report being any race, c) persons reporting two ancestries are counted in both categories. 2. Numbers in parentheses indicate the number of persons reporting this ancestry/race alone, not in combination with any other ancestry/race. 3. Refer to the Explanation of Data in the front of the book for more detailed information.

Danish	397	1.03
Dutch	570	1.49
English	2,523	6.58
European	166	0.43
Finnish	140	0.36
French, except Basque	1,341	3.50
French Canadian	263	0.69
German	18,551	48.36
Greek	240	0.63
Hawaii Native/Pacific Islander:	12	0.03
Micronesian:	1	0.00
Guamanian/Chamorro	1	0.00
Polynesian: (6)	11	0.03
Native Hawaiian (6)	9	0.02
Samoan	2	0.01
Hispanic or Latino:	595	1.56
Central American:	24	0.06
Costa Rican	3	0.01
Guatemalan	9	0.02
Honduran	9	0.02
Nicaraguan	2	0.01
Panamanian	1	0.00
Cuban	33	0.09
Mexican	322	0.84
Puerto Rican	125	0.33
South American:	31	0.08
Argentinean	6	0.02
Bolivian	2	0.01
Chilean	9	0.02
Colombian	8	0.02
Peruvian	6	0.02
Other Hispanic or Latino	60	0.16
Hungarian	391	1.02
Icelander	25	0.07
Iranian	8	0.02
Irish	4,829	12.59
Italian	2,242	5.84
Latvian	11	0.03
Lithuanian	133	0.35
Luxemburger	78	0.20
Macedonian	8	0.02
Northern European	7	0.02
Norwegian	1,881	4.90
Polish	7,025	18.31
Portuguese	20	0.05
Romanian	27	0.07
Russian	234	0.61
Scandinavian	158	0.41
Scotch-Irish	379	0.99
Scottish	382	1.00
Serbian	140	0.36
Slavic	72	0.19
Slovak	313	0.82
Slovene	191	0.50
Swedish	914	2.38
Swiss	200	0.52
Turkish	10	0.03
Ukrainian	68	0.18
United States or American	1,432	3.73
Welsh	217	0.57
West Indian, excl. Hispanic:	6	0.02
Haitian	6	0.02
White:	36,893	96.53
Not Hispanic (36,265)	36,487	95.47
Hispanic (366)	406	1.06
Yugoslavian	106	0.28

Oak Creek

Place Type: City
County: Milwaukee
Population: 28,456

Ancestry/Race	Number	%
African American/Black:	612	2.15
Not Hispanic (503)	578	2.03
Hispanic (16)	34	0.12
African, sub-Saharan:	39	0.14
African	21	0.07
Other sub-Saharan African	18	0.06
Alaska Native tribes, specified:	1	0.00
Eskimo	1	0.00
Am. Ind. or Alaska Nat., not spec.	40	0.14
Albanian	21	0.07
American Indian tribes, specified:	228	0.80
Apache (6)	6	0.02
Blackfeet (2)	5	0.02
Cherokee (6)	28	0.10
Chippewa (57)	79	0.28
Comanche (1)	1	0.00
Iroquois (44)	51	0.18
Latin American Indians	1	0.00
Menominee (7)	14	0.05
Ottawa (4)	4	0.01
Potawatomi (1)	2	0.01
Sioux (2)	5	0.02
All other tribes (12)	32	0.11
American Indian tribes, not spec.	8	0.03
Arab:	116	0.41
Arab/Arabic	46	0.16
Egyptian	43	0.15
Palestinian	27	0.09
Armenian	41	0.14
Asian:	807	2.84
Bangladeshi (1)	1	0.00
Cambodian	1	0.00
Chinese, ex. Taiwanese (72)	85	0.30
Filipino (64)	81	0.28
Hmong (23)	27	0.09
Indian (272)	293	1.03
Indonesian (4)	10	0.04
Japanese (22)	37	0.13
Korean (67)	85	0.30
Laotian (22)	30	0.11
Malaysian	3	0.01
Pakistani (18)	28	0.10
Sri Lankan (4)	6	0.02
Taiwanese (5)	8	0.03
Thai (2)	3	0.01
Vietnamese (79)	83	0.29
Other Asian, specified	1	0.00
Other Asian, not specified (16)	25	0.09
Australian	9	0.03
Austrian	192	0.67
Belgian	57	0.20
Brazilian	22	0.08
British	26	0.09
Bulgarian	12	0.04
Canadian	37	0.13
Croatian	197	0.69
Czech	535	1.88
Czechoslovakian	72	0.25
Danish	227	0.80
Dutch	296	1.04
English	1,473	5.18
Estonian	8	0.03
European	108	0.38
Finnish	140	0.49
French, except Basque	1,314	4.62
French Canadian	388	1.36
German	12,926	45.42
Greek	183	0.64
Hawaii Native/Pacific Islander:	12	0.04
Polynesian: (1)	2	0.01
Native Hawaiian (1)	1	0.00
Samoan	1	0.00
Other Pac. Isl., not spec.	10	0.04
Hispanic or Latino:	1,267	4.45
Central American:	43	0.15
Costa Rican	2	0.01
Guatemalan	7	0.02
Honduran	5	0.02
Nicaraguan	11	0.04
Panamanian	15	0.05
Salvadoran	3	0.01
Cuban	10	0.04
Dominican Republic	5	0.02
Mexican	730	2.57
Puerto Rican	294	1.03
South American:	27	0.09
Argentinean	3	0.01
Chilean	9	0.03
Colombian	11	0.04
Peruvian	4	0.01
Other Hispanic or Latino	158	0.56
Hungarian	235	0.83
Icelander	8	0.03
Iranian	27	0.09
Irish	2,829	9.94
Israeli	21	0.07
Italian	1,878	6.60
Lithuanian	128	0.45
Luxemburger	20	0.07
Northern European	6	0.02
Norwegian	1,144	4.02
Polish	7,485	26.30
Romanian	61	0.21
Russian	141	0.50
Scandinavian	53	0.19
Scotch-Irish	153	0.54
Scottish	205	0.72
Serbian	207	0.73
Slavic	34	0.12
Slovak	254	0.89
Slovene	73	0.26
Swedish	554	1.95
Swiss	142	0.50
Ukrainian	21	0.07
United States or American	772	2.71
Welsh	104	0.37
West Indian, excl. Hispanic:	16	0.06
Jamaican	16	0.06
White:	26,542	93.27
Not Hispanic (25,514)	25,791	90.63
Hispanic (655)	751	2.64
Yugoslavian	20	0.07

Oconomowoc

Place Type: City
County: Waukesha
Population: 12,382

Ancestry/Race	Number	%
African American/Black:	60	0.48
Not Hispanic (37)	56	0.45
Hispanic (1)	4	0.03
African, sub-Saharan:	8	0.06
African	8	0.06
Alaska Native tribes, specified:	1	0.01
Eskimo (1)	1	0.01
Am. Ind. or Alaska Nat., not spec.	16	0.13
American Indian tribes, specified:	44	0.36
Apache	2	0.02
Blackfeet (1)	1	0.01
Cherokee (2)	7	0.06
Cheyenne	1	0.01
Chippewa (8)	14	0.11
Latin American Indians	3	0.02
Menominee (2)	4	0.03
Navajo (1)	1	0.01
Sioux (4)	6	0.05
All other tribes (5)	5	0.04
American Indian tribes, not spec.	7	0.06
Arab:	35	0.28
Arab/Arabic	35	0.28
Armenian	17	0.14
Asian:	86	0.69
Chinese, ex. Taiwanese (23)	26	0.21
Filipino (12)	15	0.12
Hmong	4	0.03
Indian (8)	12	0.10
Japanese (6)	9	0.07
Korean (11)	12	0.10
Laotian (1)	1	0.01
Sri Lankan (3)	3	0.02
Vietnamese	1	0.01
Other Asian, not specified (1)	3	0.02
Australian	33	0.27
Austrian	52	0.42

Notes: 1. Figures in the "Number" column do not add up to the total population due to: a) Ancestry/Race overlap — e.g. persons can report being both White and Irish, b) persons of Hispanic origin can report being any race, c) persons reporting two ancestries are counted in both categories. 2. Numbers in parentheses indicate the number of persons reporting this ancestry/race alone, not in combination with any other ancestry/race. 3. Refer to the Explanation of Data in the front of the book for more detailed information.

Ancestry/Race	Number	%
Belgian	45	0.36
British	54	0.44
Canadian	14	0.11
Celtic	8	0.06
Croatian	52	0.42
Czech	127	1.03
Czechoslovakian	28	0.23
Danish	154	1.25
Dutch	310	2.51
English	1,047	8.49
European	135	1.09
Finnish	61	0.49
French, except Basque	484	3.92
French Canadian	93	0.75
German	6,773	54.91
Greek	19	0.15
Hawaii Native/Pacific Islander:	6	0.05
Polynesian: (1)	2	0.02
Native Hawaiian (1)	2	0.02
Other Pac. Isl., not spec.	4	0.03
Hispanic or Latino:	204	1.65
Central American:	2	0.02
Costa Rican	1	0.01
Other Central American	1	0.01
Mexican	152	1.23
Puerto Rican	13	0.10
South American:	5	0.04
Chilean	2	0.02
Colombian	1	0.01
Peruvian	2	0.02
Other Hispanic or Latino	32	0.26
Hungarian	61	0.49
Icelander	6	0.05
Irish	1,484	12.03
Italian	510	4.13
Luxemburger	21	0.17
Norwegian	770	6.24
Pennsylvania German	11	0.09
Polish	1,092	8.85
Russian	61	0.49
Scandinavian	27	0.22
Scotch-Irish	42	0.34
Scottish	258	2.09
Slovak	46	0.37
Slovene	71	0.58
Swedish	320	2.59
Swiss	118	0.96
Turkish	10	0.08
United States or American	274	2.22
Welsh	138	1.12
White:	12,175	98.33
Not Hispanic (11,975)	12,027	97.13
Hispanic (123)	148	1.20
Yugoslavian	12	0.10

Onalaska

Place Type: City
County: La Crosse
Population: 14,839

Ancestry/Race	Number	%
African American/Black:	126	0.85
Not Hispanic (87)	116	0.78
Hispanic (6)	10	0.07
Am. Ind. or Alaska Nat., not spec.	25	0.17
American Indian tribes, specified:	47	0.32
Cherokee (2)	7	0.05
Chickasaw	2	0.01
Chippewa (6)	13	0.09
Choctaw (2)	2	0.01
Iroquois (1)	1	0.01
Latin American Indians (2)	3	0.02
Menominee	4	0.03
Sioux (1)	1	0.01
All other tribes (5)	14	0.09
American Indian tribes, not spec.	3	0.02
Arab:	48	0.32
Lebanese	32	0.22
Moroccan	16	0.11
Asian:	495	3.34
Chinese, ex. Taiwanese (35)	42	0.28
Filipino (13)	15	0.10
Hmong (226)	253	1.70
Indian (63)	81	0.55
Indonesian	2	0.01
Japanese (2)	15	0.10
Korean (27)	35	0.24
Laotian (9)	14	0.09
Pakistani (3)	3	0.02
Thai (8)	11	0.07
Vietnamese (9)	9	0.06
Other Asian, not specified (8)	15	0.10
Austrian	20	0.13
Belgian	54	0.36
British	10	0.07
Canadian	67	0.45
Carpatho Rusyn	40	0.27
Croatian	17	0.11
Czech	306	2.06
Czechoslovakian	51	0.34
Danish	179	1.20
Dutch	195	1.31
Eastern European	14	0.09
English	1,189	8.00
Finnish	70	0.47
French, except Basque	646	4.35
French Canadian	99	0.67
German	6,870	46.23
Greek	23	0.15
Hawaii Native/Pacific Islander:	11	0.07
Micronesian:	2	0.01
Guamanian/Chamorro	2	0.01
Other Pac. Isl., not spec.	9	0.06
Hispanic or Latino:	141	0.95
Central American:	8	0.05
Guatemalan	1	0.01
Nicaraguan	2	0.01
Panamanian	1	0.01
Salvadoran	2	0.01
Other Central American	2	0.01
Cuban	4	0.03
Dominican Republic	3	0.02
Mexican	82	0.55
Puerto Rican	11	0.07
South American:	8	0.05
Chilean	1	0.01
Colombian	2	0.01
Ecuadorian	1	0.01
Peruvian	3	0.02
Venezuelan	1	0.01
Other Hispanic or Latino	25	0.17
Hungarian	44	0.30
Icelander	8	0.05
Irish	2,116	14.24
Israeli	5	0.03
Italian	311	2.09
Lithuanian	10	0.07
Luxemburger	36	0.24
Norwegian	3,407	22.93
Polish	967	6.51
Romanian	10	0.07
Russian	18	0.12
Scandinavian	79	0.53
Scotch-Irish	160	1.08
Scottish	246	1.66
Serbian	9	0.06
Slovak	4	0.03
Slovene	25	0.17
Swedish	567	3.82
Swiss	120	0.81
United States or American	432	2.91
Welsh	22	0.15
White:	14,234	95.92
Not Hispanic (14,040)	14,135	95.26
Hispanic (83)	99	0.67
Yugoslavian	7	0.05

Oshkosh

Place Type: City
County: Winnebago
Population: 62,916

Ancestry/Race	Number	%
African American/Black:	1,516	2.41
Not Hispanic (1,366)	1,497	2.38
Hispanic (10)	19	0.03
African, sub-Saharan:	92	0.15
African	53	0.08
Liberian	2	0.00
Nigerian	14	0.02
South African	11	0.02
Ugandan	5	0.01
Other sub-Saharan African	7	0.01
Alaska Native tribes, specified:	9	0.01
Aleut (6)	9	0.01
Alaska Native tribes, not specified	1	0.00
Am. Ind. or Alaska Nat., not spec.	195	0.31
American Indian tribes, specified:	316	0.50
Apache (3)	10	0.02
Blackfeet (1)	1	0.00
Cherokee (7)	24	0.04
Chippewa (53)	67	0.11
Choctaw	3	0.00
Comanche (4)	7	0.01
Creek	2	0.00
Crow	2	0.00
Delaware (1)	5	0.01
Iroquois (34)	62	0.10
Latin American Indians (3)	3	0.00
Menominee (42)	59	0.09
Navajo (2)	4	0.01
Ottawa	1	0.00
Potawatomi (5)	11	0.02
Pueblo	1	0.00
Seminole (3)	4	0.01
Shoshone (1)	2	0.00
Sioux (1)	3	0.00
All other tribes (26)	45	0.07
American Indian tribes, not spec.	15	0.02
Arab:	130	0.21
Arab/Arabic	8	0.01
Iraqi	11	0.02
Lebanese	79	0.13
Syrian	23	0.04
Other Arab	9	0.01
Armenian	34	0.05
Asian:	2,183	3.47
Chinese, ex. Taiwanese (95)	103	0.16
Filipino (47)	80	0.13
Hmong (1,288)	1,434	2.28
Indian (145)	190	0.30
Indonesian (3)	5	0.01
Japanese (31)	54	0.09
Korean (71)	77	0.12
Laotian (41)	62	0.10
Pakistani (51)	54	0.09
Sri Lankan (7)	7	0.01
Thai (7)	10	0.02
Vietnamese (26)	32	0.05
Other Asian, specified (2)	2	0.00
Other Asian, not specified (49)	73	0.12
Assyrian/Chaldean/Syriac	15	0.02
Austrian	371	0.59
Basque	6	0.01
Belgian	471	0.75
Brazilian	4	0.01
British	171	0.27
Canadian	83	0.13
Celtic	6	0.01
Croatian	63	0.10
Czech	664	1.05
Czechoslovakian	111	0.18
Danish	635	1.01
Dutch	1,665	2.65
Eastern European	5	0.01
English	4,221	6.71

Notes: 1. Figures in the "Number" column do not add up to the total population due to: a) Ancestry/Race overlap — e.g. persons can report being both White and Irish, b) persons of Hispanic origin can report being any race, c) persons reporting two ancestries are counted in both categories. 2. Numbers in parentheses indicate the number of persons reporting this ancestry/race alone, not in combination with any other ancestry/race. 3. Refer to the Explanation of Data in the front of the book for more detailed information.

Ancestry/Race	Number	%
European	156	0.25
Finnish	301	0.48
French, except Basque	2,485	3.95
French Canadian	677	1.08
German	31,287	49.71
German Russian	7	0.01
Greek	255	0.41
Hawaii Native/Pacific Islander:	63	0.10
Melanesian: (3)	3	0.00
Fijian (3)	3	0.00
Micronesian: (1)	2	0.00
Guamanian/Chamorro	1	0.00
Other Micronesian (1)	1	0.00
Polynesian: (10)	17	0.03
Native Hawaiian (4)	11	0.02
Samoan (4)	4	0.01
Other Polynesian (2)	2	0.00
Other Pac. Isl., not spec. (3)	41	0.07
Hispanic or Latino:	1,062	1.69
Central American:	29	0.05
Costa Rican	2	0.00
Guatemalan	2	0.00
Honduran	1	0.00
Nicaraguan	3	0.00
Panamanian	12	0.02
Salvadoran	8	0.01
Other Central American	1	0.00
Cuban	14	0.02
Mexican	612	0.97
Puerto Rican	86	0.14
South American:	50	0.08
Argentinean	7	0.01
Chilean	6	0.01
Colombian	5	0.01
Ecuadorian	5	0.01
Paraguayan	1	0.00
Peruvian	10	0.02
Uruguayan	4	0.01
Venezuelan	10	0.02
Other South American	2	0.00
Other Hispanic or Latino	271	0.43
Hungarian	214	0.34
Icelander	13	0.02
Iranian	34	0.05
Irish	6,156	9.78
Italian	1,492	2.37
Latvian	17	0.03
Lithuanian	97	0.15
Luxemburger	24	0.04
Maltese	7	0.01
Northern European	21	0.03
Norwegian	2,875	4.57
Pennsylvania German	9	0.01
Polish	4,339	6.89
Portuguese	10	0.02
Romanian	43	0.07
Russian	511	0.81
Scandinavian	104	0.17
Scotch-Irish	391	0.62
Scottish	647	1.03
Serbian	38	0.06
Slavic	15	0.02
Slovak	115	0.18
Slovene	44	0.07
Swedish	1,256	2.00
Swiss	436	0.69
Ukrainian	116	0.18
United States or American	2,427	3.86
Welsh	429	0.68
West Indian, excl. Hispanic:	7	0.01
Jamaican	7	0.01
White:	58,863	93.56
Not Hispanic (57,749)	58,177	92.47
Hispanic (590)	686	1.09
Yugoslavian	49	0.08

Pewaukee

Place Type: City
County: Waukesha
Population: 11,783

Ancestry/Race	Number	%
African American/Black:	62	0.53
Not Hispanic (38)	57	0.48
Hispanic (3)	5	0.04
Am. Ind. or Alaska Nat., not spec.	8	0.07
American Indian tribes, specified:	24	0.20
Cherokee (1)	8	0.07
Chippewa (1)	1	0.01
Cree	2	0.02
Iroquois (1)	4	0.03
Menominee (1)	1	0.01
Ottawa	3	0.03
Sioux (1)	1	0.01
All other tribes (2)	4	0.03
American Indian tribes, not spec.	4	0.03
Arab:	16	0.14
Palestinian	16	0.14
Armenian	28	0.24
Asian:	178	1.51
Chinese, ex. Taiwanese (39)	52	0.44
Filipino (17)	32	0.27
Indian (47)	54	0.46
Japanese (4)	13	0.11
Korean (11)	12	0.10
Laotian (1)	4	0.03
Sri Lankan (1)	4	0.03
Thai	2	0.02
Vietnamese (2)	2	0.02
Other Asian, not specified (3)	3	0.03
Australian	10	0.08
Austrian	130	1.10
Belgian	71	0.60
British	5	0.04
Croatian	84	0.71
Czech	146	1.23
Czechoslovakian	25	0.21
Danish	89	0.75
Dutch	206	1.74
Eastern European	6	0.05
English	839	7.10
European	51	0.43
Finnish	20	0.17
French, except Basque	533	4.51
French Canadian	101	0.85
German	6,196	52.41
Greek	19	0.16
Hawaii Native/Pacific Islander:	6	0.05
Polynesian:	5	0.04
Native Hawaiian	3	0.03
Tongan	1	0.01
Other Polynesian	1	0.01
Other Pac. Isl., not spec.	1	0.01
Hispanic or Latino:	153	1.30
Central American:	6	0.05
Honduran	4	0.03
Nicaraguan	2	0.02
Cuban	4	0.03
Mexican	82	0.70
Puerto Rican	19	0.16
South American:	6	0.05
Colombian	4	0.03
Peruvian	1	0.01
Other South American	1	0.01
Other Hispanic or Latino	36	0.31
Hungarian	143	1.21
Iranian	13	0.11
Irish	1,857	15.71
Italian	817	6.91
Lithuanian	32	0.27
Luxemburger	5	0.04
Norwegian	572	4.84
Pennsylvania German	10	0.08
Polish	1,388	11.74
Portuguese	11	0.09
Russian	92	0.78
Scandinavian	6	0.05
Scotch-Irish	95	0.80
Scottish	96	0.81
Serbian	28	0.24
Slavic	44	0.37
Slovak	61	0.52
Slovene	42	0.36
Swedish	311	2.63
Swiss	83	0.70
Ukrainian	5	0.04
United States or American	478	4.04
Welsh	58	0.49
White:	11,549	98.01
Not Hispanic (11,369)	11,451	97.18
Hispanic (86)	98	0.83
Yugoslavian	19	0.16

Pleasant Prairie

Place Type: Village
County: Kenosha
Population: 16,136

Ancestry/Race	Number	%
African American/Black:	309	1.91
Not Hispanic (230)	297	1.84
Hispanic (4)	12	0.07
Am. Ind. or Alaska Nat., not spec.	34	0.21
Albanian	5	0.03
American Indian tribes, specified:	103	0.64
Apache	7	0.04
Blackfeet (3)	7	0.04
Cherokee (3)	35	0.22
Chippewa (20)	28	0.17
Choctaw (1)	1	0.01
Comanche (1)	1	0.01
Iroquois (4)	6	0.04
Menominee (3)	5	0.03
Shoshone (2)	2	0.01
Sioux (3)	5	0.03
All other tribes (4)	6	0.04
American Indian tribes, not spec.	7	0.04
Arab:	35	0.22
Egyptian	15	0.09
Syrian	20	0.13
Armenian	55	0.35
Asian:	287	1.78
Chinese, ex. Taiwanese (27)	34	0.21
Filipino (75)	99	0.61
Indian (46)	51	0.32
Indonesian	1	0.01
Japanese (10)	15	0.09
Korean (34)	42	0.26
Pakistani	5	0.03
Sri Lankan (5)	5	0.03
Taiwanese (5)	5	0.03
Thai (1)	4	0.02
Vietnamese (18)	18	0.11
Other Asian, not specified (1)	8	0.05
Austrian	45	0.28
Belgian	105	0.66
British	60	0.38
Canadian	10	0.06
Celtic	6	0.04
Croatian	134	0.84
Czech	183	1.15
Czechoslovakian	54	0.34
Danish	421	2.65
Dutch	213	1.34
Eastern European	10	0.06
English	1,183	7.45
European	67	0.42
Finnish	306	1.93
French, except Basque	565	3.56
French Canadian	139	0.88
German	5,737	36.13
Greek	60	0.38
Hawaii Native/Pacific Islander:	14	0.09
Micronesian: (1)	1	0.01

Notes: 1. Figures in the "Number" column do not add up to the total population due to: a) Ancestry/Race overlap — e.g. persons can report being both White and Irish, b) persons of Hispanic origin can report being any race, c) persons reporting two ancestries are counted in both categories. 2. Numbers in parentheses indicate the number of persons reporting this ancestry/race alone, not in combination with any other ancestry/race. 3. Refer to the Explanation of Data in the front of the book for more detailed information.

Ancestry/Race	Number	%
Guamanian/Chamorro (1)	1	0.01
Polynesian: (3)	10	0.06
Native Hawaiian	6	0.04
Samoan (3)	4	0.02
Other Pac. Isl., not spec.	3	0.02
Hispanic or Latino:	544	3.37
Central American:	18	0.11
Costa Rican	1	0.01
Guatemalan	1	0.01
Honduran	5	0.03
Panamanian	8	0.05
Salvadoran	2	0.01
Other Central American	1	0.01
Cuban	13	0.08
Mexican	381	2.36
Puerto Rican	66	0.41
South American:	3	0.02
Chilean	1	0.01
Colombian	2	0.01
Other Hispanic or Latino	63	0.39
Hungarian	67	0.42
Iranian	6	0.04
Irish	2,221	13.99
Italian	1,660	10.45
Latvian	9	0.06
Lithuanian	198	1.25
Luxemburger	7	0.04
Norwegian	755	4.75
Pennsylvania German	8	0.05
Polish	1,561	9.83
Russian	117	0.74
Scandinavian	44	0.28
Scotch-Irish	174	1.10
Scottish	188	1.18
Serbian	75	0.47
Slavic	43	0.27
Slovak	103	0.65
Slovene	91	0.57
Swedish	570	3.59
Swiss	99	0.62
Ukrainian	20	0.13
United States or American	575	3.62
Welsh	93	0.59
West Indian, excl. Hispanic:	8	0.05
Dutch West Indian	8	0.05
White:	15,413	95.52
Not Hispanic (14,862)	15,043	93.23
Hispanic (319)	370	2.29
Yugoslavian	101	0.64

Plover

Place Type: Village
County: Portage
Population: 10,520

Ancestry/Race	Number	%
African American/Black:	74	0.70
Not Hispanic (45)	74	0.70
African, sub-Saharan:	7	0.07
African	7	0.07
Am. Ind. or Alaska Nat., not spec.	21	0.20
American Indian tribes, specified:	51	0.48
Apache	1	0.01
Cherokee (1)	6	0.06
Chippewa (9)	10	0.10
Choctaw (3)	4	0.04
Iroquois (1)	5	0.05
Menominee (2)	5	0.05
Potawatomi	1	0.01
Sioux (1)	5	0.05
All other tribes (12)	14	0.13
Arab:	56	0.53
Lebanese	56	0.53
Asian:	138	1.31
Cambodian (2)	3	0.03
Chinese, ex. Taiwanese (22)	32	0.30
Filipino (5)	9	0.09
Hmong (26)	29	0.28
Indian (20)	22	0.21
Japanese (1)	4	0.04
Korean (12)	20	0.19
Thai (2)	2	0.02
Vietnamese (3)	5	0.05
Other Asian, specified (1)	4	0.04
Other Asian, not specified (6)	8	0.08
Austrian	25	0.23
Belgian	49	0.46
British	7	0.07
Croatian	48	0.45
Czech	121	1.14
Czechoslovakian	36	0.34
Danish	222	2.09
Dutch	119	1.12
English	791	7.43
European	40	0.38
Finnish	75	0.70
French, except Basque	427	4.01
French Canadian	131	1.23
German	4,452	41.81
Greek	48	0.45
Hawaii Native/Pacific Islander:	11	0.10
Micronesian: (1)	3	0.03
Guamanian/Chamorro (1)	3	0.03
Polynesian: (3)	8	0.08
Native Hawaiian	3	0.03
Other Polynesian (3)	5	0.05
Hispanic or Latino:	142	1.35
Cuban	7	0.07
Mexican	102	0.97
Puerto Rican	12	0.11
South American:	3	0.03
Bolivian	1	0.01
Peruvian	2	0.02
Other Hispanic or Latino	18	0.17
Hungarian	24	0.23
Icelander	7	0.07
Irish	1,210	11.36
Italian	340	3.19
Latvian	7	0.07
Lithuanian	29	0.27
Luxemburger	7	0.07
New Zealander	16	0.15
Norwegian	824	7.74
Polish	3,002	28.20
Russian	32	0.30
Scandinavian	81	0.76
Scotch-Irish	15	0.14
Scottish	92	0.86
Slavic	4	0.04
Slovak	6	0.06
Slovene	14	0.13
Swedish	266	2.50
Swiss	40	0.38
Turkish	6	0.06
Ukrainian	9	0.08
United States or American	340	3.19
Welsh	93	0.87
White:	10,276	97.68
Not Hispanic (10,104)	10,187	96.83
Hispanic (81)	89	0.85

Port Washington

Place Type: City
County: Ozaukee
Population: 10,467

Ancestry/Race	Number	%
African American/Black:	91	0.87
Not Hispanic (71)	88	0.84
Hispanic (2)	3	0.03
Alaska Native tribes, specified:	1	0.01
Tlingit-Haida	1	0.01
Am. Ind. or Alaska Nat., not spec.	20	0.19
American Indian tribes, specified:	49	0.47
Cherokee (4)	4	0.04
Chippewa (8)	15	0.14
Creek	2	0.02
Iroquois (7)	16	0.15
Potawatomi (1)	2	0.02
All other tribes (6)	10	0.10
American Indian tribes, not spec.	2	0.02
Arab:	43	0.41
Lebanese	43	0.41
Asian:	86	0.82
Chinese, ex. Taiwanese (13)	22	0.21
Filipino (8)	12	0.11
Hmong (1)	1	0.01
Indian (5)	6	0.06
Japanese (2)	11	0.11
Korean (9)	21	0.20
Pakistani (4)	4	0.04
Vietnamese (3)	3	0.03
Other Asian, not specified	6	0.06
Austrian	47	0.45
Belgian	11	0.11
British	51	0.49
Canadian	14	0.14
Croatian	87	0.84
Czech	107	1.03
Czechoslovakian	18	0.17
Danish	147	1.42
Dutch	257	2.48
Eastern European	5	0.05
English	717	6.92
European	30	0.29
Finnish	133	1.28
French, except Basque	484	4.67
French Canadian	156	1.51
German	5,608	54.11
Greek	41	0.40
Hawaii Native/Pacific Islander:	4	0.04
Polynesian:	2	0.02
Native Hawaiian	2	0.02
Other Pac. Isl., not spec.	2	0.02
Hispanic or Latino:	168	1.61
Central American:	1	0.01
Nicaraguan	1	0.01
Cuban	1	0.01
Mexican	94	0.90
Puerto Rican	18	0.17
South American:	3	0.03
Peruvian	3	0.03
Other Hispanic or Latino	51	0.49
Hungarian	145	1.40
Irish	1,093	10.55
Italian	423	4.08
Latvian	22	0.21
Lithuanian	30	0.29
Luxemburger	551	5.32
Northern European	10	0.10
Norwegian	331	3.19
Polish	1,050	10.13
Portuguese	5	0.05
Romanian	16	0.15
Russian	41	0.40
Scandinavian	9	0.09
Scotch-Irish	79	0.76
Scottish	131	1.26
Slavic	14	0.14
Slovak	17	0.16
Slovene	45	0.43
Swedish	266	2.57
Swiss	85	0.82
Ukrainian	20	0.19
United States or American	358	3.45
Welsh	50	0.48
West Indian, excl. Hispanic:	6	0.06
Jamaican	6	0.06
White:	10,236	97.79
Not Hispanic (10,056)	10,129	96.77
Hispanic (94)	107	1.02
Yugoslavian	6	0.06

Notes: 1. Figures in the "Number" column do not add up to the total population due to: a) Ancestry/Race overlap — e.g. persons can report being both White and Irish, b) persons of Hispanic origin can report being any race, c) persons reporting two ancestries are counted in both categories. 2. Numbers in parentheses indicate the number of persons reporting this ancestry/race alone, not in combination with any other ancestry/race. 3. Refer to the Explanation of Data in the front of the book for more detailed information.

Racine

Place Type: City
County: Racine
Population: 81,855

Ancestry/Race	Number	%
African American/Black:	17,692	21.61
Not Hispanic (16,349)	17,236	21.06
Hispanic (285)	456	0.56
African, sub-Saharan:	532	0.65
African	532	0.65
Alaska Native tribes, specified:	4	0.00
Alaska Athabascan	1	0.00
Aleut (1)	2	0.00
Tlingit-Haida (1)	1	0.00
Am. Ind. or Alaska Nat., not spec.	254	0.31
American Indian tribes, specified:	464	0.57
Apache (6)	24	0.03
Blackfeet (3)	24	0.03
Cherokee (20)	91	0.11
Chickasaw	6	0.01
Chippewa (61)	107	0.13
Choctaw (3)	9	0.01
Comanche	2	0.00
Cree (2)	2	0.00
Creek	4	0.00
Delaware	1	0.00
Iroquois (14)	20	0.02
Latin American Indians (26)	46	0.06
Lumbee (3)	3	0.00
Menominee (13)	21	0.03
Navajo (1)	16	0.02
Osage (2)	2	0.00
Ottawa (7)	19	0.02
Potawatomi (3)	12	0.01
Pueblo	4	0.00
Puget Sound Salish (5)	5	0.01
Sioux (2)	6	0.01
Yaqui (3)	5	0.01
All other tribes (14)	35	0.04
American Indian tribes, not spec.	41	0.05
Arab:	101	0.12
Moroccan	9	0.01
Palestinian	92	0.11
Armenian	524	0.64
Asian:	677	0.83
Bangladeshi (1)	1	0.00
Cambodian (2)	2	0.00
Chinese, ex. Taiwanese (80)	101	0.12
Filipino (41)	73	0.09
Hmong (32)	32	0.04
Indian (122)	162	0.20
Indonesian	5	0.01
Japanese (19)	38	0.05
Korean (78)	93	0.11
Laotian (17)	21	0.03
Pakistani (7)	15	0.02
Sri Lankan (4)	4	0.00
Taiwanese (4)	6	0.01
Thai (6)	6	0.01
Vietnamese (63)	77	0.09
Other Asian, not specified (14)	41	0.05
Australian	18	0.02
Austrian	252	0.31
Basque	5	0.01
Belgian	179	0.22
British	176	0.22
Canadian	63	0.08
Celtic	15	0.02
Croatian	99	0.12
Czech	1,639	2.00
Czechoslovakian	262	0.32
Danish	5,125	6.26
Dutch	1,545	1.89
Eastern European	26	0.03
English	3,588	4.38
European	206	0.25
Finnish	362	0.44
French, except Basque	2,370	2.90
French Canadian	813	0.99
German	22,692	27.73
German Russian	14	0.02
Greek	313	0.38
Hawaii Native/Pacific Islander:	75	0.09
Micronesian: (6)	13	0.02
Guamanian/Chamorro (6)	13	0.02
Polynesian: (18)	25	0.03
Native Hawaiian (14)	18	0.02
Samoan (4)	7	0.01
Other Pac. Isl., not spec. (18)	37	0.05
Hispanic or Latino:	11,422	13.95
Central American:	39	0.05
Costa Rican	4	0.00
Guatemalan	11	0.01
Honduran	13	0.02
Panamanian	1	0.00
Salvadoran	10	0.01
Cuban	59	0.07
Dominican Republic	1	0.00
Mexican	8,939	10.92
Puerto Rican	750	0.92
South American:	45	0.05
Argentinean	6	0.01
Chilean	7	0.01
Colombian	9	0.01
Ecuadorian	1	0.00
Paraguayan	1	0.00
Peruvian	14	0.02
Venezuelan	7	0.01
Other Hispanic or Latino	1,589	1.94
Hungarian	630	0.77
Icelander	15	0.02
Iranian	9	0.01
Irish	6,333	7.74
Italian	3,780	4.62
Latvian	10	0.01
Lithuanian	401	0.49
Luxemburger	13	0.02
Macedonian	26	0.03
Northern European	18	0.02
Norwegian	3,796	4.64
Pennsylvania German	17	0.02
Polish	5,451	6.66
Portuguese	24	0.03
Romanian	21	0.03
Russian	529	0.65
Scandinavian	159	0.19
Scotch-Irish	516	0.63
Scottish	596	0.73
Serbian	224	0.27
Slavic	55	0.07
Slovak	326	0.40
Slovene	47	0.06
Swedish	1,477	1.81
Swiss	272	0.33
Turkish	57	0.07
Ukrainian	99	0.12
United States or American	1,912	2.34
Welsh	395	0.48
West Indian, excl. Hispanic:	71	0.09
Haitian	16	0.02
Jamaican	55	0.07
White:	58,214	71.12
Not Hispanic (51,962)	53,088	64.86
Hispanic (4,446)	5,126	6.26
Yugoslavian	221	0.27

Richfield

Place Type: Town
County: Washington
Population: 10,373

Ancestry/Race	Number	%
African American/Black:	31	0.30
Not Hispanic (24)	31	0.30
Am. Ind. or Alaska Nat., not spec.	10	0.10
American Indian tribes, specified:	10	0.10
Cherokee	2	0.02
Chippewa	2	0.02
Cree (1)	1	0.01
Menominee (1)	4	0.04
All other tribes (1)	1	0.01
Arab:	55	0.53
Lebanese	55	0.53
Asian:	98	0.94
Chinese, ex. Taiwanese (7)	14	0.13
Filipino (3)	3	0.03
Hmong (15)	22	0.21
Indian (9)	12	0.12
Indonesian	1	0.01
Japanese (4)	8	0.08
Korean (14)	17	0.16
Pakistani (6)	6	0.06
Thai (1)	1	0.01
Vietnamese (6)	6	0.06
Other Asian, not specified (4)	8	0.08
Austrian	59	0.57
Belgian	25	0.24
British	62	0.60
Canadian	5	0.05
Croatian	51	0.49
Czech	115	1.11
Czechoslovakian	22	0.21
Danish	45	0.43
Dutch	157	1.51
English	536	5.17
European	80	0.77
Finnish	81	0.78
French, except Basque	421	4.06
French Canadian	70	0.67
German	6,309	60.82
Greek	60	0.58
Hawaii Native/Pacific Islander:	10	0.10
Micronesian: (2)	2	0.02
Guamanian/Chamorro (2)	2	0.02
Polynesian: (1)	3	0.03
Native Hawaiian (1)	3	0.03
Other Pac. Isl., not spec. (4)	5	0.05
Hispanic or Latino:	73	0.70
Central American:	4	0.04
Costa Rican	1	0.01
Panamanian	3	0.03
Cuban	1	0.01
Mexican	40	0.39
Puerto Rican	6	0.06
South American:	2	0.02
Chilean	1	0.01
Venezuelan	1	0.01
Other Hispanic or Latino	20	0.19
Hungarian	142	1.37
Irish	982	9.47
Italian	450	4.34
Latvian	4	0.04
Lithuanian	55	0.53
Luxemburger	33	0.32
New Zealander	6	0.06
Norwegian	526	5.07
Polish	1,249	12.04
Romanian	13	0.13
Russian	123	1.19
Scandinavian	31	0.30
Scotch-Irish	61	0.59
Scottish	105	1.01
Serbian	10	0.10
Slavic	9	0.09
Slovak	75	0.72
Slovene	35	0.34
Swedish	204	1.97
Swiss	111	1.07
Ukrainian	23	0.22
United States or American	317	3.06
Welsh	18	0.17
West Indian, excl. Hispanic:	5	0.05
Trinidadian and Tobagonian	5	0.05
White:	10,250	98.81
Not Hispanic (10,146)	10,188	98.22
Hispanic (49)	62	0.60
Yugoslavian	9	0.09

Notes: 1. Figures in the "Number" column do not add up to the total population due to: a) Ancestry/Race overlap — e.g. persons can report being both White and Irish, b) persons of Hispanic origin can report being any race, c) persons reporting two ancestries are counted in both categories. 2. Numbers in parentheses indicate the number of persons reporting this ancestry/race alone, not in combination with any other ancestry/race. 3. Refer to the Explanation of Data in the front of the book for more detailed information.

River Falls

Place Type: City
County: Pierce
Population: 12,560

Ancestry/Race	Number	%
African American/Black:	106	0.84
Not Hispanic (66)	100	0.80
Hispanic	6	0.05
African, sub-Saharan:	6	0.05
African	6	0.05
Am. Ind. or Alaska Nat., not spec.	28	0.22
American Indian tribes, specified:	74	0.59
Apache	2	0.02
Blackfeet	3	0.02
Cherokee (5)	18	0.14
Chippewa (22)	27	0.21
Choctaw (1)	1	0.01
Creek	1	0.01
Iroquois (1)	1	0.01
Menominee (1)	2	0.02
Ottawa	1	0.01
Pueblo	1	0.01
Seminole	4	0.03
Sioux (2)	6	0.05
All other tribes (4)	7	0.06
American Indian tribes, not spec.	6	0.05
Asian:	171	1.36
Cambodian (3)	3	0.02
Chinese, ex. Taiwanese (14)	18	0.14
Filipino (7)	10	0.08
Hmong (20)	23	0.18
Indian (20)	24	0.19
Japanese (17)	29	0.23
Korean (30)	41	0.33
Vietnamese (11)	15	0.12
Other Asian, specified (2)	4	0.03
Other Asian, not specified (3)	4	0.03
Australian	5	0.04
Austrian	80	0.63
Belgian	67	0.53
British	59	0.47
Czech	377	2.99
Czechoslovakian	64	0.51
Danish	170	1.35
Dutch	202	1.60
Eastern European	4	0.03
English	981	7.77
European	127	1.01
Finnish	48	0.38
French, except Basque	560	4.44
French Canadian	237	1.88
German	5,375	42.60
Greek	12	0.10
Hawaii Native/Pacific Islander:	19	0.15
Micronesian: (2)	2	0.02
Guamanian/Chamorro (2)	2	0.02
Polynesian: (8)	14	0.11
Native Hawaiian (3)	6	0.05
Samoan (3)	3	0.02
Tongan (1)	4	0.03
Other Polynesian (1)	1	0.01
Other Pac. Isl., not spec. (1)	3	0.02
Hispanic or Latino:	119	0.95
Central American:	16	0.13
Costa Rican	7	0.06
Guatemalan	1	0.01
Honduran	4	0.03
Salvadoran	4	0.03
Cuban	8	0.06
Mexican	51	0.41
Puerto Rican	24	0.19
South American:	3	0.02
Bolivian	1	0.01
Chilean	2	0.02
Other Hispanic or Latino	17	0.14
Hungarian	10	0.08
Icelander	4	0.03
Iranian	28	0.22
Irish	1,553	12.31
Italian	410	3.25
Latvian	13	0.10
Lithuanian	13	0.10
Luxemburger	10	0.08
Northern European	25	0.20
Norwegian	2,617	20.74
Polish	715	5.67
Portuguese	11	0.09
Russian	66	0.52
Scandinavian	70	0.55
Scotch-Irish	138	1.09
Scottish	139	1.10
Serbian	5	0.04
Slovak	4	0.03
Swedish	1,183	9.38
Swiss	69	0.55
Turkish	6	0.05
Ukrainian	5	0.04
United States or American	278	2.20
Welsh	113	0.90
White:	12,260	97.61
Not Hispanic (12,063)	12,174	96.93
Hispanic (66)	86	0.68

Sheboygan

Place Type: City
County: Sheboygan
Population: 50,792

Ancestry/Race	Number	%
African American/Black:	575	1.13
Not Hispanic (410)	533	1.05
Hispanic (26)	42	0.08
African, sub-Saharan:	59	0.12
African	55	0.11
Ethiopian	4	0.01
Alaska Native tribes, specified:	1	0.00
Tlingit-Haida (1)	1	0.00
Am. Ind. or Alaska Nat., not spec.	138	0.27
Albanian	29	0.06
American Indian tribes, specified:	336	0.66
Apache (1)	5	0.01
Blackfeet	6	0.01
Cherokee (18)	48	0.09
Chippewa (63)	103	0.20
Comanche	1	0.00
Iroquois (18)	37	0.07
Latin American Indians (19)	23	0.05
Menominee (31)	48	0.09
Osage (5)	5	0.01
Ottawa	1	0.00
Paiute (1)	1	0.00
Potawatomi (7)	13	0.03
Shoshone	1	0.00
Sioux (6)	10	0.02
Tohono O'Odham (1)	2	0.00
All other tribes (23)	32	0.06
American Indian tribes, not spec.	9	0.02
Arab:	63	0.12
Lebanese	34	0.07
Palestinian	15	0.03
Syrian	14	0.03
Asian:	3,747	7.38
Cambodian (11)	14	0.03
Chinese, ex. Taiwanese (69)	89	0.18
Filipino (83)	122	0.24
Hmong (2,514)	2,792	5.50
Indian (82)	135	0.27
Indonesian (4)	11	0.02
Japanese (30)	45	0.09
Korean (49)	70	0.14
Laotian (169)	244	0.48
Malaysian (1)	2	0.00
Pakistani (2)	2	0.00
Sri Lankan (3)	3	0.01
Taiwanese (2)	7	0.01
Thai (3)	10	0.02
Vietnamese (25)	27	0.05
Other Asian, not specified (125)	174	0.34
Austrian	167	0.33
Belgian	161	0.32
British	85	0.17
Canadian	76	0.15
Carpatho Rusyn	17	0.03
Croatian	186	0.37
Czech	348	0.69
Czechoslovakian	45	0.09
Danish	261	0.51
Dutch	3,009	5.92
English	1,963	3.86
Estonian	6	0.01
European	282	0.56
Finnish	229	0.45
French, except Basque	1,905	3.75
French Canadian	444	0.87
German	25,596	50.38
German Russian	9	0.02
Greek	166	0.33
Hawaii Native/Pacific Islander:	114	0.22
Micronesian: (1)	1	0.00
Guamanian/Chamorro (1)	1	0.00
Polynesian: (16)	22	0.04
Native Hawaiian (13)	17	0.03
Samoan (3)	5	0.01
Other Pac. Isl., not spec. (1)	91	0.18
Hispanic or Latino:	3,034	5.97
Central American:	45	0.09
Costa Rican	3	0.01
Guatemalan	13	0.03
Honduran	5	0.01
Nicaraguan	1	0.00
Panamanian	11	0.02
Salvadoran	8	0.02
Other Central American	4	0.01
Cuban	13	0.03
Dominican Republic	3	0.01
Mexican	2,399	4.72
Puerto Rican	107	0.21
South American:	33	0.06
Argentinean	2	0.00
Chilean	3	0.01
Colombian	16	0.03
Ecuadorian	4	0.01
Peruvian	3	0.01
Uruguayan	5	0.01
Other Hispanic or Latino	434	0.85
Hungarian	117	0.23
Irish	3,667	7.22
Italian	895	1.76
Lithuanian	410	0.81
Luxemburger	137	0.27
Northern European	37	0.07
Norwegian	1,139	2.24
Polish	2,447	4.82
Romanian	25	0.05
Russian	1,809	3.56
Scandinavian	192	0.38
Scotch-Irish	185	0.36
Scottish	206	0.41
Serbian	9	0.02
Slavic	94	0.19
Slovak	100	0.20
Slovene	697	1.37
Swedish	801	1.58
Swiss	154	0.30
Turkish	35	0.07
Ukrainian	57	0.11
United States or American	1,951	3.84
Welsh	111	0.22
West Indian, excl. Hispanic:	18	0.04
Belizean	18	0.04
White:	45,108	88.81
Not Hispanic (43,189)	43,628	85.90
Hispanic (1,318)	1,480	2.91
Yugoslavian	138	0.27

Notes: 1. Figures in the "Number" column do not add up to the total population due to: a) Ancestry/Race overlap — e.g. persons can report being both White and Irish, b) persons of Hispanic origin can report being any race, c) persons reporting two ancestries are counted in both categories. 2. Numbers in parentheses indicate the number of persons reporting this ancestry/race alone, not in combination with any other ancestry/race. 3. Refer to the Explanation of Data in the front of the book for more detailed information.

Shorewood

Place Type: Village
County: Milwaukee
Population: 13,763

Ancestry/Race	Number	%
African American/Black:	428	3.11
Not Hispanic (326)	417	3.03
Hispanic (6)	11	0.08
African, sub-Saharan:	67	0.49
African	56	0.41
Other sub-Saharan African	11	0.08
Alaska Native tribes, specified:	3	0.02
Tlingit-Haida (1)	3	0.02
Am. Ind. or Alaska Nat., not spec.	19	0.14
Albanian	21	0.15
American Indian tribes, specified:	62	0.45
Apache	1	0.01
Blackfeet	2	0.01
Cherokee (1)	14	0.10
Chippewa (10)	15	0.11
Choctaw	4	0.03
Creek (1)	1	0.01
Iroquois (4)	8	0.06
Latin American Indians (3)	3	0.02
Menominee (1)	3	0.02
Navajo (1)	1	0.01
Pueblo (1)	1	0.01
Sioux (1)	1	0.01
All other tribes (4)	8	0.06
American Indian tribes, not spec.	3	0.02
Arab:	38	0.28
Egyptian	6	0.04
Iraqi	6	0.04
Lebanese	7	0.05
Palestinian	19	0.14
Armenian	42	0.31
Asian:	524	3.81
Bangladeshi (5)	5	0.04
Chinese, ex. Taiwanese (192)	199	1.45
Filipino (22)	32	0.23
Hmong (17)	17	0.12
Indian (85)	96	0.70
Indonesian (2)	2	0.01
Japanese (25)	43	0.31
Korean (39)	51	0.37
Laotian (1)	1	0.01
Pakistani (9)	11	0.08
Sri Lankan (1)	3	0.02
Taiwanese (3)	3	0.02
Thai (12)	14	0.10
Vietnamese (17)	20	0.15
Other Asian, specified (1)	4	0.03
Other Asian, not specified (5)	23	0.17
Austrian	157	1.14
Belgian	87	0.63
Brazilian	22	0.16
British	60	0.44
Canadian	58	0.42
Croatian	67	0.49
Czech	130	0.94
Czechoslovakian	39	0.28
Danish	163	1.18
Dutch	276	2.01
Eastern European	93	0.68
English	1,155	8.39
European	192	1.40
Finnish	74	0.54
French, except Basque	449	3.26
French Canadian	92	0.67
German	4,927	35.80
Greek	142	1.03
Hawaii Native/Pacific Islander:	11	0.08
Micronesian: (3)	3	0.02
Guamanian/Chamorro (3)	3	0.02
Polynesian: (2)	5	0.04
Native Hawaiian (1)	3	0.02
Samoan (1)	2	0.01
Other Pac. Isl., specified	1	0.01
Other Pac. Isl., not spec.	2	0.01
Hispanic or Latino:	345	2.51
Central American:	16	0.12
Costa Rican	2	0.01
Guatemalan	7	0.05
Honduran	3	0.02
Nicaraguan	1	0.01
Panamanian	1	0.01
Salvadoran	2	0.01
Cuban	23	0.17
Dominican Republic	1	0.01
Mexican	134	0.97
Puerto Rican	51	0.37
South American:	52	0.38
Argentinean	1	0.01
Bolivian	2	0.01
Chilean	7	0.05
Colombian	12	0.09
Ecuadorian	1	0.01
Paraguayan	3	0.02
Peruvian	11	0.08
Uruguayan	1	0.01
Venezuelan	10	0.07
Other South American	4	0.03
Other Hispanic or Latino	68	0.49
Hungarian	78	0.57
Iranian	21	0.15
Irish	2,441	17.74
Italian	1,082	7.86
Latvian	44	0.32
Lithuanian	120	0.87
Luxemburger	26	0.19
New Zealander	6	0.04
Northern European	41	0.30
Norwegian	603	4.38
Polish	1,086	7.89
Romanian	37	0.27
Russian	806	5.86
Scandinavian	51	0.37
Scotch-Irish	212	1.54
Scottish	227	1.65
Serbian	68	0.49
Slavic	11	0.08
Slovak	14	0.10
Slovene	101	0.73
Swedish	225	1.63
Swiss	116	0.84
Turkish	8	0.06
Ukrainian	150	1.09
United States or American	337	2.45
Welsh	103	0.75
West Indian, excl. Hispanic:	29	0.21
Jamaican	29	0.21
White:	12,807	93.05
Not Hispanic (12,365)	12,554	91.22
Hispanic (219)	253	1.84
Yugoslavian	26	0.19

South Milwaukee

Place Type: City
County: Milwaukee
Population: 21,256

Ancestry/Race	Number	%
African American/Black:	299	1.41
Not Hispanic (206)	275	1.29
Hispanic (16)	24	0.11
Alaska Native tribes, specified:	3	0.01
Alaska Athabascan (3)	3	0.01
Am. Ind. or Alaska Nat., not spec.	66	0.31
Albanian	229	1.08
American Indian tribes, specified:	178	0.84
Apache (4)	6	0.03
Blackfeet	5	0.02
Cherokee (2)	12	0.06
Chippewa (39)	78	0.37
Iroquois (13)	21	0.10
Latin American Indians (5)	10	0.05
Menominee (6)	15	0.07
Navajo	1	0.00
Potawatomi (1)	2	0.01
Shoshone (1)	1	0.00
Sioux (6)	8	0.04
Yaqui	1	0.00
All other tribes (11)	18	0.08
American Indian tribes, not spec.	5	0.02
Arab:	36	0.17
Egyptian	6	0.03
Lebanese	18	0.08
Syrian	5	0.02
Other Arab	7	0.03
Armenian	97	0.46
Asian:	183	0.86
Chinese, ex. Taiwanese (17)	21	0.10
Filipino (36)	42	0.20
Hmong (2)	2	0.01
Indian (45)	48	0.23
Indonesian	2	0.01
Japanese (17)	26	0.12
Korean (9)	11	0.05
Pakistani (6)	17	0.08
Thai (2)	2	0.01
Vietnamese (6)	6	0.03
Other Asian, not specified (4)	6	0.03
Australian	6	0.03
Austrian	80	0.38
Belgian	32	0.15
Bulgarian	26	0.12
Canadian	8	0.04
Croatian	122	0.58
Czech	383	1.81
Czechoslovakian	191	0.90
Danish	162	0.76
Dutch	316	1.49
English	863	4.07
European	118	0.56
Finnish	124	0.59
French, except Basque	998	4.71
French Canadian	333	1.57
German	9,177	43.30
Greek	54	0.25
Hawaii Native/Pacific Islander:	17	0.08
Micronesian: (1)	1	0.00
Guamanian/Chamorro (1)	1	0.00
Polynesian: (8)	12	0.06
Native Hawaiian (5)	7	0.03
Samoan (3)	5	0.02
Other Pac. Isl., not spec.	4	0.02
Hispanic or Latino:	852	4.01
Central American:	20	0.09
Costa Rican	5	0.02
Guatemalan	2	0.01
Honduran	5	0.02
Nicaraguan	6	0.03
Salvadoran	1	0.00
Other Central American	1	0.00
Cuban	15	0.07
Mexican	504	2.37
Puerto Rican	206	0.97
South American:	5	0.02
Chilean	1	0.00
Peruvian	1	0.00
Venezuelan	2	0.01
Other South American	1	0.00
Other Hispanic or Latino	102	0.48
Hungarian	261	1.23
Iranian	37	0.17
Irish	2,013	9.50
Italian	1,259	5.94
Latvian	7	0.03
Lithuanian	53	0.25
Luxemburger	31	0.15
Macedonian	5	0.02
Norwegian	1,106	5.22
Pennsylvania German	16	0.08
Polish	5,826	27.49
Portuguese	7	0.03
Romanian	20	0.09
Russian	154	0.73

Notes: 1. Figures in the "Number" column do not add up to the total population due to: a) Ancestry/Race overlap — e.g. persons can report being both White and Irish, b) persons of Hispanic origin can report being any race, c) persons reporting two ancestries are counted in both categories. 2. Numbers in parentheses indicate the number of persons reporting this ancestry/race alone, not in combination with any other ancestry/race. 3. Refer to the Explanation of Data in the front of the book for more detailed information.

Scandinavian	53	0.25
Scotch-Irish	98	0.46
Scottish	126	0.59
Serbian	155	0.73
Slavic	20	0.09
Slovak	198	0.93
Slovene	28	0.13
Swedish	491	2.32
Swiss	131	0.62
Turkish	13	0.06
Ukrainian	54	0.25
United States or American	737	3.48
Welsh	70	0.33
West Indian, excl. Hispanic:	17	0.08
Jamaican	17	0.08
White:	20,436	96.14
Not Hispanic (19,682)	19,906	93.65
Hispanic (471)	530	2.49
Yugoslavian	58	0.27

Stevens Point

Place Type: City
County: Portage
Population: 24,551

Ancestry/Race	Number	%
African American/Black:	181	0.74
Not Hispanic (110)	172	0.70
Hispanic (5)	9	0.04
African, sub-Saharan:	17	0.07
African	17	0.07
Alaska Native tribes, specified:	1	0.00
Eskimo (1)	1	0.00
Am. Ind. or Alaska Nat., not spec.	46	0.19
Albanian	7	0.03
American Indian tribes, specified:	155	0.63
Apache (1)	3	0.01
Blackfeet (1)	3	0.01
Cherokee (2)	10	0.04
Chippewa (25)	40	0.16
Choctaw (1)	1	0.00
Comanche	3	0.01
Cree	1	0.00
Crow	1	0.00
Iroquois (18)	30	0.12
Latin American Indians (1)	6	0.02
Lumbee (1)	1	0.00
Menominee (13)	21	0.09
Ottawa (1)	1	0.00
Potawatomi (1)	2	0.01
Shoshone	1	0.00
Sioux	6	0.02
Tohono O'Odham (2)	2	0.01
All other tribes (13)	23	0.09
American Indian tribes, not spec.	15	0.06
Arab:	15	0.06
Arab/Arabic	8	0.03
Lebanese	7	0.03
Armenian	5	0.02
Asian:	1,310	5.34
Cambodian (2)	2	0.01
Chinese, ex. Taiwanese (102)	125	0.51
Filipino (22)	28	0.11
Hmong (698)	773	3.15
Indian (35)	47	0.19
Indonesian (17)	21	0.09
Japanese (47)	63	0.26
Korean (56)	61	0.25
Laotian (47)	56	0.23
Malaysian (1)	1	0.00
Pakistani (3)	3	0.01
Sri Lankan (1)	1	0.00
Taiwanese (11)	12	0.05
Thai (5)	6	0.02
Vietnamese (38)	38	0.15
Other Asian, specified (4)	8	0.03
Other Asian, not specified (52)	65	0.26
Austrian	66	0.27
Belgian	114	0.47
Brazilian	6	0.02
British	72	0.29
Bulgarian	18	0.07
Canadian	11	0.04
Croatian	19	0.08
Czech	320	1.31
Czechoslovakian	38	0.16
Danish	192	0.78
Dutch	475	1.94
English	1,604	6.55
European	76	0.31
Finnish	184	0.75
French, except Basque	699	2.85
French Canadian	239	0.98
German	9,710	39.65
Greek	23	0.09
Hawaii Native/Pacific Islander:	68	0.28
Micronesian: (2)	4	0.02
Guamanian/Chamorro (2)	4	0.02
Polynesian: (8)	10	0.04
Native Hawaiian (8)	9	0.04
Samoan	1	0.00
Other Pac. Isl., not spec. (13)	54	0.22
Hispanic or Latino:	395	1.61
Central American:	12	0.05
Costa Rican	1	0.00
Guatemalan	1	0.00
Honduran	2	0.01
Nicaraguan	5	0.02
Panamanian	1	0.00
Salvadoran	2	0.01
Cuban	11	0.04
Dominican Republic	3	0.01
Mexican	261	1.06
Puerto Rican	14	0.06
South American:	15	0.06
Colombian	7	0.03
Ecuadorian	4	0.02
Venezuelan	2	0.01
Other South American	2	0.01
Other Hispanic or Latino	79	0.32
Hungarian	48	0.20
Iranian	9	0.04
Irish	2,365	9.66
Italian	629	2.57
Latvian	38	0.16
Lithuanian	48	0.20
Luxemburger	32	0.13
Northern European	5	0.02
Norwegian	1,570	6.41
Polish	6,529	26.66
Portuguese	4	0.02
Russian	97	0.40
Scandinavian	32	0.13
Scotch-Irish	131	0.53
Scottish	243	0.99
Serbian	13	0.05
Slavic	12	0.05
Slovak	20	0.08
Slovene	21	0.09
Swedish	643	2.63
Swiss	193	0.79
Turkish	13	0.05
Ukrainian	16	0.07
United States or American	522	2.13
Welsh	71	0.29
White:	22,936	93.42
Not Hispanic (22,479)	22,664	92.31
Hispanic (239)	272	1.11
Yugoslavian	17	0.07

Stoughton

Place Type: City
County: Dane
Population: 12,354

Ancestry/Race	Number	%
Afghan	9	0.07
African American/Black:	172	1.39
Not Hispanic (112)	165	1.34
Hispanic (2)	7	0.06
African, sub-Saharan:	10	0.08
African	6	0.05
Other sub-Saharan African	4	0.03
Am. Ind. or Alaska Nat., not spec.	20	0.16
Albanian	42	0.34
American Indian tribes, specified:	60	0.49
Apache (1)	1	0.01
Cherokee (7)	21	0.17
Chippewa (4)	9	0.07
Iroquois (4)	5	0.04
Latin American Indians (2)	2	0.02
Menominee (1)	1	0.01
Ottawa	1	0.01
Potawatomi (1)	1	0.01
Sioux (1)	8	0.06
All other tribes (7)	11	0.09
American Indian tribes, not spec.	2	0.02
Arab:	3	0.02
Lebanese	3	0.02
Armenian	8	0.06
Asian:	114	0.92
Cambodian (34)	39	0.32
Chinese, ex. Taiwanese (13)	14	0.11
Filipino (1)	6	0.05
Hmong (2)	2	0.02
Indian (8)	11	0.09
Indonesian (1)	2	0.02
Japanese (9)	17	0.14
Korean (10)	12	0.10
Laotian (1)	1	0.01
Malaysian	3	0.02
Taiwanese (1)	2	0.02
Thai (1)	1	0.01
Vietnamese (3)	4	0.03
Austrian	20	0.16
Belgian	62	0.50
British	20	0.16
Celtic	7	0.06
Croatian	15	0.12
Czech	175	1.41
Czechoslovakian	42	0.34
Danish	192	1.54
Dutch	341	2.74
English	1,206	9.70
European	18	0.14
Finnish	33	0.27
French, except Basque	381	3.06
French Canadian	87	0.70
German	4,801	38.62
Greek	55	0.44
Hawaii Native/Pacific Islander:	4	0.03
Polynesian: (2)	2	0.02
Native Hawaiian (2)	2	0.02
Other Pac. Isl., not spec.	2	0.02
Hispanic or Latino:	153	1.24
Central American:	1	0.01
Panamanian	1	0.01
Cuban	3	0.02
Mexican	93	0.75
Puerto Rican	6	0.05
South American:	10	0.08
Chilean	2	0.02
Colombian	2	0.02
Paraguayan	3	0.02
Other South American	3	0.02
Other Hispanic or Latino	40	0.32
Hungarian	28	0.23
Irish	1,765	14.20
Italian	316	2.54
Lithuanian	8	0.06
Luxemburger	8	0.06
Northern European	14	0.11
Norwegian	3,675	29.56
Pennsylvania German	8	0.06
Polish	326	2.62
Portuguese	8	0.06
Russian	39	0.31
Scandinavian	10	0.08

Notes: 1. Figures in the "Number" column do not add up to the total population due to: a) Ancestry/Race overlap — e.g. persons can report being both White and Irish, b) persons of Hispanic origin can report being any race, c) persons reporting two ancestries are counted in both categories. 2. Numbers in parentheses indicate the number of persons reporting this ancestry/race alone, not in combination with any other ancestry/race. 3. Refer to the Explanation of Data in the front of the book for more detailed information.

Scotch-Irish	136	1.09
Scottish	215	1.73
Slavic	17	0.14
Slovak	16	0.13
Swedish	351	2.82
Swiss	343	2.76
United States or American	240	1.93
Welsh	96	0.77
West Indian, excl. Hispanic:	7	0.06
West Indian	7	0.06
White:	12,068	97.68
Not Hispanic (11,854)	11,961	96.82
Hispanic (87)	107	0.87
Yugoslavian	13	0.10

Sun Prairie

Place Type: City
County: Dane
Population: 20,369

Ancestry/Race	Number	%
African American/Black:	788	3.87
Not Hispanic (623)	768	3.77
Hispanic (8)	20	0.10
African, sub-Saharan:	92	0.46
African	60	0.30
Ethiopian	32	0.16
Alaska Native tribes, specified:	1	0.00
Aleut	1	0.00
Am. Ind. or Alaska Nat., not spec.	35	0.17
American Indian tribes, specified:	105	0.52
Apache	1	0.00
Blackfeet	3	0.01
Cherokee (7)	25	0.12
Chickasaw	1	0.00
Chippewa (7)	18	0.09
Choctaw	4	0.02
Iroquois (9)	10	0.05
Kiowa (1)	1	0.00
Latin American Indians (2)	5	0.02
Lumbee (1)	2	0.01
Menominee (3)	3	0.01
Navajo (1)	3	0.01
Osage	1	0.00
Ottawa (1)	1	0.00
Potawatomi	4	0.02
Pueblo	1	0.00
Sioux (1)	4	0.02
All other tribes (10)	18	0.09
American Indian tribes, not spec.	1	0.00
Arab:	10	0.05
Lebanese	10	0.05
Asian:	331	1.63
Cambodian (2)	2	0.01
Chinese, ex. Taiwanese (38)	42	0.21
Filipino (14)	24	0.12
Hmong (105)	108	0.53
Indian (42)	48	0.24
Indonesian (2)	2	0.01
Japanese (7)	18	0.09
Korean (25)	30	0.15
Laotian (5)	7	0.03
Pakistani	2	0.01
Sri Lankan (4)	4	0.02
Taiwanese (1)	1	0.00
Thai (3)	7	0.03
Vietnamese (14)	19	0.09
Other Asian, not specified (7)	17	0.08
Austrian	78	0.39
Belgian	93	0.46
British	66	0.33
Canadian	73	0.36
Croatian	14	0.07
Czech	338	1.67
Czechoslovakian	83	0.41
Danish	144	0.71
Dutch	456	2.26
English	1,706	8.44
European	147	0.73
Finnish	208	1.03
French, except Basque	1,009	4.99
French Canadian	162	0.80
German	9,299	46.02
Greek	30	0.15
Hawaii Native/Pacific Islander:	16	0.08
Micronesian: (2)	4	0.02
Guamanian/Chamorro (2)	4	0.02
Polynesian: (5)	7	0.03
Native Hawaiian (3)	4	0.02
Samoan (2)	3	0.01
Other Pac. Isl., not spec.	5	0.02
Hispanic or Latino:	555	2.72
Central American:	29	0.14
Guatemalan	9	0.04
Honduran	3	0.01
Nicaraguan	4	0.02
Panamanian	7	0.03
Salvadoran	6	0.03
Cuban	13	0.06
Dominican Republic	6	0.03
Mexican	359	1.76
Puerto Rican	47	0.23
South American:	13	0.06
Bolivian	1	0.00
Colombian	1	0.00
Ecuadorian	2	0.01
Peruvian	6	0.03
Venezuelan	2	0.01
Other South American	1	0.00
Other Hispanic or Latino	88	0.43
Hungarian	113	0.56
Irish	2,726	13.49
Italian	759	3.76
Latvian	13	0.06
Lithuanian	42	0.21
Luxemburger	7	0.03
Norwegian	2,719	13.46
Polish	1,159	5.74
Portuguese	22	0.11
Romanian	13	0.06
Russian	41	0.20
Scandinavian	117	0.58
Scotch-Irish	196	0.97
Scottish	273	1.35
Serbian	7	0.03
Slavic	14	0.07
Slovene	11	0.05
Swedish	435	2.15
Swiss	209	1.03
Turkish	7	0.03
Ukrainian	37	0.18
United States or American	880	4.36
Welsh	195	0.97
West Indian, excl. Hispanic:	4	0.02
West Indian	4	0.02
White:	19,187	94.20
Not Hispanic (18,571)	18,818	92.39
Hispanic (306)	369	1.81
Yugoslavian	54	0.27

Superior

Place Type: City
County: Douglas
Population: 27,368

Ancestry/Race	Number	%
Afghan	7	0.03
African American/Black:	289	1.06
Not Hispanic (185)	282	1.03
Hispanic (1)	7	0.03
African, sub-Saharan:	13	0.05
African	13	0.05
Alaska Native tribes, specified:	3	0.01
Aleut	1	0.00
Eskimo	1	0.00
Tlingit-Haida	1	0.00
Am. Ind. or Alaska Nat., not spec.	257	0.94
American Indian tribes, specified:	560	2.05
Blackfeet (1)	1	0.00
Cherokee (14)	20	0.07
Cheyenne (1)	1	0.00
Chippewa (365)	491	1.79
Cree (1)	1	0.00
Creek	1	0.00
Delaware (2)	2	0.01
Iroquois (4)	10	0.04
Latin American Indians (1)	1	0.00
Navajo (3)	3	0.01
Pueblo (1)	1	0.00
Seminole (1)	1	0.00
Sioux (4)	10	0.04
Ute (1)	1	0.00
All other tribes (8)	16	0.06
American Indian tribes, not spec.	55	0.20
Arab:	20	0.07
Lebanese	8	0.03
Other Arab	12	0.04
Asian:	317	1.16
Cambodian (4)	5	0.02
Chinese, ex. Taiwanese (24)	34	0.12
Filipino (14)	32	0.12
Hmong (75)	82	0.30
Indian (24)	31	0.11
Indonesian (5)	5	0.02
Japanese (13)	20	0.07
Korean (31)	40	0.15
Laotian (2)	4	0.01
Malaysian (1)	1	0.00
Pakistani	4	0.01
Sri Lankan (11)	15	0.05
Taiwanese (1)	2	0.01
Thai (4)	8	0.03
Vietnamese (13)	18	0.07
Other Asian, not specified (6)	16	0.06
Austrian	31	0.11
Belgian	560	2.05
British	46	0.17
Canadian	25	0.09
Celtic	22	0.08
Croatian	111	0.41
Czech	301	1.10
Czechoslovakian	102	0.37
Danish	341	1.25
Dutch	312	1.14
English	1,493	5.45
European	109	0.40
Finnish	2,074	7.57
French, except Basque	1,359	4.96
French Canadian	848	3.10
German	5,656	20.66
Greek	175	0.64
Hawaii Native/Pacific Islander:	24	0.09
Polynesian: (9)	16	0.06
Native Hawaiian (5)	9	0.03
Samoan (3)	6	0.02
Other Polynesian (1)	1	0.00
Other Pac. Isl., not spec. (1)	8	0.03
Hispanic or Latino:	226	0.83
Central American:	6	0.02
Costa Rican	1	0.00
Guatemalan	1	0.00
Honduran	1	0.00
Panamanian	2	0.01
Other Central American	1	0.00
Cuban	13	0.05
Mexican	108	0.39
Puerto Rican	33	0.12
South American:	4	0.01
Peruvian	1	0.00
Venezuelan	3	0.01
Other Hispanic or Latino	62	0.23
Hungarian	43	0.16
Icelander	8	0.03
Iranian	9	0.03
Irish	3,611	13.19
Israeli	11	0.04
Italian	968	3.54
Lithuanian	89	0.33

Notes: 1. Figures in the "Number" column do not add up to the total population due to: a) Ancestry/Race overlap — e.g. persons can report being both White and Irish, b) persons of Hispanic origin can report being any race, c) persons reporting two ancestries are counted in both categories. 2. Numbers in parentheses indicate the number of persons reporting this ancestry/race alone, not in combination with any other ancestry/race. 3. Refer to the Explanation of Data in the front of the book for more detailed information.

Ancestry/Race	Number	%
Luxemburger	7	0.03
New Zealander	5	0.02
Northern European	6	0.02
Norwegian	4,171	15.23
Polish	2,554	9.33
Portuguese	4	0.01
Romanian	11	0.04
Russian	170	0.62
Scandinavian	323	1.18
Scotch-Irish	353	1.29
Scottish	326	1.19
Serbian	44	0.16
Slavic	45	0.16
Slovak	223	0.81
Slovene	37	0.14
Swedish	4,175	15.25
Swiss	135	0.49
Turkish	11	0.04
Ukrainian	61	0.22
United States or American	1,192	4.35
Welsh	100	0.37
White:	26,219	95.80
Not Hispanic (25,677)	26,074	95.27
Hispanic (120)	145	0.53
Yugoslavian	72	0.26

Two Rivers

Place Type: City
County: Manitowoc
Population: 12,639

Ancestry/Race	Number	%
African American/Black:	44	0.35
Not Hispanic (17)	41	0.32
Hispanic (3)	3	0.02
Am. Ind. or Alaska Nat., not spec.	20	0.16
American Indian tribes, specified:	68	0.54
Blackfeet (1)	1	0.01
Cherokee (2)	4	0.03
Chippewa (10)	16	0.13
Iroquois (9)	11	0.09
Menominee (16)	18	0.14
Navajo	1	0.01
Ottawa	2	0.02
Potawatomi (2)	5	0.04
Sioux (2)	3	0.02
All other tribes (4)	7	0.06
American Indian tribes, not spec.	3	0.02
Asian:	323	2.56
Chinese, ex. Taiwanese (6)	6	0.05
Filipino (5)	9	0.07
Hmong (151)	170	1.35
Indian (14)	16	0.13
Indonesian (1)	1	0.01
Japanese (5)	14	0.11
Korean (3)	3	0.02
Laotian (49)	56	0.44
Pakistani	1	0.01
Thai (3)	3	0.02
Vietnamese (9)	10	0.08
Other Asian, not specified (25)	34	0.27
Assyrian/Chaldean/Syriac	19	0.15
Australian	4	0.03
Austrian	14	0.11
Belgian	237	1.87
British	26	0.21
Canadian	9	0.07
Celtic	5	0.04
Croatian	18	0.14
Czech	1,310	10.35
Czechoslovakian	43	0.34
Danish	108	0.85
Dutch	258	2.04
English	578	4.57
Finnish	77	0.61
French, except Basque	1,034	8.17
French Canadian	576	4.55
German	5,999	47.39
German Russian	10	0.08
Greek	12	0.09
Hawaii Native/Pacific Islander:	18	0.14
Polynesian: (7)	12	0.09
Native Hawaiian (3)	8	0.06
Samoan (4)	4	0.03
Other Pac. Isl., not spec.	6	0.05
Hispanic or Latino:	170	1.35
Central American:	4	0.03
Panamanian	3	0.02
Other Central American	1	0.01
Mexican	119	0.94
Puerto Rican	3	0.02
South American:	2	0.02
Chilean	1	0.01
Peruvian	1	0.01
Other Hispanic or Latino	42	0.33
Hungarian	32	0.25
Irish	957	7.56
Italian	170	1.34
Latvian	4	0.03
Lithuanian	77	0.61
Luxemburger	5	0.04
Norwegian	464	3.67
Polish	1,853	14.64
Russian	69	0.55
Scandinavian	4	0.03
Scotch-Irish	37	0.29
Scottish	69	0.55
Slovak	8	0.06
Swedish	141	1.11
Swiss	22	0.17
Ukrainian	19	0.15
United States or American	602	4.76
Welsh	17	0.13
White:	12,193	96.47
Not Hispanic (12,011)	12,094	95.69
Hispanic (89)	99	0.78
Yugoslavian	4	0.03

Watertown

Place Type: City
County: Jefferson
Population: 21,598

Ancestry/Race	Number	%
African American/Black:	89	0.41
Not Hispanic (45)	74	0.34
Hispanic (10)	15	0.07
African, sub-Saharan:	31	0.14
African	6	0.03
Nigerian	25	0.12
Alaska Native tribes, specified:	1	0.00
Aleut (1)	1	0.00
Am. Ind. or Alaska Nat., not spec.	39	0.18
American Indian tribes, specified:	121	0.56
Apache (1)	1	0.00
Blackfeet (2)	9	0.04
Cherokee (1)	7	0.03
Chippewa (27)	41	0.19
Choctaw (6)	6	0.03
Iroquois (2)	10	0.05
Latin American Indians (8)	9	0.04
Menominee (1)	2	0.01
Ottawa (1)	5	0.02
Potawatomi (1)	1	0.00
Shoshone	1	0.00
Sioux	9	0.04
All other tribes (12)	20	0.09
American Indian tribes, not spec.	8	0.04
Arab:	9	0.04
Lebanese	9	0.04
Armenian	7	0.03
Asian:	169	0.78
Chinese, ex. Taiwanese (14)	16	0.07
Filipino (27)	32	0.15
Hmong (18)	18	0.08
Indian (18)	21	0.10
Indonesian	3	0.01
Japanese (15)	21	0.10
Korean (4)	11	0.05
Laotian (4)	4	0.02
Pakistani (18)	18	0.08
Thai (3)	7	0.03
Vietnamese (3)	3	0.01
Other Asian, specified	4	0.02
Other Asian, not specified (7)	11	0.05
Australian	13	0.06
Austrian	88	0.41
Belgian	67	0.31
Brazilian	12	0.06
British	33	0.15
Canadian	26	0.12
Croatian	17	0.08
Czech	215	1.00
Czechoslovakian	34	0.16
Danish	198	0.92
Dutch	427	1.98
English	1,031	4.77
European	88	0.41
Finnish	88	0.41
French, except Basque	565	2.62
French Canadian	173	0.80
German	12,250	56.72
Greek	72	0.33
Hawaii Native/Pacific Islander:	20	0.09
Micronesian: (6)	13	0.06
Guamanian/Chamorro (6)	13	0.06
Polynesian:	2	0.01
Native Hawaiian	1	0.00
Tongan	1	0.00
Other Pac. Isl., specified	4	0.02
Other Pac. Isl., not spec. (1)	1	0.00
Hispanic or Latino:	1,067	4.94
Cuban	7	0.03
Mexican	906	4.19
Puerto Rican	23	0.11
South American:	5	0.02
Argentinean	1	0.00
Colombian	2	0.01
Paraguayan	1	0.00
Peruvian	1	0.00
Other Hispanic or Latino	126	0.58
Hungarian	22	0.10
Irish	1,957	9.06
Italian	366	1.69
Latvian	3	0.01
Lithuanian	59	0.27
Luxemburger	2	0.01
Northern European	21	0.10
Norwegian	1,003	4.64
Pennsylvania German	7	0.03
Polish	1,134	5.25
Romanian	2	0.01
Russian	143	0.66
Scandinavian	62	0.29
Scotch-Irish	119	0.55
Scottish	177	0.82
Serbian	15	0.07
Slovak	47	0.22
Slovene	6	0.03
Swedish	482	2.23
Swiss	253	1.17
Turkish	5	0.02
Ukrainian	7	0.03
United States or American	953	4.41
Welsh	119	0.55
West Indian, excl. Hispanic:	6	0.03
Jamaican	6	0.03
White:	20,949	97.00
Not Hispanic (20,122)	20,263	93.82
Hispanic (590)	686	3.18
Yugoslavian	7	0.03

Notes: 1. Figures in the "Number" column do not add up to the total population due to: a) Ancestry/Race overlap — e.g. persons can report being both White and Irish, b) persons of Hispanic origin can report being any race, c) persons reporting two ancestries are counted in both categories. 2. Numbers in parentheses indicate the number of persons reporting this ancestry/race alone, not in combination with any other ancestry/race. 3. Refer to the Explanation of Data in the front of the book for more detailed information.

Waukesha

Place Type: City
County: Waukesha
Population: 64,825

Ancestry/Race	Number	%
African American/Black:	1,096	1.69
Not Hispanic (797)	1,031	1.59
Hispanic (34)	65	0.10
African, sub-Saharan:	76	0.12
African	68	0.11
Other sub-Saharan African	8	0.01
Am. Ind. or Alaska Nat., not spec.	153	0.24
Albanian	8	0.01
American Indian tribes, specified:	339	0.52
Apache (6)	12	0.02
Blackfeet (4)	12	0.02
Cherokee (7)	50	0.08
Cheyenne	7	0.01
Chickasaw	1	0.00
Chippewa (35)	57	0.09
Choctaw (2)	5	0.01
Comanche (1)	1	0.00
Creek (1)	1	0.00
Crow (1)	1	0.00
Delaware	3	0.00
Houma (1)	1	0.00
Iroquois (16)	35	0.05
Kiowa (1)	1	0.00
Latin American Indians (14)	39	0.06
Menominee (12)	17	0.03
Navajo (1)	4	0.01
Pima	3	0.00
Potawatomi (7)	11	0.02
Seminole	7	0.01
Sioux (8)	22	0.03
All other tribes (18)	49	0.08
American Indian tribes, not spec.	21	0.03
Arab:	54	0.08
Egyptian	18	0.03
Lebanese	9	0.01
Moroccan	20	0.03
Other Arab	7	0.01
Armenian	34	0.05
Asian:	1,645	2.54
Bangladeshi (10)	10	0.02
Cambodian (1)	1	0.00
Chinese, ex. Taiwanese (209)	243	0.37
Filipino (74)	123	0.19
Hmong (15)	16	0.02
Indian (549)	566	0.87
Indonesian (7)	16	0.02
Japanese (39)	72	0.11
Korean (86)	101	0.16
Laotian (154)	174	0.27
Pakistani (55)	75	0.12
Sri Lankan (5)	5	0.01
Taiwanese (2)	4	0.01
Thai (31)	38	0.06
Vietnamese (104)	118	0.18
Other Asian, specified (7)	10	0.02
Other Asian, not specified (38)	73	0.11
Australian	19	0.03
Austrian	288	0.45
Belgian	257	0.40
Brazilian	7	0.01
British	187	0.29
Bulgarian	9	0.01
Canadian	88	0.14
Celtic	14	0.02
Croatian	325	0.50
Czech	907	1.41
Czechoslovakian	222	0.34
Danish	733	1.14
Dutch	1,302	2.02
Eastern European	9	0.01
English	5,237	8.14
European	535	0.83
Finnish	441	0.69
French, except Basque	2,231	3.47
French Canadian	727	1.13
German	28,714	44.61
Greek	248	0.39
Guyanese	6	0.01
Hawaii Native/Pacific Islander:	53	0.08
Micronesian: (11)	13	0.02
Guamanian/Chamorro (8)	10	0.02
Other Micronesian (3)	3	0.00
Polynesian: (6)	23	0.04
Native Hawaiian (5)	20	0.03
Samoan (1)	2	0.00
Other Polynesian	1	0.00
Other Pac. Isl., specified	1	0.00
Other Pac. Isl., not spec. (6)	16	0.02
Hispanic or Latino:	5,563	8.58
Central American:	106	0.16
Costa Rican	4	0.01
Guatemalan	23	0.04
Honduran	3	0.00
Nicaraguan	55	0.08
Panamanian	16	0.02
Salvadoran	4	0.01
Other Central American	1	0.00
Cuban	37	0.06
Dominican Republic	5	0.01
Mexican	4,189	6.46
Puerto Rican	581	0.90
South American:	85	0.13
Argentinean	15	0.02
Bolivian	7	0.01
Chilean	13	0.02
Colombian	27	0.04
Ecuadorian	3	0.00
Paraguayan	2	0.00
Peruvian	4	0.01
Venezuelan	12	0.02
Other South American	2	0.00
Other Hispanic or Latino	560	0.86
Hungarian	474	0.74
Icelander	13	0.02
Iranian	8	0.01
Irish	8,080	12.55
Israeli	10	0.02
Italian	3,572	5.55
Latvian	38	0.06
Lithuanian	134	0.21
Luxemburger	41	0.06
Northern European	29	0.05
Norwegian	3,888	6.04
Pennsylvania German	13	0.02
Polish	6,708	10.42
Portuguese	62	0.10
Romanian	27	0.04
Russian	363	0.56
Scandinavian	156	0.24
Scotch-Irish	592	0.92
Scottish	639	0.99
Serbian	149	0.23
Slavic	87	0.14
Slovak	165	0.26
Slovene	177	0.27
Swedish	1,475	2.29
Swiss	615	0.96
Ukrainian	50	0.08
United States or American	2,165	3.36
Welsh	720	1.12
West Indian, excl. Hispanic:	26	0.04
Haitian	8	0.01
Jamaican	18	0.03
White:	60,113	92.73
Not Hispanic (56,191)	56,792	87.61
Hispanic (2,942)	3,321	5.12
Yugoslavian	53	0.08

Waupun

Place Type: City
County: Dodge
Population: 10,718

Ancestry/Race	Number	%
African American/Black:	1,279	11.93
Not Hispanic (1,256)	1,269	11.84
Hispanic (10)	10	0.09
Am. Ind. or Alaska Nat., not spec.	46	0.43
American Indian tribes, specified:	19	0.18
Blackfeet (1)	1	0.01
Cherokee (2)	3	0.03
Chippewa (5)	6	0.06
Navajo (1)	1	0.01
All other tribes (6)	8	0.07
American Indian tribes, not spec.	40	0.37
Asian:	38	0.35
Chinese, ex. Taiwanese	1	0.01
Filipino (9)	11	0.10
Indian (3)	3	0.03
Japanese (2)	2	0.02
Korean (6)	7	0.07
Taiwanese (7)	8	0.07
Other Asian, not specified	6	0.06
Austrian	55	0.51
Belgian	17	0.16
Brazilian	7	0.07
British	18	0.17
Czech	55	0.51
Czechoslovakian	9	0.08
Danish	89	0.83
Dutch	2,152	20.11
English	519	4.85
European	64	0.60
Finnish	29	0.27
French, except Basque	290	2.71
French Canadian	72	0.67
German	3,663	34.23
Greek	58	0.54
Hawaii Native/Pacific Islander:	14	0.13
Micronesian:	1	0.01
Guamanian/Chamorro	1	0.01
Polynesian:	1	0.01
Native Hawaiian	1	0.01
Other Pac. Isl., not spec. (5)	12	0.11
Hispanic or Latino:	304	2.84
Central American:	5	0.05
Costa Rican	4	0.04
Other Central American	1	0.01
Cuban	10	0.09
Dominican Republic	1	0.01
Mexican	80	0.75
Puerto Rican	22	0.21
South American:	1	0.01
Paraguayan	1	0.01
Other Hispanic or Latino	185	1.73
Hungarian	10	0.09
Irish	597	5.58
Italian	106	0.99
Norwegian	330	3.08
Pennsylvania German	2	0.02
Polish	415	3.88
Russian	37	0.35
Scandinavian	37	0.35
Scotch-Irish	30	0.28
Scottish	98	0.92
Slavic	2	0.02
Slovak	7	0.07
Slovene	10	0.09
Swedish	86	0.80
Swiss	92	0.86
Ukrainian	3	0.03
United States or American	353	3.30
Welsh	37	0.35
White:	9,260	86.40
Not Hispanic (8,987)	9,015	84.11
Hispanic (237)	245	2.29
Yugoslavian	5	0.05

Notes: 1. Figures in the "Number" column do not add up to the total population due to: a) Ancestry/Race overlap — e.g. persons can report being both White and Irish, b) persons of Hispanic origin can report being any race, c) persons reporting two ancestries are counted in both categories. 2. Numbers in parentheses indicate the number of persons reporting this ancestry/race alone, not in combination with any other ancestry/race. 3. Refer to the Explanation of Data in the front of the book for more detailed information.

Wausau

Place Type: City
County: Marathon
Population: 38,426

Ancestry/Race	Number	%
African American/Black:	311	0.81
Not Hispanic (205)	302	0.79
Hispanic (3)	9	0.02
African, sub-Saharan:	10	0.03
African	3	0.01
Nigerian	7	0.02
Am. Ind. or Alaska Nat., not spec.	128	0.33
American Indian tribes, specified:	270	0.70
Apache (3)	8	0.02
Blackfeet (2)	2	0.01
Cherokee (2)	22	0.06
Chippewa (50)	81	0.21
Iroquois (14)	22	0.06
Latin American Indians (1)	1	0.00
Menominee (39)	44	0.11
Navajo	4	0.01
Potawatomi (30)	34	0.09
Pueblo (1)	1	0.00
Sioux (5)	10	0.03
All other tribes (24)	41	0.11
American Indian tribes, not spec.	11	0.03
Arab:	33	0.09
Arab/Arabic	4	0.01
Egyptian	7	0.02
Palestinian	12	0.03
Syrian	10	0.03
Armenian	24	0.06
Asian:	4,704	12.24
Cambodian (9)	9	0.02
Chinese, ex. Taiwanese (63)	89	0.23
Filipino (25)	46	0.12
Hmong (3,504)	3,674	9.56
Indian (135)	190	0.49
Indonesian (1)	1	0.00
Japanese (8)	20	0.05
Korean (31)	40	0.10
Laotian (228)	264	0.69
Malaysian (1)	1	0.00
Pakistani (8)	14	0.04
Sri Lankan (4)	4	0.01
Taiwanese (9)	13	0.03
Thai (13)	18	0.05
Vietnamese (21)	29	0.08
Other Asian, specified	1	0.00
Other Asian, not specified (241)	291	0.76
Australian	9	0.02
Austrian	142	0.37
Basque	12	0.03
Belgian	138	0.36
British	63	0.16
Canadian	54	0.14
Croatian	29	0.08
Czech	447	1.16
Czechoslovakian	39	0.10
Danish	331	0.86
Dutch	660	1.72
Eastern European	14	0.04
English	1,926	5.02
European	75	0.20
Finnish	290	0.76
French, except Basque	1,752	4.56
French Canadian	472	1.23
German	17,950	46.74
German Russian	5	0.01
Greek	54	0.14
Hawaii Native/Pacific Islander:	66	0.17
Micronesian: (1)	1	0.00
Guamanian/Chamorro (1)	1	0.00
Polynesian: (4)	8	0.02
Native Hawaiian (4)	6	0.02
Samoan	2	0.01
Other Pac. Isl., specified	1	0.00
Other Pac. Isl., not spec. (10)	56	0.15
Hispanic or Latino:	398	1.04
Central American:	31	0.08
Guatemalan	11	0.03
Honduran	6	0.02
Nicaraguan	2	0.01
Panamanian	10	0.03
Salvadoran	2	0.01
Cuban	16	0.04
Dominican Republic	2	0.01
Mexican	198	0.52
Puerto Rican	37	0.10
South American:	14	0.04
Bolivian	4	0.01
Chilean	2	0.01
Colombian	4	0.01
Ecuadorian	4	0.01
Other Hispanic or Latino	100	0.26
Hungarian	135	0.35
Iranian	21	0.05
Irish	3,096	8.06
Italian	846	2.20
Latvian	62	0.16
Lithuanian	106	0.28
Macedonian	9	0.02
Northern European	15	0.04
Norwegian	2,448	6.37
Polish	4,658	12.13
Portuguese	54	0.14
Romanian	16	0.04
Russian	196	0.51
Scandinavian	100	0.26
Scotch-Irish	259	0.67
Scottish	345	0.90
Slavic	10	0.03
Slovak	100	0.26
Slovene	24	0.06
Swedish	1,090	2.84
Swiss	304	0.79
Ukrainian	54	0.14
United States or American	1,181	3.08
Welsh	170	0.44
West Indian, excl. Hispanic:	5	0.01
Trinidadian and Tobagonian	5	0.01
White:	33,343	86.77
Not Hispanic (32,802)	33,089	86.11
Hispanic (208)	254	0.66
Yugoslavian	38	0.10

Wauwatosa

Place Type: City
County: Milwaukee
Population: 47,271

Ancestry/Race	Number	%
African American/Black:	1,187	2.51
Not Hispanic (955)	1,165	2.46
Hispanic (10)	22	0.05
African, sub-Saharan:	54	0.11
African	43	0.09
Kenyan	11	0.02
Alaska Native tribes, specified:	9	0.02
Alaska Athabascan (3)	3	0.01
Eskimo (1)	6	0.01
Am. Ind. or Alaska Nat., not spec.	54	0.11
Alsatian	9	0.02
American Indian tribes, specified:	174	0.37
Apache (1)	2	0.00
Blackfeet	2	0.00
Cherokee	16	0.03
Chickasaw	4	0.01
Chippewa (26)	49	0.10
Choctaw (1)	1	0.00
Creek (2)	2	0.00
Delaware (2)	2	0.00
Iroquois (12)	28	0.06
Latin American Indians (2)	7	0.01
Menominee (13)	14	0.03
Potawatomi (3)	5	0.01
Pueblo	1	0.00
Puget Sound Salish (1)	1	0.00
Sioux (4)	7	0.01
All other tribes (23)	33	0.07
American Indian tribes, not spec.	13	0.03
Arab:	82	0.17
Egyptian	19	0.04
Lebanese	30	0.06
Syrian	11	0.02
Other Arab	22	0.05
Armenian	108	0.23
Asian:	1,126	2.38
Bangladeshi (2)	6	0.01
Cambodian (1)	1	0.00
Chinese, ex. Taiwanese (340)	384	0.81
Filipino (63)	116	0.25
Hmong (13)	13	0.03
Indian (248)	280	0.59
Indonesian (4)	9	0.02
Japanese (75)	106	0.22
Korean (66)	81	0.17
Laotian (16)	20	0.04
Malaysian (1)	1	0.00
Pakistani (18)	22	0.05
Sri Lankan	1	0.00
Taiwanese (10)	11	0.02
Thai (11)	12	0.03
Vietnamese (29)	36	0.08
Other Asian, specified (2)	4	0.01
Other Asian, not specified (9)	23	0.05
Assyrian/Chaldean/Syriac	5	0.01
Australian	20	0.04
Austrian	624	1.32
Belgian	257	0.54
British	134	0.28
Bulgarian	13	0.03
Canadian	81	0.17
Celtic	19	0.04
Croatian	474	1.00
Czech	987	2.09
Czechoslovakian	180	0.38
Danish	397	0.84
Dutch	900	1.90
Eastern European	17	0.04
English	3,811	8.06
Estonian	23	0.05
European	352	0.74
Finnish	330	0.70
French, except Basque	1,693	3.58
French Canadian	417	0.88
German	23,392	49.48
Greek	307	0.65
Hawaii Native/Pacific Islander:	59	0.12
Micronesian: (14)	19	0.04
Guamanian/Chamorro (9)	14	0.03
Other Micronesian (5)	5	0.01
Polynesian: (16)	33	0.07
Native Hawaiian (9)	26	0.06
Samoan (7)	7	0.01
Other Pac. Isl., specified	2	0.00
Other Pac. Isl., not spec. (1)	5	0.01
Hispanic or Latino:	813	1.72
Central American:	34	0.07
Costa Rican	6	0.01
Guatemalan	17	0.04
Nicaraguan	2	0.00
Panamanian	4	0.01
Salvadoran	4	0.01
Other Central American	1	0.00
Cuban	25	0.05
Dominican Republic	4	0.01
Mexican	387	0.82
Puerto Rican	163	0.34
South American:	70	0.15
Argentinean	6	0.01
Bolivian	3	0.01
Chilean	11	0.02
Colombian	12	0.03
Ecuadorian	10	0.02
Paraguayan	2	0.00
Peruvian	12	0.03

Notes: 1. Figures in the "Number" column do not add up to the total population due to: a) Ancestry/Race overlap — e.g. persons can report being both White and Irish, b) persons of Hispanic origin can report being any race, c) persons reporting two ancestries are counted in both categories. 2. Numbers in parentheses indicate the number of persons reporting this ancestry/race alone, not in combination with any other ancestry/race. 3. Refer to the Explanation of Data in the front of the book for more detailed information.

Ancestry/Race	Number	%
Venezuelan	10	0.02
Other South American	4	0.01
Other Hispanic or Latino	130	0.28
Hungarian	493	1.04
Iranian	104	0.22
Irish	7,985	16.89
Italian	2,682	5.67
Latvian	71	0.15
Lithuanian	195	0.41
Luxemburger	79	0.17
Northern European	54	0.11
Norwegian	2,475	5.24
Pennsylvania German	9	0.02
Polish	5,253	11.11
Portuguese	22	0.05
Romanian	54	0.11
Russian	241	0.51
Scandinavian	66	0.14
Scotch-Irish	440	0.93
Scottish	734	1.55
Serbian	118	0.25
Slavic	31	0.07
Slovak	285	0.60
Slovene	201	0.43
Swedish	1,070	2.26
Swiss	445	0.94
Turkish	12	0.03
Ukrainian	88	0.19
United States or American	1,445	3.06
Welsh	415	0.88
West Indian, excl. Hispanic:	21	0.04
Jamaican	17	0.04
Trinidadian and Tobagonian	4	0.01
White:	44,922	95.03
Not Hispanic (43,935)	44,347	93.81
Hispanic (487)	575	1.22
Yugoslavian	108	0.23

West Allis

Place Type: City
County: Milwaukee
Population: 61,254

Ancestry/Race	Number	%
African American/Black:	1,074	1.75
Not Hispanic (778)	1,008	1.65
Hispanic (40)	66	0.11
African, sub-Saharan:	73	0.12
African	73	0.12
Alaska Native tribes, specified:	5	0.01
Alaska Athabascan (1)	1	0.00
Eskimo (4)	4	0.01
Am. Ind. or Alaska Nat., not spec.	119	0.19
Albanian	14	0.02
American Indian tribes, specified:	576	0.94
Apache (5)	11	0.02
Blackfeet (2)	13	0.02
Cherokee (11)	48	0.08
Chickasaw	3	0.00
Chippewa (104)	156	0.25
Choctaw	1	0.00
Comanche (2)	3	0.00
Cree	3	0.00
Creek (2)	4	0.01
Iroquois (96)	124	0.20
Latin American Indians (7)	12	0.02
Lumbee	1	0.00
Menominee (40)	50	0.08
Navajo (3)	5	0.01
Osage	1	0.00
Ottawa (14)	17	0.03
Pima (3)	5	0.01
Potawatomi (16)	20	0.03
Seminole	2	0.00
Sioux (2)	11	0.02
All other tribes (54)	86	0.14
American Indian tribes, not spec.	14	0.02
Arab:	177	0.29
Arab/Arabic	52	0.08
Egyptian	36	0.06
Iraqi	8	0.01
Lebanese	37	0.06
Palestinian	26	0.04
Syrian	18	0.03
Armenian	53	0.09
Asian:	1,003	1.64
Chinese, ex. Taiwanese (130)	154	0.25
Filipino (92)	124	0.20
Hmong (9)	11	0.02
Indian (333)	359	0.59
Indonesian (1)	6	0.01
Japanese (42)	67	0.11
Korean (67)	87	0.14
Laotian (22)	39	0.06
Malaysian (2)	8	0.01
Pakistani (17)	27	0.04
Taiwanese (5)	7	0.01
Thai (10)	15	0.02
Vietnamese (55)	60	0.10
Other Asian, specified (3)	4	0.01
Other Asian, not specified (16)	35	0.06
Australian	9	0.01
Austrian	515	0.84
Belgian	127	0.21
Brazilian	3	0.00
British	89	0.15
Canadian	47	0.08
Croatian	843	1.38
Czech	1,092	1.78
Czechoslovakian	190	0.31
Danish	446	0.73
Dutch	932	1.52
Eastern European	22	0.04
English	3,134	5.11
European	244	0.40
Finnish	325	0.53
French, except Basque	2,408	3.93
French Canadian	785	1.28
German	28,100	45.84
Greek	484	0.79
Hawaii Native/Pacific Islander:	38	0.06
Micronesian: (2)	6	0.01
Guamanian/Chamorro (2)	6	0.01
Polynesian: (6)	17	0.03
Native Hawaiian (3)	10	0.02
Samoan (2)	4	0.01
Tongan (1)	1	0.00
Other Polynesian	2	0.00
Other Pac. Isl., specified	1	0.00
Other Pac. Isl., not spec. (4)	14	0.02
Hispanic or Latino:	2,155	3.52
Central American:	35	0.06
Costa Rican	2	0.00
Guatemalan	3	0.00
Honduran	13	0.02
Panamanian	4	0.01
Salvadoran	12	0.02
Other Central American	1	0.00
Cuban	42	0.07
Dominican Republic	5	0.01
Mexican	1,238	2.02
Puerto Rican	508	0.83
South American:	35	0.06
Argentinean	1	0.00
Chilean	7	0.01
Colombian	17	0.03
Ecuadorian	3	0.00
Paraguayan	1	0.00
Peruvian	5	0.01
Venezuelan	1	0.00
Other Hispanic or Latino	292	0.48
Hungarian	419	0.68
Icelander	10	0.02
Iranian	39	0.06
Irish	7,381	12.04
Italian	3,503	5.71
Latvian	79	0.13
Lithuanian	115	0.19
Luxemburger	27	0.04
Macedonian	10	0.02
Maltese	7	0.01
Northern European	6	0.01
Norwegian	2,904	4.74
Polish	12,364	20.17
Portuguese	64	0.10
Romanian	32	0.05
Russian	383	0.62
Scandinavian	87	0.14
Scotch-Irish	387	0.63
Scottish	592	0.97
Serbian	298	0.49
Slavic	127	0.21
Slovak	303	0.49
Slovene	786	1.28
Swedish	1,123	1.83
Swiss	443	0.72
Turkish	13	0.02
Ukrainian	115	0.19
United States or American	1,827	2.98
Welsh	230	0.38
West Indian, excl. Hispanic:	22	0.04
Haitian	8	0.01
Jamaican	14	0.02
White:	58,382	95.31
Not Hispanic (56,432)	57,018	93.08
Hispanic (1,168)	1,364	2.23
Yugoslavian	128	0.21

West Bend

Place Type: City
County: Washington
Population: 28,152

Ancestry/Race	Number	%
African American/Black:	142	0.50
Not Hispanic (89)	130	0.46
Hispanic (7)	12	0.04
Am. Ind. or Alaska Nat., not spec.	70	0.25
American Indian tribes, specified:	150	0.53
Blackfeet	1	0.00
Cherokee (4)	11	0.04
Cheyenne (1)	1	0.00
Chippewa (42)	53	0.19
Choctaw (1)	3	0.01
Delaware	1	0.00
Iroquois (14)	22	0.08
Kiowa	1	0.00
Latin American Indians	1	0.00
Menominee (6)	6	0.02
Ottawa (14)	17	0.06
Potawatomi (2)	2	0.01
Sioux (3)	11	0.04
All other tribes (8)	20	0.07
American Indian tribes, not spec.	2	0.01
Arab:	7	0.02
Lebanese	7	0.02
Asian:	198	0.70
Cambodian (2)	2	0.01
Chinese, ex. Taiwanese (12)	17	0.06
Filipino (61)	73	0.26
Hmong (24)	26	0.09
Indian (13)	14	0.05
Japanese (4)	8	0.03
Korean (11)	19	0.07
Laotian (3)	6	0.02
Sri Lankan (3)	3	0.01
Thai	3	0.01
Vietnamese (8)	16	0.06
Other Asian, not specified (6)	11	0.04
Australian	4	0.01
Austrian	199	0.71
Belgian	41	0.15
British	48	0.17
Bulgarian	10	0.04
Canadian	45	0.16
Croatian	51	0.18
Czech	375	1.33
Czechoslovakian	92	0.33

Notes: 1. Figures in the "Number" column do not add up to the total population due to: a) Ancestry/Race overlap — e.g. persons can report being both White and Irish, b) persons of Hispanic origin can report being any race, c) persons reporting two ancestries are counted in both categories. 2. Numbers in parentheses indicate the number of persons reporting this ancestry/race alone, not in combination with any other ancestry/race. 3. Refer to the Explanation of Data in the front of the book for more detailed information.

Ancestry/Race	Number	%
Danish	134	0.48
Dutch	638	2.27
English	1,625	5.78
Estonian	7	0.02
European	111	0.39
Finnish	118	0.42
French, except Basque	911	3.24
French Canadian	307	1.09
German	16,418	58.36
Greek	66	0.23
Hawaii Native/Pacific Islander:	13	0.05
Micronesian:	2	0.01
Guamanian/Chamorro	2	0.01
Polynesian: (2)	7	0.02
Native Hawaiian (2)	4	0.01
Samoan	3	0.01
Other Pac. Isl., not spec.	4	0.01
Hispanic or Latino:	519	1.84
Central American:	12	0.04
Costa Rican	4	0.01
Guatemalan	5	0.02
Panamanian	1	0.00
Other Central American	2	0.01
Cuban	11	0.04
Dominican Republic	1	0.00
Mexican	358	1.27
Puerto Rican	55	0.20
South American:	7	0.02
Chilean	1	0.00
Colombian	2	0.01
Ecuadorian	1	0.00
Venezuelan	3	0.01
Other Hispanic or Latino	75	0.27
Hungarian	250	0.89
Irish	3,000	10.66
Italian	781	2.78
Lithuanian	43	0.15
Luxemburger	188	0.67
Northern European	34	0.12
Norwegian	1,052	3.74
Pennsylvania German	17	0.06
Polish	2,324	8.26
Portuguese	7	0.02
Romanian	25	0.09
Russian	189	0.67
Scandinavian	50	0.18
Scotch-Irish	250	0.89
Scottish	304	1.08
Serbian	29	0.10
Slavic	19	0.07
Slovak	103	0.37
Swedish	704	2.50
Swiss	163	0.58
Ukrainian	21	0.07
United States or American	1,239	4.40
Welsh	184	0.65
White:	27,597	98.03
Not Hispanic (27,079)	27,270	96.87
Hispanic (312)	327	1.16
Yugoslavian	28	0.10

Weston

Place Type: Village
County: Marathon
Population: 12,079

Ancestry/Race	Number	%
African American/Black:	66	0.55
Not Hispanic (35)	63	0.52
Hispanic (1)	3	0.02
African, sub-Saharan:	5	0.04
African	5	0.04
Am. Ind. or Alaska Nat., not spec.	18	0.15
Albanian	27	0.22
American Indian tribes, specified:	66	0.55
Cherokee (1)	5	0.04
Chippewa (19)	21	0.17
Choctaw	1	0.01
Iroquois (1)	7	0.06
Menominee (4)	7	0.06
Navajo (1)	1	0.01
Ottawa (3)	3	0.02
Potawatomi (2)	8	0.07
Sioux	1	0.01
All other tribes (6)	12	0.10
American Indian tribes, not spec.	3	0.02
Arab:	32	0.26
Lebanese	32	0.26
Asian:	643	5.32
Cambodian (2)	4	0.03
Chinese, ex. Taiwanese (6)	7	0.06
Filipino (8)	13	0.11
Hmong (486)	523	4.33
Indian (20)	28	0.23
Indonesian (1)	1	0.01
Japanese	1	0.01
Korean (7)	11	0.09
Laotian (9)	9	0.07
Pakistani (1)	1	0.01
Taiwanese (9)	9	0.07
Thai (2)	2	0.02
Vietnamese (13)	13	0.11
Other Asian, not specified (20)	21	0.17
Austrian	59	0.48
Belgian	73	0.60
British	14	0.11
Croatian	13	0.11
Czech	173	1.41
Czechoslovakian	31	0.25
Danish	116	0.95
Dutch	335	2.73
English	717	5.85
European	20	0.16
Finnish	125	1.02
French, except Basque	522	4.26
French Canadian	181	1.48
German	6,273	51.20
Greek	8	0.07
Hawaii Native/Pacific Islander:	8	0.07
Melanesian: (1)	1	0.01
Other Melanesian (1)	1	0.01
Micronesian: (1)	1	0.01
Guamanian/Chamorro (1)	1	0.01
Polynesian:	1	0.01
Native Hawaiian	1	0.01
Other Pac. Isl., not spec.	5	0.04
Hispanic or Latino:	84	0.70
Central American:	6	0.05
Guatemalan	2	0.02
Honduran	2	0.02
Panamanian	2	0.02
Mexican	41	0.34
Puerto Rican	13	0.11
South American:	4	0.03
Argentinean	1	0.01
Bolivian	1	0.01
Colombian	2	0.02
Other Hispanic or Latino	20	0.17
Hungarian	92	0.75
Irish	979	7.99
Italian	271	2.21
Lithuanian	14	0.11
Norwegian	791	6.46
Polish	2,189	17.87
Russian	78	0.64
Scandinavian	45	0.37
Scotch-Irish	31	0.25
Scottish	146	1.19
Slavic	7	0.06
Slovak	24	0.20
Slovene	15	0.12
Swedish	402	3.28
Swiss	92	0.75
Ukrainian	44	0.36
United States or American	282	2.30
Welsh	34	0.28
White:	11,331	93.81
Not Hispanic (11,202)	11,275	93.34
Hispanic (45)	56	0.46
Yugoslavian	4	0.03

Whitefish Bay

Place Type: Village
County: Milwaukee
Population: 14,163

Ancestry/Race	Number	%
African American/Black:	183	1.29
Not Hispanic (138)	178	1.26
Hispanic (1)	5	0.04
African, sub-Saharan:	25	0.18
African	7	0.05
South African	18	0.13
Am. Ind. or Alaska Nat., not spec.	7	0.05
American Indian tribes, specified:	29	0.20
Blackfeet	2	0.01
Cherokee (1)	14	0.10
Chippewa (1)	4	0.03
Iroquois (1)	3	0.02
Latin American Indians (1)	3	0.02
Menominee (1)	1	0.01
Potawatomi (1)	1	0.01
All other tribes (1)	1	0.01
American Indian tribes, not spec.	1	0.01
Arab:	78	0.55
Lebanese	8	0.06
Palestinian	10	0.07
Other Arab	60	0.42
Armenian	13	0.09
Asian:	431	3.04
Cambodian (1)	1	0.01
Chinese, ex. Taiwanese (114)	128	0.90
Filipino (26)	37	0.26
Hmong (9)	9	0.06
Indian (71)	81	0.57
Japanese (14)	20	0.14
Korean (102)	114	0.80
Taiwanese (9)	10	0.07
Vietnamese (9)	13	0.09
Other Asian, specified (5)	6	0.04
Other Asian, not specified (3)	12	0.08
Austrian	251	1.77
Belgian	53	0.37
Brazilian	45	0.32
British	45	0.32
Canadian	19	0.13
Celtic	27	0.19
Croatian	53	0.37
Czech	157	1.11
Czechoslovakian	55	0.39
Danish	142	1.00
Dutch	281	1.98
Eastern European	49	0.35
English	1,803	12.73
European	47	0.33
Finnish	26	0.18
French, except Basque	554	3.91
French Canadian	113	0.80
German	5,509	38.90
Greek	108	0.76
Hawaii Native/Pacific Islander:	12	0.08
Polynesian: (7)	9	0.06
Native Hawaiian (5)	6	0.04
Samoan (1)	1	0.01
Other Polynesian (1)	2	0.01
Other Pac. Isl., not spec.	3	0.02
Hispanic or Latino:	221	1.56
Central American:	7	0.05
Guatemalan	5	0.04
Honduran	1	0.01
Other Central American	1	0.01
Cuban	9	0.06
Mexican	77	0.54
Puerto Rican	48	0.34
South American:	48	0.34
Argentinean	6	0.04
Chilean	2	0.01
Colombian	12	0.08

Notes: 1. Figures in the "Number" column do not add up to the total population due to: a) Ancestry/Race overlap — e.g. persons can report being both White and Irish, b) persons of Hispanic origin can report being any race, c) persons reporting two ancestries are counted in both categories. 2. Numbers in parentheses indicate the number of persons reporting this ancestry/race alone, not in combination with any other ancestry/race. 3. Refer to the Explanation of Data in the front of the book for more detailed information.

Ecuadorian	2	0.01
Paraguayan	4	0.03
Peruvian	6	0.04
Uruguayan	1	0.01
Venezuelan	6	0.04
Other South American	9	0.06
Other Hispanic or Latino	32	0.23
Hungarian	156	1.10
Icelander	7	0.05
Iranian	22	0.16
Irish	2,597	18.34
Italian	1,137	8.03
Latvian	82	0.58
Lithuanian	78	0.55
Luxemburger	46	0.32
Norwegian	567	4.00
Polish	1,376	9.72
Romanian	78	0.55
Russian	447	3.16
Scandinavian	59	0.42
Scotch-Irish	241	1.70
Scottish	345	2.44
Serbian	6	0.04
Slavic	5	0.04
Slovak	47	0.33
Slovene	35	0.25
Swedish	330	2.33
Swiss	192	1.36
Turkish	7	0.05
Ukrainian	56	0.40
United States or American	428	3.02
Welsh	110	0.78
White:	13,597	96.00
Not Hispanic (13,286)	13,406	94.66
Hispanic (181)	191	1.35
Yugoslavian	24	0.17

Whitewater

Place Type: City
County: Walworth
Population: 13,437

Ancestry/Race	Number	%
African American/Black:	353	2.63
Not Hispanic (301)	336	2.50
Hispanic (14)	17	0.13
African, sub-Saharan:	74	0.55
African	63	0.47
Sudanese	11	0.08
Alaska Native tribes, specified:	1	0.01
Eskimo (1)	1	0.01
Alaska Native tribes, not specified	1	0.01
Am. Ind. or Alaska Nat., not spec.	27	0.20
Albanian	25	0.19
American Indian tribes, specified:	43	0.32
Apache	1	0.01
Cherokee	2	0.01
Chippewa (8)	16	0.12
Creek (1)	1	0.01
Latin American Indians (6)	6	0.04
Menominee (3)	3	0.02
Osage	1	0.01
Ottawa	5	0.04
Sioux	1	0.01
All other tribes (3)	7	0.05
American Indian tribes, not spec.	1	0.01
Arab:	35	0.26
Arab/Arabic	11	0.08
Lebanese	7	0.05
Syrian	17	0.13
Armenian	13	0.10
Asian:	239	1.78
Cambodian (2)	2	0.01
Chinese, ex. Taiwanese (50)	56	0.42
Filipino (13)	20	0.15
Hmong (26)	31	0.23
Indian (33)	34	0.25
Indonesian (5)	7	0.05
Japanese (13)	16	0.12
Korean (11)	13	0.10
Laotian (13)	13	0.10
Malaysian (2)	3	0.02
Sri Lankan (4)	4	0.03
Taiwanese (4)	5	0.04
Thai (5)	5	0.04
Vietnamese (9)	20	0.15
Other Asian, not specified (5)	10	0.07
Assyrian/Chaldean/Syriac	21	0.16
Austrian	39	0.29
Belgian	52	0.39
British	32	0.24
Bulgarian	18	0.13
Canadian	11	0.08
Croatian	21	0.16
Czech	136	1.01
Czechoslovakian	37	0.28
Danish	153	1.14
Dutch	389	2.90
English	1,047	7.79
European	45	0.34
Finnish	68	0.51
French, except Basque	463	3.45
French Canadian	95	0.71
German	5,620	41.84
Greek	43	0.32
Hawaii Native/Pacific Islander:	14	0.10
Polynesian: (2)	4	0.03
Native Hawaiian (1)	3	0.02
Samoan (1)	1	0.01
Other Pac. Isl., not spec.	10	0.07
Hispanic or Latino:	873	6.50
Central American:	10	0.07
Costa Rican	1	0.01
Guatemalan	2	0.01
Honduran	2	0.01
Panamanian	1	0.01
Salvadoran	4	0.03
Cuban	5	0.04
Dominican Republic	3	0.02
Mexican	703	5.23
Puerto Rican	40	0.30
South American:	11	0.08
Colombian	3	0.02
Ecuadorian	2	0.01
Venezuelan	2	0.01
Other South American	4	0.03
Other Hispanic or Latino	101	0.75
Hungarian	53	0.39
Irish	1,737	12.93
Italian	458	3.41
Lithuanian	63	0.47
Luxemburger	3	0.02
Norwegian	1,207	8.99
Pennsylvania German	6	0.04
Polish	1,035	7.71
Portuguese	8	0.06
Romanian	17	0.13
Russian	77	0.57
Scandinavian	69	0.51
Scotch-Irish	68	0.51
Scottish	111	0.83
Slavic	3	0.02
Slovak	15	0.11
Slovene	7	0.05
Swedish	502	3.74
Swiss	207	1.54
Ukrainian	21	0.16
United States or American	231	1.72
Welsh	90	0.67
White:	12,529	93.24
Not Hispanic (11,932)	12,012	89.39
Hispanic (463)	517	3.85
Yugoslavian	25	0.19

Wisconsin Rapids

Place Type: City
County: Wood
Population: 18,435

Ancestry/Race	Number	%
African American/Black:	125	0.68
Not Hispanic (63)	125	0.68
Alaska Native tribes, specified:	6	0.03
Aleut (1)	1	0.01
Eskimo (3)	3	0.02
Tlingit-Haida	2	0.01
Am. Ind. or Alaska Nat., not spec.	46	0.25
American Indian tribes, specified:	177	0.96
Blackfeet	1	0.01
Cherokee	7	0.04
Cheyenne	1	0.01
Chippewa (11)	17	0.09
Iroquois (9)	18	0.10
Kiowa (3)	6	0.03
Latin American Indians	3	0.02
Menominee (12)	13	0.07
Ottawa (3)	3	0.02
Potawatomi (13)	15	0.08
Sioux	1	0.01
All other tribes (64)	92	0.50
American Indian tribes, not spec.	6	0.03
Asian:	678	3.68
Chinese, ex. Taiwanese (18)	22	0.12
Filipino (16)	26	0.14
Hmong (470)	489	2.65
Indian (21)	33	0.18
Japanese (5)	8	0.04
Korean (20)	21	0.11
Laotian (5)	7	0.04
Malaysian	2	0.01
Thai (2)	2	0.01
Vietnamese (20)	20	0.11
Other Asian, not specified (48)	48	0.26
Austrian	65	0.35
Belgian	21	0.11
British	44	0.24
Canadian	19	0.10
Croatian	16	0.09
Czech	333	1.81
Czechoslovakian	62	0.34
Danish	307	1.67
Dutch	504	2.75
English	1,210	6.59
European	142	0.77
Finnish	137	0.75
French, except Basque	727	3.96
French Canadian	235	1.28
German	8,180	44.58
Greek	37	0.20
Hawaii Native/Pacific Islander:	6	0.03
Micronesian: (1)	3	0.02
Guamanian/Chamorro (1)	3	0.02
Polynesian: (2)	3	0.02
Native Hawaiian (2)	3	0.02
Hispanic or Latino:	242	1.31
Central American:	4	0.02
Costa Rican	1	0.01
Honduran	2	0.01
Other Central American	1	0.01
Cuban	1	0.01
Mexican	160	0.87
Puerto Rican	28	0.15
South American:	5	0.03
Chilean	1	0.01
Ecuadorian	1	0.01
Paraguayan	2	0.01
Other South American	1	0.01
Other Hispanic or Latino	44	0.24
Hungarian	26	0.14
Irish	1,954	10.65
Italian	466	2.54
Lithuanian	7	0.04
Norwegian	1,338	7.29

Notes: 1. Figures in the "Number" column do not add up to the total population due to: a) Ancestry/Race overlap — e.g. persons can report being both White and Irish, b) persons of Hispanic origin can report being any race, c) persons reporting two ancestries are counted in both categories. 2. Numbers in parentheses indicate the number of persons reporting this ancestry/race alone, not in combination with any other ancestry/race. 3. Refer to the Explanation of Data in the front of the book for more detailed information.

Pennsylvania German	10	0.05
Polish	2,175	11.85
Russian	54	0.29
Scandinavian	65	0.35
Scotch-Irish	134	0.73
Scottish	103	0.56
Slovak	16	0.09
Swedish	557	3.04
Swiss	140	0.76
Ukrainian	6	0.03
United States or American	872	4.75
Welsh	111	0.60
West Indian, excl. Hispanic:	7	0.04
Trinidadian and Tobagonian	7	0.04
White:	17,497	94.91
Not Hispanic (17,195)	17,331	94.01
Hispanic (142)	166	0.90
Yugoslavian	28	0.15

Casper

Place Type: City
County: Natrona
Population: 49,644

Ancestry/Race	Number	%
Acadian/Cajun	7	0.01
African American/Black:	584	1.18
Not Hispanic (399)	530	1.07
Hispanic (29)	54	0.11
African, sub-Saharan:	62	0.12
African	58	0.12
Nigerian	4	0.01
Alaska Native tribes, specified:	2	0.00
Alaska Athabascan (1)	1	0.00
Eskimo (1)	1	0.00
Alaska Native tribes, not specified	1	0.00
Am. Ind. or Alaska Nat., not spec.	159	0.32
American Indian tribes, specified:	615	1.24
Apache (4)	12	0.02
Blackfeet (6)	12	0.02
Cherokee (25)	88	0.18
Cheyenne (9)	14	0.03
Chickasaw (2)	3	0.01
Chippewa (45)	60	0.12
Choctaw (3)	23	0.05
Comanche	3	0.01
Cree	1	0.00
Creek (1)	2	0.00
Crow (2)	3	0.01
Houma (2)	2	0.00
Iroquois (2)	5	0.01
Latin American Indians (7)	10	0.02
Lumbee (1)	1	0.00
Navajo (9)	23	0.05
Osage (2)	2	0.00
Ottawa	4	0.01
Paiute (1)	2	0.00
Pima (1)	1	0.00
Potawatomi (5)	5	0.01
Pueblo (4)	10	0.02
Shoshone (38)	52	0.10
Sioux (62)	83	0.17
Ute (1)	3	0.01
Yaqui	1	0.00
All other tribes (137)	190	0.38
American Indian tribes, not spec.	39	0.08
Arab:	14	0.03
Lebanese	7	0.01
Other Arab	7	0.01
Armenian	15	0.03
Asian:	349	0.70
Cambodian (11)	11	0.02
Chinese, ex. Taiwanese (55)	61	0.12
Filipino (46)	75	0.15
Indian (23)	37	0.07
Indonesian (2)	2	0.00
Japanese (16)	53	0.11
Korean (24)	29	0.06
Laotian (7)	7	0.01
Malaysian (1)	1	0.00
Pakistani (6)	9	0.02
Sri Lankan (8)	8	0.02
Taiwanese	1	0.00
Thai (14)	16	0.03
Vietnamese (7)	10	0.02
Other Asian, specified (3)	3	0.01
Other Asian, not specified (21)	26	0.05
Australian	5	0.01
Austrian	103	0.21
Basque	18	0.04
Belgian	65	0.13
British	165	0.33
Canadian	61	0.12
Celtic	35	0.07
Croatian	58	0.12
Czech	375	0.75
Czechoslovakian	130	0.26
Danish	768	1.54
Dutch	1,242	2.49
Eastern European	18	0.04
English	6,793	13.63
Estonian	9	0.02
European	355	0.71
Finnish	129	0.26
French, except Basque	2,046	4.10
French Canadian	292	0.59
German	12,384	24.84
Greek	253	0.51
Hawaii Native/Pacific Islander:	38	0.08
Melanesian: (1)	1	0.00
Fijian (1)	1	0.00
Micronesian: (3)	7	0.01
Guamanian/Chamorro (3)	7	0.01
Polynesian: (3)	20	0.04
Native Hawaiian (3)	15	0.03
Samoan	3	0.01
Other Polynesian	2	0.00
Other Pac. Isl., not spec. (3)	10	0.02
Hispanic or Latino:	2,656	5.35
Central American:	11	0.02
Costa Rican	1	0.00
Guatemalan	2	0.00
Honduran	1	0.00
Nicaraguan	3	0.01
Panamanian	4	0.01
Cuban	16	0.03
Mexican	1,728	3.48
Puerto Rican	43	0.09
South American:	8	0.02
Argentinean	1	0.00
Colombian	1	0.00
Peruvian	1	0.00
Venezuelan	4	0.01
Other South American	1	0.00
Other Hispanic or Latino	850	1.71
Hungarian	149	0.30
Icelander	23	0.05
Irish	7,330	14.70
Italian	1,843	3.70
Latvian	10	0.02
Lithuanian	53	0.11
Luxemburger	11	0.02
Northern European	50	0.10
Norwegian	2,507	5.03
Pennsylvania German	44	0.09
Polish	954	1.91
Portuguese	69	0.14
Romanian	17	0.03
Russian	202	0.41
Scandinavian	237	0.48
Scotch-Irish	1,190	2.39
Scottish	1,266	2.54
Serbian	31	0.06
Slavic	27	0.05
Slovak	41	0.08
Slovene	41	0.08
Swedish	1,423	2.85
Swiss	221	0.44
Ukrainian	44	0.09
United States or American	3,910	7.84
Welsh	696	1.40
White:	47,408	95.50
Not Hispanic (45,334)	45,861	92.38
Hispanic (1,346)	1,547	3.12
Yugoslavian	89	0.18

Cheyenne

Place Type: City
County: Laramie
Population: 53,011

Ancestry/Race	Number	%
African American/Black:	1,810	3.41
Not Hispanic (1,399)	1,667	3.14
Hispanic (73)	143	0.27
African, sub-Saharan:	113	0.21
African	75	0.14
Sudanese	38	0.07
Alaska Native tribes, specified:	7	0.01
Eskimo (1)	2	0.00
Tlingit-Haida (2)	5	0.01
Alaska Native tribes, not specified	6	0.01
Am. Ind. or Alaska Nat., not spec.	207	0.39
Albanian	6	0.01
American Indian tribes, specified:	602	1.14
Apache (17)	33	0.06
Blackfeet (7)	13	0.02
Cherokee (30)	127	0.24
Cheyenne (9)	20	0.04
Chickasaw	6	0.01
Chippewa (13)	27	0.05
Choctaw (3)	13	0.02
Comanche (1)	1	0.00
Cree	4	0.01
Creek (1)	2	0.00
Crow (1)	6	0.01
Delaware (7)	7	0.01
Iroquois (11)	18	0.03
Latin American Indians (20)	42	0.08
Lumbee (1)	1	0.00
Navajo (13)	21	0.04
Osage (1)	7	0.01
Ottawa	1	0.00
Paiute (2)	2	0.00
Potawatomi	3	0.01
Pueblo (4)	16	0.03
Puget Sound Salish	1	0.00
Shoshone (16)	20	0.04
Sioux (85)	123	0.23
Yakama	1	0.00
Yaqui	2	0.00
All other tribes (54)	85	0.16
American Indian tribes, not spec.	44	0.08
Arab:	32	0.06
Arab/Arabic	9	0.02
Egyptian	7	0.01
Lebanese	16	0.03
Asian:	899	1.70
Cambodian (3)	4	0.01
Chinese, ex. Taiwanese (60)	100	0.19
Filipino (123)	226	0.43
Indian (66)	73	0.14
Indonesian	4	0.01
Japanese (95)	172	0.32
Korean (124)	167	0.32
Pakistani (5)	5	0.01
Taiwanese (1)	1	0.00
Thai (20)	42	0.08
Vietnamese (31)	33	0.06
Other Asian, specified (2)	2	0.00
Other Asian, not specified (25)	70	0.13
Australian	27	0.05
Austrian	159	0.30
Basque	28	0.05
Belgian	37	0.07
British	178	0.34
Bulgarian	32	0.06
Canadian	71	0.13

Notes: 1. Figures in the "Number" column do not add up to the total population due to: a) Ancestry/Race overlap — e.g. persons can report being both White and Irish, b) persons of Hispanic origin can report being any race, c) persons reporting two ancestries are counted in both categories. 2. Numbers in parentheses indicate the number of persons reporting this ancestry/race alone, not in combination with any other ancestry/race. 3. Refer to the Explanation of Data in the front of the book for more detailed information.

Ancestry/Race	Number	%
Celtic	13	0.02
Croatian	21	0.04
Czech	466	0.88
Czechoslovakian	159	0.30
Danish	743	1.41
Dutch	1,238	2.35
Eastern European	42	0.08
English	7,196	13.64
Estonian	10	0.02
European	320	0.61
Finnish	148	0.28
French, except Basque	1,943	3.68
French Canadian	432	0.82
German	13,359	25.32
German Russian	57	0.11
Greek	236	0.45
Guyanese	5	0.01
Hawaii Native/Pacific Islander:	117	0.22
Micronesian: (17)	28	0.05
Guamanian/Chamorro (17)	28	0.05
Polynesian: (32)	60	0.11
Native Hawaiian (24)	48	0.09
Samoan (7)	11	0.02
Other Polynesian (1)	1	0.00
Other Pac. Isl., not spec. (9)	29	0.05
Hispanic or Latino:	6,646	12.54
Central American:	36	0.07
Costa Rican	3	0.01
Guatemalan	6	0.01
Honduran	2	0.00
Nicaraguan	3	0.01
Panamanian	19	0.04
Salvadoran	3	0.01
Cuban	38	0.07
Dominican Republic	5	0.01
Mexican	3,477	6.56
Puerto Rican	167	0.32
South American:	40	0.08
Bolivian	3	0.01
Chilean	3	0.01
Colombian	7	0.01
Ecuadorian	2	0.00
Peruvian	14	0.03
Other South American	11	0.02
Other Hispanic or Latino	2,883	5.44
Hungarian	204	0.39
Iranian	44	0.08
Irish	7,627	14.46
Italian	1,822	3.45
Latvian	19	0.04
Lithuanian	52	0.10
Luxemburger	15	0.03
Northern European	24	0.05
Norwegian	1,778	3.37
Pennsylvania German	20	0.04
Polish	969	1.84
Portuguese	82	0.16
Romanian	41	0.08
Russian	493	0.93
Scandinavian	107	0.20
Scotch-Irish	1,438	2.73
Scottish	1,671	3.17
Slavic	36	0.07
Slovak	24	0.05
Slovene	45	0.09
Swedish	1,617	3.06
Swiss	260	0.49
Turkish	22	0.04
Ukrainian	26	0.05
United States or American	3,169	6.01
Welsh	509	0.96
West Indian, excl. Hispanic:	81	0.15
British West Indian	6	0.01
Dutch West Indian	14	0.03
Jamaican	52	0.10
Trinidadian and Tobagonian	9	0.02
White:	47,948	90.45
Not Hispanic (43,146)	43,921	82.85
Hispanic (3,561)	4,027	7.60
Yugoslavian	85	0.16

Evanston

Place Type: City
County: Uinta
Population: 11,507

Ancestry/Race	Number	%
African American/Black:	39	0.34
Not Hispanic (14)	29	0.25
Hispanic (4)	10	0.09
Alaska Native tribes, specified:	8	0.07
Aleut	1	0.01
Eskimo (4)	5	0.04
Tlingit-Haida (1)	2	0.02
Am. Ind. or Alaska Nat., not spec.	68	0.59
American Indian tribes, specified:	130	1.13
Apache (2)	7	0.06
Blackfeet (3)	10	0.09
Cherokee (12)	27	0.23
Cheyenne (1)	2	0.02
Chickasaw	1	0.01
Chippewa (1)	5	0.04
Choctaw	3	0.03
Cree	3	0.03
Creek (2)	2	0.02
Crow (2)	2	0.02
Iroquois (1)	1	0.01
Latin American Indians (3)	10	0.09
Navajo (13)	15	0.13
Paiute (1)	1	0.01
Pueblo	5	0.04
Seminole	1	0.01
Shoshone (4)	10	0.09
Sioux (6)	7	0.06
Ute (3)	5	0.04
All other tribes (9)	13	0.11
American Indian tribes, not spec.	12	0.10
Arab:	7	0.06
Lebanese	7	0.06
Asian:	84	0.73
Chinese, ex. Taiwanese (11)	13	0.11
Filipino (9)	23	0.20
Indian (12)	17	0.15
Indonesian	1	0.01
Japanese (5)	9	0.08
Korean (3)	6	0.05
Thai (1)	2	0.02
Vietnamese (1)	1	0.01
Other Asian, specified (2)	8	0.07
Other Asian, not specified (2)	4	0.03
Austrian	4	0.03
Basque	33	0.29
British	39	0.34
Canadian	51	0.45
Celtic	10	0.09
Croatian	9	0.08
Czech	79	0.69
Czechoslovakian	10	0.09
Danish	324	2.83
Dutch	158	1.38
English	3,145	27.51
European	52	0.45
Finnish	128	1.12
French, except Basque	343	3.00
French Canadian	95	0.83
German	1,831	16.02
Greek	104	0.91
Hawaii Native/Pacific Islander:	21	0.18
Micronesian: (3)	3	0.03
Other Micronesian (3)	3	0.03
Polynesian: (6)	13	0.11
Native Hawaiian (1)	6	0.05
Samoan (5)	7	0.06
Other Pac. Isl., specified	3	0.03
Other Pac. Isl., not spec.	2	0.02
Hispanic or Latino:	839	7.29
Central American:	1	0.01
Panamanian	1	0.01
Cuban	4	0.03
Dominican Republic	1	0.01
Mexican	549	4.77
Puerto Rican	15	0.13
South American:	37	0.32
Chilean	9	0.08
Ecuadorian	5	0.04
Peruvian	18	0.16
Venezuelan	1	0.01
Other South American	4	0.03
Other Hispanic or Latino	232	2.02
Hungarian	21	0.18
Irish	1,038	9.08
Italian	430	3.76
Lithuanian	5	0.04
New Zealander	6	0.05
Norwegian	460	4.02
Polish	105	0.92
Portuguese	9	0.08
Romanian	6	0.05
Russian	48	0.42
Scandinavian	28	0.24
Scotch-Irish	164	1.43
Scottish	569	4.98
Serbian	20	0.17
Slavic	25	0.22
Slovak	12	0.10
Swedish	367	3.21
Swiss	63	0.55
United States or American	873	7.64
Welsh	136	1.19
White:	10,812	93.96
Not Hispanic (10,339)	10,475	91.03
Hispanic (281)	337	2.93
Yugoslavian	5	0.04

Gillette

Place Type: City
County: Campbell
Population: 19,646

Ancestry/Race	Number	%
African American/Black:	77	0.39
Not Hispanic (35)	59	0.30
Hispanic (4)	18	0.09
Alaska Native tribes, specified:	3	0.02
Aleut	3	0.02
Am. Ind. or Alaska Nat., not spec.	67	0.34
American Indian tribes, specified:	264	1.34
Apache (1)	2	0.01
Blackfeet	1	0.01
Cherokee (6)	33	0.17
Cheyenne (10)	18	0.09
Chippewa (21)	32	0.16
Choctaw (11)	16	0.08
Comanche (1)	2	0.01
Cree	5	0.03
Creek (1)	1	0.01
Crow (1)	10	0.05
Iroquois (2)	3	0.02
Latin American Indians (4)	6	0.03
Navajo (7)	9	0.05
Ottawa (1)	1	0.01
Paiute (1)	1	0.01
Potawatomi (1)	1	0.01
Puget Sound Salish (2)	2	0.01
Seminole	1	0.01
Shoshone (9)	16	0.08
Sioux (55)	87	0.44
Yuman (1)	1	0.01
All other tribes (9)	16	0.08
American Indian tribes, not spec.	12	0.06
Arab:	7	0.04
Lebanese	7	0.04
Asian:	130	0.66
Chinese, ex. Taiwanese (7)	15	0.08
Filipino (16)	31	0.16
Indian (29)	29	0.15
Indonesian	1	0.01
Japanese (14)	31	0.16
Korean (11)	14	0.07

Notes: 1. Figures in the "Number" column do not add up to the total population due to: a) Ancestry/Race overlap — e.g. persons can report being both White and Irish, b) persons of Hispanic origin can report being any race, c) persons reporting two ancestries are counted in both categories. 2. Numbers in parentheses indicate the number of persons reporting this ancestry/race alone, not in combination with any other ancestry/race. 3. Refer to the Explanation of Data in the front of the book for more detailed information.

Malaysian (1)	1	0.01
Vietnamese (2)	2	0.01
Other Asian, not specified (2)	6	0.03
Austrian	46	0.23
Basque	31	0.16
Belgian	52	0.26
British	72	0.37
Bulgarian	16	0.08
Canadian	15	0.08
Czech	271	1.38
Czechoslovakian	18	0.09
Danish	228	1.16
Dutch	536	2.72
Eastern European	6	0.03
English	2,651	13.47
European	184	0.93
Finnish	115	0.58
French, except Basque	479	2.43
French Canadian	173	0.88
German	5,672	28.82
Greek	62	0.32
Hawaii Native/Pacific Islander:	30	0.15
Micronesian: (9)	14	0.07
Guamanian/Chamorro (7)	11	0.06
Other Micronesian (2)	3	0.02
Polynesian: (5)	9	0.05
Native Hawaiian (2)	4	0.02
Samoan (3)	5	0.03
Other Pac. Isl., not spec. (6)	7	0.04
Hispanic or Latino:	774	3.94
Central American:	11	0.06
Costa Rican	3	0.02
Honduran	1	0.01
Salvadoran	7	0.04
Cuban	1	0.01
Mexican	506	2.58
Puerto Rican	5	0.03
South American:	13	0.07
Chilean	4	0.02
Colombian	3	0.02
Ecuadorian	3	0.02
Peruvian	3	0.02
Other Hispanic or Latino	238	1.21
Hungarian	30	0.15
Iranian	7	0.04
Irish	3,035	15.42
Israeli	7	0.04
Italian	435	2.21
Lithuanian	8	0.04
Norwegian	1,392	7.07
Polish	292	1.48
Romanian	12	0.06
Russian	186	0.95
Scandinavian	73	0.37
Scotch-Irish	617	3.13
Scottish	449	2.28
Serbian	19	0.10
Slavic	48	0.24
Slovene	12	0.06
Swedish	563	2.86
Swiss	54	0.27
Ukrainian	11	0.06
United States or American	1,327	6.74
Welsh	108	0.55
West Indian, excl. Hispanic:	6	0.03
Jamaican	6	0.03
White:	19,033	96.88
Not Hispanic (18,350)	18,551	94.43
Hispanic (412)	482	2.45
Yugoslavian	27	0.14

Green River

Place Type: City
County: Sweetwater
Population: 11,808

Ancestry/Race	Number	%
African American/Black:	42	0.36
Not Hispanic (32)	39	0.33
Hispanic	3	0.03
Am. Ind. or Alaska Nat., not spec.	55	0.47
American Indian tribes, specified:	141	1.19
Apache (4)	5	0.04
Blackfeet (1)	4	0.03
Cherokee (16)	28	0.24
Chickasaw (1)	1	0.01
Chippewa (6)	7	0.06
Choctaw (2)	2	0.02
Colville (1)	4	0.03
Comanche	1	0.01
Cree (1)	1	0.01
Crow (2)	5	0.04
Latin American Indians (6)	9	0.08
Navajo (37)	39	0.33
Paiute (2)	2	0.02
Shoshone (2)	5	0.04
Sioux (10)	16	0.14
All other tribes (9)	12	0.10
American Indian tribes, not spec.	21	0.18
Arab:	7	0.06
Arab/Arabic	7	0.06
Armenian	5	0.04
Asian:	65	0.55
Chinese, ex. Taiwanese (5)	7	0.06
Filipino (12)	19	0.16
Indian (1)	2	0.02
Japanese (12)	25	0.21
Korean (7)	11	0.09
Other Asian, not specified (1)	1	0.01
Australian	8	0.07
Austrian	31	0.26
Basque	88	0.75
Belgian	14	0.12
British	19	0.16
Canadian	21	0.18
Celtic	14	0.12
Czech	55	0.47
Czechoslovakian	40	0.34
Danish	445	3.77
Dutch	316	2.68
English	2,349	19.92
European	149	1.26
Finnish	83	0.70
French, except Basque	371	3.15
French Canadian	47	0.40
German	2,220	18.83
Greek	119	1.01
Hawaii Native/Pacific Islander:	10	0.08
Melanesian:	1	0.01
Fijian	1	0.01
Micronesian: (2)	2	0.02
Guamanian/Chamorro (2)	2	0.02
Polynesian: (2)	3	0.03
Native Hawaiian	1	0.01
Samoan (2)	2	0.02
Other Pac. Isl., not spec. (3)	4	0.03
Hispanic or Latino:	1,206	10.21
Central American:	3	0.03
Costa Rican	1	0.01
Guatemalan	2	0.02
Cuban	2	0.02
Mexican	697	5.90
Puerto Rican	8	0.07
South American:	3	0.03
Bolivian	1	0.01
Colombian	1	0.01
Peruvian	1	0.01
Other Hispanic or Latino	493	4.18
Hungarian	38	0.32
Icelander	16	0.14
Irish	932	7.90
Italian	301	2.55
Latvian	8	0.07
Lithuanian	19	0.16
Maltese	14	0.12
Northern European	7	0.06
Norwegian	333	2.82
Pennsylvania German	6	0.05
Polish	263	2.23
Portuguese	18	0.15
Romanian	13	0.11
Russian	41	0.35
Scandinavian	59	0.50
Scotch-Irish	223	1.89
Scottish	276	2.34
Slavic	21	0.18
Slovak	7	0.06
Slovene	14	0.12
Swedish	380	3.22
Swiss	174	1.48
United States or American	732	6.21
Welsh	183	1.55
White:	11,060	93.67
Not Hispanic (10,293)	10,387	87.97
Hispanic (586)	673	5.70
Yugoslavian	55	0.47

Laramie

Place Type: City
County: Albany
Population: 27,204

Ancestry/Race	Number	%
Acadian/Cajun	8	0.03
African American/Black:	419	1.54
Not Hispanic (305)	367	1.35
Hispanic (32)	52	0.19
African, sub-Saharan:	92	0.34
African	36	0.13
Ethiopian	7	0.03
Nigerian	29	0.11
South African	20	0.07
Alaska Native tribes, specified:	7	0.03
Alaska Athabascan (2)	2	0.01
Tlingit-Haida (1)	5	0.02
Alaska Native tribes, not specified	1	0.00
Am. Ind. or Alaska Nat., not spec.	108	0.40
American Indian tribes, specified:	347	1.28
Apache (2)	15	0.06
Blackfeet (3)	12	0.04
Cherokee (27)	78	0.29
Cheyenne (1)	4	0.01
Chickasaw	3	0.01
Chippewa (6)	11	0.04
Choctaw (5)	11	0.04
Colville (1)	1	0.00
Comanche	1	0.00
Cree	2	0.01
Crow (1)	1	0.00
Delaware (1)	1	0.00
Iroquois (1)	4	0.01
Kiowa (1)	1	0.00
Latin American Indians (7)	14	0.05
Lumbee (4)	4	0.01
Menominee	1	0.00
Navajo (10)	24	0.09
Osage (1)	4	0.01
Pima (1)	1	0.00
Potawatomi	4	0.01
Pueblo (4)	7	0.03
Puget Sound Salish (1)	1	0.00
Seminole (1)	6	0.02
Shoshone (24)	32	0.12
Sioux (11)	31	0.11
Ute	2	0.01
Yaqui (3)	3	0.01
All other tribes (53)	68	0.25
American Indian tribes, not spec.	19	0.07
Arab:	69	0.25
Egyptian	17	0.06
Lebanese	52	0.19
Asian:	638	2.35
Bangladeshi (3)	3	0.01
Cambodian (2)	2	0.01
Chinese, ex. Taiwanese (228)	250	0.92
Filipino (12)	36	0.13
Indian (87)	92	0.34
Indonesian (6)	6	0.02

Notes: 1. Figures in the "Number" column do not add up to the total population due to: a) Ancestry/Race overlap — e.g. persons can report being both White and Irish, b) persons of Hispanic origin can report being any race, c) persons reporting two ancestries are counted in both categories. 2. Numbers in parentheses indicate the number of persons reporting this ancestry/race alone, not in combination with any other ancestry/race. 3. Refer to the Explanation of Data in the front of the book for more detailed information.

Japanese (63)	97	0.36
Korean (66)	78	0.29
Malaysian (3)	7	0.03
Pakistani (8)	8	0.03
Sri Lankan (4)	4	0.01
Taiwanese	1	0.00
Thai (9)	12	0.04
Vietnamese (12)	14	0.05
Other Asian, specified (1)	3	0.01
Other Asian, not specified (13)	25	0.09
Australian	11	0.04
Austrian	109	0.40
Basque	13	0.05
Belgian	69	0.25
British	218	0.80
Canadian	100	0.37
Celtic	12	0.04
Croatian	34	0.12
Czech	237	0.87
Czechoslovakian	47	0.17
Danish	596	2.19
Dutch	445	1.64
Eastern European	22	0.08
English	4,098	15.06
Estonian	21	0.08
European	619	2.27
Finnish	215	0.79
French, except Basque	1,027	3.77
French Canadian	210	0.77
German	7,229	26.56
German Russian	10	0.04
Greek	128	0.47
Hawaii Native/Pacific Islander:	43	0.16
Micronesian: (1)	3	0.01
Guamanian/Chamorro (1)	3	0.01
Polynesian: (11)	27	0.10
Native Hawaiian (2)	18	0.07
Samoan (5)	5	0.02
Tongan (2)	2	0.01
Other Polynesian (2)	2	0.01
Other Pac. Isl., specified	2	0.01
Other Pac. Isl., not spec. (4)	11	0.04
Hispanic or Latino:	2,161	7.94
Central American:	12	0.04
Costa Rican	2	0.01
Guatemalan	1	0.00
Honduran	6	0.02
Nicaraguan	2	0.01
Salvadoran	1	0.00
Cuban	22	0.08
Dominican Republic	1	0.00
Mexican	1,320	4.85
Puerto Rican	36	0.13
South American:	18	0.07
Argentinean	1	0.00
Bolivian	1	0.00
Chilean	4	0.01
Colombian	5	0.02
Ecuadorian	2	0.01
Peruvian	3	0.01
Venezuelan	2	0.01
Other Hispanic or Latino	752	2.76
Hungarian	61	0.22
Icelander	6	0.02
Irish	3,730	13.71
Italian	1,037	3.81
Lithuanian	55	0.20
Northern European	49	0.18
Norwegian	1,359	4.99
Pennsylvania German	38	0.14
Polish	613	2.25
Portuguese	43	0.16
Romanian	19	0.07
Russian	241	0.89
Scandinavian	165	0.61
Scotch-Irish	611	2.25
Scottish	905	3.33
Serbian	40	0.15
Slavic	41	0.15
Slovak	35	0.13
Slovene	21	0.08
Swedish	1,203	4.42
Swiss	308	1.13
Turkish	8	0.03
Ukrainian	29	0.11
United States or American	1,341	4.93
Welsh	379	1.39
West Indian, excl. Hispanic:	8	0.03
Other West Indian	8	0.03
White:	25,277	92.92
Not Hispanic (23,605)	23,949	88.03
Hispanic (1,099)	1,328	4.88
Yugoslavian	29	0.11

Rock Springs

Place Type: City
County: Sweetwater
Population: 18,708

Ancestry/Race	Number	%
African American/Black:	265	1.42
Not Hispanic (196)	255	1.36
Hispanic (5)	10	0.05
African, sub-Saharan:	29	0.15
African	29	0.15
Alaska Native tribes, specified:	1	0.01
Tlingit-Haida (1)	1	0.01
Am. Ind. or Alaska Nat., not spec.	93	0.50
American Indian tribes, specified:	189	1.01
Apache (2)	5	0.03
Blackfeet (4)	5	0.03
Cherokee (20)	53	0.28
Chickasaw	6	0.03
Chippewa (5)	10	0.05
Choctaw (5)	17	0.09
Colville (1)	1	0.01
Comanche	1	0.01
Creek (2)	6	0.03
Crow (1)	3	0.02
Iroquois (1)	1	0.01
Latin American Indians (3)	5	0.03
Navajo (18)	21	0.11
Pima (1)	1	0.01
Pueblo (1)	1	0.01
Seminole	1	0.01
Shoshone (6)	8	0.04
Sioux (10)	18	0.10
Ute (1)	1	0.01
All other tribes (17)	25	0.13
American Indian tribes, not spec.	24	0.13
Arab:	12	0.06
Arab/Arabic	6	0.03
Egyptian	6	0.03
Asian:	257	1.37
Chinese, ex. Taiwanese (52)	69	0.37
Filipino (18)	32	0.17
Indian (10)	12	0.06
Indonesian (1)	1	0.01
Japanese (80)	100	0.53
Korean (23)	28	0.15
Taiwanese	1	0.01
Thai (3)	3	0.02
Vietnamese (3)	6	0.03
Other Asian, specified (1)	1	0.01
Other Asian, not specified	4	0.02
Austrian	69	0.36
Basque	113	0.60
Belgian	8	0.04
British	77	0.41
Bulgarian	9	0.05
Canadian	77	0.41
Celtic	8	0.04
Croatian	80	0.42
Czech	90	0.47
Czechoslovakian	45	0.24
Danish	447	2.36
Dutch	470	2.48
Eastern European	30	0.16
English	3,426	18.06
European	167	0.88
Finnish	275	1.45
French, except Basque	684	3.61
French Canadian	77	0.41
German	3,094	16.31
Greek	125	0.66
Hawaii Native/Pacific Islander:	19	0.10
Polynesian: (4)	14	0.07
Native Hawaiian (3)	11	0.06
Samoan (1)	2	0.01
Tongan	1	0.01
Other Pac. Isl., not spec. (2)	5	0.03
Hispanic or Latino:	1,676	8.96
Central American:	2	0.01
Guatemalan	1	0.01
Panamanian	1	0.01
Cuban	4	0.02
Mexican	993	5.31
Puerto Rican	15	0.08
South American:	15	0.08
Bolivian	6	0.03
Ecuadorian	2	0.01
Peruvian	1	0.01
Venezuelan	6	0.03
Other Hispanic or Latino	647	3.46
Hungarian	91	0.48
Icelander	19	0.10
Irish	2,036	10.73
Italian	1,527	8.05
Lithuanian	10	0.05
Northern European	54	0.28
Norwegian	870	4.59
Pennsylvania German	16	0.08
Polish	439	2.31
Portuguese	25	0.13
Russian	117	0.62
Scandinavian	96	0.51
Scotch-Irish	249	1.31
Scottish	817	4.31
Serbian	33	0.17
Slavic	186	0.98
Slovak	25	0.13
Slovene	304	1.60
Swedish	496	2.61
Swiss	102	0.54
Turkish	18	0.09
Ukrainian	40	0.21
United States or American	1,310	6.91
Welsh	372	1.96
West Indian, excl. Hispanic:	14	0.07
Jamaican	14	0.07
White:	17,548	93.80
Not Hispanic (16,239)	16,504	88.22
Hispanic (925)	1,044	5.58
Yugoslavian	302	1.59

Sheridan

Place Type: City
County: Sheridan
Population: 15,804

Ancestry/Race	Number	%
African American/Black:	66	0.42
Not Hispanic (31)	61	0.39
Hispanic (3)	5	0.03
African, sub-Saharan:	2	0.01
African	2	0.01
Alaska Native tribes, specified:	1	0.01
Alaska Athabascan (1)	1	0.01
Am. Ind. or Alaska Nat., not spec.	50	0.32
Albanian	10	0.06
American Indian tribes, specified:	181	1.15
Blackfeet (1)	3	0.02
Cherokee (5)	22	0.14
Cheyenne (12)	25	0.16
Chickasaw	1	0.01
Chippewa (7)	16	0.10
Choctaw (1)	1	0.01
Cree (1)	2	0.01

Notes: 1. Figures in the "Number" column do not add up to the total population due to: a) Ancestry/Race overlap — e.g. persons can report being both White and Irish, b) persons of Hispanic origin can report being any race, c) persons reporting two ancestries are counted in both categories. 2. Numbers in parentheses indicate the number of persons reporting this ancestry/race alone, not in combination with any other ancestry/race. 3. Refer to the Explanation of Data in the front of the book for more detailed information.

Ancestry	Number	Percent
Crow (22)	33	0.21
Iroquois (2)	2	0.01
Latin American Indians (2)	3	0.02
Navajo (6)	6	0.04
Potawatomi	1	0.01
Puget Sound Salish (1)	1	0.01
Shoshone (3)	8	0.05
Sioux (28)	38	0.24
Yaqui (1)	1	0.01
All other tribes (15)	18	0.11
American Indian tribes, not spec.	19	0.12
Arab:	19	0.12
Arab/Arabic	12	0.08
Lebanese	7	0.04
Asian:	125	0.79
Chinese, ex. Taiwanese (17)	25	0.16
Filipino (8)	25	0.16
Indian (6)	11	0.07
Japanese (6)	16	0.10
Korean (25)	31	0.20
Laotian (1)	1	0.01
Pakistani (8)	8	0.05
Vietnamese (1)	2	0.01
Other Asian, specified	3	0.02
Other Asian, not specified	3	0.02
Austrian	106	0.67
Basque	41	0.26
Belgian	4	0.03
British	84	0.53
Bulgarian	16	0.10
Canadian	24	0.15
Celtic	31	0.20
Croatian	26	0.16
Czech	121	0.76
Czechoslovakian	90	0.57
Danish	194	1.22
Dutch	507	3.20
English	2,392	15.08
European	133	0.84
Finnish	85	0.54
French, except Basque	678	4.27
French Canadian	95	0.60
German	4,385	27.64
Greek	18	0.11
Hawaii Native/Pacific Islander:	43	0.27
Micronesian: (3)	6	0.04
Guamanian/Chamorro (3)	6	0.04
Polynesian: (26)	32	0.20
Native Hawaiian (2)	7	0.04
Samoan (1)	1	0.01
Tongan (23)	24	0.15
Other Pac. Isl., specified	3	0.02
Other Pac. Isl., not spec. (2)	2	0.01
Hispanic or Latino:	417	2.64
Central American:	5	0.03
Guatemalan	1	0.01
Nicaraguan	1	0.01
Panamanian	3	0.02
Cuban	17	0.11
Mexican	247	1.56
Puerto Rican	9	0.06
South American:	2	0.01
Colombian	2	0.01
Other Hispanic or Latino	137	0.87
Hungarian	96	0.61
Icelander	8	0.05
Iranian	9	0.06
Irish	2,163	13.63
Italian	454	2.86
Lithuanian	7	0.04
Luxemburger	8	0.05
Macedonian	10	0.06
New Zealander	3	0.02
Norwegian	961	6.06
Pennsylvania German	29	0.18
Polish	813	5.12
Portuguese	50	0.32
Romanian	24	0.15
Russian	221	1.39
Scandinavian	20	0.13
Scotch-Irish	506	3.19
Scottish	425	2.68
Serbian	22	0.14
Slavic	14	0.09
Slovak	7	0.04
Swedish	589	3.71
Swiss	23	0.14
Ukrainian	6	0.04
United States or American	926	5.84
Welsh	214	1.35
White:	15,370	97.25
Not Hispanic (14,926)	15,095	95.51
Hispanic (235)	275	1.74
Yugoslavian	17	0.11

Notes: 1. Figures in the "Number" column do not add up to the total population due to: a) Ancestry/Race overlap — e.g. persons can report being both White and Irish, b) persons of Hispanic origin can report being any race, c) persons reporting two ancestries are counted in both categories. 2. Numbers in parentheses indicate the number of persons reporting this ancestry/race alone, not in combination with any other ancestry/race. 3. Refer to the Explanation of Data in the front of the book for more detailed information.

SECTION TWO:
Ranking Tables

Acadian/Cajun

Top 150 Places Sorted by Number

(Based on all places, regardless of population)

Place	Number	%
Lafayette, LA (city) Lafayette Parish	2,598	2.36
Lake Charles, LA (city) Calcasieu Parish	935	1.31
Houston, TX (city) Harris County	882	0.05
Baton Rouge, LA (city) East Baton Rouge Parish	868	0.38
New Orleans, LA (city) Orleans Parish	826	0.17
Larose, LA (cdp) Lafourche Parish	759	10.49
New Iberia, LA (city) Iberia Parish	627	1.92
Sulphur, LA (city) Calcasieu Parish	626	3.07
Abbeville, LA (city) Vermilion Parish	615	5.15
Austin, TX (city) Travis County	601	0.09
Metairie, LA (cdp) Jefferson Parish	600	0.41
Crowley, LA (city) Acadia Parish	581	4.07
Beaumont, TX (city) Jefferson County	501	0.44
Jennings, LA (city) Jefferson Davis Parish	484	4.36
Raceland, LA (cdp) Lafourche Parish	483	4.66
Cut Off, LA (cdp) Lafourche Parish	469	8.41
Scott, LA (city) Lafayette Parish	455	5.86
Houma, LA (city) Terrebonne Parish	443	1.38
Bayou Cane, LA (cdp) Terrebonne Parish	418	2.48
Port Arthur, TX (city) Jefferson County	409	0.71
New York, NY (city) New York City	382	0.00
Opelousas, LA (city) Saint Landry Parish	354	1.54
San Antonio, TX (city) Bexar County	337	0.03
Lake Arthur, LA (town) Jefferson Davis Parish	330	11.16
Morgan City, LA (city) Saint Mary Parish	330	2.53
Galliano, LA (cdp) Lafourche Parish	294	4.00
Westlake, LA (city) Calcasieu Parish	292	6.39
Eunice, LA (city) Saint Landry Parish	287	2.52
Pierre Part, LA (cdp) Assumption Parish	286	8.70
Nederland, TX (city) Jefferson County	286	1.65
Lockport, LA (town) Lafourche Parish	272	10.34
Estherwood, LA (village) Acadia Parish	261	31.41
Rayne, LA (city) Acadia Parish	252	2.97
Port Neches, TX (city) Jefferson County	244	1.80
Los Angeles, CA (city) Los Angeles County	238	0.01
Orange, TX (city) Orange County	235	1.27
Dallas, TX (city) Dallas County	221	0.02
Shreveport, LA (city) Caddo Parish	217	0.11
Breaux Bridge, LA (city) Saint Martin Parish	198	2.76
Youngsville, LA (town) Lafayette Parish	192	4.96
Westwego, LA (city) Jefferson Parish	192	1.77
Carlyss, LA (cdp) Calcasieu Parish	191	4.66
Fort Worth, TX (city) Tarrant County	191	0.04
Groves, TX (city) Jefferson County	187	1.18
Nashville-Davidson, TN (special city) Davidson County	185	0.03
Phoenix, AZ (city) Maricopa County	183	0.01
Jacksonville, FL (special city) Duval County	179	0.02
San Diego, CA (city) San Diego County	178	0.01
San Francisco, CA (city) San Francisco County	176	0.02
Bayou Vista, LA (cdp) Saint Mary Parish	175	4.36
Church Point, LA (town) Acadia Parish	167	3.62
Franklin, LA (city) Saint Mary Parish	165	1.94
Broussard, LA (town) Lafayette Parish	159	2.67
Cameron, LA (cdp) Cameron Parish	156	7.92
Kenner, LA (city) Jefferson Parish	156	0.22
Schriever, LA (cdp) Terrebonne Parish	153	2.59
Vidor, TX (city) Orange County	152	1.34
Marrero, LA (cdp) Jefferson Parish	147	0.41
Prien, LA (cdp) Calcasieu Parish	146	2.07
Bridge City, TX (city) Orange County	146	1.71
Baytown, TX (city) Harris County	144	0.22
Chackbay, LA (cdp) Lafourche Parish	140	3.56
Thibodaux, LA (city) Lafourche Parish	140	0.98
Alexandria, LA (city) Rapides Parish	140	0.30
Plano, TX (city) Collin County	139	0.06
Kaplan, LA (city) Vermilion Parish	136	2.65
Vinton, LA (town) Calcasieu Parish	130	3.89
Mathews, LA (cdp) Lafourche Parish	128	6.75
Jackson, MS (city) Hinds County	128	0.07
Jeanerette, LA (city) Iberia Parish	125	2.06
Harvey, LA (cdp) Jefferson Parish	125	0.56
Virginia Beach, VA (independent city) Virginia Beach city	121	0.03
Hammond, LA (city) Tangipahoa Parish	120	0.68
River Ridge, LA (cdp) Jefferson Parish	119	0.82
League City, TX (city) Galveston County	118	0.26
Welsh, LA (town) Jefferson Davis Parish	117	3.46
Harahan, LA (city) Jefferson Parish	117	1.19
Laplace, LA (cdp) Saint John the Baptist Parish	117	0.43
Biloxi, MS (city) Harrison County	117	0.23
Madawaska, ME (town) Aroostook County	115	2.54
De Ridder, LA (city) Beauregard Parish	115	1.18
Monroe, LA (city) Ouachita Parish	114	0.21
Chalmette, LA (cdp) Saint Bernard Parish	110	0.34
Oklahoma City, OK (city) Oklahoma County	110	0.02
Denham Springs, LA (city) Livingston Parish	109	1.26
Moss Bluff, LA (cdp) Calcasieu Parish	108	1.03
Gulfport, MS (city) Harrison County	108	0.15
Corpus Christi, TX (city) Nueces County	107	0.04
Pasadena, TX (city) Harris County	102	0.07
Erath, LA (town) Vermilion Parish	101	4.57
Montegut, LA (cdp) Terrebonne Parish	98	5.73
Central Gardens, TX (cdp) Jefferson County	97	2.31
Anchorage, AK (municipality) Anchorage Borough	97	0.04
Arnaudville, LA (town) Saint Landry Parish	96	6.89
Duson, LA (town) Lafayette Parish	95	5.67
Delcambre, LA (town) Vermilion Parish	94	4.38
Destrehan, LA (cdp) Saint Charles Parish	94	0.84
West Orange, TX (city) Orange County	93	2.22
Golden Meadow, LA (town) Lafourche Parish	92	4.31
Bunkie, LA (city) Avoyelles Parish	91	1.88
Natchitoches, LA (city) Natchitoches Parish	91	0.51
Port Barre, LA (town) Saint Landry Parish	90	3.90
Atlanta, GA (city) Fulton County	90	0.02
Patterson, LA (city) Saint Mary Parish	89	1.73
Marksville, LA (city) Avoyelles Parish	89	1.61
Bossier City, LA (city) Bossier Parish	88	0.16
Norfolk, VA (independent city) Norfolk city	88	0.04
Tulsa, OK (city) Tulsa County	88	0.02
Mandeville, LA (city) Saint Tammany Parish	87	0.81
Mermentau, LA (village) Acadia Parish	85	11.99
Seattle, WA (city) King County	84	0.01
Saint Martinville, LA (city) Saint Martin Parish	83	1.20
Gretna, LA (city) Jefferson Parish	83	0.48
Abilene, TX (city) Taylor County	83	0.07
Waggaman, LA (cdp) Jefferson Parish	82	0.87
Portland, OR (city) Multnomah County	82	0.02
Gonzales, LA (city) Ascension Parish	81	1.00
Denver, CO (city) Denver County	81	0.01
Channelview, TX (cdp) Harris County	80	0.27
Jacksonville, NC (city) Onslow County	80	0.12
College Station, TX (city) Brazos County	78	0.11
Washington, DC (city) District of Columbia	78	0.01
Rockwall, TX (city) Rockwall County	77	0.42
Slidell, LA (city) Saint Tammany Parish	76	0.30
Sherman, TX (city) Grayson County	76	0.22
Memphis, TN (city) Shelby County	76	0.01
Berwick, LA (town) Saint Mary Parish	75	1.70
Old Jefferson, LA (cdp) East Baton Rouge Parish	75	1.33
La Porte, TX (city) Harris County	75	0.24
Grand Prairie, TX (city) Dallas County	75	0.06
Arlington, TX (city) Tarrant County	74	0.02
Saint Paul, MN (city) Ramsey County	73	0.03
Colorado Springs, CO (city) El Paso County	72	0.02
Sierra Vista, AZ (city) Cochise County	71	0.19
Rowlett, TX (city) Dallas County	71	0.16
El Paso, TX (city) El Paso County	71	0.01
Mamou, LA (town) Evangeline Parish	70	1.96
Bay Saint Louis, MS (city) Hancock County	70	0.84
Lewisville, TX (city) Denton County	70	0.09
Tyler, TX (city) Smith County	70	0.08
Tallahassee, FL (city) Leon County	70	0.05
Shenandoah, LA (cdp) East Baton Rouge Parish	69	0.40
Conroe, TX (city) Montgomery County	69	0.19
Milwaukee, WI (city) Milwaukee County	69	0.01
Chicago, IL (city) Cook County	68	0.00
Terrytown, LA (cdp) Jefferson Parish	67	0.26
Euless, TX (city) Tarrant County	66	0.14
Carencro, LA (city) Lafayette Parish	64	1.07
Luling, LA (cdp) Saint Charles Parish	64	0.55
Pineville, LA (city) Rapides Parish	64	0.46

Notes: (cdp) census designated place; Refer to the Explanation of Data in the front of the book for more detailed information.

Acadian/Cajun

Top 150 Places Sorted by Percent

(Based on all places, regardless of population)

Place	Number	%
Estherwood, LA (village) Acadia Parish	261	31.41
Mermentau, LA (village) Acadia Parish	85	11.99
Lake Arthur, LA (town) Jefferson Davis Parish	330	11.16
Larose, LA (cdp) Lafourche Parish	759	10.49
Lockport, LA (town) Lafourche Parish	272	10.34
Pierre Part, LA (cdp) Assumption Parish	286	8.70
Cut Off, LA (cdp) Lafourche Parish	469	8.41
Cameron, LA (cdp) Cameron Parish	156	7.92
Westport, OK (town) Pawnee County	23	7.64
Arnaudville, LA (town) Saint Landry Parish	96	6.89
Mathews, LA (cdp) Lafourche Parish	128	6.75
Morse, LA (village) Acadia Parish	49	6.41
Westlake, LA (city) Calcasieu Parish	292	6.39
Scott, LA (city) Lafayette Parish	455	5.86
Leonville, LA (town) Saint Landry Parish	57	5.83
Fordoche, LA (town) Pointe Coupee Parish	56	5.83
Montegut, LA (cdp) Terrebonne Parish	98	5.73
Duson, LA (town) Lafayette Parish	95	5.67
Abbeville, LA (city) Vermilion Parish	615	5.15
Youngsville, LA (town) Lafayette Parish	192	4.96
Raceland, LA (cdp) Lafourche Parish	483	4.66
Carlyss, LA (cdp) Calcasieu Parish	191	4.66
Hillrose, CO (town) Morgan County	12	4.58
Erath, LA (town) Vermilion Parish	101	4.57
Cankton, LA (village) Saint Landry Parish	17	4.42
Delcambre, LA (town) Vermilion Parish	94	4.38
Jennings, LA (city) Jefferson Davis Parish	484	4.36
Bayou Vista, LA (cdp) Saint Mary Parish	175	4.36
Golden Meadow, LA (town) Lafourche Parish	92	4.31
Henderson, LA (town) Saint Martin Parish	63	4.09
Crowley, LA (city) Acadia Parish	581	4.07
Galliano, LA (cdp) Lafourche Parish	294	4.00
Frenchville, ME (town) Aroostook County	48	3.93
Port Barre, LA (town) Saint Landry Parish	90	3.90
Vinton, LA (town) Calcasieu Parish	130	3.89
Maurice, LA (village) Vermilion Parish	24	3.80
Zinc, AR (town) Boone County	3	3.70
Stowell, TX (cdp) Chambers County	58	3.65
Church Point, LA (town) Acadia Parish	167	3.62
Hardin, TX (city) Liberty County	29	3.62
Plaucheville, LA (village) Avoyelles Parish	11	3.59
Chackbay, LA (cdp) Lafourche Parish	140	3.56
Gueydan, LA (town) Vermilion Parish	56	3.53
Welsh, LA (town) Jefferson Davis Parish	117	3.46
Mapleton, KS (city) Bourbon County	4	3.45
East Thermopolis, WY (town) Hot Springs County	10	3.42
New Canada, ME (town) Aroostook County	10	3.19
Hackberry, LA (cdp) Cameron Parish	52	3.17
Etowah, AR (town) Mississippi County	11	3.13
Sulphur, LA (city) Calcasieu Parish	626	3.07
Parks, LA (village) Saint Martin Parish	17	3.04
Rayne, LA (city) Acadia Parish	252	2.97
Iota, LA (town) Acadia Parish	40	2.97
Pine Prairie, LA (village) Evangeline Parish	27	2.95
Moffat, CO (town) Saguache County	3	2.80
Breaux Bridge, LA (city) Saint Martin Parish	198	2.76
Jean Lafitte, LA (town) Jefferson Parish	59	2.76
Montz, LA (cdp) Saint Charles Parish	31	2.75
Zuehl, TX (cdp) Guadalupe County	7	2.75
Broussard, LA (town) Lafayette Parish	159	2.67
Kaplan, LA (city) Vermilion Parish	136	2.65
Pinehurst, TX (city) Orange County	62	2.61
Chenega, AK (cdp) Valdez-Cordova Census Area	2	2.60
Schriever, LA (cdp) Terrebonne Parish	153	2.59
Elton, LA (town) Jefferson Davis Parish	32	2.59
Madawaska, ME (town) Aroostook County	115	2.54
Morgan City, LA (city) Saint Mary Parish	330	2.53
Eunice, LA (city) Saint Landry Parish	287	2.52
Clio, IA (city) Wayne County	2	2.50
Labadieville, LA (cdp) Assumption Parish	45	2.49
Bayou Cane, LA (cdp) Terrebonne Parish	418	2.48
Eagle Lake, ME (town) Aroostook County	20	2.46
Talty, TX (city) Kaufman County	20	2.45
Oberlin, LA (town) Allen Parish	45	2.42
China, TX (city) Jefferson County	27	2.37
Lafayette, LA (city) Lafayette Parish	2,598	2.36
Albany, LA (village) Livingston Parish	20	2.33
Central Gardens, TX (cdp) Jefferson County	97	2.31
West Orange, TX (city) Orange County	93	2.22
Dulac, LA (cdp) Terrebonne Parish	55	2.15
Krotz Springs, LA (town) Saint Landry Parish	26	2.13
Reeves, LA (village) Allen Parish	4	2.09
Prien, LA (cdp) Calcasieu Parish	146	2.07
Jeanerette, LA (city) Iberia Parish	125	2.06
Latexo, TX (city) Houston County	6	2.02
Mamou, LA (town) Evangeline Parish	70	1.96
Westminster, LA (cdp) East Baton Rouge Parish	53	1.95
Franklin, LA (city) Saint Mary Parish	165	1.94
Livonia, LA (town) Pointe Coupee Parish	26	1.94
Greenville, IN (town) Floyd County	12	1.94
Matchwood, MI (township) Ontonagon County	2	1.94
New Iberia, LA (city) Iberia Parish	627	1.92
Des Allemands, LA (cdp) Saint Charles Parish	45	1.91
Bunkie, LA (city) Avoyelles Parish	91	1.88
Iowa, LA (town) Calcasieu Parish	48	1.81
Port Neches, TX (city) Jefferson County	244	1.80
Paradis, LA (cdp) Saint Charles Parish	25	1.79
Westwego, LA (city) Jefferson Parish	192	1.77
Circle D-KC Estates, TX (cdp) Bastrop County	36	1.76
Table Rock, MO (village) Taney County	4	1.75
Patterson, LA (city) Saint Mary Parish	89	1.73
Chauvin, LA (cdp) Terrebonne Parish	53	1.72
Bridge City, TX (city) Orange County	146	1.71
Boothville-Venice, LA (cdp) Plaquemines Parish	37	1.71
Berwick, LA (town) Saint Mary Parish	75	1.70
Lowndesboro, AL (town) Lowndes County	3	1.70
Charenton, LA (cdp) Saint Mary Parish	31	1.69
Morganza, LA (village) Pointe Coupee Parish	11	1.69
Black Springs, AR (town) Montgomery County	2	1.69
Delight, AR (city) Pike County	5	1.67
Hysham, MT (town) Treasure County	6	1.66
Nederland, TX (city) Jefferson County	286	1.65
Maple Hill, KS (city) Wabaunsee County	8	1.65
Wallagrass, ME (town) Aroostook County	9	1.62
Marksville, LA (city) Avoyelles Parish	89	1.61
Winnie, TX (cdp) Chambers County	47	1.61
Linwood, NE (village) Butler County	2	1.59
Feeley, MN (township) Itasca County	5	1.58
Rodessa, LA (village) Caddo Parish	5	1.58
Opelousas, LA (city) Saint Landry Parish	354	1.54
Pollock, LA (town) Grant Parish	6	1.54
Buchanan, GA (city) Haralson County	14	1.53
Melville, LA (town) Saint Landry Parish	21	1.52
Gramercy, LA (town) Saint James Parish	46	1.50
Ewing, NE (village) Holt County	6	1.49
Happy Valley, AK (cdp) Kenai Peninsula Borough	7	1.47
Hendrum, MN (city) Norman County	5	1.47
Mauriceville, TX (cdp) Orange County	42	1.45
Baldwin, LA (town) Saint Mary Parish	36	1.44
Silex, MO (village) Lincoln County	3	1.44
Rose Hill Acres, TX (city) Hardin County	7	1.43
Big Water, UT (town) Kane County	6	1.43
Basile, LA (town) Evangeline Parish	24	1.42
South Vacherie, LA (cdp) Saint James Parish	50	1.41
New Augusta, MS (town) Perry County	10	1.40
Houma, LA (city) Terrebonne Parish	443	1.38
Buna, TX (cdp) Jasper County	29	1.38
Simmesport, LA (town) Avoyelles Parish	30	1.37
Saint Agatha, ME (town) Aroostook County	11	1.37
Pollard, AR (town) Clay County	3	1.37
Angie, LA (village) Washington Parish	3	1.36
Asher, OK (town) Pottawatomie County	6	1.35
Vidor, TX (city) Orange County	152	1.34
Old Jefferson, LA (cdp) East Baton Rouge Parish	75	1.33
Big Sandy, TX (town) Upshur County	17	1.32
Lake Charles, LA (city) Calcasieu Parish	935	1.31
Elberta, AL (town) Baldwin County	7	1.31
Topsfield, ME (town) Washington County	3	1.29
Orange, TX (city) Orange County	235	1.27
Munford, TN (town) Tipton County	61	1.27

Notes: (cdp) census designated place; Refer to the Explanation of Data in the front of the book for more detailed information.

Acadian/Cajun

Top 150 Places Sorted by Percent

(Based on places with populations of 10,000 or more)

Place	Number	%
Abbeville, LA (city) Vermilion Parish	615	5.15
Raceland, LA (cdp) Lafourche Parish	483	4.66
Jennings, LA (city) Jefferson Davis Parish	484	4.36
Crowley, LA (city) Acadia Parish	581	4.07
Sulphur, LA (city) Calcasieu Parish	626	3.07
Morgan City, LA (city) Saint Mary Parish	330	2.53
Eunice, LA (city) Saint Landry Parish	287	2.52
Bayou Cane, LA (cdp) Terrebonne Parish	418	2.48
Lafayette, LA (city) Lafayette Parish	2,598	2.36
New Iberia, LA (city) Iberia Parish	627	1.92
Port Neches, TX (city) Jefferson County	244	1.80
Westwego, LA (city) Jefferson Parish	192	1.77
Nederland, TX (city) Jefferson County	286	1.65
Opelousas, LA (city) Saint Landry Parish	354	1.54
Houma, LA (city) Terrebonne Parish	443	1.38
Vidor, TX (city) Orange County	152	1.34
Lake Charles, LA (city) Calcasieu Parish	935	1.31
Orange, TX (city) Orange County	235	1.27
Groves, TX (city) Jefferson County	187	1.18
Moss Bluff, LA (cdp) Calcasieu Parish	108	1.03
Thibodaux, LA (city) Lafourche Parish	140	0.98
Destrehan, LA (cdp) Saint Charles Parish	94	0.84
River Ridge, LA (cdp) Jefferson Parish	119	0.82
Mandeville, LA (city) Saint Tammany Parish	87	0.81
Port Arthur, TX (city) Jefferson County	409	0.71
Hammond, LA (city) Tangipahoa Parish	120	0.68
Harvey, LA (cdp) Jefferson Parish	125	0.56
Luling, LA (cdp) Saint Charles Parish	64	0.55
Natchitoches, LA (city) Natchitoches Parish	91	0.51
Gretna, LA (city) Jefferson Parish	83	0.48
Jefferson, LA (cdp) Jefferson Parish	56	0.47
Pineville, LA (city) Rapides Parish	64	0.46
Beaumont, TX (city) Jefferson County	501	0.44
Laplace, LA (cdp) Saint John the Baptist Parish	117	0.43
Rockwall, TX (city) Rockwall County	77	0.42
Metairie, LA (cdp) Jefferson Parish	600	0.41
Marrero, LA (cdp) Jefferson Parish	147	0.41
Clute, TX (city) Brazoria County	42	0.41
Shenandoah, LA (cdp) East Baton Rouge Parish	69	0.40
Baton Rouge, LA (city) East Baton Rouge Parish	868	0.38
Jollyville, TX (cdp) Williamson County	58	0.38
Freeport, TX (city) Brazoria County	45	0.35
Zachary, LA (city) East Baton Rouge Parish	40	0.35
Chalmette, LA (cdp) Saint Bernard Parish	110	0.34
Laurel, MS (city) Jones County	63	0.34
Garden City, GA (city) Chatham County	38	0.34
Alexandria, LA (city) Rapides Parish	140	0.30
Slidell, LA (city) Saint Tammany Parish	76	0.30
Bastrop, LA (city) Morehouse Parish	40	0.30
San Anselmo, CA (town) Marin County	38	0.30
Tanque Verde, AZ (cdp) Pima County	48	0.29
Angleton, TX (city) Brazoria County	52	0.28
Harker Heights, TX (city) Bell County	49	0.28
Channelview, TX (cdp) Harris County	80	0.27
League City, TX (city) Galveston County	118	0.26
Terrytown, LA (cdp) Jefferson Parish	67	0.26
Gautier, MS (city) Jackson County	31	0.26
Gonzalez, FL (cdp) Escambia County	30	0.26
Timberlane, LA (cdp) Jefferson Parish	30	0.26
Alvin, TX (city) Brazoria County	54	0.25
Long Beach, MS (city) Harrison County	45	0.25
La Porte, TX (city) Harris County	75	0.24
Southlake, TX (city) Tarrant County	51	0.24
Burleson, TX (city) Johnson County	50	0.24
Estelle, LA (cdp) Jefferson Parish	39	0.24
Loveland, OH (city) Hamilton County	29	0.24
Meraux, LA (cdp) Saint Bernard Parish	25	0.24
Biloxi, MS (city) Harrison County	117	0.23
Rockledge, FL (city) Brevard County	47	0.23
Woodmere, LA (cdp) Jefferson Parish	30	0.23
Forestdale, AL (cdp) Jefferson County	24	0.23
Kenner, LA (city) Jefferson Parish	156	0.22
Baytown, TX (city) Harris County	144	0.22
Sherman, TX (city) Grayson County	76	0.22
Colleyville, TX (city) Tarrant County	44	0.22

Place	Number	%
Monroe, LA (city) Ouachita Parish	114	0.21
Ruston, LA (city) Lincoln Parish	43	0.21
Cedar Park, TX (city) Williamson County	51	0.20
Bellview, FL (cdp) Escambia County	42	0.20
Wade Hampton, SC (cdp) Greenville County	40	0.20
Palm Valley, FL (cdp) Saint Johns County	39	0.20
Middletown, RI (town) Newport County	34	0.20
Canyon Lake, TX (cdp) Comal County	33	0.20
Fort Leonard Wood, MO (cdp) Pulaski County	28	0.20
Effingham, IL (city) Effingham County	25	0.20
El Campo, TX (city) Wharton County	22	0.20
Sierra Vista, AZ (city) Cochise County	71	0.19
Conroe, TX (city) Montgomery County	69	0.19
Lackawanna, NY (city) Erie County	37	0.19
Piney Green, NC (cdp) Onslow County	22	0.19
Marshall, TX (city) Harrison County	42	0.18
Eufaula, AL (city) Barbour County	25	0.18
Katy, TX (city) Harris County	21	0.18
Niceville, FL (city) Okaloosa County	21	0.18
New Orleans, LA (city) Orleans Parish	826	0.17
Lake Jackson, TX (city) Brazoria County	46	0.17
Bay City, TX (city) Matagorda County	32	0.17
Mustang, OK (city) Canadian County	22	0.17
Pasadena, MD (cdp) Anne Arundel County	21	0.17
Chatham, NJ (township) Morris County	17	0.17
Bossier City, LA (city) Bossier Parish	88	0.16
Rowlett, TX (city) Dallas County	71	0.16
Spring, TX (cdp) Harris County	58	0.16
Essex, VT (town) Chittenden County	29	0.16
Ocean Springs, MS (city) Jackson County	28	0.16
Wilton Manors, FL (city) Broward County	20	0.16
Poquoson, VA (independent city) Poquoson city	19	0.16
Doraville, GA (city) De Kalb County	16	0.16
Gulfport, MS (city) Harrison County	108	0.15
Frisco, TX (city) Collin County	50	0.15
Carbondale, IL (city) Jackson County	31	0.15
Palestine, TX (city) Anderson County	27	0.15
Windham, ME (town) Cumberland County	23	0.15
Callaway, FL (city) Bay County	21	0.15
Euless, TX (city) Tarrant County	66	0.14
Hickory, NC (city) Catawba County	51	0.14
Atascocita, TX (cdp) Harris County	49	0.14
Peachtree City, GA (city) Fayette County	45	0.14
El Dorado, AR (city) Union County	29	0.14
Greensburg, PA (city) Westmoreland County	23	0.14
South Houston, TX (city) Harris County	22	0.14
Hollins, VA (cdp) Roanoke County	20	0.14
Destin, FL (city) Okaloosa County	16	0.14
Wells Branch, TX (cdp) Travis County	16	0.14
Sierra Madre, CA (city) Los Angeles County	15	0.14
Swansea, IL (village) Saint Clair County	15	0.14
Gardner, MA (city) Worcester County	27	0.13
Mountlake Terrace, WA (city) Snohomish County	27	0.13
El Segundo, CA (city) Los Angeles County	21	0.13
Brushy Creek, TX (cdp) Williamson County	20	0.13
Cayce, SC (city) Lexington County	16	0.13
Marysville, CA (city) Yuba County	16	0.13
Siloam Springs, AR (city) Benton County	14	0.13
South Miami, FL (city) Miami-Dade County	14	0.13
Mayfield, KY (city) Graves County	13	0.13
Jacksonville, NC (city) Onslow County	80	0.12
Casselberry, FL (city) Seminole County	27	0.12
Starkville, MS (city) Oktibbeha County	26	0.12
Independence, KY (city) Kenton County	18	0.12
Warrington, FL (cdp) Escambia County	18	0.12
Ferguson, PA (township) Centre County	17	0.12
Minden, LA (city) Webster Parish	16	0.12
Pecan Grove, TX (cdp) Fort Bend County	16	0.12
Fort Carson, CO (cdp) El Paso County	13	0.12
Shreveport, LA (city) Caddo Parish	217	0.11
College Station, TX (city) Brazos County	78	0.11
Midwest City, OK (city) Oklahoma County	57	0.11
Auburn, AL (city) Lee County	48	0.11
Lompoc, CA (city) Santa Barbara County	44	0.11
Wheat Ridge, CO (city) Jefferson County	37	0.11

Notes: (cdp) census designated place; Refer to the Explanation of Data in the front of the book for more detailed information.

Afghan

Top 150 Places Sorted by Number

(Based on all places, regardless of population)

Place	Number	%
New York, NY (city) New York City	5,446	0.07
Fremont, CA (city) Alameda County	3,421	1.68
Los Angeles, CA (city) Los Angeles County	2,335	0.06
Concord, CA (city) Contra Costa County	1,863	1.53
San Diego, CA (city) San Diego County	1,773	0.14
Irvine, CA (city) Orange County	1,231	0.86
Hayward, CA (city) Alameda County	1,171	0.84
Union City, CA (city) Alameda County	955	1.43
Alameda, CA (city) Alameda County	754	1.04
Alexandria, VA (independent city) Alexandria city	718	0.56
Springfield, VA (cdp) Fairfax County	708	2.34
Newark, CA (city) Alameda County	596	1.40
San Jose, CA (city) Santa Clara County	566	0.06
Burke, VA (cdp) Fairfax County	562	0.97
West Springfield, VA (cdp) Fairfax County	456	1.59
Simi Valley, CA (city) Ventura County	432	0.39
Chicago, IL (city) Cook County	381	0.01
Oyster Bay, NY (town) Nassau County	374	0.13
Centreville, VA (cdp) Fairfax County	366	0.75
Parsippany-Troy Hills, NJ (township) Morris County	361	0.71
Livermore, CA (city) Alameda County	336	0.46
Phoenix, AZ (city) Maricopa County	335	0.03
Schenectady, NY (city) Schenectady County	298	0.48
Annandale, VA (cdp) Fairfax County	294	0.53
Huntington, NY (town) Suffolk County	285	0.15
Reston, VA (cdp) Fairfax County	283	0.50
Mission Viejo, CA (city) Orange County	275	0.30
Sacramento, CA (city) Sacramento County	269	0.07
Omaha, NE (city) Douglas County	257	0.07
Saint Louis, MO (independent city) Saint Louis city	235	0.07
Castro Valley, CA (cdp) Alameda County	234	0.41
Anaheim, CA (city) Orange County	234	0.07
Hempstead, NY (town) Nassau County	223	0.03
Bostonia, CA (cdp) San Diego County	218	1.47
Orange, CA (city) Orange County	218	0.17
Newington, VA (cdp) Fairfax County	216	1.10
Hicksville, NY (cdp) Nassau County	213	0.52
Jacksonville, FL (special city) Duval County	205	0.03
Philadelphia, PA (city) Philadelphia County	201	0.01
Garden Grove, CA (city) Orange County	200	0.12
Nashville-Davidson, TN (special city) Davidson County	199	0.04
Franconia, VA (cdp) Fairfax County	194	0.61
Chantilly, VA (cdp) Fairfax County	188	0.46
Tracy, CA (city) San Joaquin County	182	0.32
Huntington Station, NY (cdp) Suffolk County	181	0.60
West Sacramento, CA (city) Yolo County	178	0.56
Laguna Niguel, CA (city) Orange County	178	0.29
Herndon, VA (town) Fairfax County	177	0.82
Antioch, CA (city) Contra Costa County	174	0.19
Walnut Creek, CA (city) Contra Costa County	172	0.27
Arlington, VA (cdp) Arlington County	165	0.09
Newark, NJ (city) Essex County	162	0.06
Lincolnia, VA (cdp) Fairfax County	161	1.01
Rancho Cucamonga, CA (city) San Bernardino County	159	0.12
Oakland, CA (city) Alameda County	159	0.04
Thousand Oaks, CA (city) Ventura County	157	0.13
Lake Forest, CA (city) Orange County	153	0.26
Raleigh, NC (city) Wake County	152	0.05
Colonie, NY (town) Albany County	148	0.19
Richardson, TX (city) Dallas County	146	0.16
Moreno Valley, CA (city) Riverside County	141	0.10
Redondo Beach, CA (city) Los Angeles County	140	0.22
La Mesa, CA (city) San Diego County	139	0.25
Glendale, CA (city) Los Angeles County	138	0.07
Plano, TX (city) Collin County	132	0.06
Rose Hill, VA (cdp) Fairfax County	131	0.88
Bailey's Crossroads, VA (cdp) Fairfax County	129	0.56
Portland, ME (city) Cumberland County	129	0.20
Aliso Viejo, CA (cdp) Orange County	125	0.31
Sunrise Manor, NV (cdp) Clark County	125	0.08
Islip, NY (town) Suffolk County	125	0.04
Westminster, CO (city) Adams County	124	0.12
Columbia, MD (cdp) Howard County	122	0.14
Oakton, VA (cdp) Fairfax County	121	0.41
Idylwood, VA (cdp) Fairfax County	118	0.73
Oceanside, CA (city) San Diego County	114	0.07
Martinez, CA (city) Contra Costa County	113	0.31
Novato, CA (city) Marin County	113	0.24
Smithtown, NY (town) Suffolk County	112	0.10
Frederick, MD (city) Frederick County	110	0.21
Santa Ana, CA (city) Orange County	110	0.03
Bloomington, IN (city) Monroe County	107	0.15
Lincoln, NE (city) Lancaster County	107	0.05
Bay Point, CA (cdp) Contra Costa County	106	0.49
Rosemead, CA (city) Los Angeles County	104	0.20
Dale City, VA (cdp) Prince William County	104	0.19
Milpitas, CA (city) Santa Clara County	104	0.17
Lemon Grove, CA (city) San Diego County	101	0.40
Fair Oaks, CA (cdp) Sacramento County	101	0.36
Temecula, CA (city) Riverside County	101	0.18
Brookhaven, NY (town) Suffolk County	101	0.02
Shoreline, WA (city) King County	100	0.19
Dublin, CA (city) Alameda County	98	0.33
Montgomery Village, MD (cdp) Montgomery County	98	0.26
Davis, CA (city) Yolo County	98	0.16
Babylon, NY (town) Suffolk County	98	0.05
Irving, TX (city) Dallas County	98	0.05
Columbus, OH (city) Franklin County	98	0.01
Harrisonburg, VA (independent city) Harrisonburg city	97	0.24
Huntington Beach, CA (city) Orange County	97	0.05
Aspen Hill, MD (cdp) Montgomery County	95	0.19
Santa Rosa, CA (city) Sonoma County	94	0.06
Las Vegas, NV (city) Clark County	91	0.02
Clinton, CT (town) Middlesex County	90	0.69
Ocean, NJ (township) Monmouth County	90	0.33
Germantown, MD (cdp) Montgomery County	90	0.16
Laguna, CA (cdp) Sacramento County	89	0.26
Spring Valley, NV (cdp) Clark County	87	0.07
Fresno, CA (city) Fresno County	87	0.02
San Francisco, CA (city) San Francisco County	87	0.01
Kings Park, NY (cdp) Suffolk County	86	0.53
Columbia Heights, MN (city) Anoka County	86	0.46
Reading, PA (city) Berks County	85	0.10
Woodbridge, VA (cdp) Prince William County	83	0.26
Dallas, TX (city) Dallas County	83	0.01
Jersey City, NJ (city) Hudson County	82	0.03
Albuquerque, NM (city) Bernalillo County	82	0.02
Torrance, CA (city) Los Angeles County	81	0.06
Rosemont, CA (cdp) Sacramento County	79	0.35
Rancho Santa Margarita, CA (city) Orange County	78	0.16
Lakewood, CA (city) Los Angeles County	78	0.10
Portland, OR (city) Multnomah County	78	0.01
Suisun City, CA (city) Solano County	76	0.29
Cottonwood Heights, UT (cdp) Salt Lake County	76	0.28
Lodi, CA (city) San Joaquin County	76	0.13
Aurora, CO (city) Arapahoe County	76	0.03
Olathe, KS (city) Johnson County	73	0.08
Melville, NY (cdp) Suffolk County	70	0.48
Cerritos, CA (city) Los Angeles County	69	0.13
Rialto, CA (city) San Bernardino County	69	0.08
North Hempstead, NY (town) Nassau County	69	0.03
Richmond, VA (independent city) Richmond city	69	0.03
Plainedge, NY (cdp) Nassau County	68	0.74
El Sobrante, CA (cdp) Contra Costa County	68	0.59
Pittsburg, CA (city) Contra Costa County	68	0.12
Haverstraw, NY (town) Rockland County	67	0.20
Bellevue, WA (city) King County	67	0.06
Salt Lake City, UT (city) Salt Lake County	67	0.04
Long Beach, CA (city) Los Angeles County	67	0.01
Montville, NJ (township) Morris County	65	0.31
South Laurel, MD (cdp) Prince George's County	65	0.31
Sunnyvale, CA (city) Santa Clara County	65	0.05
San Marcos, CA (city) San Diego County	64	0.12
Woodbridge, NJ (township) Middlesex County	64	0.07
West Haverstraw, NY (village) Rockland County	62	0.60
Thornton, CO (city) Adams County	62	0.08
Overland Park, KS (city) Johnson County	62	0.04
Detroit, MI (city) Wayne County	62	0.01
Upland, CA (city) San Bernardino County	61	0.09
Brentwood, NY (cdp) Suffolk County	60	0.11

Notes: (cdp) census designated place; Refer to the Explanation of Data in the front of the book for more detailed information.

Afghan

Top 150 Places Sorted by Percent

(Based on all places, regardless of population)

Place	Number	%
Springfield, VA (cdp) Fairfax County	708	2.34
Fremont, CA (city) Alameda County	3,421	1.68
West Springfield, VA (cdp) Fairfax County	456	1.59
Russell Gardens, NY (village) Nassau County	17	1.58
Concord, CA (city) Contra Costa County	1,863	1.53
Bostonia, CA (cdp) San Diego County	218	1.47
Union City, CA (city) Alameda County	955	1.43
Newark, CA (city) Alameda County	596	1.40
Menands, NY (village) Albany County	50	1.28
Newington, VA (cdp) Fairfax County	216	1.10
Alameda, CA (city) Alameda County	754	1.04
Lincolnia, VA (cdp) Fairfax County	161	1.01
Burke, VA (cdp) Fairfax County	562	0.97
Oregon, PA (township) Wayne County	7	0.96
Woodbury, TN (town) Cannon County	22	0.90
Rose Hill, VA (cdp) Fairfax County	131	0.88
Irvine, CA (city) Orange County	1,231	0.86
Bennington, NE (city) Douglas County	8	0.86
Hayward, CA (city) Alameda County	1,171	0.84
Maryland City, MD (cdp) Anne Arundel County	56	0.83
Herndon, VA (town) Fairfax County	177	0.82
Schlusser, PA (cdp) Cumberland County	38	0.80
Lawrenceville, NJ (cdp) Mercer County	31	0.76
Centreville, VA (cdp) Fairfax County	366	0.75
Plainedge, NY (cdp) Nassau County	68	0.74
Waldon, CA (cdp) Contra Costa County	37	0.74
Idylwood, VA (cdp) Fairfax County	118	0.73
Ocheyedan, IA (city) Osceola County	4	0.73
Parsippany-Troy Hills, NJ (township) Morris County	361	0.71
East Lansdowne, PA (borough) Delaware County	18	0.70
Clinton, CT (town) Middlesex County	90	0.69
Chester, NJ (borough) Morris County	11	0.67
East Quogue, NY (cdp) Suffolk County	28	0.66
Sudley, VA (cdp) Prince William County	52	0.65
Warrenton, VA (town) Fauquier County	42	0.64
Manhasset Hills, NY (cdp) Nassau County	23	0.63
Grifton, NC (town) Pitt County	13	0.63
Franconia, VA (cdp) Fairfax County	194	0.61
South Bristol, NY (town) Ontario County	10	0.61
Huntington Station, NY (cdp) Suffolk County	181	0.60
West Haverstraw, NY (village) Rockland County	62	0.60
El Sobrante, CA (cdp) Contra Costa County	68	0.59
Alexandria, VA (independent city) Alexandria city	718	0.56
West Sacramento, CA (city) Yolo County	178	0.56
Bailey's Crossroads, VA (cdp) Fairfax County	129	0.56
Demarest, NJ (borough) Bergen County	26	0.54
Hesston, KS (city) Harvey County	19	0.54
Annandale, VA (cdp) Fairfax County	294	0.53
Kings Park, NY (cdp) Suffolk County	86	0.53
Hicksville, NY (cdp) Nassau County	213	0.52
Reston, VA (cdp) Fairfax County	283	0.50
Bay Point, CA (cdp) Contra Costa County	106	0.49
Belle Haven, VA (cdp) Fairfax County	31	0.49
Schenectady, NY (city) Schenectady County	298	0.48
Melville, NY (cdp) Suffolk County	70	0.48
Clayton, CA (city) Contra Costa County	52	0.48
Ann Arbor, MI (township) Washtenaw County	23	0.48
Livermore, CA (city) Alameda County	336	0.46
Chantilly, VA (cdp) Fairfax County	188	0.46
Columbia Heights, MN (city) Anoka County	86	0.46
Seven Corners, VA (cdp) Fairfax County	41	0.46
Merrifield, VA (cdp) Fairfax County	49	0.44
Yorkshire, VA (cdp) Prince William County	29	0.43
Bardonia, NY (cdp) Rockland County	19	0.43
Westlake Village, CA (city) Los Angeles County	36	0.42
Castro Valley, CA (cdp) Alameda County	234	0.41
Oakton, VA (cdp) Fairfax County	121	0.41
Winslow, ME (cdp) Kennebec County	32	0.41
Lemon Grove, CA (city) San Diego County	101	0.40
Coupeville, WA (town) Island County	7	0.40
Simi Valley, CA (city) Ventura County	432	0.39
Howard Lake, MN (city) Wright County	7	0.39
Hilltop, MN (city) Anoka County	3	0.39
North Springfield, VA (cdp) Fairfax County	35	0.38
Superior, CO (town) Boulder County	34	0.38
West Bountiful, UT (city) Davis County	17	0.38
Somerville, NJ (borough) Somerset County	46	0.37
North Middleton, PA (township) Cumberland County	38	0.37
Fair Oaks, CA (cdp) Sacramento County	101	0.36
Highview, KY (cdp) Jefferson County	55	0.36
South Huntington, NY (cdp) Suffolk County	34	0.36
Rosemont, CA (cdp) Sacramento County	79	0.35
Plumsted, NJ (township) Ocean County	25	0.34
Churchville, PA (cdp) Bucks County	15	0.34
Dublin, CA (city) Alameda County	98	0.33
Ocean, NJ (township) Monmouth County	90	0.33
Rossmoor, MD (cdp) Montgomery County	25	0.33
Tracy, CA (city) San Joaquin County	182	0.32
Brookside, DE (cdp) New Castle County	47	0.32
Vienna, VA (town) Fairfax County	46	0.32
Beatyestown, NJ (cdp) Warren County	10	0.32
Lake Success, NY (village) Nassau County	9	0.32
Aliso Viejo, CA (cdp) Orange County	125	0.31
Martinez, CA (city) Contra Costa County	113	0.31
Montville, NJ (township) Morris County	65	0.31
South Laurel, MD (cdp) Prince George's County	65	0.31
Cumberland, PA (township) Adams County	18	0.31
Deer Park, IL (village) Lake County	10	0.31
Mission Viejo, CA (city) Orange County	275	0.30
Lakeside, CA (cdp) San Diego County	59	0.30
Monroe, CT (town) Fairfield County	58	0.30
La Riviera, CA (cdp) Sacramento County	31	0.30
Laguna Niguel, CA (city) Orange County	178	0.29
Suisun City, CA (city) Solano County	76	0.29
Pinole, CA (city) Contra Costa County	57	0.29
Lorton, VA (cdp) Fairfax County	51	0.29
Beckley, WV (city) Raleigh County	50	0.29
Gold River, CA (cdp) Sacramento County	24	0.29
Cottonwood Heights, UT (cdp) Salt Lake County	76	0.28
Casa de Oro-Mount Helix, CA (cdp) San Diego County	52	0.28
Walnut Creek, CA (city) Contra Costa County	172	0.27
Fairfax, VA (independent city) Fairfax city	57	0.27
Carlstadt, NJ (borough) Bergen County	16	0.27
Longview Heights, WA (cdp) Cowlitz County	9	0.27
David City, NE (city) Butler County	7	0.27
Lake Forest, CA (city) Orange County	153	0.26
Montgomery Village, MD (cdp) Montgomery County	98	0.26
Laguna, CA (cdp) Sacramento County	89	0.26
Woodbridge, VA (cdp) Prince William County	83	0.26
Wolf Trap, VA (cdp) Fairfax County	36	0.26
Marshall, MO (city) Saline County	32	0.26
La Mesa, CA (city) San Diego County	139	0.25
North Babylon, NY (cdp) Suffolk County	44	0.25
Cherryland, CA (cdp) Alameda County	35	0.25
Novato, CA (city) Marin County	113	0.24
Harrisonburg, VA (independent city) Harrisonburg city	97	0.24
South Plainfield, NJ (borough) Middlesex County	53	0.24
King of Prussia, PA (cdp) Montgomery County	44	0.24
Sunnyside, OR (cdp) Clackamas County	16	0.24
Crofton, MD (cdp) Anne Arundel County	46	0.23
Hercules, CA (city) Contra Costa County	44	0.23
Alpine, NJ (borough) Bergen County	5	0.23
Worcester, NY (town) Otsego County	5	0.23
Berkeley Lake, GA (city) Gwinnett County	4	0.23
Redondo Beach, CA (city) Los Angeles County	140	0.22
Andover, MN (city) Anoka County	59	0.22
Augusta, ME (city) Kennebec County	40	0.22
New Milford, NJ (borough) Bergen County	36	0.22
New Territory, TX (cdp) Fort Bend County	31	0.22
North Greenbush, NY (town) Rensselaer County	24	0.22
Fairview, CA (cdp) Alameda County	21	0.22
West Gate, VA (cdp) Prince William County	16	0.22
Frederick, MD (city) Frederick County	110	0.21
Plainview, NY (cdp) Nassau County	54	0.21
Avenel, NJ (cdp) Middlesex County	37	0.21
Holtsville, NY (cdp) Suffolk County	35	0.21
Secaucus, NJ (town) Hudson County	34	0.21
Rodeo, CA (cdp) Contra Costa County	18	0.21
Hodge, LA (village) Jackson Parish	1	0.21
Portland, ME (city) Cumberland County	129	0.20

Notes: (cdp) census designated place; Refer to the Explanation of Data in the front of the book for more detailed information.

Afghan

Top 150 Places Sorted by Percent

(Based on places with populations of 10,000 or more)

Place	Number	%
Springfield, VA (cdp) Fairfax County	708	2.34
Fremont, CA (city) Alameda County	3,421	1.68
West Springfield, VA (cdp) Fairfax County	456	1.59
Concord, CA (city) Contra Costa County	1,863	1.53
Bostonia, CA (cdp) San Diego County	218	1.47
Union City, CA (city) Alameda County	955	1.43
Newark, CA (city) Alameda County	596	1.40
Newington, VA (cdp) Fairfax County	216	1.10
Alameda, CA (city) Alameda County	754	1.04
Lincolnia, VA (cdp) Fairfax County	161	1.01
Burke, VA (cdp) Fairfax County	562	0.97
Rose Hill, VA (cdp) Fairfax County	131	0.88
Irvine, CA (city) Orange County	1,231	0.86
Hayward, CA (city) Alameda County	1,171	0.84
Herndon, VA (town) Fairfax County	177	0.82
Centreville, VA (cdp) Fairfax County	366	0.75
Idylwood, VA (cdp) Fairfax County	118	0.73
Parsippany-Troy Hills, NJ (township) Morris County	361	0.71
Clinton, CT (town) Middlesex County	90	0.69
Franconia, VA (cdp) Fairfax County	194	0.61
Huntington Station, NY (cdp) Suffolk County	181	0.60
West Haverstraw, NY (village) Rockland County	62	0.60
El Sobrante, CA (cdp) Contra Costa County	68	0.59
Alexandria, VA (independent city) Alexandria city	718	0.56
West Sacramento, CA (city) Yolo County	178	0.56
Bailey's Crossroads, VA (cdp) Fairfax County	129	0.56
Annandale, VA (cdp) Fairfax County	294	0.53
Kings Park, NY (cdp) Suffolk County	86	0.53
Hicksville, NY (cdp) Nassau County	213	0.52
Reston, VA (cdp) Fairfax County	283	0.50
Bay Point, CA (cdp) Contra Costa County	106	0.49
Schenectady, NY (city) Schenectady County	298	0.48
Melville, NY (cdp) Suffolk County	70	0.48
Clayton, CA (city) Contra Costa County	52	0.48
Livermore, CA (city) Alameda County	336	0.46
Chantilly, VA (cdp) Fairfax County	188	0.46
Columbia Heights, MN (city) Anoka County	86	0.46
Merrifield, VA (cdp) Fairfax County	49	0.44
Castro Valley, CA (cdp) Alameda County	234	0.41
Oakton, VA (cdp) Fairfax County	121	0.41
Lemon Grove, CA (city) San Diego County	101	0.40
Simi Valley, CA (city) Ventura County	432	0.39
Somerville, NJ (borough) Somerset County	46	0.37
North Middleton, PA (township) Cumberland County	38	0.37
Fair Oaks, CA (cdp) Sacramento County	101	0.36
Highview, KY (cdp) Jefferson County	55	0.36
Rosemont, CA (cdp) Sacramento County	79	0.35
Dublin, CA (city) Alameda County	98	0.33
Ocean, NJ (township) Monmouth County	90	0.33
Tracy, CA (city) San Joaquin County	182	0.32
Brookside, DE (cdp) New Castle County	47	0.32
Vienna, VA (town) Fairfax County	46	0.32
Aliso Viejo, CA (cdp) Orange County	125	0.31
Martinez, CA (city) Contra Costa County	113	0.31
Montville, NJ (township) Morris County	65	0.31
South Laurel, MD (cdp) Prince George's County	65	0.31
Mission Viejo, CA (city) Orange County	275	0.30
Lakeside, CA (cdp) San Diego County	59	0.30
Monroe, CT (town) Fairfield County	58	0.30
La Riviera, CA (cdp) Sacramento County	31	0.30
Laguna Niguel, CA (city) Orange County	178	0.29
Suisun City, CA (city) Solano County	76	0.29
Pinole, CA (city) Contra Costa County	57	0.29
Lorton, VA (cdp) Fairfax County	51	0.29
Beckley, WV (city) Raleigh County	50	0.29
Cottonwood Heights, UT (cdp) Salt Lake County	76	0.28
Casa de Oro-Mount Helix, CA (cdp) San Diego County	52	0.28
Walnut Creek, CA (city) Contra Costa County	172	0.27
Fairfax, VA (independent city) Fairfax city	57	0.27
Lake Forest, CA (city) Orange County	153	0.26
Montgomery Village, MD (cdp) Montgomery County	98	0.26
Laguna, CA (cdp) Sacramento County	89	0.26
Woodbridge, VA (cdp) Prince William County	83	0.26
Wolf Trap, VA (cdp) Fairfax County	36	0.26
Marshall, MO (city) Saline County	32	0.26

Place	Number	%
La Mesa, CA (city) San Diego County	139	0.25
North Babylon, NY (cdp) Suffolk County	44	0.25
Cherryland, CA (cdp) Alameda County	35	0.25
Novato, CA (city) Marin County	113	0.24
Harrisonburg, VA (independent city) Harrisonburg city	97	0.24
South Plainfield, NJ (borough) Middlesex County	53	0.24
King of Prussia, PA (cdp) Montgomery County	44	0.24
Crofton, MD (cdp) Anne Arundel County	46	0.23
Hercules, CA (city) Contra Costa County	44	0.23
Redondo Beach, CA (city) Los Angeles County	140	0.22
Andover, MN (city) Anoka County	59	0.22
Augusta, ME (city) Kennebec County	40	0.22
New Milford, NJ (borough) Bergen County	36	0.22
New Territory, TX (cdp) Fort Bend County	31	0.22
North Greenbush, NY (town) Rensselaer County	24	0.22
Frederick, MD (city) Frederick County	110	0.21
Plainview, NY (cdp) Nassau County	54	0.21
Avenel, NJ (cdp) Middlesex County	37	0.21
Holtsville, NY (cdp) Suffolk County	35	0.21
Secaucus, NJ (town) Hudson County	34	0.21
Portland, ME (city) Cumberland County	129	0.20
Rosemead, CA (city) Los Angeles County	104	0.20
Haverstraw, NY (town) Rockland County	67	0.20
Franklin Square, NY (cdp) Nassau County	59	0.20
Nutley, NJ (cdp) Essex County	55	0.20
Pullman, WA (city) Whitman County	49	0.20
Hybla Valley, VA (cdp) Fairfax County	34	0.20
Antioch, CA (city) Contra Costa County	174	0.19
Colonie, NY (town) Albany County	148	0.19
Dale City, VA (cdp) Prince William County	104	0.19
Shoreline, WA (city) King County	100	0.19
Aspen Hill, MD (cdp) Montgomery County	95	0.19
Ashland, CA (cdp) Alameda County	40	0.19
Moraga, CA (town) Contra Costa County	32	0.19
Goodlettsville, TN (city) Davidson County	26	0.19
Calverton, MD (cdp) Montgomery County	24	0.19
Temecula, CA (city) Riverside County	101	0.18
Northglenn, CO (city) Adams County	57	0.18
Saugus, MA (cdp) Essex County	46	0.18
Fords, NJ (cdp) Middlesex County	27	0.18
Orange, CA (city) Orange County	218	0.17
Milpitas, CA (city) Santa Clara County	104	0.17
Leesburg, VA (town) Loudoun County	47	0.17
Champlin, MN (city) Hennepin County	38	0.17
Fountain Hills, AZ (town) Maricopa County	35	0.17
West Bradford, PA (township) Chester County	18	0.17
Richardson, TX (city) Dallas County	146	0.16
Davis, CA (city) Yolo County	98	0.16
Germantown, MD (cdp) Montgomery County	90	0.16
Rancho Santa Margarita, CA (city) Orange County	78	0.16
Lawrence, NJ (township) Mercer County	48	0.16
Upper Merion, PA (township) Montgomery County	44	0.16
Redland, MD (cdp) Montgomery County	27	0.16
La Palma, CA (city) Orange County	24	0.16
Glenn Dale, MD (cdp) Prince George's County	20	0.16
Huntington, NY (town) Suffolk County	285	0.15
Bloomington, IN (city) Monroe County	107	0.15
Marlboro, NJ (township) Monmouth County	55	0.15
Lindenhurst, NY (village) Suffolk County	41	0.15
Cockeysville, MD (cdp) Baltimore County	30	0.15
Elmwood Park, NJ (borough) Bergen County	29	0.15
North Arlington, NJ (borough) Bergen County	23	0.15
Dyer, IN (town) Lake County	21	0.15
San Diego, CA (city) San Diego County	1,773	0.14
Columbia, MD (cdp) Howard County	122	0.14
Coram, NY (cdp) Suffolk County	49	0.14
Jefferson, VA (cdp) Fairfax County	38	0.14
Colesville, MD (cdp) Montgomery County	27	0.14
Amsterdam, NY (city) Montgomery County	25	0.14
Albany, CA (city) Alameda County	23	0.14
Wilsonville, OR (city) Clackamas County	20	0.14
Oyster Bay, NY (town) Nassau County	374	0.13
Thousand Oaks, CA (city) Ventura County	157	0.13
Lodi, CA (city) San Joaquin County	76	0.13
Cerritos, CA (city) Los Angeles County	69	0.13

Notes: (cdp) census designated place; Refer to the Explanation of Data in the front of the book for more detailed information.

African American/Black

Top 150 Places Sorted by Number

(Based on all places, regardless of population)

Place	Number	%
New York, NY (city) New York City	2,274,049	28.40
Chicago, IL (city) Cook County	1,084,221	37.44
Detroit, MI (city) Wayne County	787,687	82.80
Philadelphia, PA (city) Philadelphia County	672,162	44.29
Houston, TX (city) Harris County	505,101	25.85
Los Angeles, CA (city) Los Angeles County	444,635	12.03
Baltimore, MD (independent city) Baltimore city	424,449	65.18
Memphis, TN (city) Shelby County	402,367	61.89
Washington, DC (city) District of Columbia	350,455	61.26
New Orleans, LA (city) Orleans Parish	329,171	67.92
Dallas, TX (city) Dallas County	314,678	26.48
Atlanta, GA (city) Fulton County	258,610	62.10
Cleveland, OH (city) Cuyahoga County	249,192	52.09
Milwaukee, WI (city) Milwaukee County	230,503	38.61
Jacksonville, FL (special city) Duval County	218,451	29.70
Indianapolis, IN (special city) Marion County	206,148	26.37
Columbus, OH (city) Franklin County	185,173	26.03
Saint Louis, MO (independent city) Saint Louis city	181,503	52.13
Charlotte, NC (city) Mecklenburg County	180,371	33.35
Birmingham, AL (city) Jefferson County	179,569	73.95
Boston, MA (city) Suffolk County	163,006	27.67
Newark, NJ (city) Essex County	150,384	54.98
Oakland, CA (city) Alameda County	150,139	37.58
Nashville-Davidson, TN (special city) Davidson County	149,970	27.49
Cincinnati, OH (city) Hamilton County	145,615	43.95
Kansas City, MO (city) Jackson County	142,621	32.30
Jackson, MS (city) Hinds County	131,005	71.10
Hempstead, NY (town) Nassau County	118,490	15.67
Richmond, VA (independent city) Richmond city	114,860	58.07
Baton Rouge, LA (city) East Baton Rouge Parish	114,860	50.42
Buffalo, NY (city) Erie County	112,880	38.57
Fort Worth, TX (city) Tarrant County	111,298	20.82
San Diego, CA (city) San Diego County	109,470	8.95
Norfolk, VA (independent city) Norfolk city	106,219	45.31
Shreveport, LA (city) Caddo Parish	102,526	51.23
Montgomery, AL (city) Montgomery County	100,966	50.09
Augusta-Richmond County, GA (special city) Richmond County	100,233	51.35
Pittsburgh, PA (city) Allegheny County	93,904	28.07
Mobile, AL (city) Mobile County	92,888	46.70
Rochester, NY (city) Monroe County	89,411	40.68
Miami, FL (city) Miami-Dade County	87,857	24.24
Gary, IN (city) Lake County	87,604	85.26
Louisville, KY (city) Jefferson County	86,831	33.89
Greensboro, NC (city) Guilford County	85,634	38.25
Virginia Beach, VA (independent city) Virginia Beach city	85,216	20.04
San Antonio, TX (city) Bexar County	84,250	7.36
Durham, NC (city) Durham County	83,485	44.64
Columbus, GA (special city) Muscogee County	83,134	44.75
Oklahoma City, OK (city) Oklahoma County	83,034	16.41
Tampa, FL (city) Hillsborough County	82,470	27.18
Raleigh, NC (city) Wake County	78,844	28.56
Minneapolis, MN (city) Hennepin County	78,291	20.46
Toledo, OH (city) Lucas County	77,765	24.80
Phoenix, AZ (city) Maricopa County	76,065	5.76
Savannah, GA (city) Chatham County	75,953	57.75
Little Rock, AR (city) Pulaski County	75,026	40.97
Long Beach, CA (city) Los Angeles County	73,911	16.01
Dayton, OH (city) Montgomery County	73,552	44.26
Newport News, VA (independent city) Newport News city	73,111	40.58
Jersey City, NJ (city) Hudson County	72,080	30.03
Winston-Salem, NC (city) Forsyth County	70,434	37.91
Sacramento, CA (city) Sacramento County	70,218	17.25
Austin, TX (city) Travis County	69,943	10.65
Flint, MI (city) Genesee County	69,102	55.31
Hampton, VA (independent city) Hampton city	67,446	46.06
Denver, CO (city) Denver County	67,375	12.15
San Francisco, CA (city) San Francisco County	67,076	8.64
Tulsa, OK (city) Tulsa County	64,936	16.52
East Orange, NJ (city) Essex County	64,797	92.80
Akron, OH (city) Summit County	64,530	29.73
Macon, GA (city) Bibb County	61,185	62.91
Chesapeake, VA (independent city) Chesapeake city	58,183	29.21
Saint Petersburg, FL (city) Pinellas County	57,483	23.16
Chattanooga, TN (city) Hamilton County	57,034	36.67
Seattle, WA (city) King County	55,611	9.87
Omaha, NE (city) Douglas County	55,197	14.15
Inglewood, CA (city) Los Angeles County	54,823	48.70
Columbia, SC (city) Richland County	54,256	46.66
Las Vegas, NV (city) Clark County	53,923	11.27
Fayetteville, NC (city) Cumberland County	52,999	43.80
Beaumont, TX (city) Jefferson County	52,829	46.40
Orlando, FL (city) Orange County	52,652	28.31
Tallahassee, FL (city) Leon County	52,611	34.93
Portsmouth, VA (independent city) Portsmouth city	51,767	51.48
Irvington, NJ (cdp) Essex County	51,726	85.22
Paterson, NJ (city) Passaic County	51,663	34.62
Albany, GA (city) Dougherty County	50,177	65.22
Hartford, CT (city) Hartford County	49,412	40.64
Huntsville, AL (city) Madison County	48,913	30.92
New Haven, CT (city) New Haven County	48,604	39.32
Arlington, TX (city) Tarrant County	48,196	14.47
Fort Lauderdale, FL (city) Broward County	48,033	31.52
Bridgeport, CT (city) Fairfield County	46,281	33.17
Kansas City, KS (city) Wyandotte County	45,918	31.27
Trenton, NJ (city) Mercer County	45,762	53.58
Camden, NJ (city) Camden County	44,224	55.35
Southfield, MI (city) Oakland County	43,711	55.83
Grand Rapids, MI (city) Kent County	43,463	21.97
Wichita, KS (city) Sedgwick County	42,797	12.43
Mount Vernon, NY (city) Westchester County	42,516	62.18
Wilmington, DE (city) New Castle County	41,976	57.77
Portland, OR (city) Multnomah County	41,589	7.86
Aurora, CO (city) Arapahoe County	41,519	15.02
Syracuse, NY (city) Onondaga County	40,436	27.45
North Charleston, SC (city) Charleston County	40,093	50.34
Fresno, CA (city) Fresno County	39,362	9.20
Compton, CA (city) Los Angeles County	38,509	41.19
Saint Paul, MN (city) Ramsey County	38,402	13.37
Fort Wayne, IN (city) Allen County	38,079	18.51
Richmond, CA (city) Contra Costa County	37,543	37.84
Youngstown, OH (city) Mahoning County	37,301	45.47
San Jose, CA (city) Santa Clara County	36,928	4.13
Lexington-Fayette, KY (special city) Fayette County	36,849	14.14
Pine Bluff, AR (city) Jefferson County	36,495	66.25
Lauderhill, FL (city) Broward County	35,657	61.92
Yonkers, NY (city) Westchester County	35,421	18.06
Babylon, NY (town) Suffolk County	35,262	16.65
Springfield, MA (city) Hampden County	34,863	22.92
North Miami, FL (city) Miami-Dade County	34,778	58.08
Lake Charles, LA (city) Calcasieu Parish	34,053	47.46
Miramar, FL (city) Broward County	33,627	46.23
Tuscaloosa, AL (city) Tuscaloosa County	33,580	43.10
Charleston, SC (city) Charleston County	33,268	34.42
Pontiac, MI (city) Oakland County	33,098	49.89
San Bernardino, CA (city) San Bernardino County	32,946	17.77
Monroe, LA (city) Ouachita Parish	32,622	61.43
Islip, NY (town) Suffolk County	32,429	10.05
Carol City, FL (cdp) Miami-Dade County	31,944	53.74
Lafayette, LA (city) Lafayette Parish	31,819	28.86
Suitland-Silver Hill, MD (cdp) Prince George's County	31,625	94.36
Rocky Mount, NC (city) Nash County	31,594	56.53
Killeen, TX (city) Bell County	31,408	36.14
Redan, GA (cdp) De Kalb County	31,322	92.56
East Point, GA (city) Fulton County	31,294	79.04
Oxon Hill-Glassmanor, MD (cdp) Prince George's County	31,149	88.10
East Saint Louis, IL (city) Saint Clair County	30,983	98.23
Hempstead, NY (village) Nassau County	30,923	54.68
Alexandria, VA (independent city) Alexandria city	30,769	23.99
Moreno Valley, CA (city) Riverside County	30,752	21.60
Plainfield, NJ (city) Union County	30,557	63.89
Stockton, CA (city) San Joaquin County	30,486	12.51
Vallejo, CA (city) Solano County	30,138	25.81
Providence, RI (city) Providence County	29,700	17.11
Peoria, IL (city) Peoria County	29,553	26.17
Knoxville, TN (city) Knox County	29,286	16.84
Greenville, MS (city) Washington County	29,093	69.88
Lansing, MI (city) Ingham County	29,078	24.41
Hawthorne, CA (city) Los Angeles County	28,945	34.41
Albany, NY (city) Albany County	28,638	29.94
Chester, PA (city) Delaware County	28,329	76.87

Notes: (cdp) census designated place; Refer to the Explanation of Data in the front of the book for more detailed information.

African American/Black

Top 150 Places Sorted by Percent

(Based on all places, regardless of population)

Place	Number	%
McMullen, AL (town) Pickens County	66	100.00
Birdsong, AR (town) Mississippi County	40	100.00
Falcon, MS (town) Quitman County	316	99.68
Washington Park, FL (cdp) Broward County	1,250	99.44
Brooklyn, IL (village) Saint Clair County	671	99.26
Franklin Park, FL (cdp) Broward County	933	98.94
Moore Station, TX (city) Henderson County	182	98.91
Mound Bayou, MS (city) Bolivar County	2,078	98.86
Tollette, AR (town) Howard County	320	98.77
Lincoln Heights, OH (village) Hamilton County	4,058	98.66
Mosses, AL (town) Lowndes County	1,085	98.55
Brookdale, SC (cdp) Orangeburg County	4,655	98.54
Roosevelt Gardens, FL (cdp) Broward County	1,894	98.49
Uplands Park, MO (village) Saint Louis County	453	98.48
Coahoma, MS (town) Coahoma County	320	98.46
Velda Village Hills, MO (village) Saint Louis County	1,073	98.44
West Ken-Lark, FL (cdp) Broward County	3,358	98.42
Mitchellville, AR (city) Desha County	489	98.39
Broward Estates, FL (cdp) Broward County	3,360	98.36
Hayti Heights, MO (city) Pemiscot County	758	98.31
East Saint Louis, IL (city) Saint Clair County	30,983	98.23
White Hall, AL (town) Lowndes County	996	98.22
Saint George, FL (cdp) Broward County	2,405	98.16
Grambling, LA (town) Lincoln Parish	4,598	97.98
Alorton, IL (village) Saint Clair County	2,692	97.93
Carmody Hills-Pepper Mill Village, MD (cdp) Prince George's Co.	4,698	97.85
Reed, AR (town) Desha County	269	97.82
Winstonville, MS (town) Bolivar County	312	97.81
Fayette, MS (city) Jefferson County	2,192	97.77
Metcalfe, MS (town) Washington County	1,084	97.75
Princeville, NC (town) Edgecombe County	918	97.66
Rock Island, FL (cdp) Broward County	3,000	97.53
Glenarden, MD (city) Prince George's County	6,161	97.52
Seat Pleasant, MD (city) Prince George's County	4,764	97.52
North Courtland, AL (town) Lawrence County	779	97.50
Fairmount Heights, MD (town) Prince George's County	1,469	97.41
Panthersville, GA (cdp) De Kalb County	11,474	97.31
Bunche Park, FL (cdp) Miami-Dade County	3,863	97.26
Unionville, GA (cdp) Tift County	2,015	97.16
Kinloch, MO (city) Saint Louis County	436	97.10
Jonestown, MS (town) Coahoma County	1,651	97.06
Pine Lawn, MO (city) Saint Louis County	4,077	96.98
Memphis, AL (town) Pickens County	32	96.97
Carver Ranches, FL (cdp) Broward County	4,165	96.88
Golden Heights, FL (cdp) Broward County	485	96.81
Salem, GA (cdp) Upson County	328	96.76
Velda City, MO (city) Saint Louis County	1,563	96.72
Bucksport, SC (cdp) Horry County	1,080	96.69
Harlem, FL (cdp) Hendry County	2,636	96.56
Tchula, MS (town) Holmes County	2,250	96.48
Walker Mill, MD (cdp) Prince George's County	10,709	96.44
Neylandville, TX (town) Hunt County	54	96.43
Ford Heights, IL (village) Cook County	3,332	96.41
Anthonyville, AR (town) Crittenden County	241	96.40
Wilson City, MO (village) Mississippi County	159	96.36
Renova, MS (town) Bolivar County	600	96.31
Tuskegee, AL (city) Macon County	11,402	96.25
Centreville, IL (city) Saint Clair County	5,723	96.17
Garysburg, NC (town) Northampton County	1,206	96.17
Gresham Park, GA (cdp) De Kalb County	8,859	96.14
Beulah, MS (town) Bolivar County	454	95.98
Gordonville, AL (town) Lowndes County	305	95.91
Promised Land, SC (cdp) Greenwood County	536	95.89
Lawnside, NJ (borough) Camden County	2,580	95.84
Candler-McAfee, GA (cdp) De Kalb County	27,113	95.83
Wilkinson Heights, SC (cdp) Orangeburg County	2,939	95.80
Hillsdale, MO (village) Saint Louis County	1,415	95.80
Robbins, IL (village) Cook County	6,354	95.76
Boulevard Gardens, FL (cdp) Broward County	1,352	95.55
Langston, OK (town) Logan County	1,588	95.09
East Hodge, LA (village) Jackson Parish	348	95.08
Goodlow, TX (city) Navarro County	251	95.08
North Tunica, MS (cdp) Tunica County	1,378	95.03
Arcola, MS (town) Washington County	535	95.03
Beverly Hills, MO (city) Saint Louis County	573	95.02
Jacob City, FL (city) Jackson County	267	95.02
Lincoln Park, GA (cdp) Upson County	1,066	95.01
Edgard, LA (cdp) Saint John the Baptist Parish	2,505	94.99
Haywood City, MO (village) Scott County	227	94.98
Highland Park, MI (city) Wayne County	15,903	94.97
Phillipsburg, GA (cdp) Tift County	842	94.93
Phoenix, IL (village) Cook County	2,046	94.85
Midway, FL (city) Gadsden County	1,371	94.81
Coral Hills, MD (cdp) Prince George's County	10,162	94.79
Glendora, MS (village) Tallahatchie County	270	94.74
North Lilbourn, MO (village) New Madrid County	90	94.74
East Cleveland, OH (city) Cuyahoga County	25,752	94.62
Allport, AR (town) Lonoke County	120	94.49
Hillcrest Heights, MD (cdp) Prince George's County	15,451	94.45
Silver City, NC (cdp) Hoke County	1,082	94.42
Suitland-Silver Hill, MD (cdp) Prince George's County	31,625	94.36
Midway, FL (cdp) Seminole County	1,617	94.34
Prairie View, TX (city) Waller County	4,160	94.33
Capitol Heights, MD (town) Prince George's County	3,895	94.13
Largo, MD (cdp) Prince George's County	7,913	94.11
Venice, IL (city) Madison County	2,377	94.03
Springdale, MD (cdp) Prince George's County	2,486	93.99
Friars Point, MS (town) Coahoma County	1,391	93.99
Wallace, LA (cdp) Saint John the Baptist Parish	535	93.86
Benton Harbor, MI (city) Berrien County	10,493	93.84
Emelle, AL (town) Sumter County	29	93.55
Hopkins Park, IL (village) Kankakee County	665	93.53
Colony, AL (town) Cullman County	360	93.51
Jericho, AR (town) Crittenden County	172	93.48
Greater Landover, MD (cdp) Prince George's County	21,405	93.47
College Station, AR (cdp) Pulaski County	716	93.47
Norwood Court, MO (town) Saint Louis County	991	93.40
Northwoods, MO (city) Saint Louis County	4,336	93.39
Yellow Bluff, AL (town) Wilcox County	169	93.37
Scott Lake, FL (cdp) Miami-Dade County	13,445	93.36
East Arcadia, NC (town) Bladen County	489	93.32
Crawford, MS (town) Lowndes County	611	93.28
Pagedale, MO (city) Saint Louis County	3,372	93.25
Mount Carmel, SC (cdp) McCormick County	221	93.25
Gifford, SC (town) Hampton County	345	93.24
East Dunbar, FL (cdp) Lee County	1,804	93.23
Howardville, MO (city) New Madrid County	318	92.98
Hobson City, AL (town) Calhoun County	816	92.94
Kingstown, NC (town) Cleveland County	785	92.90
East Orange, NJ (city) Essex County	64,797	92.80
Lisman, AL (town) Choctaw County	606	92.80
Macedonia, AL (town) Pickens County	270	92.78
Fremd Village-Padgett Island, FL (cdp) Palm Beach County	2,099	92.71
Lake View, AR (city) Phillips County	492	92.66
Washington Park, IL (village) Saint Clair County	4,952	92.65
Eastover, SC (town) Richland County	769	92.65
Redan, GA (cdp) De Kalb County	31,322	92.56
Wellston, MO (city) Saint Louis County	2,277	92.56
Taft, OK (town) Muskogee County	323	92.55
Shaw, MS (city) Bolivar County	2,134	92.30
Sunset, AR (city) Crittenden County	321	92.24
Kettering, MD (cdp) Prince George's County	10,146	92.17
Carlisle, SC (town) Union County	457	92.14
Union, AL (town) Greene County	209	92.07
Brownsville, FL (cdp) Miami-Dade County	13,249	92.05
Natchez, LA (village) Natchitoches Parish	536	91.94
View Park-Windsor Hills, CA (cdp) Los Angeles County	10,061	91.81
Selmont-West Selmont, AL (cdp) Dallas County	3,215	91.80
Warrensville Heights, OH (city) Cuyahoga County	13,863	91.75
Progress Village, FL (cdp) Hillsborough County	2,277	91.74
Killona, LA (cdp) Saint Charles Parish	731	91.72
Tangipahoa, LA (village) Tangipahoa Parish	684	91.57
Shelby, MS (city) Bolivar County	2,673	91.35
Tangelo Park, FL (cdp) Orange County	2,210	90.95
Lane, SC (town) Williamsburg County	531	90.77
Merrydale, LA (cdp) East Baton Rouge Parish	9,453	90.66
Fairfield, AL (city) Jefferson County	11,215	90.58
South Sumter, SC (cdp) Sumter County	3,039	90.31
Ames, TX (city) Liberty County	974	90.27
Lake Arbor, MD (cdp) Prince George's County	7,684	90.05

Notes: (cdp) census designated place; Refer to the Explanation of Data in the front of the book for more detailed information.

African American/Black

Top 150 Places Sorted by Percent

(Based on places with populations of 10,000 or more)

Place	Number	%
East Saint Louis, IL (city) Saint Clair County	30,983	98.23
Panthersville, GA (cdp) De Kalb County	11,474	97.31
Walker Mill, MD (cdp) Prince George's County	10,709	96.44
Tuskegee, AL (city) Macon County	11,402	96.25
Candler-McAfee, GA (cdp) De Kalb County	27,113	95.83
Highland Park, MI (city) Wayne County	15,903	94.97
Coral Hills, MD (cdp) Prince George's County	10,162	94.79
East Cleveland, OH (city) Cuyahoga County	25,752	94.62
Hillcrest Heights, MD (cdp) Prince George's County	15,451	94.45
Suitland-Silver Hill, MD (cdp) Prince George's County	31,625	94.36
Benton Harbor, MI (city) Berrien County	10,493	93.84
Greater Landover, MD (cdp) Prince George's County	21,405	93.47
Scott Lake, FL (cdp) Miami-Dade County	13,445	93.36
East Orange, NJ (city) Essex County	64,797	92.80
Redan, GA (cdp) De Kalb County	31,322	92.56
Kettering, MD (cdp) Prince George's County	10,146	92.17
Brownsville, FL (cdp) Miami-Dade County	13,249	92.05
View Park-Windsor Hills, CA (cdp) Los Angeles County	10,061	91.81
Warrensville Heights, OH (city) Cuyahoga County	13,863	91.75
Merrydale, LA (cdp) East Baton Rouge Parish	9,453	90.66
Fairfield, AL (city) Jefferson County	11,215	90.58
Oxon Hill-Glassmanor, MD (cdp) Prince George's County	31,149	88.10
Riverdale, IL (village) Cook County	13,151	87.35
Forestville, MD (cdp) Prince George's County	11,093	87.30
Gary, IN (city) Lake County	87,604	85.26
Irvington, NJ (cdp) Essex County	51,726	85.22
Prichard, AL (city) Mobile County	24,369	85.11
Maywood, IL (village) Cook County	22,612	83.79
Belvedere Park, GA (cdp) De Kalb County	15,797	83.38
Country Club Hills, IL (city) Cook County	13,468	83.30
Dolton, IL (village) Cook County	21,293	83.13
College Park, GA (city) Fulton County	16,923	83.03
Detroit, MI (city) Wayne County	787,687	82.80
Bellwood, IL (village) Cook County	16,995	82.76
Yeadon, PA (borough) Delaware County	9,731	82.73
Norland, FL (cdp) Miami-Dade County	18,992	82.59
Roosevelt, NY (cdp) Nassau County	12,895	81.34
Wyandanch, NY (cdp) Suffolk County	8,523	80.82
Harvey, IL (city) Cook County	24,232	80.77
Canton, MS (city) Madison County	10,428	80.77
Milford Mill, MD (cdp) Baltimore County	21,353	80.50
East Highland Park, VA (cdp) Henrico County	10,021	80.25
Markham, IL (city) Cook County	10,089	79.94
Jennings, MO (city) Saint Louis County	12,326	79.68
Lochearn, MD (cdp) Baltimore County	20,131	79.67
Petersburg, VA (independent city) Petersburg city	26,870	79.64
Muskegon Heights, MI (city) Muskegon County	9,568	79.41
Friendly, MD (cdp) Prince George's County	8,649	79.07
East Point, GA (city) Fulton County	31,294	79.04
Orange, NJ (cdp) Essex County	25,879	78.74
Gladeview, FL (cdp) Miami-Dade County	11,323	78.26
Berkeley, MO (city) Saint Louis County	7,841	77.92
Hazel Crest, IL (village) Cook County	11,482	77.50
Chester, PA (city) Delaware County	28,329	76.87
Greater Upper Marlboro, MD (cdp) Prince George's County	14,383	76.83
Camp Springs, MD (cdp) Prince George's County	13,577	75.56
Clinton, MD (cdp) Prince George's County	19,617	75.26
Pinewood, FL (cdp) Miami-Dade County	12,422	75.18
Birmingham, AL (city) Jefferson County	179,569	73.95
Indianola, MS (city) Sunflower County	8,871	73.52
Randallstown, MD (cdp) Baltimore County	22,679	73.47
North Amityville, NY (cdp) Suffolk County	11,991	72.36
Lauderdale Lakes, FL (city) Broward County	22,834	72.02
Opa-locka, FL (city) Miami-Dade County	10,705	71.60
Jackson, MS (city) Hinds County	131,005	71.10
Moss Point, MS (city) Jackson County	11,249	70.97
Union City, GA (city) Fulton County	8,176	70.36
Golden Glades, FL (cdp) Miami-Dade County	22,922	70.26
Yazoo City, MS (city) Yazoo County	10,202	70.12
Selma, AL (city) Dallas County	14,365	70.03
Bessemer, AL (city) Jefferson County	20,758	69.96
Willingboro, NJ (township) Burlington County	23,069	69.89
Greenville, MS (city) Washington County	29,093	69.88
Opelousas, LA (city) Saint Landry Parish	15,920	69.64
Inkster, MI (city) Wayne County	20,937	69.52
Riviera Beach, FL (city) Palm Beach County	20,735	69.38
Bedford Heights, OH (city) Cuyahoga County	7,855	69.05
New Carrollton, MD (city) Prince George's County	8,680	68.95
Clarksdale, MS (city) Coahoma County	14,223	68.89
Fort Washington, MD (cdp) Prince George's County	16,400	68.78
Riverdale, GA (city) Clayton County	8,551	68.53
Wilkinsburg, PA (borough) Allegheny County	13,152	68.51
Beecher, MI (cdp) Genesee County	8,728	68.22
Orangeburg, SC (city) Orangeburg County	8,680	68.00
New Orleans, LA (city) Orleans Parish	329,171	67.92
Asbury Park, NJ (city) Monmouth County	11,240	66.39
Pine Bluff, AR (city) Jefferson County	36,495	66.25
Woodmere, LA (cdp) Jefferson Parish	8,612	65.95
Chillum, MD (cdp) Prince George's County	22,550	65.84
Greenwood, MS (city) Leflore County	12,091	65.62
Cordele, GA (city) Crisp County	7,611	65.57
Lanham-Seabrook, MD (cdp) Prince George's County	11,899	65.42
Albany, GA (city) Dougherty County	50,177	65.22
Baltimore, MD (independent city) Baltimore city	424,449	65.18
Bastrop, LA (city) Morehouse Parish	8,414	64.78
Matteson, IL (village) Cook County	8,284	64.08
Plainfield, NJ (city) Union County	30,557	63.89
Gantt, SC (cdp) Greenville County	8,902	63.76
Kinston, NC (city) Lenoir County	14,927	63.02
Macon, GA (city) Bibb County	61,185	62.91
Mount Vernon, NY (city) Westchester County	42,516	62.18
Atlanta, GA (city) Fulton County	258,610	62.10
Lauderhill, FL (city) Broward County	35,657	61.92
Memphis, TN (city) Shelby County	402,367	61.89
Darby, PA (borough) Delaware County	6,338	61.54
Forrest City, AR (city) Saint Francis County	9,079	61.45
Monroe, LA (city) Ouachita Parish	32,622	61.43
Washington, DC (city) District of Columbia	350,455	61.26
Rosaryville, MD (cdp) Prince George's County	7,530	61.11
Brownsville, TN (city) Haywood County	6,554	60.98
Vicksburg, MS (city) Warren County	16,043	60.75
Brunswick, GA (city) Glynn County	9,452	60.59
Richton Park, IL (village) Cook County	7,578	60.46
Pleasantville, NJ (city) Atlantic County	11,429	60.11
Trotwood, OH (city) Montgomery County	16,405	59.83
Henderson, NC (city) Vance County	9,591	59.59
Newburg, KY (cdp) Jefferson County	12,210	59.17
Westmont, CA (cdp) Los Angeles County	18,684	59.08
Dentsville, SC (cdp) Richland County	7,685	59.07
West Little River, FL (cdp) Miami-Dade County	19,129	58.86
McComb, MS (city) Pike County	7,825	58.67
Americus, GA (city) Sumter County	9,972	58.61
Uniondale, NY (cdp) Nassau County	13,411	58.28
North Miami, FL (city) Miami-Dade County	34,778	58.08
Richmond, VA (independent city) Richmond city	114,860	58.07
Belle Glade, FL (city) Palm Beach County	8,653	58.05
Forest Park, OH (city) Hamilton County	11,269	57.90
Wilmington, DE (city) New Castle County	41,976	57.77
Savannah, GA (city) Chatham County	75,953	57.75
Forest Hill, TX (city) Tarrant County	7,463	57.63
Harrisburg, PA (city) Dauphin County	28,123	57.45
Elizabeth City, NC (city) Pasquotank County	9,870	57.42
Buena Vista charter, MI (township) Saginaw County	5,900	57.18
Rocky Mount, NC (city) Nash County	31,594	56.53
West Point, MS (city) Clay County	6,850	56.40
Bloomfield, CT (town) Hartford County	11,035	56.34
West Memphis, AR (city) Crittenden County	15,563	56.25
Spanish Lake, MO (cdp) Saint Louis County	11,948	56.00
Southfield, MI (city) Oakland County	43,711	55.83
Thomasville, GA (city) Thomas County	10,123	55.74
Laurel, MS (city) Jones County	10,208	55.50
Pine Hills, FL (cdp) Orange County	23,135	55.39
Camden, NJ (city) Camden County	44,224	55.35
Flint, MI (city) Genesee County	69,102	55.31
Alexandria, LA (city) Rapides Parish	25,609	55.26
Newark, NJ (city) Essex County	150,384	54.98
Natchez, MS (city) Adams County	10,135	54.89
Columbus, MS (city) Lowndes County	14,235	54.87
Hempstead, NY (village) Nassau County	30,923	54.68
Meridian, MS (city) Lauderdale County	21,855	54.68

Notes: (cdp) census designated place; Refer to the Explanation of Data in the front of the book for more detailed information.

African American/Black: Not Hispanic

Top 150 Places Sorted by Number

(Based on all places, regardless of population)

Place	Number	%
New York, NY (city) New York City	2,050,764	25.61
Chicago, IL (city) Cook County	1,068,054	36.88
Detroit, MI (city) Wayne County	782,837	82.29
Philadelphia, PA (city) Philadelphia County	659,241	43.44
Houston, TX (city) Harris County	495,338	25.35
Los Angeles, CA (city) Los Angeles County	422,819	11.44
Baltimore, MD (independent city) Baltimore city	422,007	64.81
Memphis, TN (city) Shelby County	400,616	61.62
Washington, DC (city) District of Columbia	346,083	60.50
New Orleans, LA (city) Orleans Parish	326,032	67.27
Dallas, TX (city) Dallas County	310,185	26.10
Atlanta, GA (city) Fulton County	256,605	61.61
Cleveland, OH (city) Cuyahoga County	245,890	51.40
Milwaukee, WI (city) Milwaukee County	226,742	37.98
Jacksonville, FL (special city) Duval County	215,484	29.29
Indianapolis, IN (special city) Marion County	204,455	26.15
Columbus, OH (city) Franklin County	183,224	25.75
Saint Louis, MO (independent city) Saint Louis city	180,487	51.84
Birmingham, AL (city) Jefferson County	178,822	73.64
Charlotte, NC (city) Mecklenburg County	178,699	33.04
Boston, MA (city) Suffolk County	151,246	25.67
Nashville-Davidson, TN (special city) Davidson County	148,965	27.31
Oakland, CA (city) Alameda County	146,510	36.67
Newark, NJ (city) Essex County	144,900	52.97
Cincinnati, OH (city) Hamilton County	144,770	43.70
Kansas City, MO (city) Jackson County	141,182	31.97
Jackson, MS (city) Hinds County	130,387	70.76
Baton Rouge, LA (city) East Baton Rouge Parish	114,322	50.18
Richmond, VA (independent city) Richmond city	113,997	57.64
Hempstead, NY (town) Nassau County	113,317	14.99
Buffalo, NY (city) Erie County	110,334	37.70
Fort Worth, TX (city) Tarrant County	109,379	20.46
Norfolk, VA (independent city) Norfolk city	104,688	44.66
San Diego, CA (city) San Diego County	103,508	8.46
Shreveport, LA (city) Caddo Parish	101,971	50.95
Montgomery, AL (city) Montgomery County	100,479	49.85
Augusta-Richmond County, GA (special city) Richmond County	99,150	50.80
Pittsburgh, PA (city) Allegheny County	93,132	27.84
Mobile, AL (city) Mobile County	92,425	46.46
Gary, IN (city) Lake County	86,704	84.39
Louisville, KY (city) Jefferson County	86,121	33.61
Rochester, NY (city) Monroe County	85,922	39.10
Greensboro, NC (city) Guilford County	84,774	37.86
Virginia Beach, VA (independent city) Virginia Beach city	82,978	19.51
Durham, NC (city) Durham County	82,750	44.24
Columbus, GA (special city) Muscogee County	82,038	44.16
Oklahoma City, OK (city) Oklahoma County	81,714	16.14
Tampa, FL (city) Hillsborough County	79,161	26.09
San Antonio, TX (city) Bexar County	78,542	6.86
Raleigh, NC (city) Wake County	77,667	28.13
Miami, FL (city) Miami-Dade County	77,247	21.31
Minneapolis, MN (city) Hennepin County	76,672	20.04
Toledo, OH (city) Lucas County	76,563	24.41
Savannah, GA (city) Chatham County	75,441	57.37
Little Rock, AR (city) Pulaski County	74,602	40.74
Dayton, OH (city) Montgomery County	73,073	43.97
Newport News, VA (independent city) Newport News city	71,851	39.88
Long Beach, CA (city) Los Angeles County	70,935	15.37
Phoenix, AZ (city) Maricopa County	70,246	5.32
Winston-Salem, NC (city) Forsyth County	68,671	36.96
Flint, MI (city) Genesee County	68,602	54.91
Jersey City, NJ (city) Hudson County	67,172	27.98
Austin, TX (city) Travis County	67,117	10.22
Sacramento, CA (city) Sacramento County	66,927	16.44
Hampton, VA (independent city) Hampton city	66,506	45.42
Denver, CO (city) Denver County	64,370	11.61
Tulsa, OK (city) Tulsa County	64,132	16.32
Akron, OH (city) Summit County	64,073	29.52
San Francisco, CA (city) San Francisco County	64,070	8.25
East Orange, NJ (city) Essex County	63,742	91.29
Macon, GA (city) Bibb County	60,916	62.64
Chesapeake, VA (independent city) Chesapeake city	57,649	28.94
Chattanooga, TN (city) Hamilton County	56,764	36.49
Saint Petersburg, FL (city) Pinellas County	56,642	22.82
Omaha, NE (city) Douglas County	54,484	13.97
Seattle, WA (city) King County	53,869	9.56
Columbia, SC (city) Richland County	53,720	46.20
Inglewood, CA (city) Los Angeles County	53,648	47.65
Beaumont, TX (city) Jefferson County	52,461	46.07
Fayetteville, NC (city) Cumberland County	52,045	43.01
Tallahassee, FL (city) Leon County	51,926	34.47
Las Vegas, NV (city) Clark County	51,888	10.85
Portsmouth, VA (independent city) Portsmouth city	51,370	51.08
Irvington, NJ (cdp) Essex County	50,878	83.83
Orlando, FL (city) Orange County	50,745	27.29
Albany, GA (city) Dougherty County	49,941	64.91
Huntsville, AL (city) Madison County	48,462	30.63
Paterson, NJ (city) Passaic County	48,404	32.44
Fort Lauderdale, FL (city) Broward County	47,272	31.02
Arlington, TX (city) Tarrant County	47,116	14.15
New Haven, CT (city) New Haven County	46,407	37.54
Hartford, CT (city) Hartford County	46,085	37.91
Kansas City, KS (city) Wyandotte County	45,328	30.86
Trenton, NJ (city) Mercer County	44,481	52.08
Southfield, MI (city) Oakland County	43,412	55.45
Bridgeport, CT (city) Fairfield County	43,412	31.11
Grand Rapids, MI (city) Kent County	41,954	21.21
Wichita, KS (city) Sedgwick County	41,738	12.12
Mount Vernon, NY (city) Westchester County	41,372	60.50
Wilmington, DE (city) New Castle County	41,266	56.79
Camden, NJ (city) Camden County	40,651	50.87
Portland, OR (city) Multnomah County	40,209	7.60
North Charleston, SC (city) Charleston County	39,732	49.89
Aurora, CO (city) Arapahoe County	39,688	14.36
Syracuse, NY (city) Onondaga County	38,929	26.43
Compton, CA (city) Los Angeles County	37,816	40.45
Fort Wayne, IN (city) Allen County	37,523	18.24
Saint Paul, MN (city) Ramsey County	37,062	12.91
Fresno, CA (city) Fresno County	36,800	8.61
Richmond, CA (city) Contra Costa County	36,682	36.97
Youngstown, OH (city) Mahoning County	36,561	44.57
Lexington-Fayette, KY (special city) Fayette County	36,517	14.02
Pine Bluff, AR (city) Jefferson County	36,340	65.97
Lauderhill, FL (city) Broward County	35,041	60.85
Lake Charles, LA (city) Calcasieu Parish	33,830	47.15
Babylon, NY (town) Suffolk County	33,704	15.91
San Jose, CA (city) Santa Clara County	33,571	3.75
Tuscaloosa, AL (city) Tuscaloosa County	33,443	42.93
North Miami, FL (city) Miami-Dade County	33,411	55.80
Charleston, SC (city) Charleston County	33,058	34.20
Pontiac, MI (city) Oakland County	32,484	48.97
Monroe, LA (city) Ouachita Parish	32,447	61.10
Miramar, FL (city) Broward County	32,317	44.43
Yonkers, NY (city) Westchester County	32,131	16.39
Springfield, MA (city) Hampden County	31,806	20.91
Lafayette, LA (city) Lafayette Parish	31,650	28.71
San Bernardino, CA (city) San Bernardino County	31,452	16.96
Rocky Mount, NC (city) Nash County	31,437	56.24
Suitland-Silver Hill, MD (cdp) Prince George's County	31,413	93.73
East Point, GA (city) Fulton County	31,044	78.40
Redan, GA (cdp) De Kalb County	31,040	91.72
Oxon Hill-Glassmanor, MD (cdp) Prince George's County	30,900	87.40
East Saint Louis, IL (city) Saint Clair County	30,845	97.79
Alexandria, VA (independent city) Alexandria city	30,078	23.45
Carol City, FL (cdp) Miami-Dade County	30,062	50.57
Killeen, TX (city) Bell County	30,013	34.53
Hempstead, NY (village) Nassau County	29,729	52.57
Moreno Valley, CA (city) Riverside County	29,445	20.68
Plainfield, NJ (city) Union County	29,406	61.48
Vallejo, CA (city) Solano County	29,288	25.08
Peoria, IL (city) Peoria County	29,235	25.89
Islip, NY (town) Suffolk County	29,186	9.05
Knoxville, TN (city) Knox County	29,065	16.71
Greenville, MS (city) Washington County	28,971	69.59
Stockton, CA (city) San Joaquin County	28,681	11.77
Lansing, MI (city) Ingham County	28,058	23.55
Hawthorne, CA (city) Los Angeles County	28,042	33.34
Suffolk, VA (independent city) Suffolk city	27,860	43.75
Chester, PA (city) Delaware County	27,855	75.58
Athens-Clarke County, GA (special city) Clarke County	27,739	27.67

Notes: (cdp) census designated place; Refer to the Explanation of Data in the front of the book for more detailed information.

African American/Black: Not Hispanic

Top 150 Places Sorted by Percent

(Based on all places, regardless of population)

Place	Number	%
McMullen, AL (town) Pickens County	66	100.00
Birdsong, AR (town) Mississippi County	40	100.00
Falcon, MS (town) Quitman County	316	99.68
Moore Station, TX (city) Henderson County	182	98.91
Washington Park, FL (cdp) Broward County	1,243	98.89
Brooklyn, IL (village) Saint Clair County	668	98.82
Tollette, AR (town) Howard County	320	98.77
Mound Bayou, MS (city) Bolivar County	2,070	98.48
Coahoma, MS (town) Coahoma County	320	98.46
Roosevelt Gardens, FL (cdp) Broward County	1,891	98.34
Hayti Heights, MO (city) Pemiscot County	758	98.31
Lincoln Heights, OH (village) Hamilton County	4,043	98.30
Mitchellville, AR (city) Desha County	488	98.19
Brookdale, SC (cdp) Orangeburg County	4,637	98.16
Mosses, AL (town) Lowndes County	1,080	98.09
Velda Village Hills, MO (village) Saint Louis County	1,069	98.07
Franklin Park, FL (cdp) Broward County	924	97.99
Winstonville, MS (town) Bolivar County	312	97.81
East Saint Louis, IL (city) Saint Clair County	30,845	97.79
Saint George, FL (cdp) Broward County	2,394	97.71
Broward Estates, FL (cdp) Broward County	3,335	97.63
Uplands Park, MO (village) Saint Louis County	449	97.61
Carmody Hills-Pepper Mill Village, MD (cdp) Prince George's Co.	4,686	97.60
Alorton, IL (village) Saint Clair County	2,683	97.60
Grambling, LA (town) Lincoln Parish	4,580	97.59
West Ken-Lark, FL (cdp) Broward County	3,329	97.57
Reed, AR (town) Desha County	268	97.45
White Hall, AL (town) Lowndes County	988	97.44
Metcalfe, MS (town) Washington County	1,079	97.29
Rock Island, FL (cdp) Broward County	2,990	97.20
Fayette, MS (city) Jefferson County	2,178	97.15
Princeville, NC (town) Edgecombe County	913	97.13
Seat Pleasant, MD (city) Prince George's County	4,744	97.11
Fairmount Heights, MD (town) Prince George's County	1,464	97.08
Glenarden, MD (city) Prince George's County	6,131	97.04
Jonestown, MS (town) Coahoma County	1,650	97.00
Memphis, AL (town) Pickens County	32	96.97
North Courtland, AL (town) Lawrence County	773	96.75
Unionville, GA (cdp) Tift County	2,006	96.72
Bucksport, SC (cdp) Horry County	1,080	96.69
Pine Lawn, MO (city) Saint Louis County	4,064	96.67
Panthersville, GA (cdp) De Kalb County	11,377	96.49
Carver Ranches, FL (cdp) Broward County	4,146	96.44
Kinloch, MO (city) Saint Louis County	433	96.44
Neylandville, TX (town) Hunt County	54	96.43
Golden Heights, FL (cdp) Broward County	483	96.41
Anthonyville, AR (town) Crittenden County	241	96.40
Wilson City, MO (village) Mississippi County	159	96.36
Bunche Park, FL (cdp) Miami-Dade County	3,820	96.17
Garysburg, NC (town) Northampton County	1,206	96.17
Renova, MS (town) Bolivar County	599	96.15
Tchula, MS (town) Holmes County	2,239	96.01
Velda City, MO (city) Saint Louis County	1,551	95.98
Beulah, MS (town) Bolivar County	454	95.98
Walker Mill, MD (cdp) Prince George's County	10,648	95.89
Salem, GA (cdp) Upson County	325	95.87
Harlem, FL (cdp) Hendry County	2,617	95.86
Tuskegee, AL (city) Macon County	11,340	95.73
Hillsdale, MO (village) Saint Louis County	1,414	95.73
Promised Land, SC (cdp) Greenwood County	535	95.71
Centreville, IL (city) Saint Clair County	5,695	95.70
Ford Heights, IL (village) Cook County	3,305	95.63
Gresham Park, GA (cdp) De Kalb County	8,806	95.56
Candler-McAfee, GA (cdp) De Kalb County	26,972	95.33
Wilkinson Heights, SC (cdp) Orangeburg County	2,922	95.24
Robbins, IL (village) Cook County	6,317	95.21
East Hodge, LA (village) Jackson Parish	348	95.08
Jacob City, FL (city) Jackson County	267	95.02
Boulevard Gardens, FL (cdp) Broward County	1,344	94.98
Haywood City, MO (village) Scott County	227	94.98
Gordonville, AL (town) Lowndes County	302	94.97
Edgard, LA (cdp) Saint John the Baptist Parish	2,503	94.92
Beverly Hills, MO (city) Saint Louis County	572	94.86
Arcola, MS (town) Washington County	534	94.85
Phillipsburg, GA (cdp) Tift County	841	94.81
North Lilbourn, MO (village) New Madrid County	90	94.74
Goodlow, TX (city) Navarro County	250	94.70
North Tunica, MS (cdp) Tunica County	1,373	94.69
Highland Park, MI (city) Wayne County	15,850	94.65
Lawnside, NJ (borough) Camden County	2,548	94.65
Allport, AR (town) Lonoke County	120	94.49
Midway, FL (city) Gadsden County	1,366	94.47
Lincoln Park, GA (cdp) Upson County	1,058	94.30
Coral Hills, MD (cdp) Prince George's County	10,104	94.25
Midway, FL (cdp) Seminole County	1,615	94.22
Langston, OK (town) Logan County	1,573	94.19
Phoenix, IL (village) Cook County	2,031	94.16
East Cleveland, OH (city) Cuyahoga County	25,596	94.04
Silver City, NC (cdp) Hoke County	1,077	93.98
Hillcrest Heights, MD (cdp) Prince George's County	15,357	93.87
Prairie View, TX (city) Waller County	4,139	93.85
Suitland-Silver Hill, MD (cdp) Prince George's County	31,413	93.73
Wallace, LA (cdp) Saint John the Baptist Parish	534	93.68
Springdale, MD (cdp) Prince George's County	2,476	93.61
Emelle, AL (town) Sumter County	29	93.55
Benton Harbor, MI (city) Berrien County	10,457	93.52
Venice, IL (city) Madison County	2,364	93.51
Capitol Heights, MD (town) Prince George's County	3,869	93.50
Hopkins Park, IL (village) Kankakee County	664	93.39
Largo, MD (cdp) Prince George's County	7,842	93.27
Gifford, SC (town) Hampton County	345	93.24
Northwoods, MO (city) Saint Louis County	4,326	93.17
Norwood Court, MO (town) Saint Louis County	988	93.12
Colony, AL (town) Cullman County	358	92.99
College Station, AR (cdp) Pulaski County	712	92.95
Jericho, AR (town) Crittenden County	171	92.93
Pagedale, MO (city) Saint Louis County	3,360	92.92
Greater Landover, MD (cdp) Prince George's County	21,258	92.83
Crawford, MS (town) Lowndes County	608	92.82
Macedonia, AL (town) Pickens County	270	92.78
Hobson City, AL (town) Calhoun County	814	92.71
Friars Point, MS (town) Coahoma County	1,372	92.70
East Dunbar, FL (cdp) Lee County	1,793	92.66
Kingstown, NC (town) Cleveland County	783	92.66
Lake View, AR (city) Phillips County	492	92.66
Eastover, SC (town) Richland County	769	92.65
Lisman, AL (town) Choctaw County	605	92.65
Yellow Bluff, AL (town) Wilcox County	167	92.27
Taft, OK (town) Muskogee County	322	92.26
Washington Park, IL (village) Saint Clair County	4,929	92.22
Union, AL (town) Greene County	209	92.07
Fremd Village-Padgett Island, FL (cdp) Palm Beach County	2,084	92.05
Shaw, MS (city) Bolivar County	2,122	91.78
Wellston, MO (city) Saint Louis County	2,257	91.75
Carlisle, SC (town) Union County	455	91.73
Redan, GA (cdp) De Kalb County	31,040	91.72
Kettering, MD (cdp) Prince George's County	10,095	91.71
Glendora, MS (village) Tallahatchie County	261	91.58
Mount Carmel, SC (cdp) McCormick County	217	91.56
Howardville, MO (city) New Madrid County	313	91.52
Scott Lake, FL (cdp) Miami-Dade County	13,177	91.50
Tangipahoa, LA (village) Tangipahoa Parish	683	91.43
Killona, LA (cdp) Saint Charles Parish	728	91.34
Warrensville Heights, OH (city) Cuyahoga County	13,799	91.33
East Orange, NJ (city) Essex County	63,742	91.29
Natchez, LA (village) Natchitoches Parish	532	91.25
Selmont-West Selmont, AL (cdp) Dallas County	3,190	91.09
Sunset, AR (city) Crittenden County	317	91.09
Progress Village, FL (cdp) Hillsborough County	2,255	90.85
Shelby, MS (city) Bolivar County	2,658	90.84
Brownsville, FL (cdp) Miami-Dade County	13,069	90.80
View Park-Windsor Hills, CA (cdp) Los Angeles County	9,932	90.64
East Arcadia, NC (town) Bladen County	474	90.46
Merrydale, LA (cdp) East Baton Rouge Parish	9,419	90.33
Fairfield, AL (city) Jefferson County	11,175	90.26
Lane, SC (town) Williamsburg County	527	90.09
Tangelo Park, FL (cdp) Orange County	2,189	90.08
Ames, TX (city) Liberty County	972	90.08
South Sumter, SC (cdp) Sumter County	3,025	89.90
Castle Point, MO (cdp) Saint Louis County	4,089	89.69

Notes: (cdp) census designated place; Refer to the Explanation of Data in the front of the book for more detailed information.

African American/Black: Not Hispanic

Top 150 Places Sorted by Percent

(Based on places with populations of 10,000 or more)

Place	Number	%
East Saint Louis, IL (city) Saint Clair County	30,845	97.79
Panthersville, GA (cdp) De Kalb County	11,377	96.49
Walker Mill, MD (cdp) Prince George's County	10,648	95.89
Tuskegee, AL (city) Macon County	11,340	95.73
Candler-McAfee, GA (cdp) De Kalb County	26,972	95.33
Highland Park, MI (city) Wayne County	15,850	94.65
Coral Hills, MD (cdp) Prince George's County	10,104	94.25
East Cleveland, OH (city) Cuyahoga County	25,596	94.04
Hillcrest Heights, MD (cdp) Prince George's County	15,357	93.87
Suitland-Silver Hill, MD (cdp) Prince George's County	31,413	93.73
Benton Harbor, MI (city) Berrien County	10,457	93.52
Greater Landover, MD (cdp) Prince George's County	21,258	92.83
Redan, GA (cdp) De Kalb County	31,040	91.72
Kettering, MD (cdp) Prince George's County	10,095	91.71
Scott Lake, FL (cdp) Miami-Dade County	13,177	91.50
Warrensville Heights, OH (city) Cuyahoga County	13,799	91.33
East Orange, NJ (city) Essex County	63,742	91.29
Brownsville, FL (cdp) Miami-Dade County	13,069	90.80
View Park-Windsor Hills, CA (cdp) Los Angeles County	9,932	90.64
Merrydale, LA (cdp) East Baton Rouge Parish	9,419	90.33
Fairfield, AL (city) Jefferson County	11,175	90.26
Oxon Hill-Glassmanor, MD (cdp) Prince George's County	30,900	87.40
Riverdale, IL (village) Cook County	13,066	86.79
Forestville, MD (cdp) Prince George's County	11,017	86.70
Prichard, AL (city) Mobile County	24,248	84.69
Gary, IN (city) Lake County	86,704	84.39
Irvington, NJ (cdp) Essex County	50,878	83.83
Maywood, IL (village) Cook County	22,485	83.32
Belvedere Park, GA (cdp) De Kalb County	15,687	82.80
Country Club Hills, IL (city) Cook County	13,379	82.74
Dolton, IL (village) Cook County	21,159	82.61
Detroit, MI (city) Wayne County	782,837	82.29
Yeadon, PA (borough) Delaware County	9,672	82.23
College Park, GA (city) Fulton County	16,740	82.13
Bellwood, IL (village) Cook County	16,848	82.05
Canton, MS (city) Madison County	10,402	80.57
Norland, FL (cdp) Miami-Dade County	18,523	80.55
Harvey, IL (city) Cook County	24,027	80.09
Milford Mill, MD (cdp) Baltimore County	21,214	79.97
East Highland Park, VA (cdp) Henrico County	9,974	79.87
Roosevelt, NY (cdp) Nassau County	12,615	79.57
Markham, IL (city) Cook County	10,030	79.48
Jennings, MO (city) Saint Louis County	12,261	79.26
Petersburg, VA (independent city) Petersburg city	26,717	79.18
Lochearn, MD (cdp) Baltimore County	20,003	79.16
Muskegon Heights, MI (city) Muskegon County	9,503	78.87
East Point, GA (city) Fulton County	31,044	78.40
Friendly, MD (cdp) Prince George's County	8,564	78.30
Wyandanch, NY (cdp) Suffolk County	8,228	78.02
Berkeley, MO (city) Saint Louis County	7,809	77.60
Orange, NJ (cdp) Essex County	25,425	77.35
Hazel Crest, IL (village) Cook County	11,384	76.84
Gladeview, FL (cdp) Miami-Dade County	11,085	76.62
Greater Upper Marlboro, MD (cdp) Prince George's County	14,252	76.13
Chester, PA (city) Delaware County	27,855	75.58
Camp Springs, MD (cdp) Prince George's County	13,495	75.11
Clinton, MD (cdp) Prince George's County	19,484	74.75
Birmingham, AL (city) Jefferson County	178,822	73.64
Indianola, MS (city) Sunflower County	8,842	73.28
Pinewood, FL (cdp) Miami-Dade County	12,043	72.89
Randallstown, MD (cdp) Baltimore County	22,493	72.86
Lauderdale Lakes, FL (city) Broward County	22,531	71.06
Jackson, MS (city) Hinds County	130,387	70.76
Moss Point, MS (city) Jackson County	11,194	70.62
North Amityville, NY (cdp) Suffolk County	11,591	69.94
Selma, AL (city) Dallas County	14,307	69.75
Union City, GA (city) Fulton County	8,100	69.70
Bessemer, AL (city) Jefferson County	20,661	69.63
Greenville, MS (city) Washington County	28,971	69.59
Yazoo City, MS (city) Yazoo County	10,111	69.49
Opelousas, LA (city) Saint Landry Parish	15,823	69.22
Inkster, MI (city) Wayne County	20,841	69.20
Clarksdale, MS (city) Coahoma County	14,181	68.69
Riviera Beach, FL (city) Palm Beach County	20,476	68.52
Bedford Heights, OH (city) Cuyahoga County	7,793	68.51
Fort Washington, MD (cdp) Prince George's County	16,282	68.28
Willingboro, NJ (township) Burlington County	22,507	68.19
New Carrollton, MD (city) Prince George's County	8,576	68.12
Wilkinsburg, PA (borough) Allegheny County	13,040	67.93
Riverdale, GA (city) Clayton County	8,460	67.80
Opa-locka, FL (city) Miami-Dade County	10,127	67.73
Beecher, MI (cdp) Genesee County	8,660	67.69
Golden Glades, FL (cdp) Miami-Dade County	22,079	67.68
Orangeburg, SC (city) Orangeburg County	8,631	67.61
New Orleans, LA (city) Orleans Parish	326,032	67.27
Pine Bluff, AR (city) Jefferson County	36,340	65.97
Woodmere, LA (cdp) Jefferson Parish	8,559	65.55
Cordele, GA (city) Crisp County	7,564	65.16
Greenwood, MS (city) Leflore County	11,997	65.11
Albany, GA (city) Dougherty County	49,941	64.91
Lanham-Seabrook, MD (cdp) Prince George's County	11,793	64.83
Baltimore, MD (independent city) Baltimore city	422,007	64.81
Chillum, MD (cdp) Prince George's County	22,117	64.57
Bastrop, LA (city) Morehouse Parish	8,354	64.32
Asbury Park, NJ (city) Monmouth County	10,864	64.17
Gantt, SC (cdp) Greenville County	8,855	63.42
Matteson, IL (village) Cook County	8,194	63.38
Kinston, NC (city) Lenoir County	14,875	62.80
Macon, GA (city) Bibb County	60,916	62.64
Memphis, TN (city) Shelby County	400,616	61.62
Atlanta, GA (city) Fulton County	256,605	61.61
Plainfield, NJ (city) Union County	29,406	61.48
Darby, PA (borough) Delaware County	6,300	61.17
Monroe, LA (city) Ouachita Parish	32,447	61.10
Forrest City, AR (city) Saint Francis County	9,001	60.92
Lauderhill, FL (city) Broward County	35,041	60.85
Rosaryville, MD (cdp) Prince George's County	7,476	60.67
Brownsville, TN (city) Haywood County	6,518	60.64
Washington, DC (city) District of Columbia	346,083	60.50
Mount Vernon, NY (city) Westchester County	41,372	60.50
Vicksburg, MS (city) Warren County	15,970	60.48
Brunswick, GA (city) Glynn County	9,361	60.01
Richton Park, IL (village) Cook County	7,514	59.95
Trotwood, OH (city) Montgomery County	16,342	59.60
Henderson, NC (city) Vance County	9,519	59.14
Newburg, KY (cdp) Jefferson County	12,126	58.76
McComb, MS (city) Pike County	7,805	58.52
Dentsville, SC (cdp) Richland County	7,601	58.43
Americus, GA (city) Sumter County	9,905	58.22
Westmont, CA (cdp) Los Angeles County	18,363	58.07
Richmond, VA (independent city) Richmond city	113,997	57.64
Forest Park, OH (city) Hamilton County	11,216	57.63
Pleasantville, NJ (city) Atlantic County	10,927	57.47
Savannah, GA (city) Chatham County	75,441	57.37
Belle Glade, FL (city) Palm Beach County	8,546	57.33
Forest Hill, TX (city) Tarrant County	7,414	57.26
Elizabeth City, NC (city) Pasquotank County	9,821	57.14
Wilmington, DE (city) New Castle County	41,266	56.79
Rocky Mount, NC (city) Nash County	31,437	56.24
Uniondale, NY (cdp) Nassau County	12,907	56.09
Buena Vista charter, MI (township) Saginaw County	5,787	56.09
West Memphis, AR (city) Crittenden County	15,513	56.07
West Point, MS (city) Clay County	6,810	56.07
West Little River, FL (cdp) Miami-Dade County	18,206	56.02
Harrisburg, PA (city) Dauphin County	27,317	55.81
North Miami, FL (city) Miami-Dade County	33,411	55.80
Spanish Lake, MO (cdp) Saint Louis County	11,866	55.61
Southfield, MI (city) Oakland County	43,412	55.45
Bloomfield, CT (town) Hartford County	10,846	55.37
Thomasville, GA (city) Thomas County	10,043	55.30
Laurel, MS (city) Jones County	10,155	55.21
Alexandria, LA (city) Rapides Parish	25,513	55.05
Flint, MI (city) Genesee County	68,602	54.91
Columbus, MS (city) Lowndes County	14,176	54.64
Natchez, MS (city) Adams County	10,086	54.63
Meridian, MS (city) Lauderdale County	21,749	54.42
Pine Hills, FL (cdp) Orange County	22,486	53.84
Waycross, GA (city) Ware County	8,240	53.74
Calumet City, IL (city) Cook County	20,855	53.38
Ferguson, MO (city) Saint Louis County	11,958	53.37

Notes: (cdp) census designated place; Refer to the Explanation of Data in the front of the book for more detailed information.

African American/Black: Hispanic

Top 150 Places Sorted by Number

(Based on all places, regardless of population)

Place	Number	%
New York, NY (city) New York City	223,285	2.79
Los Angeles, CA (city) Los Angeles County	21,816	0.59
Chicago, IL (city) Cook County	16,167	0.56
Philadelphia, PA (city) Philadelphia County	12,921	0.85
Boston, MA (city) Suffolk County	11,760	2.00
Miami, FL (city) Miami-Dade County	10,610	2.93
Houston, TX (city) Harris County	9,763	0.50
San Diego, CA (city) San Diego County	5,962	0.49
Phoenix, AZ (city) Maricopa County	5,819	0.44
San Antonio, TX (city) Bexar County	5,708	0.50
Newark, NJ (city) Essex County	5,484	2.00
Hempstead, NY (town) Nassau County	5,173	0.68
Jersey City, NJ (city) Hudson County	4,908	2.04
Detroit, MI (city) Wayne County	4,850	0.51
Providence, RI (city) Providence County	4,610	2.66
Dallas, TX (city) Dallas County	4,493	0.38
Washington, DC (city) District of Columbia	4,372	0.76
Hialeah, FL (city) Miami-Dade County	4,321	1.91
Lawrence, MA (city) Essex County	3,786	5.26
Milwaukee, WI (city) Milwaukee County	3,761	0.63
Oakland, CA (city) Alameda County	3,629	0.91
Camden, NJ (city) Camden County	3,573	4.47
Rochester, NY (city) Monroe County	3,489	1.59
San Jose, CA (city) Santa Clara County	3,357	0.38
Hartford, CT (city) Hartford County	3,327	2.74
Tampa, FL (city) Hillsborough County	3,309	1.09
Cleveland, OH (city) Cuyahoga County	3,302	0.69
Sacramento, CA (city) Sacramento County	3,291	0.81
Yonkers, NY (city) Westchester County	3,290	1.68
Paterson, NJ (city) Passaic County	3,259	2.18
Islip, NY (town) Suffolk County	3,243	1.01
New Orleans, LA (city) Orleans Parish	3,139	0.65
Springfield, MA (city) Hampden County	3,057	2.01
San Francisco, CA (city) San Francisco County	3,006	0.39
Denver, CO (city) Denver County	3,005	0.54
Long Beach, CA (city) Los Angeles County	2,976	0.64
Jacksonville, FL (special city) Duval County	2,967	0.40
El Paso, TX (city) El Paso County	2,928	0.52
Bridgeport, CT (city) Fairfield County	2,869	2.06
Austin, TX (city) Travis County	2,826	0.43
Albuquerque, NM (city) Bernalillo County	2,595	0.58
Fresno, CA (city) Fresno County	2,562	0.60
Union City, NJ (city) Hudson County	2,559	3.81
Buffalo, NY (city) Erie County	2,546	0.87
Elizabeth, NJ (city) Union County	2,452	2.03
Baltimore, MD (independent city) Baltimore city	2,442	0.38
Tucson, AZ (city) Pima County	2,396	0.49
Virginia Beach, VA (independent city) Virginia Beach city	2,238	0.53
New Haven, CT (city) New Haven County	2,197	1.78
Santa Ana, CA (city) Orange County	2,184	0.65
Las Vegas, NV (city) Clark County	2,035	0.43
Atlanta, GA (city) Fulton County	2,005	0.48
Lynn, MA (city) Essex County	1,967	2.21
Passaic, NJ (city) Passaic County	1,958	2.89
Columbus, OH (city) Franklin County	1,949	0.27
Fort Worth, TX (city) Tarrant County	1,919	0.36
Orlando, FL (city) Orange County	1,907	1.03
Carol City, FL (cdp) Miami-Dade County	1,882	3.17
Brookhaven, NY (town) Suffolk County	1,857	0.41
Aurora, CO (city) Arapahoe County	1,831	0.66
Stockton, CA (city) San Joaquin County	1,805	0.74
Winston-Salem, NC (city) Forsyth County	1,763	0.95
Memphis, TN (city) Shelby County	1,751	0.27
Seattle, WA (city) King County	1,742	0.31
Colorado Springs, CO (city) El Paso County	1,727	0.48
Allentown, PA (city) Lehigh County	1,701	1.60
Indianapolis, IN (special city) Marion County	1,693	0.22
Reading, PA (city) Berks County	1,692	2.08
Charlotte, NC (city) Mecklenburg County	1,672	0.31
Waterbury, CT (city) New Haven County	1,619	1.51
Minneapolis, MN (city) Hennepin County	1,619	0.42
Worcester, MA (city) Worcester County	1,608	0.93
Babylon, NY (town) Suffolk County	1,558	0.74
Norfolk, VA (independent city) Norfolk city	1,531	0.65
Brentwood, NY (cdp) Suffolk County	1,513	2.81
Grand Rapids, MI (city) Kent County	1,509	0.76
Syracuse, NY (city) Onondaga County	1,507	1.02
Riverside, CA (city) Riverside County	1,502	0.59
San Bernardino, CA (city) San Bernardino County	1,494	0.81
New Brunswick, NJ (city) Middlesex County	1,487	3.06
Miami Beach, FL (city) Miami-Dade County	1,456	1.66
Kansas City, MO (city) Jackson County	1,439	0.33
West New York, NJ (town) Hudson County	1,434	3.13
Perth Amboy, NJ (city) Middlesex County	1,420	3.00
Killeen, TX (city) Bell County	1,395	1.61
Portland, OR (city) Multnomah County	1,380	0.26
North Miami, FL (city) Miami-Dade County	1,367	2.28
Saint Paul, MN (city) Ramsey County	1,340	0.47
Anaheim, CA (city) Orange County	1,329	0.41
Oklahoma City, OK (city) Oklahoma County	1,320	0.26
Lancaster, PA (city) Lancaster County	1,313	2.33
Miramar, FL (city) Broward County	1,310	1.80
Moreno Valley, CA (city) Riverside County	1,307	0.92
Trenton, NJ (city) Mercer County	1,281	1.50
Newport News, VA (independent city) Newport News city	1,260	0.70
Albany, NY (city) Albany County	1,237	1.29
Hollywood, FL (city) Broward County	1,235	0.89
New Britain, CT (city) Hartford County	1,214	1.70
Brockton, MA (city) Plymouth County	1,206	1.28
Toledo, OH (city) Lucas County	1,202	0.38
Hempstead, NY (village) Nassau County	1,194	2.11
Raleigh, NC (city) Wake County	1,177	0.43
Inglewood, CA (city) Los Angeles County	1,175	1.04
Bakersfield, CA (city) Kern County	1,155	0.47
Plainfield, NJ (city) Union County	1,151	2.41
Mount Vernon, NY (city) Westchester County	1,144	1.67
Tacoma, WA (city) Pierce County	1,101	0.57
Columbus, GA (special city) Muscogee County	1,096	0.59
Pembroke Pines, FL (city) Broward County	1,094	0.80
Augusta-Richmond County, GA (special city) Richmond County	1,083	0.55
Mesa, AZ (city) Maricopa County	1,083	0.27
Arlington, TX (city) Tarrant County	1,080	0.32
Vineland, NJ (city) Cumberland County	1,069	1.90
Oceanside, CA (city) San Diego County	1,059	0.66
Wichita, KS (city) Sedgwick County	1,059	0.31
East Orange, NJ (city) Essex County	1,055	1.51
Fontana, CA (city) San Bernardino County	1,048	0.81
North Bergen, NJ (township) Hudson County	1,041	1.79
Lorain, OH (city) Lorain County	1,039	1.51
Corpus Christi, TX (city) Nueces County	1,039	0.37
Lansing, MI (city) Ingham County	1,020	0.86
Anchorage, AK (municipality) Anchorage Borough	1,018	0.39
Saint Louis, MO (independent city) Saint Louis city	1,016	0.29
Lowell, MA (city) Middlesex County	1,013	0.96
Kissimmee, FL (city) Osceola County	1,012	2.12
Nashville-Davidson, TN (special city) Davidson County	1,005	0.18
Pasadena, CA (city) Los Angeles County	987	0.74
Atlantic City, NJ (city) Atlantic County	966	2.38
Ontario, CA (city) San Bernardino County	962	0.61
Fayetteville, NC (city) Cumberland County	954	0.79
Chula Vista, CA (city) San Diego County	944	0.54
Hayward, CA (city) Alameda County	941	0.67
Hampton, VA (independent city) Hampton city	940	0.64
Oxnard, CA (city) Ventura County	935	0.55
Freeport, NY (village) Nassau County	934	2.13
Modesto, CA (city) Stanislaus County	933	0.49
West Little River, FL (cdp) Miami-Dade County	923	2.84
Pomona, CA (city) Los Angeles County	915	0.61
Hawthorne, CA (city) Los Angeles County	903	1.07
Sunrise Manor, NV (cdp) Clark County	902	0.58
Country Club, FL (cdp) Miami-Dade County	901	2.48
Gary, IN (city) Lake County	900	0.88
New Bedford, MA (city) Bristol County	896	0.96
Palmdale, CA (city) Los Angeles County	880	0.75
South Miami Heights, FL (cdp) Miami-Dade County	876	2.61
North Hempstead, NY (town) Nassau County	872	0.39
Silver Spring, MD (cdp) Montgomery County	868	1.13
Richmond, VA (independent city) Richmond city	863	0.44
Richmond, CA (city) Contra Costa County	861	0.87
Greensboro, NC (city) Guilford County	860	0.38

Notes: (cdp) census designated place; Refer to the Explanation of Data in the front of the book for more detailed information.

African American/Black: Hispanic

Top 150 Places Sorted by Percent

(Based on all places, regardless of population)

Place	Number	%
Rio en Medio, NM (cdp) Santa Fe County	20	15.27
Maryhill, WA (cdp) Klickitat County	9	9.18
Simpson, IL (village) Johnson County	4	7.41
Morgan, GA (city) Calhoun County	90	6.15
Jefferson, SC (town) Chesterfield County	43	6.11
Lost Hills, CA (cdp) Kern County	112	5.78
Lawrence, MA (city) Essex County	3,786	5.26
Impact, TX (town) Taylor County	2	5.13
Samnorwood, TX (cdp) Collingsworth County	2	5.13
Gregg, PA (township) Union County	224	4.78
McGrath, MN (city) Aitkin County	3	4.62
Faunsdale, AL (town) Marengo County	4	4.60
Leonard, MI (village) Oakland County	15	4.52
Camden, NJ (city) Camden County	3,573	4.47
Fort Devens, MA (cdp) Worcester County	44	4.33
Foster, PA (township) Schuylkill County	47	4.18
Cotter, IA (city) Louisa County	2	4.17
Opa-locka, FL (city) Miami-Dade County	578	3.87
Elaine, AR (city) Phillips County	33	3.82
Union City, NJ (city) Hudson County	2,559	3.81
Roberts, ID (city) Jefferson County	23	3.55
Gordon Heights, NY (cdp) Suffolk County	107	3.46
Rangerville, TX (village) Cameron County	7	3.45
Linndale, OH (village) Cuyahoga County	4	3.42
Collinston, LA (village) Morehouse Parish	11	3.36
Brooksville, OK (town) Pottawatomie County	3	3.33
Ranchitos Las Lomas, TX (cdp) Webb County	11	3.29
Carol City, FL (cdp) Miami-Dade County	1,882	3.17
Glendora, MS (village) Tallahatchie County	9	3.16
Homestead Base, FL (cdp) Miami-Dade County	14	3.14
West New York, NJ (town) Hudson County	1,434	3.13
New Brunswick, NJ (city) Middlesex County	1,487	3.06
Perth Amboy, NJ (city) Middlesex County	1,420	3.00
Paradise Hill, OK (town) Sequoyah County	3	3.00
Cottage City, MD (town) Prince George's County	34	2.99
Cloud Lake, FL (town) Palm Beach County	5	2.99
Morgan City, MS (town) Leflore County	9	2.95
Miami, FL (city) Miami-Dade County	10,610	2.93
Miami Gardens, FL (cdp) Broward County	79	2.92
Stacey Street, FL (cdp) Palm Beach County	28	2.92
Passaic, NJ (city) Passaic County	1,958	2.89
East Arcadia, NC (town) Bladen County	15	2.86
West Little River, FL (cdp) Miami-Dade County	923	2.84
Brentwood, NY (cdp) Suffolk County	1,513	2.81
Wyandanch, NY (cdp) Suffolk County	295	2.80
Cope, SC (town) Orangeburg County	3	2.80
New York, NY (city) New York City	223,285	2.79
El Portal, FL (village) Miami-Dade County	70	2.79
Lamont, CA (cdp) Kern County	370	2.78
Goff, KS (city) Nemaha County	5	2.76
Hartford, CT (city) Hartford County	3,327	2.74
Oak Ridge, FL (cdp) Orange County	606	2.71
Westview, FL (cdp) Miami-Dade County	263	2.71
Del Mar Heights, TX (cdp) Cameron County	7	2.70
Timnath, CO (town) Larimer County	6	2.69
Devol, OK (town) Cotton County	4	2.67
Providence, RI (city) Providence County	4,610	2.66
East Garden City, NY (cdp) Nassau County	26	2.66
Pleasantville, NJ (city) Atlantic County	502	2.64
Monticello, NY (village) Sullivan County	171	2.63
Hillcrest, NY (cdp) Rockland County	186	2.62
South Miami Heights, FL (cdp) Miami-Dade County	876	2.61
Poinciana, FL (cdp) Osceola County	354	2.59
Golden Glades, FL (cdp) Miami-Dade County	843	2.58
Breckinridge Center, KY (cdp) Union County	48	2.56
Middletown, NY (city) Orange County	647	2.55
Yeehaw Junction, FL (cdp) Osceola County	550	2.53
Penns Grove, NJ (borough) Salem County	123	2.52
Palmetto Estates, FL (cdp) Miami-Dade County	340	2.49
Country Club, FL (cdp) Miami-Dade County	901	2.48
Ellenville, NY (village) Ulster County	102	2.47
Haverstraw, NY (village) Rockland County	249	2.46
Andover, FL (cdp) Miami-Dade County	207	2.44
Register, GA (town) Bulloch County	4	2.44
Wheatley, AR (city) Saint Francis County	9	2.42

Place	Number	%
Plainfield, NJ (city) Union County	1,151	2.41
North Amityville, NY (cdp) Suffolk County	400	2.41
Dannemora, NY (village) Clinton County	99	2.40
Atlantic City, NJ (city) Atlantic County	966	2.38
Utopia, FL (cdp) Broward County	17	2.38
Polk, PA (township) Jefferson County	7	2.38
North Bellport, NY (cdp) Suffolk County	212	2.35
Fairton, NJ (cdp) Cumberland County	53	2.35
New Cassel, NY (cdp) Nassau County	311	2.34
Lancaster, PA (city) Lancaster County	1,313	2.33
Cibola, AZ (cdp) La Paz County	4	2.33
Elwood-Magnolia, NJ (cdp) Atlantic County	32	2.30
Pinewood, FL (cdp) Miami-Dade County	379	2.29
North Miami, FL (city) Miami-Dade County	1,367	2.28
Meadow Woods, FL (cdp) Orange County	257	2.28
Chula Vista-Orason, TX (cdp) Cameron County	9	2.28
West, MS (town) Holmes County	5	2.27
New London, CT (city) New London County	578	2.25
Central Islip, NY (cdp) Suffolk County	715	2.24
Central Falls, RI (city) Providence County	424	2.24
West Perrine, FL (cdp) Miami-Dade County	192	2.23
Prospect Park, NJ (borough) Passaic County	129	2.23
McIntyre, GA (town) Wilkinson County	16	2.23
Turkey, TX (city) Hall County	11	2.23
Asbury Park, NJ (city) Monmouth County	376	2.22
Egg Harbor City, NJ (city) Atlantic County	101	2.22
Lynn, MA (city) Essex County	1,967	2.21
Uniondale, NY (cdp) Nassau County	504	2.19
Paterson, NJ (city) Passaic County	3,259	2.18
Bliss, ID (city) Gooding County	6	2.18
Creswell, NC (town) Washington County	6	2.16
Cokedale, CO (town) Las Animas County	3	2.16
Chelsea, MA (city) Suffolk County	755	2.15
Jeffersonville, GA (city) Twiggs County	26	2.15
Freeport, NY (village) Nassau County	934	2.13
Kissimmee, FL (city) Osceola County	1,012	2.12
Hempstead, NY (village) Nassau County	1,194	2.11
Fort Dix, NJ (cdp) Burlington County	157	2.10
Frankford, DE (town) Sussex County	15	2.10
North Bay Shore, NY (cdp) Suffolk County	313	2.09
Reading, PA (city) Berks County	1,692	2.08
North Miami Beach, FL (city) Miami-Dade County	848	2.08
Angie, LA (village) Washington Parish	5	2.08
Bridgeport, CT (city) Fairfield County	2,869	2.06
New Hanover, NJ (township) Burlington County	201	2.06
Opa-locka North, FL (cdp) Miami-Dade County	128	2.06
Lakeview, NY (cdp) Nassau County	115	2.05
Wheatley Heights, NY (cdp) Suffolk County	103	2.05
Jersey City, NJ (city) Hudson County	4,908	2.04
Norland, FL (cdp) Miami-Dade County	469	2.04
Elizabeth, NJ (city) Union County	2,452	2.03
Springfield, MA (city) Hampden County	3,057	2.01
Boston, MA (city) Suffolk County	11,760	2.00
Newark, NJ (city) Essex County	5,484	2.00
Norcross, GA (city) Gwinnett County	168	2.00
Dannemora, NY (town) Clinton County	103	2.00
Pemberton Heights, NJ (cdp) Burlington County	50	1.99
Lake Lucerne, FL (cdp) Miami-Dade County	181	1.98
Wheeler AFB, HI (cdp) Honolulu County	56	1.98
Patrick, SC (town) Chesterfield County	7	1.98
Mount Rainier, MD (city) Prince George's County	166	1.95
Flanders, NY (cdp) Suffolk County	71	1.95
Weehawken, NJ (township) Hudson County	260	1.93
Chula Vista, FL (cdp) Broward County	11	1.92
Belpre, KS (city) Edwards County	2	1.92
Hialeah, FL (city) Miami-Dade County	4,321	1.91
Newburgh, NY (city) Orange County	540	1.91
New Hempstead, NY (village) Rockland County	91	1.91
South Coatesville, PA (borough) Chester County	19	1.91
Everest, KS (city) Brown County	6	1.91
Vineland, NJ (city) Cumberland County	1,069	1.90
Boligee, AL (town) Greene County	7	1.90
Princeton, FL (cdp) Miami-Dade County	191	1.89
Woodbine, NJ (borough) Cape May County	51	1.88
Harlem Heights, FL (cdp) Lee County	20	1.88

Notes: (cdp) census designated place; Refer to the Explanation of Data in the front of the book for more detailed information.

African American/Black: Hispanic

Top 150 Places Sorted by Percent

(Based on places with populations of 10,000 or more)

Place	Number	%
Lawrence, MA (city) Essex County	3,786	5.26
Camden, NJ (city) Camden County	3,573	4.47
Opa-locka, FL (city) Miami-Dade County	578	3.87
Union City, NJ (city) Hudson County	2,559	3.81
Carol City, FL (cdp) Miami-Dade County	1,882	3.17
West New York, NJ (town) Hudson County	1,434	3.13
New Brunswick, NJ (city) Middlesex County	1,487	3.06
Perth Amboy, NJ (city) Middlesex County	1,420	3.00
Miami, FL (city) Miami-Dade County	10,610	2.93
Passaic, NJ (city) Passaic County	1,958	2.89
West Little River, FL (cdp) Miami-Dade County	923	2.84
Brentwood, NY (cdp) Suffolk County	1,513	2.81
Wyandanch, NY (cdp) Suffolk County	295	2.80
New York, NY (city) New York City	223,285	2.79
Lamont, CA (cdp) Kern County	370	2.78
Hartford, CT (city) Hartford County	3,327	2.74
Oak Ridge, FL (cdp) Orange County	606	2.71
Providence, RI (city) Providence County	4,610	2.66
Pleasantville, NJ (city) Atlantic County	502	2.64
South Miami Heights, FL (cdp) Miami-Dade County	876	2.61
Poinciana, FL (cdp) Osceola County	354	2.59
Golden Glades, FL (cdp) Miami-Dade County	843	2.58
Middletown, NY (city) Orange County	647	2.55
Yeehaw Junction, FL (cdp) Osceola County	550	2.53
Palmetto Estates, FL (cdp) Miami-Dade County	340	2.49
Country Club, FL (cdp) Miami-Dade County	901	2.48
Haverstraw, NY (village) Rockland County	249	2.46
Plainfield, NJ (city) Union County	1,151	2.41
North Amityville, NY (cdp) Suffolk County	400	2.41
Atlantic City, NJ (city) Atlantic County	966	2.38
New Cassel, NY (cdp) Nassau County	311	2.34
Lancaster, PA (city) Lancaster County	1,313	2.33
Pinewood, FL (cdp) Miami-Dade County	379	2.29
North Miami, FL (city) Miami-Dade County	1,367	2.28
Meadow Woods, FL (cdp) Orange County	257	2.28
New London, CT (city) New London County	578	2.25
Central Islip, NY (cdp) Suffolk County	715	2.24
Central Falls, RI (city) Providence County	424	2.24
Asbury Park, NJ (city) Monmouth County	376	2.22
Lynn, MA (city) Essex County	1,967	2.21
Uniondale, NY (cdp) Nassau County	504	2.19
Paterson, NJ (city) Passaic County	3,259	2.18
Chelsea, MA (city) Suffolk County	755	2.15
Freeport, NY (village) Nassau County	934	2.13
Kissimmee, FL (city) Osceola County	1,012	2.12
Hempstead, NY (village) Nassau County	1,194	2.11
North Bay Shore, NY (cdp) Suffolk County	313	2.09
Reading, PA (city) Berks County	1,692	2.08
North Miami Beach, FL (city) Miami-Dade County	848	2.08
Bridgeport, CT (city) Fairfield County	2,869	2.06
Jersey City, NJ (city) Hudson County	4,908	2.04
Norland, FL (cdp) Miami-Dade County	469	2.04
Elizabeth, NJ (city) Union County	2,452	2.03
Springfield, MA (city) Hampden County	3,057	2.01
Boston, MA (city) Suffolk County	11,760	2.00
Newark, NJ (city) Essex County	5,484	2.00
Weehawken, NJ (township) Hudson County	260	1.93
Hialeah, FL (city) Miami-Dade County	4,321	1.91
Newburgh, NY (city) Orange County	540	1.91
Vineland, NJ (city) Cumberland County	1,069	1.90
Princeton, FL (cdp) Miami-Dade County	191	1.89
Ives Estates, FL (cdp) Miami-Dade County	329	1.87
Scott Lake, FL (cdp) Miami-Dade County	268	1.86
Langley Park, MD (cdp) Prince George's County	297	1.83
Miramar, FL (city) Broward County	1,310	1.80
North Bergen, NJ (township) Hudson County	1,041	1.79
Peekskill, NY (city) Westchester County	401	1.79
New Haven, CT (city) New Haven County	2,197	1.78
Richmond West, FL (cdp) Miami-Dade County	498	1.77
Roosevelt, NY (cdp) Nassau County	280	1.77
Adelphi, MD (cdp) Prince George's County	265	1.77
Hialeah Gardens, FL (city) Miami-Dade County	337	1.75
New Britain, CT (city) Hartford County	1,214	1.70
Willingboro, NJ (township) Burlington County	562	1.70
Yonkers, NY (city) Westchester County	3,290	1.68
Willimantic, CT (cdp) Windham County	266	1.68
Mount Vernon, NY (city) Westchester County	1,144	1.67
Miami Beach, FL (city) Miami-Dade County	1,456	1.66
Englewood, NJ (city) Bergen County	435	1.66
Harrisburg, PA (city) Dauphin County	806	1.65
Gladeview, FL (cdp) Miami-Dade County	238	1.65
Killeen, TX (city) Bell County	1,395	1.61
York, PA (city) York County	657	1.61
Holyoke, MA (city) Hampden County	641	1.61
Beacon, NY (city) Dutchess County	222	1.61
Allentown, PA (city) Lehigh County	1,701	1.60
Rochester, NY (city) Monroe County	3,489	1.59
Schofield Barracks, HI (cdp) Honolulu County	229	1.59
Fallsburg, NY (town) Sullivan County	192	1.57
Elmont, NY (cdp) Nassau County	511	1.56
Pine Hills, FL (cdp) Orange County	649	1.55
Windham, CT (town) Windham County	353	1.54
Egypt Lake-Leto, FL (cdp) Hillsborough County	502	1.53
Roselle, NJ (borough) Union County	326	1.53
Hackensack, NJ (city) Bergen County	649	1.52
Guttenberg, NJ (town) Hudson County	164	1.52
Waterbury, CT (city) New Haven County	1,619	1.51
East Orange, NJ (city) Essex County	1,055	1.51
Lorain, OH (city) Lorain County	1,039	1.51
Bridgeton, NJ (city) Cumberland County	343	1.51
Azalea Park, FL (cdp) Orange County	167	1.51
Trenton, NJ (city) Mercer County	1,281	1.50
Long Branch, NJ (city) Monmouth County	471	1.50
Dover, NJ (town) Morris County	271	1.49
Takoma Park, MD (city) Montgomery County	256	1.48
West Haverstraw, NY (village) Rockland County	152	1.48
Haverstraw, NY (town) Rockland County	498	1.47
University, FL (cdp) Hillsborough County	452	1.47
Coolbaugh, PA (township) Monroe County	222	1.46
Poughkeepsie, NY (city) Dutchess County	427	1.43
Spring Valley, NY (village) Rockland County	364	1.43
Irvington, NJ (cdp) Essex County	848	1.40
Bay Shore, NY (cdp) Suffolk County	333	1.40
Fort Stewart, GA (cdp) Liberty County	157	1.40
Homestead, FL (city) Miami-Dade County	443	1.39
Cutler Ridge, FL (cdp) Miami-Dade County	344	1.39
Ossining, NY (village) Westchester County	333	1.39
Fort Hood, TX (cdp) Coryell County	466	1.38
Orange, NJ (cdp) Essex County	454	1.38
Leisure City, FL (cdp) Miami-Dade County	303	1.37
Thompson, NY (town) Sullivan County	193	1.36
Geneva, NY (city) Ontario County	185	1.36
Kendall West, FL (cdp) Miami-Dade County	505	1.33
North Plainfield, NJ (borough) Somerset County	281	1.33
Hoboken, NJ (city) Hudson County	509	1.32
Fountainbleau, FL (cdp) Miami-Dade County	782	1.31
Teaneck, NJ (cdp) Bergen County	513	1.31
Somerset, NJ (cdp) Somerset County	302	1.31
Malone, NY (town) Franklin County	196	1.31
Fort Bragg, NC (cdp) Cumberland County	378	1.30
Wawarsing, NY (town) Ulster County	167	1.30
Albany, NY (city) Albany County	1,237	1.29
Chester, PA (city) Delaware County	474	1.29
North Valley Stream, NY (cdp) Nassau County	203	1.29
Brockton, MA (city) Plymouth County	1,206	1.28
Westbury, NY (village) Nassau County	183	1.28
Somers, CT (town) Tolland County	133	1.28
East Chicago, IN (city) Lake County	411	1.27
Fort Benning South, GA (cdp) Chattahoochee County	149	1.27
Chillum, MD (cdp) Prince George's County	433	1.26
Palm River-Clair Mel, FL (cdp) Hillsborough County	221	1.26
Brownsville, FL (cdp) Miami-Dade County	180	1.25
South Orange, NJ (cdp) Essex County	211	1.24
Hyattsville, MD (city) Prince George's County	181	1.23
Miami Shores, FL (village) Miami-Dade County	128	1.23
Neptune, NJ (township) Monmouth County	338	1.22
Fort Campbell North, KY (cdp) Christian County	175	1.22
Freehold, NJ (borough) Monmouth County	134	1.22
Avenel, NJ (cdp) Middlesex County	213	1.21
Groton, CT (city) New London County	121	1.21

Notes: (cdp) census designated place; Refer to the Explanation of Data in the front of the book for more detailed information.

African, sub-Saharan

Top 150 Places Sorted by Number

(Based on all places, regardless of population)

Place	Number	%
New York, NY (city) New York City	122,425	1.53
Chicago, IL (city) Cook County	36,985	1.28
Los Angeles, CA (city) Los Angeles County	29,946	0.81
Houston, TX (city) Harris County	27,841	1.42
Philadelphia, PA (city) Philadelphia County	24,682	1.63
Boston, MA (city) Suffolk County	21,176	3.59
Dallas, TX (city) Dallas County	18,242	1.54
Detroit, MI (city) Wayne County	16,870	1.77
Minneapolis, MN (city) Hennepin County	16,262	4.25
Washington, DC (city) District of Columbia	16,000	2.80
Columbus, OH (city) Franklin County	15,914	2.24
San Diego, CA (city) San Diego County	13,364	1.09
Memphis, TN (city) Shelby County	10,794	1.66
Oakland, CA (city) Alameda County	10,683	2.67
Baltimore, MD (independent city) Baltimore city	10,160	1.56
Brockton, MA (city) Plymouth County	10,010	10.61
Seattle, WA (city) King County	9,987	1.77
Charlotte, NC (city) Mecklenburg County	8,902	1.64
Indianapolis, IN (special city) Marion County	8,665	1.11
Alexandria, VA (independent city) Alexandria city	8,500	6.63
Jacksonville, FL (special city) Duval County	8,010	1.09
Nashville-Davidson, TN (special city) Davidson County	7,825	1.43
New Bedford, MA (city) Bristol County	7,726	8.24
Atlanta, GA (city) Fulton County	7,699	1.85
Pawtucket, RI (city) Providence County	7,691	10.54
Milwaukee, WI (city) Milwaukee County	7,627	1.28
Providence, RI (city) Providence County	7,500	4.32
Cincinnati, OH (city) Hamilton County	7,196	2.18
Saint Paul, MN (city) Ramsey County	7,147	2.49
Newark, NJ (city) Essex County	7,114	2.60
New Orleans, LA (city) Orleans Parish	6,392	1.32
Silver Spring, MD (cdp) Montgomery County	6,076	7.92
Cleveland, OH (city) Cuyahoga County	6,075	1.27
Phoenix, AZ (city) Maricopa County	5,963	0.45
Denver, CO (city) Denver County	5,775	1.04
San Jose, CA (city) Santa Clara County	5,722	0.64
Saint Louis, MO (independent city) Saint Louis city	5,481	1.57
San Francisco, CA (city) San Francisco County	5,454	0.70
Jersey City, NJ (city) Hudson County	5,342	2.23
Arlington, TX (city) Tarrant County	5,245	1.58
Kansas City, MO (city) Jackson County	5,177	1.17
Hempstead, NY (town) Nassau County	5,025	0.66
Raleigh, NC (city) Wake County	4,922	1.78
Greensboro, NC (city) Guilford County	4,721	2.11
Austin, TX (city) Travis County	4,683	0.71
Sacramento, CA (city) Sacramento County	4,494	1.10
Fort Worth, TX (city) Tarrant County	4,417	0.82
Arlington, VA (cdp) Arlington County	4,376	2.31
Pittsburgh, PA (city) Allegheny County	4,338	1.30
Portland, OR (city) Multnomah County	4,326	0.82
Chillum, MD (cdp) Prince George's County	4,224	12.37
Rochester, NY (city) Monroe County	4,202	1.91
San Antonio, TX (city) Bexar County	4,192	0.37
Baton Rouge, LA (city) East Baton Rouge Parish	4,066	1.78
Aurora, CO (city) Arapahoe County	4,064	1.47
Worcester, MA (city) Worcester County	3,878	2.25
Buffalo, NY (city) Erie County	3,810	1.30
Durham, NC (city) Durham County	3,738	2.00
Akron, OH (city) Summit County	3,687	1.70
Oklahoma City, OK (city) Oklahoma County	3,584	0.71
Birmingham, AL (city) Jefferson County	3,519	1.45
Long Beach, CA (city) Los Angeles County	3,505	0.76
Omaha, NE (city) Douglas County	3,252	0.83
Brooklyn Park, MN (city) Hennepin County	3,232	4.80
Little Rock, AR (city) Pulaski County	3,144	1.71
Flint, MI (city) Genesee County	3,131	2.51
Fresno, CA (city) Fresno County	3,081	0.72
Las Vegas, NV (city) Clark County	3,034	0.63
Toledo, OH (city) Lucas County	2,947	0.94
Norfolk, VA (independent city) Norfolk city	2,932	1.25
Irving, TX (city) Dallas County	2,903	1.52
Richmond, VA (independent city) Richmond city	2,833	1.43
Miami, FL (city) Miami-Dade County	2,816	0.78
East Orange, NJ (city) Essex County	2,774	3.97
Tampa, FL (city) Hillsborough County	2,718	0.90

Place	Number	%
Virginia Beach, VA (independent city) Virginia Beach city	2,713	0.64
East Providence, RI (city) Providence County	2,682	5.51
Grand Rapids, MI (city) Kent County	2,645	1.34
Trenton, NJ (city) Mercer County	2,555	3.00
Columbus, GA (special city) Muscogee County	2,526	1.36
Tulsa, OK (city) Tulsa County	2,513	0.64
Garland, TX (city) Dallas County	2,497	1.16
Inglewood, CA (city) Los Angeles County	2,483	2.21
Paradise, NV (cdp) Clark County	2,435	1.31
Louisville, KY (city) Jefferson County	2,434	0.95
Irvington, NJ (cdp) Essex County	2,422	4.00
Augusta-Richmond County, GA (special city) Richmond County	2,417	1.24
Savannah, GA (city) Chatham County	2,405	1.83
Saint Petersburg, FL (city) Pinellas County	2,394	0.97
White Oak, MD (cdp) Montgomery County	2,375	11.37
Wichita, KS (city) Sedgwick County	2,344	0.68
Mobile, AL (city) Mobile County	2,268	1.14
Tallahassee, FL (city) Leon County	2,240	1.49
Yonkers, NY (city) Westchester County	2,228	1.14
Wheaton-Glenmont, MD (cdp) Montgomery County	2,223	3.85
Richmond, CA (city) Contra Costa County	2,217	2.22
Cambridge, MA (city) Middlesex County	2,190	2.16
Syracuse, NY (city) Onondaga County	2,179	1.48
Dayton, OH (city) Montgomery County	2,179	1.31
Bridgeport, CT (city) Fairfield County	2,118	1.52
Jackson, MS (city) Hinds County	2,089	1.14
Pasadena, CA (city) Los Angeles County	2,074	1.55
Southfield, MI (city) Oakland County	2,044	2.61
Shreveport, LA (city) Caddo Parish	2,039	1.02
Lexington-Fayette, KY (special city) Fayette County	2,033	0.78
Hawthorne, CA (city) Los Angeles County	2,022	2.41
Franklin, NJ (township) Somerset County	1,987	3.90
Greenbelt, MD (city) Prince George's County	1,981	9.26
Des Moines, IA (city) Polk County	1,961	0.99
Newport News, VA (independent city) Newport News city	1,955	1.09
Lincolnia, VA (cdp) Fairfax County	1,951	12.30
Montgomery, AL (city) Montgomery County	1,946	0.97
Paterson, NJ (city) Passaic County	1,930	1.29
Wilmington, DE (city) New Castle County	1,924	2.65
Tucson, AZ (city) Pima County	1,916	0.39
North Atlanta, GA (cdp) De Kalb County	1,892	4.93
Aspen Hill, MD (cdp) Montgomery County	1,888	3.76
Springfield, MA (city) Hampden County	1,858	1.22
Colorado Springs, CO (city) El Paso County	1,848	0.51
Winston-Salem, NC (city) Forsyth County	1,840	0.99
Stockton, CA (city) San Joaquin County	1,833	0.76
Fairland, MD (cdp) Montgomery County	1,823	8.45
Rochester, MN (city) Olmsted County	1,811	2.12
Albany, NY (city) Albany County	1,810	1.89
Lansing, MI (city) Ingham County	1,806	1.52
Hampton, VA (independent city) Hampton city	1,804	1.23
Fort Lauderdale, FL (city) Broward County	1,802	1.18
Tacoma, WA (city) Pierce County	1,802	0.93
Columbia, MD (cdp) Howard County	1,799	2.04
Orlando, FL (city) Orange County	1,786	0.96
Takoma Park, MD (city) Montgomery County	1,765	10.27
New Haven, CT (city) New Haven County	1,730	1.40
Bakersfield, CA (city) Kern County	1,722	0.70
Hayward, CA (city) Alameda County	1,707	1.22
Redan, GA (cdp) De Kalb County	1,696	5.01
San Bernardino, CA (city) San Bernardino County	1,686	0.91
Berkeley, CA (city) Alameda County	1,667	1.62
Sandy Springs, GA (cdp) Fulton County	1,661	1.94
Waterbury, CT (city) New Haven County	1,658	1.55
Gainesville, FL (city) Alachua County	1,630	1.70
Dale City, VA (cdp) Prince William County	1,622	2.89
Randallstown, MD (cdp) Baltimore County	1,618	5.23
Germantown, MD (cdp) Montgomery County	1,617	2.93
Fayetteville, NC (city) Cumberland County	1,606	1.33
Lanham-Seabrook, MD (cdp) Prince George's County	1,605	8.87
Lowell, MA (city) Middlesex County	1,605	1.53
Gaithersburg, MD (city) Montgomery County	1,597	3.03
Columbia, SC (city) Richland County	1,564	1.35
Wareham, MA (town) Plymouth County	1,556	7.65
Elizabeth, NJ (city) Union County	1,550	1.29

Notes: (cdp) census designated place; Refer to the Explanation of Data in the front of the book for more detailed information.

African, sub-Saharan

Top 150 Places Sorted by Percent

(Based on all places, regardless of population)

Place	Number	%
Lake Harbor, FL (cdp) Palm Beach County	29	31.18
North River, ND (city) Cass County	14	24.56
Rentiesville, OK (town) McIntosh County	16	19.51
Onset, MA (cdp) Plymouth County	261	19.11
Gilmore, AR (town) Crittenden County	62	18.56
Furman, SC (town) Hampton County	48	17.52
Anthonyville, AR (town) Crittenden County	46	17.42
Monango, ND (city) Dickey County	4	17.39
Neylandville, TX (town) Hunt County	7	17.07
Port Royal, VA (town) Caroline County	31	16.85
Clarkston, GA (city) De Kalb County	980	14.36
Siloam, GA (town) Greene County	42	13.91
Wooldridge, MO (village) Cooper County	7	12.96
Marianna, AR (city) Lee County	673	12.89
Chillum, MD (cdp) Prince George's County	4,224	12.37
Lincolnia, VA (cdp) Fairfax County	1,951	12.30
Climax, GA (city) Decatur County	36	11.80
White Oak, MD (cdp) Montgomery County	2,375	11.37
Garysburg, NC (town) Northampton County	139	11.36
Woodland, MS (village) Chickasaw County	16	11.27
Gum Springs, AR (town) Clark County	21	10.71
Woodlawn, MD (cdp) Prince George's County	661	10.64
Brockton, MA (city) Plymouth County	10,010	10.61
Pawtucket, RI (city) Providence County	7,691	10.54
West Wareham, MA (cdp) Plymouth County	189	10.54
Takoma Park, MD (city) Montgomery County	1,765	10.27
Riverdale Park, MD (town) Prince George's County	640	9.75
Goddard, MD (cdp) Prince George's County	538	9.72
Century, FL (town) Escambia County	162	9.41
Bowersville, GA (town) Hart County	30	9.40
Fate, TX (city) Rockwall County	43	9.29
Langston, OK (town) Logan County	152	9.28
Greenbelt, MD (city) Prince George's County	1,981	9.26
Fort Pierce North, FL (cdp) Saint Lucie County	673	9.17
Cundiyo, NM (cdp) Santa Fe County	11	9.17
Lanham-Seabrook, MD (cdp) Prince George's County	1,605	8.87
Cheverly, MD (town) Prince George's County	574	8.87
Adelphi, MD (cdp) Prince George's County	1,316	8.76
New Carrollton, MD (city) Prince George's County	1,117	8.70
Alexander, AR (town) Pulaski County	53	8.63
Weweantic, MA (cdp) Plymouth County	165	8.47
Fairland, MD (cdp) Montgomery County	1,823	8.45
Beauregard, MS (village) Copiah County	23	8.42
New Bedford, MA (city) Bristol County	7,726	8.24
Pulaski, GA (town) Candler County	22	8.24
Unity Village, MO (village) Jackson County	17	8.21
Beltsville, MD (cdp) Prince George's County	1,287	8.18
Frisco City, AL (town) Monroe County	125	8.17
Clarks, LA (village) Caldwell Parish	85	8.09
Genoa, CO (town) Lincoln County	14	8.09
Noxapater, MS (town) Winston County	35	8.06
White Island Shores, MA (cdp) Plymouth County	183	8.00
Silver Spring, MD (cdp) Montgomery County	6,076	7.92
Millwood, SC (cdp) Sumter County	70	7.84
Swansea, SC (town) Lexington County	41	7.84
Fort Greely, AK (cdp) Southeast Fairbanks Census Area	38	7.82
Wareham, MA (town) Plymouth County	1,556	7.65
Boston, GA (city) Thomas County	107	7.58
Mount Rainier, MD (city) Prince George's County	631	7.46
South Laurel, MD (cdp) Prince George's County	1,543	7.42
East Riverdale, MD (cdp) Prince George's County	1,126	7.32
Atlantic Beach, SC (town) Horry County	27	7.32
Turkey, NC (town) Sampson County	17	7.17
Fort Devens, MA (cdp) Worcester County	71	7.11
Brentwood, MD (town) Prince George's County	201	7.02
Cecilton, MD (town) Cecil County	33	6.92
Tildenville, FL (cdp) Orange County	34	6.85
Marion, SC (city) Marion County	478	6.75
Tignall, GA (town) Wilkes County	44	6.73
Woodbury, GA (city) Meriwether County	82	6.65
Alexandria, VA (independent city) Alexandria city	8,500	6.63
Angus, MN (township) Polk County	7	6.60
Yeadon, PA (borough) Delaware County	777	6.59
Elsah, IL (village) Jersey County	41	6.56
Cheriton, VA (town) Northampton County	33	6.43
Springdale, MD (cdp) Prince George's County	180	6.41
Cliff Village, MO (village) Newton County	3	6.38
Calverton, MD (cdp) Montgomery County	802	6.36
Augusta, AR (city) Woodruff County	170	6.36
South Brooksville, FL (cdp) Hernando County	85	6.35
Bluff City, KS (city) Harper County	4	6.35
South Coatesville, PA (borough) Chester County	63	6.33
Strong, AR (city) Union County	43	6.30
Kershaw, SC (town) Lancaster County	106	6.29
Charlack, MO (city) Saint Louis County	92	6.28
Meade, MI (township) Mason County	18	6.25
Wilberforce, OH (cdp) Greene County	89	6.24
Somerset, NJ (cdp) Somerset County	1,426	6.19
Grasonville, MD (cdp) Queen Anne's County	135	6.18
Experiment, GA (cdp) Spalding County	202	6.17
Boutte, LA (cdp) Saint Charles Parish	133	6.15
Burtonsville, MD (cdp) Montgomery County	448	6.13
Lyford South, TX (cdp) Willacy County	16	6.13
White Plains, GA (city) Greene County	21	6.09
Blenheim, SC (town) Marlboro County	7	6.03
Lake City, SC (city) Florence County	383	5.96
Cleveland, GA (city) White County	114	5.89
Oronoko charter, MI (township) Berrien County	579	5.88
Lower Oxford, PA (township) Chester County	252	5.83
Louisville, GA (city) Jefferson County	145	5.76
Humnoke, AR (city) Lonoke County	17	5.76
Gurdon, AR (city) Clark County	129	5.74
Langley Park, MD (cdp) Prince George's County	928	5.72
Camak, GA (town) Warren County	10	5.68
Coffee City, TX (town) Henderson County	10	5.65
Homestown, MO (city) Pemiscot County	10	5.62
Greater Landover, MD (cdp) Prince George's County	1,265	5.55
Phillipsburg, GA (cdp) Tift County	63	5.55
East Providence, RI (city) Providence County	2,682	5.51
Hyattsville, MD (city) Prince George's County	816	5.50
Greensboro, GA (city) Greene County	179	5.49
Emhouse, TX (town) Navarro County	9	5.49
Toco, TX (city) Lamar County	5	5.49
Central Falls, RI (city) Providence County	1,034	5.46
Travelers Rest, SC (city) Greenville County	220	5.39
Mitchellville, MD (cdp) Prince George's County	517	5.36
Olympia Fields, IL (village) Cook County	253	5.36
North Courtland, AL (town) Lawrence County	43	5.35
Catron, MO (town) New Madrid County	4	5.33
Eastover, SC (town) Richland County	46	5.31
Bladensburg, MD (town) Prince George's County	398	5.27
Woodland, GA (city) Talbot County	24	5.24
Randallstown, MD (cdp) Baltimore County	1,618	5.23
Twin Groves, AR (town) Faulkner County	14	5.15
Ellenton, GA (town) Colquitt County	20	5.14
Pulaski, IL (village) Pulaski County	15	5.14
Bloomer, MI (township) Montcalm County	157	5.12
Berrien Springs, MI (village) Berrien County	95	5.10
Franklin Park, FL (cdp) Broward County	56	5.10
Marion, MA (town) Plymouth County	261	5.09
Glenn Dale, MD (cdp) Prince George's County	651	5.08
Oglethorpe, GA (city) Macon County	61	5.07
Ghent, KY (city) Carroll County	17	5.07
Redan, GA (cdp) De Kalb County	1,696	5.01
Princess Anne, MD (town) Somerset County	120	5.00
College Park, GA (city) Fulton County	1,036	4.99
Harwich Center, MA (cdp) Barnstable County	92	4.97
South Floral Park, NY (village) Nassau County	78	4.94
North Atlanta, GA (cdp) De Kalb County	1,892	4.93
Boardman, NC (town) Columbus County	11	4.93
Meigs, GA (city) Thomas County	55	4.91
Girard, GA (town) Burke County	11	4.91
Largo, MD (cdp) Prince George's County	414	4.86
Vinita Park, MO (city) Saint Louis County	95	4.86
Brooklyn Park, MN (city) Hennepin County	3,232	4.80
Glenwood, IL (village) Cook County	434	4.80
Temple Hills, MD (cdp) Prince George's County	371	4.79
Ogema, MN (township) Pine County	15	4.76
Cloverly, MD (cdp) Montgomery County	377	4.71
Lenox, GA (town) Cook County	41	4.69

Notes: (cdp) census designated place; Refer to the Explanation of Data in the front of the book for more detailed information.

African, sub-Saharan

Top 150 Places Sorted by Percent

(Based on places with populations of 10,000 or more)

Place	Number	%
Chillum, MD (cdp) Prince George's County	4,224	12.37
Lincolnia, VA (cdp) Fairfax County	1,951	12.30
White Oak, MD (cdp) Montgomery County	2,375	11.37
Brockton, MA (city) Plymouth County	10,010	10.61
Pawtucket, RI (city) Providence County	7,691	10.54
Takoma Park, MD (city) Montgomery County	1,765	10.27
Greenbelt, MD (city) Prince George's County	1,981	9.26
Lanham-Seabrook, MD (cdp) Prince George's County	1,605	8.87
Adelphi, MD (cdp) Prince George's County	1,316	8.76
New Carrollton, MD (city) Prince George's County	1,117	8.70
Fairland, MD (cdp) Montgomery County	1,823	8.45
New Bedford, MA (city) Bristol County	7,726	8.24
Beltsville, MD (cdp) Prince George's County	1,287	8.18
Silver Spring, MD (cdp) Montgomery County	6,076	7.92
Wareham, MA (town) Plymouth County	1,556	7.65
South Laurel, MD (cdp) Prince George's County	1,543	7.42
East Riverdale, MD (cdp) Prince George's County	1,126	7.32
Alexandria, VA (independent city) Alexandria city	8,500	6.63
Yeadon, PA (borough) Delaware County	777	6.59
Calverton, MD (cdp) Montgomery County	802	6.36
Somerset, NJ (cdp) Somerset County	1,426	6.19
Langley Park, MD (cdp) Prince George's County	928	5.72
Greater Landover, MD (cdp) Prince George's County	1,265	5.55
East Providence, RI (city) Providence County	2,682	5.51
Hyattsville, MD (city) Prince George's County	816	5.50
Central Falls, RI (city) Providence County	1,034	5.46
Randallstown, MD (cdp) Baltimore County	1,618	5.23
Glenn Dale, MD (cdp) Prince George's County	651	5.08
Redan, GA (cdp) De Kalb County	1,696	5.01
College Park, GA (city) Fulton County	1,036	4.99
North Atlanta, GA (cdp) De Kalb County	1,892	4.93
Brooklyn Park, MN (city) Hennepin County	3,232	4.80
View Park-Windsor Hills, CA (cdp) Los Angeles County	510	4.65
Orange, NJ (cdp) Essex County	1,492	4.54
Brooklyn Center, MN (city) Hennepin County	1,258	4.33
Providence, RI (city) Providence County	7,500	4.32
Benton Harbor, MI (city) Berrien County	483	4.30
Brunswick, GA (city) Glynn County	660	4.28
Minneapolis, MN (city) Hennepin County	16,262	4.25
Woodlawn, MD (cdp) Baltimore County	1,527	4.23
Mount Vernon, VA (cdp) Fairfax County	1,177	4.12
Groveton, VA (cdp) Fairfax County	862	4.05
Redland, MD (cdp) Montgomery County	696	4.03
Irvington, NJ (cdp) Essex County	2,422	4.00
East Orange, NJ (city) Essex County	2,774	3.97
Randolph, MA (cdp) Norfolk County	1,214	3.92
Franklin, NJ (township) Somerset County	1,987	3.90
Justice, IL (village) Cook County	470	3.89
Bailey's Crossroads, VA (cdp) Fairfax County	886	3.88
Wheaton-Glenmont, MD (cdp) Montgomery County	2,223	3.85
Savage-Guilford, MD (cdp) Howard County	479	3.80
Aspen Hill, MD (cdp) Montgomery County	1,888	3.76
Laurel, MD (city) Prince George's County	754	3.76
Candler-McAfee, GA (cdp) De Kalb County	1,057	3.75
Newington, VA (cdp) Fairfax County	735	3.73
Boston, MA (city) Suffolk County	21,176	3.59
Milford Mill, MD (cdp) Baltimore County	914	3.45
Avenel, NJ (cdp) Middlesex County	602	3.43
Country Club Hills, IL (city) Cook County	542	3.35
Wyandanch, NY (cdp) Suffolk County	354	3.35
Morrisville, PA (borough) Bucks County	334	3.33
Fort Washington, MD (cdp) Prince George's County	800	3.31
South Orange, NJ (cdp) Essex County	560	3.30
SeaTac, WA (city) King County	838	3.28
Kettering, MD (cdp) Prince George's County	364	3.28
Riverdale, GA (city) Clayton County	403	3.24
Montgomery Village, MD (cdp) Montgomery County	1,216	3.21
New Cassel, NY (cdp) Nassau County	427	3.21
Muskegon Heights, MI (city) Muskegon County	384	3.20
Powder Springs, GA (city) Cobb County	410	3.16
Buena Vista charter, MI (township) Saginaw County	324	3.14
Cahokia, IL (village) Saint Clair County	511	3.10
Mission Bend, TX (cdp) Fort Bend County	954	3.09
Panthersville, GA (cdp) De Kalb County	361	3.09
Greater Upper Marlboro, MD (cdp) Prince George's County	576	3.08
Coatesville, PA (city) Chester County	332	3.04
Gaithersburg, MD (city) Montgomery County	1,597	3.03
Darby, PA (borough) Delaware County	310	3.01
Trenton, NJ (city) Mercer County	2,555	3.00
Benton charter, MI (township) Berrien County	482	2.94
Germantown, MD (cdp) Montgomery County	1,617	2.93
Dale City, VA (cdp) Prince William County	1,622	2.89
Wilkinsburg, PA (borough) Allegheny County	550	2.87
Addison, TX (town) Dallas County	394	2.86
Hillside, NJ (cdp) Union County	615	2.83
Hybla Valley, VA (cdp) Fairfax County	476	2.83
Statesboro, GA (city) Bulloch County	636	2.81
Washington, DC (city) District of Columbia	16,000	2.80
Forest Park, OH (city) Hamilton County	539	2.78
Chester, PA (city) Delaware County	1,021	2.77
Tukwila, WA (city) King County	474	2.76
Union City, GA (city) Fulton County	315	2.76
Hopkins, MN (city) Hennepin County	468	2.74
North Amityville, NY (cdp) Suffolk County	450	2.72
Riverdale, IL (village) Cook County	406	2.71
Oakland, CA (city) Alameda County	10,683	2.67
West Carson, CA (cdp) Los Angeles County	565	2.67
Whitehall, OH (city) Franklin County	514	2.67
Elmont, NY (cdp) Nassau County	868	2.66
Lorton, VA (cdp) Fairfax County	473	2.66
Wilmington, DE (city) New Castle County	1,924	2.65
Coral Hills, MD (cdp) Prince George's County	286	2.64
Leesburg, FL (city) Lake County	417	2.63
Bloomfield, CT (town) Hartford County	513	2.62
Southfield, MI (city) Oakland County	2,044	2.61
Newark, NJ (city) Essex County	7,114	2.60
Franconia, VA (cdp) Fairfax County	830	2.60
Springfield, VA (cdp) Fairfax County	788	2.60
Gallatin, TN (city) Sumner County	604	2.60
Falmouth, MA (town) Barnstable County	839	2.57
Parkville, MD (cdp) Baltimore County	795	2.56
Maplewood, NJ (cdp) Essex County	611	2.56
Taunton, MA (city) Bristol County	1,425	2.55
Lawrenceville, GA (city) Gwinnett County	574	2.55
Dolton, IL (village) Cook County	655	2.54
Colesville, MD (cdp) Montgomery County	502	2.53
Missouri City, TX (city) Fort Bend County	1,323	2.52
Flint, MI (city) Genesee County	3,131	2.51
Harvey, IL (city) Cook County	757	2.51
Fort Stewart, GA (cdp) Liberty County	286	2.51
North Valley Stream, NY (cdp) Nassau County	394	2.50
Saint Paul, MN (city) Ramsey County	7,147	2.49
Cedar Hill, TX (city) Dallas County	794	2.47
Roselle, NJ (borough) Union County	525	2.47
Stafford, TX (city) Fort Bend County	386	2.47
Tuskegee, AL (city) Macon County	298	2.47
Hercules, CA (city) Contra Costa County	472	2.45
Marietta, GA (city) Cobb County	1,423	2.44
Dover, DE (city) Kent County	793	2.44
South Holland, IL (village) Cook County	543	2.44
Owings Mills, MD (cdp) Baltimore County	493	2.44
Douglasville, GA (city) Douglas County	490	2.43
West Columbia, SC (city) Lexington County	322	2.43
Hawthorne, CA (city) Los Angeles County	2,022	2.41
Beecher, MI (cdp) Genesee County	309	2.39
Chelsea, MA (city) Suffolk County	835	2.38
Warrensville Heights, OH (city) Cuyahoga County	363	2.36
Rose Hill, VA (cdp) Fairfax County	353	2.36
Woodmere, LA (cdp) Jefferson Parish	308	2.35
Mashpee, MA (town) Barnstable County	304	2.35
Matteson, IL (village) Cook County	303	2.35
North Laurel, MD (cdp) Howard County	483	2.34
Carver, MA (town) Plymouth County	261	2.34
Union, NJ (cdp) Union County	1,265	2.33
Orangeburg, SC (city) Orangeburg County	302	2.33
Oxon Hill-Glassmanor, MD (cdp) Prince George's County	814	2.32
Trotwood, OH (city) Montgomery County	638	2.32
Arlington, VA (cdp) Arlington County	4,376	2.31
Clinton, MD (cdp) Prince George's County	606	2.31
Norland, FL (cdp) Miami-Dade County	531	2.31

Notes: (cdp) census designated place; Refer to the Explanation of Data in the front of the book for more detailed information.

African, sub-Saharan: African

Top 150 Places Sorted by Number

(Based on all places, regardless of population)

Place	Number	%
New York, NY (city) New York County	76,791	0.96
Chicago, IL (city) Cook County	26,959	0.93
Los Angeles, CA (city) Los Angeles County	19,718	0.53
Philadelphia, PA (city) Philadelphia County	19,570	1.29
Houston, TX (city) Harris County	15,009	0.77
Detroit, MI (city) Wayne County	14,175	1.49
Dallas, TX (city) Dallas County	10,470	0.88
Washington, DC (city) District of Columbia	9,638	1.68
Memphis, TN (city) Shelby County	9,612	1.48
Columbus, OH (city) Franklin County	8,924	1.25
Oakland, CA (city) Alameda County	7,521	1.88
Baltimore, MD (independent city) Baltimore city	7,226	1.11
Jacksonville, FL (special city) Duval County	6,995	0.95
Indianapolis, IN (special city) Marion County	6,845	0.87
Milwaukee, WI (city) Milwaukee County	6,662	1.12
Cincinnati, OH (city) Hamilton County	6,339	1.92
San Diego, CA (city) San Diego County	6,333	0.52
Boston, MA (city) Suffolk County	5,962	1.01
Cleveland, OH (city) Cuyahoga County	5,696	1.19
New Orleans, LA (city) Orleans Parish	5,660	1.17
Atlanta, GA (city) Fulton County	5,549	1.33
Nashville-Davidson, TN (special city) Davidson County	5,495	1.01
Charlotte, NC (city) Mecklenburg County	5,402	1.00
Minneapolis, MN (city) Hennepin County	5,198	1.36
Saint Louis, MO (independent city) Saint Louis city	4,172	1.20
Phoenix, AZ (city) Maricopa County	3,927	0.30
Newark, NJ (city) Essex County	3,920	1.43
Fort Worth, TX (city) Tarrant County	3,840	0.72
San Francisco, CA (city) San Francisco County	3,768	0.49
Denver, CO (city) Denver County	3,758	0.68
Pittsburgh, PA (city) Allegheny County	3,736	1.12
Sacramento, CA (city) Sacramento County	3,647	0.90
Seattle, WA (city) King County	3,585	0.64
Jersey City, NJ (city) Hudson County	3,546	1.48
Akron, OH (city) Summit County	3,525	1.62
San Antonio, TX (city) Bexar County	3,508	0.31
Kansas City, MO (city) Jackson County	3,403	0.77
Baton Rouge, LA (city) East Baton Rouge Parish	3,298	1.45
Birmingham, AL (city) Jefferson County	3,288	1.35
Rochester, NY (city) Monroe County	3,286	1.50
Flint, MI (city) Genesee County	3,081	2.47
Hempstead, NY (town) Nassau County	3,042	0.40
Saint Paul, MN (city) Ramsey County	3,032	1.06
Greensboro, NC (city) Guilford County	2,983	1.34
Raleigh, NC (city) Wake County	2,969	1.07
Austin, TX (city) Travis County	2,935	0.45
Long Beach, CA (city) Los Angeles County	2,934	0.64
Buffalo, NY (city) Erie County	2,870	0.98
Durham, NC (city) Durham County	2,767	1.48
Toledo, OH (city) Lucas County	2,668	0.85
Miami, FL (city) Miami-Dade County	2,661	0.73
Little Rock, AR (city) Pulaski County	2,660	1.45
Oklahoma City, OK (city) Oklahoma County	2,628	0.52
San Jose, CA (city) Santa Clara County	2,605	0.29
Arlington, TX (city) Tarrant County	2,568	0.77
Norfolk, VA (independent city) Norfolk city	2,478	1.06
Las Vegas, NV (city) Clark County	2,465	0.51
Aurora, CO (city) Arapahoe County	2,400	0.87
Virginia Beach, VA (independent city) Virginia Beach city	2,358	0.55
Omaha, NE (city) Douglas County	2,341	0.60
Columbus, GA (special city) Muscogee County	2,328	1.25
Alexandria, VA (independent city) Alexandria city	2,313	1.80
Richmond, VA (independent city) Richmond city	2,296	1.16
Tampa, FL (city) Hillsborough County	2,282	0.75
Fresno, CA (city) Fresno County	2,276	0.53
Savannah, GA (city) Chatham County	2,244	1.71
Portland, OR (city) Multnomah County	2,205	0.42
Silver Spring, MD (cdp) Montgomery County	2,128	2.77
Saint Petersburg, FL (city) Pinellas County	2,107	0.85
Augusta-Richmond County, GA (special city) Richmond County	2,105	1.08
Mobile, AL (city) Mobile County	2,103	1.06
Tulsa, OK (city) Tulsa County	2,063	0.52
Grand Rapids, MI (city) Kent County	2,025	1.02
Worcester, MA (city) Worcester County	2,001	1.16
Louisville, KY (city) Jefferson County	1,983	0.77
Shreveport, LA (city) Caddo Parish	1,974	0.98
Jackson, MS (city) Hinds County	1,911	1.04
Inglewood, CA (city) Los Angeles County	1,894	1.68
Providence, RI (city) Providence County	1,890	1.09
Richmond, CA (city) Contra Costa County	1,863	1.87
Wilmington, DE (city) New Castle County	1,833	2.52
Wichita, KS (city) Sedgwick County	1,804	0.52
Syracuse, NY (city) Onondaga County	1,780	1.21
Dayton, OH (city) Montgomery County	1,766	1.06
Paterson, NJ (city) Passaic County	1,733	1.16
Tallahassee, FL (city) Leon County	1,726	1.15
Newport News, VA (independent city) Newport News city	1,718	0.95
Hampton, VA (independent city) Hampton city	1,619	1.11
Montgomery, AL (city) Montgomery County	1,606	0.80
Trenton, NJ (city) Mercer County	1,603	1.88
Lexington-Fayette, KY (special city) Fayette County	1,600	0.61
East Orange, NJ (city) Essex County	1,598	2.29
Orlando, FL (city) Orange County	1,598	0.86
Fort Lauderdale, FL (city) Broward County	1,594	1.05
Stockton, CA (city) San Joaquin County	1,586	0.65
Colorado Springs, CO (city) El Paso County	1,550	0.43
Tacoma, WA (city) Pierce County	1,548	0.80
Winston-Salem, NC (city) Forsyth County	1,539	0.83
Pasadena, CA (city) Los Angeles County	1,517	1.13
Compton, CA (city) Los Angeles County	1,467	1.57
Chillum, MD (cdp) Prince George's County	1,448	4.24
Rockford, IL (city) Winnebago County	1,432	0.96
Tucson, AZ (city) Pima County	1,420	0.29
Brooklyn Park, MN (city) Hennepin County	1,396	2.07
Columbia, SC (city) Richland County	1,378	1.19
Bakersfield, CA (city) Kern County	1,378	0.56
Irvington, NJ (cdp) Essex County	1,377	2.27
Gary, IN (city) Lake County	1,372	1.34
Beaumont, TX (city) Jefferson County	1,353	1.19
Lansing, MI (city) Ingham County	1,344	1.13
San Bernardino, CA (city) San Bernardino County	1,335	0.72
Yonkers, NY (city) Westchester County	1,332	0.68
Fayetteville, NC (city) Cumberland County	1,319	1.09
Southfield, MI (city) Oakland County	1,308	1.67
Franklin, NJ (township) Somerset County	1,273	2.50
Springfield, MA (city) Hampden County	1,273	0.84
Gainesville, FL (city) Alachua County	1,249	1.31
Des Moines, IA (city) Polk County	1,243	0.63
Arlington, VA (cdp) Arlington County	1,239	0.65
Sunrise Manor, NV (cdp) Clark County	1,237	0.79
Moreno Valley, CA (city) Riverside County	1,231	0.86
Berkeley, CA (city) Alameda County	1,226	1.19
Kansas City, KS (city) Wyandotte County	1,221	0.83
Pontiac, MI (city) Oakland County	1,218	1.84
Irving, TX (city) Dallas County	1,212	0.63
New Haven, CT (city) New Haven County	1,210	0.98
Paradise, NV (cdp) Clark County	1,202	0.65
Albany, NY (city) Albany County	1,188	1.24
Hawthorne, CA (city) Los Angeles County	1,173	1.40
Woodlawn, MD (cdp) Baltimore County	1,160	3.21
Clarksville, TN (city) Montgomery County	1,147	1.11
Babylon, NY (town) Suffolk County	1,140	0.54
Garland, TX (city) Dallas County	1,127	0.52
North Las Vegas, NV (city) Clark County	1,122	0.97
Riverside, CA (city) Riverside County	1,121	0.44
Elizabeth, NJ (city) Union County	1,118	0.93
Fort Wayne, IN (city) Allen County	1,111	0.54
Charleston, SC (city) Charleston County	1,096	1.14
Hartford, CT (city) Hartford County	1,095	0.90
Fontana, CA (city) San Bernardino County	1,089	0.85
Islip, NY (town) Suffolk County	1,088	0.34
Anchorage, AK (municipality) Anchorage Borough	1,084	0.42
Portsmouth, VA (independent city) Portsmouth city	1,073	1.07
Peoria, IL (city) Peoria County	1,071	0.95
Killeen, TX (city) Bell County	1,061	1.22
Hayward, CA (city) Alameda County	1,029	0.74
Pomona, CA (city) Los Angeles County	1,016	0.68
Hempstead, NY (village) Nassau County	1,011	1.79
Vallejo, CA (city) Solano County	1,011	0.87
Camden, NJ (city) Camden County	1,006	1.26

Notes: (cdp) census designated place; Refer to the Explanation of Data in the front of the book for more detailed information.

African, sub-Saharan: African

Top 150 Places Sorted by Percent

(Based on all places, regardless of population)

Place	Number	%
Lake Harbor, FL (cdp) Palm Beach County	29	31.18
Rentiesville, OK (town) McIntosh County	16	19.51
Gilmore, AR (town) Crittenden County	62	18.56
Furman, SC (town) Hampton County	48	17.52
Anthonyville, AR (town) Crittenden County	46	17.42
Monango, ND (city) Dickey County	4	17.39
Neylandville, TX (town) Hunt County	7	17.07
Port Royal, VA (town) Caroline County	31	16.85
Siloam, GA (town) Greene County	42	13.91
Wooldridge, MO (village) Cooper County	7	12.96
Marianna, AR (city) Lee County	673	12.89
Climax, GA (city) Decatur County	36	11.80
Garysburg, NC (town) Northampton County	139	11.36
Woodland, MS (village) Chickasaw County	16	11.27
Gum Springs, AR (town) Clark County	21	10.71
Century, FL (town) Escambia County	162	9.41
Bowersville, GA (town) Hart County	30	9.40
Fate, TX (city) Rockwall County	43	9.29
Fort Pierce North, FL (cdp) Saint Lucie County	673	9.17
Cundiyo, NM (cdp) Santa Fe County	11	9.17
Alexander, AR (town) Pulaski County	53	8.63
Beauregard, MS (village) Copiah County	23	8.42
Pulaski, GA (town) Candler County	22	8.24
Unity Village, MO (village) Jackson County	17	8.21
Frisco City, AL (town) Monroe County	125	8.17
Clarks, LA (village) Caldwell Parish	85	8.09
Genoa, CO (town) Lincoln County	14	8.09
Noxapater, MS (town) Winston County	35	8.06
Millwood, SC (cdp) Sumter County	70	7.84
Swansea, SC (town) Lexington County	41	7.84
Boston, GA (city) Thomas County	107	7.58
Langston, OK (town) Logan County	122	7.45
Atlantic Beach, SC (town) Horry County	27	7.32
Turkey, NC (town) Sampson County	17	7.17
Cecilton, MD (town) Cecil County	33	6.92
Tildenville, FL (cdp) Orange County	34	6.85
Marion, SC (city) Marion County	478	6.75
Tignall, GA (town) Wilkes County	44	6.73
Woodbury, GA (city) Meriwether County	82	6.65
Cheriton, VA (town) Northampton County	33	6.43
Cliff Village, MO (village) Newton County	3	6.38
Augusta, AR (city) Woodruff County	170	6.36
Bluff City, KS (city) Harper County	4	6.35
Strong, AR (city) Union County	43	6.30
Kershaw, SC (town) Lancaster County	106	6.29
Meade, MI (township) Mason County	18	6.25
Grasonville, MD (cdp) Queen Anne's County	135	6.18
Experiment, GA (cdp) Spalding County	202	6.17
Boutte, LA (cdp) Saint Charles Parish	133	6.15
Lyford South, TX (cdp) Willacy County	16	6.13
White Plains, GA (city) Greene County	21	6.09
Blenheim, SC (town) Marlboro County	7	6.03
Fort Greely, AK (cdp) Southeast Fairbanks Census Area	29	5.97
Lake City, SC (city) Florence County	383	5.96
Charlack, MO (city) Saint Louis County	87	5.94
Louisville, GA (city) Jefferson County	145	5.76
Humnoke, AR (city) Lonoke County	17	5.76
Gurdon, AR (city) Clark County	129	5.74
Camak, GA (town) Warren County	10	5.68
Coffee City, TX (town) Henderson County	10	5.65
Homestown, MO (city) Pemiscot County	10	5.62
Springdale, MD (cdp) Prince George's County	157	5.60
Phillipsburg, GA (cdp) Tift County	63	5.55
Cleveland, GA (city) White County	107	5.53
Emhouse, TX (town) Navarro County	9	5.49
Toco, TX (city) Lamar County	5	5.49
Travelers Rest, SC (city) Greenville County	220	5.39
Greensboro, GA (city) Greene County	175	5.37
North Courtland, AL (town) Lawrence County	43	5.35
Catron, MO (town) New Madrid County	4	5.33
Eastover, SC (town) Richland County	46	5.31
Woodland, GA (city) Talbot County	24	5.24
Twin Groves, AR (town) Faulkner County	14	5.15
Ellenton, GA (town) Colquitt County	20	5.14
Pulaski, IL (village) Pulaski County	15	5.14

Place	Number	%
Bloomer, MI (township) Montcalm County	157	5.12
Franklin Park, FL (cdp) Broward County	56	5.10
Oglethorpe, GA (city) Macon County	61	5.07
Ghent, KY (city) Carroll County	17	5.07
Riverdale Park, MD (town) Prince George's County	332	5.06
Lower Oxford, PA (township) Chester County	217	5.02
Boardman, NC (town) Columbus County	11	4.93
Meigs, GA (city) Thomas County	55	4.91
Girard, GA (town) Burke County	11	4.91
Lenox, GA (town) Cook County	41	4.69
Carlisle, SC (town) Union County	22	4.61
Waverly Hall, GA (town) Harris County	30	4.60
Coleman, FL (city) Sumter County	32	4.59
Glenwood, IL (village) Cook County	414	4.58
Biscoe, NC (town) Montgomery County	77	4.58
Warwick, GA (city) Worth County	20	4.55
College Station, AR (cdp) Pulaski County	30	4.54
Hightsville, NC (cdp) New Hanover County	36	4.52
Maysville, NC (town) Jones County	45	4.48
Milner, GA (city) Lamar County	23	4.44
Makanda, IL (village) Jackson County	18	4.42
Vinita Terrace, MO (village) Saint Louis County	11	4.37
Dover, NC (town) Craven County	19	4.35
Brunswick, GA (city) Glynn County	660	4.28
Penney Farms, FL (town) Clay County	23	4.28
Taylor, MS (village) Lafayette County	13	4.28
South Apopka, FL (cdp) Orange County	259	4.26
Prado Verde, TX (cdp) El Paso County	9	4.25
Chillum, MD (cdp) Prince George's County	1,448	4.24
Graceville, FL (city) Jackson County	103	4.24
Dumas, AR (city) Desha County	225	4.23
Benton Harbor, MI (city) Berrien County	474	4.22
Camilla, GA (city) Mitchell County	236	4.22
Clio, AL (town) Barbour County	95	4.22
Light Oak, NC (cdp) Cleveland County	31	4.21
Crawford, GA (city) Oglethorpe County	33	4.20
Somerset, NJ (cdp) Somerset County	964	4.18
Chamberlayne, VA (cdp) Henrico County	184	4.18
Blue Hills, CT (cdp) Hartford County	129	4.18
Buena Vista, MI (cdp) Saginaw County	324	4.15
Parkdale, AR (city) Ashley County	17	4.14
Temple Hills, MD (cdp) Prince George's County	320	4.13
Epps, LA (village) West Carroll Parish	49	4.11
De Valls Bluff, AR (town) Prairie County	33	4.11
New Carrollton, MD (city) Prince George's County	521	4.06
Braddock, PA (borough) Allegheny County	118	4.05
Cardiff, AL (town) Jefferson County	4	4.04
Lovelady, TX (city) Houston County	24	4.01
Wilberforce, OH (cdp) Greene County	57	4.00
Flemington, GA (city) Liberty County	15	3.99
Lake Village, AR (city) Chicot County	111	3.98
Maurice River, NJ (township) Cumberland County	274	3.95
Goulding, FL (cdp) Escambia County	176	3.94
High Shoals, NC (town) Gaston County	28	3.94
Haywood City, MO (village) Scott County	10	3.94
Brundidge, AL (city) Pike County	92	3.93
Mounds, IL (city) Pulaski County	44	3.93
Supreme, LA (cdp) Assumption Parish	48	3.92
Yellow Bluff, AL (town) Wilcox County	6	3.87
De Land Southwest, FL (cdp) Volusia County	44	3.85
Liberty, TN (town) De Kalb County	15	3.81
Salem, GA (cdp) Upson County	15	3.81
Estill, SC (town) Hampton County	94	3.79
Jonesville, SC (town) Union County	36	3.77
Hedley, TX (city) Donley County	14	3.75
Argyle, GA (town) Clinch County	6	3.75
Kentwood, LA (town) Tangipahoa Parish	82	3.74
Willington, SC (cdp) McCormick County	8	3.74
Hamilton, GA (city) Harris County	9	3.72
Moline Acres, MO (city) Saint Louis County	101	3.71
Yeadon, PA (borough) Delaware County	437	3.70
Lanham-Seabrook, MD (cdp) Prince George's County	668	3.69
Gramercy, LA (town) Saint James Parish	113	3.68
Federalsburg, MD (town) Caroline County	99	3.67
Milan, GA (town) Dodge County	37	3.66

Notes: (cdp) census designated place; Refer to the Explanation of Data in the front of the book for more detailed information.

African, sub-Saharan: African

Top 150 Places Sorted by Percent

(Based on places with populations of 10,000 or more)

Place	Number	%
Brunswick, GA (city) Glynn County	660	4.28
Chillum, MD (cdp) Prince George's County	1,448	4.24
Benton Harbor, MI (city) Berrien County	474	4.22
Somerset, NJ (cdp) Somerset County	964	4.18
New Carrollton, MD (city) Prince George's County	521	4.06
Yeadon, PA (borough) Delaware County	437	3.70
Lanham-Seabrook, MD (cdp) Prince George's County	668	3.69
Beltsville, MD (cdp) Prince George's County	570	3.62
White Oak, MD (cdp) Montgomery County	743	3.56
Justice, IL (village) Cook County	431	3.56
East Riverdale, MD (cdp) Prince George's County	530	3.45
Fairland, MD (cdp) Montgomery County	713	3.30
Woodlawn, MD (cdp) Baltimore County	1,160	3.21
Buena Vista charter, MI (township) Saginaw County	324	3.14
Muskegon Heights, MI (city) Muskegon County	375	3.13
Greenbelt, MD (city) Prince George's County	668	3.12
View Park-Windsor Hills, CA (cdp) Los Angeles County	341	3.11
Cahokia, IL (village) Saint Clair County	511	3.10
Country Club Hills, IL (city) Cook County	501	3.09
Randallstown, MD (cdp) Baltimore County	930	3.01
Candler-McAfee, GA (cdp) De Kalb County	843	2.99
Savage-Guilford, MD (cdp) Howard County	364	2.89
Benton charter, MI (township) Berrien County	472	2.88
Coatesville, PA (city) Chester County	305	2.79
Greater Landover, MD (cdp) Prince George's County	635	2.78
Silver Spring, MD (cdp) Montgomery County	2,128	2.77
New Cassel, NY (cdp) Nassau County	366	2.75
Panthersville, GA (cdp) De Kalb County	314	2.69
Milford Mill, MD (cdp) Baltimore County	701	2.64
Leesburg, FL (city) Lake County	417	2.63
College Park, GA (city) Fulton County	539	2.60
North Amityville, NY (cdp) Suffolk County	422	2.56
Wilkinsburg, PA (borough) Allegheny County	486	2.53
Adelphi, MD (cdp) Prince George's County	380	2.53
Wilmington, DE (city) New Castle County	1,833	2.52
Harvey, IL (city) Cook County	757	2.51
Franklin, NJ (township) Somerset County	1,273	2.50
Flint, MI (city) Genesee County	3,081	2.47
Takoma Park, MD (city) Montgomery County	421	2.45
Orange, NJ (cdp) Essex County	801	2.44
Darby, PA (borough) Delaware County	251	2.44
Redan, GA (cdp) De Kalb County	812	2.40
Calverton, MD (cdp) Montgomery County	302	2.40
Beecher, MI (cdp) Genesee County	309	2.39
Kettering, MD (cdp) Prince George's County	265	2.39
Chester, PA (city) Delaware County	867	2.35
Wyandanch, NY (cdp) Suffolk County	248	2.34
Woodmere, LA (cdp) Jefferson Parish	304	2.32
East Orange, NJ (city) Essex County	1,598	2.29
Irvington, NJ (cdp) Essex County	1,377	2.27
Coral Hills, MD (cdp) Prince George's County	239	2.21
Avenel, NJ (cdp) Middlesex County	386	2.20
Cedar Hill, TX (city) Dallas County	703	2.19
Statesboro, GA (city) Bulloch County	493	2.18
Greater Upper Marlboro, MD (cdp) Prince George's County	408	2.18
South Laurel, MD (cdp) Prince George's County	452	2.17
Pine Hills, FL (cdp) Orange County	903	2.15
Hope, AR (city) Hempstead County	225	2.14
Warrensville Heights, OH (city) Cuyahoga County	329	2.13
Norland, FL (cdp) Miami-Dade County	487	2.12
Douglasville, GA (city) Douglas County	427	2.12
Brownsville, FL (cdp) Miami-Dade County	307	2.12
Union City, GA (city) Fulton County	242	2.12
Westmont, CA (cdp) Los Angeles County	664	2.11
Fort Washington, MD (cdp) Prince George's County	511	2.11
Lawrenceville, GA (city) Gwinnett County	472	2.10
Forestdale, AL (cdp) Jefferson County	222	2.10
Saint Andrews, SC (cdp) Richland County	455	2.09
Matteson, IL (village) Cook County	268	2.08
Brooklyn Park, MN (city) Hennepin County	1,396	2.07
Bloomfield, CT (town) Hartford County	406	2.07
Fredericksburg, VA (independent city) Fredericksburg city	395	2.05
Texas City, TX (city) Galveston County	838	2.02
Opelousas, LA (city) Saint Landry Parish	465	2.02
Pleasantville, NJ (city) Atlantic County	383	2.01
Aiken, SC (city) Aiken County	501	1.98
Ionia, MI (city) Ionia County	211	1.98
Salisbury, MD (city) Wicomico County	476	1.97
Newington, VA (cdp) Fairfax County	387	1.96
Gallatin, TN (city) Sumner County	452	1.95
Cordele, GA (city) Crisp County	223	1.94
Cincinnati, OH (city) Hamilton County	6,339	1.92
Woodlyn, PA (cdp) Delaware County	192	1.92
Statesville, NC (city) Iredell County	439	1.91
West Columbia, SC (city) Lexington County	253	1.91
Princeton, FL (cdp) Miami-Dade County	194	1.91
Mount Vernon, VA (cdp) Fairfax County	542	1.90
Corsicana, TX (city) Navarro County	465	1.90
Waycross, GA (city) Ware County	298	1.90
South Holland, IL (village) Cook County	420	1.89
Fort Stewart, GA (cdp) Liberty County	215	1.89
Oakland, CA (city) Alameda County	7,521	1.88
Trenton, NJ (city) Mercer County	1,603	1.88
East Palo Alto, CA (city) San Mateo County	553	1.88
Hyattsville, MD (city) Prince George's County	279	1.88
Richmond, CA (city) Contra Costa County	1,863	1.87
Roosevelt, NY (cdp) Nassau County	297	1.87
Pontiac, MI (city) Oakland County	1,218	1.84
Morrisville, PA (borough) Bucks County	184	1.84
Orangeburg, SC (city) Orangeburg County	236	1.82
Valdosta, GA (city) Lowndes County	793	1.81
Vidalia, GA (city) Toombs County	192	1.81
Alexandria, VA (independent city) Alexandria city	2,313	1.80
Jennings, MO (city) Saint Louis County	279	1.80
Tifton, GA (city) Tift County	268	1.80
Hempstead, NY (village) Nassau County	1,011	1.79
Laurel, MD (city) Prince George's County	358	1.79
Oxon Hill-Glassmanor, MD (cdp) Prince George's County	625	1.78
Northport, AL (city) Tuscaloosa County	336	1.76
Riverdale, IL (village) Cook County	264	1.76
Bellwood, IL (village) Cook County	359	1.75
Lexington Park, MD (cdp) Saint Mary's County	190	1.75
Trotwood, OH (city) Montgomery County	478	1.74
Groveton, VA (cdp) Fairfax County	370	1.74
Hercules, CA (city) Contra Costa County	335	1.74
Redland, MD (cdp) Montgomery County	301	1.74
Shelbyville, KY (city) Shelby County	180	1.73
Dale City, VA (cdp) Prince William County	965	1.72
Blytheville, AR (city) Mississippi County	314	1.72
Savannah, GA (city) Chatham County	2,244	1.71
Norristown, PA (borough) Montgomery County	535	1.71
La Vergne, TN (city) Rutherford County	323	1.71
Highland Park, MI (city) Wayne County	287	1.71
Martinsville, VA (independent city) Martinsville city	263	1.71
Powder Springs, GA (city) Cobb County	222	1.71
Fulton, MO (city) Callaway County	206	1.70
Glenn Dale, MD (cdp) Prince George's County	216	1.69
Friendly, MD (cdp) Prince George's County	185	1.69
Washington, DC (city) District of Columbia	9,638	1.68
Inglewood, CA (city) Los Angeles County	1,894	1.68
Southfield, MI (city) Oakland County	1,308	1.67
West Little River, FL (cdp) Miami-Dade County	539	1.67
Crestview, FL (city) Okaloosa County	247	1.67
Altadena, CA (cdp) Los Angeles County	702	1.65
Lancaster, TX (city) Dallas County	426	1.65
Seven Oaks, SC (cdp) Lexington County	261	1.65
Fort Benning South, GA (cdp) Chattahoochee County	192	1.64
Harrisburg, PA (city) Dauphin County	802	1.63
New Brunswick, NJ (city) Middlesex County	793	1.63
Athens, AL (city) Limestone County	312	1.63
Asbury Park, NJ (city) Monmouth County	276	1.63
Akron, OH (city) Summit County	3,525	1.62
El Campo, TX (city) Wharton County	175	1.62
Germantown, MD (cdp) Montgomery County	889	1.61
Sanford, FL (city) Seminole County	607	1.61
Dolton, IL (village) Cook County	414	1.61
Belvedere Park, GA (cdp) De Kalb County	306	1.61
Tuskegee, AL (city) Macon County	194	1.61
Sandusky, OH (city) Erie County	447	1.60
Spanish Lake, MO (cdp) Saint Louis County	343	1.60

Notes: (cdp) census designated place; Refer to the Explanation of Data in the front of the book for more detailed information.

African, sub-Saharan: Cape Verdean

Top 150 Places Sorted by Number

(Based on all places, regardless of population)

Place	Number	%
Boston, MA (city) Suffolk County	11,060	1.88
Brockton, MA (city) Plymouth County	8,844	9.38
New Bedford, MA (city) Bristol County	7,508	8.01
Pawtucket, RI (city) Providence County	6,243	8.56
Providence, RI (city) Providence County	3,705	2.13
East Providence, RI (city) Providence County	2,383	4.89
Wareham, MA (town) Plymouth County	1,556	7.65
Taunton, MA (city) Bristol County	1,425	2.55
Central Falls, RI (city) Providence County	961	5.08
Barnstable Town, MA (city) Barnstable County	857	1.79
New York, NY (city) New York City	848	0.01
Falmouth, MA (town) Barnstable County	831	2.54
Bridgeport, CT (city) Fairfield County	804	0.58
Waterbury, CT (city) New Haven County	696	0.65
Dartmouth, MA (town) Bristol County	679	2.21
Fall River, MA (city) Bristol County	571	0.62
Randolph, MA (cdp) Norfolk County	451	1.45
Cranston, RI (city) Providence County	400	0.50
Somerville, MA (city) Middlesex County	398	0.51
Cambridge, MA (city) Middlesex County	394	0.39
Plymouth, MA (town) Plymouth County	389	0.75
Springfield, MA (city) Hampden County	365	0.24
North Providence, RI (cdp) Providence County	345	1.06
Scituate, MA (town) Plymouth County	344	1.93
Sacramento, CA (city) Sacramento County	337	0.08
Los Angeles, CA (city) Los Angeles County	325	0.01
Philadelphia, PA (city) Philadelphia County	304	0.02
Norwich, CT (city) New London County	303	0.84
Mashpee, MA (town) Barnstable County	290	2.24
New Haven, CT (city) New Haven County	275	0.22
Bridgewater, MA (town) Plymouth County	272	1.08
Onset, MA (cdp) Plymouth County	261	19.11
Marion, MA (town) Plymouth County	261	5.09
Carver, MA (town) Plymouth County	261	2.34
Warwick, RI (city) Kent County	250	0.29
Stoughton, MA (town) Norfolk County	244	0.90
Kingston, MA (town) Plymouth County	240	2.04
Attleboro, MA (city) Bristol County	239	0.57
East Bridgewater, MA (town) Plymouth County	232	1.79
Weymouth, MA (cdp) Norfolk County	231	0.43
Oakland, CA (city) Alameda County	227	0.06
Fairhaven, MA (town) Bristol County	218	1.35
Worcester, MA (city) Worcester County	218	0.13
Harwich, MA (town) Barnstable County	214	1.73
Chelsea, MA (city) Suffolk County	212	0.60
Malden, MA (city) Middlesex County	211	0.37
Freetown, MA (town) Bristol County	202	2.38
Middleborough, MA (town) Plymouth County	198	0.99
Woonsocket, RI (city) Providence County	190	0.44
West Wareham, MA (cdp) Plymouth County	189	10.54
Cumberland, RI (town) Providence County	184	0.58
White Island Shores, MA (cdp) Plymouth County	183	8.00
Newport, RI (city) Newport County	182	0.69
Bourne, MA (town) Barnstable County	178	0.95
East Falmouth, MA (cdp) Barnstable County	167	2.53
Weweantic, MA (cdp) Plymouth County	165	8.47
West Haven, CT (city) New Haven County	161	0.31
Milton, MA (cdp) Norfolk County	160	0.61
Braintree, MA (town) Norfolk County	160	0.47
San Diego, CA (city) San Diego County	151	0.01
Everett, MA (city) Middlesex County	150	0.39
Newton, MA (city) Middlesex County	148	0.18
Brookline, MA (cdp) Norfolk County	137	0.24
Yonkers, NY (city) Westchester County	137	0.07
Raynham, MA (town) Bristol County	136	1.16
Washington, DC (city) District of Columbia	134	0.02
Northwest Harwich, MA (cdp) Barnstable County	132	3.36
Stratford, CT (cdp) Fairfield County	129	0.26
Johnston, RI (town) Providence County	124	0.44
Jersey City, NJ (city) Hudson County	124	0.05
Mattapoisett, MA (town) Plymouth County	123	1.96
Canton, MA (town) Norfolk County	123	0.59
West Warwick, RI (cdp) Kent County	116	0.39
Salem, MA (city) Essex County	116	0.29
Mansfield, MA (town) Bristol County	114	0.51
Quincy, MA (city) Norfolk County	113	0.13
Acushnet, MA (town) Bristol County	111	1.09
Rockland, MA (town) Plymouth County	109	0.62
Middleborough Center, MA (cdp) Plymouth County	107	1.55
Sandwich, MA (town) Barnstable County	106	0.53
North Attleborough, MA (town) Bristol County	104	0.38
Waltham, MA (city) Middlesex County	103	0.17
Bliss Corner, MA (cdp) Bristol County	101	1.87
Yarmouth, MA (town) Barnstable County	100	0.40
Marshfield, MA (town) Plymouth County	99	0.41
Dennis, MA (town) Barnstable County	98	0.61
Wareham Center, MA (cdp) Plymouth County	96	3.38
Laguna, CA (cdp) Sacramento County	96	0.28
Newark, NJ (city) Essex County	96	0.04
Norfolk, VA (independent city) Norfolk city	95	0.04
Poinciana, FL (cdp) Osceola County	90	0.66
Hamden, CT (town) New Haven County	90	0.16
New Britain, CT (city) Hartford County	90	0.13
Hempstead, NY (town) Nassau County	90	0.01
Amherst, MA (town) Hampshire County	89	0.26
Middletown, RI (town) Newport County	88	0.51
Lincoln, RI (town) Providence County	86	0.41
Hanson, MA (town) Plymouth County	85	0.90
Seekonk, MA (town) Bristol County	84	0.63
Orlando, FL (city) Orange County	84	0.05
Hull, MA (cdp) Plymouth County	83	0.75
Swansea, MA (town) Bristol County	83	0.52
Wheaton-Glenmont, MD (cdp) Montgomery County	83	0.14
Harwich Center, MA (cdp) Barnstable County	82	4.43
Newport East, RI (cdp) Newport County	81	0.69
Norton, MA (town) Bristol County	81	0.45
Amherst Center, MA (cdp) Hampshire County	79	0.46
Easton, MA (town) Bristol County	79	0.35
Rochester, MA (town) Plymouth County	75	1.64
Andover, MA (town) Essex County	74	0.24
Paradise, NV (cdp) Clark County	74	0.04
Indianapolis, IN (special city) Marion County	74	0.01
Ansonia, CT (city) New Haven County	73	0.39
Groton, CT (town) New London County	73	0.18
Jacksonville, FL (special city) Duval County	72	0.01
San Francisco, CA (city) San Francisco County	72	0.01
Montclair, NJ (cdp) Essex County	71	0.18
Lakewood, CO (city) Jefferson County	71	0.05
Dallas, TX (city) Dallas County	71	0.01
Framingham, MA (cdp) Middlesex County	70	0.10
Virginia Beach, VA (independent city) Virginia Beach city	68	0.02
South Yarmouth, MA (cdp) Barnstable County	67	0.57
Medford, MA (city) Middlesex County	66	0.12
Coral Springs, FL (city) Broward County	66	0.06
Augusta-Richmond County, GA (special city) Richmond County	66	0.03
Chicago, IL (city) Cook County	66	0.00
Smith Mills, MA (cdp) Bristol County	65	1.46
Woburn, MA (city) Middlesex County	65	0.17
Milford, CT (town) New Haven County	62	0.12
Milford, CT (special city) New Haven County	62	0.12
Lynnfield, MA (cdp) Essex County	61	0.53
Webster, MA (town) Worcester County	60	0.37
Mansfield Center, MA (cdp) Bristol County	59	0.83
Nashua, NH (city) Hillsborough County	59	0.07
Columbus, OH (city) Franklin County	59	0.01
Plympton, MA (town) Plymouth County	58	2.20
Pembroke, MA (town) Plymouth County	58	0.34
New Rochelle, NY (city) Westchester County	58	0.08
North Hempstead, NY (town) Nassau County	58	0.03
Cumberland Hill, RI (cdp) Providence County	57	0.74
Buzzards Bay, MA (cdp) Barnstable County	56	1.63
Lanham-Seabrook, MD (cdp) Prince George's County	56	0.31
Kissimmee, FL (city) Osceola County	56	0.12
Lawrence, MA (city) Essex County	56	0.08
Abington, MA (cdp) Plymouth County	55	0.38
Alameda, CA (city) Alameda County	55	0.08
Vacaville, CA (city) Solano County	54	0.06
Ayer, MA (town) Middlesex County	53	0.73
Bloomingdale, FL (cdp) Hillsborough County	53	0.27
Holbrook, MA (cdp) Norfolk County	52	0.48

Notes: (cdp) census designated place; Refer to the Explanation of Data in the front of the book for more detailed information.

African, sub-Saharan: Cape Verdean

Top 150 Places Sorted by Percent

(Based on all places, regardless of population)

Place	Number	%
Onset, MA (cdp) Plymouth County	261	19.11
West Wareham, MA (cdp) Plymouth County	189	10.54
Brockton, MA (city) Plymouth County	8,844	9.38
Pawtucket, RI (city) Providence County	6,243	8.56
Weweantic, MA (cdp) Plymouth County	165	8.47
New Bedford, MA (city) Bristol County	7,508	8.01
White Island Shores, MA (cdp) Plymouth County	183	8.00
Wareham, MA (town) Plymouth County	1,556	7.65
Marion, MA (town) Plymouth County	261	5.09
Central Falls, RI (city) Providence County	961	5.08
East Providence, RI (city) Providence County	2,383	4.89
Harwich Center, MA (cdp) Barnstable County	82	4.43
Fort Devens, MA (cdp) Worcester County	42	4.20
Wareham Center, MA (cdp) Plymouth County	96	3.38
Northwest Harwich, MA (cdp) Barnstable County	132	3.36
Taunton, MA (city) Bristol County	1,425	2.55
Falmouth, MA (town) Barnstable County	831	2.54
East Falmouth, MA (cdp) Barnstable County	167	2.53
Aquinnah, MA (town) Dukes County	9	2.47
Freetown, MA (town) Bristol County	202	2.38
Teaticket, MA (cdp) Barnstable County	45	2.35
Carver, MA (town) Plymouth County	261	2.34
Mashpee, MA (town) Barnstable County	290	2.24
Dartmouth, MA (town) Bristol County	679	2.21
Plympton, MA (town) Plymouth County	58	2.20
Providence, RI (city) Providence County	3,705	2.13
Kingston, MA (town) Plymouth County	240	2.04
Mattapoisett, MA (town) Plymouth County	123	1.96
Scituate, MA (town) Plymouth County	344	1.93
Boston, MA (city) Suffolk County	11,060	1.88
Bliss Corner, MA (cdp) Bristol County	101	1.87
Rice River, MN (township) Aitkin County	3	1.81
Barnstable Town, MA (city) Barnstable County	857	1.79
East Bridgewater, MA (town) Plymouth County	232	1.79
Harwich, MA (town) Barnstable County	214	1.73
Rochester, MA (town) Plymouth County	75	1.64
Buzzards Bay, MA (cdp) Barnstable County	56	1.63
Middleborough Center, MA (cdp) Plymouth County	107	1.55
Smith Mills, MA (cdp) Bristol County	65	1.46
Randolph, MA (cdp) Norfolk County	451	1.45
Fairhaven, MA (town) Bristol County	218	1.35
Dennis Port, MA (cdp) Barnstable County	45	1.25
Vineyard Haven, MA (cdp) Dukes County	24	1.25
Oak Bluffs, MA (town) Dukes County	46	1.24
Sagamore, MA (cdp) Barnstable County	42	1.18
Raynham, MA (town) Bristol County	136	1.16
North Plymouth, MA (cdp) Plymouth County	40	1.11
Acushnet, MA (town) Bristol County	111	1.09
Bridgewater, MA (town) Plymouth County	272	1.08
North Providence, RI (cdp) Providence County	345	1.06
Nantucket, MA (cdp) Nantucket County	39	1.03
Middleborough, MA (town) Plymouth County	198	0.99
North Scituate, MA (cdp) Plymouth County	51	0.98
Bourne, MA (town) Barnstable County	178	0.95
East Sandwich, MA (cdp) Barnstable County	35	0.95
Elkland, PA (borough) Tioga County	17	0.95
Stoughton, MA (town) Norfolk County	244	0.90
Hanson, MA (town) Plymouth County	85	0.90
Oxoboxo River, CT (cdp) New London County	25	0.86
West Dennis, MA (cdp) Barnstable County	22	0.86
Pocasset, MA (cdp) Barnstable County	23	0.85
Norwich, CT (city) New London County	303	0.84
South Dennis, MA (cdp) Barnstable County	31	0.84
Sandisfield, MA (town) Berkshire County	7	0.84
Mansfield Center, MA (cdp) Bristol County	59	0.83
North Falmouth, MA (cdp) Barnstable County	26	0.79
Plymouth, MA (town) Plymouth County	389	0.75
Hull, MA (cdp) Plymouth County	83	0.75
Cumberland Hill, RI (cdp) Providence County	57	0.74
Ayer, MA (town) Middlesex County	53	0.73
Poquonock Bridge, CT (cdp) New London County	11	0.71
Ava, NY (town) Oneida County	5	0.70
Newport, RI (city) Newport County	182	0.69
Newport East, RI (cdp) Newport County	81	0.69
Berkley, MA (town) Bristol County	39	0.68
Mattapoisett Center, MA (cdp) Plymouth County	20	0.68
Warren, MA (town) Worcester County	32	0.67
Poinciana, FL (cdp) Osceola County	90	0.66
Waipio Acres, HI (cdp) Honolulu County	35	0.66
Waterbury, CT (city) New Haven County	696	0.65
Tisbury, MA (town) Dukes County	24	0.64
Seekonk, MA (town) Bristol County	84	0.63
Fall River, MA (city) Bristol County	571	0.62
Rockland, MA (town) Plymouth County	109	0.62
North Westport, MA (cdp) Bristol County	29	0.62
Milton, MA (cdp) Norfolk County	160	0.61
Dennis, MA (town) Barnstable County	98	0.61
Chelsea, MA (city) Suffolk County	212	0.60
Canton, MA (town) Norfolk County	123	0.59
Bridgeport, CT (city) Fairfield County	804	0.58
Cumberland, RI (town) Providence County	184	0.58
Attleboro, MA (city) Bristol County	239	0.57
South Yarmouth, MA (cdp) Barnstable County	67	0.57
Ocean Bluff-Brant Rock, MA (cdp) Plymouth County	29	0.57
Preston, CT (town) New London County	26	0.55
Spencer, NY (village) Tioga County	4	0.55
Mashpee Neck, MA (cdp) Barnstable County	5	0.54
Sandwich, MA (town) Barnstable County	106	0.53
Lynnfield, MA (cdp) Essex County	61	0.53
Swansea, MA (town) Bristol County	83	0.52
New Hope, MS (cdp) Lowndes County	10	0.52
Somerville, MA (city) Middlesex County	398	0.51
Mansfield, MA (town) Bristol County	114	0.51
Middletown, RI (town) Newport County	88	0.51
Cranston, RI (city) Providence County	400	0.50
Moscow, TN (city) Fayette County	2	0.49
Holbrook, MA (cdp) Norfolk County	52	0.48
Braintree, MA (town) Norfolk County	160	0.47
Eielson AFB, AK (cdp) Fairbanks North Star Borough	26	0.47
Amherst Center, MA (cdp) Hampshire County	79	0.46
Acushnet Center, MA (cdp) Bristol County	15	0.46
Norton, MA (town) Bristol County	81	0.45
Dighton, MA (town) Bristol County	28	0.45
Woonsocket, RI (city) Providence County	190	0.44
Johnston, RI (town) Providence County	124	0.44
West Yarmouth, MA (cdp) Barnstable County	28	0.44
Weymouth, MA (cdp) Norfolk County	231	0.43
Tupper Lake, NY (village) Franklin County	17	0.43
Marshfield, MA (town) Plymouth County	99	0.41
Lincoln, RI (town) Providence County	86	0.41
North Smithfield, RI (town) Providence County	44	0.41
West Bridgewater, MA (town) Plymouth County	27	0.41
Sylvan Lake, MI (city) Oakland County	7	0.41
Yarmouth, MA (town) Barnstable County	100	0.40
Valley Falls, RI (cdp) Providence County	46	0.40
Sherborn, MA (town) Middlesex County	17	0.40
Cambridge, MA (city) Middlesex County	394	0.39
Everett, MA (city) Middlesex County	150	0.39
West Warwick, RI (cdp) Kent County	116	0.39
Ansonia, CT (city) New Haven County	73	0.39
North Attleborough, MA (town) Bristol County	104	0.38
Abington, MA (cdp) Plymouth County	55	0.38
Canyon Day, AZ (cdp) Gila County	4	0.38
Washington, VT (town) Orange County	4	0.38
Malden, MA (city) Middlesex County	211	0.37
Webster, MA (town) Worcester County	60	0.37
Woodbridge, CT (town) New Haven County	33	0.37
Garden City Park, NY (cdp) Nassau County	28	0.37
West Hazleton, PA (borough) Luzerne County	13	0.37
Marlborough, MO (village) Saint Louis County	8	0.36
Easton, MA (town) Bristol County	79	0.35
Putnam District, CT (cdp) Windham County	24	0.35
West Winfield, NY (village) Herkimer County	3	0.35
Pembroke, MA (town) Plymouth County	58	0.34
Conning Towers-Nautilus Park, CT (cdp) New London County	35	0.34
Wyoming, DE (town) Kent County	4	0.34
Kensington, KS (city) Smith County	2	0.34
Fort Stewart, GA (cdp) Liberty County	37	0.33
Kennebunk, ME (town) York County	35	0.33
Princeton Junction, NJ (cdp) Mercer County	8	0.33

Notes: (cdp) census designated place; Refer to the Explanation of Data in the front of the book for more detailed information.

African, sub-Saharan: Cape Verdean

Top 150 Places Sorted by Percent

(Based on places with populations of 10,000 or more)

Place	Number	%
Brockton, MA (city) Plymouth County	8,844	9.38
Pawtucket, RI (city) Providence County	6,243	8.56
New Bedford, MA (city) Bristol County	7,508	8.01
Wareham, MA (town) Plymouth County	1,556	7.65
Central Falls, RI (city) Providence County	961	5.08
East Providence, RI (city) Providence County	2,383	4.89
Taunton, MA (city) Bristol County	1,425	2.55
Falmouth, MA (town) Barnstable County	831	2.54
Carver, MA (town) Plymouth County	261	2.34
Mashpee, MA (town) Barnstable County	290	2.24
Dartmouth, MA (town) Bristol County	679	2.21
Providence, RI (city) Providence County	3,705	2.13
Kingston, MA (town) Plymouth County	240	2.04
Scituate, MA (town) Plymouth County	344	1.93
Boston, MA (city) Suffolk County	11,060	1.88
Barnstable Town, MA (city) Barnstable County	857	1.79
East Bridgewater, MA (town) Plymouth County	232	1.79
Harwich, MA (town) Barnstable County	214	1.73
Randolph, MA (cdp) Norfolk County	451	1.45
Fairhaven, MA (town) Bristol County	218	1.35
Raynham, MA (town) Bristol County	136	1.16
Acushnet, MA (town) Bristol County	111	1.09
Bridgewater, MA (town) Plymouth County	272	1.08
North Providence, RI (cdp) Providence County	345	1.06
Middleborough, MA (town) Plymouth County	198	0.99
Bourne, MA (town) Barnstable County	178	0.95
Stoughton, MA (town) Norfolk County	244	0.90
Norwich, CT (city) New London County	303	0.84
Plymouth, MA (town) Plymouth County	389	0.75
Hull, MA (cdp) Plymouth County	83	0.75
Newport, RI (city) Newport County	182	0.69
Newport East, RI (cdp) Newport County	81	0.69
Poinciana, FL (cdp) Osceola County	90	0.66
Waterbury, CT (city) New Haven County	696	0.65
Seekonk, MA (town) Bristol County	84	0.63
Fall River, MA (city) Bristol County	571	0.62
Rockland, MA (town) Plymouth County	109	0.62
Milton, MA (cdp) Norfolk County	160	0.61
Dennis, MA (town) Barnstable County	98	0.61
Chelsea, MA (city) Suffolk County	212	0.60
Canton, MA (town) Norfolk County	123	0.59
Bridgeport, CT (city) Fairfield County	804	0.58
Cumberland, RI (town) Providence County	184	0.58
Attleboro, MA (city) Bristol County	239	0.57
South Yarmouth, MA (cdp) Barnstable County	67	0.57
Sandwich, MA (town) Barnstable County	106	0.53
Lynnfield, MA (cdp) Essex County	61	0.53
Swansea, MA (town) Bristol County	83	0.52
Somerville, MA (city) Middlesex County	398	0.51
Mansfield, MA (town) Bristol County	114	0.51
Middletown, RI (town) Newport County	88	0.51
Cranston, RI (city) Providence County	400	0.50
Holbrook, MA (cdp) Norfolk County	52	0.48
Braintree, MA (town) Norfolk County	160	0.47
Amherst Center, MA (cdp) Hampshire County	79	0.46
Norton, MA (town) Bristol County	81	0.45
Woonsocket, RI (city) Providence County	190	0.44
Johnston, RI (town) Providence County	124	0.44
Weymouth, MA (cdp) Norfolk County	231	0.43
Marshfield, MA (town) Plymouth County	99	0.41
Lincoln, RI (town) Providence County	86	0.41
North Smithfield, RI (town) Providence County	44	0.41
Yarmouth, MA (town) Barnstable County	100	0.40
Valley Falls, RI (cdp) Providence County	46	0.40
Cambridge, MA (city) Middlesex County	394	0.39
Everett, MA (city) Middlesex County	150	0.39
West Warwick, RI (cdp) Kent County	116	0.39
Ansonia, CT (city) New Haven County	73	0.39
North Attleborough, MA (town) Bristol County	104	0.38
Abington, MA (cdp) Plymouth County	55	0.38
Malden, MA (city) Middlesex County	211	0.37
Webster, MA (town) Worcester County	60	0.37
Easton, MA (town) Bristol County	79	0.35
Pembroke, MA (town) Plymouth County	58	0.34
Conning Towers-Nautilus Park, CT (cdp) New London County	35	0.34
Fort Stewart, GA (cdp) Liberty County	37	0.33
Kennebunk, ME (town) York County	35	0.33
Hanover, MA (town) Plymouth County	42	0.32
West Haven, CT (city) New Haven County	161	0.31
Lanham-Seabrook, MD (cdp) Prince George's County	56	0.31
Glenn Dale, MD (cdp) Prince George's County	39	0.30
Warwick, RI (city) Kent County	250	0.29
Salem, MA (city) Essex County	116	0.29
Whitman, MA (town) Plymouth County	40	0.29
Laguna, CA (cdp) Sacramento County	96	0.28
Sharon, MA (town) Norfolk County	49	0.28
Bloomingdale, FL (cdp) Hillsborough County	53	0.27
Cayce, SC (city) Lexington County	32	0.27
Stratford, CT (cdp) Fairfield County	129	0.26
Amherst, MA (town) Hampshire County	89	0.26
East Greenwich, RI (town) Kent County	32	0.25
Upper Grand Lagoon, FL (cdp) Bay County	28	0.25
Springfield, MA (city) Hampden County	365	0.24
Brookline, MA (cdp) Norfolk County	137	0.24
Andover, MA (town) Essex County	74	0.24
Bloomfield, CT (town) Hartford County	47	0.24
Wilbraham, MA (town) Hampden County	33	0.24
Warren, RI (town) Bristol County	27	0.24
Hampton, NH (town) Rockingham County	34	0.23
New Haven, CT (city) New Haven County	275	0.22
Westerly, RI (town) Washington County	51	0.22
Montville, CT (town) New London County	41	0.22
Brattleboro, VT (town) Windham County	26	0.22
Athol, MA (town) Worcester County	25	0.22
La Riviera, CA (cdp) Sacramento County	23	0.22
Ocean Acres, NJ (cdp) Ocean County	28	0.21
Stoneham, MA (town) Middlesex County	45	0.20
Whitemarsh, PA (township) Montgomery County	33	0.20
Westport, MA (town) Bristol County	29	0.20
Arlington, NY (cdp) Dutchess County	25	0.20
Amherst, NH (town) Hillsborough County	21	0.20
Clinton, MD (cdp) Prince George's County	50	0.19
Harrison, NJ (town) Hudson County	28	0.19
Duxbury, MA (town) Plymouth County	27	0.19
Norfolk, MA (town) Norfolk County	20	0.19
Groton, CT (city) New London County	19	0.19
Newton, MA (city) Middlesex County	148	0.18
Groton, CT (town) New London County	73	0.18
Montclair, NJ (cdp) Essex County	71	0.18
Griswold, CT (town) New London County	19	0.18
Leicester, MA (town) Worcester County	19	0.18
Waltham, MA (city) Middlesex County	103	0.17
Woburn, MA (city) Middlesex County	65	0.17
Franklin, MA (city) Norfolk County	49	0.17
Bristol, RI (cdp) Bristol County	38	0.17
Citrus Park, FL (cdp) Hillsborough County	35	0.17
Somerset, MA (cdp) Bristol County	31	0.17
Bellingham, MA (town) Norfolk County	26	0.17
Hamden, CT (town) New Haven County	90	0.16
New London, CT (city) New London County	41	0.16
North Kingstown, RI (town) Washington County	41	0.16
Walpole, MA (town) Norfolk County	37	0.16
Portsmouth, RI (town) Newport County	27	0.16
North Valley Stream, NY (cdp) Nassau County	25	0.16
Cherryland, CA (cdp) Alameda County	22	0.16
Oak Grove, OR (cdp) Clackamas County	20	0.16
View Park-Windsor Hills, CA (cdp) Los Angeles County	18	0.16
Weston, MA (town) Middlesex County	18	0.16
Cheshire, CT (town) New Haven County	44	0.15
Fair Oaks, CA (cdp) Sacramento County	41	0.15
Bailey's Crossroads, VA (cdp) Fairfax County	34	0.15
West Pensacola, FL (cdp) Escambia County	32	0.15
Hudson, MA (town) Middlesex County	27	0.15
Narragansett, RI (town) Washington County	24	0.15
Wolcott, CT (town) New Haven County	23	0.15
Westbury, NY (village) Nassau County	21	0.15
Piney Green, NC (cdp) Onslow County	17	0.15
Wheaton-Glenmont, MD (cdp) Montgomery County	83	0.14
Hudson, NH (town) Hillsborough County	31	0.14
Hingham, MA (town) Plymouth County	28	0.14

Notes: (cdp) census designated place; Refer to the Explanation of Data in the front of the book for more detailed information.

African, sub-Saharan: Ethiopian

Top 150 Places Sorted by Number

(Based on all places, regardless of population)

Place	Number	%
Seattle, WA (city) King County	4,110	0.73
Dallas, TX (city) Dallas County	3,006	0.25
Los Angeles, CA (city) Los Angeles County	2,991	0.08
Alexandria, VA (independent city) Alexandria city	2,721	2.12
Minneapolis, MN (city) Hennepin County	2,259	0.59
Arlington, VA (cdp) Arlington County	2,171	1.15
Washington, DC (city) District of Columbia	2,158	0.38
New York, NY (city) New York City	1,921	0.02
San Diego, CA (city) San Diego County	1,707	0.14
Silver Spring, MD (cdp) Montgomery County	1,680	2.19
San Jose, CA (city) Santa Clara County	1,669	0.19
Saint Paul, MN (city) Ramsey County	1,279	0.45
Columbus, OH (city) Franklin County	1,241	0.17
Oakland, CA (city) Alameda County	1,195	0.30
Chicago, IL (city) Cook County	1,186	0.04
Paradise, NV (cdp) Clark County	864	0.46
Houston, TX (city) Harris County	848	0.04
North Atlanta, GA (cdp) De Kalb County	844	2.20
Portland, OR (city) Multnomah County	825	0.16
Philadelphia, PA (city) Philadelphia County	758	0.05
Denver, CO (city) Denver County	718	0.13
Wheaton-Glenmont, MD (cdp) Montgomery County	660	1.14
Boston, MA (city) Suffolk County	658	0.11
Aurora, CO (city) Arapahoe County	651	0.24
Santa Rosa, CA (city) Sonoma County	650	0.44
Charlotte, NC (city) Mecklenburg County	608	0.11
Atlanta, GA (city) Fulton County	580	0.14
Lincolnia, VA (cdp) Fairfax County	571	3.60
Takoma Park, MD (city) Montgomery County	539	3.14
Cambridge, MA (city) Middlesex County	499	0.49
San Francisco, CA (city) San Francisco County	495	0.06
Indianapolis, IN (special city) Marion County	493	0.06
Sioux Falls, SD (city) Minnehaha County	452	0.36
Nashville-Davidson, TN (special city) Davidson County	431	0.08
Phoenix, AZ (city) Maricopa County	419	0.03
Saint Louis, MO (independent city) Saint Louis city	405	0.12
Grand Rapids, MI (city) Kent County	388	0.20
Franconia, VA (cdp) Fairfax County	384	1.20
Rochester, NY (city) Monroe County	383	0.17
Springfield, VA (cdp) Fairfax County	376	1.24
Plano, TX (city) Collin County	375	0.17
Chillum, MD (cdp) Prince George's County	373	1.09
Santa Clara, CA (city) Santa Clara County	363	0.36
Kansas City, MO (city) Jackson County	351	0.08
Spring Valley, NV (cdp) Clark County	346	0.29
Annandale, VA (cdp) Fairfax County	345	0.63
Garland, TX (city) Dallas County	316	0.15
Anaheim, CA (city) Orange County	314	0.10
Detroit, MI (city) Wayne County	300	0.03
Baltimore, MD (independent city) Baltimore city	297	0.05
Fresno, CA (city) Fresno County	293	0.07
Irving, TX (city) Dallas County	286	0.15
Las Vegas, NV (city) Clark County	286	0.06
Richardson, TX (city) Dallas County	266	0.29
Austin, TX (city) Travis County	254	0.04
Newington, VA (cdp) Fairfax County	251	1.27
White Oak, MD (cdp) Montgomery County	247	1.18
Berkeley, CA (city) Alameda County	240	0.23
Jersey City, NJ (city) Hudson County	221	0.09
Aspen Hill, MD (cdp) Montgomery County	220	0.44
Tucker, GA (cdp) De Kalb County	206	0.77
Long Beach, CA (city) Los Angeles County	205	0.04
Adelphi, MD (cdp) Prince George's County	204	1.36
Pasadena, CA (city) Los Angeles County	203	0.15
Brooklyn Center, MN (city) Hennepin County	195	0.67
White Center, WA (cdp) King County	190	0.91
Saint Louis Park, MN (city) Hennepin County	185	0.42
Columbia, MD (cdp) Howard County	181	0.20
Buena Park, CA (city) Orange County	180	0.23
Malden, MA (city) Middlesex County	166	0.29
Inglewood, CA (city) Los Angeles County	166	0.15
Whitehall, OH (city) Franklin County	162	0.84
North Kensington, MD (cdp) Montgomery County	158	1.78
Kemp Mill, MD (cdp) Montgomery County	158	1.59
Bailey's Crossroads, VA (cdp) Fairfax County	157	0.69
Culver City, CA (city) Los Angeles County	155	0.40
Goddard, MD (cdp) Prince George's County	153	2.76
East Orange, NJ (city) Essex County	149	0.21
Bloomington, MN (city) Hennepin County	148	0.17
Sacramento, CA (city) Sacramento County	147	0.04
Milwaukee, WI (city) Milwaukee County	145	0.02
Cincinnati, OH (city) Hamilton County	143	0.04
Fremont, CA (city) Alameda County	136	0.07
Gainesville, FL (city) Alachua County	135	0.14
Bellevue, WA (city) King County	134	0.12
Memphis, TN (city) Shelby County	134	0.02
Tukwila, WA (city) King County	131	0.76
Burke, VA (cdp) Fairfax County	130	0.23
Brooklyn Park, MN (city) Hennepin County	130	0.19
Harrisburg, PA (city) Dauphin County	129	0.26
Babylon, NY (town) Suffolk County	126	0.06
Pomona, CA (city) Los Angeles County	125	0.08
Campbell, CA (city) Santa Clara County	123	0.32
Richfield, MN (city) Hennepin County	122	0.35
Chino Hills, CA (city) San Bernardino County	121	0.18
Hayward, CA (city) Alameda County	121	0.09
Chandler, AZ (city) Maricopa County	118	0.07
Hawthorne, CA (city) Los Angeles County	117	0.14
Redan, GA (cdp) De Kalb County	116	0.34
Addison, TX (town) Dallas County	115	0.83
San Leandro, CA (city) Alameda County	115	0.15
Sunrise Manor, NV (cdp) Clark County	115	0.07
Rose Hill, VA (cdp) Fairfax County	114	0.76
Columbia Heights, MN (city) Anoka County	113	0.61
East Lansing, MI (city) Ingham County	112	0.24
Carson, CA (city) Los Angeles County	111	0.12
San Bernardino, CA (city) San Bernardino County	111	0.06
North Decatur, GA (cdp) De Kalb County	110	0.73
Upper Darby, PA (township) Delaware County	110	0.13
Wichita, KS (city) Sedgwick County	109	0.03
Raleigh, NC (city) Wake County	107	0.04
Arlington, TX (city) Tarrant County	107	0.03
Wyandanch, NY (cdp) Suffolk County	106	1.00
Tampa, FL (city) Hillsborough County	106	0.03
SeaTac, WA (city) King County	105	0.41
Montgomery Village, MD (cdp) Montgomery County	105	0.28
Baton Rouge, LA (city) East Baton Rouge Parish	105	0.05
West Orange, NJ (cdp) Essex County	104	0.23
Gilroy, CA (city) Santa Clara County	103	0.25
Alameda, CA (city) Alameda County	102	0.14
Emeryville, CA (city) Alameda County	101	1.47
Lake Ridge, VA (cdp) Prince William County	100	0.33
Clarkston, GA (city) De Kalb County	99	1.45
Jacksonville, FL (special city) Duval County	99	0.01
Little Canada, MN (city) Ramsey County	98	1.00
Renton, WA (city) King County	98	0.20
Mount Rainier, MD (city) Prince George's County	96	1.13
Doraville, GA (city) De Kalb County	95	0.94
Shawnee, KS (city) Johnson County	95	0.20
Lancaster, PA (city) Lancaster County	95	0.17
Iowa City, IA (city) Johnson County	94	0.15
Yeadon, PA (borough) Delaware County	93	0.79
Edmonds, WA (city) Snohomish County	93	0.23
Columbia, MO (city) Boone County	92	0.11
Cary, NC (town) Wake County	91	0.10
Mobile, AL (city) Mobile County	91	0.05
Fort Washington, MD (cdp) Prince George's County	90	0.37
Randolph, MA (cdp) Norfolk County	88	0.28
Rochester, MN (city) Olmsted County	88	0.10
Scottdale, GA (cdp) De Kalb County	87	0.89
University City, MO (city) Saint Louis County	87	0.23
Hopkins, MN (city) Hennepin County	85	0.50
Mount Vernon, VA (cdp) Fairfax County	85	0.30
Des Moines, WA (city) King County	84	0.29
Norfolk, VA (independent city) Norfolk city	84	0.04
Redondo Beach, CA (city) Los Angeles County	83	0.13
Bethesda, MD (cdp) Montgomery County	82	0.15
New Rochelle, NY (city) Westchester County	82	0.11
Olathe, KS (city) Johnson County	82	0.09
Richmond, CA (city) Contra Costa County	82	0.08

Notes: (cdp) census designated place; Refer to the Explanation of Data in the front of the book for more detailed information.

African, sub-Saharan: Ethiopian

Top 150 Places Sorted by Percent

(Based on all places, regardless of population)

Place	Number	%
Angus, MN (township) Polk County	7	6.60
Lincolnia, VA (cdp) Fairfax County	571	3.60
South Haven, MN (city) Wright County	54	3.54
Vinita Park, MO (city) Saint Louis County	69	3.53
Takoma Park, MD (city) Montgomery County	539	3.14
Goddard, MD (cdp) Prince George's County	153	2.76
Boykins, VA (town) Southampton County	16	2.55
North Atlanta, GA (cdp) De Kalb County	844	2.20
Silver Spring, MD (cdp) Montgomery County	1,680	2.19
Alexandria, VA (independent city) Alexandria city	2,721	2.12
Tangelo Park, FL (cdp) Orange County	46	1.99
Esther, MN (township) Polk County	3	1.97
Cascade Valley, WA (cdp) Grant County	32	1.79
North Kensington, MD (cdp) Montgomery County	158	1.78
Kemp Mill, MD (cdp) Montgomery County	158	1.59
Barnesville, MD (town) Montgomery County	2	1.55
Emeryville, CA (city) Alameda County	101	1.47
Clarkston, GA (city) De Kalb County	99	1.45
Adelphi, MD (cdp) Prince George's County	204	1.36
Quantico, VA (town) Prince William County	7	1.33
Centerville, GA (city) Houston County	56	1.31
Louisville, TN (city) Blount County	26	1.30
Newington, VA (cdp) Fairfax County	251	1.27
Springfield, VA (cdp) Fairfax County	376	1.24
Glendale, CO (city) Arapahoe County	56	1.23
Franconia, VA (cdp) Fairfax County	384	1.20
Fairbanks, WI (town) Shawano County	8	1.20
White Oak, MD (cdp) Montgomery County	247	1.18
Ladera Heights, CA (cdp) Los Angeles County	76	1.16
Arlington, VA (cdp) Arlington County	2,171	1.15
Wheaton-Glenmont, MD (cdp) Montgomery County	660	1.14
Mount Rainier, MD (city) Prince George's County	96	1.13
Forest Glen, MD (cdp) Montgomery County	81	1.10
Chillum, MD (cdp) Prince George's County	373	1.09
Penn Forest, PA (township) Carbon County	58	1.07
Olivette, MO (city) Saint Louis County	78	1.04
Great Bend, NY (cdp) Jefferson County	8	1.03
Riverdale Park, MD (town) Prince George's County	67	1.02
Wyandanch, NY (cdp) Suffolk County	106	1.00
Little Canada, MN (city) Ramsey County	98	1.00
Doraville, GA (city) De Kalb County	95	0.94
North Chevy Chase, MD (village) Montgomery County	4	0.94
Vine Hill, CA (cdp) Contra Costa County	30	0.92
White Center, WA (cdp) King County	190	0.91
Scottdale, GA (cdp) De Kalb County	87	0.89
Kulpsville, PA (cdp) Montgomery County	70	0.87
Esto, FL (town) Holmes County	3	0.86
Whitehall, OH (city) Franklin County	162	0.84
Linden, TX (city) Cass County	19	0.84
Addison, TX (town) Dallas County	115	0.83
Yeadon, PA (borough) Delaware County	93	0.79
Tucker, GA (cdp) De Kalb County	206	0.77
University Park, NM (cdp) Dona Ana County	21	0.77
Tukwila, WA (city) King County	131	0.76
Rose Hill, VA (cdp) Fairfax County	114	0.76
Fort Washington, PA (cdp) Montgomery County	27	0.75
Bogart, GA (town) Oconee County	8	0.74
Seattle, WA (city) King County	4,110	0.73
North Decatur, GA (cdp) De Kalb County	110	0.73
Berwyn Heights, MD (town) Prince George's County	21	0.71
Bailey's Crossroads, VA (cdp) Fairfax County	157	0.69
Brooklyn Center, MN (city) Hennepin County	195	0.67
Liberty, NY (village) Sullivan County	25	0.64
Elsah, IL (village) Jersey County	4	0.64
Annandale, VA (cdp) Fairfax County	345	0.63
View Park-Windsor Hills, CA (cdp) Los Angeles County	69	0.63
Barrett, TX (cdp) Harris County	17	0.62
Fayette, IA (city) Fayette County	8	0.62
West Buechel, KY (city) Jefferson County	8	0.62
Columbia Heights, MN (city) Anoka County	113	0.61
Temple Hills, MD (cdp) Prince George's County	47	0.61
Huntington, VA (cdp) Fairfax County	51	0.60
Minneapolis, MN (city) Hennepin County	2,259	0.59
Worthington, MN (city) Nobles County	67	0.59
Flossmoor, IL (village) Cook County	55	0.59
Lilburn, GA (city) Gwinnett County	65	0.57
Springdale, MD (cdp) Prince George's County	16	0.57
Rochester, TX (town) Haskell County	2	0.56
Largo, MD (cdp) Prince George's County	46	0.54
Norwood Court, MO (town) Saint Louis County	6	0.54
Brentwood, MD (town) Prince George's County	15	0.52
Sandgate, VT (town) Bennington County	2	0.52
West Gardiner, ME (town) Kennebec County	15	0.51
Hopkins, MN (city) Hennepin County	85	0.50
Hyattsville, MD (city) Prince George's County	74	0.50
Chamblee, GA (city) De Kalb County	49	0.50
Blue Bell, PA (cdp) Montgomery County	32	0.50
Armada, MI (township) Macomb County	26	0.50
University Heights, IA (city) Johnson County	5	0.50
Cambridge, MA (city) Middlesex County	499	0.49
Bryn Mawr-Skyway, WA (cdp) King County	68	0.48
North Oaks, MN (city) Ramsey County	19	0.48
Long Hill, CT (cdp) New London County	17	0.48
Murphy, TX (city) Collin County	15	0.48
Fredonia, WI (town) Ozaukee County	14	0.48
Grant, MI (township) Huron County	4	0.48
Paradise, NV (cdp) Clark County	864	0.46
Vinings, GA (cdp) Cobb County	44	0.46
Penn Wynne, PA (cdp) Montgomery County	25	0.46
Saltville, VA (town) Smyth County	10	0.46
Loyalton, CA (city) Sierra County	4	0.46
Saint Paul, MN (city) Ramsey County	1,279	0.45
Mays Chapel, MD (cdp) Baltimore County	51	0.45
Buena Vista, CA (cdp) Santa Clara County	8	0.45
Elkhorn, CA (cdp) Monterey County	7	0.45
Lansing, MN (township) Mower County	6	0.45
Santa Rosa, CA (city) Sonoma County	650	0.44
Aspen Hill, MD (cdp) Montgomery County	220	0.44
Glenville, WV (town) Gilmer County	7	0.44
Shrewsbury, MO (city) Saint Louis County	28	0.43
Letterkenny, PA (township) Franklin County	9	0.43
Roosevelt, NJ (borough) Monmouth County	4	0.43
Saint Louis Park, MN (city) Hennepin County	185	0.42
Leland, NC (town) Brunswick County	8	0.42
SeaTac, WA (city) King County	105	0.41
West Athens, CA (cdp) Los Angeles County	38	0.41
Culver City, CA (city) Los Angeles County	155	0.40
Towamencin, PA (township) Montgomery County	70	0.40
Dentsville, SC (cdp) Richland County	51	0.40
Marion, AL (city) Perry County	14	0.40
Camp Springs, MD (cdp) Prince George's County	69	0.39
Calverton, MD (cdp) Montgomery County	49	0.39
Lake Barcroft, VA (cdp) Fairfax County	35	0.39
Washington, DC (city) District of Columbia	2,158	0.38
East Riverdale, MD (cdp) Prince George's County	58	0.38
Bull Run, VA (cdp) Prince William County	43	0.38
Fort Washington, MD (cdp) Prince George's County	90	0.37
Greenbelt, MD (city) Prince George's County	79	0.37
Langley Park, MD (cdp) Prince George's County	60	0.37
Fairview Shores, FL (cdp) Orange County	50	0.37
Morton, PA (borough) Delaware County	10	0.37
Peapack and Gladstone, NJ (borough) Somerset County	9	0.37
Orford, NH (town) Grafton County	4	0.37
Sioux Falls, SD (city) Minnehaha County	452	0.36
Santa Clara, CA (city) Santa Clara County	363	0.36
Glenarden, MD (city) Prince George's County	23	0.36
Richfield, MN (city) Hennepin County	122	0.35
Cherryland, CA (cdp) Alameda County	48	0.35
Rockford, MN (township) Wright County	12	0.35
Huachuca City, AZ (town) Cochise County	6	0.35
Redan, GA (cdp) De Kalb County	116	0.34
Burtonsville, MD (cdp) Montgomery County	25	0.34
Strawberry, CA (cdp) Marin County	18	0.34
Palmetto, GA (city) Fulton County	11	0.34
Tappahannock, VA (town) Essex County	7	0.34
Simpson, LA (village) Vernon Parish	2	0.34
Lake Ridge, VA (cdp) Prince William County	100	0.33
Gunbarrel, CO (cdp) Boulder County	32	0.33
Sudley, VA (cdp) Prince William County	26	0.33
Vandergrift, PA (borough) Westmoreland County	18	0.33

Notes: (cdp) census designated place; Refer to the Explanation of Data in the front of the book for more detailed information.

African, sub-Saharan: Ethiopian

Top 150 Places Sorted by Percent

(Based on places with populations of 10,000 or more)

Place	Number	%
Lincolnia, VA (cdp) Fairfax County	571	3.60
Takoma Park, MD (city) Montgomery County	539	3.14
North Atlanta, GA (cdp) De Kalb County	844	2.20
Silver Spring, MD (cdp) Montgomery County	1,680	2.19
Alexandria, VA (independent city) Alexandria city	2,721	2.12
Adelphi, MD (cdp) Prince George's County	204	1.36
Newington, VA (cdp) Fairfax County	251	1.27
Springfield, VA (cdp) Fairfax County	376	1.24
Franconia, VA (cdp) Fairfax County	384	1.20
White Oak, MD (cdp) Montgomery County	247	1.18
Arlington, VA (cdp) Arlington County	2,171	1.15
Wheaton-Glenmont, MD (cdp) Montgomery County	660	1.14
Chillum, MD (cdp) Prince George's County	373	1.09
Wyandanch, NY (cdp) Suffolk County	106	1.00
Doraville, GA (city) De Kalb County	95	0.94
White Center, WA (cdp) King County	190	0.91
Whitehall, OH (city) Franklin County	162	0.84
Addison, TX (town) Dallas County	115	0.83
Yeadon, PA (borough) Delaware County	93	0.79
Tucker, GA (cdp) De Kalb County	206	0.77
Tukwila, WA (city) King County	131	0.76
Rose Hill, VA (cdp) Fairfax County	114	0.76
Seattle, WA (city) King County	4,110	0.73
North Decatur, GA (cdp) De Kalb County	110	0.73
Bailey's Crossroads, VA (cdp) Fairfax County	157	0.69
Brooklyn Center, MN (city) Hennepin County	195	0.67
Annandale, VA (cdp) Fairfax County	345	0.63
View Park-Windsor Hills, CA (cdp) Los Angeles County	69	0.63
Columbia Heights, MN (city) Anoka County	113	0.61
Minneapolis, MN (city) Hennepin County	2,259	0.59
Worthington, MN (city) Nobles County	67	0.59
Lilburn, GA (city) Gwinnett County	65	0.57
Hopkins, MN (city) Hennepin County	85	0.50
Hyattsville, MD (city) Prince George's County	74	0.50
Cambridge, MA (city) Middlesex County	499	0.49
Bryn Mawr-Skyway, WA (cdp) King County	68	0.48
Paradise, NV (cdp) Clark County	864	0.46
Saint Paul, MN (city) Ramsey County	1,279	0.45
Mays Chapel, MD (cdp) Baltimore County	51	0.45
Santa Rosa, CA (city) Sonoma County	650	0.44
Aspen Hill, MD (cdp) Montgomery County	220	0.44
Saint Louis Park, MN (city) Hennepin County	185	0.42
SeaTac, WA (city) King County	105	0.41
Culver City, CA (city) Los Angeles County	155	0.40
Towamencin, PA (township) Montgomery County	70	0.40
Dentsville, SC (cdp) Richland County	51	0.40
Camp Springs, MD (cdp) Prince George's County	69	0.39
Calverton, MD (cdp) Montgomery County	49	0.39
Washington, DC (city) District of Columbia	2,158	0.38
East Riverdale, MD (cdp) Prince George's County	58	0.38
Bull Run, VA (cdp) Prince William County	43	0.38
Fort Washington, MD (cdp) Prince George's County	90	0.37
Greenbelt, MD (city) Prince George's County	79	0.37
Langley Park, MD (cdp) Prince George's County	60	0.37
Fairview Shores, FL (cdp) Orange County	50	0.37
Sioux Falls, SD (city) Minnehaha County	452	0.36
Santa Clara, CA (city) Santa Clara County	363	0.36
Richfield, MN (city) Hennepin County	122	0.35
Cherryland, CA (cdp) Alameda County	48	0.35
Redan, GA (cdp) De Kalb County	116	0.34
Lake Ridge, VA (cdp) Prince William County	100	0.33
Campbell, CA (city) Santa Clara County	123	0.32
Fairland, MD (cdp) Montgomery County	69	0.32
Groveton, VA (cdp) Fairfax County	69	0.32
Riverton-Boulevard Park, WA (cdp) King County	35	0.31
Oakland, CA (city) Alameda County	1,195	0.30
Mount Vernon, VA (cdp) Fairfax County	85	0.30
Secaucus, NJ (town) Hudson County	48	0.30
Saint Ann, MO (city) Saint Louis County	40	0.30
Guthrie, OK (city) Logan County	30	0.30
Spring Valley, NV (cdp) Clark County	346	0.29
Richardson, TX (city) Dallas County	266	0.29
Malden, MA (city) Middlesex County	166	0.29
Des Moines, WA (city) King County	84	0.29
College Park, GA (city) Fulton County	61	0.29

Place	Number	%
Powder Springs, GA (city) Cobb County	38	0.29
Montgomery Village, MD (cdp) Montgomery County	105	0.28
Randolph, MA (cdp) Norfolk County	88	0.28
Redland, MD (cdp) Montgomery County	49	0.28
New Carrollton, MD (city) Prince George's County	36	0.28
Clinton, MD (cdp) Prince George's County	70	0.27
Golden Valley, MN (city) Hennepin County	55	0.27
Rossville, MD (cdp) Baltimore County	31	0.27
Coral Hills, MD (cdp) Prince George's County	29	0.27
Harrisburg, PA (city) Dauphin County	129	0.26
Paine Field-Lake Stickney, WA (cdp) Snohomish County	64	0.26
Upper Chichester, PA (township) Delaware County	43	0.26
Holbrook, MA (cdp) Norfolk County	28	0.26
Dallas, TX (city) Dallas County	3,006	0.25
Gilroy, CA (city) Santa Clara County	103	0.25
Greater Landover, MD (cdp) Prince George's County	57	0.25
Lorton, VA (cdp) Fairfax County	45	0.25
Hillcrest Heights, MD (cdp) Prince George's County	41	0.25
El Sobrante, CA (cdp) Contra Costa County	29	0.25
Aurora, CO (city) Arapahoe County	651	0.24
East Lansing, MI (city) Ingham County	112	0.24
Ruston, LA (city) Lincoln Parish	50	0.24
Loma Linda, CA (city) San Bernardino County	45	0.24
Lanham-Seabrook, MD (cdp) Prince George's County	44	0.24
Forest Park, IL (village) Cook County	38	0.24
Cutlerville, MI (cdp) Kent County	37	0.24
Berkeley, CA (city) Alameda County	240	0.23
Buena Park, CA (city) Orange County	180	0.23
Burke, VA (cdp) Fairfax County	130	0.23
West Orange, NJ (cdp) Essex County	104	0.23
Edmonds, WA (city) Snohomish County	93	0.23
University City, MO (city) Saint Louis County	87	0.23
West Springfield, VA (cdp) Fairfax County	66	0.23
Artesia, CA (city) Los Angeles County	37	0.23
University Heights, OH (city) Cuyahoga County	33	0.23
Merrifield, VA (cdp) Fairfax County	25	0.23
Dunwoody, GA (cdp) De Kalb County	73	0.22
Picnic Point-North Lynnwood, WA (cdp) Snohomish County	51	0.22
Whitpain, PA (township) Montgomery County	42	0.22
Center, PA (township) Beaver County	25	0.22
East Orange, NJ (city) Essex County	149	0.21
Clinton, MA (town) Worcester County	28	0.21
Grand Rapids, MI (city) Kent County	388	0.20
Columbia, MD (cdp) Howard County	181	0.20
Renton, WA (city) King County	98	0.20
Shawnee, KS (city) Johnson County	95	0.20
Stillwater, OK (city) Payne County	76	0.20
Chelsea, MA (city) Suffolk County	69	0.20
College Park, MD (city) Prince George's County	48	0.20
Reisterstown, MD (cdp) Baltimore County	45	0.20
Hybla Valley, VA (cdp) Fairfax County	34	0.20
San Jose, CA (city) Santa Clara County	1,669	0.19
Brooklyn Park, MN (city) Hennepin County	130	0.19
Herndon, VA (town) Fairfax County	41	0.19
Grand Rapids charter, MI (township) Kent County	27	0.19
Chester, NY (town) Orange County	23	0.19
Darby, PA (borough) Delaware County	20	0.19
Chino Hills, CA (city) San Bernardino County	121	0.18
Winchester, NV (cdp) Clark County	49	0.18
Gaines, MI (township) Kent County	37	0.18
South Laurel, MD (cdp) Prince George's County	37	0.18
Ogden, NY (town) Monroe County	34	0.18
Phillipsburg, NJ (town) Warren County	27	0.18
Big Rapids, MI (city) Mecosta County	19	0.18
Columbus, OH (city) Franklin County	1,241	0.17
Rochester, NY (city) Monroe County	383	0.17
Plano, TX (city) Collin County	375	0.17
Bloomington, MN (city) Hennepin County	148	0.17
Lancaster, PA (city) Lancaster County	95	0.17
Everett, MA (city) Middlesex County	65	0.17
Lynnwood, WA (city) Snohomish County	59	0.17
San Pablo, CA (city) Contra Costa County	52	0.17
Jefferson, VA (cdp) Fairfax County	46	0.17
Fairfax, VA (independent city) Fairfax city	36	0.17
Arbutus, MD (cdp) Baltimore County	34	0.17

Notes: (cdp) census designated place; Refer to the Explanation of Data in the front of the book for more detailed information.

African, sub-Saharan: Ghanian

Top 150 Places Sorted by Number

(Based on all places, regardless of population)

Place	Number	%
New York, NY (city) New York City	9,921	0.12
Chicago, IL (city) Cook County	1,522	0.05
Alexandria, VA (independent city) Alexandria city	1,152	0.90
Worcester, MA (city) Worcester County	983	0.57
Newark, NJ (city) Essex County	868	0.32
Columbus, OH (city) Franklin County	731	0.10
Houston, TX (city) Harris County	532	0.03
Los Angeles, CA (city) Los Angeles County	530	0.01
Yonkers, NY (city) Westchester County	363	0.19
Chillum, MD (cdp) Prince George's County	351	1.03
Mount Vernon, VA (cdp) Fairfax County	325	1.14
Irvington, NJ (cdp) Essex County	308	0.51
Baltimore, MD (independent city) Baltimore city	306	0.05
Bolingbrook, IL (village) Will County	301	0.53
East Hartford, CT (cdp) Hartford County	298	0.60
Philadelphia, PA (city) Philadelphia County	297	0.02
Sayreville, NJ (borough) Middlesex County	289	0.72
Washington, DC (city) District of Columbia	277	0.05
Providence, RI (city) Providence County	270	0.16
White Oak, MD (cdp) Montgomery County	267	1.28
Groveton, VA (cdp) Fairfax County	265	1.25
Dale City, VA (cdp) Prince William County	264	0.47
Franklin, NJ (township) Somerset County	259	0.51
Columbia, MD (cdp) Howard County	259	0.29
Charlotte, NC (city) Mecklenburg County	245	0.05
Arlington, TX (city) Tarrant County	244	0.07
Greensboro, NC (city) Guilford County	242	0.11
Irving, TX (city) Dallas County	237	0.12
Calverton, MD (cdp) Montgomery County	232	1.84
Mableton, GA (cdp) Cobb County	217	0.73
North Brunswick Township, NJ (cdp) Middlesex County	217	0.60
East Orange, NJ (city) Essex County	217	0.31
Albany, NY (city) Albany County	210	0.22
Boston, MA (city) Suffolk County	201	0.03
Orange, NJ (cdp) Essex County	196	0.60
Hempstead, NY (town) Nassau County	193	0.03
Denver, CO (city) Denver County	192	0.03
South Laurel, MD (cdp) Prince George's County	186	0.89
Silver Spring, MD (cdp) Montgomery County	180	0.23
Dallas, TX (city) Dallas County	172	0.01
Aurora, CO (city) Arapahoe County	170	0.06
Burke, VA (cdp) Fairfax County	167	0.29
Atlanta, GA (city) Fulton County	166	0.04
Somerset, NJ (cdp) Somerset County	164	0.71
Bloomington, MN (city) Hennepin County	160	0.19
Reston, VA (cdp) Fairfax County	157	0.28
Waukegan, IL (city) Lake County	155	0.18
Greenbelt, MD (city) Prince George's County	154	0.72
Grand Prairie, TX (city) Dallas County	152	0.12
Oklahoma City, OK (city) Oklahoma County	152	0.03
Diamond Bar, CA (city) Los Angeles County	151	0.27
Pawtucket, RI (city) Providence County	150	0.21
Detroit, MI (city) Wayne County	147	0.02
Phoenix, AZ (city) Maricopa County	146	0.01
Hybla Valley, VA (cdp) Fairfax County	144	0.86
Union, NJ (cdp) Union County	143	0.26
Montgomery Village, MD (cdp) Montgomery County	142	0.37
Wheaton-Glenmont, MD (cdp) Montgomery County	141	0.24
Gaithersburg, MD (city) Montgomery County	136	0.26
Woodbridge, NJ (township) Middlesex County	134	0.14
Lowell, MA (city) Middlesex County	133	0.13
Tampa, FL (city) Hillsborough County	126	0.04
Woodbridge, VA (cdp) Prince William County	124	0.39
Edison, NJ (cdp) Middlesex County	119	0.12
Nashville-Davidson, TN (special city) Davidson County	118	0.02
Lincolnia, VA (cdp) Fairfax County	117	0.74
Paradise, NV (cdp) Clark County	117	0.06
Minneapolis, MN (city) Hennepin County	117	0.03
Fords, NJ (cdp) Middlesex County	116	0.77
Raleigh, NC (city) Wake County	115	0.04
Jersey City, NJ (city) Hudson County	114	0.05
Oakland, CA (city) Alameda County	114	0.03
Arlington, VA (cdp) Arlington County	113	0.06
Hillsborough, NJ (township) Somerset County	112	0.31
Jacksonville, FL (special city) Duval County	112	0.02
Fairland, MD (cdp) Montgomery County	109	0.51
Hillside, NJ (cdp) Union County	109	0.50
Springfield, VA (cdp) Fairfax County	108	0.36
Hartford, CT (city) Hartford County	107	0.09
Islip, NY (town) Suffolk County	106	0.03
Deerfield Beach, FL (city) Broward County	105	0.16
Saint Paul, MN (city) Ramsey County	105	0.04
Old Bridge, NJ (township) Middlesex County	102	0.17
Merrillville, IN (town) Lake County	101	0.33
Kalamazoo, MI (city) Kalamazoo County	99	0.13
East Windsor, NJ (township) Mercer County	97	0.39
New Orleans, LA (city) Orleans Parish	97	0.02
Elizabeth, NJ (city) Union County	96	0.08
Rialto, CA (city) San Bernardino County	93	0.10
Maryland City, MD (cdp) Anne Arundel County	92	1.36
Little Ferry, NJ (borough) Bergen County	91	0.84
Bailey's Crossroads, VA (cdp) Fairfax County	89	0.39
West Orange, NJ (cdp) Essex County	88	0.20
Glenn Dale, MD (cdp) Prince George's County	87	0.68
Rose Hill, VA (cdp) Fairfax County	87	0.58
Ramapo, NY (town) Rockland County	87	0.08
Roselle, NJ (borough) Union County	86	0.40
Hackensack, NJ (city) Bergen County	86	0.20
New Carrollton, MD (city) Prince George's County	85	0.66
Redland, MD (cdp) Montgomery County	82	0.48
Centreville, VA (cdp) Fairfax County	82	0.17
Tallahassee, FL (city) Leon County	82	0.05
Germantown, MD (cdp) Montgomery County	81	0.15
Brockton, MA (city) Plymouth County	81	0.09
Delran, NJ (township) Burlington County	80	0.51
Colesville, MD (cdp) Montgomery County	80	0.40
Bemidji, MN (city) Beltrami County	79	0.65
Upper Darby, PA (township) Delaware County	79	0.10
Bay Shore, NY (cdp) Suffolk County	78	0.33
Laurel, MD (city) Prince George's County	77	0.38
Tuckahoe, VA (cdp) Henrico County	76	0.18
Newington, VA (cdp) Fairfax County	75	0.38
Dover, DE (city) Kent County	74	0.23
West Haven, CT (city) New Haven County	73	0.14
Little Rock, AR (city) Pulaski County	73	0.04
Salt Lake City, UT (city) Salt Lake County	73	0.04
Belvedere Park, GA (cdp) De Kalb County	71	0.37
Gary, IN (city) Lake County	71	0.07
South Brunswick, NJ (township) Middlesex County	69	0.18
Brooklyn Park, MN (city) Hennepin County	69	0.10
Pembroke Pines, FL (city) Broward County	69	0.05
Adelphi, MD (cdp) Prince George's County	68	0.45
Randallstown, MD (cdp) Baltimore County	68	0.22
San Diego, CA (city) San Diego County	68	0.01
Maplewood, NJ (cdp) Essex County	67	0.28
Mesquite, TX (city) Dallas County	67	0.05
River Forest, IL (village) Cook County	65	0.56
Pittsburgh, PA (city) Allegheny County	65	0.02
Parkville, MD (cdp) Baltimore County	64	0.21
Aspen Hill, MD (cdp) Montgomery County	64	0.13
Goddard, MD (cdp) Prince George's County	63	1.14
Wallington, NJ (borough) Bergen County	63	0.54
Perth Amboy, NJ (city) Middlesex County	62	0.13
Missouri City, TX (city) Fort Bend County	62	0.12
Elmont, NY (cdp) Nassau County	61	0.19
Pflugerville, TX (city) Travis County	60	0.37
Renton, WA (city) King County	60	0.12
Cambridge, MA (city) Middlesex County	60	0.06
Derby, CT (city) New Haven County	59	0.48
East Riverdale, MD (cdp) Prince George's County	59	0.38
Hampton, VA (independent city) Hampton city	59	0.04
Santa Clarita, CA (city) Los Angeles County	59	0.04
Greater Upper Marlboro, MD (cdp) Prince George's County	58	0.31
Tacoma, WA (city) Pierce County	57	0.03
Catonsville, MD (cdp) Baltimore County	56	0.14
Montclair, NJ (cdp) Essex County	56	0.14
Maple Grove, MN (city) Hennepin County	56	0.11
Downey, CA (city) Los Angeles County	56	0.05
Kansas City, MO (city) Jackson County	56	0.01
Takoma Park, MD (city) Montgomery County	55	0.32

Notes: (cdp) census designated place; Refer to the Explanation of Data in the front of the book for more detailed information.

African, sub-Saharan: Ghanian

Top 150 Places Sorted by Percent

(Based on all places, regardless of population)

Place	Number	%
Smithton, MO (city) Pettis County	18	3.59
Fort Greely, AK (cdp) Southeast Fairbanks Census Area	9	1.85
Calverton, MD (cdp) Montgomery County	232	1.84
Hillsdale, MI (township) Hillsdale County	31	1.65
Strathmoor Manor, KY (city) Jefferson County	5	1.40
Maryland City, MD (cdp) Anne Arundel County	92	1.36
Hillandale, MD (cdp) Montgomery County	40	1.34
White Oak, MD (cdp) Montgomery County	267	1.28
Groveton, VA (cdp) Fairfax County	265	1.25
Chesterfield Court House, VA (cdp) Chesterfield County	43	1.21
Berkey, OH (village) Lucas County	3	1.15
Mount Vernon, VA (cdp) Fairfax County	325	1.14
Goddard, MD (cdp) Prince George's County	63	1.14
Fort Devens, MA (cdp) Worcester County	11	1.10
Chillum, MD (cdp) Prince George's County	351	1.03
East Richmond Heights, CA (cdp) Contra Costa County	32	0.92
Brentwood, MD (town) Prince George's County	26	0.91
Alexandria, VA (independent city) Alexandria city	1,152	0.90
South Laurel, MD (cdp) Prince George's County	186	0.89
Olympia Fields, IL (village) Cook County	42	0.89
Falcon Heights, MN (city) Ramsey County	48	0.87
Hybla Valley, VA (cdp) Fairfax County	144	0.86
Northeast Ithaca, NY (cdp) Tompkins County	23	0.85
Little Ferry, NJ (borough) Bergen County	91	0.84
Fords, NJ (cdp) Middlesex County	116	0.77
Lincolnia, VA (cdp) Fairfax County	117	0.74
Mableton, GA (cdp) Cobb County	217	0.73
Triangle, VA (cdp) Prince William County	41	0.73
Sayreville, NJ (borough) Middlesex County	289	0.72
Greenbelt, MD (city) Prince George's County	154	0.72
Somerset, NJ (cdp) Somerset County	164	0.71
Twin Rivers, NJ (cdp) Mercer County	53	0.71
Blessing, TX (cdp) Matagorda County	6	0.70
Glenn Dale, MD (cdp) Prince George's County	87	0.68
Burtonsville, MD (cdp) Montgomery County	50	0.68
Stanleytown, VA (cdp) Henry County	10	0.67
New Carrollton, MD (city) Prince George's County	85	0.66
Bemidji, MN (city) Beltrami County	79	0.65
Mangonia Park, FL (town) Palm Beach County	8	0.62
Coeburn, VA (town) Wise County	12	0.61
Newport, NY (village) Herkimer County	4	0.61
East Hartford, CT (cdp) Hartford County	298	0.60
North Brunswick Township, NJ (cdp) Middlesex County	217	0.60
Orange, NJ (cdp) Essex County	196	0.60
Rose Hill, VA (cdp) Fairfax County	87	0.58
Worcester, MA (city) Worcester County	983	0.57
Berwyn Heights, MD (town) Prince George's County	17	0.57
River Forest, IL (village) Cook County	65	0.56
Crete, IL (village) Will County	40	0.55
Wallington, NJ (borough) Bergen County	63	0.54
Bolingbrook, IL (village) Will County	301	0.53
Jamesburg, NJ (borough) Middlesex County	32	0.53
Irvington, NJ (cdp) Essex County	308	0.51
Franklin, NJ (township) Somerset County	259	0.51
Fairland, MD (cdp) Montgomery County	109	0.51
Delran, NJ (township) Burlington County	80	0.51
Moreland Hills, OH (village) Cuyahoga County	17	0.51
Hillside, NJ (cdp) Union County	109	0.50
New Hempstead, NY (village) Rockland County	24	0.50
Glenpool, OK (city) Tulsa County	40	0.49
Wesley Hills, NY (village) Rockland County	24	0.49
Redland, MD (cdp) Montgomery County	82	0.48
Derby, CT (city) New Haven County	59	0.48
Sun River Terrace, IL (village) Kankakee County	2	0.48
Dale City, VA (cdp) Prince William County	264	0.47
Elk, PA (township) Chester County	7	0.46
Adelphi, MD (cdp) Prince George's County	68	0.45
Lake Arbor, MD (cdp) Prince George's County	38	0.45
Coalinga, CA (city) Fresno County	49	0.42
Yeadon, PA (borough) Delaware County	49	0.42
Decorah, IA (city) Winneshiek County	34	0.41
Riverdale Park, MD (town) Prince George's County	27	0.41
Riverside, MO (city) Platte County	12	0.41
Roselle, NJ (borough) Union County	86	0.40
Colesville, MD (cdp) Montgomery County	80	0.40

Place	Number	%
South Amherst, MA (cdp) Hampshire County	20	0.40
Carmody Hills-Pepper Mill Village, MD (cdp) Prince George's Co.	19	0.40
Woodbridge, VA (cdp) Prince William County	124	0.39
East Windsor, NJ (township) Mercer County	97	0.39
Bailey's Crossroads, VA (cdp) Fairfax County	89	0.39
Laurel, MD (city) Prince George's County	77	0.38
Newington, VA (cdp) Fairfax County	75	0.38
East Riverdale, MD (cdp) Prince George's County	59	0.38
Huntington, VA (cdp) Fairfax County	32	0.38
Montgomery Village, MD (cdp) Montgomery County	142	0.37
Belvedere Park, GA (cdp) De Kalb County	71	0.37
Pflugerville, TX (city) Travis County	60	0.37
Hamilton, NY (village) Madison County	13	0.37
Alpine, NJ (borough) Bergen County	8	0.37
Springfield, VA (cdp) Fairfax County	108	0.36
Churchill, PA (borough) Allegheny County	13	0.36
Leicester, MA (town) Worcester County	37	0.35
Greenville, NY (cdp) Westchester County	30	0.35
Fairlawn, OH (city) Summit County	26	0.35
Madison Park, NJ (cdp) Middlesex County	24	0.35
Tedder, FL (cdp) Broward County	7	0.35
Manassas Park, VA (independent city) Manassas Park city	35	0.34
Kemp Mill, MD (cdp) Montgomery County	34	0.34
Swarthmore, PA (borough) Delaware County	21	0.34
Merrillville, IN (town) Lake County	101	0.33
Bay Shore, NY (cdp) Suffolk County	78	0.33
Princeton Meadows, NJ (cdp) Middlesex County	44	0.33
Windsor Locks, CT (cdp) Hartford County	40	0.33
Newark, NJ (city) Essex County	868	0.32
Takoma Park, MD (city) Montgomery County	55	0.32
Inwood, NY (cdp) Nassau County	30	0.32
Wildwood, NJ (city) Cape May County	18	0.32
East Orange, NJ (city) Essex County	217	0.31
Hillsborough, NJ (township) Somerset County	112	0.31
Greater Upper Marlboro, MD (cdp) Prince George's County	58	0.31
Bardstown, KY (city) Nelson County	32	0.31
Fort Belvoir, VA (cdp) Fairfax County	22	0.31
Oakville, WA (city) Grays Harbor County	2	0.31
Somerville, NJ (borough) Somerset County	38	0.30
Mount Rainier, MD (city) Prince George's County	25	0.30
Wheatley Heights, NY (cdp) Suffolk County	15	0.30
Troy, WI (town) Saint Croix County	11	0.30
Columbia, MD (cdp) Howard County	259	0.29
Burke, VA (cdp) Fairfax County	167	0.29
Gresham Park, GA (cdp) De Kalb County	27	0.29
Hickory Creek, TX (town) Denton County	6	0.29
Reston, VA (cdp) Fairfax County	157	0.28
Maplewood, NJ (cdp) Essex County	67	0.28
Diamond Bar, CA (city) Los Angeles County	151	0.27
Kendall Park, NJ (cdp) Middlesex County	25	0.27
Arlington Heights, PA (cdp) Monroe County	14	0.27
Kimball, WV (town) McDowell County	1	0.27
Union, NJ (cdp) Union County	143	0.26
Gaithersburg, MD (city) Montgomery County	136	0.26
Lanham-Seabrook, MD (cdp) Prince George's County	47	0.26
Poynette, WI (village) Columbia County	6	0.26
Blawnox, PA (borough) Allegheny County	4	0.26
North Laurel, MD (cdp) Howard County	51	0.25
Superior, MI (township) Washtenaw County	27	0.25
Grantley, PA (cdp) York County	9	0.25
Wheaton-Glenmont, MD (cdp) Montgomery County	141	0.24
Bound Brook, NJ (borough) Somerset County	24	0.24
East Foothills, CA (cdp) Santa Clara County	20	0.24
Silver Spring, MD (cdp) Montgomery County	180	0.23
Dover, DE (city) Kent County	74	0.23
Grosse Pointe Park, MI (city) Wayne County	29	0.23
Clemson, SC (city) Pickens County	28	0.23
Garden City, GA (city) Chatham County	26	0.23
Clarion, PA (borough) Clarion County	14	0.23
Hamilton, NY (town) Madison County	13	0.23
Chain O' Lakes-King, WI (cdp) Waupaca County	5	0.23
Greenvale, NY (cdp) Nassau County	5	0.23
Albany, NY (city) Albany County	210	0.22
Randallstown, MD (cdp) Baltimore County	68	0.22
Romeoville, IL (village) Will County	46	0.22

Notes: (cdp) census designated place; Refer to the Explanation of Data in the front of the book for more detailed information.

African, sub-Saharan: Ghanian

Top 150 Places Sorted by Percent

(Based on places with populations of 10,000 or more)

Place	Number	%
Calverton, MD (cdp) Montgomery County	232	1.84
White Oak, MD (cdp) Montgomery County	267	1.28
Groveton, VA (cdp) Fairfax County	265	1.25
Mount Vernon, VA (cdp) Fairfax County	325	1.14
Chillum, MD (cdp) Prince George's County	351	1.03
Alexandria, VA (independent city) Alexandria city	1,152	0.90
South Laurel, MD (cdp) Prince George's County	186	0.89
Hybla Valley, VA (cdp) Fairfax County	144	0.86
Little Ferry, NJ (borough) Bergen County	91	0.84
Fords, NJ (cdp) Middlesex County	116	0.77
Lincolnia, VA (cdp) Fairfax County	117	0.74
Mableton, GA (cdp) Cobb County	217	0.73
Sayreville, NJ (borough) Middlesex County	289	0.72
Greenbelt, MD (city) Prince George's County	154	0.72
Somerset, NJ (cdp) Somerset County	164	0.71
Glenn Dale, MD (cdp) Prince George's County	87	0.68
New Carrollton, MD (city) Prince George's County	85	0.66
Bemidji, MN (city) Beltrami County	79	0.65
East Hartford, CT (cdp) Hartford County	298	0.60
North Brunswick Township, NJ (cdp) Middlesex County	217	0.60
Orange, NJ (cdp) Essex County	196	0.60
Rose Hill, VA (cdp) Fairfax County	87	0.58
Worcester, MA (city) Worcester County	983	0.57
River Forest, IL (village) Cook County	65	0.56
Wallington, NJ (borough) Bergen County	63	0.54
Bolingbrook, IL (village) Will County	301	0.53
Irvington, NJ (cdp) Essex County	308	0.51
Franklin, NJ (township) Somerset County	259	0.51
Fairland, MD (cdp) Montgomery County	109	0.51
Delran, NJ (township) Burlington County	80	0.51
Hillside, NJ (cdp) Union County	109	0.50
Redland, MD (cdp) Montgomery County	82	0.48
Derby, CT (city) New Haven County	59	0.48
Dale City, VA (cdp) Prince William County	264	0.47
Adelphi, MD (cdp) Prince George's County	68	0.45
Coalinga, CA (city) Fresno County	49	0.42
Yeadon, PA (borough) Delaware County	49	0.42
Roselle, NJ (borough) Union County	86	0.40
Colesville, MD (cdp) Montgomery County	80	0.40
Woodbridge, VA (cdp) Prince William County	124	0.39
East Windsor, NJ (township) Mercer County	97	0.39
Bailey's Crossroads, VA (cdp) Fairfax County	89	0.39
Laurel, MD (city) Prince George's County	77	0.38
Newington, VA (cdp) Fairfax County	75	0.38
East Riverdale, MD (cdp) Prince George's County	59	0.38
Montgomery Village, MD (cdp) Montgomery County	142	0.37
Belvedere Park, GA (cdp) De Kalb County	71	0.37
Pflugerville, TX (city) Travis County	60	0.37
Springfield, VA (cdp) Fairfax County	108	0.36
Leicester, MA (town) Worcester County	37	0.35
Manassas Park, VA (independent city) Manassas Park city	35	0.34
Merrillville, IN (town) Lake County	101	0.33
Bay Shore, NY (cdp) Suffolk County	78	0.33
Princeton Meadows, NJ (cdp) Middlesex County	44	0.33
Windsor Locks, CT (cdp) Hartford County	40	0.33
Newark, NJ (city) Essex County	868	0.32
Takoma Park, MD (city) Montgomery County	55	0.32
East Orange, NJ (city) Essex County	217	0.31
Hillsborough, NJ (township) Somerset County	112	0.31
Greater Upper Marlboro, MD (cdp) Prince George's County	58	0.31
Bardstown, KY (city) Nelson County	32	0.31
Somerville, NJ (borough) Somerset County	38	0.30
Columbia, MD (cdp) Howard County	259	0.29
Burke, VA (cdp) Fairfax County	167	0.29
Reston, VA (cdp) Fairfax County	157	0.28
Maplewood, NJ (cdp) Essex County	67	0.28
Diamond Bar, CA (city) Los Angeles County	151	0.27
Union, NJ (cdp) Union County	143	0.26
Gaithersburg, MD (city) Montgomery County	136	0.26
Lanham-Seabrook, MD (cdp) Prince George's County	47	0.26
North Laurel, MD (cdp) Howard County	51	0.25
Superior, MI (township) Washtenaw County	27	0.25
Wheaton-Glenmont, MD (cdp) Montgomery County	141	0.24
Bound Brook, NJ (borough) Somerset County	24	0.24
Silver Spring, MD (cdp) Montgomery County	180	0.23
Dover, DE (city) Kent County	74	0.23
Grosse Pointe Park, MI (city) Wayne County	29	0.23
Clemson, SC (city) Pickens County	28	0.23
Garden City, GA (city) Chatham County	26	0.23
Albany, NY (city) Albany County	210	0.22
Randallstown, MD (cdp) Baltimore County	68	0.22
Romeoville, IL (village) Will County	46	0.22
Plainsboro, NJ (township) Middlesex County	44	0.22
Middlesex, NJ (borough) Middlesex County	30	0.22
Pawtucket, RI (city) Providence County	150	0.21
Parkville, MD (cdp) Baltimore County	64	0.21
Effingham, IL (city) Effingham County	26	0.21
West Orange, NJ (cdp) Essex County	88	0.20
Hackensack, NJ (city) Bergen County	86	0.20
Camp Springs, MD (cdp) Prince George's County	36	0.20
Oshtemo, MI (township) Kalamazoo County	34	0.20
Saint Augustine, FL (city) Saint Johns County	23	0.20
Yonkers, NY (city) Westchester County	363	0.19
Bloomington, MN (city) Hennepin County	160	0.19
Elmont, NY (cdp) Nassau County	61	0.19
Bellwood, IL (village) Cook County	39	0.19
Hazel Crest, IL (village) Cook County	28	0.19
Richton Park, IL (village) Cook County	23	0.19
Doraville, GA (city) De Kalb County	19	0.19
Waukegan, IL (city) Lake County	155	0.18
Tuckahoe, VA (cdp) Henrico County	76	0.18
South Brunswick, NJ (township) Middlesex County	69	0.18
College Park, GA (city) Fulton County	38	0.18
Apex, NC (town) Wake County	37	0.18
Wilmington Island, GA (cdp) Chatham County	26	0.18
Beaufort, SC (city) Beaufort County	23	0.18
East Bridgewater, MA (town) Plymouth County	23	0.18
Arlington, NY (cdp) Dutchess County	22	0.18
Old Bridge, NJ (township) Middlesex County	102	0.17
Centreville, VA (cdp) Fairfax County	82	0.17
Lake in the Hills, IL (village) McHenry County	39	0.17
Ithaca, NY (town) Tompkins County	31	0.17
Charlton, MA (town) Worcester County	19	0.17
Providence, RI (city) Providence County	270	0.16
Deerfield Beach, FL (city) Broward County	105	0.16
El Cerrito, CA (city) Contra Costa County	36	0.16
Hercules, CA (city) Contra Costa County	31	0.16
Colchester, VT (town) Chittenden County	27	0.16
Colonial Heights, VA (independent city) Colonial Heights city	27	0.16
Upper Gwynedd, PA (township) Montgomery County	23	0.16
Bryn Mawr-Skyway, WA (cdp) King County	22	0.16
Glasgow, DE (cdp) New Castle County	21	0.16
Germantown, MD (cdp) Montgomery County	81	0.15
Manassas, VA (independent city) Manassas city	53	0.15
Rahway, NJ (city) Union County	40	0.15
Baldwin, NY (cdp) Nassau County	35	0.15
Del City, OK (city) Oklahoma County	33	0.15
Mamaroneck, NY (village) Westchester County	28	0.15
Natchitoches, LA (city) Natchitoches Parish	27	0.15
North Bay Shore, NY (cdp) Suffolk County	23	0.15
Lincoln Park, NJ (borough) Morris County	16	0.15
Woodbridge, NJ (township) Middlesex County	134	0.14
West Haven, CT (city) New Haven County	73	0.14
Catonsville, MD (cdp) Baltimore County	56	0.14
Montclair, NJ (cdp) Essex County	56	0.14
Gadsden, AL (city) Etowah County	54	0.14
University Park, TX (city) Dallas County	32	0.14
Scotch Plains, NJ (cdp) Union County	31	0.14
Coolbaugh, PA (township) Monroe County	21	0.14
Enterprise, NV (cdp) Clark County	20	0.14
White, PA (township) Indiana County	20	0.14
Roselle Park, NJ (borough) Union County	19	0.14
Sauk Rapids, MN (city) Benton County	14	0.14
Lowell, MA (city) Middlesex County	133	0.13
Kalamazoo, MI (city) Kalamazoo County	99	0.13
Aspen Hill, MD (cdp) Montgomery County	64	0.13
Perth Amboy, NJ (city) Middlesex County	62	0.13
Willingboro, NJ (township) Burlington County	44	0.13
Jefferson, VA (cdp) Fairfax County	36	0.13
Greater Landover, MD (cdp) Prince George's County	29	0.13

Notes: (cdp) census designated place; Refer to the Explanation of Data in the front of the book for more detailed information.

African, sub-Saharan: Kenyan

Top 150 Places Sorted by Number

(Based on all places, regardless of population)

Place	Number	%
Houston, TX (city) Harris County	457	0.02
Arlington, TX (city) Tarrant County	408	0.12
Dallas, TX (city) Dallas County	361	0.03
Worcester, MA (city) Worcester County	312	0.18
Los Angeles, CA (city) Los Angeles County	247	0.01
Jersey City, NJ (city) Hudson County	209	0.09
Minneapolis, MN (city) Hennepin County	186	0.05
Marietta, GA (city) Cobb County	175	0.30
Baltimore, MD (independent city) Baltimore city	167	0.03
Wichita, KS (city) Sedgwick County	150	0.04
New York, NY (city) New York City	146	0.00
Raleigh, NC (city) Wake County	137	0.05
Silver Spring, MD (cdp) Montgomery County	133	0.17
Edison, NJ (cdp) Middlesex County	132	0.14
Kansas City, MO (city) Jackson County	132	0.03
Chicago, IL (city) Cook County	130	0.00
Oakland, CA (city) Alameda County	127	0.03
Seattle, WA (city) King County	121	0.02
Brooklyn Center, MN (city) Hennepin County	116	0.40
Parkville, MD (cdp) Baltimore County	107	0.34
Smyrna, GA (city) Cobb County	107	0.26
Homewood, AL (city) Jefferson County	104	0.42
Germantown, MD (cdp) Montgomery County	102	0.18
Irving, TX (city) Dallas County	102	0.05
Santa Rosa, CA (city) Sonoma County	97	0.07
Durham, NC (city) Durham County	96	0.05
Boston, MA (city) Suffolk County	95	0.02
Tysons Corner, VA (cdp) Fairfax County	93	0.50
Leicester, MA (town) Worcester County	90	0.86
Federal Way, WA (city) King County	87	0.10
Columbus, OH (city) Franklin County	86	0.01
Newark, NJ (city) Essex County	85	0.03
South Bend, IN (city) Saint Joseph County	84	0.08
Oronoko charter, MI (township) Berrien County	82	0.83
Portland, OR (city) Multnomah County	82	0.02
Lowell, MA (city) Middlesex County	80	0.08
Bellevue, WA (city) King County	79	0.07
Tacoma, WA (city) Pierce County	77	0.04
Saint Paul, MN (city) Ramsey County	77	0.03
Oklahoma City, OK (city) Oklahoma County	74	0.01
Athens-Clarke County, GA (special city) Clarke County	73	0.07
Philadelphia, PA (city) Philadelphia County	71	0.00
Iowa City, IA (city) Johnson County	67	0.11
Pomona, CA (city) Los Angeles County	67	0.04
Pasadena, CA (city) Los Angeles County	66	0.05
North Bethesda, MD (cdp) Montgomery County	65	0.17
Cincinnati, OH (city) Hamilton County	65	0.02
Memphis, TN (city) Shelby County	65	0.01
Shoreview, MN (city) Ramsey County	64	0.25
East Fishkill, NY (town) Dutchess County	63	0.25
La Mirada, CA (city) Los Angeles County	63	0.13
Baton Rouge, LA (city) East Baton Rouge Parish	63	0.03
Winfield, KS (city) Cowley County	61	0.50
Beltsville, MD (cdp) Prince George's County	60	0.38
Mission Bend, TX (cdp) Fort Bend County	60	0.19
Syracuse, NY (city) Onondaga County	60	0.04
Salisbury, MA (town) Essex County	59	0.75
Manhattan, KS (city) Riley County	59	0.13
Omaha, NE (city) Douglas County	59	0.02
Pittsburgh, PA (city) Allegheny County	58	0.02
Austin, TX (city) Travis County	58	0.01
Novato, CA (city) Marin County	56	0.12
Richmond, CA (city) Contra Costa County	56	0.06
Long Beach, CA (city) Los Angeles County	56	0.01
Takoma Park, MD (city) Montgomery County	55	0.32
Columbia, MD (cdp) Howard County	55	0.06
Anaheim, CA (city) Orange County	55	0.02
Fort Worth, TX (city) Tarrant County	55	0.01
Quincy, MA (city) Norfolk County	54	0.06
Ocala, FL (city) Marion County	53	0.12
Salt Lake City, UT (city) Salt Lake County	53	0.03
Birmingham, AL (city) Jefferson County	52	0.02
Franklin, IN (city) Johnson County	51	0.26
San Jose, CA (city) Santa Clara County	51	0.01
Rohnert Park, CA (city) Sonoma County	49	0.12
Potomac, MD (cdp) Montgomery County	49	0.11
Hillside, NJ (cdp) Union County	48	0.22
Montclair, NJ (cdp) Essex County	48	0.12
Nashua, NH (city) Hillsborough County	48	0.06
Lexington-Fayette, KY (special city) Fayette County	48	0.02
New Territory, TX (cdp) Fort Bend County	47	0.34
Moreno Valley, CA (city) Riverside County	47	0.03
Washington, DC (city) District of Columbia	46	0.01
Reynoldsburg, OH (city) Franklin County	45	0.14
Ramapo, NY (town) Rockland County	44	0.04
Wake Forest, NC (town) Wake County	43	0.34
Pullman, WA (city) Whitman County	43	0.17
Brooklyn Park, MN (city) Hennepin County	43	0.06
Milwaukee, WI (city) Milwaukee County	43	0.01
San Diego, CA (city) San Diego County	43	0.00
Storrs, CT (cdp) Tolland County	42	0.38
Mansfield, CT (town) Tolland County	42	0.20
Arlington, VA (cdp) Arlington County	42	0.02
Arlington, NY (cdp) Dutchess County	41	0.33
Brushy Creek, TX (cdp) Williamson County	41	0.26
Hazelwood, MO (city) Saint Louis County	41	0.16
Shaker Heights, OH (city) Cuyahoga County	41	0.14
Essex, MD (cdp) Baltimore County	41	0.10
Poughkeepsie, NY (town) Dutchess County	41	0.10
Carlstadt, NJ (borough) Bergen County	40	0.68
Indiana, PA (borough) Indiana County	40	0.27
Sandy Springs, GA (cdp) Fulton County	40	0.05
Northampton, MA (city) Hampshire County	39	0.13
Denton, TX (city) Denton County	39	0.05
Robbinsdale, MN (city) Hennepin County	38	0.27
Forest Park, IL (village) Cook County	38	0.24
West Des Moines, IA (city) Polk County	38	0.08
Duluth, MN (city) Saint Louis County	38	0.04
Garland, TX (city) Dallas County	37	0.02
Highland Falls, NY (village) Orange County	36	0.98
Arkansas City, KS (city) Cowley County	36	0.30
Highlands, NY (town) Orange County	36	0.29
Marlboro, NJ (township) Monmouth County	36	0.10
Azusa, CA (city) Los Angeles County	36	0.08
Indianapolis, IN (special city) Marion County	36	0.00
Maplewood, NJ (cdp) Essex County	35	0.15
Coon Rapids, MN (city) Anoka County	35	0.06
Rossville, MD (cdp) Baltimore County	34	0.29
Rockville, MD (city) Montgomery County	34	0.07
Yorba Linda, CA (city) Orange County	34	0.06
New Bedford, MA (city) Bristol County	34	0.04
Providence, RI (city) Providence County	34	0.02
Ithaca, NY (town) Tompkins County	33	0.18
Middle River, MD (cdp) Baltimore County	33	0.14
Chillum, MD (cdp) Prince George's County	33	0.10
Sunnyvale, CA (city) Santa Clara County	33	0.03
El Paso, TX (city) El Paso County	33	0.01
Edgewater, NJ (borough) Bergen County	32	0.42
Pelham, AL (city) Shelby County	32	0.23
Scotch Plains, NJ (cdp) Union County	32	0.14
Urbana, IL (city) Champaign County	32	0.09
Elizabeth, NJ (city) Union County	32	0.03
Norman, OK (city) Cleveland County	32	0.03
Jonesboro, GA (city) Clayton County	31	0.80
Pepper Pike, OH (city) Cuyahoga County	31	0.51
Winchester, NV (cdp) Clark County	31	0.12
North Atlanta, GA (cdp) De Kalb County	31	0.08
Fayetteville, AR (city) Washington County	31	0.05
Scranton, PA (city) Lackawanna County	31	0.04
Barrington, RI (town) Bristol County	30	0.18
Ames, IA (city) Story County	30	0.06
Cambridge, MA (city) Middlesex County	30	0.03
Gainesville, FL (city) Alachua County	30	0.03
Hayward, CA (city) Alameda County	30	0.02
Spring Valley, NY (village) Rockland County	29	0.11
Haltom City, TX (city) Tarrant County	29	0.07
Saint Louis Park, MN (city) Hennepin County	29	0.07
Longview, TX (city) Gregg County	29	0.04
Pompano Beach, FL (city) Broward County	29	0.04
Fullerton, CA (city) Orange County	29	0.02

Notes: (cdp) census designated place; Refer to the Explanation of Data in the front of the book for more detailed information.

African, sub-Saharan: Kenyan

Top 150 Places Sorted by Percent

(Based on all places, regardless of population)

Place	Number	%
College City, AR (town) Lawrence County	5	1.85
Forest Home, NY (cdp) Tompkins County	16	1.57
Round Lake, MN (city) Nobles County	6	1.48
Thunderbolt, GA (town) Chatham County	27	1.14
Princess Anne, MD (town) Somerset County	27	1.13
Highland Falls, NY (village) Orange County	36	0.98
Peapack and Gladstone, NJ (borough) Somerset County	23	0.95
Leicester, MA (town) Worcester County	90	0.86
Elbing, KS (city) Butler County	2	0.84
Oronoko charter, MI (township) Berrien County	82	0.83
Winona, KS (city) Logan County	2	0.83
Jonesboro, GA (city) Clayton County	31	0.80
Salisbury, MA (town) Essex County	59	0.75
Inwood, IA (city) Lyon County	6	0.69
Carlstadt, NJ (borough) Bergen County	40	0.68
Elsah, IL (village) Jersey County	4	0.64
Northeast Ithaca, NY (cdp) Tompkins County	17	0.63
Franklin, WV (town) Pendleton County	5	0.63
Elmer, NJ (borough) Salem County	8	0.58
Pepper Pike, OH (city) Cuyahoga County	31	0.51
Tysons Corner, VA (cdp) Fairfax County	93	0.50
Winfield, KS (city) Cowley County	61	0.50
Esperance, NY (town) Schoharie County	10	0.49
Brookmont, MD (cdp) Montgomery County	15	0.48
Hanley Hills, MO (village) Saint Louis County	9	0.44
Homewood, AL (city) Jefferson County	104	0.42
Edgewater, NJ (borough) Bergen County	32	0.42
Brooklyn Center, MN (city) Hennepin County	116	0.40
Emeryville, CA (city) Alameda County	27	0.39
Beltsville, MD (cdp) Prince George's County	60	0.38
Storrs, CT (cdp) Tolland County	42	0.38
Heathrow, FL (cdp) Seminole County	15	0.38
Upper Nyack, NY (village) Rockland County	7	0.38
Norfolk, CT (town) Litchfield County	6	0.36
Jamesburg, NJ (borough) Middlesex County	21	0.35
Parkville, MD (cdp) Baltimore County	107	0.34
New Territory, TX (cdp) Fort Bend County	47	0.34
Wake Forest, NC (town) Wake County	43	0.34
Warrenton, VA (town) Fauquier County	22	0.34
Arlington, NY (cdp) Dutchess County	41	0.33
Takoma Park, MD (city) Montgomery County	55	0.32
Bayport, MN (city) Washington County	10	0.32
Prospect, KY (city) Jefferson County	15	0.31
Richmond, MA (town) Berkshire County	5	0.31
Marietta, GA (city) Cobb County	175	0.30
Arkansas City, KS (city) Cowley County	36	0.30
Berryville, VA (town) Clarke County	9	0.30
Highlands, NY (town) Orange County	36	0.29
Rossville, MD (cdp) Baltimore County	34	0.29
Black Jack, MO (city) Saint Louis County	18	0.28
Indiana, PA (borough) Indiana County	40	0.27
Robbinsdale, MN (city) Hennepin County	38	0.27
Fairfield, IA (city) Jefferson County	26	0.27
Prairie View, TX (city) Waller County	12	0.27
Columbus Junction, IA (city) Louisa County	5	0.27
Smyrna, GA (city) Cobb County	107	0.26
Franklin, IN (city) Johnson County	51	0.26
Brushy Creek, TX (cdp) Williamson County	41	0.26
Glendale, CO (city) Arapahoe County	12	0.26
Isanti, MN (city) Isanti County	6	0.26
Shoreview, MN (city) Ramsey County	64	0.25
East Fishkill, NY (town) Dutchess County	63	0.25
Swissvale, PA (borough) Allegheny County	24	0.25
Dumbarton, VA (cdp) Henrico County	17	0.25
Forest Park, IL (village) Cook County	38	0.24
Irondale, AL (city) Jefferson County	23	0.24
Scanlon, MN (city) Carlton County	2	0.24
Stacey Street, FL (cdp) Palm Beach County	2	0.24
Pelham, AL (city) Shelby County	32	0.23
Plattsmouth, NE (city) Cass County	16	0.23
Knightdale, NC (town) Wake County	14	0.23
New Paltz, NY (village) Ulster County	14	0.23
Liberty, PA (township) McKean County	4	0.23
Hillside, NJ (cdp) Union County	48	0.22
Oberlin, OH (city) Lorain County	18	0.22
West Vincent, PA (township) Chester County	7	0.22
Bryn Athyn, PA (borough) Montgomery County	3	0.22
Miami Shores, FL (village) Miami-Dade County	22	0.21
Darby Township, PA (cdp) Delaware County	20	0.21
Richmond, RI (town) Washington County	15	0.21
Mansfield, CT (town) Tolland County	42	0.20
Lower Gwynedd, PA (township) Montgomery County	21	0.20
Forest Glen, MD (cdp) Montgomery County	15	0.20
Riverside, MD (cdp) Harford County	12	0.20
Williamsville, NY (village) Erie County	11	0.20
Berrien, MI (township) Berrien County	10	0.20
Mission Hills, KS (city) Johnson County	7	0.20
Adairsville, GA (city) Bartow County	5	0.20
Charlack, MO (city) Saint Louis County	3	0.20
West Point, IA (city) Lee County	2	0.20
Mission Bend, TX (cdp) Fort Bend County	60	0.19
Arkadelphia, AR (city) Clark County	20	0.19
Dingman, PA (township) Pike County	17	0.19
Chestnut Ridge, NY (village) Rockland County	15	0.19
Larkfield-Wikiup, CA (cdp) Sonoma County	14	0.19
Myerstown, PA (borough) Lebanon County	6	0.19
Worcester, MA (city) Worcester County	312	0.18
Germantown, MD (cdp) Montgomery County	102	0.18
Ithaca, NY (town) Tompkins County	33	0.18
Barrington, RI (town) Bristol County	30	0.18
Hyattsville, MD (city) Prince George's County	26	0.18
Wolf Trap, VA (cdp) Fairfax County	25	0.18
Forest City, FL (cdp) Seminole County	23	0.18
Kingston, PA (township) Luzerne County	13	0.18
Silver Spring, MD (cdp) Montgomery County	133	0.17
North Bethesda, MD (cdp) Montgomery County	65	0.17
Pullman, WA (city) Whitman County	43	0.17
Clive, IA (city) Polk County	22	0.17
Jefferson, OH (village) Ashtabula County	6	0.17
Hazelwood, MO (city) Saint Louis County	41	0.16
Manor, PA (township) Lancaster County	27	0.16
Marshall, MN (city) Lyon County	20	0.16
Garden City, GA (city) Chatham County	18	0.16
Magnolia, AR (city) Columbia County	17	0.16
Belle Haven, VA (cdp) Fairfax County	10	0.16
Slippery Rock, PA (borough) Butler County	5	0.16
Maplewood, NJ (cdp) Essex County	35	0.15
Rockwall, TX (city) Rockwall County	27	0.15
Ives Estates, FL (cdp) Miami-Dade County	26	0.15
Narragansett, RI (town) Washington County	25	0.15
Lakeside, VA (cdp) Henrico County	17	0.15
Nazareth, PA (borough) Northampton County	9	0.15
Gregg, PA (township) Union County	7	0.15
Edison, NJ (cdp) Middlesex County	132	0.14
Reynoldsburg, OH (city) Franklin County	45	0.14
Shaker Heights, OH (city) Cuyahoga County	41	0.14
Middle River, MD (cdp) Baltimore County	33	0.14
Scotch Plains, NJ (cdp) Union County	32	0.14
Junction City, KS (city) Geary County	26	0.14
Cedar Grove, NJ (cdp) Essex County	17	0.14
Kettering, MD (cdp) Prince George's County	16	0.14
Huntington, VA (cdp) Fairfax County	12	0.14
Mount Horeb, WI (village) Dane County	8	0.14
Hummelstown, PA (borough) Dauphin County	6	0.14
Narberth, PA (borough) Montgomery County	6	0.14
Superior, NE (city) Nuckolls County	3	0.14
Newburgh, ME (town) Penobscot County	2	0.14
La Mirada, CA (city) Los Angeles County	63	0.13
Manhattan, KS (city) Riley County	59	0.13
Northampton, MA (city) Hampshire County	39	0.13
Greenbelt, MD (city) Prince George's County	28	0.13
North Plainfield, NJ (borough) Somerset County	28	0.13
Huntington, IN (city) Huntington County	22	0.13
Covington, GA (city) Newton County	15	0.13
Media, PA (borough) Delaware County	7	0.13
Saint Joseph, MN (city) Stearns County	6	0.13
Saxon, SC (cdp) Spartanburg County	5	0.13
Flandreau, SD (city) Moody County	3	0.13
Carolina Shores, NC (town) Brunswick County	2	0.13
Arlington, TX (city) Tarrant County	408	0.12

Notes: (cdp) census designated place; Refer to the Explanation of Data in the front of the book for more detailed information.

African, sub-Saharan: Kenyan

Top 150 Places Sorted by Percent

(Based on places with populations of 10,000 or more)

Place	Number	%
Leicester, MA (town) Worcester County	90	0.86
Tysons Corner, VA (cdp) Fairfax County	93	0.50
Winfield, KS (city) Cowley County	61	0.50
Homewood, AL (city) Jefferson County	104	0.42
Brooklyn Center, MN (city) Hennepin County	116	0.40
Beltsville, MD (cdp) Prince George's County	60	0.38
Storrs, CT (cdp) Tolland County	42	0.38
Parkville, MD (cdp) Baltimore County	107	0.34
New Territory, TX (cdp) Fort Bend County	47	0.34
Wake Forest, NC (town) Wake County	43	0.34
Arlington, NY (cdp) Dutchess County	41	0.33
Takoma Park, MD (city) Montgomery County	55	0.32
Marietta, GA (city) Cobb County	175	0.30
Arkansas City, KS (city) Cowley County	36	0.30
Highlands, NY (town) Orange County	36	0.29
Rossville, MD (cdp) Baltimore County	34	0.29
Indiana, PA (borough) Indiana County	40	0.27
Robbinsdale, MN (city) Hennepin County	38	0.27
Smyrna, GA (city) Cobb County	107	0.26
Franklin, IN (city) Johnson County	51	0.26
Brushy Creek, TX (cdp) Williamson County	41	0.26
Shoreview, MN (city) Ramsey County	64	0.25
East Fishkill, NY (town) Dutchess County	63	0.25
Forest Park, IL (village) Cook County	38	0.24
Pelham, AL (city) Shelby County	32	0.23
Hillside, NJ (cdp) Union County	48	0.22
Miami Shores, FL (village) Miami-Dade County	22	0.21
Mansfield, CT (town) Tolland County	42	0.20
Lower Gwynedd, PA (township) Montgomery County	21	0.20
Mission Bend, TX (cdp) Fort Bend County	60	0.19
Arkadelphia, AR (city) Clark County	20	0.19
Worcester, MA (city) Worcester County	312	0.18
Germantown, MD (cdp) Montgomery County	102	0.18
Ithaca, NY (town) Tompkins County	33	0.18
Barrington, RI (town) Bristol County	30	0.18
Hyattsville, MD (city) Prince George's County	26	0.18
Wolf Trap, VA (cdp) Fairfax County	25	0.18
Forest City, FL (cdp) Seminole County	23	0.18
Silver Spring, MD (cdp) Montgomery County	133	0.17
North Bethesda, MD (cdp) Montgomery County	65	0.17
Pullman, WA (city) Whitman County	43	0.17
Clive, IA (city) Polk County	22	0.17
Hazelwood, MO (city) Saint Louis County	41	0.16
Manor, PA (township) Lancaster County	27	0.16
Marshall, MN (city) Lyon County	20	0.16
Garden City, GA (city) Chatham County	18	0.16
Magnolia, AR (city) Columbia County	17	0.16
Maplewood, NJ (cdp) Essex County	35	0.15
Rockwall, TX (city) Rockwall County	27	0.15
Ives Estates, FL (cdp) Miami-Dade County	26	0.15
Narragansett, RI (town) Washington County	25	0.15
Lakeside, VA (cdp) Henrico County	17	0.15
Edison, NJ (cdp) Middlesex County	132	0.14
Reynoldsburg, OH (city) Franklin County	45	0.14
Shaker Heights, OH (city) Cuyahoga County	41	0.14
Middle River, MD (cdp) Baltimore County	33	0.14
Scotch Plains, NJ (cdp) Union County	32	0.14
Junction City, KS (city) Geary County	26	0.14
Cedar Grove, NJ (cdp) Essex County	17	0.14
Kettering, MD (cdp) Prince George's County	16	0.14
La Mirada, CA (city) Los Angeles County	63	0.13
Manhattan, KS (city) Riley County	59	0.13
Northampton, MA (city) Hampshire County	39	0.13
Greenbelt, MD (city) Prince George's County	28	0.13
North Plainfield, NJ (borough) Somerset County	28	0.13
Huntington, IN (city) Huntington County	22	0.13
Covington, GA (city) Newton County	15	0.13
Arlington, TX (city) Tarrant County	408	0.12
Novato, CA (city) Marin County	56	0.12
Ocala, FL (city) Marion County	53	0.12
Rohnert Park, CA (city) Sonoma County	49	0.12
Montclair, NJ (cdp) Essex County	48	0.12
Winchester, NV (cdp) Clark County	31	0.12
Roanoke Rapids, NC (city) Halifax County	21	0.12
West Chester, PA (borough) Chester County	21	0.12
Brookside, DE (cdp) New Castle County	18	0.12
Carnot-Moon, PA (cdp) Allegheny County	13	0.12
Iowa City, IA (city) Johnson County	67	0.11
Potomac, MD (cdp) Montgomery County	49	0.11
Spring Valley, NY (village) Rockland County	29	0.11
Cockeysville, MD (cdp) Baltimore County	22	0.11
New Paltz, NY (town) Ulster County	14	0.11
Federal Way, WA (city) King County	87	0.10
Essex, MD (cdp) Baltimore County	41	0.10
Poughkeepsie, NY (town) Dutchess County	41	0.10
Marlboro, NJ (township) Monmouth County	36	0.10
Chillum, MD (cdp) Prince George's County	33	0.10
Ankeny, IA (city) Polk County	26	0.10
Kennesaw, GA (city) Cobb County	23	0.10
White Oak, MD (cdp) Montgomery County	21	0.10
Macomb, IL (city) McDonough County	19	0.10
Calverton, MD (cdp) Montgomery County	13	0.10
Canyon, TX (city) Randall County	13	0.10
Miami, OK (city) Ottawa County	13	0.10
Jersey City, NJ (city) Hudson County	209	0.09
Urbana, IL (city) Champaign County	32	0.09
Gloucester, MA (city) Essex County	27	0.09
SeaTac, WA (city) King County	24	0.09
East Hempfield, PA (township) Lancaster County	19	0.09
Wilkinsburg, PA (borough) Allegheny County	17	0.09
Langley Park, MD (cdp) Prince George's County	14	0.09
Ozark, AL (city) Dale County	13	0.09
Greenlawn, NY (cdp) Suffolk County	12	0.09
North Saint Paul, MN (city) Ramsey County	11	0.09
Montecito, CA (cdp) Santa Barbara County	9	0.09
South Bend, IN (city) Saint Joseph County	84	0.08
Lowell, MA (city) Middlesex County	80	0.08
West Des Moines, IA (city) Polk County	38	0.08
Azusa, CA (city) Los Angeles County	36	0.08
North Atlanta, GA (cdp) De Kalb County	31	0.08
Maryland Heights, MO (city) Saint Louis County	20	0.08
Starkville, MS (city) Oktibbeha County	18	0.08
New Hope, MN (city) Hennepin County	17	0.08
South Laurel, MD (cdp) Prince George's County	16	0.08
Sylvania, OH (city) Lucas County	15	0.08
Holmdel, NJ (township) Monmouth County	13	0.08
Hopkins, MN (city) Hennepin County	13	0.08
Coralville, IA (city) Johnson County	12	0.08
Saddle Brook, NJ (cdp) Bergen County	11	0.08
Central Point, OR (city) Jackson County	10	0.08
Durham, NH (town) Strafford County	10	0.08
Catskill, NY (town) Greene County	9	0.08
Shiloh, OH (cdp) Montgomery County	9	0.08
Santa Rosa, CA (city) Sonoma County	97	0.07
Bellevue, WA (city) King County	79	0.07
Athens-Clarke County, GA (special city) Clarke County	73	0.07
Rockville, MD (city) Montgomery County	34	0.07
Haltom City, TX (city) Tarrant County	29	0.07
Saint Louis Park, MN (city) Hennepin County	29	0.07
Leominster, MA (city) Worcester County	28	0.07
North Brunswick Township, NJ (cdp) Middlesex County	25	0.07
Frisco, TX (city) Collin County	23	0.07
Shawnee, OK (city) Pottawatomie County	21	0.07
Dolton, IL (village) Cook County	17	0.07
Rolling Meadows, IL (city) Cook County	17	0.07
North Laurel, MD (cdp) Howard County	15	0.07
Lanham-Seabrook, MD (cdp) Prince George's County	13	0.07
East Hampton, CT (town) Middlesex County	10	0.07
Glenn Dale, MD (cdp) Prince George's County	9	0.07
Murphysboro, IL (city) Jackson County	9	0.07
Richmond, CA (city) Contra Costa County	56	0.06
Columbia, MD (cdp) Howard County	55	0.06
Quincy, MA (city) Norfolk County	54	0.06
Nashua, NH (city) Hillsborough County	48	0.06
Brooklyn Park, MN (city) Hennepin County	43	0.06
Coon Rapids, MN (city) Anoka County	35	0.06
Yorba Linda, CA (city) Orange County	34	0.06
Ames, IA (city) Story County	30	0.06
Bedford, TX (city) Tarrant County	28	0.06
Chapel Hill, NC (town) Orange County	28	0.06

Notes: (cdp) census designated place; Refer to the Explanation of Data in the front of the book for more detailed information.

African, sub-Saharan: Liberian

Top 150 Places Sorted by Number

(Based on all places, regardless of population)

Place	Number	%
New York, NY (city) New York City	2,561	0.03
Brooklyn Park, MN (city) Hennepin County	1,079	1.60
Philadelphia, PA (city) Philadelphia County	863	0.06
Trenton, NJ (city) Mercer County	739	0.87
Providence, RI (city) Providence County	609	0.35
Charlotte, NC (city) Mecklenburg County	546	0.10
Minneapolis, MN (city) Hennepin County	484	0.13
Brooklyn Center, MN (city) Hennepin County	439	1.51
Newark, NJ (city) Essex County	427	0.16
Saint Paul, MN (city) Ramsey County	356	0.12
Pawtucket, RI (city) Providence County	325	0.45
Houston, TX (city) Harris County	251	0.01
Hempstead, NY (town) Nassau County	218	0.03
Detroit, MI (city) Wayne County	216	0.02
Indianapolis, IN (special city) Marion County	213	0.03
Columbia, MD (cdp) Howard County	188	0.21
Hamilton, NJ (township) Mercer County	187	0.21
Boston, MA (city) Suffolk County	171	0.03
Chicago, IL (city) Cook County	171	0.01
Columbus, OH (city) Franklin County	166	0.02
Redland, MD (cdp) Montgomery County	165	0.96
Bensalem, PA (township) Bucks County	165	0.28
East Orange, NJ (city) Essex County	162	0.23
Silver Spring, MD (cdp) Montgomery County	151	0.20
Chillum, MD (cdp) Prince George's County	148	0.43
Reston, VA (cdp) Fairfax County	148	0.26
Oakland, CA (city) Alameda County	144	0.04
Baltimore, MD (independent city) Baltimore city	141	0.02
Uniondale, NY (cdp) Nassau County	129	0.56
Germantown, MD (cdp) Montgomery County	123	0.22
Richmond, VA (independent city) Richmond city	122	0.06
Riverdale, IL (village) Cook County	120	0.80
Bay Point, CA (cdp) Contra Costa County	120	0.56
Lowell, MA (city) Middlesex County	111	0.11
Worcester, MA (city) Worcester County	110	0.06
Yeadon, PA (borough) Delaware County	109	0.92
Hurst, TX (city) Tarrant County	106	0.29
Atlantic City, NJ (city) Atlantic County	106	0.26
Beltsville, MD (cdp) Prince George's County	104	0.66
Southfield, MI (city) Oakland County	102	0.13
Upper Darby, PA (township) Delaware County	101	0.12
San Jose, CA (city) Santa Clara County	101	0.01
Euless, TX (city) Tarrant County	100	0.22
Gaithersburg, MD (city) Montgomery County	99	0.19
Hillcrest Heights, MD (cdp) Prince George's County	98	0.61
New Hope, MN (city) Hennepin County	98	0.47
Elizabeth, NJ (city) Union County	97	0.08
Champaign, IL (city) Champaign County	95	0.14
Syracuse, NY (city) Onondaga County	92	0.06
San Francisco, CA (city) San Francisco County	92	0.01
Stockton, CA (city) San Joaquin County	89	0.04
Salisbury, NC (city) Rowan County	87	0.33
El Cajon, CA (city) San Diego County	86	0.09
Nashville-Davidson, TN (special city) Davidson County	86	0.02
College Park, MD (city) Prince George's County	85	0.35
Boynton Beach, FL (city) Palm Beach County	85	0.14
Lynn, MA (city) Essex County	85	0.10
Cambridge, MA (city) Middlesex County	82	0.08
Washington, DC (city) District of Columbia	82	0.01
Morrisville, PA (borough) Bucks County	81	0.81
South Laurel, MD (cdp) Prince George's County	80	0.38
Oklahoma City, OK (city) Oklahoma County	80	0.02
Grandview, MO (city) Jackson County	79	0.32
Saint Louis Park, MN (city) Hennepin County	78	0.18
Winston-Salem, NC (city) Forsyth County	75	0.04
Atlanta, GA (city) Fulton County	75	0.02
Takoma Park, MD (city) Montgomery County	74	0.43
Aurora, IL (city) Kane County	74	0.05
Lanham-Seabrook, MD (cdp) Prince George's County	73	0.40
Fitchburg, WI (city) Dane County	73	0.36
Olney, MD (cdp) Montgomery County	72	0.23
Bristol, PA (township) Bucks County	72	0.13
Arlington, TX (city) Tarrant County	70	0.02
Clay, NY (town) Onondaga County	69	0.12
Wilmington, NC (city) New Hanover County	68	0.09
Raleigh, NC (city) Wake County	68	0.02
Bladensburg, MD (town) Prince George's County	66	0.87
Dale City, VA (cdp) Prince William County	66	0.12
Kansas City, MO (city) Jackson County	65	0.01
San Leandro, CA (city) Alameda County	64	0.08
Toledo, OH (city) Lucas County	64	0.02
Seattle, WA (city) King County	62	0.01
Royal Palm Beach, FL (village) Palm Beach County	61	0.28
Irvington, NJ (cdp) Essex County	59	0.10
Lexington-Fayette, KY (special city) Fayette County	59	0.02
East Windsor, NJ (township) Mercer County	58	0.23
Grand Rapids, MI (city) Kent County	58	0.03
Greater Landover, MD (cdp) Prince George's County	57	0.25
Mount Vernon, VA (cdp) Fairfax County	57	0.20
Woodlawn, MD (cdp) Baltimore County	57	0.16
Plymouth, MN (city) Hennepin County	57	0.09
Springfield, IL (city) Sangamon County	57	0.05
Montgomery Village, MD (cdp) Montgomery County	56	0.15
Paterson, NJ (city) Passaic County	56	0.04
Claymont, DE (cdp) New Castle County	55	0.60
Essex, MD (cdp) Baltimore County	55	0.14
Randolph, MA (cdp) Norfolk County	53	0.17
Cleveland Heights, OH (city) Cuyahoga County	52	0.10
Hoover, AL (city) Jefferson County	52	0.08
Rossmoor, MD (cdp) Montgomery County	51	0.67
Lake Arbor, MD (cdp) Prince George's County	51	0.60
Fridley, MN (city) Anoka County	51	0.19
Bloomington, MN (city) Hennepin County	51	0.06
Greensboro, NC (city) Guilford County	51	0.02
Monroe, NJ (township) Gloucester County	50	0.17
Jersey City, NJ (city) Hudson County	50	0.02
South Coatesville, PA (borough) Chester County	49	4.92
Hyattsville, MD (city) Prince George's County	49	0.33
Burlington, NJ (township) Burlington County	49	0.24
Ewing, NJ (cdp) Mercer County	49	0.14
Aspen Hill, MD (cdp) Montgomery County	49	0.10
Arden-Arcade, CA (cdp) Sacramento County	49	0.05
Hampton Manor, NY (cdp) Rensselaer County	48	1.82
East Greenbush, NY (town) Rensselaer County	48	0.31
Willingboro, NJ (township) Burlington County	48	0.15
Redan, GA (cdp) De Kalb County	48	0.14
Memphis, TN (city) Shelby County	48	0.01
West Haven, CT (city) New Haven County	47	0.09
Olathe, KS (city) Johnson County	47	0.05
Kansas City, KS (city) Wyandotte County	47	0.03
East Riverdale, MD (cdp) Prince George's County	46	0.30
White Oak, MD (cdp) Montgomery County	46	0.22
Potomac, MD (cdp) Montgomery County	46	0.10
South Bend, IN (city) Saint Joseph County	46	0.04
Woonsocket, RI (city) Providence County	45	0.10
East Providence, RI (city) Providence County	45	0.09
Anderson, IN (city) Madison County	45	0.08
Coon Rapids, MN (city) Anoka County	45	0.07
Madison, WI (city) Dane County	44	0.02
Spring Lake Park, MN (city) Anoka County	43	0.64
North Valley Stream, NY (cdp) Nassau County	42	0.27
Harrisburg, PA (city) Dauphin County	42	0.09
Maple Grove, MN (city) Hennepin County	42	0.08
Burnsville, MN (city) Dakota County	42	0.07
Daytona Beach, FL (city) Volusia County	41	0.06
Los Angeles, CA (city) Los Angeles County	41	0.00
Foothill Farms, CA (cdp) Sacramento County	40	0.23
Woodbridge, VA (cdp) Prince William County	40	0.13
Union City, CA (city) Alameda County	40	0.06
Cleveland, OH (city) Cuyahoga County	40	0.01
Little Canada, MN (city) Ramsey County	39	0.40
Stratford, CT (cdp) Fairfield County	39	0.08
Durham, NC (city) Durham County	39	0.02
Richardson, TX (city) Dallas County	38	0.04
Bellmore, NY (cdp) Nassau County	37	0.23
Crystal, MN (city) Hennepin County	37	0.16
Kinston, NC (city) Lenoir County	37	0.16
Kent, OH (city) Portage County	37	0.13
Lakewood, OH (city) Cuyahoga County	37	0.07
Delray Beach, FL (city) Palm Beach County	37	0.06

Notes: (cdp) census designated place; Refer to the Explanation of Data in the front of the book for more detailed information.

African, sub-Saharan: Liberian

Top 150 Places Sorted by Percent

(Based on all places, regardless of population)

Place	Number	%
South Coatesville, PA (borough) Chester County	49	4.92
Hampton Manor, NY (cdp) Rensselaer County	48	1.82
Brooklyn Park, MN (city) Hennepin County	1,079	1.60
Brooklyn Center, MN (city) Hennepin County	439	1.51
Trainer, PA (borough) Delaware County	25	1.35
Monmouth Junction, NJ (cdp) Middlesex County	32	1.32
Meadowbrook Farm, KY (city) Jefferson County	2	1.29
Colwyn, PA (borough) Delaware County	28	1.14
Redland, MD (cdp) Montgomery County	165	0.96
Yeadon, PA (borough) Delaware County	109	0.92
Trenton, NJ (city) Mercer County	739	0.87
Bladensburg, MD (town) Prince George's County	66	0.87
Harvey Cedars, NJ (borough) Ocean County	3	0.85
Morrisville, PA (borough) Bucks County	81	0.81
Riverdale, IL (village) Cook County	120	0.80
Clear Lake, MN (township) Sherburne County	11	0.69
Riverside, MO (city) Platte County	20	0.68
Amnicon, WI (town) Douglas County	7	0.68
Rossmoor, MD (cdp) Montgomery County	51	0.67
Beltsville, MD (cdp) Prince George's County	104	0.66
Spring Lake Park, MN (city) Anoka County	43	0.64
Hillcrest Heights, MD (cdp) Prince George's County	98	0.61
Claymont, DE (cdp) New Castle County	55	0.60
Lake Arbor, MD (cdp) Prince George's County	51	0.60
Uniondale, NY (cdp) Nassau County	129	0.56
Bay Point, CA (cdp) Contra Costa County	120	0.56
Hilltop, MN (city) Anoka County	4	0.52
White Sands, NM (cdp) Dona Ana County	7	0.49
Lakehurst, NJ (borough) Ocean County	12	0.48
New Hope, MN (city) Hennepin County	98	0.47
Pawtucket, RI (city) Providence County	325	0.45
North Randall, OH (village) Cuyahoga County	4	0.44
Chillum, MD (cdp) Prince George's County	148	0.43
Takoma Park, MD (city) Montgomery County	74	0.43
South Cleveland, TN (cdp) Bradley County	26	0.43
Sewaren, NJ (cdp) Middlesex County	12	0.43
Buies Creek, NC (cdp) Harnett County	9	0.41
Lanham-Seabrook, MD (cdp) Prince George's County	73	0.40
Little Canada, MN (city) Ramsey County	39	0.40
Twin Rivers, NJ (cdp) Mercer County	30	0.40
Smyrna, DE (town) Kent County	21	0.39
Simpsonville, KY (city) Shelby County	5	0.39
South Laurel, MD (cdp) Prince George's County	80	0.38
Long Lake, MN (city) Hennepin County	7	0.38
Woodlawn, MD (cdp) Prince George's County	23	0.37
Langston, OK (town) Logan County	6	0.37
Fitchburg, WI (city) Dane County	73	0.36
Dunn Loring, VA (cdp) Fairfax County	28	0.36
Providence, RI (city) Providence County	609	0.35
College Park, MD (city) Prince George's County	85	0.35
Salisbury, NC (city) Rowan County	87	0.33
Hyattsville, MD (city) Prince George's County	49	0.33
Grandview, MO (city) Jackson County	79	0.32
Crescent City North, CA (cdp) Del Norte County	13	0.32
East Greenbush, NY (town) Rensselaer County	48	0.31
Molalla, OR (city) Clackamas County	17	0.31
Wallingford, VT (town) Rutland County	7	0.31
East Riverdale, MD (cdp) Prince George's County	46	0.30
Saint Anthony, MN (city) Hennepin County	24	0.30
New Hope, TX (town) Collin County	2	0.30
Hurst, TX (city) Tarrant County	106	0.29
Perry, WI (town) Dane County	2	0.29
Bensalem, PA (township) Bucks County	165	0.28
Royal Palm Beach, FL (village) Palm Beach County	61	0.28
North Valley Stream, NY (cdp) Nassau County	42	0.27
Brigantine, NJ (city) Atlantic County	34	0.27
Cloverly, MD (cdp) Montgomery County	22	0.27
Reston, VA (cdp) Fairfax County	148	0.26
Atlantic City, NJ (city) Atlantic County	106	0.26
Downingtown, PA (borough) Chester County	20	0.26
Greater Landover, MD (cdp) Prince George's County	57	0.25
Coatesville, PA (city) Chester County	27	0.25
Madison Park, NJ (cdp) Middlesex County	17	0.25
Zebulon, NC (town) Wake County	10	0.25
Plainsboro Center, NJ (cdp) Middlesex County	6	0.25
Burlington, NJ (township) Burlington County	49	0.24
Hockinson, WA (cdp) Clark County	12	0.24
Ottawa Hills, OH (village) Lucas County	11	0.24
East Orange, NJ (city) Essex County	162	0.23
Olney, MD (cdp) Montgomery County	72	0.23
East Windsor, NJ (township) Mercer County	58	0.23
Foothill Farms, CA (cdp) Sacramento County	40	0.23
Bellmore, NY (cdp) Nassau County	37	0.23
New Cassel, NY (cdp) Nassau County	30	0.23
Rushford, MN (city) Fillmore County	4	0.23
Colo, IA (city) Story County	2	0.23
Germantown, MD (cdp) Montgomery County	123	0.22
Euless, TX (city) Tarrant County	100	0.22
White Oak, MD (cdp) Montgomery County	46	0.22
Horn Lake, MS (city) De Soto County	30	0.22
Columbia, MD (cdp) Howard County	188	0.21
Hamilton, NJ (township) Mercer County	187	0.21
Hybla Valley, VA (cdp) Fairfax County	36	0.21
Lansdowne, PA (borough) Delaware County	23	0.21
Morrisville, NC (town) Wake County	11	0.21
Arthur, MN (township) Kanabec County	4	0.21
Silver Spring, MD (cdp) Montgomery County	151	0.20
Mount Vernon, VA (cdp) Fairfax County	57	0.20
Darby, PA (borough) Delaware County	21	0.20
Maxatawny, PA (township) Berks County	12	0.20
Friendship Village, MD (cdp) Montgomery County	9	0.20
Gaithersburg, MD (city) Montgomery County	99	0.19
Fridley, MN (city) Anoka County	51	0.19
North Kensington, MD (cdp) Montgomery County	17	0.19
Oakland City, IN (city) Gibson County	5	0.19
Saint Louis Park, MN (city) Hennepin County	78	0.18
Greater Upper Marlboro, MD (cdp) Prince George's County	33	0.18
Laurel, VA (cdp) Henrico County	26	0.18
Calverton, MD (cdp) Montgomery County	23	0.18
Stone Mountain, GA (city) De Kalb County	12	0.18
Wrightsboro, NC (cdp) New Hanover County	8	0.18
Robins AFB, GA (cdp) Houston County	7	0.18
Fort Polk North, LA (cdp) Vernon Parish	6	0.18
Cottage City, MD (town) Prince George's County	2	0.18
Randolph, MA (cdp) Norfolk County	53	0.17
Monroe, NJ (township) Gloucester County	50	0.17
Brookings, SD (city) Brookings County	31	0.17
Parkland, FL (city) Broward County	24	0.17
Midway-Hardwick, GA (cdp) Baldwin County	9	0.17
Thiells, NY (cdp) Rockland County	8	0.17
Penndel, PA (borough) Bucks County	4	0.17
Sewanee, TN (cdp) Franklin County	4	0.17
Talihina, OK (town) Le Flore County	2	0.17
Newark, NJ (city) Essex County	427	0.16
Woodlawn, MD (cdp) Baltimore County	57	0.16
Crystal, MN (city) Hennepin County	37	0.16
Kinston, NC (city) Lenoir County	37	0.16
North Laurel, MD (cdp) Howard County	32	0.16
Colmar Manor, MD (town) Prince George's County	2	0.16
Duncansville, PA (borough) Blair County	2	0.16
Montgomery Village, MD (cdp) Montgomery County	56	0.15
Willingboro, NJ (township) Burlington County	48	0.15
Riverdale Park, MD (town) Prince George's County	10	0.15
Kingston, RI (cdp) Washington County	8	0.15
Champaign, IL (city) Champaign County	95	0.14
Boynton Beach, FL (city) Palm Beach County	85	0.14
Essex, MD (cdp) Baltimore County	55	0.14
Ewing, NJ (cdp) Mercer County	49	0.14
Redan, GA (cdp) De Kalb County	48	0.14
Kernersville, NC (town) Forsyth County	23	0.14
Silverdale, WA (cdp) Kitsap County	22	0.14
Quemahoning, PA (township) Somerset County	3	0.14
Minneapolis, MN (city) Hennepin County	484	0.13
Southfield, MI (city) Oakland County	102	0.13
Bristol, PA (township) Bucks County	72	0.13
Woodbridge, VA (cdp) Prince William County	40	0.13
Kent, OH (city) Portage County	37	0.13
Cumberland, MD (city) Allegany County	27	0.13
Greenlawn, NY (cdp) Suffolk County	17	0.13
Mitchellville, MD (cdp) Prince George's County	13	0.13

Notes: (cdp) census designated place; Refer to the Explanation of Data in the front of the book for more detailed information.

African, sub-Saharan: Liberian

Top 150 Places Sorted by Percent

(Based on places with populations of 10,000 or more)

Place	Number	%
Brooklyn Park, MN (city) Hennepin County	1,079	1.60
Brooklyn Center, MN (city) Hennepin County	439	1.51
Redland, MD (cdp) Montgomery County	165	0.96
Yeadon, PA (borough) Delaware County	109	0.92
Trenton, NJ (city) Mercer County	739	0.87
Morrisville, PA (borough) Bucks County	81	0.81
Riverdale, IL (village) Cook County	120	0.80
Beltsville, MD (cdp) Prince George's County	104	0.66
Hillcrest Heights, MD (cdp) Prince George's County	98	0.61
Uniondale, NY (cdp) Nassau County	129	0.56
Bay Point, CA (cdp) Contra Costa County	120	0.56
New Hope, MN (city) Hennepin County	98	0.47
Pawtucket, RI (city) Providence County	325	0.45
Chillum, MD (cdp) Prince George's County	148	0.43
Takoma Park, MD (city) Montgomery County	74	0.43
Lanham-Seabrook, MD (cdp) Prince George's County	73	0.40
South Laurel, MD (cdp) Prince George's County	80	0.38
Fitchburg, WI (city) Dane County	73	0.36
Providence, RI (city) Providence County	609	0.35
College Park, MD (city) Prince George's County	85	0.35
Salisbury, NC (city) Rowan County	87	0.33
Hyattsville, MD (city) Prince George's County	49	0.33
Grandview, MO (city) Jackson County	79	0.32
East Greenbush, NY (town) Rensselaer County	48	0.31
East Riverdale, MD (cdp) Prince George's County	46	0.30
Hurst, TX (city) Tarrant County	106	0.29
Bensalem, PA (township) Bucks County	165	0.28
Royal Palm Beach, FL (village) Palm Beach County	61	0.28
North Valley Stream, NY (cdp) Nassau County	42	0.27
Brigantine, NJ (city) Atlantic County	34	0.27
Reston, VA (cdp) Fairfax County	148	0.26
Atlantic City, NJ (city) Atlantic County	106	0.26
Greater Landover, MD (cdp) Prince George's County	57	0.25
Coatesville, PA (city) Chester County	27	0.25
Burlington, NJ (township) Burlington County	49	0.24
East Orange, NJ (city) Essex County	162	0.23
Olney, MD (cdp) Montgomery County	72	0.23
East Windsor, NJ (township) Mercer County	58	0.23
Foothill Farms, CA (cdp) Sacramento County	40	0.23
Bellmore, NY (cdp) Nassau County	37	0.23
New Cassel, NY (cdp) Nassau County	30	0.23
Germantown, MD (cdp) Montgomery County	123	0.22
Euless, TX (city) Tarrant County	100	0.22
White Oak, MD (cdp) Montgomery County	46	0.22
Horn Lake, MS (city) De Soto County	30	0.22
Columbia, MD (cdp) Howard County	188	0.21
Hamilton, NJ (township) Mercer County	187	0.21
Hybla Valley, VA (cdp) Fairfax County	36	0.21
Lansdowne, PA (borough) Delaware County	23	0.21
Silver Spring, MD (cdp) Montgomery County	151	0.20
Mount Vernon, VA (cdp) Fairfax County	57	0.20
Darby, PA (borough) Delaware County	21	0.20
Gaithersburg, MD (city) Montgomery County	99	0.19
Fridley, MN (city) Anoka County	51	0.19
Saint Louis Park, MN (city) Hennepin County	78	0.18
Greater Upper Marlboro, MD (cdp) Prince George's County	33	0.18
Laurel, VA (cdp) Henrico County	26	0.18
Calverton, MD (cdp) Montgomery County	23	0.18
Randolph, MA (cdp) Norfolk County	53	0.17
Monroe, NJ (township) Gloucester County	50	0.17
Brookings, SD (city) Brookings County	31	0.17
Parkland, FL (city) Broward County	24	0.17
Newark, NJ (city) Essex County	427	0.16
Woodlawn, MD (cdp) Baltimore County	57	0.16
Crystal, MN (city) Hennepin County	37	0.16
Kinston, NC (city) Lenoir County	37	0.16
North Laurel, MD (cdp) Howard County	32	0.16
Montgomery Village, MD (cdp) Montgomery County	56	0.15
Willingboro, NJ (township) Burlington County	48	0.15
Champaign, IL (city) Champaign County	95	0.14
Boynton Beach, FL (city) Palm Beach County	85	0.14
Essex, MD (cdp) Baltimore County	55	0.14
Ewing, NJ (cdp) Mercer County	49	0.14
Redan, GA (cdp) De Kalb County	48	0.14
Kernersville, NC (town) Forsyth County	23	0.14
Silverdale, WA (cdp) Kitsap County	22	0.14
Minneapolis, MN (city) Hennepin County	484	0.13
Southfield, MI (city) Oakland County	102	0.13
Bristol, PA (township) Bucks County	72	0.13
Woodbridge, VA (cdp) Prince William County	40	0.13
Kent, OH (city) Portage County	37	0.13
Cumberland, MD (city) Allegany County	27	0.13
Greenlawn, NY (cdp) Suffolk County	17	0.13
Saint Paul, MN (city) Ramsey County	356	0.12
Upper Darby, PA (township) Delaware County	101	0.12
Clay, NY (town) Onondaga County	69	0.12
Dale City, VA (cdp) Prince William County	66	0.12
Walpole, MA (town) Norfolk County	28	0.12
College Park, GA (city) Fulton County	25	0.12
Lowell, MA (city) Middlesex County	111	0.11
Orange, NJ (cdp) Essex County	36	0.11
Coralville, IA (city) Johnson County	17	0.11
Charlotte, NC (city) Mecklenburg County	546	0.10
Lynn, MA (city) Essex County	85	0.10
Irvington, NJ (cdp) Essex County	59	0.10
Cleveland Heights, OH (city) Cuyahoga County	52	0.10
Aspen Hill, MD (cdp) Montgomery County	49	0.10
Potomac, MD (cdp) Montgomery County	46	0.10
Woonsocket, RI (city) Providence County	45	0.10
Trotwood, OH (city) Montgomery County	27	0.10
New Brighton, MN (city) Ramsey County	23	0.10
Fairland, MD (cdp) Montgomery County	22	0.10
Laurel, MD (city) Prince George's County	21	0.10
Central Falls, RI (city) Providence County	19	0.10
Avenel, NJ (cdp) Middlesex County	18	0.10
Independence, KY (city) Kenton County	15	0.10
East Norriton, PA (cdp) Montgomery County	13	0.10
Hershey, PA (cdp) Dauphin County	13	0.10
Wake Forest, NC (town) Wake County	13	0.10
El Cajon, CA (city) San Diego County	86	0.09
Wilmington, NC (city) New Hanover County	68	0.09
Plymouth, MN (city) Hennepin County	57	0.09
West Haven, CT (city) New Haven County	47	0.09
East Providence, RI (city) Providence County	45	0.09
Harrisburg, PA (city) Dauphin County	42	0.09
Maplewood, MN (city) Ramsey County	30	0.09
Golden Valley, MN (city) Hennepin County	19	0.09
North Decatur, GA (cdp) De Kalb County	14	0.09
Orangeburg, SC (city) Orangeburg County	12	0.09
Bainbridge, GA (city) Decatur County	11	0.09
Elizabeth, NJ (city) Union County	97	0.08
Cambridge, MA (city) Middlesex County	82	0.08
San Leandro, CA (city) Alameda County	64	0.08
Hoover, AL (city) Jefferson County	52	0.08
Anderson, IN (city) Madison County	45	0.08
Maple Grove, MN (city) Hennepin County	42	0.08
Stratford, CT (cdp) Fairfield County	39	0.08
South Brunswick, NJ (township) Middlesex County	32	0.08
Manassas, VA (independent city) Manassas city	29	0.08
Richfield, MN (city) Hennepin County	28	0.08
Edgewood, MD (cdp) Harford County	19	0.08
Warrensville Heights, OH (city) Cuyahoga County	13	0.08
Tuskegee, AL (city) Macon County	10	0.08
Doraville, GA (city) De Kalb County	8	0.08
Shelbyville, KY (city) Shelby County	8	0.08
Coon Rapids, MN (city) Anoka County	45	0.07
Burnsville, MN (city) Dakota County	42	0.07
Lakewood, OH (city) Cuyahoga County	37	0.07
Frederick, MD (city) Frederick County	36	0.07
University City, MO (city) Saint Louis County	25	0.07
Cheltenham, PA (township) Montgomery County	24	0.07
Mission Bend, TX (cdp) Fort Bend County	22	0.07
Poughkeepsie, NY (city) Dutchess County	22	0.07
Gurnee, IL (village) Lake County	21	0.07
Jeffersonville, IN (city) Clark County	19	0.07
Homewood, AL (city) Jefferson County	18	0.07
Wayne, MI (city) Wayne County	13	0.07
Wilkinsburg, PA (borough) Allegheny County	13	0.07
Langley Park, MD (cdp) Prince George's County	12	0.07
Halawa, HI (cdp) Honolulu County	10	0.07

Notes: (cdp) census designated place; Refer to the Explanation of Data in the front of the book for more detailed information.

African, sub-Saharan: Nigerian

Top 150 Places Sorted by Number

(Based on all places, regardless of population)

Place	Number	%
New York, NY (city) New York City	17,928	0.22
Houston, TX (city) Harris County	8,726	0.45
Chicago, IL (city) Cook County	5,464	0.19
Los Angeles, CA (city) Los Angeles County	2,803	0.08
Dallas, TX (city) Dallas County	2,365	0.20
Washington, DC (city) District of Columbia	1,933	0.34
Boston, MA (city) Suffolk County	1,702	0.29
Baltimore, MD (independent city) Baltimore city	1,486	0.23
Detroit, MI (city) Wayne County	1,459	0.15
Philadelphia, PA (city) Philadelphia County	1,443	0.10
Newark, NJ (city) Essex County	1,325	0.48
Arlington, TX (city) Tarrant County	1,302	0.39
Hempstead, NY (town) Nassau County	1,196	0.16
Chillum, MD (cdp) Prince George's County	936	2.74
Providence, RI (city) Providence County	889	0.51
Silver Spring, MD (cdp) Montgomery County	843	1.10
Garland, TX (city) Dallas County	820	0.38
Columbus, OH (city) Franklin County	813	0.11
Nashville-Davidson, TN (special city) Davidson County	812	0.15
Saint Paul, MN (city) Ramsey County	804	0.28
Oakland, CA (city) Alameda County	801	0.20
Raleigh, NC (city) Wake County	749	0.27
Austin, TX (city) Travis County	713	0.11
Irving, TX (city) Dallas County	679	0.35
South Laurel, MD (cdp) Prince George's County	661	3.18
Atlanta, GA (city) Fulton County	630	0.15
Lanham-Seabrook, MD (cdp) Prince George's County	627	3.47
Greenbelt, MD (city) Prince George's County	599	2.80
Irvington, NJ (cdp) Essex County	598	0.99
San Jose, CA (city) Santa Clara County	594	0.07
Charlotte, NC (city) Mecklenburg County	591	0.11
Memphis, TN (city) Shelby County	591	0.09
Hawthorne, CA (city) Los Angeles County	590	0.70
Missouri City, TX (city) Fort Bend County	578	1.10
Phoenix, AZ (city) Maricopa County	572	0.04
Redan, GA (cdp) De Kalb County	564	1.67
Randallstown, MD (cdp) Baltimore County	550	1.78
Greensboro, NC (city) Guilford County	544	0.24
Indianapolis, IN (special city) Marion County	524	0.07
Union, NJ (cdp) Union County	518	0.95
Mission Bend, TX (cdp) Fort Bend County	496	1.61
San Diego, CA (city) San Diego County	496	0.04
East Orange, NJ (city) Essex County	495	0.71
San Francisco, CA (city) San Francisco County	492	0.06
Aurora, CO (city) Arapahoe County	474	0.17
Minneapolis, MN (city) Hennepin County	467	0.12
Grand Prairie, TX (city) Dallas County	462	0.36
Jersey City, NJ (city) Hudson County	449	0.19
Orange, NJ (cdp) Essex County	417	1.27
Fairland, MD (cdp) Montgomery County	407	1.89
Pawtucket, RI (city) Providence County	404	0.55
Adelphi, MD (cdp) Prince George's County	402	2.68
Oklahoma City, OK (city) Oklahoma County	400	0.08
Durham, NC (city) Durham County	396	0.21
Southfield, MI (city) Oakland County	392	0.50
Elmont, NY (cdp) Nassau County	383	1.17
Mesquite, TX (city) Dallas County	383	0.31
Fresno, CA (city) Fresno County	367	0.09
Sugar Land, TX (city) Fort Bend County	363	0.57
Kansas City, MO (city) Jackson County	358	0.08
Baton Rouge, LA (city) East Baton Rouge Parish	352	0.15
New Orleans, LA (city) Orleans Parish	350	0.07
Hayward, CA (city) Alameda County	349	0.25
Albany, GA (city) Dougherty County	347	0.45
Woodlawn, MD (cdp) Prince George's County	339	5.46
Gardena, CA (city) Los Angeles County	327	0.57
Denver, CO (city) Denver County	327	0.06
Milwaukee, WI (city) Milwaukee County	321	0.05
Brooklyn Park, MN (city) Hennepin County	319	0.47
Greater Landover, MD (cdp) Prince George's County	317	1.39
New Rochelle, NY (city) Westchester County	310	0.43
Inglewood, CA (city) Los Angeles County	308	0.27
Lynn, MA (city) Essex County	305	0.34
Portland, OR (city) Multnomah County	303	0.06
San Antonio, TX (city) Bexar County	303	0.03

Place	Number	%
Little Rock, AR (city) Pulaski County	300	0.16
Seattle, WA (city) King County	297	0.05
Saint Louis, MO (independent city) Saint Louis city	295	0.08
Langley Park, MD (cdp) Prince George's County	292	1.80
Woodbridge, NJ (township) Middlesex County	292	0.30
Hollywood, FL (city) Broward County	285	0.20
Jacksonville, FL (special city) Duval County	281	0.04
Glenn Dale, MD (cdp) Prince George's County	280	2.18
Columbia, MD (cdp) Howard County	280	0.32
Beltsville, MD (cdp) Prince George's County	279	1.77
Franklin, NJ (township) Somerset County	277	0.54
Wheaton-Glenmont, MD (cdp) Montgomery County	273	0.47
Huntsville, AL (city) Madison County	272	0.17
Miramar, FL (city) Broward County	267	0.37
Fort Worth, TX (city) Tarrant County	266	0.05
Richardson, TX (city) Dallas County	262	0.29
Rialto, CA (city) San Bernardino County	261	0.28
Tallahassee, FL (city) Leon County	250	0.17
Laurel, MD (city) Prince George's County	245	1.22
Parkville, MD (cdp) Baltimore County	245	0.79
Carson, CA (city) Los Angeles County	244	0.27
College Park, GA (city) Fulton County	241	1.16
Ramapo, NY (town) Rockland County	240	0.22
Mitchellville, MD (cdp) Prince George's County	233	2.42
Woodlawn, MD (cdp) Baltimore County	232	0.64
Alexandria, VA (independent city) Alexandria city	232	0.18
Cincinnati, OH (city) Hamilton County	232	0.07
South Orange, NJ (cdp) Essex County	231	1.36
Takoma Park, MD (city) Montgomery County	230	1.34
Owings Mills, MD (cdp) Baltimore County	229	1.13
Piscataway, NJ (township) Middlesex County	229	0.45
Dolton, IL (village) Cook County	224	0.87
Rowlett, TX (city) Dallas County	221	0.50
Greenburgh, NY (town) Westchester County	220	0.25
Hempstead, NY (village) Nassau County	219	0.39
Tulsa, OK (city) Tulsa County	216	0.05
Goddard, MD (cdp) Prince George's County	215	3.89
Plano, TX (city) Collin County	215	0.10
Colesville, MD (cdp) Montgomery County	213	1.07
Maplewood, NJ (cdp) Essex County	212	0.89
Montgomery Village, MD (cdp) Montgomery County	210	0.55
Sayreville, NJ (borough) Middlesex County	209	0.52
Palmdale, CA (city) Los Angeles County	208	0.18
Brookhaven, NY (town) Suffolk County	206	0.05
Hillside, NJ (cdp) Union County	205	0.94
East Riverdale, MD (cdp) Prince George's County	204	1.33
New Carrollton, MD (city) Prince George's County	203	1.58
Riverdale, GA (city) Clayton County	201	1.61
Randolph, MA (cdp) Norfolk County	201	0.65
Richmond, CA (city) Contra Costa County	201	0.20
Bakersfield, CA (city) Kern County	197	0.08
Montclair, NJ (cdp) Essex County	193	0.49
Montgomery, AL (city) Montgomery County	193	0.10
Richmond, VA (independent city) Richmond city	193	0.10
Hyattsville, MD (city) Prince George's County	192	1.29
Fremont, CA (city) Alameda County	189	0.09
Pembroke Pines, FL (city) Broward County	188	0.14
College Station, TX (city) Brazos County	186	0.27
Wichita, KS (city) Sedgwick County	186	0.05
Oak Park, IL (village) Cook County	185	0.35
Lewisville, TX (city) Denton County	185	0.24
Norman, OK (city) Cleveland County	185	0.19
Carrollton, TX (city) Denton County	182	0.17
White Oak, MD (cdp) Montgomery County	181	0.87
Fayetteville, NC (city) Cumberland County	181	0.15
Somerset, NJ (cdp) Somerset County	180	0.78
Calumet City, IL (city) Cook County	179	0.46
Bowie, MD (city) Prince George's County	179	0.36
Long Beach, CA (city) Los Angeles County	179	0.04
West Carson, CA (cdp) Los Angeles County	178	0.84
Germantown, MD (cdp) Montgomery County	178	0.32
Laguna, CA (cdp) Sacramento County	176	0.51
Sacramento, CA (city) Sacramento County	176	0.04
Towson, MD (cdp) Baltimore County	171	0.33
Upper Darby, PA (township) Delaware County	171	0.21

Notes: (cdp) census designated place; Refer to the Explanation of Data in the front of the book for more detailed information.

African, sub-Saharan: Nigerian

Top 150 Places Sorted by Percent

(Based on all places, regardless of population)

Place	Number	%
South Brooksville, FL (cdp) Hernando County	77	5.75
Woodlawn, MD (cdp) Prince George's County	339	5.46
Goddard, MD (cdp) Prince George's County	215	3.89
Lynnville, TN (town) Giles County	13	3.76
Four Corners, TX (cdp) Fort Bend County	105	3.55
Lanham-Seabrook, MD (cdp) Prince George's County	627	3.47
Olympia Fields, IL (village) Cook County	159	3.37
Parkdale, OR (cdp) Hood River County	6	3.28
South Laurel, MD (cdp) Prince George's County	661	3.18
Homestead Base, FL (cdp) Miami-Dade County	12	2.96
Espy, PA (cdp) Columbia County	42	2.91
Greenbelt, MD (city) Prince George's County	599	2.80
Chillum, MD (cdp) Prince George's County	936	2.74
South Floral Park, NY (village) Nassau County	43	2.72
Adelphi, MD (cdp) Prince George's County	402	2.68
Cheverly, MD (town) Prince George's County	168	2.60
Cecil, GA (town) Cook County	6	2.59
Mitchellville, MD (cdp) Prince George's County	233	2.42
Landover Hills, MD (town) Prince George's County	35	2.33
Nebo Center, CA (cdp) San Bernardino County	29	2.28
Elsah, IL (village) Jersey County	14	2.24
Bladensburg, MD (town) Prince George's County	168	2.22
Glenn Dale, MD (cdp) Prince George's County	280	2.18
Clarkston, GA (city) De Kalb County	146	2.14
New Hempstead, NY (village) Rockland County	99	2.07
Riverdale Park, MD (town) Prince George's County	133	2.03
Sibley, LA (town) Webster Parish	22	1.96
Fairland, MD (cdp) Montgomery County	407	1.89
Langley Park, MD (cdp) Prince George's County	292	1.80
Randallstown, MD (cdp) Baltimore County	550	1.78
Beltsville, MD (cdp) Prince George's County	279	1.77
Brentwood, MD (town) Prince George's County	48	1.68
Redan, GA (cdp) De Kalb County	564	1.67
Burtonsville, MD (cdp) Montgomery County	120	1.64
Woodmore, MD (cdp) Prince George's County	99	1.64
Maryland City, MD (cdp) Anne Arundel County	110	1.63
Mission Bend, TX (cdp) Fort Bend County	496	1.61
Riverdale, GA (city) Clayton County	201	1.61
New Carrollton, MD (city) Prince George's County	203	1.58
Wadley, AL (town) Randolph County	10	1.55
Wilberforce, OH (cdp) Greene County	22	1.54
Woodland, IL (village) Iroquois County	5	1.54
Glenn Heights, TX (city) Dallas County	108	1.49
Brownfields, LA (cdp) East Baton Rouge Parish	74	1.46
Largo, MD (cdp) Prince George's County	124	1.45
Tangelo Park, FL (cdp) Orange County	33	1.42
Brownville, NJ (cdp) Middlesex County	37	1.41
Greater Landover, MD (cdp) Prince George's County	317	1.39
Rock Mills, AL (cdp) Randolph County	10	1.38
Culloden, GA (city) Monroe County	3	1.38
Stoutland, MO (village) Camden County	3	1.37
South Orange, NJ (cdp) Essex County	231	1.36
Orchard, NE (village) Antelope County	5	1.36
Windemere, TX (cdp) Travis County	95	1.35
Fairview, NY (cdp) Dutchess County	81	1.35
Valley, PA (township) Chester County	69	1.35
River Falls, AL (town) Covington County	8	1.35
Takoma Park, MD (city) Montgomery County	230	1.34
Cascade Valley, WA (cdp) Grant County	24	1.34
Langston, OK (town) Logan County	22	1.34
East Riverdale, MD (cdp) Prince George's County	204	1.33
Niverville, NY (cdp) Columbia County	22	1.32
Mine Hill, NJ (township) Morris County	48	1.30
Doylestown, WI (village) Columbia County	4	1.30
Hyattsville, MD (city) Prince George's County	192	1.29
Orange, NJ (cdp) Essex County	417	1.27
Rush City, MN (city) Chisago County	26	1.27
Monticello, LA (cdp) East Baton Rouge Parish	60	1.26
Dalworthington Gardens, TX (city) Tarrant County	28	1.26
Metolius, OR (city) Jefferson County	8	1.26
Lansing, NY (village) Tompkins County	37	1.25
Fairview, CA (cdp) Alameda County	118	1.23
Laurel, MD (city) Prince George's County	245	1.22
Orange, OH (village) Cuyahoga County	39	1.21
Rice River, MN (township) Aitkin County	2	1.20

Place	Number	%
Elmont, NY (cdp) Nassau County	383	1.17
College Park, GA (city) Fulton County	241	1.16
Peeksville, WI (town) Ashland County	2	1.16
Breckenridge Hills, MO (city) Saint Louis County	58	1.15
Owings Mills, MD (cdp) Baltimore County	229	1.13
Flossmoor, IL (village) Cook County	104	1.12
Wakonda, SD (town) Clay County	4	1.11
Silver Spring, MD (cdp) Montgomery County	843	1.10
Missouri City, TX (city) Fort Bend County	578	1.10
Lake Arbor, MD (cdp) Prince George's County	94	1.10
Cloverly, MD (cdp) Montgomery County	88	1.10
Wesley Chapel, FL (cdp) Pasco County	65	1.10
Colwyn, PA (borough) Delaware County	27	1.10
Colesville, MD (cdp) Montgomery County	213	1.07
Mount Rainier, MD (city) Prince George's County	89	1.05
Austell, GA (city) Cobb County	59	1.05
Stafford, TX (city) Fort Bend County	158	1.01
Desert View Highlands, CA (cdp) Los Angeles County	21	1.01
Powder Springs, GA (city) Cobb County	130	1.00
Heathrow, FL (cdp) Seminole County	39	1.00
Irvington, NJ (cdp) Essex County	598	0.99
Frost, TX (city) Navarro County	7	0.99
Ontario, OH (village) Richland County	51	0.98
Black Jack, MO (city) Saint Louis County	62	0.96
Union, NJ (cdp) Union County	518	0.95
Hillside, NJ (cdp) Union County	205	0.94
Thorndale, PA (cdp) Chester County	34	0.94
North Valley Stream, NY (cdp) Nassau County	146	0.92
Lansing, NY (town) Tompkins County	95	0.92
Fort Gaines, GA (city) Clay County	10	0.92
Lumberton, MS (city) Lamar County	21	0.91
Fair Oaks, GA (cdp) Cobb County	77	0.90
Maplewood, NJ (cdp) Essex County	212	0.89
Lilburn, GA (city) Gwinnett County	101	0.89
Hall Park, OK (town) Cleveland County	10	0.89
Carriage Club, CO (cdp) Douglas County	9	0.89
Scott, PA (township) Columbia County	42	0.88
Dolton, IL (village) Cook County	224	0.87
White Oak, MD (cdp) Montgomery County	181	0.87
Budd Lake, NJ (cdp) Morris County	71	0.86
Cullen, LA (town) Webster Parish	11	0.86
Albany, OH (village) Athens County	7	0.85
West Carson, CA (cdp) Los Angeles County	178	0.84
Saint Anthony, MN (city) Hennepin County	67	0.84
Madison Park, NJ (cdp) Middlesex County	58	0.84
Rossville, MD (cdp) Baltimore County	95	0.82
Glenarden, MD (city) Prince George's County	52	0.82
Stockbridge, GA (city) Henry County	78	0.81
Nelson, NH (town) Cheshire County	5	0.81
Colmar Manor, MD (town) Prince George's County	10	0.80
Parkville, MD (cdp) Baltimore County	245	0.79
New Territory, TX (cdp) Fort Bend County	110	0.79
Somerset, NJ (cdp) Somerset County	180	0.78
College Place, WA (city) Walla Walla County	61	0.78
Shrewsbury, NJ (borough) Monmouth County	28	0.78
Bonanza, GA (cdp) Clayton County	22	0.78
Kinder, LA (town) Allen Parish	17	0.78
Wilkinson Heights, SC (cdp) Orangeburg County	22	0.77
Pittsville, MD (town) Wicomico County	9	0.77
Country Walk, FL (cdp) Miami-Dade County	81	0.76
Kettering, MD (cdp) Prince George's County	83	0.75
Strawberry, CA (cdp) Marin County	40	0.75
Hopewell Junction, NY (cdp) Dutchess County	19	0.75
Mendenhall, MS (city) Simpson County	19	0.75
Isola, MS (town) Humphreys County	6	0.75
Tuskegee, AL (city) Macon County	89	0.74
Gordon Heights, NY (cdp) Suffolk County	23	0.74
Hatfield, PA (borough) Montgomery County	19	0.73
Eupora, MS (city) Webster County	17	0.73
Blueberry, MN (township) Wadena County	5	0.73
Columbia, MN (township) Polk County	3	0.73
Forestville, MD (cdp) Prince George's County	92	0.72
Andover, FL (cdp) Miami-Dade County	62	0.72
Lake Shore, WA (cdp) Clark County	48	0.72
Burnham, IL (village) Cook County	30	0.72

Notes: (cdp) census designated place; Refer to the Explanation of Data in the front of the book for more detailed information.

African, sub-Saharan: Nigerian

Top 150 Places Sorted by Percent

(Based on places with populations of 10,000 or more)

Place	Number	%
Lanham-Seabrook, MD (cdp) Prince George's County	627	3.47
South Laurel, MD (cdp) Prince George's County	661	3.18
Greenbelt, MD (city) Prince George's County	599	2.80
Chillum, MD (cdp) Prince George's County	936	2.74
Adelphi, MD (cdp) Prince George's County	402	2.68
Glenn Dale, MD (cdp) Prince George's County	280	2.18
Fairland, MD (cdp) Montgomery County	407	1.89
Langley Park, MD (cdp) Prince George's County	292	1.80
Randallstown, MD (cdp) Baltimore County	550	1.78
Beltsville, MD (cdp) Prince George's County	279	1.77
Redan, GA (cdp) De Kalb County	564	1.67
Mission Bend, TX (cdp) Fort Bend County	496	1.61
Riverdale, GA (city) Clayton County	201	1.61
New Carrollton, MD (city) Prince George's County	203	1.58
Greater Landover, MD (cdp) Prince George's County	317	1.39
South Orange, NJ (cdp) Essex County	231	1.36
Takoma Park, MD (city) Montgomery County	230	1.34
East Riverdale, MD (cdp) Prince George's County	204	1.33
Hyattsville, MD (city) Prince George's County	192	1.29
Orange, NJ (cdp) Essex County	417	1.27
Laurel, MD (city) Prince George's County	245	1.22
Elmont, NY (cdp) Nassau County	383	1.17
College Park, GA (city) Fulton County	241	1.16
Owings Mills, MD (cdp) Baltimore County	229	1.13
Silver Spring, MD (cdp) Montgomery County	843	1.10
Missouri City, TX (city) Fort Bend County	578	1.10
Colesville, MD (cdp) Montgomery County	213	1.07
Stafford, TX (city) Fort Bend County	158	1.01
Powder Springs, GA (city) Cobb County	130	1.00
Irvington, NJ (cdp) Essex County	598	0.99
Union, NJ (cdp) Union County	518	0.95
Hillside, NJ (cdp) Union County	205	0.94
North Valley Stream, NY (cdp) Nassau County	146	0.92
Lansing, NY (town) Tompkins County	95	0.92
Maplewood, NJ (cdp) Essex County	212	0.89
Lilburn, GA (city) Gwinnett County	101	0.89
Dolton, IL (village) Cook County	224	0.87
White Oak, MD (cdp) Montgomery County	181	0.87
West Carson, CA (cdp) Los Angeles County	178	0.84
Rossville, MD (cdp) Baltimore County	95	0.82
Parkville, MD (cdp) Baltimore County	245	0.79
New Territory, TX (cdp) Fort Bend County	110	0.79
Somerset, NJ (cdp) Somerset County	180	0.78
Country Walk, FL (cdp) Miami-Dade County	81	0.76
Kettering, MD (cdp) Prince George's County	83	0.75
Tuskegee, AL (city) Macon County	89	0.74
Forestville, MD (cdp) Prince George's County	92	0.72
East Orange, NJ (city) Essex County	495	0.71
Hawthorne, CA (city) Los Angeles County	590	0.70
Fayetteville, GA (city) Fayette County	79	0.70
Middle River, MD (cdp) Baltimore County	164	0.69
Marshfield, WI (city) Wood County	130	0.69
Westbury, NY (village) Nassau County	98	0.69
Savage-Guilford, MD (cdp) Howard County	87	0.69
Forest Park, OH (city) Hamilton County	132	0.68
Avenel, NJ (cdp) Middlesex County	116	0.66
University Heights, OH (city) Cuyahoga County	93	0.66
Randolph, MA (cdp) Norfolk County	201	0.65
Acworth, GA (city) Cobb County	88	0.65
Woodlawn, MD (cdp) Baltimore County	232	0.64
Carbondale, IL (city) Jackson County	132	0.64
Montgomery, NJ (township) Somerset County	112	0.64
Calverton, MD (cdp) Montgomery County	79	0.63
Addison, TX (town) Dallas County	86	0.62
Stanford, CA (cdp) Santa Clara County	82	0.62
Union City, GA (city) Fulton County	66	0.58
Sugar Land, TX (city) Fort Bend County	363	0.57
Gardena, CA (city) Los Angeles County	327	0.57
Rockledge, FL (city) Brevard County	115	0.57
Pawtucket, RI (city) Providence County	404	0.55
Montgomery Village, MD (cdp) Montgomery County	210	0.55
Statesboro, GA (city) Bulloch County	125	0.55
View Park-Windsor Hills, CA (cdp) Los Angeles County	60	0.55
Franklin, NJ (township) Somerset County	277	0.54
Baldwin, NY (cdp) Nassau County	126	0.54
Hazel Crest, IL (village) Cook County	79	0.54
Cinco Ranch, TX (cdp) Fort Bend County	61	0.54
Rahway, NJ (city) Union County	140	0.53
Bergenfield, NJ (borough) Bergen County	138	0.53
North Laurel, MD (cdp) Howard County	110	0.53
Sayreville, NJ (borough) Middlesex County	209	0.52
Milford Mill, MD (cdp) Baltimore County	139	0.52
East Lyme, CT (town) New London County	95	0.52
Providence, RI (city) Providence County	889	0.51
Laguna, CA (cdp) Sacramento County	176	0.51
Southfield, MI (city) Oakland County	392	0.50
Rowlett, TX (city) Dallas County	221	0.50
Homewood, IL (village) Cook County	98	0.50
Forestville, OH (cdp) Hamilton County	55	0.50
Montclair, NJ (cdp) Essex County	193	0.49
Mableton, GA (cdp) Cobb County	145	0.49
Newark, NJ (city) Essex County	1,325	0.48
Trotwood, OH (city) Montgomery County	133	0.48
Rockaway, NJ (township) Morris County	109	0.48
Roselle, NJ (borough) Union County	103	0.48
Rosedale, MD (cdp) Baltimore County	92	0.48
Brushy Creek, TX (cdp) Williamson County	76	0.48
Brooklyn Park, MN (city) Hennepin County	319	0.47
Wheaton-Glenmont, MD (cdp) Montgomery County	273	0.47
North Plainfield, NJ (borough) Somerset County	100	0.47
Calumet City, IL (city) Cook County	179	0.46
Houston, TX (city) Harris County	8,726	0.45
Albany, GA (city) Dougherty County	347	0.45
Piscataway, NJ (township) Middlesex County	229	0.45
Milton, MA (cdp) Norfolk County	116	0.45
East Norriton, PA (cdp) Montgomery County	59	0.45
Destrehan, LA (cdp) Saint Charles Parish	51	0.45
New Rochelle, NY (city) Westchester County	310	0.43
East Windsor, NJ (township) Mercer County	107	0.43
Dover, DE (city) Kent County	137	0.42
Uniondale, NY (cdp) Nassau County	97	0.42
Los Alamitos, CA (city) Orange County	46	0.41
Coppell, TX (city) Dallas County	144	0.40
Mays Chapel, MD (cdp) Baltimore County	46	0.40
Arlington, TX (city) Tarrant County	1,302	0.39
Hempstead, NY (village) Nassau County	219	0.39
Cooper City, FL (city) Broward County	107	0.39
Clinton, MD (cdp) Prince George's County	102	0.39
Lochearn, MD (cdp) Baltimore County	98	0.39
Druid Hills, GA (cdp) De Kalb County	50	0.39
Salida, CA (cdp) Stanislaus County	49	0.39
Garland, TX (city) Dallas County	820	0.38
Solon, OH (city) Cuyahoga County	82	0.38
Rolla, MO (city) Phelps County	63	0.38
East Brainerd, TN (cdp) Hamilton County	53	0.38
Miramar, FL (city) Broward County	267	0.37
Golden Glades, FL (cdp) Miami-Dade County	118	0.37
Upper Chichester, PA (township) Delaware County	63	0.37
Cromwell, CT (town) Middlesex County	47	0.37
Grand Prairie, TX (city) Dallas County	462	0.36
Bowie, MD (city) Prince George's County	179	0.36
Stoughton, MA (town) Norfolk County	97	0.36
Arbutus, MD (cdp) Baltimore County	72	0.36
Sweetwater, FL (city) Miami-Dade County	52	0.36
Morrisville, PA (borough) Bucks County	36	0.36
Irving, TX (city) Dallas County	679	0.35
Oak Park, IL (village) Cook County	185	0.35
New Brunswick, NJ (city) Middlesex County	169	0.35
Lawndale, CA (city) Los Angeles County	111	0.35
University, FL (cdp) Hillsborough County	108	0.35
Fort Washington, MD (cdp) Prince George's County	84	0.35
Mitchell, SD (city) Davison County	52	0.35
Dyer, IN (town) Lake County	49	0.35
West Columbia, SC (city) Lexington County	47	0.35
Parker, SC (cdp) Greenville County	37	0.35
Washington, DC (city) District of Columbia	1,933	0.34
Lynn, MA (city) Essex County	305	0.34
West Orange, NJ (cdp) Essex County	154	0.34
Pittsfield charter, MI (township) Washtenaw County	101	0.34
Gantt, SC (cdp) Greenville County	47	0.34

Notes: (cdp) census designated place; Refer to the Explanation of Data in the front of the book for more detailed information.

African, sub-Saharan: Senegalese

Top 150 Places Sorted by Number

(Based on all places, regardless of population)

Place	Number	%
New York, NY (city) New York City	2,136	0.03
Washington, DC (city) District of Columbia	201	0.04
Los Angeles, CA (city) Los Angeles County	125	0.00
Jersey City, NJ (city) Hudson County	110	0.05
Silver Spring, MD (cdp) Montgomery County	108	0.14
Aspen Hill, MD (cdp) Montgomery County	107	0.21
North Atlanta, GA (cdp) De Kalb County	101	0.26
Columbus, OH (city) Franklin County	95	0.01
Detroit, MI (city) Wayne County	83	0.01
Beltsville, MD (cdp) Prince George's County	80	0.51
Oakland, CA (city) Alameda County	59	0.01
San Antonio, TX (city) Bexar County	56	0.00
Arlington, VA (cdp) Arlington County	55	0.03
Kansas City, MO (city) Jackson County	53	0.01
Pittsburgh, PA (city) Allegheny County	51	0.02
Louisville, KY (city) Jefferson County	48	0.02
Potomac, MD (cdp) Montgomery County	44	0.10
Minneapolis, MN (city) Hennepin County	40	0.01
Rossmoor, MD (cdp) Montgomery County	37	0.49
Pawtucket, RI (city) Providence County	37	0.05
Omaha, NE (city) Douglas County	35	0.01
North Potomac, MD (cdp) Montgomery County	33	0.14
Irving, TX (city) Dallas County	33	0.02
Coconut Creek, FL (city) Broward County	32	0.07
Wheaton-Glenmont, MD (cdp) Montgomery County	32	0.06
West Hartford, CT (cdp) Hartford County	32	0.05
The Village, OK (city) Oklahoma County	31	0.30
Houston, TX (city) Harris County	31	0.00
West New York, NJ (town) Hudson County	30	0.07
Ann Arbor, MI (city) Washtenaw County	30	0.03
Raleigh, NC (city) Wake County	30	0.01
Pittsfield charter, MI (township) Washtenaw County	28	0.09
Woonsocket, RI (city) Providence County	28	0.06
Arlington, TX (city) Tarrant County	28	0.01
Philadelphia, PA (city) Philadelphia County	28	0.00
East Stroudsburg, PA (borough) Monroe County	27	0.27
West Haven, CT (city) New Haven County	27	0.05
Hawthorne, CA (city) Los Angeles County	27	0.03
Oswego, IL (village) Kendall County	26	0.20
Cincinnati, OH (city) Hamilton County	26	0.01
Chicago, IL (city) Cook County	26	0.00
Atlanta, GA (city) Fulton County	25	0.01
Havelock, NC (city) Craven County	24	0.11
Montclair, NJ (cdp) Essex County	24	0.06
Pompano Beach, FL (city) Broward County	24	0.03
New Orleans, LA (city) Orleans Parish	24	0.00
Cornelius, OR (city) Washington County	23	0.24
Pikesville, MD (cdp) Baltimore County	23	0.08
View Park-Windsor Hills, CA (cdp) Los Angeles County	22	0.20
West Columbia, SC (city) Lexington County	22	0.17
Groveton, VA (cdp) Fairfax County	22	0.10
Idylwood, VA (cdp) Fairfax County	21	0.13
Beachwood, OH (city) Cuyahoga County	20	0.16
Florence, KY (city) Boone County	20	0.09
Fairborn, OH (city) Greene County	20	0.06
Lynnwood, WA (city) Snohomish County	20	0.06
Union City, NJ (city) Hudson County	20	0.03
Saint Paul, MN (city) Ramsey County	20	0.01
Denver, CO (city) Denver County	20	0.00
College Park, GA (city) Fulton County	19	0.09
White Oak, MD (cdp) Montgomery County	19	0.09
Huntsville, AL (city) Madison County	19	0.01
Phoenix, AZ (city) Maricopa County	19	0.00
Seattle, WA (city) King County	19	0.00
Tempe, AZ (city) Maricopa County	18	0.01
Boston, MA (city) Suffolk County	18	0.00
Rice Lake, WI (city) Barron County	17	0.21
Ellington, CT (town) Tolland County	17	0.13
Mount Clemens, MI (city) Macomb County	17	0.10
Fairland, MD (cdp) Montgomery County	17	0.08
Fitchburg, WI (city) Dane County	17	0.08
Jacksonville, NC (city) Onslow County	17	0.03
North Providence, RI (cdp) Providence County	16	0.05
Greensboro, NC (city) Guilford County	16	0.01
Baltimore, MD (independent city) Baltimore city	16	0.00
Newark, NJ (city) Essex County	15	0.01
San Jose, CA (city) Santa Clara County	15	0.00
Redan, GA (cdp) De Kalb County	14	0.04
Baton Rouge, LA (city) East Baton Rouge Parish	14	0.01
Milwaukee, WI (city) Milwaukee County	14	0.00
Davis, CA (city) Yolo County	13	0.02
Mount Prospect, IL (village) Cook County	13	0.02
Newport News, VA (independent city) Newport News city	13	0.01
Tukwila, WA (city) King County	12	0.07
Ferguson, MO (city) Saint Louis County	12	0.05
Moon, PA (township) Allegheny County	12	0.05
Mansfield, OH (city) Richland County	12	0.02
Yonkers, NY (city) Westchester County	12	0.01
Portland, OR (city) Multnomah County	12	0.00
San Diego, CA (city) San Diego County	12	0.00
New Bedford, MA (city) Bristol County	11	0.01
Wilberforce, OH (cdp) Greene County	10	0.70
Cayuga Heights, NY (village) Tompkins County	10	0.31
Friendship Village, MD (cdp) Montgomery County	10	0.23
Chippewa, PA (township) Beaver County	10	0.14
Jefferson, LA (cdp) Jefferson Parish	10	0.08
Ithaca, NY (town) Tompkins County	10	0.05
North Druid Hills, GA (cdp) De Kalb County	10	0.05
Danvers, MA (cdp) Essex County	10	0.04
Hoboken, NJ (city) Hudson County	10	0.03
Burke, VA (cdp) Fairfax County	10	0.02
Marietta, GA (city) Cobb County	10	0.02
Carson, CA (city) Los Angeles County	10	0.01
Fort Worth, TX (city) Tarrant County	10	0.00
Gray, ME (town) Cumberland County	9	0.13
Broadview, IL (village) Cook County	9	0.11
Gardendale, AL (city) Jefferson County	9	0.08
East Riverdale, MD (cdp) Prince George's County	9	0.06
Mercer Island, WA (city) King County	9	0.04
Chillum, MD (cdp) Prince George's County	9	0.03
Edison, NJ (cdp) Middlesex County	9	0.01
Hartford, CT (city) Hartford County	9	0.01
Mount Vernon, NY (city) Westchester County	9	0.01
Lubbock, TX (city) Lubbock County	9	0.00
Lockland, OH (village) Hamilton County	8	0.22
Village Saint George, LA (cdp) East Baton Rouge Parish	8	0.12
Washington, NJ (borough) Warren County	8	0.12
Country Club, CA (cdp) San Joaquin County	8	0.08
Martin, TN (city) Weakley County	8	0.08
Lincolnia, VA (cdp) Fairfax County	8	0.05
Takoma Park, MD (city) Montgomery County	8	0.05
Lanham-Seabrook, MD (cdp) Prince George's County	8	0.04
Pleasantville, NJ (city) Atlantic County	8	0.04
Burien, WA (city) King County	8	0.03
Montgomery Village, MD (cdp) Montgomery County	8	0.02
Rockville, MD (city) Montgomery County	8	0.02
Woodbury, MN (city) Washington County	8	0.02
Brookline, MA (cdp) Norfolk County	8	0.01
Chino, CA (city) San Bernardino County	8	0.01
Lake Forest, CA (city) Orange County	8	0.01
Pasadena, CA (city) Los Angeles County	8	0.01
Quincy, MA (city) Norfolk County	8	0.01
Indianapolis, IN (special city) Marion County	8	0.00
Madison, WI (city) Dane County	8	0.00
Mobile, AL (city) Mobile County	8	0.00
Oklahoma City, OK (city) Oklahoma County	8	0.00
Aurora, NY (village) Cayuga County	7	0.98
Ledyard, NY (town) Cayuga County	7	0.38
University Park, MD (town) Prince George's County	7	0.31
Fort Carson, CO (cdp) El Paso County	7	0.07
Carrboro, NC (town) Orange County	7	0.04
Fairhaven, MA (town) Bristol County	7	0.04
Winchester, NV (cdp) Clark County	7	0.03
Upper Arlington, OH (city) Franklin County	7	0.02
Bloomington, IN (city) Monroe County	7	0.01
Greenburgh, NY (town) Westchester County	7	0.01
Longmont, CO (city) Boulder County	7	0.01
Malden, MA (city) Middlesex County	7	0.01
Mountain View, CA (city) Santa Clara County	7	0.01
North Bergen, NJ (township) Hudson County	7	0.01

Notes: (cdp) census designated place; Refer to the Explanation of Data in the front of the book for more detailed information.

African, sub-Saharan: Senegalese

Top 150 Places Sorted by Percent

(Based on all places, regardless of population)

Place	Number	%
Glen Echo, MD (town) Montgomery County	3	1.27
Aurora, NY (village) Cayuga County	7	0.98
Wilberforce, OH (cdp) Greene County	10	0.70
Beltsville, MD (cdp) Prince George's County	80	0.51
Rossmoor, MD (cdp) Montgomery County	37	0.49
Ledyard, NY (town) Cayuga County	7	0.38
Kinnickinnic, WI (town) Saint Croix County	5	0.35
Cayuga Heights, NY (village) Tompkins County	10	0.31
University Park, MD (town) Prince George's County	7	0.31
The Village, OK (city) Oklahoma County	31	0.30
Savoonga, AK (city) Nome Census Area	2	0.28
East Stroudsburg, PA (borough) Monroe County	27	0.27
North Atlanta, GA (cdp) De Kalb County	101	0.26
Cornelius, OR (city) Washington County	23	0.24
Friendship Village, MD (cdp) Montgomery County	10	0.23
Lockland, OH (village) Hamilton County	8	0.22
Aspen Hill, MD (cdp) Montgomery County	107	0.21
Rice Lake, WI (city) Barron County	17	0.21
Oswego, IL (village) Kendall County	26	0.20
View Park-Windsor Hills, CA (cdp) Los Angeles County	22	0.20
West Windsor, VT (town) Windsor County	2	0.19
River Hills, WI (village) Milwaukee County	3	0.18
Sandstone, MN (city) Pine County	3	0.18
West Columbia, SC (city) Lexington County	22	0.17
Beachwood, OH (city) Cuyahoga County	20	0.16
Silver Spring, MD (cdp) Montgomery County	108	0.14
North Potomac, MD (cdp) Montgomery County	33	0.14
Chippewa, PA (township) Beaver County	10	0.14
Idylwood, VA (cdp) Fairfax County	21	0.13
Ellington, CT (town) Tolland County	17	0.13
Gray, ME (town) Cumberland County	9	0.13
Village Saint George, LA (cdp) East Baton Rouge Parish	8	0.12
Washington, NJ (borough) Warren County	8	0.12
Havelock, NC (city) Craven County	24	0.11
Broadview, IL (village) Cook County	9	0.11
Potomac, MD (cdp) Montgomery County	44	0.10
Groveton, VA (cdp) Fairfax County	22	0.10
Mount Clemens, MI (city) Macomb County	17	0.10
Pittsfield charter, MI (township) Washtenaw County	28	0.09
Florence, KY (city) Boone County	20	0.09
College Park, GA (city) Fulton County	19	0.09
White Oak, MD (cdp) Montgomery County	19	0.09
Pikesville, MD (cdp) Baltimore County	23	0.08
Fairland, MD (cdp) Montgomery County	17	0.08
Fitchburg, WI (city) Dane County	17	0.08
Jefferson, LA (cdp) Jefferson Parish	10	0.08
Gardendale, AL (city) Jefferson County	9	0.08
Country Club, CA (cdp) San Joaquin County	8	0.08
Martin, TN (city) Weakley County	8	0.08
Coconut Creek, FL (city) Broward County	32	0.07
West New York, NJ (town) Hudson County	30	0.07
Tukwila, WA (city) King County	12	0.07
Fort Carson, CO (cdp) El Paso County	7	0.07
Wheaton-Glenmont, MD (cdp) Montgomery County	32	0.06
Woonsocket, RI (city) Providence County	28	0.06
Montclair, NJ (cdp) Essex County	24	0.06
Fairborn, OH (city) Greene County	20	0.06
Lynnwood, WA (city) Snohomish County	20	0.06
East Riverdale, MD (cdp) Prince George's County	9	0.06
Jersey City, NJ (city) Hudson County	110	0.05
Pawtucket, RI (city) Providence County	37	0.05
West Hartford, CT (cdp) Hartford County	32	0.05
West Haven, CT (city) New Haven County	27	0.05
North Providence, RI (cdp) Providence County	16	0.05
Ferguson, MO (city) Saint Louis County	12	0.05
Moon, PA (township) Allegheny County	12	0.05
Ithaca, NY (town) Tompkins County	10	0.05
North Druid Hills, GA (cdp) De Kalb County	10	0.05
Lincolnia, VA (cdp) Fairfax County	8	0.05
Takoma Park, MD (city) Montgomery County	8	0.05
Washington, DC (city) District of Columbia	201	0.04
Redan, GA (cdp) De Kalb County	14	0.04
Danvers, MA (cdp) Essex County	10	0.04
Mercer Island, WA (city) King County	9	0.04
Lanham-Seabrook, MD (cdp) Prince George's County	8	0.04
Pleasantville, NJ (city) Atlantic County	8	0.04
Carrboro, NC (town) Orange County	7	0.04
Fairhaven, MA (town) Bristol County	7	0.04
Bessemer City, NC (city) Gaston County	2	0.04
New York, NY (city) New York City	2,136	0.03
Arlington, VA (cdp) Arlington County	55	0.03
Ann Arbor, MI (city) Washtenaw County	30	0.03
Hawthorne, CA (city) Los Angeles County	27	0.03
Pompano Beach, FL (city) Broward County	24	0.03
Union City, NJ (city) Hudson County	20	0.03
Jacksonville, NC (city) Onslow County	17	0.03
Hoboken, NJ (city) Hudson County	10	0.03
Chillum, MD (cdp) Prince George's County	9	0.03
Burien, WA (city) King County	8	0.03
Winchester, NV (cdp) Clark County	7	0.03
South Burlington, VT (city) Chittenden County	4	0.03
Pittsburgh, PA (city) Allegheny County	51	0.02
Louisville, KY (city) Jefferson County	48	0.02
Irving, TX (city) Dallas County	33	0.02
Davis, CA (city) Yolo County	13	0.02
Mount Prospect, IL (village) Cook County	13	0.02
Mansfield, OH (city) Richland County	12	0.02
Burke, VA (cdp) Fairfax County	10	0.02
Marietta, GA (city) Cobb County	10	0.02
Montgomery Village, MD (cdp) Montgomery County	8	0.02
Rockville, MD (city) Montgomery County	8	0.02
Woodbury, MN (city) Washington County	8	0.02
Upper Arlington, OH (city) Franklin County	7	0.02
Opportunity, WA (cdp) Spokane County	6	0.02
Redland, MD (cdp) Montgomery County	4	0.02
Columbus, OH (city) Franklin County	95	0.01
Detroit, MI (city) Wayne County	83	0.01
Oakland, CA (city) Alameda County	59	0.01
Kansas City, MO (city) Jackson County	53	0.01
Minneapolis, MN (city) Hennepin County	40	0.01
Omaha, NE (city) Douglas County	35	0.01
Raleigh, NC (city) Wake County	30	0.01
Arlington, TX (city) Tarrant County	28	0.01
Cincinnati, OH (city) Hamilton County	26	0.01
Atlanta, GA (city) Fulton County	25	0.01
Saint Paul, MN (city) Ramsey County	20	0.01
Huntsville, AL (city) Madison County	19	0.01
Tempe, AZ (city) Maricopa County	18	0.01
Greensboro, NC (city) Guilford County	16	0.01
Newark, NJ (city) Essex County	15	0.01
Baton Rouge, LA (city) East Baton Rouge Parish	14	0.01
Newport News, VA (independent city) Newport News city	13	0.01
Yonkers, NY (city) Westchester County	12	0.01
New Bedford, MA (city) Bristol County	11	0.01
Carson, CA (city) Los Angeles County	10	0.01
Edison, NJ (cdp) Middlesex County	9	0.01
Hartford, CT (city) Hartford County	9	0.01
Mount Vernon, NY (city) Westchester County	9	0.01
Brookline, MA (cdp) Norfolk County	8	0.01
Chino, CA (city) San Bernardino County	8	0.01
Lake Forest, CA (city) Orange County	8	0.01
Pasadena, CA (city) Los Angeles County	8	0.01
Quincy, MA (city) Norfolk County	8	0.01
Bloomington, IN (city) Monroe County	7	0.01
Greenburgh, NY (town) Westchester County	7	0.01
Longmont, CO (city) Boulder County	7	0.01
Malden, MA (city) Middlesex County	7	0.01
Mountain View, CA (city) Santa Clara County	7	0.01
North Bergen, NJ (township) Hudson County	7	0.01
Azusa, CA (city) Los Angeles County	6	0.01
Cambridge, MA (city) Middlesex County	6	0.01
Niagara Falls, NY (city) Niagara County	6	0.01
North Miami Beach, FL (city) Miami-Dade County	6	0.01
Richmond, CA (city) Contra Costa County	6	0.01
Upper Darby, PA (township) Delaware County	6	0.01
Bloomington, MN (city) Hennepin County	5	0.01
White Plains, NY (city) Westchester County	5	0.01
Willowbrook, CA (cdp) Los Angeles County	5	0.01
Yakima, WA (city) Yakima County	5	0.01
Atlantic City, NJ (city) Atlantic County	4	0.01

Notes: (cdp) census designated place; Refer to the Explanation of Data in the front of the book for more detailed information.

African, sub-Saharan: Senegalese

Top 150 Places Sorted by Percent

(Based on places with populations of 10,000 or more)

Place	Number	%
Beltsville, MD (cdp) Prince George's County	80	0.51
The Village, OK (city) Oklahoma County	31	0.30
North Atlanta, GA (cdp) De Kalb County	101	0.26
Aspen Hill, MD (cdp) Montgomery County	107	0.21
Oswego, IL (village) Kendall County	26	0.20
View Park-Windsor Hills, CA (cdp) Los Angeles County	22	0.20
West Columbia, SC (city) Lexington County	22	0.17
Beachwood, OH (city) Cuyahoga County	20	0.16
Silver Spring, MD (cdp) Montgomery County	108	0.14
North Potomac, MD (cdp) Montgomery County	33	0.14
Idylwood, VA (cdp) Fairfax County	21	0.13
Ellington, CT (town) Tolland County	17	0.13
Havelock, NC (city) Craven County	24	0.11
Potomac, MD (cdp) Montgomery County	44	0.10
Groveton, VA (cdp) Fairfax County	22	0.10
Mount Clemens, MI (city) Macomb County	17	0.10
Pittsfield charter, MI (township) Washtenaw County	28	0.09
Florence, KY (city) Boone County	20	0.09
College Park, GA (city) Fulton County	19	0.09
White Oak, MD (cdp) Montgomery County	19	0.09
Pikesville, MD (cdp) Baltimore County	23	0.08
Fairland, MD (cdp) Montgomery County	17	0.08
Fitchburg, WI (city) Dane County	17	0.08
Jefferson, LA (cdp) Jefferson Parish	10	0.08
Gardendale, AL (city) Jefferson County	9	0.08
Martin, TN (city) Weakley County	8	0.08
Coconut Creek, FL (city) Broward County	32	0.07
West New York, NJ (town) Hudson County	30	0.07
Tukwila, WA (city) King County	12	0.07
Fort Carson, CO (cdp) El Paso County	7	0.07
Wheaton-Glenmont, MD (cdp) Montgomery County	32	0.06
Woonsocket, RI (city) Providence County	28	0.06
Montclair, NJ (cdp) Essex County	24	0.06
Fairborn, OH (city) Greene County	20	0.06
Lynnwood, WA (city) Snohomish County	20	0.06
East Riverdale, MD (cdp) Prince George's County	9	0.06
Jersey City, NJ (city) Hudson County	110	0.05
Pawtucket, RI (city) Providence County	37	0.05
West Hartford, CT (cdp) Hartford County	32	0.05
West Haven, CT (city) New Haven County	27	0.05
North Providence, RI (cdp) Providence County	16	0.05
Ferguson, MO (city) Saint Louis County	12	0.05
Moon, PA (township) Allegheny County	12	0.05
Ithaca, NY (town) Tompkins County	10	0.05
North Druid Hills, GA (cdp) De Kalb County	10	0.05
Lincolnia, VA (cdp) Fairfax County	8	0.05
Takoma Park, MD (city) Montgomery County	8	0.05
Washington, DC (city) District of Columbia	201	0.04
Redan, GA (cdp) De Kalb County	14	0.04
Danvers, MA (cdp) Essex County	10	0.04
Mercer Island, WA (city) King County	9	0.04
Lanham-Seabrook, MD (cdp) Prince George's County	8	0.04
Pleasantville, NJ (city) Atlantic County	8	0.04
Carrboro, NC (town) Orange County	7	0.04
Fairhaven, MA (town) Bristol County	7	0.04
New York, NY (city) New York City	2,136	0.03
Arlington, VA (cdp) Arlington County	55	0.03
Ann Arbor, MI (city) Washtenaw County	30	0.03
Hawthorne, CA (city) Los Angeles County	27	0.03
Pompano Beach, FL (city) Broward County	24	0.03
Union City, NJ (city) Hudson County	20	0.03
Jacksonville, NC (city) Onslow County	17	0.03
Hoboken, NJ (city) Hudson County	10	0.03
Chillum, MD (cdp) Prince George's County	9	0.03
Burien, WA (city) King County	8	0.03
Winchester, NV (cdp) Clark County	7	0.03
South Burlington, VT (city) Chittenden County	4	0.03
Pittsburgh, PA (city) Allegheny County	51	0.02
Louisville, KY (city) Jefferson County	48	0.02
Irving, TX (city) Dallas County	33	0.02
Davis, CA (city) Yolo County	13	0.02
Mount Prospect, IL (village) Cook County	13	0.02
Mansfield, OH (city) Richland County	12	0.02
Burke, VA (cdp) Fairfax County	10	0.02
Marietta, GA (city) Cobb County	10	0.02
Montgomery Village, MD (cdp) Montgomery County	8	0.02
Rockville, MD (city) Montgomery County	8	0.02
Woodbury, MN (city) Washington County	8	0.02
Upper Arlington, OH (city) Franklin County	7	0.02
Opportunity, WA (cdp) Spokane County	6	0.02
Redland, MD (cdp) Montgomery County	4	0.02
Columbus, OH (city) Franklin County	95	0.01
Detroit, MI (city) Wayne County	83	0.01
Oakland, CA (city) Alameda County	59	0.01
Kansas City, MO (city) Jackson County	53	0.01
Minneapolis, MN (city) Hennepin County	40	0.01
Omaha, NE (city) Douglas County	35	0.01
Raleigh, NC (city) Wake County	30	0.01
Arlington, TX (city) Tarrant County	28	0.01
Cincinnati, OH (city) Hamilton County	26	0.01
Atlanta, GA (city) Fulton County	25	0.01
Saint Paul, MN (city) Ramsey County	20	0.01
Huntsville, AL (city) Madison County	19	0.01
Tempe, AZ (city) Maricopa County	18	0.01
Greensboro, NC (city) Guilford County	16	0.01
Newark, NJ (city) Essex County	15	0.01
Baton Rouge, LA (city) East Baton Rouge Parish	14	0.01
Newport News, VA (independent city) Newport News city	13	0.01
Yonkers, NY (city) Westchester County	12	0.01
New Bedford, MA (city) Bristol County	11	0.01
Carson, CA (city) Los Angeles County	10	0.01
Edison, NJ (cdp) Middlesex County	9	0.01
Hartford, CT (city) Hartford County	9	0.01
Mount Vernon, NY (city) Westchester County	9	0.01
Brookline, MA (cdp) Norfolk County	8	0.01
Chino, CA (city) San Bernardino County	8	0.01
Lake Forest, CA (city) Orange County	8	0.01
Pasadena, CA (city) Los Angeles County	8	0.01
Quincy, MA (city) Norfolk County	8	0.01
Bloomington, IN (city) Monroe County	7	0.01
Greenburgh, NY (town) Westchester County	7	0.01
Longmont, CO (city) Boulder County	7	0.01
Malden, MA (city) Middlesex County	7	0.01
Mountain View, CA (city) Santa Clara County	7	0.01
North Bergen, NJ (township) Hudson County	7	0.01
Azusa, CA (city) Los Angeles County	6	0.01
Cambridge, MA (city) Middlesex County	6	0.01
Niagara Falls, NY (city) Niagara County	6	0.01
North Miami Beach, FL (city) Miami-Dade County	6	0.01
Richmond, CA (city) Contra Costa County	6	0.01
Upper Darby, PA (township) Delaware County	6	0.01
Bloomington, MN (city) Hennepin County	5	0.01
White Plains, NY (city) Westchester County	5	0.01
Willowbrook, CA (cdp) Los Angeles County	5	0.01
Yakima, WA (city) Yakima County	5	0.01
Atlantic City, NJ (city) Atlantic County	4	0.01
Troy, NY (city) Rensselaer County	4	0.01
North Bethesda, MD (cdp) Montgomery County	3	0.01
Los Angeles, CA (city) Los Angeles County	125	0.00
San Antonio, TX (city) Bexar County	56	0.00
Houston, TX (city) Harris County	31	0.00
Philadelphia, PA (city) Philadelphia County	28	0.00
Chicago, IL (city) Cook County	26	0.00
New Orleans, LA (city) Orleans Parish	24	0.00
Denver, CO (city) Denver County	20	0.00
Phoenix, AZ (city) Maricopa County	19	0.00
Seattle, WA (city) King County	19	0.00
Boston, MA (city) Suffolk County	18	0.00
Baltimore, MD (independent city) Baltimore city	16	0.00
San Jose, CA (city) Santa Clara County	15	0.00
Milwaukee, WI (city) Milwaukee County	14	0.00
Portland, OR (city) Multnomah County	12	0.00
San Diego, CA (city) San Diego County	12	0.00
Fort Worth, TX (city) Tarrant County	10	0.00
Lubbock, TX (city) Lubbock County	9	0.00
Indianapolis, IN (special city) Marion County	8	0.00
Madison, WI (city) Dane County	8	0.00
Mobile, AL (city) Mobile County	8	0.00
Oklahoma City, OK (city) Oklahoma County	8	0.00
Charlotte, NC (city) Mecklenburg County	6	0.00

Notes: (cdp) census designated place; Refer to the Explanation of Data in the front of the book for more detailed information.

African, sub-Saharan: Sierra Leonean

Top 150 Places Sorted by Number

(Based on all places, regardless of population)

Place	Number	%
New York, NY (city) New York City	798	0.01
Alexandria, VA (independent city) Alexandria city	493	0.38
Washington, DC (city) District of Columbia	405	0.07
Chillum, MD (cdp) Prince George's County	290	0.85
Dallas, TX (city) Dallas County	264	0.02
Langley Park, MD (cdp) Prince George's County	212	1.31
Greenbelt, MD (city) Prince George's County	201	0.94
Boston, MA (city) Suffolk County	199	0.03
Philadelphia, PA (city) Philadelphia County	169	0.01
Lincolnia, VA (cdp) Fairfax County	168	1.06
Wheaton-Glenmont, MD (cdp) Montgomery County	168	0.29
Silver Spring, MD (cdp) Montgomery County	152	0.20
Cheverly, MD (town) Prince George's County	141	2.18
Beltsville, MD (cdp) Prince George's County	139	0.88
Charlotte, NC (city) Mecklenburg County	122	0.02
Aspen Hill, MD (cdp) Montgomery County	120	0.24
White Oak, MD (cdp) Montgomery County	115	0.55
Highland Park, NJ (borough) Middlesex County	110	0.79
Lawrence, NJ (township) Mercer County	107	0.37
Somerset, NJ (cdp) Somerset County	106	0.46
Franklin, NJ (township) Somerset County	106	0.21
East Riverdale, MD (cdp) Prince George's County	97	0.63
Pennsauken, NJ (cdp) Camden County	90	0.25
North Brunswick Township, NJ (cdp) Middlesex County	89	0.25
Indianapolis, IN (special city) Marion County	89	0.01
Columbus, OH (city) Franklin County	88	0.01
Reading, PA (city) Berks County	85	0.10
Houston, TX (city) Harris County	84	0.00
Edison, NJ (cdp) Middlesex County	81	0.08
Baltimore, MD (independent city) Baltimore city	78	0.01
New Carrollton, MD (city) Prince George's County	77	0.60
Groveton, VA (cdp) Fairfax County	75	0.35
Woodlawn, MD (cdp) Prince George's County	74	1.19
Piscataway, NJ (township) Middlesex County	74	0.15
Lowell, MA (city) Middlesex County	73	0.07
Montgomery, AL (city) Montgomery County	73	0.04
Raleigh, NC (city) Wake County	72	0.03
Fairland, MD (cdp) Montgomery County	71	0.33
Minneapolis, MN (city) Hennepin County	71	0.02
Brooklyn Park, MN (city) Hennepin County	70	0.10
San Jose, CA (city) Santa Clara County	70	0.01
Portland, OR (city) Multnomah County	69	0.01
Hyattsville, MD (city) Prince George's County	68	0.46
Ewing, NJ (cdp) Mercer County	67	0.19
Dundalk, MD (cdp) Baltimore County	67	0.11
Germantown, MD (cdp) Montgomery County	66	0.12
Inglewood, CA (city) Los Angeles County	65	0.06
Greensboro, NC (city) Guilford County	65	0.03
Bowie, MD (city) Prince George's County	64	0.13
Mesquite, TX (city) Dallas County	63	0.05
Milwaukee, WI (city) Milwaukee County	63	0.01
Redan, GA (cdp) De Kalb County	62	0.18
San Bernardino, CA (city) San Bernardino County	59	0.03
Takoma Park, MD (city) Montgomery County	58	0.34
Chicago, IL (city) Cook County	55	0.00
Plainfield, NJ (city) Union County	54	0.11
Saint Louis, MO (independent city) Saint Louis city	51	0.01
Lakeside, VA (cdp) Henrico County	50	0.45
Atlanta, GA (city) Fulton County	50	0.01
Jacksonville, FL (special city) Duval County	49	0.01
Colonial Heights, VA (independent city) Colonial Heights city	48	0.28
Palmdale, CA (city) Los Angeles County	47	0.04
Goddard, MD (cdp) Prince George's County	46	0.83
Olney, MD (cdp) Montgomery County	46	0.15
Springfield, VA (cdp) Fairfax County	46	0.15
Santa Rosa, CA (city) Sonoma County	45	0.03
Saint Paul, MN (city) Ramsey County	45	0.02
Los Angeles, CA (city) Los Angeles County	45	0.00
Calverton, MD (cdp) Montgomery County	44	0.35
Jersey City, NJ (city) Hudson County	44	0.02
Lanham-Seabrook, MD (cdp) Prince George's County	43	0.24
Upper Chichester, PA (township) Delaware County	41	0.24
Laurel, MD (city) Prince George's County	41	0.20
Lake Ridge, VA (cdp) Prince William County	41	0.13
Hempstead, NY (town) Nassau County	39	0.01
Saint Dennis, KY (cdp) Jefferson County	38	0.42
Collingswood, NJ (borough) Camden County	38	0.27
Dale City, VA (cdp) Prince William County	37	0.07
Burtonsville, MD (cdp) Montgomery County	36	0.49
College Park, GA (city) Fulton County	36	0.17
Fort Campbell North, KY (cdp) Christian County	35	0.24
Adelphi, MD (cdp) Prince George's County	35	0.23
Gaithersburg, MD (city) Montgomery County	35	0.07
Reston, VA (cdp) Fairfax County	35	0.06
Columbia, MD (cdp) Howard County	34	0.04
Aurora, CO (city) Arapahoe County	34	0.01
Sayreville, NJ (borough) Middlesex County	33	0.08
Quincy, MA (city) Norfolk County	33	0.04
Yonkers, NY (city) Westchester County	33	0.02
Bailey's Crossroads, VA (cdp) Fairfax County	32	0.14
Anaheim, CA (city) Orange County	32	0.01
Cincinnati, OH (city) Hamilton County	32	0.01
Denver, CO (city) Denver County	32	0.01
Greater Landover, MD (cdp) Prince George's County	31	0.14
East Brunswick, NJ (cdp) Middlesex County	31	0.07
East Goshen, PA (township) Chester County	30	0.18
Sanford, NC (city) Lee County	30	0.13
South Holland, IL (village) Cook County	30	0.13
Elmsford, NY (village) Westchester County	29	0.63
Kemp Mill, MD (cdp) Montgomery County	29	0.29
Fort Drum, NY (cdp) Jefferson County	29	0.24
Le Ray, NY (town) Jefferson County	29	0.15
Hackensack, NJ (city) Bergen County	29	0.07
Jonesboro, AR (city) Craighead County	29	0.05
Kendale Lakes, FL (cdp) Miami-Dade County	29	0.05
Greenburgh, NY (town) Westchester County	29	0.03
Peoria, IL (city) Peoria County	29	0.03
Kansas City, MO (city) Jackson County	29	0.01
Phoenix, AZ (city) Maricopa County	29	0.00
Euless, TX (city) Tarrant County	28	0.06
Rockville, MD (city) Montgomery County	28	0.06
Madison, WI (city) Dane County	28	0.01
Greater Upper Marlboro, MD (cdp) Prince George's County	27	0.14
Upper Darby, PA (township) Delaware County	27	0.03
Oakland, CA (city) Alameda County	27	0.01
Riverdale Park, MD (town) Prince George's County	26	0.40
College Park, MD (city) Prince George's County	26	0.11
Old Tappan, NJ (borough) Bergen County	25	0.46
Burlington, NJ (township) Burlington County	25	0.12
Roselle, NJ (borough) Union County	25	0.12
Jacksonville, NC (city) Onslow County	25	0.04
Garland, TX (city) Dallas County	25	0.01
San Francisco, CA (city) San Francisco County	25	0.00
Seattle, WA (city) King County	25	0.00
Panthersville, GA (cdp) De Kalb County	24	0.21
Lorton, VA (cdp) Fairfax County	24	0.14
Woodlawn, MD (cdp) Baltimore County	24	0.07
South Brunswick, NJ (township) Middlesex County	23	0.06
Old Bridge, NJ (township) Middlesex County	23	0.04
Sioux Falls, SD (city) Minnehaha County	23	0.02
Summerfield, NC (town) Guilford County	22	0.31
Cloverly, MD (cdp) Montgomery County	22	0.27
Teaneck, NJ (cdp) Bergen County	22	0.06
Moreno Valley, CA (city) Riverside County	22	0.02
Glendale, AZ (city) Maricopa County	22	0.01
Woodmore, MD (cdp) Prince George's County	20	0.33
Woodbury, NJ (city) Gloucester County	20	0.19
Glenn Dale, MD (cdp) Prince George's County	20	0.16
Waxahachie, TX (city) Ellis County	20	0.09
Franconia, VA (cdp) Fairfax County	20	0.06
Wheaton, IL (city) Du Page County	20	0.04
Southfield, MI (city) Oakland County	20	0.03
Richmond, VA (independent city) Richmond city	20	0.01
Annville, PA (cdp) Lebanon County	19	0.42
Montclair, NJ (cdp) Essex County	19	0.05
Irvington, NJ (cdp) Essex County	19	0.03
Arlington, VA (cdp) Arlington County	19	0.01
Sharon Hill, PA (borough) Delaware County	18	0.33
Masonboro, NC (cdp) New Hanover County	18	0.15
Cherryland, CA (cdp) Alameda County	18	0.13

Notes: (cdp) census designated place; Refer to the Explanation of Data in the front of the book for more detailed information.

African, sub-Saharan: Sierra Leonean

Top 150 Places Sorted by Percent

(Based on all places, regardless of population)

Place	Number	%
Cheverly, MD (town) Prince George's County	141	2.18
Langley Park, MD (cdp) Prince George's County	212	1.31
Woodlawn, MD (cdp) Prince George's County	74	1.19
Lincolnia, VA (cdp) Fairfax County	168	1.06
Greenbelt, MD (city) Prince George's County	201	0.94
Beltsville, MD (cdp) Prince George's County	139	0.88
Chillum, MD (cdp) Prince George's County	290	0.85
Goddard, MD (cdp) Prince George's County	46	0.83
Highland Park, NJ (borough) Middlesex County	110	0.79
East Riverdale, MD (cdp) Prince George's County	97	0.63
Elmsford, NY (village) Westchester County	29	0.63
Ault Field, WA (cdp) Island County	13	0.63
New Carrollton, MD (city) Prince George's County	77	0.60
Fairmount Heights, MD (town) Prince George's County	9	0.60
White Oak, MD (cdp) Montgomery County	115	0.55
Brandon, WI (village) Fond du Lac County	5	0.55
Burtonsville, MD (cdp) Montgomery County	36	0.49
Geneva, NY (town) Ontario County	16	0.49
Maxton, NC (town) Robeson County	13	0.49
Landover Hills, MD (town) Prince George's County	7	0.47
Somerset, NJ (cdp) Somerset County	106	0.46
Hyattsville, MD (city) Prince George's County	68	0.46
Old Tappan, NJ (borough) Bergen County	25	0.46
Lakeside, VA (cdp) Henrico County	50	0.45
Willshire, OH (village) Van Wert County	2	0.45
Saint Dennis, KY (cdp) Jefferson County	38	0.42
Annville, PA (cdp) Lebanon County	19	0.42
Riverdale Park, MD (town) Prince George's County	26	0.40
Colmar Manor, MD (town) Prince George's County	5	0.40
Alexandria, VA (independent city) Alexandria city	493	0.38
Lawrence, NJ (township) Mercer County	107	0.37
Groveton, VA (cdp) Fairfax County	75	0.35
Calverton, MD (cdp) Montgomery County	44	0.35
Takoma Park, MD (city) Montgomery County	58	0.34
Saint Michaels, MD (town) Talbot County	4	0.34
Fairland, MD (cdp) Montgomery County	71	0.33
Woodmore, MD (cdp) Prince George's County	20	0.33
Sharon Hill, PA (borough) Delaware County	18	0.33
Summerfield, NC (town) Guilford County	22	0.31
Wheaton-Glenmont, MD (cdp) Montgomery County	168	0.29
Kemp Mill, MD (cdp) Montgomery County	29	0.29
Colonial Heights, VA (independent city) Colonial Heights city	48	0.28
Austell, GA (city) Cobb County	16	0.28
Wedgefield, FL (cdp) Orange County	8	0.28
Collingswood, NJ (borough) Camden County	38	0.27
Cloverly, MD (cdp) Montgomery County	22	0.27
Bethel Springs, TN (town) McNairy County	2	0.26
Pennsauken, NJ (cdp) Camden County	90	0.25
North Brunswick Township, NJ (cdp) Middlesex County	89	0.25
Aspen Hill, MD (cdp) Montgomery County	120	0.24
Lanham-Seabrook, MD (cdp) Prince George's County	43	0.24
Upper Chichester, PA (township) Delaware County	41	0.24
Fort Campbell North, KY (cdp) Christian County	35	0.24
Fort Drum, NY (cdp) Jefferson County	29	0.24
Riverside, MO (city) Platte County	7	0.24
Adelphi, MD (cdp) Prince George's County	35	0.23
Franklin, NJ (township) Somerset County	106	0.21
Panthersville, GA (cdp) De Kalb County	24	0.21
Putnam Lake, NY (cdp) Putnam County	8	0.21
Silver Spring, MD (cdp) Montgomery County	152	0.20
Laurel, MD (city) Prince George's County	41	0.20
Hillandale, MD (cdp) Montgomery County	6	0.20
Ewing, NJ (cdp) Mercer County	67	0.19
Woodbury, NJ (city) Gloucester County	20	0.19
Huntington, VA (cdp) Fairfax County	16	0.19
Redan, GA (cdp) De Kalb County	62	0.18
East Goshen, PA (township) Chester County	30	0.18
Fairview, NY (cdp) Dutchess County	11	0.18
Tulpehocken, PA (township) Berks County	6	0.18
Cottage City, MD (town) Prince George's County	2	0.18
College Park, GA (city) Fulton County	36	0.17
Brentwood, MD (town) Prince George's County	5	0.17
Glenn Dale, MD (cdp) Prince George's County	20	0.16
Gresham Park, GA (cdp) De Kalb County	15	0.16
Bladensburg, MD (town) Prince George's County	12	0.16
Piscataway, NJ (township) Middlesex County	74	0.15
Olney, MD (cdp) Montgomery County	46	0.15
Springfield, VA (cdp) Fairfax County	46	0.15
Le Ray, NY (town) Jefferson County	29	0.15
Masonboro, NC (cdp) New Hanover County	18	0.15
Normandy, MO (city) Saint Louis County	8	0.15
Bailey's Crossroads, VA (cdp) Fairfax County	32	0.14
Greater Landover, MD (cdp) Prince George's County	31	0.14
Greater Upper Marlboro, MD (cdp) Prince George's County	27	0.14
Lorton, VA (cdp) Fairfax County	24	0.14
Forest Glen, MD (cdp) Montgomery County	10	0.14
Conley, GA (cdp) Clayton County	9	0.14
Bowie, MD (city) Prince George's County	64	0.13
Lake Ridge, VA (cdp) Prince William County	41	0.13
Sanford, NC (city) Lee County	30	0.13
South Holland, IL (village) Cook County	30	0.13
Cherryland, CA (cdp) Alameda County	18	0.13
Yeadon, PA (borough) Delaware County	15	0.13
Germantown, MD (cdp) Montgomery County	66	0.12
Burlington, NJ (township) Burlington County	25	0.12
Roselle, NJ (borough) Union County	25	0.12
Middlesex, NJ (borough) Middlesex County	16	0.12
Riverview, FL (cdp) Hillsborough County	15	0.12
Chamblee, GA (city) De Kalb County	12	0.12
Dundalk, MD (cdp) Baltimore County	67	0.11
Plainfield, NJ (city) Union County	54	0.11
College Park, MD (city) Prince George's County	26	0.11
Hybla Valley, VA (cdp) Fairfax County	18	0.11
Pine Hill, NJ (borough) Camden County	12	0.11
Fort Lee, VA (cdp) Prince George County	8	0.11
Geneseo, NY (village) Livingston County	8	0.11
Reading, PA (city) Berks County	85	0.10
Brooklyn Park, MN (city) Hennepin County	70	0.10
Stony Brook, NY (cdp) Suffolk County	13	0.10
Maryville, MO (city) Nodaway County	10	0.10
Scottdale, GA (cdp) De Kalb County	10	0.10
Aquia Harbour, VA (cdp) Stafford County	8	0.10
Vinton, VA (town) Roanoke County	8	0.10
Waxahachie, TX (city) Ellis County	20	0.09
Edison, NJ (cdp) Middlesex County	81	0.08
Sayreville, NJ (borough) Middlesex County	33	0.08
Baldwin, NY (cdp) Nassau County	18	0.08
Newington, VA (cdp) Fairfax County	15	0.08
Morton, IL (village) Tazewell County	12	0.08
Geneseo, NY (town) Livingston County	8	0.08
Woodlyn, PA (cdp) Delaware County	8	0.08
Edgewater Park, NJ (township) Burlington County	6	0.08
Dayton, NJ (cdp) Middlesex County	5	0.08
Kensington, CA (cdp) Contra Costa County	4	0.08
Glenwood Landing, NY (cdp) Nassau County	3	0.08
Washington, DC (city) District of Columbia	405	0.07
Lowell, MA (city) Middlesex County	73	0.07
Dale City, VA (cdp) Prince William County	37	0.07
Gaithersburg, MD (city) Montgomery County	35	0.07
East Brunswick, NJ (cdp) Middlesex County	31	0.07
Hackensack, NJ (city) Bergen County	29	0.07
Woodlawn, MD (cdp) Baltimore County	24	0.07
Maplewood, NJ (cdp) Essex County	16	0.07
North Valley Stream, NY (cdp) Nassau County	11	0.07
Riverdale, GA (city) Clayton County	9	0.07
Patterson, NY (town) Putnam County	8	0.07
Mechanicsburg, PA (borough) Cumberland County	6	0.07
Suttons Bay, MI (township) Leelanau County	2	0.07
Inglewood, CA (city) Los Angeles County	65	0.06
Reston, VA (cdp) Fairfax County	35	0.06
Euless, TX (city) Tarrant County	28	0.06
Rockville, MD (city) Montgomery County	28	0.06
South Brunswick, NJ (township) Middlesex County	23	0.06
Teaneck, NJ (cdp) Bergen County	22	0.06
Franconia, VA (cdp) Fairfax County	20	0.06
Candler-McAfee, GA (cdp) De Kalb County	17	0.06
Fridley, MN (city) Anoka County	16	0.06
Ithaca, NY (city) Tompkins County	16	0.06
Mansfield, MA (town) Bristol County	14	0.06
Colleyville, TX (city) Tarrant County	12	0.06

Notes: (cdp) census designated place; Refer to the Explanation of Data in the front of the book for more detailed information.

African, sub-Saharan: Sierra Leonean

Top 150 Places Sorted by Percent

(Based on places with populations of 10,000 or more)

Place	Number	%
Langley Park, MD (cdp) Prince George's County	212	1.31
Lincolnia, VA (cdp) Fairfax County	168	1.06
Greenbelt, MD (city) Prince George's County	201	0.94
Beltsville, MD (cdp) Prince George's County	139	0.88
Chillum, MD (cdp) Prince George's County	290	0.85
Highland Park, NJ (borough) Middlesex County	110	0.79
East Riverdale, MD (cdp) Prince George's County	97	0.63
New Carrollton, MD (city) Prince George's County	77	0.60
White Oak, MD (cdp) Montgomery County	115	0.55
Somerset, NJ (cdp) Somerset County	106	0.46
Hyattsville, MD (city) Prince George's County	68	0.46
Lakeside, VA (cdp) Henrico County	50	0.45
Alexandria, VA (independent city) Alexandria city	493	0.38
Lawrence, NJ (township) Mercer County	107	0.37
Groveton, VA (cdp) Fairfax County	75	0.35
Calverton, MD (cdp) Montgomery County	44	0.35
Takoma Park, MD (city) Montgomery County	58	0.34
Fairland, MD (cdp) Montgomery County	71	0.33
Wheaton-Glenmont, MD (cdp) Montgomery County	168	0.29
Colonial Heights, VA (independent city) Colonial Heights city	48	0.28
Collingswood, NJ (borough) Camden County	38	0.27
Pennsauken, NJ (cdp) Camden County	90	0.25
North Brunswick Township, NJ (cdp) Middlesex County	89	0.25
Aspen Hill, MD (cdp) Montgomery County	120	0.24
Lanham-Seabrook, MD (cdp) Prince George's County	43	0.24
Upper Chichester, PA (township) Delaware County	41	0.24
Fort Campbell North, KY (cdp) Christian County	35	0.24
Fort Drum, NY (cdp) Jefferson County	29	0.24
Adelphi, MD (cdp) Prince George's County	35	0.23
Franklin, NJ (township) Somerset County	106	0.21
Panthersville, GA (cdp) De Kalb County	24	0.21
Silver Spring, MD (cdp) Montgomery County	152	0.20
Laurel, MD (city) Prince George's County	41	0.20
Ewing, NJ (cdp) Mercer County	67	0.19
Woodbury, NJ (city) Gloucester County	20	0.19
Redan, GA (cdp) De Kalb County	62	0.18
East Goshen, PA (township) Chester County	30	0.18
College Park, GA (city) Fulton County	36	0.17
Glenn Dale, MD (cdp) Prince George's County	20	0.16
Piscataway, NJ (township) Middlesex County	74	0.15
Olney, MD (cdp) Montgomery County	46	0.15
Springfield, VA (cdp) Fairfax County	46	0.15
Le Ray, NY (town) Jefferson County	29	0.15
Masonboro, NC (cdp) New Hanover County	18	0.15
Bailey's Crossroads, VA (cdp) Fairfax County	32	0.14
Greater Landover, MD (cdp) Prince George's County	31	0.14
Greater Upper Marlboro, MD (cdp) Prince George's County	27	0.14
Lorton, VA (cdp) Fairfax County	24	0.14
Bowie, MD (city) Prince George's County	64	0.13
Lake Ridge, VA (cdp) Prince William County	41	0.13
Sanford, NC (city) Lee County	30	0.13
South Holland, IL (village) Cook County	30	0.13
Cherryland, CA (cdp) Alameda County	18	0.13
Yeadon, PA (borough) Delaware County	15	0.13
Germantown, MD (cdp) Montgomery County	66	0.12
Burlington, NJ (township) Burlington County	25	0.12
Roselle, NJ (borough) Union County	25	0.12
Middlesex, NJ (borough) Middlesex County	16	0.12
Riverview, FL (cdp) Hillsborough County	15	0.12
Dundalk, MD (cdp) Baltimore County	67	0.11
Plainfield, NJ (city) Union County	54	0.11
College Park, MD (city) Prince George's County	26	0.11
Hybla Valley, VA (cdp) Fairfax County	18	0.11
Pine Hill, NJ (borough) Camden County	12	0.11
Reading, PA (city) Berks County	85	0.10
Brooklyn Park, MN (city) Hennepin County	70	0.10
Stony Brook, NY (cdp) Suffolk County	13	0.10
Maryville, MO (city) Nodaway County	10	0.10
Waxahachie, TX (city) Ellis County	20	0.09
Edison, NJ (cdp) Middlesex County	81	0.08
Sayreville, NJ (borough) Middlesex County	33	0.08
Baldwin, NY (cdp) Nassau County	18	0.08
Newington, VA (cdp) Fairfax County	15	0.08
Morton, IL (village) Tazewell County	12	0.08
Woodlyn, PA (cdp) Delaware County	8	0.08
Washington, DC (city) District of Columbia	405	0.07
Lowell, MA (city) Middlesex County	73	0.07
Dale City, VA (cdp) Prince William County	37	0.07
Gaithersburg, MD (city) Montgomery County	35	0.07
East Brunswick, NJ (cdp) Middlesex County	31	0.07
Hackensack, NJ (city) Bergen County	29	0.07
Woodlawn, MD (cdp) Baltimore County	24	0.07
Maplewood, NJ (cdp) Essex County	16	0.07
North Valley Stream, NY (cdp) Nassau County	11	0.07
Riverdale, GA (city) Clayton County	9	0.07
Patterson, NY (town) Putnam County	8	0.07
Inglewood, CA (city) Los Angeles County	65	0.06
Reston, VA (cdp) Fairfax County	35	0.06
Euless, TX (city) Tarrant County	28	0.06
Rockville, MD (city) Montgomery County	28	0.06
South Brunswick, NJ (township) Middlesex County	23	0.06
Teaneck, NJ (cdp) Bergen County	22	0.06
Franconia, VA (cdp) Fairfax County	20	0.06
Candler-McAfee, GA (cdp) De Kalb County	17	0.06
Fridley, MN (city) Anoka County	16	0.06
Ithaca, NY (city) Tompkins County	16	0.06
Mansfield, MA (town) Bristol County	14	0.06
Colleyville, TX (city) Tarrant County	12	0.06
Lindenwold, NJ (borough) Camden County	11	0.06
Seaford, NY (cdp) Nassau County	10	0.06
Mesquite, TX (city) Dallas County	63	0.05
Jonesboro, AR (city) Craighead County	29	0.05
Kendale Lakes, FL (cdp) Miami-Dade County	29	0.05
Montclair, NJ (cdp) Essex County	19	0.05
Norwich, CT (city) New London County	17	0.05
Mount Vernon, VA (cdp) Fairfax County	14	0.05
Radnor Township, PA (cdp) Delaware County	14	0.05
South Laurel, MD (cdp) Prince George's County	11	0.05
Savage-Guilford, MD (cdp) Howard County	6	0.05
Montgomery, AL (city) Montgomery County	73	0.04
Palmdale, CA (city) Los Angeles County	47	0.04
Columbia, MD (cdp) Howard County	34	0.04
Quincy, MA (city) Norfolk County	33	0.04
Jacksonville, NC (city) Onslow County	25	0.04
Old Bridge, NJ (township) Middlesex County	23	0.04
Wheaton, IL (city) Du Page County	20	0.04
Rock Island, IL (city) Rock Island County	16	0.04
Dover, DE (city) Kent County	13	0.04
West Springfield, VA (cdp) Fairfax County	12	0.04
Clinton, MD (cdp) Prince George's County	11	0.04
New Hope, MN (city) Hennepin County	9	0.04
Golden Gate, FL (cdp) Collier County	8	0.04
North Laurel, MD (cdp) Howard County	8	0.04
Hillcrest Heights, MD (cdp) Prince George's County	7	0.04
Redland, MD (cdp) Montgomery County	7	0.04
East Highland Park, VA (cdp) Henrico County	5	0.04
Boston, MA (city) Suffolk County	199	0.03
Raleigh, NC (city) Wake County	72	0.03
Greensboro, NC (city) Guilford County	65	0.03
San Bernardino, CA (city) San Bernardino County	59	0.03
Santa Rosa, CA (city) Sonoma County	45	0.03
Greenburgh, NY (town) Westchester County	29	0.03
Peoria, IL (city) Peoria County	29	0.03
Upper Darby, PA (township) Delaware County	27	0.03
Southfield, MI (city) Oakland County	20	0.03
Irvington, NJ (cdp) Essex County	19	0.03
Penn Hills, PA (cdp) Allegheny County	15	0.03
Azusa, CA (city) Los Angeles County	13	0.03
Hurst, TX (city) Tarrant County	12	0.03
Jefferson City, MO (city) Cole County	12	0.03
York, PA (city) York County	12	0.03
Poughkeepsie, NY (town) Dutchess County	11	0.03
Brea, CA (city) Orange County	10	0.03
Egypt Lake-Leto, FL (cdp) Hillsborough County	10	0.03
McLean, VA (cdp) Fairfax County	10	0.03
Moorhead, MN (city) Clay County	10	0.03
Chelsea, MA (city) Suffolk County	9	0.03
Severn, MD (cdp) Anne Arundel County	9	0.03
Lake Magdalene, FL (cdp) Hillsborough County	8	0.03
Ridley, PA (township) Delaware County	8	0.03

Notes: (cdp) census designated place; Refer to the Explanation of Data in the front of the book for more detailed information.

African, sub-Saharan: Somalian

Top 150 Places Sorted by Number

(Based on all places, regardless of population)

Place	Number	%
Minneapolis, MN (city) Hennepin County	6,537	1.71
Columbus, OH (city) Franklin County	2,839	0.40
San Diego, CA (city) San Diego County	2,538	0.21
Rochester, MN (city) Olmsted County	1,131	1.32
Saint Paul, MN (city) Ramsey County	1,026	0.36
Seattle, WA (city) King County	786	0.14
Charlotte, NC (city) Mecklenburg County	624	0.12
Boston, MA (city) Suffolk County	614	0.10
Lincolnia, VA (cdp) Fairfax County	584	3.68
Alexandria, VA (independent city) Alexandria city	529	0.41
Buffalo, NY (city) Erie County	457	0.16
Kansas City, MO (city) Jackson County	456	0.10
Clarkston, GA (city) De Kalb County	449	6.58
Kent, WA (city) King County	444	0.56
Owatonna, MN (city) Steele County	433	1.93
Portland, OR (city) Multnomah County	390	0.07
Eden Prairie, MN (city) Hennepin County	382	0.70
Salt Lake City, UT (city) Salt Lake County	341	0.19
Saint Louis, MO (independent city) Saint Louis city	340	0.10
Nashville-Davidson, TN (special city) Davidson County	321	0.06
Greensboro, NC (city) Guilford County	313	0.14
Phoenix, AZ (city) Maricopa County	306	0.02
SeaTac, WA (city) King County	301	1.18
Houston, TX (city) Harris County	300	0.02
Portland, ME (city) Cumberland County	270	0.42
Fargo, ND (city) Cass County	258	0.28
New York, NY (city) New York City	247	0.00
Chicago, IL (city) Cook County	222	0.01
Arlington, TX (city) Tarrant County	211	0.06
Lansing, MI (city) Ingham County	203	0.17
Hopkins, MN (city) Hennepin County	195	1.14
San Jose, CA (city) Santa Clara County	186	0.02
White Center, WA (cdp) King County	185	0.89
Renton, WA (city) King County	184	0.37
Burnsville, MN (city) Dakota County	178	0.30
Rochester, NY (city) Monroe County	171	0.08
Dallas, TX (city) Dallas County	167	0.01
Raleigh, NC (city) Wake County	160	0.06
Bailey's Crossroads, VA (cdp) Fairfax County	153	0.67
Scottdale, GA (cdp) De Kalb County	146	1.50
Annandale, VA (cdp) Fairfax County	143	0.26
Louisville, KY (city) Jefferson County	142	0.06
Tukwila, WA (city) King County	137	0.80
Arlington, VA (cdp) Arlington County	136	0.07
Eagan, MN (city) Dakota County	133	0.21
Denver, CO (city) Denver County	120	0.02
Oakton, VA (cdp) Fairfax County	118	0.40
Tucson, AZ (city) Pima County	118	0.02
Memphis, TN (city) Shelby County	116	0.02
San Francisco, CA (city) San Francisco County	113	0.01
Marshall, MN (city) Lyon County	112	0.88
Marion, MN (township) Olmsted County	111	1.73
Lorton, VA (cdp) Fairfax County	111	0.63
Framingham, MA (cdp) Middlesex County	110	0.16
Willmar, MN (city) Kandiyohi County	109	0.59
Tysons Corner, VA (cdp) Fairfax County	107	0.58
Greater Landover, MD (cdp) Prince George's County	102	0.45
Saint Louis Park, MN (city) Hennepin County	96	0.22
Austin, TX (city) Travis County	94	0.01
Riverton-Boulevard Park, WA (cdp) King County	90	0.79
Washington, DC (city) District of Columbia	90	0.02
North Atlanta, GA (cdp) De Kalb County	89	0.23
Bridgeport, CT (city) Fairfield County	84	0.06
Mankato, MN (city) Blue Earth County	78	0.24
Takoma Park, MD (city) Montgomery County	77	0.45
Anaheim, CA (city) Orange County	74	0.02
Los Angeles, CA (city) Los Angeles County	68	0.00
White Bear Lake, MN (city) Ramsey County	63	0.26
De Kalb, IL (city) De Kalb County	63	0.16
Burke, VA (cdp) Fairfax County	63	0.11
Seven Corners, VA (cdp) Fairfax County	62	0.70
East Hill-Meridian, WA (cdp) King County	62	0.21
Sioux Falls, SD (city) Minnehaha County	61	0.05
Ypsilanti, MI (township) Washtenaw County	60	0.12
Ross Township, PA (cdp) Allegheny County	58	0.18
Atlanta, GA (city) Fulton County	58	0.01
Boise City, ID (city) Ada County	57	0.03
Decatur, GA (city) De Kalb County	56	0.31
Euless, TX (city) Tarrant County	55	0.12
Des Moines, WA (city) King County	54	0.18
Shoreline, WA (city) King County	54	0.10
Irving, TX (city) Dallas County	54	0.03
Faribault, MN (city) Rice County	53	0.25
East Riverdale, MD (cdp) Prince George's County	52	0.34
Detroit, MI (city) Wayne County	52	0.01
Dunwoody, GA (cdp) De Kalb County	50	0.15
Durham, NC (city) Durham County	50	0.03
Candler-McAfee, GA (cdp) De Kalb County	49	0.17
Jersey City, NJ (city) Hudson County	49	0.02
Milwaukee, WI (city) Milwaukee County	48	0.01
Oakland, CA (city) Alameda County	48	0.01
Hopkinton, MA (town) Middlesex County	47	0.35
South Salt Lake, UT (city) Salt Lake County	47	0.21
Lake Barcroft, VA (cdp) Fairfax County	46	0.51
Revere, MA (city) Suffolk County	46	0.10
Albertville, MN (city) Wright County	45	1.17
Unalaska, AK (city) Aleutians West Census Area	44	1.03
Hercules, CA (city) Contra Costa County	44	0.23
Columbia Heights, MN (city) Anoka County	43	0.23
North Mankato, MN (city) Nicollet County	42	0.36
Chelsea, MA (city) Suffolk County	42	0.12
Waterloo, IA (city) Black Hawk County	42	0.06
New Hope, MN (city) Hennepin County	41	0.20
Cascade-Fairwood, WA (cdp) King County	41	0.12
Stanton, CA (city) Orange County	39	0.11
Auburn, WA (city) King County	39	0.10
Apple Valley, MN (city) Dakota County	38	0.08
Flower Mound, TX (town) Denton County	37	0.07
Pelican Rapids, MN (city) Otter Tail County	35	1.47
Baton Rouge, LA (city) East Baton Rouge Parish	34	0.01
Pinole, CA (city) Contra Costa County	33	0.17
Bartlett, TN (city) Shelby County	33	0.08
Barron, WI (city) Barron County	32	1.00
Carmel, IN (city) Hamilton County	32	0.08
Kentwood, MI (city) Kent County	32	0.07
Hillsboro, OR (city) Washington County	32	0.05
Brockton, MA (city) Plymouth County	31	0.03
Erie, PA (city) Erie County	31	0.03
Syracuse, NY (city) Onondaga County	31	0.02
Shrewsbury, MO (city) Saint Louis County	30	0.46
Addison, TX (town) Dallas County	30	0.22
Salem, MA (city) Essex County	30	0.07
Centreville, VA (cdp) Fairfax County	29	0.06
Grand Forks, ND (city) Grand Forks County	29	0.06
Upper Darby, PA (township) Delaware County	29	0.04
Storm Lake, IA (city) Buena Vista County	28	0.28
Lake Forest Park, WA (city) King County	28	0.21
Tigard, OR (city) Washington County	28	0.07
Federal Way, WA (city) King County	28	0.03
Philadelphia, PA (city) Philadelphia County	28	0.00
Edmonds, WA (city) Snohomish County	27	0.07
Saint Peter, MN (city) Nicollet County	26	0.27
Waianae, HI (cdp) Honolulu County	26	0.24
Cambridge, MA (city) Middlesex County	26	0.03
Silver Spring, MD (cdp) Montgomery County	26	0.03
Paradise, NV (cdp) Clark County	26	0.01
Fridley, MN (city) Anoka County	25	0.09
Kenosha, WI (city) Kenosha County	25	0.03
Aurora, CO (city) Arapahoe County	25	0.01
Arlington, NY (cdp) Dutchess County	24	0.19
Poughkeepsie, NY (town) Dutchess County	24	0.06
Round Rock, TX (city) Williamson County	23	0.04
Columbus, GA (special city) Muscogee County	23	0.01
Wells, MN (city) Faribault County	22	0.93
Geneseo, NY (village) Livingston County	22	0.29
Geneseo, NY (town) Livingston County	22	0.23
Binghamton, NY (city) Broome County	22	0.05
West Hartford, CT (cdp) Hartford County	22	0.03
Pembroke Pines, FL (city) Broward County	22	0.02
Las Vegas, NV (city) Clark County	22	0.00

Notes: (cdp) census designated place; Refer to the Explanation of Data in the front of the book for more detailed information.

African, sub-Saharan: Somalian

Top 150 Places Sorted by Percent

(Based on all places, regardless of population)

Place	Number	%
Clarkston, GA (city) De Kalb County	449	6.58
Ogema, MN (township) Pine County	15	4.76
Four Bears Village, ND (cdp) McKenzie County	15	4.03
Lincolnia, VA (cdp) Fairfax County	584	3.68
Owatonna, MN (city) Steele County	433	1.93
Marion, MN (township) Olmsted County	111	1.73
Minneapolis, MN (city) Hennepin County	6,537	1.71
Scottdale, GA (cdp) De Kalb County	146	1.50
Pelican Rapids, MN (city) Otter Tail County	35	1.47
Washington Lake, MN (township) Sibley County	6	1.35
Rochester, MN (city) Olmsted County	1,131	1.32
SeaTac, WA (city) King County	301	1.18
Albertville, MN (city) Wright County	45	1.17
Hartley, IA (city) O'Brien County	20	1.15
Hopkins, MN (city) Hennepin County	195	1.14
Unalaska, AK (city) Aleutians West Census Area	44	1.03
Barron, WI (city) Barron County	32	1.00
Wells, MN (city) Faribault County	22	0.93
White Center, WA (cdp) King County	185	0.89
Marshall, MN (city) Lyon County	112	0.88
Tukwila, WA (city) King County	137	0.80
Riverton-Boulevard Park, WA (cdp) King County	90	0.79
Peapack and Gladstone, NJ (borough) Somerset County	18	0.74
Nevis, MN (township) Hubbard County	6	0.71
Commonwealth, WI (town) Florence County	3	0.71
Eden Prairie, MN (city) Hennepin County	382	0.70
Seven Corners, VA (cdp) Fairfax County	62	0.70
Fulda, MN (city) Murray County	9	0.70
Rush City, MN (city) Chisago County	14	0.68
Bailey's Crossroads, VA (cdp) Fairfax County	153	0.67
Crow Wing, MN (township) Crow Wing County	8	0.67
Lorton, VA (cdp) Fairfax County	111	0.63
Willmar, MN (city) Kandiyohi County	109	0.59
Tysons Corner, VA (cdp) Fairfax County	107	0.58
Dugway, UT (cdp) Tooele County	12	0.58
Kent, WA (city) King County	444	0.56
Lake Barcroft, VA (cdp) Fairfax County	46	0.51
Urbancrest, OH (village) Franklin County	4	0.48
Shrewsbury, MO (city) Saint Louis County	30	0.46
Webberville, MI (village) Ingham County	7	0.46
Greater Landover, MD (cdp) Prince George's County	102	0.45
Takoma Park, MD (city) Montgomery County	77	0.45
Portland, ME (city) Cumberland County	270	0.42
Alexandria, VA (independent city) Alexandria city	529	0.41
Washington Grove, MD (town) Montgomery County	2	0.41
Columbus, OH (city) Franklin County	2,839	0.40
Oakton, VA (cdp) Fairfax County	118	0.40
Renton, WA (city) King County	184	0.37
Saint Paul, MN (city) Ramsey County	1,026	0.36
North Mankato, MN (city) Nicollet County	42	0.36
Graton, CA (cdp) Sonoma County	6	0.36
Hopkinton, MA (town) Middlesex County	47	0.35
East Riverdale, MD (cdp) Prince George's County	52	0.34
Decatur, GA (city) De Kalb County	56	0.31
Burnsville, MN (city) Dakota County	178	0.30
Geneseo, NY (village) Livingston County	22	0.29
Fargo, ND (city) Cass County	258	0.28
Storm Lake, IA (city) Buena Vista County	28	0.28
Saint Peter, MN (city) Nicollet County	26	0.27
International Falls, MN (city) Koochiching County	18	0.27
Malden, MO (city) Dunklin County	13	0.27
Annandale, VA (cdp) Fairfax County	143	0.26
White Bear Lake, MN (city) Ramsey County	63	0.26
Faribault, MN (city) Rice County	53	0.25
Saint Helena, NC (village) Pender County	1	0.25
Mankato, MN (city) Blue Earth County	78	0.24
Waianae, HI (cdp) Honolulu County	26	0.24
North Atlanta, GA (cdp) De Kalb County	89	0.23
Hercules, CA (city) Contra Costa County	44	0.23
Columbia Heights, MN (city) Anoka County	43	0.23
Geneseo, NY (town) Livingston County	22	0.23
Dumfries, VA (town) Prince William County	11	0.23
Saint Louis Park, MN (city) Hennepin County	96	0.22
Addison, TX (town) Dallas County	30	0.22
San Diego, CA (city) San Diego County	2,538	0.21
Eagan, MN (city) Dakota County	133	0.21
East Hill-Meridian, WA (cdp) King County	62	0.21
South Salt Lake, UT (city) Salt Lake County	47	0.21
Lake Forest Park, WA (city) King County	28	0.21
Mishicot, WI (village) Manitowoc County	3	0.21
New Hope, MN (city) Hennepin County	41	0.20
Ladera Heights, CA (cdp) Los Angeles County	13	0.20
Butte, AK (cdp) Matanuska-Susitna Borough	5	0.20
Hansen, ID (city) Twin Falls County	2	0.20
Salt Lake City, UT (city) Salt Lake County	341	0.19
Arlington, NY (cdp) Dutchess County	24	0.19
Leroy, MI (township) Ingham County	7	0.19
Griswold, IA (city) Cass County	2	0.19
Ross Township, PA (cdp) Allegheny County	58	0.18
Des Moines, WA (city) King County	54	0.18
Merrifield, VA (cdp) Fairfax County	20	0.18
Lansing, MI (city) Ingham County	203	0.17
Candler-McAfee, GA (cdp) De Kalb County	49	0.17
Pinole, CA (city) Contra Costa County	33	0.17
Farmington, MI (city) Oakland County	18	0.17
Riverdale Park, MD (town) Prince George's County	11	0.17
Bemidji, MN (township) Beltrami County	5	0.17
Buffalo, NY (city) Erie County	457	0.16
Framingham, MA (cdp) Middlesex County	110	0.16
De Kalb, IL (city) De Kalb County	63	0.16
Dunwoody, GA (cdp) De Kalb County	50	0.15
Seattle, WA (city) King County	786	0.14
Greensboro, NC (city) Guilford County	313	0.14
Waseca, MN (city) Waseca County	12	0.14
Franklin, MI (township) Houghton County	2	0.14
Blue Ash, OH (city) Hamilton County	16	0.13
Butler, PA (township) Luzerne County	9	0.13
Vandenberg AFB, CA (cdp) Santa Barbara County	8	0.13
Charlotte, NC (city) Mecklenburg County	624	0.12
Ypsilanti, MI (township) Washtenaw County	60	0.12
Euless, TX (city) Tarrant County	55	0.12
Chelsea, MA (city) Suffolk County	42	0.12
Cascade-Fairwood, WA (cdp) King County	41	0.12
Saint Dennis, KY (cdp) Jefferson County	11	0.12
Burke, VA (cdp) Fairfax County	63	0.11
Stanton, CA (city) Orange County	39	0.11
Idylwood, VA (cdp) Fairfax County	17	0.11
Falls Church, VA (independent city) Falls Church city	11	0.11
Boston, MA (city) Suffolk County	614	0.10
Kansas City, MO (city) Jackson County	456	0.10
Saint Louis, MO (independent city) Saint Louis city	340	0.10
Shoreline, WA (city) King County	54	0.10
Revere, MA (city) Suffolk County	46	0.10
Auburn, WA (city) King County	39	0.10
South Orange, NJ (cdp) Essex County	17	0.10
Glendale, WI (city) Milwaukee County	14	0.10
Fridley, MN (city) Anoka County	25	0.09
Lawrenceville, GA (city) Gwinnett County	20	0.09
Glenside, PA (cdp) Montgomery County	7	0.09
Rochester, NY (city) Monroe County	171	0.08
Apple Valley, MN (city) Dakota County	38	0.08
Bartlett, TN (city) Shelby County	33	0.08
Carmel, IN (city) Hamilton County	32	0.08
Spring Valley, CA (cdp) San Diego County	20	0.08
Portland, OR (city) Multnomah County	390	0.07
Arlington, VA (cdp) Arlington County	136	0.07
Flower Mound, TX (town) Denton County	37	0.07
Kentwood, MI (city) Kent County	32	0.07
Salem, MA (city) Essex County	30	0.07
Tigard, OR (city) Washington County	28	0.07
Edmonds, WA (city) Snohomish County	27	0.07
Sedalia, MO (city) Pettis County	14	0.07
Glassboro, NJ (borough) Gloucester County	13	0.07
Pueblo West, CO (cdp) Pueblo County	12	0.07
Linda, CA (cdp) Yuba County	10	0.07
Shelbyville, KY (city) Shelby County	7	0.07
East Pasadena, CA (cdp) Los Angeles County	4	0.07
Nashville-Davidson, TN (special city) Davidson County	321	0.06
Arlington, TX (city) Tarrant County	211	0.06
Raleigh, NC (city) Wake County	160	0.06

Notes: (cdp) census designated place; Refer to the Explanation of Data in the front of the book for more detailed information.

African, sub-Saharan: Somalian

Top 150 Places Sorted by Percent

(Based on places with populations of 10,000 or more)

Place	Number	%
Lincolnia, VA (cdp) Fairfax County	584	3.68
Owatonna, MN (city) Steele County	433	1.93
Minneapolis, MN (city) Hennepin County	6,537	1.71
Rochester, MN (city) Olmsted County	1,131	1.32
SeaTac, WA (city) King County	301	1.18
Hopkins, MN (city) Hennepin County	195	1.14
White Center, WA (cdp) King County	185	0.89
Marshall, MN (city) Lyon County	112	0.88
Tukwila, WA (city) King County	137	0.80
Riverton-Boulevard Park, WA (cdp) King County	90	0.79
Eden Prairie, MN (city) Hennepin County	382	0.70
Bailey's Crossroads, VA (cdp) Fairfax County	153	0.67
Lorton, VA (cdp) Fairfax County	111	0.63
Willmar, MN (city) Kandiyohi County	109	0.59
Tysons Corner, VA (cdp) Fairfax County	107	0.58
Kent, WA (city) King County	444	0.56
Greater Landover, MD (cdp) Prince George's County	102	0.45
Takoma Park, MD (city) Montgomery County	77	0.45
Portland, ME (city) Cumberland County	270	0.42
Alexandria, VA (independent city) Alexandria city	529	0.41
Columbus, OH (city) Franklin County	2,839	0.40
Oakton, VA (cdp) Fairfax County	118	0.40
Renton, WA (city) King County	184	0.37
Saint Paul, MN (city) Ramsey County	1,026	0.36
North Mankato, MN (city) Nicollet County	42	0.36
Hopkinton, MA (town) Middlesex County	47	0.35
East Riverdale, MD (cdp) Prince George's County	52	0.34
Decatur, GA (city) De Kalb County	56	0.31
Burnsville, MN (city) Dakota County	178	0.30
Fargo, ND (city) Cass County	258	0.28
Storm Lake, IA (city) Buena Vista County	28	0.28
Annandale, VA (cdp) Fairfax County	143	0.26
White Bear Lake, MN (city) Ramsey County	63	0.26
Faribault, MN (city) Rice County	53	0.25
Mankato, MN (city) Blue Earth County	78	0.24
Waianae, HI (cdp) Honolulu County	26	0.24
North Atlanta, GA (cdp) De Kalb County	89	0.23
Hercules, CA (city) Contra Costa County	44	0.23
Columbia Heights, MN (city) Anoka County	43	0.23
Saint Louis Park, MN (city) Hennepin County	96	0.22
Addison, TX (town) Dallas County	30	0.22
San Diego, CA (city) San Diego County	2,538	0.21
Eagan, MN (city) Dakota County	133	0.21
East Hill-Meridian, WA (cdp) King County	62	0.21
South Salt Lake, UT (city) Salt Lake County	47	0.21
Lake Forest Park, WA (city) King County	28	0.21
New Hope, MN (city) Hennepin County	41	0.20
Salt Lake City, UT (city) Salt Lake County	341	0.19
Arlington, NY (cdp) Dutchess County	24	0.19
Ross Township, PA (cdp) Allegheny County	58	0.18
Des Moines, WA (city) King County	54	0.18
Merrifield, VA (cdp) Fairfax County	20	0.18
Lansing, MI (city) Ingham County	203	0.17
Candler-McAfee, GA (cdp) De Kalb County	49	0.17
Pinole, CA (city) Contra Costa County	33	0.17
Farmington, MI (city) Oakland County	18	0.17
Buffalo, NY (city) Erie County	457	0.16
Framingham, MA (cdp) Middlesex County	110	0.16
De Kalb, IL (city) De Kalb County	63	0.16
Dunwoody, GA (cdp) De Kalb County	50	0.15
Seattle, WA (city) King County	786	0.14
Greensboro, NC (city) Guilford County	313	0.14
Blue Ash, OH (city) Hamilton County	16	0.13
Charlotte, NC (city) Mecklenburg County	624	0.12
Ypsilanti, MI (township) Washtenaw County	60	0.12
Euless, TX (city) Tarrant County	55	0.12
Chelsea, MA (city) Suffolk County	42	0.12
Cascade-Fairwood, WA (cdp) King County	41	0.12
Burke, VA (cdp) Fairfax County	63	0.11
Stanton, CA (city) Orange County	39	0.11
Idylwood, VA (cdp) Fairfax County	17	0.11
Falls Church, VA (independent city) Falls Church city	11	0.11
Boston, MA (city) Suffolk County	614	0.10
Kansas City, MO (city) Jackson County	456	0.10
Saint Louis, MO (independent city) Saint Louis city	340	0.10

Place	Number	%
Shoreline, WA (city) King County	54	0.10
Revere, MA (city) Suffolk County	46	0.10
Auburn, WA (city) King County	39	0.10
South Orange, NJ (cdp) Essex County	17	0.10
Glendale, WI (city) Milwaukee County	14	0.10
Fridley, MN (city) Anoka County	25	0.09
Lawrenceville, GA (city) Gwinnett County	20	0.09
Rochester, NY (city) Monroe County	171	0.08
Apple Valley, MN (city) Dakota County	38	0.08
Bartlett, TN (city) Shelby County	33	0.08
Carmel, IN (city) Hamilton County	32	0.08
Spring Valley, CA (cdp) San Diego County	20	0.08
Portland, OR (city) Multnomah County	390	0.07
Arlington, VA (cdp) Arlington County	136	0.07
Flower Mound, TX (town) Denton County	37	0.07
Kentwood, MI (city) Kent County	32	0.07
Salem, MA (city) Essex County	30	0.07
Tigard, OR (city) Washington County	28	0.07
Edmonds, WA (city) Snohomish County	27	0.07
Sedalia, MO (city) Pettis County	14	0.07
Glassboro, NJ (borough) Gloucester County	13	0.07
Pueblo West, CO (cdp) Pueblo County	12	0.07
Linda, CA (cdp) Yuba County	10	0.07
Shelbyville, KY (city) Shelby County	7	0.07
Nashville-Davidson, TN (special city) Davidson County	321	0.06
Arlington, TX (city) Tarrant County	211	0.06
Raleigh, NC (city) Wake County	160	0.06
Louisville, KY (city) Jefferson County	142	0.06
Bridgeport, CT (city) Fairfield County	84	0.06
Waterloo, IA (city) Black Hawk County	42	0.06
Centreville, VA (cdp) Fairfax County	29	0.06
Grand Forks, ND (city) Grand Forks County	29	0.06
Poughkeepsie, NY (town) Dutchess County	24	0.06
Roseville, MN (city) Ramsey County	21	0.06
Burien, WA (city) King County	20	0.06
Clinton, MD (cdp) Prince George's County	17	0.06
North Platte, NE (city) Lincoln County	14	0.06
Montclair, VA (cdp) Prince William County	10	0.06
Sioux Falls, SD (city) Minnehaha County	61	0.05
Hillsboro, OR (city) Washington County	32	0.05
Binghamton, NY (city) Broome County	22	0.05
Charlottesville, VA (independent city) Charlottesville city	21	0.05
Campbell, CA (city) Santa Clara County	20	0.05
Culver City, CA (city) Los Angeles County	20	0.05
Meridian charter, MI (township) Ingham County	18	0.05
Richfield, MN (city) Hennepin County	18	0.05
Langley Park, MD (cdp) Prince George's County	8	0.05
Bexley, OH (city) Franklin County	7	0.05
Upper Darby, PA (township) Delaware County	29	0.04
Round Rock, TX (city) Williamson County	23	0.04
Woodbury, MN (city) Washington County	20	0.04
Aspen Hill, MD (cdp) Montgomery County	19	0.04
Edina, MN (city) Hennepin County	19	0.04
North Highlands, CA (cdp) Sacramento County	19	0.04
Brighton, NY (town) Monroe County	15	0.04
Burlington, VT (city) Chittenden County	15	0.04
Springfield, VA (cdp) Fairfax County	13	0.04
Tucker, GA (cdp) De Kalb County	11	0.04
Richmond, KY (city) Madison County	10	0.04
Maple Valley, WA (city) King County	6	0.04
Boise City, ID (city) Ada County	57	0.03
Irving, TX (city) Dallas County	54	0.03
Durham, NC (city) Durham County	50	0.03
Brockton, MA (city) Plymouth County	31	0.03
Erie, PA (city) Erie County	31	0.03
Federal Way, WA (city) King County	28	0.03
Cambridge, MA (city) Middlesex County	26	0.03
Silver Spring, MD (cdp) Montgomery County	26	0.03
Kenosha, WI (city) Kenosha County	25	0.03
West Hartford, CT (cdp) Hartford County	22	0.03
Bloomington, IL (city) McLean County	20	0.03
Deerfield Beach, FL (city) Broward County	18	0.03
Fountain Valley, CA (city) Orange County	15	0.03
East Lansing, MI (city) Ingham County	13	0.03
Broomfield, CO (city) Boulder County	11	0.03

Notes: (cdp) census designated place; Refer to the Explanation of Data in the front of the book for more detailed information.

African, sub-Saharan: South African

Top 150 Places Sorted by Number

(Based on all places, regardless of population)

Place	Number	%
Los Angeles, CA (city) Los Angeles County	1,982	0.05
New York, NY (city) New York City	1,399	0.02
San Diego, CA (city) San Diego County	1,250	0.10
Houston, TX (city) Harris County	764	0.04
Irvine, CA (city) Orange County	751	0.53
Dallas, TX (city) Dallas County	680	0.06
Austin, TX (city) Travis County	320	0.05
Sandy Springs, GA (cdp) Fulton County	315	0.37
Chicago, IL (city) Cook County	223	0.01
Seattle, WA (city) King County	221	0.04
Phoenix, AZ (city) Maricopa County	216	0.02
Weston, FL (city) Broward County	210	0.43
San Francisco, CA (city) San Francisco County	202	0.03
Washington, DC (city) District of Columbia	191	0.03
Newton, MA (city) Middlesex County	189	0.23
Santa Monica, CA (city) Los Angeles County	170	0.20
Plano, TX (city) Collin County	167	0.08
San Jose, CA (city) Santa Clara County	166	0.02
Boca Raton, FL (city) Palm Beach County	163	0.22
Denver, CO (city) Denver County	161	0.03
Cary, NC (town) Wake County	158	0.17
Huntington Beach, CA (city) Orange County	156	0.08
Jacksonville, FL (special city) Duval County	154	0.02
Lexington-Fayette, KY (special city) Fayette County	147	0.06
Cambridge, MA (city) Middlesex County	146	0.14
North Hempstead, NY (town) Nassau County	145	0.07
Highlands Ranch, CO (cdp) Douglas County	144	0.20
Philadelphia, PA (city) Philadelphia County	141	0.01
Charlotte, NC (city) Mecklenburg County	140	0.03
Cave Spring, VA (cdp) Roanoke County	139	0.56
Tampa, FL (city) Hillsborough County	139	0.05
Concord, PA (township) Delaware County	133	1.34
Lakewood, CO (city) Jefferson County	131	0.09
Scottsdale, AZ (city) Maricopa County	131	0.06
Boston, MA (city) Suffolk County	125	0.02
Thornton, CO (city) Adams County	121	0.15
Fort Lauderdale, FL (city) Broward County	120	0.08
Cottage Grove, MN (city) Washington County	119	0.39
Plantation, FL (city) Broward County	119	0.14
Baltimore, MD (independent city) Baltimore city	119	0.02
Provo, UT (city) Utah County	117	0.11
Coral Springs, FL (city) Broward County	114	0.10
Concord, CA (city) Contra Costa County	111	0.09
Pikesville, MD (cdp) Baltimore County	109	0.38
Reynoldsburg, OH (city) Franklin County	108	0.34
Greenburgh, NY (town) Westchester County	107	0.12
Boulder, CO (city) Boulder County	106	0.11
Indianapolis, IN (special city) Marion County	106	0.01
Deerfield Beach, FL (city) Broward County	104	0.16
West Hartford, CT (cdp) Hartford County	104	0.16
Mamaroneck, NY (town) Westchester County	100	0.35
Mission Viejo, CA (city) Orange County	100	0.11
Thousand Oaks, CA (city) Ventura County	99	0.08
Beverly Hills, CA (city) Los Angeles County	98	0.29
Alpharetta, GA (city) Fulton County	98	0.28
Newport Beach, CA (city) Orange County	98	0.14
Lake Oswego, OR (city) Clackamas County	92	0.26
Atlanta, GA (city) Fulton County	92	0.02
Castlewood, CO (cdp) Arapahoe County	90	0.35
Henderson, NV (city) Clark County	90	0.05
Salt Lake City, UT (city) Salt Lake County	90	0.05
Boca Del Mar, FL (cdp) Palm Beach County	89	0.42
Minneapolis, MN (city) Hennepin County	89	0.02
Orinda, CA (city) Contra Costa County	88	0.50
Aventura, FL (city) Miami-Dade County	88	0.35
Nashville-Davidson, TN (special city) Davidson County	88	0.02
Springfield, NJ (cdp) Union County	87	0.60
Foster City, CA (city) San Mateo County	87	0.30
Las Vegas, NV (city) Clark County	87	0.02
Sacramento, CA (city) Sacramento County	87	0.02
Portland, OR (city) Multnomah County	86	0.02
Sandalfoot Cove, FL (cdp) Palm Beach County	85	0.51
Westborough, MA (town) Worcester County	84	0.47
Schaumburg, IL (village) Cook County	84	0.11
Colorado Springs, CO (city) El Paso County	83	0.02
San Antonio, TX (city) Bexar County	83	0.01
Gainesville, FL (city) Alachua County	81	0.08
Skidaway Island, GA (cdp) Chatham County	80	1.16
Eagan, MN (city) Dakota County	78	0.12
Grapevine, TX (city) Tarrant County	77	0.18
Palo Alto, CA (city) Santa Clara County	77	0.13
Marina del Rey, CA (cdp) Los Angeles County	76	0.93
Marlborough, MA (city) Middlesex County	76	0.21
Edmond, OK (city) Oklahoma County	74	0.11
Oakland, CA (city) Alameda County	73	0.02
Tustin, CA (city) Orange County	72	0.11
Ann Arbor, MI (city) Washtenaw County	72	0.06
Milwaukee, WI (city) Milwaukee County	71	0.01
Superior, CO (town) Boulder County	69	0.77
Bethesda, MD (cdp) Montgomery County	69	0.12
Laguna Niguel, CA (city) Orange County	69	0.11
Buffalo Grove, IL (village) Lake County	68	0.16
Bridgeport, CT (city) Fairfield County	67	0.05
Paradise, NV (cdp) Clark County	67	0.04
Huntington, NY (town) Suffolk County	67	0.03
Irving, TX (city) Dallas County	67	0.03
Hempstead, NY (town) Nassau County	67	0.01
Winter Springs, FL (city) Seminole County	66	0.21
Clearwater, FL (city) Pinellas County	66	0.06
Overland Park, KS (city) Johnson County	66	0.04
North Springfield, VA (cdp) Fairfax County	65	0.71
Westport, CT (cdp) Fairfield County	65	0.25
Wheaton, IL (city) Du Page County	65	0.12
Kansas City, MO (city) Jackson County	65	0.01
Calabasas, CA (city) Los Angeles County	64	0.32
Highland Park, IL (city) Lake County	64	0.20
Montclair, NJ (cdp) Essex County	63	0.16
Poway, CA (city) San Diego County	62	0.13
Rye, NY (city) Westchester County	61	0.41
Aurora, IL (city) Kane County	61	0.04
Urbana, IL (city) Champaign County	59	0.16
Shoreline, WA (city) King County	59	0.11
Madison, WI (city) Dane County	59	0.03
Jersey City, NJ (city) Hudson County	59	0.02
Oklahoma City, OK (city) Oklahoma County	59	0.01
Newcastle, WA (city) King County	58	0.72
Westbrook, ME (city) Cumberland County	58	0.36
Lexington, MA (cdp) Middlesex County	58	0.19
Oakton, VA (cdp) Fairfax County	57	0.19
Virginia Beach, VA (independent city) Virginia Beach city	57	0.01
Deptford, NJ (township) Gloucester County	56	0.21
North Attleborough, MA (town) Bristol County	56	0.21
Cherry Hill, NJ (township) Camden County	56	0.08
Hollywood, FL (city) Broward County	56	0.04
Arlington, VA (cdp) Arlington County	56	0.03
Beachwood, OH (city) Cuyahoga County	55	0.45
Potomac, MD (cdp) Montgomery County	55	0.12
Camarillo, CA (city) Ventura County	55	0.10
Palatine, IL (village) Cook County	55	0.08
Roanoke, VA (independent city) Roanoke city	55	0.06
Costa Mesa, CA (city) Orange County	55	0.05
Anchorage, AK (municipality) Anchorage Borough	55	0.02
Raleigh, NC (city) Wake County	55	0.02
Saint Petersburg, FL (city) Pinellas County	55	0.02
Haverford, PA (township) Delaware County	54	0.11
Sugar Land, TX (city) Fort Bend County	54	0.09
Charleston, SC (city) Charleston County	54	0.06
Berkeley, CA (city) Alameda County	54	0.05
Santa Clarita, CA (city) Los Angeles County	54	0.04
Apex, NC (town) Wake County	53	0.26
Hillsboro, OR (city) Washington County	53	0.08
Vinings, GA (cdp) Cobb County	52	0.54
University Park, TX (city) Dallas County	52	0.22
Drexel Hill, PA (cdp) Delaware County	52	0.18
Greenwich, CT (town) Fairfield County	52	0.09
Upper Darby, PA (township) Delaware County	52	0.06
West Palm Beach, FL (city) Palm Beach County	52	0.06
Chandler, AZ (city) Maricopa County	52	0.03
Lincoln, NE (city) Lancaster County	52	0.02
Memphis, TN (city) Shelby County	52	0.01

Notes: (cdp) census designated place; Refer to the Explanation of Data in the front of the book for more detailed information.

African, sub-Saharan: South African

Top 150 Places Sorted by Percent

(Based on all places, regardless of population)

Place	Number	%
North River, ND (city) Cass County	14	24.56
Gotha, FL (cdp) Orange County	31	4.14
Randolph, UT (city) Rich County	12	2.54
Fairbanks Ranch, CA (cdp) San Diego County	35	1.86
Bennington, KS (city) Ottawa County	10	1.61
Saddle Rock Estates, NY (cdp) Nassau County	7	1.59
Orient, NY (cdp) Suffolk County	10	1.41
Concord, PA (township) Delaware County	133	1.34
Brisbane, CA (city) San Mateo County	46	1.31
Buhl, MN (city) Saint Louis County	13	1.31
Mannford, OK (town) Creek County	25	1.26
Bryn Athyn, PA (borough) Montgomery County	17	1.26
Argyle, MO (town) Osage County	2	1.26
Melbourne Beach, FL (town) Brevard County	41	1.24
Sturgis, MI (township) Saint Joseph County	30	1.22
Skidaway Island, GA (cdp) Chatham County	80	1.16
Stateline, NV (cdp) Douglas County	13	1.13
Cottage Grove, WI (village) Dane County	43	1.09
Elmsford, NY (village) Westchester County	49	1.06
Credit River, MN (township) Scott County	40	1.02
Martin's Additions, MD (village) Montgomery County	9	1.01
Springfield, WI (town) Saint Croix County	8	1.01
Chester Heights, PA (borough) Delaware County	25	0.99
Walden, TN (town) Hamilton County	18	0.94
Marina del Rey, CA (cdp) Los Angeles County	76	0.93
Troy, KS (city) Doniphan County	10	0.93
East Flat Rock, NC (cdp) Henderson County	38	0.91
Honeyville, UT (city) Box Elder County	11	0.91
Webster, NY (village) Monroe County	43	0.83
Flat Rock, NC (village) Henderson County	21	0.83
White Hall, AR (city) Jefferson County	40	0.82
Florence, MT (cdp) Ravalli County	21	0.80
Cottage City, MD (town) Prince George's County	9	0.79
Echo, MN (city) Yellow Medicine County	2	0.78
Superior, CO (town) Boulder County	69	0.77
Varnell, GA (city) Whitfield County	11	0.77
Nolensville, TN (town) Williamson County	24	0.75
Milford, UT (city) Beaver County	11	0.75
Harbor Bluffs, FL (cdp) Pinellas County	21	0.73
Newcastle, WA (city) King County	58	0.72
North Springfield, VA (cdp) Fairfax County	65	0.71
Belville, NC (town) Brunswick County	2	0.71
Manlius, NY (village) Onondaga County	34	0.70
Lloyd Harbor, NY (village) Suffolk County	25	0.68
Berlin, WI (town) Marathon County	6	0.68
Plymouth, IA (city) Cerro Gordo County	3	0.67
Smithton, PA (borough) Westmoreland County	3	0.67
Leverett, MA (town) Franklin County	11	0.66
Keene, NY (town) Essex County	7	0.66
Double Oak, TX (town) Denton County	14	0.65
Pupukea, HI (cdp) Honolulu County	27	0.64
Saddle Rock, NY (village) Nassau County	5	0.63
Greatwood, TX (cdp) Fort Bend County	40	0.61
Springfield, NJ (cdp) Union County	87	0.60
Acworth, NH (town) Sullivan County	5	0.60
Doolittle, MO (city) Phelps County	4	0.60
Harrisburg, NC (town) Cabarrus County	27	0.59
Amelia, OH (village) Clermont County	16	0.59
Calistoga, CA (city) Napa County	30	0.58
Cross Plains, WI (village) Dane County	18	0.58
Peninsula, OH (village) Summit County	3	0.58
Cherry Grove, MI (township) Wexford County	13	0.57
Owyhee, NV (cdp) Elko County	6	0.57
Beech Mountain, NC (town) Watauga County	2	0.57
Cave Spring, VA (cdp) Roanoke County	139	0.56
Portola Hills, CA (cdp) Orange County	36	0.56
Shelby, MI (village) Oceana County	11	0.56
Christiana, WI (town) Vernon County	5	0.56
Aspen, CO (city) Pitkin County	32	0.55
Manchester, WA (cdp) Kitsap County	27	0.55
Madisonville, TX (city) Madison County	23	0.55
Wesley Chapel South, FL (cdp) Pasco County	18	0.55
Augusta, MI (village) Kalamazoo County	5	0.55
Darnen, MN (township) Stevens County	2	0.55
Vinings, GA (cdp) Cobb County	52	0.54

Place	Number	%
East Richmond Heights, CA (cdp) Contra Costa County	19	0.54
Shorewood Hills, WI (village) Dane County	9	0.54
Great Neck Gardens, NY (cdp) Nassau County	6	0.54
Irvine, CA (city) Orange County	751	0.53
Haworth, NJ (borough) Bergen County	18	0.53
Three Oaks, FL (cdp) Lee County	12	0.53
Ainsworth, NE (city) Brown County	10	0.53
Westwood Hills, KS (city) Johnson County	2	0.53
Sandalfoot Cove, FL (cdp) Palm Beach County	85	0.51
Orinda, CA (city) Contra Costa County	88	0.50
Oak Ridge North, TX (city) Montgomery County	15	0.50
Big Coppitt Key, FL (cdp) Monroe County	13	0.50
Vail, CO (town) Eagle County	22	0.49
San Joaquin Hills, CA (cdp) Orange County	15	0.49
Hickory Creek, TX (town) Denton County	10	0.49
Adams, NY (village) Jefferson County	8	0.49
Clyde Hill, WA (city) King County	14	0.48
Berrien Springs, MI (village) Berrien County	9	0.48
Morenci, AZ (cdp) Greenlee County	9	0.48
Woodacre, CA (cdp) Marin County	7	0.48
Westborough, MA (town) Worcester County	84	0.47
Keene, TX (city) Johnson County	23	0.47
Morrow, GA (city) Clayton County	23	0.47
Kamas, UT (city) Summit County	6	0.47
Russell Gardens, NY (village) Nassau County	5	0.47
Oronoko charter, MI (township) Berrien County	45	0.46
Laguna West-Lakeside, CA (cdp) Sacramento County	39	0.46
Shirley, MA (town) Middlesex County	29	0.46
Emerald Isle, NC (town) Carteret County	16	0.46
Lake Success, NY (village) Nassau County	13	0.46
Beachwood, OH (city) Cuyahoga County	55	0.45
Norwood, PA (borough) Delaware County	27	0.45
Tyler Run-Queens Gate, PA (cdp) York County	13	0.45
Chuluota, FL (cdp) Seminole County	9	0.45
Rollingstone, MN (township) Winona County	5	0.45
North Andrews Gardens, FL (cdp) Broward County	42	0.44
Weston, FL (city) Broward County	210	0.43
Burbank, CA (cdp) Santa Clara County	23	0.43
Happy Valley, OR (city) Clackamas County	21	0.43
Lake Wildwood, CA (cdp) Nevada County	21	0.43
Ross, CA (town) Marin County	10	0.43
Delmar, DE (town) Sussex County	6	0.43
Burlington, IL (village) Kane County	2	0.43
Boca Del Mar, FL (cdp) Palm Beach County	89	0.42
Morris Plains, NJ (borough) Morris County	22	0.42
Toro Canyon, CA (cdp) Santa Barbara County	7	0.42
Beauford, MN (township) Blue Earth County	2	0.42
Rye, NY (city) Westchester County	61	0.41
Geneva, NE (city) Fillmore County	9	0.41
Sartell, MN (city) Stearns County	38	0.40
Hunters Creek, FL (cdp) Orange County	36	0.40
Yorkshire, VA (cdp) Prince William County	27	0.40
Belleville, MI (city) Wayne County	16	0.40
Stanford, NY (town) Dutchess County	14	0.40
Norton Center, MA (cdp) Bristol County	10	0.40
East Atlantic Beach, NY (cdp) Nassau County	9	0.40
Cottage Grove, MN (city) Washington County	119	0.39
Flowood, MS (city) Rankin County	19	0.39
Moreland Hills, OH (village) Cuyahoga County	13	0.39
Pikesville, MD (cdp) Baltimore County	109	0.38
New Carrollton, MD (city) Prince George's County	49	0.38
Buena Vista, CO (town) Chaffee County	8	0.38
Sandy Springs, GA (cdp) Fulton County	315	0.37
Ferndale, WA (city) Whatcom County	33	0.37
White House, TN (city) Robertson County	27	0.37
Minnetrista, MN (city) Hennepin County	16	0.37
Bradford, MN (township) Isanti County	13	0.37
Orford, NH (town) Grafton County	4	0.37
Greenwood, ME (town) Oxford County	3	0.37
Clitherall, MN (township) Otter Tail County	2	0.37
Westbrook, ME (city) Cumberland County	58	0.36
Bethel, PA (township) Delaware County	23	0.36
New Paltz, NY (village) Ulster County	22	0.36
Wailea-Makena, HI (cdp) Maui County	20	0.36
Bolton, MA (town) Worcester County	15	0.36

Notes: (cdp) census designated place; Refer to the Explanation of Data in the front of the book for more detailed information.

African, sub-Saharan: South African

Top 150 Places Sorted by Percent

(Based on places with populations of 10,000 or more)

Place	Number	%
Springfield, NJ (cdp) Union County	87	0.60
Cave Spring, VA (cdp) Roanoke County	139	0.56
Irvine, CA (city) Orange County	751	0.53
Sandalfoot Cove, FL (cdp) Palm Beach County	85	0.51
Orinda, CA (city) Contra Costa County	88	0.50
Westborough, MA (town) Worcester County	84	0.47
Beachwood, OH (city) Cuyahoga County	55	0.45
Weston, FL (city) Broward County	210	0.43
Boca Del Mar, FL (cdp) Palm Beach County	89	0.42
Rye, NY (city) Westchester County	61	0.41
Cottage Grove, MN (city) Washington County	119	0.39
Pikesville, MD (cdp) Baltimore County	109	0.38
New Carrollton, MD (city) Prince George's County	49	0.38
Sandy Springs, GA (cdp) Fulton County	315	0.37
Westbrook, ME (city) Cumberland County	58	0.36
Mamaroneck, NY (town) Westchester County	100	0.35
Castlewood, CO (cdp) Arapahoe County	90	0.35
Aventura, FL (city) Miami-Dade County	88	0.35
Lakeland Highlands, FL (cdp) Polk County	44	0.35
Reynoldsburg, OH (city) Franklin County	108	0.34
Malibu, CA (city) Los Angeles County	41	0.33
Indian Trail, NC (town) Union County	39	0.33
Calabasas, CA (city) Los Angeles County	64	0.32
Foster City, CA (city) San Mateo County	87	0.30
West University Place, TX (city) Harris County	43	0.30
Beverly Hills, CA (city) Los Angeles County	98	0.29
Niles, MI (township) Berrien County	39	0.29
Wrentham, MA (town) Norfolk County	31	0.29
Alpharetta, GA (city) Fulton County	98	0.28
Coto de Caza, CA (cdp) Orange County	37	0.28
Linganore-Bartonsville, MD (cdp) Frederick County	35	0.28
Loveland, OH (city) Hamilton County	34	0.28
Sevierville, TN (city) Sevier County	33	0.28
Conning Towers-Nautilus Park, CT (cdp) New London County	28	0.27
Doraville, GA (city) De Kalb County	27	0.27
Lake Oswego, OR (city) Clackamas County	92	0.26
Apex, NC (town) Wake County	53	0.26
Forest Park, OH (city) Hamilton County	51	0.26
Oatfield, OR (cdp) Clackamas County	41	0.26
Westport, CT (cdp) Fairfield County	65	0.25
Scarsdale, NY (village) Westchester County	44	0.25
Sunny Isles Beach, FL (city) Miami-Dade County	38	0.25
Manchester, PA (township) York County	32	0.25
Landen, OH (cdp) Warren County	31	0.25
Chesapeake Ranch Estates-Drum Point, MD (cdp) Calvert County	29	0.25
Cinco Ranch, TX (cdp) Fort Bend County	28	0.25
Richmond Heights, OH (city) Cuyahoga County	27	0.25
Tamalpais-Homestead Valley, CA (cdp) Marin County	27	0.25
Elk City, OK (city) Beckham County	25	0.24
Newton, MA (city) Middlesex County	189	0.23
Elkridge, MD (cdp) Howard County	51	0.23
Summit, NJ (city) Union County	49	0.23
Princeton, NJ (borough) Mercer County	33	0.23
Greentree, NJ (cdp) Camden County	27	0.23
Boca Raton, FL (city) Palm Beach County	163	0.22
University Park, TX (city) Dallas County	52	0.22
Ojus, FL (cdp) Miami-Dade County	36	0.22
Parkland, FL (city) Broward County	31	0.22
Stanford, CA (cdp) Santa Clara County	29	0.22
Marlborough, MA (city) Middlesex County	76	0.21
Winter Springs, FL (city) Seminole County	66	0.21
Deptford, NJ (township) Gloucester County	56	0.21
North Attleborough, MA (town) Bristol County	56	0.21
Bloomingdale, FL (cdp) Hillsborough County	41	0.21
Menasha, WI (town) Winnebago County	34	0.21
Cameron Park, CA (cdp) El Dorado County	30	0.21
Franklin Lakes, NJ (borough) Bergen County	22	0.21
Santa Monica, CA (city) Los Angeles County	170	0.20
Highlands Ranch, CO (cdp) Douglas County	144	0.20
Highland Park, IL (city) Lake County	64	0.20
South Fayette, PA (township) Allegheny County	24	0.20
Lexington, MA (cdp) Middlesex County	58	0.19
Oakton, VA (cdp) Fairfax County	57	0.19
South Windsor, CT (town) Hartford County	46	0.19
Mahwah, NJ (township) Bergen County	45	0.19
Hyattsville, MD (city) Prince George's County	28	0.19
Fostoria, OH (city) Seneca County	27	0.19
Goshen, NY (town) Orange County	24	0.19
Brown Deer, WI (village) Milwaukee County	23	0.19
Little Falls, NJ (cdp) Passaic County	21	0.19
Amherst, NH (town) Hillsborough County	20	0.19
Hillsdale, NJ (borough) Bergen County	19	0.19
Grapevine, TX (city) Tarrant County	77	0.18
Drexel Hill, PA (cdp) Delaware County	52	0.18
Ridgefield, CT (town) Fairfield County	43	0.18
Wekiwa Springs, FL (cdp) Seminole County	43	0.18
Mercer Island, WA (city) King County	40	0.18
Mountain Brook, AL (city) Jefferson County	38	0.18
Jefferson, NJ (township) Morris County	36	0.18
North Druid Hills, GA (cdp) De Kalb County	33	0.18
El Dorado Hills, CA (cdp) El Dorado County	32	0.18
Sudbury, MA (town) Middlesex County	31	0.18
Windsor, PA (township) York County	23	0.18
Medfield, MA (town) Norfolk County	22	0.18
Tyngsborough, MA (town) Middlesex County	20	0.18
Cary, NC (town) Wake County	158	0.17
Westmont, IL (village) Du Page County	42	0.17
Erlanger, KY (city) Kenton County	28	0.17
Simpsonville, SC (city) Greenville County	24	0.17
New Paltz, NY (town) Ulster County	22	0.17
Los Alamos, NM (cdp) Los Alamos County	20	0.17
Foothill Ranch, CA (cdp) Orange County	19	0.17
Deerfield Beach, FL (city) Broward County	104	0.16
West Hartford, CT (cdp) Hartford County	104	0.16
Buffalo Grove, IL (village) Lake County	68	0.16
Montclair, NJ (cdp) Essex County	63	0.16
Urbana, IL (city) Champaign County	59	0.16
Florence, SC (city) Florence County	50	0.16
Lake Magdalene, FL (cdp) Hillsborough County	47	0.16
Tarpon Springs, FL (city) Pinellas County	33	0.16
McAlester, OK (city) Pittsburg County	28	0.16
Wilton, CT (town) Fairfield County	28	0.16
Canyon Lake, TX (cdp) Comal County	27	0.16
Gulf Gate Estates, FL (cdp) Sarasota County	18	0.16
North Smithfield, RI (town) Providence County	17	0.16
Thornton, CO (city) Adams County	121	0.15
Greater Carrollwood, FL (cdp) Hillsborough County	50	0.15
Dublin, OH (city) Franklin County	47	0.15
Los Gatos, CA (town) Santa Clara County	43	0.15
Naples, FL (city) Collier County	32	0.15
Tysons Corner, VA (cdp) Fairfax County	28	0.15
Hermosa Beach, CA (city) Los Angeles County	27	0.15
Hopewell, NJ (township) Mercer County	24	0.15
Mill Valley, CA (city) Marin County	21	0.15
Jericho, NY (cdp) Nassau County	20	0.15
Mountain Park, GA (cdp) Gwinnett County	17	0.15
Newtown, PA (township) Delaware County	17	0.15
Cedarburg, WI (city) Ozaukee County	16	0.15
Bound Brook, NJ (borough) Somerset County	15	0.15
Weston, CT (town) Fairfield County	15	0.15
Cambridge, MA (city) Middlesex County	146	0.14
Plantation, FL (city) Broward County	119	0.14
Newport Beach, CA (city) Orange County	98	0.14
West Hollywood, CA (city) Los Angeles County	51	0.14
Fort Lee, NJ (borough) Bergen County	48	0.14
Ken Caryl, CO (cdp) Jefferson County	44	0.14
Hampden, PA (township) Cumberland County	34	0.14
Vernon, NJ (township) Sussex County	34	0.14
Municipality of Murrysville, PA (borough) Westmoreland County	26	0.14
Tanque Verde, AZ (cdp) Pima County	23	0.14
Fort Drum, NY (cdp) Jefferson County	17	0.14
Ringwood, NJ (borough) Passaic County	17	0.14
Gardendale, AL (city) Jefferson County	16	0.14
Hasbrouck Heights, NJ (borough) Bergen County	16	0.14
Lansing, NY (town) Tompkins County	14	0.14
Palo Alto, CA (city) Santa Clara County	77	0.13
Poway, CA (city) San Diego County	62	0.13
University City, MO (city) Saint Louis County	48	0.13
Shrewsbury, MA (town) Worcester County	41	0.13
Voorhees, NJ (township) Camden County	37	0.13

Notes: (cdp) census designated place; Refer to the Explanation of Data in the front of the book for more detailed information.

African, sub-Saharan: Sudanese

Top 150 Places Sorted by Number

(Based on all places, regardless of population)

Place	Number	%
New York, NY (city) New York City	859	0.01
Des Moines, IA (city) Polk County	481	0.24
Alexandria, VA (independent city) Alexandria city	435	0.34
San Diego, CA (city) San Diego County	346	0.03
Omaha, NE (city) Douglas County	330	0.08
Sioux Falls, SD (city) Minnehaha County	297	0.24
Salt Lake City, UT (city) Salt Lake County	293	0.16
Denver, CO (city) Denver County	267	0.05
Philadelphia, PA (city) Philadelphia County	264	0.02
Minneapolis, MN (city) Hennepin County	261	0.07
Atlanta, GA (city) Fulton County	230	0.06
Lincolnia, VA (cdp) Fairfax County	211	1.33
Greensboro, NC (city) Guilford County	196	0.09
Seattle, WA (city) King County	171	0.03
Iowa City, IA (city) Johnson County	161	0.26
Buffalo, NY (city) Erie County	161	0.06
Nashville-Davidson, TN (special city) Davidson County	158	0.03
Ames, IA (city) Story County	147	0.29
White Oak, MD (cdp) Montgomery County	146	0.70
Jersey City, NJ (city) Hudson County	146	0.06
Gallatin, TN (city) Sumner County	139	0.60
Cedar Rapids, IA (city) Linn County	129	0.11
Manchester, NH (city) Hillsborough County	118	0.11
Chicago, IL (city) Cook County	117	0.00
Dallas, TX (city) Dallas County	116	0.01
Kansas City, MO (city) Jackson County	111	0.03
Schenectady, NY (city) Schenectady County	109	0.18
Albany, NY (city) Albany County	105	0.11
Fort Washington, MD (cdp) Prince George's County	103	0.43
Fargo, ND (city) Cass County	103	0.11
Brevard, NC (city) Transylvania County	102	1.48
Washington, DC (city) District of Columbia	102	0.02
Phoenix, AZ (city) Maricopa County	102	0.01
Houston, TX (city) Harris County	99	0.01
Whitehall, OH (city) Franklin County	97	0.50
Mount Vernon, VA (cdp) Fairfax County	91	0.32
Silver Spring, MD (cdp) Montgomery County	85	0.11
Baltimore, MD (independent city) Baltimore city	83	0.01
San Antonio, TX (city) Bexar County	83	0.01
Dale City, VA (cdp) Prince William County	77	0.14
Newport News, VA (independent city) Newport News city	77	0.04
Marshalltown, IA (city) Marshall County	74	0.28
Arlington, VA (cdp) Arlington County	73	0.04
Castro Valley, CA (cdp) Alameda County	72	0.13
Council Bluffs, IA (city) Pottawattamie County	71	0.12
Saint Paul, MN (city) Ramsey County	71	0.02
Rochester, MN (city) Olmsted County	67	0.08
Durham, NC (city) Durham County	67	0.04
Brigantine, NJ (city) Atlantic County	66	0.52
Terrytown, LA (cdp) Jefferson Parish	66	0.26
Annandale, VA (cdp) Fairfax County	66	0.12
Fort Collins, CO (city) Larimer County	66	0.06
Bakersfield, CA (city) Kern County	66	0.03
Los Angeles, CA (city) Los Angeles County	65	0.00
Clarkston, GA (city) De Kalb County	64	0.94
Dunn Loring, VA (cdp) Fairfax County	64	0.82
Lake Barcroft, VA (cdp) Fairfax County	64	0.71
Jacksonville, FL (special city) Duval County	64	0.01
Bellevue, NE (city) Sarpy County	63	0.14
Anaheim, CA (city) Orange County	62	0.02
Raleigh, NC (city) Wake County	62	0.02
Fort Worth, TX (city) Tarrant County	60	0.01
Bailey's Crossroads, VA (cdp) Fairfax County	58	0.25
Chadron, NE (city) Dawes County	56	1.00
Virginia Beach, VA (independent city) Virginia Beach city	56	0.01
Binghamton, NY (city) Broome County	55	0.12
Gaithersburg, MD (city) Montgomery County	55	0.10
Lynn, MA (city) Essex County	55	0.06
Hayward, CA (city) Alameda County	52	0.04
Arlington, TX (city) Tarrant County	51	0.02
McLean, VA (cdp) Fairfax County	49	0.13
North Saint Paul, MN (city) Ramsey County	48	0.40
Centreville, VA (cdp) Fairfax County	48	0.10
Lincoln, NE (city) Lancaster County	46	0.02
Athens-Clarke County, GA (special city) Clarke County	45	0.04
Tempe, AZ (city) Maricopa County	45	0.03
Aurora, CO (city) Arapahoe County	45	0.02
Charlotte, NC (city) Mecklenburg County	45	0.01
Pembroke Pines, FL (city) Broward County	44	0.03
Glen Burnie, MD (cdp) Anne Arundel County	43	0.11
Bedford, TX (city) Tarrant County	43	0.09
Amherst Center, MA (cdp) Hampshire County	42	0.24
Amherst, MA (town) Hampshire County	42	0.12
Glendale, AZ (city) Maricopa County	42	0.02
Rochester, NY (city) Monroe County	42	0.02
Lynchburg, VA (independent city) Lynchburg city	40	0.06
Saint Ann, MO (city) Saint Louis County	39	0.29
Woodbridge, NJ (township) Middlesex County	39	0.04
Brooklyn, OH (city) Cuyahoga County	38	0.33
Riverdale, GA (city) Clayton County	38	0.31
Herndon, VA (town) Fairfax County	38	0.18
Cheyenne, WY (city) Laramie County	38	0.07
Hartford, CT (city) Hartford County	38	0.03
Lansing, MI (city) Ingham County	38	0.03
Baton Rouge, LA (city) East Baton Rouge Parish	38	0.02
Manchester, MO (city) Saint Louis County	37	0.19
Greenbelt, MD (city) Prince George's County	37	0.17
Rohnert Park, CA (city) Sonoma County	37	0.09
Boise City, ID (city) Ada County	37	0.02
Fort Wayne, IN (city) Allen County	36	0.02
Cincinnati, OH (city) Hamilton County	36	0.01
Seven Corners, VA (cdp) Fairfax County	35	0.39
Davis, CA (city) Yolo County	35	0.06
Portland, ME (city) Cumberland County	35	0.05
Long Beach, CA (city) Los Angeles County	35	0.01
Detroit, MI (city) Wayne County	35	0.00
West Springfield, VA (cdp) Fairfax County	33	0.12
Cleveland Heights, OH (city) Cuyahoga County	33	0.07
Simi Valley, CA (city) Ventura County	33	0.03
Mantua, VA (cdp) Fairfax County	32	0.43
Erie, PA (city) Erie County	31	0.03
Irving, TX (city) Dallas County	31	0.02
Boston, MA (city) Suffolk County	31	0.01
Memphis, TN (city) Shelby County	31	0.00
Princess Anne, MD (town) Somerset County	30	1.25
Justice, IL (village) Cook County	30	0.25
Westborough, MA (town) Worcester County	30	0.17
New Hope, MN (city) Hennepin County	30	0.14
Burlington, MA (cdp) Middlesex County	30	0.13
Buena Vista, CA (cdp) Santa Clara County	29	1.62
Lumberton, NC (city) Robeson County	29	0.14
Faribault, MN (city) Rice County	28	0.13
Manteca, CA (city) San Joaquin County	28	0.06
Orangeburg, SC (city) Orangeburg County	27	0.21
Langley Park, MD (cdp) Prince George's County	27	0.17
Culver City, CA (city) Los Angeles County	27	0.07
Sayre, OK (city) Beckham County	26	0.63
Statesville, NC (city) Iredell County	26	0.11
San Leandro, CA (city) Alameda County	26	0.03
Avenel, NJ (cdp) Middlesex County	25	0.14
El Cerrito, CA (city) Contra Costa County	25	0.11
Grand Rapids, MI (city) Kent County	25	0.01
Milwaukee, WI (city) Milwaukee County	25	0.00
San Jose, CA (city) Santa Clara County	25	0.00
Pismo Beach, CA (city) San Luis Obispo County	24	0.28
Northview, MI (cdp) Kent County	24	0.16
Xenia, OH (city) Greene County	24	0.10
Plainfield, MI (township) Kent County	24	0.08
Hurst, TX (city) Tarrant County	24	0.07
Richardson, TX (city) Dallas County	24	0.03
Plano, TX (city) Collin County	24	0.01
Gardere, LA (cdp) East Baton Rouge Parish	23	0.26
Keene, NH (city) Cheshire County	23	0.10
Brooklyn Park, MN (city) Hennepin County	23	0.03
Sandy Springs, GA (cdp) Fulton County	23	0.03
Woodstown, NJ (borough) Salem County	22	0.70
Princeton Meadows, NJ (cdp) Middlesex County	22	0.17
Albany, CA (city) Alameda County	22	0.13
Plainsboro, NJ (township) Middlesex County	22	0.11
Irvington, NJ (cdp) Essex County	22	0.04

Notes: (cdp) census designated place; Refer to the Explanation of Data in the front of the book for more detailed information.

African, sub-Saharan: Sudanese

Top 150 Places Sorted by Percent

(Based on all places, regardless of population)

Place	Number	%
Mitchell Heights, WV (town) Logan County	7	2.27
Hokah, MN (city) Houston County	10	1.68
Buena Vista, CA (cdp) Santa Clara County	29	1.62
Brevard, NC (city) Transylvania County	102	1.48
Lincolnia, VA (cdp) Fairfax County	211	1.33
Princess Anne, MD (town) Somerset County	30	1.25
Eagle Lake, MN (city) Blue Earth County	19	1.07
Chadron, NE (city) Dawes County	56	1.00
Clarkston, GA (city) De Kalb County	64	0.94
Dunn Loring, VA (cdp) Fairfax County	64	0.82
Lake Barcroft, VA (cdp) Fairfax County	64	0.71
White Oak, MD (cdp) Montgomery County	146	0.70
Woodstown, NJ (borough) Salem County	22	0.70
Oakland, IA (city) Pottawattamie County	10	0.68
Sayre, OK (city) Beckham County	26	0.63
Gallatin, TN (city) Sumner County	139	0.60
University Park, NM (cdp) Dona Ana County	16	0.59
Bethany, MI (township) Gratiot County	19	0.54
Brigantine, NJ (city) Atlantic County	66	0.52
Estancia, NM (town) Torrance County	8	0.51
Whitehall, OH (city) Franklin County	97	0.50
Cayuga Heights, NY (village) Tompkins County	16	0.50
Fort Washington, MD (cdp) Prince George's County	103	0.43
Mantua, VA (cdp) Fairfax County	32	0.43
North Kansas City, MO (city) Clay County	20	0.42
North Saint Paul, MN (city) Ramsey County	48	0.40
Seven Corners, VA (cdp) Fairfax County	35	0.39
Walton, IN (town) Cass County	4	0.38
Woodmere, OH (village) Cuyahoga County	3	0.36
Alexandria, VA (independent city) Alexandria city	435	0.34
Mount Pleasant, TN (city) Maury County	15	0.34
Brooklyn, OH (city) Cuyahoga County	38	0.33
Mount Vernon, VA (cdp) Fairfax County	91	0.32
Riverdale, GA (city) Clayton County	38	0.31
Stone Mountain, GA (city) De Kalb County	21	0.31
Lac du Flambeau, WI (town) Vilas County	9	0.30
Ames, IA (city) Story County	147	0.29
Saint Ann, MO (city) Saint Louis County	39	0.29
Marshalltown, IA (city) Marshall County	74	0.28
Pismo Beach, CA (city) San Luis Obispo County	24	0.28
Iowa City, IA (city) Johnson County	161	0.26
Terrytown, LA (cdp) Jefferson Parish	66	0.26
Gardere, LA (cdp) East Baton Rouge Parish	23	0.26
Haskell, AR (city) Saline County	7	0.26
Bailey's Crossroads, VA (cdp) Fairfax County	58	0.25
Justice, IL (village) Cook County	30	0.25
Day Valley, CA (cdp) Santa Cruz County	9	0.25
Des Moines, IA (city) Polk County	481	0.24
Sioux Falls, SD (city) Minnehaha County	297	0.24
Amherst Center, MA (cdp) Hampshire County	42	0.24
Fredonia, WI (town) Ozaukee County	7	0.24
Litchfield, NH (town) Hillsborough County	16	0.22
Orangeburg, SC (city) Orangeburg County	27	0.21
Arlington, VT (town) Bennington County	5	0.21
Pinetops, NC (town) Edgecombe County	3	0.21
West Pike Run, PA (township) Washington County	4	0.20
Manchester, MO (city) Saint Louis County	37	0.19
Huntington, VA (cdp) Fairfax County	16	0.19
Warren, MA (town) Worcester County	9	0.19
Schenectady, NY (city) Schenectady County	109	0.18
Herndon, VA (town) Fairfax County	38	0.18
Decatur, IN (city) Adams County	17	0.18
Greenbelt, MD (city) Prince George's County	37	0.17
Westborough, MA (town) Worcester County	30	0.17
Langley Park, MD (cdp) Prince George's County	27	0.17
Princeton Meadows, NJ (cdp) Middlesex County	22	0.17
Monongahela, PA (city) Washington County	8	0.17
Salt Lake City, UT (city) Salt Lake County	293	0.16
Northview, MI (cdp) Kent County	24	0.16
Perry, IA (city) Dallas County	12	0.16
Anamosa, IA (city) Jones County	9	0.16
Avilla, IN (town) Noble County	3	0.15
Dale City, VA (cdp) Prince William County	77	0.14
Bellevue, NE (city) Sarpy County	63	0.14
New Hope, MN (city) Hennepin County	30	0.14
Lumberton, NC (city) Robeson County	29	0.14
Avenel, NJ (cdp) Middlesex County	25	0.14
Rosemount, MN (city) Dakota County	21	0.14
Bayport, NY (cdp) Suffolk County	12	0.14
Masonville, NY (town) Delaware County	2	0.14
Preston, MN (city) Fillmore County	2	0.14
Castro Valley, CA (cdp) Alameda County	72	0.13
McLean, VA (cdp) Fairfax County	49	0.13
Burlington, MA (cdp) Middlesex County	30	0.13
Faribault, MN (city) Rice County	28	0.13
Albany, CA (city) Alameda County	22	0.13
Laurel, VA (cdp) Henrico County	19	0.13
Worthington, MN (city) Nobles County	15	0.13
Millbrook, AL (city) Elmore County	13	0.13
Mount Rainier, MD (city) Prince George's County	11	0.13
Council Bluffs, IA (city) Pottawattamie County	71	0.12
Annandale, VA (cdp) Fairfax County	66	0.12
Binghamton, NY (city) Broome County	55	0.12
Amherst, MA (town) Hampshire County	42	0.12
West Springfield, VA (cdp) Fairfax County	33	0.12
Madison, WI (town) Dane County	9	0.12
Brandon, SD (city) Minnehaha County	7	0.12
Gladstone, MI (city) Delta County	6	0.12
Cedar Rapids, IA (city) Linn County	129	0.11
Manchester, NH (city) Hillsborough County	118	0.11
Albany, NY (city) Albany County	105	0.11
Fargo, ND (city) Cass County	103	0.11
Silver Spring, MD (cdp) Montgomery County	85	0.11
Glen Burnie, MD (cdp) Anne Arundel County	43	0.11
Statesville, NC (city) Iredell County	26	0.11
El Cerrito, CA (city) Contra Costa County	25	0.11
Plainsboro, NJ (township) Middlesex County	22	0.11
North Druid Hills, GA (cdp) De Kalb County	21	0.11
Garner, NC (town) Wake County	20	0.11
Brooklyn, CT (town) Windham County	8	0.11
Denison, IA (city) Crawford County	8	0.11
Gaithersburg, MD (city) Montgomery County	55	0.10
Centreville, VA (cdp) Fairfax County	48	0.10
Xenia, OH (city) Greene County	24	0.10
Keene, NH (city) Cheshire County	23	0.10
Anoka, MN (city) Anoka County	18	0.10
Elmwood Park, NJ (borough) Bergen County	18	0.10
Lincolnton, NC (city) Lincoln County	10	0.10
Greensboro, NC (city) Guilford County	196	0.09
Bedford, TX (city) Tarrant County	43	0.09
Rohnert Park, CA (city) Sonoma County	37	0.09
Ithaca, NY (town) Tompkins County	16	0.09
Jasmine Estates, FL (cdp) Pasco County	16	0.09
Hybla Valley, VA (cdp) Fairfax County	15	0.09
East Riverdale, MD (cdp) Prince George's County	14	0.09
North Valley Stream, NY (cdp) Nassau County	14	0.09
Fenton, MI (city) Genesee County	10	0.09
Hartselle, AL (city) Morgan County	10	0.09
Houghton, MI (city) Houghton County	6	0.09
Valley City, ND (city) Barnes County	6	0.09
Omaha, NE (city) Douglas County	330	0.08
Rochester, MN (city) Olmsted County	67	0.08
Plainfield, MI (township) Kent County	24	0.08
Darien, CT (cdp) Fairfield County	15	0.08
Whitewater, WI (city) Walworth County	11	0.08
Minneapolis, MN (city) Hennepin County	261	0.07
Cheyenne, WY (city) Laramie County	38	0.07
Cleveland Heights, OH (city) Cuyahoga County	33	0.07
Culver City, CA (city) Los Angeles County	27	0.07
Hurst, TX (city) Tarrant County	24	0.07
Chili, NY (town) Monroe County	20	0.07
Inkster, MI (city) Wayne County	20	0.07
Homewood, AL (city) Jefferson County	18	0.07
Murray, KY (city) Calloway County	10	0.07
Fort Stewart, GA (cdp) Liberty County	8	0.07
Lansdowne, PA (borough) Delaware County	8	0.07
Fort Carson, CO (cdp) El Paso County	7	0.07
Atlanta, GA (city) Fulton County	230	0.06
Buffalo, NY (city) Erie County	161	0.06
Jersey City, NJ (city) Hudson County	146	0.06

Notes: (cdp) census designated place; Refer to the Explanation of Data in the front of the book for more detailed information.

African, sub-Saharan: Sudanese

Top 150 Places Sorted by Percent

(Based on places with populations of 10,000 or more)

Place	Number	%
Lincolnia, VA (cdp) Fairfax County	211	1.33
White Oak, MD (cdp) Montgomery County	146	0.70
Gallatin, TN (city) Sumner County	139	0.60
Brigantine, NJ (city) Atlantic County	66	0.52
Whitehall, OH (city) Franklin County	97	0.50
Fort Washington, MD (cdp) Prince George's County	103	0.43
North Saint Paul, MN (city) Ramsey County	48	0.40
Alexandria, VA (independent city) Alexandria city	435	0.34
Brooklyn, OH (city) Cuyahoga County	38	0.33
Mount Vernon, VA (cdp) Fairfax County	91	0.32
Riverdale, GA (city) Clayton County	38	0.31
Ames, IA (city) Story County	147	0.29
Saint Ann, MO (city) Saint Louis County	39	0.29
Marshalltown, IA (city) Marshall County	74	0.28
Iowa City, IA (city) Johnson County	161	0.26
Terrytown, LA (cdp) Jefferson Parish	66	0.26
Bailey's Crossroads, VA (cdp) Fairfax County	58	0.25
Justice, IL (village) Cook County	30	0.25
Des Moines, IA (city) Polk County	481	0.24
Sioux Falls, SD (city) Minnehaha County	297	0.24
Amherst Center, MA (cdp) Hampshire County	42	0.24
Orangeburg, SC (city) Orangeburg County	27	0.21
Manchester, MO (city) Saint Louis County	37	0.19
Schenectady, NY (city) Schenectady County	109	0.18
Herndon, VA (town) Fairfax County	38	0.18
Greenbelt, MD (city) Prince George's County	37	0.17
Westborough, MA (town) Worcester County	30	0.17
Langley Park, MD (cdp) Prince George's County	27	0.17
Princeton Meadows, NJ (cdp) Middlesex County	22	0.17
Salt Lake City, UT (city) Salt Lake County	293	0.16
Northview, MI (cdp) Kent County	24	0.16
Dale City, VA (cdp) Prince William County	77	0.14
Bellevue, NE (city) Sarpy County	63	0.14
New Hope, MN (city) Hennepin County	30	0.14
Lumberton, NC (city) Robeson County	29	0.14
Avenel, NJ (cdp) Middlesex County	25	0.14
Rosemount, MN (city) Dakota County	21	0.14
Castro Valley, CA (cdp) Alameda County	72	0.13
McLean, VA (cdp) Fairfax County	49	0.13
Burlington, MA (cdp) Middlesex County	30	0.13
Faribault, MN (city) Rice County	28	0.13
Albany, CA (city) Alameda County	22	0.13
Laurel, VA (cdp) Henrico County	19	0.13
Worthington, MN (city) Nobles County	15	0.13
Millbrook, AL (city) Elmore County	13	0.13
Council Bluffs, IA (city) Pottawattamie County	71	0.12
Annandale, VA (cdp) Fairfax County	66	0.12
Binghamton, NY (city) Broome County	55	0.12
Amherst, MA (town) Hampshire County	42	0.12
West Springfield, VA (cdp) Fairfax County	33	0.12
Cedar Rapids, IA (city) Linn County	129	0.11
Manchester, NH (city) Hillsborough County	118	0.11
Albany, NY (city) Albany County	105	0.11
Fargo, ND (city) Cass County	103	0.11
Silver Spring, MD (cdp) Montgomery County	85	0.11
Glen Burnie, MD (cdp) Anne Arundel County	43	0.11
Statesville, NC (city) Iredell County	26	0.11
El Cerrito, CA (city) Contra Costa County	25	0.11
Plainsboro, NJ (township) Middlesex County	22	0.11
North Druid Hills, GA (cdp) De Kalb County	21	0.11
Garner, NC (town) Wake County	20	0.11
Gaithersburg, MD (city) Montgomery County	55	0.10
Centreville, VA (cdp) Fairfax County	48	0.10
Xenia, OH (city) Greene County	24	0.10
Keene, NH (city) Cheshire County	23	0.10
Anoka, MN (city) Anoka County	18	0.10
Elmwood Park, NJ (borough) Bergen County	18	0.10
Greensboro, NC (city) Guilford County	196	0.09
Bedford, TX (city) Tarrant County	43	0.09
Rohnert Park, CA (city) Sonoma County	37	0.09
Ithaca, NY (town) Tompkins County	16	0.09
Jasmine Estates, FL (cdp) Pasco County	16	0.09
Hybla Valley, VA (cdp) Fairfax County	15	0.09
East Riverdale, MD (cdp) Prince George's County	14	0.09
North Valley Stream, NY (cdp) Nassau County	14	0.09
Fenton, MI (city) Genesee County	10	0.09
Hartselle, AL (city) Morgan County	10	0.09
Omaha, NE (city) Douglas County	330	0.08
Rochester, MN (city) Olmsted County	67	0.08
Plainfield, MI (township) Kent County	24	0.08
Darien, CT (cdp) Fairfield County	15	0.08
Whitewater, WI (city) Walworth County	11	0.08
Minneapolis, MN (city) Hennepin County	261	0.07
Cheyenne, WY (city) Laramie County	38	0.07
Cleveland Heights, OH (city) Cuyahoga County	33	0.07
Culver City, CA (city) Los Angeles County	27	0.07
Hurst, TX (city) Tarrant County	24	0.07
Chili, NY (town) Monroe County	20	0.07
Inkster, MI (city) Wayne County	20	0.07
Homewood, AL (city) Jefferson County	18	0.07
Murray, KY (city) Calloway County	10	0.07
Fort Stewart, GA (cdp) Liberty County	8	0.07
Lansdowne, PA (borough) Delaware County	8	0.07
Fort Carson, CO (cdp) El Paso County	7	0.07
Atlanta, GA (city) Fulton County	230	0.06
Buffalo, NY (city) Erie County	161	0.06
Jersey City, NJ (city) Hudson County	146	0.06
Fort Collins, CO (city) Larimer County	66	0.06
Lynn, MA (city) Essex County	55	0.06
Lynchburg, VA (independent city) Lynchburg city	40	0.06
Davis, CA (city) Yolo County	35	0.06
Manteca, CA (city) San Joaquin County	28	0.06
Suitland-Silver Hill, MD (cdp) Prince George's County	20	0.06
Columbia Heights, MN (city) Anoka County	12	0.06
Glen Avon, CA (cdp) Riverside County	9	0.06
Coral Hills, MD (cdp) Prince George's County	7	0.06
Denver, CO (city) Denver County	267	0.05
Portland, ME (city) Cumberland County	35	0.05
South Windsor, CT (town) Hartford County	13	0.05
Burleson, TX (city) Johnson County	10	0.05
South Orange, NJ (cdp) Essex County	8	0.05
Saginaw, TX (city) Tarrant County	6	0.05
Newport News, VA (independent city) Newport News city	77	0.04
Arlington, VA (cdp) Arlington County	73	0.04
Durham, NC (city) Durham County	67	0.04
Hayward, CA (city) Alameda County	52	0.04
Athens-Clarke County, GA (special city) Clarke County	45	0.04
Woodbridge, NJ (township) Middlesex County	39	0.04
Irvington, NJ (cdp) Essex County	22	0.04
Portage, MI (city) Kalamazoo County	20	0.04
Chesterfield, MO (city) Saint Louis County	18	0.04
Salem, MA (city) Essex County	17	0.04
Shelton, CT (city) Fairfield County	16	0.04
Mankato, MN (city) Blue Earth County	13	0.04
Southgate, MI (city) Wayne County	13	0.04
Fridley, MN (city) Anoka County	11	0.04
Sault Sainte Marie, MI (city) Chippewa County	6	0.04
Upper Gwynedd, PA (township) Montgomery County	6	0.04
Goshen, NY (town) Orange County	5	0.04
San Diego, CA (city) San Diego County	346	0.03
Seattle, WA (city) King County	171	0.03
Nashville-Davidson, TN (special city) Davidson County	158	0.03
Kansas City, MO (city) Jackson County	111	0.03
Bakersfield, CA (city) Kern County	66	0.03
Tempe, AZ (city) Maricopa County	45	0.03
Pembroke Pines, FL (city) Broward County	44	0.03
Hartford, CT (city) Hartford County	38	0.03
Lansing, MI (city) Ingham County	38	0.03
Simi Valley, CA (city) Ventura County	33	0.03
Erie, PA (city) Erie County	31	0.03
San Leandro, CA (city) Alameda County	26	0.03
Richardson, TX (city) Dallas County	24	0.03
Brooklyn Park, MN (city) Hennepin County	23	0.03
Sandy Springs, GA (cdp) Fulton County	23	0.03
Coon Rapids, MN (city) Anoka County	21	0.03
Dubuque, IA (city) Dubuque County	20	0.03
Millcreek, PA (township) Erie County	18	0.03
White Plains, NY (city) Westchester County	16	0.03
Euless, TX (city) Tarrant County	15	0.03
Troy, NY (city) Rensselaer County	14	0.03

Notes: (cdp) census designated place; Refer to the Explanation of Data in the front of the book for more detailed information.

African, sub-Saharan: Ugandan

Top 150 Places Sorted by Number

(Based on all places, regardless of population)

Place	Number	%
Los Angeles, CA (city) Los Angeles County	202	0.01
Milwaukee, WI (city) Milwaukee County	132	0.02
San Diego, CA (city) San Diego County	130	0.01
New York, NY (city) New York City	104	0.00
Seattle, WA (city) King County	85	0.02
Alexandria, VA (independent city) Alexandria city	84	0.07
White Oak, MD (cdp) Montgomery County	83	0.40
Arlington, MA (cdp) Middlesex County	73	0.17
Aurora, CO (city) Arapahoe County	69	0.03
Swatara, PA (township) Dauphin County	64	0.28
Waltham, MA (city) Middlesex County	61	0.10
Denver, CO (city) Denver County	56	0.01
Laguna Niguel, CA (city) Orange County	55	0.09
Cary, NC (town) Wake County	53	0.06
Benicia, CA (city) Solano County	51	0.19
Malden, MA (city) Middlesex County	51	0.09
Chelsea, MA (city) Suffolk County	46	0.13
Houston, TX (city) Harris County	46	0.00
Farmington Hills, MI (city) Oakland County	42	0.05
Rochester, NY (city) Monroe County	42	0.02
Oak Park, MI (city) Oakland County	41	0.14
West New York, NJ (town) Hudson County	40	0.09
Burke, VA (cdp) Fairfax County	38	0.07
Lower Merion, PA (township) Montgomery County	38	0.06
Boston, MA (city) Suffolk County	38	0.01
Redland, MD (cdp) Montgomery County	36	0.21
Lynn, MA (city) Essex County	36	0.04
Sacramento, CA (city) Sacramento County	36	0.01
Saint Paul, MN (city) Ramsey County	35	0.01
Gaithersburg, MD (city) Montgomery County	34	0.06
New Haven, CT (city) New Haven County	34	0.03
Paradise, NV (cdp) Clark County	34	0.02
Torrance, CA (city) Los Angeles County	34	0.02
Dallas, TX (city) Dallas County	34	0.00
Phoenix, AZ (city) Maricopa County	34	0.00
Melrose, MA (city) Middlesex County	33	0.12
Medford, MA (city) Middlesex County	32	0.06
Carrboro, NC (town) Orange County	30	0.18
Annapolis, MD (city) Anne Arundel County	30	0.08
Washington, DC (city) District of Columbia	30	0.01
Rockville, MD (city) Montgomery County	29	0.06
Lakewood, CA (city) Los Angeles County	29	0.04
Vancouver, WA (city) Clark County	29	0.02
Arden Hills, MN (city) Ramsey County	28	0.29
Marlborough, MA (city) Middlesex County	27	0.07
Evanston, IL (city) Cook County	27	0.04
Colesville, MD (cdp) Montgomery County	25	0.13
Simi Valley, CA (city) Ventura County	25	0.02
Watertown, MA (city) Middlesex County	24	0.07
Yorba Linda, CA (city) Orange County	24	0.04
Silver Spring, MD (cdp) Montgomery County	24	0.03
Chicago, IL (city) Cook County	24	0.00
Ferguson, PA (township) Centre County	23	0.16
Angleton, TX (city) Brazoria County	23	0.13
Cleveland Heights, OH (city) Cuyahoga County	23	0.05
Fresno, CA (city) Fresno County	23	0.01
Franklin, LA (city) Saint Mary Parish	22	0.26
Poughkeepsie, NY (city) Dutchess County	22	0.07
Taylorsville, UT (city) Salt Lake County	22	0.04
Tampa, FL (city) Hillsborough County	22	0.01
Tulsa, OK (city) Tulsa County	21	0.01
Groesbeck, OH (cdp) Hamilton County	20	0.28
Wells, ME (town) York County	20	0.21
Avenel, NJ (cdp) Middlesex County	20	0.11
North Miami Beach, FL (city) Miami-Dade County	20	0.05
Lowell, MA (city) Middlesex County	20	0.02
Woodbridge, NJ (township) Middlesex County	20	0.02
Raleigh, NC (city) Wake County	20	0.01
Wellesley, MA (cdp) Norfolk County	19	0.07
Framingham, MA (cdp) Middlesex County	19	0.03
Hamilton, OH (city) Butler County	19	0.03
Cambridge, MA (city) Middlesex County	19	0.02
Columbia, MD (cdp) Howard County	19	0.02
Somerville, MA (city) Middlesex County	19	0.02
Arlington, VA (cdp) Arlington County	19	0.01
Columbus, OH (city) Franklin County	19	0.00
Indianapolis, IN (special city) Marion County	19	0.00
Vacaville, CA (city) Solano County	18	0.02
Baltimore, MD (independent city) Baltimore city	18	0.00
North Richland Hills, TX (city) Tarrant County	17	0.03
Santa Clarita, CA (city) Los Angeles County	17	0.01
Philadelphia, PA (city) Philadelphia County	17	0.00
Cloverly, MD (cdp) Montgomery County	16	0.20
Easton, PA (city) Northampton County	16	0.06
Ithaca, NY (city) Tompkins County	16	0.06
Downey, CA (city) Los Angeles County	16	0.01
Grand Prairie, TX (city) Dallas County	16	0.01
Huntington Beach, CA (city) Orange County	16	0.01
Ayer, MA (town) Middlesex County	15	0.21
Lebanon, PA (city) Lebanon County	15	0.06
Bowie, MD (city) Prince George's County	15	0.03
Elmhurst, IL (city) Du Page County	15	0.03
Euless, TX (city) Tarrant County	15	0.03
Irving, TX (city) Dallas County	15	0.01
Lauderdale, MN (city) Ramsey County	14	0.59
Fort Valley, GA (city) Peach County	14	0.18
Gaines, MI (township) Kent County	14	0.07
Pittsford, NY (town) Monroe County	14	0.05
Concord, NH (city) Merrimack County	14	0.03
Colonie, NY (town) Albany County	14	0.02
Huntsville, AL (city) Madison County	14	0.01
Chester Township, PA (cdp) Delaware County	13	0.28
Fridley, MN (city) Anoka County	13	0.05
Atascocita, TX (cdp) Harris County	13	0.04
Mount Prospect, IL (village) Cook County	13	0.02
Albany, NY (city) Albany County	13	0.01
Fort Lauderdale, FL (city) Broward County	13	0.01
Oakland, CA (city) Alameda County	13	0.00
Spackenkill, NY (cdp) Dutchess County	12	0.26
Fairland, MD (cdp) Montgomery County	12	0.06
New London, CT (city) New London County	12	0.05
Harrisonburg, VA (independent city) Harrisonburg city	12	0.03
Poughkeepsie, NY (town) Dutchess County	12	0.03
Sayreville, NJ (borough) Middlesex County	12	0.03
Ann Arbor, MI (city) Washtenaw County	12	0.01
Arlington, TX (city) Tarrant County	12	0.00
Honolulu, HI (cdp) Honolulu County	12	0.00
Bulverde, TX (city) Comal County	11	0.29
Hood River, OR (city) Hood River County	11	0.19
Williston, VT (town) Chittenden County	11	0.14
Greenbelt, MD (city) Prince George's County	11	0.05
Wilmington, MA (cdp) Middlesex County	11	0.05
Franklin, MA (city) Norfolk County	11	0.04
Chantilly, VA (cdp) Fairfax County	11	0.03
Charlottesville, VA (independent city) Charlottesville city	11	0.02
New Brunswick, NJ (city) Middlesex County	11	0.02
Niagara Falls, NY (city) Niagara County	11	0.02
Grand Rapids, MI (city) Kent County	11	0.01
Kansas City, KS (city) Wyandotte County	11	0.01
Minneapolis, MN (city) Hennepin County	11	0.00
Riverside, MO (city) Platte County	10	0.34
Rossville, MD (cdp) Baltimore County	10	0.09
Owings Mills, MD (cdp) Baltimore County	10	0.05
Homewood, AL (city) Jefferson County	10	0.04
La Mesa, CA (city) San Diego County	10	0.02
East Orange, NJ (city) Essex County	10	0.01
Everett, WA (city) Snohomish County	10	0.01
Killeen, TX (city) Bell County	10	0.01
Lee's Summit, MO (city) Jackson County	10	0.01
Little Rock, AR (city) Pulaski County	10	0.01
Jersey City, NJ (city) Hudson County	10	0.00
Omaha, NE (city) Douglas County	10	0.00
Angwin, CA (cdp) Napa County	9	0.29
Bernardsville, NJ (borough) Somerset County	9	0.12
Robinson Township, PA (cdp) Allegheny County	9	0.07
Chillum, MD (cdp) Prince George's County	9	0.03
Ponca City, OK (city) Kay County	9	0.03
Bossier City, LA (city) Bossier Parish	9	0.02
Poway, CA (city) San Diego County	9	0.02
Woburn, MA (city) Middlesex County	9	0.02

Notes: (cdp) census designated place; Refer to the Explanation of Data in the front of the book for more detailed information.

African, sub-Saharan: Ugandan

Top 150 Places Sorted by Percent

(Based on all places, regardless of population)

Place	Number	%
Lauderdale, MN (city) Ramsey County	14	0.59
Marshfield, WI (town) Fond du Lac County	5	0.47
Whitesburg, KY (city) Letcher County	7	0.42
White Oak, MD (cdp) Montgomery County	83	0.40
Kanabec, MN (township) Kanabec County	3	0.35
Riverside, MO (city) Platte County	10	0.34
Hawaiian Ocean View, HI (cdp) Hawaii County	7	0.32
Arden Hills, MN (city) Ramsey County	28	0.29
Bulverde, TX (city) Comal County	11	0.29
Angwin, CA (cdp) Napa County	9	0.29
Shadeland, IN (town) Tippecanoe County	5	0.29
Swatara, PA (township) Dauphin County	64	0.28
Groesbeck, OH (cdp) Hamilton County	20	0.28
Chester Township, PA (cdp) Delaware County	13	0.28
Franklin, LA (city) Saint Mary Parish	22	0.26
Spackenkill, NY (cdp) Dutchess County	12	0.26
Vinita Park, MO (city) Saint Louis County	5	0.26
Redland, MD (cdp) Montgomery County	36	0.21
Wells, ME (town) York County	20	0.21
Ayer, MA (town) Middlesex County	15	0.21
Larimore, ND (city) Grand Forks County	3	0.21
Cloverly, MD (cdp) Montgomery County	16	0.20
Shippen, PA (township) Cameron County	5	0.20
Benicia, CA (city) Solano County	51	0.19
Hood River, OR (city) Hood River County	11	0.19
Hopkins, MI (township) Allegan County	5	0.19
Carrboro, NC (town) Orange County	30	0.18
Fort Valley, GA (city) Peach County	14	0.18
Barbourville, KY (city) Knox County	6	0.18
Arlington, MA (cdp) Middlesex County	73	0.17
Princess Anne, MD (town) Somerset County	4	0.17
Ferguson, PA (township) Centre County	23	0.16
Greenfield, PA (township) Erie County	3	0.16
Hughes Springs, TX (city) Cass County	3	0.16
Oak Park, MI (city) Oakland County	41	0.14
Williston, VT (town) Chittenden County	11	0.14
Quincy, PA (township) Franklin County	8	0.14
Chelsea, MA (city) Suffolk County	46	0.13
Colesville, MD (cdp) Montgomery County	25	0.13
Angleton, TX (city) Brazoria County	23	0.13
Limestone, PA (township) Union County	2	0.13
Melrose, MA (city) Middlesex County	33	0.12
Bernardsville, NJ (borough) Somerset County	9	0.12
Frankenmuth, MI (city) Saginaw County	6	0.12
Avenel, NJ (cdp) Middlesex County	20	0.11
Paxtonia, PA (cdp) Dauphin County	6	0.11
Waltham, MA (city) Middlesex County	61	0.10
Laguna Niguel, CA (city) Orange County	55	0.09
Malden, MA (city) Middlesex County	51	0.09
West New York, NJ (town) Hudson County	40	0.09
Rossville, MD (cdp) Baltimore County	10	0.09
Annapolis, MD (city) Anne Arundel County	30	0.08
Quantico Station, VA (cdp) Prince William County	5	0.08
Alexandria, VA (independent city) Alexandria city	84	0.07
Burke, VA (cdp) Fairfax County	38	0.07
Marlborough, MA (city) Middlesex County	27	0.07
Watertown, MA (city) Middlesex County	24	0.07
Poughkeepsie, NY (city) Dutchess County	22	0.07
Wellesley, MA (cdp) Norfolk County	19	0.07
Gaines, MI (township) Kent County	14	0.07
Robinson Township, PA (cdp) Allegheny County	9	0.07
Falls Church, VA (independent city) Falls Church city	7	0.07
Cary, NC (town) Wake County	53	0.06
Lower Merion, PA (township) Montgomery County	38	0.06
Gaithersburg, MD (city) Montgomery County	34	0.06
Medford, MA (city) Middlesex County	32	0.06
Rockville, MD (city) Montgomery County	29	0.06
Easton, PA (city) Northampton County	16	0.06
Ithaca, NY (city) Tompkins County	16	0.06
Lebanon, PA (city) Lebanon County	15	0.06
Fairland, MD (cdp) Montgomery County	12	0.06
Issaquah, WA (city) King County	7	0.06
Gold River, CA (cdp) Sacramento County	5	0.06
Farmington Hills, MI (city) Oakland County	42	0.05
Cleveland Heights, OH (city) Cuyahoga County	23	0.05
North Miami Beach, FL (city) Miami-Dade County	20	0.05
Pittsford, NY (town) Monroe County	14	0.05
Fridley, MN (city) Anoka County	13	0.05
New London, CT (city) New London County	12	0.05
Greenbelt, MD (city) Prince George's County	11	0.05
Wilmington, MA (cdp) Middlesex County	11	0.05
Owings Mills, MD (cdp) Baltimore County	10	0.05
Delran, NJ (township) Burlington County	7	0.05
Druid Hills, GA (cdp) De Kalb County	6	0.05
Lynn, MA (city) Essex County	36	0.04
Lakewood, CA (city) Los Angeles County	29	0.04
Evanston, IL (city) Cook County	27	0.04
Yorba Linda, CA (city) Orange County	24	0.04
Taylorsville, UT (city) Salt Lake County	22	0.04
Atascocita, TX (cdp) Harris County	13	0.04
Franklin, MA (city) Norfolk County	11	0.04
Homewood, AL (city) Jefferson County	10	0.04
Weatherford, TX (city) Parker County	8	0.04
Holly Springs, NC (town) Wake County	4	0.04
Mount Rainier, MD (city) Prince George's County	3	0.04
Highland, NY (cdp) Ulster County	2	0.04
Aurora, CO (city) Arapahoe County	69	0.03
New Haven, CT (city) New Haven County	34	0.03
Silver Spring, MD (cdp) Montgomery County	24	0.03
Framingham, MA (cdp) Middlesex County	19	0.03
Hamilton, OH (city) Butler County	19	0.03
North Richland Hills, TX (city) Tarrant County	17	0.03
Bowie, MD (city) Prince George's County	15	0.03
Elmhurst, IL (city) Du Page County	15	0.03
Euless, TX (city) Tarrant County	15	0.03
Concord, NH (city) Merrimack County	14	0.03
Harrisonburg, VA (independent city) Harrisonburg city	12	0.03
Poughkeepsie, NY (town) Dutchess County	12	0.03
Sayreville, NJ (borough) Middlesex County	12	0.03
Chantilly, VA (cdp) Fairfax County	11	0.03
Chillum, MD (cdp) Prince George's County	9	0.03
Ponca City, OK (city) Kay County	9	0.03
Wappinger, NY (town) Dutchess County	8	0.03
Harrison, NY (village) Westchester County	7	0.03
Shoreview, MN (city) Ramsey County	7	0.03
South Salt Lake, UT (city) Salt Lake County	6	0.03
Palmer, PA (township) Northampton County	5	0.03
Pepper Pike, OH (city) Cuyahoga County	2	0.03
Milwaukee, WI (city) Milwaukee County	132	0.02
Seattle, WA (city) King County	85	0.02
Rochester, NY (city) Monroe County	42	0.02
Paradise, NV (cdp) Clark County	34	0.02
Torrance, CA (city) Los Angeles County	34	0.02
Vancouver, WA (city) Clark County	29	0.02
Simi Valley, CA (city) Ventura County	25	0.02
Lowell, MA (city) Middlesex County	20	0.02
Woodbridge, NJ (township) Middlesex County	20	0.02
Cambridge, MA (city) Middlesex County	19	0.02
Columbia, MD (cdp) Howard County	19	0.02
Somerville, MA (city) Middlesex County	19	0.02
Vacaville, CA (city) Solano County	18	0.02
Colonie, NY (town) Albany County	14	0.02
Mount Prospect, IL (village) Cook County	13	0.02
Charlottesville, VA (independent city) Charlottesville city	11	0.02
New Brunswick, NJ (city) Middlesex County	11	0.02
Niagara Falls, NY (city) Niagara County	11	0.02
La Mesa, CA (city) San Diego County	10	0.02
Bossier City, LA (city) Bossier Parish	9	0.02
Poway, CA (city) San Diego County	9	0.02
Woburn, MA (city) Middlesex County	9	0.02
Centreville, VA (cdp) Fairfax County	8	0.02
Corvallis, OR (city) Benton County	8	0.02
Manhattan Beach, CA (city) Los Angeles County	8	0.02
North Bethesda, MD (cdp) Montgomery County	8	0.02
Renton, WA (city) King County	8	0.02
Hallandale, FL (city) Broward County	7	0.02
Lancaster, OH (city) Fairfield County	7	0.02
McCandless Township, PA (cdp) Allegheny County	7	0.02
Olney, MD (cdp) Montgomery County	7	0.02
York, PA (city) York County	7	0.02

Notes: (cdp) census designated place; Refer to the Explanation of Data in the front of the book for more detailed information.

African, sub-Saharan: Ugandan

Top 150 Places Sorted by Percent

(Based on places with populations of 10,000 or more)

Place	Number	%
White Oak, MD (cdp) Montgomery County	83	0.40
Swatara, PA (township) Dauphin County	64	0.28
Redland, MD (cdp) Montgomery County	36	0.21
Benicia, CA (city) Solano County	51	0.19
Carrboro, NC (town) Orange County	30	0.18
Arlington, MA (cdp) Middlesex County	73	0.17
Ferguson, PA (township) Centre County	23	0.16
Oak Park, MI (city) Oakland County	41	0.14
Chelsea, MA (city) Suffolk County	46	0.13
Colesville, MD (cdp) Montgomery County	25	0.13
Angleton, TX (city) Brazoria County	23	0.13
Melrose, MA (city) Middlesex County	33	0.12
Avenel, NJ (cdp) Middlesex County	20	0.11
Waltham, MA (city) Middlesex County	61	0.10
Laguna Niguel, CA (city) Orange County	55	0.09
Malden, MA (city) Middlesex County	51	0.09
West New York, NJ (town) Hudson County	40	0.09
Rossville, MD (cdp) Baltimore County	10	0.09
Annapolis, MD (city) Anne Arundel County	30	0.08
Alexandria, VA (independent city) Alexandria city	84	0.07
Burke, VA (cdp) Fairfax County	38	0.07
Marlborough, MA (city) Middlesex County	27	0.07
Watertown, MA (city) Middlesex County	24	0.07
Poughkeepsie, NY (city) Dutchess County	22	0.07
Wellesley, MA (cdp) Norfolk County	19	0.07
Gaines, MI (township) Kent County	14	0.07
Robinson Township, PA (cdp) Allegheny County	9	0.07
Falls Church, VA (independent city) Falls Church city	7	0.07
Cary, NC (town) Wake County	53	0.06
Lower Merion, PA (township) Montgomery County	38	0.06
Gaithersburg, MD (city) Montgomery County	34	0.06
Medford, MA (city) Middlesex County	32	0.06
Rockville, MD (city) Montgomery County	29	0.06
Easton, PA (city) Northampton County	16	0.06
Ithaca, NY (city) Tompkins County	16	0.06
Lebanon, PA (city) Lebanon County	15	0.06
Fairland, MD (cdp) Montgomery County	12	0.06
Issaquah, WA (city) King County	7	0.06
Farmington Hills, MI (city) Oakland County	42	0.05
Cleveland Heights, OH (city) Cuyahoga County	23	0.05
North Miami Beach, FL (city) Miami-Dade County	20	0.05
Pittsford, NY (town) Monroe County	14	0.05
Fridley, MN (city) Anoka County	13	0.05
New London, CT (city) New London County	12	0.05
Greenbelt, MD (city) Prince George's County	11	0.05
Wilmington, MA (cdp) Middlesex County	11	0.05
Owings Mills, MD (cdp) Baltimore County	10	0.05
Delran, NJ (township) Burlington County	7	0.05
Druid Hills, GA (cdp) De Kalb County	6	0.05
Lynn, MA (city) Essex County	36	0.04
Lakewood, CA (city) Los Angeles County	29	0.04
Evanston, IL (city) Cook County	27	0.04
Yorba Linda, CA (city) Orange County	24	0.04
Taylorsville, UT (city) Salt Lake County	22	0.04
Atascocita, TX (cdp) Harris County	13	0.04
Franklin, MA (city) Norfolk County	11	0.04
Homewood, AL (city) Jefferson County	10	0.04
Weatherford, TX (city) Parker County	8	0.04
Aurora, CO (city) Arapahoe County	69	0.03
New Haven, CT (city) New Haven County	34	0.03
Silver Spring, MD (cdp) Montgomery County	24	0.03
Framingham, MA (cdp) Middlesex County	19	0.03
Hamilton, OH (city) Butler County	19	0.03
North Richland Hills, TX (city) Tarrant County	17	0.03
Bowie, MD (city) Prince George's County	15	0.03
Elmhurst, IL (city) Du Page County	15	0.03
Euless, TX (city) Tarrant County	15	0.03
Concord, NH (city) Merrimack County	14	0.03
Harrisonburg, VA (independent city) Harrisonburg city	12	0.03
Poughkeepsie, NY (town) Dutchess County	12	0.03
Sayreville, NJ (borough) Middlesex County	12	0.03
Chantilly, VA (cdp) Fairfax County	11	0.03
Chillum, MD (cdp) Prince George's County	9	0.03
Ponca City, OK (city) Kay County	9	0.03
Wappinger, NY (town) Dutchess County	8	0.03
Harrison, NY (village) Westchester County	7	0.03
Shoreview, MN (city) Ramsey County	7	0.03
South Salt Lake, UT (city) Salt Lake County	6	0.03
Palmer, PA (township) Northampton County	5	0.03
Milwaukee, WI (city) Milwaukee County	132	0.02
Seattle, WA (city) King County	85	0.02
Rochester, NY (city) Monroe County	42	0.02
Paradise, NV (cdp) Clark County	34	0.02
Torrance, CA (city) Los Angeles County	34	0.02
Vancouver, WA (city) Clark County	29	0.02
Simi Valley, CA (city) Ventura County	25	0.02
Lowell, MA (city) Middlesex County	20	0.02
Woodbridge, NJ (township) Middlesex County	20	0.02
Cambridge, MA (city) Middlesex County	19	0.02
Columbia, MD (cdp) Howard County	19	0.02
Somerville, MA (city) Middlesex County	19	0.02
Vacaville, CA (city) Solano County	18	0.02
Colonie, NY (town) Albany County	14	0.02
Mount Prospect, IL (village) Cook County	13	0.02
Charlottesville, VA (independent city) Charlottesville city	11	0.02
New Brunswick, NJ (city) Middlesex County	11	0.02
Niagara Falls, NY (city) Niagara County	11	0.02
La Mesa, CA (city) San Diego County	10	0.02
Bossier City, LA (city) Bossier Parish	9	0.02
Poway, CA (city) San Diego County	9	0.02
Woburn, MA (city) Middlesex County	9	0.02
Centreville, VA (cdp) Fairfax County	8	0.02
Corvallis, OR (city) Benton County	8	0.02
Manhattan Beach, CA (city) Los Angeles County	8	0.02
North Bethesda, MD (cdp) Montgomery County	8	0.02
Renton, WA (city) King County	8	0.02
Hallandale, FL (city) Broward County	7	0.02
Lancaster, OH (city) Fairfield County	7	0.02
McCandless Township, PA (cdp) Allegheny County	7	0.02
Olney, MD (cdp) Montgomery County	7	0.02
York, PA (city) York County	7	0.02
Urbana, IL (city) Champaign County	6	0.02
Pullman, WA (city) Whitman County	5	0.02
Valparaiso, IN (city) Porter County	5	0.02
Vestal, NY (town) Broome County	5	0.02
West Windsor, NJ (township) Mercer County	5	0.02
Los Angeles, CA (city) Los Angeles County	202	0.01
San Diego, CA (city) San Diego County	130	0.01
Denver, CO (city) Denver County	56	0.01
Boston, MA (city) Suffolk County	38	0.01
Sacramento, CA (city) Sacramento County	36	0.01
Saint Paul, MN (city) Ramsey County	35	0.01
Washington, DC (city) District of Columbia	30	0.01
Fresno, CA (city) Fresno County	23	0.01
Tampa, FL (city) Hillsborough County	22	0.01
Tulsa, OK (city) Tulsa County	21	0.01
Raleigh, NC (city) Wake County	20	0.01
Arlington, VA (cdp) Arlington County	19	0.01
Santa Clarita, CA (city) Los Angeles County	17	0.01
Downey, CA (city) Los Angeles County	16	0.01
Grand Prairie, TX (city) Dallas County	16	0.01
Huntington Beach, CA (city) Orange County	16	0.01
Irving, TX (city) Dallas County	15	0.01
Huntsville, AL (city) Madison County	14	0.01
Albany, NY (city) Albany County	13	0.01
Fort Lauderdale, FL (city) Broward County	13	0.01
Ann Arbor, MI (city) Washtenaw County	12	0.01
Grand Rapids, MI (city) Kent County	11	0.01
Kansas City, KS (city) Wyandotte County	11	0.01
East Orange, NJ (city) Essex County	10	0.01
Everett, WA (city) Snohomish County	10	0.01
Killeen, TX (city) Bell County	10	0.01
Lee's Summit, MO (city) Jackson County	10	0.01
Little Rock, AR (city) Pulaski County	10	0.01
Brooklyn Park, MN (city) Hennepin County	9	0.01
Worcester, MA (city) Worcester County	9	0.01
Concord, NC (city) Cabarrus County	8	0.01
Fort Collins, CO (city) Larimer County	8	0.01
Lawrence, KS (city) Douglas County	8	0.01
Savannah, GA (city) Chatham County	8	0.01

Notes: (cdp) census designated place; Refer to the Explanation of Data in the front of the book for more detailed information.

African, sub-Saharan: Zairian

Top 72 Places Sorted by Number

(Based on all places, regardless of population)

Place	Number	%
Charlotte, NC (city) Mecklenburg County	116	0.02
Bedford, TX (city) Tarrant County	85	0.18
Minneapolis, MN (city) Hennepin County	77	0.02
Los Angeles, CA (city) Los Angeles County	59	0.00
Wilkes-Barre, PA (city) Luzerne County	57	0.13
Germantown, MD (cdp) Montgomery County	55	0.10
Brooklyn Center, MN (city) Hennepin County	54	0.19
Dallas, TX (city) Dallas County	52	0.00
Raleigh, NC (city) Wake County	49	0.02
Rose Hill, VA (cdp) Fairfax County	41	0.27
Irving, TX (city) Dallas County	40	0.02
Richmond, VA (independent city) Richmond city	40	0.02
Mableton, GA (cdp) Cobb County	36	0.12
North Richland Hills, TX (city) Tarrant County	36	0.06
Aspen Hill, MD (cdp) Montgomery County	35	0.07
Costa Mesa, CA (city) Orange County	28	0.03
Langley Park, MD (cdp) Prince George's County	26	0.16
Philadelphia, PA (city) Philadelphia County	26	0.00
San Francisco, CA (city) San Francisco County	23	0.00
Montgomery Village, MD (cdp) Montgomery County	22	0.06
Atlanta, GA (city) Fulton County	21	0.01
Syracuse, NY (city) Onondaga County	20	0.01
Haverhill, MA (city) Essex County	18	0.03
Terre Haute, IN (city) Vigo County	18	0.03
Teaneck, NJ (cdp) Bergen County	17	0.04
Silver Spring, MD (cdp) Montgomery County	17	0.02
Alexandria, VA (independent city) Alexandria city	17	0.01
Washington, DC (city) District of Columbia	17	0.00
Matthews, NC (town) Mecklenburg County	15	0.07
Arden-Arcade, CA (cdp) Sacramento County	15	0.02
Detroit, MI (city) Wayne County	15	0.00
Fort Worth, TX (city) Tarrant County	14	0.00
New York, NY (city) New York City	14	0.00
Burlington, NJ (township) Burlington County	13	0.06
Richardson, TX (city) Dallas County	13	0.01
Denver, CO (city) Denver County	13	0.00
Miami Beach, FL (city) Miami-Dade County	12	0.01
Acworth, GA (city) Cobb County	11	0.08
Haltom City, TX (city) Tarrant County	11	0.03
Lawrence, KS (city) Douglas County	11	0.01
Orlando, FL (city) Orange County	10	0.01
Boston, MA (city) Suffolk County	10	0.00
Cambridge, MA (city) Middlesex County	9	0.01
Huntsville, AL (city) Madison County	9	0.01
Stamford, CT (city) Fairfield County	9	0.01
San Antonio, TX (city) Bexar County	9	0.00
Lexington, VA (independent city) Lexington city	8	0.12
Fitchburg, MA (city) Worcester County	8	0.02
Rockville, MD (city) Montgomery County	8	0.02
New Orleans, LA (city) Orleans Parish	8	0.00
Newark, NJ (city) Essex County	8	0.00
Coralville, IA (city) Johnson County	7	0.05
East Point, GA (city) Fulton County	7	0.02
Mount Laurel, NJ (township) Burlington County	7	0.02
Champaign, IL (city) Champaign County	7	0.01
Grand Prairie, TX (city) Dallas County	7	0.01
Medford, MA (city) Middlesex County	7	0.01
Arlington, VA (cdp) Arlington County	7	0.00
Boise City, ID (city) Ada County	7	0.00
Miami, FL (city) Miami-Dade County	7	0.00
Seattle, WA (city) King County	7	0.00
Kemp Mill, MD (cdp) Montgomery County	6	0.06
Saks, AL (cdp) Calhoun County	6	0.06
Fairland, MD (cdp) Montgomery County	6	0.03
Ames, IA (city) Story County	6	0.01
Berkeley, CA (city) Alameda County	6	0.01
McAllen, TX (city) Hidalgo County	6	0.01
Livermore Falls, ME (town) Androscoggin County	5	0.15
Haverford, PA (township) Delaware County	5	0.01
Portland, OR (city) Multnomah County	5	0.00
Topeka, KS (city) Shawnee County	4	0.00
Palos Verdes Estates, CA (city) Los Angeles County	3	0.02

Notes: (cdp) census designated place; Refer to the Explanation of Data in the front of the book for more detailed information.

African, sub-Saharan: Zairian

Top 72 Places Sorted by Percent

(Based on all places, regardless of population)

Place	Number	%
Rose Hill, VA (cdp) Fairfax County	41	0.27
Brooklyn Center, MN (city) Hennepin County	54	0.19
Bedford, TX (city) Tarrant County	85	0.18
Langley Park, MD (cdp) Prince George's County	26	0.16
Livermore Falls, ME (town) Androscoggin County	5	0.15
Wilkes-Barre, PA (city) Luzerne County	57	0.13
Mableton, GA (cdp) Cobb County	36	0.12
Lexington, VA (independent city) Lexington city	8	0.12
Germantown, MD (cdp) Montgomery County	55	0.10
Acworth, GA (city) Cobb County	11	0.08
Aspen Hill, MD (cdp) Montgomery County	35	0.07
Matthews, NC (town) Mecklenburg County	15	0.07
North Richland Hills, TX (city) Tarrant County	36	0.06
Montgomery Village, MD (cdp) Montgomery County	22	0.06
Burlington, NJ (township) Burlington County	13	0.06
Kemp Mill, MD (cdp) Montgomery County	6	0.06
Saks, AL (cdp) Calhoun County	6	0.06
Coralville, IA (city) Johnson County	7	0.05
Teaneck, NJ (cdp) Bergen County	17	0.04
Costa Mesa, CA (city) Orange County	28	0.03
Haverhill, MA (city) Essex County	18	0.03
Terre Haute, IN (city) Vigo County	18	0.03
Haltom City, TX (city) Tarrant County	11	0.03
Fairland, MD (cdp) Montgomery County	6	0.03
Charlotte, NC (city) Mecklenburg County	116	0.02
Minneapolis, MN (city) Hennepin County	77	0.02
Raleigh, NC (city) Wake County	49	0.02
Irving, TX (city) Dallas County	40	0.02
Richmond, VA (independent city) Richmond city	40	0.02
Silver Spring, MD (cdp) Montgomery County	17	0.02
Arden-Arcade, CA (cdp) Sacramento County	15	0.02
Fitchburg, MA (city) Worcester County	8	0.02
Rockville, MD (city) Montgomery County	8	0.02
East Point, GA (city) Fulton County	7	0.02
Mount Laurel, NJ (township) Burlington County	7	0.02
Palos Verdes Estates, CA (city) Los Angeles County	3	0.02
Atlanta, GA (city) Fulton County	21	0.01
Syracuse, NY (city) Onondaga County	20	0.01
Alexandria, VA (independent city) Alexandria city	17	0.01
Richardson, TX (city) Dallas County	13	0.01
Miami Beach, FL (city) Miami-Dade County	12	0.01
Lawrence, KS (city) Douglas County	11	0.01
Orlando, FL (city) Orange County	10	0.01
Cambridge, MA (city) Middlesex County	9	0.01
Huntsville, AL (city) Madison County	9	0.01
Stamford, CT (city) Fairfield County	9	0.01
Champaign, IL (city) Champaign County	7	0.01
Grand Prairie, TX (city) Dallas County	7	0.01
Medford, MA (city) Middlesex County	7	0.01
Ames, IA (city) Story County	6	0.01
Berkeley, CA (city) Alameda County	6	0.01
McAllen, TX (city) Hidalgo County	6	0.01
Haverford, PA (township) Delaware County	5	0.01
Los Angeles, CA (city) Los Angeles County	59	0.00
Dallas, TX (city) Dallas County	52	0.00
Philadelphia, PA (city) Philadelphia County	26	0.00
San Francisco, CA (city) San Francisco County	23	0.00
Washington, DC (city) District of Columbia	17	0.00
Detroit, MI (city) Wayne County	15	0.00
Fort Worth, TX (city) Tarrant County	14	0.00
New York, NY (city) New York City	14	0.00
Denver, CO (city) Denver County	13	0.00
Boston, MA (city) Suffolk County	10	0.00
San Antonio, TX (city) Bexar County	9	0.00
New Orleans, LA (city) Orleans Parish	8	0.00
Newark, NJ (city) Essex County	8	0.00
Arlington, VA (cdp) Arlington County	7	0.00
Boise City, ID (city) Ada County	7	0.00
Miami, FL (city) Miami-Dade County	7	0.00
Seattle, WA (city) King County	7	0.00
Portland, OR (city) Multnomah County	5	0.00
Topeka, KS (city) Shawnee County	4	0.00

Notes: (cdp) census designated place; Refer to the Explanation of Data in the front of the book for more detailed information.

African, sub-Saharan: Zairian

Top 69 Places Sorted by Percent

(Based on places with populations of 10,000 or more)

Place	Number	%
Rose Hill, VA (cdp) Fairfax County	41	0.27
Brooklyn Center, MN (city) Hennepin County	54	0.19
Bedford, TX (city) Tarrant County	85	0.18
Langley Park, MD (cdp) Prince George's County	26	0.16
Wilkes-Barre, PA (city) Luzerne County	57	0.13
Mableton, GA (cdp) Cobb County	36	0.12
Germantown, MD (cdp) Montgomery County	55	0.10
Acworth, GA (city) Cobb County	11	0.08
Aspen Hill, MD (cdp) Montgomery County	35	0.07
Matthews, NC (town) Mecklenburg County	15	0.07
North Richland Hills, TX (city) Tarrant County	36	0.06
Montgomery Village, MD (cdp) Montgomery County	22	0.06
Burlington, NJ (township) Burlington County	13	0.06
Saks, AL (cdp) Calhoun County	6	0.06
Coralville, IA (city) Johnson County	7	0.05
Teaneck, NJ (cdp) Bergen County	17	0.04
Costa Mesa, CA (city) Orange County	28	0.03
Haverhill, MA (city) Essex County	18	0.03
Terre Haute, IN (city) Vigo County	18	0.03
Haltom City, TX (city) Tarrant County	11	0.03
Fairland, MD (cdp) Montgomery County	6	0.03
Charlotte, NC (city) Mecklenburg County	116	0.02
Minneapolis, MN (city) Hennepin County	77	0.02
Raleigh, NC (city) Wake County	49	0.02
Irving, TX (city) Dallas County	40	0.02
Richmond, VA (independent city) Richmond city	40	0.02
Silver Spring, MD (cdp) Montgomery County	17	0.02
Arden-Arcade, CA (cdp) Sacramento County	15	0.02
Fitchburg, MA (city) Worcester County	8	0.02
Rockville, MD (city) Montgomery County	8	0.02
East Point, GA (city) Fulton County	7	0.02
Mount Laurel, NJ (township) Burlington County	7	0.02
Palos Verdes Estates, CA (city) Los Angeles County	3	0.02
Atlanta, GA (city) Fulton County	21	0.01
Syracuse, NY (city) Onondaga County	20	0.01
Alexandria, VA (independent city) Alexandria city	17	0.01
Richardson, TX (city) Dallas County	13	0.01
Miami Beach, FL (city) Miami-Dade County	12	0.01
Lawrence, KS (city) Douglas County	11	0.01
Orlando, FL (city) Orange County	10	0.01
Cambridge, MA (city) Middlesex County	9	0.01
Huntsville, AL (city) Madison County	9	0.01
Stamford, CT (city) Fairfield County	9	0.01
Champaign, IL (city) Champaign County	7	0.01
Grand Prairie, TX (city) Dallas County	7	0.01
Medford, MA (city) Middlesex County	7	0.01
Ames, IA (city) Story County	6	0.01
Berkeley, CA (city) Alameda County	6	0.01
McAllen, TX (city) Hidalgo County	6	0.01
Haverford, PA (township) Delaware County	5	0.01
Los Angeles, CA (city) Los Angeles County	59	0.00
Dallas, TX (city) Dallas County	52	0.00
Philadelphia, PA (city) Philadelphia County	26	0.00
San Francisco, CA (city) San Francisco County	23	0.00
Washington, DC (city) District of Columbia	17	0.00
Detroit, MI (city) Wayne County	15	0.00
Fort Worth, TX (city) Tarrant County	14	0.00
New York, NY (city) New York City	14	0.00
Denver, CO (city) Denver County	13	0.00
Boston, MA (city) Suffolk County	10	0.00
San Antonio, TX (city) Bexar County	9	0.00
New Orleans, LA (city) Orleans Parish	8	0.00
Newark, NJ (city) Essex County	8	0.00
Arlington, VA (cdp) Arlington County	7	0.00
Boise City, ID (city) Ada County	7	0.00
Miami, FL (city) Miami-Dade County	7	0.00
Seattle, WA (city) King County	7	0.00
Portland, OR (city) Multnomah County	5	0.00
Topeka, KS (city) Shawnee County	4	0.00

Notes: (cdp) census designated place; Refer to the Explanation of Data in the front of the book for more detailed information.

African, sub-Saharan: Zimbabwean

Top 150 Places Sorted by Number

(Based on all places, regardless of population)

Place	Number	%
Dallas, TX (city) Dallas County	222	0.02
Oronoko charter, MI (township) Berrien County	125	1.27
Charlotte, NC (city) Mecklenburg County	98	0.02
New York, NY (city) New York City	95	0.00
Columbus, OH (city) Franklin County	82	0.01
Southglenn, CO (cdp) Arapahoe County	69	0.16
Chicago, IL (city) Cook County	64	0.00
Winfield, KS (city) Cowley County	61	0.50
White Oak, MD (cdp) Montgomery County	60	0.29
Los Angeles, CA (city) Los Angeles County	58	0.00
Phoenix, AZ (city) Maricopa County	58	0.00
Seattle, WA (city) King County	56	0.01
Beaverton, OR (city) Washington County	55	0.07
Durham, NC (city) Durham County	55	0.03
Brighton, NY (town) Monroe County	49	0.14
Annandale, VA (cdp) Fairfax County	48	0.09
Berrien Springs, MI (village) Berrien County	47	2.52
Alexandria, VA (independent city) Alexandria city	45	0.04
Irving, TX (city) Dallas County	43	0.02
Litchfield, NH (town) Hillsborough County	41	0.56
Shawnee, OK (city) Pottawatomie County	39	0.14
Collierville, TN (town) Shelby County	38	0.12
Brentwood, TN (city) Williamson County	36	0.15
Hamden, CT (town) New Haven County	36	0.06
Fort Lauderdale, FL (city) Broward County	36	0.02
Indianapolis, IN (special city) Marion County	35	0.00
San Francisco, CA (city) San Francisco County	35	0.00
Coram, NY (cdp) Suffolk County	33	0.09
Gainesville, FL (city) Alachua County	33	0.03
Lansing, MI (city) Ingham County	33	0.03
Brookhaven, NY (town) Suffolk County	33	0.01
Manteca, CA (city) San Joaquin County	32	0.07
Oakland, CA (city) Alameda County	32	0.01
Springfield, MO (city) Greene County	31	0.02
Austin, TX (city) Travis County	31	0.00
Lowell, MA (city) Middlesex County	30	0.03
Nashville-Davidson, TN (special city) Davidson County	29	0.01
Sandy Springs, GA (cdp) Fulton County	28	0.03
Dublin, CA (city) Alameda County	27	0.09
Glenview, IL (village) Cook County	27	0.06
New Orleans, LA (city) Orleans Parish	27	0.01
Hempstead, NY (town) Nassau County	27	0.00
Corona, CA (city) Riverside County	25	0.02
Downingtown, PA (borough) Chester County	24	0.32
Yonkers, NY (city) Westchester County	24	0.01
Montgomery Village, MD (cdp) Montgomery County	23	0.06
Edmond, OK (city) Oklahoma County	23	0.03
Aurora, CO (city) Arapahoe County	23	0.01
Greensboro, NC (city) Guilford County	23	0.01
East Point, GA (city) Fulton County	21	0.05
Germantown, MD (cdp) Montgomery County	21	0.04
Olivette, MO (city) Saint Louis County	20	0.27
Pulaski, TN (city) Giles County	20	0.26
Selma, AL (city) Dallas County	20	0.10
Menomonee Falls, WI (village) Waukesha County	20	0.06
Freeport, NY (village) Nassau County	19	0.04
Boulder, CO (city) Boulder County	19	0.02
Lewisville, TX (city) Denton County	19	0.02
Baton Rouge, LA (city) East Baton Rouge Parish	19	0.01
Cincinnati, OH (city) Hamilton County	19	0.01
Lakewood, CO (city) Jefferson County	19	0.01
Saint Petersburg, FL (city) Pinellas County	19	0.01
Minneapolis, MN (city) Hennepin County	19	0.00
Albany, NY (city) Albany County	18	0.02
San Antonio, TX (city) Bexar County	18	0.00
South Orange, NJ (cdp) Essex County	17	0.10
Leominster, MA (city) Worcester County	17	0.04
Haverhill, MA (city) Essex County	17	0.03
Worcester, MA (city) Worcester County	17	0.01
Fayette, MO (city) Howard County	16	0.57
Cambridge, MA (city) Middlesex County	16	0.02
Ann Arbor, MI (city) Washtenaw County	16	0.01
Long Beach, CA (city) Los Angeles County	16	0.00
Philadelphia, PA (city) Philadelphia County	16	0.00
San Diego, CA (city) San Diego County	16	0.00
Forest Park, IL (village) Cook County	15	0.10
Akron, OH (city) Summit County	15	0.01
Middlebury, VT (town) Addison County	14	0.17
New Canaan, CT (town) Fairfield County	14	0.07
State College, PA (borough) Centre County	14	0.04
Bradenton, FL (city) Manatee County	14	0.03
Tustin, CA (city) Orange County	14	0.02
Pomona, CA (city) Los Angeles County	14	0.01
South Bend, IN (city) Saint Joseph County	14	0.01
Washington, DC (city) District of Columbia	14	0.00
Rush, PA (township) Schuylkill County	13	0.33
Keene, TX (city) Johnson County	13	0.27
Silver Lake, NC (cdp) New Hanover County	13	0.23
Bozeman, MT (city) Gallatin County	13	0.05
Easton, PA (city) Northampton County	13	0.05
Cleveland Heights, OH (city) Cuyahoga County	13	0.03
Marietta, GA (city) Cobb County	13	0.02
East Bradford, PA (township) Chester County	12	0.13
North Marysville, WA (cdp) Snohomish County	12	0.06
Biloxi, MS (city) Harrison County	12	0.02
Champaign, IL (city) Champaign County	12	0.02
Mount Prospect, IL (village) Cook County	12	0.02
Miami, FL (city) Miami-Dade County	12	0.00
Omaha, NE (city) Douglas County	12	0.00
Ellsworth AFB, SD (cdp) Meade County	11	0.26
Nicholasville, KY (city) Jessamine County	11	0.06
Hoboken, NJ (city) Hudson County	11	0.03
Davis, CA (city) Yolo County	11	0.02
Norwalk, CT (city) Fairfield County	11	0.01
Hunters Creek, FL (cdp) Orange County	10	0.11
Elizabethtown, PA (borough) Lancaster County	10	0.08
Cutlerville, MI (cdp) Kent County	10	0.07
Bloomingdale, FL (cdp) Hillsborough County	10	0.05
Edwardsville, IL (city) Madison County	10	0.05
Gaines, MI (township) Kent County	10	0.05
Mableton, GA (cdp) Cobb County	10	0.03
Bolingbrook, IL (village) Will County	10	0.02
Lenexa, KS (city) Johnson County	10	0.02
Rancho Santa Margarita, CA (city) Orange County	10	0.02
Boise City, ID (city) Ada County	10	0.01
Moreno Valley, CA (city) Riverside County	10	0.01
Orem, UT (city) Utah County	10	0.01
Orlando, FL (city) Orange County	10	0.01
Salt Lake City, UT (city) Salt Lake County	10	0.01
Wilmington, DE (city) New Castle County	10	0.01
Albuquerque, NM (city) Bernalillo County	10	0.00
Fort Wayne, IN (city) Allen County	10	0.00
Oklahoma City, OK (city) Oklahoma County	10	0.00
Lewes, DE (city) Sussex County	9	0.31
Tewksbury, NJ (township) Hunterdon County	9	0.16
Grinnell, IA (city) Poweshiek County	9	0.10
Saint Joseph charter, MI (township) Berrien County	9	0.09
Beltsville, MD (cdp) Prince George's County	9	0.06
Springfield, NJ (cdp) Union County	9	0.06
Marshall, TX (city) Harrison County	9	0.04
Orcutt, CA (cdp) Santa Barbara County	9	0.03
West Springfield, MA (cdp) Hampden County	9	0.03
Potomac, MD (cdp) Montgomery County	9	0.02
Aurora, IL (city) Kane County	9	0.01
Pasadena, CA (city) Los Angeles County	9	0.01
Lauderdale, MN (city) Ramsey County	8	0.34
Morrisville, NC (town) Wake County	8	0.16
Red Lion, PA (borough) York County	8	0.13
Gettysburg, PA (borough) Adams County	8	0.11
Union charter, MI (township) Isabella County	8	0.11
Takoma Park, MD (city) Montgomery County	8	0.05
Woodmere, NY (cdp) Nassau County	8	0.05
North Druid Hills, GA (cdp) De Kalb County	8	0.04
Candler-McAfee, GA (cdp) De Kalb County	8	0.03
Harrison, NY (village) Westchester County	8	0.03
Kent, OH (city) Portage County	8	0.03
Mount Pleasant, MI (city) Isabella County	8	0.03
Woodridge, IL (village) Du Page County	8	0.03
Galesburg, IL (city) Knox County	8	0.02
Mishawaka, IN (city) Saint Joseph County	8	0.02

Notes: (cdp) census designated place; Refer to the Explanation of Data in the front of the book for more detailed information.

African, sub-Saharan: Zimbabwean

Top 150 Places Sorted by Percent

(Based on all places, regardless of population)

Place	Number	%
Berrien Springs, MI (village) Berrien County	47	2.52
Layton, FL (city) Monroe County	4	1.67
Coalton, IL (village) Montgomery County	4	1.34
Oronoko charter, MI (township) Berrien County	125	1.27
Fayette, MO (city) Howard County	16	0.57
Litchfield, NH (town) Hillsborough County	41	0.56
Winfield, KS (city) Cowley County	61	0.50
Lauderdale, MN (city) Ramsey County	8	0.34
Rush, PA (township) Schuylkill County	13	0.33
Downingtown, PA (borough) Chester County	24	0.32
Lewes, DE (city) Sussex County	9	0.31
White Oak, MD (cdp) Montgomery County	60	0.29
Olivette, MO (city) Saint Louis County	20	0.27
Keene, TX (city) Johnson County	13	0.27
Pulaski, TN (city) Giles County	20	0.26
Ellsworth AFB, SD (cdp) Meade County	11	0.26
Dolan Springs, AZ (cdp) Mohave County	5	0.26
Silver Lake, NC (cdp) New Hanover County	13	0.23
Woodsboro, MD (town) Frederick County	2	0.23
Middlesex, NY (town) Yates County	3	0.22
Lexington Hills, CA (cdp) Santa Clara County	5	0.21
Jasper, GA (city) Pickens County	4	0.19
East Caln, PA (township) Chester County	5	0.18
Warren, VT (town) Washington County	3	0.18
Middlebury, VT (town) Addison County	14	0.17
Palmer Heights, PA (cdp) Northampton County	6	0.17
Diamond Ridge, AK (cdp) Kenai Peninsula Borough	3	0.17
Mancos, CO (town) Montezuma County	2	0.17
Southglenn, CO (cdp) Arapahoe County	69	0.16
Tewksbury, NJ (township) Hunterdon County	9	0.16
Morrisville, NC (town) Wake County	8	0.16
Blandford, MA (town) Hampden County	2	0.16
Brentwood, TN (city) Williamson County	36	0.15
Brighton, NY (town) Monroe County	49	0.14
Shawnee, OK (city) Pottawatomie County	39	0.14
East Bradford, PA (township) Chester County	12	0.13
Red Lion, PA (borough) York County	8	0.13
Lakeland Village, CA (cdp) Riverside County	7	0.13
Merchantville, NJ (borough) Camden County	5	0.13
Collierville, TN (town) Shelby County	38	0.12
Bethel, NC (town) Pitt County	2	0.12
Hunters Creek, FL (cdp) Orange County	10	0.11
Gettysburg, PA (borough) Adams County	8	0.11
Union charter, MI (township) Isabella County	8	0.11
Otis Orchards-East Farms, WA (cdp) Spokane County	7	0.11
Pea Ridge, WV (cdp) Cabell County	7	0.11
Chatham, NY (village) Columbia County	2	0.11
Selma, AL (city) Dallas County	20	0.10
South Orange, NJ (cdp) Essex County	17	0.10
Forest Park, IL (village) Cook County	15	0.10
Grinnell, IA (city) Poweshiek County	9	0.10
Westford, VT (town) Chittenden County	2	0.10
Annandale, VA (cdp) Fairfax County	48	0.09
Coram, NY (cdp) Suffolk County	33	0.09
Dublin, CA (city) Alameda County	27	0.09
Saint Joseph charter, MI (township) Berrien County	9	0.09
Holly Springs, MS (city) Marshall County	7	0.09
Elizabethtown, PA (borough) Lancaster County	10	0.08
Mansfield Center, MA (cdp) Bristol County	6	0.08
Berrien, MI (township) Berrien County	4	0.08
Ward, AR (city) Lonoke County	2	0.08
Waynesville, OH (village) Warren County	2	0.08
Beaverton, OR (city) Washington County	55	0.07
Manteca, CA (city) San Joaquin County	32	0.07
New Canaan, CT (town) Fairfield County	14	0.07
Cutlerville, MI (cdp) Kent County	10	0.07
Peru, IL (city) La Salle County	7	0.07
Hamden, CT (town) New Haven County	36	0.06
Glenview, IL (village) Cook County	27	0.06
Montgomery Village, MD (cdp) Montgomery County	23	0.06
Menomonee Falls, WI (village) Waukesha County	20	0.06
North Marysville, WA (cdp) Snohomish County	12	0.06
Nicholasville, KY (city) Jessamine County	11	0.06
Beltsville, MD (cdp) Prince George's County	9	0.06
Springfield, NJ (cdp) Union County	9	0.06
Beaver Falls, PA (city) Beaver County	6	0.06
Rising Sun, MD (town) Cecil County	1	0.06
East Point, GA (city) Fulton County	21	0.05
Bozeman, MT (city) Gallatin County	13	0.05
Easton, PA (city) Northampton County	13	0.05
Bloomingdale, FL (cdp) Hillsborough County	10	0.05
Edwardsville, IL (city) Madison County	10	0.05
Gaines, MI (township) Kent County	10	0.05
Takoma Park, MD (city) Montgomery County	8	0.05
Woodmere, NY (cdp) Nassau County	8	0.05
West University Place, TX (city) Harris County	7	0.05
Chatham, NY (town) Columbia County	2	0.05
Alexandria, VA (independent city) Alexandria city	45	0.04
Germantown, MD (cdp) Montgomery County	21	0.04
Freeport, NY (village) Nassau County	19	0.04
Leominster, MA (city) Worcester County	17	0.04
State College, PA (borough) Centre County	14	0.04
Marshall, TX (city) Harrison County	9	0.04
North Druid Hills, GA (cdp) De Kalb County	8	0.04
Beckley, WV (city) Raleigh County	7	0.04
Newnan, GA (city) Coweta County	6	0.04
Palmer, PA (township) Northampton County	6	0.04
Durham, NC (city) Durham County	55	0.03
Gainesville, FL (city) Alachua County	33	0.03
Lansing, MI (city) Ingham County	33	0.03
Lowell, MA (city) Middlesex County	30	0.03
Sandy Springs, GA (cdp) Fulton County	28	0.03
Edmond, OK (city) Oklahoma County	23	0.03
Haverhill, MA (city) Essex County	17	0.03
Bradenton, FL (city) Manatee County	14	0.03
Cleveland Heights, OH (city) Cuyahoga County	13	0.03
Hoboken, NJ (city) Hudson County	11	0.03
Mableton, GA (cdp) Cobb County	10	0.03
Orcutt, CA (cdp) Santa Barbara County	9	0.03
West Springfield, MA (cdp) Hampden County	9	0.03
Candler-McAfee, GA (cdp) De Kalb County	8	0.03
Harrison, NY (village) Westchester County	8	0.03
Kent, OH (city) Portage County	8	0.03
Mount Pleasant, MI (city) Isabella County	8	0.03
Woodridge, IL (village) Du Page County	8	0.03
Coronado, CA (city) San Diego County	7	0.03
Mansfield, MA (town) Bristol County	6	0.03
Roseburg, OR (city) Douglas County	6	0.03
Durango, CO (city) La Plata County	4	0.03
Hyattsville, MD (city) Prince George's County	4	0.03
Dallas, TX (city) Dallas County	222	0.02
Charlotte, NC (city) Mecklenburg County	98	0.02
Irving, TX (city) Dallas County	43	0.02
Fort Lauderdale, FL (city) Broward County	36	0.02
Springfield, MO (city) Greene County	31	0.02
Corona, CA (city) Riverside County	25	0.02
Boulder, CO (city) Boulder County	19	0.02
Lewisville, TX (city) Denton County	19	0.02
Albany, NY (city) Albany County	18	0.02
Cambridge, MA (city) Middlesex County	16	0.02
Tustin, CA (city) Orange County	14	0.02
Marietta, GA (city) Cobb County	13	0.02
Biloxi, MS (city) Harrison County	12	0.02
Champaign, IL (city) Champaign County	12	0.02
Mount Prospect, IL (village) Cook County	12	0.02
Davis, CA (city) Yolo County	11	0.02
Bolingbrook, IL (village) Will County	10	0.02
Lenexa, KS (city) Johnson County	10	0.02
Rancho Santa Margarita, CA (city) Orange County	10	0.02
Potomac, MD (cdp) Montgomery County	9	0.02
Galesburg, IL (city) Knox County	8	0.02
Mishawaka, IN (city) Saint Joseph County	8	0.02
West Hollywood, CA (city) Los Angeles County	8	0.02
Bountiful, UT (city) Davis County	7	0.02
Elmira, NY (city) Chemung County	7	0.02
Fort Lee, NJ (borough) Bergen County	7	0.02
Kirkland, WA (city) King County	7	0.02
Mankato, MN (city) Blue Earth County	7	0.02
Randallstown, MD (cdp) Baltimore County	7	0.02
Cedar Park, TX (city) Williamson County	6	0.02

Notes: (cdp) census designated place; Refer to the Explanation of Data in the front of the book for more detailed information.

African, sub-Saharan: Zimbabwean

Top 150 Places Sorted by Percent

(Based on places with populations of 10,000 or more)

Place	Number	%
Winfield, KS (city) Cowley County	61	0.50
White Oak, MD (cdp) Montgomery County	60	0.29
Southglenn, CO (cdp) Arapahoe County	69	0.16
Brentwood, TN (city) Williamson County	36	0.15
Brighton, NY (town) Monroe County	49	0.14
Shawnee, OK (city) Pottawatomie County	39	0.14
Collierville, TN (town) Shelby County	38	0.12
Selma, AL (city) Dallas County	20	0.10
South Orange, NJ (cdp) Essex County	17	0.10
Forest Park, IL (village) Cook County	15	0.10
Annandale, VA (cdp) Fairfax County	48	0.09
Coram, NY (cdp) Suffolk County	33	0.09
Dublin, CA (city) Alameda County	27	0.09
Saint Joseph charter, MI (township) Berrien County	9	0.09
Elizabethtown, PA (borough) Lancaster County	10	0.08
Beaverton, OR (city) Washington County	55	0.07
Manteca, CA (city) San Joaquin County	32	0.07
New Canaan, CT (town) Fairfield County	14	0.07
Cutlerville, MI (cdp) Kent County	10	0.07
Hamden, CT (town) New Haven County	36	0.06
Glenview, IL (village) Cook County	27	0.06
Montgomery Village, MD (cdp) Montgomery County	23	0.06
Menomonee Falls, WI (village) Waukesha County	20	0.06
North Marysville, WA (cdp) Snohomish County	12	0.06
Nicholasville, KY (city) Jessamine County	11	0.06
Beltsville, MD (cdp) Prince George's County	9	0.06
Springfield, NJ (cdp) Union County	9	0.06
East Point, GA (city) Fulton County	21	0.05
Bozeman, MT (city) Gallatin County	13	0.05
Easton, PA (city) Northampton County	13	0.05
Bloomingdale, FL (cdp) Hillsborough County	10	0.05
Edwardsville, IL (city) Madison County	10	0.05
Gaines, MI (township) Kent County	10	0.05
Takoma Park, MD (city) Montgomery County	8	0.05
Woodmere, NY (cdp) Nassau County	8	0.05
West University Place, TX (city) Harris County	7	0.05
Alexandria, VA (independent city) Alexandria city	45	0.04
Germantown, MD (cdp) Montgomery County	21	0.04
Freeport, NY (village) Nassau County	19	0.04
Leominster, MA (city) Worcester County	17	0.04
State College, PA (borough) Centre County	14	0.04
Marshall, TX (city) Harrison County	9	0.04
North Druid Hills, GA (cdp) De Kalb County	8	0.04
Beckley, WV (city) Raleigh County	7	0.04
Newnan, GA (city) Coweta County	6	0.04
Palmer, PA (township) Northampton County	6	0.04
Durham, NC (city) Durham County	55	0.03
Gainesville, FL (city) Alachua County	33	0.03
Lansing, MI (city) Ingham County	33	0.03
Lowell, MA (city) Middlesex County	30	0.03
Sandy Springs, GA (cdp) Fulton County	28	0.03
Edmond, OK (city) Oklahoma County	23	0.03
Haverhill, MA (city) Essex County	17	0.03
Bradenton, FL (city) Manatee County	14	0.03
Cleveland Heights, OH (city) Cuyahoga County	13	0.03
Hoboken, NJ (city) Hudson County	11	0.03
Mableton, GA (cdp) Cobb County	10	0.03
Orcutt, CA (cdp) Santa Barbara County	9	0.03
West Springfield, MA (cdp) Hampden County	9	0.03
Candler-McAfee, GA (cdp) De Kalb County	8	0.03
Harrison, NY (village) Westchester County	8	0.03
Kent, OH (city) Portage County	8	0.03
Mount Pleasant, MI (city) Isabella County	8	0.03
Woodridge, IL (village) Du Page County	8	0.03
Coronado, CA (city) San Diego County	7	0.03
Mansfield, MA (town) Bristol County	6	0.03
Roseburg, OR (city) Douglas County	6	0.03
Durango, CO (city) La Plata County	4	0.03
Hyattsville, MD (city) Prince George's County	4	0.03
Dallas, TX (city) Dallas County	222	0.02
Charlotte, NC (city) Mecklenburg County	98	0.02
Irving, TX (city) Dallas County	43	0.02
Fort Lauderdale, FL (city) Broward County	36	0.02
Springfield, MO (city) Greene County	31	0.02
Corona, CA (city) Riverside County	25	0.02

Place	Number	%
Boulder, CO (city) Boulder County	19	0.02
Lewisville, TX (city) Denton County	19	0.02
Albany, NY (city) Albany County	18	0.02
Cambridge, MA (city) Middlesex County	16	0.02
Tustin, CA (city) Orange County	14	0.02
Marietta, GA (city) Cobb County	13	0.02
Biloxi, MS (city) Harrison County	12	0.02
Champaign, IL (city) Champaign County	12	0.02
Mount Prospect, IL (village) Cook County	12	0.02
Davis, CA (city) Yolo County	11	0.02
Bolingbrook, IL (village) Will County	10	0.02
Lenexa, KS (city) Johnson County	10	0.02
Rancho Santa Margarita, CA (city) Orange County	10	0.02
Potomac, MD (cdp) Montgomery County	9	0.02
Galesburg, IL (city) Knox County	8	0.02
Mishawaka, IN (city) Saint Joseph County	8	0.02
West Hollywood, CA (city) Los Angeles County	8	0.02
Bountiful, UT (city) Davis County	7	0.02
Elmira, NY (city) Chemung County	7	0.02
Fort Lee, NJ (borough) Bergen County	7	0.02
Kirkland, WA (city) King County	7	0.02
Mankato, MN (city) Blue Earth County	7	0.02
Randallstown, MD (cdp) Baltimore County	7	0.02
Cedar Park, TX (city) Williamson County	6	0.02
Kankakee, IL (city) Kankakee County	6	0.02
Lake Jackson, TX (city) Brazoria County	6	0.02
Newport, RI (city) Newport County	6	0.02
Bernards, NJ (township) Somerset County	5	0.02
Jeffersonville, IN (city) Clark County	5	0.02
Pittsfield charter, MI (township) Washtenaw County	5	0.02
Columbus, OH (city) Franklin County	82	0.01
Seattle, WA (city) King County	56	0.01
Brookhaven, NY (town) Suffolk County	33	0.01
Oakland, CA (city) Alameda County	32	0.01
Nashville-Davidson, TN (special city) Davidson County	29	0.01
New Orleans, LA (city) Orleans Parish	27	0.01
Yonkers, NY (city) Westchester County	24	0.01
Aurora, CO (city) Arapahoe County	23	0.01
Greensboro, NC (city) Guilford County	23	0.01
Baton Rouge, LA (city) East Baton Rouge Parish	19	0.01
Cincinnati, OH (city) Hamilton County	19	0.01
Lakewood, CO (city) Jefferson County	19	0.01
Saint Petersburg, FL (city) Pinellas County	19	0.01
Worcester, MA (city) Worcester County	17	0.01
Ann Arbor, MI (city) Washtenaw County	16	0.01
Akron, OH (city) Summit County	15	0.01
Pomona, CA (city) Los Angeles County	14	0.01
South Bend, IN (city) Saint Joseph County	14	0.01
Norwalk, CT (city) Fairfield County	11	0.01
Boise City, ID (city) Ada County	10	0.01
Moreno Valley, CA (city) Riverside County	10	0.01
Orem, UT (city) Utah County	10	0.01
Orlando, FL (city) Orange County	10	0.01
Salt Lake City, UT (city) Salt Lake County	10	0.01
Wilmington, DE (city) New Castle County	10	0.01
Aurora, IL (city) Kane County	9	0.01
Pasadena, CA (city) Los Angeles County	9	0.01
Chattanooga, TN (city) Hamilton County	8	0.01
Columbia, MD (cdp) Howard County	8	0.01
Port Saint Lucie, FL (city) Saint Lucie County	8	0.01
Santa Monica, CA (city) Los Angeles County	8	0.01
Concord, CA (city) Contra Costa County	7	0.01
Newton, MA (city) Middlesex County	7	0.01
West Haven, CT (city) New Haven County	7	0.01
West Palm Beach, FL (city) Palm Beach County	7	0.01
Aliso Viejo, CA (cdp) Orange County	6	0.01
Bethesda, MD (cdp) Montgomery County	6	0.01
Cary, NC (town) Wake County	6	0.01
Lower Merion, PA (township) Montgomery County	6	0.01
Palo Alto, CA (city) Santa Clara County	6	0.01
Portage, MI (city) Kalamazoo County	6	0.01
Portsmouth, VA (independent city) Portsmouth city	6	0.01
Ypsilanti, MI (township) Washtenaw County	6	0.01
Ames, IA (city) Story County	5	0.01
Claremont, CA (city) Los Angeles County	5	0.01

Notes: (cdp) census designated place; Refer to the Explanation of Data in the front of the book for more detailed information.

African, sub-Saharan: Other

Top 150 Places Sorted by Number

(Based on all places, regardless of population)

Place	Number	%
New York, NY (city) New York City	6,657	0.08
Chicago, IL (city) Cook County	756	0.03
Columbus, OH (city) Franklin County	699	0.10
Philadelphia, PA (city) Philadelphia County	687	0.05
Los Angeles, CA (city) Los Angeles County	687	0.02
Washington, DC (city) District of Columbia	682	0.12
Houston, TX (city) Harris County	665	0.03
Chillum, MD (cdp) Prince George's County	627	1.84
Silver Spring, MD (cdp) Montgomery County	492	0.64
Aspen Hill, MD (cdp) Montgomery County	458	0.91
White Oak, MD (cdp) Montgomery County	447	2.14
Minneapolis, MN (city) Hennepin County	446	0.12
Alexandria, VA (independent city) Alexandria city	429	0.33
Seattle, WA (city) King County	402	0.07
Fairland, MD (cdp) Montgomery County	369	1.71
Newark, NJ (city) Essex County	337	0.12
Raleigh, NC (city) Wake County	322	0.12
Charlotte, NC (city) Mecklenburg County	300	0.06
Arlington, VA (cdp) Arlington County	294	0.16
Boston, MA (city) Suffolk County	285	0.05
Oakland, CA (city) Alameda County	283	0.07
Detroit, MI (city) Wayne County	283	0.03
Wheaton-Glenmont, MD (cdp) Montgomery County	268	0.46
Nashville-Davidson, TN (special city) Davidson County	268	0.05
Portland, OR (city) Multnomah County	265	0.05
Dallas, TX (city) Dallas County	248	0.02
Saint Paul, MN (city) Ramsey County	242	0.08
Gaithersburg, MD (city) Montgomery County	240	0.45
Takoma Park, MD (city) Montgomery County	227	1.32
San Diego, CA (city) San Diego County	221	0.02
Adelphi, MD (cdp) Prince George's County	218	1.45
Jersey City, NJ (city) Hudson County	211	0.09
Brockton, MA (city) Plymouth County	208	0.22
Omaha, NE (city) Douglas County	202	0.05
San Jose, CA (city) Santa Clara County	196	0.02
Arlington, TX (city) Tarrant County	195	0.06
Cincinnati, OH (city) Hamilton County	193	0.06
Greenbelt, MD (city) Prince George's County	189	0.88
Baltimore, MD (independent city) Baltimore city	189	0.03
Atlanta, GA (city) Fulton County	186	0.04
North Atlanta, GA (cdp) De Kalb County	178	0.46
Upper Darby, PA (township) Delaware County	176	0.22
Austin, TX (city) Travis County	172	0.03
Durham, NC (city) Durham County	168	0.09
Jacksonville, FL (special city) Duval County	167	0.02
Greensboro, NC (city) Guilford County	162	0.07
Indianapolis, IN (special city) Marion County	161	0.02
New Orleans, LA (city) Orleans Parish	152	0.03
Greenville, SC (city) Greenville County	149	0.26
Saint Louis, MO (independent city) Saint Louis city	146	0.04
Pittsburgh, PA (city) Allegheny County	143	0.04
Potomac, MD (cdp) Montgomery County	140	0.31
New Carrollton, MD (city) Prince George's County	137	1.07
San Francisco, CA (city) San Francisco County	137	0.02
Euless, TX (city) Tarrant County	134	0.29
East Orange, NJ (city) Essex County	130	0.19
Springfield, MA (city) Hampden County	128	0.08
Plano, TX (city) Collin County	126	0.06
North Bethesda, MD (cdp) Montgomery County	125	0.32
Rockville, MD (city) Montgomery County	123	0.26
Reston, VA (cdp) Fairfax County	123	0.22
Tallahassee, FL (city) Leon County	120	0.08
Memphis, TN (city) Shelby County	118	0.02
Federal Way, WA (city) King County	114	0.14
Manchester, NH (city) Hillsborough County	113	0.11
Buffalo, NY (city) Erie County	113	0.04
South Bend, IN (city) Saint Joseph County	112	0.10
Hempstead, NY (town) Nassau County	111	0.01
Worcester, MA (city) Worcester County	110	0.06
Mount Vernon, NY (city) Westchester County	109	0.16
Dayton, OH (city) Montgomery County	104	0.06
Aurora, CO (city) Arapahoe County	103	0.04
Mount Rainier, MD (city) Prince George's County	101	1.19
Athens-Clarke County, GA (special city) Clarke County	101	0.10
Colorado Springs, CO (city) El Paso County	101	0.03
South Laurel, MD (cdp) Prince George's County	100	0.48
Lockland, OH (village) Hamilton County	99	2.67
Framingham, MA (cdp) Middlesex County	99	0.15
Anaheim, CA (city) Orange County	99	0.03
Harrisonburg, VA (independent city) Harrisonburg city	98	0.24
Marietta, GA (city) Cobb County	98	0.17
Loma Linda, CA (city) San Bernardino County	94	0.51
Sandy Springs, GA (cdp) Fulton County	94	0.11
Baton Rouge, LA (city) East Baton Rouge Parish	94	0.04
Southfield, MI (city) Oakland County	93	0.12
East Providence, RI (city) Providence County	92	0.19
Annandale, VA (cdp) Fairfax County	92	0.17
Lowell, MA (city) Middlesex County	92	0.09
Madison, WI (city) Dane County	92	0.04
Irving, TX (city) Dallas County	89	0.05
Houghton, MI (city) Houghton County	87	1.24
Bowie, MD (city) Prince George's County	87	0.17
Stamford, CT (city) Fairfield County	87	0.07
Yonkers, NY (city) Westchester County	87	0.04
Tulsa, OK (city) Tulsa County	87	0.02
New Rochelle, NY (city) Westchester County	86	0.12
Lexington-Fayette, KY (special city) Fayette County	86	0.03
Hyattsville, MD (city) Prince George's County	84	0.57
SeaTac, WA (city) King County	84	0.33
Oak Park, MI (city) Oakland County	84	0.28
Springfield, VA (cdp) Fairfax County	83	0.27
Dale City, VA (cdp) Prince William County	83	0.15
Quincy, MA (city) Norfolk County	83	0.09
Oklahoma City, OK (city) Oklahoma County	83	0.02
Brooklyn Park, MN (city) Hennepin County	81	0.12
Montgomery Village, MD (cdp) Montgomery County	80	0.21
Bailey's Crossroads, VA (cdp) Fairfax County	79	0.35
Albany, NY (city) Albany County	78	0.08
Denver, CO (city) Denver County	78	0.01
Matawan, NJ (borough) Monmouth County	77	0.86
Saint Ann, MO (city) Saint Louis County	77	0.57
College Park, GA (city) Fulton County	77	0.37
Wichita, KS (city) Sedgwick County	77	0.02
West Saint Paul, MN (city) Dakota County	76	0.39
Cambridge, MA (city) Middlesex County	76	0.07
Jeffersontown, KY (city) Jefferson County	75	0.28
Ypsilanti, MI (township) Washtenaw County	75	0.15
Columbia, MO (city) Boone County	75	0.09
Baldwin, PA (borough) Allegheny County	74	0.37
Trenton, NJ (city) Mercer County	74	0.09
Syracuse, NY (city) Onondaga County	74	0.05
Chandler, AZ (city) Maricopa County	74	0.04
Tucson, AZ (city) Pima County	73	0.02
Langley Park, MD (cdp) Prince George's County	72	0.44
Richmond, VA (independent city) Richmond city	72	0.04
Garland, TX (city) Dallas County	72	0.03
Frederick, MD (city) Frederick County	71	0.13
Waltham, MA (city) Middlesex County	71	0.12
Providence, RI (city) Providence County	71	0.04
East Lansing, MI (city) Ingham County	69	0.15
Albuquerque, NM (city) Bernalillo County	68	0.02
Olney, MD (cdp) Montgomery County	66	0.21
Ontario, CA (city) San Bernardino County	66	0.04
Northfield, MN (city) Rice County	65	0.38
Louisville, KY (city) Jefferson County	65	0.03
McLean, VA (cdp) Fairfax County	64	0.16
Cary, NC (town) Wake County	64	0.07
Fort Wayne, IN (city) Allen County	64	0.03
Newton, MA (city) Middlesex County	63	0.08
Edison, NJ (cdp) Middlesex County	63	0.06
Pasadena, CA (city) Los Angeles County	63	0.05
Newport News, VA (independent city) Newport News city	63	0.03
Carrboro, NC (town) Orange County	62	0.37
Edgewater Park, NJ (township) Burlington County	61	0.78
Herndon, VA (town) Fairfax County	61	0.28
Kansas City, MO (city) Jackson County	61	0.01
Milwaukee, WI (city) Milwaukee County	61	0.01
Calverton, MD (cdp) Montgomery County	60	0.48
Ossining, NY (village) Westchester County	60	0.25
Ossining, NY (town) Westchester County	60	0.16

Notes: (cdp) census designated place; Refer to the Explanation of Data in the front of the book for more detailed information.

African, sub-Saharan: Other

Top 150 Places Sorted by Percent

(Based on all places, regardless of population)

Place	Number	%
Lockland, OH (village) Hamilton County	99	2.67
Brunswick Station, ME (cdp) Cumberland County	38	2.59
White Oak, MD (cdp) Montgomery County	447	2.14
Kensington, MD (town) Montgomery County	36	1.92
Chillum, MD (cdp) Prince George's County	627	1.84
Fairland, MD (cdp) Montgomery County	369	1.71
Princess Anne, MD (town) Somerset County	40	1.67
Adelphi, MD (cdp) Prince George's County	218	1.45
Cayuga Heights, NY (village) Tompkins County	44	1.38
Buena Vista, CA (cdp) Santa Clara County	24	1.34
Takoma Park, MD (city) Montgomery County	227	1.32
Friendship Village, MD (cdp) Montgomery County	58	1.31
Nenana, AK (city) Yukon-Koyukuk Census Area	6	1.30
Halesite, NY (cdp) Suffolk County	32	1.25
Houghton, MI (city) Houghton County	87	1.24
Mount Rainier, MD (city) Prince George's County	101	1.19
Echo Lake, WA (cdp) Snohomish County	10	1.08
New Carrollton, MD (city) Prince George's County	137	1.07
Quinby, SC (town) Florence County	8	0.92
Aspen Hill, MD (cdp) Montgomery County	458	0.91
Greenbelt, MD (city) Prince George's County	189	0.88
Matawan, NJ (borough) Monmouth County	77	0.86
Spring Garden-Terra Verde, TX (cdp) Nueces County	6	0.83
Elsah, IL (village) Jersey County	5	0.80
Edgewater Park, NJ (township) Burlington County	61	0.78
South Nyack, NY (village) Rockland County	26	0.75
Bladensburg, MD (town) Prince George's County	55	0.73
Tilghman Island, MD (cdp) Talbot County	6	0.72
Tedder, FL (cdp) Broward County	14	0.70
Menands, NY (village) Albany County	27	0.69
Eldon, IA (city) Wapello County	7	0.69
Vienna Center, OH (cdp) Trumbull County	8	0.68
Chevy Chase, MD (town) Montgomery County	18	0.66
Hampden Sydney, VA (cdp) Prince Edward County	8	0.65
Silver Spring, MD (cdp) Montgomery County	492	0.64
Lower Oxford, PA (township) Chester County	27	0.63
Oakwood, GA (city) Hall County	16	0.60
Port Allen, LA (city) West Baton Rouge Parish	31	0.59
Hyattsville, MD (city) Prince George's County	84	0.57
Saint Ann, MO (city) Saint Louis County	77	0.57
Northeast Ithaca, NY (cdp) Tompkins County	15	0.55
Forks, PA (township) Northampton County	45	0.53
Forest Glen, MD (cdp) Montgomery County	39	0.53
Laona, MN (township) Roseau County	3	0.53
Green Lane, PA (borough) Montgomery County	3	0.52
Loma Linda, CA (city) San Bernardino County	94	0.51
North Kensington, MD (cdp) Montgomery County	45	0.51
Waipio Acres, HI (cdp) Honolulu County	27	0.51
Ledgeview, WI (town) Brown County	17	0.50
Oyster Bay Cove, NY (village) Nassau County	11	0.50
Sunnyside-Tahoe City, CA (cdp) Placer County	9	0.50
North Fork Village, OH (cdp) Ross County	8	0.50
South Laurel, MD (cdp) Prince George's County	100	0.48
Calverton, MD (cdp) Montgomery County	60	0.48
Claymont, DE (cdp) New Castle County	44	0.48
Cloverly, MD (cdp) Montgomery County	38	0.48
Mansfield, PA (borough) Tioga County	16	0.48
Doraville, GA (city) De Kalb County	48	0.47
Florence, MS (town) Rankin County	11	0.47
Halfway House, PA (cdp) Montgomery County	8	0.47
Wheaton-Glenmont, MD (cdp) Montgomery County	268	0.46
North Atlanta, GA (cdp) De Kalb County	178	0.46
Gaithersburg, MD (city) Montgomery County	240	0.45
Cheverly, MD (town) Prince George's County	29	0.45
Colwyn, PA (borough) Delaware County	11	0.45
Langley Park, MD (cdp) Prince George's County	72	0.44
Paoli, PA (cdp) Chester County	24	0.44
Mount Carmel, OH (cdp) Clermont County	19	0.44
University Park, MD (town) Prince George's County	10	0.44
Huntington, VA (cdp) Fairfax County	35	0.42
Wilder, VT (cdp) Windsor County	7	0.42
Hancock, IA (city) Pottawattamie County	1	0.42
Oronoko charter, MI (township) Berrien County	40	0.41
Riverdale Park, MD (town) Prince George's County	27	0.41
Herman, WI (town) Sheboygan County	8	0.40
West Saint Paul, MN (city) Dakota County	76	0.39
Woodbury, NY (cdp) Nassau County	35	0.39
East Lansdowne, PA (borough) Delaware County	10	0.39
Northfield, MN (city) Rice County	65	0.38
Seven Corners, VA (cdp) Fairfax County	34	0.38
College Park, GA (city) Fulton County	77	0.37
Baldwin, PA (borough) Allegheny County	74	0.37
Carrboro, NC (town) Orange County	62	0.37
Burrell, PA (township) Indiana County	14	0.37
Livermore Falls, ME (town) Androscoggin County	12	0.37
Seadrift, TX (city) Calhoun County	5	0.37
Yeadon, PA (borough) Delaware County	43	0.36
Mineral Ridge, OH (cdp) Trumbull County	13	0.36
Guilford, NY (town) Chenango County	11	0.36
Veneta, OR (city) Lane County	9	0.36
Cleveland, GA (city) White County	7	0.36
Bailey's Crossroads, VA (cdp) Fairfax County	79	0.35
River Falls, WI (town) Pierce County	8	0.35
Independence, NJ (township) Warren County	19	0.34
Shallowater, TX (city) Lubbock County	7	0.34
Fletcher, VT (town) Franklin County	4	0.34
Alexandria, VA (independent city) Alexandria city	429	0.33
SeaTac, WA (city) King County	84	0.33
Crookston, MN (city) Polk County	27	0.33
Andover, NH (town) Merrimack County	7	0.33
Fairmount Heights, MD (town) Prince George's County	5	0.33
North Bethesda, MD (cdp) Montgomery County	125	0.32
Ithaca, NY (town) Tompkins County	59	0.32
Idylwood, VA (cdp) Fairfax County	51	0.32
East Riverdale, MD (cdp) Prince George's County	49	0.32
Bull Run, VA (cdp) Prince William County	37	0.32
Woodlawn, MD (cdp) Prince George's County	20	0.32
Hawaiian Ocean View, HI (cdp) Hawaii County	7	0.32
Potomac, MD (cdp) Montgomery County	140	0.31
South Orange, NJ (cdp) Essex County	53	0.31
Cashmere, WA (city) Chelan County	9	0.31
Mitchellville, MD (cdp) Prince George's County	29	0.30
Burtonsville, MD (cdp) Montgomery County	22	0.30
Bethany, WV (town) Brooke County	3	0.30
Euless, TX (city) Tarrant County	134	0.29
Westchase, FL (cdp) Hillsborough County	32	0.29
Plantation Mobile Home Park, FL (cdp) Palm Beach County	4	0.29
Oak Park, MI (city) Oakland County	84	0.28
Jeffersontown, KY (city) Jefferson County	75	0.28
Herndon, VA (town) Fairfax County	61	0.28
Clayton, MO (city) Saint Louis County	36	0.28
Falls Church, VA (independent city) Falls Church city	29	0.28
Cotati, CA (city) Sonoma County	18	0.28
Comstock Northwest, MI (cdp) Kalamazoo County	13	0.28
Forestdale, MA (cdp) Barnstable County	11	0.28
Irasburg, VT (town) Orleans County	3	0.28
Springfield, VA (cdp) Fairfax County	83	0.27
Roselle, NJ (borough) Union County	57	0.27
Sidney, OH (city) Shelby County	54	0.27
Westwood, MI (cdp) Kalamazoo County	25	0.27
Barrington, NJ (borough) Camden County	19	0.27
Conley, GA (cdp) Clayton County	17	0.27
Pebble Creek, FL (cdp) Hillsborough County	13	0.27
Allegany, NY (village) Cattaraugus County	5	0.27
Greenville, SC (city) Greenville County	149	0.26
Rockville, MD (city) Montgomery County	123	0.26
Hybla Valley, VA (cdp) Fairfax County	43	0.26
Hooksett, NH (town) Merrimack County	30	0.26
Windemere, TX (cdp) Travis County	18	0.26
Glendale, CO (city) Arapahoe County	12	0.26
Broward Estates, FL (cdp) Broward County	9	0.26
Lebanon, IL (city) Saint Clair County	9	0.26
Walnut Springs, TX (city) Bosque County	2	0.26
Ossining, NY (village) Westchester County	60	0.25
Burlington, NJ (township) Burlington County	51	0.25
Forest Park, OH (city) Hamilton County	49	0.25
North Saint Paul, MN (city) Ramsey County	30	0.25
Springdale, MD (cdp) Prince George's County	7	0.25
Avilla, IN (town) Noble County	5	0.25
Woodburn, IN (city) Allen County	4	0.25

Notes: (cdp) census designated place; Refer to the Explanation of Data in the front of the book for more detailed information.

African, sub-Saharan: Other

Top 150 Places Sorted by Percent

(Based on places with populations of 10,000 or more)

Place	Number	%
White Oak, MD (cdp) Montgomery County	447	2.14
Chillum, MD (cdp) Prince George's County	627	1.84
Fairland, MD (cdp) Montgomery County	369	1.71
Adelphi, MD (cdp) Prince George's County	218	1.45
Takoma Park, MD (city) Montgomery County	227	1.32
New Carrollton, MD (city) Prince George's County	137	1.07
Aspen Hill, MD (cdp) Montgomery County	458	0.91
Greenbelt, MD (city) Prince George's County	189	0.88
Silver Spring, MD (cdp) Montgomery County	492	0.64
Hyattsville, MD (city) Prince George's County	84	0.57
Saint Ann, MO (city) Saint Louis County	77	0.57
Loma Linda, CA (city) San Bernardino County	94	0.51
South Laurel, MD (cdp) Prince George's County	100	0.48
Calverton, MD (cdp) Montgomery County	60	0.48
Doraville, GA (city) De Kalb County	48	0.47
Wheaton-Glenmont, MD (cdp) Montgomery County	268	0.46
North Atlanta, GA (cdp) De Kalb County	178	0.46
Gaithersburg, MD (city) Montgomery County	240	0.45
Langley Park, MD (cdp) Prince George's County	72	0.44
West Saint Paul, MN (city) Dakota County	76	0.39
Northfield, MN (city) Rice County	65	0.38
College Park, GA (city) Fulton County	77	0.37
Baldwin, PA (borough) Allegheny County	74	0.37
Carrboro, NC (town) Orange County	62	0.37
Yeadon, PA (borough) Delaware County	43	0.36
Bailey's Crossroads, VA (cdp) Fairfax County	79	0.35
Alexandria, VA (independent city) Alexandria city	429	0.33
SeaTac, WA (city) King County	84	0.33
North Bethesda, MD (cdp) Montgomery County	125	0.32
Ithaca, NY (town) Tompkins County	59	0.32
Idylwood, VA (cdp) Fairfax County	51	0.32
East Riverdale, MD (cdp) Prince George's County	49	0.32
Bull Run, VA (cdp) Prince William County	37	0.32
Potomac, MD (cdp) Montgomery County	140	0.31
South Orange, NJ (cdp) Essex County	53	0.31
Euless, TX (city) Tarrant County	134	0.29
Westchase, FL (cdp) Hillsborough County	32	0.29
Oak Park, MI (city) Oakland County	84	0.28
Jeffersontown, KY (city) Jefferson County	75	0.28
Herndon, VA (town) Fairfax County	61	0.28
Clayton, MO (city) Saint Louis County	36	0.28
Falls Church, VA (independent city) Falls Church city	29	0.28
Springfield, VA (cdp) Fairfax County	83	0.27
Roselle, NJ (borough) Union County	57	0.27
Sidney, OH (city) Shelby County	54	0.27
Greenville, SC (city) Greenville County	149	0.26
Rockville, MD (city) Montgomery County	123	0.26
Hybla Valley, VA (cdp) Fairfax County	43	0.26
Hooksett, NH (town) Merrimack County	30	0.26
Ossining, NY (village) Westchester County	60	0.25
Burlington, NJ (township) Burlington County	51	0.25
Forest Park, OH (city) Hamilton County	49	0.25
North Saint Paul, MN (city) Ramsey County	30	0.25
Harrisonburg, VA (independent city) Harrisonburg city	98	0.24
Lockhart, FL (cdp) Orange County	30	0.24
Upper Providence Township, PA (cdp) Delaware County	25	0.24
Morrisville, PA (borough) Bucks County	24	0.24
New Hartford, NY (town) Oneida County	48	0.23
Troy, AL (city) Pike County	32	0.23
Mountain Park, GA (cdp) Gwinnett County	26	0.23
Brockton, MA (city) Plymouth County	208	0.22
Upper Darby, PA (township) Delaware County	176	0.22
Reston, VA (cdp) Fairfax County	123	0.22
College Park, MD (city) Prince George's County	54	0.22
Montgomery Village, MD (cdp) Montgomery County	80	0.21
Olney, MD (cdp) Montgomery County	66	0.21
Crystal, MN (city) Hennepin County	48	0.21
Mukilteo, WA (city) Snohomish County	38	0.21
Avenel, NJ (cdp) Middlesex County	37	0.21
Oshtemo, MI (township) Kalamazoo County	35	0.21
Lincolnia, VA (cdp) Fairfax County	34	0.21
Candler-McAfee, GA (cdp) De Kalb County	55	0.20
Port Chester, NY (village) Westchester County	55	0.20
Gainesville, GA (city) Hall County	50	0.20
Elkridge, MD (cdp) Howard County	44	0.20

Place	Number	%
Whitehall, OH (city) Franklin County	38	0.20
Wake Forest, NC (town) Wake County	25	0.20
Little Ferry, NJ (borough) Bergen County	22	0.20
Woodlyn, PA (cdp) Delaware County	20	0.20
East Orange, NJ (city) Essex County	130	0.19
East Providence, RI (city) Providence County	92	0.19
Lochearn, MD (cdp) Baltimore County	45	0.18
Brunswick, ME (town) Cumberland County	38	0.18
Franklin, NJ (township) Gloucester County	28	0.18
Marietta, GA (city) Cobb County	98	0.17
Annandale, VA (cdp) Fairfax County	92	0.17
Bowie, MD (city) Prince George's County	87	0.17
Coralville, IA (city) Johnson County	26	0.17
La Palma, CA (city) Orange County	26	0.17
Murphysboro, IL (city) Jackson County	23	0.17
Arlington, VA (cdp) Arlington County	294	0.16
Mount Vernon, NY (city) Westchester County	109	0.16
McLean, VA (cdp) Fairfax County	64	0.16
Ossining, NY (town) Westchester County	60	0.16
Pittsfield charter, MI (township) Washtenaw County	47	0.16
Greater Landover, MD (cdp) Prince George's County	37	0.16
Upper Allen, PA (township) Cumberland County	25	0.16
Garfield, MI (township) Grand Traverse County	21	0.16
Lake Forest Park, WA (city) King County	21	0.16
El Sobrante, CA (cdp) Contra Costa County	18	0.16
Hillsdale, NJ (borough) Bergen County	16	0.16
Framingham, MA (cdp) Middlesex County	99	0.15
Dale City, VA (cdp) Prince William County	83	0.15
Ypsilanti, MI (township) Washtenaw County	75	0.15
East Lansing, MI (city) Ingham County	69	0.15
De Kalb, IL (city) De Kalb County	58	0.15
Randolph, MA (cdp) Norfolk County	47	0.15
Corsicana, TX (city) Navarro County	36	0.15
Zion, IL (city) Lake County	34	0.15
Rolla, MO (city) Phelps County	25	0.15
Beltsville, MD (cdp) Prince George's County	23	0.15
Rose Hill, VA (cdp) Fairfax County	23	0.15
Fountain, CO (city) El Paso County	22	0.15
Riverdale, IL (village) Cook County	22	0.15
Nether Providence Township, PA (cdp) Delaware County	20	0.15
Federal Way, WA (city) King County	114	0.14
Fitchburg, MA (city) Worcester County	55	0.14
Lawndale, CA (city) Los Angeles County	43	0.14
Frankfort, KY (city) Franklin County	38	0.14
Carbondale, IL (city) Jackson County	30	0.14
Lanham-Seabrook, MD (cdp) Prince George's County	26	0.14
Adelanto, CA (city) San Bernardino County	25	0.14
Mounds View, MN (city) Ramsey County	18	0.14
Merrifield, VA (cdp) Fairfax County	16	0.14
Forest Acres, SC (city) Richland County	15	0.14
Frederick, MD (city) Frederick County	71	0.13
Rye, NY (town) Westchester County	55	0.13
Stillwater, OK (city) Payne County	51	0.13
Teaneck, NJ (cdp) Bergen County	50	0.13
Cascade-Fairwood, WA (cdp) King County	45	0.13
Cedar Hill, TX (city) Dallas County	42	0.13
Amherst Center, MA (cdp) Hampshire County	23	0.13
Dumont, NJ (borough) Bergen County	23	0.13
New Britain, PA (township) Bucks County	14	0.13
Darby, PA (borough) Delaware County	13	0.13
Washington, DC (city) District of Columbia	682	0.12
Minneapolis, MN (city) Hennepin County	446	0.12
Newark, NJ (city) Essex County	337	0.12
Raleigh, NC (city) Wake County	322	0.12
Southfield, MI (city) Oakland County	93	0.12
New Rochelle, NY (city) Westchester County	86	0.12
Brooklyn Park, MN (city) Hennepin County	81	0.12
Waltham, MA (city) Middlesex County	71	0.12
The Hammocks, FL (cdp) Miami-Dade County	57	0.12
Cypress, CA (city) Orange County	54	0.12
Allen, TX (city) Collin County	50	0.12
Monterey, CA (city) Monterey County	35	0.12
Mount Vernon, VA (cdp) Fairfax County	34	0.12
Farmers Branch, TX (city) Dallas County	33	0.12
Stoughton, MA (town) Norfolk County	33	0.12

Notes: (cdp) census designated place; Refer to the Explanation of Data in the front of the book for more detailed information.

Alaska Native tribes, specified

Top 150 Places Sorted by Number

(Based on all places, regardless of population)

Place	Number	%
Anchorage, AK (municipality) Anchorage Borough	16,246	6.24
Juneau, AK (city and borough) Juneau Borough	4,000	13.02
Fairbanks, AK (city) Fairbanks North Star Borough	2,581	8.54
Barrow, AK (city) North Slope Borough	2,477	54.07
Bethel, AK (city) Bethel Census Area	2,448	44.75
Kotzebue, AK (city) Northwest Arctic Borough	1,804	58.53
Sitka, AK (city and borough) Sitka Borough	1,642	18.59
Nome, AK (city) Nome Census Area	1,616	46.11
Ketchikan, AK (city) Ketchikan Gateway Borough	1,427	18.01
Seattle, WA (city) King County	1,426	0.25
Metlakatla, AK (cdp) Prince of Wales-Outer Ketchikan Census Area	1,265	92.00
Dillingham, AK (city) Dillingham Census Area	1,095	44.40
College, AK (cdp) Fairbanks North Star Borough	936	8.21
Hooper Bay, AK (city) Wade Hampton Census Area	906	89.35
Emmonak, AK (city) Wade Hampton Census Area	688	89.70
Mountain Village, AK (city) Wade Hampton Census Area	677	89.67
Point Hope, AK (city) North Slope Borough	650	85.87
Unalakleet, AK (city) Nome Census Area	637	85.27
Alakanuk, AK (city) Wade Hampton Census Area	628	96.32
Kipnuk, AK (cdp) Bethel Census Area	614	95.34
Savoonga, AK (city) Nome Census Area	604	93.93
Togiak, AK (city) Dillingham Census Area	597	73.79
Gambell, AK (city) Nome Census Area	593	91.37
Noorvik, AK (city) Northwest Arctic Borough	585	92.27
Kwethluk, AK (city) Bethel Census Area	576	80.79
Kotlik, AK (city) Wade Hampton Census Area	569	96.28
Kodiak, AK (city) Kodiak Island Borough	559	8.83
Kenai, AK (city) Kenai Peninsula Borough	547	7.88
Akiachak, AK (cdp) Bethel Census Area	545	93.16
Pilot Station, AK (city) Wade Hampton Census Area	528	96.00
Hoonah, AK (city) Skagway-Hoonah-Angoon Census Area	524	60.93
Toksook Bay, AK (city) Bethel Census Area	510	95.86
Shishmaref, AK (city) Nome Census Area	510	90.75
Wainwright, AK (city) North Slope Borough	493	90.29
Kasigluk, AK (cdp) Bethel Census Area	490	90.24
Fort Yukon, AK (city) Yukon-Koyukuk Census Area	486	81.68
Stebbins, AK (city) Nome Census Area	481	87.93
Tacoma, WA (city) Pierce County	468	0.24
New Stuyahok, AK (city) Dillingham Census Area	460	97.66
Saint Paul, AK (city) Aleutians West Census Area	441	82.89
Nunapitchuk, AK (city) Bethel Census Area	436	93.56
Angoon, AK (city) Skagway-Hoonah-Angoon Census Area	425	74.30
Wrangell, AK (city) Wrangell-Petersburg Census Area	425	18.41
Galena, AK (city) Yukon-Koyukuk Census Area	418	61.93
Kake, AK (city) Wrangell-Petersburg Census Area	416	58.59
Noatak, AK (cdp) Northwest Arctic Borough	408	95.33
Saint Mary's, AK (city) Wade Hampton Census Area	399	79.80
Klawock, AK (city) Prince of Wales-Outer Ketchikan Census Area	392	45.90
Portland, OR (city) Multnomah County	391	0.07
Chefornak, AK (city) Bethel Census Area	380	96.45
Nuiqsut, AK (city) North Slope Borough	380	87.76
Napaskiak, AK (city) Bethel Census Area	373	95.64
Buckland, AK (city) Northwest Arctic Borough	370	91.13
King Cove, AK (city) Aleutians East Borough	367	46.34
Tuluksak, AK (cdp) Bethel Census Area	361	84.35
Kiana, AK (city) Northwest Arctic Borough	353	90.98
Knik-Fairview, AK (cdp) Matanuska-Susitna Borough	349	4.95
Tuntutuliak, AK (cdp) Bethel Census Area	348	94.05
Seward, AK (city) Kenai Peninsula Borough	348	12.30
Kivalina, AK (city) Northwest Arctic Borough	344	91.25
Sand Point, AK (city) Aleutians East Borough	335	35.19
Craig, AK (city) Prince of Wales-Outer Ketchikan Census Area	320	22.91
Yakutat, AK (cdp) Yakutat City and Borough	317	46.62
Saint Michael, AK (city) Nome Census Area	315	85.60
Nulato, AK (city) Yukon-Koyukuk Census Area	314	93.45
Marshall, AK (city) Wade Hampton Census Area	311	89.11
Hydaburg, AK (city) Prince of Wales-Outer Ketchikan Census Area	309	80.89
Newtok, AK (cdp) Bethel Census Area	308	95.95
Petersburg, AK (city) Wrangell-Petersburg Census Area	308	9.55
Akiak, AK (city) Bethel Census Area	300	97.09
Napakiak, AK (city) Bethel Census Area	298	84.42
Tununak, AK (cdp) Bethel Census Area	295	90.77
Saxman, AK (city) Ketchikan Gateway Borough	292	67.75
Aniak, AK (city) Bethel Census Area	292	51.05
Palmer, AK (city) Matanuska-Susitna Borough	286	6.31
Chevak, AK (city) Wade Hampton Census Area	283	36.99
Cordova, AK (city) Valdez-Cordova Census Area	282	11.49
Elim, AK (city) Nome Census Area	278	88.82
Everett, WA (city) Snohomish County	278	0.30
Lakes, AK (cdp) Matanuska-Susitna Borough	276	4.12
Valdez, AK (city) Valdez-Cordova Census Area	265	6.57
Huslia, AK (city) Yukon-Koyukuk Census Area	264	90.10
Wasilla, AK (city) Matanuska-Susitna Borough	264	4.83
Haines, AK (city) Haines Borough	257	14.19
Nikiski, AK (cdp) Kenai Peninsula Borough	257	5.94
Kwigillingok, AK (cdp) Bethel Census Area	256	75.74
Kalifornsky, AK (cdp) Kenai Peninsula Borough	255	4.36
Russian Mission, AK (city) Wade Hampton Census Area	251	84.80
Tanana, AK (city) Yukon-Koyukuk Census Area	248	80.52
Brevig Mission, AK (city) Nome Census Area	247	89.49
Unalaska, AK (city) Aleutians West Census Area	246	5.74
Selawik, AK (city) Northwest Arctic Borough	240	31.09
New York, NY (city) New York City	237	0.00
Naknek, AK (cdp) Bristol Bay Borough	233	34.37
Shungnak, AK (city) Northwest Arctic Borough	232	90.63
Koyuk, AK (city) Nome Census Area	232	78.11
Minto, AK (cdp) Yukon-Koyukuk Census Area	228	88.37
Kaktovik, AK (city) North Slope Borough	226	77.13
Atmautluak, AK (cdp) Bethel Census Area	225	76.53
Tanaina, AK (cdp) Matanuska-Susitna Borough	225	4.51
Los Angeles, CA (city) Los Angeles County	223	0.01
Teller, AK (city) Nome Census Area	218	81.34
Phoenix, AZ (city) Maricopa County	211	0.02
Point Lay, AK (cdp) North Slope Borough	209	84.62
Atqasuk, AK (city) North Slope Borough	208	91.23
Mekoryuk, AK (city) Bethel Census Area	205	97.62
Ouzinkie, AK (city) Kodiak Island Borough	204	90.67
Manokotak, AK (city) Dillingham Census Area	202	50.63
Old Harbor, AK (city) Kodiak Island Borough	199	83.97
Kaltag, AK (city) Yukon-Koyukuk Census Area	198	86.09
McGrath, AK (city) Yukon-Koyukuk Census Area	198	49.38
Ambler, AK (city) Northwest Arctic Borough	197	63.75
Goodnews Bay, AK (city) Bethel Census Area	193	83.91
Bellingham, WA (city) Whatcom County	189	0.28
Tok, AK (cdp) Southeast Fairbanks Census Area	188	13.50
Shoreline, WA (city) King County	187	0.35
Nondalton, AK (city) Lake and Peninsula Borough	185	83.71
Aleknagik, AK (city) Dillingham Census Area	182	82.35
Shaktoolik, AK (city) Nome Census Area	182	79.13
Meadow Lakes, AK (cdp) Matanuska-Susitna Borough	182	3.78
Venetie, AK (cdp) Yukon-Koyukuk Census Area	181	89.60
Kent, WA (city) King County	175	0.22
San Diego, CA (city) San Diego County	173	0.01
Nightmute, AK (city) Bethel Census Area	172	82.69
Tyonek, AK (cdp) Kenai Peninsula Borough	171	88.60
Holy Cross, AK (city) Yukon-Koyukuk Census Area	171	75.33
Edmonds, WA (city) Snohomish County	166	0.42
White Mountain, AK (city) Nome Census Area	164	80.79
Sutton-Alpine, AK (cdp) Matanuska-Susitna Borough	162	15.00
Bear Creek, AK (cdp) Kenai Peninsula Borough	158	9.04
Copper Center, AK (cdp) Valdez-Cordova Census Area	156	43.09
Vancouver, WA (city) Clark County	156	0.11
Federal Way, WA (city) King County	155	0.19
Nanwalek, AK (cdp) Kenai Peninsula Borough	152	85.88
Koliganek, AK (cdp) Dillingham Census Area	152	83.52
Port Lions, AK (city) Kodiak Island Borough	151	58.98
Ruby, AK (city) Yukon-Koyukuk Census Area	150	79.79
Newhalen, AK (city) Lake and Peninsula Borough	147	91.88
Grayling, AK (city) Yukon-Koyukuk Census Area	145	74.74
Kongiganak, AK (cdp) Bethel Census Area	142	39.55
Wales, AK (city) Nome Census Area	136	89.47
Soldotna, AK (city) Kenai Peninsula Borough	136	3.62
Saint George, AK (city) Aleutians West Census Area	132	86.84
Big Lake, AK (cdp) Matanuska-Susitna Borough	132	5.01
Arctic Village, AK (cdp) Yukon-Koyukuk Census Area	131	86.18
Golovin, AK (city) Nome Census Area	129	89.58
Sterling, AK (cdp) Kenai Peninsula Borough	129	2.74
Deering, AK (city) Northwest Arctic Borough	128	94.12
Salem, OR (city) Marion County	127	0.09
Salamatof, AK (cdp) Kenai Peninsula Borough	126	13.21

Notes: (cdp) census designated place; Refer to the Explanation of Data in the front of the book for more detailed information.

Alaska Native tribes, specified

Top 150 Places Sorted by Percent

(Based on all places, regardless of population)

Place	Number	%
Levelock, AK (cdp) Lake and Peninsula Borough	120	98.36
Oscarville, AK (cdp) Bethel Census Area	60	98.36
New Stuyahok, AK (city) Dillingham Census Area	460	97.66
Mekoryuk, AK (city) Bethel Census Area	205	97.62
Perryville, AK (cdp) Lake and Peninsula Borough	104	97.20
Akiak, AK (city) Bethel Census Area	300	97.09
Chefornak, AK (city) Bethel Census Area	380	96.45
Birch Creek, AK (cdp) Yukon-Koyukuk Census Area	27	96.43
Alakanuk, AK (city) Wade Hampton Census Area	628	96.32
Karluk, AK (cdp) Kodiak Island Borough	26	96.30
Kotlik, AK (city) Wade Hampton Census Area	569	96.28
Pilot Station, AK (city) Wade Hampton Census Area	528	96.00
Newtok, AK (cdp) Bethel Census Area	308	95.95
Toksook Bay, AK (city) Bethel Census Area	510	95.86
Napaskiak, AK (city) Bethel Census Area	373	95.64
Kipnuk, AK (cdp) Bethel Census Area	614	95.34
Noatak, AK (cdp) Northwest Arctic Borough	408	95.33
Chalkyitsik, AK (cdp) Yukon-Koyukuk Census Area	79	95.18
Platinum, AK (city) Bethel Census Area	39	95.12
Northway Village, AK (cdp) Southeast Fairbanks Census Area	101	94.39
Alatna, AK (cdp) Yukon-Koyukuk Census Area	33	94.29
Deering, AK (city) Northwest Arctic Borough	128	94.12
Tuntutuliak, AK (cdp) Bethel Census Area	348	94.05
Savoonga, AK (city) Nome Census Area	604	93.93
Ekwok, AK (city) Dillingham Census Area	122	93.85
Nunapitchuk, AK (city) Bethel Census Area	436	93.56
Nulato, AK (city) Yukon-Koyukuk Census Area	314	93.45
Akiachak, AK (cdp) Bethel Census Area	545	93.16
Tetlin, AK (cdp) Southeast Fairbanks Census Area	109	93.16
Akhiok, AK (city) Kodiak Island Borough	74	92.50
Noorvik, AK (city) Northwest Arctic Borough	585	92.27
Shageluk, AK (city) Yukon-Koyukuk Census Area	119	92.25
Metlakatla, AK (cdp) Prince of Wales-Outer Ketchikan Census Area	1,265	92.00
Stevens Village, AK (cdp) Yukon-Koyukuk Census Area	80	91.95
Newhalen, AK (city) Lake and Peninsula Borough	147	91.88
Beaver, AK (cdp) Yukon-Koyukuk Census Area	77	91.67
Gambell, AK (city) Nome Census Area	593	91.37
Kivalina, AK (city) Northwest Arctic Borough	344	91.25
Atqasuk, AK (city) North Slope Borough	208	91.23
Buckland, AK (city) Northwest Arctic Borough	370	91.13
Koyukuk, AK (city) Yukon-Koyukuk Census Area	92	91.09
Kiana, AK (city) Northwest Arctic Borough	353	90.98
Ivanof Bay, AK (cdp) Lake and Peninsula Borough	20	90.91
Tununak, AK (cdp) Bethel Census Area	295	90.77
Shishmaref, AK (city) Nome Census Area	510	90.75
Allakaket, AK (city) Yukon-Koyukuk Census Area	88	90.72
Ouzinkie, AK (city) Kodiak Island Borough	204	90.67
Shungnak, AK (city) Northwest Arctic Borough	232	90.63
Wainwright, AK (city) North Slope Borough	493	90.29
Kasigluk, AK (cdp) Bethel Census Area	490	90.24
Huslia, AK (city) Yukon-Koyukuk Census Area	264	90.10
Emmonak, AK (city) Wade Hampton Census Area	688	89.70
Mountain Village, AK (city) Wade Hampton Census Area	677	89.67
Venetie, AK (cdp) Yukon-Koyukuk Census Area	181	89.60
Golovin, AK (city) Nome Census Area	129	89.58
Brevig Mission, AK (city) Nome Census Area	247	89.49
Wales, AK (city) Nome Census Area	136	89.47
Hooper Bay, AK (city) Wade Hampton Census Area	906	89.35
Marshall, AK (city) Wade Hampton Census Area	311	89.11
Elim, AK (city) Nome Census Area	278	88.82
Tyonek, AK (cdp) Kenai Peninsula Borough	171	88.60
Minto, AK (cdp) Yukon-Koyukuk Census Area	228	88.37
Atka, AK (city) Aleutians West Census Area	81	88.04
Clark's Point, AK (city) Dillingham Census Area	66	88.00
Stebbins, AK (city) Nome Census Area	481	87.93
Nuiqsut, AK (city) North Slope Borough	380	87.76
Saint George, AK (city) Aleutians West Census Area	132	86.84
Arctic Village, AK (cdp) Yukon-Koyukuk Census Area	131	86.18
Kaltag, AK (city) Yukon-Koyukuk Census Area	198	86.09
Tatitlek, AK (cdp) Valdez-Cordova Census Area	92	85.98
Nanwalek, AK (cdp) Kenai Peninsula Borough	152	85.88
Point Hope, AK (city) North Slope Borough	650	85.87
Saint Michael, AK (city) Nome Census Area	315	85.60
Twin Hills, AK (cdp) Dillingham Census Area	59	85.51
Unalakleet, AK (city) Nome Census Area	637	85.27
Russian Mission, AK (city) Wade Hampton Census Area	251	84.80
Point Lay, AK (cdp) North Slope Borough	209	84.62
Chignik Lagoon, AK (cdp) Lake and Peninsula Borough	87	84.47
Napakiak, AK (city) Bethel Census Area	298	84.42
Tuluksak, AK (cdp) Bethel Census Area	361	84.35
Old Harbor, AK (city) Kodiak Island Borough	199	83.97
Goodnews Bay, AK (city) Bethel Census Area	193	83.91
Nondalton, AK (city) Lake and Peninsula Borough	185	83.71
Koliganek, AK (cdp) Dillingham Census Area	152	83.52
New Allakaket, AK (cdp) Yukon-Koyukuk Census Area	30	83.33
Igiugig, AK (cdp) Lake and Peninsula Borough	44	83.02
Saint Paul, AK (city) Aleutians West Census Area	441	82.89
Tanacross, AK (cdp) Southeast Fairbanks Census Area	116	82.86
Klukwan, AK (cdp) Skagway-Hoonah-Angoon Census Area	115	82.73
Nightmute, AK (city) Bethel Census Area	172	82.69
South Naknek, AK (cdp) Bristol Bay Borough	113	82.48
Aleknagik, AK (city) Dillingham Census Area	182	82.35
Fort Yukon, AK (city) Yukon-Koyukuk Census Area	486	81.68
Chignik Lake, AK (cdp) Lake and Peninsula Borough	118	81.38
Teller, AK (city) Nome Census Area	218	81.34
Hydaburg, AK (city) Prince of Wales-Outer Ketchikan Census Area	309	80.89
Kwethluk, AK (city) Bethel Census Area	576	80.79
White Mountain, AK (city) Nome Census Area	164	80.79
Tanana, AK (city) Yukon-Koyukuk Census Area	248	80.52
Circle, AK (cdp) Yukon-Koyukuk Census Area	80	80.00
Prudhoe Bay, AK (cdp) North Slope Borough	4	80.00
Kobuk, AK (city) Northwest Arctic Borough	87	79.82
Saint Mary's, AK (city) Wade Hampton Census Area	399	79.80
Ruby, AK (city) Yukon-Koyukuk Census Area	150	79.79
Nelson Lagoon, AK (cdp) Aleutians East Borough	66	79.52
Shaktoolik, AK (city) Nome Census Area	182	79.13
Northway, AK (cdp) Southeast Fairbanks Census Area	75	78.95
Pitkas Point, AK (cdp) Wade Hampton Census Area	98	78.40
Koyuk, AK (city) Nome Census Area	232	78.11
Kaktovik, AK (city) North Slope Borough	226	77.13
Pilot Point, AK (city) Lake and Peninsula Borough	77	77.00
Chenega, AK (cdp) Valdez-Cordova Census Area	66	76.74
Atmautluak, AK (cdp) Bethel Census Area	225	76.53
Dot Lake Village, AK (cdp) Southeast Fairbanks Census Area	29	76.32
Kwigillingok, AK (cdp) Bethel Census Area	256	75.74
Holy Cross, AK (city) Yukon-Koyukuk Census Area	171	75.33
Grayling, AK (city) Yukon-Koyukuk Census Area	145	74.74
Angoon, AK (city) Skagway-Hoonah-Angoon Census Area	425	74.30
Larsen Bay, AK (city) Kodiak Island Borough	85	73.91
Togiak, AK (city) Dillingham Census Area	597	73.79
Anvik, AK (city) Yukon-Koyukuk Census Area	75	72.12
Egegik, AK (city) Lake and Peninsula Borough	83	71.55
Mentasta Lake, AK (cdp) Valdez-Cordova Census Area	101	71.13
Nikolski, AK (cdp) Aleutians West Census Area	27	69.23
Chuathbaluk, AK (city) Bethel Census Area	81	68.07
Port Heiden, AK (city) Lake and Peninsula Borough	81	68.07
Saxman, AK (city) Ketchikan Gateway Borough	292	67.75
Gulkana, AK (cdp) Valdez-Cordova Census Area	59	67.05
False Pass, AK (city) Aleutians East Borough	42	65.63
Pedro Bay, AK (cdp) Lake and Peninsula Borough	32	64.00
Ambler, AK (city) Northwest Arctic Borough	197	63.75
Galena, AK (city) Yukon-Koyukuk Census Area	418	61.93
Hoonah, AK (city) Skagway-Hoonah-Angoon Census Area	524	60.93
Chistochina, AK (cdp) Valdez-Cordova Census Area	55	59.14
Nikolai, AK (city) Yukon-Koyukuk Census Area	59	59.00
Port Lions, AK (city) Kodiak Island Borough	151	58.98
Kake, AK (city) Wrangell-Petersburg Census Area	416	58.59
Kotzebue, AK (city) Northwest Arctic Borough	1,804	58.53
Northway Junction, AK (cdp) Southeast Fairbanks Census Area	42	58.33
Portage Creek, AK (cdp) Dillingham Census Area	21	58.33
Chignik, AK (city) Lake and Peninsula Borough	44	55.70
Barrow, AK (city) North Slope Borough	2,477	54.07
Evansville, AK (cdp) Yukon-Koyukuk Census Area	15	53.57
Rampart, AK (cdp) Yukon-Koyukuk Census Area	24	53.33
Diomede, AK (city) Nome Census Area	75	51.37
Aniak, AK (city) Bethel Census Area	292	51.05
Manokotak, AK (city) Dillingham Census Area	202	50.63
Port Graham, AK (cdp) Kenai Peninsula Borough	86	50.29
McGrath, AK (city) Yukon-Koyukuk Census Area	198	49.38
Yakutat, AK (cdp) Yakutat City and Borough	317	46.62

Notes: (cdp) census designated place; Refer to the Explanation of Data in the front of the book for more detailed information.

Alaska Native tribes, specified

Top 150 Places Sorted by Percent

(Based on places with populations of 10,000 or more)

Place	Number	%
Juneau, AK (city and borough) Juneau Borough	4,000	13.02
Fairbanks, AK (city) Fairbanks North Star Borough	2,581	8.54
College, AK (cdp) Fairbanks North Star Borough	936	8.21
Anchorage, AK (municipality) Anchorage Borough	16,246	6.24
Anacortes, WA (city) Skagit County	68	0.47
SeaTac, WA (city) King County	114	0.45
Mountlake Terrace, WA (city) Snohomish County	89	0.44
Edmonds, WA (city) Snohomish County	166	0.42
Durango, CO (city) La Plata County	59	0.42
Port Angeles, WA (city) Clallam County	75	0.41
White Center, WA (cdp) King County	81	0.39
Lynnwood, WA (city) Snohomish County	125	0.37
Shoreline, WA (city) King County	187	0.35
Picnic Point-North Lynnwood, WA (cdp) Snohomish County	80	0.35
Riverton-Boulevard Park, WA (cdp) King County	38	0.34
Alderwood Manor, WA (cdp) Snohomish County	49	0.32
Marysville, WA (city) Snohomish County	79	0.31
Everett, WA (city) Snohomish County	278	0.30
Burien, WA (city) King County	96	0.30
Lakeland North, WA (cdp) King County	46	0.30
Kingsgate, WA (cdp) King County	37	0.30
Des Moines, WA (city) King County	84	0.29
Bellingham, WA (city) Whatcom County	189	0.28
Auburn, WA (city) King County	114	0.28
Mukilteo, WA (city) Snohomish County	48	0.27
North Marysville, WA (cdp) Snohomish County	55	0.26
Tukwila, WA (city) King County	44	0.26
Seattle, WA (city) King County	1,426	0.25
Tacoma, WA (city) Pierce County	468	0.24
Paine Field-Lake Stickney, WA (cdp) Snohomish County	59	0.24
Ellensburg, WA (city) Kittitas County	37	0.24
Tumwater, WA (city) Thurston County	31	0.24
Kent, WA (city) King County	175	0.22
Renton, WA (city) King County	111	0.22
Mount Vernon, WA (city) Skagit County	58	0.22
Martha Lake, WA (cdp) Snohomish County	28	0.22
Lea Hill, WA (cdp) King County	24	0.22
Aberdeen, WA (city) Grays Harbor County	33	0.20
Covington, WA (city) King County	28	0.20
Federal Way, WA (city) King County	155	0.19
Bremerton, WA (city) Kitsap County	70	0.19
Bothell, WA (city) King County	58	0.19
West Lake Stevens, WA (cdp) Snohomish County	34	0.19
Clearlake, CA (city) Lake County	25	0.19
Lake Forest Park, WA (city) King County	25	0.19
Seattle Hill-Silver Firs, WA (cdp) Snohomish County	65	0.18
Puyallup, WA (city) Pierce County	59	0.18
Lacey, WA (city) Thurston County	55	0.18
North Creek, WA (cdp) Snohomish County	46	0.18
Coos Bay, OR (city) Coos County	28	0.18
Dallas, OR (city) Polk County	23	0.18
Lakewood, WA (city) Pierce County	97	0.17
Olympia, WA (city) Thurston County	71	0.17
Bryn Mawr-Skyway, WA (cdp) King County	24	0.17
South Hill, WA (cdp) Pierce County	51	0.16
Four Corners, OR (cdp) Marion County	22	0.16
East Hill-Meridian, WA (cdp) King County	44	0.15
Oak Harbor, WA (city) Island County	29	0.15
Elk Plain, WA (cdp) Pierce County	24	0.15
McKinleyville, CA (cdp) Humboldt County	20	0.15
Kelso, WA (city) Cowlitz County	18	0.15
Enumclaw, WA (city) King County	17	0.15
Cascade-Fairwood, WA (cdp) King County	47	0.14
Parkland, WA (cdp) Pierce County	33	0.14
Spanaway, WA (cdp) Pierce County	31	0.14
Camano, WA (cdp) Island County	19	0.14
East Renton Highlands, WA (cdp) King County	19	0.14
Monroe, WA (city) Snohomish County	19	0.14
Troutdale, OR (city) Multnomah County	19	0.14
Lakeland South, WA (cdp) King County	16	0.14
Saint Helens, OR (city) Columbia County	14	0.14
Oregon City, OR (city) Clackamas County	34	0.13
Orchards, WA (cdp) Clark County	24	0.13
Salmon Creek, WA (cdp) Clark County	22	0.13
Keizer, OR (city) Marion County	39	0.12
Lewiston, ID (city) Nez Perce County	36	0.12
McMinnville, OR (city) Yamhill County	31	0.12
Pullman, WA (city) Whitman County	30	0.12
Cottage Lake, WA (cdp) King County	28	0.12
Inglewood-Finn Hill, WA (cdp) King County	28	0.12
Centralia, WA (city) Lewis County	18	0.12
Maple Valley, WA (city) King County	17	0.12
West Valley, WA (cdp) Yakima County	13	0.12
Vancouver, WA (city) Clark County	156	0.11
Sammamish, WA (city) King County	39	0.11
Silverdale, WA (cdp) Kitsap County	18	0.11
Moses Lake, WA (city) Grant County	16	0.11
Red Bluff, CA (city) Tehama County	15	0.11
Redmond, OR (city) Deschutes County	15	0.11
Arlington, WA (city) Snohomish County	13	0.11
Kirkland, WA (city) King County	45	0.10
Bainbridge Island, WA (city) Kitsap County	20	0.10
Sun Valley, NV (cdp) Washoe County	19	0.10
Kihei, HI (cdp) Maui County	16	0.10
Oatfield, OR (cdp) Clackamas County	15	0.10
Prairie Ridge, WA (cdp) Pierce County	12	0.10
Dishman, WA (cdp) Spokane County	10	0.10
Salem, OR (city) Marion County	127	0.09
Springfield, OR (city) Lane County	47	0.09
Redmond, WA (city) King County	39	0.09
Longview, WA (city) Cowlitz County	30	0.09
Altamont, OR (cdp) Klamath County	18	0.09
Fort Lewis, WA (cdp) Pierce County	18	0.09
Pendleton, OR (city) Umatilla County	15	0.09
Vashon, WA (cdp) King County	9	0.09
Eugene, OR (city) Lane County	112	0.08
Gresham, OR (city) Multnomah County	70	0.08
Tigard, OR (city) Washington County	33	0.08
University Place, WA (city) Pierce County	25	0.08
Walla Walla, WA (city) Walla Walla County	25	0.08
Eureka, CA (city) Humboldt County	21	0.08
Kahului, HI (cdp) Maui County	16	0.08
Ashland, OR (city) Jackson County	15	0.08
Hayesville, OR (cdp) Marion County	15	0.08
Schofield Barracks, HI (cdp) Honolulu County	11	0.08
Canby, OR (city) Clackamas County	10	0.08
Five Corners, WA (cdp) Clark County	10	0.08
Oak Grove, OR (cdp) Clackamas County	10	0.08
Issaquah, WA (city) King County	9	0.08
Mill Creek, WA (city) Snohomish County	9	0.08
Portland, OR (city) Multnomah County	391	0.07
Bellevue, WA (city) King County	72	0.07
Hillsboro, OR (city) Washington County	50	0.07
Yakima, WA (city) Yakima County	47	0.07
Kennewick, WA (city) Benton County	40	0.07
Corvallis, OR (city) Benton County	34	0.07
Hilo, HI (cdp) Hawaii County	28	0.07
Farmington, NM (city) San Juan County	25	0.07
Fort Hood, TX (cdp) Coryell County	25	0.07
Imperial Beach, CA (city) San Diego County	20	0.07
Mililani Town, HI (cdp) Honolulu County	20	0.07
Opportunity, WA (cdp) Spokane County	17	0.07
Barstow, CA (city) San Bernardino County	14	0.07
Fort Campbell North, KY (cdp) Christian County	10	0.07
City of The Dalles, OR (city) Wasco County	9	0.07
Lebanon, OR (city) Linn County	9	0.07
Oroville, CA (city) Butte County	9	0.07
Evanston, WY (city) Uinta County	8	0.07
Grand Terrace, CA (city) San Bernardino County	8	0.07
Lincoln, CA (city) Placer County	8	0.07
Spokane, WA (city) Spokane County	121	0.06
Lawrence, KS (city) Douglas County	49	0.06
Alameda, CA (city) Alameda County	41	0.06
Chico, CA (city) Butte County	33	0.06
Bend, OR (city) Deschutes County	31	0.06
Springdale, AR (city) Washington County	29	0.06
Richland, WA (city) Benton County	24	0.06
Mercer Island, WA (city) King County	14	0.06
Gardner, MA (city) Worcester County	13	0.06
Norwood, OH (city) Hamilton County	13	0.06

Notes: (cdp) census designated place; Refer to the Explanation of Data in the front of the book for more detailed information.

Alaska Native: Alaska Athabascan

Top 150 Places Sorted by Number

(Based on all places, regardless of population)

Place	Number	%
Anchorage, AK (municipality) Anchorage Borough	3,186	1.22
Fairbanks, AK (city) Fairbanks North Star Borough	1,741	5.76
College, AK (cdp) Fairbanks North Star Borough	500	4.39
Fort Yukon, AK (city) Yukon-Koyukuk Census Area	471	79.16
Galena, AK (city) Yukon-Koyukuk Census Area	389	57.63
Nulato, AK (city) Yukon-Koyukuk Census Area	313	93.15
Kenai, AK (city) Kenai Peninsula Borough	279	4.02
Huslia, AK (city) Yukon-Koyukuk Census Area	262	89.42
Tanana, AK (city) Yukon-Koyukuk Census Area	244	79.22
Minto, AK (cdp) Yukon-Koyukuk Census Area	225	87.21
Kaltag, AK (city) Yukon-Koyukuk Census Area	194	84.35
Nondalton, AK (city) Lake and Peninsula Borough	181	81.90
Venetie, AK (cdp) Yukon-Koyukuk Census Area	177	87.62
Juneau, AK (city and borough) Juneau Borough	170	0.55
Tyonek, AK (cdp) Kenai Peninsula Borough	163	84.46
Tok, AK (cdp) Southeast Fairbanks Census Area	163	11.70
Holy Cross, AK (city) Yukon-Koyukuk Census Area	160	70.48
Copper Center, AK (cdp) Valdez-Cordova Census Area	149	41.16
Ruby, AK (city) Yukon-Koyukuk Census Area	147	78.19
McGrath, AK (city) Yukon-Koyukuk Census Area	146	36.41
Grayling, AK (city) Yukon-Koyukuk Census Area	145	74.74
Nikiski, AK (cdp) Kenai Peninsula Borough	134	3.10
Arctic Village, AK (cdp) Yukon-Koyukuk Census Area	127	83.55
Shageluk, AK (city) Yukon-Koyukuk Census Area	118	91.47
Kalifornsky, AK (cdp) Kenai Peninsula Borough	118	2.02
Tanacross, AK (cdp) Southeast Fairbanks Census Area	116	82.86
Tetlin, AK (cdp) Southeast Fairbanks Census Area	109	93.16
Nenana, AK (city) Yukon-Koyukuk Census Area	105	26.12
Northway Village, AK (cdp) Southeast Fairbanks Census Area	101	94.39
Koyukuk, AK (city) Yukon-Koyukuk Census Area	92	91.09
Mentasta Lake, AK (cdp) Valdez-Cordova Census Area	92	64.79
Knik-Fairview, AK (cdp) Matanuska-Susitna Borough	87	1.23
Allakaket, AK (city) Yukon-Koyukuk Census Area	85	87.63
Bethel, AK (city) Bethel Census Area	83	1.52
Circle, AK (cdp) Yukon-Koyukuk Census Area	80	80.00
Seattle, WA (city) King County	80	0.01
Chalkyitsik, AK (cdp) Yukon-Koyukuk Census Area	79	95.18
Beaver, AK (cdp) Yukon-Koyukuk Census Area	77	91.67
Portland, OR (city) Multnomah County	76	0.01
Northway, AK (cdp) Southeast Fairbanks Census Area	75	78.95
Ninilchik, AK (cdp) Kenai Peninsula Borough	75	9.72
Anvik, AK (city) Yukon-Koyukuk Census Area	73	70.19
Palmer, AK (city) Matanuska-Susitna Borough	68	1.50
Sitka, AK (city and borough) Sitka Borough	66	0.75
Gulkana, AK (cdp) Valdez-Cordova Census Area	58	65.91
Tanaina, AK (cdp) Matanuska-Susitna Borough	58	1.16
Seward, AK (city) Kenai Peninsula Borough	57	2.01
Nikolai, AK (city) Yukon-Koyukuk Census Area	52	52.00
Wasilla, AK (city) Matanuska-Susitna Borough	52	0.95
Chistochina, AK (cdp) Valdez-Cordova Census Area	50	53.76
Lakes, AK (cdp) Matanuska-Susitna Borough	50	0.75
New York, NY (city) New York City	49	0.00
Valdez, AK (city) Valdez-Cordova Census Area	45	1.11
Los Angeles, CA (city) Los Angeles County	44	0.00
Sterling, AK (cdp) Kenai Peninsula Borough	43	0.91
Tacoma, WA (city) Pierce County	43	0.02
Northway Junction, AK (cdp) Southeast Fairbanks Census Area	42	58.33
Sutton-Alpine, AK (cdp) Matanuska-Susitna Borough	42	3.89
Soldotna, AK (city) Kenai Peninsula Borough	41	1.09
Meadow Lakes, AK (cdp) Matanuska-Susitna Borough	39	0.81
Albuquerque, NM (city) Bernalillo County	38	0.01
Ester, AK (cdp) Fairbanks North Star Borough	37	2.20
Tazlina, AK (cdp) Valdez-Cordova Census Area	36	24.16
Cantwell, AK (cdp) Yukon-Koyukuk Census Area	36	16.22
Salamatof, AK (cdp) Kenai Peninsula Borough	36	3.77
Big Lake, AK (cdp) Matanuska-Susitna Borough	36	1.37
Edmonds, WA (city) Snohomish County	36	0.09
Bear Creek, AK (cdp) Kenai Peninsula Borough	35	2.00
Chitina, AK (cdp) Valdez-Cordova Census Area	34	27.64
Barrow, AK (city) North Slope Borough	34	0.74
Phoenix, AZ (city) Maricopa County	34	0.00
Copperville, AK (cdp) Valdez-Cordova Census Area	33	18.44
Seldovia Village, AK (cdp) Kenai Peninsula Borough	31	21.53
New Allakaket, AK (cdp) Yukon-Koyukuk Census Area	30	83.33
Eagle Village, AK (cdp) Southeast Fairbanks Census Area	30	44.12
Ridgeway, AK (cdp) Kenai Peninsula Borough	30	1.55
Alatna, AK (cdp) Yukon-Koyukuk Census Area	29	82.86
Kenny Lake, AK (cdp) Valdez-Cordova Census Area	28	6.83
Salem, OR (city) Marion County	28	0.02
Birch Creek, AK (cdp) Yukon-Koyukuk Census Area	27	96.43
Ketchikan, AK (city) Ketchikan Gateway Borough	27	0.34
Dot Lake Village, AK (cdp) Southeast Fairbanks Census Area	26	68.42
Anchor Point, AK (cdp) Kenai Peninsula Borough	26	1.41
Rampart, AK (cdp) Yukon-Koyukuk Census Area	24	53.33
Pedro Bay, AK (cdp) Lake and Peninsula Borough	24	48.00
North Pole, AK (city) Fairbanks North Star Borough	24	1.53
Everett, WA (city) Snohomish County	24	0.03
Reno, NV (city) Washoe County	24	0.01
Glennallen, AK (cdp) Valdez-Cordova Census Area	23	4.15
Butte, AK (cdp) Matanuska-Susitna Borough	23	0.90
Homer, AK (city) Kenai Peninsula Borough	23	0.58
Aniak, AK (city) Bethel Census Area	22	3.85
Kotzebue, AK (city) Northwest Arctic Borough	22	0.71
Takotna, AK (cdp) Yukon-Koyukuk Census Area	21	42.00
Kodiak, AK (city) Kodiak Island Borough	21	0.33
Dillingham, AK (city) Dillingham Census Area	20	0.81
Gateway, AK (cdp) Matanuska-Susitna Borough	20	0.68
Nome, AK (city) Nome Census Area	20	0.57
Minneapolis, MN (city) Hennepin County	20	0.01
Houston, AK (city) Matanuska-Susitna Borough	18	1.50
Spokane, WA (city) Spokane County	18	0.01
Gresham, OR (city) Multnomah County	17	0.02
Tucson, AZ (city) Pima County	17	0.00
Healy Lake, AK (cdp) Southeast Fairbanks Census Area	16	43.24
Iliamna, AK (cdp) Lake and Peninsula Borough	16	15.69
Chickaloon, AK (cdp) Matanuska-Susitna Borough	16	7.51
Gakona, AK (cdp) Valdez-Cordova Census Area	16	7.44
Bellingham, WA (city) Whatcom County	16	0.02
Kent, WA (city) King County	16	0.02
Evansville, AK (cdp) Yukon-Koyukuk Census Area	15	53.57
Seldovia, AK (city) Kenai Peninsula Borough	15	5.24
Fox, AK (cdp) Fairbanks North Star Borough	15	5.00
Haines, AK (city) Haines Borough	15	0.83
Las Vegas, NV (city) Clark County	15	0.00
Happy Valley, AK (cdp) Kenai Peninsula Borough	14	2.86
Knik River, AK (cdp) Matanuska-Susitna Borough	14	2.41
Y, AK (cdp) Matanuska-Susitna Borough	14	1.46
SeaTac, WA (city) King County	14	0.05
Vancouver, WA (city) Clark County	14	0.01
Willow Creek, AK (cdp) Valdez-Cordova Census Area	13	6.47
Two Rivers, AK (cdp) Fairbanks North Star Borough	13	2.70
Naknek, AK (cdp) Bristol Bay Borough	13	1.92
Lacey, WA (city) Thurston County	13	0.04
Lewiston, ID (city) Nez Perce County	13	0.04
Federal Way, WA (city) King County	13	0.02
Honolulu, HI (cdp) Honolulu County	13	0.00
Pleasant Valley, AK (cdp) Fairbanks North Star Borough	12	1.93
Cohoe, AK (cdp) Kenai Peninsula Borough	12	1.03
Auburn, WA (city) King County	12	0.03
Oklahoma City, OK (city) Oklahoma County	12	0.00
Wichita, KS (city) Sedgwick County	12	0.00
Hughes, AK (city) Yukon-Koyukuk Census Area	11	14.10
Picnic Point-North Lynnwood, WA (cdp) Snohomish County	11	0.05
Lynnwood, WA (city) Snohomish County	11	0.03
Springfield, OR (city) Lane County	11	0.02
San Diego, CA (city) San Diego County	11	0.00
Kokhanok, AK (cdp) Lake and Peninsula Borough	10	5.75
Adak, AK (cdp) Aleutians West Census Area	10	3.16
Kasilof, AK (cdp) Kenai Peninsula Borough	10	2.12
Angoon, AK (city) Skagway-Hoonah-Angoon Census Area	10	1.75
Delta Junction, AK (city) Southeast Fairbanks Census Area	10	1.19
Healy, AK (cdp) Yukon-Koyukuk Census Area	10	1.00
Diamond Ridge, AK (cdp) Kenai Peninsula Borough	10	0.55
Unalaska, AK (city) Aleutians West Census Area	10	0.23
Dover, NH (city) Strafford County	10	0.04
Des Moines, WA (city) King County	10	0.03
Fort Hood, TX (cdp) Coryell County	10	0.03
Olympia, WA (city) Thurston County	10	0.02
Santa Clarita, CA (city) Los Angeles County	10	0.01
Columbus, OH (city) Franklin County	10	0.00

Notes: (cdp) census designated place; Refer to the Explanation of Data in the front of the book for more detailed information.

Alaska Native: Alaska Athabascan

Top 150 Places Sorted by Percent

(Based on all places, regardless of population)

Place	Number	%
Birch Creek, AK (cdp) Yukon-Koyukuk Census Area	27	96.43
Chalkyitsik, AK (cdp) Yukon-Koyukuk Census Area	79	95.18
Northway Village, AK (cdp) Southeast Fairbanks Census Area	101	94.39
Tetlin, AK (cdp) Southeast Fairbanks Census Area	109	93.16
Nulato, AK (city) Yukon-Koyukuk Census Area	313	93.15
Beaver, AK (cdp) Yukon-Koyukuk Census Area	77	91.67
Shageluk, AK (city) Yukon-Koyukuk Census Area	118	91.47
Koyukuk, AK (city) Yukon-Koyukuk Census Area	92	91.09
Huslia, AK (city) Yukon-Koyukuk Census Area	262	89.42
Allakaket, AK (city) Yukon-Koyukuk Census Area	85	87.63
Venetie, AK (cdp) Yukon-Koyukuk Census Area	177	87.62
Minto, AK (cdp) Yukon-Koyukuk Census Area	225	87.21
Tyonek, AK (cdp) Kenai Peninsula Borough	163	84.46
Kaltag, AK (city) Yukon-Koyukuk Census Area	194	84.35
Arctic Village, AK (cdp) Yukon-Koyukuk Census Area	127	83.55
New Allakaket, AK (cdp) Yukon-Koyukuk Census Area	30	83.33
Tanacross, AK (cdp) Southeast Fairbanks Census Area	116	82.86
Alatna, AK (cdp) Yukon-Koyukuk Census Area	29	82.86
Nondalton, AK (city) Lake and Peninsula Borough	181	81.90
Circle, AK (cdp) Yukon-Koyukuk Census Area	80	80.00
Tanana, AK (city) Yukon-Koyukuk Census Area	244	79.22
Fort Yukon, AK (city) Yukon-Koyukuk Census Area	471	79.16
Northway, AK (cdp) Southeast Fairbanks Census Area	75	78.95
Ruby, AK (city) Yukon-Koyukuk Census Area	147	78.19
Grayling, AK (city) Yukon-Koyukuk Census Area	145	74.74
Holy Cross, AK (city) Yukon-Koyukuk Census Area	160	70.48
Anvik, AK (city) Yukon-Koyukuk Census Area	73	70.19
Dot Lake Village, AK (cdp) Southeast Fairbanks Census Area	26	68.42
Gulkana, AK (cdp) Valdez-Cordova Census Area	58	65.91
Mentasta Lake, AK (cdp) Valdez-Cordova Census Area	92	64.79
Northway Junction, AK (cdp) Southeast Fairbanks Census Area	42	58.33
Galena, AK (city) Yukon-Koyukuk Census Area	389	57.63
Chistochina, AK (cdp) Valdez-Cordova Census Area	50	53.76
Evansville, AK (cdp) Yukon-Koyukuk Census Area	15	53.57
Rampart, AK (cdp) Yukon-Koyukuk Census Area	24	53.33
Nikolai, AK (city) Yukon-Koyukuk Census Area	52	52.00
Pedro Bay, AK (cdp) Lake and Peninsula Borough	24	48.00
Eagle Village, AK (cdp) Southeast Fairbanks Census Area	30	44.12
Healy Lake, AK (cdp) Southeast Fairbanks Census Area	16	43.24
Takotna, AK (cdp) Yukon-Koyukuk Census Area	21	42.00
Copper Center, AK (cdp) Valdez-Cordova Census Area	149	41.16
McGrath, AK (city) Yukon-Koyukuk Census Area	146	36.41
Chitina, AK (cdp) Valdez-Cordova Census Area	34	27.64
Nenana, AK (city) Yukon-Koyukuk Census Area	105	26.12
Tazlina, AK (cdp) Valdez-Cordova Census Area	36	24.16
Four Mile Road, AK (cdp) Yukon-Koyukuk Census Area	9	23.68
Seldovia Village, AK (cdp) Kenai Peninsula Borough	31	21.53
Copperville, AK (cdp) Valdez-Cordova Census Area	33	18.44
Cantwell, AK (cdp) Yukon-Koyukuk Census Area	36	16.22
Iliamna, AK (cdp) Lake and Peninsula Borough	16	15.69
Hughes, AK (city) Yukon-Koyukuk Census Area	11	14.10
Bettles, AK (city) Yukon-Koyukuk Census Area	6	13.95
Pope-Vannoy Landing, AK (cdp) Lake and Peninsula Borough	1	12.50
Tok, AK (cdp) Southeast Fairbanks Census Area	163	11.70
Tolsona, AK (cdp) Valdez-Cordova Census Area	3	11.11
Ninilchik, AK (cdp) Kenai Peninsula Borough	75	9.72
Chickaloon, AK (cdp) Matanuska-Susitna Borough	16	7.51
Gakona, AK (cdp) Valdez-Cordova Census Area	16	7.44
Kenny Lake, AK (cdp) Valdez-Cordova Census Area	28	6.83
Willow Creek, AK (cdp) Valdez-Cordova Census Area	13	6.47
Mendeltna, AK (cdp) Valdez-Cordova Census Area	4	6.35
Fairbanks, AK (city) Fairbanks North Star Borough	1,741	5.76
Kokhanok, AK (cdp) Lake and Peninsula Borough	10	5.75
Stevens Village, AK (cdp) Yukon-Koyukuk Census Area	5	5.75
Seldovia, AK (city) Kenai Peninsula Borough	15	5.24
Fox, AK (cdp) Fairbanks North Star Borough	15	5.00
Port Alsworth, AK (cdp) Lake and Peninsula Borough	5	4.81
False Pass, AK (city) Aleutians East Borough	3	4.69
College, AK (cdp) Fairbanks North Star Borough	500	4.39
Tonsina, AK (cdp) Valdez-Cordova Census Area	4	4.35
Red Devil, AK (cdp) Bethel Census Area	2	4.17
Glennallen, AK (cdp) Valdez-Cordova Census Area	23	4.15
Slana, AK (cdp) Valdez-Cordova Census Area	5	4.03
Kenai, AK (city) Kenai Peninsula Borough	279	4.02
Saint George, AK (city) Aleutians West Census Area	6	3.95
Sutton-Alpine, AK (cdp) Matanuska-Susitna Borough	42	3.89
Aniak, AK (city) Bethel Census Area	22	3.85
Silver Springs, AK (cdp) Valdez-Cordova Census Area	5	3.85
Salamatof, AK (cdp) Kenai Peninsula Borough	36	3.77
Central, AK (cdp) Yukon-Koyukuk Census Area	5	3.73
Livengood, AK (cdp) Yukon-Koyukuk Census Area	1	3.45
Cold Bay, AK (city) Aleutians East Borough	3	3.41
Lake Louise, AK (cdp) Matanuska-Susitna Borough	3	3.41
Lower Kalskag, AK (city) Bethel Census Area	9	3.37
Whittier, AK (city) Valdez-Cordova Census Area	6	3.30
Adak, AK (cdp) Aleutians West Census Area	10	3.16
Newhalen, AK (city) Lake and Peninsula Borough	5	3.13
Lake Minchumina, AK (cdp) Yukon-Koyukuk Census Area	1	3.13
Nikiski, AK (cdp) Kenai Peninsula Borough	134	3.10
Ekwok, AK (city) Dillingham Census Area	4	3.08
Happy Valley, AK (cdp) Kenai Peninsula Borough	14	2.86
Nanwalek, AK (cdp) Kenai Peninsula Borough	5	2.82
Nelchina, AK (cdp) Valdez-Cordova Census Area	2	2.82
Two Rivers, AK (cdp) Fairbanks North Star Borough	13	2.70
Susitna, AK (cdp) Matanuska-Susitna Borough	1	2.70
Lutak, AK (cdp) Haines Borough	1	2.56
Nikolski, AK (cdp) Aleutians West Census Area	1	2.56
Point Lay, AK (cdp) North Slope Borough	6	2.43
Knik River, AK (cdp) Matanuska-Susitna Borough	14	2.41
Blaine, WI (town) Burnett County	5	2.23
Ouzinkie, AK (city) Kodiak Island Borough	5	2.22
Deering, AK (city) Northwest Arctic Borough	3	2.21
Ester, AK (cdp) Fairbanks North Star Borough	37	2.20
Crooked Creek, AK (cdp) Bethel Census Area	3	2.19
Anderson, AK (city) Yukon-Koyukuk Census Area	8	2.18
Eek, AK (city) Bethel Census Area	6	2.14
Kasilof, AK (cdp) Kenai Peninsula Borough	10	2.12
Kalifornsky, AK (cdp) Kenai Peninsula Borough	118	2.02
Seward, AK (city) Kenai Peninsula Borough	57	2.01
Bear Creek, AK (cdp) Kenai Peninsula Borough	35	2.00
Pilot Point, AK (city) Lake and Peninsula Borough	2	2.00
Pleasant Valley, AK (cdp) Fairbanks North Star Borough	12	1.93
Naknek, AK (cdp) Bristol Bay Borough	13	1.92
Angoon, AK (city) Skagway-Hoonah-Angoon Census Area	10	1.75
Port Graham, AK (cdp) Kenai Peninsula Borough	3	1.75
Egegik, AK (city) Lake and Peninsula Borough	2	1.72
Port Heiden, AK (city) Lake and Peninsula Borough	2	1.68
Ridgeway, AK (cdp) Kenai Peninsula Borough	30	1.55
Eagle, AK (city) Southeast Fairbanks Census Area	2	1.55
North Pole, AK (city) Fairbanks North Star Borough	24	1.53
Bethel, AK (city) Bethel Census Area	83	1.52
Palmer, AK (city) Matanuska-Susitna Borough	68	1.50
Houston, AK (city) Matanuska-Susitna Borough	18	1.50
Y, AK (cdp) Matanuska-Susitna Borough	14	1.46
Anchor Point, AK (cdp) Kenai Peninsula Borough	26	1.41
Saint Mary's, AK (city) Wade Hampton Census Area	7	1.40
Kachemak, AK (city) Kenai Peninsula Borough	6	1.39
Big Lake, AK (cdp) Matanuska-Susitna Borough	36	1.37
Branson, CO (town) Las Animas County	1	1.30
Quinhagak, AK (city) Bethel Census Area	7	1.26
Knik-Fairview, AK (cdp) Matanuska-Susitna Borough	87	1.23
Anchorage, AK (municipality) Anchorage Borough	3,186	1.22
Pleasant Dale, NE (village) Seward County	3	1.22
Delta Junction, AK (city) Southeast Fairbanks Census Area	10	1.19
Talkeetna, AK (cdp) Matanuska-Susitna Borough	9	1.17
Tanaina, AK (cdp) Matanuska-Susitna Borough	58	1.16
Chenega, AK (cdp) Valdez-Cordova Census Area	1	1.16
Valdez, AK (city) Valdez-Cordova Census Area	45	1.11
Soldotna, AK (city) Kenai Peninsula Borough	41	1.09
Unalakleet, AK (city) Nome Census Area	8	1.07
Anaktuvuk Pass, AK (city) North Slope Borough	3	1.06
Cohoe, AK (cdp) Kenai Peninsula Borough	12	1.03
Yakutat, AK (cdp) Yakutat City and Borough	7	1.03
Kaktovik, AK (city) North Slope Borough	3	1.02
Healy, AK (cdp) Yukon-Koyukuk Census Area	10	1.00
Wasilla, AK (city) Matanuska-Susitna Borough	52	0.95
Mahaska, KS (city) Washington County	1	0.93
Perryville, AK (cdp) Lake and Peninsula Borough	1	0.93
Kobuk, AK (city) Northwest Arctic Borough	1	0.92
Sterling, AK (cdp) Kenai Peninsula Borough	43	0.91

Notes: (cdp) census designated place; Refer to the Explanation of Data in the front of the book for more detailed information.

Alaska Native: Alaska Athabascan

Top 150 Places Sorted by Percent

(Based on places with populations of 10,000 or more)

Place	Number	%
Fairbanks, AK (city) Fairbanks North Star Borough	1,741	5.76
College, AK (cdp) Fairbanks North Star Borough	500	4.39
Anchorage, AK (municipality) Anchorage Borough	3,186	1.22
Juneau, AK (city and borough) Juneau Borough	170	0.55
Edmonds, WA (city) Snohomish County	36	0.09
Durango, CO (city) La Plata County	9	0.06
SeaTac, WA (city) King County	14	0.05
Picnic Point-North Lynnwood, WA (cdp) Snohomish County	11	0.05
Elk Plain, WA (cdp) Pierce County	8	0.05
Ellensburg, WA (city) Kittitas County	8	0.05
Lakeland North, WA (cdp) King County	7	0.05
Lacey, WA (city) Thurston County	13	0.04
Lewiston, ID (city) Nez Perce County	13	0.04
Dover, NH (city) Strafford County	10	0.04
Oatfield, OR (cdp) Clackamas County	6	0.04
Salmon Creek, WA (cdp) Clark County	6	0.04
Union Hill-Novelty Hill, WA (cdp) King County	5	0.04
Everett, WA (city) Snohomish County	24	0.03
Auburn, WA (city) King County	12	0.03
Lynnwood, WA (city) Snohomish County	11	0.03
Des Moines, WA (city) King County	10	0.03
Fort Hood, TX (cdp) Coryell County	10	0.03
Imperial Beach, CA (city) San Diego County	9	0.03
Pasco, WA (city) Franklin County	9	0.03
Seattle Hill-Silver Firs, WA (cdp) Snohomish County	9	0.03
Bothell, WA (city) King County	8	0.03
Burien, WA (city) King County	8	0.03
Marysville, WA (city) Snohomish County	7	0.03
Paine Field-Lake Stickney, WA (cdp) Snohomish County	7	0.03
Pampa, TX (city) Gray County	6	0.03
Harker Heights, TX (city) Bell County	5	0.03
Mukilteo, WA (city) Snohomish County	5	0.03
Sun Valley, NV (cdp) Washoe County	5	0.03
Tanque Verde, AZ (cdp) Pima County	5	0.03
Wyckoff, NJ (cdp) Bergen County	5	0.03
Lake Forest Park, WA (city) King County	4	0.03
San Anselmo, CA (town) Marin County	4	0.03
Troutdale, OR (city) Multnomah County	4	0.03
Tacoma, WA (city) Pierce County	43	0.02
Salem, OR (city) Marion County	28	0.02
Gresham, OR (city) Multnomah County	17	0.02
Bellingham, WA (city) Whatcom County	16	0.02
Kent, WA (city) King County	16	0.02
Federal Way, WA (city) King County	13	0.02
Springfield, OR (city) Lane County	11	0.02
Olympia, WA (city) Thurston County	10	0.02
Chico, CA (city) Butte County	9	0.02
Farmington, NM (city) San Juan County	9	0.02
Lakewood, WA (city) Pierce County	9	0.02
Rio Rancho, NM (city) Sandoval County	9	0.02
South Valley, NM (cdp) Bernalillo County	8	0.02
Belleville, IL (city) Saint Clair County	7	0.02
Hilo, HI (cdp) Hawaii County	7	0.02
Bremerton, WA (city) Kitsap County	6	0.02
Panama City, FL (city) Bay County	6	0.02
Gallup, NM (city) McKinley County	5	0.02
White Center, WA (cdp) King County	5	0.02
Bay Point, CA (cdp) Contra Costa County	4	0.02
Bedford, NH (town) Hillsborough County	4	0.02
Mount Vernon, WA (city) Skagit County	4	0.02
Mountlake Terrace, WA (city) Snohomish County	4	0.02
North Creek, WA (cdp) Snohomish County	4	0.02
Parkland, WA (cdp) Pierce County	4	0.02
Port Angeles, WA (city) Clallam County	4	0.02
Pullman, WA (city) Whitman County	4	0.02
Spanaway, WA (cdp) Pierce County	4	0.02
Tooele, UT (city) Tooele County	4	0.02
West Lake Stevens, WA (cdp) Snohomish County	4	0.02
Woodburn, OR (city) Marion County	4	0.02
Abington, MA (cdp) Plymouth County	3	0.02
Anacortes, WA (city) Skagit County	3	0.02
Bloomfield, CT (town) Hartford County	3	0.02
Centralia, WA (city) Lewis County	3	0.02
Chambersburg, PA (borough) Franklin County	3	0.02
Cudahy, WI (city) Milwaukee County	3	0.02
Dallas, OR (city) Polk County	3	0.02
East Hampton, CT (town) Middlesex County	3	0.02
East Renton Highlands, WA (cdp) King County	3	0.02
Gainesville, TX (city) Cooke County	3	0.02
Green Valley, MD (cdp) Frederick County	3	0.02
Hayesville, OR (cdp) Marion County	3	0.02
Marshfield, WI (city) Wood County	3	0.02
Mount Pleasant, TX (city) Titus County	3	0.02
North Valley Stream, NY (cdp) Nassau County	3	0.02
Orchards, WA (cdp) Clark County	3	0.02
Robinson Township, PA (cdp) Allegheny County	3	0.02
Southbridge, MA (town) Worcester County	3	0.02
Tukwila, WA (city) King County	3	0.02
West Columbia, SC (city) Lexington County	3	0.02
Baraboo, WI (city) Sauk County	2	0.02
Bonita, CA (cdp) San Diego County	2	0.02
Camas, WA (city) Clark County	2	0.02
Converse, TX (city) Bexar County	2	0.02
Dishman, WA (cdp) Spokane County	2	0.02
Fort Knox, KY (cdp) Hardin County	2	0.02
Fort Stewart, GA (cdp) Liberty County	2	0.02
Lakeland South, WA (cdp) King County	2	0.02
Lea Hill, WA (cdp) King County	2	0.02
Oak Grove, OR (cdp) Clackamas County	2	0.02
Red Bluff, CA (city) Tehama County	2	0.02
Riverdale, GA (city) Clayton County	2	0.02
Riverton-Boulevard Park, WA (cdp) King County	2	0.02
Saint Helens, OR (city) Columbia County	2	0.02
Siloam Springs, AR (city) Benton County	2	0.02
Stanford, CA (cdp) Santa Clara County	2	0.02
Town and Country, MO (city) Saint Louis County	2	0.02
Tumwater, WA (city) Thurston County	2	0.02
Valley Falls, RI (cdp) Providence County	2	0.02
Williston, ND (city) Williams County	2	0.02
Woodward, OK (city) Woodward County	2	0.02
Seattle, WA (city) King County	80	0.01
Portland, OR (city) Multnomah County	76	0.01
Albuquerque, NM (city) Bernalillo County	38	0.01
Reno, NV (city) Washoe County	24	0.01
Minneapolis, MN (city) Hennepin County	20	0.01
Spokane, WA (city) Spokane County	18	0.01
Vancouver, WA (city) Clark County	14	0.01
Santa Clarita, CA (city) Los Angeles County	10	0.01
Chula Vista, CA (city) San Diego County	9	0.01
Hillsboro, OR (city) Washington County	9	0.01
Yakima, WA (city) Yakima County	9	0.01
Battle Creek, MI (city) Calhoun County	8	0.01
Berkeley, CA (city) Alameda County	8	0.01
Eugene, OR (city) Lane County	8	0.01
Missoula, MT (city) Missoula County	8	0.01
Springfield, MO (city) Greene County	8	0.01
Bellevue, WA (city) King County	7	0.01
Fort Collins, CO (city) Larimer County	7	0.01
Bristol, PA (township) Bucks County	6	0.01
Denton, TX (city) Denton County	6	0.01
Hemet, CA (city) Riverside County	6	0.01
Lawrence, KS (city) Douglas County	6	0.01
Levittown, PA (cdp) Bucks County	6	0.01
Renton, WA (city) King County	6	0.01
Spring Valley, NV (cdp) Clark County	6	0.01
Tracy, CA (city) San Joaquin County	6	0.01
Arden-Arcade, CA (cdp) Sacramento County	5	0.01
Billings, MT (city) Yellowstone County	5	0.01
Cascade-Fairwood, WA (cdp) King County	5	0.01
Eau Claire, WI (city) Eau Claire County	5	0.01
Jackson, MI (city) Jackson County	5	0.01
Moore, OK (city) Cleveland County	5	0.01
Rapid City, SD (city) Pennington County	5	0.01
Redding, CA (city) Shasta County	5	0.01
Redmond, WA (city) King County	5	0.01
Shoreline, WA (city) King County	5	0.01
Tigard, OR (city) Washington County	5	0.01
Alexandria, LA (city) Rapides Parish	4	0.01
Aloha, OR (cdp) Washington County	4	0.01
Bozeman, MT (city) Gallatin County	4	0.01

Notes: (cdp) census designated place; Refer to the Explanation of Data in the front of the book for more detailed information.

Alaska Native: Aleut

Top 150 Places Sorted by Number

(Based on all places, regardless of population)

Place	Number	%
Anchorage, AK (municipality) Anchorage Borough	3,397	1.31
Kodiak, AK (city) Kodiak Island Borough	434	6.85
Saint Paul, AK (city) Aleutians West Census Area	426	80.08
King Cove, AK (city) Aleutians East Borough	361	45.58
Sand Point, AK (city) Aleutians East Borough	329	34.56
Seattle, WA (city) King County	269	0.05
Cordova, AK (city) Valdez-Cordova Census Area	237	9.66
Unalaska, AK (city) Aleutians West Census Area	202	4.72
Juneau, AK (city and borough) Juneau Borough	201	0.65
Old Harbor, AK (city) Kodiak Island Borough	191	80.59
Ouzinkie, AK (city) Kodiak Island Borough	189	84.00
Dillingham, AK (city) Dillingham Census Area	155	6.29
Port Lions, AK (city) Kodiak Island Borough	149	58.20
Nanwalek, AK (cdp) Kenai Peninsula Borough	132	74.58
Valdez, AK (city) Valdez-Cordova Census Area	127	3.15
Saint George, AK (city) Aleutians West Census Area	125	82.24
Chignik Lake, AK (cdp) Lake and Peninsula Borough	114	78.62
South Naknek, AK (cdp) Bristol Bay Borough	112	81.75
Kenai, AK (city) Kenai Peninsula Borough	107	1.54
Perryville, AK (cdp) Lake and Peninsula Borough	99	92.52
Naknek, AK (cdp) Bristol Bay Borough	94	13.86
Knik-Fairview, AK (cdp) Matanuska-Susitna Borough	90	1.28
Tatitlek, AK (cdp) Valdez-Cordova Census Area	89	83.18
Chignik Lagoon, AK (cdp) Lake and Peninsula Borough	84	81.55
Larsen Bay, AK (city) Kodiak Island Borough	84	73.04
Port Graham, AK (cdp) Kenai Peninsula Borough	83	48.54
Tacoma, WA (city) Pierce County	82	0.04
Atka, AK (city) Aleutians West Census Area	79	85.87
Egegik, AK (city) Lake and Peninsula Borough	79	68.10
Adak, AK (cdp) Aleutians West Census Area	79	25.00
Lakes, AK (cdp) Matanuska-Susitna Borough	79	1.18
Pilot Point, AK (city) Lake and Peninsula Borough	75	75.00
Akhiok, AK (city) Kodiak Island Borough	74	92.50
Port Heiden, AK (city) Lake and Peninsula Borough	72	60.50
Portland, OR (city) Multnomah County	69	0.01
Seward, AK (city) Kenai Peninsula Borough	68	2.40
Nelson Lagoon, AK (cdp) Aleutians East Borough	66	79.52
Levelock, AK (cdp) Lake and Peninsula Borough	65	53.28
Sitka, AK (city and borough) Sitka Borough	63	0.71
Fairbanks, AK (city) Fairbanks North Star Borough	61	0.20
Chenega, AK (cdp) Valdez-Cordova Census Area	59	68.60
King Salmon, AK (cdp) Bristol Bay Borough	59	13.35
Bellingham, WA (city) Whatcom County	56	0.08
Akutan, AK (city) Aleutians East Borough	55	7.71
Wasilla, AK (city) Matanuska-Susitna Borough	53	0.97
Vancouver, WA (city) Clark County	52	0.04
San Diego, CA (city) San Diego County	52	0.00
Meadow Lakes, AK (cdp) Matanuska-Susitna Borough	50	1.04
Tanaina, AK (cdp) Matanuska-Susitna Borough	48	0.96
Edmonds, WA (city) Snohomish County	48	0.12
Bear Creek, AK (cdp) Kenai Peninsula Borough	46	2.63
Palmer, AK (city) Matanuska-Susitna Borough	44	0.97
Ketchikan, AK (city) Ketchikan Gateway Borough	44	0.56
Everett, WA (city) Snohomish County	44	0.05
Los Angeles, CA (city) Los Angeles County	41	0.00
Chignik, AK (city) Lake and Peninsula Borough	40	50.63
Soldotna, AK (city) Kenai Peninsula Borough	40	1.06
Kalifornsky, AK (cdp) Kenai Peninsula Borough	39	0.67
Igiugig, AK (cdp) Lake and Peninsula Borough	38	71.70
Nikiski, AK (cdp) Kenai Peninsula Borough	38	0.88
Phoenix, AZ (city) Maricopa County	38	0.00
College, AK (cdp) Fairbanks North Star Borough	37	0.32
Wrangell, AK (city) Wrangell-Petersburg Census Area	35	1.52
Sterling, AK (cdp) Kenai Peninsula Borough	35	0.74
Shoreline, WA (city) King County	33	0.06
False Pass, AK (city) Aleutians East Borough	32	50.00
Homer, AK (city) Kenai Peninsula Borough	32	0.81
Eugene, OR (city) Lane County	32	0.02
Womens Bay, AK (cdp) Kodiak Island Borough	29	4.20
Sacramento, CA (city) Sacramento County	29	0.01
Spokane, WA (city) Spokane County	29	0.01
San Jose, CA (city) Santa Clara County	29	0.00
Big Lake, AK (cdp) Matanuska-Susitna Borough	28	1.06
Anacortes, WA (city) Skagit County	27	0.19
Marysville, WA (city) Snohomish County	27	0.11
Nikolski, AK (cdp) Aleutians West Census Area	26	66.67
Houston, AK (city) Matanuska-Susitna Borough	26	2.16
Picnic Point-North Lynnwood, WA (cdp) Snohomish County	26	0.11
Renton, WA (city) King County	26	0.05
Stockton, CA (city) San Joaquin County	26	0.01
Olympia, WA (city) Thurston County	25	0.06
Salem, OR (city) Marion County	25	0.02
Karluk, AK (cdp) Kodiak Island Borough	24	88.89
Ridgeway, AK (cdp) Kenai Peninsula Borough	24	1.24
Bethel, AK (city) Bethel Census Area	23	0.42
Burien, WA (city) King County	23	0.07
Lynnwood, WA (city) Snohomish County	23	0.07
Oklahoma City, OK (city) Oklahoma County	23	0.00
White Center, WA (cdp) King County	22	0.10
Bothell, WA (city) King County	22	0.07
Auburn, WA (city) King County	22	0.05
Kent, WA (city) King County	22	0.03
Boise City, ID (city) Ada County	22	0.01
San Francisco, CA (city) San Francisco County	22	0.00
Sutton-Alpine, AK (cdp) Matanuska-Susitna Borough	21	1.94
Ivanof Bay, AK (cdp) Lake and Peninsula Borough	20	90.91
Kokhanok, AK (cdp) Lake and Peninsula Borough	20	11.49
Metlakatla, AK (cdp) Prince of Wales-Outer Ketchikan Census Area	20	1.45
Willow, AK (cdp) Matanuska-Susitna Borough	20	1.21
Alderwood Manor, WA (cdp) Snohomish County	20	0.13
Federal Way, WA (city) King County	20	0.02
New York, NY (city) New York City	20	0.00
Petersburg, AK (city) Wrangell-Petersburg Census Area	19	0.59
Seattle Hill-Silver Firs, WA (cdp) Snohomish County	19	0.05
Clark's Point, AK (city) Dillingham Census Area	18	24.00
Salamatof, AK (cdp) Kenai Peninsula Borough	18	1.89
Diamond Ridge, AK (cdp) Kenai Peninsula Borough	18	1.00
Albuquerque, NM (city) Bernalillo County	18	0.00
Butte, AK (cdp) Matanuska-Susitna Borough	17	0.66
Des Moines, WA (city) King County	17	0.06
South Hill, WA (cdp) Pierce County	17	0.05
Charlotte, NC (city) Mecklenburg County	17	0.00
Port Angeles, WA (city) Clallam County	16	0.09
Las Vegas, NV (city) Clark County	16	0.00
Mesa, AZ (city) Maricopa County	16	0.00
New Stuyahok, AK (city) Dillingham Census Area	15	3.18
Ferndale, WA (city) Whatcom County	15	0.17
Beaverton, OR (city) Washington County	15	0.02
Seldovia, AK (city) Kenai Peninsula Borough	14	4.90
Gateway, AK (cdp) Matanuska-Susitna Borough	14	0.47
Bellevue, WA (city) King County	14	0.01
Seldovia Village, AK (cdp) Kenai Peninsula Borough	13	9.03
North Marysville, WA (cdp) Snohomish County	13	0.06
SeaTac, WA (city) King County	13	0.05
Santa Rosa, CA (city) Sonoma County	13	0.01
Vallejo, CA (city) Solano County	13	0.01
Port Alsworth, AK (cdp) Lake and Peninsula Borough	12	11.54
Eek, AK (city) Bethel Census Area	12	4.29
Kingsgate, WA (cdp) King County	12	0.10
Coos Bay, OR (city) Coos County	12	0.08
Oregon City, OR (city) Clackamas County	12	0.05
Lacey, WA (city) Thurston County	12	0.04
Puyallup, WA (city) Pierce County	12	0.04
Bremerton, WA (city) Kitsap County	12	0.03
Lakewood, WA (city) Pierce County	12	0.02
Springfield, OR (city) Lane County	12	0.02
San Antonio, TX (city) Bexar County	12	0.00
Wichita, KS (city) Sedgwick County	12	0.00
Newhalen, AK (city) Lake and Peninsula Borough	11	6.88
Lazy Mountain, AK (cdp) Matanuska-Susitna Borough	11	0.95
Fritz Creek, AK (cdp) Kenai Peninsula Borough	11	0.69
Anchor Point, AK (cdp) Kenai Peninsula Borough	11	0.60
Fishhook, AK (cdp) Matanuska-Susitna Borough	11	0.54
Nome, AK (city) Nome Census Area	11	0.31
Barrow, AK (city) North Slope Borough	11	0.24
Birch Bay, WA (cdp) Whatcom County	11	0.22
Lea Hill, WA (cdp) King County	11	0.10
Ellensburg, WA (city) Kittitas County	11	0.07
Mukilteo, WA (city) Snohomish County	11	0.06
Norwood, OH (city) Hamilton County	11	0.05

Notes: (cdp) census designated place; Refer to the Explanation of Data in the front of the book for more detailed information.

Alaska Native: Aleut

Top 150 Places Sorted by Percent

(Based on all places, regardless of population)

Place	Number	%
Perryville, AK (cdp) Lake and Peninsula Borough	99	92.52
Akhiok, AK (city) Kodiak Island Borough	74	92.50
Ivanof Bay, AK (cdp) Lake and Peninsula Borough	20	90.91
Karluk, AK (cdp) Kodiak Island Borough	24	88.89
Atka, AK (city) Aleutians West Census Area	79	85.87
Ouzinkie, AK (city) Kodiak Island Borough	189	84.00
Tatitlek, AK (cdp) Valdez-Cordova Census Area	89	83.18
Saint George, AK (city) Aleutians West Census Area	125	82.24
South Naknek, AK (cdp) Bristol Bay Borough	112	81.75
Chignik Lagoon, AK (cdp) Lake and Peninsula Borough	84	81.55
Old Harbor, AK (city) Kodiak Island Borough	191	80.59
Saint Paul, AK (city) Aleutians West Census Area	426	80.08
Nelson Lagoon, AK (cdp) Aleutians East Borough	66	79.52
Chignik Lake, AK (cdp) Lake and Peninsula Borough	114	78.62
Pilot Point, AK (city) Lake and Peninsula Borough	75	75.00
Nanwalek, AK (cdp) Kenai Peninsula Borough	132	74.58
Larsen Bay, AK (city) Kodiak Island Borough	84	73.04
Igiugig, AK (cdp) Lake and Peninsula Borough	38	71.70
Chenega, AK (cdp) Valdez-Cordova Census Area	59	68.60
Egegik, AK (city) Lake and Peninsula Borough	79	68.10
Nikolski, AK (cdp) Aleutians West Census Area	26	66.67
Port Heiden, AK (city) Lake and Peninsula Borough	72	60.50
Port Lions, AK (city) Kodiak Island Borough	149	58.20
Levelock, AK (cdp) Lake and Peninsula Borough	65	53.28
Chignik, AK (city) Lake and Peninsula Borough	40	50.63
False Pass, AK (city) Aleutians East Borough	32	50.00
Port Graham, AK (cdp) Kenai Peninsula Borough	83	48.54
King Cove, AK (city) Aleutians East Borough	361	45.58
Ugashik, AK (cdp) Lake and Peninsula Borough	5	45.45
Sand Point, AK (city) Aleutians East Borough	329	34.56
Adak, AK (cdp) Aleutians West Census Area	79	25.00
Clark's Point, AK (city) Dillingham Census Area	18	24.00
Naknek, AK (cdp) Bristol Bay Borough	94	13.86
King Salmon, AK (cdp) Bristol Bay Borough	59	13.35
Pedro Bay, AK (cdp) Lake and Peninsula Borough	6	12.00
Port Alsworth, AK (cdp) Lake and Peninsula Borough	12	11.54
Kokhanok, AK (cdp) Lake and Peninsula Borough	20	11.49
Cordova, AK (city) Valdez-Cordova Census Area	237	9.66
Thoms Place, AK (cdp) Wrangell-Petersburg Census Area	2	9.09
Seldovia Village, AK (cdp) Kenai Peninsula Borough	13	9.03
Cold Bay, AK (city) Aleutians East Borough	7	7.95
Akutan, AK (city) Aleutians East Borough	55	7.71
Olivet, SD (town) Hutchinson County	5	7.14
Newhalen, AK (city) Lake and Peninsula Borough	11	6.88
Kodiak, AK (city) Kodiak Island Borough	434	6.85
Dillingham, AK (city) Dillingham Census Area	155	6.29
Ekwok, AK (city) Dillingham Census Area	8	6.15
Lutak, AK (cdp) Haines Borough	2	5.13
Seldovia, AK (city) Kenai Peninsula Borough	14	4.90
Unalaska, AK (city) Aleutians West Census Area	202	4.72
Aleknagik, AK (city) Dillingham Census Area	10	4.52
Eek, AK (city) Bethel Census Area	12	4.29
Womens Bay, AK (cdp) Kodiak Island Borough	29	4.20
Petersville, AK (cdp) Matanuska-Susitna Borough	1	3.70
Chitina, AK (cdp) Valdez-Cordova Census Area	4	3.25
New Stuyahok, AK (city) Dillingham Census Area	15	3.18
Valdez, AK (city) Valdez-Cordova Census Area	127	3.15
Gakona, AK (cdp) Valdez-Cordova Census Area	6	2.79
Susitna, AK (cdp) Matanuska-Susitna Borough	1	2.70
Bear Creek, AK (cdp) Kenai Peninsula Borough	46	2.63
Akiak, AK (city) Bethel Census Area	8	2.59
Platinum, AK (city) Bethel Census Area	1	2.44
Seward, AK (city) Kenai Peninsula Borough	68	2.40
Bettles, AK (city) Yukon-Koyukuk Census Area	1	2.33
Clam Gulch, AK (cdp) Kenai Peninsula Borough	4	2.31
McGrath, AK (city) Yukon-Koyukuk Census Area	9	2.24
Houston, AK (city) Matanuska-Susitna Borough	26	2.16
Leigh, MN (township) Morrison County	4	2.08
Snoqualmie Pass, WA (cdp) Kittitas County	4	1.99
Sutton-Alpine, AK (cdp) Matanuska-Susitna Borough	21	1.94
Salamatof, AK (cdp) Kenai Peninsula Borough	18	1.89
Kenai, AK (city) Kenai Peninsula Borough	107	1.54
Wrangell, AK (city) Wrangell-Petersburg Census Area	35	1.52
Aleneva, AK (cdp) Kodiak Island Borough	1	1.47
Moose Pass, AK (cdp) Kenai Peninsula Borough	3	1.46

Place	Number	%
Metlakatla, AK (cdp) Prince of Wales-Outer Ketchikan Census Area	20	1.45
Twin Hills, AK (cdp) Dillingham Census Area	1	1.45
Anchorage, AK (municipality) Anchorage Borough	3,397	1.31
Hydaburg, AK (city) Prince of Wales-Outer Ketchikan Census Area	5	1.31
Arrowhead, MN (township) Saint Louis County	3	1.29
Knik-Fairview, AK (cdp) Matanuska-Susitna Borough	90	1.28
Ridgeway, AK (cdp) Kenai Peninsula Borough	24	1.24
Pelican, AK (city) Skagway-Hoonah-Angoon Census Area	2	1.23
Willow, AK (cdp) Matanuska-Susitna Borough	20	1.21
Kettle River, MN (city) Carlton County	2	1.19
Lakes, AK (cdp) Matanuska-Susitna Borough	79	1.18
Kotlik, AK (city) Wade Hampton Census Area	7	1.18
Ninilchik, AK (cdp) Kenai Peninsula Borough	9	1.17
Selawik, AK (city) Northwest Arctic Borough	9	1.17
Stevens Village, AK (cdp) Yukon-Koyukuk Census Area	1	1.15
Gulkana, AK (cdp) Valdez-Cordova Census Area	1	1.14
Copperville, AK (cdp) Valdez-Cordova Census Area	2	1.12
Copper Center, AK (cdp) Valdez-Cordova Census Area	4	1.10
Whittier, AK (city) Valdez-Cordova Census Area	2	1.10
Lowell Point, AK (cdp) Kenai Peninsula Borough	1	1.09
Maple Falls, WA (cdp) Whatcom County	3	1.08
Soldotna, AK (city) Kenai Peninsula Borough	40	1.06
Big Lake, AK (cdp) Matanuska-Susitna Borough	28	1.06
Meadow Lakes, AK (cdp) Matanuska-Susitna Borough	50	1.04
Coffman Cove, AK (city) Prince of Wales-Outer Ketchikan Census Area	2	1.01
Diamond Ridge, AK (cdp) Kenai Peninsula Borough	18	1.00
Iliamna, AK (cdp) Lake and Peninsula Borough	1	0.98
Wasilla, AK (city) Matanuska-Susitna Borough	53	0.97
Palmer, AK (city) Matanuska-Susitna Borough	44	0.97
Hamilton, WA (town) Skagit County	3	0.97
Tanaina, AK (cdp) Matanuska-Susitna Borough	48	0.96
Anvik, AK (city) Yukon-Koyukuk Census Area	1	0.96
Lazy Mountain, AK (cdp) Matanuska-Susitna Borough	11	0.95
Trapper Creek, AK (cdp) Matanuska-Susitna Borough	4	0.95
Mekoryuk, AK (city) Bethel Census Area	2	0.95
Kachemak, AK (city) Kenai Peninsula Borough	4	0.93
Ionia, MO (town) Benton County	1	0.93
Glennallen, AK (cdp) Valdez-Cordova Census Area	5	0.90
Nondalton, AK (city) Lake and Peninsula Borough	2	0.90
Point MacKenzie, AK (cdp) Matanuska-Susitna Borough	1	0.90
Nikiski, AK (cdp) Kenai Peninsula Borough	38	0.88
Yakutat, AK (cdp) Yakutat City and Borough	6	0.88
Happy Valley, AK (cdp) Kenai Peninsula Borough	4	0.82
Homer, AK (city) Kenai Peninsula Borough	32	0.81
Skagway, AK (city) Skagway-Hoonah-Angoon Census Area	7	0.81
French Gulch, CA (cdp) Shasta County	2	0.79
Talkeetna, AK (cdp) Matanuska-Susitna Borough	6	0.78
Cohoe, AK (cdp) Kenai Peninsula Borough	9	0.77
Roy, WA (city) Pierce County	2	0.77
Brushy, OK (cdp) Sequoyah County	6	0.76
Sterling, AK (cdp) Kenai Peninsula Borough	35	0.74
Naukati Bay, AK (cdp) Prince of Wales-Outer Ketchikan Census Area	1	0.74
Sitka, AK (city and borough) Sitka Borough	63	0.71
Hays, MT (cdp) Blaine County	5	0.71
Fritz Creek, AK (cdp) Kenai Peninsula Borough	11	0.69
Kalifornsky, AK (cdp) Kenai Peninsula Borough	39	0.67
Butte, AK (cdp) Matanuska-Susitna Borough	17	0.66
Arctic Village, AK (cdp) Yukon-Koyukuk Census Area	1	0.66
Juneau, AK (city and borough) Juneau Borough	201	0.65
Ovid, NY (village) Seneca County	4	0.65
Coleta, IL (village) Whiteside County	1	0.65
Y, AK (cdp) Matanuska-Susitna Borough	6	0.63
Anchor Point, AK (cdp) Kenai Peninsula Borough	11	0.60
Le Flore, OK (town) Le Flore County	1	0.60
Petersburg, AK (city) Wrangell-Petersburg Census Area	19	0.59
Humboldt, SD (town) Minnehaha County	3	0.58
Ketchikan, AK (city) Ketchikan Gateway Borough	44	0.56
Burdett, NY (village) Schuyler County	2	0.56
East Shore, CA (cdp) Plumas County	1	0.56
Steuben, WI (village) Crawford County	1	0.56
Koliganek, AK (cdp) Dillingham Census Area	1	0.55
Fishhook, AK (cdp) Matanuska-Susitna Borough	11	0.54
Cooper Landing, AK (cdp) Kenai Peninsula Borough	2	0.54
Knik River, AK (cdp) Matanuska-Susitna Borough	3	0.52
Tyonek, AK (cdp) Kenai Peninsula Borough	1	0.52

Notes: (cdp) census designated place; Refer to the Explanation of Data in the front of the book for more detailed information.

Alaska Native: Aleut

Top 150 Places Sorted by Percent

(Based on places with populations of 10,000 or more)

Place	Number	%
Anchorage, AK (municipality) Anchorage Borough	3,397	1.31
Juneau, AK (city and borough) Juneau Borough	201	0.65
College, AK (cdp) Fairbanks North Star Borough	37	0.32
Fairbanks, AK (city) Fairbanks North Star Borough	61	0.20
Anacortes, WA (city) Skagit County	27	0.19
Alderwood Manor, WA (cdp) Snohomish County	20	0.13
Edmonds, WA (city) Snohomish County	48	0.12
Marysville, WA (city) Snohomish County	27	0.11
Picnic Point-North Lynnwood, WA (cdp) Snohomish County	26	0.11
White Center, WA (cdp) King County	22	0.10
Kingsgate, WA (cdp) King County	12	0.10
Lea Hill, WA (cdp) King County	11	0.10
Port Angeles, WA (city) Clallam County	16	0.09
Bellingham, WA (city) Whatcom County	56	0.08
Coos Bay, OR (city) Coos County	12	0.08
East Renton Highlands, WA (cdp) King County	10	0.08
Tumwater, WA (city) Thurston County	10	0.08
Burien, WA (city) King County	23	0.07
Lynnwood, WA (city) Snohomish County	23	0.07
Bothell, WA (city) King County	22	0.07
Ellensburg, WA (city) Kittitas County	11	0.07
Shoreline, WA (city) King County	33	0.06
Olympia, WA (city) Thurston County	25	0.06
Des Moines, WA (city) King County	17	0.06
North Marysville, WA (cdp) Snohomish County	13	0.06
Mukilteo, WA (city) Snohomish County	11	0.06
Clearlake, CA (city) Lake County	8	0.06
Covington, WA (city) King County	8	0.06
Durango, CO (city) La Plata County	8	0.06
City of The Dalles, OR (city) Wasco County	7	0.06
Kelso, WA (city) Cowlitz County	7	0.06
Lincoln, CA (city) Placer County	7	0.06
Seattle, WA (city) King County	269	0.05
Everett, WA (city) Snohomish County	44	0.05
Renton, WA (city) King County	26	0.05
Auburn, WA (city) King County	22	0.05
Seattle Hill-Silver Firs, WA (cdp) Snohomish County	19	0.05
South Hill, WA (cdp) Pierce County	17	0.05
SeaTac, WA (city) King County	13	0.05
Oregon City, OR (city) Clackamas County	12	0.05
Norwood, OH (city) Hamilton County	11	0.05
Troutdale, OR (city) Multnomah County	7	0.05
Red Bluff, CA (city) Tehama County	6	0.05
Saint Helens, OR (city) Columbia County	5	0.05
Tacoma, WA (city) Pierce County	82	0.04
Vancouver, WA (city) Clark County	52	0.04
Lacey, WA (city) Thurston County	12	0.04
Puyallup, WA (city) Pierce County	12	0.04
Mount Vernon, WA (city) Skagit County	10	0.04
Parkland, WA (cdp) Pierce County	10	0.04
Gardner, MA (city) Worcester County	9	0.04
Mountlake Terrace, WA (city) Snohomish County	9	0.04
Oak Harbor, WA (city) Island County	8	0.04
Salmon Creek, WA (cdp) Clark County	7	0.04
West Lake Stevens, WA (cdp) Snohomish County	7	0.04
Elk Plain, WA (cdp) Pierce County	6	0.04
McKinleyville, CA (cdp) Humboldt County	6	0.04
Four Corners, OR (cdp) Marion County	5	0.04
Oak Grove, OR (cdp) Clackamas County	5	0.04
Riverton-Boulevard Park, WA (cdp) King County	5	0.04
Beach Park, IL (village) Lake County	4	0.04
Crestline, CA (cdp) San Bernardino County	4	0.04
Picayune, MS (city) Pearl River County	4	0.04
Kent, WA (city) King County	22	0.03
Bremerton, WA (city) Kitsap County	12	0.03
Longview, WA (city) Cowlitz County	11	0.03
Paradise, CA (town) Butte County	8	0.03
Paine Field-Lake Stickney, WA (cdp) Snohomish County	7	0.03
Pullman, WA (city) Whitman County	7	0.03
Windsor, CA (town) Sonoma County	6	0.03
Altamont, OR (cdp) Klamath County	5	0.03
Centralia, WA (city) Lewis County	5	0.03
Hayesville, OR (cdp) Marion County	5	0.03
Orchards, WA (cdp) Clark County	5	0.03
Pinole, CA (city) Contra Costa County	5	0.03
Arlington, WA (city) Snohomish County	4	0.03
Bellefontaine, OH (city) Logan County	4	0.03
Fort Campbell North, KY (cdp) Christian County	4	0.03
Lake Forest Park, WA (city) King County	4	0.03
Makakilo City, HI (cdp) Honolulu County	4	0.03
Newton, NC (city) Catawba County	4	0.03
Pineville, LA (city) Rapides Parish	4	0.03
Prairie Ridge, WA (cdp) Pierce County	4	0.03
Solana Beach, CA (city) San Diego County	4	0.03
Tillmans Corner, AL (cdp) Mobile County	4	0.03
Chowchilla, CA (city) Madera County	3	0.03
Enumclaw, WA (city) King County	3	0.03
Fortuna, CA (city) Humboldt County	3	0.03
Friendly, MD (cdp) Prince George's County	3	0.03
Garden City, ID (city) Ada County	3	0.03
Herrin, IL (city) Williamson County	3	0.03
La Vista, NE (city) Sarpy County	3	0.03
Lakeland South, WA (cdp) King County	3	0.03
Eugene, OR (city) Lane County	32	0.02
Salem, OR (city) Marion County	25	0.02
Federal Way, WA (city) King County	20	0.02
Beaverton, OR (city) Washington County	15	0.02
Lakewood, WA (city) Pierce County	12	0.02
Springfield, OR (city) Lane County	12	0.02
Kennewick, WA (city) Benton County	10	0.02
Kirkland, WA (city) King County	10	0.02
Sparks, NV (city) Washoe County	10	0.02
Chico, CA (city) Butte County	9	0.02
Rapid City, SD (city) Pennington County	9	0.02
Redmond, WA (city) King County	9	0.02
Kailua, HI (cdp) Honolulu County	8	0.02
Manteca, CA (city) San Joaquin County	8	0.02
Parkway-South Sacramento, CA (cdp) Sacramento County	7	0.02
University Place, WA (city) Pierce County	7	0.02
Alamogordo, NM (city) Otero County	6	0.02
Bullhead City, AZ (city) Mohave County	6	0.02
Gloucester, MA (city) Essex County	6	0.02
Keizer, OR (city) Marion County	6	0.02
Ardmore, OK (city) Carter County	5	0.02
East Hill-Meridian, WA (cdp) King County	5	0.02
Eureka, CA (city) Humboldt County	5	0.02
La Verne, CA (city) Los Angeles County	5	0.02
Lewiston, ID (city) Nez Perce County	5	0.02
Moscow, ID (city) Latah County	5	0.02
Bay City, TX (city) Matagorda County	4	0.02
Bay Point, CA (cdp) Contra Costa County	4	0.02
Brigham City, UT (city) Box Elder County	4	0.02
Burleson, TX (city) Johnson County	4	0.02
Foothill Farms, CA (cdp) Sacramento County	4	0.02
Germantown, WI (village) Washington County	4	0.02
Greater Upper Marlboro, MD (cdp) Prince George's County	4	0.02
Hybla Valley, VA (cdp) Fairfax County	4	0.02
Klamath Falls, OR (city) Klamath County	4	0.02
McAlester, OK (city) Pittsburg County	4	0.02
McMinnville, OR (city) Yamhill County	4	0.02
North Creek, WA (cdp) Snohomish County	4	0.02
Oakley, CA (city) Contra Costa County	4	0.02
Orinda, CA (city) Contra Costa County	4	0.02
Rexburg, ID (city) Madison County	4	0.02
Sanford, ME (town) York County	4	0.02
Sun Valley, NV (cdp) Washoe County	4	0.02
Tukwila, WA (city) King County	4	0.02
Aberdeen, WA (city) Grays Harbor County	3	0.02
Arcata, CA (city) Humboldt County	3	0.02
Camano, WA (cdp) Island County	3	0.02
Camas, WA (city) Clark County	3	0.02
Carthage, MO (city) Jasper County	3	0.02
Chickasha, OK (city) Grady County	3	0.02
Dickinson, TX (city) Galveston County	3	0.02
Five Corners, WA (cdp) Clark County	3	0.02
Front Royal, VA (town) Warren County	3	0.02
Gainesville, TX (city) Cooke County	3	0.02
Gillette, WY (city) Campbell County	3	0.02
Kenmore, WA (city) King County	3	0.02
Ladson, SC (cdp) Berkeley County	3	0.02

Notes: (cdp) census designated place; Refer to the Explanation of Data in the front of the book for more detailed information.

Alaska Native: Eskimo

Top 150 Places Sorted by Number

(Based on all places, regardless of population)

Place	Number	%
Anchorage, AK (municipality) Anchorage Borough	7,666	2.95
Barrow, AK (city) North Slope Borough	2,400	52.39
Bethel, AK (city) Bethel Census Area	2,329	42.57
Kotzebue, AK (city) Northwest Arctic Borough	1,764	57.24
Nome, AK (city) Nome Census Area	1,582	45.14
Dillingham, AK (city) Dillingham Census Area	913	37.02
Hooper Bay, AK (city) Wade Hampton Census Area	902	88.95
Fairbanks, AK (city) Fairbanks North Star Borough	714	2.36
Emmonak, AK (city) Wade Hampton Census Area	688	89.70
Mountain Village, AK (city) Wade Hampton Census Area	674	89.27
Point Hope, AK (city) North Slope Borough	648	85.60
Unalakleet, AK (city) Nome Census Area	628	84.07
Alakanuk, AK (city) Wade Hampton Census Area	627	96.17
Kipnuk, AK (cdp) Bethel Census Area	614	95.34
Savoonga, AK (city) Nome Census Area	603	93.78
Togiak, AK (city) Dillingham Census Area	595	73.55
Gambell, AK (city) Nome Census Area	593	91.37
Noorvik, AK (city) Northwest Arctic Borough	580	91.48
Kwethluk, AK (city) Bethel Census Area	576	80.79
Kotlik, AK (city) Wade Hampton Census Area	558	94.42
Akiachak, AK (cdp) Bethel Census Area	544	92.99
Pilot Station, AK (city) Wade Hampton Census Area	528	96.00
Toksook Bay, AK (city) Bethel Census Area	508	95.49
Shishmaref, AK (city) Nome Census Area	507	90.21
Wainwright, AK (city) North Slope Borough	492	90.11
Kasigluk, AK (cdp) Bethel Census Area	490	90.24
Stebbins, AK (city) Nome Census Area	480	87.75
New Stuyahok, AK (city) Dillingham Census Area	441	93.63
Nunapitchuk, AK (city) Bethel Census Area	434	93.13
Noatak, AK (cdp) Northwest Arctic Borough	407	95.09
Saint Mary's, AK (city) Wade Hampton Census Area	392	78.40
Chefornak, AK (city) Bethel Census Area	379	96.19
Nuiqsut, AK (city) North Slope Borough	378	87.30
Napaskiak, AK (city) Bethel Census Area	373	95.64
Buckland, AK (city) Northwest Arctic Borough	369	90.89
Tuluksak, AK (cdp) Bethel Census Area	360	84.11
Kiana, AK (city) Northwest Arctic Borough	353	90.98
Tuntutuliak, AK (cdp) Bethel Census Area	347	93.78
College, AK (cdp) Fairbanks North Star Borough	347	3.04
Kivalina, AK (city) Northwest Arctic Borough	344	91.25
Saint Michael, AK (city) Nome Census Area	312	84.78
Marshall, AK (city) Wade Hampton Census Area	311	89.11
Newtok, AK (cdp) Bethel Census Area	308	95.95
Napakiak, AK (city) Bethel Census Area	298	84.42
Tununak, AK (cdp) Bethel Census Area	294	90.46
Akiak, AK (city) Bethel Census Area	285	92.23
Chevak, AK (city) Wade Hampton Census Area	281	36.73
Elim, AK (city) Nome Census Area	277	88.50
Aniak, AK (city) Bethel Census Area	269	47.03
Kwigillingok, AK (cdp) Bethel Census Area	255	75.44
Russian Mission, AK (city) Wade Hampton Census Area	249	84.12
Brevig Mission, AK (city) Nome Census Area	247	89.49
Juneau, AK (city and borough) Juneau Borough	237	0.77
Koyuk, AK (city) Nome Census Area	232	78.11
Shungnak, AK (city) Northwest Arctic Borough	227	88.67
Selawik, AK (city) Northwest Arctic Borough	227	29.40
Atmautluak, AK (cdp) Bethel Census Area	225	76.53
Kaktovik, AK (city) North Slope Borough	223	76.11
Seattle, WA (city) King County	216	0.04
Teller, AK (city) Nome Census Area	213	79.48
Atqasuk, AK (city) North Slope Borough	208	91.23
Mekoryuk, AK (city) Bethel Census Area	202	96.19
Seward, AK (city) Kenai Peninsula Borough	202	7.14
Point Lay, AK (cdp) North Slope Borough	201	81.38
Manokotak, AK (city) Dillingham Census Area	201	50.38
Ambler, AK (city) Northwest Arctic Borough	195	63.11
Goodnews Bay, AK (city) Bethel Census Area	193	83.91
Shaktoolik, AK (city) Nome Census Area	182	79.13
Nightmute, AK (city) Bethel Census Area	171	82.21
Aleknagik, AK (city) Dillingham Census Area	171	77.38
White Mountain, AK (city) Nome Census Area	164	80.79
Koliganek, AK (cdp) Dillingham Census Area	150	82.42
Palmer, AK (city) Matanuska-Susitna Borough	150	3.31
Knik-Fairview, AK (cdp) Matanuska-Susitna Borough	145	2.06
Kongiganak, AK (cdp) Bethel Census Area	141	39.28
Wales, AK (city) Nome Census Area	136	89.47
Wasilla, AK (city) Matanuska-Susitna Borough	131	2.40
Newhalen, AK (city) Lake and Peninsula Borough	130	81.25
Golovin, AK (city) Nome Census Area	129	89.58
Naknek, AK (cdp) Bristol Bay Borough	126	18.58
Deering, AK (city) Northwest Arctic Borough	125	91.91
Kenai, AK (city) Kenai Peninsula Borough	121	1.74
Lakes, AK (cdp) Matanuska-Susitna Borough	118	1.76
Tacoma, WA (city) Pierce County	117	0.06
Ekwok, AK (city) Dillingham Census Area	110	84.62
Tanaina, AK (cdp) Matanuska-Susitna Borough	103	2.06
Pitkas Point, AK (cdp) Wade Hampton Census Area	98	78.40
Sitka, AK (city and borough) Sitka Borough	96	1.09
Kodiak, AK (city) Kodiak Island Borough	89	1.41
Kobuk, AK (city) Northwest Arctic Borough	86	78.90
Upper Kalskag, AK (city) Bethel Census Area	84	36.52
Portland, OR (city) Multnomah County	84	0.02
Chuathbaluk, AK (city) Bethel Census Area	80	67.23
Sutton-Alpine, AK (cdp) Matanuska-Susitna Borough	77	7.13
Diomede, AK (city) Nome Census Area	75	51.37
Stevens Village, AK (cdp) Yukon-Koyukuk Census Area	74	85.06
Scammon Bay, AK (city) Wade Hampton Census Area	70	15.05
Meadow Lakes, AK (cdp) Matanuska-Susitna Borough	68	1.41
New York, NY (city) New York City	65	0.00
Phoenix, AZ (city) Maricopa County	65	0.00
Bear Creek, AK (cdp) Kenai Peninsula Borough	64	3.66
Nikiski, AK (cdp) Kenai Peninsula Borough	62	1.43
Kalifornsky, AK (cdp) Kenai Peninsula Borough	61	1.04
Oscarville, AK (cdp) Bethel Census Area	60	98.36
Salamatof, AK (cdp) Kenai Peninsula Borough	60	6.29
Twin Hills, AK (cdp) Dillingham Census Area	58	84.06
Everett, WA (city) Snohomish County	57	0.06
Eek, AK (city) Bethel Census Area	55	19.64
Levelock, AK (cdp) Lake and Peninsula Borough	54	44.26
Homer, AK (city) Kenai Peninsula Borough	52	1.32
Valdez, AK (city) Valdez-Cordova Census Area	51	1.26
Lower Kalskag, AK (city) Bethel Census Area	50	18.73
Clark's Point, AK (city) Dillingham Census Area	48	64.00
Honolulu, HI (cdp) Honolulu County	48	0.01
Big Lake, AK (cdp) Matanuska-Susitna Borough	46	1.75
Los Angeles, CA (city) Los Angeles County	45	0.00
Gateway, AK (cdp) Matanuska-Susitna Borough	44	1.49
McGrath, AK (city) Yukon-Koyukuk Census Area	42	10.47
San Diego, CA (city) San Diego County	42	0.00
King Salmon, AK (cdp) Bristol Bay Borough	40	9.05
Soldotna, AK (city) Kenai Peninsula Borough	40	1.06
Platinum, AK (city) Bethel Census Area	38	92.68
Sterling, AK (cdp) Kenai Peninsula Borough	37	0.79
Albuquerque, NM (city) Bernalillo County	36	0.01
Kent, WA (city) King County	35	0.04
Sacramento, CA (city) Sacramento County	35	0.01
Fishhook, AK (cdp) Matanuska-Susitna Borough	34	1.67
Bellingham, WA (city) Whatcom County	32	0.05
Denver, CO (city) Denver County	32	0.01
Chicago, IL (city) Cook County	32	0.00
Colorado Springs, CO (city) El Paso County	31	0.01
Tucson, AZ (city) Pima County	31	0.01
Spokane, WA (city) Spokane County	30	0.02
Glendale, AZ (city) Maricopa County	30	0.01
Ester, AK (cdp) Fairbanks North Star Borough	29	1.73
Salem, OR (city) Marion County	29	0.02
Iliamna, AK (cdp) Lake and Peninsula Borough	28	27.45
Vancouver, WA (city) Clark County	28	0.02
Yakutat, AK (cdp) Yakutat City and Borough	27	3.97
Houston, AK (city) Matanuska-Susitna Borough	27	2.25
Springdale, AR (city) Washington County	27	0.06
San Jose, CA (city) Santa Clara County	27	0.00
Quinhagak, AK (city) Bethel Census Area	26	4.68
Willow, AK (cdp) Matanuska-Susitna Borough	26	1.57
Ketchikan, AK (city) Ketchikan Gateway Borough	26	0.33
Shoreline, WA (city) King County	26	0.05
Oklahoma City, OK (city) Oklahoma County	26	0.01
Anaktuvuk Pass, AK (city) North Slope Borough	25	8.87
Lakewood, WA (city) Pierce County	25	0.04
Redding, CA (city) Shasta County	25	0.03

Notes: (cdp) census designated place; Refer to the Explanation of Data in the front of the book for more detailed information.

Alaska Native: Eskimo

Top 150 Places Sorted by Percent

(Based on all places, regardless of population)

Place	Number	%
Oscarville, AK (cdp) Bethel Census Area	60	98.36
Chefornak, AK (city) Bethel Census Area	379	96.19
Mekoryuk, AK (city) Bethel Census Area	202	96.19
Alakanuk, AK (city) Wade Hampton Census Area	627	96.17
Pilot Station, AK (city) Wade Hampton Census Area	528	96.00
Newtok, AK (cdp) Bethel Census Area	308	95.95
Napaskiak, AK (city) Bethel Census Area	373	95.64
Toksook Bay, AK (city) Bethel Census Area	508	95.49
Kipnuk, AK (cdp) Bethel Census Area	614	95.34
Noatak, AK (cdp) Northwest Arctic Borough	407	95.09
Kotlik, AK (city) Wade Hampton Census Area	558	94.42
Savoonga, AK (city) Nome Census Area	603	93.78
Tuntutuliak, AK (cdp) Bethel Census Area	347	93.78
New Stuyahok, AK (city) Dillingham Census Area	441	93.63
Nunapitchuk, AK (city) Bethel Census Area	434	93.13
Akiachak, AK (cdp) Bethel Census Area	544	92.99
Platinum, AK (city) Bethel Census Area	38	92.68
Akiak, AK (city) Bethel Census Area	285	92.23
Deering, AK (city) Northwest Arctic Borough	125	91.91
Noorvik, AK (city) Northwest Arctic Borough	580	91.48
Gambell, AK (city) Nome Census Area	593	91.37
Kivalina, AK (city) Northwest Arctic Borough	344	91.25
Atqasuk, AK (city) North Slope Borough	208	91.23
Kiana, AK (city) Northwest Arctic Borough	353	90.98
Buckland, AK (city) Northwest Arctic Borough	369	90.89
Tununak, AK (cdp) Bethel Census Area	294	90.46
Kasigluk, AK (cdp) Bethel Census Area	490	90.24
Shishmaref, AK (city) Nome Census Area	507	90.21
Wainwright, AK (city) North Slope Borough	492	90.11
Emmonak, AK (city) Wade Hampton Census Area	688	89.70
Golovin, AK (city) Nome Census Area	129	89.58
Brevig Mission, AK (city) Nome Census Area	247	89.49
Wales, AK (city) Nome Census Area	136	89.47
Mountain Village, AK (city) Wade Hampton Census Area	674	89.27
Marshall, AK (city) Wade Hampton Census Area	311	89.11
Hooper Bay, AK (city) Wade Hampton Census Area	902	88.95
Shungnak, AK (city) Northwest Arctic Borough	227	88.67
Elim, AK (city) Nome Census Area	277	88.50
Stebbins, AK (city) Nome Census Area	480	87.75
Nuiqsut, AK (city) North Slope Borough	378	87.30
Point Hope, AK (city) North Slope Borough	648	85.60
Stevens Village, AK (cdp) Yukon-Koyukuk Census Area	74	85.06
Saint Michael, AK (city) Nome Census Area	312	84.78
Ekwok, AK (city) Dillingham Census Area	110	84.62
Napakiak, AK (city) Bethel Census Area	298	84.42
Russian Mission, AK (city) Wade Hampton Census Area	249	84.12
Tuluksak, AK (cdp) Bethel Census Area	360	84.11
Unalakleet, AK (city) Nome Census Area	628	84.07
Twin Hills, AK (cdp) Dillingham Census Area	58	84.06
Goodnews Bay, AK (city) Bethel Census Area	193	83.91
Koliganek, AK (cdp) Dillingham Census Area	150	82.42
Nightmute, AK (city) Bethel Census Area	171	82.21
Point Lay, AK (cdp) North Slope Borough	201	81.38
Newhalen, AK (city) Lake and Peninsula Borough	130	81.25
Kwethluk, AK (city) Bethel Census Area	576	80.79
White Mountain, AK (city) Nome Census Area	164	80.79
Prudhoe Bay, AK (cdp) North Slope Borough	4	80.00
Teller, AK (city) Nome Census Area	213	79.48
Shaktoolik, AK (city) Nome Census Area	182	79.13
Kobuk, AK (city) Northwest Arctic Borough	86	78.90
Saint Mary's, AK (city) Wade Hampton Census Area	392	78.40
Pitkas Point, AK (cdp) Wade Hampton Census Area	98	78.40
Koyuk, AK (city) Nome Census Area	232	78.11
Aleknagik, AK (city) Dillingham Census Area	171	77.38
Atmautluak, AK (cdp) Bethel Census Area	225	76.53
Kaktovik, AK (city) North Slope Borough	223	76.11
Kwigillingok, AK (cdp) Bethel Census Area	255	75.44
Togiak, AK (city) Dillingham Census Area	595	73.55
Chuathbaluk, AK (city) Bethel Census Area	80	67.23
Clark's Point, AK (city) Dillingham Census Area	48	64.00
Ambler, AK (city) Northwest Arctic Borough	195	63.11
Portage Creek, AK (cdp) Dillingham Census Area	21	58.33
Kotzebue, AK (city) Northwest Arctic Borough	1,764	57.24
Barrow, AK (city) North Slope Borough	2,400	52.39
Diomede, AK (city) Nome Census Area	75	51.37
Manokotak, AK (city) Dillingham Census Area	201	50.38
Aniak, AK (city) Bethel Census Area	269	47.03
Nome, AK (city) Nome Census Area	1,582	45.14
Levelock, AK (cdp) Lake and Peninsula Borough	54	44.26
Bethel, AK (city) Bethel Census Area	2,329	42.57
Red Dog Mine, AK (cdp) Northwest Arctic Borough	13	40.63
Kongiganak, AK (cdp) Bethel Census Area	141	39.28
Dillingham, AK (city) Dillingham Census Area	913	37.02
Chevak, AK (city) Wade Hampton Census Area	281	36.73
Upper Kalskag, AK (city) Bethel Census Area	84	36.52
Selawik, AK (city) Northwest Arctic Borough	227	29.40
Iliamna, AK (cdp) Lake and Peninsula Borough	28	27.45
Eek, AK (city) Bethel Census Area	55	19.64
Wiseman, AK (cdp) Yukon-Koyukuk Census Area	4	19.05
Red Devil, AK (cdp) Bethel Census Area	9	18.75
Lower Kalskag, AK (city) Bethel Census Area	50	18.73
Naknek, AK (cdp) Bristol Bay Borough	126	18.58
Scammon Bay, AK (city) Wade Hampton Census Area	70	15.05
Pope-Vannoy Landing, AK (cdp) Lake and Peninsula Borough	1	12.50
Sheldon Point, AK (city) Wade Hampton Census Area	20	12.20
Alatna, AK (cdp) Yukon-Koyukuk Census Area	4	11.43
Igiugig, AK (cdp) Lake and Peninsula Borough	6	11.32
False Pass, AK (city) Aleutians East Borough	7	10.94
McGrath, AK (city) Yukon-Koyukuk Census Area	42	10.47
King Salmon, AK (cdp) Bristol Bay Borough	40	9.05
Anaktuvuk Pass, AK (city) North Slope Borough	25	8.87
Karluk, AK (cdp) Kodiak Island Borough	2	7.41
Seward, AK (city) Kenai Peninsula Borough	202	7.14
Sutton-Alpine, AK (cdp) Matanuska-Susitna Borough	77	7.13
Nikolai, AK (city) Yukon-Koyukuk Census Area	7	7.00
Chenega, AK (cdp) Valdez-Cordova Census Area	6	6.98
Nanwalek, AK (cdp) Kenai Peninsula Borough	12	6.78
Mentasta Lake, AK (cdp) Valdez-Cordova Census Area	9	6.34
Salamatof, AK (cdp) Kenai Peninsula Borough	60	6.29
Port Heiden, AK (city) Lake and Peninsula Borough	7	5.88
Chignik, AK (city) Lake and Peninsula Borough	4	5.06
Holy Cross, AK (city) Yukon-Koyukuk Census Area	11	4.85
Quinhagak, AK (city) Bethel Census Area	26	4.68
Ouzinkie, AK (city) Kodiak Island Borough	10	4.44
Glacier View, AK (cdp) Matanuska-Susitna Borough	11	4.42
Chitina, AK (cdp) Valdez-Cordova Census Area	5	4.07
Trapper Creek, AK (cdp) Matanuska-Susitna Borough	17	4.02
Pedro Bay, AK (cdp) Lake and Peninsula Borough	2	4.00
Yakutat, AK (cdp) Yakutat City and Borough	27	3.97
Eagle, AK (city) Southeast Fairbanks Census Area	5	3.88
Seldovia, AK (city) Kenai Peninsula Borough	11	3.85
Bear Creek, AK (cdp) Kenai Peninsula Borough	64	3.66
Galena, AK (city) Yukon-Koyukuk Census Area	24	3.56
Adak, AK (cdp) Aleutians West Census Area	11	3.48
Palmer, AK (city) Matanuska-Susitna Borough	150	3.31
Allakaket, AK (city) Yukon-Koyukuk Census Area	3	3.09
Silver Springs, AK (cdp) Valdez-Cordova Census Area	4	3.08
College, AK (cdp) Fairbanks North Star Borough	347	3.04
Buffalo Soapstone, AK (cdp) Matanuska-Susitna Borough	21	3.00
Anchorage, AK (municipality) Anchorage Borough	7,666	2.95
Hope, AK (cdp) Kenai Peninsula Borough	4	2.92
Moose Pass, AK (cdp) Kenai Peninsula Borough	6	2.91
Chignik Lagoon, AK (cdp) Lake and Peninsula Borough	3	2.91
Nelchina, AK (cdp) Valdez-Cordova Census Area	2	2.82
Perryville, AK (cdp) Lake and Peninsula Borough	3	2.80
Tatitlek, AK (cdp) Valdez-Cordova Census Area	3	2.80
Chignik Lake, AK (cdp) Lake and Peninsula Borough	4	2.76
Whittier, AK (city) Valdez-Cordova Census Area	5	2.75
Nenana, AK (city) Yukon-Koyukuk Census Area	11	2.74
Dot Lake Village, AK (cdp) Southeast Fairbanks Census Area	1	2.63
Two Rivers, AK (cdp) Fairbanks North Star Borough	12	2.49
Angoon, AK (city) Skagway-Hoonah-Angoon Census Area	14	2.45
Pelican, AK (city) Skagway-Hoonah-Angoon Census Area	4	2.45
Slana, AK (cdp) Valdez-Cordova Census Area	3	2.42
Wasilla, AK (city) Matanuska-Susitna Borough	131	2.40
Fairbanks, AK (city) Fairbanks North Star Borough	714	2.36
Fort Yukon, AK (city) Yukon-Koyukuk Census Area	14	2.35
Glennallen, AK (cdp) Valdez-Cordova Census Area	13	2.35
Bettles, AK (city) Yukon-Koyukuk Census Area	1	2.33
Houston, AK (city) Matanuska-Susitna Borough	27	2.25

Notes: (cdp) census designated place; Refer to the Explanation of Data in the front of the book for more detailed information.

Alaska Native: Eskimo

Top 150 Places Sorted by Percent

(Based on places with populations of 10,000 or more)

Place	Number	%
College, AK (cdp) Fairbanks North Star Borough	347	3.04
Anchorage, AK (municipality) Anchorage Borough	7,666	2.95
Fairbanks, AK (city) Fairbanks North Star Borough	714	2.36
Juneau, AK (city and borough) Juneau Borough	237	0.77
Lakeland North, WA (cdp) King County	20	0.13
Durango, CO (city) La Plata County	18	0.13
Clearlake, CA (city) Lake County	14	0.11
Four Corners, OR (cdp) Marion County	12	0.09
Port Angeles, WA (city) Clallam County	15	0.08
Barstow, CA (city) San Bernardino County	14	0.07
Tacoma, WA (city) Pierce County	117	0.06
Everett, WA (city) Snohomish County	57	0.06
Springdale, AR (city) Washington County	27	0.06
Lynnwood, WA (city) Snohomish County	20	0.06
Fort Lewis, WA (cdp) Pierce County	12	0.06
Kahului, HI (cdp) Maui County	12	0.06
Ridgefield Park, NJ (village) Bergen County	8	0.06
Cedar Mill, OR (cdp) Washington County	7	0.06
Kelso, WA (city) Cowlitz County	7	0.06
Lea Hill, WA (cdp) King County	7	0.06
Tumwater, WA (city) Thurston County	7	0.06
Bellingham, WA (city) Whatcom County	32	0.05
Shoreline, WA (city) King County	26	0.05
Auburn, WA (city) King County	22	0.05
Marysville, WA (city) Snohomish County	13	0.05
Parkland, WA (cdp) Pierce County	12	0.05
Picnic Point-North Lynnwood, WA (cdp) Snohomish County	11	0.05
Mountlake Terrace, WA (city) Snohomish County	10	0.05
Anacortes, WA (city) Skagit County	8	0.05
Alderwood Manor, WA (cdp) Snohomish County	7	0.05
McKinleyville, CA (cdp) Humboldt County	7	0.05
Federal Heights, CO (city) Adams County	6	0.05
Riverton-Boulevard Park, WA (cdp) King County	6	0.05
Dishman, WA (cdp) Spokane County	5	0.05
Hartford, VT (town) Windsor County	5	0.05
Seattle, WA (city) King County	216	0.04
Kent, WA (city) King County	35	0.04
Lakewood, WA (city) Pierce County	25	0.04
Tigard, OR (city) Washington County	15	0.04
Bremerton, WA (city) Kitsap County	14	0.04
Farmington, NM (city) San Juan County	14	0.04
Helena, MT (city) Lewis and Clark County	10	0.04
Wallkill, NY (town) Orange County	10	0.04
Paine Field-Lake Stickney, WA (cdp) Snohomish County	9	0.04
Spanaway, WA (cdp) Pierce County	9	0.04
Altamont, OR (cdp) Klamath County	7	0.04
Sun Valley, NV (cdp) Washoe County	7	0.04
Tukwila, WA (city) King County	7	0.04
Elk River, MN (city) Sherburne County	6	0.04
Monroe, WA (city) Snohomish County	6	0.04
Poinciana, FL (cdp) Osceola County	6	0.04
Brunswick, NY (town) Rensselaer County	5	0.04
Covington, WA (city) King County	5	0.04
Enumclaw, WA (city) King County	5	0.04
Evanston, WY (city) Uinta County	5	0.04
Freeport, TX (city) Brazoria County	5	0.04
Halawa, HI (cdp) Honolulu County	5	0.04
Martha Lake, WA (cdp) Snohomish County	5	0.04
Troutdale, OR (city) Multnomah County	5	0.04
Yankton, SD (city) Yankton County	5	0.04
Fernandina Beach, FL (city) Nassau County	4	0.04
Fort Carson, CO (cdp) El Paso County	4	0.04
Holbrook, MA (cdp) Norfolk County	4	0.04
Villas, FL (cdp) Lee County	4	0.04
Redding, CA (city) Shasta County	25	0.03
Lawrence, KS (city) Douglas County	23	0.03
Enid, OK (city) Garfield County	14	0.03
Hilo, HI (cdp) Hawaii County	11	0.03
Fort Hood, TX (cdp) Coryell County	10	0.03
Keizer, OR (city) Marion County	9	0.03
Lacey, WA (city) Thurston County	9	0.03
Longview, WA (city) Cowlitz County	9	0.03
Bothell, WA (city) King County	8	0.03
Burien, WA (city) King County	8	0.03
Marina, CA (city) Monterey County	8	0.03

Place	Number	%
Commerce City, CO (city) Adams County	7	0.03
Mount Vernon, WA (city) Skagit County	7	0.03
Orangevale, CA (cdp) Sacramento County	7	0.03
White Center, WA (cdp) King County	7	0.03
Ashland, OR (city) Jackson County	6	0.03
Hayesville, OR (cdp) Marion County	6	0.03
Lakeside, CA (cdp) San Diego County	6	0.03
Lomita, CA (city) Los Angeles County	6	0.03
Loves Park, IL (city) Winnebago County	6	0.03
Oak Harbor, WA (city) Island County	6	0.03
Shelbyville, IN (city) Shelby County	6	0.03
Aberdeen, WA (city) Grays Harbor County	5	0.03
Bartow, FL (city) Polk County	5	0.03
Baywood-Los Osos, CA (cdp) San Luis Obispo County	5	0.03
Casa de Oro-Mount Helix, CA (cdp) San Diego County	5	0.03
Ellensburg, WA (city) Kittitas County	5	0.03
Forest Grove, OR (city) Washington County	5	0.03
Fredericksburg, VA (independent city) Fredericksburg city	5	0.03
Mukilteo, WA (city) Snohomish County	5	0.03
Wahiawa, HI (cdp) Honolulu County	5	0.03
West Lake Stevens, WA (cdp) Snohomish County	5	0.03
Bemidji, MN (city) Beltrami County	4	0.03
Centralia, WA (city) Lewis County	4	0.03
Coos Bay, OR (city) Coos County	4	0.03
Fort Benning South, GA (cdp) Chattahoochee County	4	0.03
Fort Campbell North, KY (cdp) Christian County	4	0.03
Fort Drum, NY (cdp) Jefferson County	4	0.03
Grand Rapids, MN (township) Itasca County	4	0.03
Lockhart, TX (city) Caldwell County	4	0.03
Makakilo City, HI (cdp) Honolulu County	4	0.03
Moses Lake, WA (city) Grant County	4	0.03
Rantoul, IL (village) Champaign County	4	0.03
Schofield Barracks, HI (cdp) Honolulu County	4	0.03
Susanville, CA (city) Lassen County	4	0.03
Berlin, NH (city) Coos County	3	0.03
Capitola, CA (city) Santa Cruz County	3	0.03
Grand Terrace, CA (city) San Bernardino County	3	0.03
Hartland, MI (township) Livingston County	3	0.03
Kingsland, GA (city) Camden County	3	0.03
Masonboro, NC (cdp) New Hanover County	3	0.03
Vashon, WA (cdp) King County	3	0.03
Portland, OR (city) Multnomah County	84	0.02
Spokane, WA (city) Spokane County	30	0.02
Salem, OR (city) Marion County	29	0.02
Vancouver, WA (city) Clark County	28	0.02
Eugene, OR (city) Lane County	24	0.02
Gresham, OR (city) Multnomah County	19	0.02
Bellevue, WA (city) King County	18	0.02
Hillsboro, OR (city) Washington County	17	0.02
Federal Way, WA (city) King County	13	0.02
Ogden, UT (city) Weber County	12	0.02
Santa Fe, NM (city) Santa Fe County	12	0.02
Yakima, WA (city) Yakima County	11	0.02
North Highlands, CA (cdp) Sacramento County	9	0.02
Aspen Hill, MD (cdp) Montgomery County	8	0.02
Olympia, WA (city) Thurston County	8	0.02
Pocatello, ID (city) Bannock County	8	0.02
Puyallup, WA (city) Pierce County	8	0.02
Roy, UT (city) Weber County	8	0.02
Albany, OR (city) Linn County	7	0.02
Butte-Silver Bow, MT (special city) Silver Bow County	7	0.02
Richland, WA (city) Benton County	7	0.02
Cottage Lake, WA (cdp) King County	6	0.02
Edmonds, WA (city) Snohomish County	6	0.02
Fort Bragg, NC (cdp) Cumberland County	6	0.02
Leavenworth, KS (city) Leavenworth County	6	0.02
Mililani Town, HI (cdp) Honolulu County	6	0.02
Opportunity, WA (cdp) Spokane County	6	0.02
Parkway-South Sacramento, CA (cdp) Sacramento County	6	0.02
Porterville, CA (city) Tulare County	6	0.02
SeaTac, WA (city) King County	6	0.02
South Hill, WA (cdp) Pierce County	6	0.02
University Place, WA (city) Pierce County	6	0.02
Benicia, CA (city) Solano County	5	0.02
Drexel Heights, AZ (cdp) Pima County	5	0.02

Notes: (cdp) census designated place; Refer to the Explanation of Data in the front of the book for more detailed information.

Alaska Native: Tlingit-Haida

Top 150 Places Sorted by Number

(Based on all places, regardless of population)

Place	Number	%
Juneau, AK (city and borough) Juneau Borough	3,272	10.65
Anchorage, AK (municipality) Anchorage Borough	1,712	0.66
Sitka, AK (city and borough) Sitka Borough	1,295	14.66
Ketchikan, AK (city) Ketchikan Gateway Borough	1,014	12.80
Seattle, WA (city) King County	692	0.12
Hoonah, AK (city) Skagway-Hoonah-Angoon Census Area	496	57.67
Angoon, AK (city) Skagway-Hoonah-Angoon Census Area	399	69.76
Kake, AK (city) Wrangell-Petersburg Census Area	397	55.92
Klawock, AK (city) Prince of Wales-Outer Ketchikan Census Area	372	43.56
Wrangell, AK (city) Wrangell-Petersburg Census Area	350	15.16
Saxman, AK (city) Ketchikan Gateway Borough	290	67.29
Hydaburg, AK (city) Prince of Wales-Outer Ketchikan Census Area	287	75.13
Craig, AK (city) Prince of Wales-Outer Ketchikan Census Area	282	20.19
Yakutat, AK (cdp) Yakutat City and Borough	277	40.74
Petersburg, AK (city) Wrangell-Petersburg Census Area	269	8.34
Haines, AK (city) Haines Borough	207	11.43
Tacoma, WA (city) Pierce County	192	0.10
Portland, OR (city) Multnomah County	138	0.03
Everett, WA (city) Snohomish County	130	0.14
Klukwan, AK (cdp) Skagway-Hoonah-Angoon Census Area	115	82.73
Shoreline, WA (city) King County	108	0.20
Federal Way, WA (city) King County	95	0.11
Metlakatla, AK (cdp) Prince of Wales-Outer Ketchikan Census Area	92	6.69
Kent, WA (city) King County	86	0.11
Los Angeles, CA (city) Los Angeles County	78	0.00
New York, NY (city) New York City	77	0.00
Edmonds, WA (city) Snohomish County	68	0.17
Bellingham, WA (city) Whatcom County	65	0.10
Phoenix, AZ (city) Maricopa County	65	0.00
San Diego, CA (city) San Diego County	63	0.01
SeaTac, WA (city) King County	60	0.24
Mountlake Terrace, WA (city) Snohomish County	58	0.28
Fairbanks, AK (city) Fairbanks North Star Borough	56	0.19
Lynnwood, WA (city) Snohomish County	55	0.16
Renton, WA (city) King County	55	0.11
Lakewood, WA (city) Pierce County	50	0.09
Vancouver, WA (city) Clark County	50	0.03
College, AK (cdp) Fairbanks North Star Borough	46	0.40
Auburn, WA (city) King County	46	0.11
Eugene, OR (city) Lane County	46	0.03
Burien, WA (city) King County	45	0.14
White Center, WA (cdp) King County	42	0.20
Salem, OR (city) Marion County	42	0.03
Des Moines, WA (city) King County	40	0.14
Spokane, WA (city) Spokane County	40	0.02
San Jose, CA (city) Santa Clara County	39	0.00
Valdez, AK (city) Valdez-Cordova Census Area	38	0.94
Mount Vernon, WA (city) Skagit County	37	0.14
North Creek, WA (cdp) Snohomish County	35	0.14
San Francisco, CA (city) San Francisco County	35	0.00
Kenai, AK (city) Kenai Peninsula Borough	34	0.49
Cascade-Fairwood, WA (cdp) King County	33	0.10
Bremerton, WA (city) Kitsap County	33	0.09
Port Angeles, WA (city) Clallam County	32	0.17
Paine Field-Lake Stickney, WA (cdp) Snohomish County	32	0.13
Puyallup, WA (city) Pierce County	32	0.10
North Marysville, WA (cdp) Snohomish County	30	0.14
Seattle Hill-Silver Firs, WA (cdp) Snohomish County	30	0.08
Stockton, CA (city) San Joaquin County	30	0.01
Kalifornsky, AK (cdp) Kenai Peninsula Borough	29	0.50
Anacortes, WA (city) Skagit County	29	0.20
Marysville, WA (city) Snohomish County	29	0.11
Sammamish, WA (city) King County	29	0.09
Picnic Point-North Lynnwood, WA (cdp) Snohomish County	28	0.12
East Hill-Meridian, WA (cdp) King County	28	0.10
Bellevue, WA (city) King County	28	0.03
Colorado Springs, CO (city) El Paso County	28	0.01
Wasilla, AK (city) Matanuska-Susitna Borough	27	0.49
Skagway, AK (city) Skagway-Hoonah-Angoon Census Area	26	3.02
South Hill, WA (cdp) Pierce County	26	0.08
Las Vegas, NV (city) Clark County	26	0.01
Ferndale, WA (city) Whatcom County	25	0.29
Riverton-Boulevard Park, WA (cdp) King County	25	0.22
Boise City, ID (city) Ada County	25	0.01
Cordova, AK (city) Valdez-Cordova Census Area	24	0.98
Lakes, AK (cdp) Matanuska-Susitna Borough	24	0.36
Meadow Lakes, AK (cdp) Matanuska-Susitna Borough	23	0.48
Knik-Fairview, AK (cdp) Matanuska-Susitna Borough	23	0.33
Tukwila, WA (city) King County	23	0.13
Gustavus, AK (cdp) Skagway-Hoonah-Angoon Census Area	22	5.13
Sutton-Alpine, AK (cdp) Matanuska-Susitna Borough	22	2.04
Palmer, AK (city) Matanuska-Susitna Borough	22	0.49
Mukilteo, WA (city) Snohomish County	22	0.12
Olympia, WA (city) Thurston County	22	0.05
Springfield, OR (city) Lane County	22	0.04
Fremont, CA (city) Alameda County	22	0.01
Big Lake, AK (cdp) Matanuska-Susitna Borough	21	0.80
Durango, CO (city) La Plata County	21	0.15
Alderwood Manor, WA (cdp) Snohomish County	21	0.14
Redmond, WA (city) King County	21	0.05
Bend, OR (city) Deschutes County	21	0.04
Alameda, CA (city) Alameda County	21	0.03
Honolulu, HI (cdp) Honolulu County	21	0.01
Ridgeway, AK (cdp) Kenai Peninsula Borough	20	1.04
Barrow, AK (city) North Slope Borough	20	0.44
Kingsgate, WA (cdp) King County	20	0.16
McMinnville, OR (city) Yamhill County	20	0.08
Corvallis, OR (city) Benton County	20	0.04
Gresham, OR (city) Multnomah County	20	0.02
Sacramento, CA (city) Sacramento County	20	0.00
Aberdeen, WA (city) Grays Harbor County	19	0.12
Kennewick, WA (city) Benton County	19	0.03
Pelican, AK (city) Skagway-Hoonah-Angoon Census Area	18	11.04
Nikiski, AK (cdp) Kenai Peninsula Borough	18	0.42
Brier, WA (city) Snohomish County	18	0.28
Keizer, OR (city) Marion County	18	0.06
Lacey, WA (city) Thurston County	18	0.06
Paradise, NV (cdp) Clark County	18	0.01
Reno, NV (city) Washoe County	18	0.01
Unalaska, AK (city) Aleutians West Census Area	17	0.40
Port Townsend, WA (city) Jefferson County	17	0.20
Lawrence, KS (city) Douglas County	17	0.02
Albuquerque, NM (city) Bernalillo County	17	0.00
Boston, MA (city) Suffolk County	17	0.00
Denver, CO (city) Denver County	17	0.00
Jacksonville, FL (special city) Duval County	17	0.00
West Lake Stevens, WA (cdp) Snohomish County	16	0.09
Inglewood-Finn Hill, WA (cdp) King County	16	0.07
Bothell, WA (city) King County	16	0.05
Lewiston, ID (city) Nez Perce County	16	0.05
Hillsboro, OR (city) Washington County	16	0.02
Fort Lauderdale, FL (city) Broward County	16	0.01
Dallas, TX (city) Dallas County	16	0.00
Mesa, AZ (city) Maricopa County	16	0.00
Kodiak Station, AK (cdp) Kodiak Island Borough	15	0.82
Tanaina, AK (cdp) Matanuska-Susitna Borough	15	0.30
East Port Orchard, WA (cdp) Kitsap County	15	0.29
Pacific, WA (city) King County	15	0.27
Dallas, OR (city) Polk County	15	0.12
Spanaway, WA (cdp) Pierce County	15	0.07
Kirkland, WA (city) King County	15	0.03
Lawton, OK (city) Comanche County	15	0.02
Yakima, WA (city) Yakima County	15	0.02
Glendale, AZ (city) Maricopa County	15	0.01
Chicago, IL (city) Cook County	15	0.00
Butte, AK (cdp) Matanuska-Susitna Borough	14	0.55
Seward, AK (city) Kenai Peninsula Borough	14	0.49
Rio Vista, CA (city) Solano County	14	0.31
Birch Bay, WA (cdp) Whatcom County	14	0.28
Walla Walla, WA (city) Walla Walla County	14	0.05
Beaverton, OR (city) Washington County	14	0.02
Long Beach, CA (city) Los Angeles County	14	0.00
Kasaan, AK (city) Prince of Wales-Outer Ketchikan Census Area	13	33.33
American Canyon, CA (city) Napa County	13	0.13
Lake Forest Park, WA (city) King County	13	0.10
Martha Lake, WA (cdp) Snohomish County	13	0.10
Bryn Mawr-Skyway, WA (cdp) King County	13	0.09
Monroe, WA (city) Snohomish County	13	0.09
Oak Harbor, WA (city) Island County	13	0.07
North Miami, FL (city) Miami-Dade County	13	0.02

Notes: (cdp) census designated place; Refer to the Explanation of Data in the front of the book for more detailed information.

Alaska Native: Tlingit-Haida

Top 150 Places Sorted by Percent

(Based on all places, regardless of population)

Place	Number	%
Klukwan, AK (cdp) Skagway-Hoonah-Angoon Census Area	115	82.73
Hydaburg, AK (city) Prince of Wales-Outer Ketchikan Census Area	287	75.13
Angoon, AK (city) Skagway-Hoonah-Angoon Census Area	399	69.76
Saxman, AK (city) Ketchikan Gateway Borough	290	67.29
Hoonah, AK (city) Skagway-Hoonah-Angoon Census Area	496	57.67
Kake, AK (city) Wrangell-Petersburg Census Area	397	55.92
Klawock, AK (city) Prince of Wales-Outer Ketchikan Census Area	372	43.56
Yakutat, AK (city) Yakutat City and Borough	277	40.74
Kasaan, AK (city) Prince of Wales-Outer Ketchikan Census Area	13	33.33
Hobart Bay, AK (cdp) Skagway-Hoonah-Angoon Census Area	1	33.33
Craig, AK (city) Prince of Wales-Outer Ketchikan Census Area	282	20.19
Wrangell, AK (city) Wrangell-Petersburg Census Area	350	15.16
Sitka, AK (city and borough) Sitka Borough	1,295	14.66
Ketchikan, AK (city) Ketchikan Gateway Borough	1,014	12.80
Haines, AK (city) Haines Borough	207	11.43
Port Alexander, AK (city) Wrangell-Petersburg Census Area	9	11.11
Pelican, AK (city) Skagway-Hoonah-Angoon Census Area	18	11.04
Juneau, AK (city and borough) Juneau Borough	3,272	10.65
Petersburg, AK (city) Wrangell-Petersburg Census Area	269	8.34
Port Protection, AK (cdp) Prince of Wales-Outer Ketchikan Census Area	5	7.94
Metlakatla, AK (cdp) Prince of Wales-Outer Ketchikan Census Area	92	6.69
Dot Lake Village, AK (cdp) Southeast Fairbanks Census Area	2	5.26
Gustavus, AK (cdp) Skagway-Hoonah-Angoon Census Area	22	5.13
Thoms Place, AK (cdp) Wrangell-Petersburg Census Area	1	4.55
Mosquito Lake, AK (cdp) Haines Borough	10	4.52
Chistochina, AK (cdp) Valdez-Cordova Census Area	4	4.30
Red Devil, AK (cdp) Bethel Census Area	2	4.17
Primrose, AK (cdp) Kenai Peninsula Borough	3	3.23
Skagway, AK (city) Skagway-Hoonah-Angoon Census Area	26	3.02
Point Baker, AK (cdp) Prince of Wales-Outer Ketchikan Census Area	1	2.86
Tyonek, AK (cdp) Kenai Peninsula Borough	5	2.59
Lutak, AK (cdp) Haines Borough	1	2.56
Mud Bay, AK (cdp) Haines Borough	3	2.19
Sutton-Alpine, AK (cdp) Matanuska-Susitna Borough	22	2.04
Chiniak, AK (cdp) Kodiak Island Borough	1	2.00
Whale Pass, AK (cdp) Prince of Wales-Outer Ketchikan Census Area	1	1.72
Nanwalek, AK (cdp) Kenai Peninsula Borough	3	1.69
Almira, WA (town) Lincoln County	5	1.66
Akiak, AK (city) Bethel Census Area	5	1.62
Teller, AK (city) Nome Census Area	4	1.49
Hollis, AK (cdp) Prince of Wales-Outer Ketchikan Census Area	2	1.44
Olivet, SD (town) Hutchinson County	1	1.43
Womens Bay, AK (cdp) Kodiak Island Borough	9	1.30
Oberon, ND (city) Benson County	1	1.23
Conway, WA (cdp) Skagit County	1	1.19
Salamatof, AK (cdp) Kenai Peninsula Borough	11	1.15
Saint Paul, AK (city) Aleutians West Census Area	6	1.13
Adair Village, OR (city) Benton County	6	1.12
Thorne Bay, AK (city) Prince of Wales-Outer Ketchikan Census Area	6	1.08
Ridgeway, AK (cdp) Kenai Peninsula Borough	20	1.04
Hyder, AK (cdp) Prince of Wales-Outer Ketchikan Census Area	1	1.03
Coffman Cove, AK (city) Prince of Wales-Outer Ketchikan Census Area	2	1.01
Cordova, AK (city) Valdez-Cordova Census Area	24	0.98
Covenant Life, AK (cdp) Haines Borough	1	0.98
Hamilton, WA (town) Skagit County	3	0.97
Tenakee Springs, AK (city) Skagway-Hoonah-Angoon Census Area	1	0.96
Adak, AK (cdp) Aleutians West Census Area	3	0.95
Valdez, AK (city) Valdez-Cordova Census Area	38	0.94
Cohoe, AK (cdp) Kenai Peninsula Borough	11	0.94
Perryville, AK (cdp) Lake and Peninsula Borough	1	0.93
Priest Point, WA (cdp) Snohomish County	7	0.90
Baring, WA (cdp) King County	2	0.86
Egegik, AK (city) Lake and Peninsula Borough	1	0.86
New Stuyahok, AK (city) Dillingham Census Area	4	0.85
Kodiak Station, AK (cdp) Kodiak Island Borough	15	0.82
Pueblo Pintado, NM (cdp) McKinley County	2	0.81
Chitina, AK (cdp) Valdez-Cordova Census Area	1	0.81
Big Lake, AK (cdp) Matanuska-Susitna Borough	21	0.80
North Pole, AK (city) Fairbanks North Star Borough	12	0.76
Galena, AK (city) Yukon-Koyukuk Census Area	5	0.74
Naukati Bay, AK (cdp) Prince of Wales-Outer Ketchikan Census Area	1	0.74
Kachemak, AK (city) Kenai Peninsula Borough	3	0.70
Bear Creek, AK (cdp) Kenai Peninsula Borough	12	0.69
Knik River, AK (cdp) Matanuska-Susitna Borough	4	0.69
Anchorage, AK (municipality) Anchorage Borough	1,712	0.66

Place	Number	%
Troy, ID (city) Latah County	5	0.63
Newhalen, AK (city) Lake and Peninsula Borough	1	0.63
Huntington, AR (city) Sebastian County	4	0.58
North Omak, WA (cdp) Okanogan County	4	0.58
Nikolaevsk, AK (cdp) Kenai Peninsula Borough	2	0.58
Grenada, CA (cdp) Siskiyou County	2	0.57
Weston, OR (city) Umatilla County	4	0.56
Butte, AK (cdp) Matanuska-Susitna Borough	14	0.55
Nevis, MN (city) Hubbard County	2	0.55
Koliganek, AK (cdp) Dillingham Census Area	1	0.55
Anchor Point, AK (cdp) Kenai Peninsula Borough	10	0.54
Glennallen, AK (cdp) Valdez-Cordova Census Area	3	0.54
Klein, MT (cdp) Musselshell County	1	0.53
Kalifornsky, AK (cdp) Kenai Peninsula Borough	29	0.50
Kenai, AK (city) Kenai Peninsula Borough	34	0.49
Wasilla, AK (city) Matanuska-Susitna Borough	27	0.49
Palmer, AK (city) Matanuska-Susitna Borough	22	0.49
Seward, AK (city) Kenai Peninsula Borough	14	0.49
Akeley, MN (city) Hubbard County	2	0.49
Moose Pass, AK (cdp) Kenai Peninsula Borough	1	0.49
Meadow Lakes, AK (cdp) Matanuska-Susitna Borough	23	0.48
Norman, AR (town) Montgomery County	2	0.47
Ocean City, WA (cdp) Grays Harbor County	1	0.46
Cheshire, OH (village) Gallia County	1	0.45
Barrow, AK (city) North Slope Borough	20	0.44
Deer River, MN (city) Itasca County	4	0.44
Wilson Creek, WA (town) Grant County	1	0.44
Sherman, ME (town) Aroostook County	4	0.43
Hammon, OK (town) Roger Mills County	2	0.43
Jacksonport, AR (town) Jackson County	1	0.43
Nikiski, AK (cdp) Kenai Peninsula Borough	18	0.42
Old Harbor, AK (city) Kodiak Island Borough	1	0.42
Ruston, WA (town) Pierce County	3	0.41
College, AK (cdp) Fairbanks North Star Borough	46	0.40
Unalaska, AK (city) Aleutians West Census Area	17	0.40
Mountain Village, AK (city) Wade Hampton Census Area	3	0.40
Marblemount, WA (cdp) Skagit County	1	0.40
Morton, WA (city) Lewis County	4	0.38
Concrete, WA (town) Skagit County	3	0.38
King Cove, AK (city) Aleutians East Borough	3	0.38
Moose Creek, AK (cdp) Fairbanks North Star Borough	2	0.37
Thorp, WA (cdp) Kittitas County	1	0.37
Woodbury, PA (borough) Bedford County	1	0.37
Lakes, AK (cdp) Matanuska-Susitna Borough	24	0.36
Ester, AK (cdp) Fairbanks North Star Borough	6	0.36
Tok, AK (cdp) Southeast Fairbanks Census Area	5	0.36
Craigmont, ID (city) Lewis County	2	0.36
Lazy Mountain, AK (cdp) Matanuska-Susitna Borough	4	0.35
Seldovia, AK (city) Kenai Peninsula Borough	1	0.35
Warm Beach, WA (cdp) Snohomish County	7	0.34
Quilcene, WA (cdp) Jefferson County	2	0.34
Knik-Fairview, AK (cdp) Matanuska-Susitna Borough	23	0.33
Westport, WA (city) Grays Harbor County	7	0.33
Thoreau, NM (cdp) McKinley County	6	0.32
Tulalip Bay, WA (cdp) Snohomish County	5	0.32
Dunes City, OR (city) Lane County	4	0.32
Bassfield, MS (town) Jefferson Davis County	1	0.32
Spirit, WI (town) Price County	1	0.32
Stantonville, TN (town) McNairy County	1	0.32
Rio Vista, CA (city) Solano County	14	0.31
Y, AK (cdp) Matanuska-Susitna Borough	3	0.31
Wishram, WA (cdp) Klickitat County	1	0.31
Tanaina, AK (cdp) Matanuska-Susitna Borough	15	0.30
Granite Falls, WA (city) Snohomish County	7	0.30
Plummer, ID (city) Benewah County	3	0.30
Kwigillingok, AK (cdp) Bethel Census Area	1	0.30
Nulato, AK (city) Yukon-Koyukuk Census Area	1	0.30
Ferndale, WA (city) Whatcom County	25	0.29
East Port Orchard, WA (cdp) Kitsap County	15	0.29
Soldotna, AK (city) Kenai Peninsula Borough	11	0.29
Mountlake Terrace, WA (city) Snohomish County	58	0.28
Brier, WA (city) Snohomish County	18	0.28
Birch Bay, WA (cdp) Whatcom County	14	0.28
La Grange, WI (town) Monroe County	5	0.28
Copper Center, AK (cdp) Valdez-Cordova Census Area	1	0.28

Notes: (cdp) census designated place; Refer to the Explanation of Data in the front of the book for more detailed information.

Alaska Native: Tlingit-Haida

Top 150 Places Sorted by Percent

(Based on places with populations of 10,000 or more)

Place	Number	%
Juneau, AK (city and borough) Juneau Borough	3,272	10.65
Anchorage, AK (municipality) Anchorage Borough	1,712	0.66
College, AK (cdp) Fairbanks North Star Borough	46	0.40
Mountlake Terrace, WA (city) Snohomish County	58	0.28
SeaTac, WA (city) King County	60	0.24
Riverton-Boulevard Park, WA (cdp) King County	25	0.22
Shoreline, WA (city) King County	108	0.20
White Center, WA (cdp) King County	42	0.20
Anacortes, WA (city) Skagit County	29	0.20
Fairbanks, AK (city) Fairbanks North Star Borough	56	0.19
Edmonds, WA (city) Snohomish County	68	0.17
Port Angeles, WA (city) Clallam County	32	0.17
Lynnwood, WA (city) Snohomish County	55	0.16
Kingsgate, WA (cdp) King County	20	0.16
Durango, CO (city) La Plata County	21	0.15
Everett, WA (city) Snohomish County	130	0.14
Burien, WA (city) King County	45	0.14
Des Moines, WA (city) King County	40	0.14
Mount Vernon, WA (city) Skagit County	37	0.14
North Creek, WA (cdp) Snohomish County	35	0.14
North Marysville, WA (cdp) Snohomish County	30	0.14
Alderwood Manor, WA (cdp) Snohomish County	21	0.14
Paine Field-Lake Stickney, WA (cdp) Snohomish County	32	0.13
Tukwila, WA (city) King County	23	0.13
Seattle, WA (city) King County	692	0.12
Picnic Point-North Lynnwood, WA (cdp) Snohomish County	28	0.12
Mukilteo, WA (city) Snohomish County	22	0.12
Aberdeen, WA (city) Grays Harbor County	19	0.12
Dallas, OR (city) Polk County	15	0.12
Federal Way, WA (city) King County	95	0.11
Kent, WA (city) King County	86	0.11
Renton, WA (city) King County	55	0.11
Auburn, WA (city) King County	46	0.11
Marysville, WA (city) Snohomish County	29	0.11
Tacoma, WA (city) Pierce County	192	0.10
Bellingham, WA (city) Whatcom County	65	0.10
Cascade-Fairwood, WA (cdp) King County	33	0.10
Puyallup, WA (city) Pierce County	32	0.10
East Hill-Meridian, WA (cdp) King County	28	0.10
Lake Forest Park, WA (city) King County	13	0.10
Martha Lake, WA (cdp) Snohomish County	13	0.10
Lakewood, WA (city) Pierce County	50	0.09
Bremerton, WA (city) Kitsap County	33	0.09
Sammamish, WA (city) King County	29	0.09
West Lake Stevens, WA (cdp) Snohomish County	16	0.09
Bryn Mawr-Skyway, WA (cdp) King County	13	0.09
Monroe, WA (city) Snohomish County	13	0.09
Seattle Hill-Silver Firs, WA (cdp) Snohomish County	30	0.08
South Hill, WA (cdp) Pierce County	26	0.08
McMinnville, OR (city) Yamhill County	20	0.08
Ellensburg, WA (city) Kittitas County	12	0.08
Camano, WA (cdp) Island County	11	0.08
Tumwater, WA (city) Thurston County	10	0.08
Enumclaw, WA (city) King County	9	0.08
Inglewood-Finn Hill, WA (cdp) King County	16	0.07
Spanaway, WA (cdp) Pierce County	15	0.07
Oak Harbor, WA (city) Island County	13	0.07
Pendleton, OR (city) Umatilla County	12	0.07
Lakeland North, WA (cdp) King County	11	0.07
Silverdale, WA (cdp) Kitsap County	11	0.07
Maple Valley, WA (city) King County	10	0.07
Redmond, OR (city) Deschutes County	10	0.07
Canby, OR (city) Clackamas County	9	0.07
Arlington, WA (city) Snohomish County	8	0.07
Issaquah, WA (city) King County	8	0.07
Lakeland South, WA (cdp) King County	8	0.07
Saint Helens, OR (city) Columbia County	7	0.07
West Valley, WA (cdp) Yakima County	7	0.07
Keizer, OR (city) Marion County	18	0.06
Lacey, WA (city) Thurston County	18	0.06
Orchards, WA (cdp) Clark County	11	0.06
Coos Bay, OR (city) Coos County	9	0.06
Elk Plain, WA (cdp) Pierce County	9	0.06
Five Corners, WA (cdp) Clark County	7	0.06
Olympia, WA (city) Thurston County	22	0.05
Redmond, WA (city) King County	21	0.05
Bothell, WA (city) King County	16	0.05
Lewiston, ID (city) Nez Perce County	16	0.05
Walla Walla, WA (city) Walla Walla County	14	0.05
Pullman, WA (city) Whitman County	12	0.05
Bainbridge Island, WA (city) Kitsap County	11	0.05
Cottage Lake, WA (cdp) King County	11	0.05
Moses Lake, WA (city) Grant County	8	0.05
Ukiah, CA (city) Mendocino County	8	0.05
Covington, WA (city) King County	7	0.05
McKinleyville, CA (cdp) Humboldt County	7	0.05
Red Bluff, CA (city) Tehama County	7	0.05
Lebanon, OR (city) Linn County	6	0.05
Nipomo, CA (cdp) San Luis Obispo County	6	0.05
Oroville, CA (city) Butte County	6	0.05
Prairie Ridge, WA (cdp) Pierce County	6	0.05
Spring Creek, NV (cdp) Elko County	5	0.05
Springfield, OR (city) Lane County	22	0.04
Bend, OR (city) Deschutes County	21	0.04
Corvallis, OR (city) Benton County	20	0.04
Eureka, CA (city) Humboldt County	11	0.04
Oregon City, OR (city) Clackamas County	11	0.04
University Place, WA (city) Pierce County	11	0.04
Kihei, HI (cdp) Maui County	7	0.04
Oatfield, OR (cdp) Clackamas County	6	0.04
Beacon, NY (city) Dutchess County	5	0.04
Four Corners, OR (cdp) Marion County	5	0.04
Kalispell, MT (city) Flathead County	5	0.04
Mill Creek, WA (city) Snohomish County	5	0.04
Niceville, FL (city) Okaloosa County	5	0.04
Beaumont, CA (city) Riverside County	4	0.04
Vashon, WA (cdp) King County	4	0.04
Portland, OR (city) Multnomah County	138	0.03
Vancouver, WA (city) Clark County	50	0.03
Eugene, OR (city) Lane County	46	0.03
Salem, OR (city) Marion County	42	0.03
Bellevue, WA (city) King County	28	0.03
Alameda, CA (city) Alameda County	21	0.03
Kennewick, WA (city) Benton County	19	0.03
Kirkland, WA (city) King County	15	0.03
Richland, WA (city) Benton County	10	0.03
Opportunity, WA (cdp) Spokane County	8	0.03
Ridgecrest, CA (city) Kern County	8	0.03
Pahrump, NV (cdp) Nye County	7	0.03
Parkland, WA (cdp) Pierce County	7	0.03
West Puente Valley, CA (cdp) Los Angeles County	7	0.03
Ypsilanti, MI (city) Washtenaw County	6	0.03
Ashland, OR (city) Jackson County	5	0.03
Centralia, WA (city) Lewis County	5	0.03
Avenal, CA (city) Kings County	4	0.03
Chickasha, OK (city) Grady County	4	0.03
East Wenatchee Bench, WA (cdp) Douglas County	4	0.03
Fountain, CO (city) El Paso County	4	0.03
Kelso, WA (city) Cowlitz County	4	0.03
Marana, AZ (town) Pima County	4	0.03
Schofield Barracks, HI (cdp) Honolulu County	4	0.03
Artesia, NM (city) Eddy County	3	0.03
Easttown, PA (township) Chester County	3	0.03
Ecorse, MI (city) Wayne County	3	0.03
Farmington, NY (town) Ontario County	3	0.03
Gladstone, OR (city) Clackamas County	3	0.03
Spokane, WA (city) Spokane County	40	0.02
Gresham, OR (city) Multnomah County	20	0.02
Lawrence, KS (city) Douglas County	17	0.02
Hillsboro, OR (city) Washington County	16	0.02
Lawton, OK (city) Comanche County	15	0.02
Yakima, WA (city) Yakima County	15	0.02
Beaverton, OR (city) Washington County	14	0.02
North Miami, FL (city) Miami-Dade County	13	0.02
Carmichael, CA (cdp) Sacramento County	12	0.02
Santa Fe, NM (city) Santa Fe County	12	0.02
Great Falls, MT (city) Cascade County	9	0.02
Hilo, HI (cdp) Hawaii County	9	0.02
Nampa, ID (city) Canyon County	9	0.02
Aloha, OR (cdp) Washington County	8	0.02

Notes: (cdp) census designated place; Refer to the Explanation of Data in the front of the book for more detailed information.

Alaska Native: All other tribes

Top 150 Places Sorted by Number

(Based on all places, regardless of population)

Place	Number	%
Metlakatla, AK (cdp) Prince of Wales-Outer Ketchikan Census Area	1,123	81.67
Ketchikan, AK (city) Ketchikan Gateway Borough	316	3.99
Anchorage, AK (municipality) Anchorage Borough	285	0.11
Seattle, WA (city) King County	169	0.03
Sitka, AK (city and borough) Sitka Borough	122	1.38
Juneau, AK (city and borough) Juneau Borough	120	0.39
Tacoma, WA (city) Pierce County	34	0.02
Wrangell, AK (city) Wrangell-Petersburg Census Area	30	1.30
New York, NY (city) New York City	26	0.00
Portland, OR (city) Multnomah County	24	0.00
Everett, WA (city) Snohomish County	23	0.03
SeaTac, WA (city) King County	21	0.08
Bellingham, WA (city) Whatcom County	20	0.03
Renton, WA (city) King County	18	0.04
Oakland, CA (city) Alameda County	17	0.00
Lynnwood, WA (city) Snohomish County	16	0.05
Kent, WA (city) King County	16	0.02
Shoreline, WA (city) King County	15	0.03
Los Angeles, CA (city) Los Angeles County	15	0.00
Sacramento, CA (city) Sacramento County	15	0.00
Klawock, AK (city) Prince of Wales-Outer Ketchikan Census Area	14	1.64
Federal Way, WA (city) King County	14	0.02
San Jose, CA (city) Santa Clara County	14	0.00
Des Moines, WA (city) King County	13	0.04
Kake, AK (city) Wrangell-Petersburg Census Area	12	1.69
Hoonah, AK (city) Skagway-Hoonah-Angoon Census Area	12	1.40
Barrow, AK (city) North Slope Borough	12	0.26
Burien, WA (city) King County	12	0.04
Auburn, WA (city) King County	12	0.03
Vancouver, WA (city) Clark County	12	0.01
Craig, AK (city) Prince of Wales-Outer Ketchikan Census Area	10	0.72
Oregon City, OR (city) Clackamas County	10	0.04
Kirkland, WA (city) King County	10	0.02
Fairbanks, AK (city) Fairbanks North Star Borough	9	0.03
Phoenix, AZ (city) Maricopa County	9	0.00
San Francisco, CA (city) San Francisco County	9	0.00
Hydaburg, AK (city) Prince of Wales-Outer Ketchikan Census Area	8	2.09
Petersburg, AK (city) Wrangell-Petersburg Census Area	8	0.25
Kalifornsky, AK (cdp) Kenai Peninsula Borough	8	0.14
Mountlake Terrace, WA (city) Snohomish County	8	0.04
Port Angeles, WA (city) Clallam County	8	0.04
Edmonds, WA (city) Snohomish County	8	0.02
Gresham, OR (city) Multnomah County	8	0.01
San Leandro, CA (city) Alameda County	8	0.01
Upland, CA (city) San Bernardino County	8	0.01
Yakima, WA (city) Yakima County	8	0.01
Mesa, AZ (city) Maricopa County	8	0.00
Seward, AK (city) Kenai Peninsula Borough	7	0.25
Martha Lake, WA (cdp) Snohomish County	7	0.06
Tukwila, WA (city) King County	7	0.04
Inglewood-Finn Hill, WA (cdp) King County	7	0.03
East Hill-Meridian, WA (cdp) King County	7	0.02
Haines, AK (city) Haines Borough	6	0.33
Omak, WA (city) Okanogan County	6	0.13
Rathdrum, ID (city) Kootenai County	6	0.12
Bethel, AK (city) Bethel Census Area	6	0.11
Kenai, AK (city) Kenai Peninsula Borough	6	0.09
College, AK (cdp) Fairbanks North Star Borough	6	0.05
Covington, WA (city) King County	6	0.04
North Marysville, WA (cdp) Snohomish County	6	0.03
Cottage Lake, WA (cdp) King County	6	0.02
Buena Park, CA (city) Orange County	6	0.01
Idaho Falls, ID (city) Bonneville County	6	0.01
Olympia, WA (city) Thurston County	6	0.01
Shungnak, AK (city) Northwest Arctic Borough	5	1.95
Ridgeway, AK (cdp) Kenai Peninsula Borough	5	0.26
Nikiski, AK (cdp) Kenai Peninsula Borough	5	0.12
Lakes, AK (cdp) Matanuska-Susitna Borough	5	0.07
Aberdeen, WA (city) Grays Harbor County	5	0.03
Lakeland North, WA (cdp) King County	5	0.03
Mukilteo, WA (city) Snohomish County	5	0.03
Mercer Island, WA (city) King County	5	0.02
Walla Walla, WA (city) Walla Walla County	5	0.02
White Center, WA (cdp) King County	5	0.02
Alameda, CA (city) Alameda County	5	0.01
Bremerton, WA (city) Kitsap County	5	0.01
Carson City, NV (special city) Carson City city	5	0.01
Vacaville, CA (city) Solano County	5	0.01
Albuquerque, NM (city) Bernalillo County	5	0.00
Bellevue, WA (city) King County	5	0.00
Long Beach, CA (city) Los Angeles County	5	0.00
San Diego, CA (city) San Diego County	5	0.00
Monona, IA (city) Clayton County	4	0.26
Grand Mound, WA (cdp) Thurston County	4	0.21
Soldotna, AK (city) Kenai Peninsula Borough	4	0.11
Valdez, AK (city) Valdez-Cordova Census Area	4	0.10
Sterling, AK (cdp) Kenai Peninsula Borough	4	0.09
Burlington, WA (city) Skagit County	4	0.06
Knik-Fairview, AK (cdp) Matanuska-Susitna Borough	4	0.06
Kodiak, AK (city) Kodiak Island Borough	4	0.06
Lake Shore, WA (cdp) Clark County	4	0.06
Lake Stevens, WA (city) Snohomish County	4	0.06
Cheney, WA (city) Spokane County	4	0.05
Cottage Grove, OR (city) Lane County	4	0.05
Washougal, WA (city) Clark County	4	0.05
Bryn Mawr-Skyway, WA (cdp) King County	4	0.03
Grand Terrace, CA (city) San Bernardino County	4	0.03
Atwater, CA (city) Merced County	4	0.02
Gallup, NM (city) McKinley County	4	0.02
Paine Field-Lake Stickney, WA (cdp) Snohomish County	4	0.02
Picnic Point-North Lynnwood, WA (cdp) Snohomish County	4	0.02
Salmon Creek, WA (cdp) Clark County	4	0.02
Apple Valley, MN (city) Dakota County	4	0.01
Bothell, WA (city) King County	4	0.01
Pekin, IL (city) Tazewell County	4	0.01
Sammamish, WA (city) King County	4	0.01
Tigard, OR (city) Washington County	4	0.01
Boston, MA (city) Suffolk County	4	0.00
Fontana, CA (city) San Bernardino County	4	0.00
Garden Grove, CA (city) Orange County	4	0.00
Lansing, MI (city) Ingham County	4	0.00
Lawton, OK (city) Comanche County	4	0.00
Orem, UT (city) Utah County	4	0.00
Santa Rosa, CA (city) Sonoma County	4	0.00
Spokane, WA (city) Spokane County	4	0.00
Naukati Bay, AK (cdp) Prince of Wales-Outer Ketchikan Census Area	3	2.22
Hollis, AK (cdp) Prince of Wales-Outer Ketchikan Census Area	3	2.16
Thorne Bay, AK (city) Prince of Wales-Outer Ketchikan Census Area	3	0.54
Metolius, OR (city) Jefferson County	3	0.47
Shaker Church, WA (cdp) Snohomish County	3	0.38
Marsing, ID (city) Owyhee County	3	0.34
Sand Point, AK (city) Aleutians East Borough	3	0.32
Minco, OK (city) Grady County	3	0.18
Willow Creek, CA (cdp) Humboldt County	3	0.17
Gervais, OR (city) Marion County	3	0.15
Dillingham, AK (city) Dillingham Census Area	3	0.12
Belgrade, ME (town) Kennebec County	3	0.10
Indianola, WA (cdp) Kitsap County	3	0.10
Kotzebue, AK (city) Northwest Arctic Borough	3	0.10
Sutter, CA (cdp) Sutter County	3	0.10
Burney, CA (cdp) Shasta County	3	0.09
Suquamish, WA (cdp) Kitsap County	3	0.09
Birch Bay, WA (cdp) Whatcom County	3	0.06
Crystal Lake, FL (cdp) Polk County	3	0.06
Raleigh Hills, OR (cdp) Washington County	3	0.05
Sidney, NE (city) Cheyenne County	3	0.05
Camp Pendleton North, CA (cdp) San Diego County	3	0.04
Harvard, IL (city) McHenry County	3	0.04
Maltby, WA (cdp) Snohomish County	3	0.04
Shelton, WA (city) Mason County	3	0.04
West Valley, WA (cdp) Yakima County	3	0.03
Dallas, OR (city) Polk County	3	0.02
Durango, CO (city) La Plata County	3	0.02
Enterprise, NV (cdp) Clark County	3	0.02
Kihei, HI (cdp) Maui County	3	0.02
Maple Valley, WA (city) King County	3	0.02
Orchards, WA (cdp) Clark County	3	0.02
Waterville, ME (city) Kennebec County	3	0.02
Bainbridge Island, WA (city) Kitsap County	3	0.01
Bozeman, MT (city) Gallatin County	3	0.01

Notes: (cdp) census designated place; Refer to the Explanation of Data in the front of the book for more detailed information.

Alaska Native: All other tribes

Top 150 Places Sorted by Percent

(Based on all places, regardless of population)

Place	Number	%
Metlakatla, AK (cdp) Prince of Wales-Outer Ketchikan Census Area	1,123	81.67
Point Baker, AK (cdp) Prince of Wales-Outer Ketchikan Census Area	2	5.71
Ketchikan, AK (city) Ketchikan Gateway Borough	316	3.99
Kasaan, AK (city) Prince of Wales-Outer Ketchikan Census Area	1	2.56
Naukati Bay, AK (cdp) Prince of Wales-Outer Ketchikan Census Area	3	2.22
Hollis, AK (cdp) Prince of Wales-Outer Ketchikan Census Area	3	2.16
Hydaburg, AK (city) Prince of Wales-Outer Ketchikan Census Area	8	2.09
Shungnak, AK (city) Northwest Arctic Borough	5	1.95
Kake, AK (city) Wrangell-Petersburg Census Area	12	1.69
Klawock, AK (city) Prince of Wales-Outer Ketchikan Census Area	14	1.64
Hoonah, AK (city) Skagway-Hoonah-Angoon Census Area	12	1.40
Sitka, AK (city and borough) Sitka Borough	122	1.38
Wrangell, AK (city) Wrangell-Petersburg Census Area	30	1.30
Chuathbaluk, AK (city) Bethel Census Area	1	0.84
Point Lay, AK (cdp) North Slope Borough	2	0.81
Shageluk, AK (city) Yukon-Koyukuk Census Area	1	0.78
Alpine Village, CA (cdp) Alpine County	1	0.74
Craig, AK (city) Prince of Wales-Outer Ketchikan Census Area	10	0.72
Adak, AK (cdp) Aleutians West Census Area	2	0.63
Pelican, AK (city) Skagway-Hoonah-Angoon Census Area	1	0.61
Thorne Bay, AK (city) Prince of Wales-Outer Ketchikan Census Area	3	0.54
Metolius, OR (city) Jefferson County	3	0.47
West Manchester, OH (village) Preble County	2	0.46
Juneau, AK (city and borough) Juneau Borough	120	0.39
Shaker Church, WA (cdp) Snohomish County	3	0.38
Eldorado, OH (village) Preble County	2	0.37
Angoon, AK (city) Skagway-Hoonah-Angoon Census Area	2	0.35
Seldovia, AK (city) Kenai Peninsula Borough	1	0.35
Marsing, ID (city) Owyhee County	3	0.34
Russian Mission, AK (city) Wade Hampton Census Area	1	0.34
Haines, AK (city) Haines Borough	6	0.33
Sand Point, AK (city) Aleutians East Borough	3	0.32
Barrow, AK (city) North Slope Borough	12	0.26
Ridgeway, AK (cdp) Kenai Peninsula Borough	5	0.26
Monona, IA (city) Clayton County	4	0.26
Petersburg, AK (city) Wrangell-Petersburg Census Area	8	0.25
Seward, AK (city) Kenai Peninsula Borough	7	0.25
Potlatch, ID (city) Latah County	2	0.25
Nenana, AK (city) Yukon-Koyukuk Census Area	1	0.25
Belmont, ME (town) Waldo County	2	0.24
Grand Mound, WA (cdp) Thurston County	4	0.21
Knute, MN (township) Polk County	1	0.20
Farm Loop, AK (cdp) Matanuska-Susitna Borough	2	0.19
Saint Paul, AK (city) Aleutians West Census Area	1	0.19
Minco, OK (city) Grady County	3	0.18
Sedgwick, ME (town) Hancock County	2	0.18
Willow Creek, CA (cdp) Humboldt County	3	0.17
Quilcene, WA (cdp) Jefferson County	1	0.17
Gervais, OR (city) Marion County	3	0.15
Kalifornsky, AK (cdp) Kenai Peninsula Borough	8	0.14
Ames Lake, WA (cdp) King County	2	0.14
Omak, WA (city) Okanogan County	6	0.13
Concrete, WA (town) Skagit County	1	0.13
Neah Bay, WA (cdp) Clallam County	1	0.13
Ninilchik, AK (cdp) Kenai Peninsula Borough	1	0.13
Palm Shores, FL (town) Brevard County	1	0.13
Point Hope, AK (city) North Slope Borough	1	0.13
Rathdrum, ID (city) Kootenai County	6	0.12
Nikiski, AK (cdp) Kenai Peninsula Borough	5	0.12
Dillingham, AK (city) Dillingham Census Area	3	0.12
Anchorage, AK (municipality) Anchorage Borough	285	0.11
Bethel, AK (city) Bethel Census Area	6	0.11
Soldotna, AK (city) Kenai Peninsula Borough	4	0.11
Deer River, MN (city) Itasca County	1	0.11
Valdez, AK (city) Valdez-Cordova Census Area	4	0.10
Belgrade, ME (town) Kennebec County	3	0.10
Indianola, WA (cdp) Kitsap County	3	0.10
Kotzebue, AK (city) Northwest Arctic Borough	3	0.10
Sutter, CA (cdp) Sutter County	3	0.10
Langdon Place, KY (city) Jefferson County	1	0.10
Salamatof, AK (cdp) Kenai Peninsula Borough	1	0.10
Kenai, AK (city) Kenai Peninsula Borough	6	0.09
Sterling, AK (cdp) Kenai Peninsula Borough	4	0.09
Burney, CA (cdp) Shasta County	3	0.09
Suquamish, WA (cdp) Kitsap County	3	0.09

Place	Number	%
Bay City, OR (city) Tillamook County	1	0.09
Gold Hill, OR (city) Jackson County	1	0.09
Lazy Mountain, AK (cdp) Matanuska-Susitna Borough	1	0.09
Yacolt, WA (town) Clark County	1	0.09
SeaTac, WA (city) King County	21	0.08
Belcourt, ND (cdp) Rolette County	2	0.08
Cordova, AK (city) Valdez-Cordova Census Area	2	0.08
Maple Heights-Lake Desire, WA (cdp) King County	2	0.08
Lakes, AK (cdp) Matanuska-Susitna Borough	5	0.07
Harrisburg, OR (city) Linn County	2	0.07
Trinity, TX (city) Trinity County	2	0.07
Brownsville, OR (city) Linn County	1	0.07
Martha Lake, WA (cdp) Snohomish County	7	0.06
Burlington, WA (city) Skagit County	4	0.06
Knik-Fairview, AK (cdp) Matanuska-Susitna Borough	4	0.06
Kodiak, AK (city) Kodiak Island Borough	4	0.06
Lake Shore, WA (cdp) Clark County	4	0.06
Lake Stevens, WA (city) Snohomish County	4	0.06
Birch Bay, WA (cdp) Whatcom County	3	0.06
Crystal Lake, FL (cdp) Polk County	3	0.06
Grangeville, ID (city) Idaho County	2	0.06
Bear Creek, AK (cdp) Kenai Peninsula Borough	1	0.06
La Center, WA (city) Clark County	1	0.06
Willow, AK (cdp) Matanuska-Susitna Borough	1	0.06
Lynnwood, WA (city) Snohomish County	16	0.05
College, AK (cdp) Fairbanks North Star Borough	6	0.05
Cheney, WA (city) Spokane County	4	0.05
Cottage Grove, OR (city) Lane County	4	0.05
Washougal, WA (city) Clark County	4	0.05
Raleigh Hills, OR (cdp) Washington County	3	0.05
Sidney, NE (city) Cheyenne County	3	0.05
Louisiana, MO (city) Pike County	2	0.05
Sequim, WA (city) Clallam County	2	0.05
Stanwood, WA (city) Snohomish County	2	0.05
Esparto, CA (cdp) Yolo County	1	0.05
Fishhook, AK (cdp) Matanuska-Susitna Borough	1	0.05
Tunkhannock, PA (borough) Wyoming County	1	0.05
White Salmon, WA (city) Klickitat County	1	0.05
Renton, WA (city) King County	18	0.04
Des Moines, WA (city) King County	13	0.04
Burien, WA (city) King County	12	0.04
Oregon City, OR (city) Clackamas County	10	0.04
Mountlake Terrace, WA (city) Snohomish County	8	0.04
Port Angeles, WA (city) Clallam County	8	0.04
Tukwila, WA (city) King County	7	0.04
Covington, WA (city) King County	6	0.04
Camp Pendleton North, CA (cdp) San Diego County	3	0.04
Harvard, IL (city) McHenry County	3	0.04
Maltby, WA (cdp) Snohomish County	3	0.04
Shelton, WA (city) Mason County	3	0.04
Ashdown, AR (city) Little River County	2	0.04
Meadow Lakes, AK (cdp) Matanuska-Susitna Borough	2	0.04
Palmer, AK (city) Matanuska-Susitna Borough	2	0.04
Port Sheldon, MI (township) Ottawa County	2	0.04
Algona, WA (city) King County	1	0.04
Big Lake, AK (cdp) Matanuska-Susitna Borough	1	0.04
Butte, AK (cdp) Matanuska-Susitna Borough	1	0.04
Carthage, IL (city) Hancock County	1	0.04
Dundee, OR (city) Yamhill County	1	0.04
Early, TX (city) Brown County	1	0.04
Littlefield, MI (township) Emmet County	1	0.04
Reynoldsville, PA (borough) Jefferson County	1	0.04
University Park, NM (cdp) Dona Ana County	1	0.04
Wedgefield, FL (cdp) Orange County	1	0.04
Whetstone, AZ (cdp) Cochise County	1	0.04
Seattle, WA (city) King County	169	0.03
Everett, WA (city) Snohomish County	23	0.03
Bellingham, WA (city) Whatcom County	20	0.03
Shoreline, WA (city) King County	15	0.03
Auburn, WA (city) King County	12	0.03
Fairbanks, AK (city) Fairbanks North Star Borough	9	0.03
Inglewood-Finn Hill, WA (cdp) King County	7	0.03
North Marysville, WA (cdp) Snohomish County	6	0.03
Aberdeen, WA (city) Grays Harbor County	5	0.03
Lakeland North, WA (cdp) King County	5	0.03

Notes: (cdp) census designated place; Refer to the Explanation of Data in the front of the book for more detailed information.

Alaska Native: All other tribes

Top 150 Places Sorted by Percent

(Based on places with populations of 10,000 or more)

Place	Number	%
Juneau, AK (city and borough) Juneau Borough	120	0.39
Anchorage, AK (municipality) Anchorage Borough	285	0.11
SeaTac, WA (city) King County	21	0.08
Martha Lake, WA (cdp) Snohomish County	7	0.06
Lynnwood, WA (city) Snohomish County	16	0.05
College, AK (cdp) Fairbanks North Star Borough	6	0.05
Renton, WA (city) King County	18	0.04
Des Moines, WA (city) King County	13	0.04
Burien, WA (city) King County	12	0.04
Oregon City, OR (city) Clackamas County	10	0.04
Mountlake Terrace, WA (city) Snohomish County	8	0.04
Port Angeles, WA (city) Clallam County	8	0.04
Tukwila, WA (city) King County	7	0.04
Covington, WA (city) King County	6	0.04
Seattle, WA (city) King County	169	0.03
Everett, WA (city) Snohomish County	23	0.03
Bellingham, WA (city) Whatcom County	20	0.03
Shoreline, WA (city) King County	15	0.03
Auburn, WA (city) King County	12	0.03
Fairbanks, AK (city) Fairbanks North Star Borough	9	0.03
Inglewood-Finn Hill, WA (cdp) King County	7	0.03
North Marysville, WA (cdp) Snohomish County	6	0.03
Aberdeen, WA (city) Grays Harbor County	5	0.03
Lakeland North, WA (cdp) King County	5	0.03
Mukilteo, WA (city) Snohomish County	5	0.03
Bryn Mawr-Skyway, WA (cdp) King County	4	0.03
Grand Terrace, CA (city) San Bernardino County	4	0.03
West Valley, WA (cdp) Yakima County	3	0.03
Tacoma, WA (city) Pierce County	34	0.02
Kent, WA (city) King County	16	0.02
Federal Way, WA (city) King County	14	0.02
Kirkland, WA (city) King County	10	0.02
Edmonds, WA (city) Snohomish County	8	0.02
East Hill-Meridian, WA (cdp) King County	7	0.02
Cottage Lake, WA (cdp) King County	6	0.02
Mercer Island, WA (city) King County	5	0.02
Walla Walla, WA (city) Walla Walla County	5	0.02
White Center, WA (cdp) King County	5	0.02
Atwater, CA (city) Merced County	4	0.02
Gallup, NM (city) McKinley County	4	0.02
Paine Field-Lake Stickney, WA (cdp) Snohomish County	4	0.02
Picnic Point-North Lynnwood, WA (cdp) Snohomish County	4	0.02
Salmon Creek, WA (cdp) Clark County	4	0.02
Dallas, OR (city) Polk County	3	0.02
Durango, CO (city) La Plata County	3	0.02
Enterprise, NV (cdp) Clark County	3	0.02
Kihei, HI (cdp) Maui County	3	0.02
Maple Valley, WA (city) King County	3	0.02
Orchards, WA (cdp) Clark County	3	0.02
Waterville, ME (city) Kennebec County	3	0.02
Azalea Park, FL (cdp) Orange County	2	0.02
Grand Haven, MI (city) Ottawa County	2	0.02
Kingsgate, WA (cdp) King County	2	0.02
Lakeland South, WA (cdp) King County	2	0.02
Lakewood Park, FL (cdp) Saint Lucie County	2	0.02
Lea Hill, WA (cdp) King County	2	0.02
Tumwater, WA (city) Thurston County	2	0.02
Vancouver, WA (city) Clark County	12	0.01
Gresham, OR (city) Multnomah County	8	0.01
San Leandro, CA (city) Alameda County	8	0.01
Upland, CA (city) San Bernardino County	8	0.01
Yakima, WA (city) Yakima County	8	0.01
Buena Park, CA (city) Orange County	6	0.01
Idaho Falls, ID (city) Bonneville County	6	0.01
Olympia, WA (city) Thurston County	6	0.01
Alameda, CA (city) Alameda County	5	0.01
Bremerton, WA (city) Kitsap County	5	0.01
Carson City, NV (special city) Carson City city	5	0.01
Vacaville, CA (city) Solano County	5	0.01
Apple Valley, MN (city) Dakota County	4	0.01
Bothell, WA (city) King County	4	0.01
Pekin, IL (city) Tazewell County	4	0.01
Sammamish, WA (city) King County	4	0.01
Tigard, OR (city) Washington County	4	0.01
Bainbridge Island, WA (city) Kitsap County	3	0.01
Bozeman, MT (city) Gallatin County	3	0.01
Coeur d'Alene, ID (city) Kootenai County	3	0.01
Keizer, OR (city) Marion County	3	0.01
Lacey, WA (city) Thurston County	3	0.01
Marysville, WA (city) Snohomish County	3	0.01
North Chicago, IL (city) Lake County	3	0.01
North Creek, WA (cdp) Snohomish County	3	0.01
Puyallup, WA (city) Pierce County	3	0.01
Seattle Hill-Silver Firs, WA (cdp) Snohomish County	3	0.01
Cascade-Fairwood, WA (cdp) King County	2	0.01
Grants Pass, OR (city) Josephine County	2	0.01
Hercules, CA (city) Contra Costa County	2	0.01
Kenmore, WA (city) King County	2	0.01
Lewiston, ID (city) Nez Perce County	2	0.01
Linda, CA (cdp) Yuba County	2	0.01
Manhattan Beach, CA (city) Los Angeles County	2	0.01
Morgan Hill, CA (city) Santa Clara County	2	0.01
Oatfield, OR (cdp) Clackamas County	2	0.01
Pasco, WA (city) Franklin County	2	0.01
Pendleton, OR (city) Umatilla County	2	0.01
Pullman, WA (city) Whitman County	2	0.01
Roseburg, OR (city) Douglas County	2	0.01
Troutdale, OR (city) Multnomah County	2	0.01
Twin Falls, ID (city) Twin Falls County	2	0.01
West Lake Stevens, WA (cdp) Snohomish County	2	0.01
Altamont, OR (cdp) Klamath County	1	0.01
Anacortes, WA (city) Skagit County	1	0.01
Black Forest, CO (cdp) El Paso County	1	0.01
Camano, WA (cdp) Island County	1	0.01
Centralia, WA (city) Lewis County	1	0.01
Coos Bay, OR (city) Coos County	1	0.01
Dishman, WA (cdp) Spokane County	1	0.01
Dudley, MA (town) Worcester County	1	0.01
Ellensburg, WA (city) Kittitas County	1	0.01
Ewa Beach, HI (cdp) Honolulu County	1	0.01
Fort Leonard Wood, MO (cdp) Pulaski County	1	0.01
Gardnerville Ranchos, NV (cdp) Douglas County	1	0.01
Greendale, WI (village) Milwaukee County	1	0.01
Hastings, MN (city) Dakota County	1	0.01
La Grande, OR (city) Union County	1	0.01
Lake Forest Park, WA (city) King County	1	0.01
Los Alamitos, CA (city) Orange County	1	0.01
Post Falls, ID (city) Kootenai County	1	0.01
San Marino, CA (city) Los Angeles County	1	0.01
Silverdale, WA (cdp) Kitsap County	1	0.01
South Yuba City, CA (cdp) Sutter County	1	0.01
Sun Lakes, AZ (cdp) Maricopa County	1	0.01
Truckee, CA (town) Nevada County	1	0.01
Vero Beach, FL (city) Indian River County	1	0.01
Wilsonville, OR (city) Clackamas County	1	0.01
New York, NY (city) New York City	26	0.00
Portland, OR (city) Multnomah County	24	0.00
Oakland, CA (city) Alameda County	17	0.00
Los Angeles, CA (city) Los Angeles County	15	0.00
Sacramento, CA (city) Sacramento County	15	0.00
San Jose, CA (city) Santa Clara County	14	0.00
Phoenix, AZ (city) Maricopa County	9	0.00
San Francisco, CA (city) San Francisco County	9	0.00
Mesa, AZ (city) Maricopa County	8	0.00
Albuquerque, NM (city) Bernalillo County	5	0.00
Bellevue, WA (city) King County	5	0.00
Long Beach, CA (city) Los Angeles County	5	0.00
San Diego, CA (city) San Diego County	5	0.00
Boston, MA (city) Suffolk County	4	0.00
Fontana, CA (city) San Bernardino County	4	0.00
Garden Grove, CA (city) Orange County	4	0.00
Lansing, MI (city) Ingham County	4	0.00
Lawton, OK (city) Comanche County	4	0.00
Orem, UT (city) Utah County	4	0.00
Santa Rosa, CA (city) Sonoma County	4	0.00
Spokane, WA (city) Spokane County	4	0.00
Arvada, CO (city) Jefferson County	3	0.00
Austin, TX (city) Travis County	3	0.00
Dallas, TX (city) Dallas County	3	0.00
Fresno, CA (city) Fresno County	3	0.00

Notes: (cdp) census designated place; Refer to the Explanation of Data in the front of the book for more detailed information.

Alaska Native tribes, not specified

Top 150 Places Sorted by Number

(Based on all places, regardless of population)

Place	Number	%
Anchorage, AK (municipality) Anchorage Borough	1,429	0.55
Selawik, AK (city) Northwest Arctic Borough	418	54.15
Bethel, AK (city) Bethel Census Area	222	4.06
Barrow, AK (city) North Slope Borough	221	4.82
Kotzebue, AK (city) Northwest Arctic Borough	203	6.59
Juneau, AK (city and borough) Juneau Borough	163	0.53
Fairbanks, AK (city) Fairbanks North Star Borough	141	0.47
Seattle, WA (city) King County	133	0.02
Manokotak, AK (city) Dillingham Census Area	125	31.33
Nome, AK (city) Nome Census Area	100	2.85
Sitka, AK (city and borough) Sitka Borough	91	1.03
College, AK (cdp) Fairbanks North Star Borough	83	0.73
Dillingham, AK (city) Dillingham Census Area	68	2.76
Ketchikan, AK (city) Ketchikan Gateway Borough	60	0.76
Seward, AK (city) Kenai Peninsula Borough	57	2.01
Chevak, AK (city) Wade Hampton Census Area	56	7.32
Nenana, AK (city) Yukon-Koyukuk Census Area	53	13.18
Akutan, AK (city) Aleutians East Borough	48	6.73
Tacoma, WA (city) Pierce County	42	0.02
Los Angeles, CA (city) Los Angeles County	42	0.00
Palmer, AK (city) Matanuska-Susitna Borough	38	0.84
Sutton-Alpine, AK (cdp) Matanuska-Susitna Borough	36	3.33
Albuquerque, NM (city) Bernalillo County	35	0.01
New York, NY (city) New York City	35	0.00
Kodiak, AK (city) Kodiak Island Borough	34	0.54
Unalaska, AK (city) Aleutians West Census Area	32	0.75
Fayetteville, AR (city) Washington County	32	0.06
Tok, AK (cdp) Southeast Fairbanks Census Area	28	2.01
Salamatof, AK (cdp) Kenai Peninsula Borough	26	2.73
Phoenix, AZ (city) Maricopa County	26	0.00
Kenai, AK (city) Kenai Peninsula Borough	25	0.36
Angoon, AK (city) Skagway-Hoonah-Angoon Census Area	24	4.20
Knik-Fairview, AK (cdp) Matanuska-Susitna Borough	24	0.34
Portland, OR (city) Multnomah County	23	0.00
San Antonio, TX (city) Bexar County	23	0.00
Quinhagak, AK (city) Bethel Census Area	21	3.78
Cordova, AK (city) Valdez-Cordova Census Area	21	0.86
Kent, WA (city) King County	21	0.03
San Diego, CA (city) San Diego County	21	0.00
Naknek, AK (cdp) Bristol Bay Borough	20	2.95
Hoonah, AK (city) Skagway-Hoonah-Angoon Census Area	20	2.33
Bellingham, WA (city) Whatcom County	19	0.03
Everett, WA (city) Snohomish County	19	0.02
Aurora, CO (city) Arapahoe County	19	0.01
Fort Worth, TX (city) Tarrant County	19	0.00
San Francisco, CA (city) San Francisco County	19	0.00
Kaktovik, AK (city) North Slope Borough	18	6.14
Scammon Bay, AK (city) Wade Hampton Census Area	18	3.87
Homer, AK (city) Kenai Peninsula Borough	17	0.43
Ridgeway, AK (cdp) Kenai Peninsula Borough	16	0.83
Nikiski, AK (cdp) Kenai Peninsula Borough	16	0.37
Gallup, NM (city) McKinley County	16	0.08
Fort Yukon, AK (city) Yukon-Koyukuk Census Area	15	2.52
Kake, AK (city) Wrangell-Petersburg Census Area	15	2.11
Big Lake, AK (cdp) Matanuska-Susitna Borough	15	0.57
Soldotna, AK (city) Kenai Peninsula Borough	15	0.40
Vancouver, WA (city) Clark County	15	0.01
Houston, TX (city) Harris County	15	0.00
Emmonak, AK (city) Wade Hampton Census Area	14	1.83
Meadow Lakes, AK (cdp) Matanuska-Susitna Borough	14	0.29
Lakes, AK (cdp) Matanuska-Susitna Borough	14	0.21
Lynnwood, WA (city) Snohomish County	14	0.04
Shoreline, WA (city) King County	14	0.03
Boise City, ID (city) Ada County	14	0.01
Dallas, TX (city) Dallas County	14	0.00
El Paso, TX (city) El Paso County	14	0.00
Omaha, NE (city) Douglas County	14	0.00
Tulsa, OK (city) Tulsa County	14	0.00
Koyuk, AK (city) Nome Census Area	13	4.38
Edmonds, WA (city) Snohomish County	13	0.03
Springfield, OR (city) Lane County	13	0.02
Austin, TX (city) Travis County	13	0.00
Honolulu, HI (cdp) Honolulu County	13	0.00
Hydaburg, AK (city) Prince of Wales-Outer Ketchikan Census Area	12	3.14
Yakutat, AK (cdp) Yakutat City and Borough	12	1.76
Klawock, AK (city) Prince of Wales-Outer Ketchikan Census Area	12	1.41
Craig, AK (city) Prince of Wales-Outer Ketchikan Census Area	12	0.86
Wrangell, AK (city) Wrangell-Petersburg Census Area	12	0.52
Tanaina, AK (cdp) Matanuska-Susitna Borough	12	0.24
Wasilla, AK (city) Matanuska-Susitna Borough	12	0.22
Burien, WA (city) King County	12	0.04
Kirkland, WA (city) King County	12	0.03
Yakima, WA (city) Yakima County	12	0.02
Yuma, AZ (city) Yuma County	12	0.02
Columbus, GA (special city) Muscogee County	12	0.01
Salem, OR (city) Marion County	12	0.01
Denver, CO (city) Denver County	12	0.00
Stockton, CA (city) San Joaquin County	12	0.00
Virginia Beach, VA (independent city) Virginia Beach city	12	0.00
Nikolai, AK (city) Yukon-Koyukuk Census Area	11	11.00
Kivalina, AK (city) Northwest Arctic Borough	11	2.92
Knik River, AK (cdp) Matanuska-Susitna Borough	11	1.89
Kwethluk, AK (city) Bethel Census Area	11	1.54
Butte, AK (cdp) Matanuska-Susitna Borough	11	0.43
Havre, MT (city) Hill County	11	0.11
Anacortes, WA (city) Skagit County	11	0.08
Durango, CO (city) La Plata County	11	0.08
Picnic Point-North Lynnwood, WA (cdp) Snohomish County	11	0.05
Spokane, WA (city) Spokane County	11	0.01
Las Vegas, NV (city) Clark County	11	0.00
Tucson, AZ (city) Pima County	11	0.00
Portage Creek, AK (cdp) Dillingham Census Area	10	27.78
Port Graham, AK (cdp) Kenai Peninsula Borough	10	5.85
Marshall, AK (city) Wade Hampton Census Area	10	2.87
Galena, AK (city) Yukon-Koyukuk Census Area	10	1.48
Petersburg, AK (city) Wrangell-Petersburg Census Area	10	0.31
Fort Lewis, WA (cdp) Pierce County	10	0.05
North Marysville, WA (cdp) Snohomish County	10	0.05
Cottage Lake, WA (cdp) King County	10	0.04
Roswell, NM (city) Chaves County	10	0.02
Boston, MA (city) Suffolk County	10	0.00
Oklahoma City, OK (city) Oklahoma County	10	0.00
Pelican, AK (city) Skagway-Hoonah-Angoon Census Area	9	5.52
Sheldon Point, AK (city) Wade Hampton Census Area	9	5.49
Napakiak, AK (city) Bethel Census Area	9	2.55
Stebbins, AK (city) Nome Census Area	9	1.65
Fritz Creek, AK (cdp) Kenai Peninsula Borough	9	0.56
Bear Creek, AK (cdp) Kenai Peninsula Borough	9	0.51
Mount Vernon, WA (city) Skagit County	9	0.03
San Marcos, TX (city) Hays County	9	0.03
Texarkana, AR (city) Miller County	9	0.03
Haverford, PA (township) Delaware County	9	0.02
Renton, WA (city) King County	9	0.02
Santa Rosa, CA (city) Sonoma County	9	0.01
South San Francisco, CA (city) San Mateo County	9	0.01
Jacksonville, FL (special city) Duval County	9	0.00
Minneapolis, MN (city) Hennepin County	9	0.00
Rochester, NY (city) Monroe County	9	0.00
Red Dog Mine, AK (cdp) Northwest Arctic Borough	8	25.00
Metlakatla, AK (cdp) Prince of Wales-Outer Ketchikan Census Area	8	0.58
Gateway, AK (cdp) Matanuska-Susitna Borough	8	0.27
Holualoa, HI (cdp) Hawaii County	8	0.13
Grants, NM (city) Cibola County	8	0.09
Bartlesville, OK (city) Washington County	8	0.02
Bremerton, WA (city) Kitsap County	8	0.02
Seattle Hill-Silver Firs, WA (cdp) Snohomish County	8	0.02
Antioch, CA (city) Contra Costa County	8	0.01
Federal Way, WA (city) King County	8	0.01
Chicago, IL (city) Cook County	8	0.00
Long Beach, CA (city) Los Angeles County	8	0.00
Philadelphia, PA (city) Philadelphia County	8	0.00
Sacramento, CA (city) Sacramento County	8	0.00
Saint Paul, MN (city) Ramsey County	8	0.00
San Jose, CA (city) Santa Clara County	8	0.00
Tampa, FL (city) Hillsborough County	8	0.00
Chuathbaluk, AK (city) Bethel Census Area	7	5.88
Chignik Lake, AK (cdp) Lake and Peninsula Borough	7	4.83
Adak, AK (cdp) Aleutians West Census Area	7	2.22
Copper Center, AK (cdp) Valdez-Cordova Census Area	7	1.93
Nisqually Indian Community, WA (cdp) Thurston County	7	1.19

Notes: (cdp) census designated place; Refer to the Explanation of Data in the front of the book for more detailed information.

Alaska Native tribes, not specified

Top 150 Places Sorted by Percent

(Based on all places, regardless of population)

Place	Number	%
Selawik, AK (city) Northwest Arctic Borough	418	54.15
Manokotak, AK (city) Dillingham Census Area	125	31.33
Portage Creek, AK (cdp) Dillingham Census Area	10	27.78
Red Dog Mine, AK (cdp) Northwest Arctic Borough	8	25.00
Nenana, AK (city) Yukon-Koyukuk Census Area	53	13.18
Nikolai, AK (city) Yukon-Koyukuk Census Area	11	11.00
Ugashik, AK (cdp) Lake and Peninsula Borough	1	9.09
Chevak, AK (city) Wade Hampton Census Area	56	7.32
Twin Hills, AK (cdp) Dillingham Census Area	5	7.25
Akutan, AK (city) Aleutians East Borough	48	6.73
Kotzebue, AK (city) Northwest Arctic Borough	203	6.59
Kaktovik, AK (city) North Slope Borough	18	6.14
Chuathbaluk, AK (city) Bethel Census Area	7	5.88
Port Graham, AK (cdp) Kenai Peninsula Borough	10	5.85
Lake Louise, AK (cdp) Matanuska-Susitna Borough	5	5.68
New Allakaket, AK (cdp) Yukon-Koyukuk Census Area	2	5.56
Pelican, AK (city) Skagway-Hoonah-Angoon Census Area	9	5.52
Sheldon Point, AK (city) Wade Hampton Census Area	9	5.49
Tonsina, AK (cdp) Valdez-Cordova Census Area	5	5.43
Chignik Lake, AK (cdp) Lake and Peninsula Borough	7	4.83
Barrow, AK (city) North Slope Borough	221	4.82
Koyuk, AK (city) Nome Census Area	13	4.38
Angoon, AK (city) Skagway-Hoonah-Angoon Census Area	24	4.20
Red Devil, AK (cdp) Bethel Census Area	2	4.17
Bethel, AK (city) Bethel Census Area	222	4.06
Scammon Bay, AK (city) Wade Hampton Census Area	18	3.87
Port Alsworth, AK (cdp) Lake and Peninsula Borough	4	3.85
Quinhagak, AK (city) Bethel Census Area	21	3.78
Beaver, AK (cdp) Yukon-Koyukuk Census Area	3	3.57
Egegik, AK (city) Lake and Peninsula Borough	4	3.45
Tetlin, AK (cdp) Southeast Fairbanks Census Area	4	3.42
Sutton-Alpine, AK (cdp) Matanuska-Susitna Borough	36	3.33
Chitina, AK (cdp) Valdez-Cordova Census Area	4	3.25
Hydaburg, AK (city) Prince of Wales-Outer Ketchikan Census Area	12	3.14
Naknek, AK (cdp) Bristol Bay Borough	20	2.95
Kivalina, AK (city) Northwest Arctic Borough	11	2.92
Marshall, AK (city) Wade Hampton Census Area	10	2.87
Kokhanok, AK (cdp) Lake and Peninsula Borough	5	2.87
Nome, AK (city) Nome Census Area	100	2.85
Dillingham, AK (city) Dillingham Census Area	68	2.76
Salamatof, AK (cdp) Kenai Peninsula Borough	26	2.73
Point MacKenzie, AK (cdp) Matanuska-Susitna Borough	3	2.70
Atqasuk, AK (city) North Slope Borough	6	2.63
Arctic Village, AK (cdp) Yukon-Koyukuk Census Area	4	2.63
Dot Lake Village, AK (cdp) Southeast Fairbanks Census Area	1	2.63
Four Mile Road, AK (cdp) Yukon-Koyukuk Census Area	1	2.63
Napakiak, AK (city) Bethel Census Area	9	2.55
Fort Yukon, AK (city) Yukon-Koyukuk Census Area	15	2.52
Clover, MN (township) Mahnomen County	3	2.44
Dripping Springs, OK (cdp) Delaware County	1	2.44
Hoonah, AK (city) Skagway-Hoonah-Angoon Census Area	20	2.33
Adak, AK (cdp) Aleutians West Census Area	7	2.22
Deering, AK (city) Northwest Arctic Borough	3	2.21
Goodnews Bay, AK (city) Bethel Census Area	5	2.17
Kake, AK (city) Wrangell-Petersburg Census Area	15	2.11
Seward, AK (city) Kenai Peninsula Borough	57	2.01
Tok, AK (cdp) Southeast Fairbanks Census Area	28	2.01
Copper Center, AK (cdp) Valdez-Cordova Census Area	7	1.93
Elim, AK (city) Nome Census Area	6	1.92
Knik River, AK (cdp) Matanuska-Susitna Borough	11	1.89
Esmond, ND (city) Benson County	3	1.89
Chickaloon, AK (cdp) Matanuska-Susitna Borough	4	1.88
Emmonak, AK (city) Wade Hampton Census Area	14	1.83
Skwentna, AK (cdp) Matanuska-Susitna Borough	2	1.80
Yakutat, AK (cdp) Yakutat City and Borough	12	1.76
Whitestone Logging Camp, AK (cdp) Skagway-Hoonah-Angoon C.A.	2	1.72
Huslia, AK (city) Yukon-Koyukuk Census Area	5	1.71
Nanwalek, AK (cdp) Kenai Peninsula Borough	3	1.69
Stebbins, AK (city) Nome Census Area	9	1.65
Ambler, AK (city) Northwest Arctic Borough	5	1.62
Port Lions, AK (city) Kodiak Island Borough	4	1.56
Kwethluk, AK (city) Bethel Census Area	11	1.54
Central, AK (cdp) Yukon-Koyukuk Census Area	2	1.49
Galena, AK (city) Yukon-Koyukuk Census Area	10	1.48
Buckland, AK (city) Northwest Arctic Borough	6	1.48
Anaktuvuk Pass, AK (city) North Slope Borough	4	1.42
Klawock, AK (city) Prince of Wales-Outer Ketchikan Census Area	12	1.41
Seldovia, AK (city) Kenai Peninsula Borough	4	1.40
Harding-Birch Lakes, AK (cdp) Fairbanks North Star Borough	3	1.39
Seldovia Village, AK (cdp) Kenai Peninsula Borough	2	1.39
Rutland, IA (city) Humboldt County	2	1.38
Mosquito Lake, AK (cdp) Haines Borough	3	1.36
Cantwell, AK (cdp) Yukon-Koyukuk Census Area	3	1.35
Saint George, AK (city) Aleutians West Census Area	2	1.32
Shaktoolik, AK (city) Nome Census Area	3	1.30
Nisqually Indian Community, WA (cdp) Thurston County	7	1.19
Shungnak, AK (city) Northwest Arctic Borough	3	1.17
Stevens Village, AK (cdp) Yukon-Koyukuk Census Area	1	1.15
Kasigluk, AK (cdp) Bethel Census Area	6	1.10
Brevig Mission, AK (city) Nome Census Area	3	1.09
Thorne Bay, AK (city) Prince of Wales-Outer Ketchikan Census Area	6	1.08
Tuntutuliak, AK (cdp) Bethel Census Area	4	1.08
Sitka, AK (city and borough) Sitka Borough	91	1.03
Atmautluak, AK (cdp) Bethel Census Area	3	1.02
Sleetmute, AK (cdp) Bethel Census Area	1	1.00
White Mountain, AK (city) Nome Census Area	2	0.99
Iliamna, AK (cdp) Lake and Peninsula Borough	1	0.98
Saint Paul, AK (city) Aleutians West Census Area	5	0.94
Savoonga, AK (city) Nome Census Area	6	0.93
Nuiqsut, AK (city) North Slope Borough	4	0.92
Ninilchik, AK (cdp) Kenai Peninsula Borough	7	0.91
Togiak, AK (city) Dillingham Census Area	7	0.87
Upper Kalskag, AK (city) Bethel Census Area	2	0.87
Cordova, AK (city) Valdez-Cordova Census Area	21	0.86
Craig, AK (city) Prince of Wales-Outer Ketchikan Census Area	12	0.86
Palmer, AK (city) Matanuska-Susitna Borough	38	0.84
Ridgeway, AK (cdp) Kenai Peninsula Borough	16	0.83
Unalakleet, AK (city) Nome Census Area	6	0.80
Pitkas Point, AK (cdp) Wade Hampton Census Area	1	0.80
Talkeetna, AK (cdp) Matanuska-Susitna Borough	6	0.78
Minto, AK (cdp) Yukon-Koyukuk Census Area	2	0.78
Napaskiak, AK (city) Bethel Census Area	3	0.77
Ketchikan, AK (city) Ketchikan Gateway Borough	60	0.76
Unalaska, AK (city) Aleutians West Census Area	32	0.75
Teller, AK (city) Nome Census Area	2	0.75
Woodbury, PA (borough) Bedford County	2	0.74
College, AK (cdp) Fairbanks North Star Borough	83	0.73
Hollis, AK (cdp) Prince of Wales-Outer Ketchikan Census Area	1	0.72
Tanacross, AK (cdp) Southeast Fairbanks Census Area	1	0.71
Akiachak, AK (cdp) Bethel Census Area	4	0.68
Treece, KS (city) Cherokee County	1	0.67
Etna, CA (city) Siskiyou County	5	0.64
Hingham, MT (town) Hill County	1	0.64
Sprague, WA (city) Lincoln County	3	0.61
Delta Junction, AK (city) Southeast Fairbanks Census Area	5	0.60
Metlakatla, AK (cdp) Prince of Wales-Outer Ketchikan Census Area	8	0.58
Houston, AK (city) Matanuska-Susitna Borough	7	0.58
Big Lake, AK (cdp) Matanuska-Susitna Borough	15	0.57
Fritz Creek, AK (cdp) Kenai Peninsula Borough	9	0.56
Anchorage, AK (municipality) Anchorage Borough	1,429	0.55
Koliganek, AK (cdp) Dillingham Census Area	1	0.55
Robeline, LA (village) Natchitoches Parish	1	0.55
Kodiak, AK (city) Kodiak Island Borough	34	0.54
Juneau, AK (city and borough) Juneau Borough	163	0.53
Sand Point, AK (city) Aleutians East Borough	5	0.53
Ruby, AK (city) Yukon-Koyukuk Census Area	1	0.53
Wrangell, AK (city) Wrangell-Petersburg Census Area	12	0.52
Bear Creek, AK (cdp) Kenai Peninsula Borough	9	0.51
Priest Point, WA (cdp) Snohomish County	4	0.51
Port Hope, MN (township) Beltrami County	3	0.51
Fairbanks, AK (city) Fairbanks North Star Borough	141	0.47
Gambell, AK (city) Nome Census Area	3	0.46
Kachemak, AK (city) Kenai Peninsula Borough	2	0.46
Ak-Chin Village, AZ (cdp) Pinal County	3	0.45
Nondalton, AK (city) Lake and Peninsula Borough	1	0.45
Homer, AK (city) Kenai Peninsula Borough	17	0.43
Butte, AK (cdp) Matanuska-Susitna Borough	11	0.43
Buffalo Soapstone, AK (cdp) Matanuska-Susitna Borough	3	0.43
Womens Bay, AK (cdp) Kodiak Island Borough	3	0.43
Happy Valley, AK (cdp) Kenai Peninsula Borough	2	0.41

Notes: (cdp) census designated place; Refer to the Explanation of Data in the front of the book for more detailed information.

Alaska Native tribes, not specified

Top 150 Places Sorted by Percent

(Based on places with populations of 10,000 or more)

Place	Number	%
College, AK (cdp) Fairbanks North Star Borough	83	0.73
Anchorage, AK (municipality) Anchorage Borough	1,429	0.55
Juneau, AK (city and borough) Juneau Borough	163	0.53
Fairbanks, AK (city) Fairbanks North Star Borough	141	0.47
Gallup, NM (city) McKinley County	16	0.08
Anacortes, WA (city) Skagit County	11	0.08
Durango, CO (city) La Plata County	11	0.08
Fayetteville, AR (city) Washington County	32	0.06
Picnic Point-North Lynnwood, WA (cdp) Snohomish County	11	0.05
Fort Lewis, WA (cdp) Pierce County	10	0.05
North Marysville, WA (cdp) Snohomish County	10	0.05
Lynnwood, WA (city) Snohomish County	14	0.04
Burien, WA (city) King County	12	0.04
Cottage Lake, WA (cdp) King County	10	0.04
Tukwila, WA (city) King County	7	0.04
Monroe, WA (city) Snohomish County	5	0.04
Issaquah, WA (city) King County	4	0.04
Kent, WA (city) King County	21	0.03
Bellingham, WA (city) Whatcom County	19	0.03
Shoreline, WA (city) King County	14	0.03
Edmonds, WA (city) Snohomish County	13	0.03
Kirkland, WA (city) King County	12	0.03
Mount Vernon, WA (city) Skagit County	9	0.03
San Marcos, TX (city) Hays County	9	0.03
Texarkana, AR (city) Miller County	8	0.03
White Center, WA (cdp) King County	7	0.03
Ardmore, OK (city) Carter County	6	0.03
Weirton, WV (city) Hancock County	6	0.03
Alderwood Manor, WA (cdp) Snohomish County	5	0.03
Ellensburg, WA (city) Kittitas County	5	0.03
Lakeland North, WA (cdp) King County	5	0.03
Sierra Vista Southeast, AZ (cdp) Cochise County	5	0.03
Arkansas City, KS (city) Cowley County	4	0.03
Camano, WA (cdp) Island County	4	0.03
Elk Plain, WA (cdp) Pierce County	4	0.03
Huron charter, MI (township) Wayne County	4	0.03
Lebanon, OR (city) Linn County	4	0.03
Cambridge, OH (city) Guernsey County	3	0.03
Enumclaw, WA (city) King County	3	0.03
Fort Carson, CO (cdp) El Paso County	3	0.03
Kelso, WA (city) Cowlitz County	3	0.03
Vashon, WA (cdp) King County	3	0.03
Seattle, WA (city) King County	133	0.02
Tacoma, WA (city) Pierce County	42	0.02
Everett, WA (city) Snohomish County	19	0.02
Springfield, OR (city) Lane County	13	0.02
Yakima, WA (city) Yakima County	12	0.02
Yuma, AZ (city) Yuma County	12	0.02
Roswell, NM (city) Chaves County	10	0.02
Haverford, PA (township) Delaware County	9	0.02
Renton, WA (city) King County	9	0.02
Bartlesville, OK (city) Washington County	8	0.02
Bremerton, WA (city) Kitsap County	8	0.02
Seattle Hill-Silver Firs, WA (cdp) Snohomish County	8	0.02
South Hill, WA (cdp) Pierce County	7	0.02
Longview, WA (city) Cowlitz County	6	0.02
Puyallup, WA (city) Pierce County	6	0.02
Waipahu, HI (cdp) Honolulu County	6	0.02
Walla Walla, WA (city) Walla Walla County	6	0.02
Hamtramck, MI (city) Wayne County	5	0.02
Marysville, WA (city) Snohomish County	5	0.02
Saratoga Springs, NY (city) Saratoga County	5	0.02
Hayesville, OR (cdp) Marion County	4	0.02
Hazlet, NJ (township) Monmouth County	4	0.02
Helena, MT (city) Lewis and Clark County	4	0.02
Rolla, MO (city) Phelps County	4	0.02
Sharon, PA (city) Mercer County	4	0.02
Canyon, TX (city) Randall County	3	0.02
Fort Drum, NY (cdp) Jefferson County	3	0.02
Kalispell, MT (city) Flathead County	3	0.02
Kenmore, WA (city) King County	3	0.02
Kingsgate, WA (cdp) King County	3	0.02
Lake Forest Park, WA (city) King County	3	0.02
Le Ray, NY (town) Jefferson County	3	0.02
Martha Lake, WA (cdp) Snohomish County	3	0.02
Pendleton, OR (city) Umatilla County	3	0.02
Blackfoot, ID (city) Bingham County	2	0.02
Brigantine, NJ (city) Atlantic County	2	0.02
Escanaba, MI (city) Delta County	2	0.02
Massena, NY (town) Saint Lawrence County	2	0.02
Mustang, OK (city) Canadian County	2	0.02
Nanakuli, HI (cdp) Honolulu County	2	0.02
Piney Green, NC (cdp) Onslow County	2	0.02
Rio Linda, CA (cdp) Sacramento County	2	0.02
Saint Helens, OR (city) Columbia County	2	0.02
Tumwater, WA (city) Thurston County	2	0.02
Waipio, HI (cdp) Honolulu County	2	0.02
West Valley, WA (cdp) Yakima County	2	0.02
Winfield, KS (city) Cowley County	2	0.02
Albuquerque, NM (city) Bernalillo County	35	0.01
Aurora, CO (city) Arapahoe County	19	0.01
Vancouver, WA (city) Clark County	15	0.01
Boise City, ID (city) Ada County	14	0.01
Columbus, GA (special city) Muscogee County	12	0.01
Salem, OR (city) Marion County	12	0.01
Spokane, WA (city) Spokane County	11	0.01
Santa Rosa, CA (city) Sonoma County	9	0.01
South San Francisco, CA (city) San Mateo County	9	0.01
Antioch, CA (city) Contra Costa County	8	0.01
Federal Way, WA (city) King County	8	0.01
Chico, CA (city) Butte County	7	0.01
Eugene, OR (city) Lane County	7	0.01
Auburn, WA (city) King County	6	0.01
Bellevue, WA (city) King County	6	0.01
Cheyenne, WY (city) Laramie County	6	0.01
Clarksville, TN (city) Montgomery County	6	0.01
Lawrence, KS (city) Douglas County	6	0.01
Lewisville, TX (city) Denton County	6	0.01
Redding, CA (city) Shasta County	6	0.01
Apple Valley, CA (town) San Bernardino County	5	0.01
Clovis, CA (city) Fresno County	5	0.01
El Cajon, CA (city) San Diego County	5	0.01
Hilo, HI (cdp) Hawaii County	5	0.01
Kalamazoo, MI (city) Kalamazoo County	5	0.01
Lawton, OK (city) Comanche County	5	0.01
Missoula, MT (city) Missoula County	5	0.01
Sammamish, WA (city) King County	5	0.01
Tulare, CA (city) Tulare County	5	0.01
Aloha, OR (cdp) Washington County	4	0.01
Apache Junction, AZ (city) Pinal County	4	0.01
Baldwin Park, CA (city) Los Angeles County	4	0.01
Bangor, ME (city) Penobscot County	4	0.01
Beaverton, OR (city) Washington County	4	0.01
Carmel, NY (town) Putnam County	4	0.01
Daytona Beach, FL (city) Volusia County	4	0.01
Farmington, NM (city) San Juan County	4	0.01
Fitchburg, MA (city) Worcester County	4	0.01
Hillsboro, OR (city) Washington County	4	0.01
Hot Springs, AR (city) Garland County	4	0.01
Lakewood, WA (city) Pierce County	4	0.01
Las Cruces, NM (city) Dona Ana County	4	0.01
Melbourne, FL (city) Brevard County	4	0.01
Newington, CT (cdp) Hartford County	4	0.01
Northglenn, CO (city) Adams County	4	0.01
Olympia, WA (city) Thurston County	4	0.01
Pine Bluff, AR (city) Jefferson County	4	0.01
Rapid City, SD (city) Pennington County	4	0.01
Saint George, UT (city) Washington County	4	0.01
Santa Fe, NM (city) Santa Fe County	4	0.01
Sherman, TX (city) Grayson County	4	0.01
West Sacramento, CA (city) Yolo County	4	0.01
Alamogordo, NM (city) Otero County	3	0.01
Barstow, CA (city) San Bernardino County	3	0.01
Bend, OR (city) Deschutes County	3	0.01
Bothell, WA (city) King County	3	0.01
Bozeman, MT (city) Gallatin County	3	0.01
Burlingame, CA (city) San Mateo County	3	0.01
Dale City, VA (cdp) Prince William County	3	0.01
East Hill-Meridian, WA (cdp) King County	3	0.01
Edinburg, TX (city) Hidalgo County	3	0.01

Notes: (cdp) census designated place; Refer to the Explanation of Data in the front of the book for more detailed information.

American Indian or Alaska Native, not specified

Top 150 Places Sorted by Number

(Based on all places, regardless of population)

Place	Number	%
New York, NY (city) New York City	43,524	0.54
Los Angeles, CA (city) Los Angeles County	22,100	0.60
Chicago, IL (city) Cook County	9,741	0.34
Phoenix, AZ (city) Maricopa County	7,404	0.56
Houston, TX (city) Harris County	7,193	0.37
San Antonio, TX (city) Bexar County	6,958	0.61
Anchorage, AK (municipality) Anchorage Borough	5,899	2.27
San Diego, CA (city) San Diego County	5,643	0.46
Philadelphia, PA (city) Philadelphia County	5,574	0.37
San Jose, CA (city) Santa Clara County	4,974	0.56
Detroit, MI (city) Wayne County	4,419	0.46
Oklahoma City, OK (city) Oklahoma County	4,355	0.86
Denver, CO (city) Denver County	4,229	0.76
Dallas, TX (city) Dallas County	4,171	0.35
Fresno, CA (city) Fresno County	4,140	0.97
Minneapolis, MN (city) Hennepin County	3,742	0.98
Seattle, WA (city) King County	3,673	0.65
Sacramento, CA (city) Sacramento County	3,551	0.87
Tulsa, OK (city) Tulsa County	3,542	0.90
Tucson, AZ (city) Pima County	3,462	0.71
Portland, OR (city) Multnomah County	3,424	0.65
San Francisco, CA (city) San Francisco County	3,403	0.44
Milwaukee, WI (city) Milwaukee County	3,074	0.51
Albuquerque, NM (city) Bernalillo County	3,056	0.68
Long Beach, CA (city) Los Angeles County	2,971	0.64
Santa Ana, CA (city) Orange County	2,903	0.86
Austin, TX (city) Travis County	2,871	0.44
El Paso, TX (city) El Paso County	2,810	0.50
Columbus, OH (city) Franklin County	2,805	0.39
Oakland, CA (city) Alameda County	2,672	0.67
Boston, MA (city) Suffolk County	2,611	0.44
Baltimore, MD (independent city) Baltimore city	2,407	0.37
Las Vegas, NV (city) Clark County	2,316	0.48
Washington, DC (city) District of Columbia	2,191	0.38
Honolulu, HI (cdp) Honolulu County	2,149	0.58
Anaheim, CA (city) Orange County	2,123	0.65
Saint Paul, MN (city) Ramsey County	2,104	0.73
Fort Worth, TX (city) Tarrant County	2,082	0.39
Indianapolis, IN (special city) Marion County	2,039	0.26
Stockton, CA (city) San Joaquin County	2,027	0.83
Bakersfield, CA (city) Kern County	1,988	0.80
Jacksonville, FL (special city) Duval County	1,954	0.27
Colorado Springs, CO (city) El Paso County	1,942	0.54
Wichita, KS (city) Sedgwick County	1,921	0.56
Cleveland, OH (city) Cuyahoga County	1,858	0.39
San Bernardino, CA (city) San Bernardino County	1,817	0.98
Kansas City, MO (city) Jackson County	1,800	0.41
Tacoma, WA (city) Pierce County	1,779	0.92
Mesa, AZ (city) Maricopa County	1,753	0.44
Riverside, CA (city) Riverside County	1,706	0.67
Hempstead, NY (town) Nassau County	1,681	0.22
Spokane, WA (city) Spokane County	1,599	0.82
Providence, RI (city) Providence County	1,568	0.90
Aurora, CO (city) Arapahoe County	1,534	0.56
Omaha, NE (city) Douglas County	1,448	0.37
Virginia Beach, VA (independent city) Virginia Beach city	1,430	0.34
Modesto, CA (city) Stanislaus County	1,411	0.75
Memphis, TN (city) Shelby County	1,406	0.22
Buffalo, NY (city) Erie County	1,386	0.47
Jersey City, NJ (city) Hudson County	1,368	0.57
Charlotte, NC (city) Mecklenburg County	1,366	0.25
Pomona, CA (city) Los Angeles County	1,358	0.91
Salinas, CA (city) Monterey County	1,292	0.86
Newark, NJ (city) Essex County	1,285	0.47
New Orleans, LA (city) Orleans Parish	1,277	0.26
Nashville-Davidson, TN (special city) Davidson County	1,257	0.23
Oxnard, CA (city) Ventura County	1,239	0.73
Escondido, CA (city) San Diego County	1,230	0.92
Corpus Christi, TX (city) Nueces County	1,229	0.44
Ontario, CA (city) San Bernardino County	1,219	0.77
Toledo, OH (city) Lucas County	1,213	0.39
Sacaton, AZ (cdp) Pinal County	1,199	75.69
El Monte, CA (city) Los Angeles County	1,169	1.01
Rochester, NY (city) Monroe County	1,166	0.53
Saint Louis, MO (independent city) Saint Louis city	1,160	0.33
Brookhaven, NY (town) Suffolk County	1,137	0.25
Arlington, TX (city) Tarrant County	1,116	0.34
Flint, MI (city) Genesee County	1,111	0.89
Pueblo, CO (city) Pueblo County	1,109	1.09
Glendale, AZ (city) Maricopa County	1,105	0.50
Syracuse, NY (city) Onondaga County	1,081	0.73
Moreno Valley, CA (city) Riverside County	1,065	0.75
Grand Rapids, MI (city) Kent County	1,058	0.53
Sioux Falls, SD (city) Minnehaha County	1,043	0.84
Cincinnati, OH (city) Hamilton County	1,033	0.31
Tampa, FL (city) Hillsborough County	1,030	0.34
East Los Angeles, CA (cdp) Los Angeles County	1,019	0.82
Reno, NV (city) Washoe County	1,016	0.56
Rapid City, SD (city) Pennington County	1,012	1.70
Atlanta, GA (city) Fulton County	1,003	0.24
Salem, OR (city) Marion County	984	0.72
Garden Grove, CA (city) Orange County	982	0.59
Oceanside, CA (city) San Diego County	968	0.60
Hayward, CA (city) Alameda County	965	0.69
Bethel, AK (city) Bethel Census Area	964	17.62
Santa Rosa, CA (city) Sonoma County	957	0.65
Fontana, CA (city) San Bernardino County	956	0.74
Pittsburgh, PA (city) Allegheny County	949	0.28
Islip, NY (town) Suffolk County	923	0.29
Paterson, NJ (city) Passaic County	918	0.62
Fremont, CA (city) Alameda County	912	0.45
Sunrise Manor, NV (cdp) Clark County	911	0.58
Kansas City, KS (city) Wyandotte County	901	0.61
Yonkers, NY (city) Westchester County	900	0.46
Duluth, MN (city) Saint Louis County	899	1.03
Lumberton, NC (city) Robeson County	897	4.31
Miami, FL (city) Miami-Dade County	897	0.25
Norfolk, VA (independent city) Norfolk city	887	0.38
Lansing, MI (city) Ingham County	883	0.74
Chula Vista, CA (city) San Diego County	879	0.51
Eugene, OR (city) Lane County	876	0.64
Vancouver, WA (city) Clark County	875	0.61
Santa Maria, CA (city) Santa Barbara County	856	1.11
Lancaster, CA (city) Los Angeles County	851	0.72
Paradise, NV (cdp) Clark County	850	0.46
Salt Lake City, UT (city) Salt Lake County	846	0.47
Great Falls, MT (city) Cascade County	842	1.49
Tempe, AZ (city) Maricopa County	836	0.53
Topeka, KS (city) Shawnee County	833	0.68
Visalia, CA (city) Tulare County	825	0.90
Lakewood, CO (city) Jefferson County	822	0.57
Raleigh, NC (city) Wake County	807	0.29
Huntington Beach, CA (city) Orange County	806	0.43
Akron, OH (city) Summit County	792	0.36
Hartford, CT (city) Hartford County	790	0.65
Pasadena, CA (city) Los Angeles County	787	0.59
Chandler, AZ (city) Maricopa County	777	0.44
Palmdale, CA (city) Los Angeles County	770	0.66
Fairbanks, AK (city) Fairbanks North Star Borough	767	2.54
Lincoln, NE (city) Lancaster County	766	0.34
Inglewood, CA (city) Los Angeles County	749	0.67
Garland, TX (city) Dallas County	745	0.35
Bridgeport, CT (city) Fairfield County	742	0.53
Springfield, MA (city) Hampden County	742	0.49
Lawton, OK (city) Comanche County	730	0.79
Amarillo, TX (city) Potter County	729	0.42
Concord, CA (city) Contra Costa County	728	0.60
Greensboro, NC (city) Guilford County	725	0.32
Billings, MT (city) Yellowstone County	722	0.80
Norwalk, CA (city) Los Angeles County	715	0.69
Worcester, MA (city) Worcester County	714	0.41
New Haven, CT (city) New Haven County	711	0.58
Corona, CA (city) Riverside County	709	0.57
Saint Petersburg, FL (city) Pinellas County	709	0.29
Vallejo, CA (city) Solano County	703	0.60
Fayetteville, NC (city) Cumberland County	702	0.58
Baldwin Park, CA (city) Los Angeles County	697	0.92
Newport News, VA (independent city) Newport News city	693	0.38
Antioch, CA (city) Contra Costa County	690	0.76
Irving, TX (city) Dallas County	689	0.36

Notes: (cdp) census designated place; Refer to the Explanation of Data in the front of the book for more detailed information.

American Indian or Alaska Native, not specified

Top 150 Places Sorted by Percent

(Based on all places, regardless of population)

Place	Number	%
Crooked Creek, AK (cdp) Bethel Census Area	125	91.24
Sleetmute, AK (cdp) Bethel Census Area	86	86.00
Santan, AZ (cdp) Pinal County	558	85.71
Quinhagak, AK (city) Bethel Census Area	472	85.05
Stony River, AK (cdp) Bethel Census Area	51	83.61
Scammon Bay, AK (city) Wade Hampton Census Area	364	78.28
Anaktuvuk Pass, AK (city) North Slope Borough	217	76.95
Sacaton, AZ (cdp) Pinal County	1,199	75.69
Lower Kalskag, AK (city) Bethel Census Area	197	73.78
Sheldon Point, AK (city) Wade Hampton Census Area	119	72.56
Eek, AK (city) Bethel Census Area	198	70.71
Kokhanok, AK (cdp) Lake and Peninsula Borough	122	70.11
Blackwater, AZ (cdp) Pinal County	335	66.47
Kongiganak, AK (cdp) Bethel Census Area	207	57.66
Upper Kalskag, AK (city) Bethel Census Area	116	50.43
Diomede, AK (city) Nome Census Area	61	41.78
Rampart, AK (cdp) Yukon-Koyukuk Census Area	16	35.56
Healy Lake, AK (cdp) Southeast Fairbanks Census Area	11	29.73
Pope-Vannoy Landing, AK (cdp) Lake and Peninsula Borough	2	25.00
White Earth, MN (township) Becker County	190	23.78
Manley Hot Springs, AK (cdp) Yukon-Koyukuk Census Area	16	22.22
Holy Cross, AK (city) Yukon-Koyukuk Census Area	49	21.59
Saint Charles, SD (cdp) Gregory County	4	21.05
Ambler, AK (city) Northwest Arctic Borough	65	21.04
Aniak, AK (city) Bethel Census Area	115	20.10
Kirkpatrick, OR (cdp) Umatilla County	34	19.77
Kwigillingok, AK (cdp) Bethel Census Area	64	18.93
Prospect, NC (cdp) Robeson County	126	18.26
Chuathbaluk, AK (city) Bethel Census Area	21	17.65
Bethel, AK (city) Bethel Census Area	964	17.62
Bullhead, SD (cdp) Corson County	54	17.53
Raemon, NC (cdp) Robeson County	37	17.45
Anvik, AK (city) Yukon-Koyukuk Census Area	18	17.31
Atmautluak, AK (cdp) Bethel Census Area	50	17.01
Bull Hollow, OK (cdp) Delaware County	14	16.67
Bathgate, ND (city) Pembina County	11	16.67
Grayling, AK (city) Yukon-Koyukuk Census Area	32	16.49
Port Graham, AK (cdp) Kenai Peninsula Borough	28	16.37
Pine Point, MN (township) Becker County	65	15.51
Old Eucha, OK (cdp) Delaware County	7	15.22
Togiak, AK (city) Dillingham Census Area	122	15.08
Maple Grove, MN (township) Becker County	60	14.81
Pitkas Point, AK (cdp) Wade Hampton Census Area	18	14.40
Bena, MN (city) Cass County	15	13.64
Callaway, MN (city) Becker County	27	13.50
La Plant, SD (cdp) Dewey County	20	13.33
Dillingham, AK (city) Dillingham Census Area	323	13.10
Dundarrach, NC (cdp) Hoke County	8	12.90
Clark, MN (township) Aitkin County	19	12.84
Kasaan, AK (city) Prince of Wales-Outer Ketchikan Census Area	5	12.82
Carter, WY (cdp) Uinta County	1	12.50
Kwethluk, AK (city) Bethel Census Area	89	12.48
La Prairie, MN (township) Clearwater County	46	12.40
Nikolai, AK (city) Yukon-Koyukuk Census Area	12	12.00
Kotzebue, AK (city) Northwest Arctic Borough	364	11.81
Ak-Chin Village, AZ (cdp) Pinal County	79	11.81
Waldron, KS (city) Harper County	2	11.76
Kake, AK (city) Wrangell-Petersburg Census Area	82	11.55
Lake Grove, MN (township) Mahnomen County	23	11.33
Wickliffe, OK (cdp) Mayes County	11	11.11
New Allakaket, AK (cdp) Yukon-Koyukuk Census Area	4	11.11
Sunrise, AK (cdp) Kenai Peninsula Borough	2	11.11
Nightmute, AK (city) Bethel Census Area	23	11.06
Nore, MN (township) Itasca County	6	10.91
White Mesa, UT (cdp) San Juan County	30	10.83
Pembroke, NC (town) Robeson County	247	10.30
Nanwalek, AK (cdp) Kenai Peninsula Borough	18	10.17
Wounded Knee, SD (cdp) Shannon County	33	10.06
Brush Creek, OK (cdp) Delaware County	4	9.76
Elrod, NC (cdp) Robeson County	43	9.75
Teller, AK (city) Nome Census Area	26	9.70
Napakiak, AK (city) Bethel Census Area	34	9.63
Causey, NM (village) Roosevelt County	5	9.62
Latimer, KS (city) Morris County	2	9.52
Koyuk, AK (city) Nome Census Area	28	9.43
Ashland, OK (town) Pittsburg County	5	9.43
Lake Minchumina, AK (cdp) Yukon-Koyukuk Census Area	3	9.38
Callaway, MN (township) Becker County	24	9.23
Peoria, OK (town) Ottawa County	13	9.22
Selawik, AK (city) Northwest Arctic Borough	71	9.20
Kobuk, AK (city) Northwest Arctic Borough	10	9.17
Naknek, AK (cdp) Bristol Bay Borough	62	9.14
Shaktoolik, AK (city) Nome Census Area	21	9.13
Russian Mission, AK (city) Wade Hampton Census Area	27	9.12
Angoon, AK (city) Skagway-Hoonah-Angoon Census Area	52	9.09
Dulac, LA (cdp) Terrebonne Parish	221	8.99
Clover, MN (township) Mahnomen County	11	8.94
Brooksville, OK (town) Pottawatomie County	8	8.89
Poospatuck Reservation, NY (reservation) Suffolk County	24	8.86
Iliamna, AK (cdp) Lake and Peninsula Borough	9	8.82
Nome, AK (city) Nome Census Area	304	8.67
Oberon, ND (city) Benson County	7	8.64
Game Creek, AK (cdp) Skagway-Hoonah-Angoon Census Area	3	8.57
Port Heiden, AK (city) Lake and Peninsula Borough	10	8.40
Rocky Ford, OK (cdp) Delaware County	5	8.33
Tuscarora Reservation, NY (reservation) Niagara County	93	8.17
Santa Clara Pueblo, NM (cdp) Rio Arriba County	79	8.06
Brumley, MO (town) Miller County	8	7.84
Goodnews Bay, AK (city) Bethel Census Area	18	7.83
Hughes, AK (city) Yukon-Koyukuk Census Area	6	7.69
Sand Point, AK (city) Aleutians East Borough	73	7.67
Kyle, SD (cdp) Shannon County	74	7.63
Sandstone, MN (township) Pine County	122	7.56
Browns Valley, MN (city) Traverse County	52	7.54
Sugar Bush, MN (township) Becker County	40	7.45
Longdale, OK (town) Blaine County	23	7.42
Dodson, MT (town) Phillips County	9	7.38
Harlem, MT (city) Blaine County	60	7.08
Pike Bay, MN (township) Cass County	116	7.06
Milton, ND (city) Cavalier County	6	7.06
Belvidere, SD (town) Jackson County	4	7.02
Paradise Hill, OK (town) Sequoyah County	7	7.00
McGrath, AK (city) Yukon-Koyukuk Census Area	28	6.98
Aullville, MO (village) Lafayette County	6	6.98
Otter Tail Peninsula, MN (township) Cass County	3	6.98
Seldovia Village, AK (cdp) Kenai Peninsula Borough	10	6.94
Box Elder, MT (cdp) Hill County	55	6.93
Lower Brule, SD (cdp) Lyman County	41	6.84
Yakutat, AK (cdp) Yakutat City and Borough	46	6.76
McDonald, NC (town) Robeson County	8	6.72
Manderson-White Horse Creek, SD (cdp) Shannon County	42	6.71
Naytahwaush, MN (cdp) Mahnomen County	39	6.69
Spring Creek, MN (township) Becker County	8	6.67
Crown Point, AK (cdp) Kenai Peninsula Borough	5	6.67
Warwick, ND (city) Benson County	5	6.67
Dunseith, ND (city) Rolette County	49	6.63
Christie, OK (cdp) Adair County	11	6.63
Long, OK (cdp) Sequoyah County	24	6.61
Klawock, AK (city) Prince of Wales-Outer Ketchikan Census Area	56	6.56
Sylvania, PA (township) Potter County	4	6.56
Middle Village, WI (cdp) Menominee County	23	6.55
Saint Michael, AK (city) Nome Census Area	24	6.52
Fruitdale, SD (town) Butte County	4	6.45
Bridgeport, OK (city) Caddo County	7	6.42
Twin Lakes, MN (township) Mahnomen County	54	6.38
Aleknagik, AK (city) Dillingham Census Area	14	6.33
Cochiti, NM (cdp) Sandoval County	32	6.31
Talala, OK (town) Rogers County	17	6.30
Ogema, MN (city) Becker County	9	6.29
Sand Lake, MN (township) Itasca County	8	6.25
Glastenbury, VT (town) Bennington County	1	6.25
Little Eagle, SD (cdp) Corson County	23	6.22
Hooper Bay, AK (city) Wade Hampton Census Area	63	6.21
Pinhook Corners, OK (cdp) Sequoyah County	10	6.21
White River, SD (city) Mellette County	37	6.19
Noble, LA (village) Sabine Parish	16	6.18
Tununak, AK (cdp) Bethel Census Area	20	6.15
Third River, MN (township) Itasca County	4	6.15
Porcupine, SD (cdp) Shannon County	25	6.14
Tuluksak, AK (cdp) Bethel Census Area	26	6.07

Notes: (cdp) census designated place; Refer to the Explanation of Data in the front of the book for more detailed information.

American Indian or Alaska Native, not specified

Top 150 Places Sorted by Percent

(Based on places with populations of 10,000 or more)

Place	Number	%
Lumberton, NC (city) Robeson County	897	4.31
Fairbanks, AK (city) Fairbanks North Star Borough	767	2.54
Tahlequah, OK (city) Cherokee County	346	2.39
Florence, AZ (town) Pinal County	388	2.28
Anchorage, AK (municipality) Anchorage Borough	5,899	2.27
Sault Sainte Marie, MI (city) Chippewa County	376	2.27
Gallup, NM (city) McKinley County	454	2.25
College, AK (cdp) Fairbanks North Star Borough	252	2.21
Bemidji, MN (city) Beltrami County	256	2.15
Laurinburg, NC (city) Scotland County	322	2.03
Juneau, AK (city and borough) Juneau Borough	616	2.01
Ada, OK (city) Pontotoc County	284	1.81
Okmulgee, OK (city) Okmulgee County	235	1.80
Claremore, OK (city) Rogers County	277	1.75
Oroville, CA (city) Butte County	226	1.74
Rapid City, SD (city) Pennington County	1,012	1.70
Linda, CA (cdp) Yuba County	229	1.70
Olivehurst, CA (cdp) Yuba County	176	1.59
Cloquet, MN (city) Carlton County	175	1.56
Miami, OK (city) Ottawa County	213	1.55
Houma, LA (city) Terrebonne Parish	500	1.54
Great Falls, MT (city) Cascade County	842	1.49
Shawnee, OK (city) Pottawatomie County	423	1.47
Nanakuli, HI (cdp) Honolulu County	156	1.44
Klamath Falls, OR (city) Klamath County	274	1.41
Susanville, CA (city) Lassen County	186	1.37
Waianae, HI (cdp) Honolulu County	142	1.35
Eureka, CA (city) Humboldt County	347	1.33
Marysville, CA (city) Yuba County	162	1.32
Durant, OK (city) Bryan County	173	1.28
Sapulpa, OK (city) Creek County	243	1.27
Muskogee, OK (city) Muskogee County	483	1.26
San Luis, AZ (city) Yuma County	193	1.26
Pierre, SD (city) Hughes County	170	1.23
Madera, CA (city) Madera County	517	1.20
Ukiah, CA (city) Mendocino County	186	1.20
Lompoc, CA (city) Santa Barbara County	485	1.18
Port Hueneme, CA (city) Ventura County	257	1.18
Ashland, CA (cdp) Alameda County	245	1.18
Chowchilla, CA (city) Madera County	131	1.18
Williston, ND (city) Williams County	147	1.17
Clearlake, CA (city) Lake County	153	1.16
Soledad, CA (city) Monterey County	127	1.13
Coffeyville, KS (city) Montgomery County	125	1.13
Citrus, CA (cdp) Los Angeles County	119	1.12
Santa Maria, CA (city) Santa Barbara County	856	1.11
Yuba City, CA (city) Sutter County	409	1.11
Parkway-South Sacramento, CA (cdp) Sacramento County	403	1.11
South Salt Lake, UT (city) Salt Lake County	245	1.11
Bremerton, WA (city) Kitsap County	409	1.10
Wahiawa, HI (cdp) Honolulu County	178	1.10
McKinleyville, CA (cdp) Humboldt County	150	1.10
Greenfield, CA (city) Monterey County	139	1.10
Lake Los Angeles, CA (cdp) Los Angeles County	127	1.10
Pueblo, CO (city) Pueblo County	1,109	1.09
Aberdeen, WA (city) Grays Harbor County	180	1.09
Farmington, NM (city) San Juan County	408	1.08
Bartlesville, OK (city) Washington County	374	1.08
White Center, WA (cdp) King County	226	1.08
Kahului, HI (cdp) Maui County	217	1.08
Desert Hot Springs, CA (city) Riverside County	179	1.08
Rio Linda, CA (cdp) Sacramento County	113	1.08
Ewa Beach, HI (cdp) Honolulu County	157	1.07
Fortuna, CA (city) Humboldt County	112	1.07
Lathrop, CA (city) San Joaquin County	112	1.07
South El Monte, CA (city) Los Angeles County	225	1.06
South San Jose Hills, CA (cdp) Los Angeles County	215	1.06
Wailuku, HI (cdp) Maui County	129	1.05
Casa Grande, AZ (city) Pinal County	262	1.04
Drexel Heights, AZ (cdp) Pima County	249	1.04
Beaumont, CA (city) Riverside County	118	1.04
Duluth, MN (city) Saint Louis County	899	1.03
Hilo, HI (cdp) Hawaii County	417	1.02
Alum Rock, CA (cdp) Santa Clara County	137	1.02
Eloy, AZ (city) Pinal County	106	1.02
El Monte, CA (city) Los Angeles County	1,169	1.01
Ardmore, OK (city) Carter County	240	1.01
San Jacinto, CA (city) Riverside County	239	1.01
Mitchell, SD (city) Davison County	147	1.01
Bell Gardens, CA (city) Los Angeles County	441	1.00
Brighton, CO (city) Adams County	209	1.00
Arkansas City, KS (city) Cowley County	120	1.00
Tehachapi, CA (city) Kern County	110	1.00
McAlester, OK (city) Pittsburg County	176	0.99
El Reno, OK (city) Canadian County	161	0.99
Welby, CO (cdp) Adams County	129	0.99
Minneapolis, MN (city) Hennepin County	3,742	0.98
San Bernardino, CA (city) San Bernardino County	1,817	0.98
Watsonville, CA (city) Santa Cruz County	434	0.98
Ponca City, OK (city) Kay County	253	0.98
Bloomington, CA (cdp) San Bernardino County	190	0.98
Coos Bay, OR (city) Coos County	151	0.98
Fresno, CA (city) Fresno County	4,140	0.97
Kaneohe, HI (cdp) Honolulu County	339	0.97
Santa Fe Springs, CA (city) Los Angeles County	169	0.97
Cherryland, CA (cdp) Alameda County	133	0.96
Monroe, WA (city) Snohomish County	133	0.96
Patterson, CA (city) Stanislaus County	111	0.96
View Park-Windsor Hills, CA (cdp) Los Angeles County	105	0.96
Saint Helens, OR (city) Columbia County	96	0.96
North Highlands, CA (cdp) Sacramento County	418	0.95
Banning, CA (city) Riverside County	223	0.95
Chickasha, OK (city) Grady County	151	0.95
Merced, CA (city) Merced County	601	0.94
Superior, WI (city) Douglas County	257	0.94
Grover Beach, CA (city) San Luis Obispo County	123	0.94
Arvin, CA (city) Kern County	122	0.94
San Fernando, CA (city) Los Angeles County	220	0.93
Adelanto, CA (city) San Bernardino County	168	0.93
Arcata, CA (city) Humboldt County	155	0.93
Tacoma, WA (city) Pierce County	1,779	0.92
Escondido, CA (city) San Diego County	1,230	0.92
Baldwin Park, CA (city) Los Angeles County	697	0.92
Montebello, CA (city) Los Angeles County	571	0.92
Selma, CA (city) Fresno County	178	0.92
Pomona, CA (city) Los Angeles County	1,358	0.91
Lakewood, WA (city) Pierce County	532	0.91
Moore, OK (city) Cleveland County	376	0.91
La Puente, CA (city) Los Angeles County	373	0.91
Bridgeton, NJ (city) Cumberland County	207	0.91
Altamont, OR (cdp) Klamath County	179	0.91
Clifton, CO (cdp) Mesa County	158	0.91
Prunedale, CA (cdp) Monterey County	150	0.91
Twentynine Palms, CA (city) San Bernardino County	135	0.91
Galena Park, TX (city) Harris County	96	0.91
Tulsa, OK (city) Tulsa County	3,542	0.90
Providence, RI (city) Providence County	1,568	0.90
Visalia, CA (city) Tulare County	825	0.90
Rosemont, CA (cdp) Sacramento County	206	0.90
Commerce City, CO (city) Adams County	189	0.90
Junction City, KS (city) Geary County	170	0.90
Glen Avon, CA (cdp) Riverside County	133	0.90
Makakilo City, HI (cdp) Honolulu County	119	0.90
Flint, MI (city) Genesee County	1,111	0.89
Gilroy, CA (city) Santa Clara County	370	0.89
Los Banos, CA (city) Merced County	229	0.89
Halawa, HI (cdp) Honolulu County	124	0.89
Riverton-Boulevard Park, WA (cdp) King County	100	0.89
Siloam Springs, AR (city) Benton County	96	0.89
Healdsburg, CA (city) Sonoma County	95	0.89
Livingston, CA (city) Merced County	93	0.89
Parkland, WA (cdp) Pierce County	211	0.88
Tukwila, WA (city) King County	152	0.88
North Amityville, NY (cdp) Suffolk County	146	0.88
Pendleton, OR (city) Umatilla County	144	0.88
Shafter, CA (city) Kern County	112	0.88
Lindsay, CA (city) Tulare County	91	0.88
Sacramento, CA (city) Sacramento County	3,551	0.87
Lynwood, CA (city) Los Angeles County	609	0.87
Pico Rivera, CA (city) Los Angeles County	554	0.87

Notes: (cdp) census designated place; Refer to the Explanation of Data in the front of the book for more detailed information.

Albanian

Top 150 Places Sorted by Number

(Based on all places, regardless of population)

Place	Number	%
New York, NY (city) New York City	24,577	0.31
Sterling Heights, MI (city) Macomb County	2,295	1.84
Waterbury, CT (city) New Haven County	2,174	2.03
Worcester, MA (city) Worcester County	2,029	1.18
Philadelphia, PA (city) Philadelphia County	1,715	0.11
Boston, MA (city) Suffolk County	1,420	0.24
Chicago, IL (city) Cook County	1,368	0.05
Yonkers, NY (city) Westchester County	1,310	0.67
Shelby, MI (cdp) Macomb County	1,180	1.81
Warren, MI (city) Macomb County	1,053	0.76
Clinton, MI (cdp) Macomb County	994	1.04
Jacksonville, FL (special city) Duval County	855	0.12
Dearborn, MI (city) Wayne County	694	0.71
Macomb, MI (township) Macomb County	652	1.29
Hamtramck, MI (city) Wayne County	635	2.76
Lakewood, OH (city) Cuyahoga County	593	1.05
Phoenix, AZ (city) Maricopa County	592	0.04
Saint Louis, MO (independent city) Saint Louis city	576	0.17
Farmington Hills, MI (city) Oakland County	509	0.62
Stamford, CT (city) Fairfield County	508	0.43
Hempstead, NY (town) Nassau County	488	0.06
Wayne, NJ (cdp) Passaic County	466	0.86
Los Angeles, CA (city) Los Angeles County	443	0.01
Manchester, NH (city) Hillsborough County	436	0.41
Hartford, CT (city) Hartford County	433	0.36
Troy, MI (city) Oakland County	410	0.51
Quincy, MA (city) Norfolk County	402	0.46
Bridgeport, CT (city) Fairfield County	386	0.28
Waterford, MI (cdp) Oakland County	373	0.51
Garfield, NJ (city) Bergen County	370	1.24
Royal Oak, MI (city) Oakland County	370	0.62
Nashville-Davidson, TN (special city) Davidson County	338	0.06
Detroit, MI (city) Wayne County	334	0.04
Largo, FL (city) Pinellas County	312	0.45
Saint Petersburg, FL (city) Pinellas County	311	0.13
Upper Darby, PA (township) Delaware County	307	0.38
Rochester Hills, MI (city) Oakland County	302	0.44
Westland, MI (city) Wayne County	301	0.35
Houston, TX (city) Harris County	301	0.02
Somerville, MA (city) Middlesex County	287	0.37
Fort Worth, TX (city) Tarrant County	279	0.05
Livonia, MI (city) Wayne County	272	0.27
Anchorage, AK (municipality) Anchorage Borough	271	0.10
Boise City, ID (city) Ada County	269	0.14
Addison, IL (village) Du Page County	267	0.75
Roseville, MI (city) Macomb County	262	0.54
Clarkstown, NY (town) Rockland County	257	0.31
Paterson, NJ (city) Passaic County	255	0.17
Kenosha, WI (city) Kenosha County	249	0.27
North Hempstead, NY (town) Nassau County	247	0.11
Lodi, NJ (borough) Bergen County	245	1.02
San Diego, CA (city) San Diego County	243	0.02
Plano, TX (city) Collin County	240	0.11
Milwaukee, WI (city) Milwaukee County	230	0.04
South Milwaukee, WI (city) Milwaukee County	229	1.08
Cleveland, OH (city) Cuyahoga County	225	0.05
Lynn, MA (city) Essex County	221	0.25
Rochester, NY (city) Monroe County	221	0.10
Grosse Pointe Park, MI (city) Wayne County	219	1.76
Washington, DC (city) District of Columbia	218	0.04
Peabody, MA (city) Essex County	214	0.44
Natick, MA (town) Middlesex County	212	0.66
Clearwater, FL (city) Pinellas County	211	0.20
Ansonia, CT (city) New Haven County	208	1.12
El Cajon, CA (city) San Diego County	208	0.22
Cudahy, WI (city) Milwaukee County	206	1.12
West Bloomfield, MI (township) Oakland County	206	0.32
Elmwood Park, IL (village) Cook County	202	0.80
Dallas, TX (city) Dallas County	202	0.02
Lincoln Park, NJ (borough) Morris County	200	1.83
Naugatuck, CT (borough) New Haven County	199	0.64
Dunedin, FL (city) Pinellas County	199	0.55
Fraser, MI (city) Macomb County	190	1.24
Naperville, IL (city) Du Page County	180	0.14
Portland, OR (city) Multnomah County	180	0.03
Chelsea, MA (city) Suffolk County	179	0.51
Concord, NH (city) Merrimack County	177	0.44
Pompton Lakes, NJ (borough) Passaic County	173	1.63
San Francisco, CA (city) San Francisco County	173	0.02
Clawson, MI (city) Oakland County	172	1.35
Cliffside Park, NJ (borough) Bergen County	172	0.75
Wixom, MI (city) Oakland County	171	1.29
New City, NY (cdp) Rockland County	171	0.50
Clifton, NJ (city) Passaic County	170	0.22
Syracuse, NY (city) Onondaga County	170	0.12
Seattle, WA (city) King County	170	0.03
Fairfield, CT (town) Fairfield County	168	0.29
Walled Lake, MI (city) Oakland County	166	2.56
Plainfield, CT (town) Windham County	166	1.14
Bedford, TX (city) Tarrant County	165	0.35
Marlborough, MA (city) Middlesex County	164	0.45
White Plains, NY (city) Westchester County	164	0.31
Akron, OH (city) Summit County	160	0.07
Watertown, CT (town) Litchfield County	159	0.73
Ossining, NY (town) Westchester County	159	0.44
Madison Heights, MI (city) Oakland County	158	0.51
Revere, MA (city) Suffolk County	158	0.33
Fort Lauderdale, FL (city) Broward County	158	0.10
Brookhaven, NY (town) Suffolk County	158	0.04
Cincinnati, OH (city) Hamilton County	155	0.05
Grand Rapids, MI (city) Kent County	152	0.08
Mansfield, OH (city) Richland County	149	0.30
Carol Stream, IL (village) Du Page County	148	0.37
Mount Prospect, IL (village) Cook County	148	0.26
Babylon, NY (town) Suffolk County	146	0.07
Baltimore, MD (independent city) Baltimore city	145	0.02
Summit, IL (village) Cook County	144	1.35
Taylor, MI (city) Wayne County	143	0.22
Ramapo, NY (town) Rockland County	143	0.13
Stoneham, MA (town) Middlesex County	141	0.63
Winthrop, MA (cdp) Suffolk County	140	0.76
Downey, CA (city) Los Angeles County	140	0.13
Tempe, AZ (city) Maricopa County	140	0.09
Yorktown, NY (town) Westchester County	138	0.38
Islip, NY (town) Suffolk County	138	0.04
Birmingham, MI (city) Oakland County	137	0.71
Prospect, CT (town) New Haven County	135	1.55
Newton, MA (city) Middlesex County	135	0.16
Stratford, CT (cdp) Fairfield County	133	0.27
Canton, MI (cdp) Wayne County	133	0.17
Columbus, OH (city) Franklin County	133	0.02
Bloomfield, MI (township) Oakland County	132	0.31
Framingham, MA (cdp) Middlesex County	129	0.19
Brockton, MA (city) Plymouth County	126	0.13
San Jose, CA (city) Santa Clara County	126	0.01
Jamestown, NY (city) Chautauqua County	123	0.39
Saint Clair Shores, MI (city) Macomb County	122	0.19
Totowa, NJ (borough) Passaic County	119	1.21
Montville, NJ (township) Morris County	117	0.56
Elgin, IL (city) Kane County	116	0.12
Allentown, PA (city) Lehigh County	116	0.11
Ventnor City, NJ (city) Atlantic County	115	0.89
Beekman, NY (town) Dutchess County	114	1.00
Orlando, FL (city) Orange County	114	0.06
Diamond Bar, CA (city) Los Angeles County	113	0.20
La Grange, NY (town) Dutchess County	111	0.74
Newtown, CT (town) Fairfield County	111	0.44
Glen Ellyn, IL (village) Du Page County	111	0.41
Shelton, CT (city) Fairfield County	111	0.29
Albany, NY (city) Albany County	111	0.12
Oyster Bay, NY (town) Nassau County	111	0.04
North Haledon, NJ (borough) Passaic County	110	1.39
Mamakating, NY (town) Sullivan County	110	1.00
North New Hyde Park, NY (cdp) Nassau County	109	0.75
Bloomfield, NJ (cdp) Essex County	109	0.23
Greenburgh, NY (town) Westchester County	109	0.13
New Brighton, MN (city) Ramsey County	108	0.49
New London, CT (city) New London County	107	0.42
Portland, ME (city) Cumberland County	107	0.17
Arlington, VA (cdp) Arlington County	107	0.06

Notes: (cdp) census designated place; Refer to the Explanation of Data in the front of the book for more detailed information.

Albanian

Top 150 Places Sorted by Percent

(Based on all places, regardless of population)

Place	Number	%
Halls Crossing, UT (cdp) San Juan County	6	6.06
Leeds, NY (cdp) Greene County	17	5.18
Scotts Corners, NY (cdp) Westchester County	22	3.82
Fairview, NC (cdp) Buncombe County	92	3.47
Walker Valley, NY (cdp) Ulster County	26	3.14
Tariffville, CT (cdp) Hartford County	38	2.85
Hamtramck, MI (city) Wayne County	635	2.76
Walled Lake, MI (city) Oakland County	166	2.56
Wauregan, CT (cdp) Windham County	25	2.40
Hindsboro, IL (village) Douglas County	8	2.25
Wausaukee, WI (village) Marinette County	13	2.20
Waterbury, CT (city) New Haven County	2,174	2.03
Brodheadsville, PA (cdp) Monroe County	29	2.00
West Buechel, KY (city) Jefferson County	26	2.00
Golden's Bridge, NY (cdp) Westchester County	30	1.94
Jamestown West, NY (cdp) Chautauqua County	48	1.91
Sterling Heights, MI (city) Macomb County	2,295	1.84
Lincoln Park, NJ (borough) Morris County	200	1.83
Spartansburg, PA (borough) Crawford County	6	1.82
Shelby, MI (cdp) Macomb County	1,180	1.81
Bardonia, NY (cdp) Rockland County	78	1.78
Grosse Pointe Park, MI (city) Wayne County	219	1.76
Newark, IL (village) Kendall County	16	1.76
Prospect Park, NJ (borough) Passaic County	101	1.75
Rock Hill, NY (cdp) Sullivan County	17	1.73
Hampton, IL (village) Rock Island County	27	1.69
Pompton Lakes, NJ (borough) Passaic County	173	1.63
Walnut Cove, NC (town) Stokes County	23	1.61
Greenup, IL (village) Cumberland County	24	1.57
Saint Olaf, IA (city) Clayton County	2	1.57
Prospect, CT (town) New Haven County	135	1.55
Eldridge, CA (cdp) Sonoma County	23	1.53
Grand View-on-Hudson, NY (village) Rockland County	4	1.41
North Haledon, NJ (borough) Passaic County	110	1.39
Bethania, NC (town) Forsyth County	5	1.38
Clawson, MI (city) Oakland County	172	1.35
Summit, IL (village) Cook County	144	1.35
Sandwich, IL (city) De Kalb County	88	1.35
Highland Mills, NY (cdp) Orange County	46	1.34
Alfred, ME (town) York County	33	1.32
Cameron, WV (city) Marshall County	16	1.32
Macomb, MI (township) Macomb County	652	1.29
Wixom, MI (city) Oakland County	171	1.29
Pomfret, CT (town) Windham County	49	1.29
Cordova, IL (village) Rock Island County	8	1.28
Salmon Brook, CT (cdp) Hartford County	31	1.25
Garfield, NJ (city) Bergen County	370	1.24
Fraser, MI (city) Macomb County	190	1.24
Briarcliff Manor, NY (village) Westchester County	94	1.23
Paxton, MA (town) Worcester County	54	1.23
Totowa, NJ (borough) Passaic County	119	1.21
Worcester, MA (city) Worcester County	2,029	1.18
Tappan, NY (cdp) Rockland County	79	1.17
Beacon Falls, CT (town) New Haven County	61	1.16
Middlebury, CT (town) New Haven County	75	1.15
Jefferson Heights, NY (cdp) Greene County	13	1.15
Bull Valley, IL (village) McHenry County	8	1.15
Plainfield, CT (town) Windham County	166	1.14
Andalusia, IL (village) Rock Island County	12	1.13
Ansonia, CT (city) New Haven County	208	1.12
Cudahy, WI (city) Milwaukee County	206	1.12
Farmington, WV (town) Marion County	4	1.12
South Duxbury, MA (cdp) Plymouth County	34	1.11
Roscoe, IL (village) Winnebago County	69	1.09
Cornwells Heights-Eddington, PA (cdp) Bucks County	36	1.09
South Milwaukee, WI (city) Milwaukee County	229	1.08
Rose, MI (township) Oakland County	67	1.08
Utica, MI (city) Macomb County	49	1.07
Chestnut Ridge, NY (village) Rockland County	82	1.06
Lakewood, OH (city) Cuyahoga County	593	1.05
Clinton, MI (cdp) Macomb County	994	1.04
Royal Oak charter, MI (township) Oakland County	56	1.03
Erma, NJ (cdp) Cape May County	22	1.03
Hillcrest, IL (village) Ogle County	12	1.03
Lodi, NJ (borough) Bergen County	245	1.02
Beekman, NY (town) Dutchess County	114	1.00
Mamakating, NY (town) Sullivan County	110	1.00
Readmond, MI (township) Emmet County	5	0.99
Enon, OH (village) Clark County	26	0.98
Kutztown, PA (borough) Berks County	49	0.97
Newland, NC (town) Avery County	7	0.96
Ford Cliff, PA (borough) Armstrong County	4	0.96
Douglas, MA (town) Worcester County	67	0.95
Danville, VT (town) Caledonia County	21	0.95
Pentwater, MI (village) Oceana County	9	0.95
Huntley, IL (village) McHenry County	53	0.93
Putnam Valley, NY (town) Putnam County	96	0.90
Ventnor City, NJ (city) Atlantic County	115	0.89
Netcong, NJ (borough) Morris County	23	0.89
Lac La Belle, WI (village) Waukesha County	3	0.89
South Woodstock, CT (cdp) Windham County	10	0.88
Provincetown, MA (town) Barnstable County	30	0.87
Wayne, NJ (cdp) Passaic County	466	0.86
Melissa, TX (city) Collin County	11	0.85
Sullivan, WI (village) Jefferson County	6	0.85
Deer Creek, PA (township) Mercer County	4	0.84
Yorktown Heights, NY (cdp) Westchester County	66	0.83
Atlantic Highlands, NJ (borough) Monmouth County	39	0.83
Center Line, MI (city) Macomb County	69	0.81
Elmwood Park, IL (village) Cook County	202	0.80
Rockaway, NJ (borough) Morris County	52	0.80
Woodcliff Lake, NJ (borough) Bergen County	46	0.80
Lake Mills, WI (city) Jefferson County	39	0.80
Plainfield Village, CT (cdp) Windham County	21	0.80
Myers Corner, NY (cdp) Dutchess County	45	0.79
Mill Neck, NY (village) Nassau County	6	0.79
West Lake Hills, TX (city) Travis County	24	0.77
Mount Carroll, IL (city) Carroll County	14	0.77
Warren, MI (city) Macomb County	1,053	0.76
Winthrop, MA (cdp) Suffolk County	140	0.76
Green Meadow, FL (cdp) Broward County	14	0.76
Addison, IL (village) Du Page County	267	0.75
Cliffside Park, NJ (borough) Bergen County	172	0.75
North New Hyde Park, NY (cdp) Nassau County	109	0.75
Dudley, MA (town) Worcester County	75	0.75
Cudjoe Key, FL (cdp) Monroe County	13	0.75
Lowden, IA (city) Cedar County	6	0.75
La Grange, NY (town) Dutchess County	111	0.74
Cresskill, NJ (borough) Bergen County	57	0.74
Lakewood, NY (village) Chautauqua County	24	0.74
Roslyn Estates, NY (village) Nassau County	9	0.74
Watertown, CT (town) Litchfield County	159	0.73
Fort Atkinson, WI (city) Jefferson County	86	0.73
Lyons, IL (village) Cook County	74	0.73
Harbor Hills, OH (cdp) Licking County	9	0.73
Loachapoka, AL (town) Lee County	1	0.73
Leland, IL (village) La Salle County	7	0.72
Elwood, UT (town) Box Elder County	5	0.72
Dearborn, MI (city) Wayne County	694	0.71
Birmingham, MI (city) Oakland County	137	0.71
Shenorock, NY (cdp) Westchester County	14	0.71
Port Hope, MI (village) Huron County	2	0.70
Closter, NJ (borough) Bergen County	58	0.69
Clayton, NJ (borough) Gloucester County	49	0.69
Lake Placid, NY (village) Essex County	18	0.69
Hastings-on-Hudson, NY (village) Westchester County	52	0.68
Bethel, AK (city) Bethel Census Area	37	0.68
Wallace, PA (township) Chester County	22	0.68
Yonkers, NY (city) Westchester County	1,310	0.67
Natick, MA (town) Middlesex County	212	0.66
Kenilworth, NJ (borough) Union County	51	0.66
Roselawn, IN (cdp) Jasper County	26	0.66
Woolwich, NJ (township) Gloucester County	20	0.66
Tobacco, MI (township) Gladwin County	17	0.66
Orangeville, IL (village) Stephenson County	5	0.66
Lansdale, PA (borough) Montgomery County	105	0.65
Atlas, MI (township) Genesee County	47	0.65
Deal, NJ (borough) Monmouth County	7	0.65
Flambeau, WI (town) Rusk County	7	0.65
Hillside, NY (cdp) Ulster County	6	0.65

Notes: (cdp) census designated place; Refer to the Explanation of Data in the front of the book for more detailed information.

Albanian

Top 150 Places Sorted by Percent

(Based on places with populations of 10,000 or more)

Place	Number	%
Hamtramck, MI (city) Wayne County	635	2.76
Waterbury, CT (city) New Haven County	2,174	2.03
Sterling Heights, MI (city) Macomb County	2,295	1.84
Lincoln Park, NJ (borough) Morris County	200	1.83
Shelby, MI (cdp) Macomb County	1,180	1.81
Grosse Pointe Park, MI (city) Wayne County	219	1.76
Pompton Lakes, NJ (borough) Passaic County	173	1.63
Clawson, MI (city) Oakland County	172	1.35
Summit, IL (village) Cook County	144	1.35
Macomb, MI (township) Macomb County	652	1.29
Wixom, MI (city) Oakland County	171	1.29
Garfield, NJ (city) Bergen County	370	1.24
Fraser, MI (city) Macomb County	190	1.24
Worcester, MA (city) Worcester County	2,029	1.18
Plainfield, CT (town) Windham County	166	1.14
Ansonia, CT (city) New Haven County	208	1.12
Cudahy, WI (city) Milwaukee County	206	1.12
South Milwaukee, WI (city) Milwaukee County	229	1.08
Lakewood, OH (city) Cuyahoga County	593	1.05
Clinton, MI (cdp) Macomb County	994	1.04
Lodi, NJ (borough) Bergen County	245	1.02
Beekman, NY (town) Dutchess County	114	1.00
Mamakating, NY (town) Sullivan County	110	1.00
Putnam Valley, NY (town) Putnam County	96	0.90
Ventnor City, NJ (city) Atlantic County	115	0.89
Wayne, NJ (cdp) Passaic County	466	0.86
Elmwood Park, IL (village) Cook County	202	0.80
Warren, MI (city) Macomb County	1,053	0.76
Winthrop, MA (cdp) Suffolk County	140	0.76
Addison, IL (village) Du Page County	267	0.75
Cliffside Park, NJ (borough) Bergen County	172	0.75
North New Hyde Park, NY (cdp) Nassau County	109	0.75
Dudley, MA (town) Worcester County	75	0.75
La Grange, NY (town) Dutchess County	111	0.74
Watertown, CT (town) Litchfield County	159	0.73
Fort Atkinson, WI (city) Jefferson County	86	0.73
Lyons, IL (village) Cook County	74	0.73
Dearborn, MI (city) Wayne County	694	0.71
Birmingham, MI (city) Oakland County	137	0.71
Yonkers, NY (city) Westchester County	1,310	0.67
Natick, MA (town) Middlesex County	212	0.66
Lansdale, PA (borough) Montgomery County	105	0.65
Naugatuck, CT (borough) New Haven County	199	0.64
Oldsmar, FL (city) Pinellas County	75	0.64
Stoneham, MA (town) Middlesex County	141	0.63
Farmington Hills, MI (city) Oakland County	509	0.62
Royal Oak, MI (city) Oakland County	370	0.62
Holden, MA (town) Worcester County	94	0.60
Montville, NJ (township) Morris County	117	0.56
Dunedin, FL (city) Pinellas County	199	0.55
Roseville, MI (city) Macomb County	262	0.54
Roselle Park, NJ (borough) Union County	72	0.54
Leicester, MA (town) Worcester County	55	0.53
Troy, MI (city) Oakland County	410	0.51
Waterford, MI (cdp) Oakland County	373	0.51
Chelsea, MA (city) Suffolk County	179	0.51
Madison Heights, MI (city) Oakland County	158	0.51
New City, NY (cdp) Rockland County	171	0.50
New Brighton, MN (city) Ramsey County	108	0.49
Jefferson Valley-Yorktown, NY (cdp) Westchester County	72	0.48
Oxford, MA (town) Worcester County	63	0.47
Justice, IL (village) Cook County	57	0.47
Catskill, NY (town) Greene County	56	0.47
Quincy, MA (city) Norfolk County	402	0.46
Lewiston, NY (town) Niagara County	75	0.46
Bridgeview, IL (village) Cook County	70	0.46
Largo, FL (city) Pinellas County	312	0.45
Marlborough, MA (city) Middlesex County	164	0.45
Fitchburg, WI (city) Dane County	93	0.45
Rochester Hills, MI (city) Oakland County	302	0.44
Peabody, MA (city) Essex County	214	0.44
Concord, NH (city) Merrimack County	177	0.44
Ossining, NY (town) Westchester County	159	0.44
Newtown, CT (town) Fairfield County	111	0.44
Stamford, CT (city) Fairfield County	508	0.43
New London, CT (city) New London County	107	0.42
Auburn, MA (town) Worcester County	67	0.42
Manchester, NH (city) Hillsborough County	436	0.41
Glen Ellyn, IL (village) Du Page County	111	0.41
Belmont, MA (cdp) Middlesex County	100	0.41
Brownstown, MI (township) Wayne County	95	0.41
Marlton, NJ (cdp) Burlington County	41	0.40
Jamestown, NY (city) Chautauqua County	123	0.39
Ossining, NY (village) Westchester County	94	0.39
Monroe, CT (town) Fairfield County	76	0.39
Palisades Park, NJ (borough) Bergen County	67	0.39
Princeton, NJ (township) Mercer County	62	0.39
Wolcott, CT (town) New Haven County	60	0.39
Fairview, NJ (borough) Bergen County	52	0.39
Upper Darby, PA (township) Delaware County	307	0.38
Yorktown, NY (town) Westchester County	138	0.38
Grafton, MA (town) Worcester County	56	0.38
Somerville, MA (city) Middlesex County	287	0.37
Carol Stream, IL (village) Du Page County	148	0.37
Washington, MI (township) Macomb County	70	0.37
Webster, MA (town) Worcester County	60	0.37
Hickory Hills, IL (city) Cook County	52	0.37
Lewisboro, NY (town) Westchester County	45	0.37
Melvindale, MI (city) Wayne County	40	0.37
Hartford, CT (city) Hartford County	433	0.36
Southbury, CT (town) New Haven County	67	0.36
Palos Hills, IL (city) Cook County	64	0.36
Wyckoff, NJ (cdp) Bergen County	60	0.36
Linganore-Bartonsville, MD (cdp) Frederick County	45	0.36
Lower Moreland, PA (township) Montgomery County	41	0.36
Fredonia, NY (village) Chautauqua County	39	0.36
Westland, MI (city) Wayne County	301	0.35
Bedford, TX (city) Tarrant County	165	0.35
Affton, MO (cdp) Saint Louis County	74	0.35
Niles, OH (city) Trumbull County	74	0.35
Dumont, NJ (borough) Bergen County	62	0.35
Secaucus, NJ (town) Hudson County	56	0.35
Duxbury, MA (town) Plymouth County	50	0.35
Stoughton, WI (city) Dane County	42	0.34
Rehoboth, MA (town) Bristol County	35	0.34
Revere, MA (city) Suffolk County	158	0.33
Wappinger, NY (town) Dutchess County	88	0.33
Ashland, MA (town) Middlesex County	48	0.33
Holliston, MA (town) Middlesex County	45	0.33
Charlton, MA (town) Worcester County	37	0.33
West Bloomfield, MI (township) Oakland County	206	0.32
Harrison, NY (village) Westchester County	77	0.32
Darien, IL (city) Du Page County	74	0.32
Villa Park, IL (village) Du Page County	71	0.32
Winchester, MA (cdp) Middlesex County	67	0.32
Franklin Park, IL (village) Cook County	62	0.32
Southbridge, MA (town) Worcester County	55	0.32
New York, NY (city) New York City	24,577	0.31
Clarkstown, NY (town) Rockland County	257	0.31
White Plains, NY (city) Westchester County	164	0.31
Bloomfield, MI (township) Oakland County	132	0.31
Lindenhurst, NY (village) Suffolk County	87	0.31
Hudson, MA (town) Middlesex County	57	0.31
Berkeley Heights, NJ (cdp) Union County	41	0.31
Fruitville, FL (cdp) Sarasota County	40	0.31
Avon, OH (city) Lorain County	35	0.31
Reading, OH (city) Hamilton County	35	0.31
Mansfield, OH (city) Richland County	149	0.30
Plymouth Township, MI (cdp) Wayne County	83	0.30
Danvers, MA (cdp) Essex County	75	0.30
Pomfret, NY (town) Chautauqua County	44	0.30
Upper, NJ (township) Cape May County	36	0.30
Calhoun, GA (city) Gordon County	31	0.30
East Rockaway, NY (village) Nassau County	31	0.30
Granby, CT (town) Hartford County	31	0.30
Fairfield, CT (town) Fairfield County	168	0.29
Shelton, CT (city) Fairfield County	111	0.29
Somers, NY (town) Westchester County	53	0.29
Town and Country, MO (city) Saint Louis County	32	0.29
Bridgeport, CT (city) Fairfield County	386	0.28

Notes: (cdp) census designated place; Refer to the Explanation of Data in the front of the book for more detailed information.

Alsatian

Top 150 Places Sorted by Number

(Based on all places, regardless of population)

Place	Number	%
San Antonio, TX (city) Bexar County	482	0.04
New York, NY (city) New York City	388	0.00
Houston, TX (city) Harris County	193	0.01
Castroville, TX (city) Medina County	168	6.29
San Francisco, CA (city) San Francisco County	156	0.02
Chicago, IL (city) Cook County	137	0.00
Los Angeles, CA (city) Los Angeles County	131	0.00
Dallas, TX (city) Dallas County	125	0.01
Seattle, WA (city) King County	97	0.02
La Coste, TX (city) Medina County	92	7.32
Austin, TX (city) Travis County	87	0.01
Hempstead, NY (town) Nassau County	87	0.01
Pittsburgh, PA (city) Allegheny County	72	0.02
Devine, TX (city) Medina County	71	1.65
Portland, OR (city) Multnomah County	70	0.01
Saint Paul, MN (city) Ramsey County	64	0.02
San Diego, CA (city) San Diego County	61	0.00
Kingsbury, TX (cdp) Guadalupe County	60	9.65
Philadelphia, PA (city) Philadelphia County	58	0.00
Boston, MA (city) Suffolk County	57	0.01
El Paso, TX (city) El Paso County	56	0.01
Flossmoor, IL (village) Cook County	55	0.59
Cambridge, MA (city) Middlesex County	55	0.05
Huntington, NY (town) Suffolk County	55	0.03
Montgomery, NJ (township) Somerset County	54	0.31
Denver, CO (city) Denver County	54	0.01
Grand Junction, CO (city) Mesa County	51	0.12
Islip, NY (town) Suffolk County	50	0.02
Indianapolis, IN (special city) Marion County	50	0.01
Phoenix, AZ (city) Maricopa County	46	0.00
Alexandria, VA (independent city) Alexandria city	44	0.03
Arlington, VA (cdp) Arlington County	44	0.02
Jacksonville, FL (special city) Duval County	43	0.01
Lowville, NY (village) Lewis County	42	1.20
Lowville, NY (town) Lewis County	42	0.92
Warwick, PA (township) Bucks County	42	0.35
Somerville, MA (city) Middlesex County	42	0.05
Eugene, OR (city) Lane County	41	0.03
Cleveland, OH (city) Cuyahoga County	41	0.01
Hamilton, NJ (township) Mercer County	40	0.05
Kerrville, TX (city) Kerr County	39	0.19
Clarence, NY (town) Erie County	39	0.15
Cheektowaga, NY (town) Erie County	38	0.04
Gainesville, FL (city) Alachua County	38	0.04
Wyckoff, NJ (cdp) Bergen County	37	0.22
Redford, MI (cdp) Wayne County	37	0.07
Albuquerque, NM (city) Bernalillo County	37	0.01
Allegheny, PA (township) Blair County	35	0.50
Akron, OH (city) Summit County	35	0.02
Brookhaven, NY (town) Suffolk County	35	0.01
Holmdel, NJ (township) Monmouth County	34	0.22
Springfield, MO (city) Greene County	34	0.02
Milwaukee, WI (city) Milwaukee County	34	0.01
Senatobia, MS (city) Tate County	33	0.48
East Longmeadow, MA (town) Hampden County	33	0.23
Butler, PA (city) Butler County	33	0.22
Rockville Centre, NY (village) Nassau County	33	0.13
Holyoke, MA (city) Hampden County	33	0.08
Scottsdale, AZ (city) Maricopa County	33	0.02
Charlotte, NC (city) Mecklenburg County	33	0.01
Washington, DC (city) District of Columbia	33	0.01
White Horse, NJ (cdp) Mercer County	31	0.32
Princeton, NJ (borough) Mercer County	31	0.22
Goshen, IN (city) Elkhart County	31	0.11
Cincinnati, OH (city) Hamilton County	31	0.01
Greenacres, FL (city) Palm Beach County	30	0.11
Costa Mesa, CA (city) Orange County	30	0.03
Naperville, IL (city) Du Page County	30	0.02
Tucson, AZ (city) Pima County	30	0.01
Tulsa, OK (city) Tulsa County	30	0.01
San Jose, CA (city) Santa Clara County	30	0.00
McLean, VA (cdp) Fairfax County	29	0.07
Huntington Beach, CA (city) Orange County	29	0.02
Oak Park, IL (village) Cook County	28	0.05
Wheaton-Glenmont, MD (cdp) Montgomery County	28	0.05
Peoria, AZ (city) Maricopa County	28	0.03
Long Beach, CA (city) Los Angeles County	28	0.01
Toledo, OH (city) Lucas County	28	0.01
Coram, NY (cdp) Suffolk County	27	0.08
Middletown, NJ (township) Monmouth County	27	0.04
Overland Park, KS (city) Johnson County	27	0.02
Villa Hills, KY (city) Kenton County	26	0.32
Pittsford, NY (town) Monroe County	26	0.10
Tonawanda, NY (town) Erie County	26	0.03
Jersey City, NJ (city) Hudson County	26	0.01
Montgomery, AL (city) Montgomery County	26	0.01
Groveland, MI (township) Oakland County	25	0.41
Brushy Creek, TX (cdp) Williamson County	25	0.16
Boulder, CO (city) Boulder County	25	0.03
Dearborn, MI (city) Wayne County	25	0.03
Webster Groves, MO (city) Saint Louis County	24	0.10
Niles, IL (village) Cook County	24	0.08
San Marcos, TX (city) Hays County	24	0.07
Victoria, TX (city) Victoria County	24	0.04
Killeen, TX (city) Bell County	24	0.03
Midland, TX (city) Midland County	24	0.03
Vancouver, WA (city) Clark County	24	0.02
Fort Wayne, IN (city) Allen County	24	0.01
Kansas City, MO (city) Jackson County	24	0.01
Oklahoma City, OK (city) Oklahoma County	24	0.00
Decatur, GA (city) De Kalb County	23	0.13
Mahwah, NJ (township) Bergen County	23	0.10
Andover, MA (town) Essex County	23	0.07
Braintree, MA (town) Norfolk County	23	0.07
Altamonte Springs, FL (city) Seminole County	23	0.06
Annapolis, MD (city) Anne Arundel County	23	0.06
Reston, VA (cdp) Fairfax County	23	0.04
Santa Rosa, CA (city) Sonoma County	23	0.02
Buffalo, NY (city) Erie County	23	0.01
Columbus, OH (city) Franklin County	23	0.00
North Falmouth, MA (cdp) Barnstable County	22	0.67
North Great River, NY (cdp) Suffolk County	22	0.56
Hudson, OH (city) Summit County	22	0.10
Scotch Plains, NJ (cdp) Union County	22	0.10
Orchard Park, NY (town) Erie County	22	0.08
Tredyffrin, PA (township) Chester County	22	0.08
Falmouth, MA (town) Barnstable County	22	0.07
Cherry Hill, NJ (township) Camden County	22	0.03
North Hempstead, NY (town) Nassau County	22	0.01
Fort Washington, PA (cdp) Montgomery County	21	0.58
Wauseon, OH (city) Fulton County	21	0.30
Princeton, IL (city) Bureau County	21	0.28
Morris, NJ (township) Morris County	21	0.10
Upper Dublin, PA (township) Montgomery County	21	0.08
Perinton, NY (town) Monroe County	21	0.05
Boynton Beach, FL (city) Palm Beach County	21	0.04
Levittown, NY (cdp) Nassau County	21	0.04
Scranton, PA (city) Lackawanna County	21	0.03
Arlington, TX (city) Tarrant County	21	0.01
Minneapolis, MN (city) Hennepin County	21	0.01
Maunawili, HI (cdp) Honolulu County	20	0.41
Clayton, MO (city) Saint Louis County	20	0.16
New Castle, NY (town) Westchester County	20	0.11
Hauppauge, NY (cdp) Suffolk County	20	0.10
Lake Forest, IL (city) Lake County	20	0.10
Bailey's Crossroads, VA (cdp) Fairfax County	20	0.09
Linden, NJ (city) Union County	20	0.05
Bryan, TX (city) Brazos County	20	0.03
Lower Merion, PA (township) Montgomery County	20	0.03
Mountain View, CA (city) Santa Clara County	20	0.03
Redwood City, CA (city) San Mateo County	20	0.03
Silver Spring, MD (cdp) Montgomery County	20	0.03
Berkeley, CA (city) Alameda County	20	0.02
Colorado Springs, CO (city) El Paso County	20	0.01
Louisville, KY (city) Jefferson County	20	0.01
Las Vegas, NV (city) Clark County	20	0.00
Lakehills, TX (cdp) Bandera County	19	0.43
Goose Creek, SC (city) Berkeley County	19	0.07
Twin Falls, ID (city) Twin Falls County	19	0.06
Flagstaff, AZ (city) Coconino County	19	0.04

Notes: (cdp) census designated place; Refer to the Explanation of Data in the front of the book for more detailed information.

Alsatian

Top 150 Places Sorted by Percent

(Based on all places, regardless of population)

Place	Number	%
Petersville, AK (cdp) Matanuska-Susitna Borough	6	50.00
Kingsbury, TX (cdp) Guadalupe County	60	9.65
La Coste, TX (city) Medina County	92	7.32
Castroville, TX (city) Medina County	168	6.29
Canada de los Alamos, NM (cdp) Santa Fe County	13	4.19
Cape May Point, NJ (borough) Cape May County	4	1.68
Devine, TX (city) Medina County	71	1.65
Otis, KS (city) Rush County	5	1.47
Huron, MI (township) Huron County	6	1.35
Elliston, MT (cdp) Powell County	3	1.29
Chester, IA (city) Howard County	2	1.27
Lowville, NY (village) Lewis County	42	1.20
Fremont, WI (town) Clark County	14	1.19
Evening Shade, OK (cdp) Sequoyah County	6	1.15
Hewlett Neck, NY (village) Nassau County	5	1.01
Lowville, NY (town) Lewis County	42	0.92
Moore, TX (cdp) Frio County	7	0.92
Bellewood, KY (city) Jefferson County	3	0.91
Silver Plume, CO (town) Clear Creek County	2	0.89
Kirtland Hills, OH (village) Lake County	5	0.83
Taylor, NY (town) Cortland County	4	0.83
Lismore, MN (city) Nobles County	2	0.78
Eek, AK (city) Bethel Census Area	2	0.77
Stanford, MT (town) Judith Basin County	3	0.75
Newbury, VT (village) Orange County	3	0.73
Straughn, IN (town) Henry County	2	0.71
North Falmouth, MA (cdp) Barnstable County	22	0.67
Niverville, NY (cdp) Columbia County	11	0.66
Ellicottville, NY (village) Cattaraugus County	3	0.63
Lake Heritage, PA (cdp) Adams County	7	0.62
Holy Cross, IA (city) Dubuque County	2	0.62
Occidental, CA (cdp) Sonoma County	9	0.60
Bromley, KY (city) Kenton County	5	0.60
Flossmoor, IL (village) Cook County	55	0.59
Kensington, MD (town) Montgomery County	11	0.59
Fort Washington, PA (cdp) Montgomery County	21	0.58
Hollywood Park, TX (town) Bexar County	15	0.58
Barataria, LA (cdp) Jefferson Parish	8	0.58
Clear Lake, WA (cdp) Skagit County	6	0.57
North Great River, NY (cdp) Suffolk County	22	0.56
Lykens, PA (township) Dauphin County	6	0.55
Contoocook, NH (cdp) Merrimack County	8	0.53
Houghton, NY (cdp) Allegany County	9	0.52
Jeffersonville, VT (village) Lamoille County	3	0.51
Allegheny, PA (township) Blair County	35	0.50
North Troy, VT (village) Orleans County	3	0.50
Carver, MN (city) Carver County	6	0.49
Senatobia, MS (city) Tate County	33	0.48
Allenhurst, GA (town) Liberty County	4	0.47
Rutledge, PA (borough) Delaware County	4	0.47
Pennsbury, PA (township) Chester County	16	0.46
Dresden, NY (town) Washington County	3	0.45
Bloomsdale, MO (city) Sainte Genevieve County	2	0.45
Yankee Springs, MI (township) Barry County	18	0.44
Lyndon, MI (township) Washtenaw County	12	0.44
North Annville, PA (township) Lebanon County	10	0.44
Lakehills, TX (cdp) Bandera County	19	0.43
Bay View, OH (village) Erie County	3	0.43
Osceola, PA (township) Tioga County	3	0.43
La Fayette, KY (city) Christian County	3	0.43
Parkway Village, KY (city) Jefferson County	3	0.42
Groveland, MI (township) Oakland County	25	0.41
Maunawili, HI (cdp) Honolulu County	20	0.41
Westhampton, MA (town) Hampshire County	6	0.41
Woodlawn, NC (cdp) Alamance County	5	0.41
Linntown, PA (cdp) Union County	6	0.40
Wilson, MN (township) Winona County	5	0.40
Bear Creek, WI (town) Sauk County	2	0.39
Blue Hill, ME (town) Hancock County	9	0.38
El Lago, TX (city) Harris County	12	0.36
Placid Lakes, FL (cdp) Highlands County	11	0.36
Warwick, PA (township) Bucks County	42	0.35
Orleans, IA (city) Dickinson County	2	0.35
Caneadea, NY (town) Allegany County	9	0.34
Gallitzin, PA (borough) Cambria County	6	0.34
Temple, ME (town) Franklin County	2	0.34
Castle Hills, TX (city) Bexar County	14	0.33
Golden Triangle, NJ (cdp) Camden County	11	0.33
White Horse, NJ (cdp) Mercer County	31	0.32
Villa Hills, KY (city) Kenton County	26	0.32
Brownsboro Village, KY (city) Jefferson County	1	0.32
Montgomery, NJ (township) Somerset County	54	0.31
Etowah, NC (cdp) Henderson County	9	0.31
Conway, PA (borough) Beaver County	7	0.31
Chevy Chase Section Five, MD (village) Montgomery County	2	0.31
Wauseon, OH (city) Fulton County	21	0.30
River Bend, NC (town) Craven County	9	0.30
Oxford, IA (city) Johnson County	2	0.30
Heritage Village, CT (cdp) New Haven County	10	0.29
Lytle, TX (city) Atascosa County	7	0.29
North Redington Beach, FL (town) Pinellas County	4	0.29
Dushore, PA (borough) Sullivan County	2	0.29
Princeton, IL (city) Bureau County	21	0.28
Jones, OK (town) Oklahoma County	7	0.28
Lebanon, NJ (borough) Hunterdon County	3	0.28
Kalihiwai, HI (cdp) Kauai County	2	0.28
Shady Hollow, TX (cdp) Travis County	15	0.27
Forked River, NJ (cdp) Ocean County	13	0.27
New Baltimore, NY (town) Greene County	9	0.27
Gastonville, PA (cdp) Washington County	8	0.27
Upland, PA (borough) Delaware County	8	0.27
Navesink, NJ (cdp) Monmouth County	5	0.27
Grabill, IN (town) Allen County	3	0.27
North Haven, NY (village) Suffolk County	2	0.27
Oak Grove, TX (town) Kaufman County	2	0.27
Waldo, ME (town) Waldo County	2	0.27
Westport, ME (town) Lincoln County	2	0.27
Callicoon, NY (town) Sullivan County	8	0.26
New Haven, MO (city) Franklin County	5	0.26
Montrose, WI (town) Dane County	3	0.26
Chevy Chase Section Three, MD (village) Montgomery County	2	0.26
Drammen, WI (town) Eau Claire County	2	0.26
Priest Point, WA (cdp) Snohomish County	2	0.26
Idyllwild-Pine Cove, CA (cdp) Riverside County	9	0.25
Sharpes, FL (cdp) Brevard County	9	0.25
Bel-Nor, MO (village) Saint Louis County	4	0.25
Woodburn, IN (city) Allen County	4	0.25
Malvern, AL (town) Geneva County	3	0.25
Jackson, NH (town) Carroll County	2	0.25
Metamora, MI (township) Lapeer County	10	0.24
Wimberley, TX (cdp) Hays County	9	0.24
South Bristol, NY (town) Ontario County	4	0.24
Aroma Park, IL (village) Kankakee County	2	0.24
East Longmeadow, MA (town) Hampden County	33	0.23
Groveport, OH (village) Franklin County	9	0.23
Silver Lake, OH (village) Summit County	7	0.23
Clinton, OH (village) Summit County	3	0.23
Colo, IA (city) Story County	2	0.23
Grantwood Village, MO (town) Saint Louis County	2	0.23
Wyckoff, NJ (cdp) Bergen County	37	0.22
Holmdel, NJ (township) Monmouth County	34	0.22
Butler, PA (city) Butler County	33	0.22
Princeton, NJ (borough) Mercer County	31	0.22
Alamosa, CO (city) Alamosa County	17	0.22
Orland, CA (city) Glenn County	14	0.22
Salida, CO (city) Chaffee County	12	0.22
Carmel-by-the-Sea, CA (city) Monterey County	9	0.22
San Antonio Heights, CA (cdp) San Bernardino County	7	0.22
Seaside Heights, NJ (borough) Ocean County	7	0.22
Chester, CA (cdp) Plumas County	5	0.22
University Park, MD (town) Prince George's County	5	0.22
Sandyston, NJ (township) Sussex County	4	0.22
Adairville, KY (city) Logan County	2	0.22
Franklin, PA (township) Lycoming County	2	0.22
Pine Island, TX (town) Waller County	2	0.22
Roseland, NJ (borough) Essex County	11	0.21
Luzerne, PA (township) Fayette County	10	0.21
Nassau Bay, TX (city) Harris County	9	0.21
Llano, TX (city) Llano County	7	0.21
Laurel Lake, NJ (cdp) Cumberland County	6	0.21

Notes: (cdp) census designated place; Refer to the Explanation of Data in the front of the book for more detailed information.

American Indian tribes, specified

Top 150 Places Sorted by Percent

(Based on all places, regardless of population)

Place	Number	%
Lodge Pole, MT (cdp) Blaine County	218	101.87
Hays, MT (cdp) Blaine County	711	101.28
Aneth, UT (cdp) San Juan County	599	100.17
Saint Pierre, MT (cdp) Hill County	289	100.00
Ojo Amarillo, NM (cdp) San Juan County	826	99.64
Steamboat, AZ (cdp) Apache County	232	99.57
Second Mesa, AZ (cdp) Navajo County	810	99.51
Huerfano, NM (cdp) San Juan County	103	99.04
Tselakai Dezza, UT (cdp) San Juan County	102	99.03
Nazlini, AZ (cdp) Apache County	393	98.99
Kaibito, AZ (cdp) Coconino County	1,589	98.88
Acomita Lake, NM (cdp) Cibola County	308	98.72
Zia Pueblo, NM (cdp) Sandoval County	636	98.45
East Fork, AZ (cdp) Navajo County	865	98.30
Pinehill, NM (cdp) Cibola County	114	98.28
Beclabito, NM (cdp) San Juan County	333	98.23
Rock Point, AZ (cdp) Apache County	711	98.20
Lechee, AZ (cdp) Coconino County	1,577	98.19
Isleta Village Proper, NM (cdp) Bernalillo County	487	98.19
Halchita, UT (cdp) San Juan County	265	98.15
Moenkopi, AZ (cdp) Coconino County	884	98.11
Little Rock, MN (cdp) Beltrami County	1,035	98.10
Oljato-Monument Valley, AZ (cdp) Navajo County	152	98.06
First Mesa, AZ (cdp) Navajo County	1,102	98.04
Bitter Springs, AZ (cdp) Coconino County	536	97.99
White Horse, SD (cdp) Todd County	176	97.78
Twin Lakes, NM (cdp) McKinley County	1,044	97.66
Nenahnezad, NM (cdp) San Juan County	709	97.66
Chuichu, AZ (cdp) Pinal County	331	97.64
Shongopovi, AZ (cdp) Navajo County	617	97.63
Nakaibito, NM (cdp) McKinley County	444	97.58
Round Rock, AZ (cdp) Apache County	585	97.34
Crystal, NM (cdp) McKinley County	337	97.12
Leupp, AZ (cdp) Coconino County	942	97.11
Sheep Springs, NM (cdp) San Juan County	230	97.05
Cameron, AZ (cdp) Coconino County	949	97.03
Upper Fruitland, NM (cdp) San Juan County	1,614	97.00
Fort Belknap Agency, MT (cdp) Blaine County	1,224	96.99
Two Strike, SD (cdp) Todd County	32	96.97
Sangrey, MT (cdp) Hill County	255	96.96
Ponemah, MN (cdp) Beltrami County	846	96.80
Houck, AZ (cdp) Apache County	1,052	96.78
Brimhall Nizhoni, NM (cdp) McKinley County	361	96.78
Church Rock, NM (cdp) McKinley County	1,042	96.75
Naschitti, NM (cdp) San Juan County	348	96.67
Tonalea, AZ (cdp) Coconino County	543	96.62
Pisinemo, AZ (cdp) Pima County	229	96.62
Peridot, AZ (cdp) Graham County	1,221	96.45
Fort Totten, ND (cdp) Benson County	918	96.43
Lukachukai, AZ (cdp) Apache County	1,508	96.36
Dilkon, AZ (cdp) Navajo County	1,218	96.28
Navajo, NM (cdp) McKinley County	2,017	96.19
Napi HQ, NM (cdp) San Juan County	679	96.18
Shiprock, NM (cdp) San Juan County	7,843	96.16
Azure, MT (cdp) Hill County	243	96.05
Encinal, NM (cdp) Cibola County	192	96.00
Rough Rock, AZ (cdp) Apache County	450	95.95
Red Lake, MN (cdp) Beltrami County	1,372	95.94
Santo Domingo Pueblo, NM (cdp) Sandoval County	2,444	95.84
Redby, MN (cdp) Beltrami County	917	95.82
Wanblee, SD (cdp) Jackson County	614	95.79
Navajo Mountain, UT (cdp) San Juan County	363	95.78
Greasewood, AZ (cdp) Navajo County	556	95.70
Canyon Day, AZ (cdp) Gila County	1,044	95.60
Mesita, NM (cdp) Cibola County	740	95.36
Zuni Pueblo, NM (cdp) McKinley County	6,061	95.19
Shell Valley, ND (cdp) Rolette County	376	95.19
Rock Springs, NM (cdp) McKinley County	531	95.16
Towaoc, CO (cdp) Montezuma County	1,042	94.99
East Dunseith, ND (cdp) Rolette County	208	94.98
Sanostee, NM (cdp) San Juan County	407	94.87
Montezuma Creek, UT (cdp) San Juan County	480	94.67
Winslow West, AZ (cdp) Coconino County	124	94.66
Nixon, NV (cdp) Washoe County	395	94.50
Santa Ana Pueblo, NM (cdp) Sandoval County	452	94.36
Whiteriver, AZ (cdp) Navajo County	4,923	94.31
Cibecue, AZ (cdp) Navajo County	1,253	94.14
Odanah, WI (cdp) Ashland County	239	94.09
Tsaile, AZ (cdp) Apache County	1,014	94.06
Whiterocks, UT (cdp) Uintah County	320	93.84
Alamo, NM (cdp) Socorro County	1,110	93.83
Turtle Lake, MT (cdp) Lake County	182	93.81
Sawmill, AZ (cdp) Apache County	574	93.79
Kykotsmovi Village, AZ (cdp) Navajo County	727	93.69
Fort Duchesne, UT (cdp) Uintah County	581	93.56
Parmelee, SD (cdp) Todd County	608	93.54
Tuba City, AZ (cdp) Coconino County	7,693	93.53
Chilchinbito, AZ (cdp) Navajo County	432	93.51
Crow Agency, MT (cdp) Big Horn County	1,451	93.49
Paguate, NM (cdp) Cibola County	443	93.46
Seama, NM (cdp) Cibola County	311	93.39
Rosebud, SD (cdp) Todd County	1,454	93.38
Santa Rosa, AZ (cdp) Pima County	409	93.38
Dennehotso, AZ (cdp) Apache County	685	93.32
Randlett, UT (cdp) Uintah County	209	93.30
Saint Regis Mohawk Reservation, NY (reservation) Franklin Co.	2,517	93.26
Fort Defiance, AZ (cdp) Apache County	3,781	93.11
Saint Francis, SD (town) Todd County	628	93.04
Little Eagle, SD (cdp) Corson County	344	92.97
Parker School, MT (cdp) Chouteau County	327	92.90
Agency, MT (cdp) Hill County	301	92.90
Jemez Pueblo, NM (cdp) Sandoval County	1,814	92.88
Neopit, WI (cdp) Menominee County	779	92.85
Oglala, SD (cdp) Shannon County	1,140	92.76
Keshena, WI (cdp) Menominee County	1,293	92.75
Teec Nos Pos, AZ (cdp) Apache County	741	92.74
Antelope, SD (cdp) Todd County	804	92.73
Laguna, NM (cdp) Cibola County	392	92.67
Taos Pueblo, NM (cdp) Taos County	1,170	92.56
San Felipe Pueblo, NM (cdp) Sandoval County	1,925	92.55
Heart Butte, MT (cdp) Pondera County	646	92.55
Skyline-Ganipa, NM (cdp) Cibola County	956	92.37
Marty, SD (cdp) Charles Mix County	388	92.16
Fort Yates, ND (city) Sioux County	210	92.11
Starr School, MT (cdp) Glacier County	228	91.94
Keams Canyon, AZ (cdp) Navajo County	239	91.92
Pueblo of Sandia Village, NM (cdp) Sandoval County	316	91.86
Oljato-Monument Valley, UT (cdp) San Juan County	792	91.67
Allen, SD (cdp) Bennett County	384	91.65
San Carlos, AZ (cdp) Gila County	3,403	91.58
Pinon, AZ (cdp) Navajo County	1,089	91.51
Window Rock, AZ (cdp) Apache County	2,799	91.50
Paraje, NM (cdp) Cibola County	612	91.48
Porcupine, SD (cdp) Shannon County	372	91.40
Nespelem Community, WA (cdp) Okanogan County	265	91.38
Green Grass, SD (cdp) Dewey County	53	91.38
Hotevilla-Bacavi, AZ (cdp) Navajo County	700	91.26
Tohatchi, NM (cdp) McKinley County	946	91.22
Manderson-White Horse Creek, SD (cdp) Shannon County	571	91.21
Tucker, MS (cdp) Neshoba County	487	91.20
Browning, MT (town) Glacier County	971	91.17
Fort Washakie, WY (cdp) Fremont County	1,345	91.06
Ethete, WY (cdp) Fremont County	1,324	91.00
North Browning, MT (cdp) Glacier County	1,997	90.77
South Browning, MT (cdp) Glacier County	1,522	90.76
Fort Thompson, SD (cdp) Buffalo County	1,248	90.76
Dulce, NM (cdp) Rio Arriba County	2,380	90.74
Birney, MT (cdp) Rosebud County	98	90.74
McDermitt, NV (cdp) Humboldt County	243	90.33
Arizona Village, AZ (cdp) Mohave County	317	90.31
Chinle, AZ (cdp) Apache County	4,843	90.25
Bogue Chitto, MS (cdp) Neshoba County	481	90.24
Cannon Ball, ND (cdp) Sioux County	779	90.16
Jeddito, AZ (cdp) Navajo County	350	89.74
Vineland, MN (cdp) Mille Lacs County	544	89.62
Santee, NE (village) Knox County	270	89.40
Whitehorse, SD (cdp) Dewey County	126	89.36
Frazer, MT (cdp) Valley County	403	89.16
Belcourt, ND (cdp) Rolette County	2,175	89.14
Burnside, AZ (cdp) Apache County	563	89.08

Notes: (cdp) census designated place; Refer to the Explanation of Data in the front of the book for more detailed information.

American Indian tribes, specified

Top 150 Places Sorted by Percent

(Based on places with populations of 10,000 or more)

Place	Number	%
Gallup, NM (city) McKinley County	7,324	36.24
Tahlequah, OK (city) Cherokee County	4,273	29.55
Miami, OK (city) Ottawa County	2,695	19.67
Ada, OK (city) Pontotoc County	3,029	19.30
Claremore, OK (city) Rogers County	2,894	18.23
Farmington, NM (city) San Juan County	6,381	16.86
Okmulgee, OK (city) Okmulgee County	2,185	16.78
Muskogee, OK (city) Muskogee County	6,410	16.73
Durant, OK (city) Bryan County	2,115	15.61
Shawnee, OK (city) Pottawatomie County	4,338	15.12
Sault Sainte Marie, MI (city) Chippewa County	2,440	14.75
McAlester, OK (city) Pittsburg County	2,374	13.35
Sapulpa, OK (city) Creek County	2,343	12.22
Ardmore, OK (city) Carter County	2,887	12.18
El Reno, OK (city) Canadian County	1,811	11.17
Bartlesville, OK (city) Washington County	3,822	11.00
Bemidji, MN (city) Beltrami County	1,243	10.43
Flagstaff, AZ (city) Coconino County	5,274	9.97
Sand Springs, OK (city) Tulsa County	1,718	9.84
Rapid City, SD (city) Pennington County	5,837	9.79
Cloquet, MN (city) Carlton County	992	8.86
Bixby, OK (city) Tulsa County	1,134	8.50
Lumberton, NC (city) Robeson County	1,755	8.44
Pierre, SD (city) Hughes County	1,166	8.40
Ponca City, OK (city) Kay County	2,169	8.37
Coffeyville, KS (city) Montgomery County	824	7.48
Owasso, OK (city) Tulsa County	1,372	7.42
Tulsa, OK (city) Tulsa County	27,263	6.94
Moore, OK (city) Cleveland County	2,856	6.94
Norman, OK (city) Cleveland County	6,089	6.36
McKinleyville, CA (cdp) Humboldt County	840	6.18
Chickasha, OK (city) Grady County	972	6.13
Broken Arrow, OK (city) Tulsa County	4,563	6.10
Del City, OK (city) Oklahoma County	1,303	5.89
Eureka, CA (city) Humboldt County	1,526	5.84
Olivehurst, CA (cdp) Yuba County	619	5.60
Siloam Springs, AR (city) Benton County	598	5.52
Midwest City, OK (city) Oklahoma County	2,960	5.47
Duncan, OK (city) Stephens County	1,218	5.41
Durango, CO (city) La Plata County	741	5.32
Mustang, OK (city) Canadian County	694	5.28
Stillwater, OK (city) Payne County	2,027	5.19
Great Falls, MT (city) Cascade County	2,866	5.06
Oklahoma City, OK (city) Oklahoma County	25,562	5.05
Klamath Falls, OR (city) Klamath County	946	4.86
Lawton, OK (city) Comanche County	4,409	4.75
Oroville, CA (city) Butte County	618	4.75
Casa Grande, AZ (city) Pinal County	1,156	4.58
Bethany, OK (city) Oklahoma County	892	4.39
The Village, OK (city) Oklahoma County	440	4.33
Altamont, OR (cdp) Klamath County	847	4.32
Ukiah, CA (city) Mendocino County	670	4.32
Eloy, AZ (city) Pinal County	443	4.27
Ledyard, CT (town) New London County	624	4.25
Aberdeen, WA (city) Grays Harbor County	681	4.14
Williston, ND (city) Williams County	514	4.11
Albuquerque, NM (city) Bernalillo County	18,309	4.08
Elk City, OK (city) Beckham County	414	3.94
Yukon, OK (city) Canadian County	811	3.85
Clearlake, CA (city) Lake County	505	3.84
Arkansas City, KS (city) Cowley County	457	3.82
Arcata, CA (city) Humboldt County	613	3.68
Billings, MT (city) Yellowstone County	3,285	3.66
Fortuna, CA (city) Humboldt County	384	3.66
Edmond, OK (city) Oklahoma County	2,479	3.63
Green Bay, WI (city) Brown County	3,661	3.58
Linda, CA (cdp) Yuba County	481	3.57
Chowchilla, CA (city) Madera County	389	3.50
Marysville, CA (city) Yuba County	427	3.48
Port Angeles, WA (city) Clallam County	624	3.39
Lawrence, KS (city) Douglas County	2,680	3.35
Mashpee, MA (town) Barnstable County	434	3.35
Coos Bay, OR (city) Coos County	508	3.30
Van Buren, AR (city) Crawford County	620	3.27
Enid, OK (city) Garfield County	1,509	3.21
Massena, NY (town) Saint Lawrence County	421	3.21
Aberdeen, SD (city) Brown County	789	3.20
Mandan, ND (city) Morton County	526	3.15
Scottsbluff, NE (city) Scotts Bluff County	459	3.12
Susanville, CA (city) Lassen County	422	3.12
Redding, CA (city) Shasta County	2,515	3.11
Oildale, CA (cdp) Kern County	855	3.07
Elko, NV (city) Elko County	509	3.05
Bismarck, ND (city) Burleigh County	1,651	2.97
Drexel Heights, AZ (cdp) Pima County	698	2.93
Cedar City, UT (city) Iron County	600	2.92
Barstow, CA (city) San Bernardino County	608	2.88
Rio Rancho, NM (city) Sandoval County	1,482	2.86
North Valley, NM (cdp) Bernalillo County	339	2.84
Bremerton, WA (city) Kitsap County	1,047	2.81
Escanaba, MI (city) Delta County	369	2.81
Kelso, WA (city) Cowlitz County	331	2.78
Banning, CA (city) Riverside County	649	2.75
Denison, TX (city) Grayson County	623	2.74
Los Lunas, NM (village) Valencia County	275	2.74
Laurinburg, NC (city) Scotland County	433	2.73
Rio Linda, CA (cdp) Sacramento County	286	2.73
Auburn, WA (city) King County	1,093	2.71
Woodward, OK (city) Woodward County	319	2.69
South Salt Lake, UT (city) Salt Lake County	591	2.68
Gardnerville Ranchos, NV (cdp) Douglas County	294	2.66
North Highlands, CA (cdp) Sacramento County	1,167	2.64
Red Bluff, CA (city) Tehama County	347	2.64
Missoula, MT (city) Missoula County	1,492	2.62
Carson City, NV (special city) Carson City city	1,375	2.62
Houma, LA (city) Terrebonne Parish	849	2.62
Mohave Valley, AZ (cdp) Mohave County	359	2.62
Grand Forks, ND (city) Grand Forks County	1,286	2.61
Blackfoot, ID (city) Bingham County	272	2.61
Fort Smith, AR (city) Sebastian County	2,074	2.58
Minot, ND (city) Ward County	944	2.58
Madera, CA (city) Madera County	1,104	2.56
Grass Valley, CA (city) Nevada County	280	2.56
San Jacinto, CA (city) Riverside County	606	2.55
Joplin, MO (city) Jasper County	1,148	2.52
New Kingman-Butler, AZ (cdp) Mohave County	370	2.50
Four Corners, OR (cdp) Marion County	348	2.50
Dallas, OR (city) Polk County	307	2.46
Spanaway, WA (cdp) Pierce County	529	2.45
Tacoma, WA (city) Pierce County	4,699	2.43
Santa Fe, NM (city) Santa Fe County	1,493	2.40
Springfield, OR (city) Lane County	1,263	2.39
Florence, AZ (town) Pinal County	406	2.38
Marana, AZ (town) Pima County	316	2.33
Beaumont, CA (city) Riverside County	265	2.33
Pendleton, OR (city) Umatilla County	379	2.32
South Sioux City, NE (city) Dakota County	277	2.32
Sun Valley, NV (cdp) Washoe County	450	2.31
Fort Carson, CO (cdp) El Paso County	244	2.31
Longview, WA (city) Cowlitz County	796	2.30
Tucson, AZ (city) Pima County	11,031	2.27
Waianae, HI (cdp) Honolulu County	237	2.26
Duluth, MN (city) Saint Louis County	1,955	2.25
Neosho, MO (city) Newton County	236	2.25
Minneapolis, MN (city) Hennepin County	8,586	2.24
West Sacramento, CA (city) Yolo County	704	2.23
Twentynine Palms, CA (city) San Bernardino County	329	2.23
Altus, OK (city) Jackson County	471	2.20
Lake Los Angeles, CA (cdp) Los Angeles County	254	2.20
Helena, MT (city) Lewis and Clark County	565	2.19
Parkway-South Sacramento, CA (cdp) Sacramento County	795	2.18
Massena, NY (village) Saint Lawrence County	244	2.18
Dishman, WA (cdp) Spokane County	218	2.17
Saint Helens, OR (city) Columbia County	217	2.17
Windsor, CA (town) Sonoma County	492	2.16
Butte-Silver Bow, MT (special city) Silver Bow County	727	2.15
Montville, CT (town) New London County	399	2.15
Prior Lake, MN (city) Scott County	342	2.15
Kingman, AZ (city) Mohave County	430	2.14
Brigham City, UT (city) Box Elder County	373	2.14

Notes: (cdp) census designated place; Refer to the Explanation of Data in the front of the book for more detailed information.

American Indian: Apache

Top 150 Places Sorted by Number

(Based on all places, regardless of population)

Place	Number	%
Whiteriver, AZ (cdp) Navajo County	4,697	89.98
San Carlos, AZ (cdp) Gila County	3,209	86.36
Dulce, NM (cdp) Rio Arriba County	2,116	80.67
Phoenix, AZ (city) Maricopa County	1,683	0.13
Los Angeles, CA (city) Los Angeles County	1,495	0.04
Cibecue, AZ (cdp) Navajo County	1,225	92.04
Peridot, AZ (cdp) Graham County	1,177	92.97
Canyon Day, AZ (cdp) Gila County	1,025	93.86
Mescalero, NM (cdp) Otero County	965	78.26
East Fork, AZ (cdp) Navajo County	856	97.27
Albuquerque, NM (city) Bernalillo County	810	0.18
San Jose, CA (city) Santa Clara County	678	0.08
Denver, CO (city) Denver County	648	0.12
San Diego, CA (city) San Diego County	626	0.05
San Antonio, TX (city) Bexar County	590	0.05
Tucson, AZ (city) Pima County	525	0.11
Mesa, AZ (city) Maricopa County	470	0.12
Sacramento, CA (city) Sacramento County	449	0.11
Fresno, CA (city) Fresno County	434	0.10
Colorado Springs, CO (city) El Paso County	430	0.12
Anadarko, OK (city) Caddo County	403	6.06
Oklahoma City, OK (city) Oklahoma County	345	0.07
New York, NY (city) New York City	342	0.00
Pueblo, CO (city) Pueblo County	332	0.33
Stockton, CA (city) San Joaquin County	300	0.12
Long Beach, CA (city) Los Angeles County	298	0.06
Houston, TX (city) Harris County	297	0.02
El Paso, TX (city) El Paso County	285	0.05
Las Vegas, NV (city) Clark County	278	0.06
Chicago, IL (city) Cook County	278	0.01
McNary, AZ (cdp) Apache County	260	74.50
Modesto, CA (city) Stanislaus County	243	0.13
San Francisco, CA (city) San Francisco County	236	0.03
Riverside, CA (city) Riverside County	235	0.09
Portland, OR (city) Multnomah County	233	0.04
Zwolle, LA (town) Sabine Parish	219	12.28
Austin, TX (city) Travis County	219	0.03
Aurora, CO (city) Arapahoe County	212	0.08
Glendale, AZ (city) Maricopa County	196	0.09
Dallas, TX (city) Dallas County	192	0.02
San Bernardino, CA (city) San Bernardino County	184	0.10
Anaheim, CA (city) Orange County	184	0.06
Tulsa, OK (city) Tulsa County	181	0.05
Lawton, OK (city) Comanche County	177	0.19
Las Cruces, NM (city) Dona Ana County	176	0.24
Bakersfield, CA (city) Kern County	176	0.07
Camp Verde, AZ (town) Yavapai County	165	1.75
Oakland, CA (city) Alameda County	164	0.04
Corpus Christi, TX (city) Nueces County	162	0.06
Fort Worth, TX (city) Tarrant County	162	0.03
Wichita, KS (city) Sedgwick County	161	0.05
Tempe, AZ (city) Maricopa County	160	0.10
Santa Ana, CA (city) Orange County	157	0.05
Fontana, CA (city) San Bernardino County	151	0.12
Seattle, WA (city) King County	147	0.03
Lancaster, CA (city) Los Angeles County	140	0.12
Santa Clarita, CA (city) Los Angeles County	138	0.09
Huntington Beach, CA (city) Orange County	137	0.07
Globe, AZ (city) Gila County	136	1.82
Moreno Valley, CA (city) Riverside County	135	0.09
Arlington, TX (city) Tarrant County	134	0.04
Thornton, CO (city) Adams County	132	0.16
Lakewood, CO (city) Jefferson County	132	0.09
Oxnard, CA (city) Ventura County	132	0.08
Honolulu, HI (cdp) Honolulu County	132	0.04
Anchorage, AK (municipality) Anchorage Borough	129	0.05
Payson, AZ (town) Gila County	124	0.91
Whittier, CA (city) Los Angeles County	121	0.14
Columbus, OH (city) Franklin County	121	0.02
Oceanside, CA (city) San Diego County	119	0.07
Westminster, CO (city) Adams County	117	0.12
Chandler, AZ (city) Maricopa County	117	0.07
Sunrise Manor, NV (cdp) Clark County	113	0.07
Apache, OK (town) Caddo County	111	6.87
Pomona, CA (city) Los Angeles County	111	0.07
Amarillo, TX (city) Potter County	108	0.06
Lubbock, TX (city) Lubbock County	107	0.05
Henderson, NV (city) Clark County	106	0.06
Ontario, CA (city) San Bernardino County	105	0.07
San Buenaventura, CA (city) Ventura County	104	0.10
Indianapolis, IN (special city) Marion County	104	0.01
Fremont, CA (city) Alameda County	103	0.05
Reno, NV (city) Washoe County	102	0.06
Virginia Beach, VA (independent city) Virginia Beach city	102	0.02
Salinas, CA (city) Monterey County	101	0.07
Paradise, NV (cdp) Clark County	101	0.05
Flagstaff, AZ (city) Coconino County	98	0.19
Norwalk, CA (city) Los Angeles County	97	0.09
Jacksonville, FL (special city) Duval County	97	0.01
Palmdale, CA (city) Los Angeles County	96	0.08
Santa Rosa, CA (city) Sonoma County	96	0.07
Corona, CA (city) Riverside County	95	0.08
Arvada, CO (city) Jefferson County	93	0.09
Orange, CA (city) Orange County	93	0.07
Santa Fe, NM (city) Santa Fe County	92	0.15
Rancho Cucamonga, CA (city) San Bernardino County	91	0.07
Garden Grove, CA (city) Orange County	91	0.06
Buena Park, CA (city) Orange County	90	0.11
Tacoma, WA (city) Pierce County	90	0.05
Kansas City, MO (city) Jackson County	90	0.02
Philadelphia, PA (city) Philadelphia County	90	0.01
South Whittier, CA (cdp) Los Angeles County	88	0.16
East Los Angeles, CA (cdp) Los Angeles County	88	0.07
Alamogordo, NM (city) Otero County	86	0.24
Rialto, CA (city) San Bernardino County	86	0.09
Concord, CA (city) Contra Costa County	86	0.07
Milwaukee, WI (city) Milwaukee County	86	0.01
Rio Rancho, NM (city) Sandoval County	83	0.16
Escondido, CA (city) San Diego County	83	0.06
El Monte, CA (city) Los Angeles County	82	0.07
Citrus Heights, CA (city) Sacramento County	81	0.10
Spokane, WA (city) Spokane County	81	0.04
Pico Rivera, CA (city) Los Angeles County	80	0.13
Fairfield, CA (city) Solano County	80	0.08
Simi Valley, CA (city) Ventura County	80	0.07
Salem, OR (city) Marion County	80	0.06
Chula Vista, CA (city) San Diego County	80	0.05
Clovis, CA (city) Fresno County	79	0.12
Fullerton, CA (city) Orange County	79	0.06
Roswell, NM (city) Chaves County	78	0.17
West Covina, CA (city) Los Angeles County	77	0.07
Fort Collins, CO (city) Larimer County	77	0.06
Hayward, CA (city) Alameda County	77	0.05
Salt Lake City, UT (city) Salt Lake County	77	0.04
Detroit, MI (city) Wayne County	76	0.01
Nashville-Davidson, TN (special city) Davidson County	75	0.01
Vallejo, CA (city) Solano County	74	0.06
Tularosa, NM (village) Otero County	73	2.55
Hesperia, CA (city) San Bernardino County	72	0.12
Gilroy, CA (city) Santa Clara County	71	0.17
Santa Maria, CA (city) Santa Barbara County	71	0.09
Downey, CA (city) Los Angeles County	71	0.07
Omaha, NE (city) Douglas County	71	0.02
Lakewood, CA (city) Los Angeles County	70	0.09
North Highlands, CA (cdp) Sacramento County	68	0.15
Abilene, TX (city) Taylor County	67	0.06
Apple Valley, CA (town) San Bernardino County	66	0.12
South San Francisco, CA (city) San Mateo County	66	0.11
Springfield, MO (city) Greene County	66	0.04
Tampa, FL (city) Hillsborough County	66	0.02
Farmington, NM (city) San Juan County	65	0.17
Grand Junction, CO (city) Mesa County	65	0.15
Merced, CA (city) Merced County	65	0.10
Santa Barbara, CA (city) Santa Barbara County	65	0.07
Arden-Arcade, CA (cdp) Sacramento County	64	0.07
Scottsdale, AZ (city) Maricopa County	64	0.03
Baltimore, MD (independent city) Baltimore city	64	0.01
Antioch, CA (city) Contra Costa County	63	0.07
Vacaville, CA (city) Solano County	63	0.07
Eugene, OR (city) Lane County	63	0.05

Notes: (cdp) census designated place; Refer to the Explanation of Data in the front of the book for more detailed information.

American Indian: Apache

Top 150 Places Sorted by Percent

(Based on all places, regardless of population)

Place	Number	%
East Fork, AZ (cdp) Navajo County	856	97.27
Canyon Day, AZ (cdp) Gila County	1,025	93.86
Peridot, AZ (cdp) Graham County	1,177	92.97
Cibecue, AZ (cdp) Navajo County	1,225	92.04
Whiteriver, AZ (cdp) Navajo County	4,697	89.98
San Carlos, AZ (cdp) Gila County	3,209	86.36
Dulce, NM (cdp) Rio Arriba County	2,116	80.67
Mescalero, NM (cdp) Otero County	965	78.26
McNary, AZ (cdp) Apache County	260	74.50
Noble, LA (village) Sabine Parish	54	20.85
Zwolle, LA (town) Sabine Parish	219	12.28
Apache, OK (town) Caddo County	111	6.87
Anadarko, OK (city) Caddo County	403	6.06
Converse, LA (village) Sabine Parish	21	5.25
Vienna, SD (town) Clark County	4	5.13
Twin Bridges, MO (village) Laclede County	2	4.76
Arna, MN (township) Pine County	4	4.65
Keams Canyon, AZ (cdp) Navajo County	11	4.23
Petersville, AK (cdp) Matanuska-Susitna Borough	1	3.70
Carnegie, OK (town) Caddo County	58	3.54
Pleasant Hill, LA (village) Sabine Parish	27	3.44
Lebam, WA (cdp) Pacific County	6	3.41
Burbank, OK (town) Osage County	5	3.23
Sams Corner, OK (cdp) Mayes County	4	3.17
Cullison, KS (city) Pratt County	3	3.06
Quail, TX (cdp) Collingsworth County	1	3.03
Nageezi, NM (cdp) San Juan County	8	2.70
Tularosa, NM (village) Otero County	73	2.55
Tallapoosa, MO (city) New Madrid County	5	2.45
Dripping Springs, OK (cdp) Delaware County	1	2.44
Stoutland, MO (village) Camden County	4	2.26
Fort Cobb, OK (town) Caddo County	15	2.25
Powhattan, KS (city) Brown County	2	2.20
Springerville, AZ (town) Apache County	42	2.13
Powhatan, LA (village) Natchitoches Parish	3	2.13
Mapleview, MN (city) Mower County	4	2.12
Banner, IL (village) Fulton County	3	2.01
Dietrich, ID (city) Lincoln County	3	2.00
First Mesa, AZ (cdp) Navajo County	22	1.96
Iliamna, AK (cdp) Lake and Peninsula Borough	2	1.96
Elgin, AZ (cdp) Santa Cruz County	6	1.94
Lodge Pole, MT (cdp) Blaine County	4	1.87
Osage, WY (cdp) Weston County	4	1.86
Aguilar, CO (town) Las Animas County	11	1.85
Gotebo, OK (town) Kiowa County	5	1.84
Globe, AZ (city) Gila County	136	1.82
Kaibab, AZ (cdp) Mohave County	5	1.82
Kykotsmovi Village, AZ (cdp) Navajo County	14	1.80
Gibson, PA (township) Cameron County	4	1.80
Randlett, UT (cdp) Uintah County	4	1.79
Ithaca, NE (village) Saunders County	3	1.79
Mitchell, OR (city) Wheeler County	3	1.76
Camp Verde, AZ (town) Yavapai County	165	1.75
Ruidoso Downs, NM (village) Lincoln County	32	1.75
Iron Post, OK (cdp) Mayes County	2	1.71
Empire, CO (town) Clear Creek County	6	1.69
Thompson, PA (borough) Susquehanna County	5	1.67
Laguna, NM (cdp) Cibola County	7	1.65
Reed Point, MT (cdp) Stillwater County	3	1.62
Wyola, MT (cdp) Big Horn County	3	1.61
Valentine, TX (town) Jeff Davis County	3	1.60
New Tulsa, OK (town) Wagoner County	9	1.58
Forestville, MI (village) Sanilac County	2	1.57
Geronimo, OK (town) Comanche County	15	1.56
Poston, AZ (cdp) La Paz County	6	1.54
Eakly, OK (town) Caddo County	4	1.45
De Tour Village, MI (village) Chippewa County	6	1.43
Chama, NM (village) Rio Arriba County	17	1.42
Arizona Village, AZ (cdp) Mohave County	5	1.42
Binger, OK (town) Caddo County	10	1.41
Oakwood, OK (town) Dewey County	1	1.39
Pepperton, MN (township) Stevens County	2	1.35
Dill City, OK (town) Washita County	7	1.33
Phillips, OK (town) Coal County	2	1.33
Bushnell, SD (town) Brookings County	1	1.33
Folsom, NM (village) Union County	1	1.33
Reserve, NM (village) Catron County	5	1.29
Houston, AR (town) Perry County	2	1.26
Brock, NE (village) Nemaha County	2	1.23
Newburg, PA (borough) Clearfield County	1	1.23
Mueller, MI (township) Schoolcraft County	3	1.22
Morristown, SD (town) Corson County	1	1.22
Vandiver, MO (village) Audrain County	1	1.20
Eagar, AZ (town) Apache County	47	1.17
Clarkdale, AZ (town) Yavapai County	40	1.17
Pueblo of Sandia Village, NM (cdp) Sandoval County	4	1.16
Bagnell, MO (town) Miller County	1	1.16
Picuris Pueblo, NM (cdp) Taos County	1	1.16
Washtucna, WA (town) Adams County	3	1.15
Esto, FL (town) Holmes County	4	1.12
Cyril, OK (town) Caddo County	13	1.11
Second Mesa, AZ (cdp) Navajo County	9	1.11
Harwood, MO (village) Vernon County	1	1.11
Goff, KS (city) Nemaha County	2	1.10
Freistatt, MO (village) Lawrence County	2	1.09
Salt Creek, CO (cdp) Pueblo County	7	1.08
Eau Claire, MI (village) Berrien County	7	1.07
Rough Rock, AZ (cdp) Apache County	5	1.07
Mehama, OR (cdp) Marion County	3	1.06
Penasco, NM (cdp) Taos County	6	1.05
Bloomfield, MI (township) Missaukee County	5	1.05
Rockaway Beach, MO (city) Taney County	6	1.04
Kirkwood, CA (cdp) Alpine County	1	1.04
Hallwood, VA (town) Accomack County	3	1.03
Nisqually Indian Community, WA (cdp) Thurston County	6	1.02
Caney, OK (town) Atoka County	2	1.01
Stanley, ID (city) Custer County	1	1.00
Darrouzett, TX (town) Lipscomb County	3	0.99
Bristow, IA (city) Butler County	2	0.99
Del Sol-Loma Linda, TX (cdp) San Patricio County	7	0.96
Claypool, IN (town) Kosciusko County	3	0.96
Shongopovi, AZ (cdp) Navajo County	6	0.95
Ainaloa, HI (cdp) Hawaii County	18	0.94
Hot Springs, MT (town) Sanders County	5	0.94
Puhi, HI (cdp) Kauai County	11	0.93
Sandia, TX (cdp) Jim Wells County	4	0.93
Sherwood, MI (village) Branch County	3	0.93
Hope, NM (village) Eddy County	1	0.93
Payson, AZ (town) Gila County	124	0.91
Thoreau, NM (cdp) McKinley County	17	0.91
Evaro, MT (cdp) Missoula County	3	0.91
Centrahoma, OK (city) Coal County	1	0.91
Haliimaile, HI (cdp) Maui County	8	0.89
North Pearsall, TX (cdp) Frio County	5	0.89
Greenville, MO (city) Wayne County	4	0.89
Chuichu, AZ (cdp) Pinal County	3	0.88
Mapleton, IL (village) Peoria County	2	0.88
Rome, IA (city) Henry County	1	0.88
Plains, KS (city) Meade County	10	0.86
Weir, TX (city) Williamson County	5	0.85
Henderson, MD (town) Caroline County	1	0.85
Paguate, NM (cdp) Cibola County	4	0.84
Pisinemo, AZ (cdp) Pima County	2	0.84
Schurz, NV (cdp) Mineral County	6	0.83
Fern Forest, HI (cdp) Hawaii County	4	0.83
Swift Trail Junction, AZ (cdp) Graham County	18	0.82
Towaoc, CO (cdp) Montezuma County	9	0.82
Santa Clara Pueblo, NM (cdp) Rio Arriba County	8	0.82
Nucla, CO (town) Montrose County	6	0.82
Traver, CA (cdp) Tulare County	6	0.82
Maggie Valley, NC (town) Haywood County	5	0.82
Callisburg, TX (city) Cooke County	3	0.82
Sharon, OK (town) Woodward County	1	0.82
Bloomington, NE (village) Franklin County	1	0.81
Greenfield, OK (town) Blaine County	1	0.81
Thayer, KS (city) Neosho County	4	0.80
Alcalde, NM (cdp) Rio Arriba County	3	0.80
Medicine Park, OK (town) Comanche County	3	0.80
Centerview, MO (city) Johnson County	2	0.80
Hillrose, CO (town) Morgan County	2	0.79

Notes: (cdp) census designated place; Refer to the Explanation of Data in the front of the book for more detailed information.

American Indian: Apache

Top 150 Places Sorted by Percent

(Based on places with populations of 10,000 or more)

Place	Number	%
Payson, AZ (town) Gila County	124	0.91
Pueblo, CO (city) Pueblo County	332	0.33
Silver City, NM (town) Grant County	32	0.30
Commerce City, CO (city) Adams County	58	0.28
Alum Rock, CA (cdp) Santa Clara County	37	0.27
Las Vegas, NM (city) San Miguel County	38	0.26
Ashland, CA (cdp) Alameda County	52	0.25
Gallup, NM (city) McKinley County	50	0.25
Las Cruces, NM (city) Dona Ana County	176	0.24
Alamogordo, NM (city) Otero County	86	0.24
Los Lunas, NM (village) Valencia County	24	0.24
Durango, CO (city) La Plata County	32	0.23
Lake Los Angeles, CA (cdp) Los Angeles County	26	0.23
Nanakuli, HI (cdp) Honolulu County	25	0.23
Fountain, CO (city) El Paso County	33	0.22
Coalinga, CA (city) Fresno County	26	0.22
Chowchilla, CA (city) Madera County	23	0.21
Olivehurst, CA (cdp) Yuba County	23	0.21
San Elizario, TX (cdp) El Paso County	22	0.20
Lawton, OK (city) Comanche County	177	0.19
Flagstaff, AZ (city) Coconino County	98	0.19
Adelanto, CA (city) San Bernardino County	35	0.19
Florence, AZ (town) Pinal County	33	0.19
Oroville, CA (city) Butte County	25	0.19
Berkley, CO (cdp) Adams County	20	0.19
Albuquerque, NM (city) Bernalillo County	810	0.18
Englewood, CO (city) Arapahoe County	58	0.18
Northglenn, CO (city) Adams County	56	0.18
Pueblo West, CO (cdp) Pueblo County	31	0.18
Cimarron Hills, CO (cdp) El Paso County	28	0.18
Rosamond, CA (cdp) Kern County	26	0.18
Roswell, NM (city) Chaves County	78	0.17
Gilroy, CA (city) Santa Clara County	71	0.17
Farmington, NM (city) San Juan County	65	0.17
La Presa, CA (cdp) San Diego County	54	0.17
Los Banos, CA (city) Merced County	44	0.17
Chickasha, OK (city) Grady County	27	0.17
Thornton, CO (city) Adams County	132	0.16
South Whittier, CA (cdp) Los Angeles County	88	0.16
Rio Rancho, NM (city) Sandoval County	83	0.16
Ridgecrest, CA (city) Kern County	39	0.16
San Fernando, CA (city) Los Angeles County	37	0.16
Canon City, CO (city) Fremont County	24	0.16
Twentynine Palms, CA (city) San Bernardino County	23	0.16
Welby, CO (cdp) Adams County	21	0.16
Federal Heights, CO (city) Adams County	19	0.16
Fort Morgan, CO (city) Morgan County	18	0.16
Santa Fe, NM (city) Santa Fe County	92	0.15
North Highlands, CA (cdp) Sacramento County	68	0.15
Grand Junction, CO (city) Mesa County	65	0.15
West Sacramento, CA (city) Yolo County	46	0.15
Carlsbad, NM (city) Eddy County	38	0.15
Wahiawa, HI (cdp) Honolulu County	25	0.15
Corcoran, CA (city) Kings County	21	0.15
North Valley, NM (cdp) Bernalillo County	18	0.15
Los Alamitos, CA (city) Orange County	17	0.15
Guymon, OK (city) Texas County	16	0.15
Whittier, CA (city) Los Angeles County	121	0.14
Lompoc, CA (city) Santa Barbara County	58	0.14
Parkway-South Sacramento, CA (cdp) Sacramento County	51	0.14
Bullhead City, AZ (city) Mohave County	48	0.14
Apache Junction, AZ (city) Pinal County	43	0.14
Banning, CA (city) Riverside County	34	0.14
Desert Hot Springs, CA (city) Riverside County	23	0.14
Dinuba, CA (city) Tulare County	23	0.14
Coos Bay, OR (city) Coos County	21	0.14
Glen Avon, CA (cdp) Riverside County	21	0.14
New Kingman-Butler, AZ (cdp) Mohave County	21	0.14
Sierra Vista Southeast, AZ (cdp) Cochise County	20	0.14
Marysville, CA (city) Yuba County	17	0.14
Waianae, HI (cdp) Honolulu County	15	0.14
Phoenix, AZ (city) Maricopa County	1,683	0.13
Modesto, CA (city) Stanislaus County	243	0.13
Pico Rivera, CA (city) Los Angeles County	80	0.13
Perris, CA (city) Riverside County	46	0.13
Morgan Hill, CA (city) Santa Clara County	45	0.13
Eureka, CA (city) Humboldt County	35	0.13
West Whittier-Los Nietos, CA (cdp) Los Angeles County	33	0.13
Casa Grande, AZ (city) Pinal County	32	0.13
San Jacinto, CA (city) Riverside County	30	0.13
Bay Point, CA (cdp) Contra Costa County	28	0.13
Santa Fe Springs, CA (city) Los Angeles County	23	0.13
Claremore, OK (city) Rogers County	20	0.13
East Hemet, CA (cdp) Riverside County	19	0.13
Clearlake, CA (city) Lake County	17	0.13
Beaumont, CA (city) Riverside County	15	0.13
Rio Linda, CA (cdp) Sacramento County	14	0.13
Eloy, AZ (city) Pinal County	13	0.13
Denver, CO (city) Denver County	648	0.12
Mesa, AZ (city) Maricopa County	470	0.12
Colorado Springs, CO (city) El Paso County	430	0.12
Stockton, CA (city) San Joaquin County	300	0.12
Fontana, CA (city) San Bernardino County	151	0.12
Lancaster, CA (city) Los Angeles County	140	0.12
Westminster, CO (city) Adams County	117	0.12
Clovis, CA (city) Fresno County	79	0.12
Hesperia, CA (city) San Bernardino County	72	0.12
Apple Valley, CA (town) San Bernardino County	66	0.12
Azusa, CA (city) Los Angeles County	54	0.12
Fort Hood, TX (cdp) Coryell County	40	0.12
Wheat Ridge, CO (city) Jefferson County	40	0.12
Rubidoux, CA (cdp) Riverside County	36	0.12
Duncan, OK (city) Stephens County	28	0.12
Barstow, CA (city) San Bernardino County	26	0.12
San Lorenzo, CA (cdp) Alameda County	26	0.12
Spanaway, WA (cdp) Pierce County	25	0.12
Clifton, CO (cdp) Mesa County	21	0.12
Pampa, TX (city) Gray County	21	0.12
Sherrelwood, CO (cdp) Adams County	21	0.12
Oakdale, CA (city) Stanislaus County	18	0.12
Troutdale, OR (city) Multnomah County	17	0.12
Fillmore, CA (city) Ventura County	16	0.12
Beecher, MI (cdp) Genesee County	15	0.12
Dallas, OR (city) Polk County	15	0.12
Montrose, CO (city) Montrose County	15	0.12
Fort Carson, CO (cdp) El Paso County	13	0.12
Tucson, AZ (city) Pima County	525	0.11
Sacramento, CA (city) Sacramento County	449	0.11
Buena Park, CA (city) Orange County	90	0.11
South San Francisco, CA (city) San Mateo County	66	0.11
Highland, CA (city) San Bernardino County	50	0.11
Bremerton, WA (city) Kitsap County	42	0.11
Ken Caryl, CO (cdp) Jefferson County	33	0.11
Garden City, KS (city) Finney County	32	0.11
Lake Elsinore, CA (city) Riverside County	32	0.11
Florin, CA (cdp) Sacramento County	31	0.11
Santa Paula, CA (city) Ventura County	31	0.11
Marina, CA (city) Monterey County	28	0.11
Lafayette, CO (city) Boulder County	26	0.11
Valinda, CA (cdp) Los Angeles County	25	0.11
Plainview, TX (city) Hale County	24	0.11
Port Hueneme, CA (city) Ventura County	24	0.11
Kingman, AZ (city) Mohave County	22	0.11
Winter Gardens, CA (cdp) San Diego County	22	0.11
Fort Lewis, WA (cdp) Pierce County	21	0.11
Yucca Valley, CA (town) San Bernardino County	19	0.11
El Reno, OK (city) Canadian County	18	0.11
El Segundo, CA (city) Los Angeles County	18	0.11
Prunedale, CA (cdp) Monterey County	18	0.11
Flowing Wells, AZ (cdp) Pima County	17	0.11
Riverbank, CA (city) Stanislaus County	17	0.11
Hawaiian Gardens, CA (city) Los Angeles County	16	0.11
Truckee, CA (town) Nevada County	15	0.11
Coffeyville, KS (city) Montgomery County	12	0.11
Magalia, CA (cdp) Butte County	12	0.11
Fresno, CA (city) Fresno County	434	0.10
San Bernardino, CA (city) San Bernardino County	184	0.10
Tempe, AZ (city) Maricopa County	160	0.10
San Buenaventura, CA (city) Ventura County	104	0.10
Citrus Heights, CA (city) Sacramento County	81	0.10

Notes: (cdp) census designated place; Refer to the Explanation of Data in the front of the book for more detailed information.

American Indian: Blackfeet

Top 150 Places Sorted by Number

(Based on all places, regardless of population)

Place	Number	%
North Browning, MT (cdp) Glacier County	1,823	82.86
New York, NY (city) New York City	1,454	0.02
South Browning, MT (cdp) Glacier County	1,411	84.14
Los Angeles, CA (city) Los Angeles County	1,037	0.03
Browning, MT (town) Glacier County	865	81.22
Great Falls, MT (city) Cascade County	699	1.23
Heart Butte, MT (cdp) Pondera County	619	88.68
Detroit, MI (city) Wayne County	565	0.06
Seattle, WA (city) King County	548	0.10
Portland, OR (city) Multnomah County	529	0.10
San Diego, CA (city) San Diego County	474	0.04
Philadelphia, PA (city) Philadelphia County	430	0.03
Sacramento, CA (city) Sacramento County	428	0.11
Chicago, IL (city) Cook County	425	0.01
Columbus, OH (city) Franklin County	407	0.06
Tacoma, WA (city) Pierce County	396	0.20
Cut Bank, MT (city) Glacier County	359	11.56
Missoula, MT (city) Missoula County	325	0.57
Spokane, WA (city) Spokane County	293	0.15
Cleveland, OH (city) Cuyahoga County	271	0.06
San Jose, CA (city) Santa Clara County	260	0.03
Oakland, CA (city) Alameda County	254	0.06
Long Beach, CA (city) Los Angeles County	243	0.05
Phoenix, AZ (city) Maricopa County	239	0.02
San Francisco, CA (city) San Francisco County	230	0.03
Anchorage, AK (municipality) Anchorage Borough	225	0.09
Baltimore, MD (independent city) Baltimore city	225	0.03
Indianapolis, IN (special city) Marion County	224	0.03
Kansas City, MO (city) Jackson County	223	0.05
Starr School, MT (cdp) Glacier County	221	89.11
Washington, DC (city) District of Columbia	218	0.04
Denver, CO (city) Denver County	212	0.04
Boston, MA (city) Suffolk County	209	0.04
Colorado Springs, CO (city) El Paso County	207	0.06
Honolulu, HI (cdp) Honolulu County	197	0.05
Jacksonville, FL (special city) Duval County	186	0.03
Milwaukee, WI (city) Milwaukee County	183	0.03
Toledo, OH (city) Lucas County	175	0.06
Virginia Beach, VA (independent city) Virginia Beach city	174	0.04
Fresno, CA (city) Fresno County	173	0.04
East Glacier Park Village, MT (cdp) Glacier County	171	43.18
Las Vegas, NV (city) Clark County	170	0.04
Houston, TX (city) Harris County	170	0.01
Oklahoma City, OK (city) Oklahoma County	169	0.03
Saint Louis, MO (independent city) Saint Louis city	164	0.05
Flint, MI (city) Genesee County	160	0.13
Aurora, CO (city) Arapahoe County	157	0.06
Akron, OH (city) Summit County	155	0.07
Wichita, KS (city) Sedgwick County	151	0.04
Billings, MT (city) Yellowstone County	150	0.17
Yakima, WA (city) Yakima County	149	0.21
San Antonio, TX (city) Bexar County	148	0.01
Cincinnati, OH (city) Hamilton County	143	0.04
Tulsa, OK (city) Tulsa County	141	0.04
Stockton, CA (city) San Joaquin County	135	0.06
Minneapolis, MN (city) Hennepin County	135	0.04
Dallas, TX (city) Dallas County	127	0.01
Lakewood, WA (city) Pierce County	124	0.21
Pittsburgh, PA (city) Allegheny County	122	0.04
Tucson, AZ (city) Pima County	119	0.02
Brookhaven, NY (town) Suffolk County	118	0.03
Salem, OR (city) Marion County	116	0.08
Bakersfield, CA (city) Kern County	115	0.05
Albuquerque, NM (city) Bernalillo County	114	0.03
Grand Rapids, MI (city) Kent County	113	0.06
Hempstead, NY (town) Nassau County	112	0.01
Norfolk, VA (independent city) Norfolk city	109	0.05
Lancaster, CA (city) Los Angeles County	108	0.09
Austin, TX (city) Travis County	108	0.02
Buffalo, NY (city) Erie County	106	0.04
Fairfield, CA (city) Solano County	105	0.11
Omaha, NE (city) Douglas County	105	0.03
San Bernardino, CA (city) San Bernardino County	102	0.06
Riverside, CA (city) Riverside County	101	0.04
Vallejo, CA (city) Solano County	99	0.08
Paradise, NV (cdp) Clark County	99	0.05
Kansas City, KS (city) Wyandotte County	96	0.07
Newark, NJ (city) Essex County	96	0.04
New Haven, CT (city) New Haven County	93	0.08
Reno, NV (city) Washoe County	93	0.05
Rochester, NY (city) Monroe County	93	0.04
Pablo, MT (cdp) Lake County	92	5.07
Vancouver, WA (city) Clark County	92	0.06
Syracuse, NY (city) Onondaga County	91	0.06
Huntington Beach, CA (city) Orange County	91	0.05
Modesto, CA (city) Stanislaus County	91	0.05
Charlotte, NC (city) Mecklenburg County	91	0.02
North Highlands, CA (cdp) Sacramento County	90	0.20
Providence, RI (city) Providence County	89	0.05
Helena, MT (city) Lewis and Clark County	88	0.34
Everett, WA (city) Snohomish County	88	0.10
Moreno Valley, CA (city) Riverside County	87	0.06
Fontana, CA (city) San Bernardino County	86	0.07
Newport News, VA (independent city) Newport News city	86	0.05
Tampa, FL (city) Hillsborough County	86	0.03
Springfield, MO (city) Greene County	85	0.06
Lansing, MI (city) Ingham County	84	0.07
Hayward, CA (city) Alameda County	83	0.06
Islip, NY (town) Suffolk County	83	0.03
Springfield, MA (city) Hampden County	82	0.05
Mesa, AZ (city) Maricopa County	82	0.02
Havre, MT (city) Hill County	81	0.84
Redding, CA (city) Shasta County	81	0.10
Rancho Cucamonga, CA (city) San Bernardino County	81	0.06
Henderson, NV (city) Clark County	81	0.05
Arden-Arcade, CA (cdp) Sacramento County	80	0.08
Independence, MO (city) Jackson County	80	0.07
Fremont, CA (city) Alameda County	80	0.04
Nashville-Davidson, TN (special city) Davidson County	80	0.01
Citrus Heights, CA (city) Sacramento County	79	0.09
Federal Way, WA (city) King County	79	0.09
Hampton, VA (independent city) Hampton city	77	0.05
Fort Worth, TX (city) Tarrant County	77	0.01
Kent, WA (city) King County	76	0.10
San Buenaventura, CA (city) Ventura County	76	0.08
Saint Petersburg, FL (city) Pinellas County	76	0.03
Eugene, OR (city) Lane County	75	0.05
Polson, MT (city) Lake County	74	1.83
Butte-Silver Bow, MT (special city) Silver Bow County	74	0.22
Sunrise Manor, NV (cdp) Clark County	74	0.05
Arlington, TX (city) Tarrant County	74	0.02
Rialto, CA (city) San Bernardino County	73	0.08
Anaheim, CA (city) Orange County	73	0.02
Battle Creek, MI (city) Calhoun County	71	0.13
Pasadena, CA (city) Los Angeles County	71	0.05
Santa Rosa, CA (city) Sonoma County	71	0.05
Boise City, ID (city) Ada County	71	0.04
Burien, WA (city) King County	70	0.22
Santa Clarita, CA (city) Los Angeles County	70	0.05
Dayton, OH (city) Montgomery County	70	0.04
Ontario, CA (city) San Bernardino County	70	0.04
Fort Wayne, IN (city) Allen County	70	0.03
Richmond, VA (independent city) Richmond city	69	0.03
Concord, CA (city) Contra Costa County	68	0.06
Oceanside, CA (city) San Diego County	68	0.04
Louisville, KY (city) Jefferson County	68	0.03
El Cajon, CA (city) San Diego County	67	0.07
White Center, WA (cdp) King County	66	0.31
Victorville, CA (city) San Bernardino County	66	0.10
Worcester, MA (city) Worcester County	66	0.04
Topeka, KS (city) Shawnee County	65	0.05
Palmdale, CA (city) Los Angeles County	64	0.05
Richmond, CA (city) Contra Costa County	63	0.06
New Orleans, LA (city) Orleans Parish	63	0.01
Auburn, WA (city) King County	62	0.15
Inglewood, CA (city) Los Angeles County	62	0.06
Lakewood, CO (city) Jefferson County	62	0.04
Rockford, IL (city) Winnebago County	62	0.04
Durham, NC (city) Durham County	62	0.03
Atlanta, GA (city) Fulton County	61	0.01

Notes: (cdp) census designated place; Refer to the Explanation of Data in the front of the book for more detailed information.

American Indian: Blackfeet

Top 150 Places Sorted by Percent

(Based on all places, regardless of population)

Place	Number	%
Starr School, MT (cdp) Glacier County	221	89.11
Heart Butte, MT (cdp) Pondera County	619	88.68
South Browning, MT (cdp) Glacier County	1,411	84.14
North Browning, MT (cdp) Glacier County	1,823	82.86
Browning, MT (town) Glacier County	865	81.22
East Glacier Park Village, MT (cdp) Glacier County	171	43.18
Ugashik, AK (cdp) Lake and Peninsula Borough	2	18.18
Cut Bank, MT (city) Glacier County	359	11.56
Evaro, MT (cdp) Missoula County	38	11.55
Valier, MT (town) Pondera County	26	5.22
Turtle Lake, MT (cdp) Lake County	10	5.15
Pablo, MT (cdp) Lake County	92	5.07
Elmo, MT (cdp) Lake County	6	4.20
Bushnell, SD (town) Brookings County	3	4.00
Arlee, MT (cdp) Lake County	23	3.82
Swan Valley, ID (city) Bonneville County	8	3.76
Zena, OK (cdp) Delaware County	4	3.25
Saint Ignatius, MT (town) Lake County	23	2.92
Alatna, AK (cdp) Yukon-Koyukuk Census Area	1	2.86
Ovando, MT (cdp) Powell County	2	2.82
Saint Pierre, MT (cdp) Hill County	8	2.77
Azure, MT (cdp) Hill County	7	2.77
Bradley, OK (town) Grady County	5	2.75
Elsmore, KS (city) Allen County	2	2.74
Mount Sterling, IA (city) Van Buren County	1	2.50
Brush Creek, OK (cdp) Delaware County	1	2.44
Simms, MT (cdp) Cascade County	9	2.41
Riverbend, MT (cdp) Mineral County	10	2.26
Keysville, GA (town) Burke County	4	2.22
Harwood, MO (village) Vernon County	2	2.22
Custer, MI (village) Mason County	7	2.20
Newburg, PA (borough) Cumberland County	8	2.15
Martin City, MT (cdp) Flathead County	7	2.11
Seldovia Village, AK (cdp) Kenai Peninsula Borough	3	2.08
Tokeland, WA (cdp) Pacific County	4	2.06
Charlo, MT (cdp) Lake County	9	2.05
Ronan, MT (city) Lake County	37	2.04
Pilot Point, AK (city) Lake and Peninsula Borough	2	2.00
Niarada, MT (cdp) Sanders County	1	2.00
Rexford, MT (town) Lincoln County	3	1.99
Purple Sage, WY (cdp) Sweetwater County	8	1.94
Hope, NM (village) Eddy County	2	1.87
Polson, MT (city) Lake County	74	1.83
Bushong, KS (city) Lyon County	1	1.82
Schurz, NV (cdp) Mineral County	13	1.80
Matchwood, MI (township) Ontonagon County	2	1.74
Ashland, MT (cdp) Rosebud County	8	1.72
Baring, WA (cdp) King County	4	1.72
Iron Post, OK (cdp) Mayes County	2	1.71
Kevin, MT (town) Toole County	3	1.69
Greenville, PA (township) Somerset County	12	1.67
White Horse, SD (cdp) Todd County	3	1.67
Kimbolton, OH (village) Guernsey County	3	1.58
Hays, MT (cdp) Blaine County	11	1.57
Big Creek, MS (village) Calhoun County	2	1.57
Ambrose, GA (city) Coffee County	5	1.56
Congress, OH (village) Wayne County	3	1.56
Unity, OR (city) Baker County	2	1.53
Winslow West, AZ (cdp) Coconino County	2	1.53
Hot Springs, MT (town) Sanders County	8	1.51
Shelby, MT (city) Toole County	47	1.46
Lonepine, MT (cdp) Sanders County	2	1.46
Sunburst, MT (town) Toole County	6	1.45
Lake Lafayette, MO (city) Lafayette County	5	1.45
Winter Harbor, ME (town) Hancock County	14	1.42
Blue Diamond, NV (cdp) Clark County	4	1.42
Nelchina, AK (cdp) Valdez-Cordova Census Area	1	1.41
Sodaville, OR (city) Linn County	4	1.38
Rosebud, MO (city) Gasconade County	5	1.37
Cleveland, VA (town) Russell County	2	1.35
New Dosey, MN (township) Pine County	1	1.35
Clark's Point, AK (city) Dillingham Census Area	1	1.33
Zinc, AR (town) Boone County	1	1.32
Beaver Crossing, NE (village) Seward County	6	1.31
Galena, OH (village) Delaware County	4	1.31

Place	Number	%
Table Rock, MO (village) Taney County	3	1.31
Lafe, AR (town) Greene County	5	1.30
Butlerville, OH (village) Warren County	3	1.30
Inez, KY (city) Martin County	6	1.29
Inchelium, WA (cdp) Ferry County	5	1.29
Bazine, KS (city) Ness County	4	1.29
Old Bennington, VT (village) Bennington County	3	1.29
Rock River, WY (town) Albany County	3	1.28
Johnstown, WY (cdp) Fremont County	3	1.27
Hodges, SC (town) Greenwood County	2	1.27
Earlton, KS (city) Neosho County	1	1.25
Sun Prairie, MT (cdp) Cascade County	22	1.24
Great Falls, MT (city) Cascade County	699	1.23
Klamath, CA (cdp) Del Norte County	8	1.23
Alsey, IL (village) Scott County	3	1.22
Scammon, KS (city) Cherokee County	6	1.21
Black Eagle, MT (cdp) Cascade County	11	1.20
Nixon, NV (cdp) Washoe County	5	1.20
Vandiver, MO (village) Audrain County	1	1.20
Kings Point, MT (cdp) Lake County	2	1.18
Ree Heights, SD (town) Hand County	1	1.18
Aullville, MO (village) Lafayette County	1	1.16
Baggs, WY (town) Carbon County	4	1.15
Minnesota Falls, MN (township) Yellow Medicine County	4	1.11
Lewistown Heights, MT (cdp) Fergus County	4	1.10
Liscomb, IA (city) Marshall County	3	1.10
Greenwater, WA (cdp) King County	1	1.10
Lake Park, GA (city) Lowndes County	6	1.09
Gilbertsville, NY (village) Otsego County	4	1.07
Crowley, CO (town) Crowley County	2	1.07
Conrad, MT (city) Pondera County	29	1.05
Armstrong, MO (city) Howard County	3	1.05
Stonewall, NC (town) Pamlico County	3	1.05
Dayton, MT (cdp) Lake County	1	1.05
Foster, WI (town) Clark County	1	1.05
Old Agency, MT (cdp) Sanders County	1	1.05
Hyder, AK (cdp) Prince of Wales-Outer Ketchikan Census Area	1	1.03
Atmautluak, AK (cdp) Bethel Census Area	3	1.02
Jefferson City, MT (cdp) Jefferson County	3	1.02
Maryhill, WA (cdp) Klickitat County	1	1.02
Tecopa, CA (cdp) Inyo County	1	1.01
Vaughn, MT (cdp) Cascade County	7	1.00
Twin Bridges, MT (town) Madison County	4	1.00
Silver Plume, CO (town) Clear Creek County	2	0.99
Brumley, MO (town) Miller County	1	0.98
Mount Calm, TX (city) Hill County	3	0.97
Nelson, MN (township) Watonwan County	3	0.97
Muddy, MT (cdp) Big Horn County	6	0.96
Masonville, IA (city) Delaware County	1	0.96
Fort Belknap Agency, MT (cdp) Blaine County	12	0.95
Powers, OR (city) Coos County	7	0.95
Birch Tree, MO (city) Shannon County	6	0.95
Le Raysville, PA (borough) Bradford County	3	0.94
Monroe, MI (township) Newaygo County	3	0.93
Paris, MI (township) Huron County	5	0.90
Coats, KS (city) Pratt County	1	0.89
Holloway, MN (city) Swift County	1	0.89
Stagecoach, TX (town) Montgomery County	4	0.88
Brandt, SD (town) Deuel County	1	0.88
Onaway, ID (city) Latah County	2	0.87
Branford, FL (town) Suwannee County	6	0.86
Busby, MT (cdp) Big Horn County	6	0.86
Delmar, WI (town) Chippewa County	8	0.85
Marshallville, OH (village) Wayne County	7	0.85
Nisqually Indian Community, WA (cdp) Thurston County	5	0.85
Havre, MT (city) Hill County	81	0.84
Walkerville, MT (town) Silver Bow County	6	0.84
Sweetwater, MI (township) Lake County	2	0.84
Ravalli, MT (cdp) Lake County	1	0.84
Houston, AK (city) Matanuska-Susitna Borough	10	0.83
Easton, KS (city) Leavenworth County	3	0.83
Otter Creek, FL (town) Levy County	1	0.83
Tower Hill, IL (village) Shelby County	5	0.82
New Douglas, IL (village) Madison County	3	0.81
Saint Mary, MO (city) Sainte Genevieve County	3	0.80

Notes: (cdp) census designated place; Refer to the Explanation of Data in the front of the book for more detailed information.

American Indian: Blackfeet

Top 150 Places Sorted by Percent

(Based on places with populations of 10,000 or more)

Place	Number	%
Great Falls, MT (city) Cascade County	699	1.23
Missoula, MT (city) Missoula County	325	0.57
Helena, MT (city) Lewis and Clark County	88	0.34
Kalispell, MT (city) Flathead County	49	0.34
White Center, WA (cdp) King County	66	0.31
Clearlake, CA (city) Lake County	39	0.30
Kelso, WA (city) Cowlitz County	32	0.27
Olivehurst, CA (cdp) Yuba County	26	0.24
Butte-Silver Bow, MT (special city) Silver Bow County	74	0.22
Burien, WA (city) King County	70	0.22
McKinleyville, CA (cdp) Humboldt County	30	0.22
Riverton-Boulevard Park, WA (cdp) King County	25	0.22
Yakima, WA (city) Yakima County	149	0.21
Lakewood, WA (city) Pierce County	124	0.21
Tacoma, WA (city) Pierce County	396	0.20
North Highlands, CA (cdp) Sacramento County	90	0.20
Bozeman, MT (city) Gallatin County	54	0.20
Spanaway, WA (cdp) Pierce County	43	0.20
Tukwila, WA (city) King County	35	0.20
Marysville, CA (city) Yuba County	24	0.20
Lake Los Angeles, CA (cdp) Los Angeles County	23	0.20
Chowchilla, CA (city) Madera County	22	0.20
Crestline, CA (cdp) San Bernardino County	20	0.20
Opportunity, WA (cdp) Spokane County	44	0.18
Foothill Farms, CA (cdp) Sacramento County	31	0.18
Elk Plain, WA (cdp) Pierce County	28	0.18
Billings, MT (city) Yellowstone County	150	0.17
Eureka, CA (city) Humboldt County	45	0.17
Parkland, WA (cdp) Pierce County	38	0.16
Coos Bay, OR (city) Coos County	25	0.16
Twentynine Palms, CA (city) San Bernardino County	23	0.16
Four Corners, OR (cdp) Marion County	22	0.16
Fort Polk South, LA (cdp) Vernon Parish	18	0.16
Spokane, WA (city) Spokane County	293	0.15
Auburn, WA (city) King County	62	0.15
Bremerton, WA (city) Kitsap County	57	0.15
Lacey, WA (city) Thurston County	47	0.15
Grandview, MO (city) Jackson County	37	0.15
Salida, CA (cdp) Stanislaus County	19	0.15
Lexington Park, MD (cdp) Saint Mary's County	17	0.15
Tehachapi, CA (city) Kern County	16	0.15
Oildale, CA (cdp) Kern County	39	0.14
Orangevale, CA (cdp) Sacramento County	37	0.14
Rosemont, CA (cdp) Sacramento County	31	0.14
Fountain, CO (city) El Paso County	22	0.14
Alderwood Manor, WA (cdp) Snohomish County	21	0.14
Bellefontaine, OH (city) Logan County	18	0.14
Ionia, MI (city) Ionia County	15	0.14
Atchison, KS (city) Atchison County	14	0.14
Dishman, WA (cdp) Spokane County	14	0.14
Flint, MI (city) Genesee County	160	0.13
Battle Creek, MI (city) Calhoun County	71	0.13
Parkway-South Sacramento, CA (cdp) Sacramento County	47	0.13
Newburgh, NY (city) Orange County	37	0.13
Fort Lewis, WA (cdp) Pierce County	25	0.13
Junction City, KS (city) Geary County	25	0.13
Oak Harbor, WA (city) Island County	25	0.13
Hayesville, OR (cdp) Marion County	23	0.13
Hillcrest Heights, MD (cdp) Prince George's County	21	0.13
Wahiawa, HI (cdp) Honolulu County	21	0.13
Forestville, MD (cdp) Prince George's County	17	0.13
El Sobrante, CA (cdp) Contra Costa County	16	0.13
Ottawa, KS (city) Franklin County	16	0.13
Emmett, MI (township) Calhoun County	15	0.13
Coatesville, PA (city) Chester County	14	0.13
Rio Linda, CA (cdp) Sacramento County	14	0.13
View Park-Windsor Hills, CA (cdp) Los Angeles County	14	0.13
Conning Towers-Nautilus Park, CT (cdp) New London County	13	0.13
Princeton, FL (cdp) Miami-Dade County	13	0.13
Vineyard, CA (cdp) Sacramento County	13	0.13
Bartlesville, OK (city) Washington County	41	0.12
Willingboro, NJ (township) Burlington County	41	0.12
Des Moines, WA (city) King County	36	0.12
Mililani Town, HI (cdp) Honolulu County	33	0.12
Benicia, CA (city) Solano County	31	0.12
Bay Point, CA (cdp) Contra Costa County	25	0.12
Greenfield, MA (town) Franklin County	21	0.12
Painesville, OH (city) Lake County	21	0.12
Mount Clemens, MI (city) Macomb County	20	0.12
Anacortes, WA (city) Skagit County	18	0.12
Beecher, MI (cdp) Genesee County	15	0.12
Gulfport, FL (city) Pinellas County	15	0.12
Muskegon Heights, MI (city) Muskegon County	14	0.12
Big Rapids, MI (city) Mecosta County	13	0.12
Fort Stewart, GA (cdp) Liberty County	13	0.12
Superior, MI (township) Washtenaw County	13	0.12
Sacramento, CA (city) Sacramento County	428	0.11
Fairfield, CA (city) Solano County	105	0.11
Springfield, OR (city) Lane County	58	0.11
Longview, WA (city) Cowlitz County	38	0.11
Lynnwood, WA (city) Snohomish County	38	0.11
Florin, CA (cdp) Sacramento County	31	0.11
Waimalu, HI (cdp) Honolulu County	31	0.11
Atascadero, CA (city) San Luis Obispo County	30	0.11
Oakley, CA (city) Contra Costa County	27	0.11
San Jacinto, CA (city) Riverside County	27	0.11
Mount Morris, MI (township) Genesee County	25	0.11
Orchards, WA (cdp) Clark County	20	0.11
Lakeland North, WA (cdp) King County	17	0.11
New Kingman-Butler, AZ (cdp) Mohave County	17	0.11
Mohave Valley, AZ (cdp) Mohave County	15	0.11
Conneaut, OH (city) Ashtabula County	14	0.11
Catskill, NY (town) Greene County	13	0.11
Waianae, HI (cdp) Honolulu County	12	0.11
Seattle, WA (city) King County	548	0.10
Portland, OR (city) Multnomah County	529	0.10
Everett, WA (city) Snohomish County	88	0.10
Redding, CA (city) Shasta County	81	0.10
Kent, WA (city) King County	76	0.10
Victorville, CA (city) San Bernardino County	66	0.10
Elyria, OH (city) Lorain County	58	0.10
Apple Valley, CA (town) San Bernardino County	54	0.10
Pittsburg, CA (city) Contra Costa County	54	0.10
Renton, WA (city) King County	49	0.10
Hilo, HI (cdp) Hawaii County	41	0.10
Hollister, CA (city) San Benito County	33	0.10
Paradise, CA (town) Butte County	26	0.10
Ashland, CA (cdp) Alameda County	20	0.10
Ashtabula, OH (city) Ashtabula County	20	0.10
Portsmouth, OH (city) Scioto County	20	0.10
Winter Gardens, CA (cdp) San Diego County	20	0.10
Klamath Falls, OR (city) Klamath County	19	0.10
Pampa, TX (city) Gray County	18	0.10
Hannibal, MO (city) Marion County	17	0.10
Live Oak, CA (cdp) Santa Cruz County	16	0.10
Willimantic, CT (cdp) Windham County	16	0.10
Tinton Falls, NJ (borough) Monmouth County	15	0.10
Callaway, FL (city) Bay County	14	0.10
Sierra Vista Southeast, AZ (cdp) Cochise County	14	0.10
Camano, WA (cdp) Island County	13	0.10
Niles, MI (township) Berrien County	13	0.10
Lakeland South, WA (cdp) King County	12	0.10
Prairie Ridge, WA (cdp) Pierce County	12	0.10
Red Bank, NJ (borough) Monmouth County	12	0.10
Browns Mills, NJ (cdp) Burlington County	11	0.10
Merriam, KS (city) Johnson County	11	0.10
Buena Vista charter, MI (township) Saginaw County	10	0.10
Millington, TN (city) Shelby County	10	0.10
Anchorage, AK (municipality) Anchorage Borough	225	0.09
Lancaster, CA (city) Los Angeles County	108	0.09
Citrus Heights, CA (city) Sacramento County	79	0.09
Federal Way, WA (city) King County	79	0.09
Medford, OR (city) Jackson County	57	0.09
Rancho Cordova, CA (cdp) Sacramento County	50	0.09
Harrisburg, PA (city) Dauphin County	42	0.09
Albany, OR (city) Linn County	36	0.09
Kailua, HI (cdp) Honolulu County	32	0.09
Martinez, CA (city) Contra Costa County	31	0.09
Winslow, NJ (township) Camden County	31	0.09
Keizer, OR (city) Marion County	30	0.09

Notes: (cdp) census designated place; Refer to the Explanation of Data in the front of the book for more detailed information.

American Indian: Cherokee

Top 150 Places Sorted by Number

(Based on all places, regardless of population)

Place	Number	%
Tulsa, OK (city) Tulsa County	14,453	3.68
New York, NY (city) New York City	6,631	0.08
Oklahoma City, OK (city) Oklahoma County	6,366	1.26
Los Angeles, CA (city) Los Angeles County	5,126	0.14
Muskogee, OK (city) Muskogee County	4,229	11.04
Tahlequah, OK (city) Cherokee County	3,426	23.70
San Diego, CA (city) San Diego County	2,643	0.22
Broken Arrow, OK (city) Tulsa County	2,538	3.39
Chicago, IL (city) Cook County	2,337	0.08
Wichita, KS (city) Sedgwick County	2,327	0.68
Bartlesville, OK (city) Washington County	2,313	6.66
Houston, TX (city) Harris County	2,159	0.11
Columbus, OH (city) Franklin County	2,100	0.30
Phoenix, AZ (city) Maricopa County	2,099	0.16
Claremore, OK (city) Rogers County	2,048	12.90
Sacramento, CA (city) Sacramento County	2,028	0.50
San Antonio, TX (city) Bexar County	1,963	0.17
Philadelphia, PA (city) Philadelphia County	1,957	0.13
Dallas, TX (city) Dallas County	1,889	0.16
Sallisaw, OK (city) Sequoyah County	1,862	23.31
San Jose, CA (city) Santa Clara County	1,781	0.20
Jacksonville, FL (special city) Duval County	1,717	0.23
Portland, OR (city) Multnomah County	1,702	0.32
Park Hill, OK (cdp) Cherokee County	1,635	41.54
Detroit, MI (city) Wayne County	1,599	0.17
Stilwell, OK (city) Adair County	1,591	48.57
Norman, OK (city) Cleveland County	1,560	1.63
Kansas City, MO (city) Jackson County	1,550	0.35
Miami, OK (city) Ottawa County	1,545	11.27
Fresno, CA (city) Fresno County	1,502	0.35
Colorado Springs, CO (city) El Paso County	1,474	0.41
Nashville-Davidson, TN (special city) Davidson County	1,443	0.26
Austin, TX (city) Travis County	1,429	0.22
Denver, CO (city) Denver County	1,390	0.25
Indianapolis, IN (special city) Marion County	1,375	0.18
San Francisco, CA (city) San Francisco County	1,352	0.17
Bakersfield, CA (city) Kern County	1,325	0.54
Seattle, WA (city) King County	1,320	0.23
Anchorage, AK (municipality) Anchorage Borough	1,296	0.50
Honolulu, HI (cdp) Honolulu County	1,286	0.35
Pryor Creek, OK (city) Mayes County	1,269	14.66
Fort Smith, AR (city) Sebastian County	1,242	1.55
Fort Worth, TX (city) Tarrant County	1,214	0.23
Virginia Beach, VA (independent city) Virginia Beach city	1,175	0.28
Modesto, CA (city) Stanislaus County	1,174	0.62
Huntsville, AL (city) Madison County	1,152	0.73
Vinita, OK (city) Craig County	1,135	17.54
Long Beach, CA (city) Los Angeles County	1,109	0.24
Albuquerque, NM (city) Bernalillo County	1,105	0.25
Tucson, AZ (city) Pima County	1,088	0.22
Las Vegas, NV (city) Clark County	1,075	0.22
Baltimore, MD (independent city) Baltimore city	1,070	0.16
Springfield, MO (city) Greene County	1,045	0.69
Arlington, TX (city) Tarrant County	1,042	0.31
Stockton, CA (city) San Joaquin County	1,035	0.42
Sand Springs, OK (city) Tulsa County	993	5.69
Wagoner, OK (city) Wagoner County	990	12.91
Cleveland, OH (city) Cuyahoga County	984	0.21
Sapulpa, OK (city) Creek County	963	5.02
Washington, DC (city) District of Columbia	929	0.16
Jay, OK (city) Delaware County	910	36.66
Oakland, CA (city) Alameda County	903	0.23
Edmond, OK (city) Oklahoma County	900	1.32
Cherry Tree, OK (cdp) Adair County	894	74.38
Owasso, OK (city) Tulsa County	886	4.79
Saint Louis, MO (independent city) Saint Louis city	883	0.25
Skiatook, OK (town) Osage County	877	16.25
Memphis, TN (city) Shelby County	870	0.13
Midwest City, OK (city) Oklahoma County	846	1.56
Aurora, CO (city) Arapahoe County	841	0.30
Moore, OK (city) Cleveland County	824	2.00
Fort Gibson, OK (town) Muskogee County	822	20.28
Riverside, CA (city) Riverside County	819	0.32
Stillwater, OK (city) Payne County	807	2.07
Charlotte, NC (city) Mecklenburg County	806	0.15

Place	Number	%
Norfolk, VA (independent city) Norfolk city	772	0.33
Toledo, OH (city) Lucas County	763	0.24
Tacoma, WA (city) Pierce County	762	0.39
Cincinnati, OH (city) Hamilton County	756	0.23
Knoxville, TN (city) Knox County	720	0.41
Independence, MO (city) Jackson County	696	0.61
Catoosa, OK (city) Rogers County	694	12.74
Huntington Beach, CA (city) Orange County	689	0.36
Milwaukee, WI (city) Milwaukee County	688	0.12
Akron, OH (city) Summit County	662	0.30
Mesa, AZ (city) Maricopa County	662	0.17
Flint, MI (city) Genesee County	660	0.53
Louisville, KY (city) Jefferson County	652	0.25
Tampa, FL (city) Hillsborough County	651	0.21
Fayetteville, AR (city) Washington County	641	1.10
Kansas City, KS (city) Wyandotte County	636	0.43
Eugene, OR (city) Lane County	633	0.46
Muldrow, OK (town) Sequoyah County	629	20.26
Hempstead, NY (town) Nassau County	627	0.08
Joplin, MO (city) Jasper County	624	1.37
San Bernardino, CA (city) San Bernardino County	623	0.34
Saint Petersburg, FL (city) Pinellas County	619	0.25
Coffeyville, KS (city) Montgomery County	617	5.60
Nowata, OK (city) Nowata County	611	15.39
Newport News, VA (independent city) Newport News city	611	0.34
Boston, MA (city) Suffolk County	609	0.10
Citrus Heights, CA (city) Sacramento County	597	0.70
Lawton, OK (city) Comanche County	596	0.64
Redding, CA (city) Shasta County	582	0.72
San Buenaventura, CA (city) Ventura County	580	0.57
Atlanta, GA (city) Fulton County	579	0.14
Corpus Christi, TX (city) Nueces County	578	0.21
Lexington-Fayette, KY (special city) Fayette County	577	0.22
Anaheim, CA (city) Orange County	576	0.18
Lancaster, CA (city) Los Angeles County	574	0.48
Spokane, WA (city) Spokane County	569	0.29
Topeka, KS (city) Shawnee County	568	0.46
Amarillo, TX (city) Potter County	557	0.32
Garland, TX (city) Dallas County	557	0.26
Enid, OK (city) Garfield County	556	1.18
Coweta, OK (city) Wagoner County	555	7.77
Salem, OR (city) Marion County	543	0.40
Grove, OK (city) Delaware County	542	10.56
Antioch, CA (city) Contra Costa County	542	0.60
Pittsburgh, PA (city) Allegheny County	542	0.16
Ponca City, OK (city) Kay County	538	2.08
Chesapeake, VA (independent city) Chesapeake city	533	0.27
Fremont, CA (city) Alameda County	530	0.26
Chattanooga, TN (city) Hamilton County	529	0.34
Arden-Arcade, CA (cdp) Sacramento County	526	0.55
Bixby, OK (city) Tulsa County	524	3.93
Vallejo, CA (city) Solano County	522	0.45
Vancouver, WA (city) Clark County	521	0.36
Shawnee, OK (city) Pottawatomie County	517	1.80
Omaha, NE (city) Douglas County	512	0.13
Brookhaven, NY (town) Suffolk County	506	0.11
Chelsea, OK (city) Rogers County	496	23.22
Siloam Springs, AR (city) Benton County	495	4.57
Henderson, NV (city) Clark County	494	0.28
Santa Rosa, CA (city) Sonoma County	491	0.33
Dayton, OH (city) Montgomery County	490	0.29
Reno, NV (city) Washoe County	489	0.27
Boise City, ID (city) Ada County	484	0.26
Eldon, OK (cdp) Cherokee County	481	48.54
Paradise, NV (cdp) Clark County	474	0.25
Hayward, CA (city) Alameda County	472	0.34
Raleigh, NC (city) Wake County	469	0.17
Glenpool, OK (city) Tulsa County	468	5.76
Lakewood, CO (city) Jefferson County	465	0.32
El Paso, TX (city) El Paso County	464	0.08
Wichita Falls, TX (city) Wichita County	462	0.44
Irving, TX (city) Dallas County	461	0.24
Concord, CA (city) Contra Costa County	458	0.38
Collinsville, OK (city) Tulsa County	455	11.16
Locust Grove, OK (town) Mayes County	454	33.24

Notes: (cdp) census designated place; Refer to the Explanation of Data in the front of the book for more detailed information.

American Indian: Cherokee

Top 150 Places Sorted by Percent

(Based on all places, regardless of population)

Place	Number	%
Oaks, OK (town) Delaware County	329	79.85
Zion, OK (cdp) Adair County	36	75.00
Cherry Tree, OK (cdp) Adair County	894	74.38
Bull Hollow, OK (cdp) Delaware County	56	66.67
Flute Springs, OK (cdp) Sequoyah County	116	63.74
Marble City, OK (town) Sequoyah County	154	63.64
Chewey, OK (cdp) Adair County	84	62.22
Sycamore, OK (cdp) Delaware County	111	60.66
Twin Oaks, OK (cdp) Delaware County	111	59.68
Dripping Springs, OK (cdp) Delaware County	24	58.54
Fairfield, OK (cdp) Adair County	214	58.31
Bell, OK (cdp) Adair County	347	57.64
Old Eucha, OK (cdp) Delaware County	26	56.52
Brush Creek, OK (cdp) Delaware County	23	56.10
Maryetta, OK (cdp) Adair County	77	55.80
Rocky Mountain, OK (cdp) Adair County	245	54.69
Lotsee, OK (town) Tulsa County	6	54.55
Peavine, OK (cdp) Adair County	191	53.35
Greasy, OK (cdp) Adair County	206	53.23
Lyons Switch, OK (cdp) Adair County	113	49.78
Hulbert, OK (town) Cherokee County	268	49.36
Stilwell, OK (city) Adair County	1,591	48.57
Eldon, OK (cdp) Cherokee County	481	48.54
Pinhook Corners, OK (cdp) Sequoyah County	78	48.45
Belfonte, OK (cdp) Sequoyah County	206	48.36
West Peavine, OK (cdp) Adair County	107	47.56
Rocky Ford, OK (cdp) Delaware County	28	46.67
Leach, OK (cdp) Delaware County	102	46.36
Salem, OK (cdp) Adair County	41	46.07
Tagg Flats, OK (cdp) Delaware County	5	45.45
Tenkiller, OK (cdp) Cherokee County	246	44.81
Kansas, OK (town) Delaware County	306	44.67
Marble City Community, OK (cdp) Sequoyah County	184	43.81
New Eucha, OK (cdp) Delaware County	129	43.00
Briggs, OK (cdp) Cherokee County	150	41.90
Park Hill, OK (cdp) Cherokee County	1,635	41.54
Welling, OK (cdp) Cherokee County	271	40.51
Jamestown, OK (town) Rogers County	4	40.00
Stony Point, OK (cdp) Sequoyah County	69	38.98
Wickliffe, OK (cdp) Mayes County	38	38.38
Zeb, OK (cdp) Cherokee County	188	37.75
Lost City, OK (cdp) Cherokee County	303	37.45
Jay, OK (city) Delaware County	910	36.66
Shady Grove, OK (cdp) Cherokee County	175	36.16
Woodall, OK (cdp) Cherokee County	263	35.49
New Alluwe, OK (town) Nowata County	33	34.74
Keys, OK (cdp) Cherokee County	157	34.28
Simms, OK (cdp) Muskogee County	101	34.24
Iron Post, OK (cdp) Mayes County	40	34.19
McKey, OK (cdp) Sequoyah County	46	34.07
Cloud Creek, OK (cdp) Delaware County	29	33.72
Duchess Landing, OK (cdp) McIntosh County	32	33.68
Vian, OK (town) Sequoyah County	453	33.26
Locust Grove, OK (town) Mayes County	454	33.24
Brushy, OK (cdp) Sequoyah County	257	32.66
Colcord, OK (town) Delaware County	267	32.60
Christie, OK (cdp) Adair County	54	32.53
Salina, OK (town) Mayes County	453	31.86
Cedar Crest, OK (cdp) Mayes County	96	31.17
Spavinaw, OK (town) Mayes County	171	30.37
Scraper, OK (cdp) Cherokee County	144	30.32
Sycamore, OK (cdp) Sequoyah County	45	30.00
Porum, OK (town) Muskogee County	217	29.93
Sour John, OK (cdp) Muskogee County	18	29.51
Dry Creek, OK (cdp) Cherokee County	62	28.70
Sams Corner, OK (cdp) Mayes County	36	28.57
Pettit, OK (cdp) Cherokee County	215	27.89
Evening Shade, OK (cdp) Sequoyah County	122	27.66
Westville, OK (town) Adair County	441	27.63
Strang, OK (town) Mayes County	27	27.00
Zena, OK (cdp) Delaware County	33	26.83
Foraker, OK (town) Osage County	6	26.09
Gore, OK (town) Sequoyah County	219	25.76
Murphy, OK (cdp) Mayes County	59	25.54
Adair, OK (town) Mayes County	176	25.00
Bluejacket, OK (town) Craig County	67	24.45
Watts Community, OK (cdp) Adair County	122	24.40
Carlile, OK (cdp) Sequoyah County	156	24.04
Webbers Falls, OK (town) Muskogee County	174	23.97
Cayuga, OK (cdp) Delaware County	25	23.81
Langley, OK (town) Mayes County	159	23.77
Tahlequah, OK (city) Cherokee County	3,426	23.70
Gans, OK (town) Sequoyah County	49	23.56
Akins, OK (cdp) Sequoyah County	105	23.39
Sallisaw, OK (city) Sequoyah County	1,862	23.31
Ballou, OK (cdp) Mayes County	33	23.24
Pump Back, OK (cdp) Mayes County	36	23.23
Chelsea, OK (city) Rogers County	496	23.22
Sand Hills, OK (cdp) Muskogee County	95	22.51
Notchietown, OK (cdp) Sequoyah County	95	22.09
Dwight Mission, OK (cdp) Sequoyah County	7	21.88
Watts, OK (town) Adair County	69	21.84
Bonanza, CO (town) Saguache County	3	21.43
North Miami, OK (town) Ottawa County	92	21.25
Short, OK (cdp) Sequoyah County	69	21.04
River Bottom, OK (cdp) Muskogee County	55	20.75
Warner, OK (town) Muskogee County	295	20.63
Fort Gibson, OK (town) Muskogee County	822	20.28
Ketchum, OK (town) Craig County	58	20.28
Muldrow, OK (town) Sequoyah County	629	20.26
Avant, OK (town) Osage County	75	20.16
Snake Creek, OK (cdp) Mayes County	60	20.13
Long, OK (cdp) Sequoyah County	73	20.11
Braggs, OK (town) Muskogee County	60	19.93
Pensacola, OK (town) Mayes County	14	19.72
Moffett, OK (town) Sequoyah County	35	19.55
Ramona, OK (town) Washington County	108	19.15
Oologah, OK (town) Rogers County	163	18.46
West Siloam Springs, OK (town) Delaware County	161	18.36
Fairland, OK (town) Ottawa County	187	18.24
Redbird Smith, OK (cdp) Sequoyah County	74	18.00
Bushyhead, OK (cdp) Rogers County	214	17.79
Big Cabin, OK (town) Craig County	52	17.75
Ochelata, OK (town) Washington County	87	17.61
Vinita, OK (city) Craig County	1,135	17.54
Wyandotte, OK (town) Ottawa County	61	16.80
Delaware, OK (town) Nowata County	76	16.67
Hallett, OK (town) Pawnee County	28	16.67
Sperry, OK (town) Tulsa County	162	16.51
Chouteau, OK (town) Mayes County	318	16.47
Galatia, KS (city) Barton County	10	16.39
Disney, OK (town) Mayes County	37	16.37
Skiatook, OK (town) Osage County	877	16.25
Lenapah, OK (town) Nowata County	48	16.11
Afton, OK (town) Ottawa County	179	16.01
Welch, OK (town) Craig County	95	15.91
Brent, OK (cdp) Sequoyah County	80	15.87
Cowlington, OK (town) Le Flore County	21	15.79
Okay, OK (town) Wagoner County	93	15.58
Talala, OK (town) Rogers County	42	15.56
Sequoyah, OK (cdp) Rogers County	104	15.50
Roland, OK (town) Sequoyah County	440	15.48
Vera, OK (town) Washington County	29	15.43
Nowata, OK (city) Nowata County	611	15.39
Paradise Hill, OK (town) Sequoyah County	15	15.00
Pin Oak Acres, OK (cdp) Mayes County	63	14.75
Webb City, OK (town) Osage County	14	14.74
Oktaha, OK (town) Muskogee County	48	14.68
Pryor Creek, OK (city) Mayes County	1,269	14.66
Wann, OK (town) Nowata County	19	14.39
Hanna, OK (town) McIntosh County	19	14.29
Picher, OK (city) Ottawa County	232	14.15
Kildare, OK (town) Kay County	13	14.13
Wynona, OK (town) Osage County	73	13.75
Justice, OK (cdp) Rogers County	176	13.42
Inola, OK (town) Rogers County	209	13.15
Wagoner, OK (city) Wagoner County	990	12.91
Claremore, OK (city) Rogers County	2,048	12.90
Catoosa, OK (city) Rogers County	694	12.74
Liberty, KS (city) Montgomery County	12	12.63

Notes: (cdp) census designated place; Refer to the Explanation of Data in the front of the book for more detailed information.

American Indian: Cherokee

Top 150 Places Sorted by Percent

(Based on places with populations of 10,000 or more)

Place	Number	%
Tahlequah, OK (city) Cherokee County	3,426	23.70
Claremore, OK (city) Rogers County	2,048	12.90
Miami, OK (city) Ottawa County	1,545	11.27
Muskogee, OK (city) Muskogee County	4,229	11.04
Bartlesville, OK (city) Washington County	2,313	6.66
Sand Springs, OK (city) Tulsa County	993	5.69
Coffeyville, KS (city) Montgomery County	617	5.60
Sapulpa, OK (city) Creek County	963	5.02
Owasso, OK (city) Tulsa County	886	4.79
Siloam Springs, AR (city) Benton County	495	4.57
Bixby, OK (city) Tulsa County	524	3.93
Tulsa, OK (city) Tulsa County	14,453	3.68
Broken Arrow, OK (city) Tulsa County	2,538	3.39
Okmulgee, OK (city) Okmulgee County	389	2.99
Olivehurst, CA (cdp) Yuba County	322	2.91
McAlester, OK (city) Pittsburg County	438	2.46
Van Buren, AR (city) Crawford County	443	2.33
Ada, OK (city) Pontotoc County	341	2.17
Ponca City, OK (city) Kay County	538	2.08
Stillwater, OK (city) Payne County	807	2.07
Durant, OK (city) Bryan County	280	2.07
Moore, OK (city) Cleveland County	824	2.00
Shawnee, OK (city) Pottawatomie County	517	1.80
Mustang, OK (city) Canadian County	221	1.68
Chickasha, OK (city) Grady County	262	1.65
Norman, OK (city) Cleveland County	1,560	1.63
Marysville, CA (city) Yuba County	197	1.61
Linda, CA (cdp) Yuba County	216	1.60
Midwest City, OK (city) Oklahoma County	846	1.56
Fort Smith, AR (city) Sebastian County	1,242	1.55
Del City, OK (city) Oklahoma County	341	1.54
Neosho, MO (city) Newton County	147	1.40
Joplin, MO (city) Jasper County	624	1.37
Waianae, HI (cdp) Honolulu County	144	1.37
Arkansas City, KS (city) Cowley County	162	1.35
Rio Linda, CA (cdp) Sacramento County	140	1.34
Edmond, OK (city) Oklahoma County	900	1.32
The Village, OK (city) Oklahoma County	134	1.32
Bethany, OK (city) Oklahoma County	264	1.30
Oildale, CA (cdp) Kern County	356	1.28
Oklahoma City, OK (city) Oklahoma County	6,366	1.26
Clearlake, CA (city) Lake County	165	1.26
Ardmore, OK (city) Carter County	297	1.25
Yukon, OK (city) Canadian County	263	1.25
Scottsboro, AL (city) Jackson County	184	1.25
Oroville, CA (city) Butte County	157	1.21
Eureka, CA (city) Humboldt County	311	1.19
Enid, OK (city) Garfield County	556	1.18
Duncan, OK (city) Stephens County	259	1.15
McKinleyville, CA (cdp) Humboldt County	155	1.14
Bentonville, AR (city) Benton County	223	1.13
Parsons, KS (city) Labette County	130	1.13
Chowchilla, CA (city) Madera County	126	1.13
Fort Payne, AL (city) De Kalb County	145	1.12
Fayetteville, AR (city) Washington County	641	1.10
El Reno, OK (city) Canadian County	166	1.02
North Highlands, CA (cdp) Sacramento County	435	0.98
Wahiawa, HI (cdp) Honolulu County	157	0.97
Carthage, MO (city) Jasper County	122	0.96
Coos Bay, OR (city) Coos County	146	0.95
Oakdale, CA (city) Stanislaus County	142	0.92
Grass Valley, CA (city) Nevada County	99	0.91
West Plains, MO (city) Howell County	99	0.91
Springdale, AR (city) Washington County	409	0.89
Pampa, TX (city) Gray County	160	0.89
Pittsburg, KS (city) Crawford County	170	0.88
Yuba City, CA (city) Sutter County	320	0.87
Borger, TX (city) Hutchinson County	125	0.87
Elk City, OK (city) Beckham County	91	0.87
Madison, AL (city) Madison County	253	0.86
Riverbank, CA (city) Stanislaus County	130	0.82
Woodward, OK (city) Woodward County	97	0.82
Denison, TX (city) Grayson County	185	0.81
Kailua, HI (cdp) Honolulu County	290	0.79
Fortuna, CA (city) Humboldt County	82	0.78
Springfield, OR (city) Lane County	405	0.77
Hartselle, AL (city) Morgan County	93	0.77
Lincoln, CA (city) Placer County	86	0.77
Warrington, FL (cdp) Escambia County	116	0.76
El Dorado, KS (city) Butler County	90	0.75
Nanakuli, HI (cdp) Honolulu County	81	0.75
Ceres, CA (city) Stanislaus County	256	0.74
Altus, OK (city) Jackson County	159	0.74
New Kingman-Butler, AZ (cdp) Mohave County	109	0.74
South Yuba City, CA (cdp) Sutter County	93	0.74
Middleburg, FL (cdp) Clay County	77	0.74
Huntsville, AL (city) Madison County	1,152	0.73
Bremerton, WA (city) Kitsap County	273	0.73
El Sobrante, CA (cdp) Contra Costa County	90	0.73
Lake Los Angeles, CA (cdp) Los Angeles County	84	0.73
Redding, CA (city) Shasta County	582	0.72
Arcata, CA (city) Humboldt County	120	0.72
Grandview, MO (city) Jackson County	176	0.71
Coalinga, CA (city) Fresno County	83	0.71
Citrus Heights, CA (city) Sacramento County	597	0.70
Hilo, HI (cdp) Hawaii County	284	0.70
Bay Point, CA (cdp) Contra Costa County	151	0.70
Springfield, MO (city) Greene County	1,045	0.69
Fairbanks, AK (city) Fairbanks North Star Borough	210	0.69
Pahrump, NV (cdp) Nye County	169	0.69
Roseburg, OR (city) Douglas County	139	0.69
Bella Vista, AR (cdp) Benton County	114	0.69
Wichita, KS (city) Sedgwick County	2,327	0.68
Klamath Falls, OR (city) Klamath County	133	0.68
Magalia, CA (cdp) Butte County	72	0.68
Rogers, AR (city) Benton County	259	0.67
Orangevale, CA (cdp) Sacramento County	178	0.67
Decatur, AL (city) Morgan County	350	0.65
Manteca, CA (city) San Joaquin County	320	0.65
Galt, CA (city) Sacramento County	126	0.65
Ottawa, KS (city) Franklin County	77	0.65
Lawton, OK (city) Comanche County	596	0.64
Rosemont, CA (cdp) Sacramento County	147	0.64
Cimarron Hills, CO (cdp) El Paso County	98	0.64
Foothill Farms, CA (cdp) Sacramento County	110	0.63
Modesto, CA (city) Stanislaus County	1,174	0.62
Hazel Park, MI (city) Oakland County	117	0.62
Poplar Bluff, MO (city) Butler County	104	0.62
Twentynine Palms, CA (city) San Bernardino County	92	0.62
Red Bluff, CA (city) Tehama County	82	0.62
Kelso, WA (city) Cowlitz County	74	0.62
Independence, MO (city) Jackson County	696	0.61
Clovis, CA (city) Fresno County	416	0.61
Longview, WA (city) Cowlitz County	211	0.61
Altamont, OR (cdp) Klamath County	119	0.61
Antioch, CA (city) Contra Costa County	542	0.60
Kaneohe, HI (cdp) Honolulu County	209	0.60
Spanaway, WA (cdp) Pierce County	130	0.60
Portsmouth, OH (city) Scioto County	126	0.60
Yucca Valley, CA (town) San Bernardino County	102	0.60
Tehachapi, CA (city) Kern County	66	0.60
Millington, TN (city) Shelby County	63	0.60
Ridgecrest, CA (city) Kern County	147	0.59
Paragould, AR (city) Greene County	129	0.59
White Settlement, TX (city) Tarrant County	87	0.59
Ladson, SC (cdp) Berkeley County	78	0.59
Winfield, KS (city) Cowley County	72	0.59
Pedley, CA (cdp) Riverside County	66	0.59
Melvindale, MI (city) Wayne County	63	0.59
Crestline, CA (cdp) San Bernardino County	60	0.59
Rancho Cordova, CA (cdp) Sacramento County	317	0.58
Desert Hot Springs, CA (city) Riverside County	96	0.58
Canon City, CO (city) Fremont County	90	0.58
Fountain, CO (city) El Paso County	88	0.58
San Buenaventura, CA (city) Ventura County	580	0.57
Albany, OR (city) Linn County	233	0.57
Florin, CA (cdp) Sacramento County	159	0.57
Oakley, CA (city) Contra Costa County	146	0.57
Newton, KS (city) Harvey County	98	0.57
Dallas, OR (city) Polk County	71	0.57

Notes: (cdp) census designated place; Refer to the Explanation of Data in the front of the book for more detailed information.

American Indian: Cheyenne

Top 150 Places Sorted by Number

(Based on all places, regardless of population)

Place	Number	%
Lame Deer, MT (cdp) Rosebud County	1,504	74.53
Busby, MT (cdp) Big Horn County	520	74.82
Billings, MT (city) Yellowstone County	487	0.54
Muddy, MT (cdp) Big Horn County	473	75.44
Oklahoma City, OK (city) Oklahoma County	459	0.09
El Reno, OK (city) Canadian County	318	1.96
Ashland, MT (cdp) Rosebud County	267	57.54
Clinton, OK (city) Custer County	246	2.79
Colstrip, MT (city) Rosebud County	235	10.02
Tulsa, OK (city) Tulsa County	141	0.04
Hammon, OK (town) Roger Mills County	123	26.23
Denver, CO (city) Denver County	121	0.02
Watonga, OK (city) Blaine County	118	2.53
Kingfisher, OK (city) Kingfisher County	97	2.21
Wichita, KS (city) Sedgwick County	96	0.03
Los Angeles, CA (city) Los Angeles County	96	0.00
Spokane, WA (city) Spokane County	90	0.05
Weatherford, OK (city) Custer County	88	0.89
Colorado Springs, CO (city) El Paso County	87	0.02
Birney, MT (cdp) Rosebud County	82	75.93
New York, NY (city) New York City	80	0.00
Albuquerque, NM (city) Bernalillo County	77	0.02
Phoenix, AZ (city) Maricopa County	77	0.01
Rapid City, SD (city) Pennington County	76	0.13
Portland, OR (city) Multnomah County	74	0.01
Elk City, OK (city) Beckham County	70	0.67
Hardin, MT (city) Big Horn County	67	1.98
Norman, OK (city) Cleveland County	66	0.07
Missoula, MT (city) Missoula County	62	0.11
Tacoma, WA (city) Pierce County	60	0.03
San Diego, CA (city) San Diego County	58	0.00
Seattle, WA (city) King County	57	0.01
Lawrence, KS (city) Douglas County	56	0.07
Seiling, OK (city) Dewey County	51	5.83
Enid, OK (city) Garfield County	46	0.10
Lawton, OK (city) Comanche County	46	0.05
Chicago, IL (city) Cook County	44	0.00
Dallas, TX (city) Dallas County	43	0.00
Geary, OK (city) Blaine County	42	3.34
Anadarko, OK (city) Caddo County	40	0.60
Sioux Falls, SD (city) Minnehaha County	38	0.03
Crow Agency, MT (cdp) Big Horn County	37	2.38
Ponca City, OK (city) Kay County	37	0.14
Sacramento, CA (city) Sacramento County	36	0.01
El Paso, TX (city) El Paso County	35	0.01
Arapahoe, WY (cdp) Fremont County	33	1.87
Midwest City, OK (city) Oklahoma County	32	0.06
Columbus, OH (city) Franklin County	32	0.00
San Antonio, TX (city) Bexar County	32	0.00
Woodward, OK (city) Woodward County	30	0.25
Salt Lake City, UT (city) Salt Lake County	30	0.02
San Francisco, CA (city) San Francisco County	30	0.00
San Jose, CA (city) Santa Clara County	30	0.00
Thomas, OK (city) Custer County	29	2.34
Ethete, WY (cdp) Fremont County	29	1.99
Anchorage, AK (municipality) Anchorage Borough	29	0.01
Fort Washakie, WY (cdp) Fremont County	28	1.90
Salem, OR (city) Marion County	28	0.02
Gallup, NM (city) McKinley County	27	0.13
Milwaukee, WI (city) Milwaukee County	27	0.00
Shawnee, OK (city) Pottawatomie County	26	0.09
Butte-Silver Bow, MT (special city) Silver Bow County	26	0.08
Great Falls, MT (city) Cascade County	26	0.05
Vancouver, WA (city) Clark County	26	0.02
Honolulu, HI (cdp) Honolulu County	26	0.01
Long Beach, CA (city) Los Angeles County	26	0.01
Sheridan, WY (city) Sheridan County	25	0.16
Mesa, AZ (city) Maricopa County	24	0.01
Helena, MT (city) Lewis and Clark County	23	0.09
Lakewood, CO (city) Jefferson County	23	0.02
Pueblo, CO (city) Pueblo County	23	0.02
Kansas City, MO (city) Jackson County	23	0.01
Pierre, SD (city) Hughes County	22	0.16
El Monte, CA (city) Los Angeles County	22	0.02
Virginia Beach, VA (independent city) Virginia Beach city	22	0.01
Houston, TX (city) Harris County	22	0.00
Longdale, OK (town) Blaine County	21	6.77
Miles City, MT (city) Custer County	21	0.25
Bozeman, MT (city) Gallatin County	21	0.08
West Valley City, UT (city) Salt Lake County	21	0.02
Springfield, MO (city) Greene County	21	0.01
Cheyenne, WY (city) Laramie County	20	0.04
Omaha, NE (city) Douglas County	20	0.01
Stockton, CA (city) San Joaquin County	20	0.01
Riverton, WY (city) Fremont County	19	0.20
Aberdeen, SD (city) Brown County	19	0.08
Everett, WA (city) Snohomish County	19	0.02
Boise City, ID (city) Ada County	19	0.01
Eugene, OR (city) Lane County	19	0.01
Cleveland, OH (city) Cuyahoga County	19	0.00
Tucson, AZ (city) Pima County	19	0.00
Lockwood, MT (cdp) Yellowstone County	18	0.42
Gillette, WY (city) Campbell County	18	0.09
Calumet, OK (town) Canadian County	17	3.18
Visalia, CA (city) Tulare County	17	0.02
Kansas City, KS (city) Wyandotte County	17	0.01
Fort Worth, TX (city) Tarrant County	17	0.00
Fresno, CA (city) Fresno County	17	0.00
Nashville-Davidson, TN (special city) Davidson County	17	0.00
Towaoc, CO (cdp) Montezuma County	16	1.46
Bethany, OK (city) Oklahoma County	16	0.08
Garden City, KS (city) Finney County	16	0.06
Stillwater, OK (city) Payne County	16	0.04
Castro Valley, CA (cdp) Alameda County	16	0.03
Greeley, CO (city) Weld County	16	0.02
Las Vegas, NV (city) Clark County	16	0.00
Minneapolis, MN (city) Hennepin County	16	0.00
Oakland, CA (city) Alameda County	16	0.00
Philadelphia, PA (city) Philadelphia County	16	0.00
Okmulgee, OK (city) Okmulgee County	15	0.12
Del City, OK (city) Oklahoma County	15	0.07
Moore, OK (city) Cleveland County	15	0.04
Muskogee, OK (city) Muskogee County	15	0.04
Aurora, CO (city) Arapahoe County	15	0.01
Modesto, CA (city) Stanislaus County	15	0.01
Austin, TX (city) Travis County	15	0.00
Jacksonville, FL (special city) Duval County	15	0.00
Casper, WY (city) Natrona County	14	0.03
Broken Arrow, OK (city) Tulsa County	14	0.02
Arvada, CO (city) Jefferson County	14	0.01
Fontana, CA (city) San Bernardino County	14	0.01
Fort Collins, CO (city) Larimer County	14	0.01
Palmdale, CA (city) Los Angeles County	14	0.01
Arapaho, OK (town) Custer County	13	1.74
Park Hill, OK (cdp) Cherokee County	13	0.33
Guymon, OK (city) Texas County	13	0.12
Ardmore, OK (city) Carter County	13	0.05
Covina, CA (city) Los Angeles County	13	0.03
Fort Smith, AR (city) Sebastian County	13	0.02
Kent, WA (city) King County	13	0.02
Gresham, OR (city) Multnomah County	13	0.01
Hayward, CA (city) Alameda County	13	0.01
Lincoln, NE (city) Lancaster County	13	0.01
Oxnard, CA (city) Ventura County	13	0.01
Reno, NV (city) Washoe County	13	0.01
Westminster, CO (city) Adams County	13	0.01
Pryor, MT (cdp) Big Horn County	12	1.91
Polson, MT (city) Lake County	12	0.30
Seminole, OK (city) Seminole County	12	0.17
Bremerton, WA (city) Kitsap County	12	0.03
Shoreline, WA (city) King County	12	0.02
Federal Way, WA (city) King County	12	0.01
Hampton, VA (independent city) Hampton city	12	0.01
Independence, MO (city) Jackson County	12	0.01
Pomona, CA (city) Los Angeles County	12	0.01
Redding, CA (city) Shasta County	12	0.01
Anaheim, CA (city) Orange County	12	0.00
Bakersfield, CA (city) Kern County	12	0.00
Knob Noster, MO (city) Johnson County	11	0.45
Alva, OK (city) Woods County	11	0.21

Notes: (cdp) census designated place; Refer to the Explanation of Data in the front of the book for more detailed information.

American Indian: Cheyenne

Top 150 Places Sorted by Percent

(Based on all places, regardless of population)

Place	Number	%
Birney, MT (cdp) Rosebud County	82	75.93
Muddy, MT (cdp) Big Horn County	473	75.44
Busby, MT (cdp) Big Horn County	520	74.82
Lame Deer, MT (cdp) Rosebud County	1,504	74.53
Ashland, MT (cdp) Rosebud County	267	57.54
Hammon, OK (town) Roger Mills County	123	26.23
Carter, WY (cdp) Uinta County	1	12.50
Colstrip, MT (city) Rosebud County	235	10.02
Longdale, OK (town) Blaine County	21	6.77
Seiling, OK (city) Dewey County	51	5.83
Topeka, IL (village) Mason County	4	4.44
Bushnell, SD (town) Brookings County	3	4.00
Springtown, AR (town) Benton County	4	3.51
Geary, OK (city) Blaine County	42	3.34
Calumet, OK (town) Canadian County	17	3.18
Hitchcock, OK (town) Blaine County	4	2.84
Clinton, OK (city) Custer County	246	2.79
Moonshine, MN (township) Big Stone County	4	2.67
Johnstown, WY (cdp) Fremont County	6	2.54
Watonga, OK (city) Blaine County	118	2.53
Crow Agency, MT (cdp) Big Horn County	37	2.38
Sharon, KS (city) Barber County	5	2.38
Foss, OK (town) Washita County	3	2.36
Thomas, OK (city) Custer County	29	2.34
Picuris Pueblo, NM (cdp) Taos County	2	2.33
Kingfisher, OK (city) Kingfisher County	97	2.21
Paradise, MT (cdp) Sanders County	4	2.17
Custer City, OK (town) Custer County	8	2.04
Ethete, WY (cdp) Fremont County	29	1.99
Hardin, MT (city) Big Horn County	67	1.98
El Reno, OK (city) Canadian County	318	1.96
Pryor, MT (cdp) Big Horn County	12	1.91
Fort Washakie, WY (cdp) Fremont County	28	1.90
Sangrey, MT (cdp) Hill County	5	1.90
Arapahoe, WY (cdp) Fremont County	33	1.87
Arapaho, OK (town) Custer County	13	1.74
Spanish Valley, UT (cdp) San Juan County	3	1.66
Taloga, OK (town) Dewey County	6	1.61
Keams Canyon, AZ (cdp) Navajo County	4	1.54
Hysham, MT (town) Treasure County	5	1.52
Towaoc, CO (cdp) Montezuma County	16	1.46
Ulysses, NE (village) Butler County	4	1.45
Nespelem, WA (town) Okanogan County	3	1.42
Colony, OK (town) Washita County	2	1.36
Lengby, MN (city) Polk County	1	1.27
Redings Mill, MO (village) Newton County	2	1.26
Evaro, MT (cdp) Missoula County	4	1.22
Buffalo Gap, SD (town) Custer County	2	1.22
Elmira, MO (village) Ray County	1	1.22
Asher, OK (town) Pottawatomie County	5	1.19
Lodge Grass, MT (town) Big Horn County	6	1.18
Draper, WI (town) Sawyer County	2	1.17
Westby, MT (town) Sheridan County	2	1.16
Heart Butte, MT (cdp) Pondera County	8	1.15
Stilesville, IN (town) Hendricks County	3	1.15
Wharton, PA (township) Potter County	1	1.10
De Soto, WI (village) Vernon County	4	1.09
Wyola, MT (cdp) Big Horn County	2	1.08
Shepherd, MT (cdp) Yellowstone County	2	1.04
McLaughlin, SD (city) Corson County	8	1.03
Turtle Lake, MT (cdp) Lake County	2	1.03
Crookston, NE (village) Cherry County	1	1.02
Tallapoosa, MO (city) New Madrid County	2	0.98
Bullhead, SD (cdp) Corson County	3	0.97
Lodge Pole, MT (cdp) Blaine County	2	0.93
McIntosh, SD (city) Corson County	2	0.92
Vilas, CO (town) Baca County	1	0.91
Weatherford, OK (city) Custer County	88	0.89
Wisdom, MT (cdp) Beaverhead County	1	0.88
Hundred, WV (town) Wetzel County	3	0.87
Hydro, OK (town) Caddo County	9	0.85
North Powder, OR (city) Union County	4	0.82
Dover, OK (town) Kingfisher County	3	0.82
Fort Smith, MT (cdp) Big Horn County	1	0.82
Levelock, AK (cdp) Lake and Peninsula Borough	1	0.82
Ordway, CO (town) Crowley County	10	0.80
Boulder Flats, WY (cdp) Fremont County	3	0.79
Azure, MT (cdp) Hill County	2	0.79
Letts, IA (city) Louisa County	3	0.77
East Glacier Park Village, MT (cdp) Glacier County	3	0.76
Ignacio, CO (town) La Plata County	5	0.75
Hartline, WA (town) Grant County	1	0.75
Macy, NE (cdp) Thurston County	7	0.73
Walker, MO (city) Vernon County	2	0.73
Lynnville, IL (village) Morgan County	1	0.73
Sparks, OK (town) Lincoln County	1	0.73
Gettysburg, OH (village) Darke County	4	0.72
Dodd City, TX (town) Fannin County	3	0.72
Salem, NE (village) Richardson County	1	0.72
Chiloquin, OR (city) Klamath County	5	0.70
Saint Pierre, MT (cdp) Hill County	2	0.69
Freeport, MI (village) Barry County	3	0.68
Greenhorn, CA (cdp) Plumas County	1	0.68
Elk City, OK (city) Beckham County	70	0.67
Florence, MT (cdp) Ravalli County	6	0.67
La Plant, SD (cdp) Dewey County	1	0.67
Browning, MT (town) Glacier County	7	0.66
Frazer, MT (cdp) Valley County	3	0.66
Rentz, GA (town) Laurens County	2	0.66
Taylorsville, CA (cdp) Plumas County	1	0.65
Shaker Church, WA (cdp) Snohomish County	5	0.64
Fort Duchesne, UT (cdp) Uintah County	4	0.64
Santa Ana Pueblo, NM (cdp) Sandoval County	3	0.63
La Rose, IL (village) Marshall County	1	0.63
Hay Springs, NE (village) Sheridan County	4	0.61
Fargo, OK (town) Ellis County	2	0.61
Preston, KS (city) Pratt County	1	0.61
Anadarko, OK (city) Caddo County	40	0.60
Maunie, IL (village) White County	1	0.56
Stony Point, OK (cdp) Sequoyah County	1	0.56
Walthill, NE (village) Thurston County	5	0.55
North Washington, CO (cdp) Adams County	3	0.55
Billings, MT (city) Yellowstone County	487	0.54
Jennings, OK (town) Pawnee County	2	0.54
Winnett, MT (town) Petroleum County	1	0.54
Bessie, OK (town) Washita County	1	0.53
Opdyke West, TX (town) Hockley County	1	0.53
Kyle, SD (cdp) Shannon County	5	0.52
Forsyth, MT (city) Rosebud County	10	0.51
Ferrelview, MO (village) Platte County	3	0.51
South Haven, KS (city) Sumner County	2	0.51
Lake Andes, SD (city) Charles Mix County	4	0.49
Limestone, NY (village) Cattaraugus County	2	0.49
Porcupine, SD (cdp) Shannon County	2	0.49
Fitzhugh, OK (town) Pontotoc County	1	0.49
Martha, OK (town) Jackson County	1	0.49
Nixon, NV (cdp) Washoe County	2	0.48
Peever, SD (town) Roberts County	1	0.48
Viola, KS (city) Sedgwick County	1	0.47
Redwater, TX (city) Bowie County	4	0.46
Fairfield, MT (town) Teton County	3	0.46
Dupree, SD (city) Ziebach County	2	0.46
Knob Noster, MO (city) Johnson County	11	0.45
Hamlin, WV (town) Lincoln County	5	0.45
Tryon, OK (town) Lincoln County	2	0.45
Dougherty, OK (town) Murray County	1	0.45
Tansem, MN (township) Clay County	1	0.45
Pablo, MT (cdp) Lake County	8	0.44
Long Creek, OR (city) Grant County	1	0.44
Swink, CO (town) Otero County	3	0.43
Baring, WA (cdp) King County	1	0.43
Lockwood, MT (cdp) Yellowstone County	18	0.42
Eau Pleine, WI (town) Marathon County	3	0.40
New Vienna, OH (village) Clinton County	5	0.39
Mokelumne Hill, CA (cdp) Calaveras County	3	0.39
Pettit, OK (cdp) Cherokee County	3	0.39
Thawville, IL (village) Iroquois County	1	0.39
Malta, MT (city) Phillips County	8	0.38
Saint Ignatius, MT (town) Lake County	3	0.38
Neola, UT (cdp) Duchesne County	2	0.38

Notes: (cdp) census designated place; Refer to the Explanation of Data in the front of the book for more detailed information.

American Indian: Cheyenne

Top 150 Places Sorted by Percent

(Based on places with populations of 10,000 or more)

Place	Number	%
El Reno, OK (city) Canadian County	318	1.96
Elk City, OK (city) Beckham County	70	0.67
Billings, MT (city) Yellowstone County	487	0.54
Woodward, OK (city) Woodward County	30	0.25
Sheridan, WY (city) Sheridan County	25	0.16
Pierre, SD (city) Hughes County	22	0.16
Ponca City, OK (city) Kay County	37	0.14
Rapid City, SD (city) Pennington County	76	0.13
Gallup, NM (city) McKinley County	27	0.13
Okmulgee, OK (city) Okmulgee County	15	0.12
Guymon, OK (city) Texas County	13	0.12
Missoula, MT (city) Missoula County	62	0.11
Enid, OK (city) Garfield County	46	0.10
Waianae, HI (cdp) Honolulu County	10	0.10
Oklahoma City, OK (city) Oklahoma County	459	0.09
Shawnee, OK (city) Pottawatomie County	26	0.09
Helena, MT (city) Lewis and Clark County	23	0.09
Gillette, WY (city) Campbell County	18	0.09
Butte-Silver Bow, MT (special city) Silver Bow County	26	0.08
Bozeman, MT (city) Gallatin County	21	0.08
Aberdeen, SD (city) Brown County	19	0.08
Bethany, OK (city) Oklahoma County	16	0.08
Tahlequah, OK (city) Cherokee County	11	0.08
Patterson, CA (city) Stanislaus County	9	0.08
Norman, OK (city) Cleveland County	66	0.07
Lawrence, KS (city) Douglas County	56	0.07
Del City, OK (city) Oklahoma County	15	0.07
Miami, OK (city) Ottawa County	10	0.07
Midwest City, OK (city) Oklahoma County	32	0.06
Garden City, KS (city) Finney County	16	0.06
Ada, OK (city) Pontotoc County	10	0.06
Fountain, CO (city) El Paso County	9	0.06
Spokane, WA (city) Spokane County	90	0.05
Lawton, OK (city) Comanche County	46	0.05
Great Falls, MT (city) Cascade County	26	0.05
Ardmore, OK (city) Carter County	13	0.05
Clifton, CO (cdp) Mesa County	9	0.05
Oak Harbor, WA (city) Island County	9	0.05
Chickasha, OK (city) Grady County	8	0.05
Scottsbluff, NE (city) Scotts Bluff County	8	0.05
La Vista, NE (city) Sarpy County	6	0.05
Mustang, OK (city) Canadian County	6	0.05
Fort Morgan, CO (city) Morgan County	5	0.05
Lexington, NE (city) Dawson County	5	0.05
Tulsa, OK (city) Tulsa County	141	0.04
Cheyenne, WY (city) Laramie County	20	0.04
Stillwater, OK (city) Payne County	16	0.04
Moore, OK (city) Cleveland County	15	0.04
Muskogee, OK (city) Muskogee County	15	0.04
Yukon, OK (city) Canadian County	9	0.04
McAlester, OK (city) Pittsburg County	7	0.04
Winter Gardens, CA (cdp) San Diego County	7	0.04
Cimarron Hills, CO (cdp) El Paso County	6	0.04
Elko, NV (city) Elko County	6	0.04
Ramona, CA (cdp) San Diego County	6	0.04
Coldwater, MI (city) Branch County	5	0.04
Durango, CO (city) La Plata County	5	0.04
Durant, OK (city) Bryan County	5	0.04
Mountain Home, ID (city) Elmore County	5	0.04
Wilsonville, OR (city) Clackamas County	5	0.04
Blackfoot, ID (city) Bingham County	4	0.04
Gonzalez, FL (cdp) Escambia County	4	0.04
Lea Hill, WA (cdp) King County	4	0.04
Lyon, MI (township) Oakland County	4	0.04
Springdale, OH (city) Hamilton County	4	0.04
Sterling, CO (city) Logan County	4	0.04
Tarboro, NC (town) Edgecombe County	4	0.04
Wood River, IL (city) Madison County	4	0.04
Wichita, KS (city) Sedgwick County	96	0.03
Tacoma, WA (city) Pierce County	60	0.03
Sioux Falls, SD (city) Minnehaha County	38	0.03
Castro Valley, CA (cdp) Alameda County	16	0.03
Casper, WY (city) Natrona County	14	0.03
Covina, CA (city) Los Angeles County	13	0.03
Bremerton, WA (city) Kitsap County	12	0.03

Place	Number	%
Bartlesville, OK (city) Washington County	11	0.03
Clinton, IA (city) Clinton County	9	0.03
La Presa, CA (cdp) San Diego County	9	0.03
Hamtramck, MI (city) Wayne County	8	0.03
Juneau, AK (city and borough) Juneau Borough	8	0.03
Brighton, CO (city) Adams County	7	0.03
Cedar City, UT (city) Iron County	7	0.03
Pahrump, NV (cdp) Nye County	7	0.03
Lafayette, CO (city) Boulder County	6	0.03
Norwood, OH (city) Hamilton County	6	0.03
Spanaway, WA (cdp) Pierce County	6	0.03
Tualatin, OR (city) Washington County	6	0.03
Brighton, MI (township) Livingston County	5	0.03
Ewa Beach, HI (cdp) Honolulu County	5	0.03
Junction City, KS (city) Geary County	5	0.03
New Kingman-Butler, AZ (cdp) Mohave County	5	0.03
Okolona, KY (cdp) Jefferson County	5	0.03
Pendleton, OR (city) Umatilla County	5	0.03
Santa Fe Springs, CA (city) Los Angeles County	5	0.03
Sapulpa, OK (city) Creek County	5	0.03
Sherrelwood, CO (cdp) Adams County	5	0.03
Clinton, UT (city) Davis County	4	0.03
Front Royal, VA (town) Warren County	4	0.03
Fulton, MO (city) Callaway County	4	0.03
Kelso, WA (city) Cowlitz County	4	0.03
Norton, OH (city) Summit County	4	0.03
Port Lavaca, TX (city) Calhoun County	4	0.03
South Ogden, UT (city) Weber County	4	0.03
Susanville, CA (city) Lassen County	4	0.03
Arkansas City, KS (city) Cowley County	3	0.03
North Auburn, CA (cdp) Placer County	3	0.03
Pontiac, IL (city) Livingston County	3	0.03
Spring Creek, NV (cdp) Elko County	3	0.03
Denver, CO (city) Denver County	121	0.02
Colorado Springs, CO (city) El Paso County	87	0.02
Albuquerque, NM (city) Bernalillo County	77	0.02
Salt Lake City, UT (city) Salt Lake County	30	0.02
Salem, OR (city) Marion County	28	0.02
Vancouver, WA (city) Clark County	26	0.02
Lakewood, CO (city) Jefferson County	23	0.02
Pueblo, CO (city) Pueblo County	23	0.02
El Monte, CA (city) Los Angeles County	22	0.02
West Valley City, UT (city) Salt Lake County	21	0.02
Everett, WA (city) Snohomish County	19	0.02
Visalia, CA (city) Tulare County	17	0.02
Greeley, CO (city) Weld County	16	0.02
Broken Arrow, OK (city) Tulsa County	14	0.02
Fort Smith, AR (city) Sebastian County	13	0.02
Kent, WA (city) King County	13	0.02
Shoreline, WA (city) King County	12	0.02
Edmond, OK (city) Oklahoma County	11	0.02
Goleta, CA (cdp) Santa Barbara County	11	0.02
Kennewick, WA (city) Benton County	11	0.02
Springfield, OR (city) Lane County	11	0.02
Colton, CA (city) San Bernardino County	10	0.02
Apple Valley, CA (town) San Bernardino County	9	0.02
Bismarck, ND (city) Burleigh County	9	0.02
Lakewood, WA (city) Pierce County	9	0.02
Pocatello, ID (city) Bannock County	9	0.02
Frederick, MD (city) Frederick County	8	0.02
Grand Forks, ND (city) Grand Forks County	8	0.02
Puyallup, WA (city) Pierce County	8	0.02
Hobbs, NM (city) Lea County	7	0.02
Hutchinson, KS (city) Reno County	7	0.02
Lawndale, CA (city) Los Angeles County	7	0.02
Moorhead, MN (city) Clay County	7	0.02
Morgan Hill, CA (city) Santa Clara County	7	0.02
Pearl City, HI (cdp) Honolulu County	7	0.02
Cedar Park, TX (city) Williamson County	6	0.02
Clearfield, UT (city) Davis County	6	0.02
Coeur d'Alene, ID (city) Kootenai County	6	0.02
Dublin, CA (city) Alameda County	6	0.02
Englewood, CO (city) Arapahoe County	6	0.02
Fairbanks, AK (city) Fairbanks North Star Borough	6	0.02
Lacey, WA (city) Thurston County	6	0.02

Notes: (cdp) census designated place; Refer to the Explanation of Data in the front of the book for more detailed information.

American Indian: Chickasaw

Top 150 Places Sorted by Number

(Based on all places, regardless of population)

Place	Number	%
Oklahoma City, OK (city) Oklahoma County	1,949	0.39
Ada, OK (city) Pontotoc County	1,189	7.58
Ardmore, OK (city) Carter County	978	4.12
Norman, OK (city) Cleveland County	577	0.60
Tulsa, OK (city) Tulsa County	444	0.11
Chevak, AK (city) Wade Hampton Census Area	371	48.50
Tishomingo, OK (city) Johnston County	364	11.51
Sulphur, OK (city) Murray County	316	6.59
Moore, OK (city) Cleveland County	300	0.73
Midwest City, OK (city) Oklahoma County	270	0.50
Durant, OK (city) Bryan County	263	1.94
Dallas, TX (city) Dallas County	236	0.02
Edmond, OK (city) Oklahoma County	230	0.34
Lone Grove, OK (city) Carter County	228	4.92
Duncan, OK (city) Stephens County	211	0.94
Phoenix, AZ (city) Maricopa County	194	0.01
Los Angeles, CA (city) Los Angeles County	191	0.01
Pauls Valley, OK (city) Garvin County	189	3.02
Lawton, OK (city) Comanche County	158	0.17
Shawnee, OK (city) Pottawatomie County	144	0.50
San Diego, CA (city) San Diego County	136	0.01
Houston, TX (city) Harris County	134	0.01
Davis, OK (city) Murray County	132	5.06
Madill, OK (city) Marshall County	131	3.84
Wichita, KS (city) Sedgwick County	130	0.04
Kingston, OK (town) Marshall County	123	8.85
Fort Worth, TX (city) Tarrant County	123	0.02
Broken Arrow, OK (city) Tulsa County	122	0.16
McAlester, OK (city) Pittsburg County	116	0.65
Tuttle, OK (city) Grady County	102	2.38
Albuquerque, NM (city) Bernalillo County	102	0.02
San Antonio, TX (city) Bexar County	102	0.01
Newcastle, OK (city) McClain County	101	1.86
Purcell, OK (city) McClain County	101	1.81
Del City, OK (city) Oklahoma County	95	0.43
Byng, OK (town) Pontotoc County	94	8.62
San Jose, CA (city) Santa Clara County	93	0.01
Muskogee, OK (city) Muskogee County	89	0.23
Mill Creek, OK (town) Johnston County	86	25.29
Garland, TX (city) Dallas County	85	0.04
New York, NY (city) New York City	85	0.00
Allen, OK (town) Pontotoc County	84	8.83
Arlington, TX (city) Tarrant County	83	0.02
Wichita Falls, TX (city) Wichita County	81	0.08
Irving, TX (city) Dallas County	79	0.04
Marlow, OK (city) Stephens County	77	1.68
Mustang, OK (city) Canadian County	76	0.58
Chickasha, OK (city) Grady County	76	0.48
Sacramento, CA (city) Sacramento County	76	0.02
Healdton, OK (city) Carter County	75	2.69
Stillwater, OK (city) Payne County	75	0.19
Austin, TX (city) Travis County	75	0.01
Modesto, CA (city) Stanislaus County	73	0.04
Ravia, OK (town) Johnston County	71	15.47
Denison, TX (city) Grayson County	71	0.31
Enid, OK (city) Garfield County	68	0.14
Stratford, OK (town) Garvin County	67	4.55
Bethany, OK (city) Oklahoma County	67	0.33
Bartlesville, OK (city) Washington County	67	0.19
Kansas City, MO (city) Jackson County	67	0.02
Fresno, CA (city) Fresno County	66	0.02
Tecumseh, OK (city) Pottawatomie County	65	1.07
Achille, OK (town) Bryan County	64	12.65
Colorado Springs, CO (city) El Paso County	64	0.02
Marietta, OK (city) Love County	63	2.58
Amarillo, TX (city) Potter County	61	0.04
Coalgate, OK (city) Coal County	60	2.99
Plano, TX (city) Collin County	60	0.03
Las Vegas, NV (city) Clark County	60	0.01
Portland, OR (city) Multnomah County	59	0.01
Anchorage, AK (municipality) Anchorage Borough	58	0.02
Sherman, TX (city) Grayson County	57	0.16
San Francisco, CA (city) San Francisco County	57	0.01
Bakersfield, CA (city) Kern County	55	0.02
Denver, CO (city) Denver County	55	0.01
Long Beach, CA (city) Los Angeles County	54	0.01
Tucson, AZ (city) Pima County	54	0.01
Grand Prairie, TX (city) Dallas County	53	0.04
Mesquite, TX (city) Dallas County	53	0.04
Slaughterville, OK (town) Cleveland County	52	1.44
Lubbock, TX (city) Lubbock County	51	0.03
Oakland, OK (town) Marshall County	50	7.42
Dickson, OK (town) Carter County	50	4.39
Sand Springs, OK (city) Tulsa County	49	0.28
Ponca City, OK (city) Kay County	49	0.19
Denton, TX (city) Denton County	48	0.06
Noble, OK (city) Cleveland County	47	0.89
Seminole, OK (city) Seminole County	47	0.68
Yukon, OK (city) Canadian County	47	0.22
Lewisville, TX (city) Denton County	46	0.06
Chicago, IL (city) Cook County	46	0.00
Wynnewood, OK (city) Garvin County	45	1.90
Stonewall, OK (town) Pontotoc County	44	9.46
Mannsville, OK (town) Johnston County	44	7.50
Choctaw, OK (city) Oklahoma County	44	0.47
Guthrie, OK (city) Logan County	44	0.44
Sapulpa, OK (city) Creek County	44	0.23
Claremore, OK (city) Rogers County	43	0.27
Riverside, CA (city) Riverside County	43	0.02
Detroit, MI (city) Wayne County	43	0.00
Blanchard, OK (city) McClain County	42	1.49
Atoka, OK (city) Atoka County	42	1.41
Mesa, AZ (city) Maricopa County	42	0.01
Nashville-Davidson, TN (special city) Davidson County	41	0.01
Okmulgee, OK (city) Okmulgee County	40	0.31
Gainesville, TX (city) Cooke County	39	0.25
Owasso, OK (city) Tulsa County	39	0.21
Oakland, CA (city) Alameda County	39	0.01
Roff, OK (town) Pontotoc County	38	5.18
North Richland Hills, TX (city) Tarrant County	37	0.07
Lawrence, KS (city) Douglas County	36	0.04
Chula Vista, CA (city) San Diego County	36	0.02
Calera, OK (town) Bryan County	35	2.01
Carrollton, TX (city) Denton County	35	0.03
Warr Acres, OK (city) Oklahoma County	34	0.35
El Reno, OK (city) Canadian County	34	0.21
Odessa, TX (city) Ector County	34	0.04
Abilene, TX (city) Taylor County	34	0.03
Anaheim, CA (city) Orange County	34	0.01
Spokane, WA (city) Spokane County	33	0.02
Burkburnett, TX (city) Wichita County	32	0.29
Tahlequah, OK (city) Cherokee County	32	0.22
Antioch, CA (city) Contra Costa County	32	0.04
Visalia, CA (city) Tulare County	32	0.03
Salinas, CA (city) Monterey County	32	0.02
Glendale, AZ (city) Maricopa County	32	0.01
Springer, OK (town) Carter County	31	5.37
Krebs, OK (city) Pittsburg County	31	1.51
Citrus Heights, CA (city) Sacramento County	31	0.04
Eugene, OR (city) Lane County	31	0.02
Huntington Beach, CA (city) Orange County	31	0.02
Meridian, OK (cdp) Stephens County	30	2.02
Anadarko, OK (city) Caddo County	30	0.45
Henderson, NV (city) Clark County	30	0.02
Fremont, CA (city) Alameda County	30	0.01
Seattle, WA (city) King County	30	0.01
Stockton, CA (city) San Joaquin County	30	0.01
Memphis, TN (city) Shelby County	30	0.00
Comanche, OK (city) Stephens County	29	1.86
Elk City, OK (city) Beckham County	29	0.28
McKinney, TX (city) Collin County	29	0.05
Honolulu, HI (cdp) Honolulu County	29	0.01
Omaha, NE (city) Douglas County	29	0.01
Bethel Acres, OK (town) Pottawatomie County	28	1.02
The Village, OK (city) Oklahoma County	28	0.28
Weatherford, OK (city) Custer County	28	0.28
Clovis, CA (city) Fresno County	28	0.04
Midland, TX (city) Midland County	28	0.03
Richardson, TX (city) Dallas County	28	0.03
Corpus Christi, TX (city) Nueces County	28	0.01

Notes: (cdp) census designated place; Refer to the Explanation of Data in the front of the book for more detailed information.

American Indian: Chickasaw

Top 150 Places Sorted by Percent

(Based on all places, regardless of population)

Place	Number	%
Chevak, AK (city) Wade Hampton Census Area	371	48.50
Mill Creek, OK (town) Johnston County	86	25.29
Ravia, OK (town) Johnston County	71	15.47
Texola, OK (town) Beckham County	6	12.77
Achille, OK (town) Bryan County	64	12.65
Tishomingo, OK (city) Johnston County	364	11.51
Mead, OK (town) Bryan County	13	10.57
Kemp, OK (town) Bryan County	15	10.42
Bromide, OK (town) Johnston County	16	9.82
Scottsville, KS (city) Mitchell County	2	9.52
Stonewall, OK (town) Pontotoc County	44	9.46
Ashland, OK (town) Pittsburg County	5	9.43
Phillips, OK (town) Coal County	14	9.33
Kingston, OK (town) Marshall County	123	8.85
Allen, OK (town) Pontotoc County	84	8.83
Byng, OK (town) Pontotoc County	94	8.62
Ada, OK (city) Pontotoc County	1,189	7.58
Mannsville, OK (town) Johnston County	44	7.50
Oakland, OK (town) Marshall County	50	7.42
Cornish, OK (town) Jefferson County	12	6.98
Sulphur, OK (city) Murray County	316	6.59
Gene Autry, OK (town) Carter County	6	6.06
Francis, OK (town) Pontotoc County	20	6.02
Hickory, OK (town) Murray County	5	5.75
Silo, OK (town) Bryan County	16	5.67
Springer, OK (town) Carter County	31	5.37
Roff, OK (town) Pontotoc County	38	5.18
Davis, OK (city) Murray County	132	5.06
Lone Grove, OK (city) Carter County	228	4.92
Sasakwa, OK (town) Seminole County	7	4.67
Stratford, OK (town) Garvin County	67	4.55
Fitzhugh, OK (town) Pontotoc County	9	4.41
Dickson, OK (town) Carter County	50	4.39
Wapanucka, OK (town) Johnston County	19	4.27
Tupelo, OK (city) Coal County	16	4.24
Ardmore, OK (city) Carter County	978	4.12
Dougherty, OK (town) Murray County	9	4.02
Byars, OK (town) McClain County	11	3.93
Milburn, OK (town) Johnston County	12	3.85
Madill, OK (city) Marshall County	131	3.84
Centrahoma, OK (city) Coal County	4	3.64
Mount Moriah, MO (town) Harrison County	5	3.50
Tatums, OK (town) Carter County	6	3.49
Hastings, OK (town) Jefferson County	5	3.23
Rocky Mound, TX (town) Camp County	3	3.23
Dibble, OK (town) McClain County	9	3.11
Rosedale, OK (town) McClain County	2	3.03
Pauls Valley, OK (city) Garvin County	189	3.02
Coalgate, OK (city) Coal County	60	2.99
Healdton, OK (city) Carter County	75	2.69
Lazy Lake, FL (village) Broward County	1	2.63
Marietta, OK (city) Love County	63	2.58
Watts, OK (town) Adair County	8	2.53
Hendrix, OK (town) Bryan County	2	2.53
Smith Village, OK (town) Oklahoma County	1	2.50
Tuttle, OK (city) Grady County	102	2.38
Foss, OK (town) Washita County	3	2.36
Council Hill, OK (town) Muskogee County	3	2.33
Ringling, OK (town) Jefferson County	26	2.29
Ratliff City, OK (town) Carter County	3	2.29
Velma, OK (town) Stephens County	15	2.26
Cole, OK (town) McClain County	10	2.11
Millstone, PA (township) Elk County	2	2.11
Meridian, OK (cdp) Stephens County	30	2.02
Calera, OK (town) Bryan County	35	2.01
Carney, OK (town) Lincoln County	13	2.00
Loco, OK (town) Stephens County	3	2.00
Colbert, OK (town) Bryan County	21	1.97
Durant, OK (city) Bryan County	263	1.94
Alderson, OK (town) Pittsburg County	5	1.92
Asher, OK (town) Pottawatomie County	8	1.91
Wynnewood, OK (city) Garvin County	45	1.90
Red Oak, OK (town) Latimer County	11	1.89
Newcastle, OK (city) McClain County	101	1.86
Comanche, OK (city) Stephens County	29	1.86
Pinhook Corners, OK (cdp) Sequoyah County	3	1.86
Longstreet, LA (village) De Soto Parish	3	1.84
Purcell, OK (city) McClain County	101	1.81
Marlow, OK (city) Stephens County	77	1.68
Goldsby, OK (town) McClain County	20	1.66
Wilson, OK (city) Carter County	26	1.64
Peru, KS (city) Chautauqua County	3	1.64
Chattanooga, OK (town) Comanche County	7	1.62
Big Creek, MS (village) Calhoun County	2	1.57
Krebs, OK (city) Pittsburg County	31	1.51
Blanchard, OK (city) McClain County	42	1.49
Thackerville, OK (town) Love County	6	1.49
Wanette, OK (town) Pottawatomie County	6	1.49
Yeager, OK (town) Hughes County	1	1.49
Chewey, OK (cdp) Adair County	2	1.48
Gotebo, OK (town) Kiowa County	4	1.47
Tribbey, OK (town) Pottawatomie County	4	1.47
Martha, OK (town) Jackson County	3	1.46
South Naknek, AK (cdp) Bristol Bay Borough	2	1.46
Slaughterville, OK (town) Cleveland County	52	1.44
Kiowa, OK (town) Pittsburg County	10	1.44
Arcadia, OK (town) Oklahoma County	4	1.43
Konawa, OK (city) Seminole County	21	1.42
Peoria, OK (town) Ottawa County	2	1.42
Atoka, OK (city) Atoka County	42	1.41
Maysville, OK (town) Garvin County	18	1.37
Oden, AR (town) Montgomery County	3	1.36
Lima, OK (town) Seminole County	1	1.35
Rosser, TX (village) Kaufman County	5	1.32
Whitefield, OK (town) Haskell County	4	1.30
Lehigh, OK (city) Coal County	4	1.27
Bray, OK (town) Stephens County	13	1.26
Alex, OK (town) Grady County	8	1.26
Bokchito, OK (town) Bryan County	7	1.24
Pink, OK (town) Pottawatomie County	14	1.20
Yale, OK (city) Payne County	16	1.19
Haswell, CO (town) Kiowa County	1	1.19
Grandfield, OK (city) Tillman County	13	1.17
Caddo, OK (town) Bryan County	11	1.17
Athens, LA (village) Claiborne Parish	3	1.15
Agra, OK (town) Lincoln County	4	1.12
Richland, NE (village) Colfax County	1	1.12
Bokoshe, OK (town) Le Flore County	5	1.11
Long, OK (cdp) Sequoyah County	4	1.10
Paoli, OK (town) Garvin County	7	1.08
Bowlegs, OK (town) Seminole County	4	1.08
Tecumseh, OK (city) Pottawatomie County	65	1.07
Indiahoma, OK (town) Comanche County	4	1.07
Pittsburg, OK (town) Pittsburg County	3	1.07
Adona, AR (town) Perry County	2	1.07
Elmore City, OK (town) Garvin County	8	1.06
Bellevue, TX (city) Clay County	4	1.04
Kenefic, OK (town) Bryan County	2	1.04
Ashland, LA (village) Natchitoches Parish	3	1.03
Bethel Acres, OK (town) Pottawatomie County	28	1.02
Wainwright, OK (town) Muskogee County	2	1.02
Ninnekah, OK (town) Grady County	10	1.02
Haileyville, OK (city) Pittsburg County	9	1.01
Abercrombie, ND (city) Richland County	3	1.01
Caney, OK (town) Atoka County	2	1.01
Latty, OH (village) Paulding County	2	1.00
Gerty, OK (town) Hughes County	1	0.99
Warner, OK (town) Muskogee County	14	0.98
Tipton, OK (town) Tillman County	9	0.98
Wayne, OK (town) McClain County	7	0.98
Texline, TX (town) Dallam County	5	0.98
Maud, OK (city) Pottawatomie County	11	0.97
Byers, TX (city) Clay County	5	0.97
Gould, OK (town) Harmon County	2	0.97
Benedict, KS (city) Wilson County	1	0.97
Grand Falls Plaza, MO (town) Newton County	1	0.96
Hartshorne, OK (city) Pittsburg County	20	0.95
Duncan, OK (city) Stephens County	211	0.94
Wright City, OK (town) McCurtain County	8	0.94
Wynona, OK (town) Osage County	5	0.94

Notes: (cdp) census designated place; Refer to the Explanation of Data in the front of the book for more detailed information.

American Indian: Chickasaw

Top 150 Places Sorted by Percent

(Based on places with populations of 10,000 or more)

Place	Number	%
Ada, OK (city) Pontotoc County	1,189	7.58
Ardmore, OK (city) Carter County	978	4.12
Durant, OK (city) Bryan County	263	1.94
Duncan, OK (city) Stephens County	211	0.94
Moore, OK (city) Cleveland County	300	0.73
McAlester, OK (city) Pittsburg County	116	0.65
Norman, OK (city) Cleveland County	577	0.60
Mustang, OK (city) Canadian County	76	0.58
Midwest City, OK (city) Oklahoma County	270	0.50
Shawnee, OK (city) Pottawatomie County	144	0.50
Chickasha, OK (city) Grady County	76	0.48
Del City, OK (city) Oklahoma County	95	0.43
Oklahoma City, OK (city) Oklahoma County	1,949	0.39
Edmond, OK (city) Oklahoma County	230	0.34
Bethany, OK (city) Oklahoma County	67	0.33
Denison, TX (city) Grayson County	71	0.31
Okmulgee, OK (city) Okmulgee County	40	0.31
Burkburnett, TX (city) Wichita County	32	0.29
Sand Springs, OK (city) Tulsa County	49	0.28
Elk City, OK (city) Beckham County	29	0.28
The Village, OK (city) Oklahoma County	28	0.28
Claremore, OK (city) Rogers County	43	0.27
Gainesville, TX (city) Cooke County	39	0.25
Muskogee, OK (city) Muskogee County	89	0.23
Sapulpa, OK (city) Creek County	44	0.23
Yukon, OK (city) Canadian County	47	0.22
Tahlequah, OK (city) Cherokee County	32	0.22
Owasso, OK (city) Tulsa County	39	0.21
El Reno, OK (city) Canadian County	34	0.21
Stillwater, OK (city) Payne County	75	0.19
Bartlesville, OK (city) Washington County	67	0.19
Ponca City, OK (city) Kay County	49	0.19
Woodward, OK (city) Woodward County	21	0.18
Lawton, OK (city) Comanche County	158	0.17
Broken Arrow, OK (city) Tulsa County	122	0.16
Sherman, TX (city) Grayson County	57	0.16
Enid, OK (city) Garfield County	68	0.14
Altus, OK (city) Jackson County	26	0.12
Bostonia, CA (cdp) San Diego County	18	0.12
Mohave Valley, AZ (cdp) Mohave County	16	0.12
Tulsa, OK (city) Tulsa County	444	0.11
Wylie, TX (city) Collin County	16	0.11
Miami, OK (city) Ottawa County	14	0.10
Arkansas City, KS (city) Cowley County	12	0.10
Mineral Wells, TX (city) Palo Pinto County	16	0.09
Pampa, TX (city) Gray County	16	0.09
Borger, TX (city) Hutchinson County	13	0.09
Bixby, OK (city) Tulsa County	12	0.09
Fortuna, CA (city) Humboldt County	9	0.09
Wichita Falls, TX (city) Wichita County	81	0.08
Oildale, CA (cdp) Kern County	23	0.08
McMinnville, OR (city) Yamhill County	20	0.08
The Colony, TX (city) Denton County	20	0.08
Derby, KS (city) Sedgwick County	14	0.08
Bellaire, TX (city) Harris County	13	0.08
McKinleyville, CA (cdp) Humboldt County	11	0.08
Levelland, TX (city) Hockley County	10	0.08
North Richland Hills, TX (city) Tarrant County	37	0.07
Frisco, TX (city) Collin County	22	0.07
Florin, CA (cdp) Sacramento County	20	0.07
Farmers Branch, TX (city) Dallas County	19	0.07
Burleson, TX (city) Johnson County	15	0.07
West Odessa, TX (cdp) Ector County	13	0.07
Yucca Valley, CA (town) San Bernardino County	11	0.07
New Kingman-Butler, AZ (cdp) Mohave County	10	0.07
Portland, TX (city) San Patricio County	10	0.07
Athens, TX (city) Henderson County	8	0.07
Snyder, TX (city) Scurry County	8	0.07
Dishman, WA (cdp) Spokane County	7	0.07
Denton, TX (city) Denton County	48	0.06
Lewisville, TX (city) Denton County	46	0.06
Grapevine, TX (city) Tarrant County	24	0.06
Hurst, TX (city) Tarrant County	20	0.06
Banning, CA (city) Riverside County	14	0.06
Ramona, CA (cdp) San Diego County	10	0.06
Dixon, CA (city) Solano County	9	0.06
Riverbank, CA (city) Stanislaus County	9	0.06
Alpine, CA (cdp) San Diego County	8	0.06
Beaumont, CA (city) Riverside County	7	0.06
El Sobrante, CA (cdp) Contra Costa County	7	0.06
Fort Knox, KY (cdp) Hardin County	7	0.06
Marysville, CA (city) Yuba County	7	0.06
Prairie Ridge, WA (cdp) Pierce County	7	0.06
McKinney, TX (city) Collin County	29	0.05
Allen, TX (city) Collin County	23	0.05
Haltom City, TX (city) Tarrant County	20	0.05
Ceres, CA (city) Stanislaus County	19	0.05
Hobbs, NM (city) Lea County	14	0.05
Keller, TX (city) Tarrant County	14	0.05
Russellville, AR (city) Pope County	11	0.05
Barstow, CA (city) San Bernardino County	10	0.05
Southlake, TX (city) Tarrant County	10	0.05
Watauga, TX (city) Tarrant County	10	0.05
Balch Springs, TX (city) Dallas County	9	0.05
Mira Loma, CA (cdp) Riverside County	9	0.05
Selma, CA (city) Fresno County	9	0.05
River Ridge, LA (cdp) Jefferson Parish	8	0.05
Twentynine Palms, CA (city) San Bernardino County	8	0.05
Brushy Creek, TX (cdp) Williamson County	7	0.05
Canon City, CO (city) Fremont County	7	0.05
Carpinteria, CA (city) Santa Barbara County	7	0.05
Ledyard, CT (town) New London County	7	0.05
Welby, CO (cdp) Adams County	7	0.05
College, AK (cdp) Fairbanks North Star Borough	6	0.05
Harrison, AR (city) Boone County	6	0.05
Vienna, MI (township) Genesee County	6	0.05
Fort Carson, CO (cdp) El Paso County	5	0.05
Siloam Springs, AR (city) Benton County	5	0.05
View Park-Windsor Hills, CA (cdp) Los Angeles County	5	0.05
Wichita, KS (city) Sedgwick County	130	0.04
Garland, TX (city) Dallas County	85	0.04
Irving, TX (city) Dallas County	79	0.04
Modesto, CA (city) Stanislaus County	73	0.04
Amarillo, TX (city) Potter County	61	0.04
Grand Prairie, TX (city) Dallas County	53	0.04
Mesquite, TX (city) Dallas County	53	0.04
Lawrence, KS (city) Douglas County	36	0.04
Odessa, TX (city) Ector County	34	0.04
Antioch, CA (city) Contra Costa County	32	0.04
Citrus Heights, CA (city) Sacramento County	31	0.04
Clovis, CA (city) Fresno County	28	0.04
Longview, TX (city) Gregg County	27	0.04
Bedford, TX (city) Tarrant County	21	0.04
Martinez, CA (city) Contra Costa County	13	0.04
Big Spring, TX (city) Howard County	11	0.04
Deer Park, TX (city) Harris County	11	0.04
Dodge City, KS (city) Ford County	11	0.04
Fairbanks, AK (city) Fairbanks North Star Borough	11	0.04
Friendswood, TX (city) Galveston County	11	0.04
Grants Pass, OR (city) Josephine County	9	0.04
Plainview, TX (city) Hale County	9	0.04
Benbrook, TX (city) Tarrant County	8	0.04
Colleyville, TX (city) Tarrant County	8	0.04
Pinole, CA (city) Contra Costa County	8	0.04
Tualatin, OR (city) Washington County	8	0.04
Van Buren, AR (city) Crawford County	8	0.04
Waxahachie, TX (city) Ellis County	8	0.04
Bentonville, AR (city) Benton County	7	0.04
Canyon Lake, TX (cdp) Comal County	7	0.04
Orinda, CA (city) Contra Costa County	7	0.04
Rockwall, TX (city) Rockwall County	7	0.04
Aberdeen, WA (city) Grays Harbor County	6	0.04
Glen Avon, CA (cdp) Riverside County	6	0.04
Pueblo West, CO (cdp) Pueblo County	6	0.04
Beecher, MI (cdp) Genesee County	5	0.04
Clearlake, CA (city) Lake County	5	0.04
Corinth, TX (city) Denton County	5	0.04
Dallas, OR (city) Polk County	5	0.04
Galion, OH (city) Crawford County	5	0.04
Kaneohe Station, HI (cdp) Honolulu County	5	0.04

Notes: (cdp) census designated place; Refer to the Explanation of Data in the front of the book for more detailed information.

American Indian: Chippewa

Top 150 Places Sorted by Number

(Based on all places, regardless of population)

Place	Number	%
Minneapolis, MN (city) Hennepin County	5,154	1.35
Sault Sainte Marie, MI (city) Chippewa County	2,257	13.64
Belcourt, ND (cdp) Rolette County	2,134	87.46
Saint Paul, MN (city) Ramsey County	1,675	0.58
Duluth, MN (city) Saint Louis County	1,637	1.88
Lac du Flambeau, WI (town) Vilas County	1,541	51.30
Milwaukee, WI (city) Milwaukee County	1,493	0.25
Red Lake, MN (cdp) Beltrami County	1,317	92.10
Bemidji, MN (city) Beltrami County	1,111	9.32
Sanborn, WI (town) Ashland County	1,020	80.19
Little Rock, MN (cdp) Beltrami County	1,008	95.55
Cloquet, MN (city) Carlton County	954	8.52
Redby, MN (cdp) Beltrami County	903	94.36
Pike Bay, MN (township) Cass County	903	54.96
Russell, WI (town) Bayfield County	850	69.90
Grand Forks, ND (city) Grand Forks County	848	1.72
Ponemah, MN (cdp) Beltrami County	840	96.11
Bass Lake, WI (town) Sawyer County	773	34.45
Little Round Lake, WI (cdp) Sawyer County	757	79.85
Hayward, WI (town) Sawyer County	676	20.62
Twin Lakes, MN (township) Mahnomen County	656	77.45
Kathio, MN (township) Mille Lacs County	647	49.43
Chicago, IL (city) Cook County	636	0.02
Kinross charter, MI (township) Chippewa County	609	10.28
Saint Ignace, MI (city) Mackinac County	607	22.67
Chippewa, MI (township) Isabella County	603	13.06
Bay Mills, MI (township) Chippewa County	601	49.51
Fargo, ND (city) Cass County	589	0.65
Minot, ND (city) Ward County	583	1.59
Ten Lake, MN (township) Beltrami County	559	55.62
Portland, OR (city) Multnomah County	539	0.10
Ashland, WI (city) Ashland County	531	6.16
Vineland, MN (cdp) Mille Lacs County	528	86.99
Cass Lake, MN (city) Cass County	507	58.95
Baraga, MI (township) Baraga County	494	13.95
Superior, WI (city) Douglas County	491	1.79
L'Anse, MI (township) Baraga County	479	12.20
Suttons Bay, MI (township) Leelanau County	478	16.03
Naytahwaush, MN (cdp) Mahnomen County	474	81.30
Great Falls, MT (city) Cascade County	470	0.83
Dunseith, ND (city) Rolette County	462	62.52
Spokane, WA (city) Spokane County	444	0.23
Grand Rapids, MI (city) Kent County	422	0.21
Chief Lake, WI (cdp) Sawyer County	412	65.92
Phoenix, AZ (city) Maricopa County	408	0.03
Detroit, MI (city) Wayne County	407	0.04
Lansing, MI (city) Ingham County	399	0.33
Rolla, ND (city) Rolette County	375	26.46
Los Angeles, CA (city) Los Angeles County	372	0.01
Shell Valley, ND (cdp) Rolette County	370	93.67
Williston, ND (city) Williams County	361	2.89
White Earth, MN (township) Becker County	355	44.43
Flint, MI (city) Genesee County	355	0.28
Bismarck, ND (city) Burleigh County	352	0.63
Tacoma, WA (city) Pierce County	351	0.18
Seattle, WA (city) King County	347	0.06
Coon Rapids, MN (city) Anoka County	342	0.56
Billings, MT (city) Yellowstone County	342	0.38
Soo, MI (township) Chippewa County	317	11.95
Moorhead, MN (city) Clay County	317	0.99
Marquette, MI (city) Marquette County	306	1.56
Baraga, MI (village) Baraga County	299	23.27
Nashville, WI (town) Forest County	294	25.41
Green Bay, WI (city) Brown County	293	0.29
Detroit Lakes, MN (city) Becker County	290	3.95
Reserve, WI (cdp) Sawyer County	283	64.91
Mount Pleasant, MI (city) Isabella County	283	1.09
Anchorage, AK (municipality) Anchorage Borough	282	0.11
Superior, MI (township) Chippewa County	279	20.99
Blaine, MN (city) Anoka County	276	0.61
Union charter, MI (township) Isabella County	275	3.61
Mahnomen, MN (city) Mahnomen County	274	22.80
Brooklyn Park, MN (city) Hennepin County	268	0.40
Saint Ignace, MI (township) Mackinac County	261	25.49
Saint Cloud, MN (city) Stearns County	256	0.43
San Diego, CA (city) San Diego County	253	0.02
Columbia Heights, MN (city) Anoka County	249	1.34
Bruce, MI (township) Chippewa County	237	12.22
Clark, MI (township) Mackinac County	235	10.68
Odanah, WI (cdp) Ashland County	233	91.73
Hunter, WI (town) Sawyer County	232	30.33
Manistique, MI (city) Schoolcraft County	223	6.22
Escanaba, MI (city) Delta County	222	1.69
Albuquerque, NM (city) Bernalillo County	222	0.05
Devils Lake, ND (city) Ramsey County	220	3.05
Cheboygan, MI (city) Cheboygan County	218	4.12
Pine Point, MN (township) Becker County	215	51.31
Shingobee, MN (township) Cass County	214	12.26
Watersmeet, MI (township) Gogebic County	213	14.47
Sugar Island, MI (township) Chippewa County	212	31.04
Brevator, MN (township) Saint Louis County	212	17.29
Bay City, MI (city) Bay County	206	0.56
Sacramento, CA (city) Sacramento County	203	0.05
East Dunseith, ND (cdp) Rolette County	200	91.32
Saint John, ND (city) Rolette County	200	55.87
New Post, WI (cdp) Sawyer County	200	54.50
La Prairie, MN (township) Clearwater County	199	53.64
Couderay, WI (town) Sawyer County	199	42.43
Eau Claire, WI (city) Eau Claire County	199	0.32
Moran, MI (township) Mackinac County	198	18.33
Denver, CO (city) Denver County	198	0.04
Fridley, MN (city) Anoka County	195	0.71
New York, NY (city) New York City	194	0.00
Warren, MI (city) Macomb County	193	0.14
Perch Lake, MN (township) Carlton County	192	19.24
Madison, WI (city) Dane County	192	0.09
Northern, MN (township) Beltrami County	190	4.73
Turtle Lake, MN (township) Cass County	186	26.61
Saginaw, MI (city) Saginaw County	182	0.29
Bloomington, MN (city) Hennepin County	181	0.21
Westland, MI (city) Wayne County	176	0.20
Bemidji, MN (township) Beltrami County	175	5.96
McMillan, MI (township) Luce County	172	4.36
Virginia, MN (city) Saint Louis County	171	1.87
Chocolay, MI (township) Marquette County	169	2.36
Munising, MI (township) Alger County	164	5.25
Everett, WA (city) Snohomish County	162	0.18
Brainerd, MN (city) Crow Wing County	161	1.22
San Jose, CA (city) Santa Clara County	160	0.02
Maple Grove, MN (township) Becker County	159	39.26
Colorado Springs, CO (city) El Paso County	158	0.04
Havre, MT (city) Hill County	157	1.63
Grand Rapids, MN (township) Itasca County	157	1.34
Tucson, AZ (city) Pima County	157	0.03
Mandan, ND (city) Morton County	156	0.93
West Allis, WI (city) Milwaukee County	156	0.25
Wyoming, MI (city) Kent County	152	0.22
Garfield, MI (township) Mackinac County	151	12.07
Brooklyn Center, MN (city) Hennepin County	151	0.52
Kenosha, WI (city) Kenosha County	150	0.17
Dafter, MI (township) Chippewa County	148	11.35
Salem, OR (city) Marion County	146	0.11
Richfield, MN (city) Hennepin County	145	0.42
Waterford, MI (cdp) Oakland County	145	0.20
International Falls, MN (city) Koochiching County	144	2.15
Port Huron, MI (city) Saint Clair County	143	0.44
Swiss, WI (town) Burnett County	138	16.93
Las Vegas, NV (city) Clark County	138	0.03
Manistique, MI (township) Schoolcraft County	137	13.01
Saint Louis Park, MN (city) Hennepin County	136	0.31
Little Elbow, MN (township) Mahnomen County	135	60.00
Helena, MT (city) Lewis and Clark County	135	0.52
Ogema, MN (township) Pine County	134	44.97
Crystal, MN (city) Hennepin County	133	0.59
Burnsville, MN (city) Dakota County	133	0.22
San Francisco, CA (city) San Francisco County	129	0.02
Greenwood, MN (township) Saint Louis County	127	14.03
Taylor, MI (city) Wayne County	127	0.19
Gresham, OR (city) Multnomah County	125	0.14
Pentland, MI (township) Luce County	124	6.94

Notes: (cdp) census designated place; Refer to the Explanation of Data in the front of the book for more detailed information.

American Indian: Chippewa

Top 150 Places Sorted by Percent

(Based on all places, regardless of population)

Place	Number	%
Ponemah, MN (cdp) Beltrami County	840	96.11
Little Rock, MN (cdp) Beltrami County	1,008	95.55
Redby, MN (cdp) Beltrami County	903	94.36
Shell Valley, ND (cdp) Rolette County	370	93.67
Red Lake, MN (cdp) Beltrami County	1,317	92.10
Odanah, WI (cdp) Ashland County	233	91.73
East Dunseith, ND (cdp) Rolette County	200	91.32
Belcourt, ND (cdp) Rolette County	2,134	87.46
Vineland, MN (cdp) Mille Lacs County	528	86.99
Naytahwaush, MN (cdp) Mahnomen County	474	81.30
Sanborn, WI (town) Ashland County	1,020	80.19
Little Round Lake, WI (cdp) Sawyer County	757	79.85
Twin Lakes, MN (township) Mahnomen County	656	77.45
Elbow Lake, MN (cdp) Becker County	77	74.04
Russell, WI (town) Bayfield County	850	69.90
Chief Lake, WI (cdp) Sawyer County	412	65.92
Reserve, WI (cdp) Sawyer County	283	64.91
Squaw Lake, MN (city) Itasca County	62	62.63
Dunseith, ND (city) Rolette County	462	62.52
Eagle View, MN (township) Becker County	101	61.21
Little Elbow, MN (township) Mahnomen County	135	60.00
Cass Lake, MN (city) Cass County	507	58.95
Bena, MN (city) Cass County	64	58.18
Saint John, ND (city) Rolette County	200	55.87
Ten Lake, MN (township) Beltrami County	559	55.62
Pike Bay, MN (township) Cass County	903	54.96
New Post, WI (cdp) Sawyer County	200	54.50
La Prairie, MN (township) Clearwater County	199	53.64
Pine Point, MN (township) Becker County	215	51.31
Lac du Flambeau, WI (town) Vilas County	1,541	51.30
Bay Mills, MI (township) Chippewa County	601	49.51
Kathio, MN (township) Mille Lacs County	647	49.43
Gould, MN (township) Cass County	123	49.40
Ogema, MN (township) Pine County	134	44.97
White Earth, MN (township) Becker County	355	44.43
Couderay, WI (town) Sawyer County	199	42.43
Round Lake, MN (township) Becker County	66	42.04
Clover, MN (township) Mahnomen County	51	41.46
Maple Grove, MN (township) Becker County	159	39.26
Spalding, MN (township) Aitkin County	89	37.55
Bass Lake, WI (town) Sawyer County	773	34.45
Sugar Island, MI (township) Chippewa County	212	31.04
Hunter, WI (town) Sawyer County	232	30.33
Hudson, MI (township) Mackinac County	62	28.97
Island Lake, MN (township) Mahnomen County	61	27.98
Waubun, MN (city) Mahnomen County	110	27.30
Turtle Lake, MN (township) Cass County	186	26.61
Ogema, MN (city) Becker County	38	26.57
Rolla, ND (city) Rolette County	375	26.46
Wilkinson, MN (township) Cass County	71	26.30
Max, MN (township) Itasca County	41	26.28
Beaulieu, MN (township) Mahnomen County	28	25.93
Saint Ignace, MI (township) Mackinac County	261	25.49
Nashville, WI (town) Forest County	294	25.41
Callaway, MN (city) Becker County	49	24.50
Baraga, MI (village) Baraga County	299	23.27
Mahnomen, MN (city) Mahnomen County	274	22.80
Federal Dam, MN (city) Cass County	23	22.77
Saint Ignace, MI (city) Mackinac County	607	22.67
Falk, MN (township) Clearwater County	58	22.22
Rolette, ND (city) Rolette County	119	22.12
Sugar Bush, MN (township) Becker County	115	21.42
Sugar Bush, MN (township) Beltrami County	41	21.24
Superior, MI (township) Chippewa County	279	20.99
Sand Lake, WI (town) Burnett County	115	20.68
Hayward, WI (town) Sawyer County	676	20.62
La Garde, MN (township) Mahnomen County	28	20.44
Oakland, MN (township) Mahnomen County	53	20.38
Mackinac Island, MI (city) Mackinac County	106	20.27
Stoney Brook, MN (township) Saint Louis County	52	19.55
Perch Lake, MN (township) Carlton County	192	19.24
Leech Lake, MN (township) Cass County	73	19.01
Leiding, MN (township) Saint Louis County	85	18.81
Bayfield, WI (city) Bayfield County	114	18.66
Bayfield, WI (town) Bayfield County	116	18.56
Moran, MI (township) Mackinac County	198	18.33
Johnstown, WI (town) Polk County	95	18.27
Good Hope, MN (township) Itasca County	14	17.72
Couderay, WI (village) Sawyer County	17	17.71
Brevator, MN (township) Saint Louis County	212	17.29
Swiss, WI (town) Burnett County	138	16.93
Popple Grove, MN (township) Mahnomen County	25	16.23
Pembina, MN (township) Mahnomen County	76	16.14
Suttons Bay, MI (township) Leelanau County	478	16.03
Sarles, ND (city) Cavalier County	4	16.00
Boy Lake, MN (township) Cass County	21	15.91
Brevort, MI (township) Mackinac County	100	15.41
Callaway, MN (township) Becker County	39	15.00
Bejou, MN (city) Mahnomen County	14	14.89
Warwick, ND (city) Benson County	11	14.67
Watersmeet, MI (township) Gogebic County	213	14.47
Chief, MN (township) Mahnomen County	19	14.39
Sand Lake, WI (town) Sawyer County	109	14.08
Greenwood, MN (township) Saint Louis County	127	14.03
Baraga, MI (township) Baraga County	494	13.95
Sault Sainte Marie, MI (city) Chippewa County	2,257	13.64
Carsonville, MN (township) Becker County	34	13.49
Maple Plain, WI (town) Barron County	116	13.24
La Follette, WI (town) Burnett County	67	13.11
Hendricks, MI (township) Mackinac County	24	13.11
Chippewa, MI (township) Isabella County	603	13.06
Manistique, MI (township) Schoolcraft County	137	13.01
Arna, MN (township) Pine County	11	12.79
Pillsbury, ND (city) Barnes County	3	12.50
Shingobee, MN (township) Cass County	214	12.26
Kego, MN (township) Cass County	57	12.26
Brookston, MN (city) Saint Louis County	12	12.24
Bruce, MI (township) Chippewa County	237	12.22
L'Anse, MI (township) Baraga County	479	12.20
Garfield, MI (township) Mackinac County	151	12.07
Soo, MI (township) Chippewa County	317	11.95
Lake Grove, MN (township) Mahnomen County	24	11.82
Mizpah, MN (city) Koochiching County	9	11.54
Dafter, MI (township) Chippewa County	148	11.35
Rice, MN (township) Clearwater County	15	11.19
De Tour Village, MI (village) Chippewa County	47	11.16
Turner, MN (township) Aitkin County	16	11.11
Heier, MN (township) Mahnomen County	17	11.04
Clark, MI (township) Mackinac County	235	10.68
Zemple, MN (city) Itasca County	8	10.67
Orr, MN (city) Saint Louis County	26	10.44
Detour, MI (township) Chippewa County	93	10.40
Hart Lake, MN (township) Hubbard County	48	10.30
Kinross charter, MI (township) Chippewa County	609	10.28
Egeland, ND (city) Towner County	5	10.20
Boy River, MN (township) Cass County	10	10.00
Thompson, MI (township) Schoolcraft County	67	9.99
Eckles, MN (township) Beltrami County	102	9.87
Deer River, MN (city) Itasca County	87	9.63
Garden, MI (village) Delta County	23	9.58
Pine Lake, MN (township) Cass County	16	9.41
Bemidji, MN (city) Beltrami County	1,111	9.32
Perley, MN (city) Norman County	11	9.09
Exeland, WI (village) Sawyer County	19	8.96
Oteneagen, MN (township) Itasca County	22	8.94
Clover, MN (township) Clearwater County	10	8.62
Strand, MN (township) Norman County	11	8.53
Cloquet, MN (city) Carlton County	954	8.52
Georgetown, WI (town) Polk County	85	8.47
Farden, MN (township) Hubbard County	84	8.45
Bagley, MN (city) Clearwater County	103	8.34
Walhalla, ND (city) Pembina County	88	8.33
Spring Creek, MN (township) Becker County	10	8.33
Dewey, WI (town) Burnett County	47	8.32
Isle, MN (city) Mille Lacs County	58	8.20
Park, MN (township) Pine County	3	8.11
Mutual, OK (town) Woodward County	6	7.89
Borup, MN (city) Norman County	7	7.69
Rudyard, MI (township) Chippewa County	101	7.68
Barry, MN (township) Pine County	45	7.67

Notes: (cdp) census designated place; Refer to the Explanation of Data in the front of the book for more detailed information.

American Indian: Chippewa

Top 150 Places Sorted by Percent

(Based on places with populations of 10,000 or more)

Place	Number	%
Sault Sainte Marie, MI (city) Chippewa County	2,257	13.64
Bemidji, MN (city) Beltrami County	1,111	9.32
Cloquet, MN (city) Carlton County	954	8.52
Williston, ND (city) Williams County	361	2.89
Duluth, MN (city) Saint Louis County	1,637	1.88
Superior, WI (city) Douglas County	491	1.79
Grand Forks, ND (city) Grand Forks County	848	1.72
Escanaba, MI (city) Delta County	222	1.69
Minot, ND (city) Ward County	583	1.59
Marquette, MI (city) Marquette County	306	1.56
Minneapolis, MN (city) Hennepin County	5,154	1.35
Columbia Heights, MN (city) Anoka County	249	1.34
Grand Rapids, MN (township) Itasca County	157	1.34
Brainerd, MN (city) Crow Wing County	161	1.22
Mount Pleasant, MI (city) Isabella County	283	1.09
Moorhead, MN (city) Clay County	317	0.99
Mandan, ND (city) Morton County	156	0.93
Garfield, MI (township) Grand Traverse County	118	0.85
Great Falls, MT (city) Cascade County	470	0.83
Traverse City, MI (city) Grand Traverse County	111	0.76
West Fargo, ND (city) Cass County	110	0.74
Fridley, MN (city) Anoka County	195	0.71
Mounds View, MN (city) Ramsey County	87	0.68
Fargo, ND (city) Cass County	589	0.65
Bismarck, ND (city) Burleigh County	352	0.63
Hibbing, MN (city) Saint Louis County	105	0.62
Blaine, MN (city) Anoka County	276	0.61
Anoka, MN (city) Anoka County	111	0.61
Crystal, MN (city) Hennepin County	133	0.59
Saint Paul, MN (city) Ramsey County	1,675	0.58
Coon Rapids, MN (city) Anoka County	342	0.56
Bay City, MI (city) Bay County	206	0.56
Brooklyn Center, MN (city) Hennepin County	151	0.52
Helena, MT (city) Lewis and Clark County	135	0.52
Lino Lakes, MN (city) Anoka County	87	0.52
Fergus Falls, MN (city) Otter Tail County	70	0.52
Bridgeport charter, MI (township) Saginaw County	55	0.47
Ramsey, MN (city) Anoka County	85	0.46
Hopkins, MN (city) Hennepin County	77	0.45
Robbinsdale, MN (city) Hennepin County	63	0.45
Port Huron, MI (city) Saint Clair County	143	0.44
Prior Lake, MN (city) Scott County	70	0.44
Jamestown, ND (city) Stutsman County	69	0.44
Saint Cloud, MN (city) Stearns County	256	0.43
Bangor, MI (township) Bay County	67	0.43
Richfield, MN (city) Hennepin County	145	0.42
New Brighton, MN (city) Ramsey County	94	0.42
Cudahy, WI (city) Milwaukee County	78	0.42
Pierre, SD (city) Hughes County	57	0.41
Buffalo, MN (city) Wright County	41	0.41
Brooklyn Park, MN (city) Hennepin County	268	0.40
East Bethel, MN (city) Anoka County	44	0.40
North Saint Paul, MN (city) Ramsey County	47	0.39
Billings, MT (city) Yellowstone County	342	0.38
Cadillac, MI (city) Wexford County	38	0.38
Genesee, MI (township) Genesee County	90	0.37
South Milwaukee, WI (city) Milwaukee County	78	0.37
Ham Lake, MN (city) Anoka County	47	0.37
Marinette, WI (city) Marinette County	43	0.37
Dishman, WA (cdp) Spokane County	37	0.37
Aberdeen, SD (city) Brown County	88	0.36
Champlin, MN (city) Hennepin County	80	0.36
Buena Vista charter, MI (township) Saginaw County	37	0.36
Andover, MN (city) Anoka County	94	0.35
South Saint Paul, MN (city) Dakota County	71	0.35
Hazel Park, MI (city) Oakland County	66	0.35
De Witt, MI (township) Clinton County	43	0.35
Alpena, MI (city) Alpena County	40	0.35
Ionia, MI (city) Ionia County	37	0.35
Shakopee, MN (city) Scott County	70	0.34
Holt, MI (cdp) Ingham County	38	0.34
Lansing, MI (city) Ingham County	399	0.33
Butte-Silver Bow, MT (special city) Silver Bow County	112	0.33
Monitor, MI (township) Bay County	33	0.33
Eau Claire, WI (city) Eau Claire County	199	0.32
Elk River, MN (city) Sherburne County	52	0.32
Saint Louis Park, MN (city) Hennepin County	136	0.31
Flint, MI (township) Genesee County	104	0.31
Green Oak, MI (township) Livingston County	49	0.31
Comstock Park, MI (cdp) Kent County	33	0.31
Delhi charter, MI (township) Ingham County	68	0.30
Faribault, MN (city) Rice County	62	0.30
Grand Haven, MI (township) Ottawa County	40	0.30
Green Bay, WI (city) Brown County	293	0.29
Saginaw, MI (city) Saginaw County	182	0.29
Maplewood, MN (city) Ramsey County	102	0.29
White Lake, MI (township) Oakland County	82	0.29
Mount Morris, MI (township) Genesee County	68	0.29
New Hope, MN (city) Hennepin County	60	0.29
Mount Clemens, MI (city) Macomb County	50	0.29
Kelso, WA (city) Cowlitz County	34	0.29
Big Rapids, MI (city) Mecosta County	32	0.29
Flint, MI (city) Genesee County	355	0.28
Midland, MI (city) Midland County	118	0.28
Oak Creek, WI (city) Milwaukee County	79	0.28
Davison, MI (township) Genesee County	50	0.28
Red Wing, MN (city) Goodhue County	45	0.28
Vienna, MI (township) Genesee County	37	0.28
Beecher, MI (cdp) Genesee County	36	0.28
Flushing, MI (township) Genesee County	29	0.28
Cottage Grove, MN (city) Washington County	83	0.27
Burton, MI (city) Genesee County	81	0.27
Springfield, MI (township) Oakland County	36	0.27
Chippewa Falls, WI (city) Chippewa County	35	0.27
Inver Grove Heights, MN (city) Dakota County	77	0.26
Wyandotte, MI (city) Wayne County	73	0.26
Ferndale, MI (city) Oakland County	58	0.26
Golden Valley, MN (city) Hennepin County	52	0.26
Alpine, MI (township) Kent County	36	0.26
Milwaukee, WI (city) Milwaukee County	1,493	0.25
West Allis, WI (city) Milwaukee County	156	0.25
Oakdale, MN (city) Washington County	67	0.25
Shoreview, MN (city) Ramsey County	65	0.25
Aberdeen, WA (city) Grays Harbor County	41	0.25
Fenton, MI (township) Genesee County	33	0.25
Spring Lake, MI (township) Ottawa County	33	0.25
Wixom, MI (city) Oakland County	33	0.25
Maple Grove, MN (city) Hennepin County	120	0.24
White Bear Lake, MN (city) Ramsey County	59	0.24
Norton Shores, MI (city) Muskegon County	53	0.24
West Saint Paul, MN (city) Dakota County	47	0.24
Wayne, MI (city) Wayne County	46	0.24
Oxford charter, MI (township) Oakland County	39	0.24
Huron charter, MI (township) Wayne County	34	0.24
Vadnais Heights, MN (city) Ramsey County	32	0.24
Hutchinson, MN (city) McLeod County	31	0.24
Spokane, WA (city) Spokane County	444	0.23
Muskegon, MI (city) Muskegon County	94	0.23
Muskegon, MI (township) Muskegon County	41	0.23
Howard, WI (village) Brown County	31	0.23
Muskegon Heights, MI (city) Muskegon County	28	0.23
Haslett, MI (cdp) Ingham County	26	0.23
Lyon, MI (township) Oakland County	25	0.23
Fenton, MI (city) Genesee County	24	0.23
South Lyon, MI (city) Oakland County	23	0.23
Wyoming, MI (city) Kent County	152	0.22
Burnsville, MN (city) Dakota County	133	0.22
Saginaw Township North, MI (cdp) Saginaw County	54	0.22
Stillwater, MN (city) Washington County	34	0.22
Kalispell, MT (city) Flathead County	32	0.22
Riverton-Boulevard Park, WA (cdp) King County	25	0.22
Antwerp, MI (township) Van Buren County	24	0.22
Grand Rapids, MI (city) Kent County	422	0.21
Bloomington, MN (city) Hennepin County	181	0.21
Missoula, MT (city) Missoula County	120	0.21
Lakeville, MN (city) Dakota County	89	0.21
Wausau, WI (city) Marathon County	81	0.21
Delta charter, MI (township) Eaton County	61	0.21
Trenton, MI (city) Wayne County	41	0.21
Elk Plain, WA (cdp) Pierce County	33	0.21

Notes: (cdp) census designated place; Refer to the Explanation of Data in the front of the book for more detailed information.

American Indian: Choctaw

Top 150 Places Sorted by Number

(Based on all places, regardless of population)

Place	Number	%
Oklahoma City, OK (city) Oklahoma County	5,576	1.10
Tulsa, OK (city) Tulsa County	2,595	0.66
Pearl River, MS (cdp) Neshoba County	2,438	77.25
McAlester, OK (city) Pittsburg County	1,422	8.00
Durant, OK (city) Bryan County	1,411	10.41
Ardmore, OK (city) Carter County	1,294	5.46
Norman, OK (city) Cleveland County	1,285	1.34
Dallas, TX (city) Dallas County	1,112	0.09
Los Angeles, CA (city) Los Angeles County	1,003	0.03
Ada, OK (city) Pontotoc County	837	5.33
Broken Bow, OK (city) McCurtain County	770	18.20
Hugo, OK (city) Choctaw County	757	13.67
Conehatta, MS (cdp) Newton County	729	73.12
Idabel, OK (city) McCurtain County	721	10.37
Moore, OK (city) Cleveland County	717	1.74
Houston, TX (city) Harris County	662	0.03
Midwest City, OK (city) Oklahoma County	652	1.21
Poteau, OK (city) Le Flore County	563	7.09
Phoenix, AZ (city) Maricopa County	561	0.04
Edmond, OK (city) Oklahoma County	554	0.81
Muskogee, OK (city) Muskogee County	511	1.33
Duncan, OK (city) Stephens County	496	2.20
San Diego, CA (city) San Diego County	495	0.04
Wichita, KS (city) Sedgwick County	489	0.14
Tucker, MS (cdp) Neshoba County	485	90.82
Bogue Chitto, MS (cdp) Neshoba County	472	88.56
Fort Worth, TX (city) Tarrant County	470	0.09
Fort Smith, AR (city) Sebastian County	455	0.57
Broken Arrow, OK (city) Tulsa County	441	0.59
Bakersfield, CA (city) Kern County	439	0.18
Lawton, OK (city) Comanche County	424	0.46
Standing Pine, MS (cdp) Leake County	414	81.34
San Antonio, TX (city) Bexar County	411	0.04
Wilburton, OK (city) Latimer County	410	13.80
Chicago, IL (city) Cook County	401	0.01
Arlington, TX (city) Tarrant County	390	0.12
Modesto, CA (city) Stanislaus County	383	0.20
Shawnee, OK (city) Pottawatomie County	382	1.33
Antlers, OK (city) Pushmataha County	375	14.69
Sacramento, CA (city) Sacramento County	373	0.09
San Jose, CA (city) Santa Clara County	370	0.04
Austin, TX (city) Travis County	366	0.06
Talihina, OK (town) Le Flore County	361	29.81
Hartshorne, OK (city) Pittsburg County	355	16.89
Fresno, CA (city) Fresno County	353	0.08
Wright City, OK (town) McCurtain County	332	39.15
Stigler, OK (city) Haskell County	326	11.94
Garland, TX (city) Dallas County	324	0.15
Albuquerque, NM (city) Bernalillo County	323	0.07
Redwater, MS (cdp) Leake County	314	76.77
Portland, OR (city) Multnomah County	311	0.06
Stillwater, OK (city) Payne County	308	0.79
Coalgate, OK (city) Coal County	306	15.26
Anchorage, AK (municipality) Anchorage Borough	302	0.12
Heavener, OK (city) Le Flore County	300	9.37
Sulphur, OK (city) Murray County	294	6.13
Amarillo, TX (city) Potter County	283	0.16
Wichita Falls, TX (city) Wichita County	281	0.27
Atoka, OK (city) Atoka County	279	9.34
Del City, OK (city) Oklahoma County	275	1.24
Denison, TX (city) Grayson County	275	1.21
Irving, TX (city) Dallas County	265	0.14
Oakland, CA (city) Alameda County	260	0.07
Mesquite, TX (city) Dallas County	257	0.21
Sherman, TX (city) Grayson County	255	0.73
New York, NY (city) New York City	255	0.00
Pauls Valley, OK (city) Garvin County	251	4.01
Chickasha, OK (city) Grady County	236	1.49
Lone Grove, OK (city) Carter County	235	5.07
Long Beach, CA (city) Los Angeles County	232	0.05
Krebs, OK (city) Pittsburg County	231	11.26
Zwolle, LA (town) Sabine Parish	230	12.90
San Francisco, CA (city) San Francisco County	225	0.03
Tahlequah, OK (city) Cherokee County	224	1.55
Plano, TX (city) Collin County	222	0.10
Mustang, OK (city) Canadian County	218	1.66
Denver, CO (city) Denver County	215	0.04
Paris, TX (city) Lamar County	212	0.82
Grand Prairie, TX (city) Dallas County	212	0.17
Colorado Springs, CO (city) El Paso County	208	0.06
Purcell, OK (city) McClain County	200	3.59
Kansas City, MO (city) Jackson County	200	0.05
Tucson, AZ (city) Pima County	198	0.04
Las Vegas, NV (city) Clark County	195	0.04
Mesa, AZ (city) Maricopa County	193	0.05
Detroit, MI (city) Wayne County	192	0.02
Seattle, WA (city) King County	190	0.03
Yukon, OK (city) Canadian County	189	0.90
Lawrence, KS (city) Douglas County	187	0.23
Bethany, OK (city) Oklahoma County	186	0.92
Sand Springs, OK (city) Tulsa County	184	1.05
Calera, OK (town) Bryan County	182	10.47
Enid, OK (city) Garfield County	181	0.38
Lubbock, TX (city) Lubbock County	179	0.09
Stockton, CA (city) San Joaquin County	177	0.07
New Orleans, LA (city) Orleans Parish	174	0.04
Memphis, TN (city) Shelby County	171	0.03
Bartlesville, OK (city) Washington County	169	0.49
Pocola, OK (town) Le Flore County	168	4.21
Shreveport, LA (city) Caddo Parish	168	0.08
Visalia, CA (city) Tulare County	162	0.18
Spiro, OK (town) Le Flore County	160	7.18
Marlow, OK (city) Stephens County	160	3.48
Choctaw, OK (city) Oklahoma County	159	1.70
Sapulpa, OK (city) Creek County	157	0.82
Huntington Beach, CA (city) Orange County	156	0.08
Okmulgee, OK (city) Okmulgee County	155	1.19
Quinton, OK (town) Pittsburg County	152	14.19
San Buenaventura, CA (city) Ventura County	149	0.15
Bixby, OK (city) Tulsa County	148	1.11
Haileyville, OK (city) Pittsburg County	147	16.50
San Bernardino, CA (city) San Bernardino County	145	0.08
Boswell, OK (town) Choctaw County	144	20.48
Seminole, OK (city) Seminole County	143	2.07
Tishomingo, OK (city) Johnston County	141	4.46
Claremore, OK (city) Rogers County	141	0.89
Philadelphia, MS (city) Neshoba County	135	1.85
Redding, CA (city) Shasta County	134	0.17
Mobile, AL (city) Mobile County	134	0.07
Tacoma, WA (city) Pierce County	134	0.07
Caddo, OK (town) Bryan County	133	14.09
Henderson, NV (city) Clark County	133	0.08
Aurora, CO (city) Arapahoe County	133	0.05
Riverside, CA (city) Riverside County	133	0.05
Madill, OK (city) Marshall County	132	3.87
El Reno, OK (city) Canadian County	131	0.81
Jacksonville, FL (special city) Duval County	131	0.02
Nashville-Davidson, TN (special city) Davidson County	130	0.02
Red Oak, OK (town) Latimer County	127	21.86
Antioch, CA (city) Contra Costa County	127	0.14
Clayton, OK (town) Pushmataha County	124	17.25
Corpus Christi, TX (city) Nueces County	122	0.04
Noble, OK (city) Cleveland County	121	2.30
Davis, OK (city) Murray County	120	4.60
Glendale, AZ (city) Maricopa County	118	0.05
Lancaster, CA (city) Los Angeles County	116	0.10
Vallejo, CA (city) Solano County	116	0.10
Fremont, CA (city) Alameda County	116	0.06
Newcastle, OK (city) McClain County	114	2.10
Ponca City, OK (city) Kay County	114	0.44
Salem, OR (city) Marion County	113	0.08
Lewisville, TX (city) Denton County	112	0.14
Carrollton, TX (city) Denton County	112	0.10
Honolulu, HI (cdp) Honolulu County	112	0.03
El Paso, TX (city) El Paso County	111	0.02
Holdenville, OK (city) Hughes County	109	2.30
Richardson, TX (city) Dallas County	108	0.12
Concord, CA (city) Contra Costa County	108	0.09
Anadarko, OK (city) Caddo County	107	1.61
Springfield, MO (city) Greene County	107	0.07

Notes: (cdp) census designated place; Refer to the Explanation of Data in the front of the book for more detailed information.

American Indian: Choctaw

Top 150 Places Sorted by Percent

(Based on all places, regardless of population)

Place	Number	%
Tucker, MS (cdp) Neshoba County	485	90.82
Bogue Chitto, MS (cdp) Neshoba County	472	88.56
Standing Pine, MS (cdp) Leake County	414	81.34
Pearl River, MS (cdp) Neshoba County	2,438	77.25
Redwater, MS (cdp) Leake County	314	76.77
Conehatta, MS (cdp) Newton County	729	73.12
Wright City, OK (town) McCurtain County	332	39.15
Bennington, OK (town) Bryan County	101	34.95
Talihina, OK (town) Le Flore County	361	29.81
Smithville, OK (town) McCurtain County	35	28.46
Armstrong, OK (town) Bryan County	38	26.95
Le Flore, OK (town) Le Flore County	40	23.81
Pittsburg, OK (town) Pittsburg County	64	22.86
Ashland, OK (town) Pittsburg County	12	22.64
Red Oak, OK (town) Latimer County	127	21.86
Phillips, OK (town) Coal County	32	21.33
Noble, LA (village) Sabine Parish	54	20.85
Soper, OK (town) Choctaw County	62	20.67
Boswell, OK (town) Choctaw County	144	20.48
Tushka, OK (town) Atoka County	68	19.71
Tupelo, OK (city) Coal County	69	18.30
Broken Bow, OK (city) McCurtain County	770	18.20
Quail, TX (cdp) Collingsworth County	6	18.18
Clayton, OK (town) Pushmataha County	124	17.25
Hartshorne, OK (city) Pittsburg County	355	16.89
Haileyville, OK (city) Pittsburg County	147	16.50
Bokchito, OK (town) Bryan County	91	16.13
Bokoshe, OK (town) Le Flore County	69	15.33
Coalgate, OK (city) Coal County	306	15.26
Fanshawe, OK (town) Le Flore County	58	15.10
Millerton, OK (town) McCurtain County	53	14.76
Antlers, OK (city) Pushmataha County	375	14.69
Sawyer, OK (town) Choctaw County	40	14.60
Kenefic, OK (town) Bryan County	28	14.58
Lehigh, OK (city) Coal County	45	14.29
Quinton, OK (town) Pittsburg County	152	14.19
Rattan, OK (town) Pushmataha County	34	14.11
Caddo, OK (town) Bryan County	133	14.09
Wilburton, OK (city) Latimer County	410	13.80
Hugo, OK (city) Choctaw County	757	13.67
Centrahoma, OK (city) Coal County	15	13.64
Alderson, OK (town) Pittsburg County	35	13.41
Achille, OK (town) Bryan County	67	13.24
Kemp, OK (town) Bryan County	19	13.19
Zwolle, LA (town) Sabine Parish	230	12.90
Caney, OK (town) Atoka County	25	12.56
Meadow Lark Lake, WY (cdp) Big Horn County	1	12.50
Stuart, OK (town) Hughes County	27	12.27
Bromide, OK (town) Johnston County	20	12.27
Stigler, OK (city) Haskell County	326	11.94
Krebs, OK (city) Pittsburg County	231	11.26
McCurtain, OK (town) Haskell County	52	11.16
Silo, OK (town) Bryan County	31	10.99
Wapanucka, OK (town) Johnston County	47	10.56
Calera, OK (town) Bryan County	182	10.47
Durant, OK (city) Bryan County	1,411	10.41
Kiowa, OK (town) Pittsburg County	72	10.39
Idabel, OK (city) McCurtain County	721	10.37
Gerty, OK (town) Hughes County	10	9.90
Scottsville, KS (city) Mitchell County	2	9.52
Keota, OK (town) Haskell County	49	9.48
Kinta, OK (town) Haskell County	23	9.47
Leon, OK (town) Love County	9	9.38
Heavener, OK (city) Le Flore County	300	9.37
Atoka, OK (city) Atoka County	279	9.34
Howe, OK (town) Le Flore County	64	9.18
Valliant, OK (town) McCurtain County	69	8.95
Canadian, OK (town) Pittsburg County	21	8.79
Wister, OK (town) Le Flore County	85	8.48
Francis, OK (town) Pontotoc County	28	8.43
Stringtown, OK (town) Atoka County	33	8.33
Zion, OK (cdp) Adair County	4	8.33
Mead, OK (town) Bryan County	10	8.13
Savanna, OK (town) Pittsburg County	59	8.08
Tamaha, OK (town) Haskell County	16	8.08

Place	Number	%
McAlester, OK (city) Pittsburg County	1,422	8.00
Panama, OK (town) Le Flore County	106	7.78
Allen, OK (town) Pontotoc County	72	7.57
Calvin, OK (town) Hughes County	21	7.53
Whitefield, OK (town) Haskell County	17	7.36
Haworth, OK (town) McCurtain County	26	7.34
Spiro, OK (town) Le Flore County	160	7.18
Maysville, OK (town) Garvin County	94	7.16
Strong City, OK (town) Roger Mills County	3	7.14
Poteau, OK (city) Le Flore County	563	7.09
Mill Creek, OK (town) Johnston County	24	7.06
Cameron, OK (town) Le Flore County	22	7.05
Cowlington, OK (town) Le Flore County	9	6.77
Shady Point, OK (town) Le Flore County	56	6.60
Stratford, OK (town) Garvin County	96	6.51
Stonewall, OK (town) Pontotoc County	30	6.45
Fitzhugh, OK (town) Pontotoc County	13	6.37
Dickson, OK (town) Carter County	72	6.32
Albion, OK (town) Pushmataha County	9	6.29
Sulphur, OK (city) Murray County	294	6.13
Mannsville, OK (town) Johnston County	36	6.13
Rock Island, OK (town) Le Flore County	43	6.06
Swink, OK (town) Choctaw County	5	6.02
Converse, LA (village) Sabine Parish	24	6.00
Meridian, OK (cdp) Stephens County	88	5.93
Tatums, OK (town) Carter County	10	5.81
Wainwright, OK (town) Muskogee County	11	5.58
Fort Towson, OK (town) Choctaw County	34	5.56
Ben Lomond, AR (town) Sevier County	7	5.56
Ardmore, OK (city) Carter County	1,294	5.46
Ada, OK (city) Pontotoc County	837	5.33
Alex, OK (town) Grady County	33	5.20
Byng, OK (town) Pontotoc County	56	5.14
Lone Grove, OK (city) Carter County	235	5.07
Dougherty, OK (town) Murray County	11	4.91
Wayne, OK (town) McClain County	35	4.90
Oakland, OK (town) Marshall County	33	4.90
Garvin, OK (town) McCurtain County	7	4.90
Velma, OK (town) Stephens County	32	4.82
Rush Springs, OK (town) Grady County	61	4.77
Roff, OK (town) Pontotoc County	35	4.77
Deer Creek, OK (town) Grant County	7	4.76
Indianola, OK (town) Pittsburg County	9	4.71
Saint Joe, AR (town) Searcy County	4	4.71
Davis, OK (city) Murray County	120	4.60
Hickory, OK (town) Murray County	4	4.60
Stony Point, OK (cdp) Sequoyah County	8	4.52
Ringling, OK (town) Jefferson County	51	4.49
Tishomingo, OK (city) Johnston County	141	4.46
Kingston, OK (town) Marshall County	61	4.39
Latham, KS (city) Butler County	7	4.27
Texola, OK (town) Beckham County	2	4.26
Pocola, OK (town) Le Flore County	168	4.21
River Bottom, OK (cdp) Muskogee County	11	4.15
Ravia, OK (town) Johnston County	19	4.14
Comanche, OK (city) Stephens County	64	4.11
Cornish, OK (town) Jefferson County	7	4.07
Zena, OK (cdp) Delaware County	5	4.07
Asher, OK (town) Pottawatomie County	17	4.06
Colbert, OK (town) Bryan County	43	4.04
Chester, AR (town) Crawford County	4	4.04
Kaw City, OK (city) Kay County	15	4.03
Pauls Valley, OK (city) Garvin County	251	4.01
Wynnewood, OK (city) Garvin County	94	3.97
Byars, OK (town) McClain County	11	3.93
Rentiesville, OK (town) McIntosh County	4	3.92
Council Hill, OK (town) Muskogee County	5	3.88
Madill, OK (city) Marshall County	132	3.87
Wilson, OK (city) Carter County	61	3.85
Bradley, OK (town) Grady County	7	3.85
Marble City Community, OK (cdp) Sequoyah County	16	3.81
Hendrix, OK (town) Bryan County	3	3.80
Pleasant Hill, LA (village) Sabine Parish	29	3.69
Fort Coffee, OK (town) Le Flore County	15	3.64
Kendrick, OK (town) Lincoln County	5	3.62

Notes: (cdp) census designated place; Refer to the Explanation of Data in the front of the book for more detailed information.

American Indian: Choctaw

Top 150 Places Sorted by Percent

(Based on places with populations of 10,000 or more)

Place	Number	%
Durant, OK (city) Bryan County	1,411	10.41
McAlester, OK (city) Pittsburg County	1,422	8.00
Ardmore, OK (city) Carter County	1,294	5.46
Ada, OK (city) Pontotoc County	837	5.33
Duncan, OK (city) Stephens County	496	2.20
Moore, OK (city) Cleveland County	717	1.74
Mustang, OK (city) Canadian County	218	1.66
Tahlequah, OK (city) Cherokee County	224	1.55
Chickasha, OK (city) Grady County	236	1.49
Norman, OK (city) Cleveland County	1,285	1.34
Muskogee, OK (city) Muskogee County	511	1.33
Shawnee, OK (city) Pottawatomie County	382	1.33
Del City, OK (city) Oklahoma County	275	1.24
Midwest City, OK (city) Oklahoma County	652	1.21
Denison, TX (city) Grayson County	275	1.21
Okmulgee, OK (city) Okmulgee County	155	1.19
Bixby, OK (city) Tulsa County	148	1.11
Oklahoma City, OK (city) Oklahoma County	5,576	1.10
Sand Springs, OK (city) Tulsa County	184	1.05
Bethany, OK (city) Oklahoma County	186	0.92
The Village, OK (city) Oklahoma County	93	0.92
Yukon, OK (city) Canadian County	189	0.90
Claremore, OK (city) Rogers County	141	0.89
Paris, TX (city) Lamar County	212	0.82
Sapulpa, OK (city) Creek County	157	0.82
Edmond, OK (city) Oklahoma County	554	0.81
El Reno, OK (city) Canadian County	131	0.81
Stillwater, OK (city) Payne County	308	0.79
Sherman, TX (city) Grayson County	255	0.73
Olivehurst, CA (cdp) Yuba County	76	0.69
Tulsa, OK (city) Tulsa County	2,595	0.66
Broken Arrow, OK (city) Tulsa County	441	0.59
Fort Smith, AR (city) Sebastian County	455	0.57
Elk City, OK (city) Beckham County	57	0.54
Owasso, OK (city) Tulsa County	98	0.53
Miami, OK (city) Ottawa County	70	0.51
Bartlesville, OK (city) Washington County	169	0.49
Lawton, OK (city) Comanche County	424	0.46
Van Buren, AR (city) Crawford County	86	0.45
Burkburnett, TX (city) Wichita County	49	0.45
Ponca City, OK (city) Kay County	114	0.44
Woodward, OK (city) Woodward County	51	0.43
Altus, OK (city) Jackson County	87	0.41
Enid, OK (city) Garfield County	181	0.38
Chowchilla, CA (city) Madera County	40	0.36
Balch Springs, TX (city) Dallas County	68	0.35
Clearlake, CA (city) Lake County	45	0.34
Borger, TX (city) Hutchinson County	47	0.33
Oildale, CA (cdp) Kern County	86	0.31
The Colony, TX (city) Denton County	81	0.31
White Settlement, TX (city) Tarrant County	43	0.29
Siloam Springs, AR (city) Benton County	31	0.29
Wylie, TX (city) Collin County	43	0.28
Wichita Falls, TX (city) Wichita County	281	0.27
Ceres, CA (city) Stanislaus County	95	0.27
Oroville, CA (city) Butte County	35	0.27
Corinth, TX (city) Denton County	31	0.27
Pampa, TX (city) Gray County	46	0.26
McKinleyville, CA (cdp) Humboldt County	36	0.26
Linda, CA (cdp) Yuba County	35	0.26
Dumas, TX (city) Moore County	35	0.25
Mount Pleasant, TX (city) Titus County	35	0.25
Fortuna, CA (city) Humboldt County	26	0.25
Gainesville, TX (city) Cooke County	37	0.24
Saraland, AL (city) Mobile County	30	0.24
Coalinga, CA (city) Fresno County	28	0.24
Lawrence, KS (city) Douglas County	187	0.23
Guymon, OK (city) Texas County	24	0.23
Picayune, MS (city) Pearl River County	23	0.22
Mesquite, TX (city) Dallas County	257	0.21
Hurst, TX (city) Tarrant County	76	0.21
Texarkana, AR (city) Miller County	56	0.21
Riverbank, CA (city) Stanislaus County	33	0.21
Vernon, TX (city) Wilbarger County	25	0.21
La Riviera, CA (cdp) Sacramento County	22	0.21
Modesto, CA (city) Stanislaus County	383	0.20
Eureka, CA (city) Humboldt County	51	0.20
Benbrook, TX (city) Tarrant County	40	0.20
Red Bluff, CA (city) Tehama County	26	0.20
Rio Linda, CA (cdp) Sacramento County	21	0.20
Casa Grande, AZ (city) Pinal County	48	0.19
Watauga, TX (city) Tarrant County	42	0.19
Bay Point, CA (cdp) Contra Costa County	40	0.19
Sulphur Springs, TX (city) Hopkins County	27	0.19
Dallas, OR (city) Polk County	24	0.19
Coffeyville, KS (city) Montgomery County	21	0.19
Bakersfield, CA (city) Kern County	439	0.18
Visalia, CA (city) Tulare County	162	0.18
Bossier City, LA (city) Bossier Parish	99	0.18
Rowlett, TX (city) Dallas County	82	0.18
Tulare, CA (city) Tulare County	79	0.18
Bentonville, AR (city) Benton County	36	0.18
Tillmans Corner, AL (cdp) Mobile County	28	0.18
Arkansas City, KS (city) Cowley County	22	0.18
Kelso, WA (city) Cowlitz County	21	0.18
Kilgore, TX (city) Gregg County	20	0.18
Vineyard, CA (cdp) Sacramento County	18	0.18
Grand Prairie, TX (city) Dallas County	212	0.17
Redding, CA (city) Shasta County	134	0.17
North Richland Hills, TX (city) Tarrant County	97	0.17
Allen, TX (city) Collin County	76	0.17
Haltom City, TX (city) Tarrant County	66	0.17
Liberal, KS (city) Seward County	33	0.17
Weatherford, TX (city) Parker County	33	0.17
Rosamond, CA (cdp) Kern County	25	0.17
La Marque, TX (city) Galveston County	23	0.17
Amarillo, TX (city) Potter County	283	0.16
Duncanville, TX (city) Dallas County	59	0.16
Oakley, CA (city) Contra Costa County	42	0.16
Paradise, CA (town) Butte County	42	0.16
Banning, CA (city) Riverside County	37	0.16
Benton, AR (city) Saline County	36	0.16
Oakdale, CA (city) Stanislaus County	25	0.16
New Kingman-Butler, AZ (cdp) Mohave County	23	0.16
Gautier, MS (city) Jackson County	19	0.16
College, AK (cdp) Fairbanks North Star Borough	18	0.16
Lake Los Angeles, CA (cdp) Los Angeles County	18	0.16
Morro Bay, CA (city) San Luis Obispo County	17	0.16
Ripon, CA (city) San Joaquin County	16	0.16
Garland, TX (city) Dallas County	324	0.15
San Buenaventura, CA (city) Ventura County	149	0.15
McKinney, TX (city) Collin County	79	0.15
Manteca, CA (city) San Joaquin County	74	0.15
Orcutt, CA (cdp) Santa Barbara County	43	0.15
Farmers Branch, TX (city) Dallas County	41	0.15
Mira Loma, CA (cdp) Riverside County	26	0.15
Arcata, CA (city) Humboldt County	25	0.15
Marysville, CA (city) Yuba County	18	0.15
Mountain Home, AR (city) Baxter County	17	0.15
Grass Valley, CA (city) Nevada County	16	0.15
Seagoville, TX (city) Dallas County	16	0.15
Wichita, KS (city) Sedgwick County	489	0.14
Irving, TX (city) Dallas County	265	0.14
Antioch, CA (city) Contra Costa County	127	0.14
Lewisville, TX (city) Denton County	112	0.14
Clovis, CA (city) Fresno County	93	0.14
Fayetteville, AR (city) Washington County	84	0.14
Rancho Cordova, CA (cdp) Sacramento County	75	0.14
Springfield, OR (city) Lane County	74	0.14
Grapevine, TX (city) Tarrant County	57	0.14
Martinez, CA (city) Contra Costa County	49	0.14
Deer Park, TX (city) Harris County	40	0.14
Lancaster, TX (city) Dallas County	36	0.14
Lemoore, CA (city) Kings County	28	0.14
Pinole, CA (city) Contra Costa County	27	0.14
Foothill Farms, CA (cdp) Sacramento County	25	0.14
Natchitoches, LA (city) Natchitoches Parish	25	0.14
Long Beach, MS (city) Harrison County	24	0.14
Durango, CO (city) La Plata County	20	0.14
Susanville, CA (city) Lassen County	19	0.14

Notes: (cdp) census designated place; Refer to the Explanation of Data in the front of the book for more detailed information.

American Indian: Colville

Top 150 Places Sorted by Number

(Based on all places, regardless of population)

Place	Number	%
Omak, WA (city) Okanogan County	613	12.98
North Omak, WA (cdp) Okanogan County	442	64.24
Spokane, WA (city) Spokane County	394	0.20
Coulee Dam, WA (town) Okanogan County	276	26.44
Inchelium, WA (cdp) Ferry County	262	67.35
Nespelem Community, WA (cdp) Okanogan County	240	82.76
Okanogan, WA (city) Okanogan County	176	7.09
Nespelem, WA (town) Okanogan County	154	72.64
Seattle, WA (city) King County	126	0.02
Tacoma, WA (city) Pierce County	93	0.05
Elmer City, WA (town) Okanogan County	85	31.84
Grand Coulee, WA (city) Grant County	74	8.25
Portland, OR (city) Multnomah County	53	0.01
Electric City, WA (town) Grant County	50	5.42
Yakima, WA (city) Yakima County	48	0.07
Wenatchee, WA (city) Chelan County	46	0.17
Colville, WA (city) Stevens County	44	0.88
Toppenish, WA (city) Yakima County	43	0.48
Auburn, WA (city) King County	40	0.10
Plummer, ID (city) Benewah County	38	3.84
Opportunity, WA (cdp) Spokane County	36	0.14
Oroville, WA (city) Okanogan County	32	1.94
Phoenix, AZ (city) Maricopa County	32	0.00
Kent, WA (city) King County	30	0.04
Kettle Falls, WA (city) Stevens County	27	1.77
Dishman, WA (cdp) Spokane County	26	0.26
White Swan, WA (cdp) Yakima County	25	0.82
Cheney, WA (city) Spokane County	24	0.27
East Wenatchee Bench, WA (cdp) Douglas County	23	0.17
Los Angeles, CA (city) Los Angeles County	22	0.00
Olympia, WA (city) Thurston County	21	0.05
Vancouver, WA (city) Clark County	21	0.01
Everett, WA (city) Snohomish County	20	0.02
Anchorage, AK (municipality) Anchorage Borough	20	0.01
Spanaway, WA (cdp) Pierce County	19	0.09
Lakewood, WA (city) Pierce County	18	0.03
Pullman, WA (city) Whitman County	17	0.07
Puyallup, WA (city) Pierce County	17	0.05
Lapwai, ID (city) Nez Perce County	15	1.32
Bridgeport, WA (city) Douglas County	15	0.73
Brewster, WA (city) Okanogan County	15	0.69
Shoreline, WA (city) King County	13	0.02
Albuquerque, NM (city) Bernalillo County	13	0.00
San Jose, CA (city) Santa Clara County	13	0.00
Chewelah, WA (city) Stevens County	12	0.55
Moses Lake North, WA (cdp) Grant County	12	0.28
Union Gap, WA (city) Yakima County	12	0.21
Bremerton, WA (city) Kitsap County	12	0.03
Eugene, OR (city) Lane County	12	0.01
Riverside, WA (town) Okanogan County	11	3.16
Skokomish, WA (cdp) Mason County	11	1.79
Wilbur, WA (town) Lincoln County	11	1.20
Republic, WA (city) Ferry County	11	1.15
Hoquiam, WA (city) Grays Harbor County	11	0.12
Ellensburg, WA (city) Kittitas County	11	0.07
Lewiston, ID (city) Nez Perce County	11	0.04
Cascade Valley, WA (cdp) Grant County	10	0.55
South Wenatchee, WA (cdp) Chelan County	10	0.50
Edgewood, WA (city) Pierce County	10	0.11
Prairie Ridge, WA (cdp) Pierce County	10	0.09
Alderwood Manor, WA (cdp) Snohomish County	10	0.07
Moses Lake, WA (city) Grant County	10	0.07
North Creek, WA (cdp) Snohomish County	10	0.04
Kirkland, WA (city) King County	10	0.02
Renton, WA (city) King County	10	0.02
Bellingham, WA (city) Whatcom County	10	0.01
Federal Way, WA (city) King County	10	0.01
Fife, WA (city) Pierce County	9	0.19
Faribault, MN (city) Rice County	9	0.04
Marysville, WA (city) Snohomish County	9	0.04
North Marysville, WA (cdp) Snohomish County	9	0.04
Coeur d'Alene, ID (city) Kootenai County	9	0.03
Juneau, AK (city and borough) Juneau Borough	9	0.03
Mount Vernon, WA (city) Skagit County	9	0.03
Long Beach, CA (city) Los Angeles County	9	0.00
Tulsa, OK (city) Tulsa County	9	0.00
Tulalip Bay, WA (cdp) Snohomish County	8	0.51
Warm Springs, OR (cdp) Jefferson County	8	0.33
Chelan, WA (city) Chelan County	8	0.23
East Wenatchee, WA (city) Douglas County	8	0.14
Tanglewilde-Thompson Place, WA (cdp) Thurston County	8	0.14
Otis Orchards-East Farms, WA (cdp) Spokane County	8	0.13
Clarkston, WA (city) Asotin County	8	0.11
Elk City, OK (city) Beckham County	8	0.08
Aberdeen, WA (city) Grays Harbor County	8	0.05
Inglewood-Finn Hill, WA (cdp) King County	8	0.04
Mountlake Terrace, WA (city) Snohomish County	8	0.04
Des Moines, WA (city) King County	8	0.03
Lynnwood, WA (city) Snohomish County	8	0.02
Pasco, WA (city) Franklin County	8	0.02
Gresham, OR (city) Multnomah County	8	0.01
Aurora, CO (city) Arapahoe County	8	0.00
Mission, OR (cdp) Umatilla County	7	0.69
Deer Park, WA (city) Spokane County	7	0.23
Airway Heights, WA (city) Spokane County	7	0.16
Redmond, OR (city) Deschutes County	7	0.05
Orchards, WA (cdp) Clark County	7	0.04
SeaTac, WA (city) King County	7	0.03
South Hill, WA (cdp) Pierce County	7	0.02
Walla Walla, WA (city) Walla Walla County	7	0.02
Bellevue, WA (city) King County	7	0.01
Kennewick, WA (city) Benton County	7	0.01
Lawrence, KS (city) Douglas County	7	0.01
Rancho Cucamonga, CA (city) San Bernardino County	7	0.01
Mesa, AZ (city) Maricopa County	7	0.00
Shaker Church, WA (cdp) Snohomish County	6	0.76
Ronan, MT (city) Lake County	6	0.33
Gleed, WA (cdp) Yakima County	6	0.20
Medical Lake, WA (city) Spokane County	6	0.16
Park Hill, OK (cdp) Cherokee County	6	0.15
Ivins, UT (town) Washington County	6	0.13
Town and Country, WA (cdp) Spokane County	6	0.13
Wapato, WA (city) Yakima County	6	0.13
Country Homes, WA (cdp) Spokane County	6	0.12
Quincy, WA (city) Grant County	6	0.12
Lakes, AK (cdp) Matanuska-Susitna Borough	6	0.09
Shelton, WA (city) Mason County	6	0.07
Pendleton, OR (city) Umatilla County	6	0.04
Picnic Point-North Lynnwood, WA (cdp) Snohomish County	6	0.03
Port Angeles, WA (city) Clallam County	6	0.03
Post Falls, ID (city) Kootenai County	6	0.03
Tukwila, WA (city) King County	6	0.03
Lacey, WA (city) Thurston County	6	0.02
Oregon City, OR (city) Clackamas County	6	0.02
Great Falls, MT (city) Cascade County	6	0.01
Tigard, OR (city) Washington County	6	0.01
Salem, OR (city) Marion County	6	0.00
Worley, ID (city) Kootenai County	5	2.24
Harrah, WA (town) Yakima County	5	0.92
Reardan, WA (town) Lincoln County	5	0.82
Rock Island, WA (city) Douglas County	5	0.58
Siletz, OR (city) Lincoln County	5	0.44
Alturas, CA (city) Modoc County	5	0.17
Soldotna, AK (city) Kenai Peninsula Borough	5	0.13
Liberty Lake, WA (cdp) Spokane County	5	0.11
Ephrata, WA (city) Grant County	5	0.07
Ferndale, WA (city) Whatcom County	5	0.06
Hartland, MI (township) Livingston County	5	0.05
Five Corners, WA (cdp) Clark County	5	0.04
Monroe, WA (city) Snohomish County	5	0.04
Forest Grove, OR (city) Washington County	5	0.03
Clearfield, UT (city) Davis County	5	0.02
Paine Field-Lake Stickney, WA (cdp) Snohomish County	5	0.02
Missoula, MT (city) Missoula County	5	0.01
Richland, WA (city) Benton County	5	0.01
Seattle Hill-Silver Firs, WA (cdp) Snohomish County	5	0.01
Bakersfield, CA (city) Kern County	5	0.00
Boise City, ID (city) Ada County	5	0.00
Fullerton, CA (city) Orange County	5	0.00
Modesto, CA (city) Stanislaus County	5	0.00

Notes: (cdp) census designated place; Refer to the Explanation of Data in the front of the book for more detailed information.

American Indian: Colville

Top 150 Places Sorted by Percent

(Based on all places, regardless of population)

Place	Number	%
Nespelem Community, WA (cdp) Okanogan County	240	82.76
Nespelem, WA (town) Okanogan County	154	72.64
Inchelium, WA (cdp) Ferry County	262	67.35
North Omak, WA (cdp) Okanogan County	442	64.24
Elmer City, WA (town) Okanogan County	85	31.84
Coulee Dam, WA (town) Okanogan County	276	26.44
Omak, WA (city) Okanogan County	613	12.98
Grand Coulee, WA (city) Grant County	74	8.25
Okanogan, WA (city) Okanogan County	176	7.09
Electric City, WA (town) Grant County	50	5.42
Plummer, ID (city) Benewah County	38	3.84
Riverside, WA (town) Okanogan County	11	3.16
Worley, ID (city) Kootenai County	5	2.24
Conconully, WA (town) Okanogan County	4	2.16
Oroville, WA (city) Okanogan County	32	1.94
Skokomish, WA (cdp) Mason County	11	1.79
Kettle Falls, WA (city) Stevens County	27	1.77
Lapwai, ID (city) Nez Perce County	15	1.32
Wilbur, WA (town) Lincoln County	11	1.20
Republic, WA (city) Ferry County	11	1.15
Almira, WA (town) Lincoln County	3	0.99
Rockport, WA (cdp) Skagit County	1	0.98
White Bird, ID (city) Idaho County	1	0.94
Harrah, WA (town) Yakima County	5	0.92
Colville, WA (city) Stevens County	44	0.88
Chehalis Village, WA (cdp) Grays Harbor County	3	0.87
Creston, WA (town) Lincoln County	2	0.86
Marcus, WA (town) Stevens County	1	0.85
White Swan, WA (cdp) Yakima County	25	0.82
Reardan, WA (town) Lincoln County	5	0.82
Shaker Church, WA (cdp) Snohomish County	6	0.76
Big Arm, MT (cdp) Lake County	1	0.76
Hartline, WA (town) Grant County	1	0.75
Bridgeport, WA (city) Douglas County	15	0.73
Thorp, WA (cdp) Kittitas County	2	0.73
Harrington, WA (city) Lincoln County	3	0.70
Brewster, WA (city) Okanogan County	15	0.69
Mission, OR (cdp) Umatilla County	7	0.69
Nisqually Indian Community, WA (cdp) Thurston County	4	0.68
Mansfield, WA (town) Douglas County	2	0.63
Metaline, WA (town) Pend Oreille County	1	0.62
Athol, ID (city) Kootenai County	4	0.59
Rock Island, WA (city) Douglas County	5	0.58
Hunter, OK (town) Garfield County	1	0.58
Chewelah, WA (city) Stevens County	12	0.55
Cascade Valley, WA (cdp) Grant County	10	0.55
Tulalip Bay, WA (cdp) Snohomish County	8	0.51
Touchet, WA (cdp) Walla Walla County	2	0.51
South Wenatchee, WA (cdp) Chelan County	10	0.50
Coulee City, WA (town) Grant County	3	0.50
Toppenish, WA (city) Yakima County	43	0.48
Deming, WA (cdp) Whatcom County	1	0.48
Malden, WA (town) Whitman County	1	0.47
Siletz, OR (city) Lincoln County	5	0.44
Stites, ID (city) Idaho County	1	0.44
Santa Ana Pueblo, NM (cdp) Sandoval County	2	0.42
Tonasket, WA (city) Okanogan County	4	0.40
Rolette, ND (city) Rolette County	2	0.37
Joseph, UT (town) Sevier County	1	0.37
Taholah, WA (cdp) Grays Harbor County	3	0.36
Clinton, WA (cdp) Island County	3	0.35
Nooksack, WA (city) Whatcom County	3	0.35
Morris, MN (township) Stevens County	2	0.35
Springdale, WA (town) Stevens County	1	0.35
Warm Springs, OR (cdp) Jefferson County	8	0.33
Ronan, MT (city) Lake County	6	0.33
Arlee, MT (cdp) Lake County	2	0.33
Entiat, WA (city) Chelan County	3	0.31
Odessa, WA (town) Lincoln County	3	0.31
Santa Clara Pueblo, NM (cdp) Rio Arriba County	3	0.31
Hauser, ID (city) Kootenai County	2	0.30
Buffalo Soapstone, AK (cdp) Matanuska-Susitna Borough	2	0.29
Moses Lake North, WA (cdp) Grant County	12	0.28
Cheney, WA (city) Spokane County	24	0.27
Simms, MT (cdp) Cascade County	1	0.27
Dishman, WA (cdp) Spokane County	26	0.26
Houston, AK (city) Matanuska-Susitna Borough	3	0.25
Neah Bay, WA (cdp) Clallam County	2	0.25
Gopher Flats, OR (cdp) Umatilla County	1	0.25
Black Rock, NM (cdp) McKinley County	3	0.24
Nixon, NV (cdp) Washoe County	1	0.24
Rockford, WA (town) Spokane County	1	0.24
Santa Cruz, NM (cdp) Santa Fe County	1	0.24
Chelan, WA (city) Chelan County	8	0.23
Deer Park, WA (city) Spokane County	7	0.23
Tutuilla, OR (cdp) Umatilla County	1	0.22
Union Gap, WA (city) Yakima County	12	0.21
Firestone, CO (town) Weld County	4	0.21
Twisp, WA (town) Okanogan County	2	0.21
North Stanwood, WA (cdp) Snohomish County	1	0.21
Spokane, WA (city) Spokane County	394	0.20
Gleed, WA (cdp) Yakima County	6	0.20
Fife, WA (city) Pierce County	9	0.19
Osburn, ID (city) Shoshone County	3	0.19
Gisela, AZ (cdp) Gila County	1	0.19
Nezperce, ID (city) Lewis County	1	0.19
Darrington, WA (town) Snohomish County	2	0.18
Lincoln, MT (cdp) Lewis and Clark County	2	0.18
Wenatchee, WA (city) Chelan County	46	0.17
East Wenatchee Bench, WA (cdp) Douglas County	23	0.17
Alturas, CA (city) Modoc County	5	0.17
Pablo, MT (cdp) Lake County	3	0.17
Sunnyside-Tahoe City, CA (cdp) Placer County	3	0.17
Homer, NE (village) Dakota County	1	0.17
Airway Heights, WA (city) Spokane County	7	0.16
Medical Lake, WA (city) Spokane County	6	0.16
Rockaway Beach, OR (city) Tillamook County	2	0.16
Moclips, WA (cdp) Grays Harbor County	1	0.16
Pateros, WA (city) Okanogan County	1	0.16
Park Hill, OK (cdp) Cherokee County	6	0.15
Lake Roesiger, WA (cdp) Snohomish County	1	0.15
Passamaquoddy Indian Twp. Res., ME (reservation) Washington Co.	1	0.15
Opportunity, WA (cdp) Spokane County	36	0.14
East Wenatchee, WA (city) Douglas County	8	0.14
Tanglewilde-Thompson Place, WA (cdp) Thurston County	8	0.14
Clyde Hill, WA (city) King County	4	0.14
North Eagle Butte, SD (cdp) Dewey County	3	0.14
Heart Butte, MT (cdp) Pondera County	1	0.14
Otis Orchards-East Farms, WA (cdp) Spokane County	8	0.13
Ivins, UT (town) Washington County	6	0.13
Town and Country, WA (cdp) Spokane County	6	0.13
Wapato, WA (city) Yakima County	6	0.13
Soldotna, AK (city) Kenai Peninsula Borough	5	0.13
Desert Shores, CA (cdp) Imperial County	1	0.13
Priest Point, WA (cdp) Snohomish County	1	0.13
Satus, WA (cdp) Yakima County	1	0.13
Hoquiam, WA (city) Grays Harbor County	11	0.12
Country Homes, WA (cdp) Spokane County	6	0.12
Quincy, WA (city) Grant County	6	0.12
Sultan, WA (city) Snohomish County	4	0.12
Bonner-West Riverside, MT (cdp) Missoula County	2	0.12
Hines, OR (city) Harney County	2	0.12
Snoqualmie, WA (city) King County	2	0.12
Soap Lake, WA (city) Grant County	2	0.12
Hoonah, AK (city) Skagway-Hoonah-Angoon Census Area	1	0.12
Edgewood, WA (city) Pierce County	10	0.11
Clarkston, WA (city) Asotin County	8	0.11
Liberty Lake, WA (cdp) Spokane County	5	0.11
Suquamish, WA (cdp) Kitsap County	4	0.11
Fort Totten, ND (cdp) Benson County	1	0.11
Poplar, MT (city) Roosevelt County	1	0.11
Weallup Lake, WA (cdp) Snohomish County	1	0.11
Auburn, WA (city) King County	40	0.10
Polson, MT (city) Lake County	4	0.10
Connell, WA (city) Franklin County	3	0.10
Y, AK (cdp) Matanuska-Susitna Borough	1	0.10
Spanaway, WA (cdp) Pierce County	19	0.09
Prairie Ridge, WA (cdp) Pierce County	10	0.09
Lakes, AK (cdp) Matanuska-Susitna Borough	6	0.09
Palmer, AK (city) Matanuska-Susitna Borough	4	0.09

Notes: (cdp) census designated place; Refer to the Explanation of Data in the front of the book for more detailed information.

American Indian: Colville

Top 150 Places Sorted by Percent

(Based on places with populations of 10,000 or more)

Place	Number	%
Dishman, WA (cdp) Spokane County	26	0.26
Spokane, WA (city) Spokane County	394	0.20
Wenatchee, WA (city) Chelan County	46	0.17
East Wenatchee Bench, WA (cdp) Douglas County	23	0.17
Opportunity, WA (cdp) Spokane County	36	0.14
Auburn, WA (city) King County	40	0.10
Spanaway, WA (cdp) Pierce County	19	0.09
Prairie Ridge, WA (cdp) Pierce County	10	0.09
Elk City, OK (city) Beckham County	8	0.08
Yakima, WA (city) Yakima County	48	0.07
Pullman, WA (city) Whitman County	17	0.07
Ellensburg, WA (city) Kittitas County	11	0.07
Alderwood Manor, WA (cdp) Snohomish County	10	0.07
Moses Lake, WA (city) Grant County	10	0.07
Tacoma, WA (city) Pierce County	93	0.05
Olympia, WA (city) Thurston County	21	0.05
Puyallup, WA (city) Pierce County	17	0.05
Aberdeen, WA (city) Grays Harbor County	8	0.05
Redmond, OR (city) Deschutes County	7	0.05
Hartland, MI (township) Livingston County	5	0.05
Kent, WA (city) King County	30	0.04
Lewiston, ID (city) Nez Perce County	11	0.04
North Creek, WA (cdp) Snohomish County	10	0.04
Faribault, MN (city) Rice County	9	0.04
Marysville, WA (city) Snohomish County	9	0.04
North Marysville, WA (cdp) Snohomish County	9	0.04
Inglewood-Finn Hill, WA (cdp) King County	8	0.04
Mountlake Terrace, WA (city) Snohomish County	8	0.04
Orchards, WA (cdp) Clark County	7	0.04
Pendleton, OR (city) Umatilla County	6	0.04
Five Corners, WA (cdp) Clark County	5	0.04
Monroe, WA (city) Snohomish County	5	0.04
Eagle, ID (city) Ada County	4	0.04
Lakewood, WA (city) Pierce County	18	0.03
Bremerton, WA (city) Kitsap County	12	0.03
Coeur d'Alene, ID (city) Kootenai County	9	0.03
Juneau, AK (city and borough) Juneau Borough	9	0.03
Mount Vernon, WA (city) Skagit County	9	0.03
Des Moines, WA (city) King County	8	0.03
SeaTac, WA (city) King County	7	0.03
Picnic Point-North Lynnwood, WA (cdp) Snohomish County	6	0.03
Port Angeles, WA (city) Clallam County	6	0.03
Post Falls, ID (city) Kootenai County	6	0.03
Tukwila, WA (city) King County	6	0.03
Forest Grove, OR (city) Washington County	5	0.03
Centralia, WA (city) Lewis County	4	0.03
Covington, WA (city) King County	4	0.03
Green River, WY (city) Sweetwater County	4	0.03
Kelso, WA (city) Cowlitz County	4	0.03
Linda, CA (cdp) Yuba County	4	0.03
Tumwater, WA (city) Thurston County	4	0.03
Lakeland South, WA (cdp) King County	3	0.03
Seattle, WA (city) King County	126	0.02
Everett, WA (city) Snohomish County	20	0.02
Shoreline, WA (city) King County	13	0.02
Kirkland, WA (city) King County	10	0.02
Renton, WA (city) King County	10	0.02
Lynnwood, WA (city) Snohomish County	8	0.02
Pasco, WA (city) Franklin County	8	0.02
South Hill, WA (cdp) Pierce County	7	0.02
Walla Walla, WA (city) Walla Walla County	7	0.02
Lacey, WA (city) Thurston County	6	0.02
Oregon City, OR (city) Clackamas County	6	0.02
Clearfield, UT (city) Davis County	5	0.02
Paine Field-Lake Stickney, WA (cdp) Snohomish County	5	0.02
Bainbridge Island, WA (city) Kitsap County	4	0.02
Kenmore, WA (city) King County	4	0.02
West Lake Stevens, WA (cdp) Snohomish County	4	0.02
West Puente Valley, CA (cdp) Los Angeles County	4	0.02
White Center, WA (cdp) King County	4	0.02
Clifton, CO (cdp) Mesa County	3	0.02
Durango, CO (city) La Plata County	3	0.02
East Renton Highlands, WA (cdp) King County	3	0.02
Elk Plain, WA (cdp) Pierce County	3	0.02
Foothill Farms, CA (cdp) Sacramento County	3	0.02
Klamath Falls, OR (city) Klamath County	3	0.02
Lake Forest Park, WA (city) King County	3	0.02
Maple Valley, WA (city) King County	3	0.02
Middleton, WI (city) Dane County	3	0.02
Red Bluff, CA (city) Tehama County	3	0.02
Sand Springs, OK (city) Tulsa County	3	0.02
Ukiah, CA (city) Mendocino County	3	0.02
College, AK (cdp) Fairbanks North Star Borough	2	0.02
Lea Hill, WA (cdp) King County	2	0.02
Lincoln, CA (city) Placer County	2	0.02
Martha Lake, WA (cdp) Snohomish County	2	0.02
Okmulgee, OK (city) Okmulgee County	2	0.02
Riverton-Boulevard Park, WA (cdp) King County	2	0.02
Speedway, IN (town) Marion County	2	0.02
Vashon, WA (cdp) King County	2	0.02
West Valley, WA (cdp) Yakima County	2	0.02
Portland, OR (city) Multnomah County	53	0.01
Vancouver, WA (city) Clark County	21	0.01
Anchorage, AK (municipality) Anchorage Borough	20	0.01
Eugene, OR (city) Lane County	12	0.01
Bellingham, WA (city) Whatcom County	10	0.01
Federal Way, WA (city) King County	10	0.01
Gresham, OR (city) Multnomah County	8	0.01
Bellevue, WA (city) King County	7	0.01
Kennewick, WA (city) Benton County	7	0.01
Lawrence, KS (city) Douglas County	7	0.01
Rancho Cucamonga, CA (city) San Bernardino County	7	0.01
Great Falls, MT (city) Cascade County	6	0.01
Tigard, OR (city) Washington County	6	0.01
Missoula, MT (city) Missoula County	5	0.01
Richland, WA (city) Benton County	5	0.01
Seattle Hill-Silver Firs, WA (cdp) Snohomish County	5	0.01
Corvallis, OR (city) Benton County	4	0.01
East Hill-Meridian, WA (cdp) King County	4	0.01
Jacksonville, NC (city) Onslow County	4	0.01
Manteca, CA (city) San Joaquin County	4	0.01
Murrieta, CA (city) Riverside County	4	0.01
Paramount, CA (city) Los Angeles County	4	0.01
Twin Falls, ID (city) Twin Falls County	4	0.01
Aloha, OR (cdp) Washington County	3	0.01
Bend, OR (city) Deschutes County	3	0.01
Bothell, WA (city) King County	3	0.01
Burien, WA (city) King County	3	0.01
Casas Adobes, AZ (cdp) Pima County	3	0.01
Cottage Lake, WA (cdp) King County	3	0.01
Edmonds, WA (city) Snohomish County	3	0.01
Farmington, NM (city) San Juan County	3	0.01
Hemet, CA (city) Riverside County	3	0.01
Lake Jackson, TX (city) Brazoria County	3	0.01
Londonderry, NH (town) Rockingham County	3	0.01
Longview, WA (city) Cowlitz County	3	0.01
Parkland, WA (cdp) Pierce County	3	0.01
Perris, CA (city) Riverside County	3	0.01
South Lake Tahoe, CA (city) El Dorado County	3	0.01
Wheat Ridge, CO (city) Jefferson County	3	0.01
Butte-Silver Bow, MT (special city) Silver Bow County	2	0.01
Camano, WA (cdp) Island County	2	0.01
Culver City, CA (city) Los Angeles County	2	0.01
Elko, NV (city) Elko County	2	0.01
Fairbanks, AK (city) Fairbanks North Star Borough	2	0.01
Fortuna Foothills, AZ (cdp) Yuma County	2	0.01
Hinesville, GA (city) Liberty County	2	0.01
Kahului, HI (cdp) Maui County	2	0.01
Lake Oswego, OR (city) Clackamas County	2	0.01
Lakeland North, WA (cdp) King County	2	0.01
Moscow, ID (city) Latah County	2	0.01
Payson, AZ (town) Gila County	2	0.01
Porterville, CA (city) Tulare County	2	0.01
Shawnee, OK (city) Pottawatomie County	2	0.01
Silverdale, WA (cdp) Kitsap County	2	0.01
Tahlequah, OK (city) Cherokee County	2	0.01
University Place, WA (city) Pierce County	2	0.01
Wilsonville, OR (city) Clackamas County	2	0.01
Anacortes, WA (city) Skagit County	1	0.01
Arcata, CA (city) Humboldt County	1	0.01

Notes: (cdp) census designated place; Refer to the Explanation of Data in the front of the book for more detailed information.

American Indian: Comanche

Top 150 Places Sorted by Number

(Based on all places, regardless of population)

Place	Number	%
Lawton, OK (city) Comanche County	1,301	1.40
Oklahoma City, OK (city) Oklahoma County	503	0.10
Cache, OK (city) Comanche County	319	13.45
Walters, OK (city) Cotton County	217	8.17
Anadarko, OK (city) Caddo County	196	2.95
Norman, OK (city) Cleveland County	160	0.17
Fort Worth, TX (city) Tarrant County	150	0.03
Los Angeles, CA (city) Los Angeles County	148	0.00
Albuquerque, NM (city) Bernalillo County	146	0.03
Dallas, TX (city) Dallas County	144	0.01
San Antonio, TX (city) Bexar County	140	0.01
Apache, OK (town) Caddo County	136	8.42
Tulsa, OK (city) Tulsa County	135	0.03
Geronimo, OK (town) Comanche County	122	12.72
Houston, TX (city) Harris County	120	0.01
Austin, TX (city) Travis County	112	0.02
Wichita, KS (city) Sedgwick County	100	0.03
San Diego, CA (city) San Diego County	98	0.01
Phoenix, AZ (city) Maricopa County	88	0.01
Arlington, TX (city) Tarrant County	84	0.03
Elgin, OK (city) Comanche County	74	6.12
Denver, CO (city) Denver County	73	0.01
Indiahoma, OK (town) Comanche County	68	18.18
New York, NY (city) New York City	65	0.00
Amarillo, TX (city) Potter County	64	0.04
Fresno, CA (city) Fresno County	63	0.01
Wichita Falls, TX (city) Wichita County	61	0.06
Colorado Springs, CO (city) El Paso County	61	0.02
Cyril, OK (town) Caddo County	60	5.14
Chickasha, OK (city) Grady County	60	0.38
Riverside, CA (city) Riverside County	55	0.02
Chicago, IL (city) Cook County	53	0.00
Corpus Christi, TX (city) Nueces County	51	0.02
Shawnee, OK (city) Pottawatomie County	49	0.17
Irving, TX (city) Dallas County	49	0.03
El Paso, TX (city) El Paso County	49	0.01
San Jose, CA (city) Santa Clara County	48	0.01
Moore, OK (city) Cleveland County	42	0.10
Long Beach, CA (city) Los Angeles County	42	0.01
Bakersfield, CA (city) Kern County	41	0.02
Garland, TX (city) Dallas County	40	0.02
Sacramento, CA (city) Sacramento County	39	0.01
Duncan, OK (city) Stephens County	38	0.17
Grand Prairie, TX (city) Dallas County	38	0.03
Anaheim, CA (city) Orange County	38	0.01
Oakland, CA (city) Alameda County	38	0.01
Midwest City, OK (city) Oklahoma County	37	0.07
Lawrence, KS (city) Douglas County	36	0.04
Mesquite, TX (city) Dallas County	36	0.03
Modesto, CA (city) Stanislaus County	34	0.02
Las Vegas, NV (city) Clark County	34	0.01
Fletcher, OK (town) Comanche County	32	3.13
Portland, OR (city) Multnomah County	32	0.01
San Francisco, CA (city) San Francisco County	32	0.00
Aurora, CO (city) Arapahoe County	31	0.01
Temple, OK (town) Cotton County	30	2.62
San Buenaventura, CA (city) Ventura County	30	0.03
Lubbock, TX (city) Lubbock County	30	0.02
Seattle, WA (city) King County	30	0.01
Tucson, AZ (city) Pima County	30	0.01
Broken Arrow, OK (city) Tulsa County	29	0.04
Edmond, OK (city) Oklahoma County	29	0.04
Odessa, TX (city) Ector County	29	0.03
Springfield, MO (city) Greene County	28	0.02
Bethany, OK (city) Oklahoma County	27	0.13
Abilene, TX (city) Taylor County	27	0.02
Chattanooga, OK (town) Comanche County	26	6.02
Anchorage, AK (municipality) Anchorage Borough	26	0.01
Spokane, WA (city) Spokane County	26	0.01
Muskogee, OK (city) Muskogee County	24	0.06
Claremore, OK (city) Rogers County	22	0.14
Del City, OK (city) Oklahoma County	22	0.10
Bedford, TX (city) Tarrant County	22	0.05
Lancaster, CA (city) Los Angeles County	22	0.02
Mesa, AZ (city) Maricopa County	22	0.01
Plano, TX (city) Collin County	22	0.01
Tacoma, WA (city) Pierce County	22	0.01
Hurst, TX (city) Tarrant County	21	0.06
Midland, TX (city) Midland County	21	0.02
Reno, NV (city) Washoe County	21	0.01
Salinas, CA (city) Monterey County	21	0.01
Kansas City, MO (city) Jackson County	21	0.00
Altus, OK (city) Jackson County	20	0.09
Euless, TX (city) Tarrant County	20	0.04
Richardson, TX (city) Dallas County	20	0.02
San Angelo, TX (city) Tom Green County	20	0.02
Weatherford, OK (city) Custer County	19	0.19
Waco, TX (city) McLennan County	19	0.02
Honolulu, HI (cdp) Honolulu County	19	0.01
Oxnard, CA (city) Ventura County	19	0.01
Pasadena, TX (city) Harris County	19	0.01
Stockton, CA (city) San Joaquin County	19	0.01
Columbus, OH (city) Franklin County	19	0.00
Fort Cobb, OK (town) Caddo County	18	2.70
Sterling, OK (town) Comanche County	18	2.36
Farmington, NM (city) San Juan County	18	0.05
Apple Valley, CA (town) San Bernardino County	18	0.03
Santa Cruz, CA (city) Santa Cruz County	18	0.03
Carrollton, TX (city) Denton County	18	0.02
Fort Collins, CO (city) Larimer County	18	0.02
Simi Valley, CA (city) Ventura County	18	0.02
Hayward, CA (city) Alameda County	18	0.01
Lakewood, CO (city) Jefferson County	18	0.01
San Bernardino, CA (city) San Bernardino County	18	0.01
Santa Rosa, CA (city) Sonoma County	18	0.01
Indianapolis, IN (special city) Marion County	18	0.00
Yukon, OK (city) Canadian County	17	0.08
North Richland Hills, TX (city) Tarrant County	17	0.03
Temple, TX (city) Bell County	17	0.03
Denton, TX (city) Denton County	17	0.02
Pueblo, CO (city) Pueblo County	17	0.02
San Leandro, CA (city) Alameda County	17	0.02
Fremont, CA (city) Alameda County	17	0.01
Garden Grove, CA (city) Orange County	17	0.01
Ontario, CA (city) San Bernardino County	17	0.01
Cement, OK (town) Caddo County	16	3.02
Ponca City, OK (city) Kay County	16	0.06
Topeka, KS (city) Shawnee County	16	0.01
Noble, OK (city) Cleveland County	15	0.29
Denison, TX (city) Grayson County	15	0.07
Bartlesville, OK (city) Washington County	15	0.04
Rio Rancho, NM (city) Sandoval County	15	0.03
Lewisville, TX (city) Denton County	15	0.02
Visalia, CA (city) Tulare County	15	0.02
Des Moines, IA (city) Polk County	15	0.01
Eugene, OR (city) Lane County	15	0.01
Glendale, AZ (city) Maricopa County	15	0.01
Rancho Cucamonga, CA (city) San Bernardino County	15	0.01
Salem, OR (city) Marion County	15	0.01
Virginia Beach, VA (independent city) Virginia Beach city	15	0.00
Guthrie, OK (city) Logan County	14	0.14
McAlester, OK (city) Pittsburg County	14	0.08
Haltom City, TX (city) Tarrant County	14	0.04
Yuba City, CA (city) Sutter County	14	0.04
Enid, OK (city) Garfield County	14	0.03
Bellflower, CA (city) Los Angeles County	14	0.02
Whittier, CA (city) Los Angeles County	14	0.02
Huntington Beach, CA (city) Orange County	14	0.01
McLoud, OK (town) Pottawatomie County	13	0.37
Newman, CA (city) Stanislaus County	13	0.18
Pryor Creek, OK (city) Mayes County	13	0.15
Port Hueneme, CA (city) Ventura County	13	0.06
Big Spring, TX (city) Howard County	13	0.05
Hesperia, CA (city) San Bernardino County	13	0.02
Yuma, AZ (city) Yuma County	13	0.02
Scottsdale, AZ (city) Maricopa County	13	0.01
Minneapolis, MN (city) Hennepin County	13	0.00
Big Pine, CA (cdp) Inyo County	12	0.89
Fort Washakie, WY (cdp) Fremont County	12	0.81
Checotah, OK (city) McIntosh County	12	0.34

Notes: (cdp) census designated place; Refer to the Explanation of Data in the front of the book for more detailed information.

American Indian: Comanche

Top 150 Places Sorted by Percent

(Based on all places, regardless of population)

Place	Number	%
Indiahoma, OK (town) Comanche County	68	18.18
Lotsee, OK (town) Tulsa County	2	18.18
Cache, OK (city) Comanche County	319	13.45
Geronimo, OK (town) Comanche County	122	12.72
Apache, OK (town) Caddo County	136	8.42
Walters, OK (city) Cotton County	217	8.17
Elgin, OK (city) Comanche County	74	6.12
Chattanooga, OK (town) Comanche County	26	6.02
Aquilla, TX (city) Hill County	7	5.15
Cyril, OK (town) Caddo County	60	5.14
Fletcher, OK (town) Comanche County	32	3.13
Thayer, IA (city) Union County	2	3.03
Cement, OK (town) Caddo County	16	3.02
Faxon, OK (town) Comanche County	4	2.99
Anadarko, OK (city) Caddo County	196	2.95
Fort Cobb, OK (town) Caddo County	18	2.70
Medicine Park, OK (town) Comanche County	10	2.68
Temple, OK (town) Cotton County	30	2.62
Sterling, OK (town) Comanche County	18	2.36
Leach, OK (cdp) Delaware County	4	1.82
Red Rock, OK (town) Noble County	5	1.71
Bartlett, KS (city) Labette County	2	1.61
Ramah, NM (cdp) McKinley County	6	1.47
Sparks, OK (town) Lincoln County	2	1.46
Lawton, OK (city) Comanche County	1,301	1.40
Johnson, OK (town) Pottawatomie County	3	1.35
Devol, OK (town) Cotton County	2	1.33
Fargo, OK (town) Ellis County	4	1.23
Mueller, MI (township) Schoolcraft County	3	1.22
Alpine Northeast, WY (cdp) Lincoln County	1	1.22
Toqua, MN (township) Big Stone County	1	1.15
Toco, TX (city) Lamar County	1	1.12
Roosevelt, OK (town) Kiowa County	3	1.07
Mountain Park, OK (town) Kiowa County	4	1.03
Maramec, OK (town) Pawnee County	1	0.96
Ninnekah, OK (town) Grady County	9	0.91
Big Pine, CA (cdp) Inyo County	12	0.89
Moffat, CO (town) Saguache County	1	0.88
Briarcliff, AR (town) Baxter County	2	0.83
Fort Washakie, WY (cdp) Fremont County	12	0.81
Richville, MN (city) Otter Tail County	1	0.81
Alpaugh, CA (cdp) Tulare County	6	0.79
Magdalena, NM (village) Socorro County	7	0.77
Meridian, OK (cdp) Stephens County	11	0.74
Kansas, OK (town) Delaware County	5	0.73
Olmitz, KS (city) Barton County	1	0.72
Comanche, OK (city) Stephens County	11	0.71
Mountain View, OK (town) Kiowa County	6	0.68
Carnegie, OK (town) Caddo County	11	0.67
Loco, OK (town) Stephens County	1	0.67
Uncertain, TX (city) Harrison County	1	0.67
Eaton, WI (town) Manitowoc County	5	0.66
Pineville, MO (town) McDonald County	5	0.65
Searsboro, IA (city) Poweshiek County	1	0.65
Rush Springs, OK (town) Grady County	8	0.63
Dwight, KS (city) Morris County	2	0.61
Bromide, OK (town) Johnston County	1	0.61
Tolar, TX (city) Hood County	3	0.60
Gracemont, OK (town) Caddo County	2	0.60
Morgan's Point, TX (city) Harris County	2	0.60
Silver Cliff, CO (town) Custer County	3	0.59
Huntsville, AR (city) Madison County	11	0.57
Nazareth, TX (city) Castro County	2	0.56
Kellyville, OK (town) Creek County	5	0.55
Camden, MI (village) Hillsdale County	3	0.55
Peru, KS (city) Chautauqua County	1	0.55
Stratford, OK (town) Garvin County	8	0.54
Gas, KS (city) Allen County	3	0.54
Snyder, OK (city) Kiowa County	8	0.53
Dickson, OK (town) Carter County	6	0.53
Davidson, OK (town) Tillman County	2	0.53
Bessie, OK (town) Washita County	1	0.53
South Coffeyville, OK (town) Nowata County	4	0.51
Warsaw, OH (village) Coshocton County	4	0.51
Meno, OK (town) Major County	1	0.51
Rye, CO (town) Pueblo County	1	0.50
Westbrook, TX (city) Mitchell County	1	0.49
Staples, MN (township) Todd County	3	0.48
Fruitvale, TX (city) Van Zandt County	2	0.48
Shiloh, GA (city) Harris County	2	0.47
Tolland, MA (town) Hampden County	2	0.47
Geuda Springs, KS (city) Sumner County	1	0.47
Smithfield, IL (village) Fulton County	1	0.47
Pawnee, OK (city) Pawnee County	10	0.45
Turtle Lake, MN (township) Beltrami County	5	0.45
Vian, OK (town) Sequoyah County	6	0.44
Olustee, OK (town) Jackson County	3	0.44
Beaver Crossing, NE (village) Seward County	2	0.44
San Ildefonso Pueblo, NM (cdp) Santa Fe County	2	0.44
Meeker, OK (town) Lincoln County	4	0.41
Amber, OK (town) Grady County	2	0.41
Braman, OK (town) Kay County	1	0.41
Kosse, TX (town) Limestone County	2	0.40
Randlett, OK (town) Cotton County	2	0.39
Basin, MT (cdp) Jefferson County	1	0.39
Ida, LA (village) Caddo Parish	1	0.39
Chickasha, OK (city) Grady County	60	0.38
Hartshorne, OK (city) Pittsburg County	8	0.38
Granite, OK (town) Greer County	7	0.38
Manistique, MI (township) Schoolcraft County	4	0.38
Shaker Church, WA (cdp) Snohomish County	3	0.38
Alderson, OK (town) Pittsburg County	1	0.38
Keams Canyon, AZ (cdp) Navajo County	1	0.38
Lostine, OR (city) Wallowa County	1	0.38
McLoud, OK (town) Pottawatomie County	13	0.37
Calumet, OK (town) Canadian County	2	0.37
Little River, KS (city) Rice County	2	0.37
Pernitas Point, TX (village) Live Oak County	1	0.37
Glenrock, WY (town) Converse County	8	0.36
Calvin, OK (town) Hughes County	1	0.36
Clatonia, NE (village) Gage County	1	0.36
Manitou, OK (town) Tillman County	1	0.36
Marland, OK (town) Noble County	1	0.36
Newcastle, TX (city) Young County	2	0.35
Norway Lake, MN (township) Kandiyohi County	1	0.35
Silo, OK (town) Bryan County	1	0.35
Checotah, OK (city) McIntosh County	12	0.34
Murchison, TX (city) Henderson County	2	0.34
Okay, OK (town) Wagoner County	2	0.34
Grays Prairie, TX (village) Kaufman County	1	0.34
Parmele, NC (town) Martin County	1	0.34
Goshen, AL (town) Pike County	1	0.33
New Eucha, OK (cdp) Delaware County	1	0.33
Soper, OK (town) Choctaw County	1	0.33
Caddo, OK (town) Bryan County	3	0.32
Cameron, OK (town) Le Flore County	1	0.32
Mount Calm, TX (city) Hill County	1	0.32
Grand Mound, WA (cdp) Thurston County	6	0.31
Morris, OK (city) Okmulgee County	4	0.31
Central High, OK (town) Stephens County	3	0.31
Santa Clara Pueblo, NM (cdp) Rio Arriba County	3	0.31
Goree, TX (city) Knox County	1	0.31
Weleetka, OK (town) Okfuskee County	3	0.30
Verden, OK (town) Grady County	2	0.30
Lakeside, TX (town) San Patricio County	1	0.30
Noble, OK (city) Cleveland County	15	0.29
Hickory Creek, TX (town) Denton County	6	0.29
Erick, OK (city) Beckham County	3	0.29
Cynthiana, IN (town) Posey County	2	0.29
Adair, OK (town) Mayes County	2	0.28
Clayton, OK (town) Pushmataha County	2	0.28
Branch, AR (city) Franklin County	1	0.28
Briggs, OK (cdp) Cherokee County	1	0.28
Naschitti, NM (cdp) San Juan County	1	0.28
Tornado, WV (cdp) Kanawha County	3	0.27
Empire City, OK (town) Stephens County	2	0.27
Roff, OK (town) Pontotoc County	2	0.27
Savanna, OK (town) Pittsburg County	2	0.27
Tioga, TX (town) Grayson County	2	0.27
McArthur, CA (cdp) Shasta County	1	0.27

Notes: (cdp) census designated place; Refer to the Explanation of Data in the front of the book for more detailed information.

American Indian: Comanche

Top 150 Places Sorted by Percent

(Based on places with populations of 10,000 or more)

Place	Number	%
Lawton, OK (city) Comanche County	1,301	1.40
Chickasha, OK (city) Grady County	60	0.38
Norman, OK (city) Cleveland County	160	0.17
Shawnee, OK (city) Pottawatomie County	49	0.17
Duncan, OK (city) Stephens County	38	0.17
Claremore, OK (city) Rogers County	22	0.14
Bethany, OK (city) Oklahoma County	27	0.13
The Village, OK (city) Oklahoma County	11	0.11
Oklahoma City, OK (city) Oklahoma County	503	0.10
Moore, OK (city) Cleveland County	42	0.10
Del City, OK (city) Oklahoma County	22	0.10
Altus, OK (city) Jackson County	20	0.09
Yukon, OK (city) Canadian County	17	0.08
McAlester, OK (city) Pittsburg County	14	0.08
Midwest City, OK (city) Oklahoma County	37	0.07
Denison, TX (city) Grayson County	15	0.07
El Reno, OK (city) Canadian County	12	0.07
Glen Avon, CA (cdp) Riverside County	10	0.07
Bixby, OK (city) Tulsa County	9	0.07
Converse, TX (city) Bexar County	8	0.07
Wichita Falls, TX (city) Wichita County	61	0.06
Muskogee, OK (city) Muskogee County	24	0.06
Hurst, TX (city) Tarrant County	21	0.06
Ponca City, OK (city) Kay County	16	0.06
Port Hueneme, CA (city) Ventura County	13	0.06
Owasso, OK (city) Tulsa County	12	0.06
Mineral Wells, TX (city) Palo Pinto County	11	0.06
Pampa, TX (city) Gray County	11	0.06
White Settlement, TX (city) Tarrant County	9	0.06
Fort Drum, NY (cdp) Jefferson County	7	0.06
Olivehurst, CA (cdp) Yuba County	7	0.06
Ottawa, KS (city) Franklin County	7	0.06
Urbana, OH (city) Champaign County	7	0.06
Sierra Madre, CA (city) Los Angeles County	6	0.06
Bedford, TX (city) Tarrant County	22	0.05
Farmington, NM (city) San Juan County	18	0.05
Big Spring, TX (city) Howard County	13	0.05
Kerrville, TX (city) Kerr County	10	0.05
Balch Springs, TX (city) Dallas County	9	0.05
Santa Fe Springs, CA (city) Los Angeles County	9	0.05
Portland, TX (city) San Patricio County	8	0.05
Pueblo West, CO (cdp) Pueblo County	8	0.05
Borger, TX (city) Hutchinson County	7	0.05
Fenton, MI (township) Genesee County	7	0.05
Miami, OK (city) Ottawa County	7	0.05
Tahlequah, OK (city) Cherokee County	7	0.05
Okmulgee, OK (city) Okmulgee County	6	0.05
Pedley, CA (cdp) Riverside County	6	0.05
Saginaw, TX (city) Tarrant County	6	0.05
Altoona, IA (city) Polk County	5	0.05
Burkburnett, TX (city) Wichita County	5	0.05
Celina, OH (city) Mercer County	5	0.05
Grass Valley, CA (city) Nevada County	5	0.05
Lexington Park, MD (cdp) Saint Mary's County	5	0.05
Amarillo, TX (city) Potter County	64	0.04
Lawrence, KS (city) Douglas County	36	0.04
Broken Arrow, OK (city) Tulsa County	29	0.04
Edmond, OK (city) Oklahoma County	29	0.04
Euless, TX (city) Tarrant County	20	0.04
Bartlesville, OK (city) Washington County	15	0.04
Haltom City, TX (city) Tarrant County	14	0.04
Yuba City, CA (city) Sutter County	14	0.04
La Presa, CA (cdp) San Diego County	12	0.04
Los Banos, CA (city) Merced County	10	0.04
Ashland, CA (cdp) Alameda County	8	0.04
Junction City, KS (city) Geary County	8	0.04
Lakeside, CA (cdp) San Diego County	8	0.04
Mountlake Terrace, WA (city) Snohomish County	8	0.04
Ada, OK (city) Pontotoc County	7	0.04
Le Ray, NY (town) Jefferson County	7	0.04
Canyon Lake, TX (cdp) Comal County	6	0.04
Coos Bay, OR (city) Coos County	6	0.04
Lansdowne-Baltimore Highlands, MD (cdp) Baltimore County	6	0.04
Live Oak, CA (cdp) Santa Cruz County	6	0.04
Troutdale, OR (city) Multnomah County	6	0.04

Place	Number	%
Addison, TX (town) Dallas County	5	0.04
Forest Hill, TX (city) Tarrant County	5	0.04
Graham, NC (city) Alamance County	5	0.04
Mustang, OK (city) Canadian County	5	0.04
Oroville, CA (city) Butte County	5	0.04
Pecan Grove, TX (cdp) Fort Bend County	5	0.04
Waipio, HI (cdp) Honolulu County	5	0.04
Crestline, CA (cdp) San Bernardino County	4	0.04
Fort Carson, CO (cdp) El Paso County	4	0.04
Griswold, CT (town) New London County	4	0.04
Rehoboth, MA (town) Bristol County	4	0.04
Siloam Springs, AR (city) Benton County	4	0.04
Tehachapi, CA (city) Kern County	4	0.04
Valle Vista, CA (cdp) Riverside County	4	0.04
Fort Worth, TX (city) Tarrant County	150	0.03
Albuquerque, NM (city) Bernalillo County	146	0.03
Tulsa, OK (city) Tulsa County	135	0.03
Wichita, KS (city) Sedgwick County	100	0.03
Arlington, TX (city) Tarrant County	84	0.03
Irving, TX (city) Dallas County	49	0.03
Grand Prairie, TX (city) Dallas County	38	0.03
Mesquite, TX (city) Dallas County	36	0.03
San Buenaventura, CA (city) Ventura County	30	0.03
Odessa, TX (city) Ector County	29	0.03
Apple Valley, CA (town) San Bernardino County	18	0.03
Santa Cruz, CA (city) Santa Cruz County	18	0.03
North Richland Hills, TX (city) Tarrant County	17	0.03
Temple, TX (city) Bell County	17	0.03
Rio Rancho, NM (city) Sandoval County	15	0.03
Enid, OK (city) Garfield County	14	0.03
Roswell, NM (city) Chaves County	12	0.03
Stillwater, OK (city) Payne County	12	0.03
Conroe, TX (city) Montgomery County	11	0.03
Gilroy, CA (city) Santa Clara County	11	0.03
Yucaipa, CA (city) San Bernardino County	11	0.03
Englewood, CO (city) Arapahoe County	10	0.03
Sherman, TX (city) Grayson County	10	0.03
Cedar Hill, TX (city) Dallas County	9	0.03
Fort Hood, TX (cdp) Coryell County	9	0.03
Winchester, NV (cdp) Clark County	9	0.03
Ardmore, OK (city) Carter County	8	0.03
Channelview, TX (cdp) Harris County	8	0.03
Cloverleaf, TX (cdp) Harris County	8	0.03
Kingsville, TX (city) Kleberg County	7	0.03
Plainview, TX (city) Hale County	7	0.03
Round Lake Beach, IL (village) Lake County	7	0.03
Colleyville, TX (city) Tarrant County	6	0.03
Columbus, NE (city) Platte County	6	0.03
Derby, KS (city) Sedgwick County	6	0.03
Ferguson, MO (city) Saint Louis County	6	0.03
Gallup, NM (city) McKinley County	6	0.03
San Jacinto, CA (city) Riverside County	6	0.03
Tukwila, WA (city) King County	6	0.03
West Odessa, TX (cdp) Ector County	6	0.03
Bourbonnais, IL (village) Kankakee County	5	0.03
Brownwood, TX (city) Brown County	5	0.03
Fort Campbell North, KY (cdp) Christian County	5	0.03
Fort Lewis, WA (cdp) Pierce County	5	0.03
Golden, CO (city) Jefferson County	5	0.03
Mukilteo, WA (city) Snohomish County	5	0.03
Ozark, AL (city) Dale County	5	0.03
Ramona, CA (cdp) San Diego County	5	0.03
Rockland, MA (town) Plymouth County	5	0.03
Stephenville, TX (city) Erath County	5	0.03
Atlantic Beach, FL (city) Duval County	4	0.03
Bonita, CA (cdp) San Diego County	4	0.03
Circleville, OH (city) Pickaway County	4	0.03
Fraser, MI (city) Macomb County	4	0.03
Jollyville, TX (cdp) Williamson County	4	0.03
La Marque, TX (city) Galveston County	4	0.03
Las Vegas, NM (city) San Miguel County	4	0.03
Moses Lake, WA (city) Grant County	4	0.03
Port Neches, TX (city) Jefferson County	4	0.03
San Anselmo, CA (town) Marin County	4	0.03
Wixom, MI (city) Oakland County	4	0.03

Notes: (cdp) census designated place; Refer to the Explanation of Data in the front of the book for more detailed information.

American Indian: Cree

Top 150 Places Sorted by Number

(Based on all places, regardless of population)

Place	Number	%
Great Falls, MT (city) Cascade County	98	0.17
New York, NY (city) New York City	94	0.00
Los Angeles, CA (city) Los Angeles County	87	0.00
Seattle, WA (city) King County	77	0.01
Chicago, IL (city) Cook County	62	0.00
Spokane, WA (city) Spokane County	56	0.03
Portland, OR (city) Multnomah County	54	0.01
Phoenix, AZ (city) Maricopa County	48	0.00
Minneapolis, MN (city) Hennepin County	38	0.01
San Jose, CA (city) Santa Clara County	36	0.00
North Browning, MT (cdp) Glacier County	31	1.41
San Francisco, CA (city) San Francisco County	31	0.00
Colorado Springs, CO (city) El Paso County	30	0.01
San Diego, CA (city) San Diego County	29	0.00
Browning, MT (town) Glacier County	27	2.54
Honolulu, HI (cdp) Honolulu County	27	0.01
Billings, MT (city) Yellowstone County	25	0.03
Butte-Silver Bow, MT (special city) Silver Bow County	24	0.07
Las Vegas, NV (city) Clark County	24	0.01
Sacramento, CA (city) Sacramento County	24	0.01
Missoula, MT (city) Missoula County	23	0.04
Oakland, CA (city) Alameda County	22	0.01
Albuquerque, NM (city) Bernalillo County	21	0.00
South Browning, MT (cdp) Glacier County	20	1.19
Eugene, OR (city) Lane County	20	0.01
Saint Paul, MN (city) Ramsey County	20	0.01
Denver, CO (city) Denver County	20	0.00
Houston, TX (city) Harris County	20	0.00
Long Beach, CA (city) Los Angeles County	20	0.00
Tucson, AZ (city) Pima County	20	0.00
Cut Bank, MT (city) Glacier County	18	0.58
Hillsboro, OR (city) Washington County	18	0.03
Detroit, MI (city) Wayne County	18	0.00
Anchorage, AK (municipality) Anchorage Borough	17	0.01
Grand Rapids, MI (city) Kent County	17	0.01
Austin, TX (city) Travis County	16	0.00
Mesa, AZ (city) Maricopa County	16	0.00
Pittsburgh, PA (city) Allegheny County	16	0.00
Wichita, KS (city) Sedgwick County	16	0.00
Fort Belknap Agency, MT (cdp) Blaine County	15	1.19
Kansas City, KS (city) Wyandotte County	15	0.01
Fresno, CA (city) Fresno County	15	0.00
Milwaukee, WI (city) Milwaukee County	15	0.00
Helena, MT (city) Lewis and Clark County	14	0.05
Aurora, CO (city) Arapahoe County	14	0.01
Boston, MA (city) Suffolk County	14	0.00
Columbus, OH (city) Franklin County	14	0.00
San Antonio, TX (city) Bexar County	14	0.00
Tulsa, OK (city) Tulsa County	14	0.00
Arlee, MT (cdp) Lake County	13	2.16
Pablo, MT (cdp) Lake County	13	0.72
Polson, MT (city) Lake County	13	0.32
Olympia, WA (city) Thurston County	13	0.03
Fort Collins, CO (city) Larimer County	13	0.01
Reno, NV (city) Washoe County	13	0.01
Vancouver, WA (city) Clark County	13	0.01
Cleveland, OH (city) Cuyahoga County	13	0.00
Havre, MT (city) Hill County	12	0.12
Fort Wayne, IN (city) Allen County	12	0.01
Newport News, VA (independent city) Newport News city	12	0.01
Paradise, NV (cdp) Clark County	12	0.01
Santa Rosa, CA (city) Sonoma County	12	0.01
Bakersfield, CA (city) Kern County	12	0.00
Lincoln, RI (town) Providence County	11	0.05
Kent, WA (city) King County	11	0.01
Salt Lake City, UT (city) Salt Lake County	11	0.01
Tacoma, WA (city) Pierce County	11	0.01
Westminster, CO (city) Adams County	11	0.01
Buffalo, NY (city) Erie County	11	0.00
Kansas City, MO (city) Jackson County	11	0.00
Philadelphia, PA (city) Philadelphia County	11	0.00
Kingsgate, WA (cdp) King County	10	0.08
Arcata, CA (city) Humboldt County	10	0.06
Claremont, CA (city) Los Angeles County	10	0.03
Moorpark, CA (city) Ventura County	10	0.03
Kennewick, WA (city) Benton County	10	0.02
Terre Haute, IN (city) Vigo County	10	0.02
Bellingham, WA (city) Whatcom County	10	0.01
Boise City, ID (city) Ada County	10	0.01
Everett, WA (city) Snohomish County	10	0.01
Huntington Beach, CA (city) Orange County	10	0.01
Jacksonville, FL (special city) Duval County	10	0.00
Nashville-Davidson, TN (special city) Davidson County	10	0.00
Oklahoma City, OK (city) Oklahoma County	10	0.00
Saint Petersburg, FL (city) Pinellas County	10	0.00
Union Gap, WA (city) Yakima County	9	0.16
SeaTac, WA (city) King County	9	0.04
Colton, CA (city) San Bernardino County	9	0.02
Saint George, UT (city) Washington County	9	0.02
Citrus Heights, CA (city) Sacramento County	9	0.01
Hayward, CA (city) Alameda County	9	0.01
Lawton, OK (city) Comanche County	9	0.01
Pasadena, CA (city) Los Angeles County	9	0.01
Richmond, CA (city) Contra Costa County	9	0.01
Salem, OR (city) Marion County	9	0.01
Akron, OH (city) Summit County	9	0.00
Anaheim, CA (city) Orange County	9	0.00
Riverside, CA (city) Riverside County	9	0.00
Tampa, FL (city) Hillsborough County	9	0.00
Lake Village, IN (cdp) Newton County	8	0.94
Dinuba, CA (city) Tulare County	8	0.05
Bremerton, WA (city) Kitsap County	8	0.02
Egypt Lake-Leto, FL (cdp) Hillsborough County	8	0.02
Muskegon, MI (city) Muskegon County	8	0.02
Placentia, CA (city) Orange County	8	0.02
Sierra Vista, AZ (city) Cochise County	8	0.02
Berkeley, CA (city) Alameda County	8	0.01
Concord, CA (city) Contra Costa County	8	0.01
Lakewood, WA (city) Pierce County	8	0.01
Nashua, NH (city) Hillsborough County	8	0.01
Henderson, NV (city) Clark County	8	0.00
Norfolk, VA (independent city) Norfolk city	8	0.00
Omaha, NE (city) Douglas County	8	0.00
Plano, TX (city) Collin County	8	0.00
Saint Louis, MO (independent city) Saint Louis city	8	0.00
San Bernardino, CA (city) San Bernardino County	8	0.00
Stockton, CA (city) San Joaquin County	8	0.00
East Glacier Park Village, MT (cdp) Glacier County	7	1.77
Sandy, OR (city) Clackamas County	7	0.13
Waite Park, MN (city) Stearns County	7	0.11
Kalispell, MT (city) Flathead County	7	0.05
Oakdale, CA (city) Stanislaus County	7	0.05
Burrillville, RI (town) Providence County	7	0.04
Port Angeles, WA (city) Clallam County	7	0.04
Bay City, MI (city) Bay County	7	0.02
Coeur d'Alene, ID (city) Kootenai County	7	0.02
Flint, MI (township) Genesee County	7	0.02
Pinellas Park, FL (city) Pinellas County	7	0.02
Alameda, CA (city) Alameda County	7	0.01
Cambridge, MA (city) Middlesex County	7	0.01
Chesterfield, MO (city) Saint Louis County	7	0.01
El Cajon, CA (city) San Diego County	7	0.01
Evansville, IN (city) Vanderburgh County	7	0.01
Greeley, CO (city) Weld County	7	0.01
Rancho Cucamonga, CA (city) San Bernardino County	7	0.01
Redding, CA (city) Shasta County	7	0.01
Shoreline, WA (city) King County	7	0.01
Visalia, CA (city) Tulare County	7	0.01
West Valley City, UT (city) Salt Lake County	7	0.01
Atlanta, GA (city) Fulton County	7	0.00
Chandler, AZ (city) Maricopa County	7	0.00
Indianapolis, IN (special city) Marion County	7	0.00
Islip, NY (town) Suffolk County	7	0.00
Lincoln, NE (city) Lancaster County	7	0.00
Louisville, KY (city) Jefferson County	7	0.00
Oceanside, CA (city) San Diego County	7	0.00
Toledo, OH (city) Lucas County	7	0.00
Floodwood, MN (city) Saint Louis County	6	1.19
Caney, KS (city) Montgomery County	6	0.29
Wolf Point, MT (city) Roosevelt County	6	0.23

Notes: (cdp) census designated place; Refer to the Explanation of Data in the front of the book for more detailed information.

American Indian: Cree

Top 150 Places Sorted by Percent

(Based on all places, regardless of population)

Place	Number	%
Port Heiden, AK (city) Lake and Peninsula Borough	4	3.36
Millville, MN (city) Wabasha County	5	2.69
Browning, MT (town) Glacier County	27	2.54
Lodge Pole, MT (cdp) Blaine County	5	2.34
East Valley, MN (township) Marshall County	1	2.22
Arlee, MT (cdp) Lake County	13	2.16
Toston, MT (cdp) Broadwater County	2	1.90
East Glacier Park Village, MT (cdp) Glacier County	7	1.77
Sangrey, MT (cdp) Hill County	4	1.52
Parker School, MT (cdp) Chouteau County	5	1.42
North Browning, MT (cdp) Glacier County	31	1.41
Hartville, WY (town) Platte County	1	1.32
Clutier, IA (city) Tama County	3	1.31
South Browning, MT (cdp) Glacier County	20	1.19
Fort Belknap Agency, MT (cdp) Blaine County	15	1.19
Floodwood, MN (city) Saint Louis County	6	1.19
Azure, MT (cdp) Hill County	3	1.19
Acme, WA (cdp) Whatcom County	3	1.14
Montgomery Creek, CA (cdp) Shasta County	1	1.04
Lake Village, IN (cdp) Newton County	8	0.94
Frazer, MT (cdp) Valley County	4	0.88
Onaway, ID (city) Latah County	2	0.87
Ashland, MT (cdp) Rosebud County	4	0.86
Fleischmanns, NY (village) Delaware County	3	0.85
Four Bears Village, ND (cdp) McKenzie County	2	0.82
Valier, MT (town) Pondera County	4	0.80
Ault, MN (township) Saint Louis County	1	0.80
Manorville, PA (borough) Armstrong County	3	0.75
Grayson, OK (town) Okmulgee County	1	0.75
Fairview, KS (city) Brown County	2	0.74
Pablo, MT (cdp) Lake County	13	0.72
Colon, NE (village) Saunders County	1	0.72
Charlo, MT (cdp) Lake County	3	0.68
Monument, OR (city) Grant County	1	0.66
Rexford, MT (town) Lincoln County	1	0.66
Index, WA (town) Snohomish County	1	0.64
Upton, KY (city) Hardin County	4	0.61
Fortine, MT (cdp) Lincoln County	1	0.59
Cut Bank, MT (city) Glacier County	18	0.58
Bellechester, MN (city) Goodhue County	1	0.58
Hays, MT (cdp) Blaine County	4	0.57
Durand, MN (township) Beltrami County	1	0.57
Reed Point, MT (cdp) Stillwater County	1	0.54
Ilwaco, WA (city) Pacific County	5	0.53
Boulder Flats, WY (cdp) Fremont County	2	0.52
Turtle Lake, MT (cdp) Lake County	1	0.52
Ten Lake, MN (township) Beltrami County	5	0.50
Birch, WI (town) Lincoln County	4	0.50
Plymouth Village, KY (city) Jefferson County	1	0.50
Rico, CO (town) Dolores County	1	0.49
Fort Duchesne, UT (cdp) Uintah County	3	0.48
North Irwin, PA (borough) Westmoreland County	4	0.46
Belfry, MT (cdp) Carbon County	1	0.46
Dixon, MT (cdp) Sanders County	1	0.46
Ocean City, WA (cdp) Grays Harbor County	1	0.46
Challis, ID (city) Custer County	4	0.44
Cedar Valley, MN (township) Saint Louis County	1	0.43
Schurz, NV (cdp) Mineral County	3	0.42
Edson, WI (town) Chippewa County	4	0.41
Vadito, NM (cdp) Taos County	1	0.41
Lodge Grass, MT (town) Big Horn County	2	0.39
Stark, NH (town) Coos County	2	0.39
Crescent Mills, CA (cdp) Plumas County	1	0.39
Miner, MO (city) Scott County	4	0.38
Box Elder, MT (cdp) Hill County	3	0.38
Potlatch, ID (city) Latah County	3	0.38
Birdsall, NY (town) Allegany County	1	0.37
Fullerton, NE (city) Nance County	5	0.36
Baudette, MN (city) Lake of the Woods County	4	0.36
Marland, OK (town) Noble County	1	0.36
Smallwood, NY (cdp) Sullivan County	2	0.35
Saint Pierre, MT (cdp) Hill County	1	0.35
McCormick, SC (town) McCormick County	5	0.34
Cato, NY (village) Cayuga County	2	0.33
Lakeside, WI (town) Douglas County	2	0.33
Eagle Nest, NM (village) Colfax County	1	0.33
Hammond, NY (village) Saint Lawrence County	1	0.33
Polson, MT (city) Lake County	13	0.32
Hungry Horse, MT (cdp) Flathead County	3	0.32
Doyle, MI (township) Schoolcraft County	2	0.32
Hermosa, SD (town) Custer County	1	0.32
Pine Mountain Club, CA (cdp) Kern County	5	0.31
Laytonville, CA (cdp) Mendocino County	4	0.31
Lempster, NH (town) Sullivan County	3	0.31
Saxeville, WI (town) Waushara County	3	0.31
Micanopy, FL (town) Alachua County	2	0.31
Agency, MT (cdp) Hill County	1	0.31
Gabbs, NV (city) Nye County	1	0.31
Mansfield, WA (town) Douglas County	1	0.31
Plumas Eureka, CA (cdp) Plumas County	1	0.31
Wrenshall, MN (township) Carlton County	1	0.31
Castlewood, SD (city) Hamlin County	2	0.30
Hauser, ID (city) Kootenai County	2	0.30
Evaro, MT (cdp) Missoula County	1	0.30
Martin City, MT (cdp) Flathead County	1	0.30
Caney, KS (city) Montgomery County	6	0.29
Marble, MN (city) Itasca County	2	0.29
Womens Bay, AK (cdp) Kodiak Island Borough	2	0.29
Cedar Fort, UT (town) Utah County	1	0.29
Culbertson, MT (town) Roosevelt County	2	0.28
Luna Pier, MI (city) Monroe County	4	0.27
Lewistown Heights, MT (cdp) Fergus County	1	0.27
Ainaloa, HI (cdp) Hawaii County	5	0.26
Hydaburg, AK (city) Prince of Wales-Outer Ketchikan Census Area	1	0.26
Olney Springs, CO (town) Crowley County	1	0.26
Wye, MT (cdp) Missoula County	1	0.26
Greenwood, MI (township) Oscoda County	3	0.25
Perry Park, CO (cdp) Douglas County	3	0.25
Startup, WA (cdp) Snohomish County	2	0.24
Big Water, UT (town) Kane County	1	0.24
Wolf Point, MT (city) Roosevelt County	6	0.23
Blessing, TX (cdp) Matagorda County	2	0.23
Fisher, MN (city) Polk County	1	0.23
Wellton, AZ (town) Yuma County	4	0.22
Birchwood, WI (town) Washburn County	1	0.22
Eyota, MN (township) Olmsted County	1	0.22
Rawson, OH (village) Hancock County	1	0.22
Ravenna, MN (township) Dakota County	5	0.21
Todd, MN (township) Hubbard County	3	0.21
Wyoming, IL (city) Stark County	3	0.21
Boulder Junction, WI (town) Vilas County	2	0.21
Union, PA (township) Tioga County	2	0.21
Bloomfield, MI (township) Missaukee County	1	0.21
Erhards Grove, MN (township) Otter Tail County	1	0.21
Okemah, OK (city) Okfuskee County	6	0.20
Belcourt, ND (cdp) Rolette County	5	0.20
Lakewood Club, MI (village) Muskegon County	2	0.20
Copalis Beach, WA (cdp) Grays Harbor County	1	0.20
Jasper, AR (city) Newton County	1	0.20
Dundee, OR (city) Yamhill County	5	0.19
Smithsburg, MD (town) Washington County	4	0.19
Darien, WI (village) Walworth County	3	0.19
Queen City, TX (city) Cass County	3	0.19
Cedar Crest, NM (cdp) Bernalillo County	2	0.19
Fayette, ME (town) Kennebec County	2	0.19
Hot Springs, MT (town) Sanders County	1	0.19
Wheatland, MI (township) Sanilac County	1	0.19
Hardin, MT (city) Big Horn County	6	0.18
Eagle, NE (village) Cass County	2	0.18
Grass Lake, MI (village) Jackson County	2	0.18
Owens Cross Roads, AL (town) Madison County	2	0.18
Turtle River, MN (township) Beltrami County	2	0.18
Clam Falls, WI (town) Polk County	1	0.18
West Shenango, PA (township) Crawford County	1	0.18
Great Falls, MT (city) Cascade County	98	0.17
Evergreen, MI (township) Montcalm County	5	0.17
Palmer, MN (township) Sherburne County	4	0.17
Biggs, CA (city) Butte County	3	0.17
Choteau, MT (city) Teton County	3	0.17
Haines, AK (city) Haines Borough	3	0.17

Notes: (cdp) census designated place; Refer to the Explanation of Data in the front of the book for more detailed information.

American Indian: Cree

Top 150 Places Sorted by Percent

(Based on places with populations of 10,000 or more)

Place	Number	%
Great Falls, MT (city) Cascade County	98	0.17
Kingsgate, WA (cdp) King County	10	0.08
Butte-Silver Bow, MT (special city) Silver Bow County	24	0.07
Arcata, CA (city) Humboldt County	10	0.06
Helena, MT (city) Lewis and Clark County	14	0.05
Lincoln, RI (town) Providence County	11	0.05
Dinuba, CA (city) Tulare County	8	0.05
Kalispell, MT (city) Flathead County	7	0.05
Oakdale, CA (city) Stanislaus County	7	0.05
Five Corners, WA (cdp) Clark County	6	0.05
Morgan City, LA (city) Saint Mary Parish	6	0.05
Tolland, CT (town) Tolland County	6	0.05
Burlington, KY (cdp) Boone County	5	0.05
Missoula, MT (city) Missoula County	23	0.04
SeaTac, WA (city) King County	9	0.04
Burrillville, RI (town) Providence County	7	0.04
Port Angeles, WA (city) Clallam County	7	0.04
Alpine, CA (cdp) San Diego County	5	0.04
Makakilo City, HI (cdp) Honolulu County	5	0.04
New Haven, IN (city) Allen County	5	0.04
Pineville, LA (city) Rapides Parish	5	0.04
Riverton-Boulevard Park, WA (cdp) King County	5	0.04
Susanville, CA (city) Lassen County	5	0.04
Magalia, CA (cdp) Butte County	4	0.04
Spokane, WA (city) Spokane County	56	0.03
Billings, MT (city) Yellowstone County	25	0.03
Hillsboro, OR (city) Washington County	18	0.03
Olympia, WA (city) Thurston County	13	0.03
Claremont, CA (city) Los Angeles County	10	0.03
Moorpark, CA (city) Ventura County	10	0.03
Gillette, WY (city) Campbell County	5	0.03
Greenfield, MA (town) Franklin County	5	0.03
Hammond, LA (city) Tangipahoa Parish	5	0.03
Laconia, NH (city) Belknap County	5	0.03
Marion, IL (city) Williamson County	5	0.03
Menomonie, WI (city) Dunn County	5	0.03
Pampa, TX (city) Gray County	5	0.03
Stillwater, MN (city) Washington County	5	0.03
Ada, OK (city) Pontotoc County	4	0.03
Bridgetown North, OH (cdp) Hamilton County	4	0.03
Catskill, NY (town) Greene County	4	0.03
Conneaut, OH (city) Ashtabula County	4	0.03
Hampton, NH (town) Rockingham County	4	0.03
Howard, WI (village) Brown County	4	0.03
Midlothian, IL (village) Cook County	4	0.03
Patterson, CA (city) Stanislaus County	4	0.03
Blackfoot, ID (city) Bingham County	3	0.03
College, AK (cdp) Fairbanks North Star Borough	3	0.03
Columbia, PA (borough) Lancaster County	3	0.03
Destin, FL (city) Okaloosa County	3	0.03
Evanston, WY (city) Uinta County	3	0.03
Fortuna, CA (city) Humboldt County	3	0.03
Granby, CT (town) Hartford County	3	0.03
Keokuk, IA (city) Lee County	3	0.03
Lakeland South, WA (cdp) King County	3	0.03
Ontario, OR (city) Malheur County	3	0.03
West Plains, MO (city) Howell County	3	0.03
White Bear, MN (township) Ramsey County	3	0.03
Worth, IL (village) Cook County	3	0.03
Kennewick, WA (city) Benton County	10	0.02
Terre Haute, IN (city) Vigo County	10	0.02
Colton, CA (city) San Bernardino County	9	0.02
Saint George, UT (city) Washington County	9	0.02
Bremerton, WA (city) Kitsap County	8	0.02
Egypt Lake-Leto, FL (cdp) Hillsborough County	8	0.02
Muskegon, MI (city) Muskegon County	8	0.02
Placentia, CA (city) Orange County	8	0.02
Sierra Vista, AZ (city) Cochise County	8	0.02
Bay City, MI (city) Bay County	7	0.02
Coeur d'Alene, ID (city) Kootenai County	7	0.02
Flint, MI (township) Genesee County	7	0.02
Pinellas Park, FL (city) Pinellas County	7	0.02
Bozeman, MT (city) Gallatin County	6	0.02
Burien, WA (city) King County	6	0.02
Cottage Grove, MN (city) Washington County	6	0.02
Morgan Hill, CA (city) Santa Clara County	6	0.02
North Royalton, OH (city) Cuyahoga County	6	0.02
Orangevale, CA (cdp) Sacramento County	6	0.02
Paine Field-Lake Stickney, WA (cdp) Snohomish County	6	0.02
Saratoga Springs, NY (city) Saratoga County	6	0.02
Spring Valley, CA (cdp) San Diego County	6	0.02
Bothell, WA (city) King County	5	0.02
Florin, CA (cdp) Sacramento County	5	0.02
Gallup, NM (city) McKinley County	5	0.02
Lacey, WA (city) Thurston County	5	0.02
North Marysville, WA (cdp) Snohomish County	5	0.02
Pearl City, HI (cdp) Honolulu County	5	0.02
Picnic Point-North Lynnwood, WA (cdp) Snohomish County	5	0.02
Tooele, UT (city) Tooele County	5	0.02
Alliance, OH (city) Stark County	4	0.02
Columbia Heights, MN (city) Anoka County	4	0.02
Cottage Lake, WA (cdp) King County	4	0.02
Elk River, MN (city) Sherburne County	4	0.02
Kerrville, TX (city) Kerr County	4	0.02
Newberg, OR (city) Yamhill County	4	0.02
Oak Harbor, WA (city) Island County	4	0.02
Papillion, NE (city) Sarpy County	4	0.02
Plattsburgh, NY (city) Clinton County	4	0.02
Somerset, MA (cdp) Bristol County	4	0.02
South Saint Paul, MN (city) Dakota County	4	0.02
Watertown, CT (town) Litchfield County	4	0.02
West Lake Stevens, WA (cdp) Snohomish County	4	0.02
Alderwood Manor, WA (cdp) Snohomish County	3	0.02
Arroyo Grande, CA (city) San Luis Obispo County	3	0.02
Beech Grove, IN (city) Marion County	3	0.02
Brookfield, IL (village) Cook County	3	0.02
Cimarron Hills, CO (cdp) El Paso County	3	0.02
Comstock, MI (township) Kalamazoo County	3	0.02
Corcoran, CA (city) Kings County	3	0.02
Daphne, AL (city) Baldwin County	3	0.02
Easthampton, MA (city) Hampshire County	3	0.02
El Dorado, KS (city) Butler County	3	0.02
Elko, NV (city) Elko County	3	0.02
Flowing Wells, AZ (cdp) Pima County	3	0.02
Frankfort, IN (city) Clinton County	3	0.02
Hatfield, PA (township) Montgomery County	3	0.02
Hopewell, NJ (township) Mercer County	3	0.02
Kihei, HI (cdp) Maui County	3	0.02
Lebanon, NH (city) Grafton County	3	0.02
Martha Lake, WA (cdp) Snohomish County	3	0.02
Milford, NH (town) Hillsborough County	3	0.02
Montclair, VA (cdp) Prince William County	3	0.02
Nicholasville, KY (city) Jessamine County	3	0.02
North Adams, MA (city) Berkshire County	3	0.02
North Bay Shore, NY (cdp) Suffolk County	3	0.02
Oakland charter, MI (township) Oakland County	3	0.02
Okmulgee, OK (city) Okmulgee County	3	0.02
Orchards, WA (cdp) Clark County	3	0.02
Palmer, MA (town) Hampden County	3	0.02
Red Wing, MN (city) Goodhue County	3	0.02
Redmond, OR (city) Deschutes County	3	0.02
Riverbank, CA (city) Stanislaus County	3	0.02
Riverdale, IL (village) Cook County	3	0.02
Rockland, MA (town) Plymouth County	3	0.02
Stonington, CT (town) New London County	3	0.02
Upper Chichester, PA (township) Delaware County	3	0.02
West Saint Paul, MN (city) Dakota County	3	0.02
Beach Park, IL (village) Lake County	2	0.02
Campbellsville, KY (city) Taylor County	2	0.02
Chenango, NY (town) Broome County	2	0.02
Clinton, CT (town) Middlesex County	2	0.02
Coldwater, MI (city) Branch County	2	0.02
Holt, MI (cdp) Ingham County	2	0.02
Madison, IN (city) Jefferson County	2	0.02
Marathon, FL (city) Monroe County	2	0.02
Marysville, CA (city) Yuba County	2	0.02
Mastic Beach, NY (cdp) Suffolk County	2	0.02
Nipomo, CA (cdp) San Luis Obispo County	2	0.02
North Mankato, MN (city) Nicollet County	2	0.02
Northbrook, OH (cdp) Hamilton County	2	0.02

Notes: (cdp) census designated place; Refer to the Explanation of Data in the front of the book for more detailed information.

American Indian: Creek

Top 150 Places Sorted by Number

(Based on all places, regardless of population)

Place	Number	%
Tulsa, OK (city) Tulsa County	4,358	1.11
Oklahoma City, OK (city) Oklahoma County	2,361	0.47
Okmulgee, OK (city) Okmulgee County	1,330	10.21
Muskogee, OK (city) Muskogee County	1,085	2.83
Sapulpa, OK (city) Creek County	857	4.47
Broken Arrow, OK (city) Tulsa County	671	0.90
Glenpool, OK (city) Tulsa County	641	7.89
Okemah, OK (city) Okfuskee County	580	19.09
Henryetta, OK (city) Okmulgee County	571	9.37
Shawnee, OK (city) Pottawatomie County	456	1.59
Holdenville, OK (city) Hughes County	437	9.23
Norman, OK (city) Cleveland County	432	0.45
Wichita, KS (city) Sedgwick County	394	0.11
Wetumka, OK (city) Hughes County	375	25.84
Eufaula, OK (city) McIntosh County	362	13.72
Los Angeles, CA (city) Los Angeles County	349	0.01
Coweta, OK (city) Wagoner County	335	4.69
Bristow, OK (city) Creek County	305	7.05
Checotah, OK (city) McIntosh County	289	8.30
Bixby, OK (city) Tulsa County	289	2.17
Midwest City, OK (city) Oklahoma County	262	0.48
Sand Springs, OK (city) Tulsa County	256	1.47
Dallas, TX (city) Dallas County	248	0.02
New York, NY (city) New York City	229	0.00
Moore, OK (city) Cleveland County	225	0.55
Weleetka, OK (town) Okfuskee County	224	22.09
Tahlequah, OK (city) Cherokee County	218	1.51
Wewoka, OK (city) Seminole County	208	5.84
Phoenix, AZ (city) Maricopa County	207	0.02
Seminole, OK (city) Seminole County	201	2.91
Edmond, OK (city) Oklahoma County	198	0.29
Claremore, OK (city) Rogers County	188	1.18
Jacksonville, FL (special city) Duval County	188	0.03
Ada, OK (city) Pontotoc County	182	1.16
Lawrence, KS (city) Douglas County	181	0.23
Stillwater, OK (city) Payne County	180	0.46
Morris, OK (city) Okmulgee County	177	13.68
Houston, TX (city) Harris County	175	0.01
San Diego, CA (city) San Diego County	173	0.01
McAlester, OK (city) Pittsburg County	163	0.92
Mobile, AL (city) Mobile County	163	0.08
Atmore, AL (city) Escambia County	161	2.10
Pensacola, FL (city) Escambia County	160	0.28
Jenks, OK (city) Tulsa County	159	1.66
Dustin, OK (town) Hughes County	153	33.85
West Pensacola, FL (cdp) Escambia County	150	0.68
Dewar, OK (town) Okmulgee County	149	16.21
Fresno, CA (city) Fresno County	149	0.03
Wagoner, OK (city) Wagoner County	145	1.89
Del City, OK (city) Oklahoma County	145	0.66
Lawton, OK (city) Comanche County	139	0.15
Bellview, FL (cdp) Escambia County	135	0.64
Owasso, OK (city) Tulsa County	132	0.71
Kansas City, MO (city) Jackson County	131	0.03
Sacramento, CA (city) Sacramento County	131	0.03
Albuquerque, NM (city) Bernalillo County	128	0.03
Ensley, FL (cdp) Escambia County	125	0.67
Bakersfield, CA (city) Kern County	121	0.05
San Antonio, TX (city) Bexar County	116	0.01
Montgomery, AL (city) Montgomery County	115	0.06
Mounds, OK (town) Creek County	114	9.89
Bartlesville, OK (city) Washington County	114	0.33
Portland, OR (city) Multnomah County	110	0.02
Ferry Pass, FL (cdp) Escambia County	108	0.40
Tallahassee, FL (city) Leon County	107	0.07
Chicago, IL (city) Cook County	102	0.00
Long Beach, CA (city) Los Angeles County	100	0.02
Brent, FL (cdp) Escambia County	98	0.44
Arlington, TX (city) Tarrant County	98	0.03
Detroit, MI (city) Wayne County	98	0.01
San Francisco, CA (city) San Francisco County	97	0.01
San Jose, CA (city) Santa Clara County	97	0.01
Oakhurst, OK (cdp) Tulsa County	96	3.52
Anchorage, AK (municipality) Anchorage Borough	95	0.04
Enid, OK (city) Garfield County	94	0.20

Place	Number	%
Denver, CO (city) Denver County	92	0.02
Haskell, OK (town) Muskogee County	90	5.10
Warrington, FL (cdp) Escambia County	89	0.59
Austin, TX (city) Travis County	89	0.01
Pace, FL (cdp) Santa Rosa County	88	1.19
Panama City, FL (city) Bay County	87	0.24
Beggs, OK (city) Okmulgee County	82	6.01
Birmingham, AL (city) Jefferson County	80	0.03
Mesa, AZ (city) Maricopa County	80	0.02
Texanna, OK (cdp) McIntosh County	78	3.74
Catoosa, OK (city) Rogers County	78	1.43
Tecumseh, OK (city) Pottawatomie County	78	1.28
Fort Worth, TX (city) Tarrant County	78	0.01
Cushing, OK (city) Payne County	77	0.92
Myrtle Grove, FL (cdp) Escambia County	76	0.44
Nashville-Davidson, TN (special city) Davidson County	76	0.01
Seattle, WA (city) King County	75	0.01
Bethany, OK (city) Oklahoma County	73	0.36
Modesto, CA (city) Stanislaus County	73	0.04
Tucson, AZ (city) Pima County	72	0.01
Gonzalez, FL (cdp) Escambia County	71	0.62
Skiatook, OK (town) Osage County	68	1.26
Ponca City, OK (city) Kay County	67	0.26
Oakland, CA (city) Alameda County	66	0.02
Atlanta, GA (city) Fulton County	65	0.02
Fort Gibson, OK (town) Muskogee County	63	1.55
Garland, TX (city) Dallas County	63	0.03
Corpus Christi, TX (city) Nueces County	63	0.02
Miami, OK (city) Ottawa County	62	0.45
Pryor Creek, OK (city) Mayes County	61	0.70
Aurora, CO (city) Arapahoe County	61	0.02
Yukon, OK (city) Canadian County	60	0.29
Ardmore, OK (city) Carter County	60	0.25
Mustang, OK (city) Canadian County	59	0.45
Fort Smith, AR (city) Sebastian County	59	0.07
San Bernardino, CA (city) San Bernardino County	57	0.03
Minneapolis, MN (city) Hennepin County	57	0.01
Columbus, GA (special city) Muscogee County	56	0.03
Tampa, FL (city) Hillsborough County	56	0.02
Paden, OK (town) Okfuskee County	55	12.33
Amarillo, TX (city) Potter County	55	0.03
Turley, OK (cdp) Tulsa County	54	1.67
McLoud, OK (town) Pottawatomie County	54	1.52
El Reno, OK (city) Canadian County	53	0.33
Huntsville, AL (city) Madison County	53	0.03
Clinton, OK (city) Custer County	52	0.59
Irving, TX (city) Dallas County	52	0.03
Colorado Springs, CO (city) El Paso County	52	0.01
Virginia Beach, VA (independent city) Virginia Beach city	52	0.01
Las Vegas, NV (city) Clark County	51	0.01
Park Hill, OK (cdp) Cherokee County	50	1.27
Chickasha, OK (city) Grady County	49	0.31
Dothan, AL (city) Houston County	49	0.08
Plano, TX (city) Collin County	49	0.02
Prague, OK (city) Lincoln County	48	2.25
Hominy, OK (city) Osage County	48	1.86
Riverside, CA (city) Riverside County	48	0.02
Kellyville, OK (town) Creek County	47	5.19
Harrah, OK (city) Oklahoma County	47	1.00
Milton, FL (city) Santa Rosa County	45	0.64
Depew, OK (town) Creek County	44	7.80
Lynn Haven, FL (city) Bay County	44	0.35
Durant, OK (city) Bryan County	44	0.32
Milwaukee, WI (city) Milwaukee County	44	0.01
Okay, OK (town) Wagoner County	43	7.20
Pawhuska, OK (city) Osage County	42	1.16
Spencer, OK (city) Oklahoma County	42	1.12
El Paso, TX (city) El Paso County	42	0.01
Philadelphia, PA (city) Philadelphia County	40	0.00
Drumright, OK (city) Creek County	39	1.34
Enterprise, AL (city) Coffee County	39	0.18
Honolulu, HI (cdp) Honolulu County	39	0.01
Vacaville, CA (city) Solano County	38	0.04
Stockton, CA (city) San Joaquin County	38	0.02
Ebro, FL (town) Washington County	37	14.80

Notes: (cdp) census designated place; Refer to the Explanation of Data in the front of the book for more detailed information.

American Indian: Creek

Top 150 Places Sorted by Percent

(Based on all places, regardless of population)

Place	Number	%
Stidham, OK (town) McIntosh County	9	39.13
Dustin, OK (town) Hughes County	153	33.85
Yeager, OK (town) Hughes County	18	26.87
Wetumka, OK (city) Hughes County	375	25.84
Blacksville, GA (cdp) Henry County	1	25.00
Weleetka, OK (town) Okfuskee County	224	22.09
Okemah, OK (city) Okfuskee County	580	19.09
Hanna, OK (town) McIntosh County	23	17.29
Grayson, OK (town) Okmulgee County	23	17.16
Dewar, OK (town) Okmulgee County	149	16.21
Ebro, FL (town) Washington County	37	14.80
Spaulding, OK (town) Hughes County	9	14.52
Clearview, OK (town) Okfuskee County	8	14.29
Eufaula, OK (city) McIntosh County	362	13.72
Morris, OK (city) Okmulgee County	177	13.68
Paden, OK (town) Okfuskee County	55	12.33
Lamar, OK (town) Hughes County	20	11.63
Castle, OK (town) Okfuskee County	13	10.66
Okmulgee, OK (city) Okmulgee County	1,330	10.21
Mounds, OK (town) Creek County	114	9.89
Henryetta, OK (city) Okmulgee County	571	9.37
Holdenville, OK (city) Hughes County	437	9.23
Liberty, OK (town) Tulsa County	16	8.70
Cromwell, OK (town) Seminole County	23	8.68
Checotah, OK (city) McIntosh County	289	8.30
Glenpool, OK (city) Tulsa County	641	7.89
Depew, OK (town) Creek County	44	7.80
Okay, OK (town) Wagoner County	43	7.20
Bristow, OK (city) Creek County	305	7.05
Slick, OK (town) Creek County	10	6.76
Beggs, OK (city) Okmulgee County	82	6.01
Wewoka, OK (city) Seminole County	208	5.84
Arcadia, OK (town) Oklahoma County	16	5.73
Boynton, OK (town) Muskogee County	15	5.47
Council Hill, OK (town) Muskogee County	7	5.43
Hoffman, OK (town) Okmulgee County	8	5.41
Kellyville, OK (town) Creek County	47	5.19
Pump Back, OK (cdp) Mayes County	8	5.16
Haskell, OK (town) Muskogee County	90	5.10
Rocky Ford, OK (cdp) Delaware County	3	5.00
Pinhook Corners, OK (cdp) Sequoyah County	8	4.97
Fair Oaks, OK (town) Wagoner County	6	4.92
Coweta, OK (city) Wagoner County	335	4.69
Sapulpa, OK (city) Creek County	857	4.47
Maryetta, OK (cdp) Adair County	6	4.35
Taft, OK (town) Muskogee County	15	4.30
Duchess Landing, OK (cdp) McIntosh County	4	4.21
Schulter, OK (town) Okmulgee County	25	4.17
Lima, OK (town) Seminole County	3	4.05
Sycamore, OK (cdp) Sequoyah County	6	4.00
Shamrock, OK (town) Creek County	5	4.00
Agra, OK (town) Lincoln County	14	3.93
Texanna, OK (cdp) McIntosh County	78	3.74
Oktaha, OK (town) Muskogee County	12	3.67
Hitchita, OK (town) McIntosh County	4	3.54
Oakhurst, OK (cdp) Tulsa County	96	3.52
Notchietown, OK (cdp) Sequoyah County	15	3.49
Kiefer, OK (town) Creek County	35	3.41
East Peru, IA (city) Madison County	5	3.27
Seward, KS (city) Stafford County	2	3.17
Indianola, OK (town) Pittsburg County	6	3.14
Taiwah, OK (cdp) Rogers County	5	3.01
Seminole, OK (city) Seminole County	201	2.91
Freeport, FL (city) Walton County	34	2.86
Muskogee, OK (city) Muskogee County	1,085	2.83
Oologah, OK (town) Rogers County	25	2.83
Libertyville, AL (town) Covington County	3	2.83
Pensacola, OK (town) Mayes County	2	2.82
Stringtown, OK (town) Atoka County	11	2.78
Flute Springs, OK (cdp) Sequoyah County	5	2.75
Campo, CO (town) Baca County	4	2.67
Gregory, OK (cdp) Rogers County	4	2.67
Argyle, GA (town) Clinch County	4	2.65
Foyil, OK (town) Rogers County	6	2.56
Lawrence Creek, OK (town) Creek County	3	2.52
Zena, OK (cdp) Delaware County	3	2.44
Ochelata, OK (town) Washington County	12	2.43
Reese Center, TX (cdp) Lubbock County	1	2.38
Snake Creek, OK (cdp) Mayes County	7	2.35
Dry Creek, OK (cdp) Cherokee County	5	2.31
Wann, OK (town) Nowata County	3	2.27
Prague, OK (city) Lincoln County	48	2.25
Konawa, OK (city) Seminole County	33	2.23
Brooksville, OK (town) Pottawatomie County	2	2.22
Bixby, OK (city) Tulsa County	289	2.17
Kendrick, OK (town) Lincoln County	3	2.17
Twin Oaks, OK (cdp) Delaware County	4	2.15
Bearden, OK (town) Okfuskee County	3	2.14
Opdyke West, TX (town) Hockley County	4	2.13
Atmore, AL (city) Escambia County	161	2.10
Canadian, OK (town) Pittsburg County	5	2.09
New Brockton, AL (town) Coffee County	26	2.08
Kenefic, OK (town) Bryan County	4	2.08
Simms, OK (cdp) Muskogee County	6	2.03
Sasakwa, OK (town) Seminole County	3	2.00
Ponce de Leon, FL (town) Holmes County	9	1.97
Esto, FL (town) Holmes County	7	1.97
Warner, OK (town) Muskogee County	28	1.96
Rentiesville, OK (town) McIntosh County	2	1.96
Cedar Vale, KS (city) Chautauqua County	14	1.94
Langley, OK (town) Mayes County	13	1.94
Locust Grove, OK (town) Mayes County	26	1.90
Lehigh, OK (city) Coal County	6	1.90
Wagoner, OK (city) Wagoner County	145	1.89
Ashland, OK (town) Pittsburg County	1	1.89
Vernon, FL (city) Washington County	14	1.88
Avant, OK (town) Osage County	7	1.88
Jennings, OK (town) Pawnee County	7	1.88
Hominy, OK (city) Osage County	48	1.86
Valley Brook, OK (town) Oklahoma County	15	1.84
Lakeview, AL (town) De Kalb County	3	1.84
Pelican, AK (city) Skagway-Hoonah-Angoon Census Area	3	1.84
Paxton, FL (town) Walton County	12	1.83
Leach, OK (cdp) Delaware County	4	1.82
Barnsdall, OK (city) Osage County	24	1.81
Greasy, OK (cdp) Adair County	7	1.81
Gate, OK (town) Beaver County	2	1.79
Keys, OK (cdp) Cherokee County	8	1.75
Sperry, OK (town) Tulsa County	17	1.73
Eldon, OK (cdp) Cherokee County	17	1.72
Woodston, KS (city) Rooks County	2	1.72
Dasher, GA (town) Lowndes County	14	1.68
Turley, OK (cdp) Tulsa County	54	1.67
Jenks, OK (city) Tulsa County	159	1.66
Winchester, OK (town) Okmulgee County	7	1.65
Justice, OK (cdp) Rogers County	21	1.60
Shawnee, OK (city) Pottawatomie County	456	1.59
Lakeville, ME (town) Penobscot County	1	1.59
Porter, OK (town) Wagoner County	9	1.57
Pittman, FL (cdp) Lake County	3	1.56
Fort Gibson, OK (town) Muskogee County	63	1.55
Salina, OK (town) Mayes County	22	1.55
Longtown, OK (cdp) Pittsburg County	37	1.54
Meno, OK (town) Major County	3	1.54
Grand Lake Towne, OK (town) Mayes County	1	1.54
Meeker, OK (town) Lincoln County	15	1.53
McLoud, OK (town) Pottawatomie County	54	1.52
Grand Ridge, FL (town) Jackson County	12	1.52
Tahlequah, OK (city) Cherokee County	218	1.51
Sentinel, OK (town) Washita County	13	1.51
River Bottom, OK (cdp) Muskogee County	4	1.51
Talala, OK (town) Rogers County	4	1.48
Chewey, OK (cdp) Adair County	2	1.48
Sand Springs, OK (city) Tulsa County	256	1.47
Byng, OK (town) Pontotoc County	16	1.47
Olustee, OK (town) Jackson County	10	1.47
Saint Louis, OK (town) Pottawatomie County	3	1.46
Sparks, OK (town) Lincoln County	2	1.46
Catoosa, OK (city) Rogers County	78	1.43
Sand Hills, OK (cdp) Muskogee County	6	1.42

Notes: (cdp) census designated place; Refer to the Explanation of Data in the front of the book for more detailed information.

American Indian: Creek

Top 150 Places Sorted by Percent

(Based on places with populations of 10,000 or more)

Place	Number	%
Okmulgee, OK (city) Okmulgee County	1,330	10.21
Sapulpa, OK (city) Creek County	857	4.47
Muskogee, OK (city) Muskogee County	1,085	2.83
Bixby, OK (city) Tulsa County	289	2.17
Shawnee, OK (city) Pottawatomie County	456	1.59
Tahlequah, OK (city) Cherokee County	218	1.51
Sand Springs, OK (city) Tulsa County	256	1.47
Claremore, OK (city) Rogers County	188	1.18
Ada, OK (city) Pontotoc County	182	1.16
Tulsa, OK (city) Tulsa County	4,358	1.11
McAlester, OK (city) Pittsburg County	163	0.92
Broken Arrow, OK (city) Tulsa County	671	0.90
Owasso, OK (city) Tulsa County	132	0.71
West Pensacola, FL (cdp) Escambia County	150	0.68
Ensley, FL (cdp) Escambia County	125	0.67
Del City, OK (city) Oklahoma County	145	0.66
Bellview, FL (cdp) Escambia County	135	0.64
Gonzalez, FL (cdp) Escambia County	71	0.62
Warrington, FL (cdp) Escambia County	89	0.59
Moore, OK (city) Cleveland County	225	0.55
Midwest City, OK (city) Oklahoma County	262	0.48
Oklahoma City, OK (city) Oklahoma County	2,361	0.47
Stillwater, OK (city) Payne County	180	0.46
Norman, OK (city) Cleveland County	432	0.45
Miami, OK (city) Ottawa County	62	0.45
Mustang, OK (city) Canadian County	59	0.45
Brent, FL (cdp) Escambia County	98	0.44
Myrtle Grove, FL (cdp) Escambia County	76	0.44
Ferry Pass, FL (cdp) Escambia County	108	0.40
Bethany, OK (city) Oklahoma County	73	0.36
Lynn Haven, FL (city) Bay County	44	0.35
The Village, OK (city) Oklahoma County	36	0.35
Bartlesville, OK (city) Washington County	114	0.33
El Reno, OK (city) Canadian County	53	0.33
Durant, OK (city) Bryan County	44	0.32
Chickasha, OK (city) Grady County	49	0.31
Edmond, OK (city) Oklahoma County	198	0.29
Yukon, OK (city) Canadian County	60	0.29
Elk City, OK (city) Beckham County	30	0.29
Pensacola, FL (city) Escambia County	160	0.28
Arkansas City, KS (city) Cowley County	33	0.28
Upper Grand Lagoon, FL (cdp) Bay County	31	0.28
Ponca City, OK (city) Kay County	67	0.26
Ardmore, OK (city) Carter County	60	0.25
Panama City, FL (city) Bay County	87	0.24
Lawrence, KS (city) Douglas County	181	0.23
Troy, AL (city) Pike County	30	0.22
Saraland, AL (city) Mobile County	27	0.22
Callaway, FL (city) Bay County	30	0.21
Enid, OK (city) Garfield County	94	0.20
Fairhope, AL (city) Baldwin County	24	0.19
Siloam Springs, AR (city) Benton County	21	0.19
Enterprise, AL (city) Coffee County	39	0.18
Tillmans Corner, AL (cdp) Mobile County	28	0.18
Woodward, OK (city) Woodward County	21	0.18
Altus, OK (city) Jackson County	37	0.17
Ozark, AL (city) Dale County	26	0.17
Crestview, FL (city) Okaloosa County	25	0.17
Duncan, OK (city) Stephens County	35	0.16
Fort Walton Beach, FL (city) Okaloosa County	31	0.16
Lawton, OK (city) Comanche County	139	0.15
Niceville, FL (city) Okaloosa County	18	0.15
Leeds, AL (city) Jefferson County	14	0.13
Prattville, AL (city) Autauga County	30	0.12
Wichita, KS (city) Sedgwick County	394	0.11
Bentonville, AR (city) Benton County	22	0.11
Selma, CA (city) Fresno County	21	0.11
Winfield, KS (city) Cowley County	14	0.11
Gautier, MS (city) Jackson County	13	0.11
Saks, AL (cdp) Calhoun County	12	0.11
Millbrook, AL (city) Elmore County	11	0.11
Pelham, AL (city) Shelby County	14	0.10
Destin, FL (city) Okaloosa County	11	0.10
Helena, AL (city) Shelby County	10	0.10
Oildale, CA (cdp) Kern County	25	0.09
Smiths, AL (cdp) Lee County	19	0.09
Oxford, AL (city) Calhoun County	13	0.09
Coffeyville, KS (city) Montgomery County	10	0.09
Mobile, AL (city) Mobile County	163	0.08
Dothan, AL (city) Houston County	49	0.08
Ceres, CA (city) Stanislaus County	28	0.08
Keller, TX (city) Tarrant County	21	0.08
Wright, FL (cdp) Okaloosa County	18	0.08
Daphne, AL (city) Baldwin County	14	0.08
Morgan City, LA (city) Saint Mary Parish	10	0.08
Ottawa, KS (city) Franklin County	10	0.08
Griswold, CT (town) New London County	9	0.08
Lea Hill, WA (cdp) King County	9	0.08
Tallahassee, FL (city) Leon County	107	0.07
Fort Smith, AR (city) Sebastian County	59	0.07
Joplin, MO (city) Jasper County	31	0.07
Haltom City, TX (city) Tarrant County	27	0.07
Lebanon, TN (city) Wilson County	14	0.07
White Center, WA (cdp) King County	14	0.07
Thomasville, GA (city) Thomas County	12	0.07
Bellair-Meadowbrook Terrace, FL (cdp) Clay County	11	0.07
Hueytown, AL (city) Jefferson County	10	0.07
Blythe, CA (city) Riverside County	9	0.07
Holly Hill, FL (city) Volusia County	9	0.07
Red Bluff, CA (city) Tehama County	9	0.07
Chowchilla, CA (city) Madera County	8	0.07
Hartselle, AL (city) Morgan County	8	0.07
Highland Village, TX (city) Denton County	8	0.07
View Park-Windsor Hills, CA (cdp) Los Angeles County	8	0.07
Guymon, OK (city) Texas County	7	0.07
Montgomery, AL (city) Montgomery County	115	0.06
Euless, TX (city) Tarrant County	26	0.06
Allen, TX (city) Collin County	24	0.06
Rogers, AR (city) Benton County	22	0.06
Juneau, AK (city and borough) Juneau Borough	17	0.06
Prichard, AL (city) Mobile County	16	0.06
Suisun City, CA (city) Solano County	16	0.06
Alabaster, AL (city) Shelby County	14	0.06
Casa Grande, AZ (city) Pinal County	14	0.06
Derby, KS (city) Sedgwick County	11	0.06
Americus, GA (city) Sumter County	10	0.06
Ocean Springs, MS (city) Jackson County	10	0.06
Bartow, FL (city) Polk County	9	0.06
Gainesville, TX (city) Cooke County	9	0.06
Horn Lake, MS (city) De Soto County	9	0.06
Portland, TX (city) San Patricio County	9	0.06
Ramona, CA (cdp) San Diego County	9	0.06
Homosassa Springs, FL (cdp) Citrus County	8	0.06
Sylacauga, AL (city) Talladega County	8	0.06
Trussville, AL (city) Jefferson County	8	0.06
Winter Garden, FL (city) Orange County	8	0.06
Auburn, CA (city) Placer County	7	0.06
Beaumont, CA (city) Riverside County	7	0.06
Corinth, TX (city) Denton County	7	0.06
El Dorado, KS (city) Butler County	7	0.06
Fort Drum, NY (cdp) Jefferson County	7	0.06
Vernon, TX (city) Wilbarger County	7	0.06
Weigelstown, PA (cdp) York County	6	0.06
West Valley, WA (cdp) Yakima County	6	0.06
Zephyrhills, FL (city) Pasco County	6	0.06
Bakersfield, CA (city) Kern County	121	0.05
Fayetteville, AR (city) Washington County	30	0.05
Lodi, CA (city) San Joaquin County	26	0.05
Grapevine, TX (city) Tarrant County	23	0.05
Warner Robins, GA (city) Houston County	23	0.05
Tulare, CA (city) Tulare County	20	0.05
Sherman, TX (city) Grayson County	19	0.05
Farmington, NM (city) San Juan County	18	0.05
Martinez, CA (city) Contra Costa County	17	0.05
Cedar Hill, TX (city) Dallas County	15	0.05
Slidell, LA (city) Saint Tammany Parish	14	0.05
Anniston, AL (city) Calhoun County	12	0.05
Casselberry, FL (city) Seminole County	12	0.05
Denison, TX (city) Grayson County	12	0.05
Eureka, CA (city) Humboldt County	12	0.05

Notes: (cdp) census designated place; Refer to the Explanation of Data in the front of the book for more detailed information.

American Indian: Crow

Top 150 Places Sorted by Number

(Based on all places, regardless of population)

Place	Number	%
Crow Agency, MT (cdp) Big Horn County	1,331	85.76
Billings, MT (city) Yellowstone County	925	1.03
Hardin, MT (city) Big Horn County	864	25.53
Pryor, MT (cdp) Big Horn County	504	80.25
Lodge Grass, MT (town) Big Horn County	406	79.61
Wyola, MT (cdp) Big Horn County	142	76.34
Lame Deer, MT (cdp) Rosebud County	109	5.40
Missoula, MT (city) Missoula County	54	0.09
Los Angeles, CA (city) Los Angeles County	52	0.00
Seattle, WA (city) King County	50	0.01
Bozeman, MT (city) Gallatin County	46	0.17
Albuquerque, NM (city) Bernalillo County	45	0.01
Ranchester, WY (town) Sheridan County	44	6.28
New York, NY (city) New York City	44	0.00
Butte-Silver Bow, MT (special city) Silver Bow County	41	0.12
Sacramento, CA (city) Sacramento County	38	0.01
Muddy, MT (cdp) Big Horn County	34	5.42
Philadelphia, PA (city) Philadelphia County	34	0.00
Sheridan, WY (city) Sheridan County	33	0.21
Spokane, WA (city) Spokane County	33	0.02
Saint Xavier, MT (cdp) Big Horn County	32	47.76
Anchorage, AK (municipality) Anchorage Borough	32	0.01
Phoenix, AZ (city) Maricopa County	32	0.00
Fort Smith, MT (cdp) Big Horn County	30	24.59
Busby, MT (cdp) Big Horn County	29	4.17
San Diego, CA (city) San Diego County	29	0.00
Lawrence, KS (city) Douglas County	26	0.03
Fort Belknap Agency, MT (cdp) Blaine County	25	1.98
Denver, CO (city) Denver County	23	0.00
Bismarck, ND (city) Burleigh County	22	0.04
Great Falls, MT (city) Cascade County	22	0.04
Chicago, IL (city) Cook County	22	0.00
Detroit, MI (city) Wayne County	22	0.00
San Antonio, TX (city) Bexar County	22	0.00
Box Elder, MT (cdp) Hill County	21	2.64
Saint Joseph, MO (city) Buchanan County	21	0.03
Tacoma, WA (city) Pierce County	21	0.01
Fresno, CA (city) Fresno County	21	0.00
Tulsa, OK (city) Tulsa County	20	0.01
Oklahoma City, OK (city) Oklahoma County	20	0.00
Lockwood, MT (cdp) Yellowstone County	19	0.44
Salem, OR (city) Marion County	19	0.01
Long Beach, CA (city) Los Angeles County	19	0.00
Toledo, OH (city) Lucas County	17	0.01
Vallejo, CA (city) Solano County	17	0.01
Milwaukee, WI (city) Milwaukee County	17	0.00
Oakland, CA (city) Alameda County	17	0.00
Anadarko, OK (city) Caddo County	16	0.24
Portland, OR (city) Multnomah County	16	0.00
Lewistown, MT (city) Fergus County	15	0.26
Havre, MT (city) Hill County	15	0.16
Reno, NV (city) Washoe County	15	0.01
Tucson, AZ (city) Pima County	15	0.00
Dayton, WY (town) Sheridan County	14	2.06
Woodland, CA (city) Yolo County	14	0.03
Aurora, CO (city) Arapahoe County	14	0.01
Mesa, AZ (city) Maricopa County	14	0.00
Boise City, ID (city) Ada County	13	0.01
San Francisco, CA (city) San Francisco County	13	0.00
Ethete, WY (cdp) Fremont County	12	0.82
North Browning, MT (cdp) Glacier County	12	0.55
Lakewood, CO (city) Jefferson County	12	0.01
Topeka, KS (city) Shawnee County	12	0.01
Honolulu, HI (cdp) Honolulu County	12	0.00
Houston, TX (city) Harris County	12	0.00
Indianapolis, IN (special city) Marion County	12	0.00
Kansas City, MO (city) Jackson County	12	0.00
San Jose, CA (city) Santa Clara County	12	0.00
Colstrip, MT (city) Rosebud County	11	0.47
Rapid City, SD (city) Pennington County	11	0.02
Austin, TX (city) Travis County	11	0.00
Baltimore, MD (independent city) Baltimore city	11	0.00
Columbus, OH (city) Franklin County	11	0.00
Dallas, TX (city) Dallas County	11	0.00
Fort Worth, TX (city) Tarrant County	11	0.00

Place	Number	%
Las Vegas, NV (city) Clark County	11	0.00
Wichita, KS (city) Sedgwick County	11	0.00
Hysham, MT (town) Treasure County	10	3.03
Harlem, MT (city) Blaine County	10	1.18
Arapahoe, WY (cdp) Fremont County	10	0.57
Gillette, WY (city) Campbell County	10	0.05
South Valley, NM (cdp) Bernalillo County	10	0.03
Lakewood, WA (city) Pierce County	10	0.02
Grand Rapids, MI (city) Kent County	10	0.01
Modesto, CA (city) Stanislaus County	10	0.01
Charlotte, NC (city) Mecklenburg County	10	0.00
Colorado Springs, CO (city) El Paso County	10	0.00
Virginia Beach, VA (independent city) Virginia Beach city	10	0.00
Washington, DC (city) District of Columbia	10	0.00
Athol, MA (town) Worcester County	9	0.08
Cleveland Heights, OH (city) Cuyahoga County	9	0.02
Citrus Heights, CA (city) Sacramento County	9	0.01
Eugene, OR (city) Lane County	9	0.01
Kent, WA (city) King County	9	0.01
Lancaster, CA (city) Los Angeles County	9	0.01
Napa, CA (city) Napa County	9	0.01
Peoria, AZ (city) Maricopa County	9	0.01
Springfield, MO (city) Greene County	9	0.01
Bakersfield, CA (city) Kern County	9	0.00
Minneapolis, MN (city) Hennepin County	9	0.00
Shreveport, LA (city) Caddo Parish	9	0.00
Agency, MT (cdp) Hill County	8	2.47
Ashland, MT (cdp) Rosebud County	8	1.72
New Town, ND (city) Mountrail County	8	0.59
Monon, IN (town) White County	8	0.46
Pablo, MT (cdp) Lake County	8	0.44
Douglas, WY (city) Converse County	8	0.15
La Puente, CA (city) Los Angeles County	8	0.02
Shoreline, WA (city) King County	8	0.02
Beaverton, OR (city) Washington County	8	0.01
Fort Collins, CO (city) Larimer County	8	0.01
North Las Vegas, NV (city) Clark County	8	0.01
Thornton, CO (city) Adams County	8	0.01
Yakima, WA (city) Yakima County	8	0.01
Akron, OH (city) Summit County	8	0.00
Anaheim, CA (city) Orange County	8	0.00
Cleveland, OH (city) Cuyahoga County	8	0.00
Nashville-Davidson, TN (special city) Davidson County	8	0.00
Riverside, CA (city) Riverside County	8	0.00
Cannon Ball, ND (cdp) Sioux County	7	0.81
Kyle, SD (cdp) Shannon County	7	0.72
Red Lodge, MT (city) Carbon County	7	0.32
Hauula, HI (cdp) Honolulu County	7	0.19
New Philadelphia, OH (city) Tuscarawas County	7	0.04
Florin, CA (cdp) Sacramento County	7	0.03
South Lake Tahoe, CA (city) El Dorado County	7	0.03
Juneau, AK (city and borough) Juneau Borough	7	0.02
Kearns, UT (cdp) Salt Lake County	7	0.02
Shawnee, OK (city) Pottawatomie County	7	0.02
Arvada, CO (city) Jefferson County	7	0.01
Bellingham, WA (city) Whatcom County	7	0.01
Boulder, CO (city) Boulder County	7	0.01
Costa Mesa, CA (city) Orange County	7	0.01
Flint, MI (city) Genesee County	7	0.01
New Haven, CT (city) New Haven County	7	0.01
Santa Fe, NM (city) Santa Fe County	7	0.01
Sioux Falls, SD (city) Minnehaha County	7	0.01
Arlington, VA (cdp) Arlington County	7	0.00
Chattanooga, TN (city) Hamilton County	7	0.00
Chula Vista, CA (city) San Diego County	7	0.00
Cincinnati, OH (city) Hamilton County	7	0.00
Hempstead, NY (town) Nassau County	7	0.00
Jacksonville, FL (special city) Duval County	7	0.00
Kansas City, KS (city) Wyandotte County	7	0.00
Salt Lake City, UT (city) Salt Lake County	7	0.00
Nixon, NV (cdp) Washoe County	6	1.44
Poplar, MT (city) Roosevelt County	6	0.66
Lapwai, ID (city) Nez Perce County	6	0.53
South Browning, MT (cdp) Glacier County	6	0.36
Cut Bank, MT (city) Glacier County	6	0.19

Notes: (cdp) census designated place; Refer to the Explanation of Data in the front of the book for more detailed information.

American Indian: Crow

Top 150 Places Sorted by Percent

(Based on all places, regardless of population)

Place	Number	%
Crow Agency, MT (cdp) Big Horn County	1,331	85.76
Pryor, MT (cdp) Big Horn County	504	80.25
Lodge Grass, MT (town) Big Horn County	406	79.61
Wyola, MT (cdp) Big Horn County	142	76.34
Saint Xavier, MT (cdp) Big Horn County	32	47.76
Hardin, MT (city) Big Horn County	864	25.53
Fort Smith, MT (cdp) Big Horn County	30	24.59
Ranchester, WY (town) Sheridan County	44	6.28
Muddy, MT (cdp) Big Horn County	34	5.42
Lame Deer, MT (cdp) Rosebud County	109	5.40
Busby, MT (cdp) Big Horn County	29	4.17
Hysham, MT (town) Treasure County	10	3.03
Arvada, WY (cdp) Sheridan County	1	3.03
Birney, MT (cdp) Rosebud County	3	2.78
Box Elder, MT (cdp) Hill County	21	2.64
Agency, MT (cdp) Hill County	8	2.47
Old Agency, MT (cdp) Sanders County	2	2.11
Dayton, WY (town) Sheridan County	14	2.06
Fort Belknap Agency, MT (cdp) Blaine County	25	1.98
Ashland, MT (cdp) Rosebud County	8	1.72
Dodson, MT (town) Phillips County	2	1.64
Nixon, NV (cdp) Washoe County	6	1.44
Parker School, MT (cdp) Chouteau County	5	1.42
White Cloud, KS (city) Doniphan County	3	1.26
Firth, ID (city) Bingham County	5	1.23
Lohrville, WI (village) Waushara County	5	1.23
Harlem, MT (city) Blaine County	10	1.18
West Brooklyn, IL (village) Lee County	2	1.15
Billings, MT (city) Yellowstone County	925	1.03
Skedee, OK (town) Pawnee County	1	0.98
Chehalis Village, WA (cdp) Grays Harbor County	3	0.87
Arlee, MT (cdp) Lake County	5	0.83
Ethete, WY (cdp) Fremont County	12	0.82
Cannon Ball, ND (cdp) Sioux County	7	0.81
Parkman, WY (cdp) Sheridan County	1	0.73
Kyle, SD (cdp) Shannon County	7	0.72
Mandaree, ND (cdp) McKenzie County	4	0.72
Thurston, OH (village) Fairfield County	4	0.72
Saint Pierre, MT (cdp) Hill County	2	0.69
Beaver, OR (cdp) Tillamook County	1	0.69
Riverbend, MT (cdp) Mineral County	3	0.68
Bygland, MN (township) Polk County	2	0.67
Poplar, MT (city) Roosevelt County	6	0.66
Monument, OR (city) Grant County	1	0.66
Bainville, MT (town) Roosevelt County	1	0.65
Iron Horse, CA (cdp) Plumas County	2	0.62
Isleta Village Proper, NM (cdp) Bernalillo County	3	0.60
Hallett, OK (town) Pawnee County	1	0.60
New Town, ND (city) Mountrail County	8	0.59
Bellechester, MN (city) Goodhue County	1	0.58
Arapahoe, WY (cdp) Fremont County	10	0.57
Altamont, UT (town) Duchesne County	1	0.56
North Browning, MT (cdp) Glacier County	12	0.55
Schurz, NV (cdp) Mineral County	4	0.55
Tordenskjold, MN (township) Otter Tail County	3	0.55
Lapwai, ID (city) Nez Perce County	6	0.53
Boneau, MT (cdp) Chouteau County	1	0.53
Joliet, MT (town) Carbon County	3	0.52
Ten Lake, MN (township) Beltrami County	5	0.50
Owyhee, NV (cdp) Elko County	5	0.49
Moose Pass, AK (cdp) Kenai Peninsula Borough	1	0.49
Sportsmen Acres, OK (town) Mayes County	1	0.49
Frannie, WY (town) Big Horn County	1	0.48
Roseville, PA (borough) Tioga County	1	0.48
Colstrip, MT (city) Rosebud County	11	0.47
Lodge Pole, MT (cdp) Blaine County	1	0.47
Monon, IN (town) White County	8	0.46
Belfry, MT (cdp) Carbon County	1	0.46
Timber Lake, SD (city) Dewey County	2	0.45
Saco, MT (town) Phillips County	1	0.45
Lockwood, MT (cdp) Yellowstone County	19	0.44
Pablo, MT (cdp) Lake County	8	0.44
Beaver Crossing, NE (village) Seward County	2	0.44
West Mineral, KS (city) Cherokee County	1	0.41
Bear River City, UT (town) Box Elder County	3	0.40
Woods Bay, MT (cdp) Lake County	3	0.40
Azure, MT (cdp) Hill County	1	0.40
Curryville, MO (city) Pike County	1	0.40
Star Valley Ranch, WY (cdp) Lincoln County	3	0.39
De Kalb, MO (town) Buchanan County	1	0.39
Saint Ignatius, MT (town) Lake County	3	0.38
Keams Canyon, AZ (cdp) Navajo County	1	0.38
Prescott, IA (city) Adams County	1	0.38
South Browning, MT (cdp) Glacier County	6	0.36
Burlington, ND (city) Ward County	4	0.36
Naco, AZ (cdp) Cochise County	3	0.36
Wellston, OK (town) Lincoln County	3	0.36
Park City, MT (cdp) Stillwater County	3	0.34
Evergreen, MN (township) Becker County	1	0.34
Cyrus, MN (city) Pope County	1	0.33
Red Lodge, MT (city) Carbon County	7	0.32
Tuscarawas, OH (village) Tuscarawas County	3	0.32
Belt, MT (city) Cascade County	2	0.32
Sherrodsville, OH (village) Carroll County	1	0.32
Lakeside, MT (cdp) Flathead County	5	0.30
Seama, NM (cdp) Cibola County	1	0.30
Fort Thompson, SD (cdp) Buffalo County	4	0.29
Coulee Dam, WA (town) Okanogan County	3	0.29
Heart Butte, MT (cdp) Pondera County	2	0.29
Womens Bay, AK (cdp) Kodiak Island Borough	2	0.29
Browning, MT (town) Glacier County	3	0.28
Colbert, OK (town) Bryan County	3	0.28
Hays, MT (cdp) Blaine County	2	0.28
Minnesota Falls, MN (township) Yellow Medicine County	1	0.28
Ganado, AZ (cdp) Apache County	4	0.27
Medicine Park, OK (town) Comanche County	1	0.27
Wakonda, SD (town) Clay County	1	0.27
Lewistown, MT (city) Fergus County	15	0.26
Roxand, MI (township) Eaton County	5	0.26
Atlanta, MI (cdp) Montmorency County	2	0.26
Boulder Flats, WY (cdp) Fremont County	1	0.26
Palermo, ME (town) Waldo County	3	0.25
Neah Bay, WA (cdp) Clallam County	2	0.25
East Glacier Park Village, MT (cdp) Glacier County	1	0.25
Anadarko, OK (city) Caddo County	16	0.24
Cambridge, IA (city) Story County	2	0.24
Hartland, WI (town) Shawano County	2	0.24
Marty, SD (cdp) Charles Mix County	1	0.24
Westcliffe, CO (town) Custer County	1	0.24
Wharton, OH (village) Wyandot County	1	0.24
Columbus, MT (town) Stillwater County	4	0.23
Boulder, MT (town) Jefferson County	3	0.23
Maywood, MN (township) Benton County	2	0.23
Cooter, MO (city) Pemiscot County	1	0.23
Raymondville, MO (town) Texas County	1	0.23
Archer City, TX (city) Archer County	4	0.22
Four Corners, MT (cdp) Gallatin County	4	0.22
La Crosse, KS (city) Rush County	3	0.22
Worcester, VT (town) Washington County	2	0.22
Eden Roc, HI (cdp) Hawaii County	1	0.22
Frazer, MT (cdp) Valley County	1	0.22
Rocky Mountain, OK (cdp) Adair County	1	0.22
Sheridan, WY (city) Sheridan County	33	0.21
San Miguel, CA (cdp) San Luis Obispo County	3	0.21
Balsam Lake, WI (village) Polk County	2	0.21
Deckerville, MI (village) Sanilac County	2	0.21
Macy, NE (cdp) Thurston County	2	0.21
Stover, MO (city) Morgan County	2	0.21
Allegheny, PA (township) Cambria County	5	0.20
Fort Pierre, SD (city) Stanley County	4	0.20
Roanoke, IL (village) Woodford County	4	0.20
Mission, OR (cdp) Umatilla County	2	0.20
Pineland, TX (city) Sabine County	2	0.20
Quapaw, OK (town) Ottawa County	2	0.20
Winter Harbor, ME (town) Hancock County	2	0.20
Ernest, PA (borough) Indiana County	1	0.20
Goodar, MI (township) Ogemaw County	1	0.20
Jackson, ME (town) Waldo County	1	0.20
Toboyne, PA (township) Perry County	1	0.20
Hauula, HI (cdp) Honolulu County	7	0.19

Notes: (cdp) census designated place; Refer to the Explanation of Data in the front of the book for more detailed information.

American Indian: Crow

Top 150 Places Sorted by Percent

(Based on places with populations of 10,000 or more)

Place	Number	%
Billings, MT (city) Yellowstone County	925	1.03
Sheridan, WY (city) Sheridan County	33	0.21
Bozeman, MT (city) Gallatin County	46	0.17
Butte-Silver Bow, MT (special city) Silver Bow County	41	0.12
Missoula, MT (city) Missoula County	54	0.09
Athol, MA (town) Worcester County	9	0.08
Excelsior Springs, MO (city) Clay County	6	0.06
Gillette, WY (city) Campbell County	10	0.05
Hanover, NH (town) Grafton County	5	0.05
Bismarck, ND (city) Burleigh County	22	0.04
Great Falls, MT (city) Cascade County	22	0.04
New Philadelphia, OH (city) Tuscarawas County	7	0.04
Black Forest, CO (cdp) El Paso County	5	0.04
Green River, WY (city) Sweetwater County	5	0.04
McKinleyville, CA (cdp) Humboldt County	5	0.04
Crestline, CA (cdp) San Bernardino County	4	0.04
Fort Carson, CO (cdp) El Paso County	4	0.04
Gages Lake, IL (cdp) Lake County	4	0.04
Vashon, WA (cdp) King County	4	0.04
Lawrence, KS (city) Douglas County	26	0.03
Saint Joseph, MO (city) Buchanan County	21	0.03
Woodland, CA (city) Yolo County	14	0.03
South Valley, NM (cdp) Bernalillo County	10	0.03
Florin, CA (cdp) Sacramento County	7	0.03
South Lake Tahoe, CA (city) El Dorado County	7	0.03
Lemoore, CA (city) Kings County	5	0.03
Antrim, PA (township) Franklin County	4	0.03
Ellensburg, WA (city) Kittitas County	4	0.03
Gorham, ME (town) Cumberland County	4	0.03
Grand Haven, MI (township) Ottawa County	4	0.03
Sierra Vista Southeast, AZ (cdp) Cochise County	4	0.03
Chesapeake Ranch Estates-Drum Point, MD (cdp) Calvert County	3	0.03
Lumberton, NJ (township) Burlington County	3	0.03
Woodlyn, PA (cdp) Delaware County	3	0.03
Spokane, WA (city) Spokane County	33	0.02
Rapid City, SD (city) Pennington County	11	0.02
Lakewood, WA (city) Pierce County	10	0.02
Cleveland Heights, OH (city) Cuyahoga County	9	0.02
La Puente, CA (city) Los Angeles County	8	0.02
Shoreline, WA (city) King County	8	0.02
Juneau, AK (city and borough) Juneau Borough	7	0.02
Kearns, UT (cdp) Salt Lake County	7	0.02
Shawnee, OK (city) Pottawatomie County	7	0.02
Bremerton, WA (city) Kitsap County	6	0.02
Chesterfield, MI (township) Macomb County	6	0.02
Eureka, CA (city) Humboldt County	6	0.02
Ashland, CA (cdp) Alameda County	5	0.02
Des Moines, WA (city) King County	5	0.02
Elmira, NY (city) Chemung County	5	0.02
Helena, MT (city) Lewis and Clark County	5	0.02
Kahului, HI (cdp) Maui County	5	0.02
La Verne, CA (city) Los Angeles County	5	0.02
Mamaroneck, NY (town) Westchester County	5	0.02
North Ridgeville, OH (city) Lorain County	5	0.02
Pahrump, NV (cdp) Nye County	5	0.02
Parkland, WA (cdp) Pierce County	5	0.02
Peekskill, NY (city) Westchester County	5	0.02
Prescott Valley, AZ (town) Yavapai County	5	0.02
Suisun City, CA (city) Solano County	5	0.02
Vernon, NJ (township) Sussex County	5	0.02
White Center, WA (cdp) King County	5	0.02
Anderson, SC (city) Anderson County	4	0.02
Grants Pass, OR (city) Josephine County	4	0.02
Lake Worth Corridor, FL (cdp) Palm Beach County	4	0.02
Norco, CA (city) Riverside County	4	0.02
Oakley, CA (city) Contra Costa County	4	0.02
Paragould, AR (city) Greene County	4	0.02
Post Falls, ID (city) Kootenai County	4	0.02
Red Wing, MN (city) Goodhue County	4	0.02
Seymour, IN (city) Jackson County	4	0.02
Sidney, OH (city) Shelby County	4	0.02
Steubenville, OH (city) Jefferson County	4	0.02
Van Buren, AR (city) Crawford County	4	0.02
Waldorf, MD (cdp) Charles County	4	0.02
Brattleboro, VT (town) Windham County	3	0.02

Place	Number	%
Brigham City, UT (city) Box Elder County	3	0.02
Cottonwood West, UT (cdp) Salt Lake County	3	0.02
Dickinson, ND (city) Stark County	3	0.02
Elko, NV (city) Elko County	3	0.02
Fairview, PA (township) York County	3	0.02
Fenton, MI (township) Genesee County	3	0.02
Fort Lewis, WA (cdp) Pierce County	3	0.02
Fort Payne, AL (city) De Kalb County	3	0.02
Hawaiian Gardens, CA (city) Los Angeles County	3	0.02
La Vergne, TN (city) Rutherford County	3	0.02
Makakilo City, HI (cdp) Honolulu County	3	0.02
Miamisburg, OH (city) Montgomery County	3	0.02
Midlothian, IL (village) Cook County	3	0.02
Newberg, OR (city) Yamhill County	3	0.02
Oswego, IL (village) Kendall County	3	0.02
Pacific Grove, CA (city) Monterey County	3	0.02
Rock Springs, WY (city) Sweetwater County	3	0.02
Sylvania, OH (city) Lucas County	3	0.02
Vandalia, OH (city) Montgomery County	3	0.02
West Fargo, ND (city) Cass County	3	0.02
Whitehall, OH (city) Franklin County	3	0.02
Winter Gardens, CA (cdp) San Diego County	3	0.02
Corinth, TX (city) Denton County	2	0.02
Evanston, WY (city) Uinta County	2	0.02
Fort Drum, NY (cdp) Jefferson County	2	0.02
Grass Valley, CA (city) Nevada County	2	0.02
Hanahan, SC (city) Berkeley County	2	0.02
Hartland, MI (township) Livingston County	2	0.02
Hermiston, OR (city) Umatilla County	2	0.02
Herrin, IL (city) Williamson County	2	0.02
Issaquah, WA (city) King County	2	0.02
Lansdowne, PA (borough) Delaware County	2	0.02
Malibu, CA (city) Los Angeles County	2	0.02
Middleburg, FL (cdp) Clay County	2	0.02
Morrisville, PA (borough) Bucks County	2	0.02
Oneida, NY (city) Madison County	2	0.02
Oroville, CA (city) Butte County	2	0.02
Picayune, MS (city) Pearl River County	2	0.02
Red Bank, TN (city) Hamilton County	2	0.02
Riverview, FL (cdp) Hillsborough County	2	0.02
Sierra Madre, CA (city) Los Angeles County	2	0.02
Soddy-Daisy, TN (city) Hamilton County	2	0.02
Springdale, OH (city) Hamilton County	2	0.02
Sturgis, MI (city) Saint Joseph County	2	0.02
Waianae, HI (cdp) Honolulu County	2	0.02
Seattle, WA (city) King County	50	0.01
Albuquerque, NM (city) Bernalillo County	45	0.01
Sacramento, CA (city) Sacramento County	38	0.01
Anchorage, AK (municipality) Anchorage Borough	32	0.01
Tacoma, WA (city) Pierce County	21	0.01
Tulsa, OK (city) Tulsa County	20	0.01
Salem, OR (city) Marion County	19	0.01
Toledo, OH (city) Lucas County	17	0.01
Vallejo, CA (city) Solano County	17	0.01
Reno, NV (city) Washoe County	15	0.01
Aurora, CO (city) Arapahoe County	14	0.01
Boise City, ID (city) Ada County	13	0.01
Lakewood, CO (city) Jefferson County	12	0.01
Topeka, KS (city) Shawnee County	12	0.01
Grand Rapids, MI (city) Kent County	10	0.01
Modesto, CA (city) Stanislaus County	10	0.01
Citrus Heights, CA (city) Sacramento County	9	0.01
Eugene, OR (city) Lane County	9	0.01
Kent, WA (city) King County	9	0.01
Lancaster, CA (city) Los Angeles County	9	0.01
Napa, CA (city) Napa County	9	0.01
Peoria, AZ (city) Maricopa County	9	0.01
Springfield, MO (city) Greene County	9	0.01
Beaverton, OR (city) Washington County	8	0.01
Fort Collins, CO (city) Larimer County	8	0.01
North Las Vegas, NV (city) Clark County	8	0.01
Thornton, CO (city) Adams County	8	0.01
Yakima, WA (city) Yakima County	8	0.01
Arvada, CO (city) Jefferson County	7	0.01
Bellingham, WA (city) Whatcom County	7	0.01

Notes: (cdp) census designated place; Refer to the Explanation of Data in the front of the book for more detailed information.

American Indian: Delaware

Top 150 Places Sorted by Number

(Based on all places, regardless of population)

Place	Number	%
Bartlesville, OK (city) Washington County	396	1.14
Tulsa, OK (city) Tulsa County	339	0.09
Oklahoma City, OK (city) Oklahoma County	281	0.06
Philadelphia, PA (city) Philadelphia County	208	0.01
Nowata, OK (city) Nowata County	150	3.78
New York, NY (city) New York City	150	0.00
Ringwood, NJ (borough) Passaic County	145	1.17
Ramapo, NY (town) Rockland County	142	0.13
Mahwah, NJ (township) Bergen County	131	0.54
Anadarko, OK (city) Caddo County	109	1.64
Hillburn, NY (village) Rockland County	104	11.80
West Milford, NJ (cdp) Passaic County	88	0.33
Canton, OH (city) Stark County	86	0.11
Los Angeles, CA (city) Los Angeles County	86	0.00
Claremore, OK (city) Rogers County	77	0.49
Norman, OK (city) Cleveland County	77	0.08
Fairfield, NJ (township) Cumberland County	76	1.21
Bridgeton, NJ (city) Cumberland County	76	0.33
Chelsea, OK (city) Rogers County	71	3.32
Wichita, KS (city) Sedgwick County	66	0.02
Dewey, OK (city) Washington County	64	2.01
Coffeyville, KS (city) Montgomery County	61	0.55
Broken Arrow, OK (city) Tulsa County	61	0.08
Vinita, OK (city) Craig County	59	0.91
Albuquerque, NM (city) Bernalillo County	52	0.01
Phoenix, AZ (city) Maricopa County	50	0.00
Millville, NJ (city) Cumberland County	48	0.18
Vineland, NJ (city) Cumberland County	47	0.08
Kansas City, MO (city) Jackson County	47	0.01
Miami, OK (city) Ottawa County	40	0.29
Warwick, NY (town) Orange County	38	0.12
Midwest City, OK (city) Oklahoma County	38	0.07
San Diego, CA (city) San Diego County	38	0.00
San Jose, CA (city) Santa Clara County	37	0.00
Kansas City, KS (city) Wyandotte County	35	0.02
Dallas, TX (city) Dallas County	35	0.00
Dover, NJ (township) Ocean County	34	0.04
Toms River, NJ (cdp) Ocean County	34	0.04
Blooming Grove, NY (town) Orange County	33	0.19
Edmond, OK (city) Oklahoma County	33	0.05
Seattle, WA (city) King County	33	0.01
Columbus, OH (city) Franklin County	32	0.00
Hopewell, NJ (township) Cumberland County	31	0.70
Aurora, CO (city) Arapahoe County	31	0.01
Detroit, MI (city) Wayne County	31	0.00
Dover, DE (city) Kent County	30	0.09
Lawrence, KS (city) Douglas County	30	0.04
Lawton, OK (city) Comanche County	30	0.03
Austin, TX (city) Travis County	30	0.00
Haverstraw, NY (town) Rockland County	29	0.09
Boise City, ID (city) Ada County	29	0.02
Moore, OK (city) Cleveland County	28	0.07
Lacombe, LA (cdp) Saint Tammany Parish	27	0.36
Wanaque, NJ (borough) Passaic County	27	0.26
Owasso, OK (city) Tulsa County	27	0.15
Overland Park, KS (city) Johnson County	27	0.02
Pawhuska, OK (city) Osage County	26	0.72
Tahlequah, OK (city) Cherokee County	26	0.18
Paterson, NJ (city) Passaic County	26	0.02
Tucson, AZ (city) Pima County	26	0.01
Chicago, IL (city) Cook County	26	0.00
Ewing, NJ (cdp) Mercer County	25	0.07
Joplin, MO (city) Jasper County	25	0.05
Allentown, PA (city) Lehigh County	25	0.02
Virginia Beach, VA (independent city) Virginia Beach city	25	0.01
Colorado Springs, CO (city) El Paso County	24	0.01
Las Vegas, NV (city) Clark County	24	0.01
Indianapolis, IN (special city) Marion County	24	0.00
Stockton, CA (city) San Joaquin County	23	0.01
Portland, OR (city) Multnomah County	23	0.00
San Antonio, TX (city) Bexar County	22	0.00
San Francisco, CA (city) San Francisco County	22	0.00
Monroe, NY (town) Orange County	21	0.07
Houston, TX (city) Harris County	21	0.00
Mamakating, NY (town) Sullivan County	20	0.18

Place	Number	%
Stony Point, NY (town) Rockland County	20	0.14
Independence, MO (city) Jackson County	20	0.02
Mesa, AZ (city) Maricopa County	20	0.01
Copan, OK (town) Washington County	19	2.39
Caney, KS (city) Montgomery County	19	0.91
Stillwater, OK (city) Payne County	19	0.05
Reading, PA (city) Berks County	19	0.02
Tacoma, WA (city) Pierce County	19	0.01
Long Beach, CA (city) Los Angeles County	19	0.00
Delaware, OK (town) Nowata County	18	3.95
Chickasha, OK (city) Grady County	18	0.11
Ponca City, OK (city) Kay County	18	0.07
Wallkill, NY (town) Orange County	18	0.07
Linden, NJ (city) Union County	18	0.05
Gloucester, NJ (township) Camden County	18	0.03
Chesapeake, VA (independent city) Chesapeake city	18	0.01
Catoosa, OK (city) Rogers County	17	0.31
Neptune, NJ (township) Monmouth County	17	0.06
Shawnee, OK (city) Pottawatomie County	17	0.06
Nampa, ID (city) Canyon County	17	0.03
Arlington, TX (city) Tarrant County	17	0.01
Binger, OK (town) Caddo County	16	2.26
Picher, OK (city) Ottawa County	16	0.98
West Haverstraw, NY (village) Rockland County	16	0.16
Camden, NJ (city) Camden County	16	0.02
Clarkstown, NY (town) Rockland County	16	0.02
Hamilton, NJ (township) Mercer County	16	0.02
Taylor, MI (city) Wayne County	16	0.02
Anchorage, AK (municipality) Anchorage Borough	16	0.01
Denver, CO (city) Denver County	16	0.00
Fresno, CA (city) Fresno County	16	0.00
Sand Springs, OK (city) Tulsa County	15	0.09
Del City, OK (city) Oklahoma County	15	0.07
New Windsor, NY (town) Orange County	15	0.07
Vernon, NJ (township) Sussex County	15	0.06
Abington, PA (township) Montgomery County	15	0.03
Bethlehem, PA (city) Northampton County	15	0.02
Passaic, NJ (city) Passaic County	15	0.02
Fremont, CA (city) Alameda County	15	0.01
Baltimore, MD (independent city) Baltimore city	15	0.00
Port Jervis, NY (city) Orange County	14	0.16
Westwood, NJ (borough) Bergen County	14	0.13
Slidell, LA (city) Saint Tammany Parish	14	0.05
Jackson, NJ (township) Ocean County	14	0.03
Wayne, NJ (cdp) Passaic County	14	0.03
Bensalem, PA (township) Bucks County	14	0.02
Amarillo, TX (city) Potter County	14	0.01
Topeka, KS (city) Shawnee County	14	0.01
Fort Worth, TX (city) Tarrant County	14	0.00
Cheswold, DE (town) Kent County	13	4.15
Fairton, NJ (cdp) Cumberland County	13	0.58
Jay, OK (city) Delaware County	13	0.52
Lawrence, NJ (township) Cumberland County	13	0.48
Skiatook, OK (town) Osage County	13	0.24
Maurice River, NJ (township) Cumberland County	13	0.19
Chester, NY (town) Orange County	13	0.11
Glassboro, NJ (borough) Gloucester County	13	0.07
Hamilton, NJ (township) Atlantic County	13	0.06
Middletown, NY (city) Orange County	13	0.05
Manchester, NJ (township) Ocean County	13	0.03
Napa, CA (city) Napa County	13	0.02
Trenton, NJ (city) Mercer County	13	0.02
Westland, MI (city) Wayne County	13	0.02
Huntington Beach, CA (city) Orange County	13	0.01
Sunrise Manor, NV (cdp) Clark County	13	0.01
Ochelata, OK (town) Washington County	12	2.43
Carneys Point, NJ (township) Salem County	12	0.16
Dingman, PA (township) Pike County	12	0.14
Wawarsing, NY (town) Ulster County	12	0.09
El Reno, OK (city) Canadian County	12	0.07
South Plainfield, NJ (borough) Middlesex County	12	0.06
Easton, PA (city) Northampton County	12	0.05
Spring Valley, NY (village) Rockland County	12	0.05
Galloway, NJ (township) Atlantic County	12	0.04
Pemberton, NJ (township) Burlington County	12	0.04

Notes: (cdp) census designated place; Refer to the Explanation of Data in the front of the book for more detailed information.

American Indian: Delaware

Top 150 Places Sorted by Percent

(Based on all places, regardless of population)

Place	Number	%
Hillburn, NY (village) Rockland County	104	11.80
New Alluwe, OK (town) Nowata County	7	7.37
Casa Colorada, NM (cdp) Valencia County	4	7.14
Cheswold, DE (town) Kent County	13	4.15
Zena, OK (cdp) Delaware County	5	4.07
Delaware, OK (town) Nowata County	18	3.95
Nowata, OK (city) Nowata County	150	3.78
Chelsea, OK (city) Rogers County	71	3.32
Wharton, PA (township) Potter County	3	3.30
Niotaze, KS (city) Chautauqua County	4	3.28
New Eucha, OK (cdp) Delaware County	8	2.67
Ochelata, OK (town) Washington County	12	2.43
Copan, OK (town) Washington County	19	2.39
Amorita, OK (town) Alfalfa County	1	2.27
Binger, OK (town) Caddo County	16	2.26
Dewey, OK (city) Washington County	64	2.01
Roseland, KS (city) Cherokee County	2	1.98
Ketchum, OK (town) Craig County	5	1.75
Lenapah, OK (town) Nowata County	5	1.68
Anadarko, OK (city) Caddo County	109	1.64
Fairview, MO (town) Newton County	6	1.52
Coyville, KS (city) Wilson County	1	1.41
Schoenchen, KS (city) Ellis County	3	1.40
Treece, KS (city) Cherokee County	2	1.34
Tyro, KS (city) Montgomery County	3	1.33
Randsburg, CA (cdp) Kern County	1	1.30
Elgin, KS (city) Chautauqua County	1	1.22
Table Rock, WY (cdp) Sweetwater County	1	1.22
Fairfield, NJ (township) Cumberland County	76	1.21
Westphalia, KS (city) Anderson County	2	1.21
Taiwah, OK (cdp) Rogers County	2	1.20
Winchester, OK (town) Okmulgee County	5	1.18
Ringwood, NJ (borough) Passaic County	145	1.17
Rockvale, CO (town) Fremont County	5	1.17
Bartlesville, OK (city) Washington County	396	1.14
Dushore, PA (borough) Sullivan County	7	1.06
Tamaha, OK (town) Haskell County	2	1.01
Strang, OK (town) Mayes County	1	1.00
Picher, OK (city) Ottawa County	16	0.98
Lehigh, PA (township) Carbon County	5	0.95
Wells, PA (township) Fulton County	5	0.95
Greenwich, NJ (township) Cumberland County	8	0.94
Calumet, OK (town) Canadian County	5	0.93
Vinita, OK (city) Craig County	59	0.91
Caney, KS (city) Montgomery County	19	0.91
South Coffeyville, OK (town) Nowata County	7	0.89
Ramona, OK (town) Washington County	5	0.89
Spavinaw, OK (town) Mayes County	5	0.89
Corbin City, NJ (city) Atlantic County	4	0.85
Welch, OK (town) Craig County	5	0.84
Sperry, OK (town) Tulsa County	8	0.82
Elkland, PA (township) Sullivan County	5	0.82
Nelliston, NY (village) Montgomery County	5	0.80
Shelocta, PA (borough) Indiana County	1	0.79
Winfield, TN (town) Scott County	1	0.77
South Haven, KS (city) Sumner County	3	0.77
Lookeba, OK (town) Caddo County	1	0.76
Wann, OK (town) Nowata County	1	0.76
Bryant, IN (town) Jay County	2	0.74
Bluejacket, OK (town) Craig County	2	0.73
Pawhuska, OK (city) Osage County	26	0.72
Hopewell, NJ (township) Cumberland County	31	0.70
Okay, OK (town) Wagoner County	4	0.67
Railroad, PA (borough) York County	2	0.67
Pomona, KS (city) Franklin County	6	0.65
Fall River, KS (city) Greenwood County	1	0.64
Great Meadows-Vienna, NJ (cdp) Warren County	8	0.63
Cedarville, NJ (cdp) Cumberland County	5	0.63
Mount Auburn, IA (city) Benton County	1	0.63
Plainfield, OH (village) Coshocton County	1	0.63
Blyn, WA (cdp) Clallam County	1	0.62
Fairton, NJ (cdp) Cumberland County	13	0.58
Bushyhead, OK (cdp) Rogers County	7	0.58
Taylor, PA (township) Fulton County	7	0.57
Stow Creek, NJ (township) Cumberland County	8	0.56
Bear Creek, TX (village) Hays County	2	0.56
Coffeyville, KS (city) Montgomery County	61	0.55
Sugar Grove, PA (township) Mercer County	5	0.55
Mahwah, NJ (township) Bergen County	131	0.54
Avant, OK (town) Osage County	2	0.54
Vera, OK (town) Washington County	1	0.53
Jay, OK (city) Delaware County	13	0.52
Centennial, WY (cdp) Albany County	1	0.52
Otisville, NY (village) Orange County	5	0.51
Corn, OK (town) Washita County	3	0.51
Little Creek, DE (town) Kent County	1	0.51
Talihina, OK (town) Le Flore County	6	0.50
Youngstown, PA (borough) Westmoreland County	2	0.50
Lake McMurray, WA (cdp) Skagit County	1	0.50
Claremore, OK (city) Rogers County	77	0.49
Hardin, MO (city) Ray County	3	0.49
Fitzhugh, OK (town) Pontotoc County	1	0.49
Leipsic, DE (town) Kent County	1	0.49
Lawrence, NJ (township) Cumberland County	13	0.48
Cameron, NY (town) Steuben County	5	0.48
Hebron, PA (township) Potter County	3	0.48
Dearing, KS (city) Montgomery County	2	0.48
New Strawn, KS (city) Coffey County	2	0.47
Haigler, NE (village) Dundy County	1	0.47
Island Park, ID (city) Fremont County	1	0.47
Saint Paul, KS (city) Neosho County	3	0.46
Melba, ID (city) Canyon County	2	0.46
Lamar Heights, MO (village) Barton County	1	0.46
Tannersville, NY (village) Greene County	2	0.45
Kirwin, KS (city) Phillips County	1	0.44
Magnolia, DE (town) Kent County	1	0.44
Cyril, OK (town) Caddo County	5	0.43
Kenton, DE (town) Kent County	1	0.42
Webbers Falls, OK (town) Muskogee County	3	0.41
Lone Wolf, OK (town) Kiowa County	2	0.40
Hooversville, PA (borough) Somerset County	3	0.39
Piney, PA (township) Clarion County	2	0.39
Rangeley, ME (town) Franklin County	4	0.38
Wynona, OK (town) Osage County	2	0.38
Westport, OK (town) Pawnee County	1	0.38
Shiloh, NJ (borough) Cumberland County	2	0.37
Tribbey, OK (town) Pottawatomie County	1	0.37
Lacombe, LA (cdp) Saint Tammany Parish	27	0.36
Afton, OK (town) Ottawa County	4	0.36
Whitley City, KY (cdp) McCreary County	4	0.36
Calvin, OK (town) Hughes County	1	0.36
Maple Falls, WA (cdp) Whatcom County	1	0.36
Sloatsburg, NY (village) Rockland County	11	0.35
Sleepy Hollow, WY (cdp) Campbell County	4	0.34
Wilmot, PA (township) Bradford County	4	0.34
Bolivar, OH (village) Tuscarawas County	3	0.34
Groom, TX (town) Carson County	2	0.34
Saint Libory, IL (village) Saint Clair County	2	0.34
Big Cabin, OK (town) Craig County	1	0.34
West Milford, NJ (cdp) Passaic County	88	0.33
Bridgeton, NJ (city) Cumberland County	76	0.33
Riverdale, CA (cdp) Fresno County	8	0.33
Westport, WA (city) Grays Harbor County	7	0.33
Cimarron, NM (village) Colfax County	3	0.33
Kellyville, OK (town) Creek County	3	0.33
Elk City, KS (city) Montgomery County	1	0.33
Galena, OH (village) Delaware County	1	0.33
Santee, NE (village) Knox County	1	0.33
Cedar Crest, OK (cdp) Mayes County	1	0.32
Catoosa, OK (city) Rogers County	17	0.31
Deerfield, NJ (township) Cumberland County	9	0.31
Downe, NJ (township) Cumberland County	5	0.31
East Canton, OH (village) Stark County	5	0.31
Justice, OK (cdp) Rogers County	4	0.31
Leon, KS (city) Butler County	2	0.31
Saint Johnsville, NY (village) Montgomery County	5	0.30
Sunol, CA (cdp) Alameda County	4	0.30
Langley, OK (town) Mayes County	2	0.30
Vici, OK (town) Dewey County	2	0.30
Hamilton, KS (city) Greenwood County	1	0.30

Notes: (cdp) census designated place; Refer to the Explanation of Data in the front of the book for more detailed information.

American Indian: Delaware

Top 150 Places Sorted by Percent

(Based on places with populations of 10,000 or more)

Place	Number	%
Ringwood, NJ (borough) Passaic County	145	1.17
Bartlesville, OK (city) Washington County	396	1.14
Coffeyville, KS (city) Montgomery County	61	0.55
Mahwah, NJ (township) Bergen County	131	0.54
Claremore, OK (city) Rogers County	77	0.49
West Milford, NJ (cdp) Passaic County	88	0.33
Bridgeton, NJ (city) Cumberland County	76	0.33
Miami, OK (city) Ottawa County	40	0.29
Wanaque, NJ (borough) Passaic County	27	0.26
Blooming Grove, NY (town) Orange County	33	0.19
Millville, NJ (city) Cumberland County	48	0.18
Tahlequah, OK (city) Cherokee County	26	0.18
Mamakating, NY (town) Sullivan County	20	0.18
West Haverstraw, NY (village) Rockland County	16	0.16
Owasso, OK (city) Tulsa County	27	0.15
Stony Point, NY (town) Rockland County	20	0.14
Ramapo, NY (town) Rockland County	142	0.13
Westwood, NJ (borough) Bergen County	14	0.13
Warwick, NY (town) Orange County	38	0.12
Canton, OH (city) Stark County	86	0.11
Chickasha, OK (city) Grady County	18	0.11
Chester, NY (town) Orange County	13	0.11
Tulsa, OK (city) Tulsa County	339	0.09
Dover, DE (city) Kent County	30	0.09
Haverstraw, NY (town) Rockland County	29	0.09
Sand Springs, OK (city) Tulsa County	15	0.09
Wawarsing, NY (town) Ulster County	12	0.09
Mount Holly, NJ (township) Burlington County	10	0.09
Norman, OK (city) Cleveland County	77	0.08
Broken Arrow, OK (city) Tulsa County	61	0.08
Vineland, NJ (city) Cumberland County	47	0.08
Logan, PA (township) Blair County	9	0.08
Middle Smithfield, PA (township) Monroe County	9	0.08
Haverstraw, NY (village) Rockland County	8	0.08
Midwest City, OK (city) Oklahoma County	38	0.07
Moore, OK (city) Cleveland County	28	0.07
Ewing, NJ (cdp) Mercer County	25	0.07
Monroe, NY (town) Orange County	21	0.07
Ponca City, OK (city) Kay County	18	0.07
Wallkill, NY (town) Orange County	18	0.07
Del City, OK (city) Oklahoma County	15	0.07
New Windsor, NY (town) Orange County	15	0.07
Glassboro, NJ (borough) Gloucester County	13	0.07
El Reno, OK (city) Canadian County	12	0.07
Borger, TX (city) Hutchinson County	10	0.07
Dryden, NY (town) Tompkins County	10	0.07
Keansburg, NJ (borough) Monmouth County	8	0.07
Oklahoma City, OK (city) Oklahoma County	281	0.06
Neptune, NJ (township) Monmouth County	17	0.06
Shawnee, OK (city) Pottawatomie County	17	0.06
Vernon, NJ (township) Sussex County	15	0.06
Hamilton, NJ (township) Atlantic County	13	0.06
South Plainfield, NJ (borough) Middlesex County	12	0.06
Golden, CO (city) Jefferson County	11	0.06
Lindenwold, NJ (borough) Camden County	11	0.06
Celina, OH (city) Mercer County	6	0.06
Hackettstown, NJ (town) Warren County	6	0.06
Edmond, OK (city) Oklahoma County	33	0.05
Joplin, MO (city) Jasper County	25	0.05
Stillwater, OK (city) Payne County	19	0.05
Linden, NJ (city) Union County	18	0.05
Slidell, LA (city) Saint Tammany Parish	14	0.05
Middletown, NY (city) Orange County	13	0.05
Easton, PA (city) Northampton County	12	0.05
Spring Valley, NY (village) Rockland County	12	0.05
Sapulpa, OK (city) Creek County	10	0.05
Nanuet, NY (cdp) Rockland County	9	0.05
Pittsburg, KS (city) Crawford County	9	0.05
Aston, PA (township) Delaware County	8	0.05
Hopewell, NJ (township) Mercer County	8	0.05
Little Egg Harbor, NJ (township) Ocean County	8	0.05
Pottsville, PA (city) Schuylkill County	8	0.05
Eatontown, NJ (borough) Monmouth County	7	0.05
Goshen, NY (town) Orange County	7	0.05
Arkansas City, KS (city) Cowley County	6	0.05
Chowchilla, CA (city) Madera County	6	0.05
Hope Mills, NC (town) Cumberland County	6	0.05
Ottawa, KS (city) Franklin County	6	0.05
Pennsville, NJ (township) Salem County	6	0.05
Red Bank, NJ (borough) Monmouth County	6	0.05
Shawangunk, NY (town) Ulster County	6	0.05
Suffern, NY (village) Rockland County	6	0.05
Fort Polk South, LA (cdp) Vernon Parish	5	0.05
Salisbury, PA (township) Lancaster County	5	0.05
Union Park, FL (cdp) Orange County	5	0.05
Dover, NJ (township) Ocean County	34	0.04
Toms River, NJ (cdp) Ocean County	34	0.04
Lawrence, KS (city) Douglas County	30	0.04
Galloway, NJ (township) Atlantic County	12	0.04
Pemberton, NJ (township) Burlington County	12	0.04
Norristown, PA (borough) Montgomery County	11	0.04
Caldwell, ID (city) Canyon County	10	0.04
Newburgh, NY (city) Orange County	10	0.04
Norco, CA (city) Riverside County	10	0.04
Wall, NJ (township) Monmouth County	10	0.04
Spring, PA (township) Berks County	8	0.04
Yukon, OK (city) Canadian County	8	0.04
Dickinson, TX (city) Galveston County	7	0.04
Jefferson, NJ (township) Morris County	7	0.04
West Deptford, NJ (township) Gloucester County	7	0.04
Franklin, NJ (township) Gloucester County	6	0.04
Mantua, NJ (township) Gloucester County	6	0.04
North Whitehall, PA (township) Lehigh County	6	0.04
Phillipsburg, NJ (town) Warren County	6	0.04
Upper Chichester, PA (township) Delaware County	6	0.04
Westminster, MD (city) Carroll County	6	0.04
Clinton, CT (town) Middlesex County	5	0.04
Dover, OH (city) Tuscarawas County	5	0.04
Elfers, FL (cdp) Pasco County	5	0.04
Endicott, NY (village) Broome County	5	0.04
Harrison, AR (city) Boone County	5	0.04
Highland Village, TX (city) Denton County	5	0.04
Hilltown, PA (township) Bucks County	5	0.04
McPherson, KS (city) McPherson County	5	0.04
Oakland, NJ (borough) Bergen County	5	0.04
Raymore, MO (city) Cass County	5	0.04
Rosaryville, MD (cdp) Prince George's County	5	0.04
Stroud, PA (township) Monroe County	5	0.04
Upper, NJ (township) Cape May County	5	0.04
Woodward, OK (city) Woodward County	5	0.04
Lower Pottsgrove, PA (township) Montgomery County	4	0.04
Morrisville, PA (borough) Bucks County	4	0.04
Pataskala, OH (city) Licking County	4	0.04
Pine Hill, NJ (borough) Camden County	4	0.04
The Village, OK (city) Oklahoma County	4	0.04
Lawton, OK (city) Comanche County	30	0.03
Gloucester, NJ (township) Camden County	18	0.03
Nampa, ID (city) Canyon County	17	0.03
Abington, PA (township) Montgomery County	15	0.03
Jackson, NJ (township) Ocean County	14	0.03
Wayne, NJ (cdp) Passaic County	14	0.03
Manchester, NJ (township) Ocean County	13	0.03
Enid, OK (city) Garfield County	12	0.03
Montclair, NJ (cdp) Essex County	12	0.03
York, PA (city) York County	11	0.03
Benicia, CA (city) Solano County	9	0.03
Brea, CA (city) Orange County	9	0.03
Deptford, NJ (township) Gloucester County	9	0.03
Englewood, NJ (city) Bergen County	8	0.03
Lawndale, CA (city) Los Angeles County	8	0.03
Liberty, MO (city) Clay County	8	0.03
Zanesville, OH (city) Muskingum County	8	0.03
Alliance, OH (city) Stark County	7	0.03
Bethany, OK (city) Oklahoma County	7	0.03
Londonderry, NH (town) Rockingham County	7	0.03
Medford, NJ (township) Burlington County	7	0.03
Montgomery, NY (town) Orange County	7	0.03
Paradise, CA (town) Butte County	7	0.03
Whitehall, PA (township) Lehigh County	7	0.03
Hamburg, MI (township) Livingston County	6	0.03

Notes: (cdp) census designated place; Refer to the Explanation of Data in the front of the book for more detailed information.

American Indian: Houma

Top 150 Places Sorted by Number

(Based on all places, regardless of population)

Place	Number	%
Houma, LA (city) Terrebonne Parish	688	2.12
Dulac, LA (cdp) Terrebonne Parish	682	27.75
Galliano, LA (cdp) Lafourche Parish	260	3.53
Bayou Cane, LA (cdp) Terrebonne Parish	217	1.27
Larose, LA (cdp) Lafourche Parish	174	2.38
Cut Off, LA (cdp) Lafourche Parish	158	2.80
Estelle, LA (cdp) Jefferson Parish	110	0.69
Morgan City, LA (city) Saint Mary Parish	105	0.83
New Orleans, LA (city) Orleans Parish	104	0.02
Metairie, LA (cdp) Jefferson Parish	95	0.07
Gray, LA (cdp) Terrebonne Parish	88	1.77
Montegut, LA (cdp) Terrebonne Parish	87	4.83
Marrero, LA (cdp) Jefferson Parish	83	0.23
Kenner, LA (city) Jefferson Parish	79	0.11
Westwego, LA (city) Jefferson Parish	76	0.71
Chalmette, LA (cdp) Saint Bernard Parish	72	0.22
Golden Meadow, LA (town) Lafourche Parish	67	3.06
Boothville-Venice, LA (cdp) Plaquemines Parish	67	3.02
Jean Lafitte, LA (town) Jefferson Parish	48	2.25
Gretna, LA (city) Jefferson Parish	47	0.27
Meraux, LA (cdp) Saint Bernard Parish	45	0.44
Terrytown, LA (cdp) Jefferson Parish	45	0.18
Chauvin, LA (cdp) Terrebonne Parish	44	1.36
Harvey, LA (cdp) Jefferson Parish	44	0.20
Raceland, LA (cdp) Lafourche Parish	43	0.42
Bridge City, LA (cdp) Jefferson Parish	41	0.49
Harahan, LA (city) Jefferson Parish	40	0.40
Slidell, LA (city) Saint Tammany Parish	38	0.15
Franklin, LA (city) Saint Mary Parish	36	0.43
Berwick, LA (town) Saint Mary Parish	35	0.79
Bayou Vista, LA (cdp) Saint Mary Parish	34	0.78
Lafitte, LA (cdp) Jefferson Parish	33	2.09
Lockport, LA (town) Lafourche Parish	30	1.14
Belle Chasse, LA (cdp) Plaquemines Parish	30	0.30
Schriever, LA (cdp) Terrebonne Parish	29	0.49
Violet, LA (cdp) Saint Bernard Parish	29	0.34
Laplace, LA (cdp) Saint John the Baptist Parish	28	0.10
Patterson, LA (city) Saint Mary Parish	23	0.45
Gulfport, MS (city) Harrison County	21	0.03
Port Sulphur, LA (cdp) Plaquemines Parish	20	0.64
Lafayette, LA (city) Lafayette Parish	20	0.02
Baton Rouge, LA (city) East Baton Rouge Parish	20	0.01
Poydras, LA (cdp) Saint Bernard Parish	19	0.49
Timberlane, LA (cdp) Jefferson Parish	19	0.17
Thibodaux, LA (city) Lafourche Parish	18	0.12
Fort Worth, TX (city) Tarrant County	18	0.00
Grand Isle, LA (town) Jefferson Parish	16	1.04
Chackbay, LA (cdp) Lafourche Parish	15	0.37
Avondale, LA (cdp) Jefferson Parish	15	0.28
New Iberia, LA (city) Iberia Parish	15	0.05
Lake Charles, LA (city) Calcasieu Parish	15	0.02
Baldwin, LA (town) Saint Mary Parish	14	0.56
Jefferson, LA (cdp) Jefferson Parish	14	0.12
Jacksonville, FL (special city) Duval County	14	0.00
Biloxi, MS (city) Harrison County	13	0.03
Charenton, LA (cdp) Saint Mary Parish	12	0.62
Delcambre, LA (town) Vermilion Parish	12	0.55
Broussard, LA (town) Lafayette Parish	12	0.20
Arabi, LA (cdp) Saint Bernard Parish	12	0.15
Amelia, LA (cdp) Saint Mary Parish	11	0.45
Waggaman, LA (cdp) Jefferson Parish	11	0.12
Abbeville, LA (city) Vermilion Parish	11	0.09
River Ridge, LA (cdp) Jefferson Parish	11	0.08
Bellview, FL (cdp) Escambia County	11	0.05
Mobile, AL (city) Mobile County	11	0.01
Los Angeles, CA (city) Los Angeles County	11	0.00
Luling, LA (cdp) Saint Charles Parish	10	0.09
Houston, TX (city) Harris County	10	0.00
New York, NY (city) New York City	10	0.00
Portland, OR (city) Multnomah County	10	0.00
Mathews, LA (cdp) Lafourche Parish	9	0.45
Dallas, TX (city) Dallas County	9	0.00
Nashville-Davidson, TN (special city) Davidson County	9	0.00
Barataria, LA (cdp) Jefferson Parish	8	0.60
Des Allemands, LA (cdp) Saint Charles Parish	8	0.32
Buras-Triumph, LA (cdp) Plaquemines Parish	8	0.24
Waveland, MS (city) Hancock County	8	0.12
Aurora, CO (city) Arapahoe County	8	0.00
Sacramento, CA (city) Sacramento County	8	0.00
Shoreline Park, MS (cdp) Hancock County	7	0.17
Prien, LA (cdp) Calcasieu Parish	7	0.10
Scott, LA (city) Lafayette Parish	7	0.09
Destrehan, LA (cdp) Saint Charles Parish	7	0.06
Columbus, GA (special city) Muscogee County	7	0.00
San Diego, CA (city) San Diego County	7	0.00
Elmwood, LA (cdp) Jefferson Parish	6	0.14
Rayville, LA (town) Richland Parish	6	0.14
Old Jefferson, LA (cdp) East Baton Rouge Parish	6	0.11
Diamondhead, MS (cdp) Hancock County	6	0.10
Bridge City, TX (city) Orange County	6	0.07
Covington, LA (city) Saint Tammany Parish	6	0.07
Woodmere, LA (cdp) Jefferson Parish	6	0.05
Phoenix, AZ (city) Maricopa County	6	0.00
Tulsa, OK (city) Tulsa County	6	0.00
Estherwood, LA (village) Acadia Parish	5	0.62
Labadieville, LA (cdp) Assumption Parish	5	0.28
Pierre Part, LA (cdp) Assumption Parish	5	0.15
New Roads, LA (city) Pointe Coupee Parish	5	0.10
Saint Rose, LA (cdp) Saint Charles Parish	5	0.08
Saint Martin, MS (cdp) Jackson County	5	0.07
Jefferson Hills, PA (borough) Allegheny County	5	0.05
Ledyard, CT (town) New London County	5	0.03
Warrington, FL (cdp) Escambia County	5	0.03
Oakley, CA (city) Contra Costa County	5	0.02
Encinitas, CA (city) San Diego County	5	0.01
Gainesville, FL (city) Alachua County	5	0.01
Jacksonville, NC (city) Onslow County	5	0.01
Chicago, IL (city) Cook County	5	0.00
Plano, TX (city) Collin County	5	0.00
Tampa, FL (city) Hillsborough County	5	0.00
Garrison, TX (city) Nacogdoches County	4	0.47
Montz, LA (cdp) Saint Charles Parish	4	0.36
Dauphin Island, AL (town) Mobile County	4	0.29
Pearlington, MS (cdp) Hancock County	4	0.24
Bayou Gauche, LA (cdp) Saint Charles Parish	4	0.23
Natalbany, LA (cdp) Tangipahoa Parish	4	0.23
Schulenburg, TX (city) Fayette County	4	0.15
Lake Darby, OH (cdp) Franklin County	4	0.11
Norco, LA (cdp) Saint Charles Parish	4	0.11
Jordan, MN (city) Scott County	4	0.10
Sparta, TN (city) White County	4	0.09
Eden Isle, LA (cdp) Saint Tammany Parish	4	0.06
Auburndale, FL (city) Polk County	4	0.04
Jennings, LA (city) Jefferson Davis Parish	4	0.04
Mandeville, LA (city) Saint Tammany Parish	4	0.04
Reserve, LA (cdp) Saint John the Baptist Parish	4	0.04
Scotts Valley, CA (city) Santa Cruz County	4	0.04
Baker, LA (city) East Baton Rouge Parish	4	0.03
Brent, FL (cdp) Escambia County	4	0.02
Forest Park, GA (city) Clayton County	4	0.02
Hammond, LA (city) Tangipahoa Parish	4	0.02
Havelock, NC (city) Craven County	4	0.02
Ocean Springs, MS (city) Jackson County	4	0.02
Spanaway, WA (cdp) Pierce County	4	0.02
West Pensacola, FL (cdp) Escambia County	4	0.02
Frederick, MD (city) Frederick County	4	0.01
Lakewood, WA (city) Pierce County	4	0.01
Rowland Heights, CA (cdp) Los Angeles County	4	0.01
Temple, TX (city) Bell County	4	0.01
Wheaton, IL (city) Du Page County	4	0.01
Anchorage, AK (municipality) Anchorage Borough	4	0.00
Canton, OH (city) Stark County	4	0.00
Corpus Christi, TX (city) Nueces County	4	0.00
Denver, CO (city) Denver County	4	0.00
El Cajon, CA (city) San Diego County	4	0.00
Eugene, OR (city) Lane County	4	0.00
Hamilton, NJ (township) Mercer County	4	0.00
Indianapolis, IN (special city) Marion County	4	0.00
San Francisco, CA (city) San Francisco County	4	0.00
San Jose, CA (city) Santa Clara County	4	0.00

Notes: (cdp) census designated place; Refer to the Explanation of Data in the front of the book for more detailed information.

American Indian: Houma

Top 150 Places Sorted by Percent

(Based on all places, regardless of population)

Place	Number	%
Dulac, LA (cdp) Terrebonne Parish	682	27.75
Montegut, LA (cdp) Terrebonne Parish	87	4.83
Galliano, LA (cdp) Lafourche Parish	260	3.53
Golden Meadow, LA (town) Lafourche Parish	67	3.06
Boothville-Venice, LA (cdp) Plaquemines Parish	67	3.02
Cut Off, LA (cdp) Lafourche Parish	158	2.80
Larose, LA (cdp) Lafourche Parish	174	2.38
Jean Lafitte, LA (town) Jefferson Parish	48	2.25
Houma, LA (city) Terrebonne Parish	688	2.12
Lafitte, LA (cdp) Jefferson Parish	33	2.09
Gray, LA (cdp) Terrebonne Parish	88	1.77
Walthall, MS (village) Webster County	3	1.76
Navarro, TX (town) Navarro County	3	1.57
Chauvin, LA (cdp) Terrebonne Parish	44	1.36
Bayou Cane, LA (cdp) Terrebonne Parish	217	1.27
Lockport, LA (town) Lafourche Parish	30	1.14
Grand Isle, LA (town) Jefferson Parish	16	1.04
Morgan City, LA (city) Saint Mary Parish	105	0.83
Berwick, LA (town) Saint Mary Parish	35	0.79
Bayou Vista, LA (cdp) Saint Mary Parish	34	0.78
Bear Bluff, WI (town) Jackson County	1	0.78
Westwego, LA (city) Jefferson Parish	76	0.71
Estelle, LA (cdp) Jefferson Parish	110	0.69
Port Sulphur, LA (cdp) Plaquemines Parish	20	0.64
Charenton, LA (cdp) Saint Mary Parish	12	0.62
Estherwood, LA (village) Acadia Parish	5	0.62
Camak, GA (town) Warren County	1	0.61
Barataria, LA (cdp) Jefferson Parish	8	0.60
Baldwin, LA (town) Saint Mary Parish	14	0.56
Turkey Creek, LA (village) Evangeline Parish	2	0.56
Delcambre, LA (town) Vermilion Parish	12	0.55
Bridge City, LA (cdp) Jefferson Parish	41	0.49
Schriever, LA (cdp) Terrebonne Parish	29	0.49
Poydras, LA (cdp) Saint Bernard Parish	19	0.49
Garrison, TX (city) Nacogdoches County	4	0.47
Junction City, LA (village) Union Parish	3	0.46
Patterson, LA (city) Saint Mary Parish	23	0.45
Amelia, LA (cdp) Saint Mary Parish	11	0.45
Mathews, LA (cdp) Lafourche Parish	9	0.45
Meraux, LA (cdp) Saint Bernard Parish	45	0.44
Franklin, LA (city) Saint Mary Parish	36	0.43
Raceland, LA (cdp) Lafourche Parish	43	0.42
Harahan, LA (city) Jefferson Parish	40	0.40
Chackbay, LA (cdp) Lafourche Parish	15	0.37
Montz, LA (cdp) Saint Charles Parish	4	0.36
Violet, LA (cdp) Saint Bernard Parish	29	0.34
Des Allemands, LA (cdp) Saint Charles Parish	8	0.32
London, AR (city) Pope County	3	0.32
Risingsun, OH (village) Wood County	2	0.32
Belle Chasse, LA (cdp) Plaquemines Parish	30	0.30
Dauphin Island, AL (town) Mobile County	4	0.29
Varnado, LA (village) Washington Parish	1	0.29
Avondale, LA (cdp) Jefferson Parish	15	0.28
Labadieville, LA (cdp) Assumption Parish	5	0.28
Culbertson, MT (town) Roosevelt County	2	0.28
Gretna, LA (city) Jefferson Parish	47	0.27
Buras-Triumph, LA (cdp) Plaquemines Parish	8	0.24
Pearlington, MS (cdp) Hancock County	4	0.24
Paradis, LA (cdp) Saint Charles Parish	3	0.24
Woodland, NC (town) Northampton County	2	0.24
Marrero, LA (cdp) Jefferson Parish	83	0.23
Bayou Gauche, LA (cdp) Saint Charles Parish	4	0.23
Natalbany, LA (cdp) Tangipahoa Parish	4	0.23
Albany, LA (village) Livingston Parish	2	0.23
Hoonah, AK (city) Skagway-Hoonah-Angoon Census Area	2	0.23
Chalmette, LA (cdp) Saint Bernard Parish	72	0.22
Willing, NY (town) Allegany County	3	0.22
Harvey, LA (cdp) Jefferson Parish	44	0.20
Broussard, LA (town) Lafayette Parish	12	0.20
Lyons, CO (town) Boulder County	3	0.19
Norris City, IL (village) White County	2	0.19
Terrytown, LA (cdp) Jefferson Parish	45	0.18
Phillips, WI (city) Price County	3	0.18
Hemphill, TX (city) Sabine County	2	0.18
Timberlane, LA (cdp) Jefferson Parish	19	0.17
Shoreline Park, MS (cdp) Hancock County	7	0.17
Zwolle, LA (town) Sabine Parish	3	0.17
Casco, WI (town) Kewaunee County	2	0.17
Simpson, LA (village) Vernon Parish	1	0.17
Sorrento, LA (town) Ascension Parish	2	0.16
Slidell, LA (city) Saint Tammany Parish	38	0.15
Arabi, LA (cdp) Saint Bernard Parish	12	0.15
Pierre Part, LA (cdp) Assumption Parish	5	0.15
Schulenburg, TX (city) Fayette County	4	0.15
Colorado City, CO (cdp) Pueblo County	3	0.15
Kiln, MS (cdp) Hancock County	3	0.15
Elmwood, LA (cdp) Jefferson Parish	6	0.14
Rayville, LA (town) Richland Parish	6	0.14
Magnolia, MS (city) Pike County	3	0.14
Riverland Village, FL (cdp) Broward County	3	0.14
Florien, LA (village) Sabine Parish	1	0.14
Brownsboro, TX (city) Henderson County	1	0.13
Thibodaux, LA (city) Lafourche Parish	18	0.12
Jefferson, LA (cdp) Jefferson Parish	14	0.12
Waggaman, LA (cdp) Jefferson Parish	11	0.12
Waveland, MS (city) Hancock County	8	0.12
Kenner, LA (city) Jefferson Parish	79	0.11
Old Jefferson, LA (cdp) East Baton Rouge Parish	6	0.11
Lake Darby, OH (cdp) Franklin County	4	0.11
Norco, LA (cdp) Saint Charles Parish	4	0.11
Iowa, LA (town) Calcasieu Parish	3	0.11
Lake Village, AR (city) Chicot County	3	0.11
Loreauville, LA (village) Iberia Parish	1	0.11
Laplace, LA (cdp) Saint John the Baptist Parish	28	0.10
Prien, LA (cdp) Calcasieu Parish	7	0.10
Diamondhead, MS (cdp) Hancock County	6	0.10
New Roads, LA (city) Pointe Coupee Parish	5	0.10
Jordan, MN (city) Scott County	4	0.10
Gramercy, LA (town) Saint James Parish	3	0.10
Many, LA (town) Sabine Parish	3	0.10
Murphy, TX (city) Collin County	3	0.10
Rome, ME (town) Kennebec County	1	0.10
Abbeville, LA (city) Vermilion Parish	11	0.09
Luling, LA (cdp) Saint Charles Parish	10	0.09
Scott, LA (city) Lafayette Parish	7	0.09
Sparta, TN (city) White County	4	0.09
Erath, LA (town) Vermilion Parish	2	0.09
Clarks, LA (village) Caldwell Parish	1	0.09
Lydia, LA (cdp) Iberia Parish	1	0.09
Merryville, LA (town) Beauregard Parish	1	0.09
River Ridge, LA (cdp) Jefferson Parish	11	0.08
Saint Rose, LA (cdp) Saint Charles Parish	5	0.08
Franklinton, LA (town) Washington Parish	3	0.08
Hartford, KY (city) Ohio County	2	0.08
Ama, LA (cdp) Saint Charles Parish	1	0.08
Buffalo, IA (city) Scott County	1	0.08
North De Land, FL (cdp) Volusia County	1	0.08
Rogersville, AL (town) Lauderdale County	1	0.08
Metairie, LA (cdp) Jefferson Parish	95	0.07
Bridge City, TX (city) Orange County	6	0.07
Covington, LA (city) Saint Tammany Parish	6	0.07
Saint Martin, MS (cdp) Jackson County	5	0.07
Arcadia, LA (town) Bienville Parish	2	0.07
Fox Island, WA (cdp) Pierce County	2	0.07
Hahnville, LA (cdp) Saint Charles Parish	2	0.07
Cecilia, LA (cdp) Saint Martin Parish	1	0.07
Decatur, MS (town) Newton County	1	0.07
Marvell, AR (city) Phillips County	1	0.07
Destrehan, LA (cdp) Saint Charles Parish	7	0.06
Eden Isle, LA (cdp) Saint Tammany Parish	4	0.06
Penn Forest, PA (township) Carbon County	3	0.06
Suquamish, WA (cdp) Kitsap County	2	0.06
Elk Rapids, MI (village) Antrim County	1	0.06
Independence, LA (town) Tangipahoa Parish	1	0.06
New Sarpy, LA (cdp) Saint Charles Parish	1	0.06
New Iberia, LA (city) Iberia Parish	15	0.05
Bellview, FL (cdp) Escambia County	11	0.05
Woodmere, LA (cdp) Jefferson Parish	6	0.05
Jefferson Hills, PA (borough) Allegheny County	5	0.05
Jeanerette, LA (city) Iberia Parish	3	0.05

Notes: (cdp) census designated place; Refer to the Explanation of Data in the front of the book for more detailed information.

American Indian: Houma

Top 150 Places Sorted by Percent

(Based on places with populations of 10,000 or more)

Place	Number	%
Houma, LA (city) Terrebonne Parish	688	2.12
Bayou Cane, LA (cdp) Terrebonne Parish	217	1.27
Morgan City, LA (city) Saint Mary Parish	105	0.83
Westwego, LA (city) Jefferson Parish	76	0.71
Estelle, LA (cdp) Jefferson Parish	110	0.69
Meraux, LA (cdp) Saint Bernard Parish	45	0.44
Raceland, LA (cdp) Lafourche Parish	43	0.42
Gretna, LA (city) Jefferson Parish	47	0.27
Marrero, LA (cdp) Jefferson Parish	83	0.23
Chalmette, LA (cdp) Saint Bernard Parish	72	0.22
Harvey, LA (cdp) Jefferson Parish	44	0.20
Terrytown, LA (cdp) Jefferson Parish	45	0.18
Timberlane, LA (cdp) Jefferson Parish	19	0.17
Slidell, LA (city) Saint Tammany Parish	38	0.15
Thibodaux, LA (city) Lafourche Parish	18	0.12
Jefferson, LA (cdp) Jefferson Parish	14	0.12
Kenner, LA (city) Jefferson Parish	79	0.11
Laplace, LA (cdp) Saint John the Baptist Parish	28	0.10
Abbeville, LA (city) Vermilion Parish	11	0.09
Luling, LA (cdp) Saint Charles Parish	10	0.09
River Ridge, LA (cdp) Jefferson Parish	11	0.08
Metairie, LA (cdp) Jefferson Parish	95	0.07
Destrehan, LA (cdp) Saint Charles Parish	7	0.06
New Iberia, LA (city) Iberia Parish	15	0.05
Bellview, FL (cdp) Escambia County	11	0.05
Woodmere, LA (cdp) Jefferson Parish	6	0.05
Auburndale, FL (city) Polk County	4	0.04
Jennings, LA (city) Jefferson Davis Parish	4	0.04
Mandeville, LA (city) Saint Tammany Parish	4	0.04
Scotts Valley, CA (city) Santa Cruz County	4	0.04
Gulfport, MS (city) Harrison County	21	0.03
Biloxi, MS (city) Harrison County	13	0.03
Ledyard, CT (town) New London County	5	0.03
Warrington, FL (cdp) Escambia County	5	0.03
Baker, LA (city) East Baton Rouge Parish	4	0.03
Brentwood, PA (borough) Allegheny County	3	0.03
Buford, GA (city) Gwinnett County	3	0.03
Hartford, VT (town) Windsor County	3	0.03
Parsons, KS (city) Labette County	3	0.03
Struthers, OH (city) Mahoning County	3	0.03
New Orleans, LA (city) Orleans Parish	104	0.02
Lafayette, LA (city) Lafayette Parish	20	0.02
Lake Charles, LA (city) Calcasieu Parish	15	0.02
Oakley, CA (city) Contra Costa County	5	0.02
Brent, FL (cdp) Escambia County	4	0.02
Forest Park, GA (city) Clayton County	4	0.02
Hammond, LA (city) Tangipahoa Parish	4	0.02
Havelock, NC (city) Craven County	4	0.02
Ocean Springs, MS (city) Jackson County	4	0.02
Spanaway, WA (cdp) Pierce County	4	0.02
West Pensacola, FL (cdp) Escambia County	4	0.02
Casa de Oro-Mount Helix, CA (cdp) San Diego County	3	0.02
Colleyville, TX (city) Tarrant County	3	0.02
Fort Lewis, WA (cdp) Pierce County	3	0.02
Killingly, CT (town) Windham County	3	0.02
Moss Point, MS (city) Jackson County	3	0.02
Myrtle Grove, FL (cdp) Escambia County	3	0.02
Shenandoah, LA (cdp) East Baton Rouge Parish	3	0.02
Lebanon, NH (city) Grafton County	2	0.02
Los Alamos, NM (cdp) Los Alamos County	2	0.02
Lynn Haven, FL (city) Bay County	2	0.02
Minden, LA (city) Webster Parish	2	0.02
Moss Bluff, LA (cdp) Calcasieu Parish	2	0.02
Tumwater, WA (city) Thurston County	2	0.02
Baton Rouge, LA (city) East Baton Rouge Parish	20	0.01
Mobile, AL (city) Mobile County	11	0.01
Encinitas, CA (city) San Diego County	5	0.01
Gainesville, FL (city) Alachua County	5	0.01
Jacksonville, NC (city) Onslow County	5	0.01
Frederick, MD (city) Frederick County	4	0.01
Lakewood, WA (city) Pierce County	4	0.01
Rowland Heights, CA (cdp) Los Angeles County	4	0.01
Temple, TX (city) Bell County	4	0.01
Wheaton, IL (city) Du Page County	4	0.01
Alvin, TX (city) Brazoria County	3	0.01
Coachella, CA (city) Riverside County	3	0.01
Drexel Heights, AZ (cdp) Pima County	3	0.01
Friendswood, TX (city) Galveston County	3	0.01
North Highlands, CA (cdp) Sacramento County	3	0.01
Pascagoula, MS (city) Jackson County	3	0.01
Ruston, LA (city) Lincoln Parish	3	0.01
Spring, TX (cdp) Harris County	3	0.01
Stillwater, OK (city) Payne County	3	0.01
Sulphur, LA (city) Calcasieu Parish	3	0.01
Texas City, TX (city) Galveston County	3	0.01
Tigard, OR (city) Washington County	3	0.01
Tracy, CA (city) San Joaquin County	3	0.01
Wellington, FL (village) Palm Beach County	3	0.01
Bayonet Point, FL (cdp) Pasco County	2	0.01
Callaway, FL (city) Bay County	2	0.01
Cedar Hill, TX (city) Dallas County	2	0.01
Citrus Park, FL (cdp) Hillsborough County	2	0.01
Clinton, MA (town) Worcester County	2	0.01
Egg Harbor, NJ (township) Atlantic County	2	0.01
Ennis, TX (city) Ellis County	2	0.01
Ensley, FL (cdp) Escambia County	2	0.01
Ferry Pass, FL (cdp) Escambia County	2	0.01
Foster City, CA (city) San Mateo County	2	0.01
Haltom City, TX (city) Tarrant County	2	0.01
Horn Lake, MS (city) De Soto County	2	0.01
Humble, TX (city) Harris County	2	0.01
La Marque, TX (city) Galveston County	2	0.01
Lafayette, CA (city) Contra Costa County	2	0.01
Langley Park, MD (cdp) Prince George's County	2	0.01
Manlius, NY (town) Onondaga County	2	0.01
Morris, NJ (township) Morris County	2	0.01
Nacogdoches, TX (city) Nacogdoches County	2	0.01
Natchitoches, LA (city) Natchitoches Parish	2	0.01
Opelika, AL (city) Lee County	2	0.01
Panama City, FL (city) Bay County	2	0.01
Pineville, LA (city) Rapides Parish	2	0.01
Ridgecrest, CA (city) Kern County	2	0.01
San Marcos, TX (city) Hays County	2	0.01
Arkadelphia, AR (city) Clark County	1	0.01
Atlantic Beach, FL (city) Duval County	1	0.01
Bastrop, LA (city) Morehouse Parish	1	0.01
Bay City, TX (city) Matagorda County	1	0.01
Berea, OH (city) Cuyahoga County	1	0.01
Bon Air, VA (cdp) Chesterfield County	1	0.01
Boone, IA (city) Boone County	1	0.01
Camp Springs, MD (cdp) Prince George's County	1	0.01
Canton, MS (city) Madison County	1	0.01
Carlisle, PA (borough) Cumberland County	1	0.01
Chalco, NE (cdp) Sarpy County	1	0.01
Coffeyville, KS (city) Montgomery County	1	0.01
Covington, GA (city) Newton County	1	0.01
Daphne, AL (city) Baldwin County	1	0.01
Eunice, LA (city) Saint Landry Parish	1	0.01
Florida Ridge, FL (cdp) Indian River County	1	0.01
Forest Grove, OR (city) Washington County	1	0.01
Fort Leonard Wood, MO (cdp) Pulaski County	1	0.01
Fort Madison, IA (city) Lee County	1	0.01
Green Haven, MD (cdp) Anne Arundel County	1	0.01
Groves, TX (city) Jefferson County	1	0.01
Healdsburg, CA (city) Sonoma County	1	0.01
Helena, AL (city) Shelby County	1	0.01
Jasper, AL (city) Walker County	1	0.01
Jollyville, TX (cdp) Williamson County	1	0.01
Kingsland, GA (city) Camden County	1	0.01
Lathrop, CA (city) San Joaquin County	1	0.01
Long Beach, MS (city) Harrison County	1	0.01
Lorton, VA (cdp) Fairfax County	1	0.01
Martin, TN (city) Weakley County	1	0.01
McComb, MS (city) Pike County	1	0.01
Merrydale, LA (cdp) East Baton Rouge Parish	1	0.01
Mustang, OK (city) Canadian County	1	0.01
North Adams, MA (city) Berkshire County	1	0.01
Picayune, MS (city) Pearl River County	1	0.01
Plainville, CT (town) Hartford County	1	0.01
Plymouth, CT (town) Litchfield County	1	0.01

Notes: (cdp) census designated place; Refer to the Explanation of Data in the front of the book for more detailed information.

American Indian: Iroquois

Top 150 Places Sorted by Number

(Based on all places, regardless of population)

Place	Number	%
Saint Regis Mohawk Reservation, NY (reservation) Franklin Co.	2,515	93.18
Green Bay, WI (city) Brown County	2,120	2.07
Buffalo, NY (city) Erie County	1,604	0.55
Syracuse, NY (city) Onondaga County	1,511	1.03
Oneida, WI (town) Outagamie County	1,396	34.89
Milwaukee, WI (city) Milwaukee County	1,209	0.20
New York, NY (city) New York City	1,069	0.01
Niagara Falls, NY (city) Niagara County	767	1.38
Hobart, WI (town) Brown County	728	14.30
Onondaga Reservation, NY (reservation) Onondaga County	698	47.39
Rochester, NY (city) Monroe County	631	0.29
Oneida, WI (cdp) Brown County	591	55.23
Salamanca, NY (city) Cattaraugus County	556	9.12
Allegany Reservation, NY (reservation) Cattaraugus County	534	48.59
Los Angeles, CA (city) Los Angeles County	417	0.01
Chicago, IL (city) Cook County	401	0.01
Massena, NY (town) Saint Lawrence County	397	3.03
Clay, NY (town) Onondaga County	280	0.48
Phoenix, AZ (city) Maricopa County	274	0.02
Detroit, MI (city) Wayne County	272	0.03
Miami, OK (city) Ottawa County	270	1.97
Tulsa, OK (city) Tulsa County	268	0.07
Onondaga, NY (town) Onondaga County	247	1.17
San Diego, CA (city) San Diego County	241	0.02
Massena, NY (village) Saint Lawrence County	223	1.99
Collins, NY (town) Erie County	218	2.62
Tonawanda, NY (town) Erie County	209	0.27
Salina, NY (town) Onondaga County	202	0.61
Greece, NY (town) Monroe County	186	0.20
Philadelphia, PA (city) Philadelphia County	184	0.01
Oklahoma City, OK (city) Oklahoma County	177	0.03
Portland, OR (city) Multnomah County	171	0.03
Albuquerque, NM (city) Bernalillo County	170	0.04
Tuscarora Reservation, NY (reservation) Niagara County	163	14.32
Jamestown, NY (city) Chautauqua County	160	0.50
Bombay, NY (town) Franklin County	157	13.17
De Pere, WI (city) Brown County	148	0.72
Cheektowaga, NY (town) Erie County	147	0.16
Niagara, NY (town) Niagara County	145	1.62
Appleton, WI (city) Outagamie County	145	0.21
Nedrow, NY (cdp) Onondaga County	138	6.09
San Jose, CA (city) Santa Clara County	136	0.02
Amherst, NY (town) Erie County	131	0.11
Brookhaven, NY (town) Suffolk County	131	0.03
Jacksonville, FL (special city) Duval County	131	0.02
San Francisco, CA (city) San Francisco County	128	0.02
Colorado Springs, CO (city) El Paso County	125	0.03
West Allis, WI (city) Milwaukee County	124	0.20
Cicero, NY (town) Onondaga County	123	0.44
Madison, WI (city) Dane County	123	0.06
De Witt, NY (town) Onondaga County	122	0.51
Virginia Beach, VA (independent city) Virginia Beach city	122	0.03
Sacramento, CA (city) Sacramento County	120	0.03
Boston, MA (city) Suffolk County	118	0.02
Columbus, OH (city) Franklin County	118	0.02
Las Vegas, NV (city) Clark County	118	0.02
Geddes, NY (town) Onondaga County	115	0.65
Tucson, AZ (city) Pima County	113	0.02
Ashwaubenon, WI (village) Brown County	112	0.64
La Fayette, NY (town) Onondaga County	110	2.28
Evans, NY (town) Erie County	109	0.62
North Tonawanda, NY (city) Niagara County	108	0.32
Minneapolis, MN (city) Hennepin County	107	0.03
Hamburg, NY (town) Erie County	105	0.19
Hempstead, NY (town) Nassau County	105	0.01
Seattle, WA (city) King County	103	0.02
San Antonio, TX (city) Bexar County	102	0.01
Albany, NY (city) Albany County	100	0.10
Kaukauna, WI (city) Outagamie County	98	0.75
Worcester, MA (city) Worcester County	98	0.06
Pittsburgh, PA (city) Allegheny County	98	0.03
Houston, TX (city) Harris County	97	0.00
Denver, CO (city) Denver County	96	0.02
Long Beach, CA (city) Los Angeles County	96	0.02
Lewiston, NY (town) Niagara County	95	0.58

Place	Number	%
Manitowoc, WI (city) Manitowoc County	95	0.28
Anchorage, AK (municipality) Anchorage Borough	95	0.04
Henrietta, NY (town) Monroe County	92	0.24
Gowanda, NY (village) Cattaraugus County	91	3.20
Cleveland, OH (city) Cuyahoga County	91	0.02
Ogdensburg, NY (city) Saint Lawrence County	89	0.72
Canton, OH (city) Stark County	89	0.11
Charlotte, NC (city) Mecklenburg County	89	0.02
Oneida, NY (city) Madison County	86	0.78
Watertown, NY (city) Jefferson County	85	0.32
West Seneca, NY (town) Erie County	85	0.19
Erie, PA (city) Erie County	85	0.08
Fort Covington, NY (town) Franklin County	84	5.11
Schenectady, NY (city) Schenectady County	83	0.13
Oakland, CA (city) Alameda County	83	0.02
Lockport, NY (city) Niagara County	80	0.36
Camillus, NY (town) Onondaga County	80	0.35
Manlius, NY (town) Onondaga County	80	0.25
Austin, TX (city) Travis County	79	0.01
Nashville-Davidson, TN (special city) Davidson County	78	0.01
Tampa, FL (city) Hillsborough County	77	0.03
Wichita, KS (city) Sedgwick County	77	0.02
Solvay, NY (village) Onondaga County	76	1.11
Islip, NY (town) Suffolk County	76	0.02
Commerce, OK (city) Ottawa County	74	2.80
Howard, WI (village) Brown County	74	0.55
Batavia, NY (city) Genesee County	74	0.46
Honolulu, HI (cdp) Honolulu County	74	0.02
Utica, NY (city) Oneida County	73	0.12
Fresno, CA (city) Fresno County	73	0.02
Westland, MI (city) Wayne County	72	0.08
Seneca, MO (city) Newton County	71	3.33
Pawhuska, OK (city) Osage County	70	1.93
Hanover, NY (town) Chautauqua County	70	0.92
Babylon, NY (town) Suffolk County	70	0.03
Norfolk, VA (independent city) Norfolk city	70	0.03
Van Buren, NY (town) Onondaga County	68	0.54
Lockport, NY (town) Niagara County	68	0.35
Chili, NY (town) Monroe County	68	0.25
Lansing, MI (city) Ingham County	68	0.06
Springfield, MA (city) Hampden County	68	0.04
Kansas City, MO (city) Jackson County	68	0.02
Joplin, MO (city) Jasper County	67	0.15
Saint Petersburg, FL (city) Pinellas County	67	0.03
Baltimore, MD (independent city) Baltimore city	67	0.01
Grove, OK (city) Delaware County	66	1.29
Lancaster, NY (town) Erie County	66	0.17
Washington, DC (city) District of Columbia	66	0.01
Indianapolis, IN (special city) Marion County	65	0.01
Mesa, AZ (city) Maricopa County	64	0.02
Tonawanda, NY (city) Erie County	63	0.39
Colonie, NY (town) Albany County	63	0.08
Sullivan, NY (town) Madison County	62	0.41
Oshkosh, WI (city) Winnebago County	62	0.10
Glendale, AZ (city) Maricopa County	62	0.03
Seymour, WI (city) Outagamie County	61	1.83
Mattydale, NY (cdp) Onondaga County	61	0.96
Norman, OK (city) Cleveland County	61	0.06
Warren, MI (city) Macomb County	61	0.04
North Syracuse, NY (village) Onondaga County	59	0.86
Dunkirk, NY (city) Chautauqua County	59	0.45
Binghamton, NY (city) Broome County	59	0.12
Irondequoit, NY (cdp) Monroe County	59	0.11
Taylor, MI (city) Wayne County	59	0.09
Neenah, WI (city) Winnebago County	58	0.24
Auburn, NY (city) Cayuga County	58	0.20
San Bernardino, CA (city) San Bernardino County	57	0.03
Aurora, CO (city) Arapahoe County	57	0.02
Kenmore, NY (village) Erie County	56	0.34
Lysander, NY (town) Onondaga County	56	0.29
Shawano, WI (city) Shawano County	55	0.66
Plattsburgh, NY (city) Clinton County	55	0.29
Greenfield, WI (city) Milwaukee County	55	0.16
Lawrence, KS (city) Douglas County	55	0.07
Eugene, OR (city) Lane County	55	0.04

Notes: (cdp) census designated place; Refer to the Explanation of Data in the front of the book for more detailed information.

American Indian: Iroquois

Top 150 Places Sorted by Percent

(Based on all places, regardless of population)

Place	Number	%
Saint Regis Mohawk Reservation, NY (reservation) Franklin Co.	2,515	93.18
Oneida, WI (cdp) Brown County	591	55.23
Allegany Reservation, NY (reservation) Cattaraugus County	534	48.59
Onondaga Reservation, NY (reservation) Onondaga County	698	47.39
Oneida, WI (town) Outagamie County	1,396	34.89
Tuscarora Reservation, NY (reservation) Niagara County	163	14.32
Hobart, WI (town) Brown County	728	14.30
Wyandotte, OK (town) Ottawa County	48	13.22
Bombay, NY (town) Franklin County	157	13.17
Salamanca, NY (city) Cattaraugus County	556	9.12
Bowmore, NC (cdp) Hoke County	10	6.90
Nedrow, NY (cdp) Onondaga County	138	6.09
Bartelme, WI (town) Shawano County	37	5.29
Fort Covington, NY (town) Franklin County	84	5.11
Nichols, WI (village) Outagamie County	15	4.89
Ogema, MN (city) Becker County	6	4.20
Perrysburg, NY (village) Cattaraugus County	16	3.92
Chautauqua, KS (city) Chautauqua County	4	3.54
Seneca, MO (city) Newton County	71	3.33
Hooper, CO (town) Alamosa County	4	3.25
Gowanda, NY (village) Cattaraugus County	91	3.20
Massena, NY (town) Saint Lawrence County	397	3.03
North Hudson, NY (town) Essex County	8	3.01
Red Springs, WI (town) Shawano County	29	2.96
Nelchina, AK (cdp) Valdez-Cordova Census Area	2	2.82
Commerce, OK (city) Ottawa County	74	2.80
Hazelton, KS (city) Barber County	4	2.78
Perrysburg, NY (town) Cattaraugus County	49	2.77
Neopit, WI (cdp) Menominee County	23	2.74
Brant, NY (town) Erie County	52	2.73
Elrod, NC (cdp) Robeson County	12	2.72
Clare, NY (town) Saint Lawrence County	3	2.68
Red House, NY (town) Cattaraugus County	1	2.63
Collins, NY (town) Erie County	218	2.62
Granger, NY (town) Allegany County	15	2.60
Pin Oak Acres, OK (cdp) Mayes County	11	2.58
McDonald, NC (town) Robeson County	3	2.52
Quapaw, OK (town) Ottawa County	24	2.44
Gresham, WI (village) Shawano County	14	2.43
Delanson, NY (village) Schenectady County	9	2.34
Callaway, MN (township) Becker County	6	2.31
Cranmoor, WI (town) Wood County	4	2.29
La Fayette, NY (town) Onondaga County	110	2.28
Alabama, NY (town) Genesee County	42	2.23
Pritchett, CO (town) Baca County	3	2.19
Dennis, OK (cdp) Delaware County	4	2.16
Millstone, PA (township) Elk County	2	2.11
Green Bay, WI (city) Brown County	2,120	2.07
Fairland, OK (town) Ottawa County	21	2.05
Keshena, WI (cdp) Menominee County	28	2.01
Big Bend, CA (cdp) Shasta County	3	2.01
Massena, NY (village) Saint Lawrence County	223	1.99
Miami, OK (city) Ottawa County	270	1.97
Lance Creek, WY (cdp) Niobrara County	1	1.96
Pawhuska, OK (city) Osage County	70	1.93
Kaukauna, WI (town) Outagamie County	22	1.93
Grugan, PA (township) Clinton County	1	1.92
Gold Hill, CO (cdp) Boulder County	4	1.90
Seymour, WI (town) Outagamie County	23	1.89
Grove, NY (town) Allegany County	10	1.88
Farnham, NY (village) Erie County	6	1.86
West Leipsic, OH (village) Putnam County	5	1.85
Brasher, NY (town) Saint Lawrence County	43	1.84
Seymour, WI (city) Outagamie County	61	1.83
Persia, NY (town) Cattaraugus County	46	1.83
Natural Bridge, NY (cdp) Jefferson County	7	1.79
Santa Clara, NY (town) Franklin County	7	1.77
Legend Lake, WI (cdp) Menominee County	27	1.76
Bowler, WI (village) Shawano County	6	1.75
Arizona Village, AZ (cdp) Mohave County	6	1.71
Sergeant, PA (township) McKean County	3	1.70
Antelope, OR (city) Wasco County	1	1.69
Cabot, VT (village) Washington County	4	1.67
Niagara, NY (town) Niagara County	145	1.62
Sams Corner, OK (cdp) Mayes County	2	1.59

Place	Number	%
Pike, NY (village) Wyoming County	6	1.57
Carrollton, NY (town) Cattaraugus County	22	1.56
Grand Lake Towne, OK (town) Mayes County	1	1.54
Almon, WI (town) Shawano County	9	1.52
Deer Park, MD (town) Garrett County	6	1.48
Salamanca, NY (town) Cattaraugus County	8	1.47
Coldspring, NY (town) Cattaraugus County	11	1.46
Shoal Creek Drive, MO (village) Newton County	5	1.45
Paxico, KS (city) Wabaunsee County	3	1.42
Peoria, OK (town) Ottawa County	2	1.42
Fabius, NY (village) Onondaga County	5	1.41
Wausaukee, WI (village) Marinette County	8	1.40
Ketchum, OK (town) Craig County	4	1.40
North Collins, NY (village) Erie County	15	1.39
Clifton, NY (town) Saint Lawrence County	11	1.39
Prue, OK (town) Osage County	6	1.39
Niagara Falls, NY (city) Niagara County	767	1.38
Westville, NY (town) Franklin County	25	1.37
Birch, WI (town) Lincoln County	11	1.37
Meadowbrook, WI (town) Sawyer County	2	1.37
Adrian, OR (city) Malheur County	2	1.36
Tajique, NM (cdp) Torrance County	2	1.35
Constable, NY (town) Franklin County	19	1.33
Cardin, OK (town) Ottawa County	2	1.33
Blue Springs, NE (city) Gage County	5	1.31
Grove, OK (city) Delaware County	66	1.29
Lincoln, WI (town) Forest County	13	1.29
Angola, NY (village) Erie County	29	1.28
Dickinson, NY (town) Franklin County	9	1.22
Clay Banks, WI (town) Door County	5	1.22
White Lake, WI (village) Langlade County	4	1.22
Windham, VT (town) Windham County	4	1.22
Napoli, NY (town) Cattaraugus County	14	1.21
East Syracuse, NY (village) Onondaga County	38	1.20
Rensselaer Falls, NY (village) Saint Lawrence County	4	1.19
Summit, WI (town) Langlade County	2	1.19
Finley, WI (town) Juneau County	1	1.19
Onondaga, NY (town) Onondaga County	247	1.17
Akron, NY (village) Erie County	36	1.17
Wyoming, NY (village) Wyoming County	6	1.17
Star Lake, NY (cdp) Saint Lawrence County	10	1.16
Sturgeon Bay, WI (town) Door County	10	1.16
Cibola, AZ (cdp) La Paz County	2	1.16
North Miami, OK (town) Ottawa County	5	1.15
Victory, NY (town) Cayuga County	21	1.14
Severn, NC (town) Northampton County	3	1.14
De Ruyter, NY (village) Madison County	6	1.13
Whiteash, IL (village) Williamson County	3	1.12
Colebrook, PA (township) Clinton County	2	1.12
Solvay, NY (village) Onondaga County	76	1.11
Brandon, NY (town) Franklin County	6	1.11
Poospatuck Reservation, NY (reservation) Suffolk County	3	1.11
Pike, NY (town) Wyoming County	12	1.10
Baring, ME (plantation) Washington County	3	1.10
Saginaw, MO (village) Newton County	3	1.09
Helix, OR (city) Umatilla County	2	1.09
Hancock, WI (village) Waushara County	5	1.08
Chistochina, AK (cdp) Valdez-Cordova Census Area	1	1.08
Osborn, WI (town) Outagamie County	11	1.07
Mattoon, WI (village) Shawano County	5	1.07
Lyndon, NY (town) Cattaraugus County	7	1.06
East Williston, FL (cdp) Levy County	10	1.04
Couderay, WI (village) Sawyer County	1	1.04
Dodge, OK (cdp) Delaware County	1	1.04
Syracuse, NY (city) Onondaga County	1,511	1.03
Kansas, OK (town) Delaware County	7	1.02
Lammers, MN (township) Beltrami County	5	1.02
Rockport, AR (town) Hot Spring County	8	1.01
Pembroke, NC (town) Robeson County	24	1.00
Franklin, NY (town) Franklin County	12	1.00
Cato, NY (village) Cayuga County	6	1.00
Ira, NY (town) Cayuga County	24	0.99
Morristown, NY (town) Saint Lawrence County	20	0.98
Ulmer, SC (town) Allendale County	1	0.98
Limestone, NY (village) Cattaraugus County	4	0.97

Notes: (cdp) census designated place; Refer to the Explanation of Data in the front of the book for more detailed information.

American Indian: Iroquois

Top 150 Places Sorted by Percent

(Based on places with populations of 10,000 or more)

Place	Number	%
Massena, NY (town) Saint Lawrence County	397	3.03
Green Bay, WI (city) Brown County	2,120	2.07
Massena, NY (village) Saint Lawrence County	223	1.99
Miami, OK (city) Ottawa County	270	1.97
Niagara Falls, NY (city) Niagara County	767	1.38
Onondaga, NY (town) Onondaga County	247	1.17
Syracuse, NY (city) Onondaga County	1,511	1.03
Oneida, NY (city) Madison County	86	0.78
Kaukauna, WI (city) Outagamie County	98	0.75
De Pere, WI (city) Brown County	148	0.72
Ogdensburg, NY (city) Saint Lawrence County	89	0.72
Geddes, NY (town) Onondaga County	115	0.65
Ashwaubenon, WI (village) Brown County	112	0.64
Evans, NY (town) Erie County	109	0.62
Salina, NY (town) Onondaga County	202	0.61
Lewiston, NY (town) Niagara County	95	0.58
Buffalo, NY (city) Erie County	1,604	0.55
Howard, WI (village) Brown County	74	0.55
Van Buren, NY (town) Onondaga County	68	0.54
De Witt, NY (town) Onondaga County	122	0.51
Jamestown, NY (city) Chautauqua County	160	0.50
Clay, NY (town) Onondaga County	280	0.48
Batavia, NY (city) Genesee County	74	0.46
Dunkirk, NY (city) Chautauqua County	59	0.45
Cicero, NY (town) Onondaga County	123	0.44
Bellevue Town, WI (cdp) Brown County	51	0.43
Sullivan, NY (town) Madison County	62	0.41
Tonawanda, NY (city) Erie County	63	0.39
Little Chute, WI (village) Outagamie County	41	0.39
Wheatfield, NY (town) Niagara County	54	0.38
Lockport, NY (city) Niagara County	80	0.36
Camillus, NY (town) Onondaga County	80	0.35
Lockport, NY (town) Niagara County	68	0.35
Fulton, NY (city) Oswego County	42	0.35
Kenmore, NY (village) Erie County	56	0.34
Fairmount, NY (cdp) Onondaga County	36	0.33
North Tonawanda, NY (city) Niagara County	108	0.32
Watertown, NY (city) Jefferson County	85	0.32
Potsdam, NY (town) Saint Lawrence County	51	0.32
Rochester, NY (city) Monroe County	631	0.29
Lysander, NY (town) Onondaga County	56	0.29
Plattsburgh, NY (city) Clinton County	55	0.29
Menasha, WI (city) Winnebago County	47	0.29
Allouez, WI (village) Brown County	45	0.29
Malone, NY (town) Franklin County	44	0.29
Pomfret, NY (town) Chautauqua County	42	0.29
Manitowoc, WI (city) Manitowoc County	95	0.28
Corning, NY (city) Steuben County	30	0.28
Tonawanda, NY (town) Erie County	209	0.27
Olean, NY (city) Cattaraugus County	41	0.27
Neosho, MO (city) Newton County	28	0.27
Manlius, NY (town) Onondaga County	80	0.25
Chili, NY (town) Monroe County	68	0.25
Oswego, NY (city) Oswego County	45	0.25
German Flatts, NY (town) Herkimer County	34	0.25
Fredonia, NY (village) Chautauqua County	27	0.25
Henrietta, NY (town) Monroe County	92	0.24
Neenah, WI (city) Winnebago County	58	0.24
Grand Island, NY (town) Erie County	44	0.24
Bath, NY (town) Steuben County	29	0.24
Canton, NY (town) Saint Lawrence County	25	0.24
Arcadia, NY (town) Wayne County	34	0.23
Lackawanna, NY (city) Erie County	41	0.22
Grosse Ile, MI (cdp) Wayne County	24	0.22
Appleton, WI (city) Outagamie County	145	0.21
Farmington, NY (town) Ontario County	22	0.21
Milwaukee, WI (city) Milwaukee County	1,209	0.20
Greece, NY (town) Monroe County	186	0.20
West Allis, WI (city) Milwaukee County	124	0.20
Auburn, NY (city) Cayuga County	58	0.20
Cortland, NY (city) Cortland County	37	0.20
Menasha, WI (town) Winnebago County	31	0.20
Hamburg, NY (town) Erie County	105	0.19
West Seneca, NY (town) Erie County	85	0.19
Ogden, NY (town) Monroe County	35	0.19
Depew, NY (village) Erie County	31	0.19
Warren, PA (city) Warren County	20	0.19
Oak Creek, WI (city) Milwaukee County	51	0.18
Cudahy, WI (city) Milwaukee County	34	0.18
Endicott, NY (village) Broome County	24	0.18
Lancaster, NY (village) Erie County	20	0.18
Lancaster, NY (town) Erie County	66	0.17
West and East Lealman, FL (cdp) Pinellas County	37	0.17
Milton, NY (town) Saratoga County	29	0.17
Melvindale, MI (city) Wayne County	18	0.17
Cheektowaga, NY (town) Erie County	147	0.16
Greenfield, WI (city) Milwaukee County	55	0.16
Hazel Park, MI (city) Oakland County	31	0.16
Gloversville, NY (city) Fulton County	24	0.16
Canandaigua, NY (city) Ontario County	18	0.16
Joplin, MO (city) Jasper County	67	0.15
Hyde Park, NY (town) Dutchess County	31	0.15
Sweden, NY (town) Monroe County	21	0.15
Dryden, NY (town) Tompkins County	20	0.15
Brunswick, NY (town) Rensselaer County	18	0.15
Catskill, NY (town) Greene County	18	0.15
Port Washington, WI (city) Ozaukee County	16	0.15
Hamburg, NY (village) Erie County	15	0.15
Rome, NY (city) Oneida County	49	0.14
Gates, NY (town) Monroe County	40	0.14
Orchard Park, NY (town) Erie County	38	0.14
Wayne, MI (city) Wayne County	26	0.14
Greenfield, MA (town) Franklin County	25	0.14
Claremore, OK (city) Rogers County	22	0.14
Browns Mills, NJ (cdp) Burlington County	16	0.14
Schenectady, NY (city) Schenectady County	83	0.13
Elmira, NY (city) Chemung County	39	0.13
Ithaca, NY (city) Tompkins County	38	0.13
Gates-North Gates, NY (cdp) Monroe County	20	0.13
Moreau, NY (town) Saratoga County	18	0.13
McKinleyville, CA (cdp) Humboldt County	17	0.13
Alden, NY (town) Erie County	14	0.13
Plattsburgh, NY (town) Clinton County	14	0.13
Southport, NY (town) Chemung County	14	0.13
Utica, NY (city) Oneida County	73	0.12
Binghamton, NY (city) Broome County	59	0.12
Webster, NY (town) Monroe County	47	0.12
Franklin, WI (city) Milwaukee County	35	0.12
Stevens Point, WI (city) Portage County	30	0.12
Tahlequah, OK (city) Cherokee County	18	0.12
Geneva, NY (city) Ontario County	17	0.12
New Paltz, NY (town) Ulster County	15	0.12
Amherst, NY (town) Erie County	131	0.11
Canton, OH (city) Stark County	89	0.11
Irondequoit, NY (cdp) Monroe County	59	0.11
Bartlesville, OK (city) Washington County	38	0.11
Rotterdam, NY (town) Schenectady County	30	0.11
Ponca City, OK (city) Kay County	29	0.11
Grand Chute, WI (town) Outagamie County	20	0.11
Halfmoon, NY (town) Saratoga County	20	0.11
Genoa, MI (township) Livingston County	17	0.11
Johnson City, NY (village) Broome County	17	0.11
Parma, NY (town) Monroe County	17	0.11
Wawarsing, NY (town) Ulster County	14	0.11
Brown Deer, WI (village) Milwaukee County	13	0.11
Chenango, NY (town) Broome County	13	0.11
Spencer, MA (town) Worcester County	13	0.11
Fort Carson, CO (cdp) El Paso County	12	0.11
Lansing, NY (town) Tompkins County	12	0.11
Albany, NY (city) Albany County	100	0.10
Oshkosh, WI (city) Winnebago County	62	0.10
Redford, MI (cdp) Wayne County	53	0.10
Troy, NY (city) Rensselaer County	48	0.10
Burlington, VT (city) Chittenden County	38	0.10
Penfield, NY (town) Monroe County	33	0.10
Garden City, MI (city) Wayne County	31	0.10
Clarence, NY (town) Erie County	26	0.10
Kingston, NY (city) Ulster County	24	0.10
South Milwaukee, WI (city) Milwaukee County	21	0.10
Horseheads, NY (town) Chemung County	19	0.10

Notes: (cdp) census designated place; Refer to the Explanation of Data in the front of the book for more detailed information.

American Indian: Kiowa

Top 150 Places Sorted by Number

(Based on all places, regardless of population)

Place	Number	%
Anadarko, OK (city) Caddo County	1,174	17.67
Oklahoma City, OK (city) Oklahoma County	1,001	0.20
Lawton, OK (city) Comanche County	721	0.78
Tulsa, OK (city) Tulsa County	327	0.08
Carnegie, OK (town) Caddo County	237	14.48
Norman, OK (city) Cleveland County	237	0.25
Wichita, KS (city) Sedgwick County	157	0.05
Hobart, OK (city) Kiowa County	109	2.73
Apache, OK (town) Caddo County	99	6.13
Dallas, TX (city) Dallas County	95	0.01
Chickasha, OK (city) Grady County	90	0.57
Albuquerque, NM (city) Bernalillo County	85	0.02
Midwest City, OK (city) Oklahoma County	83	0.15
Phoenix, AZ (city) Maricopa County	82	0.01
El Reno, OK (city) Canadian County	78	0.48
Moore, OK (city) Cleveland County	73	0.18
Mountain View, OK (town) Kiowa County	62	7.05
Del City, OK (city) Oklahoma County	59	0.27
Lawrence, KS (city) Douglas County	58	0.07
Shawnee, OK (city) Pottawatomie County	53	0.18
Cache, OK (city) Comanche County	49	2.07
Los Angeles, CA (city) Los Angeles County	47	0.00
Fort Cobb, OK (town) Caddo County	46	6.90
Fort Worth, TX (city) Tarrant County	42	0.01
Denver, CO (city) Denver County	40	0.01
Edmond, OK (city) Oklahoma County	38	0.06
Kansas City, MO (city) Jackson County	38	0.01
Muskogee, OK (city) Muskogee County	36	0.09
Yukon, OK (city) Canadian County	34	0.16
Davenport, IA (city) Scott County	34	0.03
Elgin, OK (city) Comanche County	32	2.64
Tahlequah, OK (city) Cherokee County	28	0.19
Arlington, TX (city) Tarrant County	28	0.01
Cyril, OK (town) Caddo County	27	2.31
Weatherford, OK (city) Custer County	27	0.27
Grand Prairie, TX (city) Dallas County	27	0.02
San Diego, CA (city) San Diego County	27	0.00
Claremore, OK (city) Rogers County	26	0.16
Mesa, AZ (city) Maricopa County	26	0.01
Portland, OR (city) Multnomah County	26	0.00
The Village, OK (city) Oklahoma County	25	0.25
Stillwater, OK (city) Payne County	25	0.06
Clinton, OK (city) Custer County	24	0.27
Watonga, OK (city) Blaine County	23	0.49
Bethany, OK (city) Oklahoma County	23	0.11
Ponca City, OK (city) Kay County	23	0.09
Wichita Falls, TX (city) Wichita County	23	0.02
Irving, TX (city) Dallas County	23	0.01
Ada, OK (city) Pontotoc County	22	0.14
Altus, OK (city) Jackson County	21	0.10
Glendale, AZ (city) Maricopa County	20	0.01
Okmulgee, OK (city) Okmulgee County	19	0.15
Duncan, OK (city) Stephens County	19	0.08
Sacramento, CA (city) Sacramento County	19	0.00
Walters, OK (city) Cotton County	18	0.68
Chicago, IL (city) Cook County	18	0.00
Tecumseh, OK (city) Pottawatomie County	17	0.28
Denton, TX (city) Denton County	17	0.02
Pueblo, CO (city) Pueblo County	17	0.02
Houston, TX (city) Harris County	17	0.00
Arkansas City, KS (city) Cowley County	16	0.13
McAlester, OK (city) Pittsburg County	16	0.09
Gallup, NM (city) McKinley County	16	0.08
Santa Fe, NM (city) Santa Fe County	16	0.03
Spokane, WA (city) Spokane County	16	0.01
Virginia Beach, VA (independent city) Virginia Beach city	16	0.00
Bartlesville, OK (city) Washington County	15	0.04
Broken Arrow, OK (city) Tulsa County	15	0.02
Lewisville, TX (city) Denton County	15	0.02
Bakersfield, CA (city) Kern County	15	0.01
Riverside, CA (city) Riverside County	15	0.01
Salem, OR (city) Marion County	15	0.01
Long Beach, CA (city) Los Angeles County	15	0.00
Seattle, WA (city) King County	15	0.00
Wetumka, OK (city) Hughes County	14	0.96
Amarillo, TX (city) Potter County	14	0.01
Austin, TX (city) Travis County	14	0.00
Thomas, OK (city) Custer County	13	1.05
Park Hill, OK (cdp) Cherokee County	13	0.33
San Leandro, CA (city) Alameda County	13	0.02
Tacoma, WA (city) Pierce County	13	0.01
Tempe, AZ (city) Maricopa County	13	0.01
Colorado Springs, CO (city) El Paso County	13	0.00
Fresno, CA (city) Fresno County	13	0.00
New York, NY (city) New York City	13	0.00
Pawnee, OK (city) Pawnee County	12	0.54
Cushing, OK (city) Payne County	12	0.14
Choctaw, OK (city) Oklahoma County	12	0.13
San Ramon, CA (city) Contra Costa County	12	0.03
Eugene, OR (city) Lane County	12	0.01
Mesquite, TX (city) Dallas County	12	0.01
Topeka, KS (city) Shawnee County	12	0.01
San Francisco, CA (city) San Francisco County	12	0.00
Independence, KS (city) Montgomery County	11	0.11
Warr Acres, OK (city) Oklahoma County	11	0.11
Mustang, OK (city) Canadian County	11	0.08
Oakley, CA (city) Contra Costa County	11	0.04
Farmington, NM (city) San Juan County	11	0.03
Chico, CA (city) Butte County	11	0.02
Spring Valley, NV (cdp) Clark County	11	0.01
Sunrise Manor, NV (cdp) Clark County	11	0.01
Thornton, CO (city) Adams County	11	0.01
Omaha, NE (city) Douglas County	11	0.00
Tucson, AZ (city) Pima County	11	0.00
Dennehotso, AZ (cdp) Apache County	10	1.36
Pawhuska, OK (city) Osage County	10	0.28
Piedmont, OK (city) Canadian County	10	0.27
Skiatook, OK (town) Osage County	10	0.19
Burkburnett, TX (city) Wichita County	10	0.09
Miami, OK (city) Ottawa County	10	0.07
Owasso, OK (city) Tulsa County	10	0.05
Ardmore, OK (city) Carter County	10	0.04
Rogers, AR (city) Benton County	10	0.03
Billings, MT (city) Yellowstone County	10	0.01
Columbus, OH (city) Franklin County	10	0.00
Saint Paul, MN (city) Ramsey County	10	0.00
Gracemont, OK (town) Caddo County	9	2.68
Binger, OK (town) Caddo County	9	1.27
Medford, OK (city) Grant County	9	0.77
Hominy, OK (city) Osage County	9	0.35
Taos, NM (town) Taos County	9	0.19
Pryor Creek, OK (city) Mayes County	9	0.10
Saginaw, TX (city) Tarrant County	9	0.07
Newark, CA (city) Alameda County	9	0.02
Hayward, CA (city) Alameda County	9	0.01
Lakewood, CO (city) Jefferson County	9	0.01
Overland Park, KS (city) Johnson County	9	0.01
Pico Rivera, CA (city) Los Angeles County	9	0.01
Anchorage, AK (municipality) Anchorage Borough	9	0.00
Norfolk, VA (independent city) Norfolk city	9	0.00
San Antonio, TX (city) Bexar County	9	0.00
Inola, OK (town) Rogers County	8	0.50
Tuttle, OK (city) Grady County	8	0.19
Destin, FL (city) Okaloosa County	8	0.07
Bixby, OK (city) Tulsa County	8	0.06
Sand Springs, OK (city) Tulsa County	8	0.05
Sapulpa, OK (city) Creek County	8	0.04
Copperas Cove, TX (city) Coryell County	8	0.03
Enid, OK (city) Garfield County	8	0.02
Renton, WA (city) King County	8	0.02
Rio Rancho, NM (city) Sandoval County	8	0.02
Carrollton, TX (city) Denton County	8	0.01
Fort Collins, CO (city) Larimer County	8	0.01
Killeen, TX (city) Bell County	8	0.01
Livermore, CA (city) Alameda County	8	0.01
Ontario, CA (city) San Bernardino County	8	0.01
Chandler, AZ (city) Maricopa County	8	0.00
Fremont, CA (city) Alameda County	8	0.00
Las Vegas, NV (city) Clark County	8	0.00
Lubbock, TX (city) Lubbock County	8	0.00

Notes: (cdp) census designated place; Refer to the Explanation of Data in the front of the book for more detailed information.

American Indian: Kiowa

Top 150 Places Sorted by Percent

(Based on all places, regardless of population)

Place	Number	%
Anadarko, OK (city) Caddo County	1,174	17.67
Carnegie, OK (town) Caddo County	237	14.48
Mountain View, OK (town) Kiowa County	62	7.05
Fort Cobb, OK (town) Caddo County	46	6.90
Old Eucha, OK (cdp) Delaware County	3	6.52
Apache, OK (town) Caddo County	99	6.13
Chickaloon, AK (cdp) Matanuska-Susitna Borough	7	3.29
Hobart, OK (city) Kiowa County	109	2.73
Gracemont, OK (town) Caddo County	9	2.68
Elgin, OK (city) Comanche County	32	2.64
Cyril, OK (town) Caddo County	27	2.31
Quay, OK (town) Pawnee County	1	2.13
Cache, OK (city) Comanche County	49	2.07
Gotebo, OK (town) Kiowa County	4	1.47
Sparks, OK (town) Lincoln County	2	1.46
Dennehotso, AZ (cdp) Apache County	10	1.36
Pump Back, OK (cdp) Mayes County	2	1.29
Binger, OK (town) Caddo County	9	1.27
Coyle, OK (town) Logan County	4	1.19
French Gulch, CA (cdp) Shasta County	3	1.18
Jennings, OK (town) Pawnee County	4	1.07
Thomas, OK (city) Custer County	13	1.05
Rentiesville, OK (town) McIntosh County	1	0.98
Wetumka, OK (city) Hughes County	14	0.96
Verden, OK (town) Grady County	6	0.91
Meriden, KS (city) Jefferson County	6	0.85
Iron Post, OK (cdp) Mayes County	1	0.85
Greenfield, OK (town) Blaine County	1	0.81
Highfill, AR (town) Benton County	3	0.79
Lawton, OK (city) Comanche County	721	0.78
Medford, OK (city) Grant County	9	0.77
Geronimo, OK (town) Comanche County	7	0.73
Calvin, OK (town) Hughes County	2	0.72
Buffalo, KS (city) Wilson County	2	0.70
Walters, OK (city) Cotton County	18	0.68
Red Rock, OK (town) Noble County	2	0.68
Lone Wolf, OK (town) Kiowa County	3	0.60
Tolar, TX (city) Hood County	3	0.60
Klawock, AK (city) Prince of Wales-Outer Ketchikan Census Area	5	0.59
Olustee, OK (town) Jackson County	4	0.59
Chickasha, OK (city) Grady County	90	0.57
Rocky, OK (town) Washita County	1	0.57
Geary, OK (city) Blaine County	7	0.56
Pawnee, OK (city) Pawnee County	12	0.54
Dickson, OK (town) Carter County	6	0.53
Davidson, OK (town) Tillman County	2	0.53
Cove, AR (town) Polk County	2	0.52
Inola, OK (town) Rogers County	8	0.50
Ninnekah, OK (town) Grady County	5	0.50
Colony, KS (city) Anderson County	2	0.50
Watonga, OK (city) Blaine County	23	0.49
Fletcher, OK (town) Comanche County	5	0.49
El Reno, OK (city) Canadian County	78	0.48
Wright City, OK (town) McCurtain County	4	0.47
Earlsboro, OK (town) Pottawatomie County	3	0.47
McCracken, KS (city) Rush County	1	0.47
Justice, OK (cdp) Rogers County	6	0.46
Barnsdall, OK (city) Osage County	6	0.45
Custer, MN (township) Lyon County	1	0.45
Dougherty, OK (town) Murray County	1	0.45
Johnson, OK (town) Pottawatomie County	1	0.45
Rutland, ND (city) Sargent County	1	0.45
Thrall, TX (city) Williamson County	3	0.42
Knippa, TX (cdp) Uvalde County	3	0.41
Painter, VA (town) Accomack County	1	0.41
Taos Pueblo, NM (cdp) Taos County	5	0.40
Woodall, OK (cdp) Cherokee County	3	0.40
Shinnecock Reservation, NY (reservation) Suffolk County	2	0.40
Glacier View, AK (cdp) Matanuska-Susitna Borough	1	0.40
Pueblo Pintado, NM (cdp) McKinley County	1	0.40
Rush Springs, OK (town) Grady County	5	0.39
Tulelake, CA (city) Siskiyou County	4	0.39
Winnebago, NE (village) Thurston County	3	0.39
Sacramento, KY (city) McLean County	2	0.39
Sarcoxie, MO (city) Jasper County	5	0.37
Valley Brook, OK (town) Oklahoma County	3	0.37
Calumet, OK (town) Canadian County	2	0.37
Hominy, OK (city) Osage County	9	0.35
Bennington, OK (town) Bryan County	1	0.35
Park Hill, OK (cdp) Cherokee County	13	0.33
Tangent, OR (city) Linn County	3	0.32
Cameron, OK (town) Le Flore County	1	0.32
Morris, OK (city) Okmulgee County	4	0.31
Meeker, OK (town) Lincoln County	3	0.31
Cashion, OK (town) Kingfisher County	2	0.31
Minnewaukan, ND (city) Benson County	1	0.31
Dover, AR (city) Pope County	4	0.30
Fort Supply, OK (town) Woodward County	1	0.30
Mercer, MO (town) Mercer County	1	0.29
Mill Creek, OK (town) Johnston County	1	0.29
New Germany, MN (city) Carver County	1	0.29
Tecumseh, OK (city) Pottawatomie County	17	0.28
Pawhuska, OK (city) Osage County	10	0.28
Westworth Village, TX (city) Tarrant County	6	0.28
Haworth, OK (town) McCurtain County	1	0.28
Peavine, OK (cdp) Adair County	1	0.28
Del City, OK (city) Oklahoma County	59	0.27
Weatherford, OK (city) Custer County	27	0.27
Clinton, OK (city) Custer County	24	0.27
Piedmont, OK (city) Canadian County	10	0.27
Granite, OK (town) Greer County	5	0.27
Ethete, WY (cdp) Fremont County	4	0.27
Snyder, OK (city) Kiowa County	4	0.27
Jemez Springs, NM (village) Sandoval County	1	0.27
Medicine Park, OK (town) Comanche County	1	0.27
Bethel Acres, OK (town) Pottawatomie County	7	0.26
Grand Mound, WA (cdp) Thurston County	5	0.26
Sterling, OK (town) Comanche County	2	0.26
Hydaburg, AK (city) Prince of Wales-Outer Ketchikan Census Area	1	0.26
Mountain Park, OK (town) Kiowa County	1	0.26
Oacoma, SD (town) Lyman County	1	0.26
Norman, OK (city) Cleveland County	237	0.25
The Village, OK (city) Oklahoma County	25	0.25
Roland, OK (town) Sequoyah County	7	0.25
Nicoma Park, OK (city) Oklahoma County	6	0.25
Custer City, OK (town) Custer County	1	0.25
Newbury, VT (village) Orange County	1	0.25
Winslow, AR (city) Washington County	1	0.25
Colcord, OK (town) Delaware County	2	0.24
Royal Center, IN (town) Cass County	2	0.24
Asher, OK (town) Pottawatomie County	1	0.24
Eufaula, OK (city) McIntosh County	6	0.23
Hinton, OK (town) Caddo County	5	0.23
Essex, IA (city) Page County	2	0.23
Oologah, OK (town) Rogers County	2	0.23
Wadsworth, NV (cdp) Washoe County	2	0.23
Eastman, WI (village) Crawford County	1	0.23
Morton, MN (city) Renville County	1	0.23
Oaklawn-Sunview, KS (cdp) Sedgwick County	7	0.22
Burns Flat, OK (town) Washita County	4	0.22
Mariposa, CA (cdp) Mariposa County	3	0.22
Union City, OK (town) Canadian County	3	0.22
Blair, OK (town) Jackson County	2	0.22
La Veta, CO (town) Huerfano County	2	0.22
Marine, IL (village) Madison County	2	0.22
Springdale, UT (town) Washington County	1	0.22
Charlack, MO (city) Saint Louis County	3	0.21
Lake Shore, MN (city) Cass County	2	0.21
Hammon, OK (town) Roger Mills County	1	0.21
Oklahoma City, OK (city) Oklahoma County	1,001	0.20
Dennison, OH (village) Tuscarawas County	6	0.20
Clay City, IL (village) Clay County	2	0.20
Zeb, OK (cdp) Cherokee County	1	0.20
Tahlequah, OK (city) Cherokee County	28	0.19
Skiatook, OK (town) Osage County	10	0.19
Taos, NM (town) Taos County	9	0.19
Tuttle, OK (city) Grady County	8	0.19
Lyman, MS (cdp) Harrison County	2	0.19
Canute, OK (town) Washita County	1	0.19
Cement, OK (town) Caddo County	1	0.19

Notes: (cdp) census designated place; Refer to the Explanation of Data in the front of the book for more detailed information.

American Indian: Kiowa

Top 150 Places Sorted by Percent

(Based on places with populations of 10,000 or more)

Place	Number	%
Lawton, OK (city) Comanche County	721	0.78
Chickasha, OK (city) Grady County	90	0.57
El Reno, OK (city) Canadian County	78	0.48
Del City, OK (city) Oklahoma County	59	0.27
Norman, OK (city) Cleveland County	237	0.25
The Village, OK (city) Oklahoma County	25	0.25
Oklahoma City, OK (city) Oklahoma County	1,001	0.20
Tahlequah, OK (city) Cherokee County	28	0.19
Moore, OK (city) Cleveland County	73	0.18
Shawnee, OK (city) Pottawatomie County	53	0.18
Yukon, OK (city) Canadian County	34	0.16
Claremore, OK (city) Rogers County	26	0.16
Midwest City, OK (city) Oklahoma County	83	0.15
Okmulgee, OK (city) Okmulgee County	19	0.15
Ada, OK (city) Pontotoc County	22	0.14
Arkansas City, KS (city) Cowley County	16	0.13
Bethany, OK (city) Oklahoma County	23	0.11
Altus, OK (city) Jackson County	21	0.10
Muskogee, OK (city) Muskogee County	36	0.09
Ponca City, OK (city) Kay County	23	0.09
McAlester, OK (city) Pittsburg County	16	0.09
Burkburnett, TX (city) Wichita County	10	0.09
Tulsa, OK (city) Tulsa County	327	0.08
Duncan, OK (city) Stephens County	19	0.08
Gallup, NM (city) McKinley County	16	0.08
Mustang, OK (city) Canadian County	11	0.08
Lawrence, KS (city) Douglas County	58	0.07
Miami, OK (city) Ottawa County	10	0.07
Saginaw, TX (city) Tarrant County	9	0.07
Destin, FL (city) Okaloosa County	8	0.07
Edmond, OK (city) Oklahoma County	38	0.06
Stillwater, OK (city) Payne County	25	0.06
Bixby, OK (city) Tulsa County	8	0.06
Effingham, IL (city) Effingham County	7	0.06
Wichita, KS (city) Sedgwick County	157	0.05
Owasso, OK (city) Tulsa County	10	0.05
Sand Springs, OK (city) Tulsa County	8	0.05
Avocado Heights, CA (cdp) Los Angeles County	7	0.05
Bartlesville, OK (city) Washington County	15	0.04
Oakley, CA (city) Contra Costa County	11	0.04
Ardmore, OK (city) Carter County	10	0.04
Sapulpa, OK (city) Creek County	8	0.04
Canon City, CO (city) Fremont County	6	0.04
Cherryland, CA (cdp) Alameda County	6	0.04
Four Corners, OR (cdp) Marion County	5	0.04
Plumstead, PA (township) Bucks County	5	0.04
Berkeley, MO (city) Saint Louis County	4	0.04
Elk City, OK (city) Beckham County	4	0.04
Davenport, IA (city) Scott County	34	0.03
Santa Fe, NM (city) Santa Fe County	16	0.03
San Ramon, CA (city) Contra Costa County	12	0.03
Farmington, NM (city) San Juan County	11	0.03
Rogers, AR (city) Benton County	10	0.03
Copperas Cove, TX (city) Coryell County	8	0.03
Benton, AR (city) Saline County	7	0.03
Burlington, IA (city) Des Moines County	7	0.03
Fort Lewis, WA (cdp) Pierce County	6	0.03
North Ridgeville, OH (city) Lorain County	6	0.03
Wisconsin Rapids, WI (city) Wood County	6	0.03
Desert Hot Springs, CA (city) Riverside County	5	0.03
Schofield Barracks, HI (cdp) Honolulu County	5	0.03
Cimarron Hills, CO (cdp) El Paso County	4	0.03
Durant, OK (city) Bryan County	4	0.03
Federal Heights, CO (city) Adams County	4	0.03
McPherson, KS (city) McPherson County	4	0.03
Rosamond, CA (cdp) Kern County	4	0.03
White Settlement, TX (city) Tarrant County	4	0.03
Coshocton, OH (city) Coshocton County	3	0.03
Moss Bluff, LA (cdp) Calcasieu Parish	3	0.03
Valle Vista, CA (cdp) Riverside County	3	0.03
Albuquerque, NM (city) Bernalillo County	85	0.02
Grand Prairie, TX (city) Dallas County	27	0.02
Wichita Falls, TX (city) Wichita County	23	0.02
Denton, TX (city) Denton County	17	0.02
Pueblo, CO (city) Pueblo County	17	0.02

Place	Number	%
Broken Arrow, OK (city) Tulsa County	15	0.02
Lewisville, TX (city) Denton County	15	0.02
San Leandro, CA (city) Alameda County	13	0.02
Chico, CA (city) Butte County	11	0.02
Newark, CA (city) Alameda County	9	0.02
Enid, OK (city) Garfield County	8	0.02
Renton, WA (city) King County	8	0.02
Rio Rancho, NM (city) Sandoval County	8	0.02
De Soto, TX (city) Dallas County	7	0.02
Haltom City, TX (city) Tarrant County	7	0.02
Hutchinson, KS (city) Reno County	7	0.02
Joplin, MO (city) Jasper County	7	0.02
Morgan Hill, CA (city) Santa Clara County	6	0.02
Porterville, CA (city) Tulare County	6	0.02
Cedar Park, TX (city) Williamson County	5	0.02
Farmers Branch, TX (city) Dallas County	5	0.02
Atwater, CA (city) Merced County	4	0.02
Bella Vista, AR (cdp) Benton County	4	0.02
Clearfield, UT (city) Davis County	4	0.02
Pampa, TX (city) Gray County	4	0.02
The Colony, TX (city) Denton County	4	0.02
Alderwood Manor, WA (cdp) Snohomish County	3	0.02
Ashland, OR (city) Jackson County	3	0.02
Blythe, CA (city) Riverside County	3	0.02
Bryn Mawr-Skyway, WA (cdp) King County	3	0.02
Canyon, TX (city) Randall County	3	0.02
Derby, KS (city) Sedgwick County	3	0.02
Elk Plain, WA (cdp) Pierce County	3	0.02
Fairhaven, MA (town) Bristol County	3	0.02
Fort Campbell North, KY (cdp) Christian County	3	0.02
Huntington, IN (city) Huntington County	3	0.02
Middleburg Heights, OH (city) Cuyahoga County	3	0.02
Salmon Creek, WA (cdp) Clark County	3	0.02
Susanville, CA (city) Lassen County	3	0.02
Towamencin, PA (township) Montgomery County	3	0.02
Whitney, NV (cdp) Clark County	3	0.02
Blue Ash, OH (city) Hamilton County	2	0.02
Clearlake, CA (city) Lake County	2	0.02
Endicott, NY (village) Broome County	2	0.02
Excelsior Springs, MO (city) Clay County	2	0.02
Grass Valley, CA (city) Nevada County	2	0.02
Jacinto City, TX (city) Harris County	2	0.02
Lansdowne, PA (borough) Delaware County	2	0.02
Nanakuli, HI (cdp) Honolulu County	2	0.02
Parsons, KS (city) Labette County	2	0.02
Dallas, TX (city) Dallas County	95	0.01
Phoenix, AZ (city) Maricopa County	82	0.01
Fort Worth, TX (city) Tarrant County	42	0.01
Denver, CO (city) Denver County	40	0.01
Kansas City, MO (city) Jackson County	38	0.01
Arlington, TX (city) Tarrant County	28	0.01
Mesa, AZ (city) Maricopa County	26	0.01
Irving, TX (city) Dallas County	23	0.01
Glendale, AZ (city) Maricopa County	20	0.01
Spokane, WA (city) Spokane County	16	0.01
Bakersfield, CA (city) Kern County	15	0.01
Riverside, CA (city) Riverside County	15	0.01
Salem, OR (city) Marion County	15	0.01
Amarillo, TX (city) Potter County	14	0.01
Tacoma, WA (city) Pierce County	13	0.01
Tempe, AZ (city) Maricopa County	13	0.01
Eugene, OR (city) Lane County	12	0.01
Mesquite, TX (city) Dallas County	12	0.01
Topeka, KS (city) Shawnee County	12	0.01
Spring Valley, NV (cdp) Clark County	11	0.01
Sunrise Manor, NV (cdp) Clark County	11	0.01
Thornton, CO (city) Adams County	11	0.01
Billings, MT (city) Yellowstone County	10	0.01
Hayward, CA (city) Alameda County	9	0.01
Lakewood, CO (city) Jefferson County	9	0.01
Overland Park, KS (city) Johnson County	9	0.01
Pico Rivera, CA (city) Los Angeles County	9	0.01
Carrollton, TX (city) Denton County	8	0.01
Fort Collins, CO (city) Larimer County	8	0.01
Killeen, TX (city) Bell County	8	0.01

Notes: (cdp) census designated place; Refer to the Explanation of Data in the front of the book for more detailed information.

American Indian: Latin American Indians

Top 150 Places Sorted by Number

(Based on all places, regardless of population)

Place	Number	%
New York, NY (city) New York City	22,003	0.27
Los Angeles, CA (city) Los Angeles County	11,226	0.30
Chicago, IL (city) Cook County	3,250	0.11
Houston, TX (city) Harris County	2,425	0.12
San Antonio, TX (city) Bexar County	1,624	0.14
Phoenix, AZ (city) Maricopa County	1,595	0.12
San Diego, CA (city) San Diego County	1,509	0.12
San Jose, CA (city) Santa Clara County	1,487	0.17
Santa Ana, CA (city) Orange County	1,300	0.38
Dallas, TX (city) Dallas County	1,219	0.10
Fresno, CA (city) Fresno County	1,174	0.27
San Francisco, CA (city) San Francisco County	1,080	0.14
Long Beach, CA (city) Los Angeles County	969	0.21
Denver, CO (city) Denver County	907	0.16
Tucson, AZ (city) Pima County	780	0.16
Austin, TX (city) Travis County	776	0.12
Sacramento, CA (city) Sacramento County	753	0.19
Anaheim, CA (city) Orange County	733	0.22
Madera, CA (city) Madera County	677	1.57
Oakland, CA (city) Alameda County	674	0.17
El Paso, TX (city) El Paso County	670	0.12
Oxnard, CA (city) Ventura County	652	0.38
Santa Maria, CA (city) Santa Barbara County	642	0.83
Portland, OR (city) Multnomah County	598	0.11
East Los Angeles, CA (cdp) Los Angeles County	579	0.47
Salinas, CA (city) Monterey County	567	0.38
Fort Worth, TX (city) Tarrant County	545	0.10
Boston, MA (city) Suffolk County	541	0.09
Miami, FL (city) Miami-Dade County	535	0.15
Riverside, CA (city) Riverside County	517	0.20
Philadelphia, PA (city) Philadelphia County	512	0.03
Las Vegas, NV (city) Clark County	495	0.10
Pomona, CA (city) Los Angeles County	485	0.32
Albuquerque, NM (city) Bernalillo County	477	0.11
Ontario, CA (city) San Bernardino County	470	0.30
Hempstead, NY (town) Nassau County	449	0.06
San Bernardino, CA (city) San Bernardino County	443	0.24
Mesa, AZ (city) Maricopa County	433	0.11
Escondido, CA (city) San Diego County	424	0.32
El Monte, CA (city) Los Angeles County	404	0.35
Minneapolis, MN (city) Hennepin County	402	0.11
Pasadena, CA (city) Los Angeles County	383	0.29
Stockton, CA (city) San Joaquin County	374	0.15
Watsonville, CA (city) Santa Cruz County	372	0.84
Jersey City, NJ (city) Hudson County	367	0.15
Washington, DC (city) District of Columbia	365	0.06
Bakersfield, CA (city) Kern County	364	0.15
Seattle, WA (city) King County	355	0.06
Oceanside, CA (city) San Diego County	342	0.21
Islip, NY (town) Suffolk County	336	0.10
Fontana, CA (city) San Bernardino County	334	0.26
Modesto, CA (city) Stanislaus County	320	0.17
Lake Worth, FL (city) Palm Beach County	318	0.91
Chula Vista, CA (city) San Diego County	310	0.18
Providence, RI (city) Providence County	310	0.18
Oklahoma City, OK (city) Oklahoma County	309	0.06
Vista, CA (city) San Diego County	299	0.33
Aurora, CO (city) Arapahoe County	291	0.11
South Gate, CA (city) Los Angeles County	289	0.30
Lynwood, CA (city) Los Angeles County	286	0.41
Corpus Christi, TX (city) Nueces County	282	0.10
Charlotte, NC (city) Mecklenburg County	281	0.05
Paterson, NJ (city) Passaic County	280	0.19
Baldwin Park, CA (city) Los Angeles County	278	0.37
Milwaukee, WI (city) Milwaukee County	275	0.05
Colorado Springs, CO (city) El Paso County	274	0.08
West Palm Beach, FL (city) Palm Beach County	265	0.32
Moreno Valley, CA (city) Riverside County	262	0.18
Inglewood, CA (city) Los Angeles County	261	0.23
Santa Rosa, CA (city) Sonoma County	253	0.17
Cicero, IL (town) Cook County	249	0.29
Hayward, CA (city) Alameda County	247	0.18
Yonkers, NY (city) Westchester County	244	0.12
Costa Mesa, CA (city) Orange County	243	0.22
Florence-Graham, CA (cdp) Los Angeles County	240	0.40
Arlington, VA (cdp) Arlington County	239	0.13
Orange, CA (city) Orange County	232	0.18
Union City, NJ (city) Hudson County	226	0.34
Hawthorne, CA (city) Los Angeles County	226	0.27
Tampa, FL (city) Hillsborough County	226	0.07
Palmdale, CA (city) Los Angeles County	224	0.19
Garden Grove, CA (city) Orange County	223	0.13
Pasadena, TX (city) Harris County	220	0.16
Huntington Park, CA (city) Los Angeles County	218	0.36
Newark, NJ (city) Essex County	217	0.08
Whittier, CA (city) Los Angeles County	216	0.26
Downey, CA (city) Los Angeles County	216	0.20
Brentwood, NY (cdp) Suffolk County	213	0.40
Rialto, CA (city) San Bernardino County	211	0.23
Santa Barbara, CA (city) Santa Barbara County	207	0.22
Brookhaven, NY (town) Suffolk County	207	0.05
Reno, NV (city) Washoe County	205	0.11
Compton, CA (city) Los Angeles County	204	0.22
New Bedford, MA (city) Bristol County	203	0.22
Salem, OR (city) Marion County	202	0.15
Bell Gardens, CA (city) Los Angeles County	200	0.45
Montebello, CA (city) Los Angeles County	200	0.32
Glendale, AZ (city) Maricopa County	200	0.09
Saint Paul, MN (city) Ramsey County	199	0.07
Brownsville, TX (city) Cameron County	196	0.14
Passaic, NJ (city) Passaic County	195	0.29
West Covina, CA (city) Los Angeles County	195	0.19
Gilroy, CA (city) Santa Clara County	193	0.47
Elizabeth, NJ (city) Union County	193	0.16
Parlier, CA (city) Fresno County	191	1.71
North Las Vegas, NV (city) Clark County	191	0.17
Detroit, MI (city) Wayne County	191	0.02
Richmond, CA (city) Contra Costa County	190	0.19
Pico Rivera, CA (city) Los Angeles County	188	0.30
Norwalk, CA (city) Los Angeles County	188	0.18
Grand Rapids, MI (city) Kent County	182	0.09
Salt Lake City, UT (city) Salt Lake County	181	0.10
Azusa, CA (city) Los Angeles County	180	0.40
Bellflower, CA (city) Los Angeles County	180	0.25
Hialeah, FL (city) Miami-Dade County	178	0.08
Wichita, KS (city) Sedgwick County	178	0.05
San Rafael, CA (city) Marin County	177	0.32
Laredo, TX (city) Webb County	176	0.10
Omaha, NE (city) Douglas County	175	0.04
Tulsa, OK (city) Tulsa County	174	0.04
Glendale, CA (city) Los Angeles County	172	0.09
Paramount, CA (city) Los Angeles County	171	0.31
Corona, CA (city) Riverside County	171	0.14
Garland, TX (city) Dallas County	171	0.08
Farmersville, CA (city) Tulare County	170	1.95
Pueblo, CO (city) Pueblo County	170	0.17
Merced, CA (city) Merced County	169	0.26
Silver Spring, MD (cdp) Montgomery County	168	0.22
Rancho Cucamonga, CA (city) San Bernardino County	166	0.13
Thousand Oaks, CA (city) Ventura County	165	0.14
Indianapolis, IN (special city) Marion County	165	0.02
Simi Valley, CA (city) Ventura County	164	0.15
Berkeley, CA (city) Alameda County	162	0.16
Fullerton, CA (city) Orange County	160	0.13
Columbus, OH (city) Franklin County	160	0.02
Woodburn, OR (city) Marion County	159	0.79
Concord, CA (city) Contra Costa County	158	0.13
Indiantown, FL (cdp) Martin County	156	2.79
Nashville-Davidson, TN (special city) Davidson County	156	0.03
Buena Park, CA (city) Orange County	155	0.20
San Buenaventura, CA (city) Ventura County	155	0.15
Huntington Beach, CA (city) Orange County	155	0.08
Cleveland, OH (city) Cuyahoga County	155	0.03
Perth Amboy, NJ (city) Middlesex County	152	0.32
Paradise, NV (cdp) Clark County	151	0.08
Rosemead, CA (city) Los Angeles County	150	0.28
Arlington, TX (city) Tarrant County	150	0.05
Irving, TX (city) Dallas County	149	0.08
Santa Cruz, CA (city) Santa Cruz County	148	0.27
Lawrence, MA (city) Essex County	146	0.20

Notes: (cdp) census designated place; Refer to the Explanation of Data in the front of the book for more detailed information.

American Indian: Latin American Indians

Top 150 Places Sorted by Percent

(Based on all places, regardless of population)

Place	Number	%
Vantage, WA (cdp) Kittitas County	7	10.00
Raisin City, CA (cdp) Fresno County	14	8.48
Ramah, CO (town) El Paso County	7	5.98
Dennis Acres, MO (village) Newton County	4	5.88
Bausell and Ellis, TX (cdp) Willacy County	6	5.36
Chilili, NM (cdp) Bernalillo County	5	4.42
Frankford, DE (town) Sussex County	31	4.34
Crossnore, NC (town) Avery County	10	4.13
Weedpatch, CA (cdp) Kern County	94	3.45
East Ellijay, GA (city) Gilmer County	23	3.25
Basalt, ID (city) Bingham County	13	3.10
Rio en Medio, NM (cdp) Santa Fe County	4	3.05
Indiantown, FL (cdp) Martin County	156	2.79
Elmer, MN (township) Pipestone County	7	2.55
Parksdale, CA (cdp) Madera County	68	2.53
Fairview, AL (town) Cullman County	13	2.49
Watts Mills, SC (cdp) Laurens County	34	2.30
Center Junction, IA (city) Jones County	3	2.29
Truesdale, MO (city) Warren County	9	2.27
Alamosa East, CO (cdp) Alamosa County	34	2.23
Franklin, IA (city) Lee County	3	2.21
Linn Creek, MO (city) Camden County	6	2.14
Belfonte, OK (cdp) Sequoyah County	9	2.11
Vadito, NM (cdp) Taos County	5	2.07
Latimer, IA (city) Franklin County	11	2.06
Garden City, CO (town) Weld County	7	1.96
Farmersville, CA (city) Tulare County	170	1.95
Southeast Arcadia, FL (cdp) De Soto County	118	1.95
Avalon, CA (city) Los Angeles County	61	1.95
El Indio, TX (cdp) Maverick County	5	1.90
Hope, NM (village) Eddy County	2	1.87
Sandy Hollow-Escondidas, TX (cdp) Nueces County	8	1.85
Ratamosa, TX (cdp) Cameron County	4	1.83
Taos Ski Valley, NM (village) Taos County	1	1.79
Jo Daviess, MN (township) Faribault County	5	1.78
Boone, MN (township) Lake of the Woods County	1	1.72
Vining, KS (city) Clay County	1	1.72
Parlier, CA (city) Fresno County	191	1.71
Georgetown, DE (town) Sussex County	78	1.68
Morgan, TX (city) Bosque County	8	1.65
Pelan, MN (township) Kittson County	1	1.64
Madera, CA (city) Madera County	677	1.57
Hatch, UT (town) Garfield County	2	1.57
Evant, TX (town) Coryell County	6	1.53
Lasana, TX (cdp) Cameron County	2	1.48
Mark, IL (village) Putnam County	7	1.43
Aniak, AK (city) Bethel Census Area	8	1.40
Bixby, TX (cdp) Cameron County	5	1.40
Adrian, OR (city) Malheur County	2	1.36
Long Prairie, MN (city) Todd County	40	1.32
Hickman, CA (cdp) Stanislaus County	6	1.31
Mattawa, WA (town) Grant County	34	1.30
Idanha, OR (city) Marion County	3	1.29
Salt Creek, CO (cdp) Pueblo County	8	1.23
Walnut Grove, CA (cdp) Sacramento County	8	1.20
Ashley Heights, NC (cdp) Hoke County	4	1.17
Manor, TX (city) Travis County	14	1.16
Biola, CA (cdp) Fresno County	12	1.16
Sandia, TX (cdp) Jim Wells County	5	1.16
Ballantine, MT (cdp) Yellowstone County	4	1.16
Bagnell, MO (town) Miller County	1	1.16
Willard, KS (city) Shawnee County	1	1.16
Dorris, CA (city) Siskiyou County	10	1.13
Saint Paul, OR (city) Marion County	4	1.13
Snowville, UT (town) Box Elder County	2	1.13
Boling-Iago, TX (cdp) Wharton County	14	1.10
Metolius, OR (city) Jefferson County	7	1.10
Powhattan, KS (city) Brown County	1	1.10
Terrytown, NE (village) Scotts Bluff County	7	1.08
Rennert, NC (town) Robeson County	3	1.06
Mecca, CA (cdp) Riverside County	56	1.04
Shawneetown, IL (city) Gallatin County	14	0.99
London, CA (cdp) Tulare County	18	0.97
Winterhaven, CA (cdp) Imperial County	5	0.95
Clover, WI (town) Bayfield County	2	0.95

Place	Number	%
Gove City, KS (city) Gove County	1	0.95
Avondale, CO (cdp) Pueblo County	7	0.93
Fall River Mills, CA (cdp) Shasta County	6	0.93
Sylvan Grove, KS (city) Lincoln County	3	0.93
Summitville, OH (village) Columbiana County	1	0.93
Planada, CA (cdp) Merced County	40	0.92
Cantu Addition, TX (cdp) Brooks County	2	0.92
Lake Worth, FL (city) Palm Beach County	318	0.91
Doraville, GA (city) De Kalb County	90	0.91
Liebenthal, KS (city) Rush County	1	0.90
Newport, DE (town) New Castle County	10	0.89
Eagle Lake, FL (city) Polk County	22	0.88
Chuichu, AZ (cdp) Pinal County	3	0.88
Hornet, MN (township) Beltrami County	2	0.88
Chautauqua, KS (city) Chautauqua County	1	0.88
Terra Bella, CA (cdp) Tulare County	30	0.87
Whiteface, TX (town) Cochran County	4	0.86
Hubbard, OR (city) Marion County	21	0.85
Nisqually Indian Community, WA (cdp) Thurston County	5	0.85
West Almond, NY (town) Allegany County	3	0.85
Larkspur, CO (town) Douglas County	2	0.85
Watsonville, CA (city) Santa Cruz County	372	0.84
Norcross, GA (city) Gwinnett County	71	0.84
Point Arena, CA (city) Mendocino County	4	0.84
Canada de los Alamos, NM (cdp) Santa Fe County	3	0.84
Perry Lake, MN (township) Crow Wing County	2	0.84
Santa Maria, CA (city) Santa Barbara County	642	0.83
Brunswick, NC (town) Columbus County	3	0.83
Orange Cove, CA (city) Fresno County	63	0.82
Freedom, CA (cdp) Santa Cruz County	49	0.82
Echo Lake, WA (cdp) Snohomish County	7	0.82
Conetoe, NC (town) Edgecombe County	3	0.82
Avondale, PA (borough) Chester County	9	0.81
Mountainair, NM (town) Torrance County	9	0.81
Pajaro, CA (cdp) Monterey County	27	0.80
Parachute, CO (town) Garfield County	8	0.80
Gilbert, SC (town) Lexington County	4	0.80
Woodburn, OR (city) Marion County	159	0.79
Calwa, CA (cdp) Fresno County	6	0.79
Cut and Shoot, TX (town) Montgomery County	9	0.78
Hayden, AZ (town) Gila County	7	0.78
Starkville, CO (town) Las Animas County	1	0.78
Magdalena, NM (village) Socorro County	7	0.77
Poston, AZ (cdp) La Paz County	3	0.77
Saint Charles, AR (town) Arkansas County	2	0.77
Home Garden, CA (cdp) Kings County	13	0.76
Lake City, TX (town) San Patricio County	4	0.76
O'Brien, TX (city) Haskell County	1	0.76
West Union, NY (town) Steuben County	3	0.75
Lamont, CA (cdp) Kern County	98	0.74
Guadalupe, CA (city) Santa Barbara County	42	0.74
Bellerose Terrace, NY (cdp) Nassau County	16	0.74
Sugar Bush, MN (township) Becker County	4	0.74
Wimauma, FL (cdp) Hillsborough County	31	0.73
Woodville, CA (cdp) Tulare County	12	0.72
Spring Garden-Terra Verde, TX (cdp) Nueces County	5	0.72
Elberta, AL (town) Baldwin County	4	0.72
Cokedale, CO (town) Las Animas County	1	0.72
Gore, MI (township) Huron County	1	0.72
Santa Cruz, NM (cdp) Santa Fe County	3	0.71
Hitchcock, OK (town) Blaine County	1	0.71
Redfield, KS (city) Bourbon County	1	0.71
Postville, IA (city) Allamakee County	16	0.70
Gervais, OR (city) Marion County	14	0.70
Olathe, CO (town) Montrose County	11	0.70
Thorndale, TX (city) Milam County	9	0.70
North Acomita Village, NM (cdp) Cibola County	2	0.69
Kemp, OK (town) Bryan County	1	0.69
San Saba, TX (town) San Saba County	18	0.68
Boronda, CA (cdp) Monterey County	9	0.68
Kettleman City, CA (cdp) Kings County	10	0.67
Haliimaile, HI (cdp) Maui County	6	0.67
Trout Valley, IL (village) McHenry County	4	0.67
Tice, FL (cdp) Lee County	30	0.66
Easton, CA (cdp) Fresno County	13	0.66

Notes: (cdp) census designated place; Refer to the Explanation of Data in the front of the book for more detailed information.

American Indian: Latin American Indians

Top 150 Places Sorted by Percent

(Based on places with populations of 10,000 or more)

Place	Number	%
Parlier, CA (city) Fresno County	191	1.71
Madera, CA (city) Madera County	677	1.57
Lake Worth, FL (city) Palm Beach County	318	0.91
Watsonville, CA (city) Santa Cruz County	372	0.84
Santa Maria, CA (city) Santa Barbara County	642	0.83
Woodburn, OR (city) Marion County	159	0.79
Lamont, CA (cdp) Kern County	98	0.74
Arvin, CA (city) Kern County	83	0.64
Walnut Park, CA (cdp) Los Angeles County	99	0.61
Nipomo, CA (cdp) San Luis Obispo County	71	0.56
Alum Rock, CA (cdp) Santa Clara County	71	0.53
South El Monte, CA (city) Los Angeles County	110	0.52
Morganton, NC (city) Burke County	90	0.52
Langley Park, MD (cdp) Prince George's County	81	0.50
Soledad, CA (city) Monterey County	56	0.50
San Fernando, CA (city) Los Angeles County	114	0.48
Lennox, CA (cdp) Los Angeles County	111	0.48
East Los Angeles, CA (cdp) Los Angeles County	579	0.47
Gilroy, CA (city) Santa Clara County	193	0.47
Marina, CA (city) Monterey County	117	0.47
Cudahy, CA (city) Los Angeles County	114	0.47
Takoma Park, MD (city) Montgomery County	80	0.46
Bell Gardens, CA (city) Los Angeles County	200	0.45
Selma, CA (city) Fresno County	87	0.45
East Palo Alto, CA (city) San Mateo County	130	0.44
Hawaiian Gardens, CA (city) Los Angeles County	64	0.43
Ossining, NY (village) Westchester County	100	0.42
South San Jose Hills, CA (cdp) Los Angeles County	84	0.42
Healdsburg, CA (city) Sonoma County	45	0.42
Lynwood, CA (city) Los Angeles County	286	0.41
Florence-Graham, CA (cdp) Los Angeles County	240	0.40
Brentwood, NY (cdp) Suffolk County	213	0.40
Azusa, CA (city) Los Angeles County	180	0.40
Santa Paula, CA (city) Ventura County	114	0.40
Commerce, CA (city) Los Angeles County	50	0.40
Maywood, CA (city) Los Angeles County	110	0.39
West Puente Valley, CA (cdp) Los Angeles County	88	0.39
Reedley, CA (city) Fresno County	80	0.39
Eloy, AZ (city) Pinal County	40	0.39
Santa Ana, CA (city) Orange County	1,300	0.38
Oxnard, CA (city) Ventura County	652	0.38
Salinas, CA (city) Monterey County	567	0.38
Bailey's Crossroads, VA (cdp) Fairfax County	88	0.38
Bloomington, CA (cdp) San Bernardino County	73	0.38
Carthage, MO (city) Jasper County	48	0.38
Baldwin Park, CA (city) Los Angeles County	278	0.37
West Whittier-Los Nietos, CA (cdp) Los Angeles County	92	0.37
Commerce City, CO (city) Adams County	78	0.37
Huntington Park, CA (city) Los Angeles County	218	0.36
Delano, CA (city) Kern County	141	0.36
Los Banos, CA (city) Merced County	94	0.36
El Monte, CA (city) Los Angeles County	404	0.35
La Puente, CA (city) Los Angeles County	144	0.35
Bell, CA (city) Los Angeles County	127	0.35
Lawndale, CA (city) Los Angeles County	110	0.35
Newburgh, NY (city) Orange County	99	0.35
Sanger, CA (city) Fresno County	66	0.35
Union City, NJ (city) Hudson County	226	0.34
Lake Worth Corridor, FL (cdp) Palm Beach County	64	0.34
Avocado Heights, CA (cdp) Los Angeles County	52	0.34
Vista, CA (city) San Diego County	299	0.33
Homestead, FL (city) Miami-Dade County	104	0.33
Duluth, GA (city) Gwinnett County	73	0.33
Fillmore, CA (city) Ventura County	45	0.33
Freehold, NJ (borough) Monmouth County	36	0.33
Pomona, CA (city) Los Angeles County	485	0.32
Escondido, CA (city) San Diego County	424	0.32
West Palm Beach, FL (city) Palm Beach County	265	0.32
Montebello, CA (city) Los Angeles County	200	0.32
San Rafael, CA (city) Marin County	177	0.32
Perth Amboy, NJ (city) Middlesex County	152	0.32
Perris, CA (city) Riverside County	117	0.32
Chowchilla, CA (city) Madera County	36	0.32
Lindsay, CA (city) Tulare County	33	0.32
Paramount, CA (city) Los Angeles County	171	0.31

Place	Number	%
Parkway-South Sacramento, CA (cdp) Sacramento County	113	0.31
Fallbrook, CA (cdp) San Diego County	91	0.31
Valinda, CA (cdp) Los Angeles County	68	0.31
Avenal, CA (city) Kings County	45	0.31
Greenfield, CA (city) Monterey County	39	0.31
Los Angeles, CA (city) Los Angeles County	11,226	0.30
Ontario, CA (city) San Bernardino County	470	0.30
South Gate, CA (city) Los Angeles County	289	0.30
Pico Rivera, CA (city) Los Angeles County	188	0.30
New Brunswick, NJ (city) Middlesex County	145	0.30
Stanton, CA (city) Orange County	111	0.30
Hollister, CA (city) San Benito County	103	0.30
Windsor, CA (town) Sonoma County	69	0.30
Adelanto, CA (city) San Bernardino County	55	0.30
Cherryland, CA (cdp) Alameda County	41	0.30
Fort Morgan, CO (city) Morgan County	33	0.30
Pasadena, CA (city) Los Angeles County	383	0.29
Cicero, IL (town) Cook County	249	0.29
Passaic, NJ (city) Passaic County	195	0.29
West New York, NJ (town) Hudson County	133	0.29
Duarte, CA (city) Los Angeles County	62	0.29
Santa Fe Springs, CA (city) Los Angeles County	50	0.29
Artesia, CA (city) Los Angeles County	47	0.29
Welby, CO (cdp) Adams County	38	0.29
Lincoln, CA (city) Placer County	32	0.29
Suffern, NY (village) Rockland County	32	0.29
Haverstraw, NY (village) Rockland County	29	0.29
Rosemead, CA (city) Los Angeles County	150	0.28
Ossining, NY (town) Westchester County	104	0.28
Hartselle, AL (city) Morgan County	34	0.28
Livingston, CA (city) Merced County	29	0.28
New York, NY (city) New York City	22,003	0.27
Fresno, CA (city) Fresno County	1,174	0.27
Hawthorne, CA (city) Los Angeles County	226	0.27
Santa Cruz, CA (city) Santa Cruz County	148	0.27
Brawley, CA (city) Imperial County	59	0.27
Grover Beach, CA (city) San Luis Obispo County	35	0.27
Fontana, CA (city) San Bernardino County	334	0.26
Whittier, CA (city) Los Angeles County	216	0.26
Merced, CA (city) Merced County	169	0.26
South Whittier, CA (cdp) Los Angeles County	142	0.26
Porterville, CA (city) Tulare County	104	0.26
Chillum, MD (cdp) Prince George's County	90	0.26
San Jacinto, CA (city) Riverside County	62	0.26
Bay Point, CA (cdp) Contra Costa County	57	0.26
Wildomar, CA (cdp) Riverside County	37	0.26
Patterson, CA (city) Stanislaus County	30	0.26
Bellflower, CA (city) Los Angeles County	180	0.25
North Highlands, CA (cdp) Sacramento County	110	0.25
Culver City, CA (city) Los Angeles County	97	0.25
Rubidoux, CA (cdp) Riverside County	72	0.25
Dover, NJ (town) Morris County	45	0.25
East Riverdale, MD (cdp) Prince George's County	37	0.25
East San Gabriel, CA (cdp) Los Angeles County	37	0.25
Princeton, NJ (borough) Mercer County	36	0.25
Linda, CA (cdp) Yuba County	34	0.25
Solana Beach, CA (city) San Diego County	32	0.25
San Bernardino, CA (city) San Bernardino County	443	0.24
Willowbrook, CA (cdp) Los Angeles County	81	0.24
Dalton, GA (city) Whitfield County	67	0.24
Spring Valley, NY (village) Rockland County	62	0.24
Bridgeton, NJ (city) Cumberland County	55	0.24
Coachella, CA (city) Riverside County	55	0.24
Wasco, CA (city) Kern County	50	0.24
Harrison, NJ (town) Hudson County	34	0.24
Berkley, CO (cdp) Adams County	26	0.24
Olivehurst, CA (cdp) Yuba County	26	0.24
Citrus, CA (cdp) Los Angeles County	25	0.24
Princeton, FL (cdp) Miami-Dade County	24	0.24
Inglewood, CA (city) Los Angeles County	261	0.23
Rialto, CA (city) San Bernardino County	211	0.23
Cathedral City, CA (city) Riverside County	96	0.23
Westmont, CA (cdp) Los Angeles County	72	0.23
Yeehaw Junction, FL (cdp) Osceola County	50	0.23
Live Oak, CA (cdp) Santa Cruz County	39	0.23

Notes: (cdp) census designated place; Refer to the Explanation of Data in the front of the book for more detailed information.

American Indian: Lumbee

Top 150 Places Sorted by Number

(Based on all places, regardless of population)

Place	Number	%
Lumberton, NC (city) Robeson County	1,686	8.11
Pembroke, NC (town) Robeson County	1,606	66.94
Charlotte, NC (city) Mecklenburg County	558	0.10
Prospect, NC (cdp) Robeson County	529	76.67
Fayetteville, NC (city) Cumberland County	484	0.40
Greensboro, NC (city) Guilford County	374	0.17
Baltimore, MD (independent city) Baltimore city	364	0.06
Laurinburg, NC (city) Scotland County	321	2.02
Elrod, NC (cdp) Robeson County	232	52.61
Raleigh, NC (city) Wake County	232	0.08
Red Springs, NC (town) Robeson County	194	5.55
Fairmont, NC (town) Robeson County	163	6.26
High Point, NC (city) Guilford County	149	0.17
Durham, NC (city) Durham County	129	0.07
Maxton, NC (town) Robeson County	121	4.74
Winston-Salem, NC (city) Forsyth County	121	0.07
Dundalk, MD (cdp) Baltimore County	116	0.19
Raemon, NC (cdp) Robeson County	108	50.94
Jacksonville, FL (special city) Duval County	108	0.01
Hope Mills, NC (town) Cumberland County	99	0.88
Virginia Beach, VA (independent city) Virginia Beach city	98	0.02
New York, NY (city) New York City	87	0.00
Rennert, NC (town) Robeson County	83	29.33
Philadelphia, PA (city) Philadelphia County	83	0.01
Cary, NC (town) Wake County	76	0.08
Detroit, MI (city) Wayne County	71	0.01
McColl, SC (town) Marlboro County	69	2.76
Warren, MI (city) Macomb County	66	0.05
Chapel Hill, NC (town) Orange County	63	0.13
Mint Hill, NC (town) Mecklenburg County	60	0.40
Chesapeake, VA (independent city) Chesapeake city	57	0.03
Rockingham, NC (city) Richmond County	53	0.55
Greenville, NC (city) Pitt County	53	0.09
Wilmington, NC (city) New Hanover County	53	0.07
Los Angeles, CA (city) Los Angeles County	52	0.00
Raeford, NC (city) Hoke County	51	1.51
Norfolk, VA (independent city) Norfolk city	51	0.02
Concord, NC (city) Cabarrus County	50	0.09
Barker Ten Mile, NC (cdp) Robeson County	48	4.92
McDonald, NC (town) Robeson County	47	39.50
Saint Pauls, NC (town) Robeson County	46	2.15
Indian Trail, NC (town) Union County	46	0.39
Hamlet, NC (city) Richmond County	45	0.75
Matthews, NC (town) Mecklenburg County	45	0.20
Jacksonville, NC (city) Onslow County	45	0.07
Columbus, OH (city) Franklin County	45	0.01
Shannon, NC (cdp) Robeson County	44	22.34
Rockfish, NC (cdp) Hoke County	42	1.78
Pleasant Garden, NC (town) Guilford County	39	0.83
Sterling Heights, MI (city) Macomb County	38	0.03
Hampton, VA (independent city) Hampton city	37	0.03
Essex, MD (cdp) Baltimore County	36	0.09
Sanford, NC (city) Lee County	34	0.15
Huntersville, NC (town) Mecklenburg County	34	0.14
Newport News, VA (independent city) Newport News city	33	0.02
Clinton, MI (cdp) Macomb County	31	0.03
Goldsboro, NC (city) Wayne County	30	0.08
Portsmouth, VA (independent city) Portsmouth city	30	0.03
Gibson, NC (town) Scotland County	28	4.79
Lincoln Park, MI (city) Wayne County	28	0.07
Kannapolis, NC (city) Cabarrus County	27	0.07
Ashley Heights, NC (cdp) Hoke County	26	7.62
Middle River, MD (cdp) Baltimore County	26	0.11
Taylor, MI (city) Wayne County	26	0.04
Chicago, IL (city) Cook County	26	0.00
San Diego, CA (city) San Diego County	26	0.00
Thomasville, NC (city) Davidson County	25	0.13
Monroe, NC (city) Union County	25	0.10
Tucson, AZ (city) Pima County	25	0.01
Morehead City, NC (town) Carteret County	24	0.31
Dunn, NC (city) Harnett County	24	0.26
Apex, NC (town) Wake County	24	0.12
Eastpointe, MI (city) Macomb County	24	0.07
Burlington, NC (city) Alamance County	24	0.05
Roseville, MI (city) Macomb County	24	0.05
Shelby, MI (cdp) Macomb County	23	0.04
Albuquerque, NM (city) Bernalillo County	23	0.01
San Antonio, TX (city) Bexar County	23	0.00
Rowland, NC (town) Robeson County	22	1.92
Fort Bragg, NC (cdp) Cumberland County	22	0.08
Longview, WA (city) Cowlitz County	22	0.06
Severn, MD (cdp) Anne Arundel County	22	0.06
Gastonia, NC (city) Gaston County	22	0.03
Livonia, MI (city) Wayne County	22	0.02
Knoxville, TN (city) Knox County	22	0.01
Saint Petersburg, FL (city) Pinellas County	22	0.01
Wagram, NC (town) Scotland County	21	2.62
Archdale, NC (city) Randolph County	21	0.23
Kernersville, NC (town) Forsyth County	21	0.12
Salisbury, NC (city) Rowan County	21	0.08
Colorado Springs, CO (city) El Paso County	21	0.01
Oklahoma City, OK (city) Oklahoma County	21	0.00
Trinity, NC (city) Randolph County	20	0.30
Clinton, NC (city) Sampson County	20	0.23
Rosedale, MD (cdp) Baltimore County	20	0.10
Bel Air South, MD (cdp) Harford County	20	0.05
Wilson, NC (city) Wilson County	20	0.05
North Charleston, SC (city) Charleston County	20	0.03
Huntsville, AL (city) Madison County	20	0.01
Atlanta, GA (city) Fulton County	20	0.00
Houston, TX (city) Harris County	20	0.00
Nashville-Davidson, TN (special city) Davidson County	20	0.00
Seattle, WA (city) King County	20	0.00
Dillon, SC (city) Dillon County	19	0.30
Garner, NC (town) Wake County	19	0.11
New Bern, NC (city) Craven County	19	0.08
Southgate, MI (city) Wayne County	19	0.06
Glen Burnie, MD (cdp) Anne Arundel County	19	0.05
Anchorage, AK (municipality) Anchorage Borough	19	0.01
Hempstead, NY (town) Nassau County	19	0.00
Long Beach, CA (city) Los Angeles County	19	0.00
Washington, DC (city) District of Columbia	19	0.00
Hoffman, NC (town) Richmond County	18	2.88
Chadbourn, NC (town) Columbus County	18	0.85
Canton, MI (cdp) Wayne County	18	0.02
Columbus, GA (special city) Muscogee County	18	0.01
Tampa, FL (city) Hillsborough County	18	0.01
Sacramento, CA (city) Sacramento County	18	0.00
Stallings, NC (town) Union County	17	0.53
Lake Shore, MD (cdp) Anne Arundel County	17	0.13
Lexington, NC (city) Davidson County	17	0.09
Oildale, CA (cdp) Kern County	17	0.06
Sumter, SC (city) Sumter County	17	0.04
Saint Clair Shores, MI (city) Macomb County	17	0.03
Clarksville, TN (city) Montgomery County	17	0.02
Parma, OH (city) Cuyahoga County	17	0.02
Phoenix, AZ (city) Maricopa County	17	0.00
Aberdeen, NC (town) Moore County	16	0.47
Brooklyn Park, MD (cdp) Anne Arundel County	16	0.15
Southern Pines, NC (town) Moore County	16	0.15
Joppatowne, MD (cdp) Harford County	16	0.14
Havelock, NC (city) Craven County	16	0.07
Killeen, TX (city) Bell County	16	0.02
Austin, TX (city) Travis County	16	0.00
Boiling Spring Lakes, NC (city) Brunswick County	15	0.50
Harrisburg, NC (town) Cabarrus County	15	0.33
Fuquay-Varina, NC (town) Wake County	15	0.19
Montclair, VA (cdp) Prince William County	15	0.10
Carrboro, NC (town) Orange County	15	0.09
Bel Air North, MD (cdp) Harford County	15	0.06
Harrison, MI (cdp) Macomb County	15	0.06
Chesterfield, MI (township) Macomb County	15	0.04
Bensalem, PA (township) Bucks County	15	0.03
Richmond, VA (independent city) Richmond city	15	0.01
Indianapolis, IN (special city) Marion County	15	0.00
Portland, OR (city) Multnomah County	15	0.00
Butner, NC (cdp) Granville County	14	0.24
Oak Island, NC (town) Brunswick County	14	0.21
Bennettsville, SC (city) Marlboro County	14	0.15
North Myrtle Beach, SC (city) Horry County	14	0.13

Notes: (cdp) census designated place; Refer to the Explanation of Data in the front of the book for more detailed information.

American Indian: Lumbee

Top 150 Places Sorted by Percent

(Based on all places, regardless of population)

Place	Number	%
Prospect, NC (cdp) Robeson County	529	76.67
Pembroke, NC (town) Robeson County	1,606	66.94
Elrod, NC (cdp) Robeson County	232	52.61
Raemon, NC (cdp) Robeson County	108	50.94
McDonald, NC (town) Robeson County	47	39.50
Rennert, NC (town) Robeson County	83	29.33
Shannon, NC (cdp) Robeson County	44	22.34
Raynham, NC (town) Robeson County	12	17.91
Rex, NC (cdp) Robeson County	5	9.09
Lumberton, NC (city) Robeson County	1,686	8.11
Ashley Heights, NC (cdp) Hoke County	26	7.62
Mojave Ranch Estates, AZ (cdp) Mohave County	2	7.14
Fairmont, NC (town) Robeson County	163	6.26
Red Springs, NC (town) Robeson County	194	5.55
Bowmore, NC (cdp) Hoke County	8	5.52
Barker Ten Mile, NC (cdp) Robeson County	48	4.92
Dundarrach, NC (cdp) Hoke County	3	4.84
Gibson, NC (town) Scotland County	28	4.79
Maxton, NC (town) Robeson County	121	4.74
Godwin, NC (town) Cumberland County	5	4.46
Lumber Bridge, NC (town) Robeson County	4	3.39
Port Protection, AK (cdp) Prince of Wales-Outer Ketchikan C.A.	2	3.17
Proctorville, NC (town) Robeson County	4	3.01
Hoffman, NC (town) Richmond County	18	2.88
McColl, SC (town) Marlboro County	69	2.76
Wagram, NC (town) Scotland County	21	2.62
Lake, MI (township) Macomb County	2	2.50
East Laurinburg, NC (town) Scotland County	7	2.37
Saint Pauls, NC (town) Robeson County	46	2.15
Laurinburg, NC (city) Scotland County	321	2.02
Five Points, NC (cdp) Hoke County	6	1.96
Rowland, NC (town) Robeson County	22	1.92
Rockfish, NC (cdp) Hoke County	42	1.78
Raeford, NC (city) Hoke County	51	1.51
Stedman, NC (town) Cumberland County	9	1.36
Big Woods, MN (township) Marshall County	1	1.27
Ivor, VA (town) Southampton County	4	1.25
Parkton, NC (town) Robeson County	5	1.17
Staley, NC (town) Randolph County	4	1.15
Brunswick, NC (town) Columbus County	4	1.11
Harrells, NC (town) Sampson County	2	1.07
Clio, SC (town) Marlboro County	8	1.03
Eleva, WI (village) Trempealeau County	6	0.94
Hilltop, OH (cdp) Trumbull County	5	0.94
Hope Mills, NC (town) Cumberland County	99	0.88
Claremont, VA (town) Surry County	3	0.87
Chadbourn, NC (town) Columbus County	18	0.85
Polkton, NC (town) Anson County	10	0.84
Pleasant Garden, NC (town) Guilford County	39	0.83
McArthur, CA (cdp) Shasta County	3	0.82
Linden, NC (town) Cumberland County	1	0.79
Hamlet, NC (city) Richmond County	45	0.75
Vander, NC (cdp) Cumberland County	9	0.75
Simpson, NC (village) Pitt County	3	0.65
Salemburg, NC (town) Sampson County	3	0.64
Ivyland, PA (borough) Bucks County	3	0.61
Falcon, NC (town) Cumberland County	2	0.61
Sheridan, MI (township) Mecosta County	8	0.59
Bunn, NC (town) Franklin County	2	0.56
Rockingham, NC (city) Richmond County	53	0.55
Plain View, NC (cdp) Sampson County	10	0.55
Pinebluff, NC (town) Moore County	6	0.54
Stallings, NC (town) Union County	17	0.53
Mamre, MN (township) Kandiyohi County	2	0.52
Bonnetsville, NC (cdp) Sampson County	2	0.51
Boiling Spring Lakes, NC (city) Brunswick County	15	0.50
Rancho Tehama Reserve, CA (cdp) Tehama County	7	0.50
Calypso, NC (town) Duplin County	2	0.49
Nichols, SC (town) Marion County	2	0.49
Aberdeen, NC (town) Moore County	16	0.47
Wilson's Mills, NC (town) Johnston County	6	0.46
East Bend, NC (town) Yadkin County	3	0.46
Fall River Mills, CA (cdp) Shasta County	3	0.46
Dobbins Heights, NC (town) Richmond County	4	0.43
Dwight, MI (township) Huron County	4	0.43
Hayden, AL (town) Blount County	2	0.43
Hazleton, IA (city) Buchanan County	4	0.42
Y, AK (cdp) Matanuska-Susitna Borough	4	0.42
Winter Beach, FL (cdp) Indian River County	4	0.41
Brush Creek, PA (township) Fulton County	3	0.41
Climax, MN (city) Polk County	1	0.41
Fayetteville, NC (city) Cumberland County	484	0.40
Mint Hill, NC (town) Mecklenburg County	60	0.40
Indian Trail, NC (town) Union County	46	0.39
Hinton, MI (township) Mecosta County	4	0.39
Metamora, MI (village) Lapeer County	2	0.39
Alliance, NC (town) Pamlico County	3	0.38
Lake View, SC (town) Dillon County	3	0.38
Thornton, TX (town) Limestone County	2	0.38
Turkey, NC (town) Sampson County	1	0.38
Delway, NC (cdp) Sampson County	1	0.37
Lake Placid, FL (town) Highlands County	6	0.36
Eastover, NC (cdp) Cumberland County	5	0.36
Taylortown, NC (town) Moore County	3	0.36
Silver City, NC (cdp) Hoke County	4	0.35
Sorrento, ME (town) Hancock County	1	0.34
Harrisburg, NC (town) Cabarrus County	15	0.33
East Rockingham, NC (cdp) Richmond County	13	0.33
Shrub Oak, NY (cdp) Westchester County	6	0.33
Worden, IL (village) Madison County	3	0.33
Valmeyer, IL (village) Monroe County	2	0.33
Freeport, PA (township) Greene County	1	0.33
Saxon, SC (cdp) Spartanburg County	12	0.32
New Salem, MA (town) Franklin County	3	0.32
Stoddard, NH (town) Cheshire County	3	0.32
Port Hope, MI (village) Huron County	1	0.32
Morehead City, NC (town) Carteret County	24	0.31
Davenport, FL (city) Polk County	6	0.31
White Pigeon, MI (village) Saint Joseph County	5	0.31
Trinity, NC (city) Randolph County	20	0.30
Dillon, SC (city) Dillon County	19	0.30
Maysville, NC (town) Jones County	3	0.30
Andover, NJ (borough) Sussex County	2	0.30
Northwest, NC (city) Brunswick County	2	0.30
Bridgeton, NC (town) Craven County	1	0.30
Chilhowee, MO (town) Johnson County	1	0.30
Rensselaer Falls, NY (village) Saint Lawrence County	1	0.30
Lake Park, NC (village) Union County	6	0.29
Mount Gilead, NC (town) Montgomery County	4	0.29
Branford, FL (town) Suwannee County	2	0.29
Clarks Hill, IN (town) Tippecanoe County	2	0.29
Bayshore, NC (cdp) New Hanover County	7	0.28
Gray, GA (city) Jones County	5	0.28
Richmond, NH (town) Cheshire County	3	0.28
Clarkton, NC (town) Bladen County	2	0.28
Newkirk, MI (township) Lake County	2	0.28
Fairview Park, IN (town) Vermillion County	4	0.27
Gordonsville, VA (town) Orange County	4	0.27
Castle Hayne, NC (cdp) New Hanover County	3	0.27
Memphis, MI (city) Macomb County	3	0.27
Dunn, NC (city) Harnett County	24	0.26
Bloomingdale, GA (city) Chatham County	7	0.26
Southport, NC (city) Brunswick County	6	0.26
Tyrone, PA (township) Adams County	6	0.26
Philadelphia, NY (village) Jefferson County	4	0.26
Occoquan, VA (town) Prince William County	2	0.26
Norway, SC (town) Orangeburg County	1	0.26
Enochville, NC (cdp) Rowan County	7	0.25
Huntingtown, MD (cdp) Calvert County	6	0.25
Balfour, NC (cdp) Henderson County	3	0.25
Liberty, MI (township) Wexford County	2	0.25
Star, NC (town) Montgomery County	2	0.25
Webster, FL (city) Sumter County	2	0.25
Branson West, MO (city) Stone County	1	0.25
Butner, NC (cdp) Granville County	14	0.24
North Corbin, KY (cdp) Laurel County	4	0.24
Barker Heights, NC (cdp) Henderson County	3	0.24
Archdale, NC (city) Randolph County	21	0.23
Clinton, NC (city) Sampson County	20	0.23
Rose Hill, NC (town) Duplin County	3	0.23

Notes: (cdp) census designated place; Refer to the Explanation of Data in the front of the book for more detailed information.

American Indian: Lumbee

Top 150 Places Sorted by Percent

(Based on places with populations of 10,000 or more)

Place	Number	%
Lumberton, NC (city) Robeson County	1,686	8.11
Laurinburg, NC (city) Scotland County	321	2.02
Hope Mills, NC (town) Cumberland County	99	0.88
Fayetteville, NC (city) Cumberland County	484	0.40
Mint Hill, NC (town) Mecklenburg County	60	0.40
Indian Trail, NC (town) Union County	46	0.39
Matthews, NC (town) Mecklenburg County	45	0.20
Dundalk, MD (cdp) Baltimore County	116	0.19
Greensboro, NC (city) Guilford County	374	0.17
High Point, NC (city) Guilford County	149	0.17
Sanford, NC (city) Lee County	34	0.15
Brooklyn Park, MD (cdp) Anne Arundel County	16	0.15
Southern Pines, NC (town) Moore County	16	0.15
Huntersville, NC (town) Mecklenburg County	34	0.14
Joppatowne, MD (cdp) Harford County	16	0.14
Chapel Hill, NC (town) Orange County	63	0.13
Thomasville, NC (city) Davidson County	25	0.13
Lake Shore, MD (cdp) Anne Arundel County	17	0.13
North Myrtle Beach, SC (city) Horry County	14	0.13
Apex, NC (town) Wake County	24	0.12
Kernersville, NC (town) Forsyth County	21	0.12
Middle River, MD (cdp) Baltimore County	26	0.11
Garner, NC (town) Wake County	19	0.11
Charlotte, NC (city) Mecklenburg County	558	0.10
Monroe, NC (city) Union County	25	0.10
Rosedale, MD (cdp) Baltimore County	20	0.10
Montclair, VA (cdp) Prince William County	15	0.10
Smithfield, NC (town) Johnston County	11	0.10
Greenville, NC (city) Pitt County	53	0.09
Concord, NC (city) Cabarrus County	50	0.09
Essex, MD (cdp) Baltimore County	36	0.09
Lexington, NC (city) Davidson County	17	0.09
Carrboro, NC (town) Orange County	15	0.09
Kelso, WA (city) Cowlitz County	11	0.09
Fort Stewart, GA (cdp) Liberty County	10	0.09
Fort Carson, CO (cdp) El Paso County	9	0.09
Raleigh, NC (city) Wake County	232	0.08
Cary, NC (town) Wake County	76	0.08
Goldsboro, NC (city) Wayne County	30	0.08
Fort Bragg, NC (cdp) Cumberland County	22	0.08
Salisbury, NC (city) Rowan County	21	0.08
New Bern, NC (city) Craven County	19	0.08
Harper Woods, MI (city) Wayne County	11	0.08
Cornelius, NC (town) Mecklenburg County	10	0.08
Lyon, MI (township) Oakland County	9	0.08
Masonboro, NC (cdp) New Hanover County	9	0.08
Durham, NC (city) Durham County	129	0.07
Winston-Salem, NC (city) Forsyth County	121	0.07
Wilmington, NC (city) New Hanover County	53	0.07
Jacksonville, NC (city) Onslow County	45	0.07
Lincoln Park, MI (city) Wayne County	28	0.07
Kannapolis, NC (city) Cabarrus County	27	0.07
Eastpointe, MI (city) Macomb County	24	0.07
Havelock, NC (city) Craven County	16	0.07
Hazel Park, MI (city) Oakland County	14	0.07
Rossville, MD (cdp) Baltimore County	8	0.07
Red Hill, SC (cdp) Horry County	7	0.07
Baltimore, MD (independent city) Baltimore city	364	0.06
Longview, WA (city) Cowlitz County	22	0.06
Severn, MD (cdp) Anne Arundel County	22	0.06
Southgate, MI (city) Wayne County	19	0.06
Oildale, CA (cdp) Kern County	17	0.06
Bel Air North, MD (cdp) Harford County	15	0.06
Harrison, MI (cdp) Macomb County	15	0.06
Myrtle Beach, SC (city) Horry County	13	0.06
Mooresville, NC (town) Iredell County	12	0.06
Palestine, TX (city) Anderson County	11	0.06
Washington, MI (township) Macomb County	11	0.06
Eden, NC (city) Rockingham County	9	0.06
Aberdeen, MD (city) Harford County	8	0.06
Boone, NC (town) Watauga County	8	0.06
Fostoria, OH (city) Seneca County	8	0.06
Huron charter, MI (township) Wayne County	8	0.06
Fort Benning South, GA (cdp) Chattahoochee County	7	0.06
Piney Green, NC (cdp) Onslow County	7	0.06
Warren, MI (city) Macomb County	66	0.05
Burlington, NC (city) Alamance County	24	0.05
Roseville, MI (city) Macomb County	24	0.05
Bel Air South, MD (cdp) Harford County	20	0.05
Wilson, NC (city) Wilson County	20	0.05
Glen Burnie, MD (cdp) Anne Arundel County	19	0.05
South Gate, MD (cdp) Anne Arundel County	13	0.05
Edgewood, MD (cdp) Harford County	11	0.05
Arbutus, MD (cdp) Baltimore County	10	0.05
Carrollton, GA (city) Carroll County	10	0.05
Fort Lewis, WA (cdp) Pierce County	10	0.05
Green Haven, MD (cdp) Anne Arundel County	9	0.05
Wayne, MI (city) Wayne County	9	0.05
Cocoa, FL (city) Brevard County	8	0.05
Ferndale, MD (cdp) Anne Arundel County	8	0.05
Roanoke Rapids, NC (city) Halifax County	8	0.05
Ballenger Creek, MD (cdp) Frederick County	7	0.05
Graham, NC (city) Alamance County	7	0.05
Ladson, SC (cdp) Berkeley County	7	0.05
Marana, AZ (town) Pima County	7	0.05
Socastee, SC (cdp) Horry County	7	0.05
Warrington, FL (cdp) Escambia County	7	0.05
Fulton, NY (city) Oswego County	6	0.05
Gonzalez, FL (cdp) Escambia County	6	0.05
Lebanon, NH (city) Grafton County	6	0.05
Linganore-Bartonsville, MD (cdp) Frederick County	6	0.05
Savage-Guilford, MD (cdp) Howard County	6	0.05
Bound Brook, NJ (borough) Somerset County	5	0.05
Fort Polk South, LA (cdp) Vernon Parish	5	0.05
Grosse Ile, MI (cdp) Wayne County	5	0.05
Irmo, SC (town) Richland County	5	0.05
North Middleton, PA (township) Cumberland County	5	0.05
Taylor, MI (city) Wayne County	26	0.04
Shelby, MI (cdp) Macomb County	23	0.04
Sumter, SC (city) Sumter County	17	0.04
Chesterfield, MI (township) Macomb County	15	0.04
Fort Hood, TX (cdp) Coryell County	13	0.04
Madison Heights, MI (city) Oakland County	12	0.04
Hinesville, GA (city) Liberty County	11	0.04
Wyandotte, MI (city) Wayne County	11	0.04
Eldersburg, MD (cdp) Carroll County	10	0.04
Douglasville, GA (city) Douglas County	9	0.04
Asheboro, NC (city) Randolph County	8	0.04
Ensley, FL (cdp) Escambia County	8	0.04
Albemarle, NC (city) Stanly County	6	0.04
Green Oak, MI (township) Livingston County	6	0.04
Reidsville, NC (city) Rockingham County	6	0.04
Beaufort, SC (city) Beaufort County	5	0.04
Glenn Dale, MD (cdp) Prince George's County	5	0.04
Kaneohe Station, HI (cdp) Honolulu County	5	0.04
Lynn Haven, FL (city) Bay County	5	0.04
Riviera Beach, MD (cdp) Anne Arundel County	5	0.04
Wake Forest, NC (town) Wake County	5	0.04
Williamstown, NJ (cdp) Gloucester County	5	0.04
Ecorse, MI (city) Wayne County	4	0.04
Kingsland, GA (city) Camden County	4	0.04
Tyngsborough, MA (town) Middlesex County	4	0.04
Chesapeake, VA (independent city) Chesapeake city	57	0.03
Sterling Heights, MI (city) Macomb County	38	0.03
Hampton, VA (independent city) Hampton city	37	0.03
Clinton, MI (cdp) Macomb County	31	0.03
Portsmouth, VA (independent city) Portsmouth city	30	0.03
Gastonia, NC (city) Gaston County	22	0.03
North Charleston, SC (city) Charleston County	20	0.03
Saint Clair Shores, MI (city) Macomb County	17	0.03
Bensalem, PA (township) Bucks County	15	0.03
Macomb, MI (township) Macomb County	13	0.03
Copperas Cove, TX (city) Coryell County	10	0.03
Hickory, NC (city) Catawba County	10	0.03
Lakeside, FL (cdp) Clay County	10	0.03
Mechanicsville, VA (cdp) Hanover County	10	0.03
Perry Hall, MD (cdp) Baltimore County	10	0.03
Carney, MD (cdp) Baltimore County	9	0.03
Florence, SC (city) Florence County	9	0.03
Allen Park, MI (city) Wayne County	8	0.03

Notes: (cdp) census designated place; Refer to the Explanation of Data in the front of the book for more detailed information.

American Indian: Menominee

Top 150 Places Sorted by Number

(Based on all places, regardless of population)

Place	Number	%
Keshena, WI (cdp) Menominee County	1,206	86.51
Legend Lake, WI (cdp) Menominee County	912	59.49
Neopit, WI (cdp) Menominee County	725	86.41
Green Bay, WI (city) Brown County	581	0.57
Milwaukee, WI (city) Milwaukee County	509	0.09
Shawano, WI (city) Shawano County	414	4.99
Middle Village, WI (cdp) Menominee County	232	66.10
Red Springs, WI (town) Shawano County	229	23.34
Chicago, IL (city) Cook County	183	0.01
Wescott, WI (town) Shawano County	124	3.39
Zoar, WI (cdp) Menominee County	103	83.06
Appleton, WI (city) Outagamie County	81	0.12
Oshkosh, WI (city) Winnebago County	59	0.09
Madison, WI (city) Dane County	52	0.02
West Allis, WI (city) Milwaukee County	50	0.08
Bartelme, WI (town) Shawano County	48	6.86
Sheboygan, WI (city) Sheboygan County	48	0.09
Kenosha, WI (city) Kenosha County	47	0.05
Minneapolis, MN (city) Hennepin County	47	0.01
Gresham, WI (village) Shawano County	46	8.00
Wausau, WI (city) Marathon County	44	0.11
Washington, WI (town) Shawano County	39	2.05
Richmond, WI (town) Shawano County	36	2.09
Los Angeles, CA (city) Los Angeles County	35	0.00
Underhill, WI (town) Oconto County	33	3.90
Ashwaubenon, WI (village) Brown County	33	0.19
Anchorage, AK (municipality) Anchorage Borough	26	0.01
Oneida, WI (town) Outagamie County	25	0.62
Neenah, WI (city) Winnebago County	24	0.10
How, WI (town) Oconto County	23	4.09
Manitowoc, WI (city) Manitowoc County	23	0.07
Phoenix, AZ (city) Maricopa County	23	0.00
Lac du Flambeau, WI (town) Vilas County	22	0.73
Howard, WI (village) Brown County	22	0.16
Stevens Point, WI (city) Portage County	21	0.09
Racine, WI (city) Racine County	21	0.03
Herman, WI (town) Shawano County	20	2.70
De Pere, WI (city) Brown County	20	0.10
Two Rivers, WI (city) Manitowoc County	18	0.14
Grand Chute, WI (town) Outagamie County	18	0.10
Waukesha, WI (city) Waukesha County	17	0.03
Davenport, IA (city) Scott County	17	0.02
Hobart, WI (town) Brown County	16	0.31
Antigo, WI (city) Langlade County	15	0.18
South Milwaukee, WI (city) Milwaukee County	15	0.07
Lawrence, KS (city) Douglas County	15	0.02
San Diego, CA (city) San Diego County	15	0.00
Cecil, WI (village) Shawano County	14	3.00
Menasha, WI (city) Winnebago County	14	0.09
Oak Creek, WI (city) Milwaukee County	14	0.05
Fond du Lac, WI (city) Fond du Lac County	14	0.03
La Crosse, WI (city) La Crosse County	14	0.03
Wauwatosa, WI (city) Milwaukee County	14	0.03
Gillett, WI (city) Oconto County	13	1.04
Fond du Lac, WI (town) Fond du Lac County	13	0.64
Bellevue Town, WI (cdp) Brown County	13	0.11
Wisconsin Rapids, WI (city) Wood County	13	0.07
Greenfield, WI (city) Milwaukee County	13	0.04
Eau Claire, WI (city) Eau Claire County	13	0.02
Packwaukee, WI (town) Marquette County	12	0.47
Waupaca, WI (city) Waupaca County	12	0.21
Cudahy, WI (city) Milwaukee County	12	0.07
Tucson, AZ (city) Pima County	12	0.00
Oneida, WI (cdp) Brown County	11	1.03
Center, WI (town) Outagamie County	11	0.35
Saint Francis, WI (city) Milwaukee County	11	0.13
Beloit, WI (city) Rock County	11	0.03
Anaheim, CA (city) Orange County	11	0.00
Portland, OR (city) Multnomah County	11	0.00
Suamico, WI (town) Brown County	10	0.12
Menasha, WI (town) Winnebago County	10	0.06
Lakewood, CO (city) Jefferson County	10	0.01
Las Vegas, NV (city) Clark County	10	0.00
San Jose, CA (city) Santa Clara County	10	0.00
Tulsa, OK (city) Tulsa County	10	0.00

Place	Number	%
Birch, WI (town) Lincoln County	9	1.12
Lincoln, WI (town) Forest County	9	0.90
West Milwaukee, WI (village) Milwaukee County	9	0.21
Oconto, WI (city) Oconto County	9	0.19
Prairie du Chien, WI (city) Crawford County	9	0.15
Kaukauna, WI (city) Outagamie County	9	0.07
Allouez, WI (village) Brown County	9	0.06
Franklin, WI (city) Milwaukee County	9	0.03
Menomonee Falls, WI (village) Waukesha County	9	0.03
Ann Arbor, MI (city) Washtenaw County	9	0.01
Eagan, MN (city) Dakota County	9	0.01
Springfield, IL (city) Sangamon County	9	0.01
Albuquerque, NM (city) Bernalillo County	9	0.00
Austin, TX (city) Travis County	9	0.00
Columbus, OH (city) Franklin County	9	0.00
Saint Paul, MN (city) Ramsey County	9	0.00
Seattle, WA (city) King County	9	0.00
Wichita, KS (city) Sedgwick County	9	0.00
Komensky, WI (town) Jackson County	8	1.73
Belle Plaine, WI (town) Shawano County	8	0.43
Butler, WI (village) Waukesha County	8	0.43
Black River Falls, WI (city) Jackson County	8	0.22
Freedom, WI (town) Outagamie County	8	0.15
New London, WI (city) Waupaca County	8	0.11
Menominee, MI (city) Menominee County	8	0.09
Durant, OK (city) Bryan County	8	0.06
Mount Pleasant, WI (town) Racine County	8	0.03
Paducah, KY (city) McCracken County	8	0.03
Cedar Rapids, IA (city) Linn County	8	0.01
Aurora, CO (city) Arapahoe County	8	0.00
Mesa, AZ (city) Maricopa County	8	0.00
Mattoon, WI (village) Shawano County	7	1.50
Suring, WI (village) Oconto County	7	1.16
Breed, WI (town) Oconto County	7	1.07
Waukechon, WI (town) Shawano County	7	0.75
Marinette, WI (city) Marinette County	7	0.06
Weston, WI (village) Marathon County	7	0.06
Fitchburg, WI (city) Dane County	7	0.03
Mount Pleasant, MI (city) Isabella County	7	0.03
Porterville, CA (city) Tulare County	7	0.02
Rock Island, IL (city) Rock Island County	7	0.02
Rochester, MN (city) Olmsted County	7	0.01
South Bend, IN (city) Saint Joseph County	7	0.01
Chandler, AZ (city) Maricopa County	7	0.00
Indianapolis, IN (special city) Marion County	7	0.00
Philadelphia, PA (city) Philadelphia County	7	0.00
Rockford, IL (city) Winnebago County	7	0.00
Stockton, CA (city) San Joaquin County	7	0.00
English, IN (town) Crawford County	6	0.89
Sanborn, WI (town) Ashland County	6	0.47
Bonduel, WI (village) Shawano County	6	0.42
Brillion, WI (city) Calumet County	6	0.20
Peshtigo, WI (city) Marinette County	6	0.18
Edgerton, WI (city) Rock County	6	0.12
Ashland, WI (city) Ashland County	6	0.07
Lyons, IL (village) Cook County	6	0.06
Trenton, MI (city) Wayne County	6	0.03
Brookfield, WI (city) Waukesha County	6	0.02
West Bend, WI (city) Washington County	6	0.02
Arden-Arcade, CA (cdp) Sacramento County	6	0.01
Highlands Ranch, CO (cdp) Douglas County	6	0.01
Lima, OH (city) Allen County	6	0.01
Norwalk, CA (city) Los Angeles County	6	0.01
Denver, CO (city) Denver County	6	0.00
Detroit, MI (city) Wayne County	6	0.00
Kansas City, MO (city) Jackson County	6	0.00
New York, NY (city) New York City	6	0.00
Sunrise Manor, NV (cdp) Clark County	6	0.00
Toledo, OH (city) Lucas County	6	0.00
Vancouver, WA (city) Clark County	6	0.00
Morris, WI (town) Shawano County	5	1.03
Spruce, WI (town) Oconto County	5	0.57
Green Valley, WI (town) Shawano County	5	0.49
Frederic, WI (village) Polk County	5	0.40
Wabeno, WI (town) Forest County	5	0.40

Notes: (cdp) census designated place; Refer to the Explanation of Data in the front of the book for more detailed information.

American Indian: Menominee

Top 150 Places Sorted by Percent

(Based on all places, regardless of population)

Place	Number	%
Keshena, WI (cdp) Menominee County	1,206	86.51
Neopit, WI (cdp) Menominee County	725	86.41
Zoar, WI (cdp) Menominee County	103	83.06
Middle Village, WI (cdp) Menominee County	232	66.10
Legend Lake, WI (cdp) Menominee County	912	59.49
Red Springs, WI (town) Shawano County	229	23.34
Gresham, WI (village) Shawano County	46	8.00
Bartelme, WI (town) Shawano County	48	6.86
Shawano, WI (city) Shawano County	414	4.99
How, WI (town) Oconto County	23	4.09
Underhill, WI (town) Oconto County	33	3.90
Wescott, WI (town) Shawano County	124	3.39
Cecil, WI (village) Shawano County	14	3.00
Millston, WI (town) Jackson County	4	2.94
Herman, WI (town) Shawano County	20	2.70
Richmond, WI (town) Shawano County	36	2.09
Washington, WI (town) Shawano County	39	2.05
Komensky, WI (town) Jackson County	8	1.73
Mattoon, WI (village) Shawano County	7	1.50
Suring, WI (village) Oconto County	7	1.16
Flaxville, MT (town) Daniels County	1	1.15
Fairchild, WI (town) Eau Claire County	4	1.14
Birch, WI (town) Lincoln County	9	1.12
Wyalusing, WI (town) Grant County	4	1.08
Breed, WI (town) Oconto County	7	1.07
Gillett, WI (city) Oconto County	13	1.04
Oneida, WI (cdp) Brown County	11	1.03
Morris, WI (town) Shawano County	5	1.03
Lincoln, WI (town) Forest County	9	0.90
English, IN (town) Crawford County	6	0.89
Bowler, WI (village) Shawano County	3	0.87
Matchwood, MI (township) Ontonagon County	1	0.87
Buffalo, IL (village) Sangamon County	4	0.81
Kettle River, MN (township) Pine County	4	0.81
Odanah, WI (cdp) Ashland County	2	0.79
Waukechon, WI (town) Shawano County	7	0.75
Milladore, WI (village) Wood County	2	0.75
Lac du Flambeau, WI (town) Vilas County	22	0.73
Casco, WI (village) Kewaunee County	4	0.70
Fond du Lac, WI (town) Fond du Lac County	13	0.64
Oneida, WI (town) Outagamie County	25	0.62
Green Bay, WI (city) Brown County	581	0.57
Spruce, WI (town) Oconto County	5	0.57
Hutchins, WI (town) Shawano County	3	0.56
Colburn, WI (town) Adams County	1	0.55
Dairyland, WI (town) Douglas County	1	0.54
Oconomowoc Lake, WI (village) Waukesha County	3	0.53
Seneca, WI (town) Shawano County	3	0.53
Almon, WI (town) Shawano County	3	0.51
Kinney, MN (city) Saint Louis County	1	0.50
Green Valley, WI (town) Shawano County	5	0.49
Hartland, WI (town) Shawano County	4	0.48
Weyauwega, WI (town) Waupaca County	3	0.48
Packwaukee, WI (town) Marquette County	12	0.47
Sanborn, WI (town) Ashland County	6	0.47
Harmony, WI (town) Price County	1	0.47
Mineral Hills, MI (village) Iron County	1	0.47
Maple Valley, WI (town) Oconto County	3	0.45
Norwood, WI (town) Langlade County	4	0.44
Belle Plaine, WI (town) Shawano County	8	0.43
Butler, WI (village) Waukesha County	8	0.43
Bonduel, WI (village) Shawano County	6	0.42
Little Round Lake, WI (cdp) Sawyer County	4	0.42
Birnamwood, WI (town) Shawano County	3	0.42
Hatley, WI (village) Marathon County	2	0.42
Spalding, MN (township) Aitkin County	1	0.42
Grant, WI (town) Shawano County	4	0.41
Frederic, WI (village) Polk County	5	0.40
Wabeno, WI (town) Forest County	5	0.40
Eland, WI (village) Shawano County	1	0.40
Day, WI (town) Marathon County	4	0.39
Hilltop, MN (city) Anoka County	3	0.39
Ceresco, MN (township) Blue Earth County	1	0.39
Redgranite, WI (village) Waushara County	4	0.38
Birnamwood, WI (village) Shawano County	3	0.38
Leola, WI (town) Adams County	1	0.38
Maribel, WI (village) Manitowoc County	1	0.38
Maine, WI (town) Outagamie County	3	0.36
Stetsonville, WI (village) Taylor County	2	0.36
Center, WI (town) Outagamie County	11	0.35
Catawba, WI (town) Price County	1	0.35
Grant Valley, MN (township) Beltrami County	5	0.34
Lowell, WI (town) Dodge County	3	0.34
Sister Bay, WI (village) Door County	3	0.34
Aniwa, WI (town) Shawano County	2	0.34
Chenequa, WI (village) Waukesha County	2	0.34
Neshkoro, WI (town) Marquette County	2	0.34
Waverly, KS (city) Coffey County	2	0.34
Cherry Tree, OK (cdp) Adair County	4	0.33
Holton, WI (town) Marathon County	3	0.33
Nichols, WI (village) Outagamie County	1	0.33
Bridgeport, WI (town) Crawford County	3	0.32
Hobart, WI (town) Brown County	16	0.31
Wagner, MN (township) Aitkin County	1	0.31
Black Earth, WI (village) Dane County	4	0.30
Dover, AR (city) Pope County	4	0.30
Humboldt, WI (town) Brown County	4	0.30
Eisenstein, WI (town) Price County	2	0.30
Bagley, WI (village) Grant County	1	0.29
Blackwell, WI (town) Forest County	1	0.29
Cave-In-Rock, IL (village) Hardin County	1	0.29
Centerville, WI (town) Manitowoc County	2	0.28
Masonville, MI (township) Delta County	5	0.27
Lessor, WI (town) Shawano County	3	0.27
Naselle, WA (cdp) Pacific County	1	0.27
Nevis, MN (city) Hubbard County	1	0.27
Kaukauna, WI (town) Outagamie County	3	0.26
Beecher, WI (town) Marinette County	2	0.26
Tigerton, WI (village) Shawano County	2	0.26
Cato, WI (town) Manitowoc County	4	0.25
Russell, WI (town) Bayfield County	3	0.25
Westfield, WI (village) Marquette County	3	0.25
Fountain Prairie, WI (town) Columbia County	2	0.25
Enterprise, KS (city) Dickinson County	2	0.24
Ekalaka, MT (town) Carter County	1	0.24
Gourley, MI (township) Menominee County	1	0.24
Harrison, WI (town) Marathon County	1	0.24
Navarino, WI (town) Shawano County	1	0.24
Mountain, WI (town) Oconto County	2	0.23
Eastman, WI (village) Crawford County	1	0.23
Reserve, WI (cdp) Sawyer County	1	0.23
Black River Falls, WI (city) Jackson County	8	0.22
Newton, WI (town) Manitowoc County	5	0.22
Rockland, WI (town) Manitowoc County	2	0.22
Almond, WI (village) Portage County	1	0.22
Hancock, WI (village) Waushara County	1	0.22
Highland Haven, TX (city) Burnet County	1	0.22
Waupaca, WI (city) Waupaca County	12	0.21
West Milwaukee, WI (village) Milwaukee County	9	0.21
Combined Locks, WI (village) Outagamie County	5	0.21
Mishicot, WI (town) Manitowoc County	3	0.21
Norrie, WI (town) Marathon County	2	0.21
Couderay, WI (town) Sawyer County	1	0.21
Evergreen, WI (town) Langlade County	1	0.21
Plum Lake, WI (town) Vilas County	1	0.21
Brillion, WI (city) Calumet County	6	0.20
Polar, WI (town) Langlade County	2	0.20
Seven Valleys, PA (borough) York County	1	0.20
Ashwaubenon, WI (village) Brown County	33	0.19
Oconto, WI (city) Oconto County	9	0.19
Solon, MI (township) Leelanau County	3	0.19
Farm Loop, AK (cdp) Matanuska-Susitna Borough	2	0.19
Lake, WI (town) Marinette County	2	0.19
Antigo, WI (city) Langlade County	15	0.18
Peshtigo, WI (city) Marinette County	6	0.18
Oconto Falls, WI (city) Oconto County	5	0.18
Belgium, WI (village) Ozaukee County	3	0.18
Albion, WI (town) Jackson County	2	0.18
Gaines, PA (township) Tioga County	1	0.18
Hampden, WI (town) Columbia County	1	0.18

Notes: (cdp) census designated place; Refer to the Explanation of Data in the front of the book for more detailed information.

American Indian: Menominee

Top 150 Places Sorted by Percent

(Based on places with populations of 10,000 or more)

Place	Number	%
Green Bay, WI (city) Brown County	581	0.57
Ashwaubenon, WI (village) Brown County	33	0.19
Howard, WI (village) Brown County	22	0.16
Two Rivers, WI (city) Manitowoc County	18	0.14
Appleton, WI (city) Outagamie County	81	0.12
Wausau, WI (city) Marathon County	44	0.11
Bellevue Town, WI (cdp) Brown County	13	0.11
Neenah, WI (city) Winnebago County	24	0.10
De Pere, WI (city) Brown County	20	0.10
Grand Chute, WI (town) Outagamie County	18	0.10
Milwaukee, WI (city) Milwaukee County	509	0.09
Oshkosh, WI (city) Winnebago County	59	0.09
Sheboygan, WI (city) Sheboygan County	48	0.09
Stevens Point, WI (city) Portage County	21	0.09
Menasha, WI (city) Winnebago County	14	0.09
West Allis, WI (city) Milwaukee County	50	0.08
Manitowoc, WI (city) Manitowoc County	23	0.07
South Milwaukee, WI (city) Milwaukee County	15	0.07
Wisconsin Rapids, WI (city) Wood County	13	0.07
Cudahy, WI (city) Milwaukee County	12	0.07
Kaukauna, WI (city) Outagamie County	9	0.07
Menasha, WI (town) Winnebago County	10	0.06
Allouez, WI (village) Brown County	9	0.06
Durant, OK (city) Bryan County	8	0.06
Marinette, WI (city) Marinette County	7	0.06
Weston, WI (village) Marathon County	7	0.06
Lyons, IL (village) Cook County	6	0.06
Kenosha, WI (city) Kenosha County	47	0.05
Oak Creek, WI (city) Milwaukee County	14	0.05
Barrington, IL (village) Cook County	5	0.05
Merrill, WI (city) Lincoln County	5	0.05
Monroe, WI (city) Green County	5	0.05
Plover, WI (village) Portage County	5	0.05
Greenfield, WI (city) Milwaukee County	13	0.04
Bemidji, MN (city) Beltrami County	5	0.04
Fenton, MI (township) Genesee County	5	0.04
Little Chute, WI (village) Outagamie County	4	0.04
Middleburg, FL (cdp) Clay County	4	0.04
Richfield, WI (town) Washington County	4	0.04
Racine, WI (city) Racine County	21	0.03
Waukesha, WI (city) Waukesha County	17	0.03
Fond du Lac, WI (city) Fond du Lac County	14	0.03
La Crosse, WI (city) La Crosse County	14	0.03
Wauwatosa, WI (city) Milwaukee County	14	0.03
Beloit, WI (city) Rock County	11	0.03
Franklin, WI (city) Milwaukee County	9	0.03
Menomonee Falls, WI (village) Waukesha County	9	0.03
Mount Pleasant, WI (town) Racine County	8	0.03
Paducah, KY (city) McCracken County	8	0.03
Fitchburg, WI (city) Dane County	7	0.03
Mount Pleasant, MI (city) Isabella County	7	0.03
Trenton, MI (city) Wayne County	6	0.03
Franklin Park, IL (village) Cook County	5	0.03
Pleasant Prairie, WI (village) Kenosha County	5	0.03
Cary, IL (village) McHenry County	4	0.03
Coos Bay, OR (city) Coos County	4	0.03
Laurinburg, NC (city) Scotland County	4	0.03
Middleton, WI (city) Dane County	4	0.03
Oconomowoc, WI (city) Waukesha County	4	0.03
Onalaska, WI (city) La Crosse County	4	0.03
Ottawa, KS (city) Franklin County	4	0.03
Schiller Park, IL (village) Cook County	4	0.03
Bellefontaine Neighbors, MO (city) Saint Louis County	3	0.03
Fenton, MI (city) Genesee County	3	0.03
Fort Atkinson, WI (city) Jefferson County	3	0.03
Fort Carson, CO (cdp) El Paso County	3	0.03
Grosse Ile, MI (cdp) Wayne County	3	0.03
Hartford, WI (city) Washington County	3	0.03
Madison, WI (city) Dane County	52	0.02
Davenport, IA (city) Scott County	17	0.02
Lawrence, KS (city) Douglas County	15	0.02
Eau Claire, WI (city) Eau Claire County	13	0.02
Porterville, CA (city) Tulare County	7	0.02
Rock Island, IL (city) Rock Island County	7	0.02
Brookfield, WI (city) Waukesha County	6	0.02
West Bend, WI (city) Washington County	6	0.02
Burlingame, CA (city) San Mateo County	5	0.02
Copperas Cove, TX (city) Coryell County	5	0.02
Lacey, WA (city) Thurston County	5	0.02
Balch Springs, TX (city) Dallas County	4	0.02
Columbia Heights, MN (city) Anoka County	4	0.02
Gallup, NM (city) McKinley County	4	0.02
Germantown, WI (village) Washington County	4	0.02
Norton Shores, MI (city) Muskegon County	4	0.02
Plainfield, IN (town) Hendricks County	4	0.02
Avon, CT (town) Hartford County	3	0.02
Bradley, IL (village) Kankakee County	3	0.02
Cahokia, IL (village) Saint Clair County	3	0.02
Chicago Ridge, IL (village) Cook County	3	0.02
Fort Drum, NY (cdp) Jefferson County	3	0.02
Fostoria, OH (city) Seneca County	3	0.02
Glendale, WI (city) Milwaukee County	3	0.02
Green Valley, AZ (cdp) Pima County	3	0.02
Greendale, WI (village) Milwaukee County	3	0.02
Le Ray, NY (town) Jefferson County	3	0.02
Marquette, MI (city) Marquette County	3	0.02
New Port Richey, FL (city) Pasco County	3	0.02
Norwalk, OH (city) Huron County	3	0.02
Saginaw Township South, MI (cdp) Saginaw County	3	0.02
Shorewood, WI (village) Milwaukee County	3	0.02
Whitewater, WI (city) Walworth County	3	0.02
Brown Deer, WI (village) Milwaukee County	2	0.02
Cambridge, OH (city) Guernsey County	2	0.02
Crestwood, IL (village) Cook County	2	0.02
Five Corners, WA (cdp) Clark County	2	0.02
Marysville, CA (city) Yuba County	2	0.02
River Falls, WI (city) Pierce County	2	0.02
Vidor, TX (city) Orange County	2	0.02
Worth, IL (village) Cook County	2	0.02
Chicago, IL (city) Cook County	183	0.01
Minneapolis, MN (city) Hennepin County	47	0.01
Anchorage, AK (municipality) Anchorage Borough	26	0.01
Lakewood, CO (city) Jefferson County	10	0.01
Ann Arbor, MI (city) Washtenaw County	9	0.01
Eagan, MN (city) Dakota County	9	0.01
Springfield, IL (city) Sangamon County	9	0.01
Cedar Rapids, IA (city) Linn County	8	0.01
Rochester, MN (city) Olmsted County	7	0.01
South Bend, IN (city) Saint Joseph County	7	0.01
Arden-Arcade, CA (cdp) Sacramento County	6	0.01
Highlands Ranch, CO (cdp) Douglas County	6	0.01
Lima, OH (city) Allen County	6	0.01
Norwalk, CA (city) Los Angeles County	6	0.01
Auburn, WA (city) King County	5	0.01
Berwyn, IL (city) Cook County	5	0.01
Canton, MI (cdp) Wayne County	5	0.01
Crystal Lake, IL (city) McHenry County	5	0.01
Dearborn, MI (city) Wayne County	5	0.01
Grand Forks, ND (city) Grand Forks County	5	0.01
Hammond, IN (city) Lake County	5	0.01
New Berlin, WI (city) Waukesha County	5	0.01
Streamwood, IL (village) Cook County	5	0.01
Allen Park, MI (city) Wayne County	4	0.01
Davis, CA (city) Yolo County	4	0.01
Des Plaines, IL (city) Cook County	4	0.01
Dubuque, IA (city) Dubuque County	4	0.01
Elk Grove Village, IL (village) Cook County	4	0.01
Florin, CA (cdp) Sacramento County	4	0.01
Germantown, TN (city) Shelby County	4	0.01
Haltom City, TX (city) Tarrant County	4	0.01
Janesville, WI (city) Rock County	4	0.01
Longmont, CO (city) Boulder County	4	0.01
North Little Rock, AR (city) Pulaski County	4	0.01
Saint Cloud, MN (city) Stearns County	4	0.01
Austin, MN (city) Mower County	3	0.01
Bell Gardens, CA (city) Los Angeles County	3	0.01
Burbank, IL (city) Cook County	3	0.01
Caldwell, ID (city) Canyon County	3	0.01
Caledonia, WI (town) Racine County	3	0.01
Carson City, NV (special city) Carson City city	3	0.01

Notes: (cdp) census designated place; Refer to the Explanation of Data in the front of the book for more detailed information.

American Indian: Navajo

Top 150 Places Sorted by Number

(Based on all places, regardless of population)

Place	Number	%
Phoenix, AZ (city) Maricopa County	10,143	0.77
Albuquerque, NM (city) Bernalillo County	7,889	1.76
Shiprock, NM (cdp) San Juan County	7,680	94.16
Tuba City, AZ (cdp) Coconino County	6,955	84.56
Gallup, NM (city) McKinley County	6,279	31.07
Farmington, NM (city) San Juan County	5,793	15.31
Chinle, AZ (cdp) Apache County	4,760	88.71
Kayenta, AZ (cdp) Navajo County	4,297	87.30
Flagstaff, AZ (city) Coconino County	4,069	7.69
Fort Defiance, AZ (cdp) Apache County	3,670	90.37
Kirtland, NM (cdp) San Juan County	2,845	45.96
Mesa, AZ (city) Maricopa County	2,780	0.70
Window Rock, AZ (cdp) Apache County	2,733	89.34
Crownpoint, NM (cdp) McKinley County	2,191	83.31
Navajo, NM (cdp) McKinley County	1,993	95.04
Winslow, AZ (city) Navajo County	1,786	18.76
Page, AZ (city) Coconino County	1,708	25.08
Kaibito, AZ (cdp) Coconino County	1,584	98.57
Upper Fruitland, NM (cdp) San Juan County	1,578	94.83
Lechee, AZ (cdp) Coconino County	1,564	97.38
Lukachukai, AZ (cdp) Apache County	1,506	96.23
Tucson, AZ (city) Pima County	1,387	0.28
Tempe, AZ (city) Maricopa County	1,346	0.85
Many Farms, AZ (cdp) Apache County	1,321	85.34
Thoreau, NM (cdp) McKinley County	1,262	67.74
Ganado, AZ (cdp) Apache County	1,248	82.92
Glendale, AZ (city) Maricopa County	1,208	0.55
Dilkon, AZ (cdp) Navajo County	1,200	94.86
Salt Lake City, UT (city) Salt Lake County	1,178	0.65
Saint Michaels, AZ (cdp) Apache County	1,130	87.26
Alamo, NM (cdp) Socorro County	1,103	93.24
Los Angeles, CA (city) Los Angeles County	1,089	0.03
Pinon, AZ (cdp) Navajo County	1,075	90.34
Holbrook, AZ (city) Navajo County	1,072	21.80
Twin Lakes, NM (cdp) McKinley County	1,040	97.29
Houck, AZ (cdp) Apache County	1,035	95.22
Church Rock, NM (cdp) McKinley County	1,032	95.82
Tsaile, AZ (cdp) Apache County	988	91.65
Bloomfield, NM (city) San Juan County	937	14.60
Leupp, AZ (cdp) Coconino County	923	95.15
Tohatchi, NM (cdp) McKinley County	921	88.81
Cameron, AZ (cdp) Coconino County	898	91.82
Denver, CO (city) Denver County	884	0.16
Blanding, UT (city) San Juan County	832	26.31
Ojo Amarillo, NM (cdp) San Juan County	797	96.14
Oljato-Monument Valley, UT (cdp) San Juan County	784	90.74
Teec Nos Pos, AZ (cdp) Apache County	715	89.49
Rock Point, AZ (cdp) Apache County	705	97.38
Nenahnezad, NM (cdp) San Juan County	705	97.11
West Valley City, UT (city) Salt Lake County	685	0.63
Napi HQ, NM (cdp) San Juan County	673	95.33
Dennehotso, AZ (cdp) Apache County	669	91.14
Cortez, CO (city) Montezuma County	624	7.82
Aneth, UT (cdp) San Juan County	592	99.00
Round Rock, AZ (cdp) Apache County	582	96.84
Sawmill, AZ (cdp) Apache County	569	92.97
Burnside, AZ (cdp) Apache County	561	88.77
Greasewood, AZ (cdp) Navajo County	551	94.84
Tonalea, AZ (cdp) Coconino County	538	95.73
Bitter Springs, AZ (cdp) Coconino County	534	97.62
Saint George, UT (city) Washington County	533	1.07
Rock Springs, NM (cdp) McKinley County	530	94.98
Chandler, AZ (city) Maricopa County	528	0.30
Shonto, AZ (cdp) Navajo County	491	86.44
Montezuma Creek, UT (cdp) San Juan County	474	93.49
San Diego, CA (city) San Diego County	462	0.04
Colorado Springs, CO (city) El Paso County	458	0.13
Rio Rancho, NM (city) Sandoval County	453	0.88
Nakaibito, NM (cdp) McKinley County	443	97.36
Grants, NM (city) Cibola County	434	4.93
Provo, UT (city) Utah County	434	0.41
Rough Rock, AZ (cdp) Apache County	432	92.11
Chilchinbito, AZ (cdp) Navajo County	430	93.07
Aztec, NM (city) San Juan County	417	6.54
Durango, CO (city) La Plata County	411	2.95
Sanostee, NM (cdp) San Juan County	406	94.64
Nazlini, AZ (cdp) Apache County	392	98.74
Yah-ta-hey, NM (cdp) McKinley County	373	64.31
Orem, UT (city) Utah County	369	0.44
Las Vegas, NV (city) Clark County	366	0.08
Brimhall Nizhoni, NM (cdp) McKinley County	360	96.51
Ogden, UT (city) Weber County	360	0.47
San Jose, CA (city) Santa Clara County	353	0.04
Jeddito, AZ (cdp) Navajo County	346	88.72
Naschitti, NM (cdp) San Juan County	344	95.56
Navajo Mountain, UT (cdp) San Juan County	340	89.71
Crystal, NM (cdp) McKinley County	335	96.54
Scottsdale, AZ (city) Maricopa County	332	0.16
Beclabito, NM (cdp) San Juan County	330	97.35
Newcomb, NM (cdp) San Juan County	321	82.95
South Salt Lake, UT (city) Salt Lake County	314	1.42
Santa Fe, NM (city) Santa Fe County	305	0.49
Taylorsville, UT (city) Salt Lake County	300	0.52
Sacramento, CA (city) Sacramento County	266	0.07
Halchita, UT (cdp) San Juan County	262	97.04
Cedar City, UT (city) Iron County	260	1.27
Aurora, CO (city) Arapahoe County	257	0.09
Lawrence, KS (city) Douglas County	256	0.32
Snowflake, AZ (town) Navajo County	254	5.70
Sunrise Manor, NV (cdp) Clark County	252	0.16
Long Beach, CA (city) Los Angeles County	248	0.05
Nageezi, NM (cdp) San Juan County	245	82.77
Chicago, IL (city) Cook County	245	0.01
Peoria, AZ (city) Maricopa County	244	0.23
Lakewood, CO (city) Jefferson County	235	0.16
Las Cruces, NM (city) Dona Ana County	233	0.31
Steamboat, AZ (cdp) Apache County	232	99.57
Sheep Springs, NM (cdp) San Juan County	228	96.20
South Valley, NM (cdp) Bernalillo County	224	0.57
San Francisco, CA (city) San Francisco County	223	0.03
Logan, UT (city) Cache County	221	0.52
West Jordan, UT (city) Salt Lake County	217	0.32
Oklahoma City, OK (city) Oklahoma County	214	0.04
Pueblo Pintado, NM (cdp) McKinley County	205	83.00
Pueblo, CO (city) Pueblo County	200	0.20
Stockton, CA (city) San Joaquin County	199	0.08
Oakland, CA (city) Alameda County	198	0.05
Fresno, CA (city) Fresno County	193	0.05
Gilbert, AZ (town) Maricopa County	192	0.18
Millcreek, UT (cdp) Salt Lake County	191	0.63
San Antonio, TX (city) Bexar County	191	0.02
Dallas, TX (city) Dallas County	189	0.02
Red Mesa, AZ (cdp) Apache County	187	78.90
New York, NY (city) New York City	187	0.00
Portland, OR (city) Multnomah County	184	0.03
Moab, UT (city) Grand County	182	3.81
Tulsa, OK (city) Tulsa County	180	0.05
Henderson, NV (city) Clark County	178	0.10
Show Low, AZ (city) Navajo County	175	2.27
Milan, NM (village) Cibola County	173	9.15
Tse Bonito, NM (cdp) McKinley County	171	65.52
Richfield, UT (city) Sevier County	167	2.44
Riverside, CA (city) Riverside County	167	0.07
Paradise, NV (cdp) Clark County	164	0.09
Grand Canyon Village, AZ (cdp) Coconino County	160	10.96
Thornton, CO (city) Adams County	157	0.19
Midvale, UT (city) Salt Lake County	156	0.58
Prescott, AZ (city) Yavapai County	156	0.46
Oljato-Monument Valley, AZ (cdp) Navajo County	151	97.42
Taylor, AZ (town) Navajo County	151	4.75
Brigham City, UT (city) Box Elder County	149	0.86
Seattle, WA (city) King County	148	0.03
North Valley, NM (cdp) Bernalillo County	146	1.22
Anchorage, AK (municipality) Anchorage Borough	146	0.06
Arvada, CO (city) Jefferson County	145	0.14
Anaheim, CA (city) Orange County	145	0.04
Layton, UT (city) Davis County	142	0.24
Cuba, NM (village) Sandoval County	140	23.73
Socorro, NM (city) Socorro County	140	1.58
El Paso, TX (city) El Paso County	131	0.02

Notes: (cdp) census designated place; Refer to the Explanation of Data in the front of the book for more detailed information.

American Indian: Navajo

Top 150 Places Sorted by Percent

(Based on all places, regardless of population)

Place	Number	%
Steamboat, AZ (cdp) Apache County	232	99.57
Huerfano, NM (cdp) San Juan County	103	99.04
Aneth, UT (cdp) San Juan County	592	99.00
Nazlini, AZ (cdp) Apache County	392	98.74
Kaibito, AZ (cdp) Coconino County	1,584	98.57
Bitter Springs, AZ (cdp) Coconino County	534	97.62
Oljato-Monument Valley, AZ (cdp) Navajo County	151	97.42
Lechee, AZ (cdp) Coconino County	1,564	97.38
Rock Point, AZ (cdp) Apache County	705	97.38
Nakaibito, NM (cdp) McKinley County	443	97.36
Beclabito, NM (cdp) San Juan County	330	97.35
Twin Lakes, NM (cdp) McKinley County	1,040	97.29
Nenahnezad, NM (cdp) San Juan County	705	97.11
Tselakai Dezza, UT (cdp) San Juan County	100	97.09
Halchita, UT (cdp) San Juan County	262	97.04
Round Rock, AZ (cdp) Apache County	582	96.84
Crystal, NM (cdp) McKinley County	335	96.54
Brimhall Nizhoni, NM (cdp) McKinley County	360	96.51
Lukachukai, AZ (cdp) Apache County	1,506	96.23
Sheep Springs, NM (cdp) San Juan County	228	96.20
Ojo Amarillo, NM (cdp) San Juan County	797	96.14
Church Rock, NM (cdp) McKinley County	1,032	95.82
Tonalea, AZ (cdp) Coconino County	538	95.73
Pinehill, NM (cdp) Cibola County	111	95.69
Naschitti, NM (cdp) San Juan County	344	95.56
Napi HQ, NM (cdp) San Juan County	673	95.33
Houck, AZ (cdp) Apache County	1,035	95.22
Leupp, AZ (cdp) Coconino County	923	95.15
Navajo, NM (cdp) McKinley County	1,993	95.04
Rock Springs, NM (cdp) McKinley County	530	94.98
Dilkon, AZ (cdp) Navajo County	1,200	94.86
Greasewood, AZ (cdp) Navajo County	551	94.84
Upper Fruitland, NM (cdp) San Juan County	1,578	94.83
Sanostee, NM (cdp) San Juan County	406	94.64
Shiprock, NM (cdp) San Juan County	7,680	94.16
Montezuma Creek, UT (cdp) San Juan County	474	93.49
Alamo, NM (cdp) Socorro County	1,103	93.24
Chilchinbito, AZ (cdp) Navajo County	430	93.07
Sawmill, AZ (cdp) Apache County	569	92.97
Rough Rock, AZ (cdp) Apache County	432	92.11
Cameron, AZ (cdp) Coconino County	898	91.82
Tsaile, AZ (cdp) Apache County	988	91.65
Dennehotso, AZ (cdp) Apache County	669	91.14
Oljato-Monument Valley, UT (cdp) San Juan County	784	90.74
Fort Defiance, AZ (cdp) Apache County	3,670	90.37
Pinon, AZ (cdp) Navajo County	1,075	90.34
Navajo Mountain, UT (cdp) San Juan County	340	89.71
Teec Nos Pos, AZ (cdp) Apache County	715	89.49
Window Rock, AZ (cdp) Apache County	2,733	89.34
Tohatchi, NM (cdp) McKinley County	921	88.81
Burnside, AZ (cdp) Apache County	561	88.77
Jeddito, AZ (cdp) Navajo County	346	88.72
Chinle, AZ (cdp) Apache County	4,760	88.71
Kayenta, AZ (cdp) Navajo County	4,297	87.30
Saint Michaels, AZ (cdp) Apache County	1,130	87.26
Shonto, AZ (cdp) Navajo County	491	86.44
Many Farms, AZ (cdp) Apache County	1,321	85.34
Tuba City, AZ (cdp) Coconino County	6,955	84.56
Crownpoint, NM (cdp) McKinley County	2,191	83.31
Pueblo Pintado, NM (cdp) McKinley County	205	83.00
Newcomb, NM (cdp) San Juan County	321	82.95
Ganado, AZ (cdp) Apache County	1,248	82.92
Nageezi, NM (cdp) San Juan County	245	82.77
Red Mesa, AZ (cdp) Apache County	187	78.90
Thoreau, NM (cdp) McKinley County	1,262	67.74
Tse Bonito, NM (cdp) McKinley County	171	65.52
Yah-ta-hey, NM (cdp) McKinley County	373	64.31
Kirtland, NM (cdp) San Juan County	2,845	45.96
Mexican Hat, UT (cdp) San Juan County	35	39.77
Bluff, UT (cdp) San Juan County	104	32.50
Gallup, NM (city) McKinley County	6,279	31.07
Blanding, UT (city) San Juan County	832	26.31
Page, AZ (city) Coconino County	1,708	25.08
Cuba, NM (village) Sandoval County	140	23.73
Holbrook, AZ (city) Navajo County	1,072	21.80
Halls Crossing, UT (cdp) San Juan County	19	21.35
La Sal, UT (cdp) San Juan County	71	20.94
Ramah, NM (cdp) McKinley County	82	20.15
Winslow, AZ (city) Navajo County	1,786	18.76
Manzano, NM (cdp) Torrance County	9	16.67
Farmington, NM (city) San Juan County	5,793	15.31
Keams Canyon, AZ (cdp) Navajo County	38	14.62
Bloomfield, NM (city) San Juan County	937	14.60
White Mesa, UT (cdp) San Juan County	31	11.19
Grand Canyon Village, AZ (cdp) Coconino County	160	10.96
Tusayan, AZ (cdp) Coconino County	58	10.32
Moenkopi, AZ (cdp) Coconino County	91	10.10
Towaoc, CO (cdp) Montezuma County	110	10.03
Milan, NM (village) Cibola County	173	9.15
Fredonia, AZ (town) Coconino County	93	8.98
Magdalena, NM (village) Socorro County	75	8.21
Cortez, CO (city) Montezuma County	624	7.82
Flagstaff, AZ (city) Coconino County	4,069	7.69
Arizona Village, AZ (cdp) Mohave County	26	7.41
Mountainaire, AZ (cdp) Coconino County	72	7.10
Aztec, NM (city) San Juan County	417	6.54
Regina, NM (cdp) Sandoval County	6	6.06
Snowflake, AZ (town) Navajo County	254	5.70
Monticello, UT (city) San Juan County	110	5.62
McNary, AZ (cdp) Apache County	19	5.44
Casa Colorada, NM (cdp) Valencia County	3	5.36
Grants, NM (city) Cibola County	434	4.93
Dolores, CO (town) Montezuma County	42	4.90
First Mesa, AZ (cdp) Navajo County	54	4.80
Dulce, NM (cdp) Rio Arriba County	125	4.77
Taylor, AZ (town) Navajo County	151	4.75
Randlett, UT (cdp) Uintah County	10	4.46
Ignacio, CO (town) La Plata County	29	4.33
Kykotsmovi Village, AZ (cdp) Navajo County	32	4.12
Saint Johns, AZ (city) Apache County	128	3.92
Moab, UT (city) Grand County	182	3.81
Lonepine, MT (cdp) Sanders County	5	3.65
Pueblo of Sandia Village, NM (cdp) Sandoval County	12	3.49
Second Mesa, AZ (cdp) Navajo County	28	3.44
Gulkana, AK (cdp) Valdez-Cordova Census Area	3	3.41
Kaibab, AZ (cdp) Mohave County	9	3.27
Colerain, NC (town) Bertie County	7	3.17
Paguate, NM (cdp) Cibola County	15	3.16
Brookhurst, WY (cdp) Natrona County	6	3.13
Two Strike, SD (cdp) Todd County	7	3.03
Durango, CO (city) La Plata County	411	2.95
Lamy, NM (cdp) Santa Fe County	4	2.92
Paraje, NM (cdp) Cibola County	19	2.84
Laguna, NM (cdp) Cibola County	12	2.84
University Park, NM (cdp) Dona Ana County	77	2.82
Garvin, OK (town) McCurtain County	4	2.80
Northway Village, AK (cdp) Southeast Fairbanks Census Area	3	2.80
North Acomita Village, NM (cdp) Cibola County	8	2.78
Flora Vista, NM (cdp) San Juan County	38	2.75
Parker, AZ (town) La Paz County	86	2.74
Seama, NM (cdp) Cibola County	9	2.70
Canyondam, CA (cdp) Plumas County	1	2.70
Whiterocks, UT (cdp) Uintah County	9	2.64
Fort Duchesne, UT (cdp) Uintah County	16	2.58
Alba, MN (township) Jackson County	5	2.50
Richfield, UT (city) Sevier County	167	2.44
Rico, CO (town) Dolores County	5	2.44
Springerville, AZ (town) Apache County	48	2.43
Whiteriver, AZ (cdp) Navajo County	122	2.34
Starkville, CO (town) Las Animas County	3	2.34
Picuris Pueblo, NM (cdp) Taos County	2	2.33
Lake View, ME (plantation) Piscataquis County	1	2.33
Rio en Medio, NM (cdp) Santa Fe County	3	2.29
Winslow West, AZ (cdp) Coconino County	3	2.29
Show Low, AZ (city) Navajo County	175	2.27
Wann, OK (town) Nowata County	3	2.27
Alton, UT (town) Kane County	3	2.24
Hartline, WA (town) Grant County	3	2.24
Shongopovi, AZ (cdp) Navajo County	14	2.22
Spanish Valley, UT (cdp) San Juan County	4	2.21

Notes: (cdp) census designated place; Refer to the Explanation of Data in the front of the book for more detailed information.

American Indian: Navajo

Top 150 Places Sorted by Percent

(Based on places with populations of 10,000 or more)

Place	Number	%
Gallup, NM (city) McKinley County	6,279	31.07
Farmington, NM (city) San Juan County	5,793	15.31
Flagstaff, AZ (city) Coconino County	4,069	7.69
Durango, CO (city) La Plata County	411	2.95
Albuquerque, NM (city) Bernalillo County	7,889	1.76
South Salt Lake, UT (city) Salt Lake County	314	1.42
Cedar City, UT (city) Iron County	260	1.27
North Valley, NM (cdp) Bernalillo County	146	1.22
Saint George, UT (city) Washington County	533	1.07
Las Vegas, NM (city) San Miguel County	129	0.89
Rio Rancho, NM (city) Sandoval County	453	0.88
Brigham City, UT (city) Box Elder County	149	0.86
Tempe, AZ (city) Maricopa County	1,346	0.85
Phoenix, AZ (city) Maricopa County	10,143	0.77
Los Lunas, NM (village) Valencia County	77	0.77
Mesa, AZ (city) Maricopa County	2,780	0.70
Salt Lake City, UT (city) Salt Lake County	1,178	0.65
Cottonwood-Verde Village, AZ (cdp) Yavapai County	68	0.64
West Valley City, UT (city) Salt Lake County	685	0.63
Millcreek, UT (cdp) Salt Lake County	191	0.63
Barstow, CA (city) San Bernardino County	125	0.59
Florence, AZ (town) Pinal County	100	0.59
Midvale, UT (city) Salt Lake County	156	0.58
South Valley, NM (cdp) Bernalillo County	224	0.57
Glendale, AZ (city) Maricopa County	1,208	0.55
Tooele, UT (city) Tooele County	120	0.53
Taylorsville, UT (city) Salt Lake County	300	0.52
Logan, UT (city) Cache County	221	0.52
Santa Fe, NM (city) Santa Fe County	305	0.49
Ogden, UT (city) Weber County	360	0.47
Prescott, AZ (city) Yavapai County	156	0.46
Clearfield, UT (city) Davis County	117	0.45
Magna, UT (cdp) Salt Lake County	103	0.45
Orem, UT (city) Utah County	369	0.44
Provo, UT (city) Utah County	434	0.41
Fort Carson, CO (cdp) El Paso County	43	0.41
Kingman, AZ (city) Mohave County	79	0.39
Kearns, UT (cdp) Salt Lake County	123	0.37
South Ogden, UT (city) Weber County	53	0.37
Spanish Fork, UT (city) Utah County	70	0.35
Murray, UT (city) Salt Lake County	117	0.34
Green River, WY (city) Sweetwater County	39	0.33
Artesia, NM (city) Eddy County	35	0.33
Lawrence, KS (city) Douglas County	256	0.32
West Jordan, UT (city) Salt Lake County	217	0.32
Lehi, UT (city) Utah County	61	0.32
Las Cruces, NM (city) Dona Ana County	233	0.31
Douglas, AZ (city) Cochise County	44	0.31
Portales, NM (city) Roosevelt County	34	0.31
Chandler, AZ (city) Maricopa County	528	0.30
Clinton, UT (city) Davis County	38	0.30
Tucson, AZ (city) Pima County	1,387	0.28
Oquirrh, UT (cdp) Salt Lake County	29	0.28
New Kingman-Butler, AZ (cdp) Mohave County	40	0.27
Payson, AZ (town) Gila County	37	0.27
Avondale, AZ (city) Maricopa County	93	0.26
Casa Grande, AZ (city) Pinal County	65	0.26
Prescott Valley, AZ (town) Yavapai County	60	0.25
Clifton, CO (cdp) Mesa County	43	0.25
Layton, UT (city) Davis County	142	0.24
Springville, UT (city) Utah County	49	0.24
Sherrelwood, CO (cdp) Adams County	42	0.24
Peoria, AZ (city) Maricopa County	244	0.23
Draper, UT (city) Salt Lake County	59	0.23
Schofield Barracks, HI (cdp) Honolulu County	33	0.23
Spring Creek, NV (cdp) Elko County	24	0.23
Oildale, CA (cdp) Kern County	61	0.22
Elko, NV (city) Elko County	36	0.22
Englewood, CO (city) Arapahoe County	68	0.21
Flowing Wells, AZ (cdp) Pima County	31	0.21
Pueblo, CO (city) Pueblo County	200	0.20
Apache Junction, AZ (city) Pinal County	63	0.20
Mohave Valley, AZ (cdp) Mohave County	27	0.20
Federal Heights, CO (city) Adams County	24	0.20
Thornton, CO (city) Adams County	157	0.19
Roy, UT (city) Weber County	63	0.19
Gilbert, AZ (town) Maricopa County	192	0.18
Clovis, NM (city) Curry County	59	0.18
West Carson, CA (cdp) Los Angeles County	38	0.18
Cottonwood West, UT (cdp) Salt Lake County	34	0.18
Deming, NM (city) Luna County	26	0.18
Sierra Vista Southeast, AZ (cdp) Cochise County	26	0.18
Mountain Home, ID (city) Elmore County	20	0.18
Berkley, CO (cdp) Adams County	19	0.18
Blackfoot, ID (city) Bingham County	19	0.18
Commerce City, CO (city) Adams County	36	0.17
Welby, CO (cdp) Adams County	22	0.17
Denver, CO (city) Denver County	884	0.16
Scottsdale, AZ (city) Maricopa County	332	0.16
Sunrise Manor, NV (cdp) Clark County	252	0.16
Lakewood, CO (city) Jefferson County	235	0.16
Bullhead City, AZ (city) Mohave County	55	0.16
Security-Widefield, CO (cdp) El Paso County	49	0.16
Fort Bragg, NC (cdp) Cumberland County	48	0.16
Fort Lewis, WA (cdp) Pierce County	30	0.16
Ada, OK (city) Pontotoc County	25	0.16
Fountain, CO (city) El Paso County	24	0.16
Marana, AZ (town) Pima County	22	0.16
Arkansas City, KS (city) Cowley County	19	0.16
Farmington, UT (city) Davis County	19	0.16
Cottonwood Heights, UT (cdp) Salt Lake County	41	0.15
Drexel Heights, AZ (cdp) Pima County	36	0.15
Kaysville, UT (city) Davis County	31	0.15
Silver City, NM (town) Grant County	16	0.15
Arvada, CO (city) Jefferson County	145	0.14
Apple Valley, CA (town) San Bernardino County	75	0.14
Winchester, NV (cdp) Clark County	39	0.14
Pleasant Grove, UT (city) Utah County	32	0.14
San Lorenzo, CA (cdp) Alameda County	30	0.14
Oak Harbor, WA (city) Island County	28	0.14
Twentynine Palms, CA (city) San Bernardino County	20	0.14
Blythe, CA (city) Riverside County	17	0.14
New River, AZ (cdp) Maricopa County	15	0.14
Colorado Springs, CO (city) El Paso County	458	0.13
Grand Junction, CO (city) Mesa County	54	0.13
Alamogordo, NM (city) Otero County	48	0.13
Northglenn, CO (city) Adams County	42	0.13
Goodyear, AZ (city) Maricopa County	24	0.13
Pueblo West, CO (cdp) Pueblo County	22	0.13
Riverbank, CA (city) Stanislaus County	21	0.13
Payson, UT (city) Utah County	17	0.13
Stanford, CA (cdp) Santa Clara County	17	0.13
Carthage, MO (city) Jasper County	16	0.13
Montrose, CO (city) Montrose County	16	0.13
Evanston, WY (city) Uinta County	15	0.13
Sierra Madre, CA (city) Los Angeles County	14	0.13
Sandy, UT (city) Salt Lake County	107	0.12
Longmont, CO (city) Boulder County	85	0.12
Bell Gardens, CA (city) Los Angeles County	51	0.12
Sierra Vista, AZ (city) Cochise County	46	0.12
Fort Hood, TX (cdp) Coryell County	42	0.12
Wheat Ridge, CO (city) Jefferson County	41	0.12
Imperial Beach, CA (city) San Diego County	33	0.12
American Fork, UT (city) Utah County	26	0.12
Brighton, CO (city) Adams County	26	0.12
Ashland, CA (cdp) Alameda County	25	0.12
Whitney, NV (cdp) Clark County	22	0.12
El Reno, OK (city) Canadian County	20	0.12
North Ogden, UT (city) Weber County	18	0.12
Tahlequah, OK (city) Cherokee County	18	0.12
Corcoran, CA (city) Kings County	17	0.12
Hawaiian Gardens, CA (city) Los Angeles County	17	0.12
Holladay, UT (city) Salt Lake County	17	0.12
Clearlake, CA (city) Lake County	16	0.12
Nipomo, CA (cdp) San Luis Obispo County	15	0.12
Beaumont, CA (city) Riverside County	14	0.12
Fort Benning South, GA (cdp) Chattahoochee County	14	0.12
Fort Drum, NY (cdp) Jefferson County	14	0.12
Kaneohe Station, HI (cdp) Honolulu County	14	0.12
Kelso, WA (city) Cowlitz County	14	0.12

Notes: (cdp) census designated place; Refer to the Explanation of Data in the front of the book for more detailed information.

American Indian: Osage

Top 150 Places Sorted by Number

(Based on all places, regardless of population)

Place	Number	%
Tulsa, OK (city) Tulsa County	804	0.20
Pawhuska, OK (city) Osage County	460	12.68
Bartlesville, OK (city) Washington County	342	0.98
Hominy, OK (city) Osage County	290	11.22
Oklahoma City, OK (city) Oklahoma County	269	0.05
Skiatook, OK (town) Osage County	232	4.30
Fairfax, OK (town) Osage County	204	13.12
Wichita, KS (city) Sedgwick County	188	0.05
Ponca City, OK (city) Kay County	162	0.63
Broken Arrow, OK (city) Tulsa County	119	0.16
Los Angeles, CA (city) Los Angeles County	118	0.00
Norman, OK (city) Cleveland County	107	0.11
Barnsdall, OK (city) Osage County	93	7.02
Stillwater, OK (city) Payne County	72	0.18
Phoenix, AZ (city) Maricopa County	65	0.00
Sand Springs, OK (city) Tulsa County	62	0.36
Colorado Springs, CO (city) El Paso County	59	0.02
San Diego, CA (city) San Diego County	56	0.00
Dallas, TX (city) Dallas County	53	0.00
Kansas City, MO (city) Jackson County	52	0.01
Portland, OR (city) Multnomah County	52	0.01
Edmond, OK (city) Oklahoma County	51	0.07
Houston, TX (city) Harris County	51	0.00
Albuquerque, NM (city) Bernalillo County	50	0.01
San Jose, CA (city) Santa Clara County	50	0.01
Owasso, OK (city) Tulsa County	45	0.24
Enid, OK (city) Garfield County	45	0.10
Claremore, OK (city) Rogers County	43	0.27
Seattle, WA (city) King County	43	0.01
Denver, CO (city) Denver County	42	0.01
Fresno, CA (city) Fresno County	42	0.01
New York, NY (city) New York City	40	0.00
Tahlequah, OK (city) Cherokee County	38	0.26
Springfield, MO (city) Greene County	38	0.03
Austin, TX (city) Travis County	38	0.01
Sacramento, CA (city) Sacramento County	37	0.01
Joplin, MO (city) Jasper County	36	0.08
Riverside, CA (city) Riverside County	36	0.01
Cleveland, OK (city) Pawnee County	35	1.07
Bixby, OK (city) Tulsa County	34	0.25
Moore, OK (city) Cleveland County	34	0.08
McCord, OK (cdp) Osage County	33	1.93
Anchorage, AK (municipality) Anchorage Borough	33	0.01
Las Vegas, NV (city) Clark County	30	0.01
Long Beach, CA (city) Los Angeles County	30	0.01
Eugene, OR (city) Lane County	29	0.02
Mesa, AZ (city) Maricopa County	29	0.01
San Antonio, TX (city) Bexar County	28	0.00
San Francisco, CA (city) San Francisco County	27	0.00
Muskogee, OK (city) Muskogee County	26	0.07
Miami, OK (city) Ottawa County	25	0.18
Lawton, OK (city) Comanche County	25	0.03
Coffeyville, KS (city) Montgomery County	24	0.22
Overland Park, KS (city) Johnson County	24	0.02
Arlington, TX (city) Tarrant County	24	0.01
Aurora, CO (city) Arapahoe County	24	0.01
Burbank, OK (town) Osage County	23	14.84
Independence, MO (city) Jackson County	23	0.02
Plano, TX (city) Collin County	23	0.01
Ralston, OK (town) Pawnee County	22	6.20
Nowata, OK (city) Nowata County	22	0.55
Sapulpa, OK (city) Creek County	22	0.11
Springfield, OR (city) Lane County	22	0.04
Lawrence, KS (city) Douglas County	21	0.03
Ardmore, OK (city) Carter County	20	0.08
Garland, TX (city) Dallas County	20	0.01
Kansas City, KS (city) Wyandotte County	20	0.01
Chicago, IL (city) Cook County	20	0.00
Indianapolis, IN (special city) Marion County	20	0.00
Wynona, OK (town) Osage County	19	3.58
Dewey, OK (city) Washington County	19	0.60
Turley, OK (cdp) Tulsa County	19	0.59
Tonkawa, OK (city) Kay County	19	0.58
Cushing, OK (city) Payne County	19	0.23
Richardson, TX (city) Dallas County	19	0.02
Bakersfield, CA (city) Kern County	19	0.01
Fontana, CA (city) San Bernardino County	19	0.01
Huntington Beach, CA (city) Orange County	19	0.01
Salem, OR (city) Marion County	19	0.01
Arkansas City, KS (city) Cowley County	18	0.15
Lancaster, CA (city) Los Angeles County	18	0.02
Chula Vista, CA (city) San Diego County	18	0.01
Midwest City, OK (city) Oklahoma County	17	0.03
San Buenaventura, CA (city) Ventura County	17	0.02
Fort Collins, CO (city) Larimer County	17	0.01
Santa Rosa, CA (city) Sonoma County	17	0.01
Blackwell, OK (city) Kay County	16	0.21
Pryor Creek, OK (city) Mayes County	16	0.18
Bethany, OK (city) Oklahoma County	16	0.08
Fairfield, CA (city) Solano County	16	0.02
Napa, CA (city) Napa County	16	0.02
Olathe, KS (city) Johnson County	16	0.02
Irving, TX (city) Dallas County	16	0.01
Oceanside, CA (city) San Diego County	16	0.01
Fort Worth, TX (city) Tarrant County	16	0.00
Coweta, OK (city) Wagoner County	15	0.21
Glenpool, OK (city) Tulsa County	15	0.18
McAlester, OK (city) Pittsburg County	15	0.08
Lenexa, KS (city) Johnson County	15	0.04
Vista, CA (city) San Diego County	15	0.02
Vancouver, WA (city) Clark County	15	0.01
Columbus, OH (city) Franklin County	15	0.00
Saint Louis, MO (independent city) Saint Louis city	15	0.00
Avant, OK (town) Osage County	14	3.76
Caney, KS (city) Montgomery County	14	0.67
Park Hill, OK (cdp) Cherokee County	14	0.36
Independence, KS (city) Montgomery County	14	0.14
Yukon, OK (city) Canadian County	14	0.07
Apple Valley, CA (town) San Bernardino County	14	0.03
Carlsbad, CA (city) San Diego County	14	0.02
Fayetteville, AR (city) Washington County	14	0.02
Corpus Christi, TX (city) Nueces County	14	0.01
El Cajon, CA (city) San Diego County	14	0.01
Henderson, NV (city) Clark County	14	0.01
Lakewood, CO (city) Jefferson County	14	0.01
Modesto, CA (city) Stanislaus County	14	0.01
Anaheim, CA (city) Orange County	14	0.00
Jacksonville, FL (special city) Duval County	14	0.00
Tampa, FL (city) Hillsborough County	14	0.00
Shidler, OK (city) Osage County	13	2.50
Bedford, TX (city) Tarrant County	13	0.03
Fort Smith, AR (city) Sebastian County	13	0.02
Santa Fe, NM (city) Santa Fe County	13	0.02
Irvine, CA (city) Orange County	13	0.01
Lincoln, NE (city) Lancaster County	13	0.01
Oxnard, CA (city) Ventura County	13	0.01
Pasadena, TX (city) Harris County	13	0.01
San Bernardino, CA (city) San Bernardino County	13	0.01
Spokane, WA (city) Spokane County	13	0.01
Tacoma, WA (city) Pierce County	13	0.01
Osage, OK (town) Osage County	12	6.38
Sperry, OK (town) Tulsa County	12	1.22
Vinita, OK (city) Craig County	12	0.19
San Jacinto, CA (city) Riverside County	12	0.05
West Sacramento, CA (city) Yolo County	12	0.04
Davis, CA (city) Yolo County	12	0.02
North Little Rock, AR (city) Pulaski County	12	0.02
Arden-Arcade, CA (cdp) Sacramento County	12	0.01
Everett, WA (city) Snohomish County	12	0.01
Norfolk, VA (independent city) Norfolk city	12	0.01
Simi Valley, CA (city) Ventura County	12	0.01
El Paso, TX (city) El Paso County	12	0.00
New Orleans, LA (city) Orleans Parish	12	0.00
Stockton, CA (city) San Joaquin County	12	0.00
Sedan, KS (city) Chautauqua County	11	0.82
Drumright, OK (city) Creek County	11	0.38
Muldrow, OK (town) Sequoyah County	11	0.35
Baldwin City, KS (city) Douglas County	11	0.32
Collinsville, OK (city) Tulsa County	11	0.27
Wagoner, OK (city) Wagoner County	11	0.14

Notes: (cdp) census designated place; Refer to the Explanation of Data in the front of the book for more detailed information.

American Indian: Osage

Top 150 Places Sorted by Percent

(Based on all places, regardless of population)

Place	Number	%
Burbank, OK (town) Osage County	23	14.84
Fairfax, OK (town) Osage County	204	13.12
Pawhuska, OK (city) Osage County	460	12.68
Hominy, OK (city) Osage County	290	11.22
Barnsdall, OK (city) Osage County	93	7.02
Grainola, OK (town) Osage County	2	6.45
Osage, OK (town) Osage County	12	6.38
Ralston, OK (town) Pawnee County	22	6.20
Loyal, OK (town) Kingfisher County	5	6.17
Skiatook, OK (town) Osage County	232	4.30
Randolph, MO (village) Clay County	2	4.26
Avant, OK (town) Osage County	14	3.76
Wynona, OK (town) Osage County	19	3.58
Chautauqua, KS (city) Chautauqua County	4	3.54
Shidler, OK (city) Osage County	13	2.50
Pinhook Corners, OK (cdp) Sequoyah County	4	2.48
Narcissa, OK (cdp) Ottawa County	2	2.00
Shoal Creek Estates, MO (town) Newton County	1	1.96
McCord, OK (cdp) Osage County	33	1.93
Stuart, OK (town) Hughes County	4	1.82
Niotaze, KS (city) Chautauqua County	2	1.64
Prue, OK (town) Osage County	6	1.39
Cairo, MO (village) Randolph County	4	1.37
Gregory, OK (cdp) Rogers County	2	1.33
Chignik, AK (city) Lake and Peninsula Borough	1	1.27
Sperry, OK (town) Tulsa County	12	1.22
Nikolaevsk, AK (cdp) Kenai Peninsula Borough	4	1.16
Kildare, OK (town) Kay County	1	1.09
Kaw City, OK (city) Kay County	4	1.08
Cleveland, OK (city) Pawnee County	35	1.07
Webb City, OK (town) Osage County	1	1.05
Tecopa, CA (cdp) Inyo County	1	1.01
Bartlesville, OK (city) Washington County	342	0.98
Rockport, WA (cdp) Skagit County	1	0.98
Redbird Smith, OK (cdp) Sequoyah County	4	0.97
Perryville, AK (cdp) Lake and Peninsula Borough	1	0.93
Carytown, MO (city) Jasper County	2	0.92
Foristell, MO (city) Saint Charles County	3	0.91
Ramona, OK (town) Washington County	5	0.89
Delaware, OK (town) Nowata County	4	0.88
Sedan, KS (city) Chautauqua County	11	0.82
Glacier View, AK (cdp) Matanuska-Susitna Borough	2	0.80
Lafe, AR (town) Greene County	3	0.78
Media, IL (village) Henderson County	1	0.77
Harrison, ID (city) Kootenai County	2	0.75
Hulbert, OK (town) Cherokee County	4	0.74
Kenny Lake, AK (cdp) Valdez-Cordova Census Area	3	0.73
New Strawn, KS (city) Coffey County	3	0.71
Marland, OK (town) Noble County	2	0.71
Brownville, NE (village) Nemaha County	1	0.68
Caney, KS (city) Montgomery County	14	0.67
Cameron, OK (town) Le Flore County	2	0.64
Ponca City, OK (city) Kay County	162	0.63
Lake Annette, MO (city) Cass County	1	0.61
Latham, KS (city) Butler County	1	0.61
Dewey, OK (city) Washington County	19	0.60
Turley, OK (cdp) Tulsa County	19	0.59
Tonkawa, OK (city) Kay County	19	0.58
Galva, KS (city) McPherson County	4	0.57
Nowata, OK (city) Nowata County	22	0.55
Cedar Vale, KS (city) Chautauqua County	4	0.55
Marble Hill, MO (city) Bollinger County	8	0.53
Burns Harbor, IN (town) Porter County	4	0.52
Burns Flat, OK (town) Washita County	9	0.51
Glencoe, OK (town) Payne County	3	0.51
Goldsby, OK (town) McClain County	6	0.50
Copan, OK (town) Washington County	4	0.50
Elmira, CA (cdp) Solano County	1	0.49
Tallapoosa, MO (city) New Madrid County	1	0.49
Laddonia, MO (city) Audrain County	3	0.48
Wakita, OK (town) Grant County	2	0.48
Leon, KS (city) Butler County	3	0.47
Sutton-Alpine, AK (cdp) Matanuska-Susitna Borough	5	0.46
Carney, OK (town) Lincoln County	3	0.46
East Cape Girardeau, IL (village) Alexander County	2	0.46
Harding-Birch Lakes, AK (cdp) Fairbanks North Star Borough	1	0.46
Smolan, KS (city) Saline County	1	0.46
Oologah, OK (town) Rogers County	4	0.45
Laurie, MO (village) Morgan County	3	0.45
Locust Grove, OK (town) Mayes County	6	0.44
Disney, OK (town) Mayes County	1	0.44
Oxford, KS (city) Sumner County	5	0.43
Oregon, MO (city) Holt County	4	0.43
Lamont, OK (town) Grant County	2	0.43
Arboles, CO (cdp) Archuleta County	1	0.43
Denison, KS (city) Jackson County	1	0.43
Murphy, OK (cdp) Mayes County	3	0.43
Hilshire Village, TX (city) Harris County	3	0.42
Inkom, ID (city) Bannock County	3	0.41
Scranton, KS (city) Osage County	3	0.41
Waukomis, OK (town) Garfield County	5	0.40
Gould, MN (township) Cass County	1	0.40
Sterling, OK (town) Comanche County	3	0.39
Drumright, OK (city) Creek County	11	0.38
North Enid, OK (town) Garfield County	3	0.38
Dunfermline, IL (village) Fulton County	1	0.38
Parkdale, OR (cdp) Hood River County	1	0.38
Westport, OK (town) Pawnee County	1	0.38
Apache, OK (town) Caddo County	6	0.37
Ouray, CO (city) Ouray County	3	0.37
Summersville, MO (city) Texas County	2	0.37
Latexo, TX (city) Houston County	1	0.37
Poospatuck Reservation, NY (reservation) Suffolk County	1	0.37
Sand Springs, OK (city) Tulsa County	62	0.36
Park Hill, OK (cdp) Cherokee County	14	0.36
Spavinaw, OK (town) Mayes County	2	0.36
Arcadia, OK (town) Oklahoma County	1	0.36
Muldrow, OK (town) Sequoyah County	11	0.35
Rockaway Beach, MO (city) Taney County	2	0.35
Uniontown, KS (city) Bourbon County	1	0.35
Golden City, MO (city) Barton County	3	0.34
Dustin Acres, CA (cdp) Kern County	2	0.34
Orderville, UT (town) Kane County	2	0.34
Red Rock, OK (town) Noble County	1	0.34
Sawyerville, IL (village) Macoupin County	1	0.34
Chelsea, OK (city) Rogers County	7	0.33
Elgin, OK (city) Comanche County	4	0.33
Newark, AR (city) Independence County	4	0.33
Moclips, WA (cdp) Grays Harbor County	2	0.33
Elk City, KS (city) Montgomery County	1	0.33
Baldwin City, KS (city) Douglas County	11	0.32
Montross, VA (town) Westmoreland County	1	0.32
Inola, OK (town) Rogers County	5	0.31
Winona, MO (city) Shannon County	4	0.31
Wallace, ID (city) Shoshone County	3	0.31
Queen City, MO (city) Schuyler County	2	0.31
Turtle Creek, MN (township) Todd County	1	0.31
Sarcoxie, MO (city) Jasper County	4	0.30
Eldon, OK (cdp) Cherokee County	3	0.30
Hauser, ID (city) Kootenai County	2	0.30
Forest City, MO (city) Holt County	1	0.30
Lake Almanor Peninsula, CA (cdp) Plumas County	1	0.30
Northport, WA (town) Stevens County	1	0.30
Mannford, OK (town) Creek County	6	0.29
Warsaw, MO (city) Benton County	6	0.29
Kechi, KS (city) Sedgwick County	3	0.29
Manassa, CO (town) Conejos County	3	0.29
Lake Lafayette, MO (city) Lafayette County	1	0.29
Richland Springs, TX (town) San Saba County	1	0.29
Frankfort, WI (town) Pepin County	1	0.28
Claremore, OK (city) Rogers County	43	0.27
Collinsville, OK (city) Tulsa County	11	0.27
Okarche, OK (town) Kingfisher County	3	0.27
Jennings, OK (town) Pawnee County	1	0.27
Tahlequah, OK (city) Cherokee County	38	0.26
Pine, AZ (cdp) Gila County	5	0.26
Siletz, OR (city) Lincoln County	3	0.26
Temple, OK (town) Cotton County	3	0.26
Captiva, FL (cdp) Lee County	1	0.26
Mountain Park, OK (town) Kiowa County	1	0.26

Notes: (cdp) census designated place; Refer to the Explanation of Data in the front of the book for more detailed information.

American Indian: Osage

Top 150 Places Sorted by Percent

(Based on places with populations of 10,000 or more)

Place	Number	%
Bartlesville, OK (city) Washington County	342	0.98
Ponca City, OK (city) Kay County	162	0.63
Sand Springs, OK (city) Tulsa County	62	0.36
Claremore, OK (city) Rogers County	43	0.27
Tahlequah, OK (city) Cherokee County	38	0.26
Bixby, OK (city) Tulsa County	34	0.25
Owasso, OK (city) Tulsa County	45	0.24
Coffeyville, KS (city) Montgomery County	24	0.22
Tulsa, OK (city) Tulsa County	804	0.20
Stillwater, OK (city) Payne County	72	0.18
Miami, OK (city) Ottawa County	25	0.18
Broken Arrow, OK (city) Tulsa County	119	0.16
Arkansas City, KS (city) Cowley County	18	0.15
Norman, OK (city) Cleveland County	107	0.11
Sapulpa, OK (city) Creek County	22	0.11
Enid, OK (city) Garfield County	45	0.10
Joplin, MO (city) Jasper County	36	0.08
Moore, OK (city) Cleveland County	34	0.08
Ardmore, OK (city) Carter County	20	0.08
Bethany, OK (city) Oklahoma County	16	0.08
McAlester, OK (city) Pittsburg County	15	0.08
Edmond, OK (city) Oklahoma County	51	0.07
Muskogee, OK (city) Muskogee County	26	0.07
Yukon, OK (city) Canadian County	14	0.07
El Dorado, KS (city) Butler County	9	0.07
Winfield, KS (city) Cowley County	8	0.07
Guymon, OK (city) Texas County	7	0.07
Siloam Springs, AR (city) Benton County	7	0.06
Montecito, CA (cdp) Santa Barbara County	6	0.06
Oklahoma City, OK (city) Oklahoma County	269	0.05
Wichita, KS (city) Sedgwick County	188	0.05
San Jacinto, CA (city) Riverside County	12	0.05
Sedalia, MO (city) Pettis County	11	0.05
Bentonville, AR (city) Benton County	10	0.05
Van Buren, AR (city) Crawford County	9	0.05
Ada, OK (city) Pontotoc County	8	0.05
Ashwaubenon, WI (village) Brown County	8	0.05
Chickasha, OK (city) Grady County	8	0.05
McKinleyville, CA (cdp) Humboldt County	7	0.05
Okmulgee, OK (city) Okmulgee County	7	0.05
Grover Beach, CA (city) San Luis Obispo County	6	0.05
Elk City, OK (city) Beckham County	5	0.05
Silver City, NM (town) Grant County	5	0.05
The Village, OK (city) Oklahoma County	5	0.05
Springfield, OR (city) Lane County	22	0.04
Lenexa, KS (city) Johnson County	15	0.04
West Sacramento, CA (city) Yolo County	12	0.04
Atascadero, CA (city) San Luis Obispo County	10	0.04
Klamath Falls, OR (city) Klamath County	8	0.04
West Linn, OR (city) Clackamas County	8	0.04
Pittsburg, KS (city) Crawford County	7	0.04
Borger, TX (city) Hutchinson County	6	0.04
Katy, TX (city) Harris County	5	0.04
Lebanon, MO (city) Laclede County	5	0.04
Mustang, OK (city) Canadian County	5	0.04
Nixa, MO (city) Christian County	5	0.04
Parsons, KS (city) Labette County	5	0.04
Ecorse, MI (city) Wayne County	4	0.04
Fortuna, CA (city) Humboldt County	4	0.04
Neosho, MO (city) Newton County	4	0.04
Valle Vista, CA (cdp) Riverside County	4	0.04
Zephyrhills, FL (city) Pasco County	4	0.04
Springfield, MO (city) Greene County	38	0.03
Lawton, OK (city) Comanche County	25	0.03
Lawrence, KS (city) Douglas County	21	0.03
Midwest City, OK (city) Oklahoma County	17	0.03
Apple Valley, CA (town) San Bernardino County	14	0.03
Bedford, TX (city) Tarrant County	13	0.03
Keizer, OR (city) Marion County	9	0.03
The Colony, TX (city) Denton County	9	0.03
Fallbrook, CA (cdp) San Diego County	8	0.03
Oakley, CA (city) Contra Costa County	8	0.03
Shawnee, OK (city) Pottawatomie County	8	0.03
Altus, OK (city) Jackson County	7	0.03
Benicia, CA (city) Solano County	7	0.03
Del City, OK (city) Oklahoma County	7	0.03
Gallup, NM (city) McKinley County	7	0.03
Grants Pass, OR (city) Josephine County	7	0.03
Imperial Beach, CA (city) San Diego County	7	0.03
Laguna Beach, CA (city) Orange County	7	0.03
Liberty, MO (city) Clay County	7	0.03
Spanaway, WA (cdp) Pierce County	7	0.03
Arroyo Grande, CA (city) San Luis Obispo County	5	0.03
Canyon Lake, TX (cdp) Comal County	5	0.03
Derby, KS (city) Sedgwick County	5	0.03
Desert Hot Springs, CA (city) Riverside County	5	0.03
Logansport, IN (city) Cass County	5	0.03
Rosamond, CA (cdp) Kern County	5	0.03
Silverdale, WA (cdp) Kitsap County	5	0.03
Baker, LA (city) East Baton Rouge Parish	4	0.03
Baywood-Los Osos, CA (cdp) San Luis Obispo County	4	0.03
Black Forest, CO (cdp) El Paso County	4	0.03
Dallas, OR (city) Polk County	4	0.03
Durango, CO (city) La Plata County	4	0.03
Grand Terrace, CA (city) San Bernardino County	4	0.03
Kelso, WA (city) Cowlitz County	4	0.03
Midlothian, IL (village) Cook County	4	0.03
Murray, KY (city) Calloway County	4	0.03
Welby, CO (cdp) Adams County	4	0.03
Coalinga, CA (city) Fresno County	3	0.03
Dishman, WA (cdp) Spokane County	3	0.03
Gladstone, OR (city) Clackamas County	3	0.03
Greenwood Village, CO (city) Arapahoe County	3	0.03
Henderson, TX (city) Rusk County	3	0.03
Holly, MI (township) Oakland County	3	0.03
Lakeland South, WA (cdp) King County	3	0.03
Lea Hill, WA (cdp) King County	3	0.03
Olivehurst, CA (cdp) Yuba County	3	0.03
Ontario, OR (city) Malheur County	3	0.03
Pedley, CA (cdp) Riverside County	3	0.03
Prairie Ridge, WA (cdp) Pierce County	3	0.03
Raymore, MO (city) Cass County	3	0.03
Rocky Point, NY (cdp) Suffolk County	3	0.03
Swansea, IL (village) Saint Clair County	3	0.03
Wells Branch, TX (cdp) Travis County	3	0.03
West Plains, MO (city) Howell County	3	0.03
Woodward, OK (city) Woodward County	3	0.03
Colorado Springs, CO (city) El Paso County	59	0.02
Eugene, OR (city) Lane County	29	0.02
Overland Park, KS (city) Johnson County	24	0.02
Independence, MO (city) Jackson County	23	0.02
Richardson, TX (city) Dallas County	19	0.02
Lancaster, CA (city) Los Angeles County	18	0.02
San Buenaventura, CA (city) Ventura County	17	0.02
Fairfield, CA (city) Solano County	16	0.02
Napa, CA (city) Napa County	16	0.02
Olathe, KS (city) Johnson County	16	0.02
Vista, CA (city) San Diego County	15	0.02
Carlsbad, CA (city) San Diego County	14	0.02
Fayetteville, AR (city) Washington County	14	0.02
Fort Smith, AR (city) Sebastian County	13	0.02
Santa Fe, NM (city) Santa Fe County	13	0.02
Davis, CA (city) Yolo County	12	0.02
North Little Rock, AR (city) Pulaski County	12	0.02
Redondo Beach, CA (city) Los Angeles County	11	0.02
Euless, TX (city) Tarrant County	10	0.02
Flower Mound, TX (town) Denton County	10	0.02
Missoula, MT (city) Missoula County	9	0.02
San Clemente, CA (city) Orange County	9	0.02
San Luis Obispo, CA (city) San Luis Obispo County	9	0.02
The Woodlands, TX (cdp) Montgomery County	9	0.02
Broomfield, CO (city) Boulder County	8	0.02
Coppell, TX (city) Dallas County	8	0.02
North Highlands, CA (cdp) Sacramento County	8	0.02
Tigard, OR (city) Washington County	8	0.02
Albany, OR (city) Linn County	7	0.02
Englewood, CO (city) Arapahoe County	7	0.02
Grapevine, TX (city) Tarrant County	7	0.02
Leavenworth, KS (city) Leavenworth County	7	0.02
Lombard, IL (village) Du Page County	7	0.02

Notes: (cdp) census designated place; Refer to the Explanation of Data in the front of the book for more detailed information.

American Indian: Ottawa

Top 150 Places Sorted by Number

(Based on all places, regardless of population)

Place	Number	%
Grand Rapids, MI (city) Kent County	357	0.18
Muskegon, MI (city) Muskegon County	212	0.53
Lansing, MI (city) Ingham County	192	0.16
Petoskey, MI (city) Emmet County	118	1.94
Muskegon, MI (township) Muskegon County	112	0.63
Wyoming, MI (city) Kent County	111	0.16
Norton Shores, MI (city) Muskegon County	93	0.41
Detroit, MI (city) Wayne County	83	0.01
Dalton, MI (township) Muskegon County	78	0.97
Miami, OK (city) Ottawa County	78	0.57
Egelston, MI (township) Muskegon County	71	0.74
Milwaukee, WI (city) Milwaukee County	69	0.01
Harbor Springs, MI (city) Emmet County	68	4.34
Manistee, MI (city) Manistee County	66	1.00
Bear Creek, MI (township) Emmet County	64	1.21
Littlefield, MI (township) Emmet County	61	2.19
Fruitport charter, MI (township) Muskegon County	57	0.45
Tulsa, OK (city) Tulsa County	56	0.01
Flint, MI (city) Genesee County	55	0.04
Ludington, MI (city) Mason County	47	0.56
Resort, MI (township) Emmet County	42	1.69
Kentwood, MI (city) Kent County	42	0.09
Manistee, MI (township) Manistee County	41	1.09
Chicago, IL (city) Cook County	40	0.00
Chippewa, MI (township) Isabella County	38	0.82
Mount Pleasant, MI (city) Isabella County	38	0.15
Battle Creek, MI (city) Calhoun County	37	0.07
McKinley, MI (township) Emmet County	35	2.76
Charlevoix, MI (city) Charlevoix County	35	1.17
Kalamazoo, MI (city) Kalamazoo County	35	0.05
Laketon, MI (township) Muskegon County	34	0.46
Alpine, MI (township) Kent County	34	0.24
Walker, MI (city) Kent County	34	0.16
Suttons Bay, MI (township) Leelanau County	33	1.11
Quapaw, OK (town) Ottawa County	32	3.25
Wolf Lake, MI (cdp) Muskegon County	32	0.72
Warren, MI (city) Macomb County	32	0.02
Los Angeles, CA (city) Los Angeles County	32	0.00
Cheboygan, MI (city) Cheboygan County	28	0.53
Kinross charter, MI (township) Chippewa County	28	0.47
Escanaba, MI (city) Delta County	28	0.21
Sault Sainte Marie, MI (city) Chippewa County	28	0.17
Little Traverse, MI (township) Emmet County	27	1.11
San Diego, CA (city) San Diego County	27	0.00
Pellston, MI (village) Emmet County	26	3.37
Springvale, MI (township) Emmet County	26	1.51
Comstock Park, MI (cdp) Kent County	24	0.22
Holland, MI (city) Ottawa County	24	0.07
Georgetown, MI (township) Ottawa County	24	0.06
Alanson, MI (village) Emmet County	23	2.93
Garfield, MI (township) Grand Traverse County	23	0.17
Meridian charter, MI (township) Ingham County	23	0.06
Ann Arbor, MI (city) Washtenaw County	23	0.02
Friendship, MI (township) Emmet County	22	2.61
Ferry, MI (township) Oceana County	22	1.70
De Witt, MI (township) Clinton County	22	0.18
Muskegon Heights, MI (city) Muskegon County	22	0.18
East Jordan, MI (city) Charlevoix County	21	0.84
Pittsfield charter, MI (township) Washtenaw County	21	0.07
Plainfield, MI (township) Kent County	21	0.07
Holton, MI (township) Muskegon County	20	0.79
Tuscarora, MI (township) Cheboygan County	20	0.65
McMillan, MI (township) Luce County	20	0.51
Toledo, OH (city) Lucas County	20	0.01
Phoenix, AZ (city) Maricopa County	20	0.00
Portland, OR (city) Multnomah County	20	0.00
Twin Lake, MI (cdp) Muskegon County	19	1.18
Pierson, MI (township) Montcalm County	19	0.66
Geneva, MI (township) Van Buren County	19	0.48
Shelby, MI (township) Oceana County	19	0.48
Mancelona, MI (township) Antrim County	19	0.46
Racine, WI (city) Racine County	19	0.02
Readmond, MI (township) Emmet County	18	3.65
Maple River, MI (township) Emmet County	18	1.46
Pentland, MI (township) Luce County	18	1.01
East Bay, MI (township) Grand Traverse County	18	0.18
Grand Haven, MI (city) Ottawa County	18	0.16
Holland, MI (township) Ottawa County	18	0.06
Pontiac, MI (city) Oakland County	18	0.03
Green Bay, WI (city) Brown County	18	0.02
Lancaster, CA (city) Los Angeles County	18	0.02
Albuquerque, NM (city) Bernalillo County	18	0.00
Lakewood Club, MI (village) Muskegon County	17	1.69
Shelby, MI (village) Oceana County	17	0.89
Paradise, MI (township) Grand Traverse County	17	0.41
South Haven, MI (city) Van Buren County	17	0.34
Harper Woods, MI (city) Wayne County	17	0.12
Jenison, MI (cdp) Ottawa County	17	0.10
Delhi charter, MI (township) Ingham County	17	0.08
West Bend, WI (city) Washington County	17	0.06
Portage, MI (city) Kalamazoo County	17	0.04
Shelby, MI (cdp) Macomb County	17	0.03
West Allis, WI (city) Milwaukee County	17	0.03
Springfield, MO (city) Greene County	17	0.01
Marion, MI (township) Charlevoix County	16	1.07
Fruitland, MI (township) Muskegon County	16	0.31
Windsor charter, MI (township) Eaton County	16	0.22
Traverse City, MI (city) Grand Traverse County	16	0.11
Gaines, MI (township) Kent County	16	0.08
Genesee, MI (township) Genesee County	16	0.07
Dearborn Heights, MI (city) Wayne County	16	0.03
Taylor, MI (city) Wayne County	16	0.02
Cleveland, OH (city) Cuyahoga County	16	0.00
Wichita, KS (city) Sedgwick County	16	0.00
Cross Village, MI (township) Emmet County	15	5.10
Blue Lake, MI (township) Muskegon County	15	0.75
Wilson, MI (township) Charlevoix County	15	0.74
Boyne City, MI (city) Charlevoix County	15	0.43
Kalkaska, MI (township) Kalkaska County	15	0.31
Bath, MI (township) Clinton County	15	0.20
Long Lake, MI (township) Grand Traverse County	15	0.20
Bay City, MI (city) Bay County	15	0.04
East Lansing, MI (city) Ingham County	15	0.03
Roseville, MI (city) Macomb County	15	0.03
Westland, MI (city) Wayne County	15	0.02
Houston, TX (city) Harris County	15	0.00
Sherman, MI (township) Mason County	14	1.28
West Traverse, MI (township) Emmet County	14	0.97
Newberry, MI (village) Luce County	14	0.52
Benzonia, MI (township) Benzie County	14	0.49
Grant, MI (township) Oceana County	14	0.48
Courtland, MI (township) Kent County	14	0.24
Northview, MI (cdp) Kent County	14	0.10
Byron, MI (township) Kent County	14	0.08
Hazel Park, MI (city) Oakland County	14	0.07
Okemos, MI (cdp) Ingham County	14	0.06
Delta charter, MI (township) Eaton County	14	0.05
Port Huron, MI (city) Saint Clair County	14	0.04
Joplin, MO (city) Jasper County	14	0.03
Seattle, WA (city) King County	14	0.00
Stronach, MI (township) Manistee County	13	1.62
Forest, MI (township) Cheboygan County	13	1.20
Montague, MI (township) Muskegon County	13	0.79
Hayes, MI (township) Charlevoix County	13	0.69
Bridgeton, MI (township) Newaygo County	13	0.62
Filer charter, MI (township) Manistee County	13	0.59
Newfield, MI (township) Oceana County	13	0.52
Gaylord, MI (city) Otsego County	13	0.35
Addison, MI (township) Oakland County	13	0.20
Lansing charter, MI (township) Ingham County	13	0.15
Sparta, MI (township) Kent County	13	0.15
Ferndale, MI (city) Oakland County	13	0.06
Kalamazoo, MI (township) Kalamazoo County	13	0.06
Spanaway, WA (cdp) Pierce County	13	0.06
Burton, MI (city) Genesee County	13	0.04
Garden City, MI (city) Wayne County	13	0.04
Broken Arrow, OK (city) Tulsa County	13	0.02
Saint Clair Shores, MI (city) Macomb County	13	0.02
Waterford, MI (cdp) Oakland County	13	0.02
Sterling Heights, MI (city) Macomb County	13	0.01

Notes: (cdp) census designated place; Refer to the Explanation of Data in the front of the book for more detailed information.

American Indian: Ottawa

Top 150 Places Sorted by Percent

(Based on all places, regardless of population)

Place	Number	%
Dotyville, OK (cdp) Ottawa County	3	17.65
Haynes, ND (city) Adams County	2	10.53
Cross Village, MI (township) Emmet County	15	5.10
Harbor Springs, MI (city) Emmet County	68	4.34
Readmond, MI (township) Emmet County	18	3.65
Lumber City, PA (borough) Clearfield County	3	3.49
Pellston, MI (village) Emmet County	26	3.37
Quapaw, OK (town) Ottawa County	32	3.25
Alanson, MI (village) Emmet County	23	2.93
McKinley, MI (township) Emmet County	35	2.76
Friendship, MI (township) Emmet County	22	2.61
Hulbert, MI (township) Chippewa County	5	2.37
Littlefield, MI (township) Emmet County	61	2.19
Garden, MI (village) Delta County	5	2.08
Luther, MI (village) Lake County	7	2.06
Eastlake, MI (village) Manistee County	9	2.04
Petoskey, MI (city) Emmet County	118	1.94
Ferry, MI (township) Oceana County	22	1.70
Resort, MI (township) Emmet County	42	1.69
Lakewood Club, MI (village) Muskegon County	17	1.69
Burt, MI (township) Cheboygan County	11	1.68
Stronach, MI (township) Manistee County	13	1.62
Bay de Noc, MI (township) Delta County	5	1.52
Springvale, MI (township) Emmet County	26	1.51
Maple River, MI (township) Emmet County	18	1.46
Bliss, MI (township) Emmet County	8	1.40
Newkirk, MI (township) Lake County	10	1.39
Cherry Valley, MI (township) Lake County	5	1.36
Cardin, OK (town) Ottawa County	2	1.33
Sherman, MI (township) Mason County	14	1.28
Round Lake, MN (township) Becker County	2	1.27
Jordan, MI (township) Antrim County	11	1.26
Evaro, MT (cdp) Missoula County	4	1.22
Bear Creek, MI (township) Emmet County	64	1.21
Forest, MI (township) Cheboygan County	13	1.20
Center, MI (township) Emmet County	6	1.20
Vanderbilt, MI (village) Otsego County	7	1.19
Twin Lake, MI (cdp) Muskegon County	19	1.18
Charlevoix, MI (city) Charlevoix County	35	1.17
Free Soil, MI (village) Mason County	2	1.13
Le Roy, MI (village) Osceola County	4	1.12
Suttons Bay, MI (township) Leelanau County	33	1.11
Little Traverse, MI (township) Emmet County	27	1.11
Hudson, MI (township) Charlevoix County	7	1.10
Manistee, MI (township) Manistee County	41	1.09
Marion, MI (township) Charlevoix County	16	1.07
Colfax, MI (township) Benzie County	6	1.03
Warner, MI (township) Antrim County	4	1.03
Pentland, MI (township) Luce County	18	1.01
Manistee, MI (city) Manistee County	66	1.00
Kaleva, MI (village) Manistee County	5	0.98
Tipler, WI (town) Florence County	2	0.98
Dalton, MI (township) Muskegon County	78	0.97
West Traverse, MI (township) Emmet County	14	0.97
Crystal, MI (township) Oceana County	8	0.96
Scottville, MI (city) Mason County	12	0.95
Pleasantview, MI (township) Emmet County	9	0.95
Hesperia, MI (village) Oceana County	9	0.94
Fairbanks, MI (township) Delta County	3	0.93
North Miami, OK (town) Ottawa County	4	0.92
Paris, MI (township) Huron County	5	0.90
Shelby, MI (village) Oceana County	17	0.89
Platte, MI (township) Benzie County	3	0.88
Miles, IA (city) Jackson County	4	0.87
Copemish, MI (village) Manistee County	2	0.86
East Jordan, MI (city) Charlevoix County	21	0.84
Custer, MI (township) Mason County	11	0.84
Victory, MI (township) Mason County	12	0.83
Chippewa, MI (township) Isabella County	38	0.82
Holton, MI (township) Muskegon County	20	0.79
Montague, MI (township) Muskegon County	13	0.79
Walkerville, MI (village) Oceana County	2	0.79
Blue Lake, MI (township) Muskegon County	15	0.75
Cascade, WI (village) Sheboygan County	5	0.75
Egelston, MI (township) Muskegon County	71	0.74
Wilson, MI (township) Charlevoix County	15	0.74
Carp Lake, MI (township) Emmet County	6	0.74
Garden, MI (township) Delta County	6	0.73
Wolf Lake, MI (cdp) Muskegon County	32	0.72
Eden, MI (township) Mason County	4	0.72
Leavitt, MI (township) Oceana County	6	0.71
Farwell, MI (village) Clare County	6	0.70
Brown, MI (township) Manistee County	5	0.70
Norwood, MI (township) Charlevoix County	5	0.70
Colfax, MI (township) Oceana County	4	0.70
Hayes, MI (township) Charlevoix County	13	0.69
Wellington, MI (township) Alpena County	2	0.68
Sandborn, IN (town) Knox County	3	0.67
Honor, MI (village) Benzie County	2	0.67
Pierson, MI (township) Montcalm County	19	0.66
Thompsonville, MI (village) Benzie County	3	0.66
Tuscarora, MI (township) Cheboygan County	20	0.65
South Arm, MI (township) Charlevoix County	12	0.65
Saint James, MI (township) Charlevoix County	2	0.65
Garfield, MI (township) Mackinac County	8	0.64
Muskegon, MI (township) Muskegon County	112	0.63
Harris, MI (township) Menominee County	12	0.63
Laird, MI (township) Houghton County	4	0.63
Custer, MI (village) Mason County	2	0.63
Bridgeton, MI (township) Newaygo County	13	0.62
Onekama, MI (village) Manistee County	4	0.62
Marion, MI (village) Osceola County	5	0.60
Filer charter, MI (township) Manistee County	13	0.59
Melrose, MI (township) Charlevoix County	8	0.58
Mackinaw City, MI (village) Emmet County	5	0.58
Miami, OK (city) Ottawa County	78	0.57
Mancelona, MI (village) Antrim County	8	0.57
Weldon, MI (township) Benzie County	3	0.57
Ludington, MI (city) Mason County	47	0.56
Hart, MI (city) Oceana County	11	0.56
Newton, MI (township) Mackinac County	2	0.56
Deerfield, MI (township) Mecosta County	9	0.55
Buckley, MI (village) Wexford County	3	0.55
Baraga, MI (village) Baraga County	7	0.54
Maple Grove, MI (township) Manistee County	7	0.54
Dewar, OK (town) Okmulgee County	5	0.54
Dickson, MI (township) Manistee County	5	0.54
Limestone, OK (cdp) Rogers County	4	0.54
Muskegon, MI (city) Muskegon County	212	0.53
Cheboygan, MI (city) Cheboygan County	28	0.53
Mathias, MI (township) Alger County	3	0.53
Newberry, MI (village) Luce County	14	0.52
Newfield, MI (township) Oceana County	13	0.52
Mackinaw, MI (township) Cheboygan County	3	0.52
McMillan, MI (township) Luce County	20	0.51
Denver, MI (township) Newaygo County	10	0.51
Eveline, MI (township) Charlevoix County	8	0.51
Whitefish, MI (township) Chippewa County	3	0.51
Mountain Park, OK (town) Kiowa County	2	0.51
Montague, MI (city) Muskegon County	12	0.50
Clark, MI (township) Mackinac County	11	0.50
Garden Plain, KS (city) Sedgwick County	4	0.50
Maple Ridge, MI (township) Delta County	4	0.50
Kinston, AL (town) Coffee County	3	0.50
Venetie, AK (cdp) Yukon-Koyukuk Census Area	1	0.50
Benzonia, MI (township) Benzie County	14	0.49
Aetna, MI (township) Mecosta County	10	0.49
Mentor, MI (township) Oscoda County	6	0.49
Summit, MI (township) Mason County	5	0.49
Antioch, MI (township) Wexford County	4	0.49
Gobles, MI (city) Van Buren County	4	0.49
Geneva, MI (township) Van Buren County	19	0.48
Shelby, MI (township) Oceana County	19	0.48
Grant, MI (township) Oceana County	14	0.48
Marenisco, MI (township) Gogebic County	5	0.48
Commonwealth, WI (town) Florence County	2	0.48
Gans, OK (town) Sequoyah County	1	0.48
Kinross charter, MI (township) Chippewa County	28	0.47
Columbus, MI (township) Luce County	1	0.47
Laketon, MI (township) Muskegon County	34	0.46

Notes: (cdp) census designated place; Refer to the Explanation of Data in the front of the book for more detailed information.

American Indian: Ottawa

Top 150 Places Sorted by Percent

(Based on places with populations of 10,000 or more)

Place	Number	%
Muskegon, MI (township) Muskegon County	112	0.63
Miami, OK (city) Ottawa County	78	0.57
Muskegon, MI (city) Muskegon County	212	0.53
Fruitport charter, MI (township) Muskegon County	57	0.45
Norton Shores, MI (city) Muskegon County	93	0.41
Alpine, MI (township) Kent County	34	0.24
Comstock Park, MI (cdp) Kent County	24	0.22
Escanaba, MI (city) Delta County	28	0.21
Grand Rapids, MI (city) Kent County	357	0.18
De Witt, MI (township) Clinton County	22	0.18
Muskegon Heights, MI (city) Muskegon County	22	0.18
Sault Sainte Marie, MI (city) Chippewa County	28	0.17
Garfield, MI (township) Grand Traverse County	23	0.17
Lansing, MI (city) Ingham County	192	0.16
Wyoming, MI (city) Kent County	111	0.16
Walker, MI (city) Kent County	34	0.16
Grand Haven, MI (city) Ottawa County	18	0.16
Mount Pleasant, MI (city) Isabella County	38	0.15
Harper Woods, MI (city) Wayne County	17	0.12
Traverse City, MI (city) Grand Traverse County	16	0.11
Jenison, MI (cdp) Ottawa County	17	0.10
Northview, MI (cdp) Kent County	14	0.10
Kentwood, MI (city) Kent County	42	0.09
Grand Haven, MI (township) Ottawa County	12	0.09
Fort Atkinson, WI (city) Jefferson County	11	0.09
Cadillac, MI (city) Wexford County	9	0.09
Ionia, MI (city) Ionia County	9	0.09
Delhi charter, MI (township) Ingham County	17	0.08
Gaines, MI (township) Kent County	16	0.08
Byron, MI (township) Kent County	14	0.08
Spring Lake, MI (township) Ottawa County	11	0.08
Cannon, MI (township) Kent County	10	0.08
Holt, MI (cdp) Ingham County	9	0.08
Battle Creek, MI (city) Calhoun County	37	0.07
Holland, MI (city) Ottawa County	24	0.07
Pittsfield charter, MI (township) Washtenaw County	21	0.07
Plainfield, MI (township) Kent County	21	0.07
Genesee, MI (township) Genesee County	16	0.07
Hazel Park, MI (city) Oakland County	14	0.07
Cutlerville, MI (cdp) Kent County	10	0.07
Neosho, MO (city) Newton County	7	0.07
Georgetown, MI (township) Ottawa County	24	0.06
Meridian charter, MI (township) Ingham County	23	0.06
Holland, MI (township) Ottawa County	18	0.06
West Bend, WI (city) Washington County	17	0.06
Okemos, MI (cdp) Ingham County	14	0.06
Ferndale, MI (city) Oakland County	13	0.06
Kalamazoo, MI (township) Kalamazoo County	13	0.06
Spanaway, WA (cdp) Pierce County	13	0.06
Highland, MI (township) Oakland County	11	0.06
Marquette, MI (city) Marquette County	11	0.06
Bangor, MI (township) Bay County	10	0.06
Berkley, MI (city) Oakland County	10	0.06
Desert Hot Springs, CA (city) Riverside County	10	0.06
Grandville, MI (city) Kent County	9	0.06
Green Oak, MI (township) Livingston County	9	0.06
Waverly, MI (cdp) Eaton County	9	0.06
Allendale, MI (township) Ottawa County	8	0.06
Big Rapids, MI (city) Mecosta County	6	0.06
Superior, MI (township) Washtenaw County	6	0.06
Kalamazoo, MI (city) Kalamazoo County	35	0.05
Delta charter, MI (township) Eaton County	14	0.05
Beaver Dam, WI (city) Dodge County	8	0.05
Owosso, MI (city) Shiawassee County	8	0.05
Grand Rapids charter, MI (township) Kent County	7	0.05
Clearlake, CA (city) Lake County	6	0.05
Flushing, MI (township) Genesee County	5	0.05
Lake Saint Louis, MO (city) Saint Charles County	5	0.05
Rio Linda, CA (cdp) Sacramento County	5	0.05
Flint, MI (city) Genesee County	55	0.04
Portage, MI (city) Kalamazoo County	17	0.04
Bay City, MI (city) Bay County	15	0.04
Port Huron, MI (city) Saint Clair County	14	0.04
Burton, MI (city) Genesee County	13	0.04
Garden City, MI (city) Wayne County	13	0.04

Place	Number	%
Van Buren, MI (township) Wayne County	10	0.04
Forest Hills, MI (cdp) Kent County	8	0.04
Hamburg, MI (township) Livingston County	8	0.04
Oshtemo, MI (township) Kalamazoo County	7	0.04
Wayne, MI (city) Wayne County	7	0.04
Cascade, MI (township) Kent County	6	0.04
Hereford, TX (city) Deaf Smith County	6	0.04
Oxford charter, MI (township) Oakland County	6	0.04
Scio, MI (township) Washtenaw County	6	0.04
Clawson, MI (city) Oakland County	5	0.04
Coldwater, MI (city) Branch County	5	0.04
Fort Drum, NY (cdp) Jefferson County	5	0.04
Monroe charter, MI (township) Monroe County	5	0.04
Whitewater, WI (city) Walworth County	5	0.04
Alpena, MI (city) Alpena County	4	0.04
Clute, TX (city) Brazoria County	4	0.04
Fortuna, CA (city) Humboldt County	4	0.04
Garden City, ID (city) Ada County	4	0.04
Pontiac, MI (city) Oakland County	18	0.03
Shelby, MI (cdp) Macomb County	17	0.03
West Allis, WI (city) Milwaukee County	17	0.03
Dearborn Heights, MI (city) Wayne County	16	0.03
East Lansing, MI (city) Ingham County	15	0.03
Roseville, MI (city) Macomb County	15	0.03
Joplin, MO (city) Jasper County	14	0.03
Midland, MI (city) Midland County	12	0.03
Flint, MI (township) Genesee County	11	0.03
Independence, MI (township) Oakland County	9	0.03
Brownstown, MI (township) Wayne County	8	0.03
White Bear Lake, MN (city) Ramsey County	8	0.03
Wyandotte, MI (city) Wayne County	8	0.03
Adrian, MI (city) Lenawee County	7	0.03
Angleton, TX (city) Brazoria County	6	0.03
Mount Morris, MI (township) Genesee County	6	0.03
Sylvania, OH (city) Lucas County	6	0.03
Ypsilanti, MI (city) Washtenaw County	6	0.03
Bloomington, CA (cdp) San Bernardino County	5	0.03
Claremore, OK (city) Rogers County	5	0.03
Le Ray, NY (town) Jefferson County	5	0.03
Punta Gorda, FL (city) Charlotte County	5	0.03
Ukiah, CA (city) Mendocino County	5	0.03
Comstock, MI (township) Kalamazoo County	4	0.03
Emmett, MI (township) Calhoun County	4	0.03
Fenton, MI (township) Genesee County	4	0.03
Genoa, MI (township) Livingston County	4	0.03
Haddon, NJ (township) Camden County	4	0.03
Howard, WI (village) Brown County	4	0.03
Hudson, FL (cdp) Pasco County	4	0.03
Lemont, IL (village) Cook County	4	0.03
Oakland charter, MI (township) Oakland County	4	0.03
Ottawa, KS (city) Franklin County	4	0.03
Riverbank, CA (city) Stanislaus County	4	0.03
Rosamond, CA (cdp) Kern County	4	0.03
Susanville, CA (city) Lassen County	4	0.03
Antwerp, MI (township) Van Buren County	3	0.03
Grafton, WI (village) Ozaukee County	3	0.03
Hewitt, TX (city) McLennan County	3	0.03
Holly, MI (township) Oakland County	3	0.03
Marinette, WI (city) Marinette County	3	0.03
Pewaukee, WI (city) Waukesha County	3	0.03
Texas, MI (township) Kalamazoo County	3	0.03
Warren, MI (city) Macomb County	32	0.02
Ann Arbor, MI (city) Washtenaw County	23	0.02
Racine, WI (city) Racine County	19	0.02
Green Bay, WI (city) Brown County	18	0.02
Lancaster, CA (city) Los Angeles County	18	0.02
Taylor, MI (city) Wayne County	16	0.02
Westland, MI (city) Wayne County	15	0.02
Broken Arrow, OK (city) Tulsa County	13	0.02
Saint Clair Shores, MI (city) Macomb County	13	0.02
Waterford, MI (cdp) Oakland County	13	0.02
Saginaw, MI (city) Saginaw County	12	0.02
Salina, KS (city) Saline County	11	0.02
Blue Springs, MO (city) Jackson County	10	0.02
Royal Oak, MI (city) Oakland County	10	0.02

Notes: (cdp) census designated place; Refer to the Explanation of Data in the front of the book for more detailed information.

American Indian: Paiute

Top 150 Places Sorted by Number

(Based on all places, regardless of population)

Place	Number	%
Schurz, NV (cdp) Mineral County	504	69.90
Wadsworth, NV (cdp) Washoe County	453	51.42
Reno, NV (city) Washoe County	423	0.23
Nixon, NV (cdp) Washoe County	323	77.27
Carson City, NV (special city) Carson City city	239	0.46
Cedar City, UT (city) Iron County	208	1.01
Bakersfield, CA (city) Kern County	201	0.08
Sparks, NV (city) Washoe County	168	0.25
Las Vegas, NV (city) Clark County	153	0.03
Yerington, NV (city) Lyon County	148	5.13
Sutcliffe, NV (cdp) Washoe County	116	41.28
Los Angeles, CA (city) Los Angeles County	104	0.00
Lovelock, NV (city) Pershing County	101	5.04
Susanville, CA (city) Lassen County	101	0.75
San Jose, CA (city) Santa Clara County	100	0.01
Phoenix, AZ (city) Maricopa County	98	0.01
Kaibab, AZ (cdp) Mohave County	91	33.09
Saint George, UT (city) Washington County	90	0.18
Sun Valley, NV (cdp) Washoe County	85	0.44
Fresno, CA (city) Fresno County	81	0.02
Sacramento, CA (city) Sacramento County	75	0.02
Modesto, CA (city) Stanislaus County	73	0.04
Sunrise Manor, NV (cdp) Clark County	69	0.04
Winnemucca, NV (city) Humboldt County	63	0.88
Oildale, CA (cdp) Kern County	59	0.21
San Diego, CA (city) San Diego County	53	0.00
North Las Vegas, NV (city) Clark County	49	0.04
Salt Lake City, UT (city) Salt Lake County	49	0.03
Portland, OR (city) Multnomah County	48	0.01
Fernley, NV (cdp) Lyon County	47	0.55
Oakland, CA (city) Alameda County	47	0.01
Bishop, CA (city) Inyo County	42	1.17
Enoch, UT (city) Iron County	40	1.15
Tuba City, AZ (cdp) Coconino County	39	0.47
Hayward, CA (city) Alameda County	38	0.03
Henderson, NV (city) Clark County	38	0.02
McDermitt, NV (cdp) Humboldt County	37	13.75
Fallon, NV (city) Churchill County	37	0.49
Klamath Falls, OR (city) Klamath County	35	0.18
Richfield, UT (city) Sevier County	34	0.50
Hawthorne, NV (cdp) Mineral County	31	0.94
Spanish Springs, NV (cdp) Washoe County	31	0.34
Riverside, CA (city) Riverside County	31	0.01
Ridgecrest, CA (city) Kern County	30	0.12
Anchorage, AK (municipality) Anchorage Borough	30	0.01
Long Beach, CA (city) Los Angeles County	30	0.01
Gardnerville Ranchos, NV (cdp) Douglas County	29	0.26
Eugene, OR (city) Lane County	29	0.02
Altamont, OR (cdp) Klamath County	28	0.14
North Highlands, CA (cdp) Sacramento County	28	0.06
Tracy, CA (city) San Joaquin County	28	0.05
San Francisco, CA (city) San Francisco County	28	0.00
Big Pine, CA (cdp) Inyo County	27	2.00
Antioch, CA (city) Contra Costa County	27	0.03
Lemmon Valley-Golden Valley, NV (cdp) Washoe County	26	0.38
Paradise, NV (cdp) Clark County	25	0.01
Redding, CA (city) Shasta County	24	0.03
Seattle, WA (city) King County	24	0.00
Weldon, CA (cdp) Kern County	23	0.96
Elko, NV (city) Elko County	23	0.14
Lawrence, KS (city) Douglas County	23	0.03
San Antonio, TX (city) Bexar County	22	0.00
Warm Springs, OR (cdp) Jefferson County	21	0.86
Manteca, CA (city) San Joaquin County	21	0.04
Spring Valley, NV (cdp) Clark County	21	0.02
Visalia, CA (city) Tulare County	21	0.02
Mesa, AZ (city) Maricopa County	21	0.01
Caliente, NV (city) Lincoln County	20	1.78
Burns, OR (city) Harney County	20	0.65
Nampa, ID (city) Canyon County	20	0.04
Ivins, UT (town) Washington County	19	0.43
Washington, UT (city) Washington County	19	0.23
Citrus Heights, CA (city) Sacramento County	19	0.02
Boise City, ID (city) Ada County	19	0.01
Huntington Beach, CA (city) Orange County	19	0.01
Denver, CO (city) Denver County	19	0.00
Dixon Lane-Meadow Creek, CA (cdp) Inyo County	18	0.67
Vacaville, CA (city) Solano County	18	0.02
Glendale, AZ (city) Maricopa County	18	0.01
Stockton, CA (city) San Joaquin County	18	0.01
Albuquerque, NM (city) Bernalillo County	18	0.00
Owyhee, NV (cdp) Elko County	17	1.67
Tehachapi, CA (city) Kern County	17	0.16
Pahrump, NV (cdp) Nye County	17	0.07
Merced, CA (city) Merced County	17	0.03
Roseville, CA (city) Placer County	17	0.02
Tucson, AZ (city) Pima County	17	0.00
Alameda, CA (city) Alameda County	16	0.02
Arden-Arcade, CA (cdp) Sacramento County	16	0.02
Lancaster, CA (city) Los Angeles County	16	0.01
West Bishop, CA (cdp) Inyo County	15	0.53
East Cleveland, OH (city) Cuyahoga County	15	0.06
Elk Grove, CA (cdp) Sacramento County	15	0.03
West Valley City, UT (city) Salt Lake County	15	0.01
Roosevelt, UT (city) Duchesne County	14	0.33
Fairfield, CA (city) Solano County	14	0.01
Garden Grove, CA (city) Orange County	14	0.01
Palmdale, CA (city) Los Angeles County	14	0.01
Richmond, CA (city) Contra Costa County	14	0.01
Santa Rosa, CA (city) Sonoma County	14	0.01
Tacoma, WA (city) Pierce County	14	0.01
Inyokern, CA (cdp) Kern County	13	1.32
Alturas, CA (city) Modoc County	13	0.45
Shasta Lake, CA (city) Shasta County	13	0.14
Chico, CA (city) Butte County	13	0.02
Norwalk, CA (city) Los Angeles County	13	0.01
Rancho Cucamonga, CA (city) San Bernardino County	13	0.01
Tempe, AZ (city) Maricopa County	13	0.01
Polson, MT (city) Lake County	12	0.30
Riverbank, CA (city) Stanislaus County	12	0.08
Rancho Cordova, CA (cdp) Sacramento County	12	0.02
Smith Valley, NV (cdp) Lyon County	11	0.77
Lake Isabella, CA (cdp) Kern County	11	0.33
Mesquite, NV (city) Clark County	11	0.12
Gallup, NM (city) McKinley County	11	0.05
Caldwell, ID (city) Canyon County	11	0.04
Lake Havasu City, AZ (city) Mohave County	11	0.03
Tulare, CA (city) Tulare County	11	0.03
Hesperia, CA (city) San Bernardino County	11	0.02
Chandler, AZ (city) Maricopa County	11	0.01
Concord, CA (city) Contra Costa County	11	0.01
Des Moines, IA (city) Polk County	11	0.01
Fargo, ND (city) Cass County	11	0.01
Provo, UT (city) Utah County	11	0.01
Salem, OR (city) Marion County	11	0.01
San Leandro, CA (city) Alameda County	11	0.01
Simi Valley, CA (city) Ventura County	11	0.01
Thousand Oaks, CA (city) Ventura County	11	0.01
Vancouver, WA (city) Clark County	11	0.01
Austin, TX (city) Travis County	11	0.00
Colorado Springs, CO (city) El Paso County	11	0.00
New York, NY (city) New York City	11	0.00
Navajo Mountain, UT (cdp) San Juan County	10	2.64
Fillmore, UT (city) Millard County	10	0.44
Indian Hills, NV (cdp) Douglas County	10	0.23
South Oroville, CA (cdp) Butte County	10	0.13
Lathrop, CA (city) San Joaquin County	10	0.10
Rosamond, CA (cdp) Kern County	10	0.07
Foothill Farms, CA (cdp) Sacramento County	10	0.06
Tooele, UT (city) Tooele County	10	0.04
Murrieta, CA (city) Riverside County	10	0.02
Moreno Valley, CA (city) Riverside County	10	0.01
Saint Joseph, MO (city) Buchanan County	10	0.01
Salinas, CA (city) Monterey County	10	0.01
San Buenaventura, CA (city) Ventura County	10	0.01
Chicago, IL (city) Cook County	10	0.00
Chester, CA (cdp) Plumas County	9	0.39
Wanamassa, NJ (cdp) Monmouth County	9	0.20
Madras, OR (city) Jefferson County	9	0.18
Dayton, NV (cdp) Lyon County	9	0.15

Notes: (cdp) census designated place; Refer to the Explanation of Data in the front of the book for more detailed information.

American Indian: Paiute

Top 150 Places Sorted by Percent

(Based on all places, regardless of population)

Place	Number	%
Nixon, NV (cdp) Washoe County	323	77.27
Schurz, NV (cdp) Mineral County	504	69.90
Wadsworth, NV (cdp) Washoe County	453	51.42
Sutcliffe, NV (cdp) Washoe County	116	41.28
Kaibab, AZ (cdp) Mohave County	91	33.09
McDermitt, NV (cdp) Humboldt County	37	13.75
Shoshone, CA (cdp) Inyo County	3	5.77
Nore, MN (township) Itasca County	3	5.45
Huetter, ID (city) Kootenai County	5	5.21
Yerington, NV (city) Lyon County	148	5.13
Lovelock, NV (city) Pershing County	101	5.04
Navajo Mountain, UT (cdp) San Juan County	10	2.64
Big Pine, CA (cdp) Inyo County	27	2.00
Gabbs, NV (city) Nye County	6	1.89
Caliente, NV (city) Lincoln County	20	1.78
Kevin, MT (town) Toole County	3	1.69
Owyhee, NV (cdp) Elko County	17	1.67
Alpine Village, CA (cdp) Alpine County	2	1.47
White Mesa, UT (cdp) San Juan County	4	1.44
Mesa, CA (cdp) Inyo County	3	1.40
Inyokern, CA (cdp) Kern County	13	1.32
Bishop, CA (city) Inyo County	42	1.17
Enoch, UT (city) Iron County	40	1.15
Round Valley, CA (cdp) Inyo County	3	1.08
Independence, CA (cdp) Inyo County	6	1.05
Cedar City, UT (city) Iron County	208	1.01
Weldon, CA (cdp) Kern County	23	0.96
Hawthorne, NV (cdp) Mineral County	31	0.94
Winnemucca, NV (city) Humboldt County	63	0.88
Warm Springs, OR (cdp) Jefferson County	21	0.86
Kanosh, UT (town) Millard County	4	0.82
Meadow, UT (town) Millard County	2	0.79
Smith Valley, NV (cdp) Lyon County	11	0.77
Susanville, CA (city) Lassen County	101	0.75
Alton, UT (town) Kane County	1	0.75
Thorp, WA (cdp) Kittitas County	2	0.73
Donnelly, ID (city) Valley County	1	0.72
Elsie, NE (village) Perkins County	1	0.72
Tonalea, AZ (cdp) Coconino County	4	0.71
Dixon Lane-Meadow Creek, CA (cdp) Inyo County	18	0.67
Burns, OR (city) Harney County	20	0.65
Bluff, UT (cdp) San Juan County	2	0.63
Yakutat, AK (cdp) Yakutat City and Borough	4	0.59
Fernley, NV (cdp) Lyon County	47	0.55
Mesa Vista, CA (cdp) Alpine County	1	0.55
West Bishop, CA (cdp) Inyo County	15	0.53
Lake Shore, UT (cdp) Utah County	4	0.53
Derby Acres, CA (cdp) Kern County	2	0.53
Richfield, UT (city) Sevier County	34	0.50
Fallon, NV (city) Churchill County	37	0.49
Tuba City, AZ (cdp) Coconino County	39	0.47
Malin, OR (city) Klamath County	3	0.47
Carson City, NV (special city) Carson City city	239	0.46
Kernville, CA (cdp) Kern County	8	0.46
Towaoc, CO (cdp) Montezuma County	5	0.46
Alturas, CA (city) Modoc County	13	0.45
Canyon City, OR (town) Grant County	3	0.45
Ignacio, CO (town) La Plata County	3	0.45
Sun Valley, NV (cdp) Washoe County	85	0.44
Fillmore, UT (city) Millard County	10	0.44
Little Elbow, MN (township) Mahnomen County	1	0.44
Tupman, CA (cdp) Kern County	1	0.44
Ivins, UT (town) Washington County	19	0.43
Moapa Town, NV (cdp) Clark County	4	0.43
Chiloquin, OR (city) Klamath County	3	0.42
Hollister, ID (city) Twin Falls County	1	0.42
Santa Clara Pueblo, NM (cdp) Rio Arriba County	4	0.41
Gerlach-Empire, NV (cdp) Washoe County	2	0.40
Chester, CA (cdp) Plumas County	9	0.39
Lincoln Park, TX (town) Denton County	2	0.39
Crescent Mills, CA (cdp) Plumas County	1	0.39
Lemmon Valley-Golden Valley, NV (cdp) Washoe County	26	0.38
Redmond, UT (town) Sevier County	3	0.38
Hot Sulphur Springs, CO (town) Grand County	2	0.38
Yosemite Valley, CA (cdp) Mariposa County	1	0.38
Hutchins, WI (town) Shawano County	2	0.37
Lone Pine, CA (cdp) Inyo County	6	0.36
Westwood, CA (cdp) Lassen County	7	0.35
Spanish Springs, NV (cdp) Washoe County	31	0.34
Covelo, CA (cdp) Mendocino County	4	0.34
San Juan, NM (cdp) Rio Arriba County	2	0.34
Nespelem Community, WA (cdp) Okanogan County	1	0.34
Roosevelt, UT (city) Duchesne County	14	0.33
Lake Isabella, CA (cdp) Kern County	11	0.33
Kettleman City, CA (cdp) Kings County	5	0.33
Fox, AK (cdp) Fairbanks North Star Borough	1	0.33
Greensburg, KS (city) Kiowa County	5	0.32
Buttonwillow, CA (cdp) Kern County	4	0.32
Loghill Village, CO (cdp) Ouray County	1	0.32
Bootjack, CA (cdp) Mariposa County	5	0.31
Shell Lake, WI (city) Washburn County	4	0.31
Polson, MT (city) Lake County	12	0.30
Hume, MO (town) Bates County	1	0.30
Jerome, AZ (town) Yavapai County	1	0.30
Seama, NM (cdp) Cibola County	1	0.30
Mariposa, CA (cdp) Mariposa County	4	0.29
Fredonia, AZ (town) Coconino County	3	0.29
Mission, OR (cdp) Umatilla County	3	0.29
Tulelake, CA (city) Siskiyou County	3	0.29
Keene, CA (cdp) Kern County	1	0.29
Whiterocks, UT (cdp) Uintah County	1	0.29
Lakeview, OR (town) Lake County	7	0.28
Arizona Village, AZ (cdp) Mohave County	1	0.28
Konawa, OK (city) Seminole County	4	0.27
Satus, WA (cdp) Yakima County	2	0.27
West Point, CA (cdp) Calaveras County	2	0.27
Manton, CA (cdp) Tehama County	1	0.27
McArthur, CA (cdp) Shasta County	1	0.27
Gardnerville Ranchos, NV (cdp) Douglas County	29	0.26
Beatty, NV (cdp) Nye County	3	0.26
Ringling, OK (town) Jefferson County	3	0.26
Boulder Flats, WY (cdp) Fremont County	1	0.26
Chilcoot-Vinton, CA (cdp) Plumas County	1	0.26
Culdesac, ID (city) Nez Perce County	1	0.26
Sparks, NV (city) Washoe County	168	0.25
South New Castle, PA (borough) Lawrence County	2	0.25
Reno, NV (city) Washoe County	423	0.23
Washington, UT (city) Washington County	19	0.23
Indian Hills, NV (cdp) Douglas County	10	0.23
White Swan, WA (cdp) Yakima County	7	0.23
Harbison Canyon, CA (cdp) San Diego County	8	0.22
Tutuilla, OR (cdp) Umatilla County	1	0.22
Oildale, CA (cdp) Kern County	59	0.21
Macy, NE (cdp) Thurston County	2	0.21
North Stanwood, WA (cdp) Snohomish County	1	0.21
Onyx, CA (cdp) Kern County	1	0.21
Pembina, MN (township) Mahnomen County	1	0.21
Wanamassa, NJ (cdp) Monmouth County	9	0.20
Boron, CA (cdp) Kern County	4	0.20
Everson, WA (city) Whatcom County	4	0.20
Riddle, OR (city) Douglas County	2	0.20
Marion, PA (township) Berks County	3	0.19
Tohatchi, NM (cdp) McKinley County	2	0.19
Saint George, UT (city) Washington County	90	0.18
Klamath Falls, OR (city) Klamath County	35	0.18
Madras, OR (city) Jefferson County	9	0.18
Cold Springs, NV (cdp) Washoe County	7	0.18
Bertsch-Oceanview, CA (cdp) Del Norte County	4	0.18
Cabazon, CA (cdp) Riverside County	4	0.18
Stonycreek, PA (township) Somerset County	4	0.18
Three Rivers, CA (cdp) Tulare County	4	0.18
Hines, OR (city) Harney County	3	0.18
Canyon Day, AZ (cdp) Gila County	2	0.18
Ballard, UT (town) Uintah County	1	0.18
Mandaree, ND (cdp) McKenzie County	1	0.18
Wilkerson, CA (cdp) Inyo County	1	0.18
Santaquin, UT (city) Utah County	8	0.17
Arbuckle, CA (cdp) Colusa County	4	0.17
Graton, CA (cdp) Sonoma County	3	0.17
Silt, CO (town) Garfield County	3	0.17

Notes: (cdp) census designated place; Refer to the Explanation of Data in the front of the book for more detailed information.

American Indian: Paiute

Top 150 Places Sorted by Percent

(Based on places with populations of 10,000 or more)

Place	Number	%
Cedar City, UT (city) Iron County	208	1.01
Susanville, CA (city) Lassen County	101	0.75
Carson City, NV (special city) Carson City city	239	0.46
Sun Valley, NV (cdp) Washoe County	85	0.44
Gardnerville Ranchos, NV (cdp) Douglas County	29	0.26
Sparks, NV (city) Washoe County	168	0.25
Reno, NV (city) Washoe County	423	0.23
Oildale, CA (cdp) Kern County	59	0.21
Saint George, UT (city) Washington County	90	0.18
Klamath Falls, OR (city) Klamath County	35	0.18
Tehachapi, CA (city) Kern County	17	0.16
Altamont, OR (cdp) Klamath County	28	0.14
Elko, NV (city) Elko County	23	0.14
Ridgecrest, CA (city) Kern County	30	0.12
Lathrop, CA (city) San Joaquin County	10	0.10
Spring Creek, NV (cdp) Elko County	9	0.09
Bakersfield, CA (city) Kern County	201	0.08
Riverbank, CA (city) Stanislaus County	12	0.08
Pahrump, NV (cdp) Nye County	17	0.07
Rosamond, CA (cdp) Kern County	10	0.07
Salida, CA (cdp) Stanislaus County	9	0.07
Blythe, CA (city) Riverside County	8	0.07
North Highlands, CA (cdp) Sacramento County	28	0.06
East Cleveland, OH (city) Cuyahoga County	15	0.06
Foothill Farms, CA (cdp) Sacramento County	10	0.06
Durango, CO (city) La Plata County	9	0.06
Truckee, CA (town) Nevada County	8	0.06
Tracy, CA (city) San Joaquin County	28	0.05
Gallup, NM (city) McKinley County	11	0.05
Arcata, CA (city) Humboldt County	9	0.05
Cherryland, CA (cdp) Alameda County	7	0.05
Oroville, CA (city) Butte County	7	0.05
Red Bluff, CA (city) Tehama County	7	0.05
Grass Valley, CA (city) Nevada County	6	0.05
Ontario, OR (city) Malheur County	5	0.05
Modesto, CA (city) Stanislaus County	73	0.04
Sunrise Manor, NV (cdp) Clark County	69	0.04
North Las Vegas, NV (city) Clark County	49	0.04
Manteca, CA (city) San Joaquin County	21	0.04
Nampa, ID (city) Canyon County	20	0.04
Caldwell, ID (city) Canyon County	11	0.04
Tooele, UT (city) Tooele County	10	0.04
South Salt Lake, UT (city) Salt Lake County	9	0.04
Magna, UT (cdp) Salt Lake County	8	0.04
Pendleton, OR (city) Umatilla County	7	0.04
Hawaiian Gardens, CA (city) Los Angeles County	6	0.04
Fillmore, CA (city) Ventura County	5	0.04
Grover Beach, CA (city) San Luis Obispo County	5	0.04
Lake Los Angeles, CA (cdp) Los Angeles County	5	0.04
Lamont, CA (cdp) Kern County	5	0.04
Maple Valley, WA (city) King County	5	0.04
North Auburn, CA (cdp) Placer County	5	0.04
Fortuna, CA (city) Humboldt County	4	0.04
Mountain Home, ID (city) Elmore County	4	0.04
Las Vegas, NV (city) Clark County	153	0.03
Salt Lake City, UT (city) Salt Lake County	49	0.03
Hayward, CA (city) Alameda County	38	0.03
Antioch, CA (city) Contra Costa County	27	0.03
Redding, CA (city) Shasta County	24	0.03
Lawrence, KS (city) Douglas County	23	0.03
Merced, CA (city) Merced County	17	0.03
Elk Grove, CA (cdp) Sacramento County	15	0.03
Lake Havasu City, AZ (city) Mohave County	11	0.03
Tulare, CA (city) Tulare County	11	0.03
Ocean, NJ (township) Monmouth County	9	0.03
Draper, UT (city) Salt Lake County	8	0.03
El Paso de Robles, CA (city) San Luis Obispo County	8	0.03
Florin, CA (cdp) Sacramento County	8	0.03
South Lake Tahoe, CA (city) El Dorado County	8	0.03
Atwater, CA (city) Merced County	7	0.03
Oakley, CA (city) Contra Costa County	7	0.03
Orangevale, CA (cdp) Sacramento County	7	0.03
Barstow, CA (city) San Bernardino County	6	0.03
San Fernando, CA (city) Los Angeles County	6	0.03
San Lorenzo, CA (cdp) Alameda County	6	0.03
Lemoore, CA (city) Kings County	5	0.03
Newberg, OR (city) Yamhill County	5	0.03
Tahlequah, OK (city) Cherokee County	5	0.03
Twentynine Palms, CA (city) San Bernardino County	5	0.03
Cameron Park, CA (cdp) El Dorado County	4	0.03
Canby, OR (city) Clackamas County	4	0.03
City of The Dalles, OR (city) Wasco County	4	0.03
Linda, CA (cdp) Yuba County	4	0.03
Avon, OH (city) Lorain County	3	0.03
Capitola, CA (city) Santa Cruz County	3	0.03
Chowchilla, CA (city) Madera County	3	0.03
Merrydale, LA (cdp) East Baton Rouge Parish	3	0.03
Ripon, CA (city) San Joaquin County	3	0.03
Fresno, CA (city) Fresno County	81	0.02
Sacramento, CA (city) Sacramento County	75	0.02
Henderson, NV (city) Clark County	38	0.02
Eugene, OR (city) Lane County	29	0.02
Spring Valley, NV (cdp) Clark County	21	0.02
Visalia, CA (city) Tulare County	21	0.02
Citrus Heights, CA (city) Sacramento County	19	0.02
Vacaville, CA (city) Solano County	18	0.02
Roseville, CA (city) Placer County	17	0.02
Alameda, CA (city) Alameda County	16	0.02
Arden-Arcade, CA (cdp) Sacramento County	16	0.02
Chico, CA (city) Butte County	13	0.02
Rancho Cordova, CA (cdp) Sacramento County	12	0.02
Hesperia, CA (city) San Bernardino County	11	0.02
Murrieta, CA (city) Riverside County	10	0.02
Camarillo, CA (city) Ventura County	9	0.02
Lakewood, WA (city) Pierce County	9	0.02
Parkway-South Sacramento, CA (cdp) Sacramento County	9	0.02
Perris, CA (city) Riverside County	9	0.02
Aloha, OR (cdp) Washington County	8	0.02
Monrovia, CA (city) Los Angeles County	8	0.02
San Luis Obispo, CA (city) San Luis Obispo County	8	0.02
Rohnert Park, CA (city) Sonoma County	7	0.02
Salina, KS (city) Saline County	7	0.02
Twin Falls, ID (city) Twin Falls County	7	0.02
Lawndale, CA (city) Los Angeles County	6	0.02
Millcreek, UT (cdp) Salt Lake County	6	0.02
Pleasant Hill, CA (city) Contra Costa County	6	0.02
Seaside, CA (city) Monterey County	6	0.02
Winchester, NV (cdp) Clark County	6	0.02
Yuba City, CA (city) Sutter County	6	0.02
Eureka, CA (city) Humboldt County	5	0.02
Grants Pass, OR (city) Josephine County	5	0.02
Rosemont, CA (cdp) Sacramento County	5	0.02
University Place, WA (city) Pierce County	5	0.02
Adelanto, CA (city) San Bernardino County	4	0.02
Ashland, CA (cdp) Alameda County	4	0.02
Atascadero, CA (city) San Luis Obispo County	4	0.02
Bellview, FL (cdp) Escambia County	4	0.02
Carteret, NJ (borough) Middlesex County	4	0.02
El Segundo, CA (city) Los Angeles County	4	0.02
Forest Park, OH (city) Hamilton County	4	0.02
Hayesville, OR (cdp) Marion County	4	0.02
Isla Vista, CA (cdp) Santa Barbara County	4	0.02
Kihei, HI (cdp) Maui County	4	0.02
Orange, TX (city) Orange County	4	0.02
Pampa, TX (city) Gray County	4	0.02
Riverton, UT (city) Salt Lake County	4	0.02
West Lake Stevens, WA (cdp) Snohomish County	4	0.02
Whitney, NV (cdp) Clark County	4	0.02
Windsor, CA (town) Sonoma County	4	0.02
Arvin, CA (city) Kern County	3	0.02
Clearlake, CA (city) Lake County	3	0.02
Cottonwood West, UT (cdp) Salt Lake County	3	0.02
East San Gabriel, CA (cdp) Los Angeles County	3	0.02
Harker Heights, TX (city) Bell County	3	0.02
Lehi, UT (city) Utah County	3	0.02
North Ogden, UT (city) Weber County	3	0.02
Pacific Grove, CA (city) Monterey County	3	0.02
Rutland, VT (city) Rutland County	3	0.02
San Anselmo, CA (town) Marin County	3	0.02
Thibodaux, LA (city) Lafourche Parish	3	0.02

Notes: (cdp) census designated place; Refer to the Explanation of Data in the front of the book for more detailed information.

American Indian: Pima

Top 150 Places Sorted by Number

(Based on all places, regardless of population)

Place	Number	%
Phoenix, AZ (city) Maricopa County	1,954	0.15
Mesa, AZ (city) Maricopa County	490	0.12
Chandler, AZ (city) Maricopa County	328	0.19
Tucson, AZ (city) Pima County	190	0.04
Casa Grande, AZ (city) Pinal County	187	0.74
Sacaton, AZ (cdp) Pinal County	176	11.11
Los Angeles, CA (city) Los Angeles County	165	0.00
Glendale, AZ (city) Maricopa County	164	0.07
Coolidge, AZ (city) Pinal County	119	1.53
Tempe, AZ (city) Maricopa County	111	0.07
Blackwater, AZ (cdp) Pinal County	107	21.23
Scottsdale, AZ (city) Maricopa County	68	0.03
Florence, AZ (town) Pinal County	51	0.30
Gilbert, AZ (town) Maricopa County	51	0.05
Albuquerque, NM (city) Bernalillo County	45	0.01
Riverside, CA (city) Riverside County	42	0.02
San Diego, CA (city) San Diego County	41	0.00
Oklahoma City, OK (city) Oklahoma County	36	0.01
Fresno, CA (city) Fresno County	32	0.01
Oakland, CA (city) Alameda County	31	0.01
Maricopa, AZ (cdp) Pinal County	28	2.69
Fontana, CA (city) San Bernardino County	28	0.02
San Bernardino, CA (city) San Bernardino County	28	0.02
Modesto, CA (city) Stanislaus County	27	0.01
San Carlos, AZ (cdp) Gila County	26	0.70
San Francisco, CA (city) San Francisco County	26	0.00
Norwalk, CA (city) Los Angeles County	25	0.02
San Jose, CA (city) Santa Clara County	24	0.00
Long Beach, CA (city) Los Angeles County	22	0.00
Sells, AZ (cdp) Pima County	21	0.75
Eloy, AZ (city) Pinal County	21	0.20
Chicago, IL (city) Cook County	21	0.00
Las Vegas, NV (city) Clark County	21	0.00
Bakersfield, CA (city) Kern County	20	0.01
Denver, CO (city) Denver County	20	0.00
Sacramento, CA (city) Sacramento County	20	0.00
Whiteriver, AZ (cdp) Navajo County	19	0.36
Avondale, AZ (city) Maricopa County	19	0.05
Flagstaff, AZ (city) Coconino County	19	0.04
Woodland, CA (city) Yolo County	19	0.04
Portland, OR (city) Multnomah County	19	0.00
Anaheim, CA (city) Orange County	18	0.01
Stanfield, AZ (cdp) Pinal County	17	2.61
Prescott, AZ (city) Yavapai County	17	0.05
Whittier, CA (city) Los Angeles County	17	0.02
Yuma, AZ (city) Yuma County	17	0.02
Reno, NV (city) Washoe County	17	0.01
Guadalupe, AZ (town) Maricopa County	16	0.31
Apple Valley, CA (town) San Bernardino County	16	0.03
Santa Clarita, CA (city) Los Angeles County	16	0.01
Santa Rosa, CA (city) Sonoma County	16	0.01
Sierra Vista Southeast, AZ (cdp) Cochise County	15	0.10
Colton, CA (city) San Bernardino County	15	0.03
Las Cruces, NM (city) Dona Ana County	15	0.02
Yakima, WA (city) Yakima County	15	0.02
Chuichu, AZ (cdp) Pinal County	13	3.83
Winslow, AZ (city) Navajo County	13	0.14
Port Huron, MI (city) Saint Clair County	13	0.04
Pico Rivera, CA (city) Los Angeles County	13	0.02
Oxnard, CA (city) Ventura County	13	0.01
Rancho Cucamonga, CA (city) San Bernardino County	13	0.01
Honolulu, HI (cdp) Honolulu County	13	0.00
First Mesa, AZ (cdp) Navajo County	12	1.07
Dudleyville, AZ (cdp) Pinal County	12	0.91
Pine Ridge, SD (cdp) Shannon County	12	0.38
Tuba City, AZ (cdp) Coconino County	12	0.15
Hesperia, CA (city) San Bernardino County	12	0.02
Corona, CA (city) Riverside County	12	0.01
West Covina, CA (city) Los Angeles County	12	0.01
Seattle, WA (city) King County	12	0.00
Payson, AZ (town) Gila County	11	0.08
Arden-Arcade, CA (cdp) Sacramento County	11	0.01
El Cajon, CA (city) San Diego County	11	0.01
Escondido, CA (city) San Diego County	11	0.01
Peoria, AZ (city) Maricopa County	11	0.01
Aurora, CO (city) Arapahoe County	11	0.00
San Antonio, TX (city) Bexar County	11	0.00
Shongopovi, AZ (cdp) Navajo County	10	1.58
South Tucson, AZ (city) Pima County	10	0.18
Sallisaw, OK (city) Sequoyah County	10	0.13
Camp Verde, AZ (town) Yavapai County	10	0.11
Prescott Valley, AZ (town) Yavapai County	10	0.04
Hanford, CA (city) Kings County	10	0.02
Paradise, NV (cdp) Clark County	10	0.01
Warwick, RI (city) Kent County	10	0.01
Santan, AZ (cdp) Pinal County	9	1.38
Oracle, AZ (cdp) Pinal County	9	0.25
Needles, CA (city) San Bernardino County	9	0.19
Bethel, AK (city) Bethel Census Area	9	0.16
Oregon City, OR (city) Clackamas County	9	0.03
Bell, CA (city) Los Angeles County	9	0.02
Tracy, CA (city) San Joaquin County	9	0.02
Chino, CA (city) San Bernardino County	9	0.01
Lawrence, KS (city) Douglas County	9	0.01
Monterey Park, CA (city) Los Angeles County	9	0.01
Moreno Valley, CA (city) Riverside County	9	0.01
Rialto, CA (city) San Bernardino County	9	0.01
San Buenaventura, CA (city) Ventura County	9	0.01
Corpus Christi, TX (city) Nueces County	9	0.00
Stockton, CA (city) San Joaquin County	9	0.00
Tulsa, OK (city) Tulsa County	9	0.00
Parker, AZ (town) La Paz County	8	0.25
Cottonwood, AZ (city) Yavapai County	8	0.09
Goodyear, AZ (city) Maricopa County	8	0.04
Kingman, AZ (city) Mohave County	8	0.04
Downey, CA (city) Los Angeles County	8	0.01
Flint, MI (city) Genesee County	8	0.01
Green Bay, WI (city) Brown County	8	0.01
Upland, CA (city) San Bernardino County	8	0.01
Anchorage, AK (municipality) Anchorage Borough	8	0.00
Cleveland, OH (city) Cuyahoga County	8	0.00
Irving, TX (city) Dallas County	8	0.00
Salt Lake City, UT (city) Salt Lake County	8	0.00
Moenkopi, AZ (cdp) Coconino County	7	0.78
Rio Rico Southeast, AZ (cdp) Santa Cruz County	7	0.44
Lakeland Village, CA (cdp) Riverside County	7	0.12
Winchester, NV (cdp) Clark County	7	0.03
Windsor, CA (town) Sonoma County	7	0.03
Bell Gardens, CA (city) Los Angeles County	7	0.02
Farmington, NM (city) San Juan County	7	0.02
Kearns, UT (cdp) Salt Lake County	7	0.02
Surprise, AZ (city) Maricopa County	7	0.02
Alhambra, CA (city) Los Angeles County	7	0.01
Carson City, NV (special city) Carson City city	7	0.01
Colonie, NY (town) Albany County	7	0.01
East Los Angeles, CA (cdp) Los Angeles County	7	0.01
Mountain View, CA (city) Santa Clara County	7	0.01
Visalia, CA (city) Tulare County	7	0.01
Colorado Springs, CO (city) El Paso County	7	0.00
Columbus, OH (city) Franklin County	7	0.00
Houston, TX (city) Harris County	7	0.00
Milwaukee, WI (city) Milwaukee County	7	0.00
Ontario, CA (city) San Bernardino County	7	0.00
Salinas, CA (city) Monterey County	7	0.00
Santa Ana, CA (city) Orange County	7	0.00
Parma, ID (city) Canyon County	6	0.34
Sahuarita, AZ (town) Pima County	6	0.19
Ajo, AZ (cdp) Pima County	6	0.16
City of The Dalles, OR (city) Wasco County	6	0.05
Drexel Heights, AZ (cdp) Pima County	6	0.03
Carpentersville, IL (village) Kane County	6	0.02
Chelsea, MA (city) Suffolk County	6	0.02
Clearfield, UT (city) Davis County	6	0.02
Delano, CA (city) Kern County	6	0.02
El Centro, CA (city) Imperial County	6	0.02
Sierra Vista, AZ (city) Cochise County	6	0.02
Azusa, CA (city) Los Angeles County	6	0.01
Baldwin Park, CA (city) Los Angeles County	6	0.01
Berkeley, CA (city) Alameda County	6	0.01
Buena Park, CA (city) Orange County	6	0.01

Notes: (cdp) census designated place; Refer to the Explanation of Data in the front of the book for more detailed information.

American Indian: Pima

Top 150 Places Sorted by Percent

(Based on all places, regardless of population)

Place	Number	%
Blackwater, AZ (cdp) Pinal County	107	21.23
Sacaton, AZ (cdp) Pinal County	176	11.11
Mojave Ranch Estates, AZ (cdp) Mohave County	3	10.71
Chuichu, AZ (cdp) Pinal County	13	3.83
Maricopa, AZ (cdp) Pinal County	28	2.69
Stanfield, AZ (cdp) Pinal County	17	2.61
Dublin, MN (township) Swift County	4	2.56
Shongopovi, AZ (cdp) Navajo County	10	1.58
Coolidge, AZ (city) Pinal County	119	1.53
Santan, AZ (cdp) Pinal County	9	1.38
Pisinemo, AZ (cdp) Pima County	3	1.27
First Mesa, AZ (cdp) Navajo County	12	1.07
Nixon, NV (cdp) Washoe County	4	0.96
Dudleyville, AZ (cdp) Pinal County	12	0.91
Peach Springs, AZ (cdp) Mohave County	5	0.83
Moenkopi, AZ (cdp) Coconino County	7	0.78
Poston, AZ (cdp) La Paz County	3	0.77
Sells, AZ (cdp) Pima County	21	0.75
Casa Grande, AZ (city) Pinal County	187	0.74
San Carlos, AZ (cdp) Gila County	26	0.70
Devol, OK (town) Cotton County	1	0.67
Felton, DE (town) Kent County	5	0.64
Arizona Village, AZ (cdp) Mohave County	2	0.57
Brandsville, MO (city) Howell County	1	0.57
Lanare, CA (cdp) Fresno County	3	0.56
Neola, UT (cdp) Duchesne County	3	0.56
Mesa Vista, CA (cdp) Alpine County	1	0.55
Second Mesa, AZ (cdp) Navajo County	4	0.49
Santa Rosa, AZ (cdp) Pima County	2	0.46
Ak-Chin Village, AZ (cdp) Pinal County	3	0.45
Randlett, UT (cdp) Uintah County	1	0.45
Rio Rico Southeast, AZ (cdp) Santa Cruz County	7	0.44
Allen, NY (town) Allegany County	2	0.43
Isle, MN (city) Mille Lacs County	3	0.42
Red Mesa, AZ (cdp) Apache County	1	0.42
Pine Ridge, SD (cdp) Shannon County	12	0.38
Keams Canyon, AZ (cdp) Navajo County	1	0.38
Whiteriver, AZ (cdp) Navajo County	19	0.36
Milton, IA (city) Van Buren County	2	0.36
Amado, AZ (cdp) Santa Cruz County	1	0.36
Parma, ID (city) Canyon County	6	0.34
Peridot, AZ (cdp) Graham County	4	0.32
Stratford, CA (cdp) Kings County	4	0.32
Muddy, MT (cdp) Big Horn County	2	0.32
Guadalupe, AZ (town) Maricopa County	16	0.31
Lechee, AZ (cdp) Coconino County	5	0.31
Florence, AZ (town) Pinal County	51	0.30
Brownsboro Farm, KY (city) Jefferson County	2	0.30
Little Rock, MN (cdp) Beltrami County	3	0.28
Allenhurst, NJ (borough) Monmouth County	2	0.28
Thoreau, NM (cdp) McKinley County	5	0.27
Tombstone, AZ (city) Cochise County	4	0.27
Nucla, CO (town) Montrose County	2	0.27
Kykotsmovi Village, AZ (cdp) Navajo County	2	0.26
Mesita, NM (cdp) Cibola County	2	0.26
Oracle, AZ (cdp) Pinal County	9	0.25
Parker, AZ (town) La Paz County	8	0.25
Akeley, MN (city) Hubbard County	1	0.24
McKinley, WI (town) Taylor County	1	0.24
Middletown, IL (village) Logan County	1	0.23
Big Pine, CA (cdp) Inyo County	3	0.22
Leupp, AZ (cdp) Coconino County	2	0.21
Princeton, IA (city) Scott County	2	0.21
Eloy, AZ (city) Pinal County	21	0.20
Owyhee, NV (cdp) Elko County	2	0.20
Ten Lake, MN (township) Beltrami County	2	0.20
Isleta Village Proper, NM (cdp) Bernalillo County	1	0.20
Chandler, AZ (city) Maricopa County	328	0.19
Needles, CA (city) San Bernardino County	9	0.19
Sahuarita, AZ (town) Pima County	6	0.19
Saint Paul, AK (city) Aleutians West Census Area	1	0.19
South Tucson, AZ (city) Pima County	10	0.18
Kearny, AZ (town) Pinal County	4	0.18
Glennallen, AK (cdp) Valdez-Cordova Census Area	1	0.18
Harrah, WA (town) Yakima County	1	0.18
Roseville, MN (township) Kandiyohi County	1	0.18
Wenden, AZ (cdp) La Paz County	1	0.18
Ronan, MT (city) Lake County	3	0.17
San Juan, NM (cdp) Rio Arriba County	1	0.17
Bethel, AK (city) Bethel Census Area	9	0.16
Ajo, AZ (cdp) Pima County	6	0.16
Nyssa, OR (city) Malheur County	5	0.16
Grout, MI (township) Gladwin County	3	0.16
Dilkon, AZ (cdp) Navajo County	2	0.16
Taos Pueblo, NM (cdp) Taos County	2	0.16
Pinora, MI (township) Lake County	1	0.16
Rushville, NY (village) Yates County	1	0.16
Phoenix, AZ (city) Maricopa County	1,954	0.15
Tuba City, AZ (cdp) Coconino County	12	0.15
Clifton, AZ (town) Greenlee County	4	0.15
McCloud, CA (cdp) Siskiyou County	2	0.15
Metlakatla, AK (cdp) Prince of Wales-Outer Ketchikan Census Area	2	0.15
Klamath, CA (cdp) Del Norte County	1	0.15
Saint Francis, SD (town) Todd County	1	0.15
Winslow, AZ (city) Navajo County	13	0.14
Placitas, NM (cdp) Sandoval County	5	0.14
Fort Montgomery, NY (cdp) Orange County	2	0.14
Fort Washakie, WY (cdp) Fremont County	2	0.14
Hays, MT (cdp) Blaine County	1	0.14
Junction City, AR (city) Union County	1	0.14
Van Horne, IA (city) Benton County	1	0.14
Sallisaw, OK (city) Sequoyah County	10	0.13
Litchfield Park, AZ (city) Maricopa County	5	0.13
Olton, TX (city) Lamb County	3	0.13
Hotevilla-Bacavi, AZ (cdp) Navajo County	1	0.13
McLaughlin, SD (city) Corson County	1	0.13
Mesa, AZ (city) Maricopa County	490	0.12
Lakeland Village, CA (cdp) Riverside County	7	0.12
Paulden, AZ (cdp) Yavapai County	4	0.12
Mountain View Acres, CA (cdp) San Bernardino County	3	0.12
Julian, CA (cdp) San Diego County	2	0.12
Aurora, TX (town) Wise County	1	0.12
Hoonah, AK (city) Skagway-Hoonah-Angoon Census Area	1	0.12
Pleasureville, KY (city) Henry County	1	0.12
Sonoita, AZ (cdp) Santa Cruz County	1	0.12
Camp Verde, AZ (town) Yavapai County	10	0.11
Arizona City, AZ (cdp) Pinal County	5	0.11
Golden Valley, AZ (cdp) Mohave County	5	0.11
Pinetop-Lakeside, AZ (town) Navajo County	4	0.11
Tortolita, AZ (cdp) Pima County	4	0.11
Abernathy, TX (city) Hale County	3	0.11
Crownpoint, NM (cdp) McKinley County	3	0.11
Baldwin, WI (town) Saint Croix County	1	0.11
Merrill, OR (city) Klamath County	1	0.11
Wadsworth, NV (cdp) Washoe County	1	0.11
Sierra Vista Southeast, AZ (cdp) Cochise County	15	0.10
Grove, OK (city) Delaware County	5	0.10
Oakhurst, CA (cdp) Madera County	3	0.10
Pahoa, HI (cdp) Hawaii County	1	0.10
Cottonwood, AZ (city) Yavapai County	8	0.09
San Manuel, AZ (cdp) Pinal County	4	0.09
Sonora, CA (city) Tuolumne County	4	0.09
Clarkdale, AZ (town) Yavapai County	3	0.09
Cheshire, MI (township) Allegan County	2	0.09
Canyon Day, AZ (cdp) Gila County	1	0.09
Lapwai, ID (city) Nez Perce County	1	0.09
Siletz, OR (city) Lincoln County	1	0.09
Towaoc, CO (cdp) Montezuma County	1	0.09
Payson, AZ (town) Gila County	11	0.08
Mojave, CA (cdp) Kern County	3	0.08
Big Coppitt Key, FL (cdp) Monroe County	2	0.08
Kachina Village, AZ (cdp) Coconino County	2	0.08
Valencia West, AZ (cdp) Pima County	2	0.08
Black Rock, NM (cdp) McKinley County	1	0.08
Mescalero, NM (cdp) Otero County	1	0.08
Oglala, SD (cdp) Shannon County	1	0.08
Pinon, AZ (cdp) Navajo County	1	0.08
Renovo, PA (borough) Clinton County	1	0.08
Sunol, CA (cdp) Alameda County	1	0.08
Glendale, AZ (city) Maricopa County	164	0.07

Notes: (cdp) census designated place; Refer to the Explanation of Data in the front of the book for more detailed information.

American Indian: Pima

Top 150 Places Sorted by Percent

(Based on places with populations of 10,000 or more)

Place	Number	%
Casa Grande, AZ (city) Pinal County	187	0.74
Florence, AZ (town) Pinal County	51	0.30
Eloy, AZ (city) Pinal County	21	0.20
Chandler, AZ (city) Maricopa County	328	0.19
Phoenix, AZ (city) Maricopa County	1,954	0.15
Mesa, AZ (city) Maricopa County	490	0.12
Sierra Vista Southeast, AZ (cdp) Cochise County	15	0.10
Payson, AZ (town) Gila County	11	0.08
Glendale, AZ (city) Maricopa County	164	0.07
Tempe, AZ (city) Maricopa County	111	0.07
Gilbert, AZ (town) Maricopa County	51	0.05
Avondale, AZ (city) Maricopa County	19	0.05
Prescott, AZ (city) Yavapai County	17	0.05
City of The Dalles, OR (city) Wasco County	6	0.05
Silver City, NM (town) Grant County	5	0.05
Tucson, AZ (city) Pima County	190	0.04
Flagstaff, AZ (city) Coconino County	19	0.04
Woodland, CA (city) Yolo County	19	0.04
Port Huron, MI (city) Saint Clair County	13	0.04
Prescott Valley, AZ (town) Yavapai County	10	0.04
Goodyear, AZ (city) Maricopa County	8	0.04
Kingman, AZ (city) Mohave County	8	0.04
Grand Terrace, CA (city) San Bernardino County	5	0.04
Marana, AZ (town) Pima County	5	0.04
Winfield, KS (city) Cowley County	5	0.04
Beaumont, CA (city) Riverside County	4	0.04
Scottsdale, AZ (city) Maricopa County	68	0.03
Apple Valley, CA (town) San Bernardino County	16	0.03
Colton, CA (city) San Bernardino County	15	0.03
Oregon City, OR (city) Clackamas County	9	0.03
Winchester, NV (cdp) Clark County	7	0.03
Windsor, CA (town) Sonoma County	7	0.03
Drexel Heights, AZ (cdp) Pima County	6	0.03
Douglas, AZ (city) Cochise County	5	0.03
Commerce, CA (city) Los Angeles County	4	0.03
Lake Los Angeles, CA (cdp) Los Angeles County	4	0.03
Lakeland North, WA (cdp) King County	4	0.03
Malibu, CA (city) Los Angeles County	4	0.03
Artesia, NM (city) Eddy County	3	0.03
Auburndale, FL (city) Polk County	3	0.03
Ripon, CA (city) San Joaquin County	3	0.03
Sun Lakes, AZ (cdp) Maricopa County	3	0.03
West Plains, MO (city) Howell County	3	0.03
Riverside, CA (city) Riverside County	42	0.02
Fontana, CA (city) San Bernardino County	28	0.02
San Bernardino, CA (city) San Bernardino County	28	0.02
Norwalk, CA (city) Los Angeles County	25	0.02
Whittier, CA (city) Los Angeles County	17	0.02
Yuma, AZ (city) Yuma County	17	0.02
Las Cruces, NM (city) Dona Ana County	15	0.02
Yakima, WA (city) Yakima County	15	0.02
Pico Rivera, CA (city) Los Angeles County	13	0.02
Hesperia, CA (city) San Bernardino County	12	0.02
Hanford, CA (city) Kings County	10	0.02
Bell, CA (city) Los Angeles County	9	0.02
Tracy, CA (city) San Joaquin County	9	0.02
Bell Gardens, CA (city) Los Angeles County	7	0.02
Farmington, NM (city) San Juan County	7	0.02
Kearns, UT (cdp) Salt Lake County	7	0.02
Surprise, AZ (city) Maricopa County	7	0.02
Carpentersville, IL (village) Kane County	6	0.02
Chelsea, MA (city) Suffolk County	6	0.02
Clearfield, UT (city) Davis County	6	0.02
Delano, CA (city) Kern County	6	0.02
El Centro, CA (city) Imperial County	6	0.02
Sierra Vista, AZ (city) Cochise County	6	0.02
Apache Junction, AZ (city) Pinal County	5	0.02
La Presa, CA (cdp) San Diego County	5	0.02
Lake in the Hills, IL (village) McHenry County	5	0.02
Nogales, AZ (city) Santa Cruz County	5	0.02
Pasco, WA (city) Franklin County	5	0.02
Tualatin, OR (city) Washington County	5	0.02
White Center, WA (cdp) King County	5	0.02
Banning, CA (city) Riverside County	4	0.02
Coachella, CA (city) Riverside County	4	0.02
Gallup, NM (city) McKinley County	4	0.02
Lemon Grove, CA (city) San Diego County	4	0.02
Newberg, OR (city) Yamhill County	4	0.02
Valinda, CA (cdp) Los Angeles County	4	0.02
Albany, CA (city) Alameda County	3	0.02
Altamont, OR (cdp) Klamath County	3	0.02
Alum Rock, CA (cdp) Santa Clara County	3	0.02
Brookings, SD (city) Brookings County	3	0.02
Clearlake, CA (city) Lake County	3	0.02
Clinton, MA (town) Worcester County	3	0.02
Hayesville, OR (cdp) Marion County	3	0.02
New Kingman-Butler, AZ (cdp) Mohave County	3	0.02
Orchards, WA (cdp) Clark County	3	0.02
Plainfield, IN (town) Hendricks County	3	0.02
Rosamond, CA (cdp) Kern County	3	0.02
Streetsboro, OH (city) Portage County	3	0.02
Sun Valley, NV (cdp) Washoe County	3	0.02
Van Buren, AR (city) Crawford County	3	0.02
Welby, CO (cdp) Adams County	3	0.02
Citrus, CA (cdp) Los Angeles County	2	0.02
East Bethel, MN (city) Anoka County	2	0.02
Enumclaw, WA (city) King County	2	0.02
Grand Rapids, MN (township) Itasca County	2	0.02
Highlands, NY (town) Orange County	2	0.02
Montgomeryville, PA (cdp) Montgomery County	2	0.02
Neosho, MO (city) Newton County	2	0.02
Parsons, KS (city) Labette County	2	0.02
Riverton-Boulevard Park, WA (cdp) King County	2	0.02
Shafter, CA (city) Kern County	2	0.02
West Monroe, LA (city) Ouachita Parish	2	0.02
Albuquerque, NM (city) Bernalillo County	45	0.01
Oklahoma City, OK (city) Oklahoma County	36	0.01
Fresno, CA (city) Fresno County	32	0.01
Oakland, CA (city) Alameda County	31	0.01
Modesto, CA (city) Stanislaus County	27	0.01
Bakersfield, CA (city) Kern County	20	0.01
Anaheim, CA (city) Orange County	18	0.01
Reno, NV (city) Washoe County	17	0.01
Santa Clarita, CA (city) Los Angeles County	16	0.01
Santa Rosa, CA (city) Sonoma County	16	0.01
Oxnard, CA (city) Ventura County	13	0.01
Rancho Cucamonga, CA (city) San Bernardino County	13	0.01
Corona, CA (city) Riverside County	12	0.01
West Covina, CA (city) Los Angeles County	12	0.01
Arden-Arcade, CA (cdp) Sacramento County	11	0.01
El Cajon, CA (city) San Diego County	11	0.01
Escondido, CA (city) San Diego County	11	0.01
Peoria, AZ (city) Maricopa County	11	0.01
Paradise, NV (cdp) Clark County	10	0.01
Warwick, RI (city) Kent County	10	0.01
Chino, CA (city) San Bernardino County	9	0.01
Lawrence, KS (city) Douglas County	9	0.01
Monterey Park, CA (city) Los Angeles County	9	0.01
Moreno Valley, CA (city) Riverside County	9	0.01
Rialto, CA (city) San Bernardino County	9	0.01
San Buenaventura, CA (city) Ventura County	9	0.01
Downey, CA (city) Los Angeles County	8	0.01
Flint, MI (city) Genesee County	8	0.01
Green Bay, WI (city) Brown County	8	0.01
Upland, CA (city) San Bernardino County	8	0.01
Alhambra, CA (city) Los Angeles County	7	0.01
Carson City, NV (special city) Carson City city	7	0.01
Colonie, NY (town) Albany County	7	0.01
East Los Angeles, CA (cdp) Los Angeles County	7	0.01
Mountain View, CA (city) Santa Clara County	7	0.01
Visalia, CA (city) Tulare County	7	0.01
Azusa, CA (city) Los Angeles County	6	0.01
Baldwin Park, CA (city) Los Angeles County	6	0.01
Berkeley, CA (city) Alameda County	6	0.01
Buena Park, CA (city) Orange County	6	0.01
Carson, CA (city) Los Angeles County	6	0.01
Casas Adobes, AZ (cdp) Pima County	6	0.01
Goleta, CA (cdp) Santa Barbara County	6	0.01
Hawthorne, CA (city) Los Angeles County	6	0.01
Indio, CA (city) Riverside County	6	0.01

Notes: (cdp) census designated place; Refer to the Explanation of Data in the front of the book for more detailed information.

American Indian: Potawatomi

Top 150 Places Sorted by Number

(Based on all places, regardless of population)

Place	Number	%
Oklahoma City, OK (city) Oklahoma County	758	0.15
Topeka, KS (city) Shawnee County	711	0.58
Shawnee, OK (city) Pottawatomie County	482	1.68
Harris, MI (township) Menominee County	320	16.89
Norman, OK (city) Cleveland County	240	0.25
Tulsa, OK (city) Tulsa County	240	0.06
Wabeno, WI (town) Forest County	238	18.83
Lincoln, WI (town) Forest County	207	20.60
Tecumseh, OK (city) Pottawatomie County	174	2.85
Grand Rapids, MI (city) Kent County	155	0.08
Lawrence, KS (city) Douglas County	154	0.19
Wichita, KS (city) Sedgwick County	136	0.04
Milwaukee, WI (city) Milwaukee County	131	0.02
Kansas City, MO (city) Jackson County	116	0.03
Phoenix, AZ (city) Maricopa County	112	0.01
Moore, OK (city) Cleveland County	106	0.26
Chicago, IL (city) Cook County	105	0.00
Midwest City, OK (city) Oklahoma County	104	0.19
Los Angeles, CA (city) Los Angeles County	104	0.00
Dowagiac, MI (city) Cass County	103	1.68
Edmond, OK (city) Oklahoma County	99	0.14
Battle Creek, MI (city) Calhoun County	97	0.18
South Bend, IN (city) Saint Joseph County	95	0.09
Wyoming, MI (city) Kent County	84	0.12
Dallas, TX (city) Dallas County	81	0.01
Hartford, MI (city) Van Buren County	76	3.07
San Diego, CA (city) San Diego County	76	0.01
Escanaba, MI (city) Delta County	70	0.53
Holton, KS (city) Jackson County	67	2.00
Kalamazoo, MI (city) Kalamazoo County	67	0.09
San Jose, CA (city) Santa Clara County	67	0.01
Bakersfield, CA (city) Kern County	63	0.03
Crandon, WI (city) Forest County	61	3.11
Slaughterville, OK (town) Cleveland County	59	1.63
Choctaw, OK (city) Oklahoma County	59	0.63
Denver, CO (city) Denver County	58	0.01
Broken Arrow, OK (city) Tulsa County	56	0.07
Indianapolis, IN (special city) Marion County	56	0.01
Bethel Acres, OK (town) Pottawatomie County	55	2.01
Ada, OK (city) Pontotoc County	53	0.34
Fresno, CA (city) Fresno County	53	0.01
Fort Worth, TX (city) Tarrant County	50	0.01
Green Bay, WI (city) Brown County	49	0.05
Albuquerque, NM (city) Bernalillo County	49	0.01
Noble, OK (city) Cleveland County	48	0.91
Kansas City, KS (city) Wyandotte County	48	0.03
Las Vegas, NV (city) Clark County	48	0.01
Stockton, CA (city) San Joaquin County	47	0.02
Sacramento, CA (city) Sacramento County	45	0.01
Houston, TX (city) Harris County	45	0.00
Lansing, MI (city) Ingham County	44	0.04
Seattle, WA (city) King County	43	0.01
San Antonio, TX (city) Bexar County	42	0.00
Hominy, OK (city) Osage County	41	1.59
Jackson, MI (city) Jackson County	41	0.11
Austin, TX (city) Travis County	41	0.01
Horton, KS (city) Brown County	40	2.03
Hartford, MI (township) Van Buren County	40	1.27
Niles, MI (township) Berrien County	40	0.30
Stillwater, OK (city) Payne County	40	0.10
Lexington, OK (city) Cleveland County	39	1.87
Purcell, OK (city) McClain County	38	0.68
Minneapolis, MN (city) Hennepin County	38	0.01
Detroit, MI (city) Wayne County	38	0.00
Neenah, WI (city) Winnebago County	37	0.15
Silver Creek, MI (township) Cass County	36	1.03
Pawhuska, OK (city) Osage County	36	0.99
Portage, MI (city) Kalamazoo County	36	0.08
Colorado Springs, CO (city) El Paso County	36	0.01
Portland, OR (city) Multnomah County	36	0.01
Mayetta, KS (city) Jackson County	35	11.22
Enid, OK (city) Garfield County	35	0.07
El Reno, OK (city) Canadian County	34	0.21
Bartlesville, OK (city) Washington County	34	0.10
Wausau, WI (city) Marathon County	34	0.09

Place	Number	%
Del City, OK (city) Oklahoma County	33	0.15
Muskegon, MI (city) Muskegon County	33	0.08
Manhattan, KS (city) Riley County	33	0.07
Reno, NV (city) Washoe County	33	0.02
Gourley, MI (township) Menominee County	32	7.82
Kentwood, MI (city) Kent County	32	0.07
Wayne, MI (township) Cass County	31	1.08
Lawton, OK (city) Comanche County	31	0.03
Anchorage, AK (municipality) Anchorage Borough	31	0.01
Long Beach, CA (city) Los Angeles County	31	0.01
Muskogee, OK (city) Muskogee County	30	0.08
Mishawaka, IN (city) Saint Joseph County	30	0.06
Tucson, AZ (city) Pima County	30	0.01
Eugene, OR (city) Lane County	29	0.02
Huntington Beach, CA (city) Orange County	29	0.02
Omaha, NE (city) Douglas County	29	0.01
Tacoma, WA (city) Pierce County	29	0.01
Grand Haven, MI (township) Ottawa County	28	0.21
Visalia, CA (city) Tulare County	28	0.03
Aurora, CO (city) Arapahoe County	28	0.01
Plano, TX (city) Collin County	28	0.01
New York, NY (city) New York City	27	0.00
Lac du Flambeau, WI (town) Vilas County	26	0.87
Harrah, OK (city) Oklahoma County	26	0.55
Pauls Valley, OK (city) Garvin County	26	0.42
Arkansas City, KS (city) Cowley County	26	0.22
Bethany, OK (city) Oklahoma County	26	0.13
Madison, WI (city) Dane County	26	0.01
Seminole, OK (city) Seminole County	25	0.36
Niles, MI (city) Berrien County	25	0.20
Mesquite, TX (city) Dallas County	25	0.02
Arlington, TX (city) Tarrant County	25	0.01
San Francisco, CA (city) San Francisco County	25	0.00
Ontwa, MI (township) Cass County	24	0.41
Blackwell, OK (city) Kay County	24	0.31
Yukon, OK (city) Canadian County	24	0.11
Henderson, NV (city) Clark County	24	0.01
Maud, OK (city) Pottawatomie County	23	2.02
Paw Paw, MI (township) Van Buren County	23	0.32
Benton charter, MI (township) Berrien County	23	0.14
Shawnee, KS (city) Johnson County	23	0.05
San Angelo, TX (city) Tom Green County	23	0.03
Springfield, MO (city) Greene County	23	0.02
Westminster, CO (city) Adams County	23	0.02
Boise City, ID (city) Ada County	23	0.01
Fort Wayne, IN (city) Allen County	23	0.01
Lubbock, TX (city) Lubbock County	23	0.01
Bark River, MI (township) Delta County	22	1.33
Watervliet, MI (township) Berrien County	22	0.65
Newcastle, OK (city) McClain County	22	0.40
Mustang, OK (city) Canadian County	22	0.17
Ardmore, OK (city) Carter County	22	0.09
Ponca City, OK (city) Kay County	22	0.08
Georgetown, MI (township) Ottawa County	22	0.05
Odessa, TX (city) Ector County	22	0.02
Rossville, KS (city) Shawnee County	21	2.07
Gaines, MI (township) Kent County	21	0.10
Anaheim, CA (city) Orange County	21	0.01
Saint Louis, OK (town) Pottawatomie County	20	9.71
Monterey, MI (township) Allegan County	20	0.97
Athens, MI (township) Calhoun County	20	0.78
Keeler, MI (township) Van Buren County	20	0.77
McLoud, OK (town) Pottawatomie County	20	0.56
Menominee, MI (city) Menominee County	20	0.22
Duncan, OK (city) Stephens County	20	0.09
Bloomington, IL (city) McLean County	20	0.03
West Allis, WI (city) Milwaukee County	20	0.03
Independence, MO (city) Jackson County	20	0.02
Glendale, AZ (city) Maricopa County	20	0.01
Seneca, WI (town) Wood County	19	1.58
Laona, WI (town) Forest County	19	1.39
Saint Marys, KS (city) Pottawatomie County	19	0.86
Cutlerville, MI (cdp) Kent County	19	0.13
Lee's Summit, MO (city) Jackson County	19	0.03
Napa, CA (city) Napa County	19	0.03

Notes: (cdp) census designated place; Refer to the Explanation of Data in the front of the book for more detailed information.

American Indian: Potawatomi

Top 150 Places Sorted by Percent

(Based on all places, regardless of population)

Place	Number	%
Lincoln, WI (town) Forest County	207	20.60
Wabeno, WI (town) Forest County	238	18.83
Harris, MI (township) Menominee County	320	16.89
Grainola, OK (town) Osage County	4	12.90
Mayetta, KS (city) Jackson County	35	11.22
Saint Louis, OK (town) Pottawatomie County	20	9.71
Delia, KS (city) Jackson County	16	8.94
Gourley, MI (township) Menominee County	32	7.82
Willis, KS (city) Brown County	4	5.80
Brooksville, OK (town) Pottawatomie County	4	4.44
Powhattan, KS (city) Brown County	4	4.40
Centrahoma, OK (city) Coal County	4	3.64
Wheaton, KS (city) Pottawatomie County	3	3.26
Circleville, KS (city) Jackson County	6	3.24
Pittsburg, OK (town) Pittsburg County	9	3.21
Hoyt, KS (city) Jackson County	18	3.15
Crandon, WI (city) Forest County	61	3.11
Asher, OK (town) Pottawatomie County	13	3.10
Hartford, MI (city) Van Buren County	76	3.07
Breedsville, MI (village) Van Buren County	7	2.98
Sparks, OK (town) Lincoln County	4	2.92
Tecumseh, OK (city) Pottawatomie County	174	2.85
Earlsboro, OK (town) Pottawatomie County	18	2.84
Wanette, OK (town) Pottawatomie County	11	2.74
Emmett, KS (city) Pottawatomie County	7	2.53
Soldier, KS (city) Jackson County	3	2.46
Whiting, KS (city) Jackson County	5	2.43
Carter, OK (town) Beckham County	6	2.36
Dora, NM (village) Roosevelt County	3	2.31
Lipscomb, TX (cdp) Lipscomb County	1	2.27
Milburn, OK (town) Johnston County	7	2.24
Dougherty, OK (town) Murray County	5	2.23
Rossville, KS (city) Shawnee County	21	2.07
Horton, KS (city) Brown County	40	2.03
Maud, OK (city) Pottawatomie County	23	2.02
Bethel Acres, OK (town) Pottawatomie County	55	2.01
Holton, KS (city) Jackson County	67	2.00
Caswell, WI (town) Forest County	2	1.96
Manchester, KS (city) Dickinson County	2	1.96
Shidler, OK (city) Osage County	10	1.92
Lexington, OK (city) Cleveland County	39	1.87
Tribbey, OK (town) Pottawatomie County	5	1.83
Westphalia, KS (city) Anderson County	3	1.82
Lecompton, KS (city) Douglas County	11	1.81
Eckley, CO (town) Yuma County	5	1.80
Stringtown, OK (town) Atoka County	7	1.77
Corning, KS (city) Nemaha County	3	1.76
Cibola, AZ (cdp) La Paz County	3	1.74
Denison, KS (city) Jackson County	4	1.73
Lonsdale, AR (town) Garland County	2	1.69
Shawnee, OK (city) Pottawatomie County	482	1.68
Dowagiac, MI (city) Cass County	103	1.68
Slaughterville, OK (town) Cleveland County	59	1.63
Crandon, WI (town) Forest County	10	1.63
Gould, MN (township) Cass County	4	1.61
Lakewood, WI (town) Oconto County	14	1.60
Hominy, OK (city) Osage County	41	1.59
Seneca, WI (town) Wood County	19	1.58
Partridge, KS (city) Reno County	4	1.54
Wann, OK (town) Nowata County	2	1.52
Sheridan Lake, CO (town) Kiowa County	1	1.52
Armstrong Creek, WI (town) Forest County	7	1.51
Caney, OK (town) Atoka County	3	1.51
Muscotah, KS (city) Atchison County	3	1.50
Hiles, WI (town) Forest County	6	1.49
Nashville, WI (town) Forest County	17	1.47
Kiowa, OK (town) Pittsburg County	10	1.44
Middle Village, WI (cdp) Menominee County	5	1.42
Laona, WI (town) Forest County	19	1.39
Billings, OK (town) Noble County	6	1.38
Viking, MN (township) Marshall County	2	1.38
Bark River, MI (township) Delta County	22	1.33
Hartford, MI (township) Van Buren County	40	1.27
Norwich, KS (city) Kingman County	7	1.27
Bear Lake, MI (village) Manistee County	4	1.26
White Cloud, KS (city) Doniphan County	3	1.26
Clayton, OK (town) Pushmataha County	9	1.25
Kinta, OK (town) Haskell County	3	1.23
Follett, TX (city) Lipscomb County	5	1.21
Higgins, TX (city) Lipscomb County	5	1.18
Kappa, IL (village) Woodford County	2	1.18
Okay, OK (town) Wagoner County	7	1.17
Little Round Lake, WI (cdp) Sawyer County	11	1.16
Havana, KS (city) Montgomery County	1	1.16
Lawrence, MI (village) Van Buren County	12	1.13
Wynona, OK (town) Osage County	6	1.13
Pink, OK (town) Pottawatomie County	13	1.12
Wayne, MI (township) Cass County	31	1.08
Arcadia, OK (town) Oklahoma County	3	1.08
Linwood, KS (city) Leavenworth County	4	1.07
Dibble, OK (town) McClain County	3	1.04
Silver Creek, MI (township) Cass County	36	1.03
Yale, IL (village) Jasper County	1	1.03
Stratford, OK (town) Garvin County	15	1.02
Reserve, KS (city) Brown County	1	1.00
Pawhuska, OK (city) Osage County	36	0.99
Meriden, KS (city) Jefferson County	7	0.99
Wayne, OK (town) McClain County	7	0.98
Monterey, MI (township) Allegan County	20	0.97
Nickerson, NE (village) Dodge County	4	0.93
Noble, OK (city) Cleveland County	48	0.91
Vilas, CO (town) Baca County	1	0.91
Topsfield, ME (town) Washington County	2	0.89
Silver Lake, KS (city) Shawnee County	12	0.88
Kansas, OK (town) Delaware County	6	0.88
Tyro, KS (city) Montgomery County	2	0.88
Atwood, OK (town) Hughes County	1	0.88
Lac du Flambeau, WI (town) Vilas County	26	0.87
Edwardsburg, MI (village) Cass County	10	0.87
Ravia, OK (town) Johnston County	4	0.87
Saint Marys, KS (city) Pottawatomie County	19	0.86
Kingdom City, MO (village) Callaway County	1	0.83
Perley, MN (city) Norman County	1	0.83
West Mineral, KS (city) Cherokee County	2	0.82
Avant, OK (town) Osage County	3	0.81
South Prairie, WA (town) Pierce County	3	0.79
Forestville, MI (village) Sanilac County	1	0.79
Athens, MI (township) Calhoun County	20	0.78
Bates, MI (township) Iron County	8	0.78
Keeler, MI (township) Van Buren County	20	0.77
Bloomingdale, MI (village) Van Buren County	4	0.76
Pyote, TX (town) Ward County	1	0.76
Cassopolis, MI (village) Cass County	13	0.75
Cromwell, OK (town) Seminole County	2	0.75
Cowlington, OK (town) Le Flore County	1	0.75
Valley Brook, OK (town) Oklahoma County	6	0.73
Murry, WI (town) Rusk County	2	0.73
Cedarville, MI (township) Menominee County	2	0.72
Cross Timber, TX (town) Johnson County	2	0.72
Norman, AR (town) Montgomery County	3	0.71
Byars, OK (town) McClain County	2	0.71
Stephenson, MI (township) Menominee County	5	0.70
Vandalia, MI (village) Cass County	3	0.70
Wolbach, NE (village) Greeley County	2	0.70
Garvin, OK (town) McCurtain County	1	0.70
Martin, MI (village) Allegan County	3	0.69
Purcell, OK (city) McClain County	38	0.68
Penn, MI (township) Cass County	13	0.68
Davenport, OK (town) Lincoln County	6	0.68
Hopkins, MI (village) Allegan County	4	0.68
Merrill, MI (township) Newaygo County	4	0.68
Devol, OK (town) Cotton County	1	0.67
Herndon, KS (city) Rawlins County	1	0.67
Lake Michigan Beach, MI (cdp) Berrien County	10	0.66
Goldsby, OK (town) McClain County	8	0.66
Elmore City, OK (town) Garvin County	5	0.66
Watervliet, MI (township) Berrien County	22	0.65
Bayfield, WI (city) Bayfield County	4	0.65
Hill City, SD (city) Pennington County	5	0.64
Everest, KS (city) Brown County	2	0.64

Notes: (cdp) census designated place; Refer to the Explanation of Data in the front of the book for more detailed information.

American Indian: Potawatomi

Top 150 Places Sorted by Percent

(Based on places with populations of 10,000 or more)

Place	Number	%
Shawnee, OK (city) Pottawatomie County	482	1.68
Topeka, KS (city) Shawnee County	711	0.58
Escanaba, MI (city) Delta County	70	0.53
Ada, OK (city) Pontotoc County	53	0.34
Niles, MI (township) Berrien County	40	0.30
Moore, OK (city) Cleveland County	106	0.26
Norman, OK (city) Cleveland County	240	0.25
Arkansas City, KS (city) Cowley County	26	0.22
El Reno, OK (city) Canadian County	34	0.21
Grand Haven, MI (township) Ottawa County	28	0.21
Niles, MI (city) Berrien County	25	0.20
Lawrence, KS (city) Douglas County	154	0.19
Midwest City, OK (city) Oklahoma County	104	0.19
Battle Creek, MI (city) Calhoun County	97	0.18
Mustang, OK (city) Canadian County	22	0.17
The Village, OK (city) Oklahoma County	17	0.17
Oklahoma City, OK (city) Oklahoma County	758	0.15
Neenah, WI (city) Winnebago County	37	0.15
Del City, OK (city) Oklahoma County	33	0.15
Edmond, OK (city) Oklahoma County	99	0.14
Benton charter, MI (township) Berrien County	23	0.14
Saint Joseph charter, MI (township) Berrien County	14	0.14
Bethany, OK (city) Oklahoma County	26	0.13
Cutlerville, MI (cdp) Kent County	19	0.13
Comstock Park, MI (cdp) Kent County	14	0.13
Wyoming, MI (city) Kent County	84	0.12
Anacortes, WA (city) Skagit County	17	0.12
Lincoln charter, MI (township) Berrien County	17	0.12
Grand Haven, MI (city) Ottawa County	13	0.12
Ionia, MI (city) Ionia County	13	0.12
Jackson, MI (city) Jackson County	41	0.11
Yukon, OK (city) Canadian County	24	0.11
Chickasha, OK (city) Grady County	17	0.11
Alpine, MI (township) Kent County	15	0.11
Emmett, MI (township) Calhoun County	13	0.11
Stillwater, OK (city) Payne County	40	0.10
Bartlesville, OK (city) Washington County	34	0.10
Gaines, MI (township) Kent County	21	0.10
Sault Sainte Marie, MI (city) Chippewa County	17	0.10
Corcoran, CA (city) Kings County	14	0.10
Durant, OK (city) Bryan County	13	0.10
Beatrice, NE (city) Gage County	12	0.10
Winfield, KS (city) Cowley County	12	0.10
Coffeyville, KS (city) Montgomery County	11	0.10
South Bend, IN (city) Saint Joseph County	95	0.09
Kalamazoo, MI (city) Kalamazoo County	67	0.09
Wausau, WI (city) Marathon County	34	0.09
Ardmore, OK (city) Carter County	22	0.09
Duncan, OK (city) Stephens County	20	0.09
Oshtemo, MI (township) Kalamazoo County	16	0.09
Sand Springs, OK (city) Tulsa County	16	0.09
Comstock, MI (township) Kalamazoo County	12	0.09
Cadillac, MI (city) Wexford County	9	0.09
Grand Rapids, MI (city) Kent County	155	0.08
Portage, MI (city) Kalamazoo County	36	0.08
Muskegon, MI (city) Muskegon County	33	0.08
Muskogee, OK (city) Muskogee County	30	0.08
Ponca City, OK (city) Kay County	22	0.08
Marshfield, WI (city) Wood County	15	0.08
Wisconsin Rapids, WI (city) Wood County	15	0.08
Jenison, MI (cdp) Ottawa County	13	0.08
Northview, MI (cdp) Kent County	12	0.08
Grover Beach, CA (city) San Luis Obispo County	10	0.08
Alpena, MI (city) Alpena County	9	0.08
Chowchilla, CA (city) Madera County	9	0.08
Grass Valley, CA (city) Nevada County	9	0.08
Marinette, WI (city) Marinette County	9	0.08
Merriam, KS (city) Johnson County	9	0.08
Moberly, MO (city) Randolph County	9	0.08
Ottawa, KS (city) Franklin County	9	0.08
Broken Arrow, OK (city) Tulsa County	56	0.07
Enid, OK (city) Garfield County	35	0.07
Manhattan, KS (city) Riley County	33	0.07
Kentwood, MI (city) Kent County	32	0.07
Gladstone, MO (city) Clay County	18	0.07
Kalamazoo, MI (township) Kalamazoo County	15	0.07
Norton Shores, MI (city) Muskegon County	15	0.07
Sun Valley, NV (cdp) Washoe County	14	0.07
McPherson, KS (city) McPherson County	10	0.07
Coldwater, MI (city) Branch County	9	0.07
Miami, OK (city) Ottawa County	9	0.07
Texas, MI (township) Kalamazoo County	8	0.07
Weston, WI (village) Marathon County	8	0.07
Tulsa, OK (city) Tulsa County	240	0.06
Mishawaka, IN (city) Saint Joseph County	30	0.06
Plainfield, MI (township) Kent County	18	0.06
Emporia, KS (city) Lyon County	16	0.06
Marquette, MI (city) Marquette County	12	0.06
Milwaukie, OR (city) Clackamas County	12	0.06
Byron, MI (township) Kent County	11	0.06
Weatherford, TX (city) Parker County	11	0.06
Claremore, OK (city) Rogers County	10	0.06
Grandville, MI (city) Kent County	10	0.06
Borger, TX (city) Hutchinson County	9	0.06
Bixby, OK (city) Tulsa County	8	0.06
Okmulgee, OK (city) Okmulgee County	8	0.06
Tahlequah, OK (city) Cherokee County	8	0.06
Antwerp, MI (township) Van Buren County	7	0.06
Katy, TX (city) Harris County	7	0.06
Los Alamos, NM (cdp) Los Alamos County	7	0.06
Woodward, OK (city) Woodward County	7	0.06
Elk City, OK (city) Beckham County	6	0.06
Excelsior Springs, MO (city) Clay County	6	0.06
Green Bay, WI (city) Brown County	49	0.05
Shawnee, KS (city) Johnson County	23	0.05
Georgetown, MI (township) Ottawa County	22	0.05
McMinnville, OR (city) Yamhill County	13	0.05
Walker, MI (city) Kent County	12	0.05
Delhi charter, MI (township) Ingham County	11	0.05
Bentonville, AR (city) Benton County	10	0.05
Sapulpa, OK (city) Creek County	10	0.05
Selma, CA (city) Fresno County	10	0.05
Fredericksburg, VA (independent city) Fredericksburg city	9	0.05
Flowing Wells, AZ (cdp) Pima County	8	0.05
Muskegon, MI (township) Muskegon County	8	0.05
Oroville, CA (city) Butte County	7	0.05
Clawson, MI (city) Oakland County	6	0.05
Coalinga, CA (city) Fresno County	6	0.05
De Witt, MI (township) Clinton County	6	0.05
Marysville, CA (city) Yuba County	6	0.05
Sumpter, MI (township) Wayne County	6	0.05
Hartford, WI (city) Washington County	5	0.05
Olivehurst, CA (cdp) Yuba County	5	0.05
Rio Linda, CA (cdp) Sacramento County	5	0.05
Wichita, KS (city) Sedgwick County	136	0.04
Lansing, MI (city) Ingham County	44	0.04
Hutchinson, KS (city) Reno County	16	0.04
Hollister, CA (city) San Benito County	15	0.04
Laguna, CA (cdp) Sacramento County	14	0.04
Leavenworth, KS (city) Leavenworth County	13	0.04
Granger, IN (cdp) Saint Joseph County	12	0.04
Independence, MI (township) Oakland County	12	0.04
Burton, MI (city) Genesee County	11	0.04
Harrison, MI (cdp) Macomb County	11	0.04
Liberty, MO (city) Clay County	10	0.04
Mount Pleasant, MI (city) Isabella County	10	0.04
Oildale, CA (cdp) Kern County	10	0.04
Van Buren, MI (township) Wayne County	9	0.04
Liberal, KS (city) Seward County	8	0.04
Altamont, OR (cdp) Klamath County	7	0.04
McAlester, OK (city) Pittsburg County	7	0.04
Mount Clemens, MI (city) Macomb County	7	0.04
Owasso, OK (city) Tulsa County	7	0.04
Menasha, WI (city) Winnebago County	6	0.04
Ramona, CA (cdp) San Diego County	6	0.04
South Elgin, IL (village) Kane County	6	0.04
Alpine, CA (cdp) San Diego County	5	0.04
Enumclaw, WA (city) King County	5	0.04
Goldenrod, FL (cdp) Seminole County	5	0.04
Ham Lake, MN (city) Anoka County	5	0.04

Notes: (cdp) census designated place; Refer to the Explanation of Data in the front of the book for more detailed information.

American Indian: Pueblo

Top 150 Places Sorted by Number

(Based on all places, regardless of population)

Place	Number	%
Zuni Pueblo, NM (cdp) McKinley County	5,946	93.39
Albuquerque, NM (city) Bernalillo County	4,695	1.05
Santo Domingo Pueblo, NM (cdp) Sandoval County	2,434	95.45
Phoenix, AZ (city) Maricopa County	2,089	0.16
San Felipe Pueblo, NM (cdp) Sandoval County	1,915	92.07
Jemez Pueblo, NM (cdp) Sandoval County	1,772	90.73
New York, NY (city) New York City	1,162	0.01
Taos Pueblo, NM (cdp) Taos County	1,102	87.18
Black Rock, NM (cdp) McKinley County	1,077	86.02
First Mesa, AZ (cdp) Navajo County	968	86.12
Skyline-Ganipa, NM (cdp) Cibola County	942	91.01
El Paso, TX (city) El Paso County	910	0.16
Moenkopi, AZ (cdp) Coconino County	760	84.35
Second Mesa, AZ (cdp) Navajo County	737	90.54
Mesita, NM (cdp) Cibola County	719	92.65
Santa Clara Pueblo, NM (cdp) Rio Arriba County	686	70.00
Hotevilla-Bacavi, AZ (cdp) Navajo County	671	87.48
Los Angeles, CA (city) Los Angeles County	668	0.02
Kykotsmovi Village, AZ (cdp) Navajo County	663	85.44
Zia Pueblo, NM (cdp) Sandoval County	634	98.14
Gallup, NM (city) McKinley County	624	3.09
Flagstaff, AZ (city) Coconino County	608	1.15
Paraje, NM (cdp) Cibola County	581	86.85
Shongopovi, AZ (cdp) Navajo County	573	90.66
Tuba City, AZ (cdp) Coconino County	500	6.08
Isleta Village Proper, NM (cdp) Bernalillo County	476	95.97
San Juan, NM (cdp) Rio Arriba County	466	78.72
Santa Ana Pueblo, NM (cdp) Sandoval County	442	92.28
Grants, NM (city) Cibola County	421	4.78
Paguate, NM (cdp) Cibola County	420	88.61
Cochiti, NM (cdp) Sandoval County	413	81.46
Santa Fe, NM (city) Santa Fe County	409	0.66
Mesa, AZ (city) Maricopa County	401	0.10
Rio Rancho, NM (city) Sandoval County	375	0.72
Laguna, NM (cdp) Cibola County	371	87.71
Las Cruces, NM (city) Dona Ana County	332	0.45
Winslow, AZ (city) Navajo County	328	3.45
San Ildefonso Pueblo, NM (cdp) Santa Fe County	321	70.09
Acomita Lake, NM (cdp) Cibola County	304	97.44
Tucson, AZ (city) Pima County	300	0.06
Pueblo of Sandia Village, NM (cdp) Sandoval County	295	85.76
Seama, NM (cdp) Cibola County	291	87.39
Denver, CO (city) Denver County	277	0.05
North Acomita Village, NM (cdp) Cibola County	236	81.94
San Diego, CA (city) San Diego County	219	0.02
South Valley, NM (cdp) Bernalillo County	207	0.53
Glendale, AZ (city) Maricopa County	195	0.09
Encinal, NM (cdp) Cibola County	188	94.00
Barstow, CA (city) San Bernardino County	168	0.80
Socorro, TX (city) El Paso County	165	0.61
Keams Canyon, AZ (cdp) Navajo County	162	62.31
San Jose, CA (city) Santa Clara County	156	0.02
Pojoaque, NM (cdp) Santa Fe County	148	11.74
Tempe, AZ (city) Maricopa County	143	0.09
Chandler, AZ (city) Maricopa County	130	0.07
Bernalillo, NM (town) Sandoval County	124	1.88
Riverside, CA (city) Riverside County	122	0.05
Long Beach, CA (city) Los Angeles County	122	0.03
Winslow West, AZ (cdp) Coconino County	119	90.84
San Antonio, TX (city) Bexar County	115	0.01
Los Lunas, NM (village) Valencia County	111	1.11
Colorado Springs, CO (city) El Paso County	111	0.03
San Francisco, CA (city) San Francisco County	108	0.01
Taos, NM (town) Taos County	103	2.19
Espanola, NM (city) Rio Arriba County	103	1.06
Oklahoma City, OK (city) Oklahoma County	103	0.02
Chicago, IL (city) Cook County	103	0.00
Scottsdale, AZ (city) Maricopa County	101	0.05
Farmington, NM (city) San Juan County	97	0.26
Oakland, CA (city) Alameda County	97	0.02
Anchorage, AK (municipality) Anchorage Borough	96	0.04
Las Vegas, NV (city) Clark County	94	0.02
Portland, OR (city) Multnomah County	89	0.02
Sacramento, CA (city) Sacramento County	86	0.02
Lakewood, CO (city) Jefferson County	85	0.06
Anaheim, CA (city) Orange County	83	0.03
Houston, TX (city) Harris County	83	0.00
Carson City, NV (special city) Carson City city	78	0.15
Lawrence, KS (city) Douglas County	74	0.09
Aurora, CO (city) Arapahoe County	74	0.03
Whittier, CA (city) Los Angeles County	73	0.09
Dallas, TX (city) Dallas County	73	0.01
San Bernardino, CA (city) San Bernardino County	71	0.04
Honolulu, HI (cdp) Honolulu County	71	0.02
Santa Ana, CA (city) Orange County	69	0.02
Milan, NM (village) Cibola County	67	3.54
Camp Verde, AZ (town) Yavapai County	66	0.70
Yonkers, NY (city) Westchester County	65	0.03
Boston, MA (city) Suffolk County	65	0.01
Meadow Lake, NM (cdp) Valencia County	64	1.43
Fontana, CA (city) San Bernardino County	63	0.05
Dulce, NM (cdp) Rio Arriba County	61	2.33
North Valley, NM (cdp) Bernalillo County	61	0.51
Pueblo, CO (city) Pueblo County	61	0.06
Holbrook, AZ (city) Navajo County	59	1.20
Rialto, CA (city) San Bernardino County	59	0.06
Picuris Pueblo, NM (cdp) Taos County	56	65.12
Seattle, WA (city) King County	56	0.01
Norwalk, CA (city) Los Angeles County	54	0.05
Ontario, CA (city) San Bernardino County	54	0.03
Philadelphia, PA (city) Philadelphia County	54	0.00
Peoria, AZ (city) Maricopa County	53	0.05
Page, AZ (city) Coconino County	52	0.76
Modesto, CA (city) Stanislaus County	51	0.03
Gilbert, AZ (town) Maricopa County	50	0.05
Parker, AZ (town) La Paz County	49	1.56
Lancaster, CA (city) Los Angeles County	49	0.04
Apple Valley, CA (town) San Bernardino County	48	0.09
Fresno, CA (city) Fresno County	48	0.01
Orem, UT (city) Utah County	47	0.06
Sunrise Manor, NV (cdp) Clark County	47	0.03
Grand Canyon Village, AZ (cdp) Coconino County	46	3.15
Hesperia, CA (city) San Bernardino County	46	0.07
Austin, TX (city) Travis County	46	0.01
Tulsa, OK (city) Tulsa County	46	0.01
Durango, CO (city) La Plata County	45	0.32
Corona, CA (city) Riverside County	45	0.04
Paterson, NJ (city) Passaic County	45	0.03
Henderson, NV (city) Clark County	44	0.03
West Valley City, UT (city) Salt Lake County	43	0.04
Hayward, CA (city) Alameda County	43	0.03
Miami, FL (city) Miami-Dade County	42	0.01
Cameron, AZ (cdp) Coconino County	41	4.19
Provo, UT (city) Utah County	41	0.04
Rancho Cucamonga, CA (city) San Bernardino County	41	0.03
Garden Grove, CA (city) Orange County	41	0.02
Reno, NV (city) Washoe County	41	0.02
Stockton, CA (city) San Joaquin County	41	0.02
Wichita, KS (city) Sedgwick County	41	0.01
Roswell, NM (city) Chaves County	40	0.09
Bakersfield, CA (city) Kern County	40	0.02
Huntington Beach, CA (city) Orange County	40	0.02
Salt Lake City, UT (city) Salt Lake County	40	0.02
Alamogordo, NM (city) Otero County	39	0.11
Thornton, CO (city) Adams County	39	0.05
Fort Worth, TX (city) Tarrant County	39	0.01
Belen, NM (city) Valencia County	38	0.55
Palmdale, CA (city) Los Angeles County	38	0.03
Fremont, CA (city) Alameda County	38	0.02
Tacoma, WA (city) Pierce County	37	0.02
Perth Amboy, NJ (city) Middlesex County	36	0.08
Westminster, CA (city) Orange County	36	0.04
Amarillo, TX (city) Potter County	36	0.02
Shiprock, NM (cdp) San Juan County	35	0.43
Kingman, AZ (city) Mohave County	35	0.17
Victorville, CA (city) San Bernardino County	35	0.05
Norman, OK (city) Cleveland County	34	0.04
Spring Valley, NV (cdp) Clark County	34	0.03
Glendale, CA (city) Los Angeles County	34	0.02
Pomona, CA (city) Los Angeles County	34	0.02

Notes: (cdp) census designated place; Refer to the Explanation of Data in the front of the book for more detailed information.

American Indian: Pueblo

Top 150 Places Sorted by Percent

(Based on all places, regardless of population)

Place	Number	%
Zia Pueblo, NM (cdp) Sandoval County	634	98.14
Acomita Lake, NM (cdp) Cibola County	304	97.44
Isleta Village Proper, NM (cdp) Bernalillo County	476	95.97
Santo Domingo Pueblo, NM (cdp) Sandoval County	2,434	95.45
Encinal, NM (cdp) Cibola County	188	94.00
Zuni Pueblo, NM (cdp) McKinley County	5,946	93.39
Mesita, NM (cdp) Cibola County	719	92.65
Santa Ana Pueblo, NM (cdp) Sandoval County	442	92.28
San Felipe Pueblo, NM (cdp) Sandoval County	1,915	92.07
Skyline-Ganipa, NM (cdp) Cibola County	942	91.01
Winslow West, AZ (cdp) Coconino County	119	90.84
Jemez Pueblo, NM (cdp) Sandoval County	1,772	90.73
Shongopovi, AZ (cdp) Navajo County	573	90.66
Second Mesa, AZ (cdp) Navajo County	737	90.54
Paguate, NM (cdp) Cibola County	420	88.61
Laguna, NM (cdp) Cibola County	371	87.71
Hotevilla-Bacavi, AZ (cdp) Navajo County	671	87.48
Seama, NM (cdp) Cibola County	291	87.39
Taos Pueblo, NM (cdp) Taos County	1,102	87.18
Paraje, NM (cdp) Cibola County	581	86.85
First Mesa, AZ (cdp) Navajo County	968	86.12
Black Rock, NM (cdp) McKinley County	1,077	86.02
Pueblo of Sandia Village, NM (cdp) Sandoval County	295	85.76
Kykotsmovi Village, AZ (cdp) Navajo County	663	85.44
Moenkopi, AZ (cdp) Coconino County	760	84.35
North Acomita Village, NM (cdp) Cibola County	236	81.94
Cochiti, NM (cdp) Sandoval County	413	81.46
San Juan, NM (cdp) Rio Arriba County	466	78.72
San Ildefonso Pueblo, NM (cdp) Santa Fe County	321	70.09
Santa Clara Pueblo, NM (cdp) Rio Arriba County	686	70.00
Picuris Pueblo, NM (cdp) Taos County	56	65.12
Keams Canyon, AZ (cdp) Navajo County	162	62.31
Pojoaque, NM (cdp) Santa Fe County	148	11.74
San Ysidro, NM (village) Sandoval County	18	7.56
Tuba City, AZ (cdp) Coconino County	500	6.08
Grants, NM (city) Cibola County	421	4.78
Cameron, AZ (cdp) Coconino County	41	4.19
Ponderosa, NM (cdp) Sandoval County	13	4.19
Rio en Medio, NM (cdp) Santa Fe County	5	3.82
Milan, NM (village) Cibola County	67	3.54
Winslow, AZ (city) Navajo County	328	3.45
Yah-ta-hey, NM (cdp) McKinley County	19	3.28
Grand Canyon Village, AZ (cdp) Coconino County	46	3.15
Gallup, NM (city) McKinley County	624	3.09
Navajo Mountain, UT (cdp) San Juan County	11	2.90
Ruby, AK (city) Yukon-Koyukuk Census Area	5	2.66
Rio Lucio, NM (cdp) Taos County	10	2.64
Pinehill, NM (cdp) Cibola County	3	2.59
Pena Blanca, NM (cdp) Sandoval County	17	2.57
Dulce, NM (cdp) Rio Arriba County	61	2.33
Humptulips, WA (cdp) Grays Harbor County	5	2.31
Headrick, OK (town) Jackson County	3	2.31
Ramah, NM (cdp) McKinley County	9	2.21
Taos, NM (town) Taos County	103	2.19
Oakland, MN (township) Mahnomen County	5	1.92
Algodones, NM (cdp) Sandoval County	13	1.89
Yosemite Valley, CA (cdp) Mariposa County	5	1.89
Bernalillo, NM (town) Sandoval County	124	1.88
Santan, AZ (cdp) Pinal County	12	1.84
Casa Colorada, NM (cdp) Valencia County	1	1.79
Taos Ski Valley, NM (village) Taos County	1	1.79
La Puebla, NM (cdp) Santa Fe County	22	1.70
Jemez Springs, NM (village) Sandoval County	6	1.60
Parker, AZ (town) La Paz County	49	1.56
Starkville, CO (town) Las Animas County	2	1.56
Tse Bonito, NM (cdp) McKinley County	4	1.53
Meadow Lake, NM (cdp) Valencia County	64	1.43
Elmo, MT (cdp) Lake County	2	1.40
Mescalero, NM (cdp) Otero County	17	1.38
Rock Island Arsenal, IL (cdp) Rock Island County	2	1.38
El Valle de Arroyo Seco, NM (cdp) Santa Fe County	15	1.31
Kicking Horse, MT (cdp) Lake County	1	1.25
Penasco, NM (cdp) Taos County	7	1.22
Holbrook, AZ (city) Navajo County	59	1.20
Nelson Lagoon, AK (cdp) Aleutians East Borough	1	1.20
Ranchos de Taos, NM (cdp) Taos County	28	1.17
Lake Sumner, NM (cdp) De Baca County	1	1.16
Flagstaff, AZ (city) Coconino County	608	1.15
Los Lunas, NM (village) Valencia County	111	1.11
Espanola, NM (city) Rio Arriba County	103	1.06
Albuquerque, NM (city) Bernalillo County	4,695	1.05
Cuba, NM (village) Sandoval County	6	1.02
Mayview, MO (city) Lafayette County	3	1.02
Caney, OK (town) Atoka County	2	1.01
Regina, NM (cdp) Sandoval County	1	1.01
Chamisal, NM (cdp) Taos County	3	1.00
Blackwater, AZ (cdp) Pinal County	5	0.99
Thoreau, NM (cdp) McKinley County	18	0.97
Harrold, SD (town) Hughes County	2	0.96
Mayfield, UT (town) Sanpete County	4	0.95
Leupp, AZ (cdp) Coconino County	9	0.93
Hope, NM (village) Eddy County	1	0.93
Point Hope, AK (city) North Slope Borough	7	0.92
Towaoc, CO (cdp) Montezuma County	10	0.91
Ignacio, CO (town) La Plata County	6	0.90
Crownpoint, NM (cdp) McKinley County	23	0.87
Kego, MN (township) Cass County	4	0.86
Window Rock, AZ (cdp) Apache County	26	0.85
Edgewood, NM (town) Santa Fe County	16	0.85
Ojo Amarillo, NM (cdp) San Juan County	7	0.84
Neck City, MO (city) Jasper County	1	0.84
Tsaile, AZ (cdp) Apache County	9	0.83
Peach Springs, AZ (cdp) Mohave County	5	0.83
Naschitti, NM (cdp) San Juan County	3	0.83
Bluewater, AZ (cdp) La Paz County	6	0.82
Soldier, KS (city) Jackson County	1	0.82
Sombrillo, NM (cdp) Santa Fe County	4	0.81
Barstow, CA (city) San Bernardino County	168	0.80
Fort Defiance, AZ (cdp) Apache County	32	0.79
Eagle, AK (city) Southeast Fairbanks Census Area	1	0.78
Saint Michaels, AZ (cdp) Apache County	10	0.77
Page, AZ (city) Coconino County	52	0.76
Sacaton, AZ (cdp) Pinal County	12	0.76
Teec Nos Pos, AZ (cdp) Apache County	6	0.75
Los Trujillos-Gabaldon, NM (cdp) Valencia County	16	0.74
Moriarty, NM (city) Torrance County	13	0.74
Agua Fria, NM (cdp) Santa Fe County	15	0.73
Royalton, PA (borough) Dauphin County	7	0.73
Medicine Bow, WY (town) Carbon County	2	0.73
Rio Rancho, NM (city) Sandoval County	375	0.72
Cuyamungue, NM (cdp) Santa Fe County	3	0.71
Camp Verde, AZ (town) Yavapai County	66	0.70
San Carlos, AZ (cdp) Gila County	26	0.70
Shonto, AZ (cdp) Navajo County	4	0.70
Teton, ID (city) Fremont County	4	0.70
Dennehotso, AZ (cdp) Apache County	5	0.68
Nisqually Indian Community, WA (cdp) Thurston County	4	0.68
Santa Fe, NM (city) Santa Fe County	409	0.66
Modale, IA (city) Harrison County	2	0.66
Romoland, CA (cdp) Riverside County	18	0.65
Kayenta, AZ (cdp) Navajo County	31	0.63
Smyer, TX (town) Hockley County	3	0.63
Bluff, UT (cdp) San Juan County	2	0.63
Chupadero, NM (cdp) Santa Fe County	2	0.63
Socorro, TX (city) El Paso County	165	0.61
Peralta, NM (cdp) Valencia County	23	0.61
Pine, PA (township) Lycoming County	2	0.61
Valencia, NM (cdp) Valencia County	27	0.60
Loving, NM (village) Eddy County	8	0.60
Jackson, ME (town) Waldo County	3	0.59
Tropic, UT (town) Garfield County	3	0.59
El Cerro-Monterey Park, NM (cdp) Valencia County	32	0.58
Tohatchi, NM (cdp) McKinley County	6	0.58
Crystal, NM (cdp) McKinley County	2	0.58
Torrey, UT (town) Wayne County	1	0.58
Navajo, NM (cdp) McKinley County	12	0.57
Napi HQ, NM (cdp) San Juan County	4	0.57
Arbyrd, MO (city) Dunklin County	3	0.57
Arizona Village, AZ (cdp) Mohave County	2	0.57
Parker School, MT (cdp) Chouteau County	2	0.57

Notes: (cdp) census designated place: Refer to the Explanation of Data in the front of the book for more detailed information.

American Indian: Pueblo

Top 150 Places Sorted by Percent

(Based on places with populations of 10,000 or more)

Place	Number	%
Gallup, NM (city) McKinley County	624	3.09
Flagstaff, AZ (city) Coconino County	608	1.15
Los Lunas, NM (village) Valencia County	111	1.11
Albuquerque, NM (city) Bernalillo County	4,695	1.05
Barstow, CA (city) San Bernardino County	168	0.80
Rio Rancho, NM (city) Sandoval County	375	0.72
Santa Fe, NM (city) Santa Fe County	409	0.66
Socorro, TX (city) El Paso County	165	0.61
South Valley, NM (cdp) Bernalillo County	207	0.53
North Valley, NM (cdp) Bernalillo County	61	0.51
Las Cruces, NM (city) Dona Ana County	332	0.45
Durango, CO (city) La Plata County	45	0.32
Farmington, NM (city) San Juan County	97	0.26
San Elizario, TX (cdp) El Paso County	28	0.25
Las Vegas, NM (city) San Miguel County	32	0.22
Brigham City, UT (city) Box Elder County	32	0.18
Los Alamos, NM (cdp) Los Alamos County	22	0.18
Kingman, AZ (city) Mohave County	35	0.17
Phoenix, AZ (city) Maricopa County	2,089	0.16
El Paso, TX (city) El Paso County	910	0.16
Carson City, NV (special city) Carson City city	78	0.15
Portales, NM (city) Roosevelt County	17	0.15
Deming, NM (city) Luna County	18	0.13
Carlsbad, NM (city) Eddy County	30	0.12
Ashland, CA (cdp) Alameda County	25	0.12
New Kingman-Butler, AZ (cdp) Mohave County	18	0.12
Sierra Vista Southeast, AZ (cdp) Cochise County	17	0.12
Guymon, OK (city) Texas County	13	0.12
Alamogordo, NM (city) Otero County	39	0.11
Mohave Valley, AZ (cdp) Mohave County	15	0.11
Mesa, AZ (city) Maricopa County	401	0.10
Adelanto, CA (city) San Bernardino County	18	0.10
Vincent, CA (cdp) Los Angeles County	15	0.10
Silver City, NM (town) Grant County	11	0.10
Glendale, AZ (city) Maricopa County	195	0.09
Tempe, AZ (city) Maricopa County	143	0.09
Lawrence, KS (city) Douglas County	74	0.09
Whittier, CA (city) Los Angeles County	73	0.09
Apple Valley, CA (town) San Bernardino County	48	0.09
Roswell, NM (city) Chaves County	40	0.09
Prescott, AZ (city) Yavapai County	32	0.09
Lomita, CA (city) Los Angeles County	18	0.09
Twentynine Palms, CA (city) San Bernardino County	14	0.09
Ventnor City, NJ (city) Atlantic County	12	0.09
Artesia, NM (city) Eddy County	10	0.09
Clayton, CA (city) Contra Costa County	10	0.09
Valle Vista, CA (cdp) Riverside County	9	0.09
Perth Amboy, NJ (city) Middlesex County	36	0.08
Northglenn, CO (city) Adams County	25	0.08
Lake Elsinore, CA (city) Riverside County	22	0.08
Montrose, CO (city) Montrose County	10	0.08
Chandler, AZ (city) Maricopa County	130	0.07
Hesperia, CA (city) San Bernardino County	46	0.07
North Highlands, CA (cdp) Sacramento County	30	0.07
Stanton, CA (city) Orange County	25	0.07
West Whittier-Los Nietos, CA (cdp) Los Angeles County	18	0.07
Tooele, UT (city) Tooele County	16	0.07
Cedar City, UT (city) Iron County	15	0.07
South El Monte, CA (city) Los Angeles County	14	0.07
Florence, AZ (town) Pinal County	12	0.07
Pinewood, FL (cdp) Miami-Dade County	12	0.07
Elk Plain, WA (cdp) Pierce County	11	0.07
Glen Avon, CA (cdp) Riverside County	11	0.07
Salmon Creek, WA (cdp) Clark County	11	0.07
Fort Leonard Wood, MO (cdp) Pulaski County	10	0.07
South Ogden, UT (city) Weber County	10	0.07
Commerce, CA (city) Los Angeles County	9	0.07
Federal Heights, CO (city) Adams County	9	0.07
Beaumont, CA (city) Riverside County	8	0.07
Dickson, TN (city) Dickson County	8	0.07
Ecorse, MI (city) Wayne County	8	0.07
Enumclaw, WA (city) King County	8	0.07
Los Alamitos, CA (city) Orange County	8	0.07
Red Bank, NJ (borough) Monmouth County	8	0.07
Tucson, AZ (city) Pima County	300	0.06
Lakewood, CO (city) Jefferson County	85	0.06
Pueblo, CO (city) Pueblo County	61	0.06
Rialto, CA (city) San Bernardino County	59	0.06
Orem, UT (city) Utah County	47	0.06
La Mirada, CA (city) Los Angeles County	27	0.06
La Puente, CA (city) Los Angeles County	23	0.06
Perris, CA (city) Riverside County	20	0.06
Security-Widefield, CO (cdp) El Paso County	18	0.06
Juneau, AK (city and borough) Juneau Borough	17	0.06
Rubidoux, CA (cdp) Riverside County	17	0.06
West Springfield, VA (cdp) Fairfax County	17	0.06
Lemon Grove, CA (city) San Diego County	16	0.06
Drexel Heights, AZ (cdp) Pima County	15	0.06
San Fernando, CA (city) Los Angeles County	15	0.06
Casa Grande, AZ (city) Pinal County	14	0.06
Del City, OK (city) Oklahoma County	14	0.06
Prescott Valley, AZ (town) Yavapai County	13	0.06
Brighton, CO (city) Adams County	12	0.06
Galt, CA (city) Sacramento County	12	0.06
Hermosa Beach, CA (city) Los Angeles County	12	0.06
Alum Rock, CA (cdp) Santa Clara County	8	0.06
Fort Campbell North, KY (cdp) Christian County	8	0.06
Central Point, OR (city) Jackson County	7	0.06
College, AK (cdp) Fairbanks North Star Borough	7	0.06
Fort Morgan, CO (city) Morgan County	7	0.06
Cottonwood-Verde Village, AZ (cdp) Yavapai County	6	0.06
Crestline, CA (cdp) San Bernardino County	6	0.06
Kingsland, GA (city) Camden County	6	0.06
Denver, CO (city) Denver County	277	0.05
Riverside, CA (city) Riverside County	122	0.05
Scottsdale, AZ (city) Maricopa County	101	0.05
Fontana, CA (city) San Bernardino County	63	0.05
Norwalk, CA (city) Los Angeles County	54	0.05
Peoria, AZ (city) Maricopa County	53	0.05
Gilbert, AZ (town) Maricopa County	50	0.05
Thornton, CO (city) Adams County	39	0.05
Victorville, CA (city) San Bernardino County	35	0.05
Tracy, CA (city) San Joaquin County	31	0.05
Gardena, CA (city) Los Angeles County	27	0.05
Brentwood, NY (cdp) Suffolk County	26	0.05
National City, CA (city) San Diego County	25	0.05
Madera, CA (city) Madera County	20	0.05
Avondale, AZ (city) Maricopa County	19	0.05
Culver City, CA (city) Los Angeles County	19	0.05
San Dimas, CA (city) Los Angeles County	18	0.05
Clovis, NM (city) Curry County	17	0.05
Montclair, CA (city) San Bernardino County	17	0.05
Dublin, CA (city) Alameda County	16	0.05
Hobbs, NM (city) Lea County	15	0.05
Benicia, CA (city) Solano County	13	0.05
Clearfield, UT (city) Davis County	13	0.05
Magna, UT (cdp) Salt Lake County	11	0.05
South Salt Lake, UT (city) Salt Lake County	10	0.05
Spanaway, WA (cdp) Pierce County	10	0.05
Whitney, NV (cdp) Clark County	10	0.05
Bloomington, CA (cdp) San Bernardino County	9	0.05
Golden, CO (city) Jefferson County	9	0.05
Goodyear, AZ (city) Maricopa County	9	0.05
Yucca Valley, CA (town) San Bernardino County	9	0.05
Flowing Wells, AZ (cdp) Pima County	8	0.05
Live Oak, CA (cdp) Santa Cruz County	8	0.05
Mira Loma, CA (cdp) Riverside County	8	0.05
Roosevelt, NY (cdp) Nassau County	8	0.05
Ukiah, CA (city) Mendocino County	8	0.05
Bostonia, CA (cdp) San Diego County	7	0.05
Cimarron Hills, CO (cdp) El Paso County	7	0.05
Douglas, AZ (city) Cochise County	7	0.05
Fountain, CO (city) El Paso County	7	0.05
Hazel Crest, IL (village) Cook County	7	0.05
Lockport, IL (city) Will County	7	0.05
Stephenville, TX (city) Erath County	7	0.05
Sunland Park, NM (city) Dona Ana County	7	0.05
Tahlequah, OK (city) Cherokee County	7	0.05
Bemidji, MN (city) Beltrami County	6	0.05
Hope Mills, NC (town) Cumberland County	6	0.05

Notes: (cdp) census designated place; Refer to the Explanation of Data in the front of the book for more detailed information.

American Indian: Puget Sound Salish

Top 150 Places Sorted by Number

(Based on all places, regardless of population)

Place	Number	%
Tacoma, WA (city) Pierce County	956	0.49
Tulalip Bay, WA (cdp) Snohomish County	408	26.14
Skokomish, WA (cdp) Mason County	400	64.94
Auburn, WA (city) King County	381	0.95
Seattle, WA (city) King County	315	0.06
Nisqually Indian Community, WA (cdp) Thurston County	270	45.92
Everett, WA (city) Snohomish County	245	0.27
Suquamish, WA (cdp) Kitsap County	231	6.58
Shaker Church, WA (cdp) Snohomish County	197	25.03
Bellingham, WA (city) Whatcom County	135	0.20
Shelton, WA (city) Mason County	116	1.37
Marysville, WA (city) Snohomish County	116	0.46
Lakewood, WA (city) Pierce County	112	0.19
Fife, WA (city) Pierce County	97	2.03
North Marysville, WA (cdp) Snohomish County	89	0.42
Waller, WA (cdp) Pierce County	87	0.95
Portland, OR (city) Multnomah County	87	0.02
Kent, WA (city) King County	80	0.10
Indianola, WA (cdp) Kitsap County	76	2.51
Priest Point, WA (cdp) Snohomish County	68	8.73
Bremerton, WA (city) Kitsap County	64	0.17
Anacortes, WA (city) Skagit County	63	0.43
Lacey, WA (city) Thurston County	63	0.20
Federal Way, WA (city) King County	62	0.07
Olympia, WA (city) Thurston County	61	0.14
Bainbridge Island, WA (city) Kitsap County	60	0.30
Spanaway, WA (cdp) Pierce County	56	0.26
Puyallup, WA (city) Pierce County	55	0.17
Yakima, WA (city) Yakima County	53	0.07
Mount Vernon, WA (city) Skagit County	52	0.20
Spokane, WA (city) Spokane County	52	0.03
South Hill, WA (cdp) Pierce County	50	0.16
John Sam Lake, WA (cdp) Snohomish County	48	6.37
Midland, WA (cdp) Pierce County	42	0.57
Sedro-Woolley, WA (city) Skagit County	42	0.49
Port Angeles, WA (city) Clallam County	40	0.22
Aberdeen, WA (city) Grays Harbor County	39	0.24
Sumner, WA (city) Pierce County	38	0.45
Chehalis Village, WA (cdp) Grays Harbor County	36	10.40
White Center, WA (cdp) King County	34	0.16
Anchorage, AK (municipality) Anchorage Borough	34	0.01
SeaTac, WA (city) King County	33	0.13
Los Angeles, CA (city) Los Angeles County	33	0.00
West Lake Stevens, WA (cdp) Snohomish County	32	0.18
Burien, WA (city) King County	32	0.10
Summit, WA (cdp) Pierce County	29	0.36
Paine Field-Lake Stickney, WA (cdp) Snohomish County	28	0.11
Seattle Hill-Silver Firs, WA (cdp) Snohomish County	28	0.08
Vancouver, WA (city) Clark County	28	0.02
North Creek, WA (cdp) Snohomish County	27	0.10
Des Moines, WA (city) King County	27	0.09
Ferndale, WA (city) Whatcom County	25	0.29
Parkland, WA (cdp) Pierce County	25	0.10
Cascade-Fairwood, WA (cdp) King County	24	0.07
Port Hadlock-Irondale, WA (cdp) Jefferson County	23	0.66
University Place, WA (city) Pierce County	23	0.08
Shoreline, WA (city) King County	23	0.04
Las Vegas, NV (city) Clark County	23	0.00
San Diego, CA (city) San Diego County	23	0.00
East Hill-Meridian, WA (cdp) King County	22	0.08
Edmonds, WA (city) Snohomish County	22	0.06
Kennewick, WA (city) Benton County	22	0.04
Graham, WA (cdp) Pierce County	21	0.24
Tumwater, WA (city) Thurston County	21	0.17
Tanglewilde-Thompson Place, WA (cdp) Thurston County	20	0.35
Edgewood, WA (city) Pierce County	20	0.22
Covington, WA (city) King County	20	0.15
Mukilteo, WA (city) Snohomish County	20	0.11
Picnic Point-North Lynnwood, WA (cdp) Snohomish County	20	0.09
Bellevue, WA (city) King County	20	0.02
Taholah, WA (cdp) Grays Harbor County	19	2.31
Peaceful Valley, WA (cdp) Whatcom County	19	0.78
Port Townsend, WA (city) Jefferson County	19	0.23
Maple Valley, WA (city) King County	19	0.13
Pullman, WA (city) Whitman County	19	0.08
Algona, WA (city) King County	18	0.73
White Swan, WA (cdp) Yakima County	18	0.59
Yelm, WA (city) Thurston County	18	0.55
Marietta-Alderwood, WA (cdp) Whatcom County	18	0.50
Burlington, WA (city) Skagit County	18	0.27
Snohomish, WA (city) Snohomish County	18	0.21
Klamath Falls, OR (city) Klamath County	18	0.09
Oakville, WA (city) Grays Harbor County	17	2.52
Everson, WA (city) Whatcom County	17	0.84
Enumclaw, WA (city) King County	17	0.15
Monroe, WA (city) Snohomish County	17	0.12
Richland, WA (city) Benton County	17	0.04
Renton, WA (city) King County	17	0.03
Manchester, WA (cdp) Kitsap County	16	0.32
Hoquiam, WA (city) Grays Harbor County	16	0.18
Bonney Lake, WA (city) Pierce County	16	0.17
Arlington, WA (city) Snohomish County	16	0.14
Bothell, WA (city) King County	16	0.05
Granite Falls, WA (city) Snohomish County	15	0.64
Erlands Point-Kitsap Lake, WA (cdp) Kitsap County	15	0.55
Omak, WA (city) Okanogan County	15	0.32
Port Orchard, WA (city) Kitsap County	15	0.19
Artondale, WA (cdp) Pierce County	15	0.17
Tukwila, WA (city) King County	15	0.09
Fresno, CA (city) Fresno County	15	0.00
Tulsa, OK (city) Tulsa County	15	0.00
Centralia, WA (city) Lewis County	14	0.09
Wenatchee, WA (city) Chelan County	14	0.05
Darrington, WA (town) Snohomish County	13	1.14
Snoqualmie, WA (city) King County	13	0.80
Sultan, WA (city) Snohomish County	13	0.39
Kirkland, WA (city) King County	13	0.03
Phoenix, AZ (city) Maricopa County	13	0.00
Stimson Crossing, WA (cdp) Snohomish County	12	1.55
Milton, WA (city) Pierce County	12	0.21
Dallas, OR (city) Polk County	12	0.10
Bryn Mawr-Skyway, WA (cdp) King County	12	0.09
Sammamish, WA (city) King County	12	0.04
North Yelm, WA (cdp) Thurston County	11	0.39
Stanwood, WA (city) Snohomish County	11	0.28
Buckley, WA (city) Pierce County	11	0.27
East Port Orchard, WA (cdp) Kitsap County	11	0.22
Steilacoom, WA (town) Pierce County	11	0.18
Prairie Ridge, WA (cdp) Pierce County	11	0.09
Oak Harbor, WA (city) Island County	11	0.06
Lynnwood, WA (city) Snohomish County	11	0.03
Tigard, OR (city) Washington County	11	0.03
Corpus Christi, TX (city) Nueces County	11	0.00
Sacramento, CA (city) Sacramento County	11	0.00
Haines, AK (city) Haines Borough	10	0.55
Eatonville, WA (town) Pierce County	10	0.50
Ocean Shores, WA (city) Grays Harbor County	10	0.26
Union Hill-Novelty Hill, WA (cdp) King County	10	0.09
Kelso, WA (city) Cowlitz County	10	0.08
Camano, WA (cdp) Island County	10	0.07
Elk Plain, WA (cdp) Pierce County	10	0.06
Cottage Lake, WA (cdp) King County	10	0.04
Inglewood-Finn Hill, WA (cdp) King County	10	0.04
Longview, WA (city) Cowlitz County	10	0.03
Aloha, OR (cdp) Washington County	10	0.02
North Las Vegas, NV (city) Clark County	10	0.01
Salt Lake City, UT (city) Salt Lake County	10	0.01
Colorado Springs, CO (city) El Paso County	10	0.00
Denver, CO (city) Denver County	10	0.00
Honolulu, HI (cdp) Honolulu County	10	0.00
Oakland, CA (city) Alameda County	10	0.00
Cathan, WA (cdp) Snohomish County	9	1.71
Wapato, WA (city) Yakima County	9	0.20
Frederickson, WA (cdp) Pierce County	9	0.16
Poulsbo, WA (city) Kitsap County	9	0.13
Lake Morton-Berrydale, WA (cdp) King County	9	0.09
Vashon, WA (cdp) King County	9	0.09
Riverton-Boulevard Park, WA (cdp) King County	9	0.08
East Renton Highlands, WA (cdp) King County	9	0.07
Mountlake Terrace, WA (city) Snohomish County	9	0.04

Notes: (cdp) census designated place; Refer to the Explanation of Data in the front of the book for more detailed information.

American Indian: Puget Sound Salish

Top 150 Places Sorted by Percent

(Based on all places, regardless of population)

Place	Number	%
Skokomish, WA (cdp) Mason County	400	64.94
Nisqually Indian Community, WA (cdp) Thurston County	270	45.92
Tulalip Bay, WA (cdp) Snohomish County	408	26.14
Shaker Church, WA (cdp) Snohomish County	197	25.03
Chehalis Village, WA (cdp) Grays Harbor County	36	10.40
Priest Point, WA (cdp) Snohomish County	68	8.73
Suquamish, WA (cdp) Kitsap County	231	6.58
John Sam Lake, WA (cdp) Snohomish County	48	6.37
Oakville, WA (city) Grays Harbor County	17	2.52
Indianola, WA (cdp) Kitsap County	76	2.51
Nespelem, WA (town) Okanogan County	5	2.36
Taholah, WA (cdp) Grays Harbor County	19	2.31
Fife, WA (city) Pierce County	97	2.03
Cathan, WA (cdp) Snohomish County	9	1.71
Stimson Crossing, WA (cdp) Snohomish County	12	1.55
Naukati Bay, AK (cdp) Prince of Wales-Outer Ketchikan Census Area	2	1.48
Shelton, WA (city) Mason County	116	1.37
Marblemount, WA (cdp) Skagit County	3	1.20
Kirkpatrick, OR (cdp) Umatilla County	2	1.16
Washtucna, WA (town) Adams County	3	1.15
Darrington, WA (town) Snohomish County	13	1.14
Elmer City, WA (town) Okanogan County	3	1.12
Quilcene, WA (cdp) Jefferson County	6	1.02
Lake Bosworth, WA (cdp) Snohomish County	2	0.98
Auburn, WA (city) King County	381	0.95
Waller, WA (cdp) Pierce County	87	0.95
Deming, WA (cdp) Whatcom County	2	0.95
Kachemak, AK (city) Kenai Peninsula Borough	4	0.93
North Omak, WA (cdp) Okanogan County	6	0.87
Everson, WA (city) Whatcom County	17	0.84
Anderson, AK (city) Yukon-Koyukuk Census Area	3	0.82
Dodson, MT (town) Phillips County	1	0.82
Smithville, OK (town) McCurtain County	1	0.81
Snoqualmie, WA (city) King County	13	0.80
Peaceful Valley, WA (cdp) Whatcom County	19	0.78
Biola, CA (cdp) Fresno County	8	0.77
Wilkeson, WA (town) Pierce County	3	0.76
Edison, WA (cdp) Skagit County	1	0.75
Algona, WA (city) King County	18	0.73
Sumas, WA (city) Whatcom County	7	0.73
Lyman, WA (town) Skagit County	3	0.73
Bear Creek, WI (village) Outagamie County	3	0.72
Maple Falls, WA (cdp) Whatcom County	2	0.72
Macdoel, CA (cdp) Siskiyou County	1	0.71
Port Hadlock-Irondale, WA (cdp) Jefferson County	23	0.66
La Conner, WA (town) Skagit County	5	0.66
Moclips, WA (cdp) Grays Harbor County	4	0.65
Granite Falls, WA (city) Snohomish County	15	0.64
Hunker, PA (borough) Westmoreland County	2	0.61
White Swan, WA (cdp) Yakima County	18	0.59
Clinton, WA (cdp) Island County	5	0.58
Waumandee, WI (town) Buffalo County	3	0.58
Midland, WA (cdp) Pierce County	42	0.57
Yelm, WA (city) Thurston County	18	0.55
Erlands Point-Kitsap Lake, WA (cdp) Kitsap County	15	0.55
Haines, AK (city) Haines Borough	10	0.55
Harrah, WA (town) Yakima County	3	0.55
Carlton, OR (city) Yamhill County	8	0.53
Turtle Lake, MT (cdp) Lake County	1	0.52
Marietta-Alderwood, WA (cdp) Whatcom County	18	0.50
Eatonville, WA (town) Pierce County	10	0.50
Neah Bay, WA (cdp) Clallam County	4	0.50
Plymouth Village, KY (city) Jefferson County	1	0.50
Tacoma, WA (city) Pierce County	956	0.49
Sedro-Woolley, WA (city) Skagit County	42	0.49
Ravensdale, WA (cdp) King County	4	0.49
Marrowstone, WA (cdp) Jefferson County	4	0.48
Rainier, WA (town) Thurston County	7	0.47
Marysville, WA (city) Snohomish County	116	0.46
Fairfield, MT (town) Teton County	3	0.46
Sumner, WA (city) Pierce County	38	0.45
Mosquito Lake, AK (cdp) Haines Borough	1	0.45
Anacortes, WA (city) Skagit County	63	0.43
North Stanwood, WA (cdp) Snohomish County	2	0.43
North Marysville, WA (cdp) Snohomish County	89	0.42
Y, AK (cdp) Matanuska-Susitna Borough	4	0.42
Thompsons, TX (town) Fort Bend County	1	0.42
Glacier View, AK (cdp) Matanuska-Susitna Borough	1	0.40
Sultan, WA (city) Snohomish County	13	0.39
North Yelm, WA (cdp) Thurston County	11	0.39
Roy, WA (city) Pierce County	1	0.38
Wilmot, SD (city) Roberts County	2	0.37
Ashford, WA (cdp) Pierce County	1	0.37
Summit, WA (cdp) Pierce County	29	0.36
Tanglewilde-Thompson Place, WA (cdp) Thurston County	20	0.35
Friday Harbor, WA (town) San Juan County	7	0.35
Big Lake, WA (cdp) Skagit County	4	0.35
Carlsborg, WA (cdp) Clallam County	3	0.35
Echo Lake, WA (cdp) Snohomish County	3	0.35
McCleary, WA (city) Grays Harbor County	5	0.34
Sleepy Hollow, WY (cdp) Campbell County	4	0.34
Dorris, CA (city) Siskiyou County	3	0.34
Manchester, WA (cdp) Kitsap County	16	0.32
Omak, WA (city) Okanogan County	15	0.32
Smokey Point, WA (cdp) Snohomish County	5	0.32
Twisp, WA (town) Okanogan County	3	0.32
Delight, AR (city) Pike County	1	0.32
Bainbridge Island, WA (city) Kitsap County	60	0.30
Freeland, WA (cdp) Island County	4	0.30
Martin City, MT (cdp) Flathead County	1	0.30
Ferndale, WA (city) Whatcom County	25	0.29
Fox Island, WA (cdp) Pierce County	8	0.29
Bridgeport, WA (city) Douglas County	6	0.29
Winthrop, WA (town) Okanogan County	1	0.29
Stanwood, WA (city) Snohomish County	11	0.28
South Bend, WA (city) Pacific County	5	0.28
South Mansfield, LA (village) De Soto Parish	1	0.28
Everett, WA (city) Snohomish County	245	0.27
Burlington, WA (city) Skagit County	18	0.27
Buckley, WA (city) Pierce County	11	0.27
Raymond, WA (city) Pacific County	8	0.27
Rochester, WA (cdp) Thurston County	5	0.27
Bell Hill, WA (cdp) Clallam County	2	0.27
Ruston, WA (town) Pierce County	2	0.27
Bombay Beach, CA (cdp) Imperial County	1	0.27
Spanaway, WA (cdp) Pierce County	56	0.26
Ocean Shores, WA (city) Grays Harbor County	10	0.26
Jordan Road-Canyon Creek, WA (cdp) Snohomish County	6	0.26
South Prairie, WA (town) Pierce County	1	0.26
Warm Beach, WA (cdp) Snohomish County	5	0.25
Yatesville, GA (town) Upson County	1	0.25
Aberdeen, WA (city) Grays Harbor County	39	0.24
Graham, WA (cdp) Pierce County	21	0.24
Arlington Heights, WA (cdp) Snohomish County	6	0.24
Willow, AK (cdp) Matanuska-Susitna Borough	4	0.24
Port Townsend, WA (city) Jefferson County	19	0.23
King Salmon, AK (cdp) Bristol Bay Borough	1	0.23
Port Angeles, WA (city) Clallam County	40	0.22
Edgewood, WA (city) Pierce County	20	0.22
East Port Orchard, WA (cdp) Kitsap County	11	0.22
Cascade Valley, WA (cdp) Grant County	4	0.22
River Road, WA (cdp) Clallam County	1	0.22
Springdale, UT (town) Washington County	1	0.22
Snohomish, WA (city) Snohomish County	18	0.21
Milton, WA (city) Pierce County	12	0.21
Whetstone, AZ (cdp) Cochise County	5	0.21
Gold Beach, OR (city) Curry County	4	0.21
Craig, AK (city) Prince of Wales-Outer Ketchikan Census Area	3	0.21
Falls City, OR (city) Polk County	2	0.21
Salamatof, AK (cdp) Kenai Peninsula Borough	2	0.21
Burt, MI (township) Alger County	1	0.21
Fern Forest, HI (cdp) Hawaii County	1	0.21
Bellingham, WA (city) Whatcom County	135	0.20
Lacey, WA (city) Thurston County	63	0.20
Mount Vernon, WA (city) Skagit County	52	0.20
Wapato, WA (city) Yakima County	9	0.20
Central Park, WA (cdp) Grays Harbor County	5	0.20
Westwood, CA (cdp) Lassen County	4	0.20
Todd, PA (township) Fulton County	3	0.20
Roslyn, WA (city) Kittitas County	2	0.20

Notes: (cdp) census designated place; Refer to the Explanation of Data in the front of the book for more detailed information.

American Indian: Puget Sound Salish

Top 150 Places Sorted by Percent

(Based on places with populations of 10,000 or more)

Place	Number	%
Auburn, WA (city) King County	381	0.95
Tacoma, WA (city) Pierce County	956	0.49
Marysville, WA (city) Snohomish County	116	0.46
Anacortes, WA (city) Skagit County	63	0.43
North Marysville, WA (cdp) Snohomish County	89	0.42
Bainbridge Island, WA (city) Kitsap County	60	0.30
Everett, WA (city) Snohomish County	245	0.27
Spanaway, WA (cdp) Pierce County	56	0.26
Aberdeen, WA (city) Grays Harbor County	39	0.24
Port Angeles, WA (city) Clallam County	40	0.22
Bellingham, WA (city) Whatcom County	135	0.20
Lacey, WA (city) Thurston County	63	0.20
Mount Vernon, WA (city) Skagit County	52	0.20
Lakewood, WA (city) Pierce County	112	0.19
West Lake Stevens, WA (cdp) Snohomish County	32	0.18
Bremerton, WA (city) Kitsap County	64	0.17
Puyallup, WA (city) Pierce County	55	0.17
Tumwater, WA (city) Thurston County	21	0.17
South Hill, WA (cdp) Pierce County	50	0.16
White Center, WA (cdp) King County	34	0.16
Covington, WA (city) King County	20	0.15
Enumclaw, WA (city) King County	17	0.15
Olympia, WA (city) Thurston County	61	0.14
Arlington, WA (city) Snohomish County	16	0.14
SeaTac, WA (city) King County	33	0.13
Maple Valley, WA (city) King County	19	0.13
Monroe, WA (city) Snohomish County	17	0.12
Paine Field-Lake Stickney, WA (cdp) Snohomish County	28	0.11
Mukilteo, WA (city) Snohomish County	20	0.11
Kent, WA (city) King County	80	0.10
Burien, WA (city) King County	32	0.10
North Creek, WA (cdp) Snohomish County	27	0.10
Parkland, WA (cdp) Pierce County	25	0.10
Dallas, OR (city) Polk County	12	0.10
Des Moines, WA (city) King County	27	0.09
Picnic Point-North Lynnwood, WA (cdp) Snohomish County	20	0.09
Klamath Falls, OR (city) Klamath County	18	0.09
Tukwila, WA (city) King County	15	0.09
Centralia, WA (city) Lewis County	14	0.09
Bryn Mawr-Skyway, WA (cdp) King County	12	0.09
Prairie Ridge, WA (cdp) Pierce County	11	0.09
Union Hill-Novelty Hill, WA (cdp) King County	10	0.09
Vashon, WA (cdp) King County	9	0.09
Seattle Hill-Silver Firs, WA (cdp) Snohomish County	28	0.08
University Place, WA (city) Pierce County	23	0.08
East Hill-Meridian, WA (cdp) King County	22	0.08
Pullman, WA (city) Whitman County	19	0.08
Kelso, WA (city) Cowlitz County	10	0.08
Riverton-Boulevard Park, WA (cdp) King County	9	0.08
Federal Way, WA (city) King County	62	0.07
Yakima, WA (city) Yakima County	53	0.07
Cascade-Fairwood, WA (cdp) King County	24	0.07
Camano, WA (cdp) Island County	10	0.07
East Renton Highlands, WA (cdp) King County	9	0.07
Lakeland South, WA (cdp) King County	8	0.07
Dishman, WA (cdp) Spokane County	7	0.07
Seattle, WA (city) King County	315	0.06
Edmonds, WA (city) Snohomish County	22	0.06
Oak Harbor, WA (city) Island County	11	0.06
Elk Plain, WA (cdp) Pierce County	10	0.06
Lea Hill, WA (cdp) King County	6	0.06
Bothell, WA (city) King County	16	0.05
Wenatchee, WA (city) Chelan County	14	0.05
Lakeland North, WA (cdp) King County	8	0.05
Silverdale, WA (cdp) Kitsap County	8	0.05
McKinleyville, CA (cdp) Humboldt County	7	0.05
Kingsgate, WA (cdp) King County	6	0.05
Saint Helens, OR (city) Columbia County	5	0.05
West Valley, WA (cdp) Yakima County	5	0.05
Shoreline, WA (city) King County	23	0.04
Kennewick, WA (city) Benton County	22	0.04
Richland, WA (city) Benton County	17	0.04
Sammamish, WA (city) King County	12	0.04
Cottage Lake, WA (cdp) King County	10	0.04
Inglewood-Finn Hill, WA (cdp) King County	10	0.04
Mountlake Terrace, WA (city) Snohomish County	9	0.04
Kenmore, WA (city) King County	7	0.04
Alderwood Manor, WA (cdp) Snohomish County	6	0.04
East Wenatchee Bench, WA (cdp) Douglas County	6	0.04
Ellensburg, WA (city) Kittitas County	6	0.04
Camas, WA (city) Clark County	5	0.04
Kalispell, MT (city) Flathead County	5	0.04
Fort Carson, CO (cdp) El Paso County	4	0.04
Spokane, WA (city) Spokane County	52	0.03
Renton, WA (city) King County	17	0.03
Kirkland, WA (city) King County	13	0.03
Lynnwood, WA (city) Snohomish County	11	0.03
Tigard, OR (city) Washington County	11	0.03
Longview, WA (city) Cowlitz County	10	0.03
Juneau, AK (city and borough) Juneau Borough	9	0.03
Atwater, CA (city) Merced County	7	0.03
Woodburn, OR (city) Marion County	7	0.03
Bellview, FL (cdp) Escambia County	6	0.03
Bloomingdale, FL (cdp) Hillsborough County	6	0.03
Altamont, OR (cdp) Klamath County	5	0.03
Post Falls, ID (city) Kootenai County	5	0.03
Five Corners, WA (cdp) Clark County	4	0.03
Kingston, PA (borough) Luzerne County	4	0.03
Shafter, CA (city) Kern County	4	0.03
College, AK (cdp) Fairbanks North Star Borough	3	0.03
New River, AZ (cdp) Maricopa County	3	0.03
Spring Creek, NV (cdp) Elko County	3	0.03
Portland, OR (city) Multnomah County	87	0.02
Vancouver, WA (city) Clark County	28	0.02
Bellevue, WA (city) King County	20	0.02
Aloha, OR (cdp) Washington County	10	0.02
Keizer, OR (city) Marion County	8	0.02
Redmond, WA (city) King County	8	0.02
Springfield, OR (city) Lane County	8	0.02
Midvale, UT (city) Salt Lake County	6	0.02
Ponca City, OK (city) Kay County	6	0.02
Twin Falls, ID (city) Twin Falls County	6	0.02
Moscow, ID (city) Latah County	5	0.02
Northglenn, CO (city) Adams County	5	0.02
Walla Walla, WA (city) Walla Walla County	5	0.02
Grants Pass, OR (city) Josephine County	4	0.02
Medford, NJ (township) Burlington County	4	0.02
Milwaukie, OR (city) Clackamas County	4	0.02
Radcliff, KY (city) Hardin County	4	0.02
Springville, UT (city) Utah County	4	0.02
Buckingham, PA (township) Bucks County	3	0.02
Coto de Caza, CA (cdp) Orange County	3	0.02
Foothill Farms, CA (cdp) Sacramento County	3	0.02
Geneva, NY (city) Ontario County	3	0.02
Grover Beach, CA (city) San Luis Obispo County	3	0.02
Hermiston, OR (city) Umatilla County	3	0.02
La Grande, OR (city) Union County	3	0.02
Lake Forest Park, WA (city) King County	3	0.02
Martha Lake, WA (cdp) Snohomish County	3	0.02
Newberg, OR (city) Yamhill County	3	0.02
Oroville, CA (city) Butte County	3	0.02
Tullahoma, TN (city) Coffee County	3	0.02
Issaquah, WA (city) King County	2	0.02
Marysville, CA (city) Yuba County	2	0.02
Sedona, AZ (city) Yavapai County	2	0.02
Wabash, IN (city) Wabash County	2	0.02
Washington, MO (city) Franklin County	2	0.02
Anchorage, AK (municipality) Anchorage Borough	34	0.01
North Las Vegas, NV (city) Clark County	10	0.01
Salt Lake City, UT (city) Salt Lake County	10	0.01
Eugene, OR (city) Lane County	9	0.01
Moreno Valley, CA (city) Riverside County	9	0.01
Fairfield, CA (city) Solano County	7	0.01
Medford, OR (city) Jackson County	7	0.01
San Mateo, CA (city) San Mateo County	7	0.01
Appleton, WI (city) Outagamie County	6	0.01
Arden-Arcade, CA (cdp) Sacramento County	6	0.01
Bend, OR (city) Deschutes County	6	0.01
Manteca, CA (city) San Joaquin County	6	0.01
Missoula, MT (city) Missoula County	6	0.01

Notes: (cdp) census designated place; Refer to the Explanation of Data in the front of the book for more detailed information.

American Indian: Seminole

Top 150 Places Sorted by Number

(Based on all places, regardless of population)

Place	Number	%
Oklahoma City, OK (city) Oklahoma County	1,486	0.29
Seminole, OK (city) Seminole County	784	11.36
Shawnee, OK (city) Pottawatomie County	656	2.29
Wewoka, OK (city) Seminole County	583	16.37
Tulsa, OK (city) Tulsa County	469	0.12
New York, NY (city) New York City	374	0.00
Los Angeles, CA (city) Los Angeles County	259	0.01
Konawa, OK (city) Seminole County	239	16.16
Norman, OK (city) Cleveland County	231	0.24
Ada, OK (city) Pontotoc County	223	1.42
Holdenville, OK (city) Hughes County	185	3.91
Midwest City, OK (city) Oklahoma County	152	0.28
Tecumseh, OK (city) Pottawatomie County	147	2.41
Philadelphia, PA (city) Philadelphia County	134	0.01
Jacksonville, FL (special city) Duval County	124	0.02
Immokalee, FL (cdp) Collier County	123	0.62
Wichita, KS (city) Sedgwick County	121	0.04
Moore, OK (city) Cleveland County	114	0.28
Del City, OK (city) Oklahoma County	107	0.48
Maud, OK (city) Pottawatomie County	105	9.24
San Antonio, TX (city) Bexar County	104	0.01
Lawrence, KS (city) Douglas County	94	0.12
Chicago, IL (city) Cook County	81	0.00
Dallas, TX (city) Dallas County	79	0.01
San Diego, CA (city) San Diego County	78	0.01
Okmulgee, OK (city) Okmulgee County	74	0.57
Tampa, FL (city) Hillsborough County	74	0.02
Albuquerque, NM (city) Bernalillo County	73	0.02
Lawton, OK (city) Comanche County	71	0.08
Seattle, WA (city) King County	67	0.01
Muskogee, OK (city) Muskogee County	66	0.17
San Jose, CA (city) Santa Clara County	65	0.01
Houston, TX (city) Harris County	61	0.00
Detroit, MI (city) Wayne County	58	0.01
Edmond, OK (city) Oklahoma County	57	0.08
Honolulu, HI (cdp) Honolulu County	56	0.02
Okemah, OK (city) Okfuskee County	55	1.81
Ardmore, OK (city) Carter County	55	0.23
Oakland, CA (city) Alameda County	55	0.01
Denver, CO (city) Denver County	54	0.01
San Francisco, CA (city) San Francisco County	54	0.01
Portland, OR (city) Multnomah County	53	0.01
Sacramento, CA (city) Sacramento County	52	0.01
Phoenix, AZ (city) Maricopa County	52	0.00
Virginia Beach, VA (independent city) Virginia Beach city	48	0.01
Wetumka, OK (city) Hughes County	45	3.10
Kansas City, MO (city) Jackson County	45	0.01
Glenpool, OK (city) Tulsa County	44	0.54
McAlester, OK (city) Pittsburg County	44	0.25
Fort Worth, TX (city) Tarrant County	44	0.01
Las Vegas, NV (city) Clark County	44	0.01
McLoud, OK (town) Pottawatomie County	43	1.21
Anchorage, AK (municipality) Anchorage Borough	43	0.02
Aurora, CO (city) Arapahoe County	43	0.02
Baltimore, MD (independent city) Baltimore city	43	0.01
Saint Petersburg, FL (city) Pinellas County	41	0.02
Cleveland, OH (city) Cuyahoga County	41	0.01
Long Beach, CA (city) Los Angeles County	41	0.01
Broken Arrow, OK (city) Tulsa County	40	0.05
Washington, DC (city) District of Columbia	39	0.01
Hollywood, FL (city) Broward County	38	0.03
Lancaster, CA (city) Los Angeles County	38	0.03
Tahlequah, OK (city) Cherokee County	37	0.26
Hempstead, NY (town) Nassau County	37	0.00
El Reno, OK (city) Canadian County	36	0.22
Stillwater, OK (city) Payne County	36	0.09
Orlando, FL (city) Orange County	36	0.02
East Lake-Orient Park, FL (cdp) Hillsborough County	35	0.61
Yukon, OK (city) Canadian County	35	0.17
Rochester, NY (city) Monroe County	35	0.02
Columbus, OH (city) Franklin County	35	0.00
Sapulpa, OK (city) Creek County	34	0.18
Bowlegs, OK (town) Seminole County	33	8.89
Fresno, CA (city) Fresno County	33	0.01
Claremore, OK (city) Rogers County	32	0.20
Visalia, CA (city) Tulare County	32	0.03
Brookhaven, NY (town) Suffolk County	32	0.01
Nashville-Davidson, TN (special city) Davidson County	31	0.01
Henryetta, OK (city) Okmulgee County	30	0.49
Arlington, TX (city) Tarrant County	30	0.01
Boston, MA (city) Suffolk County	30	0.01
Minneapolis, MN (city) Hennepin County	30	0.01
Austin, TX (city) Travis County	30	0.00
Sasakwa, OK (town) Seminole County	29	19.33
Bakersfield, CA (city) Kern County	29	0.01
Colorado Springs, CO (city) El Paso County	29	0.01
Newark, NJ (city) Essex County	29	0.01
Modesto, CA (city) Stanislaus County	28	0.01
Park Hill, OK (cdp) Cherokee County	27	0.69
Davie, FL (town) Broward County	27	0.04
Toledo, OH (city) Lucas County	27	0.01
North Highlands, CA (cdp) Sacramento County	26	0.06
Brandon, FL (cdp) Hillsborough County	26	0.03
Charlotte, NC (city) Mecklenburg County	26	0.00
Cromwell, OK (town) Seminole County	25	9.43
Choctaw, OK (city) Oklahoma County	25	0.27
Bethany, OK (city) Oklahoma County	25	0.12
Berkeley, CA (city) Alameda County	25	0.02
Riverside, CA (city) Riverside County	25	0.01
Saint Louis, MO (independent city) Saint Louis city	25	0.01
Bartlesville, OK (city) Washington County	24	0.07
Columbus, GA (special city) Muscogee County	24	0.01
Corpus Christi, TX (city) Nueces County	24	0.01
Hampton, VA (independent city) Hampton city	23	0.02
Fremont, CA (city) Alameda County	23	0.01
Garland, TX (city) Dallas County	23	0.01
Oceanside, CA (city) San Diego County	23	0.01
Tucson, AZ (city) Pima County	23	0.00
Okeechobee, FL (city) Okeechobee County	22	0.41
Ponca City, OK (city) Kay County	22	0.08
Pittsburg, CA (city) Contra Costa County	22	0.04
Buffalo, NY (city) Erie County	22	0.01
Tallahassee, FL (city) Leon County	22	0.01
Mustang, OK (city) Canadian County	21	0.16
Eugene, OR (city) Lane County	21	0.02
Gainesville, FL (city) Alachua County	21	0.02
Irving, TX (city) Dallas County	21	0.01
Springfield, MO (city) Greene County	21	0.01
Tacoma, WA (city) Pierce County	21	0.01
Tempe, AZ (city) Maricopa County	21	0.01
Palm Bay, FL (city) Brevard County	20	0.03
Independence, MO (city) Jackson County	20	0.02
Boise City, ID (city) Ada County	20	0.01
Mesa, AZ (city) Maricopa County	20	0.01
Paradise, NV (cdp) Clark County	20	0.01
Indianapolis, IN (special city) Marion County	20	0.00
Byng, OK (town) Pontotoc County	19	1.74
The Village, OK (city) Oklahoma County	19	0.19
Kerrville, TX (city) Kerr County	19	0.09
Enid, OK (city) Garfield County	19	0.04
Fullerton, CA (city) Orange County	19	0.02
Richmond, CA (city) Contra Costa County	19	0.02
Garden Grove, CA (city) Orange County	19	0.01
Milwaukee, WI (city) Milwaukee County	19	0.00
Weleetka, OK (town) Okfuskee County	18	1.78
Hawthorne, CA (city) Los Angeles County	18	0.02
Palmdale, CA (city) Los Angeles County	18	0.02
Cincinnati, OH (city) Hamilton County	18	0.01
Concord, CA (city) Contra Costa County	18	0.01
Flint, MI (city) Genesee County	18	0.01
New Haven, CT (city) New Haven County	18	0.01
Pittsburgh, PA (city) Allegheny County	18	0.01
Oakhurst, OK (cdp) Tulsa County	17	0.62
Bristow, OK (city) Creek County	17	0.39
Blackwell, OK (city) Kay County	17	0.22
Daytona Beach, FL (city) Volusia County	17	0.03
Fayetteville, AR (city) Washington County	17	0.03
Merced, CA (city) Merced County	17	0.03
Gulfport, MS (city) Harrison County	17	0.02
Port Saint Lucie, FL (city) Saint Lucie County	17	0.02

Notes: (cdp) census designated place; Refer to the Explanation of Data in the front of the book for more detailed information.

American Indian: Seminole

Top 150 Places Sorted by Percent

(Based on all places, regardless of population)

Place	Number	%
Sasakwa, OK (town) Seminole County	29	19.33
Wewoka, OK (city) Seminole County	583	16.37
Konawa, OK (city) Seminole County	239	16.16
Yeager, OK (town) Hughes County	9	13.43
Seminole, OK (city) Seminole County	784	11.36
Shady Grove, OK (town) Pawnee County	5	11.36
Lima, OK (town) Seminole County	7	9.46
Cromwell, OK (town) Seminole County	25	9.43
Maud, OK (city) Pottawatomie County	105	9.24
Bowlegs, OK (town) Seminole County	33	8.89
Horntown, OK (town) Hughes County	5	8.20
Elbert, TX (cdp) Throckmorton County	3	5.36
Holdenville, OK (city) Hughes County	185	3.91
Cantwell, AK (cdp) Yukon-Koyukuk Census Area	8	3.60
Dustin, OK (town) Hughes County	15	3.32
Rocky Mound, TX (town) Camp County	3	3.23
Wetumka, OK (city) Hughes County	45	3.10
Red Rock, OK (town) Noble County	8	2.73
Dripping Springs, OK (cdp) Delaware County	1	2.44
Saint Louis, OK (town) Pottawatomie County	5	2.43
Tecumseh, OK (city) Pottawatomie County	147	2.41
Shawnee, OK (city) Pottawatomie County	656	2.29
Batesland, SD (town) Shannon County	2	2.27
Brooksville, OK (town) Pottawatomie County	2	2.22
Niarada, MT (cdp) Sanders County	1	2.00
Eagle Harbor, MD (town) Prince George's County	1	1.82
Okemah, OK (city) Okfuskee County	55	1.81
Clearview, OK (town) Okfuskee County	1	1.79
Weleetka, OK (town) Okfuskee County	18	1.78
Byng, OK (town) Pontotoc County	19	1.74
Earlsboro, OK (town) Pottawatomie County	11	1.74
Asher, OK (town) Pottawatomie County	7	1.67
Spaulding, OK (town) Hughes County	1	1.61
Douglas, ND (city) Ward County	1	1.56
Colony, KS (city) Anderson County	6	1.51
Valley Brook, OK (town) Oklahoma County	12	1.47
Tushka, OK (town) Atoka County	5	1.45
Ada, OK (city) Pontotoc County	223	1.42
Colony, OK (town) Washita County	2	1.36
Tupelo, OK (city) Coal County	5	1.33
Loco, OK (town) Stephens County	2	1.33
Redbird, OK (town) Wagoner County	2	1.31
Riley, KS (city) Riley County	11	1.24
McLoud, OK (town) Pottawatomie County	43	1.21
Lamar, OK (town) Hughes County	2	1.16
Morley, IA (city) Jones County	1	1.14
Arcadia, OK (town) Oklahoma County	3	1.08
Byars, OK (town) McClain County	3	1.07
Cole, OK (town) McClain County	5	1.06
Meeker, OK (town) Lincoln County	10	1.02
Gene Autry, OK (town) Carter County	1	1.01
Strang, OK (town) Mayes County	1	1.00
Lost City, OK (cdp) Cherokee County	8	0.99
Dry Creek, OK (cdp) Cherokee County	2	0.93
Johnson, OK (town) Pottawatomie County	2	0.90
Elk Falls, KS (city) Elk County	1	0.89
Two Rivers, AK (cdp) Fairbanks North Star Borough	4	0.83
Rattan, OK (town) Pushmataha County	2	0.83
Castle, OK (town) Okfuskee County	1	0.82
Geary, OK (city) Blaine County	10	0.79
Forestville, MI (village) Sanilac County	1	0.79
Cove, AR (town) Polk County	3	0.78
Grandfalls, TX (town) Ward County	3	0.77
Melrose, IA (city) Monroe County	1	0.77
Prague, OK (city) Lincoln County	16	0.75
Alpine Village, CA (cdp) Alpine County	1	0.74
Boynton, OK (town) Muskogee County	2	0.73
La Crosse, FL (town) Alachua County	1	0.70
Park Hill, OK (cdp) Cherokee County	27	0.69
Cohutta, GA (town) Whitfield County	4	0.69
Davenport, OK (town) Lincoln County	6	0.68
Helena, OK (town) Alfalfa County	3	0.68
Tryon, OK (town) Lincoln County	3	0.67
Talihina, OK (town) Le Flore County	8	0.66
Fort Greely, AK (cdp) Southeast Fairbanks Census Area	3	0.65
Fellows, CA (cdp) Kern County	1	0.65
Immokalee, FL (cdp) Collier County	123	0.62
Oakhurst, OK (cdp) Tulsa County	17	0.62
Metaline, WA (town) Pend Oreille County	1	0.62
East Lake-Orient Park, FL (cdp) Hillsborough County	35	0.61
Eufaula, OK (city) McIntosh County	16	0.61
Lake Annette, MO (city) Cass County	1	0.61
Francis, OK (town) Pontotoc County	2	0.60
Pickstown, SD (town) Charles Mix County	1	0.60
Locust Grove, OK (town) Mayes County	8	0.59
Colma, CA (town) San Mateo County	7	0.59
Tatums, OK (town) Carter County	1	0.58
Okmulgee, OK (city) Okmulgee County	74	0.57
Dill City, OK (town) Washita County	3	0.57
Binger, OK (town) Caddo County	1	0.56
Hulbert, OK (town) Cherokee County	3	0.55
Glenpool, OK (city) Tulsa County	44	0.54
Dewar, OK (town) Okmulgee County	5	0.54
Roff, OK (town) Pontotoc County	4	0.54
Miller, MO (city) Lawrence County	4	0.53
Reddick, FL (town) Marion County	3	0.53
Davidson, OK (town) Tillman County	2	0.53
Pink, OK (town) Pottawatomie County	6	0.52
Fanshawe, OK (town) Le Flore County	2	0.52
Turtle Lake, MT (cdp) Lake County	2	0.52
Concord, MN (township) Dodge County	3	0.51
Akron, MN (township) Big Stone County	1	0.51
Henryetta, OK (city) Okmulgee County	30	0.49
Krebs, OK (city) Pittsburg County	10	0.49
Sanford, TX (town) Hutchinson County	1	0.49
Del City, OK (city) Oklahoma County	107	0.48
Thomas, OK (city) Custer County	6	0.48
Chickaloon, AK (cdp) Matanuska-Susitna Borough	1	0.47
Riverdale, NE (village) Buffalo County	1	0.47
Schoenchen, KS (city) Ellis County	1	0.47
Morris, OK (city) Okmulgee County	6	0.46
Strong, AR (city) Union County	3	0.46
Crowder, OK (town) Pittsburg County	2	0.46
New Hope, TX (town) Collin County	3	0.45
Velma, OK (town) Stephens County	3	0.45
Paden, OK (town) Okfuskee County	2	0.45
Kellyville, OK (town) Creek County	4	0.44
Stagecoach, TX (town) Montgomery County	2	0.44
Spencer, OK (city) Oklahoma County	16	0.43
Stonewall, OK (town) Pontotoc County	2	0.43
Fostoria, IA (city) Clay County	1	0.43
Goodsprings, NV (cdp) Clark County	1	0.43
Larkspur, CO (town) Douglas County	1	0.43
Allen, OK (town) Pontotoc County	4	0.42
Hillcrest, TX (village) Brazoria County	3	0.42
Okeechobee, FL (city) Okeechobee County	22	0.41
Paisley, FL (cdp) Lake County	3	0.41
Bradford, WI (town) Rock County	4	0.40
Double Springs, AL (town) Winston County	4	0.40
Achille, OK (town) Bryan County	2	0.40
Emmet, AR (city) Nevada County	2	0.40
Meta, MO (city) Osage County	1	0.40
Bristow, OK (city) Creek County	17	0.39
New Cordell, OK (city) Washita County	11	0.38
Forest Park, OK (town) Oklahoma County	4	0.38
Lyle, WA (cdp) Klickitat County	2	0.38
Saint Paul, AK (city) Aleutians West Census Area	2	0.38
Silas, AL (town) Choctaw County	2	0.38
Hebron, MD (town) Wicomico County	3	0.37
Study Butte-Terlingua, TX (cdp) Brewster County	1	0.37
Haleiwa, HI (cdp) Honolulu County	8	0.36
Boley, OK (town) Okfuskee County	4	0.36
Mountain City, GA (town) Rabun County	3	0.36
Scottsville, VA (town) Albemarle County	2	0.36
Calvin, OK (town) Hughes County	1	0.36
East Thermopolis, WY (town) Hot Springs County	1	0.36
Marland, OK (town) Noble County	1	0.36
Sutcliffe, NV (cdp) Washoe County	1	0.36
Clintondale, NY (cdp) Ulster County	5	0.35
Salina, OK (town) Mayes County	5	0.35

Notes: (cdp) census designated place; Refer to the Explanation of Data in the front of the book for more detailed information.

American Indian: Seminole

Top 150 Places Sorted by Percent

(Based on places with populations of 10,000 or more)

Place	Number	%
Shawnee, OK (city) Pottawatomie County	656	2.29
Ada, OK (city) Pontotoc County	223	1.42
Immokalee, FL (cdp) Collier County	123	0.62
Okmulgee, OK (city) Okmulgee County	74	0.57
Del City, OK (city) Oklahoma County	107	0.48
Oklahoma City, OK (city) Oklahoma County	1,486	0.29
Midwest City, OK (city) Oklahoma County	152	0.28
Moore, OK (city) Cleveland County	114	0.28
Tahlequah, OK (city) Cherokee County	37	0.26
McAlester, OK (city) Pittsburg County	44	0.25
Norman, OK (city) Cleveland County	231	0.24
Ardmore, OK (city) Carter County	55	0.23
El Reno, OK (city) Canadian County	36	0.22
Claremore, OK (city) Rogers County	32	0.20
The Village, OK (city) Oklahoma County	19	0.19
Sapulpa, OK (city) Creek County	34	0.18
Muskogee, OK (city) Muskogee County	66	0.17
Yukon, OK (city) Canadian County	35	0.17
Mustang, OK (city) Canadian County	21	0.16
Tulsa, OK (city) Tulsa County	469	0.12
Lawrence, KS (city) Douglas County	94	0.12
Bethany, OK (city) Oklahoma County	25	0.12
Bixby, OK (city) Tulsa County	14	0.10
Arkansas City, KS (city) Cowley County	12	0.10
Stillwater, OK (city) Payne County	36	0.09
Kerrville, TX (city) Kerr County	19	0.09
Lawton, OK (city) Comanche County	71	0.08
Edmond, OK (city) Oklahoma County	57	0.08
Ponca City, OK (city) Kay County	22	0.08
Bartlesville, OK (city) Washington County	24	0.07
Owasso, OK (city) Tulsa County	13	0.07
Durant, OK (city) Bryan County	10	0.07
Blythe, CA (city) Riverside County	9	0.07
Holly Hill, FL (city) Volusia County	8	0.07
View Park-Windsor Hills, CA (cdp) Los Angeles County	8	0.07
North Highlands, CA (cdp) Sacramento County	26	0.06
Ocoee, FL (city) Orange County	14	0.06
Duncan, OK (city) Stephens County	13	0.06
Roosevelt, NY (cdp) Nassau County	10	0.06
Avocado Heights, CA (cdp) Los Angeles County	9	0.06
Chickasha, OK (city) Grady County	9	0.06
Hammonton, NJ (town) Atlantic County	7	0.06
Riverview, FL (cdp) Hillsborough County	7	0.06
Lake Wales, FL (city) Polk County	6	0.06
Middleburg, FL (cdp) Clay County	6	0.06
Broken Arrow, OK (city) Tulsa County	40	0.05
Bloomfield, CT (town) Hartford County	10	0.05
Wilkinsburg, PA (borough) Allegheny County	10	0.05
Jacksonville, IL (city) Morgan County	9	0.05
Selma, CA (city) Fresno County	9	0.05
Cameron Park, CA (cdp) El Dorado County	8	0.05
Mastic, NY (cdp) Suffolk County	8	0.05
Ladson, SC (cdp) Berkeley County	7	0.05
Miami, OK (city) Ottawa County	7	0.05
Oroville, CA (city) Butte County	7	0.05
Schofield Barracks, HI (cdp) Honolulu County	7	0.05
Taylor, TX (city) Williamson County	7	0.05
Universal City, TX (city) Bexar County	7	0.05
Cocoa Beach, FL (city) Brevard County	6	0.05
Corinth, TX (city) Denton County	6	0.05
Lexington Park, MD (cdp) Saint Mary's County	6	0.05
Garden City, ID (city) Ada County	5	0.05
Holly, MI (township) Oakland County	5	0.05
Upper Grand Lagoon, FL (cdp) Bay County	5	0.05
Wichita, KS (city) Sedgwick County	121	0.04
Davie, FL (town) Broward County	27	0.04
Pittsburg, CA (city) Contra Costa County	22	0.04
Enid, OK (city) Garfield County	19	0.04
Hilo, HI (cdp) Hawaii County	15	0.04
Sanford, FL (city) Seminole County	15	0.04
Del Rio, TX (city) Val Verde County	14	0.04
Kailua, HI (cdp) Honolulu County	13	0.04
Clovis, NM (city) Curry County	12	0.04
Englewood, CO (city) Arapahoe County	12	0.04
Saint Cloud, FL (city) Osceola County	9	0.04

Place	Number	%
Altus, OK (city) Jackson County	8	0.04
Port Angeles, WA (city) Clallam County	8	0.04
Selden, NY (cdp) Suffolk County	8	0.04
West Pensacola, FL (cdp) Escambia County	8	0.04
Hybla Valley, VA (cdp) Fairfax County	7	0.04
Ocean Springs, MS (city) Jackson County	7	0.04
Whitney, NV (cdp) Clark County	7	0.04
Winter Gardens, CA (cdp) San Diego County	7	0.04
Boulder City, NV (city) Clark County	6	0.04
Flowing Wells, AZ (cdp) Pima County	6	0.04
Ukiah, CA (city) Mendocino County	6	0.04
Walnut Park, CA (cdp) Los Angeles County	6	0.04
Atlantic Beach, FL (city) Duval County	5	0.04
Colonial Park, PA (cdp) Dauphin County	5	0.04
Forest Hill, TX (city) Tarrant County	5	0.04
Fort Stewart, GA (cdp) Liberty County	5	0.04
Geneva, NY (city) Ontario County	5	0.04
Hudson, FL (cdp) Pasco County	5	0.04
McPherson, KS (city) McPherson County	5	0.04
Mounds View, MN (city) Ramsey County	5	0.04
Ulster, NY (town) Ulster County	5	0.04
Coatesville, PA (city) Chester County	4	0.04
Fort Polk South, LA (cdp) Vernon Parish	4	0.04
Olivehurst, CA (cdp) Yuba County	4	0.04
Palatka, FL (city) Putnam County	4	0.04
Pine Hill, NJ (borough) Camden County	4	0.04
Wyandanch, NY (cdp) Suffolk County	4	0.04
Hollywood, FL (city) Broward County	38	0.03
Lancaster, CA (city) Los Angeles County	38	0.03
Visalia, CA (city) Tulare County	32	0.03
Brandon, FL (cdp) Hillsborough County	26	0.03
Palm Bay, FL (city) Brevard County	20	0.03
Daytona Beach, FL (city) Volusia County	17	0.03
Fayetteville, AR (city) Washington County	17	0.03
Merced, CA (city) Merced County	17	0.03
Dothan, AL (city) Houston County	16	0.03
Altadena, CA (cdp) Los Angeles County	14	0.03
Kaneohe, HI (cdp) Honolulu County	12	0.03
Fort Bragg, NC (cdp) Cumberland County	10	0.03
Oxon Hill-Glassmanor, MD (cdp) Prince George's County	10	0.03
Pacifica, CA (city) San Mateo County	10	0.03
Benicia, CA (city) Solano County	9	0.03
Fairbanks, AK (city) Fairbanks North Star Borough	9	0.03
Lakeside, FL (cdp) Clay County	9	0.03
McMinnville, OR (city) Yamhill County	9	0.03
Ferry Pass, FL (cdp) Escambia County	8	0.03
Fort Washington, MD (cdp) Prince George's County	8	0.03
Cedar Park, TX (city) Williamson County	7	0.03
Cleburne, TX (city) Johnson County	7	0.03
Edgewood, MD (cdp) Harford County	7	0.03
Maplewood, NJ (cdp) Essex County	7	0.03
Spring Valley, CA (cdp) San Diego County	7	0.03
Wallkill, NY (town) Orange County	7	0.03
Alice, TX (city) Jim Wells County	6	0.03
Baldwin, NY (cdp) Nassau County	6	0.03
Enterprise, AL (city) Coffee County	6	0.03
Foothill Farms, CA (cdp) Sacramento County	6	0.03
Highland, MI (township) Oakland County	6	0.03
Orange, TX (city) Orange County	6	0.03
Sherrelwood, CO (cdp) Adams County	6	0.03
Steubenville, OH (city) Jefferson County	6	0.03
Van Buren, AR (city) Crawford County	6	0.03
Arroyo Grande, CA (city) San Luis Obispo County	5	0.03
Branchburg, NJ (township) Somerset County	5	0.03
Brownsville, FL (cdp) Miami-Dade County	5	0.03
Casa de Oro-Mount Helix, CA (cdp) San Diego County	5	0.03
Cocoa, FL (city) Brevard County	5	0.03
Galt, CA (city) Sacramento County	5	0.03
Leesburg, FL (city) Lake County	5	0.03
Montclair, VA (cdp) Prince William County	5	0.03
North Amityville, NY (cdp) Suffolk County	5	0.03
Sand Springs, OK (city) Tulsa County	5	0.03
Brigantine, NJ (city) Atlantic County	4	0.03
Bryn Mawr-Skyway, WA (cdp) King County	4	0.03
Carthage, MO (city) Jasper County	4	0.03

Notes: (cdp) census designated place; Refer to the Explanation of Data in the front of the book for more detailed information.

American Indian: Shoshone

Top 150 Places Sorted by Number

(Based on all places, regardless of population)

Place	Number	%
Fort Washakie, WY (cdp) Fremont County	954	64.59
Elko, NV (city) Elko County	189	1.13
Reno, NV (city) Washoe County	162	0.09
Lander, WY (city) Fremont County	140	2.04
Boulder Flats, WY (cdp) Fremont County	139	36.48
Los Angeles, CA (city) Los Angeles County	128	0.00
Riverton, WY (city) Fremont County	120	1.29
Ethete, WY (cdp) Fremont County	107	7.35
Ely, NV (city) White Pine County	84	2.08
Sacramento, CA (city) Sacramento County	74	0.02
Pocatello, ID (city) Bannock County	70	0.14
Ogden, UT (city) Weber County	68	0.09
Boise City, ID (city) Ada County	67	0.04
Phoenix, AZ (city) Maricopa County	67	0.01
Albuquerque, NM (city) Bernalillo County	59	0.01
Owyhee, NV (cdp) Elko County	57	5.60
Salt Lake City, UT (city) Salt Lake County	55	0.03
Brigham City, UT (city) Box Elder County	54	0.31
Casper, WY (city) Natrona County	52	0.10
Seattle, WA (city) King County	52	0.01
Crowheart, WY (cdp) Fremont County	50	30.67
Johnstown, WY (cdp) Fremont County	47	19.92
Blackfoot, ID (city) Bingham County	47	0.45
Denver, CO (city) Denver County	47	0.01
San Diego, CA (city) San Diego County	46	0.00
Fort Hall, ID (cdp) Bannock County	45	1.41
Portland, OR (city) Multnomah County	45	0.01
San Jose, CA (city) Santa Clara County	44	0.00
Las Vegas, NV (city) Clark County	43	0.01
Carson City, NV (special city) Carson City city	42	0.08
Sun Valley, NV (cdp) Washoe County	35	0.18
Anchorage, AK (municipality) Anchorage Borough	35	0.01
Arapahoe, WY (cdp) Fremont County	33	1.87
Vernal, UT (city) Uintah County	33	0.43
Laramie, WY (city) Albany County	32	0.12
Battle Mountain, NV (cdp) Lander County	30	1.04
West Valley City, UT (city) Salt Lake County	30	0.03
Fallon, NV (city) Churchill County	29	0.38
Chubbuck, ID (city) Bannock County	27	0.28
Henderson, NV (city) Clark County	27	0.02
Glendale, AZ (city) Maricopa County	26	0.01
Oakland, CA (city) Alameda County	25	0.01
Stockton, CA (city) San Joaquin County	25	0.01
Furnace Creek, CA (cdp) Inyo County	24	77.42
Roosevelt, UT (city) Duchesne County	24	0.56
New York, NY (city) New York City	24	0.00
Aurora, CO (city) Arapahoe County	23	0.01
Nampa, ID (city) Canyon County	22	0.04
Wendover, UT (city) Tooele County	21	1.37
West Wendover, NV (city) Elko County	21	0.44
Idaho Falls, ID (city) Bonneville County	21	0.04
Sparks, NV (city) Washoe County	21	0.03
Arden-Arcade, CA (cdp) Sacramento County	21	0.02
Salem, OR (city) Marion County	21	0.02
Bakersfield, CA (city) Kern County	21	0.01
Riverside, CA (city) Riverside County	21	0.01
Spokane, WA (city) Spokane County	21	0.01
Oklahoma City, OK (city) Oklahoma County	21	0.00
McGill, NV (cdp) White Pine County	20	1.90
Cheyenne, WY (city) Laramie County	20	0.04
Corona, CA (city) Riverside County	20	0.02
Redding, CA (city) Shasta County	20	0.02
Spring Valley, NV (cdp) Clark County	20	0.02
Fresno, CA (city) Fresno County	20	0.00
Grantsville, UT (city) Tooele County	19	0.32
Taylorsville, UT (city) Salt Lake County	19	0.03
Billings, MT (city) Yellowstone County	19	0.02
Colorado Springs, CO (city) El Paso County	19	0.01
Santa Ana, CA (city) Orange County	19	0.01
Tacoma, WA (city) Pierce County	19	0.01
Tucson, AZ (city) Pima County	19	0.00
Lemmon Valley-Golden Valley, NV (cdp) Washoe County	18	0.26
Tooele, UT (city) Tooele County	18	0.08
Santa Fe, NM (city) Santa Fe County	18	0.03
Mesa, AZ (city) Maricopa County	18	0.00
South Salt Lake, UT (city) Salt Lake County	17	0.08
Clearfield, UT (city) Davis County	17	0.07
Twin Falls, ID (city) Twin Falls County	17	0.05
Norwalk, CA (city) Los Angeles County	17	0.02
West Jordan, UT (city) Salt Lake County	17	0.02
Anaheim, CA (city) Orange County	17	0.01
Sunrise Manor, NV (cdp) Clark County	17	0.01
Gillette, WY (city) Campbell County	16	0.08
Orem, UT (city) Utah County	16	0.02
Eugene, OR (city) Lane County	16	0.01
Lancaster, CA (city) Los Angeles County	16	0.01
Vancouver, WA (city) Clark County	16	0.01
San Francisco, CA (city) San Francisco County	16	0.00
Wells, NV (city) Elko County	15	1.11
Thermopolis, WY (town) Hot Springs County	15	0.47
Spring Creek, NV (cdp) Elko County	15	0.14
Sandy, UT (city) Salt Lake County	15	0.02
Victorville, CA (city) San Bernardino County	15	0.02
Lakewood, CO (city) Jefferson County	15	0.01
Oceanside, CA (city) San Diego County	15	0.01
Paradise, NV (cdp) Clark County	15	0.01
Rancho Cucamonga, CA (city) San Bernardino County	15	0.01
Chicago, IL (city) Cook County	15	0.00
Wichita, KS (city) Sedgwick County	15	0.00
West Point, UT (city) Davis County	14	0.23
Winnemucca, NV (city) Humboldt County	14	0.20
Fairfield, CA (city) Solano County	14	0.01
Long Beach, CA (city) Los Angeles County	14	0.00
Minneapolis, MN (city) Hennepin County	14	0.00
Fort Duchesne, UT (cdp) Uintah County	13	2.09
Pahrump, NV (cdp) Nye County	13	0.05
Fontana, CA (city) San Bernardino County	13	0.01
Palmdale, CA (city) Los Angeles County	13	0.01
Dallas, TX (city) Dallas County	13	0.00
Houston, TX (city) Harris County	13	0.00
Carlin, NV (city) Elko County	12	0.56
Bishop, CA (city) Inyo County	12	0.34
Morrilton, AR (city) Conway County	12	0.18
Syracuse, UT (city) Davis County	12	0.13
Kearns, UT (cdp) Salt Lake County	12	0.04
Bremerton, WA (city) Kitsap County	12	0.03
Gilroy, CA (city) Santa Clara County	12	0.03
North Highlands, CA (cdp) Sacramento County	12	0.03
Lakewood, WA (city) Pierce County	12	0.02
Rapid City, SD (city) Pennington County	12	0.02
Huntington Beach, CA (city) Orange County	12	0.01
Inglewood, CA (city) Los Angeles County	12	0.01
San Bernardino, CA (city) San Bernardino County	12	0.01
Tempe, AZ (city) Maricopa County	12	0.01
Memphis, TN (city) Shelby County	12	0.00
San Antonio, TX (city) Bexar County	12	0.00
Hardin, MT (city) Big Horn County	11	0.33
Susanville, CA (city) Lassen County	11	0.08
Butte-Silver Bow, MT (special city) Silver Bow County	11	0.03
Coeur d'Alene, ID (city) Kootenai County	11	0.03
Northglenn, CO (city) Adams County	11	0.03
Chino, CA (city) San Bernardino County	11	0.02
Citrus Heights, CA (city) Sacramento County	11	0.01
Lawton, OK (city) Comanche County	11	0.01
Springfield, MO (city) Greene County	11	0.01
Thornton, CO (city) Adams County	11	0.01
Vacaville, CA (city) Solano County	11	0.01
West Covina, CA (city) Los Angeles County	11	0.01
Honolulu, HI (cdp) Honolulu County	11	0.00
Philadelphia, PA (city) Philadelphia County	11	0.00
Hawthorne, NV (cdp) Mineral County	10	0.30
Evanston, WY (city) Uinta County	10	0.09
Roy, UT (city) Weber County	10	0.03
Missoula, MT (city) Missoula County	10	0.02
Rancho Cordova, CA (cdp) Sacramento County	10	0.02
Kent, WA (city) King County	10	0.01
Austin, TX (city) Travis County	10	0.00
Fort Worth, TX (city) Tarrant County	10	0.00
Schurz, NV (cdp) Mineral County	9	1.25
Anadarko, OK (city) Caddo County	9	0.14

Notes: (cdp) census designated place; Refer to the Explanation of Data in the front of the book for more detailed information.

American Indian: Shoshone

Top 150 Places Sorted by Percent

(Based on all places, regardless of population)

Place	Number	%
Furnace Creek, CA (cdp) Inyo County	24	77.42
Fort Washakie, WY (cdp) Fremont County	954	64.59
Boulder Flats, WY (cdp) Fremont County	139	36.48
Crowheart, WY (cdp) Fremont County	50	30.67
Johnstown, WY (cdp) Fremont County	47	19.92
Ethete, WY (cdp) Fremont County	107	7.35
Owyhee, NV (cdp) Elko County	57	5.60
Bloomington, ID (city) Bear Lake County	6	2.39
Gabbs, NV (city) Nye County	7	2.20
Fort Duchesne, UT (cdp) Uintah County	13	2.09
Ely, NV (city) White Pine County	84	2.08
Lander, WY (city) Fremont County	140	2.04
McGill, NV (cdp) White Pine County	20	1.90
Arapahoe, WY (cdp) Fremont County	33	1.87
Saint Xavier, MT (cdp) Big Horn County	1	1.49
Sutcliffe, NV (cdp) Washoe County	4	1.42
Fort Hall, ID (cdp) Bannock County	45	1.41
Lost Springs, KS (city) Marion County	1	1.41
Wendover, UT (city) Tooele County	21	1.37
South Flat, WY (cdp) Washakie County	5	1.34
Randlett, UT (cdp) Uintah County	3	1.34
Lincolnville, KS (city) Marion County	3	1.33
La Crosse, WA (town) Whitman County	5	1.32
Riverton, WY (city) Fremont County	120	1.29
Schurz, NV (cdp) Mineral County	9	1.25
Kicking Horse, MT (cdp) Lake County	1	1.25
Acme, WA (cdp) Whatcom County	3	1.14
Elko, NV (city) Elko County	189	1.13
Wells, NV (city) Elko County	15	1.11
Grand Ronde, OR (cdp) Polk County	3	1.11
East Thermopolis, WY (town) Hot Springs County	3	1.09
Lead Hill, AR (town) Boone County	3	1.05
Battle Mountain, NV (cdp) Lander County	30	1.04
Tecopa, CA (cdp) Inyo County	1	1.01
Purple Sage, WY (cdp) Sweetwater County	4	0.97
Deming, WA (cdp) Whatcom County	2	0.95
Jeffrey City, WY (cdp) Fremont County	1	0.94
Mesa, CA (cdp) Inyo County	2	0.93
Wounded Knee, SD (cdp) Shannon County	3	0.91
Liberal, MO (city) Barton County	7	0.90
Stagecoach, TX (town) Montgomery County	4	0.88
Vernon, UT (town) Tooele County	2	0.85
Indiahoma, OK (town) Comanche County	3	0.80
Wadsworth, NV (cdp) Washoe County	7	0.79
Oaks, OK (town) Delaware County	1	0.73
Diamondville, WY (town) Lincoln County	5	0.70
La Barge, WY (town) Lincoln County	3	0.70
Powers, OR (city) Coos County	5	0.68
Dustin Acres, CA (cdp) Kern County	4	0.68
Tazlina, AK (cdp) Valdez-Cordova Census Area	2	0.67
Rexford, MT (town) Lincoln County	1	0.66
Manila, UT (town) Daggett County	2	0.65
Vega, MN (township) Marshall County	1	0.65
West River, WY (cdp) Washakie County	2	0.62
Inyokern, CA (cdp) Kern County	6	0.61
Lingle, WY (town) Goshen County	3	0.59
Whiterocks, UT (cdp) Uintah County	2	0.59
Roosevelt, UT (city) Duchesne County	24	0.56
Carlin, NV (city) Elko County	12	0.56
Moapa Town, NV (cdp) Clark County	5	0.54
Circleville, KS (city) Jackson County	1	0.54
Dubois, WY (town) Fremont County	5	0.52
Markleeville, CA (cdp) Alpine County	1	0.51
Duchesne, UT (city) Duchesne County	7	0.50
Picher, OK (city) Ottawa County	8	0.49
Mission, OR (cdp) Umatilla County	5	0.49
Hudson, WY (town) Fremont County	2	0.49
Nixon, NV (cdp) Washoe County	2	0.48
Thermopolis, WY (town) Hot Springs County	15	0.47
Shoshoni, WY (town) Fremont County	3	0.47
Homa Hills, WY (cdp) Natrona County	5	0.47
East Dunseith, ND (cdp) Rolette County	1	0.46
Blackfoot, ID (city) Bingham County	47	0.45
Grand Coulee, WA (city) Grant County	4	0.45
Sequoyah, OK (cdp) Rogers County	3	0.45
Knox City, MO (city) Knox County	1	0.45
West Wendover, NV (city) Elko County	21	0.44
Elwood, UT (town) Box Elder County	3	0.44
Naknek, AK (cdp) Bristol Bay Borough	3	0.44
South Cle Elum, WA (town) Kittitas County	2	0.44
Peetz, CO (town) Logan County	1	0.44
Vernal, UT (city) Uintah County	33	0.43
Hildale, UT (city) Washington County	8	0.42
Milan, NM (village) Cibola County	8	0.42
Lone Pine, CA (cdp) Inyo County	7	0.42
Hollister, ID (city) Twin Falls County	1	0.42
Brookville, KS (city) Saline County	1	0.39
Crescent Mills, CA (cdp) Plumas County	1	0.39
Fallon, NV (city) Churchill County	29	0.38
Tse Bonito, NM (cdp) McKinley County	1	0.38
Raymond, MN (city) Kandiyohi County	3	0.37
Myton, UT (city) Duchesne County	2	0.37
McDermitt, NV (cdp) Humboldt County	1	0.37
Mud Lake, ID (city) Jefferson County	1	0.37
Edmundson, MO (city) Saint Louis County	3	0.36
Echo, MN (city) Yellow Medicine County	1	0.36
Maxwell, NM (village) Colfax County	1	0.36
Wallsburg, UT (town) Wasatch County	1	0.36
Beatty, NV (cdp) Nye County	4	0.35
Oljato-Monument Valley, UT (cdp) San Juan County	3	0.35
Lewellen, NE (village) Garden County	1	0.35
Saint Pierre, MT (cdp) Hill County	1	0.35
Stockport, IA (city) Van Buren County	1	0.35
Bishop, CA (city) Inyo County	12	0.34
Loma Rica, CA (cdp) Yuba County	7	0.34
Hardin, MT (city) Big Horn County	11	0.33
Peach Springs, AZ (cdp) Mohave County	2	0.33
Grantsville, UT (city) Tooele County	19	0.32
Arbon Valley, ID (cdp) Power County	2	0.32
Keystone, SD (town) Pennington County	1	0.32
Mayetta, KS (city) Jackson County	1	0.32
Brigham City, UT (city) Box Elder County	54	0.31
Montgomery, MA (town) Hampden County	2	0.31
Hawthorne, NV (cdp) Mineral County	10	0.30
Plymouth, UT (town) Box Elder County	1	0.30
Honaunau-Napoopoo, HI (cdp) Hawaii County	7	0.29
Shoshone, ID (city) Lincoln County	4	0.29
Busby, MT (cdp) Big Horn County	2	0.29
Dayton, WY (town) Sheridan County	2	0.29
Keystone, IA (city) Benton County	2	0.29
Chubbuck, ID (city) Bannock County	27	0.28
Yerington, NV (city) Lyon County	8	0.28
Rancho Tehama Reserve, CA (cdp) Tehama County	4	0.28
Parker School, MT (cdp) Chouteau County	1	0.28
Evansville, WY (town) Natrona County	6	0.27
Searles Valley, CA (cdp) San Bernardino County	5	0.27
Caliente, NV (city) Lincoln County	3	0.27
Lincoln, MT (cdp) Lewis and Clark County	3	0.27
Satus, WA (cdp) Yakima County	2	0.27
Eastbrook, ME (town) Hancock County	1	0.27
Peeples Valley, AZ (cdp) Yavapai County	1	0.27
Lemmon Valley-Golden Valley, NV (cdp) Washoe County	18	0.26
Ninilchik, AK (cdp) Kenai Peninsula Borough	2	0.26
Eden, WY (cdp) Sweetwater County	1	0.26
Highfill, AR (town) Benton County	1	0.26
Pinon, AZ (cdp) Navajo County	3	0.25
Second Mesa, AZ (cdp) Navajo County	2	0.25
Webster, FL (city) Sumter County	2	0.25
Firth, ID (city) Bingham County	1	0.25
Fort Bridger, WY (cdp) Uinta County	1	0.25
Holden, UT (town) Millard County	1	0.25
Nenana, AK (city) Yukon-Koyukuk Census Area	1	0.25
Ramah, NM (cdp) McKinley County	1	0.25
Harlem, MT (city) Blaine County	2	0.24
West Point, UT (city) Davis County	14	0.23
Tonopah, NV (cdp) Nye County	6	0.23
Lewiston, CA (cdp) Trinity County	3	0.23
Honokaa, HI (cdp) Hawaii County	5	0.22
Warsaw, PA (township) Jefferson County	3	0.22
Surrey, ND (city) Ward County	2	0.22

Notes: (cdp) census designated place; Refer to the Explanation of Data in the front of the book for more detailed information.

American Indian: Shoshone

Top 150 Places Sorted by Percent

(Based on places with populations of 10,000 or more)

Place	Number	%
Elko, NV (city) Elko County	189	1.13
Blackfoot, ID (city) Bingham County	47	0.45
Brigham City, UT (city) Box Elder County	54	0.31
Sun Valley, NV (cdp) Washoe County	35	0.18
Pocatello, ID (city) Bannock County	70	0.14
Spring Creek, NV (cdp) Elko County	15	0.14
Laramie, WY (city) Albany County	32	0.12
Casper, WY (city) Natrona County	52	0.10
Reno, NV (city) Washoe County	162	0.09
Ogden, UT (city) Weber County	68	0.09
Evanston, WY (city) Uinta County	10	0.09
Carson City, NV (special city) Carson City city	42	0.08
Tooele, UT (city) Tooele County	18	0.08
South Salt Lake, UT (city) Salt Lake County	17	0.08
Gillette, WY (city) Campbell County	16	0.08
Susanville, CA (city) Lassen County	11	0.08
Elizabethtown, PA (borough) Lancaster County	9	0.08
Mountain Home, ID (city) Elmore County	9	0.08
Clearfield, UT (city) Davis County	17	0.07
East Renton Highlands, WA (cdp) King County	9	0.07
Boulder City, NV (city) Clark County	9	0.06
Four Corners, OR (cdp) Marion County	8	0.06
Gardnerville Ranchos, NV (cdp) Douglas County	7	0.06
Kingsgate, WA (cdp) King County	7	0.06
Twin Falls, ID (city) Twin Falls County	17	0.05
Pahrump, NV (cdp) Nye County	13	0.05
Sheridan, WY (city) Sheridan County	8	0.05
Garden City, ID (city) Ada County	5	0.05
Lathrop, CA (city) San Joaquin County	5	0.05
Silver City, NM (town) Grant County	5	0.05
Boise City, ID (city) Ada County	67	0.04
Nampa, ID (city) Canyon County	22	0.04
Idaho Falls, ID (city) Bonneville County	21	0.04
Cheyenne, WY (city) Laramie County	20	0.04
Kearns, UT (cdp) Salt Lake County	12	0.04
Cedar City, UT (city) Iron County	9	0.04
Rock Springs, WY (city) Sweetwater County	8	0.04
White Center, WA (cdp) King County	8	0.04
Lakeland North, WA (cdp) King County	6	0.04
Green River, WY (city) Sweetwater County	5	0.04
Longwood, FL (city) Seminole County	5	0.04
Sunnyside, WA (city) Yakima County	5	0.04
Truckee, CA (town) Nevada County	5	0.04
Crestline, CA (cdp) San Bernardino County	4	0.04
Enumclaw, WA (city) King County	4	0.04
Mexico, MO (city) Audrain County	4	0.04
Ontario, OR (city) Malheur County	4	0.04
Salt Lake City, UT (city) Salt Lake County	55	0.03
West Valley City, UT (city) Salt Lake County	30	0.03
Sparks, NV (city) Washoe County	21	0.03
Taylorsville, UT (city) Salt Lake County	19	0.03
Santa Fe, NM (city) Santa Fe County	18	0.03
Bremerton, WA (city) Kitsap County	12	0.03
Gilroy, CA (city) Santa Clara County	12	0.03
North Highlands, CA (cdp) Sacramento County	12	0.03
Butte-Silver Bow, MT (special city) Silver Bow County	11	0.03
Coeur d'Alene, ID (city) Kootenai County	11	0.03
Northglenn, CO (city) Adams County	11	0.03
Roy, UT (city) Weber County	10	0.03
Eureka, CA (city) Humboldt County	9	0.03
Midvale, UT (city) Salt Lake County	9	0.03
Lafayette, CO (city) Boulder County	8	0.03
Draper, UT (city) Salt Lake County	7	0.03
Hamilton, NJ (township) Atlantic County	6	0.03
Oak Harbor, WA (city) Island County	6	0.03
Selma, CA (city) Fresno County	6	0.03
South Laurel, MD (cdp) Prince George's County	6	0.03
Van Buren, MI (township) Wayne County	6	0.03
Whitney, NV (cdp) Clark County	6	0.03
Fountain, CO (city) El Paso County	5	0.03
Post Falls, ID (city) Kootenai County	5	0.03
Prunedale, CA (cdp) Monterey County	5	0.03
Sharon, MA (town) Norfolk County	5	0.03
South Ogden, UT (city) Weber County	5	0.03
Ukiah, CA (city) Mendocino County	5	0.03

Place	Number	%
Vincent, CA (cdp) Los Angeles County	5	0.03
Ada, OK (city) Pontotoc County	4	0.03
Coos Bay, OR (city) Coos County	4	0.03
Durango, CO (city) La Plata County	4	0.03
Grover Beach, CA (city) San Luis Obispo County	4	0.03
Hampton Bays, NY (cdp) Suffolk County	4	0.03
North Auburn, CA (cdp) Placer County	4	0.03
North Ogden, UT (city) Weber County	4	0.03
Payson, AZ (town) Gila County	4	0.03
Redmond, OR (city) Deschutes County	4	0.03
Forestville, OH (cdp) Hamilton County	3	0.03
Helena, AL (city) Shelby County	3	0.03
Iona, FL (cdp) Lee County	3	0.03
Lake Los Angeles, CA (cdp) Los Angeles County	3	0.03
Oldsmar, FL (city) Pinellas County	3	0.03
Stafford, CT (town) Tolland County	3	0.03
Sacramento, CA (city) Sacramento County	74	0.02
Henderson, NV (city) Clark County	27	0.02
Arden-Arcade, CA (cdp) Sacramento County	21	0.02
Salem, OR (city) Marion County	21	0.02
Corona, CA (city) Riverside County	20	0.02
Redding, CA (city) Shasta County	20	0.02
Spring Valley, NV (cdp) Clark County	20	0.02
Billings, MT (city) Yellowstone County	19	0.02
Norwalk, CA (city) Los Angeles County	17	0.02
West Jordan, UT (city) Salt Lake County	17	0.02
Orem, UT (city) Utah County	16	0.02
Sandy, UT (city) Salt Lake County	15	0.02
Victorville, CA (city) San Bernardino County	15	0.02
Lakewood, WA (city) Pierce County	12	0.02
Rapid City, SD (city) Pennington County	12	0.02
Chino, CA (city) San Bernardino County	11	0.02
Missoula, MT (city) Missoula County	10	0.02
Rancho Cordova, CA (cdp) Sacramento County	10	0.02
Highland, CA (city) San Bernardino County	9	0.02
Tigard, OR (city) Washington County	9	0.02
Atascocita, TX (cdp) Harris County	8	0.02
Bullhead City, AZ (city) Mohave County	8	0.02
Muskogee, OK (city) Muskogee County	8	0.02
Fairbanks, AK (city) Fairbanks North Star Borough	7	0.02
Granite City, IL (city) Madison County	7	0.02
Joplin, MO (city) Jasper County	7	0.02
Meridian, ID (city) Ada County	7	0.02
Porterville, CA (city) Tulare County	7	0.02
West Sacramento, CA (city) Yolo County	7	0.02
Burien, WA (city) King County	6	0.02
Fair Oaks, CA (cdp) Sacramento County	6	0.02
Fort Dodge, IA (city) Webster County	6	0.02
Millcreek, UT (cdp) Salt Lake County	6	0.02
Norco, CA (city) Riverside County	6	0.02
Orangevale, CA (cdp) Sacramento County	6	0.02
Belton, MO (city) Cass County	5	0.02
Castle Rock, CO (town) Douglas County	5	0.02
Grants Pass, OR (city) Josephine County	5	0.02
Lewiston, ID (city) Nez Perce County	5	0.02
Mableton, GA (cdp) Cobb County	5	0.02
Pleasant Grove, UT (city) Utah County	5	0.02
Rosemont, CA (cdp) Sacramento County	5	0.02
Aberdeen, SD (city) Brown County	4	0.02
American Fork, UT (city) Utah County	4	0.02
Carlsbad, NM (city) Eddy County	4	0.02
Champlin, MN (city) Hennepin County	4	0.02
Kalamazoo, MI (township) Kalamazoo County	4	0.02
New Smyrna Beach, FL (city) Volusia County	4	0.02
Paine Field-Lake Stickney, WA (cdp) Snohomish County	4	0.02
Pendleton, OR (city) Umatilla County	4	0.02
Pittsburg, KS (city) Crawford County	4	0.02
Ponca City, OK (city) Kay County	4	0.02
Round Lake Beach, IL (village) Lake County	4	0.02
SeaTac, WA (city) King County	4	0.02
Aberdeen, WA (city) Grays Harbor County	3	0.02
Beatrice, NE (city) Gage County	3	0.02
Cherryland, CA (cdp) Alameda County	3	0.02
Cockeysville, MD (cdp) Baltimore County	3	0.02
Delran, NJ (township) Burlington County	3	0.02

Notes: (cdp) census designated place; Refer to the Explanation of Data in the front of the book for more detailed information.

American Indian: Sioux

Top 150 Places Sorted by Number

(Based on all places, regardless of population)

Place	Number	%
Rapid City, SD (city) Pennington County	5,256	8.82
Pine Ridge, SD (cdp) Shannon County	2,633	83.03
North Eagle Butte, SD (cdp) Dewey County	1,863	86.13
Sioux Falls, SD (city) Minnehaha County	1,775	1.43
Rosebud, SD (cdp) Todd County	1,406	90.30
Minneapolis, MN (city) Hennepin County	1,395	0.36
Fort Thompson, SD (cdp) Buffalo County	1,220	88.73
Denver, CO (city) Denver County	1,155	0.21
Oglala, SD (cdp) Shannon County	1,120	91.13
Pierre, SD (city) Hughes County	996	7.18
Sisseton, SD (city) Roberts County	973	37.83
Sioux City, IA (city) Woodbury County	832	0.98
Saint Paul, MN (city) Ramsey County	827	0.29
Los Angeles, CA (city) Los Angeles County	817	0.02
Fort Totten, ND (cdp) Benson County	814	85.50
Bismarck, ND (city) Burleigh County	814	1.47
Antelope, SD (cdp) Todd County	796	91.81
Portland, OR (city) Multnomah County	740	0.14
Cannon Ball, ND (cdp) Sioux County	739	85.53
Kyle, SD (cdp) Shannon County	714	73.61
Phoenix, AZ (city) Maricopa County	689	0.05
Omaha, NE (city) Douglas County	651	0.17
Mission, SD (city) Todd County	645	71.35
Saint Francis, SD (town) Todd County	617	91.41
Wanblee, SD (cdp) Jackson County	606	94.54
Parmelee, SD (cdp) Todd County	601	92.46
Albuquerque, NM (city) Bernalillo County	577	0.13
Aberdeen, SD (city) Brown County	566	2.30
Manderson-White Horse Creek, SD (cdp) Shannon County	563	89.94
Mobridge, SD (city) Walworth County	543	15.19
Lincoln, NE (city) Lancaster County	541	0.24
Wagner, SD (city) Charles Mix County	535	31.94
Seattle, WA (city) King County	511	0.09
Lower Brule, SD (cdp) Lyman County	507	84.64
Flandreau, SD (city) Moody County	473	19.91
Eagle Butte, SD (city) Dewey County	463	74.80
Martin, SD (city) Bennett County	452	40.87
Chicago, IL (city) Cook County	439	0.02
New York, NY (city) New York City	437	0.01
Billings, MT (city) Yellowstone County	430	0.48
Wolf Point, MT (city) Roosevelt County	410	15.40
Scottsbluff, NE (city) Scotts Bluff County	392	2.66
Colorado Springs, CO (city) El Paso County	392	0.11
Allen, SD (cdp) Bennett County	381	90.93
Marty, SD (cdp) Charles Mix County	376	89.31
McLaughlin, SD (city) Corson County	373	48.13
San Diego, CA (city) San Diego County	372	0.03
Porcupine, SD (cdp) Shannon County	366	89.93
Poplar, MT (city) Roosevelt County	364	39.96
Aurora, CO (city) Arapahoe County	341	0.12
Little Eagle, SD (cdp) Corson County	339	91.62
Lake Andes, SD (city) Charles Mix County	320	39.07
Rapid Valley, SD (cdp) Pennington County	310	4.40
Watertown, SD (city) Codington County	310	1.53
Hot Springs, SD (city) Fall River County	297	7.19
Sacramento, CA (city) Sacramento County	295	0.07
Wounded Knee, SD (cdp) Shannon County	287	87.50
Mandan, ND (city) Morton County	287	1.72
Dupree, SD (city) Ziebach County	285	65.67
Vermillion, SD (city) Clay County	285	2.92
Lakewood, CO (city) Jefferson County	284	0.20
Tulsa, OK (city) Tulsa County	278	0.07
San Jose, CA (city) Santa Clara County	277	0.03
Fargo, ND (city) Cass County	276	0.30
Winner, SD (city) Tripp County	275	8.77
Devils Lake, ND (city) Ramsey County	274	3.79
Las Vegas, NV (city) Clark County	258	0.05
Tacoma, WA (city) Pierce County	251	0.13
Prior Lake, MN (city) Scott County	250	1.57
Santee, NE (village) Knox County	249	82.45
Gordon, NE (city) Sheridan County	247	14.07
Spokane, WA (city) Spokane County	243	0.12
Tucson, AZ (city) Pima County	243	0.05
Alliance, NE (city) Box Butte County	242	2.70
Anchorage, AK (municipality) Anchorage Borough	239	0.09
Bullhead, SD (cdp) Corson County	238	77.27
Oklahoma City, OK (city) Oklahoma County	237	0.05
Wichita, KS (city) Sedgwick County	235	0.07
White River, SD (city) Mellette County	233	38.96
Red Wing, MN (city) Goodhue County	233	1.45
Mitchell, SD (city) Davison County	232	1.59
Grand Forks, ND (city) Grand Forks County	222	0.45
Lawrence, KS (city) Douglas County	220	0.27
San Francisco, CA (city) San Francisco County	214	0.03
San Antonio, TX (city) Bexar County	203	0.02
Moorhead, MN (city) Clay County	202	0.63
Fort Yates, ND (city) Sioux County	199	87.28
Indianapolis, IN (special city) Marion County	192	0.02
Norfolk, NE (city) Madison County	190	0.81
Milwaukee, WI (city) Milwaukee County	190	0.03
Oakland, CA (city) Alameda County	188	0.05
Kansas City, MO (city) Jackson County	187	0.04
Redwood Falls, MN (city) Redwood County	186	3.41
Rushville, NE (city) Sheridan County	179	17.92
Brockton, MT (town) Roosevelt County	178	72.65
Columbus, OH (city) Franklin County	178	0.03
Chamberlain, SD (city) Brule County	176	7.53
Thornton, CO (city) Adams County	175	0.21
Salem, OR (city) Marion County	175	0.13
Mesa, AZ (city) Maricopa County	175	0.04
Chadron, NE (city) Dawes County	174	3.09
Des Moines, IA (city) Polk County	173	0.09
Yankton, SD (city) Yankton County	172	1.27
Houston, TX (city) Harris County	169	0.01
Dallas, TX (city) Dallas County	168	0.01
White Horse, SD (cdp) Todd County	166	92.22
Spearfish, SD (city) Lawrence County	165	1.92
Vancouver, WA (city) Clark County	165	0.11
Paxton, MN (township) Redwood County	164	28.42
Honolulu, HI (cdp) Honolulu County	157	0.04
Waubay, SD (city) Day County	156	23.56
Box Elder, SD (city) Pennington County	155	5.46
Sturgis, SD (city) Meade County	149	2.31
Stockton, CA (city) San Joaquin County	149	0.06
Fresno, CA (city) Fresno County	145	0.03
Granite Falls, MN (city) Yellow Medicine County	144	4.69
Long Beach, CA (city) Los Angeles County	144	0.03
Timber Lake, SD (city) Dewey County	141	31.83
Great Falls, MT (city) Cascade County	141	0.25
Cleveland, OH (city) Cuyahoga County	140	0.03
Valentine, NE (city) Cherry County	138	4.89
Philadelphia, PA (city) Philadelphia County	136	0.01
Peever, SD (town) Roberts County	135	64.59
Brookings, SD (city) Brookings County	135	0.73
Minot, ND (city) Ward County	127	0.35
Westminster, CO (city) Adams County	127	0.13
Whitehorse, SD (cdp) Dewey County	125	88.65
Cheyenne, WY (city) Laramie County	123	0.23
Modesto, CA (city) Stanislaus County	113	0.06
Sherman, MN (township) Redwood County	112	37.21
Selfridge, ND (city) Sioux County	110	49.33
Pipestone, MN (city) Pipestone County	110	2.57
Redding, CA (city) Shasta County	108	0.13
Jacksonville, FL (special city) Duval County	108	0.01
Tempe, AZ (city) Maricopa County	107	0.07
Austin, TX (city) Travis County	107	0.02
La Plant, SD (cdp) Dewey County	106	70.67
Everett, WA (city) Snohomish County	106	0.12
Independence, MO (city) Jackson County	106	0.09
Riverside, CA (city) Riverside County	106	0.04
Eugene, OR (city) Lane County	104	0.08
Springfield, MO (city) Greene County	104	0.07
Salt Lake City, UT (city) Salt Lake County	104	0.06
Fort Collins, CO (city) Larimer County	100	0.08
Reno, NV (city) Washoe County	100	0.06
Fort Pierre, SD (city) Stanley County	99	4.97
Huron, SD (city) Beadle County	99	0.83
Arvada, CO (city) Jefferson County	99	0.10
Boise City, ID (city) Ada County	98	0.05
Glendale, AZ (city) Maricopa County	97	0.04

Notes: (cdp) census designated place; Refer to the Explanation of Data in the front of the book for more detailed information.

American Indian: Sioux

Top 150 Places Sorted by Percent

(Based on all places, regardless of population)

Place	Number	%
Wanblee, SD (cdp) Jackson County	606	94.54
Two Strike, SD (cdp) Todd County	31	93.94
Parmelee, SD (cdp) Todd County	601	92.46
White Horse, SD (cdp) Todd County	166	92.22
Antelope, SD (cdp) Todd County	796	91.81
Little Eagle, SD (cdp) Corson County	339	91.62
Saint Francis, SD (town) Todd County	617	91.41
Oglala, SD (cdp) Shannon County	1,120	91.13
Allen, SD (cdp) Bennett County	381	90.93
Rosebud, SD (cdp) Todd County	1,406	90.30
Manderson-White Horse Creek, SD (cdp) Shannon County	563	89.94
Porcupine, SD (cdp) Shannon County	366	89.93
Green Grass, SD (cdp) Dewey County	52	89.66
Marty, SD (cdp) Charles Mix County	376	89.31
Fort Thompson, SD (cdp) Buffalo County	1,220	88.73
Whitehorse, SD (cdp) Dewey County	125	88.65
Wounded Knee, SD (cdp) Shannon County	287	87.50
Fort Yates, ND (city) Sioux County	199	87.28
North Eagle Butte, SD (cdp) Dewey County	1,863	86.13
Cannon Ball, ND (cdp) Sioux County	739	85.53
Fort Totten, ND (cdp) Benson County	814	85.50
Lower Brule, SD (cdp) Lyman County	507	84.64
Batesland, SD (town) Shannon County	74	84.09
Pine Ridge, SD (cdp) Shannon County	2,633	83.03
Santee, NE (village) Knox County	249	82.45
Bullhead, SD (cdp) Corson County	238	77.27
Eagle Butte, SD (city) Dewey County	463	74.80
Kyle, SD (cdp) Shannon County	714	73.61
Brockton, MT (town) Roosevelt County	178	72.65
Mission, SD (city) Todd County	645	71.35
La Plant, SD (cdp) Dewey County	106	70.67
Spring Creek, SD (cdp) Todd County	91	66.91
Dupree, SD (city) Ziebach County	285	65.67
Peever, SD (town) Roberts County	135	64.59
Ravinia, SD (town) Charles Mix County	50	63.29
Pine Ridge, NE (cdp) Sheridan County	8	57.14
Solen, ND (city) Sioux County	49	56.98
Selfridge, ND (city) Sioux County	110	49.33
McLaughlin, SD (city) Corson County	373	48.13
Martin, SD (city) Bennett County	452	40.87
Poplar, MT (city) Roosevelt County	364	39.96
Lake Andes, SD (city) Charles Mix County	320	39.07
White River, SD (city) Mellette County	233	38.96
Interior, SD (town) Jackson County	30	38.96
Sisseton, SD (city) Roberts County	973	37.83
Sherman, MN (township) Redwood County	112	37.21
Wagner, SD (city) Charles Mix County	535	31.94
Timber Lake, SD (city) Dewey County	141	31.83
Wood, SD (town) Mellette County	20	30.30
Isabel, SD (town) Dewey County	71	29.71
Paxton, MN (township) Redwood County	164	28.42
Minnesota Falls, MN (township) Yellow Medicine County	87	24.10
Warwick, ND (city) Benson County	18	24.00
Waubay, SD (city) Day County	156	23.56
New Effington, SD (town) Roberts County	54	23.18
McIntosh, SD (city) Corson County	45	20.74
Flandreau, SD (city) Moody County	473	19.91
Rushville, NE (city) Sheridan County	179	17.92
Okaton, SD (cdp) Jones County	5	17.24
Oberon, ND (city) Benson County	13	16.05
Wolf Point, MT (city) Roosevelt County	410	15.40
Mobridge, SD (city) Walworth County	543	15.19
Oelrichs, SD (town) Fall River County	22	15.17
Marvin, SD (town) Grant County	10	15.15
Veblen, SD (city) Marshall County	40	14.23
Gordon, NE (city) Sheridan County	247	14.07
Kadoka, SD (city) Jackson County	92	13.03
Ortley, SD (town) Roberts County	7	12.96
Summit, SD (town) Roberts County	31	11.03
Belvidere, SD (town) Jackson County	6	10.53
Kilgore, NE (village) Cherry County	10	10.10
Sheyenne, ND (city) Eddy County	32	10.06
Ward, SD (town) Moody County	4	9.76
Akaska, SD (town) Walworth County	3	9.68
Pickstown, SD (town) Charles Mix County	16	9.52

Place	Number	%
Kennebec, SD (town) Lyman County	27	9.44
Rapid City, SD (city) Pennington County	5,256	8.82
Faith, SD (city) Meade County	43	8.79
Winner, SD (city) Tripp County	275	8.77
Dante, SD (town) Charles Mix County	7	8.54
Niobrara, NE (village) Knox County	32	8.44
Claire City, SD (town) Roberts County	7	8.24
Kenneth, MN (city) Rock County	5	8.20
Browns Valley, MN (city) Traverse County	55	7.97
Chamberlain, SD (city) Brule County	176	7.53
Delmont, SD (city) Douglas County	19	7.22
Hot Springs, SD (city) Fall River County	297	7.19
Pierre, SD (city) Hughes County	996	7.18
Dallas, SD (town) Gregory County	10	6.94
Walthill, NE (village) Thurston County	63	6.93
Ashland, MT (cdp) Rosebud County	32	6.90
Quinn, SD (town) Pennington County	3	6.82
Ashland Heights, SD (cdp) Pennington County	57	6.81
Buffalo Gap, SD (town) Custer County	11	6.71
Morton, MN (city) Renville County	28	6.33
Wilmot, SD (city) Roberts County	34	6.26
Turtle Lake, MT (cdp) Lake County	12	6.19
Wall, SD (town) Pennington County	50	6.11
Frazer, MT (cdp) Valley County	27	5.97
Merriman, NE (village) Cherry County	7	5.93
Utica, SD (town) Yankton County	5	5.81
Farmer, SD (town) Hanson County	1	5.56
Box Elder, SD (city) Pennington County	155	5.46
White Shield, ND (cdp) McLean County	19	5.46
Reliance, SD (town) Lyman County	11	5.34
Aldrich, MO (village) Polk County	4	5.33
Bushnell, SD (town) Brookings County	4	5.33
Saint Charles, SD (cdp) Gregory County	1	5.26
Winnebago, NE (village) Thurston County	39	5.08
Bonesteel, SD (city) Gregory County	15	5.05
Fort Pierre, SD (city) Stanley County	99	4.97
Valentine, NE (city) Cherry County	138	4.89
New Underwood, SD (city) Pennington County	30	4.87
Edgemont, SD (city) Fall River County	42	4.84
Mound City, SD (town) Campbell County	4	4.76
Hay Springs, NE (village) Sheridan County	31	4.75
Granite Falls, MN (city) Yellow Medicine County	144	4.69
Birney, MT (cdp) Rosebud County	5	4.63
Andover, IA (city) Clinton County	4	4.60
Rosholt, SD (town) Roberts County	19	4.53
Leshara, NE (village) Saunders County	5	4.50
Rapid Valley, SD (cdp) Pennington County	310	4.40
Terrytown, NE (village) Scotts Bluff County	28	4.33
Culver, KS (city) Ottawa County	7	4.27
Plaza, ND (city) Mountrail County	7	4.19
Sangrey, MT (cdp) Hill County	11	4.18
Colome, SD (city) Tripp County	14	4.12
Crookston, NE (village) Cherry County	4	4.08
New Holland, SD (cdp) Douglas County	3	3.85
York, ND (city) Benson County	1	3.85
Devils Lake, ND (city) Ramsey County	274	3.79
Egan, SD (city) Moody County	10	3.77
Earlton, KS (city) Neosho County	3	3.75
Darwin, CA (cdp) Inyo County	2	3.70
Aurora, IA (city) Buchanan County	7	3.61
Belgium, MN (township) Polk County	4	3.60
Corona, SD (town) Roberts County	4	3.57
Sutcliffe, NV (cdp) Washoe County	10	3.56
Java, SD (town) Walworth County	7	3.55
Hermosa, SD (town) Custer County	11	3.49
Oto, IA (city) Woodbury County	5	3.45
Lake Alice, MN (township) Hubbard County	3	3.45
Livengood, AK (cdp) Yukon-Koyukuk Census Area	1	3.45
New Town, ND (city) Mountrail County	47	3.44
Redwood Falls, MN (city) Redwood County	186	3.41
Bristow, NE (village) Boyd County	3	3.41
Danville, KS (city) Harper County	2	3.39
Springfield, SD (city) Bon Homme County	26	3.28
Green Valley, SD (cdp) Pennington County	25	3.26
Blunt, SD (city) Hughes County	12	3.24

Notes: (cdp) census designated place; Refer to the Explanation of Data in the front of the book for more detailed information.

American Indian: Sioux

Top 150 Places Sorted by Percent

(Based on places with populations of 10,000 or more)

Place	Number	%
Rapid City, SD (city) Pennington County	5,256	8.82
Pierre, SD (city) Hughes County	996	7.18
Scottsbluff, NE (city) Scotts Bluff County	392	2.66
Aberdeen, SD (city) Brown County	566	2.30
Mandan, ND (city) Morton County	287	1.72
Mitchell, SD (city) Davison County	232	1.59
Prior Lake, MN (city) Scott County	250	1.57
Watertown, SD (city) Codington County	310	1.53
Bismarck, ND (city) Burleigh County	814	1.47
Red Wing, MN (city) Goodhue County	233	1.45
Sioux Falls, SD (city) Minnehaha County	1,775	1.43
Yankton, SD (city) Yankton County	172	1.27
Sioux City, IA (city) Woodbury County	832	0.98
Huron, SD (city) Beadle County	99	0.83
Norfolk, NE (city) Madison County	190	0.81
South Sioux City, NE (city) Dakota County	94	0.79
Brookings, SD (city) Brookings County	135	0.73
Moorhead, MN (city) Clay County	202	0.63
Williston, ND (city) Williams County	65	0.52
Billings, MT (city) Yellowstone County	430	0.48
Bemidji, MN (city) Beltrami County	55	0.46
Grand Forks, ND (city) Grand Forks County	222	0.45
Gillette, WY (city) Campbell County	87	0.44
Dickinson, ND (city) Stark County	61	0.38
Minneapolis, MN (city) Hennepin County	1,395	0.36
Shakopee, MN (city) Scott County	74	0.36
Minot, ND (city) Ward County	127	0.35
Welby, CO (cdp) Adams County	40	0.31
Dallas, OR (city) Polk County	38	0.31
Fargo, ND (city) Cass County	276	0.30
Commerce City, CO (city) Adams County	62	0.30
Sterling, CO (city) Logan County	34	0.30
Saint Paul, MN (city) Ramsey County	827	0.29
Lawrence, KS (city) Douglas County	220	0.27
Great Falls, MT (city) Cascade County	141	0.25
Lexington, NE (city) Dawson County	25	0.25
Lincoln, NE (city) Lancaster County	541	0.24
El Reno, OK (city) Canadian County	39	0.24
Sheridan, WY (city) Sheridan County	38	0.24
Jamestown, ND (city) Stutsman County	37	0.24
Cheyenne, WY (city) Laramie County	123	0.23
Bremerton, WA (city) Kitsap County	84	0.23
Fairbanks, AK (city) Fairbanks North Star Borough	70	0.23
North Platte, NE (city) Lincoln County	55	0.23
Kelso, WA (city) Cowlitz County	27	0.23
Kearney, NE (city) Buffalo County	60	0.22
Berkley, CO (cdp) Adams County	24	0.22
Denver, CO (city) Denver County	1,155	0.21
Thornton, CO (city) Adams County	175	0.21
Brigham City, UT (city) Box Elder County	36	0.21
Coos Bay, OR (city) Coos County	33	0.21
Durango, CO (city) La Plata County	29	0.21
Fort Carson, CO (cdp) El Paso County	22	0.21
Lakewood, CO (city) Jefferson County	284	0.20
West Saint Paul, MN (city) Dakota County	38	0.20
Beatrice, NE (city) Gage County	25	0.20
North Saint Paul, MN (city) Ramsey County	24	0.20
Wheat Ridge, CO (city) Jefferson County	61	0.19
Fridley, MN (city) Anoka County	51	0.19
Brighton, CO (city) Adams County	39	0.19
Gallup, NM (city) McKinley County	39	0.19
Columbia Heights, MN (city) Anoka County	35	0.19
Alum Rock, CA (cdp) Santa Clara County	26	0.19
Crestline, CA (cdp) San Bernardino County	19	0.19
Longview, WA (city) Cowlitz County	63	0.18
Golden, CO (city) Jefferson County	31	0.18
McKinleyville, CA (cdp) Humboldt County	24	0.18
North Valley, NM (cdp) Bernalillo County	22	0.18
San Elizario, TX (cdp) El Paso County	20	0.18
Waianae, HI (cdp) Honolulu County	19	0.18
Saint Helens, OR (city) Columbia County	18	0.18
Omaha, NE (city) Douglas County	651	0.17
Casper, WY (city) Natrona County	83	0.17
Columbus, NE (city) Platte County	35	0.17
Sherrelwood, CO (cdp) Adams County	30	0.17
Hermiston, OR (city) Umatilla County	23	0.17
Gladstone, OR (city) Clackamas County	19	0.17
Grass Valley, CA (city) Nevada County	19	0.17
Pocatello, ID (city) Bannock County	81	0.16
Farmington, NM (city) San Juan County	62	0.16
Englewood, CO (city) Arapahoe County	51	0.16
Hastings, MN (city) Dakota County	29	0.16
Ada, OK (city) Pontotoc County	25	0.16
Four Corners, OR (cdp) Marion County	22	0.16
Mounds View, MN (city) Ramsey County	20	0.16
Missoula, MT (city) Missoula County	83	0.15
Auburn, WA (city) King County	61	0.15
Maplewood, MN (city) Ramsey County	52	0.15
Eureka, CA (city) Humboldt County	40	0.15
SeaTac, WA (city) King County	39	0.15
Pahrump, NV (cdp) Nye County	37	0.15
Hastings, NE (city) Adams County	35	0.15
Lakeside, CA (cdp) San Diego County	30	0.15
Hayesville, OR (cdp) Marion County	27	0.15
Arcata, CA (city) Humboldt County	25	0.15
Fountain, CO (city) El Paso County	23	0.15
Brainerd, MN (city) Crow Wing County	20	0.15
Ottawa, KS (city) Franklin County	18	0.15
Cloquet, MN (city) Carlton County	17	0.15
Buffalo, MN (city) Wright County	15	0.15
Portland, OR (city) Multnomah County	740	0.14
Saint Cloud, MN (city) Stearns County	82	0.14
Broomfield, CO (city) Boulder County	52	0.14
Butte-Silver Bow, MT (special city) Silver Bow County	49	0.14
Keizer, OR (city) Marion County	45	0.14
Northglenn, CO (city) Adams County	44	0.14
Orangevale, CA (cdp) Sacramento County	37	0.14
Helena, MT (city) Lewis and Clark County	36	0.14
South Salt Lake, UT (city) Salt Lake County	30	0.14
Lomita, CA (city) Los Angeles County	28	0.14
Newberg, OR (city) Yamhill County	25	0.14
Lino Lakes, MN (city) Anoka County	23	0.14
Marshall, MN (city) Lyon County	18	0.14
Oroville, CA (city) Butte County	18	0.14
Green River, WY (city) Sweetwater County	16	0.14
Lakeland South, WA (cdp) King County	16	0.14
Worthington, MN (city) Nobles County	16	0.14
Albuquerque, NM (city) Bernalillo County	577	0.13
Tacoma, WA (city) Pierce County	251	0.13
Salem, OR (city) Marion County	175	0.13
Westminster, CO (city) Adams County	127	0.13
Redding, CA (city) Shasta County	108	0.13
Loveland, CO (city) Larimer County	68	0.13
Bellevue, NE (city) Sarpy County	57	0.13
Brooklyn Center, MN (city) Hennepin County	39	0.13
Fremont, NE (city) Dodge County	33	0.13
Spanaway, WA (cdp) Pierce County	28	0.13
Klamath Falls, OR (city) Klamath County	25	0.13
Anoka, MN (city) Anoka County	23	0.13
Wahiawa, HI (cdp) Honolulu County	21	0.13
Rosemount, MN (city) Dakota County	19	0.13
Tahlequah, OK (city) Cherokee County	19	0.13
Robbinsdale, MN (city) Hennepin County	18	0.13
Fergus Falls, MN (city) Otter Tail County	17	0.13
Federal Heights, CO (city) Adams County	16	0.13
Chalco, NE (cdp) Sarpy County	14	0.13
Ontario, OR (city) Malheur County	14	0.13
Dishman, WA (cdp) Spokane County	13	0.13
Aurora, CO (city) Arapahoe County	341	0.12
Spokane, WA (city) Spokane County	243	0.12
Everett, WA (city) Snohomish County	106	0.12
Longmont, CO (city) Boulder County	84	0.12
Lakewood, WA (city) Pierce County	67	0.12
Grand Island, NE (city) Hall County	51	0.12
Juneau, AK (city and borough) Juneau Borough	37	0.12
Lewiston, ID (city) Nez Perce County	37	0.12
Fort Bragg, NC (cdp) Cumberland County	36	0.12
Clearfield, UT (city) Davis County	32	0.12
Ponca City, OK (city) Kay County	32	0.12
White Bear Lake, MN (city) Ramsey County	28	0.12

Notes: (cdp) census designated place; Refer to the Explanation of Data in the front of the book for more detailed information.

American Indian: Tohono O'Odham

Top 150 Places Sorted by Number

(Based on all places, regardless of population)

Place	Number	%
Sells, AZ (cdp) Pima County	2,380	85.03
Tucson, AZ (city) Pima County	2,355	0.48
Phoenix, AZ (city) Maricopa County	1,013	0.08
Casa Grande, AZ (city) Pinal County	548	2.17
Ak-Chin Village, AZ (cdp) Pinal County	463	69.21
Santa Rosa, AZ (cdp) Pima County	400	91.32
Chuichu, AZ (cdp) Pinal County	304	89.68
Eloy, AZ (city) Pinal County	255	2.46
Pisinemo, AZ (cdp) Pima County	223	94.09
Los Angeles, CA (city) Los Angeles County	201	0.01
Drexel Heights, AZ (cdp) Pima County	187	0.78
Ajo, AZ (cdp) Pima County	182	4.91
South Tucson, AZ (city) Pima County	176	3.21
Mesa, AZ (city) Maricopa County	155	0.04
Gila Bend, AZ (town) Maricopa County	148	7.47
Glendale, AZ (city) Maricopa County	95	0.04
Tempe, AZ (city) Maricopa County	89	0.06
Florence, AZ (town) Pinal County	81	0.47
Chandler, AZ (city) Maricopa County	79	0.04
Sacaton, AZ (cdp) Pinal County	78	4.92
Coolidge, AZ (city) Pinal County	69	0.89
Fresno, CA (city) Fresno County	68	0.02
San Jose, CA (city) Santa Clara County	58	0.01
Stanfield, AZ (cdp) Pinal County	54	8.29
Guadalupe, AZ (town) Maricopa County	51	0.98
New York, NY (city) New York City	43	0.00
Arizona City, AZ (cdp) Pinal County	40	0.91
Marana, AZ (town) Pima County	35	0.26
Riverside, CA (city) Riverside County	35	0.01
Flowing Wells, AZ (cdp) Pima County	34	0.23
Yuma, AZ (city) Yuma County	34	0.04
Scottsdale, AZ (city) Maricopa County	33	0.02
San Diego, CA (city) San Diego County	32	0.00
Peoria, AZ (city) Maricopa County	30	0.03
San Francisco, CA (city) San Francisco County	29	0.00
West Covina, CA (city) Los Angeles County	28	0.03
Avondale, AZ (city) Maricopa County	27	0.08
Casas Adobes, AZ (cdp) Pima County	26	0.05
San Buenaventura, CA (city) Ventura County	26	0.03
El Paso, TX (city) El Paso County	25	0.00
Avra Valley, AZ (cdp) Pima County	24	0.48
Colorado Springs, CO (city) El Paso County	24	0.01
Portland, OR (city) Multnomah County	24	0.00
Denver, CO (city) Denver County	22	0.00
Long Beach, CA (city) Los Angeles County	21	0.00
Three Points, AZ (cdp) Pima County	20	0.38
Montebello, CA (city) Los Angeles County	20	0.03
Maricopa, AZ (cdp) Pinal County	19	1.83
Buckeye, AZ (town) Maricopa County	19	0.29
Oakland, CA (city) Alameda County	19	0.00
Fontana, CA (city) San Bernardino County	18	0.01
Modesto, CA (city) Stanislaus County	18	0.01
Flagstaff, AZ (city) Coconino County	17	0.03
Gilbert, AZ (town) Maricopa County	17	0.02
Albuquerque, NM (city) Bernalillo County	17	0.00
Dallas, TX (city) Dallas County	17	0.00
Drexel-Alvernon, AZ (cdp) Pima County	16	0.38
Montclair, CA (city) San Bernardino County	16	0.05
Corona, CA (city) Riverside County	16	0.01
Lancaster, CA (city) Los Angeles County	16	0.01
Las Vegas, NV (city) Clark County	16	0.00
Blackwater, AZ (cdp) Pinal County	15	2.98
Sierra Vista, AZ (city) Cochise County	15	0.04
Glendale, CA (city) Los Angeles County	15	0.01
San Antonio, TX (city) Bexar County	15	0.00
Woodburn, OR (city) Marion County	14	0.07
Alhambra, CA (city) Los Angeles County	14	0.02
Carson, CA (city) Los Angeles County	14	0.02
Sacramento, CA (city) Sacramento County	14	0.00
Santa Ana, CA (city) Orange County	14	0.00
Avocado Heights, CA (cdp) Los Angeles County	13	0.09
La Quinta, CA (city) Riverside County	13	0.05
Catalina Foothills, AZ (cdp) Pima County	13	0.02
Oklahoma City, OK (city) Oklahoma County	13	0.00
Santan, AZ (cdp) Pinal County	12	1.84
Clifton, AZ (town) Greenlee County	12	0.46
Tucson Estates, AZ (cdp) Pima County	12	0.12
Apache Junction, AZ (city) Pinal County	12	0.04
Covina, CA (city) Los Angeles County	12	0.03
Glendora, CA (city) Los Angeles County	12	0.02
Fremont, CA (city) Alameda County	12	0.01
Tolleson, AZ (city) Maricopa County	11	0.22
Picture Rocks, AZ (cdp) Pima County	11	0.14
Los Banos, CA (city) Merced County	11	0.04
Hacienda Heights, CA (cdp) Los Angeles County	11	0.02
Burbank, CA (city) Los Angeles County	11	0.01
Orange, CA (city) Orange County	11	0.01
Pomona, CA (city) Los Angeles County	11	0.01
San Bernardino, CA (city) San Bernardino County	11	0.01
Bakersfield, CA (city) Kern County	11	0.00
Chicago, IL (city) Cook County	11	0.00
Valencia West, AZ (cdp) Pima County	10	0.42
Pine Ridge, SD (cdp) Shannon County	10	0.32
Whiteriver, AZ (cdp) Navajo County	10	0.19
La Habra, CA (city) Orange County	10	0.02
Yucaipa, CA (city) San Bernardino County	10	0.02
Alameda, CA (city) Alameda County	10	0.01
Garden Grove, CA (city) Orange County	10	0.01
Moreno Valley, CA (city) Riverside County	10	0.01
Palmdale, CA (city) Los Angeles County	10	0.01
Santa Rosa, CA (city) Sonoma County	10	0.01
Stockton, CA (city) San Joaquin County	10	0.00
Catalina, AZ (cdp) Pima County	9	0.13
Calexico, CA (city) Imperial County	9	0.03
Colton, CA (city) San Bernardino County	9	0.02
Downey, CA (city) Los Angeles County	9	0.01
Florence-Graham, CA (cdp) Los Angeles County	9	0.01
Norwalk, CA (city) Los Angeles County	9	0.01
Santa Fe, NM (city) Santa Fe County	9	0.01
Anaheim, CA (city) Orange County	9	0.00
Cleveland, OH (city) Cuyahoga County	9	0.00
Kansas City, MO (city) Jackson County	9	0.00
Seattle, WA (city) King County	9	0.00
Seama, NM (cdp) Cibola County	8	2.40
First Mesa, AZ (cdp) Navajo County	8	0.71
Sahuarita, AZ (town) Pima County	8	0.25
San Carlos, AZ (cdp) Gila County	8	0.22
Summit, AZ (cdp) Pima County	8	0.22
Muscoy, CA (cdp) San Bernardino County	8	0.09
Silver City, NM (town) Grant County	8	0.08
Commerce, CA (city) Los Angeles County	8	0.06
Gallup, NM (city) McKinley County	8	0.04
Port Hueneme, CA (city) Ventura County	8	0.04
Hanford, CA (city) Kings County	8	0.02
San Dimas, CA (city) Los Angeles County	8	0.02
Santee, CA (city) San Diego County	8	0.02
Troy, NY (city) Rensselaer County	8	0.02
East Los Angeles, CA (cdp) Los Angeles County	8	0.01
Escondido, CA (city) San Diego County	8	0.01
Gresham, OR (city) Multnomah County	8	0.01
La Mesa, CA (city) San Diego County	8	0.01
Ontario, CA (city) San Bernardino County	8	0.01
Pasadena, CA (city) Los Angeles County	8	0.01
Redding, CA (city) Shasta County	8	0.01
Redlands, CA (city) San Bernardino County	8	0.01
South Whittier, CA (cdp) Los Angeles County	8	0.01
Tracy, CA (city) San Joaquin County	8	0.01
Whittier, CA (city) Los Angeles County	8	0.01
Arlington, VA (cdp) Arlington County	8	0.00
Oxnard, CA (city) Ventura County	8	0.00
Shongopovi, AZ (cdp) Navajo County	7	1.11
Upper Fruitland, NM (cdp) San Juan County	7	0.42
Miami, AZ (town) Gila County	7	0.36
Big Coppitt Key, FL (cdp) Monroe County	7	0.27
San Manuel, AZ (cdp) Pinal County	7	0.16
Douglas, AZ (city) Cochise County	7	0.05
Altamont, OR (cdp) Klamath County	7	0.04
Arcata, CA (city) Humboldt County	7	0.04
Citrus Heights, CA (city) Sacramento County	7	0.01
Diamond Bar, CA (city) Los Angeles County	7	0.01

Notes: (cdp) census designated place; Refer to the Explanation of Data in the front of the book for more detailed information.

American Indian: Tohono O'Odham

Top 150 Places Sorted by Percent

(Based on all places, regardless of population)

Place	Number	%
Pisinemo, AZ (cdp) Pima County	223	94.09
Santa Rosa, AZ (cdp) Pima County	400	91.32
Chuichu, AZ (cdp) Pinal County	304	89.68
Sells, AZ (cdp) Pima County	2,380	85.03
Ak-Chin Village, AZ (cdp) Pinal County	463	69.21
Stanfield, AZ (cdp) Pinal County	54	8.29
Gila Bend, AZ (town) Maricopa County	148	7.47
Sacaton, AZ (cdp) Pinal County	78	4.92
Ajo, AZ (cdp) Pima County	182	4.91
South Tucson, AZ (city) Pima County	176	3.21
Blackwater, AZ (cdp) Pinal County	15	2.98
Eloy, AZ (city) Pinal County	255	2.46
Seama, NM (cdp) Cibola County	8	2.40
Casa Grande, AZ (city) Pinal County	548	2.17
Santan, AZ (cdp) Pinal County	12	1.84
Maricopa, AZ (cdp) Pinal County	19	1.83
Pleasant Plains, AR (town) Independence County	3	1.12
Shongopovi, AZ (cdp) Navajo County	7	1.11
Guadalupe, AZ (town) Maricopa County	51	0.98
Arizona City, AZ (cdp) Pinal County	40	0.91
Coolidge, AZ (city) Pinal County	69	0.89
Drexel Heights, AZ (cdp) Pima County	187	0.78
East Glacier Park Village, MT (cdp) Glacier County	3	0.76
First Mesa, AZ (cdp) Navajo County	8	0.71
Crowheart, WY (cdp) Fremont County	1	0.61
Whiterocks, UT (cdp) Uintah County	2	0.59
Hoonah, AK (city) Skagway-Hoonah-Angoon Census Area	5	0.58
Tacna, AZ (cdp) Yuma County	3	0.54
Boneau, MT (cdp) Chouteau County	1	0.53
Greenville, CA (cdp) Plumas County	6	0.52
Tucson, AZ (city) Pima County	2,355	0.48
Avra Valley, AZ (cdp) Pima County	24	0.48
Florence, AZ (town) Pinal County	81	0.47
Clifton, AZ (town) Greenlee County	12	0.46
Valencia West, AZ (cdp) Pima County	10	0.42
Upper Fruitland, NM (cdp) San Juan County	7	0.42
Bluewater, AZ (cdp) La Paz County	3	0.41
Raymond, MN (township) Stearns County	1	0.39
Three Points, AZ (cdp) Pima County	20	0.38
Drexel-Alvernon, AZ (cdp) Pima County	16	0.38
Keams Canyon, AZ (cdp) Navajo County	1	0.38
Halchita, UT (cdp) San Juan County	1	0.37
Miami, AZ (town) Gila County	7	0.36
Hurley, NM (town) Grant County	5	0.34
Red Rock, OK (town) Noble County	1	0.34
Pine Ridge, SD (cdp) Shannon County	10	0.32
Peridot, AZ (cdp) Graham County	4	0.32
Village of Lake Isabella, MI (village) Isabella County	4	0.32
Buckeye, AZ (town) Maricopa County	19	0.29
Big Coppitt Key, FL (cdp) Monroe County	7	0.27
Boyne Falls, MI (village) Charlevoix County	1	0.27
Marana, AZ (town) Pima County	35	0.26
Hotevilla-Bacavi, AZ (cdp) Navajo County	2	0.26
Kykotsmovi Village, AZ (cdp) Navajo County	2	0.26
Sahuarita, AZ (town) Pima County	8	0.25
Broomfield, MI (township) Isabella County	4	0.25
Buena Vista, WI (town) Portage County	3	0.25
Second Mesa, AZ (cdp) Navajo County	2	0.25
Mountain View Acres, CA (cdp) San Bernardino County	6	0.24
Salome, AZ (cdp) La Paz County	4	0.24
Flowing Wells, AZ (cdp) Pima County	34	0.23
Nuiqsut, AK (city) North Slope Borough	1	0.23
Salesville, AR (city) Baxter County	1	0.23
Tolleson, AZ (city) Maricopa County	11	0.22
San Carlos, AZ (cdp) Gila County	8	0.22
Summit, AZ (cdp) Pima County	8	0.22
Claypool, AZ (cdp) Gila County	4	0.22
Frazer, MT (cdp) Valley County	1	0.22
Paguate, NM (cdp) Cibola County	1	0.21
Licking Creek, PA (township) Fulton County	3	0.20
Littletown, AZ (cdp) Pima County	2	0.20
Isleta Village Proper, NM (cdp) Bernalillo County	1	0.20
Whiteriver, AZ (cdp) Navajo County	10	0.19
Winterhaven, CA (cdp) Imperial County	1	0.19
La Center, WA (city) Clark County	3	0.18
Cottage City, MD (town) Prince George's County	2	0.18
Teton, ID (city) Fremont County	1	0.18
Mechanicsville, IA (city) Cedar County	2	0.17
Nassau, NY (village) Rensselaer County	2	0.17
Glencoe, OK (town) Payne County	1	0.17
Searchlight, NV (cdp) Clark County	1	0.17
San Manuel, AZ (cdp) Pinal County	7	0.16
Blanding, UT (city) San Juan County	5	0.16
Morenci, AZ (cdp) Greenlee County	3	0.16
Mescalero, NM (cdp) Otero County	2	0.16
Wanblee, SD (cdp) Jackson County	1	0.16
Cibecue, AZ (cdp) Navajo County	2	0.15
Alna, ME (town) Lincoln County	1	0.15
Picture Rocks, AZ (cdp) Pima County	11	0.14
Caruthers, CA (cdp) Fresno County	3	0.14
East Sahuarita, AZ (cdp) Pima County	2	0.14
Catalina, AZ (cdp) Pima County	9	0.13
Southport, NC (city) Brunswick County	3	0.13
Tucson Estates, AZ (cdp) Pima County	12	0.12
Humboldt Hill, CA (cdp) Humboldt County	4	0.12
Myrtle Point, OR (city) Coos County	3	0.12
Lakeview, CA (cdp) Riverside County	2	0.12
Aurora, TX (town) Wise County	1	0.12
Cass Lake, MN (city) Cass County	1	0.12
Corona de Tucson, AZ (cdp) Pima County	1	0.12
Shoreham, MI (village) Berrien County	1	0.12
Chinle, AZ (cdp) Apache County	6	0.11
Homeland, CA (cdp) Riverside County	4	0.11
Central Heights-Midland City, AZ (cdp) Gila County	3	0.11
Mammoth, AZ (town) Pinal County	2	0.11
Pablo, MT (cdp) Lake County	2	0.11
Hillburn, NY (village) Rockland County	1	0.11
Moenkopi, AZ (cdp) Coconino County	1	0.11
Madras, OR (city) Jefferson County	5	0.10
East Dundee, IL (village) Kane County	3	0.10
Kotzebue, AK (city) Northwest Arctic Borough	3	0.10
Lumberland, NY (town) Sullivan County	2	0.10
Swedesboro, NJ (borough) Gloucester County	2	0.10
Basye-Bryce Mountain, VA (cdp) Shenandoah County	1	0.10
Gadsden, AZ (cdp) Yuma County	1	0.10
Mission, OR (cdp) Umatilla County	1	0.10
Avocado Heights, CA (cdp) Los Angeles County	13	0.09
Muscoy, CA (cdp) San Bernardino County	8	0.09
Laie, HI (cdp) Honolulu County	4	0.09
Idyllwild-Pine Cove, CA (cdp) Riverside County	3	0.09
Lenwood, CA (cdp) San Bernardino County	3	0.09
Rose Hill, KS (city) Butler County	3	0.09
Superior, AZ (town) Pinal County	3	0.09
Vernonia, OR (city) Columbia County	2	0.09
Boles Acres, NM (cdp) Otero County	1	0.09
Canyon Day, AZ (cdp) Gila County	1	0.09
Church Rock, NM (cdp) McKinley County	1	0.09
Houck, AZ (cdp) Apache County	1	0.09
Kamiah, ID (city) Lewis County	1	0.09
Niland, CA (cdp) Imperial County	1	0.09
Westfield Center, OH (village) Medina County	1	0.09
Phoenix, AZ (city) Maricopa County	1,013	0.08
Avondale, AZ (city) Maricopa County	27	0.08
Silver City, NM (town) Grant County	8	0.08
Ruidoso, NM (village) Lincoln County	6	0.08
El Rio, CA (cdp) Ventura County	5	0.08
Running Springs, CA (cdp) San Bernardino County	4	0.08
Day Valley, CA (cdp) Santa Cruz County	3	0.08
El Verano, CA (cdp) Sonoma County	3	0.08
Tortolita, AZ (cdp) Pima County	3	0.08
Hubbard, OR (city) Marion County	2	0.08
Boyne Valley, MI (township) Charlevoix County	1	0.08
Calverton Park, MO (village) Saint Louis County	1	0.08
Cherry Tree, OK (cdp) Adair County	1	0.08
Elliston-Lafayette, VA (cdp) Montgomery County	1	0.08
Luck, WI (village) Polk County	1	0.08
Morningside, MD (town) Prince George's County	1	0.08
Plantation Mobile Home Park, FL (cdp) Palm Beach County	1	0.08
Taos Pueblo, NM (cdp) Taos County	1	0.08
Woodburn, OR (city) Marion County	14	0.07

Notes: (cdp) census designated place; Refer to the Explanation of Data in the front of the book for more detailed information.

American Indian: Tohono O'Odham

Top 150 Places Sorted by Percent

(Based on places with populations of 10,000 or more)

Place	Number	%
Eloy, AZ (city) Pinal County	255	2.46
Casa Grande, AZ (city) Pinal County	548	2.17
Drexel Heights, AZ (cdp) Pima County	187	0.78
Tucson, AZ (city) Pima County	2,355	0.48
Florence, AZ (town) Pinal County	81	0.47
Marana, AZ (town) Pima County	35	0.26
Flowing Wells, AZ (cdp) Pima County	34	0.23
Avocado Heights, CA (cdp) Los Angeles County	13	0.09
Phoenix, AZ (city) Maricopa County	1,013	0.08
Avondale, AZ (city) Maricopa County	27	0.08
Silver City, NM (town) Grant County	8	0.08
Woodburn, OR (city) Marion County	14	0.07
Tempe, AZ (city) Maricopa County	89	0.06
Commerce, CA (city) Los Angeles County	8	0.06
Casas Adobes, AZ (cdp) Pima County	26	0.05
Montclair, CA (city) San Bernardino County	16	0.05
La Quinta, CA (city) Riverside County	13	0.05
Douglas, AZ (city) Cochise County	7	0.05
Beaumont, CA (city) Riverside County	6	0.05
Mountain Home, ID (city) Elmore County	6	0.05
Buffalo, MN (city) Wright County	5	0.05
Crestline, CA (cdp) San Bernardino County	5	0.05
Mesa, AZ (city) Maricopa County	155	0.04
Glendale, AZ (city) Maricopa County	95	0.04
Chandler, AZ (city) Maricopa County	79	0.04
Yuma, AZ (city) Yuma County	34	0.04
Sierra Vista, AZ (city) Cochise County	15	0.04
Apache Junction, AZ (city) Pinal County	12	0.04
Los Banos, CA (city) Merced County	11	0.04
Gallup, NM (city) McKinley County	8	0.04
Port Hueneme, CA (city) Ventura County	8	0.04
Altamont, OR (cdp) Klamath County	7	0.04
Arcata, CA (city) Humboldt County	7	0.04
Twentynine Palms, CA (city) San Bernardino County	6	0.04
Cherryland, CA (cdp) Alameda County	5	0.04
Fort Polk South, LA (cdp) Vernon Parish	4	0.04
Spring Creek, NV (cdp) Elko County	4	0.04
Valle Vista, CA (cdp) Riverside County	4	0.04
Peoria, AZ (city) Maricopa County	30	0.03
West Covina, CA (city) Los Angeles County	28	0.03
San Buenaventura, CA (city) Ventura County	26	0.03
Montebello, CA (city) Los Angeles County	20	0.03
Flagstaff, AZ (city) Coconino County	17	0.03
Covina, CA (city) Los Angeles County	12	0.03
Calexico, CA (city) Imperial County	9	0.03
Cabot, AR (city) Lonoke County	4	0.03
Catskill, NY (town) Greene County	4	0.03
East Norriton, PA (cdp) Montgomery County	4	0.03
Grover Beach, CA (city) San Luis Obispo County	4	0.03
Patterson, CA (city) Stanislaus County	4	0.03
Vincent, CA (cdp) Los Angeles County	4	0.03
Artesia, NM (city) Eddy County	3	0.03
Newberry, SC (town) Newberry County	3	0.03
Riverton-Boulevard Park, WA (cdp) King County	3	0.03
The Village, OK (city) Oklahoma County	3	0.03
Fresno, CA (city) Fresno County	68	0.02
Scottsdale, AZ (city) Maricopa County	33	0.02
Gilbert, AZ (town) Maricopa County	17	0.02
Alhambra, CA (city) Los Angeles County	14	0.02
Carson, CA (city) Los Angeles County	14	0.02
Catalina Foothills, AZ (cdp) Pima County	13	0.02
Glendora, CA (city) Los Angeles County	12	0.02
Hacienda Heights, CA (cdp) Los Angeles County	11	0.02
La Habra, CA (city) Orange County	10	0.02
Yucaipa, CA (city) San Bernardino County	10	0.02
Colton, CA (city) San Bernardino County	9	0.02
Hanford, CA (city) Kings County	8	0.02
San Dimas, CA (city) Los Angeles County	8	0.02
Santee, CA (city) San Diego County	8	0.02
Troy, NY (city) Rensselaer County	8	0.02
El Centro, CA (city) Imperial County	6	0.02
Maywood, CA (city) Los Angeles County	6	0.02
Security-Widefield, CO (cdp) El Paso County	6	0.02
Burien, WA (city) King County	5	0.02
Mount Vernon, WA (city) Skagit County	5	0.02
West Sacramento, CA (city) Yolo County	5	0.02
Westmont, CA (cdp) Los Angeles County	5	0.02
Adelanto, CA (city) San Bernardino County	4	0.02
Asbury Park, NJ (city) Monmouth County	4	0.02
Banning, CA (city) Riverside County	4	0.02
Clifton, CO (cdp) Mesa County	4	0.02
Fortuna Foothills, AZ (cdp) Yuma County	4	0.02
Goodyear, AZ (city) Maricopa County	4	0.02
Kingman, AZ (city) Mohave County	4	0.02
Lemon Grove, CA (city) San Diego County	4	0.02
Reedley, CA (city) Fresno County	4	0.02
Rosemont, CA (cdp) Sacramento County	4	0.02
Santa Fe Springs, CA (city) Los Angeles County	4	0.02
Alum Rock, CA (cdp) Santa Clara County	3	0.02
Blythe, CA (city) Riverside County	3	0.02
Brigham City, UT (city) Box Elder County	3	0.02
Camp Springs, MD (cdp) Prince George's County	3	0.02
Cartersville, GA (city) Bartow County	3	0.02
Desert Hot Springs, CA (city) Riverside County	3	0.02
Dickinson, ND (city) Stark County	3	0.02
Fort Knox, KY (cdp) Hardin County	3	0.02
Franklin, IN (city) Johnson County	3	0.02
Poinciana, FL (cdp) Osceola County	3	0.02
Tanque Verde, AZ (cdp) Pima County	3	0.02
Guilford, PA (township) Franklin County	2	0.02
Marysville, CA (city) Yuba County	2	0.02
North Auburn, CA (cdp) Placer County	2	0.02
Okmulgee, OK (city) Okmulgee County	2	0.02
Stanford, CA (cdp) Santa Clara County	2	0.02
Los Angeles, CA (city) Los Angeles County	201	0.01
San Jose, CA (city) Santa Clara County	58	0.01
Riverside, CA (city) Riverside County	35	0.01
Colorado Springs, CO (city) El Paso County	24	0.01
Fontana, CA (city) San Bernardino County	18	0.01
Modesto, CA (city) Stanislaus County	18	0.01
Corona, CA (city) Riverside County	16	0.01
Lancaster, CA (city) Los Angeles County	16	0.01
Glendale, CA (city) Los Angeles County	15	0.01
Fremont, CA (city) Alameda County	12	0.01
Burbank, CA (city) Los Angeles County	11	0.01
Orange, CA (city) Orange County	11	0.01
Pomona, CA (city) Los Angeles County	11	0.01
San Bernardino, CA (city) San Bernardino County	11	0.01
Alameda, CA (city) Alameda County	10	0.01
Garden Grove, CA (city) Orange County	10	0.01
Moreno Valley, CA (city) Riverside County	10	0.01
Palmdale, CA (city) Los Angeles County	10	0.01
Santa Rosa, CA (city) Sonoma County	10	0.01
Downey, CA (city) Los Angeles County	9	0.01
Florence-Graham, CA (cdp) Los Angeles County	9	0.01
Norwalk, CA (city) Los Angeles County	9	0.01
Santa Fe, NM (city) Santa Fe County	9	0.01
East Los Angeles, CA (cdp) Los Angeles County	8	0.01
Escondido, CA (city) San Diego County	8	0.01
Gresham, OR (city) Multnomah County	8	0.01
La Mesa, CA (city) San Diego County	8	0.01
Ontario, CA (city) San Bernardino County	8	0.01
Pasadena, CA (city) Los Angeles County	8	0.01
Redding, CA (city) Shasta County	8	0.01
Redlands, CA (city) San Bernardino County	8	0.01
South Whittier, CA (cdp) Los Angeles County	8	0.01
Tracy, CA (city) San Joaquin County	8	0.01
Whittier, CA (city) Los Angeles County	8	0.01
Citrus Heights, CA (city) Sacramento County	7	0.01
Diamond Bar, CA (city) Los Angeles County	7	0.01
Hemet, CA (city) Riverside County	7	0.01
Lawrence, KS (city) Douglas County	7	0.01
Nampa, ID (city) Canyon County	7	0.01
Altadena, CA (cdp) Los Angeles County	6	0.01
El Cajon, CA (city) San Diego County	6	0.01
El Monte, CA (city) Los Angeles County	6	0.01
Inglewood, CA (city) Los Angeles County	6	0.01
Lompoc, CA (city) Santa Barbara County	6	0.01
Midland, TX (city) Midland County	6	0.01
Pico Rivera, CA (city) Los Angeles County	6	0.01

Notes: (cdp) census designated place; Refer to the Explanation of Data in the front of the book for more detailed information.

American Indian: Ute

Top 150 Places Sorted by Number

(Based on all places, regardless of population)

Place	Number	%
Towaoc, CO (cdp) Montezuma County	853	77.76
Fort Duchesne, UT (cdp) Uintah County	519	83.57
Whiterocks, UT (cdp) Uintah County	292	85.63
Roosevelt, UT (city) Duchesne County	274	6.37
White Mesa, UT (cdp) San Juan County	196	70.76
Randlett, UT (cdp) Uintah County	187	83.48
Salt Lake City, UT (city) Salt Lake County	159	0.09
Denver, CO (city) Denver County	139	0.03
Colorado Springs, CO (city) El Paso County	111	0.03
Ignacio, CO (town) La Plata County	91	13.60
Albuquerque, NM (city) Bernalillo County	87	0.02
Cortez, CO (city) Montezuma County	86	1.08
Vernal, UT (city) Uintah County	82	1.06
West Valley City, UT (city) Salt Lake County	63	0.06
Ogden, UT (city) Weber County	58	0.08
Los Angeles, CA (city) Los Angeles County	56	0.00
Myton, UT (city) Duchesne County	53	9.83
Durango, CO (city) La Plata County	51	0.37
Phoenix, AZ (city) Maricopa County	48	0.00
Neola, UT (cdp) Duchesne County	42	7.88
Farmington, NM (city) San Juan County	41	0.11
Lakewood, CO (city) Jefferson County	36	0.02
Aurora, CO (city) Arapahoe County	34	0.01
Saint George, UT (city) Washington County	32	0.06
Portland, OR (city) Multnomah County	31	0.01
Mesa, AZ (city) Maricopa County	29	0.01
Millcreek, UT (cdp) Salt Lake County	28	0.09
Tucson, AZ (city) Pima County	28	0.01
Kearns, UT (cdp) Salt Lake County	26	0.08
Pueblo, CO (city) Pueblo County	26	0.03
Magna, UT (cdp) Salt Lake County	25	0.11
Taylorsville, UT (city) Salt Lake County	24	0.04
Cedar City, UT (city) Iron County	23	0.11
Tooele, UT (city) Tooele County	23	0.10
San Diego, CA (city) San Diego County	23	0.00
Grand Junction, CO (city) Mesa County	22	0.05
Orem, UT (city) Utah County	22	0.03
Clearfield, UT (city) Davis County	21	0.08
Draper, UT (city) Salt Lake County	21	0.08
Thornton, CO (city) Adams County	21	0.03
San Jose, CA (city) Santa Clara County	21	0.00
South Salt Lake, UT (city) Salt Lake County	20	0.09
Las Vegas, NV (city) Clark County	20	0.00
Glendale, AZ (city) Maricopa County	19	0.01
Riverside, CA (city) Riverside County	19	0.01
Rio Rancho, NM (city) Sandoval County	18	0.03
West Jordan, UT (city) Salt Lake County	18	0.03
Sacramento, CA (city) Sacramento County	18	0.00
Blanding, UT (city) San Juan County	17	0.54
Vallejo, CA (city) Solano County	17	0.01
San Francisco, CA (city) San Francisco County	17	0.00
Provo, UT (city) Utah County	16	0.02
Maeser, UT (cdp) Uintah County	15	0.53
Kirtland, NM (cdp) San Juan County	15	0.24
Security-Widefield, CO (cdp) El Paso County	15	0.05
Fort Collins, CO (city) Larimer County	15	0.01
Fremont, CA (city) Alameda County	15	0.01
Long Beach, CA (city) Los Angeles County	15	0.00
Tulsa, OK (city) Tulsa County	15	0.00
Ballard, UT (town) Uintah County	14	2.47
Berthoud, CO (town) Larimer County	14	0.29
Clifton, CO (cdp) Mesa County	14	0.08
Lancaster, CA (city) Los Angeles County	14	0.01
Westminster, CO (city) Adams County	14	0.01
Stratmoor, CO (cdp) El Paso County	13	0.20
Santa Rosa, CA (city) Sonoma County	13	0.01
Rangely, CO (town) Rio Blanco County	12	0.57
Gallup, NM (city) McKinley County	12	0.06
Redding, CA (city) Shasta County	12	0.01
Sandy, UT (city) Salt Lake County	12	0.01
Tempe, AZ (city) Maricopa County	12	0.01
Austin, TX (city) Travis County	12	0.00
Chicago, IL (city) Cook County	12	0.00
Seattle, WA (city) King County	12	0.00
Parker School, MT (cdp) Chouteau County	11	3.13
Alamosa, CO (city) Alamosa County	11	0.14
Montrose, CO (city) Montrose County	11	0.09
Sherrelwood, CO (cdp) Adams County	11	0.06
Logan, UT (city) Cache County	11	0.03
Longmont, CO (city) Boulder County	11	0.02
Boise City, ID (city) Ada County	11	0.01
Simi Valley, CA (city) Ventura County	11	0.01
Oakland, CA (city) Alameda County	11	0.00
Oklahoma City, OK (city) Oklahoma County	11	0.00
Saguache, CO (town) Saguache County	10	1.73
Bosque Farms, NM (village) Valencia County	10	0.25
Derby, CO (cdp) Adams County	10	0.16
Brigham City, UT (city) Box Elder County	10	0.06
Roy, UT (city) Weber County	10	0.03
Southglenn, CO (cdp) Arapahoe County	10	0.02
Billings, MT (city) Yellowstone County	10	0.01
Corona, CA (city) Riverside County	10	0.01
Modesto, CA (city) Stanislaus County	10	0.01
Bayfield, CO (town) La Plata County	9	0.58
Richfield, UT (city) Sevier County	9	0.13
Idaho Falls, ID (city) Bonneville County	9	0.02
Layton, UT (city) Davis County	9	0.02
Arvada, CO (city) Jefferson County	9	0.01
Concord, CA (city) Contra Costa County	9	0.01
Spring Valley, NV (cdp) Clark County	9	0.01
Anchorage, AK (municipality) Anchorage Borough	9	0.00
Reno, NV (city) Washoe County	9	0.00
Mancos, CO (town) Montezuma County	8	0.71
Sedro-Woolley, WA (city) Skagit County	8	0.09
El Segundo, CA (city) Los Angeles County	8	0.05
Sulphur Springs, TX (city) Hopkins County	8	0.05
Brighton, CO (city) Adams County	8	0.04
Commerce City, CO (city) Adams County	8	0.04
Lafayette, CO (city) Boulder County	8	0.03
West Sacramento, CA (city) Yolo County	8	0.03
Loveland, CO (city) Larimer County	8	0.02
Bismarck, ND (city) Burleigh County	8	0.01
Eugene, OR (city) Lane County	8	0.01
Great Falls, MT (city) Cascade County	8	0.01
Las Cruces, NM (city) Dona Ana County	8	0.01
Palmdale, CA (city) Los Angeles County	8	0.01
Rancho Cucamonga, CA (city) San Bernardino County	8	0.01
Rialto, CA (city) San Bernardino County	8	0.01
Sunrise Manor, NV (cdp) Clark County	8	0.01
Chandler, AZ (city) Maricopa County	8	0.00
Honolulu, HI (cdp) Honolulu County	8	0.00
New York, NY (city) New York City	8	0.00
Oxnard, CA (city) Ventura County	8	0.00
Virginia Beach, VA (independent city) Virginia Beach city	8	0.00
Gunnison, UT (city) Sanpete County	7	0.29
Vail, CO (town) Eagle County	7	0.15
Bloomfield, NM (city) San Juan County	7	0.11
Lander, WY (city) Fremont County	7	0.10
Shiprock, NM (cdp) San Juan County	7	0.09
Washington Terrace, UT (city) Weber County	7	0.08
American Fork, UT (city) Utah County	7	0.03
Milwaukie, OR (city) Clackamas County	7	0.03
SeaTac, WA (city) King County	7	0.03
Greeley, CO (city) Weld County	7	0.01
Lodi, CA (city) San Joaquin County	7	0.01
Midland, TX (city) Midland County	7	0.01
San Angelo, TX (city) Tom Green County	7	0.01
San Buenaventura, CA (city) Ventura County	7	0.01
San Leandro, CA (city) Alameda County	7	0.01
Santa Fe, NM (city) Santa Fe County	7	0.01
Santa Maria, CA (city) Santa Barbara County	7	0.01
Sparks, NV (city) Washoe County	7	0.01
Torrance, CA (city) Los Angeles County	7	0.01
San Antonio, TX (city) Bexar County	7	0.00
Scottsdale, AZ (city) Maricopa County	7	0.00
Springfield, MO (city) Greene County	7	0.00
Stockton, CA (city) San Joaquin County	7	0.00
Pecos, NM (village) San Miguel County	6	0.42
Pima, AZ (town) Graham County	6	0.30
Moab, UT (city) Grand County	6	0.13

Notes: (cdp) census designated place; Refer to the Explanation of Data in the front of the book for more detailed information.

American Indian: Ute

Top 150 Places Sorted by Percent

(Based on all places, regardless of population)

Place	Number	%
Whiterocks, UT (cdp) Uintah County	292	85.63
Fort Duchesne, UT (cdp) Uintah County	519	83.57
Randlett, UT (cdp) Uintah County	187	83.48
Towaoc, CO (cdp) Montezuma County	853	77.76
White Mesa, UT (cdp) San Juan County	196	70.76
Ignacio, CO (town) La Plata County	91	13.60
Myton, UT (city) Duchesne County	53	9.83
Neola, UT (cdp) Duchesne County	42	7.88
Roosevelt, UT (city) Duchesne County	274	6.37
Parker School, MT (cdp) Chouteau County	11	3.13
Ballard, UT (town) Uintah County	14	2.47
Antimony, UT (town) Garfield County	3	2.46
Altamont, UT (town) Duchesne County	4	2.25
Moffat, CO (town) Saguache County	2	1.75
Saguache, CO (town) Saguache County	10	1.73
Arboles, CO (cdp) Archuleta County	4	1.72
Alton, UT (town) Kane County	2	1.49
Magnet, NE (village) Cedar County	1	1.27
Aquinnah, MA (town) Dukes County	4	1.16
Keams Canyon, AZ (cdp) Navajo County	3	1.15
Garden City, UT (town) Rich County	4	1.12
Success, AR (town) Clay County	2	1.11
Kaibab, AZ (cdp) Mohave County	3	1.09
Cortez, CO (city) Montezuma County	86	1.08
Vernal, UT (city) Uintah County	82	1.06
Pilot Point, AK (city) Lake and Peninsula Borough	1	1.00
White Mountain, AK (city) Nome Census Area	2	0.99
Tselakai Dezza, UT (cdp) San Juan County	1	0.97
Muddy, MT (cdp) Big Horn County	5	0.80
Mancos, CO (town) Montezuma County	8	0.71
Tabiona, UT (town) Duchesne County	1	0.67
Corona, NM (village) Lincoln County	1	0.61
Doerun, GA (city) Colquitt County	5	0.60
Angus, TX (city) Navarro County	2	0.60
La Sal, UT (cdp) San Juan County	2	0.59
Bayfield, CO (town) La Plata County	9	0.58
Rangely, CO (town) Rio Blanco County	12	0.57
Blanding, UT (city) San Juan County	17	0.54
Maeser, UT (cdp) Uintah County	15	0.53
Iona, MN (township) Murray County	1	0.51
Saratoga Springs, UT (town) Utah County	5	0.50
Swan Valley, ID (city) Bonneville County	1	0.47
Asbury, MO (city) Jasper County	1	0.46
Wilhoit, AZ (cdp) Yavapai County	3	0.45
Fort Yates, ND (city) Sioux County	1	0.44
Glendo, WY (town) Platte County	1	0.44
Kamrar, IA (city) Hamilton County	1	0.44
Busby, MT (cdp) Big Horn County	3	0.43
Pecos, NM (village) San Miguel County	6	0.42
Hollister, ID (city) Twin Falls County	1	0.42
Mescalero, NM (cdp) Otero County	5	0.41
Arriba, CO (town) Lincoln County	1	0.41
Durango, CO (city) La Plata County	51	0.37
Fort Washakie, WY (cdp) Fremont County	5	0.34
Kamiah, ID (city) Lewis County	4	0.34
Hamden, OH (village) Vinton County	3	0.34
Pagosa Springs, CO (town) Archuleta County	5	0.31
Splendora, TX (city) Montgomery County	4	0.31
Naturita, CO (town) Montrose County	2	0.31
Pima, AZ (town) Graham County	6	0.30
Berthoud, CO (town) Larimer County	14	0.29
Gunnison, UT (city) Sanpete County	7	0.29
Arco, ID (city) Butte County	3	0.29
Skyline-Ganipa, NM (cdp) Cibola County	3	0.29
Pueblo of Sandia Village, NM (cdp) Sandoval County	1	0.29
Duchesne, UT (city) Duchesne County	4	0.28
Ethete, WY (cdp) Fremont County	4	0.27
Sligo, PA (borough) Clarion County	2	0.27
East Pleasant View, CO (cdp) Jefferson County	1	0.27
Weirgor, WI (town) Sawyer County	1	0.27
Beulah Valley, CO (cdp) Pueblo County	3	0.26
Kykotsmovi Village, AZ (cdp) Navajo County	2	0.26
Mesita, NM (cdp) Cibola County	2	0.26
Talkeetna, AK (cdp) Matanuska-Susitna Borough	2	0.26
Chilcoot-Vinton, CA (cdp) Plumas County	1	0.26
Bosque Farms, NM (village) Valencia County	10	0.25
Westville, OK (town) Adair County	4	0.25
Teec Nos Pos, AZ (cdp) Apache County	2	0.25
Ramah, NM (cdp) McKinley County	1	0.25
Sadler, TX (city) Grayson County	1	0.25
Kirtland, NM (cdp) San Juan County	15	0.24
Cobb, CA (cdp) Lake County	4	0.24
Ojo Amarillo, NM (cdp) San Juan County	2	0.24
Hodgkins, IL (village) Cook County	5	0.23
Dolores, CO (town) Montezuma County	2	0.23
West Siloam Springs, OK (town) Delaware County	2	0.23
La Barge, WY (town) Lincoln County	1	0.23
Sigurd, UT (town) Sevier County	1	0.23
Monroe, UT (city) Sevier County	4	0.22
Keshena, WI (cdp) Menominee County	3	0.22
Fraser, CO (town) Grand County	2	0.22
De Beque, CO (town) Mesa County	1	0.22
Eden Roc, HI (cdp) Hawaii County	1	0.22
Hoback, WY (cdp) Teton County	3	0.21
Kibler, AR (city) Crawford County	2	0.21
Stratmoor, CO (cdp) El Paso County	13	0.20
River Heights, UT (city) Cache County	3	0.20
Dahlgren, VA (cdp) King George County	2	0.20
Montezuma Creek, UT (cdp) San Juan County	1	0.20
Crow Agency, MT (cdp) Big Horn County	3	0.19
Hampton, NJ (borough) Hunterdon County	3	0.19
Centerfield, UT (town) Sanpete County	2	0.19
Mount Pleasant, UT (city) Sanpete County	5	0.18
Upper Fruitland, NM (cdp) San Juan County	3	0.18
Cripple Creek, CO (city) Teller County	2	0.18
First Mesa, AZ (cdp) Navajo County	2	0.18
Rail Road Flat, CA (cdp) Calaveras County	1	0.18
Lazy Mountain, AK (cdp) Matanuska-Susitna Borough	2	0.17
Aneth, UT (cdp) San Juan County	1	0.17
Beech Bottom, WV (village) Brooke County	1	0.17
Peach Springs, AZ (cdp) Mohave County	1	0.17
San Juan, NM (cdp) Rio Arriba County	1	0.17
Derby, CO (cdp) Adams County	10	0.16
Fort Hall, ID (cdp) Bannock County	5	0.16
Three Rivers, OR (cdp) Deschutes County	4	0.16
Royal City, WA (city) Grant County	3	0.16
Taos Pueblo, NM (cdp) Taos County	2	0.16
New Underwood, SD (city) Pennington County	1	0.16
Pleasant Valley, AK (cdp) Fairbanks North Star Borough	1	0.16
Skokomish, WA (cdp) Mason County	1	0.16
Vail, CO (town) Eagle County	7	0.15
Dulce, NM (cdp) Rio Arriba County	4	0.15
Wellington, CO (town) Larimer County	4	0.15
Hay Springs, NE (village) Sheridan County	1	0.15
Levan, UT (town) Juab County	1	0.15
Rosalia, WA (town) Whitman County	1	0.15
Alamosa, CO (city) Alamosa County	11	0.14
Tularosa, NM (village) Otero County	4	0.14
Nederland, CO (town) Boulder County	2	0.14
Dell Grove, MN (township) Pine County	1	0.14
San Luis, CO (town) Costilla County	1	0.14
Schurz, NV (cdp) Mineral County	1	0.14
Walkerville, MT (town) Silver Bow County	1	0.14
Richfield, UT (city) Sevier County	9	0.13
Moab, UT (city) Grand County	6	0.13
White Swan, WA (cdp) Yakima County	4	0.13
Tool, TX (city) Henderson County	3	0.13
Volcano, HI (cdp) Hawaii County	3	0.13
Alamosa East, CO (cdp) Alamosa County	2	0.13
Bear River City, UT (town) Box Elder County	1	0.13
Eagar, AZ (town) Apache County	5	0.12
Deer Lodge, MT (city) Powell County	4	0.12
Fort Polk North, LA (cdp) Vernon Parish	4	0.12
Bangs, TX (city) Brown County	2	0.12
Ferron, UT (city) Emery County	2	0.12
Hayden, CO (town) Routt County	2	0.12
Lakeview, CA (cdp) Riverside County	2	0.12
Rainier, OR (city) Columbia County	2	0.12
Wellington, UT (city) Carbon County	2	0.12
Lexington, NY (town) Greene County	1	0.12

Notes: (cdp) census designated place; Refer to the Explanation of Data in the front of the book for more detailed information.

American Indian: Ute

Top 150 Places Sorted by Percent

(Based on places with populations of 10,000 or more)

Place	Number	%
Durango, CO (city) La Plata County	51	0.37
Farmington, NM (city) San Juan County	41	0.11
Magna, UT (cdp) Salt Lake County	25	0.11
Cedar City, UT (city) Iron County	23	0.11
Tooele, UT (city) Tooele County	23	0.10
Salt Lake City, UT (city) Salt Lake County	159	0.09
Millcreek, UT (cdp) Salt Lake County	28	0.09
South Salt Lake, UT (city) Salt Lake County	20	0.09
Montrose, CO (city) Montrose County	11	0.09
Ogden, UT (city) Weber County	58	0.08
Kearns, UT (cdp) Salt Lake County	26	0.08
Clearfield, UT (city) Davis County	21	0.08
Draper, UT (city) Salt Lake County	21	0.08
Clifton, CO (cdp) Mesa County	14	0.08
West Valley City, UT (city) Salt Lake County	63	0.06
Saint George, UT (city) Washington County	32	0.06
Gallup, NM (city) McKinley County	12	0.06
Sherrelwood, CO (cdp) Adams County	11	0.06
Brigham City, UT (city) Box Elder County	10	0.06
Grand Junction, CO (city) Mesa County	22	0.05
Security-Widefield, CO (cdp) El Paso County	15	0.05
El Segundo, CA (city) Los Angeles County	8	0.05
Sulphur Springs, TX (city) Hopkins County	8	0.05
Dallas, OR (city) Polk County	6	0.05
Taylorsville, UT (city) Salt Lake County	24	0.04
Brighton, CO (city) Adams County	8	0.04
Commerce City, CO (city) Adams County	8	0.04
Cimarron Hills, CO (cdp) El Paso County	6	0.04
East San Gabriel, CA (cdp) Los Angeles County	6	0.04
Fountain, CO (city) El Paso County	6	0.04
Evanston, WY (city) Uinta County	5	0.04
Payson, UT (city) Utah County	5	0.04
Welby, CO (cdp) Adams County	5	0.04
Denver, CO (city) Denver County	139	0.03
Colorado Springs, CO (city) El Paso County	111	0.03
Pueblo, CO (city) Pueblo County	26	0.03
Orem, UT (city) Utah County	22	0.03
Thornton, CO (city) Adams County	21	0.03
Rio Rancho, NM (city) Sandoval County	18	0.03
West Jordan, UT (city) Salt Lake County	18	0.03
Logan, UT (city) Cache County	11	0.03
Roy, UT (city) Weber County	10	0.03
Lafayette, CO (city) Boulder County	8	0.03
West Sacramento, CA (city) Yolo County	8	0.03
American Fork, UT (city) Utah County	7	0.03
Milwaukie, OR (city) Clackamas County	7	0.03
SeaTac, WA (city) King County	7	0.03
Cottonwood West, UT (cdp) Salt Lake County	6	0.03
Kaysville, UT (city) Davis County	6	0.03
Canon City, CO (city) Fremont County	5	0.03
El Reno, OK (city) Canadian County	5	0.03
South Ogden, UT (city) Weber County	5	0.03
Federal Heights, CO (city) Adams County	4	0.03
North Valley, NM (cdp) Bernalillo County	4	0.03
Artesia, NM (city) Eddy County	3	0.03
Berkley, CO (cdp) Adams County	3	0.03
Blackfoot, ID (city) Bingham County	3	0.03
Elk City, OK (city) Beckham County	3	0.03
Farmington, NY (town) Ontario County	3	0.03
Lea Hill, WA (cdp) King County	3	0.03
Oquirrh, UT (cdp) Salt Lake County	3	0.03
Upper Grand Lagoon, FL (cdp) Bay County	3	0.03
Albuquerque, NM (city) Bernalillo County	87	0.02
Lakewood, CO (city) Jefferson County	36	0.02
Provo, UT (city) Utah County	16	0.02
Longmont, CO (city) Boulder County	11	0.02
Southglenn, CO (cdp) Arapahoe County	10	0.02
Idaho Falls, ID (city) Bonneville County	9	0.02
Layton, UT (city) Davis County	9	0.02
Loveland, CO (city) Larimer County	8	0.02
Bozeman, MT (city) Gallatin County	6	0.02
Englewood, CO (city) Arapahoe County	6	0.02
Martinez, CA (city) Contra Costa County	6	0.02
Midvale, UT (city) Salt Lake County	6	0.02
Banning, CA (city) Riverside County	5	0.02

Place	Number	%
Oro Valley, AZ (town) Pima County	5	0.02
Parker, CO (town) Douglas County	5	0.02
Spanish Fork, UT (city) Utah County	5	0.02
Springville, UT (city) Utah County	5	0.02
Brook Park, OH (city) Cuyahoga County	4	0.02
Caldwell, ID (city) Canyon County	4	0.02
Drexel Heights, AZ (cdp) Pima County	4	0.02
Galt, CA (city) Sacramento County	4	0.02
Hinsdale, IL (village) Du Page County	4	0.02
Prairie Village, KS (city) Johnson County	4	0.02
Suisun City, CA (city) Solano County	4	0.02
Wall, NJ (township) Monmouth County	4	0.02
Arcata, CA (city) Humboldt County	3	0.02
Artesia, CA (city) Los Angeles County	3	0.02
Brushy Creek, TX (cdp) Williamson County	3	0.02
Flowing Wells, AZ (cdp) Pima County	3	0.02
Hopkins, MN (city) Hennepin County	3	0.02
Lakeside, CA (cdp) San Diego County	3	0.02
Las Vegas, NM (city) San Miguel County	3	0.02
Lebanon, OR (city) Linn County	3	0.02
Lorton, VA (cdp) Fairfax County	3	0.02
Louisville, CO (city) Boulder County	3	0.02
Makakilo City, HI (cdp) Honolulu County	3	0.02
Marshall, MO (city) Saline County	3	0.02
Mastic, NY (cdp) Suffolk County	3	0.02
Munhall, PA (borough) Allegheny County	3	0.02
Poinciana, FL (cdp) Osceola County	3	0.02
Streetsboro, OH (city) Portage County	3	0.02
Thomasville, NC (city) Davidson County	3	0.02
Wahiawa, HI (cdp) Honolulu County	3	0.02
Chowchilla, CA (city) Madera County	2	0.02
Citrus, CA (cdp) Los Angeles County	2	0.02
Fort Benning South, GA (cdp) Chattahoochee County	2	0.02
Fort Carson, CO (cdp) El Paso County	2	0.02
Fort Drum, NY (cdp) Jefferson County	2	0.02
Garden City, ID (city) Ada County	2	0.02
Grand Terrace, CA (city) San Bernardino County	2	0.02
Grass Valley, CA (city) Nevada County	2	0.02
Kaneohe Station, HI (cdp) Honolulu County	2	0.02
Lebanon, NH (city) Grafton County	2	0.02
Lexington Park, MD (cdp) Saint Mary's County	2	0.02
Parsons, KS (city) Labette County	2	0.02
Somersworth, NH (city) Strafford County	2	0.02
Spencer, MA (town) Worcester County	2	0.02
Sterling, CO (city) Logan County	2	0.02
View Park-Windsor Hills, CA (cdp) Los Angeles County	2	0.02
Wilton, NY (town) Saratoga County	2	0.02
Woodhaven, MI (city) Wayne County	2	0.02
Aurora, CO (city) Arapahoe County	34	0.01
Portland, OR (city) Multnomah County	31	0.01
Mesa, AZ (city) Maricopa County	29	0.01
Tucson, AZ (city) Pima County	28	0.01
Glendale, AZ (city) Maricopa County	19	0.01
Riverside, CA (city) Riverside County	19	0.01
Vallejo, CA (city) Solano County	17	0.01
Fort Collins, CO (city) Larimer County	15	0.01
Fremont, CA (city) Alameda County	15	0.01
Lancaster, CA (city) Los Angeles County	14	0.01
Westminster, CO (city) Adams County	14	0.01
Santa Rosa, CA (city) Sonoma County	13	0.01
Redding, CA (city) Shasta County	12	0.01
Sandy, UT (city) Salt Lake County	12	0.01
Tempe, AZ (city) Maricopa County	12	0.01
Boise City, ID (city) Ada County	11	0.01
Simi Valley, CA (city) Ventura County	11	0.01
Billings, MT (city) Yellowstone County	10	0.01
Corona, CA (city) Riverside County	10	0.01
Modesto, CA (city) Stanislaus County	10	0.01
Arvada, CO (city) Jefferson County	9	0.01
Concord, CA (city) Contra Costa County	9	0.01
Spring Valley, NV (cdp) Clark County	9	0.01
Bismarck, ND (city) Burleigh County	8	0.01
Eugene, OR (city) Lane County	8	0.01
Great Falls, MT (city) Cascade County	8	0.01
Las Cruces, NM (city) Dona Ana County	8	0.01

Notes: (cdp) census designated place; Refer to the Explanation of Data in the front of the book for more detailed information.

American Indian: Yakama

Top 150 Places Sorted by Number

(Based on all places, regardless of population)

Place	Number	%
White Swan, WA (cdp) Yakima County	1,533	50.54
Toppenish, WA (city) Yakima County	475	5.31
Yakima, WA (city) Yakima County	390	0.54
Wapato, WA (city) Yakima County	303	6.61
Satus, WA (cdp) Yakima County	227	30.43
Portland, OR (city) Multnomah County	150	0.03
Seattle, WA (city) King County	146	0.03
Tacoma, WA (city) Pierce County	143	0.07
Goldendale, WA (city) Klickitat County	112	2.98
Warm Springs, OR (cdp) Jefferson County	97	3.99
Harrah, WA (town) Yakima County	83	15.31
Mission, OR (cdp) Umatilla County	69	6.77
Union Gap, WA (city) Yakima County	52	0.93
Spokane, WA (city) Spokane County	50	0.03
Lapwai, ID (city) Nez Perce County	39	3.44
Everett, WA (city) Snohomish County	38	0.04
West Valley, WA (cdp) Yakima County	36	0.35
City of The Dalles, OR (city) Wasco County	33	0.27
Auburn, WA (city) King County	32	0.08
Ahtanum, WA (cdp) Yakima County	29	0.69
Vancouver, WA (city) Clark County	27	0.02
Lakewood, WA (city) Pierce County	24	0.04
Kennewick, WA (city) Benton County	23	0.04
Zillah, WA (city) Yakima County	21	0.96
Longview, WA (city) Cowlitz County	21	0.06
Olympia, WA (city) Thurston County	19	0.04
Los Angeles, CA (city) Los Angeles County	19	0.00
Bingen, WA (city) Klickitat County	18	2.68
Dallesport, WA (cdp) Klickitat County	18	1.52
Omak, WA (city) Okanogan County	18	0.38
Pendleton, OR (city) Umatilla County	18	0.11
Shoreline, WA (city) King County	18	0.03
Klickitat, WA (cdp) Klickitat County	17	4.08
Burien, WA (city) King County	17	0.05
Renton, WA (city) King County	17	0.03
Selah, WA (city) Yakima County	16	0.25
Sunnyside, WA (city) Yakima County	16	0.12
Anchorage, AK (municipality) Anchorage Borough	16	0.01
Carson River Valley, WA (cdp) Skamania County	15	0.71
Terrace Heights, WA (cdp) Yakima County	15	0.23
Sedro-Woolley, WA (city) Skagit County	15	0.17
Lewiston, ID (city) Nez Perce County	15	0.05
Bellingham, WA (city) Whatcom County	15	0.02
Chenoweth, OR (cdp) Wasco County	14	0.41
Aberdeen, WA (city) Grays Harbor County	14	0.09
Federal Way, WA (city) King County	14	0.02
Eugene, OR (city) Lane County	14	0.01
Salem, OR (city) Marion County	14	0.01
Sacramento, CA (city) Sacramento County	14	0.00
Wishram, WA (cdp) Klickitat County	13	4.01
Waller, WA (cdp) Pierce County	13	0.14
Spanaway, WA (cdp) Pierce County	13	0.06
Ellensburg, WA (city) Kittitas County	12	0.08
Kailua, HI (cdp) Honolulu County	12	0.03
San Jose, CA (city) Santa Clara County	12	0.00
Roslyn, WA (city) Kittitas County	11	1.08
Granger, WA (town) Yakima County	11	0.43
Madras, OR (city) Jefferson County	11	0.22
Grandview, WA (city) Yakima County	11	0.13
Pullman, WA (city) Whitman County	11	0.04
South Hill, WA (cdp) Pierce County	11	0.03
Kent, WA (city) King County	11	0.01
Kirkpatrick, OR (cdp) Umatilla County	10	5.81
Athena, OR (city) Umatilla County	10	0.82
Tulalip Bay, WA (cdp) Snohomish County	10	0.64
West Clarkston-Highland, WA (cdp) Asotin County	10	0.21
Richland, WA (city) Benton County	10	0.03
Bend, OR (city) Deschutes County	10	0.02
Gresham, OR (city) Multnomah County	10	0.01
Sunrise Manor, NV (cdp) Clark County	10	0.01
Phoenix, AZ (city) Maricopa County	10	0.00
Tucson, AZ (city) Pima County	10	0.00
Tutuilla, OR (cdp) Umatilla County	9	1.96
Fife, WA (city) Pierce County	9	0.19
Maltby, WA (cdp) Snohomish County	9	0.11
Prairie Ridge, WA (cdp) Pierce County	9	0.08
Tigard, OR (city) Washington County	9	0.02
Billings, MT (city) Yellowstone County	9	0.01
Slana, AK (cdp) Valdez-Cordova Census Area	8	6.45
Skokomish, WA (cdp) Mason County	8	1.30
Tieton, WA (town) Yakima County	8	0.69
Okanogan, WA (city) Okanogan County	8	0.32
Gleed, WA (cdp) Yakima County	8	0.27
Parkwood, WA (cdp) Kitsap County	8	0.11
Redmond, OR (city) Deschutes County	8	0.06
Elk Plain, WA (cdp) Pierce County	8	0.05
Des Moines, WA (city) King County	8	0.03
Wenatchee, WA (city) Chelan County	8	0.03
Bremerton, WA (city) Kitsap County	8	0.02
Lynnwood, WA (city) Snohomish County	8	0.02
Bellevue, WA (city) King County	8	0.01
Lawrence, KS (city) Douglas County	8	0.01
Las Vegas, NV (city) Clark County	8	0.00
Minneapolis, MN (city) Hennepin County	8	0.00
Modesto, CA (city) Stanislaus County	8	0.00
Lyle, WA (cdp) Klickitat County	7	1.32
Shaker Church, WA (cdp) Snohomish County	7	0.89
Milton-Freewater, OR (city) Umatilla County	7	0.11
Midland, WA (cdp) Pierce County	7	0.09
Oak Grove, OR (cdp) Clackamas County	7	0.05
Orchards, WA (cdp) Clark County	7	0.04
Marysville, WA (city) Snohomish County	7	0.03
McMinnville, OR (city) Yamhill County	7	0.03
Opportunity, WA (cdp) Spokane County	7	0.03
Lacey, WA (city) Thurston County	7	0.02
Clovis, CA (city) Fresno County	7	0.01
Manteca, CA (city) San Joaquin County	7	0.01
Santee, CA (city) San Diego County	7	0.01
Mesa, AZ (city) Maricopa County	7	0.00
Nisqually Indian Community, WA (cdp) Thurston County	6	1.02
Priest River, ID (city) Bonner County	6	0.34
Shelton, WA (city) Mason County	6	0.07
Enumclaw, WA (city) King County	6	0.05
Centralia, WA (city) Lewis County	6	0.04
Mountlake Terrace, WA (city) Snohomish County	6	0.03
Port Angeles, WA (city) Clallam County	6	0.03
Puyallup, WA (city) Pierce County	6	0.02
Seattle Hill-Silver Firs, WA (cdp) Snohomish County	6	0.02
Winchester, NV (cdp) Clark County	6	0.02
Aloha, OR (cdp) Washington County	6	0.01
Fort Myers, FL (city) Lee County	6	0.01
Las Cruces, NM (city) Dona Ana County	6	0.01
Rapid City, SD (city) Pennington County	6	0.01
Bakersfield, CA (city) Kern County	6	0.00
San Francisco, CA (city) San Francisco County	6	0.00
Maupin, OR (city) Wasco County	5	1.22
Ignacio, CO (town) La Plata County	5	0.75
Taholah, WA (cdp) Grays Harbor County	5	0.61
Kamiah, ID (city) Lewis County	5	0.43
White Salmon, WA (city) Klickitat County	5	0.23
Indianola, WA (cdp) Kitsap County	5	0.17
Forks, WA (city) Clallam County	5	0.16
Medical Lake, WA (city) Spokane County	5	0.13
Buckley, WA (city) Pierce County	5	0.12
Hood River, OR (city) Hood River County	5	0.09
Edgewood, WA (city) Pierce County	5	0.06
Hoquiam, WA (city) Grays Harbor County	5	0.05
Kelso, WA (city) Cowlitz County	5	0.04
Hayesville, OR (cdp) Marion County	5	0.03
Oak Harbor, WA (city) Island County	5	0.03
Tukwila, WA (city) King County	5	0.03
Juneau, AK (city and borough) Juneau Borough	5	0.02
Carmichael, CA (cdp) Sacramento County	5	0.01
Boise City, ID (city) Ada County	5	0.00
Dallas, TX (city) Dallas County	5	0.00
Oklahoma City, OK (city) Oklahoma County	5	0.00
Saint Paul, MN (city) Ramsey County	5	0.00
San Diego, CA (city) San Diego County	5	0.00
Santa Rosa, CA (city) Sonoma County	5	0.00
Sunnyvale, CA (city) Santa Clara County	5	0.00

Notes: (cdp) census designated place; Refer to the Explanation of Data in the front of the book for more detailed information.

American Indian: Yakama

Top 150 Places Sorted by Percent

(Based on all places, regardless of population)

Place	Number	%
White Swan, WA (cdp) Yakima County	1,533	50.54
Satus, WA (cdp) Yakima County	227	30.43
Harrah, WA (town) Yakima County	83	15.31
Mission, OR (cdp) Umatilla County	69	6.77
Wapato, WA (city) Yakima County	303	6.61
Slana, AK (cdp) Valdez-Cordova Census Area	8	6.45
Kirkpatrick, OR (cdp) Umatilla County	10	5.81
Toppenish, WA (city) Yakima County	475	5.31
Klickitat, WA (cdp) Klickitat County	17	4.08
Wishram, WA (cdp) Klickitat County	13	4.01
Warm Springs, OR (cdp) Jefferson County	97	3.99
Lapwai, ID (city) Nez Perce County	39	3.44
Goldendale, WA (city) Klickitat County	112	2.98
Bingen, WA (city) Klickitat County	18	2.68
Bickleton, WA (cdp) Klickitat County	3	2.65
Tutuilla, OR (cdp) Umatilla County	9	1.96
Dallesport, WA (cdp) Klickitat County	18	1.52
Deming, WA (cdp) Whatcom County	3	1.43
Lyle, WA (cdp) Klickitat County	7	1.32
Skokomish, WA (cdp) Mason County	8	1.30
Maupin, OR (city) Wasco County	5	1.22
Chehalis Village, WA (cdp) Grays Harbor County	4	1.16
Roslyn, WA (city) Kittitas County	11	1.08
Nisqually Indian Community, WA (cdp) Thurston County	6	1.02
Gopher Flats, OR (cdp) Umatilla County	4	1.00
Zillah, WA (city) Yakima County	21	0.96
Nespelem, WA (town) Okanogan County	2	0.94
Union Gap, WA (city) Yakima County	52	0.93
Shaker Church, WA (cdp) Snohomish County	7	0.89
Athena, OR (city) Umatilla County	10	0.82
Ignacio, CO (town) La Plata County	5	0.75
Carson River Valley, WA (cdp) Skamania County	15	0.71
Ahtanum, WA (cdp) Yakima County	29	0.69
Tieton, WA (town) Yakima County	8	0.69
Owendale, MI (village) Huron County	2	0.68
Tulalip Bay, WA (cdp) Snohomish County	10	0.64
Fossil, OR (city) Wheeler County	3	0.64
Taholah, WA (cdp) Grays Harbor County	5	0.61
Bedford, WY (cdp) Lincoln County	1	0.59
Kansas, OK (town) Delaware County	4	0.58
Whittier, AK (city) Valdez-Cordova Census Area	1	0.55
Yakima, WA (city) Yakima County	390	0.54
Conconully, WA (town) Okanogan County	1	0.54
Naselle, WA (cdp) Pacific County	2	0.53
Oyehut-Hogans Corner, WA (cdp) Grays Harbor County	1	0.53
Richey, MT (town) Dawson County	1	0.53
Stimson Crossing, WA (cdp) Snohomish County	4	0.52
Wasco, OR (city) Sherman County	2	0.52
Moclips, WA (cdp) Grays Harbor County	3	0.49
Humptulips, WA (cdp) Grays Harbor County	1	0.46
Ocean City, WA (cdp) Grays Harbor County	1	0.46
Tygh Valley, OR (cdp) Wasco County	1	0.45
North Omak, WA (cdp) Okanogan County	3	0.44
Granger, WA (town) Yakima County	11	0.43
Kamiah, ID (city) Lewis County	5	0.43
Arrowsic, ME (town) Sagadahoc County	2	0.42
Chenoweth, OR (cdp) Wasco County	14	0.41
East Cathlamet, WA (cdp) Wahkiakum County	2	0.41
Omak, WA (city) Okanogan County	18	0.38
Coulee Dam, WA (town) Okanogan County	4	0.38
Elmer City, WA (town) Okanogan County	1	0.37
Grand Ronde, OR (cdp) Polk County	1	0.37
West Valley, WA (cdp) Yakima County	36	0.35
Priest River, ID (city) Bonner County	6	0.34
Adams, OR (city) Umatilla County	1	0.34
Kaktovik, AK (city) North Slope Borough	1	0.34
Nespelem Community, WA (cdp) Okanogan County	1	0.34
Grand Coulee, WA (city) Grant County	3	0.33
Okanogan, WA (city) Okanogan County	8	0.32
Cohassett Beach, WA (cdp) Grays Harbor County	2	0.32
Lakeside, OR (city) Coos County	4	0.29
Weston, OR (city) Umatilla County	2	0.28
City of The Dalles, OR (city) Wasco County	33	0.27
Gleed, WA (cdp) Yakima County	8	0.27
Bell Hill, WA (cdp) Clallam County	2	0.27
Alberton, MT (town) Mineral County	1	0.27
Murphy, NC (town) Cherokee County	4	0.26
Pilot Rock, OR (city) Umatilla County	4	0.26
Selah, WA (city) Yakima County	16	0.25
Snoqualmie, WA (city) King County	4	0.25
Fort Belknap Agency, MT (cdp) Blaine County	3	0.24
Pine Hollow, OR (cdp) Wasco County	1	0.24
Terrace Heights, WA (cdp) Yakima County	15	0.23
White Salmon, WA (city) Klickitat County	5	0.23
Alta Vista, KS (city) Wabaunsee County	1	0.23
Charlo, MT (cdp) Lake County	1	0.23
Madras, OR (city) Jefferson County	11	0.22
Locust Grove, OK (town) Mayes County	3	0.22
Metlakatla, AK (cdp) Prince of Wales-Outer Ketchikan Census Area	3	0.22
Brookfield, MI (township) Huron County	2	0.22
Summitview, WA (cdp) Yakima County	2	0.22
South Cle Elum, WA (town) Kittitas County	1	0.22
West Clarkston-Highland, WA (cdp) Asotin County	10	0.21
Rough Rock, AZ (cdp) Apache County	1	0.21
Stanfield, OR (city) Umatilla County	4	0.20
Carlton, OR (city) Yamhill County	3	0.20
Fife, WA (city) Pierce County	9	0.19
Cascade Locks, OR (city) Hood River County	2	0.18
Houck, AZ (cdp) Apache County	2	0.18
Riverdale Park, CA (cdp) Stanislaus County	2	0.18
Manzanita, OR (city) Tillamook County	1	0.18
Tordenskjold, MN (township) Otter Tail County	1	0.18
Sedro-Woolley, WA (city) Skagit County	15	0.17
Indianola, WA (cdp) Kitsap County	5	0.17
Cascade Valley, WA (cdp) Grant County	3	0.17
South Bend, WA (city) Pacific County	3	0.17
Forks, WA (city) Clallam County	5	0.16
Rio Grande, NJ (cdp) Cape May County	4	0.16
Waterville, MN (city) Le Sueur County	3	0.16
Rockaway Beach, OR (city) Tillamook County	2	0.16
Manderson-White Horse Creek, SD (cdp) Shannon County	1	0.16
Minnetonka Beach, MN (city) Hennepin County	1	0.16
Tioga, PA (borough) Tioga County	1	0.16
Colley, PA (township) Sullivan County	1	0.15
Hauser, ID (city) Kootenai County	1	0.15
Waller, WA (cdp) Pierce County	13	0.14
Connell, WA (city) Franklin County	4	0.14
North Browning, MT (cdp) Glacier County	3	0.14
Big Sandy, MT (town) Chouteau County	1	0.14
Busby, MT (cdp) Big Horn County	1	0.14
Chiloquin, OR (city) Klamath County	1	0.14
Kake, AK (city) Wrangell-Petersburg Census Area	1	0.14
Scio, OR (city) Linn County	1	0.14
Grandview, WA (city) Yakima County	11	0.13
Medical Lake, WA (city) Spokane County	5	0.13
Sacaton, AZ (cdp) Pinal County	2	0.13
McLaughlin, SD (city) Corson County	1	0.13
Neah Bay, WA (cdp) Clallam County	1	0.13
Priest Point, WA (cdp) Snohomish County	1	0.13
Sunnyside, WA (city) Yakima County	16	0.12
Buckley, WA (city) Pierce County	5	0.12
Woodstock, VT (town) Windsor County	4	0.12
Algona, WA (city) King County	3	0.12
Homedale, ID (city) Owyhee County	3	0.12
Fall City, WA (cdp) King County	2	0.12
South Browning, MT (cdp) Glacier County	2	0.12
Moxee, WA (city) Yakima County	1	0.12
Ojo Amarillo, NM (cdp) San Juan County	1	0.12
Wallowa, OR (city) Wallowa County	1	0.12
Pendleton, OR (city) Umatilla County	18	0.11
Maltby, WA (cdp) Snohomish County	9	0.11
Parkwood, WA (cdp) Kitsap County	8	0.11
Milton-Freewater, OR (city) Umatilla County	7	0.11
Barview, OR (cdp) Coos County	2	0.11
Cle Elum, WA (city) Kittitas County	2	0.11
Davenport, OK (town) Lincoln County	1	0.11
Electric City, WA (town) Grant County	1	0.11
Garibaldi, OR (city) Tillamook County	1	0.11
Haileyville, OK (city) Pittsburg County	1	0.11
Haliimaile, HI (cdp) Maui County	1	0.11

Notes: (cdp) census designated place; Refer to the Explanation of Data in the front of the book for more detailed information.

American Indian: Yakama

Top 150 Places Sorted by Percent

(Based on places with populations of 10,000 or more)

Place	Number	%
Yakima, WA (city) Yakima County	390	0.54
West Valley, WA (cdp) Yakima County	36	0.35
City of The Dalles, OR (city) Wasco County	33	0.27
Sunnyside, WA (city) Yakima County	16	0.12
Pendleton, OR (city) Umatilla County	18	0.11
Aberdeen, WA (city) Grays Harbor County	14	0.09
Auburn, WA (city) King County	32	0.08
Ellensburg, WA (city) Kittitas County	12	0.08
Prairie Ridge, WA (cdp) Pierce County	9	0.08
Tacoma, WA (city) Pierce County	143	0.07
Longview, WA (city) Cowlitz County	21	0.06
Spanaway, WA (cdp) Pierce County	13	0.06
Redmond, OR (city) Deschutes County	8	0.06
Burien, WA (city) King County	17	0.05
Lewiston, ID (city) Nez Perce County	15	0.05
Elk Plain, WA (cdp) Pierce County	8	0.05
Oak Grove, OR (cdp) Clackamas County	7	0.05
Enumclaw, WA (city) King County	6	0.05
Everett, WA (city) Snohomish County	38	0.04
Lakewood, WA (city) Pierce County	24	0.04
Kennewick, WA (city) Benton County	23	0.04
Olympia, WA (city) Thurston County	19	0.04
Pullman, WA (city) Whitman County	11	0.04
Orchards, WA (cdp) Clark County	7	0.04
Centralia, WA (city) Lewis County	6	0.04
Kelso, WA (city) Cowlitz County	5	0.04
Waianae, HI (cdp) Honolulu County	4	0.04
Portland, OR (city) Multnomah County	150	0.03
Seattle, WA (city) King County	146	0.03
Spokane, WA (city) Spokane County	50	0.03
Shoreline, WA (city) King County	18	0.03
Renton, WA (city) King County	17	0.03
Kailua, HI (cdp) Honolulu County	12	0.03
South Hill, WA (cdp) Pierce County	11	0.03
Richland, WA (city) Benton County	10	0.03
Des Moines, WA (city) King County	8	0.03
Wenatchee, WA (city) Chelan County	8	0.03
Marysville, WA (city) Snohomish County	7	0.03
McMinnville, OR (city) Yamhill County	7	0.03
Opportunity, WA (cdp) Spokane County	7	0.03
Mountlake Terrace, WA (city) Snohomish County	6	0.03
Port Angeles, WA (city) Clallam County	6	0.03
Hayesville, OR (cdp) Marion County	5	0.03
Oak Harbor, WA (city) Island County	5	0.03
Tukwila, WA (city) King County	5	0.03
Anacortes, WA (city) Skagit County	4	0.03
Coldwater, MI (city) Branch County	4	0.03
East Wenatchee Bench, WA (cdp) Douglas County	4	0.03
Four Corners, OR (cdp) Marion County	4	0.03
Moses Lake, WA (city) Grant County	4	0.03
Issaquah, WA (city) King County	3	0.03
Kaneohe Station, HI (cdp) Honolulu County	3	0.03
Saint Helens, OR (city) Columbia County	3	0.03
Vancouver, WA (city) Clark County	27	0.02
Bellingham, WA (city) Whatcom County	15	0.02
Federal Way, WA (city) King County	14	0.02
Bend, OR (city) Deschutes County	10	0.02
Tigard, OR (city) Washington County	9	0.02
Bremerton, WA (city) Kitsap County	8	0.02
Lynnwood, WA (city) Snohomish County	8	0.02
Lacey, WA (city) Thurston County	7	0.02
Puyallup, WA (city) Pierce County	6	0.02
Seattle Hill-Silver Firs, WA (cdp) Snohomish County	6	0.02
Winchester, NV (cdp) Clark County	6	0.02
Juneau, AK (city and borough) Juneau Borough	5	0.02
Belmont, CA (city) San Mateo County	4	0.02
Havelock, NC (city) Craven County	4	0.02
Kenmore, WA (city) King County	4	0.02
Middle, NJ (township) Cape May County	4	0.02
Mount Vernon, WA (city) Skagit County	4	0.02
Oregon City, OR (city) Clackamas County	4	0.02
Parkland, WA (cdp) Pierce County	4	0.02
Salmon Creek, WA (cdp) Clark County	4	0.02
Shakopee, MN (city) Scott County	4	0.02
Altamont, OR (cdp) Klamath County	3	0.02
Claremore, OK (city) Rogers County	3	0.02
Durango, CO (city) La Plata County	3	0.02
Highview, KY (cdp) Jefferson County	3	0.02
Linda, CA (cdp) Yuba County	3	0.02
Live Oak, CA (cdp) Santa Cruz County	3	0.02
Martha Lake, WA (cdp) Snohomish County	3	0.02
Post Falls, ID (city) Kootenai County	3	0.02
Sun Valley, NV (cdp) Washoe County	3	0.02
Tumwater, WA (city) Thurston County	3	0.02
Canby, OR (city) Clackamas County	2	0.02
Cedar Mill, OR (cdp) Washington County	2	0.02
Dallas, OR (city) Polk County	2	0.02
East Renton Highlands, WA (cdp) King County	2	0.02
Fort Polk South, LA (cdp) Vernon Parish	2	0.02
Kingsgate, WA (cdp) King County	2	0.02
Lea Hill, WA (cdp) King County	2	0.02
Red Bluff, CA (city) Tehama County	2	0.02
Anchorage, AK (municipality) Anchorage Borough	16	0.01
Eugene, OR (city) Lane County	14	0.01
Salem, OR (city) Marion County	14	0.01
Kent, WA (city) King County	11	0.01
Gresham, OR (city) Multnomah County	10	0.01
Sunrise Manor, NV (cdp) Clark County	10	0.01
Billings, MT (city) Yellowstone County	9	0.01
Bellevue, WA (city) King County	8	0.01
Lawrence, KS (city) Douglas County	8	0.01
Clovis, CA (city) Fresno County	7	0.01
Manteca, CA (city) San Joaquin County	7	0.01
Santee, CA (city) San Diego County	7	0.01
Aloha, OR (cdp) Washington County	6	0.01
Fort Myers, FL (city) Lee County	6	0.01
Las Cruces, NM (city) Dona Ana County	6	0.01
Rapid City, SD (city) Pennington County	6	0.01
Carmichael, CA (cdp) Sacramento County	5	0.01
Albany, OR (city) Linn County	4	0.01
Appleton, WI (city) Outagamie County	4	0.01
Elk Grove, CA (cdp) Sacramento County	4	0.01
Flower Mound, TX (town) Denton County	4	0.01
Keizer, OR (city) Marion County	4	0.01
Lauderdale Lakes, FL (city) Broward County	4	0.01
Madera, CA (city) Madera County	4	0.01
Martinez, CA (city) Contra Costa County	4	0.01
Ogden, UT (city) Weber County	4	0.01
Oildale, CA (cdp) Kern County	4	0.01
Redmond, WA (city) King County	4	0.01
Rio Rancho, NM (city) Sandoval County	4	0.01
Springfield, OR (city) Lane County	4	0.01
Atascadero, CA (city) San Luis Obispo County	3	0.01
Bothell, WA (city) King County	3	0.01
Corvallis, OR (city) Benton County	3	0.01
Folsom, CA (city) Sacramento County	3	0.01
Hollister, CA (city) San Benito County	3	0.01
Inglewood-Finn Hill, WA (cdp) King County	3	0.01
Milwaukie, OR (city) Clackamas County	3	0.01
North Creek, WA (cdp) Snohomish County	3	0.01
Paramount, CA (city) Los Angeles County	3	0.01
Picnic Point-North Lynnwood, WA (cdp) Snohomish County	3	0.01
Rancho Cordova, CA (cdp) Sacramento County	3	0.01
Rocklin, CA (city) Placer County	3	0.01
Rubidoux, CA (cdp) Riverside County	3	0.01
Saint George, UT (city) Washington County	3	0.01
Sanford, FL (city) Seminole County	3	0.01
SeaTac, WA (city) King County	3	0.01
Tooele, UT (city) Tooele County	3	0.01
West Whittier-Los Nietos, CA (cdp) Los Angeles County	3	0.01
White Center, WA (cdp) King County	3	0.01
Yuba City, CA (city) Sutter County	3	0.01
Albany, CA (city) Alameda County	2	0.01
Arroyo Grande, CA (city) San Luis Obispo County	2	0.01
Bullhead City, AZ (city) Mohave County	2	0.01
Camano, WA (cdp) Island County	2	0.01
East Hill-Meridian, WA (cdp) King County	2	0.01
Eureka, CA (city) Humboldt County	2	0.01
Ewa Beach, HI (cdp) Honolulu County	2	0.01
Fairbanks, AK (city) Fairbanks North Star Borough	2	0.01

Notes: (cdp) census designated place; Refer to the Explanation of Data in the front of the book for more detailed information.

American Indian: Yaqui

Top 150 Places Sorted by Number

(Based on all places, regardless of population)

Place	Number	%
Tucson, AZ (city) Pima County	2,634	0.54
Guadalupe, AZ (town) Maricopa County	2,113	40.42
Phoenix, AZ (city) Maricopa County	1,112	0.08
Los Angeles, CA (city) Los Angeles County	480	0.01
Tempe, AZ (city) Maricopa County	354	0.22
Mesa, AZ (city) Maricopa County	322	0.08
Drexel Heights, AZ (cdp) Pima County	272	1.14
Fresno, CA (city) Fresno County	260	0.06
San Jose, CA (city) Santa Clara County	232	0.03
San Diego, CA (city) San Diego County	232	0.02
South Tucson, AZ (city) Pima County	218	3.97
Chandler, AZ (city) Maricopa County	206	0.12
Scottsdale, AZ (city) Maricopa County	183	0.09
Sacramento, CA (city) Sacramento County	173	0.04
Marana, AZ (town) Pima County	107	0.79
Coolidge, AZ (city) Pinal County	106	1.36
Yuma, AZ (city) Yuma County	94	0.12
Bakersfield, CA (city) Kern County	93	0.04
Riverside, CA (city) Riverside County	86	0.03
Casa Grande, AZ (city) Pinal County	82	0.33
Fontana, CA (city) San Bernardino County	77	0.06
Long Beach, CA (city) Los Angeles County	76	0.02
Oxnard, CA (city) Ventura County	75	0.04
Glendale, AZ (city) Maricopa County	75	0.03
San Francisco, CA (city) San Francisco County	74	0.01
Avondale, AZ (city) Maricopa County	71	0.20
San Bernardino, CA (city) San Bernardino County	71	0.04
Eloy, AZ (city) Pinal County	66	0.64
Chula Vista, CA (city) San Diego County	66	0.04
Ontario, CA (city) San Bernardino County	66	0.04
Stockton, CA (city) San Joaquin County	65	0.03
San Buenaventura, CA (city) Ventura County	63	0.06
Oakland, CA (city) Alameda County	61	0.02
San Antonio, TX (city) Bexar County	61	0.01
Santa Barbara, CA (city) Santa Barbara County	56	0.06
Anaheim, CA (city) Orange County	55	0.02
Rialto, CA (city) San Bernardino County	53	0.06
Salinas, CA (city) Monterey County	51	0.03
Rancho Cucamonga, CA (city) San Bernardino County	49	0.04
Gilbert, AZ (town) Maricopa County	48	0.04
El Paso, TX (city) El Paso County	48	0.01
Denver, CO (city) Denver County	45	0.01
El Cajon, CA (city) San Diego County	42	0.04
Modesto, CA (city) Stanislaus County	42	0.02
Three Points, AZ (cdp) Pima County	41	0.78
Escondido, CA (city) San Diego County	41	0.03
Montebello, CA (city) Los Angeles County	40	0.06
Albuquerque, NM (city) Bernalillo County	40	0.01
Portland, OR (city) Multnomah County	40	0.01
Drexel-Alvernon, AZ (cdp) Pima County	38	0.91
Simi Valley, CA (city) Ventura County	37	0.03
Pomona, CA (city) Los Angeles County	37	0.02
Victorville, CA (city) San Bernardino County	36	0.06
Huntington Beach, CA (city) Orange County	36	0.02
Las Vegas, NV (city) Clark County	35	0.01
Santa Ana, CA (city) Orange County	35	0.01
Tucson Estates, AZ (cdp) Pima County	34	0.35
South Whittier, CA (cdp) Los Angeles County	34	0.06
Corona, CA (city) Riverside County	34	0.03
El Monte, CA (city) Los Angeles County	34	0.03
Hayward, CA (city) Alameda County	34	0.02
Summit, AZ (cdp) Pima County	32	0.86
Whittier, CA (city) Los Angeles County	32	0.04
East Los Angeles, CA (cdp) Los Angeles County	32	0.03
Visalia, CA (city) Tulare County	32	0.03
Houston, TX (city) Harris County	31	0.00
Cathedral City, CA (city) Riverside County	30	0.07
Tulare, CA (city) Tulare County	30	0.07
Redlands, CA (city) San Bernardino County	30	0.05
Santa Maria, CA (city) Santa Barbara County	30	0.04
Santa Clarita, CA (city) Los Angeles County	30	0.02
Casas Adobes, AZ (cdp) Pima County	29	0.05
New York, NY (city) New York City	29	0.00
Lake Elsinore, CA (city) Riverside County	28	0.10
Yucaipa, CA (city) San Bernardino County	28	0.07
Merced, CA (city) Merced County	28	0.04
Garden Grove, CA (city) Orange County	28	0.02
Lancaster, CA (city) Los Angeles County	28	0.02
Paradise, NV (cdp) Clark County	28	0.02
Morgan Hill, CA (city) Santa Clara County	27	0.08
Chino, CA (city) San Bernardino County	27	0.04
Pico Rivera, CA (city) Los Angeles County	27	0.04
Fullerton, CA (city) Orange County	27	0.02
Orange, CA (city) Orange County	27	0.02
Valencia West, AZ (cdp) Pima County	26	1.09
National City, CA (city) San Diego County	26	0.05
Austin, TX (city) Travis County	26	0.00
Flowing Wells, AZ (cdp) Pima County	25	0.17
Alhambra, CA (city) Los Angeles County	25	0.03
Sunnyvale, CA (city) Santa Clara County	25	0.02
West Covina, CA (city) Los Angeles County	25	0.02
La Puente, CA (city) Los Angeles County	24	0.06
Madera, CA (city) Madera County	24	0.06
Colton, CA (city) San Bernardino County	24	0.05
Catalina Foothills, AZ (cdp) Pima County	24	0.04
Antioch, CA (city) Contra Costa County	24	0.03
Citrus Heights, CA (city) Sacramento County	24	0.03
Moreno Valley, CA (city) Riverside County	24	0.02
Colorado Springs, CO (city) El Paso County	24	0.01
Florence, AZ (town) Pinal County	23	0.13
Baldwin Park, CA (city) Los Angeles County	23	0.03
Downey, CA (city) Los Angeles County	23	0.02
Palmdale, CA (city) Los Angeles County	23	0.02
Pasadena, CA (city) Los Angeles County	23	0.02
Santa Rosa, CA (city) Sonoma County	23	0.02
Avra Valley, AZ (cdp) Pima County	22	0.44
Picture Rocks, AZ (cdp) Pima County	22	0.27
Brawley, CA (city) Imperial County	22	0.10
Upland, CA (city) San Bernardino County	22	0.03
Fremont, CA (city) Alameda County	22	0.01
Lubbock, TX (city) Lubbock County	22	0.01
Sunrise Manor, NV (cdp) Clark County	22	0.01
Seattle, WA (city) King County	22	0.00
San Fernando, CA (city) Los Angeles County	21	0.09
Redondo Beach, CA (city) Los Angeles County	21	0.03
Eugene, OR (city) Lane County	21	0.02
Norwalk, CA (city) Los Angeles County	21	0.02
Clovis, CA (city) Fresno County	20	0.03
Berkeley, CA (city) Alameda County	20	0.02
Santa Clara, CA (city) Santa Clara County	20	0.02
Indio, CA (city) Riverside County	19	0.04
Santee, CA (city) San Diego County	19	0.04
Arden-Arcade, CA (cdp) Sacramento County	19	0.02
Aurora, CO (city) Arapahoe County	19	0.01
Wichita, KS (city) Sedgwick County	19	0.01
Parkway-South Sacramento, CA (cdp) Sacramento County	18	0.05
Woodland, CA (city) Yolo County	18	0.04
Hesperia, CA (city) San Bernardino County	18	0.03
Torrance, CA (city) Los Angeles County	18	0.01
Ceres, CA (city) Stanislaus County	17	0.05
Highland, CA (city) San Bernardino County	17	0.04
Chino Hills, CA (city) San Bernardino County	17	0.03
La Habra, CA (city) Orange County	17	0.03
Costa Mesa, CA (city) Orange County	17	0.02
Lakewood, CA (city) Los Angeles County	17	0.02
Nogales, AZ (city) Santa Cruz County	16	0.08
Calexico, CA (city) Imperial County	16	0.06
Eureka, CA (city) Humboldt County	16	0.06
Apache Junction, AZ (city) Pinal County	16	0.05
Concord, CA (city) Contra Costa County	16	0.01
Glendale, CA (city) Los Angeles County	16	0.01
Oceanside, CA (city) San Diego County	16	0.01
Commerce, CA (city) Los Angeles County	15	0.12
La Quinta, CA (city) Riverside County	15	0.06
Hollister, CA (city) San Benito County	15	0.04
Lompoc, CA (city) Santa Barbara County	15	0.04
Porterville, CA (city) Tulare County	15	0.04
Covina, CA (city) Los Angeles County	15	0.03
Lynwood, CA (city) Los Angeles County	15	0.02
Union City, CA (city) Alameda County	15	0.02

Notes: (cdp) census designated place; Refer to the Explanation of Data in the front of the book for more detailed information.

American Indian: Yaqui

Top 150 Places Sorted by Percent

(Based on all places, regardless of population)

Place	Number	%
Guadalupe, AZ (town) Maricopa County	2,113	40.42
Oxford, ID (city) Franklin County	3	5.66
South Tucson, AZ (city) Pima County	218	3.97
Elgin, AZ (cdp) Santa Cruz County	9	2.91
Montgomery Creek, CA (cdp) Shasta County	2	2.08
Tennant, CA (cdp) Siskiyou County	1	1.59
Cromberg, CA (cdp) Plumas County	4	1.38
Coolidge, AZ (city) Pinal County	106	1.36
Drexel Heights, AZ (cdp) Pima County	272	1.14
Valencia West, AZ (cdp) Pima County	26	1.09
Millstone, PA (township) Elk County	1	1.05
Elk Mountain, WY (town) Carbon County	2	1.04
Littletown, AZ (cdp) Pima County	10	0.99
Winterhaven, CA (cdp) Imperial County	5	0.95
Drexel-Alvernon, AZ (cdp) Pima County	38	0.91
Maricopa, AZ (cdp) Pinal County	9	0.87
Summit, AZ (cdp) Pima County	32	0.86
Marana, AZ (town) Pima County	107	0.79
Three Points, AZ (cdp) Pima County	41	0.78
Covelo, CA (cdp) Mendocino County	9	0.77
Arlee, MT (cdp) Lake County	4	0.66
New Lothrop, MI (village) Shiawassee County	4	0.66
Eloy, AZ (city) Pinal County	66	0.64
Lewisville, ID (city) Jefferson County	3	0.64
East Sahuarita, AZ (cdp) Pima County	9	0.63
Naco, AZ (cdp) Cochise County	5	0.60
Pickstown, SD (town) Charles Mix County	1	0.60
Tucson, AZ (city) Pima County	2,634	0.54
Morenci, AZ (cdp) Greenlee County	10	0.53
Escalante, UT (city) Garfield County	4	0.49
Baudette, MN (city) Lake of the Woods County	5	0.45
Avra Valley, AZ (cdp) Pima County	22	0.44
Arboles, CO (cdp) Archuleta County	1	0.43
Blackwater, AZ (cdp) Pinal County	2	0.40
Litchfield, MN (township) Meeker County	3	0.37
Woodville, CA (cdp) Tulare County	6	0.36
Norwood, MO (city) Wright County	2	0.36
Tucson Estates, AZ (cdp) Pima County	34	0.35
San Miguel, CA (cdp) San Luis Obispo County	5	0.35
Casa Grande, AZ (city) Pinal County	82	0.33
Moenkopi, AZ (cdp) Coconino County	3	0.33
Ajo, AZ (cdp) Pima County	12	0.32
Tanana, AK (city) Yukon-Koyukuk Census Area	1	0.32
Jerome, AZ (town) Yavapai County	1	0.30
Top-of-the-World, AZ (cdp) Gila County	1	0.30
Sells, AZ (cdp) Pima County	8	0.29
Arapahoe, WY (cdp) Fremont County	5	0.28
Mammoth, AZ (town) Pinal County	5	0.28
Ronan, MT (city) Lake County	5	0.28
Wayne, OK (town) McClain County	2	0.28
Arizona Village, AZ (cdp) Mohave County	1	0.28
Picture Rocks, AZ (cdp) Pima County	22	0.27
Sunol-Midtown, CA (cdp) Santa Clara County	2	0.27
Mission Hills, CA (cdp) Santa Barbara County	8	0.25
Saint Ignatius, MT (town) Lake County	2	0.25
Teec Nos Pos, AZ (cdp) Apache County	2	0.25
Home Garden, CA (cdp) Kings County	4	0.24
Sonoita, AZ (cdp) Santa Cruz County	2	0.24
Mesilla, NM (town) Dona Ana County	5	0.23
Patagonia, AZ (town) Santa Cruz County	2	0.23
Tempe, AZ (city) Maricopa County	354	0.22
Tolleson, AZ (city) Maricopa County	11	0.22
Sahuarita, AZ (town) Pima County	7	0.22
Dixon Lane-Meadow Creek, CA (cdp) Inyo County	6	0.22
Bodfish, CA (cdp) Kern County	4	0.22
Graton, CA (cdp) Sonoma County	4	0.22
Hayden, AZ (town) Gila County	2	0.22
Tortolita, AZ (cdp) Pima County	8	0.21
Spaulding, MI (township) Saginaw County	5	0.21
Chester, WI (town) Dodge County	2	0.21
Martensdale, IA (city) Warren County	1	0.21
Avondale, AZ (city) Maricopa County	71	0.20
Holcomb, KS (city) Finney County	4	0.20
Addyston, OH (village) Hamilton County	2	0.20
Gerlach-Empire, NV (cdp) Washoe County	1	0.20
Winchester, CA (cdp) Riverside County	4	0.19
Sacaton, AZ (cdp) Pinal County	3	0.19
Westville, OK (town) Adair County	3	0.19
Kiowa, KS (city) Barber County	2	0.19
Nanawale Estates, HI (cdp) Hawaii County	2	0.19
Sugar Bush, MN (township) Becker County	1	0.19
Paulden, AZ (cdp) Yavapai County	6	0.18
Hazelton, MI (township) Shiawassee County	4	0.18
Swift Trail Junction, AZ (cdp) Graham County	4	0.18
Akron, CO (town) Washington County	3	0.18
Grandfield, OK (city) Tillman County	2	0.18
Parks, AZ (cdp) Coconino County	2	0.18
Scottsville, VA (town) Albemarle County	1	0.18
Tumacacori-Carmen, AZ (cdp) Santa Cruz County	1	0.18
Flowing Wells, AZ (cdp) Pima County	25	0.17
Catalina, AZ (cdp) Pima County	12	0.17
Chamberlain, SD (city) Brule County	4	0.17
Tecumseh, NE (city) Johnson County	3	0.17
Nisqually Indian Community, WA (cdp) Thurston County	1	0.17
Peach Springs, AZ (cdp) Mohave County	1	0.17
Arizona City, AZ (cdp) Pinal County	7	0.16
Celina, TX (town) Collin County	3	0.16
Selma, MI (township) Wexford County	3	0.16
North Edwards, CA (cdp) Kern County	2	0.16
Rushville, NY (village) Yates County	1	0.16
Golden Hills, CA (cdp) Kern County	11	0.15
Thatcher, AZ (town) Graham County	6	0.15
Benton City, WA (city) Benton County	4	0.15
Dansville, NY (town) Steuben County	3	0.15
Gila Bend, AZ (town) Maricopa County	3	0.15
Ak-Chin Village, AZ (cdp) Pinal County	1	0.15
Bingen, WA (city) Klickitat County	1	0.15
Fort Jones, CA (city) Siskiyou County	1	0.15
Santan, AZ (cdp) Pinal County	1	0.15
Stanfield, AZ (cdp) Pinal County	1	0.15
Guadalupe, CA (city) Santa Barbara County	8	0.14
Harbison Canyon, CA (cdp) San Diego County	5	0.14
Oracle, AZ (cdp) Pinal County	5	0.14
Littlerock, CA (cdp) Los Angeles County	2	0.14
Kake, AK (city) Wrangell-Petersburg Census Area	1	0.14
Menan, ID (city) Jefferson County	1	0.14
Florence, AZ (town) Pinal County	23	0.13
Lincoln City, OR (city) Lincoln County	10	0.13
Bystrom, CA (cdp) Stanislaus County	6	0.13
Parker, AZ (town) La Paz County	4	0.13
Cabazon, CA (cdp) Riverside County	3	0.13
Olton, TX (city) Lamb County	3	0.13
Bootjack, CA (cdp) Mariposa County	2	0.13
Pirtleville, AZ (cdp) Cochise County	2	0.13
Wilson, OK (city) Carter County	2	0.13
Alpaugh, CA (cdp) Tulare County	1	0.13
Etna, CA (city) Siskiyou County	1	0.13
Glasgow, WV (town) Kanawha County	1	0.13
Chandler, AZ (city) Maricopa County	206	0.12
Yuma, AZ (city) Yuma County	94	0.12
Commerce, CA (city) Los Angeles County	15	0.12
Coalinga, CA (city) Fresno County	14	0.12
California City, CA (city) Kern County	10	0.12
Mentone, CA (cdp) San Bernardino County	9	0.12
Buckeye, AZ (town) Maricopa County	8	0.12
Gardnerville, NV (cdp) Douglas County	4	0.12
Hawthorne, NV (cdp) Mineral County	4	0.12
Mountain View, CA (cdp) Contra Costa County	3	0.12
Three Rivers, OR (cdp) Deschutes County	3	0.12
Vail, AZ (cdp) Pima County	3	0.12
Sandstone, MN (township) Pine County	2	0.12
Farwell, MI (village) Clare County	1	0.12
Queen Valley, AZ (cdp) Pinal County	1	0.12
East Foothills, CA (cdp) Santa Clara County	9	0.11
El Mirage, AZ (city) Maricopa County	8	0.11
Keyes, CA (cdp) Stanislaus County	5	0.11
Big Lake, AK (cdp) Matanuska-Susitna Borough	3	0.11
Bowdoin, ME (town) Sagadahoc County	3	0.11
Curwensville, PA (borough) Clearfield County	3	0.11
Haughton, LA (town) Bossier Parish	3	0.11

Notes: (cdp) census designated place; Refer to the Explanation of Data in the front of the book for more detailed information.

American Indian: Yaqui

Top 150 Places Sorted by Percent

(Based on places with populations of 10,000 or more)

Place	Number	%
Drexel Heights, AZ (cdp) Pima County	272	1.14
Marana, AZ (town) Pima County	107	0.79
Eloy, AZ (city) Pinal County	66	0.64
Tucson, AZ (city) Pima County	2,634	0.54
Casa Grande, AZ (city) Pinal County	82	0.33
Tempe, AZ (city) Maricopa County	354	0.22
Avondale, AZ (city) Maricopa County	71	0.20
Flowing Wells, AZ (cdp) Pima County	25	0.17
Florence, AZ (town) Pinal County	23	0.13
Chandler, AZ (city) Maricopa County	206	0.12
Yuma, AZ (city) Yuma County	94	0.12
Commerce, CA (city) Los Angeles County	15	0.12
Coalinga, CA (city) Fresno County	14	0.12
Lake Elsinore, CA (city) Riverside County	28	0.10
Brawley, CA (city) Imperial County	22	0.10
Fillmore, CA (city) Ventura County	13	0.10
Scottsdale, AZ (city) Maricopa County	183	0.09
San Fernando, CA (city) Los Angeles County	21	0.09
Douglas, AZ (city) Cochise County	13	0.09
Blythe, CA (city) Riverside County	11	0.09
Phoenix, AZ (city) Maricopa County	1,112	0.08
Mesa, AZ (city) Maricopa County	322	0.08
Morgan Hill, CA (city) Santa Clara County	27	0.08
Nogales, AZ (city) Santa Cruz County	16	0.08
East Hemet, CA (cdp) Riverside County	12	0.08
Clearlake, CA (city) Lake County	11	0.08
Susanville, CA (city) Lassen County	11	0.08
Cathedral City, CA (city) Riverside County	30	0.07
Tulare, CA (city) Tulare County	30	0.07
Yucaipa, CA (city) San Bernardino County	28	0.07
Yucca Valley, CA (town) San Bernardino County	11	0.07
San Luis, AZ (city) Yuma County	10	0.07
Alum Rock, CA (cdp) Santa Clara County	9	0.07
Chowchilla, CA (city) Madera County	8	0.07
Magalia, CA (cdp) Butte County	7	0.07
Fresno, CA (city) Fresno County	260	0.06
Fontana, CA (city) San Bernardino County	77	0.06
San Buenaventura, CA (city) Ventura County	63	0.06
Santa Barbara, CA (city) Santa Barbara County	56	0.06
Rialto, CA (city) San Bernardino County	53	0.06
Montebello, CA (city) Los Angeles County	40	0.06
Victorville, CA (city) San Bernardino County	36	0.06
South Whittier, CA (cdp) Los Angeles County	34	0.06
La Puente, CA (city) Los Angeles County	24	0.06
Madera, CA (city) Madera County	24	0.06
Calexico, CA (city) Imperial County	16	0.06
Eureka, CA (city) Humboldt County	16	0.06
La Quinta, CA (city) Riverside County	15	0.06
West Puente Valley, CA (cdp) Los Angeles County	13	0.06
Lemoore, CA (city) Kings County	12	0.06
Winter Gardens, CA (cdp) San Diego County	11	0.06
Adelanto, CA (city) San Bernardino County	10	0.06
Moses Lake, WA (city) Grant County	9	0.06
Sierra Vista Southeast, AZ (cdp) Cochise County	9	0.06
Twentynine Palms, CA (city) San Bernardino County	9	0.06
Grover Beach, CA (city) San Luis Obispo County	8	0.06
Mohave Valley, AZ (cdp) Mohave County	8	0.06
Citrus, CA (cdp) Los Angeles County	6	0.06
Los Lunas, NM (village) Valencia County	6	0.06
Redlands, CA (city) San Bernardino County	30	0.05
Casas Adobes, AZ (cdp) Pima County	29	0.05
National City, CA (city) San Diego County	26	0.05
Colton, CA (city) San Bernardino County	24	0.05
Parkway-South Sacramento, CA (cdp) Sacramento County	18	0.05
Ceres, CA (city) Stanislaus County	17	0.05
Apache Junction, AZ (city) Pinal County	16	0.05
Lemon Grove, CA (city) San Diego County	13	0.05
Port Hueneme, CA (city) Ventura County	12	0.05
San Jacinto, CA (city) Riverside County	12	0.05
Banning, CA (city) Riverside County	11	0.05
Casselberry, FL (city) Seminole County	11	0.05
Rancho San Diego, CA (cdp) San Diego County	10	0.05
Selma, CA (city) Fresno County	10	0.05
Vincent, CA (cdp) Los Angeles County	8	0.05
Avocado Heights, CA (cdp) Los Angeles County	7	0.05
Fountain, CO (city) El Paso County	7	0.05
Payson, AZ (town) Gila County	7	0.05
Marysville, CA (city) Yuba County	6	0.05
Nipomo, CA (cdp) San Luis Obispo County	6	0.05
Crestline, CA (cdp) San Bernardino County	5	0.05
Sacramento, CA (city) Sacramento County	173	0.04
Bakersfield, CA (city) Kern County	93	0.04
Oxnard, CA (city) Ventura County	75	0.04
San Bernardino, CA (city) San Bernardino County	71	0.04
Chula Vista, CA (city) San Diego County	66	0.04
Ontario, CA (city) San Bernardino County	66	0.04
Rancho Cucamonga, CA (city) San Bernardino County	49	0.04
Gilbert, AZ (town) Maricopa County	48	0.04
El Cajon, CA (city) San Diego County	42	0.04
Whittier, CA (city) Los Angeles County	32	0.04
Santa Maria, CA (city) Santa Barbara County	30	0.04
Merced, CA (city) Merced County	28	0.04
Chino, CA (city) San Bernardino County	27	0.04
Pico Rivera, CA (city) Los Angeles County	27	0.04
Catalina Foothills, AZ (cdp) Pima County	24	0.04
Indio, CA (city) Riverside County	19	0.04
Santee, CA (city) San Diego County	19	0.04
Woodland, CA (city) Yolo County	18	0.04
Highland, CA (city) San Bernardino County	17	0.04
Hollister, CA (city) San Benito County	15	0.04
Lompoc, CA (city) Santa Barbara County	15	0.04
Porterville, CA (city) Tulare County	15	0.04
Lawndale, CA (city) Los Angeles County	14	0.04
Laguna, CA (cdp) Sacramento County	13	0.04
Rubidoux, CA (cdp) Riverside County	11	0.04
West Whittier-Los Nietos, CA (cdp) Los Angeles County	10	0.04
Coachella, CA (city) Riverside County	8	0.04
Duarte, CA (city) Los Angeles County	8	0.04
Isla Vista, CA (cdp) Santa Barbara County	8	0.04
South San Jose Hills, CA (cdp) Los Angeles County	8	0.04
Valinda, CA (cdp) Los Angeles County	8	0.04
Lakeside, CA (cdp) San Diego County	7	0.04
Mira Loma, CA (cdp) Riverside County	7	0.04
Arcata, CA (city) Humboldt County	6	0.04
Ferndale, MD (cdp) Anne Arundel County	6	0.04
Salida, CA (cdp) Stanislaus County	5	0.04
Shafter, CA (city) Kern County	5	0.04
Beaumont, CA (city) Riverside County	4	0.04
Capitola, CA (city) Santa Cruz County	4	0.04
Groton, CT (city) New London County	4	0.04
Healdsburg, CA (city) Sonoma County	4	0.04
Morro Bay, CA (city) San Luis Obispo County	4	0.04
San Jose, CA (city) Santa Clara County	232	0.03
Riverside, CA (city) Riverside County	86	0.03
Glendale, AZ (city) Maricopa County	75	0.03
Stockton, CA (city) San Joaquin County	65	0.03
Salinas, CA (city) Monterey County	51	0.03
Escondido, CA (city) San Diego County	41	0.03
Simi Valley, CA (city) Ventura County	37	0.03
Corona, CA (city) Riverside County	34	0.03
El Monte, CA (city) Los Angeles County	34	0.03
East Los Angeles, CA (cdp) Los Angeles County	32	0.03
Visalia, CA (city) Tulare County	32	0.03
Alhambra, CA (city) Los Angeles County	25	0.03
Antioch, CA (city) Contra Costa County	24	0.03
Citrus Heights, CA (city) Sacramento County	24	0.03
Baldwin Park, CA (city) Los Angeles County	23	0.03
Upland, CA (city) San Bernardino County	22	0.03
Redondo Beach, CA (city) Los Angeles County	21	0.03
Clovis, CA (city) Fresno County	20	0.03
Hesperia, CA (city) San Bernardino County	18	0.03
Chino Hills, CA (city) San Bernardino County	17	0.03
La Habra, CA (city) Orange County	17	0.03
Covina, CA (city) Los Angeles County	15	0.03
Apple Valley, CA (town) San Bernardino County	14	0.03
Glendora, CA (city) Los Angeles County	14	0.03
Santa Cruz, CA (city) Santa Cruz County	14	0.03
Turlock, CA (city) Stanislaus County	14	0.03
Altadena, CA (cdp) Los Angeles County	13	0.03
Hanford, CA (city) Kings County	13	0.03

Notes: (cdp) census designated place; Refer to the Explanation of Data in the front of the book for more detailed information.

American Indian: Yuman

Top 150 Places Sorted by Number

(Based on all places, regardless of population)

Place	Number	%
Peach Springs, AZ (cdp) Mohave County	461	76.83
Phoenix, AZ (city) Maricopa County	398	0.03
Yuma, AZ (city) Yuma County	310	0.40
Needles, CA (city) San Bernardino County	285	5.90
Arizona Village, AZ (cdp) Mohave County	267	76.07
Parker, AZ (town) La Paz County	138	4.39
Mohave Valley, AZ (cdp) Mohave County	116	0.85
Los Angeles, CA (city) Los Angeles County	100	0.00
Mesa, AZ (city) Maricopa County	95	0.02
Kingman, AZ (city) Mohave County	72	0.36
Camp Verde, AZ (town) Yavapai County	66	0.70
Tucson, AZ (city) Pima County	64	0.01
San Diego, CA (city) San Diego County	53	0.00
Flagstaff, AZ (city) Coconino County	50	0.09
Riverside, CA (city) Riverside County	49	0.02
Albuquerque, NM (city) Bernalillo County	47	0.01
Long Beach, CA (city) Los Angeles County	42	0.01
Chandler, AZ (city) Maricopa County	40	0.02
Tempe, AZ (city) Maricopa County	39	0.02
Glendale, AZ (city) Maricopa County	37	0.02
Prescott, AZ (city) Yavapai County	31	0.09
Grand Canyon Village, AZ (cdp) Coconino County	26	1.78
Clarkdale, AZ (town) Yavapai County	25	0.73
Bullhead City, AZ (city) Mohave County	25	0.07
New Kingman-Butler, AZ (cdp) Mohave County	23	0.16
Avondale, AZ (city) Maricopa County	23	0.06
Fresno, CA (city) Fresno County	23	0.01
Sunrise Manor, NV (cdp) Clark County	22	0.01
Denver, CO (city) Denver County	19	0.00
Sacramento, CA (city) Sacramento County	19	0.00
Second Mesa, AZ (cdp) Navajo County	18	2.21
Lawrence, KS (city) Douglas County	18	0.02
Stockton, CA (city) San Joaquin County	18	0.01
Sacaton, AZ (cdp) Pinal County	17	1.07
San Bernardino, CA (city) San Bernardino County	17	0.01
New York, NY (city) New York City	16	0.00
San Francisco, CA (city) San Francisco County	16	0.00
Lake Havasu City, AZ (city) Mohave County	15	0.04
Norwalk, CA (city) Los Angeles County	15	0.01
Las Vegas, NV (city) Clark County	15	0.00
San Jose, CA (city) Santa Clara County	15	0.00
Poston, AZ (cdp) La Paz County	14	3.60
Winterhaven, CA (cdp) Imperial County	14	2.65
Somerton, AZ (city) Yuma County	14	0.19
Azusa, CA (city) Los Angeles County	14	0.03
Oklahoma City, OK (city) Oklahoma County	14	0.00
Pico Rivera, CA (city) Los Angeles County	13	0.02
Downey, CA (city) Los Angeles County	13	0.01
Shasta Lake, CA (city) Shasta County	12	0.13
Cottonwood-Verde Village, AZ (cdp) Yavapai County	12	0.11
Florence, AZ (town) Pinal County	12	0.07
Barstow, CA (city) San Bernardino County	12	0.06
Carson City, NV (special city) Carson City city	12	0.02
Fontana, CA (city) San Bernardino County	12	0.01
Anchorage, AK (municipality) Anchorage Borough	12	0.00
Oakland, CA (city) Alameda County	12	0.00
Casa Grande, AZ (city) Pinal County	11	0.04
Chula Vista, CA (city) San Diego County	11	0.01
Lancaster, CA (city) Los Angeles County	11	0.01
Moreno Valley, CA (city) Riverside County	11	0.01
Rancho Cucamonga, CA (city) San Bernardino County	11	0.01
San Carlos, AZ (cdp) Gila County	10	0.27
Bloomington, CA (cdp) San Bernardino County	10	0.05
Escondido, CA (city) San Diego County	10	0.01
Paradise, NV (cdp) Clark County	10	0.01
Peoria, AZ (city) Maricopa County	10	0.01
Redding, CA (city) Shasta County	10	0.01
Anaheim, CA (city) Orange County	10	0.00
Dallas, TX (city) Dallas County	10	0.00
Houston, TX (city) Harris County	10	0.00
Moenkopi, AZ (cdp) Coconino County	9	1.00
First Mesa, AZ (cdp) Navajo County	9	0.80
Bell, CA (city) Los Angeles County	9	0.02
Baldwin Park, CA (city) Los Angeles County	9	0.01
El Cajon, CA (city) San Diego County	9	0.01
Oceanside, CA (city) San Diego County	9	0.01
Rialto, CA (city) San Bernardino County	9	0.01
Upland, CA (city) San Bernardino County	9	0.01
Colorado Springs, CO (city) El Paso County	9	0.00
Seward, AK (city) Kenai Peninsula Borough	8	0.28
Anadarko, OK (city) Caddo County	8	0.12
Buckeye, AZ (town) Maricopa County	8	0.12
Longview, WA (city) Cowlitz County	8	0.02
Manteca, CA (city) San Joaquin County	8	0.02
Berkeley, CA (city) Alameda County	8	0.01
Corona, CA (city) Riverside County	8	0.01
Redwood City, CA (city) San Mateo County	8	0.01
Rosemead, CA (city) Los Angeles County	8	0.01
Vallejo, CA (city) Solano County	8	0.01
West Covina, CA (city) Los Angeles County	8	0.01
Portland, OR (city) Multnomah County	8	0.00
Scottsdale, AZ (city) Maricopa County	8	0.00
Kykotsmovi Village, AZ (cdp) Navajo County	7	0.90
Arapahoe, WY (cdp) Fremont County	7	0.40
Sells, AZ (cdp) Pima County	7	0.25
Parker Strip, AZ (cdp) La Paz County	7	0.21
Tuba City, AZ (cdp) Coconino County	7	0.09
Village Park, HI (cdp) Honolulu County	7	0.07
Gallup, NM (city) McKinley County	7	0.03
El Centro, CA (city) Imperial County	7	0.02
Beaumont, TX (city) Jefferson County	7	0.01
Buena Park, CA (city) Orange County	7	0.01
Concord, CA (city) Contra Costa County	7	0.01
Lawton, OK (city) Comanche County	7	0.01
Chicago, IL (city) Cook County	7	0.00
Henderson, NV (city) Clark County	7	0.00
Modesto, CA (city) Stanislaus County	7	0.00
Mojave Ranch Estates, AZ (cdp) Mohave County	6	21.43
Salton City, CA (cdp) Imperial County	6	0.61
Ajo, AZ (cdp) Pima County	6	0.16
Coolidge, AZ (city) Pinal County	6	0.08
Mukilteo, WA (city) Snohomish County	6	0.03
Winchester, NV (cdp) Clark County	6	0.02
Appleton, WI (city) Outagamie County	6	0.01
El Monte, CA (city) Los Angeles County	6	0.01
Monterey Park, CA (city) Los Angeles County	6	0.01
Palmdale, CA (city) Los Angeles County	6	0.01
Santa Maria, CA (city) Santa Barbara County	6	0.01
Fremont, CA (city) Alameda County	6	0.00
Indianapolis, IN (special city) Marion County	6	0.00
Reno, NV (city) Washoe County	6	0.00
Santa Ana, CA (city) Orange County	6	0.00
Wadsworth, NV (cdp) Washoe County	5	0.57
Big River, CA (cdp) San Bernardino County	5	0.39
Tulalip Bay, WA (cdp) Snohomish County	5	0.32
Lakeland Village, CA (cdp) Riverside County	5	0.09
Carrollton, MI (cdp) Saginaw County	5	0.08
West Plains, MO (city) Howell County	5	0.05
Arvin, CA (city) Kern County	5	0.04
Marana, AZ (town) Pima County	5	0.04
Cameron Park, CA (cdp) El Dorado County	5	0.03
Douglas, AZ (city) Cochise County	5	0.03
Winter Gardens, CA (cdp) San Diego County	5	0.03
Elizabethtown, KY (city) Hardin County	5	0.02
Prescott Valley, AZ (town) Yavapai County	5	0.02
San Fernando, CA (city) Los Angeles County	5	0.02
Security-Widefield, CO (cdp) El Paso County	5	0.02
Claremont, CA (city) Los Angeles County	5	0.01
Dana Point, CA (city) Orange County	5	0.01
Folsom, CA (city) Sacramento County	5	0.01
Gilroy, CA (city) Santa Clara County	5	0.01
Novato, CA (city) Marin County	5	0.01
Pittsburg, CA (city) Contra Costa County	5	0.01
Rancho Cordova, CA (cdp) Sacramento County	5	0.01
San Dimas, CA (city) Los Angeles County	5	0.01
San Luis Obispo, CA (city) San Luis Obispo County	5	0.01
Santa Monica, CA (city) Los Angeles County	5	0.01
Santee, CA (city) San Diego County	5	0.01
Stanton, CA (city) Orange County	5	0.01
East Los Angeles, CA (cdp) Los Angeles County	5	0.00

Notes: (cdp) census designated place; Refer to the Explanation of Data in the front of the book for more detailed information.

American Indian: Yuman

Top 150 Places Sorted by Percent

(Based on all places, regardless of population)

Place	Number	%
Peach Springs, AZ (cdp) Mohave County	461	76.83
Arizona Village, AZ (cdp) Mohave County	267	76.07
Mojave Ranch Estates, AZ (cdp) Mohave County	6	21.43
Needles, CA (city) San Bernardino County	285	5.90
Parker, AZ (town) La Paz County	138	4.39
Poston, AZ (cdp) La Paz County	14	3.60
Winterhaven, CA (cdp) Imperial County	14	2.65
Second Mesa, AZ (cdp) Navajo County	18	2.21
Grand Canyon Village, AZ (cdp) Coconino County	26	1.78
Sacaton, AZ (cdp) Pinal County	17	1.07
Moenkopi, AZ (cdp) Coconino County	9	1.00
Sanford, TX (town) Hutchinson County	2	0.99
Jerome, AZ (town) Yavapai County	3	0.91
Kykotsmovi Village, AZ (cdp) Navajo County	7	0.90
Mohave Valley, AZ (cdp) Mohave County	116	0.85
First Mesa, AZ (cdp) Navajo County	9	0.80
Ebro, FL (town) Washington County	2	0.80
Keams Canyon, AZ (cdp) Navajo County	2	0.77
Clarkdale, AZ (town) Yavapai County	25	0.73
Camp Verde, AZ (town) Yavapai County	66	0.70
Willow Valley, AZ (cdp) Mohave County	4	0.68
Salton City, CA (cdp) Imperial County	6	0.61
Santan, AZ (cdp) Pinal County	4	0.61
Wadsworth, NV (cdp) Washoe County	5	0.57
Bluewater, AZ (cdp) La Paz County	4	0.55
Saint Michael, AK (city) Nome Census Area	2	0.54
Hotevilla-Bacavi, AZ (cdp) Navajo County	4	0.52
Encinal, NM (cdp) Cibola County	1	0.50
Elmira, CA (cdp) Solano County	1	0.49
Seligman, AZ (cdp) Yavapai County	2	0.44
Yuma, AZ (city) Yuma County	310	0.40
Arapahoe, WY (cdp) Fremont County	7	0.40
Big River, CA (cdp) San Bernardino County	5	0.39
Kingman, AZ (city) Mohave County	72	0.36
San Juan, NM (cdp) Rio Arriba County	2	0.34
Tulalip Bay, WA (cdp) Snohomish County	5	0.32
Shongopovi, AZ (cdp) Navajo County	2	0.32
Beckwourth, CA (cdp) Plumas County	1	0.29
Seward, AK (city) Kenai Peninsula Borough	8	0.28
San Carlos, AZ (cdp) Gila County	10	0.27
Bombay Beach, CA (cdp) Imperial County	1	0.27
Stewartsville, MO (city) De Kalb County	2	0.26
Sells, AZ (cdp) Pima County	7	0.25
Neah Bay, WA (cdp) Clallam County	2	0.25
Town of Pines, IN (town) Porter County	2	0.25
East Glacier Park Village, MT (cdp) Glacier County	1	0.25
Nichols, SC (town) Marion County	1	0.25
Seven Trees, CA (cdp) Santa Clara County	4	0.24
Truman, MN (city) Martin County	3	0.24
Valley Brook, OK (town) Oklahoma County	2	0.24
Akeley, MN (city) Hubbard County	1	0.24
Hamden, NY (town) Delaware County	3	0.23
Portage, OH (village) Wood County	1	0.23
Fort Thompson, SD (cdp) Buffalo County	3	0.22
Challis, ID (city) Custer County	2	0.22
Frazer, MT (cdp) Valley County	1	0.22
Parker Strip, AZ (cdp) La Paz County	7	0.21
Paguate, NM (cdp) Cibola County	1	0.21
Pima, AZ (town) Graham County	4	0.20
Owyhee, NV (cdp) Elko County	2	0.20
Ten Lake, MN (township) Beltrami County	2	0.20
Somerton, AZ (city) Yuma County	14	0.19
Bayfield, CO (town) La Plata County	3	0.19
Seaman, OH (village) Adams County	2	0.19
Shishmaref, AK (city) Nome Census Area	1	0.18
Tecumseh, NE (city) Johnson County	3	0.17
Yah-ta-hey, NM (cdp) McKinley County	1	0.17
New Kingman-Butler, AZ (cdp) Mohave County	23	0.16
Ajo, AZ (cdp) Pima County	6	0.16
Walla Walla East, WA (cdp) Walla Walla County	4	0.16
Peridot, AZ (cdp) Graham County	2	0.16
Reardan, WA (town) Lincoln County	1	0.16
Clifton, AZ (town) Greenlee County	4	0.15
Conway, MI (township) Livingston County	4	0.15
Lame Deer, MT (cdp) Rosebud County	3	0.15
Cibecue, AZ (cdp) Navajo County	2	0.15
Ignacio, CO (town) La Plata County	1	0.15
Wilhoit, AZ (cdp) Yavapai County	1	0.15
Yakutat, AK (cdp) Yakutat City and Borough	1	0.15
Shasta Lake, CA (city) Shasta County	12	0.13
Crow Agency, MT (cdp) Big Horn County	2	0.13
La Conner, WA (town) Skagit County	1	0.13
Mesita, NM (cdp) Cibola County	1	0.13
Teec Nos Pos, AZ (cdp) Apache County	1	0.13
Anadarko, OK (city) Caddo County	8	0.12
Buckeye, AZ (town) Maricopa County	8	0.12
Lenwood, CA (cdp) San Bernardino County	4	0.12
Lakeview, CA (cdp) Riverside County	2	0.12
Lechee, AZ (cdp) Coconino County	2	0.12
Pike Bay, MN (township) Cass County	2	0.12
Clinton, WA (cdp) Island County	1	0.12
Cottonwood-Verde Village, AZ (cdp) Yavapai County	12	0.11
Mountain View, HI (cdp) Hawaii County	3	0.11
Stigler, OK (city) Haskell County	3	0.11
West Bishop, CA (cdp) Inyo County	3	0.11
Bear Creek, AK (cdp) Kenai Peninsula Borough	2	0.11
Taft Heights, CA (cdp) Kern County	2	0.11
Little Round Lake, WI (cdp) Sawyer County	1	0.11
Dovre, MN (township) Kandiyohi County	2	0.10
New Summerfield, TX (city) Cherokee County	1	0.10
Strawberry, AZ (cdp) Gila County	1	0.10
Flagstaff, AZ (city) Coconino County	50	0.09
Prescott, AZ (city) Yavapai County	31	0.09
Tuba City, AZ (cdp) Coconino County	7	0.09
Lakeland Village, CA (cdp) Riverside County	5	0.09
Lake Montezuma, AZ (cdp) Yavapai County	3	0.09
Hayfork, CA (cdp) Trinity County	2	0.09
Winchester, CA (cdp) Riverside County	2	0.09
Houck, AZ (cdp) Apache County	1	0.09
Lincoln, MT (cdp) Lewis and Clark County	1	0.09
Oconto Falls, WI (town) Oconto County	1	0.09
Parks, AZ (cdp) Coconino County	1	0.09
Towaoc, CO (cdp) Montezuma County	1	0.09
Coolidge, AZ (city) Pinal County	6	0.08
Carrollton, MI (cdp) Saginaw County	5	0.08
Los Ranchos de Albuquerque, NM (village) Bernalillo County	4	0.08
McGregor, TX (city) McLennan County	4	0.08
Tolleson, AZ (city) Maricopa County	4	0.08
Wrightwood, CA (cdp) San Bernardino County	3	0.08
Sterling, KS (city) Rice County	2	0.08
Wolf Point, MT (city) Roosevelt County	2	0.08
Black Rock, NM (cdp) McKinley County	1	0.08
Mescalero, NM (cdp) Otero County	1	0.08
Talihina, OK (town) Le Flore County	1	0.08
Washington Heights, NY (cdp) Orange County	1	0.08
Bullhead City, AZ (city) Mohave County	25	0.07
Florence, AZ (town) Pinal County	12	0.07
Village Park, HI (cdp) Honolulu County	7	0.07
Catoosa, OK (city) Rogers County	4	0.07
Frederickson, WA (cdp) Pierce County	4	0.07
McCloud, CA (cdp) Siskiyou County	1	0.07
Avondale, AZ (city) Maricopa County	23	0.06
Barstow, CA (city) San Bernardino County	12	0.06
Hawaiian Paradise Park, HI (cdp) Hawaii County	4	0.06
Kirtland, NM (cdp) San Juan County	4	0.06
Zuni Pueblo, NM (cdp) McKinley County	4	0.06
Pine Ridge, SD (cdp) Shannon County	2	0.06
Lone Pine, CA (cdp) Inyo County	1	0.06
Maine Prairie, MN (township) Stearns County	1	0.06
Morrison, WI (town) Brown County	1	0.06
Olathe, CO (town) Montrose County	1	0.06
Upper Fruitland, NM (cdp) San Juan County	1	0.06
Wagner, SD (city) Charles Mix County	1	0.06
Woodville, CA (cdp) Tulare County	1	0.06
Bloomington, CA (cdp) San Bernardino County	10	0.05
West Plains, MO (city) Howell County	5	0.05
El Mirage, AZ (city) Maricopa County	4	0.05
West Penn, PA (township) Schuylkill County	2	0.05
Cortland, IL (town) De Kalb County	1	0.05
Fords Prairie, WA (cdp) Lewis County	1	0.05

Notes: (cdp) census designated place; Refer to the Explanation of Data in the front of the book for more detailed information.

American Indian: Yuman

Top 150 Places Sorted by Percent

(Based on places with populations of 10,000 or more)

Place	Number	%
Mohave Valley, AZ (cdp) Mohave County	116	0.85
Yuma, AZ (city) Yuma County	310	0.40
Kingman, AZ (city) Mohave County	72	0.36
New Kingman-Butler, AZ (cdp) Mohave County	23	0.16
Cottonwood-Verde Village, AZ (cdp) Yavapai County	12	0.11
Flagstaff, AZ (city) Coconino County	50	0.09
Prescott, AZ (city) Yavapai County	31	0.09
Bullhead City, AZ (city) Mohave County	25	0.07
Florence, AZ (town) Pinal County	12	0.07
Avondale, AZ (city) Maricopa County	23	0.06
Barstow, CA (city) San Bernardino County	12	0.06
Bloomington, CA (cdp) San Bernardino County	10	0.05
West Plains, MO (city) Howell County	5	0.05
Lake Havasu City, AZ (city) Mohave County	15	0.04
Casa Grande, AZ (city) Pinal County	11	0.04
Arvin, CA (city) Kern County	5	0.04
Marana, AZ (town) Pima County	5	0.04
Beaumont, CA (city) Riverside County	4	0.04
Hope, AR (city) Hempstead County	4	0.04
Phoenix, AZ (city) Maricopa County	398	0.03
Azusa, CA (city) Los Angeles County	14	0.03
Gallup, NM (city) McKinley County	7	0.03
Mukilteo, WA (city) Snohomish County	6	0.03
Cameron Park, CA (cdp) El Dorado County	5	0.03
Douglas, AZ (city) Cochise County	5	0.03
Winter Gardens, CA (cdp) San Diego County	5	0.03
Dallas, OR (city) Polk County	4	0.03
Ukiah, CA (city) Mendocino County	4	0.03
Valle Vista, CA (cdp) Riverside County	3	0.03
Mesa, AZ (city) Maricopa County	95	0.02
Riverside, CA (city) Riverside County	49	0.02
Chandler, AZ (city) Maricopa County	40	0.02
Tempe, AZ (city) Maricopa County	39	0.02
Glendale, AZ (city) Maricopa County	37	0.02
Lawrence, KS (city) Douglas County	18	0.02
Pico Rivera, CA (city) Los Angeles County	13	0.02
Carson City, NV (special city) Carson City city	12	0.02
Bell, CA (city) Los Angeles County	9	0.02
Longview, WA (city) Cowlitz County	8	0.02
Manteca, CA (city) San Joaquin County	8	0.02
El Centro, CA (city) Imperial County	7	0.02
Winchester, NV (cdp) Clark County	6	0.02
Elizabethtown, KY (city) Hardin County	5	0.02
Prescott Valley, AZ (town) Yavapai County	5	0.02
San Fernando, CA (city) Los Angeles County	5	0.02
Security-Widefield, CO (cdp) El Paso County	5	0.02
Bay Point, CA (cdp) Contra Costa County	4	0.02
Dickinson, TX (city) Galveston County	4	0.02
Elko, NV (city) Elko County	4	0.02
Fountain Hills, AZ (town) Maricopa County	4	0.02
Willmar, MN (city) Kandiyohi County	4	0.02
Durango, CO (city) La Plata County	3	0.02
Fountain, CO (city) El Paso County	3	0.02
Louisville, CO (city) Boulder County	3	0.02
Mandan, ND (city) Morton County	3	0.02
Pierre, SD (city) Hughes County	3	0.02
Solana Beach, CA (city) San Diego County	3	0.02
South Yuba City, CA (cdp) Sutter County	3	0.02
Tahlequah, OK (city) Cherokee County	3	0.02
Chowchilla, CA (city) Madera County	2	0.02
Los Lunas, NM (village) Valencia County	2	0.02
Monroe, WI (city) Green County	2	0.02
Walker Mill, MD (cdp) Prince George's County	2	0.02
Tucson, AZ (city) Pima County	64	0.01
Albuquerque, NM (city) Bernalillo County	47	0.01
Long Beach, CA (city) Los Angeles County	42	0.01
Fresno, CA (city) Fresno County	23	0.01
Sunrise Manor, NV (cdp) Clark County	22	0.01
Stockton, CA (city) San Joaquin County	18	0.01
San Bernardino, CA (city) San Bernardino County	17	0.01
Norwalk, CA (city) Los Angeles County	15	0.01
Downey, CA (city) Los Angeles County	13	0.01
Fontana, CA (city) San Bernardino County	12	0.01
Chula Vista, CA (city) San Diego County	11	0.01
Lancaster, CA (city) Los Angeles County	11	0.01
Moreno Valley, CA (city) Riverside County	11	0.01
Rancho Cucamonga, CA (city) San Bernardino County	11	0.01
Escondido, CA (city) San Diego County	10	0.01
Paradise, NV (cdp) Clark County	10	0.01
Peoria, AZ (city) Maricopa County	10	0.01
Redding, CA (city) Shasta County	10	0.01
Baldwin Park, CA (city) Los Angeles County	9	0.01
El Cajon, CA (city) San Diego County	9	0.01
Oceanside, CA (city) San Diego County	9	0.01
Rialto, CA (city) San Bernardino County	9	0.01
Upland, CA (city) San Bernardino County	9	0.01
Berkeley, CA (city) Alameda County	8	0.01
Corona, CA (city) Riverside County	8	0.01
Redwood City, CA (city) San Mateo County	8	0.01
Rosemead, CA (city) Los Angeles County	8	0.01
Vallejo, CA (city) Solano County	8	0.01
West Covina, CA (city) Los Angeles County	8	0.01
Beaumont, TX (city) Jefferson County	7	0.01
Buena Park, CA (city) Orange County	7	0.01
Concord, CA (city) Contra Costa County	7	0.01
Lawton, OK (city) Comanche County	7	0.01
Appleton, WI (city) Outagamie County	6	0.01
El Monte, CA (city) Los Angeles County	6	0.01
Monterey Park, CA (city) Los Angeles County	6	0.01
Palmdale, CA (city) Los Angeles County	6	0.01
Santa Maria, CA (city) Santa Barbara County	6	0.01
Claremont, CA (city) Los Angeles County	5	0.01
Dana Point, CA (city) Orange County	5	0.01
Folsom, CA (city) Sacramento County	5	0.01
Gilroy, CA (city) Santa Clara County	5	0.01
Novato, CA (city) Marin County	5	0.01
Pittsburg, CA (city) Contra Costa County	5	0.01
Rancho Cordova, CA (cdp) Sacramento County	5	0.01
San Dimas, CA (city) Los Angeles County	5	0.01
San Luis Obispo, CA (city) San Luis Obispo County	5	0.01
Santa Monica, CA (city) Los Angeles County	5	0.01
Santee, CA (city) San Diego County	5	0.01
Stanton, CA (city) Orange County	5	0.01
Altadena, CA (cdp) Los Angeles County	4	0.01
Bell Gardens, CA (city) Los Angeles County	4	0.01
Carmichael, CA (cdp) Sacramento County	4	0.01
Casas Adobes, AZ (cdp) Pima County	4	0.01
Colton, CA (city) San Bernardino County	4	0.01
Covina, CA (city) Los Angeles County	4	0.01
Glendora, CA (city) Los Angeles County	4	0.01
Hollister, CA (city) San Benito County	4	0.01
Milpitas, CA (city) Santa Clara County	4	0.01
Rowland Heights, CA (cdp) Los Angeles County	4	0.01
San Leandro, CA (city) Alameda County	4	0.01
Aberdeen, SD (city) Brown County	3	0.01
Apple Valley, CA (town) San Bernardino County	3	0.01
Burke, VA (cdp) Fairfax County	3	0.01
Campbell, CA (city) Santa Clara County	3	0.01
Florin, CA (cdp) Sacramento County	3	0.01
Fortuna Foothills, AZ (cdp) Yuma County	3	0.01
Highland, CA (city) San Bernardino County	3	0.01
Jackson, NJ (township) Ocean County	3	0.01
Kearns, UT (cdp) Salt Lake County	3	0.01
La Verne, CA (city) Los Angeles County	3	0.01
Lake Elsinore, CA (city) Riverside County	3	0.01
Lawndale, CA (city) Los Angeles County	3	0.01
Rio Rancho, NM (city) Sandoval County	3	0.01
Rubidoux, CA (cdp) Riverside County	3	0.01
Santa Paula, CA (city) Ventura County	3	0.01
Sierra Vista, AZ (city) Cochise County	3	0.01
Temecula, CA (city) Riverside County	3	0.01
Westmont, CA (cdp) Los Angeles County	3	0.01
Adelanto, CA (city) San Bernardino County	2	0.01
Apache Junction, AZ (city) Pinal County	2	0.01
Bailey's Crossroads, VA (cdp) Fairfax County	2	0.01
Banning, CA (city) Riverside County	2	0.01
Bowling Green, OH (city) Wood County	2	0.01
Brawley, CA (city) Imperial County	2	0.01
Calexico, CA (city) Imperial County	2	0.01
Casa de Oro-Mount Helix, CA (cdp) San Diego County	2	0.01

Notes: (cdp) census designated place; Refer to the Explanation of Data in the front of the book for more detailed information.

American Indian: All other tribes

Top 150 Places Sorted by Number

(Based on all places, regardless of population)

Place	Number	%
Oklahoma City, OK (city) Oklahoma County	2,703	0.53
Los Angeles, CA (city) Los Angeles County	2,431	0.07
New York, NY (city) New York City	2,182	0.03
Portland, OR (city) Multnomah County	2,080	0.39
Fort Hall, ID (cdp) Bannock County	2,021	63.29
Warm Springs, OR (cdp) Jefferson County	1,853	76.22
Sacramento, CA (city) Sacramento County	1,671	0.41
Fresno, CA (city) Fresno County	1,577	0.37
Seattle, WA (city) King County	1,453	0.26
Shawnee, OK (city) Pottawatomie County	1,413	4.92
Spokane, WA (city) Spokane County	1,406	0.72
Tulsa, OK (city) Tulsa County	1,391	0.35
Santa Rosa, CA (city) Sonoma County	1,341	0.91
San Diego, CA (city) San Diego County	1,312	0.11
Phoenix, AZ (city) Maricopa County	1,245	0.09
Redding, CA (city) Shasta County	1,201	1.49
Omaha, NE (city) Douglas County	1,199	0.31
Arapahoe, WY (cdp) Fremont County	1,193	67.55
Great Falls, MT (city) Cascade County	1,191	2.10
Fort Belknap Agency, MT (cdp) Blaine County	1,102	87.32
Ethete, WY (cdp) Fremont County	1,090	74.91
Providence, RI (city) Providence County	1,081	0.62
San Jose, CA (city) Santa Clara County	1,043	0.12
Ponca City, OK (city) Kay County	971	3.75
Tacoma, WA (city) Pierce County	931	0.48
Eureka, CA (city) Humboldt County	852	3.26
El Reno, OK (city) Canadian County	819	5.05
Salem, OR (city) Marion County	805	0.59
Macy, NE (cdp) Thurston County	804	84.10
Lapwai, ID (city) Nez Perce County	802	70.72
Norman, OK (city) Cleveland County	773	0.81
Sioux City, IA (city) Woodbury County	731	0.86
Anadarko, OK (city) Caddo County	719	10.82
Albuquerque, NM (city) Bernalillo County	710	0.16
Milwaukee, WI (city) Milwaukee County	709	0.12
Pablo, MT (cdp) Lake County	696	38.37
San Francisco, CA (city) San Francisco County	687	0.09
Anchorage, AK (municipality) Anchorage Borough	671	0.26
Taholah, WA (cdp) Grays Harbor County	665	80.70
Box Elder, MT (cdp) Hill County	651	81.99
Boston, MA (city) Suffolk County	650	0.11
Bakersfield, CA (city) Kern County	638	0.26
Hays, MT (cdp) Blaine County	636	90.60
Lincoln, NE (city) Lancaster County	632	0.28
Wichita, KS (city) Sedgwick County	623	0.18
Billings, MT (city) Yellowstone County	621	0.69
Neah Bay, WA (cdp) Clallam County	615	77.46
Chicago, IL (city) Cook County	612	0.02
Riverside, CA (city) Riverside County	611	0.24
Klamath Falls, OR (city) Klamath County	610	3.13
Winnebago, NE (village) Thurston County	608	79.17
Owyhee, NV (cdp) Elko County	606	59.59
Philadelphia, PA (city) Philadelphia County	601	0.04
Mission, OR (cdp) Umatilla County	594	58.29
Houston, TX (city) Harris County	555	0.03
Passamaquoddy Pleasant Pt. Res., ME (reservation) Washington Co.	552	86.25
Altamont, OR (cdp) Klamath County	552	2.82
Passamaquoddy Indian Twp. Res., ME (reservation) Washington Co.	551	81.51
Denver, CO (city) Denver County	547	0.10
San Antonio, TX (city) Bexar County	543	0.05
Stockton, CA (city) San Joaquin County	536	0.22
Missoula, MT (city) Missoula County	530	0.93
Walthill, NE (village) Thurston County	528	58.09
Eugene, OR (city) Lane County	523	0.38
Riverton, WY (city) Fremont County	517	5.55
Polson, MT (city) Lake County	511	12.65
Miami, OK (city) Ottawa County	506	3.69
Carson City, NV (special city) Carson City city	504	0.96
Pawnee, OK (city) Pawnee County	503	22.56
Reno, NV (city) Washoe County	502	0.28
McKinleyville, CA (cdp) Humboldt County	498	3.66
Oakland, CA (city) Alameda County	496	0.12
Ledyard, CT (town) New London County	495	3.37
Lawrence, KS (city) Douglas County	493	0.62
Havre, MT (city) Hill County	481	5.00
New Town, ND (city) Mountrail County	475	34.75
Ukiah, CA (city) Mendocino County	468	3.02
Ronan, MT (city) Lake County	463	25.55
Bellingham, WA (city) Whatcom County	461	0.69
Chico, CA (city) Butte County	459	0.77
Las Vegas, NV (city) Clark County	457	0.10
Penobscot Indian Island Res., ME (reservation) Penobscot County	445	79.18
Wolf Point, MT (city) Roosevelt County	444	16.67
South Kingstown, RI (town) Washington County	444	1.59
Norwich, CT (city) New London County	444	1.23
Escondido, CA (city) San Diego County	442	0.33
Tucson, AZ (city) Pima County	441	0.09
Vancouver, WA (city) Clark County	438	0.31
Oxnard, CA (city) Ventura County	435	0.26
Brookhaven, NY (town) Suffolk County	430	0.10
Shinnecock Reservation, NY (reservation) Suffolk County	428	84.92
Clovis, CA (city) Fresno County	428	0.63
Aberdeen, WA (city) Grays Harbor County	426	2.59
San Buenaventura, CA (city) Ventura County	423	0.42
Santa Ana, CA (city) Orange County	423	0.13
Bartelme, WI (town) Shawano County	421	60.14
Santa Barbara, CA (city) Santa Barbara County	413	0.45
Mandaree, ND (cdp) McKenzie County	412	73.84
San Bernardino, CA (city) San Bernardino County	408	0.22
Minneapolis, MN (city) Hennepin County	407	0.11
Boise City, ID (city) Ada County	404	0.22
Springfield, OR (city) Lane County	398	0.75
Worcester, MA (city) Worcester County	396	0.23
Rosita South, TX (cdp) Maverick County	392	15.23
Saint Paul, MN (city) Ramsey County	391	0.14
Dallas, TX (city) Dallas County	383	0.03
New Bedford, MA (city) Bristol County	382	0.41
Yreka, CA (city) Siskiyou County	379	5.20
Mashpee, MA (town) Barnstable County	378	2.92
Long Beach, CA (city) Los Angeles County	378	0.08
Port Angeles, WA (city) Clallam County	377	2.05
Arden-Arcade, CA (cdp) Sacramento County	372	0.39
Green Bay, WI (city) Brown County	369	0.36
Parker, AZ (town) La Paz County	365	11.62
Colorado Springs, CO (city) El Paso County	365	0.10
Bismarck, ND (city) Burleigh County	361	0.65
Pocatello, ID (city) Bannock County	360	0.70
Mesa, AZ (city) Maricopa County	359	0.09
Virginia Beach, VA (independent city) Virginia Beach city	356	0.08
Frazer, MT (cdp) Valley County	354	78.32
Banning, CA (city) Riverside County	353	1.50
Lewiston, ID (city) Nez Perce County	353	1.14
Columbus, OH (city) Franklin County	353	0.05
Brockway, WI (town) Jackson County	350	13.57
Chiloquin, OR (city) Klamath County	348	48.60
Anaheim, CA (city) Orange County	343	0.10
Indianapolis, IN (special city) Marion County	343	0.04
Lawton, OK (city) Comanche County	338	0.36
Covelo, CA (cdp) Mendocino County	334	28.43
Modesto, CA (city) Stanislaus County	333	0.18
Groton, CT (town) New London County	327	0.82
Washington, DC (city) District of Columbia	322	0.06
Citrus Heights, CA (city) Sacramento County	311	0.37
Plummer, ID (city) Benewah County	306	30.91
Arcata, CA (city) Humboldt County	306	1.84
Gresham, OR (city) Multnomah County	306	0.34
Stillwater, OK (city) Payne County	305	0.78
Medford, OR (city) Jackson County	304	0.48
Montville, CT (town) New London County	302	1.63
Fort Wayne, IN (city) Allen County	301	0.15
Porterville, CA (city) Tulare County	299	0.75
Saint Ignatius, MT (town) Lake County	296	37.56
Parker School, MT (cdp) Chouteau County	294	83.52
East Providence, RI (city) Providence County	293	0.60
Babylon, NY (town) Suffolk County	292	0.14
Aurora, CO (city) Arapahoe County	292	0.11
Hempstead, NY (town) Nassau County	290	0.04
Oroville, CA (city) Butte County	289	2.22
Wakefield-Peacedale, RI (cdp) Washington County	286	3.38
Oceanside, CA (city) San Diego County	286	0.18

Notes: (cdp) census designated place; Refer to the Explanation of Data in the front of the book for more detailed information.

American Indian: All other tribes

Top 150 Places Sorted by Percent

(Based on all places, regardless of population)

Place	Number	%
Lodge Pole, MT (cdp) Blaine County	203	94.86
Hays, MT (cdp) Blaine County	636	90.60
Azure, MT (cdp) Hill County	227	89.72
Fort Belknap Agency, MT (cdp) Blaine County	1,102	87.32
Sangrey, MT (cdp) Hill County	229	87.07
Saint Pierre, MT (cdp) Hill County	251	86.85
Passamaquoddy Pleasant Pt. Res., ME (reservation) Washington Co.	552	86.25
Agency, MT (cdp) Hill County	278	85.80
Shinnecock Reservation, NY (reservation) Suffolk County	428	84.92
Macy, NE (cdp) Thurston County	804	84.10
Boneau, MT (cdp) Chouteau County	159	83.68
Parker School, MT (cdp) Chouteau County	294	83.52
Box Elder, MT (cdp) Hill County	651	81.99
Passamaquoddy Indian Twp. Res., ME (reservation) Washington Co.	551	81.51
Taholah, WA (cdp) Grays Harbor County	665	80.70
Penobscot Indian Island Res., ME (reservation) Penobscot Co.	445	79.18
Winnebago, NE (village) Thurston County	608	79.17
Frazer, MT (cdp) Valley County	354	78.32
Neah Bay, WA (cdp) Clallam County	615	77.46
Old Agency, MT (cdp) Sanders County	73	76.84
Warm Springs, OR (cdp) Jefferson County	1,853	76.22
Ethete, WY (cdp) Fremont County	1,090	74.91
McDermitt, NV (cdp) Humboldt County	200	74.35
Mandaree, ND (cdp) McKenzie County	412	73.84
Turtle Lake, MT (cdp) Lake County	143	73.71
White Shield, ND (cdp) McLean County	256	73.56
Lapwai, ID (city) Nez Perce County	802	70.72
Arapahoe, WY (cdp) Fremont County	1,193	67.55
Chehalis Village, WA (cdp) Grays Harbor County	226	63.32
Fort Hall, ID (cdp) Bannock County	2,021	63.29
Red Rock, OK (town) Noble County	183	62.46
Elmo, MT (cdp) Lake County	89	62.24
Bartelme, WI (town) Shawano County	421	60.14
Owyhee, NV (cdp) Elko County	606	59.59
Mission, OR (cdp) Umatilla County	594	58.29
Walthill, NE (village) Thurston County	528	58.09
Four Bears Village, ND (cdp) McKenzie County	206	56.59
Poospatuck Reservation, NY (reservation) Suffolk County	153	56.46
Komensky, WI (town) Jackson County	234	50.65
Chiloquin, OR (city) Klamath County	348	48.60
Cayuse, OR (cdp) Umatilla County	27	45.76
Kicking Horse, MT (cdp) Lake County	36	45.00
Arlee, MT (cdp) Lake County	254	42.19
Pablo, MT (cdp) Lake County	696	38.37
Saint Ignatius, MT (town) Lake County	296	37.56
Marland, OK (town) Noble County	105	37.50
Aquinnah, MA (town) Dukes County	128	37.21
New Town, ND (city) Mountrail County	475	34.75
Evaro, MT (cdp) Missoula County	104	31.61
Harlem, MT (city) Blaine County	267	31.49
Plummer, ID (city) Benewah County	306	30.91
Dodson, MT (town) Phillips County	37	30.33
Niarada, MT (cdp) Sanders County	15	30.00
Covelo, CA (cdp) Mendocino County	334	28.43
Johnstown, WY (cdp) Fremont County	65	27.54
Big Arm, MT (cdp) Lake County	36	27.48
Klamath, CA (cdp) Del Norte County	173	26.57
Alpine Village, CA (cdp) Alpine County	36	26.47
Tutuilla, OR (cdp) Umatilla County	121	26.30
Kirkpatrick, OR (cdp) Umatilla County	45	26.16
Ronan, MT (city) Lake County	463	25.55
Ravalli, MT (cdp) Lake County	30	25.21
Rulo, NE (village) Richardson County	55	24.34
Boulder Flats, WY (cdp) Fremont County	87	22.83
Moclips, WA (cdp) Grays Harbor County	139	22.60
Pawnee, OK (city) Pawnee County	503	22.56
Parshall, ND (city) Mountrail County	206	21.00
Fort Washakie, WY (cdp) Fremont County	273	18.48
Siletz, OR (city) Lincoln County	200	17.65
Port Graham, AK (cdp) Kenai Peninsula Borough	29	16.96
Wolf Point, MT (city) Roosevelt County	444	16.67
Red Devil, AK (cdp) Bethel Census Area	8	16.67
Geary, OK (city) Blaine County	205	16.30
Dixon, MT (cdp) Sanders County	35	16.20
Preston, NE (village) Richardson County	8	16.00
Tensed, ID (city) Benewah County	20	15.87
Grand Ronde, OR (cdp) Polk County	42	15.50
Gresham, WI (village) Shawano County	89	15.48
Worley, ID (city) Kootenai County	34	15.25
Rosita South, TX (cdp) Maverick County	392	15.23
Bay Center, WA (cdp) Pacific County	26	14.94
Bowler, WI (village) Shawano County	49	14.29
Alcan Border, AK (cdp) Southeast Fairbanks Census Area	3	14.29
Laytonville, CA (cdp) Mendocino County	184	14.14
Crowheart, WY (cdp) Fremont County	23	14.11
Brockway, WI (town) Jackson County	350	13.57
Red Springs, WI (town) Shawano County	132	13.46
White Cloud, KS (city) Doniphan County	32	13.39
Charenton, LA (cdp) Saint Mary Parish	250	12.86
Poplar, MT (city) Roosevelt County	116	12.73
Polson, MT (city) Lake County	511	12.65
Finley Point, MT (cdp) Lake County	61	12.37
Lyndon, WI (town) Juneau County	146	12.00
Parker, AZ (town) La Paz County	365	11.62
Johnson, OK (town) Pottawatomie County	25	11.21
Poston, AZ (cdp) La Paz County	43	11.05
Charlo, MT (cdp) Lake County	48	10.93
Anadarko, OK (city) Caddo County	719	10.82
Kings Point, MT (cdp) Lake County	18	10.65
Peoria, OK (town) Ottawa County	15	10.64
Brockton, MT (town) Roosevelt County	26	10.61
Montgomery Creek, CA (cdp) Shasta County	10	10.42
Perry, ME (town) Washington County	86	10.15
Reserve, KS (city) Brown County	10	10.00
Kaw City, OK (city) Kay County	37	9.95
Round Mountain, CA (cdp) Shasta County	12	9.84
Gopher Flats, OR (cdp) Umatilla County	39	9.73
Longdale, OK (town) Blaine County	30	9.68
Grainola, OK (town) Osage County	3	9.68
Quapaw, OK (town) Ottawa County	95	9.65
Canton, OK (town) Blaine County	53	8.58
Decatur, NE (village) Burt County	52	8.41
Nixon, NV (cdp) Washoe County	35	8.37
Gracemont, OK (town) Caddo County	28	8.33
Canyondam, CA (cdp) Plumas County	3	8.11
Cranmoor, WI (town) Wood County	14	8.00
Hersey, ME (town) Aroostook County	5	7.94
Willow Creek, CA (cdp) Humboldt County	137	7.86
Macdoel, CA (cdp) Siskiyou County	11	7.86
Fall River Mills, CA (cdp) Shasta County	50	7.72
Dering Harbor, NY (village) Suffolk County	1	7.69
Nisqually Indian Community, WA (cdp) Thurston County	45	7.65
Seiling, OK (city) Dewey County	66	7.54
Binger, OK (town) Caddo County	53	7.49
Birney, MT (cdp) Rosebud County	8	7.41
Willamina, OR (city) Yamhill County	136	7.38
Bertsch-Oceanview, CA (cdp) Del Norte County	164	7.33
Calumet, OK (town) Canadian County	39	7.29
Willis, KS (city) Brown County	5	7.25
Rosalie, NE (village) Thurston County	14	7.22
Selfridge, ND (city) Sioux County	16	7.17
State Line, ID (city) Kootenai County	2	7.14
McLoud, OK (town) Pottawatomie County	250	7.05
Noble, LA (village) Sabine Parish	18	6.95
Hot Springs, MT (town) Sanders County	36	6.78
Byron, WI (town) Monroe County	94	6.74
West Point, CA (cdp) Calaveras County	50	6.70
Brooksville, OK (town) Pottawatomie County	6	6.67
Dellona, WI (town) Sauk County	79	6.59
Kaibab, AZ (cdp) Mohave County	18	6.55
Kendrick, OK (town) Lincoln County	9	6.52
Crescent City North, CA (cdp) Del Norte County	257	6.38
Tolley, ND (city) Renville County	4	6.35
Santee, NE (village) Knox County	19	6.29
Big Bend, CA (cdp) Shasta County	9	6.04
Greenville, CA (cdp) Plumas County	70	6.03
Hammon, OK (town) Roger Mills County	28	5.97
Birnamwood, WI (town) Shawano County	42	5.91
Dotyville, OK (cdp) Ottawa County	1	5.88
Shoshone, CA (cdp) Inyo County	3	5.77

Notes: (cdp) census designated place; Refer to the Explanation of Data in the front of the book for more detailed information.

American Indian: All other tribes

Top 150 Places Sorted by Percent

(Based on places with populations of 10,000 or more)

Place	Number	%
El Reno, OK (city) Canadian County	819	5.05
Shawnee, OK (city) Pottawatomie County	1,413	4.92
Ponca City, OK (city) Kay County	971	3.75
Miami, OK (city) Ottawa County	506	3.69
McKinleyville, CA (cdp) Humboldt County	498	3.66
Ledyard, CT (town) New London County	495	3.37
Eureka, CA (city) Humboldt County	852	3.26
Klamath Falls, OR (city) Klamath County	610	3.13
Ukiah, CA (city) Mendocino County	468	3.02
Mashpee, MA (town) Barnstable County	378	2.92
Altamont, OR (cdp) Klamath County	552	2.82
Aberdeen, WA (city) Grays Harbor County	426	2.59
Oroville, CA (city) Butte County	289	2.22
Great Falls, MT (city) Cascade County	1,191	2.10
Port Angeles, WA (city) Clallam County	377	2.05
Fortuna, CA (city) Humboldt County	198	1.89
Arcata, CA (city) Humboldt County	306	1.84
Montville, CT (town) New London County	302	1.63
South Kingstown, RI (town) Washington County	444	1.59
Gardnerville Ranchos, NV (cdp) Douglas County	173	1.57
Banning, CA (city) Riverside County	353	1.50
Redding, CA (city) Shasta County	1,201	1.49
Peru, IN (city) Miami County	184	1.42
Blackfoot, ID (city) Bingham County	145	1.39
Griswold, CT (town) New London County	140	1.30
South Sioux City, NE (city) Dakota County	151	1.27
Pendleton, OR (city) Umatilla County	205	1.25
Norwich, CT (city) New London County	444	1.23
Coos Bay, OR (city) Coos County	189	1.23
Mastic, NY (cdp) Suffolk County	180	1.17
Lewiston, ID (city) Nez Perce County	353	1.14
Susanville, CA (city) Lassen County	150	1.11
Red Bluff, CA (city) Tehama County	144	1.10
Claremore, OK (city) Rogers County	166	1.05
Clearlake, CA (city) Lake County	129	0.98
Four Corners, OR (cdp) Marion County	135	0.97
Carson City, NV (special city) Carson City city	504	0.96
Windsor, CA (town) Sonoma County	217	0.95
Narragansett, RI (town) Washington County	156	0.95
Healdsburg, CA (city) Sonoma County	102	0.95
Missoula, MT (city) Missoula County	530	0.93
New London, CT (city) New London County	239	0.93
San Jacinto, CA (city) Riverside County	222	0.93
Santa Rosa, CA (city) Sonoma County	1,341	0.91
Wabash, IN (city) Wabash County	105	0.89
Bangor, ME (city) Penobscot County	276	0.88
Sioux City, IA (city) Woodbury County	731	0.86
Tahlequah, OK (city) Cherokee County	123	0.85
Arkansas City, KS (city) Cowley County	101	0.84
Sapulpa, OK (city) Creek County	159	0.83
Beaumont, CA (city) Riverside County	94	0.83
Groton, CT (town) New London County	327	0.82
Groton, CT (city) New London County	82	0.82
Norman, OK (city) Cleveland County	773	0.81
North Amityville, NY (cdp) Suffolk County	133	0.80
East Hemet, CA (cdp) Riverside County	118	0.80
Linda, CA (cdp) Yuba County	108	0.80
Butte-Silver Bow, MT (special city) Silver Bow County	268	0.79
Elko, NV (city) Elko County	132	0.79
Stillwater, OK (city) Payne County	305	0.78
Chico, CA (city) Butte County	459	0.77
Hayesville, OR (cdp) Marion County	139	0.76
Springfield, OR (city) Lane County	398	0.75
Porterville, CA (city) Tulare County	299	0.75
Olivehurst, CA (cdp) Yuba County	83	0.75
Spokane, WA (city) Spokane County	1,406	0.72
Keizer, OR (city) Marion County	233	0.72
Marysville, CA (city) Yuba County	88	0.72
West Sacramento, CA (city) Yolo County	223	0.71
Elk City, OK (city) Beckham County	75	0.71
Spring Creek, NV (cdp) Elko County	75	0.71
Saint Helens, OR (city) Columbia County	71	0.71
Pocatello, ID (city) Bannock County	360	0.70
Parkway-South Sacramento, CA (cdp) Sacramento County	255	0.70
Billings, MT (city) Yellowstone County	621	0.69
Bellingham, WA (city) Whatcom County	461	0.69
Bremerton, WA (city) Kitsap County	252	0.68
Dallas, OR (city) Polk County	85	0.68
Grass Valley, CA (city) Nevada County	74	0.68
Norfolk, NE (city) Madison County	158	0.67
Helena, MT (city) Lewis and Clark County	169	0.66
Bismarck, ND (city) Burleigh County	361	0.65
Lemoore, CA (city) Kings County	128	0.65
Lebanon, OR (city) Linn County	84	0.65
Clovis, CA (city) Fresno County	428	0.63
Okmulgee, OK (city) Okmulgee County	82	0.63
Valle Vista, CA (cdp) Riverside County	66	0.63
Providence, RI (city) Providence County	1,081	0.62
Lawrence, KS (city) Douglas County	493	0.62
Chowchilla, CA (city) Madera County	69	0.62
Newport, RI (city) Newport County	162	0.61
Westerly, RI (town) Washington County	139	0.61
Del City, OK (city) Oklahoma County	134	0.61
East Providence, RI (city) Providence County	293	0.60
McMinnville, OR (city) Yamhill County	159	0.60
Salem, OR (city) Marion County	805	0.59
North Auburn, CA (cdp) Placer County	70	0.59
Longview, WA (city) Cowlitz County	202	0.58
Plainfield, CT (town) Windham County	85	0.58
White Center, WA (cdp) King County	119	0.57
Centralia, WA (city) Lewis County	83	0.56
Williston, ND (city) Williams County	70	0.56
Enid, OK (city) Garfield County	254	0.54
Lompoc, CA (city) Santa Barbara County	224	0.54
Ashland, OR (city) Jackson County	106	0.54
Kalispell, MT (city) Flathead County	77	0.54
Kelso, WA (city) Cowlitz County	64	0.54
Dishman, WA (cdp) Spokane County	54	0.54
Oklahoma City, OK (city) Oklahoma County	2,703	0.53
Roseburg, OR (city) Douglas County	106	0.53
Florin, CA (cdp) Sacramento County	140	0.51
Chickasha, OK (city) Grady County	81	0.51
Baraboo, WI (city) Sauk County	55	0.51
Bethany, OK (city) Oklahoma County	102	0.50
Bourne, MA (town) Barnstable County	93	0.50
Wisconsin Rapids, WI (city) Wood County	92	0.50
Redmond, OR (city) Deschutes County	68	0.50
Barnstable Town, MA (city) Barnstable County	233	0.49
Killingly, CT (town) Windham County	81	0.49
Madison Heights, VA (cdp) Amherst County	57	0.49
Tacoma, WA (city) Pierce County	931	0.48
Medford, OR (city) Jackson County	304	0.48
North Kingstown, RI (town) Washington County	126	0.48
Waterville, ME (city) Kennebec County	75	0.48
Windham, ME (town) Cumberland County	71	0.48
Minot, ND (city) Ward County	172	0.47
San Juan Capistrano, CA (city) Orange County	160	0.47
Waterford, CT (town) New London County	90	0.47
Augusta, ME (city) Kennebec County	87	0.47
Elk Grove, CA (cdp) Sacramento County	277	0.46
Moore, OK (city) Cleveland County	188	0.46
Ramona, CA (cdp) San Diego County	72	0.46
La Grande, OR (city) Union County	57	0.46
Santa Barbara, CA (city) Santa Barbara County	413	0.45
Goleta, CA (cdp) Santa Barbara County	249	0.45
Midwest City, OK (city) Oklahoma County	242	0.45
Lacey, WA (city) Thurston County	142	0.45
Foothill Farms, CA (cdp) Sacramento County	78	0.45
Pierre, SD (city) Hughes County	63	0.45
Woodward, OK (city) Woodward County	53	0.45
Orcutt, CA (cdp) Santa Barbara County	128	0.44
Grants Pass, OR (city) Josephine County	102	0.44
Sand Springs, OK (city) Tulsa County	76	0.44
Hemet, CA (city) Riverside County	255	0.43
Temecula, CA (city) Riverside County	250	0.43
Olympia, WA (city) Thurston County	183	0.43
Saint Charles, MD (cdp) Charles County	142	0.43
Biddeford, ME (city) York County	91	0.43
Central Point, OR (city) Jackson County	54	0.43
Tumwater, WA (city) Thurston County	54	0.43

Notes: (cdp) census designated place; Refer to the Explanation of Data in the front of the book for more detailed information.

American Indian tribes, not specified

Top 150 Places Sorted by Number

(Based on all places, regardless of population)

Place	Number	%
New York, NY (city) New York City	7,090	0.09
Los Angeles, CA (city) Los Angeles County	3,258	0.09
Phoenix, AZ (city) Maricopa County	1,672	0.13
San Antonio, TX (city) Bexar County	1,664	0.15
Chicago, IL (city) Cook County	1,394	0.05
Albuquerque, NM (city) Bernalillo County	1,151	0.26
Houston, TX (city) Harris County	1,141	0.06
Tucson, AZ (city) Pima County	1,136	0.23
Denver, CO (city) Denver County	840	0.15
San Diego, CA (city) San Diego County	827	0.07
Dallas, TX (city) Dallas County	797	0.07
Philadelphia, PA (city) Philadelphia County	779	0.05
San Jose, CA (city) Santa Clara County	756	0.08
Tulsa, OK (city) Tulsa County	704	0.18
Fresno, CA (city) Fresno County	644	0.15
Oklahoma City, OK (city) Oklahoma County	608	0.12
Detroit, MI (city) Wayne County	555	0.06
Austin, TX (city) Travis County	548	0.08
Seattle, WA (city) King County	524	0.09
Sacramento, CA (city) Sacramento County	502	0.12
San Francisco, CA (city) San Francisco County	478	0.06
Minneapolis, MN (city) Hennepin County	473	0.12
Mesa, AZ (city) Maricopa County	469	0.12
Portland, OR (city) Multnomah County	468	0.09
Long Beach, CA (city) Los Angeles County	465	0.10
El Paso, TX (city) El Paso County	462	0.08
Gallup, NM (city) McKinley County	454	2.25
Baltimore, MD (independent city) Baltimore city	417	0.06
Las Vegas, NV (city) Clark County	404	0.08
Bakersfield, CA (city) Kern County	385	0.16
Milwaukee, WI (city) Milwaukee County	378	0.06
Flagstaff, AZ (city) Coconino County	368	0.70
Indianapolis, IN (special city) Marion County	365	0.05
Colorado Springs, CO (city) El Paso County	363	0.10
Oakland, CA (city) Alameda County	361	0.09
Hempstead, NY (town) Nassau County	360	0.05
Stockton, CA (city) San Joaquin County	353	0.14
Santa Ana, CA (city) Orange County	353	0.10
Rapid City, SD (city) Pennington County	341	0.57
Fort Worth, TX (city) Tarrant County	331	0.06
Columbus, OH (city) Franklin County	329	0.05
Providence, RI (city) Providence County	325	0.19
Boston, MA (city) Suffolk County	321	0.05
Washington, DC (city) District of Columbia	320	0.06
Anaheim, CA (city) Orange County	319	0.10
New Town, ND (city) Mountrail County	301	22.02
Jacksonville, FL (special city) Duval County	288	0.04
Nashville-Davidson, TN (special city) Davidson County	281	0.05
Anchorage, AK (municipality) Anchorage Borough	280	0.11
San Bernardino, CA (city) San Bernardino County	277	0.15
Farmington, NM (city) San Juan County	276	0.73
Tacoma, WA (city) Pierce County	276	0.14
Riverside, CA (city) Riverside County	267	0.10
Modesto, CA (city) Stanislaus County	252	0.13
Parshall, ND (city) Mountrail County	251	25.59
Kansas City, MO (city) Jackson County	251	0.06
Buffalo, NY (city) Erie County	249	0.09
Tahlequah, OK (city) Cherokee County	247	1.71
Pueblo, CO (city) Pueblo County	247	0.24
Virginia Beach, VA (independent city) Virginia Beach city	246	0.06
Arlington, TX (city) Tarrant County	244	0.07
Glendale, AZ (city) Maricopa County	241	0.11
Cleveland, OH (city) Cuyahoga County	238	0.05
Aurora, CO (city) Arapahoe County	230	0.08
Reno, NV (city) Washoe County	227	0.13
Wichita, KS (city) Sedgwick County	225	0.07
Pine Ridge, SD (cdp) Shannon County	224	7.06
Saint Paul, MN (city) Ramsey County	224	0.08
White Swan, WA (cdp) Yakima County	218	7.19
Corpus Christi, TX (city) Nueces County	215	0.08
Tempe, AZ (city) Maricopa County	211	0.13
Salt Lake City, UT (city) Salt Lake County	207	0.11
Pomona, CA (city) Los Angeles County	203	0.14
Norman, OK (city) Cleveland County	200	0.21
Warm Springs, OR (cdp) Jefferson County	194	7.98
Memphis, TN (city) Shelby County	192	0.03
Honolulu, HI (cdp) Honolulu County	190	0.05
Lakewood, CO (city) Jefferson County	189	0.13
Jersey City, NJ (city) Hudson County	188	0.08
Pittsburgh, PA (city) Allegheny County	186	0.06
Omaha, NE (city) Douglas County	186	0.05
Charlotte, NC (city) Mecklenburg County	186	0.03
Dugway, UT (cdp) Tooele County	184	9.13
Newark, NJ (city) Essex County	180	0.07
Lubbock, TX (city) Lubbock County	179	0.09
Toledo, OH (city) Lucas County	179	0.06
Spokane, WA (city) Spokane County	177	0.09
Sunrise Manor, NV (cdp) Clark County	176	0.11
Amarillo, TX (city) Potter County	176	0.10
Rochester, NY (city) Monroe County	176	0.08
Salinas, CA (city) Monterey County	173	0.11
Oxnard, CA (city) Ventura County	172	0.10
Tampa, FL (city) Hillsborough County	172	0.06
Santa Fe, NM (city) Santa Fe County	169	0.27
Laredo, TX (city) Webb County	169	0.10
Islip, NY (town) Suffolk County	169	0.05
Brookhaven, NY (town) Suffolk County	169	0.04
El Monte, CA (city) Los Angeles County	167	0.14
Yonkers, NY (city) Westchester County	162	0.08
Oneida, WI (town) Outagamie County	160	4.00
East Los Angeles, CA (cdp) Los Angeles County	160	0.13
Yuma, AZ (city) Yuma County	158	0.20
Baldwin Park, CA (city) Los Angeles County	157	0.21
Norfolk, VA (independent city) Norfolk city	157	0.07
Miami, FL (city) Miami-Dade County	157	0.04
Tuba City, AZ (cdp) Coconino County	156	1.90
Hayward, CA (city) Alameda County	155	0.11
Santa Rosa, CA (city) Sonoma County	155	0.11
Ontario, CA (city) San Bernardino County	155	0.10
Muskogee, OK (city) Muskogee County	152	0.40
Las Cruces, NM (city) Dona Ana County	152	0.20
Fontana, CA (city) San Bernardino County	151	0.12
Window Rock, AZ (cdp) Apache County	150	4.90
Atlanta, GA (city) Fulton County	150	0.04
Kayenta, AZ (cdp) Navajo County	149	3.03
Topeka, KS (city) Shawnee County	149	0.12
Grand Rapids, MI (city) Kent County	149	0.08
Salem, OR (city) Marion County	148	0.11
Lincoln, NE (city) Lancaster County	146	0.06
Chula Vista, CA (city) San Diego County	145	0.08
Moreno Valley, CA (city) Riverside County	144	0.10
Ramapo, NY (town) Rockland County	141	0.13
Paradise, NV (cdp) Clark County	141	0.08
Escondido, CA (city) San Diego County	140	0.10
Shiprock, NM (cdp) San Juan County	139	1.70
Casa Grande, AZ (city) Pinal County	139	0.55
Duluth, MN (city) Saint Louis County	138	0.16
Palmdale, CA (city) Los Angeles County	138	0.12
Eugene, OR (city) Lane County	138	0.10
Oceanside, CA (city) San Diego County	138	0.09
Kansas City, KS (city) Wyandotte County	137	0.09
Irving, TX (city) Dallas County	137	0.07
Cincinnati, OH (city) Hamilton County	135	0.04
Saint Louis, MO (independent city) Saint Louis city	134	0.04
Lumberton, NC (city) Robeson County	131	0.63
San Felipe Pueblo, NM (cdp) Sandoval County	130	6.25
Norwalk, CA (city) Los Angeles County	130	0.13
Syracuse, NY (city) Onondaga County	130	0.09
Fremont, CA (city) Alameda County	130	0.06
Sells, AZ (cdp) Pima County	128	4.57
Grand Prairie, TX (city) Dallas County	128	0.10
Bridgeport, CT (city) Fairfield County	127	0.09
Des Moines, IA (city) Polk County	125	0.06
Montgomery, AL (city) Montgomery County	125	0.06
Garden Grove, CA (city) Orange County	123	0.07
Carson City, NV (special city) Carson City city	122	0.23
Garland, TX (city) Dallas County	122	0.06
Four Bears Village, ND (cdp) McKenzie County	121	33.24
Waco, TX (city) McLennan County	120	0.11
New Orleans, LA (city) Orleans Parish	120	0.02

Notes: (cdp) census designated place; Refer to the Explanation of Data in the front of the book for more detailed information.

American Indian tribes, not specified

Top 150 Places Sorted by Percent

(Based on all places, regardless of population)

Place	Number	%
Hughes, AK (city) Yukon-Koyukuk Census Area	44	56.41
Four Bears Village, ND (cdp) McKenzie County	121	33.24
Spring Creek, SD (cdp) Todd County	42	30.88
Parshall, ND (city) Mountrail County	251	25.59
New Town, ND (city) Mountrail County	301	22.02
Maza, ND (city) Towner County	1	20.00
Mexican Hat, UT (cdp) San Juan County	16	18.18
White Shield, ND (cdp) McLean County	57	16.38
Mandaree, ND (cdp) McKenzie County	89	15.95
Middle Village, WI (cdp) Menominee County	56	15.95
Reserve, WI (cdp) Sawyer County	65	14.91
Manzano, NM (cdp) Torrance County	8	14.81
Poospatuck Reservation, NY (reservation) Suffolk County	39	14.39
La Plant, SD (cdp) Dewey County	20	13.33
Boy River, MN (city) Cass County	5	13.16
Ayr, ND (city) Cass County	3	13.04
Manokotak, AK (city) Dillingham Census Area	50	12.53
Couderay, WI (town) Sawyer County	58	12.37
Nageezi, NM (cdp) San Juan County	35	11.82
Hillburn, NY (village) Rockland County	104	11.80
Kyle, SD (cdp) Shannon County	110	11.34
Gopher Flats, OR (cdp) Umatilla County	45	11.22
La Prairie, MN (township) Clearwater County	41	11.05
Komensky, WI (town) Jackson County	48	10.39
Shonto, AZ (cdp) Navajo County	56	9.86
Dwight Mission, OK (cdp) Sequoyah County	3	9.38
Cloud Creek, OK (cdp) Delaware County	8	9.30
Dugway, UT (cdp) Tooele County	184	9.13
Boneau, MT (cdp) Chouteau County	17	8.95
La Follette, WI (town) Burnett County	45	8.81
North Acomita Village, NM (cdp) Cibola County	25	8.68
Green Grass, SD (cdp) Dewey County	5	8.62
Columbia, VA (town) Fluvanna County	4	8.16
Zoar, WI (cdp) Menominee County	10	8.06
Warm Springs, OR (cdp) Jefferson County	194	7.98
Peach Springs, AZ (cdp) Mohave County	46	7.67
Pine Point, MN (township) Becker County	31	7.40
Red Springs, WI (town) Shawano County	72	7.34
San Ildefonso Pueblo, NM (cdp) Santa Fe County	33	7.21
White Swan, WA (cdp) Yakima County	218	7.19
Pine Ridge, NE (cdp) Sheridan County	1	7.14
White Earth, MN (township) Becker County	57	7.13
Pine Ridge, SD (cdp) Shannon County	224	7.06
Covelo, CA (cdp) Mendocino County	83	7.06
Kaibab, AZ (cdp) Mohave County	19	6.91
Cochiti, NM (cdp) Sandoval County	35	6.90
Pike Bay, MN (township) Cass County	113	6.88
Little Round Lake, WI (cdp) Sawyer County	65	6.86
Corral City, TX (town) Denton County	6	6.74
McDermitt, NV (cdp) Humboldt County	18	6.69
Ak-Chin Village, AZ (cdp) Pinal County	44	6.58
Onondaga Reservation, NY (reservation) Onondaga County	96	6.52
Busby, MT (cdp) Big Horn County	45	6.47
White Earth, ND (city) Mountrail County	4	6.35
San Felipe Pueblo, NM (cdp) Sandoval County	130	6.25
Tusayan, AZ (cdp) Coconino County	35	6.23
Teec Nos Pos, AZ (cdp) Apache County	49	6.13
Rio en Medio, NM (cdp) Santa Fe County	8	6.11
Chief Lake, WI (cdp) Sawyer County	38	6.08
Skyline-Ganipa, NM (cdp) Cibola County	61	5.89
McDonald, NC (town) Robeson County	7	5.88
Oglala, SD (cdp) Shannon County	72	5.86
Tuscarora Reservation, NY (reservation) Niagara County	66	5.80
Dennehotso, AZ (cdp) Apache County	42	5.72
Seama, NM (cdp) Cibola County	19	5.71
Oneida, WI (cdp) Brown County	61	5.70
Yah-ta-hey, NM (cdp) McKinley County	33	5.69
Halls Crossing, UT (cdp) San Juan County	5	5.62
Zemple, MN (city) Itasca County	4	5.33
Mescalero, NM (cdp) Otero County	65	5.27
Shaktoolik, AK (city) Nome Census Area	12	5.22
Shaker Church, WA (cdp) Snohomish County	41	5.21
Rockwell, MN (township) Norman County	4	5.13
Tulalip Bay, WA (cdp) Snohomish County	80	5.12
Muddy, MT (cdp) Big Horn County	32	5.10
Penobscot Indian Island Res., ME (reservation) Penobscot County	28	4.98
Whitehorse, SD (cdp) Dewey County	7	4.96
Ramah, NM (cdp) McKinley County	20	4.91
Window Rock, AZ (cdp) Apache County	150	4.90
Santa Clara Pueblo, NM (cdp) Rio Arriba County	48	4.90
Elgin, KS (city) Chautauqua County	4	4.88
Gould, MN (township) Cass County	12	4.82
Jemez Pueblo, NM (cdp) Sandoval County	93	4.76
Meyers Chuck, AK (cdp) Prince of Wales-Outer Ketchikan C.A.	1	4.76
Taholah, WA (cdp) Grays Harbor County	39	4.73
Hotevilla-Bacavi, AZ (cdp) Navajo County	36	4.69
Rock Springs, NM (cdp) McKinley County	26	4.66
Sanostee, NM (cdp) San Juan County	20	4.66
Wadsworth, NV (cdp) Washoe County	41	4.65
Paguate, NM (cdp) Cibola County	22	4.64
Maple Ridge, MN (township) Beltrami County	5	4.63
Tse Bonito, NM (cdp) McKinley County	12	4.60
Winslow West, AZ (cdp) Coconino County	6	4.58
Sells, AZ (cdp) Pima County	128	4.57
Legend Lake, WI (cdp) Menominee County	70	4.57
North Browning, MT (cdp) Glacier County	100	4.55
Stony River, MN (township) Lake County	8	4.47
Little Elbow, MN (township) Mahnomen County	10	4.44
Orr, MN (city) Saint Louis County	11	4.42
McNary, AZ (cdp) Apache County	15	4.30
Parker School, MT (cdp) Chouteau County	15	4.26
Navajo Mountain, UT (cdp) San Juan County	16	4.22
Spalding, MN (township) Aitkin County	10	4.22
Taos Pueblo, NM (cdp) Taos County	53	4.19
Mason, WI (village) Bayfield County	3	4.17
Fort Thompson, SD (cdp) Buffalo County	57	4.15
Bogue Chitto, MS (cdp) Neshoba County	22	4.13
Fort Smith, MT (cdp) Big Horn County	5	4.10
Allegany Reservation, NY (reservation) Cattaraugus County	45	4.09
New Post, WI (cdp) Sawyer County	15	4.09
Brookston, MN (city) Saint Louis County	4	4.08
Grand Ronde, OR (cdp) Polk County	11	4.06
South Browning, MT (cdp) Glacier County	68	4.05
Worley, ID (city) Kootenai County	9	4.04
Laguna, NM (cdp) Cibola County	17	4.02
Oneida, WI (town) Outagamie County	160	4.00
Russell, WI (town) Bayfield County	48	3.95
Cass Lake, MN (city) Cass County	34	3.95
Maple Grove, MN (township) Becker County	16	3.95
Pembroke, NC (town) Robeson County	94	3.92
San Juan, NM (cdp) Rio Arriba County	23	3.89
Crownpoint, NM (cdp) McKinley County	102	3.88
Hartly, DE (town) Kent County	3	3.85
Towaoc, CO (cdp) Montezuma County	42	3.83
Vineland, MN (cdp) Mille Lacs County	23	3.79
Rocky Mountain, OK (cdp) Adair County	17	3.79
Ashland, OK (town) Pittsburg County	2	3.77
Poplar, MT (city) Roosevelt County	34	3.73
Oteneagen, MN (township) Itasca County	9	3.66
La Garde, MN (township) Mahnomen County	5	3.65
Rosalie, NE (village) Thurston County	7	3.61
Belgium, MN (township) Polk County	4	3.60
Neopit, WI (cdp) Menominee County	30	3.58
Dunseith, ND (city) Rolette County	26	3.52
Havana, KS (city) Montgomery County	3	3.49
Ten Lake, MN (township) Beltrami County	35	3.48
Chilchinbito, AZ (cdp) Navajo County	16	3.46
Gaylord, KS (city) Smith County	5	3.45
Red Rock, OK (town) Noble County	10	3.41
Moose Lake, MN (township) Beltrami County	7	3.41
Saint Michaels, AZ (cdp) Apache County	44	3.40
Cayuse, OR (cdp) Umatilla County	2	3.39
Santa Ana Pueblo, NM (cdp) Sandoval County	16	3.34
Longville, MN (city) Cass County	6	3.33
Lame Deer, MT (cdp) Rosebud County	67	3.32
Cameron, AZ (cdp) Coconino County	32	3.27
Satus, WA (cdp) Yakima County	24	3.22
Max, MN (township) Itasca County	5	3.21
Ganado, AZ (cdp) Apache County	48	3.19
Laguna Seca, TX (cdp) Hidalgo County	8	3.19

Notes: (cdp) census designated place; Refer to the Explanation of Data in the front of the book for more detailed information.

American Indian tribes, not specified

Top 150 Places Sorted by Percent

(Based on places with populations of 10,000 or more)

Place	Number	%
Gallup, NM (city) McKinley County	454	2.25
Tahlequah, OK (city) Cherokee County	247	1.71
Farmington, NM (city) San Juan County	276	0.73
Flagstaff, AZ (city) Coconino County	368	0.70
Claremore, OK (city) Rogers County	109	0.69
Lumberton, NC (city) Robeson County	131	0.63
Miami, OK (city) Ottawa County	86	0.63
Ada, OK (city) Pontotoc County	94	0.60
Rapid City, SD (city) Pennington County	341	0.57
Casa Grande, AZ (city) Pinal County	139	0.55
Bemidji, MN (city) Beltrami County	59	0.50
Oneida, NY (city) Madison County	49	0.45
Oroville, CA (city) Butte County	57	0.44
Shawnee, OK (city) Pottawatomie County	118	0.41
Muskogee, OK (city) Muskogee County	152	0.40
Eloy, AZ (city) Pinal County	41	0.40
Sault Sainte Marie, MI (city) Chippewa County	64	0.39
Pierre, SD (city) Hughes County	53	0.38
Waupun, WI (city) Dodge County	40	0.37
Altamont, OR (cdp) Klamath County	71	0.36
Las Vegas, NM (city) San Miguel County	53	0.36
McKinleyville, CA (cdp) Humboldt County	47	0.35
Chowchilla, CA (city) Madera County	39	0.35
Siloam Springs, AR (city) Benton County	38	0.35
Lathrop, CA (city) San Joaquin County	37	0.35
Los Lunas, NM (village) Valencia County	35	0.35
Kingman, AZ (city) Mohave County	69	0.34
Mastic, NY (cdp) Suffolk County	52	0.34
Deming, NM (city) Luna County	46	0.33
Morgan Hill, CA (city) Santa Clara County	108	0.32
Eureka, CA (city) Humboldt County	84	0.32
Ledyard, CT (town) New London County	45	0.31
Linda, CA (cdp) Yuba County	42	0.31
Drexel Heights, AZ (cdp) Pima County	71	0.30
Clearlake, CA (city) Lake County	39	0.30
Portales, NM (city) Roosevelt County	33	0.30
Okmulgee, OK (city) Okmulgee County	38	0.29
McAlester, OK (city) Pittsburg County	50	0.28
Twentynine Palms, CA (city) San Bernardino County	41	0.28
North Valley, NM (cdp) Bernalillo County	33	0.28
Cloquet, MN (city) Carlton County	31	0.28
Gardnerville Ranchos, NV (cdp) Douglas County	31	0.28
Santa Fe, NM (city) Santa Fe County	169	0.27
Bartlesville, OK (city) Washington County	95	0.27
Houma, LA (city) Terrebonne Parish	86	0.27
Klamath Falls, OR (city) Klamath County	53	0.27
Scottsbluff, NE (city) Scotts Bluff County	40	0.27
Durango, CO (city) La Plata County	37	0.27
Mohave Valley, AZ (cdp) Mohave County	37	0.27
Olivehurst, CA (cdp) Yuba County	30	0.27
Berkley, CO (cdp) Adams County	29	0.27
Albuquerque, NM (city) Bernalillo County	1,151	0.26
West Sacramento, CA (city) Yolo County	83	0.26
Oildale, CA (cdp) Kern County	73	0.26
Sanger, CA (city) Fresno County	50	0.26
Ponca City, OK (city) Kay County	66	0.25
Bay City, TX (city) Matagorda County	46	0.25
Florence, AZ (town) Pinal County	43	0.25
Coos Bay, OR (city) Coos County	38	0.25
Lexington Park, MD (cdp) Saint Mary's County	28	0.25
Pueblo, CO (city) Pueblo County	247	0.24
Ardmore, OK (city) Carter County	58	0.24
Commerce City, CO (city) Adams County	51	0.24
Barstow, CA (city) San Bernardino County	50	0.24
Bethany, OK (city) Oklahoma County	48	0.24
El Sobrante, CA (cdp) Contra Costa County	29	0.24
Tucson, AZ (city) Pima County	1,136	0.23
Carson City, NV (special city) Carson City city	122	0.23
Sapulpa, OK (city) Creek County	44	0.23
Adelanto, CA (city) San Bernardino County	41	0.23
Sierra Vista Southeast, AZ (cdp) Cochise County	33	0.23
Camano, WA (cdp) Island County	31	0.23
Levelland, TX (city) Hockley County	30	0.23
Woodland, CA (city) Yolo County	109	0.22
Manteca, CA (city) San Joaquin County	107	0.22

Place	Number	%
South Valley, NM (cdp) Bernalillo County	85	0.22
South Salt Lake, UT (city) Salt Lake County	48	0.22
Arcata, CA (city) Humboldt County	36	0.22
Fort Campbell North, KY (cdp) Christian County	31	0.22
Marana, AZ (town) Pima County	30	0.22
Welby, CO (cdp) Adams County	28	0.22
Beaumont, CA (city) Riverside County	25	0.22
Norman, OK (city) Cleveland County	200	0.21
Baldwin Park, CA (city) Los Angeles County	157	0.21
Great Falls, MT (city) Cascade County	117	0.21
Tulare, CA (city) Tulare County	92	0.21
Madera, CA (city) Madera County	90	0.21
Auburn, WA (city) King County	83	0.21
Clifton, CO (cdp) Mesa County	37	0.21
Pendleton, OR (city) Umatilla County	35	0.21
Ukiah, CA (city) Mendocino County	32	0.21
Bixby, OK (city) Tulsa County	28	0.21
Issaquah, WA (city) King County	24	0.21
Wyandanch, NY (cdp) Suffolk County	22	0.21
Yuma, AZ (city) Yuma County	158	0.20
Las Cruces, NM (city) Dona Ana County	152	0.20
Rio Rancho, NM (city) Sandoval County	104	0.20
Superior, WI (city) Douglas County	55	0.20
Isla Vista, CA (cdp) Santa Barbara County	37	0.20
Whitney, NV (cdp) Clark County	36	0.20
Sand Springs, OK (city) Tulsa County	35	0.20
Alum Rock, CA (cdp) Santa Clara County	27	0.20
Kelso, WA (city) Cowlitz County	24	0.20
Arlington, WA (city) Snohomish County	23	0.20
Fort Morgan, CO (city) Morgan County	22	0.20
Nanakuli, HI (cdp) Honolulu County	22	0.20
Providence, RI (city) Providence County	325	0.19
Minot, ND (city) Ward County	71	0.19
Paine Field-Lake Stickney, WA (cdp) Snohomish County	47	0.19
Banning, CA (city) Riverside County	44	0.19
Brawley, CA (city) Imperial County	43	0.19
Brent, FL (cdp) Escambia County	43	0.19
Owasso, OK (city) Tulsa County	35	0.19
Langley Park, MD (cdp) Prince George's County	31	0.19
Covington, WA (city) King County	26	0.19
Arvin, CA (city) Kern County	25	0.19
North Auburn, CA (cdp) Placer County	22	0.19
Hope Mills, NC (town) Cumberland County	21	0.19
Healdsburg, CA (city) Sonoma County	20	0.19
Waianae, HI (cdp) Honolulu County	20	0.19
Crestline, CA (cdp) San Bernardino County	19	0.19
Tulsa, OK (city) Tulsa County	704	0.18
Merced, CA (city) Merced County	112	0.18
Lakewood, WA (city) Pierce County	105	0.18
Hempstead, NY (village) Nassau County	99	0.18
Olympia, WA (city) Thurston County	75	0.18
Stillwater, OK (city) Payne County	70	0.18
Bremerton, WA (city) Kitsap County	66	0.18
Fort Hood, TX (cdp) Coryell County	59	0.18
Carlsbad, NM (city) Eddy County	45	0.18
Hayesville, OR (cdp) Marion County	33	0.18
Glen Avon, CA (cdp) Riverside County	26	0.18
Peru, IN (city) Miami County	23	0.18
Green River, WY (city) Sweetwater County	21	0.18
College, AK (cdp) Fairbanks North Star Borough	20	0.18
Lindsay, CA (city) Tulare County	19	0.18
Bismarck, ND (city) Burleigh County	95	0.17
Roswell, NM (city) Chaves County	76	0.17
Parkway-South Sacramento, CA (cdp) Sacramento County	62	0.17
Ceres, CA (city) Stanislaus County	60	0.17
Los Banos, CA (city) Merced County	45	0.17
Tooele, UT (city) Tooele County	39	0.17
North Marysville, WA (cdp) Snohomish County	36	0.17
Bainbridge Island, WA (city) Kitsap County	35	0.17
Tukwila, WA (city) King County	29	0.17
Wahiawa, HI (cdp) Honolulu County	27	0.17
Carpinteria, CA (city) Santa Barbara County	24	0.17
Marysville, CA (city) Yuba County	21	0.17
Coalinga, CA (city) Fresno County	20	0.17
Coffeyville, KS (city) Montgomery County	19	0.17

Notes: (cdp) census designated place; Refer to the Explanation of Data in the front of the book for more detailed information.

Arab

Top 150 Places Sorted by Number

(Based on all places, regardless of population)

Place	Number	%
New York, NY (city) New York City	70,965	0.89
Dearborn, MI (city) Wayne County	29,344	30.01
Los Angeles, CA (city) Los Angeles County	25,937	0.70
Chicago, IL (city) Cook County	14,971	0.52
Houston, TX (city) Harris County	11,322	0.58
Detroit, MI (city) Wayne County	8,300	0.87
San Diego, CA (city) San Diego County	7,448	0.61
Jersey City, NJ (city) Hudson County	6,764	2.82
Boston, MA (city) Suffolk County	5,955	1.01
Jacksonville, FL (special city) Duval County	5,861	0.80
San Francisco, CA (city) San Francisco County	5,430	0.70
Philadelphia, PA (city) Philadelphia County	5,271	0.35
Phoenix, AZ (city) Maricopa County	5,172	0.39
Nashville-Davidson, TN (special city) Davidson County	4,761	0.87
Sterling Heights, MI (city) Macomb County	4,598	3.69
Dearborn Heights, MI (city) Wayne County	4,578	7.86
Columbus, OH (city) Franklin County	4,512	0.63
San Jose, CA (city) Santa Clara County	4,302	0.48
Dallas, TX (city) Dallas County	4,137	0.35
Glendale, CA (city) Los Angeles County	4,054	2.08
San Antonio, TX (city) Bexar County	3,787	0.33
Toledo, OH (city) Lucas County	3,668	1.17
Anaheim, CA (city) Orange County	3,494	1.07
Warren, MI (city) Macomb County	3,478	2.52
Arlington, VA (cdp) Arlington County	3,433	1.81
Charlotte, NC (city) Mecklenburg County	3,342	0.62
Hempstead, NY (town) Nassau County	3,264	0.43
Austin, TX (city) Travis County	3,177	0.48
Washington, DC (city) District of Columbia	3,120	0.55
Cleveland, OH (city) Cuyahoga County	2,916	0.61
Arlington, TX (city) Tarrant County	2,741	0.82
Yonkers, NY (city) Westchester County	2,697	1.38
Clifton, NJ (city) Passaic County	2,641	3.36
Allentown, PA (city) Lehigh County	2,638	2.47
Paterson, NJ (city) Passaic County	2,634	1.77
Raleigh, NC (city) Wake County	2,577	0.93
Troy, MI (city) Oakland County	2,570	3.17
El Cajon, CA (city) San Diego County	2,463	2.60
Bailey's Crossroads, VA (cdp) Fairfax County	2,443	10.69
Burbank, CA (city) Los Angeles County	2,434	2.43
Oklahoma City, OK (city) Oklahoma County	2,404	0.48
Pittsburgh, PA (city) Allegheny County	2,374	0.71
Lakewood, OH (city) Cuyahoga County	2,371	4.19
Bayonne, NJ (city) Hudson County	2,345	3.79
Seattle, WA (city) King County	2,321	0.41
Worcester, MA (city) Worcester County	2,292	1.33
Wichita, KS (city) Sedgwick County	2,228	0.65
Denver, CO (city) Denver County	2,193	0.40
Minneapolis, MN (city) Hennepin County	2,192	0.57
Hamtramck, MI (city) Wayne County	2,158	9.39
Portland, OR (city) Multnomah County	2,144	0.41
Oak Lawn, IL (village) Cook County	2,142	3.87
El Paso, TX (city) El Paso County	2,105	0.37
West Bloomfield, MI (township) Oakland County	2,092	3.23
Farmington Hills, MI (city) Oakland County	2,082	2.54
Tulsa, OK (city) Tulsa County	1,991	0.51
Alexandria, VA (independent city) Alexandria city	1,979	1.54
Indianapolis, IN (special city) Marion County	1,973	0.25
Livonia, MI (city) Wayne County	1,972	1.96
Huntington Beach, CA (city) Orange County	1,966	1.04
Methuen, MA (city) Essex County	1,936	4.42
Milwaukee, WI (city) Milwaukee County	1,879	0.31
Virginia Beach, VA (independent city) Virginia Beach city	1,876	0.44
Clinton, MI (cdp) Macomb County	1,869	1.95
Rancho Cucamonga, CA (city) San Bernardino County	1,866	1.46
Miami, FL (city) Miami-Dade County	1,864	0.51
Las Vegas, NV (city) Clark County	1,844	0.39
Albuquerque, NM (city) Bernalillo County	1,838	0.41
Memphis, TN (city) Shelby County	1,837	0.28
North Bergen, NJ (township) Hudson County	1,830	3.14
Ann Arbor, MI (city) Washtenaw County	1,795	1.57
Daly City, CA (city) San Mateo County	1,794	1.73
Plano, TX (city) Collin County	1,777	0.80
North Hempstead, NY (town) Nassau County	1,768	0.79
Buffalo, NY (city) Erie County	1,737	0.59
Downey, CA (city) Los Angeles County	1,724	1.61
Tucson, AZ (city) Pima County	1,715	0.35
Irvine, CA (city) Orange County	1,714	1.20
Orlando, FL (city) Orange County	1,693	0.91
Saint Clair Shores, MI (city) Macomb County	1,677	2.66
Saint Louis, MO (independent city) Saint Louis city	1,643	0.47
Torrance, CA (city) Los Angeles County	1,642	1.19
Long Beach, CA (city) Los Angeles County	1,624	0.35
Southfield, MI (city) Oakland County	1,607	2.05
Peoria, IL (city) Peoria County	1,576	1.40
Omaha, NE (city) Douglas County	1,574	0.40
Fresno, CA (city) Fresno County	1,574	0.37
Riverside, CA (city) Riverside County	1,556	0.61
Kansas City, MO (city) Jackson County	1,545	0.35
Fremont, CA (city) Alameda County	1,519	0.75
Brookhaven, NY (town) Suffolk County	1,513	0.34
Richardson, TX (city) Dallas County	1,506	1.64
Fort Worth, TX (city) Tarrant County	1,475	0.28
Baton Rouge, LA (city) East Baton Rouge Parish	1,466	0.64
Glendora, CA (city) Los Angeles County	1,456	2.93
Akron, OH (city) Summit County	1,453	0.67
Wayne, NJ (cdp) Passaic County	1,448	2.68
Canton, MI (cdp) Wayne County	1,448	1.90
Corona, CA (city) Riverside County	1,444	1.16
Annandale, VA (cdp) Fairfax County	1,418	2.58
Metairie, LA (cdp) Jefferson Parish	1,403	0.96
Quincy, MA (city) Norfolk County	1,388	1.58
Pasadena, CA (city) Los Angeles County	1,384	1.03
Parma, OH (city) Cuyahoga County	1,381	1.61
Cambridge, MA (city) Middlesex County	1,374	1.36
Sacramento, CA (city) Sacramento County	1,372	0.34
Scottsdale, AZ (city) Maricopa County	1,345	0.66
Aurora, CO (city) Arapahoe County	1,329	0.48
Kendall, FL (cdp) Miami-Dade County	1,315	1.75
Utica, NY (city) Oneida County	1,313	2.16
East Brunswick, NJ (cdp) Middlesex County	1,307	2.80
Baltimore, MD (independent city) Baltimore city	1,298	0.20
Lawrence, MA (city) Essex County	1,290	1.79
Burbank, IL (city) Cook County	1,273	4.58
Bloomfield, MI (township) Oakland County	1,272	2.96
Danbury, CT (city) Fairfield County	1,248	1.67
Grand Rapids, MI (city) Kent County	1,248	0.63
Coral Springs, FL (city) Broward County	1,247	1.06
Saint Paul, MN (city) Ramsey County	1,239	0.43
McLean, VA (cdp) Fairfax County	1,233	3.16
Pembroke Pines, FL (city) Broward County	1,230	0.90
Saint Petersburg, FL (city) Pinellas County	1,229	0.50
Lexington-Fayette, KY (special city) Fayette County	1,227	0.47
Oyster Bay, NY (town) Nassau County	1,217	0.41
Stockton, CA (city) San Joaquin County	1,214	0.50
Henderson, NV (city) Clark County	1,210	0.69
Tysons Corner, VA (cdp) Fairfax County	1,208	6.53
Lincoln, NE (city) Lancaster County	1,208	0.54
Louisville, KY (city) Jefferson County	1,203	0.47
Mission Viejo, CA (city) Orange County	1,189	1.28
Tempe, AZ (city) Maricopa County	1,187	0.75
Hollywood, FL (city) Broward County	1,183	0.85
Chula Vista, CA (city) San Diego County	1,180	0.68
Fullerton, CA (city) Orange County	1,170	0.93
Paradise, NV (cdp) Clark County	1,168	0.63
Orange, CA (city) Orange County	1,163	0.91
Santa Clarita, CA (city) Los Angeles County	1,162	0.77
Bakersfield, CA (city) Kern County	1,161	0.47
South San Francisco, CA (city) San Mateo County	1,152	1.90
Shelby, MI (cdp) Macomb County	1,147	1.76
Old Bridge, NJ (township) Middlesex County	1,140	1.89
Rochester Hills, MI (city) Oakland County	1,137	1.65
Tampa, FL (city) Hillsborough County	1,118	0.37
Lackawanna, NY (city) Erie County	1,111	5.83
Mesa, AZ (city) Maricopa County	1,109	0.28
Bridgeview, IL (village) Cook County	1,104	7.18
Charleston, WV (city) Kanawha County	1,104	2.08
Santa Clara, CA (city) Santa Clara County	1,104	1.08
Westland, MI (city) Wayne County	1,099	1.27
Lafayette, LA (city) Lafayette Parish	1,088	0.99

Notes: (cdp) census designated place; Refer to the Explanation of Data in the front of the book for more detailed information.

Arab

Top 150 Places Sorted by Percent

(Based on all places, regardless of population)

Place	Number	%
Dearborn, MI (city) Wayne County	29,344	30.01
Deal, NJ (borough) Monmouth County	242	22.62
Dunes Road, FL (cdp) Palm Beach County	104	21.99
C-Road, CA (cdp) Plumas County	21	15.11
Graf, IA (city) Dubuque County	15	15.00
Highland, ME (plantation) Somerset County	10	14.49
Bailey's Crossroads, VA (cdp) Fairfax County	2,443	10.69
Grosse Pointe, MI (township) Wayne County	266	9.70
Grosse Pointe Shores, MI (village) Wayne County	266	9.52
Hamtramck, MI (city) Wayne County	2,158	9.39
Saddle Rock, NY (village) Nassau County	74	9.36
Salix-Beauty Line Park, PA (cdp) Cambria County	105	8.76
Carrick, CA (cdp) Siskiyou County	13	8.55
Haledon, NJ (borough) Passaic County	699	8.47
Blakeslee, OH (village) Williams County	10	8.26
Smithfield, WV (town) Wetzel County	16	7.88
Dearborn Heights, MI (city) Wayne County	4,578	7.86
Hepler, KS (city) Crawford County	12	7.84
Bridgeview, IL (village) Cook County	1,104	7.18
Sholes, NE (village) Wayne County	2	7.14
Chicago Ridge, IL (village) Cook County	963	6.94
McIntosh, AL (town) Washington County	17	6.94
Clinton, NE (village) Sheridan County	2	6.67
Tysons Corner, VA (cdp) Fairfax County	1,208	6.53
Brian Head, UT (town) Iron County	6	6.52
Stratton, VT (town) Windham County	9	6.43
Pottawattamie Park, IN (town) La Porte County	19	6.31
Carlsbad North, NM (cdp) Eddy County	72	5.87
Masury, OH (cdp) Trumbull County	161	5.85
Lackawanna, NY (city) Erie County	1,111	5.83
Fullerton, PA (cdp) Lehigh County	793	5.58
McGregor, MN (township) Aitkin County	6	5.56
Hickory Hills, IL (city) Cook County	763	5.48
Whitestone Logging Camp, AK (cdp) Skagway-Hoonah-Angoon C.A.	6	5.45
Wilbur Park, MO (village) Saint Louis County	27	5.44
Rice River, MN (township) Aitkin County	9	5.42
Gilbertown, AL (town) Choctaw County	10	5.38
Grosse Pointe Woods, MI (city) Wayne County	912	5.34
Oak Park, CA (cdp) Ventura County	131	5.34
Prospect Park, NJ (borough) Passaic County	305	5.28
Foundryville, PA (cdp) Columbia County	14	5.28
Great Neck Gardens, NY (cdp) Nassau County	58	5.19
Orchard Lake Village, MI (city) Oakland County	113	5.10
Fairlawn, OH (city) Summit County	356	4.86
Salton Sea Beach, CA (cdp) Imperial County	21	4.77
Friendship Village, MD (cdp) Montgomery County	211	4.76
Madison Park, NJ (cdp) Middlesex County	327	4.75
North Kansas City, MO (city) Clay County	224	4.74
Rancho San Diego, CA (cdp) San Diego County	942	4.70
Terlton, OK (town) Pawnee County	4	4.65
Burbank, IL (city) Cook County	1,273	4.58
Methuen, MA (city) Essex County	1,936	4.42
Totowa, NJ (borough) Passaic County	422	4.29
Fairview, NJ (borough) Bergen County	565	4.26
Oak Brook, IL (village) Du Page County	358	4.24
Lakewood, OH (city) Cuyahoga County	2,371	4.19
Justice, IL (village) Cook County	507	4.19
Hoople, ND (city) Walsh County	12	4.17
Ithaca, NE (village) Saunders County	6	4.17
Dedham, MA (cdp) Norfolk County	965	4.10
Climax, MN (city) Polk County	10	4.08
Cloud Lake, FL (town) Palm Beach County	5	4.07
Hills and Dales, KY (city) Jefferson County	5	4.03
Dunn Loring, VA (cdp) Fairfax County	314	4.00
Freedom, OK (town) Woods County	10	4.00
Davis, SD (town) Turner County	4	3.96
Ephraim, WI (village) Door County	13	3.94
Crownsville, MD (cdp) Anne Arundel County	67	3.93
Holiday City, OH (village) Williams County	2	3.92
Matinicus Isle, ME (plantation) Knox County	2	3.92
Gates Mills, OH (village) Cuyahoga County	95	3.88
Belleair Beach, FL (city) Pinellas County	65	3.88
Oak Lawn, IL (village) Cook County	2,142	3.87
Sibley, ND (city) Barnes County	2	3.85
Moreland Hills, OH (village) Cuyahoga County	126	3.82
Bayonne, NJ (city) Hudson County	2,345	3.79
Norwood, MA (cdp) Norfolk County	1,070	3.74
Springdale, WA (town) Stevens County	12	3.72
Clay Center, OH (village) Ottawa County	11	3.72
Crescent Mills, CA (cdp) Plumas County	10	3.72
Bloomfield Hills, MI (city) Oakland County	146	3.71
Sterling Heights, MI (city) Macomb County	4,598	3.69
Pulawski, MI (township) Presque Isle County	14	3.64
Midvale, ID (city) Washington County	7	3.61
Elco, PA (borough) Washington County	14	3.57
Washington Township, NJ (cdp) Bergen County	316	3.54
Beaux Arts Village, WA (town) King County	11	3.53
Crossgate, KY (city) Jefferson County	9	3.53
Alvo, NE (village) Cass County	5	3.50
New Ashford, MA (town) Berkshire County	8	3.45
West Middletown, PA (borough) Washington County	5	3.45
Clark Mills, NY (cdp) Oneida County	48	3.44
Crandon Lakes, NJ (cdp) Sussex County	43	3.44
North Seekonk, MA (cdp) Bristol County	90	3.41
Millbrae, CA (city) San Mateo County	705	3.40
Gibraltar, MI (city) Wayne County	145	3.40
Moodus, CT (cdp) Middlesex County	47	3.40
New York Mills, NY (village) Oneida County	109	3.39
Clyde, CA (cdp) Contra Costa County	23	3.38
Glen Echo, MD (town) Montgomery County	8	3.38
Upper Brookville, NY (village) Nassau County	61	3.37
Clifton, NJ (city) Passaic County	2,641	3.36
Whitehall, PA (township) Lehigh County	834	3.35
Lavallette, NJ (borough) Ocean County	89	3.34
Sugar Bush Knolls, OH (village) Portage County	7	3.32
Ottawa Hills, OH (village) Lucas County	150	3.30
Bingham Farms, MI (village) Oakland County	34	3.30
Lake Belvedere Estates, FL (cdp) Palm Beach County	49	3.28
Otis, ME (town) Hancock County	18	3.28
Tierra Verde, FL (cdp) Pinellas County	116	3.27
Palos Hills, IL (city) Cook County	578	3.26
Lincolnia, VA (cdp) Fairfax County	518	3.26
Harvard, NE (city) Clay County	33	3.26
Plover, IA (city) Pocahontas County	3	3.26
New Hartford, NY (town) Oneida County	688	3.25
Hanover, PA (township) Luzerne County	372	3.25
Portville, NY (village) Cattaraugus County	34	3.24
West Bloomfield, MI (township) Oakland County	2,092	3.23
Novi, MI (township) Oakland County	6	3.23
Sasakwa, OK (town) Seminole County	5	3.21
Hanna City, IL (village) Peoria County	32	3.18
Gulf Stream, FL (town) Palm Beach County	22	3.18
Troy, MI (city) Oakland County	2,570	3.17
Lohman, MO (city) Cole County	6	3.17
McLean, VA (cdp) Fairfax County	1,233	3.16
Wesley Chapel, FL (cdp) Pasco County	186	3.16
North Bergen, NJ (township) Hudson County	1,830	3.14
Westlake, TX (town) Tarrant County	7	3.14
Wolf Trap, VA (cdp) Fairfax County	434	3.13
Doctor Phillips, FL (cdp) Orange County	302	3.13
Brandt, MN (township) Polk County	2	3.13
Lake Barcroft, VA (cdp) Fairfax County	281	3.11
Westwood, MA (town) Norfolk County	436	3.09
Grosse Pointe Park, MI (city) Wayne County	385	3.09
Mockingbird Valley, KY (city) Jefferson County	6	3.09
North Olmsted, OH (city) Cuyahoga County	1,050	3.08
East Pasadena, CA (cdp) Los Angeles County	186	3.08
Morada, CA (cdp) San Joaquin County	110	3.04
Park Ridge, NJ (borough) Bergen County	263	3.02
Falcon Heights, MN (city) Ramsey County	166	3.02
Cripple Creek, CO (city) Teller County	34	3.02
Wampsville, NY (village) Madison County	17	3.02
Saddle River, NJ (borough) Bergen County	96	3.00
Pittsfield charter, MI (township) Washtenaw County	902	2.99
Atlantic Beach, SC (town) Horry County	11	2.98
Monmouth Junction, NJ (cdp) Middlesex County	72	2.97
Bloomfield, MI (township) Oakland County	1,272	2.96
Idylwood, VA (cdp) Fairfax County	475	2.96
Olean, NY (town) Cattaraugus County	60	2.96
Lake Marcel-Stillwater, WA (cdp) King County	42	2.95

Notes: (cdp) census designated place; Refer to the Explanation of Data in the front of the book for more detailed information.

Arab

Top 150 Places Sorted by Percent

(Based on places with populations of 10,000 or more)

Place	Number	%
Dearborn, MI (city) Wayne County	29,344	30.01
Bailey's Crossroads, VA (cdp) Fairfax County	2,443	10.69
Hamtramck, MI (city) Wayne County	2,158	9.39
Dearborn Heights, MI (city) Wayne County	4,578	7.86
Bridgeview, IL (village) Cook County	1,104	7.18
Chicago Ridge, IL (village) Cook County	963	6.94
Tysons Corner, VA (cdp) Fairfax County	1,208	6.53
Lackawanna, NY (city) Erie County	1,111	5.83
Fullerton, PA (cdp) Lehigh County	793	5.58
Hickory Hills, IL (city) Cook County	763	5.48
Grosse Pointe Woods, MI (city) Wayne County	912	5.34
Rancho San Diego, CA (cdp) San Diego County	942	4.70
Burbank, IL (city) Cook County	1,273	4.58
Methuen, MA (city) Essex County	1,936	4.42
Fairview, NJ (borough) Bergen County	565	4.26
Lakewood, OH (city) Cuyahoga County	2,371	4.19
Justice, IL (village) Cook County	507	4.19
Dedham, MA (cdp) Norfolk County	965	4.10
Oak Lawn, IL (village) Cook County	2,142	3.87
Bayonne, NJ (city) Hudson County	2,345	3.79
Norwood, MA (cdp) Norfolk County	1,070	3.74
Sterling Heights, MI (city) Macomb County	4,598	3.69
Millbrae, CA (city) San Mateo County	705	3.40
Clifton, NJ (city) Passaic County	2,641	3.36
Whitehall, PA (township) Lehigh County	834	3.35
Palos Hills, IL (city) Cook County	578	3.26
Lincolnia, VA (cdp) Fairfax County	518	3.26
New Hartford, NY (town) Oneida County	688	3.25
Hanover, PA (township) Luzerne County	372	3.25
West Bloomfield, MI (township) Oakland County	2,092	3.23
Troy, MI (city) Oakland County	2,570	3.17
McLean, VA (cdp) Fairfax County	1,233	3.16
North Bergen, NJ (township) Hudson County	1,830	3.14
Wolf Trap, VA (cdp) Fairfax County	434	3.13
Westwood, MA (town) Norfolk County	436	3.09
Grosse Pointe Park, MI (city) Wayne County	385	3.09
North Olmsted, OH (city) Cuyahoga County	1,050	3.08
Pittsfield charter, MI (township) Washtenaw County	902	2.99
Bloomfield, MI (township) Oakland County	1,272	2.96
Idylwood, VA (cdp) Fairfax County	475	2.96
Little Falls, NJ (cdp) Passaic County	319	2.94
Glendora, CA (city) Los Angeles County	1,456	2.93
Westlake, OH (city) Cuyahoga County	926	2.91
Hawthorne, NJ (borough) Passaic County	521	2.86
Jersey City, NJ (city) Hudson County	6,764	2.82
East Brunswick, NJ (cdp) Middlesex County	1,307	2.80
Brooklyn, OH (city) Cuyahoga County	317	2.74
West Paterson, NJ (borough) Passaic County	298	2.71
Foxborough, MA (town) Norfolk County	438	2.70
Wayne, NJ (cdp) Passaic County	1,448	2.68
Saint Clair Shores, MI (city) Macomb County	1,677	2.66
Olean, NY (city) Cattaraugus County	408	2.66
Oak Park, MI (city) Oakland County	780	2.62
El Cajon, CA (city) San Diego County	2,463	2.60
Saddle Brook, NJ (cdp) Bergen County	342	2.60
Annandale, VA (cdp) Fairfax County	1,418	2.58
Mays Chapel, MD (cdp) Baltimore County	295	2.58
Worth, IL (village) Cook County	288	2.58
Wanaque, NJ (borough) Passaic County	264	2.57
Ocean, NJ (township) Monmouth County	687	2.55
Farmington Hills, MI (city) Oakland County	2,082	2.54
Hazel Park, MI (city) Oakland County	482	2.54
Warren, MI (city) Macomb County	3,478	2.52
Melvindale, MI (city) Wayne County	268	2.50
Pinecrest, FL (village) Miami-Dade County	477	2.49
Sunny Isles Beach, FL (city) Miami-Dade County	380	2.49
Allentown, PA (city) Lehigh County	2,638	2.47
Burbank, CA (city) Los Angeles County	2,434	2.43
Fraser, MI (city) Macomb County	369	2.41
Oakton, VA (cdp) Fairfax County	692	2.35
Harper Woods, MI (city) Wayne County	328	2.30
Coldwater, MI (city) Branch County	292	2.30
Lincoln, RI (town) Providence County	477	2.28
Garfield, NJ (city) Bergen County	676	2.27
New Kensington, PA (city) Westmoreland County	331	2.25
North Brunswick Township, NJ (cdp) Middlesex County	809	2.23
New Milford, NJ (borough) Bergen County	362	2.21
Rosemont, CA (cdp) Sacramento County	501	2.19
Ojus, FL (cdp) Miami-Dade County	365	2.19
Wilkes-Barre, PA (city) Luzerne County	934	2.17
Utica, NY (city) Oneida County	1,313	2.16
Watertown, MA (city) Middlesex County	708	2.15
Rocky River, OH (city) Cuyahoga County	444	2.14
Merrifield, VA (cdp) Fairfax County	237	2.14
Salem, NH (town) Rockingham County	600	2.13
Aliquippa, PA (city) Beaver County	249	2.13
Secaucus, NJ (town) Hudson County	336	2.12
Paramus, NJ (borough) Bergen County	542	2.11
Cliffside Park, NJ (borough) Bergen County	483	2.10
Ridgefield Park, NJ (village) Bergen County	270	2.10
Glendale, CA (city) Los Angeles County	4,054	2.08
Charleston, WV (city) Kanawha County	1,104	2.08
Avenel, NJ (cdp) Middlesex County	363	2.07
Waterville, ME (city) Kennebec County	323	2.07
Southfield, MI (city) Oakland County	1,607	2.05
Temple Terrace, FL (city) Hillsborough County	428	2.05
Sharon, MA (town) Norfolk County	356	2.05
Foothill Ranch, CA (cdp) Orange County	221	2.03
Spring Valley, CA (cdp) San Diego County	537	2.02
Casa de Oro-Mount Helix, CA (cdp) San Diego County	382	2.02
Aventura, FL (city) Miami-Dade County	505	2.00
Schiller Park, IL (village) Cook County	234	1.99
Southfield, MI (township) Oakland County	284	1.97
Livonia, MI (city) Wayne County	1,972	1.96
San Bruno, CA (city) San Mateo County	786	1.96
Madison Heights, MI (city) Oakland County	609	1.96
Clinton, MI (cdp) Macomb County	1,869	1.95
Alsip, IL (village) Cook County	388	1.95
Beverly Hills, MI (village) Oakland County	204	1.95
Rochester, MI (city) Oakland County	204	1.95
Lodi, NJ (borough) Bergen County	466	1.94
New Castle, PA (city) Lawrence County	507	1.93
Whitestown, NY (town) Oneida County	358	1.92
Springfield, VA (cdp) Fairfax County	577	1.91
Canton, MI (cdp) Wayne County	1,448	1.90
South San Francisco, CA (city) San Mateo County	1,152	1.90
Fairview Park, OH (city) Cuyahoga County	333	1.90
Ridgefield, NJ (borough) Bergen County	206	1.90
Old Bridge, NJ (township) Middlesex County	1,140	1.89
Fountain Valley, CA (city) Orange County	1,039	1.89
Flint, MI (township) Genesee County	638	1.89
Orland Park, IL (village) Cook County	960	1.88
East Grand Rapids, MI (city) Kent County	202	1.87
Eastpointe, MI (city) Macomb County	631	1.85
Harrison, MI (cdp) Macomb County	453	1.85
Colts Neck, NJ (township) Monmouth County	228	1.85
Brecksville, OH (city) Cuyahoga County	245	1.84
Los Alamitos, CA (city) Orange County	207	1.84
Arlington, VA (cdp) Arlington County	3,433	1.81
Parma Heights, OH (city) Cuyahoga County	389	1.80
East Hanover, NJ (township) Morris County	205	1.80
Lawrence, MA (city) Essex County	1,290	1.79
Plymouth Township, MI (cdp) Wayne County	494	1.79
Duarte, CA (city) Los Angeles County	385	1.79
Paterson, NJ (city) Passaic County	2,634	1.77
Shelby, MI (cdp) Macomb County	1,147	1.76
Kendall, FL (cdp) Miami-Dade County	1,315	1.75
Cypress, CA (city) Orange County	814	1.75
Franconia, VA (cdp) Fairfax County	561	1.75
Miami Lakes, FL (cdp) Miami-Dade County	396	1.74
Northville, MI (township) Wayne County	367	1.74
Farmington, MI (city) Oakland County	181	1.74
Daly City, CA (city) San Mateo County	1,794	1.73
Easton, PA (city) Northampton County	455	1.73
Herndon, VA (town) Fairfax County	375	1.73
North Arlington, NJ (borough) Bergen County	262	1.73
Center, PA (township) Beaver County	199	1.73
South Brunswick, NJ (township) Middlesex County	650	1.72
Ives Estates, FL (cdp) Miami-Dade County	297	1.71
Scott Township, PA (cdp) Allegheny County	294	1.70

Notes: (cdp) census designated place; Refer to the Explanation of Data in the front of the book for more detailed information.

Arab: Arab/Arabic

Top 150 Places Sorted by Number

(Based on all places, regardless of population)

Place	Number	%
New York, NY (city) New York City	14,572	0.18
Chicago, IL (city) Cook County	5,458	0.19
Dearborn, MI (city) Wayne County	5,027	5.14
Detroit, MI (city) Wayne County	3,614	0.38
Los Angeles, CA (city) Los Angeles County	3,002	0.08
Houston, TX (city) Harris County	2,728	0.14
Jacksonville, FL (special city) Duval County	1,602	0.22
San Diego, CA (city) San Diego County	1,375	0.11
San Francisco, CA (city) San Francisco County	1,311	0.17
Hamtramck, MI (city) Wayne County	1,285	5.59
Phoenix, AZ (city) Maricopa County	1,246	0.09
Paterson, NJ (city) Passaic County	1,171	0.78
Oak Lawn, IL (village) Cook County	1,070	1.93
San Antonio, TX (city) Bexar County	1,011	0.09
Philadelphia, PA (city) Philadelphia County	1,002	0.07
Columbus, OH (city) Franklin County	921	0.13
Milwaukee, WI (city) Milwaukee County	893	0.15
Boston, MA (city) Suffolk County	871	0.15
Yonkers, NY (city) Westchester County	854	0.44
Rancho Cucamonga, CA (city) San Bernardino County	853	0.67
Dearborn Heights, MI (city) Wayne County	826	1.42
Dallas, TX (city) Dallas County	824	0.07
Bailey's Crossroads, VA (cdp) Fairfax County	817	3.57
Cleveland, OH (city) Cuyahoga County	805	0.17
Burbank, IL (city) Cook County	788	2.83
Charlotte, NC (city) Mecklenburg County	783	0.14
Sterling Heights, MI (city) Macomb County	775	0.62
Jersey City, NJ (city) Hudson County	770	0.32
San Jose, CA (city) Santa Clara County	768	0.09
Warren, MI (city) Macomb County	753	0.54
Bridgeview, IL (village) Cook County	743	4.83
Clifton, NJ (city) Passaic County	729	0.93
Lakewood, OH (city) Cuyahoga County	721	1.27
Arlington, TX (city) Tarrant County	645	0.19
Lackawanna, NY (city) Erie County	617	3.24
Anaheim, CA (city) Orange County	617	0.19
Daly City, CA (city) San Mateo County	588	0.57
Tysons Corner, VA (cdp) Fairfax County	581	3.14
Arlington, VA (cdp) Arlington County	573	0.30
El Cajon, CA (city) San Diego County	568	0.60
Alexandria, VA (independent city) Alexandria city	553	0.43
Fresno, CA (city) Fresno County	546	0.13
Chicago Ridge, IL (village) Cook County	539	3.88
Irvine, CA (city) Orange County	527	0.37
Allentown, PA (city) Lehigh County	524	0.49
Raleigh, NC (city) Wake County	523	0.19
Oklahoma City, OK (city) Oklahoma County	523	0.10
Buffalo, NY (city) Erie County	522	0.18
Austin, TX (city) Travis County	496	0.08
Oakland, CA (city) Alameda County	495	0.12
Washington, DC (city) District of Columbia	491	0.09
Southfield, MI (city) Oakland County	479	0.61
Memphis, TN (city) Shelby County	476	0.07
Portland, OR (city) Multnomah County	467	0.09
Hempstead, NY (town) Nassau County	460	0.06
Richardson, TX (city) Dallas County	447	0.49
Tucson, AZ (city) Pima County	446	0.09
Bakersfield, CA (city) Kern County	432	0.17
Fort Worth, TX (city) Tarrant County	431	0.08
Moreno Valley, CA (city) Riverside County	425	0.30
North Bergen, NJ (township) Hudson County	416	0.71
Seattle, WA (city) King County	409	0.07
Orland Park, IL (village) Cook County	401	0.78
Livonia, MI (city) Wayne County	396	0.39
Albuquerque, NM (city) Bernalillo County	394	0.09
West Bloomfield, MI (township) Oakland County	392	0.60
Tulsa, OK (city) Tulsa County	391	0.10
Wichita, KS (city) Sedgwick County	389	0.11
Hickory Hills, IL (city) Cook County	381	2.73
Nashville-Davidson, TN (special city) Davidson County	379	0.07
Syracuse, NY (city) Onondaga County	370	0.25
Fremont, CA (city) Alameda County	368	0.18
Farmington Hills, MI (city) Oakland County	366	0.45
Westland, MI (city) Wayne County	366	0.42
Aurora, CO (city) Arapahoe County	366	0.13
Denver, CO (city) Denver County	364	0.07
Toledo, OH (city) Lucas County	359	0.11
Rancho San Diego, CA (cdp) San Diego County	358	1.79
San Bernardino, CA (city) San Bernardino County	357	0.19
Rochester, NY (city) Monroe County	351	0.16
Cambridge, MA (city) Middlesex County	342	0.34
Kansas City, MO (city) Jackson County	342	0.08
Stockton, CA (city) San Joaquin County	341	0.14
Alsip, IL (village) Cook County	338	1.70
North Olmsted, OH (city) Cuyahoga County	335	0.98
Tempe, AZ (city) Maricopa County	335	0.21
Tampa, FL (city) Hillsborough County	333	0.11
Miami, FL (city) Miami-Dade County	333	0.09
Tinley Park, IL (village) Cook County	324	0.67
Pittsburgh, PA (city) Allegheny County	324	0.10
Burbank, CA (city) Los Angeles County	322	0.32
South San Francisco, CA (city) San Mateo County	321	0.53
Canton, MI (cdp) Wayne County	313	0.41
Modesto, CA (city) Stanislaus County	310	0.16
Garden Grove, CA (city) Orange County	296	0.18
Glendale, CA (city) Los Angeles County	294	0.15
Durham, NC (city) Durham County	292	0.16
Justice, IL (village) Cook County	290	2.40
Long Beach, CA (city) Los Angeles County	283	0.06
Westminster, CA (city) Orange County	281	0.32
Santa Clara, CA (city) Santa Clara County	281	0.28
Riverside, CA (city) Riverside County	280	0.11
Ypsilanti, MI (township) Washtenaw County	279	0.57
Las Vegas, NV (city) Clark County	279	0.06
Louisville, KY (city) Jefferson County	277	0.11
Mesa, AZ (city) Maricopa County	275	0.07
Annandale, VA (cdp) Fairfax County	271	0.49
Chula Vista, CA (city) San Diego County	269	0.15
Spring Valley, NV (cdp) Clark County	268	0.23
Spokane, WA (city) Spokane County	264	0.13
Miami Lakes, FL (cdp) Miami-Dade County	261	1.15
San Bruno, CA (city) San Mateo County	258	0.64
El Paso, TX (city) El Paso County	257	0.05
Glendale, AZ (city) Maricopa County	256	0.12
Lancaster, CA (city) Los Angeles County	254	0.21
Metairie, LA (cdp) Jefferson Parish	254	0.17
Orlando, FL (city) Orange County	254	0.14
Palos Hills, IL (city) Cook County	253	1.42
Akron, OH (city) Summit County	248	0.11
Haledon, NJ (borough) Passaic County	247	2.99
Lincoln, NE (city) Lancaster County	245	0.11
Lexington-Fayette, KY (special city) Fayette County	245	0.09
Downey, CA (city) Los Angeles County	243	0.23
Paradise, NV (cdp) Clark County	242	0.13
Pasadena, CA (city) Los Angeles County	240	0.18
San Mateo, CA (city) San Mateo County	239	0.26
Rocky Mount, NC (city) Nash County	238	0.42
Westlake, OH (city) Cuyahoga County	237	0.74
Troy, MI (city) Oakland County	236	0.29
Sacramento, CA (city) Sacramento County	236	0.06
Ann Arbor, MI (city) Washtenaw County	235	0.21
Oak Park, MI (city) Oakland County	233	0.78
Temple Terrace, FL (city) Hillsborough County	231	1.11
Shelby, MI (cdp) Macomb County	230	0.35
Minneapolis, MN (city) Hennepin County	230	0.06
Fontana, CA (city) San Bernardino County	229	0.18
Irving, TX (city) Dallas County	229	0.12
Rohnert Park, CA (city) Sonoma County	228	0.54
Torrance, CA (city) Los Angeles County	228	0.17
Palm Bay, FL (city) Brevard County	226	0.28
Fullerton, CA (city) Orange County	225	0.18
Virginia Beach, VA (independent city) Virginia Beach city	225	0.05
Pittsfield charter, MI (township) Washtenaw County	224	0.74
Fort Collins, CO (city) Larimer County	223	0.19
Berwyn, IL (city) Cook County	222	0.41
Buena Park, CA (city) Orange County	220	0.28
Pembroke Pines, FL (city) Broward County	220	0.16
Corona, CA (city) Riverside County	216	0.17
Saint Paul, MN (city) Ramsey County	214	0.07
Everett, WA (city) Snohomish County	212	0.23

Notes: (cdp) census designated place; Refer to the Explanation of Data in the front of the book for more detailed information.

Arab: Arab/Arabic

Top 150 Places Sorted by Percent

(Based on all places, regardless of population)

Place	Number	%
Graf, IA (city) Dubuque County	11	11.00
Hepler, KS (city) Crawford County	12	7.84
Hamtramck, MI (city) Wayne County	1,285	5.59
Dearborn, MI (city) Wayne County	5,027	5.14
Bridgeview, IL (village) Cook County	743	4.83
Salton Sea Beach, CA (cdp) Imperial County	21	4.77
Oak Park, CA (cdp) Ventura County	96	3.91
Chicago Ridge, IL (village) Cook County	539	3.88
Springdale, WA (town) Stevens County	12	3.72
Bailey's Crossroads, VA (cdp) Fairfax County	817	3.57
Alvo, NE (village) Cass County	5	3.50
Moodus, CT (cdp) Middlesex County	47	3.40
Prospect Park, NJ (borough) Passaic County	194	3.36
Lackawanna, NY (city) Erie County	617	3.24
Novi, MI (township) Oakland County	6	3.23
Tysons Corner, VA (cdp) Fairfax County	581	3.14
Haledon, NJ (borough) Passaic County	247	2.99
Parnell, MN (township) Traverse County	2	2.94
Burbank, IL (city) Cook County	788	2.83
Westmanland, ME (town) Aroostook County	2	2.78
Buttonwillow, CA (cdp) Kern County	35	2.76
Hickory Hills, IL (city) Cook County	381	2.73
Thompsons, TX (town) Fort Bend County	6	2.59
Topeka, IN (town) La Grange County	29	2.50
Justice, IL (village) Cook County	290	2.40
Fredericktown-Millsboro, PA (cdp) Washington County	26	2.32
Metaline, WA (town) Pend Oreille County	4	2.23
Chester, TX (town) Tyler County	6	2.19
Dunn Loring, VA (cdp) Fairfax County	165	2.10
Orland Hills, IL (village) Cook County	140	2.04
Kennedy, CA (cdp) San Joaquin County	74	2.04
Davis Junction, IL (village) Ogle County	9	1.98
Watermill, NY (cdp) Suffolk County	33	1.96
Oak Lawn, IL (village) Cook County	1,070	1.93
Oak Ridge, TX (town) Kaufman County	8	1.91
Dalworthington Gardens, TX (city) Tarrant County	42	1.90
Wilburton Number One, PA (cdp) Columbia County	5	1.88
Rivergrove, OR (city) Clackamas County	6	1.86
Lanare, CA (cdp) Fresno County	10	1.85
Accord, NY (cdp) Ulster County	13	1.84
Orchard Lake Village, MI (city) Oakland County	40	1.81
Worth, IL (village) Cook County	201	1.80
Rancho San Diego, CA (cdp) San Diego County	358	1.79
Port La Belle, FL (cdp) Hendry County	58	1.79
Glenaire, MO (city) Clay County	10	1.79
Chauncey, OH (village) Athens County	19	1.77
Albion, WA (town) Whitman County	10	1.72
Ewington, MN (township) Jackson County	4	1.71
Alsip, IL (village) Cook County	338	1.70
Austwell, TX (city) Refugio County	3	1.68
Rose Hill Acres, TX (city) Hardin County	8	1.63
Clyde, CA (cdp) Contra Costa County	11	1.62
Circleville, KS (city) Jackson County	3	1.62
Lenox, GA (town) Cook County	14	1.60
Broad Fields, KY (city) Jefferson County	4	1.52
Coldwater, MI (city) Branch County	185	1.46
Wesley Chapel, FL (cdp) Pasco County	86	1.46
Lavallette, NJ (borough) Ocean County	39	1.46
Channel Lake, IL (cdp) Lake County	26	1.46
Cassville, WV (cdp) Monongalia County	23	1.44
Dearborn Heights, MI (city) Wayne County	826	1.42
Palos Hills, IL (city) Cook County	253	1.42
Piney Point Village, TX (city) Harris County	48	1.42
Friendship, AR (town) Hot Spring County	3	1.42
Miramiguoa Park, MO (village) Franklin County	2	1.41
Palm Shores, FL (town) Brevard County	11	1.39
Galeville, NY (cdp) Onondaga County	60	1.36
Brownsdale, MN (city) Mower County	10	1.36
Davy, WV (town) McDowell County	5	1.35
Seven Corners, VA (cdp) Fairfax County	118	1.33
Park Ridge, NJ (borough) Bergen County	116	1.33
Coldwater, MI (township) Branch County	47	1.30
Lakewood, OH (city) Cuyahoga County	721	1.27
Fairview, NJ (borough) Bergen County	169	1.27
Lewisburg, WV (city) Greenbrier County	47	1.27
Rice, MN (township) Clearwater County	2	1.27
Xenia, IL (village) Clay County	5	1.25
Morada, CA (cdp) San Joaquin County	45	1.24
Massanutten, VA (cdp) Rockingham County	24	1.24
West Buechel, KY (city) Jefferson County	16	1.23
Walthill, NE (village) Thurston County	11	1.23
Tranquillity, CA (cdp) Fresno County	10	1.23
Fort Greely, AK (cdp) Southeast Fairbanks Census Area	6	1.23
West Burke, VT (village) Caledonia County	4	1.23
Oak Brook, IL (village) Du Page County	102	1.21
Westvale, NY (cdp) Onondaga County	62	1.20
Colma, CA (town) San Mateo County	14	1.20
Amity, NY (town) Allegany County	26	1.17
Melvindale, MI (city) Wayne County	124	1.16
Placid Lakes, FL (cdp) Highlands County	35	1.16
Gulf Stream, FL (town) Palm Beach County	8	1.16
Traver, CA (cdp) Tulare County	8	1.16
Miami Lakes, FL (cdp) Miami-Dade County	261	1.15
Gateway, FL (cdp) Lee County	35	1.15
Hazel, KY (city) Calloway County	5	1.13
Shady Hills, FL (cdp) Pasco County	87	1.12
Castine, ME (town) Hancock County	15	1.12
Temple Terrace, FL (city) Hillsborough County	231	1.11
Quilcene, WA (cdp) Jefferson County	7	1.11
Wallace, NC (town) Duplin County	36	1.10
Bass Lake, WI (town) Washburn County	6	1.10
Richfield, OH (village) Summit County	36	1.09
Kaanapali, HI (cdp) Maui County	15	1.09
Harrisburg, MO (town) Boone County	2	1.09
Bedford Park, IL (village) Cook County	6	1.07
Liberty, NJ (township) Warren County	29	1.06
Bloomfield Hills, MI (city) Oakland County	41	1.04
Manorhaven, NY (village) Nassau County	63	1.03
East Bethlehem, PA (township) Washington County	26	1.03
East Haddam, CT (town) Middlesex County	84	1.01
Keego Harbor, MI (city) Oakland County	28	1.01
Waucoma, IA (city) Fayette County	3	1.01
Greatwood, TX (cdp) Fort Bend County	65	0.99
North Olmsted, OH (city) Cuyahoga County	335	0.98
Haverhill, FL (town) Palm Beach County	15	0.98
Calabash, NC (town) Brunswick County	7	0.98
Hendren, WI (town) Clark County	5	0.97
Lake Providence, LA (town) East Carroll Parish	48	0.96
Pere Marquette charter, MI (township) Mason County	21	0.96
Los Alamitos, CA (city) Orange County	107	0.95
Lyncourt, NY (cdp) Onondaga County	41	0.94
Lake Belvedere Estates, FL (cdp) Palm Beach County	14	0.94
Greene, PA (township) Mercer County	11	0.94
Byers, TX (city) Clay County	5	0.94
Clifton, NJ (city) Passaic County	729	0.93
Secaucus, NJ (town) Hudson County	148	0.93
Green Valley, CA (cdp) Solano County	18	0.93
Valley View, TX (town) Cooke County	7	0.93
Rosiclare, IL (city) Hardin County	11	0.90
Martin's Additions, MD (village) Montgomery County	8	0.90
Upper Freehold, NJ (township) Monmouth County	38	0.89
Brodheadsville, PA (cdp) Monroe County	13	0.89
Olga, FL (cdp) Lee County	13	0.88
Saint Louisville, OH (village) Licking County	3	0.88
Fullerton, PA (cdp) Lehigh County	124	0.87
Bel-Ridge, MO (village) Saint Louis County	27	0.87
Empire, LA (cdp) Plaquemines Parish	18	0.87
Lehigh, PA (township) Northampton County	84	0.86
Saltillo, TN (town) Hardin County	3	0.86
Willis, TX (city) Montgomery County	35	0.85
Virginia Gardens, FL (village) Miami-Dade County	20	0.85
Shenandoah, VA (town) Page County	16	0.85
Hurstbourne Acres, KY (city) Jefferson County	13	0.84
Danvers, IL (village) McLean County	10	0.84
Inyokern, CA (cdp) Kern County	8	0.84
Gurley, NE (village) Cheyenne County	2	0.84
Marshall, IL (city) Clark County	31	0.83
Thorndale, PA (cdp) Chester County	30	0.83
Ben Lomond, CA (cdp) Santa Cruz County	19	0.83
Villa Park, CA (city) Orange County	50	0.82

Notes: (cdp) census designated place; Refer to the Explanation of Data in the front of the book for more detailed information.

Arab: Arab/Arabic

Top 150 Places Sorted by Percent

(Based on places with populations of 10,000 or more)

Place	Number	%
Hamtramck, MI (city) Wayne County	1,285	5.59
Dearborn, MI (city) Wayne County	5,027	5.14
Bridgeview, IL (village) Cook County	743	4.83
Chicago Ridge, IL (village) Cook County	539	3.88
Bailey's Crossroads, VA (cdp) Fairfax County	817	3.57
Lackawanna, NY (city) Erie County	617	3.24
Tysons Corner, VA (cdp) Fairfax County	581	3.14
Burbank, IL (city) Cook County	788	2.83
Hickory Hills, IL (city) Cook County	381	2.73
Justice, IL (village) Cook County	290	2.40
Oak Lawn, IL (village) Cook County	1,070	1.93
Worth, IL (village) Cook County	201	1.80
Rancho San Diego, CA (cdp) San Diego County	358	1.79
Alsip, IL (village) Cook County	338	1.70
Coldwater, MI (city) Branch County	185	1.46
Dearborn Heights, MI (city) Wayne County	826	1.42
Palos Hills, IL (city) Cook County	253	1.42
Lakewood, OH (city) Cuyahoga County	721	1.27
Fairview, NJ (borough) Bergen County	169	1.27
Melvindale, MI (city) Wayne County	124	1.16
Miami Lakes, FL (cdp) Miami-Dade County	261	1.15
Temple Terrace, FL (city) Hillsborough County	231	1.11
North Olmsted, OH (city) Cuyahoga County	335	0.98
Los Alamitos, CA (city) Orange County	107	0.95
Clifton, NJ (city) Passaic County	729	0.93
Secaucus, NJ (town) Hudson County	148	0.93
Fullerton, PA (cdp) Lehigh County	124	0.87
Windsor Locks, CT (cdp) Hartford County	98	0.81
Arlington, NY (cdp) Dutchess County	99	0.80
Paterson, NJ (city) Passaic County	1,171	0.78
Orland Park, IL (village) Cook County	401	0.78
Oak Park, MI (city) Oakland County	233	0.78
Belle Glade, FL (city) Palm Beach County	115	0.77
Schiller Park, IL (village) Cook County	91	0.77
Oak Forest, IL (city) Cook County	211	0.75
West Paterson, NJ (borough) Passaic County	82	0.75
Westlake, OH (city) Cuyahoga County	237	0.74
Pittsfield charter, MI (township) Washtenaw County	224	0.74
Ives Estates, FL (cdp) Miami-Dade County	127	0.73
Grosse Pointe Woods, MI (city) Wayne County	124	0.73
North Bergen, NJ (township) Hudson County	416	0.71
Idylwood, VA (cdp) Fairfax County	112	0.70
Millbrae, CA (city) San Mateo County	143	0.69
Merrifield, VA (cdp) Fairfax County	77	0.69
Rancho Cucamonga, CA (city) San Bernardino County	853	0.67
Tinley Park, IL (village) Cook County	324	0.67
Tyngsborough, MA (town) Middlesex County	74	0.67
Bloomingdale, IL (village) Du Page County	142	0.66
West Carrollton City, OH (city) Montgomery County	92	0.66
Milford, MI (township) Oakland County	100	0.65
Wolf Trap, VA (cdp) Fairfax County	90	0.65
Guttenberg, NJ (town) Hudson County	69	0.65
San Bruno, CA (city) San Mateo County	258	0.64
Sterling Heights, MI (city) Macomb County	775	0.62
Lincolnwood, IL (village) Cook County	77	0.62
Martin, TN (city) Weakley County	65	0.62
Southfield, MI (city) Oakland County	479	0.61
Griffin, GA (city) Spalding County	144	0.61
Oneida, NY (city) Madison County	67	0.61
El Cajon, CA (city) San Diego County	568	0.60
West Bloomfield, MI (township) Oakland County	392	0.60
Hazel Park, MI (city) Oakland County	114	0.60
Roselle, IL (village) Du Page County	138	0.59
Herndon, VA (town) Fairfax County	127	0.59
New Territory, TX (cdp) Fort Bend County	82	0.59
Barstow, CA (city) San Bernardino County	121	0.58
Sunny Isles Beach, FL (city) Miami-Dade County	88	0.58
Daly City, CA (city) San Mateo County	588	0.57
Ypsilanti, MI (township) Washtenaw County	279	0.57
Garfield, NJ (city) Bergen County	171	0.57
Elmwood Park, IL (village) Cook County	144	0.57
Chalmette, LA (cdp) Saint Bernard Parish	181	0.56
Vienna, MI (township) Genesee County	73	0.56
Fairmount, NY (cdp) Onondaga County	59	0.55
Warren, MI (city) Macomb County	753	0.54
Rohnert Park, CA (city) Sonoma County	228	0.54
Salina, NY (town) Onondaga County	179	0.54
Springfield, VA (cdp) Fairfax County	163	0.54
Sunset, FL (cdp) Miami-Dade County	92	0.54
South San Francisco, CA (city) San Mateo County	321	0.53
Whitehall, PA (township) Lehigh County	131	0.53
Wixom, MI (city) Oakland County	70	0.53
McLean, VA (cdp) Fairfax County	201	0.52
Flint, MI (township) Genesee County	176	0.52
West Linn, OR (city) Clackamas County	115	0.52
Teays Valley, WV (cdp) Putnam County	66	0.52
Lyons, IL (village) Cook County	53	0.52
Franklin, WI (city) Milwaukee County	152	0.51
Wade Hampton, SC (cdp) Greenville County	103	0.51
Rolla, MO (city) Phelps County	84	0.51
Timberlane, LA (cdp) Jefferson Parish	58	0.51
Allentown, PA (city) Lehigh County	524	0.49
Richardson, TX (city) Dallas County	447	0.49
Annandale, VA (cdp) Fairfax County	271	0.49
Palisades Park, NJ (borough) Bergen County	83	0.49
Conway, FL (cdp) Orange County	70	0.49
North Valley, NM (cdp) Bernalillo County	60	0.49
Canyon Rim, UT (cdp) Salt Lake County	52	0.49
Bensenville, IL (village) Du Page County	99	0.48
Wallington, NJ (borough) Bergen County	56	0.48
Lodi, NJ (borough) Bergen County	112	0.47
Albany, CA (city) Alameda County	77	0.47
North Arlington, NJ (borough) Bergen County	72	0.47
White, PA (township) Indiana County	66	0.47
San Gabriel, CA (city) Los Angeles County	180	0.46
Cooper City, FL (city) Broward County	127	0.46
Alpena, MI (city) Alpena County	51	0.46
Farmington Hills, MI (city) Oakland County	366	0.45
Westerville, OH (city) Franklin County	159	0.45
Franconia, VA (cdp) Fairfax County	144	0.45
Elmwood Park, NJ (borough) Bergen County	86	0.45
Mokena, IL (village) Will County	66	0.45
Yonkers, NY (city) Westchester County	854	0.44
West New York, NJ (town) Hudson County	203	0.44
Kentwood, MI (city) Kent County	199	0.44
Alexandria, VA (independent city) Alexandria city	553	0.43
Bell, CA (city) Los Angeles County	158	0.43
Spring Valley, CA (cdp) San Diego County	114	0.43
Genesee, MI (township) Genesee County	103	0.43
Ferndale, MI (city) Oakland County	94	0.43
South Laurel, MD (cdp) Prince George's County	90	0.43
Highland, MI (township) Oakland County	82	0.43
Sanger, CA (city) Fresno County	81	0.43
Goodings Grove, IL (cdp) Will County	73	0.43
Westland, MI (city) Wayne County	366	0.42
Rocky Mount, NC (city) Nash County	238	0.42
Kissimmee, FL (city) Osceola County	201	0.42
The Hammocks, FL (cdp) Miami-Dade County	199	0.42
Duncanville, TX (city) Dallas County	152	0.42
Middleburg Heights, OH (city) Cuyahoga County	66	0.42
South Houston, TX (city) Harris County	66	0.42
Forest City, FL (cdp) Seminole County	53	0.42
Big Rapids, MI (city) Mecosta County	45	0.42
Willistown, PA (township) Chester County	42	0.42
Canton, MI (cdp) Wayne County	313	0.41
Berwyn, IL (city) Cook County	222	0.41
Bloomfield, MI (township) Oakland County	176	0.41
Chantilly, VA (cdp) Fairfax County	168	0.41
Grand Blanc, MI (township) Genesee County	123	0.41
Superior, MI (township) Washtenaw County	44	0.41
Wanaque, NJ (borough) Passaic County	42	0.41
Centreville, VA (cdp) Fairfax County	192	0.40
South Plainfield, NJ (borough) Middlesex County	87	0.40
Fairland, MD (cdp) Montgomery County	86	0.40
Prospect Heights, IL (city) Cook County	70	0.40
Sharon, PA (city) Mercer County	65	0.40
Azalea Park, FL (cdp) Orange County	44	0.40
Suffern, NY (village) Rockland County	44	0.40
Flushing, MI (township) Genesee County	41	0.40
Livonia, MI (city) Wayne County	396	0.39

Notes: (cdp) census designated place; Refer to the Explanation of Data in the front of the book for more detailed information.

Arab: Egyptian

Top 150 Places Sorted by Number

(Based on all places, regardless of population)

Place	Number	%
New York, NY (city) New York City	17,223	0.22
Los Angeles, CA (city) Los Angeles County	5,792	0.16
Jersey City, NJ (city) Hudson County	4,820	2.01
Bayonne, NJ (city) Hudson County	1,958	3.17
Houston, TX (city) Harris County	1,286	0.07
East Brunswick, NJ (cdp) Middlesex County	1,128	2.41
Hempstead, NY (town) Nassau County	965	0.13
Nashville-Davidson, TN (special city) Davidson County	918	0.17
Old Bridge, NJ (township) Middlesex County	900	1.49
Downey, CA (city) Los Angeles County	898	0.84
Philadelphia, PA (city) Philadelphia County	893	0.06
Anaheim, CA (city) Orange County	764	0.23
Huntington Beach, CA (city) Orange County	693	0.36
San Jose, CA (city) Santa Clara County	638	0.07
Edison, NJ (cdp) Middlesex County	562	0.58
Woodbridge, NJ (township) Middlesex County	562	0.58
San Diego, CA (city) San Diego County	561	0.05
Chicago, IL (city) Cook County	556	0.02
Brookhaven, NY (town) Suffolk County	552	0.12
Washington, DC (city) District of Columbia	526	0.09
Indianapolis, IN (special city) Marion County	519	0.07
Torrance, CA (city) Los Angeles County	499	0.36
Columbus, OH (city) Franklin County	491	0.07
Bellflower, CA (city) Los Angeles County	488	0.67
Minneapolis, MN (city) Hennepin County	488	0.13
North Bergen, NJ (township) Hudson County	485	0.83
Glendale, CA (city) Los Angeles County	467	0.24
Burbank, CA (city) Los Angeles County	454	0.45
North Hempstead, NY (town) Nassau County	431	0.19
San Francisco, CA (city) San Francisco County	423	0.05
West Covina, CA (city) Los Angeles County	387	0.37
Oyster Bay, NY (town) Nassau County	373	0.13
South Brunswick, NJ (township) Middlesex County	363	0.96
Boston, MA (city) Suffolk County	363	0.06
Sayreville, NJ (borough) Middlesex County	355	0.88
Troy, MI (city) Oakland County	355	0.44
Raleigh, NC (city) Wake County	348	0.13
Arlington, VA (cdp) Arlington County	336	0.18
Phoenix, AZ (city) Maricopa County	336	0.03
Cleveland, OH (city) Cuyahoga County	329	0.07
Islip, NY (town) Suffolk County	318	0.10
Baltimore, MD (independent city) Baltimore city	318	0.05
Corona, CA (city) Riverside County	309	0.25
Virginia Beach, VA (independent city) Virginia Beach city	306	0.07
Irvine, CA (city) Orange County	303	0.21
Huntington, NY (town) Suffolk County	303	0.16
Charlotte, NC (city) Mecklenburg County	303	0.06
Hamilton, NJ (township) Mercer County	301	0.34
Bloomfield, NJ (cdp) Essex County	300	0.63
Ann Arbor, MI (city) Washtenaw County	299	0.26
Riverside, CA (city) Riverside County	293	0.11
North Brunswick Township, NJ (cdp) Middlesex County	292	0.80
Madison Park, NJ (cdp) Middlesex County	286	4.15
Franklin, NJ (township) Somerset County	285	0.56
Rancho Cucamonga, CA (city) San Bernardino County	285	0.22
Diamond Bar, CA (city) Los Angeles County	278	0.49
Pittsburgh, PA (city) Allegheny County	278	0.08
Oakton, VA (cdp) Fairfax County	276	0.94
Arcadia, CA (city) Los Angeles County	275	0.52
Alexandria, VA (independent city) Alexandria city	273	0.21
Columbia, MD (cdp) Howard County	272	0.31
Colton, CA (city) San Bernardino County	266	0.55
Mission Viejo, CA (city) Orange County	266	0.29
Santa Monica, CA (city) Los Angeles County	261	0.31
Avenel, NJ (cdp) Middlesex County	259	1.48
Plano, TX (city) Collin County	257	0.12
Madison, WI (city) Dane County	248	0.12
Parsippany-Troy Hills, NJ (township) Morris County	244	0.48
Henderson, NV (city) Clark County	242	0.14
Cerritos, CA (city) Los Angeles County	240	0.47
Santa Clara, CA (city) Santa Clara County	231	0.23
Pasadena, CA (city) Los Angeles County	231	0.17
Clifton, NJ (city) Passaic County	228	0.29
Valley Stream, NY (village) Nassau County	226	0.62
Hackensack, NJ (city) Bergen County	223	0.52
Costa Mesa, CA (city) Orange County	221	0.20
Sterling Heights, MI (city) Macomb County	221	0.18
Dallas, TX (city) Dallas County	218	0.02
Palmdale, CA (city) Los Angeles County	217	0.19
Santa Clarita, CA (city) Los Angeles County	217	0.14
Seattle, WA (city) King County	215	0.04
Dana Point, CA (city) Orange County	213	0.61
Fridley, MN (city) Anoka County	212	0.77
Fullerton, CA (city) Orange County	207	0.16
Dearborn, MI (city) Wayne County	206	0.21
Altamonte Springs, FL (city) Seminole County	204	0.49
Rowland Heights, CA (cdp) Los Angeles County	204	0.42
San Antonio, TX (city) Bexar County	203	0.02
Bailey's Crossroads, VA (cdp) Fairfax County	202	0.88
Kearny, NJ (town) Hudson County	202	0.50
Laguna Niguel, CA (city) Orange County	202	0.33
Aliso Viejo, CA (cdp) Orange County	201	0.50
Long Beach, CA (city) Los Angeles County	200	0.04
Moorpark, CA (city) Ventura County	195	0.62
Greensboro, NC (city) Guilford County	193	0.09
Fountain Valley, CA (city) Orange County	191	0.35
Sugar Land, TX (city) Fort Bend County	190	0.30
Wayne, NJ (cdp) Passaic County	189	0.35
Coral Springs, FL (city) Broward County	189	0.16
Yonkers, NY (city) Westchester County	183	0.09
West Orange, NJ (cdp) Essex County	181	0.40
Orange, CA (city) Orange County	181	0.14
Sacramento, CA (city) Sacramento County	181	0.04
La Mirada, CA (city) Los Angeles County	179	0.38
Fresno, CA (city) Fresno County	179	0.04
Rutherford, NJ (borough) Bergen County	174	0.96
Smithtown, NY (town) Suffolk County	174	0.15
Las Vegas, NV (city) Clark County	174	0.04
Annandale, VA (cdp) Fairfax County	173	0.31
Arlington, TX (city) Tarrant County	173	0.05
Belleville, NJ (cdp) Essex County	172	0.48
Scotch Plains, NJ (cdp) Union County	170	0.75
Elizabeth, NJ (city) Union County	170	0.14
Cary, NC (town) Wake County	168	0.18
West Windsor, NJ (township) Mercer County	167	0.76
Temple City, CA (city) Los Angeles County	167	0.50
Culver City, CA (city) Los Angeles County	167	0.43
Allentown, PA (city) Lehigh County	167	0.16
Jacksonville, FL (special city) Duval County	167	0.02
Victorville, CA (city) San Bernardino County	166	0.26
Aurora, CO (city) Arapahoe County	165	0.06
Ojus, FL (cdp) Miami-Dade County	164	0.98
Framingham, MA (cdp) Middlesex County	164	0.25
East Windsor, NJ (township) Mercer County	163	0.65
Garfield, NJ (city) Bergen County	163	0.55
Glendora, CA (city) Los Angeles County	163	0.33
Burke, VA (cdp) Fairfax County	162	0.28
Fremont, CA (city) Alameda County	162	0.08
Ridgefield Park, NJ (village) Bergen County	161	1.25
Secaucus, NJ (town) Hudson County	159	1.00
Hawthorne, CA (city) Los Angeles County	159	0.19
Walnut Creek, CA (city) Contra Costa County	158	0.24
Clarkstown, NY (town) Rockland County	158	0.19
Durham, NC (city) Durham County	157	0.08
Scottsdale, AZ (city) Maricopa County	157	0.08
Pittsfield charter, MI (township) Washtenaw County	155	0.51
Bakersfield, CA (city) Kern County	155	0.06
Denver, CO (city) Denver County	155	0.03
New Brunswick, NJ (city) Middlesex County	154	0.32
Pico Rivera, CA (city) Los Angeles County	154	0.24
Piscataway, NJ (township) Middlesex County	153	0.30
Reston, VA (cdp) Fairfax County	153	0.27
Somerset, NJ (cdp) Somerset County	152	0.66
Ellicott City, MD (cdp) Howard County	152	0.27
West New York, NJ (town) Hudson County	150	0.33
Concord, CA (city) Contra Costa County	150	0.12
Honolulu, HI (cdp) Honolulu County	150	0.04
Towson, MD (cdp) Baltimore County	149	0.29
Gloucester, NJ (township) Camden County	148	0.23
Revere, MA (city) Suffolk County	147	0.31

Notes: (cdp) census designated place; Refer to the Explanation of Data in the front of the book for more detailed information.

Arab: Egyptian

Top 150 Places Sorted by Percent

(Based on all places, regardless of population)

Place	Number	%
Madison Park, NJ (cdp) Middlesex County	286	4.15
Crandon Lakes, NJ (cdp) Sussex County	43	3.44
Bayonne, NJ (city) Hudson County	1,958	3.17
Belleair Beach, FL (city) Pinellas County	46	2.75
Monmouth Junction, NJ (cdp) Middlesex County	66	2.73
East Brunswick, NJ (cdp) Middlesex County	1,128	2.41
Brownville, NJ (cdp) Middlesex County	62	2.37
Plainsboro Center, NJ (cdp) Middlesex County	52	2.19
Espy, PA (cdp) Columbia County	31	2.15
Jersey City, NJ (city) Hudson County	4,820	2.01
Morris, WI (town) Shawano County	11	1.97
Lemont, PA (cdp) Centre County	43	1.93
Boydton, VA (town) Mecklenburg County	9	1.90
Sudden Valley, WA (cdp) Whatcom County	76	1.82
Poquonock Bridge, CT (cdp) New London County	28	1.82
Bear Valley Springs, CA (cdp) Kern County	78	1.81
Dayton, NJ (cdp) Middlesex County	111	1.73
Woodridge, NY (village) Sullivan County	15	1.68
Gold River, CA (cdp) Sacramento County	140	1.67
Hayesville, NC (town) Clay County	5	1.67
Fanwood, NJ (borough) Union County	119	1.66
Rolling Oaks, FL (cdp) Broward County	23	1.62
Golden's Bridge, NY (cdp) Westchester County	25	1.61
Rockaway, NJ (borough) Morris County	103	1.59
Islandia, NY (village) Suffolk County	48	1.57
Manalapan, FL (town) Palm Beach County	5	1.55
Falcon Heights, MN (city) Ramsey County	84	1.53
Old Bridge, NJ (township) Middlesex County	900	1.49
Avenel, NJ (cdp) Middlesex County	259	1.48
New Auburn, MN (township) Sibley County	7	1.46
Haviland, NY (cdp) Dutchess County	53	1.42
Butler Beach, FL (cdp) Saint Johns County	63	1.39
South Hooksett, NH (cdp) Merrimack County	72	1.37
Sanctuary, TX (town) Parker County	4	1.37
Lake Barcroft, VA (cdp) Fairfax County	123	1.36
Seaside Heights, NJ (borough) Ocean County	43	1.36
Friendship Village, MD (cdp) Montgomery County	59	1.33
Riverdale, NJ (borough) Morris County	33	1.32
Oak Brook, IL (village) Du Page County	109	1.29
Chadds Ford, PA (township) Delaware County	41	1.29
Beaux Arts Village, WA (town) King County	4	1.28
Ridgefield Park, NJ (village) Bergen County	161	1.25
Valencia West, AZ (cdp) Pima County	30	1.22
Eagleville, PA (cdp) Montgomery County	51	1.16
Canton Valley, CT (cdp) Hartford County	19	1.16
South Russell, OH (village) Geauga County	46	1.14
Hornick, IA (city) Woodbury County	3	1.12
Fairview, NJ (borough) Bergen County	141	1.06
Ottawa Hills, OH (village) Lucas County	48	1.06
Montebello, NY (village) Rockland County	38	1.05
Portland, PA (borough) Northampton County	6	1.05
La Habra Heights, CA (city) Los Angeles County	56	1.04
Stillwater, NJ (township) Sussex County	43	1.01
Lincoln Park, NY (cdp) Ulster County	23	1.01
Rio Grande, OH (village) Gallia County	9	1.01
Secaucus, NJ (town) Hudson County	159	1.00
Pepper Pike, OH (city) Cuyahoga County	60	0.99
Ojus, FL (cdp) Miami-Dade County	164	0.98
Bedminster, NJ (township) Somerset County	81	0.98
Mount Pocono, PA (borough) Monroe County	27	0.98
Willow Springs, IL (village) Cook County	48	0.97
South Brunswick, NJ (township) Middlesex County	363	0.96
Rutherford, NJ (borough) Bergen County	174	0.96
Tierra Verde, FL (cdp) Pinellas County	34	0.96
Berger, MO (city) Franklin County	2	0.96
Fern Park, FL (cdp) Seminole County	79	0.95
Spotswood, NJ (borough) Middlesex County	75	0.95
Schroeder, MN (township) Cook County	2	0.95
Oakton, VA (cdp) Fairfax County	276	0.94
Kendall Park, NJ (cdp) Middlesex County	86	0.94
Milltown, NJ (borough) Middlesex County	66	0.94
Manorhaven, NY (village) Nassau County	58	0.94
Manhasset Hills, NY (cdp) Nassau County	34	0.93
Riceboro, GA (city) Liberty County	7	0.92
Searingtown, NY (cdp) Nassau County	46	0.91

Place	Number	%
Redington Beach, FL (town) Pinellas County	15	0.91
Marshallton, PA (cdp) Northumberland County	13	0.90
New London, PA (township) Chester County	41	0.89
Trappe, MD (town) Talbot County	10	0.89
Crystal Lake Park, MO (city) Saint Louis County	4	0.89
Sayreville, NJ (borough) Middlesex County	355	0.88
Bailey's Crossroads, VA (cdp) Fairfax County	202	0.88
Lincolnia, VA (cdp) Fairfax County	140	0.88
Warrenton, NC (town) Warren County	7	0.88
Melville, NY (cdp) Suffolk County	125	0.86
Kendall Green, FL (cdp) Broward County	27	0.86
Bechtelsville, PA (borough) Berks County	8	0.86
New Braintree, MA (town) Worcester County	8	0.86
Eastampton, NJ (township) Burlington County	53	0.85
Pittstown, NY (town) Rensselaer County	48	0.85
Harbor Isle, NY (cdp) Nassau County	12	0.85
Downey, CA (city) Los Angeles County	898	0.84
Raritan, NJ (borough) Somerset County	53	0.84
Monticello, IN (city) White County	47	0.84
North Bergen, NJ (township) Hudson County	485	0.83
Cocoa Beach, FL (city) Brevard County	103	0.83
Wolf Trap, VA (cdp) Fairfax County	113	0.81
Potsdam, NY (village) Saint Lawrence County	77	0.81
North Brunswick Township, NJ (cdp) Middlesex County	292	0.80
Montville, ME (town) Waldo County	8	0.80
Farwell, MI (village) Clare County	7	0.80
Westwood, MI (cdp) Kalamazoo County	72	0.79
East Rutherford, NJ (borough) Bergen County	69	0.79
Premont, TX (city) Jim Wells County	22	0.79
Crescent Springs, KY (city) Kenton County	28	0.78
Heritage Village, CT (cdp) New Haven County	27	0.78
Fridley, MN (city) Anoka County	212	0.77
Wanaque, NJ (borough) Passaic County	79	0.77
Ralston, NE (city) Douglas County	48	0.77
East Freehold, NJ (cdp) Monmouth County	39	0.77
Pomona, NJ (cdp) Atlantic County	31	0.77
Pennsbury, PA (township) Chester County	27	0.77
Butterfield, MO (village) Barry County	3	0.77
West Windsor, NJ (township) Mercer County	167	0.76
Roscoe, IL (village) Winnebago County	48	0.76
Scotch Plains, NJ (cdp) Union County	170	0.75
Pulaski, NY (village) Oswego County	18	0.75
Bartonville, TX (town) Denton County	9	0.75
Cockeysville, MD (cdp) Baltimore County	144	0.74
Saint John, IN (town) Lake County	62	0.74
Ventnor City, NJ (city) Atlantic County	94	0.73
South Amboy, NJ (city) Middlesex County	58	0.73
Bermuda Dunes, CA (cdp) Riverside County	44	0.73
Leetsdale, PA (borough) Allegheny County	9	0.73
North Springfield, VA (cdp) Fairfax County	66	0.72
Woodmere, OH (village) Cuyahoga County	6	0.72
Lake Butter, FL (cdp) Orange County	50	0.71
Woodmore, MD (cdp) Prince George's County	43	0.71
Washington, NJ (township) Mercer County	72	0.70
Washington, CT (town) Litchfield County	25	0.70
North Plainfield, NJ (borough) Somerset County	145	0.69
The Village of Indian Hill, OH (city) Hamilton County	40	0.69
Bal Harbour, FL (village) Miami-Dade County	23	0.69
Bound Brook, NJ (borough) Somerset County	69	0.68
Dunn Loring, VA (cdp) Fairfax County	53	0.68
Atlantic Highlands, NJ (borough) Monmouth County	32	0.68
Nassau Bay, TX (city) Harris County	29	0.68
Luna Pier, MI (city) Monroe County	10	0.68
Port Republic, NJ (city) Atlantic County	7	0.68
Bellflower, CA (city) Los Angeles County	488	0.67
Millstone, NJ (township) Monmouth County	60	0.67
Pine Bush, NY (cdp) Orange County	10	0.67
Almond, NY (village) Allegany County	3	0.67
Somerset, NJ (cdp) Somerset County	152	0.66
Helmetta, NJ (borough) Middlesex County	12	0.66
Golden Heights, FL (cdp) Broward County	4	0.66
East Windsor, NJ (township) Mercer County	163	0.65
Holmdel, NJ (township) Monmouth County	103	0.65
Sleepy Hollow, NY (village) Westchester County	60	0.65
Twin Rivers, NJ (cdp) Mercer County	48	0.65

Notes: (cdp) census designated place; Refer to the Explanation of Data in the front of the book for more detailed information.

Arab: Egyptian

Top 150 Places Sorted by Percent

(Based on places with populations of 10,000 or more)

Place	Number	%
Bayonne, NJ (city) Hudson County	1,958	3.17
East Brunswick, NJ (cdp) Middlesex County	1,128	2.41
Jersey City, NJ (city) Hudson County	4,820	2.01
Old Bridge, NJ (township) Middlesex County	900	1.49
Avenel, NJ (cdp) Middlesex County	259	1.48
Ridgefield Park, NJ (village) Bergen County	161	1.25
Fairview, NJ (borough) Bergen County	141	1.06
Secaucus, NJ (town) Hudson County	159	1.00
Ojus, FL (cdp) Miami-Dade County	164	0.98
South Brunswick, NJ (township) Middlesex County	363	0.96
Rutherford, NJ (borough) Bergen County	174	0.96
Oakton, VA (cdp) Fairfax County	276	0.94
Sayreville, NJ (borough) Middlesex County	355	0.88
Bailey's Crossroads, VA (cdp) Fairfax County	202	0.88
Lincolnia, VA (cdp) Fairfax County	140	0.88
Melville, NY (cdp) Suffolk County	125	0.86
Downey, CA (city) Los Angeles County	898	0.84
North Bergen, NJ (township) Hudson County	485	0.83
Cocoa Beach, FL (city) Brevard County	103	0.83
Wolf Trap, VA (cdp) Fairfax County	113	0.81
North Brunswick Township, NJ (cdp) Middlesex County	292	0.80
Fridley, MN (city) Anoka County	212	0.77
Wanaque, NJ (borough) Passaic County	79	0.77
West Windsor, NJ (township) Mercer County	167	0.76
Scotch Plains, NJ (cdp) Union County	170	0.75
Cockeysville, MD (cdp) Baltimore County	144	0.74
Ventnor City, NJ (city) Atlantic County	94	0.73
Washington, NJ (township) Mercer County	72	0.70
North Plainfield, NJ (borough) Somerset County	145	0.69
Bound Brook, NJ (borough) Somerset County	69	0.68
Bellflower, CA (city) Los Angeles County	488	0.67
Somerset, NJ (cdp) Somerset County	152	0.66
East Windsor, NJ (township) Mercer County	163	0.65
Holmdel, NJ (township) Monmouth County	103	0.65
Clark, NJ (cdp) Union County	94	0.64
Clemson, SC (city) Pickens County	78	0.64
Bloomfield, NJ (cdp) Essex County	300	0.63
Valley Stream, NY (village) Nassau County	226	0.62
Moorpark, CA (city) Ventura County	195	0.62
Washington, NJ (township) Morris County	109	0.62
Burr Ridge, IL (village) Du Page County	64	0.62
Dana Point, CA (city) Orange County	213	0.61
North Arlington, NJ (borough) Bergen County	92	0.61
Hooksett, NH (town) Merrimack County	72	0.61
Edison, NJ (cdp) Middlesex County	562	0.58
Woodbridge, NJ (township) Middlesex County	562	0.58
Colts Neck, NJ (township) Monmouth County	71	0.58
Seaford, NY (cdp) Nassau County	90	0.57
Sunny Isles Beach, FL (city) Miami-Dade County	87	0.57
Franklin, NJ (township) Somerset County	285	0.56
North Ogden, UT (city) Weber County	84	0.56
Colton, CA (city) San Bernardino County	266	0.55
Garfield, NJ (city) Bergen County	163	0.55
Duarte, CA (city) Los Angeles County	117	0.54
Arcadia, CA (city) Los Angeles County	275	0.52
Hackensack, NJ (city) Bergen County	223	0.52
Mercerville-Hamilton Square, NJ (cdp) Mercer County	137	0.52
Montgomery, NJ (township) Somerset County	91	0.52
Vienna, VA (town) Fairfax County	75	0.52
Pittsfield charter, MI (township) Washtenaw County	155	0.51
Kearny, NJ (town) Hudson County	202	0.50
Aliso Viejo, CA (cdp) Orange County	201	0.50
Temple City, CA (city) Los Angeles County	167	0.50
Carteret, NJ (borough) Middlesex County	104	0.50
Diamond Bar, CA (city) Los Angeles County	278	0.49
Altamonte Springs, FL (city) Seminole County	204	0.49
South Saint Paul, MN (city) Dakota County	99	0.49
South Middleton, PA (township) Cumberland County	63	0.49
Parsippany-Troy Hills, NJ (township) Morris County	244	0.48
Belleville, NJ (cdp) Essex County	172	0.48
Plainsboro, NJ (township) Middlesex County	97	0.48
Potsdam, NY (town) Saint Lawrence County	77	0.48
South River, NJ (borough) Middlesex County	74	0.48
Roselle Park, NJ (borough) Union County	64	0.48
Morganville, NJ (cdp) Monmouth County	54	0.48
Cerritos, CA (city) Los Angeles County	240	0.47
Orange, CT (cdp) New Haven County	62	0.47
Wallington, NJ (borough) Bergen County	54	0.47
Burbank, CA (city) Los Angeles County	454	0.45
Tustin Foothills, CA (cdp) Orange County	107	0.45
Parma Heights, OH (city) Cuyahoga County	98	0.45
Isla Vista, CA (cdp) Santa Barbara County	82	0.45
South Orange, NJ (cdp) Essex County	76	0.45
River Forest, IL (village) Cook County	52	0.45
Troy, MI (city) Oakland County	355	0.44
Duluth, GA (city) Gwinnett County	99	0.44
Hazlet, NJ (township) Monmouth County	93	0.44
Glenn Dale, MD (cdp) Prince George's County	56	0.44
Culver City, CA (city) Los Angeles County	167	0.43
Franconia, VA (cdp) Fairfax County	136	0.43
Lawndale, CA (city) Los Angeles County	136	0.43
Nutley, NJ (cdp) Essex County	118	0.43
Roselle, NJ (borough) Union County	91	0.43
East San Gabriel, CA (cdp) Los Angeles County	63	0.43
Little Ferry, NJ (borough) Bergen County	46	0.43
Rowland Heights, CA (cdp) Los Angeles County	204	0.42
Herndon, VA (town) Fairfax County	90	0.42
North Branford, CT (town) New Haven County	59	0.42
Selden, NY (cdp) Suffolk County	90	0.41
Fords, NJ (cdp) Middlesex County	62	0.41
Tenafly, NJ (borough) Bergen County	56	0.41
Stanford, CA (cdp) Santa Clara County	54	0.41
Justice, IL (village) Cook County	50	0.41
West Orange, NJ (cdp) Essex County	181	0.40
Manalapan, NJ (township) Monmouth County	135	0.40
Eustis, FL (city) Lake County	62	0.40
Pinecrest, FL (village) Miami-Dade County	74	0.39
Wantage, NJ (township) Sussex County	41	0.39
La Mirada, CA (city) Los Angeles County	179	0.38
La Verne, CA (city) Los Angeles County	122	0.38
Walnut, CA (city) Los Angeles County	114	0.38
Monterey, CA (city) Monterey County	113	0.38
Palos Hills, IL (city) Cook County	68	0.38
Kings Park, NY (cdp) Suffolk County	62	0.38
Druid Hills, GA (cdp) De Kalb County	48	0.38
Somerville, NJ (borough) Somerset County	48	0.38
East Hanover, NJ (township) Morris County	43	0.38
West Covina, CA (city) Los Angeles County	387	0.37
Picnic Point-North Lynnwood, WA (cdp) Snohomish County	85	0.37
Mayfield Heights, OH (city) Cuyahoga County	71	0.37
Lake Wales, FL (city) Polk County	38	0.37
Huntington Beach, CA (city) Orange County	693	0.36
Torrance, CA (city) Los Angeles County	499	0.36
Teaneck, NJ (cdp) Bergen County	143	0.36
Stroud, PA (township) Monroe County	50	0.36
Colonial Park, PA (cdp) Dauphin County	47	0.36
Cypress Lake, FL (cdp) Lee County	44	0.36
West Paterson, NJ (borough) Passaic County	40	0.36
Town and Country, MO (city) Saint Louis County	39	0.36
Fountain Valley, CA (city) Orange County	191	0.35
Wayne, NJ (cdp) Passaic County	189	0.35
Laguna Hills, CA (city) Orange County	108	0.35
New Providence, NJ (borough) Union County	42	0.35
Groton, CT (city) New London County	35	0.35
Hamilton, NJ (township) Mercer County	301	0.34
Colleyville, TX (city) Tarrant County	66	0.34
Aberdeen, NJ (township) Monmouth County	59	0.34
Ocean City, NJ (city) Cape May County	52	0.34
Grand Terrace, CA (city) San Bernardino County	40	0.34
Laguna Niguel, CA (city) Orange County	202	0.33
Glendora, CA (city) Los Angeles County	163	0.33
West New York, NJ (town) Hudson County	150	0.33
Jackson, NJ (township) Ocean County	143	0.33
Ormond Beach, FL (city) Volusia County	119	0.33
Long Branch, NJ (city) Monmouth County	104	0.33
Livingston, NJ (cdp) Essex County	91	0.33
Kalamazoo, MI (township) Kalamazoo County	72	0.33
Hillside, NJ (cdp) Union County	71	0.33
Raritan, NJ (township) Hunterdon County	65	0.33
Albany, CA (city) Alameda County	54	0.33

Notes: (cdp) census designated place; Refer to the Explanation of Data in the front of the book for more detailed information.

Arab: Iraqi

Top 150 Places Sorted by Number

(Based on all places, regardless of population)

Place	Number	%
Dearborn, MI (city) Wayne County	2,042	2.09
Sterling Heights, MI (city) Macomb County	1,384	1.11
El Cajon, CA (city) San Diego County	1,237	1.30
West Bloomfield, MI (township) Oakland County	973	1.50
Detroit, MI (city) Wayne County	966	0.10
New York, NY (city) New York City	957	0.01
Chicago, IL (city) Cook County	931	0.03
Warren, MI (city) Macomb County	906	0.66
Los Angeles, CA (city) Los Angeles County	812	0.02
Southfield, MI (city) Oakland County	753	0.96
Nashville-Davidson, TN (special city) Davidson County	598	0.11
San Diego, CA (city) San Diego County	579	0.05
Farmington Hills, MI (city) Oakland County	499	0.61
Phoenix, AZ (city) Maricopa County	460	0.03
Glendale, CA (city) Los Angeles County	453	0.23
Rancho San Diego, CA (cdp) San Diego County	448	2.24
Troy, MI (city) Oakland County	438	0.54
Oak Park, MI (city) Oakland County	412	1.38
North Hempstead, NY (town) Nassau County	334	0.15
San Jose, CA (city) Santa Clara County	320	0.04
Saint Louis, MO (independent city) Saint Louis city	318	0.09
Spring Valley, CA (cdp) San Diego County	271	1.02
Philadelphia, PA (city) Philadelphia County	264	0.02
Skokie, IL (village) Cook County	244	0.39
Madison Heights, MI (city) Oakland County	237	0.76
Houston, TX (city) Harris County	227	0.01
Lincoln, NE (city) Lancaster County	214	0.09
Bloomfield, MI (township) Oakland County	209	0.49
Ann Arbor, MI (city) Washtenaw County	195	0.17
Hazel Park, MI (city) Oakland County	188	0.99
Arlington, TX (city) Tarrant County	187	0.06
Casa de Oro-Mount Helix, CA (cdp) San Diego County	178	0.94
Jacksonville, FL (special city) Duval County	169	0.02
Dallas, TX (city) Dallas County	168	0.01
La Mesa, CA (city) San Diego County	164	0.30
Everett, WA (city) Snohomish County	158	0.17
Bostonia, CA (cdp) San Diego County	154	1.04
Wichita, KS (city) Sedgwick County	152	0.04
Annandale, VA (cdp) Fairfax County	138	0.25
Memphis, TN (city) Shelby County	130	0.02
Hempstead, NY (town) Nassau County	127	0.02
Rochester Hills, MI (city) Oakland County	125	0.18
Minneapolis, MN (city) Hennepin County	123	0.03
Toledo, OH (city) Lucas County	121	0.04
Glendale, AZ (city) Maricopa County	118	0.05
North Kansas City, MO (city) Clay County	113	2.39
Chula Vista, CA (city) San Diego County	113	0.06
Hamtramck, MI (city) Wayne County	111	0.48
Columbus, OH (city) Franklin County	111	0.02
San Francisco, CA (city) San Francisco County	110	0.01
Royal Oak, MI (city) Oakland County	109	0.18
Erie, PA (city) Erie County	109	0.11
Louisville, KY (city) Jefferson County	109	0.04
Santa Clara, CA (city) Santa Clara County	108	0.11
Modesto, CA (city) Stanislaus County	106	0.06
Cedar Rapids, IA (city) Linn County	105	0.09
Baltimore, MD (independent city) Baltimore city	105	0.02
Escondido, CA (city) San Diego County	98	0.07
Washington, DC (city) District of Columbia	97	0.02
Bridgeport, CT (city) Fairfield County	96	0.07
Mishawaka, IN (city) Saint Joseph County	93	0.20
Newport Beach, CA (city) Orange County	92	0.13
Miami, FL (city) Miami-Dade County	89	0.02
Virginia Beach, VA (independent city) Virginia Beach city	89	0.02
Columbia, MO (city) Boone County	87	0.10
Oak Hills Place, LA (cdp) East Baton Rouge Parish	86	1.08
Beverly Hills, CA (city) Los Angeles County	86	0.25
Kansas City, MO (city) Jackson County	84	0.02
Henderson, NV (city) Clark County	83	0.05
Fremont, CA (city) Alameda County	83	0.04
Atlanta, GA (city) Fulton County	80	0.02
Shelby, MI (cdp) Macomb County	79	0.12
Fort Worth, TX (city) Tarrant County	79	0.01
Jamul, CA (cdp) San Diego County	77	1.29
Millcreek, UT (cdp) Salt Lake County	77	0.25
Kent, WA (city) King County	77	0.10
Boston, MA (city) Suffolk County	77	0.01
South Amherst, MA (cdp) Hampshire County	75	1.49
Amherst, MA (town) Hampshire County	75	0.22
Lansing, MI (city) Ingham County	75	0.06
Olean, NY (city) Cattaraugus County	72	0.47
Portland, OR (city) Multnomah County	72	0.01
University Gardens, NY (cdp) Nassau County	71	1.71
Columbia, MD (cdp) Howard County	71	0.08
Mount Morris, MI (township) Genesee County	70	0.29
Macomb, MI (township) Macomb County	69	0.14
Eagan, MN (city) Dakota County	69	0.11
Oceanside, CA (city) San Diego County	69	0.04
Roanoke, VA (independent city) Roanoke city	68	0.07
Springfield, IL (city) Sangamon County	68	0.06
Moreno Valley, CA (city) Riverside County	68	0.05
Mesa, AZ (city) Maricopa County	68	0.02
Orange, CA (city) Orange County	67	0.05
Salt Lake City, UT (city) Salt Lake County	67	0.04
Irving, TX (city) Dallas County	64	0.03
Foothill Ranch, CA (cdp) Orange County	63	0.58
Tarrytown, NY (village) Westchester County	62	0.56
McKinney, TX (city) Collin County	62	0.11
Canton, MI (cdp) Wayne County	62	0.08
Greenburgh, NY (town) Westchester County	62	0.07
Manchester, NH (city) Hillsborough County	61	0.06
Harrison, NY (village) Westchester County	60	0.25
Denver, CO (city) Denver County	60	0.01
Affton, MO (cdp) Saint Louis County	59	0.28
Sunnyvale, CA (city) Santa Clara County	59	0.04
Albuquerque, NM (city) Bernalillo County	59	0.01
Moorhead, MN (city) Clay County	58	0.18
Des Plaines, IL (city) Cook County	58	0.10
Coon Rapids, MN (city) Anoka County	58	0.09
Bakersfield, CA (city) Kern County	58	0.02
Princeton, NJ (township) Mercer County	57	0.36
McLean, VA (cdp) Fairfax County	56	0.14
Milpitas, CA (city) Santa Clara County	56	0.09
Gilbert, AZ (town) Maricopa County	56	0.05
Oyster Bay, NY (town) Nassau County	56	0.02
Dearborn Heights, MI (city) Wayne County	55	0.09
Passaic, NJ (city) Passaic County	55	0.08
Newtown, PA (township) Delaware County	53	0.45
Whitemarsh, PA (township) Montgomery County	53	0.32
Calabasas, CA (city) Los Angeles County	53	0.26
Niles, IL (village) Cook County	52	0.17
Riverside, CA (city) Riverside County	52	0.02
Charlotte, NC (city) Mecklenburg County	52	0.01
Seattle, WA (city) King County	52	0.01
Southfield, MI (township) Oakland County	51	0.35
Rancho Santa Margarita, CA (city) Orange County	51	0.11
Burke, VA (cdp) Fairfax County	51	0.09
Turlock, CA (city) Stanislaus County	51	0.09
Swarthmore, PA (borough) Delaware County	50	0.81
Boise City, ID (city) Ada County	50	0.03
Scottsdale, AZ (city) Maricopa County	50	0.02
Oklahoma City, OK (city) Oklahoma County	50	0.01
Rochester, MI (city) Oakland County	48	0.46
Wixom, MI (city) Oakland County	48	0.36
Lorton, VA (cdp) Fairfax County	48	0.27
Tustin Foothills, CA (cdp) Orange County	47	0.20
Grand Blanc, MI (township) Genesee County	47	0.16
Sioux Falls, SD (city) Minnehaha County	47	0.04
Aurora, CO (city) Arapahoe County	47	0.02
Cedarhurst, NY (village) Nassau County	46	0.75
Mayfield Heights, OH (city) Cuyahoga County	46	0.24
Newton, MA (city) Middlesex County	46	0.05
Amarillo, TX (city) Potter County	46	0.03
Chattanooga, TN (city) Hamilton County	46	0.03
Holly, MI (village) Oakland County	45	0.73
Holly, MI (township) Oakland County	45	0.45
Beverly Hills, MI (village) Oakland County	45	0.43
Maryland Heights, MO (city) Saint Louis County	45	0.17
Utica, NY (city) Oneida County	45	0.07
Palmdale, CA (city) Los Angeles County	45	0.04

Notes: (cdp) census designated place; Refer to the Explanation of Data in the front of the book for more detailed information.

Arab: Iraqi

Top 150 Places Sorted by Percent

(Based on all places, regardless of population)

Place	Number	%
Carrick, CA (cdp) Siskiyou County	13	8.55
Sholes, NE (village) Wayne County	2	7.14
Saddle Rock, NY (village) Nassau County	34	4.30
Great Neck Gardens, NY (cdp) Nassau County	30	2.69
McFarland, KS (city) Wabaunsee County	7	2.67
North Kansas City, MO (city) Clay County	113	2.39
Rancho San Diego, CA (cdp) San Diego County	448	2.24
Lee, IL (village) Lee County	6	2.21
Gilgo-Oak Beach-Captree, NY (cdp) Suffolk County	7	2.17
Dearborn, MI (city) Wayne County	2,042	2.09
University Gardens, NY (cdp) Nassau County	71	1.71
Saddle Rock Estates, NY (cdp) Nassau County	7	1.59
Orchard Lake Village, MI (city) Oakland County	34	1.53
West Bloomfield, MI (township) Oakland County	973	1.50
South Amherst, MA (cdp) Hampshire County	75	1.49
Oak Park, MI (city) Oakland County	412	1.38
El Cajon, CA (city) San Diego County	1,237	1.30
Village of Clarkston, MI (city) Oakland County	13	1.30
Jamul, CA (cdp) San Diego County	77	1.29
Crest, CA (cdp) San Diego County	32	1.15
Sterling Heights, MI (city) Macomb County	1,384	1.11
Oak Hills Place, LA (cdp) East Baton Rouge Parish	86	1.08
Elysburg, PA (cdp) Northumberland County	22	1.08
Bostonia, CA (cdp) San Diego County	154	1.04
Spring Valley, CA (cdp) San Diego County	271	1.02
Hazel Park, MI (city) Oakland County	188	0.99
Southfield, MI (city) Oakland County	753	0.96
Casa de Oro-Mount Helix, CA (cdp) San Diego County	178	0.94
Samak, UT (cdp) Summit County	2	0.87
Haworth, NJ (borough) Bergen County	29	0.86
Williamston, MI (city) Ingham County	28	0.84
Swarthmore, PA (borough) Delaware County	50	0.81
Searingtown, NY (cdp) Nassau County	39	0.77
Madison Heights, MI (city) Oakland County	237	0.76
Cedarhurst, NY (village) Nassau County	46	0.75
Rio Communities North, NM (cdp) Valencia County	12	0.74
Holly, MI (village) Oakland County	45	0.73
Great Neck Estates, NY (village) Nassau County	20	0.71
Warren, MI (city) Macomb County	906	0.66
Russell Gardens, NY (village) Nassau County	7	0.65
Greencastle, PA (borough) Franklin County	24	0.64
Lawrence, MI (township) Van Buren County	20	0.62
Farmington Hills, MI (city) Oakland County	499	0.61
Portage, PA (borough) Cambria County	17	0.60
Wormleysburg, PA (borough) Cumberland County	16	0.60
Belle Terre, NY (village) Suffolk County	5	0.60
Foothill Ranch, CA (cdp) Orange County	63	0.58
Ralpho, PA (township) Northumberland County	22	0.58
Yantis, TX (town) Wood County	2	0.58
Leet, PA (township) Allegheny County	9	0.57
Tarrytown, NY (village) Westchester County	62	0.56
Conrad, IA (city) Grundy County	6	0.56
Troy, MI (city) Oakland County	438	0.54
Olmsted Falls, OH (city) Cuyahoga County	40	0.51
Medina, WA (city) King County	15	0.50
Bloomfield, MI (township) Oakland County	209	0.49
Frankenmuth, MI (township) Saginaw County	10	0.49
Langston, OK (town) Logan County	8	0.49
Kensington, NY (village) Nassau County	6	0.49
Oakview, MO (village) Clay County	2	0.49
Hamtramck, MI (city) Wayne County	111	0.48
Monte Sereno, CA (city) Santa Clara County	17	0.48
Olean, NY (city) Cattaraugus County	72	0.47
Chadds Ford, PA (township) Delaware County	15	0.47
Summerfield, MI (township) Clare County	2	0.47
Rochester, MI (city) Oakland County	48	0.46
Kingsley, KY (city) Jefferson County	2	0.46
Newtown, PA (township) Delaware County	53	0.45
Holly, MI (township) Oakland County	45	0.45
Garden City South, NY (cdp) Nassau County	18	0.45
Beverly Hills, MI (village) Oakland County	45	0.43
North Salem, NY (town) Westchester County	22	0.43
Waimanalo Beach, HI (cdp) Honolulu County	18	0.42
Deer Park, CA (cdp) Napa County	6	0.41
Manassas Park, VA (independent city) Manassas Park city	41	0.40
Skokie, IL (village) Cook County	244	0.39
Great Neck, NY (village) Nassau County	36	0.38
Great Falls, VA (cdp) Fairfax County	32	0.37
Dilworth, MN (city) Clay County	11	0.37
Deal, NJ (borough) Monmouth County	4	0.37
Strattanville, PA (borough) Clarion County	2	0.37
Princeton, NJ (township) Mercer County	57	0.36
Wixom, MI (city) Oakland County	48	0.36
Sea Ranch Lakes, FL (village) Broward County	5	0.36
Southfield, MI (township) Oakland County	51	0.35
Bethany, CT (town) New Haven County	17	0.34
Hampton, MD (cdp) Baltimore County	17	0.34
Hedwig Village, TX (city) Harris County	8	0.34
Cocoa Beach, FL (city) Brevard County	41	0.33
Whitemarsh, PA (township) Montgomery County	53	0.32
South Nyack, NY (village) Rockland County	11	0.32
Hewlett Harbor, NY (village) Nassau County	4	0.32
Tiburon, CA (town) Marin County	27	0.31
Royal Oak charter, MI (township) Oakland County	17	0.31
La Mesa, CA (city) San Diego County	164	0.30
Kings Point, NY (village) Nassau County	15	0.30
Munfordville, KY (city) Hart County	5	0.30
Mount Morris, MI (township) Genesee County	70	0.29
West Paterson, NJ (borough) Passaic County	32	0.29
Platteville, WI (town) Grant County	4	0.29
Browns Valley, MN (city) Traverse County	2	0.29
Affton, MO (cdp) Saint Louis County	59	0.28
Larkfield-Wikiup, CA (cdp) Sonoma County	21	0.28
Lorton, VA (cdp) Fairfax County	48	0.27
Saginaw Township South, MI (cdp) Saginaw County	37	0.27
Camas, WA (city) Clark County	34	0.27
Tahoe Vista, CA (cdp) Placer County	5	0.27
Alexandria Bay, NY (village) Jefferson County	3	0.27
Calabasas, CA (city) Los Angeles County	53	0.26
Middle Valley, TN (cdp) Hamilton County	31	0.26
Meadow Woods, FL (cdp) Orange County	30	0.26
Lake Murray of Richland, SC (cdp) Richland County	9	0.26
West Simsbury, CT (cdp) Hartford County	6	0.26
Annandale, VA (cdp) Fairfax County	138	0.25
Beverly Hills, CA (city) Los Angeles County	86	0.25
Millcreek, UT (cdp) Salt Lake County	77	0.25
Harrison, NY (village) Westchester County	60	0.25
Sachse, TX (city) Dallas County	24	0.25
Oakwood, OH (village) Cuyahoga County	9	0.25
Ames, TX (city) Liberty County	3	0.25
Mayfield Heights, OH (city) Cuyahoga County	46	0.24
Woodsburgh, NY (village) Nassau County	2	0.24
Glendale, CA (city) Los Angeles County	453	0.23
Yorktown Heights, NY (cdp) Westchester County	18	0.23
Four Corners, MT (cdp) Gallatin County	4	0.23
Amherst, MA (town) Hampshire County	75	0.22
Dunn Loring, VA (cdp) Fairfax County	17	0.22
Village Shires, PA (cdp) Bucks County	9	0.22
Kennebunkport, ME (town) York County	8	0.22
Cutchogue, NY (cdp) Suffolk County	6	0.22
La Canada Flintridge, CA (city) Los Angeles County	43	0.21
Miami Springs, FL (city) Miami-Dade County	29	0.21
Excelsior Springs, MO (city) Clay County	23	0.21
Clayton, MI (township) Genesee County	16	0.21
Helotes, TX (city) Bexar County	9	0.21
North Wales, PA (borough) Montgomery County	7	0.21
East Dundee, IL (village) Kane County	6	0.21
Hewlett Bay Park, NY (village) Nassau County	1	0.21
Mishawaka, IN (city) Saint Joseph County	93	0.20
Tustin Foothills, CA (cdp) Orange County	47	0.20
Palm Beach, FL (town) Palm Beach County	21	0.20
Washington, NJ (township) Mercer County	21	0.20
Cedar Hills, OR (cdp) Washington County	18	0.20
Golf Manor, OH (village) Hamilton County	8	0.20
Armonk, NY (cdp) Westchester County	7	0.20
Hancock, NY (town) Delaware County	7	0.20
Franklin, MI (village) Oakland County	6	0.20
Malvern, PA (borough) Chester County	6	0.20
Montague, CA (city) Siskiyou County	3	0.20
Cliffside Park, NJ (borough) Bergen County	43	0.19

Notes: (cdp) census designated place; Refer to the Explanation of Data in the front of the book for more detailed information.

Arab: Iraqi

Top 150 Places Sorted by Percent

(Based on places with populations of 10,000 or more)

Place	Number	%
Rancho San Diego, CA (cdp) San Diego County	448	2.24
Dearborn, MI (city) Wayne County	2,042	2.09
West Bloomfield, MI (township) Oakland County	973	1.50
Oak Park, MI (city) Oakland County	412	1.38
El Cajon, CA (city) San Diego County	1,237	1.30
Sterling Heights, MI (city) Macomb County	1,384	1.11
Bostonia, CA (cdp) San Diego County	154	1.04
Spring Valley, CA (cdp) San Diego County	271	1.02
Hazel Park, MI (city) Oakland County	188	0.99
Southfield, MI (city) Oakland County	753	0.96
Casa de Oro-Mount Helix, CA (cdp) San Diego County	178	0.94
Madison Heights, MI (city) Oakland County	237	0.76
Warren, MI (city) Macomb County	906	0.66
Farmington Hills, MI (city) Oakland County	499	0.61
Foothill Ranch, CA (cdp) Orange County	63	0.58
Tarrytown, NY (village) Westchester County	62	0.56
Troy, MI (city) Oakland County	438	0.54
Bloomfield, MI (township) Oakland County	209	0.49
Hamtramck, MI (city) Wayne County	111	0.48
Olean, NY (city) Cattaraugus County	72	0.47
Rochester, MI (city) Oakland County	48	0.46
Newtown, PA (township) Delaware County	53	0.45
Holly, MI (township) Oakland County	45	0.45
Beverly Hills, MI (village) Oakland County	45	0.43
Manassas Park, VA (independent city) Manassas Park city	41	0.40
Skokie, IL (village) Cook County	244	0.39
Princeton, NJ (township) Mercer County	57	0.36
Wixom, MI (city) Oakland County	48	0.36
Southfield, MI (township) Oakland County	51	0.35
Cocoa Beach, FL (city) Brevard County	41	0.33
Whitemarsh, PA (township) Montgomery County	53	0.32
La Mesa, CA (city) San Diego County	164	0.30
Mount Morris, MI (township) Genesee County	70	0.29
West Paterson, NJ (borough) Passaic County	32	0.29
Affton, MO (cdp) Saint Louis County	59	0.28
Lorton, VA (cdp) Fairfax County	48	0.27
Saginaw Township South, MI (cdp) Saginaw County	37	0.27
Camas, WA (city) Clark County	34	0.27
Calabasas, CA (city) Los Angeles County	53	0.26
Middle Valley, TN (cdp) Hamilton County	31	0.26
Meadow Woods, FL (cdp) Orange County	30	0.26
Annandale, VA (cdp) Fairfax County	138	0.25
Beverly Hills, CA (city) Los Angeles County	86	0.25
Millcreek, UT (cdp) Salt Lake County	77	0.25
Harrison, NY (village) Westchester County	60	0.25
Mayfield Heights, OH (city) Cuyahoga County	46	0.24
Glendale, CA (city) Los Angeles County	453	0.23
Amherst, MA (town) Hampshire County	75	0.22
La Canada Flintridge, CA (city) Los Angeles County	43	0.21
Miami Springs, FL (city) Miami-Dade County	29	0.21
Excelsior Springs, MO (city) Clay County	23	0.21
Mishawaka, IN (city) Saint Joseph County	93	0.20
Tustin Foothills, CA (cdp) Orange County	47	0.20
Palm Beach, FL (town) Palm Beach County	21	0.20
Washington, NJ (township) Mercer County	21	0.20
Cliffside Park, NJ (borough) Bergen County	43	0.19
Mineola, NY (village) Nassau County	37	0.19
Lincolnia, VA (cdp) Fairfax County	30	0.19
Rochester Hills, MI (city) Oakland County	125	0.18
Royal Oak, MI (city) Oakland County	109	0.18
Moorhead, MN (city) Clay County	58	0.18
Morton Grove, IL (village) Cook County	41	0.18
Romeoville, IL (village) Will County	39	0.18
Piedmont, CA (city) Alameda County	20	0.18
Leicester, MA (town) Worcester County	19	0.18
Melvindale, MI (city) Wayne County	19	0.18
Ann Arbor, MI (city) Washtenaw County	195	0.17
Everett, WA (city) Snohomish County	158	0.17
Niles, IL (village) Cook County	52	0.17
Maryland Heights, MO (city) Saint Louis County	45	0.17
Lemon Grove, CA (city) San Diego County	42	0.17
Smyrna, TN (town) Rutherford County	42	0.17
Duarte, CA (city) Los Angeles County	36	0.17
Millbrae, CA (city) San Mateo County	35	0.17
Rye, NY (city) Westchester County	26	0.17
Five Corners, WA (cdp) Clark County	20	0.17
Grand Blanc, MI (township) Genesee County	47	0.16
Casa Grande, AZ (city) Pinal County	40	0.16
Paramus, NJ (borough) Bergen County	40	0.16
Bailey's Crossroads, VA (cdp) Fairfax County	36	0.16
Berlin, CT (town) Hartford County	30	0.16
East Islip, NY (cdp) Suffolk County	22	0.16
Irmo, SC (town) Richland County	18	0.16
North Hempstead, NY (town) Nassau County	334	0.15
Farmers Branch, TX (city) Dallas County	42	0.15
Acton, MA (town) Middlesex County	31	0.15
Columbus, NE (city) Platte County	31	0.15
Clayton, OH (city) Montgomery County	20	0.15
Beachwood, OH (city) Cuyahoga County	18	0.15
Lea Hill, WA (cdp) King County	16	0.15
Macomb, MI (township) Macomb County	69	0.14
McLean, VA (cdp) Fairfax County	56	0.14
Pittsfield charter, MI (township) Washtenaw County	42	0.14
Jefferson, VA (cdp) Fairfax County	37	0.14
Parma Heights, OH (city) Cuyahoga County	31	0.14
Cockeysville, MD (cdp) Baltimore County	27	0.14
Loma Linda, CA (city) San Bernardino County	26	0.14
Riverdale, IL (village) Cook County	21	0.14
Somerset, KY (city) Pulaski County	16	0.14
Newport Beach, CA (city) Orange County	92	0.13
Ridgewood, NJ (village) Bergen County	33	0.13
Niskayuna, NY (town) Schenectady County	27	0.13
Glen Rock, NJ (borough) Bergen County	15	0.13
Hartland, MI (township) Livingston County	14	0.13
Shelby, MI (cdp) Macomb County	79	0.12
Pleasant Hill, CA (city) Contra Costa County	40	0.12
Walnut, CA (city) Los Angeles County	37	0.12
Cooper City, FL (city) Broward County	32	0.12
South Salt Lake, UT (city) Salt Lake County	27	0.12
Hercules, CA (city) Contra Costa County	23	0.12
Idylwood, VA (cdp) Fairfax County	19	0.12
Palos Verdes Estates, CA (city) Los Angeles County	16	0.12
Jericho, NY (cdp) Nassau County	15	0.12
Lebanon, NH (city) Grafton County	15	0.12
Nashville-Davidson, TN (special city) Davidson County	598	0.11
Erie, PA (city) Erie County	109	0.11
Santa Clara, CA (city) Santa Clara County	108	0.11
Eagan, MN (city) Dakota County	69	0.11
McKinney, TX (city) Collin County	62	0.11
Rancho Santa Margarita, CA (city) Orange County	51	0.11
Chantilly, VA (cdp) Fairfax County	44	0.11
Franconia, VA (cdp) Fairfax County	34	0.11
University Place, WA (city) Pierce County	33	0.11
Cottonwood Heights, UT (cdp) Salt Lake County	31	0.11
Aventura, FL (city) Miami-Dade County	27	0.11
Dania Beach, FL (city) Broward County	22	0.11
Setauket-East Setauket, NY (cdp) Suffolk County	18	0.11
Potsdam, NY (town) Saint Lawrence County	17	0.11
Weehawken, NJ (township) Hudson County	15	0.11
Riverton-Boulevard Park, WA (cdp) King County	12	0.11
Detroit, MI (city) Wayne County	966	0.10
Columbia, MO (city) Boone County	87	0.10
Kent, WA (city) King County	77	0.10
Des Plaines, IL (city) Cook County	58	0.10
Oakton, VA (cdp) Fairfax County	30	0.10
Bedford, MI (township) Monroe County	28	0.10
Imperial Beach, CA (city) San Diego County	28	0.10
Norco, CA (city) Riverside County	24	0.10
Prairie Village, KS (city) Johnson County	23	0.10
Lynbrook, NY (village) Nassau County	19	0.10
Hawthorne, NJ (borough) Passaic County	18	0.10
Cocoa, FL (city) Brevard County	16	0.10
Brecksville, OH (city) Cuyahoga County	13	0.10
Millbrook, AL (city) Elmore County	10	0.10
Saint Louis, MO (independent city) Saint Louis city	318	0.09
Lincoln, NE (city) Lancaster County	214	0.09
Cedar Rapids, IA (city) Linn County	105	0.09
Coon Rapids, MN (city) Anoka County	58	0.09
Milpitas, CA (city) Santa Clara County	56	0.09
Dearborn Heights, MI (city) Wayne County	55	0.09

Notes: (cdp) census designated place; Refer to the Explanation of Data in the front of the book for more detailed information.

Arab: Jordanian

Top 150 Places Sorted by Number

(Based on all places, regardless of population)

Place	Number	%
Yonkers, NY (city) Westchester County	1,093	0.56
Chicago, IL (city) Cook County	1,078	0.04
New York, NY (city) New York City	897	0.01
Los Angeles, CA (city) Los Angeles County	836	0.02
Houston, TX (city) Harris County	567	0.03
Dearborn, MI (city) Wayne County	501	0.51
Phoenix, AZ (city) Maricopa County	430	0.03
Dallas, TX (city) Dallas County	379	0.03
South San Francisco, CA (city) San Mateo County	282	0.46
San Francisco, CA (city) San Francisco County	266	0.03
Anaheim, CA (city) Orange County	255	0.08
San Bernardino, CA (city) San Bernardino County	252	0.14
San Antonio, TX (city) Bexar County	236	0.02
Sterling Heights, MI (city) Macomb County	226	0.18
Riverside, CA (city) Riverside County	215	0.08
Oak Lawn, IL (village) Cook County	194	0.35
Chicago Ridge, IL (village) Cook County	192	1.38
Hempstead, NY (town) Nassau County	191	0.03
Morton Grove, IL (village) Cook County	189	0.84
San Rafael, CA (city) Marin County	182	0.32
Grand Rapids, MI (city) Kent County	182	0.09
Toledo, OH (city) Lucas County	174	0.06
Buena Park, CA (city) Orange County	173	0.22
Metairie, LA (cdp) Jefferson Parish	169	0.12
Arlington, TX (city) Tarrant County	169	0.05
Paterson, NJ (city) Passaic County	165	0.11
Akron, OH (city) Summit County	150	0.07
Livonia, MI (city) Wayne County	147	0.15
Columbus, OH (city) Franklin County	146	0.02
Tempe, AZ (city) Maricopa County	144	0.09
Clifton, NJ (city) Passaic County	143	0.18
Jersey City, NJ (city) Hudson County	143	0.06
Milwaukee, WI (city) Milwaukee County	140	0.02
Oak Forest, IL (city) Cook County	138	0.49
West Haven, CT (city) New Haven County	138	0.26
Fullerton, CA (city) Orange County	137	0.11
Plano, TX (city) Collin County	136	0.06
San Jose, CA (city) Santa Clara County	136	0.02
Cleveland, OH (city) Cuyahoga County	135	0.03
Lexington-Fayette, KY (special city) Fayette County	130	0.05
Corona, CA (city) Riverside County	129	0.10
Memphis, TN (city) Shelby County	122	0.02
Fort Worth, TX (city) Tarrant County	121	0.02
North Bergen, NJ (township) Hudson County	120	0.21
Pasadena, CA (city) Los Angeles County	119	0.09
Raleigh, NC (city) Wake County	119	0.04
Scottsdale, AZ (city) Maricopa County	115	0.06
Philadelphia, PA (city) Philadelphia County	115	0.01
Warren, MI (city) Macomb County	114	0.08
Fairfield, CA (city) Solano County	111	0.12
Dearborn Heights, MI (city) Wayne County	110	0.19
Fountain Valley, CA (city) Orange County	109	0.20
Garland, TX (city) Dallas County	107	0.05
Bakersfield, CA (city) Kern County	107	0.04
Lakewood, OH (city) Cuyahoga County	106	0.19
Iowa City, IA (city) Johnson County	106	0.17
Santa Clara, CA (city) Santa Clara County	105	0.10
Nashville-Davidson, TN (special city) Davidson County	105	0.02
Des Plaines, IL (city) Cook County	104	0.18
El Cajon, CA (city) San Diego County	104	0.11
Hyde Park, NY (town) Dutchess County	103	0.49
Palos Hills, IL (city) Cook County	102	0.57
Westminster, CA (city) Orange County	102	0.12
Mesquite, TX (city) Dallas County	102	0.08
Tulsa, OK (city) Tulsa County	101	0.03
Austin, TX (city) Travis County	101	0.02
Hollywood, FL (city) Broward County	100	0.07
Aurora, CO (city) Arapahoe County	98	0.04
Sacramento, CA (city) Sacramento County	98	0.02
Burbank, IL (city) Cook County	96	0.35
Glendale, CA (city) Los Angeles County	96	0.05
Overland Park, KS (city) Johnson County	95	0.06
Washington, DC (city) District of Columbia	94	0.02
Bayonne, NJ (city) Hudson County	93	0.15
Knoxville, TN (city) Knox County	93	0.05
Nashville, NC (town) Nash County	92	2.15
Burbank, CA (city) Los Angeles County	92	0.09
Detroit, MI (city) Wayne County	92	0.01
Ojus, FL (cdp) Miami-Dade County	91	0.55
Miamisburg, OH (city) Montgomery County	91	0.46
Daly City, CA (city) San Mateo County	91	0.09
Naperville, IL (city) Du Page County	91	0.07
North Arlington, NJ (borough) Bergen County	90	0.59
Reston, VA (cdp) Fairfax County	90	0.16
Niles, IL (village) Cook County	89	0.30
Orland Park, IL (village) Cook County	89	0.17
El Paso, TX (city) El Paso County	89	0.02
San Diego, CA (city) San Diego County	89	0.01
Oneida, NY (city) Madison County	88	0.80
Chandler, AZ (city) Maricopa County	87	0.05
Boston, MA (city) Suffolk County	87	0.01
Hemet, CA (city) Riverside County	85	0.14
Rancho Cucamonga, CA (city) San Bernardino County	84	0.07
Santa Clarita, CA (city) Los Angeles County	84	0.06
Chula Vista, CA (city) San Diego County	84	0.05
Wichita, KS (city) Sedgwick County	84	0.02
Sugar Land, TX (city) Fort Bend County	83	0.13
Lucas Valley-Marinwood, CA (cdp) Marin County	82	1.30
Hickory Hills, IL (city) Cook County	82	0.59
Garfield, NJ (city) Bergen County	82	0.28
Chantilly, VA (cdp) Fairfax County	82	0.20
Omaha, NE (city) Douglas County	81	0.02
Jacksonville, FL (special city) Duval County	81	0.01
Mount Prospect, IL (village) Cook County	80	0.14
Hawthorne, NJ (borough) Passaic County	79	0.43
Rancho San Diego, CA (cdp) San Diego County	79	0.39
Downey, CA (city) Los Angeles County	79	0.07
San Dimas, CA (city) Los Angeles County	78	0.22
Westminster, CO (city) Adams County	78	0.08
Oklahoma City, OK (city) Oklahoma County	78	0.02
Fairfield, OH (city) Butler County	77	0.18
Orange, CA (city) Orange County	77	0.06
Spring, TX (cdp) Harris County	76	0.21
Redondo Beach, CA (city) Los Angeles County	75	0.12
Berwyn, IL (city) Cook County	74	0.14
Kansas City, MO (city) Jackson County	74	0.02
Pedley, CA (cdp) Riverside County	73	0.66
Calumet City, IL (city) Cook County	73	0.19
Culver City, CA (city) Los Angeles County	73	0.19
Arden-Arcade, CA (cdp) Sacramento County	73	0.08
Cary, NC (town) Wake County	72	0.08
Richardson, TX (city) Dallas County	72	0.08
Long Beach, CA (city) Los Angeles County	72	0.02
Worcester, MA (city) Worcester County	71	0.04
Albuquerque, NM (city) Bernalillo County	71	0.02
Holland, MI (city) Ottawa County	70	0.20
Glendora, CA (city) Los Angeles County	70	0.14
Brookhaven, NY (town) Suffolk County	69	0.02
Tucson, AZ (city) Pima County	69	0.01
Upper Providence, PA (township) Montgomery County	68	0.44
Topeka, KS (city) Shawnee County	68	0.06
Sullivan, NY (town) Madison County	67	0.45
Costa Mesa, CA (city) Orange County	66	0.06
Lafayette, LA (city) Lafayette Parish	66	0.06
Arlington, VA (cdp) Arlington County	66	0.03
Bridgeview, IL (village) Cook County	65	0.42
East Fishkill, NY (town) Dutchess County	65	0.25
Lakes by the Bay, FL (cdp) Miami-Dade County	64	0.71
Brea, CA (city) Orange County	64	0.18
Poughkeepsie, NY (town) Dutchess County	64	0.15
Arlington Heights, IL (village) Cook County	64	0.08
Lenox, NY (town) Madison County	63	0.73
Bedford, TX (city) Tarrant County	63	0.13
Farmington Hills, MI (city) Oakland County	63	0.08
Hammond, IN (city) Lake County	63	0.08
Columbia, MO (city) Boone County	63	0.07
Irving, TX (city) Dallas County	63	0.03
Hacienda Heights, CA (cdp) Los Angeles County	62	0.12
Shelby, MI (cdp) Macomb County	62	0.10
Cicero, IL (town) Cook County	62	0.07

Notes: (cdp) census designated place; Refer to the Explanation of Data in the front of the book for more detailed information.

Arab: Jordanian

Top 150 Places Sorted by Percent

(Based on all places, regardless of population)

Place	Number	%
Pulawski, MI (township) Presque Isle County	14	3.64
Wampsville, NY (village) Madison County	16	2.85
Lake Belvedere Estates, FL (cdp) Palm Beach County	35	2.34
Hillman, MN (township) Morrison County	4	2.25
Nashville, NC (town) Nash County	92	2.15
Granite, UT (cdp) Salt Lake County	47	2.14
Lincoln Park, NY (cdp) Ulster County	38	1.67
Rochester, KY (city) Butler County	3	1.63
Saint Helena, NC (village) Pender County	6	1.48
Chicago Ridge, IL (village) Cook County	192	1.38
Lucas Valley-Marinwood, CA (cdp) Marin County	82	1.30
Canastota, NY (village) Madison County	47	1.11
Marvin, NC (village) Union County	13	1.06
Emerald Lake Hills, CA (cdp) San Mateo County	37	0.95
Cedarhurst, NY (village) Nassau County	56	0.91
Southgate, KY (city) Campbell County	32	0.91
Beaver, WV (cdp) Raleigh County	12	0.89
Savanna, IL (city) Carroll County	31	0.88
University Park, NM (cdp) Dona Ana County	24	0.88
Morton Grove, IL (village) Cook County	189	0.84
Mayo, MD (cdp) Anne Arundel County	27	0.84
Haviland, NY (cdp) Dutchess County	30	0.81
Oneida, NY (city) Madison County	88	0.80
Murphy, TX (city) Collin County	25	0.80
Dexter, MI (village) Washtenaw County	19	0.79
Crown Heights, NY (cdp) Dutchess County	23	0.77
Lenox, NY (town) Madison County	63	0.73
Marlborough, NY (town) Ulster County	60	0.72
Middlebury, CT (town) New Haven County	47	0.72
Lakes by the Bay, FL (cdp) Miami-Dade County	64	0.71
Sudley, VA (cdp) Prince William County	55	0.69
Greenhills, OH (village) Hamilton County	28	0.69
Fair Haven, NY (village) Cayuga County	6	0.68
Pedley, CA (cdp) Riverside County	73	0.66
Richland, MI (township) Montcalm County	18	0.62
North Arlington, NJ (borough) Bergen County	90	0.59
Hickory Hills, IL (city) Cook County	82	0.59
Odell, IL (village) Livingston County	6	0.59
Spackenkill, NY (cdp) Dutchess County	27	0.58
Brinckerhoff, NY (cdp) Dutchess County	16	0.58
West Taylor, PA (township) Cambria County	5	0.58
Gulf Stream, FL (town) Palm Beach County	4	0.58
Palos Hills, IL (city) Cook County	102	0.57
Yonkers, NY (city) Westchester County	1,093	0.56
Ojus, FL (cdp) Miami-Dade County	91	0.55
Mount Morris, MI (city) Genesee County	18	0.55
Timberwood Park, TX (cdp) Bexar County	30	0.53
Putnam Valley, NY (town) Putnam County	56	0.52
Dearborn, MI (city) Wayne County	501	0.51
Lincolnshire, IL (village) Lake County	31	0.50
Old Westbury, NY (village) Nassau County	21	0.50
Colfax, MI (township) Mecosta County	10	0.50
Oak Forest, IL (city) Cook County	138	0.49
Hyde Park, NY (town) Dutchess County	103	0.49
Barclay-Kingston, NJ (cdp) Camden County	53	0.49
Jamul, CA (cdp) San Diego County	28	0.47
Gap, PA (cdp) Lancaster County	28	0.47
South San Francisco, CA (city) San Mateo County	282	0.46
Miamisburg, OH (city) Montgomery County	91	0.46
Pleasantville, NY (village) Westchester County	33	0.46
Sullivan, NY (town) Madison County	67	0.45
Upper Providence, PA (township) Montgomery County	68	0.44
Moulton, AL (city) Lawrence County	14	0.44
Park Hills, KY (city) Kenton County	13	0.44
Hawthorne, NJ (borough) Passaic County	79	0.43
Warrenton, VA (town) Fauquier County	28	0.43
Hunters Creek Village, TX (city) Harris County	19	0.43
Bridgeview, IL (village) Cook County	65	0.42
Town and Country, MO (city) Saint Louis County	46	0.42
Dayton, NJ (cdp) Middlesex County	27	0.42
Pelham, AL (city) Shelby County	56	0.40
Keansburg, NJ (borough) Monmouth County	43	0.40
Clarkston, GA (city) De Kalb County	27	0.40
Rancho San Diego, CA (cdp) San Diego County	79	0.39
Wallington, NJ (borough) Bergen County	45	0.39
Echelon, NJ (cdp) Camden County	40	0.39
Huntington Woods, MI (city) Oakland County	24	0.39
Bainbridge, NY (town) Chenango County	13	0.39
Lake Goodwin, WA (cdp) Snohomish County	12	0.38
Mulberry, OH (cdp) Clermont County	12	0.38
Upper Oxford, PA (township) Chester County	8	0.38
Lake Carmel, NY (cdp) Putnam County	32	0.37
Elberta, AL (town) Baldwin County	2	0.37
Idylwood, VA (cdp) Fairfax County	57	0.36
North Auburn, CA (cdp) Placer County	43	0.36
Mount Holly, NC (city) Gaston County	35	0.36
Osceola, NY (town) Lewis County	1	0.36
Oak Lawn, IL (village) Cook County	194	0.35
Burbank, IL (city) Cook County	96	0.35
Montgomery, OH (city) Hamilton County	35	0.35
Bow, NH (town) Merrimack County	25	0.35
Charter Oak, CA (cdp) Los Angeles County	31	0.34
Newton, NJ (town) Sussex County	28	0.34
Solvay, NY (village) Onondaga County	23	0.34
Point Pleasant Beach, NJ (borough) Ocean County	18	0.34
Ogdensburg, NJ (borough) Sussex County	9	0.34
Middle Island, NY (cdp) Suffolk County	32	0.33
Golden Lakes, FL (cdp) Palm Beach County	22	0.33
San Rafael, CA (city) Marin County	182	0.32
Avon, OH (city) Lorain County	37	0.32
Hasbrouck Heights, NJ (borough) Bergen County	37	0.32
Devon-Berwyn, PA (cdp) Chester County	16	0.32
Niles, IL (village) Cook County	89	0.30
Lake Shore, MD (cdp) Anne Arundel County	40	0.30
Ulster, NY (town) Ulster County	38	0.30
Los Alamitos, CA (city) Orange County	34	0.30
Cottonwood-Verde Village, AZ (cdp) Yavapai County	32	0.30
Millersville, PA (borough) Lancaster County	24	0.30
Magnolia, OH (village) Stark County	3	0.30
Roslyn Harbor, NY (village) Nassau County	3	0.30
Pompton Lakes, NJ (borough) Passaic County	31	0.29
Seabrook, TX (city) Harris County	26	0.29
Prospect Park, NJ (borough) Passaic County	17	0.29
South Barrington, IL (village) Cook County	11	0.29
Breed, WI (town) Oconto County	2	0.29
Garfield, NJ (city) Bergen County	82	0.28
Milford, MI (township) Oakland County	42	0.28
Landen, OH (cdp) Warren County	35	0.28
Schiller Park, IL (village) Cook County	33	0.28
Berlin, MI (township) Saint Clair County	9	0.28
East Syracuse, NY (village) Onondaga County	9	0.28
Upper Brookville, NY (village) Nassau County	5	0.28
Star City, WV (town) Monongalia County	4	0.28
Duarte, CA (city) Los Angeles County	58	0.27
Carbondale, IL (city) Jackson County	56	0.27
Delmar, NY (cdp) Albany County	22	0.27
Wahneta, FL (cdp) Polk County	13	0.27
West Haven, CT (city) New Haven County	138	0.26
New Milford, NJ (borough) Bergen County	42	0.26
Brooklyn, OH (city) Cuyahoga County	30	0.26
West Bradford, PA (township) Chester County	28	0.26
Soquel, CA (cdp) Santa Cruz County	13	0.26
Umatilla, OR (city) Umatilla County	13	0.26
East Fishkill, NY (town) Dutchess County	65	0.25
Summit, IL (village) Cook County	27	0.25
Lyons, IL (village) Cook County	25	0.25
South Gastonia, NC (cdp) Gaston County	14	0.25
Selby-on-the-Bay, MD (cdp) Anne Arundel County	9	0.25
Council, ID (city) Adams County	2	0.25
Matthews, NC (town) Mecklenburg County	53	0.24
Halfmoon, NY (town) Saratoga County	44	0.24
Douglas, GA (city) Coffee County	24	0.24
Woodbridge, CT (town) New Haven County	22	0.24
Warrensburg, MO (city) Johnson County	37	0.23
Kent, NY (town) Putnam County	32	0.23
Glasgow, DE (cdp) New Castle County	29	0.23
Montgomeryville, PA (cdp) Montgomery County	27	0.23
Columbus AFB, MS (cdp) Lowndes County	5	0.23
Medicine Lodge, KS (city) Barber County	5	0.23
Goodland, MI (township) Lapeer County	4	0.23

Notes: (cdp) census designated place; Refer to the Explanation of Data in the front of the book for more detailed information.

Arab: Jordanian

Top 150 Places Sorted by Percent

(Based on places with populations of 10,000 or more)

Place	Number	%
Chicago Ridge, IL (village) Cook County	192	1.38
Morton Grove, IL (village) Cook County	189	0.84
Oneida, NY (city) Madison County	88	0.80
Pedley, CA (cdp) Riverside County	73	0.66
North Arlington, NJ (borough) Bergen County	90	0.59
Hickory Hills, IL (city) Cook County	82	0.59
Palos Hills, IL (city) Cook County	102	0.57
Yonkers, NY (city) Westchester County	1,093	0.56
Ojus, FL (cdp) Miami-Dade County	91	0.55
Putnam Valley, NY (town) Putnam County	56	0.52
Dearborn, MI (city) Wayne County	501	0.51
Oak Forest, IL (city) Cook County	138	0.49
Hyde Park, NY (town) Dutchess County	103	0.49
Barclay-Kingston, NJ (cdp) Camden County	53	0.49
South San Francisco, CA (city) San Mateo County	282	0.46
Miamisburg, OH (city) Montgomery County	91	0.46
Sullivan, NY (town) Madison County	67	0.45
Upper Providence, PA (township) Montgomery County	68	0.44
Hawthorne, NJ (borough) Passaic County	79	0.43
Bridgeview, IL (village) Cook County	65	0.42
Town and Country, MO (city) Saint Louis County	46	0.42
Pelham, AL (city) Shelby County	56	0.40
Keansburg, NJ (borough) Monmouth County	43	0.40
Rancho San Diego, CA (cdp) San Diego County	79	0.39
Wallington, NJ (borough) Bergen County	45	0.39
Echelon, NJ (cdp) Camden County	40	0.39
Idylwood, VA (cdp) Fairfax County	57	0.36
North Auburn, CA (cdp) Placer County	43	0.36
Oak Lawn, IL (village) Cook County	194	0.35
Burbank, IL (city) Cook County	96	0.35
Montgomery, OH (city) Hamilton County	35	0.35
San Rafael, CA (city) Marin County	182	0.32
Avon, OH (city) Lorain County	37	0.32
Hasbrouck Heights, NJ (borough) Bergen County	37	0.32
Niles, IL (village) Cook County	89	0.30
Lake Shore, MD (cdp) Anne Arundel County	40	0.30
Ulster, NY (town) Ulster County	38	0.30
Los Alamitos, CA (city) Orange County	34	0.30
Cottonwood-Verde Village, AZ (cdp) Yavapai County	32	0.30
Pompton Lakes, NJ (borough) Passaic County	31	0.29
Garfield, NJ (city) Bergen County	82	0.28
Milford, MI (township) Oakland County	42	0.28
Landen, OH (cdp) Warren County	35	0.28
Schiller Park, IL (village) Cook County	33	0.28
Duarte, CA (city) Los Angeles County	58	0.27
Carbondale, IL (city) Jackson County	56	0.27
West Haven, CT (city) New Haven County	138	0.26
New Milford, NJ (borough) Bergen County	42	0.26
Brooklyn, OH (city) Cuyahoga County	30	0.26
West Bradford, PA (township) Chester County	28	0.26
East Fishkill, NY (town) Dutchess County	65	0.25
Summit, IL (village) Cook County	27	0.25
Lyons, IL (village) Cook County	25	0.25
Matthews, NC (town) Mecklenburg County	53	0.24
Halfmoon, NY (town) Saratoga County	44	0.24
Douglas, GA (city) Coffee County	24	0.24
Warrensburg, MO (city) Johnson County	37	0.23
Kent, NY (town) Putnam County	32	0.23
Glasgow, DE (cdp) New Castle County	29	0.23
Montgomeryville, PA (cdp) Montgomery County	27	0.23
Buena Park, CA (city) Orange County	173	0.22
San Dimas, CA (city) Los Angeles County	78	0.22
Bailey's Crossroads, VA (cdp) Fairfax County	50	0.22
Little Falls, NJ (cdp) Passaic County	24	0.22
North Bergen, NJ (township) Hudson County	120	0.21
Spring, TX (cdp) Harris County	76	0.21
Valinda, CA (cdp) Los Angeles County	46	0.21
North Plainfield, NJ (borough) Somerset County	44	0.21
Bay Village, OH (city) Cuyahoga County	33	0.21
Fountain Valley, CA (city) Orange County	109	0.20
Chantilly, VA (cdp) Fairfax County	82	0.20
Holland, MI (city) Ottawa County	70	0.20
Ferry Pass, FL (cdp) Escambia County	55	0.20
Oviedo, FL (city) Seminole County	55	0.20
Lake in the Hills, IL (village) McHenry County	47	0.20
Rosemont, CA (cdp) Sacramento County	45	0.20
Evergreen Park, IL (village) Cook County	42	0.20
Bon Air, VA (cdp) Chesterfield County	33	0.20
Rye, NY (city) Westchester County	30	0.20
Athens, TX (city) Henderson County	23	0.20
Rochester, MI (city) Oakland County	21	0.20
Rocky Point, NY (cdp) Suffolk County	20	0.20
Dearborn Heights, MI (city) Wayne County	110	0.19
Lakewood, OH (city) Cuyahoga County	106	0.19
Calumet City, IL (city) Cook County	73	0.19
Culver City, CA (city) Los Angeles County	73	0.19
Millbrae, CA (city) San Mateo County	40	0.19
Patton, PA (township) Centre County	22	0.19
Sterling Heights, MI (city) Macomb County	226	0.18
Clifton, NJ (city) Passaic County	143	0.18
Des Plaines, IL (city) Cook County	104	0.18
Fairfield, OH (city) Butler County	77	0.18
Brea, CA (city) Orange County	64	0.18
Foothill Farms, CA (cdp) Sacramento County	31	0.18
Bellmore, NY (cdp) Nassau County	30	0.18
Goodings Grove, IL (cdp) Will County	30	0.18
Simpsonville, SC (city) Greenville County	26	0.18
Guttenberg, NJ (town) Hudson County	19	0.18
Bound Brook, NJ (borough) Somerset County	18	0.18
Iowa City, IA (city) Johnson County	106	0.17
Orland Park, IL (village) Cook County	89	0.17
Manchester, MO (city) Saint Louis County	33	0.17
Sweetwater, FL (city) Miami-Dade County	24	0.17
Reston, VA (cdp) Fairfax County	90	0.16
Yuba City, CA (city) Sutter County	57	0.16
Temple City, CA (city) Los Angeles County	54	0.16
Watertown, MA (city) Middlesex County	53	0.16
Madison Heights, MI (city) Oakland County	51	0.16
Wyandotte, MI (city) Wayne County	46	0.16
Lansing, IL (village) Cook County	45	0.16
Plymouth Township, MI (cdp) Wayne County	43	0.16
Lakeside, CA (cdp) San Diego County	31	0.16
Fairview Park, OH (city) Cuyahoga County	28	0.16
River Edge, NJ (borough) Bergen County	17	0.16
Easttown, PA (township) Chester County	16	0.16
Livonia, MI (city) Wayne County	147	0.15
Bayonne, NJ (city) Hudson County	93	0.15
Poughkeepsie, NY (town) Dutchess County	64	0.15
McLean, VA (cdp) Fairfax County	57	0.15
Springfield, VA (cdp) Fairfax County	45	0.15
Emporia, KS (city) Lyon County	41	0.15
Weirton, WV (city) Hancock County	31	0.15
Hinsdale, IL (village) Du Page County	27	0.15
Artesia, CA (city) Los Angeles County	25	0.15
Brentwood, PA (borough) Allegheny County	16	0.15
San Bernardino, CA (city) San Bernardino County	252	0.14
Hemet, CA (city) Riverside County	85	0.14
Mount Prospect, IL (village) Cook County	80	0.14
Berwyn, IL (city) Cook County	74	0.14
Glendora, CA (city) Los Angeles County	70	0.14
Pacifica, CA (city) San Mateo County	55	0.14
Elmont, NY (cdp) Nassau County	46	0.14
University, FL (cdp) Hillsborough County	44	0.14
Garden City, MI (city) Wayne County	41	0.14
Voorhees, NJ (township) Camden County	40	0.14
Upper Dublin, PA (township) Montgomery County	36	0.14
Ocoee, FL (city) Orange County	32	0.14
South Salt Lake, UT (city) Salt Lake County	32	0.14
Norridge, IL (village) Cook County	20	0.14
Fairview, NJ (borough) Bergen County	19	0.14
La Grange Park, IL (village) Cook County	19	0.14
Vineyard, CA (cdp) Sacramento County	14	0.14
Sugar Land, TX (city) Fort Bend County	83	0.13
Bedford, TX (city) Tarrant County	63	0.13
Wilson, NC (city) Wilson County	58	0.13
Carmel, NY (town) Putnam County	44	0.13
Winter Springs, FL (city) Seminole County	42	0.13
Lawndale, CA (city) Los Angeles County	41	0.13
Mamaroneck, NY (town) Westchester County	39	0.13
East Windsor, NJ (township) Mercer County	33	0.13

Notes: (cdp) census designated place; Refer to the Explanation of Data in the front of the book for more detailed information.

Arab: Lebanese

Top 150 Places Sorted by Number

(Based on all places, regardless of population)

Place	Number	%
Dearborn, MI (city) Wayne County	17,305	17.70
New York, NY (city) New York City	11,419	0.14
Los Angeles, CA (city) Los Angeles County	7,769	0.21
Dearborn Heights, MI (city) Wayne County	3,136	5.38
Houston, TX (city) Harris County	3,052	0.16
Boston, MA (city) Suffolk County	2,901	0.49
San Diego, CA (city) San Diego County	2,367	0.19
Toledo, OH (city) Lucas County	2,048	0.65
Chicago, IL (city) Cook County	2,027	0.07
Detroit, MI (city) Wayne County	1,925	0.20
Glendale, CA (city) Los Angeles County	1,849	0.95
Phoenix, AZ (city) Maricopa County	1,826	0.14
Methuen, MA (city) Essex County	1,751	4.00
Austin, TX (city) Travis County	1,748	0.27
Jacksonville, FL (special city) Duval County	1,623	0.22
Sterling Heights, MI (city) Macomb County	1,598	1.28
San Antonio, TX (city) Bexar County	1,389	0.12
Worcester, MA (city) Worcester County	1,373	0.80
Dallas, TX (city) Dallas County	1,341	0.11
Peoria, IL (city) Peoria County	1,300	1.15
Columbus, OH (city) Franklin County	1,291	0.18
Oklahoma City, OK (city) Oklahoma County	1,287	0.25
Clinton, MI (cdp) Macomb County	1,284	1.34
Saint Clair Shores, MI (city) Macomb County	1,182	1.87
Warren, MI (city) Macomb County	1,152	0.83
El Paso, TX (city) El Paso County	1,142	0.20
Lawrence, MA (city) Essex County	1,133	1.57
San Francisco, CA (city) San Francisco County	1,120	0.14
San Jose, CA (city) Santa Clara County	1,086	0.12
Charlotte, NC (city) Mecklenburg County	1,083	0.20
Pittsburgh, PA (city) Allegheny County	1,065	0.32
Wichita, KS (city) Sedgwick County	1,039	0.30
Troy, MI (city) Oakland County	1,036	1.28
Philadelphia, PA (city) Philadelphia County	1,029	0.07
Cleveland, OH (city) Cuyahoga County	1,004	0.21
Danbury, CT (city) Fairfield County	958	1.28
Parma, OH (city) Cuyahoga County	958	1.12
Utica, NY (city) Oneida County	945	1.56
Tulsa, OK (city) Tulsa County	921	0.23
Livonia, MI (city) Wayne County	897	0.89
Omaha, NE (city) Douglas County	897	0.23
Albuquerque, NM (city) Bernalillo County	893	0.20
Las Vegas, NV (city) Clark County	882	0.18
Miami, FL (city) Miami-Dade County	855	0.24
Anaheim, CA (city) Orange County	846	0.26
Virginia Beach, VA (independent city) Virginia Beach city	845	0.20
Akron, OH (city) Summit County	834	0.38
Quincy, MA (city) Norfolk County	821	0.93
Fall River, MA (city) Bristol County	820	0.89
Minneapolis, MN (city) Hennepin County	807	0.21
Charleston, WV (city) Kanawha County	805	1.51
Buffalo, NY (city) Erie County	801	0.27
Baton Rouge, LA (city) East Baton Rouge Parish	792	0.35
Dedham, MA (cdp) Norfolk County	763	3.25
Saint Louis, MO (independent city) Saint Louis city	758	0.22
Kendall, FL (cdp) Miami-Dade County	755	1.00
Washington, DC (city) District of Columbia	747	0.13
Seattle, WA (city) King County	740	0.13
Arlington, VA (cdp) Arlington County	731	0.39
Portland, OR (city) Multnomah County	730	0.14
Norwood, MA (cdp) Norfolk County	725	2.54
Farmington Hills, MI (city) Oakland County	716	0.87
Raleigh, NC (city) Wake County	711	0.26
Saint Paul, MN (city) Ramsey County	666	0.23
Amherst, NY (town) Erie County	664	0.57
Waterbury, CT (city) New Haven County	663	0.62
Plano, TX (city) Collin County	652	0.29
Grosse Pointe Woods, MI (city) Wayne County	649	3.80
Lakewood, OH (city) Cuyahoga County	645	1.14
Cedar Rapids, IA (city) Linn County	637	0.53
Rochester Hills, MI (city) Oakland County	619	0.90
Lansing, MI (city) Ingham County	615	0.52
Scranton, PA (city) Lackawanna County	608	0.80
Salem, NH (town) Rockingham County	594	2.11
Tucson, AZ (city) Pima County	594	0.12
Louisville, KY (city) Jefferson County	588	0.23
Orlando, FL (city) Orange County	587	0.32
Burbank, CA (city) Los Angeles County	580	0.58
Springfield, MA (city) Hampden County	575	0.38
Kansas City, MO (city) Jackson County	573	0.13
Denver, CO (city) Denver County	571	0.10
Canton, MI (cdp) Wayne County	570	0.75
Brockton, MA (city) Plymouth County	569	0.60
Nashville-Davidson, TN (special city) Davidson County	568	0.10
Saint Petersburg, FL (city) Pinellas County	565	0.23
Indianapolis, IN (special city) Marion County	563	0.07
Grand Rapids, MI (city) Kent County	561	0.28
Cincinnati, OH (city) Hamilton County	559	0.17
New Hartford, NY (town) Oneida County	554	2.62
Lafayette, LA (city) Lafayette Parish	552	0.50
Shelby, MI (cdp) Macomb County	544	0.84
Torrance, CA (city) Los Angeles County	544	0.39
Pasadena, CA (city) Los Angeles County	543	0.41
Wilkes-Barre, PA (city) Luzerne County	527	1.22
Sacramento, CA (city) Sacramento County	527	0.13
Long Beach, CA (city) Los Angeles County	526	0.11
Coral Springs, FL (city) Broward County	511	0.43
Macomb, MI (township) Macomb County	500	0.99
Mobile, AL (city) Mobile County	499	0.25
Birmingham, AL (city) Jefferson County	498	0.20
Hempstead, NY (town) Nassau County	498	0.07
Huntington Beach, CA (city) Orange County	489	0.26
Arlington, TX (city) Tarrant County	489	0.15
Glendora, CA (city) Los Angeles County	488	0.98
Scottsdale, AZ (city) Maricopa County	483	0.24
Strongsville, OH (city) Cuyahoga County	478	1.09
Carrollton, TX (city) Denton County	478	0.44
Stockton, CA (city) San Joaquin County	471	0.19
Westland, MI (city) Wayne County	469	0.54
Overland Park, KS (city) Johnson County	469	0.32
McLean, VA (cdp) Fairfax County	465	1.19
Alexandria, VA (independent city) Alexandria city	465	0.36
New Orleans, LA (city) Orleans Parish	461	0.10
Colorado Springs, CO (city) El Paso County	457	0.13
Haverhill, MA (city) Essex County	452	0.77
Wheeling, WV (city) Ohio County	447	1.43
Henderson, NV (city) Clark County	447	0.25
Ann Arbor, MI (city) Washtenaw County	446	0.39
Michigan City, IN (city) La Porte County	444	1.35
Atlanta, GA (city) Fulton County	444	0.11
Boardman, OH (cdp) Mahoning County	441	1.18
Downey, CA (city) Los Angeles County	440	0.41
Cambridge, MA (city) Middlesex County	438	0.43
New Bedford, MA (city) Bristol County	429	0.46
Hialeah, FL (city) Miami-Dade County	429	0.19
Manchester, NH (city) Hillsborough County	424	0.40
Lexington-Fayette, KY (special city) Fayette County	423	0.16
Orange, CA (city) Orange County	422	0.33
Eastpointe, MI (city) Macomb County	421	1.24
Pembroke Pines, FL (city) Broward County	421	0.31
Paradise, NV (cdp) Clark County	417	0.22
Providence, RI (city) Providence County	415	0.24
Bloomfield, MI (township) Oakland County	413	0.96
Roseville, MI (city) Macomb County	406	0.84
Fremont, CA (city) Alameda County	405	0.20
Coral Gables, FL (city) Miami-Dade County	402	0.95
Franklin, NJ (township) Somerset County	394	0.77
Hollywood, FL (city) Broward County	394	0.28
Metairie, LA (cdp) Jefferson Parish	391	0.27
Memphis, TN (city) Shelby County	390	0.06
Niagara Falls, NY (city) Niagara County	388	0.70
Watertown, MA (city) Middlesex County	387	1.17
Jersey City, NJ (city) Hudson County	387	0.16
Laguna Niguel, CA (city) Orange County	385	0.62
Brookhaven, NY (town) Suffolk County	385	0.09
North Brunswick Township, NJ (cdp) Middlesex County	381	1.05
Irvine, CA (city) Orange County	379	0.26
Shrewsbury, MA (town) Worcester County	378	1.19
Bell, CA (city) Los Angeles County	378	1.03
Boca Raton, FL (city) Palm Beach County	375	0.50

Notes: (cdp) census designated place; Refer to the Explanation of Data in the front of the book for more detailed information.

Arab: Lebanese

Top 150 Places Sorted by Percent

(Based on all places, regardless of population)

Place	Number	%
Dearborn, MI (city) Wayne County	17,305	17.70
C-Road, CA (cdp) Plumas County	21	15.11
Highland, ME (plantation) Somerset County	10	14.49
Grosse Pointe, MI (township) Wayne County	235	8.57
Grosse Pointe Shores, MI (village) Wayne County	235	8.41
Stratton, VT (town) Windham County	9	6.43
Pottawattamie Park, IN (town) La Porte County	19	6.31
Carlsbad North, NM (cdp) Eddy County	72	5.87
McGregor, MN (township) Aitkin County	6	5.56
Rice River, MN (township) Aitkin County	9	5.42
Dearborn Heights, MI (city) Wayne County	3,136	5.38
Gilbertown, AL (town) Choctaw County	10	5.38
Foundryville, PA (cdp) Columbia County	14	5.28
Terlton, OK (town) Pawnee County	4	4.65
Climax, MN (city) Polk County	10	4.08
Cloud Lake, FL (town) Palm Beach County	5	4.07
Hills and Dales, KY (city) Jefferson County	5	4.03
Methuen, MA (city) Essex County	1,751	4.00
Freedom, OK (town) Woods County	10	4.00
Crownsville, MD (cdp) Anne Arundel County	67	3.93
Holiday City, OH (village) Williams County	2	3.92
Sibley, ND (city) Barnes County	2	3.85
Deal, NJ (borough) Monmouth County	41	3.83
Grosse Pointe Woods, MI (city) Wayne County	649	3.80
Crescent Mills, CA (cdp) Plumas County	10	3.72
Midvale, ID (city) Washington County	7	3.61
Crossgate, KY (city) Jefferson County	9	3.53
Fairlawn, OH (city) Summit County	255	3.48
New Ashford, MA (town) Berkshire County	8	3.45
Glen Echo, MD (town) Montgomery County	8	3.38
Otis, ME (town) Hancock County	18	3.28
Brian Head, UT (town) Iron County	3	3.26
Dedham, MA (cdp) Norfolk County	763	3.25
Portville, NY (village) Cattaraugus County	34	3.24
Sasakwa, OK (town) Seminole County	5	3.21
Hanna City, IL (village) Peoria County	32	3.18
Lohman, MO (city) Cole County	6	3.17
Clark Mills, NY (cdp) Oneida County	44	3.16
North Seekonk, MA (cdp) Bristol County	83	3.15
Brandt, MN (township) Polk County	2	3.13
Mockingbird Valley, KY (city) Jefferson County	6	3.09
Olean, NY (town) Cattaraugus County	60	2.96
Lake Marcel-Stillwater, WA (cdp) King County	42	2.95
Glenview Manor, KY (city) Jefferson County	6	2.93
New Hartford, NY (village) Oneida County	55	2.92
Pocono Pines, PA (cdp) Monroe County	30	2.81
Gibraltar, MI (city) Wayne County	119	2.79
Allensville, KY (city) Todd County	4	2.78
Hopewell, PA (borough) Bedford County	6	2.76
Upper Brookville, NY (village) Nassau County	48	2.65
New Hartford, NY (town) Oneida County	554	2.62
Wilbur Park, MO (village) Saint Louis County	13	2.62
Westwood, MA (town) Norfolk County	365	2.59
Deerfield, NY (town) Oneida County	101	2.59
East Pasadena, CA (cdp) Los Angeles County	155	2.57
Nelson Lagoon, AK (cdp) Aleutians East Borough	2	2.56
Norwood, MA (cdp) Norfolk County	725	2.54
Leonardo, NJ (cdp) Monmouth County	72	2.51
Lynchburg, SC (town) Lee County	14	2.49
Fox, AK (cdp) Fairbanks North Star Borough	7	2.45
Schuyler, NY (town) Herkimer County	83	2.44
Paris, NY (town) Oneida County	112	2.43
Avery, CA (cdp) Calaveras County	15	2.43
Chancellor, SD (town) Turner County	8	2.42
Cedar Rock, NC (village) Caldwell County	7	2.42
Boyd, MN (city) Lac qui Parle County	5	2.42
Dallas, PA (borough) Luzerne County	61	2.39
Eastborough, KS (city) Sedgwick County	19	2.33
New Baltimore, MI (city) Macomb County	172	2.32
West Swanzey, NH (cdp) Cheshire County	25	2.32
Frankfort, NY (town) Herkimer County	173	2.31
Forty Fort, PA (borough) Luzerne County	106	2.31
Leisureville, FL (cdp) Broward County	25	2.31
Bell, WI (town) Bayfield County	5	2.31
Vinco, PA (cdp) Cambria County	31	2.29

Place	Number	%
Four Corners, TX (cdp) Fort Bend County	67	2.27
Copeland, KS (city) Gray County	8	2.27
Niederwald, TX (town) Hays County	14	2.24
Wynantskill, NY (cdp) Rensselaer County	70	2.23
Reliance, SD (town) Lyman County	5	2.23
Sweden, ME (town) Oxford County	7	2.22
Menallen, PA (township) Fayette County	102	2.20
Grosse Pointe Park, MI (city) Wayne County	272	2.19
Magnolia, IL (village) Putnam County	7	2.19
Despard, WV (cdp) Harrison County	24	2.14
Bingham Farms, MI (village) Oakland County	22	2.14
Cragsmoor, NY (cdp) Ulster County	10	2.14
Salem, NH (town) Rockingham County	594	2.11
Whitesboro, NY (village) Oneida County	85	2.11
Montrose-Ghent, OH (cdp) Summit County	105	2.10
Tierra Verde, FL (cdp) Pinellas County	74	2.09
New York Mills, NY (village) Oneida County	67	2.08
Hopwood, PA (cdp) Fayette County	41	2.04
Olean, NY (city) Cattaraugus County	310	2.02
Foxborough, MA (town) Norfolk County	326	2.01
Waterville, ME (city) Kennebec County	314	2.01
Yorkville, NY (village) Oneida County	54	2.01
Corfu, NY (village) Genesee County	16	2.01
Barton Hills, MI (village) Washtenaw County	7	2.01
Southport, IN (city) Marion County	39	2.00
Mountainhome, PA (cdp) Monroe County	25	1.99
Denton, KS (city) Doniphan County	4	1.99
Height of Land, MN (township) Becker County	12	1.98
Weston, NE (village) Saunders County	6	1.98
Wyandotte, MN (township) Pennington County	2	1.98
Bee Cave, TX (village) Travis County	12	1.97
Gates Mills, OH (village) Cuyahoga County	48	1.96
Fellows, CA (cdp) Kern County	3	1.94
Grosse Pointe Farms, MI (city) Wayne County	188	1.93
Gulivoire Park, IN (cdp) Saint Joseph County	57	1.93
Ramblewood, PA (cdp) Centre County	19	1.93
Clarksburg, MA (town) Berkshire County	32	1.90
Saddle Rock, NY (village) Nassau County	15	1.90
Matoaka, WV (town) Mercer County	6	1.90
Skyline, MN (city) Blue Earth County	7	1.89
Lavallette, NJ (borough) Ocean County	50	1.88
Saint Clair Shores, MI (city) Macomb County	1,182	1.87
Biscayne Park, FL (village) Miami-Dade County	62	1.87
Bella Villa, MO (city) Saint Louis County	12	1.87
Washington Township, NJ (cdp) Bergen County	166	1.86
East Side, PA (borough) Carbon County	5	1.85
Penn Lake Park, PA (borough) Luzerne County	5	1.85
Wareham Center, MA (cdp) Plymouth County	52	1.83
San Joaquin Hills, CA (cdp) Orange County	56	1.82
Fisher, MN (township) Polk County	4	1.81
Jemez Springs, NM (village) Sandoval County	9	1.80
Sutton, MA (town) Worcester County	148	1.79
Frankfort, NY (village) Herkimer County	45	1.78
Big Horn, WY (cdp) Sheridan County	3	1.78
Patterson Heights, PA (borough) Beaver County	12	1.77
Woodbury, PA (borough) Bedford County	5	1.76
Lake Hamilton, AR (cdp) Garland County	27	1.75
Rio Rico Southeast, AZ (cdp) Santa Cruz County	31	1.74
Haverhill, IA (city) Marshall County	3	1.74
East Grand Rapids, MI (city) Kent County	184	1.71
Heath, MA (town) Franklin County	14	1.71
Danby, NY (town) Tompkins County	52	1.70
Yatesville, PA (borough) Luzerne County	11	1.69
Wheatland, MI (township) Hillsdale County	21	1.68
Zephyr Cove-Round Hill Village, NV (cdp) Douglas County	28	1.66
Country Knolls, NY (cdp) Saratoga County	35	1.65
Housatonic, MA (cdp) Berkshire County	22	1.64
Green Tree, PA (borough) Allegheny County	77	1.63
Thompsonville, PA (cdp) Washington County	57	1.63
Camp Wood, TX (city) Real County	13	1.63
Whitestown, NY (town) Oneida County	301	1.62
Pine, PA (township) Crawford County	8	1.62
McGregor, MN (city) Aitkin County	7	1.62
Summerland, CA (cdp) Santa Barbara County	24	1.61
Eatons Neck, NY (cdp) Suffolk County	22	1.61

Notes: (cdp) census designated place; Refer to the Explanation of Data in the front of the book for more detailed information.

Arab: Lebanese

Top 150 Places Sorted by Percent

(Based on places with populations of 10,000 or more)

Place	Number	%
Dearborn, MI (city) Wayne County	17,305	17.70
Dearborn Heights, MI (city) Wayne County	3,136	5.38
Methuen, MA (city) Essex County	1,751	4.00
Grosse Pointe Woods, MI (city) Wayne County	649	3.80
Dedham, MA (cdp) Norfolk County	763	3.25
New Hartford, NY (town) Oneida County	554	2.62
Westwood, MA (town) Norfolk County	365	2.59
Norwood, MA (cdp) Norfolk County	725	2.54
Grosse Pointe Park, MI (city) Wayne County	272	2.19
Salem, NH (town) Rockingham County	594	2.11
Olean, NY (city) Cattaraugus County	310	2.02
Foxborough, MA (town) Norfolk County	326	2.01
Waterville, ME (city) Kennebec County	314	2.01
Saint Clair Shores, MI (city) Macomb County	1,182	1.87
East Grand Rapids, MI (city) Kent County	184	1.71
Whitestown, NY (town) Oneida County	301	1.62
Lawrence, MA (city) Essex County	1,133	1.57
Utica, NY (city) Oneida County	945	1.56
Fraser, MI (city) Macomb County	237	1.55
Aliquippa, PA (city) Beaver County	179	1.53
Charleston, WV (city) Kanawha County	805	1.51
Harper Woods, MI (city) Wayne County	214	1.50
Fullerton, PA (cdp) Lehigh County	213	1.50
Wheeling, WV (city) Ohio County	447	1.43
Center, PA (township) Beaver County	162	1.41
Michigan City, IN (city) La Porte County	444	1.35
North Attleborough Center, MA (cdp) Bristol County	228	1.35
Clinton, MI (cdp) Macomb County	1,284	1.34
Easton, PA (city) Northampton County	348	1.33
Brooklyn, OH (city) Cuyahoga County	154	1.33
Somerset, MA (cdp) Bristol County	239	1.31
North Adams, MA (city) Berkshire County	193	1.31
West Saint Paul, MN (city) Dakota County	251	1.29
Sterling Heights, MI (city) Macomb County	1,598	1.28
Troy, MI (city) Oakland County	1,036	1.28
Danbury, CT (city) Fairfield County	958	1.28
Hampton, NH (town) Rockingham County	189	1.27
Eastpointe, MI (city) Macomb County	421	1.24
Wilkes-Barre, PA (city) Luzerne County	527	1.22
Dover, NH (city) Strafford County	327	1.22
Brecksville, OH (city) Cuyahoga County	161	1.21
Mendota Heights, MN (city) Dakota County	137	1.21
McLean, VA (cdp) Fairfax County	465	1.19
Shrewsbury, MA (town) Worcester County	378	1.19
Boardman, OH (cdp) Mahoning County	441	1.18
Watertown, MA (city) Middlesex County	387	1.17
Pottsville, PA (city) Schuylkill County	182	1.17
Woodhaven, MI (city) Wayne County	146	1.17
South Charleston, WV (city) Kanawha County	158	1.16
Peoria, IL (city) Peoria County	1,300	1.15
Sharon, MA (town) Norfolk County	200	1.15
Seekonk, MA (town) Bristol County	155	1.15
Lakewood, OH (city) Cuyahoga County	645	1.14
Hanover, PA (township) Luzerne County	130	1.13
Parma, OH (city) Cuyahoga County	958	1.12
Agawam, MA (city) Hampden County	314	1.12
Harrison, MI (cdp) Macomb County	273	1.12
Uniontown, PA (city) Fayette County	138	1.11
Doral, FL (cdp) Miami-Dade County	225	1.10
Strongsville, OH (city) Cuyahoga County	478	1.09
Pinecrest, FL (village) Miami-Dade County	209	1.09
Kirkland, NY (town) Oneida County	111	1.09
Parma Heights, OH (city) Cuyahoga County	233	1.08
Sylvania, OH (city) Lucas County	201	1.07
Derry, NH (town) Rockingham County	361	1.06
North Brunswick Township, NJ (cdp) Middlesex County	381	1.05
Canton, MA (town) Norfolk County	217	1.04
Birmingham, MI (city) Oakland County	202	1.04
Little Falls, NJ (cdp) Passaic County	113	1.04
Bell, CA (city) Los Angeles County	378	1.03
Medway, MA (town) Norfolk County	127	1.02
Melvindale, MI (city) Wayne County	110	1.02
North Andover, MA (town) Essex County	276	1.01
Kendall, FL (cdp) Miami-Dade County	755	1.00
Vashon, WA (cdp) King County	101	1.00

Place	Number	%
Macomb, MI (township) Macomb County	500	0.99
Grand Island, NY (town) Erie County	185	0.99
Raynham, MA (town) Bristol County	116	0.99
Glendora, CA (city) Los Angeles County	488	0.98
Delta charter, MI (township) Eaton County	291	0.98
Vestavia Hills, AL (city) Jefferson County	241	0.97
Bloomfield, MI (township) Oakland County	413	0.96
Andover, MA (town) Essex County	301	0.96
Whitehall, PA (township) Lehigh County	240	0.96
Walpole, MA (town) Norfolk County	218	0.96
Saginaw Township South, MI (cdp) Saginaw County	132	0.96
Glendale, CA (city) Los Angeles County	1,849	0.95
Coral Gables, FL (city) Miami-Dade County	402	0.95
Westlake, OH (city) Cuyahoga County	304	0.95
Acushnet, MA (town) Bristol County	97	0.95
Somersworth, NH (city) Strafford County	108	0.94
Quincy, MA (city) Norfolk County	821	0.93
Torrington, CT (city) Litchfield County	329	0.93
Broadview Heights, OH (city) Cuyahoga County	148	0.93
North Greenbush, NY (town) Rensselaer County	100	0.93
Hillsdale, NJ (borough) Bergen County	94	0.93
Southfield, MI (township) Oakland County	133	0.92
Plymouth Township, MI (cdp) Wayne County	252	0.91
Bridgewater, MA (town) Plymouth County	229	0.91
Wilbraham, MA (town) Hampden County	122	0.91
Rochester Hills, MI (city) Oakland County	619	0.90
Idylwood, VA (cdp) Fairfax County	144	0.90
Forestville, OH (cdp) Hamilton County	100	0.90
Livonia, MI (city) Wayne County	897	0.89
Fall River, MA (city) Bristol County	820	0.89
New Castle, PA (city) Lawrence County	235	0.89
Tysons Corner, VA (cdp) Fairfax County	165	0.89
Northville, MI (township) Wayne County	185	0.88
South Union, PA (township) Fayette County	99	0.88
Farmington Hills, MI (city) Oakland County	716	0.87
North Attleborough, MA (town) Bristol County	237	0.87
Rocky River, OH (city) Cuyahoga County	180	0.87
Gloucester, MA (city) Essex County	260	0.86
Mansfield, MA (town) Bristol County	192	0.86
East Hanover, NJ (township) Morris County	98	0.86
Fenton, MI (city) Genesee County	91	0.86
North Union, PA (township) Fayette County	120	0.85
Foothill Ranch, CA (cdp) Orange County	93	0.85
Shelby, MI (cdp) Macomb County	544	0.84
Roseville, MI (city) Macomb County	406	0.84
Waverly, MI (cdp) Eaton County	135	0.84
Swansea, MA (town) Bristol County	133	0.84
Warren, MI (city) Macomb County	1,152	0.83
North Olmsted, OH (city) Cuyahoga County	282	0.83
Lake Magdalene, FL (cdp) Hillsborough County	235	0.82
East Peoria, IL (city) Tazewell County	187	0.82
Easton, MA (town) Bristol County	183	0.82
Middleburg Heights, OH (city) Cuyahoga County	127	0.82
Duxbury, MA (town) Plymouth County	117	0.82
Grand Rapids charter, MI (township) Kent County	115	0.82
Wolf Trap, VA (cdp) Fairfax County	114	0.82
Mays Chapel, MD (cdp) Baltimore County	94	0.82
Bailey's Crossroads, VA (cdp) Fairfax County	186	0.81
Peters, PA (township) Washington County	143	0.81
Holden, MA (town) Worcester County	127	0.81
Wolcott, CT (town) New Haven County	124	0.81
Crowley, LA (city) Acadia Parish	115	0.81
Seven Hills, OH (city) Cuyahoga County	101	0.81
Kingston, MA (town) Plymouth County	96	0.81
South Yarmouth, MA (cdp) Barnstable County	95	0.81
Farmington, MI (city) Oakland County	84	0.81
Worcester, MA (city) Worcester County	1,373	0.80
Scranton, PA (city) Lackawanna County	608	0.80
Bellingham, MA (town) Norfolk County	122	0.80
Beverly Hills, MI (village) Oakland County	84	0.80
Wanaque, NJ (borough) Passaic County	82	0.80
North Royalton, OH (city) Cuyahoga County	226	0.79
Pittsfield, MA (city) Berkshire County	356	0.78
Colchester, VT (town) Chittenden County	133	0.78
Haverhill, MA (city) Essex County	452	0.77

Notes: (cdp) census designated place; Refer to the Explanation of Data in the front of the book for more detailed information.

Arab: Moroccan

Top 150 Places Sorted by Number

(Based on all places, regardless of population)

Place	Number	%
New York, NY (city) New York City	5,116	0.06
Los Angeles, CA (city) Los Angeles County	1,412	0.04
Arlington, VA (cdp) Arlington County	762	0.40
Chicago, IL (city) Cook County	733	0.03
Philadelphia, PA (city) Philadelphia County	579	0.04
Washington, DC (city) District of Columbia	473	0.08
San Francisco, CA (city) San Francisco County	350	0.05
San Diego, CA (city) San Diego County	330	0.03
Boston, MA (city) Suffolk County	321	0.05
Alexandria, VA (independent city) Alexandria city	304	0.24
Denver, CO (city) Denver County	290	0.05
Revere, MA (city) Suffolk County	289	0.61
Houston, TX (city) Harris County	284	0.01
Orlando, FL (city) Orange County	272	0.15
Hempstead, NY (town) Nassau County	258	0.03
Kissimmee, FL (city) Osceola County	249	0.52
Dallas, TX (city) Dallas County	239	0.02
Jersey City, NJ (city) Hudson County	223	0.09
Seattle, WA (city) King County	209	0.04
Oklahoma City, OK (city) Oklahoma County	198	0.04
Indianapolis, IN (special city) Marion County	197	0.03
Baltimore, MD (independent city) Baltimore city	186	0.03
North Hempstead, NY (town) Nassau County	183	0.08
Malden, MA (city) Middlesex County	175	0.31
Aurora, CO (city) Arapahoe County	173	0.06
Everett, MA (city) Middlesex County	166	0.44
Aspen Hill, MD (cdp) Montgomery County	165	0.33
Detroit, MI (city) Wayne County	156	0.02
Virginia Beach, VA (independent city) Virginia Beach city	142	0.03
Lorton, VA (cdp) Fairfax County	133	0.75
Cleveland, OH (city) Cuyahoga County	133	0.03
Sarasota, FL (city) Sarasota County	128	0.24
Kansas City, MO (city) Jackson County	126	0.03
Columbus, OH (city) Franklin County	121	0.02
Miami Beach, FL (city) Miami-Dade County	120	0.14
Silver Spring, MD (cdp) Montgomery County	116	0.15
Paterson, NJ (city) Passaic County	115	0.08
Kinross charter, MI (township) Chippewa County	114	1.93
Raleigh, NC (city) Wake County	112	0.04
Atlanta, GA (city) Fulton County	109	0.03
Sunny Isles Beach, FL (city) Miami-Dade County	108	0.71
Hollywood, FL (city) Broward County	107	0.08
Chandler, AZ (city) Maricopa County	106	0.06
Somerville, MA (city) Middlesex County	100	0.13
Pembroke Pines, FL (city) Broward County	99	0.07
Vancouver, WA (city) Clark County	99	0.07
Huntington, NY (town) Suffolk County	99	0.05
Colorado Springs, CO (city) El Paso County	99	0.03
West Orange, NJ (cdp) Essex County	98	0.22
Brookline, MA (cdp) Norfolk County	98	0.17
Wichita, KS (city) Sedgwick County	97	0.03
Clearwater, FL (city) Pinellas County	96	0.09
San Antonio, TX (city) Bexar County	96	0.01
Jacksonville, FL (special city) Duval County	94	0.01
Jefferson City, MO (city) Cole County	93	0.24
Youngstown, OH (city) Mahoning County	92	0.11
Paradise, NV (cdp) Clark County	91	0.05
Bailey's Crossroads, VA (cdp) Fairfax County	90	0.39
Lakewood, NJ (township) Ocean County	88	0.15
Saint Petersburg, FL (city) Pinellas County	87	0.04
Norfolk, VA (independent city) Norfolk city	86	0.04
Lauderhill, FL (city) Broward County	84	0.15
Tampa, FL (city) Hillsborough County	84	0.03
Centreville, VA (cdp) Fairfax County	83	0.17
Harrisburg, PA (city) Dauphin County	83	0.17
Annandale, VA (cdp) Fairfax County	83	0.15
Phoenix, AZ (city) Maricopa County	83	0.01
Charlotte, NC (city) Mecklenburg County	81	0.01
Miami, FL (city) Miami-Dade County	80	0.02
Wallingford, CT (town) New Haven County	79	0.18
Cherry Hill, NJ (township) Camden County	78	0.11
Williamsburg, FL (cdp) Orange County	76	1.10
Aventura, FL (city) Miami-Dade County	76	0.30
North Miami Beach, FL (city) Miami-Dade County	76	0.19
Waltham, MA (city) Middlesex County	74	0.12
Madison, WI (city) Dane County	74	0.04
Pittsburgh, PA (city) Allegheny County	74	0.02
Irvine, CA (city) Orange County	73	0.05
Hallandale, FL (city) Broward County	72	0.21
Cambridge, MA (city) Middlesex County	72	0.07
Long Beach, CA (city) Los Angeles County	71	0.02
Saint Louis, MO (independent city) Saint Louis city	70	0.02
South Yarmouth, MA (cdp) Barnstable County	69	0.59
Bexley, OH (city) Franklin County	69	0.52
Yarmouth, MA (town) Barnstable County	69	0.28
Muskegon, MI (city) Muskegon County	69	0.17
Medford, MA (city) Middlesex County	69	0.12
Richmond, VA (independent city) Richmond city	69	0.03
Lincolnia, VA (cdp) Fairfax County	68	0.43
Oyster Bay, NY (town) Nassau County	68	0.02
Skokie, IL (village) Cook County	67	0.11
Oakland, CA (city) Alameda County	66	0.02
Daytona Beach, FL (city) Volusia County	65	0.10
Austin, TX (city) Travis County	65	0.01
Cary, NC (town) Wake County	64	0.07
Huntington Beach, CA (city) Orange County	64	0.03
Las Vegas, NV (city) Clark County	64	0.01
Dale City, VA (cdp) Prince William County	63	0.11
New Rochelle, NY (city) Westchester County	63	0.09
Sunnyvale, CA (city) Santa Clara County	63	0.05
Minneapolis, MN (city) Hennepin County	63	0.02
Babylon, NY (town) Suffolk County	62	0.03
Lisle, IL (village) Du Page County	60	0.28
Franklin, NJ (township) Somerset County	58	0.11
Cliffside Park, NJ (borough) Bergen County	57	0.25
Tucker, GA (cdp) De Kalb County	57	0.21
Muncie, IN (city) Delaware County	57	0.08
Seven Corners, VA (cdp) Fairfax County	56	0.63
Plantation, FL (city) Broward County	56	0.07
Ramapo, NY (town) Rockland County	56	0.05
Albuquerque, NM (city) Bernalillo County	56	0.01
Carlisle, IN (town) Sullivan County	55	2.15
South Huntington, NY (cdp) Suffolk County	55	0.58
Glendale, CA (city) Los Angeles County	55	0.03
North New Hyde Park, NY (cdp) Nassau County	54	0.37
Jefferson, VA (cdp) Fairfax County	54	0.20
Bloomer, MI (township) Montcalm County	53	1.73
Rockville, MD (city) Montgomery County	53	0.11
Deerfield Beach, FL (city) Broward County	53	0.08
Chelsea, MA (city) Suffolk County	52	0.15
Potomac, MD (cdp) Montgomery County	52	0.12
Quincy, MA (city) Norfolk County	52	0.06
Guttenberg, NJ (town) Hudson County	51	0.48
East Meadow, NY (cdp) Nassau County	51	0.14
Flint, MI (city) Genesee County	51	0.04
Plano, TX (city) Collin County	51	0.02
North Bergen, NJ (township) Hudson County	50	0.09
Oak Lawn, IL (village) Cook County	50	0.09
Bridgeport, CT (city) Fairfield County	50	0.04
Indian Harbour Beach, FL (city) Brevard County	49	0.60
Ionia, MI (city) Ionia County	49	0.46
Land O' Lakes, FL (cdp) Pasco County	49	0.24
Teaneck, NJ (cdp) Bergen County	49	0.12
Portsmouth, VA (independent city) Portsmouth city	49	0.05
Pelham Manor, NY (village) Westchester County	48	0.88
Pelham, NY (town) Westchester County	48	0.40
Mount Vernon, VA (cdp) Fairfax County	48	0.17
Chester, PA (city) Delaware County	48	0.13
Weymouth, MA (cdp) Norfolk County	48	0.09
Fort Wayne, IN (city) Allen County	48	0.02
Greensboro, NC (city) Guilford County	48	0.02
Redondo Beach, CA (city) Los Angeles County	46	0.07
Arlington, TX (city) Tarrant County	46	0.01
Bethany, MI (township) Gratiot County	45	1.27
Elkridge, MD (cdp) Howard County	45	0.20
Woodlawn, MD (cdp) Baltimore County	45	0.12
Berwyn, IL (city) Cook County	45	0.08
Viola, NY (cdp) Rockland County	44	0.74
Plymouth Township, MI (cdp) Wayne County	44	0.16
Carlsbad, CA (city) San Diego County	44	0.06

Notes: (cdp) census designated place; Refer to the Explanation of Data in the front of the book for more detailed information.

Arab: Moroccan

Top 150 Places Sorted by Percent

(Based on all places, regardless of population)

Place	Number	%
Graf, IA (city) Dubuque County	4	4.00
Atlantic Beach, SC (town) Horry County	11	2.98
Carlisle, IN (town) Sullivan County	55	2.15
Kinross charter, MI (township) Chippewa County	114	1.93
Bloomer, MI (township) Montcalm County	53	1.73
Centre Island, NY (village) Nassau County	7	1.57
Lakeshore Gardens-Hidden Acres, TX (cdp) San Patricio County	9	1.33
Ten Broeck, KY (city) Jefferson County	2	1.33
Big Sky, MT (cdp) Gallatin County	16	1.32
Packwaukee, WI (town) Marquette County	33	1.29
Bethany, MI (township) Gratiot County	45	1.27
Saddle Rock, NY (village) Nassau County	10	1.26
Marenisco, MI (township) Gogebic County	13	1.21
Williamsburg, FL (cdp) Orange County	76	1.10
Seaside Heights, NJ (borough) Ocean County	34	1.08
Union, WI (town) Waupaca County	8	0.97
Bluewater, CA (cdp) San Bernardino County	2	0.97
Thomaston, NY (village) Nassau County	25	0.96
Fayetteville, PA (cdp) Franklin County	26	0.93
Manistee, MI (township) Manistee County	34	0.91
Denmark, ME (town) Oxford County	9	0.90
Roslyn Harbor, NY (village) Nassau County	9	0.90
Pelham Manor, NY (village) Westchester County	48	0.88
Clyde, CA (cdp) Contra Costa County	6	0.88
Parkers Crossroads, TN (city) Henderson County	2	0.87
Greendale, MO (city) Saint Louis County	6	0.86
Culbertson, NE (village) Hitchcock County	5	0.82
Bay Harbor Islands, FL (town) Miami-Dade County	41	0.80
Berwyn Heights, MD (town) Prince George's County	23	0.77
Lorton, VA (cdp) Fairfax County	133	0.75
Viola, NY (cdp) Rockland County	44	0.74
Tipton, MO (city) Moniteau County	24	0.74
Viburnum, MO (city) Iron County	6	0.73
Montevallo, AL (city) Shelby County	35	0.72
Sunny Isles Beach, FL (city) Miami-Dade County	108	0.71
Eagle Harbor, MI (township) Keweenaw County	2	0.71
Woodside, PA (cdp) Bucks County	19	0.70
Schoharie, NY (village) Schoharie County	7	0.68
Spring House, PA (cdp) Montgomery County	22	0.67
Hastings, FL (town) Saint Johns County	3	0.64
Seven Corners, VA (cdp) Fairfax County	56	0.63
Saint Louis, MI (city) Gratiot County	28	0.63
Hewlett Harbor, NY (village) Nassau County	8	0.63
Revere, MA (city) Suffolk County	289	0.61
Indian Harbour Beach, FL (city) Brevard County	49	0.60
Berlin, MI (township) Ionia County	17	0.60
Newberry, MI (village) Luce County	16	0.60
Shrub Oak, NY (cdp) Westchester County	11	0.60
Pine Mountain Club, CA (cdp) Kern County	10	0.60
South Yarmouth, MA (cdp) Barnstable County	69	0.59
South Huntington, NY (cdp) Suffolk County	55	0.58
Pine, PA (township) Allegheny County	43	0.56
Walnut Grove, WA (cdp) Clark County	41	0.56
Wrightstown, NJ (borough) Burlington County	4	0.54
Wye, MT (cdp) Missoula County	2	0.54
Kissimmee, FL (city) Osceola County	249	0.52
Bexley, OH (city) Franklin County	69	0.52
Hurstbourne Acres, KY (city) Jefferson County	8	0.52
Rochelle Park, NJ (cdp) Bergen County	28	0.51
Bal Harbour, FL (village) Miami-Dade County	17	0.51
Estancia, NM (town) Torrance County	8	0.51
Lake George, NY (village) Warren County	5	0.51
Bardwell, TX (city) Ellis County	3	0.51
Laguna West-Lakeside, CA (cdp) Sacramento County	43	0.50
Littlestown, PA (borough) Adams County	20	0.50
West Gate, VA (cdp) Prince William County	36	0.49
Atlantic Highlands, NJ (borough) Monmouth County	23	0.49
Saint Leo, FL (town) Pasco County	3	0.49
Guttenberg, NJ (town) Hudson County	51	0.48
Berlin, MD (town) Worcester County	17	0.48
Yanceyville, NC (town) Caswell County	10	0.48
Crane, TX (city) Crane County	15	0.47
Ionia, MI (city) Ionia County	49	0.46
Everett, MA (city) Middlesex County	166	0.44
Panton, VT (town) Addison County	3	0.44
Lincolnia, VA (cdp) Fairfax County	68	0.43
Ayer, MA (town) Middlesex County	31	0.43
Chocolay, MI (township) Marquette County	31	0.43
Patterson, LA (city) Saint Mary Parish	22	0.43
Bodfish, CA (cdp) Kern County	8	0.43
Briarcliff, AR (town) Baxter County	2	0.43
Kahaluu-Keauhou, HI (cdp) Hawaii County	10	0.42
Calumet-Norvelt, PA (cdp) Westmoreland County	7	0.42
Millbourne, PA (borough) Delaware County	4	0.42
Briarcliffe Acres, SC (town) Horry County	2	0.42
Wantage, NJ (township) Sussex County	43	0.41
Las Flores, CA (cdp) Orange County	23	0.41
Allenhurst, NJ (borough) Monmouth County	3	0.41
Arlington, VA (cdp) Arlington County	762	0.40
Pelham, NY (town) Westchester County	48	0.40
McMillan, MI (township) Luce County	16	0.40
Adams, MI (township) Houghton County	11	0.40
Clio, AL (town) Barbour County	9	0.40
Bailey's Crossroads, VA (cdp) Fairfax County	90	0.39
Mount Kisco, NY (village) Westchester County	39	0.39
Three Lakes, FL (cdp) Miami-Dade County	27	0.39
Denton, MD (town) Caroline County	11	0.39
Hobe Sound, FL (cdp) Martin County	42	0.38
Country Walk, FL (cdp) Miami-Dade County	41	0.38
The Meadows, FL (cdp) Sarasota County	17	0.38
Marietta-Alderwood, WA (cdp) Whatcom County	15	0.38
North New Hyde Park, NY (cdp) Nassau County	54	0.37
South Padre Island, TX (town) Cameron County	9	0.37
Deal, NJ (borough) Monmouth County	4	0.37
Elba, AL (city) Coffee County	15	0.36
Imperial-Enlow, PA (cdp) Allegheny County	13	0.36
Port Ludlow, WA (cdp) Jefferson County	7	0.36
Leonia, NJ (borough) Bergen County	31	0.35
Adams, PA (township) Butler County	24	0.35
Chester, CT (town) Middlesex County	13	0.35
Northwest Harbor, NY (cdp) Suffolk County	11	0.35
Wenonah, NJ (borough) Gloucester County	8	0.35
Butterfield, MN (city) Watonwan County	2	0.35
Kellyville, OK (town) Creek County	3	0.34
Pepin, WI (village) Pepin County	3	0.34
Aspen Hill, MD (cdp) Montgomery County	165	0.33
Lenox, MI (township) Macomb County	28	0.33
Southchase, FL (cdp) Orange County	15	0.33
Hope, IN (town) Bartholomew County	7	0.33
Fairmount Heights, MD (town) Prince George's County	5	0.33
Bayport, MN (city) Washington County	10	0.32
Colmesneil, TX (city) Tyler County	2	0.32
Malden, MA (city) Middlesex County	175	0.31
University Gardens, NY (cdp) Nassau County	13	0.31
Munising, MI (township) Alger County	10	0.31
Iron River, MI (township) Iron County	5	0.31
Brookside, OH (village) Belmont County	2	0.31
Aventura, FL (city) Miami-Dade County	76	0.30
Covington, VA (independent city) Covington city	19	0.30
Poinciana, FL (cdp) Osceola County	39	0.29
West Bradford, PA (township) Chester County	31	0.29
Taylor Creek, FL (cdp) Okeechobee County	13	0.29
Brookmont, MD (cdp) Montgomery County	9	0.29
Kendall Green, FL (cdp) Broward County	9	0.29
Mission Bay, FL (cdp) Palm Beach County	9	0.29
Bushnell, MI (township) Montcalm County	6	0.29
Yarmouth, MA (town) Barnstable County	69	0.28
Lisle, IL (village) Du Page County	60	0.28
Little Ferry, NJ (borough) Bergen County	30	0.28
Irondale, GA (cdp) Clayton County	22	0.28
Downingtown, PA (borough) Chester County	21	0.28
Lawrence, NY (village) Nassau County	18	0.28
Spring Lake, NJ (borough) Monmouth County	10	0.28
Adairsville, GA (city) Bartow County	7	0.28
Rossville, MD (cdp) Baltimore County	32	0.27
Kemp Mill, MD (cdp) Montgomery County	27	0.27
Tiburon, CA (town) Marin County	24	0.27
Johnson Lane, NV (cdp) Douglas County	13	0.27
Kingsbury, NV (cdp) Douglas County	7	0.27
New Ellenton, SC (town) Aiken County	6	0.27

Notes: (cdp) census designated place; Refer to the Explanation of Data in the front of the book for more detailed information.

Arab: Moroccan

Top 150 Places Sorted by Percent

(Based on places with populations of 10,000 or more)

Place	Number	%
Lorton, VA (cdp) Fairfax County	133	0.75
Sunny Isles Beach, FL (city) Miami-Dade County	108	0.71
Revere, MA (city) Suffolk County	289	0.61
South Yarmouth, MA (cdp) Barnstable County	69	0.59
Kissimmee, FL (city) Osceola County	249	0.52
Bexley, OH (city) Franklin County	69	0.52
Guttenberg, NJ (town) Hudson County	51	0.48
Ionia, MI (city) Ionia County	49	0.46
Everett, MA (city) Middlesex County	166	0.44
Lincolnia, VA (cdp) Fairfax County	68	0.43
Wantage, NJ (township) Sussex County	43	0.41
Arlington, VA (cdp) Arlington County	762	0.40
Pelham, NY (town) Westchester County	48	0.40
Bailey's Crossroads, VA (cdp) Fairfax County	90	0.39
Hobe Sound, FL (cdp) Martin County	42	0.38
Country Walk, FL (cdp) Miami-Dade County	41	0.38
North New Hyde Park, NY (cdp) Nassau County	54	0.37
Aspen Hill, MD (cdp) Montgomery County	165	0.33
Malden, MA (city) Middlesex County	175	0.31
Aventura, FL (city) Miami-Dade County	76	0.30
Poinciana, FL (cdp) Osceola County	39	0.29
West Bradford, PA (township) Chester County	31	0.29
Yarmouth, MA (town) Barnstable County	69	0.28
Lisle, IL (village) Du Page County	60	0.28
Little Ferry, NJ (borough) Bergen County	30	0.28
Rossville, MD (cdp) Baltimore County	32	0.27
Cliffside Park, NJ (borough) Bergen County	57	0.25
Beaufort, SC (city) Beaufort County	32	0.25
Coldwater, MI (city) Branch County	32	0.25
Alexandria, VA (independent city) Alexandria city	304	0.24
Sarasota, FL (city) Sarasota County	128	0.24
Jefferson City, MO (city) Cole County	93	0.24
Land O' Lakes, FL (cdp) Pasco County	49	0.24
Citrus Ridge, FL (cdp) Lake County	27	0.24
Wallingford Center, CT (cdp) New Haven County	41	0.23
Cherry Hill Mall, NJ (cdp) Camden County	31	0.23
West Orange, NJ (cdp) Essex County	98	0.22
Sault Sainte Marie, MI (city) Chippewa County	36	0.22
Ventnor City, NJ (city) Atlantic County	28	0.22
South Miami, FL (city) Miami-Dade County	24	0.22
Hallandale, FL (city) Broward County	72	0.21
Tucker, GA (cdp) De Kalb County	57	0.21
Millburn, NJ (cdp) Essex County	42	0.21
Greene, PA (township) Franklin County	26	0.21
Greentree, NJ (cdp) Camden County	24	0.21
Lower Gwynedd, PA (township) Montgomery County	22	0.21
Jefferson, VA (cdp) Fairfax County	54	0.20
Elkridge, MD (cdp) Howard County	45	0.20
Roselle, NJ (borough) Union County	43	0.20
Georgetown, KY (city) Scott County	37	0.20
North Miami Beach, FL (city) Miami-Dade County	76	0.19
Boca Del Mar, FL (cdp) Palm Beach County	41	0.19
Calabasas, CA (city) Los Angeles County	39	0.19
Pleasantville, NJ (city) Atlantic County	37	0.19
Wallingford, CT (town) New Haven County	79	0.18
Burlington, MA (cdp) Middlesex County	42	0.18
Mineola, NY (village) Nassau County	35	0.18
Phoenixville, PA (borough) Chester County	26	0.18
North Reading, MA (town) Middlesex County	25	0.18
Grover Beach, CA (city) San Luis Obispo County	24	0.18
Hamptons at Boca Raton, FL (cdp) Palm Beach County	20	0.18
Brookline, MA (cdp) Norfolk County	98	0.17
Centreville, VA (cdp) Fairfax County	83	0.17
Harrisburg, PA (city) Dauphin County	83	0.17
Muskegon, MI (city) Muskegon County	69	0.17
Mount Vernon, VA (cdp) Fairfax County	48	0.17
Newington, VA (cdp) Fairfax County	34	0.17
Wilkinsburg, PA (borough) Allegheny County	33	0.17
North Druid Hills, GA (cdp) De Kalb County	32	0.17
Ojus, FL (cdp) Miami-Dade County	28	0.17
Plymouth Township, MI (cdp) Wayne County	44	0.16
Mount Juliet, TN (city) Wilson County	20	0.16
Englewood, OH (city) Montgomery County	19	0.16
Merrifield, VA (cdp) Fairfax County	18	0.16
Orlando, FL (city) Orange County	272	0.15
Silver Spring, MD (cdp) Montgomery County	116	0.15
Lakewood, NJ (township) Ocean County	88	0.15
Lauderhill, FL (city) Broward County	84	0.15
Annandale, VA (cdp) Fairfax County	83	0.15
Chelsea, MA (city) Suffolk County	52	0.15
Fridley, MN (city) Anoka County	41	0.15
South Euclid, OH (city) Cuyahoga County	35	0.15
Pearl, MS (city) Rankin County	33	0.15
Washington, NJ (township) Morris County	26	0.15
Hackettstown, NJ (town) Warren County	16	0.15
Miami Beach, FL (city) Miami-Dade County	120	0.14
East Meadow, NY (cdp) Nassau County	51	0.14
Unity, PA (township) Westmoreland County	30	0.14
Lanham-Seabrook, MD (cdp) Prince George's County	26	0.14
Colonial Park, PA (cdp) Dauphin County	18	0.14
Somerville, MA (city) Middlesex County	100	0.13
Chester, PA (city) Delaware County	48	0.13
Franconia, VA (cdp) Fairfax County	41	0.13
Faribault, MN (city) Rice County	28	0.13
Fullerton, PA (cdp) Lehigh County	19	0.13
Hyattsville, MD (city) Prince George's County	19	0.13
Farmington, MO (city) Saint Francois County	18	0.13
Waltham, MA (city) Middlesex County	74	0.12
Medford, MA (city) Middlesex County	69	0.12
Potomac, MD (cdp) Montgomery County	52	0.12
Teaneck, NJ (cdp) Bergen County	49	0.12
Woodlawn, MD (cdp) Baltimore County	45	0.12
West Hollywood, CA (city) Los Angeles County	43	0.12
Suitland-Silver Hill, MD (cdp) Prince George's County	40	0.12
North Plainfield, NJ (borough) Somerset County	25	0.12
Upper Southampton, PA (township) Bucks County	19	0.12
Riverdale, GA (city) Clayton County	15	0.12
Oldsmar, FL (city) Pinellas County	14	0.12
Panthersville, GA (cdp) De Kalb County	14	0.12
Palm Beach, FL (town) Palm Beach County	12	0.12
Youngstown, OH (city) Mahoning County	92	0.11
Cherry Hill, NJ (township) Camden County	78	0.11
Skokie, IL (village) Cook County	67	0.11
Dale City, VA (cdp) Prince William County	63	0.11
Franklin, NJ (township) Somerset County	58	0.11
Rockville, MD (city) Montgomery County	53	0.11
Holland, MI (city) Ottawa County	38	0.11
Fair Lawn, NJ (borough) Bergen County	34	0.11
Pittsfield charter, MI (township) Washtenaw County	33	0.11
Deer Park, NY (cdp) Suffolk County	30	0.11
Kingsville, TX (city) Kleberg County	29	0.11
Agoura Hills, CA (city) Los Angeles County	23	0.11
Fairview Park, OH (city) Cuyahoga County	20	0.11
Onalaska, WI (city) La Crosse County	16	0.11
Harper Woods, MI (city) Wayne County	15	0.11
Parkland, FL (city) Broward County	15	0.11
Wayland, MA (town) Middlesex County	14	0.11
Freehold, NJ (borough) Monmouth County	12	0.11
Daytona Beach, FL (city) Volusia County	65	0.10
Pennsauken, NJ (cdp) Camden County	36	0.10
Clearfield, UT (city) Davis County	26	0.10
Plainview, NY (cdp) Nassau County	26	0.10
Merrimack, NH (town) Hillsborough County	25	0.10
Cutler Ridge, FL (cdp) Miami-Dade County	24	0.10
Mercer Island, WA (city) King County	22	0.10
Laurel, VA (cdp) Henrico County	15	0.10
New Paltz, NY (town) Ulster County	13	0.10
Saint Marys, GA (city) Camden County	13	0.10
Muscle Shoals, AL (city) Colbert County	12	0.10
Barclay-Kingston, NJ (cdp) Camden County	11	0.10
Browns Mills, NJ (cdp) Burlington County	11	0.10
Coventry, CT (town) Tolland County	11	0.10
River Grove, IL (village) Cook County	11	0.10
Buena Vista charter, MI (township) Saginaw County	10	0.10
Jersey City, NJ (city) Hudson County	223	0.09
Clearwater, FL (city) Pinellas County	96	0.09
New Rochelle, NY (city) Westchester County	63	0.09
North Bergen, NJ (township) Hudson County	50	0.09
Oak Lawn, IL (village) Cook County	50	0.09
Weymouth, MA (cdp) Norfolk County	48	0.09

Notes: (cdp) census designated place; Refer to the Explanation of Data in the front of the book for more detailed information.

Arab: Palestinian

Top 150 Places Sorted by Number

(Based on all places, regardless of population)

Place	Number	%
New York, NY (city) New York City	3,184	0.04
Chicago, IL (city) Cook County	2,052	0.07
Houston, TX (city) Harris County	1,135	0.06
Los Angeles, CA (city) Los Angeles County	1,009	0.03
Dearborn, MI (city) Wayne County	953	0.97
San Francisco, CA (city) San Francisco County	877	0.11
Jacksonville, FL (special city) Duval County	789	0.11
Daly City, CA (city) San Mateo County	770	0.74
Philadelphia, PA (city) Philadelphia County	741	0.05
San Diego, CA (city) San Diego County	704	0.06
Arlington, TX (city) Tarrant County	622	0.19
San Jose, CA (city) Santa Clara County	621	0.07
Oak Lawn, IL (village) Cook County	577	1.04
Paterson, NJ (city) Passaic County	556	0.37
Columbus, OH (city) Franklin County	510	0.07
San Bruno, CA (city) San Mateo County	479	1.19
Lakewood, OH (city) Cuyahoga County	473	0.84
Charlotte, NC (city) Mecklenburg County	406	0.07
Raleigh, NC (city) Wake County	404	0.15
Orland Park, IL (village) Cook County	394	0.77
Anaheim, CA (city) Orange County	376	0.11
North Olmsted, OH (city) Cuyahoga County	354	1.04
North Bergen, NJ (township) Hudson County	354	0.61
South San Francisco, CA (city) San Mateo County	349	0.57
Livonia, MI (city) Wayne County	325	0.32
Toledo, OH (city) Lucas County	322	0.10
Burbank, IL (city) Cook County	311	1.12
Clifton, NJ (city) Passaic County	298	0.38
Millbrae, CA (city) San Mateo County	294	1.42
Memphis, TN (city) Shelby County	288	0.04
Bailey's Crossroads, VA (cdp) Fairfax County	275	1.20
Milwaukee, WI (city) Milwaukee County	257	0.04
Fremont, CA (city) Alameda County	254	0.12
Cleveland, OH (city) Cuyahoga County	244	0.05
Detroit, MI (city) Wayne County	234	0.02
Tulsa, OK (city) Tulsa County	226	0.06
Greensboro, NC (city) Guilford County	223	0.10
Dearborn Heights, MI (city) Wayne County	220	0.38
Lexington-Fayette, KY (special city) Fayette County	208	0.08
Passaic, NJ (city) Passaic County	207	0.31
Hickory Hills, IL (city) Cook County	203	1.46
Pasadena, TX (city) Harris County	200	0.14
Fresno, CA (city) Fresno County	199	0.05
Annandale, VA (cdp) Fairfax County	194	0.35
San Antonio, TX (city) Bexar County	184	0.02
Chicago Ridge, IL (village) Cook County	183	1.32
Portland, OR (city) Multnomah County	179	0.03
Arlington, VA (cdp) Arlington County	178	0.09
Yonkers, NY (city) Westchester County	177	0.09
Warren, MI (city) Macomb County	174	0.13
Islip, NY (town) Suffolk County	174	0.05
Missouri City, TX (city) Fort Bend County	171	0.33
Mission Viejo, CA (city) Orange County	171	0.18
Canton, MI (cdp) Wayne County	170	0.22
Burke, VA (cdp) Fairfax County	169	0.29
Orlando, FL (city) Orange County	169	0.09
Metairie, LA (cdp) Jefferson Parish	163	0.11
Irving, TX (city) Dallas County	160	0.08
Plantation, FL (city) Broward County	156	0.19
Palos Hills, IL (city) Cook County	155	0.87
Sugar Land, TX (city) Fort Bend County	153	0.24
Long Beach, CA (city) Los Angeles County	153	0.03
Lincolnia, VA (cdp) Fairfax County	152	0.96
Bloomfield, MI (township) Oakland County	151	0.35
Minneapolis, MN (city) Hennepin County	150	0.04
Brandon, FL (cdp) Hillsborough County	149	0.19
West Palm Beach, FL (city) Palm Beach County	149	0.18
Dallas, TX (city) Dallas County	149	0.01
Montgomery Village, MD (cdp) Montgomery County	147	0.39
Baton Rouge, LA (city) East Baton Rouge Parish	146	0.06
Westminster, CA (city) Orange County	145	0.16
Saddle Brook, NJ (cdp) Bergen County	143	1.09
Mesquite, TX (city) Dallas County	143	0.11
Riverside, CA (city) Riverside County	142	0.06
Bridgeview, IL (village) Cook County	141	0.92
New Orleans, LA (city) Orleans Parish	135	0.03
Hempstead, NY (town) Nassau County	133	0.02
Fairfield, CA (city) Solano County	130	0.14
Orange, CA (city) Orange County	130	0.10
Nashville-Davidson, TN (special city) Davidson County	130	0.02
Germantown, MD (cdp) Montgomery County	127	0.23
Saint Petersburg, FL (city) Pinellas County	127	0.05
Blacksburg, VA (town) Montgomery County	125	0.32
Washington, DC (city) District of Columbia	125	0.02
Garfield, NJ (city) Bergen County	121	0.41
Aurora, CO (city) Arapahoe County	121	0.04
Fairview, NJ (borough) Bergen County	120	0.91
Scottsdale, AZ (city) Maricopa County	120	0.06
West Bloomfield, MI (township) Oakland County	119	0.18
Highlands Ranch, CO (cdp) Douglas County	119	0.17
Kenner, LA (city) Jefferson Parish	119	0.17
Miami, FL (city) Miami-Dade County	119	0.03
Boston, MA (city) Suffolk County	118	0.02
Manlius, NY (town) Onondaga County	117	0.37
San Mateo, CA (city) San Mateo County	117	0.13
Pasadena, CA (city) Los Angeles County	117	0.09
Laguna, CA (cdp) Sacramento County	116	0.34
Upland, CA (city) San Bernardino County	116	0.17
Alameda, CA (city) Alameda County	116	0.16
Baltimore, MD (independent city) Baltimore city	116	0.02
El Paso, TX (city) El Paso County	115	0.02
Troy, MI (city) Oakland County	114	0.14
Sunnyvale, CA (city) Santa Clara County	114	0.09
Phoenix, AZ (city) Maricopa County	114	0.01
West Springfield, VA (cdp) Fairfax County	113	0.40
Ypsilanti, MI (township) Washtenaw County	113	0.23
The Hammocks, FL (cdp) Miami-Dade County	112	0.24
Goodings Grove, IL (cdp) Will County	111	0.65
Glendale, AZ (city) Maricopa County	110	0.05
Cambridge, MA (city) Middlesex County	109	0.11
Mount Pleasant, MI (city) Isabella County	108	0.41
Ramapo, NY (town) Rockland County	108	0.10
Denver, CO (city) Denver County	108	0.02
Farmington Hills, MI (city) Oakland County	107	0.13
Ann Arbor, MI (city) Washtenaw County	107	0.09
Summit, IL (village) Cook County	106	1.00
Rocky River, OH (city) Cuyahoga County	106	0.51
Foster City, CA (city) San Mateo County	106	0.37
Chattanooga, TN (city) Hamilton County	106	0.07
Huntington Beach, CA (city) Orange County	106	0.06
Modesto, CA (city) Stanislaus County	106	0.06
Birmingham, AL (city) Jefferson County	106	0.04
Salix-Beauty Line Park, PA (cdp) Cambria County	105	8.76
Adams, PA (township) Cambria County	105	1.62
Terrytown, LA (cdp) Jefferson Parish	105	0.41
Palm Harbor, FL (cdp) Pinellas County	105	0.18
Dunes Road, FL (cdp) Palm Beach County	104	21.99
Pearland, TX (city) Brazoria County	104	0.28
Euless, TX (city) Tarrant County	104	0.23
Colesville, MD (cdp) Montgomery County	102	0.51
Wichita, KS (city) Sedgwick County	102	0.03
Camillus, NY (town) Onondaga County	101	0.44
Glendora, CA (city) Los Angeles County	101	0.20
Lodi, CA (city) San Joaquin County	101	0.18
Hawthorne, CA (city) Los Angeles County	100	0.12
Centreville, VA (cdp) Fairfax County	99	0.20
Henderson, NV (city) Clark County	99	0.06
Pittsfield charter, MI (township) Washtenaw County	98	0.33
Westlake, OH (city) Cuyahoga County	98	0.31
Fountainbleau, FL (cdp) Miami-Dade County	98	0.16
Tinley Park, IL (village) Cook County	97	0.20
Garland, TX (city) Dallas County	97	0.04
Richmond, CA (city) Contra Costa County	95	0.10
Newton, NJ (town) Sussex County	94	1.14
Justice, IL (village) Cook County	94	0.78
Mount Morris, MI (township) Genesee County	94	0.39
Racine, WI (city) Racine County	92	0.11
Seattle, WA (city) King County	91	0.02
Petaluma, CA (city) Sonoma County	90	0.17
Chantilly, VA (cdp) Fairfax County	89	0.22

Notes: (cdp) census designated place; Refer to the Explanation of Data in the front of the book for more detailed information.

Arab: Palestinian

Top 150 Places Sorted by Percent

(Based on all places, regardless of population)

Place	Number	%
Dunes Road, FL (cdp) Palm Beach County	104	21.99
Salix-Beauty Line Park, PA (cdp) Cambria County	105	8.76
McIntosh, AL (town) Washington County	17	6.94
Downsville, LA (village) Union Parish	3	2.24
Cripple Creek, CO (city) Teller County	24	2.14
Dunlap, IL (village) Peoria County	19	2.11
Callao, MO (city) Macon County	5	1.82
Williamstown, MI (township) Ingham County	81	1.63
Adams, PA (township) Cambria County	105	1.62
Shannon, GA (cdp) Floyd County	28	1.57
Bastrop, TX (city) Bastrop County	86	1.56
Hickory Hills, IL (city) Cook County	203	1.46
Millbrae, CA (city) San Mateo County	294	1.42
Chicago Ridge, IL (village) Cook County	183	1.32
Molino, FL (cdp) Escambia County	18	1.27
White Sands, NM (cdp) Dona Ana County	18	1.26
Santa Teresa, NM (cdp) Dona Ana County	32	1.23
Bailey's Crossroads, VA (cdp) Fairfax County	275	1.20
San Bruno, CA (city) San Mateo County	479	1.19
Newton, NJ (town) Sussex County	94	1.14
Burbank, IL (city) Cook County	311	1.12
Heathcote, NJ (cdp) Middlesex County	51	1.11
Fayetteville, NY (village) Onondaga County	47	1.11
Saddle Brook, NJ (cdp) Bergen County	143	1.09
Sturtevant, WI (village) Racine County	57	1.07
Oak Lawn, IL (village) Cook County	577	1.04
North Olmsted, OH (city) Cuyahoga County	354	1.04
Long Grove, IL (village) Lake County	68	1.03
Summit, IL (village) Cook County	106	1.00
Dearborn, MI (city) Wayne County	953	0.97
Jamestown, NC (town) Guilford County	28	0.97
Lincolnia, VA (cdp) Fairfax County	152	0.96
Bridgeview, IL (village) Cook County	141	0.92
Fairview, NJ (borough) Bergen County	120	0.91
Haledon, NJ (borough) Passaic County	74	0.90
Palos Hills, IL (city) Cook County	155	0.87
Taylor Lake Village, TX (city) Harris County	32	0.87
Oak Park, CA (cdp) Ventura County	21	0.86
Lakewood, OH (city) Cuyahoga County	473	0.84
Gurley, NE (village) Cheyenne County	2	0.84
Doctor Phillips, FL (cdp) Orange County	80	0.83
Wesley Chapel, FL (cdp) Pasco County	48	0.82
Green Valley, CA (cdp) Solano County	16	0.82
Middletown, KY (city) Jefferson County	48	0.81
Valencia, NM (cdp) Valencia County	36	0.80
Foxfield, CO (town) Arapahoe County	6	0.79
Justice, IL (village) Cook County	94	0.78
Mechanicsville, PA (cdp) Montour County	25	0.78
Orland Park, IL (village) Cook County	394	0.77
Friendship Village, MD (cdp) Montgomery County	34	0.77
Daly City, CA (city) San Mateo County	770	0.74
Delmar, MD (town) Wicomico County	13	0.74
Rosemont, IL (village) Cook County	30	0.72
Bay Hill, FL (cdp) Orange County	38	0.71
Sorrento, ME (town) Hancock County	2	0.70
Ottawa Hills, OH (village) Lucas County	31	0.68
Lower Heidelberg, PA (township) Berks County	29	0.67
Goodings Grove, IL (cdp) Will County	111	0.65
Cherry Valley, NY (village) Otsego County	4	0.65
Schiller Park, IL (village) Cook County	75	0.64
Murphy, TX (city) Collin County	20	0.64
Bay Pines, FL (cdp) Pinellas County	21	0.63
Pleasant Gap, PA (cdp) Centre County	11	0.63
North Bergen, NJ (township) Hudson County	354	0.61
Prospect Park, NJ (borough) Passaic County	35	0.61
Morada, CA (cdp) San Joaquin County	22	0.61
Mayflower Village, CA (cdp) Los Angeles County	30	0.60
Plainview, TN (city) Union County	12	0.60
Mahoning, PA (township) Montour County	25	0.59
Flying Hills, PA (cdp) Berks County	7	0.59
Trimble, TN (town) Dyer County	4	0.58
Odessa, DE (town) New Castle County	2	0.58
South San Francisco, CA (city) San Mateo County	349	0.57
Orland Hills, IL (village) Cook County	39	0.57
Sudley, VA (cdp) Prince William County	44	0.55
West Salem, WI (village) La Crosse County	25	0.55
Wallace, NC (town) Duplin County	18	0.55
Grand Terrace, CA (city) San Bernardino County	64	0.54
Fairmount, NY (cdp) Onondaga County	58	0.54
Flossmoor, IL (village) Cook County	50	0.54
Providence, NY (town) Saratoga County	10	0.54
Hoschton, GA (city) Jackson County	6	0.54
Old Jefferson, LA (cdp) East Baton Rouge Parish	30	0.53
Surfside, FL (town) Miami-Dade County	27	0.53
Rocky River, OH (city) Cuyahoga County	106	0.51
Colesville, MD (cdp) Montgomery County	102	0.51
North Bay Shore, NY (cdp) Suffolk County	77	0.51
Happy Valley, OR (city) Clackamas County	25	0.51
East Oakdale, CA (cdp) Stanislaus County	14	0.51
Mission Canyon, CA (cdp) Santa Barbara County	13	0.51
Campbell, OH (city) Mahoning County	47	0.50
Edgemont Park, MI (cdp) Ingham County	12	0.50
Ridgefield, NJ (borough) Bergen County	53	0.49
Emeryville, CA (city) Alameda County	34	0.49
Auburn, MI (city) Bay County	10	0.49
Rankin, IL (village) Vermilion County	3	0.49
East La Mirada, CA (cdp) Los Angeles County	46	0.48
Worth, IL (village) Cook County	52	0.47
Umatilla, OR (city) Umatilla County	23	0.47
Esperance, WA (cdp) Snohomish County	17	0.47
Lowellville, OH (village) Mahoning County	6	0.47
Bear Creek, TX (village) Hays County	2	0.47
East Pikeland, PA (township) Chester County	30	0.46
Hybla Valley, VA (cdp) Fairfax County	75	0.45
Jenkintown, PA (borough) Montgomery County	20	0.45
Indian Springs Village, AL (town) Shelby County	10	0.45
Camillus, NY (town) Onondaga County	101	0.44
Fort Gratiot, MI (township) Saint Clair County	47	0.44
Waihee-Waiehu, HI (cdp) Maui County	32	0.44
Holden Heights, FL (cdp) Orange County	17	0.44
Vinton, IA (city) Benton County	22	0.43
Woodlynne, NJ (borough) Camden County	12	0.43
Edgecliff Village, TX (town) Tarrant County	11	0.43
Ben Lomond, CA (cdp) Santa Cruz County	10	0.43
Au Train, MI (township) Alger County	5	0.43
Brooklyn, OH (city) Cuyahoga County	49	0.42
Rochelle, IL (city) Ogle County	39	0.42
Woodside, CA (town) San Mateo County	22	0.42
Nevada City, CA (city) Nevada County	12	0.42
Garfield, NJ (city) Bergen County	121	0.41
Mount Pleasant, MI (city) Isabella County	108	0.41
Terrytown, LA (cdp) Jefferson Parish	105	0.41
Tysons Corner, VA (cdp) Fairfax County	75	0.41
Mount Juliet, TN (city) Wilson County	50	0.41
Masonboro, NC (cdp) New Hanover County	49	0.41
Hunters Creek Village, TX (city) Harris County	18	0.41
Orchard Lake Village, MI (city) Oakland County	9	0.41
West Springfield, VA (cdp) Fairfax County	113	0.40
South Daytona, FL (city) Volusia County	53	0.40
Fruitville, FL (cdp) Sarasota County	52	0.40
Great Falls, VA (cdp) Fairfax County	34	0.40
Fairview, OR (city) Multnomah County	31	0.40
Point, TX (city) Rains County	3	0.40
Montgomery Village, MD (cdp) Montgomery County	147	0.39
Mount Morris, MI (township) Genesee County	94	0.39
Monsey, NY (cdp) Rockland County	58	0.39
Paradise Valley, AZ (town) Maricopa County	53	0.39
Rockcreek, OR (cdp) Washington County	37	0.39
Lansing charter, MI (township) Ingham County	33	0.39
Wedgefield, FL (cdp) Orange County	11	0.39
Clifton, NJ (city) Passaic County	298	0.38
Dearborn Heights, MI (city) Wayne County	220	0.38
Meadow Woods, FL (cdp) Orange County	44	0.38
Hanover, PA (township) Luzerne County	43	0.38
Travilah, MD (cdp) Montgomery County	29	0.38
Geneseo, IL (city) Henry County	25	0.38
Barton Creek, TX (cdp) Travis County	6	0.38
Arlington, OR (city) Gilliam County	2	0.38
Broad Fields, KY (city) Jefferson County	1	0.38
Cabery, IL (village) Ford County	1	0.38

Notes: (cdp) census designated place; Refer to the Explanation of Data in the front of the book for more detailed information.

Arab: Palestinian

Top 150 Places Sorted by Percent

(Based on places with populations of 10,000 or more)

Place	Number	%
Hickory Hills, IL (city) Cook County	203	1.46
Millbrae, CA (city) San Mateo County	294	1.42
Chicago Ridge, IL (village) Cook County	183	1.32
Bailey's Crossroads, VA (cdp) Fairfax County	275	1.20
San Bruno, CA (city) San Mateo County	479	1.19
Burbank, IL (city) Cook County	311	1.12
Saddle Brook, NJ (cdp) Bergen County	143	1.09
Oak Lawn, IL (village) Cook County	577	1.04
North Olmsted, OH (city) Cuyahoga County	354	1.04
Summit, IL (village) Cook County	106	1.00
Dearborn, MI (city) Wayne County	953	0.97
Lincolnia, VA (cdp) Fairfax County	152	0.96
Bridgeview, IL (village) Cook County	141	0.92
Fairview, NJ (borough) Bergen County	120	0.91
Palos Hills, IL (city) Cook County	155	0.87
Lakewood, OH (city) Cuyahoga County	473	0.84
Justice, IL (village) Cook County	94	0.78
Orland Park, IL (village) Cook County	394	0.77
Daly City, CA (city) San Mateo County	770	0.74
Goodings Grove, IL (cdp) Will County	111	0.65
Schiller Park, IL (village) Cook County	75	0.64
North Bergen, NJ (township) Hudson County	354	0.61
South San Francisco, CA (city) San Mateo County	349	0.57
Grand Terrace, CA (city) San Bernardino County	64	0.54
Fairmount, NY (cdp) Onondaga County	58	0.54
Rocky River, OH (city) Cuyahoga County	106	0.51
Colesville, MD (cdp) Montgomery County	102	0.51
North Bay Shore, NY (cdp) Suffolk County	77	0.51
Ridgefield, NJ (borough) Bergen County	53	0.49
Worth, IL (village) Cook County	52	0.47
Hybla Valley, VA (cdp) Fairfax County	75	0.45
Camillus, NY (town) Onondaga County	101	0.44
Fort Gratiot, MI (township) Saint Clair County	47	0.44
Brooklyn, OH (city) Cuyahoga County	49	0.42
Garfield, NJ (city) Bergen County	121	0.41
Mount Pleasant, MI (city) Isabella County	108	0.41
Terrytown, LA (cdp) Jefferson Parish	105	0.41
Tysons Corner, VA (cdp) Fairfax County	75	0.41
Mount Juliet, TN (city) Wilson County	50	0.41
Masonboro, NC (cdp) New Hanover County	49	0.41
West Springfield, VA (cdp) Fairfax County	113	0.40
South Daytona, FL (city) Volusia County	53	0.40
Fruitville, FL (cdp) Sarasota County	52	0.40
Montgomery Village, MD (cdp) Montgomery County	147	0.39
Mount Morris, MI (township) Genesee County	94	0.39
Monsey, NY (cdp) Rockland County	58	0.39
Paradise Valley, AZ (town) Maricopa County	53	0.39
Clifton, NJ (city) Passaic County	298	0.38
Dearborn Heights, MI (city) Wayne County	220	0.38
Meadow Woods, FL (cdp) Orange County	44	0.38
Hanover, PA (township) Luzerne County	43	0.38
Paterson, NJ (city) Passaic County	556	0.37
Manlius, NY (town) Onondaga County	117	0.37
Foster City, CA (city) San Mateo County	106	0.37
Orinda, CA (city) Contra Costa County	65	0.37
Evergreen Park, IL (village) Cook County	75	0.36
Annandale, VA (cdp) Fairfax County	194	0.35
Bloomfield, MI (township) Oakland County	151	0.35
Elmwood Park, NJ (borough) Bergen County	67	0.35
Montgomery, OH (city) Hamilton County	35	0.35
Laguna, CA (cdp) Sacramento County	116	0.34
Northville, MI (township) Wayne County	71	0.34
Idylwood, VA (cdp) Fairfax County	54	0.34
Fenton, MI (city) Genesee County	36	0.34
Missouri City, TX (city) Fort Bend County	171	0.33
Pittsfield charter, MI (township) Washtenaw County	98	0.33
Marco Island, FL (city) Collier County	49	0.33
Hillsdale, NJ (borough) Bergen County	33	0.33
Livonia, MI (city) Wayne County	325	0.32
Blacksburg, VA (town) Montgomery County	125	0.32
Selma, CA (city) Fresno County	61	0.32
Passaic, NJ (city) Passaic County	207	0.31
Westlake, OH (city) Cuyahoga County	98	0.31
Burlingame, CA (city) San Mateo County	87	0.31
Belmont, CA (city) San Mateo County	78	0.31

Place	Number	%
Grand Island, NY (town) Erie County	58	0.31
South Elgin, IL (village) Kane County	49	0.31
Aliquippa, PA (city) Beaver County	36	0.31
Crestline, CA (cdp) San Bernardino County	32	0.31
Laurel, VA (cdp) Henrico County	44	0.30
Mays Chapel, MD (cdp) Baltimore County	34	0.30
Burke, VA (cdp) Fairfax County	169	0.29
Texas, MI (township) Kalamazoo County	32	0.29
Pearland, TX (city) Brazoria County	104	0.28
Springfield, VA (cdp) Fairfax County	86	0.28
West Lafayette, IN (city) Tippecanoe County	81	0.28
Suisun City, CA (city) Solano County	72	0.28
Coral Terrace, FL (cdp) Miami-Dade County	69	0.28
Duarte, CA (city) Los Angeles County	61	0.28
Issaquah, WA (city) King County	31	0.28
Blue Island, IL (city) Cook County	64	0.27
Villa Park, IL (village) Du Page County	60	0.27
Greater Northdale, FL (cdp) Hillsborough County	55	0.27
Scottsboro, AL (city) Jackson County	40	0.27
Mantua, NJ (township) Gloucester County	39	0.27
Punta Gorda, FL (city) Charlotte County	39	0.27
Foothill Ranch, CA (cdp) Orange County	29	0.27
Silver Spring, PA (township) Cumberland County	29	0.27
Bound Brook, NJ (borough) Somerset County	28	0.27
Parkland, FL (city) Broward County	37	0.26
Sunnyside, WA (city) Yakima County	37	0.26
San Dimas, CA (city) Los Angeles County	88	0.25
Cliffside Park, NJ (borough) Bergen County	58	0.25
Charleston, IL (city) Coles County	52	0.25
Fords, NJ (cdp) Middlesex County	38	0.25
Sugar Land, TX (city) Fort Bend County	153	0.24
The Hammocks, FL (cdp) Miami-Dade County	112	0.24
Swampscott, MA (cdp) Essex County	34	0.24
Wolf Trap, VA (cdp) Fairfax County	33	0.24
Landen, OH (cdp) Warren County	30	0.24
Germantown, MD (cdp) Montgomery County	127	0.23
Ypsilanti, MI (township) Washtenaw County	113	0.23
Euless, TX (city) Tarrant County	104	0.23
Egypt Lake-Leto, FL (cdp) Hillsborough County	75	0.23
Paramus, NJ (borough) Bergen County	59	0.23
Niskayuna, NY (town) Schenectady County	46	0.23
El Dorado Hills, CA (cdp) El Dorado County	41	0.23
Ives Estates, FL (cdp) Miami-Dade County	40	0.23
Merrifield, VA (cdp) Fairfax County	25	0.23
Washington, NJ (township) Mercer County	24	0.23
Canton, MI (cdp) Wayne County	170	0.22
Chantilly, VA (cdp) Fairfax County	89	0.22
Greenbelt, MD (city) Prince George's County	48	0.22
Sherwood, AR (city) Pulaski County	48	0.22
Sharon, MA (town) Norfolk County	38	0.22
Bellaire, TX (city) Harris County	35	0.22
Alamo, CA (cdp) Contra Costa County	33	0.22
Weehawken, NJ (township) Hudson County	30	0.22
McLean, VA (cdp) Fairfax County	83	0.21
Duncanville, TX (city) Dallas County	75	0.21
Niles, IL (village) Cook County	64	0.21
Hazelwood, MO (city) Saint Louis County	54	0.21
Dania Beach, FL (city) Broward County	43	0.21
Mountlake Terrace, WA (city) Snohomish County	42	0.21
Tallmadge, OH (city) Summit County	35	0.21
La Palma, CA (city) Orange County	32	0.21
Cypress Lake, FL (cdp) Lee County	25	0.21
Terryville, NY (cdp) Suffolk County	22	0.21
Glendora, CA (city) Los Angeles County	101	0.20
Centreville, VA (cdp) Fairfax County	99	0.20
Tinley Park, IL (village) Cook County	97	0.20
Aliso Viejo, CA (cdp) Orange County	82	0.20
Fridley, MN (city) Anoka County	55	0.20
Alsip, IL (village) Cook County	39	0.20
Fairview Park, OH (city) Cuyahoga County	36	0.20
Yucca Valley, CA (town) San Bernardino County	33	0.20
Fairfield, AL (city) Jefferson County	25	0.20
Grosse Pointe Park, MI (city) Wayne County	25	0.20
Lincolnwood, IL (village) Cook County	25	0.20
Hasbrouck Heights, NJ (borough) Bergen County	23	0.20

Notes: (cdp) census designated place; Refer to the Explanation of Data in the front of the book for more detailed information.

Arab: Syrian

Top 150 Places Sorted by Number

(Based on all places, regardless of population)

Place	Number	%
New York, NY (city) New York City	10,985	0.14
Los Angeles, CA (city) Los Angeles County	2,995	0.08
Allentown, PA (city) Lehigh County	1,708	1.60
Jacksonville, FL (special city) Duval County	1,182	0.16
Chicago, IL (city) Cook County	1,124	0.04
Clifton, NJ (city) Passaic County	1,010	1.28
Wayne, NJ (cdp) Passaic County	853	1.58
Houston, TX (city) Harris County	849	0.04
Burbank, CA (city) Los Angeles County	831	0.83
Boston, MA (city) Suffolk County	709	0.12
Glendale, CA (city) Los Angeles County	598	0.31
Dearborn, MI (city) Wayne County	567	0.58
San Diego, CA (city) San Diego County	563	0.05
Worcester, MA (city) Worcester County	559	0.32
Pittsburgh, PA (city) Allegheny County	447	0.13
Glendora, CA (city) Los Angeles County	442	0.89
Phoenix, AZ (city) Maricopa County	442	0.03
Hempstead, NY (town) Nassau County	424	0.06
Whitehall, PA (township) Lehigh County	421	1.69
Fullerton, PA (cdp) Lehigh County	414	2.91
Pawtucket, RI (city) Providence County	388	0.53
San Jose, CA (city) Santa Clara County	384	0.04
Dallas, TX (city) Dallas County	382	0.03
Columbus, OH (city) Franklin County	381	0.05
Haledon, NJ (borough) Passaic County	371	4.50
Wilkes-Barre, PA (city) Luzerne County	362	0.84
Portland, OR (city) Multnomah County	353	0.07
El Paso, TX (city) El Paso County	352	0.06
Indianapolis, IN (special city) Marion County	346	0.04
Anaheim, CA (city) Orange County	341	0.10
Ocean, NJ (township) Monmouth County	337	1.25
Kendall, FL (cdp) Miami-Dade County	335	0.45
Lincoln, RI (town) Providence County	333	1.59
Paterson, NJ (city) Passaic County	329	0.22
San Francisco, CA (city) San Francisco County	314	0.04
Cumberland, RI (town) Providence County	306	0.96
Toledo, OH (city) Lucas County	304	0.10
Las Vegas, NV (city) Clark County	297	0.06
Troy, MI (city) Oakland County	294	0.36
Totowa, NJ (borough) Passaic County	287	2.91
Canton, OH (city) Stark County	278	0.34
Austin, TX (city) Travis County	270	0.04
Huntington Beach, CA (city) Orange County	269	0.14
Hawthorne, NJ (borough) Passaic County	266	1.46
Warren, MI (city) Macomb County	266	0.19
Sterling Heights, MI (city) Macomb County	265	0.21
Saint Clair Shores, MI (city) Macomb County	264	0.42
Rancho Cucamonga, CA (city) San Bernardino County	259	0.20
San Antonio, TX (city) Bexar County	256	0.02
Clinton, MI (cdp) Macomb County	255	0.27
New Kensington, PA (city) Westmoreland County	254	1.72
Arlington, VA (cdp) Arlington County	254	0.13
Philadelphia, PA (city) Philadelphia County	254	0.02
Norwood, MA (cdp) Norfolk County	245	0.86
Farmington Hills, MI (city) Oakland County	245	0.30
Denver, CO (city) Denver County	242	0.04
Spring Hill, FL (cdp) Hernando County	239	0.35
Miami, FL (city) Miami-Dade County	236	0.07
Lancaster, CA (city) Los Angeles County	234	0.20
Cranston, RI (city) Providence County	224	0.28
Santa Clarita, CA (city) Los Angeles County	219	0.14
New Castle, PA (city) Lawrence County	218	0.83
Lodi, NJ (borough) Bergen County	215	0.90
San Buenaventura, CA (city) Ventura County	214	0.21
Lakewood, OH (city) Cuyahoga County	213	0.38
Brookhaven, NY (town) Suffolk County	208	0.05
Grand Rapids, MI (city) Kent County	207	0.10
Orlando, FL (city) Orange County	204	0.11
Hanover, PA (township) Luzerne County	199	1.74
Arlington, TX (city) Tarrant County	197	0.06
Omaha, NE (city) Douglas County	196	0.05
Lafayette, LA (city) Lafayette Parish	195	0.18
Virginia Beach, VA (independent city) Virginia Beach city	194	0.05
Detroit, MI (city) Wayne County	193	0.02
Terre Haute, IN (city) Vigo County	188	0.32
Cleveland, OH (city) Cuyahoga County	187	0.04
Hollywood, FL (city) Broward County	186	0.13
Stratford, CT (cdp) Fairfield County	185	0.37
Seattle, WA (city) King County	183	0.03
Aventura, FL (city) Miami-Dade County	182	0.72
Jersey City, NJ (city) Hudson County	181	0.08
Deal, NJ (borough) Monmouth County	180	16.82
Shelby, MI (cdp) Macomb County	179	0.28
Charlotte, NC (city) Mecklenburg County	179	0.03
Johnston, RI (town) Providence County	177	0.63
Fullerton, CA (city) Orange County	177	0.14
Middletown, NJ (township) Monmouth County	176	0.27
Livonia, MI (city) Wayne County	176	0.18
Alexandria, LA (city) Rapides Parish	174	0.37
Little Falls, NJ (cdp) Passaic County	173	1.59
Long Branch, NJ (city) Monmouth County	173	0.55
La Verne, CA (city) Los Angeles County	173	0.54
Woonsocket, RI (city) Providence County	170	0.39
Parsippany-Troy Hills, NJ (township) Morris County	170	0.34
Gresham, OR (city) Multnomah County	170	0.19
Fairfield, CT (town) Fairfield County	169	0.29
Corona, CA (city) Riverside County	169	0.14
Orange, CA (city) Orange County	169	0.13
Torrance, CA (city) Los Angeles County	168	0.12
Stockton, CA (city) San Joaquin County	168	0.07
New Milford, NJ (borough) Bergen County	167	1.02
Hempfield, PA (township) Westmoreland County	166	0.41
Providence, RI (city) Providence County	163	0.09
Oyster Bay, NY (town) Nassau County	163	0.06
Quincy, MA (city) Norfolk County	162	0.18
Richardson, TX (city) Dallas County	162	0.18
Toms River, NJ (cdp) Ocean County	161	0.19
Dover, NJ (township) Ocean County	161	0.18
Plano, TX (city) Collin County	160	0.07
Charleston, WV (city) Kanawha County	158	0.30
Canton, MI (cdp) Wayne County	158	0.21
Fresno, CA (city) Fresno County	157	0.04
Westlake, OH (city) Cuyahoga County	156	0.49
Bloomfield, MI (township) Oakland County	156	0.36
Paramus, NJ (borough) Bergen County	155	0.60
Sugar Land, TX (city) Fort Bend County	155	0.24
Pembroke Pines, FL (city) Broward County	155	0.11
West Bloomfield, MI (township) Oakland County	154	0.24
Saint Petersburg, FL (city) Pinellas County	153	0.06
Walpole, MA (town) Norfolk County	152	0.67
Freehold, NJ (township) Monmouth County	150	0.48
Bethlehem, PA (city) Northampton County	150	0.21
Huntington, NY (town) Suffolk County	149	0.08
Lower Burrell, PA (city) Westmoreland County	148	1.17
Valley Falls, RI (cdp) Providence County	147	1.27
Syracuse, NY (city) Onondaga County	147	0.10
Glendale, AZ (city) Maricopa County	147	0.07
Camarillo, CA (city) Ventura County	146	0.26
Utica, NY (city) Oneida County	146	0.24
Mission Viejo, CA (city) Orange County	146	0.16
Tempe, AZ (city) Maricopa County	146	0.09
Pontiac, MI (city) Oakland County	145	0.22
North Smithfield, RI (town) Providence County	144	1.36
Macomb, MI (township) Macomb County	144	0.29
Mesa, AZ (city) Maricopa County	144	0.04
Bailey's Crossroads, VA (cdp) Fairfax County	143	0.63
Warwick, RI (city) Kent County	143	0.17
Chandler, AZ (city) Maricopa County	142	0.08
Wichita, KS (city) Sedgwick County	141	0.04
Central Falls, RI (city) Providence County	140	0.74
Sacramento, CA (city) Sacramento County	140	0.03
North Huntingdon, PA (township) Westmoreland County	137	0.47
Bethel Park, PA (borough) Allegheny County	136	0.41
Henderson, NV (city) Clark County	136	0.08
East Providence, RI (city) Providence County	135	0.28
Tustin, CA (city) Orange County	135	0.20
Bridgeport, CT (city) Fairfield County	135	0.10
Mays Chapel, MD (cdp) Baltimore County	133	1.16
Alexandria, VA (independent city) Alexandria city	133	0.10
Ann Arbor, MI (city) Washtenaw County	132	0.12

Notes: (cdp) census designated place; Refer to the Explanation of Data in the front of the book for more detailed information.

Arab: Syrian

Top 150 Places Sorted by Percent

(Based on all places, regardless of population)

Place	Number	%
Deal, NJ (borough) Monmouth County	180	16.82
Blakeslee, OH (village) Williams County	10	8.26
Smithfield, WV (town) Wetzel County	16	7.88
Clinton, NE (village) Sheridan County	2	6.67
Whitestone Logging Camp, AK (cdp) Skagway-Hoonah-Angoon C.A.	6	5.45
Haledon, NJ (borough) Passaic County	371	4.50
Hoople, ND (city) Walsh County	12	4.17
Ithaca, NE (village) Saunders County	6	4.17
Davis, SD (town) Turner County	4	3.96
Ephraim, WI (village) Door County	13	3.94
Matinicus Isle, ME (plantation) Knox County	2	3.92
Clay Center, OH (village) Ottawa County	11	3.72
West Middletown, PA (borough) Washington County	5	3.45
Harvard, NE (city) Clay County	33	3.26
Brian Head, UT (town) Iron County	3	3.26
Plover, IA (city) Pocahontas County	3	3.26
Westlake, TX (town) Tarrant County	7	3.14
Fullerton, PA (cdp) Lehigh County	414	2.91
Totowa, NJ (borough) Passaic County	287	2.91
Sugar Bush Knolls, OH (village) Portage County	6	2.84
Wilbur Park, MO (village) Saint Louis County	14	2.82
Heidelberg, PA (township) Lehigh County	93	2.70
Stony Prairie, OH (cdp) Sandusky County	24	2.68
Dahlgren, VA (cdp) King George County	24	2.45
Saddle River, NJ (borough) Bergen County	76	2.37
Paxico, KS (city) Wabaunsee County	5	2.35
College Springs, IA (city) Page County	6	2.34
Warren City, TX (city) Gregg County	8	2.29
Mount Croghan, SC (town) Chesterfield County	3	2.26
Eau Claire, PA (borough) Butler County	8	2.22
Halden, MN (township) Saint Louis County	3	2.19
Pinehurst, TX (city) Orange County	51	2.15
Elco, PA (borough) Washington County	8	2.04
Moreland Hills, OH (village) Cuyahoga County	67	2.03
Manchester, NY (village) Ontario County	29	1.97
Gates Mills, OH (village) Cuyahoga County	47	1.92
West Newton, PA (borough) Westmoreland County	57	1.85
Bear Creek Village, PA (borough) Luzerne County	5	1.79
Waldo, OH (village) Marion County	6	1.78
Medicine Lake, MT (town) Sheridan County	5	1.77
Athens, LA (village) Claiborne Parish	4	1.77
Hanover, PA (township) Luzerne County	199	1.74
Lehr, ND (city) McIntosh County	2	1.74
New Kensington, PA (city) Westmoreland County	254	1.72
Edmore, ND (city) Ramsey County	4	1.72
Walkerville, MT (town) Silver Bow County	12	1.71
Alden, KS (city) Rice County	3	1.71
Whitehall, PA (township) Lehigh County	421	1.69
North Catasauqua, PA (borough) Northampton County	47	1.67
Tesuque, NM (cdp) Santa Fe County	14	1.66
Franksville, WI (cdp) Racine County	28	1.65
Merriman, NE (village) Cherry County	2	1.63
Baneberry, TN (city) Jefferson County	6	1.62
Allentown, PA (city) Lehigh County	1,708	1.60
Lincoln, RI (town) Providence County	333	1.59
Little Falls, NJ (cdp) Passaic County	173	1.59
Springfield, NE (city) Sarpy County	23	1.59
Wayne, NJ (cdp) Passaic County	853	1.58
Burt, MI (township) Alger County	7	1.58
Big Flats Airport, NY (cdp) Chemung County	35	1.53
Southwest Greensburg, PA (borough) Westmoreland County	36	1.50
Portersville, PA (borough) Butler County	4	1.50
Hawthorne, NJ (borough) Passaic County	266	1.46
Bronson, IA (city) Woodbury County	4	1.44
Ledyard, IA (city) Kossuth County	2	1.44
Harrietta, MI (village) Wexford County	2	1.39
Greenville, KY (city) Muhlenberg County	58	1.38
Sands Point, NY (village) Nassau County	38	1.38
Cabazon, CA (cdp) Riverside County	32	1.37
Lake Norden, SD (city) Hamlin County	6	1.37
North Smithfield, RI (town) Providence County	144	1.36
Greenwich, NJ (township) Warren County	59	1.35
Atlantis, FL (city) Palm Beach County	28	1.32
Geneva, NY (town) Ontario County	43	1.31
Seminary, MS (town) Covington County	4	1.31

Place	Number	%
Wolfdale, PA (cdp) Washington County	38	1.30
Fossil, OR (city) Wheeler County	6	1.30
Allen, PA (township) Northampton County	34	1.29
Clifton, NJ (city) Passaic County	1,010	1.28
Valley Falls, RI (cdp) Providence County	147	1.27
Sheridan, MI (village) Montcalm County	9	1.26
Ocean, NJ (township) Monmouth County	337	1.25
North Haledon, NJ (borough) Passaic County	99	1.25
Union, PA (township) Lawrence County	63	1.24
Ashland, KS (city) Clark County	12	1.23
Collier, PA (township) Allegheny County	64	1.22
Shortsville, NY (village) Ontario County	17	1.22
Republic, PA (cdp) Fayette County	17	1.21
Bloomfield Hills, MI (city) Oakland County	47	1.19
Noble, MI (township) Branch County	6	1.19
Mill Village, PA (borough) Erie County	5	1.19
Lower Burrell, PA (city) Westmoreland County	148	1.17
Mays Chapel, MD (cdp) Baltimore County	133	1.16
Bradbury, CA (city) Los Angeles County	10	1.16
Neshannock, PA (township) Lawrence County	104	1.13
Lowhill, PA (township) Lehigh County	21	1.12
Cokeburg, PA (borough) Washington County	8	1.12
Ho-Ho-Kus, NJ (borough) Bergen County	45	1.11
Casa Conejo, CA (cdp) Ventura County	38	1.11
Home, MI (township) Newaygo County	3	1.10
New Avon, MN (township) Redwood County	3	1.10
Shueyville, IA (city) Johnson County	3	1.10
Holyoke, MN (township) Carlton County	2	1.10
Lake George, NY (town) Warren County	39	1.09
Slocum, PA (township) Luzerne County	12	1.09
Catasauqua, PA (borough) Lehigh County	70	1.06
Sherwood, OH (cdp) Hamilton County	41	1.06
Colts Neck, NJ (township) Monmouth County	130	1.05
Meridian, PA (cdp) Butler County	39	1.05
Prospect, PA (borough) Butler County	13	1.05
Gayle Mill, SC (cdp) Chester County	12	1.05
Van Etten, NY (village) Chemung County	6	1.05
Jefferson, PA (township) Butler County	59	1.04
Louisville, NY (town) Saint Lawrence County	33	1.03
New Milford, NJ (borough) Bergen County	167	1.02
Boylston, MA (town) Worcester County	41	1.02
Logan, WV (city) Logan County	16	1.02
How, WI (town) Oconto County	6	1.02
Markleysburg, PA (borough) Fayette County	3	1.02
Shenango, PA (township) Lawrence County	77	1.01
Savoy, MA (town) Berkshire County	7	1.01
Akron, NY (village) Erie County	31	0.99
Grosse Ile, MI (cdp) Wayne County	107	0.98
Surfside, FL (town) Miami-Dade County	50	0.98
Westmoreland, NY (town) Oneida County	60	0.97
Bath, PA (borough) Northampton County	26	0.97
Cumberland, RI (town) Providence County	306	0.96
Jeannette, PA (city) Westmoreland County	103	0.96
Washington Township, NJ (cdp) Bergen County	86	0.96
Duncansville, PA (borough) Blair County	12	0.96
Aleppo, PA (township) Allegheny County	10	0.96
Elmer, MN (township) Pipestone County	3	0.96
Carnegie, PA (borough) Allegheny County	80	0.95
Ottawa Hills, OH (village) Lucas County	43	0.95
Chinook, MT (city) Blaine County	13	0.95
Marion Heights, PA (borough) Northumberland County	7	0.95
West Dundee, IL (village) Kane County	50	0.93
Many, LA (town) Sabine Parish	27	0.93
Manalapan, FL (town) Palm Beach County	3	0.93
Glens Falls, NY (city) Warren County	131	0.91
South Snyderville Basin, UT (cdp) Summit County	32	0.91
Wilmington, PA (township) Lawrence County	25	0.91
Chapman, PA (township) Snyder County	13	0.91
Hopewell, PA (township) Washington County	9	0.91
North Irwin, PA (borough) Westmoreland County	8	0.91
Stamford, NE (village) Harlan County	2	0.91
Lodi, NJ (borough) Bergen County	215	0.90
Glendora, CA (city) Los Angeles County	442	0.89
Osage, IA (city) Mitchell County	31	0.89
Sugar Notch, PA (borough) Luzerne County	9	0.89

Notes: (cdp) census designated place; Refer to the Explanation of Data in the front of the book for more detailed information.

Arab: Syrian

Top 150 Places Sorted by Percent

(Based on places with populations of 10,000 or more)

Place	Number	%
Fullerton, PA (cdp) Lehigh County	414	2.91
Hanover, PA (township) Luzerne County	199	1.74
New Kensington, PA (city) Westmoreland County	254	1.72
Whitehall, PA (township) Lehigh County	421	1.69
Allentown, PA (city) Lehigh County	1,708	1.60
Lincoln, RI (town) Providence County	333	1.59
Little Falls, NJ (cdp) Passaic County	173	1.59
Wayne, NJ (cdp) Passaic County	853	1.58
Hawthorne, NJ (borough) Passaic County	266	1.46
North Smithfield, RI (town) Providence County	144	1.36
Clifton, NJ (city) Passaic County	1,010	1.28
Valley Falls, RI (cdp) Providence County	147	1.27
Ocean, NJ (township) Monmouth County	337	1.25
Lower Burrell, PA (city) Westmoreland County	148	1.17
Mays Chapel, MD (cdp) Baltimore County	133	1.16
Colts Neck, NJ (township) Monmouth County	130	1.05
New Milford, NJ (borough) Bergen County	167	1.02
Grosse Ile, MI (cdp) Wayne County	107	0.98
Cumberland, RI (town) Providence County	306	0.96
Jeannette, PA (city) Westmoreland County	103	0.96
Glens Falls, NY (city) Warren County	131	0.91
Lodi, NJ (borough) Bergen County	215	0.90
Glendora, CA (city) Los Angeles County	442	0.89
Salisbury, PA (township) Lehigh County	117	0.87
Norwood, MA (cdp) Norfolk County	245	0.86
Wilkes-Barre, PA (city) Luzerne County	362	0.84
Scituate, RI (town) Providence County	87	0.84
Burbank, CA (city) Los Angeles County	831	0.83
New Castle, PA (city) Lawrence County	218	0.83
Hopewell, PA (township) Beaver County	108	0.81
Grosse Pointe Woods, MI (city) Wayne County	131	0.77
Paradise Valley, AZ (town) Maricopa County	105	0.77
West Freehold, NJ (cdp) Monmouth County	97	0.77
Bedford, MA (town) Middlesex County	96	0.76
Central Falls, RI (city) Providence County	140	0.74
Saddle Brook, NJ (cdp) Bergen County	97	0.74
Amherst, OH (city) Lorain County	88	0.74
Aventura, FL (city) Miami-Dade County	182	0.72
Plains, PA (township) Luzerne County	76	0.70
Ridgefield, NJ (borough) Bergen County	74	0.68
Walpole, MA (town) Norfolk County	152	0.67
Tinton Falls, NJ (borough) Monmouth County	98	0.65
West Paterson, NJ (borough) Passaic County	71	0.65
Franklin Lakes, NJ (borough) Bergen County	68	0.65
Johnston, RI (town) Providence County	177	0.63
Bailey's Crossroads, VA (cdp) Fairfax County	143	0.63
Westborough, MA (town) Worcester County	110	0.61
Paramus, NJ (borough) Bergen County	155	0.60
Pequannock, NJ (township) Morris County	83	0.60
Bridgeview, IL (village) Cook County	91	0.59
Millbury, MA (town) Worcester County	75	0.59
Dearborn, MI (city) Wayne County	567	0.58
Mountain Top, PA (cdp) Luzerne County	85	0.56
East Hanover, NJ (township) Morris County	64	0.56
Long Branch, NJ (city) Monmouth County	173	0.55
Plymouth, PA (township) Montgomery County	88	0.55
Oldsmar, FL (city) Pinellas County	65	0.55
Burr Ridge, IL (village) Du Page County	57	0.55
La Verne, CA (city) Los Angeles County	173	0.54
Dedham, MA (cdp) Norfolk County	126	0.54
New Hartford, NY (town) Oneida County	114	0.54
Pawtucket, RI (city) Providence County	388	0.53
Holiday, FL (cdp) Pasco County	117	0.53
South Whitehall, PA (township) Lehigh County	95	0.53
Seekonk, MA (town) Bristol County	71	0.53
Munhall, PA (borough) Allegheny County	63	0.51
Wyckoff, NJ (cdp) Bergen County	82	0.50
Westlake, OH (city) Cuyahoga County	156	0.49
Upper Saint Clair, PA (cdp) Allegheny County	99	0.49
Washington, PA (city) Washington County	75	0.49
Geneva, NY (city) Ontario County	67	0.49
Westwood, NJ (borough) Bergen County	54	0.49
Freehold, NJ (township) Monmouth County	150	0.48
Harper Woods, MI (city) Wayne County	68	0.48
North Huntingdon, PA (township) Westmoreland County	137	0.47
East Bridgewater, MA (town) Plymouth County	61	0.47
Hasbrouck Heights, NJ (borough) Bergen County	55	0.47
Morganville, NJ (cdp) Monmouth County	52	0.47
Salisbury, NY (cdp) Nassau County	57	0.46
Kendall, FL (cdp) Miami-Dade County	335	0.45
La Crescenta-Montrose, CA (cdp) Los Angeles County	83	0.45
Dumont, NJ (borough) Bergen County	79	0.45
Tonawanda, NY (city) Erie County	73	0.45
Lynn Haven, FL (city) Bay County	55	0.45
South Fayette, PA (township) Allegheny County	54	0.44
Randolph, NJ (township) Morris County	108	0.43
Warren, NJ (township) Somerset County	62	0.43
Saint Clair Shores, MI (city) Macomb County	264	0.42
Back Mountain, PA (cdp) Luzerne County	112	0.42
Ives Estates, FL (cdp) Miami-Dade County	74	0.42
Westwood, MA (town) Norfolk County	59	0.42
Oroville, CA (city) Butte County	54	0.42
North Fayette, PA (township) Allegheny County	52	0.42
Merrifield, VA (cdp) Fairfax County	46	0.42
North Strabane, PA (township) Washington County	42	0.42
Hempfield, PA (township) Westmoreland County	166	0.41
Bethel Park, PA (borough) Allegheny County	136	0.41
Lower Macungie, PA (township) Lehigh County	79	0.41
Fair Lawn, NJ (borough) Bergen County	126	0.40
East Lake, FL (cdp) Pinellas County	117	0.40
Bernards, NJ (township) Somerset County	99	0.40
Harrison, MI (cdp) Macomb County	98	0.40
Wekiwa Springs, FL (cdp) Seminole County	93	0.40
Peters, PA (township) Washington County	70	0.40
East Longmeadow, MA (town) Hampden County	57	0.40
Ringwood, NJ (borough) Passaic County	49	0.40
Woonsocket, RI (city) Providence County	170	0.39
Sandwich, MA (town) Barnstable County	78	0.39
Mount Clemens, MI (city) Macomb County	68	0.39
Butler, PA (township) Butler County	67	0.39
Lakewood, OH (city) Cuyahoga County	213	0.38
New Castle, NY (town) Westchester County	66	0.38
Derry, PA (township) Westmoreland County	56	0.38
Brecksville, OH (city) Cuyahoga County	50	0.38
Beecher, MI (cdp) Genesee County	49	0.38
Lansing, NY (town) Tompkins County	39	0.38
Morro Bay, CA (city) San Luis Obispo County	39	0.38
Chatham, NJ (township) Morris County	38	0.38
Montgomery, OH (city) Hamilton County	38	0.38
Stratford, CT (cdp) Fairfield County	185	0.37
Alexandria, LA (city) Rapides Parish	174	0.37
Sunny Isles Beach, FL (city) Miami-Dade County	57	0.37
Baywood-Los Osos, CA (cdp) San Luis Obispo County	52	0.37
Troy, MI (city) Oakland County	294	0.36
Bloomfield, MI (township) Oakland County	156	0.36
Florence, KY (city) Boone County	84	0.36
Greensburg, PA (city) Westmoreland County	57	0.36
Upper Macungie, PA (township) Lehigh County	50	0.36
Spring Hill, FL (cdp) Hernando County	239	0.35
Mount Lebanon, PA (cdp) Allegheny County	114	0.35
West Linn, OR (city) Clackamas County	77	0.35
Wolf Trap, VA (cdp) Fairfax County	49	0.35
Longwood, FL (city) Seminole County	48	0.35
Hartland, MI (township) Livingston County	38	0.35
Wanaque, NJ (borough) Passaic County	36	0.35
Canton, OH (city) Stark County	278	0.34
Parsippany-Troy Hills, NJ (township) Morris County	170	0.34
Sparta, NJ (township) Sussex County	61	0.34
Fairview Park, OH (city) Cuyahoga County	60	0.34
North Whitehall, PA (township) Lehigh County	50	0.34
Oakland, NJ (borough) Bergen County	42	0.34
Rehoboth, MA (town) Bristol County	35	0.34
Mansfield, MA (town) Bristol County	73	0.33
Herndon, VA (town) Fairfax County	71	0.33
Baldwin, PA (borough) Allegheny County	66	0.33
Sylvania, OH (city) Lucas County	62	0.33
Rye, NY (city) Westchester County	49	0.33
Newton, NC (city) Catawba County	42	0.33
Franklin Park, PA (borough) Allegheny County	37	0.33
Nanticoke, PA (city) Luzerne County	36	0.33

Notes: (cdp) census designated place; Refer to the Explanation of Data in the front of the book for more detailed information.

Arab: Other

Top 150 Places Sorted by Number

(Based on all places, regardless of population)

Place	Number	%
New York, NY (city) New York City	6,612	0.08
Dearborn, MI (city) Wayne County	2,701	2.76
Los Angeles, CA (city) Los Angeles County	2,310	0.06
Nashville-Davidson, TN (special city) Davidson County	1,925	0.35
Houston, TX (city) Harris County	1,194	0.06
Chicago, IL (city) Cook County	1,012	0.03
Detroit, MI (city) Wayne County	1,010	0.11
San Diego, CA (city) San Diego County	880	0.07
San Francisco, CA (city) San Francisco County	659	0.08
Bailey's Crossroads, VA (cdp) Fairfax County	644	2.82
Hamtramck, MI (city) Wayne County	541	2.35
Columbus, OH (city) Franklin County	540	0.08
Arlington, VA (cdp) Arlington County	526	0.28
Boston, MA (city) Suffolk County	508	0.09
Lackawanna, NY (city) Erie County	478	2.51
Washington, DC (city) District of Columbia	458	0.08
Dallas, TX (city) Dallas County	437	0.04
Charlotte, NC (city) Mecklenburg County	413	0.08
San Antonio, TX (city) Bexar County	407	0.04
Philadelphia, PA (city) Philadelphia County	394	0.03
Seattle, WA (city) King County	376	0.07
El Cajon, CA (city) San Diego County	373	0.39
Denver, CO (city) Denver County	373	0.07
Ann Arbor, MI (city) Washtenaw County	321	0.28
San Jose, CA (city) Santa Clara County	320	0.04
Lincoln, NE (city) Lancaster County	309	0.14
Plano, TX (city) Collin County	307	0.14
North Hempstead, NY (town) Nassau County	301	0.14
Tucson, AZ (city) Pima County	290	0.06
Richardson, TX (city) Dallas County	286	0.31
Tysons Corner, VA (cdp) Fairfax County	268	1.45
Anaheim, CA (city) Orange County	261	0.08
Salt Lake City, UT (city) Salt Lake County	259	0.14
Austin, TX (city) Travis County	249	0.04
Raleigh, NC (city) Wake County	246	0.09
Phoenix, AZ (city) Maricopa County	235	0.02
Minneapolis, MN (city) Hennepin County	234	0.06
Toledo, OH (city) Lucas County	228	0.07
Annandale, VA (cdp) Fairfax County	226	0.41
Arlington, TX (city) Tarrant County	213	0.06
Fort Worth, TX (city) Tarrant County	209	0.04
Hempstead, NY (town) Nassau County	208	0.03
Irvine, CA (city) Orange County	204	0.14
Memphis, TN (city) Shelby County	202	0.03
Corona, CA (city) Riverside County	200	0.16
Fort Collins, CO (city) Larimer County	194	0.16
Jersey City, NJ (city) Hudson County	192	0.08
Long Beach, CA (city) Los Angeles County	187	0.04
Boulder, CO (city) Boulder County	185	0.20
Saint Louis, MO (independent city) Saint Louis city	185	0.05
Moorhead, MN (city) Clay County	184	0.57
Cupertino, CA (city) Santa Clara County	184	0.36
Franklin, TN (city) Williamson County	181	0.43
Daly City, CA (city) San Mateo County	178	0.17
Buffalo, NY (city) Erie County	178	0.06
Auburn, WA (city) King County	176	0.44
Glendale, CA (city) Los Angeles County	172	0.09
Columbia, MO (city) Boone County	163	0.19
Ashland, CA (cdp) Alameda County	161	0.78
Portland, OR (city) Multnomah County	160	0.03
Federal Way, WA (city) King County	159	0.19
Cary, NC (town) Wake County	159	0.17
Masury, OH (cdp) Trumbull County	157	5.70
Hayward, CA (city) Alameda County	156	0.11
Cambridge, MA (city) Middlesex County	155	0.15
Santa Monica, CA (city) Los Angeles County	154	0.18
Jacksonville, FL (special city) Duval County	154	0.02
Metairie, LA (cdp) Jefferson Parish	153	0.10
Berkeley, CA (city) Alameda County	152	0.15
Chula Vista, CA (city) San Diego County	152	0.09
Milwaukee, WI (city) Milwaukee County	152	0.03
Alexandria, VA (independent city) Alexandria city	150	0.12
Manchester, NH (city) Hillsborough County	146	0.14
Tempe, AZ (city) Maricopa County	145	0.09
Norman, OK (city) Cleveland County	143	0.15
Pembroke Pines, FL (city) Broward County	142	0.10
Miami Beach, FL (city) Miami-Dade County	138	0.16
Canton, MI (cdp) Wayne County	137	0.18
Binghamton, NY (city) Broome County	134	0.28
Saint Paul, MN (city) Ramsey County	134	0.05
McLean, VA (cdp) Fairfax County	133	0.34
Malden, MA (city) Middlesex County	133	0.24
Baton Rouge, LA (city) East Baton Rouge Parish	131	0.06
Colorado Springs, CO (city) El Paso County	131	0.04
Tampa, FL (city) Hillsborough County	131	0.04
Rosemont, CA (cdp) Sacramento County	129	0.57
Ocean, NJ (township) Monmouth County	129	0.48
Indianapolis, IN (special city) Marion County	128	0.02
Torrance, CA (city) Los Angeles County	127	0.09
Potomac, MD (cdp) Montgomery County	125	0.28
Aurora, CO (city) Arapahoe County	125	0.05
Norfolk, VA (independent city) Norfolk city	123	0.05
College Station, TX (city) Brazos County	122	0.18
Jefferson, VA (cdp) Fairfax County	121	0.44
Concord, CA (city) Contra Costa County	121	0.10
Fremont, CA (city) Alameda County	120	0.06
Oakland, CA (city) Alameda County	120	0.03
Burbank, CA (city) Los Angeles County	119	0.12
La Mesa, CA (city) San Diego County	118	0.22
Beaverton, OR (city) Washington County	118	0.16
Bellevue, WA (city) King County	118	0.11
Dayton, OH (city) Montgomery County	118	0.07
Huntington Beach, CA (city) Orange County	118	0.06
Rose Hill, VA (cdp) Fairfax County	117	0.78
Bridgeport, CT (city) Fairfield County	116	0.08
Tacoma, WA (city) Pierce County	116	0.06
Lawrence, KS (city) Douglas County	115	0.14
Beverly Hills, CA (city) Los Angeles County	114	0.34
Lodi, NJ (borough) Bergen County	113	0.47
Wheaton-Glenmont, MD (cdp) Montgomery County	113	0.20
Silver Spring, MD (cdp) Montgomery County	113	0.15
Pittsburgh, PA (city) Allegheny County	113	0.03
Groveton, VA (cdp) Fairfax County	112	0.53
Mission Bend, TX (cdp) Fort Bend County	112	0.36
Paradise, NV (cdp) Clark County	112	0.06
Tara Hills, CA (cdp) Contra Costa County	111	2.07
Coral Springs, FL (city) Broward County	111	0.09
Fairfax, VA (independent city) Fairfax city	110	0.51
Sunnyvale, CA (city) Santa Clara County	110	0.08
Scottsdale, AZ (city) Maricopa County	110	0.05
Ypsilanti, MI (township) Washtenaw County	109	0.22
Quincy, MA (city) Norfolk County	109	0.12
Tulsa, OK (city) Tulsa County	109	0.03
San Mateo, CA (city) San Mateo County	107	0.12
Clay, NY (town) Onondaga County	106	0.18
Burke, VA (cdp) Fairfax County	104	0.18
Baltimore, MD (independent city) Baltimore city	104	0.02
Pinehurst, MA (cdp) Middlesex County	103	1.49
Billerica, MA (town) Middlesex County	103	0.26
Modesto, CA (city) Stanislaus County	103	0.05
Wichita, KS (city) Sedgwick County	102	0.03
Edison, NJ (cdp) Middlesex County	101	0.10
West Springfield, VA (cdp) Fairfax County	100	0.35
Bremerton, WA (city) Kitsap County	99	0.27
Fontana, CA (city) San Bernardino County	99	0.08
Stockton, CA (city) San Joaquin County	99	0.04
Temple Terrace, FL (city) Hillsborough County	98	0.47
Lafayette, LA (city) Lafayette Parish	98	0.09
Lakewood, CO (city) Jefferson County	98	0.07
Mesa, AZ (city) Maricopa County	98	0.02
Arden-Arcade, CA (cdp) Sacramento County	97	0.10
Orlando, FL (city) Orange County	97	0.05
Brooklyn Park, MN (city) Hennepin County	96	0.14
Oakton, VA (cdp) Fairfax County	95	0.32
Overland Park, KS (city) Johnson County	95	0.06
Melbourne, FL (city) Brevard County	94	0.13
Ramapo, NY (town) Rockland County	94	0.09
Montgomery Village, MD (cdp) Montgomery County	93	0.25
Kalamazoo, MI (city) Kalamazoo County	93	0.12
Irving, TX (city) Dallas County	93	0.05

Notes: (cdp) census designated place; Refer to the Explanation of Data in the front of the book for more detailed information.

Arab: Other

Top 150 Places Sorted by Percent

(Based on all places, regardless of population)

Place	Number	%
Masury, OH (cdp) Trumbull County	157	5.70
Hillside, NY (cdp) Ulster County	26	2.83
Bailey's Crossroads, VA (cdp) Fairfax County	644	2.82
Dearborn, MI (city) Wayne County	2,701	2.76
Lackawanna, NY (city) Erie County	478	2.51
Great Neck Gardens, NY (cdp) Nassau County	28	2.51
Hamtramck, MI (city) Wayne County	541	2.35
Tara Hills, CA (cdp) Contra Costa County	111	2.07
Courtland, MN (city) Nicollet County	10	1.86
Leavenworth, IN (town) Crawford County	6	1.74
Saddle Rock, NY (village) Nassau County	13	1.64
Beaux Arts Village, WA (town) King County	5	1.60
Pinehurst, MA (cdp) Middlesex County	103	1.49
Tysons Corner, VA (cdp) Fairfax County	268	1.45
North Kansas City, MO (city) Clay County	64	1.36
Woodmere, OH (village) Cuyahoga County	11	1.33
Lyons, PA (borough) Berks County	6	1.32
Tiskilwa, IL (village) Bureau County	10	1.27
Akron, MN (township) Wilkin County	2	1.27
Standard, IL (village) Putnam County	3	1.16
Wilkes-Barre Township, PA (cdp) Luzerne County	37	1.14
Golden Beach, FL (town) Miami-Dade County	12	1.14
Carson River Valley, WA (cdp) Skamania County	23	1.10
Laupahoehoe, HI (cdp) Hawaii County	5	1.08
Antrim, MN (township) Watonwan County	3	1.04
Chevy Chase Section Three, MD (village) Montgomery County	8	1.03
Cedarhurst, NY (village) Nassau County	62	1.01
Shepherdstown, WV (town) Jefferson County	8	1.01
Rockland, MI (township) Ontonagon County	3	1.00
Bingham Farms, MI (village) Oakland County	10	0.97
Willow Creek, CA (cdp) Humboldt County	16	0.93
Lerna, IL (village) Coles County	3	0.93
Stigler, OK (city) Haskell County	25	0.92
Saint Florian, AL (town) Lauderdale County	3	0.92
Bystrom, CA (cdp) Stanislaus County	41	0.91
Lake City, PA (borough) Erie County	25	0.89
Clyde, CA (cdp) Contra Costa County	6	0.88
Fairlawn, OH (city) Summit County	63	0.86
Glen Ellen, CA (cdp) Sonoma County	8	0.86
Riverdale Park, CA (cdp) Stanislaus County	9	0.82
Silver, MN (township) Carlton County	3	0.81
Ashland, CA (cdp) Alameda County	161	0.78
Rose Hill, VA (cdp) Fairfax County	117	0.78
Roslyn Heights, NY (cdp) Nassau County	47	0.75
Middletown, KY (city) Jefferson County	44	0.74
Port Monmouth, NJ (cdp) Monmouth County	27	0.74
Kensington, NY (village) Nassau County	9	0.74
Richland, MI (township) Kalamazoo County	47	0.72
Viola, NY (cdp) Rockland County	43	0.72
Dunn Loring, VA (cdp) Fairfax County	56	0.71
Riverbend, WA (cdp) King County	16	0.71
Henry Clay, PA (township) Fayette County	14	0.71
Huntington, VA (cdp) Fairfax County	59	0.70
Marina del Rey, CA (cdp) Los Angeles County	57	0.70
Dover, MA (town) Norfolk County	39	0.70
North Lewisburg, OH (village) Champaign County	11	0.69
Forest Home, NY (cdp) Tompkins County	7	0.69
White House, TN (city) Robertson County	47	0.65
Milford, ME (town) Penobscot County	19	0.64
Asharoken, NY (village) Suffolk County	4	0.62
Yankeetown, FL (town) Levy County	4	0.62
Fountain, MN (township) Fillmore County	2	0.62
South Huntington, NY (cdp) Suffolk County	58	0.61
El Verano, CA (cdp) Sonoma County	24	0.59
Lawrenceville, NJ (cdp) Mercer County	24	0.59
Pelican Rapids, MN (city) Otter Tail County	14	0.59
Baldwinville, MA (cdp) Worcester County	11	0.59
Vernon Valley, NJ (cdp) Sussex County	10	0.58
Day, WI (town) Marathon County	6	0.58
Moorhead, MN (city) Clay County	184	0.57
Rosemont, CA (cdp) Sacramento County	129	0.57
Watchung, NJ (borough) Somerset County	32	0.57
Great Neck, NY (village) Nassau County	53	0.56
Worcester, PA (township) Montgomery County	43	0.56
Twin Rivers, NJ (cdp) Mercer County	41	0.55
Brooklyn, OH (city) Cuyahoga County	62	0.54
Pearlington, MS (cdp) Hancock County	10	0.54
Groveton, VA (cdp) Fairfax County	112	0.53
Fayetteville, GA (city) Fayette County	60	0.53
Great Neck Estates, NY (village) Nassau County	15	0.53
Spring Grove, MN (township) Houston County	2	0.53
Richland, PA (township) Allegheny County	48	0.52
Lambertville, NJ (city) Hunterdon County	20	0.52
Hanover, PA (township) Lehigh County	10	0.52
Fairfax, VA (independent city) Fairfax city	110	0.51
North Haledon, NJ (borough) Passaic County	40	0.51
Bear Valley Springs, CA (cdp) Kern County	22	0.51
Oakhurst, NJ (cdp) Monmouth County	21	0.51
Cypress Lakes, FL (cdp) Palm Beach County	7	0.51
Point Blank, TX (city) San Jacinto County	3	0.51
Justice, IL (village) Cook County	60	0.50
Fair Oaks Ranch, TX (city) Bexar County	24	0.50
Dilworth, MN (city) Clay County	15	0.50
Copperopolis, CA (cdp) Calaveras County	12	0.50
Trophy Club, TX (town) Denton County	32	0.49
Eldorado at Santa Fe, NM (cdp) Santa Fe County	28	0.49
Meadows Place, TX (city) Fort Bend County	24	0.49
Ocean, NJ (township) Monmouth County	129	0.48
Alpena, MI (city) Alpena County	53	0.48
Scottsville, KY (city) Allen County	21	0.48
Edgewood, PA (borough) Allegheny County	16	0.48
New Britain, PA (borough) Bucks County	15	0.48
Upper Nyack, NY (village) Rockland County	9	0.48
Lodi, NJ (borough) Bergen County	113	0.47
Temple Terrace, FL (city) Hillsborough County	98	0.47
West Haven-Sylvan, OR (cdp) Washington County	33	0.47
Little Silver, NJ (borough) Monmouth County	29	0.47
North Hills, NY (village) Nassau County	20	0.47
Spencer, NY (town) Tioga County	14	0.47
Lonsdale, MN (city) Rice County	7	0.47
Alondra Park, CA (cdp) Los Angeles County	39	0.46
Anahuac, TX (city) Chambers County	10	0.46
Rome, IL (cdp) Peoria County	8	0.46
Shields, MI (cdp) Saginaw County	30	0.45
Pikeville, KY (city) Pike County	28	0.45
Hagar, MI (township) Berrien County	18	0.45
Auburn, WA (city) King County	176	0.44
Jefferson, VA (cdp) Fairfax County	121	0.44
Coldwater, MI (city) Branch County	56	0.44
Willowbrook, IL (village) Du Page County	40	0.44
Parkville, MO (city) Platte County	17	0.44
Groton Long Point, CT (borough) New London County	3	0.44
Emery, SD (city) Hanson County	2	0.44
Franklin, TN (city) Williamson County	181	0.43
Lyons, IL (village) Cook County	44	0.43
Durham, OR (city) Washington County	6	0.43
Whitefish Bay, WI (village) Milwaukee County	60	0.42
Eatontown, NJ (borough) Monmouth County	59	0.42
Vinings, GA (cdp) Cobb County	40	0.42
Pelham, NY (village) Westchester County	27	0.42
Las Flores, CA (cdp) Orange County	24	0.42
Thomaston, NY (village) Nassau County	11	0.42
Herriman, UT (town) Salt Lake County	7	0.42
Coburg, OR (city) Lane County	4	0.42
Annandale, VA (cdp) Fairfax County	226	0.41
Azalea Park, FL (cdp) Orange County	46	0.41
Lucas Valley-Marinwood, CA (cdp) Marin County	26	0.41
Chalfont, PA (borough) Bucks County	16	0.41
Wellington, CO (town) Larimer County	11	0.41
Hanalei, HI (cdp) Kauai County	2	0.41
Montclair, VA (cdp) Prince William County	63	0.40
Santa Venetia, CA (cdp) Marin County	17	0.40
El Cajon, CA (city) San Diego County	373	0.39
Westborough, MA (town) Worcester County	71	0.39
Yorkshire, VA (cdp) Prince William County	26	0.39
Maywood Park, OR (city) Multnomah County	3	0.39
Edgewater, NJ (borough) Bergen County	29	0.38
Fairwood, WA (cdp) Spokane County	26	0.38
Earlimart, CA (cdp) Tulare County	25	0.38
Algoma, WI (town) Winnebago County	22	0.38

Notes: (cdp) census designated place; Refer to the Explanation of Data in the front of the book for more detailed information.

Arab: Other

Top 150 Places Sorted by Percent

(Based on places with populations of 10,000 or more)

Place	Number	%
Bailey's Crossroads, VA (cdp) Fairfax County	644	2.82
Dearborn, MI (city) Wayne County	2,701	2.76
Lackawanna, NY (city) Erie County	478	2.51
Hamtramck, MI (city) Wayne County	541	2.35
Tysons Corner, VA (cdp) Fairfax County	268	1.45
Ashland, CA (cdp) Alameda County	161	0.78
Rose Hill, VA (cdp) Fairfax County	117	0.78
Moorhead, MN (city) Clay County	184	0.57
Rosemont, CA (cdp) Sacramento County	129	0.57
Brooklyn, OH (city) Cuyahoga County	62	0.54
Groveton, VA (cdp) Fairfax County	112	0.53
Fayetteville, GA (city) Fayette County	60	0.53
Fairfax, VA (independent city) Fairfax city	110	0.51
Justice, IL (village) Cook County	60	0.50
Ocean, NJ (township) Monmouth County	129	0.48
Alpena, MI (city) Alpena County	53	0.48
Lodi, NJ (borough) Bergen County	113	0.47
Temple Terrace, FL (city) Hillsborough County	98	0.47
Auburn, WA (city) King County	176	0.44
Jefferson, VA (cdp) Fairfax County	121	0.44
Coldwater, MI (city) Branch County	56	0.44
Franklin, TN (city) Williamson County	181	0.43
Lyons, IL (village) Cook County	44	0.43
Whitefish Bay, WI (village) Milwaukee County	60	0.42
Eatontown, NJ (borough) Monmouth County	59	0.42
Annandale, VA (cdp) Fairfax County	226	0.41
Azalea Park, FL (cdp) Orange County	46	0.41
Montclair, VA (cdp) Prince William County	63	0.40
El Cajon, CA (city) San Diego County	373	0.39
Westborough, MA (town) Worcester County	71	0.39
West Paterson, NJ (borough) Passaic County	41	0.37
Cupertino, CA (city) Santa Clara County	184	0.36
Mission Bend, TX (cdp) Fort Bend County	112	0.36
Nashville-Davidson, TN (special city) Davidson County	1,925	0.35
West Springfield, VA (cdp) Fairfax County	100	0.35
Rolla, MO (city) Phelps County	58	0.35
McLean, VA (cdp) Fairfax County	133	0.34
Beverly Hills, CA (city) Los Angeles County	114	0.34
Cliffside Park, NJ (borough) Bergen County	78	0.34
Mauldin, SC (city) Greenville County	51	0.34
North Potomac, MD (cdp) Montgomery County	75	0.33
Athens, OH (city) Athens County	69	0.33
Oakton, VA (cdp) Fairfax County	95	0.32
Foster City, CA (city) San Mateo County	92	0.32
Manchester, MO (city) Saint Louis County	61	0.32
Glenvar Heights, FL (cdp) Miami-Dade County	51	0.32
Arvin, CA (city) Kern County	41	0.32
Richardson, TX (city) Dallas County	286	0.31
Carbondale, IL (city) Jackson County	65	0.31
Macomb, IL (city) McDonough County	57	0.31
Pittsfield charter, MI (township) Washtenaw County	91	0.30
Burlingame, CA (city) San Mateo County	85	0.30
Foxborough, MA (town) Norfolk County	49	0.30
Maryland Heights, MO (city) Saint Louis County	74	0.29
Arlington, VA (cdp) Arlington County	526	0.28
Ann Arbor, MI (city) Washtenaw County	321	0.28
Binghamton, NY (city) Broome County	134	0.28
Potomac, MD (cdp) Montgomery County	125	0.28
Paramus, NJ (borough) Bergen County	72	0.28
Glendale, WI (city) Milwaukee County	38	0.28
Mounds View, MN (city) Ramsey County	36	0.28
Bremerton, WA (city) Kitsap County	99	0.27
Farragut, TN (town) Knox County	49	0.27
Scott Township, PA (cdp) Allegheny County	46	0.27
Weehawken, NJ (township) Hudson County	37	0.27
Fort Drum, NY (cdp) Jefferson County	33	0.27
Wells Branch, TX (cdp) Travis County	30	0.27
Vineyard, CA (cdp) Sacramento County	27	0.27
Billerica, MA (town) Middlesex County	103	0.26
Fort Lee, NJ (borough) Bergen County	91	0.26
Hallandale, FL (city) Broward County	89	0.26
Lower Allen, PA (township) Cumberland County	46	0.26
Lilburn, GA (city) Gwinnett County	30	0.26
Montgomery Village, MD (cdp) Montgomery County	93	0.25
South River, NJ (borough) Middlesex County	39	0.25
Dyer, IN (town) Lake County	35	0.25
Wolf Trap, VA (cdp) Fairfax County	35	0.25
Thomas, MI (township) Saginaw County	30	0.25
Malden, MA (city) Middlesex County	133	0.24
Belmont, CA (city) San Mateo County	61	0.24
Lemon Grove, CA (city) San Diego County	60	0.24
Lakeside, VA (cdp) Henrico County	27	0.24
Upper Grand Lagoon, FL (cdp) Bay County	26	0.24
Lawndale, CA (city) Los Angeles County	72	0.23
Boca Del Mar, FL (cdp) Palm Beach County	49	0.23
Rocky Hill, CT (town) Hartford County	42	0.23
Myrtle Grove, FL (cdp) Escambia County	40	0.23
Jollyville, TX (cdp) Williamson County	35	0.23
Highland Park, NJ (borough) Middlesex County	32	0.23
Pelham, NY (town) Westchester County	27	0.23
Mays Chapel, MD (cdp) Baltimore County	26	0.23
Coral Hills, MD (cdp) Prince George's County	25	0.23
Dobbs Ferry, NY (village) Westchester County	24	0.23
La Mesa, CA (city) San Diego County	118	0.22
Ypsilanti, MI (township) Washtenaw County	109	0.22
Rome, GA (city) Floyd County	78	0.22
Trumbull, CT (cdp) Fairfield County	77	0.22
Springfield, VA (cdp) Fairfax County	66	0.22
Madison, AL (city) Madison County	63	0.22
Hampden, PA (township) Cumberland County	53	0.22
Pinecrest, FL (village) Miami-Dade County	43	0.22
Saco, ME (city) York County	37	0.22
Saint Matthews, KY (city) Jefferson County	35	0.22
Vienna, VA (town) Fairfax County	32	0.22
Lower Salford, PA (township) Montgomery County	28	0.22
Grosse Pointe Park, MI (city) Wayne County	27	0.22
West Hollywood, CA (city) Los Angeles County	76	0.21
Watertown, MA (city) Middlesex County	70	0.21
South Pasadena, CA (city) Los Angeles County	52	0.21
Seguin, TX (city) Guadalupe County	45	0.21
Ruston, LA (city) Lincoln Parish	43	0.21
Colleyville, TX (city) Tarrant County	41	0.21
Hatfield, PA (township) Montgomery County	35	0.21
Whitemarsh, PA (township) Montgomery County	35	0.21
Pflugerville, TX (city) Travis County	34	0.21
Martha Lake, WA (cdp) Snohomish County	27	0.21
Ulster, NY (town) Ulster County	26	0.21
Boulder, CO (city) Boulder County	185	0.20
Wheaton-Glenmont, MD (cdp) Montgomery County	113	0.20
Auburn Hills, MI (city) Oakland County	40	0.20
Upper Southampton, PA (township) Bucks County	31	0.20
Waycross, GA (city) Ware County	31	0.20
Wixom, MI (city) Oakland County	27	0.20
Blue Ash, OH (city) Hamilton County	25	0.20
Sturgis, MI (city) Saint Joseph County	23	0.20
Cloquet, MN (city) Carlton County	22	0.20
Westwood, NJ (borough) Bergen County	22	0.20
Columbia, MO (city) Boone County	163	0.19
Federal Way, WA (city) King County	159	0.19
The Hammocks, FL (cdp) Miami-Dade County	91	0.19
Mount Lebanon, PA (cdp) Allegheny County	63	0.19
Westlake, OH (city) Cuyahoga County	61	0.19
Kenmore, WA (city) King County	36	0.19
Alderwood Manor, WA (cdp) Snohomish County	29	0.19
Enterprise, NV (cdp) Clark County	27	0.19
Simpsonville, SC (city) Greenville County	27	0.19
Savage-Guilford, MD (cdp) Howard County	24	0.19
Santa Monica, CA (city) Los Angeles County	154	0.18
Canton, MI (cdp) Wayne County	137	0.18
College Station, TX (city) Brazos County	122	0.18
Clay, NY (town) Onondaga County	106	0.18
Burke, VA (cdp) Fairfax County	104	0.18
Bartlett, IL (village) Du Page County	67	0.18
Vestal, NY (town) Broome County	47	0.18
El Cerrito, CA (city) Contra Costa County	42	0.18
Inglewood-Finn Hill, WA (cdp) King County	41	0.18
Kaysville, UT (city) Davis County	37	0.18
Newington, VA (cdp) Fairfax County	35	0.18
Pittsburg, KS (city) Crawford County	34	0.18
Hybla Valley, VA (cdp) Fairfax County	31	0.18

Notes: (cdp) census designated place; Refer to the Explanation of Data in the front of the book for more detailed information.

Armenian

Top 150 Places Sorted by Number

(Based on all places, regardless of population)

Place	Number	%
Los Angeles, CA (city) Los Angeles County	64,997	1.76
Glendale, CA (city) Los Angeles County	53,840	27.60
New York, NY (city) New York City	10,360	0.13
Burbank, CA (city) Los Angeles County	8,312	8.29
Fresno, CA (city) Fresno County	6,024	1.41
Pasadena, CA (city) Los Angeles County	4,400	3.29
Montebello, CA (city) Los Angeles County	2,736	4.42
Watertown, MA (city) Middlesex County	2,708	8.21
San Francisco, CA (city) San Francisco County	2,528	0.33
Altadena, CA (cdp) Los Angeles County	2,134	5.02
San Diego, CA (city) San Diego County	1,839	0.15
Chicago, IL (city) Cook County	1,674	0.06
Cranston, RI (city) Providence County	1,555	1.96
La Crescenta-Montrose, CA (cdp) Los Angeles County	1,382	7.51
Worcester, MA (city) Worcester County	1,306	0.76
Hempstead, NY (town) Nassau County	1,270	0.17
Phoenix, AZ (city) Maricopa County	1,215	0.09
San Jose, CA (city) Santa Clara County	1,197	0.13
Belmont, MA (cdp) Middlesex County	1,165	4.82
Providence, RI (city) Providence County	1,092	0.63
Waltham, MA (city) Middlesex County	1,091	1.84
Boston, MA (city) Suffolk County	1,080	0.18
Farmington Hills, MI (city) Oakland County	1,009	1.23
Rancho Cordova, CA (cdp) Sacramento County	957	1.75
Livonia, MI (city) Wayne County	928	0.92
Dearborn, MI (city) Wayne County	895	0.92
Cliffside Park, NJ (borough) Bergen County	879	3.82
Oyster Bay, NY (town) Nassau County	877	0.30
Warwick, RI (city) Kent County	872	1.02
Philadelphia, PA (city) Philadelphia County	842	0.06
Whittier, CA (city) Los Angeles County	795	0.95
Arlington, MA (cdp) Middlesex County	763	1.80
Houston, TX (city) Harris County	761	0.04
Irvine, CA (city) Orange County	757	0.53
North Hempstead, NY (town) Nassau County	717	0.32
Brookhaven, NY (town) Suffolk County	694	0.15
Huntington Beach, CA (city) Orange County	693	0.36
Clovis, CA (city) Fresno County	684	1.00
Torrance, CA (city) Los Angeles County	672	0.49
Santa Clarita, CA (city) Los Angeles County	664	0.44
Las Vegas, NV (city) Clark County	661	0.14
La Canada Flintridge, CA (city) Los Angeles County	656	3.22
Bellevue, WA (city) King County	650	0.60
Newton, MA (city) Middlesex County	640	0.76
Upper Darby, PA (township) Delaware County	632	0.77
Huntington, NY (town) Suffolk County	621	0.32
Haverhill, MA (city) Essex County	607	1.03
Long Beach, CA (city) Los Angeles County	597	0.13
Seattle, WA (city) King County	597	0.11
Fort Lee, NJ (borough) Bergen County	582	1.64
West Bloomfield, MI (township) Oakland County	564	0.87
Anaheim, CA (city) Orange County	563	0.17
Racine, WI (city) Racine County	524	0.64
Rosemont, CA (cdp) Sacramento County	481	2.11
Bloomfield, MI (township) Oakland County	479	1.11
Palmdale, CA (city) Los Angeles County	475	0.41
Thousand Oaks, CA (city) Ventura County	474	0.41
Bakersfield, CA (city) Kern County	472	0.19
Sacramento, CA (city) Sacramento County	472	0.12
North Providence, RI (cdp) Providence County	471	1.45
Southfield, MI (city) Oakland County	468	0.60
Lexington, MA (cdp) Middlesex County	457	1.51
Riverside, CA (city) Riverside County	454	0.18
Paramus, NJ (borough) Bergen County	445	1.73
Spring Valley, NV (cdp) Clark County	440	0.37
Henderson, NV (city) Clark County	440	0.25
Newport Beach, CA (city) Orange County	439	0.63
Duarte, CA (city) Los Angeles County	431	2.01
Scottsdale, AZ (city) Maricopa County	422	0.21
La Verne, CA (city) Los Angeles County	421	1.32
Portland, OR (city) Multnomah County	407	0.08
Medford, MA (city) Middlesex County	405	0.73
Arden-Arcade, CA (cdp) Sacramento County	404	0.42
Redondo Beach, CA (city) Los Angeles County	403	0.64
Colonie, NY (town) Albany County	398	0.50
Jacksonville, FL (special city) Duval County	397	0.05
Oakland, CA (city) Alameda County	395	0.10
Burlington, MA (cdp) Middlesex County	389	1.70
Methuen, MA (city) Essex County	384	0.88
Arcadia, CA (city) Los Angeles County	380	0.72
Santa Monica, CA (city) Los Angeles County	377	0.45
Novi, MI (city) Oakland County	374	0.79
Billerica, MA (town) Middlesex County	373	0.96
Washington, DC (city) District of Columbia	372	0.07
New Milford, NJ (borough) Bergen County	367	2.24
Laguna Niguel, CA (city) Orange County	366	0.59
Troy, NY (city) Rensselaer County	364	0.74
Visalia, CA (city) Tulare County	354	0.39
Santa Clara, CA (city) Santa Clara County	354	0.35
Nashua, NH (city) Hillsborough County	350	0.40
Cambridge, MA (city) Middlesex County	342	0.34
Concord, CA (city) Contra Costa County	340	0.28
Winchester, MA (cdp) Middlesex County	339	1.63
Sterling Heights, MI (city) Macomb County	337	0.27
Modesto, CA (city) Stanislaus County	335	0.18
Fountain Valley, CA (city) Orange County	334	0.61
Haverford, PA (township) Delaware County	333	0.69
Dearborn Heights, MI (city) Wayne County	333	0.57
Tucson, AZ (city) Pima County	331	0.07
Canton, MI (cdp) Wayne County	330	0.43
Sunnyvale, CA (city) Santa Clara County	329	0.25
Islip, NY (town) Suffolk County	329	0.10
Simi Valley, CA (city) Ventura County	323	0.29
Fairview, NJ (borough) Bergen County	320	2.41
Palisades Park, NJ (borough) Bergen County	320	1.87
Lowell, MA (city) Middlesex County	317	0.30
Ann Arbor, MI (city) Washtenaw County	316	0.28
Paradise, NV (cdp) Clark County	314	0.17
San Antonio, TX (city) Bexar County	314	0.03
Springfield, MA (city) Hampden County	311	0.20
Dallas, TX (city) Dallas County	311	0.03
Salem, NH (town) Rockingham County	310	1.10
Northbridge, MA (town) Worcester County	309	2.34
Wayne, NJ (cdp) Passaic County	309	0.57
Oradell, NJ (borough) Bergen County	307	3.82
Troy, MI (city) Oakland County	307	0.38
Yorba Linda, CA (city) Orange County	306	0.52
Fremont, CA (city) Alameda County	306	0.15
Denver, CO (city) Denver County	304	0.05
Milwaukee, WI (city) Milwaukee County	302	0.05
Skokie, IL (village) Cook County	301	0.48
Ridgefield, NJ (borough) Bergen County	294	2.71
Temple City, CA (city) Los Angeles County	294	0.88
Andover, MA (town) Essex County	292	0.93
Rancho Palos Verdes, CA (city) Los Angeles County	292	0.71
Hacienda Heights, CA (cdp) Los Angeles County	289	0.54
Garden Grove, CA (city) Orange County	289	0.17
Niagara Falls, NY (city) Niagara County	287	0.52
Framingham, MA (cdp) Middlesex County	287	0.43
Arlington, VA (cdp) Arlington County	286	0.15
Carlsbad, CA (city) San Diego County	284	0.36
Walnut Creek, CA (city) Contra Costa County	282	0.44
Marple, PA (township) Delaware County	281	1.18
Carmichael, CA (cdp) Sacramento County	279	0.56
Cypress, CA (city) Orange County	278	0.60
Diamond Bar, CA (city) Los Angeles County	278	0.49
New Britain, CT (city) Hartford County	277	0.39
Drexel Hill, PA (cdp) Delaware County	275	0.94
Montgomery, PA (township) Montgomery County	272	1.23
North Bergen, NJ (township) Hudson County	269	0.46
Costa Mesa, CA (city) Orange County	266	0.24
Berkeley, CA (city) Alameda County	265	0.26
Nashville-Davidson, TN (special city) Davidson County	265	0.05
Glendora, CA (city) Los Angeles County	261	0.52
Downey, CA (city) Los Angeles County	261	0.24
Royal Oak, MI (city) Oakland County	259	0.43
North Andover, MA (town) Essex County	258	0.95
Rancho Santa Margarita, CA (city) Orange County	252	0.53
Waukegan, IL (city) Lake County	252	0.29
Austin, TX (city) Travis County	252	0.04

Notes: (cdp) census designated place; Refer to the Explanation of Data in the front of the book for more detailed information.

Armenian

Top 150 Places Sorted by Percent

(Based on all places, regardless of population)

Place	Number	%
Glendale, CA (city) Los Angeles County	53,840	27.60
Ridgely, MO (village) Platte County	10	14.08
Madrid, NM (cdp) Santa Fe County	13	12.26
Bowles, CA (cdp) Fresno County	17	10.76
Seboeis, ME (plantation) Penobscot County	3	8.57
Burbank, CA (city) Los Angeles County	8,312	8.29
Rowena, OR (cdp) Wasco County	14	8.28
Watertown, MA (city) Middlesex County	2,708	8.21
La Crescenta-Montrose, CA (cdp) Los Angeles County	1,382	7.51
Cleveland, ND (city) Stutsman County	7	6.09
Carleton, NE (village) Thayer County	7	5.15
Altadena, CA (cdp) Los Angeles County	2,134	5.02
Hillsboro, VA (town) Loudoun County	4	5.00
Belmont, MA (cdp) Middlesex County	1,165	4.82
Echo Lake, WA (cdp) Snohomish County	44	4.75
Blyn, WA (cdp) Clallam County	6	4.51
Montebello, CA (city) Los Angeles County	2,736	4.42
Kirkland, NC (cdp) New Hanover County	23	4.41
Pippa Passes, KY (city) Knott County	12	4.26
Harbor Hills, NY (cdp) Nassau County	23	4.01
Volant, PA (borough) Lawrence County	4	3.96
Cliffside Park, NJ (borough) Bergen County	879	3.82
Oradell, NJ (borough) Bergen County	307	3.82
East Pasadena, CA (cdp) Los Angeles County	223	3.69
Whitinsville, MA (cdp) Worcester County	235	3.68
Cordaville, MA (cdp) Worcester County	97	3.67
West Leipsic, OH (village) Putnam County	9	3.49
Englewood Cliffs, NJ (borough) Bergen County	184	3.46
Galatia, IL (village) Saline County	36	3.44
Menominee, IL (village) Jo Daviess County	8	3.31
Pasadena, CA (city) Los Angeles County	4,400	3.29
La Canada Flintridge, CA (city) Los Angeles County	656	3.22
Malverne Park Oaks, NY (cdp) Nassau County	16	3.21
Munsey Park, NY (village) Nassau County	80	3.04
Fairbanks Ranch, CA (cdp) San Diego County	57	3.04
Dana, IA (city) Greene County	2	2.94
Tipton, PA (cdp) Blair County	35	2.88
Sunol-Midtown, CA (cdp) Santa Clara County	22	2.86
Riverton, MN (township) Clay County	12	2.81
Stafford, MN (township) Roseau County	8	2.81
Emerson, NJ (borough) Bergen County	200	2.78
Demarest, NJ (borough) Bergen County	133	2.75
Boylston, NY (town) Oswego County	15	2.74
Clearwater, NE (village) Antelope County	12	2.73
Medora, ND (city) Billings County	4	2.72
Ridgefield, NJ (borough) Bergen County	294	2.71
La Habra Heights, CA (city) Los Angeles County	145	2.68
West Union, NY (town) Steuben County	10	2.45
Fairview, NJ (borough) Bergen County	320	2.41
Radom, IL (village) Washington County	10	2.40
Plandome Manor, NY (village) Nassau County	20	2.39
Wind Point, WI (village) Racine County	43	2.35
Northbridge, MA (town) Worcester County	309	2.34
Old Tappan, NJ (borough) Bergen County	128	2.33
Southborough, MA (town) Worcester County	199	2.27
Plandome Heights, NY (village) Nassau County	22	2.27
New Milford, NJ (borough) Bergen County	367	2.24
Paxton, MA (town) Worcester County	95	2.17
Allendale, NJ (borough) Bergen County	145	2.16
Golva, ND (city) Golden Valley County	2	2.15
Sierra Madre, CA (city) Los Angeles County	226	2.14
Rosemont, CA (cdp) Sacramento County	481	2.11
Covelo, CA (cdp) Mendocino County	25	2.09
Duarte, CA (city) Los Angeles County	431	2.01
Cranston, RI (city) Providence County	1,555	1.96
Washington Township, NJ (cdp) Bergen County	173	1.94
Baldwinville, MA (cdp) Worcester County	36	1.94
Leicester, MA (town) Worcester County	202	1.93
Shinnecock Hills, NY (cdp) Suffolk County	34	1.89
Blue Ridge, AL (cdp) Elmore County	26	1.89
Skyline, MN (city) Blue Earth County	7	1.89
Land, MN (township) Grant County	5	1.89
Palisades Park, NJ (borough) Bergen County	320	1.87
Murrieta Hot Springs, CA (cdp) Riverside County	55	1.87
North Falmouth, MA (cdp) Barnstable County	61	1.85
Waltham, MA (city) Middlesex County	1,091	1.84
Desert View Highlands, CA (cdp) Los Angeles County	38	1.83
Elmwood Park, WI (village) Racine County	9	1.83
Forest Meadows, CA (cdp) Calaveras County	24	1.82
Arlington, MA (cdp) Middlesex County	763	1.80
Los Angeles, CA (city) Los Angeles County	64,997	1.76
Rancho Cordova, CA (cdp) Sacramento County	957	1.75
Searsburg, VT (town) Bennington County	2	1.75
Alpine, NJ (borough) Bergen County	38	1.74
Paramus, NJ (borough) Bergen County	445	1.73
Banks, AL (town) Pike County	4	1.73
Burlington, MA (cdp) Middlesex County	389	1.70
Conesville, NY (town) Schoharie County	12	1.70
Tenafly, NJ (borough) Bergen County	229	1.66
Fort Lee, NJ (borough) Bergen County	582	1.64
Winchester, MA (cdp) Middlesex County	339	1.63
Newtown, PA (township) Delaware County	188	1.61
Upton-West Upton, MA (cdp) Worcester County	40	1.61
Atkinson, NH (town) Rockingham County	98	1.59
Saddle River, NJ (borough) Bergen County	51	1.59
Napavine, WA (city) Lewis County	21	1.59
Upton, MA (town) Worcester County	89	1.58
Middletown, PA (township) Susquehanna County	5	1.58
North Bay, WI (village) Racine County	4	1.57
Rockville, IN (town) Parke County	42	1.53
Grant, WI (town) Rusk County	11	1.53
Kenilworth, IL (village) Cook County	38	1.52
Wellington, KY (city) Jefferson County	8	1.52
Lexington, MA (cdp) Middlesex County	457	1.51
Alamo, CA (cdp) Contra Costa County	229	1.51
Newfield Hamlet, NY (cdp) Tompkins County	12	1.51
Jenkins, MN (city) Crow Wing County	4	1.50
Amador City, CA (city) Amador County	3	1.49
Newfane, VT (village) Windham County	2	1.49
Mohnton, PA (borough) Berks County	44	1.48
Old Brookville, NY (village) Nassau County	32	1.47
North Providence, RI (cdp) Providence County	471	1.45
Granville, VT (town) Addison County	5	1.45
Weldon, CA (cdp) Kern County	35	1.42
Fresno, CA (city) Fresno County	6,024	1.41
Harrington Park, NJ (borough) Bergen County	67	1.41
Felton, MN (city) Clay County	3	1.41
Fort Washington, PA (cdp) Montgomery County	50	1.39
Henning, MN (township) Otter Tail County	6	1.39
Avon, MA (town) Norfolk County	61	1.37
Kent Narrows, MD (cdp) Queen Anne's County	8	1.37
West Boylston, MA (town) Worcester County	102	1.36
Sheridan, MI (township) Huron County	10	1.36
West Chester, IA (city) Washington County	2	1.35
River Edge, NJ (borough) Bergen County	147	1.34
Verona, MN (township) Faribault County	5	1.34
Holden, MA (town) Worcester County	208	1.33
Marion, MI (township) Livingston County	90	1.33
Old Bethpage, NY (cdp) Nassau County	72	1.33
Edgmont, PA (township) Delaware County	52	1.33
La Verne, CA (city) Los Angeles County	421	1.32
Wolverine Lake, MI (village) Oakland County	59	1.32
Bandon, OR (city) Coos County	38	1.32
Maalaea, HI (cdp) Maui County	6	1.32
Leonia, NJ (borough) Bergen County	117	1.31
Closter, NJ (borough) Bergen County	109	1.30
Westwood, NJ (borough) Bergen County	142	1.29
South Hampton, NH (town) Rockingham County	11	1.29
Greenville, RI (cdp) Providence County	110	1.27
Hamler, OH (village) Henry County	8	1.27
Bingham Farms, MI (village) Oakland County	13	1.26
Rochelle Park, NJ (cdp) Bergen County	69	1.25
Boxborough, MA (town) Middlesex County	61	1.25
East Nassau, NY (village) Rensselaer County	3	1.25
Littlerock, CA (cdp) Los Angeles County	16	1.24
Farmington Hills, MI (city) Oakland County	1,009	1.23
Montgomery, PA (township) Montgomery County	272	1.23
San Marino, CA (city) Los Angeles County	160	1.23
Victory Lakes, NJ (cdp) Gloucester County	25	1.23
Kingsburg, CA (city) Fresno County	112	1.22

Notes: (cdp) census designated place; Refer to the Explanation of Data in the front of the book for more detailed information.

Armenian

Top 150 Places Sorted by Percent

(Based on places with populations of 10,000 or more)

Place	Number	%
Glendale, CA (city) Los Angeles County	53,840	27.60
Burbank, CA (city) Los Angeles County	8,312	8.29
Watertown, MA (city) Middlesex County	2,708	8.21
La Crescenta-Montrose, CA (cdp) Los Angeles County	1,382	7.51
Altadena, CA (cdp) Los Angeles County	2,134	5.02
Belmont, MA (cdp) Middlesex County	1,165	4.82
Montebello, CA (city) Los Angeles County	2,736	4.42
Cliffside Park, NJ (borough) Bergen County	879	3.82
Pasadena, CA (city) Los Angeles County	4,400	3.29
La Canada Flintridge, CA (city) Los Angeles County	656	3.22
Ridgefield, NJ (borough) Bergen County	294	2.71
Fairview, NJ (borough) Bergen County	320	2.41
Northbridge, MA (town) Worcester County	309	2.34
New Milford, NJ (borough) Bergen County	367	2.24
Sierra Madre, CA (city) Los Angeles County	226	2.14
Rosemont, CA (cdp) Sacramento County	481	2.11
Duarte, CA (city) Los Angeles County	431	2.01
Cranston, RI (city) Providence County	1,555	1.96
Leicester, MA (town) Worcester County	202	1.93
Palisades Park, NJ (borough) Bergen County	320	1.87
Waltham, MA (city) Middlesex County	1,091	1.84
Arlington, MA (cdp) Middlesex County	763	1.80
Los Angeles, CA (city) Los Angeles County	64,997	1.76
Rancho Cordova, CA (cdp) Sacramento County	957	1.75
Paramus, NJ (borough) Bergen County	445	1.73
Burlington, MA (cdp) Middlesex County	389	1.70
Tenafly, NJ (borough) Bergen County	229	1.66
Fort Lee, NJ (borough) Bergen County	582	1.64
Winchester, MA (cdp) Middlesex County	339	1.63
Newtown, PA (township) Delaware County	188	1.61
Lexington, MA (cdp) Middlesex County	457	1.51
Alamo, CA (cdp) Contra Costa County	229	1.51
North Providence, RI (cdp) Providence County	471	1.45
Fresno, CA (city) Fresno County	6,024	1.41
River Edge, NJ (borough) Bergen County	147	1.34
Holden, MA (town) Worcester County	208	1.33
La Verne, CA (city) Los Angeles County	421	1.32
Westwood, NJ (borough) Bergen County	142	1.29
Farmington Hills, MI (city) Oakland County	1,009	1.23
Montgomery, PA (township) Montgomery County	272	1.23
San Marino, CA (city) Los Angeles County	160	1.23
Birmingham, MI (city) Oakland County	231	1.19
Wyckoff, NJ (cdp) Bergen County	196	1.19
Hillsdale, NJ (borough) Bergen County	120	1.19
Marple, PA (township) Delaware County	281	1.18
Lake Forest, IL (city) Lake County	234	1.17
Lake Mary, FL (city) Seminole County	132	1.17
Windham, NH (town) Rockingham County	124	1.16
Brunswick, NY (town) Rensselaer County	132	1.13
Bloomfield, MI (township) Oakland County	479	1.11
Salem, NH (town) Rockingham County	310	1.10
Medfield, MA (town) Norfolk County	135	1.10
Martha Lake, WA (cdp) Snohomish County	137	1.08
Moraga, CA (town) Contra Costa County	178	1.07
Auburn, MA (town) Worcester County	169	1.06
Haverhill, MA (city) Essex County	607	1.03
Warwick, RI (city) Kent County	872	1.02
Lower Moreland, PA (township) Montgomery County	115	1.02
Clovis, CA (city) Fresno County	684	1.00
Southfield, MI (township) Oakland County	145	1.00
Broomall, PA (cdp) Delaware County	109	0.98
West Whittier-Los Nietos, CA (cdp) Los Angeles County	245	0.97
Kingston, MA (town) Plymouth County	114	0.97
Beverly Hills, MI (village) Oakland County	101	0.97
Billerica, MA (town) Middlesex County	373	0.96
Ashland, MA (town) Middlesex County	141	0.96
Whittier, CA (city) Los Angeles County	795	0.95
North Andover, MA (town) Essex County	258	0.95
Drexel Hill, PA (cdp) Delaware County	275	0.94
Andover, MA (town) Essex County	292	0.93
Hasbrouck Heights, NJ (borough) Bergen County	109	0.93
Livonia, MI (city) Wayne County	928	0.92
Dearborn, MI (city) Wayne County	895	0.92
Westwood, MA (town) Norfolk County	130	0.92
Oakland charter, MI (township) Oakland County	116	0.89
Methuen, MA (city) Essex County	384	0.88
Temple City, CA (town) Los Angeles County	294	0.88
Hillsborough, CA (town) San Mateo County	95	0.88
West Bloomfield, MI (township) Oakland County	564	0.87
Palos Verdes Estates, CA (city) Los Angeles County	116	0.87
Garden City, NY (village) Nassau County	186	0.86
Watervliet, NY (city) Albany County	88	0.86
Franklin, MA (city) Norfolk County	247	0.84
Needham, MA (cdp) Norfolk County	242	0.84
Bergenfield, NJ (borough) Bergen County	221	0.84
Oxford, MA (town) Worcester County	112	0.84
Cottonwood Heights, UT (cdp) Salt Lake County	228	0.83
Stoneham, MA (town) Middlesex County	182	0.82
Northville, MI (township) Wayne County	172	0.82
Hanover, MA (town) Plymouth County	108	0.82
Springfield, PA (cdp) Delaware County	191	0.81
Loma Linda, CA (city) San Bernardino County	151	0.81
Dumont, NJ (borough) Bergen County	142	0.81
Reading, MA (cdp) Middlesex County	190	0.80
Hampton, NH (town) Rockingham County	120	0.80
Novi, MI (city) Oakland County	374	0.79
Farmington, CT (town) Hartford County	187	0.79
Lincolnwood, IL (village) Cook County	98	0.79
Dudley, MA (town) Worcester County	79	0.79
Baywood-Los Osos, CA (cdp) San Luis Obispo County	111	0.78
Melvindale, MI (city) Wayne County	84	0.78
Upper Darby, PA (township) Delaware County	632	0.77
Allen Park, MI (city) Wayne County	226	0.77
Worcester, MA (city) Worcester County	1,306	0.76
Newton, MA (city) Middlesex County	640	0.76
Morton Grove, IL (village) Cook County	169	0.75
Parkland, FL (city) Broward County	105	0.75
East Greenwich, RI (town) Kent County	97	0.75
Lynnfield, MA (cdp) Essex County	87	0.75
Hanover, NH (town) Grafton County	81	0.75
Troy, NY (city) Rensselaer County	364	0.74
Shrewsbury, MA (town) Worcester County	235	0.74
Concord, MA (town) Middlesex County	126	0.74
Medford, MA (city) Middlesex County	405	0.73
Millcreek, UT (cdp) Salt Lake County	224	0.73
Wayland, MA (town) Middlesex County	96	0.73
Woodhaven, MI (city) Wayne County	92	0.73
North Greenbush, NY (town) Rensselaer County	78	0.73
Scituate, RI (town) Providence County	75	0.73
Rehoboth, MA (town) Bristol County	74	0.73
Arcadia, CA (city) Los Angeles County	380	0.72
Barrington, RI (town) Bristol County	121	0.72
Rancho Palos Verdes, CA (city) Los Angeles County	292	0.71
Saugus, MA (cdp) Essex County	185	0.71
Caledonia, WI (town) Racine County	168	0.71
Harper Woods, MI (city) Wayne County	101	0.71
Belmont, CA (city) San Mateo County	176	0.70
Tustin Foothills, CA (cdp) Orange County	168	0.70
Weehawken, NJ (township) Hudson County	95	0.70
Haverford, PA (township) Delaware County	333	0.69
Smithfield, RI (town) Providence County	143	0.69
South Yarmouth, MA (cdp) Barnstable County	81	0.69
Franklin Lakes, NJ (borough) Bergen County	72	0.69
Weston, CT (town) Fairfield County	69	0.69
Seekonk, MA (town) Bristol County	91	0.68
Mahwah, NJ (township) Bergen County	161	0.67
Piedmont, CA (city) Alameda County	73	0.67
San Dimas, CA (city) Los Angeles County	230	0.66
Newington, CT (cdp) Hartford County	192	0.66
North Kingstown, RI (town) Washington County	173	0.66
Calabasas, CA (city) Los Angeles County	132	0.66
Hopkinton, MA (town) Middlesex County	88	0.66
Bedford, MA (town) Middlesex County	83	0.66
Lafayette, CA (city) Contra Costa County	152	0.65
Buckingham, PA (township) Bucks County	107	0.65
Collingswood, NJ (borough) Camden County	93	0.65
Pequannock, NJ (township) Morris County	90	0.65
Ridgefield Park, NJ (village) Bergen County	84	0.65
Montgomeryville, PA (cdp) Montgomery County	78	0.65
Upper Providence Township, PA (cdp) Delaware County	68	0.65

Notes: (cdp) census designated place; Refer to the Explanation of Data in the front of the book for more detailed information.

Asian

Top 150 Places Sorted by Number

(Based on all places, regardless of population)

Place	Number	%
New York, NY (city) New York City	889,642	11.11
Los Angeles, CA (city) Los Angeles County	417,435	11.30
Honolulu, HI (cdp) Honolulu County	279,450	75.19
San Jose, CA (city) Santa Clara County	263,819	29.48
San Francisco, CA (city) San Francisco County	259,403	33.40
San Diego, CA (city) San Diego County	194,228	15.88
Chicago, IL (city) Cook County	143,175	4.94
Houston, TX (city) Harris County	116,608	5.97
Seattle, WA (city) King County	87,550	15.54
Fremont, CA (city) Alameda County	82,664	40.64
Sacramento, CA (city) Sacramento County	79,286	19.48
Philadelphia, PA (city) Philadelphia County	76,421	5.04
Oakland, CA (city) Alameda County	68,311	17.10
Long Beach, CA (city) Los Angeles County	65,538	14.20
Stockton, CA (city) San Joaquin County	57,387	23.54
Daly City, CA (city) San Mateo County	56,690	54.71
Fresno, CA (city) Fresno County	55,436	12.96
Garden Grove, CA (city) Orange County	54,134	32.77
Boston, MA (city) Suffolk County	48,469	8.23
Irvine, CA (city) Orange County	47,527	33.22
Sunnyvale, CA (city) Santa Clara County	45,822	34.78
Anaheim, CA (city) Orange County	44,343	13.52
Torrance, CA (city) Los Angeles County	44,265	32.09
Alhambra, CA (city) Los Angeles County	43,951	51.22
Jersey City, NJ (city) Hudson County	42,849	17.85
Portland, OR (city) Multnomah County	40,844	7.72
Monterey Park, CA (city) Los Angeles County	39,783	66.25
Saint Paul, MN (city) Ramsey County	39,586	13.79
Dallas, TX (city) Dallas County	37,458	3.15
Austin, TX (city) Travis County	35,922	5.47
Westminster, CA (city) Orange County	35,517	40.27
Glendale, CA (city) Los Angeles County	34,903	17.90
Milpitas, CA (city) Santa Clara County	34,713	55.37
Phoenix, AZ (city) Maricopa County	34,060	2.58
Santa Clara, CA (city) Santa Clara County	32,707	31.95
Santa Ana, CA (city) Orange County	32,629	9.65
Vallejo, CA (city) Solano County	32,449	27.79
Union City, CA (city) Alameda County	32,098	48.00
Cerritos, CA (city) Los Angeles County	32,023	62.20
Hayward, CA (city) Alameda County	31,255	22.32
Hempstead, NY (town) Nassau County	31,057	4.11
Hilo, HI (cdp) Hawaii County	30,372	74.52
Las Vegas, NV (city) Clark County	29,987	6.27
Edison, NJ (cdp) Middlesex County	29,669	30.37
Columbus, OH (city) Franklin County	28,624	4.02
Rosemead, CA (city) Los Angeles County	28,376	53.03
Waipahu, HI (cdp) Honolulu County	28,120	84.93
Minneapolis, MN (city) Hennepin County	27,217	7.11
Rowland Heights, CA (cdp) Los Angeles County	26,380	54.33
West Covina, CA (city) Los Angeles County	26,276	25.01
Diamond Bar, CA (city) Los Angeles County	26,012	46.21
Arcadia, CA (city) Los Angeles County	25,838	48.70
Kaneohe, HI (cdp) Honolulu County	25,800	73.78
Virginia Beach, VA (independent city) Virginia Beach city	25,796	6.07
Jacksonville, FL (special city) Duval County	25,465	3.46
Plano, TX (city) Collin County	24,816	11.18
Pearl City, HI (cdp) Honolulu County	24,718	79.80
San Antonio, TX (city) Bexar County	24,633	2.15
Waimalu, HI (cdp) Honolulu County	24,215	82.45
Cupertino, CA (city) Santa Clara County	23,808	47.10
El Monte, CA (city) Los Angeles County	23,258	20.06
Chula Vista, CA (city) San Diego County	23,250	13.40
Mililani Town, HI (cdp) Honolulu County	23,130	80.85
Arlington, TX (city) Tarrant County	22,456	6.74
Fullerton, CA (city) Orange County	22,406	17.78
Carson, CA (city) Los Angeles County	22,205	24.75
North Hempstead, NY (town) Nassau County	22,196	9.97
Bellevue, WA (city) King County	21,547	19.67
Alameda, CA (city) Alameda County	21,513	29.77
Huntington Beach, CA (city) Orange County	21,200	11.18
San Gabriel, CA (city) Los Angeles County	20,988	52.73
Hacienda Heights, CA (cdp) Los Angeles County	20,921	39.38
Charlotte, NC (city) Mecklenburg County	20,813	3.85
Oklahoma City, OK (city) Oklahoma County	20,661	4.08
Milwaukee, WI (city) Milwaukee County	20,659	3.46
San Leandro, CA (city) Alameda County	20,206	25.43
Berkeley, CA (city) Alameda County	19,911	19.38
South San Francisco, CA (city) San Mateo County	19,696	32.53
Denver, CO (city) Denver County	19,513	3.52
Tacoma, WA (city) Pierce County	19,459	10.05
Lowell, MA (city) Middlesex County	19,238	18.29
Arlington, VA (cdp) Arlington County	19,135	10.10
Anchorage, AK (municipality) Anchorage Borough	18,974	7.29
Washington, DC (city) District of Columbia	18,345	3.21
Buena Park, CA (city) Orange County	18,247	23.31
Walnut, CA (city) Los Angeles County	17,975	59.91
Riverside, CA (city) Riverside County	17,596	6.90
Garland, TX (city) Dallas County	17,401	8.06
Irving, TX (city) Dallas County	17,357	9.06
Gardena, CA (city) Los Angeles County	17,122	29.65
Kailua, HI (cdp) Honolulu County	17,087	46.80
Kahului, HI (cdp) Maui County	16,742	83.10
Chino Hills, CA (city) San Bernardino County	16,655	24.94
Fort Worth, TX (city) Tarrant County	16,613	3.11
San Mateo, CA (city) San Mateo County	16,363	17.69
Mountain View, CA (city) Santa Clara County	16,219	22.94
Sugar Land, TX (city) Fort Bend County	16,206	25.59
Nashville-Davidson, TN (special city) Davidson County	15,972	2.93
Wichita, KS (city) Sedgwick County	15,933	4.63
Tucson, AZ (city) Pima County	15,823	3.25
Fountain Valley, CA (city) Orange County	15,675	28.51
Pasadena, CA (city) Los Angeles County	15,648	11.68
Oyster Bay, NY (town) Nassau County	15,630	5.32
Spring Valley, NV (cdp) Clark County	15,596	13.29
Paradise, NV (cdp) Clark County	15,488	8.32
Brookhaven, NY (town) Suffolk County	15,288	3.41
Ann Arbor, MI (city) Washtenaw County	15,128	13.27
Woodbridge, NJ (township) Middlesex County	15,042	15.47
Modesto, CA (city) Stanislaus County	15,041	7.96
Aurora, CO (city) Arapahoe County	15,009	5.43
Oxnard, CA (city) Ventura County	14,898	8.75
Skokie, IL (village) Cook County	14,565	22.99
Concord, CA (city) Contra Costa County	14,482	11.89
Colorado Springs, CO (city) El Paso County	14,326	3.97
Quincy, MA (city) Norfolk County	14,195	16.13
Richmond, CA (city) Contra Costa County	14,183	14.30
Temple City, CA (city) Los Angeles County	14,064	42.14
Fairfield, CA (city) Solano County	13,967	14.52
Indianapolis, IN (special city) Marion County	13,902	1.78
Madison, WI (city) Dane County	13,804	6.63
Orange, CA (city) Orange County	13,719	10.65
Cambridge, MA (city) Middlesex County	13,516	13.34
Bakersfield, CA (city) Kern County	13,405	5.43
Naperville, IL (city) Du Page County	13,377	10.42
Albuquerque, NM (city) Bernalillo County	13,290	2.96
Wahiawa, HI (cdp) Honolulu County	13,282	82.24
Norwalk, CA (city) Los Angeles County	13,194	12.77
Piscataway, NJ (township) Middlesex County	13,167	26.08
Carrollton, TX (city) Denton County	13,140	11.99
Lakewood, CA (city) Los Angeles County	12,751	16.07
Detroit, MI (city) Wayne County	12,733	1.34
Pomona, CA (city) Los Angeles County	12,603	8.43
Providence, RI (city) Providence County	12,530	7.22
Elk Grove, CA (cdp) Sacramento County	12,461	20.77
New Orleans, LA (city) Orleans Parish	12,370	2.55
Davis, CA (city) Yolo County	12,327	20.44
Federal Way, WA (city) King County	12,293	14.76
Oceanside, CA (city) San Diego County	12,242	7.60
Baltimore, MD (independent city) Baltimore city	12,088	1.86
Salinas, CA (city) Monterey County	11,887	7.87
Ewa Beach, HI (cdp) Honolulu County	11,864	80.98
Rancho Palos Verdes, CA (city) Los Angeles County	11,817	28.72
Richardson, TX (city) Dallas County	11,800	12.85
Reno, NV (city) Washoe County	11,722	6.49
Annandale, VA (cdp) Fairfax County	11,590	21.08
Corona, CA (city) Riverside County	11,588	9.27
Fort Lee, NJ (borough) Bergen County	11,548	32.57
Palo Alto, CA (city) Santa Clara County	11,454	19.55
Troy, MI (city) Oakland County	11,419	14.10
Schaumburg, IL (village) Cook County	11,373	15.09

Notes: (cdp) census designated place; Refer to the Explanation of Data in the front of the book for more detailed information.

Asian

Top 150 Places Sorted by Percent

(Based on all places, regardless of population)

Place	Number	%
Ewa Villages, HI (cdp) Honolulu County	4,802	101.29
Kaumakani, HI (cdp) Kauai County	604	99.51
Whitmore Village, HI (cdp) Honolulu County	3,813	93.99
Eleele, HI (cdp) Kauai County	1,897	92.99
Hanamaulu, HI (cdp) Kauai County	3,022	92.36
Puhi, HI (cdp) Kauai County	1,087	91.65
Keaau, HI (cdp) Hawaii County	1,831	91.09
Pahala, HI (cdp) Hawaii County	1,231	89.33
Lanai City, HI (cdp) Maui County	2,804	88.62
Waipio, HI (cdp) Honolulu County	10,342	88.61
Village Park, HI (cdp) Honolulu County	8,449	87.78
Pepeekeo, HI (cdp) Hawaii County	1,458	85.92
Ewa Gentry, HI (cdp) Honolulu County	4,243	85.91
Waialua, HI (cdp) Honolulu County	3,203	85.16
Waipahu, HI (cdp) Honolulu County	28,120	84.93
Aiea, HI (cdp) Honolulu County	7,637	84.68
Halaula, HI (cdp) Hawaii County	419	84.65
Paauilo, HI (cdp) Hawaii County	483	84.59
Hanapepe, HI (cdp) Kauai County	1,797	83.46
Kahului, HI (cdp) Maui County	16,742	83.10
Waimalu, HI (cdp) Honolulu County	24,215	82.45
Wahiawa, HI (cdp) Honolulu County	13,282	82.24
Waimea, HI (cdp) Kauai County	1,465	81.98
Kapaau, HI (cdp) Hawaii County	941	81.19
Ewa Beach, HI (cdp) Honolulu County	11,864	80.98
Mililani Town, HI (cdp) Honolulu County	23,130	80.85
Pearl City, HI (cdp) Honolulu County	24,718	79.80
Wainaku, HI (cdp) Hawaii County	977	79.63
Hawi, HI (cdp) Hawaii County	742	79.10
Waikapu, HI (cdp) Maui County	871	78.12
Lihue, HI (cdp) Kauai County	4,413	77.78
Halawa, HI (cdp) Honolulu County	10,705	77.06
Kurtistown, HI (cdp) Hawaii County	889	76.84
Kekaha, HI (cdp) Kauai County	2,428	76.47
Waihee-Waiehu, HI (cdp) Maui County	5,562	76.09
Honolulu, HI (cdp) Honolulu County	279,450	75.19
Naalehu, HI (cdp) Hawaii County	691	75.19
Honokaa, HI (cdp) Hawaii County	1,674	74.97
Hilo, HI (cdp) Hawaii County	30,372	74.52
Wailuku, HI (cdp) Maui County	9,111	74.10
Kaneohe, HI (cdp) Honolulu County	25,800	73.78
Waipio Acres, HI (cdp) Honolulu County	3,892	73.46
Pahoa, HI (cdp) Hawaii County	705	73.28
Ahuimanu, HI (cdp) Honolulu County	6,141	72.20
Heeia, HI (cdp) Honolulu County	3,551	71.82
Papaikou, HI (cdp) Hawaii County	1,015	71.78
Koloa, HI (cdp) Kauai County	1,393	71.73
Honomu, HI (cdp) Hawaii County	384	70.98
Haleiwa, HI (cdp) Honolulu County	1,571	70.61
Kealakekua, HI (cdp) Hawaii County	1,135	69.00
Kukuihaele, HI (cdp) Hawaii County	218	68.77
Makakilo City, HI (cdp) Honolulu County	9,001	68.42
Monterey Park, CA (city) Los Angeles County	39,783	66.25
Waimanalo, HI (cdp) Honolulu County	2,423	66.13
Haliimaile, HI (cdp) Maui County	587	65.59
Wailua, HI (cdp) Kauai County	1,358	65.19
Kapaa, HI (cdp) Kauai County	6,157	65.00
Lawai, HI (cdp) Kauai County	1,271	64.06
Pakala Village, HI (cdp) Kauai County	306	64.02
Kaunakakai, HI (cdp) Maui County	1,726	63.32
Waianae, HI (cdp) Honolulu County	6,628	63.09
Lahaina, HI (cdp) Maui County	5,687	62.37
Kahuku, HI (cdp) Honolulu County	1,308	62.37
Cerritos, CA (city) Los Angeles County	32,023	62.20
Maili, HI (cdp) Honolulu County	3,686	62.02
Paukaa, HI (cdp) Hawaii County	306	61.82
Captain Cook, HI (cdp) Hawaii County	1,967	61.35
Laupahoehoe, HI (cdp) Hawaii County	289	61.10
Pukalani, HI (cdp) Maui County	4,467	60.53
Walnut, CA (city) Los Angeles County	17,975	59.91
Mountain View, HI (cdp) Hawaii County	1,675	59.84
Paia, HI (cdp) Maui County	1,462	58.50
Millbourne, PA (borough) Delaware County	544	57.69
Kalaheo, HI (cdp) Kauai County	2,242	57.30
Hawaiian Paradise Park, HI (cdp) Hawaii County	4,039	57.28
Hawaiian Beaches, HI (cdp) Hawaii County	2,113	56.97
Kahaluu, HI (cdp) Honolulu County	1,666	56.76
Waikane, HI (cdp) Honolulu County	410	56.47
Makaha, HI (cdp) Honolulu County	4,334	55.90
Makaha Valley, HI (cdp) Honolulu County	716	55.55
Milpitas, CA (city) Santa Clara County	34,713	55.37
Nanawale Estates, HI (cdp) Hawaii County	590	54.99
Maunawili, HI (cdp) Honolulu County	2,676	54.96
Daly City, CA (city) San Mateo County	56,690	54.71
Rowland Heights, CA (cdp) Los Angeles County	26,380	54.33
Honalo, HI (cdp) Hawaii County	1,063	53.50
Wailua Homesteads, HI (cdp) Kauai County	2,434	53.30
Rosemead, CA (city) Los Angeles County	28,376	53.03
Omao, HI (cdp) Kauai County	645	52.83
San Gabriel, CA (city) Los Angeles County	20,988	52.73
San Marino, CA (city) Los Angeles County	6,754	52.17
Waimea, HI (cdp) Hawaii County	3,658	52.05
Makawao, HI (cdp) Maui County	3,246	51.30
Alhambra, CA (city) Los Angeles County	43,951	51.22
Ainaloa, HI (cdp) Hawaii County	969	50.73
Orchidlands Estates, HI (cdp) Hawaii County	874	50.49
Kualapuu, HI (cdp) Maui County	952	49.17
Nanakuli, HI (cdp) Honolulu County	5,293	48.95
Arcadia, CA (city) Los Angeles County	25,838	48.70
Union City, CA (city) Alameda County	32,098	48.00
La Palma, CA (city) Orange County	7,377	47.88
Cupertino, CA (city) Santa Clara County	23,808	47.10
Kailua, HI (cdp) Hawaii County	4,648	47.09
South San Gabriel, CA (cdp) Los Angeles County	3,572	47.03
Maunaloa, HI (cdp) Maui County	108	46.96
Honaunau-Napoopoo, HI (cdp) Hawaii County	1,133	46.93
Waikoloa Village, HI (cdp) Hawaii County	2,253	46.88
Kailua, HI (cdp) Honolulu County	17,087	46.80
Diamond Bar, CA (city) Los Angeles County	26,012	46.21
Hercules, CA (city) Contra Costa County	9,005	46.21
Kilauea, HI (cdp) Kauai County	958	45.79
East San Gabriel, CA (cdp) Los Angeles County	6,423	44.26
Hana, HI (cdp) Maui County	308	43.44
Kihei, HI (cdp) Maui County	7,176	42.84
Palisades Park, NJ (borough) Bergen County	7,259	42.52
Temple City, CA (city) Los Angeles County	14,064	42.14
Forest Home, NY (cdp) Tompkins County	387	41.13
Kalaoa, HI (cdp) Hawaii County	2,785	40.99
Fremont, CA (city) Alameda County	82,664	40.64
Plainsboro Center, NJ (cdp) Middlesex County	890	40.29
Westminster, CA (city) Orange County	35,517	40.27
Akutan, AK (city) Aleutians East Borough	282	39.55
Hacienda Heights, CA (cdp) Los Angeles County	20,921	39.38
Hanalei, HI (cdp) Kauai County	186	38.91
Broadmoor, CA (cdp) San Mateo County	1,561	38.77
Punaluu, HI (cdp) Honolulu County	333	37.80
Fern Acres, HI (cdp) Hawaii County	279	36.90
Hauula, HI (cdp) Honolulu County	1,339	36.67
Society Hill, NJ (cdp) Middlesex County	1,357	35.67
Foster City, CA (city) San Mateo County	10,258	35.61
Pupukea, HI (cdp) Honolulu County	1,502	35.34
Sunnyvale, CA (city) Santa Clara County	45,822	34.78
Bayou La Batre, AL (city) Mobile County	801	34.63
Eden Roc, HI (cdp) Hawaii County	156	34.59
Haiku-Pauwela, HI (cdp) Maui County	2,234	33.96
Kodiak, AK (city) Kodiak Island Borough	2,145	33.86
San Francisco, CA (city) San Francisco County	259,403	33.40
Champ, MO (village) Saint Louis County	4	33.33
Irvine, CA (city) Orange County	47,527	33.22
Unalaska, AK (city) Aleutians West Census Area	1,416	33.06
Garden Grove, CA (city) Orange County	54,134	32.77
Holualoa, HI (cdp) Hawaii County	2,001	32.77
Volcano, HI (cdp) Hawaii County	730	32.72
Anahola, HI (cdp) Kauai County	631	32.66
Fort Lee, NJ (borough) Bergen County	11,548	32.57
South San Francisco, CA (city) San Mateo County	19,696	32.53
Merrifield, VA (cdp) Fairfax County	3,610	32.32
Hawaiian Acres, HI (cdp) Hawaii County	572	32.21
Torrance, CA (city) Los Angeles County	44,265	32.09
Santa Clara, CA (city) Santa Clara County	32,707	31.95

Notes: (cdp) census designated place; Refer to the Explanation of Data in the front of the book for more detailed information.

Asian

Top 150 Places Sorted by Percent

(Based on places with populations of 10,000 or more)

Place	Number	%
Waipio, HI (cdp) Honolulu County	10,342	88.61
Waipahu, HI (cdp) Honolulu County	28,120	84.93
Kahului, HI (cdp) Maui County	16,742	83.10
Waimalu, HI (cdp) Honolulu County	24,215	82.45
Wahiawa, HI (cdp) Honolulu County	13,282	82.24
Ewa Beach, HI (cdp) Honolulu County	11,864	80.98
Mililani Town, HI (cdp) Honolulu County	23,130	80.85
Pearl City, HI (cdp) Honolulu County	24,718	79.80
Halawa, HI (cdp) Honolulu County	10,705	77.06
Honolulu, HI (cdp) Honolulu County	279,450	75.19
Hilo, HI (cdp) Hawaii County	30,372	74.52
Wailuku, HI (cdp) Maui County	9,111	74.10
Kaneohe, HI (cdp) Honolulu County	25,800	73.78
Makakilo City, HI (cdp) Honolulu County	9,001	68.42
Monterey Park, CA (city) Los Angeles County	39,783	66.25
Waianae, HI (cdp) Honolulu County	6,628	63.09
Cerritos, CA (city) Los Angeles County	32,023	62.20
Walnut, CA (city) Los Angeles County	17,975	59.91
Milpitas, CA (city) Santa Clara County	34,713	55.37
Daly City, CA (city) San Mateo County	56,690	54.71
Rowland Heights, CA (cdp) Los Angeles County	26,380	54.33
Rosemead, CA (city) Los Angeles County	28,376	53.03
San Gabriel, CA (city) Los Angeles County	20,988	52.73
San Marino, CA (city) Los Angeles County	6,754	52.17
Alhambra, CA (city) Los Angeles County	43,951	51.22
Nanakuli, HI (cdp) Honolulu County	5,293	48.95
Arcadia, CA (city) Los Angeles County	25,838	48.70
Union City, CA (city) Alameda County	32,098	48.00
La Palma, CA (city) Orange County	7,377	47.88
Cupertino, CA (city) Santa Clara County	23,808	47.10
Kailua, HI (cdp) Honolulu County	17,087	46.80
Diamond Bar, CA (city) Los Angeles County	26,012	46.21
Hercules, CA (city) Contra Costa County	9,005	46.21
East San Gabriel, CA (cdp) Los Angeles County	6,423	44.26
Kihei, HI (cdp) Maui County	7,176	42.84
Palisades Park, NJ (borough) Bergen County	7,259	42.52
Temple City, CA (city) Los Angeles County	14,064	42.14
Fremont, CA (city) Alameda County	82,664	40.64
Westminster, CA (city) Orange County	35,517	40.27
Hacienda Heights, CA (cdp) Los Angeles County	20,921	39.38
Foster City, CA (city) San Mateo County	10,258	35.61
Sunnyvale, CA (city) Santa Clara County	45,822	34.78
San Francisco, CA (city) San Francisco County	259,403	33.40
Irvine, CA (city) Orange County	47,527	33.22
Garden Grove, CA (city) Orange County	54,134	32.77
Fort Lee, NJ (borough) Bergen County	11,548	32.57
South San Francisco, CA (city) San Mateo County	19,696	32.53
Merrifield, VA (cdp) Fairfax County	3,610	32.32
Torrance, CA (city) Los Angeles County	44,265	32.09
Santa Clara, CA (city) Santa Clara County	32,707	31.95
Plainsboro, NJ (township) Middlesex County	6,432	31.82
Princeton Meadows, NJ (cdp) Middlesex County	4,211	31.34
Saratoga, CA (city) Santa Clara County	9,341	31.30
Edison, NJ (cdp) Middlesex County	29,669	30.37
Millbrae, CA (city) San Mateo County	6,190	29.88
South Pasadena, CA (city) Los Angeles County	7,250	29.85
Alameda, CA (city) Alameda County	21,513	29.77
Gardena, CA (city) Los Angeles County	17,122	29.65
Artesia, CA (city) Los Angeles County	4,843	29.57
San Jose, CA (city) Santa Clara County	263,819	29.48
North Potomac, MD (cdp) Montgomery County	6,793	29.48
Stanford, CA (cdp) Santa Clara County	3,841	28.85
Rancho Palos Verdes, CA (city) Los Angeles County	11,817	28.72
Albany, CA (city) Alameda County	4,708	28.63
Fountain Valley, CA (city) Orange County	15,675	28.51
New Territory, TX (cdp) Fort Bend County	3,900	28.14
West Carson, CA (cdp) Los Angeles County	5,920	28.01
Loma Linda, CA (city) San Bernardino County	5,215	27.92
Vallejo, CA (city) Solano County	32,449	27.79
El Cerrito, CA (city) Contra Costa County	6,415	27.69
Hillsborough, CA (town) San Mateo County	2,881	26.61
Iselin, NJ (cdp) Middlesex County	4,409	26.40
Piscataway, NJ (township) Middlesex County	13,167	26.08
Sugar Land, TX (city) Fort Bend County	16,206	25.59
San Leandro, CA (city) Alameda County	20,206	25.43
South Yuba City, CA (cdp) Sutter County	3,210	25.37
Bryn Mawr-Skyway, WA (cdp) King County	3,523	25.21
Pinole, CA (city) Contra Costa County	4,770	25.05
West Covina, CA (city) Los Angeles County	26,276	25.01
Chino Hills, CA (city) San Bernardino County	16,655	24.94
Newark, CA (city) Alameda County	10,583	24.92
Carson, CA (city) Los Angeles County	22,205	24.75
West Windsor, NJ (township) Mercer County	5,268	24.05
White Center, WA (cdp) King County	5,009	23.88
Morton Grove, IL (village) Cook County	5,345	23.81
Stockton, CA (city) San Joaquin County	57,387	23.54
Cypress, CA (city) Orange County	10,853	23.48
Buena Park, CA (city) Orange County	18,247	23.31
La Canada Flintridge, CA (city) Los Angeles County	4,681	23.04
Skokie, IL (village) Cook County	14,565	22.99
Mountain View, CA (city) Santa Clara County	16,219	22.94
Springfield, VA (cdp) Fairfax County	6,979	22.94
Lincolnwood, IL (village) Cook County	2,822	22.83
Florin, CA (cdp) Sacramento County	6,281	22.71
San Bruno, CA (city) San Mateo County	9,056	22.55
Hayward, CA (city) Alameda County	31,255	22.32
Suisun City, CA (city) Solano County	5,774	22.11
Laguna, CA (cdp) Sacramento County	7,558	22.03
Bergenfield, NJ (borough) Bergen County	5,678	21.63
Stafford, TX (city) Fort Bend County	3,376	21.53
Marina, CA (city) Monterey County	5,348	21.31
Glendale Heights, IL (village) Du Page County	6,764	21.29
Annandale, VA (cdp) Fairfax County	11,590	21.08
Idylwood, VA (cdp) Fairfax County	3,364	21.02
Linda, CA (cdp) Yuba County	2,820	20.93
Elk Grove, CA (cdp) Sacramento County	12,461	20.77
Avenel, NJ (cdp) Middlesex County	3,640	20.74
Tysons Corner, VA (cdp) Fairfax County	3,834	20.68
Jefferson, VA (cdp) Fairfax County	5,669	20.67
National City, CA (city) San Diego County	11,161	20.57
La Crescenta-Montrose, CA (cdp) Los Angeles County	3,803	20.52
Parkway-South Sacramento, CA (cdp) Sacramento County	7,461	20.46
Davis, CA (city) Yolo County	12,327	20.44
Tenafly, NJ (borough) Bergen County	2,791	20.22
El Monte, CA (city) Los Angeles County	23,258	20.06
Bellevue, WA (city) King County	21,547	19.67
Palos Verdes Estates, CA (city) Los Angeles County	2,622	19.66
Palo Alto, CA (city) Santa Clara County	11,454	19.55
Parsippany-Troy Hills, NJ (township) Morris County	9,870	19.49
Sacramento, CA (city) Sacramento County	79,286	19.48
Colesville, MD (cdp) Montgomery County	3,843	19.40
Berkeley, CA (city) Alameda County	19,911	19.38
Pacifica, CA (city) San Mateo County	7,416	19.32
Vineyard, CA (cdp) Sacramento County	1,936	19.15
South Brunswick, NJ (township) Middlesex County	7,160	18.97
Piedmont, CA (city) Alameda County	2,077	18.96
Blackhawk-Camino Tassajara, CA (cdp) Contra Costa County	1,898	18.89
San Pablo, CA (city) Contra Costa County	5,686	18.82
Mission Bend, TX (cdp) Fort Bend County	5,793	18.79
Little Ferry, NJ (borough) Bergen County	2,015	18.66
Holmdel, NJ (township) Monmouth County	2,909	18.43
Lowell, MA (city) Middlesex County	19,238	18.29
Paramus, NJ (borough) Bergen County	4,681	18.19
Belmont, CA (city) San Mateo County	4,568	18.18
San Lorenzo, CA (cdp) Alameda County	3,979	18.17
Ridgefield, NJ (borough) Bergen County	1,962	18.12
Chantilly, VA (cdp) Fairfax County	7,410	18.06
Glendale, CA (city) Los Angeles County	34,903	17.90
Jersey City, NJ (city) Hudson County	42,849	17.85
Calverton, MD (cdp) Montgomery County	2,251	17.85
Delano, CA (city) Kern County	6,910	17.80
Fullerton, CA (city) Orange County	22,406	17.78
San Mateo, CA (city) San Mateo County	16,363	17.69
Los Altos, CA (city) Santa Clara County	4,887	17.65
San Ramon, CA (city) Contra Costa County	7,860	17.58
Lincolnia, VA (cdp) Fairfax County	2,768	17.53
Foothill Ranch, CA (cdp) Orange County	1,911	17.53
Redland, MD (cdp) Montgomery County	2,962	17.43
Ashland, CA (cdp) Alameda County	3,619	17.40
East Brunswick, NJ (cdp) Middlesex County	8,027	17.17

Notes: (cdp) census designated place; Refer to the Explanation of Data in the front of the book for more detailed information.

Asian: Bangladeshi

Top 150 Places Sorted by Number

(Based on all places, regardless of population)

Place	Number	%
New York, NY (city) New York City	28,269	0.35
Los Angeles, CA (city) Los Angeles County	1,629	0.04
Detroit, MI (city) Wayne County	1,131	0.12
Hamtramck, MI (city) Wayne County	1,034	4.50
Paterson, NJ (city) Passaic County	729	0.49
Arlington, VA (cdp) Arlington County	527	0.28
Houston, TX (city) Harris County	464	0.02
Chicago, IL (city) Cook County	376	0.01
Dallas, TX (city) Dallas County	325	0.03
Atlantic City, NJ (city) Atlantic County	303	0.75
North Atlanta, GA (cdp) De Kalb County	276	0.72
Irving, TX (city) Dallas County	270	0.14
Alexandria, VA (independent city) Alexandria city	228	0.18
San Jose, CA (city) Santa Clara County	224	0.03
Philadelphia, PA (city) Philadelphia County	209	0.01
Arlington, TX (city) Tarrant County	197	0.06
Columbus, OH (city) Franklin County	194	0.03
Jersey City, NJ (city) Hudson County	182	0.08
Reno, NV (city) Washoe County	170	0.09
North Hempstead, NY (town) Nassau County	159	0.07
Austin, TX (city) Travis County	157	0.02
Plano, TX (city) Collin County	154	0.07
Cambridge, MA (city) Middlesex County	152	0.15
Washington, DC (city) District of Columbia	151	0.03
Hempstead, NY (town) Nassau County	150	0.02
Oklahoma City, OK (city) Oklahoma County	146	0.03
Atlanta, GA (city) Fulton County	144	0.03
Silver Spring, MD (cdp) Montgomery County	130	0.17
Hatfield, PA (township) Montgomery County	126	0.75
Lansdale, PA (borough) Montgomery County	125	0.78
Brookhaven, NY (town) Suffolk County	120	0.03
Glendale, CA (city) Los Angeles County	118	0.06
Wichita, KS (city) Sedgwick County	115	0.03
Boston, MA (city) Suffolk County	113	0.02
Fremont, CA (city) Alameda County	112	0.06
Richardson, TX (city) Dallas County	111	0.12
Long Beach, CA (city) Los Angeles County	102	0.02
Stamford, CT (city) Fairfield County	100	0.09
Phoenix, AZ (city) Maricopa County	96	0.01
Manchester, CT (town) Hartford County	95	0.17
Reston, VA (cdp) Fairfax County	95	0.17
Anaheim, CA (city) Orange County	88	0.03
Edison, NJ (cdp) Middlesex County	87	0.09
Chamblee, GA (city) De Kalb County	85	0.89
Chandler, AZ (city) Maricopa County	82	0.05
Oyster Bay, NY (town) Nassau County	82	0.03
Gaithersburg, MD (city) Montgomery County	81	0.15
Indianapolis, IN (special city) Marion County	79	0.01
Nashville-Davidson, TN (special city) Davidson County	79	0.01
Islip, NY (town) Suffolk County	78	0.02
Hudson, NY (city) Columbia County	77	1.02
Sunnyvale, CA (city) Santa Clara County	77	0.06
Babylon, NY (town) Suffolk County	76	0.04
Raleigh, NC (city) Wake County	73	0.03
Elizabeth, NJ (city) Union County	72	0.06
San Diego, CA (city) San Diego County	72	0.01
Rockville, MD (city) Montgomery County	71	0.15
Tempe, AZ (city) Maricopa County	71	0.04
Hatfield, PA (borough) Montgomery County	69	2.65
Bridgeport, CT (city) Fairfield County	67	0.05
Newark, NJ (city) Essex County	67	0.02
Garland, TX (city) Dallas County	65	0.03
Ventnor City, NJ (city) Atlantic County	64	0.50
College Station, TX (city) Brazos County	64	0.09
Fort Worth, TX (city) Tarrant County	64	0.01
Central Manchester, CT (cdp) Hartford County	63	0.21
Danbury, CT (city) Fairfield County	63	0.08
Tulsa, OK (city) Tulsa County	63	0.02
Herndon, VA (town) Fairfax County	62	0.29
Springfield, VA (cdp) Fairfax County	61	0.20
Woodlawn, MD (cdp) Baltimore County	61	0.17
Hybla Valley, VA (cdp) Fairfax County	60	0.36
Upper Darby, PA (township) Delaware County	60	0.07
Baltimore, MD (independent city) Baltimore city	60	0.01
Edmond, OK (city) Oklahoma County	59	0.09

Place	Number	%
San Francisco, CA (city) San Francisco County	57	0.01
Warren, MI (city) Macomb County	56	0.04
Aspen Hill, MD (cdp) Montgomery County	55	0.11
Mobile, AL (city) Mobile County	55	0.03
Yonkers, NY (city) Westchester County	55	0.03
Lincolnia, VA (cdp) Fairfax County	54	0.34
Bailey's Crossroads, VA (cdp) Fairfax County	54	0.23
Franconia, VA (cdp) Fairfax County	50	0.16
Boynton Beach, FL (city) Palm Beach County	50	0.08
Fargo, ND (city) Cass County	50	0.06
Woodbridge, NJ (township) Middlesex County	50	0.05
Hyattsville, MD (city) Prince George's County	49	0.33
Delray Beach, FL (city) Palm Beach County	49	0.08
Miami Beach, FL (city) Miami-Dade County	49	0.06
Carrollton, TX (city) Denton County	49	0.04
Lexington-Fayette, KY (special city) Fayette County	49	0.02
Saint Cloud, MN (city) Stearns County	48	0.08
Tustin, CA (city) Orange County	48	0.07
Montclair, NJ (cdp) Essex County	47	0.12
Hackensack, NJ (city) Bergen County	47	0.11
Buena Park, CA (city) Orange County	47	0.06
Beaumont, TX (city) Jefferson County	47	0.04
North Decatur, GA (cdp) De Kalb County	44	0.29
Lindenwold, NJ (borough) Camden County	44	0.25
Lake Worth Corridor, FL (cdp) Palm Beach County	44	0.24
Montgomery Village, MD (cdp) Montgomery County	44	0.12
Kissimmee, FL (city) Osceola County	44	0.09
San Antonio, TX (city) Bexar County	44	0.00
Germantown, MD (cdp) Montgomery County	43	0.08
Haledon, NJ (borough) Passaic County	42	0.51
Santa Clara, CA (city) Santa Clara County	42	0.04
Durham, NC (city) Durham County	42	0.02
Pittsburgh, PA (city) Allegheny County	42	0.01
Troy, MI (city) Oakland County	41	0.05
Greensboro, NC (city) Guilford County	41	0.02
Hicksville, NY (cdp) Nassau County	40	0.10
Lynn, MA (city) Essex County	40	0.04
Huntington, NY (town) Suffolk County	40	0.02
Elmwood Park, NJ (borough) Bergen County	39	0.21
Norman, OK (city) Cleveland County	39	0.04
Fullerton, CA (city) Orange County	39	0.03
North Bethesda, MD (cdp) Montgomery County	38	0.10
Potomac, MD (cdp) Montgomery County	38	0.08
Wheaton-Glenmont, MD (cdp) Montgomery County	38	0.07
Norwalk, CT (city) Fairfield County	38	0.05
Mesa, AZ (city) Maricopa County	38	0.01
Jefferson, VA (cdp) Fairfax County	37	0.13
Syracuse, NY (city) Onondaga County	37	0.03
North Miami Beach, FL (city) Miami-Dade County	36	0.09
Centreville, VA (cdp) Fairfax County	36	0.07
Loma Linda, CA (city) San Bernardino County	35	0.19
Somerville, MA (city) Middlesex County	35	0.05
Lubbock, TX (city) Lubbock County	35	0.02
Deerfield Beach, FL (city) Broward County	34	0.05
Kenner, LA (city) Jefferson Parish	34	0.05
Fort Lauderdale, FL (city) Broward County	34	0.02
Albuquerque, NM (city) Bernalillo County	34	0.01
Seattle, WA (city) King County	34	0.01
Ronkonkoma, NY (cdp) Suffolk County	33	0.16
Mount Vernon, VA (cdp) Fairfax County	33	0.12
Chantilly, VA (cdp) Fairfax County	33	0.08
Roswell, GA (city) Fulton County	33	0.04
Ontario, CA (city) San Bernardino County	33	0.02
Burke, VA (cdp) Fairfax County	32	0.06
Old Bridge, NJ (township) Middlesex County	32	0.05
Skokie, IL (village) Cook County	32	0.05
Columbia, MD (cdp) Howard County	32	0.04
Hawthorne, CA (city) Los Angeles County	32	0.04
Pompano Beach, FL (city) Broward County	32	0.04
New Haven, CT (city) New Haven County	32	0.03
Santa Clarita, CA (city) Los Angeles County	32	0.02
Scottdale, GA (cdp) De Kalb County	30	0.31
Brigantine, NJ (city) Atlantic County	30	0.24
Denton, TX (city) Denton County	30	0.04
Plantation, FL (city) Broward County	30	0.04

Notes: (cdp) census designated place; Refer to the Explanation of Data in the front of the book for more detailed information.

Asian: Bangladeshi

Top 150 Places Sorted by Percent

(Based on all places, regardless of population)

Place	Number	%
Hamtramck, MI (city) Wayne County	1,034	4.50
Hatfield, PA (borough) Montgomery County	69	2.65
Pine Hill, NY (cdp) Ulster County	5	1.62
Millbourne, PA (borough) Delaware County	14	1.48
Hudson, NY (city) Columbia County	77	1.02
Chamblee, GA (city) De Kalb County	85	0.89
Lansdale, PA (borough) Montgomery County	125	0.78
Atlantic City, NJ (city) Atlantic County	303	0.75
Hatfield, PA (township) Montgomery County	126	0.75
North Atlanta, GA (cdp) De Kalb County	276	0.72
Northville, NY (village) Fulton County	6	0.53
Haledon, NJ (borough) Passaic County	42	0.51
Ventnor City, NJ (city) Atlantic County	64	0.50
Paterson, NJ (city) Passaic County	729	0.49
Bally, PA (borough) Berks County	5	0.47
Searingtown, NY (cdp) Nassau County	22	0.44
Bethlehem, GA (town) Barrow County	3	0.42
Loyall, KY (city) Harlan County	3	0.39
Whitesburg, KY (city) Letcher County	6	0.38
Washington Heights, NY (cdp) Orange County	5	0.38
Jellico, TN (city) Campbell County	9	0.37
Bellerose Terrace, NY (cdp) Nassau County	8	0.37
Hybla Valley, VA (cdp) Fairfax County	60	0.36
New York, NY (city) New York City	28,269	0.35
North Hills, NY (village) Nassau County	15	0.35
Lincolnia, VA (cdp) Fairfax County	54	0.34
Herricks, NY (cdp) Nassau County	14	0.34
North Brooksville, FL (cdp) Hernando County	5	0.34
Hyattsville, MD (city) Prince George's County	49	0.33
Monmouth Junction, NJ (cdp) Middlesex County	9	0.33
Newtown, CT (borough) Fairfield County	6	0.33
Society Hill, NJ (cdp) Middlesex County	12	0.32
Scottdale, GA (cdp) De Kalb County	30	0.31
Wilkes-Barre Township, PA (cdp) Luzerne County	10	0.31
Bordentown, NJ (city) Burlington County	12	0.30
Baxter Estates, NY (village) Nassau County	3	0.30
Bingen, WA (city) Klickitat County	2	0.30
Herndon, VA (town) Fairfax County	62	0.29
North Decatur, GA (cdp) De Kalb County	44	0.29
Doraville, GA (city) De Kalb County	29	0.29
Pompano Beach Highlands, FL (cdp) Broward County	19	0.29
Berlin, NJ (borough) Camden County	18	0.29
Manorhaven, NY (village) Nassau County	18	0.29
Arlington, VA (cdp) Arlington County	527	0.28
Loch Lomond, FL (cdp) Broward County	10	0.28
Twin Lakes, FL (cdp) Broward County	5	0.27
Lindenwold, NJ (borough) Camden County	44	0.25
Seven Corners, VA (cdp) Fairfax County	22	0.25
Carle Place, NY (cdp) Nassau County	13	0.25
Brooklawn, NJ (borough) Camden County	6	0.25
Lucasville, OH (cdp) Scioto County	4	0.25
Lake Worth Corridor, FL (cdp) Palm Beach County	44	0.24
Brigantine, NJ (city) Atlantic County	30	0.24
Lilburn, GA (city) Gwinnett County	27	0.24
Absecon, NJ (city) Atlantic County	18	0.24
Bellville, TX (city) Austin County	9	0.24
Pine Island, TX (town) Waller County	2	0.24
Clermont, GA (town) Hall County	1	0.24
Bailey's Crossroads, VA (cdp) Fairfax County	54	0.23
Islandia, NY (village) Suffolk County	7	0.23
Cabin John, MD (cdp) Montgomery County	4	0.23
Holland, OH (village) Lucas County	3	0.23
Dansville, MI (village) Ingham County	1	0.23
Chambers Estates, FL (cdp) Broward County	8	0.22
Northampton, NY (town) Fulton County	6	0.22
Matamoras, PA (borough) Pike County	5	0.22
Central Manchester, CT (cdp) Hartford County	63	0.21
Elmwood Park, NJ (borough) Bergen County	39	0.21
Garden City Park, NY (cdp) Nassau County	16	0.21
Broadview-Pompano Park, FL (cdp) Broward County	11	0.21
Huntingtown, MD (cdp) Calvert County	5	0.21
Edgewood, FL (city) Orange County	4	0.21
Romney, WV (city) Hampshire County	4	0.21
Forest Home, NY (cdp) Tompkins County	2	0.21
Springfield, VA (cdp) Fairfax County	61	0.20
Merrifield, VA (cdp) Fairfax County	22	0.20
Echelon, NJ (cdp) Camden County	21	0.20
Mount Hope, NY (town) Orange County	13	0.20
Calvert Beach-Long Beach, MD (cdp) Calvert County	5	0.20
Hypoluxo, FL (town) Palm Beach County	4	0.20
Chevy Chase Heights, PA (cdp) Indiana County	3	0.20
Loma Linda, CA (city) San Bernardino County	35	0.19
South Barrington, IL (village) Cook County	7	0.19
Fredonia, KS (city) Wilson County	5	0.19
Roslyn, NY (village) Nassau County	5	0.19
Harlan, KY (city) Harlan County	4	0.19
Valley, PA (township) Montour County	4	0.19
Hill, MI (township) Ogemaw County	3	0.19
Alexandria, VA (independent city) Alexandria city	228	0.18
Westville, NJ (borough) Gloucester County	8	0.18
Dover, FL (cdp) Hillsborough County	5	0.18
Silver Spring, MD (cdp) Montgomery County	130	0.17
Manchester, CT (town) Hartford County	95	0.17
Reston, VA (cdp) Fairfax County	95	0.17
Woodlawn, MD (cdp) Baltimore County	61	0.17
West Haverstraw, NY (village) Rockland County	18	0.17
Norcross, GA (city) Gwinnett County	14	0.17
Cloverly, MD (cdp) Montgomery County	13	0.17
Berwyn Heights, MD (town) Prince George's County	5	0.17
Philippi, WV (city) Barbour County	5	0.17
Melville, RI (cdp) Newport County	4	0.17
Leisureville, FL (cdp) Broward County	2	0.17
Saint Leo, FL (town) Pasco County	1	0.17
Franconia, VA (cdp) Fairfax County	50	0.16
Ronkonkoma, NY (cdp) Suffolk County	33	0.16
Burtonsville, MD (cdp) Montgomery County	12	0.16
Forest Glen, MD (cdp) Montgomery County	12	0.16
Maybrook, NY (village) Orange County	5	0.16
Mechanicsville, PA (cdp) Montour County	5	0.16
Frankenlust, MI (township) Bay County	4	0.16
New Egypt, NJ (cdp) Ocean County	4	0.16
West Union, IA (city) Fayette County	4	0.16
Claycomo, MO (village) Clay County	2	0.16
Plandome, NY (village) Nassau County	2	0.16
Cambridge, MA (city) Middlesex County	152	0.15
Gaithersburg, MD (city) Montgomery County	81	0.15
Rockville, MD (city) Montgomery County	71	0.15
Oak Hills, OR (cdp) Washington County	14	0.15
South Huntington, NY (cdp) Suffolk County	14	0.15
Dunn Loring, VA (cdp) Fairfax County	12	0.15
Menands, NY (village) Albany County	6	0.15
Lakeside Green, FL (cdp) Palm Beach County	5	0.15
Shandaken, NY (town) Ulster County	5	0.15
Brownville, NJ (cdp) Middlesex County	4	0.15
Morton, PA (borough) Delaware County	4	0.15
Wilder, KY (city) Campbell County	4	0.15
Muldraugh, KY (city) Meade County	2	0.15
Berry Hill, TN (city) Davidson County	1	0.15
Irving, TX (city) Dallas County	270	0.14
Tuskegee, AL (city) Macon County	16	0.14
Signal Hill, CA (city) Los Angeles County	13	0.14
Bridgeport, PA (borough) Montgomery County	6	0.14
Chatham, NY (town) Columbia County	6	0.14
Lake Clarke Shores, FL (town) Palm Beach County	5	0.14
Manhasset Hills, NY (cdp) Nassau County	5	0.14
Gorham, NH (town) Coos County	4	0.14
San Joaquin Hills, CA (cdp) Orange County	4	0.14
Jefferson, VA (cdp) Fairfax County	37	0.13
Avenel, NJ (cdp) Middlesex County	22	0.13
Sandalfoot Cove, FL (cdp) Palm Beach County	22	0.13
Highland Park, NJ (borough) Middlesex County	18	0.13
Totowa, NJ (borough) Passaic County	13	0.13
Moraine, OH (city) Montgomery County	9	0.13
Powell, OH (village) Delaware County	8	0.13
Berlin, NJ (township) Camden County	7	0.13
Ebensburg, PA (borough) Cambria County	4	0.13
Sag Harbor, NY (village) Suffolk County	3	0.13
Blawnox, PA (borough) Allegheny County	2	0.13
Sand Lake, WI (town) Sawyer County	1	0.13
Detroit, MI (city) Wayne County	1,131	0.12

Notes: (cdp) census designated place; Refer to the Explanation of Data in the front of the book for more detailed information.

Asian: Bangladeshi

Top 150 Places Sorted by Percent

(Based on places with populations of 10,000 or more)

Place	Number	%
Hamtramck, MI (city) Wayne County	1,034	4.50
Lansdale, PA (borough) Montgomery County	125	0.78
Atlantic City, NJ (city) Atlantic County	303	0.75
Hatfield, PA (township) Montgomery County	126	0.75
North Atlanta, GA (cdp) De Kalb County	276	0.72
Ventnor City, NJ (city) Atlantic County	64	0.50
Paterson, NJ (city) Passaic County	729	0.49
Hybla Valley, VA (cdp) Fairfax County	60	0.36
New York, NY (city) New York City	28,269	0.35
Lincolnia, VA (cdp) Fairfax County	54	0.34
Hyattsville, MD (city) Prince George's County	49	0.33
Herndon, VA (town) Fairfax County	62	0.29
North Decatur, GA (cdp) De Kalb County	44	0.29
Arlington, VA (cdp) Arlington County	527	0.28
Lindenwold, NJ (borough) Camden County	44	0.25
Lake Worth Corridor, FL (cdp) Palm Beach County	44	0.24
Brigantine, NJ (city) Atlantic County	30	0.24
Lilburn, GA (city) Gwinnett County	27	0.24
Bailey's Crossroads, VA (cdp) Fairfax County	54	0.23
Central Manchester, CT (cdp) Hartford County	63	0.21
Elmwood Park, NJ (borough) Bergen County	39	0.21
Springfield, VA (cdp) Fairfax County	61	0.20
Merrifield, VA (cdp) Fairfax County	22	0.20
Echelon, NJ (cdp) Camden County	21	0.20
Loma Linda, CA (city) San Bernardino County	35	0.19
Alexandria, VA (independent city) Alexandria city	228	0.18
Silver Spring, MD (cdp) Montgomery County	130	0.17
Manchester, CT (town) Hartford County	95	0.17
Reston, VA (cdp) Fairfax County	95	0.17
Woodlawn, MD (cdp) Baltimore County	61	0.17
West Haverstraw, NY (village) Rockland County	18	0.17
Franconia, VA (cdp) Fairfax County	50	0.16
Ronkonkoma, NY (cdp) Suffolk County	33	0.16
Cambridge, MA (city) Middlesex County	152	0.15
Gaithersburg, MD (city) Montgomery County	81	0.15
Rockville, MD (city) Montgomery County	71	0.15
Irving, TX (city) Dallas County	270	0.14
Tuskegee, AL (city) Macon County	16	0.14
Jefferson, VA (cdp) Fairfax County	37	0.13
Avenel, NJ (cdp) Middlesex County	22	0.13
Sandalfoot Cove, FL (cdp) Palm Beach County	22	0.13
Highland Park, NJ (borough) Middlesex County	18	0.13
Detroit, MI (city) Wayne County	1,131	0.12
Richardson, TX (city) Dallas County	111	0.12
Montclair, NJ (cdp) Essex County	47	0.12
Montgomery Village, MD (cdp) Montgomery County	44	0.12
Mount Vernon, VA (cdp) Fairfax County	33	0.12
Copiague, NY (cdp) Suffolk County	26	0.12
New Territory, TX (cdp) Fort Bend County	17	0.12
Westbury, NY (village) Nassau County	17	0.12
Aspen Hill, MD (cdp) Montgomery County	55	0.11
Hackensack, NJ (city) Bergen County	47	0.11
Burlington, MA (cdp) Middlesex County	26	0.11
Oak Ridge, FL (cdp) Orange County	25	0.11
Lumberton, NJ (township) Burlington County	11	0.11
Hicksville, NY (cdp) Nassau County	40	0.10
North Bethesda, MD (cdp) Montgomery County	38	0.10
West Springfield, VA (cdp) Fairfax County	29	0.10
Deer Park, NY (cdp) Suffolk County	27	0.10
Ocean, NJ (township) Monmouth County	27	0.10
Wappinger, NY (town) Dutchess County	25	0.10
West Windsor, NJ (township) Mercer County	22	0.10
North Druid Hills, GA (cdp) De Kalb County	18	0.10
Langley Park, MD (cdp) Prince George's County	17	0.10
Indiana, PA (borough) Indiana County	15	0.10
Princeton Meadows, NJ (cdp) Middlesex County	13	0.10
Bellmawr, NJ (borough) Camden County	11	0.10
Morganville, NJ (cdp) Monmouth County	11	0.10
Reno, NV (city) Washoe County	170	0.09
Stamford, CT (city) Fairfield County	100	0.09
Edison, NJ (cdp) Middlesex County	87	0.09
College Station, TX (city) Brazos County	64	0.09
Edmond, OK (city) Oklahoma County	59	0.09
Kissimmee, FL (city) Osceola County	44	0.09
North Miami Beach, FL (city) Miami-Dade County	36	0.09

Place	Number	%
Voorhees, NJ (township) Camden County	24	0.09
Tucker, GA (cdp) De Kalb County	23	0.09
Newtown, CT (town) Fairfield County	22	0.09
Cliffside Park, NJ (borough) Bergen County	21	0.09
White Oak, MD (cdp) Montgomery County	19	0.09
Carbondale, IL (city) Jackson County	18	0.09
Plainsboro, NJ (township) Middlesex County	18	0.09
Hopkins, MN (city) Hennepin County	16	0.09
Iselin, NJ (cdp) Middlesex County	15	0.09
Adelphi, MD (cdp) Prince George's County	14	0.09
Idylwood, VA (cdp) Fairfax County	14	0.09
Longwood, FL (city) Seminole County	13	0.09
Montgomeryville, PA (cdp) Montgomery County	11	0.09
Country Walk, FL (cdp) Miami-Dade County	10	0.09
Jersey City, NJ (city) Hudson County	182	0.08
Danbury, CT (city) Fairfield County	63	0.08
Boynton Beach, FL (city) Palm Beach County	50	0.08
Delray Beach, FL (city) Palm Beach County	49	0.08
Saint Cloud, MN (city) Stearns County	48	0.08
Germantown, MD (cdp) Montgomery County	43	0.08
Potomac, MD (cdp) Montgomery County	38	0.08
Chantilly, VA (cdp) Fairfax County	33	0.08
Egg Harbor, NJ (township) Atlantic County	26	0.08
Oakland Park, FL (city) Broward County	26	0.08
Lexington, MA (cdp) Middlesex County	25	0.08
Greenacres, FL (city) Palm Beach County	23	0.08
Dix Hills, NY (cdp) Suffolk County	22	0.08
Cooper City, FL (city) Broward County	21	0.08
North Potomac, MD (cdp) Montgomery County	18	0.08
Derry, PA (township) Dauphin County	17	0.08
Colesville, MD (cdp) Montgomery County	15	0.08
Brookings, SD (city) Brookings County	14	0.08
Nanuet, NY (cdp) Rockland County	13	0.08
Setauket-East Setauket, NY (cdp) Suffolk County	13	0.08
Pearl River, NY (cdp) Rockland County	12	0.08
Harrison, NJ (town) Hudson County	11	0.08
North New Hyde Park, NY (cdp) Nassau County	11	0.08
White, PA (township) Indiana County	11	0.08
Hershey, PA (cdp) Dauphin County	10	0.08
New Carrollton, MD (city) Prince George's County	10	0.08
Wilton Manors, FL (city) Broward County	10	0.08
Terryville, NY (cdp) Suffolk County	8	0.08
North Hempstead, NY (town) Nassau County	159	0.07
Plano, TX (city) Collin County	154	0.07
Upper Darby, PA (township) Delaware County	60	0.07
Tustin, CA (city) Orange County	48	0.07
Wheaton-Glenmont, MD (cdp) Montgomery County	38	0.07
Centreville, VA (cdp) Fairfax County	36	0.07
Blacksburg, VA (town) Montgomery County	26	0.07
Haverstraw, NY (town) Rockland County	24	0.07
North Brunswick Township, NJ (cdp) Middlesex County	24	0.07
Madison Heights, MI (city) Oakland County	23	0.07
Woodbridge, VA (cdp) Prince William County	22	0.07
Greenbelt, MD (city) Prince George's County	15	0.07
Groveton, VA (cdp) Fairfax County	15	0.07
Merrick, NY (cdp) Nassau County	15	0.07
Newington, VA (cdp) Fairfax County	14	0.07
Bethel, CT (town) Fairfield County	12	0.07
Redland, MD (cdp) Montgomery County	12	0.07
Laurel, VA (cdp) Henrico County	11	0.07
Brecksville, OH (city) Cuyahoga County	10	0.07
Durant, OK (city) Bryan County	10	0.07
Fullerton, PA (cdp) Lehigh County	10	0.07
North Bay Shore, NY (cdp) Suffolk County	10	0.07
Somerville, NJ (borough) Somerset County	9	0.07
Bedford Heights, OH (city) Cuyahoga County	8	0.07
Darby, PA (borough) Delaware County	7	0.07
Lake Grove, NY (village) Suffolk County	7	0.07
Arlington, TX (city) Tarrant County	197	0.06
Glendale, CA (city) Los Angeles County	118	0.06
Fremont, CA (city) Alameda County	112	0.06
Sunnyvale, CA (city) Santa Clara County	77	0.06
Elizabeth, NJ (city) Union County	72	0.06
Fargo, ND (city) Cass County	50	0.06
Miami Beach, FL (city) Miami-Dade County	49	0.06

Notes: (cdp) census designated place; Refer to the Explanation of Data in the front of the book for more detailed information.

Asian: Cambodian

Top 150 Places Sorted by Number

(Based on all places, regardless of population)

Place	Number	%
Long Beach, CA (city) Los Angeles County	20,262	4.39
Lowell, MA (city) Middlesex County	10,904	10.37
Stockton, CA (city) San Joaquin County	10,202	4.19
Philadelphia, PA (city) Philadelphia County	7,761	0.51
San Jose, CA (city) Santa Clara County	4,886	0.55
San Diego, CA (city) San Diego County	4,545	0.37
Fresno, CA (city) Fresno County	4,522	1.06
Los Angeles, CA (city) Los Angeles County	4,364	0.12
Providence, RI (city) Providence County	3,758	2.16
Lynn, MA (city) Essex County	3,748	4.21
Tacoma, WA (city) Pierce County	3,569	1.84
Oakland, CA (city) Alameda County	3,237	0.81
Modesto, CA (city) Stanislaus County	2,880	1.52
Seattle, WA (city) King County	2,866	0.51
New York, NY (city) New York City	2,296	0.03
Santa Ana, CA (city) Orange County	2,013	0.60
Chicago, IL (city) Cook County	1,751	0.06
Columbus, OH (city) Franklin County	1,366	0.19
Saint Paul, MN (city) Ramsey County	1,358	0.47
San Francisco, CA (city) San Francisco County	1,358	0.17
Fall River, MA (city) Bristol County	1,344	1.46
Revere, MA (city) Suffolk County	1,214	2.57
Pomona, CA (city) Los Angeles County	1,100	0.74
San Bernardino, CA (city) San Bernardino County	1,070	0.58
Jacksonville, FL (special city) Duval County	1,064	0.14
Cranston, RI (city) Providence County	987	1.25
Portland, OR (city) Multnomah County	975	0.18
Dallas, TX (city) Dallas County	968	0.08
White Center, WA (cdp) King County	967	4.61
Rochester, MN (city) Olmsted County	945	1.10
Danbury, CT (city) Fairfield County	909	1.21
Houston, TX (city) Harris County	907	0.05
Carrollton, TX (city) Denton County	848	0.77
Lakewood, CA (city) Los Angeles County	820	1.03
West Valley City, UT (city) Salt Lake County	805	0.74
Signal Hill, CA (city) Los Angeles County	772	8.27
Charlotte, NC (city) Mecklenburg County	761	0.14
Rosemead, CA (city) Los Angeles County	720	1.35
Santa Rosa, CA (city) Sonoma County	654	0.44
Boston, MA (city) Suffolk County	651	0.11
Attleboro, MA (city) Bristol County	643	1.53
Portland, ME (city) Cumberland County	624	0.97
Norwalk, CA (city) Los Angeles County	623	0.60
Monterey Park, CA (city) Los Angeles County	597	0.99
Lawrence, MA (city) Essex County	570	0.79
Bloomington, MN (city) Hennepin County	552	0.65
Bakersfield, CA (city) Kern County	548	0.22
Bridgeport, CT (city) Fairfield County	546	0.39
Garden Grove, CA (city) Orange County	546	0.33
Wichita, KS (city) Sedgwick County	541	0.16
Saint Petersburg, FL (city) Pinellas County	538	0.22
Memphis, TN (city) Shelby County	533	0.08
Bellflower, CA (city) Los Angeles County	521	0.71
El Monte, CA (city) Los Angeles County	520	0.45
Denver, CO (city) Denver County	513	0.09
Sacramento, CA (city) Sacramento County	511	0.13
Anaheim, CA (city) Orange County	509	0.16
Everett, WA (city) Snohomish County	507	0.55
Greensboro, NC (city) Guilford County	474	0.21
Nashville-Davidson, TN (special city) Davidson County	472	0.09
Garland, TX (city) Dallas County	471	0.22
Fort Worth, TX (city) Tarrant County	467	0.09
Holland, MI (township) Ottawa County	439	1.52
Arlington, VA (cdp) Arlington County	434	0.23
Vancouver, WA (city) Clark County	429	0.30
Minneapolis, MN (city) Hennepin County	404	0.11
Phoenix, AZ (city) Maricopa County	393	0.03
Cleveland, OH (city) Cuyahoga County	391	0.08
Alhambra, CA (city) Los Angeles County	388	0.45
Holland, MI (city) Ottawa County	387	1.10
Lexington, NC (city) Davidson County	386	1.93
Moreno Valley, CA (city) Riverside County	386	0.27
Des Moines, IA (city) Polk County	374	0.19
Aurora, CO (city) Arapahoe County	365	0.13
Bellevue, WA (city) King County	358	0.33

Place	Number	%
Aloha, OR (cdp) Washington County	334	0.80
Madison, WI (city) Dane County	331	0.16
Beaverton, OR (city) Washington County	322	0.42
Paramount, CA (city) Los Angeles County	321	0.58
Kent, WA (city) King County	318	0.40
Kansas City, MO (city) Jackson County	318	0.07
Worcester, MA (city) Worcester County	313	0.18
Rochester, NY (city) Monroe County	311	0.14
Silver Spring, MD (cdp) Montgomery County	304	0.40
Westminster, CA (city) Orange County	301	0.34
Chelsea, MA (city) Suffolk County	299	0.85
Federal Way, WA (city) King County	296	0.36
Seattle Hill-Silver Firs, WA (cdp) Snohomish County	291	0.82
Tukwila, WA (city) King County	287	1.67
Riverside, CA (city) Riverside County	285	0.11
SeaTac, WA (city) King County	284	1.11
Lacey, WA (city) Thurston County	283	0.91
Burnsville, MN (city) Dakota County	277	0.46
Rialto, CA (city) San Bernardino County	270	0.29
Camden, NJ (city) Camden County	267	0.33
Tempe, AZ (city) Maricopa County	261	0.16
Parkway-South Sacramento, CA (cdp) Sacramento County	258	0.71
Amherst, MA (town) Hampshire County	249	0.71
Buena Park, CA (city) Orange County	242	0.31
Orange, CA (city) Orange County	241	0.19
Riverton-Boulevard Park, WA (cdp) King County	236	2.11
Sanford, ME (town) York County	236	1.13
Savage, MN (city) Scott County	235	1.11
San Gabriel, CA (city) Los Angeles County	234	0.59
Fontana, CA (city) San Bernardino County	232	0.18
Cincinnati, OH (city) Hamilton County	229	0.07
Columbia, MO (city) Boone County	228	0.27
Ontario, CA (city) San Bernardino County	227	0.14
Corona, CA (city) Riverside County	224	0.18
Brockton, MA (city) Plymouth County	220	0.23
Lancaster, PA (city) Lancaster County	218	0.39
Burien, WA (city) King County	217	0.68
Florin, CA (cdp) Sacramento County	215	0.78
Lynnwood, WA (city) Snohomish County	215	0.64
Las Vegas, NV (city) Clark County	214	0.04
Austin, TX (city) Travis County	214	0.03
Wheaton-Glenmont, MD (cdp) Montgomery County	213	0.37
Richmond, VA (independent city) Richmond city	211	0.11
Upper Darby, PA (township) Delaware County	210	0.26
Janesville, WI (city) Rock County	209	0.35
Renton, WA (city) King County	207	0.41
Annandale, VA (cdp) Fairfax County	205	0.37
Sioux City, IA (city) Woodbury County	204	0.24
Des Moines, WA (city) King County	198	0.68
Tustin, CA (city) Orange County	194	0.29
East Hill-Meridian, WA (cdp) King County	193	0.66
Hillsboro, OR (city) Washington County	192	0.27
Eagan, MN (city) Dakota County	191	0.30
Carson, CA (city) Los Angeles County	190	0.21
Longview, WA (city) Cowlitz County	189	0.55
Irvine, CA (city) Orange County	183	0.13
Eden Prairie, MN (city) Hennepin County	182	0.33
Chandler, AZ (city) Maricopa County	181	0.10
Riverdale, GA (city) Clayton County	180	1.44
Faribault, MN (city) Rice County	180	0.86
Malden, MA (city) Middlesex County	180	0.32
Richfield, MN (city) Hennepin County	178	0.52
Fullerton, CA (city) Orange County	176	0.14
Kingsgate, WA (cdp) King County	175	1.43
Logan, UT (city) Cache County	174	0.41
Midland, WA (cdp) Pierce County	171	2.31
West Sacramento, CA (city) Yolo County	171	0.54
Newport News, VA (independent city) Newport News city	169	0.09
Baldwin Park, CA (city) Los Angeles County	168	0.22
Hayward, CA (city) Alameda County	167	0.12
Dracut, MA (town) Middlesex County	166	0.58
Longmont, CO (city) Boulder County	166	0.23
San Leandro, CA (city) Alameda County	165	0.21
Brooklyn Park, MN (city) Hennepin County	164	0.24
Honolulu, HI (cdp) Honolulu County	163	0.04

Notes: (cdp) census designated place; Refer to the Explanation of Data in the front of the book for more detailed information.

Asian: Cambodian

Top 150 Places Sorted by Percent

(Based on all places, regardless of population)

Place	Number	%
Lowell, MA (city) Middlesex County	10,904	10.37
Signal Hill, CA (city) Los Angeles County	772	8.27
Urbancrest, OH (village) Franklin County	58	6.68
Bayou La Batre, AL (city) Mobile County	135	5.84
Iowa Colony, TX (village) Brazoria County	45	5.60
White Center, WA (cdp) King County	967	4.61
Long Beach, CA (city) Los Angeles County	20,262	4.39
Pleasant View, MN (township) Norman County	6	4.29
Cascade, MN (township) Olmsted County	135	4.24
Lynn, MA (city) Essex County	3,748	4.21
Stockton, CA (city) San Joaquin County	10,202	4.19
Campobello, SC (town) Spartanburg County	17	3.79
Burkittsville, MD (town) Frederick County	6	3.51
Byron, ME (town) Oxford County	4	3.31
Bensley, VA (cdp) Chesterfield County	153	2.82
Grand Ronde, OR (cdp) Polk County	7	2.58
Revere, MA (city) Suffolk County	1,214	2.57
Buras-Triumph, LA (cdp) Plaquemines Parish	86	2.56
Midland, WA (cdp) Pierce County	171	2.31
Providence, RI (city) Providence County	3,758	2.16
Newton, UT (town) Cache County	15	2.15
Tenino, WA (city) Thurston County	31	2.14
Riverton-Boulevard Park, WA (cdp) King County	236	2.11
Wheatland, CA (city) Yuba County	48	2.11
South Amherst, MA (cdp) Hampshire County	102	2.02
Lexington, NC (city) Davidson County	386	1.93
Tacoma, WA (city) Pierce County	3,569	1.84
Valleyview, OH (village) Franklin County	11	1.83
Satsop, WA (cdp) Grays Harbor County	11	1.78
West Modesto, CA (cdp) Stanislaus County	103	1.69
Butterfield, MN (township) Watonwan County	5	1.68
Tukwila, WA (city) King County	287	1.67
Bellwood, VA (cdp) Chesterfield County	99	1.66
Roseland, CA (cdp) Sonoma County	104	1.63
Garland, UT (city) Box Elder County	31	1.60
Bonney, TX (village) Brazoria County	6	1.56
Attleboro, MA (city) Bristol County	643	1.53
Modesto, CA (city) Stanislaus County	2,880	1.52
Holland, MI (township) Ottawa County	439	1.52
Angus, TX (city) Navarro County	5	1.50
Fall River, MA (city) Bristol County	1,344	1.46
Tanglewilde-Thompson Place, WA (cdp) Thurston County	82	1.45
Riverdale, GA (city) Clayton County	180	1.44
Kingsgate, WA (cdp) King County	175	1.43
Springvale, ME (cdp) York County	49	1.40
Rosemead, CA (city) Los Angeles County	720	1.35
Boothville-Venice, LA (cdp) Plaquemines Parish	30	1.35
Kingston, RI (cdp) Washington County	69	1.27
Cranston, RI (city) Providence County	987	1.25
Raymond, WA (city) Pacific County	37	1.24
Danbury, CT (city) Fairfield County	909	1.21
South Sanford, ME (cdp) York County	50	1.20
Beechwood, MI (cdp) Ottawa County	35	1.18
Sanford, ME (town) York County	236	1.13
Martha Lake, WA (cdp) Snohomish County	143	1.13
Barker Heights, NC (cdp) Henderson County	14	1.13
Oaklawn-Sunview, KS (cdp) Sedgwick County	35	1.12
SeaTac, WA (city) King County	284	1.11
Savage, MN (city) Scott County	235	1.11
Rochester, MN (city) Olmsted County	945	1.10
Holland, MI (city) Ottawa County	387	1.10
East Lansdowne, PA (borough) Delaware County	28	1.08
Fresno, CA (city) Fresno County	4,522	1.06
Lakewood, CA (city) Los Angeles County	820	1.03
Niederwald, TX (town) Hays County	6	1.03
Inman, SC (city) Spartanburg County	19	1.01
Bristol, IN (town) Elkhart County	14	1.01
Woodlynne, NJ (borough) Camden County	28	1.00
Monterey Park, CA (city) Los Angeles County	597	0.99
Fife, WA (city) Pierce County	47	0.98
Portland, ME (city) Cumberland County	624	0.97
Martin, GA (town) Stephens County	3	0.96
South Bend, WA (city) Pacific County	17	0.94
Sumas, WA (city) Whatcom County	9	0.94
Lacey, WA (city) Thurston County	283	0.91

Place	Number	%
Elma, WA (city) Grays Harbor County	27	0.89
Mayfield, KS (city) Sumner County	1	0.88
Faribault, MN (city) Rice County	180	0.86
Woodland, ME (town) Aroostook County	12	0.86
Chelsea, MA (city) Suffolk County	299	0.85
Yreka, CA (city) Siskiyou County	62	0.85
Onset, MA (cdp) Plymouth County	11	0.85
Calvin, LA (village) Winn Parish	2	0.85
North Springfield, VA (cdp) Fairfax County	77	0.84
Easthampton, MA (city) Hampshire County	133	0.83
Royalton, PA (borough) Dauphin County	8	0.83
Sharon, NH (town) Hillsborough County	3	0.83
Seattle Hill-Silver Firs, WA (cdp) Snohomish County	291	0.82
Tremonton, UT (city) Box Elder County	46	0.82
Oakland, CA (city) Alameda County	3,237	0.81
Lansdale, PA (borough) Montgomery County	130	0.81
Aloha, OR (cdp) Washington County	334	0.80
West Longview, WA (cdp) Cowlitz County	23	0.80
Lawrence, MA (city) Essex County	570	0.79
Bunkerville, NV (cdp) Clark County	8	0.79
Florin, CA (cdp) Sacramento County	215	0.78
Carrollton, TX (city) Denton County	848	0.77
Mill Plain, WA (cdp) Clark County	56	0.76
Pomona, CA (city) Los Angeles County	1,100	0.74
West Valley City, UT (city) Salt Lake County	805	0.74
Riverside, UT (cdp) Box Elder County	5	0.74
Haleiwa, HI (cdp) Honolulu County	16	0.72
Bellflower, CA (city) Los Angeles County	521	0.71
Parkway-South Sacramento, CA (cdp) Sacramento County	258	0.71
Amherst, MA (town) Hampshire County	249	0.71
Fillmore, UT (city) Millard County	16	0.71
Walnut Grove, WA (cdp) Clark County	50	0.70
Cleona, PA (borough) Lebanon County	15	0.70
Burien, WA (city) King County	217	0.68
Des Moines, WA (city) King County	198	0.68
East Hill-Meridian, WA (cdp) King County	193	0.66
Hapeville, GA (city) Fulton County	41	0.66
Valley Hill, NC (cdp) Henderson County	14	0.66
Clinton Falls, MN (township) Steele County	3	0.66
Bloomington, MN (city) Hennepin County	552	0.65
Welcome, NC (cdp) Davidson County	23	0.65
Chester Center, CT (cdp) Middlesex County	10	0.65
Lynnwood, WA (city) Snohomish County	215	0.64
Annville, PA (cdp) Lebanon County	29	0.64
Orchards, WA (cdp) Clark County	113	0.63
Bryn Mawr-Skyway, WA (cdp) King County	88	0.63
Dumbarton, VA (cdp) Henrico County	42	0.63
Leacock-Leola-Bareville, PA (cdp) Lancaster County	42	0.63
Oronoco, MN (township) Olmsted County	14	0.63
Five Corners, WA (cdp) Clark County	76	0.62
Herndon, VA (town) Fairfax County	133	0.61
South San Gabriel, CA (cdp) Los Angeles County	46	0.61
Morrow, GA (city) Clayton County	30	0.61
Empire, CA (cdp) Stanislaus County	24	0.61
Santa Ana, CA (city) Orange County	2,013	0.60
Norwalk, CA (city) Los Angeles County	623	0.60
Park City, IL (city) Lake County	40	0.60
Leverett, MA (town) Franklin County	10	0.60
Pleasant Lake, MN (city) Stearns County	3	0.60
San Gabriel, CA (city) Los Angeles County	234	0.59
Doraville, GA (city) De Kalb County	58	0.59
Woodinville, WA (city) King County	54	0.59
Kenneth City, FL (town) Pinellas County	26	0.59
Duncan, SC (town) Spartanburg County	17	0.59
Pelican Rapids, MN (city) Otter Tail County	14	0.59
East Ithaca, NY (cdp) Tompkins County	13	0.59
East Mahoning, PA (township) Indiana County	7	0.59
Cologne, MN (city) Carver County	6	0.59
Payne Springs, TX (town) Henderson County	4	0.59
San Bernardino, CA (city) San Bernardino County	1,070	0.58
Paramount, CA (city) Los Angeles County	321	0.58
Dracut, MA (town) Middlesex County	166	0.58
Lincolnia, VA (cdp) Fairfax County	92	0.58
Artesia, CA (city) Los Angeles County	93	0.57
Kemp Mill, MD (cdp) Montgomery County	57	0.57

Notes: (cdp) census designated place; Refer to the Explanation of Data in the front of the book for more detailed information.

Asian: Cambodian

Top 150 Places Sorted by Percent

(Based on places with populations of 10,000 or more)

Place	Number	%
Lowell, MA (city) Middlesex County	10,904	10.37
White Center, WA (cdp) King County	967	4.61
Long Beach, CA (city) Los Angeles County	20,262	4.39
Lynn, MA (city) Essex County	3,748	4.21
Stockton, CA (city) San Joaquin County	10,202	4.19
Revere, MA (city) Suffolk County	1,214	2.57
Providence, RI (city) Providence County	3,758	2.16
Riverton-Boulevard Park, WA (cdp) King County	236	2.11
Lexington, NC (city) Davidson County	386	1.93
Tacoma, WA (city) Pierce County	3,569	1.84
Tukwila, WA (city) King County	287	1.67
Attleboro, MA (city) Bristol County	643	1.53
Modesto, CA (city) Stanislaus County	2,880	1.52
Holland, MI (township) Ottawa County	439	1.52
Fall River, MA (city) Bristol County	1,344	1.46
Riverdale, GA (city) Clayton County	180	1.44
Kingsgate, WA (cdp) King County	175	1.43
Rosemead, CA (city) Los Angeles County	720	1.35
Cranston, RI (city) Providence County	987	1.25
Danbury, CT (city) Fairfield County	909	1.21
Sanford, ME (town) York County	236	1.13
Martha Lake, WA (cdp) Snohomish County	143	1.13
SeaTac, WA (city) King County	284	1.11
Savage, MN (city) Scott County	235	1.11
Rochester, MN (city) Olmsted County	945	1.10
Holland, MI (city) Ottawa County	387	1.10
Fresno, CA (city) Fresno County	4,522	1.06
Lakewood, CA (city) Los Angeles County	820	1.03
Monterey Park, CA (city) Los Angeles County	597	0.99
Portland, ME (city) Cumberland County	624	0.97
Lacey, WA (city) Thurston County	283	0.91
Faribault, MN (city) Rice County	180	0.86
Chelsea, MA (city) Suffolk County	299	0.85
Easthampton, MA (city) Hampshire County	133	0.83
Seattle Hill-Silver Firs, WA (cdp) Snohomish County	291	0.82
Oakland, CA (city) Alameda County	3,237	0.81
Lansdale, PA (borough) Montgomery County	130	0.81
Aloha, OR (cdp) Washington County	334	0.80
Lawrence, MA (city) Essex County	570	0.79
Florin, CA (cdp) Sacramento County	215	0.78
Carrollton, TX (city) Denton County	848	0.77
Pomona, CA (city) Los Angeles County	1,100	0.74
West Valley City, UT (city) Salt Lake County	805	0.74
Bellflower, CA (city) Los Angeles County	521	0.71
Parkway-South Sacramento, CA (cdp) Sacramento County	258	0.71
Amherst, MA (town) Hampshire County	249	0.71
Burien, WA (city) King County	217	0.68
Des Moines, WA (city) King County	198	0.68
East Hill-Meridian, WA (cdp) King County	193	0.66
Bloomington, MN (city) Hennepin County	552	0.65
Lynnwood, WA (city) Snohomish County	215	0.64
Orchards, WA (cdp) Clark County	113	0.63
Bryn Mawr-Skyway, WA (cdp) King County	88	0.63
Five Corners, WA (cdp) Clark County	76	0.62
Herndon, VA (town) Fairfax County	133	0.61
Santa Ana, CA (city) Orange County	2,013	0.60
Norwalk, CA (city) Los Angeles County	623	0.60
San Gabriel, CA (city) Los Angeles County	234	0.59
San Bernardino, CA (city) San Bernardino County	1,070	0.58
Paramount, CA (city) Los Angeles County	321	0.58
Dracut, MA (town) Middlesex County	166	0.58
Lincolnia, VA (cdp) Fairfax County	92	0.58
Artesia, CA (city) Los Angeles County	93	0.57
Aberdeen, WA (city) Grays Harbor County	92	0.56
San Jose, CA (city) Santa Clara County	4,886	0.55
Everett, WA (city) Snohomish County	507	0.55
Longview, WA (city) Cowlitz County	189	0.55
Paine Field-Lake Stickney, WA (cdp) Snohomish County	135	0.55
Redland, MD (cdp) Montgomery County	94	0.55
Alderwood Manor, WA (cdp) Snohomish County	85	0.55
Hawaiian Gardens, CA (city) Los Angeles County	82	0.55
West Sacramento, CA (city) Yolo County	171	0.54
Bethel, CT (town) Fairfield County	95	0.53
Richfield, MN (city) Hennepin County	178	0.52
Philadelphia, PA (city) Philadelphia County	7,761	0.51
Seattle, WA (city) King County	2,866	0.51
Springfield, VA (cdp) Fairfax County	156	0.51
Bailey's Crossroads, VA (cdp) Fairfax County	119	0.51
Jefferson, VA (cdp) Fairfax County	138	0.50
Colesville, MD (cdp) Montgomery County	99	0.50
Tyngsborough, MA (town) Middlesex County	55	0.50
Amherst Center, MA (cdp) Hampshire County	82	0.48
Salida, CA (cdp) Stanislaus County	60	0.48
Saint Paul, MN (city) Ramsey County	1,358	0.47
Picnic Point-North Lynnwood, WA (cdp) Snohomish County	107	0.47
Burnsville, MN (city) Dakota County	277	0.46
Shakopee, MN (city) Scott County	95	0.46
El Monte, CA (city) Los Angeles County	520	0.45
Alhambra, CA (city) Los Angeles County	388	0.45
Santa Rosa, CA (city) Sonoma County	654	0.44
Ceres, CA (city) Stanislaus County	153	0.44
Mountlake Terrace, WA (city) Snohomish County	90	0.44
Hayesville, OR (cdp) Marion County	80	0.44
Loma Linda, CA (city) San Bernardino County	80	0.43
Beaverton, OR (city) Washington County	322	0.42
Renton, WA (city) King County	207	0.41
Logan, UT (city) Cache County	174	0.41
Kent, WA (city) King County	318	0.40
Silver Spring, MD (cdp) Montgomery County	304	0.40
York, PA (city) York County	162	0.40
Groveton, VA (cdp) Fairfax County	85	0.40
Bridgeport, CT (city) Fairfield County	546	0.39
Lancaster, PA (city) Lancaster County	218	0.39
Lake Elsinore, CA (city) Riverside County	112	0.39
North Creek, WA (cdp) Snohomish County	101	0.39
Chanhassen, MN (city) Carver County	77	0.38
San Diego, CA (city) San Diego County	4,545	0.37
Wheaton-Glenmont, MD (cdp) Montgomery County	213	0.37
Annandale, VA (cdp) Fairfax County	205	0.37
Biddeford, ME (city) York County	77	0.37
East Riverdale, MD (cdp) Prince George's County	56	0.37
Federal Way, WA (city) King County	296	0.36
Calverton, MD (cdp) Montgomery County	46	0.36
Janesville, WI (city) Rock County	209	0.35
Chelmsford, MA (town) Middlesex County	119	0.35
Westminster, CA (city) Orange County	301	0.34
Woonsocket, RI (city) Providence County	146	0.34
Pennsauken, NJ (cdp) Camden County	122	0.34
Cascade-Fairwood, WA (cdp) King County	116	0.34
Fairfax, VA (independent city) Fairfax city	74	0.34
Hercules, CA (city) Contra Costa County	66	0.34
Hopkins, MN (city) Hennepin County	59	0.34
La Palma, CA (city) Orange County	53	0.34
Lilburn, GA (city) Gwinnett County	39	0.34
Garden Grove, CA (city) Orange County	546	0.33
Bellevue, WA (city) King County	358	0.33
Camden, NJ (city) Camden County	267	0.33
Eden Prairie, MN (city) Hennepin County	182	0.33
Highland, CA (city) San Bernardino County	146	0.33
Mankato, MN (city) Blue Earth County	107	0.33
Hershey, PA (cdp) Dauphin County	42	0.33
New Carrollton, MD (city) Prince George's County	42	0.33
Malden, MA (city) Middlesex County	180	0.32
Redmond, WA (city) King County	144	0.32
Lakeville, MN (city) Dakota County	138	0.32
Adelanto, CA (city) San Bernardino County	58	0.32
Pineville, LA (city) Rapides Parish	44	0.32
Stoughton, WI (city) Dane County	39	0.32
North Lebanon, PA (township) Lebanon County	34	0.32
Buena Park, CA (city) Orange County	242	0.31
Northampton, MA (city) Hampshire County	90	0.31
Tucker, GA (cdp) De Kalb County	83	0.31
Vancouver, WA (city) Clark County	429	0.30
Eagan, MN (city) Dakota County	191	0.30
Inglewood-Finn Hill, WA (cdp) King County	69	0.30
West and East Lealman, FL (cdp) Pinellas County	65	0.30
Derry, PA (township) Dauphin County	63	0.30
Alum Rock, CA (cdp) Santa Clara County	40	0.30
Rialto, CA (city) San Bernardino County	270	0.29
Tustin, CA (city) Orange County	194	0.29

Notes: (cdp) census designated place; Refer to the Explanation of Data in the front of the book for more detailed information.

Asian: Chinese, except Taiwanese

Top 150 Places Sorted by Number

(Based on all places, regardless of population)

Place	Number	%
New York, NY (city) New York City	374,321	4.67
San Francisco, CA (city) San Francisco County	160,113	20.61
Los Angeles, CA (city) Los Angeles County	69,668	1.89
Honolulu, HI (cdp) Honolulu County	68,070	18.32
San Jose, CA (city) Santa Clara County	55,543	6.21
Oakland, CA (city) Alameda County	34,139	8.55
Chicago, IL (city) Cook County	33,701	1.16
Fremont, CA (city) Alameda County	29,145	14.33
Alhambra, CA (city) Los Angeles County	29,139	33.96
San Diego, CA (city) San Diego County	26,016	2.13
Monterey Park, CA (city) Los Angeles County	25,411	42.32
Houston, TX (city) Harris County	24,695	1.26
Seattle, WA (city) King County	21,886	3.88
Sacramento, CA (city) Sacramento County	21,450	5.27
Boston, MA (city) Suffolk County	20,370	3.46
Philadelphia, PA (city) Philadelphia County	19,205	1.27
Rosemead, CA (city) Los Angeles County	16,995	31.76
Daly City, CA (city) San Mateo County	15,185	14.65
Arcadia, CA (city) Los Angeles County	14,945	28.17
Irvine, CA (city) Orange County	13,620	9.52
San Gabriel, CA (city) Los Angeles County	13,417	33.71
Sunnyvale, CA (city) Santa Clara County	13,063	9.91
El Monte, CA (city) Los Angeles County	12,506	10.78
Rowland Heights, CA (cdp) Los Angeles County	12,445	25.63
Cupertino, CA (city) Santa Clara County	11,867	23.48
Hacienda Heights, CA (cdp) Los Angeles County	10,394	19.57
Quincy, MA (city) Norfolk County	9,511	10.80
Plano, TX (city) Collin County	9,477	4.27
Alameda, CA (city) Alameda County	8,833	12.22
Diamond Bar, CA (city) Los Angeles County	8,785	15.61
Portland, OR (city) Multnomah County	8,613	1.63
Temple City, CA (city) Los Angeles County	8,534	25.57
Austin, TX (city) Travis County	8,470	1.29
Milpitas, CA (city) Santa Clara County	8,446	13.47
San Leandro, CA (city) Alameda County	8,418	10.60
Berkeley, CA (city) Alameda County	8,255	8.03
West Covina, CA (city) Los Angeles County	7,579	7.21
Walnut, CA (city) Los Angeles County	7,571	25.23
Kaneohe, HI (cdp) Honolulu County	6,965	19.92
Phoenix, AZ (city) Maricopa County	6,956	0.53
Bellevue, WA (city) King County	6,696	6.11
Hempstead, NY (town) Nassau County	6,607	0.87
Torrance, CA (city) Los Angeles County	6,524	4.73
San Mateo, CA (city) San Mateo County	6,451	6.98
Union City, CA (city) Alameda County	6,438	9.63
Cerritos, CA (city) Los Angeles County	6,378	12.39
Dallas, TX (city) Dallas County	6,114	0.51
North Hempstead, NY (town) Nassau County	6,003	2.70
Sugar Land, TX (city) Fort Bend County	5,997	9.47
Columbus, OH (city) Franklin County	5,977	0.84
Mountain View, CA (city) Santa Clara County	5,931	8.39
Edison, NJ (cdp) Middlesex County	5,824	5.96
Palo Alto, CA (city) Santa Clara County	5,740	9.80
Hilo, HI (cdp) Hawaii County	5,709	14.01
Santa Clara, CA (city) Santa Clara County	5,644	5.51
Davis, CA (city) Yolo County	5,270	8.74
Saratoga, CA (city) Santa Clara County	5,237	17.55
South San Francisco, CA (city) San Mateo County	5,229	8.64
Brookhaven, NY (town) Suffolk County	5,140	1.15
Anaheim, CA (city) Orange County	5,133	1.56
Stockton, CA (city) San Joaquin County	5,114	2.10
Long Beach, CA (city) Los Angeles County	5,076	1.10
Ann Arbor, MI (city) Washtenaw County	5,021	4.40
Kailua, HI (cdp) Honolulu County	5,000	13.69
Cambridge, MA (city) Middlesex County	4,969	4.90
Foster City, CA (city) San Mateo County	4,921	17.09
Pasadena, CA (city) Los Angeles County	4,686	3.50
Hayward, CA (city) Alameda County	4,674	3.34
Malden, MA (city) Middlesex County	4,660	8.27
Spring Valley, NV (cdp) Clark County	4,571	3.89
Oyster Bay, NY (town) Nassau County	4,286	1.46
Waimalu, HI (cdp) Honolulu County	4,253	14.48
Mililani Town, HI (cdp) Honolulu County	4,194	14.66
San Marino, CA (city) Los Angeles County	4,186	32.34
Fresno, CA (city) Fresno County	4,181	0.98
Castro Valley, CA (cdp) Alameda County	4,179	7.29
Washington, DC (city) District of Columbia	4,173	0.73
Newton, MA (city) Middlesex County	4,164	4.97
Pearl City, HI (cdp) Honolulu County	4,131	13.34
Naperville, IL (city) Du Page County	4,072	3.17
Chino Hills, CA (city) San Bernardino County	4,007	6.00
San Antonio, TX (city) Bexar County	3,972	0.35
Las Vegas, NV (city) Clark County	3,929	0.82
South Pasadena, CA (city) Los Angeles County	3,874	15.95
East San Gabriel, CA (cdp) Los Angeles County	3,829	26.39
Jersey City, NJ (city) Hudson County	3,811	1.59
Huntington Beach, CA (city) Orange County	3,785	2.00
Tucson, AZ (city) Pima County	3,599	0.74
Richmond, CA (city) Contra Costa County	3,586	3.61
Brookline, MA (cdp) Norfolk County	3,579	6.27
Madison, WI (city) Dane County	3,566	1.71
Millbrae, CA (city) San Mateo County	3,558	17.17
Richardson, TX (city) Dallas County	3,548	3.86
Baldwin Park, CA (city) Los Angeles County	3,306	4.36
East Brunswick, NJ (cdp) Middlesex County	3,245	6.94
Concord, CA (city) Contra Costa County	3,188	2.62
North Potomac, MD (cdp) Montgomery County	3,186	13.83
Rancho Palos Verdes, CA (city) Los Angeles County	3,166	7.69
Fullerton, CA (city) Orange County	3,153	2.50
Pleasanton, CA (city) Alameda County	3,132	4.92
Glendale, CA (city) Los Angeles County	3,114	1.60
Riverside, CA (city) Riverside County	3,083	1.21
Arlington, VA (cdp) Arlington County	3,053	1.61
El Cerrito, CA (city) Contra Costa County	3,050	13.16
Arlington, TX (city) Tarrant County	3,008	0.90
Redwood City, CA (city) San Mateo County	3,004	3.98
Rockville, MD (city) Montgomery County	2,963	6.25
Pittsburgh, PA (city) Allegheny County	2,953	0.88
San Ramon, CA (city) Contra Costa County	2,931	6.55
Montebello, CA (city) Los Angeles County	2,905	4.67
Parsippany-Troy Hills, NJ (township) Morris County	2,870	5.67
Garden Grove, CA (city) Orange County	2,827	1.71
Minneapolis, MN (city) Hennepin County	2,822	0.74
Troy, MI (city) Oakland County	2,821	3.48
Walnut Creek, CA (city) Contra Costa County	2,800	4.35
Denver, CO (city) Denver County	2,757	0.50
Charlotte, NC (city) Mecklenburg County	2,677	0.49
Waipahu, HI (cdp) Honolulu County	2,669	8.06
Thousand Oaks, CA (city) Ventura County	2,557	2.19
Baltimore, MD (independent city) Baltimore city	2,535	0.39
Santa Ana, CA (city) Orange County	2,533	0.75
San Bruno, CA (city) San Mateo County	2,501	6.23
Piscataway, NJ (township) Middlesex County	2,478	4.91
Indianapolis, IN (special city) Marion County	2,461	0.31
Fountain Valley, CA (city) Orange County	2,460	4.47
Potomac, MD (cdp) Montgomery County	2,458	5.48
Pomona, CA (city) Los Angeles County	2,446	1.64
Gaithersburg, MD (city) Montgomery County	2,428	4.61
Westminster, CA (city) Orange County	2,423	2.75
Albuquerque, NM (city) Bernalillo County	2,414	0.54
Los Altos, CA (city) Santa Clara County	2,367	8.55
Albany, CA (city) Alameda County	2,351	14.30
Paradise, NV (cdp) Clark County	2,308	1.24
Chandler, AZ (city) Maricopa County	2,304	1.30
Laguna, CA (cdp) Sacramento County	2,299	6.70
Tempe, AZ (city) Maricopa County	2,270	1.43
Cleveland, OH (city) Cuyahoga County	2,231	0.47
Elk Grove, CA (cdp) Sacramento County	2,208	3.68
Marlboro, NJ (township) Monmouth County	2,206	6.06
Oklahoma City, OK (city) Oklahoma County	2,173	0.43
Reno, NV (city) Washoe County	2,151	1.19
Kahului, HI (cdp) Maui County	2,103	10.44
Halawa, HI (cdp) Honolulu County	2,102	15.13
Raleigh, NC (city) Wake County	2,102	0.76
Wahiawa, HI (cdp) Honolulu County	2,084	12.90
Durham, NC (city) Durham County	2,083	1.11
Cary, NC (town) Wake County	2,061	2.18
Wheaton-Glenmont, MD (cdp) Montgomery County	2,059	3.57
Lexington-Fayette, KY (special city) Fayette County	2,057	0.79
Nashville-Davidson, TN (special city) Davidson County	2,049	0.38

Notes: (cdp) census designated place; Refer to the Explanation of Data in the front of the book for more detailed information.

Asian: Chinese, except Taiwanese

Top 150 Places Sorted by Percent

(Based on all places, regardless of population)

Place	Number	%
Monterey Park, CA (city) Los Angeles County	25,411	42.32
Alhambra, CA (city) Los Angeles County	29,139	33.96
San Gabriel, CA (city) Los Angeles County	13,417	33.71
San Marino, CA (city) Los Angeles County	4,186	32.34
Rosemead, CA (city) Los Angeles County	16,995	31.76
Arcadia, CA (city) Los Angeles County	14,945	28.17
East San Gabriel, CA (cdp) Los Angeles County	3,829	26.39
Rowland Heights, CA (cdp) Los Angeles County	12,445	25.63
Temple City, CA (city) Los Angeles County	8,534	25.57
Walnut, CA (city) Los Angeles County	7,571	25.23
Cupertino, CA (city) Santa Clara County	11,867	23.48
South San Gabriel, CA (cdp) Los Angeles County	1,731	22.79
Hawi, HI (cdp) Hawaii County	207	22.07
Kahaluu, HI (cdp) Honolulu County	612	20.85
Ahuimanu, HI (cdp) Honolulu County	1,767	20.77
San Francisco, CA (city) San Francisco County	160,113	20.61
Kaneohe, HI (cdp) Honolulu County	6,965	19.92
Hana, HI (cdp) Maui County	140	19.75
Hacienda Heights, CA (cdp) Los Angeles County	10,394	19.57
Waianae, HI (cdp) Honolulu County	2,024	19.27
Waimanalo, HI (cdp) Honolulu County	704	19.21
Heeia, HI (cdp) Honolulu County	939	18.99
Hillsborough, CA (town) San Mateo County	2,000	18.48
Makaha Valley, HI (cdp) Honolulu County	237	18.39
Punaluu, HI (cdp) Honolulu County	162	18.39
Honolulu, HI (cdp) Honolulu County	68,070	18.32
Nanakuli, HI (cdp) Honolulu County	1,956	18.09
Maunawili, HI (cdp) Honolulu County	875	17.97
Kapaau, HI (cdp) Hawaii County	205	17.69
Saratoga, CA (city) Santa Clara County	5,237	17.55
Millbrae, CA (city) San Mateo County	3,558	17.17
Foster City, CA (city) San Mateo County	4,921	17.09
Kukuihaele, HI (cdp) Hawaii County	54	17.03
Halaula, HI (cdp) Hawaii County	84	16.97
North El Monte, CA (cdp) Los Angeles County	621	16.77
Waimanalo Beach, HI (cdp) Honolulu County	702	16.44
South Pasadena, CA (city) Los Angeles County	3,874	15.95
Maili, HI (cdp) Honolulu County	947	15.93
Makaha, HI (cdp) Honolulu County	1,227	15.83
Hauula, HI (cdp) Honolulu County	578	15.83
Diamond Bar, CA (city) Los Angeles County	8,785	15.61
Hawaiian Beaches, HI (cdp) Hawaii County	578	15.58
Waikane, HI (cdp) Honolulu County	111	15.29
Waipio, HI (cdp) Honolulu County	1,770	15.16
Haleiwa, HI (cdp) Honolulu County	337	15.15
Halawa, HI (cdp) Honolulu County	2,102	15.13
Kurtistown, HI (cdp) Hawaii County	174	15.04
Mountain View, HI (cdp) Hawaii County	419	14.97
Mililani Town, HI (cdp) Honolulu County	4,194	14.66
Daly City, CA (city) San Mateo County	15,185	14.65
Waipio Acres, HI (cdp) Honolulu County	773	14.59
Waimalu, HI (cdp) Honolulu County	4,253	14.48
Fremont, CA (city) Alameda County	29,145	14.33
Kahuku, HI (cdp) Honolulu County	300	14.31
Albany, CA (city) Alameda County	2,351	14.30
Makakilo City, HI (cdp) Honolulu County	1,855	14.10
Aiea, HI (cdp) Honolulu County	1,272	14.10
Forest Home, NY (cdp) Tompkins County	132	14.03
Hilo, HI (cdp) Hawaii County	5,709	14.01
Nanawale Estates, HI (cdp) Hawaii County	149	13.89
North Potomac, MD (cdp) Montgomery County	3,186	13.83
Kailua, HI (cdp) Honolulu County	5,000	13.69
Ewa Gentry, HI (cdp) Honolulu County	674	13.65
Milpitas, CA (city) Santa Clara County	8,446	13.47
Pearl City, HI (cdp) Honolulu County	4,131	13.34
Highlands-Baywood Park, CA (cdp) San Mateo County	560	13.30
El Cerrito, CA (city) Contra Costa County	3,050	13.16
Stanford, CA (cdp) Santa Clara County	1,740	13.07
Los Altos Hills, CA (town) Santa Clara County	1,030	13.03
Wahiawa, HI (cdp) Honolulu County	2,084	12.90
Ewa Beach, HI (cdp) Honolulu County	1,888	12.89
Eden Roc, HI (cdp) Hawaii County	58	12.86
Waikoloa Village, HI (cdp) Hawaii County	608	12.65
Piedmont, CA (city) Alameda County	1,378	12.58
Pahala, HI (cdp) Hawaii County	172	12.48
Cerritos, CA (city) Los Angeles County	6,378	12.39
Hawaiian Paradise Park, HI (cdp) Hawaii County	873	12.38
Kealakekua, HI (cdp) Hawaii County	203	12.34
Wailuku, HI (cdp) Maui County	1,514	12.31
Alameda, CA (city) Alameda County	8,833	12.22
Waihee-Waiehu, HI (cdp) Maui County	891	12.19
Fern Acres, HI (cdp) Hawaii County	92	12.17
Laie, HI (cdp) Honolulu County	557	12.15
Keaau, HI (cdp) Hawaii County	244	12.14
Pepeekeo, HI (cdp) Hawaii County	206	12.14
Kaunakakai, HI (cdp) Maui County	328	12.03
Lawai, HI (cdp) Kauai County	238	12.00
Makawao, HI (cdp) Maui County	755	11.93
Waimea, HI (cdp) Hawaii County	838	11.92
Waimea, HI (cdp) Kauai County	211	11.81
Kailua, HI (cdp) Hawaii County	1,154	11.69
Ainaloa, HI (cdp) Hawaii County	223	11.68
Village Park, HI (cdp) Honolulu County	1,123	11.67
Honomu, HI (cdp) Hawaii County	63	11.65
Hanalei, HI (cdp) Kauai County	55	11.51
Waialua, HI (cdp) Honolulu County	432	11.49
Kualapuu, HI (cdp) Maui County	221	11.42
Honaunau-Napoopoo, HI (cdp) Hawaii County	274	11.35
Honalo, HI (cdp) Hawaii County	225	11.32
Captain Cook, HI (cdp) Hawaii County	362	11.29
Kapaa, HI (cdp) Kauai County	1,068	11.28
Paauilo, HI (cdp) Hawaii County	64	11.21
Laupahoehoe, HI (cdp) Hawaii County	53	11.21
Honokaa, HI (cdp) Hawaii County	246	11.02
Paia, HI (cdp) Maui County	275	11.00
Wainaku, HI (cdp) Hawaii County	134	10.92
Orchidlands Estates, HI (cdp) Hawaii County	188	10.86
Waikapu, HI (cdp) Maui County	121	10.85
Quincy, MA (city) Norfolk County	9,511	10.80
Broadmoor, CA (cdp) San Mateo County	435	10.80
El Monte, CA (city) Los Angeles County	12,506	10.78
Kalaoa, HI (cdp) Hawaii County	732	10.77
East Pasadena, CA (cdp) Los Angeles County	651	10.77
Pukalani, HI (cdp) Maui County	791	10.72
San Leandro, CA (city) Alameda County	8,418	10.60
Ewa Villages, HI (cdp) Honolulu County	500	10.55
Kahului, HI (cdp) Maui County	2,103	10.44
Hanapepe, HI (cdp) Kauai County	224	10.40
Naalehu, HI (cdp) Hawaii County	95	10.34
Emeryville, CA (city) Alameda County	701	10.19
Laguna West-Lakeside, CA (cdp) Sacramento County	850	10.10
Hercules, CA (city) Contra Costa County	1,946	9.99
Lihue, HI (cdp) Kauai County	566	9.98
Holmdel, NJ (township) Monmouth County	1,574	9.97
Lanai City, HI (cdp) Maui County	314	9.92
Sunnyvale, CA (city) Santa Clara County	13,063	9.91
Palo Alto, CA (city) Santa Clara County	5,740	9.80
Union City, CA (city) Alameda County	6,438	9.63
Anahola, HI (cdp) Kauai County	186	9.63
Hanamaulu, HI (cdp) Kauai County	312	9.54
Irvine, CA (city) Orange County	13,620	9.52
Kaaawa, HI (cdp) Honolulu County	126	9.52
Wailua Homesteads, HI (cdp) Kauai County	434	9.50
Sugar Land, TX (city) Fort Bend County	5,997	9.47
Falcon Heights, MN (city) Ramsey County	516	9.26
La Habra Heights, CA (city) Los Angeles County	524	9.17
Wailua, HI (cdp) Kauai County	191	9.17
Kekaha, HI (cdp) Kauai County	290	9.13
Lansing, NY (village) Tompkins County	309	9.04
Haiku-Pauwela, HI (cdp) Maui County	589	8.95
Mayflower Village, CA (cdp) Los Angeles County	452	8.90
Fern Forest, HI (cdp) Hawaii County	42	8.75
Davis, CA (city) Yolo County	5,270	8.74
Pupukea, HI (cdp) Honolulu County	371	8.73
Volcano, HI (cdp) Hawaii County	194	8.70
South San Francisco, CA (city) San Mateo County	5,229	8.64
Oakland, CA (city) Alameda County	34,139	8.55
Los Altos, CA (city) Santa Clara County	2,367	8.55
Plainsboro, NJ (township) Middlesex County	1,729	8.55
Great Pond, ME (town) Hancock County	4	8.51

Notes: (cdp) census designated place; Refer to the Explanation of Data in the front of the book for more detailed information.

Asian: Chinese, except Taiwanese

Top 150 Places Sorted by Percent

(Based on places with populations of 10,000 or more)

Place	Number	%
Monterey Park, CA (city) Los Angeles County	25,411	42.32
Alhambra, CA (city) Los Angeles County	29,139	33.96
San Gabriel, CA (city) Los Angeles County	13,417	33.71
San Marino, CA (city) Los Angeles County	4,186	32.34
Rosemead, CA (city) Los Angeles County	16,995	31.76
Arcadia, CA (city) Los Angeles County	14,945	28.17
East San Gabriel, CA (cdp) Los Angeles County	3,829	26.39
Rowland Heights, CA (cdp) Los Angeles County	12,445	25.63
Temple City, CA (city) Los Angeles County	8,534	25.57
Walnut, CA (city) Los Angeles County	7,571	25.23
Cupertino, CA (city) Santa Clara County	11,867	23.48
San Francisco, CA (city) San Francisco County	160,113	20.61
Kaneohe, HI (cdp) Honolulu County	6,965	19.92
Hacienda Heights, CA (cdp) Los Angeles County	10,394	19.57
Waianae, HI (cdp) Honolulu County	2,024	19.27
Hillsborough, CA (town) San Mateo County	2,000	18.48
Honolulu, HI (cdp) Honolulu County	68,070	18.32
Nanakuli, HI (cdp) Honolulu County	1,956	18.09
Saratoga, CA (city) Santa Clara County	5,237	17.55
Millbrae, CA (city) San Mateo County	3,558	17.17
Foster City, CA (city) San Mateo County	4,921	17.09
South Pasadena, CA (city) Los Angeles County	3,874	15.95
Diamond Bar, CA (city) Los Angeles County	8,785	15.61
Waipio, HI (cdp) Honolulu County	1,770	15.16
Halawa, HI (cdp) Honolulu County	2,102	15.13
Mililani Town, HI (cdp) Honolulu County	4,194	14.66
Daly City, CA (city) San Mateo County	15,185	14.65
Waimalu, HI (cdp) Honolulu County	4,253	14.48
Fremont, CA (city) Alameda County	29,145	14.33
Albany, CA (city) Alameda County	2,351	14.30
Makakilo City, HI (cdp) Honolulu County	1,855	14.10
Hilo, HI (cdp) Hawaii County	5,709	14.01
North Potomac, MD (cdp) Montgomery County	3,186	13.83
Kailua, HI (cdp) Honolulu County	5,000	13.69
Milpitas, CA (city) Santa Clara County	8,446	13.47
Pearl City, HI (cdp) Honolulu County	4,131	13.34
El Cerrito, CA (city) Contra Costa County	3,050	13.16
Stanford, CA (cdp) Santa Clara County	1,740	13.07
Wahiawa, HI (cdp) Honolulu County	2,084	12.90
Ewa Beach, HI (cdp) Honolulu County	1,888	12.89
Piedmont, CA (city) Alameda County	1,378	12.58
Cerritos, CA (city) Los Angeles County	6,378	12.39
Wailuku, HI (cdp) Maui County	1,514	12.31
Alameda, CA (city) Alameda County	8,833	12.22
Quincy, MA (city) Norfolk County	9,511	10.80
El Monte, CA (city) Los Angeles County	12,506	10.78
San Leandro, CA (city) Alameda County	8,418	10.60
Kahului, HI (cdp) Maui County	2,103	10.44
Hercules, CA (city) Contra Costa County	1,946	9.99
Holmdel, NJ (township) Monmouth County	1,574	9.97
Sunnyvale, CA (city) Santa Clara County	13,063	9.91
Palo Alto, CA (city) Santa Clara County	5,740	9.80
Union City, CA (city) Alameda County	6,438	9.63
Irvine, CA (city) Orange County	13,620	9.52
Sugar Land, TX (city) Fort Bend County	5,997	9.47
Davis, CA (city) Yolo County	5,270	8.74
South San Francisco, CA (city) San Mateo County	5,229	8.64
Oakland, CA (city) Alameda County	34,139	8.55
Los Altos, CA (city) Santa Clara County	2,367	8.55
Plainsboro, NJ (township) Middlesex County	1,729	8.55
Mountain View, CA (city) Santa Clara County	5,931	8.39
West Windsor, NJ (township) Mercer County	1,820	8.31
Malden, MA (city) Middlesex County	4,660	8.27
Blackhawk-Camino Tassajara, CA (cdp) Contra Costa County	821	8.17
Waipahu, HI (cdp) Honolulu County	2,669	8.06
Berkeley, CA (city) Alameda County	8,255	8.03
Belmont, CA (city) San Mateo County	1,966	7.83
Moraga, CA (town) Contra Costa County	1,268	7.78
Princeton Meadows, NJ (cdp) Middlesex County	1,037	7.72
Rancho Palos Verdes, CA (city) Los Angeles County	3,166	7.69
La Palma, CA (city) Orange County	1,142	7.41
Castro Valley, CA (cdp) Alameda County	4,179	7.29
Harrison, NJ (town) Hudson County	1,042	7.22
West Covina, CA (city) Los Angeles County	7,579	7.21
San Mateo, CA (city) San Mateo County	6,451	6.98
East Brunswick, NJ (cdp) Middlesex County	3,245	6.94
Laguna, CA (cdp) Sacramento County	2,299	6.70
Burlingame, CA (city) San Mateo County	1,852	6.58
San Ramon, CA (city) Contra Costa County	2,931	6.55
Kihei, HI (cdp) Maui County	1,072	6.40
New Territory, TX (cdp) Fort Bend County	873	6.30
Livingston, NJ (cdp) Essex County	1,723	6.29
Brookline, MA (cdp) Norfolk County	3,579	6.27
Rockville, MD (city) Montgomery County	2,963	6.25
San Bruno, CA (city) San Mateo County	2,501	6.23
Orinda, CA (city) Contra Costa County	1,094	6.22
San Jose, CA (city) Santa Clara County	55,543	6.21
Bellevue, WA (city) King County	6,696	6.11
Marlboro, NJ (township) Monmouth County	2,206	6.06
Chino Hills, CA (city) San Bernardino County	4,007	6.00
Pinole, CA (city) Contra Costa County	1,138	5.98
Edison, NJ (cdp) Middlesex County	5,824	5.96
Palos Verdes Estates, CA (city) Los Angeles County	790	5.92
Montgomery, NJ (township) Somerset County	1,023	5.85
Ithaca, NY (city) Tompkins County	1,700	5.80
Parsippany-Troy Hills, NJ (township) Morris County	2,870	5.67
Urbana, IL (city) Champaign County	2,034	5.59
Mercer Island, WA (city) King County	1,229	5.58
Fort Lee, NJ (borough) Bergen County	1,971	5.56
Santa Clara, CA (city) Santa Clara County	5,644	5.51
Lexington, MA (cdp) Middlesex County	1,670	5.50
Potomac, MD (cdp) Montgomery County	2,458	5.48
La Canada Flintridge, CA (city) Los Angeles County	1,087	5.35
Sacramento, CA (city) Sacramento County	21,450	5.27
Montville, NJ (township) Morris County	1,098	5.27
Ashland, CA (cdp) Alameda County	1,093	5.26
San Lorenzo, CA (cdp) Alameda County	1,143	5.22
Highland Park, NJ (borough) Middlesex County	731	5.22
Randolph, MA (cdp) Norfolk County	1,592	5.14
Tenafly, NJ (borough) Bergen County	698	5.06
Pacifica, CA (city) San Mateo County	1,926	5.02
Morganville, NJ (cdp) Monmouth County	565	5.02
Newton, MA (city) Middlesex County	4,164	4.97
Pleasanton, CA (city) Alameda County	3,132	4.92
Piscataway, NJ (township) Middlesex County	2,478	4.91
Cambridge, MA (city) Middlesex County	4,969	4.90
Danville, CA (town) Contra Costa County	1,988	4.77
Newark, CA (city) Alameda County	2,017	4.75
Warren, NJ (township) Somerset County	677	4.75
Torrance, CA (city) Los Angeles County	6,524	4.73
New York, NY (city) New York City	374,321	4.67
Montebello, CA (city) Los Angeles County	2,905	4.67
Lafayette, CA (city) Contra Costa County	1,115	4.66
Isla Vista, CA (cdp) Santa Barbara County	853	4.65
Gaithersburg, MD (city) Montgomery County	2,428	4.61
South El Monte, CA (city) Los Angeles County	975	4.61
North New Hyde Park, NY (cdp) Nassau County	669	4.60
East Hanover, NJ (township) Morris County	524	4.60
Princeton, NJ (township) Mercer County	731	4.56
Redland, MD (cdp) Montgomery County	773	4.55
Setauket-East Setauket, NY (cdp) Suffolk County	721	4.53
Bryn Mawr-Skyway, WA (cdp) King County	626	4.48
Fountain Valley, CA (city) Orange County	2,460	4.47
Artesia, CA (city) Los Angeles County	728	4.44
Hanover, NJ (township) Morris County	571	4.43
Ann Arbor, MI (city) Washtenaw County	5,021	4.40
Merrifield, VA (cdp) Fairfax County	492	4.40
Baldwin Park, CA (city) Los Angeles County	3,306	4.36
Walnut Creek, CA (city) Contra Costa County	2,800	4.35
Syosset, NY (cdp) Nassau County	803	4.33
Plano, TX (city) Collin County	9,477	4.27
Colesville, MD (cdp) Montgomery County	843	4.26
Redmond, WA (city) King County	1,904	4.21
South Brunswick, NJ (township) Middlesex County	1,583	4.20
Greentree, NJ (cdp) Camden County	482	4.18
North Bethesda, MD (cdp) Montgomery County	1,603	4.15
Claremont, CA (city) Los Angeles County	1,411	4.15
Princeton, NJ (borough) Mercer County	588	4.14
San Carlos, CA (city) San Mateo County	1,143	4.12
Acton, MA (town) Middlesex County	838	4.12

Notes: (cdp) census designated place; Refer to the Explanation of Data in the front of the book for more detailed information.

Asian: Filipino

Top 150 Places Sorted by Number

(Based on all places, regardless of population)

Place	Number	%
Los Angeles, CA (city) Los Angeles County	113,793	3.08
San Diego, CA (city) San Diego County	86,920	7.10
New York, NY (city) New York City	62,058	0.77
Honolulu, HI (cdp) Honolulu County	60,922	16.39
San Jose, CA (city) Santa Clara County	55,120	6.16
San Francisco, CA (city) San Francisco County	45,793	5.90
Daly City, CA (city) San Mateo County	35,099	33.87
Chicago, IL (city) Cook County	32,266	1.11
Vallejo, CA (city) Solano County	27,098	23.21
Long Beach, CA (city) Los Angeles County	21,502	4.66
Waipahu, HI (cdp) Honolulu County	19,727	59.58
Seattle, WA (city) King County	19,567	3.47
Stockton, CA (city) San Joaquin County	19,232	7.89
Carson, CA (city) Los Angeles County	18,223	20.31
Virginia Beach, VA (independent city) Virginia Beach city	17,429	4.10
Jersey City, NJ (city) Hudson County	16,777	6.99
Chula Vista, CA (city) San Diego County	15,001	8.64
Hayward, CA (city) Alameda County	14,443	10.31
Las Vegas, NV (city) Clark County	14,139	2.96
Fremont, CA (city) Alameda County	13,863	6.82
Union City, CA (city) Alameda County	13,716	20.51
Jacksonville, FL (special city) Duval County	12,295	1.67
Glendale, CA (city) Los Angeles County	12,099	6.21
Sacramento, CA (city) Sacramento County	11,156	2.74
South San Francisco, CA (city) San Mateo County	11,127	18.38
West Covina, CA (city) Los Angeles County	10,469	9.96
Milpitas, CA (city) Santa Clara County	10,265	16.37
National City, CA (city) San Diego County	10,207	18.81
Oxnard, CA (city) Ventura County	9,907	5.82
Anaheim, CA (city) Orange County	9,655	2.94
Houston, TX (city) Harris County	9,276	0.47
Kahului, HI (cdp) Maui County	8,940	44.38
Oakland, CA (city) Alameda County	8,191	2.05
Ewa Beach, HI (cdp) Honolulu County	7,835	53.48
Fairfield, CA (city) Solano County	7,534	7.83
Anchorage, AK (municipality) Anchorage Borough	7,481	2.87
Salinas, CA (city) Monterey County	7,345	4.86
Hilo, HI (cdp) Hawaii County	7,329	17.98
San Leandro, CA (city) Alameda County	7,153	9.00
Phoenix, AZ (city) Maricopa County	6,996	0.53
Sunnyvale, CA (city) Santa Clara County	6,880	5.22
Paradise, NV (cdp) Clark County	6,743	3.62
Santa Clara, CA (city) Santa Clara County	6,592	6.44
Cerritos, CA (city) Los Angeles County	6,560	12.74
Pearl City, HI (cdp) Honolulu County	6,460	20.85
Alameda, CA (city) Alameda County	6,406	8.87
Oceanside, CA (city) San Diego County	6,390	3.97
Delano, CA (city) Kern County	6,372	16.41
Mililani Town, HI (cdp) Honolulu County	6,134	21.44
Sunrise Manor, NV (cdp) Clark County	5,971	3.82
Waimalu, HI (cdp) Honolulu County	5,951	20.26
Pittsburg, CA (city) Contra Costa County	5,764	10.15
Chino Hills, CA (city) San Bernardino County	5,738	8.59
San Antonio, TX (city) Bexar County	5,580	0.49
Buena Park, CA (city) Orange County	5,570	7.12
Lakewood, CA (city) Los Angeles County	5,372	6.77
Wahiawa, HI (cdp) Honolulu County	5,362	33.20
Fresno, CA (city) Fresno County	5,264	1.23
Hercules, CA (city) Contra Costa County	5,246	26.92
Philadelphia, PA (city) Philadelphia County	5,232	0.34
Norfolk, VA (independent city) Norfolk city	5,182	2.21
Norwalk, CA (city) Los Angeles County	5,019	4.86
Concord, CA (city) Contra Costa County	5,016	4.12
Moreno Valley, CA (city) Riverside County	4,970	3.49
Reno, NV (city) Washoe County	4,889	2.71
Spring Valley, NV (cdp) Clark County	4,813	4.10
Antioch, CA (city) Contra Costa County	4,775	5.27
Village Park, HI (cdp) Honolulu County	4,732	49.16
Hempstead, NY (town) Nassau County	4,712	0.62
Kaneohe, HI (cdp) Honolulu County	4,513	12.91
Portland, OR (city) Multnomah County	4,262	0.81
Kihei, HI (cdp) Maui County	4,246	25.35
Irvine, CA (city) Orange County	4,223	2.95
Makakilo City, HI (cdp) Honolulu County	4,112	31.26
Newark, CA (city) Alameda County	4,078	9.60
Corona, CA (city) Riverside County	4,055	3.24
Torrance, CA (city) Los Angeles County	4,048	2.93
Henderson, NV (city) Clark County	4,040	2.30
Riverside, CA (city) Riverside County	3,952	1.55
Pacifica, CA (city) San Mateo County	3,925	10.22
Walnut, CA (city) Los Angeles County	3,912	13.04
Burbank, CA (city) Los Angeles County	3,860	3.85
Bellflower, CA (city) Los Angeles County	3,787	5.20
Bakersfield, CA (city) Kern County	3,767	1.52
Halawa, HI (cdp) Honolulu County	3,735	26.89
Richmond, CA (city) Contra Costa County	3,705	3.73
Elk Grove, CA (cdp) Sacramento County	3,661	6.10
Santa Clarita, CA (city) Los Angeles County	3,652	2.42
San Bruno, CA (city) San Mateo County	3,634	9.05
Suisun City, CA (city) Solano County	3,597	13.77
Lahaina, HI (cdp) Maui County	3,596	39.44
Skokie, IL (village) Cook County	3,594	5.67
Baldwin Park, CA (city) Los Angeles County	3,591	4.74
Waipio, HI (cdp) Honolulu County	3,535	30.29
Ewa Villages, HI (cdp) Honolulu County	3,480	73.40
San Mateo, CA (city) San Mateo County	3,478	3.76
Rowland Heights, CA (cdp) Los Angeles County	3,425	7.05
La Presa, CA (cdp) San Diego County	3,404	10.40
Fontana, CA (city) San Bernardino County	3,381	2.62
Pasadena, CA (city) Los Angeles County	3,367	2.51
Garden Grove, CA (city) Orange County	3,349	2.03
Pomona, CA (city) Los Angeles County	3,335	2.23
Santa Maria, CA (city) Santa Barbara County	3,306	4.27
Diamond Bar, CA (city) Los Angeles County	3,298	5.86
Bergenfield, NJ (borough) Bergen County	3,254	12.40
Tacoma, WA (city) Pierce County	3,158	1.63
Waihee-Waiehu, HI (cdp) Maui County	3,106	42.49
Palmdale, CA (city) Los Angeles County	3,094	2.65
Rancho Cucamonga, CA (city) San Bernardino County	3,050	2.39
Escondido, CA (city) San Diego County	3,039	2.28
Wailuku, HI (cdp) Maui County	3,001	24.41
Whitmore Village, HI (cdp) Honolulu County	2,980	73.45
Waianae, HI (cdp) Honolulu County	2,970	28.27
Kailua, HI (cdp) Honolulu County	2,969	8.13
Kapaa, HI (cdp) Kauai County	2,965	31.30
North Las Vegas, NV (city) Clark County	2,916	2.52
Tracy, CA (city) San Joaquin County	2,891	5.08
Huntington Beach, CA (city) Orange County	2,717	1.43
Washington, DC (city) District of Columbia	2,714	0.47
Tucson, AZ (city) Pima County	2,697	0.55
Modesto, CA (city) Stanislaus County	2,695	1.43
Santa Ana, CA (city) Orange County	2,693	0.80
Dallas, TX (city) Dallas County	2,680	0.23
Vacaville, CA (city) Solano County	2,674	3.02
Ontario, CA (city) San Bernardino County	2,662	1.68
Mountain View, CA (city) Santa Clara County	2,638	3.73
Chesapeake, VA (independent city) Chesapeake city	2,637	1.32
Colorado Springs, CO (city) El Paso County	2,628	0.73
West Carson, CA (cdp) Los Angeles County	2,584	12.22
Lancaster, CA (city) Los Angeles County	2,556	2.15
Edison, NJ (cdp) Middlesex County	2,516	2.58
Cypress, CA (city) Orange County	2,463	5.33
San Bernardino, CA (city) San Bernardino County	2,416	1.30
Downey, CA (city) Los Angeles County	2,407	2.24
Laguna, CA (cdp) Sacramento County	2,402	7.00
Arlington, VA (cdp) Arlington County	2,388	1.26
Federal Way, WA (city) King County	2,386	2.87
Hawthorne, CA (city) Los Angeles County	2,373	2.82
Gardena, CA (city) Los Angeles County	2,320	4.02
Orange, CA (city) Orange County	2,311	1.79
Nanakuli, HI (cdp) Honolulu County	2,289	21.17
Woodbridge, NJ (township) Middlesex County	2,284	2.35
La Mirada, CA (city) Los Angeles County	2,281	4.88
Austin, TX (city) Travis County	2,269	0.35
Fort Washington, MD (cdp) Prince George's County	2,242	9.40
Simi Valley, CA (city) Ventura County	2,239	2.01
Piscataway, NJ (township) Middlesex County	2,235	4.43
Belleville, NJ (cdp) Essex County	2,224	6.19
Kent, WA (city) King County	2,224	2.80
Hanamaulu, HI (cdp) Kauai County	2,188	66.87

Notes: (cdp) census designated place; Refer to the Explanation of Data in the front of the book for more detailed information.

Asian: Filipino

Top 150 Places Sorted by Percent

(Based on all places, regardless of population)

Place	Number	%
Kaumakani, HI (cdp) Kauai County	486	80.07
Whitmore Village, HI (cdp) Honolulu County	2,980	73.45
Ewa Villages, HI (cdp) Honolulu County	3,480	73.40
Puhi, HI (cdp) Kauai County	804	67.79
Hanamaulu, HI (cdp) Kauai County	2,188	66.87
Lanai City, HI (cdp) Maui County	2,007	63.43
Waipahu, HI (cdp) Honolulu County	19,727	59.58
Eleele, HI (cdp) Kauai County	1,148	56.27
Pahala, HI (cdp) Hawaii County	765	55.52
Paauilo, HI (cdp) Hawaii County	313	54.82
Ewa Beach, HI (cdp) Honolulu County	7,835	53.48
Waialua, HI (cdp) Honolulu County	1,923	51.13
Keaau, HI (cdp) Hawaii County	995	49.50
Naalehu, HI (cdp) Hawaii County	452	49.18
Village Park, HI (cdp) Honolulu County	4,732	49.16
Halaula, HI (cdp) Hawaii County	239	48.28
Kekaha, HI (cdp) Kauai County	1,502	47.31
Kahului, HI (cdp) Maui County	8,940	44.38
Pepeekeo, HI (cdp) Hawaii County	740	43.61
Haliimaile, HI (cdp) Maui County	385	43.02
Honokaa, HI (cdp) Hawaii County	954	42.72
Hanapepe, HI (cdp) Kauai County	915	42.50
Waihee-Waiehu, HI (cdp) Maui County	3,106	42.49
Wainaku, HI (cdp) Hawaii County	509	41.48
Ewa Gentry, HI (cdp) Honolulu County	2,048	41.47
Koloa, HI (cdp) Kauai County	805	41.45
Lahaina, HI (cdp) Maui County	3,596	39.44
Pahoa, HI (cdp) Hawaii County	379	39.40
Kaunakakai, HI (cdp) Maui County	1,024	37.56
Akutan, AK (city) Aleutians East Borough	263	36.89
Papaikou, HI (cdp) Hawaii County	512	36.21
Hawi, HI (cdp) Hawaii County	338	36.03
Pakala Village, HI (cdp) Kauai County	169	35.36
Kapaau, HI (cdp) Hawaii County	401	34.60
Kahuku, HI (cdp) Honolulu County	715	34.10
Daly City, CA (city) San Mateo County	35,099	33.87
Maili, HI (cdp) Honolulu County	2,004	33.72
Maunaloa, HI (cdp) Maui County	77	33.48
Wahiawa, HI (cdp) Honolulu County	5,362	33.20
Waikapu, HI (cdp) Maui County	359	32.20
Kapaa, HI (cdp) Kauai County	2,965	31.30
Makakilo City, HI (cdp) Honolulu County	4,112	31.26
Waimanalo, HI (cdp) Honolulu County	1,145	31.25
Kodiak, AK (city) Kodiak Island Borough	1,940	30.63
Waipio, HI (cdp) Honolulu County	3,535	30.29
Paia, HI (cdp) Maui County	750	30.01
Waimea, HI (cdp) Kauai County	536	29.99
Nanawale Estates, HI (cdp) Hawaii County	316	29.45
Waipio Acres, HI (cdp) Honolulu County	1,537	29.01
Haleiwa, HI (cdp) Honolulu County	631	28.36
Waianae, HI (cdp) Honolulu County	2,970	28.27
Hawaiian Paradise Park, HI (cdp) Hawaii County	1,939	27.50
Makaha, HI (cdp) Honolulu County	2,096	27.03
Hercules, CA (city) Contra Costa County	5,246	26.92
Halawa, HI (cdp) Honolulu County	3,735	26.89
Kilauea, HI (cdp) Kauai County	562	26.86
Storla, SD (cdp) Aurora County	4	26.67
Orchidlands Estates, HI (cdp) Hawaii County	461	26.63
Lihue, HI (cdp) Kauai County	1,500	26.44
King Cove, AK (city) Aleutians East Borough	208	26.26
Hawaiian Beaches, HI (cdp) Hawaii County	973	26.23
Omao, HI (cdp) Kauai County	316	25.88
Kihei, HI (cdp) Maui County	4,246	25.35
Laupahoehoe, HI (cdp) Hawaii County	118	24.95
Honomu, HI (cdp) Hawaii County	134	24.77
Ainaloa, HI (cdp) Hawaii County	473	24.76
Kualapuu, HI (cdp) Maui County	476	24.59
Wailuku, HI (cdp) Maui County	3,001	24.41
Kalaheo, HI (cdp) Kauai County	921	23.54
Vallejo, CA (city) Solano County	27,098	23.21
Kurtistown, HI (cdp) Hawaii County	267	23.08
Aiea, HI (cdp) Honolulu County	2,077	23.03
Makaha Valley, HI (cdp) Honolulu County	289	22.42
Colma, CA (town) San Mateo County	265	22.25
Wailua, HI (cdp) Kauai County	462	22.18
Waikane, HI (cdp) Honolulu County	161	22.18
Broadmoor, CA (cdp) San Mateo County	877	21.78
Unalaska, AK (city) Aleutians West Census Area	931	21.74
Sand Point, AK (city) Aleutians East Borough	207	21.74
Mililani Town, HI (cdp) Honolulu County	6,134	21.44
Nanakuli, HI (cdp) Honolulu County	2,289	21.17
Kukuihaele, HI (cdp) Hawaii County	67	21.14
Kealakekua, HI (cdp) Hawaii County	346	21.03
Pearl City, HI (cdp) Honolulu County	6,460	20.85
Union City, CA (city) Alameda County	13,716	20.51
Carson, CA (city) Los Angeles County	18,223	20.31
Wailua Homesteads, HI (cdp) Kauai County	927	20.30
Waimea, HI (cdp) Hawaii County	1,426	20.29
Kailua, HI (cdp) Hawaii County	2,002	20.28
Waimalu, HI (cdp) Honolulu County	5,951	20.26
Pukalani, HI (cdp) Maui County	1,492	20.22
Lawai, HI (cdp) Kauai County	401	20.21
Makawao, HI (cdp) Maui County	1,267	20.03
Paukaa, HI (cdp) Hawaii County	99	20.00
Mountain View, HI (cdp) Hawaii County	557	19.90
Waikoloa Village, HI (cdp) Hawaii County	920	19.14
Captain Cook, HI (cdp) Hawaii County	611	19.06
National City, CA (city) San Diego County	10,207	18.81
South San Francisco, CA (city) San Mateo County	11,127	18.38
Hilo, HI (cdp) Hawaii County	7,329	17.98
Napili-Honokowai, HI (cdp) Maui County	1,182	17.41
Delano, CA (city) Kern County	6,372	16.41
Honolulu, HI (cdp) Honolulu County	60,922	16.39
Milpitas, CA (city) Santa Clara County	10,265	16.37
Honaunau-Napoopoo, HI (cdp) Hawaii County	393	16.28
Poplar-Cotton Center, CA (cdp) Tulare County	241	16.11
Honalo, HI (cdp) Hawaii County	317	15.95
Hana, HI (cdp) Maui County	111	15.66
Walnut Grove, CA (cdp) Sacramento County	102	15.25
Rollingwood, CA (cdp) Contra Costa County	436	15.03
Pupukea, HI (cdp) Honolulu County	624	14.68
Mokuleia, HI (cdp) Honolulu County	268	14.57
American Canyon, CA (city) Napa County	1,399	14.31
Suisun City, CA (city) Solano County	3,597	13.77
Kalaoa, HI (cdp) Hawaii County	917	13.50
Port Tobacco Village, MD (town) Charles County	2	13.33
Ahuimanu, HI (cdp) Honolulu County	1,123	13.20
Walnut, CA (city) Los Angeles County	3,912	13.04
Kaneohe, HI (cdp) Honolulu County	4,513	12.91
Cerritos, CA (city) Los Angeles County	6,560	12.74
Fern Acres, HI (cdp) Hawaii County	95	12.57
Carter, WY (cdp) Uinta County	1	12.50
Anahola, HI (cdp) Kauai County	240	12.42
Bergenfield, NJ (borough) Bergen County	3,254	12.40
Kahaluu, HI (cdp) Honolulu County	359	12.23
West Carson, CA (cdp) Los Angeles County	2,584	12.22
Holualoa, HI (cdp) Hawaii County	741	12.13
Lathrop, CA (city) San Joaquin County	1,251	11.98
Eden Roc, HI (cdp) Hawaii County	54	11.97
Haiku-Pauwela, HI (cdp) Maui County	743	11.30
Pinole, CA (city) Contra Costa County	2,144	11.26
Artesia, CA (city) Los Angeles County	1,806	11.03
Hawaiian Ocean View, HI (cdp) Hawaii County	239	10.97
Kapalua, HI (cdp) Maui County	51	10.92
Rodeo, CA (cdp) Contra Costa County	947	10.86
Leilani Estates, HI (cdp) Hawaii County	113	10.80
Boronda, CA (cdp) Monterey County	143	10.79
Adak, AK (cdp) Aleutians West Census Area	33	10.44
Hawaiian Acres, HI (cdp) Hawaii County	185	10.42
La Presa, CA (cdp) San Diego County	3,404	10.40
Hayward, CA (city) Alameda County	14,443	10.31
Silverdale, WA (cdp) Kitsap County	1,628	10.29
Pacifica, CA (city) San Mateo County	3,925	10.22
Pittsburg, CA (city) Contra Costa County	5,764	10.15
Cordova, AK (city) Valdez-Cordova Census Area	248	10.11
Colmar Manor, MD (town) Prince George's County	127	10.10
Volcano, HI (cdp) Hawaii County	225	10.09
Oak Harbor, WA (city) Island County	1,976	9.98
West Covina, CA (city) Los Angeles County	10,469	9.96
Lemoore Station, CA (cdp) Kings County	572	9.95

Notes: (cdp) census designated place; Refer to the Explanation of Data in the front of the book for more detailed information.

Asian: Filipino

Top 150 Places Sorted by Percent

(Based on places with populations of 10,000 or more)

Place	Number	%
Waipahu, HI (cdp) Honolulu County	19,727	59.58
Ewa Beach, HI (cdp) Honolulu County	7,835	53.48
Kahului, HI (cdp) Maui County	8,940	44.38
Daly City, CA (city) San Mateo County	35,099	33.87
Wahiawa, HI (cdp) Honolulu County	5,362	33.20
Makakilo City, HI (cdp) Honolulu County	4,112	31.26
Waipio, HI (cdp) Honolulu County	3,535	30.29
Waianae, HI (cdp) Honolulu County	2,970	28.27
Hercules, CA (city) Contra Costa County	5,246	26.92
Halawa, HI (cdp) Honolulu County	3,735	26.89
Kihei, HI (cdp) Maui County	4,246	25.35
Wailuku, HI (cdp) Maui County	3,001	24.41
Vallejo, CA (city) Solano County	27,098	23.21
Mililani Town, HI (cdp) Honolulu County	6,134	21.44
Nanakuli, HI (cdp) Honolulu County	2,289	21.17
Pearl City, HI (cdp) Honolulu County	6,460	20.85
Union City, CA (city) Alameda County	13,716	20.51
Carson, CA (city) Los Angeles County	18,223	20.31
Waimalu, HI (cdp) Honolulu County	5,951	20.26
National City, CA (city) San Diego County	10,207	18.81
South San Francisco, CA (city) San Mateo County	11,127	18.38
Hilo, HI (cdp) Hawaii County	7,329	17.98
Delano, CA (city) Kern County	6,372	16.41
Honolulu, HI (cdp) Honolulu County	60,922	16.39
Milpitas, CA (city) Santa Clara County	10,265	16.37
Suisun City, CA (city) Solano County	3,597	13.77
Walnut, CA (city) Los Angeles County	3,912	13.04
Kaneohe, HI (cdp) Honolulu County	4,513	12.91
Cerritos, CA (city) Los Angeles County	6,560	12.74
Bergenfield, NJ (borough) Bergen County	3,254	12.40
West Carson, CA (cdp) Los Angeles County	2,584	12.22
Lathrop, CA (city) San Joaquin County	1,251	11.98
Pinole, CA (city) Contra Costa County	2,144	11.26
Artesia, CA (city) Los Angeles County	1,806	11.03
La Presa, CA (cdp) San Diego County	3,404	10.40
Hayward, CA (city) Alameda County	14,443	10.31
Silverdale, WA (cdp) Kitsap County	1,628	10.29
Pacifica, CA (city) San Mateo County	3,925	10.22
Pittsburg, CA (city) Contra Costa County	5,764	10.15
Oak Harbor, WA (city) Island County	1,976	9.98
West Covina, CA (city) Los Angeles County	10,469	9.96
Newark, CA (city) Alameda County	4,078	9.60
Fort Washington, MD (cdp) Prince George's County	2,242	9.40
San Bruno, CA (city) San Mateo County	3,634	9.05
San Leandro, CA (city) Alameda County	7,153	9.00
Alameda, CA (city) Alameda County	6,406	8.87
Chula Vista, CA (city) San Diego County	15,001	8.64
Bryn Mawr-Skyway, WA (cdp) King County	1,203	8.61
Chino Hills, CA (city) San Bernardino County	5,738	8.59
Loma Linda, CA (city) San Bernardino County	1,574	8.43
Lemoore, CA (city) Kings County	1,635	8.29
San Lorenzo, CA (cdp) Alameda County	1,793	8.19
Kailua, HI (cdp) Honolulu County	2,969	8.13
La Palma, CA (city) Orange County	1,220	7.92
Stockton, CA (city) San Joaquin County	19,232	7.89
Fairfield, CA (city) Solano County	7,534	7.83
Marina, CA (city) Monterey County	1,831	7.29
Buena Park, CA (city) Orange County	5,570	7.12
Duarte, CA (city) Los Angeles County	1,530	7.12
San Diego, CA (city) San Diego County	86,920	7.10
Imperial Beach, CA (city) San Diego County	1,910	7.08
Bay Point, CA (cdp) Contra Costa County	1,525	7.08
Rowland Heights, CA (cdp) Los Angeles County	3,425	7.05
Laguna, CA (cdp) Sacramento County	2,402	7.00
Jersey City, NJ (city) Hudson County	16,777	6.99
Morton Grove, IL (village) Cook County	1,569	6.99
San Pablo, CA (city) Contra Costa County	2,086	6.90
Fremont, CA (city) Alameda County	13,863	6.82
Ashland, CA (cdp) Alameda County	1,418	6.82
New Milford, NJ (borough) Bergen County	1,119	6.82
Lakewood, CA (city) Los Angeles County	5,372	6.77
Seaside, CA (city) Monterey County	2,074	6.54
Vineyard, CA (cdp) Sacramento County	654	6.47
Santa Clara, CA (city) Santa Clara County	6,592	6.44
Bonita, CA (cdp) San Diego County	778	6.27
Glendale, CA (city) Los Angeles County	12,099	6.21
Belleville, NJ (cdp) Essex County	2,224	6.19
San Jose, CA (city) Santa Clara County	55,120	6.16
Elk Grove, CA (cdp) Sacramento County	3,661	6.10
Glendale Heights, IL (village) Du Page County	1,926	6.06
San Francisco, CA (city) San Francisco County	45,793	5.90
Diamond Bar, CA (city) Los Angeles County	3,298	5.86
Oxnard, CA (city) Ventura County	9,907	5.82
Skokie, IL (village) Cook County	3,594	5.67
Bremerton, WA (city) Kitsap County	2,086	5.60
Port Hueneme, CA (city) Ventura County	1,200	5.49
Cypress, CA (city) Orange County	2,463	5.33
Valinda, CA (cdp) Los Angeles County	1,153	5.29
Antioch, CA (city) Contra Costa County	4,775	5.27
Sunnyvale, CA (city) Santa Clara County	6,880	5.22
Bellflower, CA (city) Los Angeles County	3,787	5.20
Cherryland, CA (cdp) Alameda County	707	5.11
Tracy, CA (city) San Joaquin County	2,891	5.08
Dumont, NJ (borough) Bergen County	884	5.05
Florin, CA (cdp) Sacramento County	1,390	5.03
Benicia, CA (city) Solano County	1,331	4.95
South Lake Tahoe, CA (city) El Dorado County	1,168	4.95
La Mirada, CA (city) Los Angeles County	2,281	4.88
Salinas, CA (city) Monterey County	7,345	4.86
Norwalk, CA (city) Los Angeles County	5,019	4.86
Juneau, AK (city and borough) Juneau Borough	1,478	4.81
Baldwin Park, CA (city) Los Angeles County	3,591	4.74
Long Beach, CA (city) Los Angeles County	21,502	4.66
Lincolnwood, IL (village) Cook County	575	4.65
Friendly, MD (cdp) Prince George's County	493	4.51
Fords, NJ (cdp) Middlesex County	677	4.50
Foothill Ranch, CA (cdp) Orange County	487	4.47
Piscataway, NJ (township) Middlesex County	2,235	4.43
Kaneohe Station, HI (cdp) Honolulu County	523	4.42
Millbrae, CA (city) San Mateo County	913	4.41
Cascade-Fairwood, WA (cdp) King County	1,511	4.37
Santa Maria, CA (city) Santa Barbara County	3,306	4.27
Foster City, CA (city) San Mateo County	1,208	4.19
Lemon Grove, CA (city) San Diego County	1,044	4.19
El Sobrante, CA (cdp) Contra Costa County	508	4.14
Concord, CA (city) Contra Costa County	5,016	4.12
Virginia Beach, VA (independent city) Virginia Beach city	17,429	4.10
Spring Valley, NV (cdp) Clark County	4,813	4.10
South San Jose Hills, CA (cdp) Los Angeles County	829	4.10
Darien, IL (city) Du Page County	930	4.07
East Hill-Meridian, WA (cdp) King County	1,180	4.03
Gardena, CA (city) Los Angeles County	2,320	4.02
Union, NJ (cdp) Union County	2,184	4.01
Spring Valley, CA (cdp) San Diego County	1,068	4.01
Oceanside, CA (city) San Diego County	6,390	3.97
Myrtle Grove, FL (cdp) Escambia County	683	3.97
Citrus, CA (cdp) Los Angeles County	414	3.91
Alum Rock, CA (cdp) Santa Clara County	525	3.89
Poway, CA (city) San Diego County	1,858	3.87
Burbank, CA (city) Los Angeles County	3,860	3.85
Baywood-Los Osos, CA (cdp) San Luis Obispo County	551	3.84
Sunrise Manor, NV (cdp) Clark County	5,971	3.82
San Mateo, CA (city) San Mateo County	3,478	3.76
Richmond, CA (city) Contra Costa County	3,705	3.73
Mountain View, CA (city) Santa Clara County	2,638	3.73
Covina, CA (city) Los Angeles County	1,707	3.64
Mountlake Terrace, WA (city) Snohomish County	741	3.64
Paradise, NV (cdp) Clark County	6,743	3.62
Renton, WA (city) King County	1,805	3.61
Bloomfield, NJ (cdp) Essex County	1,714	3.59
Enterprise, NV (cdp) Clark County	524	3.57
Shoreline, WA (city) King County	1,871	3.53
Temecula, CA (city) Riverside County	2,034	3.52
Moreno Valley, CA (city) Riverside County	4,970	3.49
Seattle, WA (city) King County	19,567	3.47
Twentynine Palms, CA (city) San Bernardino County	512	3.47
Azusa, CA (city) Los Angeles County	1,545	3.46
Secaucus, NJ (town) Hudson County	549	3.45
Stafford, TX (city) Fort Bend County	533	3.40
Gurnee, IL (village) Lake County	977	3.39

Notes: (cdp) census designated place; Refer to the Explanation of Data in the front of the book for more detailed information.

Asian: Hmong

Top 150 Places Sorted by Number

(Based on all places, regardless of population)

Place	Number	%
Saint Paul, MN (city) Ramsey County	26,509	9.23
Fresno, CA (city) Fresno County	20,390	4.77
Sacramento, CA (city) Sacramento County	12,610	3.10
Minneapolis, MN (city) Hennepin County	10,489	2.74
Milwaukee, WI (city) Milwaukee County	8,418	1.41
Stockton, CA (city) San Joaquin County	5,401	2.22
Merced, CA (city) Merced County	4,464	6.99
Wausau, WI (city) Marathon County	3,674	9.56
Green Bay, WI (city) Brown County	2,858	2.79
Sheboygan, WI (city) Sheboygan County	2,792	5.50
Appleton, WI (city) Outagamie County	2,645	3.77
Parkway-South Sacramento, CA (cdp) Sacramento County	2,553	7.00
Linda, CA (cdp) Yuba County	2,174	16.13
Madison, WI (city) Dane County	2,053	0.99
La Crosse, WI (city) La Crosse County	1,893	3.65
Detroit, MI (city) Wayne County	1,882	0.20
Eau Claire, WI (city) Eau Claire County	1,776	2.88
Clovis, CA (city) Fresno County	1,728	2.52
San Diego, CA (city) San Diego County	1,518	0.12
Brooklyn Center, MN (city) Hennepin County	1,448	4.96
Oshkosh, WI (city) Winnebago County	1,434	2.28
Portland, OR (city) Multnomah County	1,342	0.25
Brooklyn Park, MN (city) Hennepin County	1,292	1.92
Westminster, CO (city) Adams County	1,123	1.11
Manitowoc, WI (city) Manitowoc County	1,042	3.06
Kansas City, KS (city) Wyandotte County	986	0.67
Florin, CA (cdp) Sacramento County	950	3.44
Providence, RI (city) Providence County	946	0.54
Chico, CA (city) Butte County	921	1.54
Pontiac, MI (city) Oakland County	884	1.33
Lansing, MI (city) Ingham County	798	0.67
Charlotte, NC (city) Mecklenburg County	797	0.15
Warren, MI (city) Macomb County	780	0.56
Stevens Point, WI (city) Portage County	773	3.15
Maplewood, MN (city) Ramsey County	714	2.04
Hickory, NC (city) Catawba County	705	1.89
Visalia, CA (city) Tulare County	700	0.76
Fitchburg, MA (city) Worcester County	688	1.76
South Oroville, CA (cdp) Butte County	682	8.86
Thermalito, CA (cdp) Butte County	614	10.16
Banning, CA (city) Riverside County	595	2.53
Oroville, CA (city) Butte County	574	4.41
Weston, WI (village) Marathon County	523	4.33
Modesto, CA (city) Stanislaus County	513	0.27
Atwater, CA (city) Merced County	505	2.18
Wisconsin Rapids, WI (city) Wood County	489	2.65
Santa Ana, CA (city) Orange County	467	0.14
Lompoc, CA (city) Santa Barbara County	445	1.08
Willows, CA (city) Glenn County	431	6.93
Olivehurst, CA (cdp) Yuba County	416	3.76
Long Beach, CA (city) Los Angeles County	416	0.09
Fond du Lac, WI (city) Fond du Lac County	408	0.97
Tulsa, OK (city) Tulsa County	407	0.10
Albemarle, NC (city) Stanly County	395	2.52
Eureka, CA (city) Humboldt County	352	1.35
Elk Grove, CA (cdp) Sacramento County	343	0.57
Rancho Cordova, CA (cdp) Sacramento County	326	0.59
Spokane, WA (city) Spokane County	318	0.16
Anchorage, AK (municipality) Anchorage Borough	299	0.11
Menomonie, WI (city) Dunn County	293	1.96
Woodbury, MN (city) Washington County	291	0.63
Thornton, CO (city) Adams County	288	0.35
Akron, OH (city) Summit County	280	0.13
Statesville, NC (city) Iredell County	275	1.18
Arden-Arcade, CA (cdp) Sacramento County	271	0.28
Winton, CA (cdp) Merced County	270	3.06
Broomfield, CO (city) Boulder County	268	0.70
Brockton, MA (city) Plymouth County	259	0.27
Kaukauna, WI (city) Outagamie County	256	1.97
Onalaska, WI (city) La Crosse County	253	1.70
West Sacramento, CA (city) Yolo County	249	0.79
Gresham, OR (city) Multnomah County	249	0.28
Marysville, CA (city) Yuba County	240	1.96
North Highlands, CA (cdp) Sacramento County	232	0.53
Rochester, MN (city) Olmsted County	230	0.27
Vadnais Heights, MN (city) Ramsey County	228	1.74
Winona, MN (city) Winona County	227	0.84
Oakdale, MN (city) Washington County	219	0.82
Porterville, CA (city) Tulare County	216	0.55
Arvada, CO (city) Jefferson County	215	0.21
Menomonie, WI (town) Dunn County	208	6.55
Kennedy, CA (cdp) San Joaquin County	207	6.32
Newton, NC (city) Catawba County	206	1.64
Federal Heights, CO (city) Adams County	203	1.68
Tracy, MN (city) Lyon County	189	8.33
Menasha, WI (city) Winnebago County	189	1.16
Blaine, MN (city) Anoka County	188	0.42
Garden Grove, CA (city) Orange County	188	0.11
Garden Acres, CA (cdp) San Joaquin County	182	1.87
Des Moines, IA (city) Polk County	177	0.09
Syracuse, NY (city) Onondaga County	174	0.12
Chicago, IL (city) Cook County	173	0.01
Two Rivers, WI (city) Manitowoc County	170	1.35
Holmen, WI (village) La Crosse County	165	2.66
Lafayette, CO (city) Boulder County	160	0.69
Duluth, MN (city) Saint Louis County	157	0.18
Berkley, CO (cdp) Adams County	156	1.45
San Jose, CA (city) Santa Clara County	156	0.02
Tulare, CA (city) Tulare County	153	0.35
Menasha, WI (town) Winnebago County	152	0.96
Northglenn, CO (city) Adams County	145	0.46
East Cocalico, PA (township) Lancaster County	142	1.43
Crescent City North, CA (cdp) Del Norte County	140	3.48
Philadelphia, PA (city) Philadelphia County	140	0.01
Suisun City, CA (city) Solano County	136	0.52
Sherrelwood, CO (cdp) Adams County	135	0.76
Seattle, WA (city) King County	132	0.02
Valdese, NC (town) Burke County	131	2.92
Auburn, GA (city) Barrow County	128	1.85
Little Canada, MN (city) Ramsey County	128	1.31
Fitchburg, WI (city) Dane County	127	0.62
Mount Airy, NC (city) Surry County	123	1.45
Cottage Grove, MN (city) Washington County	122	0.40
Roseville, MN (city) Ramsey County	122	0.36
Riverton-Boulevard Park, WA (cdp) King County	121	1.08
Leominster, MA (city) Worcester County	120	0.29
Long View, NC (town) Catawba County	119	2.52
Rib Mountain, WI (town) Marathon County	119	1.57
Columbia Heights, MN (city) Anoka County	119	0.64
White Bear Lake, MN (city) Ramsey County	118	0.49
Taft Mosswood, CA (cdp) San Joaquin County	117	8.43
Conover, NC (city) Catawba County	116	1.76
Inver Grove Heights, MN (city) Dakota County	115	0.39
Connelly Springs, NC (town) Burke County	114	6.28
Glen Alpine, NC (town) Burke County	110	10.09
Fridley, MN (city) Anoka County	110	0.40
Sun Prairie, WI (city) Dane County	108	0.53
Missoula, MT (city) Missoula County	108	0.19
Eagan, MN (city) Dakota County	107	0.17
SeaTac, WA (city) King County	106	0.42
Crescent City, CA (city) Del Norte County	105	2.62
Sheboygan, WI (town) Sheboygan County	105	1.79
Neenah, WI (city) Winnebago County	105	0.43
Goleta, CA (cdp) Santa Barbara County	104	0.19
Home Garden, CA (cdp) Kings County	102	5.99
Salem, OR (city) Marion County	101	0.07
Rothschild, WI (village) Marathon County	100	2.01
Saint Stephens, NC (cdp) Catawba County	100	1.06
Coon Rapids, MN (city) Anoka County	100	0.16
Los Angeles, CA (city) Los Angeles County	100	0.00
Morganton, NC (city) Burke County	98	0.57
Davis, CA (city) Yolo County	98	0.16
Aurora, IL (city) Kane County	95	0.07
Fremont, CA (city) Alameda County	95	0.05
Palermo, CA (cdp) Butte County	93	1.63
Springfield, MA (city) Hampden County	93	0.06
Moreno Valley, CA (city) Riverside County	92	0.06
Bellevue Town, WI (cdp) Brown County	91	0.77
Anaheim, CA (city) Orange County	89	0.03
Turlock, CA (city) Stanislaus County	88	0.16

Notes: (cdp) census designated place; Refer to the Explanation of Data in the front of the book for more detailed information.

Asian: Hmong

Top 150 Places Sorted by Percent

(Based on all places, regardless of population)

Place	Number	%
Linda, CA (cdp) Yuba County	2,174	16.13
Thermalito, CA (cdp) Butte County	614	10.16
Popple River, WI (town) Forest County	8	10.13
Glen Alpine, NC (town) Burke County	110	10.09
Wausau, WI (city) Marathon County	3,674	9.56
Parrish, WI (town) Langlade County	10	9.26
Saint Paul, MN (city) Ramsey County	26,509	9.23
South Oroville, CA (cdp) Butte County	682	8.86
Taft Mosswood, CA (cdp) San Joaquin County	117	8.43
Tracy, MN (city) Lyon County	189	8.33
Parkway-South Sacramento, CA (cdp) Sacramento County	2,553	7.00
Merced, CA (city) Merced County	4,464	6.99
Willows, CA (city) Glenn County	431	6.93
Menomonie, WI (town) Dunn County	208	6.55
Kennedy, CA (cdp) San Joaquin County	207	6.32
Connelly Springs, NC (town) Burke County	114	6.28
Home Garden, CA (cdp) Kings County	102	5.99
Taylors Falls, MN (city) Chisago County	57	5.99
Sheboygan, WI (city) Sheboygan County	2,792	5.50
Kekoskee, WI (village) Dodge County	9	5.33
Brooklyn Center, MN (city) Hennepin County	1,448	4.96
Fresno, CA (city) Fresno County	20,390	4.77
Portage, MN (township) Saint Louis County	8	4.52
Oroville, CA (city) Butte County	574	4.41
Weston, WI (village) Marathon County	523	4.33
Wilson, WI (village) Saint Croix County	7	3.98
Drexel, NC (town) Burke County	74	3.82
Appleton, WI (city) Outagamie County	2,645	3.77
Olivehurst, CA (cdp) Yuba County	416	3.76
Coates, MN (city) Dakota County	6	3.68
La Crosse, WI (city) La Crosse County	1,893	3.65
Peru, WI (town) Dunn County	9	3.64
Hildebran, NC (town) Burke County	53	3.60
Crescent City North, CA (cdp) Del Norte County	140	3.48
Clifton, MN (township) Lyon County	10	3.47
Florin, CA (cdp) Sacramento County	950	3.44
Otter Creek, WI (town) Eau Claire County	18	3.39
Port Edwards, WI (village) Wood County	63	3.24
Brookford, NC (town) Catawba County	14	3.23
Stevens Point, WI (city) Portage County	773	3.15
Braselton, GA (town) Jackson County	38	3.15
Swede Grove, MN (township) Meeker County	13	3.14
Sacramento, CA (city) Sacramento County	12,610	3.10
Manitowoc, WI (city) Manitowoc County	1,042	3.06
Winton, CA (cdp) Merced County	270	3.06
Watterstown, WI (town) Grant County	11	3.04
Rutherford College, NC (town) Burke County	39	3.02
Valdese, NC (town) Burke County	131	2.92
Eau Claire, WI (city) Eau Claire County	1,776	2.88
Whiting, WI (village) Portage County	50	2.84
Green Bay, WI (city) Brown County	2,858	2.79
Minneapolis, MN (city) Hennepin County	10,489	2.74
Holmen, WI (village) La Crosse County	165	2.66
Wisconsin Rapids, WI (city) Wood County	489	2.65
Crescent City, CA (city) Del Norte County	105	2.62
Banning, CA (city) Riverside County	595	2.53
Clovis, CA (city) Fresno County	1,728	2.52
Albemarle, NC (city) Stanly County	395	2.52
Long View, NC (town) Catawba County	119	2.52
Bear Lake, MI (village) Manistee County	8	2.52
Elk Grove, WI (town) Lafayette County	11	2.38
Oshkosh, WI (city) Winnebago County	1,434	2.28
Cary, WI (town) Wood County	11	2.26
Union, WI (town) Eau Claire County	54	2.25
Jefferson, WI (town) Monroe County	18	2.25
Central Pacolet, SC (town) Spartanburg County	6	2.25
Stockton, CA (city) San Joaquin County	5,401	2.22
Hortonville, WI (village) Outagamie County	52	2.21
Atwater, CA (city) Merced County	505	2.18
Leslie, MN (township) Todd County	15	2.17
Rudolph, WI (town) Wood County	25	2.15
Rudolph, WI (village) Wood County	9	2.13
Star Prairie, WI (village) Saint Croix County	12	2.09
Maplewood, MN (city) Ramsey County	714	2.04
Rothschild, WI (village) Marathon County	100	2.01
Clinton Falls, MN (township) Steele County	9	1.99
Fairchild, WI (town) Eau Claire County	7	1.99
Hamburg, WI (town) Marathon County	18	1.98
Kaukauna, WI (city) Outagamie County	256	1.97
Menomonie, WI (city) Dunn County	293	1.96
Marysville, CA (city) Yuba County	240	1.96
Wheatland, CA (city) Yuba County	44	1.93
Blooming Prairie, MN (township) Steele County	10	1.93
Brooklyn Park, MN (city) Hennepin County	1,292	1.92
Elk Mound, WI (village) Dunn County	15	1.91
Portland, WI (town) Monroe County	13	1.90
Hickory, NC (city) Catawba County	705	1.89
Garden Acres, CA (cdp) San Joaquin County	182	1.87
Elk Mound, WI (town) Dunn County	21	1.87
Auburn, GA (city) Barrow County	128	1.85
Holland, WI (town) La Crosse County	55	1.81
Sheboygan, WI (town) Sheboygan County	105	1.79
Mount Calvary, WI (village) Fond du Lac County	17	1.78
Fitchburg, MA (city) Worcester County	688	1.76
Conover, NC (city) Catawba County	116	1.76
Mountain View, NC (cdp) Catawba County	66	1.75
Seneca, WI (town) Wood County	21	1.75
Plover, WI (town) Marathon County	12	1.75
Vadnais Heights, MN (city) Ramsey County	228	1.74
Salem, NC (cdp) Burke County	51	1.74
Stettin, WI (town) Marathon County	38	1.73
Onalaska, WI (city) La Crosse County	253	1.70
Carnation, WA (city) King County	32	1.69
Federal Heights, CO (city) Adams County	203	1.68
Mount Gilead, NC (town) Montgomery County	23	1.66
Dover, WI (town) Buffalo County	8	1.65
Newton, NC (city) Catawba County	206	1.64
Palermo, CA (cdp) Butte County	93	1.63
Peachland, NC (town) Anson County	9	1.62
Springfield, WI (town) Saint Croix County	13	1.61
Maine, MN (township) Otter Tail County	11	1.60
Wausau, WI (town) Marathon County	35	1.58
Rib Mountain, WI (town) Marathon County	119	1.57
Bertsch-Oceanview, CA (cdp) Del Norte County	35	1.56
Kingston, WI (town) Green Lake County	14	1.56
Chico, CA (city) Butte County	921	1.54
Kingstown, NC (town) Cleveland County	13	1.54
Bethlehem, GA (town) Barrow County	11	1.54
Boon Lake, MN (township) Renville County	6	1.50
Plover, WI (town) Portage County	36	1.49
Easton, CA (cdp) Fresno County	29	1.48
Tranquillity, CA (cdp) Fresno County	12	1.48
Brighton, WI (town) Marathon County	9	1.47
Schofield, WI (city) Marathon County	31	1.46
Berkley, CO (cdp) Adams County	156	1.45
Mount Airy, NC (city) Surry County	123	1.45
Lyons, MN (township) Lyon County	3	1.44
East Cocalico, PA (township) Lancaster County	142	1.43
Milwaukee, WI (city) Milwaukee County	8,418	1.41
New Tulsa, OK (town) Wagoner County	8	1.41
Rock Creek, WI (town) Dunn County	11	1.39
Richfield, NC (town) Stanly County	7	1.36
Eureka, CA (city) Humboldt County	352	1.35
Two Rivers, WI (city) Manitowoc County	170	1.35
Pontiac, MI (city) Oakland County	884	1.33
Little Canada, MN (city) Ramsey County	128	1.31
Richfield, WI (town) Wood County	20	1.31
Jackson, WI (town) Burnett County	10	1.31
Warner, WI (town) Clark County	8	1.28
Oshkosh, WI (town) Winnebago County	41	1.27
Weston, WI (town) Dunn County	8	1.27
Birnamwood, WI (village) Shawano County	10	1.26
Dane, WI (village) Dane County	10	1.25
Grant, WI (town) Shawano County	12	1.23
Easton, WI (town) Marathon County	13	1.22
Hallie, WI (town) Chippewa County	57	1.21
Unity, WI (town) Clark County	9	1.21
Wyocena, WI (village) Columbia County	8	1.20
Pine Springs, MN (city) Washington County	5	1.19
Statesville, NC (city) Iredell County	275	1.18

Notes: (cdp) census designated place; Refer to the Explanation of Data in the front of the book for more detailed information.

Asian: Hmong

Top 150 Places Sorted by Percent

(Based on places with populations of 10,000 or more)

Place	Number	%
Linda, CA (cdp) Yuba County	2,174	16.13
Wausau, WI (city) Marathon County	3,674	9.56
Saint Paul, MN (city) Ramsey County	26,509	9.23
Parkway-South Sacramento, CA (cdp) Sacramento County	2,553	7.00
Merced, CA (city) Merced County	4,464	6.99
Sheboygan, WI (city) Sheboygan County	2,792	5.50
Brooklyn Center, MN (city) Hennepin County	1,448	4.96
Fresno, CA (city) Fresno County	20,390	4.77
Oroville, CA (city) Butte County	574	4.41
Weston, WI (village) Marathon County	523	4.33
Appleton, WI (city) Outagamie County	2,645	3.77
Olivehurst, CA (cdp) Yuba County	416	3.76
La Crosse, WI (city) La Crosse County	1,893	3.65
Florin, CA (cdp) Sacramento County	950	3.44
Stevens Point, WI (city) Portage County	773	3.15
Sacramento, CA (city) Sacramento County	12,610	3.10
Manitowoc, WI (city) Manitowoc County	1,042	3.06
Eau Claire, WI (city) Eau Claire County	1,776	2.88
Green Bay, WI (city) Brown County	2,858	2.79
Minneapolis, MN (city) Hennepin County	10,489	2.74
Wisconsin Rapids, WI (city) Wood County	489	2.65
Banning, CA (city) Riverside County	595	2.53
Clovis, CA (city) Fresno County	1,728	2.52
Albemarle, NC (city) Stanly County	395	2.52
Oshkosh, WI (city) Winnebago County	1,434	2.28
Stockton, CA (city) San Joaquin County	5,401	2.22
Atwater, CA (city) Merced County	505	2.18
Maplewood, MN (city) Ramsey County	714	2.04
Kaukauna, WI (city) Outagamie County	256	1.97
Menomonie, WI (city) Dunn County	293	1.96
Marysville, CA (city) Yuba County	240	1.96
Brooklyn Park, MN (city) Hennepin County	1,292	1.92
Hickory, NC (city) Catawba County	705	1.89
Fitchburg, MA (city) Worcester County	688	1.76
Vadnais Heights, MN (city) Ramsey County	228	1.74
Onalaska, WI (city) La Crosse County	253	1.70
Federal Heights, CO (city) Adams County	203	1.68
Newton, NC (city) Catawba County	206	1.64
Chico, CA (city) Butte County	921	1.54
Berkley, CO (cdp) Adams County	156	1.45
Milwaukee, WI (city) Milwaukee County	8,418	1.41
Eureka, CA (city) Humboldt County	352	1.35
Two Rivers, WI (city) Manitowoc County	170	1.35
Pontiac, MI (city) Oakland County	884	1.33
Statesville, NC (city) Iredell County	275	1.18
Menasha, WI (city) Winnebago County	189	1.16
Westminster, CO (city) Adams County	1,123	1.11
Lompoc, CA (city) Santa Barbara County	445	1.08
Riverton-Boulevard Park, WA (cdp) King County	121	1.08
Madison, WI (city) Dane County	2,053	0.99
Fond du Lac, WI (city) Fond du Lac County	408	0.97
Menasha, WI (town) Winnebago County	152	0.96
Winona, MN (city) Winona County	227	0.84
Oakdale, MN (city) Washington County	219	0.82
West Sacramento, CA (city) Yolo County	249	0.79
Bellevue Town, WI (cdp) Brown County	91	0.77
Visalia, CA (city) Tulare County	700	0.76
Sherrelwood, CO (cdp) Adams County	135	0.76
Broomfield, CO (city) Boulder County	268	0.70
Lafayette, CO (city) Boulder County	160	0.69
Livingston, CA (city) Merced County	72	0.69
Kansas City, KS (city) Wyandotte County	986	0.67
Lansing, MI (city) Ingham County	798	0.67
North Saint Paul, MN (city) Ramsey County	79	0.66
Rio Linda, CA (cdp) Sacramento County	69	0.66
Columbia Heights, MN (city) Anoka County	119	0.64
Woodbury, MN (city) Washington County	291	0.63
Kingsgate, WA (cdp) King County	77	0.63
Fitchburg, WI (city) Dane County	127	0.62
Rancho Cordova, CA (cdp) Sacramento County	326	0.59
Elk Grove, CA (cdp) Sacramento County	343	0.57
Morganton, NC (city) Burke County	98	0.57
Mounds View, MN (city) Ramsey County	73	0.57
Warren, MI (city) Macomb County	780	0.56
Porterville, CA (city) Tulare County	216	0.55
Providence, RI (city) Providence County	946	0.54
North Highlands, CA (cdp) Sacramento County	232	0.53
Sun Prairie, WI (city) Dane County	108	0.53
Suisun City, CA (city) Solano County	136	0.52
White Bear Lake, MN (city) Ramsey County	118	0.49
Troutdale, OR (city) Multnomah County	66	0.48
Northglenn, CO (city) Adams County	145	0.46
Grand Chute, WI (town) Outagamie County	81	0.44
Little Chute, WI (village) Outagamie County	46	0.44
Neenah, WI (city) Winnebago County	105	0.43
Hazel Park, MI (city) Oakland County	82	0.43
Blaine, MN (city) Anoka County	188	0.42
SeaTac, WA (city) King County	106	0.42
Ashwaubenon, WI (village) Brown County	72	0.41
Cottage Grove, MN (city) Washington County	122	0.40
Fridley, MN (city) Anoka County	110	0.40
Winder, GA (city) Barrow County	41	0.40
Inver Grove Heights, MN (city) Dakota County	115	0.39
Roseville, MN (city) Ramsey County	122	0.36
Robbinsdale, MN (city) Hennepin County	51	0.36
Thornton, CO (city) Adams County	288	0.35
Tulare, CA (city) Tulare County	153	0.35
Howard, WI (village) Brown County	47	0.35
Crystal, MN (city) Hennepin County	74	0.33
Lilburn, GA (city) Gwinnett County	37	0.33
Superior, WI (city) Douglas County	82	0.30
Four Corners, OR (cdp) Marion County	42	0.30
Leominster, MA (city) Worcester County	120	0.29
West Saint Paul, MN (city) Dakota County	57	0.29
Arden-Arcade, CA (cdp) Sacramento County	271	0.28
Gresham, OR (city) Multnomah County	249	0.28
Owatonna, MN (city) Steele County	63	0.28
Golden Valley, MN (city) Hennepin County	57	0.28
Marshall, MN (city) Lyon County	36	0.28
Plover, WI (village) Portage County	29	0.28
Modesto, CA (city) Stanislaus County	513	0.27
Brockton, MA (city) Plymouth County	259	0.27
Rochester, MN (city) Olmsted County	230	0.27
Rosemont, CA (cdp) Sacramento County	59	0.26
White Bear, MN (township) Ramsey County	29	0.26
Portland, OR (city) Multnomah County	1,342	0.25
Faribault, MN (city) Rice County	51	0.24
Whitewater, WI (city) Walworth County	31	0.23
Chippewa Falls, WI (city) Chippewa County	29	0.22
Stafford, CT (town) Tolland County	25	0.22
Arvada, CO (city) Jefferson County	215	0.21
Bay City, MI (city) Bay County	78	0.21
Lathrop, CA (city) San Joaquin County	22	0.21
Richfield, WI (town) Washington County	22	0.21
Detroit, MI (city) Wayne County	1,882	0.20
Shoreview, MN (city) Ramsey County	51	0.20
Arcata, CA (city) Humboldt County	33	0.20
Bryn Mawr-Skyway, WA (cdp) King County	28	0.20
Glendale, WI (city) Milwaukee County	27	0.20
De Witt, MI (township) Clinton County	24	0.20
Missoula, MT (city) Missoula County	108	0.19
Goleta, CA (cdp) Santa Barbara County	104	0.19
South Saint Paul, MN (city) Dakota County	39	0.19
Lino Lakes, MN (city) Anoka County	32	0.19
Ephrata, PA (borough) Lancaster County	25	0.19
Salida, CA (cdp) Stanislaus County	24	0.19
South Yuba City, CA (cdp) Sutter County	24	0.19
Duluth, MN (city) Saint Louis County	157	0.18
Aloha, OR (cdp) Washington County	76	0.18
Yuba City, CA (city) Sutter County	65	0.18
Belvedere Park, GA (cdp) De Kalb County	35	0.18
Ham Lake, MN (city) Anoka County	23	0.18
River Falls, WI (city) Pierce County	23	0.18
Brown Deer, WI (village) Milwaukee County	22	0.18
Salisbury, PA (township) Lancaster County	18	0.18
Eagan, MN (city) Dakota County	107	0.17
Ramsey, MN (city) Anoka County	32	0.17
East Renton Highlands, WA (cdp) King County	23	0.17
Spokane, WA (city) Spokane County	318	0.16
Coon Rapids, MN (city) Anoka County	100	0.16

Notes: (cdp) census designated place; Refer to the Explanation of Data in the front of the book for more detailed information.

Asian: Indian

Top 150 Places Sorted by Number

(Based on all places, regardless of population)

Place	Number	%
New York, NY (city) New York City	206,228	2.58
Los Angeles, CA (city) Los Angeles County	29,604	0.80
San Jose, CA (city) Santa Clara County	28,301	3.16
Chicago, IL (city) Cook County	27,889	0.96
Houston, TX (city) Harris County	22,549	1.15
Fremont, CA (city) Alameda County	21,618	10.63
Edison, NJ (cdp) Middlesex County	17,343	17.75
Jersey City, NJ (city) Hudson County	14,206	5.92
Philadelphia, PA (city) Philadelphia County	14,191	0.94
Sunnyvale, CA (city) Santa Clara County	13,443	10.20
Hempstead, NY (town) Nassau County	11,966	1.58
Santa Clara, CA (city) Santa Clara County	9,163	8.95
Woodbridge, NJ (township) Middlesex County	8,937	9.19
Dallas, TX (city) Dallas County	8,625	0.73
Austin, TX (city) Travis County	8,330	1.27
North Hempstead, NY (town) Nassau County	7,951	3.57
San Diego, CA (city) San Diego County	7,936	0.65
Columbus, OH (city) Franklin County	7,025	0.99
Sacramento, CA (city) Sacramento County	6,838	1.68
Plano, TX (city) Collin County	6,644	2.99
San Francisco, CA (city) San Francisco County	6,616	0.85
Irving, TX (city) Dallas County	6,594	3.44
Piscataway, NJ (township) Middlesex County	6,307	12.49
Union City, CA (city) Alameda County	6,195	9.26
Oyster Bay, NY (town) Nassau County	5,415	1.84
Naperville, IL (city) Du Page County	5,261	4.10
Phoenix, AZ (city) Maricopa County	5,169	0.39
Boston, MA (city) Suffolk County	5,154	0.87
Hayward, CA (city) Alameda County	5,141	3.67
Charlotte, NC (city) Mecklenburg County	5,017	0.93
Yonkers, NY (city) Westchester County	5,008	2.55
Schaumburg, IL (village) Cook County	5,006	6.64
Fresno, CA (city) Fresno County	4,993	1.17
Troy, MI (city) Oakland County	4,789	5.92
Irvine, CA (city) Orange County	4,762	3.33
Carrollton, TX (city) Denton County	4,625	4.22
Sugar Land, TX (city) Fort Bend County	4,573	7.22
Cupertino, CA (city) Santa Clara County	4,546	8.99
Milpitas, CA (city) Santa Clara County	4,495	7.17
Anaheim, CA (city) Orange County	4,415	1.35
Parsippany-Troy Hills, NJ (township) Morris County	4,251	8.39
Skokie, IL (village) Cook County	4,142	6.54
South Brunswick, NJ (township) Middlesex County	3,954	10.48
San Antonio, TX (city) Bexar County	3,927	0.34
Arlington, VA (cdp) Arlington County	3,845	2.03
Brookhaven, NY (town) Suffolk County	3,738	0.83
Indianapolis, IN (special city) Marion County	3,728	0.48
Detroit, MI (city) Wayne County	3,700	0.39
Seattle, WA (city) King County	3,680	0.65
Franklin, NJ (township) Somerset County	3,574	7.02
Ann Arbor, MI (city) Washtenaw County	3,527	3.09
Canton, MI (cdp) Wayne County	3,523	4.61
Bakersfield, CA (city) Kern County	3,521	1.43
Washington, DC (city) District of Columbia	3,507	0.61
Farmington Hills, MI (city) Oakland County	3,482	4.24
Arlington, TX (city) Tarrant County	3,439	1.03
Plainsboro, NJ (township) Middlesex County	3,431	16.97
Cary, NC (town) Wake County	3,379	3.57
Hoffman Estates, IL (village) Cook County	3,371	6.81
Islip, NY (town) Suffolk County	3,360	1.04
Mount Prospect, IL (village) Cook County	3,325	5.91
Garland, TX (city) Dallas County	3,321	1.54
Oklahoma City, OK (city) Oklahoma County	3,249	0.64
Old Bridge, NJ (township) Middlesex County	3,219	5.32
Mountain View, CA (city) Santa Clara County	3,206	4.53
Jacksonville, FL (special city) Duval County	3,163	0.43
North Brunswick Township, NJ (cdp) Middlesex County	3,158	8.70
Bellevue, WA (city) King County	3,069	2.80
Cerritos, CA (city) Los Angeles County	3,017	5.86
Cambridge, MA (city) Middlesex County	3,001	2.96
Modesto, CA (city) Stanislaus County	2,982	1.58
Nashville-Davidson, TN (special city) Davidson County	2,962	0.54
Fort Worth, TX (city) Tarrant County	2,922	0.55
Iselin, NJ (cdp) Middlesex County	2,912	17.44
Stockton, CA (city) San Joaquin County	2,892	1.19
Glendale Heights, IL (village) Du Page County	2,840	8.94
Raleigh, NC (city) Wake County	2,813	1.02
North Bergen, NJ (township) Hudson County	2,796	4.81
Stamford, CT (city) Fairfield County	2,779	2.37
Milwaukee, WI (city) Milwaukee County	2,779	0.47
South Yuba City, CA (cdp) Sutter County	2,713	21.44
Passaic, NJ (city) Passaic County	2,692	3.97
East Brunswick, NJ (cdp) Middlesex County	2,662	5.69
Sayreville, NJ (borough) Middlesex County	2,657	6.58
Richardson, TX (city) Dallas County	2,640	2.88
Yuba City, CA (city) Sutter County	2,636	7.17
Atlanta, GA (city) Fulton County	2,617	0.63
Lowell, MA (city) Middlesex County	2,616	2.49
Clarkstown, NY (town) Rockland County	2,596	3.16
Sterling Heights, MI (city) Macomb County	2,581	2.07
Denver, CO (city) Denver County	2,578	0.46
Bensalem, PA (township) Bucks County	2,570	4.40
Durham, NC (city) Durham County	2,551	1.36
Torrance, CA (city) Los Angeles County	2,523	1.83
Clifton, NJ (city) Passaic County	2,503	3.18
Memphis, TN (city) Shelby County	2,487	0.38
Greenburgh, NY (town) Westchester County	2,481	2.86
Baltimore, MD (independent city) Baltimore city	2,432	0.37
Diamond Bar, CA (city) Los Angeles County	2,403	4.27
Avenel, NJ (cdp) Middlesex County	2,395	13.65
Mesquite, TX (city) Dallas County	2,378	1.91
Minneapolis, MN (city) Hennepin County	2,369	0.62
Des Plaines, IL (city) Cook County	2,339	3.98
Oakland, CA (city) Alameda County	2,321	0.58
Hanover Park, IL (village) Cook County	2,313	6.04
Princeton Meadows, NJ (cdp) Middlesex County	2,305	17.16
Pembroke Pines, FL (city) Broward County	2,237	1.63
Palatine, IL (village) Cook County	2,229	3.40
Pittsburgh, PA (city) Allegheny County	2,204	0.66
Reston, VA (cdp) Fairfax County	2,197	3.89
Rochester Hills, MI (city) Oakland County	2,169	3.15
Overland Park, KS (city) Johnson County	2,168	1.45
Buena Park, CA (city) Orange County	2,162	2.76
Ramapo, NY (town) Rockland County	2,157	1.98
Huntington, NY (town) Suffolk County	2,156	1.10
Gaithersburg, MD (city) Montgomery County	2,151	4.09
Portland, OR (city) Multnomah County	2,151	0.41
Coral Springs, FL (city) Broward County	2,149	1.83
Upper Darby, PA (township) Delaware County	2,132	2.61
Elmont, NY (cdp) Nassau County	2,113	6.47
Germantown, MD (cdp) Montgomery County	2,073	3.74
Carol Stream, IL (village) Du Page County	2,063	5.10
Amherst, NY (town) Erie County	2,055	1.76
Missouri City, TX (city) Fort Bend County	2,042	3.86
San Mateo, CA (city) San Mateo County	2,039	2.20
Berkeley, CA (city) Alameda County	2,021	1.97
West Bloomfield, MI (township) Oakland County	2,000	3.08
Madison, WI (city) Dane County	1,984	0.95
West Windsor, NJ (township) Mercer County	1,973	9.01
Tampa, FL (city) Hillsborough County	1,955	0.64
Tulsa, OK (city) Tulsa County	1,933	0.49
Colorado Springs, CO (city) El Paso County	1,908	0.53
Fullerton, CA (city) Orange County	1,903	1.51
Long Beach, CA (city) Los Angeles County	1,897	0.41
Pleasanton, CA (city) Alameda County	1,894	2.98
Concord, CA (city) Contra Costa County	1,891	1.55
Montgomery Village, MD (cdp) Montgomery County	1,889	4.96
Omaha, NE (city) Douglas County	1,889	0.48
Columbia, MD (cdp) Howard County	1,886	2.14
Bridgewater, NJ (township) Somerset County	1,885	4.39
Hicksville, NY (cdp) Nassau County	1,876	4.55
Newark, CA (city) Alameda County	1,875	4.41
Alexandria, VA (independent city) Alexandria city	1,872	1.46
Tempe, AZ (city) Maricopa County	1,843	1.16
Aurora, IL (city) Kane County	1,841	1.29
Centreville, VA (cdp) Fairfax County	1,837	3.78
Chantilly, VA (cdp) Fairfax County	1,806	4.40
Babylon, NY (town) Suffolk County	1,779	0.84
Paterson, NJ (city) Passaic County	1,775	1.19
Woodridge, IL (village) Du Page County	1,769	5.72

Notes: (cdp) census designated place; Refer to the Explanation of Data in the front of the book for more detailed information.

Asian: Indian

Top 150 Places Sorted by Percent

(Based on all places, regardless of population)

Place	Number	%
Millbourne, PA (borough) Delaware County	402	42.63
Plainsboro Center, NJ (cdp) Middlesex County	603	27.30
South Yuba City, CA (cdp) Sutter County	2,713	21.44
Society Hill, NJ (cdp) Middlesex County	713	18.74
Edison, NJ (cdp) Middlesex County	17,343	17.75
Iselin, NJ (cdp) Middlesex County	2,912	17.44
Princeton Meadows, NJ (cdp) Middlesex County	2,305	17.16
Plainsboro, NJ (township) Middlesex County	3,431	16.97
Dayton, NJ (cdp) Middlesex County	980	15.72
Madison Park, NJ (cdp) Middlesex County	985	14.22
Avenel, NJ (cdp) Middlesex County	2,395	13.65
Livingston, CA (city) Merced County	1,366	13.04
Manhasset Hills, NY (cdp) Nassau County	474	12.95
Herricks, NY (cdp) Nassau County	521	12.78
Norman, NC (town) Richmond County	9	12.50
Piscataway, NJ (township) Middlesex County	6,307	12.49
Garden City Park, NY (cdp) Nassau County	941	12.46
New Territory, TX (cdp) Fort Bend County	1,725	12.44
Searingtown, NY (cdp) Nassau County	616	12.24
New Morgan, PA (borough) Berks County	4	11.43
Oak Brook, IL (village) Du Page County	949	10.91
Muttontown, NY (village) Nassau County	365	10.70
Fremont, CA (city) Alameda County	21,618	10.63
South Brunswick, NJ (township) Middlesex County	3,954	10.48
Bellerose Terrace, NY (cdp) Nassau County	224	10.38
Helen, GA (city) White County	44	10.23
Sunnyvale, CA (city) Santa Clara County	13,443	10.20
Union City, CA (city) Alameda County	6,195	9.26
Woodbridge, NJ (township) Middlesex County	8,937	9.19
West Windsor, NJ (township) Mercer County	1,973	9.01
Cupertino, CA (city) Santa Clara County	4,546	8.99
Santa Clara, CA (city) Santa Clara County	9,163	8.95
Glendale Heights, IL (village) Du Page County	2,840	8.94
North Brunswick Township, NJ (cdp) Middlesex County	3,158	8.70
Albertson, NY (cdp) Nassau County	451	8.67
Fords, NJ (cdp) Middlesex County	1,290	8.58
Parsippany-Troy Hills, NJ (township) Morris County	4,251	8.39
Live Oak, CA (city) Sutter County	522	8.38
Tierra Buena, CA (cdp) Sutter County	382	8.33
Merrifield, VA (cdp) Fairfax County	917	8.21
Monmouth Junction, NJ (cdp) Middlesex County	217	7.98
Burtonsville, MD (cdp) Montgomery County	582	7.97
Kerman, CA (city) Fresno County	680	7.95
Farmington, MI (city) Oakland County	813	7.80
Stafford, TX (city) Fort Bend County	1,219	7.77
New Hyde Park, NY (village) Nassau County	739	7.76
North New Hyde Park, NY (cdp) Nassau County	1,122	7.72
Heathcote, NJ (cdp) Middlesex County	357	7.51
Lake, MI (township) Macomb County	6	7.50
South Barrington, IL (village) Cook County	273	7.26
Sugar Land, TX (city) Fort Bend County	4,573	7.22
Scottdale, GA (cdp) De Kalb County	707	7.21
Cloud Lake, FL (town) Palm Beach County	12	7.19
Milpitas, CA (city) Santa Clara County	4,495	7.17
Yuba City, CA (city) Sutter County	2,636	7.17
Burlington, MA (cdp) Middlesex County	1,608	7.03
Franklin, NJ (township) Somerset County	3,574	7.02
Morton Grove, IL (village) Cook County	1,565	6.97
Hoffman Estates, IL (village) Cook County	3,371	6.81
Roselle Park, NJ (borough) Union County	896	6.75
Hamtramck, MI (city) Wayne County	1,537	6.69
Echelon, NJ (cdp) Camden County	695	6.66
Schaumburg, IL (village) Cook County	5,006	6.64
Sayreville, NJ (borough) Middlesex County	2,657	6.58
Idylwood, VA (cdp) Fairfax County	1,051	6.57
Skokie, IL (village) Cook County	4,142	6.54
Kendall Park, NJ (cdp) Middlesex County	589	6.54
Elmont, NY (cdp) Nassau County	2,113	6.47
Lincolnwood, IL (village) Cook County	795	6.43
Burr Ridge, IL (village) Du Page County	664	6.38
Carteret, NJ (borough) Middlesex County	1,311	6.33
Emeryville, CA (city) Alameda County	433	6.29
Caruthers, CA (cdp) Fresno County	132	6.28
Bergenfield, NJ (borough) Bergen County	1,602	6.10
East Windsor, NJ (township) Mercer County	1,520	6.10
Raisin City, CA (cdp) Fresno County	10	6.06
Hanover Park, IL (village) Cook County	2,313	6.04
Four Corners, TX (cdp) Fort Bend County	178	6.03
Foster City, CA (city) San Mateo County	1,720	5.97
Jersey City, NJ (city) Hudson County	14,206	5.92
Troy, MI (city) Oakland County	4,789	5.92
Mount Prospect, IL (village) Cook County	3,325	5.91
Herndon, VA (town) Fairfax County	1,276	5.89
Biola, CA (cdp) Fresno County	61	5.88
Cerritos, CA (city) Los Angeles County	3,017	5.86
Bay Hill, FL (cdp) Orange County	303	5.85
Old Westbury, NY (village) Nassau County	247	5.84
North Potomac, MD (cdp) Montgomery County	1,339	5.81
Cloverly, MD (cdp) Montgomery County	452	5.77
Woodridge, IL (village) Du Page County	1,769	5.72
Oakbrook Terrace, IL (city) Du Page County	131	5.70
East Brunswick, NJ (cdp) Middlesex County	2,662	5.69
Forest Home, NY (cdp) Tompkins County	52	5.53
Lower Salem, OH (village) Washington County	6	5.50
Lodi, NJ (borough) Bergen County	1,317	5.49
Voorhees, NJ (township) Camden County	1,532	5.45
Westmont, IL (village) Du Page County	1,317	5.36
Travilah, MD (cdp) Montgomery County	399	5.36
Hatfield, PA (township) Montgomery County	892	5.34
Elmsford, NY (village) Westchester County	249	5.33
Old Bridge, NJ (township) Middlesex County	3,219	5.32
Scott Township, PA (cdp) Allegheny County	920	5.32
Hurstbourne Acres, KY (city) Jefferson County	80	5.32
Little Flock, AR (city) Benton County	136	5.26
Bradbury, CA (city) Los Angeles County	45	5.26
Hillcrest, NY (cdp) Rockland County	368	5.18
King of Prussia, PA (cdp) Montgomery County	956	5.16
South Valley Stream, NY (cdp) Nassau County	291	5.16
Englewood Cliffs, NJ (borough) Bergen County	273	5.13
Randolph, NJ (township) Morris County	1,271	5.12
Carol Stream, IL (village) Du Page County	2,063	5.10
Ivanhoe Estates, FL (cdp) Broward County	14	5.02
Mission Bend, TX (cdp) Fort Bend County	1,537	4.99
Hatfield, PA (borough) Montgomery County	130	4.99
Montgomery Village, MD (cdp) Montgomery County	1,889	4.96
Tysons Corner, VA (cdp) Fairfax County	919	4.96
Highland Park, NJ (borough) Middlesex County	694	4.96
Sportsmen Acres, OK (town) Mayes County	10	4.90
Artesia, CA (city) Los Angeles County	799	4.88
Ardencroft, DE (village) New Castle County	13	4.87
Fairland, MD (cdp) Montgomery County	1,054	4.85
Calverton, MD (cdp) Montgomery County	610	4.84
Stanford, CA (cdp) Santa Clara County	642	4.82
North Bergen, NJ (township) Hudson County	2,796	4.81
Pomona, NJ (cdp) Atlantic County	192	4.78
Elmwood Park, NJ (borough) Bergen County	903	4.77
Addison, IL (village) Du Page County	1,711	4.76
North Valley Stream, NY (cdp) Nassau County	752	4.76
Paramus, NJ (borough) Bergen County	1,199	4.66
Goddard, MD (cdp) Prince George's County	259	4.66
Canton, MI (cdp) Wayne County	3,523	4.61
Niles, IL (village) Cook County	1,380	4.59
Mountain Park, GA (cdp) Gwinnett County	540	4.59
Morrisville, NC (town) Wake County	238	4.57
Hicksville, NY (cdp) Nassau County	1,876	4.55
Mountain View, CA (city) Santa Clara County	3,206	4.53
Marlboro, NJ (township) Monmouth County	1,634	4.49
Congers, NY (cdp) Rockland County	371	4.47
Colesville, MD (cdp) Montgomery County	883	4.46
Redland, MD (cdp) Montgomery County	758	4.46
Los Altos Hills, CA (town) Santa Clara County	350	4.43
Newark, CA (city) Alameda County	1,875	4.41
Bensalem, PA (township) Bucks County	2,570	4.40
Chantilly, VA (cdp) Fairfax County	1,806	4.40
Bridgewater, NJ (township) Somerset County	1,885	4.39
Greenville, NY (cdp) Westchester County	375	4.34
Greentree, NJ (cdp) Camden County	498	4.32
Waldon, CA (cdp) Contra Costa County	221	4.31
South Floral Park, NY (village) Nassau County	68	4.31
Diamond Bar, CA (city) Los Angeles County	2,403	4.27

Notes: (cdp) census designated place; Refer to the Explanation of Data in the front of the book for more detailed information.

Asian: Indian

Top 150 Places Sorted by Percent

(Based on places with populations of 10,000 or more)

Place	Number	%
South Yuba City, CA (cdp) Sutter County	2,713	21.44
Edison, NJ (cdp) Middlesex County	17,343	17.75
Iselin, NJ (cdp) Middlesex County	2,912	17.44
Princeton Meadows, NJ (cdp) Middlesex County	2,305	17.16
Plainsboro, NJ (township) Middlesex County	3,431	16.97
Avenel, NJ (cdp) Middlesex County	2,395	13.65
Livingston, CA (city) Merced County	1,366	13.04
Piscataway, NJ (township) Middlesex County	6,307	12.49
New Territory, TX (cdp) Fort Bend County	1,725	12.44
Fremont, CA (city) Alameda County	21,618	10.63
South Brunswick, NJ (township) Middlesex County	3,954	10.48
Sunnyvale, CA (city) Santa Clara County	13,443	10.20
Union City, CA (city) Alameda County	6,195	9.26
Woodbridge, NJ (township) Middlesex County	8,937	9.19
West Windsor, NJ (township) Mercer County	1,973	9.01
Cupertino, CA (city) Santa Clara County	4,546	8.99
Santa Clara, CA (city) Santa Clara County	9,163	8.95
Glendale Heights, IL (village) Du Page County	2,840	8.94
North Brunswick Township, NJ (cdp) Middlesex County	3,158	8.70
Fords, NJ (cdp) Middlesex County	1,290	8.58
Parsippany-Troy Hills, NJ (township) Morris County	4,251	8.39
Merrifield, VA (cdp) Fairfax County	917	8.21
Farmington, MI (city) Oakland County	813	7.80
Stafford, TX (city) Fort Bend County	1,219	7.77
North New Hyde Park, NY (cdp) Nassau County	1,122	7.72
Sugar Land, TX (city) Fort Bend County	4,573	7.22
Milpitas, CA (city) Santa Clara County	4,495	7.17
Yuba City, CA (city) Sutter County	2,636	7.17
Burlington, MA (cdp) Middlesex County	1,608	7.03
Franklin, NJ (township) Somerset County	3,574	7.02
Morton Grove, IL (village) Cook County	1,565	6.97
Hoffman Estates, IL (village) Cook County	3,371	6.81
Roselle Park, NJ (borough) Union County	896	6.75
Hamtramck, MI (city) Wayne County	1,537	6.69
Echelon, NJ (cdp) Camden County	695	6.66
Schaumburg, IL (village) Cook County	5,006	6.64
Sayreville, NJ (borough) Middlesex County	2,657	6.58
Idylwood, VA (cdp) Fairfax County	1,051	6.57
Skokie, IL (village) Cook County	4,142	6.54
Elmont, NY (cdp) Nassau County	2,113	6.47
Lincolnwood, IL (village) Cook County	795	6.43
Burr Ridge, IL (village) Du Page County	664	6.38
Carteret, NJ (borough) Middlesex County	1,311	6.33
Bergenfield, NJ (borough) Bergen County	1,602	6.10
East Windsor, NJ (township) Mercer County	1,520	6.10
Hanover Park, IL (village) Cook County	2,313	6.04
Foster City, CA (city) San Mateo County	1,720	5.97
Jersey City, NJ (city) Hudson County	14,206	5.92
Troy, MI (city) Oakland County	4,789	5.92
Mount Prospect, IL (village) Cook County	3,325	5.91
Herndon, VA (town) Fairfax County	1,276	5.89
Cerritos, CA (city) Los Angeles County	3,017	5.86
North Potomac, MD (cdp) Montgomery County	1,339	5.81
Woodridge, IL (village) Du Page County	1,769	5.72
East Brunswick, NJ (cdp) Middlesex County	2,662	5.69
Lodi, NJ (borough) Bergen County	1,317	5.49
Voorhees, NJ (township) Camden County	1,532	5.45
Westmont, IL (village) Du Page County	1,317	5.36
Hatfield, PA (township) Montgomery County	892	5.34
Old Bridge, NJ (township) Middlesex County	3,219	5.32
Scott Township, PA (cdp) Allegheny County	920	5.32
King of Prussia, PA (cdp) Montgomery County	956	5.16
Randolph, NJ (township) Morris County	1,271	5.12
Carol Stream, IL (village) Du Page County	2,063	5.10
Mission Bend, TX (cdp) Fort Bend County	1,537	4.99
Montgomery Village, MD (cdp) Montgomery County	1,889	4.96
Tysons Corner, VA (cdp) Fairfax County	919	4.96
Highland Park, NJ (borough) Middlesex County	694	4.96
Artesia, CA (city) Los Angeles County	799	4.88
Fairland, MD (cdp) Montgomery County	1,054	4.85
Calverton, MD (cdp) Montgomery County	610	4.84
Stanford, CA (cdp) Santa Clara County	642	4.82
North Bergen, NJ (township) Hudson County	2,796	4.81
Elmwood Park, NJ (borough) Bergen County	903	4.77
Addison, IL (village) Du Page County	1,711	4.76
North Valley Stream, NY (cdp) Nassau County	752	4.76
Paramus, NJ (borough) Bergen County	1,199	4.66
Canton, MI (cdp) Wayne County	3,523	4.61
Niles, IL (village) Cook County	1,380	4.59
Mountain Park, GA (cdp) Gwinnett County	540	4.59
Hicksville, NY (cdp) Nassau County	1,876	4.55
Mountain View, CA (city) Santa Clara County	3,206	4.53
Marlboro, NJ (township) Monmouth County	1,634	4.49
Colesville, MD (cdp) Montgomery County	883	4.46
Redland, MD (cdp) Montgomery County	758	4.46
Newark, CA (city) Alameda County	1,875	4.41
Bensalem, PA (township) Bucks County	2,570	4.40
Chantilly, VA (cdp) Fairfax County	1,806	4.40
Bridgewater, NJ (township) Somerset County	1,885	4.39
Greentree, NJ (cdp) Camden County	498	4.32
Diamond Bar, CA (city) Los Angeles County	2,403	4.27
Wheeling, IL (village) Cook County	1,472	4.27
Saratoga, CA (city) Santa Clara County	1,269	4.25
Darien, IL (city) Du Page County	972	4.25
Westborough, MA (town) Worcester County	764	4.25
Farmington Hills, MI (city) Oakland County	3,482	4.24
Carrollton, TX (city) Denton County	4,625	4.22
Wells Branch, TX (cdp) Travis County	467	4.14
Naperville, IL (city) Du Page County	5,261	4.10
Gaithersburg, MD (city) Montgomery County	2,151	4.09
Little Ferry, NJ (borough) Bergen County	438	4.06
Montville, NJ (township) Morris County	843	4.05
Duluth, GA (city) Gwinnett County	887	4.01
Beltsville, MD (cdp) Prince George's County	629	4.01
Adelphi, MD (cdp) Prince George's County	601	4.01
Upper Merion, PA (township) Montgomery County	1,073	3.99
Des Plaines, IL (city) Cook County	2,339	3.98
Guttenberg, NJ (town) Hudson County	430	3.98
Passaic, NJ (city) Passaic County	2,692	3.97
New Milford, NJ (borough) Bergen County	651	3.97
La Palma, CA (city) Orange County	611	3.97
Lilburn, GA (city) Gwinnett County	449	3.97
Lisle, IL (village) Du Page County	831	3.92
Somerset, NJ (cdp) Somerset County	898	3.90
Reston, VA (cdp) Fairfax County	2,197	3.89
Missouri City, TX (city) Fort Bend County	2,042	3.86
Bloomingdale, IL (village) Du Page County	835	3.85
Lawrence, NJ (township) Mercer County	1,119	3.84
Bensenville, IL (village) Du Page County	794	3.84
Nanuet, NY (cdp) Rockland County	639	3.82
Shrewsbury, MA (town) Worcester County	1,204	3.81
Hercules, CA (city) Contra Costa County	742	3.81
Centreville, VA (cdp) Fairfax County	1,837	3.78
Greenbelt, MD (city) Prince George's County	807	3.76
Holmdel, NJ (township) Monmouth County	591	3.75
Germantown, MD (cdp) Montgomery County	2,073	3.74
Lombard, IL (village) Du Page County	1,564	3.70
Auburn Hills, MI (city) Oakland County	734	3.70
Blackhawk-Camino Tassajara, CA (cdp) Contra Costa County	371	3.69
Hayward, CA (city) Alameda County	5,141	3.67
North Hempstead, NY (town) Nassau County	7,951	3.57
Cary, NC (town) Wake County	3,379	3.57
West Lafayette, IN (city) Tippecanoe County	1,027	3.57
Coppell, TX (city) Dallas County	1,281	3.56
Salisbury, NY (cdp) Nassau County	439	3.56
El Sobrante, CA (cdp) Contra Costa County	434	3.54
Secaucus, NJ (town) Hudson County	559	3.51
Maryland Heights, MO (city) Saint Louis County	896	3.48
Okemos, MI (cdp) Ingham County	788	3.46
Irving, TX (city) Dallas County	6,594	3.44
Palatine, IL (village) Cook County	2,229	3.40
Belmont, CA (city) San Mateo County	855	3.40
Glenn Dale, MD (cdp) Prince George's County	428	3.39
Wallington, NJ (borough) Bergen County	390	3.37
Springfield, VA (cdp) Fairfax County	1,021	3.36
Montgomery, NJ (township) Somerset County	585	3.35
Elk Grove Village, IL (village) Cook County	1,161	3.34
Irvine, CA (city) Orange County	4,762	3.33
Pittsfield charter, MI (township) Washtenaw County	1,004	3.33
Redmond, WA (city) King County	1,486	3.28

Notes: (cdp) census designated place; Refer to the Explanation of Data in the front of the book for more detailed information.

Asian: Indonesian

Top 150 Places Sorted by Number

(Based on all places, regardless of population)

Place	Number	%
Los Angeles, CA (city) Los Angeles County	3,258	0.09
New York, NY (city) New York City	3,017	0.04
San Francisco, CA (city) San Francisco County	1,142	0.15
San Jose, CA (city) Santa Clara County	767	0.09
Loma Linda, CA (city) San Bernardino County	728	3.90
Houston, TX (city) Harris County	709	0.04
San Diego, CA (city) San Diego County	634	0.05
Philadelphia, PA (city) Philadelphia County	601	0.04
San Bernardino, CA (city) San Bernardino County	597	0.32
Seattle, WA (city) King County	554	0.10
Columbus, OH (city) Franklin County	490	0.07
Anaheim, CA (city) Orange County	477	0.15
Alhambra, CA (city) Los Angeles County	475	0.55
Denver, CO (city) Denver County	406	0.07
Rancho Cucamonga, CA (city) San Bernardino County	380	0.30
Arcadia, CA (city) Los Angeles County	378	0.71
Chicago, IL (city) Cook County	359	0.01
Colton, CA (city) San Bernardino County	347	0.73
Diamond Bar, CA (city) Los Angeles County	342	0.61
Daly City, CA (city) San Mateo County	340	0.33
Ontario, CA (city) San Bernardino County	332	0.21
Upland, CA (city) San Bernardino County	326	0.48
Fullerton, CA (city) Orange County	317	0.25
Redlands, CA (city) San Bernardino County	306	0.48
West Covina, CA (city) Los Angeles County	306	0.29
Rowland Heights, CA (cdp) Los Angeles County	305	0.63
Portland, OR (city) Multnomah County	292	0.06
Montclair, CA (city) San Bernardino County	288	0.87
Pasadena, CA (city) Los Angeles County	284	0.21
Fremont, CA (city) Alameda County	284	0.14
Monterey Park, CA (city) Los Angeles County	283	0.47
Chino Hills, CA (city) San Bernardino County	277	0.41
Honolulu, HI (cdp) Honolulu County	267	0.07
Sacramento, CA (city) Sacramento County	262	0.06
Long Beach, CA (city) Los Angeles County	256	0.06
Boston, MA (city) Suffolk County	255	0.04
Irvine, CA (city) Orange County	251	0.18
Huntington Beach, CA (city) Orange County	243	0.13
Madison, WI (city) Dane County	243	0.12
Fontana, CA (city) San Bernardino County	239	0.19
Everett, WA (city) Snohomish County	236	0.26
Pomona, CA (city) Los Angeles County	232	0.16
Austin, TX (city) Travis County	229	0.03
Washington, DC (city) District of Columbia	225	0.04
Riverside, CA (city) Riverside County	224	0.09
Phoenix, AZ (city) Maricopa County	220	0.02
Walnut, CA (city) Los Angeles County	208	0.69
Arlington, VA (cdp) Arlington County	207	0.11
Fresno, CA (city) Fresno County	204	0.05
Cerritos, CA (city) Los Angeles County	203	0.39
Torrance, CA (city) Los Angeles County	199	0.14
Wheaton-Glenmont, MD (cdp) Montgomery County	196	0.34
Ames, IA (city) Story County	195	0.38
Edison, NJ (cdp) Middlesex County	182	0.19
Hayward, CA (city) Alameda County	181	0.13
Garden Grove, CA (city) Orange County	181	0.11
Eugene, OR (city) Lane County	180	0.13
Dallas, TX (city) Dallas County	176	0.01
Covina, CA (city) Los Angeles County	175	0.37
Oakland, CA (city) Alameda County	171	0.04
Temple City, CA (city) Los Angeles County	164	0.49
Aurora, CO (city) Arapahoe County	164	0.06
Lakewood, CA (city) Los Angeles County	163	0.21
Oklahoma City, OK (city) Oklahoma County	162	0.03
San Gabriel, CA (city) Los Angeles County	154	0.39
Woodbridge, NJ (township) Middlesex County	154	0.16
Bellevue, WA (city) King County	153	0.14
Simi Valley, CA (city) Ventura County	152	0.14
Hacienda Heights, CA (cdp) Los Angeles County	151	0.28
South San Francisco, CA (city) San Mateo County	143	0.24
Tempe, AZ (city) Maricopa County	141	0.09
West Lafayette, IN (city) Tippecanoe County	139	0.48
Glendale, CA (city) Los Angeles County	139	0.07
Concord, CA (city) Contra Costa County	138	0.11
Sunnyvale, CA (city) Santa Clara County	138	0.10
Tucson, AZ (city) Pima County	137	0.03
Corona, CA (city) Riverside County	136	0.11
Arlington, TX (city) Tarrant County	135	0.04
Union City, CA (city) Alameda County	134	0.20
Orange, CA (city) Orange County	134	0.10
Moreno Valley, CA (city) Riverside County	132	0.09
Santa Clarita, CA (city) Los Angeles County	130	0.09
Santa Clara, CA (city) Santa Clara County	127	0.12
Dover, NH (city) Strafford County	125	0.46
College Station, TX (city) Brazos County	123	0.18
Corvallis, OR (city) Benton County	121	0.25
Westminster, CA (city) Orange County	120	0.14
Lexington-Fayette, KY (special city) Fayette County	119	0.05
Yorba Linda, CA (city) Orange County	118	0.20
Glendora, CA (city) Los Angeles County	117	0.24
Tulsa, OK (city) Tulsa County	112	0.03
Milwaukee, WI (city) Milwaukee County	112	0.02
Mission Viejo, CA (city) Orange County	111	0.12
Irving, TX (city) Dallas County	111	0.06
Paine Field-Lake Stickney, WA (cdp) Snohomish County	110	0.45
Santa Ana, CA (city) Orange County	109	0.03
Avenel, NJ (cdp) Middlesex County	108	0.62
Roswell, GA (city) Fulton County	108	0.14
Bloomington, IN (city) Monroe County	105	0.15
Pittsburgh, PA (city) Allegheny County	105	0.03
Costa Mesa, CA (city) Orange County	104	0.10
Stillwater, OK (city) Payne County	103	0.26
Minneapolis, MN (city) Hennepin County	102	0.03
Tustin, CA (city) Orange County	100	0.15
Palmdale, CA (city) Los Angeles County	100	0.09
Laguna Niguel, CA (city) Orange County	99	0.16
Chino, CA (city) San Bernardino County	99	0.15
Las Vegas, NV (city) Clark County	99	0.02
Silver Spring, MD (cdp) Montgomery County	97	0.13
Bellflower, CA (city) Los Angeles County	96	0.13
Azusa, CA (city) Los Angeles County	94	0.21
Beaverton, OR (city) Washington County	94	0.12
Plano, TX (city) Collin County	94	0.04
Milpitas, CA (city) Santa Clara County	92	0.15
Redondo Beach, CA (city) Los Angeles County	92	0.15
Ann Arbor, MI (city) Washtenaw County	92	0.08
Aspen Hill, MD (cdp) Montgomery County	91	0.18
Buena Park, CA (city) Orange County	91	0.12
San Mateo, CA (city) San Mateo County	91	0.10
Mesa, AZ (city) Maricopa County	90	0.02
Rialto, CA (city) San Bernardino County	89	0.10
Richmond, CA (city) Contra Costa County	89	0.09
Monrovia, CA (city) Los Angeles County	88	0.24
San Dimas, CA (city) Los Angeles County	87	0.25
Norwalk, CA (city) Los Angeles County	87	0.08
Oceanside, CA (city) San Diego County	86	0.05
Antioch, CA (city) Contra Costa County	86	0.09
Henderson, NV (city) Clark County	85	0.05
Redwood City, CA (city) San Mateo County	83	0.11
North Bethesda, MD (cdp) Montgomery County	82	0.21
Gresham, OR (city) Multnomah County	82	0.09
Mountain View, CA (city) Santa Clara County	81	0.11
Paradise, NV (cdp) Clark County	81	0.04
Highland, CA (city) San Bernardino County	80	0.18
Fountain Valley, CA (city) Orange County	80	0.15
Berkeley, CA (city) Alameda County	80	0.08
Cambridge, MA (city) Middlesex County	80	0.08
Charlotte, NC (city) Mecklenburg County	80	0.01
Lake Forest, CA (city) Orange County	79	0.13
Thousand Oaks, CA (city) Ventura County	79	0.07
Wichita, KS (city) Sedgwick County	79	0.02
Oronoko charter, MI (township) Berrien County	78	0.79
Urbana, IL (city) Champaign County	77	0.21
El Monte, CA (city) Los Angeles County	77	0.07
Shoreline, WA (city) King County	76	0.14
La Habra, CA (city) Orange County	76	0.13
Bakersfield, CA (city) Kern County	74	0.03
Cypress, CA (city) Orange County	73	0.16
East Lansing, MI (city) Ingham County	73	0.16
Colorado Springs, CO (city) El Paso County	73	0.02

Notes: (cdp) census designated place; Refer to the Explanation of Data in the front of the book for more detailed information.

Asian: Indonesian

Top 150 Places Sorted by Percent

(Based on all places, regardless of population)

Place	Number	%
Loma Linda, CA (city) San Bernardino County	728	3.90
Pringle, SD (town) Custer County	4	3.20
Pelan, MN (township) Kittson County	1	1.64
Forest Home, NY (cdp) Tompkins County	15	1.59
Ogema, MN (township) Pine County	4	1.34
York Haven, PA (borough) York County	9	1.11
Knollwood, TX (village) Grayson County	4	1.07
Nanawale Estates, HI (cdp) Hawaii County	11	1.03
Lake Aluma, OK (town) Oklahoma County	1	1.03
Neponset, IL (village) Bureau County	5	0.96
Goshen, VT (town) Addison County	2	0.88
Montclair, CA (city) San Bernardino County	288	0.87
Saint Libory, IL (village) Saint Clair County	5	0.86
Oronoko charter, MI (township) Berrien County	78	0.79
Kremlin, MT (cdp) Hill County	3	0.79
Pineville, NC (town) Mecklenburg County	27	0.78
Colton, CA (city) San Bernardino County	347	0.73
Bonanza, OR (town) Klamath County	3	0.72
Camp Three, MT (cdp) Musselshell County	1	0.72
Gore, MI (township) Huron County	1	0.72
Arcadia, CA (city) Los Angeles County	378	0.71
Walnut, CA (city) Los Angeles County	208	0.69
North Union, PA (township) Schuylkill County	8	0.65
Rowland Heights, CA (cdp) Los Angeles County	305	0.63
Desert Shores, CA (cdp) Imperial County	5	0.63
Avenel, NJ (cdp) Middlesex County	108	0.62
Diamond Bar, CA (city) Los Angeles County	342	0.61
Kevin, MT (town) Toole County	1	0.56
Alhambra, CA (city) Los Angeles County	475	0.55
Grand Terrace, CA (city) San Bernardino County	63	0.54
Talmage, CA (cdp) Mendocino County	6	0.53
Edgar Springs, MO (city) Phelps County	1	0.53
San Juan Bautista, CA (city) San Benito County	8	0.52
Arlee, MT (cdp) Lake County	3	0.50
Temple City, CA (city) Los Angeles County	164	0.49
North El Monte, CA (cdp) Los Angeles County	18	0.49
Upland, CA (city) San Bernardino County	326	0.48
Redlands, CA (city) San Bernardino County	306	0.48
West Lafayette, IN (city) Tippecanoe County	139	0.48
San Marino, CA (city) Los Angeles County	62	0.48
Westcliffe, CO (town) Custer County	2	0.48
Monterey Park, CA (city) Los Angeles County	283	0.47
Mentone, CA (cdp) San Bernardino County	37	0.47
La Habra Heights, CA (city) Los Angeles County	27	0.47
Mayflower Village, CA (cdp) Los Angeles County	24	0.47
Elsah, IL (village) Jersey County	3	0.47
Dover, NH (city) Strafford County	125	0.46
Smelterville, ID (city) Shoshone County	3	0.46
Paine Field-Lake Stickney, WA (cdp) Snohomish County	110	0.45
Piney Point Village, TX (city) Harris County	15	0.44
Oakhurst, TX (city) San Jacinto County	1	0.43
East San Gabriel, CA (cdp) Los Angeles County	61	0.42
Kalihiwai, HI (cdp) Kauai County	3	0.42
Galena, MN (township) Martin County	1	0.42
Roxbury, NH (town) Cheshire County	1	0.42
Chino Hills, CA (city) San Bernardino County	277	0.41
Casa Conejo, CA (cdp) Ventura County	13	0.41
Vincent, CA (cdp) Los Angeles County	61	0.40
Cerritos, CA (city) Los Angeles County	203	0.39
San Gabriel, CA (city) Los Angeles County	154	0.39
Del Aire, CA (cdp) Los Angeles County	35	0.39
Ames, IA (city) Story County	195	0.38
Covina, CA (city) Los Angeles County	175	0.37
Forest Glen, MD (cdp) Montgomery County	27	0.37
Broadmoor, CA (cdp) San Mateo County	15	0.37
Concow, CA (cdp) Butte County	4	0.37
Middletown, IA (city) Des Moines County	2	0.37
New Millford, IL (village) Winnebago County	2	0.37
Kaanapali, HI (cdp) Maui County	5	0.36
Crookston, MN (township) Polk County	2	0.36
Laytonsville, MD (town) Montgomery County	1	0.36
Citrus, CA (cdp) Los Angeles County	37	0.35
Epworth, IA (city) Dubuque County	5	0.35
Colo, IA (city) Story County	3	0.35
Wheaton-Glenmont, MD (cdp) Montgomery County	196	0.34
Dunn Loring, VA (cdp) Fairfax County	27	0.34
Severance, CO (town) Weld County	2	0.34
Daly City, CA (city) San Mateo County	340	0.33
Sylva, NC (town) Jackson County	8	0.33
Sea Bright, NJ (borough) Monmouth County	6	0.33
San Bernardino, CA (city) San Bernardino County	597	0.32
Wailea-Makena, HI (cdp) Maui County	18	0.32
Angwin, CA (cdp) Napa County	10	0.32
Berrien Springs, MI (village) Berrien County	6	0.32
Northfield, VT (village) Washington County	10	0.31
Union, KY (city) Boone County	9	0.31
Koloa, HI (cdp) Kauai County	6	0.31
Holly Pond, AL (town) Cullman County	2	0.31
Dillon Beach, CA (cdp) Marin County	1	0.31
Yantis, TX (town) Wood County	1	0.31
Rancho Cucamonga, CA (city) San Bernardino County	380	0.30
East Pasadena, CA (cdp) Los Angeles County	18	0.30
Cortland West, NY (cdp) Cortland County	4	0.30
West Covina, CA (city) Los Angeles County	306	0.29
Ferndale, CA (city) Humboldt County	4	0.29
Hacienda Heights, CA (cdp) Los Angeles County	151	0.28
Secaucus, NJ (town) Hudson County	44	0.28
Stockton, WI (town) Portage County	8	0.28
Poipu, HI (cdp) Kauai County	3	0.28
Rich Valley, MN (township) McLeod County	2	0.28
Mokuleia, HI (cdp) Honolulu County	5	0.27
Snowmass Village, CO (town) Pitkin County	5	0.27
Francestown, NH (town) Hillsborough County	4	0.27
Everett, WA (city) Snohomish County	236	0.26
Stillwater, OK (city) Payne County	103	0.26
South Pasadena, CA (city) Los Angeles County	63	0.26
Artesia, CA (city) Los Angeles County	42	0.26
Merrifield, VA (cdp) Fairfax County	29	0.26
Seven Corners, VA (cdp) Fairfax County	23	0.26
Oak Park, CA (cdp) Ventura County	6	0.26
Leisureville, FL (cdp) Broward County	3	0.26
Rafter J Ranch, WY (cdp) Teton County	3	0.26
Derby Line, VT (village) Orleans County	2	0.26
Fullerton, CA (city) Orange County	317	0.25
Corvallis, OR (city) Benton County	121	0.25
San Dimas, CA (city) Los Angeles County	87	0.25
Duarte, CA (city) Los Angeles County	54	0.25
Tysons Corner, VA (cdp) Fairfax County	46	0.25
Brisbane, CA (city) San Mateo County	9	0.25
Ferron, UT (city) Emery County	4	0.25
Gibbon, MN (city) Sibley County	2	0.25
South San Francisco, CA (city) San Mateo County	143	0.24
Glendora, CA (city) Los Angeles County	117	0.24
Monrovia, CA (city) Los Angeles County	88	0.24
Pacific Grove, CA (city) Monterey County	37	0.24
Chamblee, GA (city) De Kalb County	23	0.24
Glendale, CO (city) Arapahoe County	11	0.24
Highlands-Baywood Park, CA (cdp) San Mateo County	10	0.24
Lake City, GA (city) Clayton County	7	0.24
Alma, NY (town) Allegany County	2	0.24
Metuchen, NJ (borough) Middlesex County	30	0.23
Farmingdale, NY (village) Nassau County	19	0.23
Morrow, GA (city) Clayton County	11	0.23
Lansing, NY (village) Tompkins County	8	0.23
Hawaiian Acres, HI (cdp) Hawaii County	4	0.23
Rush Springs, OK (town) Grady County	3	0.23
Bradbury, CA (city) Los Angeles County	2	0.23
Luck, WI (town) Polk County	2	0.23
Pleasant Hill, CA (city) Contra Costa County	72	0.22
La Verne, CA (city) Los Angeles County	71	0.22
El Segundo, CA (city) Los Angeles County	36	0.22
Havana, IL (city) Mason County	8	0.22
La Veta, CO (town) Huerfano County	2	0.22
Buffalo Gap, TX (town) Taylor County	1	0.22
Norbourne Estates, KY (city) Jefferson County	1	0.22
Ontario, CA (city) San Bernardino County	332	0.21
Pasadena, CA (city) Los Angeles County	284	0.21
Lakewood, CA (city) Los Angeles County	163	0.21
Azusa, CA (city) Los Angeles County	94	0.21
North Bethesda, MD (cdp) Montgomery County	82	0.21

Notes: (cdp) census designated place; Refer to the Explanation of Data in the front of the book for more detailed information.

Asian: Indonesian

Top 150 Places Sorted by Percent

(Based on places with populations of 10,000 or more)

Place	Number	%
Loma Linda, CA (city) San Bernardino County	728	3.90
Montclair, CA (city) San Bernardino County	288	0.87
Colton, CA (city) San Bernardino County	347	0.73
Arcadia, CA (city) Los Angeles County	378	0.71
Walnut, CA (city) Los Angeles County	208	0.69
Rowland Heights, CA (cdp) Los Angeles County	305	0.63
Avenel, NJ (cdp) Middlesex County	108	0.62
Diamond Bar, CA (city) Los Angeles County	342	0.61
Alhambra, CA (city) Los Angeles County	475	0.55
Grand Terrace, CA (city) San Bernardino County	63	0.54
Temple City, CA (city) Los Angeles County	164	0.49
Upland, CA (city) San Bernardino County	326	0.48
Redlands, CA (city) San Bernardino County	306	0.48
West Lafayette, IN (city) Tippecanoe County	139	0.48
San Marino, CA (city) Los Angeles County	62	0.48
Monterey Park, CA (city) Los Angeles County	283	0.47
Dover, NH (city) Strafford County	125	0.46
Paine Field-Lake Stickney, WA (cdp) Snohomish County	110	0.45
East San Gabriel, CA (cdp) Los Angeles County	61	0.42
Chino Hills, CA (city) San Bernardino County	277	0.41
Vincent, CA (cdp) Los Angeles County	61	0.40
Cerritos, CA (city) Los Angeles County	203	0.39
San Gabriel, CA (city) Los Angeles County	154	0.39
Ames, IA (city) Story County	195	0.38
Covina, CA (city) Los Angeles County	175	0.37
Citrus, CA (cdp) Los Angeles County	37	0.35
Wheaton-Glenmont, MD (cdp) Montgomery County	196	0.34
Daly City, CA (city) San Mateo County	340	0.33
San Bernardino, CA (city) San Bernardino County	597	0.32
Rancho Cucamonga, CA (city) San Bernardino County	380	0.30
West Covina, CA (city) Los Angeles County	306	0.29
Hacienda Heights, CA (cdp) Los Angeles County	151	0.28
Secaucus, NJ (town) Hudson County	44	0.28
Everett, WA (city) Snohomish County	236	0.26
Stillwater, OK (city) Payne County	103	0.26
South Pasadena, CA (city) Los Angeles County	63	0.26
Artesia, CA (city) Los Angeles County	42	0.26
Merrifield, VA (cdp) Fairfax County	29	0.26
Fullerton, CA (city) Orange County	317	0.25
Corvallis, OR (city) Benton County	121	0.25
San Dimas, CA (city) Los Angeles County	87	0.25
Duarte, CA (city) Los Angeles County	54	0.25
Tysons Corner, VA (cdp) Fairfax County	46	0.25
South San Francisco, CA (city) San Mateo County	143	0.24
Glendora, CA (city) Los Angeles County	117	0.24
Monrovia, CA (city) Los Angeles County	88	0.24
Pacific Grove, CA (city) Monterey County	37	0.24
Metuchen, NJ (borough) Middlesex County	30	0.23
Pleasant Hill, CA (city) Contra Costa County	72	0.22
La Verne, CA (city) Los Angeles County	71	0.22
El Segundo, CA (city) Los Angeles County	36	0.22
Ontario, CA (city) San Bernardino County	332	0.21
Pasadena, CA (city) Los Angeles County	284	0.21
Lakewood, CA (city) Los Angeles County	163	0.21
Azusa, CA (city) Los Angeles County	94	0.21
North Bethesda, MD (cdp) Montgomery County	82	0.21
Urbana, IL (city) Champaign County	77	0.21
Iselin, NJ (cdp) Middlesex County	35	0.21
Union City, CA (city) Alameda County	134	0.20
Yorba Linda, CA (city) Orange County	118	0.20
Lawndale, CA (city) Los Angeles County	62	0.20
Rochester, NH (city) Strafford County	57	0.20
Portsmouth, NH (city) Rockingham County	41	0.20
Fontana, CA (city) San Bernardino County	239	0.19
Edison, NJ (cdp) Middlesex County	182	0.19
Laguna Hills, CA (city) Orange County	59	0.19
Calabasas, CA (city) Los Angeles County	38	0.19
Golden, CO (city) Jefferson County	32	0.19
Irvine, CA (city) Orange County	251	0.18
College Station, TX (city) Brazos County	123	0.18
Aspen Hill, MD (cdp) Montgomery County	91	0.18
Highland, CA (city) San Bernardino County	80	0.18
Aliso Viejo, CA (cdp) Orange County	72	0.18
Sierra Madre, CA (city) Los Angeles County	19	0.18
San Bruno, CA (city) San Mateo County	69	0.17

Place	Number	%
Pomona, CA (city) Los Angeles County	232	0.16
Woodbridge, NJ (township) Middlesex County	154	0.16
Laguna Niguel, CA (city) Orange County	99	0.16
Cypress, CA (city) Orange County	73	0.16
East Lansing, MI (city) Ingham County	73	0.16
Monterey, CA (city) Monterey County	46	0.16
El Cerrito, CA (city) Contra Costa County	36	0.16
Idylwood, VA (cdp) Fairfax County	26	0.16
San Francisco, CA (city) San Francisco County	1,142	0.15
Anaheim, CA (city) Orange County	477	0.15
Bloomington, IN (city) Monroe County	105	0.15
Tustin, CA (city) Orange County	100	0.15
Chino, CA (city) San Bernardino County	99	0.15
Milpitas, CA (city) Santa Clara County	92	0.15
Redondo Beach, CA (city) Los Angeles County	92	0.15
Fountain Valley, CA (city) Orange County	80	0.15
Placentia, CA (city) Orange County	72	0.15
Rockville, MD (city) Montgomery County	72	0.15
San Ramon, CA (city) Contra Costa County	68	0.15
Claremont, CA (city) Los Angeles County	50	0.15
Jefferson, VA (cdp) Fairfax County	42	0.15
West Carson, CA (cdp) Los Angeles County	31	0.15
Ithaca, NY (town) Tompkins County	28	0.15
La Crescenta-Montrose, CA (cdp) Los Angeles County	28	0.15
Fremont, CA (city) Alameda County	284	0.14
Torrance, CA (city) Los Angeles County	199	0.14
Bellevue, WA (city) King County	153	0.14
Simi Valley, CA (city) Ventura County	152	0.14
Westminster, CA (city) Orange County	120	0.14
Roswell, GA (city) Fulton County	108	0.14
Shoreline, WA (city) King County	76	0.14
Newark, CA (city) Alameda County	61	0.14
Lynnwood, WA (city) Snohomish County	49	0.14
Beverly Hills, CA (city) Los Angeles County	46	0.14
Belmont, CA (city) San Mateo County	35	0.14
Starkville, MS (city) Oktibbeha County	30	0.14
Pinole, CA (city) Contra Costa County	27	0.14
Middlesex, NJ (borough) Middlesex County	19	0.14
Huntington Beach, CA (city) Orange County	243	0.13
Hayward, CA (city) Alameda County	181	0.13
Eugene, OR (city) Lane County	180	0.13
Silver Spring, MD (cdp) Montgomery County	97	0.13
Bellflower, CA (city) Los Angeles County	96	0.13
Lake Forest, CA (city) Orange County	79	0.13
La Habra, CA (city) Orange County	76	0.13
Rosemead, CA (city) Los Angeles County	70	0.13
Pacifica, CA (city) San Mateo County	51	0.13
McLean, VA (cdp) Fairfax County	49	0.13
Ithaca, NY (city) Tompkins County	39	0.13
Bailey's Crossroads, VA (cdp) Fairfax County	30	0.13
North Potomac, MD (cdp) Montgomery County	29	0.13
Herndon, VA (town) Fairfax County	28	0.13
South Plainfield, NJ (borough) Middlesex County	28	0.13
Lomita, CA (city) Los Angeles County	27	0.13
Redland, MD (cdp) Montgomery County	22	0.13
Makakilo City, HI (cdp) Honolulu County	17	0.13
Lea Hill, WA (cdp) King County	14	0.13
Madison, WI (city) Dane County	243	0.12
Santa Clara, CA (city) Santa Clara County	127	0.12
Mission Viejo, CA (city) Orange County	111	0.12
Beaverton, OR (city) Washington County	94	0.12
Buena Park, CA (city) Orange County	91	0.12
Rancho Santa Margarita, CA (city) Orange County	57	0.12
La Mirada, CA (city) Los Angeles County	56	0.12
La Canada Flintridge, CA (city) Los Angeles County	24	0.12
Newington, VA (cdp) Fairfax County	23	0.12
Albany, CA (city) Alameda County	20	0.12
La Palma, CA (city) Orange County	19	0.12
Hillsborough, CA (town) San Mateo County	13	0.12
Arlington, VA (cdp) Arlington County	207	0.11
Garden Grove, CA (city) Orange County	181	0.11
Concord, CA (city) Contra Costa County	138	0.11
Corona, CA (city) Riverside County	136	0.11
Redwood City, CA (city) San Mateo County	83	0.11
Mountain View, CA (city) Santa Clara County	81	0.11

Notes: (cdp) census designated place; Refer to the Explanation of Data in the front of the book for more detailed information.

Asian: Japanese

Top 150 Places Sorted by Number

(Based on all places, regardless of population)

Place	Number	%
Honolulu, HI (cdp) Honolulu County	112,778	30.34
Los Angeles, CA (city) Los Angeles County	45,176	1.22
New York, NY (city) New York City	26,419	0.33
Torrance, CA (city) Los Angeles County	16,048	11.63
Hilo, HI (cdp) Hawaii County	15,639	38.37
San Jose, CA (city) Santa Clara County	15,353	1.72
San Francisco, CA (city) San Francisco County	14,618	1.88
San Diego, CA (city) San Diego County	13,953	1.14
Kaneohe, HI (cdp) Honolulu County	12,518	35.80
Pearl City, HI (cdp) Honolulu County	12,499	40.35
Seattle, WA (city) King County	12,113	2.15
Waimalu, HI (cdp) Honolulu County	11,537	39.28
Mililani Town, HI (cdp) Honolulu County	10,739	37.54
Sacramento, CA (city) Sacramento County	8,710	2.14
Kailua, HI (cdp) Honolulu County	7,534	20.63
Gardena, CA (city) Los Angeles County	7,445	12.89
Chicago, IL (city) Cook County	7,114	0.25
Irvine, CA (city) Orange County	6,075	4.25
Kahului, HI (cdp) Maui County	5,087	25.25
Wahiawa, HI (cdp) Honolulu County	4,888	30.26
Waipahu, HI (cdp) Honolulu County	4,874	14.72
Monterey Park, CA (city) Los Angeles County	4,856	8.09
Long Beach, CA (city) Los Angeles County	4,363	0.95
Sunnyvale, CA (city) Santa Clara County	4,261	3.23
Portland, OR (city) Multnomah County	4,207	0.80
Waipio, HI (cdp) Honolulu County	4,205	36.03
Huntington Beach, CA (city) Orange County	4,174	2.20
Wailuku, HI (cdp) Maui County	3,984	32.40
Halawa, HI (cdp) Honolulu County	3,911	28.15
Las Vegas, NV (city) Clark County	3,751	0.78
Aiea, HI (cdp) Honolulu County	3,735	41.41
Rancho Palos Verdes, CA (city) Los Angeles County	3,679	8.94
Fresno, CA (city) Fresno County	3,629	0.85
Bellevue, WA (city) King County	3,538	3.23
Houston, TX (city) Harris County	3,277	0.17
Chula Vista, CA (city) San Diego County	3,252	1.87
Anaheim, CA (city) Orange County	3,164	0.96
Oakland, CA (city) Alameda County	3,162	0.79
Berkeley, CA (city) Alameda County	3,084	3.00
Fremont, CA (city) Alameda County	3,002	1.48
Phoenix, AZ (city) Maricopa County	2,989	0.23
Denver, CO (city) Denver County	2,846	0.51
Boston, MA (city) Suffolk County	2,817	0.48
Ahuimanu, HI (cdp) Honolulu County	2,787	32.77
Pasadena, CA (city) Los Angeles County	2,670	1.99
San Mateo, CA (city) San Mateo County	2,668	2.88
Cupertino, CA (city) Santa Clara County	2,660	5.26
Columbus, OH (city) Franklin County	2,458	0.35
San Antonio, TX (city) Bexar County	2,414	0.21
Makakilo City, HI (cdp) Honolulu County	2,318	17.62
Stockton, CA (city) San Joaquin County	2,253	0.92
Lihue, HI (cdp) Kauai County	2,175	38.33
Fort Lee, NJ (borough) Bergen County	2,161	6.09
Redondo Beach, CA (city) Los Angeles County	2,125	3.36
Santa Clara, CA (city) Santa Clara County	2,103	2.05
Montebello, CA (city) Los Angeles County	2,095	3.37
Oceanside, CA (city) San Diego County	2,079	1.29
Village Park, HI (cdp) Honolulu County	2,064	21.44
Tacoma, WA (city) Pierce County	2,054	1.06
Cerritos, CA (city) Los Angeles County	2,044	3.97
Mountain View, CA (city) Santa Clara County	2,040	2.89
Santa Monica, CA (city) Los Angeles County	1,928	2.29
Glendale, CA (city) Los Angeles County	1,920	0.98
Paradise, NV (cdp) Clark County	1,907	1.02
Greenburgh, NY (town) Westchester County	1,894	2.18
Colorado Springs, CO (city) El Paso County	1,888	0.52
Pukalani, HI (cdp) Maui County	1,864	25.26
Kapaa, HI (cdp) Kauai County	1,850	19.53
Heeia, HI (cdp) Honolulu County	1,839	37.20
Fountain Valley, CA (city) Orange County	1,809	3.29
Austin, TX (city) Travis County	1,807	0.28
Tucson, AZ (city) Pima County	1,805	0.37
Alhambra, CA (city) Los Angeles County	1,758	2.05
Anchorage, AK (municipality) Anchorage Borough	1,735	0.67
Ewa Beach, HI (cdp) Honolulu County	1,731	11.82
Palo Alto, CA (city) Santa Clara County	1,703	2.91
Philadelphia, PA (city) Philadelphia County	1,695	0.11
Costa Mesa, CA (city) Orange County	1,671	1.54
Santa Clarita, CA (city) Los Angeles County	1,657	1.10
Fullerton, CA (city) Orange County	1,635	1.30
Hacienda Heights, CA (cdp) Los Angeles County	1,606	3.02
Culver City, CA (city) Los Angeles County	1,604	4.13
Albuquerque, NM (city) Bernalillo County	1,593	0.36
Cypress, CA (city) Orange County	1,570	3.40
Foster City, CA (city) San Mateo County	1,555	5.40
Orange, CA (city) Orange County	1,553	1.21
Oxnard, CA (city) Ventura County	1,551	0.91
Eugene, OR (city) Lane County	1,549	1.12
Mission Viejo, CA (city) Orange County	1,528	1.64
West Bloomfield, MI (township) Oakland County	1,511	2.33
Greenwich, CT (town) Fairfield County	1,506	2.46
Henderson, NV (city) Clark County	1,506	0.86
Fairfield, CA (city) Solano County	1,483	1.54
Washington, DC (city) District of Columbia	1,471	0.26
Riverside, CA (city) Riverside County	1,460	0.57
Ann Arbor, MI (city) Washtenaw County	1,450	1.27
Garden Grove, CA (city) Orange County	1,447	0.88
Davis, CA (city) Yolo County	1,439	2.39
El Paso, TX (city) El Paso County	1,436	0.25
Hayward, CA (city) Alameda County	1,431	1.02
Aurora, CO (city) Arapahoe County	1,412	0.51
Brookline, MA (cdp) Norfolk County	1,406	2.46
Thousand Oaks, CA (city) Ventura County	1,404	1.20
Spokane, WA (city) Spokane County	1,365	0.70
Kihei, HI (cdp) Maui County	1,362	8.13
Alameda, CA (city) Alameda County	1,329	1.84
Waianae, HI (cdp) Honolulu County	1,317	12.54
Dallas, TX (city) Dallas County	1,307	0.11
Concord, CA (city) Contra Costa County	1,306	1.07
Salt Lake City, UT (city) Salt Lake County	1,293	0.71
Arcadia, CA (city) Los Angeles County	1,290	2.43
El Cerrito, CA (city) Contra Costa County	1,288	5.56
Westminster, CA (city) Orange County	1,284	1.46
Arlington, VA (cdp) Arlington County	1,284	0.68
Waihee-Waiehu, HI (cdp) Maui County	1,278	17.48
Virginia Beach, VA (independent city) Virginia Beach city	1,275	0.30
Diamond Bar, CA (city) Los Angeles County	1,264	2.25
Lahaina, HI (cdp) Maui County	1,262	13.84
Salinas, CA (city) Monterey County	1,245	0.82
Waipio Acres, HI (cdp) Honolulu County	1,244	23.48
Spring Valley, NV (cdp) Clark County	1,236	1.05
Ewa Gentry, HI (cdp) Honolulu County	1,235	25.01
Maunawili, HI (cdp) Honolulu County	1,223	25.12
Kailua, HI (cdp) Hawaii County	1,223	12.39
Schaumburg, IL (village) Cook County	1,214	1.61
Santa Ana, CA (city) Orange County	1,209	0.36
Richmond, CA (city) Contra Costa County	1,193	1.20
Daly City, CA (city) San Mateo County	1,188	1.15
Novi, MI (city) Oakland County	1,185	2.50
Waimea, HI (cdp) Hawaii County	1,183	16.83
Lexington-Fayette, KY (special city) Fayette County	1,174	0.45
Reno, NV (city) Washoe County	1,171	0.65
Beaverton, OR (city) Washington County	1,155	1.52
Cambridge, MA (city) Middlesex County	1,155	1.14
Carson, CA (city) Los Angeles County	1,154	1.29
North Hempstead, NY (town) Nassau County	1,130	0.51
Yorba Linda, CA (city) Orange County	1,114	1.89
Eastchester, NY (town) Westchester County	1,110	3.54
Arlington Heights, IL (village) Cook County	1,108	1.46
West Covina, CA (city) Los Angeles County	1,106	1.05
West Carson, CA (cdp) Los Angeles County	1,093	5.17
Tustin, CA (city) Orange County	1,079	1.60
Carlsbad, CA (city) San Diego County	1,069	1.37
Laguna Niguel, CA (city) Orange County	1,068	1.73
Lakewood, CA (city) Los Angeles County	1,066	1.34
Buena Park, CA (city) Orange County	1,054	1.35
Indianapolis, IN (special city) Marion County	1,043	0.13
Chino Hills, CA (city) San Bernardino County	1,039	1.56
Minneapolis, MN (city) Hennepin County	1,032	0.27
Camarillo, CA (city) Ventura County	1,031	1.81

Notes: (cdp) census designated place; Refer to the Explanation of Data in the front of the book for more detailed information.

Asian: Japanese

Top 150 Places Sorted by Percent

(Based on all places, regardless of population)

Place	Number	%
Aiea, HI (cdp) Honolulu County	3,735	41.41
Pearl City, HI (cdp) Honolulu County	12,499	40.35
Waimalu, HI (cdp) Honolulu County	11,537	39.28
Hilo, HI (cdp) Hawaii County	15,639	38.37
Lihue, HI (cdp) Kauai County	2,175	38.33
Waimea, HI (cdp) Kauai County	672	37.60
Mililani Town, HI (cdp) Honolulu County	10,739	37.54
Heeia, HI (cdp) Honolulu County	1,839	37.20
Waipio, HI (cdp) Honolulu County	4,205	36.03
Kaneohe, HI (cdp) Honolulu County	12,518	35.80
Kurtistown, HI (cdp) Hawaii County	393	33.97
Kealakekua, HI (cdp) Hawaii County	545	33.13
Ahuimanu, HI (cdp) Honolulu County	2,787	32.77
Wailuku, HI (cdp) Maui County	3,984	32.40
Wailua, HI (cdp) Kauai County	671	32.21
Honomu, HI (cdp) Hawaii County	173	31.98
Saint Charles, SD (cdp) Gregory County	6	31.58
Waikapu, HI (cdp) Maui County	349	31.30
Honolulu, HI (cdp) Honolulu County	112,778	30.34
Wahiawa, HI (cdp) Honolulu County	4,888	30.26
Paukaa, HI (cdp) Hawaii County	149	30.10
Lawai, HI (cdp) Kauai County	593	29.89
Captain Cook, HI (cdp) Hawaii County	934	29.13
Kukuihaele, HI (cdp) Hawaii County	90	28.39
Halawa, HI (cdp) Honolulu County	3,911	28.15
Hanapepe, HI (cdp) Kauai County	601	27.91
Papaikou, HI (cdp) Hawaii County	391	27.65
Eleele, HI (cdp) Kauai County	556	27.25
Pepeekeo, HI (cdp) Hawaii County	460	27.11
Keaau, HI (cdp) Hawaii County	528	26.27
Kapaau, HI (cdp) Hawaii County	300	25.88
Pukalani, HI (cdp) Maui County	1,864	25.26
Kahului, HI (cdp) Maui County	5,087	25.25
Maunawili, HI (cdp) Honolulu County	1,223	25.12
Ewa Gentry, HI (cdp) Honolulu County	1,235	25.01
Pahoa, HI (cdp) Hawaii County	234	24.32
Wainaku, HI (cdp) Hawaii County	296	24.12
Kalaheo, HI (cdp) Kauai County	937	23.95
Honalo, HI (cdp) Hawaii County	467	23.50
Waipio Acres, HI (cdp) Honolulu County	1,244	23.48
Laupahoehoe, HI (cdp) Hawaii County	105	22.20
Mountain View, HI (cdp) Hawaii County	611	21.83
Hanalei, HI (cdp) Kauai County	103	21.55
Village Park, HI (cdp) Honolulu County	2,064	21.44
Wailua Homesteads, HI (cdp) Kauai County	950	20.80
Koloa, HI (cdp) Kauai County	404	20.80
Kailua, HI (cdp) Honolulu County	7,534	20.63
Pahala, HI (cdp) Hawaii County	284	20.61
Pakala Village, HI (cdp) Kauai County	97	20.29
Honokaa, HI (cdp) Hawaii County	452	20.24
Waialua, HI (cdp) Honolulu County	755	20.07
Kapaa, HI (cdp) Kauai County	1,850	19.53
Haleiwa, HI (cdp) Honolulu County	434	19.51
Kahaluu, HI (cdp) Honolulu County	551	18.77
Omao, HI (cdp) Kauai County	223	18.26
Hawi, HI (cdp) Hawaii County	169	18.02
Makakilo City, HI (cdp) Honolulu County	2,318	17.62
Kekaha, HI (cdp) Kauai County	556	17.51
Waihee-Waiehu, HI (cdp) Maui County	1,278	17.48
Halaula, HI (cdp) Hawaii County	85	17.17
Honaunau-Napoopoo, HI (cdp) Hawaii County	407	16.86
Waimea, HI (cdp) Hawaii County	1,183	16.83
Paauilo, HI (cdp) Hawaii County	96	16.81
Makawao, HI (cdp) Maui County	1,010	15.96
Puhi, HI (cdp) Kauai County	185	15.60
Naalehu, HI (cdp) Hawaii County	140	15.23
Haliimaile, HI (cdp) Maui County	136	15.20
Paia, HI (cdp) Maui County	379	15.17
Kalaoa, HI (cdp) Hawaii County	1,002	14.75
Waipahu, HI (cdp) Honolulu County	4,874	14.72
Waikane, HI (cdp) Honolulu County	105	14.46
Hanamaulu, HI (cdp) Kauai County	463	14.15
Hawaiian Paradise Park, HI (cdp) Hawaii County	995	14.11
Lahaina, HI (cdp) Maui County	1,262	13.84
Kaumakani, HI (cdp) Kauai County	83	13.67
Hawaiian Beaches, HI (cdp) Hawaii County	495	13.35
Poipu, HI (cdp) Kauai County	143	13.30
Ewa Villages, HI (cdp) Honolulu County	622	13.12
Gardena, CA (city) Los Angeles County	7,445	12.89
Kaunakakai, HI (cdp) Maui County	346	12.69
Waimanalo, HI (cdp) Honolulu County	464	12.66
Lanai City, HI (cdp) Maui County	399	12.61
Waianae, HI (cdp) Honolulu County	1,317	12.54
Kailua, HI (cdp) Hawaii County	1,223	12.39
Waikoloa Village, HI (cdp) Hawaii County	588	12.23
Ewa Beach, HI (cdp) Honolulu County	1,731	11.82
Ainaloa, HI (cdp) Hawaii County	225	11.78
Torrance, CA (city) Los Angeles County	16,048	11.63
Holualoa, HI (cdp) Hawaii County	709	11.61
Volcano, HI (cdp) Hawaii County	255	11.43
Puako, HI (cdp) Hawaii County	49	11.42
Kualapuu, HI (cdp) Maui County	218	11.26
Haiku-Pauwela, HI (cdp) Maui County	728	11.07
Kahuku, HI (cdp) Honolulu County	231	11.02
Kaaawa, HI (cdp) Honolulu County	144	10.88
Fern Forest, HI (cdp) Hawaii County	52	10.83
Makaha Valley, HI (cdp) Honolulu County	135	10.47
Kahaluu-Keauhou, HI (cdp) Hawaii County	250	10.36
Kilauea, HI (cdp) Kauai County	215	10.28
Punaluu, HI (cdp) Honolulu County	89	10.10
South San Gabriel, CA (cdp) Los Angeles County	764	10.06
Whitmore Village, HI (cdp) Honolulu County	405	9.98
Makaha, HI (cdp) Honolulu County	773	9.97
Pupukea, HI (cdp) Honolulu County	409	9.62
Maili, HI (cdp) Honolulu County	567	9.54
Fern Acres, HI (cdp) Hawaii County	72	9.52
Nanawale Estates, HI (cdp) Hawaii County	101	9.41
Hawaiian Acres, HI (cdp) Hawaii County	164	9.23
Orchidlands Estates, HI (cdp) Hawaii County	159	9.19
Anahola, HI (cdp) Kauai County	175	9.06
Rancho Palos Verdes, CA (city) Los Angeles County	3,679	8.94
Rolling Hills Estates, CA (city) Los Angeles County	670	8.73
Hauula, HI (cdp) Honolulu County	306	8.38
Hamer, ID (city) Jefferson County	1	8.33
Kihei, HI (cdp) Maui County	1,362	8.13
Monterey Park, CA (city) Los Angeles County	4,856	8.09
Nanakuli, HI (cdp) Honolulu County	861	7.96
Greenville, NY (cdp) Westchester County	684	7.91
Maunaloa, HI (cdp) Maui County	18	7.83
Eden Roc, HI (cdp) Hawaii County	35	7.76
Mokuleia, HI (cdp) Honolulu County	138	7.50
Kapalua, HI (cdp) Maui County	34	7.28
Bonanza, CO (town) Saguache County	1	7.14
Napili-Honokowai, HI (cdp) Maui County	474	6.98
Salem, WV (city) Harrison County	140	6.98
Belknap, IL (village) Johnson County	9	6.77
Waimanalo Beach, HI (cdp) Honolulu County	284	6.65
Forest Home, NY (cdp) Tompkins County	62	6.59
Wailea-Makena, HI (cdp) Maui County	361	6.37
Fort Lee, NJ (borough) Bergen County	2,161	6.09
Maalaea, HI (cdp) Maui County	27	5.95
Laie, HI (cdp) Honolulu County	268	5.85
Tuckahoe, NY (village) Westchester County	359	5.78
Hana, HI (cdp) Maui County	41	5.78
El Cerrito, CA (city) Contra Costa County	1,288	5.56
Kaanapali, HI (cdp) Maui County	76	5.53
La Palma, CA (city) Orange County	847	5.50
Foster City, CA (city) San Mateo County	1,555	5.40
Cupertino, CA (city) Santa Clara County	2,660	5.26
West Carson, CA (cdp) Los Angeles County	1,093	5.17
Palos Verdes Estates, CA (city) Los Angeles County	681	5.10
Hawaiian Ocean View, HI (cdp) Hawaii County	111	5.10
Walnut Grove, CA (cdp) Sacramento County	34	5.08
Alcova, WY (cdp) Natrona County	1	5.00
Alcan Border, AK (cdp) Southeast Fairbanks Census Area	1	4.76
Leilani Estates, HI (cdp) Hawaii County	48	4.59
Newcastle, WA (city) King County	352	4.55
Barbers Point Housing, HI (cdp) Honolulu County	3	4.48
Vining, MN (city) Otter Tail County	3	4.41
Manorhaven, NY (village) Nassau County	269	4.38

Notes: (cdp) census designated place; Refer to the Explanation of Data in the front of the book for more detailed information.

Asian: Japanese

Top 150 Places Sorted by Percent

(Based on places with populations of 10,000 or more)

Place	Number	%
Pearl City, HI (cdp) Honolulu County	12,499	40.35
Waimalu, HI (cdp) Honolulu County	11,537	39.28
Hilo, HI (cdp) Hawaii County	15,639	38.37
Mililani Town, HI (cdp) Honolulu County	10,739	37.54
Waipio, HI (cdp) Honolulu County	4,205	36.03
Kaneohe, HI (cdp) Honolulu County	12,518	35.80
Wailuku, HI (cdp) Maui County	3,984	32.40
Honolulu, HI (cdp) Honolulu County	112,778	30.34
Wahiawa, HI (cdp) Honolulu County	4,888	30.26
Halawa, HI (cdp) Honolulu County	3,911	28.15
Kahului, HI (cdp) Maui County	5,087	25.25
Kailua, HI (cdp) Honolulu County	7,534	20.63
Makakilo City, HI (cdp) Honolulu County	2,318	17.62
Waipahu, HI (cdp) Honolulu County	4,874	14.72
Gardena, CA (city) Los Angeles County	7,445	12.89
Waianae, HI (cdp) Honolulu County	1,317	12.54
Ewa Beach, HI (cdp) Honolulu County	1,731	11.82
Torrance, CA (city) Los Angeles County	16,048	11.63
Rancho Palos Verdes, CA (city) Los Angeles County	3,679	8.94
Kihei, HI (cdp) Maui County	1,362	8.13
Monterey Park, CA (city) Los Angeles County	4,856	8.09
Nanakuli, HI (cdp) Honolulu County	861	7.96
Fort Lee, NJ (borough) Bergen County	2,161	6.09
El Cerrito, CA (city) Contra Costa County	1,288	5.56
La Palma, CA (city) Orange County	847	5.50
Foster City, CA (city) San Mateo County	1,555	5.40
Cupertino, CA (city) Santa Clara County	2,660	5.26
West Carson, CA (cdp) Los Angeles County	1,093	5.17
Palos Verdes Estates, CA (city) Los Angeles County	681	5.10
Irvine, CA (city) Orange County	6,075	4.25
Culver City, CA (city) Los Angeles County	1,604	4.13
South Pasadena, CA (city) Los Angeles County	998	4.11
Rye, NY (city) Westchester County	611	4.09
Scarsdale, NY (village) Westchester County	728	4.08
Albany, CA (city) Alameda County	654	3.98
Cerritos, CA (city) Los Angeles County	2,044	3.97
Eastchester, NY (town) Westchester County	1,110	3.54
Bryn Mawr-Skyway, WA (cdp) King County	490	3.51
Lomita, CA (city) Los Angeles County	699	3.49
Mercer Island, WA (city) King County	762	3.46
Cypress, CA (city) Orange County	1,570	3.40
Montebello, CA (city) Los Angeles County	2,095	3.37
Redondo Beach, CA (city) Los Angeles County	2,125	3.36
Los Altos, CA (city) Santa Clara County	920	3.32
Fountain Valley, CA (city) Orange County	1,809	3.29
East San Gabriel, CA (cdp) Los Angeles County	477	3.29
Sunnyvale, CA (city) Santa Clara County	4,261	3.23
Bellevue, WA (city) King County	3,538	3.23
Hacienda Heights, CA (cdp) Los Angeles County	1,606	3.02
Berkeley, CA (city) Alameda County	3,084	3.00
Saratoga, CA (city) Santa Clara County	896	3.00
Marina, CA (city) Monterey County	744	2.96
Palo Alto, CA (city) Santa Clara County	1,703	2.91
Millbrae, CA (city) San Mateo County	600	2.90
Mountain View, CA (city) Santa Clara County	2,040	2.89
San Mateo, CA (city) San Mateo County	2,668	2.88
Harrison, NY (village) Westchester County	694	2.87
San Marino, CA (city) Los Angeles County	359	2.77
Dublin, OH (city) Franklin County	855	2.72
Monterey, CA (city) Monterey County	802	2.70
La Canada Flintridge, CA (city) Los Angeles County	545	2.68
Belmont, CA (city) San Mateo County	667	2.65
Campbell, CA (city) Santa Clara County	1,004	2.63
Manhattan Beach, CA (city) Los Angeles County	879	2.60
Walnut, CA (city) Los Angeles County	767	2.56
Novi, MI (city) Oakland County	1,185	2.50
Burlingame, CA (city) San Mateo County	696	2.47
Greenwich, CT (town) Fairfield County	1,506	2.46
Brookline, MA (cdp) Norfolk County	1,406	2.46
Laguna, CA (cdp) Sacramento County	842	2.45
Moraga, CA (town) Contra Costa County	398	2.44
Arcadia, CA (city) Los Angeles County	1,290	2.43
Ontario, OR (city) Malheur County	265	2.41
Davis, CA (city) Yolo County	1,439	2.39
West Bloomfield, MI (township) Oakland County	1,511	2.33

Place	Number	%
Reedley, CA (city) Fresno County	481	2.32
Piedmont, CA (city) Alameda County	253	2.31
Seaside, CA (city) Monterey County	729	2.30
Rossmoor, CA (cdp) Orange County	237	2.30
Santa Monica, CA (city) Los Angeles County	1,928	2.29
Diamond Bar, CA (city) Los Angeles County	1,264	2.25
Huntington Beach, CA (city) Orange County	4,174	2.20
Stanford, CA (cdp) Santa Clara County	293	2.20
Hillsborough, CA (town) San Mateo County	238	2.20
Redmond, WA (city) King County	989	2.19
Aliso Viejo, CA (cdp) Orange County	881	2.19
Ellensburg, WA (city) Kittitas County	338	2.19
Greenburgh, NY (town) Westchester County	1,894	2.18
Seattle, WA (city) King County	12,113	2.15
Sacramento, CA (city) Sacramento County	8,710	2.14
Cascade-Fairwood, WA (cdp) King County	724	2.09
Foothill Ranch, CA (cdp) Orange County	228	2.09
Seal Beach, CA (city) Orange County	497	2.06
Santa Clara, CA (city) Santa Clara County	2,103	2.05
Alhambra, CA (city) Los Angeles County	1,758	2.05
Tenafly, NJ (borough) Bergen County	282	2.04
Los Gatos, CA (town) Santa Clara County	576	2.01
Pasadena, CA (city) Los Angeles County	2,670	1.99
Elk Grove Village, IL (village) Cook County	676	1.95
Rowland Heights, CA (cdp) Los Angeles County	937	1.93
Hermosa Beach, CA (city) Los Angeles County	359	1.93
Temple City, CA (city) Los Angeles County	640	1.92
Menlo Park, CA (city) San Mateo County	591	1.92
La Riviera, CA (cdp) Sacramento County	195	1.90
Yorba Linda, CA (city) Orange County	1,114	1.89
San Francisco, CA (city) San Francisco County	14,618	1.88
Isla Vista, CA (cdp) Santa Barbara County	344	1.88
Chula Vista, CA (city) San Diego County	3,252	1.87
San Gabriel, CA (city) Los Angeles County	745	1.87
Pullman, WA (city) Whitman County	461	1.87
Lafayette, CA (city) Contra Costa County	444	1.86
Alameda, CA (city) Alameda County	1,329	1.84
Cliffside Park, NJ (borough) Bergen County	424	1.84
Pacific Grove, CA (city) Monterey County	285	1.84
Kaneohe Station, HI (cdp) Honolulu County	218	1.84
Vineyard, CA (cdp) Sacramento County	184	1.82
Camarillo, CA (city) Ventura County	1,031	1.81
San Bruno, CA (city) San Mateo County	725	1.81
Port Washington, NY (cdp) Nassau County	276	1.81
Bonita, CA (cdp) San Diego County	223	1.80
East Hill-Meridian, WA (cdp) King County	521	1.78
Sammamish, WA (city) King County	602	1.77
Pleasant Hill, CA (city) Contra Costa County	582	1.77
Lakewood, WA (city) Pierce County	1,011	1.74
Laguna Niguel, CA (city) Orange County	1,068	1.73
San Jose, CA (city) Santa Clara County	15,353	1.72
Sierra Madre, CA (city) Los Angeles County	181	1.71
San Ramon, CA (city) Contra Costa County	760	1.70
Ridgewood, NJ (village) Bergen County	423	1.70
Avocado Heights, CA (cdp) Los Angeles County	257	1.70
Orinda, CA (city) Contra Costa County	298	1.69
Tustin Foothills, CA (cdp) Orange County	403	1.68
Parkland, WA (cdp) Pierce County	402	1.67
Mill Creek, WA (city) Snohomish County	193	1.67
Rosemead, CA (city) Los Angeles County	887	1.66
Pinole, CA (city) Contra Costa County	316	1.66
Los Alamitos, CA (city) Orange County	191	1.66
Mission Viejo, CA (city) Orange County	1,528	1.64
Renton, WA (city) King County	815	1.63
El Segundo, CA (city) Los Angeles County	262	1.63
Altadena, CA (cdp) Los Angeles County	692	1.62
Rosemont, CA (cdp) Sacramento County	372	1.62
Dobbs Ferry, NY (village) Westchester County	172	1.62
Schaumburg, IL (village) Cook County	1,214	1.61
Hoffman Estates, IL (village) Cook County	796	1.61
Tustin, CA (city) Orange County	1,079	1.60
La Crescenta-Montrose, CA (cdp) Los Angeles County	296	1.60
Tamalpais-Homestead Valley, CA (cdp) Marin County	170	1.59
Hercules, CA (city) Contra Costa County	308	1.58
Lake Forest Park, WA (city) King County	207	1.58

Notes: (cdp) census designated place; Refer to the Explanation of Data in the front of the book for more detailed information.

Asian: Korean

Top 150 Places Sorted by Number

(Based on all places, regardless of population)

Place	Number	%
Los Angeles, CA (city) Los Angeles County	95,106	2.57
New York, NY (city) New York City	90,208	1.13
Honolulu, HI (cdp) Honolulu County	21,576	5.81
Chicago, IL (city) Cook County	12,867	0.44
Glendale, CA (city) Los Angeles County	12,800	6.57
San Jose, CA (city) Santa Clara County	10,393	1.16
Torrance, CA (city) Los Angeles County	9,864	7.15
Fullerton, CA (city) Orange County	9,301	7.38
Cerritos, CA (city) Los Angeles County	9,109	17.69
San Francisco, CA (city) San Francisco County	8,706	1.12
San Diego, CA (city) San Diego County	8,339	0.68
Irvine, CA (city) Orange County	7,913	5.53
Philadelphia, PA (city) Philadelphia County	7,059	0.47
Garden Grove, CA (city) Orange County	6,439	3.90
Anaheim, CA (city) Orange County	6,426	1.96
Palisades Park, NJ (borough) Bergen County	6,211	36.38
Houston, TX (city) Harris County	6,172	0.32
Fort Lee, NJ (borough) Bergen County	6,091	17.18
Seattle, WA (city) King County	5,808	1.03
Diamond Bar, CA (city) Los Angeles County	5,742	10.20
Buena Park, CA (city) Orange County	5,115	6.53
Federal Way, WA (city) King County	4,740	5.69
Anchorage, AK (municipality) Anchorage Borough	4,084	1.57
Austin, TX (city) Travis County	4,006	0.61
Colorado Springs, CO (city) El Paso County	3,944	1.09
Rowland Heights, CA (cdp) Los Angeles County	3,821	7.87
Annandale, VA (cdp) Fairfax County	3,752	6.82
Gardena, CA (city) Los Angeles County	3,748	6.49
Aurora, CO (city) Arapahoe County	3,641	1.32
Dallas, TX (city) Dallas County	3,578	0.30
Tacoma, WA (city) Pierce County	3,552	1.84
Fremont, CA (city) Alameda County	3,464	1.70
North Hempstead, NY (town) Nassau County	3,425	1.54
Burke, VA (cdp) Fairfax County	3,383	5.86
Downey, CA (city) Los Angeles County	3,359	3.13
Hacienda Heights, CA (cdp) Los Angeles County	3,055	5.75
San Antonio, TX (city) Bexar County	2,957	0.26
Columbus, OH (city) Franklin County	2,930	0.41
Ellicott City, MD (cdp) Howard County	2,876	5.10
Norwalk, CA (city) Los Angeles County	2,831	2.74
Lakewood, WA (city) Pierce County	2,777	4.77
Boston, MA (city) Suffolk County	2,753	0.47
Irving, TX (city) Dallas County	2,688	1.40
La Palma, CA (city) Orange County	2,685	17.43
Sunnyvale, CA (city) Santa Clara County	2,618	1.99
La Crescenta-Montrose, CA (cdp) Los Angeles County	2,596	14.01
Killeen, TX (city) Bell County	2,587	2.98
Ann Arbor, MI (city) Washtenaw County	2,581	2.26
Hempstead, NY (town) Nassau County	2,559	0.34
Skokie, IL (village) Cook County	2,557	4.04
Cypress, CA (city) Orange County	2,548	5.51
Oyster Bay, NY (town) Nassau County	2,505	0.85
Santa Clara, CA (city) Santa Clara County	2,471	2.41
Phoenix, AZ (city) Maricopa County	2,462	0.19
Portland, OR (city) Multnomah County	2,398	0.45
La Mirada, CA (city) Los Angeles County	2,365	5.06
Bellevue, WA (city) King County	2,351	2.15
La Canada Flintridge, CA (city) Los Angeles County	2,297	11.31
Burbank, CA (city) Los Angeles County	2,295	2.29
Cupertino, CA (city) Santa Clara County	2,193	4.34
Centreville, VA (cdp) Fairfax County	2,152	4.42
Oakland, CA (city) Alameda County	2,131	0.53
Rancho Palos Verdes, CA (city) Los Angeles County	2,130	5.18
El Paso, TX (city) El Paso County	2,108	0.37
Las Vegas, NV (city) Clark County	2,080	0.43
Berkeley, CA (city) Alameda County	2,076	2.02
Riverside, CA (city) Riverside County	2,008	0.79
Baltimore, MD (independent city) Baltimore city	2,008	0.31
Cambridge, MA (city) Middlesex County	1,993	1.97
Charlotte, NC (city) Mecklenburg County	1,936	0.36
Minneapolis, MN (city) Hennepin County	1,934	0.51
Glenview, IL (village) Cook County	1,929	4.61
Plano, TX (city) Collin County	1,916	0.86
Long Beach, CA (city) Los Angeles County	1,911	0.41
Huntington Beach, CA (city) Orange County	1,822	0.96
Nashville-Davidson, TN (special city) Davidson County	1,810	0.33
Arcadia, CA (city) Los Angeles County	1,775	3.35
Spring Valley, NV (cdp) Clark County	1,768	1.51
Arlington, VA (cdp) Arlington County	1,758	0.93
Madison, WI (city) Dane County	1,740	0.84
Chula Vista, CA (city) San Diego County	1,723	0.99
Columbia, MD (cdp) Howard County	1,714	1.94
Waimalu, HI (cdp) Honolulu County	1,708	5.82
Denver, CO (city) Denver County	1,702	0.31
Brookhaven, NY (town) Suffolk County	1,689	0.38
Lakewood, CA (city) Los Angeles County	1,677	2.11
Edison, NJ (cdp) Middlesex County	1,647	1.69
Chino Hills, CA (city) San Bernardino County	1,641	2.46
Schaumburg, IL (village) Cook County	1,641	2.18
Cliffside Park, NJ (borough) Bergen County	1,620	7.04
West Springfield, VA (cdp) Fairfax County	1,570	5.53
Newport News, VA (independent city) Newport News city	1,554	0.86
Ridgefield, NJ (borough) Bergen County	1,550	14.31
Alameda, CA (city) Alameda County	1,545	2.14
Clarksville, TN (city) Montgomery County	1,538	1.49
Leonia, NJ (borough) Bergen County	1,537	17.24
Northbrook, IL (village) Cook County	1,520	4.55
Jersey City, NJ (city) Hudson County	1,507	0.63
Carrollton, TX (city) Denton County	1,504	1.37
Lawton, OK (city) Comanche County	1,499	1.62
Tucson, AZ (city) Pima County	1,498	0.31
Shoreline, WA (city) King County	1,475	2.78
Alexandria, VA (independent city) Alexandria city	1,454	1.13
Aspen Hill, MD (cdp) Montgomery County	1,451	2.89
Orange, CA (city) Orange County	1,451	1.13
Pasadena, CA (city) Los Angeles County	1,435	1.07
Paradise, NV (cdp) Clark County	1,423	0.76
Mililani Town, HI (cdp) Honolulu County	1,413	4.94
Cherry Hill, NJ (township) Camden County	1,409	2.01
Beaverton, OR (city) Washington County	1,393	1.83
Indianapolis, IN (special city) Marion County	1,385	0.18
Raleigh, NC (city) Wake County	1,367	0.50
Jacksonville, FL (special city) Duval County	1,366	0.19
Huntington, NY (town) Suffolk County	1,352	0.69
Chantilly, VA (cdp) Fairfax County	1,348	3.28
Cheltenham, PA (township) Montgomery County	1,346	3.65
Oklahoma City, OK (city) Oklahoma County	1,342	0.27
Tenafly, NJ (borough) Bergen County	1,332	9.65
Marina, CA (city) Monterey County	1,313	5.23
Walnut, CA (city) Los Angeles County	1,307	4.36
University Place, WA (city) Pierce County	1,286	4.30
Troy, MI (city) Oakland County	1,283	1.58
Washington, DC (city) District of Columbia	1,273	0.22
Augusta-Richmond County, GA (special city) Richmond County	1,258	0.64
Paramus, NJ (borough) Bergen County	1,253	4.87
Fort Worth, TX (city) Tarrant County	1,253	0.23
Columbus, GA (special city) Muscogee County	1,252	0.67
Virginia Beach, VA (independent city) Virginia Beach city	1,237	0.29
Tustin, CA (city) Orange County	1,234	1.83
Mount Prospect, IL (village) Cook County	1,232	2.19
Fountain Valley, CA (city) Orange County	1,221	2.22
Naperville, IL (city) Du Page County	1,215	0.95
Bakersfield, CA (city) Kern County	1,212	0.49
Greenburgh, NY (town) Westchester County	1,196	1.38
Fayetteville, NC (city) Cumberland County	1,187	0.98
Eugene, OR (city) Lane County	1,179	0.86
Oakton, VA (cdp) Fairfax County	1,167	3.98
Fresno, CA (city) Fresno County	1,155	0.27
Amherst, NY (town) Erie County	1,145	0.98
Hoffman Estates, IL (village) Cook County	1,144	2.31
Santa Clarita, CA (city) Los Angeles County	1,140	0.75
Sacramento, CA (city) Sacramento County	1,140	0.28
Urbana, IL (city) Champaign County	1,139	3.13
Buffalo Grove, IL (village) Lake County	1,135	2.65
Richardson, TX (city) Dallas County	1,133	1.23
North Potomac, MD (cdp) Montgomery County	1,130	4.90
Albuquerque, NM (city) Bernalillo County	1,125	0.25
Garland, TX (city) Dallas County	1,115	0.52
Pittsburgh, PA (city) Allegheny County	1,113	0.33
Lynnwood, WA (city) Snohomish County	1,103	3.26

Notes: (cdp) census designated place; Refer to the Explanation of Data in the front of the book for more detailed information.

Asian: Korean

Top 150 Places Sorted by Percent

(Based on all places, regardless of population)

Place	Number	%
Palisades Park, NJ (borough) Bergen County	6,211	36.38
Cerritos, CA (city) Los Angeles County	9,109	17.69
La Palma, CA (city) Orange County	2,685	17.43
Leonia, NJ (borough) Bergen County	1,537	17.24
Fort Lee, NJ (borough) Bergen County	6,091	17.18
Ridgefield, NJ (borough) Bergen County	1,550	14.31
La Crescenta-Montrose, CA (cdp) Los Angeles County	2,596	14.01
Closter, NJ (borough) Bergen County	1,069	12.75
Norwood, NJ (borough) Bergen County	730	12.69
Edgewater, NJ (borough) Bergen County	908	11.83
Englewood Cliffs, NJ (borough) Bergen County	626	11.76
La Canada Flintridge, CA (city) Los Angeles County	2,297	11.31
Demarest, NJ (borough) Bergen County	508	10.49
Diamond Bar, CA (city) Los Angeles County	5,742	10.20
Cresskill, NJ (borough) Bergen County	784	10.12
Old Tappan, NJ (borough) Bergen County	552	10.07
Tenafly, NJ (borough) Bergen County	1,332	9.65
Alpine, NJ (borough) Bergen County	205	9.39
Northvale, NJ (borough) Bergen County	394	8.83
Harrington Park, NJ (borough) Bergen County	406	8.57
Little Ferry, NJ (borough) Bergen County	865	8.01
Rowland Heights, CA (cdp) Los Angeles County	3,821	7.87
Merrifield, VA (cdp) Fairfax County	879	7.87
Fullerton, CA (city) Orange County	9,301	7.38
Lake Success, NY (village) Nassau County	204	7.29
Forest Home, NY (cdp) Tompkins County	68	7.23
Torrance, CA (city) Los Angeles County	9,864	7.15
Lansing, NY (village) Tompkins County	241	7.05
Cliffside Park, NJ (borough) Bergen County	1,620	7.04
Mantua, VA (cdp) Fairfax County	525	7.01
Annandale, VA (cdp) Fairfax County	3,752	6.82
Elliott, ND (city) Ransom County	3	6.82
Belknap, IL (village) Johnson County	9	6.77
Glendale, CA (city) Los Angeles County	12,800	6.57
Buena Park, CA (city) Orange County	5,115	6.53
Gardena, CA (city) Los Angeles County	3,748	6.49
Gully, MN (township) Polk County	6	6.06
Panola, IL (village) Woodford County	2	6.06
East Rutherford, NJ (borough) Bergen County	525	6.02
Burke, VA (cdp) Fairfax County	3,383	5.86
Waimalu, HI (cdp) Honolulu County	1,708	5.82
Honolulu, HI (cdp) Honolulu County	21,576	5.81
Hacienda Heights, CA (cdp) Los Angeles County	3,055	5.75
Federal Way, WA (city) King County	4,740	5.69
Van Tassell, WY (town) Niobrara County	1	5.56
Irvine, CA (city) Orange County	7,913	5.53
West Springfield, VA (cdp) Fairfax County	1,570	5.53
Cypress, CA (city) Orange County	2,548	5.51
Rutherford, NJ (borough) Bergen County	995	5.49
Mukilteo, WA (city) Snohomish County	985	5.47
Colesville, MD (cdp) Montgomery County	1,076	5.43
University Gardens, NY (cdp) Nassau County	219	5.29
Marina, CA (city) Monterey County	1,313	5.23
Savoy, IL (village) Champaign County	233	5.21
Rancho Palos Verdes, CA (city) Los Angeles County	2,130	5.18
Hawaiian Gardens, CA (city) Los Angeles County	761	5.15
Ellicott City, MD (cdp) Howard County	2,876	5.10
Searingtown, NY (cdp) Nassau County	256	5.09
La Mirada, CA (city) Los Angeles County	2,365	5.06
River Edge, NJ (borough) Bergen County	553	5.05
Mililani Town, HI (cdp) Honolulu County	1,413	4.94
North Potomac, MD (cdp) Montgomery County	1,130	4.90
Mill Creek, WA (city) Snohomish County	565	4.90
Paramus, NJ (borough) Bergen County	1,253	4.87
Lakewood, WA (city) Pierce County	2,777	4.77
Johnsville, CA (cdp) Plumas County	1	4.76
Morton Grove, IL (village) Cook County	1,065	4.74
Lincolnwood, IL (village) Cook County	586	4.74
Manorhaven, NY (village) Nassau County	290	4.72
Lake Sumner, NM (cdp) De Baca County	4	4.65
Saltaire, NY (village) Suffolk County	2	4.65
Burtonsville, MD (cdp) Montgomery County	338	4.63
Glenview, IL (village) Cook County	1,929	4.61
West Carson, CA (cdp) Los Angeles County	973	4.60
Waipio, HI (cdp) Honolulu County	534	4.58
Tysons Corner, VA (cdp) Fairfax County	848	4.57
Artesia, CA (city) Los Angeles County	748	4.57
Northbrook, IL (village) Cook County	1,520	4.55
Blind Lake, MN (township) Cass County	4	4.55
Barbers Point Housing, HI (cdp) Honolulu County	3	4.48
Calverton, MD (cdp) Montgomery County	562	4.46
Hedwig Village, TX (city) Harris County	104	4.46
Centreville, VA (cdp) Fairfax County	2,152	4.42
Walnut, CA (city) Los Angeles County	1,307	4.36
Millward, MN (township) Aitkin County	3	4.35
Cupertino, CA (city) Santa Clara County	2,193	4.34
Albany, CA (city) Alameda County	710	4.32
University Place, WA (city) Pierce County	1,286	4.30
Fairland, MD (cdp) Montgomery County	930	4.28
Cockeysville, MD (cdp) Baltimore County	830	4.28
Picnic Point-North Lynnwood, WA (cdp) Snohomish County	973	4.24
Du Pont, WA (city) Pierce County	104	4.24
Angwin, CA (cdp) Napa County	132	4.19
Northeast Ithaca, NY (cdp) Tompkins County	111	4.18
Wahiawa, HI (cdp) Honolulu County	668	4.14
Saint Robert, MO (city) Pulaski County	114	4.13
Manhasset Hills, NY (cdp) Nassau County	151	4.12
Jericho, NY (cdp) Nassau County	535	4.10
Skokie, IL (village) Cook County	2,557	4.04
Oak Hills, OR (cdp) Washington County	364	4.02
Oakton, VA (cdp) Fairfax County	1,167	3.98
Aiea, HI (cdp) Honolulu County	358	3.97
Stanford, CA (cdp) Santa Clara County	522	3.92
Garden Grove, CA (city) Orange County	6,439	3.90
Whitpain, PA (township) Montgomery County	716	3.86
Broomall, PA (cdp) Delaware County	426	3.86
Rolling Hills Estates, CA (city) Los Angeles County	296	3.86
Tappan, NY (cdp) Rockland County	260	3.85
Louisburg, MN (city) Lac qui Parle County	1	3.85
Beaver, IA (city) Boone County	2	3.77
South Pasadena, CA (city) Los Angeles County	913	3.76
North Springfield, VA (cdp) Fairfax County	345	3.76
Dunn Loring, VA (cdp) Fairfax County	293	3.73
Spanaway, WA (cdp) Pierce County	804	3.72
Parkland, WA (cdp) Pierce County	893	3.71
Heeia, HI (cdp) Honolulu County	183	3.70
Syosset, NY (cdp) Nassau County	685	3.69
Cheltenham, PA (township) Montgomery County	1,346	3.65
Paukaa, HI (cdp) Hawaii County	18	3.64
Haworth, NJ (borough) Bergen County	121	3.57
North Hills, NY (village) Nassau County	153	3.56
Duluth, GA (city) Gwinnett County	785	3.55
Waipio Acres, HI (cdp) Honolulu County	185	3.49
Udell, IA (city) Appanoose County	2	3.45
Livengood, AK (cdp) Yukon-Koyukuk Census Area	1	3.45
Montgomery, PA (township) Montgomery County	755	3.43
Los Alamitos, CA (city) Orange County	390	3.38
Halawa, HI (cdp) Honolulu County	468	3.37
Marlborough, MO (village) Saint Louis County	75	3.36
Arcadia, CA (city) Los Angeles County	1,775	3.35
Cabin John, MD (cdp) Montgomery County	58	3.34
Wailuku, HI (cdp) Maui County	410	3.33
Gold River, CA (cdp) Sacramento County	266	3.32
Greenbelt, MD (city) Prince George's County	706	3.29
Chantilly, VA (cdp) Fairfax County	1,348	3.28
Blue Bell, PA (cdp) Montgomery County	210	3.28
Lynnwood, WA (city) Snohomish County	1,103	3.26
Mays Chapel, MD (cdp) Baltimore County	373	3.26
Fort Ritchie, MD (cdp) Washington County	9	3.26
Tonsina, AK (cdp) Valdez-Cordova Census Area	3	3.26
Greenville, NY (cdp) Westchester County	281	3.25
Greentree, NJ (cdp) Camden County	374	3.24
Ewa Gentry, HI (cdp) Honolulu County	160	3.24
White Oak, MD (cdp) Montgomery County	678	3.23
Tanglewilde-Thompson Place, WA (cdp) Thurston County	182	3.21
Pittsville, MD (town) Wicomico County	38	3.21
South Valley Stream, NY (cdp) Nassau County	180	3.19
Loma Linda, CA (city) San Bernardino County	594	3.18
Niles, IL (village) Cook County	949	3.16
Ridgefield Park, NJ (village) Bergen County	407	3.16

Notes: (cdp) census designated place; Refer to the Explanation of Data in the front of the book for more detailed information.

Asian: Korean

Top 150 Places Sorted by Percent

(Based on places with populations of 10,000 or more)

Place	Number	%
Palisades Park, NJ (borough) Bergen County	6,211	36.38
Cerritos, CA (city) Los Angeles County	9,109	17.69
La Palma, CA (city) Orange County	2,685	17.43
Fort Lee, NJ (borough) Bergen County	6,091	17.18
Ridgefield, NJ (borough) Bergen County	1,550	14.31
La Crescenta-Montrose, CA (cdp) Los Angeles County	2,596	14.01
La Canada Flintridge, CA (city) Los Angeles County	2,297	11.31
Diamond Bar, CA (city) Los Angeles County	5,742	10.20
Tenafly, NJ (borough) Bergen County	1,332	9.65
Little Ferry, NJ (borough) Bergen County	865	8.01
Rowland Heights, CA (cdp) Los Angeles County	3,821	7.87
Merrifield, VA (cdp) Fairfax County	879	7.87
Fullerton, CA (city) Orange County	9,301	7.38
Torrance, CA (city) Los Angeles County	9,864	7.15
Cliffside Park, NJ (borough) Bergen County	1,620	7.04
Annandale, VA (cdp) Fairfax County	3,752	6.82
Glendale, CA (city) Los Angeles County	12,800	6.57
Buena Park, CA (city) Orange County	5,115	6.53
Gardena, CA (city) Los Angeles County	3,748	6.49
Burke, VA (cdp) Fairfax County	3,383	5.86
Waimalu, HI (cdp) Honolulu County	1,708	5.82
Honolulu, HI (cdp) Honolulu County	21,576	5.81
Hacienda Heights, CA (cdp) Los Angeles County	3,055	5.75
Federal Way, WA (city) King County	4,740	5.69
Irvine, CA (city) Orange County	7,913	5.53
West Springfield, VA (cdp) Fairfax County	1,570	5.53
Cypress, CA (city) Orange County	2,548	5.51
Rutherford, NJ (borough) Bergen County	995	5.49
Mukilteo, WA (city) Snohomish County	985	5.47
Colesville, MD (cdp) Montgomery County	1,076	5.43
Marina, CA (city) Monterey County	1,313	5.23
Rancho Palos Verdes, CA (city) Los Angeles County	2,130	5.18
Hawaiian Gardens, CA (city) Los Angeles County	761	5.15
Ellicott City, MD (cdp) Howard County	2,876	5.10
La Mirada, CA (city) Los Angeles County	2,365	5.06
River Edge, NJ (borough) Bergen County	553	5.05
Mililani Town, HI (cdp) Honolulu County	1,413	4.94
North Potomac, MD (cdp) Montgomery County	1,130	4.90
Mill Creek, WA (city) Snohomish County	565	4.90
Paramus, NJ (borough) Bergen County	1,253	4.87
Lakewood, WA (city) Pierce County	2,777	4.77
Morton Grove, IL (village) Cook County	1,065	4.74
Lincolnwood, IL (village) Cook County	586	4.74
Glenview, IL (village) Cook County	1,929	4.61
West Carson, CA (cdp) Los Angeles County	973	4.60
Waipio, HI (cdp) Honolulu County	534	4.58
Tysons Corner, VA (cdp) Fairfax County	848	4.57
Artesia, CA (city) Los Angeles County	748	4.57
Northbrook, IL (village) Cook County	1,520	4.55
Calverton, MD (cdp) Montgomery County	562	4.46
Centreville, VA (cdp) Fairfax County	2,152	4.42
Walnut, CA (city) Los Angeles County	1,307	4.36
Cupertino, CA (city) Santa Clara County	2,193	4.34
Albany, CA (city) Alameda County	710	4.32
University Place, WA (city) Pierce County	1,286	4.30
Fairland, MD (cdp) Montgomery County	930	4.28
Cockeysville, MD (cdp) Baltimore County	830	4.28
Picnic Point-North Lynnwood, WA (cdp) Snohomish County	973	4.24
Wahiawa, HI (cdp) Honolulu County	668	4.14
Jericho, NY (cdp) Nassau County	535	4.10
Skokie, IL (village) Cook County	2,557	4.04
Oakton, VA (cdp) Fairfax County	1,167	3.98
Stanford, CA (cdp) Santa Clara County	522	3.92
Garden Grove, CA (city) Orange County	6,439	3.90
Whitpain, PA (township) Montgomery County	716	3.86
Broomall, PA (cdp) Delaware County	426	3.86
South Pasadena, CA (city) Los Angeles County	913	3.76
Spanaway, WA (cdp) Pierce County	804	3.72
Parkland, WA (cdp) Pierce County	893	3.71
Syosset, NY (cdp) Nassau County	685	3.69
Cheltenham, PA (township) Montgomery County	1,346	3.65
Duluth, GA (city) Gwinnett County	785	3.55
Montgomery, PA (township) Montgomery County	755	3.43
Los Alamitos, CA (city) Orange County	390	3.38
Halawa, HI (cdp) Honolulu County	468	3.37
Arcadia, CA (city) Los Angeles County	1,775	3.35
Wailuku, HI (cdp) Maui County	410	3.33
Greenbelt, MD (city) Prince George's County	706	3.29
Chantilly, VA (cdp) Fairfax County	1,348	3.28
Lynnwood, WA (city) Snohomish County	1,103	3.26
Mays Chapel, MD (cdp) Baltimore County	373	3.26
Greentree, NJ (cdp) Camden County	374	3.24
White Oak, MD (cdp) Montgomery County	678	3.23
Loma Linda, CA (city) San Bernardino County	594	3.18
Niles, IL (village) Cook County	949	3.16
Ridgefield Park, NJ (village) Bergen County	407	3.16
Upper Dublin, PA (township) Montgomery County	816	3.15
Downey, CA (city) Los Angeles County	3,359	3.13
Urbana, IL (city) Champaign County	1,139	3.13
Newington, VA (cdp) Fairfax County	618	3.12
Vernon Hills, IL (village) Lake County	626	3.11
Makakilo City, HI (cdp) Honolulu County	409	3.11
Pearl City, HI (cdp) Honolulu County	953	3.08
Kaneohe, HI (cdp) Honolulu County	1,054	3.01
Fairfax, VA (independent city) Fairfax city	644	3.00
Killeen, TX (city) Bell County	2,587	2.98
Cherry Hill Mall, NJ (cdp) Camden County	395	2.98
South Gate, MD (cdp) Anne Arundel County	836	2.92
Aspen Hill, MD (cdp) Montgomery County	1,451	2.89
Carney, MD (cdp) Baltimore County	810	2.87
Springfield, VA (cdp) Fairfax County	867	2.85
Shoreline, WA (city) King County	1,475	2.78
Mountlake Terrace, WA (city) Snohomish County	562	2.76
Norwalk, CA (city) Los Angeles County	2,831	2.74
Ridgewood, NJ (village) Bergen County	681	2.73
Marple, PA (township) Delaware County	647	2.73
Springdale, NJ (cdp) Camden County	389	2.70
Palos Verdes Estates, CA (city) Los Angeles County	358	2.68
Fairview, NJ (borough) Bergen County	355	2.68
Buffalo Grove, IL (village) Lake County	1,135	2.65
Lincolnia, VA (cdp) Fairfax County	419	2.65
Hilo, HI (cdp) Hawaii County	1,068	2.62
Junction City, KS (city) Geary County	494	2.62
Millbrae, CA (city) San Mateo County	541	2.61
Franconia, VA (cdp) Fairfax County	824	2.58
Los Angeles, CA (city) Los Angeles County	95,106	2.57
Kailua, HI (cdp) Honolulu County	933	2.56
Radcliff, KY (city) Hardin County	562	2.56
Beverly Hills, CA (city) Los Angeles County	862	2.55
Montgomeryville, PA (cdp) Montgomery County	307	2.55
Wilmette, IL (village) Cook County	701	2.54
Livingston, NJ (cdp) Essex County	696	2.54
Lansing, NY (town) Tompkins County	265	2.52
McLean, VA (cdp) Fairfax County	962	2.47
Lacey, WA (city) Thurston County	771	2.47
Chino Hills, CA (city) San Bernardino County	1,641	2.46
Santa Clara, CA (city) Santa Clara County	2,471	2.41
Campbell, CA (city) Santa Clara County	911	2.39
Potomac, MD (cdp) Montgomery County	1,060	2.36
Severn, MD (cdp) Anne Arundel County	824	2.35
West Windsor, NJ (township) Mercer County	514	2.35
Upper Gwynedd, PA (township) Montgomery County	335	2.35
Hoffman Estates, IL (village) Cook County	1,144	2.31
Burbank, CA (city) Los Angeles County	2,295	2.29
Idylwood, VA (cdp) Fairfax County	366	2.29
Lomita, CA (city) Los Angeles County	456	2.27
Ann Arbor, MI (city) Washtenaw County	2,581	2.26
East Lansing, MI (city) Ingham County	1,051	2.26
Harker Heights, TX (city) Bell County	391	2.26
Coppell, TX (city) Dallas County	802	2.23
Lyndhurst, NJ (cdp) Bergen County	433	2.23
Fountain Valley, CA (city) Orange County	1,221	2.22
North Laurel, MD (cdp) Howard County	455	2.22
Scarsdale, NY (village) Westchester County	394	2.21
Redland, MD (cdp) Montgomery County	375	2.21
Mount Prospect, IL (village) Cook County	1,232	2.19
Glen Rock, NJ (borough) Bergen County	253	2.19
Schaumburg, IL (village) Cook County	1,641	2.18
Brea, CA (city) Orange County	772	2.18
Horsham, PA (township) Montgomery County	525	2.17

Notes: (cdp) census designated place; Refer to the Explanation of Data in the front of the book for more detailed information.

Asian: Laotian

Top 150 Places Sorted by Number

(Based on all places, regardless of population)

Place	Number	%
San Diego, CA (city) San Diego County	7,003	0.57
Sacramento, CA (city) Sacramento County	6,876	1.69
Fresno, CA (city) Fresno County	6,575	1.54
Stockton, CA (city) San Joaquin County	3,367	1.38
Seattle, WA (city) King County	3,267	0.58
Oakland, CA (city) Alameda County	3,206	0.80
Portland, OR (city) Multnomah County	2,999	0.57
Minneapolis, MN (city) Hennepin County	2,522	0.66
Milwaukee, WI (city) Milwaukee County	2,236	0.37
Richmond, CA (city) Contra Costa County	2,108	2.12
Nashville-Davidson, TN (special city) Davidson County	2,045	0.37
Visalia, CA (city) Tulare County	1,962	2.14
Des Moines, IA (city) Polk County	1,939	0.98
Merced, CA (city) Merced County	1,846	2.89
San Jose, CA (city) Santa Clara County	1,813	0.20
Lowell, MA (city) Middlesex County	1,750	1.66
Providence, RI (city) Providence County	1,718	0.99
Fort Smith, AR (city) Sebastian County	1,557	1.94
Elgin, IL (city) Kane County	1,507	1.59
Redding, CA (city) Shasta County	1,437	1.78
Saint Paul, MN (city) Ramsey County	1,426	0.50
Parkway-South Sacramento, CA (cdp) Sacramento County	1,401	3.84
Honolulu, HI (cdp) Honolulu County	1,399	0.38
Anchorage, AK (municipality) Anchorage Borough	1,385	0.53
Modesto, CA (city) Stanislaus County	1,369	0.72
Brooklyn Park, MN (city) Hennepin County	1,299	1.93
Woonsocket, RI (city) Providence County	1,293	2.99
San Pablo, CA (city) Contra Costa County	1,290	4.27
Columbus, OH (city) Franklin County	1,290	0.18
Charlotte, NC (city) Mecklenburg County	1,211	0.22
Saint Petersburg, FL (city) Pinellas County	1,178	0.47
Dallas, TX (city) Dallas County	1,169	0.10
Amarillo, TX (city) Potter County	1,137	0.65
Philadelphia, PA (city) Philadelphia County	1,123	0.07
Rockford, IL (city) Winnebago County	1,085	0.72
Haltom City, TX (city) Tarrant County	1,017	2.61
Fort Worth, TX (city) Tarrant County	984	0.18
Wichita, KS (city) Sedgwick County	940	0.27
Rochester, NY (city) Monroe County	933	0.42
Holland, MI (township) Ottawa County	932	3.22
Long Beach, CA (city) Los Angeles County	916	0.20
Murfreesboro, TN (city) Rutherford County	884	1.28
Westminster, CO (city) Adams County	884	0.88
Santa Ana, CA (city) Orange County	813	0.24
Los Angeles, CA (city) Los Angeles County	812	0.02
Anaheim, CA (city) Orange County	799	0.24
West Valley City, UT (city) Salt Lake County	794	0.73
Santa Rosa, CA (city) Sonoma County	753	0.51
West Sacramento, CA (city) Yolo County	714	2.26
San Francisco, CA (city) San Francisco County	707	0.09
Oklahoma City, OK (city) Oklahoma County	686	0.14
Storm Lake, IA (city) Buena Vista County	643	6.38
Garland, TX (city) Dallas County	629	0.29
Bridgeport, CT (city) Fairfield County	601	0.43
Kansas City, KS (city) Wyandotte County	537	0.37
New Iberia, LA (city) Iberia Parish	535	1.64
Rochester, MN (city) Olmsted County	522	0.61
Chicago, IL (city) Cook County	517	0.02
Akron, OH (city) Summit County	516	0.24
Worthington, MN (city) Nobles County	510	4.52
Detroit, MI (city) Wayne County	504	0.05
High Point, NC (city) Guilford County	502	0.58
Grand Prairie, TX (city) Dallas County	499	0.39
Springdale, AR (city) Washington County	484	1.06
Irving, TX (city) Dallas County	480	0.25
Las Vegas, NV (city) Clark County	478	0.10
Madison, WI (city) Dane County	476	0.23
Olathe, KS (city) Johnson County	471	0.51
North Highlands, CA (cdp) Sacramento County	464	1.05
Fitchburg, MA (city) Worcester County	463	1.18
Brooklyn Center, MN (city) Hennepin County	462	1.58
Phoenix, AZ (city) Maricopa County	454	0.03
Escondido, CA (city) San Diego County	429	0.32
Sunrise Manor, NV (cdp) Clark County	415	0.27
Green Bay, WI (city) Brown County	413	0.40
Riverside, CA (city) Riverside County	408	0.16
Florin, CA (cdp) Sacramento County	407	1.47
Euless, TX (city) Tarrant County	407	0.88
Banning, CA (city) Riverside County	402	1.71
Moreno Valley, CA (city) Riverside County	393	0.28
South Elgin, IL (village) Kane County	380	2.36
Greensboro, NC (city) Guilford County	380	0.17
New Britain, CT (city) Hartford County	375	0.52
Garden Grove, CA (city) Orange County	372	0.23
Tacoma, WA (city) Pierce County	371	0.19
Oaklawn-Sunview, KS (cdp) Sedgwick County	366	11.67
Eagan, MN (city) Dakota County	366	0.58
Fairfield, CA (city) Solano County	359	0.37
Winfield, KS (city) Cowley County	348	2.85
Houston, TX (city) Harris County	346	0.02
Albuquerque, NM (city) Bernalillo County	344	0.08
Sioux City, IA (city) Woodbury County	335	0.39
Fort Wayne, IN (city) Allen County	335	0.16
Pomona, CA (city) Los Angeles County	333	0.22
Buffalo, NY (city) Erie County	332	0.11
Memphis, TN (city) Shelby County	330	0.05
Saint Cloud, MN (city) Stearns County	327	0.55
Everett, WA (city) Snohomish County	327	0.36
Arvada, CO (city) Jefferson County	325	0.32
Richfield, MN (city) Hennepin County	320	0.93
Bryn Mawr-Skyway, WA (cdp) King County	319	2.28
Saint Louis, MO (independent city) Saint Louis city	317	0.09
Union, NY (town) Broome County	316	0.56
New York, NY (city) New York City	316	0.00
Gresham, OR (city) Multnomah County	312	0.35
Lynn, MA (city) Essex County	310	0.35
West Jordan, UT (city) Salt Lake County	306	0.45
Van Buren, AR (city) Crawford County	305	1.61
Elk Grove, CA (cdp) Sacramento County	302	0.50
East Hartford, CT (cdp) Hartford County	297	0.60
Pinellas Park, FL (city) Pinellas County	296	0.65
Porterville, CA (city) Tulare County	289	0.73
South Oroville, CA (cdp) Butte County	286	3.72
Boise City, ID (city) Ada County	284	0.15
Bloomington, MN (city) Hennepin County	283	0.33
Aloha, OR (cdp) Washington County	276	0.66
Jacksonville, FL (special city) Duval County	273	0.04
Bellevue, WA (city) King County	272	0.25
Suisun City, CA (city) Solano County	268	1.03
Wausau, WI (city) Marathon County	264	0.69
Tulare, CA (city) Tulare County	262	0.60
Tucson, AZ (city) Pima County	262	0.05
Springfield, VA (cdp) Fairfax County	261	0.86
Warren, MI (city) Macomb County	258	0.19
Renton, WA (city) King County	250	0.50
Sheboygan, WI (city) Sheboygan County	244	0.48
Grand Island, NE (city) Hall County	232	0.54
Sioux Falls, SD (city) Minnehaha County	228	0.18
Joliet, IL (city) Will County	222	0.21
Johnson City, NY (village) Broome County	220	1.42
Eureka, CA (city) Humboldt County	220	0.84
Chico, CA (city) Butte County	220	0.37
Danbury, CT (city) Fairfield County	216	0.29
Lansing, MI (city) Ingham County	213	0.18
Holland, MI (city) Ottawa County	210	0.60
Leominster, MA (city) Worcester County	209	0.51
Des Moines, WA (city) King County	206	0.70
North Richland Hills, TX (city) Tarrant County	206	0.37
Burnsville, MN (city) Dakota County	205	0.34
Salina, KS (city) Saline County	204	0.45
Arlington, VA (cdp) Arlington County	204	0.11
Hickory, NC (city) Catawba County	203	0.55
Montgomery, AL (city) Montgomery County	202	0.10
Binghamton, NY (city) Broome County	200	0.42
Clovis, CA (city) Fresno County	195	0.28
Upper Darby, PA (township) Delaware County	195	0.24
Vancouver, WA (city) Clark County	193	0.13
Watauga, TX (city) Tarrant County	192	0.88
Taylorsville, UT (city) Salt Lake County	190	0.33
Bakersfield, CA (city) Kern County	186	0.08

Notes: (cdp) census designated place; Refer to the Explanation of Data in the front of the book for more detailed information.

Asian: Laotian

Top 150 Places Sorted by Percent

(Based on all places, regardless of population)

Place	Number	%
Oaklawn-Sunview, KS (cdp) Sedgwick County	366	11.67
Magnolia, MN (city) Rock County	22	9.95
Warroad, MN (city) Roseau County	147	8.54
Belleville, AR (city) Yell County	31	8.36
Mountain Lake, MN (city) Cottonwood County	170	8.17
Tecumseh, NE (city) Johnson County	111	6.47
Storm Lake, IA (city) Buena Vista County	643	6.38
Vandalia, MI (village) Cass County	27	6.29
Butterfield, MN (city) Watonwan County	35	6.21
Lakeside, IA (city) Buena Vista County	30	6.20
Alto, GA (town) Habersham County	52	5.94
Macdoel, CA (cdp) Siskiyou County	8	5.71
Raymond, WA (city) Pacific County	163	5.48
Worthington, MN (city) Nobles County	510	4.52
Venus, TX (town) Johnson County	41	4.51
San Pablo, CA (city) Contra Costa County	1,290	4.27
Cornelia, GA (city) Habersham County	153	4.16
Lake, MN (township) Roseau County	86	4.12
Parkway-South Sacramento, CA (cdp) Sacramento County	1,401	3.84
Weed, CA (city) Siskiyou County	114	3.83
South Oroville, CA (cdp) Butte County	286	3.72
Jackson, MN (city) Jackson County	121	3.46
Rollingwood, CA (cdp) Contra Costa County	97	3.34
Holland, MI (township) Ottawa County	932	3.22
Bayview-Montalvin, CA (cdp) Contra Costa County	159	3.18
Prior, MN (township) Big Stone County	7	3.14
Bayou La Batre, AL (city) Mobile County	72	3.11
Cassopolis, MI (village) Cass County	54	3.10
Westside, MN (township) Nobles County	8	3.10
Haleiwa, HI (cdp) Honolulu County	67	3.01
Woonsocket, RI (city) Providence County	1,293	2.99
Saint Charles, MN (city) Winona County	97	2.94
Selma, MN (township) Cottonwood County	6	2.94
Burchard, NE (village) Pawnee County	3	2.91
Merced, CA (city) Merced County	1,846	2.89
Connell, WA (city) Franklin County	85	2.88
Winfield, KS (city) Cowley County	348	2.85
Willows, CA (city) Glenn County	174	2.80
Cottonwood, CA (cdp) Shasta County	83	2.80
Haltom City, TX (city) Tarrant County	1,017	2.61
Glen Alpine, NC (town) Burke County	28	2.57
Leesburg, IN (town) Kosciusko County	16	2.56
South Elgin, IL (village) Kane County	380	2.36
Long Lake, MN (township) Watonwan County	8	2.31
Bryn Mawr-Skyway, WA (cdp) King County	319	2.28
West Sacramento, CA (city) Yolo County	714	2.26
Danielson, CT (borough) Windham County	96	2.25
Bethel Heights, AR (town) Benton County	16	2.24
Darfur, MN (city) Watonwan County	3	2.19
South Bend, WA (city) Pacific County	39	2.16
Visalia, CA (city) Tulare County	1,962	2.14
Newmarket, NH (town) Rockingham County	172	2.14
Richmond, CA (city) Contra Costa County	2,108	2.12
Brookford, NC (town) Catawba County	9	2.07
West Liberty, IA (city) Muscatine County	68	2.04
Butterfield, MN (township) Watonwan County	6	2.02
Midway, MN (township) Cottonwood County	6	2.02
Braselton, GA (town) Jackson County	24	1.99
Webster City, IA (city) Hamilton County	162	1.98
De Pue, IL (village) Bureau County	36	1.95
Fort Smith, AR (city) Sebastian County	1,557	1.94
Brooklyn Park, MN (city) Hennepin County	1,299	1.93
Maywood Park, OR (city) Multnomah County	15	1.93
La Grange, MI (township) Cass County	63	1.89
Penn, MI (township) Cass County	35	1.84
Algona, WA (city) King County	45	1.83
Drexel, NC (town) Burke County	35	1.81
Havana, AR (city) Yell County	7	1.79
Redding, CA (city) Shasta County	1,437	1.78
Elk, MN (township) Nobles County	5	1.76
Baldwin, GA (city) Habersham County	42	1.73
Banning, CA (city) Riverside County	402	1.71
Kawela Bay, HI (cdp) Honolulu County	7	1.71
Lake Fremont, MN (township) Martin County	3	1.71
Sacramento, CA (city) Sacramento County	6,876	1.69
Mount Pleasant, IA (city) Henry County	148	1.69
Swanville, MN (township) Morrison County	9	1.69
Rosendale, MN (township) Watonwan County	6	1.68
Lowell, MA (city) Middlesex County	1,750	1.66
Two Rivers, AK (cdp) Fairbanks North Star Borough	8	1.66
New Iberia, LA (city) Iberia Parish	535	1.64
Van Buren, AR (city) Crawford County	305	1.61
Elgin, IL (city) Kane County	1,507	1.59
Alpha, MN (city) Jackson County	2	1.59
Brooklyn Center, MN (city) Hennepin County	462	1.58
Fresno, CA (city) Fresno County	6,575	1.54
Carey, OH (village) Wyandot County	59	1.51
Roseland, CA (cdp) Sonoma County	94	1.48
Ogilvie, MN (city) Kanabec County	7	1.48
Florin, CA (cdp) Sacramento County	407	1.47
Mount Holly, NC (city) Gaston County	139	1.45
East Porterville, CA (cdp) Tulare County	96	1.43
Johnson City, NY (village) Broome County	220	1.42
Ullin, IL (village) Pulaski County	11	1.41
Stockton, CA (city) San Joaquin County	3,367	1.38
Danville, AR (city) Yell County	33	1.38
Linda, CA (cdp) Yuba County	183	1.36
Kahuku, HI (cdp) Honolulu County	28	1.34
Elk Mound, WI (town) Dunn County	15	1.34
Kibler, AR (city) Crawford County	13	1.34
Oroville, CA (city) Butte County	173	1.33
Anderson, CA (city) Shasta County	120	1.33
Mount Airy, GA (town) Habersham County	8	1.32
Kamrar, IA (city) Hamilton County	3	1.31
Carson, MN (township) Cottonwood County	4	1.29
Murfreesboro, TN (city) Rutherford County	884	1.28
Tustin, MI (village) Osceola County	3	1.27
Riverdale, GA (city) Clayton County	157	1.26
Dakota City, NE (city) Dakota County	23	1.26
Carnation, WA (city) King County	23	1.22
Burke, MN (township) Pipestone County	3	1.22
Thermalito, CA (cdp) Butte County	72	1.19
Fitchburg, MA (city) Worcester County	463	1.18
Newton, NC (city) Catawba County	148	1.18
South Sioux City, NE (city) Dakota County	139	1.17
Bystrom, CA (cdp) Stanislaus County	53	1.17
Sultan, WA (city) Snohomish County	39	1.17
Kistler, PA (borough) Mifflin County	4	1.16
King Cove, AK (city) Aleutians East Borough	9	1.14
McCloud, CA (cdp) Siskiyou County	15	1.12
Central Pacolet, SC (town) Spartanburg County	3	1.12
Montpelier, OH (village) Williams County	48	1.11
Beechwood, MI (cdp) Ottawa County	33	1.11
Killingly, CT (town) Windham County	179	1.09
Kings Mountain, NC (city) Cleveland County	106	1.09
Tara Hills, CA (cdp) Contra Costa County	58	1.09
Sergeant Bluff, IA (city) Woodbury County	36	1.08
McCurtain, OK (town) Haskell County	5	1.07
Springdale, AR (city) Washington County	484	1.06
Saybrook Manor, CT (cdp) Middlesex County	12	1.06
Goessel, KS (city) Marion County	6	1.06
North Highlands, CA (cdp) Sacramento County	464	1.05
Cherry Valley, IL (village) Winnebago County	23	1.05
York Springs, PA (borough) Adams County	6	1.05
Fanshawe, OK (town) Le Flore County	4	1.04
Suisun City, CA (city) Solano County	268	1.03
Enstrom, MN (township) Roseau County	6	1.03
Sharpsburg, IA (city) Taylor County	1	1.02
Womens Bay, AK (cdp) Kodiak Island Borough	7	1.01
Providence, RI (city) Providence County	1,718	0.99
Federal Dam, MN (city) Cass County	1	0.99
Des Moines, IA (city) Polk County	1,939	0.98
Cleveland, MN (township) Le Sueur County	6	0.98
Southbridge, MA (town) Worcester County	165	0.96
Remington, VA (town) Fauquier County	6	0.96
Millbourne, PA (borough) Delaware County	9	0.95
Arlington, IL (village) Bureau County	2	0.95
McNary, LA (village) Rapides Parish	2	0.95
Orland, CA (city) Glenn County	59	0.94
Connelly Springs, NC (town) Burke County	17	0.94

Notes: (cdp) census designated place; Refer to the Explanation of Data in the front of the book for more detailed information.

Asian: Laotian

Top 150 Places Sorted by Percent

(Based on places with populations of 10,000 or more)

Place	Number	%
Storm Lake, IA (city) Buena Vista County	643	6.38
Worthington, MN (city) Nobles County	510	4.52
San Pablo, CA (city) Contra Costa County	1,290	4.27
Parkway-South Sacramento, CA (cdp) Sacramento County	1,401	3.84
Holland, MI (township) Ottawa County	932	3.22
Woonsocket, RI (city) Providence County	1,293	2.99
Merced, CA (city) Merced County	1,846	2.89
Winfield, KS (city) Cowley County	348	2.85
Haltom City, TX (city) Tarrant County	1,017	2.61
South Elgin, IL (village) Kane County	380	2.36
Bryn Mawr-Skyway, WA (cdp) King County	319	2.28
West Sacramento, CA (city) Yolo County	714	2.26
Visalia, CA (city) Tulare County	1,962	2.14
Richmond, CA (city) Contra Costa County	2,108	2.12
Fort Smith, AR (city) Sebastian County	1,557	1.94
Brooklyn Park, MN (city) Hennepin County	1,299	1.93
Redding, CA (city) Shasta County	1,437	1.78
Banning, CA (city) Riverside County	402	1.71
Sacramento, CA (city) Sacramento County	6,876	1.69
Lowell, MA (city) Middlesex County	1,750	1.66
New Iberia, LA (city) Iberia Parish	535	1.64
Van Buren, AR (city) Crawford County	305	1.61
Elgin, IL (city) Kane County	1,507	1.59
Brooklyn Center, MN (city) Hennepin County	462	1.58
Fresno, CA (city) Fresno County	6,575	1.54
Florin, CA (cdp) Sacramento County	407	1.47
Johnson City, NY (village) Broome County	220	1.42
Stockton, CA (city) San Joaquin County	3,367	1.38
Linda, CA (cdp) Yuba County	183	1.36
Oroville, CA (city) Butte County	173	1.33
Murfreesboro, TN (city) Rutherford County	884	1.28
Riverdale, GA (city) Clayton County	157	1.26
Fitchburg, MA (city) Worcester County	463	1.18
Newton, NC (city) Catawba County	148	1.18
South Sioux City, NE (city) Dakota County	139	1.17
Killingly, CT (town) Windham County	179	1.09
Springdale, AR (city) Washington County	484	1.06
North Highlands, CA (cdp) Sacramento County	464	1.05
Suisun City, CA (city) Solano County	268	1.03
Providence, RI (city) Providence County	1,718	0.99
Des Moines, IA (city) Polk County	1,939	0.98
Southbridge, MA (town) Worcester County	165	0.96
Richfield, MN (city) Hennepin County	320	0.93
Berkley, CO (cdp) Adams County	99	0.92
Riverton-Boulevard Park, WA (cdp) King County	102	0.91
Westminster, CO (city) Adams County	884	0.88
Euless, TX (city) Tarrant County	407	0.88
Watauga, TX (city) Tarrant County	192	0.88
Kingsgate, WA (cdp) King County	107	0.88
Springfield, VA (cdp) Fairfax County	261	0.86
Park, MI (township) Ottawa County	151	0.86
Eureka, CA (city) Humboldt County	220	0.84
Aldine, TX (cdp) Harris County	113	0.81
Oakland, CA (city) Alameda County	3,206	0.80
Forest Park, GA (city) Clayton County	160	0.75
West Valley City, UT (city) Salt Lake County	794	0.73
Porterville, CA (city) Tulare County	289	0.73
Dumas, TX (city) Moore County	100	0.73
Modesto, CA (city) Stanislaus County	1,369	0.72
Rockford, IL (city) Winnebago County	1,085	0.72
Troutdale, OR (city) Multnomah County	99	0.72
Des Moines, WA (city) King County	206	0.70
Wausau, WI (city) Marathon County	264	0.69
Tukwila, WA (city) King County	118	0.69
Minneapolis, MN (city) Hennepin County	2,522	0.66
Aloha, OR (cdp) Washington County	276	0.66
Amarillo, TX (city) Potter County	1,137	0.65
Pinellas Park, FL (city) Pinellas County	296	0.65
White Center, WA (cdp) King County	135	0.64
Lawrenceville, GA (city) Gwinnett County	139	0.62
Savage, MN (city) Scott County	131	0.62
Rochester, MN (city) Olmsted County	522	0.61
Garden City, KS (city) Finney County	174	0.61
Albemarle, NC (city) Stanly County	96	0.61
East Hartford, CT (cdp) Hartford County	297	0.60
Tulare, CA (city) Tulare County	262	0.60
Holland, MI (city) Ottawa County	210	0.60
Smyrna, TN (town) Rutherford County	151	0.59
Seattle, WA (city) King County	3,267	0.58
High Point, NC (city) Guilford County	502	0.58
Eagan, MN (city) Dakota County	366	0.58
Crystal, MN (city) Hennepin County	131	0.58
Shakopee, MN (city) Scott County	120	0.58
San Diego, CA (city) San Diego County	7,003	0.57
Portland, OR (city) Multnomah County	2,999	0.57
Union, NY (town) Broome County	316	0.56
Austin, MN (city) Mower County	130	0.56
Saint Cloud, MN (city) Stearns County	327	0.55
Hickory, NC (city) Catawba County	203	0.55
West and East Lealman, FL (cdp) Pinellas County	120	0.55
Grand Island, NE (city) Hall County	232	0.54
Anchorage, AK (municipality) Anchorage Borough	1,385	0.53
Ceres, CA (city) Stanislaus County	184	0.53
Liberal, KS (city) Seward County	105	0.53
La Vergne, TN (city) Rutherford County	99	0.53
North Aurora, IL (village) Kane County	56	0.53
New Britain, CT (city) Hartford County	375	0.52
Hercules, CA (city) Contra Costa County	102	0.52
Orchards, WA (cdp) Clark County	92	0.52
Santa Rosa, CA (city) Sonoma County	753	0.51
Olathe, KS (city) Johnson County	471	0.51
Leominster, MA (city) Worcester County	209	0.51
Saint Paul, MN (city) Ramsey County	1,426	0.50
Elk Grove, CA (cdp) Sacramento County	302	0.50
Renton, WA (city) King County	250	0.50
Gardner, MA (city) Worcester County	103	0.50
Sheboygan, WI (city) Sheboygan County	244	0.48
Oquirrh, UT (cdp) Salt Lake County	50	0.48
Saint Petersburg, FL (city) Pinellas County	1,178	0.47
Robbinsdale, MN (city) Hennepin County	66	0.47
Chanhassen, MN (city) Carver County	93	0.46
West Jordan, UT (city) Salt Lake County	306	0.45
Salina, KS (city) Saline County	204	0.45
Kearns, UT (cdp) Salt Lake County	153	0.45
Central Manchester, CT (cdp) Hartford County	134	0.44
Sherrelwood, CO (cdp) Adams County	77	0.44
Two Rivers, WI (city) Manitowoc County	56	0.44
Bridgeport, CT (city) Fairfield County	601	0.43
Rochester, NY (city) Monroe County	933	0.42
Binghamton, NY (city) Broome County	200	0.42
Pasco, WA (city) Franklin County	133	0.41
Lathrop, CA (city) San Joaquin County	43	0.41
Rio Linda, CA (cdp) Sacramento County	43	0.41
Waianae, HI (cdp) Honolulu County	43	0.41
Green Bay, WI (city) Brown County	413	0.40
SeaTac, WA (city) King County	101	0.40
Grand Prairie, TX (city) Dallas County	499	0.39
Sioux City, IA (city) Woodbury County	335	0.39
Burlington, NC (city) Alamance County	174	0.39
Opelika, AL (city) Lee County	91	0.39
New Hope, MN (city) Hennepin County	81	0.39
Whitehall, OH (city) Franklin County	75	0.39
Merriam, KS (city) Johnson County	43	0.39
Honolulu, HI (cdp) Honolulu County	1,399	0.38
Hanover Park, IL (village) Cook County	147	0.38
Milwaukee, WI (city) Milwaukee County	2,236	0.37
Nashville-Davidson, TN (special city) Davidson County	2,045	0.37
Kansas City, KS (city) Wyandotte County	537	0.37
Fairfield, CA (city) Solano County	359	0.37
Chico, CA (city) Butte County	220	0.37
North Richland Hills, TX (city) Tarrant County	206	0.37
Gates-North Gates, NY (cdp) Monroe County	56	0.37
Everett, WA (city) Snohomish County	327	0.36
Broomfield, CO (city) Boulder County	137	0.36
Emporia, KS (city) Lyon County	97	0.36
Hopkins, MN (city) Hennepin County	62	0.36
Alum Rock, CA (cdp) Santa Clara County	48	0.36
Union City, GA (city) Fulton County	42	0.36
Gresham, OR (city) Multnomah County	312	0.35
Lynn, MA (city) Essex County	310	0.35

Notes: (cdp) census designated place; Refer to the Explanation of Data in the front of the book for more detailed information.

Asian: Malaysian

Top 150 Places Sorted by Number

(Based on all places, regardless of population)

Place	Number	%
New York, NY (city) New York City	2,287	0.03
Los Angeles, CA (city) Los Angeles County	355	0.01
San Diego, CA (city) San Diego County	294	0.02
San Francisco, CA (city) San Francisco County	244	0.03
San Jose, CA (city) Santa Clara County	198	0.02
Chicago, IL (city) Cook County	186	0.01
Houston, TX (city) Harris County	182	0.01
Honolulu, HI (cdp) Honolulu County	138	0.04
Ames, IA (city) Story County	102	0.20
Oklahoma City, OK (city) Oklahoma County	101	0.02
Philadelphia, PA (city) Philadelphia County	101	0.01
Stillwater, OK (city) Payne County	100	0.26
Dallas, TX (city) Dallas County	96	0.01
Seattle, WA (city) King County	94	0.02
Kalamazoo, MI (city) Kalamazoo County	91	0.12
Alhambra, CA (city) Los Angeles County	91	0.11
West Haven, CT (city) New Haven County	87	0.17
Wichita, KS (city) Sedgwick County	87	0.03
Fremont, CA (city) Alameda County	85	0.04
Edmond, OK (city) Oklahoma County	80	0.12
Boston, MA (city) Suffolk County	79	0.01
Minneapolis, MN (city) Hennepin County	78	0.02
Fort Wayne, IN (city) Allen County	77	0.04
Norman, OK (city) Cleveland County	75	0.08
Arlington, TX (city) Tarrant County	70	0.02
Kansas City, MO (city) Jackson County	70	0.02
Austin, TX (city) Travis County	70	0.01
Fayetteville, AR (city) Washington County	68	0.12
Long Beach, CA (city) Los Angeles County	67	0.01
Madison, WI (city) Dane County	66	0.03
Columbus, OH (city) Franklin County	66	0.01
Washington, DC (city) District of Columbia	66	0.01
Anaheim, CA (city) Orange County	65	0.02
Lexington-Fayette, KY (special city) Fayette County	61	0.02
West Lafayette, IN (city) Tippecanoe County	60	0.21
Arlington, VA (cdp) Arlington County	60	0.03
Fresno, CA (city) Fresno County	58	0.01
Knoxville, TN (city) Knox County	57	0.03
Jersey City, NJ (city) Hudson County	56	0.02
Jacksonville, FL (special city) Duval County	56	0.01
Carbondale, IL (city) Jackson County	55	0.27
Lincoln, NE (city) Lancaster County	55	0.02
Monterey Park, CA (city) Los Angeles County	51	0.08
Saint Cloud, MN (city) Stearns County	50	0.08
Colorado Springs, CO (city) El Paso County	50	0.01
Oakland, CA (city) Alameda County	50	0.01
Portland, OR (city) Multnomah County	50	0.01
Daly City, CA (city) San Mateo County	49	0.05
Vallejo, CA (city) Solano County	49	0.04
Sunnyvale, CA (city) Santa Clara County	48	0.04
Pittsburgh, PA (city) Allegheny County	48	0.01
Chandler, AZ (city) Maricopa County	47	0.03
Virginia Beach, VA (independent city) Virginia Beach city	47	0.01
Winona, MN (city) Winona County	45	0.17
Milpitas, CA (city) Santa Clara County	45	0.07
Fort Worth, TX (city) Tarrant County	45	0.01
Milwaukee, WI (city) Milwaukee County	45	0.01
Cambridge, MA (city) Middlesex County	43	0.04
Mobile, AL (city) Mobile County	43	0.02
Nashville-Davidson, TN (special city) Davidson County	43	0.01
Toledo, OH (city) Lucas County	43	0.01
McLean, VA (cdp) Fairfax County	42	0.11
Torrance, CA (city) Los Angeles County	42	0.03
Phoenix, AZ (city) Maricopa County	42	0.00
Oxnard, CA (city) Ventura County	41	0.02
Indianapolis, IN (special city) Marion County	41	0.01
Lawrence, KS (city) Douglas County	40	0.05
Richmond, CA (city) Contra Costa County	40	0.04
Providence, RI (city) Providence County	40	0.02
South Bend, IN (city) Saint Joseph County	39	0.04
Baton Rouge, LA (city) East Baton Rouge Parish	39	0.02
Chula Vista, CA (city) San Diego County	38	0.02
Fairview, OR (city) Multnomah County	37	0.49
West Covina, CA (city) Los Angeles County	37	0.04
Columbia, MO (city) Boone County	36	0.04
Denver, CO (city) Denver County	36	0.01
East Lansing, MI (city) Ingham County	35	0.08
Ann Arbor, MI (city) Washtenaw County	35	0.03
Sacramento, CA (city) Sacramento County	35	0.01
Pasadena, CA (city) Los Angeles County	34	0.03
Plano, TX (city) Collin County	34	0.02
Tulsa, OK (city) Tulsa County	34	0.01
Houghton, MI (city) Houghton County	33	0.47
Urbana, IL (city) Champaign County	33	0.09
El Monte, CA (city) Los Angeles County	32	0.03
Syracuse, NY (city) Onondaga County	32	0.02
Speedway, IN (town) Marion County	31	0.24
Rowland Heights, CA (cdp) Los Angeles County	31	0.06
Irvine, CA (city) Orange County	31	0.02
Norfolk, VA (independent city) Norfolk city	31	0.01
Oceanside, CA (city) San Diego County	30	0.02
Aurora, CO (city) Arapahoe County	30	0.01
Baltimore, MD (independent city) Baltimore city	30	0.00
Memphis, TN (city) Shelby County	30	0.00
Walnut, CA (city) Los Angeles County	29	0.10
Temple City, CA (city) Los Angeles County	29	0.09
Midland, MI (city) Midland County	29	0.07
Arden-Arcade, CA (cdp) Sacramento County	29	0.03
Charlotte, NC (city) Mecklenburg County	29	0.01
Troutdale, OR (city) Multnomah County	28	0.20
Troy, NY (city) Rensselaer County	28	0.06
Diamond Bar, CA (city) Los Angeles County	28	0.05
Bloomington, IN (city) Monroe County	28	0.04
Bellevue, WA (city) King County	28	0.03
Sandy Springs, GA (cdp) Fulton County	28	0.03
Durham, NC (city) Durham County	28	0.01
Tucson, AZ (city) Pima County	28	0.01
San Antonio, TX (city) Bexar County	28	0.00
Arcadia, CA (city) Los Angeles County	27	0.05
Terre Haute, IN (city) Vigo County	27	0.05
Champaign, IL (city) Champaign County	27	0.04
Fort Collins, CO (city) Larimer County	27	0.02
Paradise, NV (cdp) Clark County	27	0.01
Everett, WA (city) Snohomish County	26	0.03
Las Vegas, NV (city) Clark County	26	0.01
Saint Paul, MN (city) Ramsey County	26	0.01
Talmage, CA (cdp) Mendocino County	25	2.19
Dunn Loring, VA (cdp) Fairfax County	25	0.32
Athens, OH (city) Athens County	25	0.12
Ithaca, NY (city) Tompkins County	25	0.09
Blacksburg, VA (town) Montgomery County	25	0.06
Newark, CA (city) Alameda County	25	0.06
Bridgeport, CT (city) Fairfield County	25	0.02
Lubbock, TX (city) Lubbock County	25	0.01
San Gabriel, CA (city) Los Angeles County	24	0.06
Carson, CA (city) Los Angeles County	24	0.03
Richardson, TX (city) Dallas County	24	0.03
Santa Clara, CA (city) Santa Clara County	24	0.02
Tysons Corner, VA (cdp) Fairfax County	23	0.12
Jefferson, VA (cdp) Fairfax County	23	0.08
Sugar Land, TX (city) Fort Bend County	23	0.04
Athens-Clarke County, GA (special city) Clarke County	23	0.02
Hayward, CA (city) Alameda County	23	0.02
Lafayette, LA (city) Lafayette Parish	23	0.02
Tustin, CA (city) Orange County	22	0.03
Spring Valley, NV (cdp) Clark County	22	0.02
Irving, TX (city) Dallas County	22	0.01
Riverside, CA (city) Riverside County	22	0.01
Saint Louis, MO (independent city) Saint Louis city	22	0.01
Bozeman, MT (city) Gallatin County	21	0.08
Berkeley, CA (city) Alameda County	21	0.02
Gainesville, FL (city) Alachua County	21	0.02
San Mateo, CA (city) San Mateo County	21	0.02
Anchorage, AK (municipality) Anchorage Borough	21	0.01
Glendale, CA (city) Los Angeles County	21	0.01
Raleigh, NC (city) Wake County	21	0.01
Reno, NV (city) Washoe County	21	0.01
Tempe, AZ (city) Maricopa County	21	0.01
Oronoko charter, MI (township) Berrien County	20	0.20
Folsom, CA (city) Sacramento County	20	0.04

Notes: (cdp) census designated place; Refer to the Explanation of Data in the front of the book for more detailed information.

Asian: Malaysian

Top 150 Places Sorted by Percent

(Based on all places, regardless of population)

Place	Number	%
Talmage, CA (cdp) Mendocino County	25	2.19
Fairview, OR (city) Multnomah County	37	0.49
Houghton, MI (city) Houghton County	33	0.47
Eileen, WI (town) Bayfield County	3	0.47
Davis Junction, IL (village) Ogle County	2	0.41
Berrien Springs, MI (village) Berrien County	7	0.38
Solon Springs, WI (town) Douglas County	3	0.37
Kampsville, IL (village) Calhoun County	1	0.33
Dunn Loring, VA (cdp) Fairfax County	25	0.32
Northport, MI (village) Leelanau County	2	0.31
West Terre Haute, IN (town) Vigo County	7	0.30
Carbondale, IL (city) Jackson County	55	0.27
Valley View, TX (town) Cooke County	2	0.27
Boyne Falls, MI (village) Charlevoix County	1	0.27
Stillwater, OK (city) Payne County	100	0.26
Speedway, IN (town) Marion County	31	0.24
Woodmere, OH (village) Cuyahoga County	2	0.24
Kerhonkson, NY (cdp) Ulster County	4	0.23
Tyrone, OK (town) Texas County	2	0.23
South Toms River, NJ (borough) Ocean County	8	0.22
West Lafayette, IN (city) Tippecanoe County	60	0.21
Glen Gardner, NJ (borough) Hunterdon County	4	0.21
New Johnsonville, TN (city) Humphreys County	4	0.21
Pembina, MN (township) Mahnomen County	1	0.21
Ames, IA (city) Story County	102	0.20
Troutdale, OR (city) Multnomah County	28	0.20
Oronoko charter, MI (township) Berrien County	20	0.20
Holualoa, HI (cdp) Hawaii County	12	0.20
Park Ridge, WI (village) Portage County	1	0.20
Angola, IN (city) Steuben County	14	0.19
Normandy, MO (city) Saint Louis County	10	0.19
Poquonock Bridge, CT (cdp) New London County	3	0.19
Damon, TX (cdp) Brazoria County	1	0.19
Page Park, FL (cdp) Lee County	1	0.19
Spring Hill, KS (city) Johnson County	5	0.18
Hawaiian Ocean View, HI (cdp) Hawaii County	4	0.18
Decatur, WI (town) Green County	3	0.18
West Haven, CT (city) New Haven County	87	0.17
Winona, MN (city) Winona County	45	0.17
Dawson Springs, KY (city) Hopkins County	5	0.17
Desert View Highlands, CA (cdp) Los Angeles County	4	0.17
Biggs, CA (city) Butte County	3	0.17
Stubbs, WI (town) Rusk County	1	0.17
Coats, NC (town) Harnett County	3	0.16
Hampton Falls, NH (town) Rockingham County	3	0.16
Naches, WA (town) Yakima County	1	0.16
Putnam, NY (town) Washington County	1	0.16
Englewood Cliffs, NJ (borough) Bergen County	8	0.15
Eastgate, WA (cdp) King County	7	0.15
Monfort Heights East, OH (cdp) Hamilton County	6	0.15
Clarkson Valley, MO (city) Saint Louis County	4	0.15
Wedgefield, FL (cdp) Orange County	4	0.15
Cold Spring, NY (village) Putnam County	3	0.15
Hopewell, NJ (borough) Mercer County	3	0.15
Dysart, IA (city) Tama County	2	0.15
Kaanapali, HI (cdp) Maui County	2	0.15
Munson, MN (township) Stearns County	2	0.15
Saint Joseph, LA (town) Tensas Parish	2	0.15
East Butler, PA (borough) Butler County	1	0.15
Helotes, TX (city) Bexar County	6	0.14
Excelsior, WI (town) Sauk County	2	0.14
Frankford, DE (town) Sussex County	1	0.14
Turbotville, PA (borough) Northumberland County	1	0.14
Whitelaw, WI (village) Manitowoc County	1	0.14
Seven Corners, VA (cdp) Fairfax County	11	0.13
Madison, WI (town) Dane County	9	0.13
Fruit Heights, UT (city) Davis County	6	0.13
Greentown, OH (cdp) Stark County	4	0.13
Saint Augusta, MN (township) Stearns County	4	0.13
Wakefield, MN (township) Stearns County	4	0.13
Lauderdale, MN (city) Ramsey County	3	0.13
Pagosa Springs, CO (town) Archuleta County	2	0.13
Bainbridge, IN (town) Putnam County	1	0.13
Bluffs, IL (village) Scott County	1	0.13
Kalamazoo, MI (city) Kalamazoo County	91	0.12
Edmond, OK (city) Oklahoma County	80	0.12
Fayetteville, AR (city) Washington County	68	0.12
Athens, OH (city) Athens County	25	0.12
Tysons Corner, VA (cdp) Fairfax County	23	0.12
Westwood, MI (cdp) Kalamazoo County	11	0.12
Spring House, PA (cdp) Montgomery County	4	0.12
Pepeekeo, HI (cdp) Hawaii County	2	0.12
Zephyr Cove-Round Hill Village, NV (cdp) Douglas County	2	0.12
Carlsborg, WA (cdp) Clallam County	1	0.12
Far Hills, NJ (borough) Somerset County	1	0.12
Alhambra, CA (city) Los Angeles County	91	0.11
McLean, VA (cdp) Fairfax County	42	0.11
Oshtemo, MI (township) Kalamazoo County	18	0.11
Park Forest Village, PA (cdp) Centre County	10	0.11
Elmsford, NY (village) Westchester County	5	0.11
Green Oaks, IL (village) Lake County	4	0.11
Forest Home, NY (cdp) Tompkins County	1	0.11
Walnut, CA (city) Los Angeles County	29	0.10
Loma Linda, CA (city) San Bernardino County	19	0.10
East San Gabriel, CA (cdp) Los Angeles County	15	0.10
Albertson, NY (cdp) Nassau County	5	0.10
Murphy, TX (city) Collin County	3	0.10
Pelican, WI (town) Oneida County	3	0.10
Sedco Hills, CA (cdp) Riverside County	3	0.10
Plandome Heights, NY (village) Nassau County	1	0.10
Rapid River, MI (township) Kalkaska County	1	0.10
Urbana, IL (city) Champaign County	33	0.09
Temple City, CA (city) Los Angeles County	29	0.09
Ithaca, NY (city) Tompkins County	25	0.09
Great Falls, VA (cdp) Fairfax County	8	0.09
Oak Hills, OR (cdp) Washington County	8	0.09
Cloverly, MD (cdp) Montgomery County	7	0.09
Saint Anthony, MN (city) Hennepin County	7	0.09
Broadview Park, FL (cdp) Broward County	6	0.09
Kodiak, AK (city) Kodiak Island Borough	6	0.09
Marion, KY (city) Crittenden County	3	0.09
Orangeburg, NY (cdp) Rockland County	3	0.09
Coal Creek, CO (cdp) Boulder County	2	0.09
Horseshoe Bend, AR (city) Izard County	2	0.09
Leelanau, MI (township) Leelanau County	2	0.09
Marlborough, MO (village) Saint Louis County	2	0.09
Wallingford, VT (town) Rutland County	2	0.09
Beatty, NV (cdp) Nye County	1	0.09
Cherry, PA (township) Butler County	1	0.09
Great Neck Gardens, NY (cdp) Nassau County	1	0.09
Northville, NY (village) Fulton County	1	0.09
Norman, OK (city) Cleveland County	75	0.08
Monterey Park, CA (city) Los Angeles County	51	0.08
Saint Cloud, MN (city) Stearns County	50	0.08
East Lansing, MI (city) Ingham County	35	0.08
Jefferson, VA (cdp) Fairfax County	23	0.08
Bozeman, MT (city) Gallatin County	21	0.08
Golden, CO (city) Jefferson County	13	0.08
Redland, MD (cdp) Montgomery County	13	0.08
Ewa Beach, HI (cdp) Honolulu County	11	0.08
Ferguson, PA (township) Centre County	11	0.08
San Marino, CA (city) Los Angeles County	10	0.08
Clute, TX (city) Brazoria County	8	0.08
Little Canada, MN (city) Ramsey County	8	0.08
Briarcliff Manor, NY (village) Westchester County	6	0.08
Irvington, NY (village) Westchester County	5	0.08
Kennett, PA (township) Chester County	5	0.08
North Amherst, MA (cdp) Hampshire County	5	0.08
Pimmit Hills, VA (cdp) Fairfax County	5	0.08
Bay Hill, FL (cdp) Orange County	4	0.08
Berrien, MI (township) Berrien County	4	0.08
Cahaba Heights, AL (cdp) Jefferson County	4	0.08
Ewa Gentry, HI (cdp) Honolulu County	4	0.08
Omak, WA (city) Okanogan County	4	0.08
Chalfont, PA (borough) Bucks County	3	0.08
Breckenridge, CO (town) Summit County	2	0.08
Gates Mills, OH (village) Cuyahoga County	2	0.08
New Egypt, NJ (cdp) Ocean County	2	0.08
Adams, WI (town) Jackson County	1	0.08
Boston Heights, OH (village) Summit County	1	0.08

Notes: (cdp) census designated place; Refer to the Explanation of Data in the front of the book for more detailed information.

Asian: Malaysian

Top 150 Places Sorted by Percent

(Based on places with populations of 10,000 or more)

Place	Number	%
Carbondale, IL (city) Jackson County	55	0.27
Stillwater, OK (city) Payne County	100	0.26
Speedway, IN (town) Marion County	31	0.24
West Lafayette, IN (city) Tippecanoe County	60	0.21
Ames, IA (city) Story County	102	0.20
Troutdale, OR (city) Multnomah County	28	0.20
West Haven, CT (city) New Haven County	87	0.17
Winona, MN (city) Winona County	45	0.17
Kalamazoo, MI (city) Kalamazoo County	91	0.12
Edmond, OK (city) Oklahoma County	80	0.12
Fayetteville, AR (city) Washington County	68	0.12
Athens, OH (city) Athens County	25	0.12
Tysons Corner, VA (cdp) Fairfax County	23	0.12
Alhambra, CA (city) Los Angeles County	91	0.11
McLean, VA (cdp) Fairfax County	42	0.11
Oshtemo, MI (township) Kalamazoo County	18	0.11
Walnut, CA (city) Los Angeles County	29	0.10
Loma Linda, CA (city) San Bernardino County	19	0.10
East San Gabriel, CA (cdp) Los Angeles County	15	0.10
Urbana, IL (city) Champaign County	33	0.09
Temple City, CA (city) Los Angeles County	29	0.09
Ithaca, NY (city) Tompkins County	25	0.09
Norman, OK (city) Cleveland County	75	0.08
Monterey Park, CA (city) Los Angeles County	51	0.08
Saint Cloud, MN (city) Stearns County	50	0.08
East Lansing, MI (city) Ingham County	35	0.08
Jefferson, VA (cdp) Fairfax County	23	0.08
Bozeman, MT (city) Gallatin County	21	0.08
Golden, CO (city) Jefferson County	13	0.08
Redland, MD (cdp) Montgomery County	13	0.08
Ewa Beach, HI (cdp) Honolulu County	11	0.08
Ferguson, PA (township) Centre County	11	0.08
San Marino, CA (city) Los Angeles County	10	0.08
Clute, TX (city) Brazoria County	8	0.08
Milpitas, CA (city) Santa Clara County	45	0.07
Midland, MI (city) Midland County	29	0.07
West Carson, CA (cdp) Los Angeles County	14	0.07
Warrensburg, MO (city) Johnson County	11	0.07
Durham, NH (town) Strafford County	9	0.07
Marshall, MN (city) Lyon County	9	0.07
Bemidji, MN (city) Beltrami County	8	0.07
Hampton Bays, NY (cdp) Suffolk County	8	0.07
River Edge, NJ (borough) Bergen County	8	0.07
Rowland Heights, CA (cdp) Los Angeles County	31	0.06
Troy, NY (city) Rensselaer County	28	0.06
Blacksburg, VA (town) Montgomery County	25	0.06
Newark, CA (city) Alameda County	25	0.06
San Gabriel, CA (city) Los Angeles County	24	0.06
Sammamish, WA (city) King County	19	0.06
Waimalu, HI (cdp) Honolulu County	19	0.06
Oakton, VA (cdp) Fairfax County	17	0.06
Starkville, MS (city) Oktibbeha County	14	0.06
Kalamazoo, MI (township) Kalamazoo County	12	0.06
Whitney, NV (cdp) Clark County	11	0.06
Wahiawa, HI (cdp) Honolulu County	10	0.06
Addison, TX (town) Dallas County	9	0.06
Indiana, PA (borough) Indiana County	9	0.06
Moraga, CA (town) Contra Costa County	9	0.06
Atlantic Beach, FL (city) Duval County	8	0.06
Halawa, HI (cdp) Honolulu County	8	0.06
Stanford, CA (cdp) Santa Clara County	8	0.06
Hartford, VT (town) Windsor County	6	0.06
Daly City, CA (city) San Mateo County	49	0.05
Lawrence, KS (city) Douglas County	40	0.05
Diamond Bar, CA (city) Los Angeles County	28	0.05
Arcadia, CA (city) Los Angeles County	27	0.05
Terre Haute, IN (city) Vigo County	27	0.05
De Kalb, IL (city) De Kalb County	18	0.05
Fort Lee, NJ (borough) Bergen County	16	0.05
Foster City, CA (city) San Mateo County	15	0.05
Waipahu, HI (cdp) Honolulu County	15	0.05
Suisun City, CA (city) Solano County	12	0.05
Agoura Hills, CA (city) Los Angeles County	11	0.05
Lisle, IL (village) Du Page County	11	0.05
Ypsilanti, MI (city) Washtenaw County	11	0.05
Greenbelt, MD (city) Prince George's County	10	0.05
Hercules, CA (city) Contra Costa County	10	0.05
Macomb, IL (city) McDonough County	10	0.05
Lakeland North, WA (cdp) King County	8	0.05
Druid Hills, GA (cdp) De Kalb County	7	0.05
Upper Macungie, PA (township) Lehigh County	7	0.05
Vienna, VA (town) Fairfax County	7	0.05
Wolf Trap, VA (cdp) Fairfax County	7	0.05
Waipio, HI (cdp) Honolulu County	6	0.05
Rossmoor, CA (cdp) Orange County	5	0.05
South Miami, FL (city) Miami-Dade County	5	0.05
Honolulu, HI (cdp) Honolulu County	138	0.04
Fremont, CA (city) Alameda County	85	0.04
Fort Wayne, IN (city) Allen County	77	0.04
Vallejo, CA (city) Solano County	49	0.04
Sunnyvale, CA (city) Santa Clara County	48	0.04
Cambridge, MA (city) Middlesex County	43	0.04
Richmond, CA (city) Contra Costa County	40	0.04
South Bend, IN (city) Saint Joseph County	39	0.04
West Covina, CA (city) Los Angeles County	37	0.04
Columbia, MO (city) Boone County	36	0.04
Bloomington, IN (city) Monroe County	28	0.04
Champaign, IL (city) Champaign County	27	0.04
Sugar Land, TX (city) Fort Bend County	23	0.04
Folsom, CA (city) Sacramento County	20	0.04
Cupertino, CA (city) Santa Clara County	19	0.04
Logan, UT (city) Cache County	18	0.04
East Brunswick, NJ (cdp) Middlesex County	17	0.04
Beverly Hills, CA (city) Los Angeles County	14	0.04
Bremerton, WA (city) Kitsap County	14	0.04
North Bethesda, MD (cdp) Montgomery County	14	0.04
Rocklin, CA (city) Placer County	13	0.04
Winchester, NV (cdp) Clark County	11	0.04
Dover, NH (city) Strafford County	10	0.04
Morgantown, WV (city) Monongalia County	10	0.04
Paramus, NJ (borough) Bergen County	10	0.04
Bellview, FL (cdp) Escambia County	9	0.04
Rolling Meadows, IL (city) Cook County	9	0.04
Duluth, GA (city) Gwinnett County	8	0.04
North Druid Hills, GA (cdp) De Kalb County	8	0.04
Oak Harbor, WA (city) Island County	8	0.04
Brookings, SD (city) Brookings County	7	0.04
Nanuet, NY (cdp) Rockland County	7	0.04
Rolla, MO (city) Phelps County	7	0.04
Albany, CA (city) Alameda County	6	0.04
El Segundo, CA (city) Los Angeles County	6	0.04
Forest Park, IL (village) Cook County	6	0.04
Fullerton, PA (cdp) Lehigh County	6	0.04
Maumee, OH (city) Lucas County	6	0.04
Middleton, WI (city) Dane County	6	0.04
North Valley Stream, NY (cdp) Nassau County	6	0.04
Justice, IL (village) Cook County	5	0.04
Longwood, FL (city) Seminole County	5	0.04
Cinco Ranch, TX (cdp) Fort Bend County	4	0.04
Elwood, NY (cdp) Suffolk County	4	0.04
Gages Lake, IL (cdp) Lake County	4	0.04
Herrin, IL (city) Williamson County	4	0.04
Issaquah, WA (city) King County	4	0.04
Lower Gwynedd, PA (township) Montgomery County	4	0.04
Magnolia, AR (city) Columbia County	4	0.04
Merriam, KS (city) Johnson County	4	0.04
Monroe, WI (city) Green County	4	0.04
New York, NY (city) New York City	2,287	0.03
San Francisco, CA (city) San Francisco County	244	0.03
Wichita, KS (city) Sedgwick County	87	0.03
Madison, WI (city) Dane County	66	0.03
Arlington, VA (cdp) Arlington County	60	0.03
Knoxville, TN (city) Knox County	57	0.03
Chandler, AZ (city) Maricopa County	47	0.03
Torrance, CA (city) Los Angeles County	42	0.03
Ann Arbor, MI (city) Washtenaw County	35	0.03
Pasadena, CA (city) Los Angeles County	34	0.03
El Monte, CA (city) Los Angeles County	32	0.03
Arden-Arcade, CA (cdp) Sacramento County	29	0.03
Bellevue, WA (city) King County	28	0.03

Notes: (cdp) census designated place; Refer to the Explanation of Data in the front of the book for more detailed information.

Asian: Pakistani

Top 150 Places Sorted by Number

(Based on all places, regardless of population)

Place	Number	%
New York, NY (city) New York City	34,310	0.43
Chicago, IL (city) Cook County	7,606	0.26
Houston, TX (city) Harris County	6,490	0.33
Jersey City, NJ (city) Hudson County	2,617	1.09
Los Angeles, CA (city) Los Angeles County	2,423	0.07
Hempstead, NY (town) Nassau County	2,039	0.27
Fremont, CA (city) Alameda County	1,294	0.64
San Jose, CA (city) Santa Clara County	1,252	0.14
Philadelphia, PA (city) Philadelphia County	1,096	0.07
Carrollton, TX (city) Denton County	1,083	0.99
Dallas, TX (city) Dallas County	1,062	0.09
Sugar Land, TX (city) Fort Bend County	1,032	1.63
Sacramento, CA (city) Sacramento County	1,004	0.25
Arlington, VA (cdp) Arlington County	959	0.51
Brookhaven, NY (town) Suffolk County	869	0.19
Stockton, CA (city) San Joaquin County	822	0.34
Austin, TX (city) Travis County	818	0.12
Skokie, IL (village) Cook County	804	1.27
Arlington, TX (city) Tarrant County	788	0.24
Woodbridge, NJ (township) Middlesex County	755	0.78
Islip, NY (town) Suffolk County	755	0.23
Edison, NJ (cdp) Middlesex County	737	0.75
Torrance, CA (city) Los Angeles County	717	0.52
Lodi, CA (city) San Joaquin County	707	1.24
Irving, TX (city) Dallas County	681	0.36
Alexandria, VA (independent city) Alexandria city	658	0.51
San Francisco, CA (city) San Francisco County	636	0.08
Richardson, TX (city) Dallas County	627	0.68
Anaheim, CA (city) Orange County	601	0.18
Huntington, NY (town) Suffolk County	600	0.31
Irvine, CA (city) Orange County	581	0.41
Plano, TX (city) Collin County	578	0.26
Oyster Bay, NY (town) Nassau County	578	0.20
Euless, TX (city) Tarrant County	562	1.22
Yonkers, NY (city) Westchester County	553	0.28
Old Bridge, NJ (township) Middlesex County	526	0.87
High Point, NC (city) Guilford County	517	0.60
Santa Clara, CA (city) Santa Clara County	491	0.48
San Diego, CA (city) San Diego County	489	0.04
Mission Bend, TX (cdp) Fort Bend County	481	1.56
North Hempstead, NY (town) Nassau County	462	0.21
San Antonio, TX (city) Bexar County	456	0.04
Springfield, VA (cdp) Fairfax County	438	1.44
Columbus, OH (city) Franklin County	434	0.06
Lincolnia, VA (cdp) Fairfax County	427	2.70
Garland, TX (city) Dallas County	424	0.20
Dale City, VA (cdp) Prince William County	422	0.75
Woodland, CA (city) Yolo County	409	0.83
Madison Park, NJ (cdp) Middlesex County	406	5.86
Bailey's Crossroads, VA (cdp) Fairfax County	406	1.75
Naperville, IL (city) Du Page County	403	0.31
Boston, MA (city) Suffolk County	390	0.07
Indianapolis, IN (special city) Marion County	389	0.05
Babylon, NY (town) Suffolk County	387	0.18
Herndon, VA (town) Fairfax County	383	1.77
Metairie, LA (cdp) Jefferson Parish	377	0.26
Annandale, VA (cdp) Fairfax County	366	0.67
Mount Vernon, VA (cdp) Fairfax County	358	1.25
Piscataway, NJ (township) Middlesex County	355	0.70
Glendale Heights, IL (village) Du Page County	354	1.11
Hanover Park, IL (village) Cook County	351	0.92
Hoffman Estates, IL (village) Cook County	351	0.71
Reston, VA (cdp) Fairfax County	350	0.62
Stafford, TX (city) Fort Bend County	348	2.22
Garden Grove, CA (city) Orange County	348	0.21
Groveton, VA (cdp) Fairfax County	341	1.60
Burke, VA (cdp) Fairfax County	338	0.59
Avenel, NJ (cdp) Middlesex County	330	1.88
Schaumburg, IL (village) Cook County	326	0.43
Centreville, VA (cdp) Fairfax County	324	0.67
New Territory, TX (cdp) Fort Bend County	316	2.28
Canton, MI (cdp) Wayne County	312	0.41
Atlantic City, NJ (city) Atlantic County	309	0.76
Colonie, NY (town) Albany County	309	0.39
Pembroke Pines, FL (city) Broward County	307	0.22
Woodlawn, MD (cdp) Baltimore County	306	0.85
Troy, MI (city) Oakland County	306	0.38
East Meadow, NY (cdp) Nassau County	302	0.81
Fort Worth, TX (city) Tarrant County	301	0.06
Boonton, NJ (town) Morris County	300	3.53
Tulsa, OK (city) Tulsa County	299	0.08
Milwaukee, WI (city) Milwaukee County	299	0.05
Sayreville, NJ (borough) Middlesex County	297	0.74
Missouri City, TX (city) Fort Bend County	294	0.56
Lombard, IL (village) Du Page County	285	0.67
Brownstown, MI (township) Wayne County	277	1.20
Washington, DC (city) District of Columbia	276	0.05
Aurora, CO (city) Arapahoe County	271	0.10
Hamilton, NJ (township) Mercer County	270	0.31
Oklahoma City, OK (city) Oklahoma County	265	0.05
Sterling Heights, MI (city) Macomb County	261	0.21
Union City, CA (city) Alameda County	260	0.39
Corona, CA (city) Riverside County	257	0.21
Bolingbrook, IL (village) Will County	256	0.45
Upper Darby, PA (township) Delaware County	255	0.31
Cary, NC (town) Wake County	255	0.27
Detroit, MI (city) Wayne County	255	0.03
Ellicott City, MD (cdp) Howard County	252	0.45
Durham, NC (city) Durham County	251	0.13
Valley Stream, NY (village) Nassau County	248	0.68
Franklin, NJ (township) Somerset County	247	0.49
Wichita, KS (city) Sedgwick County	247	0.07
Newington, VA (cdp) Fairfax County	246	1.24
North Brunswick Township, NJ (cdp) Middlesex County	245	0.68
Carol Stream, IL (village) Du Page County	245	0.61
Elmont, NY (cdp) Nassau County	243	0.74
Germantown, MD (cdp) Montgomery County	242	0.44
Bayonne, NJ (city) Hudson County	242	0.39
Ramapo, NY (town) Rockland County	242	0.22
Newark, NJ (city) Essex County	242	0.09
Chino Hills, CA (city) San Bernardino County	241	0.36
Baltimore, MD (independent city) Baltimore city	240	0.04
Coral Springs, FL (city) Broward County	239	0.20
Hawthorne, CA (city) Los Angeles County	238	0.28
Chantilly, VA (cdp) Fairfax County	237	0.58
Albany, NY (city) Albany County	236	0.25
Sunnyvale, CA (city) Santa Clara County	234	0.18
Woodbridge, VA (cdp) Prince William County	231	0.72
Diamond Bar, CA (city) Los Angeles County	227	0.40
Smithtown, NY (town) Suffolk County	227	0.20
Hybla Valley, VA (cdp) Fairfax County	223	1.33
Farmington Hills, MI (city) Oakland County	223	0.27
Franconia, VA (cdp) Fairfax County	221	0.69
Charlotte, NC (city) Mecklenburg County	221	0.04
Gaithersburg, MD (city) Montgomery County	219	0.42
Fullerton, CA (city) Orange County	219	0.17
Ann Arbor, MI (city) Washtenaw County	216	0.19
Parsippany-Troy Hills, NJ (township) Morris County	212	0.42
Palatine, IL (village) Cook County	212	0.32
Walnut, CA (city) Los Angeles County	209	0.70
Raleigh, NC (city) Wake County	206	0.07
South Brunswick, NJ (township) Middlesex County	204	0.54
Overland Park, KS (city) Johnson County	204	0.14
Lincolnwood, IL (village) Cook County	203	1.64
Daly City, CA (city) San Mateo County	203	0.20
Milpitas, CA (city) Santa Clara County	202	0.32
Columbia, MD (cdp) Howard County	201	0.23
Elgin, IL (city) Kane County	198	0.21
Stamford, CT (city) Fairfield County	196	0.17
Rancho Cucamonga, CA (city) San Bernardino County	196	0.15
Kansas City, MO (city) Jackson County	195	0.04
Berkeley, CA (city) Alameda County	194	0.19
Hicksville, NY (cdp) Nassau County	193	0.47
Brentwood, NY (cdp) Suffolk County	193	0.36
Phoenix, AZ (city) Maricopa County	193	0.01
Montgomery Village, MD (cdp) Montgomery County	191	0.50
Orlando, FL (city) Orange County	190	0.10
Dearborn, MI (city) Wayne County	188	0.19
Bensenville, IL (village) Du Page County	187	0.90
Danbury, CT (city) Fairfield County	187	0.25

Notes: (cdp) census designated place; Refer to the Explanation of Data in the front of the book for more detailed information.

Asian: Pakistani

Top 150 Places Sorted by Percent

(Based on all places, regardless of population)

Place	Number	%
Champ, MO (village) Saint Louis County	4	33.33
Saltaire, NY (village) Suffolk County	7	16.28
Templeville, MD (town) Queen Anne's County	7	8.75
Madison Park, NJ (cdp) Middlesex County	406	5.86
Boonton, NJ (town) Morris County	300	3.53
Lincolnia, VA (cdp) Fairfax County	427	2.70
Barkeyville, PA (borough) Venango County	6	2.53
Four Corners, TX (cdp) Fort Bend County	71	2.40
New Territory, TX (cdp) Fort Bend County	316	2.28
Stafford, TX (city) Fort Bend County	348	2.22
Glenview Manor, KY (city) Jefferson County	4	2.09
Sycamore, KY (city) Jefferson County	3	1.89
Avenel, NJ (cdp) Middlesex County	330	1.88
Manor Creek, KY (city) Jefferson County	4	1.81
Millbourne, PA (borough) Delaware County	17	1.80
Herndon, VA (town) Fairfax County	383	1.77
Bailey's Crossroads, VA (cdp) Fairfax County	406	1.75
Tierra Buena, CA (cdp) Sutter County	79	1.72
Sagaponack, NY (cdp) Suffolk County	10	1.72
Lincolnwood, IL (village) Cook County	203	1.64
Sugar Land, TX (city) Fort Bend County	1,032	1.63
Groveton, VA (cdp) Fairfax County	341	1.60
Seven Corners, VA (cdp) Fairfax County	138	1.59
Mission Bend, TX (cdp) Fort Bend County	481	1.56
Barton Hills, MI (village) Washtenaw County	5	1.49
White, PA (township) Cambria County	12	1.48
Mount Cory, OH (village) Hancock County	3	1.48
Columbia, LA (town) Caldwell Parish	7	1.47
Springfield, VA (cdp) Fairfax County	438	1.44
Hybla Valley, VA (cdp) Fairfax County	223	1.33
Jupiter Island, FL (town) Martin County	8	1.29
Skokie, IL (village) Cook County	804	1.27
Rockville, CT (cdp) Tolland County	97	1.26
Mount Vernon, VA (cdp) Fairfax County	358	1.25
Lodi, CA (city) San Joaquin County	707	1.24
Newington, VA (cdp) Fairfax County	246	1.24
Oak Brook, IL (village) Du Page County	107	1.23
Euless, TX (city) Tarrant County	562	1.22
Brownstown, MI (township) Wayne County	277	1.20
Bay Hill, FL (cdp) Orange County	62	1.20
Harrison, NJ (town) Hudson County	168	1.16
River Hills, WI (village) Milwaukee County	19	1.16
Huntington, VA (cdp) Fairfax County	96	1.15
Monmouth Junction, NJ (cdp) Middlesex County	31	1.14
Glendale Heights, IL (village) Du Page County	354	1.11
Herricks, NY (cdp) Nassau County	45	1.10
Jersey City, NJ (city) Hudson County	2,617	1.09
Saint Lawrence, MN (township) Scott County	5	1.06
Lake Katrine, NY (cdp) Ulster County	24	1.00
Carrollton, TX (city) Denton County	1,083	0.99
North Springfield, VA (cdp) Fairfax County	91	0.99
Secretary, MD (town) Dorchester County	5	0.99
Iselin, NJ (cdp) Middlesex County	164	0.98
North Valley Stream, NY (cdp) Nassau County	151	0.96
Deer Lake, PA (borough) Schuylkill County	5	0.95
Hesperia, MI (village) Oceana County	9	0.94
Dune Acres, IN (town) Porter County	2	0.94
Burr Ridge, IL (village) Du Page County	97	0.93
August, CA (cdp) San Joaquin County	73	0.93
East Lansdowne, PA (borough) Delaware County	24	0.93
Hanover Park, IL (village) Cook County	351	0.92
Live Oak, CA (city) Sutter County	57	0.92
Bensenville, IL (village) Du Page County	187	0.90
Roseland, FL (cdp) Indian River County	16	0.90
Rose Hill, VA (cdp) Fairfax County	134	0.89
Bellmawr, NJ (borough) Camden County	100	0.89
Brigantine, NJ (city) Atlantic County	111	0.88
Heathcote, NJ (cdp) Middlesex County	42	0.88
Old Bridge, NJ (township) Middlesex County	526	0.87
Sewaren, NJ (cdp) Middlesex County	24	0.86
Woodlawn, MD (cdp) Baltimore County	306	0.85
South Valley Stream, NY (cdp) Nassau County	48	0.85
Malverne Park Oaks, NY (cdp) Nassau County	4	0.85
Woodland, CA (city) Yolo County	409	0.83
Oakbrook Terrace, IL (city) Du Page County	19	0.83
Hilshire Village, TX (city) Harris County	6	0.83
Hewlett Bay Park, NY (village) Nassau County	4	0.83
North Bellmore, NY (cdp) Nassau County	164	0.82
East Meadow, NY (cdp) Nassau County	302	0.81
North Plainfield, NJ (borough) Somerset County	170	0.81
Algonquin, MD (cdp) Dorchester County	11	0.81
Whitewright, TX (town) Grayson County	14	0.80
Saint Mary's, AK (city) Wade Hampton Census Area	4	0.80
Hamtramck, MI (city) Wayne County	181	0.79
Bluefield, VA (town) Tazewell County	40	0.79
Woodbridge, NJ (township) Middlesex County	755	0.78
Hughesville, MD (cdp) Charles County	12	0.78
Pine Bush, NY (cdp) Orange County	12	0.78
Merrifield, VA (cdp) Fairfax County	86	0.77
Stone Ridge, NY (cdp) Ulster County	9	0.77
Hawley, TX (city) Jones County	5	0.77
Atlantic City, NJ (city) Atlantic County	309	0.76
West Carthage, NY (village) Jefferson County	16	0.76
Arcola, TX (city) Fort Bend County	8	0.76
Edison, NJ (cdp) Middlesex County	737	0.75
Dale City, VA (cdp) Prince William County	422	0.75
Lorton, VA (cdp) Fairfax County	133	0.75
Garden City Park, NY (cdp) Nassau County	57	0.75
Quioque, NY (cdp) Suffolk County	6	0.75
Sayreville, NJ (borough) Middlesex County	297	0.74
Elmont, NY (cdp) Nassau County	243	0.74
Elmwood Park, NJ (borough) Bergen County	140	0.74
East Farmingdale, NY (cdp) Suffolk County	40	0.74
Gazelle, CA (cdp) Siskiyou County	1	0.74
Laurel, MD (city) Prince George's County	146	0.73
Woodbridge, VA (cdp) Prince William County	231	0.72
Hoffman Estates, IL (village) Cook County	351	0.71
Nesconset, NY (cdp) Suffolk County	85	0.71
South Huntington, NY (cdp) Suffolk County	67	0.71
Piscataway, NJ (township) Middlesex County	355	0.70
Walnut, CA (city) Los Angeles County	209	0.70
Fairland, MD (cdp) Montgomery County	152	0.70
El Sobrante, CA (cdp) Contra Costa County	86	0.70
Town and Country, MO (city) Saint Louis County	76	0.70
Franconia, VA (cdp) Fairfax County	221	0.69
Islandia, NY (village) Suffolk County	21	0.69
Hardy, AR (city) Sharp County	4	0.69
Richardson, TX (city) Dallas County	627	0.68
Valley Stream, NY (village) Nassau County	248	0.68
North Brunswick Township, NJ (cdp) Middlesex County	245	0.68
Cloverly, MD (cdp) Montgomery County	53	0.68
Searingtown, NY (cdp) Nassau County	34	0.68
Cleveland, MO (city) Cass County	4	0.68
Annandale, VA (cdp) Fairfax County	366	0.67
Centreville, VA (cdp) Fairfax County	324	0.67
Lombard, IL (village) Du Page County	285	0.67
Blackhawk-Camino Tassajara, CA (cdp) Contra Costa County	67	0.67
Greatwood, TX (cdp) Fort Bend County	44	0.66
Cashtown-McKnightstown, PA (cdp) Adams County	5	0.66
Morton Grove, IL (village) Cook County	146	0.65
Ventnor City, NJ (city) Atlantic County	84	0.65
Pomona, NJ (cdp) Atlantic County	26	0.65
Fremont, CA (city) Alameda County	1,294	0.64
Glen Ellyn, IL (village) Du Page County	174	0.64
Manchester, MO (city) Saint Louis County	122	0.64
Burtonsville, MD (cdp) Montgomery County	47	0.64
Petersburgh, NY (town) Rensselaer County	10	0.64
Willards, MD (town) Wicomico County	6	0.64
Reston, VA (cdp) Fairfax County	350	0.62
Albertson, NY (cdp) Nassau County	32	0.62
Carol Stream, IL (village) Du Page County	245	0.61
Jefferson, VA (cdp) Fairfax County	168	0.61
West Brunswick, PA (township) Schuylkill County	21	0.61
Upper Brookville, NY (village) Nassau County	11	0.61
Cressona, PA (borough) Schuylkill County	10	0.61
Stephens City, VA (town) Frederick County	7	0.61
Fincastle, KY (city) Jefferson County	5	0.61
High Point, NC (city) Guilford County	517	0.60
Colesville, MD (cdp) Montgomery County	118	0.60
Wayne, NY (town) Steuben County	7	0.60

Notes: (cdp) census designated place; Refer to the Explanation of Data in the front of the book for more detailed information.

Asian: Pakistani

Top 150 Places Sorted by Percent

(Based on places with populations of 10,000 or more)

Place	Number	%
Lincolnia, VA (cdp) Fairfax County	427	2.70
New Territory, TX (cdp) Fort Bend County	316	2.28
Stafford, TX (city) Fort Bend County	348	2.22
Avenel, NJ (cdp) Middlesex County	330	1.88
Herndon, VA (town) Fairfax County	383	1.77
Bailey's Crossroads, VA (cdp) Fairfax County	406	1.75
Lincolnwood, IL (village) Cook County	203	1.64
Sugar Land, TX (city) Fort Bend County	1,032	1.63
Groveton, VA (cdp) Fairfax County	341	1.60
Mission Bend, TX (cdp) Fort Bend County	481	1.56
Springfield, VA (cdp) Fairfax County	438	1.44
Hybla Valley, VA (cdp) Fairfax County	223	1.33
Skokie, IL (village) Cook County	804	1.27
Mount Vernon, VA (cdp) Fairfax County	358	1.25
Lodi, CA (city) San Joaquin County	707	1.24
Newington, VA (cdp) Fairfax County	246	1.24
Euless, TX (city) Tarrant County	562	1.22
Brownstown, MI (township) Wayne County	277	1.20
Harrison, NJ (town) Hudson County	168	1.16
Glendale Heights, IL (village) Du Page County	354	1.11
Jersey City, NJ (city) Hudson County	2,617	1.09
Carrollton, TX (city) Denton County	1,083	0.99
Iselin, NJ (cdp) Middlesex County	164	0.98
North Valley Stream, NY (cdp) Nassau County	151	0.96
Burr Ridge, IL (village) Du Page County	97	0.93
Hanover Park, IL (village) Cook County	351	0.92
Bensenville, IL (village) Du Page County	187	0.90
Rose Hill, VA (cdp) Fairfax County	134	0.89
Bellmawr, NJ (borough) Camden County	100	0.89
Brigantine, NJ (city) Atlantic County	111	0.88
Old Bridge, NJ (township) Middlesex County	526	0.87
Woodlawn, MD (cdp) Baltimore County	306	0.85
Woodland, CA (city) Yolo County	409	0.83
North Bellmore, NY (cdp) Nassau County	164	0.82
East Meadow, NY (cdp) Nassau County	302	0.81
North Plainfield, NJ (borough) Somerset County	170	0.81
Hamtramck, MI (city) Wayne County	181	0.79
Woodbridge, NJ (township) Middlesex County	755	0.78
Merrifield, VA (cdp) Fairfax County	86	0.77
Atlantic City, NJ (city) Atlantic County	309	0.76
Edison, NJ (cdp) Middlesex County	737	0.75
Dale City, VA (cdp) Prince William County	422	0.75
Lorton, VA (cdp) Fairfax County	133	0.75
Sayreville, NJ (borough) Middlesex County	297	0.74
Elmont, NY (cdp) Nassau County	243	0.74
Elmwood Park, NJ (borough) Bergen County	140	0.74
Laurel, MD (city) Prince George's County	146	0.73
Woodbridge, VA (cdp) Prince William County	231	0.72
Hoffman Estates, IL (village) Cook County	351	0.71
Nesconset, NY (cdp) Suffolk County	85	0.71
Piscataway, NJ (township) Middlesex County	355	0.70
Walnut, CA (city) Los Angeles County	209	0.70
Fairland, MD (cdp) Montgomery County	152	0.70
El Sobrante, CA (cdp) Contra Costa County	86	0.70
Town and Country, MO (city) Saint Louis County	76	0.70
Franconia, VA (cdp) Fairfax County	221	0.69
Richardson, TX (city) Dallas County	627	0.68
Valley Stream, NY (village) Nassau County	248	0.68
North Brunswick Township, NJ (cdp) Middlesex County	245	0.68
Annandale, VA (cdp) Fairfax County	366	0.67
Centreville, VA (cdp) Fairfax County	324	0.67
Lombard, IL (village) Du Page County	285	0.67
Blackhawk-Camino Tassajara, CA (cdp) Contra Costa County	67	0.67
Morton Grove, IL (village) Cook County	146	0.65
Ventnor City, NJ (city) Atlantic County	84	0.65
Fremont, CA (city) Alameda County	1,294	0.64
Glen Ellyn, IL (village) Du Page County	174	0.64
Manchester, MO (city) Saint Louis County	122	0.64
Reston, VA (cdp) Fairfax County	350	0.62
Carol Stream, IL (village) Du Page County	245	0.61
Jefferson, VA (cdp) Fairfax County	168	0.61
High Point, NC (city) Guilford County	517	0.60
Colesville, MD (cdp) Montgomery County	118	0.60
Burke, VA (cdp) Fairfax County	338	0.59
Chantilly, VA (cdp) Fairfax County	237	0.58
Redland, MD (cdp) Montgomery County	97	0.57
Princeton Meadows, NJ (cdp) Middlesex County	77	0.57
Missouri City, TX (city) Fort Bend County	294	0.56
Niles, IL (village) Cook County	167	0.56
Vernon, CT (town) Tolland County	158	0.56
East Windsor, NJ (township) Mercer County	140	0.56
Little Ferry, NJ (borough) Bergen County	61	0.56
South Laurel, MD (cdp) Prince George's County	113	0.55
Dobbs Ferry, NY (village) Westchester County	58	0.55
South Brunswick, NJ (township) Middlesex County	204	0.54
West Sacramento, CA (city) Yolo County	170	0.54
Ives Estates, FL (cdp) Miami-Dade County	93	0.53
Corinth, TX (city) Denton County	60	0.53
Torrance, CA (city) Los Angeles County	717	0.52
Riverdale, GA (city) Clayton County	65	0.52
Arlington, VA (cdp) Arlington County	959	0.51
Alexandria, VA (independent city) Alexandria city	658	0.51
Huntington Station, NY (cdp) Suffolk County	153	0.51
Dix Hills, NY (cdp) Suffolk County	132	0.51
West Windsor, NJ (township) Mercer County	111	0.51
Montgomery Village, MD (cdp) Montgomery County	191	0.50
Plainsboro, NJ (township) Middlesex County	101	0.50
Wells Branch, TX (cdp) Travis County	56	0.50
Franklin, NJ (township) Somerset County	247	0.49
Bartlett, IL (village) Du Page County	179	0.49
Spring Valley, NY (village) Rockland County	125	0.49
Loma Linda, CA (city) San Bernardino County	92	0.49
Santa Clara, CA (city) Santa Clara County	491	0.48
Woodridge, IL (village) Du Page County	150	0.48
West Springfield, VA (cdp) Fairfax County	136	0.48
Fairfax, VA (independent city) Fairfax city	104	0.48
Hicksville, NY (cdp) Nassau County	193	0.47
Teaneck, NJ (cdp) Bergen County	186	0.47
Bloomingdale, IL (village) Du Page County	102	0.47
Tysons Corner, VA (cdp) Fairfax County	87	0.47
North Bay Shore, NY (cdp) Suffolk County	71	0.47
Melville, NY (cdp) Suffolk County	69	0.47
Humble, TX (city) Harris County	68	0.47
Addison, IL (village) Du Page County	167	0.46
Lake Ridge, VA (cdp) Prince William County	140	0.46
Bolingbrook, IL (village) Will County	256	0.45
Ellicott City, MD (cdp) Howard County	252	0.45
Fords, NJ (cdp) Middlesex County	67	0.45
Salisbury, NY (cdp) Nassau County	56	0.45
North Lindenhurst, NY (cdp) Suffolk County	53	0.45
Farmington, MI (city) Oakland County	47	0.45
Germantown, MD (cdp) Montgomery County	242	0.44
Galloway, NJ (township) Atlantic County	138	0.44
Pittsford, NY (town) Monroe County	121	0.44
Greenbelt, MD (city) Prince George's County	94	0.44
New York, NY (city) New York City	34,310	0.43
Schaumburg, IL (village) Cook County	326	0.43
Bridgeview, IL (village) Cook County	66	0.43
Somerville, NJ (borough) Somerset County	53	0.43
Bull Run, VA (cdp) Prince William County	49	0.43
Gaithersburg, MD (city) Montgomery County	219	0.42
Parsippany-Troy Hills, NJ (township) Morris County	212	0.42
Hillsborough, NJ (township) Somerset County	155	0.42
Roselle, IL (village) Du Page County	98	0.42
Arbutus, MD (cdp) Baltimore County	84	0.42
Ferndale, MD (cdp) Anne Arundel County	67	0.42
Addison, TX (town) Dallas County	60	0.42
Metuchen, NJ (borough) Middlesex County	54	0.42
North Merrick, NY (cdp) Nassau County	50	0.42
Irvine, CA (city) Orange County	581	0.41
Canton, MI (cdp) Wayne County	312	0.41
Westmont, IL (village) Du Page County	101	0.41
Lomita, CA (city) Los Angeles County	83	0.41
Woodmere, NY (cdp) Nassau County	67	0.41
Idylwood, VA (cdp) Fairfax County	66	0.41
Forest Park, IL (village) Cook County	64	0.41
Greenlawn, NY (cdp) Suffolk County	54	0.41
Diamond Bar, CA (city) Los Angeles County	227	0.40
Lawndale, CA (city) Los Angeles County	127	0.40
Secaucus, NJ (town) Hudson County	64	0.40

Notes: (cdp) census designated place; Refer to the Explanation of Data in the front of the book for more detailed information.

Asian: Sri Lankan

Top 150 Places Sorted by Number

(Based on all places, regardless of population)

Place	Number	%
New York, NY (city) New York City	2,640	0.03
Los Angeles, CA (city) Los Angeles County	1,800	0.05
Houston, TX (city) Harris County	220	0.01
Wheaton-Glenmont, MD (cdp) Montgomery County	184	0.32
Anaheim, CA (city) Orange County	167	0.05
Washington, DC (city) District of Columbia	157	0.03
Austin, TX (city) Travis County	156	0.02
Torrance, CA (city) Los Angeles County	152	0.11
San Jose, CA (city) Santa Clara County	150	0.02
San Diego, CA (city) San Diego County	144	0.01
Chicago, IL (city) Cook County	144	0.00
Arlington, VA (cdp) Arlington County	132	0.07
Aspen Hill, MD (cdp) Montgomery County	124	0.25
Pasadena, CA (city) Los Angeles County	121	0.09
Honolulu, HI (cdp) Honolulu County	118	0.03
Columbus, OH (city) Franklin County	116	0.02
Irvine, CA (city) Orange County	112	0.08
Long Beach, CA (city) Los Angeles County	112	0.02
Bethesda, MD (cdp) Montgomery County	104	0.19
Rockville, MD (city) Montgomery County	97	0.20
San Francisco, CA (city) San Francisco County	96	0.01
Burbank, CA (city) Los Angeles County	89	0.09
Phoenix, AZ (city) Maricopa County	88	0.01
Fremont, CA (city) Alameda County	86	0.04
Plano, TX (city) Collin County	84	0.04
Cerritos, CA (city) Los Angeles County	82	0.16
Boston, MA (city) Suffolk County	80	0.01
Lancaster, CA (city) Los Angeles County	78	0.07
West Covina, CA (city) Los Angeles County	76	0.07
Riverside, CA (city) Riverside County	69	0.03
South Brunswick, NJ (township) Middlesex County	68	0.18
Las Vegas, NV (city) Clark County	66	0.01
Philadelphia, PA (city) Philadelphia County	66	0.00
Cincinnati, OH (city) Hamilton County	65	0.02
Seattle, WA (city) King County	65	0.01
Lexington-Fayette, KY (special city) Fayette County	64	0.02
Hempstead, NY (town) Nassau County	64	0.01
Montgomery Village, MD (cdp) Montgomery County	63	0.17
Sunnyvale, CA (city) Santa Clara County	63	0.05
North Bethesda, MD (cdp) Montgomery County	61	0.16
Tucson, AZ (city) Pima County	59	0.01
Dallas, TX (city) Dallas County	59	0.00
Paradise, NV (cdp) Clark County	58	0.03
Portland, OR (city) Multnomah County	58	0.01
Germantown, MD (cdp) Montgomery County	56	0.10
Federal Way, WA (city) King County	55	0.07
Woodbridge, NJ (township) Middlesex County	55	0.06
Elizabeth, NJ (city) Union County	55	0.05
Edison, NJ (cdp) Middlesex County	54	0.06
Amherst, NY (town) Erie County	54	0.05
Cambridge, MA (city) Middlesex County	54	0.05
Santa Clara, CA (city) Santa Clara County	53	0.05
Santa Clarita, CA (city) Los Angeles County	53	0.04
Davis, CA (city) Yolo County	52	0.09
Mountain View, CA (city) Santa Clara County	52	0.07
Bloomington, MN (city) Hennepin County	50	0.06
Glendale, CA (city) Los Angeles County	50	0.03
Raleigh, NC (city) Wake County	50	0.02
Arcadia, CA (city) Los Angeles County	49	0.09
Palmdale, CA (city) Los Angeles County	49	0.04
Olney, MD (cdp) Montgomery County	47	0.15
Gaithersburg, MD (city) Montgomery County	47	0.09
Santa Barbara, CA (city) Santa Barbara County	47	0.05
San Antonio, TX (city) Bexar County	47	0.00
Urbana, IL (city) Champaign County	46	0.13
Lake Forest, CA (city) Orange County	46	0.08
Framingham, MA (cdp) Middlesex County	46	0.07
Silver Spring, MD (cdp) Montgomery County	46	0.06
Arlington, TX (city) Tarrant County	46	0.01
Wichita, KS (city) Sedgwick County	45	0.01
Palm Springs, CA (city) Riverside County	44	0.10
Spring Valley, NV (cdp) Clark County	44	0.04
Madison, WI (city) Dane County	44	0.02
New Rochelle, NY (city) Westchester County	43	0.06
Minneapolis, MN (city) Hennepin County	43	0.01
Saint Paul, MN (city) Ramsey County	42	0.01
Garden Grove, CA (city) Orange County	40	0.02
Lubbock, TX (city) Lubbock County	40	0.02
Newark, NJ (city) Essex County	40	0.01
Oakland, CA (city) Alameda County	40	0.01
Tustin, CA (city) Orange County	39	0.06
Lakewood, CA (city) Los Angeles County	39	0.05
Downey, CA (city) Los Angeles County	39	0.04
Chandler, AZ (city) Maricopa County	39	0.02
Virginia Beach, VA (independent city) Virginia Beach city	39	0.01
North Brunswick Township, NJ (cdp) Middlesex County	38	0.10
Gardena, CA (city) Los Angeles County	38	0.07
Hawthorne, CA (city) Los Angeles County	38	0.05
Alhambra, CA (city) Los Angeles County	38	0.04
Simi Valley, CA (city) Ventura County	38	0.03
Brookhaven, NY (town) Suffolk County	38	0.01
Covina, CA (city) Los Angeles County	37	0.08
Rancho Cucamonga, CA (city) San Bernardino County	37	0.03
Vancouver, WA (city) Clark County	37	0.03
Indianapolis, IN (special city) Marion County	37	0.00
Piscataway, NJ (township) Middlesex County	36	0.07
San Buenaventura, CA (city) Ventura County	36	0.04
Huntington Beach, CA (city) Orange County	36	0.02
Irving, TX (city) Dallas County	36	0.02
Baltimore, MD (independent city) Baltimore city	36	0.01
Buffalo, NY (city) Erie County	36	0.01
Fort Worth, TX (city) Tarrant County	36	0.01
Milwaukee, WI (city) Milwaukee County	36	0.01
Detroit, MI (city) Wayne County	36	0.00
San Ramon, CA (city) Contra Costa County	35	0.08
Buena Park, CA (city) Orange County	35	0.04
Whittier, CA (city) Los Angeles County	35	0.04
Berkeley, CA (city) Alameda County	35	0.03
Corona, CA (city) Riverside County	35	0.03
Albuquerque, NM (city) Bernalillo County	35	0.01
Denver, CO (city) Denver County	35	0.01
Cupertino, CA (city) Santa Clara County	34	0.07
Cary, NC (town) Wake County	34	0.04
Richfield, MN (city) Hennepin County	33	0.10
Coppell, TX (city) Dallas County	33	0.09
Ames, IA (city) Story County	33	0.07
Jersey City, NJ (city) Hudson County	33	0.01
Malden, MA (city) Middlesex County	32	0.06
Columbia, MO (city) Boone County	32	0.04
Baton Rouge, LA (city) East Baton Rouge Parish	32	0.01
Fresno, CA (city) Fresno County	32	0.01
Sacramento, CA (city) Sacramento County	32	0.01
Lawrence, NJ (township) Mercer County	31	0.11
McLean, VA (cdp) Fairfax County	31	0.08
Old Bridge, NJ (township) Middlesex County	31	0.05
Pittsburgh, PA (city) Allegheny County	31	0.01
Ellicott City, MD (cdp) Howard County	30	0.05
Ann Arbor, MI (city) Washtenaw County	30	0.03
Stamford, CT (city) Fairfield County	30	0.03
Thousand Oaks, CA (city) Ventura County	30	0.03
Omaha, NE (city) Douglas County	30	0.01
Beaverton, OR (city) Washington County	29	0.04
Rochester Hills, MI (city) Oakland County	29	0.04
Mission Viejo, CA (city) Orange County	29	0.03
Lomita, CA (city) Los Angeles County	28	0.14
East Brunswick, NJ (cdp) Middlesex County	28	0.06
Southfield, MI (city) Oakland County	28	0.04
Ramapo, NY (town) Rockland County	28	0.03
Fort Collins, CO (city) Larimer County	28	0.02
San Bernardino, CA (city) San Bernardino County	28	0.02
Greensboro, NC (city) Guilford County	28	0.01
North Kensington, MD (cdp) Montgomery County	27	0.30
Burlington, MA (cdp) Middlesex County	27	0.12
Reading, MA (cdp) Middlesex County	27	0.11
Stanton, CA (city) Orange County	27	0.07
Medford, MA (city) Middlesex County	27	0.05
Reston, VA (cdp) Fairfax County	27	0.05
Carson, CA (city) Los Angeles County	27	0.03
Farmington Hills, MI (city) Oakland County	27	0.03
Jacksonville, FL (special city) Duval County	27	0.00

Notes: (cdp) census designated place; Refer to the Explanation of Data in the front of the book for more detailed information.

Asian: Sri Lankan

Top 150 Places Sorted by Percent

(Based on all places, regardless of population)

Place	Number	%
Covenant Life, AK (cdp) Haines Borough	2	1.96
Glenview, KY (city) Jefferson County	4	0.72
Coldspring, NY (town) Cattaraugus County	4	0.53
Tuscumbia, MO (town) Miller County	1	0.46
Lebanon, NJ (borough) Hunterdon County	4	0.38
Fairfax, OH (village) Hamilton County	7	0.36
Blue Diamond, NV (cdp) Clark County	1	0.35
Cromberg, CA (cdp) Plumas County	1	0.34
Pippa Passes, KY (city) Knott County	1	0.34
Wheaton-Glenmont, MD (cdp) Montgomery County	184	0.32
Poquott, NY (village) Suffolk County	3	0.31
North Kensington, MD (cdp) Montgomery County	27	0.30
Randolph, NY (village) Cattaraugus County	4	0.30
Cassadaga, NY (village) Chautauqua County	2	0.30
Rancho Viejo, TX (town) Cameron County	5	0.29
Mettawa, IL (village) Lake County	1	0.27
Barnegat Light, NJ (borough) Ocean County	2	0.26
Aspen Hill, MD (cdp) Montgomery County	124	0.25
Worthington Hills, KY (city) Jefferson County	4	0.25
Forks, PA (township) Sullivan County	1	0.25
Hillsboro Pines, FL (cdp) Broward County	1	0.25
Gates Mills, OH (village) Cuyahoga County	6	0.24
Slayton, MN (city) Murray County	5	0.24
Castanea, PA (township) Clinton County	3	0.24
Fruitvale, TX (city) Van Zandt County	1	0.24
Lansing, NY (village) Tompkins County	8	0.23
Slippery Rock, PA (borough) Butler County	7	0.23
Stewartstown, PA (borough) York County	4	0.23
Sea Breeze, NC (cdp) New Hanover County	3	0.23
Anderson Mill, TX (cdp) Williamson County	20	0.22
Haines, AK (city) Haines Borough	4	0.22
Wind Point, WI (village) Racine County	4	0.22
Las Flores, CA (cdp) Orange County	12	0.21
Heathcote, NJ (cdp) Middlesex County	10	0.21
East Richmond Heights, CA (cdp) Contra Costa County	7	0.21
Bald Eagle, PA (township) Clinton County	4	0.21
Kensington, MD (town) Montgomery County	4	0.21
Rollingwood, TX (city) Travis County	3	0.21
Rockville, MD (city) Montgomery County	97	0.20
Kendall Park, NJ (cdp) Middlesex County	18	0.20
Friendship Village, MD (cdp) Montgomery County	9	0.20
Seven Fields, PA (borough) Butler County	4	0.20
Bethesda, MD (cdp) Montgomery County	104	0.19
Ann Arbor, MI (township) Washtenaw County	9	0.19
Springetts Manor-Yorklyn, PA (cdp) York County	8	0.19
Freeland, PA (borough) Luzerne County	7	0.19
Bethlehem, WV (village) Ohio County	5	0.19
Marysville, MN (township) Wright County	4	0.19
South Brunswick, NJ (township) Middlesex County	68	0.18
East Pasadena, CA (cdp) Los Angeles County	11	0.18
New Cumberland, WV (city) Hancock County	2	0.18
Montgomery Village, MD (cdp) Montgomery County	63	0.17
Pebble Creek, FL (cdp) Hillsborough County	8	0.17
Medina, WA (city) King County	5	0.17
Tyler Run-Queens Gate, PA (cdp) York County	5	0.17
Greenville, DE (cdp) New Castle County	4	0.17
Parma, ID (city) Canyon County	3	0.17
Cerritos, CA (city) Los Angeles County	82	0.16
North Bethesda, MD (cdp) Montgomery County	61	0.16
Mayflower Village, CA (cdp) Los Angeles County	8	0.16
Bonnie Lock-Woodsetter North, FL (cdp) Broward County	7	0.16
Brookmont, MD (cdp) Montgomery County	5	0.16
Midway, TN (cdp) Washington County	4	0.16
Olney, MD (cdp) Montgomery County	47	0.15
Princeton, MA (town) Worcester County	5	0.15
Grosse Pointe, MI (township) Wayne County	4	0.15
Randolph, NY (town) Cattaraugus County	4	0.15
Clifton, IL (village) Iroquois County	2	0.15
Lomita, CA (city) Los Angeles County	28	0.14
Iselin, NJ (cdp) Middlesex County	23	0.14
East San Gabriel, CA (cdp) Los Angeles County	20	0.14
Farmington, MI (city) Oakland County	15	0.14
Forest Glen, MD (cdp) Montgomery County	10	0.14
Mountain Lakes, NJ (borough) Morris County	6	0.14
Berwyn Heights, MD (town) Prince George's County	4	0.14
Dunstable, MA (town) Middlesex County	4	0.14
Grosse Pointe Shores, MI (village) Wayne County	4	0.14
Tedder, FL (cdp) Broward County	3	0.14
Urbana, IL (city) Champaign County	46	0.13
Redland, MD (cdp) Montgomery County	22	0.13
Los Alamitos, CA (city) Orange County	15	0.13
Pedley, CA (cdp) Riverside County	15	0.13
Rockcreek, OR (cdp) Washington County	12	0.13
Seven Corners, VA (cdp) Fairfax County	11	0.13
Rossmoor, MD (cdp) Montgomery County	10	0.13
South Kensington, MD (cdp) Montgomery County	10	0.13
Fairfield, NJ (cdp) Essex County	9	0.13
Dayton, NJ (cdp) Middlesex County	8	0.13
Ramtown, NJ (cdp) Monmouth County	8	0.13
Excelsior, MN (city) Hennepin County	3	0.13
Germany, PA (township) Adams County	3	0.13
Ross, CA (town) Marin County	3	0.13
Big Delta, AK (cdp) Southeast Fairbanks Census Area	1	0.13
Juno Ridge, FL (cdp) Palm Beach County	1	0.13
Burlington, MA (cdp) Middlesex County	27	0.12
Winchester, MA (cdp) Middlesex County	25	0.12
Westborough, MA (town) Worcester County	22	0.12
Mount Kisco, NY (village) Westchester County	12	0.12
Leonia, NJ (borough) Bergen County	11	0.12
Farmington, ME (town) Franklin County	9	0.12
Nyack, NY (village) Rockland County	8	0.12
Orange Lake, NY (cdp) Orange County	7	0.12
Lawrenceville, NJ (cdp) Mercer County	5	0.12
Mount Repose, OH (cdp) Clermont County	5	0.12
Windy Hills, KY (city) Jefferson County	3	0.12
Hines, OR (city) Harney County	2	0.12
Kortright, NY (town) Delaware County	2	0.12
Ritzville, WA (city) Adams County	2	0.12
Tyrone, NY (town) Schuyler County	2	0.12
Enigma, GA (town) Berrien County	1	0.12
Lincoln, WI (town) Trempealeau County	1	0.12
Matinecock, NY (village) Nassau County	1	0.12
Torrance, CA (city) Los Angeles County	152	0.11
Lawrence, NJ (township) Mercer County	31	0.11
Reading, MA (cdp) Middlesex County	27	0.11
Montgomery, NJ (township) Somerset County	19	0.11
San Marino, CA (city) Los Angeles County	14	0.11
Swarthmore, PA (borough) Delaware County	7	0.11
Woodlawn, MD (cdp) Prince George's County	7	0.11
Slippery Rock, PA (township) Butler County	6	0.11
Bayside, WI (village) Milwaukee County	5	0.11
Savoy, IL (village) Champaign County	5	0.11
Esperance, WA (cdp) Snohomish County	4	0.11
Long Hill, CT (cdp) New London County	4	0.11
Osage Beach, MO (city) Camden County	4	0.11
Spring Lake, MN (township) Scott County	4	0.11
East Caln, PA (township) Chester County	3	0.11
Wrightstown, PA (township) Bucks County	3	0.11
Alta, IA (city) Buena Vista County	2	0.11
Tipton, CA (cdp) Tulare County	2	0.11
Garrett Park, MD (town) Montgomery County	1	0.11
Martin's Additions, MD (village) Montgomery County	1	0.11
Sweetser, IN (town) Grant County	1	0.11
Germantown, MD (cdp) Montgomery County	56	0.10
Palm Springs, CA (city) Riverside County	44	0.10
North Brunswick Township, NJ (cdp) Middlesex County	38	0.10
Richfield, MN (city) Hennepin County	33	0.10
White Oak, MD (cdp) Montgomery County	20	0.10
Scarsdale, NY (village) Westchester County	17	0.10
Princeton Meadows, NJ (cdp) Middlesex County	14	0.10
O'Hara Township, PA (cdp) Allegheny County	9	0.10
Los Altos Hills, CA (town) Santa Clara County	8	0.10
Demarest, NJ (borough) Bergen County	5	0.10
Bloomfield Hills, MI (city) Oakland County	4	0.10
Fox Run, PA (cdp) Butler County	3	0.10
Franklin, MI (village) Oakland County	3	0.10
Kahaluu, HI (cdp) Honolulu County	3	0.10
Monument, CO (town) El Paso County	2	0.10
Oakes, ND (city) Dickey County	2	0.10
Fifield, WI (town) Price County	1	0.10

Notes: (cdp) census designated place; Refer to the Explanation of Data in the front of the book for more detailed information.

Asian: Sri Lankan

Top 150 Places Sorted by Percent

(Based on places with populations of 10,000 or more)

Place	Number	%
Wheaton-Glenmont, MD (cdp) Montgomery County	184	0.32
Aspen Hill, MD (cdp) Montgomery County	124	0.25
Rockville, MD (city) Montgomery County	97	0.20
Bethesda, MD (cdp) Montgomery County	104	0.19
South Brunswick, NJ (township) Middlesex County	68	0.18
Montgomery Village, MD (cdp) Montgomery County	63	0.17
Cerritos, CA (city) Los Angeles County	82	0.16
North Bethesda, MD (cdp) Montgomery County	61	0.16
Olney, MD (cdp) Montgomery County	47	0.15
Lomita, CA (city) Los Angeles County	28	0.14
Iselin, NJ (cdp) Middlesex County	23	0.14
East San Gabriel, CA (cdp) Los Angeles County	20	0.14
Farmington, MI (city) Oakland County	15	0.14
Urbana, IL (city) Champaign County	46	0.13
Redland, MD (cdp) Montgomery County	22	0.13
Los Alamitos, CA (city) Orange County	15	0.13
Pedley, CA (cdp) Riverside County	15	0.13
Burlington, MA (cdp) Middlesex County	27	0.12
Winchester, MA (cdp) Middlesex County	25	0.12
Westborough, MA (town) Worcester County	22	0.12
Torrance, CA (city) Los Angeles County	152	0.11
Lawrence, NJ (township) Mercer County	31	0.11
Reading, MA (cdp) Middlesex County	27	0.11
Montgomery, NJ (township) Somerset County	19	0.11
San Marino, CA (city) Los Angeles County	14	0.11
Germantown, MD (cdp) Montgomery County	56	0.10
Palm Springs, CA (city) Riverside County	44	0.10
North Brunswick Township, NJ (cdp) Middlesex County	38	0.10
Richfield, MN (city) Hennepin County	33	0.10
White Oak, MD (cdp) Montgomery County	20	0.10
Scarsdale, NY (village) Westchester County	17	0.10
Princeton Meadows, NJ (cdp) Middlesex County	14	0.10
Pasadena, CA (city) Los Angeles County	121	0.09
Burbank, CA (city) Los Angeles County	89	0.09
Davis, CA (city) Yolo County	52	0.09
Arcadia, CA (city) Los Angeles County	49	0.09
Gaithersburg, MD (city) Montgomery County	47	0.09
Coppell, TX (city) Dallas County	33	0.09
Bergenfield, NJ (borough) Bergen County	23	0.09
South Pasadena, CA (city) Los Angeles County	22	0.09
El Cerrito, CA (city) Contra Costa County	21	0.09
West Windsor, NJ (township) Mercer County	19	0.09
La Canada Flintridge, CA (city) Los Angeles County	18	0.09
Plainsboro, NJ (township) Middlesex County	18	0.09
Whitpain, PA (township) Montgomery County	16	0.09
Albany, CA (city) Alameda County	14	0.09
Stanford, CA (cdp) Santa Clara County	12	0.09
Jefferson, LA (cdp) Jefferson Parish	11	0.09
Lansing, NY (town) Tompkins County	9	0.09
Irvine, CA (city) Orange County	112	0.08
Lake Forest, CA (city) Orange County	46	0.08
Covina, CA (city) Los Angeles County	37	0.08
San Ramon, CA (city) Contra Costa County	35	0.08
McLean, VA (cdp) Fairfax County	31	0.08
Claremont, CA (city) Los Angeles County	26	0.08
Walnut, CA (city) Los Angeles County	24	0.08
Jefferson, VA (cdp) Fairfax County	23	0.08
Spring Valley, NY (village) Rockland County	20	0.08
Tustin Foothills, CA (cdp) Orange County	20	0.08
Tysons Corner, VA (cdp) Fairfax County	14	0.08
Arlington, VA (cdp) Arlington County	132	0.07
Lancaster, CA (city) Los Angeles County	78	0.07
West Covina, CA (city) Los Angeles County	76	0.07
Federal Way, WA (city) King County	55	0.07
Mountain View, CA (city) Santa Clara County	52	0.07
Framingham, MA (cdp) Middlesex County	46	0.07
Gardena, CA (city) Los Angeles County	38	0.07
Piscataway, NJ (township) Middlesex County	36	0.07
Cupertino, CA (city) Santa Clara County	34	0.07
Ames, IA (city) Story County	33	0.07
Stanton, CA (city) Orange County	27	0.07
Shrewsbury, MA (town) Worcester County	21	0.07
West Lafayette, IN (city) Tippecanoe County	19	0.07
Millbrae, CA (city) San Mateo County	15	0.07
West Carson, CA (cdp) Los Angeles County	15	0.07
Amherst Center, MA (cdp) Hampshire County	12	0.07
Artesia, CA (city) Los Angeles County	12	0.07
Rolla, MO (city) Phelps County	11	0.07
New Fairfield, CT (town) Fairfield County	10	0.07
Beacon, NY (city) Dutchess County	9	0.07
East Hampton, CT (town) Middlesex County	9	0.07
Fairview, NJ (borough) Bergen County	9	0.07
Glenn Dale, MD (cdp) Prince George's County	9	0.07
Orange, CT (cdp) New Haven County	9	0.07
Clayton, CA (city) Contra Costa County	8	0.07
Clemson, SC (city) Pickens County	8	0.07
Oneida, NY (city) Madison County	8	0.07
River Forest, IL (village) Cook County	8	0.07
Town and Country, MO (city) Saint Louis County	8	0.07
Franklin Lakes, NJ (borough) Bergen County	7	0.07
Rossmoor, CA (cdp) Orange County	7	0.07
Woodbridge, NJ (township) Middlesex County	55	0.06
Edison, NJ (cdp) Middlesex County	54	0.06
Bloomington, MN (city) Hennepin County	50	0.06
Silver Spring, MD (cdp) Montgomery County	46	0.06
New Rochelle, NY (city) Westchester County	43	0.06
Tustin, CA (city) Orange County	39	0.06
Malden, MA (city) Middlesex County	32	0.06
East Brunswick, NJ (cdp) Middlesex County	28	0.06
Aloha, OR (cdp) Washington County	26	0.06
Bloomfield, MI (township) Oakland County	25	0.06
Potomac, MD (cdp) Montgomery County	25	0.06
Woburn, MA (city) Middlesex County	24	0.06
Stillwater, OK (city) Payne County	23	0.06
Blacksburg, VA (town) Montgomery County	22	0.06
Campbell, CA (city) Santa Clara County	22	0.06
Monrovia, CA (city) Los Angeles County	22	0.06
Penfield, NY (town) Monroe County	22	0.06
State College, PA (borough) Centre County	22	0.06
Amherst, MA (town) Hampshire County	21	0.06
University, FL (cdp) Hillsborough County	19	0.06
La Verne, CA (city) Los Angeles County	18	0.06
Ithaca, NY (city) Tompkins County	17	0.06
Emporia, KS (city) Lyon County	16	0.06
Hilliard, OH (city) Franklin County	15	0.06
Pullman, WA (city) Whitman County	15	0.06
Randolph, NJ (township) Morris County	15	0.06
Duarte, CA (city) Los Angeles County	13	0.06
Niskayuna, NY (town) Schenectady County	13	0.06
North Plainfield, NJ (borough) Somerset County	13	0.06
Apex, NC (town) Wake County	12	0.06
Louisville, CO (city) Boulder County	12	0.06
Hopkins, MN (city) Hennepin County	11	0.06
Avon, CT (town) Hartford County	10	0.06
East Lyme, CT (town) New London County	10	0.06
Kirksville, MO (city) Adair County	10	0.06
La Palma, CA (city) Orange County	10	0.06
Rocky Hill, CT (town) Hartford County	10	0.06
South Orange, NJ (cdp) Essex County	10	0.06
Fords, NJ (cdp) Middlesex County	9	0.06
Mauldin, SC (city) Greenville County	9	0.06
Monsey, NY (cdp) Rockland County	8	0.06
Princeton, NJ (borough) Mercer County	8	0.06
Ramsey, NJ (borough) Bergen County	8	0.06
Saddle Brook, NJ (cdp) Bergen County	8	0.06
Blue Ash, OH (city) Hamilton County	7	0.06
Wallington, NJ (borough) Bergen County	7	0.06
Los Angeles, CA (city) Los Angeles County	1,800	0.05
Anaheim, CA (city) Orange County	167	0.05
Sunnyvale, CA (city) Santa Clara County	63	0.05
Elizabeth, NJ (city) Union County	55	0.05
Amherst, NY (town) Erie County	54	0.05
Cambridge, MA (city) Middlesex County	54	0.05
Santa Clara, CA (city) Santa Clara County	53	0.05
Santa Barbara, CA (city) Santa Barbara County	47	0.05
Lakewood, CA (city) Los Angeles County	39	0.05
Hawthorne, CA (city) Los Angeles County	38	0.05
Old Bridge, NJ (township) Middlesex County	31	0.05
Ellicott City, MD (cdp) Howard County	30	0.05
Medford, MA (city) Middlesex County	27	0.05

Notes: (cdp) census designated place; Refer to the Explanation of Data in the front of the book for more detailed information.

Asian: Taiwanese

Top 150 Places Sorted by Number

(Based on all places, regardless of population)

Place	Number	%
New York, NY (city) New York City	5,488	0.07
Arcadia, CA (city) Los Angeles County	4,731	8.92
Los Angeles, CA (city) Los Angeles County	4,200	0.11
Irvine, CA (city) Orange County	3,341	2.34
Rowland Heights, CA (cdp) Los Angeles County	3,295	6.79
Hacienda Heights, CA (cdp) Los Angeles County	3,157	5.94
Diamond Bar, CA (city) Los Angeles County	2,611	4.64
San Jose, CA (city) Santa Clara County	2,431	0.27
Fremont, CA (city) Alameda County	2,372	1.17
Cerritos, CA (city) Los Angeles County	2,333	4.53
Walnut, CA (city) Los Angeles County	2,028	6.76
Alhambra, CA (city) Los Angeles County	1,960	2.28
Houston, TX (city) Harris County	1,846	0.09
San Diego, CA (city) San Diego County	1,793	0.15
Temple City, CA (city) Los Angeles County	1,735	5.20
San Marino, CA (city) Los Angeles County	1,542	11.91
Monterey Park, CA (city) Los Angeles County	1,399	2.33
Torrance, CA (city) Los Angeles County	1,344	0.97
San Gabriel, CA (city) Los Angeles County	1,164	2.92
West Covina, CA (city) Los Angeles County	1,105	1.05
Bellevue, WA (city) King County	1,056	0.96
Seattle, WA (city) King County	974	0.17
Cupertino, CA (city) Santa Clara County	910	1.80
Sugar Land, TX (city) Fort Bend County	836	1.32
San Francisco, CA (city) San Francisco County	834	0.11
Anaheim, CA (city) Orange County	832	0.25
Rancho Palos Verdes, CA (city) Los Angeles County	813	1.98
Honolulu, HI (cdp) Honolulu County	779	0.21
Austin, TX (city) Travis County	760	0.12
East San Gabriel, CA (cdp) Los Angeles County	708	4.88
Plano, TX (city) Collin County	702	0.32
Chino Hills, CA (city) San Bernardino County	693	1.04
Chicago, IL (city) Cook County	669	0.02
Fountain Valley, CA (city) Orange County	667	1.21
El Monte, CA (city) Los Angeles County	646	0.56
Sunnyvale, CA (city) Santa Clara County	628	0.48
Fullerton, CA (city) Orange County	612	0.49
Huntington Beach, CA (city) Orange County	571	0.30
Saratoga, CA (city) Santa Clara County	543	1.82
Tustin, CA (city) Orange County	536	0.79
Ann Arbor, MI (city) Washtenaw County	523	0.46
Pasadena, CA (city) Los Angeles County	475	0.35
Berkeley, CA (city) Alameda County	469	0.46
Philadelphia, PA (city) Philadelphia County	467	0.03
Edison, NJ (cdp) Middlesex County	465	0.48
Naperville, IL (city) Du Page County	455	0.35
Rosemead, CA (city) Los Angeles County	446	0.83
Columbus, OH (city) Franklin County	435	0.06
Orange, CA (city) Orange County	431	0.33
Boston, MA (city) Suffolk County	430	0.07
Upland, CA (city) San Bernardino County	425	0.62
Troy, MI (city) Oakland County	419	0.52
North Hempstead, NY (town) Nassau County	418	0.19
Riverside, CA (city) Riverside County	414	0.16
Yorba Linda, CA (city) Orange County	412	0.70
Cypress, CA (city) Orange County	409	0.88
Dallas, TX (city) Dallas County	407	0.03
Parsippany-Troy Hills, NJ (township) Morris County	400	0.79
Cambridge, MA (city) Middlesex County	397	0.39
Madison, WI (city) Dane County	389	0.19
North Potomac, MD (cdp) Montgomery County	374	1.62
Arlington, TX (city) Tarrant County	365	0.11
Buena Park, CA (city) Orange County	362	0.46
Milpitas, CA (city) Santa Clara County	342	0.55
Claremont, CA (city) Los Angeles County	330	0.97
South Pasadena, CA (city) Los Angeles County	322	1.33
Placentia, CA (city) Orange County	321	0.69
La Palma, CA (city) Orange County	315	2.04
Thousand Oaks, CA (city) Ventura County	312	0.27
Palo Alto, CA (city) Santa Clara County	308	0.53
Palos Verdes Estates, CA (city) Los Angeles County	300	2.25
Redmond, WA (city) King County	298	0.66
Potomac, MD (cdp) Montgomery County	287	0.64
East Brunswick, NJ (cdp) Middlesex County	285	0.61
Richardson, TX (city) Dallas County	285	0.31
Pittsburgh, PA (city) Allegheny County	270	0.08
Livingston, NJ (cdp) Essex County	269	0.98
Urbana, IL (city) Champaign County	260	0.71
Santa Monica, CA (city) Los Angeles County	260	0.31
West Windsor, NJ (township) Mercer County	253	1.15
Long Beach, CA (city) Los Angeles County	251	0.05
Hempstead, NY (town) Nassau County	248	0.03
San Dimas, CA (city) Los Angeles County	233	0.67
Cary, NC (town) Wake County	229	0.24
Laguna Niguel, CA (city) Orange County	226	0.37
Artesia, CA (city) Los Angeles County	224	1.37
Covina, CA (city) Los Angeles County	224	0.48
Rancho Cucamonga, CA (city) San Bernardino County	223	0.17
San Antonio, TX (city) Bexar County	223	0.02
Holmdel, NJ (township) Monmouth County	216	1.37
El Cerrito, CA (city) Contra Costa County	216	0.93
Santa Clara, CA (city) Santa Clara County	215	0.21
Mission Viejo, CA (city) Orange County	209	0.22
Stanford, CA (cdp) Santa Clara County	200	1.50
Baltimore, MD (independent city) Baltimore city	197	0.03
Baldwin Park, CA (city) Los Angeles County	195	0.26
Arlington, VA (cdp) Arlington County	191	0.10
Brookhaven, NY (town) Suffolk County	191	0.04
Montville, NJ (township) Morris County	187	0.90
Laguna Hills, CA (city) Orange County	187	0.60
Union City, CA (city) Alameda County	184	0.28
Mercer Island, WA (city) King County	182	0.83
Lexington, MA (cdp) Middlesex County	182	0.60
Davis, CA (city) Yolo County	182	0.30
College Station, TX (city) Brazos County	181	0.27
Tustin Foothills, CA (cdp) Orange County	179	0.74
Durham, NC (city) Durham County	179	0.10
Piscataway, NJ (township) Middlesex County	178	0.35
Pomona, CA (city) Los Angeles County	178	0.12
Brookline, MA (cdp) Norfolk County	177	0.31
Mountain View, CA (city) Santa Clara County	176	0.25
Spring Valley, NV (cdp) Clark County	173	0.15
La Habra Heights, CA (city) Los Angeles County	169	2.96
Newton, MA (city) Middlesex County	169	0.20
Los Altos, CA (city) Santa Clara County	168	0.61
Sacramento, CA (city) Sacramento County	168	0.04
Bridgewater, NJ (township) Somerset County	167	0.39
Rockville, MD (city) Montgomery County	166	0.35
Las Vegas, NV (city) Clark County	165	0.03
Evanston, IL (city) Cook County	161	0.22
Oyster Bay, NY (town) Nassau County	161	0.05
Raleigh, NC (city) Wake County	158	0.06
East Lansing, MI (city) Ingham County	157	0.34
Cherry Hill, NJ (township) Camden County	156	0.22
Syracuse, NY (city) Onondaga County	155	0.11
Phoenix, AZ (city) Maricopa County	154	0.01
East Pasadena, CA (cdp) Los Angeles County	152	2.51
Sammamish, WA (city) King County	152	0.45
Chesterfield, MO (city) Saint Louis County	152	0.32
Oklahoma City, OK (city) Oklahoma County	150	0.03
Poway, CA (city) San Diego County	149	0.31
Tempe, AZ (city) Maricopa County	149	0.09
Denver, CO (city) Denver County	147	0.03
Brea, CA (city) Orange County	146	0.41
Rochester Hills, MI (city) Oakland County	145	0.21
Glendora, CA (city) Los Angeles County	144	0.29
Providence, RI (city) Providence County	144	0.08
Ames, IA (city) Story County	143	0.28
Port Lavaca, TX (city) Calhoun County	142	1.18
Newport Beach, CA (city) Orange County	142	0.20
Gaithersburg, MD (city) Montgomery County	140	0.27
Lakewood, CA (city) Los Angeles County	140	0.18
Jersey City, NJ (city) Hudson County	140	0.06
Eugene, OR (city) Lane County	139	0.10
Marlboro, NJ (township) Monmouth County	138	0.38
Downey, CA (city) Los Angeles County	138	0.13
Baton Rouge, LA (city) East Baton Rouge Parish	137	0.06
Portland, OR (city) Multnomah County	136	0.03
Montgomery, NJ (township) Somerset County	134	0.77
Foster City, CA (city) San Mateo County	134	0.47

Notes: (cdp) census designated place; Refer to the Explanation of Data in the front of the book for more detailed information.

Asian: Taiwanese

Top 150 Places Sorted by Percent

(Based on all places, regardless of population)

Place	Number	%
San Marino, CA (city) Los Angeles County	1,542	11.91
West Hampton Dunes, NY (village) Suffolk County	1	9.09
Arcadia, CA (city) Los Angeles County	4,731	8.92
Talmage, CA (cdp) Mendocino County	97	8.50
Rowland Heights, CA (cdp) Los Angeles County	3,295	6.79
Walnut, CA (city) Los Angeles County	2,028	6.76
Hacienda Heights, CA (cdp) Los Angeles County	3,157	5.94
Temple City, CA (city) Los Angeles County	1,735	5.20
East San Gabriel, CA (cdp) Los Angeles County	708	4.88
Diamond Bar, CA (city) Los Angeles County	2,611	4.64
Cerritos, CA (city) Los Angeles County	2,333	4.53
Forest Home, NY (cdp) Tompkins County	35	3.72
Bradbury, CA (city) Los Angeles County	27	3.16
La Habra Heights, CA (city) Los Angeles County	169	2.96
San Gabriel, CA (city) Los Angeles County	1,164	2.92
East Pasadena, CA (cdp) Los Angeles County	152	2.51
Irvine, CA (city) Orange County	3,341	2.34
Monterey Park, CA (city) Los Angeles County	1,399	2.33
Alhambra, CA (city) Los Angeles County	1,960	2.28
Palos Verdes Estates, CA (city) Los Angeles County	300	2.25
Rolling Hills, CA (city) Los Angeles County	40	2.14
La Palma, CA (city) Orange County	315	2.04
Mayflower Village, CA (cdp) Los Angeles County	101	1.99
Rancho Palos Verdes, CA (city) Los Angeles County	813	1.98
Villa Park, CA (city) Orange County	117	1.95
Saratoga, CA (city) Santa Clara County	543	1.82
Cupertino, CA (city) Santa Clara County	910	1.80
Newport Coast, CA (cdp) Orange County	46	1.72
North El Monte, CA (cdp) Los Angeles County	61	1.65
North Potomac, MD (cdp) Montgomery County	374	1.62
Stanford, CA (cdp) Santa Clara County	200	1.50
Rolling Hills Estates, CA (city) Los Angeles County	115	1.50
Fairbanks Ranch, CA (cdp) San Diego County	33	1.47
Artesia, CA (city) Los Angeles County	224	1.37
Holmdel, NJ (township) Monmouth County	216	1.37
South Pasadena, CA (city) Los Angeles County	322	1.33
Sugar Land, TX (city) Fort Bend County	836	1.32
Benezette, PA (township) Elk County	3	1.32
Old Field, NY (village) Suffolk County	12	1.27
Fountain Valley, CA (city) Orange County	667	1.21
Russell Gardens, NY (village) Nassau County	13	1.21
Port Lavaca, TX (city) Calhoun County	142	1.18
Berkeley Lake, GA (city) Gwinnett County	20	1.18
Fremont, CA (city) Alameda County	2,372	1.17
East Hanover, NJ (township) Morris County	133	1.17
Godfrey Road, FL (cdp) Broward County	7	1.16
West Windsor, NJ (township) Mercer County	253	1.15
Point Comfort, TX (city) Calhoun County	9	1.15
Hillsborough, CA (town) San Mateo County	122	1.13
Greenvale, NY (cdp) Nassau County	24	1.08
Flemington, GA (city) Liberty County	4	1.08
West Covina, CA (city) Los Angeles County	1,105	1.05
Chino Hills, CA (city) San Bernardino County	693	1.04
Los Altos Hills, CA (town) Santa Clara County	78	0.99
Livingston, NJ (cdp) Essex County	269	0.98
Loyola, CA (cdp) Santa Clara County	34	0.98
Torrance, CA (city) Los Angeles County	1,344	0.97
Claremont, CA (city) Los Angeles County	330	0.97
Emeryville, CA (city) Alameda County	67	0.97
Bellevue, WA (city) King County	1,056	0.96
Duncan, PA (township) Tioga County	2	0.94
El Cerrito, CA (city) Contra Costa County	216	0.93
Ann Arbor, MI (township) Washtenaw County	43	0.91
North Hills, NY (village) Nassau County	39	0.91
Montville, NJ (township) Morris County	187	0.90
Piney Point Village, TX (city) Harris County	30	0.89
Cypress, CA (city) Orange County	409	0.88
Oak Brook, IL (village) Du Page County	77	0.88
Manhasset Hills, NY (cdp) Nassau County	31	0.85
San Joaquin Hills, CA (cdp) Orange County	25	0.84
Thomaston, NY (village) Nassau County	22	0.84
Rosemead, CA (city) Los Angeles County	446	0.83
Mercer Island, WA (city) King County	182	0.83
Great Neck Gardens, NY (cdp) Nassau County	9	0.83
Tustin, CA (city) Orange County	536	0.79
Parsippany-Troy Hills, NJ (township) Morris County	400	0.79
Hanover, NJ (township) Morris County	102	0.79
Montgomery, NJ (township) Somerset County	134	0.77
Northeast Ithaca, NY (cdp) Tompkins County	20	0.75
Tustin Foothills, CA (cdp) Orange County	179	0.74
Bunker Hill Village, TX (city) Harris County	27	0.74
East Ithaca, NY (cdp) Tompkins County	16	0.73
Urbana, IL (city) Champaign County	260	0.71
Yorba Linda, CA (city) Orange County	412	0.70
Placentia, CA (city) Orange County	321	0.69
South Barrington, IL (village) Cook County	26	0.69
Hedwig Village, TX (city) Harris County	16	0.69
Lake Success, NY (village) Nassau County	19	0.68
Lauderdale, MN (city) Ramsey County	16	0.68
San Dimas, CA (city) Los Angeles County	233	0.67
Lansing, NY (village) Tompkins County	23	0.67
Clarkson Valley, MO (city) Saint Louis County	18	0.67
Redmond, WA (city) King County	298	0.66
Lebanon, NJ (borough) Hunterdon County	7	0.66
Cranbury, NJ (township) Middlesex County	21	0.65
Potomac, MD (cdp) Montgomery County	287	0.64
Rossmoor, CA (cdp) Orange County	66	0.64
North Star, DE (cdp) New Castle County	53	0.64
Thornburg, PA (borough) Allegheny County	3	0.64
Princeton Junction, NJ (cdp) Mercer County	15	0.63
Upland, CA (city) San Bernardino County	425	0.62
East Brunswick, NJ (cdp) Middlesex County	285	0.61
Los Altos, CA (city) Santa Clara County	168	0.61
Bellaire, TX (city) Harris County	96	0.61
Laguna Hills, CA (city) Orange County	187	0.60
Lexington, MA (cdp) Middlesex County	182	0.60
Greentree, NJ (cdp) Camden County	69	0.60
Cordaville, MA (cdp) Worcester County	15	0.60
Albany, CA (city) Alameda County	97	0.59
Cayuga Heights, NY (village) Tompkins County	19	0.58
Millbrae, CA (city) San Mateo County	118	0.57
Mill Creek, WA (city) Snohomish County	66	0.57
Cheney, WA (city) Spokane County	50	0.57
El Monte, CA (city) Los Angeles County	646	0.56
Abington, PA (township) Lackawanna County	9	0.56
Clarkesville, GA (city) Habersham County	7	0.56
Milpitas, CA (city) Santa Clara County	342	0.55
Society Hill, NJ (cdp) Middlesex County	21	0.55
Blackhawk-Camino Tassajara, CA (cdp) Contra Costa County	54	0.54
Woods Hole, MA (cdp) Barnstable County	5	0.54
Palo Alto, CA (city) Santa Clara County	308	0.53
Ithaca, NY (town) Tompkins County	97	0.53
Moraga, CA (town) Contra Costa County	86	0.53
Warren, NJ (township) Somerset County	76	0.53
New Territory, TX (cdp) Fort Bend County	74	0.53
Cinco Bayou, FL (town) Okaloosa County	2	0.53
Troy, MI (city) Oakland County	419	0.52
Evendale, OH (village) Hamilton County	16	0.52
Paramus, NJ (borough) Bergen County	132	0.51
Englewood Cliffs, NJ (borough) Bergen County	27	0.51
North Caldwell, NJ (borough) Essex County	37	0.50
Birmingham, PA (township) Chester County	21	0.50
Highlands-Baywood Park, CA (cdp) San Mateo County	21	0.50
Fullerton, CA (city) Orange County	612	0.49
Plainsboro, NJ (township) Middlesex County	99	0.49
Gould, OK (town) Harmon County	1	0.49
Sunnyvale, CA (city) Santa Clara County	628	0.48
Edison, NJ (cdp) Middlesex County	465	0.48
Covina, CA (city) Los Angeles County	224	0.48
Foothill Ranch, CA (cdp) Orange County	52	0.48
Town and Country, MO (city) Saint Louis County	52	0.48
Shawnee Hills, OH (village) Delaware County	2	0.48
Foster City, CA (city) San Mateo County	134	0.47
Travilah, MD (cdp) Montgomery County	35	0.47
Cedar Crest, NM (cdp) Bernalillo County	5	0.47
Mount Sterling, WI (village) Crawford County	1	0.47
Ann Arbor, MI (city) Washtenaw County	523	0.46
Berkeley, CA (city) Alameda County	469	0.46
Buena Park, CA (city) Orange County	362	0.46
Cloverly, MD (cdp) Montgomery County	36	0.46

Notes: (cdp) census designated place; Refer to the Explanation of Data in the front of the book for more detailed information.

Asian: Taiwanese

Top 150 Places Sorted by Percent

(Based on places with populations of 10,000 or more)

Place	Number	%
San Marino, CA (city) Los Angeles County	1,542	11.91
Arcadia, CA (city) Los Angeles County	4,731	8.92
Rowland Heights, CA (cdp) Los Angeles County	3,295	6.79
Walnut, CA (city) Los Angeles County	2,028	6.76
Hacienda Heights, CA (cdp) Los Angeles County	3,157	5.94
Temple City, CA (city) Los Angeles County	1,735	5.20
East San Gabriel, CA (cdp) Los Angeles County	708	4.88
Diamond Bar, CA (city) Los Angeles County	2,611	4.64
Cerritos, CA (city) Los Angeles County	2,333	4.53
San Gabriel, CA (city) Los Angeles County	1,164	2.92
Irvine, CA (city) Orange County	3,341	2.34
Monterey Park, CA (city) Los Angeles County	1,399	2.33
Alhambra, CA (city) Los Angeles County	1,960	2.28
Palos Verdes Estates, CA (city) Los Angeles County	300	2.25
La Palma, CA (city) Orange County	315	2.04
Rancho Palos Verdes, CA (city) Los Angeles County	813	1.98
Saratoga, CA (city) Santa Clara County	543	1.82
Cupertino, CA (city) Santa Clara County	910	1.80
North Potomac, MD (cdp) Montgomery County	374	1.62
Stanford, CA (cdp) Santa Clara County	200	1.50
Artesia, CA (city) Los Angeles County	224	1.37
Holmdel, NJ (township) Monmouth County	216	1.37
South Pasadena, CA (city) Los Angeles County	322	1.33
Sugar Land, TX (city) Fort Bend County	836	1.32
Fountain Valley, CA (city) Orange County	667	1.21
Port Lavaca, TX (city) Calhoun County	142	1.18
Fremont, CA (city) Alameda County	2,372	1.17
East Hanover, NJ (township) Morris County	133	1.17
West Windsor, NJ (township) Mercer County	253	1.15
Hillsborough, CA (town) San Mateo County	122	1.13
West Covina, CA (city) Los Angeles County	1,105	1.05
Chino Hills, CA (city) San Bernardino County	693	1.04
Livingston, NJ (cdp) Essex County	269	0.98
Torrance, CA (city) Los Angeles County	1,344	0.97
Claremont, CA (city) Los Angeles County	330	0.97
Bellevue, WA (city) King County	1,056	0.96
El Cerrito, CA (city) Contra Costa County	216	0.93
Montville, NJ (township) Morris County	187	0.90
Cypress, CA (city) Orange County	409	0.88
Rosemead, CA (city) Los Angeles County	446	0.83
Mercer Island, WA (city) King County	182	0.83
Tustin, CA (city) Orange County	536	0.79
Parsippany-Troy Hills, NJ (township) Morris County	400	0.79
Hanover, NJ (township) Morris County	102	0.79
Montgomery, NJ (township) Somerset County	134	0.77
Tustin Foothills, CA (cdp) Orange County	179	0.74
Urbana, IL (city) Champaign County	260	0.71
Yorba Linda, CA (city) Orange County	412	0.70
Placentia, CA (city) Orange County	321	0.69
San Dimas, CA (city) Los Angeles County	233	0.67
Redmond, WA (city) King County	298	0.66
Potomac, MD (cdp) Montgomery County	287	0.64
Rossmoor, CA (cdp) Orange County	66	0.64
Upland, CA (city) San Bernardino County	425	0.62
East Brunswick, NJ (cdp) Middlesex County	285	0.61
Los Altos, CA (city) Santa Clara County	168	0.61
Bellaire, TX (city) Harris County	96	0.61
Laguna Hills, CA (city) Orange County	187	0.60
Lexington, MA (cdp) Middlesex County	182	0.60
Greentree, NJ (cdp) Camden County	69	0.60
Albany, CA (city) Alameda County	97	0.59
Millbrae, CA (city) San Mateo County	118	0.57
Mill Creek, WA (city) Snohomish County	66	0.57
El Monte, CA (city) Los Angeles County	646	0.56
Milpitas, CA (city) Santa Clara County	342	0.55
Blackhawk-Camino Tassajara, CA (cdp) Contra Costa County	54	0.54
Palo Alto, CA (city) Santa Clara County	308	0.53
Ithaca, NY (town) Tompkins County	97	0.53
Moraga, CA (town) Contra Costa County	86	0.53
Warren, NJ (township) Somerset County	76	0.53
New Territory, TX (cdp) Fort Bend County	74	0.53
Troy, MI (city) Oakland County	419	0.52
Paramus, NJ (borough) Bergen County	132	0.51
Fullerton, CA (city) Orange County	612	0.49
Plainsboro, NJ (township) Middlesex County	99	0.49
Sunnyvale, CA (city) Santa Clara County	628	0.48
Edison, NJ (cdp) Middlesex County	465	0.48
Covina, CA (city) Los Angeles County	224	0.48
Foothill Ranch, CA (cdp) Orange County	52	0.48
Town and Country, MO (city) Saint Louis County	52	0.48
Foster City, CA (city) San Mateo County	134	0.47
Ann Arbor, MI (city) Washtenaw County	523	0.46
Berkeley, CA (city) Alameda County	469	0.46
Buena Park, CA (city) Orange County	362	0.46
Sammamish, WA (city) King County	152	0.45
Princeton, NJ (township) Mercer County	69	0.43
La Canada Flintridge, CA (city) Los Angeles County	86	0.42
Millburn, NJ (cdp) Essex County	84	0.42
Brea, CA (city) Orange County	146	0.41
Wolf Trap, VA (cdp) Fairfax County	56	0.40
Cambridge, MA (city) Middlesex County	397	0.39
Bridgewater, NJ (township) Somerset County	167	0.39
Marlboro, NJ (township) Monmouth County	138	0.38
Laguna Niguel, CA (city) Orange County	226	0.37
Fort Lee, NJ (borough) Bergen County	132	0.37
West Lafayette, IN (city) Tippecanoe County	105	0.36
Loma Linda, CA (city) San Bernardino County	67	0.36
Princeton Meadows, NJ (cdp) Middlesex County	49	0.36
Cedar Grove, NJ (cdp) Essex County	44	0.36
Pasadena, CA (city) Los Angeles County	475	0.35
Naperville, IL (city) Du Page County	455	0.35
Piscataway, NJ (township) Middlesex County	178	0.35
Rockville, MD (city) Montgomery County	166	0.35
Vestal, NY (town) Broome County	94	0.35
Scarsdale, NY (village) Westchester County	63	0.35
Issaquah, WA (city) King County	39	0.35
Martin, TN (city) Weakley County	37	0.35
Sierra Madre, CA (city) Los Angeles County	37	0.35
East Lansing, MI (city) Ingham County	157	0.34
Ithaca, NY (city) Tompkins County	101	0.34
Tenafly, NJ (borough) Bergen County	47	0.34
Berkeley Heights, NJ (cdp) Union County	45	0.34
Orange, CA (city) Orange County	431	0.33
Monrovia, CA (city) Los Angeles County	121	0.33
Lomita, CA (city) Los Angeles County	66	0.33
Plano, TX (city) Collin County	702	0.32
Chesterfield, MO (city) Saint Louis County	152	0.32
Okemos, MI (cdp) Ingham County	72	0.32
Lake Forest Park, WA (city) King County	42	0.32
Lilburn, GA (city) Gwinnett County	36	0.32
Franklin Lakes, NJ (borough) Bergen County	33	0.32
Richardson, TX (city) Dallas County	285	0.31
Santa Monica, CA (city) Los Angeles County	260	0.31
Brookline, MA (cdp) Norfolk County	177	0.31
Poway, CA (city) San Diego County	149	0.31
Danville, CA (town) Contra Costa County	129	0.31
McLean, VA (cdp) Fairfax County	122	0.31
Upper Arlington, OH (city) Franklin County	103	0.31
Lisle, IL (village) Du Page County	66	0.31
Hockessin, DE (cdp) New Castle County	40	0.31
Huntington Beach, CA (city) Orange County	571	0.30
Davis, CA (city) Yolo County	182	0.30
Fairland, MD (cdp) Montgomery County	65	0.30
Jollyville, TX (cdp) Williamson County	48	0.30
Fulton, MO (city) Callaway County	36	0.30
Glendora, CA (city) Los Angeles County	144	0.29
Aliso Viejo, CA (cdp) Orange County	115	0.29
Harrison, NJ (town) Hudson County	42	0.29
Springdale, NJ (cdp) Camden County	42	0.29
Union City, CA (city) Alameda County	184	0.28
Ames, IA (city) Story County	143	0.28
Wellesley, MA (cdp) Norfolk County	74	0.28
Tucker, GA (cdp) De Kalb County	73	0.28
Highland Park, NJ (borough) Middlesex County	39	0.28
Lansing, NY (town) Tompkins County	29	0.28
San Jose, CA (city) Santa Clara County	2,431	0.27
Thousand Oaks, CA (city) Ventura County	312	0.27
College Station, TX (city) Brazos County	181	0.27
Gaithersburg, MD (city) Montgomery County	140	0.27
State College, PA (borough) Centre County	105	0.27

Notes: (cdp) census designated place; Refer to the Explanation of Data in the front of the book for more detailed information.

Asian: Thai

Top 150 Places Sorted by Number

(Based on all places, regardless of population)

Place	Number	%
Los Angeles, CA (city) Los Angeles County	11,398	0.31
New York, NY (city) New York City	5,002	0.06
Chicago, IL (city) Cook County	2,385	0.08
San Francisco, CA (city) San Francisco County	1,638	0.21
San Diego, CA (city) San Diego County	1,300	0.11
Las Vegas, NV (city) Clark County	1,226	0.26
Seattle, WA (city) King County	1,139	0.20
Long Beach, CA (city) Los Angeles County	967	0.21
Houston, TX (city) Harris County	928	0.05
Honolulu, HI (cdp) Honolulu County	852	0.23
San Jose, CA (city) Santa Clara County	776	0.09
San Antonio, TX (city) Bexar County	725	0.06
Cerritos, CA (city) Los Angeles County	694	1.35
Glendale, CA (city) Los Angeles County	669	0.34
Austin, TX (city) Travis County	666	0.10
Dallas, TX (city) Dallas County	656	0.06
Des Moines, IA (city) Polk County	643	0.32
Sunrise Manor, NV (cdp) Clark County	628	0.40
Anchorage, AK (municipality) Anchorage Borough	607	0.23
Phoenix, AZ (city) Maricopa County	545	0.04
Arlington, VA (cdp) Arlington County	523	0.28
Spring Valley, NV (cdp) Clark County	519	0.44
Anaheim, CA (city) Orange County	515	0.16
West Covina, CA (city) Los Angeles County	513	0.49
Portland, OR (city) Multnomah County	495	0.09
Irvine, CA (city) Orange County	493	0.34
Alhambra, CA (city) Los Angeles County	486	0.57
Paradise, NV (cdp) Clark County	472	0.25
Columbus, OH (city) Franklin County	472	0.07
Monterey Park, CA (city) Los Angeles County	470	0.78
Denver, CO (city) Denver County	457	0.08
Tucson, AZ (city) Pima County	455	0.09
Boston, MA (city) Suffolk County	454	0.08
Oklahoma City, OK (city) Oklahoma County	438	0.09
Bellflower, CA (city) Los Angeles County	436	0.60
Philadelphia, PA (city) Philadelphia County	401	0.03
Aurora, CO (city) Arapahoe County	400	0.14
Tampa, FL (city) Hillsborough County	376	0.12
Torrance, CA (city) Los Angeles County	373	0.27
Sacramento, CA (city) Sacramento County	362	0.09
North Las Vegas, NV (city) Clark County	351	0.30
Moreno Valley, CA (city) Riverside County	351	0.25
Nashville-Davidson, TN (special city) Davidson County	350	0.06
Fort Worth, TX (city) Tarrant County	349	0.07
Burbank, CA (city) Los Angeles County	340	0.34
Colorado Springs, CO (city) El Paso County	340	0.09
Lakewood, CA (city) Los Angeles County	329	0.41
Madison, WI (city) Dane County	316	0.15
Fresno, CA (city) Fresno County	314	0.07
Norwalk, CA (city) Los Angeles County	313	0.30
Wheaton-Glenmont, MD (cdp) Montgomery County	309	0.54
Riverside, CA (city) Riverside County	308	0.12
Downey, CA (city) Los Angeles County	307	0.29
Arlington, TX (city) Tarrant County	306	0.09
Tacoma, WA (city) Pierce County	305	0.16
Minneapolis, MN (city) Hennepin County	299	0.08
Walnut, CA (city) Los Angeles County	298	0.99
Fairfield, CA (city) Solano County	297	0.31
Henderson, NV (city) Clark County	297	0.17
San Bernardino, CA (city) San Bernardino County	297	0.16
Irving, TX (city) Dallas County	297	0.15
Fremont, CA (city) Alameda County	291	0.14
Oakland, CA (city) Alameda County	285	0.07
Springfield, VA (cdp) Fairfax County	283	0.93
Chino Hills, CA (city) San Bernardino County	283	0.42
Bellevue, WA (city) King County	277	0.25
Berkeley, CA (city) Alameda County	276	0.27
Jacksonville, FL (special city) Duval County	271	0.04
Aspen Hill, MD (cdp) Montgomery County	269	0.54
Wichita, KS (city) Sedgwick County	264	0.08
Washington, DC (city) District of Columbia	261	0.05
Rancho Cucamonga, CA (city) San Bernardino County	256	0.20
Hempstead, NY (town) Nassau County	255	0.03
Santa Clarita, CA (city) Los Angeles County	254	0.17
Glendale, AZ (city) Maricopa County	252	0.12
Plano, TX (city) Collin County	249	0.11
Albuquerque, NM (city) Bernalillo County	248	0.06
Yonkers, NY (city) Westchester County	246	0.13
Reno, NV (city) Washoe County	244	0.14
Skokie, IL (village) Cook County	243	0.38
Pittsburgh, PA (city) Allegheny County	243	0.07
Rowland Heights, CA (cdp) Los Angeles County	242	0.50
Huntington Beach, CA (city) Orange County	242	0.13
Pomona, CA (city) Los Angeles County	240	0.16
Arcadia, CA (city) Los Angeles County	239	0.45
Buena Park, CA (city) Orange County	237	0.30
Daly City, CA (city) San Mateo County	235	0.23
Alexandria, VA (independent city) Alexandria city	226	0.18
Ann Arbor, MI (city) Washtenaw County	225	0.20
Fullerton, CA (city) Orange County	220	0.17
Mesa, AZ (city) Maricopa County	220	0.06
Simi Valley, CA (city) Ventura County	213	0.19
Indianapolis, IN (special city) Marion County	213	0.03
Stockton, CA (city) San Joaquin County	205	0.08
Pasadena, CA (city) Los Angeles County	204	0.15
Hacienda Heights, CA (cdp) Los Angeles County	202	0.38
Milwaukee, WI (city) Milwaukee County	194	0.03
Wright, FL (cdp) Okaloosa County	193	0.89
Charlotte, NC (city) Mecklenburg County	193	0.04
Kansas City, MO (city) Jackson County	192	0.04
Saint Petersburg, FL (city) Pinellas County	191	0.08
Diamond Bar, CA (city) Los Angeles County	189	0.34
Killeen, TX (city) Bell County	189	0.22
Rosemead, CA (city) Los Angeles County	188	0.35
Virginia Beach, VA (independent city) Virginia Beach city	188	0.04
El Monte, CA (city) Los Angeles County	187	0.16
Baltimore, MD (independent city) Baltimore city	186	0.03
Richmond, CA (city) Contra Costa County	181	0.18
Cambridge, MA (city) Middlesex County	178	0.18
Omaha, NE (city) Douglas County	178	0.05
Garland, TX (city) Dallas County	177	0.08
Santa Ana, CA (city) Orange County	176	0.05
Jersey City, NJ (city) Hudson County	171	0.07
Atlanta, GA (city) Fulton County	171	0.04
Corvallis, OR (city) Benton County	170	0.34
Garden Grove, CA (city) Orange County	170	0.10
Baldwin Park, CA (city) Los Angeles County	168	0.22
Bakersfield, CA (city) Kern County	167	0.07
Abilene, TX (city) Taylor County	166	0.14
Fayetteville, NC (city) Cumberland County	166	0.14
Temple City, CA (city) Los Angeles County	165	0.49
Silver Spring, MD (cdp) Montgomery County	162	0.21
San Gabriel, CA (city) Los Angeles County	160	0.40
Melbourne, FL (city) Brevard County	158	0.22
Raleigh, NC (city) Wake County	158	0.06
Boulder, CO (city) Boulder County	157	0.17
Providence, RI (city) Providence County	156	0.09
Lowell, MA (city) Middlesex County	155	0.15
Eugene, OR (city) Lane County	155	0.11
Hampton, VA (independent city) Hampton city	155	0.11
Loma Linda, CA (city) San Bernardino County	153	0.82
Lakewood, WA (city) Pierce County	152	0.26
Lancaster, CA (city) Los Angeles County	150	0.13
Cypress, CA (city) Orange County	149	0.32
Lexington-Fayette, KY (special city) Fayette County	149	0.06
Denton, TX (city) Denton County	148	0.18
Hayward, CA (city) Alameda County	148	0.11
San Mateo, CA (city) San Mateo County	147	0.16
Norfolk, VA (independent city) Norfolk city	147	0.06
Saint Paul, MN (city) Ramsey County	147	0.05
Gardena, CA (city) Los Angeles County	146	0.25
Layton, UT (city) Davis County	145	0.25
Oceanside, CA (city) San Diego County	144	0.09
Tempe, AZ (city) Maricopa County	143	0.09
Newport News, VA (independent city) Newport News city	143	0.08
Brookhaven, NY (town) Suffolk County	143	0.03
Columbia, MO (city) Boone County	141	0.17
Augusta-Richmond County, GA (special city) Richmond County	141	0.07
Brandon, FL (cdp) Hillsborough County	140	0.18
Covina, CA (city) Los Angeles County	139	0.30

Notes: (cdp) census designated place; Refer to the Explanation of Data in the front of the book for more detailed information.

Asian: Thai

Top 150 Places Sorted by Percent

(Based on all places, regardless of population)

Place	Number	%
Brocket, ND (city) Ramsey County	4	6.15
Johnstown, NE (village) Brown County	3	5.66
Crown Point, AK (cdp) Kenai Peninsula Borough	2	2.67
Leipsic, DE (town) Kent County	5	2.46
Effie, MN (city) Itasca County	2	2.20
Colburn, WI (town) Adams County	3	1.66
Cuney, TX (town) Cherokee County	2	1.38
Cerritos, CA (city) Los Angeles County	694	1.35
Big Bend, CA (cdp) Shasta County	2	1.34
Butte City, ID (city) Butte County	1	1.32
Dolliver, IA (city) Emmet County	1	1.30
Marlborough, MO (village) Saint Louis County	28	1.25
Mansfield, WA (town) Douglas County	4	1.25
Slater, MN (township) Cass County	3	1.20
Dow City, IA (city) Crawford County	6	1.19
Ocean City, FL (cdp) Okaloosa County	64	1.14
Bixby, TX (cdp) Cameron County	4	1.12
Moffett, OK (town) Sequoyah County	2	1.12
East Ithaca, NY (cdp) Tompkins County	24	1.09
Allegheny, PA (township) Venango County	3	1.07
Union Grove, AL (town) Marshall County	1	1.06
Elm Springs, AR (city) Washington County	11	1.05
Ramona, SD (town) Lake County	2	1.05
Marion, TX (city) Guadalupe County	11	1.00
Walnut, CA (city) Los Angeles County	298	0.99
Cleveland, MN (township) Le Sueur County	6	0.98
Springfield, VA (cdp) Fairfax County	283	0.93
Pateros, WA (city) Okanogan County	6	0.93
Lake Arthur, NM (town) Chaves County	4	0.93
Bear Creek, MN (township) Clearwater County	1	0.93
Tatitlek, AK (cdp) Valdez-Cordova Census Area	1	0.93
Wright, FL (cdp) Okaloosa County	193	0.89
Broadmoor, CA (cdp) San Mateo County	36	0.89
Stanton, ND (city) Mercer County	3	0.87
Laupahoehoe, HI (cdp) Hawaii County	4	0.85
Rockwood, MN (township) Hubbard County	4	0.85
Barrow, AK (city) North Slope Borough	38	0.83
Mount Airy, GA (town) Habersham County	5	0.83
Prairie Farm, WI (town) Barron County	5	0.83
Loma Linda, CA (city) San Bernardino County	153	0.82
Cherry Valley, MI (township) Lake County	3	0.82
Damiansville, IL (village) Clinton County	3	0.82
North Buena Vista, IA (city) Clayton County	1	0.81
Urich, MO (city) Henry County	4	0.80
Monterey Park, CA (city) Los Angeles County	470	0.78
Iola, PA (cdp) Columbia County	1	0.78
Hybla Valley, VA (cdp) Fairfax County	129	0.77
Mary Esther, FL (city) Okaloosa County	31	0.76
Scottsville, TX (city) Harrison County	2	0.76
Faxon, OK (town) Comanche County	1	0.75
Wilma, MN (township) Pine County	1	0.73
Hollis, AK (cdp) Prince of Wales-Outer Ketchikan Census Area	1	0.72
Butterfield, MN (city) Watonwan County	4	0.71
Quantico, VA (town) Prince William County	4	0.71
Duncan, MI (township) Houghton County	2	0.71
Saint Robert, MO (city) Pulaski County	19	0.69
Rodney Village, DE (cdp) Kent County	11	0.69
Evergreen, MN (township) Becker County	2	0.69
Kemp Mill, MD (cdp) Montgomery County	68	0.68
Big Cabin, OK (town) Craig County	2	0.68
Fort Walton Beach, FL (city) Okaloosa County	133	0.67
Wrightstown, NJ (borough) Burlington County	5	0.67
Trimble, MO (city) Clinton County	3	0.67
Riverton, IA (city) Fremont County	2	0.66
La Palma, CA (city) Orange County	100	0.65
Man, WV (town) Logan County	5	0.65
Hickam Housing, HI (cdp) Honolulu County	35	0.64
Forest Home, NY (cdp) Tompkins County	6	0.64
Etna, CA (city) Siskiyou County	5	0.64
Loghill Village, CO (cdp) Ouray County	2	0.64
Viola, DE (town) Kent County	1	0.64
Haleiwa, HI (cdp) Honolulu County	14	0.63
Palm Shores, FL (town) Brevard County	5	0.63
Bluffton, MN (township) Otter Tail County	3	0.63
Rivergrove, OR (city) Clackamas County	2	0.62
Marcus, IA (city) Cherokee County	7	0.61
Skyline, MN (city) Blue Earth County	2	0.61
Loachapoka, AL (town) Lee County	1	0.61
Bellflower, CA (city) Los Angeles County	436	0.60
Moody AFB, GA (cdp) Lowndes County	6	0.60
Riverlea, OH (village) Franklin County	3	0.60
Dunn Loring, VA (cdp) Fairfax County	46	0.59
Littletown, AZ (cdp) Pima County	6	0.59
Emerado, ND (city) Grand Forks County	3	0.59
Avocado Heights, CA (cdp) Los Angeles County	88	0.58
Lake Lafayette, MO (city) Lafayette County	2	0.58
Clam Gulch, AK (cdp) Kenai Peninsula Borough	1	0.58
Cornish, OK (town) Jefferson County	1	0.58
Alhambra, CA (city) Los Angeles County	486	0.57
South San Gabriel, CA (cdp) Los Angeles County	43	0.57
Lowry Crossing, TX (city) Collin County	7	0.57
Fairmount, MD (cdp) Somerset County	3	0.56
Wheaton-Glenmont, MD (cdp) Montgomery County	309	0.54
Aspen Hill, MD (cdp) Montgomery County	269	0.54
Springfield, FL (city) Bay County	48	0.54
Flemington, GA (city) Liberty County	2	0.54
Hunters Hollow, KY (city) Bullitt County	2	0.54
Callaway, FL (city) Bay County	76	0.53
Lake Lorraine, FL (cdp) Okaloosa County	38	0.53
Cinco Bayou, FL (town) Okaloosa County	2	0.53
Mokane, MO (city) Callaway County	1	0.53
Riverside, OR (cdp) Umatilla County	1	0.53
Tecumseh, NE (city) Johnson County	9	0.52
Vienna, VA (town) Fairfax County	73	0.51
Niceville, FL (city) Okaloosa County	60	0.51
Elroy, NC (cdp) Wayne County	20	0.51
Boles Acres, NM (cdp) Otero County	6	0.51
Norwood, KY (city) Jefferson County	2	0.51
Petersburg, ND (city) Nelson County	1	0.51
Rowland Heights, CA (cdp) Los Angeles County	242	0.50
Lincolnwood, IL (village) Cook County	62	0.50
Hiland Park, FL (cdp) Bay County	5	0.50
Maysville, NC (town) Jones County	5	0.50
Kirtland Hills, OH (village) Lake County	3	0.50
West Covina, CA (city) Los Angeles County	513	0.49
Temple City, CA (city) Los Angeles County	165	0.49
Clearfield, UT (city) Davis County	126	0.49
West Wendover, NV (city) Elko County	23	0.49
Greenvale, NY (cdp) Nassau County	11	0.49
Kealakekua, HI (cdp) Hawaii County	8	0.49
Kawela Bay, HI (cdp) Honolulu County	2	0.49
Dorrance, KS (city) Russell County	1	0.49
East Pasadena, CA (cdp) Los Angeles County	29	0.48
Wall Lake, IA (city) Sac County	4	0.48
Pillager, MN (city) Cass County	2	0.48
Boyd, MN (city) Lac qui Parle County	1	0.48
Gold Hill, CO (cdp) Boulder County	1	0.48
Valparaiso, FL (city) Okaloosa County	30	0.47
Sienna Plantation, TX (cdp) Fort Bend County	9	0.47
Stateburg, SC (cdp) Sumter County	6	0.47
Puako, HI (cdp) Hawaii County	2	0.47
Bailey, TX (city) Fannin County	1	0.47
Nespelem, WA (town) Okanogan County	1	0.47
Panama, IA (city) Shelby County	1	0.47
East San Gabriel, CA (cdp) Los Angeles County	67	0.46
West Nyack, NY (cdp) Rockland County	15	0.46
Box Elder, SD (city) Pennington County	13	0.46
Meadowlakes, TX (city) Burnet County	6	0.46
Crowder, OK (town) Pittsburg County	2	0.46
Arcadia, CA (city) Los Angeles County	239	0.45
Emeryville, CA (city) Alameda County	31	0.45
Oaklawn-Sunview, KS (cdp) Sedgwick County	14	0.45
Hebron Estates, KY (city) Bullitt County	5	0.45
Mondovi, WI (town) Buffalo County	2	0.45
Nash, OK (town) Grant County	1	0.45
Spring Valley, NV (cdp) Clark County	519	0.44
Tukwila, WA (city) King County	76	0.44
Browns Mills, NJ (cdp) Burlington County	49	0.44
Holualoa, HI (cdp) Hawaii County	27	0.44
Parker, TX (city) Collin County	6	0.44

Notes: (cdp) census designated place; Refer to the Explanation of Data in the front of the book for more detailed information.

Asian: Thai

Top 150 Places Sorted by Percent

(Based on places with populations of 10,000 or more)

Place	Number	%
Cerritos, CA (city) Los Angeles County	694	1.35
Walnut, CA (city) Los Angeles County	298	0.99
Springfield, VA (cdp) Fairfax County	283	0.93
Wright, FL (cdp) Okaloosa County	193	0.89
Loma Linda, CA (city) San Bernardino County	153	0.82
Monterey Park, CA (city) Los Angeles County	470	0.78
Hybla Valley, VA (cdp) Fairfax County	129	0.77
Fort Walton Beach, FL (city) Okaloosa County	133	0.67
La Palma, CA (city) Orange County	100	0.65
Bellflower, CA (city) Los Angeles County	436	0.60
Avocado Heights, CA (cdp) Los Angeles County	88	0.58
Alhambra, CA (city) Los Angeles County	486	0.57
Wheaton-Glenmont, MD (cdp) Montgomery County	309	0.54
Aspen Hill, MD (cdp) Montgomery County	269	0.54
Callaway, FL (city) Bay County	76	0.53
Vienna, VA (town) Fairfax County	73	0.51
Niceville, FL (city) Okaloosa County	60	0.51
Rowland Heights, CA (cdp) Los Angeles County	242	0.50
Lincolnwood, IL (village) Cook County	62	0.50
West Covina, CA (city) Los Angeles County	513	0.49
Temple City, CA (city) Los Angeles County	165	0.49
Clearfield, UT (city) Davis County	126	0.49
East San Gabriel, CA (cdp) Los Angeles County	67	0.46
Arcadia, CA (city) Los Angeles County	239	0.45
Spring Valley, NV (cdp) Clark County	519	0.44
Tukwila, WA (city) King County	76	0.44
Browns Mills, NJ (cdp) Burlington County	49	0.44
Morton Grove, IL (village) Cook County	97	0.43
Makakilo City, HI (cdp) Honolulu County	56	0.43
Citrus, CA (cdp) Los Angeles County	45	0.43
Chino Hills, CA (city) San Bernardino County	283	0.42
Suisun City, CA (city) Solano County	111	0.42
Lakewood, CA (city) Los Angeles County	329	0.41
Sunrise Manor, NV (cdp) Clark County	628	0.40
San Gabriel, CA (city) Los Angeles County	160	0.40
Franconia, VA (cdp) Fairfax County	127	0.40
Skokie, IL (village) Cook County	243	0.38
Hacienda Heights, CA (cdp) Los Angeles County	202	0.38
Claremont, CA (city) Los Angeles County	129	0.38
Winchester, NV (cdp) Clark County	102	0.38
Herndon, VA (town) Fairfax County	82	0.38
Ithaca, NY (city) Tompkins County	109	0.37
Rosamond, CA (cdp) Kern County	53	0.37
SeaTac, WA (city) King County	91	0.36
Duarte, CA (city) Los Angeles County	77	0.36
Rosemead, CA (city) Los Angeles County	188	0.35
Darien, IL (city) Du Page County	79	0.35
Merrifield, VA (cdp) Fairfax County	39	0.35
Storm Lake, IA (city) Buena Vista County	35	0.35
Glendale, CA (city) Los Angeles County	669	0.34
Irvine, CA (city) Orange County	493	0.34
Burbank, CA (city) Los Angeles County	340	0.34
Diamond Bar, CA (city) Los Angeles County	189	0.34
Corvallis, OR (city) Benton County	170	0.34
Rose Hill, VA (cdp) Fairfax County	51	0.34
Converse, TX (city) Bexar County	39	0.34
Mililani Town, HI (cdp) Honolulu County	93	0.33
Wilmette, IL (village) Cook County	91	0.33
Marina, CA (city) Monterey County	82	0.33
Atwater, CA (city) Merced County	76	0.33
Des Moines, IA (city) Polk County	643	0.32
Cypress, CA (city) Orange County	149	0.32
Lincolnia, VA (cdp) Fairfax County	50	0.32
Linda, CA (cdp) Yuba County	43	0.32
Los Angeles, CA (city) Los Angeles County	11,398	0.31
Fairfield, CA (city) Solano County	297	0.31
South Pasadena, CA (city) Los Angeles County	75	0.31
Stanford, CA (cdp) Santa Clara County	41	0.31
North Las Vegas, NV (city) Clark County	351	0.30
Norwalk, CA (city) Los Angeles County	313	0.30
Buena Park, CA (city) Orange County	237	0.30
Covina, CA (city) Los Angeles County	139	0.30
Sierra Vista, AZ (city) Cochise County	113	0.30
El Cerrito, CA (city) Contra Costa County	70	0.30
Halawa, HI (cdp) Honolulu County	42	0.30

Place	Number	%
Downey, CA (city) Los Angeles County	307	0.29
Blacksburg, VA (town) Montgomery County	114	0.29
Pemberton, NJ (township) Burlington County	82	0.29
Murray, KY (city) Calloway County	44	0.29
Clemson, SC (city) Pickens County	35	0.29
Arlington, VA (cdp) Arlington County	523	0.28
Highland, CA (city) San Bernardino County	127	0.28
Lorton, VA (cdp) Fairfax County	50	0.28
Socastee, SC (cdp) Horry County	40	0.28
Calverton, MD (cdp) Montgomery County	35	0.28
Kingsgate, WA (cdp) King County	34	0.28
Grand Terrace, CA (city) San Bernardino County	33	0.28
Mountain Home, ID (city) Elmore County	31	0.28
Torrance, CA (city) Los Angeles County	373	0.27
Berkeley, CA (city) Alameda County	276	0.27
Bellevue, NE (city) Sarpy County	119	0.27
Jacksonville, AR (city) Pulaski County	82	0.27
Waimalu, HI (cdp) Honolulu County	79	0.27
Newington, VA (cdp) Fairfax County	53	0.27
Forest Park, IL (village) Cook County	43	0.27
Worthington, MN (city) Nobles County	31	0.27
Las Vegas, NV (city) Clark County	1,226	0.26
Lakewood, WA (city) Pierce County	152	0.26
Pittsfield charter, MI (township) Washtenaw County	79	0.26
Spanaway, WA (cdp) Pierce County	57	0.26
Foothill Farms, CA (cdp) Sacramento County	46	0.26
River Edge, NJ (borough) Bergen County	28	0.26
Paradise, NV (cdp) Clark County	472	0.25
Moreno Valley, CA (city) Riverside County	351	0.25
Bellevue, WA (city) King County	277	0.25
Gardena, CA (city) Los Angeles County	146	0.25
Layton, UT (city) Davis County	145	0.25
Paramount, CA (city) Los Angeles County	138	0.25
Shoreline, WA (city) King County	130	0.25
North Highlands, CA (cdp) Sacramento County	111	0.25
Urbana, IL (city) Champaign County	92	0.25
Fairbanks, AK (city) Fairbanks North Star Borough	77	0.25
Oakton, VA (cdp) Fairfax County	73	0.25
Ithaca, NY (town) Tompkins County	46	0.25
Montclair, CA (city) San Bernardino County	80	0.24
Woodbridge, VA (cdp) Prince William County	77	0.24
Olney, MD (cdp) Montgomery County	74	0.24
Mount Vernon, VA (cdp) Fairfax County	68	0.24
Scarsdale, NY (village) Westchester County	43	0.24
Artesia, CA (city) Los Angeles County	39	0.24
Coralville, IA (city) Johnson County	36	0.24
Crestview, FL (city) Okaloosa County	36	0.24
Destin, FL (city) Okaloosa County	27	0.24
Honolulu, HI (cdp) Honolulu County	852	0.23
Anchorage, AK (municipality) Anchorage Borough	607	0.23
Daly City, CA (city) San Mateo County	235	0.23
Rockville, MD (city) Montgomery County	111	0.23
Monrovia, CA (city) Los Angeles County	86	0.23
Severn, MD (cdp) Anne Arundel County	79	0.23
Dover, DE (city) Kent County	73	0.23
Pullman, WA (city) Whitman County	56	0.23
Groveton, VA (cdp) Fairfax County	49	0.23
West Carson, CA (cdp) Los Angeles County	49	0.23
North Druid Hills, GA (cdp) De Kalb County	44	0.23
Albany, CA (city) Alameda County	38	0.23
Wilton Manors, FL (city) Broward County	29	0.23
Los Alamitos, CA (city) Orange County	27	0.23
Palm Springs, FL (village) Palm Beach County	27	0.23
Killeen, TX (city) Bell County	189	0.22
Baldwin Park, CA (city) Los Angeles County	168	0.22
Melbourne, FL (city) Brevard County	158	0.22
Redlands, CA (city) San Bernardino County	139	0.22
East Lansing, MI (city) Ingham County	104	0.22
Redmond, WA (city) King County	98	0.22
Haltom City, TX (city) Tarrant County	86	0.22
Copperas Cove, TX (city) Coryell County	66	0.22
Security-Widefield, CO (cdp) El Paso County	66	0.22
Jefferson, VA (cdp) Fairfax County	61	0.22
Bailey's Crossroads, VA (cdp) Fairfax County	52	0.22
Fairfax, VA (independent city) Fairfax city	47	0.22

Notes: (cdp) census designated place; Refer to the Explanation of Data in the front of the book for more detailed information.

Asian: Vietnamese

Top 150 Places Sorted by Number

(Based on all places, regardless of population)

Place	Number	%
San Jose, CA (city) Santa Clara County	82,834	9.26
Garden Grove, CA (city) Orange County	36,532	22.11
Houston, TX (city) Harris County	33,922	1.74
San Diego, CA (city) San Diego County	29,665	2.42
Westminster, CA (city) Orange County	27,887	31.62
Los Angeles, CA (city) Los Angeles County	22,156	0.60
Santa Ana, CA (city) Orange County	19,919	5.89
Seattle, WA (city) King County	13,032	2.31
New York, NY (city) New York City	13,010	0.16
Philadelphia, PA (city) Philadelphia County	12,968	0.85
San Francisco, CA (city) San Francisco County	12,874	1.66
Portland, OR (city) Multnomah County	11,404	2.16
Boston, MA (city) Suffolk County	11,376	1.93
Anaheim, CA (city) Orange County	10,559	3.22
Arlington, TX (city) Tarrant County	9,954	2.99
Oakland, CA (city) Alameda County	9,658	2.42
Chicago, IL (city) Cook County	8,925	0.31
Oklahoma City, OK (city) Oklahoma County	8,652	1.71
Milpitas, CA (city) Santa Clara County	8,566	13.66
Dallas, TX (city) Dallas County	8,084	0.68
Fountain Valley, CA (city) Orange County	7,358	13.38
New Orleans, LA (city) Orleans Parish	7,327	1.51
Wichita, KS (city) Sedgwick County	7,273	2.11
Honolulu, HI (cdp) Honolulu County	7,227	1.94
Rosemead, CA (city) Los Angeles County	7,175	13.41
Garland, TX (city) Dallas County	7,023	3.25
El Monte, CA (city) Los Angeles County	6,766	5.83
Sacramento, CA (city) Sacramento County	6,753	1.66
Austin, TX (city) Travis County	6,426	0.98
Phoenix, AZ (city) Maricopa County	5,770	0.44
Stockton, CA (city) San Joaquin County	5,755	2.36
Huntington Beach, CA (city) Orange County	5,706	3.01
Long Beach, CA (city) Los Angeles County	5,697	1.23
Fort Worth, TX (city) Tarrant County	5,666	1.06
Alhambra, CA (city) Los Angeles County	5,390	6.28
Worcester, MA (city) Worcester County	5,061	2.93
Santa Clara, CA (city) Santa Clara County	5,046	4.93
Denver, CO (city) Denver County	4,849	0.87
Irvine, CA (city) Orange County	4,734	3.31
Charlotte, NC (city) Mecklenburg County	4,709	0.87
Fremont, CA (city) Alameda County	4,459	2.19
Orange, CA (city) Orange County	3,940	3.06
Lincoln, NE (city) Lancaster County	3,925	1.74
Tacoma, WA (city) Pierce County	3,911	2.02
Monterey Park, CA (city) Los Angeles County	3,850	6.41
Sunnyvale, CA (city) Santa Clara County	3,478	2.64
Saint Louis, MO (independent city) Saint Louis city	3,464	0.99
Kansas City, MO (city) Jackson County	3,386	0.77
Annandale, VA (cdp) Fairfax County	3,308	6.02
San Gabriel, CA (city) Los Angeles County	3,179	7.99
Stanton, CA (city) Orange County	3,117	8.33
Albuquerque, NM (city) Bernalillo County	3,058	0.68
Hayward, CA (city) Alameda County	2,979	2.13
Saint Paul, MN (city) Ramsey County	2,915	1.02
Port Arthur, TX (city) Jefferson County	2,869	4.97
Riverside, CA (city) Riverside County	2,830	1.11
Baton Rouge, LA (city) East Baton Rouge Parish	2,718	1.19
Memphis, TN (city) Shelby County	2,707	0.42
Elk Grove, CA (cdp) Sacramento County	2,682	4.47
West Covina, CA (city) Los Angeles County	2,619	2.49
Minneapolis, MN (city) Hennepin County	2,612	0.68
Aurora, CO (city) Arapahoe County	2,592	0.94
Grand Prairie, TX (city) Dallas County	2,589	2.03
Jacksonville, FL (special city) Duval County	2,566	0.35
Jefferson, VA (cdp) Fairfax County	2,469	9.00
San Antonio, TX (city) Bexar County	2,453	0.21
Carrollton, TX (city) Denton County	2,442	2.23
Des Moines, IA (city) Polk County	2,346	1.18
Greensboro, NC (city) Guilford County	2,340	1.05
Union City, CA (city) Alameda County	2,309	3.45
Tustin, CA (city) Orange County	2,300	3.41
Costa Mesa, CA (city) Orange County	2,299	2.11
White Center, WA (cdp) King County	2,294	10.94
Arlington, VA (cdp) Arlington County	2,255	1.19
Fresno, CA (city) Fresno County	2,175	0.51
Tucson, AZ (city) Pima County	2,148	0.44
Nashville-Davidson, TN (special city) Davidson County	2,134	0.39
Saint Petersburg, FL (city) Pinellas County	2,108	0.85
Columbus, OH (city) Franklin County	2,089	0.29
Fullerton, CA (city) Orange County	2,060	1.63
Washington, DC (city) District of Columbia	2,035	0.36
Silver Spring, MD (cdp) Montgomery County	2,023	2.64
Brooklyn Park, MN (city) Hennepin County	1,989	2.95
Springfield, VA (cdp) Fairfax County	1,960	6.44
West Valley City, UT (city) Salt Lake County	1,933	1.78
Richardson, TX (city) Dallas County	1,903	2.07
Plano, TX (city) Collin County	1,900	0.86
San Bernardino, CA (city) San Bernardino County	1,881	1.01
Atlanta, GA (city) Fulton County	1,881	0.45
Irving, TX (city) Dallas County	1,880	0.98
Quincy, MA (city) Norfolk County	1,850	2.10
Louisville, KY (city) Jefferson County	1,818	0.71
Salt Lake City, UT (city) Salt Lake County	1,811	1.00
Pomona, CA (city) Los Angeles County	1,782	1.19
Biloxi, MS (city) Harrison County	1,774	3.50
Tulsa, OK (city) Tulsa County	1,771	0.45
Lowell, MA (city) Middlesex County	1,769	1.68
Fort Smith, AR (city) Sebastian County	1,758	2.19
Torrance, CA (city) Los Angeles County	1,724	1.25
Jersey City, NJ (city) Hudson County	1,701	0.71
Renton, WA (city) King County	1,688	3.37
Tampa, FL (city) Hillsborough County	1,677	0.55
Grand Rapids, MI (city) Kent County	1,651	0.83
Bellevue, WA (city) King County	1,627	1.48
Raleigh, NC (city) Wake County	1,627	0.59
Upper Darby, PA (township) Delaware County	1,618	1.98
Corona, CA (city) Riverside County	1,604	1.28
Springfield, MA (city) Hampden County	1,601	1.05
Syracuse, NY (city) Onondaga County	1,600	1.09
Hawthorne, CA (city) Los Angeles County	1,569	1.87
Alameda, CA (city) Alameda County	1,529	2.12
Sioux City, IA (city) Woodbury County	1,524	1.79
Lawndale, CA (city) Los Angeles County	1,500	4.73
Lake Forest, CA (city) Orange County	1,498	2.55
Florin, CA (cdp) Sacramento County	1,491	5.39
Gardena, CA (city) Los Angeles County	1,469	2.54
Mission Bend, TX (cdp) Fort Bend County	1,468	4.76
Vancouver, WA (city) Clark County	1,460	1.02
Amarillo, TX (city) Potter County	1,459	0.84
Wyoming, MI (city) Kent County	1,449	2.09
Malden, MA (city) Middlesex County	1,434	2.55
Everett, WA (city) Snohomish County	1,432	1.57
Kent, WA (city) King County	1,407	1.77
Buffalo, NY (city) Erie County	1,402	0.48
Baldwin Park, CA (city) Los Angeles County	1,398	1.84
Rochester, NY (city) Monroe County	1,390	0.63
Haltom City, TX (city) Tarrant County	1,386	3.55
San Leandro, CA (city) Alameda County	1,371	1.73
Lakewood, CO (city) Jefferson County	1,357	0.94
Milwaukee, WI (city) Milwaukee County	1,357	0.23
Ontario, CA (city) San Bernardino County	1,353	0.86
Atlantic City, NJ (city) Atlantic County	1,352	3.34
Camden, NJ (city) Camden County	1,344	1.68
Sugar Land, TX (city) Fort Bend County	1,341	2.12
Chantilly, VA (cdp) Fairfax County	1,325	3.23
Lansing, MI (city) Ingham County	1,324	1.11
Mobile, AL (city) Mobile County	1,285	0.65
Buena Park, CA (city) Orange County	1,284	1.64
Montclair, CA (city) San Bernardino County	1,269	3.84
Virginia Beach, VA (independent city) Virginia Beach city	1,268	0.30
Bridgeport, CT (city) Fairfield County	1,259	0.90
Lynn, MA (city) Essex County	1,255	1.41
Westminster, CO (city) Adams County	1,246	1.23
Kentwood, MI (city) Kent County	1,240	2.74
Wheaton-Glenmont, MD (cdp) Montgomery County	1,237	2.14
Indianapolis, IN (special city) Marion County	1,227	0.16
Davenport, IA (city) Scott County	1,222	1.24
Escondido, CA (city) San Diego County	1,221	0.91
Burke, VA (cdp) Fairfax County	1,213	2.10
Cleveland, OH (city) Cuyahoga County	1,186	0.25

Notes: (cdp) census designated place; Refer to the Explanation of Data in the front of the book for more detailed information.

Asian: Vietnamese

Top 150 Places Sorted by Percent

(Based on all places, regardless of population)

Place	Number	%
Westminster, CA (city) Orange County	27,887	31.62
Bayou La Batre, AL (city) Mobile County	543	23.48
Amelia, LA (cdp) Saint Mary Parish	545	22.49
Garden Grove, CA (city) Orange County	36,532	22.11
Henderson, LA (town) Saint Martin Parish	243	15.87
Milpitas, CA (city) Santa Clara County	8,566	13.66
Rosemead, CA (city) Los Angeles County	7,175	13.41
Fountain Valley, CA (city) Orange County	7,358	13.38
Palacios, TX (city) Matagorda County	609	11.82
Avondale, LA (cdp) Jefferson Parish	638	11.73
White Center, WA (cdp) King County	2,294	10.94
Chamblee, GA (city) De Kalb County	1,034	10.82
Buras-Triumph, LA (cdp) Plaquemines Parish	359	10.69
Clarkston, GA (city) De Kalb County	752	10.40
Seven Corners, VA (cdp) Fairfax County	860	9.88
Seadrift, TX (city) Calhoun County	132	9.76
San Jose, CA (city) Santa Clara County	82,834	9.26
Jefferson, VA (cdp) Fairfax County	2,469	9.00
Texola, OK (town) Beckham County	4	8.51
Stanton, CA (city) Orange County	3,117	8.33
Morrow, GA (city) Clayton County	397	8.13
San Gabriel, CA (city) Los Angeles County	3,179	7.99
Lake City, GA (city) Clayton County	227	7.87
Fulton, TX (town) Aransas County	122	7.86
Spencer Mountain, NC (town) Gaston County	4	7.84
Woodlynne, NJ (borough) Camden County	211	7.55
San Leon, TX (cdp) Galveston County	302	6.92
Hapeville, GA (city) Fulton County	405	6.55
Alondra Park, CA (cdp) Los Angeles County	564	6.54
Springfield, VA (cdp) Fairfax County	1,960	6.44
Monterey Park, CA (city) Los Angeles County	3,850	6.41
North Springfield, VA (cdp) Fairfax County	586	6.39
Panorama Park, IA (city) Scott County	7	6.31
Alhambra, CA (city) Los Angeles County	5,390	6.28
Merrifield, VA (cdp) Fairfax County	676	6.05
Thunderbolt, GA (town) Chatham County	141	6.03
Annandale, VA (cdp) Fairfax County	3,308	6.02
South San Gabriel, CA (cdp) Los Angeles County	455	5.99
Santa Ana, CA (city) Orange County	19,919	5.89
El Monte, CA (city) Los Angeles County	6,766	5.83
Saint Martin, MS (cdp) Jackson County	387	5.80
D'Iberville, MS (city) Harrison County	439	5.77
Seven Trees, CA (cdp) Santa Clara County	94	5.64
Florin, CA (cdp) Sacramento County	1,491	5.39
Doraville, GA (city) De Kalb County	528	5.35
Seven Oaks, TX (city) Polk County	7	5.34
Abbeville, LA (city) Vermilion Parish	599	5.04
Port Arthur, TX (city) Jefferson County	2,869	4.97
Santa Clara, CA (city) Santa Clara County	5,046	4.93
Woodmere, LA (cdp) Jefferson Parish	641	4.91
Unalaska, AK (city) Aleutians West Census Area	209	4.88
Pitkin, CO (town) Gunnison County	6	4.84
Mission Bend, TX (cdp) Fort Bend County	1,468	4.76
Lawndale, CA (city) Los Angeles County	1,500	4.73
Gulf Hills, MS (cdp) Jackson County	277	4.69
Forest Park, GA (city) Clayton County	965	4.50
Elk Grove, CA (cdp) Sacramento County	2,682	4.47
Barling, AR (city) Sebastian County	186	4.45
Epworth, IA (city) Dubuque County	60	4.20
Bryn Mawr-Skyway, WA (cdp) King County	586	4.19
Lincolnia, VA (cdp) Fairfax County	654	4.14
Bailey's Crossroads, VA (cdp) Fairfax County	954	4.12
Moonshine, MN (township) Big Stone County	6	4.00
Winooski, VT (city) Chittenden County	259	3.95
Idylwood, VA (cdp) Fairfax County	627	3.92
Montclair, CA (city) San Bernardino County	1,269	3.84
Lake Barcroft, VA (cdp) Fairfax County	339	3.81
Bridge City, LA (cdp) Jefferson Parish	315	3.78
Harvey, LA (cdp) Jefferson Parish	801	3.60
Haltom City, TX (city) Tarrant County	1,386	3.55
Murphy, TX (city) Collin County	110	3.55
Summit, OK (town) Muskogee County	8	3.54
Rollingwood, CA (cdp) Contra Costa County	102	3.52
Biloxi, MS (city) Harrison County	1,774	3.50
Vineyard, CA (cdp) Sacramento County	351	3.47
Conley, GA (cdp) Clayton County	214	3.46
Union City, CA (city) Alameda County	2,309	3.45
Four Corners, TX (cdp) Fort Bend County	102	3.45
Erath, LA (town) Vermilion Parish	75	3.43
Tustin, CA (city) Orange County	2,300	3.41
Renton, WA (city) King County	1,688	3.37
Atlantic City, NJ (city) Atlantic County	1,352	3.34
Irvine, CA (city) Orange County	4,734	3.31
Saint Joseph, MN (township) Stearns County	81	3.31
Garland, TX (city) Dallas County	7,023	3.25
Mount Calvary, WI (village) Fond du Lac County	31	3.24
Chantilly, VA (cdp) Fairfax County	1,325	3.23
Stafford, TX (city) Fort Bend County	506	3.23
Anaheim, CA (city) Orange County	10,559	3.22
Whitemarsh Island, GA (cdp) Chatham County	185	3.18
Hillandale, MD (cdp) Montgomery County	97	3.18
Mapleview, MN (city) Mower County	6	3.17
Oak Ridge, FL (cdp) Orange County	706	3.16
Telford, PA (borough) Montgomery County	147	3.14
Truxton, MO (village) Lincoln County	3	3.13
South El Monte, CA (city) Los Angeles County	659	3.12
East Foothills, CA (cdp) Santa Clara County	253	3.11
Alum Rock, CA (cdp) Santa Clara County	416	3.09
Souderton, PA (borough) Montgomery County	207	3.08
Riverton-Boulevard Park, WA (cdp) King County	344	3.07
Orange, CA (city) Orange County	3,940	3.06
Lynnwood, WA (city) Snohomish County	1,028	3.04
Marina, CA (city) Monterey County	761	3.03
Rockport, TX (city) Aransas County	224	3.03
Timberlane, LA (cdp) Jefferson Parish	344	3.02
Pass Christian, MS (city) Harrison County	199	3.02
Huntington Beach, CA (city) Orange County	5,706	3.01
Newport Coast, CA (cdp) Orange County	80	3.00
Narcissa, OK (cdp) Ottawa County	3	3.00
Arlington, TX (city) Tarrant County	9,954	2.99
Brooklyn Park, MN (city) Hennepin County	1,989	2.95
Temple City, CA (city) Los Angeles County	985	2.95
Worcester, MA (city) Worcester County	5,061	2.93
Lilburn, GA (city) Gwinnett County	331	2.93
Mackenzie, MO (village) Saint Louis County	4	2.92
Meadows Place, TX (city) Fort Bend County	143	2.91
Riverdale, GA (city) Clayton County	361	2.89
Springfield, FL (city) Bay County	254	2.88
Kenneth City, FL (town) Pinellas County	124	2.82
East Hill-Meridian, WA (cdp) King County	812	2.77
Estelle, LA (cdp) Jefferson Parish	437	2.75
McDonald Chapel, AL (cdp) Jefferson County	29	2.75
Kentwood, MI (city) Kent County	1,240	2.74
Dunn Loring, VA (cdp) Fairfax County	215	2.74
Bacliff, TX (cdp) Galveston County	190	2.73
Hancock, MN (township) Carver County	10	2.72
Parkway-South Sacramento, CA (cdp) Sacramento County	984	2.70
West and East Lealman, FL (cdp) Pinellas County	584	2.68
Empire, LA (cdp) Plaquemines Parish	59	2.67
Monhegan, ME (plantation) Lincoln County	2	2.67
Kemp Mill, MD (cdp) Montgomery County	264	2.65
Sunnyvale, CA (city) Santa Clara County	3,478	2.64
Silver Spring, MD (cdp) Montgomery County	2,023	2.64
Foothill Ranch, CA (cdp) Orange County	284	2.61
Windemere, TX (cdp) Travis County	178	2.59
Chelsea, MA (city) Suffolk County	901	2.57
Saint Vincent, MN (city) Kittson County	3	2.56
Lake Forest, CA (city) Orange County	1,498	2.55
Malden, MA (city) Middlesex County	1,434	2.55
Garden City, KS (city) Finney County	726	2.55
Gretna, LA (city) Jefferson Parish	444	2.55
Newcastle, WA (city) King County	197	2.55
Gardena, CA (city) Los Angeles County	1,469	2.54
Campbell, CA (city) Santa Clara County	969	2.54
Olympia, WA (city) Thurston County	1,074	2.53
Glendale Heights, IL (village) Du Page County	805	2.53
Federal Heights, CO (city) Adams County	303	2.51
West Covina, CA (city) Los Angeles County	2,619	2.49
Pennsauken, NJ (cdp) Camden County	883	2.47
Randolph, MA (cdp) Norfolk County	762	2.46

Notes: (cdp) census designated place; Refer to the Explanation of Data in the front of the book for more detailed information.

Asian: Vietnamese

Top 150 Places Sorted by Percent

(Based on places with populations of 10,000 or more)

Place	Number	%
Westminster, CA (city) Orange County	27,887	31.62
Garden Grove, CA (city) Orange County	36,532	22.11
Milpitas, CA (city) Santa Clara County	8,566	13.66
Rosemead, CA (city) Los Angeles County	7,175	13.41
Fountain Valley, CA (city) Orange County	7,358	13.38
White Center, WA (cdp) King County	2,294	10.94
San Jose, CA (city) Santa Clara County	82,834	9.26
Jefferson, VA (cdp) Fairfax County	2,469	9.00
Stanton, CA (city) Orange County	3,117	8.33
San Gabriel, CA (city) Los Angeles County	3,179	7.99
Springfield, VA (cdp) Fairfax County	1,960	6.44
Monterey Park, CA (city) Los Angeles County	3,850	6.41
Alhambra, CA (city) Los Angeles County	5,390	6.28
Merrifield, VA (cdp) Fairfax County	676	6.05
Annandale, VA (cdp) Fairfax County	3,308	6.02
Santa Ana, CA (city) Orange County	19,919	5.89
El Monte, CA (city) Los Angeles County	6,766	5.83
Florin, CA (cdp) Sacramento County	1,491	5.39
Abbeville, LA (city) Vermilion Parish	599	5.04
Port Arthur, TX (city) Jefferson County	2,869	4.97
Santa Clara, CA (city) Santa Clara County	5,046	4.93
Woodmere, LA (cdp) Jefferson Parish	641	4.91
Mission Bend, TX (cdp) Fort Bend County	1,468	4.76
Lawndale, CA (city) Los Angeles County	1,500	4.73
Forest Park, GA (city) Clayton County	965	4.50
Elk Grove, CA (cdp) Sacramento County	2,682	4.47
Bryn Mawr-Skyway, WA (cdp) King County	586	4.19
Lincolnia, VA (cdp) Fairfax County	654	4.14
Bailey's Crossroads, VA (cdp) Fairfax County	954	4.12
Idylwood, VA (cdp) Fairfax County	627	3.92
Montclair, CA (city) San Bernardino County	1,269	3.84
Harvey, LA (cdp) Jefferson Parish	801	3.60
Haltom City, TX (city) Tarrant County	1,386	3.55
Biloxi, MS (city) Harrison County	1,774	3.50
Vineyard, CA (cdp) Sacramento County	351	3.47
Union City, CA (city) Alameda County	2,309	3.45
Tustin, CA (city) Orange County	2,300	3.41
Renton, WA (city) King County	1,688	3.37
Atlantic City, NJ (city) Atlantic County	1,352	3.34
Irvine, CA (city) Orange County	4,734	3.31
Garland, TX (city) Dallas County	7,023	3.25
Chantilly, VA (cdp) Fairfax County	1,325	3.23
Stafford, TX (city) Fort Bend County	506	3.23
Anaheim, CA (city) Orange County	10,559	3.22
Oak Ridge, FL (cdp) Orange County	706	3.16
South El Monte, CA (city) Los Angeles County	659	3.12
Alum Rock, CA (cdp) Santa Clara County	416	3.09
Riverton-Boulevard Park, WA (cdp) King County	344	3.07
Orange, CA (city) Orange County	3,940	3.06
Lynnwood, WA (city) Snohomish County	1,028	3.04
Marina, CA (city) Monterey County	761	3.03
Timberlane, LA (cdp) Jefferson Parish	344	3.02
Huntington Beach, CA (city) Orange County	5,706	3.01
Arlington, TX (city) Tarrant County	9,954	2.99
Brooklyn Park, MN (city) Hennepin County	1,989	2.95
Temple City, CA (city) Los Angeles County	985	2.95
Worcester, MA (city) Worcester County	5,061	2.93
Lilburn, GA (city) Gwinnett County	331	2.93
Riverdale, GA (city) Clayton County	361	2.89
East Hill-Meridian, WA (cdp) King County	812	2.77
Estelle, LA (cdp) Jefferson Parish	437	2.75
Kentwood, MI (city) Kent County	1,240	2.74
Parkway-South Sacramento, CA (cdp) Sacramento County	984	2.70
West and East Lealman, FL (cdp) Pinellas County	584	2.68
Sunnyvale, CA (city) Santa Clara County	3,478	2.64
Silver Spring, MD (cdp) Montgomery County	2,023	2.64
Foothill Ranch, CA (cdp) Orange County	284	2.61
Chelsea, MA (city) Suffolk County	901	2.57
Lake Forest, CA (city) Orange County	1,498	2.55
Malden, MA (city) Middlesex County	1,434	2.55
Garden City, KS (city) Finney County	726	2.55
Gretna, LA (city) Jefferson Parish	444	2.55
Gardena, CA (city) Los Angeles County	1,469	2.54
Campbell, CA (city) Santa Clara County	969	2.54
Olympia, WA (city) Thurston County	1,074	2.53
Glendale Heights, IL (village) Du Page County	805	2.53
Federal Heights, CO (city) Adams County	303	2.51
West Covina, CA (city) Los Angeles County	2,619	2.49
Pennsauken, NJ (cdp) Camden County	883	2.47
Randolph, MA (cdp) Norfolk County	762	2.46
West Springfield, VA (cdp) Fairfax County	697	2.46
San Diego, CA (city) San Diego County	29,665	2.42
Oakland, CA (city) Alameda County	9,658	2.42
Bay Point, CA (cdp) Contra Costa County	516	2.40
White Oak, MD (cdp) Montgomery County	501	2.39
Rosemont, CA (cdp) Sacramento County	544	2.38
Stockton, CA (city) San Joaquin County	5,755	2.36
Aloha, OR (cdp) Washington County	984	2.36
Seattle, WA (city) King County	13,032	2.31
Terrytown, LA (cdp) Jefferson Parish	586	2.30
New Territory, TX (cdp) Fort Bend County	318	2.29
Placentia, CA (city) Orange County	1,053	2.27
Carrollton, TX (city) Denton County	2,442	2.23
Pflugerville, TX (city) Travis County	362	2.22
Cascade-Fairwood, WA (cdp) King County	765	2.21
Laguna, CA (cdp) Sacramento County	756	2.20
Fremont, CA (city) Alameda County	4,459	2.19
Fort Smith, AR (city) Sebastian County	1,758	2.19
Marrero, LA (cdp) Jefferson Parish	787	2.18
Tukwila, WA (city) King County	374	2.18
Highland, CA (city) San Bernardino County	966	2.17
SeaTac, WA (city) King County	553	2.17
Hatfield, PA (township) Montgomery County	362	2.17
Portland, OR (city) Multnomah County	11,404	2.16
Wheaton-Glenmont, MD (cdp) Montgomery County	1,237	2.14
San Pablo, CA (city) Contra Costa County	647	2.14
Hayward, CA (city) Alameda County	2,979	2.13
Liberal, KS (city) Seward County	419	2.13
Alameda, CA (city) Alameda County	1,529	2.12
Sugar Land, TX (city) Fort Bend County	1,341	2.12
Calverton, MD (cdp) Montgomery County	267	2.12
Wichita, KS (city) Sedgwick County	7,273	2.11
Costa Mesa, CA (city) Orange County	2,299	2.11
West Puente Valley, CA (cdp) Los Angeles County	477	2.11
Quincy, MA (city) Norfolk County	1,850	2.10
Burke, VA (cdp) Fairfax County	1,213	2.10
Burien, WA (city) King County	669	2.10
Wyoming, MI (city) Kent County	1,449	2.09
Newark, CA (city) Alameda County	887	2.09
Richardson, TX (city) Dallas County	1,903	2.07
Grand Prairie, TX (city) Dallas County	2,589	2.03
Cerritos, CA (city) Los Angeles County	1,045	2.03
Gainesville, GA (city) Hall County	519	2.03
Tacoma, WA (city) Pierce County	3,911	2.02
Fairfax, VA (independent city) Fairfax city	433	2.01
Harrisburg, PA (city) Dauphin County	972	1.99
Upper Darby, PA (township) Delaware County	1,618	1.98
East San Gabriel, CA (cdp) Los Angeles County	285	1.96
Honolulu, HI (cdp) Honolulu County	7,227	1.94
Boston, MA (city) Suffolk County	11,376	1.93
Everett, MA (city) Middlesex County	736	1.93
Herndon, VA (town) Fairfax County	417	1.93
Wade Hampton, SC (cdp) Greenville County	394	1.93
Davis, CA (city) Yolo County	1,156	1.92
Walnut, CA (city) Los Angeles County	574	1.91
Ventnor City, NJ (city) Atlantic County	245	1.90
Franconia, VA (cdp) Fairfax County	600	1.88
West Pensacola, FL (cdp) Escambia County	412	1.88
Hawthorne, CA (city) Los Angeles County	1,569	1.87
Watauga, TX (city) Tarrant County	407	1.86
Pearland, TX (city) Brazoria County	697	1.85
Newington, VA (cdp) Fairfax County	366	1.85
Baldwin Park, CA (city) Los Angeles County	1,398	1.84
Pinellas Park, FL (city) Pinellas County	839	1.84
Aliso Viejo, CA (cdp) Orange County	741	1.84
Des Moines, WA (city) King County	538	1.84
Martha Lake, WA (cdp) Snohomish County	233	1.84
Centreville, VA (cdp) Fairfax County	888	1.82
Halawa, HI (cdp) Honolulu County	250	1.80
Sioux City, IA (city) Woodbury County	1,524	1.79

Notes: (cdp) census designated place; Refer to the Explanation of Data in the front of the book for more detailed information.

Asian: Other Asian, specified

Top 150 Places Sorted by Number

(Based on all places, regardless of population)

Place	Number	%
New York, NY (city) New York City	3,921	0.05
Honolulu, HI (cdp) Honolulu County	2,560	0.69
San Francisco, CA (city) San Francisco County	1,134	0.15
Los Angeles, CA (city) Los Angeles County	1,095	0.03
Daly City, CA (city) San Mateo County	659	0.64
Fremont, CA (city) Alameda County	510	0.25
Fort Wayne, IN (city) Allen County	476	0.23
Chicago, IL (city) Cook County	404	0.01
San Jose, CA (city) Santa Clara County	397	0.04
Kaneohe, HI (cdp) Honolulu County	389	1.11
Houston, TX (city) Harris County	357	0.02
Waimalu, HI (cdp) Honolulu County	297	1.01
San Diego, CA (city) San Diego County	293	0.02
Alhambra, CA (city) Los Angeles County	263	0.31
Seattle, WA (city) King County	261	0.05
Mililani Town, HI (cdp) Honolulu County	252	0.88
Kailua, HI (cdp) Honolulu County	244	0.67
Washington, DC (city) District of Columbia	225	0.04
Hilo, HI (cdp) Hawaii County	222	0.54
Irving, TX (city) Dallas County	222	0.12
Arlington, VA (cdp) Arlington County	221	0.12
Dallas, TX (city) Dallas County	219	0.02
Pearl City, HI (cdp) Honolulu County	217	0.70
Portland, OR (city) Multnomah County	217	0.04
Boston, MA (city) Suffolk County	186	0.03
Rosemead, CA (city) Los Angeles County	168	0.31
San Gabriel, CA (city) Los Angeles County	164	0.41
Philadelphia, PA (city) Philadelphia County	159	0.01
Phoenix, AZ (city) Maricopa County	158	0.01
Jacksonville, FL (special city) Duval County	152	0.02
Austin, TX (city) Travis County	147	0.02
Monterey Park, CA (city) Los Angeles County	146	0.24
Denver, CO (city) Denver County	142	0.03
Omaha, NE (city) Douglas County	136	0.03
Long Beach, CA (city) Los Angeles County	135	0.03
Bakersfield, CA (city) Kern County	132	0.05
Saint Paul, MN (city) Ramsey County	130	0.05
Union City, CA (city) Alameda County	126	0.19
Baltimore, MD (independent city) Baltimore city	126	0.02
Waipio, HI (cdp) Honolulu County	125	1.07
Diamond Bar, CA (city) Los Angeles County	125	0.22
Indianapolis, IN (special city) Marion County	119	0.02
Oakland, CA (city) Alameda County	116	0.03
Wheaton-Glenmont, MD (cdp) Montgomery County	113	0.20
Somerville, MA (city) Middlesex County	113	0.15
Makakilo City, HI (cdp) Honolulu County	111	0.84
Fort Worth, TX (city) Tarrant County	111	0.02
Atlanta, GA (city) Fulton County	110	0.03
Detroit, MI (city) Wayne County	108	0.01
Tulsa, OK (city) Tulsa County	107	0.03
Torrance, CA (city) Los Angeles County	106	0.08
Las Vegas, NV (city) Clark County	104	0.02
Sunnyvale, CA (city) Santa Clara County	103	0.08
Madison, WI (city) Dane County	103	0.05
Columbus, OH (city) Franklin County	103	0.01
Hempstead, NY (town) Nassau County	102	0.01
San Antonio, TX (city) Bexar County	101	0.01
Gaithersburg, MD (city) Montgomery County	100	0.19
Wahiawa, HI (cdp) Honolulu County	98	0.61
New Orleans, LA (city) Orleans Parish	94	0.02
Arcadia, CA (city) Los Angeles County	93	0.18
Davis, CA (city) Yolo County	93	0.15
Waipahu, HI (cdp) Honolulu County	89	0.27
Arlington, TX (city) Tarrant County	88	0.03
Tucson, AZ (city) Pima County	88	0.02
Rowland Heights, CA (cdp) Los Angeles County	87	0.18
El Monte, CA (city) Los Angeles County	87	0.08
Charlotte, NC (city) Mecklenburg County	86	0.02
Aiea, HI (cdp) Honolulu County	85	0.94
South San Francisco, CA (city) San Mateo County	85	0.14
Boulder, CO (city) Boulder County	85	0.09
Berkeley, CA (city) Alameda County	83	0.08
Cambridge, MA (city) Middlesex County	83	0.08
West Covina, CA (city) Los Angeles County	83	0.08
Halawa, HI (cdp) Honolulu County	82	0.59
Bellevue, NE (city) Sarpy County	82	0.18
Pittsburgh, PA (city) Allegheny County	82	0.02
Rockville, MD (city) Montgomery County	81	0.17
Mountain View, CA (city) Santa Clara County	81	0.11
Saint Louis, MO (independent city) Saint Louis city	80	0.02
Minneapolis, MN (city) Hennepin County	79	0.02
Village Park, HI (cdp) Honolulu County	78	0.81
Idylwood, VA (cdp) Fairfax County	78	0.49
Colorado Springs, CO (city) El Paso County	76	0.02
Oakton, VA (cdp) Fairfax County	75	0.26
Heeia, HI (cdp) Honolulu County	73	1.48
Kapaa, HI (cdp) Kauai County	73	0.77
Pasadena, CA (city) Los Angeles County	73	0.05
Fresno, CA (city) Fresno County	72	0.02
Santa Clara, CA (city) Santa Clara County	71	0.07
Albuquerque, NM (city) Bernalillo County	70	0.02
Concord, CA (city) Contra Costa County	69	0.06
Riverside, CA (city) Riverside County	69	0.03
Irvine, CA (city) Orange County	68	0.05
Raleigh, NC (city) Wake County	68	0.02
Brookhaven, NY (town) Suffolk County	65	0.01
Pukalani, HI (cdp) Maui County	64	0.87
Frederick, MD (city) Frederick County	63	0.12
Bethesda, MD (cdp) Montgomery County	63	0.11
Oceanside, CA (city) San Diego County	63	0.04
Plano, TX (city) Collin County	63	0.03
Sacramento, CA (city) Sacramento County	63	0.02
Milpitas, CA (city) Santa Clara County	62	0.10
Santa Clarita, CA (city) Los Angeles County	62	0.04
Augusta-Richmond County, GA (special city) Richmond County	62	0.03
Jersey City, NJ (city) Hudson County	62	0.03
Virginia Beach, VA (independent city) Virginia Beach city	62	0.01
Memphis, TN (city) Shelby County	61	0.01
Germantown, MD (cdp) Montgomery County	60	0.11
Wichita, KS (city) Sedgwick County	60	0.02
Buffalo, NY (city) Erie County	59	0.02
Ahuimanu, HI (cdp) Honolulu County	58	0.68
Silver Spring, MD (cdp) Montgomery County	57	0.07
Anaheim, CA (city) Orange County	57	0.02
Lexington-Fayette, KY (special city) Fayette County	57	0.02
Tacoma, WA (city) Pierce County	56	0.03
Lincoln, NE (city) Lancaster County	56	0.02
Walnut, CA (city) Los Angeles County	55	0.18
Edmond, OK (city) Oklahoma County	55	0.08
Baldwin Park, CA (city) Los Angeles County	54	0.07
Alexandria, VA (independent city) Alexandria city	54	0.04
Durham, NC (city) Durham County	54	0.03
Paradise, NV (cdp) Clark County	54	0.03
Mesa, AZ (city) Maricopa County	54	0.01
Kahului, HI (cdp) Maui County	53	0.26
Aspen Hill, MD (cdp) Montgomery County	53	0.11
Shreveport, LA (city) Caddo Parish	53	0.03
Oklahoma City, OK (city) Oklahoma County	53	0.01
Ithaca, NY (city) Tompkins County	52	0.18
Fountain Valley, CA (city) Orange County	51	0.09
Pleasanton, CA (city) Alameda County	51	0.08
Milwaukee, WI (city) Milwaukee County	51	0.01
Wailuku, HI (cdp) Maui County	50	0.41
Temple City, CA (city) Los Angeles County	50	0.15
Battle Creek, MI (city) Calhoun County	50	0.09
Chino Hills, CA (city) San Bernardino County	50	0.07
Bellevue, WA (city) King County	50	0.05
San Mateo, CA (city) San Mateo County	50	0.05
Aurora, CO (city) Arapahoe County	49	0.02
Fullerton, CA (city) Orange County	48	0.04
Kansas City, MO (city) Jackson County	48	0.01
Makawao, HI (cdp) Maui County	47	0.74
Merrifield, VA (cdp) Fairfax County	47	0.42
Ann Arbor, MI (city) Washtenaw County	47	0.04
Rochester, NY (city) Monroe County	47	0.02
Hayward, CA (city) Alameda County	46	0.03
Birmingham, AL (city) Jefferson County	46	0.02
Maunawili, HI (cdp) Honolulu County	45	0.92
Waipio Acres, HI (cdp) Honolulu County	45	0.85
North Bethesda, MD (cdp) Montgomery County	45	0.12

Notes: (cdp) census designated place; Refer to the Explanation of Data in the front of the book for more detailed information.

Asian: Other Asian, specified

Top 150 Places Sorted by Percent

(Based on all places, regardless of population)

Place	Number	%
Alcan Border, AK (cdp) Southeast Fairbanks Census Area	1	4.76
Mount Carmel, SC (cdp) McCormick County	8	3.38
Hickory Hill, KY (city) Jefferson County	3	2.08
Eldora, CO (cdp) Boulder County	3	1.76
Warren City, TX (city) Gregg County	6	1.75
Trenton, KY (city) Todd County	7	1.67
Yantis, TX (town) Wood County	5	1.56
Rockleigh, NJ (borough) Bergen County	6	1.53
Heeia, HI (cdp) Honolulu County	73	1.48
Waikane, HI (cdp) Honolulu County	10	1.38
Crown Point, AK (cdp) Kenai Peninsula Borough	1	1.33
Kirby, VT (town) Caledonia County	6	1.32
Kurtistown, HI (cdp) Hawaii County	15	1.30
Omao, HI (cdp) Kauai County	15	1.23
Elizabeth, LA (town) Allen Parish	7	1.22
Frankfort, OH (village) Ross County	12	1.19
Kaneohe, HI (cdp) Honolulu County	389	1.11
Rancho Viejo, TX (town) Cameron County	19	1.08
Waipio, HI (cdp) Honolulu County	125	1.07
Oconee, GA (city) Washington County	3	1.07
Waimalu, HI (cdp) Honolulu County	297	1.01
Harleyville, SC (town) Dorchester County	6	1.01
Greenview, CA (cdp) Siskiyou County	2	1.00
Arco, MN (city) Lincoln County	1	1.00
Aiea, HI (cdp) Honolulu County	85	0.94
Tuttle, ND (city) Kidder County	1	0.94
Maunawili, HI (cdp) Honolulu County	45	0.92
Coram, MT (cdp) Flathead County	3	0.89
Mililani Town, HI (cdp) Honolulu County	252	0.88
Pukalani, HI (cdp) Maui County	64	0.87
Millen, MI (township) Alcona County	4	0.86
Waipio Acres, HI (cdp) Honolulu County	45	0.85
Shorter, AL (town) Macon County	3	0.85
Makakilo City, HI (cdp) Honolulu County	111	0.84
Pahoa, HI (cdp) Hawaii County	8	0.83
Village Park, HI (cdp) Honolulu County	78	0.81
Hawaiian Acres, HI (cdp) Hawaii County	14	0.79
Rosser, TX (village) Kaufman County	3	0.79
Kapaau, HI (cdp) Hawaii County	9	0.78
Kapaa, HI (cdp) Kauai County	73	0.77
Wealthwood, MN (township) Aitkin County	2	0.76
Makawao, HI (cdp) Maui County	47	0.74
Seven Mile, OH (village) Butler County	5	0.74
San Isidro, TX (cdp) Starr County	2	0.74
Pearl City, HI (cdp) Honolulu County	217	0.70
Makaha Valley, HI (cdp) Honolulu County	9	0.70
Honolulu, HI (cdp) Honolulu County	2,560	0.69
Ewa Gentry, HI (cdp) Honolulu County	34	0.69
Ahuimanu, HI (cdp) Honolulu County	58	0.68
Kailua, HI (cdp) Honolulu County	244	0.67
Beseman, MN (township) Carlton County	1	0.67
Fern Acres, HI (cdp) Hawaii County	5	0.66
Lihue, HI (cdp) Kauai County	37	0.65
Washington, PA (township) Cambria County	6	0.65
Cleveland, MN (township) Le Sueur County	4	0.65
Daly City, CA (city) San Mateo County	659	0.64
Papaikou, HI (cdp) Hawaii County	9	0.64
Parrott, GA (town) Terrell County	1	0.64
Springville, CA (cdp) Tulare County	7	0.63
Paoli, OK (town) Garvin County	4	0.62
Wahiawa, HI (cdp) Honolulu County	98	0.61
Kahaluu, HI (cdp) Honolulu County	18	0.61
Halaula, HI (cdp) Hawaii County	3	0.61
Paukaa, HI (cdp) Hawaii County	3	0.61
Monroe, SD (town) Turner County	1	0.61
Kekaha, HI (cdp) Kauai County	19	0.60
Bassett, AR (town) Mississippi County	1	0.60
Halawa, HI (cdp) Honolulu County	82	0.59
Ewa Villages, HI (cdp) Honolulu County	28	0.59
Thornton, AR (city) Calhoun County	3	0.58
Mountain View, HI (cdp) Hawaii County	16	0.57
Queen Anne, MD (town) Queen Anne's County	1	0.57
Haliimaile, HI (cdp) Maui County	5	0.56
Hilo, HI (cdp) Hawaii County	222	0.54
Waikapu, HI (cdp) Maui County	6	0.54
Belleville, AR (city) Yell County	2	0.54
New Eagle, PA (borough) Washington County	12	0.53
Loris, SC (city) Horry County	11	0.53
Kaaawa, HI (cdp) Honolulu County	7	0.53
Clarendon, PA (borough) Warren County	3	0.53
Paauilo, HI (cdp) Hawaii County	3	0.53
Broadmoor, CA (cdp) San Mateo County	21	0.52
Hawaiian Paradise Park, HI (cdp) Hawaii County	36	0.51
Carrollton, AL (town) Pickens County	5	0.51
Buckner, AR (city) Lafayette County	2	0.51
Rensselaer, NY (city) Rensselaer County	39	0.50
Wailua Homesteads, HI (cdp) Kauai County	23	0.50
Braselton, GA (town) Jackson County	6	0.50
Idylwood, VA (cdp) Fairfax County	78	0.49
Leipsic, DE (town) Kent County	1	0.49
Aloha, MI (township) Cheboygan County	5	0.48
Gold Hill, CO (cdp) Boulder County	1	0.48
Haiku-Pauwela, HI (cdp) Maui County	31	0.47
Summerton, SC (town) Clarendon County	5	0.47
Sweet Home, AR (cdp) Pulaski County	5	0.47
Paia, HI (cdp) Maui County	11	0.44
Mokuleia, HI (cdp) Honolulu County	8	0.44
Flippin, AR (city) Marion County	6	0.44
Linn, MO (city) Osage County	6	0.44
Chinook, WA (cdp) Pacific County	2	0.44
Winona, KS (city) Logan County	1	0.44
Waialua, HI (cdp) Honolulu County	16	0.43
Waverly, VA (town) Sussex County	10	0.43
Murphy, OK (cdp) Mayes County	1	0.43
Olney, MN (township) Nobles County	1	0.43
Merrifield, VA (cdp) Fairfax County	47	0.42
Hanapepe, HI (cdp) Kauai County	9	0.42
Minonk, IL (city) Woodford County	9	0.42
Kalihiwai, HI (cdp) Kauai County	3	0.42
Ridgway, CO (town) Ouray County	3	0.42
San Gabriel, CA (city) Los Angeles County	164	0.41
Wailuku, HI (cdp) Maui County	50	0.41
Wainaku, HI (cdp) Hawaii County	5	0.41
Marlow, NH (town) Cheshire County	3	0.40
Coffee Springs, AL (town) Geneva County	1	0.40
Springfield, MI (city) Calhoun County	20	0.39
McLaughlin, SD (city) Corson County	3	0.39
Algoma, MS (town) Pontotoc County	2	0.39
Copperhill, TN (city) Polk County	2	0.39
South San Gabriel, CA (cdp) Los Angeles County	29	0.38
Highgrove, CA (cdp) Riverside County	13	0.38
Readlyn, IA (city) Bremer County	3	0.38
Philadelphia, TN (city) Loudon County	2	0.38
Maili, HI (cdp) Honolulu County	22	0.37
Hanamaulu, HI (cdp) Kauai County	12	0.37
Ainaloa, HI (cdp) Hawaii County	7	0.37
Ellaville, GA (city) Schley County	6	0.37
Honomu, HI (cdp) Hawaii County	2	0.37
Baudette, MN (city) Lake of the Woods County	4	0.36
Marthasville, MO (city) Warren County	3	0.36
Laytonsville, MD (town) Montgomery County	1	0.36
Lawai, HI (cdp) Kauai County	7	0.35
North Bennington, VT (village) Bennington County	5	0.35
Glorieta, NM (cdp) Santa Fe County	3	0.35
Burns, WY (town) Laramie County	1	0.35
West Harrison, IN (town) Dearborn County	1	0.35
Wailua, HI (cdp) Kauai County	7	0.34
Gruver, TX (city) Hansford County	4	0.34
Corning, OH (village) Perry County	2	0.34
Cromberg, CA (cdp) Plumas County	1	0.34
Homer, MI (township) Calhoun County	10	0.33
Slippery Rock, PA (borough) Butler County	10	0.33
Pineville, KY (city) Bell County	7	0.33
Buffalo, TX (city) Leon County	6	0.33
Richland, GA (city) Stewart County	6	0.33
Fairmount, PA (township) Luzerne County	4	0.33
Naalehu, HI (cdp) Hawaii County	3	0.33
Rio Grande, OH (village) Gallia County	3	0.33
Kaumakani, HI (cdp) Kauai County	2	0.33
Moclips, WA (cdp) Grays Harbor County	2	0.33

Notes: (cdp) census designated place; Refer to the Explanation of Data in the front of the book for more detailed information.

Asian: Other Asian, specified

Top 150 Places Sorted by Percent

(Based on places with populations of 10,000 or more)

Place	Number	%
Kaneohe, HI (cdp) Honolulu County	389	1.11
Waipio, HI (cdp) Honolulu County	125	1.07
Waimalu, HI (cdp) Honolulu County	297	1.01
Mililani Town, HI (cdp) Honolulu County	252	0.88
Makakilo City, HI (cdp) Honolulu County	111	0.84
Pearl City, HI (cdp) Honolulu County	217	0.70
Honolulu, HI (cdp) Honolulu County	2,560	0.69
Kailua, HI (cdp) Honolulu County	244	0.67
Daly City, CA (city) San Mateo County	659	0.64
Wahiawa, HI (cdp) Honolulu County	98	0.61
Halawa, HI (cdp) Honolulu County	82	0.59
Hilo, HI (cdp) Hawaii County	222	0.54
Idylwood, VA (cdp) Fairfax County	78	0.49
Merrifield, VA (cdp) Fairfax County	47	0.42
San Gabriel, CA (city) Los Angeles County	164	0.41
Wailuku, HI (cdp) Maui County	50	0.41
Alhambra, CA (city) Los Angeles County	263	0.31
Rosemead, CA (city) Los Angeles County	168	0.31
Waipahu, HI (cdp) Honolulu County	89	0.27
Ewa Beach, HI (cdp) Honolulu County	40	0.27
Oakton, VA (cdp) Fairfax County	75	0.26
Kahului, HI (cdp) Maui County	53	0.26
Fremont, CA (city) Alameda County	510	0.25
Kihei, HI (cdp) Maui County	42	0.25
Monterey Park, CA (city) Los Angeles County	146	0.24
Fort Wayne, IN (city) Allen County	476	0.23
Diamond Bar, CA (city) Los Angeles County	125	0.22
Wheaton-Glenmont, MD (cdp) Montgomery County	113	0.20
Union City, CA (city) Alameda County	126	0.19
Gaithersburg, MD (city) Montgomery County	100	0.19
Macomb, IL (city) McDonough County	35	0.19
Arcadia, CA (city) Los Angeles County	93	0.18
Rowland Heights, CA (cdp) Los Angeles County	87	0.18
Bellevue, NE (city) Sarpy County	82	0.18
Walnut, CA (city) Los Angeles County	55	0.18
Ithaca, NY (city) Tompkins County	52	0.18
Redland, MD (cdp) Montgomery County	31	0.18
Rockville, MD (city) Montgomery County	81	0.17
Fairfax, VA (independent city) Fairfax city	37	0.17
East Riverdale, MD (cdp) Prince George's County	24	0.16
San Francisco, CA (city) San Francisco County	1,134	0.15
Somerville, MA (city) Middlesex County	113	0.15
Davis, CA (city) Yolo County	93	0.15
Temple City, CA (city) Los Angeles County	50	0.15
Herndon, VA (town) Fairfax County	32	0.15
Carrboro, NC (town) Orange County	25	0.15
San Marino, CA (city) Los Angeles County	20	0.15
Stanford, CA (cdp) Santa Clara County	20	0.15
Garden City, GA (city) Chatham County	17	0.15
South San Francisco, CA (city) San Mateo County	85	0.14
Vienna, VA (town) Fairfax County	20	0.14
Piney Green, NC (cdp) Onslow County	16	0.14
Rossville, MD (cdp) Baltimore County	16	0.14
El Cerrito, CA (city) Contra Costa County	29	0.13
Bay Point, CA (cdp) Contra Costa County	27	0.13
Loma Linda, CA (city) San Bernardino County	24	0.13
Golden, CO (city) Jefferson County	23	0.13
Hyattsville, MD (city) Prince George's County	19	0.13
Irving, TX (city) Dallas County	222	0.12
Arlington, VA (cdp) Arlington County	221	0.12
Frederick, MD (city) Frederick County	63	0.12
North Bethesda, MD (cdp) Montgomery County	45	0.12
Kearney, NE (city) Buffalo County	33	0.12
Griffin, GA (city) Spalding County	28	0.12
Cockeysville, MD (cdp) Baltimore County	23	0.12
Tysons Corner, VA (cdp) Fairfax County	22	0.12
Mountain View, CA (city) Santa Clara County	81	0.11
Bethesda, MD (cdp) Montgomery County	63	0.11
Germantown, MD (cdp) Montgomery County	60	0.11
Aspen Hill, MD (cdp) Montgomery County	53	0.11
Fairland, MD (cdp) Montgomery County	24	0.11
Ithaca, NY (town) Tompkins County	20	0.11
Scarsdale, NY (village) Westchester County	19	0.11
Powder Springs, GA (city) Cobb County	14	0.11
Ventnor City, NJ (city) Atlantic County	14	0.11
Nanakuli, HI (cdp) Honolulu County	12	0.11
Waianae, HI (cdp) Honolulu County	12	0.11
Milpitas, CA (city) Santa Clara County	62	0.10
Newark, CA (city) Alameda County	44	0.10
McLean, VA (cdp) Fairfax County	39	0.10
Culver City, CA (city) Los Angeles County	38	0.10
Mankato, MN (city) Blue Earth County	33	0.10
East Hill-Meridian, WA (cdp) King County	30	0.10
Monterey, CA (city) Monterey County	29	0.10
Jefferson, VA (cdp) Fairfax County	27	0.10
Spanaway, WA (cdp) Pierce County	21	0.10
Valinda, CA (cdp) Los Angeles County	21	0.10
Pinole, CA (city) Contra Costa County	19	0.10
Albany, CA (city) Alameda County	17	0.10
East San Gabriel, CA (cdp) Los Angeles County	15	0.10
Moultrie, GA (city) Colquitt County	14	0.10
West Point, MS (city) Clay County	12	0.10
Franklin, OH (city) Warren County	11	0.10
Vineyard, CA (cdp) Sacramento County	10	0.10
Boulder, CO (city) Boulder County	85	0.09
Fountain Valley, CA (city) Orange County	51	0.09
Battle Creek, MI (city) Calhoun County	50	0.09
Potomac, MD (cdp) Montgomery County	41	0.09
East Brunswick, NJ (cdp) Middlesex County	40	0.09
Claremont, CA (city) Los Angeles County	30	0.09
College Park, MD (city) Prince George's County	21	0.09
Gallup, NM (city) McKinley County	19	0.09
Mansfield, CT (town) Tolland County	19	0.09
West Carson, CA (cdp) Los Angeles County	19	0.09
Troutdale, OR (city) Multnomah County	12	0.09
Hanover, NJ (township) Morris County	11	0.09
Springboro, OH (city) Warren County	11	0.09
Dobbs Ferry, NY (village) Westchester County	10	0.09
Woodstock, GA (city) Cherokee County	9	0.09
Torrance, CA (city) Los Angeles County	106	0.08
Sunnyvale, CA (city) Santa Clara County	103	0.08
El Monte, CA (city) Los Angeles County	87	0.08
Berkeley, CA (city) Alameda County	83	0.08
Cambridge, MA (city) Middlesex County	83	0.08
West Covina, CA (city) Los Angeles County	83	0.08
Edmond, OK (city) Oklahoma County	55	0.08
Pleasanton, CA (city) Alameda County	51	0.08
Reston, VA (cdp) Fairfax County	45	0.08
Covina, CA (city) Los Angeles County	39	0.08
Concord, NH (city) Merrimack County	34	0.08
Smyrna, GA (city) Cobb County	32	0.08
Pacifica, CA (city) San Mateo County	31	0.08
University City, MO (city) Saint Louis County	30	0.08
Brighton, NY (town) Monroe County	28	0.08
Fort Lee, NJ (borough) Bergen County	28	0.08
Amherst, MA (town) Hampshire County	27	0.08
Pleasant Hill, CA (city) Contra Costa County	27	0.08
Randolph, MA (cdp) Norfolk County	26	0.08
East Palo Alto, CA (city) San Mateo County	24	0.08
Benicia, CA (city) Solano County	22	0.08
Homewood, AL (city) Jefferson County	20	0.08
South Salt Lake, UT (city) Salt Lake County	18	0.08
Greenbelt, MD (city) Prince George's County	17	0.08
Ashland, CA (cdp) Alameda County	16	0.08
Forest Grove, OR (city) Washington County	15	0.08
Amherst Center, MA (cdp) Hampshire County	13	0.08
Humble, TX (city) Harris County	12	0.08
North Decatur, GA (cdp) De Kalb County	12	0.08
Addison, TX (town) Dallas County	11	0.08
New Territory, TX (cdp) Fort Bend County	11	0.08
Druid Hills, GA (cdp) De Kalb County	10	0.08
Glenn Dale, MD (cdp) Prince George's County	10	0.08
Lake Forest Park, WA (city) King County	10	0.08
Speedway, IN (town) Marion County	10	0.08
Iona, FL (cdp) Lee County	9	0.08
Lexington Park, MD (cdp) Saint Mary's County	9	0.08
Little Ferry, NJ (borough) Bergen County	9	0.08
Mays Chapel, MD (cdp) Baltimore County	9	0.08
Palm Springs, FL (village) Palm Beach County	9	0.08
Storrs, CT (cdp) Tolland County	9	0.08

Notes: (cdp) census designated place; Refer to the Explanation of Data in the front of the book for more detailed information.

Asian: Other Asian, not specified

Top 150 Places Sorted by Number

(Based on all places, regardless of population)

Place	Number	%
New York, NY (city) New York City	29,826	0.37
Los Angeles, CA (city) Los Angeles County	10,498	0.28
Chicago, IL (city) Cook County	5,843	0.20
Houston, TX (city) Harris County	4,262	0.22
Philadelphia, PA (city) Philadelphia County	3,947	0.26
San Diego, CA (city) San Diego County	3,314	0.27
San Jose, CA (city) Santa Clara County	3,225	0.36
San Francisco, CA (city) San Francisco County	2,804	0.36
Dallas, TX (city) Dallas County	1,919	0.16
Seattle, WA (city) King County	1,904	0.34
Nashville-Davidson, TN (special city) Davidson County	1,734	0.32
Fremont, CA (city) Alameda County	1,713	0.84
Fresno, CA (city) Fresno County	1,589	0.37
Washington, DC (city) District of Columbia	1,567	0.27
Long Beach, CA (city) Los Angeles County	1,480	0.32
Stockton, CA (city) San Joaquin County	1,407	0.58
Detroit, MI (city) Wayne County	1,370	0.14
Saint Paul, MN (city) Ramsey County	1,368	0.48
Boston, MA (city) Suffolk County	1,367	0.23
Phoenix, AZ (city) Maricopa County	1,363	0.10
Oakland, CA (city) Alameda County	1,359	0.34
San Antonio, TX (city) Bexar County	1,327	0.12
Columbus, OH (city) Franklin County	1,315	0.18
Sacramento, CA (city) Sacramento County	1,310	0.32
Austin, TX (city) Travis County	1,266	0.19
Minneapolis, MN (city) Hennepin County	1,251	0.33
Honolulu, HI (cdp) Honolulu County	1,218	0.33
Baltimore, MD (independent city) Baltimore city	1,121	0.17
Denver, CO (city) Denver County	1,118	0.20
Jacksonville, FL (special city) Duval County	1,110	0.15
Portland, OR (city) Multnomah County	1,109	0.21
Pittsburgh, PA (city) Allegheny County	1,099	0.33
Arlington, VA (cdp) Arlington County	1,094	0.58
Hempstead, NY (town) Nassau County	1,091	0.14
Glendale, CA (city) Los Angeles County	1,071	0.55
Tucson, AZ (city) Pima County	1,056	0.22
Charlotte, NC (city) Mecklenburg County	1,045	0.19
Jersey City, NJ (city) Hudson County	1,025	0.43
Irvine, CA (city) Orange County	1,017	0.71
Milwaukee, WI (city) Milwaukee County	983	0.16
Arlington, TX (city) Tarrant County	911	0.27
Santa Ana, CA (city) Orange County	891	0.26
Las Vegas, NV (city) Clark County	862	0.18
Oklahoma City, OK (city) Oklahoma County	839	0.17
North Hempstead, NY (town) Nassau County	837	0.38
Dearborn, MI (city) Wayne County	824	0.84
Anaheim, CA (city) Orange County	792	0.24
Fort Worth, TX (city) Tarrant County	773	0.14
Alexandria, VA (independent city) Alexandria city	735	0.57
Providence, RI (city) Providence County	721	0.42
Hayward, CA (city) Alameda County	719	0.51
Indianapolis, IN (special city) Marion County	716	0.09
Plano, TX (city) Collin County	709	0.32
Concord, CA (city) Contra Costa County	691	0.57
Union City, CA (city) Alameda County	668	1.00
New Haven, CT (city) New Haven County	663	0.54
Lowell, MA (city) Middlesex County	636	0.60
Wichita, KS (city) Sedgwick County	634	0.18
Memphis, TN (city) Shelby County	621	0.10
Ithaca, NY (city) Tompkins County	620	2.12
Aurora, CO (city) Arapahoe County	607	0.22
Albuquerque, NM (city) Bernalillo County	583	0.13
Kansas City, MO (city) Jackson County	583	0.13
Virginia Beach, VA (independent city) Virginia Beach city	573	0.13
Brookhaven, NY (town) Suffolk County	570	0.13
Irving, TX (city) Dallas County	565	0.29
Garden Grove, CA (city) Orange County	555	0.34
College Park, MD (city) Prince George's County	553	2.24
Sunnyvale, CA (city) Santa Clara County	545	0.41
Greensboro, NC (city) Guilford County	541	0.24
Torrance, CA (city) Los Angeles County	531	0.38
Tacoma, WA (city) Pierce County	528	0.27
Raleigh, NC (city) Wake County	520	0.19
Cleveland, OH (city) Cuyahoga County	518	0.11
Yonkers, NY (city) Westchester County	513	0.26
Cambridge, MA (city) Middlesex County	512	0.51
Pomona, CA (city) Los Angeles County	507	0.34
Des Moines, IA (city) Polk County	499	0.25
Tempe, AZ (city) Maricopa County	490	0.31
Riverside, CA (city) Riverside County	489	0.19
Anchorage, AK (municipality) Anchorage Borough	488	0.19
Saint Louis, MO (independent city) Saint Louis city	488	0.14
Colorado Springs, CO (city) El Paso County	486	0.13
Tulsa, OK (city) Tulsa County	484	0.12
Modesto, CA (city) Stanislaus County	469	0.25
Alhambra, CA (city) Los Angeles County	451	0.53
Newark, NJ (city) Essex County	450	0.16
El Paso, TX (city) El Paso County	450	0.08
Garland, TX (city) Dallas County	449	0.21
Bakersfield, CA (city) Kern County	446	0.18
Spring Valley, NV (cdp) Clark County	443	0.38
Tampa, FL (city) Hillsborough County	441	0.15
Lynn, MA (city) Essex County	435	0.49
Islip, NY (town) Suffolk County	426	0.13
Berkeley, CA (city) Alameda County	424	0.41
Buffalo, NY (city) Erie County	421	0.14
Paradise, NV (cdp) Clark County	417	0.22
Madison, WI (city) Dane County	417	0.20
New Orleans, LA (city) Orleans Parish	412	0.09
Santa Clara, CA (city) Santa Clara County	408	0.40
Saint Petersburg, FL (city) Pinellas County	407	0.16
Toledo, OH (city) Lucas County	399	0.13
Lincoln, NE (city) Lancaster County	398	0.18
Bridgeport, CT (city) Fairfield County	396	0.28
Ann Arbor, MI (city) Washtenaw County	395	0.35
Daly City, CA (city) San Mateo County	394	0.38
Burke, VA (cdp) Fairfax County	393	0.68
Oyster Bay, NY (town) Nassau County	389	0.13
Richardson, TX (city) Dallas County	385	0.42
Beverly Hills, CA (city) Los Angeles County	383	1.13
Norfolk, VA (independent city) Norfolk city	383	0.16
Rancho Cucamonga, CA (city) San Bernardino County	382	0.30
Mesa, AZ (city) Maricopa County	380	0.10
Carrollton, TX (city) Denton County	379	0.35
Atlanta, GA (city) Fulton County	379	0.09
Alameda, CA (city) Alameda County	377	0.52
Omaha, NE (city) Douglas County	377	0.10
Springfield, VA (cdp) Fairfax County	376	1.24
Sugar Land, TX (city) Fort Bend County	375	0.59
Monterey Park, CA (city) Los Angeles County	372	0.62
Skokie, IL (village) Cook County	372	0.59
Orlando, FL (city) Orange County	368	0.20
Paterson, NJ (city) Passaic County	367	0.25
San Bernardino, CA (city) San Bernardino County	367	0.20
Chandler, AZ (city) Maricopa County	366	0.21
Huntington Beach, CA (city) Orange County	361	0.19
Salt Lake City, UT (city) Salt Lake County	351	0.19
Parsippany-Troy Hills, NJ (township) Morris County	349	0.69
Corona, CA (city) Riverside County	348	0.28
Worcester, MA (city) Worcester County	347	0.20
Bellevue, WA (city) King County	345	0.31
Richmond, VA (independent city) Richmond city	344	0.17
Cincinnati, OH (city) Hamilton County	341	0.10
Rochester, NY (city) Monroe County	338	0.15
Sunrise Manor, NV (cdp) Clark County	337	0.22
Pasadena, CA (city) Los Angeles County	334	0.25
Reno, NV (city) Washoe County	334	0.19
Tysons Corner, VA (cdp) Fairfax County	329	1.77
Richmond, CA (city) Contra Costa County	329	0.33
Warren, MI (city) Macomb County	328	0.24
Fullerton, CA (city) Orange County	327	0.26
Spokane, WA (city) Spokane County	325	0.17
Annandale, VA (cdp) Fairfax County	318	0.58
Westminster, CA (city) Orange County	317	0.36
Burbank, CA (city) Los Angeles County	317	0.32
Lancaster, CA (city) Los Angeles County	317	0.27
Durham, NC (city) Durham County	315	0.17
Huntington, NY (town) Suffolk County	314	0.16
Newark, CA (city) Alameda County	313	0.74
Hamtramck, MI (city) Wayne County	312	1.36

Notes: (cdp) census designated place; Refer to the Explanation of Data in the front of the book for more detailed information.

Asian: Other Asian, not specified

Top 150 Places Sorted by Percent

(Based on all places, regardless of population)

Place	Number	%
Ellenton, GA (town) Colquitt County	17	5.06
Sandyville, IA (city) Warren County	3	4.92
Kupreanof, AK (city) Wrangell-Petersburg Census Area	1	4.35
Urbancrest, OH (village) Franklin County	34	3.92
Laketown, UT (town) Rich County	7	3.72
Unalaska, AK (city) Aleutians West Census Area	158	3.69
Vanleer, TN (town) Dickson County	11	3.55
Vernonburg, GA (town) Chatham County	4	2.90
Smoaks, SC (town) Colleton County	4	2.86
McKittrick, MO (town) Montgomery County	2	2.78
Emhouse, TX (town) Navarro County	4	2.52
College Park, MD (city) Prince George's County	553	2.24
Swift Trail Junction, AZ (cdp) Graham County	48	2.19
Iroquois, SD (city) Kingsbury County	6	2.16
Ithaca, NY (city) Tompkins County	620	2.12
Manley, NE (village) Cass County	4	2.09
Rosebud, MN (township) Polk County	7	2.04
Woods Landing-Jelm, WY (cdp) Albany County	2	2.00
Fort Riley-Camp Whiteside, KS (cdp) Geary County	2	1.94
Bannockburn, IL (village) Lake County	27	1.89
Johnstown, NE (village) Brown County	1	1.89
Taos Ski Valley, NM (village) Taos County	1	1.79
Tysons Corner, VA (cdp) Fairfax County	329	1.77
Buies Creek, NC (cdp) Harnett County	39	1.76
Grand View-on-Hudson, NY (village) Rockland County	5	1.76
Drew, ME (plantation) Penobscot County	1	1.75
Carlton, GA (city) Madison County	4	1.72
Kings Point, NY (village) Nassau County	86	1.69
Topeka, IN (town) La Grange County	19	1.64
South San Gabriel, CA (cdp) Los Angeles County	122	1.61
Alpaugh, CA (cdp) Tulare County	12	1.58
Gregg, PA (township) Union County	73	1.56
Barton Hills, MI (village) Washtenaw County	5	1.49
Bandon, MN (township) Renville County	3	1.49
Springerton, IL (village) White County	2	1.49
Fort Devens, MA (cdp) Worcester County	15	1.47
Lyons, MN (township) Lyon County	3	1.44
Butterfield, MN (city) Watonwan County	8	1.42
Saddle Rock Estates, NY (cdp) Nassau County	6	1.42
Bethania, NC (town) Forsyth County	5	1.41
Rutland, IA (city) Humboldt County	2	1.38
Viking, MN (township) Marshall County	2	1.38
Cairo, MO (village) Randolph County	4	1.37
Greenhorn, CA (cdp) Plumas County	2	1.37
Hamtramck, MI (city) Wayne County	312	1.36
Spring Brook, MN (township) Kittson County	1	1.35
Lincolnia, VA (cdp) Fairfax County	211	1.34
Newberry, MI (village) Luce County	36	1.34
Bailey's Crossroads, VA (cdp) Fairfax County	309	1.33
Cromwell, IN (town) Noble County	6	1.33
Lime Lake, MN (township) Murray County	3	1.33
Girard, GA (town) Burke County	3	1.32
Searingtown, NY (cdp) Nassau County	65	1.29
Great Neck Gardens, NY (cdp) Nassau County	14	1.29
Ridgeville, AL (town) Etowah County	2	1.27
Great Neck, NY (village) Nassau County	119	1.25
Springfield, VA (cdp) Fairfax County	376	1.24
Glendale, CO (city) Arapahoe County	56	1.23
New London, NC (town) Stanly County	4	1.23
McCaskill, AR (city) Hempstead County	1	1.19
Haddam, KS (city) Washington County	2	1.18
Owatonna, MN (township) Steele County	9	1.17
Tatums, OK (town) Carter County	2	1.16
Aullville, MO (village) Lafayette County	1	1.16
Garland, AR (town) Miller County	4	1.14
Beverly Hills, CA (city) Los Angeles County	383	1.13
Birnamwood, WI (town) Shawano County	8	1.13
Coleridge, NE (village) Cedar County	6	1.11
Honomu, HI (cdp) Hawaii County	6	1.11
Merrifield, VA (cdp) Fairfax County	123	1.10
Glen Alpine, NC (town) Burke County	12	1.10
Vernon, CA (city) Los Angeles County	1	1.10
Parker, TX (city) Collin County	15	1.09
Washington, VA (town) Rappahannock County	2	1.09
Glen Flora, WI (village) Rusk County	1	1.08
French Camp, CA (cdp) San Joaquin County	44	1.07
Sawyer, ND (city) Ward County	4	1.06
Vera, OK (town) Washington County	2	1.06
Clarkston, GA (city) De Kalb County	76	1.05
Beaver, AR (town) Carroll County	1	1.05
North Lilbourn, MO (village) New Madrid County	1	1.05
Oakdale, LA (city) Allen Parish	84	1.03
Greenvale, NY (cdp) Nassau County	23	1.03
Chauncey, OH (village) Athens County	11	1.03
Lake Harbor, FL (cdp) Palm Beach County	2	1.03
Arcadia, KS (city) Crawford County	4	1.02
Augsburg, MN (township) Marshall County	1	1.02
Postville, IA (city) Allamakee County	23	1.01
Lenapah, OK (town) Nowata County	3	1.01
Gene Autry, OK (town) Carter County	1	1.01
Union City, CA (city) Alameda County	668	1.00
Benson, NY (town) Hamilton County	2	1.00
Oaklawn-Sunview, KS (cdp) Sedgwick County	31	0.99
Venus, TX (town) Johnson County	9	0.99
Canton, WI (town) Buffalo County	3	0.99
Ensign, KS (city) Gray County	2	0.99
East Richmond Heights, CA (cdp) Contra Costa County	33	0.98
Hamilton, GA (city) Harris County	3	0.98
Inkster, ND (city) Grand Forks County	1	0.98
Newington, VA (cdp) Fairfax County	192	0.97
Stanford, CA (cdp) Santa Clara County	129	0.97
Cordova, MN (township) Le Sueur County	5	0.97
Fire Island, NY (cdp) Suffolk County	3	0.97
Pleasant Valley, MN (township) Mower County	3	0.97
Trenton, NC (town) Jones County	2	0.97
Mountain View, WY (cdp) Natrona County	1	0.97
Nezperce, ID (city) Lewis County	5	0.96
Lehigh, OK (city) Coal County	3	0.95
Dunn Loring, VA (cdp) Fairfax County	74	0.94
Upper Brookville, NY (village) Nassau County	17	0.94
Berkeley Lake, GA (city) Gwinnett County	16	0.94
Troutville, VA (town) Botetourt County	4	0.93
Felton, MN (township) Clay County	1	0.93
Seven Corners, VA (cdp) Fairfax County	80	0.92
South Hill, NY (cdp) Tompkins County	55	0.92
University Park, NM (cdp) Dona Ana County	25	0.92
Bode, IA (city) Humboldt County	3	0.92
McMillan, MI (township) Luce County	36	0.91
Kensington, NY (village) Nassau County	11	0.91
Booneville, KY (city) Owsley County	1	0.90
Leshara, NE (village) Saunders County	1	0.90
North Kansas City, MO (city) Clay County	42	0.89
Ouzinkie, AK (city) Kodiak Island Borough	2	0.89
Springtown, AR (town) Benton County	1	0.88
Lawrence, MI (township) Van Buren County	29	0.87
Stem, NC (town) Granville County	2	0.87
West Paterson, NJ (borough) Passaic County	94	0.86
Marenisco, MI (township) Gogebic County	9	0.86
Minneiska, MN (city) Wabasha County	1	0.86
Almon, WI (town) Shawano County	5	0.85
Alton, KS (city) Osborne County	1	0.85
Fremont, CA (city) Alameda County	1,713	0.84
Dearborn, MI (city) Wayne County	824	0.84
Williamsburg, VA (independent city) Williamsburg city	101	0.84
Little Ferry, NJ (borough) Bergen County	91	0.84
Dugway, UT (cdp) Tooele County	17	0.84
Herndon, VA (town) Fairfax County	179	0.83
Lackland AFB, TX (cdp) Bexar County	58	0.81
Thomaston, NY (village) Nassau County	21	0.81
Jewell Junction, IA (city) Hamilton County	10	0.81
Vergennes, IL (village) Jackson County	4	0.81
Roe, AR (town) Monroe County	1	0.81
Slana, AK (cdp) Valdez-Cordova Census Area	1	0.81
Bethany, MI (township) Gratiot County	28	0.80
Fairgrove, MI (village) Tuscola County	5	0.80
Lake Barcroft, VA (cdp) Fairfax County	70	0.79
Bellerose Terrace, NY (cdp) Nassau County	17	0.79
Mound Station, IL (village) Brown County	1	0.79
West Springfield, VA (cdp) Fairfax County	220	0.78
Prospect Park, NJ (borough) Passaic County	45	0.78

Notes: (cdp) census designated place; Refer to the Explanation of Data in the front of the book for more detailed information.

Asian: Other Asian, not specified

Top 150 Places Sorted by Percent

(Based on places with populations of 10,000 or more)

Place	Number	%
College Park, MD (city) Prince George's County	553	2.24
Ithaca, NY (city) Tompkins County	620	2.12
Tysons Corner, VA (cdp) Fairfax County	329	1.77
Hamtramck, MI (city) Wayne County	312	1.36
Lincolnia, VA (cdp) Fairfax County	211	1.34
Bailey's Crossroads, VA (cdp) Fairfax County	309	1.33
Springfield, VA (cdp) Fairfax County	376	1.24
Beverly Hills, CA (city) Los Angeles County	383	1.13
Merrifield, VA (cdp) Fairfax County	123	1.10
Union City, CA (city) Alameda County	668	1.00
Newington, VA (cdp) Fairfax County	192	0.97
Stanford, CA (cdp) Santa Clara County	129	0.97
West Paterson, NJ (borough) Passaic County	94	0.86
Fremont, CA (city) Alameda County	1,713	0.84
Dearborn, MI (city) Wayne County	824	0.84
Williamsburg, VA (independent city) Williamsburg city	101	0.84
Little Ferry, NJ (borough) Bergen County	91	0.84
Herndon, VA (town) Fairfax County	179	0.83
West Springfield, VA (cdp) Fairfax County	220	0.78
Groveton, VA (cdp) Fairfax County	163	0.77
Idylwood, VA (cdp) Fairfax County	123	0.77
Hanover, NH (town) Grafton County	84	0.77
Wausau, WI (city) Marathon County	291	0.76
Franconia, VA (cdp) Fairfax County	238	0.75
East San Gabriel, CA (cdp) Los Angeles County	109	0.75
Newark, CA (city) Alameda County	313	0.74
Irvine, CA (city) Orange County	1,017	0.71
Ionia, MI (city) Ionia County	75	0.71
Parsippany-Troy Hills, NJ (township) Morris County	349	0.69
Claremont, CA (city) Los Angeles County	236	0.69
Lincolnwood, IL (village) Cook County	85	0.69
Burke, VA (cdp) Fairfax County	393	0.68
Dublin, CA (city) Alameda County	195	0.65
Mission Bend, TX (cdp) Fort Bend County	196	0.64
Lorton, VA (cdp) Fairfax County	113	0.64
Oakton, VA (cdp) Fairfax County	186	0.63
Justice, IL (village) Cook County	77	0.63
Monterey Park, CA (city) Los Angeles County	372	0.62
Rose Hill, VA (cdp) Fairfax County	92	0.61
New Territory, TX (cdp) Fort Bend County	84	0.61
Lowell, MA (city) Middlesex County	636	0.60
Avenel, NJ (cdp) Middlesex County	106	0.60
Hybla Valley, VA (cdp) Fairfax County	100	0.60
Sugar Land, TX (city) Fort Bend County	375	0.59
Skokie, IL (village) Cook County	372	0.59
Chantilly, VA (cdp) Fairfax County	243	0.59
Lathrop, CA (city) San Joaquin County	62	0.59
Stockton, CA (city) San Joaquin County	1,407	0.58
Arlington, VA (cdp) Arlington County	1,094	0.58
Annandale, VA (cdp) Fairfax County	318	0.58
North Valley Stream, NY (cdp) Nassau County	92	0.58
Alexandria, VA (independent city) Alexandria city	735	0.57
Concord, CA (city) Contra Costa County	691	0.57
White Center, WA (cdp) King County	120	0.57
Montgomery Village, MD (cdp) Montgomery County	214	0.56
Mount Vernon, VA (cdp) Fairfax County	161	0.56
Glendale, CA (city) Los Angeles County	1,071	0.55
San Gabriel, CA (city) Los Angeles County	218	0.55
New Haven, CT (city) New Haven County	663	0.54
Centreville, VA (cdp) Fairfax County	261	0.54
McLean, VA (cdp) Fairfax County	209	0.54
North Potomac, MD (cdp) Montgomery County	124	0.54
Alhambra, CA (city) Los Angeles County	451	0.53
State College, PA (borough) Centre County	203	0.53
Alameda, CA (city) Alameda County	377	0.52
Rosemead, CA (city) Los Angeles County	279	0.52
Stafford, TX (city) Fort Bend County	81	0.52
Hayward, CA (city) Alameda County	719	0.51
Cambridge, MA (city) Middlesex County	512	0.51
West Sacramento, CA (city) Yolo County	161	0.51
Jefferson, VA (cdp) Fairfax County	139	0.51
San Pablo, CA (city) Contra Costa County	152	0.50
Fairfax, VA (independent city) Fairfax city	108	0.50
Isla Vista, CA (cdp) Santa Barbara County	92	0.50
Vienna, VA (town) Fairfax County	72	0.50
Chicago Ridge, IL (village) Cook County	71	0.50
Bull Run, VA (cdp) Prince William County	57	0.50
Lynn, MA (city) Essex County	435	0.49
Corvallis, OR (city) Benton County	240	0.49
Tukwila, WA (city) King County	84	0.49
Saint Paul, MN (city) Ramsey County	1,368	0.48
Arcadia, CA (city) Los Angeles County	253	0.48
North Bethesda, MD (cdp) Montgomery County	184	0.48
Walnut, CA (city) Los Angeles County	145	0.48
Pittsfield charter, MI (township) Washtenaw County	144	0.48
El Sobrante, CA (cdp) Contra Costa County	58	0.47
Storm Lake, IA (city) Buena Vista County	47	0.47
Temple City, CA (city) Los Angeles County	152	0.46
Woodbridge, VA (cdp) Prince William County	147	0.46
Pullman, WA (city) Whitman County	113	0.46
Riverton-Boulevard Park, WA (cdp) King County	51	0.46
Rockville, MD (city) Montgomery County	211	0.45
Aliso Viejo, CA (cdp) Orange County	182	0.45
SeaTac, WA (city) King County	115	0.45
Brookside, DE (cdp) New Castle County	66	0.45
Merced, CA (city) Merced County	281	0.44
Reston, VA (cdp) Fairfax County	250	0.44
Dale City, VA (cdp) Prince William County	249	0.44
Gaithersburg, MD (city) Montgomery County	231	0.44
Paramus, NJ (borough) Bergen County	114	0.44
El Cerrito, CA (city) Contra Costa County	102	0.44
Ithaca, NY (town) Tompkins County	80	0.44
Redland, MD (cdp) Montgomery County	75	0.44
Wolf Trap, VA (cdp) Fairfax County	61	0.44
Manassas Park, VA (independent city) Manassas Park city	45	0.44
Blackhawk-Camino Tassajara, CA (cdp) Contra Costa County	44	0.44
Jersey City, NJ (city) Hudson County	1,025	0.43
Bloomington, IN (city) Monroe County	296	0.43
Germantown, MD (cdp) Montgomery County	240	0.43
Fort Lee, NJ (borough) Bergen County	154	0.43
Dix Hills, NY (cdp) Suffolk County	111	0.43
Laurel, MD (city) Prince George's County	86	0.43
Loma Linda, CA (city) San Bernardino County	80	0.43
Albemarle, NC (city) Stanly County	67	0.43
La Palma, CA (city) Orange County	66	0.43
Cherry Hill Mall, NJ (cdp) Camden County	57	0.43
Providence, RI (city) Providence County	721	0.42
Richardson, TX (city) Dallas County	385	0.42
Wheaton-Glenmont, MD (cdp) Montgomery County	244	0.42
Laguna Hills, CA (city) Orange County	131	0.42
Falls Church, VA (independent city) Falls Church city	44	0.42
Sunnyvale, CA (city) Santa Clara County	545	0.41
Berkeley, CA (city) Alameda County	424	0.41
Brookline, MA (cdp) Norfolk County	234	0.41
Blacksburg, VA (town) Montgomery County	163	0.41
Amherst, MA (town) Hampshire County	142	0.41
Radnor Township, PA (cdp) Delaware County	127	0.41
Florin, CA (cdp) Sacramento County	113	0.41
Santa Clara, CA (city) Santa Clara County	408	0.40
North Bergen, NJ (township) Hudson County	232	0.40
Dearborn Heights, MI (city) Wayne County	231	0.40
Rowland Heights, CA (cdp) Los Angeles County	193	0.40
Euless, TX (city) Tarrant County	182	0.40
Harrisonburg, VA (independent city) Harrisonburg city	161	0.40
Pinole, CA (city) Contra Costa County	76	0.40
Amherst Center, MA (cdp) Hampshire County	68	0.40
Calverton, MD (cdp) Montgomery County	51	0.40
Laguna Niguel, CA (city) Orange County	240	0.39
Renton, WA (city) King County	195	0.39
Potomac, MD (cdp) Montgomery County	173	0.39
Stillwater, OK (city) Payne County	151	0.39
Holland, MI (township) Ottawa County	114	0.39
Ives Estates, FL (cdp) Miami-Dade County	69	0.39
Linda, CA (cdp) Yuba County	53	0.39
North Hempstead, NY (town) Nassau County	837	0.38
Torrance, CA (city) Los Angeles County	531	0.38
Spring Valley, NV (cdp) Clark County	443	0.38
Daly City, CA (city) San Mateo County	394	0.38
Schenectady, NY (city) Schenectady County	232	0.38
Cupertino, CA (city) Santa Clara County	192	0.38

Notes: (cdp) census designated place; Refer to the Explanation of Data in the front of the book for more detailed information.

Assyrian/Chaldean/Syriac

Top 150 Places Sorted by Number

(Based on all places, regardless of population)

Place	Number	%
Chicago, IL (city) Cook County	7,121	0.25
Sterling Heights, MI (city) Macomb County	5,515	4.43
West Bloomfield, MI (township) Oakland County	4,874	7.52
Southfield, MI (city) Oakland County	3,684	4.71
Modesto, CA (city) Stanislaus County	2,967	1.57
Turlock, CA (city) Stanislaus County	2,871	5.17
Warren, MI (city) Macomb County	2,625	1.90
El Cajon, CA (city) San Diego County	2,522	2.66
Farmington Hills, MI (city) Oakland County	2,499	3.04
Skokie, IL (village) Cook County	2,381	3.76
San Jose, CA (city) Santa Clara County	2,200	0.25
Troy, MI (city) Oakland County	2,047	2.53
Los Angeles, CA (city) Los Angeles County	2,031	0.05
Detroit, MI (city) Wayne County	1,963	0.21
Oak Park, MI (city) Oakland County	1,864	6.26
Madison Heights, MI (city) Oakland County	1,428	4.59
Phoenix, AZ (city) Maricopa County	822	0.06
Rancho San Diego, CA (cdp) San Diego County	686	3.42
San Diego, CA (city) San Diego County	633	0.05
Bloomfield, MI (township) Oakland County	513	1.19
Hazel Park, MI (city) Oakland County	512	2.70
Morton Grove, IL (village) Cook County	496	2.21
Shelby, MI (cdp) Macomb County	493	0.76
Bostonia, CA (cdp) San Diego County	474	3.19
Niles, IL (village) Cook County	458	1.52
Lincolnwood, IL (village) Cook County	438	3.54
Waterford, MI (cdp) Oakland County	413	0.56
Ceres, CA (city) Stanislaus County	395	1.14
Glendale, CA (city) Los Angeles County	352	0.18
Elgin, IL (city) Kane County	334	0.36
San Francisco, CA (city) San Francisco County	308	0.04
New York, NY (city) New York City	300	0.00
Commerce, MI (township) Oakland County	298	0.85
Spring Valley, CA (cdp) San Diego County	277	1.04
Schaumburg, IL (village) Cook County	272	0.37
Glendale, AZ (city) Maricopa County	268	0.12
Rochester Hills, MI (city) Oakland County	265	0.38
Southfield, MI (township) Oakland County	264	1.83
Scottsdale, AZ (city) Maricopa County	245	0.12
Beverly Hills, MI (village) Oakland County	242	2.32
Orchard Lake Village, MI (city) Oakland County	241	10.88
Fremont, CA (city) Alameda County	234	0.12
Clinton, MI (cdp) Macomb County	225	0.24
Anaheim, CA (city) Orange County	223	0.07
Mount Prospect, IL (village) Cook County	220	0.39
Casa de Oro-Mount Helix, CA (cdp) San Diego County	207	1.10
Royal Oak, MI (city) Oakland County	206	0.34
Glenview, IL (village) Cook County	203	0.49
Santa Clarita, CA (city) Los Angeles County	200	0.13
Macomb, MI (township) Macomb County	196	0.39
New Britain, CT (city) Hartford County	190	0.27
Ferndale, MI (city) Oakland County	182	0.82
Yonkers, NY (city) Westchester County	179	0.09
Elk Grove Village, IL (village) Cook County	169	0.49
Burbank, CA (city) Los Angeles County	167	0.17
Novi, MI (city) Oakland County	164	0.35
Streamwood, IL (village) Cook County	161	0.44
Long Beach, CA (city) Los Angeles County	153	0.03
Des Plaines, IL (city) Cook County	152	0.26
Pontiac, MI (city) Oakland County	143	0.22
Peoria, AZ (city) Maricopa County	143	0.13
Campbell, CA (city) Santa Clara County	139	0.36
Park Ridge, IL (city) Cook County	137	0.36
Flint, MI (city) Genesee County	123	0.10
Livonia, MI (city) Wayne County	115	0.11
Orange, CA (city) Orange County	115	0.09
Burton, MI (city) Genesee County	109	0.36
Jamul, CA (cdp) San Diego County	108	1.81
Carlsbad, CA (city) San Diego County	108	0.14
Gilbert, AZ (town) Maricopa County	108	0.10
Hoffman Estates, IL (village) Cook County	100	0.20
Corona, CA (city) Riverside County	97	0.08
Dearborn, MI (city) Wayne County	96	0.10
Clayton, MI (township) Genesee County	95	1.27
Oakland charter, MI (township) Oakland County	93	0.71
Riverside, CA (city) Riverside County	93	0.04
Lathrup Village, MI (city) Oakland County	92	2.17
La Mesa, CA (city) San Diego County	92	0.17
Fullerton, CA (city) Orange County	91	0.07
Rancho Cucamonga, CA (city) San Bernardino County	91	0.07
Marysville, MI (city) Saint Clair County	88	0.90
New Milford, NJ (borough) Bergen County	88	0.54
Bartlett, IL (village) Du Page County	88	0.24
Palmdale, CA (city) Los Angeles County	86	0.07
Bedford, MI (township) Monroe County	85	0.30
Saint Clair Shores, MI (city) Macomb County	84	0.13
Escondido, CA (city) San Diego County	83	0.06
Milford, MI (township) Oakland County	82	0.54
Santa Clara, CA (city) Santa Clara County	82	0.08
Huntington Beach, CA (city) Orange County	82	0.04
Arlington Heights, IL (village) Cook County	79	0.10
Ossining, NY (town) Westchester County	78	0.21
Wayne, NJ (cdp) Passaic County	77	0.14
Norton Shores, MI (city) Muskegon County	76	0.34
Grand Blanc, MI (township) Genesee County	76	0.25
La Riviera, CA (cdp) Sacramento County	75	0.73
Saginaw Township North, MI (cdp) Saginaw County	75	0.30
Saginaw charter, MI (township) Saginaw County	75	0.19
North Miami Beach, FL (city) Miami-Dade County	75	0.18
Berkley, MI (city) Oakland County	74	0.48
Lambertville, MI (cdp) Monroe County	73	0.79
Buffalo Grove, IL (village) Lake County	73	0.17
Chester, CT (town) Middlesex County	72	1.92
Farmington, MI (city) Oakland County	72	0.69
Harrison, MI (cdp) Macomb County	72	0.29
Spring Valley, NV (cdp) Clark County	72	0.06
Providence, RI (city) Providence County	71	0.04
Charlotte, NC (city) Mecklenburg County	71	0.01
Springfield, NJ (cdp) Union County	70	0.49
Carpentersville, IL (village) Kane County	70	0.23
Little Rock, AR (city) Pulaski County	68	0.04
Evanston, IL (city) Cook County	67	0.09
Redwood City, CA (city) San Mateo County	67	0.09
Oakland, CA (city) Alameda County	67	0.02
Flushing, MI (township) Genesee County	66	0.65
Rolling Meadows, IL (city) Cook County	66	0.27
Palatine, IL (village) Cook County	64	0.10
Arden-Arcade, CA (cdp) Sacramento County	64	0.07
Chula Vista, CA (city) San Diego County	64	0.04
Sunnyvale, CA (city) Santa Clara County	62	0.05
El Dorado Hills, CA (cdp) El Dorado County	61	0.34
Eastpointe, MI (city) Macomb County	61	0.18
Ann Arbor, MI (city) Washtenaw County	61	0.05
Upper Saddle River, NJ (borough) Bergen County	60	0.78
Surprise, AZ (city) Maricopa County	60	0.19
Lyon, MI (township) Oakland County	59	0.54
Ypsilanti, MI (township) Washtenaw County	58	0.12
Naperville, IL (city) Du Page County	58	0.05
Lake Elsinore, CA (city) Riverside County	56	0.19
Santee, CA (city) San Diego County	56	0.11
Merrillville, IN (town) Lake County	55	0.18
Buena Park, CA (city) Orange County	55	0.07
Canton, MI (cdp) Wayne County	55	0.07
Wilmette, IL (village) Cook County	54	0.20
Burke, VA (cdp) Fairfax County	54	0.09
Elizabeth, NJ (city) Union County	54	0.04
Pittsfield charter, MI (township) Washtenaw County	53	0.18
Crystal Lake, IL (city) McHenry County	53	0.14
Petaluma, CA (city) Sonoma County	53	0.10
Fresno, CA (city) Fresno County	53	0.01
Flushing, MI (city) Genesee County	52	0.62
East Bay, MI (township) Grand Traverse County	52	0.52
Wixom, MI (city) Oakland County	52	0.39
Plymouth Township, MI (cdp) Wayne County	52	0.19
Sunrise Manor, NV (cdp) Clark County	52	0.03
Itasca, IL (village) Du Page County	51	0.62
Prospect Heights, IL (city) Cook County	51	0.29
Perris, CA (city) Riverside County	51	0.14
Hanover Park, IL (village) Cook County	51	0.13
Walled Lake, MI (city) Oakland County	50	0.77

Notes: (cdp) census designated place; Refer to the Explanation of Data in the front of the book for more detailed information.

Assyrian/Chaldean/Syriac

Top 150 Places Sorted by Percent

(Based on all places, regardless of population)

Place	Number	%
Orchard Lake Village, MI (city) Oakland County	241	10.88
West Bloomfield, MI (township) Oakland County	4,874	7.52
Oak Park, MI (city) Oakland County	1,864	6.26
Turlock, CA (city) Stanislaus County	2,871	5.17
Southfield, MI (city) Oakland County	3,684	4.71
Madison Heights, MI (city) Oakland County	1,428	4.59
Sterling Heights, MI (city) Macomb County	5,515	4.43
Timber Lakes, UT (cdp) Wasatch County	13	4.39
Skokie, IL (village) Cook County	2,381	3.76
Lincolnwood, IL (village) Cook County	438	3.54
Rancho San Diego, CA (cdp) San Diego County	686	3.42
Bostonia, CA (cdp) San Diego County	474	3.19
Farmington Hills, MI (city) Oakland County	2,499	3.04
Golf, IL (village) Cook County	13	2.88
Hazel Park, MI (city) Oakland County	512	2.70
El Cajon, CA (city) San Diego County	2,522	2.66
Henderson, IL (village) Knox County	9	2.54
Troy, MI (city) Oakland County	2,047	2.53
Beverly Hills, MI (village) Oakland County	242	2.32
Morton Grove, IL (village) Cook County	496	2.21
Lathrup Village, MI (city) Oakland County	92	2.17
Chester, CT (town) Middlesex County	72	1.92
Warren, MI (city) Macomb County	2,625	1.90
Southfield, MI (township) Oakland County	264	1.83
Jamul, CA (cdp) San Diego County	108	1.81
Modesto, CA (city) Stanislaus County	2,967	1.57
Felton, CA (cdp) Santa Cruz County	17	1.56
Niles, IL (village) Cook County	458	1.52
Bingham Farms, MI (village) Oakland County	15	1.46
Port Sanilac, MI (village) Sanilac County	9	1.37
Clayton, MI (township) Genesee County	95	1.27
Bloomfield, MI (township) Oakland County	513	1.19
Keego Harbor, MI (city) Oakland County	32	1.16
Ceres, CA (city) Stanislaus County	395	1.14
Casa de Oro-Mount Helix, CA (cdp) San Diego County	207	1.10
Spring Valley, CA (cdp) San Diego County	277	1.04
Mettawa, IL (village) Lake County	3	0.93
Marysville, MI (city) Saint Clair County	88	0.90
Newtown Grant, PA (cdp) Bucks County	36	0.90
North Star, MI (township) Gratiot County	9	0.90
Palmyra, MI (township) Lenawee County	20	0.86
Commerce, MI (township) Oakland County	298	0.85
Oxford, IN (town) Benton County	11	0.85
Ferndale, MI (city) Oakland County	182	0.82
Keyes, CA (cdp) Stanislaus County	36	0.81
Pleasant Hills, MD (cdp) Harford County	23	0.80
Keene, CA (cdp) Kern County	2	0.80
Lambertville, MI (cdp) Monroe County	73	0.79
Upper Saddle River, NJ (borough) Bergen County	60	0.78
Walled Lake, MI (city) Oakland County	50	0.77
Marlette, MI (township) Sanilac County	16	0.77
Shelby, MI (cdp) Macomb County	493	0.76
Big Pine Key, FL (cdp) Monroe County	38	0.75
La Riviera, CA (cdp) Sacramento County	75	0.73
Park, MI (township) Saint Joseph County	20	0.73
Oakland charter, MI (township) Oakland County	93	0.71
Farmington, MI (city) Oakland County	72	0.69
Flushing, MI (township) Genesee County	66	0.65
Acme, MI (township) Grand Traverse County	28	0.64
Buel, MI (township) Sanilac County	8	0.64
Flushing, MI (city) Genesee County	52	0.62
Itasca, IL (village) Du Page County	51	0.62
Willow Springs, IL (village) Cook County	29	0.59
Manitowish Waters, WI (town) Vilas County	4	0.59
Waterford, MI (cdp) Oakland County	413	0.56
Woodbourne, PA (cdp) Bucks County	19	0.56
Whitewater, MI (township) Grand Traverse County	14	0.56
Winfield, IL (village) Du Page County	49	0.55
Grand Blanc, MI (city) Genesee County	45	0.55
New Milford, NJ (borough) Bergen County	88	0.54
Milford, MI (township) Oakland County	82	0.54
Lyon, MI (township) Oakland County	59	0.54
Delhi, CA (cdp) Merced County	44	0.54
Birch Run, MI (village) Saginaw County	9	0.53
Oxford, MD (town) Talbot County	4	0.53
East Bay, MI (township) Grand Traverse County	52	0.52
South Monroe, MI (cdp) Monroe County	32	0.52
De Witt, MI (city) Clinton County	25	0.52
Valhalla, NY (cdp) Westchester County	27	0.51
Cambrian Park, CA (cdp) Santa Clara County	17	0.51
Glenview, IL (village) Cook County	203	0.49
Elk Grove Village, IL (village) Cook County	169	0.49
Springfield, NJ (cdp) Union County	70	0.49
Wheatfield, MI (township) Ingham County	8	0.49
Berkley, MI (city) Oakland County	74	0.48
Rosemont, IL (village) Cook County	20	0.48
Toro Canyon, CA (cdp) Santa Barbara County	8	0.48
El Verano, CA (cdp) Sonoma County	19	0.47
Denair, CA (cdp) Stanislaus County	17	0.47
Hamilton, NY (village) Madison County	16	0.46
Manannah, MN (township) Meeker County	3	0.46
Hilmar-Irwin, CA (cdp) Merced County	22	0.45
Empire, CA (cdp) Stanislaus County	17	0.45
North Barrington, IL (village) Lake County	13	0.45
Ringwood, IL (village) McHenry County	2	0.45
Streamwood, IL (village) Cook County	161	0.44
Putnam, MI (township) Livingston County	33	0.44
Utica, MI (city) Macomb County	20	0.44
Fairfax, CA (town) Marin County	31	0.43
Hadley, MI (township) Lapeer County	20	0.43
Dexter, MI (township) Washtenaw County	22	0.42
Pistakee Highlands, IL (cdp) McHenry County	16	0.42
Troy, WI (town) Saint Croix County	15	0.41
Kenilworth, IL (village) Cook County	10	0.40
Mount Prospect, IL (village) Cook County	220	0.39
Macomb, MI (township) Macomb County	196	0.39
Wixom, MI (city) Oakland County	52	0.39
Ortonville, MI (village) Oakland County	6	0.39
Rochester Hills, MI (city) Oakland County	265	0.38
Burns Harbor, IN (town) Porter County	3	0.38
Schaumburg, IL (village) Cook County	272	0.37
West Paterson, NJ (borough) Passaic County	41	0.37
Round Lake, IL (village) Lake County	21	0.37
Sodus, MI (township) Berrien County	8	0.37
Elgin, IL (city) Kane County	334	0.36
Campbell, CA (city) Santa Clara County	139	0.36
Park Ridge, IL (city) Cook County	137	0.36
Burton, MI (city) Genesee County	109	0.36
El Sobrante, CA (cdp) Contra Costa County	42	0.36
Washington Township, NJ (cdp) Bergen County	32	0.36
Westbrook Center, CT (cdp) Middlesex County	8	0.36
Novi, MI (city) Oakland County	164	0.35
Saint Augustine Shores, FL (cdp) Saint Johns County	18	0.35
Sanilac, MI (township) Sanilac County	9	0.35
Sylvan Lake, MI (city) Oakland County	6	0.35
Royal Oak, MI (city) Oakland County	206	0.34
Norton Shores, MI (city) Muskegon County	76	0.34
El Dorado Hills, CA (cdp) El Dorado County	61	0.34
Newman, CA (city) Stanislaus County	24	0.34
Hazardville, CT (cdp) Hartford County	16	0.33
Wrens, GA (city) Jefferson County	8	0.33
Pine Island, TX (town) Waller County	3	0.33
Toquerville, UT (town) Washington County	3	0.33
Williamsfield, IL (village) Knox County	2	0.33
Almira, MI (township) Benzie County	9	0.32
Middlefield, OH (village) Geauga County	7	0.32
Riverbank, CA (city) Stanislaus County	49	0.31
River Rouge, MI (city) Wayne County	31	0.31
Kensington, CT (cdp) Hartford County	26	0.31
Hebron, IN (town) Porter County	11	0.31
Brightwaters, NY (village) Suffolk County	10	0.31
Bedford, MI (township) Monroe County	85	0.30
Saginaw Township North, MI (cdp) Saginaw County	75	0.30
Atlas, MI (township) Genesee County	22	0.30
Shannon Hills, AR (city) Saline County	6	0.30
Burt, MI (township) Cheboygan County	2	0.30
Washington, WI (town) Door County	2	0.30
Harrison, MI (cdp) Macomb County	72	0.29
Prospect Heights, IL (city) Cook County	51	0.29
Center Line, MI (city) Macomb County	25	0.29

Notes: (cdp) census designated place; Refer to the Explanation of Data in the front of the book for more detailed information.

Assyrian/Chaldean/Syriac

Top 150 Places Sorted by Percent

(Based on places with populations of 10,000 or more)

Place	Number	%
West Bloomfield, MI (township) Oakland County	4,874	7.52
Oak Park, MI (city) Oakland County	1,864	6.26
Turlock, CA (city) Stanislaus County	2,871	5.17
Southfield, MI (city) Oakland County	3,684	4.71
Madison Heights, MI (city) Oakland County	1,428	4.59
Sterling Heights, MI (city) Macomb County	5,515	4.43
Skokie, IL (village) Cook County	2,381	3.76
Lincolnwood, IL (village) Cook County	438	3.54
Rancho San Diego, CA (cdp) San Diego County	686	3.42
Bostonia, CA (cdp) San Diego County	474	3.19
Farmington Hills, MI (city) Oakland County	2,499	3.04
Hazel Park, MI (city) Oakland County	512	2.70
El Cajon, CA (city) San Diego County	2,522	2.66
Troy, MI (city) Oakland County	2,047	2.53
Beverly Hills, MI (village) Oakland County	242	2.32
Morton Grove, IL (village) Cook County	496	2.21
Warren, MI (city) Macomb County	2,625	1.90
Southfield, MI (township) Oakland County	264	1.83
Modesto, CA (city) Stanislaus County	2,967	1.57
Niles, IL (village) Cook County	458	1.52
Bloomfield, MI (township) Oakland County	513	1.19
Ceres, CA (city) Stanislaus County	395	1.14
Casa de Oro-Mount Helix, CA (cdp) San Diego County	207	1.10
Spring Valley, CA (cdp) San Diego County	277	1.04
Commerce, MI (township) Oakland County	298	0.85
Ferndale, MI (city) Oakland County	182	0.82
Shelby, MI (cdp) Macomb County	493	0.76
La Riviera, CA (cdp) Sacramento County	75	0.73
Oakland charter, MI (township) Oakland County	93	0.71
Farmington, MI (city) Oakland County	72	0.69
Flushing, MI (township) Genesee County	66	0.65
Waterford, MI (cdp) Oakland County	413	0.56
New Milford, NJ (borough) Bergen County	88	0.54
Milford, MI (township) Oakland County	82	0.54
Lyon, MI (township) Oakland County	59	0.54
Glenview, IL (village) Cook County	203	0.49
Elk Grove Village, IL (village) Cook County	169	0.49
Springfield, NJ (cdp) Union County	70	0.49
Berkley, MI (city) Oakland County	74	0.48
Streamwood, IL (village) Cook County	161	0.44
Mount Prospect, IL (village) Cook County	220	0.39
Macomb, MI (township) Macomb County	196	0.39
Wixom, MI (city) Oakland County	52	0.39
Rochester Hills, MI (city) Oakland County	265	0.38
Schaumburg, IL (village) Cook County	272	0.37
West Paterson, NJ (borough) Passaic County	41	0.37
Elgin, IL (city) Kane County	334	0.36
Campbell, CA (city) Santa Clara County	139	0.36
Park Ridge, IL (city) Cook County	137	0.36
Burton, MI (city) Genesee County	109	0.36
El Sobrante, CA (cdp) Contra Costa County	42	0.36
Novi, MI (city) Oakland County	164	0.35
Royal Oak, MI (city) Oakland County	206	0.34
Norton Shores, MI (city) Muskegon County	76	0.34
El Dorado Hills, CA (cdp) El Dorado County	61	0.34
Riverbank, CA (city) Stanislaus County	49	0.31
Bedford, MI (township) Monroe County	85	0.30
Saginaw Township North, MI (cdp) Saginaw County	75	0.30
Harrison, MI (cdp) Macomb County	72	0.29
Prospect Heights, IL (city) Cook County	51	0.29
Holden, MA (town) Worcester County	43	0.28
New Britain, CT (city) Hartford County	190	0.27
Rolling Meadows, IL (city) Cook County	66	0.27
Grafton, MA (town) Worcester County	40	0.27
Des Plaines, IL (city) Cook County	152	0.26
Berlin, CT (town) Hartford County	48	0.26
Plainville, CT (town) Hartford County	45	0.26
Chicago, IL (city) Cook County	7,121	0.25
San Jose, CA (city) Santa Clara County	2,200	0.25
Grand Blanc, MI (township) Genesee County	76	0.25
Grayslake, IL (village) Lake County	47	0.25
Davison, MI (township) Genesee County	44	0.25
Salida, CA (cdp) Stanislaus County	31	0.25
Clinton, MI (cdp) Macomb County	225	0.24
Bartlett, IL (village) Du Page County	88	0.24
Monroe charter, MI (township) Monroe County	32	0.24
Newtown, PA (township) Delaware County	28	0.24
Carpentersville, IL (village) Kane County	70	0.23
Buckingham, PA (township) Bucks County	37	0.23
Hickory Hills, IL (city) Cook County	32	0.23
Ridgefield, NJ (borough) Bergen County	25	0.23
Kirkland, NY (town) Oneida County	23	0.23
Pontiac, MI (city) Oakland County	143	0.22
Calabasas, CA (city) Los Angeles County	45	0.22
Wyckoff, NJ (cdp) Bergen County	37	0.22
Detroit, MI (city) Wayne County	1,963	0.21
Ossining, NY (town) Westchester County	78	0.21
Millbrae, CA (city) San Mateo County	44	0.21
Highland, MI (township) Oakland County	40	0.21
Piedmont, CA (city) Alameda County	23	0.21
Hoffman Estates, IL (village) Cook County	100	0.20
Wilmette, IL (village) Cook County	54	0.20
Newtown, PA (township) Bucks County	36	0.20
Vienna, MI (township) Genesee County	26	0.20
Martin, TN (city) Weakley County	21	0.20
Saginaw charter, MI (township) Saginaw County	75	0.19
Surprise, AZ (city) Maricopa County	60	0.19
Lake Elsinore, CA (city) Riverside County	56	0.19
Plymouth Township, MI (cdp) Wayne County	52	0.19
Hobart, IN (city) Lake County	49	0.19
Rocky River, OH (city) Cuyahoga County	39	0.19
La Palma, CA (city) Orange County	28	0.19
River Grove, IL (village) Cook County	20	0.19
Glendale, CA (city) Los Angeles County	352	0.18
North Miami Beach, FL (city) Miami-Dade County	75	0.18
Eastpointe, MI (city) Macomb County	61	0.18
Merrillville, IN (town) Lake County	55	0.18
Pittsfield charter, MI (township) Washtenaw County	53	0.18
Brownstown, MI (township) Wayne County	41	0.18
Manchester, MO (city) Saint Louis County	34	0.18
Cary, IL (village) McHenry County	28	0.18
Rosamond, CA (cdp) Kern County	26	0.18
Fenton, MI (township) Genesee County	23	0.18
Burbank, CA (city) Los Angeles County	167	0.17
La Mesa, CA (city) San Diego County	92	0.17
Buffalo Grove, IL (village) Lake County	73	0.17
Adrian, MI (city) Lenawee County	37	0.17
Northville, MI (township) Wayne County	36	0.17
Duxbury, MA (town) Plymouth County	24	0.17
Little Falls, NJ (cdp) Passaic County	18	0.17
Melvindale, MI (city) Wayne County	18	0.17
Menlo Park, CA (city) San Mateo County	48	0.16
Glen Ellyn, IL (village) Du Page County	42	0.16
Deerfield, IL (village) Lake County	30	0.16
South Elgin, IL (village) Kane County	25	0.16
Clinton, MA (town) Worcester County	21	0.16
Whitewater, WI (city) Walworth County	21	0.16
Marquette, MI (city) Marquette County	30	0.15
Two Rivers, WI (city) Manitowoc County	19	0.15
Carlsbad, CA (city) San Diego County	108	0.14
Wayne, NJ (cdp) Passaic County	77	0.14
Crystal Lake, IL (city) McHenry County	53	0.14
Perris, CA (city) Riverside County	51	0.14
Lake Zurich, IL (village) Lake County	25	0.14
Nederland, TX (city) Jefferson County	24	0.14
Riverdale, IL (village) Cook County	21	0.14
Los Alamitos, CA (city) Orange County	16	0.14
Santa Clarita, CA (city) Los Angeles County	200	0.13
Peoria, AZ (city) Maricopa County	143	0.13
Saint Clair Shores, MI (city) Macomb County	84	0.13
Hanover Park, IL (village) Cook County	51	0.13
Shrewsbury, MA (town) Worcester County	40	0.13
Los Altos, CA (city) Santa Clara County	35	0.13
Catskill, NY (town) Greene County	15	0.13
Glendale, AZ (city) Maricopa County	268	0.12
Scottsdale, AZ (city) Maricopa County	245	0.12
Fremont, CA (city) Alameda County	234	0.12
Ypsilanti, MI (township) Washtenaw County	58	0.12
Cortlandt, NY (town) Westchester County	47	0.12
De Kalb, IL (city) De Kalb County	47	0.12

Notes: (cdp) census designated place; Refer to the Explanation of Data in the front of the book for more detailed information.

Australian

Top 150 Places Sorted by Number

(Based on all places, regardless of population)

Place	Number	%
New York, NY (city) New York City	3,155	0.04
Los Angeles, CA (city) Los Angeles County	1,515	0.04
San Francisco, CA (city) San Francisco County	820	0.11
San Diego, CA (city) San Diego County	766	0.06
Houston, TX (city) Harris County	614	0.03
Seattle, WA (city) King County	507	0.09
Chicago, IL (city) Cook County	486	0.02
San Jose, CA (city) Santa Clara County	474	0.05
Phoenix, AZ (city) Maricopa County	450	0.03
Portland, OR (city) Multnomah County	375	0.07
Dallas, TX (city) Dallas County	312	0.03
Austin, TX (city) Travis County	306	0.05
Virginia Beach, VA (independent city) Virginia Beach city	265	0.06
Columbus, OH (city) Franklin County	262	0.04
Washington, DC (city) District of Columbia	257	0.04
Brookhaven, NY (town) Suffolk County	250	0.06
Boston, MA (city) Suffolk County	246	0.04
Provo, UT (city) Utah County	230	0.22
Indianapolis, IN (special city) Marion County	221	0.03
Santa Monica, CA (city) Los Angeles County	213	0.25
Honolulu, HI (cdp) Honolulu County	204	0.05
Denver, CO (city) Denver County	199	0.04
Scottsdale, AZ (city) Maricopa County	191	0.09
Charlotte, NC (city) Mecklenburg County	190	0.04
Colorado Springs, CO (city) El Paso County	181	0.05
Tucson, AZ (city) Pima County	178	0.04
Las Vegas, NV (city) Clark County	177	0.04
Berkeley, CA (city) Alameda County	174	0.17
Nashville-Davidson, TN (special city) Davidson County	174	0.03
Irvine, CA (city) Orange County	172	0.12
New Orleans, LA (city) Orleans Parish	168	0.03
Palmdale, CA (city) Los Angeles County	165	0.14
Palo Alto, CA (city) Santa Clara County	162	0.28
Glendale, CA (city) Los Angeles County	158	0.08
Greenwich, CT (town) Fairfield County	156	0.26
Santa Clarita, CA (city) Los Angeles County	156	0.10
San Antonio, TX (city) Bexar County	156	0.01
Albuquerque, NM (city) Bernalillo County	152	0.03
Plano, TX (city) Collin County	151	0.07
Newport Beach, CA (city) Orange County	150	0.21
Cambridge, MA (city) Middlesex County	149	0.15
Huntington Beach, CA (city) Orange County	147	0.08
Burke, VA (cdp) Fairfax County	146	0.25
Arlington, TX (city) Tarrant County	146	0.04
Reno, NV (city) Washoe County	144	0.08
Oklahoma City, OK (city) Oklahoma County	141	0.03
Philadelphia, PA (city) Philadelphia County	139	0.01
Jacksonville, FL (special city) Duval County	137	0.02
Brookline, MA (cdp) Norfolk County	136	0.24
Santa Barbara, CA (city) Santa Barbara County	124	0.13
Kansas City, MO (city) Jackson County	124	0.03
Temecula, CA (city) Riverside County	123	0.21
Cary, NC (town) Wake County	123	0.13
Orem, UT (city) Utah County	121	0.14
Bellevue, WA (city) King County	121	0.11
Raleigh, NC (city) Wake County	120	0.04
Cupertino, CA (city) Santa Clara County	118	0.23
Long Beach, CA (city) Los Angeles County	118	0.03
San Rafael, CA (city) Marin County	117	0.21
Aurora, CO (city) Arapahoe County	116	0.04
Mesa, AZ (city) Maricopa County	116	0.03
Petaluma, CA (city) Sonoma County	115	0.21
Sunnyvale, CA (city) Santa Clara County	115	0.09
Oyster Bay, NY (town) Nassau County	115	0.04
Foster City, CA (city) San Mateo County	114	0.40
Eagan, MN (city) Dakota County	114	0.18
Columbia, MD (cdp) Howard County	111	0.13
Torrance, CA (city) Los Angeles County	111	0.08
Salt Lake City, UT (city) Salt Lake County	110	0.06
Oakland, CA (city) Alameda County	110	0.03
Vacaville, CA (city) Solano County	109	0.12
Baltimore, MD (independent city) Baltimore city	109	0.02
Stockton, CA (city) San Joaquin County	108	0.04
Bloomfield, MI (township) Oakland County	107	0.25
Toledo, OH (city) Lucas County	107	0.03
Irving, TX (city) Dallas County	105	0.05
Davis, CA (city) Yolo County	104	0.17
Santa Clara, CA (city) Santa Clara County	102	0.10
Anchorage, AK (municipality) Anchorage Borough	102	0.04
Orinda, CA (city) Contra Costa County	100	0.57
Fremont, CA (city) Alameda County	99	0.05
Wichita, KS (city) Sedgwick County	99	0.03
Atlanta, GA (city) Fulton County	99	0.02
Walnut Creek, CA (city) Contra Costa County	98	0.15
Annandale, VA (cdp) Fairfax County	97	0.18
Arlington, VA (cdp) Arlington County	97	0.05
Richardson, TX (city) Dallas County	95	0.10
Athens-Clarke County, GA (special city) Clarke County	94	0.09
Fort Lauderdale, FL (city) Broward County	94	0.06
Miami, FL (city) Miami-Dade County	94	0.03
Alameda, CA (city) Alameda County	92	0.13
Gresham, OR (city) Multnomah County	92	0.10
Arden-Arcade, CA (cdp) Sacramento County	91	0.09
Jacksonville, NC (city) Onslow County	90	0.13
Carlsbad, CA (city) San Diego County	90	0.12
Durham, NC (city) Durham County	90	0.05
San Mateo, CA (city) San Mateo County	89	0.10
El Cajon, CA (city) San Diego County	89	0.09
Oceanside, CA (city) San Diego County	89	0.06
Sacramento, CA (city) Sacramento County	89	0.02
Mamaroneck, NY (town) Westchester County	88	0.30
Reston, VA (cdp) Fairfax County	88	0.16
Saratoga, CA (city) Santa Clara County	87	0.29
Antioch, CA (city) Contra Costa County	87	0.10
Rancho Cucamonga, CA (city) San Bernardino County	87	0.07
Salem, OR (city) Marion County	87	0.06
Tallahassee, FL (city) Leon County	86	0.06
West Hollywood, CA (city) Los Angeles County	85	0.24
Hempstead, NY (town) Nassau County	85	0.01
Paradise, NV (cdp) Clark County	84	0.05
Saint Petersburg, FL (city) Pinellas County	84	0.03
Fort Worth, TX (city) Tarrant County	83	0.02
Belmont, MA (cdp) Middlesex County	82	0.34
McLean, VA (cdp) Fairfax County	82	0.21
Santee, CA (city) San Diego County	81	0.15
Corpus Christi, TX (city) Nueces County	81	0.03
Minneapolis, MN (city) Hennepin County	81	0.02
Westminster, CO (city) Adams County	80	0.08
Spring Valley, NV (cdp) Clark County	79	0.07
Thousand Oaks, CA (city) Ventura County	79	0.07
Omaha, NE (city) Douglas County	79	0.02
Littleton, CO (city) Arapahoe County	78	0.19
Vancouver, WA (city) Clark County	78	0.05
Columbus, GA (special city) Muscogee County	78	0.04
Yonkers, NY (city) Westchester County	78	0.04
Lincoln, NE (city) Lancaster County	78	0.03
Saint Paul, MN (city) Ramsey County	78	0.03
Hayward, CA (city) Alameda County	77	0.06
Chantilly, VA (cdp) Fairfax County	76	0.18
Rio Rancho, NM (city) Sandoval County	76	0.15
Pasadena, CA (city) Los Angeles County	75	0.06
Jersey City, NJ (city) Hudson County	75	0.03
Mastic Beach, NY (cdp) Suffolk County	74	0.64
Winchester, MA (cdp) Middlesex County	74	0.36
Ridgewood, NJ (village) Bergen County	74	0.30
Burbank, CA (city) Los Angeles County	74	0.07
Costa Mesa, CA (city) Orange County	74	0.07
Eugene, OR (city) Lane County	74	0.05
Malibu, CA (city) Los Angeles County	73	0.58
Redmond, WA (city) King County	71	0.16
Escondido, CA (city) San Diego County	71	0.05
Sunrise Manor, NV (cdp) Clark County	71	0.05
Rochester, MN (city) Olmsted County	70	0.08
Clearwater, FL (city) Pinellas County	70	0.06
Spokane, WA (city) Spokane County	70	0.04
Tacoma, WA (city) Pierce County	70	0.04
Madison, WI (city) Dane County	70	0.03
Lebanon, ME (town) York County	69	1.36
Cortlandt, NY (town) Westchester County	69	0.18
Boise City, ID (city) Ada County	69	0.04

Notes: (cdp) census designated place; Refer to the Explanation of Data in the front of the book for more detailed information.

Australian

Top 150 Places Sorted by Percent

(Based on all places, regardless of population)

Place	Number	%
Bonanza, CO (town) Saguache County	2	8.70
McCarthy, AK (cdp) Valdez-Cordova Census Area	2	6.06
Stratton, VT (town) Windham County	8	5.71
Rossie, IA (city) Clay County	4	5.41
Cal-Nev-Ari, NV (cdp) Clark County	12	4.20
Glen Echo, MD (town) Montgomery County	9	3.80
Waverly, AL (town) Chambers County	6	3.51
Corona de Tucson, AZ (cdp) Pima County	28	3.37
Concow, CA (cdp) Butte County	34	3.06
Neilton, WA (cdp) Grays Harbor County	10	2.91
Keystone, CO (cdp) Summit County	22	2.84
Diablo, CA (cdp) Contra Costa County	27	2.73
Leonard, ND (city) Cass County	7	2.68
Bannockburn, IL (village) Lake County	37	2.60
Swaledale, IA (city) Cerro Gordo County	5	2.59
Belgrade, NE (village) Nance County	3	2.42
Young Harris, GA (city) Towns County	15	2.41
North Bay, WI (village) Racine County	6	2.36
Echo, MN (city) Yellow Medicine County	6	2.35
Kawela Bay, HI (cdp) Honolulu County	10	2.33
Mesa Vista, CA (cdp) Alpine County	4	2.21
Greenwood, MN (city) Hennepin County	16	2.16
Black Hawk, CO (city) Gilpin County	3	2.16
West Perry, PA (township) Snyder County	21	2.02
Auberry, CA (cdp) Fresno County	42	2.00
Kendrick, ID (city) Latah County	7	1.75
Buckland, AK (city) Northwest Arctic Borough	7	1.70
Kirkpatrick, OR (cdp) Umatilla County	3	1.70
Oneida, PA (cdp) Schuylkill County	3	1.64
Molino, FL (cdp) Escambia County	23	1.62
Woodland, UT (cdp) Summit County	5	1.61
McEwensville, PA (borough) Northumberland County	5	1.60
Lava Hot Springs, ID (city) Bannock County	8	1.59
Rose Bud, AR (town) White County	6	1.58
Washta, IA (city) Cherokee County	5	1.56
Jewett, NY (town) Greene County	15	1.55
Newton, UT (town) Cache County	11	1.55
Yampa, CO (town) Routt County	7	1.54
Dublin, IN (town) Wayne County	11	1.50
Brownington, MO (town) Henry County	2	1.50
Halden, MN (township) Saint Louis County	2	1.46
Hatch, UT (town) Garfield County	2	1.46
Westwood, MO (village) Saint Louis County	4	1.45
Tyringham, MA (town) Berkshire County	5	1.42
Rye, CO (town) Pueblo County	3	1.42
Vineyard Haven, MA (cdp) Dukes County	27	1.40
Lebanon, ME (town) York County	69	1.36
Dollar Point, CA (cdp) Placer County	21	1.34
Weston, WI (town) Dunn County	9	1.33
Hollywood Park, TX (town) Bexar County	34	1.32
Alna, ME (town) Lincoln County	9	1.32
Wayne Heights, PA (cdp) Franklin County	24	1.31
Wales, UT (town) Sanpete County	3	1.29
Middletown, PA (township) Susquehanna County	4	1.27
Old Saybrook Center, CT (cdp) Middlesex County	23	1.26
Hanalei, HI (cdp) Kauai County	6	1.24
Phoenicia, NY (cdp) Ulster County	5	1.24
Spring Creek, PA (township) Elk County	3	1.24
Navesink, NJ (cdp) Monmouth County	23	1.23
Monroe, SD (town) Turner County	2	1.23
Atlantis, FL (city) Palm Beach County	26	1.22
Cudjoe Key, FL (cdp) Monroe County	21	1.21
Tijeras, NM (village) Bernalillo County	5	1.21
Hillsmere Shores, MD (cdp) Anne Arundel County	34	1.20
Sunnyside, UT (city) Carbon County	5	1.18
Wallace, NE (village) Lincoln County	4	1.18
Waldron, MI (village) Hillsdale County	7	1.16
Eagle-Vail, CO (cdp) Eagle County	34	1.15
Munsey Park, NY (village) Nassau County	30	1.14
Gibbon, MN (city) Sibley County	9	1.14
New Milford, PA (borough) Susquehanna County	10	1.13
Callao, MO (city) Macon County	3	1.09
Reed, PA (township) Dauphin County	2	1.09
Fox Run, PA (cdp) Butler County	33	1.06
Vail, CO (town) Eagle County	47	1.04

Place	Number	%
Coupeville, WA (town) Island County	18	1.04
Sunol-Midtown, CA (cdp) Santa Clara County	8	1.04
Nesbitt, TX (town) Harrison County	3	1.03
Martin's Additions, MD (village) Montgomery County	9	1.01
Trout Valley, IL (village) McHenry County	6	1.01
Cave Junction, OR (city) Josephine County	14	1.00
Sudden Valley, WA (cdp) Whatcom County	41	0.98
Montara, CA (cdp) San Mateo County	29	0.97
Midway, PA (cdp) Adams County	23	0.97
Cleveland, MO (city) Cass County	6	0.97
Folsom, LA (village) Saint Tammany Parish	5	0.97
Crested Butte, CO (town) Gunnison County	15	0.95
Plymouth, ME (town) Penobscot County	12	0.95
Trenton, KY (city) Todd County	4	0.95
Bazine, KS (city) Ness County	3	0.95
Upper Brookville, NY (village) Nassau County	17	0.94
Gilsum, NH (town) Cheshire County	7	0.94
Elkhart, IA (city) Polk County	3	0.94
Savoy, IL (village) Champaign County	40	0.93
Bow Mar, CO (town) Arapahoe County	8	0.93
Bradbury, CA (city) Los Angeles County	8	0.93
Mettawa, IL (village) Lake County	3	0.93
Washington, CT (town) Litchfield County	33	0.92
Essex, MA (town) Essex County	30	0.92
Westwood, KS (city) Johnson County	14	0.91
Rocky Hill, NJ (borough) Somerset County	6	0.91
Hannibal, NY (village) Oswego County	5	0.91
Larchmont, NY (village) Westchester County	58	0.89
Ridgeway, AK (cdp) Kenai Peninsula Borough	17	0.86
Breckenridge, CO (town) Summit County	20	0.85
Kensington, MD (town) Montgomery County	16	0.85
Wellston, OK (town) Lincoln County	7	0.85
Eidsvold, MN (township) Lyon County	2	0.85
Saugerties South, NY (cdp) Ulster County	19	0.84
Lowry City, MO (city) Saint Clair County	6	0.84
Bliss, MI (township) Emmet County	5	0.84
Genesee, CO (cdp) Jefferson County	30	0.83
Tyndall AFB, FL (cdp) Bay County	23	0.83
West Menlo Park, CA (cdp) San Mateo County	30	0.82
Aquinnah, MA (town) Dukes County	3	0.82
Sturgeon Lake, MN (city) Pine County	3	0.82
Upper Nyack, NY (village) Rockland County	15	0.81
Brunswick, WI (town) Eau Claire County	13	0.81
Ovid, NY (village) Seneca County	5	0.81
Hills and Dales, KY (city) Jefferson County	5	0.81
Greenwood Lake, NY (village) Orange County	27	0.80
Tracyton, WA (cdp) Kitsap County	26	0.80
Rosebud, MO (city) Gasconade County	3	0.80
Corona, NM (village) Lincoln County	2	0.79
Croton-on-Hudson, NY (village) Westchester County	59	0.78
Liberty, MN (township) Beltrami County	5	0.78
Marshfield, ME (town) Washington County	4	0.77
Springport, NY (town) Cayuga County	17	0.76
Sunshine Acres, FL (cdp) Broward County	8	0.76
Argyle, MN (city) Marshall County	5	0.76
Wellsboro, PA (borough) Tioga County	25	0.75
Malvern, PA (borough) Chester County	23	0.75
Madison Center, CT (cdp) New Haven County	17	0.75
West Windsor, VT (town) Windsor County	8	0.75
Sampson, WI (town) Chippewa County	7	0.75
Watauga, TN (city) Carter County	3	0.75
Woodbury Heights, NJ (borough) Gloucester County	22	0.74
Ben Lomond, CA (cdp) Santa Cruz County	17	0.74
Burlington, ND (city) Ward County	8	0.74
Pacific City, OR (cdp) Tillamook County	7	0.74
Evant, TX (town) Coryell County	3	0.74
Putnam, PA (township) Tioga County	3	0.74
Blue Lake, MI (township) Muskegon County	15	0.73
Cleveland, NC (town) Rowan County	6	0.73
Tisbury, MA (town) Dukes County	27	0.72
Mount Hope, KS (city) Sedgwick County	6	0.72
Bunker Hill Village, TX (city) Harris County	26	0.71
Sewickley Heights, PA (borough) Allegheny County	7	0.71
Accord, NY (cdp) Ulster County	5	0.71
Lima, WI (town) Pepin County	5	0.71

Notes: (cdp) census designated place; Refer to the Explanation of Data in the front of the book for more detailed information.

Australian

Top 150 Places Sorted by Percent

(Based on places with populations of 10,000 or more)

Place	Number	%
Mastic Beach, NY (cdp) Suffolk County	74	0.64
Malibu, CA (city) Los Angeles County	73	0.58
Orinda, CA (city) Contra Costa County	100	0.57
Sedona, AZ (city) Yavapai County	55	0.54
Washington, IL (city) Tazewell County	50	0.46
Palos Verdes Estates, CA (city) Los Angeles County	56	0.42
Beachwood, OH (city) Cuyahoga County	50	0.41
Larkspur, CA (city) Marin County	49	0.41
Foster City, CA (city) San Mateo County	114	0.40
San Marino, CA (city) Los Angeles County	49	0.38
Lake Shore, MD (cdp) Anne Arundel County	48	0.37
Gardnerville Ranchos, NV (cdp) Douglas County	41	0.37
Winchester, MA (cdp) Middlesex County	74	0.36
West University Place, TX (city) Harris County	51	0.36
Clayton, MO (city) Saint Louis County	46	0.36
Sumpter, MI (township) Wayne County	42	0.35
Belmont, MA (cdp) Middlesex County	82	0.34
Birmingham, MI (city) Oakland County	66	0.34
Mount Vernon, OH (city) Knox County	50	0.34
Lake Mary, FL (city) Seminole County	38	0.34
Darien, CT (cdp) Fairfield County	65	0.33
Key Biscayne, FL (village) Miami-Dade County	35	0.33
Cottonwood West, UT (cdp) Salt Lake County	59	0.32
Stanford, CA (cdp) Santa Clara County	43	0.32
Magalia, CA (cdp) Butte County	34	0.32
Potsdam, NY (town) Saint Lawrence County	49	0.31
Derry, PA (township) Westmoreland County	45	0.31
Grosse Pointe Park, MI (city) Wayne County	38	0.31
Montgomeryville, PA (cdp) Montgomery County	37	0.31
Capitola, CA (city) Santa Cruz County	32	0.31
Mamaroneck, NY (town) Westchester County	88	0.30
Ridgewood, NJ (village) Bergen County	74	0.30
La Canada Flintridge, CA (city) Los Angeles County	61	0.30
Princeton, NJ (borough) Mercer County	42	0.30
Fort Benning South, GA (cdp) Chattahoochee County	35	0.30
Saratoga, CA (city) Santa Clara County	87	0.29
University Park, TX (city) Dallas County	67	0.29
Rye, NY (city) Westchester County	43	0.29
Lebanon, NH (city) Grafton County	36	0.29
Valle Vista, CA (cdp) Riverside County	31	0.29
Palo Alto, CA (city) Santa Clara County	162	0.28
Bristol, RI (cdp) Bristol County	64	0.28
Robinson Township, PA (cdp) Allegheny County	34	0.28
Belmont, CA (city) San Mateo County	67	0.27
Ridgefield, CT (town) Fairfield County	65	0.27
Wright, FL (cdp) Okaloosa County	59	0.27
Lockport, IL (city) Will County	40	0.27
Tolland, CT (town) Tolland County	36	0.27
Oconomowoc, WI (city) Waukesha County	33	0.27
Old Saybrook, CT (town) Middlesex County	28	0.27
Greenwich, CT (town) Fairfield County	156	0.26
New Fairfield, CT (town) Fairfield County	36	0.26
Glendale, WI (city) Milwaukee County	35	0.26
Santa Monica, CA (city) Los Angeles County	213	0.25
Burke, VA (cdp) Fairfax County	146	0.25
Bloomfield, MI (township) Oakland County	107	0.25
Morris, NJ (township) Morris County	54	0.25
Ardmore, PA (cdp) Montgomery County	32	0.25
Levelland, TX (city) Hockley County	32	0.25
Brookline, MA (cdp) Norfolk County	136	0.24
West Hollywood, CA (city) Los Angeles County	85	0.24
New Windsor, NY (town) Orange County	54	0.24
Setauket-East Setauket, NY (cdp) Suffolk County	38	0.24
Loveland, OH (city) Hamilton County	29	0.24
Cupertino, CA (city) Santa Clara County	118	0.23
Eureka, CA (city) Humboldt County	59	0.23
Maryland Heights, MO (city) Saint Louis County	59	0.23
Solon, OH (city) Cuyahoga County	51	0.23
North Druid Hills, GA (cdp) De Kalb County	44	0.23
Doylestown, PA (township) Bucks County	40	0.23
North Ogden, UT (city) Weber County	34	0.23
Provo, UT (city) Utah County	230	0.22
Moorestown, NJ (township) Burlington County	42	0.22
Holmdel, NJ (township) Monmouth County	34	0.22
Ballenger Creek, MD (cdp) Frederick County	30	0.22
Fairview Shores, FL (cdp) Orange County	30	0.22
San Anselmo, CA (town) Marin County	28	0.22
Newport Beach, CA (city) Orange County	150	0.21
Temecula, CA (city) Riverside County	123	0.21
San Rafael, CA (city) Marin County	117	0.21
Petaluma, CA (city) Sonoma County	115	0.21
McLean, VA (cdp) Fairfax County	82	0.21
Palm Valley, FL (cdp) Saint Johns County	41	0.21
Worthington, OH (city) Franklin County	30	0.21
Payson, UT (city) Utah County	27	0.21
Clinton, UT (city) Davis County	26	0.21
Pelham, NY (town) Westchester County	25	0.21
Washington, PA (township) Franklin County	24	0.21
Melvindale, MI (city) Wayne County	23	0.21
Lathrop, CA (city) San Joaquin County	22	0.21
Weston, CT (town) Fairfield County	21	0.21
Amherst Center, MA (cdp) Hampshire County	35	0.20
Sierra Vista Southeast, AZ (cdp) Cochise County	30	0.20
Solana Beach, CA (city) San Diego County	26	0.20
Arlington, WA (city) Snohomish County	24	0.20
Kingsgate, WA (cdp) King County	24	0.20
Cinco Ranch, TX (cdp) Fort Bend County	22	0.20
Los Alamitos, CA (city) Orange County	22	0.20
Falls Church, VA (independent city) Falls Church city	21	0.20
Littleton, CO (city) Arapahoe County	78	0.19
Alpharetta, GA (city) Fulton County	67	0.19
Salisbury, NC (city) Rowan County	51	0.19
Burlington, IA (city) Des Moines County	50	0.19
Pahrump, NV (cdp) Nye County	47	0.19
Laguna Beach, CA (city) Orange County	44	0.19
Oak Harbor, WA (city) Island County	38	0.19
South Orange, NJ (cdp) Essex County	32	0.19
Live Oak, CA (cdp) Santa Cruz County	31	0.19
Scio, MI (township) Washtenaw County	29	0.19
Addison, TX (town) Dallas County	26	0.19
Lebanon, OR (city) Linn County	25	0.19
Kaneohe Station, HI (cdp) Honolulu County	23	0.19
Destin, FL (city) Okaloosa County	21	0.19
Montecito, CA (cdp) Santa Barbara County	19	0.19
Eagan, MN (city) Dakota County	114	0.18
Annandale, VA (cdp) Fairfax County	97	0.18
Chantilly, VA (cdp) Fairfax County	76	0.18
Cortlandt, NY (town) Westchester County	69	0.18
Sammamish, WA (city) King County	61	0.18
Falmouth, MA (town) Barnstable County	58	0.18
Menlo Park, CA (city) San Mateo County	55	0.18
Shaker Heights, OH (city) Cuyahoga County	54	0.18
Noblesville, IN (city) Hamilton County	52	0.18
Coronado, CA (city) San Diego County	44	0.18
North Potomac, MD (cdp) Montgomery County	41	0.18
White Center, WA (cdp) King County	37	0.18
Brigham City, UT (city) Box Elder County	32	0.18
Pueblo West, CO (cdp) Pueblo County	31	0.18
Milton, NY (town) Saratoga County	30	0.18
Phoenixville, PA (borough) Chester County	27	0.18
Endicott, NY (village) Broome County	24	0.18
Mill Valley, CA (city) Marin County	24	0.18
Succasunna-Kenvil, NJ (cdp) Morris County	22	0.18
Issaquah, WA (city) King County	20	0.18
Berkeley, CA (city) Alameda County	174	0.17
Davis, CA (city) Yolo County	104	0.17
Lake Oswego, OR (city) Clackamas County	60	0.17
Des Moines, WA (city) King County	50	0.17
Los Gatos, CA (town) Santa Clara County	48	0.17
Ferry Pass, FL (cdp) Escambia County	47	0.17
Huntersville, NC (town) Mecklenburg County	42	0.17
Cranberry, PA (township) Butler County	41	0.17
Parker, CO (town) Douglas County	40	0.17
Montgomery, PA (township) Montgomery County	37	0.17
Fortuna Foothills, AZ (cdp) Yuma County	36	0.17
Menasha, WI (town) Winnebago County	27	0.17
Clark, NJ (cdp) Union County	25	0.17
Mantua, NJ (township) Gloucester County	24	0.17
Wolf Trap, VA (cdp) Fairfax County	23	0.17
Oskaloosa, IA (city) Mahaska County	18	0.17

Notes: (cdp) census designated place; Refer to the Explanation of Data in the front of the book for more detailed information.

Austrian

Top 150 Places Sorted by Number

(Based on all places, regardless of population)

Place	Number	%
New York, NY (city) New York City	33,605	0.42
Los Angeles, CA (city) Los Angeles County	11,430	0.31
Chicago, IL (city) Cook County	8,080	0.28
Hempstead, NY (town) Nassau County	6,437	0.85
San Diego, CA (city) San Diego County	3,865	0.32
Oyster Bay, NY (town) Nassau County	3,802	1.29
Philadelphia, PA (city) Philadelphia County	3,787	0.25
Brookhaven, NY (town) Suffolk County	3,427	0.76
Phoenix, AZ (city) Maricopa County	3,103	0.23
North Hempstead, NY (town) Nassau County	2,795	1.26
San Francisco, CA (city) San Francisco County	2,772	0.36
Seattle, WA (city) King County	2,705	0.48
Milwaukee, WI (city) Milwaukee County	2,477	0.41
Houston, TX (city) Harris County	2,041	0.10
Huntington, NY (town) Suffolk County	2,004	1.03
Portland, OR (city) Multnomah County	1,985	0.38
Denver, CO (city) Denver County	1,838	0.33
Saint Paul, MN (city) Ramsey County	1,761	0.61
Washington, DC (city) District of Columbia	1,703	0.30
Dallas, TX (city) Dallas County	1,599	0.13
Islip, NY (town) Suffolk County	1,537	0.48
Pittsburgh, PA (city) Allegheny County	1,517	0.45
San Jose, CA (city) Santa Clara County	1,514	0.17
Columbus, OH (city) Franklin County	1,483	0.21
Allentown, PA (city) Lehigh County	1,461	1.37
Scottsdale, AZ (city) Maricopa County	1,351	0.67
Boston, MA (city) Suffolk County	1,346	0.23
Colorado Springs, CO (city) El Paso County	1,344	0.37
Tucson, AZ (city) Pima County	1,258	0.26
Minneapolis, MN (city) Hennepin County	1,250	0.33
San Antonio, TX (city) Bexar County	1,199	0.10
Austin, TX (city) Travis County	1,198	0.18
Las Vegas, NV (city) Clark County	1,187	0.25
Indianapolis, IN (special city) Marion County	1,127	0.14
Greenburgh, NY (town) Westchester County	1,111	1.28
Smithtown, NY (town) Suffolk County	1,088	0.94
Jacksonville, FL (special city) Duval County	1,086	0.15
Whitehall, PA (township) Lehigh County	1,065	4.28
Babylon, NY (town) Suffolk County	1,006	0.48
Virginia Beach, VA (independent city) Virginia Beach city	976	0.23
Omaha, NE (city) Douglas County	974	0.25
Charlotte, NC (city) Mecklenburg County	956	0.18
Albuquerque, NM (city) Bernalillo County	953	0.21
Madison, WI (city) Dane County	933	0.45
Saint Petersburg, FL (city) Pinellas County	931	0.38
Clarkstown, NY (town) Rockland County	927	1.13
Ramapo, NY (town) Rockland County	926	0.85
Butte-Silver Bow, MT (special city) Silver Bow County	914	2.70
Santa Monica, CA (city) Los Angeles County	908	1.08
Oakland, CA (city) Alameda County	907	0.23
Baltimore, MD (independent city) Baltimore city	886	0.14
Huntington Beach, CA (city) Orange County	873	0.46
Tamarac, FL (city) Broward County	862	1.54
Long Beach, CA (city) Los Angeles County	838	0.18
Pembroke Pines, FL (city) Broward County	837	0.61
Yonkers, NY (city) Westchester County	829	0.42
Mesa, AZ (city) Maricopa County	822	0.21
Coral Springs, FL (city) Broward County	821	0.70
Miami Beach, FL (city) Miami-Dade County	816	0.93
Fort Lauderdale, FL (city) Broward County	816	0.54
Arlington, VA (cdp) Arlington County	810	0.43
Naperville, IL (city) Du Page County	806	0.63
Cincinnati, OH (city) Hamilton County	804	0.24
Clifton, NJ (city) Passaic County	799	1.02
Hollywood, FL (city) Broward County	790	0.57
Boca Raton, FL (city) Palm Beach County	786	1.04
Aurora, CO (city) Arapahoe County	786	0.28
Greenwich, CT (town) Fairfield County	773	1.27
Thousand Oaks, CA (city) Ventura County	772	0.66
Bethlehem, PA (city) Northampton County	758	1.06
Manalapan, NJ (township) Monmouth County	753	2.25
Cleveland, OH (city) Cuyahoga County	749	0.16
Amherst, NY (town) Erie County	748	0.64
Plantation, FL (city) Broward County	735	0.88
Saint Louis, MO (independent city) Saint Louis city	733	0.21

Place	Number	%
Anchorage, AK (municipality) Anchorage Borough	724	0.28
Arlington Heights, IL (village) Cook County	712	0.94
Santa Rosa, CA (city) Sonoma County	701	0.48
Stamford, CT (city) Fairfield County	692	0.59
Kansas City, MO (city) Jackson County	691	0.16
Marlboro, NJ (township) Monmouth County	682	1.87
Anaheim, CA (city) Orange County	669	0.20
Boulder, CO (city) Boulder County	668	0.71
Tacoma, WA (city) Pierce County	667	0.35
Plano, TX (city) Collin County	663	0.30
Monroe, NJ (township) Middlesex County	656	2.34
Bethesda, MD (cdp) Montgomery County	653	1.18
Cherry Hill, NJ (township) Camden County	648	0.93
Sacramento, CA (city) Sacramento County	648	0.16
Henderson, NV (city) Clark County	644	0.37
Torrance, CA (city) Los Angeles County	641	0.46
Schaumburg, IL (village) Cook County	640	0.86
Orland Park, IL (village) Cook County	628	1.23
Wauwatosa, WI (city) Milwaukee County	624	1.32
Arlington, TX (city) Tarrant County	624	0.19
Plainview, NY (cdp) Nassau County	621	2.42
Oak Lawn, IL (village) Cook County	619	1.12
West Hartford, CT (cdp) Hartford County	613	0.96
Lower Merion, PA (township) Montgomery County	609	1.02
Farmington Hills, MI (city) Oakland County	603	0.73
Akron, OH (city) Summit County	602	0.28
New Orleans, LA (city) Orleans Parish	599	0.12
Nashville-Davidson, TN (special city) Davidson County	593	0.11
El Paso, TX (city) El Paso County	591	0.10
Fairfield, CT (town) Fairfield County	589	1.03
Tampa, FL (city) Hillsborough County	585	0.19
Cambridge, MA (city) Middlesex County	580	0.57
Lakewood, CO (city) Jefferson County	579	0.40
Wayne, NJ (cdp) Passaic County	578	1.07
Tulsa, OK (city) Tulsa County	574	0.15
Sunrise, FL (city) Broward County	573	0.67
Ann Arbor, MI (city) Washtenaw County	569	0.50
Fort Worth, TX (city) Tarrant County	565	0.11
Deerfield Beach, FL (city) Broward County	563	0.87
New Rochelle, NY (city) Westchester County	556	0.77
Berkeley, CA (city) Alameda County	555	0.54
Brookline, MA (cdp) Norfolk County	554	0.97
Palo Alto, CA (city) Santa Clara County	554	0.94
Northampton, PA (borough) Northampton County	552	5.87
Honolulu, HI (cdp) Honolulu County	551	0.15
Newton, MA (city) Middlesex County	549	0.65
Bellevue, WA (city) King County	549	0.50
Yorktown, NY (town) Westchester County	547	1.51
East Brunswick, NJ (cdp) Middlesex County	546	1.17
Buffalo, NY (city) Erie County	545	0.19
Reno, NV (city) Washoe County	544	0.30
Simi Valley, CA (city) Ventura County	543	0.49
Sandy Springs, GA (cdp) Fulton County	541	0.63
Paradise, NV (cdp) Clark County	540	0.29
Boise City, ID (city) Ada County	537	0.29
Overland Park, KS (city) Johnson County	525	0.35
Middletown, NJ (township) Monmouth County	520	0.78
Spokane, WA (city) Spokane County	520	0.27
Irvine, CA (city) Orange County	518	0.36
West Allis, WI (city) Milwaukee County	515	0.84
Northbrook, IL (village) Cook County	510	1.53
Eau Claire, WI (city) Eau Claire County	510	0.83
Atlanta, GA (city) Fulton County	509	0.12
Mamaroneck, NY (town) Westchester County	508	1.75
Fullerton, PA (cdp) Lehigh County	507	3.57
Warren, MI (city) Macomb County	507	0.37
Glendale, AZ (city) Maricopa County	507	0.23
New Berlin, WI (city) Waukesha County	506	1.32
Raleigh, NC (city) Wake County	505	0.18
Edison, NJ (cdp) Middlesex County	503	0.51
Orangetown, NY (town) Rockland County	502	1.05
Livingston, NJ (cdp) Essex County	500	1.83
Tempe, AZ (city) Maricopa County	500	0.32
South Whitehall, PA (township) Lehigh County	497	2.76
Coconut Creek, FL (city) Broward County	491	1.13

Notes: (cdp) census designated place; Refer to the Explanation of Data in the front of the book for more detailed information.

Austrian

Top 150 Places Sorted by Percent

(Based on all places, regardless of population)

Place	Number	%
Chase, AK (cdp) Matanuska-Susitna Borough	7	100.00
West Hampton Dunes, NY (village) Suffolk County	6	75.00
Boulder, WY (cdp) Sublette County	4	33.33
Lima, WI (town) Pepin County	218	30.88
Peru, WI (town) Dunn County	53	22.08
Durand, WI (town) Pepin County	142	20.55
Canyondam, CA (cdp) Plumas County	7	20.00
Canton, WI (town) Buffalo County	55	18.39
Scofield, UT (town) Carbon County	4	18.18
Eden, SD (town) Marshall County	17	17.00
Whaleyville, MD (cdp) Worcester County	20	16.53
Maxville, WI (town) Buffalo County	58	15.98
Waterville, WI (town) Pepin County	138	15.74
Waubeek, WI (town) Pepin County	52	14.05
Coplay, PA (borough) Lehigh County	390	11.51
Mondovi, WI (town) Buffalo County	47	11.49
Indian Village, IN (town) Saint Joseph County	15	10.71
Newfane, VT (village) Windham County	14	10.45
Albany, WI (town) Pepin County	66	10.41
Eau Galle, WI (town) Dunn County	82	10.39
Padroni, CO (cdp) Logan County	8	10.39
West Havre, MT (cdp) Hill County	31	10.23
Durand, WI (city) Pepin County	200	10.17
Fingal, ND (city) Barnes County	14	9.86
Amorita, OK (town) Alfalfa County	5	9.80
Parrish, WI (town) Langlade County	8	9.41
Old Appleton, MO (town) Cape Girardeau County	6	9.23
Seven Springs, PA (borough) Fayette County	6	9.23
Longford, KS (city) Clay County	7	8.64
Fort Smith, MT (cdp) Big Horn County	9	8.49
Hokendauqua, PA (cdp) Lehigh County	296	8.41
Bucyrus, ND (city) Adams County	3	8.33
Marlin, PA (cdp) Schuylkill County	52	8.16
Mulligan, MN (township) Brown County	20	8.06
Sheppton, PA (cdp) Schuylkill County	18	7.63
Meridian, CO (cdp) Douglas County	12	7.55
Scotts Mills, OR (city) Marion County	21	7.19
Maiden Rock, WI (town) Pierce County	45	7.13
Oneida, PA (cdp) Schuylkill County	13	7.10
Whittingham, NJ (cdp) Middlesex County	171	7.00
Westphalia, IA (city) Shelby County	10	6.99
Rock Creek, WI (town) Dunn County	58	6.90
Gem, KS (city) Thomas County	5	6.76
West Mineral, KS (city) Cherokee County	17	6.67
Taos Ski Valley, NM (village) Taos County	6	6.67
Nelson, WI (town) Buffalo County	37	6.64
Haverhill, IA (city) Marshall County	11	6.40
Frankfort, WI (town) Pepin County	21	6.33
Poplar Grove, MN (township) Roseau County	5	6.25
Rock Elm, WI (town) Pierce County	33	6.17
Modena, WI (town) Buffalo County	22	6.15
Donegal, PA (borough) Westmoreland County	10	6.06
Tuscarora, PA (cdp) Schuylkill County	55	6.00
Dibble, OK (town) McClain County	19	5.96
Indian Creek, FL (village) Miami-Dade County	2	5.88
Northampton, PA (borough) Northampton County	552	5.87
Meadowbrook Farm, KY (city) Jefferson County	9	5.81
Great Scott, MN (township) Saint Louis County	35	5.78
Edna Bay, AK (cdp) Prince of Wales-Outer Ketchikan Census Area	3	5.77
Drammen, WI (town) Eau Claire County	44	5.73
Oak Point, FL (cdp) Broward County	9	5.70
Herndon, KS (city) Rawlins County	10	5.59
Van Buren, MN (township) Saint Louis County	9	5.59
Elmer, MN (township) Saint Louis County	10	5.52
Olmitz, KS (city) Barton County	9	5.52
Wallace, IN (town) Fountain County	6	5.50
Nekoma, ND (city) Cavalier County	2	5.41
Union, WI (town) Pierce County	30	5.40
Allen, PA (township) Northampton County	141	5.36
Palenville, NY (cdp) Greene County	63	5.20
Curtiss, WI (village) Clark County	10	5.15
Grand Island, MI (township) Alger County	2	5.13
Glen Flora, WI (village) Rusk County	3	5.08
Ravalli, MT (cdp) Lake County	5	5.00
Cloverdale, OR (cdp) Tillamook County	12	4.98
Mondovi, WI (city) Buffalo County	131	4.96
Ouray, CO (city) Ouray County	41	4.96
Sharon, NH (town) Hillsborough County	17	4.96
Hill View Heights, WY (cdp) Weston County	9	4.92
Lumber, PA (township) Cameron County	9	4.92
Concordia, NJ (cdp) Middlesex County	181	4.90
North Catasauqua, PA (borough) Northampton County	138	4.90
Schuylkill, PA (township) Schuylkill County	55	4.90
Frankfort, SD (city) Spink County	9	4.89
White Mountain, AK (city) Nome Census Area	10	4.76
Cusick, WA (town) Pend Oreille County	10	4.74
Mount Carbon, PA (borough) Schuylkill County	4	4.71
Hewlett Neck, NY (village) Nassau County	23	4.66
Bruceton Mills, WV (town) Preston County	3	4.62
Eastlawn Gardens, PA (cdp) Northampton County	132	4.60
Saddle Rock Estates, NY (cdp) Nassau County	20	4.56
Baltimore, VT (town) Windsor County	13	4.56
Bessie, OK (town) Washita County	9	4.55
Crestone, CO (town) Saguache County	3	4.55
De Borgia, MT (cdp) Mineral County	3	4.55
Bloomingburg, NY (village) Sullivan County	14	4.52
Auburn, IA (city) Sac County	14	4.46
La Crosse, MN (township) Jackson County	9	4.46
Burnt Prairie, IL (village) White County	2	4.35
Upper Nazareth, PA (township) Northampton County	192	4.34
Seven Mile Creek, WI (town) Juneau County	14	4.31
Newry, PA (borough) Blair County	10	4.31
Whitehall, PA (township) Lehigh County	1,065	4.28
French Gulch, CA (cdp) Shasta County	11	4.28
Great Neck Plaza, NY (village) Nassau County	267	4.21
Highland Beach, FL (town) Palm Beach County	152	4.21
Gibson, PA (township) Cameron County	10	4.18
Golf, FL (village) Palm Beach County	10	4.18
Rowena, OR (cdp) Wasco County	7	4.14
Stark, KS (city) Neosho County	5	4.10
Sylvania, PA (township) Potter County	2	4.08
Masonville, IA (city) Delaware County	4	4.04
Eschbach, WA (cdp) Yakima County	17	4.01
Hometown, PA (cdp) Schuylkill County	56	3.98
Brunswick, WI (town) Eau Claire County	64	3.97
Ronald, WA (cdp) Kittitas County	7	3.95
Washington, VA (town) Rappahannock County	7	3.91
Roseland, KS (city) Cherokee County	3	3.90
Hancock, WI (town) Waushara County	21	3.87
Stamford, VT (town) Bennington County	32	3.86
Ringwood, IL (village) McHenry County	17	3.83
Plum City, WI (village) Pierce County	23	3.82
Cove Neck, NY (village) Nassau County	10	3.82
Miesville, MN (city) Dakota County	5	3.82
Fairbanks, MN (township) Saint Louis County	3	3.80
Arma, KS (city) Crawford County	58	3.79
High Point, FL (cdp) Palm Beach County	83	3.76
Ramey, PA (borough) Clearfield County	19	3.76
Harbor Isle, NY (cdp) Nassau County	53	3.75
Indian Hills, CO (cdp) Jefferson County	42	3.75
Tuscarawas, OH (village) Tuscarawas County	36	3.75
Indian Beach, NC (town) Carteret County	3	3.75
Mead, WI (town) Clark County	11	3.73
Westport, SD (town) Brown County	5	3.73
Russell Gardens, NY (village) Nassau County	40	3.72
Prompton, PA (borough) Wayne County	10	3.68
Tripp, WI (town) Bayfield County	7	3.68
Villages of Oriole, FL (cdp) Palm Beach County	174	3.67
Clearbrook Park, NJ (cdp) Middlesex County	112	3.66
East Union, PA (township) Schuylkill County	52	3.66
McKinley, MN (city) Saint Louis County	3	3.66
Reed Point, MT (cdp) Stillwater County	6	3.59
Spooner, MN (township) Lake of the Woods County	10	3.58
Fullerton, PA (cdp) Lehigh County	507	3.57
Forrestville, PA (cdp) Schuylkill County	14	3.56
Sherry, WI (town) Wood County	29	3.52
Barnett, PA (township) Forest County	13	3.51
Butler, PA (township) Luzerne County	250	3.49
Tony, WI (village) Rusk County	3	3.49
Nazareth, PA (borough) Northampton County	208	3.45

Notes: (cdp) census designated place; Refer to the Explanation of Data in the front of the book for more detailed information.

Austrian

Top 150 Places Sorted by Percent

(Based on places with populations of 10,000 or more)

Place	Number	%
Whitehall, PA (township) Lehigh County	1,065	4.28
Fullerton, PA (cdp) Lehigh County	507	3.57
Hamptons at Boca Raton, FL (cdp) Palm Beach County	391	3.42
Kings Point, FL (cdp) Palm Beach County	420	3.39
Jericho, NY (cdp) Nassau County	407	3.13
South Whitehall, PA (township) Lehigh County	497	2.76
Butte-Silver Bow, MT (special city) Silver Bow County	914	2.70
Morganville, NJ (cdp) Monmouth County	299	2.69
Salisbury, PA (township) Lehigh County	356	2.64
Upper Saucon, PA (township) Lehigh County	303	2.54
North Whitehall, PA (township) Lehigh County	365	2.48
Millburn, NJ (cdp) Essex County	482	2.44
Plainview, NY (cdp) Nassau County	621	2.42
Monroe, NJ (township) Middlesex County	656	2.34
Emmaus, PA (borough) Lehigh County	263	2.34
Syosset, NY (cdp) Nassau County	423	2.28
Manalapan, NJ (township) Monmouth County	753	2.25
Palm Beach, FL (town) Palm Beach County	224	2.16
West Freehold, NJ (cdp) Monmouth County	267	2.13
Westwood, NJ (borough) Bergen County	234	2.13
Dobbs Ferry, NY (village) Westchester County	224	2.11
Glen Rock, NJ (borough) Bergen County	241	2.09
Merrick, NY (cdp) Nassau County	461	2.03
Lower Macungie, PA (township) Lehigh County	378	1.97
Hazleton, PA (city) Luzerne County	450	1.93
Scarsdale, NY (village) Westchester County	336	1.89
Marlboro, NJ (township) Monmouth County	682	1.87
Salisbury, NY (cdp) Nassau County	229	1.86
Livingston, NJ (cdp) Essex County	500	1.83
Pinecrest, FL (village) Miami-Dade County	351	1.83
Somers, NY (town) Westchester County	334	1.82
Whitefish Bay, WI (village) Milwaukee County	251	1.77
Mamaroneck, NY (town) Westchester County	508	1.75
Warren, NJ (township) Somerset County	247	1.73
Jefferson Valley-Yorktown, NY (cdp) Westchester County	255	1.71
Deerfield, IL (village) Lake County	312	1.69
Aventura, FL (city) Miami-Dade County	422	1.67
Palos Heights, IL (city) Cook County	188	1.66
Saint James, NY (cdp) Suffolk County	217	1.64
Beachwood, OH (city) Cuyahoga County	198	1.62
Agoura Hills, CA (city) Los Angeles County	325	1.60
Bellmore, NY (cdp) Nassau County	263	1.60
Little Falls, NJ (cdp) Passaic County	174	1.60
Springdale, NJ (cdp) Camden County	226	1.57
Oakland, NJ (borough) Bergen County	195	1.56
Tamarac, FL (city) Broward County	862	1.54
Laguna Woods, CA (city) Orange County	251	1.54
Northbrook, IL (village) Cook County	510	1.53
Tinton Falls, NJ (borough) Monmouth County	231	1.53
Yorktown, NY (town) Westchester County	547	1.51
Montgomery, NJ (township) Somerset County	264	1.51
Moraga, CA (town) Contra Costa County	252	1.51
North Wantagh, NY (cdp) Nassau County	184	1.51
Westport, CT (cdp) Fairfield County	384	1.49
Clinton, NJ (township) Hunterdon County	193	1.49
New Castle, NY (town) Westchester County	257	1.47
Highland Park, IL (city) Lake County	456	1.45
Randolph, NJ (township) Morris County	358	1.44
North Castle, NY (town) Westchester County	155	1.43
Putnam Valley, NY (town) Putnam County	153	1.43
Montecito, CA (cdp) Santa Barbara County	144	1.43
Hallandale, FL (city) Broward County	490	1.42
Springfield, NJ (cdp) Union County	200	1.39
Lewisboro, NY (town) Westchester County	171	1.39
Robinson Township, PA (cdp) Allegheny County	169	1.38
Crestwood, IL (village) Cook County	155	1.38
Allentown, PA (city) Lehigh County	1,461	1.37
Rockville Centre, NY (village) Nassau County	336	1.37
Woodmere, NY (cdp) Nassau County	223	1.36
Malibu, CA (city) Los Angeles County	169	1.35
Tamalpais-Homestead Valley, CA (cdp) Marin County	143	1.35
Evergreen Park, IL (village) Cook County	280	1.34
Setauket-East Setauket, NY (cdp) Suffolk County	213	1.34
Pearl River, NY (cdp) Rockland County	208	1.34
Calabasas, CA (city) Los Angeles County	267	1.33
Weston, CT (town) Fairfield County	133	1.33
Wauwatosa, WI (city) Milwaukee County	624	1.32
New Berlin, WI (city) Waukesha County	506	1.32
Boca Del Mar, FL (cdp) Palm Beach County	281	1.31
Glendale, WI (city) Milwaukee County	175	1.31
New Canaan, CT (town) Fairfield County	253	1.30
Hanover, NH (town) Grafton County	141	1.30
Grafton, WI (village) Ozaukee County	134	1.30
Oyster Bay, NY (town) Nassau County	3,802	1.29
New City, NY (cdp) Rockland County	440	1.29
Dix Hills, NY (cdp) Suffolk County	336	1.29
Sudbury, MA (town) Middlesex County	217	1.29
North New Hyde Park, NY (cdp) Nassau County	187	1.29
Greenburgh, NY (town) Westchester County	1,111	1.28
Carmel, NY (town) Putnam County	424	1.28
Wilton, CT (town) Fairfield County	225	1.28
Chestnuthill, PA (township) Monroe County	185	1.28
Greenwich, CT (town) Fairfield County	773	1.27
Montville, NJ (township) Morris County	264	1.27
Sandalfoot Cove, FL (cdp) Palm Beach County	210	1.27
Melville, NY (cdp) Suffolk County	184	1.27
Princeton Meadows, NJ (cdp) Middlesex County	168	1.27
Cornwall, NY (town) Orange County	156	1.27
North Hempstead, NY (town) Nassau County	2,795	1.26
Ocean, NJ (township) Monmouth County	341	1.26
Plainsboro, NJ (township) Middlesex County	254	1.26
West Hempstead, NY (cdp) Nassau County	236	1.26
Freehold, NJ (township) Monmouth County	393	1.25
Paramus, NJ (borough) Bergen County	321	1.25
North Merrick, NY (cdp) Nassau County	148	1.25
Trumbull, CT (cdp) Fairfield County	424	1.24
Ridgewood, NJ (village) Bergen County	309	1.24
Scotch Plains, NJ (cdp) Union County	281	1.24
Mamaroneck, NY (village) Westchester County	233	1.24
Bedford, NY (town) Westchester County	225	1.24
Wood Dale, IL (city) Du Page County	173	1.24
Orland Park, IL (village) Cook County	628	1.23
Tenafly, NJ (borough) Bergen County	170	1.23
Oceanside, NY (cdp) Nassau County	397	1.21
Wyckoff, NJ (cdp) Bergen County	200	1.21
Menomonie, WI (city) Dunn County	181	1.21
Farmingville, NY (cdp) Suffolk County	198	1.20
Buckingham, PA (township) Bucks County	197	1.20
Princeton, NJ (township) Mercer County	190	1.19
Coal, PA (township) Northumberland County	127	1.19
Bethesda, MD (cdp) Montgomery County	653	1.18
Rancho Mirage, CA (city) Riverside County	153	1.18
East Brunswick, NJ (cdp) Middlesex County	546	1.17
Ridgefield, CT (town) Fairfield County	276	1.17
Upper Gwynedd, PA (township) Montgomery County	167	1.17
Cherry Hill Mall, NJ (cdp) Camden County	158	1.17
Larkspur, CA (city) Marin County	140	1.17
Blooming Grove, NY (town) Orange County	201	1.16
Oak Forest, IL (city) Cook County	321	1.15
Metuchen, NJ (borough) Middlesex County	148	1.15
Pelham, NY (town) Westchester County	137	1.15
Mendota Heights, MN (city) Dakota County	131	1.15
Long Beach, NY (city) Nassau County	404	1.14
Hickory Hills, IL (city) Cook County	159	1.14
Shorewood, WI (village) Milwaukee County	157	1.14
Warrenville, IL (city) Du Page County	151	1.14
Clarkstown, NY (town) Rockland County	927	1.13
Coconut Creek, FL (city) Broward County	491	1.13
Fort Lee, NJ (borough) Bergen County	400	1.13
Mount Lebanon, PA (cdp) Allegheny County	372	1.13
Mahwah, NJ (township) Bergen County	271	1.13
Ramsey, NJ (borough) Bergen County	162	1.13
Stony Brook, NY (cdp) Suffolk County	155	1.13
Leisure Village West-Pine Lake Park, NJ (cdp) Ocean County	125	1.13
Oak Lawn, IL (village) Cook County	619	1.12
White Bear Lake, MN (city) Ramsey County	273	1.12
Cudahy, WI (city) Milwaukee County	207	1.12
Ringwood, NJ (borough) Passaic County	139	1.12
Cortlandt, NY (town) Westchester County	426	1.11
Franklin, WI (city) Milwaukee County	328	1.11

Notes: (cdp) census designated place; Refer to the Explanation of Data in the front of the book for more detailed information.

Basque

Top 150 Places Sorted by Number

(Based on all places, regardless of population)

Place	Number	%
Boise City, ID (city) Ada County	1,965	1.06
Reno, NV (city) Washoe County	1,226	0.68
Los Angeles, CA (city) Los Angeles County	1,197	0.03
Elko, NV (city) Elko County	642	3.87
New York, NY (city) New York City	596	0.01
Bakersfield, CA (city) Kern County	562	0.23
San Francisco, CA (city) San Francisco County	549	0.07
San Diego, CA (city) San Diego County	479	0.04
Fresno, CA (city) Fresno County	457	0.11
Sparks, NV (city) Washoe County	440	0.66
Meridian, ID (city) Ada County	433	1.24
Winnemucca, NV (city) Humboldt County	339	4.67
Stockton, CA (city) San Joaquin County	333	0.14
Phoenix, AZ (city) Maricopa County	327	0.02
Caldwell, ID (city) Canyon County	322	1.25
Seattle, WA (city) King County	319	0.06
San Jose, CA (city) Santa Clara County	311	0.03
Portland, OR (city) Multnomah County	290	0.05
Nampa, ID (city) Canyon County	284	0.54
Carson City, NV (special city) Carson City city	278	0.53
Tucson, AZ (city) Pima County	267	0.05
Sacramento, CA (city) Sacramento County	258	0.06
Las Vegas, NV (city) Clark County	248	0.05
Denver, CO (city) Denver County	239	0.04
Twin Falls, ID (city) Twin Falls County	216	0.63
Rancho Cucamonga, CA (city) San Bernardino County	209	0.16
Albuquerque, NM (city) Bernalillo County	205	0.05
Long Beach, CA (city) Los Angeles County	193	0.04
Susanville, CA (city) Lassen County	189	1.39
San Antonio, TX (city) Bexar County	189	0.02
Oildale, CA (cdp) Kern County	181	0.65
Washington, DC (city) District of Columbia	180	0.03
Salt Lake City, UT (city) Salt Lake County	175	0.10
Ontario, OR (city) Malheur County	145	1.30
Huntington Beach, CA (city) Orange County	145	0.08
Riverside, CA (city) Riverside County	143	0.06
San Buenaventura, CA (city) Ventura County	141	0.14
Chicago, IL (city) Cook County	141	0.00
Eagle, ID (city) Ada County	140	1.26
Clovis, CA (city) Fresno County	140	0.21
Houston, TX (city) Harris County	138	0.01
Santa Rosa, CA (city) Sonoma County	135	0.09
Henderson, NV (city) Clark County	134	0.08
Chino, CA (city) San Bernardino County	133	0.20
San Mateo, CA (city) San Mateo County	130	0.14
Los Banos, CA (city) Merced County	127	0.49
Battle Mountain, NV (cdp) Lander County	124	4.18
Gooding, ID (city) Gooding County	124	3.68
Modesto, CA (city) Stanislaus County	124	0.07
Paradise, NV (cdp) Clark County	123	0.07
Arlington, VA (cdp) Arlington County	123	0.06
Mission Viejo, CA (city) Orange County	121	0.13
Taylorsville, UT (city) Salt Lake County	120	0.21
Anaheim, CA (city) Orange County	118	0.04
Miami, FL (city) Miami-Dade County	118	0.03
Orange, CA (city) Orange County	117	0.09
Pacifica, CA (city) San Mateo County	116	0.30
Spring Creek, NV (cdp) Elko County	115	1.05
San Luis Obispo, CA (city) San Luis Obispo County	114	0.26
Rock Springs, WY (city) Sweetwater County	113	0.60
Burbank, CA (city) Los Angeles County	106	0.11
Buffalo, WY (city) Johnson County	102	2.71
Spanish Springs, NV (cdp) Washoe County	102	1.16
Ontario, CA (city) San Bernardino County	102	0.06
Dallas, TX (city) Dallas County	102	0.01
Spokane, WA (city) Spokane County	101	0.05
Fallon, NV (city) Churchill County	100	1.34
Cypress, CA (city) Orange County	99	0.21
West Valley City, UT (city) Salt Lake County	99	0.09
Santa Clarita, CA (city) Los Angeles County	98	0.06
Cutler, FL (cdp) Miami-Dade County	96	0.54
Eugene, OR (city) Lane County	96	0.07
Moreno Valley, CA (city) Riverside County	96	0.07
Irvine, CA (city) Orange County	95	0.07
Austin, TX (city) Travis County	94	0.01
Chico, CA (city) Butte County	93	0.16
Encinitas, CA (city) San Diego County	92	0.16
Hempstead, NY (town) Nassau County	91	0.01
Tracy, CA (city) San Joaquin County	90	0.16
Santa Barbara, CA (city) Santa Barbara County	90	0.10
Woodridge, IL (village) Du Page County	89	0.29
Novato, CA (city) Marin County	89	0.19
Fairfield, CA (city) Solano County	89	0.09
Green River, WY (city) Sweetwater County	88	0.75
Camarillo, CA (city) Ventura County	88	0.15
Simi Valley, CA (city) Ventura County	87	0.08
Anchorage, AK (municipality) Anchorage Borough	86	0.03
Redwood City, CA (city) San Mateo County	85	0.11
Pomona, CA (city) Los Angeles County	85	0.06
Rosedale, CA (cdp) Kern County	84	0.99
Santa Monica, CA (city) Los Angeles County	84	0.10
Spring Valley, NV (cdp) Clark County	84	0.07
Mesa, AZ (city) Maricopa County	84	0.02
Coral Gables, FL (city) Miami-Dade County	82	0.19
Vacaville, CA (city) Solano County	82	0.09
Oxnard, CA (city) Ventura County	82	0.05
Aurora, CO (city) Arapahoe County	82	0.03
Burlingame, CA (city) San Mateo County	81	0.29
Rupert, ID (city) Minidoka County	80	1.41
Lompoc, CA (city) Santa Barbara County	80	0.19
Chula Vista, CA (city) San Diego County	80	0.05
San Carlos, CA (city) San Mateo County	79	0.29
Woodland, CA (city) Yolo County	79	0.16
Goleta, CA (cdp) Santa Barbara County	79	0.14
Berkeley, CA (city) Alameda County	78	0.08
Vancouver, WA (city) Clark County	78	0.05
Miles City, MT (city) Custer County	77	0.91
Fairbanks, AK (city) Fairbanks North Star Borough	77	0.25
San Rafael, CA (city) Marin County	77	0.14
Miami Beach, FL (city) Miami-Dade County	77	0.09
Costa Mesa, CA (city) Orange County	77	0.07
Fullerton, CA (city) Orange County	77	0.06
Yakima, WA (city) Yakima County	76	0.11
Tampa, FL (city) Hillsborough County	76	0.03
Federal Way, WA (city) King County	74	0.09
Antioch, CA (city) Contra Costa County	74	0.08
Arden-Arcade, CA (cdp) Sacramento County	74	0.08
Visalia, CA (city) Tulare County	74	0.08
El Paso, TX (city) El Paso County	74	0.01
Minden, NV (cdp) Douglas County	73	2.51
Pocatello, ID (city) Bannock County	73	0.14
Fort Collins, CO (city) Larimer County	73	0.06
Westminster, CO (city) Adams County	71	0.07
Thousand Oaks, CA (city) Ventura County	71	0.06
Lakewood, CO (city) Jefferson County	71	0.05
Enterprise, NV (cdp) Clark County	70	0.48
Grand Junction, CO (city) Mesa County	70	0.17
Corvallis, OR (city) Benton County	70	0.14
Alameda, CA (city) Alameda County	70	0.10
Whittier, CA (city) Los Angeles County	70	0.08
Doral, FL (cdp) Miami-Dade County	69	0.34
Kendall, FL (cdp) Miami-Dade County	69	0.09
Escondido, CA (city) San Diego County	69	0.05
Boston, MA (city) Suffolk County	69	0.01
Chino Hills, CA (city) San Bernardino County	68	0.10
Salem, OR (city) Marion County	68	0.05
Torrance, CA (city) Los Angeles County	68	0.05
Scottsdale, AZ (city) Maricopa County	68	0.03
Danville, CA (town) Contra Costa County	66	0.16
Davis, CA (city) Yolo County	66	0.11
Laguna Niguel, CA (city) Orange County	66	0.11
Santee, CA (city) San Diego County	65	0.12
Hesperia, CA (city) San Bernardino County	65	0.10
New Orleans, LA (city) Orleans Parish	65	0.01
Gardnerville, NV (cdp) Douglas County	64	1.89
San Clemente, CA (city) Orange County	64	0.13
Upland, CA (city) San Bernardino County	64	0.09
Carmichael, CA (cdp) Sacramento County	63	0.13
Tempe, AZ (city) Maricopa County	63	0.04
Mountain Home, ID (city) Elmore County	60	0.52

Notes: (cdp) census designated place; Refer to the Explanation of Data in the front of the book for more detailed information.

Basque

Top 150 Places Sorted by Percent

(Based on all places, regardless of population)

Place	Number	%
Jordan Valley, OR (city) Malheur County	46	18.47
Atlantic City, WY (cdp) Fremont County	5	15.63
Lamy, NM (cdp) Santa Fe County	21	13.04
Washam, WY (cdp) Sweetwater County	6	12.50
Airport Road, WY (cdp) Washakie County	20	6.62
Port Costa, CA (cdp) Contra Costa County	15	6.20
Ashford, WA (cdp) Pierce County	15	5.79
Eden, WY (cdp) Sweetwater County	27	5.34
Winnemucca, NV (city) Humboldt County	339	4.67
Battle Mountain, NV (cdp) Lander County	124	4.18
Elko, NV (city) Elko County	642	3.87
Gooding, ID (city) Gooding County	124	3.68
Shoshone, ID (city) Lincoln County	49	3.48
Long Creek, OR (city) Grant County	7	3.41
Cascade, ID (city) Valley County	33	3.37
Gerlach-Empire, NV (cdp) Washoe County	16	3.03
Sun Valley, TX (city) Lamar County	2	3.03
Dodson, MT (town) Phillips County	4	2.96
Fortine, MT (cdp) Lincoln County	5	2.78
Bloomington, NE (village) Franklin County	3	2.75
Buffalo, WY (city) Johnson County	102	2.71
Maywood, NE (village) Frontier County	9	2.69
Dietrich, ID (city) Lincoln County	5	2.58
Minden, NV (cdp) Douglas County	73	2.51
Clearview Acres, WY (cdp) Sweetwater County	17	2.43
Carey, ID (city) Blaine County	14	2.41
Portage, UT (town) Box Elder County	6	2.37
Shongaloo, LA (village) Webster Parish	3	2.26
Unity, OR (city) Baker County	2	2.11
Gardnerville, NV (cdp) Douglas County	64	1.89
Hines, OR (city) Harney County	30	1.78
Washakie Ten, WY (cdp) Washakie County	9	1.78
Tacna, AZ (cdp) Yuma County	10	1.77
Fisher Island, FL (cdp) Miami-Dade County	6	1.77
Idaho City, ID (city) Boise County	8	1.74
Onaway, ID (city) Latah County	4	1.63
Bellerose, NY (village) Nassau County	19	1.62
Westfir, OR (city) Lane County	5	1.61
Burns, OR (city) Harney County	46	1.56
New Plymouth, ID (city) Payette County	22	1.55
Hagerman, ID (city) Gooding County	10	1.55
Mi-Wuk Village, CA (cdp) Tuolumne County	21	1.45
Rupert, ID (city) Minidoka County	80	1.41
Minidoka, ID (city) Minidoka County	2	1.41
Susanville, CA (city) Lassen County	189	1.39
Oak Park, CA (cdp) Ventura County	34	1.39
Fallon, NV (city) Churchill County	100	1.34
Kingsbury, NV (cdp) Douglas County	35	1.33
Castleford, ID (city) Twin Falls County	3	1.33
Marsing, ID (city) Owyhee County	12	1.31
Ontario, OR (city) Malheur County	145	1.30
Vale, OR (city) Malheur County	26	1.30
Moss Beach, CA (cdp) San Mateo County	24	1.27
Roy, NM (village) Harding County	4	1.27
Eagle, ID (city) Ada County	140	1.26
Caldwell, ID (city) Canyon County	322	1.25
Bodfish, CA (cdp) Kern County	23	1.25
Story, WY (cdp) Sheridan County	12	1.25
Meridian, ID (city) Ada County	433	1.24
North Rock Springs, WY (cdp) Sweetwater County	23	1.23
Bonsall, CA (cdp) San Diego County	42	1.22
Canyon City, OR (town) Grant County	8	1.21
North Woodbridge, CA (cdp) San Joaquin County	15	1.20
Saco, MT (town) Phillips County	3	1.20
Palouse, WA (city) Whitman County	12	1.17
Mount Vernon, OR (city) Grant County	7	1.17
Spanish Springs, NV (cdp) Washoe County	102	1.16
Ryegate, MT (town) Golden Valley County	3	1.16
Ruskin, NE (village) Nuckolls County	2	1.14
Melba, ID (city) Canyon County	5	1.11
Homedale, ID (city) Owyhee County	28	1.10
Mitchell, OR (city) Wheeler County	2	1.10
Craigmont, ID (city) Lewis County	6	1.09
Plymouth, VT (town) Windsor County	6	1.07
Boise City, ID (city) Ada County	1,965	1.06
Salton City, CA (cdp) Imperial County	10	1.06
Tubac, AZ (cdp) Santa Cruz County	9	1.06
Spring Creek, NV (cdp) Elko County	115	1.05
Riverside, UT (cdp) Box Elder County	7	1.04
Fruitland, ID (city) Payette County	39	1.03
Murrieta Hot Springs, CA (cdp) Riverside County	30	1.02
Rosedale, CA (cdp) Kern County	84	0.99
Notus, ID (city) Canyon County	4	0.98
Bliss, ID (city) Gooding County	3	0.97
Mojave, CA (cdp) Kern County	35	0.96
Sweden, ME (town) Oxford County	3	0.95
Roanoke, TX (city) Denton County	27	0.94
Woodsboro, MD (town) Frederick County	8	0.94
Long Beach, WA (city) Pacific County	12	0.93
Paulden, AZ (cdp) Yavapai County	31	0.92
Poipu, HI (cdp) Kauai County	10	0.92
Nashua, MT (town) Valley County	3	0.92
Miles City, MT (city) Custer County	77	0.91
Bellevue, ID (city) Blaine County	17	0.91
Filer, ID (city) Twin Falls County	15	0.91
Guerneville, CA (cdp) Sonoma County	22	0.89
Electric City, WA (town) Grant County	8	0.89
Kelseyville, CA (cdp) Lake County	25	0.88
Sugar Hill, NH (town) Grafton County	5	0.88
Cold Springs, NV (cdp) Washoe County	33	0.86
Saratoga Springs, UT (town) Utah County	8	0.86
Noxon, MT (cdp) Sanders County	2	0.86
Littlerock, CA (cdp) Los Angeles County	11	0.85
Hailey, ID (city) Blaine County	51	0.84
Alturas, CA (city) Modoc County	25	0.84
Cle Elum, WA (city) Kittitas County	15	0.84
Kaycee, WY (town) Johnson County	2	0.84
Wendell, ID (city) Gooding County	18	0.83
North Troy, VT (village) Orleans County	5	0.83
Carlin, NV (city) Elko County	18	0.82
Toledo, OR (city) Lincoln County	28	0.81
Bayview, CA (cdp) Humboldt County	19	0.81
Glenns Ferry, ID (city) Elmore County	13	0.80
East Sonora, CA (cdp) Tuolumne County	16	0.79
Elizabeth, CO (town) Elbert County	12	0.79
Schaller, IA (city) Sac County	6	0.79
French Gulch, CA (cdp) Shasta County	2	0.78
Johnson Lane, NV (cdp) Douglas County	36	0.76
Green River, WY (city) Sweetwater County	88	0.75
Glendo, WY (town) Platte County	2	0.74
Idyllwild-Pine Cove, CA (cdp) Riverside County	26	0.73
Dolan Springs, AZ (cdp) Mohave County	14	0.73
Culbertson, MT (town) Roosevelt County	5	0.73
Lemmon Valley-Golden Valley, NV (cdp) Washoe County	49	0.72
Paul, ID (city) Minidoka County	7	0.72
Bladen, NE (village) Webster County	2	0.72
Mount Hood Village, OR (cdp) Clackamas County	23	0.71
Payette, ID (city) Payette County	49	0.70
Liberty Lake, WA (cdp) Spokane County	33	0.69
Nyssa, OR (city) Malheur County	22	0.69
Thorne Bay, AK (city) Prince of Wales-Outer Ketchikan C.A.	4	0.69
Reno, NV (city) Washoe County	1,226	0.68
Burbank, WA (cdp) Walla Walla County	23	0.68
Jamestown, CA (cdp) Tuolumne County	21	0.68
McDermitt, NV (cdp) Humboldt County	15	0.68
Kuna, ID (city) Ada County	37	0.67
Sparks, NV (city) Washoe County	440	0.66
Oildale, CA (cdp) Kern County	181	0.65
Malvern, PA (borough) Chester County	20	0.65
Heppner, OR (city) Morrow County	9	0.65
Irasburg, VT (town) Orleans County	7	0.65
Lemon Cove, CA (cdp) Tulare County	2	0.65
Brookline, MO (village) Greene County	2	0.64
Twin Falls, ID (city) Twin Falls County	216	0.63
Woodside, CA (town) San Mateo County	33	0.63
Buhl, ID (city) Twin Falls County	25	0.63
Huntsville, UT (town) Weber County	4	0.63
Harpers Ferry, WV (town) Jefferson County	2	0.63
Troy, MT (city) Lincoln County	6	0.62
Prosser, WA (city) Benton County	28	0.61

Notes: (cdp) census designated place; Refer to the Explanation of Data in the front of the book for more detailed information.

Basque

Top 150 Places Sorted by Percent

(Based on places with populations of 10,000 or more)

Place	Number	%
Elko, NV (city) Elko County	642	3.87
Susanville, CA (city) Lassen County	189	1.39
Ontario, OR (city) Malheur County	145	1.30
Eagle, ID (city) Ada County	140	1.26
Caldwell, ID (city) Canyon County	322	1.25
Meridian, ID (city) Ada County	433	1.24
Boise City, ID (city) Ada County	1,965	1.06
Spring Creek, NV (cdp) Elko County	115	1.05
Green River, WY (city) Sweetwater County	88	0.75
Reno, NV (city) Washoe County	1,226	0.68
Sparks, NV (city) Washoe County	440	0.66
Oildale, CA (cdp) Kern County	181	0.65
Twin Falls, ID (city) Twin Falls County	216	0.63
Rock Springs, WY (city) Sweetwater County	113	0.60
Nampa, ID (city) Canyon County	284	0.54
Cutler, FL (cdp) Miami-Dade County	96	0.54
Carson City, NV (special city) Carson City city	278	0.53
Mountain Home, ID (city) Elmore County	60	0.52
Los Banos, CA (city) Merced County	127	0.49
Enterprise, NV (cdp) Clark County	70	0.48
Putnam Valley, NY (town) Putnam County	46	0.43
Larkspur, CA (city) Marin County	46	0.38
Piedmont, CA (city) Alameda County	42	0.38
Healdsburg, CA (city) Sonoma County	40	0.38
Doral, FL (cdp) Miami-Dade County	69	0.34
Baywood-Los Osos, CA (cdp) San Luis Obispo County	48	0.34
La Grande, OR (city) Union County	40	0.33
Key Biscayne, FL (village) Miami-Dade County	35	0.33
Nipomo, CA (cdp) San Luis Obispo County	40	0.32
Mira Loma, CA (cdp) Riverside County	56	0.31
Pacifica, CA (city) San Mateo County	116	0.30
Little Falls, NJ (cdp) Passaic County	33	0.30
Woodridge, IL (village) Du Page County	89	0.29
Burlingame, CA (city) San Mateo County	81	0.29
San Carlos, CA (city) San Mateo County	79	0.29
Evanston, WY (city) Uinta County	33	0.29
Valle Vista, CA (cdp) Riverside County	31	0.29
Gardnerville Ranchos, NV (cdp) Douglas County	30	0.27
West Paterson, NJ (borough) Passaic County	30	0.27
San Luis Obispo, CA (city) San Luis Obispo County	114	0.26
Sheridan, WY (city) Sheridan County	41	0.26
McKinleyville, CA (cdp) Humboldt County	35	0.26
Central Point, OR (city) Jackson County	32	0.26
Garden City, ID (city) Ada County	28	0.26
Fortuna, CA (city) Humboldt County	27	0.26
Fairbanks, AK (city) Fairbanks North Star Borough	77	0.25
Magna, UT (cdp) Salt Lake County	57	0.25
Calabasas, CA (city) Los Angeles County	50	0.25
Mill Valley, CA (city) Marin County	34	0.25
Moscow, ID (city) Latah County	51	0.24
Selma, CA (city) Fresno County	47	0.24
Marysville, CA (city) Yuba County	30	0.24
Bakersfield, CA (city) Kern County	562	0.23
Coalinga, CA (city) Fresno County	27	0.23
Lathrop, CA (city) San Joaquin County	24	0.23
Sierra Madre, CA (city) Los Angeles County	24	0.23
La Riviera, CA (cdp) Sacramento County	23	0.22
Clovis, CA (city) Fresno County	140	0.21
Taylorsville, UT (city) Salt Lake County	120	0.21
Cypress, CA (city) Orange County	99	0.21
Grants Pass, OR (city) Josephine County	49	0.21
Brighton, CO (city) Adams County	43	0.21
Chino, CA (city) San Bernardino County	133	0.20
Laguna Beach, CA (city) Orange County	46	0.20
Arcata, CA (city) Humboldt County	33	0.20
Pacific Grove, CA (city) Monterey County	31	0.20
Novato, CA (city) Marin County	89	0.19
Coral Gables, FL (city) Miami-Dade County	82	0.19
Lompoc, CA (city) Santa Barbara County	80	0.19
McMinnville, OR (city) Yamhill County	50	0.19
Helena, MT (city) Lewis and Clark County	49	0.19
Riverton, UT (city) Salt Lake County	48	0.19
Oak Harbor, WA (city) Island County	38	0.19
Dixon, CA (city) Solano County	31	0.19
Glenvar Heights, FL (cdp) Miami-Dade County	31	0.19
Boulder City, NV (city) Clark County	28	0.19
Tenafly, NJ (borough) Bergen County	26	0.19
Weehawken, NJ (township) Hudson County	26	0.19
Hudson, NH (town) Hillsborough County	41	0.18
Clifton, CO (cdp) Mesa County	31	0.18
Hopkins, MN (city) Hennepin County	30	0.18
Arroyo Grande, CA (city) San Luis Obispo County	29	0.18
Rose Hill, VA (cdp) Fairfax County	27	0.18
Grand Junction, CO (city) Mesa County	70	0.17
Benicia, CA (city) Solano County	45	0.17
Casa Grande, AZ (city) Pinal County	44	0.17
Milford, NH (town) Hillsborough County	23	0.17
Babylon, NY (village) Suffolk County	22	0.17
Kelso, WA (city) Cowlitz County	21	0.17
Rancho Cucamonga, CA (city) San Bernardino County	209	0.16
Chico, CA (city) Butte County	93	0.16
Encinitas, CA (city) San Diego County	92	0.16
Tracy, CA (city) San Joaquin County	90	0.16
Woodland, CA (city) Yolo County	79	0.16
Danville, CA (town) Contra Costa County	66	0.16
Dana Point, CA (city) Orange County	55	0.16
Orangevale, CA (cdp) Sacramento County	44	0.16
Gillette, WY (city) Campbell County	31	0.16
River Ridge, LA (cdp) Jefferson Parish	23	0.16
Solana Beach, CA (city) San Diego County	21	0.16
South Yuba City, CA (cdp) Sutter County	21	0.16
Stanford, CA (cdp) Santa Clara County	21	0.16
Camarillo, CA (city) Ventura County	88	0.15
Woodburn, OR (city) Marion County	31	0.15
Wilton, CT (town) Fairfield County	27	0.15
Montrose, CO (city) Montrose County	19	0.15
Issaquah, WA (city) King County	17	0.15
Oquirrh, UT (cdp) Salt Lake County	16	0.15
Stockton, CA (city) San Joaquin County	333	0.14
San Buenaventura, CA (city) Ventura County	141	0.14
San Mateo, CA (city) San Mateo County	130	0.14
Goleta, CA (cdp) Santa Barbara County	79	0.14
San Rafael, CA (city) Marin County	77	0.14
Pocatello, ID (city) Bannock County	73	0.14
Corvallis, OR (city) Benton County	70	0.14
Kearny, NJ (town) Hudson County	55	0.14
Edmonds, WA (city) Snohomish County	54	0.14
Milwaukie, OR (city) Clackamas County	30	0.14
Goodyear, AZ (city) Maricopa County	27	0.14
Cameron Park, CA (cdp) El Dorado County	20	0.14
Blythe, CA (city) Riverside County	17	0.14
Foothill Ranch, CA (cdp) Orange County	15	0.14
Siloam Springs, AR (city) Benton County	15	0.14
Fernandina Beach, FL (city) Nassau County	14	0.14
Mission Viejo, CA (city) Orange County	121	0.13
San Clemente, CA (city) Orange County	64	0.13
Carmichael, CA (cdp) Sacramento County	63	0.13
Campbell, CA (city) Santa Clara County	49	0.13
San Juan Capistrano, CA (city) Orange County	44	0.13
Highland Park, IL (city) Lake County	40	0.13
Monterey, CA (city) Monterey County	40	0.13
Millcreek, UT (cdp) Salt Lake County	39	0.13
Des Moines, WA (city) King County	37	0.13
Pullman, WA (city) Whitman County	33	0.13
Winter Park, FL (city) Orange County	31	0.13
Mineola, NY (village) Nassau County	25	0.13
Bridgeton, MO (city) Saint Louis County	20	0.13
East Greenbush, NY (town) Rensselaer County	20	0.13
Marco Island, FL (city) Collier County	19	0.13
Enumclaw, WA (city) King County	15	0.13
Lakeland South, WA (cdp) King County	15	0.13
Reading, OH (city) Hamilton County	15	0.13
Hull, MA (cdp) Plymouth County	14	0.13
Santee, CA (city) San Diego County	65	0.12
Martinez, CA (city) Contra Costa County	44	0.12
Prescott, AZ (city) Yavapai County	42	0.12
Fair Oaks, CA (cdp) Sacramento County	33	0.12
Los Gatos, CA (town) Santa Clara County	33	0.12
Columbine, CO (cdp) Jefferson County	30	0.12
Genesee, MI (township) Genesee County	30	0.12

Notes: (cdp) census designated place; Refer to the Explanation of Data in the front of the book for more detailed information.

Belgian

Top 150 Places Sorted by Number

(Based on all places, regardless of population)

Place	Number	%
Green Bay, WI (city) Brown County	10,101	9.87
New York, NY (city) New York City	3,426	0.04
Moline, IL (city) Rock Island County	2,686	6.14
Chicago, IL (city) Cook County	2,366	0.08
Clinton, MI (cdp) Macomb County	2,337	2.44
Los Angeles, CA (city) Los Angeles County	2,151	0.06
Saint Clair Shores, MI (city) Macomb County	2,150	3.41
Bellevue Town, WI (cdp) Brown County	2,053	17.24
Sterling Heights, MI (city) Macomb County	1,931	1.55
Warren, MI (city) Macomb County	1,825	1.32
De Pere, WI (city) Brown County	1,756	8.55
Allouez, WI (village) Brown County	1,652	10.70
Mishawaka, IN (city) Saint Joseph County	1,595	3.41
Shelby, MI (cdp) Macomb County	1,525	2.34
Phoenix, AZ (city) Maricopa County	1,520	0.12
East Moline, IL (city) Rock Island County	1,490	7.32
Rock Island, IL (city) Rock Island County	1,480	3.73
South Bend, IN (city) Saint Joseph County	1,423	1.33
Howard, WI (village) Brown County	1,388	10.25
Ashwaubenon, WI (village) Brown County	1,384	7.83
Macomb, MI (township) Macomb County	1,322	2.62
Davenport, IA (city) Scott County	1,131	1.15
Milwaukee, WI (city) Milwaukee County	1,100	0.18
Suamico, WI (town) Brown County	1,085	12.50
Marshall, MN (city) Lyon County	1,043	8.18
Madison, WI (city) Dane County	1,023	0.49
Roseville, MI (city) Macomb County	1,002	2.08
Seattle, WA (city) King County	994	0.18
Appleton, WI (city) Outagamie County	967	1.38
Houston, TX (city) Harris County	967	0.05
Sturgeon Bay, WI (city) Door County	959	10.12
San Diego, CA (city) San Diego County	951	0.08
Eastpointe, MI (city) Macomb County	852	2.50
Chesterfield, MI (township) Macomb County	844	2.25
Red River, WI (town) Kewaunee County	837	55.76
San Francisco, CA (city) San Francisco County	823	0.11
Kewanee, IL (city) Henry County	805	6.22
Scott, WI (town) Brown County	776	21.63
Luxemburg, WI (village) Kewaunee County	761	40.41
Kansas City, MO (city) Jackson County	759	0.17
Minneapolis, MN (city) Hennepin County	751	0.20
Detroit, MI (city) Wayne County	727	0.08
San Antonio, TX (city) Bexar County	726	0.06
Green Bay, WI (town) Brown County	715	39.74
Troy, MI (city) Oakland County	669	0.83
Shawnee, KS (city) Johnson County	664	1.38
Luxemburg, WI (town) Kewaunee County	656	44.90
Jacksonville, FL (special city) Duval County	645	0.09
Portland, OR (city) Multnomah County	644	0.12
Harrison, MI (cdp) Macomb County	637	2.60
Geneseo, IL (city) Henry County	635	9.68
Grosse Pointe Woods, MI (city) Wayne County	630	3.69
Washington, DC (city) District of Columbia	623	0.11
Omaha, NE (city) Douglas County	614	0.16
Granger, IN (cdp) Saint Joseph County	607	2.15
Rochester Hills, MI (city) Oakland County	603	0.88
Scottsdale, AZ (city) Maricopa County	592	0.29
Indianapolis, IN (special city) Marion County	576	0.07
Hobart, WI (town) Brown County	563	11.12
Algoma, WI (city) Kewaunee County	562	16.76
Superior, WI (city) Douglas County	560	2.05
Denver, CO (city) Denver County	552	0.10
Humboldt, WI (town) Brown County	549	41.81
Brussels, WI (town) Door County	542	47.80
San Jose, CA (city) Santa Clara County	528	0.06
Dallas, TX (city) Dallas County	528	0.04
Austin, TX (city) Travis County	524	0.08
Columbus, OH (city) Franklin County	510	0.07
Washington, MI (township) Macomb County	507	2.65
Union, WI (town) Door County	476	52.48
Silvis, IL (city) Rock Island County	476	6.51
Oshkosh, WI (city) Winnebago County	471	0.75
Philadelphia, PA (city) Philadelphia County	466	0.03
Colorado Springs, CO (city) El Paso County	461	0.13
Livonia, MI (city) Wayne County	460	0.46
Toledo, OH (city) Lucas County	458	0.15
Manitowoc, WI (city) Manitowoc County	456	1.34
Saint Paul, MN (city) Ramsey County	456	0.16
Kewaunee, WI (city) Kewaunee County	449	16.15
Alexandria, LA (city) Rapides Parish	417	0.89
Overland Park, KS (city) Johnson County	417	0.28
Brookhaven, NY (town) Suffolk County	415	0.09
Little Suamico, WI (town) Oconto County	411	10.57
Fraser, MI (city) Macomb County	407	2.66
Mesa, AZ (city) Maricopa County	401	0.10
Tucson, AZ (city) Pima County	398	0.08
Armada, MI (township) Macomb County	395	7.53
Escanaba, MI (city) Delta County	392	2.98
Bettendorf, IA (city) Scott County	392	1.25
Las Vegas, NV (city) Clark County	387	0.08
Lincoln, WI (town) Kewaunee County	383	40.83
Peoria, IL (city) Peoria County	380	0.34
Plano, TX (city) Collin County	376	0.17
Royal Oak, MI (city) Oakland County	364	0.61
Ledgeview, WI (town) Brown County	363	10.70
Eaton, WI (town) Brown County	357	25.25
New Baltimore, MI (city) Macomb County	354	4.78
Casco, WI (town) Kewaunee County	344	30.15
Harper Woods, MI (city) Wayne County	343	2.41
Charlotte, NC (city) Mecklenburg County	343	0.06
Minneota, MN (city) Lyon County	342	23.57
Boston, MA (city) Suffolk County	342	0.06
Atkinson, IL (town) Henry County	340	33.86
Ann Arbor, MI (city) Washtenaw County	340	0.30
Cedar Rapids, IA (city) Linn County	340	0.28
Marquette, MI (city) Marquette County	338	1.72
Mount Clemens, MI (city) Macomb County	337	1.95
Albuquerque, NM (city) Bernalillo County	337	0.08
Virginia Beach, VA (independent city) Virginia Beach city	332	0.08
Sioux Falls, SD (city) Minnehaha County	331	0.27
Chandler, AZ (city) Maricopa County	326	0.18
Nasewaupee, WI (town) Door County	325	17.58
Rockford, IL (city) Winnebago County	325	0.22
Orion, MI (township) Oakland County	323	0.96
Hempstead, NY (town) Nassau County	321	0.04
Billings, MT (city) Yellowstone County	316	0.35
Westland, MI (city) Wayne County	315	0.36
Irondequoit, NY (cdp) Monroe County	306	0.58
Bruce, MI (township) Macomb County	304	3.75
Marinette, WI (city) Marinette County	302	2.58
Des Moines, IA (city) Polk County	301	0.15
Huntington Beach, CA (city) Orange County	297	0.16
Clay, MI (township) Saint Clair County	295	3.05
Annawan, IL (town) Henry County	290	33.56
Gladstone, MI (city) Delta County	290	5.75
Longmont, CO (city) Boulder County	290	0.41
Grand Chute, WI (town) Outagamie County	287	1.57
Bakersfield, CA (city) Kern County	287	0.12
Forestville, WI (town) Door County	286	26.43
Oconto, WI (city) Oconto County	285	6.10
Canton, MI (cdp) Wayne County	274	0.36
Greece, NY (town) Monroe County	273	0.29
Anaheim, CA (city) Orange County	272	0.08
Kaukauna, WI (city) Outagamie County	270	2.08
Aurora, IL (city) Kane County	270	0.19
Olathe, KS (city) Johnson County	269	0.29
Saint Petersburg, FL (city) Pinellas County	269	0.11
Casco, WI (village) Kewaunee County	268	46.37
Novi, MI (city) Oakland County	265	0.56
Waterford, MI (cdp) Oakland County	262	0.36
Grand Rapids, MI (city) Kent County	262	0.13
Montpelier, WI (town) Kewaunee County	260	21.21
Colona, IL (city) Henry County	260	5.08
Kansas City, KS (city) Wyandotte County	259	0.18
Oyster Bay, NY (town) Nassau County	259	0.09
Sevastopol, WI (town) Door County	258	9.62
Wauwatosa, WI (city) Milwaukee County	257	0.54
Waukesha, WI (city) Waukesha County	257	0.40
Coal Valley, IL (village) Rock Island County	256	7.06
Spokane, WA (city) Spokane County	256	0.13

Notes: (cdp) census designated place; Refer to the Explanation of Data in the front of the book for more detailed information.

Belgian

Top 150 Places Sorted by Percent

(Based on all places, regardless of population)

Place	Number	%
Red River, WI (town) Kewaunee County	837	55.76
Union, WI (town) Door County	476	52.48
Buels, VT (gore) Chittenden County	3	50.00
Brussels, WI (town) Door County	542	47.80
Grandview, MN (township) Lyon County	146	47.40
Casco, WI (village) Kewaunee County	268	46.37
Luxemburg, WI (town) Kewaunee County	656	44.90
Humboldt, WI (town) Brown County	549	41.81
Lincoln, WI (town) Kewaunee County	383	40.83
Luxemburg, WI (village) Kewaunee County	761	40.41
Green Bay, WI (town) Brown County	715	39.74
Eidsvold, MN (township) Lyon County	90	38.14
Westerheim, MN (township) Lyon County	109	37.33
Atkinson, IL (town) Henry County	340	33.86
Annawan, IL (town) Henry County	290	33.56
Pointe Aux Barques, MI (township) Huron County	4	33.33
Nordland, MN (township) Lyon County	88	31.43
Casco, WI (town) Kewaunee County	344	30.15
Swede Prairie, MN (township) Yellow Medicine County	49	28.82
Stanley, MN (township) Lyon County	78	28.16
Ghent, MN (city) Lyon County	84	27.63
Forestville, WI (town) Door County	286	26.43
Clifton, MN (township) Lyon County	73	26.07
Vallers, MN (township) Lyon County	63	25.30
Eaton, WI (town) Brown County	357	25.25
Burton, MN (township) Yellow Medicine County	42	23.73
Sodus, MN (township) Lyon County	62	23.66
Minneota, MN (city) Lyon County	342	23.57
Lake Marshall, MN (township) Lyon County	117	21.99
Scott, WI (town) Brown County	776	21.63
Fairview, MN (township) Lyon County	98	21.35
Ahnapee, WI (town) Kewaunee County	219	21.30
Mineral, IL (village) Bureau County	58	21.25
Montpelier, WI (town) Kewaunee County	260	21.21
Gardner, WI (town) Door County	247	21.11
Taunton, MN (city) Lyon County	34	19.43
Saint Leo, MN (city) Yellow Medicine County	20	19.05
Normania, MN (township) Yellow Medicine County	34	18.78
Forestville, WI (village) Door County	81	18.62
Lynd, MN (township) Lyon County	90	18.60
Beaver, IA (city) Boone County	10	18.18
Lucas, MN (township) Lyon County	45	17.79
Nasewaupee, WI (town) Door County	325	17.58
Bellevue Town, WI (cdp) Brown County	2,053	17.24
Alta Vista, MN (township) Lincoln County	33	17.19
Algoma, WI (city) Kewaunee County	562	16.76
Westline, MN (township) Redwood County	36	16.74
Island Lake, MN (township) Lyon County	36	16.67
Brandt, SD (town) Deuel County	14	16.47
Kewaunee, WI (city) Kewaunee County	449	16.15
Limestone, MN (township) Lincoln County	23	15.86
Guernsey, IA (city) Poweshiek County	8	15.38
Lone Elm, KS (city) Anderson County	2	15.38
Monroe, MN (township) Lyon County	39	15.06
Clay Banks, WI (town) Door County	57	14.92
Pierce, WI (town) Kewaunee County	130	14.84
West Kewaunee, WI (town) Kewaunee County	202	14.79
Gales, MN (township) Redwood County	24	14.04
Glenmore, WI (town) Brown County	163	13.92
Ash Lake, MN (township) Lincoln County	25	13.81
Wergeland, MN (township) Yellow Medicine County	26	13.54
Carlton, WI (town) Kewaunee County	133	13.05
Suamico, WI (town) Brown County	1,085	12.50
Shaniko, OR (city) Wasco County	3	12.50
New Denmark, WI (town) Brown County	175	12.03
Franklin, WI (town) Kewaunee County	124	11.97
Deer Grove, IL (village) Whiteside County	6	11.32
Hobart, WI (town) Brown County	563	11.12
Vesta, MN (township) Redwood County	22	11.06
West Union, MN (city) Todd County	10	10.99
Gourley, MI (township) Menominee County	47	10.96
Doty, WI (town) Oconto County	27	10.89
Florida, MN (township) Yellow Medicine County	18	10.84
Underwood, MN (township) Redwood County	23	10.80
Allouez, WI (village) Brown County	1,652	10.70

Place	Number	%
Ledgeview, WI (town) Brown County	363	10.70
Lyons, MN (township) Lyon County	23	10.65
Rose Dell, MN (township) Rock County	22	10.58
Little Suamico, WI (town) Oconto County	411	10.57
Oconto, WI (town) Oconto County	135	10.56
Johnsonville, MN (township) Redwood County	15	10.56
Knik River, AK (cdp) Matanuska-Susitna Borough	64	10.39
Sturgeon Bay, WI (town) Door County	89	10.37
Coon Creek, MN (township) Lyon County	32	10.32
Howard, WI (village) Brown County	1,388	10.25
Lawrence, WI (town) Brown County	156	10.20
Cape Meares, OR (cdp) Tillamook County	5	10.20
Sturgeon Bay, WI (city) Door County	959	10.12
Milroy, MN (city) Redwood County	26	10.04
Green Bay, WI (city) Brown County	10,101	9.87
Sheridan, MN (township) Redwood County	27	9.82
Victor, IA (city) Iowa County	96	9.81
Geneseo, IL (city) Henry County	635	9.68
Lena, WI (town) Oconto County	82	9.67
Amiret, MN (township) Lyon County	22	9.65
Sevastopol, WI (town) Door County	258	9.62
Wrightstown, WI (town) Brown County	196	9.57
Ruthton, MN (city) Pipestone County	29	9.48
Sherrard, IL (village) Mercer County	65	9.45
Cottonwood, MN (city) Lyon County	106	9.25
Rockland, WI (town) Brown County	141	9.22
Sandnes, MN (township) Yellow Medicine County	19	9.22
Valier, MT (town) Pondera County	47	9.20
Hooppole, IL (village) Henry County	15	9.20
Abrams, WI (town) Oconto County	166	9.19
Holly, MN (township) Murray County	17	9.19
Port Costa, CA (cdp) Contra Costa County	22	9.09
Hodges, MN (township) Stevens County	24	9.06
Southbrook, MN (township) Cottonwood County	12	9.02
Wells, MI (township) Marquette County	24	8.82
De Pere, WI (city) Brown County	1,756	8.55
Breen, MI (township) Dickinson County	40	8.55
Sheffield, IL (village) Bureau County	79	8.49
Stiles, WI (town) Oconto County	124	8.48
Spruce, WI (town) Oconto County	66	8.37
Calamus, IA (city) Clinton County	34	8.25
Tyro, MN (township) Yellow Medicine County	16	8.25
Apple River, IL (village) Jo Daviess County	33	8.21
Marshall, MN (city) Lyon County	1,043	8.18
Waucedah, MI (township) Dickinson County	65	8.10
Custer, MN (township) Lyon County	16	8.08
Cornell, MI (township) Delta County	44	7.99
Reynolds, IL (village) Rock Island County	40	7.98
Lena, WI (village) Oconto County	37	7.91
Ashwaubenon, WI (village) Brown County	1,384	7.83
Maribel, WI (village) Manitowoc County	19	7.82
Manfred, MN (township) Lac qui Parle County	8	7.62
Brampton, MI (township) Delta County	83	7.61
Marble, MN (township) Lincoln County	15	7.61
Armada, MI (township) Macomb County	395	7.53
Wrightstown, WI (village) Brown County	142	7.51
Pittsfield, WI (town) Brown County	179	7.43
Rapids City, IL (village) Rock Island County	67	7.42
Niagara, WI (town) Marinette County	70	7.36
Prairie Rose, ND (city) Cass County	5	7.35
East Moline, IL (city) Rock Island County	1,490	7.32
Kent, IA (city) Union County	3	7.32
Popple River, WI (town) Forest County	4	7.27
Norman, MN (township) Yellow Medicine County	21	7.22
Springdale, MN (township) Redwood County	14	7.22
Russell, MN (city) Lyon County	27	7.12
Denmark, WI (village) Brown County	141	7.10
Coal Valley, IL (village) Rock Island County	256	7.06
Midway, PA (borough) Washington County	69	7.03
Lynd, MN (city) Lyon County	22	6.94
New Albany, KS (city) Wilson County	5	6.94
Pensaukee, WI (town) Oconto County	79	6.88
Chase, WI (town) Oconto County	142	6.83
Cleveland, IL (village) Henry County	17	6.77
Omro, MN (township) Yellow Medicine County	13	6.74

Notes: (cdp) census designated place; Refer to the Explanation of Data in the front of the book for more detailed information.

Belgian

Top 150 Places Sorted by Percent

(Based on places with populations of 10,000 or more)

Place	Number	%
Bellevue Town, WI (cdp) Brown County	2,053	17.24
Allouez, WI (village) Brown County	1,652	10.70
Howard, WI (village) Brown County	1,388	10.25
Green Bay, WI (city) Brown County	10,101	9.87
De Pere, WI (city) Brown County	1,756	8.55
Marshall, MN (city) Lyon County	1,043	8.18
Ashwaubenon, WI (village) Brown County	1,384	7.83
East Moline, IL (city) Rock Island County	1,490	7.32
Kewanee, IL (city) Henry County	805	6.22
Moline, IL (city) Rock Island County	2,686	6.14
Rock Island, IL (city) Rock Island County	1,480	3.73
Grosse Pointe Woods, MI (city) Wayne County	630	3.69
Saint Clair Shores, MI (city) Macomb County	2,150	3.41
Mishawaka, IN (city) Saint Joseph County	1,595	3.41
Escanaba, MI (city) Delta County	392	2.98
Fraser, MI (city) Macomb County	407	2.66
Washington, MI (township) Macomb County	507	2.65
Macomb, MI (township) Macomb County	1,322	2.62
Harrison, MI (cdp) Macomb County	637	2.60
Marinette, WI (city) Marinette County	302	2.58
Eastpointe, MI (city) Macomb County	852	2.50
Clinton, MI (cdp) Macomb County	2,337	2.44
Harper Woods, MI (city) Wayne County	343	2.41
Shelby, MI (cdp) Macomb County	1,525	2.34
Chesterfield, MI (township) Macomb County	844	2.25
Granger, IN (cdp) Saint Joseph County	607	2.15
Roseville, MI (city) Macomb County	1,002	2.08
Kaukauna, WI (city) Outagamie County	270	2.08
Superior, WI (city) Douglas County	560	2.05
Mount Clemens, MI (city) Macomb County	337	1.95
Two Rivers, WI (city) Manitowoc County	237	1.87
Little Chute, WI (village) Outagamie County	192	1.84
Marquette, MI (city) Marquette County	338	1.72
Grand Chute, WI (town) Outagamie County	287	1.57
Rochester, MI (city) Oakland County	163	1.56
Sterling Heights, MI (city) Macomb County	1,931	1.55
Menasha, WI (town) Winnebago County	231	1.45
Appleton, WI (city) Outagamie County	967	1.38
Shawnee, KS (city) Johnson County	664	1.38
Manitowoc, WI (city) Manitowoc County	456	1.34
South Fayette, PA (township) Allegheny County	164	1.34
South Bend, IN (city) Saint Joseph County	1,423	1.33
Warren, MI (city) Macomb County	1,825	1.32
Bettendorf, IA (city) Scott County	392	1.25
North Fayette, PA (township) Allegheny County	148	1.21
Davenport, IA (city) Scott County	1,131	1.15
Geneva, IL (city) Kane County	222	1.14
Grosse Pointe Park, MI (city) Wayne County	141	1.13
Monroe charter, MI (township) Monroe County	147	1.10
New Kensington, PA (city) Westmoreland County	151	1.03
Menasha, WI (city) Winnebago County	164	1.00
Oxford charter, MI (township) Oakland County	160	1.00
Orion, MI (township) Oakland County	323	0.96
Harrison Township, PA (cdp) Allegheny County	101	0.92
Fort Gratiot, MI (township) Saint Clair County	98	0.92
Oakland charter, MI (township) Oakland County	119	0.91
Monroe, MI (city) Monroe County	201	0.90
Alexandria, LA (city) Rapides Parish	417	0.89
Frenchtown, MI (township) Monroe County	184	0.89
Rochester Hills, MI (city) Oakland County	603	0.88
Neenah, WI (city) Winnebago County	211	0.87
Brighton, MI (township) Livingston County	154	0.87
Menomonie, WI (city) Dunn County	129	0.86
Troy, MI (city) Oakland County	669	0.83
Farragut, TN (town) Knox County	149	0.83
Saint Charles, IL (city) Kane County	229	0.82
Oswego, IL (village) Kendall County	109	0.82
Comstock Park, MI (cdp) Kent County	87	0.82
Summit, MI (township) Jackson County	175	0.81
Brandon, MI (township) Oakland County	120	0.81
Springfield, MI (township) Oakland County	108	0.81
Sault Sainte Marie, MI (city) Chippewa County	127	0.77
Milford, MI (township) Oakland County	116	0.76
Oshkosh, WI (city) Winnebago County	471	0.75
Winnetka, IL (village) Cook County	92	0.74
North Mankato, MN (city) Nicollet County	86	0.73
Grand Haven, MI (township) Ottawa County	97	0.72
Grand Haven, MI (city) Ottawa County	80	0.72
Bedford, MI (township) Monroe County	203	0.71
Mount Pleasant, WI (town) Racine County	164	0.71
Southfield, MI (township) Oakland County	103	0.71
Los Alamos, NM (cdp) Los Alamos County	85	0.71
Berkley, MI (city) Oakland County	108	0.70
South Lyon, MI (city) Oakland County	70	0.70
Rolling Meadows, IL (city) Cook County	170	0.69
Germantown, WI (village) Washington County	125	0.69
Wixom, MI (city) Oakland County	91	0.69
Okemos, MI (cdp) Ingham County	155	0.68
Fenton, MI (township) Genesee County	86	0.67
Pleasant Prairie, WI (village) Kenosha County	105	0.66
South Venice, FL (cdp) Sarasota County	89	0.66
Payson, AZ (town) Gila County	90	0.64
Shorewood, WI (village) Milwaukee County	87	0.63
Niles, MI (township) Berrien County	84	0.63
Windham, NH (town) Rockingham County	68	0.63
Alpine, MI (township) Kent County	87	0.62
Upper, NJ (township) Cape May County	75	0.62
Royal Oak, MI (city) Oakland County	364	0.61
South Miami, FL (city) Miami-Dade County	67	0.61
Cypress Lake, FL (cdp) Lee County	73	0.60
Weston, WI (village) Marathon County	73	0.60
Pewaukee, WI (city) Waukesha County	71	0.60
Brookings, SD (city) Brookings County	110	0.59
Farmington, MI (city) Oakland County	61	0.59
Irondequoit, NY (cdp) Monroe County	306	0.58
Ankeny, IA (city) Polk County	156	0.58
Trenton, MI (city) Wayne County	114	0.58
West Lake Stevens, WA (cdp) Snohomish County	103	0.58
Bloomfield, MI (township) Oakland County	247	0.57
Midland, MI (city) Midland County	239	0.57
Port Huron, MI (city) Saint Clair County	186	0.57
Atlantic Beach, FL (city) Duval County	77	0.57
Hasbrouck Heights, NJ (borough) Bergen County	67	0.57
Novi, MI (city) Oakland County	265	0.56
Meridian charter, MI (township) Ingham County	220	0.56
White Lake, MI (township) Oakland County	159	0.56
Watertown, SD (city) Codington County	113	0.56
Lenexa, KS (city) Johnson County	220	0.55
Lake Zurich, IL (village) Lake County	99	0.55
Altoona, IA (city) Polk County	56	0.55
Wauwatosa, WI (city) Milwaukee County	257	0.54
Urbandale, IA (city) Polk County	157	0.54
Mount Pleasant, MI (city) Isabella County	141	0.54
Northville, MI (township) Wayne County	114	0.54
Hinsdale, IL (village) Du Page County	95	0.54
River Falls, WI (city) Pierce County	67	0.53
Haslett, MI (cdp) Ingham County	60	0.53
Beverly Hills, MI (village) Oakland County	55	0.53
Port Saint John, FL (cdp) Brevard County	62	0.52
Streamwood, IL (village) Cook County	189	0.51
Delta charter, MI (township) Eaton County	153	0.51
Plymouth Township, MI (cdp) Wayne County	140	0.51
Lake Forest, IL (city) Lake County	103	0.51
Scio, MI (township) Washtenaw County	80	0.51
Bixby, OK (city) Tulsa County	67	0.51
Lower Burrell, PA (city) Westmoreland County	65	0.51
Hartford, WI (city) Washington County	56	0.51
Zephyrhills, FL (city) Pasco County	55	0.51
East Lansing, MI (city) Ingham County	234	0.50
Madison Heights, MI (city) Oakland County	154	0.50
Guilford, CT (town) New Haven County	107	0.50
Stoughton, WI (city) Dane County	62	0.50
Pelham, NY (town) Westchester County	59	0.50
Jensen Beach, FL (cdp) Martin County	56	0.50
Madison, WI (city) Dane County	1,023	0.49
Brown Deer, WI (village) Milwaukee County	60	0.49
River Forest, IL (village) Cook County	57	0.49
Spencer, IA (city) Clay County	56	0.49
Commerce, MI (township) Oakland County	168	0.48
Independence, MI (township) Oakland County	157	0.48

Notes: (cdp) census designated place; Refer to the Explanation of Data in the front of the book for more detailed information.

Brazilian

Top 150 Places Sorted by Number

(Based on all places, regardless of population)

Place	Number	%
New York, NY (city) New York City	12,176	0.15
Newark, NJ (city) Essex County	5,805	2.12
Danbury, CT (city) Fairfield County	4,133	5.52
Somerville, MA (city) Middlesex County	3,870	4.99
Boston, MA (city) Suffolk County	3,594	0.61
Framingham, MA (cdp) Middlesex County	3,500	5.23
Los Angeles, CA (city) Los Angeles County	2,758	0.07
Deerfield Beach, FL (city) Broward County	2,307	3.56
Miami Beach, FL (city) Miami-Dade County	1,949	2.21
Lowell, MA (city) Middlesex County	1,820	1.73
Kearny, NJ (town) Hudson County	1,629	4.02
Bridgeport, CT (city) Fairfield County	1,611	1.15
San Diego, CA (city) San Diego County	1,449	0.12
Marlborough, MA (city) Middlesex County	1,388	3.83
Orlando, FL (city) Orange County	1,355	0.73
Elizabeth, NJ (city) Union County	1,349	1.12
Everett, MA (city) Middlesex County	1,278	3.36
San Francisco, CA (city) San Francisco County	1,112	0.14
Worcester, MA (city) Worcester County	1,099	0.64
Philadelphia, PA (city) Philadelphia County	1,083	0.07
Malden, MA (city) Middlesex County	1,027	1.82
Mount Vernon, NY (city) Westchester County	991	1.45
Houston, TX (city) Harris County	980	0.05
Barnstable Town, MA (city) Barnstable County	930	1.94
Pompano Beach, FL (city) Broward County	919	1.17
Fort Lauderdale, FL (city) Broward County	917	0.60
Coral Springs, FL (city) Broward County	901	0.77
Long Branch, NJ (city) Monmouth County	890	2.84
Revere, MA (city) Suffolk County	846	1.79
Chicago, IL (city) Cook County	833	0.03
Miami, FL (city) Miami-Dade County	802	0.22
Boca Raton, FL (city) Palm Beach County	788	1.04
Pembroke Pines, FL (city) Broward County	751	0.55
Washington, DC (city) District of Columbia	734	0.13
Hollywood, FL (city) Broward County	731	0.52
Harrison, NJ (town) Hudson County	726	5.03
Sandy Springs, GA (cdp) Fulton County	720	0.84
Oakland Park, FL (city) Broward County	704	2.26
Cambridge, MA (city) Middlesex County	694	0.68
Kendall, FL (cdp) Miami-Dade County	680	0.90
Sunrise, FL (city) Broward County	617	0.72
Naugatuck, CT (borough) New Haven County	595	1.92
Fall River, MA (city) Bristol County	595	0.65
Coconut Creek, FL (city) Broward County	589	1.36
Hempstead, NY (town) Nassau County	581	0.08
Daly City, CA (city) San Mateo County	541	0.52
Doral, FL (cdp) Miami-Dade County	535	2.61
Medford, MA (city) Middlesex County	520	0.93
Cliffside Park, NJ (borough) Bergen County	503	2.19
Milford, MA (town) Worcester County	495	1.85
Hudson, MA (town) Middlesex County	487	2.69
Weston, FL (city) Broward County	471	0.96
Loch Lomond, FL (cdp) Broward County	469	14.12
Hillside, NJ (cdp) Union County	469	2.16
Aventura, FL (city) Miami-Dade County	463	1.83
Aspen Hill, MD (cdp) Montgomery County	463	0.92
Dallas, TX (city) Dallas County	451	0.04
Brockton, MA (city) Plymouth County	441	0.47
Austin, TX (city) Travis County	440	0.07
Waterbury, CT (city) New Haven County	420	0.39
North Bay Village, FL (city) Miami-Dade County	419	6.22
Chelsea, MA (city) Suffolk County	415	1.18
Stamford, CT (city) Fairfield County	395	0.34
North Bergen, NJ (township) Hudson County	384	0.66
New Rochelle, NY (city) Westchester County	384	0.53
New Bedford, MA (city) Bristol County	377	0.40
South River, NJ (borough) Middlesex County	376	2.45
Quincy, MA (city) Norfolk County	375	0.43
Tampa, FL (city) Hillsborough County	366	0.12
Seattle, WA (city) King County	364	0.06
The Crossings, FL (cdp) Miami-Dade County	362	1.54
San Jose, CA (city) Santa Clara County	356	0.04
Yarmouth, MA (town) Barnstable County	352	1.42
Plantation, FL (city) Broward County	349	0.42
Las Vegas, NV (city) Clark County	343	0.07
Port Chester, NY (village) Westchester County	342	1.23
Rye, NY (town) Westchester County	342	0.78
Sandalfoot Cove, FL (cdp) Palm Beach County	340	2.05
Phoenix, AZ (city) Maricopa County	337	0.03
North Miami Beach, FL (city) Miami-Dade County	335	0.82
Union, NJ (cdp) Union County	331	0.61
North Hempstead, NY (town) Nassau County	316	0.14
Nashua, NH (city) Hillsborough County	315	0.36
Davie, FL (town) Broward County	305	0.40
Oakland, CA (city) Alameda County	301	0.08
Alpharetta, GA (city) Fulton County	298	0.86
East Providence, RI (city) Providence County	292	0.60
Kissimmee, FL (city) Osceola County	291	0.61
Leominster, MA (city) Worcester County	289	0.70
Fountainbleau, FL (cdp) Miami-Dade County	286	0.48
San Rafael, CA (city) Marin County	285	0.51
North Lauderdale, FL (city) Broward County	283	0.88
North Miami, FL (city) Miami-Dade County	276	0.46
Columbus, OH (city) Franklin County	272	0.04
Peabody, MA (city) Essex County	270	0.56
Ojus, FL (cdp) Miami-Dade County	268	1.61
Fairview, NJ (borough) Bergen County	261	1.97
Charlotte, NC (city) Mecklenburg County	260	0.05
Bethesda, MD (cdp) Montgomery County	259	0.47
Margate, FL (city) Broward County	258	0.48
Mamaroneck, NY (town) Westchester County	257	0.89
Jersey City, NJ (city) Hudson County	256	0.11
Weymouth, MA (cdp) Norfolk County	253	0.47
Oyster Bay, NY (town) Nassau County	253	0.09
Redondo Beach, CA (city) Los Angeles County	249	0.39
West Yarmouth, MA (cdp) Barnstable County	246	3.89
Wheaton-Glenmont, MD (cdp) Montgomery County	244	0.42
Miramar, FL (city) Broward County	242	0.33
Greenwich, CT (town) Fairfield County	239	0.39
Bonnie Lock-Woodsetter North, FL (cdp) Broward County	238	5.52
Belleville, NJ (cdp) Essex County	236	0.66
Arlington, VA (cdp) Arlington County	236	0.12
Natick, MA (town) Middlesex County	229	0.71
Portland, OR (city) Multnomah County	227	0.04
Ann Arbor, MI (city) Washtenaw County	226	0.20
Sunny Isles Beach, FL (city) Miami-Dade County	222	1.45
Rockville, MD (city) Montgomery County	221	0.47
Delran, NJ (township) Burlington County	217	1.40
Torrance, CA (city) Los Angeles County	216	0.16
Kendale Lakes, FL (cdp) Miami-Dade County	215	0.38
Riverside, CA (city) Riverside County	212	0.08
Greenburgh, NY (town) Westchester County	210	0.24
Plano, TX (city) Collin County	209	0.09
Indianapolis, IN (special city) Marion County	208	0.03
Ashland, MA (town) Middlesex County	207	1.41
Woburn, MA (city) Middlesex County	207	0.56
The Hammocks, FL (cdp) Miami-Dade County	206	0.43
Shrewsbury, MA (town) Worcester County	203	0.64
Coral Gables, FL (city) Miami-Dade County	198	0.47
Hartford, CT (city) Hartford County	197	0.16
Irvine, CA (city) Orange County	197	0.14
Winthrop, MA (cdp) Suffolk County	196	1.07
Norwalk, CT (city) Fairfield County	195	0.24
Grand Prairie, TX (city) Dallas County	195	0.15
Brookhaven, NY (town) Suffolk County	195	0.04
Berkeley, CA (city) Alameda County	191	0.19
Doctor Phillips, FL (cdp) Orange County	189	1.96
North Bethesda, MD (cdp) Montgomery County	187	0.48
Bethel, CT (town) Fairfield County	185	1.02
Long Beach, CA (city) Los Angeles County	185	0.04
Honolulu, HI (cdp) Honolulu County	181	0.05
Key Biscayne, FL (village) Miami-Dade County	180	1.72
Tucson, AZ (city) Pima County	180	0.04
Pompano Beach Highlands, FL (cdp) Broward County	178	2.74
Brookline, MA (cdp) Norfolk County	177	0.31
Pinecrest, FL (village) Miami-Dade County	175	0.91
Richmond, CA (city) Contra Costa County	175	0.18
West Palm Beach, FL (city) Palm Beach County	174	0.21
Gainesville, FL (city) Alachua County	172	0.18
Denver, CO (city) Denver County	172	0.03

Notes: (cdp) census designated place; Refer to the Explanation of Data in the front of the book for more detailed information.

Brazilian

Top 150 Places Sorted by Percent

(Based on all places, regardless of population)

Place	Number	%
Loch Lomond, FL (cdp) Broward County	469	14.12
Indian Creek, FL (village) Miami-Dade County	4	11.76
East Newark, NJ (borough) Hudson County	154	6.48
Alamo, IN (town) Montgomery County	7	6.48
North Bay Village, FL (city) Miami-Dade County	419	6.22
Coleta, IL (village) Whiteside County	9	5.63
Danbury, CT (city) Fairfield County	4,133	5.52
Bonnie Lock-Woodsetter North, FL (cdp) Broward County	238	5.52
Granville South, OH (cdp) Licking County	64	5.26
Framingham, MA (cdp) Middlesex County	3,500	5.23
Harrison, NJ (town) Hudson County	726	5.03
Somerville, MA (city) Middlesex County	3,870	4.99
Vineyard Haven, MA (cdp) Dukes County	96	4.99
Kawela Bay, HI (cdp) Honolulu County	20	4.66
Kearny, NJ (town) Hudson County	1,629	4.02
West Yarmouth, MA (cdp) Barnstable County	246	3.89
Marlborough, MA (city) Middlesex County	1,388	3.83
Deerfield Beach, FL (city) Broward County	2,307	3.56
Ridgeway, OH (village) Hardin County	12	3.45
Everett, MA (city) Middlesex County	1,278	3.36
Harbor Hills, NY (cdp) Nassau County	19	3.32
Edgartown, MA (town) Dukes County	125	3.31
Kirkwood, CA (cdp) Alpine County	3	3.13
Oak Bluffs, MA (town) Dukes County	113	3.04
Long Branch, NJ (city) Monmouth County	890	2.84
Tisbury, MA (town) Dukes County	106	2.82
Pompano Beach Highlands, FL (cdp) Broward County	178	2.74
Hudson, MA (town) Middlesex County	487	2.69
Doral, FL (cdp) Miami-Dade County	535	2.61
Palm Aire, FL (cdp) Broward County	34	2.60
Country Estates, FL (cdp) Broward County	48	2.58
South River, NJ (borough) Middlesex County	376	2.45
Forest Home, NY (cdp) Tompkins County	24	2.36
Kendall Green, FL (cdp) Broward County	73	2.32
Cottonwood, CO (cdp) Douglas County	23	2.31
Oakland Park, FL (city) Broward County	704	2.26
Scotts Corners, NY (cdp) Westchester County	13	2.26
Miami Beach, FL (city) Miami-Dade County	1,949	2.21
Cliffside Park, NJ (borough) Bergen County	503	2.19
Schall Circle, FL (cdp) Palm Beach County	24	2.17
Hillside, NJ (cdp) Union County	469	2.16
Uehling, NE (village) Dodge County	6	2.13
Newark, NJ (city) Essex County	5,805	2.12
Sandalfoot Cove, FL (cdp) Palm Beach County	340	2.05
Westbrook Center, CT (cdp) Middlesex County	45	2.05
Sea Ranch Lakes, FL (village) Broward County	28	2.03
Weston, ME (town) Aroostook County	4	2.03
Juno Ridge, FL (cdp) Palm Beach County	15	1.99
Fairview, NJ (borough) Bergen County	261	1.97
Doctor Phillips, FL (cdp) Orange County	189	1.96
Barnstable Town, MA (city) Barnstable County	930	1.94
Naugatuck, CT (borough) New Haven County	595	1.92
Saint Leo, MN (city) Yellow Medicine County	2	1.90
Milford, MA (town) Worcester County	495	1.85
Oakland Acres, IA (city) Jasper County	3	1.84
Aventura, FL (city) Miami-Dade County	463	1.83
Malden, MA (city) Middlesex County	1,027	1.82
Riverside, NJ (township) Burlington County	144	1.82
Surfside, FL (town) Miami-Dade County	93	1.81
Revere, MA (city) Suffolk County	846	1.79
Lowell, MA (city) Middlesex County	1,820	1.73
Key Biscayne, FL (village) Miami-Dade County	180	1.72
Zeeland, ND (city) McIntosh County	2	1.71
Avondale Estates, GA (city) De Kalb County	43	1.68
Dennis Port, MA (cdp) Barnstable County	60	1.67
South Lancaster, MA (cdp) Worcester County	29	1.63
Ojus, FL (cdp) Miami-Dade County	268	1.61
Fountain, MI (village) Mason County	3	1.60
The Crossings, FL (cdp) Miami-Dade County	362	1.54
Keene, TX (city) Johnson County	75	1.54
Bergman, AR (town) Boone County	6	1.49
Rolling Oaks, FL (cdp) Broward County	21	1.48
Del Rio, CA (cdp) Stanislaus County	17	1.47
La Grange, WY (town) Goshen County	5	1.46
Mount Vernon, NY (city) Westchester County	991	1.45
Sunny Isles Beach, FL (city) Miami-Dade County	222	1.45
Great River, NY (cdp) Suffolk County	22	1.44
Yarmouth, MA (town) Barnstable County	352	1.42
Friendship, AR (town) Hot Spring County	3	1.42
Ashland, MA (town) Middlesex County	207	1.41
Grand View-on-Hudson, NY (village) Rockland County	4	1.41
Delran, NJ (township) Burlington County	217	1.40
Big Pine Key, FL (cdp) Monroe County	70	1.39
Corte Madera, CA (town) Marin County	126	1.38
Brookmont, MD (cdp) Montgomery County	43	1.38
Coconut Creek, FL (city) Broward County	589	1.36
Laymantown, VA (cdp) Botetourt County	25	1.32
Taylorsville, GA (town) Bartow County	3	1.29
Belle Isle, FL (city) Orange County	74	1.28
Strawberry, CA (cdp) Marin County	68	1.27
Ivesdale, IL (village) Champaign County	4	1.26
Holden Heights, FL (cdp) Orange County	48	1.24
Chesterfield, IL (village) Macoupin County	3	1.24
Port Chester, NY (village) Westchester County	342	1.23
Trenton, FL (city) Gilchrist County	19	1.23
Boca Pointe, FL (cdp) Palm Beach County	40	1.21
Clermont, GA (town) Hall County	5	1.21
Chelsea, MA (city) Suffolk County	415	1.18
Halaula, HI (cdp) Hawaii County	6	1.18
Pompano Beach, FL (city) Broward County	919	1.17
Shinnecock Hills, NY (cdp) Suffolk County	21	1.17
Bridgeport, CT (city) Fairfield County	1,611	1.15
Heritage Hills, NY (cdp) Westchester County	44	1.15
Barker Heights, NC (cdp) Henderson County	14	1.14
Sibley, MN (township) Sibley County	4	1.14
Nunez, GA (town) Emanuel County	2	1.14
Elizabeth, NJ (city) Union County	1,349	1.12
Roseland, NJ (borough) Essex County	59	1.11
Maalaea, HI (cdp) Maui County	5	1.10
Michiana, MI (village) Berrien County	2	1.09
Winthrop, MA (cdp) Suffolk County	196	1.07
Collier Manor-Cresthaven, FL (cdp) Broward County	84	1.06
North Sea, NY (cdp) Suffolk County	48	1.05
Saybrook Manor, CT (cdp) Middlesex County	12	1.05
Harwood, MO (village) Vernon County	1	1.05
Boca Raton, FL (city) Palm Beach County	788	1.04
Friendship Village, MD (cdp) Montgomery County	46	1.04
Nyack, NY (village) Rockland County	69	1.03
Bethel, CT (town) Fairfield County	185	1.02
North Catasauqua, PA (borough) Northampton County	28	1.00
Riverview, DE (cdp) Kent County	15	0.99
Larchmont, NY (village) Westchester County	63	0.97
Pebble Creek, FL (cdp) Hillsborough County	47	0.97
Bath, PA (borough) Northampton County	26	0.97
Navy Yard City, WA (cdp) Kitsap County	26	0.97
Weston, FL (city) Broward County	471	0.96
Fairfield, NJ (cdp) Essex County	68	0.96
Empire, CA (cdp) Stanislaus County	36	0.95
Mission Canyon, CA (cdp) Santa Barbara County	24	0.95
Berwyn Heights, MD (town) Prince George's County	28	0.94
Melville, RI (cdp) Newport County	21	0.94
Medford, MA (city) Middlesex County	520	0.93
South Fallsburg, NY (cdp) Sullivan County	21	0.93
Chatham, MI (village) Alger County	2	0.93
Aspen Hill, MD (cdp) Montgomery County	463	0.92
Ives Estates, FL (cdp) Miami-Dade County	161	0.92
Madisonville, LA (town) Saint Tammany Parish	6	0.92
Pinecrest, FL (village) Miami-Dade County	175	0.91
Williamsburg, FL (cdp) Orange County	63	0.91
Manorhaven, NY (village) Nassau County	56	0.91
Spillertown, IL (village) Williamson County	2	0.91
Kendall, FL (cdp) Miami-Dade County	680	0.90
South Yarmouth, MA (cdp) Barnstable County	106	0.90
Hope, NJ (township) Warren County	17	0.90
Mamaroneck, NY (town) Westchester County	257	0.89
Northeast Ithaca, NY (cdp) Tompkins County	24	0.89
Bronson, MI (township) Branch County	13	0.89
North Lauderdale, FL (city) Broward County	283	0.88
Palisades Park, NJ (borough) Bergen County	150	0.88
Bethel, NY (town) Sullivan County	38	0.88

Notes: (cdp) census designated place; Refer to the Explanation of Data in the front of the book for more detailed information.

Brazilian

Top 150 Places Sorted by Percent

(Based on places with populations of 10,000 or more)

Place	Number	%
Danbury, CT (city) Fairfield County	4,133	5.52
Framingham, MA (cdp) Middlesex County	3,500	5.23
Harrison, NJ (town) Hudson County	726	5.03
Somerville, MA (city) Middlesex County	3,870	4.99
Kearny, NJ (town) Hudson County	1,629	4.02
Marlborough, MA (city) Middlesex County	1,388	3.83
Deerfield Beach, FL (city) Broward County	2,307	3.56
Everett, MA (city) Middlesex County	1,278	3.36
Long Branch, NJ (city) Monmouth County	890	2.84
Hudson, MA (town) Middlesex County	487	2.69
Doral, FL (cdp) Miami-Dade County	535	2.61
South River, NJ (borough) Middlesex County	376	2.45
Oakland Park, FL (city) Broward County	704	2.26
Miami Beach, FL (city) Miami-Dade County	1,949	2.21
Cliffside Park, NJ (borough) Bergen County	503	2.19
Hillside, NJ (cdp) Union County	469	2.16
Newark, NJ (city) Essex County	5,805	2.12
Sandalfoot Cove, FL (cdp) Palm Beach County	340	2.05
Fairview, NJ (borough) Bergen County	261	1.97
Barnstable Town, MA (city) Barnstable County	930	1.94
Naugatuck, CT (borough) New Haven County	595	1.92
Milford, MA (town) Worcester County	495	1.85
Aventura, FL (city) Miami-Dade County	463	1.83
Malden, MA (city) Middlesex County	1,027	1.82
Revere, MA (city) Suffolk County	846	1.79
Lowell, MA (city) Middlesex County	1,820	1.73
Key Biscayne, FL (village) Miami-Dade County	180	1.72
Ojus, FL (cdp) Miami-Dade County	268	1.61
The Crossings, FL (cdp) Miami-Dade County	362	1.54
Mount Vernon, NY (city) Westchester County	991	1.45
Sunny Isles Beach, FL (city) Miami-Dade County	222	1.45
Yarmouth, MA (town) Barnstable County	352	1.42
Ashland, MA (town) Middlesex County	207	1.41
Delran, NJ (township) Burlington County	217	1.40
Coconut Creek, FL (city) Broward County	589	1.36
Port Chester, NY (village) Westchester County	342	1.23
Chelsea, MA (city) Suffolk County	415	1.18
Pompano Beach, FL (city) Broward County	919	1.17
Bridgeport, CT (city) Fairfield County	1,611	1.15
Elizabeth, NJ (city) Union County	1,349	1.12
Winthrop, MA (cdp) Suffolk County	196	1.07
Boca Raton, FL (city) Palm Beach County	788	1.04
Bethel, CT (town) Fairfield County	185	1.02
Weston, FL (city) Broward County	471	0.96
Medford, MA (city) Middlesex County	520	0.93
Aspen Hill, MD (cdp) Montgomery County	463	0.92
Ives Estates, FL (cdp) Miami-Dade County	161	0.92
Pinecrest, FL (village) Miami-Dade County	175	0.91
Kendall, FL (cdp) Miami-Dade County	680	0.90
South Yarmouth, MA (cdp) Barnstable County	106	0.90
Mamaroneck, NY (town) Westchester County	257	0.89
North Lauderdale, FL (city) Broward County	283	0.88
Palisades Park, NJ (borough) Bergen County	150	0.88
Alpharetta, GA (city) Fulton County	298	0.86
Sandy Springs, GA (cdp) Fulton County	720	0.84
North Miami Beach, FL (city) Miami-Dade County	335	0.82
Boca Del Mar, FL (cdp) Palm Beach County	171	0.80
Guttenberg, NJ (town) Hudson County	86	0.80
Palm Springs, FL (village) Palm Beach County	93	0.79
Rye, NY (town) Westchester County	342	0.78
Westborough, MA (town) Worcester County	141	0.78
Coral Springs, FL (city) Broward County	901	0.77
Orlando, FL (city) Orange County	1,355	0.73
Sunrise, FL (city) Broward County	617	0.72
Oak Ridge, FL (cdp) Orange County	161	0.72
Beltsville, MD (cdp) Prince George's County	113	0.72
North Arlington, NJ (borough) Bergen County	110	0.72
Natick, MA (town) Middlesex County	229	0.71
Leominster, MA (city) Worcester County	289	0.70
Cambridge, MA (city) Middlesex County	694	0.68
Scarsdale, NY (village) Westchester County	119	0.67
Clinton, MA (town) Worcester County	90	0.67
North Bergen, NJ (township) Hudson County	384	0.66
Belleville, NJ (cdp) Essex County	236	0.66
Fall River, MA (city) Bristol County	595	0.65
Worcester, MA (city) Worcester County	1,099	0.64
Shrewsbury, MA (town) Worcester County	203	0.64
Maynard, MA (cdp) Middlesex County	67	0.64
Cutler, FL (cdp) Miami-Dade County	110	0.62
Glenvar Heights, FL (cdp) Miami-Dade County	100	0.62
Larkspur, CA (city) Marin County	75	0.62
Boston, MA (city) Suffolk County	3,594	0.61
Union, NJ (cdp) Union County	331	0.61
Kissimmee, FL (city) Osceola County	291	0.61
Fort Lauderdale, FL (city) Broward County	917	0.60
East Providence, RI (city) Providence County	292	0.60
Miami Lakes, FL (cdp) Miami-Dade County	133	0.59
South Laurel, MD (cdp) Prince George's County	120	0.58
Mamaroneck, NY (village) Westchester County	107	0.57
Dennis, MA (town) Barnstable County	91	0.57
Suffern, NY (village) Rockland County	63	0.57
Peabody, MA (city) Essex County	270	0.56
Woburn, MA (city) Middlesex County	207	0.56
Pembroke Pines, FL (city) Broward County	751	0.55
Maplewood, NJ (cdp) Essex County	129	0.54
Country Walk, FL (cdp) Miami-Dade County	57	0.54
New Rochelle, NY (city) Westchester County	384	0.53
Hollywood, FL (city) Broward County	731	0.52
Daly City, CA (city) San Mateo County	541	0.52
Parkland, FL (city) Broward County	73	0.52
San Rafael, CA (city) Marin County	285	0.51
White Oak, MD (cdp) Montgomery County	107	0.51
Dania Beach, FL (city) Broward County	102	0.51
Lodi, NJ (borough) Bergen County	121	0.50
Scotch Plains, NJ (cdp) Union County	113	0.50
Agoura Hills, CA (city) Los Angeles County	101	0.50
New Providence, NJ (borough) Union County	59	0.50
West Caldwell, NJ (cdp) Essex County	56	0.50
Palmetto Estates, FL (cdp) Miami-Dade County	67	0.49
Fountainbleau, FL (cdp) Miami-Dade County	286	0.48
Margate, FL (city) Broward County	258	0.48
North Bethesda, MD (cdp) Montgomery County	187	0.48
Wethersfield, CT (cdp) Hartford County	126	0.48
Metuchen, NJ (borough) Middlesex County	62	0.48
Villas, FL (cdp) Lee County	54	0.48
Lansing, NY (town) Tompkins County	49	0.48
Brockton, MA (city) Plymouth County	441	0.47
Bethesda, MD (cdp) Montgomery County	259	0.47
Weymouth, MA (cdp) Norfolk County	253	0.47
Rockville, MD (city) Montgomery County	221	0.47
Coral Gables, FL (city) Miami-Dade County	198	0.47
Gulf Gate Estates, FL (cdp) Sarasota County	54	0.47
North Miami, FL (city) Miami-Dade County	276	0.46
Oquirrh, UT (cdp) Salt Lake County	48	0.46
Bailey's Crossroads, VA (cdp) Fairfax County	102	0.45
Rockland, MA (town) Plymouth County	79	0.45
Miami Springs, FL (city) Miami-Dade County	62	0.45
Miami Shores, FL (village) Miami-Dade County	47	0.45
Marshfield, MA (town) Plymouth County	108	0.44
Acton, MA (town) Middlesex County	90	0.44
Ithaca, NY (town) Tompkins County	81	0.44
Quincy, MA (city) Norfolk County	375	0.43
The Hammocks, FL (cdp) Miami-Dade County	206	0.43
Hamptons at Boca Raton, FL (cdp) Palm Beach County	49	0.43
Plantation, FL (city) Broward County	349	0.42
Wheaton-Glenmont, MD (cdp) Montgomery County	244	0.42
Bethpage, NY (cdp) Nassau County	70	0.42
Clark, NJ (cdp) Union County	61	0.42
New Cassel, NY (cdp) Nassau County	56	0.42
Pelham, NH (town) Hillsborough County	46	0.42
Linden, NJ (city) Union County	162	0.41
Myrtle Beach, SC (city) Horry County	93	0.41
Whitney, NV (cdp) Clark County	72	0.41
Highland Park, NJ (borough) Middlesex County	58	0.41
Hampton Bays, NY (cdp) Suffolk County	50	0.41
Dobbs Ferry, NY (village) Westchester County	44	0.41
Ridgefield, NJ (borough) Bergen County	44	0.41
Winchester, CT (town) Litchfield County	44	0.41
New Bedford, MA (city) Bristol County	377	0.40
Davie, FL (town) Broward County	305	0.40

Notes: (cdp) census designated place; Refer to the Explanation of Data in the front of the book for more detailed information.

British

Top 150 Places Sorted by Number

(Based on all places, regardless of population)

Place	Number	%
New York, NY (city) New York City	17,030	0.21
Los Angeles, CA (city) Los Angeles County	11,653	0.32
Houston, TX (city) Harris County	7,483	0.38
San Diego, CA (city) San Diego County	6,848	0.56
Seattle, WA (city) King County	5,408	0.96
San Francisco, CA (city) San Francisco County	5,144	0.66
Phoenix, AZ (city) Maricopa County	4,768	0.36
Austin, TX (city) Travis County	4,753	0.72
Chicago, IL (city) Cook County	4,653	0.16
Dallas, TX (city) Dallas County	4,278	0.36
Portland, OR (city) Multnomah County	4,122	0.78
Indianapolis, IN (special city) Marion County	3,585	0.46
Nashville-Davidson, TN (special city) Davidson County	3,480	0.64
Washington, DC (city) District of Columbia	3,402	0.59
San Jose, CA (city) Santa Clara County	3,299	0.37
Columbus, OH (city) Franklin County	3,186	0.45
Jacksonville, FL (special city) Duval County	3,160	0.43
Virginia Beach, VA (independent city) Virginia Beach city	3,127	0.74
Charlotte, NC (city) Mecklenburg County	2,999	0.55
Salt Lake City, UT (city) Salt Lake County	2,956	1.63
San Antonio, TX (city) Bexar County	2,833	0.25
Philadelphia, PA (city) Philadelphia County	2,599	0.17
Denver, CO (city) Denver County	2,584	0.47
Tucson, AZ (city) Pima County	2,533	0.52
Raleigh, NC (city) Wake County	2,494	0.90
Provo, UT (city) Utah County	2,487	2.36
Boston, MA (city) Suffolk County	2,405	0.41
Colorado Springs, CO (city) El Paso County	2,388	0.66
Arlington, VA (cdp) Arlington County	2,288	1.21
Albuquerque, NM (city) Bernalillo County	2,265	0.50
Atlanta, GA (city) Fulton County	2,174	0.52
Mesa, AZ (city) Maricopa County	1,985	0.50
Fort Worth, TX (city) Tarrant County	1,938	0.36
Tulsa, OK (city) Tulsa County	1,881	0.48
Lexington-Fayette, KY (special city) Fayette County	1,858	0.71
Las Vegas, NV (city) Clark County	1,846	0.39
Plano, TX (city) Collin County	1,802	0.81
Minneapolis, MN (city) Hennepin County	1,795	0.47
Orem, UT (city) Utah County	1,730	2.05
Anchorage, AK (municipality) Anchorage Borough	1,631	0.63
Saint Petersburg, FL (city) Pinellas County	1,607	0.65
Arlington, TX (city) Tarrant County	1,568	0.47
Hempstead, NY (town) Nassau County	1,552	0.21
Memphis, TN (city) Shelby County	1,542	0.24
Tampa, FL (city) Hillsborough County	1,535	0.51
Baltimore, MD (independent city) Baltimore city	1,512	0.23
Long Beach, CA (city) Los Angeles County	1,464	0.32
Oklahoma City, OK (city) Oklahoma County	1,433	0.28
Sacramento, CA (city) Sacramento County	1,426	0.35
Kansas City, MO (city) Jackson County	1,420	0.32
Oakland, CA (city) Alameda County	1,416	0.35
Scottsdale, AZ (city) Maricopa County	1,379	0.68
Boise City, ID (city) Ada County	1,360	0.73
Durham, NC (city) Durham County	1,340	0.72
Wichita, KS (city) Sedgwick County	1,338	0.39
Sandy, UT (city) Salt Lake County	1,326	1.50
Cary, NC (town) Wake County	1,302	1.38
New Orleans, LA (city) Orleans Parish	1,287	0.27
Greensboro, NC (city) Guilford County	1,279	0.57
Ann Arbor, MI (city) Washtenaw County	1,277	1.12
Cambridge, MA (city) Middlesex County	1,251	1.23
Berkeley, CA (city) Alameda County	1,239	1.21
Eugene, OR (city) Lane County	1,231	0.89
Bellevue, WA (city) King County	1,227	1.12
Omaha, NE (city) Douglas County	1,218	0.31
Cincinnati, OH (city) Hamilton County	1,188	0.36
Huntington Beach, CA (city) Orange County	1,186	0.62
Chesapeake, VA (independent city) Chesapeake city	1,186	0.60
Santa Monica, CA (city) Los Angeles County	1,171	1.39
Brookhaven, NY (town) Suffolk County	1,167	0.26
Boulder, CO (city) Boulder County	1,162	1.23
Aurora, CO (city) Arapahoe County	1,140	0.41
Fort Collins, CO (city) Larimer County	1,138	0.96
Huntsville, AL (city) Madison County	1,138	0.72
Tallahassee, FL (city) Leon County	1,136	0.75
Alexandria, VA (independent city) Alexandria city	1,134	0.88
Irvine, CA (city) Orange County	1,126	0.79
Richmond, VA (independent city) Richmond city	1,115	0.56
Greenwich, CT (town) Fairfield County	1,114	1.82
Chandler, AZ (city) Maricopa County	1,105	0.63
Madison, WI (city) Dane County	1,095	0.53
Santa Barbara, CA (city) Santa Barbara County	1,089	1.18
Orlando, FL (city) Orange County	1,080	0.58
Thousand Oaks, CA (city) Ventura County	1,077	0.92
Norfolk, VA (independent city) Norfolk city	1,051	0.45
Riverside, CA (city) Riverside County	1,037	0.41
Palo Alto, CA (city) Santa Clara County	1,035	1.76
Santa Clarita, CA (city) Los Angeles County	1,021	0.67
El Paso, TX (city) El Paso County	1,018	0.18
Pittsburgh, PA (city) Allegheny County	993	0.30
Overland Park, KS (city) Johnson County	975	0.66
Reno, NV (city) Washoe County	973	0.54
Tacoma, WA (city) Pierce County	973	0.50
Louisville, KY (city) Jefferson County	973	0.38
Knoxville, TN (city) Knox County	966	0.56
Montgomery, AL (city) Montgomery County	958	0.48
Bountiful, UT (city) Davis County	953	2.30
Taylorsville, UT (city) Salt Lake County	944	1.63
Spokane, WA (city) Spokane County	928	0.47
Salem, OR (city) Marion County	910	0.67
Henderson, NV (city) Clark County	902	0.51
West Valley City, UT (city) Salt Lake County	900	0.83
Little Rock, AR (city) Pulaski County	895	0.49
Glendale, CA (city) Los Angeles County	889	0.46
Fort Lauderdale, FL (city) Broward County	882	0.58
Clearwater, FL (city) Pinellas County	877	0.81
Honolulu, HI (cdp) Honolulu County	875	0.24
The Woodlands, TX (cdp) Montgomery County	857	1.54
Bakersfield, CA (city) Kern County	857	0.35
Lubbock, TX (city) Lubbock County	853	0.43
Sunrise Manor, NV (cdp) Clark County	848	0.54
Newport Beach, CA (city) Orange County	843	1.20
Athens-Clarke County, GA (special city) Clarke County	842	0.84
Vancouver, WA (city) Clark County	842	0.59
Oceanside, CA (city) San Diego County	839	0.52
Anaheim, CA (city) Orange County	831	0.25
Torrance, CA (city) Los Angeles County	829	0.60
Fremont, CA (city) Alameda County	828	0.41
Asheville, NC (city) Buncombe County	822	1.19
Oyster Bay, NY (town) Nassau County	817	0.28
Chapel Hill, NC (town) Orange County	816	1.67
Sunnyvale, CA (city) Santa Clara County	815	0.62
Mission Viejo, CA (city) Orange County	814	0.88
Saint Paul, MN (city) Ramsey County	812	0.28
Tempe, AZ (city) Maricopa County	808	0.51
Newport News, VA (independent city) Newport News city	802	0.45
Bloomington, IN (city) Monroe County	798	1.15
Irving, TX (city) Dallas County	785	0.41
Santa Rosa, CA (city) Sonoma County	784	0.53
Roswell, GA (city) Fulton County	772	0.97
Mobile, AL (city) Mobile County	765	0.38
Carlsbad, CA (city) San Diego County	760	0.97
Gainesville, FL (city) Alachua County	759	0.79
Lakewood, CO (city) Jefferson County	755	0.52
Winston-Salem, NC (city) Forsyth County	750	0.40
West Jordan, UT (city) Salt Lake County	749	1.10
Towson, MD (cdp) Baltimore County	748	1.44
Columbia, SC (city) Richland County	743	0.64
Huntington, NY (town) Suffolk County	736	0.38
Glendale, AZ (city) Maricopa County	736	0.34
Lincoln, NE (city) Lancaster County	726	0.32
Norman, OK (city) Cleveland County	716	0.75
Columbia, MD (cdp) Howard County	714	0.81
Reston, VA (cdp) Fairfax County	713	1.26
Charleston, SC (city) Charleston County	713	0.74
Naperville, IL (city) Du Page County	711	0.55
Redmond, WA (city) King County	710	1.56
Chattanooga, TN (city) Hamilton County	708	0.46
Hampton, VA (independent city) Hampton city	707	0.48
Paradise, NV (cdp) Clark County	707	0.38

Notes: (cdp) census designated place; Refer to the Explanation of Data in the front of the book for more detailed information.

British

Top 150 Places Sorted by Percent

(Based on all places, regardless of population)

Place	Number	%
Seconsett Island, MA (cdp) Barnstable County	5	20.83
Grand Pass, MO (village) Saline County	13	18.06
Yorktown, VA (cdp) York County	30	16.67
Liverpool, IL (village) Fulton County	10	10.53
Wheatland, ND (cdp) Cass County	4	10.53
Heidelberg, MN (city) Le Sueur County	7	10.00
Ohiopyle, PA (borough) Fayette County	7	9.72
Vernonburg, GA (town) Chatham County	16	9.64
La Sal, UT (cdp) San Juan County	36	9.11
Stony Creek, VA (town) Sussex County	17	9.04
Ward, CO (town) Boulder County	6	8.45
Goshen, VT (town) Addison County	16	8.29
Bishop, GA (town) Oconee County	12	8.28
Peru, VT (town) Bennington County	36	7.89
Hill View Heights, WY (cdp) Weston County	14	7.65
Indian Beach, NC (town) Carteret County	6	7.50
Severance, KS (city) Doniphan County	8	7.34
Upton, ME (town) Oxford County	4	7.27
Paradise, UT (town) Cache County	57	7.26
Spring Lake, UT (cdp) Utah County	30	7.19
Turnerville, WY (cdp) Lincoln County	8	7.08
Lake Alice, MN (township) Hubbard County	6	6.98
Gadsden, TN (town) Crockett County	40	6.97
JAARS, NC (cdp) Union County	18	6.87
Old Bennington, VT (village) Bennington County	16	6.84
Avon, UT (cdp) Cache County	18	6.57
Hebo, OR (cdp) Tillamook County	18	6.55
Moffat, CO (town) Saguache County	7	6.54
Newfield Hamlet, NY (cdp) Tompkins County	51	6.40
Glen Echo, MD (town) Montgomery County	15	6.33
Livonia, MO (village) Putnam County	8	6.30
Kirkwood, CA (cdp) Alpine County	6	6.25
Kingdom City, MO (village) Callaway County	7	6.14
Quamba, MN (city) Kanabec County	6	6.12
West Mountain, UT (cdp) Utah County	48	6.11
Norton, VT (town) Essex County	5	6.10
Herriman, UT (town) Salt Lake County	101	6.01
New Salem, IL (village) Pike County	9	6.00
Clarksburg, MD (cdp) Montgomery County	113	5.98
Waxhaw, NC (town) Union County	158	5.94
Lake Santeetlah, NC (town) Graham County	4	5.88
Elk, PA (township) Tioga County	3	5.88
Montezuma, CO (town) Summit County	2	5.88
Saint Charles, ID (city) Bear Lake County	8	5.84
Spirit, WI (town) Price County	15	5.75
Griffin, IN (town) Posey County	8	5.52
Pineland, FL (cdp) Lee County	26	5.49
Falcon, NC (town) Cumberland County	19	5.49
Boardman, NC (town) Columbus County	12	5.38
Byron, CA (cdp) Contra Costa County	47	5.32
Johannesburg, CA (cdp) Kern County	7	5.30
Mission Woods, KS (city) Johnson County	8	5.26
Fairview Beach, VA (cdp) King George County	13	5.24
Power, MT (cdp) Teton County	9	5.17
Silverton, CO (town) San Juan County	27	5.00
Forest, LA (village) West Carroll Parish	14	5.00
Chilcoot-Vinton, CA (cdp) Plumas County	14	4.81
South Willard, UT (cdp) Box Elder County	28	4.72
Walshville, IL (village) Montgomery County	4	4.71
Cedar Grove, NM (cdp) Santa Fe County	32	4.69
Benson, UT (cdp) Cache County	66	4.63
Gilliam, LA (village) Caddo Parish	7	4.58
Riverside, WY (town) Carbon County	3	4.55
Grayson, GA (city) Gwinnett County	35	4.49
Wilson Creek, WA (town) Grant County	9	4.48
Murchison, TX (city) Henderson County	28	4.45
Parkersburg, IL (village) Richland County	8	4.41
Greensboro, IN (town) Henry County	8	4.40
Woodbury Center, CT (cdp) Litchfield County	58	4.38
Oak Grove, TX (town) Kaufman County	33	4.38
Brookville, KS (city) Saline County	13	4.35
Slana, AK (cdp) Valdez-Cordova Census Area	5	4.35
Maidstone, VT (town) Essex County	4	4.35
Gateway, AR (town) Benton County	3	4.35
Etowah, OK (town) Cleveland County	6	4.29
Cathay, ND (city) Wells County	3	4.29
Pease, MN (city) Mille Lacs County	8	4.28
Sorrento, ME (town) Hancock County	12	4.23
Julian, NE (village) Nemaha County	3	4.23
Jupiter Island, FL (town) Martin County	26	4.19
Norwich, VT (town) Windsor County	148	4.18
Leavenworth, WA (city) Chelan County	85	4.17
Barbers Point Housing, HI (cdp) Honolulu County	3	4.17
White Rock, NM (cdp) Los Alamos County	250	4.15
Avondale Estates, GA (city) De Kalb County	106	4.15
Sterling, UT (town) Sanpete County	9	4.15
Pine Grove, WV (town) Wetzel County	23	4.12
Hancock, WI (village) Waushara County	20	4.12
Reliance, WY (cdp) Sweetwater County	27	4.09
Lumber City, PA (borough) Clearfield County	4	4.08
Indian River Shores, FL (town) Indian River County	133	4.04
South Park View, KY (city) Jefferson County	8	4.02
Rensselaer Falls, NY (village) Saint Lawrence County	13	4.00
Panama, NE (village) Lancaster County	11	3.94
Morrison, MO (city) Gasconade County	5	3.94
Essex Village, CT (cdp) Middlesex County	100	3.92
Matinicus Isle, ME (plantation) Knox County	2	3.92
Washington, VA (town) Rappahannock County	7	3.91
Wilson, WY (cdp) Teton County	51	3.89
Point Reyes Station, CA (cdp) Marin County	33	3.89
River Heights, UT (city) Cache County	59	3.87
Highland, UT (city) Utah County	305	3.83
Marvin, NC (village) Union County	47	3.83
Scotts Corners, NY (cdp) Westchester County	22	3.82
Poplar, MN (township) Cass County	6	3.82
Timken, KS (city) Rush County	3	3.80
Iona, ID (city) Bonneville County	46	3.79
Golf, FL (village) Palm Beach County	9	3.77
Hemby Bridge, NC (town) Union County	35	3.76
Galway, NY (village) Saratoga County	8	3.76
Maryhill Estates, KY (city) Jefferson County	7	3.76
Del Sol-Loma Linda, TX (cdp) San Patricio County	27	3.75
Chillicothe, IA (city) Wapello County	3	3.75
Rushmere, VA (cdp) Isle of Wight County	40	3.73
Washington Grove, MD (town) Montgomery County	18	3.73
Princeton, KS (city) Franklin County	12	3.73
Desert View Highlands, CA (cdp) Los Angeles County	77	3.71
Houghton, NY (cdp) Allegany County	64	3.70
Lakeview, AL (town) De Kalb County	6	3.70
Andover, SD (town) Day County	3	3.70
Fairdale, ND (city) Walsh County	2	3.70
Mount Olympus, UT (cdp) Salt Lake County	250	3.66
Dorset, VT (town) Bennington County	74	3.63
Goldston, NC (town) Chatham County	11	3.62
Centre Island, NY (village) Nassau County	16	3.60
Bannockburn, IL (village) Lake County	51	3.58
Randolph, NH (town) Coos County	12	3.57
Chevy Chase, MD (cdp) Montgomery County	334	3.56
Adrian, TX (city) Oldham County	5	3.55
Westover Hills, TX (town) Tarrant County	23	3.54
Teton Village, WY (cdp) Teton County	9	3.52
La Plata, MO (city) Macon County	52	3.51
Lakeville, ME (town) Penobscot County	2	3.51
Point Arena, CA (city) Mendocino County	17	3.50
Canyon City, OR (town) Grant County	23	3.49
Old Washington, OH (village) Guernsey County	10	3.48
Holliday, MO (village) Monroe County	5	3.47
Todd Mission, TX (city) Grimes County	5	3.47
Hyde Park, UT (city) Cache County	102	3.46
Jonesville, IN (town) Bartholomew County	8	3.45
Greenhorn, CA (cdp) Plumas County	6	3.45
Manila, UT (town) Daggett County	11	3.44
Harrisville, MI (city) Alcona County	20	3.42
Chestonia, MI (township) Antrim County	18	3.42
Chamois, MO (city) Osage County	16	3.41
Lowndesboro, AL (town) Lowndes County	6	3.41
Oyehut-Hogans Corner, WA (cdp) Grays Harbor County	7	3.40
Cedar Hills, UT (town) Utah County	105	3.39
Lansford, ND (city) Bottineau County	8	3.38
Magnolia, DE (town) Kent County	8	3.38

Notes: (cdp) census designated place; Refer to the Explanation of Data in the front of the book for more detailed information.

British

Top 150 Places Sorted by Percent

(Based on places with populations of 10,000 or more)

Place	Number	%
Farmington, UT (city) Davis County	383	3.14
Kaysville, UT (city) Davis County	625	3.02
Holladay, UT (city) Salt Lake County	422	2.90
Cinco Ranch, TX (cdp) Fort Bend County	290	2.58
Cottonwood Heights, UT (cdp) Salt Lake County	674	2.46
Saint Simons, GA (cdp) Glynn County	331	2.46
Provo, UT (city) Utah County	2,487	2.36
Rexburg, ID (city) Madison County	398	2.31
Bountiful, UT (city) Davis County	953	2.30
Canyon Rim, UT (cdp) Salt Lake County	237	2.24
Union Hill-Novelty Hill, WA (cdp) King County	248	2.22
Tamalpais-Homestead Valley, CA (cdp) Marin County	226	2.13
Palos Verdes Estates, CA (city) Los Angeles County	281	2.11
Clemson, SC (city) Pickens County	254	2.10
Orem, UT (city) Utah County	1,730	2.05
American Fork, UT (city) Utah County	445	2.03
Centerville, UT (city) Davis County	292	2.03
Laguna Beach, CA (city) Orange County	461	1.98
East Millcreek, UT (cdp) Salt Lake County	423	1.98
Amherst, NH (town) Hillsborough County	213	1.98
Berkeley Heights, NJ (cdp) Union County	262	1.95
Highland Village, TX (city) Denton County	237	1.95
Fort Hunt, VA (cdp) Fairfax County	242	1.89
Falls Church, VA (independent city) Falls Church city	196	1.89
North Druid Hills, GA (cdp) De Kalb County	354	1.88
Hanover, NH (town) Grafton County	203	1.87
Greenwich, CT (town) Fairfield County	1,114	1.82
Chatham, NJ (township) Morris County	184	1.82
Draper, UT (city) Salt Lake County	453	1.78
Palo Alto, CA (city) Santa Clara County	1,035	1.76
University Park, TX (city) Dallas County	412	1.76
Sudbury, MA (town) Middlesex County	297	1.76
Half Moon Bay, CA (city) San Mateo County	211	1.76
Vestavia Hills, AL (city) Jefferson County	434	1.75
Druid Hills, GA (cdp) De Kalb County	222	1.75
San Anselmo, CA (town) Marin County	219	1.75
Ithaca, NY (town) Tompkins County	319	1.73
Durham, NH (town) Strafford County	219	1.73
Larkspur, CA (city) Marin County	207	1.72
Los Gatos, CA (town) Santa Clara County	487	1.70
Wellesley, MA (cdp) Norfolk County	451	1.69
Concord, MA (town) Middlesex County	285	1.68
Chapel Hill, NC (town) Orange County	816	1.67
Murray, UT (city) Salt Lake County	568	1.67
Montecito, CA (cdp) Santa Barbara County	168	1.67
Riverton, UT (city) Salt Lake County	418	1.66
Springville, UT (city) Utah County	341	1.66
McLean, VA (cdp) Fairfax County	643	1.65
Salt Lake City, UT (city) Salt Lake County	2,956	1.63
Taylorsville, UT (city) Salt Lake County	944	1.63
Darien, CT (cdp) Fairfield County	320	1.63
Lighthouse Point, FL (city) Broward County	173	1.62
Wayland, MA (town) Middlesex County	211	1.61
Kingsgate, WA (cdp) King County	194	1.61
Sierra Madre, CA (city) Los Angeles County	170	1.61
Easttown, PA (township) Chester County	163	1.59
Stanford, CA (cdp) Santa Clara County	210	1.58
Redmond, WA (city) King County	710	1.56
Saratoga, CA (city) Santa Clara County	466	1.56
Orinda, CA (city) Contra Costa County	272	1.56
Marblehead, MA (cdp) Essex County	315	1.55
Pacific Grove, CA (city) Monterey County	239	1.55
The Woodlands, TX (cdp) Montgomery County	857	1.54
Bainbridge Island, WA (city) Kitsap County	312	1.54
Arlington, NY (cdp) Dutchess County	191	1.54
Princeton, NJ (township) Mercer County	245	1.53
Black Forest, CO (cdp) El Paso County	202	1.53
Citrus Ridge, FL (cdp) Lake County	175	1.53
Pleasant Grove, UT (city) Utah County	356	1.51
Rancho San Diego, CA (cdp) San Diego County	302	1.51
West University Place, TX (city) Harris County	214	1.51
Sandy, UT (city) Salt Lake County	1,326	1.50
Moberly, MO (city) Randolph County	180	1.50
Lake Oswego, OR (city) Clackamas County	526	1.49
Madison, NJ (borough) Morris County	247	1.49
Auburn, CA (city) Placer County	186	1.49
Pecan Grove, TX (cdp) Fort Bend County	199	1.48
Kirkland, WA (city) King County	663	1.47
Ithaca, NY (city) Tompkins County	425	1.47
New Canaan, CT (town) Fairfield County	283	1.46
North Ogden, UT (city) Weber County	216	1.45
Towson, MD (cdp) Baltimore County	748	1.44
Winter Park, FL (city) Orange County	348	1.44
Vashon, WA (cdp) King County	145	1.43
Lafayette, CA (city) Contra Costa County	333	1.42
Montclair, VA (cdp) Prince William County	225	1.42
Cedar Mill, OR (cdp) Washington County	182	1.42
Logan, UT (city) Cache County	603	1.41
New Providence, NJ (borough) Union County	168	1.41
Santa Monica, CA (city) Los Angeles County	1,171	1.39
Tredyffrin, PA (township) Chester County	405	1.39
Wolf Trap, VA (cdp) Fairfax County	193	1.39
Cary, NC (town) Wake County	1,302	1.38
Blacksburg, VA (town) Montgomery County	540	1.37
Mountain Brook, AL (city) Jefferson County	287	1.37
South Ogden, UT (city) Weber County	198	1.37
Guilford, CT (town) New Haven County	292	1.36
Lake Saint Louis, MO (city) Saint Charles County	137	1.36
North Decatur, GA (cdp) De Kalb County	204	1.35
Port Neches, TX (city) Jefferson County	183	1.35
Vero Beach, FL (city) Indian River County	239	1.34
Princeton, NJ (borough) Mercer County	190	1.34
Goodlettsville, TN (city) Davidson County	186	1.34
Cottonwood West, UT (cdp) Salt Lake County	248	1.33
Moraga, CA (town) Contra Costa County	222	1.33
McKinleyville, CA (cdp) Humboldt County	180	1.32
Chesapeake Ranch Estates-Drum Point, MD (cdp) Calvert County	153	1.32
Inglewood-Finn Hill, WA (cdp) King County	297	1.31
Pinecrest, FL (village) Miami-Dade County	249	1.30
Frankfort, IN (city) Clinton County	217	1.30
Mill Valley, CA (city) Marin County	175	1.29
Malibu, CA (city) Los Angeles County	161	1.29
Sun Lakes, AZ (cdp) Maricopa County	154	1.29
College Park, MD (city) Prince George's County	313	1.27
Hudson, OH (city) Summit County	285	1.27
Idylwood, VA (cdp) Fairfax County	204	1.27
Reston, VA (cdp) Fairfax County	713	1.26
Peachtree City, GA (city) Fayette County	401	1.26
Apex, NC (town) Wake County	250	1.25
Snellville, GA (city) Gwinnett County	187	1.25
Lexington, MA (cdp) Middlesex County	375	1.24
Oakton, VA (cdp) Fairfax County	365	1.24
Tooele, UT (city) Tooele County	280	1.24
Sunny Isles Beach, FL (city) Miami-Dade County	189	1.24
Cambridge, MA (city) Middlesex County	1,251	1.23
Boulder, CO (city) Boulder County	1,162	1.23
Westport, CT (cdp) Fairfield County	313	1.22
Casa de Oro-Mount Helix, CA (cdp) San Diego County	231	1.22
Punta Gorda, FL (city) Charlotte County	176	1.22
Antrim, PA (township) Franklin County	153	1.22
Arlington, VA (cdp) Arlington County	2,288	1.21
Berkeley, CA (city) Alameda County	1,239	1.21
Bethesda, MD (cdp) Montgomery County	669	1.21
Daphne, AL (city) Baldwin County	204	1.21
Carrboro, NC (town) Orange County	202	1.21
Bellaire, TX (city) Harris County	189	1.21
Ipswich, MA (town) Essex County	157	1.21
Bedford, MA (town) Middlesex County	152	1.21
Newport Beach, CA (city) Orange County	843	1.20
South Hill, WA (cdp) Pierce County	382	1.20
South Jordan, UT (city) Salt Lake County	354	1.20
Los Altos, CA (city) Santa Clara County	330	1.20
Takoma Park, MD (city) Montgomery County	207	1.20
Haddonfield, NJ (borough) Camden County	140	1.20
Montgomery, OH (city) Hamilton County	121	1.20
Asheville, NC (city) Buncombe County	822	1.19
Matthews, NC (town) Mecklenburg County	266	1.19
Cedar City, UT (city) Iron County	244	1.19
Sierra Vista Southeast, AZ (cdp) Cochise County	176	1.19
Upper Providence Township, PA (cdp) Delaware County	125	1.19

Notes: (cdp) census designated place; Refer to the Explanation of Data in the front of the book for more detailed information.

Bulgarian

Top 150 Places Sorted by Number

(Based on all places, regardless of population)

Place	Number	%
New York, NY (city) New York City	3,826	0.05
Chicago, IL (city) Cook County	2,045	0.07
Los Angeles, CA (city) Los Angeles County	1,479	0.04
Phoenix, AZ (city) Maricopa County	506	0.04
San Diego, CA (city) San Diego County	432	0.04
Seattle, WA (city) King County	354	0.06
Las Vegas, NV (city) Clark County	297	0.06
Houston, TX (city) Harris County	295	0.02
Saint Petersburg, FL (city) Pinellas County	268	0.11
Glendale, CA (city) Los Angeles County	262	0.13
Paradise, NV (cdp) Clark County	256	0.14
Schiller Park, IL (village) Cook County	244	2.07
San Jose, CA (city) Santa Clara County	233	0.03
Dallas, TX (city) Dallas County	219	0.02
Columbus, OH (city) Franklin County	217	0.03
Skokie, IL (village) Cook County	208	0.33
Washington, DC (city) District of Columbia	207	0.04
Denver, CO (city) Denver County	194	0.03
Bellevue, WA (city) King County	187	0.17
Indianapolis, IN (special city) Marion County	175	0.02
Toledo, OH (city) Lucas County	167	0.05
Mount Prospect, IL (village) Cook County	164	0.29
Lakewood, CO (city) Jefferson County	162	0.11
Virginia Beach, VA (independent city) Virginia Beach city	162	0.04
Boston, MA (city) Suffolk County	159	0.03
Spokane, WA (city) Spokane County	156	0.08
Wixom, MI (city) Oakland County	154	1.16
Irvine, CA (city) Orange County	150	0.10
Portland, OR (city) Multnomah County	150	0.03
Des Plaines, IL (city) Cook County	149	0.25
Austin, TX (city) Travis County	149	0.02
Greenburgh, NY (town) Westchester County	147	0.17
Colorado Springs, CO (city) El Paso County	147	0.04
San Francisco, CA (city) San Francisco County	146	0.02
Lynnwood, WA (city) Snohomish County	145	0.43
Modesto, CA (city) Stanislaus County	145	0.08
Concord, CA (city) Contra Costa County	144	0.12
Minneapolis, MN (city) Hennepin County	136	0.04
Brookhaven, NY (town) Suffolk County	130	0.03
Greater Carrollwood, FL (cdp) Hillsborough County	129	0.38
Spring Valley, NV (cdp) Clark County	128	0.11
Arlington, TX (city) Tarrant County	125	0.04
Rosemont, IL (village) Cook County	119	2.85
Lexington-Fayette, KY (special city) Fayette County	111	0.04
Cockeysville, MD (cdp) Baltimore County	109	0.56
Sunnyvale, CA (city) Santa Clara County	108	0.08
Milwaukee, WI (city) Milwaukee County	107	0.02
Elmwood Park, IL (village) Cook County	106	0.42
Cincinnati, OH (city) Hamilton County	106	0.03
Charlotte, NC (city) Mecklenburg County	106	0.02
Mount Lebanon, PA (cdp) Allegheny County	105	0.32
Hartsdale, NY (cdp) Westchester County	104	1.06
Santa Monica, CA (city) Los Angeles County	104	0.12
Schaumburg, IL (village) Cook County	103	0.14
Tulsa, OK (city) Tulsa County	103	0.03
Albuquerque, NM (city) Bernalillo County	103	0.02
Baltimore, MD (independent city) Baltimore city	102	0.02
Hempstead, NY (town) Nassau County	102	0.01
Mesa, AZ (city) Maricopa County	98	0.02
Fairwood, WA (cdp) Spokane County	96	1.42
Salem, OR (city) Marion County	94	0.07
Euless, TX (city) Tarrant County	91	0.20
Miami Beach, FL (city) Miami-Dade County	91	0.10
Rancho Cucamonga, CA (city) San Bernardino County	91	0.07
Roselle, IL (village) Du Page County	89	0.38
Wethersfield, CT (cdp) Hartford County	88	0.34
Stamford, CT (city) Fairfield County	88	0.08
Greenwich, CT (town) Fairfield County	86	0.14
Long Beach, CA (city) Los Angeles County	86	0.02
Alexandria, VA (independent city) Alexandria city	85	0.07
Thousand Oaks, CA (city) Ventura County	85	0.07
Fort Lauderdale, FL (city) Broward County	85	0.06
Cambridge, MA (city) Middlesex County	84	0.08
Brigantine, NJ (city) Atlantic County	83	0.66
Naperville, IL (city) Du Page County	83	0.06
Bryans Road, MD (cdp) Charles County	82	1.66
River Grove, IL (village) Cook County	82	0.77
Waterford, MI (cdp) Oakland County	82	0.11
Detroit, MI (city) Wayne County	82	0.01
Rochester, NY (city) Monroe County	81	0.04
Oyster Bay, NY (town) Nassau County	81	0.03
Newark, DE (city) New Castle County	80	0.28
Gainesville, FL (city) Alachua County	80	0.08
Tacoma, WA (city) Pierce County	80	0.04
Walnut Creek, CA (city) Contra Costa County	79	0.12
Cleveland, OH (city) Cuyahoga County	79	0.02
Honolulu, HI (cdp) Honolulu County	79	0.02
Ken Caryl, CO (cdp) Jefferson County	78	0.25
Hillsboro, OR (city) Washington County	78	0.11
Corpus Christi, TX (city) Nueces County	78	0.03
La Mesa, CA (city) San Diego County	75	0.14
Boca Raton, FL (city) Palm Beach County	75	0.10
Utica, NY (city) Oneida County	74	0.12
Miami, FL (city) Miami-Dade County	74	0.02
Northglenn, CO (city) Adams County	73	0.23
Waterloo, IA (city) Black Hawk County	73	0.11
Santa Barbara, CA (city) Santa Barbara County	73	0.08
Greensboro, NC (city) Guilford County	73	0.03
Islip, NY (town) Suffolk County	73	0.02
Kent, WA (city) King County	72	0.09
Newton, MA (city) Middlesex County	72	0.09
Raleigh, NC (city) Wake County	72	0.03
Evanston, IL (city) Cook County	71	0.10
Newport Beach, CA (city) Orange County	71	0.10
Arlington, VA (cdp) Arlington County	71	0.04
Philadelphia, PA (city) Philadelphia County	71	0.00
Bedford, MI (township) Monroe County	70	0.24
Eugene, OR (city) Lane County	70	0.05
Bethesda, MD (cdp) Montgomery County	69	0.12
Tonawanda, NY (town) Erie County	69	0.09
Palmdale, CA (city) Los Angeles County	69	0.06
Elk Grove Village, IL (village) Cook County	68	0.20
Plano, TX (city) Collin County	68	0.03
Wheeling, IL (village) Cook County	67	0.19
Provo, UT (city) Utah County	67	0.06
Akron, OH (city) Summit County	67	0.03
Kansas City, MO (city) Jackson County	67	0.02
Aurora, CO (city) Arapahoe County	66	0.02
Omaha, NE (city) Douglas County	66	0.02
Stony Brook, NY (cdp) Suffolk County	65	0.48
Addison, IL (village) Du Page County	65	0.18
State College, PA (borough) Centre County	65	0.17
Syracuse, NY (city) Onondaga County	65	0.04
Grayslake, IL (village) Lake County	64	0.35
Brookline, MA (cdp) Norfolk County	64	0.11
Oregon, OH (city) Lucas County	63	0.33
Wichita, KS (city) Sedgwick County	63	0.02
Moore, OK (city) Cleveland County	62	0.15
Elgin, IL (city) Kane County	62	0.07
Tempe, AZ (city) Maricopa County	62	0.04
Portland, ME (city) Cumberland County	61	0.09
Westminster, CO (city) Adams County	61	0.06
Tampa, FL (city) Hillsborough County	61	0.02
Crozet, VA (cdp) Albemarle County	60	2.11
Hopkins, MN (city) Hennepin County	60	0.35
West Sacramento, CA (city) Yolo County	60	0.19
Rancho Mirage, CA (city) Riverside County	59	0.45
Renton, WA (city) King County	59	0.12
Arvada, CO (city) Jefferson County	59	0.06
Madison, WI (city) Dane County	59	0.03
Pittsburgh, PA (city) Allegheny County	59	0.02
Saint Paul, MN (city) Ramsey County	59	0.02
Granite City, IL (city) Madison County	58	0.18
Oakville, MO (cdp) Saint Louis County	58	0.16
Palm Springs, CA (city) Riverside County	58	0.14
Germantown, MD (cdp) Montgomery County	58	0.11
Clearwater, FL (city) Pinellas County	58	0.05
Hollywood, FL (city) Broward County	58	0.04
Berkeley, CA (city) Alameda County	57	0.06
South Bend, IN (city) Saint Joseph County	57	0.05

Notes: (cdp) census designated place; Refer to the Explanation of Data in the front of the book for more detailed information.

Bulgarian

Top 150 Places Sorted by Percent

(Based on all places, regardless of population)

Place	Number	%
Rantoul, KS (city) Franklin County	21	8.47
Bucyrus, ND (city) Adams County	3	8.33
Galway, NY (village) Saratoga County	11	5.16
Portland, PA (borough) Northampton County	29	5.07
Old Harbor, AK (city) Kodiak Island Borough	7	2.87
Rosemont, IL (village) Cook County	119	2.85
Point Reyes Station, CA (cdp) Marin County	24	2.83
Burbank, OH (village) Wayne County	7	2.48
Linndale, OH (village) Cuyahoga County	3	2.48
Granville, ND (city) McHenry County	7	2.39
Crozet, VA (cdp) Albemarle County	60	2.11
Schiller Park, IL (village) Cook County	244	2.07
Bowdon, GA (city) Carroll County	41	2.06
Bear Valley, CA (cdp) Alpine County	2	2.02
Nelson, IL (village) Lee County	3	2.00
Ashford, WA (cdp) Pierce County	5	1.93
Steele, ND (city) Kidder County	13	1.72
Des Lacs, ND (city) Ward County	4	1.68
Bryans Road, MD (cdp) Charles County	82	1.66
Fairfield, NY (town) Herkimer County	27	1.64
New Diggings, WI (town) Lafayette County	7	1.59
Washburn, WI (town) Bayfield County	8	1.49
Holy Cross, MN (township) Clay County	2	1.49
New Avon, MN (township) Redwood County	4	1.47
Fairwood, WA (cdp) Spokane County	96	1.42
West Middletown, PA (borough) Washington County	2	1.38
Lake Shore, UT (cdp) Utah County	10	1.33
Crooked Creek, MN (township) Houston County	4	1.31
Richland, WI (town) Rusk County	3	1.31
Lake Angelus, MI (city) Oakland County	4	1.23
Oakwood Park, MO (village) Clay County	2	1.21
Watkinsville, GA (town) Oconee County	25	1.19
Chambers Estates, FL (cdp) Broward County	42	1.18
French Gulch, CA (cdp) Shasta County	3	1.17
Wixom, MI (city) Oakland County	154	1.16
Spring Hill, MN (township) Stearns County	5	1.14
Folden, MN (township) Otter Tail County	3	1.09
Keys, OK (cdp) Cherokee County	4	1.08
Hartsdale, NY (cdp) Westchester County	104	1.06
Stony Creek, VA (town) Sussex County	2	1.06
Vance, AL (town) Tuscaloosa County	5	1.04
Perrysburg, NY (village) Cattaraugus County	4	1.04
Vassar, MI (township) Tuscola County	44	1.02
Buckeye, MI (township) Gladwin County	14	1.02
Lehigh, IA (city) Webster County	5	1.01
Iron Ridge, WI (village) Dodge County	10	1.00
Franklin, WI (town) Sauk County	7	1.00
Stanford, MT (town) Judith Basin County	4	1.00
Streeter, ND (city) Stutsman County	2	0.98
Ogden, IL (village) Champaign County	7	0.95
Chamisal, NM (cdp) Taos County	3	0.92
Burnt Store Marina, FL (cdp) Lee County	11	0.91
Lyons, OH (village) Fulton County	5	0.90
Choconut, PA (township) Susquehanna County	7	0.89
Sherwood, OH (cdp) Hamilton County	34	0.88
Grow, WI (town) Rusk County	5	0.87
Kenton, DE (town) Kent County	2	0.87
Lake Wylie, SC (cdp) York County	27	0.86
Elliston, MT (cdp) Powell County	2	0.86
Sebeka, MN (city) Wadena County	6	0.83
Roselawn, IN (cdp) Jasper County	32	0.82
Bay City, WI (village) Pierce County	4	0.82
Bovey, MN (city) Itasca County	5	0.80
Raleigh Hills, OR (cdp) Washington County	45	0.79
Saint Paul, OR (city) Marion County	3	0.79
Bates, MI (township) Iron County	8	0.78
River Grove, IL (village) Cook County	82	0.77
Lake Meade, PA (cdp) Adams County	14	0.77
Hanover, IL (village) Jo Daviess County	6	0.76
Rancho Viejo, TX (town) Cameron County	13	0.74
Foxhome, MN (city) Wilkin County	1	0.74
Penn Wynne, PA (cdp) Montgomery County	39	0.72
Plainsboro Center, NJ (cdp) Middlesex County	17	0.72
Minetto, NY (town) Oswego County	12	0.72
Lenox, IA (city) Taylor County	10	0.72
Quapaw, OK (town) Ottawa County	7	0.71
Glen, MN (township) Aitkin County	3	0.71
Chino Valley, AZ (town) Yavapai County	56	0.70
Freedom, MI (township) Washtenaw County	11	0.70
Edwardsburg, MI (village) Cass County	8	0.70
Hellam, PA (township) York County	41	0.69
Northfield, IL (village) Cook County	38	0.69
East Pittsburgh, PA (borough) Allegheny County	14	0.69
Bethlehem, NJ (township) Hunterdon County	26	0.68
Frenchtown, NJ (borough) Hunterdon County	10	0.67
Brigantine, NJ (city) Atlantic County	83	0.66
Stambaugh, MI (city) Iron County	8	0.66
Garfield, WA (town) Whitman County	4	0.66
Loghill Village, CO (cdp) Ouray County	2	0.66
Princeville, HI (cdp) Kauai County	11	0.65
East Richmond Heights, CA (cdp) Contra Costa County	22	0.63
New London, OH (village) Huron County	17	0.63
Wrightsville, PA (borough) York County	14	0.63
Lynd, MN (city) Lyon County	2	0.63
Fruit Hill, OH (cdp) Hamilton County	24	0.62
Little Falls-South Windham, ME (cdp) Cumberland County	10	0.62
Gillett, WI (town) Oconto County	7	0.62
Union, PA (township) Berks County	21	0.61
Fairmont, IL (cdp) Will County	16	0.61
Solana, FL (cdp) Charlotte County	6	0.61
Sulphur, OK (city) Murray County	29	0.60
Benton, WI (town) Lafayette County	3	0.60
Scraper, OK (cdp) Cherokee County	3	0.60
Gaastra, MI (city) Iron County	2	0.60
Batavia, NY (town) Genesee County	35	0.59
Garner, IA (city) Hancock County	17	0.58
Oakland, NE (city) Burt County	8	0.58
Peck, WI (town) Langlade County	2	0.58
Pleasant Hill, IA (city) Polk County	29	0.57
Waterville, OH (village) Lucas County	27	0.57
Randall, MN (city) Morrison County	3	0.57
Cockeysville, MD (cdp) Baltimore County	109	0.56
Uniontown, OH (cdp) Stark County	16	0.56
Kenilworth, IL (village) Cook County	14	0.56
Haines, AK (city) Haines Borough	10	0.56
Richmond, MN (township) Winona County	4	0.56
Bristol, SD (city) Day County	2	0.54
Brownsville, WI (village) Dodge County	3	0.53
Kickapoo, WI (town) Vernon County	3	0.53
Willard, OH (city) Huron County	35	0.51
Ada, OH (village) Hardin County	28	0.51
Berkeley, IL (village) Cook County	27	0.51
Devine, TX (city) Medina County	22	0.51
Ely, MN (city) Saint Louis County	19	0.51
Whitehouse, OH (village) Lucas County	14	0.51
West Yellowstone, MT (town) Gallatin County	6	0.51
Stroudsburg, PA (borough) Monroe County	29	0.50
Dell Prairie, WI (town) Adams County	7	0.50
Cylon, WI (town) Saint Croix County	3	0.50
Chamblee, GA (city) De Kalb County	48	0.49
Decorah, IA (city) Winneshiek County	40	0.49
Klacking, MI (township) Ogemaw County	3	0.49
Stony Brook, NY (cdp) Suffolk County	65	0.48
Palmerton, PA (borough) Carbon County	25	0.48
Sunnyvale, TX (town) Dallas County	13	0.48
North Eagle Butte, SD (cdp) Dewey County	10	0.48
West Carroll, PA (township) Cambria County	7	0.48
Bouse, AZ (cdp) La Paz County	4	0.48
Richmond, MI (city) Macomb County	23	0.47
Amherst, VA (town) Amherst County	11	0.47
Reminderville, OH (village) Summit County	11	0.47
Manattee Road, FL (cdp) Levy County	10	0.47
Stambaugh, MI (township) Iron County	6	0.47
Orbisonia, PA (borough) Huntingdon County	2	0.47
Pioneer, MI (township) Missaukee County	2	0.47
Newcastle, WA (city) King County	37	0.46
Ladysmith, WI (city) Rusk County	18	0.46
Paw Paw, MI (village) Van Buren County	15	0.46
Dows, IA (city) Wright County	3	0.46
Shoshoni, WY (town) Fremont County	3	0.46

Notes: (cdp) census designated place; Refer to the Explanation of Data in the front of the book for more detailed information.

Bulgarian

Top 150 Places Sorted by Percent

(Based on places with populations of 10,000 or more)

Place	Number	%
Schiller Park, IL (village) Cook County	244	2.07
Wixom, MI (city) Oakland County	154	1.16
River Grove, IL (village) Cook County	82	0.77
Brigantine, NJ (city) Atlantic County	83	0.66
Cockeysville, MD (cdp) Baltimore County	109	0.56
Stony Brook, NY (cdp) Suffolk County	65	0.48
Rancho Mirage, CA (city) Riverside County	59	0.45
Lynnwood, WA (city) Snohomish County	145	0.43
Elmwood Park, IL (village) Cook County	106	0.42
Greater Carrollwood, FL (cdp) Hillsborough County	129	0.38
Roselle, IL (village) Du Page County	89	0.38
York, ME (town) York County	48	0.37
Merrifield, VA (cdp) Fairfax County	40	0.36
Marathon, FL (city) Monroe County	37	0.36
Grayslake, IL (village) Lake County	64	0.35
Hopkins, MN (city) Hennepin County	60	0.35
Wethersfield, CT (cdp) Hartford County	88	0.34
North Castle, NY (town) Westchester County	37	0.34
Skokie, IL (village) Cook County	208	0.33
Oregon, OH (city) Lucas County	63	0.33
Mount Lebanon, PA (cdp) Allegheny County	105	0.32
Washington, NJ (township) Mercer County	32	0.31
Pleasant Grove, AL (city) Jefferson County	31	0.31
La Crescenta-Montrose, CA (cdp) Los Angeles County	56	0.30
Elkton, MD (town) Cecil County	36	0.30
Palm Springs, FL (village) Palm Beach County	35	0.30
Mount Prospect, IL (village) Cook County	164	0.29
Newark, DE (city) New Castle County	80	0.28
Wood Dale, IL (city) Du Page County	39	0.28
Lebanon, OH (city) Warren County	45	0.27
Federal Heights, CO (city) Adams County	32	0.27
Burr Ridge, IL (village) Du Page County	28	0.27
Glen Carbon, IL (village) Madison County	28	0.27
Lake Saint Louis, MO (city) Saint Charles County	27	0.27
Forest Park, IL (village) Cook County	41	0.26
Ventnor City, NJ (city) Atlantic County	33	0.26
Falls Church, VA (independent city) Falls Church city	27	0.26
Des Plaines, IL (city) Cook County	149	0.25
Ken Caryl, CO (cdp) Jefferson County	78	0.25
Carbondale, IL (city) Jackson County	51	0.25
Rocky River, OH (city) Cuyahoga County	51	0.25
Maitland, FL (city) Orange County	30	0.25
Bedford, MI (township) Monroe County	70	0.24
Fairview Park, OH (city) Cuyahoga County	43	0.24
Winter Garden, FL (city) Orange County	33	0.24
Clawson, MI (city) Oakland County	30	0.24
Lea Hill, WA (cdp) King County	26	0.24
Farmington, MI (city) Oakland County	25	0.24
Northglenn, CO (city) Adams County	73	0.23
Mamaroneck, NY (village) Westchester County	44	0.23
Mount Vernon, OH (city) Knox County	34	0.23
Warrenville, IL (city) Du Page County	31	0.23
Sylvania, OH (city) Lucas County	42	0.22
Sunny Isles Beach, FL (city) Miami-Dade County	34	0.22
Harper Woods, MI (city) Wayne County	32	0.22
Apopka, FL (city) Orange County	55	0.21
Kenmore, NY (village) Erie County	35	0.21
Fort Madison, IA (city) Lee County	23	0.21
Mountain Home, AR (city) Baxter County	23	0.21
Euless, TX (city) Tarrant County	91	0.20
Elk Grove Village, IL (village) Cook County	68	0.20
Duluth, GA (city) Gwinnett County	45	0.20
Wheeling, IL (village) Cook County	67	0.19
West Sacramento, CA (city) Yolo County	60	0.19
Oakley, CA (city) Contra Costa County	49	0.19
Massapequa, NY (cdp) Nassau County	44	0.19
Casa de Oro-Mount Helix, CA (cdp) San Diego County	35	0.19
Seven Oaks, SC (cdp) Lexington County	30	0.19
Enterprise, NV (cdp) Clark County	27	0.19
Brown Deer, WI (village) Milwaukee County	23	0.19
Sterling, CO (city) Logan County	22	0.19
Worth, IL (village) Cook County	21	0.19
Manville, NJ (borough) Somerset County	20	0.19
Lyons, IL (village) Cook County	19	0.19
Addison, IL (village) Du Page County	65	0.18
Granite City, IL (city) Madison County	58	0.18
Massillon, OH (city) Stark County	56	0.18
Merrillville, IN (town) Lake County	55	0.18
Randolph, NJ (township) Morris County	44	0.18
Hauppauge, NY (cdp) Suffolk County	37	0.18
Auburn Hills, MI (city) Oakland County	35	0.18
Tysons Corner, VA (cdp) Fairfax County	33	0.18
Bethel, CT (town) Fairfield County	32	0.18
Hinsdale, IL (village) Du Page County	32	0.18
Desert Hot Springs, CA (city) Riverside County	30	0.18
New Port Richey, FL (city) Pasco County	29	0.18
Gulf Gate Estates, FL (cdp) Sarasota County	21	0.18
Vashon, WA (cdp) King County	18	0.18
Bellevue, WA (city) King County	187	0.17
Greenburgh, NY (town) Westchester County	147	0.17
State College, PA (borough) Centre County	65	0.17
Monterey, CA (city) Monterey County	51	0.17
East Hill-Meridian, WA (cdp) King County	50	0.17
Agoura Hills, CA (city) Los Angeles County	35	0.17
Derby, KS (city) Sedgwick County	30	0.17
Holladay, UT (city) Salt Lake County	25	0.17
Whitehall, PA (borough) Allegheny County	24	0.17
Ephrata, PA (borough) Lancaster County	23	0.17
Grand Rapids, MN (township) Itasca County	20	0.17
Meadow Woods, FL (cdp) Orange County	20	0.17
Avon, OH (city) Lorain County	19	0.17
Sturgis, MI (city) Saint Joseph County	19	0.17
Alden, NY (town) Erie County	18	0.17
Marlton, NJ (cdp) Burlington County	17	0.17
Oakville, MO (cdp) Saint Louis County	58	0.16
Gurnee, IL (village) Lake County	46	0.16
Pikesville, MD (cdp) Baltimore County	45	0.16
Harrison, NY (village) Westchester County	39	0.16
Lodi, NJ (borough) Bergen County	39	0.16
Manchester, MO (city) Saint Louis County	30	0.16
Grosse Pointe Woods, MI (city) Wayne County	27	0.16
Tukwila, WA (city) King County	27	0.16
Aurora, NY (town) Erie County	22	0.16
Forest City, FL (cdp) Seminole County	20	0.16
Crestwood, MO (city) Saint Louis County	19	0.16
Middle Valley, TN (cdp) Hamilton County	19	0.16
South Miami, FL (city) Miami-Dade County	18	0.16
Moundsville, WV (city) Marshall County	16	0.16
Moore, OK (city) Cleveland County	62	0.15
Woburn, MA (city) Middlesex County	56	0.15
Dana Point, CA (city) Orange County	54	0.15
Mamaroneck, NY (town) Westchester County	44	0.15
Lafayette, CO (city) Boulder County	36	0.15
De Land, FL (city) Volusia County	31	0.15
New Milford, NJ (borough) Bergen County	25	0.15
Princeton, NJ (borough) Mercer County	22	0.15
Blue Ash, OH (city) Hamilton County	19	0.15
Munhall, PA (borough) Allegheny County	18	0.15
Beaumont, CA (city) Riverside County	17	0.15
Paradise, NV (cdp) Clark County	256	0.14
Schaumburg, IL (village) Cook County	103	0.14
Greenwich, CT (town) Fairfield County	86	0.14
La Mesa, CA (city) San Diego County	75	0.14
Palm Springs, CA (city) Riverside County	58	0.14
Melrose, MA (city) Middlesex County	37	0.14
Cottage Lake, WA (cdp) King County	35	0.14
Morton Grove, IL (village) Cook County	32	0.14
Picnic Point-North Lynnwood, WA (cdp) Snohomish County	32	0.14
West Windsor, NJ (township) Mercer County	31	0.14
Millbrae, CA (city) San Mateo County	29	0.14
Mountlake Terrace, WA (city) Snohomish County	29	0.14
Defiance, OH (city) Defiance County	23	0.14
Laguna Woods, CA (city) Orange County	22	0.14
Laurel, VA (cdp) Henrico County	20	0.14
Weston, CT (town) Fairfield County	14	0.14
Glendale, CA (city) Los Angeles County	262	0.13
Mount Pleasant, NY (town) Westchester County	56	0.13
Edmonds, WA (city) Snohomish County	52	0.13
Dunedin, FL (city) Pinellas County	45	0.13
Wilmette, IL (village) Cook County	37	0.13

Notes: (cdp) census designated place; Refer to the Explanation of Data in the front of the book for more detailed information.

Canadian

Top 150 Places Sorted by Number

(Based on all places, regardless of population)

Place	Number	%
New York, NY (city) New York City	9,744	0.12
Los Angeles, CA (city) Los Angeles County	8,181	0.22
San Diego, CA (city) San Diego County	4,036	0.33
Phoenix, AZ (city) Maricopa County	3,611	0.27
Boston, MA (city) Suffolk County	3,178	0.54
Seattle, WA (city) King County	2,761	0.49
Houston, TX (city) Harris County	2,420	0.12
San Jose, CA (city) Santa Clara County	2,112	0.24
Portland, OR (city) Multnomah County	2,088	0.39
Chicago, IL (city) Cook County	2,050	0.07
San Francisco, CA (city) San Francisco County	1,980	0.25
Las Vegas, NV (city) Clark County	1,969	0.41
Scottsdale, AZ (city) Maricopa County	1,706	0.84
Manchester, NH (city) Hillsborough County	1,570	1.47
Jacksonville, FL (special city) Duval County	1,400	0.19
Virginia Beach, VA (independent city) Virginia Beach city	1,383	0.33
San Antonio, TX (city) Bexar County	1,379	0.12
Dallas, TX (city) Dallas County	1,377	0.12
Tucson, AZ (city) Pima County	1,335	0.27
Mesa, AZ (city) Maricopa County	1,332	0.34
Hempstead, NY (town) Nassau County	1,319	0.17
Charlotte, NC (city) Mecklenburg County	1,269	0.23
Quincy, MA (city) Norfolk County	1,191	1.35
Brookhaven, NY (town) Suffolk County	1,179	0.26
Austin, TX (city) Travis County	1,170	0.18
Hollywood, FL (city) Broward County	1,156	0.83
Huntington Beach, CA (city) Orange County	1,141	0.60
Detroit, MI (city) Wayne County	1,094	0.12
Waltham, MA (city) Middlesex County	1,086	1.83
Albuquerque, NM (city) Bernalillo County	1,086	0.24
Anchorage, AK (municipality) Anchorage Borough	1,072	0.41
Philadelphia, PA (city) Philadelphia County	1,059	0.07
Denver, CO (city) Denver County	1,057	0.19
Long Beach, CA (city) Los Angeles County	1,036	0.22
Columbus, OH (city) Franklin County	1,034	0.15
Plano, TX (city) Collin County	1,014	0.46
Colorado Springs, CO (city) El Paso County	991	0.27
Amherst, NY (town) Erie County	985	0.85
Nashua, NH (city) Hillsborough County	980	1.13
Saint Petersburg, FL (city) Pinellas County	963	0.39
Washington, DC (city) District of Columbia	948	0.17
Bellevue, WA (city) King County	936	0.86
Livonia, MI (city) Wayne County	910	0.91
Spokane, WA (city) Spokane County	894	0.46
Cambridge, MA (city) Middlesex County	880	0.87
Indianapolis, IN (special city) Marion County	873	0.11
Santa Clarita, CA (city) Los Angeles County	871	0.58
Warren, MI (city) Macomb County	861	0.62
Newton, MA (city) Middlesex County	845	1.01
Raleigh, NC (city) Wake County	836	0.30
Anaheim, CA (city) Orange County	834	0.25
Irvine, CA (city) Orange County	795	0.56
Weymouth, MA (cdp) Norfolk County	781	1.45
Somerville, MA (city) Middlesex County	779	1.01
Thousand Oaks, CA (city) Ventura County	773	0.66
Troy, MI (city) Oakland County	771	0.95
Riverside, CA (city) Riverside County	757	0.30
Buffalo, NY (city) Erie County	753	0.26
Farmington Hills, MI (city) Oakland County	739	0.90
Nashville-Davidson, TN (special city) Davidson County	726	0.13
Canton, MI (cdp) Wayne County	721	0.94
Sacramento, CA (city) Sacramento County	717	0.18
Deerfield Beach, FL (city) Broward County	708	1.09
Westland, MI (city) Wayne County	705	0.81
Simi Valley, CA (city) Ventura County	703	0.63
Eugene, OR (city) Lane County	700	0.51
Largo, FL (city) Pinellas County	699	1.01
Springfield, MA (city) Hampden County	688	0.45
Ann Arbor, MI (city) Washtenaw County	682	0.60
Toledo, OH (city) Lucas County	682	0.22
Glendale, AZ (city) Maricopa County	674	0.31
Fort Lauderdale, FL (city) Broward County	655	0.43
Aurora, CO (city) Arapahoe County	654	0.24
Fremont, CA (city) Alameda County	649	0.32
Malden, MA (city) Middlesex County	646	1.15
Oakland, CA (city) Alameda County	639	0.16
Kansas City, MO (city) Jackson County	638	0.14
Waterford, MI (cdp) Oakland County	635	0.87
Costa Mesa, CA (city) Orange County	630	0.58
Durham, NC (city) Durham County	628	0.34
Henderson, NV (city) Clark County	627	0.36
Bellingham, WA (city) Whatcom County	625	0.94
Lynn, MA (city) Essex County	622	0.70
Worcester, MA (city) Worcester County	619	0.36
Sterling Heights, MI (city) Macomb County	614	0.49
Fort Worth, TX (city) Tarrant County	606	0.11
Royal Oak, MI (city) Oakland County	604	1.01
Coral Springs, FL (city) Broward County	599	0.51
Tacoma, WA (city) Pierce County	599	0.31
Minneapolis, MN (city) Hennepin County	598	0.16
Salt Lake City, UT (city) Salt Lake County	594	0.33
Rochester Hills, MI (city) Oakland County	593	0.86
Oklahoma City, OK (city) Oklahoma County	593	0.12
Fresno, CA (city) Fresno County	592	0.14
Pasadena, CA (city) Los Angeles County	586	0.44
Medford, MA (city) Middlesex County	584	1.05
Oyster Bay, NY (town) Nassau County	583	0.20
Islip, NY (town) Suffolk County	583	0.18
Boca Raton, FL (city) Palm Beach County	582	0.77
Clinton, MI (cdp) Macomb County	581	0.61
Reno, NV (city) Washoe County	580	0.32
Grand Rapids, MI (city) Kent County	580	0.29
Santa Rosa, CA (city) Sonoma County	576	0.39
Billerica, MA (town) Middlesex County	574	1.47
Clearwater, FL (city) Pinellas County	570	0.53
Chandler, AZ (city) Maricopa County	570	0.32
Vancouver, WA (city) Clark County	567	0.40
Paradise, NV (cdp) Clark County	561	0.30
Atlanta, GA (city) Fulton County	556	0.13
Naperville, IL (city) Du Page County	554	0.43
Escondido, CA (city) San Diego County	553	0.41
Lewiston, ME (city) Androscoggin County	550	1.54
Brookline, MA (cdp) Norfolk County	549	0.96
Pembroke Pines, FL (city) Broward County	544	0.40
Arlington, VA (cdp) Arlington County	541	0.29
Glendale, CA (city) Los Angeles County	540	0.28
Framingham, MA (cdp) Middlesex County	539	0.81
Oceanside, CA (city) San Diego County	537	0.33
Gilbert, AZ (town) Maricopa County	532	0.48
Lexington-Fayette, KY (special city) Fayette County	531	0.20
Tampa, FL (city) Hillsborough County	531	0.17
Beaverton, OR (city) Washington County	530	0.70
Arlington, MA (cdp) Middlesex County	529	1.25
Plantation, FL (city) Broward County	528	0.63
Saint Clair Shores, MI (city) Macomb County	522	0.83
Cary, NC (town) Wake County	518	0.55
Madison, WI (city) Dane County	518	0.25
Pompano Beach, FL (city) Broward County	516	0.66
Greece, NY (town) Monroe County	516	0.55
Sunnyvale, CA (city) Santa Clara County	515	0.39
Peabody, MA (city) Essex County	514	1.07
Orange, CA (city) Orange County	513	0.40
Torrance, CA (city) Los Angeles County	511	0.37
Corona, CA (city) Riverside County	509	0.41
Cape Coral, FL (city) Lee County	508	0.50
Natick, MA (town) Middlesex County	507	1.58
West Bloomfield, MI (township) Oakland County	507	0.78
Tulsa, OK (city) Tulsa County	507	0.13
Tempe, AZ (city) Maricopa County	506	0.32
Everett, MA (city) Middlesex County	505	1.33
Carlsbad, CA (city) San Diego County	503	0.64
Bakersfield, CA (city) Kern County	503	0.20
Chesapeake, VA (independent city) Chesapeake city	500	0.25
Midland, MI (city) Midland County	495	1.19
Mission Viejo, CA (city) Orange County	495	0.53
Novi, MI (city) Oakland County	494	1.04
Spring Valley, NV (cdp) Clark County	493	0.42
Rochester, NY (city) Monroe County	492	0.22
Greensboro, NC (city) Guilford County	489	0.22
Plymouth, MA (town) Plymouth County	488	0.94

Notes: (cdp) census designated place; Refer to the Explanation of Data in the front of the book for more detailed information.

Canadian

Top 150 Places Sorted by Percent

(Based on all places, regardless of population)

Place	Number	%
Parc, NY (cdp) Clinton County	11	22.45
Hyder, AK (cdp) Prince of Wales-Outer Ketchikan Census Area	20	20.41
Shoal Creek Estates, MO (town) Newton County	7	15.91
Oto, IA (city) Woodbury County	19	13.29
Centerville, ME (town) Washington County	4	12.90
Humboldt, MN (city) Kittson County	5	10.87
Ravenswood Estates, FL (cdp) Broward County	100	10.72
Game Creek, AK (cdp) Skagway-Hoonah-Angoon Census Area	3	10.71
Victory, VT (town) Essex County	11	10.38
Pekin, ND (city) Nelson County	7	9.59
Kendall, WA (cdp) Whatcom County	6	9.09
Scotts Mills, OR (city) Marion County	26	8.90
Rogers, MN (township) Cass County	4	8.89
Muir Beach, CA (cdp) Marin County	24	8.70
Clio, IA (city) Wayne County	10	8.33
Zilwaukee, MI (township) Saginaw County	5	8.33
Mason, WI (village) Bayfield County	3	8.33
Blaine, ME (town) Aroostook County	62	7.76
Village Park, FL (cdp) Broward County	82	7.56
Nome, ND (city) Barnes County	6	7.50
Lonetree, WY (cdp) Uinta County	6	7.41
Glacier View, AK (cdp) Matanuska-Susitna Borough	18	7.29
Westdale, TX (cdp) Jim Wells County	24	6.78
Timber Hills, PA (cdp) Lebanon County	23	6.53
Eldora, CO (cdp) Boulder County	14	6.31
Shady Grove, OK (town) Pawnee County	2	6.06
Clifford, ND (city) Traill County	3	6.00
Vanceboro, ME (town) Washington County	9	5.92
Seboeis, ME (plantation) Penobscot County	2	5.71
Brewster Hill, NY (cdp) Putnam County	121	5.54
Almont, ND (city) Morton County	6	5.50
North Beach, FL (cdp) Indian River County	12	5.43
La Fargeville, NY (cdp) Jefferson County	32	5.38
Mars Hill-Blaine, ME (cdp) Aroostook County	73	5.12
Smyrna, NY (village) Chenango County	12	5.11
Coplin, ME (plantation) Franklin County	9	5.08
Lubec, ME (town) Washington County	82	5.06
Crawford, ME (town) Washington County	5	5.00
Greensboro, VT (town) Orleans County	38	4.99
Sims, IL (village) Wayne County	13	4.98
Monticello, ME (town) Aroostook County	39	4.96
Mapleton, ME (town) Aroostook County	94	4.94
Derby Line, VT (village) Orleans County	39	4.92
Shambaugh, IA (city) Page County	9	4.81
Gann, OH (village) Knox County	7	4.76
Mooers, NY (cdp) Clinton County	19	4.73
New Middletown, IN (town) Harrison County	3	4.69
Birch Bay, WA (cdp) Whatcom County	230	4.63
Tamarack, MN (city) Aitkin County	3	4.55
Newcomb, NY (town) Essex County	22	4.53
Chilhowee, MO (town) Johnson County	15	4.49
Jackson Center, PA (borough) Mercer County	10	4.48
Fairfield Harbour, NC (cdp) Craven County	82	4.40
Bridgewater, ME (town) Aroostook County	27	4.39
Lyons Switch, OK (cdp) Adair County	9	4.33
Meadow Acres, WY (cdp) Natrona County	10	4.26
Dunes Road, FL (cdp) Palm Beach County	20	4.23
Fort Fairfield, ME (town) Aroostook County	151	4.22
Mars Hill, ME (town) Aroostook County	62	4.17
Bondsville, MA (cdp) Hampden County	74	4.09
Maxfield, ME (town) Penobscot County	3	4.05
Saint Francis, AR (city) Clay County	10	4.03
Dennysville, ME (town) Washington County	13	3.99
Long Island, ME (town) Cumberland County	8	3.98
Copake Lake, NY (cdp) Columbia County	32	3.96
Morehouse, NY (town) Hamilton County	5	3.91
Troy, VT (town) Orleans County	61	3.89
Hope, ID (city) Bonner County	3	3.85
Isle La Motte, VT (town) Grand Isle County	19	3.82
Baring, ME (plantation) Washington County	10	3.80
Acton, CA (cdp) Los Angeles County	82	3.79
Westfield, ME (town) Aroostook County	21	3.76
Metamora, MI (village) Lapeer County	21	3.74
Redwood, NY (cdp) Jefferson County	24	3.70
Gull Lake, WI (town) Washburn County	5	3.68
Champlain, NY (village) Clinton County	44	3.66
Wessington, SD (city) Beadle County	10	3.64
Woodland, ME (cdp) Washington County	38	3.60
Merrill, ME (town) Aroostook County	9	3.60
Estates of Fort Lauderdale, FL (cdp) Broward County	66	3.58
Saint John, ME (plantation) Aroostook County	10	3.56
Clio, SC (town) Marlboro County	28	3.54
Westbrook, TX (city) Mitchell County	8	3.51
East Merrimack, NH (cdp) Hillsborough County	130	3.49
Dexter, WI (town) Wood County	14	3.46
Iron Horse, CA (cdp) Plumas County	12	3.46
Gorham, NH (town) Coos County	100	3.45
Gorton, MN (township) Grant County	2	3.45
Washington, VT (town) Orange County	36	3.44
Willow Valley, AZ (cdp) Mohave County	19	3.44
Island Pond, VT (cdp) Essex County	29	3.40
Bay View, WA (cdp) Skagit County	15	3.39
Blaine, WA (city) Whatcom County	125	3.37
Stewartstown, NH (town) Coos County	33	3.26
Richford, VT (town) Franklin County	75	3.23
Perham, ME (town) Aroostook County	14	3.23
Gratz, KY (city) Owen County	3	3.23
Arriba, CO (town) Lincoln County	4	3.19
Smithland, IA (city) Woodbury County	7	3.18
Jupiter, MN (township) Kittson County	4	3.17
Mooers, NY (town) Clinton County	107	3.14
Canaan, VT (town) Essex County	34	3.11
Goshen, VT (town) Addison County	6	3.11
Henderson, MI (township) Wexford County	5	3.11
Wallagrass, ME (town) Aroostook County	17	3.07
Caswell, ME (town) Aroostook County	9	3.07
Ulysses, NE (village) Butler County	7	3.06
North Yarmouth, ME (town) Cumberland County	98	3.05
Andrews, FL (cdp) Levy County	23	3.05
Rouses Point, NY (village) Clinton County	70	3.03
Baileyville, ME (town) Washington County	51	3.02
Cesar Chavez, TX (cdp) Hidalgo County	42	3.02
Elliston, MT (cdp) Powell County	7	3.02
Pembroke Park, FL (town) Broward County	191	3.01
Newark, VT (town) Caledonia County	14	3.00
Round Lake, MN (township) Becker County	5	2.98
Calais, ME (city) Washington County	101	2.93
Hunts Point, WA (town) King County	13	2.93
Alvarado, MN (city) Marshall County	10	2.92
Melvin, MI (village) Sanilac County	4	2.92
Lyon Mountain, NY (cdp) Clinton County	14	2.90
Cuba, AL (town) Sumter County	12	2.90
Broughton, OH (village) Paulding County	6	2.90
Champlain, NY (town) Clinton County	167	2.88
Hypoluxo, FL (town) Palm Beach County	58	2.87
Berkshire, VT (town) Franklin County	40	2.87
Grant, MI (township) Grand Traverse County	27	2.87
Piercefield, NY (town) Saint Lawrence County	9	2.87
Carmine, TX (city) Fayette County	6	2.84
Spurr, MI (township) Baraga County	6	2.84
Rock Falls, IA (city) Cerro Gordo County	5	2.84
Salome, AZ (cdp) La Paz County	32	2.82
Sorrento, ME (town) Hancock County	8	2.82
Grass Range, MT (town) Fergus County	4	2.82
Brighton, VT (town) Essex County	35	2.78
Ripley, ME (town) Somerset County	11	2.77
Hartford, OH (village) Licking County	11	2.76
Winterport, ME (town) Waldo County	99	2.75
Vista West, WY (cdp) Natrona County	25	2.75
Bryn Athyn, PA (borough) Montgomery County	37	2.74
Ames Lake, WA (cdp) King County	39	2.73
Granville, ND (city) McHenry County	8	2.73
Alta, WY (cdp) Teton County	12	2.69
Eastport, ME (city) Washington County	44	2.68
Bliss, MI (township) Emmet County	16	2.68
Bridgewater, NH (town) Grafton County	26	2.67
Butte City, ID (city) Butte County	2	2.67
Port Royal, PA (borough) Juniata County	26	2.66
Presque Isle, ME (city) Aroostook County	252	2.65
Snowville, UT (town) Box Elder County	5	2.65

Notes: (cdp) census designated place; Refer to the Explanation of Data in the front of the book for more detailed information.

Canadian

Top 150 Places Sorted by Percent

(Based on places with populations of 10,000 or more)

Place	Number	%
Maynard, MA (cdp) Middlesex County	213	2.04
Reading, MA (cdp) Middlesex County	463	1.95
Goffstown, NH (town) Hillsborough County	322	1.90
Wayland, MA (town) Middlesex County	248	1.89
Bedford, NH (town) Hillsborough County	344	1.88
Waltham, MA (city) Middlesex County	1,086	1.83
Fort Gratiot, MI (township) Saint Clair County	193	1.81
Lewiston, NY (town) Niagara County	291	1.79
Bedford, MA (town) Middlesex County	225	1.79
Pembroke, MA (town) Plymouth County	302	1.78
Merrimack, NH (town) Hillsborough County	442	1.76
Berlin, NH (city) Coos County	180	1.74
Melrose, MA (city) Middlesex County	465	1.71
North Reading, MA (town) Middlesex County	229	1.65
Wilmington, MA (cdp) Middlesex County	345	1.61
Southbridge, MA (town) Worcester County	276	1.60
Oakland charter, MI (township) Oakland County	209	1.60
Salem, NH (town) Rockingham County	446	1.59
Somersworth, NH (city) Strafford County	182	1.59
Natick, MA (town) Middlesex County	507	1.58
Tewksbury, MA (town) Middlesex County	454	1.57
Brighton, MI (township) Livingston County	278	1.57
Rockland, MA (town) Plymouth County	277	1.57
South Burlington, VT (city) Chittenden County	248	1.57
Northborough, MA (town) Worcester County	220	1.57
Saint Simons, GA (cdp) Glynn County	209	1.55
Windham, NH (town) Rockingham County	166	1.55
Lewiston, ME (city) Androscoggin County	550	1.54
Rancho Mirage, CA (city) Riverside County	197	1.52
Englewood, FL (cdp) Sarasota County	244	1.50
Norwood, MA (cdp) Norfolk County	424	1.48
Manchester, NH (city) Hillsborough County	1,570	1.47
Billerica, MA (town) Middlesex County	574	1.47
Plainfield, CT (town) Windham County	215	1.47
Grand Island, NY (town) Erie County	272	1.46
Weymouth, MA (cdp) Norfolk County	781	1.45
Watertown, MA (city) Middlesex County	477	1.45
Norfolk, MA (town) Norfolk County	152	1.45
Ogdensburg, NY (city) Saint Lawrence County	178	1.44
Hooksett, NH (town) Merrimack County	169	1.44
Ipswich, MA (town) Essex County	185	1.42
Athol, MA (town) Worcester County	161	1.42
Pepperell, MA (town) Middlesex County	156	1.40
Massena, NY (town) Saint Lawrence County	182	1.39
Gloucester, MA (city) Essex County	419	1.38
North Smithfield, RI (town) Providence County	147	1.38
Hallandale, FL (city) Broward County	475	1.37
Dedham, MA (cdp) Norfolk County	321	1.37
Bellingham, MA (town) Norfolk County	209	1.36
Swampscott, MA (cdp) Essex County	196	1.36
South Yarmouth, MA (cdp) Barnstable County	160	1.36
Mill Creek, WA (city) Snohomish County	156	1.36
Quincy, MA (city) Norfolk County	1,191	1.35
Darien, CT (cdp) Fairfield County	265	1.35
Everett, MA (city) Middlesex County	505	1.33
Hanover, MA (town) Plymouth County	175	1.33
Walpole, MA (town) Norfolk County	299	1.31
Easton, MA (town) Bristol County	292	1.31
Stoneham, MA (town) Middlesex County	289	1.30
Colchester, VT (town) Chittenden County	220	1.30
Massena, NY (village) Saint Lawrence County	146	1.30
Abington, MA (cdp) Plymouth County	189	1.29
Lynnfield, MA (cdp) Essex County	149	1.29
Hudson, NH (town) Hillsborough County	293	1.28
Braintree, MA (town) Norfolk County	431	1.27
Chelmsford, MA (town) Middlesex County	429	1.27
Calabasas, CA (city) Los Angeles County	256	1.27
Lebanon, NH (city) Grafton County	159	1.27
Ashland, MA (town) Middlesex County	185	1.26
North Palm Beach, FL (village) Palm Beach County	153	1.26
Arlington, MA (cdp) Middlesex County	529	1.25
East Lake, FL (cdp) Pinellas County	369	1.25
Biddeford, ME (city) York County	262	1.25
Northville, MI (township) Wayne County	262	1.25
Medfield, MA (town) Norfolk County	154	1.25
Derry, NH (town) Rockingham County	421	1.24
Palmer, MA (town) Hampden County	155	1.24
Half Moon Bay, CA (city) San Mateo County	148	1.24
Dracut, MA (town) Middlesex County	351	1.23
Sanford, ME (town) York County	256	1.23
Canton, NY (town) Saint Lawrence County	127	1.23
Sudbury, MA (town) Middlesex County	206	1.22
Sammamish, WA (city) King County	413	1.21
Franklin, MA (city) Norfolk County	355	1.20
Whitman, MA (town) Plymouth County	166	1.20
Midland, MI (city) Midland County	495	1.19
Plattsburgh, NY (town) Clinton County	132	1.19
Kennebunk, ME (town) York County	125	1.19
Laguna Beach, CA (city) Orange County	275	1.18
Winthrop, MA (cdp) Suffolk County	216	1.18
Hudson, FL (cdp) Pasco County	149	1.17
Edmonds, WA (city) Snohomish County	459	1.16
Sandwich, MA (town) Barnstable County	234	1.16
Easthampton, MA (city) Hampshire County	185	1.16
Malden, MA (city) Middlesex County	646	1.15
East Bridgewater, MA (town) Plymouth County	149	1.15
Healdsburg, CA (city) Sonoma County	122	1.15
Gardner, MA (city) Worcester County	237	1.14
Portsmouth, NH (city) Rockingham County	236	1.14
Nashua, NH (city) Hillsborough County	980	1.13
Danvers, MA (cdp) Essex County	286	1.13
Princeton, NJ (borough) Mercer County	160	1.13
Marlborough, MA (city) Middlesex County	406	1.12
Acton, MA (town) Middlesex County	227	1.12
Madison Heights, MI (city) Oakland County	344	1.11
Wareham, MA (town) Plymouth County	225	1.11
Lyon, MI (township) Oakland County	122	1.11
Wakefield, MA (cdp) Middlesex County	274	1.10
South Hadley, MA (town) Hampshire County	189	1.10
Wolf Trap, VA (cdp) Fairfax County	152	1.10
Carver, MA (town) Plymouth County	123	1.10
Deerfield Beach, FL (city) Broward County	708	1.09
Wellesley, MA (cdp) Norfolk County	290	1.09
Watertown, NY (city) Jefferson County	289	1.08
Marshfield, MA (town) Plymouth County	262	1.08
Saco, ME (city) York County	182	1.08
Foxborough, MA (town) Norfolk County	175	1.08
Hartford, VT (town) Windsor County	112	1.08
Peabody, MA (city) Essex County	514	1.07
Mercer Island, WA (city) King County	235	1.07
Hamburg, MI (township) Livingston County	219	1.07
Exeter, NH (town) Rockingham County	150	1.07
Leominster, MA (city) Worcester County	437	1.06
Stoughton, MA (town) Norfolk County	287	1.06
Birmingham, MI (city) Oakland County	206	1.06
Union Hill-Novelty Hill, WA (cdp) King County	118	1.06
Medford, MA (city) Middlesex County	584	1.05
Yarmouth, MA (town) Barnstable County	261	1.05
Auburn, ME (city) Androscoggin County	243	1.05
Londonderry, NH (town) Rockingham County	243	1.05
Laconia, NH (city) Belknap County	173	1.05
Novi, MI (city) Oakland County	494	1.04
Redmond, WA (city) King County	473	1.04
Dunedin, FL (city) Pinellas County	374	1.04
Holiday, FL (cdp) Pasco County	227	1.04
Newburyport, MA (city) Essex County	179	1.04
Rye, NY (city) Westchester County	155	1.04
Fenton, MI (township) Genesee County	134	1.04
Rochester, MI (city) Oakland County	109	1.04
Bloomfield, MI (township) Oakland County	444	1.03
Woburn, MA (city) Middlesex County	382	1.03
Davison, MI (township) Genesee County	182	1.03
Grafton, MA (town) Worcester County	154	1.03
Mill Valley, CA (city) Marin County	139	1.03
Coventry, CT (town) Tolland County	119	1.03
Newton, MA (city) Middlesex County	845	1.01
Somerville, MA (city) Middlesex County	779	1.01
Largo, FL (city) Pinellas County	699	1.01
Royal Oak, MI (city) Oakland County	604	1.01
Bainbridge Island, WA (city) Kitsap County	206	1.01

Notes: (cdp) census designated place; Refer to the Explanation of Data in the front of the book for more detailed information.

Carpatho Rusyn

Top 150 Places Sorted by Number

(Based on all places, regardless of population)

Place	Number	%
New York, NY (city) New York City	138	0.00
Pittsburgh, PA (city) Allegheny County	116	0.03
Johnstown, PA (city) Cambria County	67	0.28
Union, NY (town) Broome County	62	0.11
Uniontown, PA (city) Fayette County	54	0.43
Binghamton, NY (city) Broome County	52	0.11
McKees Rocks, PA (borough) Allegheny County	51	0.77
Akron, OH (city) Summit County	51	0.02
Baidland, PA (cdp) Washington County	50	3.09
Carroll, PA (township) Washington County	50	0.88
Cleveland, OH (city) Cuyahoga County	48	0.01
Minneapolis, MN (city) Hennepin County	48	0.01
West Hanover, PA (township) Dauphin County	47	0.72
Municipality of Monroeville, PA (borough) Allegheny County	47	0.16
Stamford, CT (city) Fairfield County	47	0.04
Los Angeles, CA (city) Los Angeles County	44	0.00
Glen Burnie, MD (cdp) Anne Arundel County	42	0.11
Columbus, OH (city) Franklin County	41	0.01
Onalaska, WI (city) La Crosse County	40	0.27
Denver, CO (city) Denver County	40	0.01
Idaho Falls, ID (city) Bonneville County	39	0.08
Owego, NY (town) Tioga County	38	0.19
Plum, PA (borough) Allegheny County	38	0.14
El Paso, TX (city) El Paso County	38	0.01
Lower Paxton, PA (township) Dauphin County	37	0.08
Fort Worth, TX (city) Tarrant County	37	0.01
Chicago, IL (city) Cook County	37	0.00
Mount Lebanon, PA (cdp) Allegheny County	36	0.11
Scranton, PA (city) Lackawanna County	36	0.05
North Laurel, MD (cdp) Howard County	35	0.17
Warren, MI (city) Macomb County	35	0.03
Lower Yoder, PA (township) Cambria County	34	1.12
Duquesne, PA (city) Allegheny County	34	0.46
West Mifflin, PA (borough) Allegheny County	34	0.15
McKeesport, PA (city) Allegheny County	34	0.14
North Royalton, OH (city) Cuyahoga County	34	0.12
Parma, OH (city) Cuyahoga County	34	0.04
Taylor, PA (borough) Lackawanna County	33	0.51
Colonia, NJ (cdp) Middlesex County	33	0.19
Stratford, CT (cdp) Fairfield County	33	0.07
Woodbridge, NJ (township) Middlesex County	33	0.03
Aspen Hill, MD (cdp) Montgomery County	31	0.06
Fox Run, PA (cdp) Butler County	30	0.96
Brooklyn, OH (city) Cuyahoga County	30	0.26
Amherst, OH (city) Lorain County	30	0.25
Weehawken, NJ (township) Hudson County	30	0.22
Johnson City, NY (village) Broome County	30	0.19
Cranberry, PA (township) Butler County	30	0.13
Moon, PA (township) Allegheny County	30	0.13
Chesapeake, VA (independent city) Chesapeake city	30	0.02
Trumbull, CT (cdp) Fairfield County	29	0.08
Fruitland, MD (city) Wicomico County	28	0.75
Forest Hills, PA (borough) Allegheny County	27	0.40
Jefferson, NJ (township) Morris County	27	0.14
Ross Township, PA (cdp) Allegheny County	27	0.08
Dallas, TX (city) Dallas County	27	0.00
Albuquerque, NM (city) Bernalillo County	26	0.01
Freeland, PA (borough) Luzerne County	25	0.69
New Baltimore, NY (town) Greene County	24	0.71
Monaca, PA (borough) Beaver County	24	0.38
Wilson, PA (borough) Northampton County	24	0.31
Butler, PA (township) Butler County	24	0.14
Bridgeport, CT (city) Fairfield County	24	0.02
Anchorage, AK (municipality) Anchorage Borough	24	0.01
Scott, PA (township) Lackawanna County	23	0.47
Stowe Township, PA (cdp) Allegheny County	23	0.34
Bristol, PA (township) Bucks County	23	0.04
Glassport, PA (borough) Allegheny County	22	0.44
Colonial Park, PA (cdp) Dauphin County	22	0.17
Saratoga, CA (city) Santa Clara County	22	0.07
Charlotte, NC (city) Mecklenburg County	22	0.00
White Oak, PA (borough) Allegheny County	21	0.25
Mount Pleasant, PA (township) Westmoreland County	21	0.19
Perrysburg, OH (city) Wood County	21	0.12
Parma Heights, OH (city) Cuyahoga County	21	0.10

Place	Number	%
Warren, OH (city) Trumbull County	21	0.04
Reade, PA (township) Cambria County	20	1.15
Donora, PA (borough) Washington County	20	0.35
Chenango, NY (town) Broome County	20	0.17
Endwell, NY (cdp) Broome County	20	0.17
Tenafly, NJ (borough) Bergen County	20	0.14
Bethel Park, PA (borough) Allegheny County	20	0.06
McLean, VA (cdp) Fairfax County	20	0.05
Sewickley, PA (township) Westmoreland County	19	0.31
Macedonia, OH (city) Summit County	19	0.21
Dormont, PA (borough) Allegheny County	19	0.20
Hanover, NJ (township) Morris County	19	0.15
Garfield, NJ (city) Bergen County	19	0.06
Linden, NJ (city) Union County	19	0.05
Silver Spring, MD (cdp) Montgomery County	19	0.02
Bardonia, NY (cdp) Rockland County	18	0.41
Bedford, OH (city) Cuyahoga County	18	0.13
Ferndale, MI (city) Oakland County	18	0.08
Bristol, CT (city) Hartford County	18	0.03
Clarkstown, NY (town) Rockland County	18	0.02
Phoenix, AZ (city) Maricopa County	18	0.00
Orchard Hills, PA (cdp) Armstrong County	17	0.79
Kiskiminetas, PA (township) Armstrong County	17	0.34
Georges, PA (township) Fayette County	17	0.24
Solebury, PA (township) Bucks County	17	0.22
Dunmore, PA (borough) Lackawanna County	17	0.12
New Castle, PA (city) Lawrence County	17	0.06
Ballwin, MO (city) Saint Louis County	17	0.05
Sheboygan, WI (city) Sheboygan County	17	0.03
Orlando, FL (city) Orange County	17	0.01
Boston, MA (city) Suffolk County	17	0.00
Detroit, MI (city) Wayne County	17	0.00
Alpharetta, GA (city) Fulton County	16	0.05
Wilkes-Barre, PA (city) Luzerne County	16	0.04
Franklin, NJ (township) Somerset County	16	0.03
Yorba Linda, CA (city) Orange County	16	0.03
Port Saint Lucie, FL (city) Saint Lucie County	16	0.02
Perryopolis, PA (borough) Fayette County	15	0.85
Nesquehoning, PA (borough) Carbon County	15	0.47
Upper Yoder, PA (township) Cambria County	15	0.26
Kennedy Township, PA (cdp) Allegheny County	15	0.20
Chatham, NJ (borough) Morris County	15	0.18
Campbell, OH (city) Mahoning County	15	0.16
Hobe Sound, FL (cdp) Martin County	15	0.13
Westchester, IL (village) Cook County	15	0.09
Ashland, OR (city) Jackson County	15	0.08
Willoughby, OH (city) Lake County	15	0.07
Harrisburg, PA (city) Dauphin County	15	0.03
Lakewood, OH (city) Cuyahoga County	15	0.03
Trenton, NJ (city) Mercer County	15	0.02
Ben Avon, PA (borough) Allegheny County	14	0.73
Chester, NY (village) Orange County	14	0.39
Ellwood City, PA (borough) Lawrence County	14	0.16
Chester, NY (town) Orange County	14	0.12
Cherry Hill Mall, NJ (cdp) Camden County	14	0.10
Derry, PA (township) Westmoreland County	14	0.10
Kingston, PA (borough) Luzerne County	14	0.10
Hermitage, PA (city) Mercer County	14	0.09
Solon, OH (city) Cuyahoga County	14	0.06
Colton, CA (city) San Bernardino County	14	0.03
Cherry Hill, NJ (township) Camden County	14	0.02
Allentown, PA (city) Lehigh County	14	0.01
Foster, PA (township) Luzerne County	13	0.38
Monessen, PA (city) Westmoreland County	13	0.15
Idylwood, VA (cdp) Fairfax County	13	0.08
Randolph, NJ (township) Morris County	13	0.05
McCandless Township, PA (cdp) Allegheny County	13	0.04
Millcreek, UT (cdp) Salt Lake County	13	0.04
Piscataway, NJ (township) Middlesex County	13	0.03
Boulder, CO (city) Boulder County	13	0.01
Providence, RI (city) Providence County	13	0.01
East McKeesport, PA (borough) Allegheny County	12	0.51
Sharpsville, PA (borough) Mercer County	12	0.27
Edwardsville, PA (borough) Luzerne County	12	0.24
Cambria, PA (township) Cambria County	12	0.19

Notes: (cdp) census designated place; Refer to the Explanation of Data in the front of the book for more detailed information.

Carpatho Rusyn

Top 150 Places Sorted by Percent

(Based on all places, regardless of population)

Place	Number	%
Baidland, PA (cdp) Washington County	50	3.09
Reade, PA (township) Cambria County	20	1.15
Lower Yoder, PA (township) Cambria County	34	1.12
Vance Creek, WI (town) Barron County	7	1.00
Herminie, PA (cdp) Westmoreland County	7	0.98
Fox Run, PA (cdp) Butler County	30	0.96
Colburn, WI (town) Chippewa County	7	0.94
Franklin, PA (borough) Cambria County	4	0.91
Carroll, PA (township) Washington County	50	0.88
Perryopolis, PA (borough) Fayette County	15	0.85
Ernest, PA (borough) Indiana County	4	0.80
Orchard Hills, PA (cdp) Armstrong County	17	0.79
McKees Rocks, PA (borough) Allegheny County	51	0.77
Barkeyville, PA (borough) Venango County	2	0.77
Fruitland, MD (city) Wicomico County	28	0.75
Ben Avon, PA (borough) Allegheny County	14	0.73
West Hanover, PA (township) Dauphin County	47	0.72
New Castle, PA (township) Schuylkill County	3	0.72
Bear Creek Village, PA (borough) Luzerne County	2	0.72
New Baltimore, NY (town) Greene County	24	0.71
Osborne, PA (borough) Allegheny County	4	0.71
Freeland, PA (borough) Luzerne County	25	0.69
Gilberton, PA (borough) Schuylkill County	6	0.69
Wall, PA (borough) Allegheny County	5	0.68
Blawnox, PA (borough) Allegheny County	10	0.65
Roseland, FL (cdp) Indian River County	11	0.61
East Pittsburgh, PA (borough) Allegheny County	11	0.55
Allenport, PA (borough) Washington County	3	0.52
Ben Avon Heights, PA (borough) Allegheny County	2	0.52
Taylor, PA (borough) Lackawanna County	33	0.51
East McKeesport, PA (borough) Allegheny County	12	0.51
Banks, PA (township) Carbon County	7	0.51
Lincoln, PA (borough) Allegheny County	6	0.50
Walden, VT (town) Caledonia County	4	0.50
Fairfield Harbour, NC (cdp) Craven County	9	0.48
Briny Breezes, FL (town) Palm Beach County	2	0.48
Scott, PA (township) Lackawanna County	23	0.47
Nesquehoning, PA (borough) Carbon County	15	0.47
Duquesne, PA (city) Allegheny County	34	0.46
Youngstown, NY (village) Niagara County	9	0.46
Paint, PA (borough) Somerset County	5	0.45
Glassport, PA (borough) Allegheny County	22	0.44
Uniontown, PA (city) Fayette County	54	0.43
Falls Creek, PA (borough) Jefferson County	4	0.42
Whitney Point, NY (village) Broome County	4	0.42
Bardonia, NY (cdp) Rockland County	18	0.41
Beaver Meadows, PA (borough) Carbon County	3	0.41
Forest Hills, PA (borough) Allegheny County	27	0.40
Chester, NY (village) Orange County	14	0.39
Brownsville, PA (township) Fayette County	3	0.39
Monaca, PA (borough) Beaver County	24	0.38
Foster, PA (township) Luzerne County	13	0.38
Wilson, WY (cdp) Teton County	5	0.38
Hot Sulphur Springs, CO (town) Grand County	2	0.38
Ortonville, MN (city) Big Stone County	8	0.37
Belle Valley, OH (village) Noble County	1	0.37
Grand Isle, VT (town) Grand Isle County	7	0.36
Leaf River, IL (village) Ogle County	2	0.36
Donora, PA (borough) Washington County	20	0.35
Ortonville, MN (township) Big Stone County	8	0.35
Versailles, PA (borough) Allegheny County	6	0.35
West Shenango, PA (township) Crawford County	2	0.35
Stowe Township, PA (cdp) Allegheny County	23	0.34
Kiskiminetas, PA (township) Armstrong County	17	0.34
Buffalo, PA (township) Union County	11	0.34
Saint Clair, PA (borough) Schuylkill County	11	0.34
Weidman, MI (cdp) Isabella County	3	0.34
Heidelberg, PA (borough) Allegheny County	4	0.33
Pine Island, TX (town) Waller County	3	0.33
Alpha, NJ (borough) Warren County	8	0.32
West Homestead, PA (borough) Allegheny County	7	0.32
Washington, PA (township) Cambria County	3	0.32
Wilson, PA (borough) Northampton County	24	0.31
Sewickley, PA (township) Westmoreland County	19	0.31
Huntington, PA (township) Adams County	7	0.31
Colley, PA (township) Sullivan County	2	0.31
Etna Green, IN (town) Kosciusko County	2	0.31
Bentleyville, PA (borough) Washington County	7	0.29
Boyd, WI (village) Chippewa County	2	0.29
Johnstown, PA (city) Cambria County	67	0.28
Cloverdale, VA (cdp) Botetourt County	8	0.28
Mount Olive, IL (city) Macoupin County	6	0.28
North Charleroi, PA (borough) Washington County	4	0.28
Onalaska, WI (city) La Crosse County	40	0.27
Sharpsville, PA (borough) Mercer County	12	0.27
Bridgewater, PA (borough) Beaver County	2	0.27
Brooklyn, OH (city) Cuyahoga County	30	0.26
Upper Yoder, PA (township) Cambria County	15	0.26
Nockamixon, PA (township) Bucks County	9	0.26
Skaneateles, NY (village) Onondaga County	7	0.26
Coaldale, PA (borough) Schuylkill County	6	0.26
Greene, PA (township) Mercer County	3	0.26
Bassett, NE (city) Rock County	2	0.26
North Abington, PA (township) Lackawanna County	2	0.26
Washingtonville, OH (village) Columbiana County	2	0.26
Amherst, OH (city) Lorain County	30	0.25
White Oak, PA (borough) Allegheny County	21	0.25
Patterson Township, PA (cdp) Beaver County	8	0.25
Dunkard, PA (township) Greene County	6	0.25
Roaring Brook, PA (township) Lackawanna County	4	0.25
Georges, PA (township) Fayette County	17	0.24
Edwardsville, PA (borough) Luzerne County	12	0.24
Hollis, ME (town) York County	10	0.24
Eastlawn Gardens, PA (cdp) Northampton County	7	0.24
Cross Creek, PA (township) Washington County	4	0.24
Conneautville, PA (borough) Crawford County	2	0.24
Shawnee Hills, OH (village) Delaware County	1	0.24
Brownstown, PA (borough) Cambria County	2	0.23
Weehawken, NJ (township) Hudson County	30	0.22
Solebury, PA (township) Bucks County	17	0.22
Bolton, MA (town) Worcester County	9	0.22
Wilkes-Barre Township, PA (cdp) Luzerne County	7	0.22
Glade, PA (township) Warren County	5	0.22
Bowmanstown, PA (borough) Carbon County	2	0.22
Chester Hill, PA (borough) Clearfield County	2	0.22
Interlaken, NJ (borough) Monmouth County	2	0.22
Macedonia, OH (city) Summit County	19	0.21
Baden, PA (borough) Beaver County	9	0.21
Melrose Park, NY (cdp) Cayuga County	5	0.21
Newburgh Heights, OH (village) Cuyahoga County	5	0.21
Sherburne, NY (village) Chenango County	3	0.21
Walker, PA (township) Schuylkill County	2	0.21
Parryville, PA (borough) Carbon County	1	0.21
Dormont, PA (borough) Allegheny County	19	0.20
Kennedy Township, PA (cdp) Allegheny County	15	0.20
Ford City, PA (borough) Armstrong County	7	0.20
Geistown, PA (borough) Cambria County	5	0.20
Folly Beach, SC (city) Charleston County	5	0.20
Gwinn, MI (cdp) Marquette County	4	0.20
South Waverly, PA (borough) Bradford County	2	0.20
Owego, NY (town) Tioga County	38	0.19
Colonia, NJ (cdp) Middlesex County	33	0.19
Johnson City, NY (village) Broome County	30	0.19
Mount Pleasant, PA (township) Westmoreland County	21	0.19
Cambria, PA (township) Cambria County	12	0.19
Benld, IL (city) Macoupin County	3	0.19
Leet, PA (township) Allegheny County	3	0.19
Aleppo, PA (township) Allegheny County	2	0.19
Chatham, NJ (borough) Morris County	15	0.18
Jackson, PA (township) Luzerne County	8	0.18
Roxborough Park, CO (cdp) Douglas County	8	0.18
Washington, PA (township) Fayette County	8	0.18
Windber, PA (borough) Somerset County	8	0.18
Fairbury, IL (city) Livingston County	7	0.18
Baldwin, PA (township) Allegheny County	4	0.18
Southmont, PA (borough) Cambria County	4	0.18
North Laurel, MD (cdp) Howard County	35	0.17
Colonial Park, PA (cdp) Dauphin County	22	0.17
Chenango, NY (town) Broome County	20	0.17
Endwell, NY (cdp) Broome County	20	0.17

Notes: (cdp) census designated place; Refer to the Explanation of Data in the front of the book for more detailed information.

Carpatho Rusyn

Top 150 Places Sorted by Percent

(Based on places with populations of 10,000 or more)

Place	Number	%
Uniontown, PA (city) Fayette County	54	0.43
Johnstown, PA (city) Cambria County	67	0.28
Onalaska, WI (city) La Crosse County	40	0.27
Brooklyn, OH (city) Cuyahoga County	30	0.26
Amherst, OH (city) Lorain County	30	0.25
Weehawken, NJ (township) Hudson County	30	0.22
Owego, NY (town) Tioga County	38	0.19
Colonia, NJ (cdp) Middlesex County	33	0.19
Johnson City, NY (village) Broome County	30	0.19
Mount Pleasant, PA (township) Westmoreland County	21	0.19
North Laurel, MD (cdp) Howard County	35	0.17
Colonial Park, PA (cdp) Dauphin County	22	0.17
Chenango, NY (town) Broome County	20	0.17
Endwell, NY (cdp) Broome County	20	0.17
Municipality of Monroeville, PA (borough) Allegheny County	47	0.16
West Mifflin, PA (borough) Allegheny County	34	0.15
Hanover, NJ (township) Morris County	19	0.15
Plum, PA (borough) Allegheny County	38	0.14
McKeesport, PA (city) Allegheny County	34	0.14
Jefferson, NJ (township) Morris County	27	0.14
Butler, PA (township) Butler County	24	0.14
Tenafly, NJ (borough) Bergen County	20	0.14
Cranberry, PA (township) Butler County	30	0.13
Moon, PA (township) Allegheny County	30	0.13
Bedford, OH (city) Cuyahoga County	18	0.13
Hobe Sound, FL (cdp) Martin County	15	0.13
North Royalton, OH (city) Cuyahoga County	34	0.12
Perrysburg, OH (city) Wood County	21	0.12
Dunmore, PA (borough) Lackawanna County	17	0.12
Chester, NY (town) Orange County	14	0.12
Union, NY (town) Broome County	62	0.11
Binghamton, NY (city) Broome County	52	0.11
Glen Burnie, MD (cdp) Anne Arundel County	42	0.11
Mount Lebanon, PA (cdp) Allegheny County	36	0.11
Parma Heights, OH (city) Cuyahoga County	21	0.10
Cherry Hill Mall, NJ (cdp) Camden County	14	0.10
Derry, PA (township) Westmoreland County	14	0.10
Kingston, PA (borough) Luzerne County	14	0.10
Westchester, IL (village) Cook County	15	0.09
Hermitage, PA (city) Mercer County	14	0.09
Endicott, NY (village) Broome County	12	0.09
Brentwood, PA (borough) Allegheny County	9	0.09
Farmington, MI (city) Oakland County	9	0.09
Idaho Falls, ID (city) Bonneville County	39	0.08
Lower Paxton, PA (township) Dauphin County	37	0.08
Trumbull, CT (cdp) Fairfield County	29	0.08
Ross Township, PA (cdp) Allegheny County	27	0.08
Ferndale, MI (city) Oakland County	18	0.08
Ashland, OR (city) Jackson County	15	0.08
Idylwood, VA (cdp) Fairfax County	13	0.08
North Union, PA (township) Fayette County	11	0.08
East Hanover, NJ (township) Morris County	9	0.08
Stratford, CT (cdp) Fairfield County	33	0.07
Saratoga, CA (city) Santa Clara County	22	0.07
Willoughby, OH (city) Lake County	15	0.07
Port Neches, TX (city) Jefferson County	10	0.07
Issaquah, WA (city) King County	8	0.07
Patton, PA (township) Centre County	8	0.07
Worthington, MN (city) Nobles County	8	0.07
Carnot-Moon, PA (cdp) Allegheny County	7	0.07
Chesterton, IN (town) Porter County	7	0.07
Florence, NJ (township) Burlington County	7	0.07
Warren, PA (city) Warren County	7	0.07
Aspen Hill, MD (cdp) Montgomery County	31	0.06
Bethel Park, PA (borough) Allegheny County	20	0.06
Garfield, NJ (city) Bergen County	19	0.06
New Castle, PA (city) Lawrence County	17	0.06
Solon, OH (city) Cuyahoga County	14	0.06
Readington, NJ (township) Hunterdon County	10	0.06
Bay Village, OH (city) Cuyahoga County	9	0.06
Clark, NJ (cdp) Union County	9	0.06
Pottsville, PA (city) Schuylkill County	9	0.06
Sharon, PA (city) Mercer County	9	0.06
Sterling, IL (city) Whiteside County	9	0.06
Richland, PA (township) Cambria County	8	0.06
Franklin Park, PA (borough) Allegheny County	7	0.06
Hilltown, PA (township) Bucks County	7	0.06
Munhall, PA (borough) Allegheny County	7	0.06
Robinson Township, PA (cdp) Allegheny County	7	0.06
Schodack, NY (town) Rensselaer County	7	0.06
Vermilion, OH (city) Lorain County	7	0.06
Amherst, NH (town) Hillsborough County	6	0.06
Pompton Lakes, NJ (borough) Passaic County	6	0.06
Scranton, PA (city) Lackawanna County	36	0.05
McLean, VA (cdp) Fairfax County	20	0.05
Linden, NJ (city) Union County	19	0.05
Ballwin, MO (city) Saint Louis County	17	0.05
Alpharetta, GA (city) Fulton County	16	0.05
Randolph, NJ (township) Morris County	13	0.05
Cranford, NJ (cdp) Union County	12	0.05
Middletown, NY (city) Orange County	12	0.05
Upper Dublin, PA (township) Montgomery County	12	0.05
Waldorf, MD (cdp) Charles County	11	0.05
Upper Saint Clair, PA (cdp) Allegheny County	10	0.05
Concord, MO (cdp) Saint Louis County	9	0.05
Upper Providence, PA (township) Montgomery County	8	0.05
Elizabeth, PA (township) Allegheny County	7	0.05
Jasper, AL (city) Walker County	7	0.05
Whitehall, PA (borough) Allegheny County	7	0.05
Winter Garden, FL (city) Orange County	7	0.05
Brecksville, OH (city) Cuyahoga County	6	0.05
Hartland, MI (township) Livingston County	6	0.05
Rostraver, PA (township) Westmoreland County	6	0.05
Stamford, CT (city) Fairfield County	47	0.04
Parma, OH (city) Cuyahoga County	34	0.04
Bristol, PA (township) Bucks County	23	0.04
Warren, OH (city) Trumbull County	21	0.04
Wilkes-Barre, PA (city) Luzerne County	16	0.04
McCandless Township, PA (cdp) Allegheny County	13	0.04
Millcreek, UT (cdp) Salt Lake County	13	0.04
Brooklyn Center, MN (city) Hennepin County	12	0.04
Garfield Heights, OH (city) Cuyahoga County	12	0.04
Shaler Township, PA (cdp) Allegheny County	12	0.04
Newtown, CT (town) Fairfield County	11	0.04
North Huntingdon, PA (township) Westmoreland County	11	0.04
Pittsfield charter, MI (township) Washtenaw County	11	0.04
Bernards, NJ (township) Somerset County	10	0.04
East Hempfield, PA (township) Lancaster County	9	0.04
Greenbelt, MD (city) Prince George's County	9	0.04
Carlisle, PA (borough) Cumberland County	8	0.04
South Whitehall, PA (township) Lehigh County	8	0.04
Brookfield, CT (town) Fairfield County	7	0.04
Greensburg, PA (city) Westmoreland County	7	0.04
Hampton Township, PA (cdp) Allegheny County	7	0.04
King of Prussia, PA (cdp) Montgomery County	7	0.04
Peters, PA (township) Washington County	7	0.04
Kings Park, NY (cdp) Suffolk County	6	0.04
New Milford, NJ (borough) Bergen County	6	0.04
North Whitehall, PA (township) Lehigh County	6	0.04
Socastee, SC (cdp) Horry County	6	0.04
Springfield, NJ (cdp) Union County	6	0.04
Harper Woods, MI (city) Wayne County	5	0.04
New Britain, PA (township) Bucks County	4	0.04
Pittsburgh, PA (city) Allegheny County	116	0.03
Warren, MI (city) Macomb County	35	0.03
Woodbridge, NJ (township) Middlesex County	33	0.03
Bristol, CT (city) Hartford County	18	0.03
Sheboygan, WI (city) Sheboygan County	17	0.03
Franklin, NJ (township) Somerset County	16	0.03
Yorba Linda, CA (city) Orange County	16	0.03
Harrisburg, PA (city) Dauphin County	15	0.03
Lakewood, OH (city) Cuyahoga County	15	0.03
Colton, CA (city) San Bernardino County	14	0.03
Piscataway, NJ (township) Middlesex County	13	0.03
Montgomery Village, MD (cdp) Montgomery County	12	0.03
Perth Amboy, NJ (city) Middlesex County	12	0.03
South Brunswick, NJ (township) Middlesex County	11	0.03
Crystal Lake, IL (city) McHenry County	10	0.03
Keizer, OR (city) Marion County	10	0.03
Olney, MD (cdp) Montgomery County	10	0.03

Notes: (cdp) census designated place; Refer to the Explanation of Data in the front of the book for more detailed information.

Celtic

Top 150 Places Sorted by Number

(Based on all places, regardless of population)

Place	Number	%
New York, NY (city) New York City	836	0.01
Los Angeles, CA (city) Los Angeles County	809	0.02
San Francisco, CA (city) San Francisco County	569	0.07
Seattle, WA (city) King County	500	0.09
Portland, OR (city) Multnomah County	475	0.09
San Diego, CA (city) San Diego County	427	0.03
Austin, TX (city) Travis County	383	0.06
Albuquerque, NM (city) Bernalillo County	337	0.08
Phoenix, AZ (city) Maricopa County	335	0.03
San Antonio, TX (city) Bexar County	314	0.03
San Jose, CA (city) Santa Clara County	283	0.03
Chicago, IL (city) Cook County	269	0.01
Dallas, TX (city) Dallas County	267	0.02
Houston, TX (city) Harris County	255	0.01
Tucson, AZ (city) Pima County	235	0.05
Philadelphia, PA (city) Philadelphia County	232	0.02
Columbus, OH (city) Franklin County	222	0.03
Sacramento, CA (city) Sacramento County	196	0.05
Jacksonville, FL (special city) Duval County	195	0.03
Denver, CO (city) Denver County	182	0.03
Anchorage, AK (municipality) Anchorage Borough	174	0.07
Lexington-Fayette, KY (special city) Fayette County	168	0.06
Colorado Springs, CO (city) El Paso County	164	0.05
Boston, MA (city) Suffolk County	162	0.03
Nashville-Davidson, TN (special city) Davidson County	162	0.03
Tempe, AZ (city) Maricopa County	161	0.10
Oklahoma City, OK (city) Oklahoma County	161	0.03
Berkeley, CA (city) Alameda County	156	0.15
Oakland, CA (city) Alameda County	151	0.04
Vancouver, WA (city) Clark County	144	0.10
Salt Lake City, UT (city) Salt Lake County	144	0.08
Virginia Beach, VA (independent city) Virginia Beach city	144	0.03
Tacoma, WA (city) Pierce County	141	0.07
Memphis, TN (city) Shelby County	140	0.02
Indianapolis, IN (special city) Marion County	139	0.02
Saint Paul, MN (city) Ramsey County	131	0.05
Santa Cruz, CA (city) Santa Cruz County	129	0.24
El Paso, TX (city) El Paso County	127	0.02
Washington, DC (city) District of Columbia	126	0.02
Tallahassee, FL (city) Leon County	125	0.08
Las Vegas, NV (city) Clark County	118	0.02
Lakewood, CO (city) Jefferson County	114	0.08
Weymouth, MA (cdp) Norfolk County	111	0.21
Tampa, FL (city) Hillsborough County	111	0.04
Norfolk, VA (independent city) Norfolk city	109	0.05
Fort Worth, TX (city) Tarrant County	109	0.02
Concord, CA (city) Contra Costa County	108	0.09
Eugene, OR (city) Lane County	108	0.08
Minneapolis, MN (city) Hennepin County	108	0.03
Syracuse, NY (city) Onondaga County	106	0.07
Arlington, TX (city) Tarrant County	106	0.03
Omaha, NE (city) Douglas County	106	0.03
Salinas, CA (city) Monterey County	105	0.07
Tyler, TX (city) Smith County	102	0.12
Charlotte, NC (city) Mecklenburg County	99	0.02
Brookhaven, NY (town) Suffolk County	98	0.02
Beaumont, TX (city) Jefferson County	97	0.09
Spokane, WA (city) Spokane County	97	0.05
Plano, TX (city) Collin County	95	0.04
Garland, TX (city) Dallas County	94	0.04
Mesa, AZ (city) Maricopa County	94	0.02
Palo Alto, CA (city) Santa Clara County	93	0.16
Huntsville, AL (city) Madison County	93	0.06
Atlanta, GA (city) Fulton County	93	0.02
Bremerton, WA (city) Kitsap County	92	0.25
Bend, OR (city) Deschutes County	92	0.18
Chandler, AZ (city) Maricopa County	91	0.05
Madison, WI (city) Dane County	91	0.04
Santa Rosa, CA (city) Sonoma County	90	0.06
Salem, OR (city) Marion County	89	0.07
Carmichael, CA (cdp) Sacramento County	88	0.18
Denton, TX (city) Denton County	88	0.11
Antioch, CA (city) Contra Costa County	88	0.10
Boise City, ID (city) Ada County	88	0.05
Dale City, VA (cdp) Prince William County	87	0.16
Gainesville, FL (city) Alachua County	86	0.09
Knoxville, TN (city) Knox County	85	0.05
Reno, NV (city) Washoe County	85	0.05
Paradise, NV (cdp) Clark County	83	0.04
Townsend, MA (town) Middlesex County	82	0.89
Catlettsburg, KY (city) Boyd County	81	3.88
San Clemente, CA (city) Orange County	81	0.16
Shreveport, LA (city) Caddo Parish	81	0.04
Fresno, CA (city) Fresno County	81	0.02
Burke, VA (cdp) Fairfax County	80	0.14
Oceanside, CA (city) San Diego County	80	0.05
Rochester, NY (city) Monroe County	80	0.04
Hillsboro, OR (city) Washington County	79	0.11
Pittsburgh, PA (city) Allegheny County	79	0.02
New Orleans, LA (city) Orleans Parish	78	0.02
Hempstead, NY (town) Nassau County	78	0.01
Chesapeake, VA (independent city) Chesapeake city	77	0.04
Corpus Christi, TX (city) Nueces County	77	0.03
Boulder, CO (city) Boulder County	76	0.08
San Buenaventura, CA (city) Ventura County	76	0.08
Shoreline, WA (city) King County	74	0.14
Sunnyvale, CA (city) Santa Clara County	74	0.06
Durham, NC (city) Durham County	73	0.04
Flagstaff, AZ (city) Coconino County	72	0.14
Richmond, VA (independent city) Richmond city	72	0.04
Lincoln, NE (city) Lancaster County	71	0.03
Woodmoor, CO (cdp) El Paso County	70	0.99
Middleborough, MA (town) Plymouth County	70	0.35
Vestavia Hills, AL (city) Jefferson County	70	0.28
Murrieta, CA (city) Riverside County	70	0.16
Arlington, VA (cdp) Arlington County	70	0.04
Fremont, CA (city) Alameda County	70	0.03
Pasadena, CA (city) Los Angeles County	69	0.05
Long Beach, CA (city) Los Angeles County	69	0.01
Albany, NY (city) Albany County	68	0.07
Beaverton, OR (city) Washington County	67	0.09
Cincinnati, OH (city) Hamilton County	67	0.02
Longmont, CO (city) Boulder County	66	0.09
Topeka, KS (city) Shawnee County	66	0.05
Bakersfield, CA (city) Kern County	66	0.03
Buffalo, NY (city) Erie County	65	0.02
Baltimore, MD (independent city) Baltimore city	65	0.01
Kansas City, MO (city) Jackson County	65	0.01
Callaway, FL (city) Bay County	64	0.45
Littleton, CO (city) Arapahoe County	64	0.16
Irving, TX (city) Dallas County	64	0.03
Plaistow, NH (town) Rockingham County	63	0.81
Bangor, ME (city) Penobscot County	63	0.20
Lakewood, WA (city) Pierce County	63	0.11
Santa Fe, NM (city) Santa Fe County	63	0.10
Bethlehem, PA (city) Northampton County	63	0.09
Nashua, NH (city) Hillsborough County	63	0.07
McAllen, TX (city) Hidalgo County	63	0.06
Springfield, MO (city) Greene County	63	0.04
Exeter, NH (town) Rockingham County	62	0.44
Amarillo, TX (city) Potter County	62	0.04
Hayward, CA (city) Alameda County	61	0.04
Newport News, VA (independent city) Newport News city	61	0.03
Honolulu, HI (cdp) Honolulu County	61	0.02
Horseheads, NY (town) Chemung County	60	0.31
Kent, WA (city) King County	60	0.08
Islip, NY (town) Suffolk County	60	0.02
Cahokia, IL (village) Saint Clair County	59	0.36
Bedford, TX (city) Tarrant County	59	0.13
Aurora, CO (city) Arapahoe County	59	0.02
Chuluota, FL (cdp) Seminole County	58	2.92
Northport, AL (city) Tuscaloosa County	57	0.30
Eureka, CA (city) Humboldt County	57	0.22
Davis, CA (city) Yolo County	57	0.09
Cambridge, MA (city) Middlesex County	57	0.06
Oyster Bay, NY (town) Nassau County	57	0.02
Half Moon Bay, CA (city) San Mateo County	56	0.47
Livermore, CA (city) Alameda County	56	0.08
Billings, MT (city) Yellowstone County	56	0.06
Glendale, AZ (city) Maricopa County	56	0.03

Notes: (cdp) census designated place; Refer to the Explanation of Data in the front of the book for more detailed information.

Celtic

Top 150 Places Sorted by Percent

(Based on all places, regardless of population)

Place	Number	%
Lake Minchumina, AK (cdp) Yukon-Koyukuk Census Area	2	6.25
Roosevelt, WI (town) Burnett County	10	5.03
Crestone, CO (town) Saguache County	3	4.55
Little Meadows, PA (borough) Susquehanna County	13	4.28
Yorktown, VA (cdp) York County	7	3.89
Catlettsburg, KY (city) Boyd County	81	3.88
Tecopa, CA (cdp) Inyo County	5	3.45
Fairburn, SD (town) Custer County	2	3.33
Accord, NY (cdp) Ulster County	22	3.11
Lessor, MN (township) Polk County	7	3.11
Centerport, PA (borough) Berks County	10	3.06
Chuluota, FL (cdp) Seminole County	58	2.92
Geneseo, KS (city) Rice County	7	2.82
Meadow, UT (town) Millard County	8	2.80
Galisteo, NM (cdp) Santa Fe County	9	2.70
Laurel Mountain, PA (borough) Westmoreland County	5	2.70
Bowersville, OH (village) Greene County	8	2.56
Creekside, KY (city) Jefferson County	8	2.49
Melrose, IA (city) Monroe County	3	2.34
Picuris Pueblo, NM (cdp) Taos County	2	2.30
Onota, MI (township) Alger County	7	2.29
Burt, MI (township) Alger County	10	2.26
Bath, NC (town) Beaufort County	6	2.24
Sunset Valley, TX (city) Travis County	8	2.17
Bell Buckle, TN (town) Bedford County	8	2.16
Alvo, NE (village) Cass County	3	2.10
Bell Hill, WA (cdp) Clallam County	17	2.05
Saint Leo, FL (town) Pasco County	12	1.97
Ardenhurst, MN (township) Itasca County	3	1.90
Rock River, MI (township) Alger County	23	1.89
Verplanck, NY (cdp) Westchester County	14	1.89
Bellerose, NY (village) Nassau County	22	1.88
Belle Valley, OH (village) Noble County	5	1.87
Poncha Springs, CO (town) Chaffee County	8	1.72
Westminster, VT (village) Windham County	5	1.68
India Hook, SC (cdp) York County	25	1.65
Weston, TX (city) Collin County	11	1.61
Newborn, GA (town) Newton County	9	1.55
Goodrich, TX (city) Polk County	4	1.54
North Sultan, WA (cdp) Snohomish County	6	1.53
Horseheads North, NY (cdp) Chemung County	44	1.52
Huntley, MT (cdp) Yellowstone County	7	1.47
Home, MI (township) Newaygo County	4	1.47
Judson, SC (cdp) Greenville County	35	1.45
Soso, MS (town) Jones County	5	1.44
Moorland, IA (city) Webster County	3	1.42
Makoti, ND (city) Ward County	2	1.41
Melissa, TX (city) Collin County	18	1.39
Kent Narrows, MD (cdp) Queen Anne's County	8	1.37
Lakewood Village, TX (city) Denton County	5	1.37
Creedmoor, TX (city) Travis County	3	1.37
Montgomery, NY (village) Orange County	48	1.35
Monson Center, MA (cdp) Hampden County	26	1.35
Railroad, PA (borough) York County	4	1.33
Princeton, IA (city) Scott County	13	1.32
Brooklin, ME (town) Hancock County	11	1.29
Noank, CT (cdp) New London County	22	1.26
Brushton, NY (village) Franklin County	6	1.25
Alexander, NY (village) Genesee County	6	1.24
Chapmanville, WV (town) Logan County	15	1.22
Red River, WI (town) Kewaunee County	18	1.20
Black Hammer, MN (township) Houston County	4	1.20
Thornhill, KY (city) Jefferson County	2	1.18
Bearinger, MI (township) Presque Isle County	4	1.17
Sherwood, OH (cdp) Hamilton County	45	1.16
Castle Hayne, NC (cdp) New Hanover County	13	1.15
Loxley, AL (town) Baldwin County	15	1.11
Ellsworth, IL (village) McLean County	3	1.11
Acres Green, CO (cdp) Douglas County	34	1.10
Jay, FL (town) Santa Rosa County	6	1.10
Candor, NC (town) Montgomery County	9	1.09
Wells, NY (town) Hamilton County	8	1.09
Ballantine, MT (cdp) Yellowstone County	4	1.09
Corralitos, CA (cdp) Santa Cruz County	31	1.08
Pine Mountain Club, CA (cdp) Kern County	18	1.08
Hauser, ID (city) Kootenai County	7	1.08
Cabin John, MD (cdp) Montgomery County	18	1.07
Tatamy, PA (borough) Northampton County	10	1.07
Clyde, WI (town) Iowa County	3	1.05
New Denmark, WI (town) Brown County	15	1.03
Riceland, MN (township) Freeborn County	5	1.03
Fayette, PA (township) Juniata County	33	1.01
Koyuk, AK (city) Nome Census Area	3	1.00
Oak Ridge, TX (town) Cooke County	2	1.00
Timberlane, IL (village) Boone County	2	1.00
Woodmoor, CO (cdp) El Paso County	70	0.99
Wynantskill, NY (cdp) Rensselaer County	31	0.99
Pantego, TX (town) Tarrant County	23	0.99
Corinna, ME (town) Penobscot County	21	0.98
Trappe, MD (town) Talbot County	11	0.98
Proctorville, OH (village) Lawrence County	6	0.98
Vader, WA (city) Lewis County	6	0.97
Casstown, OH (village) Miami County	3	0.97
Hubbardton, VT (town) Rutland County	7	0.95
Bazine, KS (city) Ness County	3	0.95
South Beach, FL (cdp) Indian River County	32	0.94
Montgomery, PA (borough) Lycoming County	16	0.94
Sand Ridge, NY (cdp) Oswego County	8	0.94
Zearing, IA (city) Story County	6	0.94
Lerna, IL (village) Coles County	3	0.93
Littleton, NC (town) Halifax County	6	0.92
West Bradenton, FL (cdp) Manatee County	41	0.91
Craig, AK (city) Prince of Wales-Outer Ketchikan Census Area	13	0.91
Rock Island, WA (city) Douglas County	8	0.91
Center City, MN (city) Chisago County	6	0.91
Brookfield, VT (town) Orange County	11	0.90
La Conner, WA (town) Skagit County	7	0.90
Huntington, AR (city) Sebastian County	6	0.90
Elba, NE (village) Howard County	2	0.90
Townsend, MA (town) Middlesex County	82	0.89
Harbor Hills, OH (cdp) Licking County	11	0.89
Melbourne Village, FL (town) Brevard County	6	0.89
Swans Island, ME (town) Hancock County	3	0.89
Baring, WA (cdp) King County	2	0.89
Sardis, TN (town) Henderson County	4	0.88
Castle Valley, UT (town) Grand County	3	0.88
Pecan Gap, TX (city) Delta County	2	0.88
Pewamo, MI (village) Ionia County	5	0.87
Platte, MI (township) Benzie County	3	0.87
Napeague, NY (cdp) Suffolk County	2	0.87
Tupman, CA (cdp) Kern County	2	0.87
Bedford, VA (independent city) Bedford city	54	0.86
Nisqually Indian Community, WA (cdp) Thurston County	5	0.85
Richlawn, KY (city) Jefferson County	4	0.85
Woods, MN (township) Chippewa County	2	0.85
Ashford, CT (town) Windham County	34	0.83
Orford, NH (town) Grafton County	9	0.83
Washington Grove, MD (town) Montgomery County	4	0.83
Lake City, CO (town) Hinsdale County	3	0.83
Gleneagle, CO (cdp) El Paso County	35	0.82
Lagunitas-Forest Knolls, CA (cdp) Marin County	15	0.82
Andover, ME (town) Oxford County	7	0.82
Plaistow, NH (town) Rockingham County	63	0.81
Wyndmoor, PA (cdp) Montgomery County	45	0.81
Red Bud, IL (city) Randolph County	27	0.81
Baileys Harbor, WI (town) Door County	8	0.81
Darling, MN (township) Morrison County	5	0.81
Mosby, MO (city) Clay County	2	0.81
Bethel Island, CA (cdp) Contra Costa County	18	0.80
Easton, NH (town) Grafton County	2	0.80
Towanda, PA (borough) Bradford County	24	0.79
Aromas, CA (cdp) San Benito County	23	0.79
Laurens, NY (town) Otsego County	19	0.79
Saint George, FL (cdp) Broward County	19	0.79
Little Compton, RI (town) Newport County	28	0.78
Franklin, PA (township) Columbia County	5	0.78
Woodlawn, KY (city) Campbell County	2	0.77
Cayucos, CA (cdp) San Luis Obispo County	22	0.76
Briarcliff, TX (village) Travis County	7	0.76
Summitview, WA (cdp) Yakima County	6	0.76

Notes: (cdp) census designated place; Refer to the Explanation of Data in the front of the book for more detailed information.

Celtic

Top 150 Places Sorted by Percent

(Based on places with populations of 10,000 or more)

Place	Number	%
Half Moon Bay, CA (city) San Mateo County	56	0.47
Callaway, FL (city) Bay County	64	0.45
Exeter, NH (town) Rockingham County	62	0.44
Kingsland, GA (city) Camden County	41	0.39
Cahokia, IL (village) Saint Clair County	59	0.36
Middleborough, MA (town) Plymouth County	70	0.35
Wylie, TX (city) Collin County	52	0.35
San Anselmo, CA (town) Marin County	44	0.35
Morro Bay, CA (city) San Luis Obispo County	35	0.34
Parole, MD (cdp) Anne Arundel County	44	0.32
Horseheads, NY (town) Chemung County	60	0.31
Malibu, CA (city) Los Angeles County	39	0.31
Maynard, MA (cdp) Middlesex County	32	0.31
Northport, AL (city) Tuscaloosa County	57	0.30
Cameron Park, CA (cdp) El Dorado County	44	0.30
McKinleyville, CA (cdp) Humboldt County	41	0.30
King City, CA (city) Monterey County	34	0.30
Soddy-Daisy, TN (city) Hamilton County	34	0.30
North Greenbush, NY (town) Rensselaer County	31	0.29
Vestavia Hills, AL (city) Jefferson County	70	0.28
Masonboro, NC (cdp) New Hanover County	33	0.28
Bainbridge Island, WA (city) Kitsap County	54	0.27
Saint Augustine, FL (city) Saint Johns County	31	0.27
Concord, MA (town) Middlesex County	45	0.26
Hockessin, DE (cdp) New Castle County	33	0.26
Sierra Madre, CA (city) Los Angeles County	27	0.26
Bremerton, WA (city) Kitsap County	92	0.25
Druid Hills, GA (cdp) De Kalb County	32	0.25
Lakeland Highlands, FL (cdp) Polk County	32	0.25
Tamalpais-Homestead Valley, CA (cdp) Marin County	27	0.25
Santa Cruz, CA (city) Santa Cruz County	129	0.24
Mountain Brook, AL (city) Jefferson County	51	0.24
Tanque Verde, AZ (cdp) Pima County	39	0.24
Easton, MD (town) Talbot County	28	0.24
Montgomery, NY (town) Orange County	48	0.23
Altamont, OR (cdp) Klamath County	45	0.23
Springfield, PA (township) Montgomery County	45	0.23
Dyersburg, TN (city) Dyer County	40	0.23
Sterling, CO (city) Logan County	26	0.23
Siloam Springs, AR (city) Benton County	25	0.23
Eureka, CA (city) Humboldt County	57	0.22
West Odessa, TX (cdp) Ector County	40	0.22
Portsmouth, RI (town) Newport County	37	0.22
Murray, KY (city) Calloway County	33	0.22
Endicott, NY (village) Broome County	29	0.22
Weymouth, MA (cdp) Norfolk County	111	0.21
Mount Olive, NJ (township) Morris County	51	0.21
Woodstock, IL (city) McHenry County	42	0.21
Lower Southampton, PA (township) Bucks County	40	0.21
Van Wert, OH (city) Van Wert County	22	0.21
Bangor, ME (city) Penobscot County	63	0.20
Starkville, MS (city) Oktibbeha County	43	0.20
Sand Springs, OK (city) Tulsa County	36	0.20
Leesburg, FL (city) Lake County	31	0.20
Sheridan, WY (city) Sheridan County	31	0.20
Lancaster, PA (township) Lancaster County	28	0.20
Stony Brook, NY (cdp) Suffolk County	27	0.20
Medfield, MA (town) Norfolk County	25	0.20
Bellmawr, NJ (borough) Camden County	23	0.20
Rossmoor, CA (cdp) Orange County	21	0.20
Chatham, NJ (township) Morris County	20	0.20
Homewood, AL (city) Jefferson County	47	0.19
Lawrenceville, GA (city) Gwinnett County	43	0.19
South Salt Lake, UT (city) Salt Lake County	41	0.19
Crawfordsville, IN (city) Montgomery County	29	0.19
Whitefish Bay, WI (village) Milwaukee County	27	0.19
Mill Valley, CA (city) Marin County	26	0.19
Lansdowne, PA (borough) Delaware County	21	0.19
Holly, MI (township) Oakland County	19	0.19
Bend, OR (city) Deschutes County	92	0.18
Carmichael, CA (cdp) Sacramento County	88	0.18
Dover, NH (city) Strafford County	49	0.18
Hauppauge, NY (cdp) Suffolk County	37	0.18
La Canada Flintridge, CA (city) Los Angeles County	37	0.18
Taylors, SC (cdp) Greenville County	36	0.18
Grand Chute, WI (town) Outagamie County	33	0.18
Yucca Valley, CA (town) San Bernardino County	30	0.18
Coos Bay, OR (city) Coos County	28	0.18
Aurora, OH (city) Portage County	25	0.18
Auburn, CA (city) Placer County	22	0.18
Green Valley, MD (cdp) Frederick County	22	0.18
South Yarmouth, MA (cdp) Barnstable County	21	0.18
Tarrytown, NY (village) Westchester County	20	0.18
Frankfort, KY (city) Franklin County	46	0.17
Parker, CO (town) Douglas County	40	0.17
South Portland, ME (city) Cumberland County	40	0.17
Watauga, TX (city) Tarrant County	38	0.17
Olive Branch, MS (city) De Soto County	37	0.17
Portsmouth, NH (city) Rockingham County	36	0.17
South Saint Paul, MN (city) Dakota County	34	0.17
Raritan, NJ (township) Hunterdon County	33	0.17
Kenmore, WA (city) King County	32	0.17
New Lenox, IL (village) Will County	30	0.17
Whitemarsh, PA (township) Montgomery County	29	0.17
Beltsville, MD (cdp) Prince George's County	26	0.17
Orange, CT (cdp) New Haven County	23	0.17
Saint James, NY (cdp) Suffolk County	23	0.17
Canby, OR (city) Clackamas County	22	0.17
Clemson, SC (city) Pickens County	21	0.17
Fort Knox, KY (cdp) Hardin County	21	0.17
Lockhart, FL (cdp) Orange County	21	0.17
Corning, NY (city) Steuben County	18	0.17
Palo Alto, CA (city) Santa Clara County	93	0.16
Dale City, VA (cdp) Prince William County	87	0.16
San Clemente, CA (city) Orange County	81	0.16
Murrieta, CA (city) Riverside County	70	0.16
Littleton, CO (city) Arapahoe County	64	0.16
Ken Caryl, CO (cdp) Jefferson County	50	0.16
Peachtree City, GA (city) Fayette County	50	0.16
Henderson, KY (city) Henderson County	45	0.16
Marshfield, MA (town) Plymouth County	38	0.16
Radcliff, KY (city) Hardin County	34	0.16
Castle Rock, CO (town) Douglas County	33	0.16
Cortland, NY (city) Cortland County	30	0.16
Moraga, CA (town) Contra Costa County	26	0.16
Sullivan, NY (town) Madison County	24	0.16
Cinnaminson, NJ (township) Burlington County	23	0.16
Black Forest, CO (cdp) El Paso County	21	0.16
Marana, AZ (town) Pima County	21	0.16
Haddonfield, NJ (borough) Camden County	19	0.16
Manville, NJ (borough) Somerset County	17	0.16
The Village, OK (city) Oklahoma County	16	0.16
Berkeley, CA (city) Alameda County	156	0.15
North Creek, WA (cdp) Snohomish County	39	0.15
Edgewood, MD (cdp) Harford County	35	0.15
El Cerrito, CA (city) Contra Costa County	34	0.15
Augusta, ME (city) Kennebec County	27	0.15
Elk Plain, WA (cdp) Pierce County	23	0.15
Portland, TX (city) San Patricio County	23	0.15
Tillmans Corner, AL (cdp) Mobile County	23	0.15
Belton, TX (city) Bell County	22	0.15
North Decatur, GA (cdp) De Kalb County	22	0.15
West University Place, TX (city) Harris County	21	0.15
Canton, MS (city) Madison County	20	0.15
Dumas, TX (city) Moore County	20	0.15
Springfield, MI (township) Oakland County	20	0.15
Brattleboro, VT (town) Windham County	18	0.15
Hartselle, AL (city) Morgan County	18	0.15
Holly Hill, FL (city) Volusia County	18	0.15
Shawangunk, NY (town) Ulster County	18	0.15
Athens, TX (city) Henderson County	17	0.15
Weston, MA (town) Middlesex County	17	0.15
Hackettstown, NJ (town) Warren County	16	0.15
Sedona, AZ (city) Yavapai County	15	0.15
Burke, VA (cdp) Fairfax County	80	0.14
Shoreline, WA (city) King County	74	0.14
Flagstaff, AZ (city) Coconino County	72	0.14
Amherst, MA (town) Hampshire County	50	0.14
Chelmsford, MA (town) Middlesex County	49	0.14
Mansfield, TX (city) Tarrant County	41	0.14

Notes: (cdp) census designated place; Refer to the Explanation of Data in the front of the book for more detailed information.

Croatian

Top 150 Places Sorted by Number

(Based on all places, regardless of population)

Place	Number	%
New York, NY (city) New York City	11,948	0.15
Chicago, IL (city) Cook County	7,819	0.27
Los Angeles, CA (city) Los Angeles County	5,425	0.15
Pittsburgh, PA (city) Allegheny County	2,981	0.89
Milwaukee, WI (city) Milwaukee County	2,272	0.38
Cleveland, OH (city) Cuyahoga County	2,219	0.46
Kansas City, KS (city) Wyandotte County	2,001	1.36
Phoenix, AZ (city) Maricopa County	1,848	0.14
Euclid, OH (city) Cuyahoga County	1,705	3.23
Joliet, IL (city) Will County	1,536	1.45
Seattle, WA (city) King County	1,432	0.25
San Diego, CA (city) San Diego County	1,379	0.11
Shaler Township, PA (cdp) Allegheny County	1,338	4.50
San Jose, CA (city) Santa Clara County	1,336	0.15
Omaha, NE (city) Douglas County	1,273	0.33
San Francisco, CA (city) San Francisco County	1,272	0.16
Hammond, IN (city) Lake County	1,221	1.47
Mentor, OH (city) Lake County	1,173	2.33
Columbus, OH (city) Franklin County	1,117	0.16
Hempstead, NY (town) Nassau County	1,092	0.14
Portland, OR (city) Multnomah County	1,079	0.20
Oyster Bay, NY (town) Nassau County	1,051	0.36
Youngstown, OH (city) Mahoning County	1,013	1.23
Eastlake, OH (city) Lake County	901	4.47
Orland Park, IL (village) Cook County	868	1.70
Boardman, OH (cdp) Mahoning County	864	2.32
Akron, OH (city) Summit County	856	0.39
Parma, OH (city) Cuyahoga County	851	0.99
West Allis, WI (city) Milwaukee County	843	1.38
Lorain, OH (city) Lorain County	830	1.21
Las Vegas, NV (city) Clark County	829	0.17
Kansas City, MO (city) Jackson County	827	0.19
Saint Louis, MO (independent city) Saint Louis city	811	0.23
Overland Park, KS (city) Johnson County	717	0.48
Oak Lawn, IL (village) Cook County	713	1.29
Schererville, IN (town) Lake County	683	2.75
Naperville, IL (city) Du Page County	680	0.53
Denver, CO (city) Denver County	671	0.12
North Hempstead, NY (town) Nassau County	667	0.30
Cliffside Park, NJ (borough) Bergen County	662	2.87
Minneapolis, MN (city) Hennepin County	661	0.17
Jacksonville, FL (special city) Duval County	659	0.09
North Huntingdon, PA (township) Westmoreland County	652	2.23
Houston, TX (city) Harris County	648	0.03
McCandless Township, PA (cdp) Allegheny County	642	2.21
Philadelphia, PA (city) Philadelphia County	637	0.04
Hobart, IN (city) Lake County	630	2.48
Fairview, NJ (borough) Bergen County	607	4.58
Swatara, PA (township) Dauphin County	595	2.63
Sacramento, CA (city) Sacramento County	584	0.14
Rancho Palos Verdes, CA (city) Los Angeles County	579	1.40
Ross Township, PA (cdp) Allegheny County	568	1.74
Lansing, IL (village) Cook County	564	2.00
Hibbing, MN (city) Saint Louis County	561	3.29
Shawnee, KS (city) Johnson County	558	1.16
Salt Lake City, UT (city) Salt Lake County	557	0.31
Willowick, OH (city) Lake County	555	3.85
Hampton Township, PA (cdp) Allegheny County	546	3.12
Indianapolis, IN (special city) Marion County	545	0.07
Tinley Park, IL (village) Cook County	543	1.12
West Mifflin, PA (borough) Allegheny County	542	2.41
Palisades Park, NJ (borough) Bergen County	541	3.17
McKeesport, PA (city) Allegheny County	541	2.25
Lakewood, OH (city) Cuyahoga County	536	0.95
Brookhaven, NY (town) Suffolk County	533	0.12
Sunnyvale, CA (city) Santa Clara County	528	0.40
Long Beach, CA (city) Los Angeles County	524	0.11
Merrillville, IN (town) Lake County	514	1.67
Hopewell, PA (township) Beaver County	512	3.84
Highland, IN (town) Lake County	509	2.16
Washington, DC (city) District of Columbia	508	0.09
Struthers, OH (city) Mahoning County	506	4.30
Crown Point, IN (city) Lake County	497	2.54
Scottsdale, AZ (city) Maricopa County	496	0.24
Downers Grove, IL (village) Du Page County	488	1.00

Place	Number	%
Mesa, AZ (city) Maricopa County	488	0.12
Austintown, OH (cdp) Mahoning County	486	1.54
Dallas, TX (city) Dallas County	479	0.04
New Orleans, LA (city) Orleans Parish	477	0.10
New Berlin, WI (city) Waukesha County	475	1.24
Wauwatosa, WI (city) Milwaukee County	474	1.00
Hermitage, PA (city) Mercer County	473	2.93
Tucson, AZ (city) Pima County	470	0.10
Duluth, MN (city) Saint Louis County	469	0.54
Huntington Beach, CA (city) Orange County	466	0.25
Des Moines, IA (city) Polk County	464	0.23
Hamburg, NY (town) Erie County	458	0.82
Lenexa, KS (city) Johnson County	452	1.13
Munster, IN (town) Lake County	446	2.07
Strongsville, OH (city) Cuyahoga County	446	1.02
Colorado Springs, CO (city) El Paso County	446	0.12
Portage, IN (city) Porter County	445	1.33
Madison, WI (city) Dane County	441	0.21
Crest Hill, IL (city) Will County	437	3.35
Tacoma, WA (city) Pierce County	430	0.22
Chandler, AZ (city) Maricopa County	429	0.24
Willoughby, OH (city) Lake County	425	1.88
Sterling Heights, MI (city) Macomb County	425	0.34
Paradise, NV (cdp) Clark County	424	0.23
Austin, TX (city) Travis County	421	0.06
Municipality of Monroeville, PA (borough) Allegheny County	419	1.43
Hempfield, PA (township) Westmoreland County	417	1.02
Berwyn, IL (city) Cook County	415	0.77
Charlotte, NC (city) Mecklenburg County	414	0.08
Albuquerque, NM (city) Bernalillo County	412	0.09
San Antonio, TX (city) Bexar County	409	0.04
Moon, PA (township) Allegheny County	404	1.81
Griffith, IN (town) Lake County	400	2.31
North Olmsted, OH (city) Cuyahoga County	400	1.17
North Versailles, PA (cdp) Allegheny County	399	3.59
Warren, MI (city) Macomb County	398	0.29
Huntington, NY (town) Suffolk County	398	0.20
Cranberry, PA (township) Butler County	396	1.68
Glendale, CA (city) Los Angeles County	396	0.20
Fort Lee, NJ (borough) Bergen County	395	1.11
West Deer, PA (township) Allegheny County	393	3.40
North Royalton, OH (city) Cuyahoga County	390	1.36
Johnstown, PA (city) Cambria County	389	1.63
Willoughby Hills, OH (city) Lake County	383	4.42
Oakland, CA (city) Alameda County	380	0.10
Granite City, IL (city) Madison County	378	1.19
Elizabeth, PA (township) Allegheny County	377	2.72
Wheaton, IL (city) Du Page County	377	0.68
Arlington, VA (cdp) Arlington County	376	0.20
Bethel Park, PA (borough) Allegheny County	374	1.11
Center, PA (township) Beaver County	373	3.25
Rochester Hills, MI (city) Oakland County	372	0.54
Kenosha, WI (city) Kenosha County	367	0.40
Ridgefield, NJ (borough) Bergen County	366	3.38
Buffalo, NY (city) Erie County	363	0.12
Troy, MI (city) Oakland County	355	0.44
Cuyahoga Falls, OH (city) Summit County	352	0.71
Palos Hills, IL (city) Cook County	351	1.98
Penn Hills, PA (cdp) Allegheny County	350	0.75
Greenfield, WI (city) Milwaukee County	349	0.98
Virginia Beach, VA (independent city) Virginia Beach city	343	0.08
Tonawanda, NY (town) Erie County	338	0.43
Niles, OH (city) Trumbull County	337	1.61
San Mateo, CA (city) San Mateo County	336	0.36
Escanaba, MI (city) Delta County	330	2.51
Seven Hills, OH (city) Cuyahoga County	329	2.72
Lower Paxton, PA (township) Dauphin County	328	0.74
Hubbard, OH (city) Trumbull County	326	3.95
North Bergen, NJ (township) Hudson County	325	0.56
Waukesha, WI (city) Waukesha County	325	0.50
Franklin, WI (city) Milwaukee County	323	1.09
Virginia, MN (city) Saint Louis County	322	3.52
Livonia, MI (city) Wayne County	322	0.32
Shelby, MI (cdp) Macomb County	321	0.49
Economy, PA (borough) Beaver County	319	3.41

Notes: (cdp) census designated place; Refer to the Explanation of Data in the front of the book for more detailed information.

Croatian

Top 150 Places Sorted by Percent

(Based on all places, regardless of population)

Place	Number	%
McCook, IL (village) Cook County	37	16.30
Yankee Lake, OH (village) Trumbull County	13	14.61
Eileen, WI (town) Bayfield County	83	12.95
Kelly, WI (town) Bayfield County	47	12.21
Bessemer, PA (borough) Lawrence County	141	12.04
Rathbun, IA (city) Appanoose County	9	10.23
Coal Center, PA (borough) Washington County	12	8.89
Mason, WI (town) Bayfield County	30	8.47
Versailles, PA (borough) Allegheny County	140	8.09
Lake McMurray, WA (cdp) Skagit County	14	7.87
Fallston, PA (borough) Beaver County	24	7.82
Mount Clare, IL (village) Macoupin County	31	7.58
Bressler-Enhaut-Oberlin, PA (cdp) Dauphin County	214	7.54
Ellsworth, PA (borough) Washington County	81	7.48
Braddock Hills, PA (borough) Allegheny County	149	7.46
Norris, IL (village) Fulton County	16	7.27
Saint David, IL (village) Fulton County	42	6.94
Bentleyville, PA (borough) Washington County	165	6.81
Etna, PA (borough) Allegheny County	264	6.73
Reserve Township, PA (cdp) Allegheny County	259	6.72
Wilma, MN (township) Pine County	11	6.71
Sawyerville, IL (village) Macoupin County	21	6.60
Novi, MI (township) Oakland County	12	6.45
Shooks, MN (township) Beltrami County	12	6.38
Nebish, MN (township) Beltrami County	22	6.21
Empire, LA (cdp) Plaquemines Parish	127	6.12
South Cle Elum, WA (town) Kittitas County	28	6.09
Cokeburg, PA (borough) Washington County	43	6.02
Aquilla, OH (village) Geauga County	22	5.99
Oceanside, OR (cdp) Tillamook County	21	5.98
Marengo, WI (town) Ashland County	22	5.91
Roslyn, WA (city) Kittitas County	59	5.82
Trafford, PA (borough) Westmoreland County	181	5.60
South Range, MI (village) Houghton County	42	5.58
Mason, WI (village) Bayfield County	2	5.56
Shelocta, PA (borough) Indiana County	7	5.51
Barksdale, WI (town) Bayfield County	42	5.45
Steelton, PA (borough) Dauphin County	316	5.44
Gingles, WI (town) Ashland County	35	5.32
Thorpe, MN (township) Hubbard County	2	5.26
Conway, PA (borough) Beaver County	120	5.24
Adams, MI (township) Houghton County	142	5.16
Mead, WI (town) Clark County	15	5.08
Ensign, MI (township) Delta County	39	5.05
Republic, PA (cdp) Fayette County	70	4.99
Saint Michael-Sidman, PA (cdp) Cambria County	47	4.94
East Rochester, PA (borough) Beaver County	30	4.89
Ahmeek, MI (village) Keweenaw County	8	4.85
Chalfant, PA (borough) Allegheny County	42	4.83
Daugherty, PA (township) Beaver County	166	4.82
Farmington, WV (town) Marion County	17	4.76
Vanport, PA (township) Beaver County	70	4.73
Shanagolden, WI (town) Ashland County	7	4.70
Freedom, PA (borough) Beaver County	83	4.69
Matherville, IL (village) Mercer County	36	4.67
Chest Springs, PA (borough) Cambria County	5	4.63
West Sunbury, PA (borough) Butler County	5	4.63
Gilbert, MN (city) Saint Louis County	85	4.60
Fairview, NJ (borough) Bergen County	607	4.58
White City, IL (village) Macoupin County	9	4.57
Port Vue, PA (borough) Allegheny County	193	4.56
Keewatin, MN (city) Itasca County	53	4.55
Cincinnati, IA (city) Appanoose County	19	4.51
Shaler Township, PA (cdp) Allegheny County	1,338	4.50
Industry, PA (borough) Beaver County	86	4.48
Eastlake, OH (city) Lake County	901	4.47
Numa, IA (city) Appanoose County	5	4.46
South Versailles, PA (township) Allegheny County	15	4.44
Willoughby Hills, OH (city) Lake County	383	4.42
Hagali, MN (township) Beltrami County	14	4.40
Napeague, NY (cdp) Suffolk County	10	4.33
Struthers, OH (city) Mahoning County	506	4.30
Basehor, KS (city) Leavenworth County	97	4.30
Heath, PA (township) Jefferson County	6	4.29
Dunfermline, IL (village) Fulton County	11	4.28
Powers, MI (village) Menominee County	16	4.27
Masury, OH (cdp) Trumbull County	117	4.25
Allouez, MI (township) Keweenaw County	67	4.20
Baden, PA (borough) Beaver County	183	4.18
Beatty, MN (township) Saint Louis County	17	4.18
Carp Lake, MI (township) Ontonagon County	36	4.13
Ogden Dunes, IN (town) Porter County	54	4.12
Bryant, IL (village) Fulton County	12	4.08
Wells, MI (township) Delta County	204	4.03
Calumet, MI (township) Houghton County	278	3.98
Hubbard, OH (city) Trumbull County	326	3.95
Raccoon, PA (township) Beaver County	134	3.94
Escanaba, MI (township) Delta County	139	3.90
Cuyuna, MN (city) Crow Wing County	9	3.90
Eveleth, MN (city) Saint Louis County	150	3.88
Perry, PA (township) Armstrong County	14	3.87
Willowick, OH (city) Lake County	555	3.85
Mount Olive, IL (city) Macoupin County	83	3.85
Hopewell, PA (township) Beaver County	512	3.84
Poland, OH (village) Mahoning County	110	3.84
Eagle River, WI (city) Vilas County	55	3.79
Rankin, PA (borough) Allegheny County	87	3.76
Flambeau, WI (town) Price County	21	3.75
Kimball, WI (town) Iron County	20	3.75
Whiting, IN (city) Lake County	189	3.68
Potter, PA (township) Beaver County	21	3.66
McDonald, OH (village) Trumbull County	126	3.64
Laurium, MI (village) Houghton County	77	3.61
Neihart, MT (town) Cascade County	3	3.61
North Versailles, PA (cdp) Allegheny County	399	3.59
Jackson Center, PA (borough) Mercer County	8	3.59
Lincoln, PA (borough) Allegheny County	43	3.58
Fruitdale, CA (cdp) Santa Clara County	25	3.57
Aleppo, PA (township) Allegheny County	37	3.56
Ambridge, PA (borough) Beaver County	274	3.53
Lakes of the Four Seasons, IN (cdp) Lake County	258	3.53
Kirtland, OH (city) Lake County	236	3.53
Virginia, MN (city) Saint Louis County	322	3.52
Timberlake, OH (village) Lake County	27	3.52
South Heights, PA (borough) Beaver County	19	3.50
Crabtree, PA (cdp) Westmoreland County	13	3.50
Balkan, MN (township) Saint Louis County	28	3.48
Chisholm, MN (city) Saint Louis County	171	3.45
Lone Pine, MN (township) Itasca County	19	3.45
Washington, PA (township) Fayette County	154	3.44
Bolindale, OH (cdp) Trumbull County	84	3.43
Economy, PA (borough) Beaver County	319	3.41
West Deer, PA (township) Allegheny County	393	3.40
Fredericktown-Millsboro, PA (cdp) Washington County	38	3.40
Millston, WI (town) Jackson County	5	3.40
Ridgefield, NJ (borough) Bergen County	366	3.38
Benld, IL (city) Macoupin County	52	3.38
Grant, MI (township) Keweenaw County	5	3.38
Hubbell, MI (cdp) Houghton County	37	3.36
Crest Hill, IL (city) Will County	437	3.35
Walton Hills, OH (village) Cuyahoga County	80	3.34
Eagarville, IL (village) Macoupin County	4	3.33
East Pittsburgh, PA (borough) Allegheny County	67	3.32
Hibbing, MN (city) Saint Louis County	561	3.29
Tipton, PA (cdp) Blair County	40	3.29
Millvale, PA (borough) Allegheny County	132	3.28
Ontonagon, MI (township) Ontonagon County	97	3.28
Shenango, PA (township) Mercer County	132	3.27
Bergland, MI (township) Ontonagon County	19	3.27
Bearville, MN (township) Itasca County	5	3.27
Monaca, PA (borough) Beaver County	205	3.26
Center, PA (township) Beaver County	373	3.25
Wheatland, PA (borough) Mercer County	24	3.24
Fall Lake, MN (township) Lake County	18	3.24
Euclid, OH (city) Cuyahoga County	1,705	3.23
New Brighton, PA (borough) Beaver County	214	3.22
Yeagertown, PA (cdp) Mifflin County	35	3.20
Campbell, OH (city) Mahoning County	302	3.19
Palisades Park, NJ (borough) Bergen County	541	3.17
Pulaski, PA (township) Beaver County	53	3.17

Notes: (cdp) census designated place; Refer to the Explanation of Data in the front of the book for more detailed information.

Croatian

Top 150 Places Sorted by Percent

(Based on places with populations of 10,000 or more)

Place	Number	%
Fairview, NJ (borough) Bergen County	607	4.58
Shaler Township, PA (cdp) Allegheny County	1,338	4.50
Eastlake, OH (city) Lake County	901	4.47
Struthers, OH (city) Mahoning County	506	4.30
Willowick, OH (city) Lake County	555	3.85
Hopewell, PA (township) Beaver County	512	3.84
North Versailles, PA (cdp) Allegheny County	399	3.59
West Deer, PA (township) Allegheny County	393	3.40
Ridgefield, NJ (borough) Bergen County	366	3.38
Crest Hill, IL (city) Will County	437	3.35
Hibbing, MN (city) Saint Louis County	561	3.29
Center, PA (township) Beaver County	373	3.25
Euclid, OH (city) Cuyahoga County	1,705	3.23
Palisades Park, NJ (borough) Bergen County	541	3.17
Hampton Township, PA (cdp) Allegheny County	546	3.12
Hermitage, PA (city) Mercer County	473	2.93
Cliffside Park, NJ (borough) Bergen County	661	2.87
Schererville, IN (town) Lake County	683	2.75
Elizabeth, PA (township) Allegheny County	377	2.72
Seven Hills, OH (city) Cuyahoga County	329	2.72
Swatara, PA (township) Dauphin County	595	2.63
Crown Point, IN (city) Lake County	497	2.54
Escanaba, MI (city) Delta County	330	2.51
Hobart, IN (city) Lake County	630	2.48
West Mifflin, PA (borough) Allegheny County	542	2.41
Fernway, PA (cdp) Butler County	291	2.39
Mentor, OH (city) Lake County	1,173	2.33
Boardman, OH (cdp) Mahoning County	864	2.32
Griffith, IN (town) Lake County	400	2.31
Richmond Heights, OH (city) Cuyahoga County	252	2.30
McKeesport, PA (city) Allegheny County	541	2.25
North Huntingdon, PA (township) Westmoreland County	652	2.23
McCandless Township, PA (cdp) Allegheny County	642	2.21
Highland, IN (town) Lake County	509	2.16
Munster, IN (town) Lake County	446	2.07
Lansing, IL (village) Cook County	564	2.00
Palos Hills, IL (city) Cook County	351	1.98
Wickliffe, OH (city) Lake County	260	1.93
Amherst, OH (city) Lorain County	226	1.90
Willoughby, OH (city) Lake County	425	1.88
Goodings Grove, IL (cdp) Will County	316	1.85
Moon, PA (township) Allegheny County	404	1.81
Ross Township, PA (cdp) Allegheny County	568	1.74
Canton, IL (city) Fulton County	264	1.73
Franklin Park, PA (borough) Allegheny County	195	1.72
Crestwood, IL (village) Cook County	193	1.72
Richland, PA (township) Cambria County	216	1.71
Avon, OH (city) Lorain County	196	1.71
Orland Park, IL (village) Cook County	868	1.70
Rostraver, PA (township) Westmoreland County	197	1.69
Cranberry, PA (township) Butler County	396	1.68
Sauk Village, IL (village) Cook County	175	1.68
Merrillville, IN (town) Lake County	514	1.67
Johnstown, PA (city) Cambria County	389	1.63
Brecksville, OH (city) Cuyahoga County	217	1.63
Niles, OH (city) Trumbull County	337	1.61
North Strabane, PA (township) Washington County	159	1.58
Dyer, IN (town) Lake County	218	1.57
Municipality of Murrysville, PA (borough) Westmoreland County	295	1.56
Aliquippa, PA (city) Beaver County	181	1.55
Lyons, IL (village) Cook County	157	1.55
Austintown, OH (cdp) Mahoning County	486	1.54
Lemont, IL (village) Cook County	202	1.53
Texas, MI (township) Kalamazoo County	165	1.51
Munhall, PA (borough) Allegheny County	181	1.48
Hammond, IN (city) Lake County	1,221	1.47
Joliet, IL (city) Will County	1,536	1.45
Penn, PA (township) Westmoreland County	283	1.44
Frankfort, IL (village) Will County	148	1.44
Municipality of Monroeville, PA (borough) Allegheny County	419	1.43
Lackawanna, NY (city) Erie County	273	1.43
Jeannette, PA (city) Westmoreland County	150	1.41
Rancho Palos Verdes, CA (city) Los Angeles County	579	1.40
Sharon, PA (city) Mercer County	227	1.39
West Allis, WI (city) Milwaukee County	843	1.38
Kansas City, KS (city) Wyandotte County	2,001	1.36
North Royalton, OH (city) Cuyahoga County	390	1.36
Whitehall, PA (borough) Allegheny County	193	1.34
Portage, IN (city) Porter County	445	1.33
Western Springs, IL (village) Cook County	167	1.32
Girard, OH (city) Trumbull County	147	1.32
Little Ferry, NJ (borough) Bergen County	143	1.32
Peters, PA (township) Washington County	230	1.31
Oak Lawn, IL (village) Cook County	713	1.29
Derry, PA (township) Westmoreland County	188	1.28
New Berlin, WI (city) Waukesha County	475	1.24
Youngstown, OH (city) Mahoning County	1,013	1.23
Greendale, WI (village) Milwaukee County	177	1.23
Lorain, OH (city) Lorain County	830	1.21
Baldwin, PA (borough) Allegheny County	239	1.20
Anacortes, WA (city) Skagit County	176	1.20
Robinson Township, PA (cdp) Allegheny County	147	1.20
Granite City, IL (city) Madison County	378	1.19
South Park Township, PA (cdp) Allegheny County	171	1.19
Worth, IL (village) Cook County	132	1.18
North Olmsted, OH (city) Cuyahoga County	400	1.17
Lincolnwood, IL (village) Cook County	144	1.17
Shawnee, KS (city) Johnson County	558	1.16
Plum, PA (borough) Allegheny County	313	1.16
Westchester, IL (village) Cook County	191	1.15
Alsip, IL (village) Cook County	227	1.14
Lockport, IL (city) Will County	169	1.14
Chesterton, IN (town) Porter County	119	1.14
Lenexa, KS (city) Johnson County	452	1.13
Tinley Park, IL (village) Cook County	543	1.12
Mokena, IL (village) Will County	164	1.12
Brooklyn, OH (city) Cuyahoga County	130	1.12
Fort Lee, NJ (borough) Bergen County	395	1.11
Bethel Park, PA (borough) Allegheny County	374	1.11
Franklin, WI (city) Milwaukee County	323	1.09
Mehlville, MO (cdp) Saint Louis County	314	1.09
North Fayette, PA (township) Allegheny County	134	1.09
Weirton, WV (city) Hancock County	219	1.07
South Euclid, OH (city) Cuyahoga County	249	1.06
Twinsburg, OH (city) Summit County	177	1.05
Burr Ridge, IL (village) Du Page County	108	1.05
Brookfield, IL (village) Cook County	197	1.04
Aberdeen, WA (city) Grays Harbor County	171	1.04
South Union, PA (township) Fayette County	117	1.04
Uniontown, PA (city) Fayette County	128	1.03
Strongsville, OH (city) Cuyahoga County	446	1.02
Hempfield, PA (township) Westmoreland County	417	1.02
Green, OH (city) Summit County	231	1.01
Downers Grove, IL (village) Du Page County	488	1.00
Wauwatosa, WI (city) Milwaukee County	474	1.00
Evergreen Park, IL (village) Cook County	209	1.00
Parma, OH (city) Cuyahoga County	851	0.99
Darien, IL (city) Du Page County	228	0.99
New Lenox, IL (village) Will County	174	0.99
Greenfield, WI (city) Milwaukee County	349	0.98
Garfield Heights, OH (city) Cuyahoga County	301	0.98
Hudson, OH (city) Summit County	220	0.98
Middleburg Heights, OH (city) Cuyahoga County	150	0.97
Lakewood, OH (city) Cuyahoga County	536	0.95
Woodridge, IL (village) Du Page County	294	0.95
Upper Saint Clair, PA (cdp) Allegheny County	190	0.95
River Forest, IL (village) Cook County	111	0.95
Mayfield Heights, OH (city) Cuyahoga County	183	0.94
Scott Township, PA (cdp) Allegheny County	161	0.93
Palos Heights, IL (city) Cook County	105	0.93
Concord, MO (cdp) Saint Louis County	151	0.91
Colonial Park, PA (cdp) Dauphin County	118	0.90
Pittsburgh, PA (city) Allegheny County	2,981	0.89
Hickory Hills, IL (city) Cook County	122	0.88
Lyndhurst, OH (city) Cuyahoga County	133	0.87
North Ridgeville, OH (city) Lorain County	193	0.86
Mount Pleasant, PA (township) Westmoreland County	96	0.86
Brentwood, PA (borough) Allegheny County	90	0.86
Parma Heights, OH (city) Cuyahoga County	183	0.84
Muskego, WI (city) Waukesha County	179	0.84

Notes: (cdp) census designated place; Refer to the Explanation of Data in the front of the book for more detailed information.

Cypriot

Top 150 Places Sorted by Number

(Based on all places, regardless of population)

Place	Number	%
New York, NY (city) New York City	1,397	0.02
Hempstead, NY (town) Nassau County	203	0.03
Oyster Bay, NY (town) Nassau County	165	0.06
Brookhaven, NY (town) Suffolk County	137	0.03
Huntington, NY (town) Suffolk County	120	0.06
Annapolis, MD (city) Anne Arundel County	99	0.28
Paramus, NJ (borough) Bergen County	96	0.37
Virginia Beach, VA (independent city) Virginia Beach city	84	0.02
North Hempstead, NY (town) Nassau County	76	0.03
South Brunswick, NJ (township) Middlesex County	73	0.19
Yonkers, NY (city) Westchester County	73	0.04
Hicksville, NY (cdp) Nassau County	72	0.17
Norfolk, VA (independent city) Norfolk city	69	0.03
Los Angeles, CA (city) Los Angeles County	63	0.00
Oakley, CA (city) Contra Costa County	59	0.23
Fairfield, NJ (cdp) Essex County	57	0.81
Phoenix, AZ (city) Maricopa County	55	0.00
East Brunswick, NJ (cdp) Middlesex County	52	0.11
Boca Raton, FL (city) Palm Beach County	52	0.07
Chicago, IL (city) Cook County	52	0.00
Salisbury, NY (cdp) Nassau County	51	0.41
Akron, OH (city) Summit County	51	0.02
Upper Darby, PA (township) Delaware County	48	0.06
Greenburgh, NY (town) Westchester County	47	0.05
Austin, TX (city) Travis County	46	0.01
Tucson, AZ (city) Pima County	44	0.01
San Jose, CA (city) Santa Clara County	44	0.00
Raritan, NJ (township) Hunterdon County	42	0.21
West Springfield, MA (cdp) Hampden County	40	0.14
Cinco Ranch, TX (cdp) Fort Bend County	39	0.35
Seaford, NY (cdp) Nassau County	39	0.25
West Orange, NJ (cdp) Essex County	38	0.08
Southampton, NY (village) Suffolk County	37	0.93
Parole, MD (cdp) Anne Arundel County	37	0.27
Glen Cove, NY (city) Nassau County	37	0.14
Southampton, NY (town) Suffolk County	37	0.07
Colesville, MD (cdp) Montgomery County	36	0.18
Shelby, MI (cdp) Macomb County	36	0.06
Allentown, PA (city) Lehigh County	36	0.03
Hammond, IN (city) Lake County	35	0.04
Garland, TX (city) Dallas County	35	0.02
Jacksonville, FL (special city) Duval County	35	0.00
Burtonsville, MD (cdp) Montgomery County	34	0.47
North Brunswick Township, NJ (cdp) Middlesex County	34	0.09
Hillsboro, OR (city) Washington County	34	0.05
Dix Hills, NY (cdp) Suffolk County	33	0.13
Houston, TX (city) Harris County	33	0.00
Cary, NC (town) Wake County	32	0.03
Brittany Farms-Highlands, PA (cdp) Bucks County	31	0.96
New Britain, PA (township) Bucks County	31	0.29
Saint Louis, MO (independent city) Saint Louis city	31	0.01
Holtsville, NY (cdp) Suffolk County	30	0.18
Jamestown, NY (city) Chautauqua County	30	0.09
Palm Harbor, FL (cdp) Pinellas County	30	0.05
Tempe, AZ (city) Maricopa County	29	0.02
University Gardens, NY (cdp) Nassau County	28	0.68
Ridge, NY (cdp) Suffolk County	28	0.21
Granger, IN (cdp) Saint Joseph County	28	0.10
Kirkland, WA (city) King County	28	0.06
Union City, NJ (city) Hudson County	28	0.04
Oradell, NJ (borough) Bergen County	27	0.34
Plainview, NY (cdp) Nassau County	27	0.11
Levittown, NY (cdp) Nassau County	27	0.05
Columbus, OH (city) Franklin County	27	0.00
Inglewood-Finn Hill, WA (cdp) King County	26	0.11
Charlottesville, VA (independent city) Charlottesville city	26	0.06
Canton, MI (cdp) Wayne County	26	0.03
Montgomery, AL (city) Montgomery County	26	0.01
Indianapolis, IN (special city) Marion County	26	0.00
Hartsdale, NY (cdp) Westchester County	25	0.25
Oldsmar, FL (city) Pinellas County	25	0.21
Carbondale, IL (city) Jackson County	25	0.12
Nashua, NH (city) Hillsborough County	25	0.03
Richardson, TX (city) Dallas County	25	0.03
Huntington Beach, CA (city) Orange County	25	0.01
Philadelphia, PA (city) Philadelphia County	25	0.00
Leonia, NJ (borough) Bergen County	24	0.27
Arlington, MA (cdp) Middlesex County	24	0.06
Gaithersburg, MD (city) Montgomery County	24	0.05
Howell, NJ (township) Monmouth County	24	0.05
Providence, RI (city) Providence County	24	0.01
Toledo, OH (city) Lucas County	24	0.01
Shenandoah, LA (cdp) East Baton Rouge Parish	23	0.13
Ann Arbor, MI (city) Washtenaw County	23	0.02
Babylon, NY (town) Suffolk County	23	0.01
Airmont, NY (village) Rockland County	22	0.28
East Rockaway, NY (village) Nassau County	22	0.21
Lake Grove, NY (village) Suffolk County	22	0.21
Vienna, VA (town) Fairfax County	22	0.15
Lutherville-Timonium, MD (cdp) Baltimore County	22	0.14
Dumont, NJ (borough) Bergen County	22	0.13
Syosset, NY (cdp) Nassau County	22	0.12
East Northport, NY (cdp) Suffolk County	22	0.11
Ridgewood, NJ (village) Bergen County	22	0.09
Ramapo, NY (town) Rockland County	22	0.02
San Buenaventura, CA (city) Ventura County	22	0.02
Louisville, KY (city) Jefferson County	22	0.01
Boston, MA (city) Suffolk County	22	0.00
Clarion, PA (borough) Clarion County	21	0.34
Groton, MA (town) Middlesex County	21	0.22
Thompson, NY (town) Sullivan County	21	0.15
Charleston, WV (city) Kanawha County	21	0.04
Cambridge, MA (city) Middlesex County	21	0.02
Edison, NJ (cdp) Middlesex County	21	0.02
Newtown, PA (township) Delaware County	20	0.17
Fort Hunt, VA (cdp) Fairfax County	20	0.16
Brecksville, OH (city) Cuyahoga County	20	0.15
Hopewell, VA (independent city) Hopewell city	20	0.09
Wellington, FL (village) Palm Beach County	20	0.05
Chula Vista, CA (city) San Diego County	20	0.01
New Orleans, LA (city) Orleans Parish	20	0.00
Cottage Lake, WA (cdp) King County	19	0.08
Mercerville-Hamilton Square, NJ (cdp) Mercer County	19	0.07
Commack, NY (cdp) Suffolk County	19	0.05
Clarkstown, NY (town) Rockland County	19	0.02
Hamilton, NJ (township) Mercer County	19	0.02
Mission Viejo, CA (city) Orange County	19	0.02
Rochester, MN (city) Olmsted County	19	0.02
Sound Beach, NY (cdp) Suffolk County	18	0.18
Lincolnwood, IL (village) Cook County	18	0.15
Cherry Hill Mall, NJ (cdp) Camden County	18	0.13
Warren, NJ (township) Somerset County	18	0.13
Bedford, NY (town) Westchester County	18	0.10
Brookfield, IL (village) Cook County	18	0.09
Shirley, NY (cdp) Suffolk County	18	0.07
Boardman, OH (cdp) Mahoning County	18	0.05
Biloxi, MS (city) Harrison County	18	0.04
Rye, NY (town) Westchester County	18	0.04
Cherry Hill, NJ (township) Camden County	18	0.03
College Station, TX (city) Brazos County	18	0.03
Wilmington, NC (city) New Hanover County	18	0.02
Syracuse, NY (city) Onondaga County	18	0.01
Washington, DC (city) District of Columbia	18	0.00
West Hills, NY (cdp) Suffolk County	17	0.30
Spartanburg, SC (city) Spartanburg County	17	0.04
West Babylon, NY (cdp) Suffolk County	17	0.04
Des Plaines, IL (city) Cook County	17	0.03
Brandon, FL (cdp) Hillsborough County	17	0.02
Bryn Mawr, PA (cdp) Montgomery County	16	0.36
Arcata, CA (city) Humboldt County	16	0.10
West Hollywood, CA (city) Los Angeles County	16	0.04
Lower Merion, PA (township) Montgomery County	16	0.03
Palm Bay, FL (city) Brevard County	16	0.02
Paradise, NV (cdp) Clark County	16	0.01
Raleigh, NC (city) Wake County	16	0.01
Pittsburgh, PA (city) Allegheny County	16	0.00
Murphysboro, IL (city) Jackson County	15	0.11
Massapequa Park, NY (village) Nassau County	15	0.09
Greenwood, IN (city) Johnson County	15	0.04
Fountain Valley, CA (city) Orange County	15	0.03

Notes: (cdp) census designated place; Refer to the Explanation of Data in the front of the book for more detailed information.

Cypriot

Top 150 Places Sorted by Percent

(Based on all places, regardless of population)

Place	Number	%
Lake Alice, MN (township) Hubbard County	4	4.65
Rock Hill, NY (cdp) Sullivan County	12	1.22
Brittany Farms-Highlands, PA (cdp) Bucks County	31	0.96
Southampton, NY (village) Suffolk County	37	0.93
Fairfield, NJ (cdp) Essex County	57	0.81
University Gardens, NY (cdp) Nassau County	28	0.68
Atlantic Beach, NY (village) Nassau County	12	0.61
Alna, ME (town) Lincoln County	4	0.59
Maybee, MI (village) Monroe County	3	0.57
Burtonsville, MD (cdp) Montgomery County	34	0.47
Barnum Island, NY (cdp) Nassau County	11	0.46
Salisbury, NY (cdp) Nassau County	51	0.41
South Hempstead, NY (cdp) Nassau County	12	0.38
Paramus, NJ (borough) Bergen County	96	0.37
Bryn Mawr, PA (cdp) Montgomery County	16	0.36
Nelsonville, NY (village) Putnam County	2	0.36
Cinco Ranch, TX (cdp) Fort Bend County	39	0.35
Oradell, NJ (borough) Bergen County	27	0.34
Clarion, PA (borough) Clarion County	21	0.34
Munsey Park, NY (village) Nassau County	9	0.34
East Nantmeal, PA (township) Chester County	6	0.34
Wallace, ID (city) Shoshone County	3	0.32
West Hills, NY (cdp) Suffolk County	17	0.30
New Britain, PA (township) Bucks County	31	0.29
Annapolis, MD (city) Anne Arundel County	99	0.28
Airmont, NY (village) Rockland County	22	0.28
Hillsmere Shores, MD (cdp) Anne Arundel County	8	0.28
Parole, MD (cdp) Anne Arundel County	37	0.27
Leonia, NJ (borough) Bergen County	24	0.27
Osprey, FL (cdp) Sarasota County	11	0.27
Roslyn, NY (village) Nassau County	7	0.27
Clintwood, VA (town) Dickenson County	4	0.26
Mill Neck, NY (village) Nassau County	2	0.26
Seaford, NY (cdp) Nassau County	39	0.25
Hartsdale, NY (cdp) Westchester County	25	0.25
Mattituck, NY (cdp) Suffolk County	10	0.24
East Dundee, IL (village) Kane County	7	0.24
Plandome, NY (village) Nassau County	3	0.24
Oakley, CA (city) Contra Costa County	59	0.23
Middleburgh, NY (town) Schoharie County	8	0.23
Medina, WA (city) King County	7	0.23
Groton, MA (town) Middlesex County	21	0.22
Red Hook, NY (village) Dutchess County	4	0.22
Raritan, NJ (township) Hunterdon County	42	0.21
Ridge, NY (cdp) Suffolk County	28	0.21
Oldsmar, FL (city) Pinellas County	25	0.21
East Rockaway, NY (village) Nassau County	22	0.21
Lake Grove, NY (village) Suffolk County	22	0.21
Plandome Heights, NY (village) Nassau County	2	0.21
Highlands, NJ (borough) Monmouth County	10	0.20
Garland, ME (town) Penobscot County	2	0.20
Roslyn Harbor, NY (village) Nassau County	2	0.20
South Brunswick, NJ (township) Middlesex County	73	0.19
Colesville, MD (cdp) Montgomery County	36	0.18
Holtsville, NY (cdp) Suffolk County	30	0.18
Sound Beach, NY (cdp) Suffolk County	18	0.18
Hicksville, NY (cdp) Nassau County	72	0.17
Newtown, PA (township) Delaware County	20	0.17
Durham, CT (town) Middlesex County	11	0.17
Centerport, NY (cdp) Suffolk County	9	0.17
Fort Hunt, VA (cdp) Fairfax County	20	0.16
Palermo, ME (town) Waldo County	2	0.16
Vienna, VA (town) Fairfax County	22	0.15
Thompson, NY (town) Sullivan County	21	0.15
Brecksville, OH (city) Cuyahoga County	20	0.15
Lincolnwood, IL (village) Cook County	18	0.15
Great Neck, NY (village) Nassau County	14	0.15
Exeter, RI (town) Washington County	9	0.15
Glen Head, NY (cdp) Nassau County	7	0.15
West Springfield, MA (cdp) Hampden County	40	0.14
Glen Cove, NY (city) Nassau County	37	0.14
Lutherville-Timonium, MD (cdp) Baltimore County	22	0.14
Emerson, NJ (borough) Bergen County	10	0.14
Fremont, NH (town) Rockingham County	5	0.14
Cramerton, NC (town) Gaston County	4	0.14

Place	Number	%
Dix Hills, NY (cdp) Suffolk County	33	0.13
Shenandoah, LA (cdp) East Baton Rouge Parish	23	0.13
Dumont, NJ (borough) Bergen County	22	0.13
Cherry Hill Mall, NJ (cdp) Camden County	18	0.13
Warren, NJ (township) Somerset County	18	0.13
Marlton, NJ (cdp) Burlington County	13	0.13
South Huntington, NY (cdp) Suffolk County	12	0.13
Lake Worth, TX (city) Tarrant County	6	0.13
Lewiston, MN (city) Winona County	2	0.13
Carbondale, IL (city) Jackson County	25	0.12
Syosset, NY (cdp) Nassau County	22	0.12
Pelham, NY (village) Westchester County	8	0.12
Herricks, NY (cdp) Nassau County	5	0.12
Sandisfield, MA (town) Berkshire County	1	0.12
East Brunswick, NJ (township) Middlesex County	52	0.11
Plainview, NY (cdp) Nassau County	27	0.11
Inglewood-Finn Hill, WA (cdp) King County	26	0.11
East Northport, NY (cdp) Suffolk County	22	0.11
Murphysboro, IL (city) Jackson County	15	0.11
Vermillion, SD (city) Clay County	11	0.11
Salisbury, MA (town) Essex County	9	0.11
Garden City Park, NY (cdp) Nassau County	8	0.11
Northport, NY (village) Suffolk County	8	0.11
Hurley, NY (town) Ulster County	7	0.11
Morris Plains, NJ (borough) Morris County	6	0.11
Brecknock, PA (township) Berks County	5	0.11
Granger, IN (cdp) Saint Joseph County	28	0.10
Bedford, NY (town) Westchester County	18	0.10
Arcata, CA (city) Humboldt County	16	0.10
Washington, NJ (township) Mercer County	10	0.10
Kenilworth, NJ (borough) Union County	8	0.10
North Star, DE (cdp) New Castle County	8	0.10
Canterbury, NH (town) Merrimack County	2	0.10
West Nantmeal, PA (township) Chester County	2	0.10
Walhalla, ND (city) Pembina County	1	0.10
North Brunswick Township, NJ (cdp) Middlesex County	34	0.09
Jamestown, NY (city) Chautauqua County	30	0.09
Ridgewood, NJ (village) Bergen County	22	0.09
Hopewell, VA (independent city) Hopewell city	20	0.09
Brookfield, IL (village) Cook County	18	0.09
Massapequa Park, NY (village) Nassau County	15	0.09
Cinnaminson, NJ (township) Burlington County	13	0.09
Milton, VT (town) Chittenden County	9	0.09
Woodbury, NY (cdp) Nassau County	8	0.09
Monroe, NY (village) Orange County	7	0.09
Belvedere, CA (city) Marin County	2	0.09
Jean Lafitte, LA (town) Jefferson Parish	2	0.09
West Orange, NJ (cdp) Essex County	38	0.08
Cottage Lake, WA (cdp) King County	19	0.08
Nanuet, NY (cdp) Rockland County	13	0.08
Kingsland, GA (city) Camden County	8	0.08
Pleasant Hills, PA (borough) Allegheny County	7	0.08
Lakes of the Four Seasons, IN (cdp) Lake County	6	0.08
Exeter, MI (township) Monroe County	3	0.08
Boca Raton, FL (city) Palm Beach County	52	0.07
Southampton, NY (town) Suffolk County	37	0.07
Mercerville-Hamilton Square, NJ (cdp) Mercer County	19	0.07
Shirley, NY (cdp) Suffolk County	18	0.07
Lyndhurst, NJ (cdp) Bergen County	13	0.07
Idylwood, VA (cdp) Fairfax County	11	0.07
South Farmingdale, NY (cdp) Nassau County	10	0.07
Grosse Pointe Park, MI (city) Wayne County	9	0.07
Patton, PA (township) Centre County	8	0.07
Pelham, NY (town) Westchester County	8	0.07
Port Saint John, FL (cdp) Brevard County	8	0.07
Miami Shores, FL (village) Miami-Dade County	7	0.07
Congers, NY (cdp) Rockland County	6	0.07
Highland Park, TX (town) Dallas County	6	0.07
Kendall Park, NJ (cdp) Middlesex County	6	0.07
Redwood, OR (cdp) Josephine County	4	0.07
Pendleton, SC (town) Anderson County	2	0.07
Oyster Bay, NY (town) Nassau County	165	0.06
Huntington, NY (town) Suffolk County	120	0.06
Upper Darby, PA (township) Delaware County	48	0.06
Shelby, MI (cdp) Macomb County	36	0.06

Notes: (cdp) census designated place; Refer to the Explanation of Data in the front of the book for more detailed information.

Cypriot

Top 150 Places Sorted by Percent

(Based on places with populations of 10,000 or more)

Place	Number	%
Salisbury, NY (cdp) Nassau County	51	0.41
Paramus, NJ (borough) Bergen County	96	0.37
Cinco Ranch, TX (cdp) Fort Bend County	39	0.35
New Britain, PA (township) Bucks County	31	0.29
Annapolis, MD (city) Anne Arundel County	99	0.28
Parole, MD (cdp) Anne Arundel County	37	0.27
Seaford, NY (cdp) Nassau County	39	0.25
Oakley, CA (city) Contra Costa County	59	0.23
Raritan, NJ (township) Hunterdon County	42	0.21
Ridge, NY (cdp) Suffolk County	28	0.21
Oldsmar, FL (city) Pinellas County	25	0.21
East Rockaway, NY (village) Nassau County	22	0.21
Lake Grove, NY (village) Suffolk County	22	0.21
South Brunswick, NJ (township) Middlesex County	73	0.19
Colesville, MD (cdp) Montgomery County	36	0.18
Holtsville, NY (cdp) Suffolk County	30	0.18
Hicksville, NY (cdp) Nassau County	72	0.17
Newtown, PA (township) Delaware County	20	0.17
Fort Hunt, VA (cdp) Fairfax County	20	0.16
Vienna, VA (town) Fairfax County	22	0.15
Thompson, NY (town) Sullivan County	21	0.15
Brecksville, OH (city) Cuyahoga County	20	0.15
Lincolnwood, IL (village) Cook County	18	0.15
West Springfield, MA (cdp) Hampden County	40	0.14
Glen Cove, NY (city) Nassau County	37	0.14
Lutherville-Timonium, MD (cdp) Baltimore County	22	0.14
Dix Hills, NY (cdp) Suffolk County	33	0.13
Shenandoah, LA (cdp) East Baton Rouge Parish	23	0.13
Dumont, NJ (borough) Bergen County	22	0.13
Cherry Hill Mall, NJ (cdp) Camden County	18	0.13
Warren, NJ (township) Somerset County	18	0.13
Marlton, NJ (cdp) Burlington County	13	0.13
Carbondale, IL (city) Jackson County	25	0.12
Syosset, NY (cdp) Nassau County	22	0.12
East Brunswick, NJ (cdp) Middlesex County	52	0.11
Plainview, NY (cdp) Nassau County	27	0.11
Inglewood-Finn Hill, WA (cdp) King County	26	0.11
East Northport, NY (cdp) Suffolk County	22	0.11
Murphysboro, IL (city) Jackson County	15	0.11
Granger, IN (cdp) Saint Joseph County	28	0.10
Bedford, NY (town) Westchester County	18	0.10
Arcata, CA (city) Humboldt County	16	0.10
Washington, NJ (township) Mercer County	10	0.10
North Brunswick Township, NJ (cdp) Middlesex County	34	0.09
Jamestown, NY (city) Chautauqua County	30	0.09
Ridgewood, NJ (village) Bergen County	22	0.09
Hopewell, VA (independent city) Hopewell city	20	0.09
Brookfield, IL (village) Cook County	18	0.09
Massapequa Park, NY (village) Nassau County	15	0.09
Cinnaminson, NJ (township) Burlington County	13	0.09
West Orange, NJ (cdp) Essex County	38	0.08
Cottage Lake, WA (cdp) King County	19	0.08
Nanuet, NY (cdp) Rockland County	13	0.08
Kingsland, GA (city) Camden County	8	0.08
Boca Raton, FL (city) Palm Beach County	52	0.07
Southampton, NY (town) Suffolk County	37	0.07
Mercerville-Hamilton Square, NJ (cdp) Mercer County	19	0.07
Shirley, NY (cdp) Suffolk County	18	0.07
Lyndhurst, NJ (cdp) Bergen County	13	0.07
Idylwood, VA (cdp) Fairfax County	11	0.07
South Farmingdale, NY (cdp) Nassau County	10	0.07
Grosse Pointe Park, MI (city) Wayne County	9	0.07
Patton, PA (township) Centre County	8	0.07
Pelham, NY (town) Westchester County	8	0.07
Port Saint John, FL (cdp) Brevard County	8	0.07
Miami Shores, FL (village) Miami-Dade County	7	0.07
Oyster Bay, NY (town) Nassau County	165	0.06
Huntington, NY (town) Suffolk County	120	0.06
Upper Darby, PA (township) Delaware County	48	0.06
Shelby, MI (cdp) Macomb County	36	0.06
Kirkland, WA (city) King County	28	0.06
Charlottesville, VA (independent city) Charlottesville city	26	0.06
Arlington, MA (cdp) Middlesex County	24	0.06
Horsham, PA (township) Montgomery County	14	0.06
Boca Del Mar, FL (cdp) Palm Beach County	12	0.06
Muhlenberg, PA (township) Berks County	9	0.06
Highland Village, TX (city) Denton County	7	0.06
Mounds View, MN (city) Ramsey County	7	0.06
Greenburgh, NY (town) Westchester County	47	0.05
Hillsboro, OR (city) Washington County	34	0.05
Palm Harbor, FL (cdp) Pinellas County	30	0.05
Levittown, NY (cdp) Nassau County	27	0.05
Gaithersburg, MD (city) Montgomery County	24	0.05
Howell, NJ (township) Monmouth County	24	0.05
Wellington, FL (village) Palm Beach County	20	0.05
Commack, NY (cdp) Suffolk County	19	0.05
Boardman, OH (cdp) Mahoning County	18	0.05
Englewood, NJ (city) Bergen County	14	0.05
Maplewood, NJ (cdp) Essex County	12	0.05
Newington, VA (cdp) Fairfax County	10	0.05
Southold, NY (town) Suffolk County	10	0.05
East Lyme, CT (town) New London County	9	0.05
Farmingville, NY (cdp) Suffolk County	9	0.05
Green Haven, MD (cdp) Anne Arundel County	8	0.05
Coos Bay, OR (city) Coos County	7	0.05
Ellington, CT (town) Tolland County	6	0.05
La Grange Park, IL (village) Cook County	6	0.05
North Lindenhurst, NY (cdp) Suffolk County	6	0.05
Hartford, VT (town) Windsor County	5	0.05
Yonkers, NY (city) Westchester County	73	0.04
Hammond, IN (city) Lake County	35	0.04
Union City, NJ (city) Hudson County	28	0.04
Charleston, WV (city) Kanawha County	21	0.04
Biloxi, MS (city) Harrison County	18	0.04
Rye, NY (town) Westchester County	18	0.04
Spartanburg, SC (city) Spartanburg County	17	0.04
West Babylon, NY (cdp) Suffolk County	17	0.04
West Hollywood, CA (city) Los Angeles County	16	0.04
Greenwood, IN (city) Johnson County	15	0.04
Eastpointe, MI (city) Macomb County	13	0.04
Freehold, NJ (township) Monmouth County	13	0.04
Bonita Springs, FL (city) Lee County	12	0.04
Bowling Green, OH (city) Wood County	12	0.04
Menomonee Falls, WI (village) Waukesha County	12	0.04
Port Chester, NY (village) Westchester County	12	0.04
Helena, MT (city) Lewis and Clark County	10	0.04
White Oak, MD (cdp) Montgomery County	9	0.04
Montville, NJ (township) Morris County	8	0.04
Rosedale, MD (cdp) Baltimore County	8	0.04
Farragut, TN (town) Knox County	7	0.04
Lynbrook, NY (village) Nassau County	7	0.04
Scio, MI (township) Washtenaw County	7	0.04
Goodlettsville, TN (city) Davidson County	6	0.04
West Freehold, NJ (cdp) Monmouth County	5	0.04
Red Hook, NY (town) Dutchess County	4	0.04
Hempstead, NY (town) Nassau County	203	0.03
Brookhaven, NY (town) Suffolk County	137	0.03
North Hempstead, NY (town) Nassau County	76	0.03
Norfolk, VA (independent city) Norfolk city	69	0.03
Allentown, PA (city) Lehigh County	36	0.03
Cary, NC (town) Wake County	32	0.03
Canton, MI (cdp) Wayne County	26	0.03
Nashua, NH (city) Hillsborough County	25	0.03
Richardson, TX (city) Dallas County	25	0.03
Cherry Hill, NJ (township) Camden County	18	0.03
College Station, TX (city) Brazos County	18	0.03
Des Plaines, IL (city) Cook County	17	0.03
Lower Merion, PA (township) Montgomery County	16	0.03
Fountain Valley, CA (city) Orange County	15	0.03
Evesham, NJ (township) Burlington County	13	0.03
Valley Stream, NY (village) Nassau County	12	0.03
Hallandale, FL (city) Broward County	11	0.03
Monroe, NY (town) Orange County	11	0.03
Mount Laurel, NJ (township) Burlington County	11	0.03
Oakland Park, FL (city) Broward County	9	0.03
Fairfax, VA (independent city) Fairfax city	7	0.03
Queensbury, NY (town) Warren County	7	0.03
Kingston, NY (city) Ulster County	6	0.03
Mamaroneck, NY (village) Westchester County	6	0.03
Palisades Park, NJ (borough) Bergen County	5	0.03

Notes: (cdp) census designated place; Refer to the Explanation of Data in the front of the book for more detailed information.

Czech

Top 150 Places Sorted by Number

(Based on all places, regardless of population)

Place	Number	%
Omaha, NE (city) Douglas County	16,796	4.31
Chicago, IL (city) Cook County	13,790	0.48
Lincoln, NE (city) Lancaster County	11,510	5.11
New York, NY (city) New York City	10,659	0.13
Houston, TX (city) Harris County	9,545	0.49
Cedar Rapids, IA (city) Linn County	7,934	6.58
Austin, TX (city) Travis County	6,299	0.96
Los Angeles, CA (city) Los Angeles County	5,900	0.16
Phoenix, AZ (city) Maricopa County	5,279	0.40
San Antonio, TX (city) Bexar County	4,622	0.40
Minneapolis, MN (city) Hennepin County	4,522	1.18
Milwaukee, WI (city) Milwaukee County	3,940	0.66
San Diego, CA (city) San Diego County	3,804	0.31
Dallas, TX (city) Dallas County	3,598	0.30
Cleveland, OH (city) Cuyahoga County	3,580	0.75
Saint Paul, MN (city) Ramsey County	3,310	1.15
Manitowoc, WI (city) Manitowoc County	3,004	8.84
Berwyn, IL (city) Cook County	2,982	5.52
Madison, WI (city) Dane County	2,821	1.36
Seattle, WA (city) King County	2,812	0.50
Naperville, IL (city) Du Page County	2,803	2.18
Portland, OR (city) Multnomah County	2,786	0.53
Downers Grove, IL (village) Du Page County	2,563	5.27
Parma, OH (city) Cuyahoga County	2,554	2.98
Colorado Springs, CO (city) El Paso County	2,521	0.70
Green Bay, WI (city) Brown County	2,520	2.46
Corpus Christi, TX (city) Nueces County	2,337	0.84
Denver, CO (city) Denver County	2,316	0.42
Bellevue, NE (city) Sarpy County	2,288	5.16
Columbus, OH (city) Franklin County	2,232	0.31
Brookhaven, NY (town) Suffolk County	2,115	0.47
Victoria, TX (city) Victoria County	2,089	3.46
San Francisco, CA (city) San Francisco County	2,062	0.27
Oklahoma City, OK (city) Oklahoma County	2,021	0.40
Arlington, TX (city) Tarrant County	2,008	0.60
Hempstead, NY (town) Nassau County	1,842	0.24
Tucson, AZ (city) Pima County	1,820	0.37
Saint Louis, MO (independent city) Saint Louis city	1,819	0.52
Brookfield, IL (village) Cook County	1,802	9.48
Albuquerque, NM (city) Bernalillo County	1,801	0.40
Baltimore, MD (independent city) Baltimore city	1,773	0.27
Mesa, AZ (city) Maricopa County	1,732	0.44
Cicero, IL (town) Cook County	1,714	2.00
Wichita, KS (city) Sedgwick County	1,671	0.49
Islip, NY (town) Suffolk County	1,662	0.52
Bloomington, MN (city) Hennepin County	1,650	1.94
Racine, WI (city) Racine County	1,639	2.00
Iowa City, IA (city) Johnson County	1,587	2.54
San Jose, CA (city) Santa Clara County	1,578	0.18
Las Vegas, NV (city) Clark County	1,574	0.33
Kansas City, MO (city) Jackson County	1,553	0.35
Sioux Falls, SD (city) Minnehaha County	1,537	1.24
Bolingbrook, IL (village) Will County	1,532	2.71
Grand Island, NE (city) Hall County	1,519	3.55
Fort Worth, TX (city) Tarrant County	1,513	0.28
Fargo, ND (city) Cass County	1,479	1.63
Philadelphia, PA (city) Philadelphia County	1,466	0.10
Garfield Heights, OH (city) Cuyahoga County	1,445	4.72
Grand Forks, ND (city) Grand Forks County	1,442	2.93
College Station, TX (city) Brazos County	1,398	2.06
Woodridge, IL (village) Du Page County	1,396	4.49
Plano, TX (city) Collin County	1,380	0.62
Scottsdale, AZ (city) Maricopa County	1,378	0.68
Columbus, NE (city) Platte County	1,377	6.56
Owatonna, MN (city) Steele County	1,376	6.14
Wheaton, IL (city) Du Page County	1,366	2.46
Schaumburg, IL (village) Cook County	1,356	1.82
Virginia Beach, VA (independent city) Virginia Beach city	1,344	0.32
Temple, TX (city) Bell County	1,342	2.47
Indianapolis, IN (special city) Marion County	1,332	0.17
Bryan, TX (city) Brazos County	1,330	2.01
La Crosse, WI (city) La Crosse County	1,318	2.55
Two Rivers, WI (city) Manitowoc County	1,310	10.35
Fremont, NE (city) Dodge County	1,289	5.12
Oyster Bay, NY (town) Nassau County	1,287	0.44
Washington, DC (city) District of Columbia	1,274	0.22
Rochester, MN (city) Olmsted County	1,252	1.47
Jacksonville, FL (special city) Duval County	1,244	0.17
Oak Lawn, IL (village) Cook County	1,233	2.23
Lombard, IL (village) Du Page County	1,229	2.94
Fort Collins, CO (city) Larimer County	1,222	1.03
Rosenberg, TX (city) Fort Bend County	1,202	4.97
Joliet, IL (city) Will County	1,201	1.13
Westchester, IL (village) Cook County	1,194	7.17
Lakeville, MN (city) Dakota County	1,183	2.74
Strongsville, OH (city) Cuyahoga County	1,180	2.69
El Campo, TX (city) Wharton County	1,176	10.87
Darien, IL (city) Du Page County	1,176	5.12
Des Moines, IA (city) Polk County	1,176	0.59
Taylor, TX (city) Williamson County	1,175	8.67
Eau Claire, WI (city) Eau Claire County	1,163	1.89
Pittsburgh, PA (city) Allegheny County	1,141	0.34
Orland Park, IL (village) Cook County	1,138	2.23
Elmhurst, IL (city) Du Page County	1,128	2.63
Dickinson, ND (city) Stark County	1,118	7.06
Aurora, IL (city) Kane County	1,112	0.77
Anchorage, AK (municipality) Anchorage Borough	1,104	0.42
West Allis, WI (city) Milwaukee County	1,092	1.78
New Prague, MN (city) Scott County	1,085	24.13
Westmont, IL (village) Du Page County	1,085	4.46
Boise City, ID (city) Ada County	1,080	0.58
Marion, IA (city) Linn County	1,078	4.07
La Grange Park, IL (village) Cook County	1,072	8.10
Overland Park, KS (city) Johnson County	1,064	0.71
Eagan, MN (city) Dakota County	1,055	1.66
Oak Park, IL (village) Cook County	1,044	1.99
Norfolk, NE (city) Madison County	1,042	4.43
Tinley Park, IL (village) Cook County	1,038	2.15
Waco, TX (city) McLennan County	1,030	0.90
Aurora, CO (city) Arapahoe County	1,021	0.37
Lakewood, OH (city) Cuyahoga County	1,014	1.79
Huntington, NY (town) Suffolk County	1,006	0.52
Council Bluffs, IA (city) Pottawattamie County	1,003	1.72
Glendale, AZ (city) Maricopa County	996	0.46
Arlington Heights, IL (village) Cook County	995	1.31
Sugar Land, TX (city) Fort Bend County	993	1.56
Charlotte, NC (city) Mecklenburg County	993	0.18
Lyons, IL (village) Cook County	991	9.78
Mentor, OH (city) Lake County	990	1.97
Saint Petersburg, FL (city) Pinellas County	990	0.40
Wauwatosa, WI (city) Milwaukee County	987	2.09
Yankton, SD (city) Yankton County	979	7.28
Faribault, MN (city) Rice County	973	4.67
Apple Valley, MN (city) Dakota County	968	2.13
Maple Heights, OH (city) Cuyahoga County	964	3.69
Woodbury, MN (city) Washington County	956	2.06
North Royalton, OH (city) Cuyahoga County	949	3.31
West, TX (city) McLennan County	945	34.24
Garland, TX (city) Dallas County	945	0.44
Tulsa, OK (city) Tulsa County	945	0.24
Ennis, TX (city) Ellis County	942	5.88
Henderson, NV (city) Clark County	939	0.53
Rapid City, SD (city) Pennington County	938	1.58
Wahoo, NE (city) Saunders County	937	23.73
Carol Stream, IL (village) Du Page County	935	2.35
Lakewood, CO (city) Jefferson County	926	0.64
Schuyler, NE (city) Colfax County	922	17.41
Janesville, WI (city) Rock County	922	1.55
Pasadena, TX (city) Harris County	922	0.65
Appleton, WI (city) Outagamie County	908	1.29
Waukesha, WI (city) Waukesha County	907	1.41
Santa Clarita, CA (city) Los Angeles County	907	0.60
Arlington, VA (cdp) Arlington County	906	0.48
Nashville-Davidson, TN (special city) Davidson County	881	0.16
Tempe, AZ (city) Maricopa County	880	0.56
Plymouth, MN (city) Hennepin County	879	1.33
Davenport, IA (city) Scott County	874	0.89
Boston, MA (city) Suffolk County	866	0.15
Eugene, OR (city) Lane County	863	0.63
Eden Prairie, MN (city) Hennepin County	860	1.57

Notes: (cdp) census designated place; Refer to the Explanation of Data in the front of the book for more detailed information.

Czech

Top 150 Places Sorted by Percent

(Based on all places, regardless of population)

Place	Number	%
Conway, ND (city) Walsh County	16	55.17
Pisek, ND (city) Walsh County	47	54.02
Prague, NE (village) Saunders County	173	53.89
Dwight, NE (village) Butler County	114	50.67
Milligan, NE (village) Fillmore County	151	50.00
Bruno, NE (village) Butler County	47	46.53
Verdigre, NE (village) Knox County	235	45.90
Protivin, IA (city) Howard County	138	45.10
Clarkson, NE (city) Colfax County	301	44.99
Spillville, IA (city) Winneshiek County	167	44.41
Vining, IA (city) Tama County	35	43.75
Abie, NE (village) Butler County	59	41.84
Yuba, WI (village) Richland County	41	41.00
Tabor, SD (town) Bon Homme County	170	40.87
Brainard, NE (village) Butler County	152	40.64
Henryville, MN (township) Renville County	81	38.94
Clutier, IA (city) Tama County	93	38.91
Weston, NE (village) Saunders County	115	37.95
Howells, NE (village) Colfax County	241	37.08
Valparaiso, NE (village) Saunders County	212	36.93
Fayetteville, TX (city) Fayette County	103	36.79
Wilber, NE (city) Saline County	624	35.33
Denham, MN (city) Pine County	18	35.29
Franklin, WI (town) Kewaunee County	365	35.23
Morse Bluff, NE (village) Saunders County	47	35.07
Linwood, NE (village) Butler County	44	34.92
West, TX (city) McLennan County	945	34.24
Munden, KS (city) Republic County	46	33.82
Jackson Junction, IA (city) Winneshiek County	23	33.82
Octavia, NE (village) Butler County	49	32.89
Fullerton, ND (city) Dickey County	25	32.89
Reese Center, TX (cdp) Lubbock County	15	32.61
Abbott, TX (city) Hill County	95	32.31
Tabor, MN (township) Polk County	52	31.90
Two Creeks, WI (town) Manitowoc County	176	31.04
Tyndall, SD (city) Bon Homme County	387	30.74
Hazard, NE (village) Sherman County	26	29.89
Lonsdale, MN (city) Rice County	447	29.86
Carlton, WI (town) Kewaunee County	300	29.44
Lankin, ND (city) Walsh County	35	29.41
David City, NE (city) Butler County	769	29.15
Montgomery, MN (township) Le Sueur County	226	29.12
Moulton, TX (town) Lavaca County	275	29.01
Wheatland, MN (township) Rice County	381	28.80
Cuba, KS (city) Republic County	62	28.18
Shiner, TX (city) Lavaca County	584	28.16
Verdel, NE (village) Knox County	13	27.66
Castle Rock, WI (town) Grant County	83	27.48
Ross, TX (city) McLennan County	68	26.98
Montgomery, MN (city) Le Sueur County	741	26.67
Wirt, MN (township) Itasca County	29	26.61
Swanton, NE (village) Saline County	22	26.51
Thurston, NE (village) Thurston County	31	26.27
Geddes, SD (city) Charles Mix County	62	25.73
Lanesburgh, MN (township) Le Sueur County	526	25.65
Poplar Grove, MN (township) Roseau County	20	25.00
Chelsea, SD (town) Faulk County	4	25.00
Conrath, WI (village) Rusk County	15	24.59
Brislet, MN (township) Polk County	13	24.53
West Kewaunee, WI (town) Kewaunee County	334	24.45
Hale, MN (township) McLeod County	227	24.25
New Prague, MN (city) Scott County	1,085	24.13
Thief Lake, MN (township) Marshall County	12	24.00
East Bernard, TX (cdp) Wharton County	401	23.77
Snook, TX (city) Burleson County	131	23.77
Wahoo, NE (city) Saunders County	937	23.73
Ben Wade, MN (township) Pope County	66	23.66
Elyria, NE (village) Valley County	15	23.44
Clatonia, NE (village) Gage County	64	23.10
Brocket, ND (city) Ramsey County	14	22.95
Montpelier, WI (town) Kewaunee County	281	22.92
Gibson, WI (town) Manitowoc County	300	22.81
Schulenburg, TX (city) Fayette County	601	22.59
Kewaunee, WI (city) Kewaunee County	623	22.40
Sandsville, MN (township) Polk County	15	22.39
Malmo, NE (village) Saunders County	25	22.32
Granger, TX (city) Williamson County	292	22.31
Kossuth, WI (town) Manitowoc County	459	22.25
Lexington, MN (township) Le Sueur County	180	21.95
Maribel, WI (village) Manitowoc County	53	21.81
Colon, NE (village) Saunders County	29	21.80
Fort Atkinson, IA (city) Winneshiek County	85	21.68
Norfolk, MN (township) Renville County	49	21.59
Spring Creek, MN (township) Norman County	11	21.57
Wallis, TX (city) Austin County	255	21.41
Rich Valley, MN (township) McLeod County	158	21.24
Erin, MN (township) Rice County	170	21.07
Aurora, MN (township) Steele County	136	20.92
Haugen, WI (village) Barron County	55	20.68
Dorchester, NE (village) Saline County	127	20.58
Summit, MN (township) Steele County	104	20.43
Lesterville, SD (town) Yankton County	36	20.34
Mishicot, WI (town) Manitowoc County	286	20.28
Hallettsville, TX (city) Lavaca County	475	20.26
Chelsea, IA (city) Tama County	59	20.21
Bellwood, NE (village) Butler County	94	20.04
Emery, WI (town) Price County	68	20.00
Richland, NE (village) Colfax County	17	20.00
Kellnersville, WI (village) Manitowoc County	77	19.95
Franklin, WI (town) Manitowoc County	256	19.72
Middletown, MN (township) Jackson County	44	19.64
Western, NE (village) Saline County	57	19.59
Point Baker, AK (cdp) Prince of Wales-Outer Ketchikan Census Area	8	19.51
Lawrence, NE (village) Nuckolls County	63	19.44
Bee, NE (village) Seward County	39	19.40
Daykin, NE (village) Jefferson County	29	19.33
Hillsboro, WI (city) Vernon County	254	19.26
Brownell, KS (city) Ness County	10	19.23
Ulysses, NE (village) Butler County	44	19.21
Owatonna, MN (township) Steele County	147	19.19
Sullivan, MN (township) Polk County	34	19.10
North Bend, NE (city) Dodge County	230	18.87
Somerset, MN (township) Steele County	159	18.86
Penelope, TX (town) Hill County	43	18.86
Ree Heights, SD (town) Hand County	15	18.75
Atlantic City, WY (cdp) Fremont County	6	18.75
Silver Lake, MN (city) McLeod County	142	18.59
Kilkenny, MN (city) Le Sueur County	31	18.56
Orchard, TX (city) Fort Bend County	77	18.47
Lake Mary, MN (township) Douglas County	177	18.38
Keystone, MN (township) Polk County	18	18.37
Spring Creek, MN (township) Becker County	18	18.18
Latimer, KS (city) Morris County	2	18.18
Flatonia, TX (town) Fayette County	248	18.16
Wilson, KS (city) Ellsworth County	142	18.16
Garland, NE (village) Seward County	46	17.97
Hollenberg, KS (city) Washington County	5	17.86
Swisher, IA (city) Johnson County	149	17.84
Helena, MN (township) Scott County	270	17.82
Winnetoon, NE (village) Knox County	14	17.72
Whitelaw, WI (village) Manitowoc County	125	17.61
Narka, KS (city) Republic County	14	17.50
Schuyler, NE (city) Colfax County	922	17.41
Loma, ND (city) Cavalier County	5	17.24
Spencer, NE (village) Boyd County	89	17.21
Union, WI (town) Vernon County	87	17.19
Heidelberg, MN (city) Le Sueur County	12	17.14
Mishicot, WI (village) Manitowoc County	243	17.05
Union Center, WI (village) Juneau County	39	17.03
Waucoma, IA (city) Fayette County	50	16.89
Hackett, WI (town) Price County	31	16.85
Merton, MN (township) Steele County	63	16.84
Tobias, NE (village) Saline County	27	16.77
Wauzeka, WI (town) Crawford County	61	16.76
Northland, MN (township) Polk County	31	16.76
Bird Island, MN (township) Renville County	39	16.74
Bear Lake, WI (town) Barron County	96	16.72
Seaforth, MN (city) Redwood County	11	16.67
Fairdale, ND (city) Walsh County	9	16.67
Eastman, WI (village) Crawford County	71	16.59

Notes: (cdp) census designated place; Refer to the Explanation of Data in the front of the book for more detailed information.

Czech

Top 150 Places Sorted by Percent

(Based on places with populations of 10,000 or more)

Place	Number	%
El Campo, TX (city) Wharton County	1,176	10.87
Two Rivers, WI (city) Manitowoc County	1,310	10.35
Lyons, IL (village) Cook County	991	9.78
Brookfield, IL (village) Cook County	1,802	9.48
Manitowoc, WI (city) Manitowoc County	3,004	8.84
Taylor, TX (city) Williamson County	1,175	8.67
La Grange Park, IL (village) Cook County	1,072	8.10
Yankton, SD (city) Yankton County	979	7.28
Westchester, IL (village) Cook County	1,194	7.17
Dickinson, ND (city) Stark County	1,118	7.06
La Vista, NE (city) Sarpy County	791	6.75
Cedar Rapids, IA (city) Linn County	7,934	6.58
Columbus, NE (city) Platte County	1,377	6.56
Owatonna, MN (city) Steele County	1,376	6.14
Ennis, TX (city) Ellis County	942	5.88
Seven Hills, OH (city) Cuyahoga County	704	5.83
Berwyn, IL (city) Cook County	2,982	5.52
La Grange, IL (village) Cook County	853	5.42
Chalco, NE (cdp) Sarpy County	569	5.31
Downers Grove, IL (village) Du Page County	2,563	5.27
Bellevue, NE (city) Sarpy County	2,288	5.16
Papillion, NE (city) Sarpy County	835	5.14
Fremont, NE (city) Dodge County	1,289	5.12
Darien, IL (city) Du Page County	1,176	5.12
Lincoln, NE (city) Lancaster County	11,510	5.11
Rosenberg, TX (city) Fort Bend County	1,202	4.97
Burr Ridge, IL (village) Du Page County	493	4.77
Garfield Heights, OH (city) Cuyahoga County	1,445	4.72
Faribault, MN (city) Rice County	973	4.67
Pecan Grove, TX (cdp) Fort Bend County	608	4.52
Woodridge, IL (village) Du Page County	1,396	4.49
Westmont, IL (village) Du Page County	1,085	4.46
Norfolk, NE (city) Madison County	1,042	4.43
Omaha, NE (city) Douglas County	16,796	4.31
Brecksville, OH (city) Cuyahoga County	568	4.26
Western Springs, IL (village) Cook County	518	4.10
Marion, IA (city) Linn County	1,078	4.07
Shakopee, MN (city) Scott County	814	3.97
Broadview Heights, OH (city) Cuyahoga County	610	3.82
Beatrice, NE (city) Gage County	464	3.72
Bellevue Town, WI (cdp) Brown County	442	3.71
Maple Heights, OH (city) Cuyahoga County	964	3.69
Bridgeview, IL (village) Cook County	557	3.62
Palos Hills, IL (city) Cook County	633	3.57
Plainfield, IL (village) Will County	464	3.57
Grand Island, NE (city) Hall County	1,519	3.55
Romeoville, IL (village) Will County	744	3.52
Prior Lake, MN (city) Scott County	561	3.52
Solon, OH (city) Cuyahoga County	757	3.47
Victoria, TX (city) Victoria County	2,089	3.46
Goodings Grove, IL (cdp) Will County	592	3.46
Caledonia, WI (town) Racine County	787	3.33
North Royalton, OH (city) Cuyahoga County	949	3.31
Lisle, IL (village) Du Page County	689	3.26
Austin, MN (city) Mower County	756	3.25
Ashwaubenon, WI (village) Brown County	575	3.25
Hopkins, MN (city) Hennepin County	543	3.18
Mokena, IL (village) Will County	466	3.18
Kearney, NE (city) Buffalo County	848	3.14
Worth, IL (village) Cook County	350	3.14
Hinsdale, IL (village) Du Page County	547	3.13
Middleburg Heights, OH (city) Cuyahoga County	484	3.11
Oswego, IL (village) Kendall County	414	3.11
Hastings, NE (city) Adams County	742	3.08
Aurora, OH (city) Portage County	412	3.04
Brooklyn, OH (city) Cuyahoga County	350	3.02
Northfield, MN (city) Rice County	514	3.00
Hickory Hills, IL (city) Cook County	417	2.99
Pierre, SD (city) Hughes County	417	2.99
Brenham, TX (city) Washington County	402	2.99
River Falls, WI (city) Pierce County	377	2.99
Parma, OH (city) Cuyahoga County	2,554	2.98
Villa Park, IL (village) Du Page County	661	2.97
Lombard, IL (village) Du Page County	1,229	2.94
Grand Forks, ND (city) Grand Forks County	1,442	2.93
Coralville, IA (city) Johnson County	424	2.80
Allouez, WI (village) Brown County	431	2.79
Bedford, OH (city) Cuyahoga County	396	2.79
Lockport, IL (city) Will County	410	2.77
Lakeville, MN (city) Dakota County	1,183	2.74
Bolingbrook, IL (village) Will County	1,532	2.71
Strongsville, OH (city) Cuyahoga County	1,180	2.69
Palos Heights, IL (city) Cook County	301	2.66
Howard, WI (village) Brown County	359	2.65
Lemont, IL (village) Cook County	349	2.65
Elmhurst, IL (city) Du Page County	1,128	2.63
Mitchell, SD (city) Davison County	385	2.62
Parma Heights, OH (city) Cuyahoga County	561	2.59
Burbank, IL (city) Cook County	712	2.56
La Crosse, WI (city) La Crosse County	1,318	2.55
Iowa City, IA (city) Johnson County	1,587	2.54
Warrenville, IL (city) Du Page County	335	2.54
Hutchinson, MN (city) McLeod County	331	2.54
Glen Ellyn, IL (village) Du Page County	684	2.53
Marinette, WI (city) Marinette County	293	2.50
Temple, TX (city) Bell County	1,342	2.47
Twinsburg, OH (city) Summit County	417	2.47
Green Bay, WI (city) Brown County	2,520	2.46
Wheaton, IL (city) Du Page County	1,366	2.46
New Ulm, MN (city) Brown County	332	2.45
Brook Park, OH (city) Cuyahoga County	517	2.44
De Pere, WI (city) Brown County	496	2.41
Albert Lea, MN (city) Freeborn County	433	2.36
Carol Stream, IL (village) Du Page County	935	2.35
Bay City, TX (city) Matagorda County	438	2.35
Cary, IL (village) McHenry County	362	2.35
Lake Jackson, TX (city) Brazoria County	618	2.33
Chicago Ridge, IL (village) Cook County	322	2.32
Lino Lakes, MN (city) Anoka County	386	2.30
Algonquin, IL (village) McHenry County	528	2.25
Port Lavaca, TX (city) Calhoun County	269	2.24
Oak Lawn, IL (village) Cook County	1,233	2.23
Orland Park, IL (village) Cook County	1,138	2.23
Midlothian, IL (village) Cook County	317	2.23
Streetsboro, OH (city) Portage County	275	2.23
Brunswick, OH (city) Medina County	738	2.21
Fairview Park, OH (city) Cuyahoga County	389	2.21
Naperville, IL (city) Du Page County	2,803	2.18
Richmond, TX (city) Fort Bend County	241	2.18
Evergreen Park, IL (village) Cook County	452	2.17
Chanhassen, MN (city) Carver County	439	2.16
Tinley Park, IL (village) Cook County	1,038	2.15
Owosso, MI (city) Shiawassee County	335	2.14
Bellaire, TX (city) Harris County	334	2.14
Apple Valley, MN (city) Dakota County	968	2.13
Cinco Ranch, TX (cdp) Fort Bend County	239	2.13
Baraboo, WI (city) Sauk County	228	2.12
Wauwatosa, WI (city) Milwaukee County	987	2.09
Winona, MN (city) Winona County	563	2.09
Fort Dodge, IA (city) Webster County	521	2.07
Overlea, MD (cdp) Baltimore County	248	2.07
College Station, TX (city) Brazos County	1,398	2.06
Woodbury, MN (city) Washington County	956	2.06
Middleton, WI (city) Dane County	320	2.06
Onalaska, WI (city) La Crosse County	306	2.06
Mandan, ND (city) Morton County	341	2.04
Mason City, IA (city) Cerro Gordo County	593	2.03
Bryan, TX (city) Brazos County	1,330	2.01
Concord, MO (cdp) Saint Louis County	335	2.01
Crestwood, IL (village) Cook County	225	2.01
Cicero, IL (town) Cook County	1,714	2.00
Racine, WI (city) Racine County	1,639	2.00
Mehlville, MO (cdp) Saint Louis County	577	2.00
Oak Park, IL (village) Cook County	1,044	1.99
Georgetown, TX (city) Williamson County	561	1.99
Oak Forest, IL (city) Cook County	556	1.99
New Lenox, IL (village) Will County	350	1.99
Mentor, OH (city) Lake County	990	1.97
North Platte, NE (city) Lincoln County	465	1.95
Bloomington, MN (city) Hennepin County	1,650	1.94

Notes: (cdp) census designated place; Refer to the Explanation of Data in the front of the book for more detailed information.

Czechoslovakian

Top 150 Places Sorted by Number

(Based on all places, regardless of population)

Place	Number	%
New York, NY (city) New York City	8,154	0.10
Los Angeles, CA (city) Los Angeles County	3,493	0.09
Chicago, IL (city) Cook County	3,296	0.11
Phoenix, AZ (city) Maricopa County	2,424	0.18
Houston, TX (city) Harris County	2,148	0.11
Omaha, NE (city) Douglas County	2,106	0.54
San Diego, CA (city) San Diego County	2,012	0.16
Lincoln, NE (city) Lancaster County	1,632	0.72
Austin, TX (city) Travis County	1,604	0.24
Hempstead, NY (town) Nassau County	1,549	0.20
Cedar Rapids, IA (city) Linn County	1,448	1.20
Dallas, TX (city) Dallas County	1,285	0.11
Brookhaven, NY (town) Suffolk County	1,281	0.29
Minneapolis, MN (city) Hennepin County	1,226	0.32
San Antonio, TX (city) Bexar County	1,141	0.10
Columbus, OH (city) Franklin County	1,125	0.16
Cleveland, OH (city) Cuyahoga County	1,096	0.23
Portland, OR (city) Multnomah County	1,048	0.20
Milwaukee, WI (city) Milwaukee County	964	0.16
Oklahoma City, OK (city) Oklahoma County	957	0.19
Seattle, WA (city) King County	957	0.17
Philadelphia, PA (city) Philadelphia County	955	0.06
Colorado Springs, CO (city) El Paso County	941	0.26
Pittsburgh, PA (city) Allegheny County	935	0.28
Islip, NY (town) Suffolk County	922	0.29
San Francisco, CA (city) San Francisco County	869	0.11
Denver, CO (city) Denver County	858	0.15
Naperville, IL (city) Du Page County	827	0.64
Saint Paul, MN (city) Ramsey County	823	0.29
Oyster Bay, NY (town) Nassau County	823	0.28
Parma, OH (city) Cuyahoga County	766	0.89
Indianapolis, IN (special city) Marion County	759	0.10
Tucson, AZ (city) Pima County	741	0.15
Jacksonville, FL (special city) Duval County	741	0.10
Albuquerque, NM (city) Bernalillo County	733	0.16
Berwyn, IL (city) Cook County	717	1.33
Union, NY (town) Broome County	709	1.26
San Jose, CA (city) Santa Clara County	706	0.08
Fort Worth, TX (city) Tarrant County	690	0.13
Madison, WI (city) Dane County	667	0.32
Corpus Christi, TX (city) Nueces County	660	0.24
Mesa, AZ (city) Maricopa County	649	0.16
Lakewood, CO (city) Jefferson County	639	0.44
Las Vegas, NV (city) Clark County	633	0.13
Huntington, NY (town) Suffolk County	631	0.32
Virginia Beach, VA (independent city) Virginia Beach city	623	0.15
Toledo, OH (city) Lucas County	569	0.18
Arlington, TX (city) Tarrant County	568	0.17
Akron, OH (city) Summit County	563	0.26
Wichita, KS (city) Sedgwick County	550	0.16
Scottsdale, AZ (city) Maricopa County	532	0.26
Tulsa, OK (city) Tulsa County	521	0.13
North Hempstead, NY (town) Nassau County	517	0.23
Aurora, CO (city) Arapahoe County	501	0.18
Saint Petersburg, FL (city) Pinellas County	493	0.20
Nashville-Davidson, TN (special city) Davidson County	483	0.09
Charlotte, NC (city) Mecklenburg County	480	0.09
Babylon, NY (town) Suffolk County	474	0.22
Hamilton, NJ (township) Mercer County	465	0.53
Long Beach, CA (city) Los Angeles County	460	0.10
Saint Louis, MO (independent city) Saint Louis city	456	0.13
Fort Collins, CO (city) Larimer County	454	0.38
Yonkers, NY (city) Westchester County	453	0.23
Lakewood, OH (city) Cuyahoga County	446	0.79
Kansas City, MO (city) Jackson County	445	0.10
Santa Clarita, CA (city) Los Angeles County	440	0.29
Plano, TX (city) Collin County	436	0.20
Boise City, ID (city) Ada County	434	0.23
Baltimore, MD (independent city) Baltimore city	433	0.07
Tacoma, WA (city) Pierce County	419	0.22
Raleigh, NC (city) Wake County	410	0.15
Glendale, AZ (city) Maricopa County	400	0.18
Anchorage, AK (municipality) Anchorage Borough	400	0.15
Woodbridge, NJ (township) Middlesex County	399	0.41
Sacramento, CA (city) Sacramento County	385	0.09
Bellevue, NE (city) Sarpy County	377	0.85
Bloomington, MN (city) Hennepin County	375	0.44
Downers Grove, IL (village) Du Page County	374	0.77
Warren, MI (city) Macomb County	370	0.27
Tempe, AZ (city) Maricopa County	368	0.23
Shelton, CT (city) Fairfield County	365	0.96
Paradise, NV (cdp) Clark County	365	0.20
Edison, NJ (cdp) Middlesex County	364	0.37
Stratford, CT (cdp) Fairfield County	357	0.71
Anaheim, CA (city) Orange County	355	0.11
Boston, MA (city) Suffolk County	355	0.06
Fresno, CA (city) Fresno County	351	0.08
Spokane, WA (city) Spokane County	348	0.18
Arlington, VA (cdp) Arlington County	343	0.18
Waco, TX (city) McLennan County	340	0.30
Allentown, PA (city) Lehigh County	338	0.32
Strongsville, OH (city) Cuyahoga County	334	0.76
Henderson, NV (city) Clark County	332	0.19
Hollywood, FL (city) Broward County	330	0.24
Spring Hill, FL (cdp) Hernando County	327	0.47
Redding, CA (city) Shasta County	319	0.39
Brookfield, IL (village) Cook County	318	1.67
Smithtown, NY (town) Suffolk County	318	0.27
Binghamton, NY (city) Broome County	314	0.66
Thousand Oaks, CA (city) Ventura County	313	0.27
Huntington Beach, CA (city) Orange County	313	0.16
Oceanside, CA (city) San Diego County	310	0.19
Tampa, FL (city) Hillsborough County	308	0.10
Eagan, MN (city) Dakota County	307	0.48
Fargo, ND (city) Cass County	306	0.34
Irving, TX (city) Dallas County	306	0.16
Brick, NJ (township) Ocean County	304	0.40
Washington, DC (city) District of Columbia	304	0.05
Burnsville, MN (city) Dakota County	299	0.50
Oakland, CA (city) Alameda County	298	0.07
Buffalo, NY (city) Erie County	297	0.10
Arlington Heights, IL (village) Cook County	292	0.38
Troy, MI (city) Oakland County	292	0.36
Temple, TX (city) Bell County	290	0.53
Clearwater, FL (city) Pinellas County	289	0.27
Wheaton, IL (city) Du Page County	288	0.52
Rochester Hills, MI (city) Oakland County	287	0.42
Sterling Heights, MI (city) Macomb County	286	0.23
Garland, TX (city) Dallas County	286	0.13
Lee's Summit, MO (city) Jackson County	283	0.40
Grand Forks, ND (city) Grand Forks County	282	0.57
Aurora, IL (city) Kane County	282	0.20
Westlake, OH (city) Cuyahoga County	281	0.88
Dover, NJ (township) Ocean County	280	0.31
Ramapo, NY (town) Rockland County	277	0.25
Norfolk, VA (independent city) Norfolk city	276	0.12
Eugene, OR (city) Lane County	275	0.20
Apple Valley, MN (city) Dakota County	274	0.60
Linden, NJ (city) Union County	273	0.69
Shelby, MI (cdp) Macomb County	271	0.42
Reno, NV (city) Washoe County	271	0.15
Fremont, CA (city) Alameda County	270	0.13
Overland Park, KS (city) Johnson County	268	0.18
Millcreek, PA (township) Erie County	266	0.51
Victoria, TX (city) Victoria County	266	0.44
Toms River, NJ (cdp) Ocean County	266	0.31
Elgin, IL (city) Kane County	265	0.28
Orange, CA (city) Orange County	265	0.21
Rancho Cucamonga, CA (city) San Bernardino County	265	0.21
College Station, TX (city) Brazos County	264	0.39
Chandler, AZ (city) Maricopa County	264	0.15
Livonia, MI (city) Wayne County	263	0.26
Trumbull, CT (cdp) Fairfield County	262	0.77
Ames, IA (city) Story County	262	0.52
Racine, WI (city) Racine County	262	0.32
Simi Valley, CA (city) Ventura County	262	0.23
Gilbert, AZ (town) Maricopa County	261	0.24
Santa Rosa, CA (city) Sonoma County	261	0.18
Westchester, IL (village) Cook County	260	1.56
Billings, MT (city) Yellowstone County	260	0.29

Notes: (cdp) census designated place; Refer to the Explanation of Data in the front of the book for more detailed information.

Czechoslovakian

Top 150 Places Sorted by Percent

(Based on all places, regardless of population)

Place	Number	%
Cedar Rapids, WI (town) Rusk County	11	22.92
Marblemount, WA (cdp) Skagit County	56	17.13
Heidelberg, MN (city) Le Sueur County	11	15.71
Dante, SD (town) Charles Mix County	9	14.29
Lankin, ND (city) Walsh County	16	13.45
Primrose, AK (cdp) Kenai Peninsula Borough	24	13.33
Dunes Road, FL (cdp) Palm Beach County	62	13.11
Elmer, MN (township) Saint Louis County	23	12.71
Montgomery, MN (township) Le Sueur County	89	11.47
Port Costa, CA (cdp) Contra Costa County	27	11.16
Henryville, MN (township) Renville County	21	10.10
East Bernard, TX (cdp) Wharton County	170	10.08
Polonia, MN (township) Roseau County	3	9.68
Alvwood, MN (township) Itasca County	7	9.21
Cuba, KS (city) Republic County	20	9.09
Erin, MN (township) Rice County	73	9.05
Harmony, WI (town) Price County	19	8.96
Lonsdale, MN (city) Rice County	134	8.95
Wheatland, MN (township) Rice County	117	8.84
Chilgren, MN (township) Lake of the Woods County	18	8.07
Pisek, ND (city) Walsh County	7	8.05
Thief Lake, MN (township) Marshall County	4	8.00
Clutier, IA (city) Tama County	19	7.95
Zippel, MN (township) Lake of the Woods County	8	7.77
Soler, MN (township) Roseau County	9	7.69
Deer, MN (township) Roseau County	6	7.59
Lanesburgh, MN (township) Le Sueur County	155	7.56
Meadowlands, MN (township) Saint Louis County	24	7.43
Milligan, NE (village) Fillmore County	22	7.28
Twin Hills, AK (cdp) Dillingham Census Area	3	6.98
Catawba, WI (town) Price County	20	6.94
Morse Bluff, NE (village) Saunders County	9	6.72
Moose Park, MN (township) Itasca County	4	6.45
Benton, IA (city) Ringgold County	2	6.45
Silverton, MN (township) Pennington County	13	6.37
Tabor, SD (town) Bon Homme County	26	6.25
Hampden, MN (township) Kittson County	2	6.25
Westdale, TX (cdp) Jim Wells County	22	6.21
Peck, WI (town) Langlade County	21	6.12
Boxville, MN (township) Marshall County	2	6.06
Worcester, WI (town) Price County	104	5.88
Eldora, CO (cdp) Boulder County	13	5.86
Euclid, MN (township) Polk County	10	5.65
Hubbard, WI (town) Rusk County	10	5.59
Tornado, WV (cdp) Kanawha County	65	5.57
Taos Ski Valley, NM (village) Taos County	5	5.56
Burchard, NE (village) Pawnee County	4	5.48
Hunter, KS (city) Mitchell County	4	5.33
Lawrence, WI (town) Rusk County	13	5.31
Penelope, TX (town) Hill County	12	5.26
Junction City, WA (cdp) Grays Harbor County	3	5.26
Morristown, OH (village) Belmont County	16	5.25
Moodus, CT (cdp) Middlesex County	72	5.21
Grand Island, MI (township) Alger County	2	5.13
Lazy Lake, FL (village) Broward County	2	5.13
Viola, DE (town) Kent County	6	5.08
C-Road, CA (cdp) Plumas County	7	5.04
Narka, KS (city) Republic County	4	5.00
New Prague, MN (city) Scott County	224	4.98
Goodland, FL (cdp) Collier County	11	4.98
Dwight, NE (village) Butler County	11	4.89
Northland, MN (township) Polk County	9	4.86
Cromberg, CA (cdp) Plumas County	15	4.78
Oketo, KS (city) Marshall County	3	4.76
Gilead, NE (village) Thayer County	2	4.76
Lawton, ND (city) Ramsey County	2	4.76
Offerle, KS (city) Edwards County	10	4.74
Wilber, NE (city) Saline County	83	4.70
West, TX (city) McLennan County	128	4.64
Webster, MN (township) Rice County	85	4.63
Ocean Beach, NY (village) Suffolk County	6	4.62
Garrison, NE (village) Butler County	3	4.62
Black Diamond, FL (cdp) Citrus County	30	4.60
Protivin, IA (city) Howard County	14	4.58
Montgomery, MN (city) Le Sueur County	127	4.57
Lake Grove, MN (township) Mahnomen County	9	4.55
Riverside, WY (town) Carbon County	3	4.55
Mission Creek, MN (township) Pine County	27	4.51
Lake Almanor Country Club, CA (cdp) Plumas County	38	4.42
Okahumpka, FL (cdp) Lake County	9	4.41
Munden, KS (city) Republic County	6	4.41
Michigan City, ND (city) Nelson County	16	4.37
Prague, NE (village) Saunders County	14	4.36
Kasaan, AK (city) Prince of Wales-Outer Ketchikan Census Area	2	4.35
Two Inlets, MN (township) Becker County	7	4.32
Zuehl, TX (cdp) Guadalupe County	11	4.31
Tabor, MN (township) Polk County	7	4.29
Mount Moriah, MO (town) Harrison County	7	4.27
Dorchester, NE (village) Saline County	26	4.21
Walhalla, MN (township) Lake of the Woods County	6	4.20
Clarkson, NE (city) Colfax County	28	4.19
Ferndale, FL (cdp) Lake County	12	4.17
Hungerford, TX (cdp) Wharton County	25	4.15
Emery, WI (town) Price County	14	4.12
Metamora, OH (village) Fulton County	23	4.07
Cloud Lake, FL (town) Palm Beach County	5	4.07
Shieldsville, MN (township) Rice County	46	4.06
Oakland, MN (township) Freeborn County	19	4.00
Cedar Lake, MN (township) Scott County	88	3.99
Blooming Prairie, MN (township) Steele County	21	3.99
Barnes, KS (city) Washington County	6	3.97
Weston, NE (village) Saunders County	12	3.96
Hingham, MT (town) Hill County	8	3.92
Elk, PA (township) Tioga County	2	3.92
Oxbow, ME (plantation) Aroostook County	2	3.92
Tyndall, SD (city) Bon Homme County	49	3.89
Megargel, TX (town) Archer County	10	3.86
Barnett, MN (township) Roseau County	6	3.85
Mullen, NE (village) Hooker County	19	3.84
Parkline, ID (city) Benewah County	3	3.80
David City, NE (city) Butler County	100	3.79
Hamilton, MI (township) Gratiot County	17	3.78
Malden, WA (town) Whitman County	8	3.76
Nesquehoning, PA (borough) Carbon County	119	3.72
South Canal, OH (cdp) Trumbull County	50	3.71
Coal Center, PA (borough) Washington County	5	3.70
Courtenay, ND (city) Stutsman County	2	3.70
Fairdale, ND (city) Walsh County	2	3.70
Aastad, MN (township) Otter Tail County	7	3.61
Highlanding, MN (township) Pennington County	7	3.61
Swanton, NE (village) Saline County	3	3.61
Ross, TX (city) McLennan County	9	3.57
Abie, NE (village) Butler County	5	3.55
Lausanne, PA (township) Carbon County	8	3.54
Norfolk, MN (township) Renville County	8	3.52
Deerfield, MO (village) Vernon County	3	3.49
Lyons, MN (township) Wadena County	5	3.42
Lowndesboro, AL (town) Lowndes County	6	3.41
Oso, WA (cdp) Snohomish County	7	3.40
Glen Flora, WI (village) Rusk County	2	3.39
Hansonville, MN (township) Lincoln County	3	3.37
Orchard, TX (city) Fort Bend County	14	3.36
Hart Lake, MN (township) Hubbard County	13	3.32
Stickney, IL (village) Cook County	203	3.30
Elberon, IA (city) Tama County	7	3.29
Hale's, NH (location) Carroll County	2	3.28
Spivey, KS (city) Kingman County	2	3.28
Hackett, WI (town) Price County	6	3.26
Wisconsin, MN (township) Jackson County	9	3.25
Vega, MN (township) Marshall County	5	3.23
Foster, PA (township) Luzerne County	109	3.21
Warrenton, MN (township) Marshall County	4	3.20
Spillville, IA (city) Winneshiek County	12	3.19
Hayward, MN (township) Freeborn County	15	3.17
Manhattan Beach, MN (city) Crow Wing County	2	3.17
Union, WI (town) Vernon County	16	3.16
Niobrara, NE (village) Knox County	11	3.16
Chesaning, MI (township) Saginaw County	153	3.15
Pierpont, SD (town) Day County	4	3.15
Wahoo, NE (city) Saunders County	124	3.14

Notes: (cdp) census designated place; Refer to the Explanation of Data in the front of the book for more detailed information.

Czechoslovakian

Top 150 Places Sorted by Percent

(Based on places with populations of 10,000 or more)

Place	Number	%
La Grange Park, IL (village) Cook County	250	1.89
Brookfield, IL (village) Cook County	318	1.67
Burr Ridge, IL (village) Du Page County	170	1.65
Lyons, IL (village) Cook County	164	1.62
Westchester, IL (village) Cook County	260	1.56
Yankton, SD (city) Yankton County	194	1.44
Brecksville, OH (city) Cuyahoga County	184	1.38
Endwell, NY (cdp) Broome County	157	1.34
Berwyn, IL (city) Cook County	717	1.33
Ennis, TX (city) Ellis County	205	1.28
Union, NY (town) Broome County	709	1.26
Owosso, MI (city) Shiawassee County	189	1.21
Brooklyn, OH (city) Cuyahoga County	140	1.21
Cedar Rapids, IA (city) Linn County	1,448	1.20
Johnson City, NY (village) Broome County	182	1.17
El Campo, TX (city) Wharton County	125	1.16
Manville, NJ (borough) Somerset County	119	1.15
Robinson Township, PA (cdp) Allegheny County	139	1.13
Taylor, TX (city) Williamson County	148	1.09
Pasadena, MD (cdp) Anne Arundel County	130	1.08
Chenango, NY (town) Broome County	121	1.06
Seven Hills, OH (city) Cuyahoga County	127	1.05
Western Springs, IL (village) Cook County	131	1.04
Harrison Township, PA (cdp) Allegheny County	114	1.04
Green Haven, MD (cdp) Anne Arundel County	179	1.03
La Grange, IL (village) Cook County	159	1.01
Indiana, PA (borough) Indiana County	148	0.99
Darien, IL (city) Du Page County	225	0.98
New Kensington, PA (city) Westmoreland County	144	0.98
Mundy, MI (township) Genesee County	119	0.98
Upper Providence Township, PA (cdp) Delaware County	103	0.98
Shelton, CT (city) Fairfield County	365	0.96
Broadview Heights, OH (city) Cuyahoga County	153	0.96
Crestwood, MO (city) Saint Louis County	112	0.96
Chesterton, IN (town) Porter County	100	0.96
Fremont, NE (city) Dodge County	238	0.95
Cudahy, WI (city) Milwaukee County	175	0.95
Northfield, MN (city) Rice County	161	0.94
Uniontown, PA (city) Fayette County	117	0.94
Morrisville, PA (borough) Bucks County	94	0.94
Fernway, PA (cdp) Butler County	113	0.93
Seminole, FL (city) Pinellas County	100	0.93
Bedford, OH (city) Cuyahoga County	130	0.91
Patton, PA (township) Centre County	104	0.91
South Milwaukee, WI (city) Milwaukee County	191	0.90
Seymour, CT (town) New Haven County	139	0.90
Parma, OH (city) Cuyahoga County	766	0.89
Stafford, CT (town) Tolland County	101	0.89
Vermilion, OH (city) Lorain County	97	0.89
Westlake, OH (city) Cuyahoga County	281	0.88
Villa Park, IL (village) Du Page County	197	0.88
Faribault, MN (city) Rice County	181	0.87
Vadnais Heights, MN (city) Ramsey County	113	0.87
North Union, PA (township) Fayette County	122	0.86
North Strabane, PA (township) Washington County	86	0.86
Bellevue, NE (city) Sarpy County	377	0.85
Columbus, NE (city) Platte County	178	0.85
Municipality of Murrysville, PA (borough) Westmoreland County	160	0.85
Saint Simons, GA (cdp) Glynn County	114	0.85
North Huntingdon, PA (township) Westmoreland County	245	0.84
Endicott, NY (village) Broome County	109	0.84
Munhall, PA (borough) Allegheny County	103	0.84
Avon, OH (city) Lorain County	96	0.84
Warren, RI (town) Bristol County	94	0.83
Marion, IA (city) Linn County	216	0.82
Flushing, MI (township) Genesee County	84	0.82
Mount Pleasant, PA (township) Westmoreland County	91	0.81
East Goshen, PA (township) Chester County	135	0.80
Concord, MO (cdp) Saint Louis County	133	0.80
Stony Brook, NY (cdp) Suffolk County	109	0.80
Plainfield, IL (village) Will County	104	0.80
Lakewood, OH (city) Cuyahoga County	446	0.79
Vestal, NY (town) Broome County	209	0.79
Lake Jackson, TX (city) Brazoria County	207	0.78
Hazleton, PA (city) Luzerne County	181	0.78
Parma Heights, OH (city) Cuyahoga County	170	0.78
Brookings, SD (city) Brookings County	144	0.78
Middleburg Heights, OH (city) Cuyahoga County	121	0.78
Tolland, CT (town) Tolland County	102	0.78
Downers Grove, IL (village) Du Page County	374	0.77
Trumbull, CT (cdp) Fairfield County	262	0.77
Lisle, IL (village) Du Page County	162	0.77
Strongsville, OH (city) Cuyahoga County	334	0.76
Milton, NY (town) Saratoga County	130	0.76
Upper Saucon, PA (township) Lehigh County	91	0.76
Glen Ellyn, IL (village) Du Page County	203	0.75
Owego, NY (town) Tioga County	152	0.75
Weirton, WV (city) Hancock County	152	0.75
South Union, PA (township) Fayette County	85	0.75
North Royalton, OH (city) Cuyahoga County	210	0.73
Montville, NJ (township) Morris County	152	0.73
Lincoln, NE (city) Lancaster County	1,632	0.72
Mineola, NY (village) Nassau County	139	0.72
Stratford, CT (cdp) Fairfield County	357	0.71
Solon, OH (city) Cuyahoga County	155	0.71
Ringwood, NJ (borough) Passaic County	88	0.71
Glenville, NY (town) Schenectady County	197	0.70
Joppatowne, MD (cdp) Harford County	79	0.70
Linden, NJ (city) Union County	273	0.69
Rosemount, MN (city) Dakota County	101	0.69
Norton, OH (city) Summit County	79	0.69
Richmond Heights, OH (city) Cuyahoga County	75	0.69
Garden City, NY (village) Nassau County	148	0.68
Bethel, CT (town) Fairfield County	122	0.68
Setauket-East Setauket, NY (cdp) Suffolk County	108	0.68
Metuchen, NJ (borough) Middlesex County	87	0.68
Antwerp, MI (township) Van Buren County	72	0.68
Westmont, IL (village) Du Page County	164	0.67
Upper Saint Clair, PA (cdp) Allegheny County	135	0.67
Marquette, MI (city) Marquette County	132	0.67
Hickory Hills, IL (city) Cook County	94	0.67
Wells Branch, TX (cdp) Travis County	75	0.67
Lighthouse Point, FL (city) Broward County	71	0.67
Silver City, NM (town) Grant County	71	0.67
Binghamton, NY (city) Broome County	314	0.66
Spring, PA (township) Berks County	144	0.66
Brookfield, CT (town) Fairfield County	103	0.66
Cedar Mill, OR (cdp) Washington County	84	0.66
Owatonna, MN (city) Steele County	146	0.65
Savage, MN (city) Scott County	137	0.65
Shakopee, MN (city) Scott County	133	0.65
Twinsburg, OH (city) Summit County	109	0.65
Corning, NY (city) Steuben County	71	0.65
Naperville, IL (city) Du Page County	827	0.64
McCandless Township, PA (cdp) Allegheny County	186	0.64
West Mifflin, PA (borough) Allegheny County	143	0.64
Raritan, NJ (township) Hunterdon County	127	0.64
Westtown, PA (township) Chester County	66	0.64
Bernards, NJ (township) Somerset County	156	0.63
Sun City, CA (cdp) Riverside County	113	0.63
Streator, IL (city) La Salle County	89	0.63
University Heights, OH (city) Cuyahoga County	89	0.63
Hasbrouck Heights, NJ (borough) Bergen County	73	0.63
North Olmsted, OH (city) Cuyahoga County	210	0.62
Saratoga Springs, NY (city) Saratoga County	163	0.62
Ramsey, NJ (borough) Bergen County	89	0.62
Hillsdale, NJ (borough) Bergen County	63	0.62
Hempfield, PA (township) Westmoreland County	248	0.61
Stafford, NJ (township) Ocean County	138	0.61
La Canada Flintridge, CA (city) Los Angeles County	124	0.61
Birmingham, MI (city) Oakland County	119	0.61
Lakeside, CA (cdp) San Diego County	119	0.61
Hutchinson, MN (city) McLeod County	80	0.61
Beachwood, OH (city) Cuyahoga County	74	0.61
La Vista, NE (city) Sarpy County	71	0.61
Apple Valley, MN (city) Dakota County	274	0.60
Wildwood, MO (city) Saint Louis County	200	0.60
Newtown, CT (town) Fairfield County	149	0.60
Grayslake, IL (village) Lake County	110	0.60
Avon Lake, OH (city) Lorain County	109	0.60

Notes: (cdp) census designated place; Refer to the Explanation of Data in the front of the book for more detailed information.

Danish

Top 150 Places Sorted by Number

(Based on all places, regardless of population)

Place	Number	%
Omaha, NE (city) Douglas County	11,367	2.91
Los Angeles, CA (city) Los Angeles County	10,270	0.28
Salt Lake City, UT (city) Salt Lake County	7,874	4.34
Provo, UT (city) Utah County	7,627	7.25
New York, NY (city) New York City	7,460	0.09
Phoenix, AZ (city) Maricopa County	7,129	0.54
Seattle, WA (city) King County	7,100	1.26
San Diego, CA (city) San Diego County	6,923	0.57
Orem, UT (city) Utah County	6,324	7.50
Sandy, UT (city) Salt Lake County	6,065	6.87
Chicago, IL (city) Cook County	5,922	0.20
Lincoln, NE (city) Lancaster County	5,832	2.59
Portland, OR (city) Multnomah County	5,786	1.09
Minneapolis, MN (city) Hennepin County	5,355	1.40
Mesa, AZ (city) Maricopa County	5,297	1.33
Racine, WI (city) Racine County	5,125	6.26
West Valley City, UT (city) Salt Lake County	4,813	4.42
West Jordan, UT (city) Salt Lake County	4,415	6.47
San Jose, CA (city) Santa Clara County	4,326	0.48
San Francisco, CA (city) San Francisco County	3,970	0.51
Boise City, ID (city) Ada County	3,900	2.10
Bountiful, UT (city) Davis County	3,842	9.28
Sioux Falls, SD (city) Minnehaha County	3,800	3.06
Las Vegas, NV (city) Clark County	3,763	0.79
Denver, CO (city) Denver County	3,379	0.61
Taylorsville, UT (city) Salt Lake County	3,263	5.64
Council Bluffs, IA (city) Pottawattamie County	3,149	5.41
Saint Paul, MN (city) Ramsey County	3,116	1.09
Colorado Springs, CO (city) El Paso County	3,068	0.85
Layton, UT (city) Davis County	3,019	5.15
Logan, UT (city) Cache County	2,985	6.99
Tucson, AZ (city) Pima County	2,849	0.59
Houston, TX (city) Harris County	2,804	0.14
Des Moines, IA (city) Polk County	2,775	1.40
Fresno, CA (city) Fresno County	2,763	0.65
Madison, WI (city) Dane County	2,688	1.30
Saint George, UT (city) Washington County	2,644	5.33
Milwaukee, WI (city) Milwaukee County	2,596	0.43
Austin, TX (city) Travis County	2,590	0.39
Ogden, UT (city) Weber County	2,533	3.28
Albuquerque, NM (city) Bernalillo County	2,399	0.53
Murray, UT (city) Salt Lake County	2,380	7.02
Pocatello, ID (city) Bannock County	2,370	4.60
Scottsdale, AZ (city) Maricopa County	2,354	1.16
Sioux City, IA (city) Woodbury County	2,334	2.74
Eugene, OR (city) Lane County	2,269	1.65
Anchorage, AK (municipality) Anchorage Borough	2,239	0.86
Dallas, TX (city) Dallas County	2,205	0.19
Kenosha, WI (city) Kenosha County	2,189	2.41
San Antonio, TX (city) Bexar County	2,166	0.19
Idaho Falls, ID (city) Bonneville County	2,158	4.27
Salem, OR (city) Marion County	2,130	1.56
Spokane, WA (city) Spokane County	2,121	1.08
Mount Pleasant, WI (town) Racine County	2,117	9.16
Santa Rosa, CA (city) Sonoma County	2,108	1.43
Reno, NV (city) Washoe County	2,089	1.16
East Millcreek, UT (cdp) Salt Lake County	2,078	9.71
Brigham City, UT (city) Box Elder County	2,076	11.93
Sacramento, CA (city) Sacramento County	2,069	0.51
Fort Collins, CO (city) Larimer County	2,053	1.73
Long Beach, CA (city) Los Angeles County	2,042	0.44
Aurora, CO (city) Arapahoe County	2,027	0.73
South Jordan, UT (city) Salt Lake County	2,002	6.80
Henderson, NV (city) Clark County	1,932	1.10
Spanish Fork, UT (city) Utah County	1,872	9.23
Kaysville, UT (city) Davis County	1,839	8.88
Kansas City, MO (city) Jackson County	1,794	0.41
Huntington Beach, CA (city) Orange County	1,770	0.93
Bloomington, MN (city) Hennepin County	1,765	2.07
Roy, UT (city) Weber County	1,764	5.39
Cedar Rapids, IA (city) Linn County	1,714	1.42
Caledonia, WI (town) Racine County	1,711	7.23
Gilbert, AZ (town) Maricopa County	1,707	1.55
Cedar Falls, IA (city) Black Hawk County	1,702	4.69
Draper, UT (city) Salt Lake County	1,693	6.66

Place	Number	%
American Fork, UT (city) Utah County	1,672	7.63
Brookhaven, NY (town) Suffolk County	1,660	0.37
Vancouver, WA (city) Clark County	1,658	1.16
Glendale, AZ (city) Maricopa County	1,639	0.75
Lakewood, CO (city) Jefferson County	1,633	1.13
Rochester, MN (city) Olmsted County	1,630	1.91
Wichita, KS (city) Sedgwick County	1,630	0.47
Springville, UT (city) Utah County	1,629	7.94
Cottonwood Heights, UT (cdp) Salt Lake County	1,624	5.93
Santa Clarita, CA (city) Los Angeles County	1,621	1.07
Pleasant Grove, UT (city) Utah County	1,614	6.86
Indianapolis, IN (special city) Marion County	1,573	0.20
Tacoma, WA (city) Pierce County	1,571	0.81
Riverton, UT (city) Salt Lake County	1,559	6.20
Grand Island, NE (city) Hall County	1,557	3.64
Albert Lea, MN (city) Freeborn County	1,533	8.35
Millcreek, UT (cdp) Salt Lake County	1,532	5.02
Billings, MT (city) Yellowstone County	1,524	1.71
Lehi, UT (city) Utah County	1,516	7.92
Paradise, NV (cdp) Clark County	1,495	0.80
Chandler, AZ (city) Maricopa County	1,458	0.83
Oakland, CA (city) Alameda County	1,453	0.36
Waterloo, IA (city) Black Hawk County	1,437	2.09
Fargo, ND (city) Cass County	1,434	1.58
Tempe, AZ (city) Maricopa County	1,417	0.89
Anaheim, CA (city) Orange County	1,394	0.43
Fremont, CA (city) Alameda County	1,384	0.68
Centerville, UT (city) Davis County	1,373	9.55
Oklahoma City, OK (city) Oklahoma County	1,373	0.27
Jacksonville, FL (special city) Duval County	1,337	0.18
Naperville, IL (city) Du Page County	1,328	1.04
Fremont, NE (city) Dodge County	1,323	5.26
Thousand Oaks, CA (city) Ventura County	1,312	1.12
Arvada, CO (city) Jefferson County	1,309	1.28
Duluth, MN (city) Saint Louis County	1,298	1.50
Hempstead, NY (town) Nassau County	1,279	0.17
Bakersfield, CA (city) Kern County	1,261	0.51
Kearns, UT (cdp) Salt Lake County	1,204	3.58
Coon Rapids, MN (city) Anoka County	1,187	1.93
Rexburg, ID (city) Madison County	1,183	6.88
Oceanside, CA (city) San Diego County	1,179	0.73
Cottonwood West, UT (cdp) Salt Lake County	1,175	6.31
Eden Prairie, MN (city) Hennepin County	1,172	2.13
Modesto, CA (city) Stanislaus County	1,165	0.61
Tulsa, OK (city) Tulsa County	1,164	0.30
Bellevue, WA (city) King County	1,159	1.06
Plano, TX (city) Collin County	1,157	0.52
Blair, NE (city) Washington County	1,155	15.28
Beaverton, OR (city) Washington County	1,153	1.52
Cedar City, UT (city) Iron County	1,140	5.54
Kearney, NE (city) Buffalo County	1,128	4.17
Nashville-Davidson, TN (special city) Davidson County	1,128	0.21
Tooele, UT (city) Tooele County	1,127	5.01
Livermore, CA (city) Alameda County	1,124	1.53
Iowa City, IA (city) Johnson County	1,122	1.80
Irvine, CA (city) Orange County	1,109	0.78
Richfield, UT (city) Sevier County	1,108	16.09
Holladay, UT (city) Salt Lake County	1,107	7.61
Virginia Beach, VA (independent city) Virginia Beach city	1,106	0.26
Pleasanton, CA (city) Alameda County	1,099	1.73
Plymouth, MN (city) Hennepin County	1,098	1.67
Atlantic, IA (city) Cass County	1,092	14.98
Westminster, CO (city) Adams County	1,084	1.07
Ames, IA (city) Story County	1,076	2.12
Rapid City, SD (city) Pennington County	1,074	1.80
Maple Grove, MN (city) Hennepin County	1,065	2.12
Walnut Creek, CA (city) Contra Costa County	1,050	1.63
Washington, DC (city) District of Columbia	1,047	0.18
North Ogden, UT (city) Weber County	1,042	6.98
Edina, MN (city) Hennepin County	1,042	2.19
Midvale, UT (city) Salt Lake County	1,038	3.84
Napa, CA (city) Napa County	1,033	1.42
Highland, UT (city) Utah County	1,032	12.96
Green Bay, WI (city) Brown County	1,031	1.01
Burnsville, MN (city) Dakota County	1,029	1.71

Notes: (cdp) census designated place; Refer to the Explanation of Data in the front of the book for more detailed information.

Danish

Top 150 Places Sorted by Percent

(Based on all places, regardless of population)

Place	Number	%
Hibberts, ME (gore) Lincoln County	2	100.00
Esterbrook, WY (cdp) Converse County	10	58.82
Kimballton, IA (city) Audubon County	180	58.06
Bergen, ND (city) McHenry County	2	50.00
Hope, MN (township) Lincoln County	148	45.40
Cache, UT (cdp) Cache County	8	44.44
Elk Horn, IA (city) Shelby County	283	42.88
Exira, IA (city) Audubon County	304	36.94
Brayton, IA (city) Audubon County	52	33.55
Leamington, UT (town) Millard County	71	32.72
Audubon, IA (city) Audubon County	731	30.88
Viborg, SD (city) Turner County	253	30.52
Hetland, SD (town) Kingsbury County	18	30.51
Elsinore, UT (town) Sevier County	230	30.26
Elmo, UT (town) Emery County	100	29.59
Badger, SD (town) Kingsbury County	39	29.32
Cotesfield, NE (village) Howard County	20	28.57
Bear River City, UT (town) Box Elder County	189	26.36
Marshfield, MN (township) Lincoln County	51	26.15
Centerfield, UT (town) Sanpete County	272	25.59
Lynndyl, UT (town) Millard County	34	25.37
Spring City, UT (city) Sanpete County	246	25.26
Turin, IA (city) Monona County	22	25.00
Mayfield, UT (town) Sanpete County	114	24.78
Mantua, UT (town) Box Elder County	187	24.32
Deweyville, UT (town) Box Elder County	65	24.25
Marne, IA (city) Cass County	30	24.00
Ringsted, IA (city) Emmet County	94	23.68
Partridge, MN (township) Pine County	127	23.61
Cleveland, UT (town) Emery County	122	23.51
Lake Louise, AK (cdp) Matanuska-Susitna Borough	7	23.33
Levan, UT (town) Juab County	163	22.96
Cordova, NE (village) Seward County	27	22.88
Newton, UT (town) Cache County	162	22.78
Fountain Green, UT (city) Sanpete County	209	22.59
Moroni, UT (city) Sanpete County	280	21.60
Benson, UT (cdp) Cache County	307	21.54
Tyler, MN (city) Lincoln County	255	21.45
Eola, OR (cdp) Polk County	10	21.28
Obert, NE (village) Cedar County	10	21.28
Reserve, MT (cdp) Sheridan County	7	21.21
Dannebrog, NE (village) Howard County	70	20.83
Broadland, SD (town) Beadle County	7	20.59
Aurora, UT (city) Sevier County	187	19.94
Hurley, SD (city) Turner County	80	19.85
Scipio, UT (town) Millard County	58	19.73
Cornlea, NE (village) Platte County	8	19.51
Elwood, UT (town) Box Elder County	134	19.39
Oak City, UT (town) Millard County	125	18.97
Elyria, NE (village) Valley County	12	18.75
Glenwood, UT (town) Sevier County	85	18.64
Florence, MN (city) Lyon County	8	18.60
Flaxton, ND (city) Burke County	14	18.42
Alta, WY (cdp) Teton County	82	18.39
Antelope, MT (cdp) Sheridan County	9	18.37
Redmond, UT (town) Sevier County	148	18.32
Fairview, UT (city) Sanpete County	208	18.25
Askov, MN (city) Pine County	71	18.16
Royal, IA (city) Clay County	86	18.14
Lake Benton, MN (township) Lincoln County	51	18.02
Mount Pleasant, UT (city) Sanpete County	462	17.89
Gray, IA (city) Audubon County	15	17.86
Marble, CO (town) Gunnison County	26	17.81
Irene, SD (city) Turner County	77	17.66
Kingston, UT (town) Piute County	24	17.52
Rodney, IA (city) Monona County	12	17.14
Clontarf, MN (township) Swift County	12	16.90
Howell, UT (town) Box Elder County	38	16.89
Peter, UT (cdp) Cache County	37	16.82
Benjamin, UT (cdp) Utah County	155	16.68
Washam, WY (cdp) Sweetwater County	8	16.67
Minnie, MN (township) Beltrami County	2	16.67
South Red River, MN (township) Kittson County	2	16.67
Portage, UT (town) Box Elder County	42	16.60
Sterling, UT (town) Sanpete County	36	16.59
Fayette, UT (town) Sanpete County	34	16.59
Donnybrook, ND (city) Ward County	13	16.46
Monroe, UT (city) Sevier County	300	16.39
Wales, UT (town) Sanpete County	38	16.31
Emery, UT (town) Emery County	50	16.29
Washington, WI (town) Door County	107	16.26
Richfield, UT (city) Sevier County	1,108	16.09
Bath, MN (township) Freeborn County	74	16.09
Moorhead, IA (city) Monona County	37	16.09
Shelburne, MN (township) Lyon County	26	16.05
Robertson, WY (cdp) Uinta County	10	15.87
Joseph, UT (town) Sevier County	41	15.71
Hyde Park, UT (city) Cache County	462	15.68
Manti, UT (city) Sanpete County	478	15.66
Homer, NE (village) Dakota County	91	15.64
Castle Dale, UT (city) Emery County	257	15.59
Corinne, UT (city) Box Elder County	99	15.57
Ruskin, NE (village) Nuckolls County	27	15.43
Wiota, IA (city) Cass County	22	15.38
Agassiz, MN (township) Lac qui Parle County	12	15.38
Arlington, SD (city) Kingsbury County	154	15.34
Blair, NE (city) Washington County	1,155	15.28
Altamont, UT (town) Duchesne County	29	15.26
Luck, WI (village) Polk County	179	15.11
Dunnell, MN (city) Martin County	30	15.08
Atlantic, IA (city) Cass County	1,092	14.98
Dayton, ID (city) Franklin County	73	14.87
Elba, NE (village) Howard County	33	14.86
McClelland, IA (city) Pottawattamie County	19	14.84
Minden, NE (city) Kearney County	441	14.81
Weston, ID (city) Franklin County	51	14.78
Brookfield, MN (township) Renville County	26	14.77
Ruthton, MN (city) Pipestone County	45	14.71
Clawson, UT (town) Emery County	24	14.55
Laketown, WI (town) Polk County	130	14.53
Ortley, SD (town) Roberts County	9	14.52
Kennard, NE (village) Washington County	56	14.47
Lake Stay, MN (township) Lincoln County	23	14.47
Kilgore, NE (village) Cherry County	12	14.29
Atomic City, ID (city) Bingham County	3	14.29
Bickleton, WA (cdp) Klickitat County	14	14.14
River Heights, UT (city) Cache County	215	14.12
Luck, WI (town) Polk County	126	14.06
Holden, UT (town) Millard County	55	13.99
Luverne, ND (city) Steele County	6	13.95
Manchester, MN (township) Freeborn County	70	13.94
Salina, UT (city) Sevier County	333	13.93
Franksville, WI (cdp) Racine County	236	13.92
Riverside, UT (cdp) Box Elder County	94	13.91
Primrose, AK (cdp) Kenai Peninsula Borough	25	13.89
Bushnell, NE (village) Kimball County	23	13.86
Hinckley, UT (town) Millard County	94	13.80
McKinnon, WY (cdp) Sweetwater County	8	13.79
Harlan, IA (city) Shelby County	722	13.71
Rockville, NE (village) Sherman County	13	13.68
Kirkman, IA (city) Shelby County	11	13.58
Magnet, NE (village) Cedar County	11	13.58
Hayward, MN (township) Freeborn County	64	13.53
Oxford, ID (city) Franklin County	5	13.51
Dawson, IA (city) Dallas County	22	13.41
Anita, IA (city) Cass County	142	13.40
Dietrich, ID (city) Lincoln County	26	13.40
Carlston, MN (township) Freeborn County	45	13.39
Wallsburg, UT (town) Wasatch County	41	13.36
Halibut Cove, AK (cdp) Kenai Peninsula Borough	8	13.33
Tennant, IA (city) Shelby County	8	13.33
Smithfield, NE (village) Gosper County	9	13.24
Riceland, MN (township) Freeborn County	64	13.22
Blooming Prairie, MN (township) Steele County	69	13.12
Bancroft, MN (township) Freeborn County	142	13.11
Norman, NE (village) Kearney County	8	13.11
Sanford, CO (town) Conejos County	105	13.04
Ephraim, UT (city) Sanpete County	583	13.03
Highland, UT (city) Utah County	1,032	12.96
Strandquist, MN (city) Marshall County	11	12.94

Notes: (cdp) census designated place; Refer to the Explanation of Data in the front of the book for more detailed information.

Danish

Top 150 Places Sorted by Percent

(Based on places with populations of 10,000 or more)

Place	Number	%
Brigham City, UT (city) Box Elder County	2,076	11.93
East Millcreek, UT (cdp) Salt Lake County	2,078	9.71
Centerville, UT (city) Davis County	1,373	9.55
Bountiful, UT (city) Davis County	3,842	9.28
Spanish Fork, UT (city) Utah County	1,872	9.23
Mount Pleasant, WI (town) Racine County	2,117	9.16
Kaysville, UT (city) Davis County	1,839	8.88
Albert Lea, MN (city) Freeborn County	1,533	8.35
Springville, UT (city) Utah County	1,629	7.94
Lehi, UT (city) Utah County	1,516	7.92
Canyon Rim, UT (cdp) Salt Lake County	812	7.68
American Fork, UT (city) Utah County	1,672	7.63
Holladay, UT (city) Salt Lake County	1,107	7.61
Orem, UT (city) Utah County	6,324	7.50
Clinton, UT (city) Davis County	935	7.39
Farmington, UT (city) Davis County	889	7.28
Provo, UT (city) Utah County	7,627	7.25
Caledonia, WI (town) Racine County	1,711	7.23
Murray, UT (city) Salt Lake County	2,380	7.02
Logan, UT (city) Cache County	2,985	6.99
North Ogden, UT (city) Weber County	1,042	6.98
Rexburg, ID (city) Madison County	1,183	6.88
Sandy, UT (city) Salt Lake County	6,065	6.87
Pleasant Grove, UT (city) Utah County	1,614	6.86
South Jordan, UT (city) Salt Lake County	2,002	6.80
Draper, UT (city) Salt Lake County	1,693	6.66
Payson, UT (city) Utah County	843	6.57
West Jordan, UT (city) Salt Lake County	4,415	6.47
Cottonwood West, UT (cdp) Salt Lake County	1,175	6.31
Racine, WI (city) Racine County	5,125	6.26
South Ogden, UT (city) Weber County	897	6.22
Riverton, UT (city) Salt Lake County	1,559	6.20
Blackfoot, ID (city) Bingham County	632	6.06
Cottonwood Heights, UT (cdp) Salt Lake County	1,624	5.93
Yankton, SD (city) Yankton County	797	5.92
Taylorsville, UT (city) Salt Lake County	3,263	5.64
Oquirrh, UT (cdp) Salt Lake County	582	5.62
Cedar City, UT (city) Iron County	1,140	5.54
Council Bluffs, IA (city) Pottawattamie County	3,149	5.41
Roy, UT (city) Weber County	1,764	5.39
Saint George, UT (city) Washington County	2,644	5.33
Fremont, NE (city) Dodge County	1,323	5.26
Layton, UT (city) Davis County	3,019	5.15
Spencer, IA (city) Clay County	581	5.09
Millcreek, UT (cdp) Salt Lake County	1,532	5.02
Tooele, UT (city) Tooele County	1,127	5.01
Cedar Falls, IA (city) Black Hawk County	1,702	4.69
Pocatello, ID (city) Bannock County	2,370	4.60
West Valley City, UT (city) Salt Lake County	4,813	4.42
Salt Lake City, UT (city) Salt Lake County	7,874	4.34
Idaho Falls, ID (city) Bonneville County	2,158	4.27
Kearney, NE (city) Buffalo County	1,128	4.17
Chalco, NE (cdp) Sarpy County	437	4.08
Midvale, UT (city) Salt Lake County	1,038	3.84
Marshall, MN (city) Lyon County	481	3.77
Green River, WY (city) Sweetwater County	445	3.77
Grand Island, NE (city) Hall County	1,557	3.64
Kearns, UT (cdp) Salt Lake County	1,204	3.58
Brookings, SD (city) Brookings County	655	3.53
Clearfield, UT (city) Davis County	898	3.46
Ogden, UT (city) Weber County	2,533	3.28
Shoreview, MN (city) Ramsey County	851	3.28
Hutchinson, MN (city) McLeod County	427	3.27
Austin, MN (city) Mower County	760	3.26
South Salt Lake, UT (city) Salt Lake County	720	3.25
Pierre, SD (city) Hughes County	445	3.19
Papillion, NE (city) Sarpy County	502	3.09
Sioux Falls, SD (city) Minnehaha County	3,800	3.06
Magna, UT (cdp) Salt Lake County	696	3.06
Norfolk, NE (city) Madison County	714	3.03
Stillwater, MN (city) Washington County	448	2.95
Omaha, NE (city) Douglas County	11,367	2.91
Clinton, IA (city) Clinton County	804	2.89
Mason City, IA (city) Cerro Gordo County	837	2.87
Alderwood Manor, WA (cdp) Snohomish County	436	2.86
Hastings, NE (city) Adams County	682	2.83
Evanston, WY (city) Uinta County	324	2.83
Storm Lake, IA (city) Buena Vista County	286	2.82
North Mankato, MN (city) Nicollet County	329	2.79
Sioux City, IA (city) Woodbury County	2,334	2.74
Clive, IA (city) Polk County	351	2.73
Owatonna, MN (city) Steele County	606	2.70
Mendota Heights, MN (city) Dakota County	307	2.70
Pleasant Prairie, WI (village) Kenosha County	421	2.65
La Vista, NE (city) Sarpy County	311	2.65
Sterling, CO (city) Logan County	300	2.65
Warren, PA (city) Warren County	270	2.63
Carroll, IA (city) Carroll County	262	2.61
Lincoln, NE (city) Lancaster County	5,832	2.59
Ramsey, MN (city) Anoka County	467	2.53
Spring Creek, NV (cdp) Elko County	278	2.53
Northfield, MN (city) Rice County	432	2.52
Eagle, ID (city) Ada County	281	2.52
Hermiston, OR (city) Umatilla County	334	2.49
Twin Falls, ID (city) Twin Falls County	847	2.48
Boone, IA (city) Boone County	316	2.47
Camas, WA (city) Clark County	313	2.47
Neenah, WI (city) Winnebago County	588	2.42
Kenosha, WI (city) Kenosha County	2,189	2.41
Seal Beach, CA (city) Orange County	585	2.41
Louisville, CO (city) Boulder County	448	2.37
Rock Springs, WY (city) Sweetwater County	447	2.36
Issaquah, WA (city) King County	264	2.36
Tamalpais-Homestead Valley, CA (cdp) Marin County	249	2.35
Anacortes, WA (city) Skagit County	344	2.34
Milwaukie, OR (city) Clackamas County	486	2.33
Central Point, OR (city) Jackson County	282	2.27
Marion, IA (city) Linn County	597	2.25
Rossmoor, CA (cdp) Orange County	231	2.25
North Platte, NE (city) Lincoln County	529	2.22
Kalispell, MT (city) Flathead County	314	2.22
Moscow, ID (city) Latah County	468	2.21
Lakeville, MN (city) Dakota County	947	2.20
Edina, MN (city) Hennepin County	1,042	2.19
Laramie, WY (city) Albany County	596	2.19
Williston, ND (city) Williams County	274	2.18
Coralville, IA (city) Johnson County	328	2.17
Sammamish, WA (city) King County	736	2.16
Cameron Park, CA (cdp) El Dorado County	315	2.16
Willmar, MN (city) Kandiyohi County	396	2.15
Eden Prairie, MN (city) Hennepin County	1,172	2.13
Ames, IA (city) Story County	1,076	2.12
Maple Grove, MN (city) Hennepin County	1,065	2.12
Ankeny, IA (city) Polk County	571	2.12
Savage, MN (city) Scott County	448	2.11
Boise City, ID (city) Ada County	3,900	2.10
West Des Moines, IA (city) Polk County	971	2.10
Lino Lakes, MN (city) Anoka County	353	2.10
Waterloo, IA (city) Black Hawk County	1,437	2.09
Brainerd, MN (city) Crow Wing County	272	2.09
Plover, WI (village) Portage County	222	2.09
Bloomington, MN (city) Hennepin County	1,765	2.07
El Campo, TX (city) Wharton County	224	2.07
Fort Dodge, IA (city) Webster County	518	2.06
Urbandale, IA (city) Polk County	594	2.04
Brentwood, CA (city) Contra Costa County	475	2.04
Farmington, MN (city) Dakota County	255	2.04
South Sioux City, NE (city) Dakota County	242	2.02
Fergus Falls, MN (city) Otter Tail County	271	2.01
New Brighton, MN (city) Ramsey County	443	1.99
Meridian, ID (city) Ada County	686	1.97
Garden City, ID (city) Ada County	215	1.97
Minnetonka, MN (city) Hennepin County	1,006	1.96
Coon Rapids, MN (city) Anoka County	1,187	1.93
Windsor, CA (town) Sonoma County	444	1.93
Crystal, MN (city) Hennepin County	441	1.93
Seattle Hill-Silver Firs, WA (cdp) Snohomish County	684	1.92
Mounds View, MN (city) Ramsey County	244	1.92
Rochester, MN (city) Olmsted County	1,630	1.91
Roseville, MN (city) Ramsey County	645	1.91

Notes: (cdp) census designated place; Refer to the Explanation of Data in the front of the book for more detailed information.

Dutch

Top 150 Places Sorted by Number

(Based on all places, regardless of population)

Place	Number	%
Grand Rapids, MI (city) Kent County	31,050	15.69
New York, NY (city) New York City	19,402	0.24
Phoenix, AZ (city) Maricopa County	18,765	1.42
Los Angeles, CA (city) Los Angeles County	18,200	0.49
Georgetown, MI (township) Ottawa County	17,780	42.68
Wyoming, MI (city) Kent County	15,679	22.60
San Diego, CA (city) San Diego County	12,943	1.06
Indianapolis, IN (special city) Marion County	12,223	1.56
Chicago, IL (city) Cook County	11,906	0.41
Portland, OR (city) Multnomah County	10,986	2.08
Holland, MI (city) Ottawa County	10,564	30.00
Seattle, WA (city) King County	10,415	1.85
Columbus, OH (city) Franklin County	9,831	1.38
Houston, TX (city) Harris County	9,822	0.50
Holland, MI (township) Ottawa County	9,446	33.01
Oklahoma City, OK (city) Oklahoma County	8,567	1.69
Denver, CO (city) Denver County	8,133	1.47
Kentwood, MI (city) Kent County	8,098	17.90
San Jose, CA (city) Santa Clara County	7,920	0.89
Sioux Falls, SD (city) Minnehaha County	7,841	6.32
Jacksonville, FL (special city) Duval County	7,635	1.04
Tulsa, OK (city) Tulsa County	7,616	1.94
Mesa, AZ (city) Maricopa County	7,461	1.88
Jenison, MI (cdp) Ottawa County	7,218	41.88
Dallas, TX (city) Dallas County	7,159	0.60
Des Moines, IA (city) Polk County	7,129	3.59
San Antonio, TX (city) Bexar County	7,096	0.62
Colorado Springs, CO (city) El Paso County	6,959	1.93
Omaha, NE (city) Douglas County	6,897	1.77
Las Vegas, NV (city) Clark County	6,663	1.39
Austin, TX (city) Travis County	6,591	1.00
Wichita, KS (city) Sedgwick County	6,570	1.91
Tucson, AZ (city) Pima County	6,485	1.33
Byron, MI (township) Kent County	6,469	36.73
Gaines, MI (township) Kent County	6,410	31.96
San Francisco, CA (city) San Francisco County	6,319	0.81
Park, MI (township) Ottawa County	6,249	35.57
Grandville, MI (city) Kent County	6,073	37.34
Nashville-Davidson, TN (special city) Davidson County	6,005	1.10
Kalamazoo, MI (city) Kalamazoo County	5,969	7.74
Virginia Beach, VA (independent city) Virginia Beach city	5,860	1.38
Albuquerque, NM (city) Bernalillo County	5,833	1.30
Plainfield, MI (township) Kent County	5,800	19.27
Kansas City, MO (city) Jackson County	5,678	1.29
Lincoln, NE (city) Lancaster County	5,651	2.51
Walker, MI (city) Kent County	5,470	25.10
Philadelphia, PA (city) Philadelphia County	5,444	0.36
Charlotte, NC (city) Mecklenburg County	5,410	1.00
Portage, MI (city) Kalamazoo County	5,388	11.99
Fort Worth, TX (city) Tarrant County	5,231	0.98
Minneapolis, MN (city) Hennepin County	5,083	1.33
Appleton, WI (city) Outagamie County	4,977	7.10
Aurora, CO (city) Arapahoe County	4,901	1.78
Anchorage, AK (municipality) Anchorage Borough	4,888	1.88
Green Bay, WI (city) Brown County	4,812	4.70
Boise City, ID (city) Ada County	4,673	2.51
Arlington, TX (city) Tarrant County	4,586	1.38
Pella, IA (city) Marion County	4,462	45.77
Long Beach, CA (city) Los Angeles County	4,420	0.96
Madison, WI (city) Dane County	4,352	2.10
Toledo, OH (city) Lucas County	4,309	1.37
Sioux Center, IA (city) Sioux County	4,272	70.53
Brookhaven, NY (town) Suffolk County	4,271	0.95
Hudsonville, MI (city) Ottawa County	4,268	58.18
Forest Hills, MI (cdp) Kent County	4,256	20.33
Cutlerville, MI (cdp) Kent County	4,219	27.87
Modesto, CA (city) Stanislaus County	4,194	2.21
Milwaukee, WI (city) Milwaukee County	4,097	0.69
Scottsdale, AZ (city) Maricopa County	4,081	2.01
Spokane, WA (city) Spokane County	4,047	2.06
Saint Petersburg, FL (city) Pinellas County	4,000	1.61
Hempstead, NY (town) Nassau County	3,964	0.52
Zeeland charter, MI (township) Ottawa County	3,933	51.96
Huntington Beach, CA (city) Orange County	3,898	2.05
Lansing, IL (village) Cook County	3,857	13.70
Sacramento, CA (city) Sacramento County	3,823	0.94
Eugene, OR (city) Lane County	3,809	2.76
Allendale, MI (township) Ottawa County	3,719	28.30
Memphis, TN (city) Shelby County	3,655	0.56
Sioux City, IA (city) Woodbury County	3,633	4.27
Rochester, NY (city) Monroe County	3,627	1.65
Fresno, CA (city) Fresno County	3,595	0.84
Henderson, NV (city) Clark County	3,576	2.03
Fort Wayne, IN (city) Allen County	3,576	1.74
Riverside, CA (city) Riverside County	3,564	1.40
Lexington-Fayette, KY (special city) Fayette County	3,561	1.37
Saint Paul, MN (city) Ramsey County	3,499	1.22
Zeeland, MI (city) Ottawa County	3,455	58.62
Glendale, AZ (city) Maricopa County	3,455	1.58
Salt Lake City, UT (city) Salt Lake County	3,421	1.89
Grand Haven, MI (township) Ottawa County	3,397	25.28
Springfield, MO (city) Greene County	3,362	2.21
Anaheim, CA (city) Orange County	3,361	1.03
Salem, OR (city) Marion County	3,346	2.45
Cedar Rapids, IA (city) Linn County	3,345	2.77
Little Chute, WI (village) Outagamie County	3,277	31.36
Reno, NV (city) Washoe County	3,274	1.81
Norton Shores, MI (city) Muskegon County	3,253	14.44
Lansing, MI (city) Ingham County	3,248	2.73
Blendon, MI (township) Ottawa County	3,238	57.09
Tacoma, WA (city) Pierce County	3,136	1.62
Bakersfield, CA (city) Kern County	3,070	1.24
Kalamazoo, MI (township) Kalamazoo County	3,068	14.12
Jamestown charter, MI (township) Ottawa County	3,054	61.36
Akron, OH (city) Summit County	3,053	1.41
Knoxville, TN (city) Knox County	3,052	1.76
Tampa, FL (city) Hillsborough County	3,035	1.00
Cincinnati, OH (city) Hamilton County	3,032	0.92
Baltimore, MD (independent city) Baltimore city	3,024	0.46
Sheboygan, WI (city) Sheboygan County	3,009	5.92
Chandler, AZ (city) Maricopa County	2,995	1.70
Northview, MI (cdp) Kent County	2,977	20.29
Grand Rapids charter, MI (township) Kent County	2,972	21.18
Orange City, IA (city) Sioux County	2,940	52.66
Spring Lake, MI (township) Ottawa County	2,922	22.23
Washington, DC (city) District of Columbia	2,879	0.50
Vancouver, WA (city) Clark County	2,870	2.00
Louisville, KY (city) Jefferson County	2,863	1.12
Colonie, NY (town) Albany County	2,859	3.61
Cleveland, OH (city) Cuyahoga County	2,847	0.60
Lakewood, CO (city) Jefferson County	2,817	1.96
Naperville, IL (city) Du Page County	2,808	2.19
Lynden, WA (city) Whatcom County	2,790	30.68
Greece, NY (town) Monroe County	2,776	2.95
Cascade, MI (township) Kent County	2,768	18.32
Santa Rosa, CA (city) Sonoma County	2,767	1.88
Overland Park, KS (city) Johnson County	2,749	1.85
Kaukauna, WI (city) Outagamie County	2,735	21.05
Tempe, AZ (city) Maricopa County	2,729	1.72
South Holland, IL (village) Cook County	2,718	12.20
Santa Clarita, CA (city) Los Angeles County	2,713	1.79
Arcadia, NY (town) Wayne County	2,672	17.80
Plano, TX (city) Collin County	2,671	1.20
Muskegon, MI (city) Muskegon County	2,669	6.65
Ann Arbor, MI (city) Washtenaw County	2,661	2.33
Amarillo, TX (city) Potter County	2,655	1.53
Independence, MO (city) Jackson County	2,636	2.33
Allentown, PA (city) Lehigh County	2,614	2.45
Fort Collins, CO (city) Larimer County	2,608	2.20
Raleigh, NC (city) Wake County	2,599	0.94
Islip, NY (town) Suffolk County	2,588	0.80
Grand Haven, MI (city) Ottawa County	2,586	23.17
Tinley Park, IL (village) Cook County	2,566	5.31
Laketown, MI (township) Allegan County	2,525	46.30
West Valley City, UT (city) Salt Lake County	2,508	2.30
Boston, MA (city) Suffolk County	2,495	0.42
Saint Louis, MO (independent city) Saint Louis city	2,450	0.70
Ontario, CA (city) San Bernardino County	2,436	1.55
Muskegon, MI (township) Muskegon County	2,410	13.62
Bellflower, CA (city) Los Angeles County	2,410	3.31

Notes: (cdp) census designated place; Refer to the Explanation of Data in the front of the book for more detailed information.

Dutch

Top 150 Places Sorted by Percent

(Based on all places, regardless of population)

Place	Number	%
Leota, MN (township) Nobles County	367	79.78
Maurice, IA (city) Sioux County	192	76.19
Osborne, MN (township) Pipestone County	239	76.11
Doon, IA (city) Lyon County	389	75.24
Prinsburg, MN (city) Kandiyohi County	317	71.56
Moulton, MN (township) Murray County	180	70.59
Sioux Center, IA (city) Sioux County	4,272	70.53
Leighton, IA (city) Mahaska County	123	69.89
Sully, IA (city) Jasper County	631	69.88
Edgerton, MN (city) Pipestone County	701	66.51
Hull, IA (city) Sioux County	1,296	66.06
Rock Valley, IA (city) Sioux County	1,756	65.38
New Holland, SD (cdp) Douglas County	50	64.94
Overisel, MI (township) Allegan County	1,635	62.40
Jamestown charter, MI (township) Ottawa County	3,054	61.36
Zeeland, MI (city) Ottawa County	3,455	58.62
Hudsonville, MI (city) Ottawa County	4,268	58.18
Blendon, MI (township) Ottawa County	3,238	57.09
Burke, MN (township) Pipestone County	138	56.79
Oostburg, WI (village) Sheboygan County	1,423	55.03
Boyden, IA (city) Sioux County	356	54.02
Corsica, SD (city) Douglas County	363	53.78
Orange City, IA (city) Sioux County	2,940	52.66
Holland, MN (township) Kandiyohi County	202	52.60
Zeeland charter, MI (township) Ottawa County	3,933	51.96
Alto, WI (town) Fond du Lac County	566	51.31
McBain, MI (city) Missaukee County	289	50.26
Islandia, FL (city) Miami-Dade County	3	50.00
Randolph, WI (town) Columbia County	334	48.90
Steen, MN (city) Rock County	82	48.81
Battle Plain, MN (township) Rock County	120	48.78
Elmer, MN (township) Pipestone County	150	48.23
Chandler, MN (city) Murray County	130	47.97
Richland, MI (township) Missaukee County	704	47.96
Woodstock, MN (city) Pipestone County	60	47.24
Clam Union, MI (township) Missaukee County	451	47.18
Amsterdam-Churchill, MT (cdp) Gallatin County	345	46.81
Alvord, IA (city) Lyon County	95	46.80
Chanarambie, MN (township) Murray County	100	46.73
Laketown, MI (township) Allegan County	2,525	46.30
Ireton, IA (city) Sioux County	268	46.13
Pella, IA (city) Marion County	4,462	45.77
Cold Spring, PA (township) Lebanon County	35	45.45
Fillmore, MI (township) Allegan County	1,270	45.39
Matlock, IA (city) Sioux County	36	44.44
Hospers, IA (city) Sioux County	303	43.72
Friesland, WI (village) Columbia County	142	43.56
Byron Center, MI (cdp) Kent County	1,614	43.42
Clinton, MN (township) Rock County	112	42.75
Georgetown, MI (township) Ottawa County	17,780	42.68
Cedar Grove, WI (village) Sheboygan County	800	42.46
Heath, MI (township) Allegan County	1,291	42.15
Jenison, MI (cdp) Ottawa County	7,218	41.88
Martin, MN (township) Rock County	188	41.23
Rock, MN (township) Pipestone County	79	40.93
Kupreanof, AK (city) Wrangell-Petersburg Census Area	13	40.63
Vandenbroek, WI (town) Outagamie County	535	40.41
Sanborn, IA (city) O'Brien County	540	40.24
Riverside, MI (township) Missaukee County	426	39.85
Prairie View, KS (city) Phillips County	49	39.52
Archer, IA (city) O'Brien County	50	39.37
Olive, MI (township) Ottawa County	1,877	39.16
Polkton, MI (township) Ottawa County	911	39.01
Manlius, MI (township) Allegan County	1,044	38.67
Fenton, MN (township) Murray County	82	38.14
Hollandale, MN (city) Freeborn County	101	38.11
Prattville, CA (cdp) Plumas County	8	38.10
Grandville, MI (city) Kent County	6,073	37.34
Fulton, IL (city) Whiteside County	1,451	37.29
Byron, MI (township) Kent County	6,469	36.73
Inwood, IA (city) Lyon County	315	36.33
Ellsworth, MI (village) Antrim County	171	36.23
Rose Dell, MN (township) Rock County	75	36.06
Port Sheldon, MI (township) Ottawa County	1,571	35.70
Holland, WI (town) Sheboygan County	856	35.65
Park, MI (township) Ottawa County	6,249	35.57
Leighton, MI (township) Allegan County	1,300	35.44
Rock Rapids, IA (city) Lyon County	911	35.28
Tallmadge, MI (township) Ottawa County	2,409	35.01
Platte, SD (city) Charles Mix County	478	34.99
Aetna, MI (township) Missaukee County	159	34.72
Struble, IA (city) Plymouth County	27	34.62
Lester, IA (city) Lyon County	83	34.44
Alton, IA (city) Sioux County	373	33.85
Salem, MI (township) Allegan County	1,170	33.62
Morehouse, NY (town) Hamilton County	43	33.59
Randolph, WI (village) Dodge County	624	33.53
Sheldon, IA (city) O'Brien County	1,630	33.35
Holland, MI (township) Ottawa County	9,446	33.01
Waupun, WI (town) Fond du Lac County	455	32.59
Trosky, MN (city) Pipestone County	29	32.22
Gaines, MI (township) Kent County	6,410	31.96
Roseland, MN (township) Kandiyohi County	154	31.62
Buckhorn, PA (cdp) Columbia County	42	31.58
Spring Lake, MI (village) Ottawa County	750	31.53
Little Chute, WI (village) Outagamie County	3,277	31.36
Kimberly, WI (village) Outagamie County	1,943	31.30
Lima, WI (town) Sheboygan County	931	31.18
Beechwood, MI (cdp) Ottawa County	915	31.12
Lynden, WA (city) Whatcom County	2,790	30.68
Acme, WA (cdp) Whatcom County	51	30.54
Owl Creek, WY (cdp) Hot Springs County	16	30.19
Holland, MI (city) Ottawa County	10,564	30.00
Duchess Landing, OK (cdp) McIntosh County	12	30.00
Valley Park, OK (town) Rogers County	3	30.00
Stickney, SD (town) Aurora County	105	29.91
Denver, MN (township) Rock County	63	29.86
Mound, MN (township) Rock County	78	29.21
Kaukauna, WI (town) Outagamie County	345	29.19
Pioneer, IA (city) Humboldt County	7	29.17
Arrowhead Springs, WY (cdp) Sweetwater County	30	28.85
Southbrook, MN (township) Cottonwood County	38	28.57
Kinbrae, MN (city) Nobles County	8	28.57
Allendale, MI (township) Ottawa County	3,719	28.30
Elk, MN (township) Nobles County	86	28.29
Gregory, MN (township) Mahnomen County	30	28.04
Corning, MO (town) Holt County	7	28.00
Cutlerville, MI (cdp) Kent County	4,219	27.87
Harrison, SD (cdp) Douglas County	17	27.87
Beaver Creek, MN (township) Rock County	103	27.84
Magnolia, MN (township) Rock County	70	27.67
Holland, WI (town) Brown County	370	27.65
Freedom, WI (town) Outagamie County	1,446	27.59
Edwards, MN (township) Kandiyohi County	77	27.50
Indian Falls, CA (cdp) Plumas County	6	27.27
Hills, MN (city) Rock County	156	27.23
Combined Locks, WI (village) Outagamie County	670	27.20
Dorr, MI (township) Allegan County	1,773	26.95
Highland, MI (township) Osceola County	331	26.93
Heckscherville, PA (cdp) Schuylkill County	19	26.76
Butler, MN (township) Otter Tail County	80	26.58
Robinson, MI (township) Ottawa County	1,443	26.43
Hudson, SD (town) Lincoln County	112	26.11
Vienna, MN (township) Rock County	42	26.09
Martin, MI (township) Allegan County	658	25.95
Dayton, MI (township) Newaygo County	527	25.88
Kanaranzi, MN (township) Rock County	79	25.65
Springwater, MN (township) Rock County	75	25.60
Sherman, SD (town) Minnehaha County	16	25.40
Grand Haven, MI (township) Ottawa County	3,397	25.28
Forestville, MN (township) Fillmore County	102	25.19
Walker, MI (city) Kent County	5,470	25.10
Clymer, NY (town) Chautauqua County	390	25.00
Lake Wilson, MN (city) Murray County	69	25.00
Santa Monica, TX (cdp) Willacy County	24	25.00
Ronneby, MN (city) Benton County	3	25.00
Leeds, MN (township) Murray County	57	24.89
Alamo, MI (township) Kalamazoo County	947	24.79
Chester, WI (town) Dodge County	238	24.61
New Era, MI (village) Oceana County	115	24.47

Notes: (cdp) census designated place; Refer to the Explanation of Data in the front of the book for more detailed information.

Dutch

Top 150 Places Sorted by Percent

(Based on places with populations of 10,000 or more)

Place	Number	%
Georgetown, MI (township) Ottawa County	17,780	42.68
Jenison, MI (cdp) Ottawa County	7,218	41.88
Grandville, MI (city) Kent County	6,073	37.34
Byron, MI (township) Kent County	6,469	36.73
Park, MI (township) Ottawa County	6,249	35.57
Holland, MI (township) Ottawa County	9,446	33.01
Gaines, MI (township) Kent County	6,410	31.96
Little Chute, WI (village) Outagamie County	3,277	31.36
Holland, MI (city) Ottawa County	10,564	30.00
Allendale, MI (township) Ottawa County	3,719	28.30
Cutlerville, MI (cdp) Kent County	4,219	27.87
Grand Haven, MI (township) Ottawa County	3,397	25.28
Walker, MI (city) Kent County	5,470	25.10
Grand Haven, MI (city) Ottawa County	2,586	23.17
Wyoming, MI (city) Kent County	15,679	22.60
Spring Lake, MI (township) Ottawa County	2,922	22.23
Grand Rapids charter, MI (township) Kent County	2,972	21.18
Kaukauna, WI (city) Outagamie County	2,735	21.05
Forest Hills, MI (cdp) Kent County	4,256	20.33
Northview, MI (cdp) Kent County	2,977	20.29
Waupun, WI (city) Dodge County	2,152	20.11
Plainfield, MI (township) Kent County	5,800	19.27
Cannon, MI (township) Kent County	2,281	18.87
Cascade, MI (township) Kent County	2,768	18.32
Kentwood, MI (city) Kent County	8,098	17.90
Arcadia, NY (town) Wayne County	2,672	17.80
Fruitport charter, MI (township) Muskegon County	2,202	17.57
East Grand Rapids, MI (city) Kent County	1,787	16.57
Grand Rapids, MI (city) Kent County	31,050	15.69
Alpine, MI (township) Kent County	2,156	15.30
Norton Shores, MI (city) Muskegon County	3,253	14.44
Oskaloosa, IA (city) Mahaska County	1,571	14.40
Comstock Park, MI (cdp) Kent County	1,519	14.30
Comstock, MI (township) Kalamazoo County	1,967	14.23
Kalamazoo, MI (township) Kalamazoo County	3,068	14.12
Lansing, IL (village) Cook County	3,857	13.70
Muskegon, MI (township) Muskegon County	2,410	13.62
Texas, MI (township) Kalamazoo County	1,463	13.40
Oshtemo, MI (township) Kalamazoo County	2,212	13.01
Ripon, CA (city) San Joaquin County	1,260	12.43
South Holland, IL (village) Cook County	2,718	12.20
Portage, MI (city) Kalamazoo County	5,388	11.99
De Pere, WI (city) Brown County	2,309	11.24
Antwerp, MI (township) Van Buren County	1,194	11.21
Hawthorne, NJ (borough) Passaic County	2,014	11.06
Coal, PA (township) Northumberland County	1,159	10.91
Newton, IA (city) Jasper County	1,566	10.04
Berwick, PA (borough) Columbia County	1,035	9.67
Palos Heights, IL (city) Cook County	1,032	9.12
Wantage, NJ (township) Sussex County	946	9.11
Spencer, IA (city) Clay County	981	8.59
Wyckoff, NJ (cdp) Bergen County	1,374	8.32
Pottsville, PA (city) Schuylkill County	1,282	8.25
Pequannock, NJ (township) Morris County	1,141	8.22
Grand Chute, WI (town) Outagamie County	1,421	7.79
Kalamazoo, MI (city) Kalamazoo County	5,969	7.74
Saugerties, NY (town) Ulster County	1,508	7.63
Schodack, NY (town) Rensselaer County	945	7.54
Bellevue Town, WI (cdp) Brown County	897	7.53
Pompton Lakes, NJ (borough) Passaic County	792	7.44
Dyer, IN (town) Lake County	1,004	7.25
Appleton, WI (city) Outagamie County	4,977	7.10
Menasha, WI (town) Winnebago County	1,111	6.97
Worthington, MN (city) Nobles County	781	6.92
Highland, IN (town) Lake County	1,598	6.79
Muskegon, MI (city) Muskegon County	2,669	6.65
Ashwaubenon, WI (village) Brown County	1,168	6.61
Northbridge, MA (town) Worcester County	861	6.52
Vernon, NJ (township) Sussex County	1,593	6.45
Canandaigua, NY (city) Ontario County	717	6.37
Sioux Falls, SD (city) Minnehaha County	7,841	6.32
West Milford, NJ (cdp) Passaic County	1,668	6.32
Phillipsburg, NJ (town) Warren County	938	6.18
Allouez, WI (village) Brown County	936	6.06
Wanaque, NJ (borough) Passaic County	621	6.05
Gloversville, NY (city) Fulton County	930	6.03
Ulster, NY (town) Ulster County	749	5.97
Sheboygan, WI (city) Sheboygan County	3,009	5.92
Farmington, NY (town) Ontario County	623	5.89
Willmar, MN (city) Kandiyohi County	1,072	5.83
Schererville, IN (town) Lake County	1,445	5.82
Sunbury, PA (city) Northumberland County	614	5.79
Clinton, IA (city) Clinton County	1,600	5.75
Catskill, NY (town) Greene County	659	5.56
Hazleton, PA (city) Luzerne County	1,271	5.46
Rotterdam, NY (town) Schenectady County	1,538	5.42
Oakland, NJ (borough) Bergen County	676	5.42
Mitchell, SD (city) Davison County	795	5.41
Neenah, WI (city) Winnebago County	1,300	5.34
Menasha, WI (city) Winnebago County	875	5.34
Tinley Park, IL (village) Cook County	2,566	5.31
East Greenbush, NY (town) Rensselaer County	827	5.30
Altoona, IA (city) Polk County	544	5.29
Dallas, OR (city) Polk County	645	5.19
Oak Forest, IL (city) Cook County	1,439	5.15
Griffith, IN (town) Lake County	873	5.04
Howard, WI (village) Brown County	683	5.04
Glenville, NY (town) Schenectady County	1,412	5.03
Munster, IN (town) Lake County	1,083	5.03
Wawarsing, NY (town) Ulster County	647	5.02
German Flatts, NY (town) Herkimer County	682	4.99
Pottstown, PA (borough) Montgomery County	1,082	4.97
Delta charter, MI (township) Eaton County	1,475	4.96
Jefferson, NJ (township) Morris County	975	4.94
West Des Moines, IA (city) Polk County	2,281	4.93
Marshall, MN (city) Lyon County	626	4.91
Franklin Lakes, NJ (borough) Bergen County	509	4.88
Ottumwa, IA (city) Wapello County	1,208	4.85
Urbandale, IA (city) Polk County	1,401	4.82
Kingston, NY (city) Ulster County	1,127	4.82
Dryden, NY (town) Tompkins County	661	4.82
Sullivan, NY (town) Madison County	721	4.81
Crestline, CA (cdp) San Bernardino County	491	4.81
Delhi charter, MI (township) Ingham County	1,088	4.80
Garfield, MI (township) Grand Traverse County	648	4.80
Clinton, UT (city) Davis County	608	4.80
Oquirrh, UT (cdp) Salt Lake County	491	4.74
Big Rapids, MI (city) Mecosta County	502	4.73
Traverse City, MI (city) Grand Traverse County	685	4.71
Green Bay, WI (city) Brown County	4,812	4.70
Moreau, NY (town) Saratoga County	650	4.70
Clive, IA (city) Polk County	596	4.64
Frankfort, IL (village) Will County	474	4.63
Chestnuthill, PA (township) Monroe County	666	4.62
De Witt, MI (township) Clinton County	556	4.62
Bloomsburg, PA (town) Columbia County	574	4.61
Artesia, CA (city) Los Angeles County	747	4.56
Indianola, IA (city) Warren County	591	4.56
Webster, NY (town) Monroe County	1,716	4.52
Bethlehem, NY (town) Albany County	1,407	4.49
Niles, MI (township) Berrien County	602	4.49
Brunswick, NY (town) Rensselaer County	526	4.49
Worth, IL (village) Cook County	500	4.48
Guilderland, NY (town) Albany County	1,455	4.45
Hyde Park, NY (town) Dutchess County	928	4.45
Brookings, SD (city) Brookings County	825	4.45
Waverly, MI (cdp) Eaton County	717	4.44
North Greenbush, NY (town) Rensselaer County	478	4.44
Shawangunk, NY (town) Ulster County	534	4.43
Saint Joseph charter, MI (township) Berrien County	449	4.41
Ankeny, IA (city) Polk County	1,185	4.40
Haslett, MI (cdp) Ingham County	493	4.37
Montgomery, NY (town) Orange County	908	4.35
North Union, PA (township) Fayette County	610	4.31
Easton, PA (city) Northampton County	1,125	4.28
Sioux City, IA (city) Woodbury County	3,633	4.27
Watertown, SD (city) Codington County	868	4.27
Ringwood, NJ (borough) Passaic County	529	4.27
Exeter, PA (township) Berks County	903	4.26
Canyon Lake, CA (city) Riverside County	434	4.25

Notes: (cdp) census designated place; Refer to the Explanation of Data in the front of the book for more detailed information.

Eastern European

Top 150 Places Sorted by Number

(Based on all places, regardless of population)

Place	Number	%
New York, NY (city) New York City	30,570	0.38
Los Angeles, CA (city) Los Angeles County	8,891	0.24
Hempstead, NY (town) Nassau County	3,765	0.50
Chicago, IL (city) Cook County	3,388	0.12
San Francisco, CA (city) San Francisco County	2,626	0.34
Philadelphia, PA (city) Philadelphia County	2,551	0.17
North Hempstead, NY (town) Nassau County	2,251	1.01
Washington, DC (city) District of Columbia	2,160	0.38
Oyster Bay, NY (town) Nassau County	2,156	0.73
Newton, MA (city) Middlesex County	1,817	2.17
San Diego, CA (city) San Diego County	1,616	0.13
Boston, MA (city) Suffolk County	1,398	0.24
Lower Merion, PA (township) Montgomery County	1,389	2.32
Greenburgh, NY (town) Westchester County	1,338	1.54
Potomac, MD (cdp) Montgomery County	1,306	2.91
Ramapo, NY (town) Rockland County	1,193	1.10
Brookline, MA (cdp) Norfolk County	1,184	2.07
Huntington, NY (town) Suffolk County	1,175	0.60
Seattle, WA (city) King County	1,173	0.21
Bethesda, MD (cdp) Montgomery County	1,127	2.04
Berkeley, CA (city) Alameda County	1,055	1.03
Cambridge, MA (city) Middlesex County	942	0.93
Denver, CO (city) Denver County	915	0.16
Baltimore, MD (independent city) Baltimore city	898	0.14
Dallas, TX (city) Dallas County	879	0.07
Cherry Hill, NJ (township) Camden County	876	1.25
Pittsburgh, PA (city) Allegheny County	865	0.26
Brookhaven, NY (town) Suffolk County	836	0.19
Houston, TX (city) Harris County	833	0.04
Portland, OR (city) Multnomah County	827	0.16
Oakland, CA (city) Alameda County	820	0.21
Clarkstown, NY (town) Rockland County	818	1.00
Highland Park, IL (city) Lake County	797	2.54
Phoenix, AZ (city) Maricopa County	767	0.06
Livingston, NJ (cdp) Essex County	743	2.71
Teaneck, NJ (cdp) Bergen County	734	1.87
New Rochelle, NY (city) Westchester County	703	0.97
New Castle, NY (town) Westchester County	689	3.94
Arlington, VA (cdp) Arlington County	686	0.36
North Bethesda, MD (cdp) Montgomery County	679	1.76
Plainview, NY (cdp) Nassau County	652	2.54
Scarsdale, NY (village) Westchester County	647	3.63
Columbia, MD (cdp) Howard County	635	0.72
Ann Arbor, MI (city) Washtenaw County	635	0.56
West Bloomfield, MI (township) Oakland County	630	0.97
Skokie, IL (village) Cook County	603	0.95
Beverly Hills, CA (city) Los Angeles County	601	1.78
Pikesville, MD (cdp) Baltimore County	599	2.07
Needham, MA (cdp) Norfolk County	596	2.06
New City, NY (cdp) Rockland County	594	1.74
Stamford, CT (city) Fairfield County	591	0.50
Evanston, IL (city) Cook County	585	0.79
Boulder, CO (city) Boulder County	578	0.61
Silver Spring, MD (cdp) Montgomery County	576	0.75
Austin, TX (city) Travis County	571	0.09
North Potomac, MD (cdp) Montgomery County	555	2.42
Mamaroneck, NY (town) Westchester County	527	1.82
Marlboro, NJ (township) Monmouth County	525	1.44
Plantation, FL (city) Broward County	525	0.63
Buffalo Grove, IL (village) Lake County	521	1.22
Boca Raton, FL (city) Palm Beach County	518	0.69
Santa Monica, CA (city) Los Angeles County	518	0.62
Minneapolis, MN (city) Hennepin County	513	0.13
Westport, CT (cdp) Fairfield County	508	1.97
Coral Springs, FL (city) Broward County	508	0.43
Upper Dublin, PA (township) Montgomery County	502	1.94
Sharon, MA (town) Norfolk County	498	2.86
Millburn, NJ (cdp) Essex County	495	2.50
Hollywood, FL (city) Broward County	494	0.35
Lakewood, NJ (township) Ocean County	493	0.82
San Jose, CA (city) Santa Clara County	492	0.06
Palo Alto, CA (city) Santa Clara County	491	0.84
West Orange, NJ (cdp) Essex County	489	1.09
Haverford, PA (township) Delaware County	488	1.01
Cheltenham, PA (township) Montgomery County	484	1.31
White Plains, NY (city) Westchester County	480	0.90
Providence, RI (city) Providence County	478	0.28
Smithtown, NY (town) Suffolk County	473	0.41
Scottsdale, AZ (city) Maricopa County	470	0.23
Albuquerque, NM (city) Bernalillo County	470	0.10
Atlanta, GA (city) Fulton County	465	0.11
Framingham, MA (cdp) Middlesex County	453	0.68
Irvine, CA (city) Orange County	452	0.32
Deerfield, IL (village) Lake County	444	2.40
Woodmere, NY (cdp) Nassau County	441	2.68
Springdale, NJ (cdp) Camden County	434	3.01
Farmington Hills, MI (city) Oakland County	433	0.53
Columbus, OH (city) Franklin County	428	0.06
Rye, NY (town) Westchester County	423	0.96
Rockville, MD (city) Montgomery County	422	0.89
Miami Beach, FL (city) Miami-Dade County	414	0.47
Madison, WI (city) Dane County	408	0.20
Sandy Springs, GA (cdp) Fulton County	401	0.47
Westfield, NJ (town) Union County	398	1.34
Edison, NJ (cdp) Middlesex County	395	0.40
Somerville, MA (city) Middlesex County	393	0.51
Beachwood, OH (city) Cuyahoga County	391	3.21
Thousand Oaks, CA (city) Ventura County	390	0.33
Glencoe, IL (village) Cook County	387	4.38
East Brunswick, NJ (cdp) Middlesex County	387	0.83
West Windsor, NJ (township) Mercer County	386	1.76
Jericho, NY (cdp) Nassau County	377	2.90
Shaker Heights, OH (city) Cuyahoga County	372	1.26
West Hartford, CT (cdp) Hartford County	370	0.58
Rye Brook, NY (village) Westchester County	368	4.27
Islip, NY (town) Suffolk County	363	0.11
Tucson, AZ (city) Pima County	362	0.07
Chappaqua, NY (cdp) Westchester County	360	3.82
Long Beach, CA (city) Los Angeles County	357	0.08
Randolph, NJ (township) Morris County	352	1.42
Montclair, NJ (cdp) Essex County	340	0.87
Merrick, NY (cdp) Nassau County	339	1.49
Wilmette, IL (village) Cook County	338	1.22
San Antonio, TX (city) Bexar County	336	0.03
Culver City, CA (city) Los Angeles County	335	0.86
Northbrook, IL (village) Cook County	331	0.99
Durham, NC (city) Durham County	331	0.18
Larchmont, NY (village) Westchester County	330	5.09
Weston, FL (city) Broward County	328	0.67
New Haven, CT (city) New Haven County	327	0.26
Cleveland Heights, OH (city) Cuyahoga County	323	0.65
Jacksonville, FL (special city) Duval County	323	0.04
Plano, TX (city) Collin County	319	0.14
Kendall, FL (cdp) Miami-Dade County	316	0.42
Highland Park, NJ (borough) Middlesex County	315	2.25
Amherst, NY (town) Erie County	314	0.27
Virginia Beach, VA (independent city) Virginia Beach city	314	0.07
Lexington, MA (cdp) Middlesex County	307	1.01
Oceanside, NY (cdp) Nassau County	307	0.94
Dunwoody, GA (cdp) De Kalb County	304	0.93
Greenville, NY (cdp) Westchester County	303	3.54
Olney, MD (cdp) Montgomery County	302	0.95
Englewood, NJ (city) Bergen County	298	1.14
Agoura Hills, CA (city) Los Angeles County	297	1.46
Aventura, FL (city) Miami-Dade County	297	1.18
Cortlandt, NY (town) Westchester County	295	0.77
Chesterfield, MO (city) Saint Louis County	295	0.63
Abington, PA (township) Montgomery County	288	0.51
East Hills, NY (village) Nassau County	287	4.18
Weston, CT (town) Fairfield County	287	2.86
Alexandria, VA (independent city) Alexandria city	286	0.22
Colorado Springs, CO (city) El Paso County	286	0.08
Wayne, NJ (cdp) Passaic County	285	0.53
Long Beach, NY (city) Nassau County	283	0.80
East Meadow, NY (cdp) Nassau County	283	0.75
Memphis, TN (city) Shelby County	279	0.04
Aspen Hill, MD (cdp) Montgomery County	278	0.55
Charlotte, NC (city) Mecklenburg County	277	0.05
Syosset, NY (cdp) Nassau County	269	1.45
Lower Makefield, PA (township) Bucks County	269	0.82

Notes: (cdp) census designated place; Refer to the Explanation of Data in the front of the book for more detailed information.

Eastern European

Top 150 Places Sorted by Percent

(Based on all places, regardless of population)

Place	Number	%
Smithfield, IL (village) Fulton County	15	7.18
Kensington, NY (village) Nassau County	82	6.75
Sands Point, NY (village) Nassau County	159	5.76
Hills and Dales, OH (village) Stark County	16	5.48
Larchmont, NY (village) Westchester County	330	5.09
Hillside, NY (cdp) Ulster County	42	4.58
Scotts Corners, NY (cdp) Westchester County	26	4.51
Russell Gardens, NY (village) Nassau County	48	4.47
El Valle de Arroyo Seco, NM (cdp) Santa Fe County	38	4.45
North Chevy Chase, MD (village) Montgomery County	19	4.45
Glencoe, IL (village) Cook County	387	4.38
Muir Beach, CA (cdp) Marin County	12	4.35
Rye Brook, NY (village) Westchester County	368	4.27
East Hills, NY (village) Nassau County	287	4.18
Hewlett Bay Park, NY (village) Nassau County	20	4.12
New Castle, NY (town) Westchester County	689	3.94
Roslyn Estates, NY (village) Nassau County	48	3.93
Martin's Additions, MD (village) Montgomery County	35	3.92
Teton Village, WY (cdp) Teton County	10	3.91
Hewlett Neck, NY (village) Nassau County	19	3.85
Chappaqua, NY (cdp) Westchester County	360	3.82
Chevy Chase, MD (town) Montgomery County	103	3.78
Garrett Park, MD (town) Montgomery County	33	3.68
Scarsdale, NY (village) Westchester County	647	3.63
Hewlett Harbor, NY (village) Nassau County	46	3.62
New Hempstead, NY (village) Rockland County	170	3.55
Greenville, NY (cdp) Westchester County	303	3.54
Westwood, MO (village) Saint Louis County	9	3.26
Viola, NY (cdp) Rockland County	192	3.23
Beachwood, OH (city) Cuyahoga County	391	3.21
Thomaston, NY (village) Nassau County	82	3.16
Huntington Woods, MI (city) Oakland County	192	3.12
Woodside, PA (cdp) Bucks County	84	3.08
Bear Valley, CA (cdp) Alpine County	3	3.03
Springdale, NJ (cdp) Camden County	434	3.01
Roslyn Harbor, NY (village) Nassau County	30	3.00
Wells, MI (township) Marquette County	8	2.94
Montebello, NY (village) Rockland County	106	2.92
Potomac, MD (cdp) Montgomery County	1,306	2.91
Jericho, NY (cdp) Nassau County	377	2.90
Sharon, MA (town) Norfolk County	498	2.86
Weston, CT (town) Fairfield County	287	2.86
Orange, OH (village) Cuyahoga County	92	2.84
Fort Washington, PA (cdp) Montgomery County	101	2.81
Harbor Hills, NY (cdp) Nassau County	16	2.79
Crossgate, KY (city) Jefferson County	7	2.75
Hyden, KY (city) Leslie County	6	2.74
Aurora, ME (town) Hancock County	3	2.73
Livingston, NJ (cdp) Essex County	743	2.71
Woodmere, NY (cdp) Nassau County	441	2.68
Franklin, MI (village) Oakland County	77	2.62
Roosevelt, NJ (borough) Monmouth County	24	2.59
Highland Park, IL (city) Lake County	797	2.54
Plainview, NY (cdp) Nassau County	652	2.54
Monhegan, ME (plantation) Lincoln County	2	2.53
Woodcliff Lake, NJ (borough) Bergen County	145	2.52
Millburn, NJ (cdp) Essex County	495	2.50
Hewlett, NY (cdp) Nassau County	175	2.48
Manhasset Hills, NY (cdp) Nassau County	90	2.46
Princeton Junction, NJ (cdp) Mercer County	58	2.43
North Potomac, MD (cdp) Montgomery County	555	2.42
Deerfield, IL (village) Lake County	444	2.40
Lake Success, NY (village) Nassau County	67	2.40
Saint Clair, PA (borough) Schuylkill County	77	2.36
Ardsley, NY (village) Westchester County	100	2.34
Pittsfield, VT (town) Rutland County	10	2.33
Lower Merion, PA (township) Montgomery County	1,389	2.32
Amberley, OH (village) Hamilton County	79	2.32
Chevy Chase Village, MD (town) Montgomery County	47	2.29
North Castle, NY (town) Westchester County	247	2.28
Mission Bay, FL (cdp) Palm Beach County	70	2.28
Highland Park, NJ (borough) Middlesex County	315	2.25
Roslyn, NY (village) Nassau County	58	2.24
Great Neck Plaza, NY (village) Nassau County	141	2.22
Hastings-on-Hudson, NY (village) Westchester County	169	2.21
Bardonia, NY (cdp) Rockland County	96	2.19
Marlboro, VT (town) Windham County	21	2.18
Newton, MA (city) Middlesex County	1,817	2.17
Westover Hills, TX (town) Tarrant County	14	2.16
Turners Falls, MA (cdp) Franklin County	93	2.15
Plandome Manor, NY (village) Nassau County	18	2.15
Chestnut Ridge, NY (village) Rockland County	164	2.12
Sheppton, PA (cdp) Schuylkill County	5	2.12
Laurel Hollow, NY (village) Nassau County	43	2.10
Wesley, ME (town) Washington County	2	2.08
Brookline, MA (cdp) Norfolk County	1,184	2.07
Pikesville, MD (cdp) Baltimore County	599	2.07
Wesley Hills, NY (village) Rockland County	102	2.07
North Hills, NY (village) Nassau County	89	2.07
Needham, MA (cdp) Norfolk County	596	2.06
Chevy Chase Section Three, MD (village) Montgomery County	16	2.06
Cherry Hills Village, CO (city) Arapahoe County	122	2.05
East Ithaca, NY (cdp) Tompkins County	47	2.05
Enchanted Oaks, TX (town) Henderson County	10	2.05
Bethesda, MD (cdp) Montgomery County	1,127	2.04
Saddle Rock, NY (village) Nassau County	16	2.02
Chickamaw Beach, MN (city) Cass County	3	2.01
Cedarhurst, NY (village) Nassau County	123	2.00
Swarthmore, PA (borough) Delaware County	122	1.98
Holly Grove, AR (city) Monroe County	15	1.98
Westport, CT (cdp) Fairfield County	508	1.97
Great Neck, NY (village) Nassau County	187	1.96
Roslyn Heights, NY (cdp) Nassau County	123	1.95
South Fallsburg, NY (cdp) Sullivan County	44	1.95
Upper Dublin, PA (township) Montgomery County	502	1.94
Newtown Grant, PA (cdp) Bucks County	77	1.93
Glen Ellen, CA (cdp) Sonoma County	18	1.93
Cragsmoor, NY (cdp) Ulster County	9	1.92
Chatham, NH (town) Carroll County	5	1.92
Irvington, NY (village) Westchester County	126	1.90
Cabin John, MD (cdp) Montgomery County	32	1.90
Woodsburgh, NY (village) Nassau County	16	1.90
Hartsdale, NY (cdp) Westchester County	185	1.88
Bermuda Run, NC (town) Davie County	29	1.88
Teaneck, NJ (cdp) Bergen County	734	1.87
West Brownsville, PA (borough) Washington County	20	1.86
Woodbridge, CT (town) New Haven County	166	1.85
Lewisboro, NY (town) Westchester County	226	1.83
Mamaroneck, NY (town) Westchester County	527	1.82
Beverly Hills, CA (city) Los Angeles County	601	1.78
Upper Saddle River, NJ (borough) Bergen County	138	1.78
Alford, MA (town) Berkshire County	7	1.78
Seltzer, PA (cdp) Schuylkill County	5	1.77
North Bethesda, MD (cdp) Montgomery County	679	1.76
West Windsor, NJ (township) Mercer County	386	1.76
Armonk, NY (cdp) Westchester County	62	1.76
Celebration, FL (cdp) Osceola County	48	1.75
New City, NY (cdp) Rockland County	594	1.74
Brookville, NY (village) Nassau County	37	1.72
Moro, ME (plantation) Aroostook County	1	1.72
Monsey, NY (cdp) Rockland County	251	1.71
Great Neck Gardens, NY (cdp) Nassau County	19	1.70
Tenafly, NJ (borough) Bergen County	234	1.69
Bexley, OH (city) Franklin County	223	1.69
Pound Ridge, NY (town) Westchester County	80	1.69
Rose Valley, PA (borough) Delaware County	16	1.69
Glen Echo, MD (town) Montgomery County	4	1.69
Melville, NY (cdp) Suffolk County	244	1.68
Penn Wynne, PA (cdp) Montgomery County	91	1.68
Wilsonville, NE (village) Furnas County	2	1.68
Boca Pointe, FL (cdp) Palm Beach County	55	1.67
Gates Mills, OH (village) Cuyahoga County	41	1.67
Briarcliff Manor, NY (village) Westchester County	126	1.65
Lagunitas-Forest Knolls, CA (cdp) Marin County	30	1.65
Moreland Hills, OH (village) Cuyahoga County	54	1.64
Wardsboro, VT (town) Windham County	14	1.64
Clyde Hill, WA (city) King County	47	1.63
Spring House, PA (cdp) Montgomery County	53	1.62
Cumberland Center, ME (cdp) Cumberland County	42	1.62
Bryn Mawr, PA (cdp) Montgomery County	71	1.61

Notes: (cdp) census designated place; Refer to the Explanation of Data in the front of the book for more detailed information.

Eastern European

Top 150 Places Sorted by Percent

(Based on places with populations of 10,000 or more)

Place	Number	%
New Castle, NY (town) Westchester County	689	3.94
Scarsdale, NY (village) Westchester County	647	3.63
Beachwood, OH (city) Cuyahoga County	391	3.21
Springdale, NJ (cdp) Camden County	434	3.01
Potomac, MD (cdp) Montgomery County	1,306	2.91
Jericho, NY (cdp) Nassau County	377	2.90
Sharon, MA (town) Norfolk County	498	2.86
Weston, CT (town) Fairfield County	287	2.86
Livingston, NJ (cdp) Essex County	743	2.71
Woodmere, NY (cdp) Nassau County	441	2.68
Highland Park, IL (city) Lake County	797	2.54
Plainview, NY (cdp) Nassau County	652	2.54
Millburn, NJ (cdp) Essex County	495	2.50
North Potomac, MD (cdp) Montgomery County	555	2.42
Deerfield, IL (village) Lake County	444	2.40
Lower Merion, PA (township) Montgomery County	1,389	2.32
North Castle, NY (town) Westchester County	247	2.28
Highland Park, NJ (borough) Middlesex County	315	2.25
Newton, MA (city) Middlesex County	1,817	2.17
Brookline, MA (cdp) Norfolk County	1,184	2.07
Pikesville, MD (cdp) Baltimore County	599	2.07
Needham, MA (cdp) Norfolk County	596	2.06
Bethesda, MD (cdp) Montgomery County	1,127	2.04
Westport, CT (cdp) Fairfield County	508	1.97
Upper Dublin, PA (township) Montgomery County	502	1.94
Teaneck, NJ (cdp) Bergen County	734	1.87
Lewisboro, NY (town) Westchester County	226	1.83
Mamaroneck, NY (town) Westchester County	527	1.82
Beverly Hills, CA (city) Los Angeles County	601	1.78
North Bethesda, MD (cdp) Montgomery County	679	1.76
West Windsor, NJ (township) Mercer County	386	1.76
New City, NY (cdp) Rockland County	594	1.74
Monsey, NY (cdp) Rockland County	251	1.71
Tenafly, NJ (borough) Bergen County	234	1.69
Bexley, OH (city) Franklin County	223	1.69
Melville, NY (cdp) Suffolk County	244	1.68
Port Washington, NY (cdp) Nassau County	243	1.60
Greenburgh, NY (town) Westchester County	1,338	1.54
Morganville, NJ (cdp) Monmouth County	172	1.54
Merrick, NY (cdp) Nassau County	339	1.49
Wayland, MA (town) Middlesex County	193	1.47
Agoura Hills, CA (city) Los Angeles County	297	1.46
Syosset, NY (cdp) Nassau County	269	1.45
Warren, NJ (township) Somerset County	207	1.45
Marlboro, NJ (township) Monmouth County	525	1.44
Weston, MA (town) Middlesex County	165	1.44
Randolph, NJ (township) Morris County	352	1.42
University Heights, OH (city) Cuyahoga County	198	1.40
Westfield, NJ (town) Union County	398	1.34
Newtown, PA (township) Bucks County	245	1.34
Greentree, NJ (cdp) Camden County	152	1.32
Cheltenham, PA (township) Montgomery County	484	1.31
Calabasas, CA (city) Los Angeles County	261	1.30
West Caldwell, NJ (cdp) Essex County	146	1.30
Bellmore, NY (cdp) Nassau County	212	1.29
Shaker Heights, OH (city) Cuyahoga County	372	1.26
Cherry Hill, NJ (township) Camden County	876	1.25
Marblehead, MA (cdp) Essex County	254	1.25
Tarrytown, NY (village) Westchester County	136	1.23
Buffalo Grove, IL (village) Lake County	521	1.22
Wilmette, IL (village) Cook County	338	1.22
Aventura, FL (city) Miami-Dade County	297	1.18
Berkeley Heights, NJ (cdp) Union County	158	1.18
Boca Del Mar, FL (cdp) Palm Beach County	250	1.17
Clayton, MO (city) Saint Louis County	150	1.17
Birmingham, MI (city) Oakland County	224	1.16
Bedford, NY (town) Westchester County	210	1.16
Susquehanna, PA (township) Dauphin County	249	1.15
Englewood, NJ (city) Bergen County	298	1.14
Paradise Valley, AZ (town) Maricopa County	151	1.11
Ramapo, NY (town) Rockland County	1,193	1.10
Mendota Heights, MN (city) Dakota County	125	1.10
West Orange, NJ (cdp) Essex County	489	1.09
Sudbury, MA (town) Middlesex County	184	1.09
Lincolnwood, IL (village) Cook County	133	1.08
Dobbs Ferry, NY (village) Westchester County	114	1.07
Berkeley, CA (city) Alameda County	1,055	1.03
Upper Saint Clair, PA (cdp) Allegheny County	206	1.03
Dix Hills, NY (cdp) Suffolk County	267	1.02
North Hempstead, NY (town) Nassau County	2,251	1.01
Haverford, PA (township) Delaware County	488	1.01
Lexington, MA (cdp) Middlesex County	307	1.01
Clarkstown, NY (town) Rockland County	818	1.00
Northbrook, IL (village) Cook County	331	0.99
Maplewood, NJ (cdp) Essex County	237	0.99
Orange, CT (cdp) New Haven County	131	0.99
Morris, NJ (township) Morris County	213	0.98
New Rochelle, NY (city) Westchester County	703	0.97
West Bloomfield, MI (township) Oakland County	630	0.97
West Hempstead, NY (cdp) Nassau County	181	0.97
Rye, NY (town) Westchester County	423	0.96
Skokie, IL (village) Cook County	603	0.95
Olney, MD (cdp) Montgomery County	302	0.95
Takoma Park, MD (city) Montgomery County	163	0.95
Oceanside, NY (cdp) Nassau County	307	0.94
Ojus, FL (cdp) Miami-Dade County	157	0.94
Cambridge, MA (city) Middlesex County	942	0.93
Dunwoody, GA (cdp) De Kalb County	304	0.93
Winnetka, IL (village) Cook County	115	0.93
Lower Gwynedd, PA (township) Montgomery County	97	0.93
Voorhees, NJ (township) Camden County	259	0.92
Wilton, CT (town) Fairfield County	163	0.92
Solon, OH (city) Cuyahoga County	198	0.91
North Bellmore, NY (cdp) Nassau County	182	0.91
White Plains, NY (city) Westchester County	480	0.90
South Orange, NJ (cdp) Essex County	153	0.90
Rockville, MD (city) Montgomery County	422	0.89
Longmeadow, MA (cdp) Hampden County	139	0.89
Glendale, WI (city) Milwaukee County	119	0.89
Montclair, NJ (cdp) Essex County	340	0.87
Belmont, MA (cdp) Middlesex County	210	0.87
Culver City, CA (city) Los Angeles County	335	0.86
Mamaroneck, NY (village) Westchester County	162	0.86
Springfield, NJ (cdp) Union County	124	0.86
Ardmore, PA (cdp) Montgomery County	108	0.86
South Whitehall, PA (township) Lehigh County	153	0.85
Palo Alto, CA (city) Santa Clara County	491	0.84
Fair Lawn, NJ (borough) Bergen County	267	0.84
Druid Hills, GA (cdp) De Kalb County	107	0.84
East Brunswick, NJ (cdp) Middlesex County	387	0.83
Lakewood, NJ (township) Ocean County	493	0.82
Lower Makefield, PA (township) Bucks County	269	0.82
Rye, NY (city) Westchester County	122	0.82
Lower Moreland, PA (township) Montgomery County	93	0.82
Greenwood Village, CO (city) Arapahoe County	91	0.82
Falmouth, ME (town) Cumberland County	84	0.81
Long Beach, NY (city) Nassau County	283	0.80
West Freehold, NJ (cdp) Monmouth County	100	0.80
Evanston, IL (city) Cook County	585	0.79
Cherry Hill Mall, NJ (cdp) Camden County	106	0.79
Ithaca, NY (city) Tompkins County	225	0.78
Whitemarsh, PA (township) Montgomery County	130	0.78
Sandalfoot Cove, FL (cdp) Palm Beach County	129	0.78
Southfield, MI (township) Oakland County	112	0.78
Cortlandt, NY (town) Westchester County	295	0.77
Wantagh, NY (cdp) Nassau County	147	0.77
Lower Macungie, PA (township) Lehigh County	146	0.76
Amherst Center, MA (cdp) Hampshire County	130	0.76
Stony Brook, NY (cdp) Suffolk County	104	0.76
Piedmont, CA (city) Alameda County	83	0.76
Silver Spring, MD (cdp) Montgomery County	576	0.75
East Meadow, NY (cdp) Nassau County	283	0.75
Amherst, MA (town) Hampshire County	263	0.75
Wellesley, MA (cdp) Norfolk County	200	0.75
Ridgewood, NJ (village) Bergen County	188	0.75
Cutler, FL (cdp) Miami-Dade County	132	0.75
Wyckoff, NJ (cdp) Bergen County	123	0.75
Jefferson Valley-Yorktown, NY (cdp) Westchester County	110	0.74
Stanford, CA (cdp) Santa Clara County	98	0.74
Maitland, FL (city) Orange County	88	0.74

Notes: (cdp) census designated place; Refer to the Explanation of Data in the front of the book for more detailed information.

English

Top 150 Places Sorted by Number

(Based on all places, regardless of population)

Place	Number	%
Los Angeles, CA (city) Los Angeles County	127,632	3.45
New York, NY (city) New York City	124,821	1.56
Phoenix, AZ (city) Maricopa County	105,835	8.01
Houston, TX (city) Harris County	98,067	5.02
San Diego, CA (city) San Diego County	97,807	8.00
Dallas, TX (city) Dallas County	68,355	5.75
Seattle, WA (city) King County	63,869	11.34
Jacksonville, FL (special city) Duval County	62,798	8.54
Portland, OR (city) Multnomah County	61,707	11.66
Indianapolis, IN (special city) Marion County	60,562	7.74
Chicago, IL (city) Cook County	57,579	1.99
Austin, TX (city) Travis County	57,443	8.75
San Antonio, TX (city) Bexar County	57,099	4.99
Columbus, OH (city) Franklin County	55,990	7.87
Mesa, AZ (city) Maricopa County	54,554	13.73
San Jose, CA (city) Santa Clara County	50,448	5.64
Virginia Beach, VA (independent city) Virginia Beach city	50,343	11.84
Nashville-Davidson, TN (special city) Davidson County	49,163	9.01
San Francisco, CA (city) San Francisco County	47,221	6.08
Charlotte, NC (city) Mecklenburg County	46,020	8.49
Denver, CO (city) Denver County	45,841	8.27
Colorado Springs, CO (city) El Paso County	44,805	12.42
Philadelphia, PA (city) Philadelphia County	44,513	2.93
Oklahoma City, OK (city) Oklahoma County	43,049	8.51
Las Vegas, NV (city) Clark County	40,378	8.43
Albuquerque, NM (city) Bernalillo County	40,280	8.98
Tucson, AZ (city) Pima County	40,147	8.25
Tulsa, OK (city) Tulsa County	39,603	10.08
Salt Lake City, UT (city) Salt Lake County	37,879	20.88
Kansas City, MO (city) Jackson County	35,525	8.05
Fort Worth, TX (city) Tarrant County	34,747	6.49
Memphis, TN (city) Shelby County	34,030	5.24
Wichita, KS (city) Sedgwick County	33,544	9.75
Omaha, NE (city) Douglas County	33,296	8.53
Raleigh, NC (city) Wake County	33,044	11.95
Lexington-Fayette, KY (special city) Fayette County	32,399	12.44
Boise City, ID (city) Ada County	32,070	17.25
Provo, UT (city) Utah County	32,044	30.44
Arlington, TX (city) Tarrant County	28,838	8.67
Orem, UT (city) Utah County	28,796	34.15
Saint Petersburg, FL (city) Pinellas County	27,556	11.12
Sandy, UT (city) Salt Lake County	27,315	30.95
Scottsdale, AZ (city) Maricopa County	27,262	13.45
Brookhaven, NY (town) Suffolk County	26,741	5.97
Plano, TX (city) Collin County	26,546	11.94
Boston, MA (city) Suffolk County	26,384	4.48
Anchorage, AK (municipality) Anchorage Borough	26,123	10.04
Long Beach, CA (city) Los Angeles County	25,747	5.58
Sacramento, CA (city) Sacramento County	25,698	6.31
Washington, DC (city) District of Columbia	25,214	4.41
Lincoln, NE (city) Lancaster County	24,766	10.99
Atlanta, GA (city) Fulton County	24,686	5.93
Aurora, CO (city) Arapahoe County	24,340	8.82
Hempstead, NY (town) Nassau County	23,832	3.15
Spokane, WA (city) Spokane County	23,755	12.11
Minneapolis, MN (city) Hennepin County	23,356	6.11
Tampa, FL (city) Hillsborough County	23,319	7.68
Fresno, CA (city) Fresno County	23,236	5.44
West Valley City, UT (city) Salt Lake County	22,692	20.85
Huntington Beach, CA (city) Orange County	22,467	11.83
Greensboro, NC (city) Guilford County	21,970	9.84
Arlington, VA (cdp) Arlington County	21,855	11.54
Overland Park, KS (city) Johnson County	21,483	14.43
Baltimore, MD (independent city) Baltimore city	21,015	3.23
Chesapeake, VA (independent city) Chesapeake city	20,988	10.54
Reno, NV (city) Washoe County	20,590	11.40
Eugene, OR (city) Lane County	20,348	14.77
Madison, WI (city) Dane County	20,330	9.80
Henderson, NV (city) Clark County	20,088	11.41
Glendale, AZ (city) Maricopa County	20,069	9.18
Louisville, KY (city) Jefferson County	19,923	7.77
Riverside, CA (city) Riverside County	19,858	7.78
Lakewood, CO (city) Jefferson County	19,497	13.53
Toledo, OH (city) Lucas County	18,854	6.01
West Jordan, UT (city) Salt Lake County	18,772	27.52
Des Moines, IA (city) Polk County	18,465	9.29
Santa Clarita, CA (city) Los Angeles County	18,423	12.17
Lubbock, TX (city) Lubbock County	18,417	9.23
Santa Rosa, CA (city) Sonoma County	18,380	12.46
Cincinnati, OH (city) Hamilton County	18,016	5.45
Chandler, AZ (city) Maricopa County	18,004	10.21
Winston-Salem, NC (city) Forsyth County	17,913	9.66
Anaheim, CA (city) Orange County	17,891	5.47
Tempe, AZ (city) Maricopa County	17,735	11.19
Knoxville, TN (city) Knox County	17,674	10.18
Bakersfield, CA (city) Kern County	17,663	7.14
Tacoma, WA (city) Pierce County	17,406	9.01
Layton, UT (city) Davis County	17,067	29.09
Huntsville, AL (city) Madison County	17,031	10.79
Richmond, VA (independent city) Richmond city	16,881	8.53
Fort Collins, CO (city) Larimer County	16,836	14.21
New Orleans, LA (city) Orleans Parish	16,562	3.42
Springfield, MO (city) Greene County	16,555	10.90
Salem, OR (city) Marion County	16,443	12.03
Vancouver, WA (city) Clark County	16,374	11.43
Ogden, UT (city) Weber County	16,190	20.96
Arvada, CO (city) Jefferson County	16,157	15.76
Norfolk, VA (independent city) Norfolk city	16,152	6.89
Thousand Oaks, CA (city) Ventura County	16,126	13.82
Little Rock, AR (city) Pulaski County	16,116	8.78
Oakland, CA (city) Alameda County	15,991	4.00
Modesto, CA (city) Stanislaus County	15,931	8.41
Corpus Christi, TX (city) Nueces County	15,884	5.72
Garland, TX (city) Dallas County	15,829	7.33
Milwaukee, WI (city) Milwaukee County	15,742	2.64
Akron, OH (city) Summit County	15,720	7.24
El Paso, TX (city) El Paso County	15,719	2.79
Fort Wayne, IN (city) Allen County	15,638	7.59
Oceanside, CA (city) San Diego County	15,479	9.62
Gilbert, AZ (town) Maricopa County	15,391	14.00
Pittsburgh, PA (city) Allegheny County	15,352	4.59
Amarillo, TX (city) Potter County	15,309	8.82
Saint George, UT (city) Washington County	15,290	30.81
Saint Paul, MN (city) Ramsey County	15,261	5.31
Durham, NC (city) Durham County	15,222	8.13
Paradise, NV (cdp) Clark County	15,008	8.08
Taylorsville, UT (city) Salt Lake County	14,950	25.83
Newport News, VA (independent city) Newport News city	14,950	8.30
Independence, MO (city) Jackson County	14,823	13.09
Bountiful, UT (city) Davis County	14,764	35.67
Irvine, CA (city) Orange County	14,694	10.27
Orlando, FL (city) Orange County	14,663	7.88
Islip, NY (town) Suffolk County	14,592	4.52
Baton Rouge, LA (city) East Baton Rouge Parish	14,461	6.34
Warwick, RI (city) Kent County	14,450	16.84
Boulder, CO (city) Boulder County	14,243	15.07
Honolulu, HI (cdp) Honolulu County	14,124	3.80
Bellevue, WA (city) King County	13,993	12.82
Tallahassee, FL (city) Leon County	13,888	9.22
Mobile, AL (city) Mobile County	13,865	6.97
Grand Rapids, MI (city) Kent County	13,683	6.92
Montgomery, AL (city) Montgomery County	13,567	6.73
Ann Arbor, MI (city) Washtenaw County	13,521	11.85
Fremont, CA (city) Alameda County	13,514	6.64
Cary, NC (town) Wake County	13,498	14.28
Topeka, KS (city) Shawnee County	13,494	11.06
Alexandria, VA (independent city) Alexandria city	13,465	10.50
Saint Louis, MO (independent city) Saint Louis city	13,435	3.86
San Buenaventura, CA (city) Ventura County	13,417	13.26
Shreveport, LA (city) Caddo Parish	13,348	6.66
Springfield, IL (city) Sangamon County	13,288	11.84
Oyster Bay, NY (town) Nassau County	13,218	4.50
Cleveland, OH (city) Cuyahoga County	13,169	2.75
Clearwater, FL (city) Pinellas County	12,820	11.88
Irving, TX (city) Dallas County	12,800	6.68
Newport Beach, CA (city) Orange County	12,707	18.15
Rochester, NY (city) Monroe County	12,677	5.77
Naperville, IL (city) Du Page County	12,672	9.88
Simi Valley, CA (city) Ventura County	12,657	11.35
Mission Viejo, CA (city) Orange County	12,595	13.58

Notes: (cdp) census designated place; Refer to the Explanation of Data in the front of the book for more detailed information.

English

Top 150 Places Sorted by Percent

(Based on all places, regardless of population)

Place	Number	%
Point of Rocks, WY (cdp) Sweetwater County	20	100.00
Esterbrook, WY (cdp) Converse County	17	100.00
Dotyville, OK (cdp) Ottawa County	12	100.00
Sweeney Ranch, WY (cdp) Sweetwater County	6	100.00
Baker, MO (village) Stoddard County	2	100.00
Cottonwood, SD (town) Jackson County	2	100.00
Hanaford, IL (village) Franklin County	2	100.00
Rocky Ridge, UT (town) Juab County	393	94.47
Buels, VT (gore) Chittenden County	5	83.33
Lincoln, ME (plantation) Oxford County	26	76.47
Champ, MO (village) Saint Louis County	16	76.19
Cardwell, MT (cdp) Jefferson County	22	70.97
Miltonsburg, OH (village) Monroe County	14	70.00
Ophir, UT (town) Tooele County	11	68.75
Bayport, FL (cdp) Hernando County	16	66.67
Jamestown, OK (town) Rogers County	10	66.67
Stow, ME (town) Oxford County	162	65.85
Tropic, UT (town) Garfield County	352	65.06
Hildale, UT (city) Washington County	1,287	64.93
Osborn, ME (town) Hancock County	53	64.63
Garfield, ME (plantation) Aroostook County	45	61.64
Cannonville, UT (town) Garfield County	79	58.96
Lynndyl, UT (town) Millard County	79	58.96
Millsfield, NH (township) Coos County	11	57.89
Cedar, KS (city) Smith County	13	56.52
Susank, KS (city) Barton County	31	56.36
Laketown, UT (town) Rich County	112	56.28
Reed, ME (plantation) Aroostook County	126	56.00
Warm River, ID (city) Fremont County	5	55.56
Wentworth, NH (location) Coos County	27	55.10
Table Rock, WY (cdp) Sweetwater County	52	54.74
Palmyra, UT (cdp) Utah County	256	54.58
Thurmond, WV (town) Fayette County	6	54.55
Scipio, UT (town) Millard County	160	54.42
Oakfield, ME (town) Aroostook County	398	54.22
Shoshone, CA (cdp) Inyo County	45	53.57
Galt, IA (city) Wright County	15	53.57
Loraine, ND (city) Renville County	16	53.33
Ocean City, WA (cdp) Grays Harbor County	95	53.07
Lyman, UT (town) Wayne County	135	52.33
Orient, ME (town) Aroostook County	84	52.17
Evansville, AK (cdp) Yukon-Koyukuk Census Area	24	52.17
Wallsburg, UT (town) Wasatch County	160	52.12
New Harmony, UT (town) Washington County	100	52.08
Topsfield, ME (town) Washington County	120	51.72
Thoms Place, AK (cdp) Wrangell-Petersburg Census Area	15	51.72
Bloomington, ID (city) Bear Lake County	148	51.57
Canyondam, CA (cdp) Plumas County	18	51.43
Vanceboro, ME (town) Washington County	78	51.32
Mona, UT (town) Juab County	428	51.20
Huntley, WY (cdp) Goshen County	26	50.98
Haynesville, ME (town) Aroostook County	63	50.81
Carthage, ME (town) Franklin County	253	50.10
McKinnon, WY (cdp) Sweetwater County	29	50.00
Spring Garden, CA (cdp) Plumas County	13	50.00
Willowbrook, KS (city) Reno County	13	50.00
Laconia, IN (town) Harrison County	12	50.00
Van Tassell, WY (town) Niobrara County	7	50.00
Nora, NE (village) Nuckolls County	5	50.00
Ellsworth, NH (town) Grafton County	31	49.21
Woodlawn Heights, IN (town) Madison County	26	49.06
Escalante, UT (city) Garfield County	393	48.88
Powder River, WY (cdp) Natrona County	19	48.72
Tulsita, TX (cdp) Bee County	12	48.00
Bonanza, CO (town) Saguache County	11	47.83
Henefer, UT (town) Summit County	323	47.02
Alexander, ME (town) Washington County	229	47.02
Swans Island, ME (town) Hancock County	158	46.88
Hampden, MN (township) Kittson County	15	46.88
Halibut Cove, AK (cdp) Kenai Peninsula Borough	28	46.67
Meyers Chuck, AK (cdp) Prince of Wales-Outer Ketchikan C.A.	7	46.67
Holden, UT (town) Millard County	183	46.56
Pinesdale, MT (town) Ravalli County	348	46.52
Vineyard, UT (town) Utah County	89	46.35
Oak City, UT (town) Millard County	305	46.28
Lake Shore, UT (cdp) Utah County	347	46.27
Waite, ME (town) Washington County	55	45.83
Deblois, ME (town) Washington County	16	45.71
Orleans, VT (village) Orleans County	374	45.55
Glastenbury, VT (town) Bennington County	5	45.45
Henrieville, UT (town) Garfield County	79	45.40
Talmadge, ME (town) Washington County	29	45.31
Grandfather, NC (village) Avery County	37	45.12
Matinicus Isle, ME (plantation) Knox County	23	45.10
Leamington, UT (town) Millard County	97	44.70
Spring Lake, UT (cdp) Utah County	186	44.60
Smoot, WY (cdp) Lincoln County	82	44.57
Cache, UT (cdp) Cache County	8	44.44
Kicking Horse, MT (cdp) Lake County	35	44.30
Dennysville, ME (town) Washington County	143	43.87
Cranberry Isles, ME (town) Hancock County	56	43.75
Atlantic City, WY (cdp) Fremont County	14	43.75
Clifton, ID (city) Franklin County	99	43.61
Hyde Park, UT (city) Cache County	1,281	43.47
Kanosh, UT (town) Millard County	227	43.40
Highland, UT (city) Utah County	3,435	43.12
Short Pump, VA (cdp) Henrico County	49	42.98
Riverside, UT (cdp) Box Elder County	290	42.90
Port Clarence, AK (cdp) Nome Census Area	9	42.86
Bucks Lake, CA (cdp) Plumas County	6	42.86
Nephi, UT (city) Juab County	2,054	42.76
Farmington, UT (city) Davis County	5,217	42.74
Centerville, UT (city) Davis County	6,138	42.71
Huntsville, UT (town) Weber County	271	42.41
Fruit Heights, UT (city) Davis County	1,986	42.39
Harrington, ME (town) Washington County	373	42.29
Fayette, UT (town) Sanpete County	86	41.95
Gilead, ME (town) Oxford County	70	41.92
Peck, ID (city) Nez Perce County	92	41.82
Dayton, ID (city) Franklin County	205	41.75
Pointe Aux Barques, MI (township) Huron County	5	41.67
Amity, ME (town) Aroostook County	82	41.62
Oceanside, OR (cdp) Tillamook County	146	41.60
Antimony, UT (town) Garfield County	52	41.60
Lake View, ME (plantation) Piscataquis County	12	41.38
Strafford, VT (town) Orange County	432	41.34
Dames Quarter, MD (cdp) Somerset County	96	41.20
Weston, ID (city) Franklin County	142	41.16
Sandwich, NH (town) Carroll County	529	41.14
Glendale, UT (town) Kane County	137	41.02
Crawford, ME (town) Washington County	41	41.00
Kaysville, UT (city) Davis County	8,488	40.99
Kittery Point, ME (cdp) York County	456	40.79
Elberta, UT (cdp) Utah County	88	40.74
Dyer Brook, ME (town) Aroostook County	81	40.70
Meadow, UT (town) Millard County	87	40.65
Panguitch, UT (city) Garfield County	655	40.63
Douglas, OK (town) Garfield County	15	40.54
Milbridge, ME (town) Washington County	518	40.50
Great Pond, ME (town) Hancock County	17	40.48
Peter, UT (cdp) Cache County	89	40.45
Crystal, ME (town) Aroostook County	113	40.36
Enterprise, UT (city) Washington County	519	40.17
Randolph, UT (city) Rich County	190	40.17
Newdale, ID (city) Fremont County	160	40.10
Annabella, UT (town) Sevier County	238	40.00
Aurora, ME (town) Hancock County	44	40.00
Bancroft, ME (town) Aroostook County	16	40.00
Opal, WY (town) Lincoln County	37	39.78
North Haven, ME (town) Knox County	154	39.69
Neola, UT (cdp) Duchesne County	210	39.62
Fielding, UT (town) Box Elder County	187	39.62
Cedar Hills, UT (town) Utah County	1,226	39.57
Caratunk, ME (town) Somerset County	49	39.52
Gosnold, MA (town) Dukes County	32	39.51
Marriott-Slaterville, UT (city) Weber County	587	39.42
Paris, ID (city) Bear Lake County	221	39.39
Carroll, ME (plantation) Penobscot County	50	39.37
Franconia, NH (town) Grafton County	362	39.26
Minersville, UT (town) Beaver County	318	39.26

Notes: (cdp) census designated place; Refer to the Explanation of Data in the front of the book for more detailed information.

English

Top 150 Places Sorted by Percent

(Based on places with populations of 10,000 or more)

Place	Number	%
Farmington, UT (city) Davis County	5,217	42.74
Centerville, UT (city) Davis County	6,138	42.71
Kaysville, UT (city) Davis County	8,488	40.99
East Millcreek, UT (cdp) Salt Lake County	8,210	38.36
South Jordan, UT (city) Salt Lake County	10,774	36.57
Canyon Rim, UT (cdp) Salt Lake County	3,844	36.37
Holladay, UT (city) Salt Lake County	5,285	36.32
North Ogden, UT (city) Weber County	5,344	35.79
Pleasant Grove, UT (city) Utah County	8,406	35.71
Bountiful, UT (city) Davis County	14,764	35.67
American Fork, UT (city) Utah County	7,753	35.36
Lehi, UT (city) Utah County	6,596	34.44
Orem, UT (city) Utah County	28,796	34.15
Springville, UT (city) Utah County	6,915	33.70
Spanish Fork, UT (city) Utah County	6,623	32.67
South Ogden, UT (city) Weber County	4,657	32.30
Brigham City, UT (city) Box Elder County	5,576	32.04
Murray, UT (city) Salt Lake County	10,768	31.75
Cottonwood West, UT (cdp) Salt Lake County	5,867	31.53
Riverton, UT (city) Salt Lake County	7,846	31.21
Sandy, UT (city) Salt Lake County	27,315	30.95
Saint George, UT (city) Washington County	15,290	30.81
Cottonwood Heights, UT (cdp) Salt Lake County	8,428	30.79
Cedar City, UT (city) Iron County	6,290	30.57
Provo, UT (city) Utah County	32,044	30.44
Payson, UT (city) Utah County	3,804	29.66
Layton, UT (city) Davis County	17,067	29.09
Logan, UT (city) Cache County	12,176	28.50
Rexburg, ID (city) Madison County	4,890	28.43
Draper, UT (city) Salt Lake County	7,200	28.31
Kennebunk, ME (town) York County	2,935	28.02
Mountain Brook, AL (city) Jefferson County	5,864	27.95
West Jordan, UT (city) Salt Lake County	18,772	27.52
Evanston, WY (city) Uinta County	3,145	27.51
Roy, UT (city) Weber County	8,817	26.93
Clinton, UT (city) Davis County	3,324	26.26
Taylorsville, UT (city) Salt Lake County	14,950	25.83
Tooele, UT (city) Tooele County	5,786	25.71
Brewster, MA (town) Barnstable County	2,594	25.70
Falmouth, ME (town) Cumberland County	2,635	25.56
Harwich, MA (town) Barnstable County	3,159	25.50
York, ME (town) York County	3,272	25.46
Windham, ME (town) Cumberland County	3,753	25.18
Millcreek, UT (cdp) Salt Lake County	7,657	25.08
Green Valley, AZ (cdp) Pima County	4,342	25.05
Poquoson, VA (independent city) Poquoson city	2,786	24.09
Scarborough, ME (town) Cumberland County	4,080	24.04
Exeter, NH (town) Rockingham County	3,370	23.97
Saint Simons, GA (cdp) Glynn County	3,196	23.77
Concord, MA (town) Middlesex County	4,016	23.63
Oquirrh, UT (cdp) Salt Lake County	2,411	23.27
Idaho Falls, ID (city) Bonneville County	11,718	23.21
Gorham, ME (town) Cumberland County	3,245	22.95
Ipswich, MA (town) Essex County	2,956	22.76
Magna, UT (cdp) Salt Lake County	5,145	22.59
Midvale, UT (city) Salt Lake County	6,102	22.57
Bainbridge Island, WA (city) Kitsap County	4,548	22.40
Pocatello, ID (city) Bannock County	11,533	22.37
Clearfield, UT (city) Davis County	5,787	22.33
Rehoboth, MA (town) Bristol County	2,257	22.19
Tuckahoe, VA (cdp) Henrico County	9,532	22.07
Bon Air, VA (cdp) Chesterfield County	3,569	22.04
South Portland, ME (city) Cumberland County	5,123	21.96
Blackfoot, ID (city) Bingham County	2,283	21.88
North Kingstown, RI (town) Washington County	5,702	21.66
Darien, CT (cdp) Fairfield County	4,239	21.62
Amherst, NH (town) Hillsborough County	2,318	21.52
Duxbury, MA (town) Plymouth County	3,063	21.50
Montecito, CA (cdp) Santa Barbara County	2,166	21.47
Brattleboro, VT (town) Windham County	2,567	21.38
Brentwood, TN (city) Williamson County	5,085	21.34
Barrington, RI (town) Bristol County	3,587	21.33
Marblehead, MA (cdp) Essex County	4,326	21.23
University Park, TX (city) Dallas County	4,954	21.22
Hanover, NH (town) Grafton County	2,293	21.13
Ogden, UT (city) Weber County	16,190	20.96
Ledyard, CT (town) New London County	3,076	20.95
Salt Lake City, UT (city) Salt Lake County	37,879	20.88
West Valley City, UT (city) Salt Lake County	22,692	20.85
Baywood-Los Osos, CA (cdp) San Luis Obispo County	2,918	20.62
Greater Sun Center, FL (cdp) Hillsborough County	3,336	20.48
Hampton, NH (town) Rockingham County	3,059	20.48
Parma, NY (town) Monroe County	3,027	20.40
Sun City West, AZ (cdp) Maricopa County	5,333	20.31
Palos Verdes Estates, CA (city) Los Angeles County	2,708	20.30
Granby, CT (town) Hartford County	2,100	20.30
Middleborough, MA (town) Plymouth County	4,037	20.24
Farragut, TN (town) Knox County	3,605	20.16
Dryden, NY (town) Tompkins County	2,752	20.09
Sandwich, MA (town) Barnstable County	4,029	20.00
New Canaan, CT (town) Fairfield County	3,874	19.97
Green River, WY (city) Sweetwater County	2,349	19.92
Vestavia Hills, AL (city) Jefferson County	4,944	19.89
Sullivan, NY (town) Madison County	2,979	19.87
Durham, NH (town) Strafford County	2,511	19.83
Piedmont, CA (city) Alameda County	2,170	19.81
Rochester, NH (city) Strafford County	5,635	19.80
Lafayette, CA (city) Contra Costa County	4,640	19.78
Wolf Trap, VA (cdp) Fairfax County	2,741	19.75
Kearns, UT (cdp) Salt Lake County	6,630	19.72
Fort Hunt, VA (cdp) Fairfax County	2,523	19.67
Concord, NH (city) Merrimack County	7,982	19.62
Dennis, MA (town) Barnstable County	3,133	19.61
Prairie Village, KS (city) Johnson County	4,316	19.58
Lysander, NY (town) Onondaga County	3,756	19.48
Cottage Lake, WA (cdp) King County	4,713	19.40
Hartford, VT (town) Windsor County	2,007	19.36
Portsmouth, NH (city) Rockingham County	4,018	19.33
Englewood, FL (cdp) Sarasota County	3,140	19.32
Brunswick, ME (town) Cumberland County	4,089	19.31
Haddonfield, NJ (borough) Camden County	2,251	19.31
Waterville, ME (city) Kennebec County	3,010	19.29
Scituate, RI (town) Providence County	1,989	19.27
Upper Arlington, OH (city) Franklin County	6,462	19.23
Yarmouth, MA (town) Barnstable County	4,759	19.18
East Greenwich, RI (town) Kent County	2,484	19.18
Portland, ME (city) Cumberland County	12,320	19.17
Twin Falls, ID (city) Twin Falls County	6,529	19.11
Pepperell, MA (town) Middlesex County	2,128	19.10
Newburyport, MA (city) Essex County	3,291	19.09
Mill Valley, CA (city) Marin County	2,589	19.09
Farmington, NY (town) Ontario County	2,020	19.08
Venice, FL (city) Sarasota County	3,402	19.06
Madison, CT (town) New Haven County	3,402	19.05
Worthington, OH (city) Franklin County	2,728	19.05
Southglenn, CO (cdp) Arapahoe County	8,285	19.04
East Grand Rapids, MI (city) Kent County	2,051	19.02
Sun Lakes, AZ (cdp) Maricopa County	2,263	18.94
Canandaigua, NY (city) Ontario County	2,131	18.92
Westbrook, ME (city) Cumberland County	3,051	18.90
West University Place, TX (city) Harris County	2,686	18.90
Narragansett, RI (town) Washington County	3,091	18.89
Masonboro, NC (cdp) New Hanover County	2,259	18.89
Germantown, TN (city) Shelby County	7,013	18.81
East Goshen, PA (township) Chester County	3,163	18.80
Bella Vista, AR (cdp) Benton County	3,091	18.80
Vashon, WA (cdp) King County	1,901	18.78
Stonington, CT (town) New London County	3,360	18.76
Dover, NH (city) Strafford County	5,041	18.75
Carver, MA (town) Plymouth County	2,092	18.74
Fairhope, AL (city) Baldwin County	2,283	18.69
Naples, FL (city) Collier County	3,920	18.68
Old Saybrook, CT (town) Middlesex County	1,936	18.67
Bangor, ME (city) Penobscot County	5,872	18.66
South Kingstown, RI (town) Washington County	5,206	18.65
Beverly, MA (city) Essex County	7,429	18.64
Greenwood Village, CO (city) Arapahoe County	2,060	18.61
Coto de Caza, CA (cdp) Orange County	2,420	18.53
Eagle, ID (city) Ada County	2,065	18.53
Portsmouth, RI (town) Newport County	3,173	18.50

Notes: (cdp) census designated place; Refer to the Explanation of Data in the front of the book for more detailed information.

Estonian

Top 150 Places Sorted by Number

(Based on all places, regardless of population)

Place	Number	%
New York, NY (city) New York City	883	0.01
Los Angeles, CA (city) Los Angeles County	492	0.01
Chicago, IL (city) Cook County	233	0.01
Seattle, WA (city) King County	228	0.04
Hempstead, NY (town) Nassau County	203	0.03
Brookhaven, NY (town) Suffolk County	161	0.04
Lakewood, NJ (township) Ocean County	160	0.27
San Francisco, CA (city) San Francisco County	155	0.02
Baltimore, MD (independent city) Baltimore city	145	0.02
Portland, OR (city) Multnomah County	143	0.03
Arlington, VA (cdp) Arlington County	133	0.07
Jackson, NJ (township) Ocean County	126	0.29
Boston, MA (city) Suffolk County	112	0.02
San Diego, CA (city) San Diego County	109	0.01
Washington, DC (city) District of Columbia	100	0.02
Bellevue, WA (city) King County	93	0.09
Aspen Hill, MD (cdp) Montgomery County	89	0.18
Palo Alto, CA (city) Santa Clara County	87	0.15
Minneapolis, MN (city) Hennepin County	79	0.02
West Orange, NJ (cdp) Essex County	78	0.17
Old Bridge, NJ (township) Middlesex County	74	0.12
Nashville-Davidson, TN (special city) Davidson County	71	0.01
Everett, WA (city) Snohomish County	70	0.08
Indianapolis, IN (special city) Marion County	69	0.01
Clarence, NY (town) Erie County	62	0.24
Cary, NC (town) Wake County	62	0.07
Elkridge, MD (cdp) Howard County	60	0.27
Perinton, NY (town) Monroe County	60	0.13
Lawrence, KS (city) Douglas County	58	0.07
Medford, MA (city) Middlesex County	57	0.10
Amherst, NY (town) Erie County	57	0.05
Oyster Bay, NY (town) Nassau County	56	0.02
Houston, TX (city) Harris County	56	0.00
Crestwood, IL (village) Cook County	55	0.49
Renton, WA (city) King County	55	0.11
Towson, MD (cdp) Baltimore County	55	0.11
Philadelphia, PA (city) Philadelphia County	55	0.00
Phoenix, AZ (city) Maricopa County	55	0.00
Edison, NJ (cdp) Middlesex County	53	0.05
Tulsa, OK (city) Tulsa County	53	0.01
Middletown, CT (city) Middlesex County	51	0.12
Garden Home-Whitford, OR (cdp) Washington County	50	0.72
Wellington, FL (village) Palm Beach County	49	0.13
North Hempstead, NY (town) Nassau County	49	0.02
Albuquerque, NM (city) Bernalillo County	49	0.01
Charlotte, NC (city) Mecklenburg County	48	0.01
Islip, NY (town) Suffolk County	48	0.01
Plymouth, MA (town) Plymouth County	47	0.09
Scottsdale, AZ (city) Maricopa County	47	0.02
Arlington Heights, IL (village) Cook County	46	0.06
Bellflower, CA (city) Los Angeles County	46	0.06
Clarkstown, NY (town) Rockland County	46	0.06
Richmond, VA (independent city) Richmond city	46	0.02
Kent, WA (city) King County	45	0.06
Naperville, IL (city) Du Page County	45	0.04
Babylon, NY (town) Suffolk County	45	0.02
Huntington, NY (town) Suffolk County	45	0.02
Hillsborough, CA (town) San Mateo County	44	0.41
Broadview Heights, OH (city) Cuyahoga County	44	0.28
East Goshen, PA (township) Chester County	44	0.26
Glen Ellyn, IL (village) Du Page County	44	0.16
Vineland, NJ (city) Cumberland County	44	0.08
Columbia, MD (cdp) Howard County	44	0.05
Dania Beach, FL (city) Broward County	43	0.21
Summit, NJ (city) Union County	43	0.20
Kirkland, WA (city) King County	43	0.10
Redwood City, CA (city) San Mateo County	43	0.06
Denver, CO (city) Denver County	42	0.01
Bernards, NJ (township) Somerset County	41	0.17
Hackensack, NJ (city) Bergen County	41	0.10
Berkeley, CA (city) Alameda County	41	0.04
Fairfield, CA (city) Solano County	41	0.04
Alexandria, VA (independent city) Alexandria city	41	0.03
Saint Louis Park, MN (city) Hennepin County	40	0.09
Farmington Hills, MI (city) Oakland County	40	0.05
Santa Monica, CA (city) Los Angeles County	40	0.05
Jamestown, RI (town) Newport County	39	0.69
Beverly Hills, CA (city) Los Angeles County	39	0.12
Lakewood, OH (city) Cuyahoga County	39	0.07
Tacoma, WA (city) Pierce County	39	0.02
Waynesboro, VA (independent city) Waynesboro city	38	0.19
McLean, VA (cdp) Fairfax County	38	0.10
Cambridge, MA (city) Middlesex County	38	0.04
Vancouver, WA (city) Clark County	38	0.03
Orlando, FL (city) Orange County	38	0.02
Lomita, CA (city) Los Angeles County	37	0.19
Franklin, MA (city) Norfolk County	37	0.13
Oceanside, NY (cdp) Nassau County	37	0.11
Bethesda, MD (cdp) Montgomery County	37	0.07
Irvine, CA (city) Orange County	37	0.03
Aurora, CO (city) Arapahoe County	37	0.01
Upper Deerfield, NJ (township) Cumberland County	36	0.48
Brunswick, NY (town) Rensselaer County	36	0.31
Orangetown, NY (town) Rockland County	36	0.08
Dallas, TX (city) Dallas County	36	0.00
Salem, NJ (city) Salem County	35	0.60
Westwood, NJ (borough) Bergen County	35	0.32
Powder Springs, GA (city) Cobb County	35	0.27
Grayslake, IL (village) Lake County	35	0.19
North Kingstown, RI (town) Washington County	35	0.13
Washington, NJ (township) Gloucester County	35	0.07
Oakland, CA (city) Alameda County	35	0.01
San Jose, CA (city) Santa Clara County	35	0.00
College Station, TX (city) Brazos County	34	0.05
Parma, OH (city) Cuyahoga County	34	0.04
Erie, PA (city) Erie County	34	0.03
Wetherington, OH (cdp) Butler County	33	3.24
Denville, NJ (township) Morris County	33	0.21
Burlingame, CA (city) San Mateo County	33	0.12
Deer Park, NY (cdp) Suffolk County	33	0.12
Shrewsbury, MA (town) Worcester County	33	0.10
Newport Beach, CA (city) Orange County	33	0.05
Tonawanda, NY (town) Erie County	33	0.04
Warwick, RI (city) Kent County	33	0.04
Smithtown, NY (town) Suffolk County	33	0.03
Eugene, OR (city) Lane County	33	0.02
Paradise, NV (cdp) Clark County	33	0.02
Tappan, NY (cdp) Rockland County	32	0.48
Ridley Park, PA (borough) Delaware County	32	0.44
Laguna Beach, CA (city) Orange County	32	0.14
Bay Shore, NY (cdp) Suffolk County	32	0.13
Amherst, MA (town) Hampshire County	32	0.09
Novato, CA (city) Marin County	32	0.07
Potomac, MD (cdp) Montgomery County	32	0.07
Ann Arbor, MI (city) Washtenaw County	32	0.03
Warren, MI (city) Macomb County	32	0.02
Worcester, MA (city) Worcester County	32	0.02
Newport, ME (town) Penobscot County	31	1.03
Danielson, CT (borough) Windham County	31	0.74
Marshfield, MO (city) Webster County	31	0.53
Killingly, CT (town) Windham County	31	0.19
Uwchlan, PA (township) Chester County	31	0.19
De Witt, NY (town) Onondaga County	31	0.13
Parsippany-Troy Hills, NJ (township) Morris County	31	0.06
Yorba Linda, CA (city) Orange County	31	0.05
Schaumburg, IL (village) Cook County	31	0.04
Pasadena, CA (city) Los Angeles County	31	0.02
Milwaukee, WI (city) Milwaukee County	31	0.01
Waterford, CA (city) Stanislaus County	30	0.44
Scio, MI (township) Washtenaw County	30	0.19
East Hampton, NY (town) Suffolk County	30	0.15
Lynbrook, NY (village) Nassau County	30	0.15
Howell, NJ (township) Monmouth County	30	0.06
Bethlehem, PA (city) Northampton County	30	0.04
Evanston, IL (city) Cook County	30	0.04
Somerville, MA (city) Middlesex County	30	0.04
Provo, UT (city) Utah County	30	0.03
Garden Grove, CA (city) Orange County	30	0.02
Echelon, NJ (cdp) Camden County	29	0.28
Brooklyn Park, MD (cdp) Anne Arundel County	29	0.27

Notes: (cdp) census designated place; Refer to the Explanation of Data in the front of the book for more detailed information.

Estonian

Top 150 Places Sorted by Percent

(Based on all places, regardless of population)

Place	Number	%
Edison, WA (cdp) Skagit County	8	5.63
Willimantic, ME (town) Piscataquis County	7	5.04
Darwin, CA (cdp) Inyo County	3	4.35
Wetherington, OH (cdp) Butler County	33	3.24
Rudyard, MT (cdp) Hill County	6	2.21
Wheatfield, IN (town) Jasper County	15	1.92
Cantwell, AK (cdp) Yukon-Koyukuk Census Area	4	1.64
Preston, NY (town) Chenango County	13	1.36
North Granby, CT (cdp) Hartford County	23	1.33
Scotland, CT (town) Windham County	18	1.16
Garfield, WI (town) Jackson County	6	1.11
Shelter Island, NY (town) Suffolk County	24	1.08
Newport, ME (town) Penobscot County	31	1.03
Almena, WI (village) Barron County	7	1.00
Paddock, MN (township) Otter Tail County	3	0.97
East Penn, PA (township) Carbon County	23	0.93
Hallowell, ME (city) Kennebec County	23	0.93
Sauk City, WI (village) Sauk County	27	0.91
Sunol, CA (cdp) Alameda County	12	0.90
Hamilton, PA (township) Tioga County	4	0.90
Monmouth Junction, NJ (cdp) Middlesex County	21	0.87
Chamois, MO (city) Osage County	4	0.85
Tenhassen, MN (township) Martin County	2	0.82
Russell, MN (city) Lyon County	3	0.79
Chester, MT (town) Liberty County	7	0.78
Rockford, IA (city) Floyd County	7	0.76
Danielson, CT (borough) Windham County	31	0.74
Helvetia, WI (town) Waupaca County	5	0.74
Verona, ME (town) Hancock County	4	0.74
Garden Home-Whitford, OR (cdp) Washington County	50	0.72
Sherwood, OH (cdp) Hamilton County	28	0.72
Wakeman, OH (village) Huron County	7	0.72
Jamestown, RI (town) Newport County	39	0.69
Northlakes, NC (cdp) Caldwell County	9	0.69
Cohoctah, MI (township) Livingston County	24	0.68
Greenport West, NY (cdp) Suffolk County	11	0.66
Nelson, NH (town) Cheshire County	4	0.65
Greenwood Lake, NY (village) Orange County	21	0.63
Arendahl, MN (township) Fillmore County	2	0.63
Anson, ME (town) Somerset County	16	0.62
Shinnecock Hills, NY (cdp) Suffolk County	9	0.61
Salem, NJ (city) Salem County	35	0.60
Warren Park, IN (town) Marion County	10	0.60
Windham, VT (town) Windham County	2	0.60
Medina, ND (city) Stutsman County	2	0.59
Deerfield, NJ (township) Cumberland County	17	0.58
Chester, CA (cdp) Plumas County	13	0.58
Bellemeade, KY (city) Jefferson County	5	0.58
Fairview, MT (town) Richland County	4	0.58
Girard, MN (township) Otter Tail County	4	0.58
Somerset, NY (town) Niagara County	16	0.56
Millbrook, NY (village) Dutchess County	8	0.56
Fair Haven, NY (village) Cayuga County	5	0.56
Cibolo, TX (city) Guadalupe County	17	0.54
Freedom, NH (town) Carroll County	7	0.54
Marshfield, MO (city) Webster County	31	0.53
Third Lake, IL (village) Lake County	7	0.52
Rock Falls, WI (town) Lincoln County	3	0.52
West Side Highway, WA (cdp) Cowlitz County	23	0.51
Shelter Island Heights, NY (cdp) Suffolk County	5	0.51
Day Valley, CA (cdp) Santa Cruz County	18	0.50
Fox Island, WA (cdp) Pierce County	14	0.50
Mason, TX (city) Mason County	11	0.50
Crestwood, IL (village) Cook County	55	0.49
Dorset, VT (town) Bennington County	10	0.49
Upper Deerfield, NJ (township) Cumberland County	36	0.48
Tappan, NY (cdp) Rockland County	32	0.48
Chenoweth, OR (cdp) Wasco County	16	0.48
Sag Harbor, NY (village) Suffolk County	11	0.48
Cadiz, WI (town) Green County	4	0.48
Rancho Viejo, TX (town) Cameron County	8	0.46
Madbury, NH (town) Strafford County	7	0.46
Watchung, NJ (borough) Somerset County	25	0.45
Yaphank, NY (cdp) Suffolk County	23	0.45
Lake Pocotopaug, CT (cdp) Middlesex County	14	0.45
Lyme, CT (town) New London County	9	0.45
Cross Mountain, TX (cdp) Bexar County	7	0.45
Ridley Park, PA (borough) Delaware County	32	0.44
Waterford, CA (city) Stanislaus County	30	0.44
Meridianville, AL (cdp) Madison County	18	0.44
Maineville, OH (village) Warren County	4	0.44
Fleming, CO (town) Logan County	2	0.44
Mahoning, PA (township) Carbon County	17	0.43
Blaine, WA (city) Whatcom County	16	0.43
Dacono, CO (city) Weld County	13	0.43
Riverton, NJ (borough) Burlington County	12	0.43
Beechwood Village, KY (city) Jefferson County	5	0.43
Lionville-Marchwood, PA (cdp) Chester County	26	0.42
Spring Lake Heights, NJ (borough) Monmouth County	22	0.42
Boylston, MA (town) Worcester County	17	0.42
Lawrenceville, NJ (cdp) Mercer County	17	0.42
Cornwall, CT (town) Litchfield County	6	0.42
Bentleyville, OH (village) Cuyahoga County	4	0.42
Hillsborough, CA (town) San Mateo County	44	0.41
Lebanon, CT (town) New London County	28	0.41
Churchville, PA (cdp) Bucks County	18	0.41
Del Mar, CA (city) San Diego County	18	0.41
Newtown, OH (village) Hamilton County	10	0.41
Sylva, NC (town) Jackson County	10	0.41
Lake Mills, IA (city) Winnebago County	9	0.41
Sheldon, VT (town) Franklin County	8	0.41
Fox Chapel, PA (borough) Allegheny County	22	0.40
Harris Hill, NY (cdp) Erie County	19	0.40
Andover, CT (town) Tolland County	12	0.40
Medina, WA (city) King County	12	0.40
Holly Grove, AR (city) Monroe County	3	0.40
Cabot, VT (village) Washington County	1	0.40
Laurel Lake, NJ (cdp) Cumberland County	11	0.39
New Egypt, NJ (cdp) Ocean County	10	0.39
Brownsboro, TX (city) Henderson County	3	0.39
Columbia, CT (town) Tolland County	19	0.38
Mountain Lakes, NJ (borough) Morris County	16	0.38
Ashley, PA (borough) Luzerne County	11	0.38
Empire, WI (town) Fond du Lac County	10	0.38
North Hero, VT (town) Grand Isle County	3	0.38
Demarest, NJ (borough) Bergen County	18	0.37
Downe, NJ (township) Cumberland County	6	0.37
Harrisville, NH (town) Cheshire County	4	0.37
Preston, PA (township) Wayne County	4	0.37
Brooklyn, CT (town) Windham County	26	0.36
Ocean, NJ (township) Ocean County	23	0.36
Lindale, GA (cdp) Floyd County	15	0.36
Mullan, ID (city) Shoshone County	3	0.36
Dahlonega, GA (city) Lumpkin County	13	0.35
Oxoboxo River, CT (cdp) New London County	10	0.35
Flat Rock, NC (village) Henderson County	9	0.35
Tracy, MN (city) Lyon County	8	0.35
East Palatka, FL (cdp) Putnam County	6	0.35
Republic, MI (township) Marquette County	4	0.35
Hamilton, VA (town) Loudoun County	2	0.35
Watson, PA (township) Warren County	2	0.35
Barrington Hills, IL (village) Cook County	14	0.34
Colstrip, MT (city) Rosebud County	8	0.34
Englishtown, NJ (borough) Monmouth County	6	0.34
Lowell, MI (township) Kent County	17	0.33
Lordstown, OH (village) Trumbull County	12	0.33
Red Hook, NY (village) Dutchess County	6	0.33
Round Lake, NY (village) Saratoga County	2	0.33
Westwood, NJ (borough) Bergen County	35	0.32
Lower Grand Lagoon, FL (cdp) Bay County	13	0.32
Orting, WA (city) Pierce County	12	0.32
Caroline, NY (town) Tompkins County	9	0.32
Birch Lake, MN (township) Cass County	2	0.32
Minnesott Beach, NC (town) Pamlico County	1	0.32
Brunswick, NY (town) Rensselaer County	36	0.31
Washington Township, NJ (cdp) Bergen County	28	0.31
Glencoe, IL (village) Cook County	27	0.31
New Hanover, PA (township) Montgomery County	23	0.31
Hudson, WI (town) Saint Croix County	20	0.31
Groveland, MA (town) Essex County	19	0.31

Notes: (cdp) census designated place; Refer to the Explanation of Data in the front of the book for more detailed information.

Estonian

Top 150 Places Sorted by Percent

(Based on places with populations of 10,000 or more)

Place	Number	%
Crestwood, IL (village) Cook County	55	0.49
Hillsborough, CA (town) San Mateo County	44	0.41
Westwood, NJ (borough) Bergen County	35	0.32
Brunswick, NY (town) Rensselaer County	36	0.31
Jackson, NJ (township) Ocean County	126	0.29
Broadview Heights, OH (city) Cuyahoga County	44	0.28
Echelon, NJ (cdp) Camden County	29	0.28
Lakewood, NJ (township) Ocean County	160	0.27
Elkridge, MD (cdp) Howard County	60	0.27
Powder Springs, GA (city) Cobb County	35	0.27
Brooklyn Park, MD (cdp) Anne Arundel County	29	0.27
East Goshen, PA (township) Chester County	44	0.26
Old Saybrook, CT (town) Middlesex County	27	0.26
Rochester, MI (city) Oakland County	26	0.25
Washington, NJ (township) Mercer County	26	0.25
Clarence, NY (town) Erie County	62	0.24
Oakland, NJ (borough) Bergen County	29	0.23
Schodack, NY (town) Rensselaer County	29	0.23
Vashon, WA (cdp) King County	23	0.23
Burr Ridge, IL (village) Du Page County	23	0.22
Granby, CT (town) Hartford County	23	0.22
Dania Beach, FL (city) Broward County	43	0.21
Denville, NJ (township) Morris County	33	0.21
Troutdale, OR (city) Multnomah County	28	0.21
Capitola, CA (city) Santa Cruz County	21	0.21
Summit, NJ (city) Union County	43	0.20
Half Moon Bay, CA (city) San Mateo County	24	0.20
Waynesboro, VA (independent city) Waynesboro city	38	0.19
Lomita, CA (city) Los Angeles County	37	0.19
Grayslake, IL (village) Lake County	35	0.19
Killingly, CT (town) Windham County	31	0.19
Uwchlan, PA (township) Chester County	31	0.19
Scio, MI (township) Washtenaw County	30	0.19
Holden, MA (town) Worcester County	29	0.19
West Caldwell, NJ (cdp) Essex County	21	0.19
Aspen Hill, MD (cdp) Montgomery County	89	0.18
Plainfield, CT (town) Windham County	27	0.18
Westport, MA (town) Bristol County	26	0.18
West Orange, NJ (cdp) Essex County	78	0.17
Bernards, NJ (township) Somerset County	41	0.17
Jefferson Valley-Yorktown, NY (cdp) Westchester County	25	0.17
Tamalpais-Homestead Valley, CA (cdp) Marin County	18	0.17
Glen Ellyn, IL (village) Du Page County	44	0.16
Wyckoff, NJ (cdp) Bergen County	26	0.16
La Grange, IL (village) Cook County	25	0.16
Lansdale, PA (borough) Montgomery County	25	0.16
Sunny Isles Beach, FL (city) Miami-Dade County	25	0.16
New Fairfield, CT (town) Fairfield County	23	0.16
Milford, NH (town) Hillsborough County	21	0.16
Hockessin, DE (cdp) New Castle County	20	0.16
Palo Alto, CA (city) Santa Clara County	87	0.15
East Hampton, NY (town) Suffolk County	30	0.15
Lynbrook, NY (village) Nassau County	30	0.15
Stony Brook, NY (cdp) Suffolk County	21	0.15
Cypress Lake, FL (cdp) Lee County	18	0.15
Superior, MI (township) Washtenaw County	16	0.15
Laguna Beach, CA (city) Orange County	32	0.14
Colonial Heights, VA (independent city) Colonial Heights city	24	0.14
Barrington, RI (town) Bristol County	23	0.14
Perinton, NY (town) Monroe County	60	0.13
Wellington, FL (village) Palm Beach County	49	0.13
Franklin, MA (city) Norfolk County	37	0.13
North Kingstown, RI (town) Washington County	35	0.13
Bay Shore, NY (cdp) Suffolk County	32	0.13
De Witt, NY (town) Onondaga County	31	0.13
New Milford, NJ (borough) Bergen County	21	0.13
Kings Point, FL (cdp) Palm Beach County	16	0.13
Catskill, NY (town) Greene County	15	0.13
Franconia, PA (township) Montgomery County	15	0.13
Old Bridge, NJ (township) Middlesex County	74	0.12
Middletown, CT (city) Middlesex County	51	0.12
Beverly Hills, CA (city) Los Angeles County	39	0.12
Burlingame, CA (city) San Mateo County	33	0.12
Deer Park, NY (cdp) Suffolk County	33	0.12
La Canada Flintridge, CA (city) Los Angeles County	25	0.12
Rosedale, MD (cdp) Baltimore County	23	0.12
Amherst Center, MA (cdp) Hampshire County	20	0.12
Idylwood, VA (cdp) Fairfax County	20	0.12
Palisades Park, NJ (borough) Bergen County	20	0.12
Tonawanda, NY (city) Erie County	19	0.12
Moorestown-Lenola, NJ (cdp) Burlington County	17	0.12
Hamburg, NY (village) Erie County	12	0.12
Merrill, WI (city) Lincoln County	12	0.12
Renton, WA (city) King County	55	0.11
Towson, MD (cdp) Baltimore County	55	0.11
Oceanside, NY (cdp) Nassau County	37	0.11
Spanaway, WA (cdp) Pierce County	24	0.11
Woodstock, IL (city) McHenry County	23	0.11
Mamaroneck, NY (village) Westchester County	21	0.11
Westborough, MA (town) Worcester County	20	0.11
Kihei, HI (cdp) Maui County	19	0.11
Saco, ME (city) York County	18	0.11
Oneonta, NY (city) Otsego County	15	0.11
Lewisboro, NY (town) Westchester County	14	0.11
Medford, MA (city) Middlesex County	57	0.10
Kirkland, WA (city) King County	43	0.10
Hackensack, NJ (city) Bergen County	41	0.10
McLean, VA (cdp) Fairfax County	38	0.10
Shrewsbury, MA (town) Worcester County	33	0.10
Voorhees, NJ (township) Camden County	29	0.10
Salisbury, NC (city) Rowan County	28	0.10
Newtown, CT (town) Fairfield County	26	0.10
North Attleborough, MA (town) Bristol County	26	0.10
Bel Air North, MD (cdp) Harford County	25	0.10
Burlington, MA (cdp) Middlesex County	22	0.10
Mineola, NY (village) Nassau County	19	0.10
Point Pleasant, NJ (borough) Ocean County	19	0.10
West Deptford, NJ (township) Gloucester County	19	0.10
Washington, NJ (township) Morris County	18	0.10
Wilton, CT (town) Fairfield County	17	0.10
Canton, IL (city) Fulton County	16	0.10
Berkley, MI (city) Oakland County	15	0.10
Lutherville-Timonium, MD (cdp) Baltimore County	15	0.10
East Hampton, CT (town) Middlesex County	14	0.10
Kelso, WA (city) Cowlitz County	12	0.10
Lilburn, GA (city) Gwinnett County	11	0.10
Mayfield, KY (city) Graves County	10	0.10
Bellevue, WA (city) King County	93	0.09
Plymouth, MA (town) Plymouth County	47	0.09
Saint Louis Park, MN (city) Hennepin County	40	0.09
Amherst, MA (town) Hampshire County	32	0.09
Mundelein, IL (village) Lake County	26	0.09
Franklin Square, NY (cdp) Nassau County	25	0.09
Bergenfield, NJ (borough) Bergen County	24	0.09
Wellesley, MA (cdp) Norfolk County	23	0.09
Lafayette, CO (city) Boulder County	22	0.09
Simsbury, CT (town) Hartford County	20	0.09
Parma Heights, OH (city) Cuyahoga County	19	0.09
Pike Creek, DE (cdp) New Castle County	18	0.09
Moorestown, NJ (township) Burlington County	17	0.09
Venice, FL (city) Sarasota County	16	0.09
Nanuet, NY (cdp) Rockland County	15	0.09
Pembroke, MA (town) Plymouth County	15	0.09
Portsmouth, RI (town) Newport County	15	0.09
Towamencin, PA (township) Montgomery County	15	0.09
Dryden, NY (town) Tompkins County	12	0.09
McKinleyville, CA (cdp) Humboldt County	12	0.09
Metuchen, NJ (borough) Middlesex County	12	0.09
Riviera Beach, MD (cdp) Anne Arundel County	12	0.09
Weehawken, NJ (township) Hudson County	12	0.09
West Lampeter, PA (township) Lancaster County	12	0.09
Riverview, FL (cdp) Hillsborough County	11	0.09
Rossville, MD (cdp) Baltimore County	11	0.09
Western Springs, IL (village) Cook County	11	0.09
Mamakating, NY (town) Sullivan County	10	0.09
Ridgefield, NJ (borough) Bergen County	10	0.09
Beachwood, NJ (borough) Ocean County	9	0.09
Palm Beach, FL (town) Palm Beach County	9	0.09
Everett, WA (city) Snohomish County	70	0.08
Vineland, NJ (city) Cumberland County	44	0.08

Notes: (cdp) census designated place; Refer to the Explanation of Data in the front of the book for more detailed information.

European

Top 150 Places Sorted by Number

(Based on all places, regardless of population)

Place	Number	%
New York, NY (city) New York City	32,892	0.41
Los Angeles, CA (city) Los Angeles County	22,598	0.61
San Diego, CA (city) San Diego County	13,053	1.07
Seattle, WA (city) King County	11,656	2.07
Portland, OR (city) Multnomah County	11,371	2.15
Houston, TX (city) Harris County	8,720	0.45
Phoenix, AZ (city) Maricopa County	8,624	0.65
San Francisco, CA (city) San Francisco County	8,448	1.09
San Jose, CA (city) Santa Clara County	8,366	0.94
Chicago, IL (city) Cook County	7,652	0.26
Indianapolis, IN (special city) Marion County	6,617	0.85
Austin, TX (city) Travis County	6,347	0.97
Dallas, TX (city) Dallas County	5,739	0.48
Nashville-Davidson, TN (special city) Davidson County	5,242	0.96
Columbus, OH (city) Franklin County	5,217	0.73
Jacksonville, FL (special city) Duval County	5,173	0.70
Colorado Springs, CO (city) El Paso County	5,005	1.39
Denver, CO (city) Denver County	4,893	0.88
Charlotte, NC (city) Mecklenburg County	4,624	0.85
Tucson, AZ (city) Pima County	4,388	0.90
San Antonio, TX (city) Bexar County	4,343	0.38
Memphis, TN (city) Shelby County	4,163	0.64
Minneapolis, MN (city) Hennepin County	3,925	1.03
Long Beach, CA (city) Los Angeles County	3,799	0.82
Wichita, KS (city) Sedgwick County	3,770	1.10
Mesa, AZ (city) Maricopa County	3,744	0.94
Tulsa, OK (city) Tulsa County	3,739	0.95
Anchorage, AK (municipality) Anchorage Borough	3,717	1.43
Boise City, ID (city) Ada County	3,594	1.93
Albuquerque, NM (city) Bernalillo County	3,535	0.79
Oklahoma City, OK (city) Oklahoma County	3,528	0.70
Philadelphia, PA (city) Philadelphia County	3,502	0.23
Oakland, CA (city) Alameda County	3,490	0.87
Raleigh, NC (city) Wake County	3,466	1.25
Virginia Beach, VA (independent city) Virginia Beach city	3,454	0.81
Sacramento, CA (city) Sacramento County	3,453	0.85
Washington, DC (city) District of Columbia	3,445	0.60
Hempstead, NY (town) Nassau County	3,388	0.45
Salt Lake City, UT (city) Salt Lake County	3,363	1.85
Arlington, VA (cdp) Arlington County	3,036	1.60
Orem, UT (city) Utah County	3,017	3.58
Atlanta, GA (city) Fulton County	3,012	0.72
Lexington-Fayette, KY (special city) Fayette County	2,971	1.14
Tacoma, WA (city) Pierce County	2,891	1.50
Kansas City, MO (city) Jackson County	2,891	0.66
Plano, TX (city) Collin County	2,884	1.30
Fort Worth, TX (city) Tarrant County	2,871	0.54
Eugene, OR (city) Lane County	2,822	2.05
Provo, UT (city) Utah County	2,803	2.66
Fresno, CA (city) Fresno County	2,727	0.64
Saint Paul, MN (city) Ramsey County	2,676	0.93
Las Vegas, NV (city) Clark County	2,634	0.55
Berkeley, CA (city) Alameda County	2,593	2.52
Boston, MA (city) Suffolk County	2,588	0.44
Aurora, CO (city) Arapahoe County	2,577	0.93
Overland Park, KS (city) Johnson County	2,435	1.64
Madison, WI (city) Dane County	2,358	1.14
Lincoln, NE (city) Lancaster County	2,335	1.04
Anaheim, CA (city) Orange County	2,305	0.70
Greensboro, NC (city) Guilford County	2,279	1.02
Omaha, NE (city) Douglas County	2,220	0.57
Spokane, WA (city) Spokane County	2,218	1.13
Santa Rosa, CA (city) Sonoma County	2,189	1.48
Springfield, MO (city) Greene County	2,187	1.44
Cincinnati, OH (city) Hamilton County	2,175	0.66
New Orleans, LA (city) Orleans Parish	2,154	0.44
Fremont, CA (city) Alameda County	2,147	1.06
Baltimore, MD (independent city) Baltimore city	2,147	0.33
Boulder, CO (city) Boulder County	2,130	2.25
Huntington Beach, CA (city) Orange County	2,127	1.12
Durham, NC (city) Durham County	2,117	1.13
Santa Clarita, CA (city) Los Angeles County	2,110	1.39
Davis, CA (city) Yolo County	2,104	3.49
Ann Arbor, MI (city) Washtenaw County	2,104	1.84
Arlington, TX (city) Tarrant County	2,084	0.63
Tempe, AZ (city) Maricopa County	2,053	1.30
Fort Collins, CO (city) Larimer County	2,036	1.72
Irvine, CA (city) Orange County	2,029	1.42
Louisville, KY (city) Jefferson County	2,029	0.79
Bellevue, WA (city) King County	2,019	1.85
San Buenaventura, CA (city) Ventura County	2,003	1.98
Tampa, FL (city) Hillsborough County	1,958	0.65
Glendale, AZ (city) Maricopa County	1,935	0.89
Milwaukee, WI (city) Milwaukee County	1,935	0.32
Oyster Bay, NY (town) Nassau County	1,925	0.65
Scottsdale, AZ (city) Maricopa County	1,919	0.95
Salem, OR (city) Marion County	1,918	1.40
Lakewood, CO (city) Jefferson County	1,885	1.31
Vancouver, WA (city) Clark County	1,831	1.28
Pittsburgh, PA (city) Allegheny County	1,818	0.54
Riverside, CA (city) Riverside County	1,812	0.71
Little Rock, AR (city) Pulaski County	1,808	0.98
Cary, NC (town) Wake County	1,791	1.89
Modesto, CA (city) Stanislaus County	1,783	0.94
El Paso, TX (city) El Paso County	1,776	0.31
Winston-Salem, NC (city) Forsyth County	1,773	0.96
Bakersfield, CA (city) Kern County	1,761	0.71
Ramapo, NY (town) Rockland County	1,745	1.60
Concord, CA (city) Contra Costa County	1,729	1.42
Newport News, VA (independent city) Newport News city	1,703	0.95
West Valley City, UT (city) Salt Lake County	1,697	1.56
Huntsville, AL (city) Madison County	1,667	1.06
Athens-Clarke County, GA (special city) Clarke County	1,639	1.63
Sunnyvale, CA (city) Santa Clara County	1,631	1.24
Sandy, UT (city) Salt Lake County	1,627	1.84
Garland, TX (city) Dallas County	1,626	0.75
Rancho Cucamonga, CA (city) San Bernardino County	1,610	1.26
Richmond, VA (independent city) Richmond city	1,591	0.80
Henderson, NV (city) Clark County	1,584	0.90
Montgomery, AL (city) Montgomery County	1,571	0.78
Livermore, CA (city) Alameda County	1,558	2.12
West Jordan, UT (city) Salt Lake County	1,539	2.26
Knoxville, TN (city) Knox County	1,538	0.89
Lawrence, KS (city) Douglas County	1,517	1.89
Gilbert, AZ (town) Maricopa County	1,494	1.36
Thousand Oaks, CA (city) Ventura County	1,474	1.26
Layton, UT (city) Davis County	1,462	2.49
Taylorsville, UT (city) Salt Lake County	1,461	2.52
Norman, OK (city) Cleveland County	1,441	1.51
Columbus, GA (special city) Muscogee County	1,440	0.78
Chula Vista, CA (city) San Diego County	1,435	0.83
Alexandria, VA (independent city) Alexandria city	1,434	1.12
Fullerton, CA (city) Orange County	1,428	1.13
Baton Rouge, LA (city) East Baton Rouge Parish	1,426	0.63
Bellingham, WA (city) Whatcom County	1,416	2.12
Tallahassee, FL (city) Leon County	1,416	0.94
Norfolk, VA (independent city) Norfolk city	1,414	0.60
Hillsboro, OR (city) Washington County	1,410	2.02
Mission Viejo, CA (city) Orange County	1,399	1.51
North Hempstead, NY (town) Nassau County	1,399	0.63
Olathe, KS (city) Johnson County	1,395	1.50
Torrance, CA (city) Los Angeles County	1,387	1.01
Chandler, AZ (city) Maricopa County	1,379	0.78
Saint Petersburg, FL (city) Pinellas County	1,372	0.55
Reno, NV (city) Washoe County	1,366	0.76
Mobile, AL (city) Mobile County	1,362	0.68
Corvallis, OR (city) Benton County	1,354	2.75
Oceanside, CA (city) San Diego County	1,353	0.84
Cambridge, MA (city) Middlesex County	1,346	1.33
Des Moines, IA (city) Polk County	1,341	0.67
Pleasanton, CA (city) Alameda County	1,335	2.10
Santa Clara, CA (city) Santa Clara County	1,328	1.30
Honolulu, HI (cdp) Honolulu County	1,323	0.36
Santa Cruz, CA (city) Santa Cruz County	1,322	2.43
Stockton, CA (city) San Joaquin County	1,312	0.54
Arden-Arcade, CA (cdp) Sacramento County	1,304	1.36
Saint Louis, MO (independent city) Saint Louis city	1,304	0.37
Shreveport, LA (city) Caddo Parish	1,293	0.64
Corpus Christi, TX (city) Nueces County	1,287	0.46
Poway, CA (city) San Diego County	1,285	2.66

Notes: (cdp) census designated place; Refer to the Explanation of Data in the front of the book for more detailed information.

European

Top 150 Places Sorted by Percent

(Based on all places, regardless of population)

Place	Number	%
Lotsee, OK (town) Tulsa County	3	50.00
Huntley, WY (cdp) Goshen County	13	25.49
Silvana, WA (cdp) Snohomish County	22	22.92
Warm River, ID (city) Fremont County	2	22.22
Rea, MO (city) Andrew County	10	21.74
Oakley, WY (cdp) Lincoln County	4	21.05
Four Mile Road, AK (cdp) Yukon-Koyukuk Census Area	10	20.41
Furnace Creek, CA (cdp) Inyo County	9	18.75
Port Alsworth, AK (cdp) Lake and Peninsula Borough	21	17.50
Snoqualmie Pass, WA (cdp) Kittitas County	37	17.45
Tensed, ID (city) Benewah County	23	17.42
Muscotah, KS (city) Atchison County	38	17.12
Neskowin, OR (cdp) Tillamook County	35	16.59
Roopville, GA (town) Carroll County	32	15.92
Bruceville, IN (town) Knox County	71	15.74
Gunn City, MO (village) Cass County	17	15.74
Peter, UT (cdp) Cache County	33	15.00
Learned, MS (town) Hinds County	8	14.29
Bethel, DE (town) Sussex County	28	13.93
Markham, WA (cdp) Grays Harbor County	10	13.70
Maple Rapids, MI (village) Clinton County	85	13.67
Scofield, UT (town) Carbon County	3	13.64
Tracy, MO (city) Platte County	28	13.27
Comer, GA (city) Madison County	135	13.15
Monterey, VA (town) Highland County	22	12.94
Port Heiden, AK (city) Lake and Peninsula Borough	12	12.90
Barbers Point Housing, HI (cdp) Honolulu County	9	12.50
Ostrander, OH (village) Delaware County	42	11.63
Gazelle, CA (cdp) Siskiyou County	15	11.28
Jordan Valley, OR (city) Malheur County	28	11.24
Antimony, UT (town) Garfield County	14	11.20
Berkley, IA (city) Boone County	3	11.11
Edgewater, FL (cdp) Broward County	78	11.00
Nelson, MO (city) Saline County	22	10.43
Morrison Bluff, AR (town) Logan County	8	10.39
Leadore, ID (city) Lemhi County	9	10.34
Blue Springs, MS (village) Union County	13	10.32
Big Bend, CA (cdp) Shasta County	15	10.27
Springtown, AR (town) Benton County	11	10.19
Ronald, WA (cdp) Kittitas County	18	10.17
Round Valley, CA (cdp) Inyo County	25	10.16
Gail Lake, MN (township) Crow Wing County	9	9.78
North Snyderville Basin, UT (cdp) Summit County	182	9.68
Grainola, OK (town) Osage County	3	9.68
Leavenworth, IN (town) Crawford County	33	9.57
Prescott, OR (city) Columbia County	9	9.57
Cleveland, IL (village) Henry County	24	9.56
Taylorsville, CA (cdp) Plumas County	16	9.14
Bolinas, CA (cdp) Marin County	114	9.13
Halls Crossing, UT (cdp) San Juan County	9	9.09
Admire, KS (city) Lyon County	17	9.04
Essex, MI (township) Clinton County	166	9.01
Limestone, OK (cdp) Rogers County	62	8.99
Greenbush, MI (township) Clinton County	190	8.98
Christie, OK (cdp) Adair County	13	8.84
Cottage Grove, TN (town) Henry County	9	8.74
Promise City, IA (city) Wayne County	9	8.74
Cantwell, AK (cdp) Yukon-Koyukuk Census Area	21	8.61
Gentry, MO (village) Gentry County	9	8.57
Bettles, AK (city) Yukon-Koyukuk Census Area	4	8.51
New Hudson, NY (town) Allegany County	62	8.45
Keeler, CA (cdp) Inyo County	6	8.45
Ward, CO (town) Boulder County	6	8.45
Stilesville, IN (town) Hendricks County	24	8.42
Mendocino, CA (cdp) Mendocino County	64	8.41
Elfin Cove, AK (cdp) Skagway-Hoonah-Angoon Census Area	3	8.33
Rutledge, MO (town) Scotland County	6	8.22
Parkdale, OR (cdp) Hood River County	15	8.20
Oxford, ID (city) Franklin County	3	8.11
Cove, UT (cdp) Cache County	33	8.05
Runnells, IA (city) Polk County	28	7.98
Hundred, WV (town) Wetzel County	26	7.98
Dorchester, TX (town) Grayson County	10	7.94
Chinook, WA (cdp) Pacific County	33	7.91
Hunts Point, WA (town) King County	35	7.88
Alpine Northwest, WY (cdp) Lincoln County	12	7.84
Pine, PA (township) Armstrong County	38	7.80
Rockville, UT (town) Washington County	22	7.80
Bradford, MN (township) Wilkin County	9	7.76
Ripton, VT (town) Addison County	45	7.61
Monhegan, ME (plantation) Lincoln County	6	7.59
Medicine Bow, WY (town) Carbon County	21	7.58
Knightstown, IN (town) Henry County	162	7.57
Boones Mill, VA (town) Franklin County	21	7.53
Centerville, NC (town) Franklin County	7	7.53
Ivanhoe Estates, FL (cdp) Broward County	19	7.51
Alton, UT (town) Kane County	11	7.48
Woodacre, CA (cdp) Marin County	108	7.46
Solway, MN (city) Beltrami County	5	7.35
Lebanon, MI (township) Clinton County	49	7.27
McFarland, KS (city) Wabaunsee County	19	7.25
Eldora, CO (cdp) Boulder County	16	7.21
Willow Creek, MT (cdp) Gallatin County	17	7.17
North High Shoals, GA (town) Oconee County	33	7.16
Portola Valley, CA (town) San Mateo County	330	7.14
Spokane, MO (cdp) Christian County	11	7.10
March AFB, CA (cdp) Riverside County	28	7.05
Johnsonville, MN (township) Redwood County	10	7.04
Ellsworth, IA (city) Hamilton County	37	7.03
Polkville, MS (village) Smith County	9	7.03
Bellerive, MO (village) Saint Louis County	16	7.02
Geneva, GA (town) Talbot County	8	7.02
Arimo, ID (city) Bannock County	26	6.99
Westmoreland, KS (city) Pottawatomie County	45	6.97
Williams, IA (city) Hamilton County	31	6.95
Clontarf, MN (city) Swift County	13	6.88
Faxon, OK (town) Comanche County	11	6.88
New Providence, IA (city) Hardin County	16	6.84
Blyn, WA (cdp) Clallam County	9	6.77
Tulare, SD (town) Spink County	13	6.74
Centerville, WA (cdp) Klickitat County	7	6.73
Chewey, OK (cdp) Adair County	11	6.67
Fairburn, SD (town) Custer County	4	6.67
Larson, ND (city) Burke County	2	6.67
Tumacacori-Carmen, AZ (cdp) Santa Cruz County	34	6.65
Kaser, NY (village) Rockland County	219	6.64
McCord Bend, MO (village) Stone County	20	6.62
Marseilles, OH (village) Wyandot County	9	6.62
Garden City, UT (town) Rich County	21	6.60
Fern, MN (township) Hubbard County	14	6.60
Marion Center, MA (cdp) Plymouth County	72	6.55
Frog Creek, WI (town) Washburn County	11	6.55
Emery, UT (town) Emery County	20	6.51
McKinley Park, AK (cdp) Denali Census Area	9	6.47
Talladega Springs, AL (town) Talladega County	6	6.45
Orwell, NY (town) Oswego County	81	6.42
La Fargeville, NY (cdp) Jefferson County	38	6.39
Marcus, WA (town) Stevens County	9	6.38
Aurora, ME (town) Hancock County	7	6.36
Brookeville, MD (town) Montgomery County	7	6.36
San Antonio, FL (city) Pasco County	39	6.34
Floyd, NM (village) Roosevelt County	5	6.33
Ketchum, OK (town) Craig County	18	6.32
Partridge, KS (city) Reno County	17	6.32
Allensville, KY (city) Todd County	9	6.25
Elmira, MO (village) Ray County	6	6.25
Kechi, KS (city) Sedgwick County	64	6.22
Danby, NY (town) Tompkins County	190	6.20
Lagunitas-Forest Knolls, CA (cdp) Marin County	113	6.20
Troy, SC (town) Greenwood County	6	6.19
Hill Country Village, TX (city) Bexar County	64	6.18
Donnelsville, OH (village) Clark County	15	6.17
La Verkin, UT (city) Washington County	209	6.16
Wellfleet, NE (village) Lincoln County	4	6.15
Sky Valley, GA (city) Rabun County	14	6.14
Glade, KS (city) Phillips County	7	6.14
Brandonville, WV (town) Preston County	6	6.12
Danbury, NE (village) Red Willow County	8	6.11
North Chevy Chase, MD (village) Montgomery County	26	6.09
Bluff, UT (cdp) San Juan County	22	6.09

Notes: (cdp) census designated place; Refer to the Explanation of Data in the front of the book for more detailed information.

European

Top 150 Places Sorted by Percent

(Based on places with populations of 10,000 or more)

Place	Number	%
Lea Hill, WA (cdp) King County	490	4.59
Monsey, NY (cdp) Rockland County	662	4.51
Durango, CO (city) La Plata County	544	3.88
Pleasant Grove, UT (city) Utah County	908	3.86
Canyon Lake, CA (city) Riverside County	394	3.86
Canyon Rim, UT (cdp) Salt Lake County	400	3.78
Arcata, CA (city) Humboldt County	629	3.76
Ashland, OR (city) Jackson County	725	3.72
Springville, UT (city) Utah County	739	3.60
Orem, UT (city) Utah County	3,017	3.58
Riverton, UT (city) Salt Lake County	894	3.56
Davis, CA (city) Yolo County	2,104	3.49
Benicia, CA (city) Solano County	933	3.46
Morro Bay, CA (city) San Luis Obispo County	353	3.42
Scotts Valley, CA (city) Santa Cruz County	392	3.40
Covington, WA (city) King County	443	3.22
Spanish Fork, UT (city) Utah County	642	3.17
Rexburg, ID (city) Madison County	541	3.14
Montecito, CA (cdp) Santa Barbara County	308	3.05
Kaysville, UT (city) Davis County	630	3.04
Orinda, CA (city) Contra Costa County	528	3.03
El Dorado Hills, CA (cdp) El Dorado County	543	3.00
Bountiful, UT (city) Davis County	1,233	2.98
Bainbridge Island, WA (city) Kitsap County	605	2.98
Weston, MA (town) Middlesex County	336	2.93
Vashon, WA (cdp) King County	295	2.91
Richland, WA (city) Benton County	1,110	2.87
Martin, TN (city) Weakley County	303	2.87
Moscow, ID (city) Latah County	604	2.85
McKinleyville, CA (cdp) Humboldt County	384	2.82
Clayton, CA (city) Contra Costa County	303	2.81
Centerville, UT (city) Davis County	401	2.79
Cedar Mill, OR (cdp) Washington County	352	2.76
Corvallis, OR (city) Benton County	1,354	2.75
Los Gatos, CA (town) Santa Clara County	787	2.74
Holladay, UT (city) Salt Lake County	396	2.72
Statesville, NC (city) Iredell County	624	2.71
North Ogden, UT (city) Weber County	405	2.71
Pullman, WA (city) Whitman County	669	2.70
Lake Oswego, OR (city) Clackamas County	949	2.69
Cedar City, UT (city) Iron County	553	2.69
West University Place, TX (city) Harris County	380	2.67
Wood River, IL (city) Madison County	299	2.67
Provo, UT (city) Utah County	2,803	2.66
Poway, CA (city) San Diego County	1,285	2.66
Lacey, WA (city) Thurston County	828	2.66
American Fork, UT (city) Utah County	578	2.64
Moraga, CA (town) Contra Costa County	440	2.64
Piedmont, CA (city) Alameda County	286	2.61
El Segundo, CA (city) Los Angeles County	415	2.60
West Valley, WA (cdp) Yakima County	262	2.60
Winnetka, IL (village) Cook County	321	2.59
Deerfield, IL (village) Lake County	478	2.58
Boone, NC (town) Watauga County	345	2.57
Newberg, OR (city) Yamhill County	462	2.55
Laguna Beach, CA (city) Orange County	592	2.54
Lehi, UT (city) Utah County	487	2.54
Woodmere, NY (cdp) Nassau County	418	2.54
Godfrey, IL (village) Madison County	415	2.54
Wayland, MA (town) Middlesex County	333	2.54
Kearns, UT (cdp) Salt Lake County	850	2.53
Concord, MA (town) Middlesex County	430	2.53
Berkeley, CA (city) Alameda County	2,593	2.52
Taylorsville, UT (city) Salt Lake County	1,461	2.52
Layton, UT (city) Davis County	1,462	2.49
Mercer Island, WA (city) King County	549	2.49
Lake Forest Park, WA (city) King County	335	2.49
Agoura Hills, CA (city) Los Angeles County	503	2.47
Pendleton, OR (city) Umatilla County	401	2.47
Capitola, CA (city) Santa Cruz County	251	2.46
Forest Grove, OR (city) Washington County	429	2.45
Santa Cruz, CA (city) Santa Cruz County	1,322	2.43
Garden City, ID (city) Ada County	262	2.40
Danville, CA (town) Contra Costa County	1,008	2.39
Oak Grove, OR (cdp) Clackamas County	301	2.39
Rocklin, CA (city) Placer County	869	2.38
Louisville, CO (city) Boulder County	450	2.38
Atascadero, CA (city) San Luis Obispo County	627	2.37
Tualatin, OR (city) Washington County	536	2.37
Juneau, AK (city and borough) Juneau Borough	724	2.36
Kenmore, WA (city) King County	438	2.36
Roy, UT (city) Weber County	769	2.35
Brigham City, UT (city) Box Elder County	409	2.35
Siloam Springs, AR (city) Benton County	254	2.35
Tenafly, NJ (borough) Bergen County	321	2.33
Larkspur, CA (city) Marin County	280	2.33
Maple Valley, WA (city) King County	333	2.32
Logan, UT (city) Cache County	985	2.31
New Castle, NY (town) Westchester County	404	2.31
Tamalpais-Homestead Valley, CA (cdp) Marin County	245	2.31
Apex, NC (town) Wake County	461	2.30
Mill Valley, CA (city) Marin County	312	2.30
Laramie, WY (city) Albany County	619	2.27
West Jordan, UT (city) Salt Lake County	1,539	2.26
Calabasas, CA (city) Los Angeles County	454	2.26
Albany, CA (city) Alameda County	371	2.26
Mountain Park, GA (cdp) Gwinnett County	260	2.26
Lilburn, GA (city) Gwinnett County	257	2.26
Altoona, IA (city) Polk County	232	2.26
Boulder, CO (city) Boulder County	2,130	2.25
Redmond, WA (city) King County	1,018	2.24
Sammamish, WA (city) King County	765	2.24
Oak Ridge, TN (city) Anderson County	612	2.23
Fairborn, OH (city) Greene County	709	2.22
La Canada Flintridge, CA (city) Los Angeles County	452	2.22
Draper, UT (city) Salt Lake County	562	2.21
Casa de Oro-Mount Helix, CA (cdp) San Diego County	417	2.21
Carrboro, NC (town) Orange County	369	2.21
Idaho Falls, ID (city) Bonneville County	1,109	2.20
Rockwall, TX (city) Rockwall County	403	2.20
Los Altos, CA (city) Santa Clara County	601	2.18
Clearfield, UT (city) Davis County	566	2.18
Decatur, GA (city) De Kalb County	396	2.18
Auburn, AL (city) Lee County	930	2.17
Ithaca, NY (city) Tompkins County	630	2.17
Portland, OR (city) Multnomah County	11,371	2.15
Troutdale, OR (city) Multnomah County	293	2.15
Palo Alto, CA (city) Santa Clara County	1,255	2.13
University Park, TX (city) Dallas County	498	2.13
Niceville, FL (city) Okaloosa County	251	2.13
Oxford, MS (city) Lafayette County	251	2.13
Livermore, CA (city) Alameda County	1,558	2.12
Bellingham, WA (city) Whatcom County	1,416	2.12
Pleasanton, CA (city) Alameda County	1,335	2.10
South Jordan, UT (city) Salt Lake County	619	2.10
Hayesville, OR (cdp) Marion County	378	2.10
Pacific Grove, CA (city) Monterey County	324	2.10
Baywood-Los Osos, CA (cdp) San Luis Obispo County	297	2.10
Druid Hills, GA (cdp) De Kalb County	267	2.10
Farmington, UT (city) Davis County	256	2.10
Auburn, WA (city) King County	842	2.09
West Linn, OR (city) Clackamas County	465	2.09
Stillwater, OK (city) Payne County	809	2.08
Acton, MA (town) Middlesex County	422	2.08
Seattle, WA (city) King County	11,656	2.07
Lafayette, CA (city) Contra Costa County	486	2.07
Maitland, FL (city) Orange County	247	2.07
Manhattan, KS (city) Riley County	922	2.06
Olympia, WA (city) Thurston County	873	2.06
Eugene, OR (city) Lane County	2,822	2.05
Truckee, CA (town) Nevada County	287	2.05
Los Alamos, NM (cdp) Los Alamos County	244	2.05
East Renton Highlands, WA (cdp) King County	267	2.04
San Anselmo, CA (town) Marin County	255	2.04
Crestline, CA (cdp) San Bernardino County	208	2.04
Shoreline, WA (city) King County	1,073	2.03
Germantown, TN (city) Shelby County	756	2.03
Inglewood-Finn Hill, WA (cdp) King County	459	2.03
Hillsboro, OR (city) Washington County	1,410	2.02
Bethesda, MD (cdp) Montgomery County	1,115	2.02

Notes: (cdp) census designated place; Refer to the Explanation of Data in the front of the book for more detailed information.

Finnish

Top 150 Places Sorted by Number

(Based on all places, regardless of population)

Place	Number	%
Duluth, MN (city) Saint Louis County	6,593	7.59
Minneapolis, MN (city) Hennepin County	4,069	1.06
Portland, OR (city) Multnomah County	3,894	0.74
New York, NY (city) New York City	3,466	0.04
Seattle, WA (city) King County	3,320	0.59
Los Angeles, CA (city) Los Angeles County	3,079	0.08
Calumet, MI (township) Houghton County	2,791	39.95
Marquette, MI (city) Marquette County	2,654	13.54
Phoenix, AZ (city) Maricopa County	2,620	0.20
San Diego, CA (city) San Diego County	2,531	0.21
Hibbing, MN (city) Saint Louis County	2,350	13.77
Saint Paul, MN (city) Ramsey County	2,206	0.77
Chicago, IL (city) Cook County	2,163	0.07
Superior, WI (city) Douglas County	2,074	7.57
Ishpeming, MI (city) Marquette County	1,940	29.50
Virginia, MN (city) Saint Louis County	1,923	21.00
Cloquet, MN (city) Carlton County	1,755	15.73
San Francisco, CA (city) San Francisco County	1,617	0.21
Fitchburg, MA (city) Worcester County	1,593	4.07
Ironwood, MI (city) Gogebic County	1,552	24.67
Milwaukee, WI (city) Milwaukee County	1,506	0.25
Brooklyn Park, MN (city) Hennepin County	1,446	2.15
Plymouth, MN (city) Hennepin County	1,428	2.17
Hancock, MI (city) Houghton County	1,392	32.35
Negaunee, MI (city) Marquette County	1,339	29.55
Anchorage, AK (municipality) Anchorage Borough	1,328	0.51
Livonia, MI (city) Wayne County	1,323	1.32
Coon Rapids, MN (city) Anoka County	1,310	2.13
Ishpeming, MI (township) Marquette County	1,232	34.16
Adams, MI (township) Houghton County	1,228	44.59
Maple Grove, MN (city) Hennepin County	1,205	2.39
San Jose, CA (city) Santa Clara County	1,192	0.13
Vancouver, WA (city) Clark County	1,180	0.82
Blaine, MN (city) Anoka County	1,119	2.49
Negaunee, MI (township) Marquette County	1,114	40.19
Thomson, MN (township) Carlton County	1,107	25.36
Portage, MI (township) Houghton County	1,078	34.73
Farmington Hills, MI (city) Oakland County	1,044	1.27
L'Anse, MI (township) Baraga County	1,038	25.76
Lake Worth, FL (city) Palm Beach County	1,026	2.91
Forsyth, MI (township) Marquette County	1,024	21.01
Ann Arbor, MI (city) Washtenaw County	1,012	0.89
Worcester, MA (city) Worcester County	1,012	0.59
Green Bay, WI (city) Brown County	1,010	0.99
Westland, MI (city) Wayne County	999	1.15
Gardner, MA (city) Worcester County	964	4.64
Redford, MI (cdp) Wayne County	963	1.87
Tucson, AZ (city) Pima County	959	0.20
West Ishpeming, MI (cdp) Marquette County	953	34.02
Chassell, MI (township) Houghton County	951	51.54
Butte-Silver Bow, MT (special city) Silver Bow County	950	2.80
Chocolay, MI (township) Marquette County	932	13.04
Baraga, MI (township) Baraga County	914	26.09
Madison, WI (city) Dane County	911	0.44
Canton, MI (cdp) Wayne County	900	1.18
Kenosha, WI (city) Kenosha County	897	0.99
Bloomington, MN (city) Hennepin County	896	1.05
Colorado Springs, CO (city) El Paso County	894	0.25
Grand Rapids, MN (township) Itasca County	886	7.57
Houghton, MI (city) Houghton County	878	12.50
Ashtabula, OH (city) Ashtabula County	878	4.21
Brookhaven, NY (town) Suffolk County	872	0.19
Denver, CO (city) Denver County	870	0.16
Mesa, AZ (city) Maricopa County	860	0.22
Mountain Iron, MN (city) Saint Louis County	854	28.24
Saint Louis Park, MN (city) Hennepin County	854	1.94
Saint Cloud, MN (city) Stearns County	853	1.45
Houston, TX (city) Harris County	844	0.04
Eugene, OR (city) Lane County	836	0.61
New Ipswich, NH (town) Hillsborough County	832	19.40
White, MN (township) Saint Louis County	830	23.78
Gloucester, MA (city) Essex County	830	2.74
Laurium, MI (village) Houghton County	824	38.59
Columbus, OH (city) Franklin County	822	0.12
Warren, MI (city) Macomb County	820	0.59
Sterling Heights, MI (city) Macomb County	816	0.66
Troy, MI (city) Oakland County	810	1.00
Hermantown, MN (city) Saint Louis County	808	10.79
Longview, WA (city) Cowlitz County	805	2.31
Royal Oak, MI (city) Oakland County	802	1.34
Austin, TX (city) Travis County	798	0.12
Boise City, ID (city) Ada County	797	0.43
Las Vegas, NV (city) Clark County	796	0.17
Ontonagon, MI (township) Ontonagon County	778	26.30
Ironwood, MI (township) Gogebic County	763	33.15
Boston, MA (city) Suffolk County	756	0.13
Spokane, WA (city) Spokane County	754	0.38
Allouez, MI (township) Keweenaw County	749	46.93
Conneaut, OH (city) Ashtabula County	741	5.92
Albuquerque, NM (city) Bernalillo County	740	0.16
Apple Valley, MN (city) Dakota County	738	1.62
Minnetonka, MN (city) Hennepin County	736	1.43
Franklin, MI (township) Houghton County	730	52.52
Osceola, MI (township) Houghton County	723	39.23
Ely, MI (township) Marquette County	720	36.04
Detroit, MI (city) Wayne County	720	0.08
Andover, MN (city) Anoka County	716	2.69
Champlin, MN (city) Hennepin County	715	3.20
Fargo, ND (city) Cass County	705	0.78
Stanton, MI (township) Houghton County	700	55.07
Eden Prairie, MN (city) Hennepin County	695	1.27
Novi, MI (city) Oakland County	693	1.46
Barnstable Town, MA (city) Barnstable County	688	1.44
Chisholm, MN (city) Saint Louis County	680	13.71
Burnsville, MN (city) Dakota County	674	1.12
Jacksonville, FL (special city) Duval County	665	0.09
Waterford, MI (cdp) Oakland County	660	0.90
Bellevue, WA (city) King County	660	0.60
Chandler, AZ (city) Maricopa County	660	0.37
Tacoma, WA (city) Pierce County	658	0.34
Cokato, MN (city) Wright County	654	23.82
Eveleth, MN (city) Saint Louis County	645	16.69
Westminster, MA (town) Worcester County	637	9.22
Waukegan, IL (city) Lake County	635	0.72
Iron Mountain, MI (city) Dickinson County	631	7.83
Fridley, MN (city) Anoka County	631	2.30
Everett, WA (city) Snohomish County	614	0.67
Aurora, CO (city) Arapahoe County	613	0.22
Garden City, MI (city) Wayne County	612	2.04
Gresham, OR (city) Multnomah County	610	0.68
Indianapolis, IN (special city) Marion County	610	0.08
Ashland, WI (city) Ashland County	608	7.07
Charlotte, NC (city) Mecklenburg County	606	0.11
Marquette, MI (township) Marquette County	601	17.99
Long Beach, CA (city) Los Angeles County	601	0.13
Billings, MT (city) Yellowstone County	596	0.67
Wakefield, MI (city) Gogebic County	592	28.59
Lansing, MI (city) Ingham County	592	0.50
Clinton, MI (cdp) Macomb County	591	0.62
Grand Rapids, MN (city) Itasca County	575	7.45
Missoula, MT (city) Missoula County	575	1.01
Hempstead, NY (town) Nassau County	574	0.08
Leominster, MA (city) Worcester County	572	1.38
Scottsdale, AZ (city) Maricopa County	572	0.28
Lantana, FL (town) Palm Beach County	570	5.97
Washington, DC (city) District of Columbia	568	0.10
Brighton, MI (township) Livingston County	567	3.20
L'Anse, MI (village) Baraga County	565	26.35
Lakeville, MN (city) Dakota County	556	1.29
Santa Rosa, CA (city) Sonoma County	553	0.37
Escanaba, MI (city) Delta County	549	4.18
Commerce, MI (township) Oakland County	549	1.57
Rochester, MN (city) Olmsted County	549	0.64
Astoria, OR (city) Clatsop County	548	5.59
Huntington Beach, CA (city) Orange County	547	0.29
Torch Lake, MI (township) Houghton County	543	28.64
Sacramento, CA (city) Sacramento County	539	0.13
Rindge, NH (town) Cheshire County	536	9.83
Great Falls, MT (city) Cascade County	533	0.94
Eagan, MN (city) Dakota County	531	0.83

Notes: (cdp) census designated place; Refer to the Explanation of Data in the front of the book for more detailed information.

Finnish

Top 150 Places Sorted by Percent

(Based on all places, regardless of population)

Place	Number	%
Wolf Lake, MN (city) Becker County	29	74.36
Wolf Lake, MN (township) Becker County	127	61.06
Covington, MI (township) Baraga County	356	60.44
Brookston, MN (city) Saint Louis County	45	60.00
Chatham, MI (village) Alger County	123	57.21
Copper City, MI (village) Houghton County	114	57.00
Humboldt, MI (township) Marquette County	250	55.43
Stanton, MI (township) Houghton County	700	55.07
Bohemia, MI (township) Ontonagon County	39	53.42
Franklin, MI (township) Houghton County	730	52.52
Laird, MI (township) Houghton County	344	52.28
Stannard, MI (township) Ontonagon County	410	51.64
Chassell, MI (township) Houghton County	951	51.54
Floodwood, MN (city) Saint Louis County	246	50.51
Salo, MN (township) Aitkin County	37	50.00
Paddock, MN (township) Otter Tail County	152	49.03
Elm River, MI (township) Houghton County	73	47.10
Allouez, MI (township) Keweenaw County	749	46.93
Hancock, MI (township) Houghton County	183	46.33
South Range, MI (village) Houghton County	343	45.55
Greenland, MI (township) Ontonagon County	407	45.37
Cedar Valley, MN (township) Saint Louis County	112	45.16
Adams, MI (township) Houghton County	1,228	44.59
Sherman, MI (township) Keweenaw County	24	43.64
Richmond, MI (township) Marquette County	424	43.13
Spruce Grove, MN (township) Becker County	158	43.05
Floodwood, MN (township) Saint Louis County	135	42.45
Oulu, WI (town) Bayfield County	216	42.44
Maple, WI (town) Douglas County	279	42.08
Republic, MI (township) Marquette County	476	42.01
Palmer, MI (cdp) Marquette County	185	41.48
Tilden, MI (township) Marquette County	418	41.14
Negaunee, MI (township) Marquette County	1,114	40.19
Calumet, MI (township) Houghton County	2,791	39.95
Runeberg, MN (township) Becker County	174	39.91
Menahga, MN (city) Wadena County	482	39.31
Osceola, MI (township) Houghton County	723	39.23
Quincy, MI (township) Houghton County	106	39.11
Vermilion Lake, MN (township) Saint Louis County	131	38.87
Eagle, MN (township) Carlton County	199	38.72
Colvin, MN (township) Saint Louis County	132	38.60
Laurium, MI (village) Houghton County	824	38.59
Wuori, MN (township) Saint Louis County	197	38.40
Interior, MI (township) Ontonagon County	144	38.10
Rock River, MI (township) Alger County	464	38.06
Erwin, MI (township) Gogebic County	143	37.63
Spurr, MI (township) Baraga County	79	37.44
Van Buren, MN (township) Saint Louis County	60	37.27
Cokato, MN (township) Wright County	450	37.07
Knight, WI (town) Iron County	99	36.94
Kalevala, MN (township) Carlton County	106	36.55
White River, WI (town) Ashland County	320	36.12
Ely, MI (township) Marquette County	720	36.04
Brule, WI (town) Douglas County	206	35.95
Sturgeon, MN (township) Saint Louis County	48	35.82
Ahmeek, MI (village) Keweenaw County	59	35.76
Kugler, MN (township) Saint Louis County	64	35.75
Pike, MN (township) Saint Louis County	168	35.74
Blueberry, MN (township) Wadena County	245	35.71
Ewing, MI (township) Marquette County	54	35.53
McMillan, MI (township) Ontonagon County	218	35.33
Kimball, WI (town) Iron County	187	35.02
Portage, MI (township) Houghton County	1,078	34.73
Marengo, WI (town) Ashland County	129	34.68
Kettle River, MN (city) Carlton County	57	34.55
Rice River, MN (township) Aitkin County	57	34.34
Ishpeming, MI (township) Marquette County	1,232	34.16
West Ishpeming, MI (cdp) Marquette County	953	34.02
Fine Lakes, MN (township) Saint Louis County	39	33.91
Grant, MI (township) Keweenaw County	50	33.78
Cromwell, MN (city) Carlton County	43	33.59
Lutak, AK (cdp) Haines Borough	12	33.33
Cherry, MN (township) Saint Louis County	305	33.22
Ironwood, MI (township) Gogebic County	763	33.15
Green Valley, MN (township) Becker County	94	33.10
Halden, MN (township) Saint Louis County	45	32.85
Red Eye, MN (township) Wadena County	134	32.76
Hematite, MI (township) Iron County	112	32.56
Hancock, MI (city) Houghton County	1,392	32.35
Kingston, MN (city) Meeker County	51	32.28
Wakefield, MI (township) Gogebic County	127	32.15
Knox, WI (town) Price County	125	32.05
Automba, MN (township) Carlton County	46	31.94
Scofield, UT (town) Carbon County	7	31.82
Turin, MI (township) Marquette County	46	31.51
Ault, MN (township) Saint Louis County	38	30.89
Champion, MI (township) Marquette County	83	30.63
Ashland, WI (town) Ashland County	177	30.31
Tower, MN (city) Saint Louis County	142	30.28
Mathias, MI (township) Alger County	170	30.20
Newton, MN (township) Otter Tail County	215	30.03
Angora, MN (township) Saint Louis County	95	29.69
Negaunee, MI (city) Marquette County	1,339	29.55
Clinton, MN (township) Saint Louis County	307	29.55
Ishpeming, MI (city) Marquette County	1,940	29.50
Tripp, WI (town) Bayfield County	56	29.47
Sandy, MN (township) Saint Louis County	121	29.37
Calumet, MI (village) Houghton County	269	29.27
Embarrass, MN (township) Saint Louis County	200	29.15
Bessemer, MI (township) Gogebic County	359	29.09
Alango, MN (township) Saint Louis County	88	28.76
Torch Lake, MI (township) Houghton County	543	28.64
Wakefield, MI (city) Gogebic County	592	28.59
Mountain Iron, MN (city) Saint Louis County	854	28.24
Lavell, MN (township) Saint Louis County	103	27.99
Naselle, WA (cdp) Pacific County	100	27.70
Oteneagen, MN (township) Itasca County	66	27.27
Waasa, MN (township) Saint Louis County	84	27.18
Sebeka, MN (city) Wadena County	197	27.17
Schoolcraft, MI (township) Houghton County	495	26.81
Lakeside, WI (town) Douglas County	167	26.76
Otto, MN (township) Otter Tail County	134	26.69
Carsonville, MN (township) Becker County	57	26.64
L'Anse, MI (village) Baraga County	565	26.35
Ontonagon, MI (township) Ontonagon County	778	26.30
Bergland, MI (township) Ontonagon County	152	26.16
Baraga, MI (township) Baraga County	914	26.09
Anderson, WI (town) Iron County	12	26.09
Rockland, MI (township) Ontonagon County	78	26.00
L'Anse, MI (township) Baraga County	1,038	25.76
Lake Linden, MI (village) Houghton County	275	25.53
Bassett, MN (township) Saint Louis County	12	25.53
Alpha, MI (village) Iron County	51	25.50
Toivola, MN (township) Saint Louis County	45	25.42
Thomson, MN (township) Carlton County	1,107	25.36
Hubbell, MI (cdp) Houghton County	279	25.36
Beseman, MN (township) Carlton County	45	25.28
Biwabik, MN (township) Saint Louis County	230	25.14
Split Rock, MN (township) Carlton County	34	25.00
Haight, MI (township) Ontonagon County	61	24.80
Ironwood, MI (city) Gogebic County	1,552	24.67
Baraga, MI (village) Baraga County	319	24.54
Ontonagon, MI (village) Ontonagon County	433	24.49
Clark, MN (township) Aitkin County	31	24.41
Carey, WI (town) Iron County	48	24.37
Silver, MN (township) Carlton County	90	24.32
Lakeview, MN (township) Carlton County	49	24.26
Gwinn, MI (cdp) Marquette County	482	23.99
Cokato, MN (city) Wright County	654	23.82
White, MN (township) Saint Louis County	830	23.78
Linden Grove, MN (township) Saint Louis County	30	23.62
New York Mills, MN (city) Otter Tail County	274	23.54
Field, MN (township) Saint Louis County	96	23.36
Breitung, MN (township) Saint Louis County	160	23.26
Bessemer, MI (city) Gogebic County	501	22.97
Hurley, WI (city) Iron County	414	22.86
Carp Lake, MI (township) Ontonagon County	199	22.85
Duncan, MI (township) Houghton County	62	22.63
Camp 5, MN (township) Saint Louis County	7	22.58
Michigamme, MI (township) Marquette County	87	22.42

Notes: (cdp) census designated place; Refer to the Explanation of Data in the front of the book for more detailed information.

Finnish

Top 150 Places Sorted by Percent

(Based on places with populations of 10,000 or more)

Place	Number	%
Cloquet, MN (city) Carlton County	1,755	15.73
Hibbing, MN (city) Saint Louis County	2,350	13.77
Marquette, MI (city) Marquette County	2,654	13.54
Duluth, MN (city) Saint Louis County	6,593	7.59
Superior, WI (city) Douglas County	2,074	7.57
Grand Rapids, MN (township) Itasca County	886	7.57
Conneaut, OH (city) Ashtabula County	741	5.92
Gardner, MA (city) Worcester County	964	4.64
Ashtabula, OH (city) Ashtabula County	878	4.21
Escanaba, MI (city) Delta County	549	4.18
Fitchburg, MA (city) Worcester County	1,593	4.07
Maynard, MA (cdp) Middlesex County	391	3.75
Lyon, MI (township) Oakland County	362	3.28
Champlin, MN (city) Hennepin County	715	3.20
Brighton, MI (township) Livingston County	567	3.20
Lake Worth, FL (city) Palm Beach County	1,026	2.91
Butte-Silver Bow, MT (special city) Silver Bow County	950	2.80
Buffalo, MN (city) Wright County	282	2.78
Gloucester, MA (city) Essex County	830	2.74
Ramsey, MN (city) Anoka County	504	2.73
Andover, MN (city) Anoka County	716	2.69
Sault Sainte Marie, MI (city) Chippewa County	444	2.69
Lino Lakes, MN (city) Anoka County	448	2.67
Brainerd, MN (city) Crow Wing County	348	2.67
White Bear, MN (township) Ramsey County	292	2.61
Blaine, MN (city) Anoka County	1,119	2.49
Maple Grove, MN (city) Hennepin County	1,205	2.39
Longview, WA (city) Cowlitz County	805	2.31
Crystal, MN (city) Hennepin County	528	2.31
Fridley, MN (city) Anoka County	631	2.30
Bemidji, MN (city) Beltrami County	277	2.29
Milford, MI (township) Oakland County	345	2.26
Plymouth, MN (city) Hennepin County	1,428	2.17
Brooklyn Park, MN (city) Hennepin County	1,446	2.15
Coon Rapids, MN (city) Anoka County	1,310	2.13
White Bear Lake, MN (city) Ramsey County	513	2.10
Aberdeen, WA (city) Grays Harbor County	344	2.09
Mounds View, MN (city) Ramsey County	264	2.08
East Bethel, MN (city) Anoka County	226	2.07
Genoa, MI (township) Livingston County	330	2.06
Robbinsdale, MN (city) Hennepin County	289	2.05
Garden City, MI (city) Wayne County	612	2.04
Elk River, MN (city) Sherburne County	332	2.02
Berkley, MI (city) Oakland County	312	2.01
Kelso, WA (city) Cowlitz County	239	1.99
Saint Louis Park, MN (city) Hennepin County	854	1.94
Orchards, WA (cdp) Clark County	346	1.93
Pleasant Prairie, WI (village) Kenosha County	306	1.93
Green Oak, MI (township) Livingston County	296	1.89
Ham Lake, MN (city) Anoka County	241	1.89
Redford, MI (cdp) Wayne County	963	1.87
Zion, IL (city) Lake County	423	1.84
Savage, MN (city) Scott County	384	1.81
South Lyon, MI (city) Oakland County	181	1.80
Prior Lake, MN (city) Scott County	286	1.79
Brooklyn Center, MN (city) Hennepin County	513	1.77
New Hope, MN (city) Hennepin County	369	1.77
Highland, MI (township) Oakland County	337	1.76
Hartland, MI (township) Livingston County	191	1.74
Golden Valley, MN (city) Hennepin County	349	1.72
Farmington, MI (city) Oakland County	175	1.68
Ashwaubenon, WI (village) Brown County	293	1.66
Painesville, OH (city) Lake County	289	1.65
Ferndale, MI (city) Oakland County	363	1.64
Apple Valley, MN (city) Dakota County	738	1.62
Vadnais Heights, MN (city) Ramsey County	211	1.62
Clawson, MI (city) Oakland County	206	1.62
Howard, WI (village) Brown County	216	1.60
Commerce, MI (township) Oakland County	549	1.57
Anoka, MN (city) Anoka County	283	1.57
Spring Lake, MI (township) Ottawa County	207	1.57
New Brighton, MN (city) Ramsey County	344	1.55
Traverse City, MI (city) Grand Traverse County	226	1.55
Wixom, MI (city) Oakland County	203	1.53
Plainfield, CT (town) Windham County	222	1.52
Carver, MA (town) Plymouth County	170	1.52
Athol, MA (town) Worcester County	171	1.51
Keene, NH (city) Cheshire County	339	1.50
Spencer, MA (town) Worcester County	174	1.49
Leicester, MA (town) Worcester County	155	1.48
Troutdale, OR (city) Multnomah County	200	1.47
Novi, MI (city) Oakland County	693	1.46
Stillwater, MN (city) Washington County	222	1.46
Saint Cloud, MN (city) Stearns County	853	1.45
Independence, MI (township) Oakland County	472	1.45
Rock Springs, WY (city) Sweetwater County	275	1.45
Barnstable Town, MA (city) Barnstable County	688	1.44
Minnetonka, MN (city) Hennepin County	736	1.43
Chanhassen, MN (city) Carver County	291	1.43
Centralia, WA (city) Lewis County	210	1.43
Five Corners, WA (cdp) Clark County	168	1.39
Leominster, MA (city) Worcester County	572	1.38
Richfield, MN (city) Hennepin County	477	1.38
Fergus Falls, MN (city) Otter Tail County	185	1.37
Hazel Park, MI (city) Oakland County	258	1.36
Chaska, MN (city) Carver County	238	1.36
Royal Oak, MI (city) Oakland County	802	1.34
Gurnee, IL (village) Lake County	384	1.34
Pittsfield charter, MI (township) Washtenaw County	400	1.33
Livonia, MI (city) Wayne County	1,323	1.32
Plymouth Township, MI (cdp) Wayne County	365	1.32
Shoreview, MN (city) Ramsey County	343	1.32
Madison Heights, MI (city) Oakland County	408	1.31
Columbia Heights, MN (city) Anoka County	243	1.31
Oatfield, OR (cdp) Clackamas County	205	1.31
Cottage Grove, MN (city) Washington County	398	1.30
Lakeville, MN (city) Dakota County	556	1.29
Port Washington, WI (city) Ozaukee County	133	1.28
Farmington Hills, MI (city) Oakland County	1,044	1.27
Eden Prairie, MN (city) Hennepin County	695	1.27
Waverly, MI (cdp) Eaton County	205	1.27
Milford, NH (town) Hillsborough County	169	1.25
Moorhead, MN (city) Clay County	400	1.24
South Saint Paul, MN (city) Dakota County	248	1.23
Grand Chute, WI (town) Outagamie County	222	1.22
Marinette, WI (city) Marinette County	143	1.22
Big Rapids, MI (city) Mecosta County	130	1.22
Northfield, MN (city) Rice County	205	1.20
Aberdeen, SD (city) Brown County	292	1.19
Bellevue Town, WI (cdp) Brown County	142	1.19
Canton, MI (cdp) Wayne County	900	1.18
Millbury, MA (town) Worcester County	150	1.17
Westland, MI (city) Wayne County	999	1.15
Mill Creek, WA (city) Snohomish County	132	1.15
Allouez, WI (village) Brown County	176	1.14
Hopkinton, MA (town) Middlesex County	152	1.14
Prairie Ridge, WA (cdp) Pierce County	131	1.14
Fenton, MI (city) Genesee County	121	1.14
Burnsville, MN (city) Dakota County	674	1.12
Evanston, WY (city) Uinta County	128	1.12
Shakopee, MN (city) Scott County	228	1.11
Cascade, MI (township) Kent County	168	1.11
Mundy, MI (township) Genesee County	135	1.11
Red Wing, MN (city) Goodhue County	178	1.10
Gages Lake, IL (cdp) Lake County	114	1.09
Flushing, MI (township) Genesee County	112	1.09
Minneapolis, MN (city) Hennepin County	4,069	1.06
Bloomington, MN (city) Hennepin County	896	1.05
Northville, MI (township) Wayne County	220	1.05
Inglewood-Finn Hill, WA (cdp) King County	235	1.04
Moraga, CA (town) Contra Costa County	173	1.04
Killingly, CT (town) Windham County	172	1.04
East Hampton, CT (town) Middlesex County	139	1.04
Sun Prairie, WI (city) Dane County	208	1.03
Hopkins, MN (city) Hennepin County	176	1.03
Plymouth, MA (town) Plymouth County	525	1.02
Hamburg, MI (township) Livingston County	209	1.02
Pembroke, MA (town) Plymouth County	173	1.02
Weston, WI (village) Marathon County	125	1.02
Missoula, MT (city) Missoula County	575	1.01

Notes: (cdp) census designated place; Refer to the Explanation of Data in the front of the book for more detailed information.

French, except Basque

Top 150 Places Sorted by Number

(Based on all places, regardless of population)

Place	Number	%
New York, NY (city) New York City	52,907	0.66
Los Angeles, CA (city) Los Angeles County	49,284	1.33
Houston, TX (city) Harris County	36,790	1.88
Metairie, LA (cdp) Jefferson Parish	33,209	22.77
Phoenix, AZ (city) Maricopa County	31,941	2.42
San Diego, CA (city) San Diego County	28,937	2.37
New Orleans, LA (city) Orleans Parish	27,187	5.61
Chicago, IL (city) Cook County	24,043	0.83
Baton Rouge, LA (city) East Baton Rouge Parish	20,340	8.92
San Antonio, TX (city) Bexar County	19,624	1.71
Manchester, NH (city) Hillsborough County	19,235	17.98
Seattle, WA (city) King County	18,743	3.33
Lafayette, LA (city) Lafayette Parish	18,647	16.91
Portland, OR (city) Multnomah County	18,441	3.49
Dallas, TX (city) Dallas County	18,072	1.52
San Francisco, CA (city) San Francisco County	17,957	2.31
Worcester, MA (city) Worcester County	17,719	10.26
Austin, TX (city) Travis County	17,520	2.67
Jacksonville, FL (special city) Duval County	16,196	2.20
San Jose, CA (city) Santa Clara County	15,953	1.78
Indianapolis, IN (special city) Marion County	15,444	1.97
Toledo, OH (city) Lucas County	14,382	4.59
Columbus, OH (city) Franklin County	13,588	1.91
Denver, CO (city) Denver County	13,568	2.45
Tucson, AZ (city) Pima County	13,250	2.72
Las Vegas, NV (city) Clark County	13,241	2.77
Mesa, AZ (city) Maricopa County	12,835	3.23
Minneapolis, MN (city) Hennepin County	12,685	3.32
Springfield, MA (city) Hampden County	12,437	8.18
Colorado Springs, CO (city) El Paso County	12,418	3.44
Virginia Beach, VA (independent city) Virginia Beach city	12,388	2.91
Fall River, MA (city) Bristol County	12,343	13.43
Milwaukee, WI (city) Milwaukee County	11,751	1.97
Nashua, NH (city) Hillsborough County	11,651	13.45
Lowell, MA (city) Middlesex County	11,607	11.04
Albuquerque, NM (city) Bernalillo County	11,529	2.57
Philadelphia, PA (city) Philadelphia County	11,258	0.74
Oklahoma City, OK (city) Oklahoma County	11,253	2.22
Bristol, CT (city) Hartford County	11,082	18.45
Kenner, LA (city) Jefferson Parish	11,064	15.69
Chicopee, MA (city) Hampden County	10,946	20.03
Boston, MA (city) Suffolk County	10,903	1.85
Saint Paul, MN (city) Ramsey County	10,853	3.78
Tulsa, OK (city) Tulsa County	10,718	2.73
Warwick, RI (city) Kent County	10,713	12.48
Woonsocket, RI (city) Providence County	9,902	22.91
Omaha, NE (city) Douglas County	9,878	2.53
Nashville-Davidson, TN (special city) Davidson County	9,867	1.81
Fort Worth, TX (city) Tarrant County	9,741	1.82
Charlotte, NC (city) Mecklenburg County	9,675	1.78
Pawtucket, RI (city) Providence County	9,574	13.12
Wichita, KS (city) Sedgwick County	9,523	2.77
Kansas City, MO (city) Jackson County	9,441	2.14
Saint Petersburg, FL (city) Pinellas County	9,438	3.81
Brookhaven, NY (town) Suffolk County	9,044	2.02
Anchorage, AK (municipality) Anchorage Borough	8,842	3.40
Chalmette, LA (cdp) Saint Bernard Parish	8,818	27.49
Hempstead, NY (town) Nassau County	8,604	1.14
Long Beach, CA (city) Los Angeles County	8,562	1.86
New Bedford, MA (city) Bristol County	8,529	9.10
Arlington, TX (city) Tarrant County	8,434	2.54
Sacramento, CA (city) Sacramento County	8,389	2.06
Spokane, WA (city) Spokane County	8,384	4.27
Saint Louis, MO (independent city) Saint Louis city	8,376	2.41
Lake Charles, LA (city) Calcasieu Parish	8,065	11.28
Haverhill, MA (city) Essex County	7,842	13.30
Fort Wayne, IN (city) Allen County	7,836	3.80
Shreveport, LA (city) Caddo Parish	7,652	3.82
Aurora, CO (city) Arapahoe County	7,482	2.71
Memphis, TN (city) Shelby County	7,464	1.15
Scottsdale, AZ (city) Maricopa County	7,445	3.67
Fresno, CA (city) Fresno County	7,321	1.71
Warren, MI (city) Macomb County	7,314	5.29
Fitchburg, MA (city) Worcester County	7,289	18.64
Tampa, FL (city) Hillsborough County	7,198	2.37
Huntington Beach, CA (city) Orange County	7,021	3.70
Washington, DC (city) District of Columbia	6,909	1.21
Leominster, MA (city) Worcester County	6,803	16.47
Portland, ME (city) Cumberland County	6,741	10.49
Boise City, ID (city) Ada County	6,701	3.60
Houma, LA (city) Terrebonne Parish	6,659	20.73
Plano, TX (city) Collin County	6,617	2.98
Enfield, CT (town) Hartford County	6,587	14.57
Providence, RI (city) Providence County	6,551	3.77
Coventry, RI (town) Kent County	6,548	19.47
Lewiston, ME (city) Androscoggin County	6,536	18.31
Madison, WI (city) Dane County	6,509	3.14
Glendale, AZ (city) Maricopa County	6,434	2.94
Attleboro, MA (city) Bristol County	6,310	15.00
Reno, NV (city) Washoe County	6,302	3.49
Lincoln, NE (city) Lancaster County	6,258	2.78
Syracuse, NY (city) Onondaga County	6,203	4.21
Tacoma, WA (city) Pierce County	6,181	3.20
Cranston, RI (city) Providence County	6,157	7.77
Green Bay, WI (city) Brown County	6,130	5.99
Waterbury, CT (city) New Haven County	6,087	5.67
Pittsfield, MA (city) Berkshire County	6,083	13.28
Riverside, CA (city) Riverside County	6,069	2.38
Anaheim, CA (city) Orange County	6,052	1.85
Henderson, NV (city) Clark County	6,032	3.43
Raleigh, NC (city) Wake County	5,891	2.13
Taunton, MA (city) Bristol County	5,851	10.45
Westfield, MA (city) Hampden County	5,813	14.51
Concord, NH (city) Merrimack County	5,797	14.25
Sterling Heights, MI (city) Macomb County	5,744	4.61
Santa Rosa, CA (city) Sonoma County	5,739	3.89
Clinton, MI (cdp) Macomb County	5,707	5.97
Marrero, LA (cdp) Jefferson Parish	5,658	15.68
El Paso, TX (city) El Paso County	5,608	0.99
Eugene, OR (city) Lane County	5,606	4.07
Cincinnati, OH (city) Hamilton County	5,602	1.69
Rochester, NH (city) Strafford County	5,586	19.63
Lakewood, CO (city) Jefferson County	5,570	3.87
Paradise, NV (cdp) Clark County	5,555	2.99
Livonia, MI (city) Wayne County	5,485	5.46
West Warwick, RI (cdp) Kent County	5,473	18.50
Vancouver, WA (city) Clark County	5,446	3.80
Cumberland, RI (town) Providence County	5,378	16.89
New Iberia, LA (city) Iberia Parish	5,354	16.42
Corpus Christi, TX (city) Nueces County	5,327	1.92
Lexington-Fayette, KY (special city) Fayette County	5,316	2.04
Oakland, CA (city) Alameda County	5,302	1.33
Buffalo, NY (city) Erie County	5,292	1.81
Colonie, NY (town) Albany County	5,256	6.63
Grand Rapids, MI (city) Kent County	5,217	2.64
Chandler, AZ (city) Maricopa County	5,201	2.95
Overland Park, KS (city) Johnson County	5,181	3.48
Dracut, MA (town) Middlesex County	5,165	18.08
Bakersfield, CA (city) Kern County	5,147	2.08
Detroit, MI (city) Wayne County	5,130	0.54
Lynn, MA (city) Essex County	5,112	5.74
Laplace, LA (cdp) Saint John the Baptist Parish	5,085	18.48
Southington, CT (town) Hartford County	5,061	12.74
Oceanside, CA (city) San Diego County	5,050	3.14
Derry, NH (town) Rockingham County	5,029	14.78
Atlanta, GA (city) Fulton County	4,984	1.20
Islip, NY (town) Suffolk County	4,982	1.54
Burlington, VT (city) Chittenden County	4,945	12.72
Honolulu, HI (cdp) Honolulu County	4,931	1.33
Fort Collins, CO (city) Larimer County	4,906	4.14
Modesto, CA (city) Stanislaus County	4,901	2.59
Beaumont, TX (city) Jefferson County	4,891	4.29
Manchester, CT (town) Hartford County	4,882	8.92
Agawam, MA (city) Hampden County	4,839	17.19
Santa Clarita, CA (city) Los Angeles County	4,837	3.20
Des Moines, IA (city) Polk County	4,783	2.41
Mobile, AL (city) Mobile County	4,763	2.39
Springfield, MO (city) Greene County	4,728	3.11
Westland, MI (city) Wayne County	4,722	5.45
Baltimore, MD (independent city) Baltimore city	4,721	0.73

Notes: (cdp) census designated place; Refer to the Explanation of Data in the front of the book for more detailed information.

French, except Basque

Top 150 Places Sorted by Percent

(Based on all places, regardless of population)

Place	Number	%
Hamlin, ME (town) Aroostook County	183	66.06
Nashville, ME (plantation) Aroostook County	35	64.81
Wallagrass, ME (town) Aroostook County	356	64.26
Eagle Lake, ME (town) Aroostook County	519	63.84
Winterville, ME (plantation) Aroostook County	119	59.50
Codyville, ME (plantation) Washington County	11	57.89
Cyr, ME (plantation) Aroostook County	69	57.02
Cache, UT (cdp) Cache County	10	55.56
Lambert, OK (town) Alfalfa County	5	55.56
Bellmont, NY (town) Franklin County	783	54.22
New Canada, ME (town) Aroostook County	165	52.72
Stockholm, ME (town) Aroostook County	144	51.25
Tupper Lake, NY (village) Franklin County	1,962	50.14
Tagg Flats, OK (cdp) Delaware County	9	47.37
North Grosvenor Dale, CT (cdp) Windham County	690	47.20
Duane, NY (town) Franklin County	65	47.10
Bloomfield, VT (town) Essex County	150	46.58
West Forks, ME (plantation) Somerset County	22	45.83
Roxbury, ME (town) Oxford County	191	45.58
Altamont, NY (town) Franklin County	2,789	45.45
Krupp, WA (town) Grant County	35	44.87
Saint Agatha, ME (town) Aroostook County	346	42.98
Parker, MN (township) Marshall County	18	42.86
Garfield, ME (plantation) Aroostook County	31	42.47
Barton, VT (village) Orleans County	303	42.14
Chesterfield, NY (town) Essex County	1,009	41.88
Brandon, NY (town) Franklin County	223	41.68
Waverly, NY (town) Franklin County	456	41.53
Portage Lake, ME (town) Aroostook County	145	40.73
Jean Lafitte, LA (town) Jefferson Parish	849	39.75
Milan, NH (town) Coos County	522	39.58
Byron, ME (town) Oxford County	34	39.53
Browns Creek, MN (township) Red Lake County	28	39.44
Coventry, VT (town) Orleans County	383	37.77
Ophir, UT (town) Tooele County	6	37.50
Livonia, LA (town) Pointe Coupee Parish	493	36.87
Columbia, NH (town) Coos County	270	36.49
Dickinson, NY (town) Franklin County	270	36.19
Bay Lake, FL (city) Orange County	14	35.90
Brushton, NY (village) Franklin County	171	35.63
Russia, OH (village) Shelby County	202	35.56
Gorham, NH (town) Coos County	1,025	35.34
Sawpit, CO (town) San Miguel County	6	35.29
Fairbanks, MI (township) Delta County	111	35.02
Miltonsburg, OH (village) Monroe County	7	35.00
Harrisville, NY (village) Lewis County	232	34.99
Berwick, LA (town) Saint Mary Parish	1,544	34.95
Dummer, NH (town) Coos County	118	34.20
Saint John, ME (plantation) Aroostook County	96	34.16
Moose River, ME (town) Somerset County	84	34.15
Brighton, VT (town) Essex County	430	34.13
Canaan, VT (town) Essex County	371	33.88
Jay, NY (town) Essex County	780	33.82
South Ashburnham, MA (cdp) Worcester County	342	33.73
Terrebonne, MN (township) Red Lake County	43	33.59
Harrisville, RI (cdp) Providence County	511	33.55
Alburg, VT (village) Grand Isle County	168	33.47
Parnell, MN (township) Polk County	25	33.33
Saint Francis, ME (town) Aroostook County	193	33.05
Clinton, NY (town) Clinton County	247	32.89
Island Pond, VT (cdp) Essex County	280	32.86
Barton, VT (town) Orleans County	913	32.84
Lyon Mountain, NY (cdp) Clinton County	158	32.78
Beaver, IA (city) Boone County	18	32.73
Harahan, LA (city) Jefferson Parish	3,215	32.60
North Hudson, NY (town) Essex County	87	32.46
Ellenburg, NY (town) Clinton County	579	32.38
Musselshell, MT (cdp) Musselshell County	22	32.35
Roxbury, VT (town) Washington County	184	32.22
Diana, NY (town) Lewis County	533	31.99
Lewis, NY (town) Essex County	379	31.96
Ashland, ME (town) Aroostook County	476	31.63
Merrill, ME (town) Aroostook County	79	31.60
Wauregan, CT (cdp) Windham County	326	31.35
Eden, VT (town) Lamoille County	361	31.34
Paradis, LA (cdp) Saint Charles Parish	436	31.28
Black Brook, NY (town) Clinton County	519	31.25
Concord, VT (town) Essex County	372	31.10
Louisville, MN (township) Red Lake County	62	31.00
Wellington, ME (town) Piscataquis County	75	30.99
Prairie du Rocher, IL (village) Randolph County	191	30.96
Waite, ME (town) Washington County	37	30.83
Milltown, SD (cdp) Hutchinson County	4	30.77
Caribou, ME (city) Aroostook County	2,539	30.59
Keeseville, NY (village) Clinton County	565	30.56
Norton, VT (town) Essex County	25	30.49
Caswell, ME (town) Aroostook County	89	30.38
Constable, NY (town) Franklin County	433	30.32
Dennistown, ME (plantation) Somerset County	10	30.30
Overly, ND (city) Bottineau County	10	30.30
Golden Meadow, LA (town) Lafourche Parish	640	30.00
Port Barre, LA (town) Saint Landry Parish	690	29.90
South Woodstock, CT (cdp) Windham County	341	29.86
Clarksburg, MA (town) Berkshire County	502	29.77
Millinocket, ME (town) Penobscot County	1,548	29.75
Jackman, ME (town) Somerset County	210	29.75
Westfield, VT (town) Orleans County	144	29.75
Northumberland, NH (town) Coos County	724	29.70
Macwahoc, ME (plantation) Aroostook County	27	29.67
Cankton, LA (village) Saint Landry Parish	114	29.61
Andover, MN (township) Polk County	47	29.56
Orleans, VT (village) Orleans County	242	29.48
Lafitte, LA (cdp) Jefferson Parish	486	29.45
Au Sable Forks, NY (cdp) Clinton County	196	29.43
Bingham, ME (town) Somerset County	291	29.42
Saranac Lake, NY (village) Franklin County	1,491	29.38
Norco, LA (cdp) Saint Charles Parish	1,023	29.25
Brooks, MN (city) Red Lake County	42	29.17
Zippel, MN (township) Lake of the Woods County	30	29.13
Masardis, ME (town) Aroostook County	79	29.04
Burrillville, RI (town) Providence County	4,579	28.99
Arabi, LA (cdp) Saint Bernard Parish	2,344	28.93
Covington, PA (township) Clearfield County	182	28.93
Onstad, MN (township) Polk County	17	28.81
Labadieville, LA (cdp) Assumption Parish	519	28.69
Stewartstown, NH (town) Coos County	290	28.66
Meraux, LA (cdp) Saint Bernard Parish	2,938	28.62
Hardwick, VT (town) Caledonia County	908	28.61
Dorchester, NH (town) Grafton County	104	28.49
Lunenburg, VT (town) Essex County	382	28.46
East Brooklyn, CT (cdp) Windham County	376	28.42
Shelburne, NH (town) Coos County	107	28.31
Stark, NH (town) Coos County	150	28.30
Bangor, NY (town) Franklin County	609	28.19
Monson Center, MA (cdp) Hampden County	543	28.18
Allagash, ME (town) Aroostook County	76	28.04
Landaff, NH (town) Grafton County	111	27.89
Lambert, MN (township) Red Lake County	41	27.89
Lowell, VT (town) Orleans County	207	27.86
Sheffield, VT (town) Caledonia County	190	27.82
Chapman, ME (town) Aroostook County	131	27.81
Saint George, VT (town) Chittenden County	193	27.65
Alpine Northeast, WY (cdp) Lincoln County	29	27.62
Savoy, MA (town) Berkshire County	191	27.60
Destrehan, LA (cdp) Saint Charles Parish	3,095	27.59
Thompson, CT (town) Windham County	2,449	27.59
Madrid, ME (town) Franklin County	40	27.59
Isle La Motte, VT (town) Grand Isle County	137	27.51
Frenchville, ME (town) Aroostook County	336	27.50
Chalmette, LA (cdp) Saint Bernard Parish	8,818	27.49
Morgan City, LA (city) Saint Mary Parish	3,587	27.46
Mooers, NY (cdp) Clinton County	110	27.36
Danielson, CT (borough) Windham County	1,139	27.31
Orange, NH (town) Grafton County	83	27.30
Upton, ME (town) Oxford County	15	27.27
Biehle, MO (village) Perry County	3	27.27
Glastenbury, VT (town) Bennington County	3	27.27
Gramercy, LA (town) Saint James Parish	836	27.23
Perham, ME (town) Aroostook County	118	27.19
Plaucheville, LA (village) Avoyelles Parish	83	27.12

Notes: (cdp) census designated place; Refer to the Explanation of Data in the front of the book for more detailed information.

French, except Basque

Top 150 Places Sorted by Percent

(Based on places with populations of 10,000 or more)

Place	Number	%
Burrillville, RI (town) Providence County	4,579	28.99
Meraux, LA (cdp) Saint Bernard Parish	2,938	28.62
Destrehan, LA (cdp) Saint Charles Parish	3,095	27.59
Chalmette, LA (cdp) Saint Bernard Parish	8,818	27.49
Morgan City, LA (city) Saint Mary Parish	3,587	27.46
Bayou Cane, LA (cdp) Terrebonne Parish	4,384	25.99
Killingly, CT (town) Windham County	4,273	25.94
Massena, NY (village) Saint Lawrence County	2,901	25.85
Massena, NY (town) Saint Lawrence County	3,373	25.71
Dudley, MA (town) Worcester County	2,565	25.56
North Adams, MA (city) Berkshire County	3,706	25.25
Westwego, LA (city) Jefferson Parish	2,685	24.77
Palmer, MA (town) Hampden County	3,043	24.35
Plattsburgh, NY (town) Clinton County	2,705	24.31
Luling, LA (cdp) Saint Charles Parish	2,809	24.27
Oxford, MA (town) Worcester County	3,195	23.93
Spencer, MA (town) Worcester County	2,796	23.92
Southbridge, MA (town) Worcester County	4,103	23.84
Plainfield, CT (town) Windham County	3,460	23.67
North Smithfield, RI (town) Providence County	2,495	23.50
Woonsocket, RI (city) Providence County	9,902	22.91
Metairie, LA (cdp) Jefferson Parish	33,209	22.77
Raceland, LA (cdp) Lafourche Parish	2,340	22.57
Charlton, MA (town) Worcester County	2,520	22.37
Millbury, MA (town) Worcester County	2,768	21.65
Estelle, LA (cdp) Jefferson Parish	3,435	21.49
Biddeford, ME (city) York County	4,482	21.40
River Ridge, LA (cdp) Jefferson Parish	3,077	21.07
Pelham, NH (town) Hillsborough County	2,271	20.81
Ogdensburg, NY (city) Saint Lawrence County	2,571	20.80
Houma, LA (city) Terrebonne Parish	6,659	20.73
Leicester, MA (town) Worcester County	2,164	20.67
Athol, MA (town) Worcester County	2,331	20.63
Kingsbury, NY (town) Washington County	2,289	20.49
Plattsburgh, NY (city) Clinton County	3,840	20.48
Auburn, ME (city) Androscoggin County	4,700	20.26
Saco, ME (city) York County	3,407	20.25
Escanaba, MI (city) Delta County	2,659	20.25
Webster, MA (town) Worcester County	3,308	20.15
Somersworth, NH (city) Strafford County	2,311	20.14
Berlin, NH (city) Coos County	2,071	20.05
Chicopee, MA (city) Hampden County	10,946	20.03
Sanford, ME (town) York County	4,140	19.90
Rochester, NH (city) Strafford County	5,586	19.63
Claremont, NH (city) Sullivan County	2,567	19.52
Coventry, RI (town) Kent County	6,548	19.47
Easthampton, MA (city) Hampshire County	3,096	19.36
Thibodaux, LA (city) Lafourche Parish	2,759	19.27
Jefferson, LA (cdp) Jefferson Parish	2,287	19.26
Cohoes, NY (city) Albany County	2,984	19.23
Sulphur, LA (city) Calcasieu Parish	3,877	19.01
Griswold, CT (town) New London County	2,043	18.90
Mandeville, LA (city) Saint Tammany Parish	2,022	18.88
Auburn, MA (town) Worcester County	3,000	18.87
Gardner, MA (city) Worcester County	3,915	18.85
Stafford, CT (town) Tolland County	2,111	18.67
Fitchburg, MA (city) Worcester County	7,289	18.64
Eunice, LA (city) Saint Landry Parish	2,116	18.60
Swansea, MA (town) Bristol County	2,956	18.59
Timberlane, LA (cdp) Jefferson Parish	2,124	18.53
Crowley, LA (city) Acadia Parish	2,643	18.52
West Warwick, RI (cdp) Kent County	5,473	18.50
Laplace, LA (cdp) Saint John the Baptist Parish	5,085	18.48
Bristol, CT (city) Hartford County	11,082	18.45
Shenandoah, LA (cdp) East Baton Rouge Parish	3,140	18.35
Lewiston, ME (city) Androscoggin County	6,536	18.31
Waterville, ME (city) Kennebec County	2,831	18.14
Dracut, MA (town) Middlesex County	5,165	18.08
Groves, TX (city) Jefferson County	2,864	18.08
Rutland, VT (city) Rutland County	3,121	18.05
Belchertown, MA (town) Hampshire County	2,337	18.02
Manchester, NH (city) Hillsborough County	19,235	17.98
Plymouth, CT (town) Litchfield County	2,092	17.98
Augusta, ME (city) Kennebec County	3,296	17.76
Acushnet, MA (town) Bristol County	1,791	17.63
Uxbridge, MA (town) Worcester County	1,951	17.52
Malone, NY (town) Franklin County	2,620	17.49
Windham, ME (town) Cumberland County	2,587	17.36
Agawam, MA (city) Hampden County	4,839	17.19
Glens Falls, NY (city) Warren County	2,450	16.96
Lafayette, LA (city) Lafayette Parish	18,647	16.91
Cumberland, RI (town) Providence County	5,378	16.89
Port Neches, TX (city) Jefferson County	2,281	16.84
Tyngsborough, MA (town) Middlesex County	1,857	16.76
Westbrook, ME (city) Cumberland County	2,686	16.64
Leominster, MA (city) Worcester County	6,803	16.47
New Iberia, LA (city) Iberia Parish	5,354	16.42
Moreau, NY (town) Saratoga County	2,248	16.26
Bangor, MI (township) Bay County	2,516	16.18
Colchester, VT (town) Chittenden County	2,745	16.16
Laconia, NH (city) Belknap County	2,643	16.11
Hudson, NH (town) Hillsborough County	3,688	16.09
Lincoln, RI (town) Providence County	3,362	16.09
Goffstown, NH (town) Hillsborough County	2,696	15.93
Valley Falls, RI (cdp) Providence County	1,835	15.91
Westport, MA (town) Bristol County	2,247	15.84
Kenner, LA (city) Jefferson Parish	11,064	15.69
Marrero, LA (cdp) Jefferson Parish	5,658	15.68
Hooksett, NH (town) Merrimack County	1,826	15.58
South Hadley, MA (town) Hampshire County	2,678	15.57
Fairhaven, MA (town) Bristol County	2,514	15.56
Somerset, MA (cdp) Bristol County	2,835	15.55
Moss Bluff, LA (cdp) Calcasieu Parish	1,637	15.54
Northbridge, MA (town) Worcester County	2,050	15.53
Harvey, LA (cdp) Jefferson Parish	3,439	15.45
Warren, RI (town) Bristol County	1,731	15.24
Gorham, ME (town) Cumberland County	2,149	15.20
Jennings, LA (city) Jefferson Davis Parish	1,679	15.12
Salem, NH (town) Rockingham County	4,220	15.01
Attleboro, MA (city) Bristol County	6,310	15.00
Dover, NH (city) Strafford County	4,031	14.99
Scituate, RI (town) Providence County	1,547	14.98
North Attleborough Center, MA (cdp) Bristol County	2,515	14.94
Milford, NH (town) Hillsborough County	2,009	14.84
Amesbury, MA (town) Essex County	2,426	14.80
Derry, NH (town) Rockingham County	5,029	14.78
Bennington, VT (town) Bennington County	2,339	14.78
Slidell, LA (city) Saint Tammany Parish	3,777	14.76
Plainville, CT (town) Hartford County	2,529	14.59
Enfield, CT (town) Hartford County	6,587	14.57
Westfield, MA (city) Hampden County	5,813	14.51
Ludlow, MA (town) Hampden County	3,068	14.47
Tiverton, RI (town) Newport County	2,205	14.45
Seekonk, MA (town) Bristol County	1,928	14.36
Bellingham, MA (town) Norfolk County	2,198	14.35
Greenfield, MA (town) Franklin County	2,606	14.34
Grafton, MA (town) Worcester County	2,129	14.29
Wolcott, CT (town) New Haven County	2,172	14.28
Concord, NH (city) Merrimack County	5,797	14.25
Alpena, MI (city) Alpena County	1,588	14.23
Rehoboth, MA (town) Bristol County	1,447	14.23
Ellington, CT (town) Tolland County	1,812	14.02
West Springfield, MA (cdp) Hampden County	3,877	13.90
Merrimack, NH (town) Hillsborough County	3,481	13.86
Coventry, CT (town) Tolland County	1,591	13.83
Queensbury, NY (town) Warren County	3,497	13.79
Gretna, LA (city) Jefferson Parish	2,379	13.72
Bradley, IL (village) Kankakee County	1,713	13.46
Nashua, NH (city) Hillsborough County	11,651	13.45
Winchester, CT (town) Litchfield County	1,434	13.45
Fall River, MA (city) Bristol County	12,343	13.43
Haverhill, MA (city) Essex County	7,842	13.30
Pittsfield, MA (city) Berkshire County	6,083	13.28
Keene, NH (city) Cheshire County	2,984	13.23
North Attleborough, MA (town) Bristol County	3,579	13.19
Pawtucket, RI (city) Providence County	9,574	13.12
Terrytown, LA (cdp) Jefferson Parish	3,306	13.02
Nederland, TX (city) Jefferson County	2,252	13.01
Marquette, MI (city) Marquette County	2,539	12.96
Holden, MA (town) Worcester County	2,024	12.96

Notes: (cdp) census designated place; Refer to the Explanation of Data in the front of the book for more detailed information.

French Canadian

Top 150 Places Sorted by Number

(Based on all places, regardless of population)

Place	Number	%
Manchester, NH (city) Hillsborough County	17,681	16.52
Nashua, NH (city) Hillsborough County	11,038	12.75
New York, NY (city) New York City	10,645	0.13
Lewiston, ME (city) Androscoggin County	10,497	29.41
Woonsocket, RI (city) Providence County	10,008	23.15
Lowell, MA (city) Middlesex County	8,846	8.41
Los Angeles, CA (city) Los Angeles County	7,940	0.21
Chicopee, MA (city) Hampden County	7,827	14.32
Phoenix, AZ (city) Maricopa County	7,735	0.59
Worcester, MA (city) Worcester County	7,394	4.28
Boston, MA (city) Suffolk County	7,145	1.21
Springfield, MA (city) Hampden County	6,656	4.38
Lafayette, LA (city) Lafayette Parish	6,633	6.02
San Diego, CA (city) San Diego County	6,337	0.52
New Bedford, MA (city) Bristol County	5,557	5.93
Biddeford, ME (city) York County	5,505	26.29
Fall River, MA (city) Bristol County	5,445	5.92
Pawtucket, RI (city) Providence County	5,427	7.44
Houston, TX (city) Harris County	5,419	0.28
Chicago, IL (city) Cook County	4,945	0.17
Bristol, CT (city) Hartford County	4,766	7.94
Fitchburg, MA (city) Worcester County	4,702	12.02
Haverhill, MA (city) Essex County	4,657	7.90
Leominster, MA (city) Worcester County	4,627	11.20
Cumberland, RI (town) Providence County	4,612	14.48
Dracut, MA (town) Middlesex County	4,522	15.83
Portland, OR (city) Multnomah County	4,456	0.84
Jacksonville, FL (special city) Duval County	4,238	0.58
Warwick, RI (city) Kent County	4,233	4.93
Concord, NH (city) Merrimack County	4,150	10.20
Virginia Beach, VA (independent city) Virginia Beach city	4,063	0.96
Berlin, NH (city) Coos County	4,022	38.93
Auburn, ME (city) Androscoggin County	3,956	17.05
Seattle, WA (city) King County	3,891	0.69
Methuen, MA (city) Essex County	3,833	8.75
Lynn, MA (city) Essex County	3,826	4.29
Gardner, MA (city) Worcester County	3,734	17.98
Attleboro, MA (city) Bristol County	3,627	8.62
Baton Rouge, LA (city) East Baton Rouge Parish	3,531	1.55
Sanford, ME (town) York County	3,507	16.86
Enfield, CT (town) Hartford County	3,499	7.74
San Antonio, TX (city) Bexar County	3,493	0.31
Lincoln, RI (town) Providence County	3,485	16.68
Warren, MI (city) Macomb County	3,469	2.51
Minneapolis, MN (city) Hennepin County	3,457	0.90
Burlington, VT (city) Chittenden County	3,419	8.79
Tucson, AZ (city) Pima County	3,416	0.70
Waltham, MA (city) Middlesex County	3,395	5.73
Rochester, NH (city) Strafford County	3,366	11.83
Salem, MA (city) Essex County	3,309	8.19
Goffstown, NH (town) Hillsborough County	3,300	19.49
Saint Paul, MN (city) Ramsey County	3,286	1.14
Lawrence, MA (city) Essex County	3,175	4.41
Milwaukee, WI (city) Milwaukee County	3,161	0.53
Las Vegas, NV (city) Clark County	3,158	0.66
Portland, ME (city) Cumberland County	3,154	4.91
Green Bay, WI (city) Brown County	3,154	3.08
San Jose, CA (city) Santa Clara County	3,115	0.35
Hudson, NH (town) Hillsborough County	3,113	13.58
San Francisco, CA (city) San Francisco County	3,099	0.40
Westfield, MA (city) Hampden County	3,078	7.68
Colorado Springs, CO (city) El Paso County	3,002	0.83
Saco, ME (city) York County	2,991	17.78
Merrimack, NH (town) Hillsborough County	2,982	11.87
Agawam, MA (city) Hampden County	2,909	10.34
Coventry, RI (town) Kent County	2,876	8.55
Burrillville, RI (town) Providence County	2,866	18.14
Taunton, MA (city) Bristol County	2,836	5.07
North Smithfield, RI (town) Providence County	2,821	26.57
Mesa, AZ (city) Maricopa County	2,821	0.71
Austin, TX (city) Travis County	2,821	0.43
Lake Charles, LA (city) Calcasieu Parish	2,802	3.92
Derry, NH (town) Rockingham County	2,790	8.20
West Warwick, RI (cdp) Kent County	2,779	9.39
Anchorage, AK (municipality) Anchorage Borough	2,775	1.07
Waterbury, CT (city) New Haven County	2,757	2.57
Brookhaven, NY (town) Suffolk County	2,741	0.61
Providence, RI (city) Providence County	2,735	1.58
Colchester, VT (town) Chittenden County	2,700	15.90
Augusta, ME (city) Kennebec County	2,680	14.44
Sterling Heights, MI (city) Macomb County	2,679	2.15
Livonia, MI (city) Wayne County	2,637	2.62
Metairie, LA (cdp) Jefferson Parish	2,612	1.79
Toledo, OH (city) Lucas County	2,604	0.83
North Attleborough, MA (town) Bristol County	2,602	9.59
Manchester, CT (town) Hartford County	2,577	4.71
Denver, CO (city) Denver County	2,544	0.46
Syracuse, NY (city) Onondaga County	2,539	1.72
Norwich, CT (city) New London County	2,528	7.00
Saint Petersburg, FL (city) Pinellas County	2,528	1.02
Dallas, TX (city) Dallas County	2,527	0.21
New Orleans, LA (city) Orleans Parish	2,501	0.52
Waterville, ME (city) Kennebec County	2,493	15.98
Laconia, NH (city) Belknap County	2,484	15.14
Colonie, NY (town) Albany County	2,452	3.09
Killingly, CT (town) Windham County	2,428	14.74
Albuquerque, NM (city) Bernalillo County	2,425	0.54
Holyoke, MA (city) Hampden County	2,397	6.02
Southbridge, MA (town) Worcester County	2,385	13.86
Brockton, MA (city) Plymouth County	2,376	2.52
Cranston, RI (city) Providence County	2,343	2.96
Houma, LA (city) Terrebonne Parish	2,339	7.28
Salem, NH (town) Rockingham County	2,323	8.26
Billerica, MA (town) Middlesex County	2,323	5.96
Meriden, CT (city) New Haven County	2,280	3.91
Dover, NH (city) Strafford County	2,270	8.44
Chelmsford, MA (town) Middlesex County	2,268	6.70
Quincy, MA (city) Norfolk County	2,264	2.57
Clinton, MI (cdp) Macomb County	2,258	2.36
Marlborough, MA (city) Middlesex County	2,252	6.21
Spokane, WA (city) Spokane County	2,230	1.14
Bedford, NH (town) Hillsborough County	2,222	12.16
Southington, CT (town) Hartford County	2,215	5.58
Detroit, MI (city) Wayne County	2,181	0.23
Peabody, MA (city) Essex County	2,153	4.47
West Springfield, MA (cdp) Hampden County	2,137	7.66
East Hartford, CT (cdp) Hartford County	2,094	4.22
Madawaska, ME (town) Aroostook County	2,069	45.63
South Hadley, MA (town) Hampshire County	2,058	11.97
Indianapolis, IN (special city) Marion County	2,041	0.26
Pittsfield, MA (city) Berkshire County	2,025	4.42
Columbus, OH (city) Franklin County	2,010	0.28
Easthampton, MA (city) Hampshire County	2,005	12.54
Westland, MI (city) Wayne County	1,998	2.31
Framingham, MA (cdp) Middlesex County	1,973	2.95
Hempstead, NY (town) Nassau County	1,971	0.26
Philadelphia, PA (city) Philadelphia County	1,971	0.13
Essex, VT (town) Chittenden County	1,967	10.56
Taylor, MI (city) Wayne County	1,962	2.98
Hooksett, NH (town) Merrimack County	1,961	16.73
Blackstone, MA (town) Worcester County	1,955	22.21
Barnstable Town, MA (city) Barnstable County	1,937	4.05
Smithfield, RI (town) Providence County	1,904	9.25
Charlotte, NC (city) Mecklenburg County	1,901	0.35
Tampa, FL (city) Hillsborough County	1,892	0.62
Saint Clair Shores, MI (city) Macomb County	1,888	2.99
Weymouth, MA (cdp) Norfolk County	1,866	3.46
Waterford, MI (cdp) Oakland County	1,866	2.55
Somerville, MA (city) Middlesex County	1,858	2.40
New Iberia, LA (city) Iberia Parish	1,848	5.67
Keene, NH (city) Cheshire County	1,839	8.15
Beverly, MA (city) Essex County	1,837	4.61
Tacoma, WA (city) Pierce County	1,822	0.94
Brunswick, ME (town) Cumberland County	1,816	8.58
Cumberland Hill, RI (cdp) Providence County	1,805	23.42
Ludlow, MA (town) Hampden County	1,799	8.48
Northampton, MA (city) Hampshire County	1,791	6.18
Vernon, CT (town) Tolland County	1,788	6.37
New Britain, CT (city) Hartford County	1,775	2.48
Tewksbury, MA (town) Middlesex County	1,771	6.13

Notes: (cdp) census designated place; Refer to the Explanation of Data in the front of the book for more detailed information.

French Canadian

Top 150 Places Sorted by Percent

(Based on all places, regardless of population)

Place	Number	%
Madawaska, ME (town) Aroostook County	2,069	45.63
Barada, NE (village) Richardson County	11	44.00
Damar, KS (city) Rooks County	72	42.86
Van Buren, ME (town) Aroostook County	1,061	40.33
Frenchville, ME (town) Aroostook County	485	39.69
Berlin, NH (city) Coos County	4,022	38.93
Grand Isle, ME (town) Aroostook County	200	38.61
Fort Kent, ME (town) Aroostook County	1,620	38.27
Ferdinand, VT (town) Essex County	17	37.78
Parc, NY (cdp) Clinton County	17	34.69
Lewiston, ME (city) Androscoggin County	10,497	29.41
New Canada, ME (town) Aroostook County	92	29.39
Saint Agatha, ME (town) Aroostook County	234	29.07
Sabattus, ME (town) Androscoggin County	1,279	28.51
Chisholm, ME (cdp) Franklin County	401	28.38
North Smithfield, RI (town) Providence County	2,821	26.57
Biddeford, ME (city) York County	5,505	26.29
Greene, ME (town) Androscoggin County	1,032	25.32
Errol, NH (town) Coos County	79	25.16
Maurice, LA (village) Vermilion Parish	150	23.73
Kertsonville, MN (township) Polk County	24	23.53
Cumberland Hill, RI (cdp) Providence County	1,805	23.42
Woonsocket, RI (city) Providence County	10,008	23.15
Pinardville, NH (cdp) Hillsborough County	1,299	23.12
Estherwood, LA (village) Acadia Parish	190	22.86
Blackstone, MA (town) Worcester County	1,955	22.21
Newport, VT (town) Orleans County	330	21.90
Frenchboro, ME (town) Hancock County	6	21.43
Arcola, MO (village) Dade County	10	21.28
Whiting, VT (town) Addison County	76	21.17
Mooers, NY (town) Clinton County	718	21.09
Rouses Point, NY (village) Clinton County	484	20.95
Caswell, ME (town) Aroostook County	60	20.48
Winslow, ME (cdp) Kennebec County	1,580	20.41
Sheldon, VT (town) Franklin County	401	20.40
Berkshire, VT (town) Franklin County	284	20.39
Hamer, ID (city) Jefferson County	3	20.00
Lydia, LA (cdp) Iberia Parish	224	19.98
Putnam District, CT (cdp) Windham County	1,360	19.96
Swanton, VT (town) Franklin County	1,227	19.78
Champlain, NY (town) Clinton County	1,135	19.60
Goffstown, NH (town) Hillsborough County	3,300	19.49
Putnam, CT (town) Windham County	1,752	19.46
Arundel, ME (town) York County	695	19.46
Gentilly, MN (township) Polk County	64	19.45
Slater, WY (cdp) Platte County	12	19.35
Highgate, VT (town) Franklin County	655	19.28
Pierre Part, LA (cdp) Assumption Parish	628	19.11
Mathews, LA (cdp) Lafourche Parish	361	19.04
Maxfield, ME (town) Penobscot County	14	18.92
Suncook, NH (cdp) Merrimack County	986	18.85
Golden Meadow, LA (town) Lafourche Parish	401	18.80
Piercefield, NY (town) Saint Lawrence County	59	18.79
New Haven, VT (town) Addison County	311	18.67
Dummer, NH (town) Coos County	64	18.55
Derby, VT (town) Orleans County	856	18.48
Burrillville, RI (town) Providence County	2,866	18.14
Champlain, NY (village) Clinton County	218	18.14
Stannard, VT (town) Caledonia County	36	18.09
Winooski, VT (city) Chittenden County	1,185	18.06
Allenstown, NH (town) Merrimack County	872	18.01
Gardner, MA (city) Worcester County	3,734	17.98
Lake Arthur, LA (town) Jefferson Davis Parish	531	17.95
Derby Center, VT (village) Orleans County	118	17.91
Granby, MA (town) Hampshire County	1,092	17.81
Polk Centre, MN (township) Pennington County	13	17.81
Saco, ME (city) York County	2,991	17.78
Rumford, ME (town) Oxford County	1,141	17.63
Enosburg Falls, VT (village) Franklin County	258	17.62
Harrisville, RI (cdp) Providence County	267	17.53
Hanover, ME (town) Oxford County	42	17.43
Wales, ME (town) Androscoggin County	230	17.40
Sprague, CT (town) New London County	515	17.33
Milton, VT (village) Chittenden County	266	17.31
Fort Covington, NY (town) Franklin County	285	17.28
Saint Albans, VT (city) Franklin County	1,317	17.22
Irasburg, VT (town) Orleans County	186	17.22
Newport, VT (city) Orleans County	855	17.18
Auburn, ME (city) Androscoggin County	3,956	17.05
Depauville, NY (cdp) Jefferson County	84	16.97
Lyman, ME (town) York County	642	16.92
South Barre, VT (cdp) Washington County	195	16.88
Sanford, ME (town) York County	3,507	16.86
Loreauville, LA (village) Iberia Parish	162	16.80
Acushnet Center, MA (cdp) Bristol County	549	16.77
Hooksett, NH (town) Merrimack County	1,961	16.73
Auburn, NH (town) Rockingham County	783	16.72
Lincoln, RI (town) Providence County	3,485	16.68
Cut Off, LA (cdp) Lafourche Parish	930	16.68
Niarada, MT (cdp) Sanders County	7	16.67
Shoreham, VT (town) Addison County	203	16.61
East Brooklyn, CT (cdp) Windham County	219	16.55
Sidney, ME (town) Kennebec County	581	16.53
Manchester, NH (city) Hillsborough County	17,681	16.52
Clinton, NY (town) Clinton County	124	16.51
Aurora, KS (city) Cloud County	11	16.42
Jay, ME (town) Franklin County	813	16.31
Sterling, CT (town) Windham County	503	16.23
Reeves, LA (village) Allen Parish	31	16.23
Jefferson, OK (town) Grant County	6	16.22
Chauvin, LA (cdp) Terrebonne Parish	495	16.10
Canaan, VT (town) Essex County	176	16.07
Derby Line, VT (village) Orleans County	127	16.04
Stark, NH (town) Coos County	85	16.04
Quinebaug, CT (cdp) Windham County	173	16.03
Saint Albans, VT (town) Franklin County	814	16.00
Waterville, ME (city) Kennebec County	2,493	15.98
Nahma, MI (township) Delta County	81	15.98
Escanaba, MI (township) Delta County	568	15.94
Colchester, VT (town) Chittenden County	2,700	15.90
Norton, VT (town) Essex County	13	15.85
Dracut, MA (town) Middlesex County	4,522	15.83
Rollinsford, NH (town) Strafford County	418	15.79
Minot, ME (town) Androscoggin County	355	15.79
Bloomer, MN (township) Marshall County	12	15.79
Effie, MN (city) Itasca County	15	15.63
Chaplin, CT (town) Windham County	350	15.56
South Hooksett, NH (cdp) Merrimack County	819	15.54
Moosup, CT (cdp) Windham County	509	15.47
Dayton, ME (town) York County	279	15.46
Thompson, CT (town) Windham County	1,366	15.39
Somersworth, NH (city) Strafford County	1,761	15.34
South Sanford, ME (cdp) York County	633	15.26
Erath, LA (town) Vermilion Parish	337	15.26
Lisbon, ME (town) Androscoggin County	1,382	15.23
Wheaton, KS (city) Pottawatomie County	17	15.18
Dennistown, ME (plantation) Somerset County	5	15.15
Laconia, NH (city) Belknap County	2,484	15.14
Enosburg, VT (town) Franklin County	421	15.13
Barre, VT (town) Washington County	1,149	15.11
Chackbay, LA (cdp) Lafourche Parish	589	14.97
Saranac, NY (town) Clinton County	621	14.91
North Grosvenor Dale, CT (cdp) Windham County	218	14.91
Isle La Motte, VT (town) Grand Isle County	74	14.86
Killingly, CT (town) Windham County	2,428	14.74
Alburg, VT (village) Grand Isle County	74	14.74
Plaucheville, LA (village) Avoyelles Parish	45	14.71
Acushnet, MA (town) Bristol County	1,492	14.68
Lake Linden, MI (village) Houghton County	158	14.67
Ashburnham, MA (town) Worcester County	813	14.66
Jaffrey, NH (town) Cheshire County	802	14.65
Litchfield, NH (town) Hillsborough County	1,077	14.63
Milan, NH (town) Coos County	193	14.63
Franklin, VT (town) Franklin County	189	14.63
Gorham, NH (town) Coos County	424	14.62
Galliano, LA (cdp) Lafourche Parish	1,069	14.56
Cumberland, RI (town) Providence County	4,612	14.48
Augusta, ME (city) Kennebec County	2,680	14.44
Springvale, ME (cdp) York County	494	14.43
Chazy, NY (town) Clinton County	603	14.42

Notes: (cdp) census designated place; Refer to the Explanation of Data in the front of the book for more detailed information.

French Canadian

Top 150 Places Sorted by Percent

(Based on places with populations of 10,000 or more)

Place	Number	%
Berlin, NH (city) Coos County	4,022	38.93
Lewiston, ME (city) Androscoggin County	10,497	29.41
North Smithfield, RI (town) Providence County	2,821	26.57
Biddeford, ME (city) York County	5,505	26.29
Woonsocket, RI (city) Providence County	10,008	23.15
Goffstown, NH (town) Hillsborough County	3,300	19.49
Burrillville, RI (town) Providence County	2,866	18.14
Gardner, MA (city) Worcester County	3,734	17.98
Saco, ME (city) York County	2,991	17.78
Auburn, ME (city) Androscoggin County	3,956	17.05
Sanford, ME (town) York County	3,507	16.86
Hooksett, NH (town) Merrimack County	1,961	16.73
Lincoln, RI (town) Providence County	3,485	16.68
Manchester, NH (city) Hillsborough County	17,681	16.52
Waterville, ME (city) Kennebec County	2,493	15.98
Colchester, VT (town) Chittenden County	2,700	15.90
Dracut, MA (town) Middlesex County	4,522	15.83
Somersworth, NH (city) Strafford County	1,761	15.34
Laconia, NH (city) Belknap County	2,484	15.14
Killingly, CT (town) Windham County	2,428	14.74
Acushnet, MA (town) Bristol County	1,492	14.68
Cumberland, RI (town) Providence County	4,612	14.48
Augusta, ME (city) Kennebec County	2,680	14.44
Chicopee, MA (city) Hampden County	7,827	14.32
Plattsburgh, NY (town) Clinton County	1,554	13.97
Southbridge, MA (town) Worcester County	2,385	13.86
Hudson, NH (town) Hillsborough County	3,113	13.58
Spencer, MA (town) Worcester County	1,581	13.52
Belchertown, MA (town) Hampshire County	1,715	13.22
Nashua, NH (city) Hillsborough County	11,038	12.75
Pelham, NH (town) Hillsborough County	1,374	12.59
Athol, MA (town) Worcester County	1,419	12.56
Easthampton, MA (city) Hampshire County	2,005	12.54
Bedford, NH (town) Hillsborough County	2,222	12.16
Fitchburg, MA (city) Worcester County	4,702	12.02
South Hadley, MA (town) Hampshire County	2,058	11.97
Plainfield, CT (town) Windham County	1,747	11.95
Merrimack, NH (town) Hillsborough County	2,982	11.87
Rochester, NH (city) Strafford County	3,366	11.83
Claremont, NH (city) Sullivan County	1,504	11.44
Jennings, LA (city) Jefferson Davis Parish	1,261	11.36
Uxbridge, MA (town) Worcester County	1,255	11.27
Leominster, MA (city) Worcester County	4,627	11.20
South Burlington, VT (city) Chittenden County	1,765	11.16
Grafton, MA (town) Worcester County	1,662	11.16
Millbury, MA (town) Worcester County	1,403	10.97
Essex, VT (town) Chittenden County	1,967	10.56
Bellingham, MA (town) Norfolk County	1,615	10.55
Escanaba, MI (city) Delta County	1,386	10.55
Valley Falls, RI (cdp) Providence County	1,217	10.55
Agawam, MA (city) Hampden County	2,909	10.34
Massena, NY (village) Saint Lawrence County	1,154	10.28
Concord, NH (city) Merrimack County	4,150	10.20
Tyngsborough, MA (town) Middlesex County	1,122	10.13
Palmer, MA (town) Hampden County	1,235	9.88
Northbridge, MA (town) Worcester County	1,294	9.80
North Attleborough Center, MA (cdp) Bristol County	1,634	9.71
Griswold, CT (town) New London County	1,048	9.70
Massena, NY (town) Saint Lawrence County	1,265	9.64
North Attleborough, MA (town) Bristol County	2,602	9.59
Dudley, MA (town) Worcester County	957	9.54
Bayou Cane, LA (cdp) Terrebonne Parish	1,608	9.53
Amesbury, MA (town) Essex County	1,553	9.47
Westport, MA (town) Bristol County	1,339	9.44
West Warwick, RI (cdp) Kent County	2,779	9.39
Somerset, MA (cdp) Bristol County	1,706	9.36
Smithfield, RI (town) Providence County	1,904	9.25
Webster, MA (town) Worcester County	1,461	8.90
Crowley, LA (city) Acadia Parish	1,259	8.82
Burlington, VT (city) Chittenden County	3,419	8.79
Lebanon, NH (city) Grafton County	1,104	8.78
Methuen, MA (city) Essex County	3,833	8.75
Plattsburgh, NY (city) Clinton County	1,622	8.65
Attleboro, MA (city) Bristol County	3,627	8.62
Malone, NY (town) Franklin County	1,292	8.62
Milford, NH (town) Hillsborough County	1,165	8.61
Brunswick, ME (town) Cumberland County	1,816	8.58
Wrentham, MA (town) Norfolk County	906	8.58
Coventry, RI (town) Kent County	2,876	8.55
Tiverton, RI (town) Newport County	1,298	8.51
Fairhaven, MA (town) Bristol County	1,372	8.49
Ludlow, MA (town) Hampden County	1,799	8.48
Dover, NH (city) Strafford County	2,270	8.44
Lowell, MA (city) Middlesex County	8,846	8.41
Hampton, NH (town) Rockingham County	1,251	8.38
Rehoboth, MA (town) Bristol County	851	8.37
Auburn, MA (town) Worcester County	1,330	8.36
Exeter, NH (town) Rockingham County	1,168	8.31
Westbrook, ME (city) Cumberland County	1,340	8.30
Salem, NH (town) Rockingham County	2,323	8.26
Derry, NH (town) Rockingham County	2,790	8.20
Salem, MA (city) Essex County	3,309	8.19
Swansea, MA (town) Bristol County	1,299	8.17
North Adams, MA (city) Berkshire County	1,198	8.16
Keene, NH (city) Cheshire County	1,839	8.15
Ogdensburg, NY (city) Saint Lawrence County	996	8.06
Windham, NH (town) Rockingham County	851	7.95
Bristol, CT (city) Hartford County	4,766	7.94
Greenfield, MA (town) Franklin County	1,441	7.93
Haverhill, MA (city) Essex County	4,657	7.90
Scarborough, ME (town) Cumberland County	1,338	7.88
Gorham, ME (town) Cumberland County	1,098	7.76
Enfield, CT (town) Hartford County	3,499	7.74
Westfield, MA (city) Hampden County	3,078	7.68
West Springfield, MA (cdp) Hampden County	2,137	7.66
Eunice, LA (city) Saint Landry Parish	869	7.64
Cohoes, NY (city) Albany County	1,177	7.58
Tolland, CT (town) Tolland County	987	7.51
Colchester, CT (town) New London County	1,092	7.50
Thibodaux, LA (city) Lafourche Parish	1,074	7.50
Pawtucket, RI (city) Providence County	5,427	7.44
Londonderry, NH (town) Rockingham County	1,717	7.39
Raceland, LA (cdp) Lafourche Parish	762	7.35
Wilbraham, MA (town) Hampden County	988	7.33
Leicester, MA (town) Worcester County	766	7.32
Oxford, MA (town) Worcester County	976	7.31
Houma, LA (city) Terrebonne Parish	2,339	7.28
South Windsor, CT (town) Hartford County	1,768	7.22
Charlton, MA (town) Worcester County	811	7.20
Durham, NH (town) Strafford County	897	7.08
Plymouth, CT (town) Litchfield County	817	7.02
Norwich, CT (city) New London County	2,528	7.00
South Portland, ME (city) Cumberland County	1,607	6.89
Central Falls, RI (city) Providence County	1,305	6.89
Kennebunk, ME (town) York County	713	6.81
Marinette, WI (city) Marinette County	797	6.80
East Longmeadow, MA (town) Hampden County	956	6.78
Northborough, MA (town) Worcester County	948	6.77
Scituate, RI (town) Providence County	696	6.74
Warren, RI (town) Bristol County	762	6.71
Chelmsford, MA (town) Middlesex County	2,268	6.70
Bennington, VT (town) Bennington County	1,053	6.65
Windham, CT (town) Windham County	1,518	6.64
Norton, MA (town) Bristol County	1,191	6.60
Abbeville, LA (city) Vermilion Parish	779	6.53
Willimantic, CT (cdp) Windham County	1,032	6.52
Amherst, NH (town) Hillsborough County	702	6.52
Westford, MA (town) Middlesex County	1,334	6.43
Vernon, CT (town) Tolland County	1,788	6.37
Seekonk, MA (town) Bristol County	854	6.36
Danvers, MA (cdp) Essex County	1,578	6.26
Marlborough, MA (city) Middlesex County	2,252	6.21
Northampton, MA (city) Hampshire County	1,791	6.18
North Kingstown, RI (town) Washington County	1,620	6.15
Tewksbury, MA (town) Middlesex County	1,771	6.13
Hartford, VT (town) Windsor County	632	6.10
Longmeadow, MA (cdp) Hampden County	950	6.08
Sulphur, LA (city) Calcasieu Parish	1,234	6.05
Plainville, CT (town) Hartford County	1,045	6.03
Coventry, CT (town) Tolland County	694	6.03

Notes: (cdp) census designated place; Refer to the Explanation of Data in the front of the book for more detailed information.

German

Top 150 Places Sorted by Number

(Based on all places, regardless of population)

Place	Number	%
New York, NY (city) New York City	255,536	3.19
Chicago, IL (city) Cook County	189,618	6.55
Phoenix, AZ (city) Maricopa County	181,124	13.71
Los Angeles, CA (city) Los Angeles County	167,160	4.52
Columbus, OH (city) Franklin County	137,761	19.36
San Diego, CA (city) San Diego County	131,592	10.76
Indianapolis, IN (special city) Marion County	130,045	16.62
Milwaukee, WI (city) Milwaukee County	124,484	20.85
Philadelphia, PA (city) Philadelphia County	123,058	8.11
Houston, TX (city) Harris County	118,564	6.07
Omaha, NE (city) Douglas County	112,024	28.72
San Antonio, TX (city) Bexar County	103,366	9.03
Portland, OR (city) Multnomah County	99,715	18.85
Lincoln, NE (city) Lancaster County	89,621	39.75
Brookhaven, NY (town) Suffolk County	87,375	19.49
Hempstead, NY (town) Nassau County	87,201	11.54
Seattle, WA (city) King County	85,484	15.17
Austin, TX (city) Travis County	84,350	12.85
Minneapolis, MN (city) Hennepin County	82,283	21.51
Colorado Springs, CO (city) El Paso County	79,290	21.98
Denver, CO (city) Denver County	76,686	13.83
Madison, WI (city) Dane County	74,418	35.86
Toledo, OH (city) Lucas County	73,482	23.43
Saint Paul, MN (city) Ramsey County	73,265	25.51
Dallas, TX (city) Dallas County	73,062	6.15
Wichita, KS (city) Sedgwick County	71,197	20.70
Jacksonville, FL (special city) Duval County	70,440	9.58
Tucson, AZ (city) Pima County	69,909	14.37
Mesa, AZ (city) Maricopa County	68,647	17.28
Kansas City, MO (city) Jackson County	67,780	15.36
San Jose, CA (city) Santa Clara County	67,712	7.57
Pittsburgh, PA (city) Allegheny County	65,976	19.72
Cincinnati, OH (city) Hamilton County	65,659	19.86
San Francisco, CA (city) San Francisco County	60,176	7.75
Oklahoma City, OK (city) Oklahoma County	59,379	11.74
Virginia Beach, VA (independent city) Virginia Beach city	58,303	13.71
Las Vegas, NV (city) Clark County	58,288	12.17
Fort Wayne, IN (city) Allen County	56,716	27.54
Albuquerque, NM (city) Bernalillo County	56,320	12.55
Charlotte, NC (city) Mecklenburg County	54,861	10.12
Tulsa, OK (city) Tulsa County	51,994	13.23
Saint Louis, MO (independent city) Saint Louis city	50,575	14.53
Sioux Falls, SD (city) Minnehaha County	50,520	40.71
Aurora, CO (city) Arapahoe County	50,449	18.28
Baltimore, MD (independent city) Baltimore city	48,423	7.44
Nashville-Davidson, TN (special city) Davidson County	48,035	8.80
Islip, NY (town) Suffolk County	47,823	14.82
Anchorage, AK (municipality) Anchorage Borough	45,770	17.58
Spokane, WA (city) Spokane County	44,829	22.86
Cleveland, OH (city) Cuyahoga County	44,172	9.23
Des Moines, IA (city) Polk County	42,755	21.52
Cedar Rapids, IA (city) Linn County	42,747	35.46
Oyster Bay, NY (town) Nassau County	42,703	14.53
Scottsdale, AZ (city) Maricopa County	41,695	20.57
Overland Park, KS (city) Johnson County	41,281	27.73
Buffalo, NY (city) Erie County	39,692	13.56
Fort Worth, TX (city) Tarrant County	39,403	7.36
Akron, OH (city) Summit County	39,203	18.06
Louisville, KY (city) Jefferson County	38,979	15.20
Boise City, ID (city) Ada County	38,259	20.58
Arlington, TX (city) Tarrant County	37,847	11.38
Fargo, ND (city) Cass County	36,827	40.56
Fresno, CA (city) Fresno County	36,751	8.60
Saint Petersburg, FL (city) Pinellas County	36,327	14.66
Plano, TX (city) Collin County	36,276	16.32
Lakewood, CO (city) Jefferson County	36,219	25.14
Glendale, AZ (city) Maricopa County	36,070	16.50
Green Bay, WI (city) Brown County	35,842	35.01
Lexington-Fayette, KY (special city) Fayette County	35,189	13.51
Appleton, WI (city) Outagamie County	34,776	49.59
Naperville, IL (city) Du Page County	34,638	27.00
Sacramento, CA (city) Sacramento County	34,198	8.40
Fort Collins, CO (city) Larimer County	34,007	28.71
Long Beach, CA (city) Los Angeles County	33,634	7.29
Chandler, AZ (city) Maricopa County	32,987	18.71
Davenport, IA (city) Scott County	32,389	32.93
Bismarck, ND (city) Burleigh County	32,138	58.13
Babylon, NY (town) Suffolk County	31,723	14.98
Huntington Beach, CA (city) Orange County	31,677	16.68
Huntington, NY (town) Suffolk County	31,620	16.19
Oshkosh, WI (city) Winnebago County	31,287	49.71
Rochester, MN (city) Olmsted County	30,572	35.80
Tacoma, WA (city) Pierce County	30,433	15.75
Henderson, NV (city) Clark County	30,027	17.06
Evansville, IN (city) Vanderburgh County	29,976	24.60
Amherst, NY (town) Erie County	29,827	25.60
Topeka, KS (city) Shawnee County	29,471	24.15
Rockford, IL (city) Winnebago County	29,443	19.67
Billings, MT (city) Yellowstone County	29,442	32.95
Saint Cloud, MN (city) Stearns County	28,762	48.77
Reno, NV (city) Washoe County	28,740	15.91
Waukesha, WI (city) Waukesha County	28,714	44.61
Kenosha, WI (city) Kenosha County	28,533	31.47
Springfield, MO (city) Greene County	28,331	18.66
Cheektowaga, NY (town) Erie County	28,147	29.94
Warren, MI (city) Macomb County	28,146	20.35
West Allis, WI (city) Milwaukee County	28,100	45.84
Tempe, AZ (city) Maricopa County	28,042	17.70
Tampa, FL (city) Hillsborough County	27,990	9.22
Anaheim, CA (city) Orange County	27,971	8.54
Eugene, OR (city) Lane County	27,948	20.28
Arvada, CO (city) Jefferson County	27,865	27.18
Raleigh, NC (city) Wake County	27,737	10.03
Bloomington, MN (city) Hennepin County	27,642	32.44
Washington, DC (city) District of Columbia	27,415	4.79
Springfield, IL (city) Sangamon County	27,385	24.41
Grand Rapids, MI (city) Kent County	27,296	13.80
Memphis, TN (city) Shelby County	27,044	4.16
Vancouver, WA (city) Clark County	26,975	18.83
Dubuque, IA (city) Dubuque County	26,901	46.81
Metairie, LA (cdp) Jefferson Parish	26,485	18.16
Salem, OR (city) Marion County	26,477	19.37
Sioux City, IA (city) Woodbury County	26,416	31.06
New Orleans, LA (city) Orleans Parish	26,404	5.45
Riverside, CA (city) Riverside County	26,216	10.28
Olathe, KS (city) Johnson County	26,173	28.14
El Paso, TX (city) El Paso County	25,770	4.57
Eau Claire, WI (city) Eau Claire County	25,659	41.71
Sheboygan, WI (city) Sheboygan County	25,596	50.38
Bakersfield, CA (city) Kern County	25,541	10.32
Tonawanda, NY (town) Erie County	25,522	32.66
Erie, PA (city) Erie County	25,279	24.37
Westminster, CO (city) Adams County	25,117	24.82
Aurora, IL (city) Kane County	25,070	17.46
Sterling Heights, MI (city) Macomb County	24,814	19.94
Peoria, IL (city) Peoria County	24,774	21.94
Greece, NY (town) Monroe County	24,689	26.23
Corpus Christi, TX (city) Nueces County	24,611	8.87
Boston, MA (city) Suffolk County	24,426	4.15
Janesville, WI (city) Rock County	24,329	40.98
Dayton, OH (city) Montgomery County	23,990	14.44
Arlington, VA (cdp) Arlington County	23,893	12.61
Rochester, NY (city) Monroe County	23,892	10.87
Independence, MO (city) Jackson County	23,598	20.85
Santa Clarita, CA (city) Los Angeles County	23,526	15.54
Gilbert, AZ (town) Maricopa County	23,504	21.38
Wauwatosa, WI (city) Milwaukee County	23,392	49.48
Eagan, MN (city) Dakota County	23,246	36.53
Clinton, MI (cdp) Macomb County	22,997	24.04
Fond du Lac, WI (city) Fond du Lac County	22,946	54.25
Livonia, MI (city) Wayne County	22,822	22.70
Saint Charles, MO (city) Saint Charles County	22,743	37.91
Allentown, PA (city) Lehigh County	22,715	21.30
Racine, WI (city) Racine County	22,692	27.73
Santa Rosa, CA (city) Sonoma County	22,672	15.37
Ann Arbor, MI (city) Washtenaw County	22,546	19.76
Coon Rapids, MN (city) Anoka County	22,440	36.41
Paradise, NV (cdp) Clark County	22,417	12.06
Plymouth, MN (city) Hennepin County	22,230	33.73
Waterloo, IA (city) Black Hawk County	21,994	32.04

Notes: (cdp) census designated place; Refer to the Explanation of Data in the front of the book for more detailed information.

German

Top 150 Places Sorted by Percent

(Based on all places, regardless of population)

Place	Number	%
Blacksville, GA (cdp) Henry County	52	100.00
Fults, IL (village) Monroe County	38	100.00
Alcova, WY (cdp) Natrona County	31	100.00
Biehle, MO (village) Perry County	11	100.00
Thurmond, WV (town) Fayette County	11	100.00
Forest Area, MN (township) Lake of the Woods County	10	100.00
Artas, SD (town) Campbell County	7	100.00
Cave, MO (town) Lincoln County	5	100.00
Anoka, NE (village) Boyd County	4	100.00
Grano, ND (city) Renville County	4	100.00
Hanaford, IL (village) Franklin County	2	100.00
Hibberts, ME (gore) Lincoln County	2	100.00
Maza, ND (city) Towner County	2	100.00
Tenney, MN (city) Wilkin County	1	100.00
Greenwald, MN (city) Stearns County	197	95.17
Graf, IA (city) Dubuque County	92	92.00
Saint Helena, NE (village) Cedar County	71	88.75
Elrosa, MN (city) Stearns County	123	88.49
Akaska, SD (town) Walworth County	33	86.84
Lastrup, MN (city) Morrison County	102	85.71
Argyle, MO (town) Osage County	136	85.53
Willey, IA (city) Carroll County	94	85.45
Saint Martin, MN (city) Stearns County	225	85.23
McLean, NE (village) Pierce County	27	84.38
Nilsen, MN (township) Wilkin County	37	84.09
Bazile Mills, NE (village) Knox County	21	84.00
Grove, MN (township) Stearns County	395	83.86
Spring Hill, MN (city) Stearns County	35	83.33
Mulligan, MN (township) Brown County	206	83.06
Fredonia, ND (city) Logan County	49	83.05
Lake George, MN (township) Stearns County	337	83.00
Mantador, ND (city) Richland County	56	82.35
Alexandria, OH (village) Licking County	14	82.35
Saint Martin, MN (township) Stearns County	409	82.29
Slater, WY (cdp) Platte County	51	82.26
Moyer, MN (township) Swift County	124	82.12
Frederick, KS (city) Rice County	9	81.82
Yetter, IA (city) Calhoun County	26	81.25
Luxemburg, MN (township) Stearns County	569	80.82
Halbur, IA (city) Carroll County	175	80.28
Dimock, SD (town) Hutchinson County	118	80.27
Saint Thomas, MO (town) Cole County	221	80.07
Lowry, SD (town) Walworth County	8	80.00
Washington Lake, MN (township) Sibley County	354	79.91
Westphalia, IA (city) Shelby County	114	79.72
Brighton, MN (township) Nicollet County	145	79.67
Meire Grove, MN (city) Stearns County	129	79.63
Green Isle, MN (township) Sibley County	463	79.55
New Trier, MN (city) Dakota County	97	79.51
Saint Anthony, MN (city) Stearns County	80	79.21
Melrose, MN (township) Stearns County	592	79.14
Penn, MN (township) McLeod County	226	79.02
Cobden, MN (city) Brown County	60	78.95
Sioux Valley, MN (township) Jackson County	224	78.87
Great Bend, ND (city) Richland County	84	78.50
Farming, MN (township) Stearns County	690	78.14
Prairieville, MN (township) Brown County	252	78.02
Fenwood, WI (village) Marathon County	138	77.97
Ottoville, OH (village) Putnam County	677	77.91
Calio, ND (city) Cavalier County	14	77.78
Belfast, MN (township) Murray County	138	77.53
Cottonwood, MN (township) Brown County	730	77.49
Glandorf, OH (village) Putnam County	719	77.48
Regal, MN (city) Kandiyohi County	24	77.42
Rockland, WI (town) Manitowoc County	668	77.40
Miesville, MN (city) Dakota County	101	77.10
New Leipzig, ND (city) Grant County	210	76.92
Krupp, WA (town) Grant County	60	76.92
Walter, MN (township) Lac qui Parle County	156	76.85
Lake Henry, MN (township) Stearns County	246	76.64
Cold Spring, PA (township) Lebanon County	59	76.62
Spring Hill, MN (township) Stearns County	336	76.54
Farmer, SD (town) Hanson County	13	76.47
Hamburg, MN (city) Carver County	435	76.45
Sentinel Butte, ND (city) Golden Valley County	42	76.36
Harbine, NE (village) Jefferson County	45	76.27
Saint Cloud, WI (village) Fond du Lac County	379	76.26
Ridgely, MN (township) Nicollet County	83	76.15
Charlestown, WI (town) Calumet County	591	75.96
Grant, WI (town) Shawano County	738	75.93
Glasgow, MN (township) Wabasha County	236	75.88
Bankston, IA (city) Dubuque County	22	75.86
Hart, MN (township) Winona County	210	75.81
Gascoyne, ND (city) Bowman County	25	75.76
Lomira, WI (town) Dodge County	999	75.74
Cornlea, NE (village) Platte County	31	75.61
Minster, OH (village) Auglaize County	2,131	75.43
Tennyson, WI (village) Grant County	248	75.38
Young America, MN (township) Carver County	618	75.37
Buchanan, ND (city) Stutsman County	64	75.29
Fort Jennings, OH (village) Putnam County	349	75.22
Marshfield, WI (town) Fond du Lac County	794	75.19
Brothertown, WI (town) Calumet County	1,051	75.07
New Riegel, OH (village) Seneca County	165	75.00
Alba, MN (township) Jackson County	126	75.00
Chelsea, SD (town) Faulk County	12	75.00
Saint Charles, SD (cdp) Gregory County	9	75.00
Vail, MN (township) Redwood County	218	74.91
Waverly, MN (township) Martin County	173	74.89
Dryden, MN (township) Sibley County	241	74.84
Marathon, WI (town) Marathon County	813	74.79
Enterprise, WI (town) Oneida County	234	74.76
Mercer, ND (city) McLean County	71	74.74
Amboy, MN (township) Cottonwood County	115	74.68
Dollymount, MN (township) Traverse County	59	74.68
Westport, SD (town) Brown County	100	74.63
Susank, KS (city) Barton County	41	74.55
Pleasant Mound, MN (township) Blue Earth County	204	74.45
Berlin, WI (town) Marathon County	660	74.41
Burkettsville, OH (village) Mercer County	189	74.41
Westford, MN (township) Martin County	264	74.37
Wishek, ND (city) McIntosh County	824	74.30
Eau Pleine, WI (town) Marathon County	559	74.24
Beulah, ND (city) Mercer County	2,343	74.08
Hillman, MN (city) Morrison County	20	74.07
Milford, MN (township) Brown County	619	74.04
Arlington, MN (township) Sibley County	399	74.03
Kelso, MN (township) Sibley County	268	74.03
Petersburg, NE (village) Boone County	279	74.01
Hamburg, WI (town) Marathon County	678	73.94
Lushton, NE (village) York County	17	73.91
Albany, MN (township) Stearns County	644	73.85
Pierz, MN (township) Morrison County	364	73.83
Goodrich, ND (city) Sheridan County	121	73.78
Worthington, IA (city) Dubuque County	286	73.71
New Holstein, WI (town) Calumet County	1,073	73.70
Westphalia, MO (city) Osage County	201	73.63
Osgood, OH (village) Darke County	198	73.61
Coldwater, OH (village) Mercer County	3,392	73.55
Horton, MN (township) Stevens County	200	73.53
Green Meadow, MN (township) Norman County	83	73.45
Sigel, MN (township) Brown County	306	73.38
Germantown, WI (town) Washington County	223	73.36
South Branch, MN (township) Watonwan County	228	73.31
Cedar Mills, MN (township) Meeker County	366	73.20
Leith, ND (city) Grant County	30	73.17
New Holstein, WI (city) Calumet County	2,431	73.16
Saint Henry, OH (village) Mercer County	1,683	73.14
Lincoln, WI (town) Buffalo County	136	73.12
Herman, WI (town) Dodge County	891	73.09
Strang, NE (village) Fillmore County	19	73.08
Ossian, IA (city) Winneshiek County	610	73.05
Rosedale, MN (township) Mahnomen County	111	73.03
Lynn, MN (township) McLeod County	454	72.99
West Newton, MN (township) Nicollet County	381	72.99
Rose Hill, MN (township) Cottonwood County	135	72.97
Houghton, IA (city) Lee County	94	72.87
Morristown, SD (town) Corson County	59	72.84
Honey Creek, WI (town) Sauk County	555	72.83
Forest, WI (town) Fond du Lac County	825	72.82

Notes: (cdp) census designated place; Refer to the Explanation of Data in the front of the book for more detailed information.

German

Top 150 Places Sorted by Percent

(Based on places with populations of 10,000 or more)

Place	Number	%
New Ulm, MN (city) Brown County	8,926	65.86
Carroll, IA (city) Carroll County	6,151	61.28
Mandan, ND (city) Morton County	10,244	61.20
Richfield, WI (town) Washington County	6,309	60.82
West Bend, WI (city) Washington County	16,418	58.36
Bismarck, ND (city) Burleigh County	32,138	58.13
Germantown, WI (village) Washington County	10,413	57.11
Bridgetown North, OH (cdp) Hamilton County	7,249	56.98
Watertown, WI (city) Jefferson County	12,250	56.72
Saint Marys, PA (city) Elk County	8,226	56.72
Marshfield, WI (city) Wood County	10,510	55.88
Menomonee Falls, WI (village) Waukesha County	18,204	55.76
Sauk Rapids, MN (city) Benton County	5,642	55.41
Hutchinson, MN (city) McLeod County	7,209	55.22
Beaver Dam, WI (city) Dodge County	8,278	55.03
Oconomowoc, WI (city) Waukesha County	6,773	54.91
Merrill, WI (city) Lincoln County	5,567	54.89
Dickinson, ND (city) Stark County	8,665	54.69
North Mankato, MN (city) Nicollet County	6,446	54.59
Menasha, WI (town) Winnebago County	8,699	54.57
Jasper, IN (city) Dubois County	6,497	54.30
Fond du Lac, WI (city) Fond du Lac County	22,946	54.25
Jamestown, ND (city) Stutsman County	8,386	54.20
Neenah, WI (city) Winnebago County	13,179	54.15
Port Washington, WI (city) Ozaukee County	5,608	54.11
Aberdeen, SD (city) Brown County	13,206	53.66
Hartford, WI (city) Washington County	5,890	53.65
Grafton, WI (village) Ozaukee County	5,532	53.61
Grand Chute, WI (town) Outagamie County	9,747	53.44
Menasha, WI (city) Winnebago County	8,718	53.21
Cedarburg, WI (city) Ozaukee County	5,678	52.70
Pewaukee, WI (city) Waukesha County	6,196	52.41
Fairmont, MN (city) Martin County	5,579	51.25
Weston, WI (village) Marathon County	6,273	51.20
Muskego, WI (city) Waukesha County	10,874	50.83
Sheboygan, WI (city) Sheboygan County	25,596	50.38
Watertown, SD (city) Codington County	10,182	50.14
Fort Atkinson, WI (city) Jefferson County	5,850	49.97
Norfolk, NE (city) Madison County	11,730	49.83
Manitowoc, WI (city) Manitowoc County	16,910	49.74
Oshkosh, WI (city) Winnebago County	31,287	49.71
Washington, MO (city) Franklin County	6,498	49.63
Appleton, WI (city) Outagamie County	34,776	49.59
Wauwatosa, WI (city) Milwaukee County	23,392	49.48
Kaukauna, WI (city) Outagamie County	6,424	49.44
Concord, MO (cdp) Saint Louis County	8,212	49.24
West Fargo, ND (city) Cass County	7,152	48.88
Celina, OH (city) Mercer County	5,089	48.85
Saint Cloud, MN (city) Stearns County	28,762	48.77
New Berlin, WI (city) Waukesha County	18,551	48.36
Huron, SD (city) Beadle County	5,767	48.13
White Oak, OH (cdp) Hamilton County	6,375	48.11
Oakville, MO (cdp) Saint Louis County	16,930	47.83
Shakopee, MN (city) Scott County	9,784	47.73
Beatrice, NE (city) Gage County	5,929	47.50
Two Rivers, WI (city) Manitowoc County	5,999	47.39
Mitchell, SD (city) Davison County	6,917	47.08
Dubuque, IA (city) Dubuque County	26,901	46.81
Hastings, MN (city) Dakota County	8,512	46.75
Wausau, WI (city) Marathon County	17,950	46.74
Columbus, NE (city) Platte County	9,746	46.43
Greendale, WI (village) Milwaukee County	6,683	46.39
Onalaska, WI (city) La Crosse County	6,870	46.23
Chippewa Falls, WI (city) Chippewa County	5,988	46.15
Brookfield, WI (city) Waukesha County	17,899	46.12
Sun Prairie, WI (city) Dane County	9,299	46.02
Crestwood, MO (city) Saint Louis County	5,394	46.02
Baraboo, WI (city) Sauk County	4,940	46.00
West Allis, WI (city) Milwaukee County	28,100	45.84
Mankato, MN (city) Blue Earth County	14,801	45.74
Hays, KS (city) Ellis County	9,101	45.43
Oak Creek, WI (city) Milwaukee County	12,926	45.42
Middleton, WI (city) Dane County	7,007	45.01
Chaska, MN (city) Carver County	7,830	44.89
Fremont, NE (city) Dodge County	11,267	44.79
Howard, WI (village) Brown County	6,061	44.77
Waukesha, WI (city) Waukesha County	28,714	44.61
Wisconsin Rapids, WI (city) Wood County	8,180	44.58
Fort Thomas, KY (city) Campbell County	7,409	44.52
Manchester, PA (township) York County	5,648	44.48
Brookings, SD (city) Brookings County	8,241	44.40
Elk River, MN (city) Sherburne County	7,297	44.37
Chalco, NE (cdp) Sarpy County	4,750	44.34
Dover, PA (township) York County	8,008	44.31
Tiffin, OH (city) Seneca County	8,025	44.25
Warwick, PA (township) Lancaster County	6,845	44.23
Manor, PA (township) Lancaster County	7,269	44.22
Windsor, PA (township) York County	5,608	43.79
Cedar Falls, IA (city) Black Hawk County	15,740	43.41
Greenfield, WI (city) Milwaukee County	15,390	43.38
Ephrata, PA (borough) Lancaster County	5,721	43.36
Winona, MN (city) Winona County	11,693	43.33
Weigelstown, PA (cdp) York County	4,373	43.31
South Milwaukee, WI (city) Milwaukee County	9,177	43.30
Cottage Grove, MN (city) Washington County	13,219	43.26
York, PA (township) York County	10,192	43.12
Lino Lakes, MN (city) Anoka County	7,228	43.10
West Lampeter, PA (township) Lancaster County	5,641	43.03
Affton, MO (cdp) Saint Louis County	8,982	42.97
Little Chute, WI (village) Outagamie County	4,470	42.78
Franklin, WI (city) Milwaukee County	12,640	42.77
De Pere, WI (city) Brown County	8,781	42.74
Red Wing, MN (city) Goodhue County	6,879	42.63
Buffalo, MN (city) Wright County	4,318	42.62
River Falls, WI (city) Pierce County	5,375	42.60
Rosemount, MN (city) Dakota County	6,193	42.37
Caledonia, WI (town) Racine County	9,995	42.26
Yankton, SD (city) Yankton County	5,681	42.23
Owatonna, MN (city) Steele County	9,461	42.21
North Lebanon, PA (township) Lebanon County	4,483	42.18
Hanover, PA (borough) York County	6,130	42.17
Farmington, MN (city) Dakota County	5,256	42.14
Muhlenberg, PA (township) Berks County	6,849	42.06
Kearney, NE (city) Buffalo County	11,344	41.96
La Crosse, WI (city) La Crosse County	21,617	41.86
Whitewater, WI (city) Walworth County	5,620	41.84
Mehlville, MO (cdp) Saint Louis County	12,035	41.82
Plover, WI (village) Portage County	4,452	41.81
Mequon, WI (city) Ozaukee County	9,130	41.79
Eau Claire, WI (city) Eau Claire County	25,659	41.71
Hastings, NE (city) Adams County	10,009	41.58
Maumee, OH (city) Lucas County	6,330	41.57
Oakdale, MN (city) Washington County	11,078	41.54
Penn, PA (township) York County	6,050	41.46
Chanhassen, MN (city) Carver County	8,422	41.43
Elizabethtown, PA (borough) Lancaster County	4,908	41.31
West Hempfield, PA (township) Lancaster County	6,251	41.28
Spencer, IA (city) Clay County	4,714	41.28
Lakeville, MN (city) Dakota County	17,770	41.20
Janesville, WI (city) Rock County	24,329	40.98
Menomonie, WI (city) Dunn County	6,140	40.95
Savage, MN (city) Scott County	8,666	40.91
Minot, ND (city) Ward County	14,913	40.77
Ramsey, MN (city) Anoka County	7,539	40.77
East Hempfield, PA (township) Lancaster County	8,667	40.76
Sioux Falls, SD (city) Minnehaha County	50,520	40.71
Monroe, WI (city) Green County	4,398	40.68
Fargo, ND (city) Cass County	36,827	40.56
Pierre, SD (city) Hughes County	5,666	40.56
Lake Saint Louis, MO (city) Saint Charles County	4,075	40.51
Marinette, WI (city) Marinette County	4,734	40.40
Prior Lake, MN (city) Scott County	6,435	40.38
Logan, PA (township) Blair County	4,812	40.36
Morton, IL (village) Tazewell County	6,055	40.25
Newberry, PA (township) York County	5,766	40.25
Mason City, IA (city) Cerro Gordo County	11,732	40.21
Brentwood, PA (borough) Allegheny County	4,205	40.18
Champlin, MN (city) Hennepin County	8,976	40.14
Cudahy, WI (city) Milwaukee County	7,397	40.14
Upper Saucon, PA (township) Lehigh County	4,779	40.03

Notes: (cdp) census designated place; Refer to the Explanation of Data in the front of the book for more detailed information.

German Russian

Top 150 Places Sorted by Number

(Based on all places, regardless of population)

Place	Number	%
Hays, KS (city) Ellis County	420	2.10
Portland, OR (city) Multnomah County	176	0.03
Los Angeles, CA (city) Los Angeles County	134	0.00
Bismarck, ND (city) Burleigh County	131	0.24
Milwaukee, WI (city) Milwaukee County	112	0.02
New York, NY (city) New York City	110	0.00
Fargo, ND (city) Cass County	103	0.11
Lincoln, NE (city) Lancaster County	99	0.04
Phoenix, AZ (city) Maricopa County	98	0.01
Fort Collins, CO (city) Larimer County	90	0.08
Dickinson, ND (city) Stark County	88	0.56
Grand Forks, ND (city) Grand Forks County	84	0.17
San Diego, CA (city) San Diego County	83	0.01
Topeka, KS (city) Shawnee County	77	0.06
Kansas City, MO (city) Jackson County	74	0.02
Chicago, IL (city) Cook County	73	0.00
Seattle, WA (city) King County	72	0.01
Detroit, MI (city) Wayne County	69	0.01
Denver, CO (city) Denver County	62	0.01
Colorado Springs, CO (city) El Paso County	60	0.02
Jennings, MO (city) Saint Louis County	57	0.37
Cheyenne, WY (city) Laramie County	57	0.11
Hutchinson, KS (city) Reno County	54	0.13
Orangevale, CA (cdp) Sacramento County	53	0.20
Teaneck, NJ (cdp) Bergen County	53	0.13
Las Vegas, NV (city) Clark County	53	0.01
Jamestown, ND (city) Stutsman County	49	0.32
Minneapolis, MN (city) Hennepin County	48	0.01
Aliso Viejo, CA (cdp) Orange County	47	0.12
Springfield, MO (city) Greene County	47	0.03
Pittsburgh, PA (city) Allegheny County	47	0.01
Aurora, CO (city) Arapahoe County	46	0.02
Montgomery, AL (city) Montgomery County	44	0.02
Newport News, VA (independent city) Newport News city	42	0.02
Clinton, OK (city) Custer County	40	0.45
Fresno, CA (city) Fresno County	40	0.01
Omaha, NE (city) Douglas County	40	0.01
Lawrence, KS (city) Douglas County	39	0.05
Riverside, CA (city) Riverside County	39	0.02
Mandan, ND (city) Morton County	38	0.23
Fairfield, CA (city) Solano County	38	0.04
El Paso, TX (city) El Paso County	37	0.01
Arvada, CO (city) Jefferson County	35	0.03
Victoria, KS (city) Ellis County	34	2.80
Modesto, CA (city) Stanislaus County	34	0.02
Richfield, MN (city) Hennepin County	31	0.09
The Colony, TX (city) Denton County	30	0.11
Pasco, WA (city) Franklin County	30	0.09
Salina, KS (city) Saline County	30	0.07
Killeen, TX (city) Bell County	30	0.03
Melrose Park, FL (cdp) Broward County	29	0.41
Inglewood, CA (city) Los Angeles County	29	0.03
Summit, WA (cdp) Pierce County	28	0.34
Lakewood, WA (city) Pierce County	28	0.05
Santa Rosa, CA (city) Sonoma County	28	0.02
Grand Rapids, MI (city) Kent County	28	0.01
Duncan, OK (city) Stephens County	27	0.12
Aberdeen, SD (city) Brown County	27	0.11
Dallas, TX (city) Dallas County	27	0.00
Columbia, MD (cdp) Howard County	26	0.03
Indianapolis, IN (special city) Marion County	26	0.00
Washington, DC (city) District of Columbia	26	0.00
Horseheads North, NY (cdp) Chemung County	25	0.86
Rockton, IL (village) Winnebago County	25	0.47
Eagle Mountain, TX (cdp) Tarrant County	25	0.38
Fountain, CO (city) El Paso County	25	0.17
Horseheads, NY (town) Chemung County	25	0.13
Willingboro, NJ (township) Burlington County	25	0.08
Stockton, CA (city) San Joaquin County	25	0.01
WaKeeney, KS (city) Trego County	24	1.28
Dillon, MT (city) Beaverhead County	24	0.64
Kirby, TX (city) Bexar County	24	0.28
Green Haven, MD (cdp) Anne Arundel County	24	0.14
Lodi, CA (city) San Joaquin County	24	0.04
Kansas City, KS (city) Wyandotte County	24	0.02
Paradise, NV (cdp) Clark County	24	0.01
Philadelphia, PA (city) Philadelphia County	24	0.00
San Francisco, CA (city) San Francisco County	24	0.00
Tucson, AZ (city) Pima County	24	0.00
Maryland Heights, MO (city) Saint Louis County	23	0.09
Greeley, CO (city) Weld County	23	0.03
Kent, WA (city) King County	23	0.03
Salinas, CA (city) Monterey County	23	0.02
Columbus, OH (city) Franklin County	23	0.00
San Antonio, TX (city) Bexar County	23	0.00
Wheat Ridge, CO (city) Jefferson County	22	0.07
Germantown, MD (cdp) Montgomery County	22	0.04
Brooklyn Park, MN (city) Hennepin County	22	0.03
Yakima, WA (city) Yakima County	22	0.03
Chattanooga, TN (city) Hamilton County	22	0.01
Knoxville, TN (city) Knox County	22	0.01
Sunrise Manor, NV (cdp) Clark County	22	0.01
Virginia Beach, VA (independent city) Virginia Beach city	22	0.01
Presidential Lakes Estates, NJ (cdp) Burlington County	21	0.87
Burlington, WA (city) Skagit County	21	0.32
Rosamond, CA (cdp) Kern County	21	0.15
Pemberton, NJ (township) Burlington County	21	0.07
Visalia, CA (city) Tulare County	21	0.02
Westminster, CO (city) Adams County	21	0.02
Charlestown, IN (city) Clark County	20	0.33
Euclid, OH (city) Cuyahoga County	20	0.04
Hollywood, FL (city) Broward County	20	0.01
Windsor, CO (town) Weld County	19	0.19
Sterling, CO (city) Logan County	19	0.17
Buffalo Grove, IL (village) Lake County	19	0.04
Thornton, CO (city) Adams County	19	0.02
Torrance, CA (city) Los Angeles County	19	0.01
Wichita, KS (city) Sedgwick County	19	0.01
Macon, MS (city) Noxubee County	18	0.73
Wilson, WI (town) Sheboygan County	18	0.59
Devils Lake, ND (city) Ramsey County	18	0.25
Lindenwold, NJ (borough) Camden County	18	0.10
Elizabethtown, KY (city) Hardin County	18	0.08
Bellevue, NE (city) Sarpy County	18	0.04
Appleton, WI (city) Outagamie County	18	0.03
Hempstead, NY (village) Nassau County	18	0.03
Lorain, OH (city) Lorain County	18	0.03
Hempstead, NY (town) Nassau County	18	0.00
Mesa, AZ (city) Maricopa County	18	0.00
West Longview, WA (cdp) Cowlitz County	17	0.59
Beulah, ND (city) Mercer County	17	0.54
Roeland Park, KS (city) Johnson County	17	0.25
Asbury Park, NJ (city) Monmouth County	17	0.10
Copperas Cove, TX (city) Coryell County	17	0.06
Jacksonville, AR (city) Pulaski County	17	0.06
Hallandale, FL (city) Broward County	17	0.05
Bowie, MD (city) Prince George's County	17	0.03
Bloomington, MN (city) Hennepin County	17	0.02
Gresham, OR (city) Multnomah County	17	0.02
Hillsboro, OR (city) Washington County	17	0.02
Reading, PA (city) Berks County	17	0.02
Houston, TX (city) Harris County	17	0.00
Hettinger, ND (city) Adams County	16	1.23
Canfield, OH (city) Mahoning County	16	0.21
Cottage Grove, OR (city) Lane County	16	0.19
North Bend, OR (city) Coos County	16	0.17
Dentsville, SC (cdp) Richland County	16	0.12
Manhattan, KS (city) Riley County	16	0.04
North Chicago, IL (city) Lake County	16	0.04
Middletown, OH (city) Butler County	16	0.03
Lakewood, CA (city) Los Angeles County	16	0.02
Akron, OH (city) Summit County	16	0.01
Rancho Cucamonga, CA (city) San Bernardino County	16	0.01
Albuquerque, NM (city) Bernalillo County	16	0.00
Hillburn, NY (village) Rockland County	15	1.91
Ashley, ND (city) McIntosh County	15	1.71
Clyde, OH (city) Sandusky County	15	0.25
Welby, CO (cdp) Adams County	15	0.12
Bridgewater, NJ (township) Somerset County	15	0.03
Columbia, MO (city) Boone County	15	0.02

Notes: (cdp) census designated place; Refer to the Explanation of Data in the front of the book for more detailed information.

German Russian

Top 150 Places Sorted by Percent

(Based on all places, regardless of population)

Place	Number	%
Balta, ND (city) Pierce County	9	10.71
Alexander, KS (city) Rush County	4	5.80
Roscoe, SD (city) Edmunds County	14	4.46
Zap, ND (city) Mercer County	7	3.45
Mound City, SD (town) Campbell County	3	3.45
Wallace, KS (city) Wallace County	2	3.45
Iuka, KS (city) Pratt County	6	3.30
Christine, ND (city) Richland County	5	2.92
Victoria, KS (city) Ellis County	34	2.80
Ramona, SD (town) Lake County	4	2.42
McCracken, KS (city) Rush County	6	2.34
Java, SD (town) Walworth County	4	2.33
Bazine, KS (city) Ness County	7	2.22
New Leipzig, ND (city) Grant County	6	2.20
Hazelton, ND (city) Emmons County	5	2.17
Hays, KS (city) Ellis County	420	2.10
Hosmer, SD (city) Edmunds County	6	2.10
Gate, OK (town) Beaver County	2	2.04
Hillburn, NY (village) Rockland County	15	1.91
Center, ND (city) Oliver County	13	1.90
Halliday, ND (city) Dunn County	4	1.76
Ashley, ND (city) McIntosh County	15	1.71
Gorham, KS (city) Russell County	6	1.60
Terrebonne, MN (township) Red Lake County	2	1.56
Medina, ND (city) Stutsman County	5	1.47
Gackle, ND (city) Logan County	5	1.42
Hunter, ND (city) Cass County	4	1.36
Taylor, ND (city) Stark County	2	1.34
WaKeeney, KS (city) Trego County	24	1.28
Quinter, KS (city) Gove County	12	1.24
Carson, ND (city) Grant County	4	1.24
Hettinger, ND (city) Adams County	16	1.23
Chinook, WA (cdp) Pacific County	5	1.20
Kulm, ND (city) La Moure County	5	1.18
Echo, MN (city) Yellow Medicine County	3	1.18
Wishek, ND (city) McIntosh County	13	1.17
McVille, ND (city) Nelson County	5	1.07
Medicine Lake, MT (town) Sheridan County	3	1.06
Lind, WA (town) Adams County	6	1.03
Brady, PA (township) Butler County	14	1.00
Hebron, ND (city) Morton County	8	1.00
New Market, MN (city) Scott County	3	1.00
Schoenchen, KS (city) Ellis County	2	1.00
Crookston, MN (township) Polk County	5	0.97
Le Roy, MN (city) Mower County	9	0.95
McClusky, ND (city) Sheridan County	4	0.94
Leola, SD (city) McPherson County	4	0.90
Presidential Lakes Estates, NJ (cdp) Burlington County	21	0.87
Horseheads North, NY (cdp) Chemung County	25	0.86
Schneider, IN (town) Lake County	3	0.86
Gladstone, ND (city) Stark County	2	0.85
Holyrood, KS (city) Ellsworth County	4	0.84
Eureka, SD (city) McPherson County	9	0.82
Prentice, WI (town) Price County	4	0.81
Washakie Ten, WY (cdp) Washakie County	4	0.79
Shell Lake, WI (city) Washburn County	10	0.77
Linton, ND (city) Emmons County	10	0.76
Macon, MS (city) Noxubee County	18	0.73
Odessa, WA (town) Lincoln County	7	0.72
Henderson, NE (city) York County	7	0.71
Napoleon, ND (city) Logan County	6	0.68
Bayard, NE (city) Morrill County	8	0.65
Dillon, MT (city) Beaverhead County	24	0.64
Thackerville, OK (town) Love County	3	0.63
Anamoose, ND (city) McHenry County	2	0.63
Onsted, MI (village) Lenawee County	5	0.62
Elgin, ND (city) Grant County	4	0.61
Wilson, WI (town) Sheboygan County	18	0.59
West Longview, WA (cdp) Cowlitz County	17	0.59
Moltke, MI (township) Presque Isle County	2	0.59
Sylvan Grove, KS (city) Lincoln County	2	0.59
Kellerton, IA (city) Ringgold County	2	0.58
Dickinson, ND (city) Stark County	88	0.56
Beulah, ND (city) Mercer County	17	0.54
Freeman, SD (city) Hutchinson County	7	0.54
New England, ND (city) Hettinger County	3	0.54
Osborne, PA (borough) Allegheny County	3	0.53
Mackay, ID (city) Custer County	3	0.52
Veneta, OR (city) Lane County	13	0.51
Belle, MO (city) Maries County	7	0.51
Middleburgh, NY (village) Schoharie County	7	0.50
Talihina, OK (town) Le Flore County	6	0.50
Fessenden, ND (city) Wells County	3	0.49
Malcolm, NE (village) Lancaster County	2	0.49
Dorrance, KS (city) Russell County	1	0.49
Kachemak, AK (city) Kenai Peninsula Borough	2	0.48
Rockton, IL (village) Winnebago County	25	0.47
Paxton, NE (village) Keith County	3	0.47
Breckenridge, MN (township) Wilkin County	1	0.47
Keenesburg, CO (town) Weld County	4	0.46
Clinton, OK (city) Custer County	40	0.45
China Lake Acres, CA (cdp) Kern County	8	0.45
Maupin, OR (city) Wasco County	2	0.44
Melrose Park, FL (cdp) Broward County	29	0.41
Clancy, MT (cdp) Jefferson County	6	0.41
Kismet, KS (city) Seward County	2	0.41
Yelm, WA (city) Thurston County	13	0.39
Eagle Mountain, TX (cdp) Tarrant County	25	0.38
Salford, PA (township) Montgomery County	9	0.38
Jennings, MO (city) Saint Louis County	57	0.37
Cherokee, OK (city) Alfalfa County	6	0.37
Brownton, MN (city) McLeod County	3	0.37
Ropesville, TX (city) Hockley County	2	0.37
Trinidad, TX (city) Henderson County	4	0.36
Benton, KS (city) Butler County	3	0.36
Maple Valley, MI (township) Sanilac County	4	0.35
Metcalfe, MS (town) Washington County	4	0.35
Summit, WA (cdp) Pierce County	28	0.34
Corn, OK (town) Washita County	2	0.34
Charlestown, IN (city) Clark County	20	0.33
Jamestown, ND (city) Stutsman County	49	0.32
Burlington, WA (city) Skagit County	21	0.32
Morningside, MD (town) Prince George's County	4	0.31
Log Lane Village, CO (town) Morgan County	3	0.31
Alturas, CA (city) Modoc County	9	0.30
Clear Lake, SD (city) Deuel County	4	0.30
Garrison, ND (city) McLean County	4	0.30
Fairview, OK (city) Major County	8	0.29
Kirby, TX (city) Bexar County	24	0.28
Spirit Lake, IA (city) Dickinson County	12	0.28
Chester, NY (village) Orange County	10	0.28
Wheeler AFB, HI (cdp) Honolulu County	8	0.28
Swansboro, NC (town) Onslow County	4	0.28
West Brownsville, PA (borough) Washington County	3	0.28
Tomahawk, WI (city) Lincoln County	10	0.27
Holiday Lakes, TX (town) Brazoria County	3	0.27
Rockville, MN (city) Stearns County	2	0.27
Sterling, OK (town) Comanche County	2	0.27
Steele, ND (city) Kidder County	2	0.26
Devils Lake, ND (city) Ramsey County	18	0.25
Roeland Park, KS (city) Johnson County	17	0.25
Clyde, OH (city) Sandusky County	15	0.25
Alma, NE (city) Harlan County	3	0.25
Underwood, ND (city) McLean County	2	0.25
Bismarck, ND (city) Burleigh County	131	0.24
Erie, MN (township) Becker County	4	0.24
Tyndall, SD (city) Bon Homme County	3	0.24
Washington, KS (city) Washington County	3	0.24
Spearville, KS (city) Ford County	2	0.24
Mandan, ND (city) Morton County	38	0.23
Rugby, ND (city) Pierce County	7	0.23
Springfield, GA (city) Effingham County	4	0.23
Leighton, AL (town) Colbert County	2	0.23
Skagway, AK (city) Skagway-Hoonah-Angoon Census Area	2	0.23
Granite, OK (town) Greer County	4	0.22
Deadwood, SD (city) Lawrence County	3	0.22
East Machias, ME (town) Washington County	3	0.22
Maple Bluff, WI (village) Dane County	3	0.22
Americus, KS (city) Lyon County	2	0.22
Canfield, OH (city) Mahoning County	16	0.21

Notes: (cdp) census designated place; Refer to the Explanation of Data in the front of the book for more detailed information.

German Russian

Top 150 Places Sorted by Percent

(Based on places with populations of 10,000 or more)

Place	Number	%
Hays, KS (city) Ellis County	420	2.10
Dickinson, ND (city) Stark County	88	0.56
Jennings, MO (city) Saint Louis County	57	0.37
Jamestown, ND (city) Stutsman County	49	0.32
Bismarck, ND (city) Burleigh County	131	0.24
Mandan, ND (city) Morton County	38	0.23
Orangevale, CA (cdp) Sacramento County	53	0.20
Windsor, CO (town) Weld County	19	0.19
Grand Forks, ND (city) Grand Forks County	84	0.17
Fountain, CO (city) El Paso County	25	0.17
Sterling, CO (city) Logan County	19	0.17
Rosamond, CA (cdp) Kern County	21	0.15
Green Haven, MD (cdp) Anne Arundel County	24	0.14
Hutchinson, KS (city) Reno County	54	0.13
Teaneck, NJ (cdp) Bergen County	53	0.13
Horseheads, NY (town) Chemung County	25	0.13
Aliso Viejo, CA (cdp) Orange County	47	0.12
Duncan, OK (city) Stephens County	27	0.12
Dentsville, SC (cdp) Richland County	16	0.12
Welby, CO (cdp) Adams County	15	0.12
Greenwood Village, CO (city) Arapahoe County	13	0.12
Fargo, ND (city) Cass County	103	0.11
Cheyenne, WY (city) Laramie County	57	0.11
The Colony, TX (city) Denton County	30	0.11
Aberdeen, SD (city) Brown County	27	0.11
Franklin Park, PA (borough) Allegheny County	12	0.11
West Haverstraw, NY (village) Rockland County	11	0.11
Lindenwold, NJ (borough) Camden County	18	0.10
Asbury Park, NJ (city) Monmouth County	17	0.10
Richfield, MN (city) Hennepin County	31	0.09
Pasco, WA (city) Franklin County	30	0.09
Maryland Heights, MO (city) Saint Louis County	23	0.09
Manor, PA (township) Lancaster County	14	0.09
Fort Leonard Wood, MO (cdp) Pulaski County	12	0.09
Marshall, MN (city) Lyon County	12	0.09
Williston, ND (city) Williams County	11	0.09
Lower Pottsgrove, PA (township) Montgomery County	10	0.09
Spencer, MA (town) Worcester County	10	0.09
Fort Collins, CO (city) Larimer County	90	0.08
Willingboro, NJ (township) Burlington County	25	0.08
Elizabethtown, KY (city) Hardin County	18	0.08
Salmon Creek, WA (cdp) Clark County	14	0.08
Whitney, NV (cdp) Clark County	14	0.08
Oatfield, OR (cdp) Clackamas County	13	0.08
Baywood-Los Osos, CA (cdp) San Luis Obispo County	12	0.08
Mitchell, SD (city) Davison County	12	0.08
Chester, NY (town) Orange County	10	0.08
Two Rivers, WI (city) Manitowoc County	10	0.08
Antwerp, MI (township) Van Buren County	9	0.08
Fort Atkinson, WI (city) Jefferson County	9	0.08
Mastic Beach, NY (cdp) Suffolk County	9	0.08
Mill Creek, WA (city) Snohomish County	9	0.08
Salina, KS (city) Saline County	30	0.07
Wheat Ridge, CO (city) Jefferson County	22	0.07
Pemberton, NJ (township) Burlington County	21	0.07
Alamo, TX (city) Hidalgo County	10	0.07
Dumas, TX (city) Moore County	10	0.07
Twentynine Palms, CA (city) San Bernardino County	10	0.07
Beacon, NY (city) Dutchess County	9	0.07
Brown Deer, WI (village) Milwaukee County	9	0.07
Mohave Valley, AZ (cdp) Mohave County	9	0.07
Tuskegee, AL (city) Macon County	8	0.07
Burr Ridge, IL (village) Du Page County	7	0.07
Storm Lake, IA (city) Buena Vista County	7	0.07
Topeka, KS (city) Shawnee County	77	0.06
Copperas Cove, TX (city) Coryell County	17	0.06
Jacksonville, AR (city) Pulaski County	17	0.06
Lakeland North, WA (cdp) King County	9	0.06
Leesburg, FL (city) Lake County	9	0.06
Midlothian, IL (village) Cook County	9	0.06
Scottsbluff, NE (city) Scotts Bluff County	9	0.06
Corcoran, CA (city) Kings County	8	0.06
Four Corners, OR (cdp) Marion County	8	0.06
Grover Beach, CA (city) San Luis Obispo County	8	0.06
McPherson, KS (city) McPherson County	8	0.06
Red Hook, NY (town) Dutchess County	6	0.06
Lawrence, KS (city) Douglas County	39	0.05
Lakewood, WA (city) Pierce County	28	0.05
Hallandale, FL (city) Broward County	17	0.05
Parkland, WA (cdp) Pierce County	12	0.05
Bellwood, IL (village) Cook County	11	0.05
Roseburg, OR (city) Douglas County	11	0.05
Shakopee, MN (city) Scott County	11	0.05
Herndon, VA (town) Fairfax County	10	0.05
Bella Vista, AR (cdp) Benton County	9	0.05
Crown Point, IN (city) Lake County	9	0.05
Forest Grove, OR (city) Washington County	9	0.05
Mukilteo, WA (city) Snohomish County	9	0.05
Owasso, OK (city) Tulsa County	9	0.05
Thomasville, NC (city) Davidson County	9	0.05
Golden, CO (city) Jefferson County	8	0.05
New Milford, NJ (borough) Bergen County	8	0.05
Newton, KS (city) Harvey County	8	0.05
Great Bend, KS (city) Barton County	7	0.05
Willowick, OH (city) Lake County	7	0.05
City of The Dalles, OR (city) Wasco County	6	0.05
Piedmont, CA (city) Alameda County	6	0.05
Herrin, IL (city) Williamson County	5	0.05
Lincoln, NE (city) Lancaster County	99	0.04
Fairfield, CA (city) Solano County	38	0.04
Lodi, CA (city) San Joaquin County	24	0.04
Germantown, MD (cdp) Montgomery County	22	0.04
Euclid, OH (city) Cuyahoga County	20	0.04
Buffalo Grove, IL (village) Lake County	19	0.04
Bellevue, NE (city) Sarpy County	18	0.04
Manhattan, KS (city) Riley County	16	0.04
North Chicago, IL (city) Lake County	16	0.04
Northglenn, CO (city) Adams County	13	0.04
Des Moines, WA (city) King County	11	0.04
Hazelwood, MO (city) Saint Louis County	10	0.04
Laramie, WY (city) Albany County	10	0.04
Upper Dublin, PA (township) Montgomery County	10	0.04
Wenatchee, WA (city) Chelan County	10	0.04
Ypsilanti, MI (city) Washtenaw County	10	0.04
Park Forest, IL (village) Cook County	9	0.04
West Linn, OR (city) Clackamas County	9	0.04
Laurel, MD (city) Prince George's County	8	0.04
Yukon, OK (city) Canadian County	8	0.04
Casa de Oro-Mount Helix, CA (cdp) San Diego County	7	0.04
Lemoore, CA (city) Kings County	7	0.04
Waynesboro, VA (independent city) Waynesboro city	7	0.04
Alamo, CA (cdp) Contra Costa County	6	0.04
Fort Campbell North, KY (cdp) Christian County	6	0.04
Hybla Valley, VA (cdp) Fairfax County	6	0.04
Pierre, SD (city) Hughes County	6	0.04
Robbinsdale, MN (city) Hennepin County	6	0.04
West Fargo, ND (city) Cass County	6	0.04
Gulfport, FL (city) Pinellas County	5	0.04
Marana, AZ (town) Pima County	5	0.04
Merriam, KS (city) Johnson County	5	0.04
Portland, OR (city) Multnomah County	176	0.03
Springfield, MO (city) Greene County	47	0.03
Arvada, CO (city) Jefferson County	35	0.03
Killeen, TX (city) Bell County	30	0.03
Inglewood, CA (city) Los Angeles County	29	0.03
Columbia, MD (cdp) Howard County	26	0.03
Greeley, CO (city) Weld County	23	0.03
Kent, WA (city) King County	23	0.03
Brooklyn Park, MN (city) Hennepin County	22	0.03
Yakima, WA (city) Yakima County	22	0.03
Appleton, WI (city) Outagamie County	18	0.03
Hempstead, NY (village) Nassau County	18	0.03
Lorain, OH (city) Lorain County	18	0.03
Bowie, MD (city) Prince George's County	17	0.03
Middletown, OH (city) Butler County	16	0.03
Bridgewater, NJ (township) Somerset County	15	0.03
La Mesa, CA (city) San Diego County	14	0.03
Lenexa, KS (city) Johnson County	13	0.03
Grand Island, NE (city) Hall County	12	0.03
Coeur d'Alene, ID (city) Kootenai County	11	0.03

Notes: (cdp) census designated place; Refer to the Explanation of Data in the front of the book for more detailed information.

Greek

Top 150 Places Sorted by Number

(Based on all places, regardless of population)

Place	Number	%
New York, NY (city) New York City	80,145	1.00
Chicago, IL (city) Cook County	18,249	0.63
Los Angeles, CA (city) Los Angeles County	11,016	0.30
Hempstead, NY (town) Nassau County	10,576	1.40
Brookhaven, NY (town) Suffolk County	6,580	1.47
Oyster Bay, NY (town) Nassau County	5,932	2.02
San Diego, CA (city) San Diego County	5,588	0.46
Boston, MA (city) Suffolk County	5,325	0.90
Phoenix, AZ (city) Maricopa County	4,770	0.36
Philadelphia, PA (city) Philadelphia County	4,414	0.29
Houston, TX (city) Harris County	3,980	0.20
San Francisco, CA (city) San Francisco County	3,831	0.49
San Jose, CA (city) Santa Clara County	3,734	0.42
Charlotte, NC (city) Mecklenburg County	3,612	0.67
North Hempstead, NY (town) Nassau County	3,529	1.59
Huntington, NY (town) Suffolk County	3,492	1.79
Manchester, NH (city) Hillsborough County	3,066	2.87
Islip, NY (town) Suffolk County	2,970	0.92
Lowell, MA (city) Middlesex County	2,815	2.68
Seattle, WA (city) King County	2,812	0.50
Columbus, OH (city) Franklin County	2,702	0.38
Baltimore, MD (independent city) Baltimore city	2,693	0.41
Lynn, MA (city) Essex County	2,527	2.84
Tarpon Springs, FL (city) Pinellas County	2,479	11.77
Virginia Beach, VA (independent city) Virginia Beach city	2,463	0.58
Portland, OR (city) Multnomah County	2,452	0.46
Worcester, MA (city) Worcester County	2,431	1.41
Peabody, MA (city) Essex County	2,391	4.97
Las Vegas, NV (city) Clark County	2,380	0.50
Denver, CO (city) Denver County	2,321	0.42
Jacksonville, FL (special city) Duval County	2,314	0.31
Babylon, NY (town) Suffolk County	2,273	1.07
Sacramento, CA (city) Sacramento County	2,203	0.54
Dallas, TX (city) Dallas County	2,119	0.18
Stamford, CT (city) Fairfield County	2,100	1.79
Indianapolis, IN (special city) Marion County	2,074	0.27
San Antonio, TX (city) Bexar County	2,060	0.18
Clearwater, FL (city) Pinellas County	1,934	1.79
Washington, DC (city) District of Columbia	1,893	0.33
Smithtown, NY (town) Suffolk County	1,843	1.59
Pittsburgh, PA (city) Allegheny County	1,833	0.55
Orland Park, IL (village) Cook County	1,797	3.52
Palm Harbor, FL (cdp) Pinellas County	1,707	2.89
Skokie, IL (village) Cook County	1,706	2.69
Norwalk, CT (city) Fairfield County	1,691	2.04
Albuquerque, NM (city) Bernalillo County	1,679	0.37
Long Beach, CA (city) Los Angeles County	1,667	0.36
Mount Prospect, IL (village) Cook County	1,654	2.92
Salt Lake City, UT (city) Salt Lake County	1,630	0.90
Naperville, IL (city) Du Page County	1,606	1.25
Upper Darby, PA (township) Delaware County	1,605	1.96
Milwaukee, WI (city) Milwaukee County	1,576	0.26
Yonkers, NY (city) Westchester County	1,563	0.80
Toledo, OH (city) Lucas County	1,554	0.50
Haverhill, MA (city) Essex County	1,549	2.63
Tucson, AZ (city) Pima County	1,463	0.30
Arlington Heights, IL (village) Cook County	1,442	1.89
Austin, TX (city) Travis County	1,437	0.22
Saint Petersburg, FL (city) Pinellas County	1,436	0.58
Des Plaines, IL (city) Cook County	1,423	2.42
Nashua, NH (city) Hillsborough County	1,422	1.64
Scottsdale, AZ (city) Maricopa County	1,422	0.70
Glenview, IL (village) Cook County	1,420	3.41
Arlington, MA (cdp) Middlesex County	1,418	3.35
Dracut, MA (town) Middlesex County	1,401	4.91
Cleveland, OH (city) Cuyahoga County	1,385	0.29
Oak Lawn, IL (village) Cook County	1,378	2.49
Fort Lee, NJ (borough) Bergen County	1,346	3.80
Arlington, VA (cdp) Arlington County	1,310	0.69
Aurora, CO (city) Arapahoe County	1,302	0.47
Park Ridge, IL (city) Cook County	1,288	3.41
Akron, OH (city) Summit County	1,267	0.58
Levittown, NY (cdp) Nassau County	1,259	2.37
Watertown, MA (city) Middlesex County	1,257	3.81
Somerville, MA (city) Middlesex County	1,252	1.62

Place	Number	%
Holiday, FL (cdp) Pasco County	1,247	5.69
Newton, MA (city) Middlesex County	1,244	1.48
Huntington Beach, CA (city) Orange County	1,197	0.63
Salem, MA (city) Essex County	1,188	2.94
Schaumburg, IL (village) Cook County	1,152	1.55
Mesa, AZ (city) Maricopa County	1,149	0.29
Palos Hills, IL (city) Cook County	1,141	6.43
Oakland, CA (city) Alameda County	1,122	0.28
Minneapolis, MN (city) Hennepin County	1,107	0.29
Hicksville, NY (cdp) Nassau County	1,103	2.67
Hollywood, FL (city) Broward County	1,097	0.79
Sterling Heights, MI (city) Macomb County	1,086	0.87
Commack, NY (cdp) Suffolk County	1,083	2.98
Livonia, MI (city) Wayne County	1,079	1.07
Cambridge, MA (city) Middlesex County	1,069	1.05
Boca Raton, FL (city) Palm Beach County	1,065	1.41
Brockton, MA (city) Plymouth County	1,061	1.13
Canton, OH (city) Stark County	1,059	1.31
Anaheim, CA (city) Orange County	1,057	0.32
Henderson, NV (city) Clark County	1,048	0.60
Cincinnati, OH (city) Hamilton County	1,040	0.31
Fort Lauderdale, FL (city) Broward County	1,038	0.68
Warren, OH (city) Trumbull County	1,033	2.20
Norfolk, VA (independent city) Norfolk city	1,028	0.44
Springfield, MA (city) Hampden County	1,026	0.67
Tampa, FL (city) Hillsborough County	1,022	0.34
Oklahoma City, OK (city) Oklahoma County	1,021	0.20
Jersey City, NJ (city) Hudson County	1,011	0.42
Reno, NV (city) Washoe County	1,006	0.56
Joliet, IL (city) Will County	1,005	0.95
Troy, MI (city) Oakland County	1,003	1.24
Saint Louis, MO (independent city) Saint Louis city	994	0.29
Niles, IL (village) Cook County	990	3.28
Edison, NJ (cdp) Middlesex County	990	1.01
Paradise, NV (cdp) Clark County	989	0.53
Campbell, OH (city) Mahoning County	981	10.37
Warren, MI (city) Macomb County	977	0.71
Coral Springs, FL (city) Broward County	976	0.83
Spring Valley, NV (cdp) Clark County	965	0.82
Lincolnwood, IL (village) Cook County	963	7.79
Colorado Springs, CO (city) El Paso County	960	0.27
Cherry Hill, NJ (township) Camden County	959	1.37
Clarkstown, NY (town) Rockland County	954	1.16
Omaha, NE (city) Douglas County	950	0.24
Raleigh, NC (city) Wake County	942	0.34
Medford, MA (city) Middlesex County	940	1.69
Buffalo, NY (city) Erie County	937	0.32
Saint Clair Shores, MI (city) Macomb County	935	1.48
Aurora, IL (city) Kane County	935	0.65
Ann Arbor, MI (city) Washtenaw County	934	0.82
Greenburgh, NY (town) Westchester County	927	1.07
Plano, TX (city) Collin County	926	0.42
Madison, WI (city) Dane County	922	0.44
Quincy, MA (city) Norfolk County	919	1.04
Atlanta, GA (city) Fulton County	913	0.22
Cranston, RI (city) Providence County	910	1.15
Modesto, CA (city) Stanislaus County	909	0.48
Amherst, NY (town) Erie County	904	0.78
Fresno, CA (city) Fresno County	901	0.21
Nashville-Davidson, TN (special city) Davidson County	901	0.17
Sandy, UT (city) Salt Lake County	889	1.01
Torrance, CA (city) Los Angeles County	887	0.64
Chelmsford, MA (town) Middlesex County	872	2.58
East Lake, FL (cdp) Pinellas County	868	2.95
Parma, OH (city) Cuyahoga County	867	1.01
Clinton, MI (cdp) Macomb County	867	0.91
Morton Grove, IL (village) Cook County	859	3.83
Chandler, AZ (city) Maricopa County	857	0.49
Brookline, MA (cdp) Norfolk County	854	1.50
Kansas City, MO (city) Jackson County	851	0.19
Marple, PA (township) Delaware County	849	3.58
Metairie, LA (cdp) Jefferson Parish	844	0.58
Anchorage, AK (municipality) Anchorage Borough	843	0.32
Dover, NJ (township) Ocean County	840	0.94
San Mateo, CA (city) San Mateo County	839	0.91

Notes: (cdp) census designated place; Refer to the Explanation of Data in the front of the book for more detailed information.

Greek

Top 150 Places Sorted by Percent

(Based on all places, regardless of population)

Place	Number	%
Jeddo, PA (borough) Luzerne County	24	16.67
Malden, NY (cdp) Ulster County	64	13.11
Spring Hill, IN (town) Marion County	16	12.80
Falman-County Acres, TX (cdp) San Patricio County	30	12.30
Tarpon Springs, FL (city) Pinellas County	2,479	11.77
Fruitdale, SD (town) Butte County	8	11.27
Gore, MI (township) Huron County	15	10.79
Campbell, OH (city) Mahoning County	981	10.37
River Bend, MO (village) Jackson County	1	10.00
Lake, MI (township) Macomb County	5	9.62
Plandome Manor, NY (village) Nassau County	79	9.43
Madrid, NM (cdp) Santa Fe County	10	9.43
Gold Hill, CO (cdp) Boulder County	19	9.09
Allenwood, NJ (cdp) Monmouth County	70	8.58
East Valley, MN (township) Marshall County	4	8.51
Halcott, NY (town) Greene County	18	8.41
Kingston, MN (city) Meeker County	13	8.23
Huntleigh, MO (city) Saint Louis County	25	8.20
Lincolnwood, IL (village) Cook County	963	7.79
Greenwood, IL (village) McHenry County	20	7.55
Stark, KS (city) Neosho County	9	7.38
South Barrington, IL (village) Cook County	274	7.35
Englewood Cliffs, NJ (borough) Bergen County	386	7.25
New Boston-Morea, PA (cdp) Schuylkill County	33	7.21
Del Rio, CA (cdp) Stanislaus County	78	6.75
East Marion, NY (cdp) Suffolk County	52	6.70
Denver, MO (village) Worth County	2	6.67
Winifred, MT (town) Fergus County	12	6.52
Munsey Park, NY (village) Nassau County	171	6.50
Palos Hills, IL (city) Cook County	1,141	6.43
Duncan, PA (township) Tioga County	13	6.28
Grosse Pointe Shores, MI (village) Wayne County	175	6.26
Grosse Pointe, MI (township) Wayne County	170	6.20
Brandonville, WV (town) Preston County	6	6.12
Palos Park, IL (village) Cook County	276	6.10
Nahant, MA (cdp) Essex County	221	6.08
Bedford Park, IL (village) Cook County	33	5.87
Fernan Lake Village, ID (city) Kootenai County	10	5.85
Holiday, FL (cdp) Pasco County	1,247	5.69
Harbor Isle, NY (cdp) Nassau County	79	5.59
Teachey, NC (town) Duplin County	5	5.59
Hartville, WY (town) Platte County	5	5.56
Great Neck Gardens, NY (cdp) Nassau County	62	5.55
Vallecito, CA (cdp) Calaveras County	32	5.55
Yosemite Valley, CA (cdp) Mariposa County	12	5.38
Lake Dalecarlia, IN (cdp) Lake County	67	5.32
Fisher Island, FL (cdp) Miami-Dade County	18	5.31
Fairview Beach, VA (cdp) King George County	13	5.24
Alpine, NJ (borough) Bergen County	114	5.22
Lynndyl, UT (town) Millard County	7	5.22
Brighton, ME (plantation) Somerset County	5	5.21
Upper Brookville, NY (village) Nassau County	94	5.20
New Seabury, MA (cdp) Barnstable County	41	5.07
Soldier, KS (city) Jackson County	5	5.05
Ocean City, WA (cdp) Grays Harbor County	9	5.03
Barnum Island, NY (cdp) Nassau County	121	5.02
North Woodbridge, CA (cdp) San Joaquin County	62	4.98
Peabody, MA (city) Essex County	2,391	4.97
Dracut, MA (town) Middlesex County	1,401	4.91
Braddyville, IA (city) Page County	8	4.91
Oak Ridge, LA (village) Morehouse Parish	7	4.86
Thorp, WA (cdp) Kittitas County	14	4.84
Tannersville, NY (village) Greene County	22	4.78
Cleveland, IL (village) Henry County	12	4.78
Shoshone, CA (cdp) Inyo County	4	4.76
Glasgow, PA (borough) Beaver County	3	4.76
Porter, PA (township) Pike County	18	4.74
Mount Carbon, PA (borough) Schuylkill County	4	4.71
Little Grant, WI (town) Grant County	12	4.69
Plandome, NY (village) Nassau County	59	4.64
Livingston Manor, NY (cdp) Sullivan County	62	4.62
Harding-Birch Lakes, AK (cdp) Fairbanks North Star Borough	8	4.60
Fort Indiantown Gap, PA (cdp) Lebanon County	4	4.60
Heron, MT (cdp) Sanders County	7	4.55
Oak Brook, IL (village) Du Page County	383	4.53
Onley, VA (town) Accomack County	22	4.51
Ipswich, MA (town) Essex County	583	4.49
Popponesset, MA (cdp) Barnstable County	19	4.47
Garden City South, NY (cdp) Nassau County	176	4.43
Malverne Park Oaks, NY (cdp) Nassau County	22	4.42
Lausanne, PA (township) Carbon County	10	4.42
Windham, NY (town) Greene County	73	4.40
Yorkville, OH (village) Jefferson County	55	4.40
Grove, PA (township) Cameron County	7	4.40
Trommald, MN (city) Crow Wing County	6	4.38
Monte Sereno, CA (city) Santa Clara County	155	4.36
Vista Center, NJ (cdp) Ocean County	31	4.36
Oyster Bay Cove, NY (village) Nassau County	95	4.35
Harwood Heights, IL (village) Cook County	357	4.34
University Gardens, NY (cdp) Nassau County	180	4.34
Oakhurst, NJ (cdp) Monmouth County	177	4.29
Delano, PA (township) Schuylkill County	21	4.29
Terryville, NY (cdp) Suffolk County	453	4.28
Chinese Camp, CA (cdp) Tuolumne County	6	4.26
Broomall, PA (cdp) Delaware County	475	4.25
Long Grove, IL (village) Lake County	280	4.23
Wellington, UT (city) Carbon County	73	4.17
Harmony Township, PA (cdp) Beaver County	140	4.15
Cope, SC (town) Orangeburg County	5	4.07
Centre Island, NY (village) Nassau County	18	4.04
Manhasset, NY (cdp) Nassau County	337	4.03
Groveland, MA (town) Essex County	243	4.02
Hiller, PA (cdp) Fayette County	49	4.02
Plandome Heights, NY (village) Nassau County	39	4.02
Fredericksburg, PA (cdp) Crawford County	47	4.00
Dutchtown, MO (village) Cape Girardeau County	4	4.00
Banks, PA (township) Carbon County	55	3.99
Quinebaug, CT (cdp) Windham County	43	3.99
Crystal Lake, CT (cdp) Tolland County	57	3.98
Point Arena, CA (city) Mendocino County	19	3.91
Teton Village, WY (cdp) Teton County	10	3.91
Manchester, KS (city) Dickinson County	4	3.88
Rudy, AR (town) Crawford County	2	3.85
Erma, NJ (cdp) Cape May County	82	3.84
Morton Grove, IL (village) Cook County	859	3.83
Stanhope, NJ (borough) Sussex County	135	3.83
Ferris, IL (village) Hancock County	7	3.83
Watertown, MA (city) Middlesex County	1,257	3.81
Ravensdale, WA (cdp) King County	29	3.81
Alta, WY (cdp) Teton County	17	3.81
Butteville, OR (cdp) Marion County	8	3.81
Fort Lee, NJ (borough) Bergen County	1,346	3.80
Monhegan, ME (plantation) Lincoln County	3	3.80
Norridge, IL (village) Cook County	556	3.78
Flower Hill, NY (village) Nassau County	168	3.73
Zinc, AR (town) Boone County	3	3.70
Mount Olympus, UT (cdp) Salt Lake County	252	3.69
Graeagle, CA (cdp) Plumas County	34	3.66
Verona, PA (borough) Allegheny County	114	3.65
Golden Triangle, NJ (cdp) Camden County	123	3.64
Robinson, KS (city) Brown County	8	3.60
Fox River Grove, IL (village) McHenry County	176	3.59
Mahanoy, PA (township) Schuylkill County	40	3.59
Marple, PA (township) Delaware County	849	3.58
Kitzmiller, MD (town) Garrett County	10	3.58
Palisades Park, NJ (borough) Bergen County	610	3.57
Stockdale, PA (borough) Washington County	19	3.57
Orland Park, IL (village) Cook County	1,797	3.52
Lynnfield, MA (cdp) Essex County	405	3.51
Kline, PA (township) Schuylkill County	56	3.51
Lyman, UT (town) Wayne County	9	3.49
Topsfield, MA (town) Essex County	214	3.48
Winfield, IN (town) Lake County	79	3.48
Truxton, MO (village) Lincoln County	4	3.48
Wilmington, MN (township) Houston County	16	3.47
Bethpage, NY (cdp) Nassau County	573	3.46
Napeague, NY (cdp) Suffolk County	8	3.46
Irondale, MO (city) Washington County	16	3.45
Grosse Pointe Woods, MI (city) Wayne County	586	3.43
River Edge, NJ (borough) Bergen County	375	3.43

Notes: (cdp) census designated place; Refer to the Explanation of Data in the front of the book for more detailed information.

Greek

Top 150 Places Sorted by Percent

(Based on places with populations of 10,000 or more)

Place	Number	%
Tarpon Springs, FL (city) Pinellas County	2,479	11.77
Lincolnwood, IL (village) Cook County	963	7.79
Palos Hills, IL (city) Cook County	1,141	6.43
Holiday, FL (cdp) Pasco County	1,247	5.69
Peabody, MA (city) Essex County	2,391	4.97
Dracut, MA (town) Middlesex County	1,401	4.91
Ipswich, MA (town) Essex County	583	4.49
Terryville, NY (cdp) Suffolk County	453	4.28
Broomall, PA (cdp) Delaware County	475	4.25
Morton Grove, IL (village) Cook County	859	3.83
Watertown, MA (city) Middlesex County	1,257	3.81
Fort Lee, NJ (borough) Bergen County	1,346	3.80
Norridge, IL (village) Cook County	556	3.78
Marple, PA (township) Delaware County	849	3.58
Palisades Park, NJ (borough) Bergen County	610	3.57
Orland Park, IL (village) Cook County	1,797	3.52
Lynnfield, MA (cdp) Essex County	405	3.51
Bethpage, NY (cdp) Nassau County	573	3.46
Grosse Pointe Woods, MI (city) Wayne County	586	3.43
River Edge, NJ (borough) Bergen County	375	3.43
Glenview, IL (village) Cook County	1,420	3.41
Park Ridge, IL (city) Cook County	1,288	3.41
Arlington, MA (cdp) Middlesex County	1,418	3.35
Niles, IL (village) Cook County	990	3.28
Danvers, MA (cdp) Essex County	827	3.28
Garden City, NY (village) Nassau County	691	3.19
Belmont, MA (cdp) Middlesex County	752	3.11
Hillsborough, CA (town) San Mateo County	324	2.99
Commack, NY (cdp) Suffolk County	1,083	2.98
Grosse Pointe Park, MI (city) Wayne County	370	2.97
Tyngsborough, MA (town) Middlesex County	329	2.97
East Lake, FL (cdp) Pinellas County	868	2.95
Westchester, IL (village) Cook County	491	2.95
Salem, MA (city) Essex County	1,188	2.94
Lake Forest, IL (city) Lake County	586	2.93
Mount Prospect, IL (village) Cook County	1,654	2.92
Rosedale, MD (cdp) Baltimore County	560	2.92
Weirton, WV (city) Hancock County	592	2.91
Palm Harbor, FL (cdp) Pinellas County	1,707	2.89
Manchester, NH (city) Hillsborough County	3,066	2.87
Lynn, MA (city) Essex County	2,527	2.84
Alsip, IL (village) Cook County	563	2.83
Hickory Hills, IL (city) Cook County	392	2.81
Palos Heights, IL (city) Cook County	315	2.78
Skokie, IL (village) Cook County	1,706	2.69
Lowell, MA (city) Middlesex County	2,815	2.68
Hicksville, NY (cdp) Nassau County	1,103	2.67
North Bellmore, NY (cdp) Nassau County	533	2.65
Haverhill, MA (city) Essex County	1,549	2.63
Miller Place, NY (cdp) Suffolk County	281	2.63
Crown Point, IN (city) Lake County	509	2.60
Lutherville-Timonium, MD (cdp) Baltimore County	404	2.59
Chelmsford, MA (town) Middlesex County	872	2.58
Canton, MA (town) Norfolk County	536	2.58
Syosset, NY (cdp) Nassau County	478	2.58
Seven Hills, OH (city) Cuyahoga County	310	2.57
Goodings Grove, IL (cdp) Will County	438	2.56
Dedham, MA (cdp) Norfolk County	600	2.55
Salisbury, NY (cdp) Nassau County	313	2.54
Waterford, CT (town) New London County	481	2.51
Oak Lawn, IL (village) Cook County	1,378	2.49
Rocky Point, NY (cdp) Suffolk County	252	2.46
Swampscott, MA (cdp) Essex County	350	2.43
Des Plaines, IL (city) Cook County	1,423	2.42
Longmeadow, MA (cdp) Hampden County	379	2.42
Westwood, MA (town) Norfolk County	341	2.42
Levittown, NY (cdp) Nassau County	1,259	2.37
Merrillville, IN (town) Lake County	729	2.37
Elmwood Park, IL (village) Cook County	598	2.35
Dyer, IN (town) Lake County	326	2.35
Windham, NH (town) Rockingham County	252	2.35
Wood Dale, IL (city) Du Page County	326	2.33
Ridgefield, NJ (borough) Bergen County	252	2.33
Newburyport, MA (city) Essex County	399	2.31
Lemont, IL (village) Cook County	304	2.31
Millbrae, CA (city) San Mateo County	476	2.30
Plainview, NY (cdp) Nassau County	586	2.29
New Milford, NJ (borough) Bergen County	373	2.27
Saco, ME (city) York County	381	2.26
Hazleton, PA (city) Luzerne County	521	2.24
Bloomingdale, IL (village) Du Page County	484	2.24
Warren, OH (city) Trumbull County	1,033	2.20
Damascus, MD (cdp) Montgomery County	249	2.20
Addison, IL (village) Du Page County	783	2.19
Wilmette, IL (village) Cook County	606	2.19
Massapequa, NY (cdp) Nassau County	495	2.19
Franklin Square, NY (cdp) Nassau County	639	2.18
Westford, MA (town) Middlesex County	452	2.18
West Hempstead, NY (cdp) Nassau County	407	2.18
Bedford, NH (town) Hillsborough County	399	2.18
Frankfort, IL (village) Will County	219	2.14
Cliffside Park, NJ (borough) Bergen County	489	2.13
Dix Hills, NY (cdp) Suffolk County	553	2.12
Wantagh, NY (cdp) Nassau County	403	2.12
Barrington, IL (village) Cook County	210	2.10
Scarsdale, NY (village) Westchester County	372	2.09
Lynbrook, NY (village) Nassau County	414	2.08
North Strabane, PA (township) Washington County	209	2.08
Burr Ridge, IL (village) Du Page County	214	2.07
Marlborough, MA (city) Middlesex County	748	2.06
Norwalk, CT (city) Fairfield County	1,691	2.04
Chesterton, IN (town) Porter County	213	2.04
Westlake, OH (city) Cuyahoga County	647	2.03
Oyster Bay, NY (town) Nassau County	5,932	2.02
Westport, CT (cdp) Fairfield County	521	2.02
Setauket-East Setauket, NY (cdp) Suffolk County	322	2.02
Prospect Heights, IL (city) Cook County	352	2.01
Bridgeview, IL (village) Cook County	309	2.01
Holtsville, NY (cdp) Suffolk County	336	1.98
Ventnor City, NJ (city) Atlantic County	255	1.98
Dumont, NJ (borough) Bergen County	344	1.97
Upper Darby, PA (township) Delaware County	1,605	1.96
Dover, NH (city) Strafford County	528	1.96
Merrick, NY (cdp) Nassau County	446	1.96
East Northport, NY (cdp) Suffolk County	408	1.96
Lakewood Park, FL (cdp) Saint Lucie County	204	1.96
Ashland, MA (town) Middlesex County	286	1.95
Wall, NJ (township) Monmouth County	484	1.92
Easton, MA (town) Bristol County	429	1.92
Perry Hall, MD (cdp) Baltimore County	546	1.91
River Forest, IL (village) Cook County	222	1.91
Wheeling, WV (city) Ohio County	596	1.90
Weston, MA (town) Middlesex County	218	1.90
Arlington Heights, IL (village) Cook County	1,442	1.89
Darien, CT (cdp) Fairfield County	370	1.89
Farmingville, NY (cdp) Suffolk County	312	1.89
North Arlington, NJ (borough) Bergen County	287	1.89
Northbrook, IL (village) Cook County	628	1.88
Bellmore, NY (cdp) Nassau County	309	1.88
Beverly, MA (city) Essex County	741	1.86
Rolling Meadows, IL (city) Cook County	459	1.86
Monroe, CT (town) Fairfield County	358	1.86
Pelham, NH (town) Hillsborough County	203	1.86
New Port Richey East, FL (cdp) Pasco County	188	1.86
Olney, MD (cdp) Montgomery County	584	1.85
North Babylon, NY (cdp) Suffolk County	328	1.85
Valley Stream, NY (village) Nassau County	668	1.84
Southgate, MI (city) Wayne County	551	1.83
Hooksett, NH (town) Merrimack County	214	1.83
Burlington, MA (cdp) Middlesex County	416	1.82
Needham, MA (cdp) Norfolk County	523	1.81
Riverview, MI (city) Wayne County	240	1.81
Brooklyn, OH (city) Cuyahoga County	208	1.80
Huntington, NY (town) Suffolk County	3,492	1.79
Stamford, CT (city) Fairfield County	2,100	1.79
Clearwater, FL (city) Pinellas County	1,934	1.79
Ocean, NJ (township) Monmouth County	482	1.79
Tenafly, NJ (borough) Bergen County	247	1.79
Portsmouth, NH (city) Rockingham County	371	1.78
Harper Woods, MI (city) Wayne County	252	1.77

Notes: (cdp) census designated place; Refer to the Explanation of Data in the front of the book for more detailed information.

Guyanese

Top 150 Places Sorted by Number

(Based on all places, regardless of population)

Place	Number	%
New York, NY (city) New York City	99,537	1.24
Hempstead, NY (town) Nassau County	3,420	0.45
Jersey City, NJ (city) Hudson County	1,986	0.83
East Orange, NJ (city) Essex County	1,460	2.09
Newark, NJ (city) Essex County	1,313	0.48
Irvington, NJ (cdp) Essex County	920	1.52
Orange, NJ (cdp) Essex County	821	2.50
Washington, DC (city) District of Columbia	709	0.12
Elmont, NY (cdp) Nassau County	603	1.85
Mount Vernon, NY (city) Westchester County	568	0.83
Islip, NY (town) Suffolk County	553	0.17
Los Angeles, CA (city) Los Angeles County	549	0.01
Pembroke Pines, FL (city) Broward County	508	0.37
Hempstead, NY (village) Nassau County	503	0.89
Babylon, NY (town) Suffolk County	502	0.24
Miramar, FL (city) Broward County	469	0.65
Yonkers, NY (city) Westchester County	426	0.22
Brookhaven, NY (town) Suffolk County	423	0.09
Bloomfield, NJ (cdp) Essex County	394	0.83
Hartford, CT (city) Hartford County	390	0.32
Pine Hills, FL (cdp) Orange County	385	0.92
Boston, MA (city) Suffolk County	381	0.06
Minneapolis, MN (city) Hennepin County	373	0.10
Chicago, IL (city) Cook County	370	0.01
Jacksonville, FL (special city) Duval County	358	0.05
Schenectady, NY (city) Schenectady County	355	0.57
Town 'n' Country, FL (cdp) Hillsborough County	354	0.49
North Hempstead, NY (town) Nassau County	346	0.16
South Plainfield, NJ (borough) Middlesex County	342	1.57
South Miami Heights, FL (cdp) Miami-Dade County	337	1.00
Philadelphia, PA (city) Philadelphia County	331	0.02
Freeport, NY (village) Nassau County	326	0.74
Union, NJ (cdp) Union County	314	0.58
Englewood, NJ (city) Bergen County	306	1.17
Silver Spring, MD (cdp) Montgomery County	293	0.38
Waterbury, CT (city) New Haven County	281	0.26
Hollywood, FL (city) Broward County	281	0.20
Wheaton-Glenmont, MD (cdp) Montgomery County	280	0.49
Piscataway, NJ (township) Middlesex County	269	0.53
Uniondale, NY (cdp) Nassau County	268	1.16
Central Islip, NY (cdp) Suffolk County	244	0.77
Oyster Bay, NY (town) Nassau County	238	0.08
North Valley Stream, NY (cdp) Nassau County	236	1.49
Albany, NY (city) Albany County	235	0.25
Chillum, MD (cdp) Prince George's County	226	0.66
Montclair, NJ (cdp) Essex County	221	0.57
Tampa, FL (city) Hillsborough County	220	0.07
Sunrise, FL (city) Broward County	218	0.25
Lauderhill, FL (city) Broward County	217	0.38
Maplewood, NJ (cdp) Essex County	216	0.90
Virginia Beach, VA (independent city) Virginia Beach city	216	0.05
Palm Bay, FL (city) Brevard County	211	0.27
Woodbridge, NJ (township) Middlesex County	206	0.21
Teaneck, NJ (cdp) Bergen County	205	0.52
Roselle, NJ (borough) Union County	202	0.95
Long Beach, NY (city) Nassau County	202	0.57
Houston, TX (city) Harris County	202	0.01
New Brunswick, NJ (city) Middlesex County	201	0.41
West Orange, NJ (cdp) Essex County	199	0.44
Paterson, NJ (city) Passaic County	193	0.13
Valley Stream, NY (village) Nassau County	185	0.51
Lanham-Seabrook, MD (cdp) Prince George's County	170	0.94
East Hartford, CT (cdp) Hartford County	170	0.34
Ramapo, NY (town) Rockland County	169	0.16
Baltimore, MD (independent city) Baltimore city	168	0.03
East Riverdale, MD (cdp) Prince George's County	167	1.09
Charlotte, NC (city) Mecklenburg County	166	0.03
Lauderdale Lakes, FL (city) Broward County	163	0.52
Saint Petersburg, FL (city) Pinellas County	161	0.06
Edison, NJ (cdp) Middlesex County	160	0.16
Cleveland, OH (city) Cuyahoga County	159	0.03
Plantation, FL (city) Broward County	158	0.19
Roosevelt, NY (cdp) Nassau County	156	0.98
Carol City, FL (cdp) Miami-Dade County	155	0.26
New Carrollton, MD (city) Prince George's County	151	1.18
Plainfield, NJ (city) Union County	149	0.31
Brooklyn Park, MN (city) Hennepin County	149	0.22
Coral Springs, FL (city) Broward County	147	0.13
Langley Park, MD (cdp) Prince George's County	145	0.89
East Meadow, NY (cdp) Nassau County	140	0.37
Richmond West, FL (cdp) Miami-Dade County	139	0.50
Windsor, CT (town) Hartford County	139	0.49
Deer Park, NY (cdp) Suffolk County	137	0.48
Davie, FL (town) Broward County	136	0.18
Missouri City, TX (city) Fort Bend County	134	0.26
Coolbaugh, PA (township) Monroe County	131	0.86
Franklin, NJ (township) Somerset County	131	0.26
Orlando, FL (city) Orange County	131	0.07
Adelphi, MD (cdp) Prince George's County	129	0.86
San Jose, CA (city) Santa Clara County	128	0.01
Greenburgh, NY (town) Westchester County	127	0.15
Germantown, MD (cdp) Montgomery County	126	0.23
Rochester, NY (city) Monroe County	126	0.06
Nashville-Davidson, TN (special city) Davidson County	126	0.02
Port Charlotte, FL (cdp) Charlotte County	125	0.27
Hillside, NJ (cdp) Union County	123	0.57
Huntington, NY (town) Suffolk County	123	0.06
Redan, GA (cdp) De Kalb County	122	0.36
Bowie, MD (city) Prince George's County	122	0.24
North Plainfield, NJ (borough) Somerset County	121	0.57
Linden, NJ (city) Union County	121	0.31
Kissimmee, FL (city) Osceola County	120	0.25
Deltona, FL (city) Volusia County	120	0.17
Palmdale, CA (city) Los Angeles County	120	0.10
North Amityville, NY (cdp) Suffolk County	119	0.72
San Antonio, TX (city) Bexar County	118	0.01
Detroit, MI (city) Wayne County	117	0.01
South Orange, NJ (cdp) Essex County	116	0.68
Bayonne, NJ (city) Hudson County	116	0.19
North Miami, FL (city) Miami-Dade County	116	0.19
Tallahassee, FL (city) Leon County	116	0.08
Palm Coast, FL (city) Flagler County	115	0.34
Concord, CA (city) Contra Costa County	115	0.09
Palmetto Estates, FL (cdp) Miami-Dade County	113	0.83
Bloomfield, CT (town) Hartford County	112	0.57
Gaithersburg, MD (city) Montgomery County	112	0.21
Passaic, NJ (city) Passaic County	112	0.17
Olney, MD (cdp) Montgomery County	111	0.35
Elmwood Park, NJ (borough) Bergen County	107	0.57
Memphis, TN (city) Shelby County	106	0.02
Citrus Park, FL (cdp) Hillsborough County	105	0.52
Fairland, MD (cdp) Montgomery County	105	0.49
Worcester, MA (city) Worcester County	105	0.06
Stamford, CT (city) Fairfield County	104	0.09
Temple Terrace, FL (city) Hillsborough County	102	0.49
Baldwin, NY (cdp) Nassau County	102	0.43
Pine Castle, FL (cdp) Orange County	100	1.22
Takoma Park, MD (city) Montgomery County	99	0.58
New Rochelle, NY (city) Westchester County	99	0.14
South Laurel, MD (cdp) Prince George's County	97	0.47
Golden Glades, FL (cdp) Miami-Dade County	96	0.30
Alexandria, VA (independent city) Alexandria city	96	0.07
Aurora, CO (city) Arapahoe County	95	0.03
White Plains, NY (city) Westchester County	93	0.18
Fresno, CA (city) Fresno County	93	0.02
Wedgefield, FL (cdp) Orange County	91	3.23
East Brunswick, NJ (cdp) Middlesex County	91	0.19
South Valley Stream, NY (cdp) Nassau County	90	1.60
Garland, TX (city) Dallas County	90	0.04
Westbury, NY (village) Nassau County	89	0.62
Willingboro, NJ (township) Burlington County	89	0.27
Montgomery Village, MD (cdp) Montgomery County	89	0.23
Franklin Square, NY (cdp) Nassau County	87	0.30
South Brunswick, NJ (township) Middlesex County	87	0.23
Hawthorne, CA (city) Los Angeles County	87	0.10
North Lauderdale, FL (city) Broward County	84	0.26
Aspen Hill, MD (cdp) Montgomery County	81	0.16
Greenbelt, MD (city) Prince George's County	80	0.37
Old Bridge, NJ (township) Middlesex County	80	0.13
San Diego, CA (city) San Diego County	80	0.01

Notes: (cdp) census designated place; Refer to the Explanation of Data in the front of the book for more detailed information.

Guyanese

Top 150 Places Sorted by Percent

(Based on all places, regardless of population)

Place	Number	%
Fort Ritchie, MD (cdp) Washington County	34	16.27
East Garden City, NY (cdp) Nassau County	47	4.72
North Lynbrook, NY (cdp) Nassau County	22	3.36
Wedgefield, FL (cdp) Orange County	91	3.23
Orange, NJ (cdp) Essex County	821	2.50
Bellerose Terrace, NY (cdp) Nassau County	54	2.50
East Orange, NJ (city) Essex County	1,460	2.09
Gordon Heights, NY (cdp) Suffolk County	64	2.07
North Brentwood, MD (town) Prince George's County	9	1.93
Elmont, NY (cdp) Nassau County	603	1.85
Ashton-Sandy Spring, MD (cdp) Montgomery County	59	1.74
South Floral Park, NY (village) Nassau County	26	1.65
Brentwood, MD (town) Prince George's County	47	1.64
Bay Park, NY (cdp) Nassau County	37	1.64
South Valley Stream, NY (cdp) Nassau County	90	1.60
Sewaren, NJ (cdp) Middlesex County	45	1.60
Pavo, GA (city) Thomas County	11	1.59
South Plainfield, NJ (borough) Middlesex County	342	1.57
Irvington, NJ (cdp) Essex County	920	1.52
North Valley Stream, NY (cdp) Nassau County	236	1.49
Broadview-Pompano Park, FL (cdp) Broward County	72	1.40
Lexington, MN (city) Anoka County	30	1.35
South Hempstead, NY (cdp) Nassau County	42	1.32
High Falls, NY (cdp) Ulster County	8	1.32
Crown Heights, NY (cdp) Dutchess County	39	1.30
Glen Echo, MD (town) Montgomery County	3	1.27
New York, NY (city) New York City	99,537	1.24
Pine Castle, FL (cdp) Orange County	100	1.22
Fairview, NY (cdp) Westchester County	36	1.20
Southchase, FL (cdp) Orange County	54	1.19
New Carrollton, MD (city) Prince George's County	151	1.18
Hillandale, MD (cdp) Montgomery County	35	1.18
Englewood, NJ (city) Bergen County	306	1.17
Uniondale, NY (cdp) Nassau County	268	1.16
Woodlawn, MD (cdp) Prince George's County	71	1.14
University Park, IL (village) Will County	74	1.12
Colmar Manor, MD (town) Prince George's County	14	1.11
East Riverdale, MD (cdp) Prince George's County	167	1.09
South Miami Heights, FL (cdp) Miami-Dade County	337	1.00
Roosevelt, NY (cdp) Nassau County	156	0.98
Riverland Village, FL (cdp) Broward County	20	0.97
Roselle, NJ (borough) Union County	202	0.95
Lanham-Seabrook, MD (cdp) Prince George's County	170	0.94
Thompsonville, CT (cdp) Hartford County	75	0.94
Pine Hills, FL (cdp) Orange County	385	0.92
Melrose Park, FL (cdp) Broward County	65	0.92
Silver Springs Shores, FL (cdp) Marion County	60	0.92
Mount Rainier, MD (city) Prince George's County	77	0.91
Maplewood, NJ (cdp) Essex County	216	0.90
Hempstead, NY (village) Nassau County	503	0.89
Langley Park, MD (cdp) Prince George's County	145	0.89
Springdale, MD (cdp) Prince George's County	25	0.89
Eau Claire, MI (village) Berrien County	6	0.89
West Salem, PA (township) Mercer County	31	0.87
Coolbaugh, PA (township) Monroe County	131	0.86
Adelphi, MD (cdp) Prince George's County	129	0.86
West Middlesex, PA (borough) Mercer County	5	0.86
Lithonia, GA (city) De Kalb County	19	0.85
Selbyville, DE (town) Sussex County	14	0.85
Pomona, NY (village) Rockland County	23	0.84
Jersey City, NJ (city) Hudson County	1,986	0.83
Mount Vernon, NY (city) Westchester County	568	0.83
Bloomfield, NJ (cdp) Essex County	394	0.83
Palmetto Estates, FL (cdp) Miami-Dade County	113	0.83
Tanglewilde-Thompson Place, WA (cdp) Thurston County	47	0.82
Dalton City, IL (village) Moultrie County	5	0.82
June Park, FL (cdp) Brevard County	38	0.81
Goulds, FL (cdp) Miami-Dade County	61	0.80
Hillcrest, NY (cdp) Rockland County	57	0.80
Loch Lomond, FL (cdp) Broward County	26	0.78
Central Islip, NY (cdp) Suffolk County	244	0.77
Gantt, AL (town) Covington County	2	0.77
Riverdale Park, MD (town) Prince George's County	49	0.75
Roosevelt, NJ (borough) Monmouth County	7	0.75
Freeport, NY (village) Nassau County	326	0.74
East Perrine, FL (cdp) Miami-Dade County	51	0.74
Bonnie Lock-Woodsetter North, FL (cdp) Broward County	32	0.74
Cortland, IL (town) De Kalb County	15	0.73
Landover Hills, MD (town) Prince George's County	11	0.73
North Amityville, NY (cdp) Suffolk County	119	0.72
McGuire AFB, NJ (cdp) Burlington County	47	0.72
Medicine Lake, MT (town) Sheridan County	2	0.71
Searingtown, NY (cdp) Nassau County	35	0.69
Bloomfield Hills, MI (city) Oakland County	27	0.69
Morrisville, NY (village) Madison County	15	0.69
South Orange, NJ (cdp) Essex County	116	0.68
Chillum, MD (cdp) Prince George's County	226	0.66
Pebble Creek, FL (cdp) Hillsborough County	32	0.66
Mountain View, NC (cdp) Catawba County	26	0.66
Miramar, FL (city) Broward County	469	0.65
Cheverly, MD (town) Prince George's County	42	0.65
Wheatley Heights, NY (cdp) Suffolk County	32	0.64
Westbury, NY (village) Nassau County	89	0.62
Clermont, FL (city) Lake County	58	0.60
Dundee, FL (town) Polk County	17	0.59
Union, NJ (cdp) Union County	314	0.58
Takoma Park, MD (city) Montgomery County	99	0.58
Rosaryville, MD (cdp) Prince George's County	70	0.58
Goddard, MD (cdp) Prince George's County	32	0.58
Loch Lomond, VA (cdp) Prince William County	20	0.58
Schenectady, NY (city) Schenectady County	355	0.57
Montclair, NJ (cdp) Essex County	221	0.57
Long Beach, NY (city) Nassau County	202	0.57
Hillside, NJ (cdp) Union County	123	0.57
North Plainfield, NJ (borough) Somerset County	121	0.57
Bloomfield, CT (town) Hartford County	112	0.57
Elmwood Park, NJ (borough) Bergen County	107	0.57
Country Club Estates, GA (cdp) Glynn County	43	0.56
Grimes, IA (city) Polk County	28	0.55
Conyers, GA (city) Rockdale County	61	0.54
Kemp Mill, MD (cdp) Montgomery County	54	0.54
Blauvelt, NY (cdp) Rockland County	28	0.54
Pleasant Garden, NC (town) Guilford County	26	0.54
Piscataway, NJ (township) Middlesex County	269	0.53
Franklinton, NC (town) Franklin County	9	0.53
Center Hill, FL (city) Sumter County	5	0.53
Teaneck, NJ (cdp) Bergen County	205	0.52
Lauderdale Lakes, FL (city) Broward County	163	0.52
Citrus Park, FL (cdp) Hillsborough County	105	0.52
Poinciana, FL (cdp) Osceola County	70	0.52
Wyandanch, NY (cdp) Suffolk County	55	0.52
Irondale, GA (cdp) Clayton County	40	0.52
Broadview Park, FL (cdp) Broward County	35	0.52
Pelham, NY (village) Westchester County	33	0.52
Lathrup Village, MI (city) Oakland County	22	0.52
Valley Stream, NY (village) Nassau County	185	0.51
Lincroft, NJ (cdp) Monmouth County	32	0.51
Pine Manor, FL (cdp) Lee County	20	0.51
Newport, NC (town) Carteret County	17	0.51
Edmonston, MD (town) Prince George's County	5	0.51
Richmond West, FL (cdp) Miami-Dade County	139	0.50
Kettering, MD (cdp) Prince George's County	56	0.50
Great Neck Plaza, NY (village) Nassau County	32	0.50
Calcium, NY (cdp) Jefferson County	16	0.50
Town 'n' Country, FL (cdp) Hillsborough County	354	0.49
Wheaton-Glenmont, MD (cdp) Montgomery County	280	0.49
Windsor, CT (town) Hartford County	139	0.49
Fairland, MD (cdp) Montgomery County	105	0.49
Temple Terrace, FL (city) Hillsborough County	102	0.49
Harrison, NJ (town) Hudson County	70	0.49
Hunters Creek, FL (cdp) Orange County	44	0.49
Sea Cliff, NY (village) Nassau County	25	0.49
Newark, NJ (city) Essex County	1,313	0.48
Deer Park, NY (cdp) Suffolk County	137	0.48
Bay Hill, FL (cdp) Orange County	26	0.48
Delaware, NY (town) Sullivan County	13	0.48
Pearlington, MS (cdp) Hancock County	9	0.48
South Laurel, MD (cdp) Prince George's County	97	0.47
Grand Terrace, CA (city) San Bernardino County	56	0.47
River Vale, NJ (cdp) Bergen County	44	0.47

Notes: (cdp) census designated place; Refer to the Explanation of Data in the front of the book for more detailed information.

Guyanese

Top 150 Places Sorted by Percent

(Based on places with populations of 10,000 or more)

Place	Number	%
Orange, NJ (cdp) Essex County	821	2.50
East Orange, NJ (city) Essex County	1,460	2.09
Elmont, NY (cdp) Nassau County	603	1.85
South Plainfield, NJ (borough) Middlesex County	342	1.57
Irvington, NJ (cdp) Essex County	920	1.52
North Valley Stream, NY (cdp) Nassau County	236	1.49
New York, NY (city) New York City	99,537	1.24
New Carrollton, MD (city) Prince George's County	151	1.18
Englewood, NJ (city) Bergen County	306	1.17
Uniondale, NY (cdp) Nassau County	268	1.16
East Riverdale, MD (cdp) Prince George's County	167	1.09
South Miami Heights, FL (cdp) Miami-Dade County	337	1.00
Roosevelt, NY (cdp) Nassau County	156	0.98
Roselle, NJ (borough) Union County	202	0.95
Lanham-Seabrook, MD (cdp) Prince George's County	170	0.94
Pine Hills, FL (cdp) Orange County	385	0.92
Maplewood, NJ (cdp) Essex County	216	0.90
Hempstead, NY (village) Nassau County	503	0.89
Langley Park, MD (cdp) Prince George's County	145	0.89
Coolbaugh, PA (township) Monroe County	131	0.86
Adelphi, MD (cdp) Prince George's County	129	0.86
Jersey City, NJ (city) Hudson County	1,986	0.83
Mount Vernon, NY (city) Westchester County	568	0.83
Bloomfield, NJ (cdp) Essex County	394	0.83
Palmetto Estates, FL (cdp) Miami-Dade County	113	0.83
Central Islip, NY (cdp) Suffolk County	244	0.77
Freeport, NY (village) Nassau County	326	0.74
North Amityville, NY (cdp) Suffolk County	119	0.72
South Orange, NJ (cdp) Essex County	116	0.68
Chillum, MD (cdp) Prince George's County	226	0.66
Miramar, FL (city) Broward County	469	0.65
Westbury, NY (village) Nassau County	89	0.62
Union, NJ (cdp) Union County	314	0.58
Takoma Park, MD (city) Montgomery County	99	0.58
Rosaryville, MD (cdp) Prince George's County	70	0.58
Schenectady, NY (city) Schenectady County	355	0.57
Montclair, NJ (cdp) Essex County	221	0.57
Long Beach, NY (city) Nassau County	202	0.57
Hillside, NJ (cdp) Union County	123	0.57
North Plainfield, NJ (borough) Somerset County	121	0.57
Bloomfield, CT (town) Hartford County	112	0.57
Elmwood Park, NJ (borough) Bergen County	107	0.57
Conyers, GA (city) Rockdale County	61	0.54
Piscataway, NJ (township) Middlesex County	269	0.53
Teaneck, NJ (cdp) Bergen County	205	0.52
Lauderdale Lakes, FL (city) Broward County	163	0.52
Citrus Park, FL (cdp) Hillsborough County	105	0.52
Poinciana, FL (cdp) Osceola County	70	0.52
Wyandanch, NY (cdp) Suffolk County	55	0.52
Valley Stream, NY (village) Nassau County	185	0.51
Richmond West, FL (cdp) Miami-Dade County	139	0.50
Kettering, MD (cdp) Prince George's County	56	0.50
Town 'n' Country, FL (cdp) Hillsborough County	354	0.49
Wheaton-Glenmont, MD (cdp) Montgomery County	280	0.49
Windsor, CT (town) Hartford County	139	0.49
Fairland, MD (cdp) Montgomery County	105	0.49
Temple Terrace, FL (city) Hillsborough County	102	0.49
Harrison, NJ (town) Hudson County	70	0.49
Newark, NJ (city) Essex County	1,313	0.48
Deer Park, NY (cdp) Suffolk County	137	0.48
South Laurel, MD (cdp) Prince George's County	97	0.47
Grand Terrace, CA (city) San Bernardino County	56	0.47
Hempstead, NY (town) Nassau County	3,420	0.45
Beltsville, MD (cdp) Prince George's County	70	0.45
Glenn Dale, MD (cdp) Prince George's County	58	0.45
Walker Mill, MD (cdp) Prince George's County	51	0.45
West Orange, NJ (cdp) Essex County	199	0.44
Ives Estates, FL (cdp) Miami-Dade County	76	0.44
Elizabethtown, PA (borough) Lancaster County	52	0.44
Baldwin, NY (cdp) Nassau County	102	0.43
Powder Springs, GA (city) Cobb County	55	0.42
Lilburn, GA (city) Gwinnett County	48	0.42
New Brunswick, NJ (city) Middlesex County	201	0.41
Parkland, FL (city) Broward County	57	0.41
Lockhart, FL (cdp) Orange County	51	0.41
Silver Spring, MD (cdp) Montgomery County	293	0.38
Lauderhill, FL (city) Broward County	217	0.38
White Oak, MD (cdp) Montgomery County	79	0.38
Pembroke Pines, FL (city) Broward County	508	0.37
East Meadow, NY (cdp) Nassau County	140	0.37
Greenbelt, MD (city) Prince George's County	80	0.37
Iselin, NJ (cdp) Middlesex County	62	0.37
Woodmere, NY (cdp) Nassau County	61	0.37
North Bay Shore, NY (cdp) Suffolk County	55	0.37
Little Ferry, NJ (borough) Bergen County	40	0.37
Redan, GA (cdp) De Kalb County	122	0.36
Olney, MD (cdp) Montgomery County	111	0.35
Casselberry, FL (city) Seminole County	77	0.35
South Farmingdale, NY (cdp) Nassau County	53	0.35
Browns Mills, NJ (cdp) Burlington County	40	0.35
East Hartford, CT (cdp) Hartford County	170	0.34
Palm Coast, FL (city) Flagler County	115	0.34
North Babylon, NY (cdp) Suffolk County	60	0.34
Dobbs Ferry, NY (village) Westchester County	36	0.34
Bay Shore, NY (cdp) Suffolk County	78	0.33
Hyattsville, MD (city) Prince George's County	49	0.33
Springfield, NJ (cdp) Union County	47	0.33
Hartford, CT (city) Hartford County	390	0.32
Mount Olive, NJ (township) Morris County	78	0.32
Plainfield, NJ (city) Union County	149	0.31
Linden, NJ (city) Union County	121	0.31
Laurel, MD (city) Prince George's County	62	0.31
Golden Glades, FL (cdp) Miami-Dade County	96	0.30
Franklin Square, NY (cdp) Nassau County	87	0.30
Bergenfield, NJ (borough) Bergen County	78	0.30
East Windsor, NJ (township) Mercer County	74	0.30
Hazlet, NJ (township) Monmouth County	65	0.30
Colesville, MD (cdp) Montgomery County	59	0.30
Hackettstown, NJ (town) Warren County	31	0.30
Garden City, NY (village) Nassau County	63	0.29
Calverton, MD (cdp) Montgomery County	36	0.29
Pelham, NY (town) Westchester County	33	0.28
Azalea Park, FL (cdp) Orange County	31	0.28
North Greenbush, NY (town) Rensselaer County	30	0.28
Palm Bay, FL (city) Brevard County	211	0.27
Port Charlotte, FL (cdp) Charlotte County	125	0.27
Willingboro, NJ (township) Burlington County	89	0.27
Boca Del Mar, FL (cdp) Palm Beach County	57	0.27
Vincent, CA (cdp) Los Angeles County	40	0.27
Forestville, MD (cdp) Prince George's County	35	0.27
Riverview, FL (cdp) Hillsborough County	33	0.27
Waterbury, CT (city) New Haven County	281	0.26
Carol City, FL (cdp) Miami-Dade County	155	0.26
Missouri City, TX (city) Fort Bend County	134	0.26
Franklin, NJ (township) Somerset County	131	0.26
North Lauderdale, FL (city) Broward County	84	0.26
Somerset, NJ (cdp) Somerset County	61	0.26
Matthews, NC (town) Mecklenburg County	59	0.26
North Decatur, GA (cdp) De Kalb County	39	0.26
Conway, FL (cdp) Orange County	37	0.26
Albany, NY (city) Albany County	235	0.25
Sunrise, FL (city) Broward County	218	0.25
Kissimmee, FL (city) Osceola County	120	0.25
Lodi, NJ (borough) Bergen County	60	0.25
North Laurel, MD (cdp) Howard County	51	0.25
East Massapequa, NY (cdp) Nassau County	49	0.25
Saint Simons, GA (cdp) Glynn County	33	0.25
Manorville, NY (cdp) Suffolk County	28	0.25
Babylon, NY (town) Suffolk County	502	0.24
Bowie, MD (city) Prince George's County	122	0.24
Shakopee, MN (city) Scott County	49	0.24
North Bellmore, NY (cdp) Nassau County	48	0.24
Fountain, CO (city) El Paso County	36	0.24
Cedar Grove, NJ (cdp) Essex County	30	0.24
Meadow Woods, FL (cdp) Orange County	28	0.24
Germantown, MD (cdp) Montgomery County	126	0.23
Montgomery Village, MD (cdp) Montgomery County	89	0.23
South Brunswick, NJ (township) Middlesex County	87	0.23
Channelview, TX (cdp) Harris County	68	0.23
Carteret, NJ (borough) Middlesex County	48	0.23

Notes: (cdp) census designated place; Refer to the Explanation of Data in the front of the book for more detailed information.

Hawaii Native/Pacific Islander

Top 150 Places Sorted by Number

(Based on all places, regardless of population)

Place	Number	%
Honolulu, HI (cdp) Honolulu County	60,586	16.30
New York, NY (city) New York City	19,313	0.24
Hilo, HI (cdp) Hawaii County	14,401	35.33
Los Angeles, CA (city) Los Angeles County	13,390	0.36
Kaneohe, HI (cdp) Honolulu County	11,296	32.30
San Diego, CA (city) San Diego County	10,911	0.89
Kailua, HI (cdp) Honolulu County	9,341	25.58
Nanakuli, HI (cdp) Honolulu County	8,684	80.30
Long Beach, CA (city) Los Angeles County	8,022	1.74
Waipahu, HI (cdp) Honolulu County	7,867	23.76
San Jose, CA (city) Santa Clara County	7,252	0.81
Sacramento, CA (city) Sacramento County	6,961	1.71
Waianae, HI (cdp) Honolulu County	6,839	65.10
San Francisco, CA (city) San Francisco County	6,369	0.82
Pearl City, HI (cdp) Honolulu County	5,775	18.64
Kahului, HI (cdp) Maui County	5,547	27.53
Mililani Town, HI (cdp) Honolulu County	5,331	18.63
Seattle, WA (city) King County	5,096	0.90
Wahiawa, HI (cdp) Honolulu County	4,951	30.65
Waimalu, HI (cdp) Honolulu County	4,888	16.64
Hayward, CA (city) Alameda County	4,814	3.44
Chicago, IL (city) Cook County	4,661	0.16
Ewa Beach, HI (cdp) Honolulu County	4,529	30.91
Las Vegas, NV (city) Clark County	4,440	0.93
Salt Lake City, UT (city) Salt Lake County	4,433	2.44
Makaha, HI (cdp) Honolulu County	4,361	56.25
West Valley City, UT (city) Salt Lake County	4,017	3.69
Makakilo City, HI (cdp) Honolulu County	3,947	30.00
Wailuku, HI (cdp) Maui County	3,813	31.01
Anchorage, AK (municipality) Anchorage Borough	3,804	1.46
Portland, OR (city) Multnomah County	3,732	0.71
Phoenix, AZ (city) Maricopa County	3,554	0.27
Carson, CA (city) Los Angeles County	3,541	3.95
Maili, HI (cdp) Honolulu County	3,499	58.88
Halawa, HI (cdp) Honolulu County	3,488	25.11
Waimanalo Beach, HI (cdp) Honolulu County	3,393	79.44
Kailua, HI (cdp) Hawaii County	3,368	34.12
Oakland, CA (city) Alameda County	3,339	0.84
Laie, HI (cdp) Honolulu County	3,172	69.18
Oceanside, CA (city) San Diego County	3,152	1.96
Kihei, HI (cdp) Maui County	3,116	18.60
Tacoma, WA (city) Pierce County	2,980	1.54
Houston, TX (city) Harris County	2,899	0.15
Waimea, HI (cdp) Hawaii County	2,870	40.84
Hauula, HI (cdp) Honolulu County	2,861	78.36
Kapaa, HI (cdp) Kauai County	2,859	30.18
Ahuimanu, HI (cdp) Honolulu County	2,711	31.87
East Palo Alto, CA (city) San Mateo County	2,599	8.81
Waihee-Waiehu, HI (cdp) Maui County	2,493	34.10
Stockton, CA (city) San Joaquin County	2,477	1.02
Anaheim, CA (city) Orange County	2,445	0.75
Vallejo, CA (city) Solano County	2,413	2.07
Philadelphia, PA (city) Philadelphia County	2,379	0.16
Hawaiian Paradise Park, HI (cdp) Hawaii County	2,326	32.99
San Mateo, CA (city) San Mateo County	2,295	2.48
Modesto, CA (city) Stanislaus County	2,281	1.21
Waipio, HI (cdp) Honolulu County	2,211	18.94
Paradise, NV (cdp) Clark County	2,201	1.18
San Antonio, TX (city) Bexar County	2,093	0.18
Waimanalo, HI (cdp) Honolulu County	2,090	57.04
Lahaina, HI (cdp) Maui County	2,042	22.40
Fremont, CA (city) Alameda County	2,039	1.00
Village Park, HI (cdp) Honolulu County	2,015	20.94
Pukalani, HI (cdp) Maui County	1,989	26.95
Kalaoa, HI (cdp) Hawaii County	1,962	28.88
Makawao, HI (cdp) Maui County	1,929	30.49
Chula Vista, CA (city) San Diego County	1,872	1.08
Santa Ana, CA (city) Orange County	1,841	0.54
San Bruno, CA (city) San Mateo County	1,832	4.56
Riverside, CA (city) Riverside County	1,813	0.71
Daly City, CA (city) San Mateo County	1,766	1.70
Fairfield, CA (city) Solano County	1,740	1.81
Hawaiian Beaches, HI (cdp) Hawaii County	1,693	45.65
Henderson, NV (city) Clark County	1,687	0.96
Mesa, AZ (city) Maricopa County	1,679	0.42
Garden Grove, CA (city) Orange County	1,671	1.01
Provo, UT (city) Utah County	1,646	1.57
Fresno, CA (city) Fresno County	1,635	0.38
Lakewood, WA (city) Pierce County	1,627	2.80
Colorado Springs, CO (city) El Paso County	1,619	0.45
Kaunakakai, HI (cdp) Maui County	1,600	58.69
Reno, NV (city) Washoe County	1,600	0.89
Boston, MA (city) Suffolk County	1,576	0.27
Haiku-Pauwela, HI (cdp) Maui County	1,556	23.65
Sunrise Manor, NV (cdp) Clark County	1,532	0.98
South San Francisco, CA (city) San Mateo County	1,514	2.50
Tucson, AZ (city) Pima County	1,509	0.31
Aiea, HI (cdp) Honolulu County	1,500	16.63
Dallas, TX (city) Dallas County	1,483	0.12
Anahola, HI (cdp) Kauai County	1,417	73.34
Waipio Acres, HI (cdp) Honolulu County	1,416	26.73
Federal Way, WA (city) King County	1,408	1.69
Waikoloa Village, HI (cdp) Hawaii County	1,389	28.90
Kualapuu, HI (cdp) Maui County	1,384	71.49
Denver, CO (city) Denver County	1,380	0.25
Vancouver, WA (city) Clark County	1,363	0.95
Moreno Valley, CA (city) Riverside County	1,351	0.95
Jacksonville, FL (special city) Duval County	1,290	0.18
Saint Paul, MN (city) Ramsey County	1,284	0.45
Kahaluu, HI (cdp) Honolulu County	1,281	43.65
Maunawili, HI (cdp) Honolulu County	1,262	25.92
San Leandro, CA (city) Alameda County	1,262	1.59
Union City, CA (city) Alameda County	1,261	1.89
Killeen, TX (city) Bell County	1,260	1.45
Oxnard, CA (city) Ventura County	1,260	0.74
Kahuku, HI (cdp) Honolulu County	1,243	59.28
Concord, CA (city) Contra Costa County	1,236	1.01
Taylorsville, UT (city) Salt Lake County	1,235	2.15
Heeia, HI (cdp) Honolulu County	1,231	24.90
Orem, UT (city) Utah County	1,207	1.43
Compton, CA (city) Los Angeles County	1,184	1.27
North Las Vegas, NV (city) Clark County	1,175	1.02
Holualoa, HI (cdp) Hawaii County	1,166	19.09
Mountain View, HI (cdp) Hawaii County	1,162	41.51
Torrance, CA (city) Los Angeles County	1,153	0.84
Spring Valley, NV (cdp) Clark County	1,148	0.98
Virginia Beach, VA (independent city) Virginia Beach city	1,140	0.27
Napili-Honokowai, HI (cdp) Maui County	1,119	16.48
Huntington Beach, CA (city) Orange County	1,114	0.59
San Bernardino, CA (city) San Bernardino County	1,103	0.59
Lihue, HI (cdp) Kauai County	1,096	19.32
Austin, TX (city) Travis County	1,082	0.16
Kent, WA (city) King County	1,073	1.35
Wailua Homesteads, HI (cdp) Kauai County	1,071	23.45
Vista, CA (city) San Diego County	1,066	1.19
Aurora, CO (city) Arapahoe County	1,065	0.39
El Paso, TX (city) El Paso County	1,064	0.19
Hawthorne, CA (city) Los Angeles County	1,044	1.24
Kekaha, HI (cdp) Kauai County	1,040	32.76
Euless, TX (city) Tarrant County	1,010	2.20
Costa Mesa, CA (city) Orange County	1,009	0.93
Redwood City, CA (city) San Mateo County	992	1.32
Salem, OR (city) Marion County	987	0.72
Albuquerque, NM (city) Bernalillo County	982	0.22
Columbus, OH (city) Franklin County	974	0.14
Minneapolis, MN (city) Hennepin County	953	0.25
Ewa Gentry, HI (cdp) Honolulu County	951	19.25
Lakewood, CA (city) Los Angeles County	949	1.20
Kansas City, MO (city) Jackson County	942	0.21
Honaunau-Napoopoo, HI (cdp) Hawaii County	936	38.77
Santa Clara, CA (city) Santa Clara County	929	0.91
Ontario, CA (city) San Bernardino County	929	0.59
Alameda, CA (city) Alameda County	927	1.28
Ewa Villages, HI (cdp) Honolulu County	925	19.51
West Jordan, UT (city) Salt Lake County	921	1.35
Marina, CA (city) Monterey County	911	3.63
Kearns, UT (cdp) Salt Lake County	908	2.70
Springdale, AR (city) Washington County	904	1.97
Sunnyvale, CA (city) Santa Clara County	900	0.68
Whitmore Village, HI (cdp) Honolulu County	890	21.94

Notes: (cdp) census designated place; Refer to the Explanation of Data in the front of the book for more detailed information.

Hawaii Native/Pacific Islander

Top 150 Places Sorted by Percent

(Based on all places, regardless of population)

Place	Number	%
Nanakuli, HI (cdp) Honolulu County	8,684	80.30
Waimanalo Beach, HI (cdp) Honolulu County	3,393	79.44
Hauula, HI (cdp) Honolulu County	2,861	78.36
Hana, HI (cdp) Maui County	548	77.29
Anahola, HI (cdp) Kauai County	1,417	73.34
Kualapuu, HI (cdp) Maui County	1,384	71.49
Laie, HI (cdp) Honolulu County	3,172	69.18
Maunaloa, HI (cdp) Maui County	152	66.09
Waianae, HI (cdp) Honolulu County	6,839	65.10
Makaha Valley, HI (cdp) Honolulu County	806	62.53
Waikane, HI (cdp) Honolulu County	436	60.06
Kahuku, HI (cdp) Honolulu County	1,243	59.28
Maili, HI (cdp) Honolulu County	3,499	58.88
Kaunakakai, HI (cdp) Maui County	1,600	58.69
Waimanalo, HI (cdp) Honolulu County	2,090	57.04
Makaha, HI (cdp) Honolulu County	4,361	56.25
Punaluu, HI (cdp) Honolulu County	479	54.37
Kaaawa, HI (cdp) Honolulu County	632	47.73
Hawaiian Beaches, HI (cdp) Hawaii County	1,693	45.65
Pakala Village, HI (cdp) Kauai County	210	43.93
Kukuihaele, HI (cdp) Hawaii County	139	43.85
Kahaluu, HI (cdp) Honolulu County	1,281	43.65
Hawi, HI (cdp) Hawaii County	400	42.64
Ainaloa, HI (cdp) Hawaii County	809	42.36
Nanawale Estates, HI (cdp) Hawaii County	452	42.12
Mountain View, HI (cdp) Hawaii County	1,162	41.51
Waimea, HI (cdp) Hawaii County	2,870	40.84
Naalehu, HI (cdp) Hawaii County	373	40.59
Honaunau-Napoopoo, HI (cdp) Hawaii County	936	38.77
Halaula, HI (cdp) Hawaii County	185	37.37
Waimea, HI (cdp) Kauai County	639	35.76
Haleiwa, HI (cdp) Honolulu County	794	35.69
Pahala, HI (cdp) Hawaii County	489	35.49
Hilo, HI (cdp) Hawaii County	14,401	35.33
Kapaau, HI (cdp) Hawaii County	407	35.12
Haliimaile, HI (cdp) Maui County	313	34.97
Kailua, HI (cdp) Hawaii County	3,368	34.12
Waihee-Waiehu, HI (cdp) Maui County	2,493	34.10
Hawaiian Paradise Park, HI (cdp) Hawaii County	2,326	32.99
Eden Roc, HI (cdp) Hawaii County	148	32.82
Kekaha, HI (cdp) Kauai County	1,040	32.76
Fern Acres, HI (cdp) Hawaii County	246	32.54
Kaneohe, HI (cdp) Honolulu County	11,296	32.30
Ahuimanu, HI (cdp) Honolulu County	2,711	31.87
Honalo, HI (cdp) Hawaii County	631	31.76
Volcano, HI (cdp) Hawaii County	707	31.69
Pahoa, HI (cdp) Hawaii County	302	31.39
Orchidlands Estates, HI (cdp) Hawaii County	543	31.37
Wailuku, HI (cdp) Maui County	3,813	31.01
Paauilo, HI (cdp) Hawaii County	177	31.00
Ewa Beach, HI (cdp) Honolulu County	4,529	30.91
Wahiawa, HI (cdp) Honolulu County	4,951	30.65
Makawao, HI (cdp) Maui County	1,929	30.49
Kapaa, HI (cdp) Kauai County	2,859	30.18
Makakilo City, HI (cdp) Honolulu County	3,947	30.00
Kealakekua, HI (cdp) Hawaii County	479	29.12
Waikoloa Village, HI (cdp) Hawaii County	1,389	28.90
Kalaoa, HI (cdp) Hawaii County	1,962	28.88
Paia, HI (cdp) Maui County	719	28.77
Waikapu, HI (cdp) Maui County	310	27.80
Kahului, HI (cdp) Maui County	5,547	27.53
Laupahoehoe, HI (cdp) Hawaii County	130	27.48
Pukalani, HI (cdp) Maui County	1,989	26.95
Fern Forest, HI (cdp) Hawaii County	129	26.88
Kurtistown, HI (cdp) Hawaii County	310	26.79
Waipio Acres, HI (cdp) Honolulu County	1,416	26.73
Hawaiian Ocean View, HI (cdp) Hawaii County	573	26.31
Papaikou, HI (cdp) Hawaii County	369	26.10
Captain Cook, HI (cdp) Hawaii County	836	26.08
Maunawili, HI (cdp) Honolulu County	1,262	25.92
Hawaiian Acres, HI (cdp) Hawaii County	455	25.62
Kailua, HI (cdp) Honolulu County	9,341	25.58
Hanapepe, HI (cdp) Kauai County	548	25.45
Honomu, HI (cdp) Hawaii County	136	25.14
Halawa, HI (cdp) Honolulu County	3,488	25.11

Place	Number	%
Heeia, HI (cdp) Honolulu County	1,231	24.90
Kapalua, HI (cdp) Maui County	116	24.84
Wailua, HI (cdp) Kauai County	507	24.34
Koloa, HI (cdp) Kauai County	467	24.05
Waipahu, HI (cdp) Honolulu County	7,867	23.76
Haiku-Pauwela, HI (cdp) Maui County	1,556	23.65
Wailua Homesteads, HI (cdp) Kauai County	1,071	23.45
Waialua, HI (cdp) Honolulu County	879	23.37
Honokaa, HI (cdp) Hawaii County	506	22.66
Wainaku, HI (cdp) Hawaii County	275	22.41
Lahaina, HI (cdp) Maui County	2,042	22.40
Lawai, HI (cdp) Kauai County	438	22.08
Whitmore Village, HI (cdp) Honolulu County	890	21.94
Eleele, HI (cdp) Kauai County	435	21.32
Hanamaulu, HI (cdp) Kauai County	696	21.27
Pepeekeo, HI (cdp) Hawaii County	356	20.98
Omao, HI (cdp) Kauai County	256	20.97
Village Park, HI (cdp) Honolulu County	2,015	20.94
Mokuleia, HI (cdp) Honolulu County	385	20.94
Lanai City, HI (cdp) Maui County	661	20.89
Keaau, HI (cdp) Hawaii County	411	20.45
Leilani Estates, HI (cdp) Hawaii County	208	19.89
Ewa Villages, HI (cdp) Honolulu County	925	19.51
Lihue, HI (cdp) Kauai County	1,096	19.32
Ewa Gentry, HI (cdp) Honolulu County	951	19.25
Holualoa, HI (cdp) Hawaii County	1,166	19.09
Waipio, HI (cdp) Honolulu County	2,211	18.94
Pearl City, HI (cdp) Honolulu County	5,775	18.64
Mililani Town, HI (cdp) Honolulu County	5,331	18.63
Kihei, HI (cdp) Maui County	3,116	18.60
Pupukea, HI (cdp) Honolulu County	789	18.56
Kalaheo, HI (cdp) Kauai County	707	18.07
Hanalei, HI (cdp) Kauai County	86	17.99
Kahaluu-Keauhou, HI (cdp) Hawaii County	407	16.86
Waimalu, HI (cdp) Honolulu County	4,888	16.64
Aiea, HI (cdp) Honolulu County	1,500	16.63
Napili-Honokowai, HI (cdp) Maui County	1,119	16.48
Honolulu, HI (cdp) Honolulu County	60,586	16.30
Paukaa, HI (cdp) Hawaii County	79	15.96
Kilauea, HI (cdp) Kauai County	323	15.44
Puhi, HI (cdp) Kauai County	170	14.33
Kaumakani, HI (cdp) Kauai County	81	13.34
Puako, HI (cdp) Hawaii County	50	11.66
Appleton, MN (city) Swift County	331	11.53
Kalihiwai, HI (cdp) Kauai County	79	11.02
Kawela Bay, HI (cdp) Honolulu County	37	9.02
East Palo Alto, CA (city) San Mateo County	2,599	8.81
Leon, OK (town) Love County	8	8.33
Poipu, HI (cdp) Kauai County	85	7.91
Princeville, HI (cdp) Kauai County	129	7.60
Tampa, KS (city) Marion County	10	6.94
Wailea-Makena, HI (cdp) Maui County	383	6.75
Kimmswick, MO (city) Jefferson County	6	6.38
Kirkwood, CA (cdp) Alpine County	6	6.25
Elfin Cove, AK (cdp) Skagway-Hoonah-Angoon Census Area	2	6.25
Doran, MN (city) Wilkin County	3	5.08
Watonga, OK (city) Blaine County	224	4.81
Mulhall, OK (town) Logan County	11	4.60
San Bruno, CA (city) San Mateo County	1,832	4.56
Kaanapali, HI (cdp) Maui County	58	4.22
Mifflintown, PA (borough) Juniata County	35	4.07
Maalaea, HI (cdp) Maui County	18	3.96
Carson, CA (city) Los Angeles County	3,541	3.95
Fort Greely, AK (cdp) Southeast Fairbanks Census Area	18	3.90
Shoshone, CA (cdp) Inyo County	2	3.85
Belmont, OH (village) Belmont County	20	3.76
Ranchette Estates, TX (cdp) Willacy County	5	3.76
Nisqually Indian Community, WA (cdp) Thurston County	22	3.74
Petersville, AK (cdp) Matanuska-Susitna Borough	1	3.70
West Valley City, UT (city) Salt Lake County	4,017	3.69
Rex, NC (cdp) Robeson County	2	3.64
Marina, CA (city) Monterey County	911	3.63
Avon, UT (cdp) Cache County	11	3.59
Wheeler AFB, HI (cdp) Honolulu County	101	3.57
Roosevelt, OK (town) Kiowa County	10	3.57

Notes: (cdp) census designated place; Refer to the Explanation of Data in the front of the book for more detailed information.

Hawaii Native/Pacific Islander

Top 150 Places Sorted by Percent

(Based on places with populations of 10,000 or more)

Place	Number	%
Nanakuli, HI (cdp) Honolulu County	8,684	80.30
Waianae, HI (cdp) Honolulu County	6,839	65.10
Hilo, HI (cdp) Hawaii County	14,401	35.33
Kaneohe, HI (cdp) Honolulu County	11,296	32.30
Wailuku, HI (cdp) Maui County	3,813	31.01
Ewa Beach, HI (cdp) Honolulu County	4,529	30.91
Wahiawa, HI (cdp) Honolulu County	4,951	30.65
Makakilo City, HI (cdp) Honolulu County	3,947	30.00
Kahului, HI (cdp) Maui County	5,547	27.53
Kailua, HI (cdp) Honolulu County	9,341	25.58
Halawa, HI (cdp) Honolulu County	3,488	25.11
Waipahu, HI (cdp) Honolulu County	7,867	23.76
Waipio, HI (cdp) Honolulu County	2,211	18.94
Pearl City, HI (cdp) Honolulu County	5,775	18.64
Mililani Town, HI (cdp) Honolulu County	5,331	18.63
Kihei, HI (cdp) Maui County	3,116	18.60
Waimalu, HI (cdp) Honolulu County	4,888	16.64
Honolulu, HI (cdp) Honolulu County	60,586	16.30
East Palo Alto, CA (city) San Mateo County	2,599	8.81
San Bruno, CA (city) San Mateo County	1,832	4.56
Carson, CA (city) Los Angeles County	3,541	3.95
West Valley City, UT (city) Salt Lake County	4,017	3.69
Marina, CA (city) Monterey County	911	3.63
SeaTac, WA (city) King County	882	3.46
Hayward, CA (city) Alameda County	4,814	3.44
White Center, WA (cdp) King County	668	3.18
Schofield Barracks, HI (cdp) Honolulu County	443	3.07
Spanaway, WA (cdp) Pierce County	658	3.05
Fort Lewis, WA (cdp) Pierce County	536	2.81
Lakewood, WA (city) Pierce County	1,627	2.80
Kaneohe Station, HI (cdp) Honolulu County	324	2.74
Kearns, UT (cdp) Salt Lake County	908	2.70
Riverton-Boulevard Park, WA (cdp) King County	299	2.67
Tukwila, WA (city) King County	457	2.66
Parkland, WA (cdp) Pierce County	620	2.58
Twentynine Palms, CA (city) San Bernardino County	376	2.55
South San Francisco, CA (city) San Mateo County	1,514	2.50
San Mateo, CA (city) San Mateo County	2,295	2.48
Salt Lake City, UT (city) Salt Lake County	4,433	2.44
Seaside, CA (city) Monterey County	751	2.37
Suisun City, CA (city) Solano County	618	2.37
Ashland, CA (cdp) Alameda County	476	2.29
Euless, TX (city) Tarrant County	1,010	2.20
Taylorsville, UT (city) Salt Lake County	1,235	2.15
Elk Plain, WA (cdp) Pierce County	336	2.14
Oquirrh, UT (cdp) Salt Lake County	221	2.13
Vallejo, CA (city) Solano County	2,413	2.07
Cherryland, CA (cdp) Alameda County	287	2.07
Newark, CA (city) Alameda County	857	2.02
La Presa, CA (cdp) San Diego County	647	1.98
Springdale, AR (city) Washington County	904	1.97
Oceanside, CA (city) San Diego County	3,152	1.96
West Carson, CA (cdp) Los Angeles County	415	1.96
Silverdale, WA (cdp) Kitsap County	304	1.92
Union City, CA (city) Alameda County	1,261	1.89
Magna, UT (cdp) Salt Lake County	420	1.84
Des Moines, WA (city) King County	533	1.82
Fairfield, CA (city) Solano County	1,740	1.81
Fort Campbell North, KY (cdp) Christian County	251	1.75
Long Beach, CA (city) Los Angeles County	8,022	1.74
Burien, WA (city) King County	551	1.73
Lennox, CA (cdp) Los Angeles County	394	1.72
Sacramento, CA (city) Sacramento County	6,961	1.71
Florin, CA (cdp) Sacramento County	473	1.71
Millbrae, CA (city) San Mateo County	354	1.71
Daly City, CA (city) San Mateo County	1,766	1.70
Federal Way, WA (city) King County	1,408	1.69
Bremerton, WA (city) Kitsap County	630	1.69
Menlo Park, CA (city) San Mateo County	517	1.68
South Salt Lake, UT (city) Salt Lake County	355	1.61
North Fair Oaks, CA (cdp) San Mateo County	248	1.61
San Leandro, CA (city) Alameda County	1,262	1.59
Provo, UT (city) Utah County	1,646	1.57
Lemon Grove, CA (city) San Diego County	390	1.57
Lacey, WA (city) Thurston County	488	1.56
Pittsburg, CA (city) Contra Costa County	880	1.55
Tacoma, WA (city) Pierce County	2,980	1.54
Pacifica, CA (city) San Mateo County	593	1.54
Parkway-South Sacramento, CA (cdp) Sacramento County	561	1.54
Oak Harbor, WA (city) Island County	300	1.52
Bay Point, CA (cdp) Contra Costa County	316	1.47
Anchorage, AK (municipality) Anchorage Borough	3,804	1.46
Fort Bragg, NC (cdp) Cumberland County	426	1.46
Killeen, TX (city) Bell County	1,260	1.45
Orem, UT (city) Utah County	1,207	1.43
Fort Hood, TX (cdp) Coryell County	480	1.42
Barstow, CA (city) San Bernardino County	297	1.41
Stanton, CA (city) Orange County	522	1.40
Gardena, CA (city) Los Angeles County	791	1.37
Imperial Beach, CA (city) San Diego County	370	1.37
Fort Carson, CO (cdp) El Paso County	144	1.36
Kent, WA (city) King County	1,073	1.35
West Jordan, UT (city) Salt Lake County	921	1.35
East Hill-Meridian, WA (cdp) King County	396	1.35
Spring Valley, CA (cdp) San Diego County	361	1.35
San Lorenzo, CA (cdp) Alameda County	292	1.33
Redwood City, CA (city) San Mateo County	992	1.32
Elk Grove, CA (cdp) Sacramento County	786	1.31
West Sacramento, CA (city) Yolo County	415	1.31
Lathrop, CA (city) San Joaquin County	135	1.29
Alameda, CA (city) Alameda County	927	1.28
Compton, CA (city) Los Angeles County	1,184	1.27
National City, CA (city) San Diego County	691	1.27
Hawthorne, CA (city) Los Angeles County	1,044	1.24
Lawndale, CA (city) Los Angeles County	393	1.24
Four Corners, OR (cdp) Marion County	171	1.23
Rancho Cordova, CA (cdp) Sacramento County	669	1.22
Modesto, CA (city) Stanislaus County	2,281	1.21
Milpitas, CA (city) Santa Clara County	759	1.21
Lakewood, CA (city) Los Angeles County	949	1.20
University Place, WA (city) Pierce County	358	1.20
Vista, CA (city) San Diego County	1,066	1.19
Neosho, MO (city) Newton County	125	1.19
Paradise, NV (cdp) Clark County	2,201	1.18
La Grande, OR (city) Union County	145	1.18
Fort Drum, NY (cdp) Jefferson County	143	1.18
Tracy, CA (city) San Joaquin County	664	1.17
Security-Widefield, CO (cdp) El Paso County	348	1.17
Bryn Mawr-Skyway, WA (cdp) King County	164	1.17
Susanville, CA (city) Lassen County	158	1.17
Mountlake Terrace, WA (city) Snohomish County	236	1.16
Fort Polk South, LA (cdp) Vernon Parish	126	1.15
San Pablo, CA (city) Contra Costa County	345	1.14
Hawaiian Gardens, CA (city) Los Angeles County	166	1.12
Lomita, CA (city) Los Angeles County	221	1.10
Hayesville, OR (cdp) Marion County	201	1.10
Bellflower, CA (city) Los Angeles County	792	1.09
Saint George, UT (city) Washington County	542	1.09
Belmont, CA (city) San Mateo County	275	1.09
Chula Vista, CA (city) San Diego County	1,872	1.08
Enterprise, NV (cdp) Clark County	159	1.08
North Highlands, CA (cdp) Sacramento County	475	1.07
Paramount, CA (city) Los Angeles County	585	1.06
Foster City, CA (city) San Mateo County	306	1.06
Fountain, CO (city) El Paso County	161	1.06
Millcreek, UT (cdp) Salt Lake County	319	1.05
Castro Valley, CA (cdp) Alameda County	589	1.03
Rohnert Park, CA (city) Sonoma County	433	1.03
Laguna, CA (cdp) Sacramento County	355	1.03
Fort Leonard Wood, MO (cdp) Pulaski County	141	1.03
Stockton, CA (city) San Joaquin County	2,477	1.02
North Las Vegas, NV (city) Clark County	1,175	1.02
Auburn, WA (city) King County	413	1.02
Fairbanks, AK (city) Fairbanks North Star Borough	307	1.02
Orchards, WA (cdp) Clark County	182	1.02
Artesia, CA (city) Los Angeles County	167	1.02
Garden Grove, CA (city) Orange County	1,671	1.01
Concord, CA (city) Contra Costa County	1,236	1.01
Fremont, CA (city) Alameda County	2,039	1.00
Vacaville, CA (city) Solano County	884	1.00

Notes: (cdp) census designated place; Refer to the Explanation of Data in the front of the book for more detailed information.

Hawaii Native/Pacific Islander: Melanesian

Top 150 Places Sorted by Number

(Based on all places, regardless of population)

Place	Number	%
Sacramento, CA (city) Sacramento County	1,254	0.31
Hayward, CA (city) Alameda County	1,149	0.82
Modesto, CA (city) Stanislaus County	454	0.24
San Bruno, CA (city) San Mateo County	353	0.88
New York, NY (city) New York City	339	0.00
Los Angeles, CA (city) Los Angeles County	327	0.01
San Jose, CA (city) Santa Clara County	302	0.03
San Mateo, CA (city) San Mateo County	281	0.30
San Francisco, CA (city) San Francisco County	218	0.03
South San Francisco, CA (city) San Mateo County	210	0.35
East Palo Alto, CA (city) San Mateo County	203	0.69
Union City, CA (city) Alameda County	196	0.29
Portland, OR (city) Multnomah County	177	0.03
Seattle, WA (city) King County	155	0.03
Stockton, CA (city) San Joaquin County	152	0.06
Rancho Cordova, CA (cdp) Sacramento County	151	0.27
Vallejo, CA (city) Solano County	147	0.13
Newark, CA (city) Alameda County	144	0.34
Arden-Arcade, CA (cdp) Sacramento County	143	0.15
Seaside, CA (city) Monterey County	133	0.42
Honolulu, HI (cdp) Honolulu County	130	0.03
Elk Grove, CA (cdp) Sacramento County	129	0.22
Fremont, CA (city) Alameda County	121	0.06
Parkway-South Sacramento, CA (cdp) Sacramento County	115	0.32
Daly City, CA (city) San Mateo County	115	0.11
Florin, CA (cdp) Sacramento County	114	0.41
Oakland, CA (city) Alameda County	111	0.03
West Sacramento, CA (city) Yolo County	107	0.34
Redwood City, CA (city) San Mateo County	87	0.12
North Highlands, CA (cdp) Sacramento County	83	0.19
Pittsburg, CA (city) Contra Costa County	76	0.13
Davis, CA (city) Yolo County	75	0.12
Kent, WA (city) King County	73	0.09
Fairfield, CA (city) Solano County	70	0.07
San Leandro, CA (city) Alameda County	66	0.08
Lynnwood, WA (city) Snohomish County	64	0.19
Richmond, CA (city) Contra Costa County	64	0.06
Woodland, CA (city) Yolo County	63	0.13
Castro Valley, CA (cdp) Alameda County	61	0.11
Antioch, CA (city) Contra Costa County	59	0.07
East Hill-Meridian, WA (cdp) King County	56	0.19
Shoreline, WA (city) King County	55	0.10
Inglewood, CA (city) Los Angeles County	55	0.05
San Pablo, CA (city) Contra Costa County	54	0.18
Hawthorne, CA (city) Los Angeles County	49	0.06
Mountlake Terrace, WA (city) Snohomish County	47	0.23
Vancouver, WA (city) Clark County	47	0.03
Laie, HI (cdp) Honolulu County	46	1.00
Millbrae, CA (city) San Mateo County	46	0.22
Marina, CA (city) Monterey County	46	0.18
Ashland, CA (cdp) Alameda County	45	0.22
Santa Clara, CA (city) Santa Clara County	45	0.04
Hilo, HI (cdp) Hawaii County	44	0.11
Tracy, CA (city) San Joaquin County	44	0.08
Turlock, CA (city) Stanislaus County	43	0.08
San Diego, CA (city) San Diego County	43	0.00
Edmonds, WA (city) Snohomish County	42	0.11
Laguna, CA (cdp) Sacramento County	41	0.12
Concord, CA (city) Contra Costa County	41	0.03
Menlo Park, CA (city) San Mateo County	40	0.13
Foster City, CA (city) San Mateo County	38	0.13
Everett, WA (city) Snohomish County	38	0.04
Houston, TX (city) Harris County	37	0.00
Cherryland, CA (cdp) Alameda County	35	0.25
Culver City, CA (city) Los Angeles County	33	0.09
Folsom, CA (city) Sacramento County	33	0.06
Bellflower, CA (city) Los Angeles County	33	0.05
Sunnyvale, CA (city) Santa Clara County	33	0.03
Paine Field-Lake Stickney, WA (cdp) Snohomish County	32	0.13
Kaneohe, HI (cdp) Honolulu County	32	0.09
Renton, WA (city) King County	32	0.06
San Rafael, CA (city) Marin County	32	0.06
Rohnert Park, CA (city) Sonoma County	30	0.07
Federal Way, WA (city) King County	30	0.04
Mountain View, CA (city) Santa Clara County	30	0.04

Place	Number	%
Anaheim, CA (city) Orange County	30	0.01
Pacifica, CA (city) San Mateo County	29	0.08
Beaverton, OR (city) Washington County	29	0.04
Riverside, CA (city) Riverside County	29	0.01
Hercules, CA (city) Contra Costa County	28	0.14
Bay Point, CA (cdp) Contra Costa County	28	0.13
Aloha, OR (cdp) Washington County	28	0.07
Milpitas, CA (city) Santa Clara County	27	0.04
Fresno, CA (city) Fresno County	27	0.01
Tacoma, WA (city) Pierce County	27	0.01
Rosemont, CA (cdp) Sacramento County	26	0.11
Del Aire, CA (cdp) Los Angeles County	25	0.28
West Valley City, UT (city) Salt Lake County	25	0.02
Paradise, NV (cdp) Clark County	25	0.01
Alderwood Manor, WA (cdp) Snohomish County	24	0.16
Tukwila, WA (city) King County	24	0.14
Carmichael, CA (cdp) Sacramento County	24	0.05
Costa Mesa, CA (city) Orange County	24	0.02
Burlingame, CA (city) San Mateo County	23	0.08
West Covina, CA (city) Los Angeles County	23	0.02
Chicago, IL (city) Cook County	23	0.00
Laguna West-Lakeside, CA (cdp) Sacramento County	22	0.26
SeaTac, WA (city) King County	22	0.09
Wichita, KS (city) Sedgwick County	22	0.01
El Cerrito, CA (city) Contra Costa County	21	0.09
North Creek, WA (cdp) Snohomish County	21	0.08
Santa Monica, CA (city) Los Angeles County	21	0.02
Phoenix, AZ (city) Maricopa County	21	0.00
Colusa, CA (city) Colusa County	20	0.37
Carson, CA (city) Los Angeles County	20	0.02
Corona, CA (city) Riverside County	20	0.02
Downey, CA (city) Los Angeles County	20	0.02
Santa Clarita, CA (city) Los Angeles County	20	0.01
North Fair Oaks, CA (cdp) San Mateo County	19	0.12
San Carlos, CA (city) San Mateo County	19	0.07
Buena Park, CA (city) Orange County	19	0.02
Citrus Heights, CA (city) Sacramento County	19	0.02
Santa Rosa, CA (city) Sonoma County	19	0.01
Galt, CA (city) Sacramento County	18	0.09
Ceres, CA (city) Stanislaus County	18	0.05
Manteca, CA (city) San Joaquin County	18	0.04
Bellevue, WA (city) King County	18	0.02
Henderson, NV (city) Clark County	18	0.01
Cascade-Fairwood, WA (cdp) King County	17	0.05
Lodi, CA (city) San Joaquin County	17	0.03
Hillsboro, OR (city) Washington County	17	0.02
Reno, NV (city) Washoe County	17	0.01
Dallas, TX (city) Dallas County	17	0.00
San Ramon, CA (city) Contra Costa County	16	0.04
Rialto, CA (city) San Bernardino County	16	0.02
Eugene, OR (city) Lane County	16	0.01
Salt Lake City, UT (city) Salt Lake County	16	0.01
Kapaa, HI (cdp) Kauai County	15	0.16
Grants Pass, OR (city) Josephine County	15	0.07
Bothell, WA (city) King County	15	0.05
Pearl City, HI (cdp) Honolulu County	15	0.05
San Bernardino, CA (city) San Bernardino County	15	0.01
Hauula, HI (cdp) Honolulu County	14	0.38
American Canyon, CA (city) Napa County	14	0.14
Gardena, CA (city) Los Angeles County	14	0.02
Orem, UT (city) Utah County	14	0.02
Nashville-Davidson, TN (special city) Davidson County	14	0.00
Ferndale, WA (city) Whatcom County	13	0.15
Scotts Valley, CA (city) Santa Cruz County	13	0.11
Belmont, CA (city) San Mateo County	13	0.05
Suisun City, CA (city) Solano County	13	0.05
Novato, CA (city) Marin County	13	0.03
Long Beach, CA (city) Los Angeles County	13	0.00
Kahuku, HI (cdp) Honolulu County	12	0.57
Blaine, WA (city) Whatcom County	12	0.32
Atherton, CA (town) San Mateo County	12	0.17
Vineyard, CA (cdp) Sacramento County	12	0.12
Picnic Point-North Lynnwood, WA (cdp) Snohomish County	12	0.05
Monterey, CA (city) Monterey County	12	0.04
Kailua, HI (cdp) Honolulu County	12	0.03

Notes: (cdp) census designated place; Refer to the Explanation of Data in the front of the book for more detailed information.

Hawaii Native/Pacific Islander: Melanesian

Top 150 Places Sorted by Percent

(Based on all places, regardless of population)

Place	Number	%
Lake Bosworth, WA (cdp) Snohomish County	3	1.47
Charlestown, MN (township) Redwood County	3	1.38
Laie, HI (cdp) Honolulu County	46	1.00
San Bruno, CA (city) San Mateo County	353	0.88
Waikane, HI (cdp) Honolulu County	6	0.83
Hayward, CA (city) Alameda County	1,149	0.82
Strasburg, MO (city) Cass County	1	0.74
East Palo Alto, CA (city) San Mateo County	203	0.69
Lore City, OH (village) Guernsey County	2	0.66
Kahuku, HI (cdp) Honolulu County	12	0.57
Kawela Bay, HI (cdp) Honolulu County	2	0.49
East Gillespie, IL (village) Macoupin County	1	0.43
Seaside, CA (city) Monterey County	133	0.42
Florin, CA (cdp) Sacramento County	114	0.41
Tetonia, ID (city) Teton County	1	0.40
Hauula, HI (cdp) Honolulu County	14	0.38
Colusa, CA (city) Colusa County	20	0.37
South San Francisco, CA (city) San Mateo County	210	0.35
Newark, CA (city) Alameda County	144	0.34
West Sacramento, CA (city) Yolo County	107	0.34
Parkway-South Sacramento, CA (cdp) Sacramento County	115	0.32
Blaine, WA (city) Whatcom County	12	0.32
Trinidad, CA (city) Humboldt County	1	0.32
Sacramento, CA (city) Sacramento County	1,254	0.31
San Mateo, CA (city) San Mateo County	281	0.30
Penns Creek, PA (cdp) Snyder County	2	0.30
Evaro, MT (cdp) Missoula County	1	0.30
Union City, CA (city) Alameda County	196	0.29
Del Aire, CA (cdp) Los Angeles County	25	0.28
Rancho Cordova, CA (cdp) Sacramento County	151	0.27
Laguna West-Lakeside, CA (cdp) Sacramento County	22	0.26
Cherryland, CA (cdp) Alameda County	35	0.25
Hancock, MI (township) Houghton County	1	0.25
Modesto, CA (city) Stanislaus County	454	0.24
Mountlake Terrace, WA (city) Snohomish County	47	0.23
Kaaawa, HI (cdp) Honolulu County	3	0.23
San Geronimo, CA (cdp) Marin County	1	0.23
Elk Grove, CA (cdp) Sacramento County	129	0.22
Millbrae, CA (city) San Mateo County	46	0.22
Ashland, CA (cdp) Alameda County	45	0.22
French Camp, CA (cdp) San Joaquin County	9	0.22
Eden Roc, HI (cdp) Hawaii County	1	0.22
Mountain View, HI (cdp) Hawaii County	6	0.21
Wood Village, OR (city) Multnomah County	6	0.21
Paukaa, HI (cdp) Hawaii County	1	0.20
Torning, MN (township) Swift County	1	0.20
North Highlands, CA (cdp) Sacramento County	83	0.19
Lynnwood, WA (city) Snohomish County	64	0.19
East Hill-Meridian, WA (cdp) King County	56	0.19
Brisbane, CA (city) San Mateo County	7	0.19
San Pablo, CA (city) Contra Costa County	54	0.18
Marina, CA (city) Monterey County	46	0.18
East Richmond Heights, CA (cdp) Contra Costa County	6	0.18
Logan, NM (village) Quay County	2	0.18
Atherton, CA (town) San Mateo County	12	0.17
Keyes, CA (cdp) Stanislaus County	8	0.17
Hawaiian Acres, HI (cdp) Hawaii County	3	0.17
Alderwood Manor, WA (cdp) Snohomish County	24	0.16
Kapaa, HI (cdp) Kauai County	15	0.16
Pupukea, HI (cdp) Honolulu County	7	0.16
Arden-Arcade, CA (cdp) Sacramento County	143	0.15
Ferndale, WA (city) Whatcom County	13	0.15
Hercules, CA (city) Contra Costa County	28	0.14
Tukwila, WA (city) King County	24	0.14
American Canyon, CA (city) Napa County	14	0.14
Rollingwood, CA (cdp) Contra Costa County	4	0.14
Vallejo, CA (city) Solano County	147	0.13
Pittsburg, CA (city) Contra Costa County	76	0.13
Woodland, CA (city) Yolo County	63	0.13
Menlo Park, CA (city) San Mateo County	40	0.13
Foster City, CA (city) San Mateo County	38	0.13
Paine Field-Lake Stickney, WA (cdp) Snohomish County	32	0.13
Bay Point, CA (cdp) Contra Costa County	28	0.13
Falcon Heights, MN (city) Ramsey County	7	0.13
Empire, CA (cdp) Stanislaus County	5	0.13
Hughson, CA (city) Stanislaus County	5	0.13
Salina, UT (city) Sevier County	3	0.13
Redwood City, CA (city) San Mateo County	87	0.12
Davis, CA (city) Yolo County	75	0.12
Laguna, CA (cdp) Sacramento County	41	0.12
North Fair Oaks, CA (cdp) San Mateo County	19	0.12
Vineyard, CA (cdp) Sacramento County	12	0.12
North Amherst, MA (cdp) Hampshire County	7	0.12
White City, UT (cdp) Salt Lake County	7	0.12
Heeia, HI (cdp) Honolulu County	6	0.12
Okanogan, WA (city) Okanogan County	3	0.12
Paia, HI (cdp) Maui County	3	0.12
Carbon Cliff, IL (village) Rock Island County	2	0.12
Daly City, CA (city) San Mateo County	115	0.11
Castro Valley, CA (cdp) Alameda County	61	0.11
Hilo, HI (cdp) Hawaii County	44	0.11
Edmonds, WA (city) Snohomish County	42	0.11
Rosemont, CA (cdp) Sacramento County	26	0.11
Scotts Valley, CA (city) Santa Cruz County	13	0.11
Fairview, CA (cdp) Alameda County	10	0.11
Waihee-Waiehu, HI (cdp) Maui County	8	0.11
Strawberry, CA (cdp) Marin County	6	0.11
Carlisle, MA (town) Middlesex County	5	0.11
Marietta-Alderwood, WA (cdp) Whatcom County	4	0.11
Ridgemark, CA (cdp) San Benito County	3	0.11
Kentland, IN (town) Newton County	2	0.11
Punaluu, HI (cdp) Honolulu County	1	0.11
Shoreline, WA (city) King County	55	0.10
North Bend, OR (city) Coos County	10	0.10
Willows, CA (city) Glenn County	6	0.10
Bayview-Montalvin, CA (cdp) Contra Costa County	5	0.10
Birch Bay, WA (cdp) Whatcom County	5	0.10
Mountain Village, CO (town) San Miguel County	1	0.10
Kent, WA (city) King County	73	0.09
Culver City, CA (city) Los Angeles County	33	0.09
Kaneohe, HI (cdp) Honolulu County	32	0.09
SeaTac, WA (city) King County	22	0.09
El Cerrito, CA (city) Contra Costa County	21	0.09
Galt, CA (city) Sacramento County	18	0.09
Gig Harbor, WA (city) Pierce County	6	0.09
Whitemarsh Island, GA (cdp) Chatham County	5	0.09
Hanamaulu, HI (cdp) Kauai County	3	0.09
Lockeford, CA (cdp) San Joaquin County	3	0.09
Suquamish, WA (cdp) Kitsap County	3	0.09
Center, PA (township) Snyder County	2	0.09
San Leandro, CA (city) Alameda County	66	0.08
Tracy, CA (city) San Joaquin County	44	0.08
Turlock, CA (city) Stanislaus County	43	0.08
Pacifica, CA (city) San Mateo County	29	0.08
Burlingame, CA (city) San Mateo County	23	0.08
North Creek, WA (cdp) Snohomish County	21	0.08
Makaha, HI (cdp) Honolulu County	6	0.08
Maunawili, HI (cdp) Honolulu County	4	0.08
Litchfield Park, AZ (city) Maricopa County	3	0.08
Wrightwood, CA (cdp) San Bernardino County	3	0.08
Osceola, WI (village) Polk County	2	0.08
Dassel, MN (city) Meeker County	1	0.08
Stateline, NV (cdp) Douglas County	1	0.08
Fairfield, CA (city) Solano County	70	0.07
Antioch, CA (city) Contra Costa County	59	0.07
Rohnert Park, CA (city) Sonoma County	30	0.07
Aloha, OR (cdp) Washington County	28	0.07
San Carlos, CA (city) San Mateo County	19	0.07
Grants Pass, OR (city) Josephine County	15	0.07
Kihei, HI (cdp) Maui County	11	0.07
Martha Lake, WA (cdp) Snohomish County	9	0.07
Mill Valley, CA (city) Marin County	9	0.07
Lathrop, CA (city) San Joaquin County	7	0.07
Ahuimanu, HI (cdp) Honolulu County	6	0.07
Gonzales, CA (city) Monterey County	5	0.07
Minnehaha, WA (cdp) Clark County	5	0.07
Pacific, WA (city) King County	4	0.07
Ely, NV (city) White Pine County	3	0.07
Happy Valley, OR (city) Clackamas County	3	0.07
Kaunakakai, HI (cdp) Maui County	2	0.07

Notes: (cdp) census designated place; Refer to the Explanation of Data in the front of the book for more detailed information.

Hawaii Native/Pacific Islander: Melanesian

Top 150 Places Sorted by Percent

(Based on places with populations of 10,000 or more)

Place	Number	%
San Bruno, CA (city) San Mateo County	353	0.88
Hayward, CA (city) Alameda County	1,149	0.82
East Palo Alto, CA (city) San Mateo County	203	0.69
Seaside, CA (city) Monterey County	133	0.42
Florin, CA (cdp) Sacramento County	114	0.41
South San Francisco, CA (city) San Mateo County	210	0.35
Newark, CA (city) Alameda County	144	0.34
West Sacramento, CA (city) Yolo County	107	0.34
Parkway-South Sacramento, CA (cdp) Sacramento County	115	0.32
Sacramento, CA (city) Sacramento County	1,254	0.31
San Mateo, CA (city) San Mateo County	281	0.30
Union City, CA (city) Alameda County	196	0.29
Rancho Cordova, CA (cdp) Sacramento County	151	0.27
Cherryland, CA (cdp) Alameda County	35	0.25
Modesto, CA (city) Stanislaus County	454	0.24
Mountlake Terrace, WA (city) Snohomish County	47	0.23
Elk Grove, CA (cdp) Sacramento County	129	0.22
Millbrae, CA (city) San Mateo County	46	0.22
Ashland, CA (cdp) Alameda County	45	0.22
North Highlands, CA (cdp) Sacramento County	83	0.19
Lynnwood, WA (city) Snohomish County	64	0.19
East Hill-Meridian, WA (cdp) King County	56	0.19
San Pablo, CA (city) Contra Costa County	54	0.18
Marina, CA (city) Monterey County	46	0.18
Alderwood Manor, WA (cdp) Snohomish County	24	0.16
Arden-Arcade, CA (cdp) Sacramento County	143	0.15
Hercules, CA (city) Contra Costa County	28	0.14
Tukwila, WA (city) King County	24	0.14
Vallejo, CA (city) Solano County	147	0.13
Pittsburg, CA (city) Contra Costa County	76	0.13
Woodland, CA (city) Yolo County	63	0.13
Menlo Park, CA (city) San Mateo County	40	0.13
Foster City, CA (city) San Mateo County	38	0.13
Paine Field-Lake Stickney, WA (cdp) Snohomish County	32	0.13
Bay Point, CA (cdp) Contra Costa County	28	0.13
Redwood City, CA (city) San Mateo County	87	0.12
Davis, CA (city) Yolo County	75	0.12
Laguna, CA (cdp) Sacramento County	41	0.12
North Fair Oaks, CA (cdp) San Mateo County	19	0.12
Vineyard, CA (cdp) Sacramento County	12	0.12
Daly City, CA (city) San Mateo County	115	0.11
Castro Valley, CA (cdp) Alameda County	61	0.11
Hilo, HI (cdp) Hawaii County	44	0.11
Edmonds, WA (city) Snohomish County	42	0.11
Rosemont, CA (cdp) Sacramento County	26	0.11
Scotts Valley, CA (city) Santa Cruz County	13	0.11
Shoreline, WA (city) King County	55	0.10
Kent, WA (city) King County	73	0.09
Culver City, CA (city) Los Angeles County	33	0.09
Kaneohe, HI (cdp) Honolulu County	32	0.09
SeaTac, WA (city) King County	22	0.09
El Cerrito, CA (city) Contra Costa County	21	0.09
Galt, CA (city) Sacramento County	18	0.09
San Leandro, CA (city) Alameda County	66	0.08
Tracy, CA (city) San Joaquin County	44	0.08
Turlock, CA (city) Stanislaus County	43	0.08
Pacifica, CA (city) San Mateo County	29	0.08
Burlingame, CA (city) San Mateo County	23	0.08
North Creek, WA (cdp) Snohomish County	21	0.08
Fairfield, CA (city) Solano County	70	0.07
Antioch, CA (city) Contra Costa County	59	0.07
Rohnert Park, CA (city) Sonoma County	30	0.07
Aloha, OR (cdp) Washington County	28	0.07
San Carlos, CA (city) San Mateo County	19	0.07
Grants Pass, OR (city) Josephine County	15	0.07
Kihei, HI (cdp) Maui County	11	0.07
Martha Lake, WA (cdp) Snohomish County	9	0.07
Mill Valley, CA (city) Marin County	9	0.07
Lathrop, CA (city) San Joaquin County	7	0.07
Stockton, CA (city) San Joaquin County	152	0.06
Fremont, CA (city) Alameda County	121	0.06
Richmond, CA (city) Contra Costa County	64	0.06
Hawthorne, CA (city) Los Angeles County	49	0.06
Folsom, CA (city) Sacramento County	33	0.06
Renton, WA (city) King County	32	0.06
San Rafael, CA (city) Marin County	32	0.06
Hannibal, MO (city) Marion County	11	0.06
Mukilteo, WA (city) Snohomish County	11	0.06
Bryn Mawr-Skyway, WA (cdp) King County	8	0.06
Eloy, AZ (city) Pinal County	6	0.06
La Riviera, CA (cdp) Sacramento County	6	0.06
Lea Hill, WA (cdp) King County	6	0.06
Inglewood, CA (city) Los Angeles County	55	0.05
Bellflower, CA (city) Los Angeles County	33	0.05
Carmichael, CA (cdp) Sacramento County	24	0.05
Ceres, CA (city) Stanislaus County	18	0.05
Cascade-Fairwood, WA (cdp) King County	17	0.05
Bothell, WA (city) King County	15	0.05
Pearl City, HI (cdp) Honolulu County	15	0.05
Belmont, CA (city) San Mateo County	13	0.05
Suisun City, CA (city) Solano County	13	0.05
Picnic Point-North Lynnwood, WA (cdp) Snohomish County	12	0.05
Brentwood, CA (city) Contra Costa County	11	0.05
Bostonia, CA (cdp) San Diego County	8	0.05
Coos Bay, OR (city) Coos County	8	0.05
Lakeland North, WA (cdp) King County	8	0.05
Cannon, MI (township) Kent County	6	0.05
Hobe Sound, FL (cdp) Martin County	6	0.05
Oak Grove, OR (cdp) Clackamas County	6	0.05
Nanakuli, HI (cdp) Honolulu County	5	0.05
Oquirrh, UT (cdp) Salt Lake County	5	0.05
Santa Clara, CA (city) Santa Clara County	45	0.04
Everett, WA (city) Snohomish County	38	0.04
Federal Way, WA (city) King County	30	0.04
Mountain View, CA (city) Santa Clara County	30	0.04
Beaverton, OR (city) Washington County	29	0.04
Milpitas, CA (city) Santa Clara County	27	0.04
Manteca, CA (city) San Joaquin County	18	0.04
San Ramon, CA (city) Contra Costa County	16	0.04
Monterey, CA (city) Monterey County	12	0.04
Fair Oaks, CA (cdp) Sacramento County	11	0.04
Orangevale, CA (cdp) Sacramento County	10	0.04
Milwaukie, OR (city) Clackamas County	9	0.04
San Lorenzo, CA (cdp) Alameda County	9	0.04
Valinda, CA (cdp) Los Angeles County	9	0.04
Windsor, CA (town) Sonoma County	9	0.04
Pinole, CA (city) Contra Costa County	7	0.04
Rexburg, ID (city) Madison County	7	0.04
Albany, CA (city) Alameda County	6	0.04
Fountain, CO (city) El Paso County	6	0.04
Linda, CA (cdp) Yuba County	5	0.04
Merrifield, VA (cdp) Fairfax County	5	0.04
Mill Creek, WA (city) Snohomish County	5	0.04
Patterson, CA (city) Stanislaus County	5	0.04
Wailuku, HI (cdp) Maui County	5	0.04
Wildomar, CA (cdp) Riverside County	5	0.04
Blackhawk-Camino Tassajara, CA (cdp) Contra Costa County	4	0.04
Falls Church, VA (independent city) Falls Church city	4	0.04
Lincoln, CA (city) Placer County	4	0.04
Rossmoor, CA (cdp) Orange County	4	0.04
Sauk Village, IL (village) Cook County	4	0.04
Sterling, CO (city) Logan County	4	0.04
San Jose, CA (city) Santa Clara County	302	0.03
San Francisco, CA (city) San Francisco County	218	0.03
Portland, OR (city) Multnomah County	177	0.03
Seattle, WA (city) King County	155	0.03
Honolulu, HI (cdp) Honolulu County	130	0.03
Oakland, CA (city) Alameda County	111	0.03
Vancouver, WA (city) Clark County	47	0.03
Concord, CA (city) Contra Costa County	41	0.03
Sunnyvale, CA (city) Santa Clara County	33	0.03
Lodi, CA (city) San Joaquin County	17	0.03
Novato, CA (city) Marin County	13	0.03
Kailua, HI (cdp) Honolulu County	12	0.03
Yuba City, CA (city) Sutter County	11	0.03
Burien, WA (city) King County	10	0.03
Pleasant Hill, CA (city) Contra Costa County	10	0.03
Waipahu, HI (cdp) Honolulu County	9	0.03
Imperial Beach, CA (city) San Diego County	8	0.03
Oakley, CA (city) Contra Costa County	7	0.03

Notes: (cdp) census designated place; Refer to the Explanation of Data in the front of the book for more detailed information.

Hawaii Native/Pacific Islander: Native Hawaiian

Top 150 Places Sorted by Percent

(Based on all places, regardless of population)

Place	Number	%
Hana, HI (cdp) Maui County	537	75.74
Waimanalo Beach, HI (cdp) Honolulu County	3,229	75.60
Anahola, HI (cdp) Kauai County	1,385	71.69
Kualapuu, HI (cdp) Maui County	1,337	69.06
Nanakuli, HI (cdp) Honolulu County	7,171	66.31
Waianae, HI (cdp) Honolulu County	6,021	57.31
Maunaloa, HI (cdp) Maui County	131	56.96
Kaunakakai, HI (cdp) Maui County	1,534	56.27
Makaha Valley, HI (cdp) Honolulu County	700	54.31
Waikane, HI (cdp) Honolulu County	385	53.03
Waimanalo, HI (cdp) Honolulu County	1,893	51.66
Hauula, HI (cdp) Honolulu County	1,797	49.22
Maili, HI (cdp) Honolulu County	2,899	48.78
Makaha, HI (cdp) Honolulu County	3,714	47.90
Kukuihaele, HI (cdp) Hawaii County	139	43.85
Pakala Village, HI (cdp) Kauai County	208	43.51
Punaluu, HI (cdp) Honolulu County	380	43.13
Hawi, HI (cdp) Hawaii County	385	41.04
Hawaiian Beaches, HI (cdp) Hawaii County	1,488	40.12
Kahaluu, HI (cdp) Honolulu County	1,175	40.03
Kaaawa, HI (cdp) Honolulu County	522	39.43
Naalehu, HI (cdp) Hawaii County	362	39.39
Mountain View, HI (cdp) Hawaii County	1,082	38.66
Waimea, HI (cdp) Hawaii County	2,701	38.43
Ainaloa, HI (cdp) Hawaii County	728	38.12
Halaula, HI (cdp) Hawaii County	181	36.57
Nanawale Estates, HI (cdp) Hawaii County	391	36.44
Honaunau-Napoopoo, HI (cdp) Hawaii County	836	34.63
Waimea, HI (cdp) Kauai County	606	33.91
Pahala, HI (cdp) Hawaii County	467	33.89
Kapaau, HI (cdp) Hawaii County	390	33.65
Haleiwa, HI (cdp) Honolulu County	731	32.85
Waihee-Waiehu, HI (cdp) Maui County	2,327	31.83
Hilo, HI (cdp) Hawaii County	12,951	31.77
Kahuku, HI (cdp) Honolulu County	641	30.57
Kailua, HI (cdp) Hawaii County	2,970	30.09
Fern Acres, HI (cdp) Hawaii County	227	30.03
Hawaiian Paradise Park, HI (cdp) Hawaii County	2,099	29.77
Kekaha, HI (cdp) Kauai County	944	29.73
Volcano, HI (cdp) Hawaii County	656	29.40
Honalo, HI (cdp) Hawaii County	579	29.14
Pahoa, HI (cdp) Hawaii County	279	29.00
Kaneohe, HI (cdp) Honolulu County	10,067	28.79
Ahuimanu, HI (cdp) Honolulu County	2,439	28.67
Paauilo, HI (cdp) Hawaii County	163	28.55
Eden Roc, HI (cdp) Hawaii County	127	28.16
Wailuku, HI (cdp) Maui County	3,453	28.08
Makawao, HI (cdp) Maui County	1,770	27.98
Kealakekua, HI (cdp) Hawaii County	458	27.84
Kapaa, HI (cdp) Kauai County	2,592	27.36
Paia, HI (cdp) Maui County	673	26.93
Kalaoa, HI (cdp) Hawaii County	1,742	25.64
Laupahoehoe, HI (cdp) Hawaii County	121	25.58
Kurtistown, HI (cdp) Hawaii County	292	25.24
Pukalani, HI (cdp) Maui County	1,828	24.77
Laie, HI (cdp) Honolulu County	1,135	24.75
Orchidlands Estates, HI (cdp) Hawaii County	427	24.67
Fern Forest, HI (cdp) Hawaii County	118	24.58
Waikoloa Village, HI (cdp) Hawaii County	1,180	24.55
Makakilo City, HI (cdp) Honolulu County	3,188	24.23
Waikapu, HI (cdp) Maui County	269	24.13
Papaikou, HI (cdp) Hawaii County	341	24.12
Captain Cook, HI (cdp) Hawaii County	773	24.11
Hanapepe, HI (cdp) Kauai County	518	24.06
Ewa Beach, HI (cdp) Honolulu County	3,473	23.71
Maunawili, HI (cdp) Honolulu County	1,149	23.60
Wahiawa, HI (cdp) Honolulu County	3,776	23.38
Wailua, HI (cdp) Kauai County	485	23.28
Kailua, HI (cdp) Honolulu County	8,390	22.98
Kahului, HI (cdp) Maui County	4,566	22.66
Koloa, HI (cdp) Kauai County	435	22.40
Kapalua, HI (cdp) Maui County	104	22.27
Hawaiian Acres, HI (cdp) Hawaii County	395	22.24
Heeia, HI (cdp) Honolulu County	1,099	22.23
Hawaiian Ocean View, HI (cdp) Hawaii County	483	22.18
Haiku-Pauwela, HI (cdp) Maui County	1,450	22.04
Honomu, HI (cdp) Hawaii County	119	22.00
Haliimaile, HI (cdp) Maui County	195	21.79
Wailua Homesteads, HI (cdp) Kauai County	986	21.59
Honokaa, HI (cdp) Hawaii County	480	21.50
Waipio Acres, HI (cdp) Honolulu County	1,118	21.10
Waialua, HI (cdp) Honolulu County	789	20.98
Lawai, HI (cdp) Kauai County	406	20.46
Lanai City, HI (cdp) Maui County	625	19.75
Hanamaulu, HI (cdp) Kauai County	646	19.74
Wainaku, HI (cdp) Hawaii County	242	19.72
Eleele, HI (cdp) Kauai County	400	19.61
Keaau, HI (cdp) Hawaii County	390	19.40
Omao, HI (cdp) Kauai County	235	19.25
Mokuleia, HI (cdp) Honolulu County	346	18.81
Pepeekeo, HI (cdp) Hawaii County	316	18.62
Lahaina, HI (cdp) Maui County	1,686	18.49
Leilani Estates, HI (cdp) Hawaii County	190	18.16
Lihue, HI (cdp) Kauai County	1,020	17.98
Hanalei, HI (cdp) Kauai County	84	17.57
Kalaheo, HI (cdp) Kauai County	650	16.61
Holualoa, HI (cdp) Hawaii County	998	16.34
Whitmore Village, HI (cdp) Honolulu County	660	16.27
Halawa, HI (cdp) Honolulu County	2,245	16.16
Ewa Gentry, HI (cdp) Honolulu County	793	16.06
Mililani Town, HI (cdp) Honolulu County	4,483	15.67
Pupukea, HI (cdp) Honolulu County	664	15.62
Waipio, HI (cdp) Honolulu County	1,799	15.41
Village Park, HI (cdp) Honolulu County	1,438	14.94
Ewa Villages, HI (cdp) Honolulu County	708	14.93
Kihei, HI (cdp) Maui County	2,487	14.85
Pearl City, HI (cdp) Honolulu County	4,596	14.84
Kahaluu-Keauhou, HI (cdp) Hawaii County	353	14.62
Paukaa, HI (cdp) Hawaii County	72	14.55
Kilauea, HI (cdp) Kauai County	300	14.34
Aiea, HI (cdp) Honolulu County	1,289	14.29
Puhi, HI (cdp) Kauai County	159	13.41
Waimalu, HI (cdp) Honolulu County	3,746	12.75
Kaumakani, HI (cdp) Kauai County	76	12.52
Waipahu, HI (cdp) Honolulu County	4,006	12.10
Honolulu, HI (cdp) Honolulu County	43,363	11.67
Napili-Honokowai, HI (cdp) Maui County	761	11.21
Puako, HI (cdp) Hawaii County	47	10.96
Kalihiwai, HI (cdp) Kauai County	77	10.74
Appleton, MN (city) Swift County	241	8.39
Leon, OK (town) Love County	8	8.33
Kawela Bay, HI (cdp) Honolulu County	32	7.80
Tampa, KS (city) Marion County	10	6.94
Princeville, HI (cdp) Kauai County	112	6.60
Poipu, HI (cdp) Kauai County	70	6.51
Elfin Cove, AK (cdp) Skagway-Hoonah-Angoon Census Area	2	6.25
Wailea-Makena, HI (cdp) Maui County	316	5.57
Doran, MN (city) Wilkin County	3	5.08
Mulhall, OK (town) Logan County	11	4.60
Ranchette Estates, TX (cdp) Willacy County	5	3.76
Watonga, OK (city) Blaine County	174	3.74
Morken, MN (township) Clay County	7	3.45
Roosevelt, OK (town) Kiowa County	9	3.21
Indian Beach, NC (town) Carteret County	3	3.16
Kirkwood, CA (cdp) Alpine County	3	3.13
Barbers Point Housing, HI (cdp) Honolulu County	2	2.99
Brandonville, WV (town) Preston County	3	2.94
Maalaea, HI (cdp) Maui County	13	2.86
Seney, MI (township) Schoolcraft County	5	2.78
Bode, IA (city) Humboldt County	9	2.75
Inman, NE (village) Holt County	4	2.70
Carrier, OK (town) Garfield County	2	2.60
Gorman, MN (township) Otter Tail County	10	2.51
Gulf Port, IL (village) Henderson County	5	2.42
Nisqually Indian Community, WA (cdp) Thurston County	14	2.38
Yoder, WY (town) Goshen County	4	2.37
Kaanapali, HI (cdp) Maui County	32	2.33
Cold Bay, AK (city) Aleutians East Borough	2	2.27
Freeman Spur, IL (village) Franklin County	6	2.20
Glen Flora, WI (village) Rusk County	2	2.15

Notes: (cdp) census designated place; Refer to the Explanation of Data in the front of the book for more detailed information.

Hawaii Native/Pacific Islander: Fijian

Top 150 Places Sorted by Number

(Based on all places, regardless of population)

Place	Number	%
Sacramento, CA (city) Sacramento County	1,253	0.31
Hayward, CA (city) Alameda County	1,149	0.82
Modesto, CA (city) Stanislaus County	454	0.24
San Bruno, CA (city) San Mateo County	352	0.88
Los Angeles, CA (city) Los Angeles County	320	0.01
San Jose, CA (city) Santa Clara County	302	0.03
New York, NY (city) New York City	302	0.00
San Mateo, CA (city) San Mateo County	281	0.30
San Francisco, CA (city) San Francisco County	215	0.03
South San Francisco, CA (city) San Mateo County	210	0.35
East Palo Alto, CA (city) San Mateo County	203	0.69
Union City, CA (city) Alameda County	196	0.29
Portland, OR (city) Multnomah County	174	0.03
Seattle, WA (city) King County	154	0.03
Rancho Cordova, CA (cdp) Sacramento County	151	0.27
Stockton, CA (city) San Joaquin County	151	0.06
Vallejo, CA (city) Solano County	147	0.13
Newark, CA (city) Alameda County	144	0.34
Arden-Arcade, CA (cdp) Sacramento County	141	0.15
Seaside, CA (city) Monterey County	133	0.42
Elk Grove, CA (cdp) Sacramento County	129	0.22
Honolulu, HI (cdp) Honolulu County	121	0.03
Fremont, CA (city) Alameda County	120	0.06
Parkway-South Sacramento, CA (cdp) Sacramento County	115	0.32
Daly City, CA (city) San Mateo County	115	0.11
Florin, CA (cdp) Sacramento County	114	0.41
West Sacramento, CA (city) Yolo County	107	0.34
Oakland, CA (city) Alameda County	105	0.03
Redwood City, CA (city) San Mateo County	86	0.11
North Highlands, CA (cdp) Sacramento County	83	0.19
Pittsburg, CA (city) Contra Costa County	76	0.13
Davis, CA (city) Yolo County	75	0.12
Kent, WA (city) King County	73	0.09
Fairfield, CA (city) Solano County	70	0.07
San Leandro, CA (city) Alameda County	66	0.08
Lynnwood, WA (city) Snohomish County	64	0.19
Richmond, CA (city) Contra Costa County	64	0.06
Woodland, CA (city) Yolo County	63	0.13
Castro Valley, CA (cdp) Alameda County	61	0.11
Antioch, CA (city) Contra Costa County	59	0.07
East Hill-Meridian, WA (cdp) King County	56	0.19
Shoreline, WA (city) King County	55	0.10
Inglewood, CA (city) Los Angeles County	55	0.05
San Pablo, CA (city) Contra Costa County	54	0.18
Hawthorne, CA (city) Los Angeles County	49	0.06
Mountlake Terrace, WA (city) Snohomish County	47	0.23
Vancouver, WA (city) Clark County	47	0.03
Laie, HI (cdp) Honolulu County	46	1.00
Millbrae, CA (city) San Mateo County	46	0.22
Marina, CA (city) Monterey County	46	0.18
Ashland, CA (cdp) Alameda County	45	0.22
Tracy, CA (city) San Joaquin County	44	0.08
Santa Clara, CA (city) Santa Clara County	44	0.04
Turlock, CA (city) Stanislaus County	43	0.08
Edmonds, WA (city) Snohomish County	42	0.11
Laguna, CA (cdp) Sacramento County	41	0.12
Hilo, HI (cdp) Hawaii County	41	0.10
Menlo Park, CA (city) San Mateo County	40	0.13
Concord, CA (city) Contra Costa County	39	0.03
Foster City, CA (city) San Mateo County	38	0.13
Everett, WA (city) Snohomish County	38	0.04
San Diego, CA (city) San Diego County	37	0.00
Cherryland, CA (cdp) Alameda County	34	0.25
Culver City, CA (city) Los Angeles County	33	0.09
Bellflower, CA (city) Los Angeles County	33	0.05
Houston, TX (city) Harris County	33	0.00
Paine Field-Lake Stickney, WA (cdp) Snohomish County	32	0.13
Renton, WA (city) King County	32	0.06
San Rafael, CA (city) Marin County	32	0.06
Sunnyvale, CA (city) Santa Clara County	32	0.02
Kaneohe, HI (cdp) Honolulu County	31	0.09
Rohnert Park, CA (city) Sonoma County	30	0.07
Folsom, CA (city) Sacramento County	30	0.06
Federal Way, WA (city) King County	30	0.04
Mountain View, CA (city) Santa Clara County	30	0.04

Place	Number	%
Anaheim, CA (city) Orange County	30	0.01
Pacifica, CA (city) San Mateo County	29	0.08
Riverside, CA (city) Riverside County	29	0.01
Hercules, CA (city) Contra Costa County	28	0.14
Bay Point, CA (cdp) Contra Costa County	28	0.13
Beaverton, OR (city) Washington County	28	0.04
Milpitas, CA (city) Santa Clara County	27	0.04
Rosemont, CA (cdp) Sacramento County	26	0.11
Aloha, OR (cdp) Washington County	26	0.06
Tacoma, WA (city) Pierce County	26	0.01
Del Aire, CA (cdp) Los Angeles County	25	0.28
West Valley City, UT (city) Salt Lake County	25	0.02
Fresno, CA (city) Fresno County	25	0.01
Paradise, NV (cdp) Clark County	25	0.01
Tukwila, WA (city) King County	24	0.14
Carmichael, CA (cdp) Sacramento County	24	0.05
Costa Mesa, CA (city) Orange County	24	0.02
Alderwood Manor, WA (cdp) Snohomish County	23	0.15
Burlingame, CA (city) San Mateo County	23	0.08
West Covina, CA (city) Los Angeles County	23	0.02
Laguna West-Lakeside, CA (cdp) Sacramento County	22	0.26
SeaTac, WA (city) King County	22	0.09
Wichita, KS (city) Sedgwick County	22	0.01
El Cerrito, CA (city) Contra Costa County	21	0.09
North Creek, WA (cdp) Snohomish County	21	0.08
Santa Monica, CA (city) Los Angeles County	21	0.02
Colusa, CA (city) Colusa County	20	0.37
Carson, CA (city) Los Angeles County	20	0.02
Corona, CA (city) Riverside County	20	0.02
Santa Clarita, CA (city) Los Angeles County	20	0.01
Phoenix, AZ (city) Maricopa County	20	0.00
North Fair Oaks, CA (cdp) San Mateo County	19	0.12
San Carlos, CA (city) San Mateo County	19	0.07
Buena Park, CA (city) Orange County	19	0.02
Citrus Heights, CA (city) Sacramento County	19	0.02
Downey, CA (city) Los Angeles County	19	0.02
Chicago, IL (city) Cook County	19	0.00
Galt, CA (city) Sacramento County	18	0.09
Ceres, CA (city) Stanislaus County	18	0.05
Manteca, CA (city) San Joaquin County	18	0.04
Bellevue, WA (city) King County	18	0.02
Henderson, NV (city) Clark County	18	0.01
Santa Rosa, CA (city) Sonoma County	18	0.01
Cascade-Fairwood, WA (cdp) King County	17	0.05
Lodi, CA (city) San Joaquin County	17	0.03
Hillsboro, OR (city) Washington County	17	0.02
Reno, NV (city) Washoe County	17	0.01
San Ramon, CA (city) Contra Costa County	16	0.04
Rialto, CA (city) San Bernardino County	16	0.02
Dallas, TX (city) Dallas County	16	0.00
Grants Pass, OR (city) Josephine County	15	0.07
Bothell, WA (city) King County	15	0.05
Pearl City, HI (cdp) Honolulu County	15	0.05
Eugene, OR (city) Lane County	15	0.01
Salt Lake City, UT (city) Salt Lake County	15	0.01
San Bernardino, CA (city) San Bernardino County	15	0.01
Hauula, HI (cdp) Honolulu County	14	0.38
American Canyon, CA (city) Napa County	14	0.14
Gardena, CA (city) Los Angeles County	14	0.02
Orem, UT (city) Utah County	14	0.02
Ferndale, WA (city) Whatcom County	13	0.15
Scotts Valley, CA (city) Santa Cruz County	13	0.11
Belmont, CA (city) San Mateo County	13	0.05
Suisun City, CA (city) Solano County	13	0.05
Kahuku, HI (cdp) Honolulu County	12	0.57
Blaine, WA (city) Whatcom County	12	0.32
Atherton, CA (town) San Mateo County	12	0.17
Vineyard, CA (cdp) Sacramento County	12	0.12
Picnic Point-North Lynnwood, WA (cdp) Snohomish County	12	0.05
Monterey, CA (city) Monterey County	12	0.04
Kailua, HI (cdp) Honolulu County	12	0.03
Livermore, CA (city) Alameda County	12	0.02
Taylorsville, UT (city) Salt Lake County	12	0.02
Provo, UT (city) Utah County	12	0.01
Santa Ana, CA (city) Orange County	12	0.00

Notes: (cdp) census designated place; Refer to the Explanation of Data in the front of the book for more detailed information.

Hawaii Native/Pacific Islander: Fijian

Top 150 Places Sorted by Percent

(Based on all places, regardless of population)

Place	Number	%
Lake Bosworth, WA (cdp) Snohomish County	3	1.47
Laie, HI (cdp) Honolulu County	46	1.00
San Bruno, CA (city) San Mateo County	352	0.88
Waikane, HI (cdp) Honolulu County	6	0.83
Hayward, CA (city) Alameda County	1,149	0.82
East Palo Alto, CA (city) San Mateo County	203	0.69
Lore City, OH (village) Guernsey County	2	0.66
Kahuku, HI (cdp) Honolulu County	12	0.57
Kawela Bay, HI (cdp) Honolulu County	2	0.49
Seaside, CA (city) Monterey County	133	0.42
Florin, CA (cdp) Sacramento County	114	0.41
Tetonia, ID (city) Teton County	1	0.40
Hauula, HI (cdp) Honolulu County	14	0.38
Colusa, CA (city) Colusa County	20	0.37
South San Francisco, CA (city) San Mateo County	210	0.35
Newark, CA (city) Alameda County	144	0.34
West Sacramento, CA (city) Yolo County	107	0.34
Parkway-South Sacramento, CA (cdp) Sacramento County	115	0.32
Blaine, WA (city) Whatcom County	12	0.32
Trinidad, CA (city) Humboldt County	1	0.32
Sacramento, CA (city) Sacramento County	1,253	0.31
San Mateo, CA (city) San Mateo County	281	0.30
Evaro, MT (cdp) Missoula County	1	0.30
Union City, CA (city) Alameda County	196	0.29
Del Aire, CA (cdp) Los Angeles County	25	0.28
Rancho Cordova, CA (cdp) Sacramento County	151	0.27
Laguna West-Lakeside, CA (cdp) Sacramento County	22	0.26
Cherryland, CA (cdp) Alameda County	34	0.25
Modesto, CA (city) Stanislaus County	454	0.24
Mountlake Terrace, WA (city) Snohomish County	47	0.23
Kaaawa, HI (cdp) Honolulu County	3	0.23
San Geronimo, CA (cdp) Marin County	1	0.23
Elk Grove, CA (cdp) Sacramento County	129	0.22
Millbrae, CA (city) San Mateo County	46	0.22
Ashland, CA (cdp) Alameda County	45	0.22
French Camp, CA (cdp) San Joaquin County	9	0.22
Eden Roc, HI (cdp) Hawaii County	1	0.22
Mountain View, HI (cdp) Hawaii County	6	0.21
Wood Village, OR (city) Multnomah County	6	0.21
Paukaa, HI (cdp) Hawaii County	1	0.20
Torning, MN (township) Swift County	1	0.20
North Highlands, CA (cdp) Sacramento County	83	0.19
Lynnwood, WA (city) Snohomish County	64	0.19
East Hill-Meridian, WA (cdp) King County	56	0.19
Brisbane, CA (city) San Mateo County	7	0.19
San Pablo, CA (city) Contra Costa County	54	0.18
Marina, CA (city) Monterey County	46	0.18
East Richmond Heights, CA (cdp) Contra Costa County	6	0.18
Atherton, CA (town) San Mateo County	12	0.17
Keyes, CA (cdp) Stanislaus County	8	0.17
Hawaiian Acres, HI (cdp) Hawaii County	3	0.17
Pupukea, HI (cdp) Honolulu County	7	0.16
Arden-Arcade, CA (cdp) Sacramento County	141	0.15
Alderwood Manor, WA (cdp) Snohomish County	23	0.15
Ferndale, WA (city) Whatcom County	13	0.15
Hercules, CA (city) Contra Costa County	28	0.14
Tukwila, WA (city) King County	24	0.14
American Canyon, CA (city) Napa County	14	0.14
Rollingwood, CA (cdp) Contra Costa County	4	0.14
Vallejo, CA (city) Solano County	147	0.13
Pittsburg, CA (city) Contra Costa County	76	0.13
Woodland, CA (city) Yolo County	63	0.13
Menlo Park, CA (city) San Mateo County	40	0.13
Foster City, CA (city) San Mateo County	38	0.13
Paine Field-Lake Stickney, WA (cdp) Snohomish County	32	0.13
Bay Point, CA (cdp) Contra Costa County	28	0.13
Empire, CA (cdp) Stanislaus County	5	0.13
Hughson, CA (city) Stanislaus County	5	0.13
Salina, UT (city) Sevier County	3	0.13
Davis, CA (city) Yolo County	75	0.12
Laguna, CA (cdp) Sacramento County	41	0.12
North Fair Oaks, CA (cdp) San Mateo County	19	0.12
Vineyard, CA (cdp) Sacramento County	12	0.12
White City, UT (cdp) Salt Lake County	7	0.12
Heeia, HI (cdp) Honolulu County	6	0.12
Okanogan, WA (city) Okanogan County	3	0.12
Paia, HI (cdp) Maui County	3	0.12
Carbon Cliff, IL (village) Rock Island County	2	0.12
Daly City, CA (city) San Mateo County	115	0.11
Redwood City, CA (city) San Mateo County	86	0.11
Castro Valley, CA (cdp) Alameda County	61	0.11
Edmonds, WA (city) Snohomish County	42	0.11
Rosemont, CA (cdp) Sacramento County	26	0.11
Scotts Valley, CA (city) Santa Cruz County	13	0.11
Fairview, CA (cdp) Alameda County	10	0.11
Waihee-Waiehu, HI (cdp) Maui County	8	0.11
Strawberry, CA (cdp) Marin County	6	0.11
Carlisle, MA (town) Middlesex County	5	0.11
Marietta-Alderwood, WA (cdp) Whatcom County	4	0.11
Ridgemark, CA (cdp) San Benito County	3	0.11
Kentland, IN (town) Newton County	2	0.11
Punaluu, HI (cdp) Honolulu County	1	0.11
Shoreline, WA (city) King County	55	0.10
Hilo, HI (cdp) Hawaii County	41	0.10
North Bend, OR (city) Coos County	10	0.10
Willows, CA (city) Glenn County	6	0.10
Bayview-Montalvin, CA (cdp) Contra Costa County	5	0.10
Birch Bay, WA (cdp) Whatcom County	5	0.10
Mountain Village, CO (town) San Miguel County	1	0.10
Kent, WA (city) King County	73	0.09
Culver City, CA (city) Los Angeles County	33	0.09
Kaneohe, HI (cdp) Honolulu County	31	0.09
SeaTac, WA (city) King County	22	0.09
El Cerrito, CA (city) Contra Costa County	21	0.09
Galt, CA (city) Sacramento County	18	0.09
Gig Harbor, WA (city) Pierce County	6	0.09
Whitemarsh Island, GA (cdp) Chatham County	5	0.09
Lockeford, CA (cdp) San Joaquin County	3	0.09
Suquamish, WA (cdp) Kitsap County	3	0.09
San Leandro, CA (city) Alameda County	66	0.08
Tracy, CA (city) San Joaquin County	44	0.08
Turlock, CA (city) Stanislaus County	43	0.08
Pacifica, CA (city) San Mateo County	29	0.08
Burlingame, CA (city) San Mateo County	23	0.08
North Creek, WA (cdp) Snohomish County	21	0.08
Makaha, HI (cdp) Honolulu County	6	0.08
Maunawili, HI (cdp) Honolulu County	4	0.08
Litchfield Park, AZ (city) Maricopa County	3	0.08
Wrightwood, CA (cdp) San Bernardino County	3	0.08
Dassel, MN (city) Meeker County	1	0.08
Stateline, NV (cdp) Douglas County	1	0.08
Fairfield, CA (city) Solano County	70	0.07
Antioch, CA (city) Contra Costa County	59	0.07
Rohnert Park, CA (city) Sonoma County	30	0.07
San Carlos, CA (city) San Mateo County	19	0.07
Grants Pass, OR (city) Josephine County	15	0.07
Kihei, HI (cdp) Maui County	11	0.07
Martha Lake, WA (cdp) Snohomish County	9	0.07
Lathrop, CA (city) San Joaquin County	7	0.07
Ahuimanu, HI (cdp) Honolulu County	6	0.07
Gonzales, CA (city) Monterey County	5	0.07
Minnehaha, WA (cdp) Clark County	5	0.07
Pacific, WA (city) King County	4	0.07
Ely, NV (city) White Pine County	3	0.07
Happy Valley, OR (city) Clackamas County	3	0.07
Kaunakakai, HI (cdp) Maui County	2	0.07
Bunker Hill, OR (cdp) Coos County	1	0.07
Greenfield, MO (city) Dade County	1	0.07
Midway, LA (cdp) La Salle Parish	1	0.07
Stockton, CA (city) San Joaquin County	151	0.06
Fremont, CA (city) Alameda County	120	0.06
Richmond, CA (city) Contra Costa County	64	0.06
Hawthorne, CA (city) Los Angeles County	49	0.06
Renton, WA (city) King County	32	0.06
San Rafael, CA (city) Marin County	32	0.06
Folsom, CA (city) Sacramento County	30	0.06
Aloha, OR (cdp) Washington County	26	0.06
Hannibal, MO (city) Marion County	11	0.06
Mukilteo, WA (city) Snohomish County	11	0.06
Bryn Mawr-Skyway, WA (cdp) King County	8	0.06

Notes: (cdp) census designated place; Refer to the Explanation of Data in the front of the book for more detailed information.

Hawaii Native/Pacific Islander: Fijian

Top 150 Places Sorted by Percent

(Based on places with populations of 10,000 or more)

Place	Number	%
San Bruno, CA (city) San Mateo County	352	0.88
Hayward, CA (city) Alameda County	1,149	0.82
East Palo Alto, CA (city) San Mateo County	203	0.69
Seaside, CA (city) Monterey County	133	0.42
Florin, CA (cdp) Sacramento County	114	0.41
South San Francisco, CA (city) San Mateo County	210	0.35
Newark, CA (city) Alameda County	144	0.34
West Sacramento, CA (city) Yolo County	107	0.34
Parkway-South Sacramento, CA (cdp) Sacramento County	115	0.32
Sacramento, CA (city) Sacramento County	1,253	0.31
San Mateo, CA (city) San Mateo County	281	0.30
Union City, CA (city) Alameda County	196	0.29
Rancho Cordova, CA (cdp) Sacramento County	151	0.27
Cherryland, CA (cdp) Alameda County	34	0.25
Modesto, CA (city) Stanislaus County	454	0.24
Mountlake Terrace, WA (city) Snohomish County	47	0.23
Elk Grove, CA (cdp) Sacramento County	129	0.22
Millbrae, CA (city) San Mateo County	46	0.22
Ashland, CA (cdp) Alameda County	45	0.22
North Highlands, CA (cdp) Sacramento County	83	0.19
Lynnwood, WA (city) Snohomish County	64	0.19
East Hill-Meridian, WA (cdp) King County	56	0.19
San Pablo, CA (city) Contra Costa County	54	0.18
Marina, CA (city) Monterey County	46	0.18
Arden-Arcade, CA (cdp) Sacramento County	141	0.15
Alderwood Manor, WA (cdp) Snohomish County	23	0.15
Hercules, CA (city) Contra Costa County	28	0.14
Tukwila, WA (city) King County	24	0.14
Vallejo, CA (city) Solano County	147	0.13
Pittsburg, CA (city) Contra Costa County	76	0.13
Woodland, CA (city) Yolo County	63	0.13
Menlo Park, CA (city) San Mateo County	40	0.13
Foster City, CA (city) San Mateo County	38	0.13
Paine Field-Lake Stickney, WA (cdp) Snohomish County	32	0.13
Bay Point, CA (cdp) Contra Costa County	28	0.13
Davis, CA (city) Yolo County	75	0.12
Laguna, CA (cdp) Sacramento County	41	0.12
North Fair Oaks, CA (cdp) San Mateo County	19	0.12
Vineyard, CA (cdp) Sacramento County	12	0.12
Daly City, CA (city) San Mateo County	115	0.11
Redwood City, CA (city) San Mateo County	86	0.11
Castro Valley, CA (cdp) Alameda County	61	0.11
Edmonds, WA (city) Snohomish County	42	0.11
Rosemont, CA (cdp) Sacramento County	26	0.11
Scotts Valley, CA (city) Santa Cruz County	13	0.11
Shoreline, WA (city) King County	55	0.10
Hilo, HI (cdp) Hawaii County	41	0.10
Kent, WA (city) King County	73	0.09
Culver City, CA (city) Los Angeles County	33	0.09
Kaneohe, HI (cdp) Honolulu County	31	0.09
SeaTac, WA (city) King County	22	0.09
El Cerrito, CA (city) Contra Costa County	21	0.09
Galt, CA (city) Sacramento County	18	0.09
San Leandro, CA (city) Alameda County	66	0.08
Tracy, CA (city) San Joaquin County	44	0.08
Turlock, CA (city) Stanislaus County	43	0.08
Pacifica, CA (city) San Mateo County	29	0.08
Burlingame, CA (city) San Mateo County	23	0.08
North Creek, WA (cdp) Snohomish County	21	0.08
Fairfield, CA (city) Solano County	70	0.07
Antioch, CA (city) Contra Costa County	59	0.07
Rohnert Park, CA (city) Sonoma County	30	0.07
San Carlos, CA (city) San Mateo County	19	0.07
Grants Pass, OR (city) Josephine County	15	0.07
Kihei, HI (cdp) Maui County	11	0.07
Martha Lake, WA (cdp) Snohomish County	9	0.07
Lathrop, CA (city) San Joaquin County	7	0.07
Stockton, CA (city) San Joaquin County	151	0.06
Fremont, CA (city) Alameda County	120	0.06
Richmond, CA (city) Contra Costa County	64	0.06
Hawthorne, CA (city) Los Angeles County	49	0.06
Renton, WA (city) King County	32	0.06
San Rafael, CA (city) Marin County	32	0.06
Folsom, CA (city) Sacramento County	30	0.06
Aloha, OR (cdp) Washington County	26	0.06
Hannibal, MO (city) Marion County	11	0.06
Mukilteo, WA (city) Snohomish County	11	0.06
Bryn Mawr-Skyway, WA (cdp) King County	8	0.06
Eloy, AZ (city) Pinal County	6	0.06
La Riviera, CA (cdp) Sacramento County	6	0.06
Lea Hill, WA (cdp) King County	6	0.06
Inglewood, CA (city) Los Angeles County	55	0.05
Bellflower, CA (city) Los Angeles County	33	0.05
Carmichael, CA (cdp) Sacramento County	24	0.05
Ceres, CA (city) Stanislaus County	18	0.05
Cascade-Fairwood, WA (cdp) King County	17	0.05
Bothell, WA (city) King County	15	0.05
Pearl City, HI (cdp) Honolulu County	15	0.05
Belmont, CA (city) San Mateo County	13	0.05
Suisun City, CA (city) Solano County	13	0.05
Picnic Point-North Lynnwood, WA (cdp) Snohomish County	12	0.05
Brentwood, CA (city) Contra Costa County	11	0.05
Bostonia, CA (cdp) San Diego County	8	0.05
Coos Bay, OR (city) Coos County	8	0.05
Lakeland North, WA (cdp) King County	8	0.05
Cannon, MI (township) Kent County	6	0.05
Oak Grove, OR (cdp) Clackamas County	6	0.05
Nanakuli, HI (cdp) Honolulu County	5	0.05
Oquirrh, UT (cdp) Salt Lake County	5	0.05
Santa Clara, CA (city) Santa Clara County	44	0.04
Everett, WA (city) Snohomish County	38	0.04
Federal Way, WA (city) King County	30	0.04
Mountain View, CA (city) Santa Clara County	30	0.04
Beaverton, OR (city) Washington County	28	0.04
Milpitas, CA (city) Santa Clara County	27	0.04
Manteca, CA (city) San Joaquin County	18	0.04
San Ramon, CA (city) Contra Costa County	16	0.04
Monterey, CA (city) Monterey County	12	0.04
Fair Oaks, CA (cdp) Sacramento County	11	0.04
Orangevale, CA (cdp) Sacramento County	10	0.04
Milwaukie, OR (city) Clackamas County	9	0.04
San Lorenzo, CA (cdp) Alameda County	9	0.04
Valinda, CA (cdp) Los Angeles County	9	0.04
Windsor, CA (town) Sonoma County	9	0.04
Pinole, CA (city) Contra Costa County	7	0.04
Rexburg, ID (city) Madison County	7	0.04
Albany, CA (city) Alameda County	6	0.04
Fountain, CO (city) El Paso County	6	0.04
Mill Valley, CA (city) Marin County	6	0.04
Linda, CA (cdp) Yuba County	5	0.04
Merrifield, VA (cdp) Fairfax County	5	0.04
Mill Creek, WA (city) Snohomish County	5	0.04
Patterson, CA (city) Stanislaus County	5	0.04
Wailuku, HI (cdp) Maui County	5	0.04
Wildomar, CA (cdp) Riverside County	5	0.04
Blackhawk-Camino Tassajara, CA (cdp) Contra Costa County	4	0.04
Lincoln, CA (city) Placer County	4	0.04
Rossmoor, CA (cdp) Orange County	4	0.04
Sauk Village, IL (village) Cook County	4	0.04
Sterling, CO (city) Logan County	4	0.04
San Jose, CA (city) Santa Clara County	302	0.03
San Francisco, CA (city) San Francisco County	215	0.03
Portland, OR (city) Multnomah County	174	0.03
Seattle, WA (city) King County	154	0.03
Honolulu, HI (cdp) Honolulu County	121	0.03
Oakland, CA (city) Alameda County	105	0.03
Vancouver, WA (city) Clark County	47	0.03
Concord, CA (city) Contra Costa County	39	0.03
Lodi, CA (city) San Joaquin County	17	0.03
Kailua, HI (cdp) Honolulu County	12	0.03
Yuba City, CA (city) Sutter County	11	0.03
Burien, WA (city) King County	10	0.03
Pleasant Hill, CA (city) Contra Costa County	10	0.03
Waipahu, HI (cdp) Honolulu County	9	0.03
Imperial Beach, CA (city) San Diego County	7	0.03
Oakley, CA (city) Contra Costa County	7	0.03
Foothill Farms, CA (cdp) Sacramento County	6	0.03
White Center, WA (cdp) King County	6	0.03
La Palma, CA (city) Orange County	5	0.03
Port Washington, NY (cdp) Nassau County	5	0.03

Notes: (cdp) census designated place; Refer to the Explanation of Data in the front of the book for more detailed information.

Hawaii Native/Pacific Islander: Other Melanesian

Top 150 Places Sorted by Number

(Based on all places, regardless of population)

Place	Number	%
New York, NY (city) New York City	37	0.00
Kapaa, HI (cdp) Kauai County	14	0.15
Cincinnati, OH (city) Hamilton County	11	0.00
Tulsa, OK (city) Tulsa County	11	0.00
Honolulu, HI (cdp) Honolulu County	9	0.00
Washington, DC (city) District of Columbia	8	0.00
Falcon Heights, MN (city) Ramsey County	7	0.13
North Amherst, MA (cdp) Hampshire County	7	0.12
Amherst, MA (town) Hampshire County	7	0.02
Los Angeles, CA (city) Los Angeles County	7	0.00
Nashville-Davidson, TN (special city) Davidson County	7	0.00
Hobe Sound, FL (cdp) Martin County	6	0.05
Roseville, MN (city) Ramsey County	6	0.02
Aspen Hill, MD (cdp) Montgomery County	6	0.01
Iowa City, IA (city) Johnson County	6	0.01
Silver Spring, MD (cdp) Montgomery County	6	0.01
Oakland, CA (city) Alameda County	6	0.00
San Diego, CA (city) San Diego County	6	0.00
Fontana, CA (city) San Bernardino County	5	0.00
Milwaukee, WI (city) Milwaukee County	5	0.00
Falls Church, VA (independent city) Falls Church city	4	0.04
Setauket-East Setauket, NY (cdp) Suffolk County	4	0.03
Lacey, WA (city) Thurston County	4	0.01
Portland, ME (city) Cumberland County	4	0.01
State College, PA (borough) Centre County	4	0.01
Brookhaven, NY (town) Suffolk County	4	0.00
Chicago, IL (city) Cook County	4	0.00
Clarksville, TN (city) Montgomery County	4	0.00
Houston, TX (city) Harris County	4	0.00
Minneapolis, MN (city) Hennepin County	4	0.00
Charlestown, MN (township) Redwood County	3	1.38
Hanamaulu, HI (cdp) Kauai County	3	0.09
La Habra Heights, CA (city) Los Angeles County	3	0.05
Fairview Shores, FL (cdp) Orange County	3	0.02
Isla Vista, CA (cdp) Santa Barbara County	3	0.02
Mill Valley, CA (city) Marin County	3	0.02
North Valley Stream, NY (cdp) Nassau County	3	0.02
Tysons Corner, VA (cdp) Fairfax County	3	0.02
Avondale, AZ (city) Maricopa County	3	0.01
Brent, FL (cdp) Escambia County	3	0.01
Danville, CA (town) Contra Costa County	3	0.01
De Kalb, IL (city) De Kalb County	3	0.01
East Point, GA (city) Fulton County	3	0.01
Folsom, CA (city) Sacramento County	3	0.01
Fort Hood, TX (cdp) Coryell County	3	0.01
Hilo, HI (cdp) Hawaii County	3	0.01
Littleton, CO (city) Arapahoe County	3	0.01
Mankato, MN (city) Blue Earth County	3	0.01
Minnetonka, MN (city) Hennepin County	3	0.01
Newtown, CT (town) Fairfield County	3	0.01
North Bethesda, MD (cdp) Montgomery County	3	0.01
Anchorage, AK (municipality) Anchorage Borough	3	0.00
Arlington, TX (city) Tarrant County	3	0.00
Chula Vista, CA (city) San Diego County	3	0.00
Hempstead, NY (town) Nassau County	3	0.00
Muncie, IN (city) Delaware County	3	0.00
Portland, OR (city) Multnomah County	3	0.00
San Francisco, CA (city) San Francisco County	3	0.00
Springfield, MO (city) Greene County	3	0.00
West Palm Beach, FL (city) Palm Beach County	3	0.00
Penns Creek, PA (cdp) Snyder County	2	0.30
Logan, NM (village) Quay County	2	0.18
Center, PA (township) Snyder County	2	0.09
Osceola, WI (village) Polk County	2	0.08
East Drumore, PA (township) Lancaster County	2	0.06
Lansing, NY (village) Tompkins County	2	0.06
Wailua Homesteads, HI (cdp) Kauai County	2	0.04
Cambria, CA (cdp) San Luis Obispo County	2	0.03
Fircrest, WA (city) Pierce County	2	0.03
Arkadelphia, AR (city) Clark County	2	0.02
Lansing, NY (town) Tompkins County	2	0.02
Larkspur, CA (city) Marin County	2	0.02
Millington, TN (city) Shelby County	2	0.02
Mount Dora, FL (city) Lake County	2	0.02
New Carrollton, MD (city) Prince George's County	2	0.02
Dublin, OH (city) Franklin County	2	0.01
Fitchburg, WI (city) Dane County	2	0.01
Franconia, VA (cdp) Fairfax County	2	0.01
Ithaca, NY (town) Tompkins County	2	0.01
Marlborough, MA (city) Middlesex County	2	0.01
Palm Coast, FL (city) Flagler County	2	0.01
Scarsdale, NY (village) Westchester County	2	0.01
Security-Widefield, CO (cdp) El Paso County	2	0.01
Aloha, OR (cdp) Washington County	2	0.00
Arden-Arcade, CA (cdp) Sacramento County	2	0.00
Carlsbad, CA (city) San Diego County	2	0.00
Charlotte, NC (city) Mecklenburg County	2	0.00
Concord, CA (city) Contra Costa County	2	0.00
Fort Collins, CO (city) Larimer County	2	0.00
Fountain Valley, CA (city) Orange County	2	0.00
Fresno, CA (city) Fresno County	2	0.00
Harrisburg, PA (city) Dauphin County	2	0.00
Jackson, MS (city) Hinds County	2	0.00
Kansas City, MO (city) Jackson County	2	0.00
Long Beach, CA (city) Los Angeles County	2	0.00
Lubbock, TX (city) Lubbock County	2	0.00
Metairie, LA (cdp) Jefferson Parish	2	0.00
Novato, CA (city) Marin County	2	0.00
Ontario, CA (city) San Bernardino County	2	0.00
Overland Park, KS (city) Johnson County	2	0.00
Philadelphia, PA (city) Philadelphia County	2	0.00
Rancho Cucamonga, CA (city) San Bernardino County	2	0.00
Reston, VA (cdp) Fairfax County	2	0.00
San Antonio, TX (city) Bexar County	2	0.00
Ypsilanti, MI (township) Washtenaw County	2	0.00
Strasburg, MO (city) Cass County	1	0.74
East Gillespie, IL (village) Macoupin County	1	0.43
Hancock, MI (township) Houghton County	1	0.25
Holloman AFB, NM (cdp) Otero County	1	0.05
Starksboro, VT (town) Addison County	1	0.05
Baldwin, WI (village) Saint Croix County	1	0.04
Northeast Ithaca, NY (cdp) Tompkins County	1	0.04
Pumpkin Center, NC (cdp) Onslow County	1	0.04
South Hutchinson, KS (city) Reno County	1	0.04
Cayuga Heights, NY (village) Tompkins County	1	0.03
Fruitland, ID (city) Payette County	1	0.03
New Hampton, IA (city) Chickasaw County	1	0.03
Bay Hill, FL (cdp) Orange County	1	0.02
Eagle Point, OR (city) Jackson County	1	0.02
Fruita, CO (city) Mesa County	1	0.02
Grambling, LA (town) Lincoln Parish	1	0.02
Holly, MI (village) Oakland County	1	0.02
Shippensburg, PA (borough) Cumberland County	1	0.02
Sterling, AK (cdp) Kenai Peninsula Borough	1	0.02
Swarthmore, PA (borough) Delaware County	1	0.02
Ticonderoga, NY (town) Essex County	1	0.02
Tuscola, IL (city) Douglas County	1	0.02
Vandercook Lake, MI (cdp) Jackson County	1	0.02
Woodlawn, MD (cdp) Prince George's County	1	0.02
Alderwood Manor, WA (cdp) Snohomish County	1	0.01
Beaver Falls, PA (city) Beaver County	1	0.01
Belton, TX (city) Bell County	1	0.01
Butler, PA (city) Butler County	1	0.01
Cherryland, CA (cdp) Alameda County	1	0.01
Christiansburg, VA (town) Montgomery County	1	0.01
Clemson, SC (city) Pickens County	1	0.01
Crawfordsville, IN (city) Montgomery County	1	0.01
Dunn Loring, VA (cdp) Fairfax County	1	0.01
Ellensburg, WA (city) Kittitas County	1	0.01
Fort Lee, VA (cdp) Prince George County	1	0.01
Four Corners, OR (cdp) Marion County	1	0.01
Heber, UT (city) Wasatch County	1	0.01
Hershey, PA (cdp) Dauphin County	1	0.01
Holly, MI (township) Oakland County	1	0.01
Kailua, HI (cdp) Hawaii County	1	0.01
Keyport, NJ (borough) Monmouth County	1	0.01
Ladue, MO (city) Saint Louis County	1	0.01
Lemoore, CA (city) Kings County	1	0.01
Loma Linda, CA (city) San Bernardino County	1	0.01
Montrose, CO (city) Montrose County	1	0.01

Notes: (cdp) census designated place; Refer to the Explanation of Data in the front of the book for more detailed information.

Hawaii Native/Pacific Islander: Other Melanesian

Top 150 Places Sorted by Percent

(Based on all places, regardless of population)

Place	Number	%
Charlestown, MN (township) Redwood County	3	1.38
Strasburg, MO (city) Cass County	1	0.74
East Gillespie, IL (village) Macoupin County	1	0.43
Penns Creek, PA (cdp) Snyder County	2	0.30
Hancock, MI (township) Houghton County	1	0.25
Logan, NM (village) Quay County	2	0.18
Kapaa, HI (cdp) Kauai County	14	0.15
Falcon Heights, MN (city) Ramsey County	7	0.13
North Amherst, MA (cdp) Hampshire County	7	0.12
Hanamaulu, HI (cdp) Kauai County	3	0.09
Center, PA (township) Snyder County	2	0.09
Osceola, WI (village) Polk County	2	0.08
East Drumore, PA (township) Lancaster County	2	0.06
Lansing, NY (village) Tompkins County	2	0.06
Hobe Sound, FL (cdp) Martin County	6	0.05
La Habra Heights, CA (city) Los Angeles County	3	0.05
Holloman AFB, NM (cdp) Otero County	1	0.05
Starksboro, VT (town) Addison County	1	0.05
Falls Church, VA (independent city) Falls Church city	4	0.04
Wailua Homesteads, HI (cdp) Kauai County	2	0.04
Baldwin, WI (village) Saint Croix County	1	0.04
Northeast Ithaca, NY (cdp) Tompkins County	1	0.04
Pumpkin Center, NC (cdp) Onslow County	1	0.04
South Hutchinson, KS (city) Reno County	1	0.04
Setauket-East Setauket, NY (cdp) Suffolk County	4	0.03
Cambria, CA (cdp) San Luis Obispo County	2	0.03
Fircrest, WA (city) Pierce County	2	0.03
Cayuga Heights, NY (village) Tompkins County	1	0.03
Fruitland, ID (city) Payette County	1	0.03
New Hampton, IA (city) Chickasaw County	1	0.03
Amherst, MA (town) Hampshire County	7	0.02
Roseville, MN (city) Ramsey County	6	0.02
Fairview Shores, FL (cdp) Orange County	3	0.02
Isla Vista, CA (cdp) Santa Barbara County	3	0.02
Mill Valley, CA (city) Marin County	3	0.02
North Valley Stream, NY (cdp) Nassau County	3	0.02
Tysons Corner, VA (cdp) Fairfax County	3	0.02
Arkadelphia, AR (city) Clark County	2	0.02
Lansing, NY (town) Tompkins County	2	0.02
Larkspur, CA (city) Marin County	2	0.02
Millington, TN (city) Shelby County	2	0.02
Mount Dora, FL (city) Lake County	2	0.02
New Carrollton, MD (city) Prince George's County	2	0.02
Bay Hill, FL (cdp) Orange County	1	0.02
Eagle Point, OR (city) Jackson County	1	0.02
Fruita, CO (city) Mesa County	1	0.02
Grambling, LA (town) Lincoln Parish	1	0.02
Holly, MI (village) Oakland County	1	0.02
Shippensburg, PA (borough) Cumberland County	1	0.02
Sterling, AK (cdp) Kenai Peninsula Borough	1	0.02
Swarthmore, PA (borough) Delaware County	1	0.02
Ticonderoga, NY (town) Essex County	1	0.02
Tuscola, IL (city) Douglas County	1	0.02
Vandercook Lake, MI (cdp) Jackson County	1	0.02
Woodlawn, MD (cdp) Prince George's County	1	0.02
Aspen Hill, MD (cdp) Montgomery County	6	0.01
Iowa City, IA (city) Johnson County	6	0.01
Silver Spring, MD (cdp) Montgomery County	6	0.01
Lacey, WA (city) Thurston County	4	0.01
Portland, ME (city) Cumberland County	4	0.01
State College, PA (borough) Centre County	4	0.01
Avondale, AZ (city) Maricopa County	3	0.01
Brent, FL (cdp) Escambia County	3	0.01
Danville, CA (town) Contra Costa County	3	0.01
De Kalb, IL (city) De Kalb County	3	0.01
East Point, GA (city) Fulton County	3	0.01
Folsom, CA (city) Sacramento County	3	0.01
Fort Hood, TX (cdp) Coryell County	3	0.01
Hilo, HI (cdp) Hawaii County	3	0.01
Littleton, CO (city) Arapahoe County	3	0.01
Mankato, MN (city) Blue Earth County	3	0.01
Minnetonka, MN (city) Hennepin County	3	0.01
Newtown, CT (town) Fairfield County	3	0.01
North Bethesda, MD (cdp) Montgomery County	3	0.01
Dublin, OH (city) Franklin County	2	0.01
Fitchburg, WI (city) Dane County	2	0.01
Franconia, VA (cdp) Fairfax County	2	0.01
Ithaca, NY (town) Tompkins County	2	0.01
Marlborough, MA (city) Middlesex County	2	0.01
Palm Coast, FL (city) Flagler County	2	0.01
Scarsdale, NY (village) Westchester County	2	0.01
Security-Widefield, CO (cdp) El Paso County	2	0.01
Alderwood Manor, WA (cdp) Snohomish County	1	0.01
Beaver Falls, PA (city) Beaver County	1	0.01
Belton, TX (city) Bell County	1	0.01
Butler, PA (city) Butler County	1	0.01
Cherryland, CA (cdp) Alameda County	1	0.01
Christiansburg, VA (town) Montgomery County	1	0.01
Clemson, SC (city) Pickens County	1	0.01
Crawfordsville, IN (city) Montgomery County	1	0.01
Dunn Loring, VA (cdp) Fairfax County	1	0.01
Ellensburg, WA (city) Kittitas County	1	0.01
Fort Lee, VA (cdp) Prince George County	1	0.01
Four Corners, OR (cdp) Marion County	1	0.01
Heber, UT (city) Wasatch County	1	0.01
Hershey, PA (cdp) Dauphin County	1	0.01
Holly, MI (township) Oakland County	1	0.01
Kailua, HI (cdp) Hawaii County	1	0.01
Keyport, NJ (borough) Monmouth County	1	0.01
Ladue, MO (city) Saint Louis County	1	0.01
Lemoore, CA (city) Kings County	1	0.01
Loma Linda, CA (city) San Bernardino County	1	0.01
Montrose, CO (city) Montrose County	1	0.01
Oswego, NY (city) Oswego County	1	0.01
Portland, TX (city) San Patricio County	1	0.01
Prairie Ridge, WA (cdp) Pierce County	1	0.01
Sebring, FL (city) Highlands County	1	0.01
Sedro-Woolley, WA (city) Skagit County	1	0.01
Shasta Lake, CA (city) Shasta County	1	0.01
South Daytona, FL (city) Volusia County	1	0.01
South Hadley, MA (town) Hampshire County	1	0.01
Standish, ME (town) Cumberland County	1	0.01
Sugar Hill, GA (city) Gwinnett County	1	0.01
Sun City, CA (cdp) Riverside County	1	0.01
Swissvale, PA (borough) Allegheny County	1	0.01
Universal City, TX (city) Bexar County	1	0.01
Village Park, HI (cdp) Honolulu County	1	0.01
Weatherford, OK (city) Custer County	1	0.01
Weston, WI (village) Marathon County	1	0.01
New York, NY (city) New York City	37	0.00
Cincinnati, OH (city) Hamilton County	11	0.00
Tulsa, OK (city) Tulsa County	11	0.00
Honolulu, HI (cdp) Honolulu County	9	0.00
Washington, DC (city) District of Columbia	8	0.00
Los Angeles, CA (city) Los Angeles County	7	0.00
Nashville-Davidson, TN (special city) Davidson County	7	0.00
Oakland, CA (city) Alameda County	6	0.00
San Diego, CA (city) San Diego County	6	0.00
Fontana, CA (city) San Bernardino County	5	0.00
Milwaukee, WI (city) Milwaukee County	5	0.00
Brookhaven, NY (town) Suffolk County	4	0.00
Chicago, IL (city) Cook County	4	0.00
Clarksville, TN (city) Montgomery County	4	0.00
Houston, TX (city) Harris County	4	0.00
Minneapolis, MN (city) Hennepin County	4	0.00
Anchorage, AK (municipality) Anchorage Borough	3	0.00
Arlington, TX (city) Tarrant County	3	0.00
Chula Vista, CA (city) San Diego County	3	0.00
Hempstead, NY (town) Nassau County	3	0.00
Muncie, IN (city) Delaware County	3	0.00
Portland, OR (city) Multnomah County	3	0.00
San Francisco, CA (city) San Francisco County	3	0.00
Springfield, MO (city) Greene County	3	0.00
West Palm Beach, FL (city) Palm Beach County	3	0.00
Aloha, OR (cdp) Washington County	2	0.00
Arden-Arcade, CA (cdp) Sacramento County	2	0.00
Carlsbad, CA (city) San Diego County	2	0.00
Charlotte, NC (city) Mecklenburg County	2	0.00
Concord, CA (city) Contra Costa County	2	0.00
Fort Collins, CO (city) Larimer County	2	0.00

Notes: (cdp) census designated place; Refer to the Explanation of Data in the front of the book for more detailed information.

Hawaii Native/Pacific Islander: Other Melanesian

Top 150 Places Sorted by Percent

(Based on places with populations of 10,000 or more)

Place	Number	%
Hobe Sound, FL (cdp) Martin County	6	0.05
Falls Church, VA (independent city) Falls Church city	4	0.04
Setauket-East Setauket, NY (cdp) Suffolk County	4	0.03
Amherst, MA (town) Hampshire County	7	0.02
Roseville, MN (city) Ramsey County	6	0.02
Fairview Shores, FL (cdp) Orange County	3	0.02
Isla Vista, CA (cdp) Santa Barbara County	3	0.02
Mill Valley, CA (city) Marin County	3	0.02
North Valley Stream, NY (cdp) Nassau County	3	0.02
Tysons Corner, VA (cdp) Fairfax County	3	0.02
Arkadelphia, AR (city) Clark County	2	0.02
Lansing, NY (town) Tompkins County	2	0.02
Larkspur, CA (city) Marin County	2	0.02
Millington, TN (city) Shelby County	2	0.02
New Carrollton, MD (city) Prince George's County	2	0.02
Aspen Hill, MD (cdp) Montgomery County	6	0.01
Iowa City, IA (city) Johnson County	6	0.01
Silver Spring, MD (cdp) Montgomery County	6	0.01
Lacey, WA (city) Thurston County	4	0.01
Portland, ME (city) Cumberland County	4	0.01
State College, PA (borough) Centre County	4	0.01
Avondale, AZ (city) Maricopa County	3	0.01
Brent, FL (cdp) Escambia County	3	0.01
Danville, CA (town) Contra Costa County	3	0.01
De Kalb, IL (city) De Kalb County	3	0.01
East Point, GA (city) Fulton County	3	0.01
Folsom, CA (city) Sacramento County	3	0.01
Fort Hood, TX (cdp) Coryell County	3	0.01
Hilo, HI (cdp) Hawaii County	3	0.01
Littleton, CO (city) Arapahoe County	3	0.01
Mankato, MN (city) Blue Earth County	3	0.01
Minnetonka, MN (city) Hennepin County	3	0.01
Newtown, CT (town) Fairfield County	3	0.01
North Bethesda, MD (cdp) Montgomery County	3	0.01
Dublin, OH (city) Franklin County	2	0.01
Fitchburg, WI (city) Dane County	2	0.01
Franconia, VA (cdp) Fairfax County	2	0.01
Ithaca, NY (town) Tompkins County	2	0.01
Marlborough, MA (city) Middlesex County	2	0.01
Palm Coast, FL (city) Flagler County	2	0.01
Scarsdale, NY (village) Westchester County	2	0.01
Security-Widefield, CO (cdp) El Paso County	2	0.01
Alderwood Manor, WA (cdp) Snohomish County	1	0.01
Belton, TX (city) Bell County	1	0.01
Butler, PA (city) Butler County	1	0.01
Cherryland, CA (cdp) Alameda County	1	0.01
Christiansburg, VA (town) Montgomery County	1	0.01
Clemson, SC (city) Pickens County	1	0.01
Crawfordsville, IN (city) Montgomery County	1	0.01
Ellensburg, WA (city) Kittitas County	1	0.01
Four Corners, OR (cdp) Marion County	1	0.01
Hershey, PA (cdp) Dauphin County	1	0.01
Holly, MI (township) Oakland County	1	0.01
Lemoore, CA (city) Kings County	1	0.01
Loma Linda, CA (city) San Bernardino County	1	0.01
Montrose, CO (city) Montrose County	1	0.01
Oswego, NY (city) Oswego County	1	0.01
Portland, TX (city) San Patricio County	1	0.01
Prairie Ridge, WA (cdp) Pierce County	1	0.01
South Daytona, FL (city) Volusia County	1	0.01
South Hadley, MA (town) Hampshire County	1	0.01
Sugar Hill, GA (city) Gwinnett County	1	0.01
Sun City, CA (cdp) Riverside County	1	0.01
Universal City, TX (city) Bexar County	1	0.01
Weston, WI (village) Marathon County	1	0.01
New York, NY (city) New York City	37	0.00
Cincinnati, OH (city) Hamilton County	11	0.00
Tulsa, OK (city) Tulsa County	11	0.00
Honolulu, HI (cdp) Honolulu County	9	0.00
Washington, DC (city) District of Columbia	8	0.00
Los Angeles, CA (city) Los Angeles County	7	0.00
Nashville-Davidson, TN (special city) Davidson County	7	0.00
Oakland, CA (city) Alameda County	6	0.00
San Diego, CA (city) San Diego County	6	0.00
Fontana, CA (city) San Bernardino County	5	0.00

Place	Number	%
Milwaukee, WI (city) Milwaukee County	5	0.00
Brookhaven, NY (town) Suffolk County	4	0.00
Chicago, IL (city) Cook County	4	0.00
Clarksville, TN (city) Montgomery County	4	0.00
Houston, TX (city) Harris County	4	0.00
Minneapolis, MN (city) Hennepin County	4	0.00
Anchorage, AK (municipality) Anchorage Borough	3	0.00
Arlington, TX (city) Tarrant County	3	0.00
Chula Vista, CA (city) San Diego County	3	0.00
Hempstead, NY (town) Nassau County	3	0.00
Muncie, IN (city) Delaware County	3	0.00
Portland, OR (city) Multnomah County	3	0.00
San Francisco, CA (city) San Francisco County	3	0.00
Springfield, MO (city) Greene County	3	0.00
West Palm Beach, FL (city) Palm Beach County	3	0.00
Aloha, OR (cdp) Washington County	2	0.00
Arden-Arcade, CA (cdp) Sacramento County	2	0.00
Carlsbad, CA (city) San Diego County	2	0.00
Charlotte, NC (city) Mecklenburg County	2	0.00
Concord, CA (city) Contra Costa County	2	0.00
Fort Collins, CO (city) Larimer County	2	0.00
Fountain Valley, CA (city) Orange County	2	0.00
Fresno, CA (city) Fresno County	2	0.00
Harrisburg, PA (city) Dauphin County	2	0.00
Jackson, MS (city) Hinds County	2	0.00
Kansas City, MO (city) Jackson County	2	0.00
Long Beach, CA (city) Los Angeles County	2	0.00
Lubbock, TX (city) Lubbock County	2	0.00
Metairie, LA (cdp) Jefferson Parish	2	0.00
Novato, CA (city) Marin County	2	0.00
Ontario, CA (city) San Bernardino County	2	0.00
Overland Park, KS (city) Johnson County	2	0.00
Philadelphia, PA (city) Philadelphia County	2	0.00
Rancho Cucamonga, CA (city) San Bernardino County	2	0.00
Reston, VA (cdp) Fairfax County	2	0.00
San Antonio, TX (city) Bexar County	2	0.00
Ypsilanti, MI (township) Washtenaw County	2	0.00
Altoona, PA (city) Blair County	1	0.00
Ann Arbor, MI (city) Washtenaw County	1	0.00
Atlanta, GA (city) Fulton County	1	0.00
Austin, TX (city) Travis County	1	0.00
Beaverton, OR (city) Washington County	1	0.00
Bellevue, NE (city) Sarpy County	1	0.00
Berkeley, CA (city) Alameda County	1	0.00
Berwyn, IL (city) Cook County	1	0.00
Bloomington, IN (city) Monroe County	1	0.00
Boston, MA (city) Suffolk County	1	0.00
Brighton, NY (town) Monroe County	1	0.00
Brockton, MA (city) Plymouth County	1	0.00
Charleston, WV (city) Kanawha County	1	0.00
Charleston, SC (city) Charleston County	1	0.00
Chillicothe, OH (city) Ross County	1	0.00
Cliffside Park, NJ (borough) Bergen County	1	0.00
Dallas, TX (city) Dallas County	1	0.00
Derry, PA (township) Dauphin County	1	0.00
Detroit, MI (city) Wayne County	1	0.00
Downey, CA (city) Los Angeles County	1	0.00
Duncanville, TX (city) Dallas County	1	0.00
East Orange, NJ (city) Essex County	1	0.00
El Cajon, CA (city) San Diego County	1	0.00
Elizabeth, NJ (city) Union County	1	0.00
Encinitas, CA (city) San Diego County	1	0.00
Eugene, OR (city) Lane County	1	0.00
Fairfax, VA (independent city) Fairfax city	1	0.00
Ferry Pass, FL (cdp) Escambia County	1	0.00
Fort Wayne, IN (city) Allen County	1	0.00
Fountainbleau, FL (cdp) Miami-Dade County	1	0.00
Freehold, NJ (township) Monmouth County	1	0.00
Fremont, CA (city) Alameda County	1	0.00
Garden Grove, CA (city) Orange County	1	0.00
Gary, IN (city) Lake County	1	0.00
Grand Prairie, TX (city) Dallas County	1	0.00
Hamilton, NJ (township) Mercer County	1	0.00
Imperial Beach, CA (city) San Diego County	1	0.00
Independence, MO (city) Jackson County	1	0.00

Notes: (cdp) census designated place; Refer to the Explanation of Data in the front of the book for more detailed information.

Hawaii Native/Pacific Islander: Micronesian

Top 150 Places Sorted by Number

(Based on all places, regardless of population)

Place	Number	%
Honolulu, HI (cdp) Honolulu County	5,327	1.43
San Diego, CA (city) San Diego County	3,657	0.30
Los Angeles, CA (city) Los Angeles County	1,604	0.04
New York, NY (city) New York City	1,552	0.02
San Jose, CA (city) Santa Clara County	1,257	0.14
Vallejo, CA (city) Solano County	914	0.78
Portland, OR (city) Multnomah County	909	0.17
Chula Vista, CA (city) San Diego County	880	0.51
Long Beach, CA (city) Los Angeles County	863	0.19
Seattle, WA (city) King County	806	0.14
Fairfield, CA (city) Solano County	742	0.77
Springdale, AR (city) Washington County	731	1.60
Chicago, IL (city) Cook County	663	0.02
Phoenix, AZ (city) Maricopa County	662	0.05
Las Vegas, NV (city) Clark County	586	0.12
Hayward, CA (city) Alameda County	577	0.41
San Antonio, TX (city) Bexar County	573	0.05
Hilo, HI (cdp) Hawaii County	564	1.38
Tacoma, WA (city) Pierce County	563	0.29
Killeen, TX (city) Bell County	541	0.62
Sacramento, CA (city) Sacramento County	523	0.13
Waipahu, HI (cdp) Honolulu County	521	1.57
San Francisco, CA (city) San Francisco County	496	0.06
Salem, OR (city) Marion County	491	0.36
Houston, TX (city) Harris County	475	0.02
Kahului, HI (cdp) Maui County	467	2.32
Oceanside, CA (city) San Diego County	457	0.28
Tucson, AZ (city) Pima County	413	0.08
Colorado Springs, CO (city) El Paso County	389	0.11
Fremont, CA (city) Alameda County	382	0.19
Waimalu, HI (cdp) Honolulu County	373	1.27
Costa Mesa, CA (city) Orange County	372	0.34
Lakewood, WA (city) Pierce County	370	0.64
National City, CA (city) San Diego County	356	0.66
Sunrise Manor, NV (cdp) Clark County	347	0.22
Vancouver, WA (city) Clark County	334	0.23
El Paso, TX (city) El Paso County	328	0.06
Santa Ana, CA (city) Orange County	323	0.10
Bremerton, WA (city) Kitsap County	317	0.85
Stockton, CA (city) San Joaquin County	317	0.13
Spanaway, WA (cdp) Pierce County	316	1.46
Virginia Beach, VA (independent city) Virginia Beach city	313	0.07
Marina, CA (city) Monterey County	312	1.24
San Leandro, CA (city) Alameda County	308	0.39
Moreno Valley, CA (city) Riverside County	302	0.21
Anaheim, CA (city) Orange County	302	0.09
Jacksonville, FL (special city) Duval County	300	0.04
Riverside, CA (city) Riverside County	285	0.11
Parkland, WA (cdp) Pierce County	283	1.18
Denver, CO (city) Denver County	283	0.05
Carson, CA (city) Los Angeles County	270	0.30
La Presa, CA (cdp) San Diego County	269	0.82
Enid, OK (city) Garfield County	268	0.57
Vacaville, CA (city) Solano County	268	0.30
El Cajon, CA (city) San Diego County	268	0.28
Alameda, CA (city) Alameda County	263	0.36
Paradise, NV (cdp) Clark County	262	0.14
Suisun City, CA (city) Solano County	259	0.99
Federal Way, WA (city) King County	258	0.31
Salinas, CA (city) Monterey County	254	0.17
Wahiawa, HI (cdp) Honolulu County	250	1.55
Pearl City, HI (cdp) Honolulu County	247	0.80
Oklahoma City, OK (city) Oklahoma County	237	0.05
Spokane, WA (city) Spokane County	236	0.12
Lakewood, CA (city) Los Angeles County	234	0.29
Garden Grove, CA (city) Orange County	231	0.14
Milpitas, CA (city) Santa Clara County	230	0.37
Oxnard, CA (city) Ventura County	226	0.13
Oakland, CA (city) Alameda County	223	0.06
Anchorage, AK (municipality) Anchorage Borough	220	0.08
Reno, NV (city) Washoe County	218	0.12
Dallas, TX (city) Dallas County	217	0.02
Aurora, CO (city) Arapahoe County	213	0.08
Halawa, HI (cdp) Honolulu County	208	1.50
Mililani Town, HI (cdp) Honolulu County	208	0.73
Modesto, CA (city) Stanislaus County	208	0.11
North Las Vegas, NV (city) Clark County	204	0.18
Fresno, CA (city) Fresno County	199	0.05
Kansas City, MO (city) Jackson County	199	0.05
Albuquerque, NM (city) Bernalillo County	195	0.04
Fort Lewis, WA (cdp) Pierce County	194	1.02
Grand Rapids, MI (city) Kent County	193	0.10
Elk Grove, CA (cdp) Sacramento County	191	0.32
Tempe, AZ (city) Maricopa County	191	0.12
Lacey, WA (city) Thurston County	190	0.61
Kailua, HI (cdp) Honolulu County	188	0.51
Providence, RI (city) Providence County	188	0.11
Philadelphia, PA (city) Philadelphia County	187	0.01
Lawton, OK (city) Comanche County	183	0.20
Kaneohe, HI (cdp) Honolulu County	182	0.52
Escondido, CA (city) San Diego County	180	0.13
Austin, TX (city) Travis County	180	0.03
Tigard, OR (city) Washington County	179	0.43
Antioch, CA (city) Contra Costa County	176	0.19
Fayetteville, NC (city) Cumberland County	174	0.14
Huntington Beach, CA (city) Orange County	174	0.09
Vista, CA (city) San Diego County	173	0.19
Fort Hood, TX (cdp) Coryell County	170	0.50
La Mesa, CA (city) San Diego County	168	0.31
Tampa, FL (city) Hillsborough County	168	0.06
Henderson, NV (city) Clark County	167	0.10
San Bernardino, CA (city) San Bernardino County	167	0.09
Clarksville, TN (city) Montgomery County	164	0.16
Spring Valley, CA (cdp) San Diego County	162	0.61
Elk Plain, WA (cdp) Pierce County	160	1.02
Santee, CA (city) San Diego County	160	0.30
Mesa, AZ (city) Maricopa County	160	0.04
Lemon Grove, CA (city) San Diego County	158	0.63
Trenton, NJ (city) Mercer County	158	0.19
Boise City, ID (city) Ada County	157	0.08
Fort Worth, TX (city) Tarrant County	156	0.03
Sunnyvale, CA (city) Santa Clara County	155	0.12
Augusta-Richmond County, GA (special city) Richmond County	152	0.08
Columbus, GA (special city) Muscogee County	152	0.08
Union City, CA (city) Alameda County	150	0.22
Concord, CA (city) Contra Costa County	150	0.12
Arlington, TX (city) Tarrant County	150	0.05
Fort Bragg, NC (cdp) Cumberland County	148	0.51
Newark, CA (city) Alameda County	148	0.35
Kent, WA (city) King County	146	0.18
Ewa Beach, HI (cdp) Honolulu County	145	0.99
Corona, CA (city) Riverside County	145	0.12
Buena Park, CA (city) Orange County	144	0.18
Norfolk, VA (independent city) Norfolk city	144	0.06
Seaside, CA (city) Monterey County	140	0.44
Everett, WA (city) Snohomish County	140	0.15
Spring Valley, NV (cdp) Clark County	138	0.12
Makakilo City, HI (cdp) Honolulu County	137	1.04
Memphis, TN (city) Shelby County	137	0.02
Indianapolis, IN (special city) Marion County	136	0.02
Morganton, NC (city) Burke County	133	0.77
Oak Harbor, WA (city) Island County	133	0.67
Bakersfield, CA (city) Kern County	133	0.05
West Valley City, UT (city) Salt Lake County	132	0.12
Security-Widefield, CO (cdp) El Paso County	131	0.44
Sierra Vista, AZ (city) Cochise County	130	0.34
Citrus Heights, CA (city) Sacramento County	130	0.15
Gresham, OR (city) Multnomah County	129	0.14
Wailuku, HI (cdp) Maui County	128	1.04
Barstow, CA (city) San Bernardino County	128	0.61
Wichita, KS (city) Sedgwick County	126	0.04
Columbus, OH (city) Franklin County	126	0.02
Waipio Acres, HI (cdp) Honolulu County	123	2.32
Temecula, CA (city) Riverside County	123	0.21
Glendale, AZ (city) Maricopa County	123	0.06
Daly City, CA (city) San Mateo County	122	0.12
Tracy, CA (city) San Joaquin County	121	0.21
Eugene, OR (city) Lane County	120	0.09
Chattanooga, TN (city) Hamilton County	120	0.08
Cypress, CA (city) Orange County	119	0.26

Notes: (cdp) census designated place; Refer to the Explanation of Data in the front of the book for more detailed information.

Hawaii Native/Pacific Islander: Micronesian

Top 150 Places Sorted by Percent

(Based on all places, regardless of population)

Place	Number	%
Haliimaile, HI (cdp) Maui County	89	9.94
Maunaloa, HI (cdp) Maui County	9	3.91
Rex, NC (cdp) Robeson County	2	3.64
Mifflintown, PA (borough) Juniata County	31	3.60
Okaton, SD (cdp) Jones County	1	3.45
Orchidlands Estates, HI (cdp) Hawaii County	54	3.12
Adair Village, OR (city) Benton County	16	2.99
East Ellijay, GA (city) Gilmer County	21	2.97
Cavour, SD (town) Beadle County	4	2.84
Oliver, GA (city) Screven County	7	2.77
Livingston, SC (town) Orangeburg County	4	2.70
Eden Roc, HI (cdp) Hawaii County	12	2.66
Retreat, TX (town) Navarro County	9	2.65
Alto Bonito, TX (cdp) Starr County	15	2.64
Kapalua, HI (cdp) Maui County	12	2.57
Ramah, CO (town) El Paso County	3	2.56
Honaunau-Napoopoo, HI (cdp) Hawaii County	61	2.53
Orrum, NC (town) Robeson County	2	2.53
Kahului, HI (cdp) Maui County	467	2.32
Waipio Acres, HI (cdp) Honolulu County	123	2.32
Keene, TX (city) Johnson County	113	2.26
Hauula, HI (cdp) Honolulu County	82	2.25
Delway, NC (cdp) Sampson County	6	2.22
Hawaiian Ocean View, HI (cdp) Hawaii County	47	2.16
Hedgesville, WV (town) Berkeley County	5	2.08
Ainaloa, HI (cdp) Hawaii County	39	2.04
Lone Rock, IA (city) Kossuth County	3	1.91
Waikoloa Village, HI (cdp) Hawaii County	90	1.87
Nanawale Estates, HI (cdp) Hawaii County	20	1.86
Bradley, SD (town) Clark County	2	1.79
Fort Greely, AK (cdp) Southeast Fairbanks Census Area	8	1.74
Havelock, IA (city) Pocahontas County	3	1.69
Hawaiian Beaches, HI (cdp) Hawaii County	61	1.64
Honalo, HI (cdp) Hawaii County	32	1.61
Waikapu, HI (cdp) Maui County	18	1.61
Springdale, AR (city) Washington County	731	1.60
Waipahu, HI (cdp) Honolulu County	521	1.57
Pine Island, FL (cdp) Hernando County	1	1.56
Wahiawa, HI (cdp) Honolulu County	250	1.55
Perry, KS (city) Jefferson County	14	1.55
Gays, IL (village) Moultrie County	4	1.54
McGrath, MN (city) Aitkin County	1	1.54
Halawa, HI (cdp) Honolulu County	208	1.50
Laupahoehoe, HI (cdp) Hawaii County	7	1.48
Meigs, GA (city) Thomas County	16	1.47
Spanaway, WA (cdp) Pierce County	316	1.46
Tracyton, WA (cdp) Kitsap County	47	1.44
Honolulu, HI (cdp) Honolulu County	5,327	1.43
Vantage, WA (cdp) Kittitas County	1	1.43
Hilo, HI (cdp) Hawaii County	564	1.38
Papaikou, HI (cdp) Hawaii County	19	1.34
Dixville, NH (township) Coos County	1	1.33
Troy Grove, IL (village) La Salle County	4	1.31
Pepeekeo, HI (cdp) Hawaii County	22	1.30
Albion, WA (town) Whitman County	8	1.30
East Port Orchard, WA (cdp) Kitsap County	66	1.29
Kekaha, HI (cdp) Kauai County	41	1.29
Waimalu, HI (cdp) Honolulu County	373	1.27
Chignik, AK (city) Lake and Peninsula Borough	1	1.27
Marina, CA (city) Monterey County	312	1.24
Waikane, HI (cdp) Honolulu County	9	1.24
Rattan, OK (town) Pushmataha County	3	1.24
Paauilo, HI (cdp) Hawaii County	7	1.23
Torreon, NM (cdp) Torrence County	3	1.23
Ebro, FL (town) Washington County	3	1.20
Bingham Lake, MN (city) Cottonwood County	2	1.20
Parkland, WA (cdp) Pierce County	283	1.18
Corning, KS (city) Nemaha County	2	1.18
Pahoa, HI (cdp) Hawaii County	11	1.14
American Canyon, CA (city) Napa County	110	1.13
Bird Island, MN (township) Renville County	3	1.12
Medicine Lake, MT (town) Sheridan County	3	1.12
Kailua, HI (cdp) Hawaii County	110	1.11
Copper Center, AK (cdp) Valdez-Cordova Census Area	4	1.10
Primrose, AK (cdp) Kenai Peninsula Borough	1	1.08
Malone-Porter, WA (cdp) Grays Harbor County	5	1.06
Delaware, IA (city) Delaware County	2	1.06
Makakilo City, HI (cdp) Honolulu County	137	1.04
Wailuku, HI (cdp) Maui County	128	1.04
Port Orchard, WA (city) Kitsap County	80	1.04
Kahaluu-Keauhou, HI (cdp) Hawaii County	25	1.04
Fern Forest, HI (cdp) Hawaii County	5	1.04
Fort Lewis, WA (cdp) Pierce County	194	1.02
Elk Plain, WA (cdp) Pierce County	160	1.02
Tanglewilde-Thompson Place, WA (cdp) Thurston County	58	1.02
Navy Yard City, WA (cdp) Kitsap County	27	1.02
Nisqually Indian Community, WA (cdp) Thurston County	6	1.02
Maryhill, WA (cdp) Klickitat County	1	1.02
Ocotillo, CA (cdp) Imperial County	3	1.01
Glenford, OH (village) Perry County	2	1.01
Suisun City, CA (city) Solano County	259	0.99
Ewa Beach, HI (cdp) Honolulu County	145	0.99
Indiantown, FL (cdp) Martin County	55	0.98
Parkwood, WA (cdp) Kitsap County	70	0.97
Captain Cook, HI (cdp) Hawaii County	31	0.97
Parkville, MO (city) Platte County	39	0.96
Butler, MN (township) Otter Tail County	3	0.95
Noma, FL (town) Holmes County	2	0.94
Stanfield, AZ (cdp) Pinal County	6	0.92
Honomu, HI (cdp) Hawaii County	5	0.92
Wainaku, HI (cdp) Hawaii County	11	0.90
Neosho, MO (city) Newton County	93	0.89
Jadis, MN (township) Roseau County	5	0.89
Hawaiian Paradise Park, HI (cdp) Hawaii County	62	0.88
Springdale, UT (town) Washington County	4	0.88
Summit, OK (town) Muskogee County	2	0.88
Baldwin, GA (city) Habersham County	21	0.87
Blythedale, MO (village) Harrison County	2	0.86
Bremerton, WA (city) Kitsap County	317	0.85
Kealakekua, HI (cdp) Hawaii County	14	0.85
Makaha Valley, HI (cdp) Honolulu County	11	0.85
North Stanwood, WA (cdp) Snohomish County	4	0.85
La Presa, CA (cdp) San Diego County	269	0.82
Ault Field, WA (cdp) Island County	17	0.82
Highland, WI (town) Douglas County	2	0.82
Valley Hi, OH (village) Logan County	2	0.82
Waipio, HI (cdp) Honolulu County	95	0.81
Wheeler AFB, HI (cdp) Honolulu County	23	0.81
Pearl City, HI (cdp) Honolulu County	247	0.80
Lowell, AR (city) Benton County	40	0.80
Redstone Arsenal, AL (cdp) Madison County	19	0.80
Dunkerton, IA (city) Black Hawk County	6	0.80
Milford, KS (city) Geary County	4	0.80
Hersey, MI (village) Osceola County	3	0.80
La Grande, OR (city) Union County	97	0.79
Norwich, PA (township) McKean County	5	0.79
Vallejo, CA (city) Solano County	914	0.78
Eleele, HI (cdp) Kauai County	16	0.78
Hamilton, NC (town) Martin County	4	0.78
Formoso, KS (city) Jewell County	1	0.78
Fairfield, CA (city) Solano County	742	0.77
Morganton, NC (city) Burke County	133	0.77
Waialua, HI (cdp) Honolulu County	29	0.77
Forest, WI (town) Richland County	3	0.77
Four Corners, OR (cdp) Marion County	106	0.76
Whitmore Village, HI (cdp) Honolulu County	31	0.76
Palm Shores, FL (town) Brevard County	6	0.76
Evant, TX (town) Coryell County	3	0.76
Village Park, HI (cdp) Honolulu County	72	0.75
Kalaoa, HI (cdp) Hawaii County	51	0.75
Loami, IL (village) Sangamon County	6	0.75
Centralia, KS (city) Nemaha County	4	0.75
North Hero, VT (town) Grand Isle County	6	0.74
Yakutat, AK (cdp) Yakutat City and Borough	5	0.74
Mililani Town, HI (cdp) Honolulu County	208	0.73
Schofield Barracks, HI (cdp) Honolulu County	105	0.73
Manchester, WA (cdp) Kitsap County	36	0.73
Laie, HI (cdp) Honolulu County	33	0.72
Pumpkin Center, NC (cdp) Onslow County	16	0.72
Colfax, MN (township) Kandiyohi County	4	0.72

Notes: (cdp) census designated place; Refer to the Explanation of Data in the front of the book for more detailed information.

Hawaii Native/Pacific Islander: Micronesian

Top 150 Places Sorted by Percent

(Based on places with populations of 10,000 or more)

Place	Number	%
Kahului, HI (cdp) Maui County	467	2.32
Springdale, AR (city) Washington County	731	1.60
Waipahu, HI (cdp) Honolulu County	521	1.57
Wahiawa, HI (cdp) Honolulu County	250	1.55
Halawa, HI (cdp) Honolulu County	208	1.50
Spanaway, WA (cdp) Pierce County	316	1.46
Honolulu, HI (cdp) Honolulu County	5,327	1.43
Hilo, HI (cdp) Hawaii County	564	1.38
Waimalu, HI (cdp) Honolulu County	373	1.27
Marina, CA (city) Monterey County	312	1.24
Parkland, WA (cdp) Pierce County	283	1.18
Makakilo City, HI (cdp) Honolulu County	137	1.04
Wailuku, HI (cdp) Maui County	128	1.04
Fort Lewis, WA (cdp) Pierce County	194	1.02
Elk Plain, WA (cdp) Pierce County	160	1.02
Suisun City, CA (city) Solano County	259	0.99
Ewa Beach, HI (cdp) Honolulu County	145	0.99
Neosho, MO (city) Newton County	93	0.89
Bremerton, WA (city) Kitsap County	317	0.85
La Presa, CA (cdp) San Diego County	269	0.82
Waipio, HI (cdp) Honolulu County	95	0.81
Pearl City, HI (cdp) Honolulu County	247	0.80
La Grande, OR (city) Union County	97	0.79
Vallejo, CA (city) Solano County	914	0.78
Fairfield, CA (city) Solano County	742	0.77
Morganton, NC (city) Burke County	133	0.77
Four Corners, OR (cdp) Marion County	106	0.76
Mililani Town, HI (cdp) Honolulu County	208	0.73
Schofield Barracks, HI (cdp) Honolulu County	105	0.73
Kaneohe Station, HI (cdp) Honolulu County	84	0.71
Silverdale, WA (cdp) Kitsap County	107	0.68
Oak Harbor, WA (city) Island County	133	0.67
National City, CA (city) San Diego County	356	0.66
Waianae, HI (cdp) Honolulu County	68	0.65
Lakewood, WA (city) Pierce County	370	0.64
Nanakuli, HI (cdp) Honolulu County	69	0.64
Lemon Grove, CA (city) San Diego County	158	0.63
Killeen, TX (city) Bell County	541	0.62
Lacey, WA (city) Thurston County	190	0.61
Spring Valley, CA (cdp) San Diego County	162	0.61
Barstow, CA (city) San Bernardino County	128	0.61
Enid, OK (city) Garfield County	268	0.57
Fort Campbell North, KY (cdp) Christian County	78	0.54
Susanville, CA (city) Lassen County	73	0.54
Hayesville, OR (cdp) Marion County	97	0.53
Kaneohe, HI (cdp) Honolulu County	182	0.52
Fort Polk South, LA (cdp) Vernon Parish	57	0.52
Chula Vista, CA (city) San Diego County	880	0.51
Kailua, HI (cdp) Honolulu County	188	0.51
Fort Bragg, NC (cdp) Cumberland County	148	0.51
Fort Hood, TX (cdp) Coryell County	170	0.50
Orchards, WA (cdp) Clark County	85	0.48
Kihei, HI (cdp) Maui County	80	0.48
Fountain, CO (city) El Paso County	71	0.47
Twentynine Palms, CA (city) San Bernardino County	67	0.45
Seaside, CA (city) Monterey County	140	0.44
Security-Widefield, CO (cdp) El Paso County	131	0.44
Bonita, CA (cdp) San Diego County	54	0.44
Tigard, OR (city) Washington County	179	0.43
SeaTac, WA (city) King County	109	0.43
Riverton-Boulevard Park, WA (cdp) King County	48	0.43
Altoona, IA (city) Polk County	43	0.42
Hayward, CA (city) Alameda County	577	0.41
San Leandro, CA (city) Alameda County	308	0.39
Imperial Beach, CA (city) San Diego County	104	0.39
Fort Carson, CO (cdp) El Paso County	41	0.39
Ridgecrest, CA (city) Kern County	95	0.38
Bostonia, CA (cdp) San Diego County	58	0.38
Milpitas, CA (city) Santa Clara County	230	0.37
Salem, OR (city) Marion County	491	0.36
Alameda, CA (city) Alameda County	263	0.36
Radcliff, KY (city) Hardin County	80	0.36
Newark, CA (city) Alameda County	148	0.35
Ashland, CA (cdp) Alameda County	73	0.35
Five Corners, WA (cdp) Clark County	43	0.35
Costa Mesa, CA (city) Orange County	372	0.34
Sierra Vista, AZ (city) Cochise County	130	0.34
Fort Drum, NY (cdp) Jefferson County	41	0.34
Easton, MD (town) Talbot County	40	0.34
Fort Benning South, GA (cdp) Chattahoochee County	40	0.34
Elk Grove, CA (cdp) Sacramento County	191	0.32
Federal Way, WA (city) King County	258	0.31
La Mesa, CA (city) San Diego County	168	0.31
Corsicana, TX (city) Navarro County	75	0.31
Bay Point, CA (cdp) Contra Costa County	66	0.31
Rio Linda, CA (cdp) Sacramento County	32	0.31
San Diego, CA (city) San Diego County	3,657	0.30
Carson, CA (city) Los Angeles County	270	0.30
Vacaville, CA (city) Solano County	268	0.30
Santee, CA (city) San Diego County	160	0.30
Des Moines, WA (city) King County	89	0.30
Fort Leonard Wood, MO (cdp) Pulaski County	41	0.30
Marshall, MO (city) Saline County	37	0.30
Tacoma, WA (city) Pierce County	563	0.29
Lakewood, CA (city) Los Angeles County	234	0.29
South Hill, WA (cdp) Pierce County	93	0.29
University Place, WA (city) Pierce County	86	0.29
Spring Valley, NY (village) Rockland County	73	0.29
Brent, FL (cdp) Escambia County	64	0.29
Oceanside, CA (city) San Diego County	457	0.28
El Cajon, CA (city) San Diego County	268	0.28
Benicia, CA (city) Solano County	75	0.28
Casa de Oro-Mount Helix, CA (cdp) San Diego County	52	0.28
Enterprise, NV (cdp) Clark County	41	0.28
Lathrop, CA (city) San Joaquin County	29	0.28
Cypress, CA (city) Orange County	119	0.26
Copperas Cove, TX (city) Coryell County	76	0.26
Vineyard, CA (cdp) Sacramento County	26	0.26
Port Hueneme, CA (city) Ventura County	54	0.25
Harker Heights, TX (city) Bell County	44	0.25
Miami, OK (city) Ottawa County	34	0.25
Fort Knox, KY (cdp) Hardin County	31	0.25
Lompoc, CA (city) Santa Barbara County	97	0.24
Los Banos, CA (city) Merced County	61	0.24
Atwater, CA (city) Merced County	56	0.24
San Lorenzo, CA (cdp) Alameda County	52	0.24
Los Alamitos, CA (city) Orange County	28	0.24
Fort Morgan, CO (city) Morgan County	26	0.24
Vancouver, WA (city) Clark County	334	0.23
Fairbanks, AK (city) Fairbanks North Star Borough	70	0.23
Mountlake Terrace, WA (city) Snohomish County	47	0.23
Tukwila, WA (city) King County	40	0.23
Cocoa, FL (city) Brevard County	38	0.23
Cherryland, CA (cdp) Alameda County	32	0.23
Sunrise Manor, NV (cdp) Clark County	347	0.22
Union City, CA (city) Alameda County	150	0.22
Le Ray, NY (town) Jefferson County	44	0.22
Portland, TX (city) San Patricio County	32	0.22
Sierra Vista Southeast, AZ (cdp) Cochise County	32	0.22
Moreno Valley, CA (city) Riverside County	302	0.21
Temecula, CA (city) Riverside County	123	0.21
Tracy, CA (city) San Joaquin County	121	0.21
Poway, CA (city) San Diego County	103	0.21
Laguna, CA (cdp) Sacramento County	72	0.21
Coronado, CA (city) San Diego County	50	0.21
Altus, OK (city) Jackson County	45	0.21
Immokalee, FL (cdp) Collier County	41	0.21
Carthage, MO (city) Jasper County	27	0.21
South Yuba City, CA (cdp) Sutter County	26	0.21
Prairie Ridge, WA (cdp) Pierce County	25	0.21
Gladstone, OR (city) Clackamas County	24	0.21
Lawton, OK (city) Comanche County	183	0.20
Hinesville, GA (city) Liberty County	61	0.20
Monterey, CA (city) Monterey County	59	0.20
Oakley, CA (city) Contra Costa County	51	0.20
Junction City, KS (city) Geary County	37	0.20
Alpine, CA (cdp) San Diego County	26	0.20
Arlington, WA (city) Snohomish County	23	0.20
Fort Stewart, GA (cdp) Liberty County	22	0.20
Guymon, OK (city) Texas County	21	0.20

Notes: (cdp) census designated place; Refer to the Explanation of Data in the front of the book for more detailed information.

Hawaii Native/Pacific Islander: Guamanian or Chamorro

Top 150 Places Sorted by Number

(Based on all places, regardless of population)

Place	Number	%
San Diego, CA (city) San Diego County	3,450	0.28
Los Angeles, CA (city) Los Angeles County	1,563	0.04
New York, NY (city) New York City	1,486	0.02
Honolulu, HI (cdp) Honolulu County	1,221	0.33
San Jose, CA (city) Santa Clara County	1,174	0.13
Vallejo, CA (city) Solano County	890	0.76
Chula Vista, CA (city) San Diego County	838	0.48
Long Beach, CA (city) Los Angeles County	833	0.18
Fairfield, CA (city) Solano County	731	0.76
Seattle, WA (city) King County	721	0.13
Chicago, IL (city) Cook County	637	0.02
Phoenix, AZ (city) Maricopa County	551	0.04
San Antonio, TX (city) Bexar County	540	0.05
Tacoma, WA (city) Pierce County	536	0.28
Las Vegas, NV (city) Clark County	531	0.11
Hayward, CA (city) Alameda County	530	0.38
Killeen, TX (city) Bell County	516	0.59
San Francisco, CA (city) San Francisco County	460	0.06
Houston, TX (city) Harris County	442	0.02
Sacramento, CA (city) Sacramento County	438	0.11
Oceanside, CA (city) San Diego County	426	0.26
Fremont, CA (city) Alameda County	373	0.18
Colorado Springs, CO (city) El Paso County	363	0.10
National City, CA (city) San Diego County	351	0.65
Lakewood, WA (city) Pierce County	331	0.57
Sunrise Manor, NV (cdp) Clark County	327	0.21
Portland, OR (city) Multnomah County	321	0.06
El Paso, TX (city) El Paso County	310	0.05
Vancouver, WA (city) Clark County	306	0.21
Spanaway, WA (cdp) Pierce County	304	1.41
Tucson, AZ (city) Pima County	300	0.06
Anaheim, CA (city) Orange County	299	0.09
Marina, CA (city) Monterey County	289	1.15
Santa Ana, CA (city) Orange County	289	0.09
Bremerton, WA (city) Kitsap County	285	0.76
Virginia Beach, VA (independent city) Virginia Beach city	285	0.07
Riverside, CA (city) Riverside County	283	0.11
Moreno Valley, CA (city) Riverside County	282	0.20
San Leandro, CA (city) Alameda County	274	0.34
Stockton, CA (city) San Joaquin County	272	0.11
Parkland, WA (cdp) Pierce County	269	1.12
Carson, CA (city) Los Angeles County	264	0.29
La Presa, CA (cdp) San Diego County	263	0.80
Jacksonville, FL (special city) Duval County	263	0.04
Vacaville, CA (city) Solano County	259	0.29
El Cajon, CA (city) San Diego County	259	0.27
Suisun City, CA (city) Solano County	257	0.98
Alameda, CA (city) Alameda County	257	0.36
Salinas, CA (city) Monterey County	250	0.17
Paradise, NV (cdp) Clark County	238	0.13
Milpitas, CA (city) Santa Clara County	228	0.36
Lakewood, CA (city) Los Angeles County	228	0.29
Oklahoma City, OK (city) Oklahoma County	225	0.04
Garden Grove, CA (city) Orange County	222	0.13
Oxnard, CA (city) Ventura County	219	0.13
Oakland, CA (city) Alameda County	212	0.05
North Las Vegas, NV (city) Clark County	203	0.18
Dallas, TX (city) Dallas County	201	0.02
Modesto, CA (city) Stanislaus County	200	0.11
Federal Way, WA (city) King County	189	0.23
Grand Rapids, MI (city) Kent County	188	0.10
Providence, RI (city) Providence County	187	0.11
Elk Grove, CA (cdp) Sacramento County	186	0.31
Anchorage, AK (municipality) Anchorage Borough	184	0.07
Aurora, CO (city) Arapahoe County	182	0.07
Denver, CO (city) Denver County	182	0.03
Fresno, CA (city) Fresno County	180	0.04
Albuquerque, NM (city) Bernalillo County	177	0.04
Philadelphia, PA (city) Philadelphia County	176	0.01
Escondido, CA (city) San Diego County	171	0.13
Lacey, WA (city) Thurston County	169	0.54
La Mesa, CA (city) San Diego County	168	0.31
Spokane, WA (city) Spokane County	166	0.08
Antioch, CA (city) Contra Costa County	165	0.18
Mililani Town, HI (cdp) Honolulu County	163	0.57
Vista, CA (city) San Diego County	162	0.18
Fayetteville, NC (city) Cumberland County	162	0.13
Spring Valley, CA (cdp) San Diego County	161	0.60
Elk Plain, WA (cdp) Pierce County	160	1.02
Austin, TX (city) Travis County	159	0.02
Lemon Grove, CA (city) San Diego County	158	0.63
Trenton, NJ (city) Mercer County	158	0.19
Santee, CA (city) San Diego County	157	0.30
Henderson, NV (city) Clark County	155	0.09
Sunnyvale, CA (city) Santa Clara County	152	0.12
Union City, CA (city) Alameda County	150	0.22
Fort Worth, TX (city) Tarrant County	150	0.03
Lawton, OK (city) Comanche County	149	0.16
Fort Lewis, WA (cdp) Pierce County	142	0.74
Buena Park, CA (city) Orange County	142	0.18
Huntington Beach, CA (city) Orange County	141	0.07
Newark, CA (city) Alameda County	140	0.33
Seaside, CA (city) Monterey County	137	0.43
Kailua, HI (cdp) Honolulu County	137	0.38
Corona, CA (city) Riverside County	136	0.11
Memphis, TN (city) Shelby County	136	0.02
Waimalu, HI (cdp) Honolulu County	135	0.46
Augusta-Richmond County, GA (special city) Richmond County	134	0.07
Morganton, NC (city) Burke County	133	0.77
Norfolk, VA (independent city) Norfolk city	132	0.06
Columbus, GA (special city) Muscogee County	131	0.07
Clarksville, TN (city) Montgomery County	130	0.13
Security-Widefield, CO (cdp) El Paso County	128	0.43
Fort Hood, TX (cdp) Coryell County	126	0.37
Spring Valley, NV (cdp) Clark County	126	0.11
Barstow, CA (city) San Bernardino County	125	0.59
Indianapolis, IN (special city) Marion County	125	0.02
Sierra Vista, AZ (city) Cochise County	124	0.33
Reno, NV (city) Washoe County	124	0.07
Oak Harbor, WA (city) Island County	123	0.62
Temecula, CA (city) Riverside County	122	0.21
Citrus Heights, CA (city) Sacramento County	122	0.14
Boise City, ID (city) Ada County	122	0.07
Tracy, CA (city) San Joaquin County	121	0.21
Chattanooga, TN (city) Hamilton County	120	0.08
San Bernardino, CA (city) San Bernardino County	120	0.06
Cypress, CA (city) Orange County	118	0.26
Concord, CA (city) Contra Costa County	118	0.10
Arlington, TX (city) Tarrant County	117	0.04
Bakersfield, CA (city) Kern County	116	0.05
Columbus, OH (city) Franklin County	116	0.02
Richmond, VA (independent city) Richmond city	115	0.06
Mesa, AZ (city) Maricopa County	114	0.03
Pearl City, HI (cdp) Honolulu County	113	0.36
Kent, WA (city) King County	111	0.14
Daly City, CA (city) San Mateo County	111	0.11
American Canyon, CA (city) Napa County	110	1.13
Pittsburg, CA (city) Contra Costa County	107	0.19
Wichita, KS (city) Sedgwick County	107	0.03
Milwaukee, WI (city) Milwaukee County	106	0.02
Santa Clara, CA (city) Santa Clara County	105	0.10
Glendale, AZ (city) Maricopa County	105	0.05
Norwalk, CA (city) Los Angeles County	104	0.10
Washington, DC (city) District of Columbia	104	0.02
Silverdale, WA (cdp) Kitsap County	103	0.65
Omaha, NE (city) Douglas County	103	0.03
Makakilo City, HI (cdp) Honolulu County	102	0.78
Fort Bragg, NC (cdp) Cumberland County	101	0.35
Victorville, CA (city) San Bernardino County	101	0.16
Lancaster, CA (city) Los Angeles County	100	0.08
Detroit, MI (city) Wayne County	100	0.01
Wahiawa, HI (cdp) Honolulu County	99	0.61
Imperial Beach, CA (city) San Diego County	99	0.37
West Palm Beach, FL (city) Palm Beach County	98	0.12
Poway, CA (city) San Diego County	97	0.20
Hilo, HI (cdp) Hawaii County	95	0.23
Lompoc, CA (city) Santa Barbara County	94	0.23
South Hill, WA (cdp) Pierce County	93	0.29
Livermore, CA (city) Alameda County	92	0.13
Tempe, AZ (city) Maricopa County	92	0.06

Notes: (cdp) census designated place; Refer to the Explanation of Data in the front of the book for more detailed information.

Hawaii Native/Pacific Islander: Guamanian or Chamorro

Top 150 Places Sorted by Percent

(Based on all places, regardless of population)

Place	Number	%
Maunaloa, HI (cdp) Maui County	9	3.91
Rex, NC (cdp) Robeson County	2	3.64
Mifflintown, PA (borough) Juniata County	31	3.60
Okaton, SD (cdp) Jones County	1	3.45
East Ellijay, GA (city) Gilmer County	21	2.97
Oliver, GA (city) Screven County	7	2.77
Livingston, SC (town) Orangeburg County	4	2.70
Ramah, CO (town) El Paso County	3	2.56
Orrum, NC (town) Robeson County	2	2.53
Delway, NC (cdp) Sampson County	6	2.22
Hedgesville, WV (town) Berkeley County	5	2.08
Lone Rock, IA (city) Kossuth County	3	1.91
Bradley, SD (town) Clark County	2	1.79
Fort Greely, AK (cdp) Southeast Fairbanks Census Area	8	1.74
Havelock, IA (city) Pocahontas County	3	1.69
Pine Island, FL (cdp) Hernando County	1	1.56
Perry, KS (city) Jefferson County	14	1.55
Gays, IL (village) Moultrie County	4	1.54
McGrath, MN (city) Aitkin County	1	1.54
Meigs, GA (city) Thomas County	16	1.47
Hawaiian Beaches, HI (cdp) Hawaii County	53	1.43
Vantage, WA (cdp) Kittitas County	1	1.43
Spanaway, WA (cdp) Pierce County	304	1.41
Dixville, NH (township) Coos County	1	1.33
Troy Grove, IL (village) La Salle County	4	1.31
Tracyton, WA (cdp) Kitsap County	42	1.29
Waipio Acres, HI (cdp) Honolulu County	68	1.28
Chignik, AK (city) Lake and Peninsula Borough	1	1.27
Rattan, OK (town) Pushmataha County	3	1.24
Paauilo, HI (cdp) Hawaii County	7	1.23
Torreon, NM (cdp) Torrence County	3	1.23
Ebro, FL (town) Washington County	3	1.20
Bingham Lake, MN (city) Cottonwood County	2	1.20
Corning, KS (city) Nemaha County	2	1.18
East Port Orchard, WA (cdp) Kitsap County	60	1.17
Kekaha, HI (cdp) Kauai County	37	1.17
Marina, CA (city) Monterey County	289	1.15
American Canyon, CA (city) Napa County	110	1.13
Parkland, WA (cdp) Pierce County	269	1.12
Bird Island, MN (township) Renville County	3	1.12
Copper Center, AK (cdp) Valdez-Cordova Census Area	4	1.10
Primrose, AK (cdp) Kenai Peninsula Borough	1	1.08
Malone-Porter, WA (cdp) Grays Harbor County	5	1.06
Delaware, IA (city) Delaware County	2	1.06
Orchidlands Estates, HI (cdp) Hawaii County	18	1.04
Fern Forest, HI (cdp) Hawaii County	5	1.04
Elk Plain, WA (cdp) Pierce County	160	1.02
Tanglewilde-Thompson Place, WA (cdp) Thurston County	58	1.02
Nisqually Indian Community, WA (cdp) Thurston County	6	1.02
Maryhill, WA (cdp) Klickitat County	1	1.02
Ocotillo, CA (cdp) Imperial County	3	1.01
Glenford, OH (village) Perry County	2	1.01
Port Orchard, WA (city) Kitsap County	76	0.99
Suisun City, CA (city) Solano County	257	0.98
Indiantown, FL (cdp) Martin County	55	0.98
Parkwood, WA (cdp) Kitsap County	69	0.96
Waikane, HI (cdp) Honolulu County	7	0.96
Navy Yard City, WA (cdp) Kitsap County	25	0.95
Noma, FL (town) Holmes County	2	0.94
Stanfield, AZ (cdp) Pinal County	6	0.92
Springdale, UT (town) Washington County	4	0.88
Summit, OK (town) Muskogee County	2	0.88
Blythedale, MO (village) Harrison County	2	0.86
North Stanwood, WA (cdp) Snohomish County	4	0.85
Ault Field, WA (cdp) Island County	17	0.82
Highland, WI (town) Douglas County	2	0.82
La Presa, CA (cdp) San Diego County	263	0.80
Milford, KS (city) Geary County	4	0.80
Hersey, MI (village) Osceola County	3	0.80
Norwich, PA (township) McKean County	5	0.79
Makakilo City, HI (cdp) Honolulu County	102	0.78
Hamilton, NC (town) Martin County	4	0.78
Formoso, KS (city) Jewell County	1	0.78
Morganton, NC (city) Burke County	133	0.77
Forest, WI (town) Richland County	3	0.77
Vallejo, CA (city) Solano County	890	0.76
Fairfield, CA (city) Solano County	731	0.76
Bremerton, WA (city) Kitsap County	285	0.76
Redstone Arsenal, AL (cdp) Madison County	18	0.76
Palm Shores, FL (town) Brevard County	6	0.76
Evant, TX (town) Coryell County	3	0.76
Loami, IL (village) Sangamon County	6	0.75
Centralia, KS (city) Nemaha County	4	0.75
Fort Lewis, WA (cdp) Pierce County	142	0.74
North Hero, VT (town) Grand Isle County	6	0.74
Yakutat, AK (cdp) Yakutat City and Borough	5	0.74
Manchester, WA (cdp) Kitsap County	36	0.73
Henlopen Acres, DE (town) Sussex County	1	0.72
Wentworth, MO (village) Newton County	1	0.71
Makaha Valley, HI (cdp) Honolulu County	9	0.70
Rainbow, CA (cdp) San Diego County	14	0.69
Paradise Heights, FL (cdp) Orange County	9	0.69
Jordan, MI (township) Antrim County	6	0.69
Bangor Trident Base, WA (cdp) Kitsap County	49	0.68
Hillburn, NY (village) Rockland County	6	0.68
Yelm, WA (city) Thurston County	22	0.67
Wheeler AFB, HI (cdp) Honolulu County	19	0.67
Pumpkin Center, NC (cdp) Onslow County	15	0.67
Sherman, MN (township) Redwood County	2	0.66
National City, CA (city) San Diego County	351	0.65
Silverdale, WA (cdp) Kitsap County	103	0.65
Taft Mosswood, CA (cdp) San Joaquin County	9	0.65
Mendon, MI (village) Saint Joseph County	6	0.65
Grayson, GA (city) Gwinnett County	5	0.65
Albion, WA (town) Whitman County	4	0.65
Aberdeen Proving Ground, MD (cdp) Harford County	20	0.64
North Yelm, WA (cdp) Thurston County	18	0.64
Dixon, MO (city) Pulaski County	10	0.64
Nescopeck, PA (township) Luzerne County	6	0.64
Erhards Grove, MN (township) Otter Tail County	3	0.64
Lemon Grove, CA (city) San Diego County	158	0.63
Fort Belvoir, VA (cdp) Fairfax County	45	0.63
McChord AFB, WA (cdp) Pierce County	26	0.63
Ellijay, GA (city) Gilmer County	10	0.63
Gabbs, NV (city) Nye County	2	0.63
Redings Mill, MO (village) Newton County	1	0.63
Oak Harbor, WA (city) Island County	123	0.62
Newtown, IN (town) Fountain County	1	0.62
Wahiawa, HI (cdp) Honolulu County	99	0.61
Paukaa, HI (cdp) Hawaii County	3	0.61
Spring Valley, CA (cdp) San Diego County	161	0.60
Remsenburg-Speonk, NY (cdp) Suffolk County	16	0.60
Sidney, IN (town) Kosciusko County	1	0.60
Valley Springs, AR (town) Boone County	1	0.60
Killeen, TX (city) Bell County	516	0.59
Barstow, CA (city) San Bernardino County	125	0.59
Warsaw, NC (town) Duplin County	18	0.59
Skidmore, TX (cdp) Bee County	6	0.59
Valley Acres, CA (cdp) Kern County	3	0.59
Luther, MI (village) Lake County	2	0.59
Ewa Beach, HI (cdp) Honolulu County	85	0.58
Waialua, HI (cdp) Honolulu County	22	0.58
Baldwin, GA (city) Habersham County	14	0.58
Haleiwa, HI (cdp) Honolulu County	13	0.58
Ainaloa, HI (cdp) Hawaii County	11	0.58
Iona, MN (city) Murray County	1	0.58
Lakewood, WA (city) Pierce County	331	0.57
Mililani Town, HI (cdp) Honolulu County	163	0.57
Schofield Barracks, HI (cdp) Honolulu County	82	0.57
Kaneohe Station, HI (cdp) Honolulu County	68	0.57
Whitmore Village, HI (cdp) Honolulu County	23	0.57
Du Pont, WA (city) Pierce County	14	0.57
North Edwards, CA (cdp) Kern County	7	0.57
Queen Anne, MD (town) Queen Anne's County	1	0.57
Lemoore Station, CA (cdp) Kings County	32	0.56
Nanawale Estates, HI (cdp) Hawaii County	6	0.56
Selbyville, DE (town) Sussex County	9	0.55
Fallon Station, NV (cdp) Churchill County	7	0.55
Driggs, ID (city) Teton County	6	0.55
Lacey, WA (city) Thurston County	169	0.54

Notes: (cdp) census designated place; Refer to the Explanation of Data in the front of the book for more detailed information.

Hawaii Native/Pacific Islander: Guamanian or Chamorro

Top 150 Places Sorted by Percent

(Based on places with populations of 10,000 or more)

Place	Number	%
Spanaway, WA (cdp) Pierce County	304	1.41
Marina, CA (city) Monterey County	289	1.15
Parkland, WA (cdp) Pierce County	269	1.12
Elk Plain, WA (cdp) Pierce County	160	1.02
Suisun City, CA (city) Solano County	257	0.98
La Presa, CA (cdp) San Diego County	263	0.80
Makakilo City, HI (cdp) Honolulu County	102	0.78
Morganton, NC (city) Burke County	133	0.77
Vallejo, CA (city) Solano County	890	0.76
Fairfield, CA (city) Solano County	731	0.76
Bremerton, WA (city) Kitsap County	285	0.76
Fort Lewis, WA (cdp) Pierce County	142	0.74
National City, CA (city) San Diego County	351	0.65
Silverdale, WA (cdp) Kitsap County	103	0.65
Lemon Grove, CA (city) San Diego County	158	0.63
Oak Harbor, WA (city) Island County	123	0.62
Wahiawa, HI (cdp) Honolulu County	99	0.61
Spring Valley, CA (cdp) San Diego County	161	0.60
Killeen, TX (city) Bell County	516	0.59
Barstow, CA (city) San Bernardino County	125	0.59
Ewa Beach, HI (cdp) Honolulu County	85	0.58
Lakewood, WA (city) Pierce County	331	0.57
Mililani Town, HI (cdp) Honolulu County	163	0.57
Schofield Barracks, HI (cdp) Honolulu County	82	0.57
Kaneohe Station, HI (cdp) Honolulu County	68	0.57
Lacey, WA (city) Thurston County	169	0.54
Chula Vista, CA (city) San Diego County	838	0.48
Halawa, HI (cdp) Honolulu County	66	0.48
Orchards, WA (cdp) Clark County	84	0.47
Waipio, HI (cdp) Honolulu County	55	0.47
Waimalu, HI (cdp) Honolulu County	135	0.46
Fort Campbell North, KY (cdp) Christian County	66	0.46
Fountain, CO (city) El Paso County	68	0.45
Twentynine Palms, CA (city) San Bernardino County	67	0.45
Seaside, CA (city) Monterey County	137	0.43
Security-Widefield, CO (cdp) El Paso County	128	0.43
Bonita, CA (cdp) San Diego County	53	0.43
Fort Polk South, LA (cdp) Vernon Parish	47	0.43
Waianae, HI (cdp) Honolulu County	42	0.40
Hayward, CA (city) Alameda County	530	0.38
Kailua, HI (cdp) Honolulu County	137	0.38
Bostonia, CA (cdp) San Diego County	58	0.38
Fort Hood, TX (cdp) Coryell County	126	0.37
Imperial Beach, CA (city) San Diego County	99	0.37
Alameda, CA (city) Alameda County	257	0.36
Milpitas, CA (city) Santa Clara County	228	0.36
Pearl City, HI (cdp) Honolulu County	113	0.36
Radcliff, KY (city) Hardin County	80	0.36
Fort Bragg, NC (cdp) Cumberland County	101	0.35
Ridgecrest, CA (city) Kern County	87	0.35
Five Corners, WA (cdp) Clark County	43	0.35
Nanakuli, HI (cdp) Honolulu County	38	0.35
San Leandro, CA (city) Alameda County	274	0.34
Honolulu, HI (cdp) Honolulu County	1,221	0.33
Newark, CA (city) Alameda County	140	0.33
Sierra Vista, AZ (city) Cochise County	124	0.33
Easton, MD (town) Talbot County	37	0.32
Elk Grove, CA (cdp) Sacramento County	186	0.31
La Mesa, CA (city) San Diego County	168	0.31
Rio Linda, CA (cdp) Sacramento County	32	0.31
Santee, CA (city) San Diego County	157	0.30
Carson, CA (city) Los Angeles County	264	0.29
Vacaville, CA (city) Solano County	259	0.29
Lakewood, CA (city) Los Angeles County	228	0.29
South Hill, WA (cdp) Pierce County	93	0.29
Spring Valley, NY (village) Rockland County	73	0.29
Bay Point, CA (cdp) Contra Costa County	63	0.29
Ashland, CA (cdp) Alameda County	60	0.29
Fort Leonard Wood, MO (cdp) Pulaski County	40	0.29
San Diego, CA (city) San Diego County	3,450	0.28
Tacoma, WA (city) Pierce County	536	0.28
SeaTac, WA (city) King County	71	0.28
Kihei, HI (cdp) Maui County	47	0.28
Lathrop, CA (city) San Joaquin County	29	0.28
El Cajon, CA (city) San Diego County	259	0.27
Benicia, CA (city) Solano County	73	0.27
Casa de Oro-Mount Helix, CA (cdp) San Diego County	51	0.27
Fort Carson, CO (cdp) El Paso County	28	0.27
Oceanside, CA (city) San Diego County	426	0.26
Cypress, CA (city) Orange County	118	0.26
Kaneohe, HI (cdp) Honolulu County	90	0.26
Vineyard, CA (cdp) Sacramento County	25	0.25
Waipahu, HI (cdp) Honolulu County	78	0.24
Copperas Cove, TX (city) Coryell County	72	0.24
San Lorenzo, CA (cdp) Alameda County	52	0.24
Harker Heights, TX (city) Bell County	42	0.24
Los Alamitos, CA (city) Orange County	28	0.24
Fort Morgan, CO (city) Morgan County	26	0.24
Federal Way, WA (city) King County	189	0.23
Hilo, HI (cdp) Hawaii County	95	0.23
Lompoc, CA (city) Santa Barbara County	94	0.23
Atwater, CA (city) Merced County	54	0.23
Cocoa, FL (city) Brevard County	38	0.23
Fort Knox, KY (cdp) Hardin County	29	0.23
Fort Benning South, GA (cdp) Chattahoochee County	27	0.23
Union City, CA (city) Alameda County	150	0.22
University Place, WA (city) Pierce County	67	0.22
Los Banos, CA (city) Merced County	58	0.22
Enterprise, NV (cdp) Clark County	32	0.22
Sierra Vista Southeast, AZ (cdp) Cochise County	32	0.22
Wailuku, HI (cdp) Maui County	27	0.22
Sunrise Manor, NV (cdp) Clark County	327	0.21
Vancouver, WA (city) Clark County	306	0.21
Temecula, CA (city) Riverside County	122	0.21
Tracy, CA (city) San Joaquin County	121	0.21
Fairbanks, AK (city) Fairbanks North Star Borough	63	0.21
Port Hueneme, CA (city) Ventura County	46	0.21
Immokalee, FL (cdp) Collier County	41	0.21
Fort Drum, NY (cdp) Jefferson County	25	0.21
Prairie Ridge, WA (cdp) Pierce County	25	0.21
Moreno Valley, CA (city) Riverside County	282	0.20
Poway, CA (city) San Diego County	97	0.20
Brent, FL (cdp) Escambia County	44	0.20
Junction City, KS (city) Geary County	37	0.20
Portland, TX (city) San Patricio County	30	0.20
Cherryland, CA (cdp) Alameda County	28	0.20
Alpine, CA (cdp) San Diego County	26	0.20
Carthage, MO (city) Jasper County	25	0.20
Guymon, OK (city) Texas County	21	0.20
Trenton, NJ (city) Mercer County	158	0.19
Pittsburg, CA (city) Contra Costa County	107	0.19
Yuba City, CA (city) Sutter County	69	0.19
Oakley, CA (city) Contra Costa County	48	0.19
Rancho San Diego, CA (cdp) San Diego County	38	0.19
Tukwila, WA (city) King County	33	0.19
Dixon, CA (city) Solano County	30	0.19
Cimarron Hills, CO (cdp) El Paso County	29	0.19
Long Beach, CA (city) Los Angeles County	833	0.18
Fremont, CA (city) Alameda County	373	0.18
North Las Vegas, NV (city) Clark County	203	0.18
Antioch, CA (city) Contra Costa County	165	0.18
Vista, CA (city) San Diego County	162	0.18
Buena Park, CA (city) Orange County	142	0.18
Pacifica, CA (city) San Mateo County	68	0.18
Cookeville, TN (city) Putnam County	43	0.18
Lakeside, CA (cdp) San Diego County	35	0.18
Tumwater, WA (city) Thurston County	23	0.18
Salinas, CA (city) Monterey County	250	0.17
Manteca, CA (city) San Joaquin County	85	0.17
Rome, GA (city) Floyd County	60	0.17
Laguna, CA (cdp) Sacramento County	58	0.17
Dublin, CA (city) Alameda County	51	0.17
Des Moines, WA (city) King County	50	0.17
Paine Field-Lake Stickney, WA (cdp) Snohomish County	42	0.17
Kahului, HI (cdp) Maui County	35	0.17
Lomita, CA (city) Los Angeles County	34	0.17
Lakeland North, WA (cdp) King County	25	0.17
South Yuba City, CA (cdp) Sutter County	22	0.17
Mountain Home, ID (city) Elmore County	19	0.17
Riverton-Boulevard Park, WA (cdp) King County	19	0.17

Notes: (cdp) census designated place; Refer to the Explanation of Data in the front of the book for more detailed information.

Hawaii Native/Pacific Islander: Other Micronesian

Top 150 Places Sorted by Number

(Based on all places, regardless of population)

Place	Number	%
Honolulu, HI (cdp) Honolulu County	4,106	1.10
Springdale, AR (city) Washington County	719	1.57
Portland, OR (city) Multnomah County	588	0.11
Hilo, HI (cdp) Hawaii County	469	1.15
Waipahu, HI (cdp) Honolulu County	443	1.34
Kahului, HI (cdp) Maui County	432	2.14
Salem, OR (city) Marion County	418	0.31
Costa Mesa, CA (city) Orange County	301	0.28
Enid, OK (city) Garfield County	256	0.54
Waimalu, HI (cdp) Honolulu County	238	0.81
San Diego, CA (city) San Diego County	207	0.02
Wahiawa, HI (cdp) Honolulu County	151	0.93
Halawa, HI (cdp) Honolulu County	142	1.02
Tigard, OR (city) Washington County	136	0.33
Pearl City, HI (cdp) Honolulu County	134	0.43
Kansas City, MO (city) Jackson County	130	0.03
West Valley City, UT (city) Salt Lake County	117	0.11
Keene, TX (city) Johnson County	113	2.26
Tucson, AZ (city) Pima County	113	0.02
Phoenix, AZ (city) Maricopa County	111	0.01
Wailuku, HI (cdp) Maui County	101	0.82
Denver, CO (city) Denver County	101	0.02
Tempe, AZ (city) Maricopa County	99	0.06
Four Corners, OR (cdp) Marion County	97	0.70
Tampa, FL (city) Hillsborough County	96	0.03
Kailua, HI (cdp) Hawaii County	94	0.95
Reno, NV (city) Washoe County	94	0.05
Neosho, MO (city) Newton County	92	0.88
Kaneohe, HI (cdp) Honolulu County	92	0.26
Haliimaile, HI (cdp) Maui County	89	9.94
Sacramento, CA (city) Sacramento County	85	0.02
Seattle, WA (city) King County	85	0.02
San Jose, CA (city) Santa Clara County	83	0.01
La Grande, OR (city) Union County	78	0.63
Hauula, HI (cdp) Honolulu County	75	2.05
Corsicana, TX (city) Navarro County	75	0.31
Waikoloa Village, HI (cdp) Hawaii County	73	1.52
Susanville, CA (city) Lassen County	72	0.53
Hayesville, OR (cdp) Marion County	70	0.38
Spokane, WA (city) Spokane County	70	0.04
Federal Way, WA (city) King County	69	0.08
New York, NY (city) New York City	66	0.00
Honaunau-Napoopoo, HI (cdp) Hawaii County	60	2.49
Ewa Beach, HI (cdp) Honolulu County	60	0.41
Everett, WA (city) Snohomish County	59	0.06
Fayetteville, AR (city) Washington County	58	0.10
Springfield, OR (city) Lane County	57	0.11
Waipio Acres, HI (cdp) Honolulu County	55	1.04
Las Vegas, NV (city) Clark County	55	0.01
Fort Lewis, WA (cdp) Pierce County	52	0.27
Kailua, HI (cdp) Honolulu County	51	0.14
Gresham, OR (city) Multnomah County	49	0.05
Fort Bragg, NC (cdp) Cumberland County	47	0.16
Auburn, WA (city) King County	47	0.12
Hayward, CA (city) Alameda County	47	0.03
San Bernardino, CA (city) San Bernardino County	47	0.03
Mesa, AZ (city) Maricopa County	46	0.01
Mililani Town, HI (cdp) Honolulu County	45	0.16
Stockton, CA (city) San Joaquin County	45	0.02
Hawaiian Ocean View, HI (cdp) Hawaii County	44	2.02
Fort Hood, TX (cdp) Coryell County	44	0.13
Altoona, IA (city) Polk County	43	0.42
Springfield, MO (city) Greene County	43	0.03
Chula Vista, CA (city) San Diego County	42	0.02
Gladstone, MO (city) Clay County	41	0.16
Los Angeles, CA (city) Los Angeles County	41	0.00
Waipio, HI (cdp) Honolulu County	40	0.34
Parkville, MO (city) Platte County	39	0.96
Lowell, AR (city) Benton County	39	0.78
Des Moines, WA (city) King County	39	0.13
Lakewood, WA (city) Pierce County	39	0.07
SeaTac, WA (city) King County	38	0.15
Orlando, FL (city) Orange County	38	0.02
Kalaoa, HI (cdp) Hawaii County	37	0.54
Hawaiian Paradise Park, HI (cdp) Hawaii County	37	0.52
Marshall, MO (city) Saline County	37	0.30
Jacksonville, FL (special city) Duval County	37	0.01
Orchidlands Estates, HI (cdp) Hawaii County	36	2.08
Cleburne, TX (city) Johnson County	36	0.14
Anchorage, AK (municipality) Anchorage Borough	36	0.01
San Francisco, CA (city) San Francisco County	36	0.00
Waihee-Waiehu, HI (cdp) Maui County	35	0.48
Monmouth, OR (city) Polk County	35	0.45
Makakilo City, HI (cdp) Honolulu County	35	0.27
Kent, WA (city) King County	35	0.04
Eugene, OR (city) Lane County	35	0.03
Boise City, ID (city) Ada County	35	0.02
Lincoln, NE (city) Lancaster County	35	0.02
Holualoa, HI (cdp) Hawaii County	34	0.56
Beaverton, OR (city) Washington County	34	0.04
Lawton, OK (city) Comanche County	34	0.04
San Leandro, CA (city) Alameda County	34	0.04
Clarksville, TN (city) Montgomery County	34	0.03
Santa Ana, CA (city) Orange County	34	0.01
Kihei, HI (cdp) Maui County	33	0.20
Huntington Beach, CA (city) Orange County	33	0.02
Arlington, TX (city) Tarrant County	33	0.01
Houston, TX (city) Harris County	33	0.00
San Antonio, TX (city) Bexar County	33	0.00
Raytown, MO (city) Jackson County	32	0.11
Bremerton, WA (city) Kitsap County	32	0.09
Cedar Rapids, IA (city) Linn County	32	0.03
Concord, CA (city) Contra Costa County	32	0.03
Durham, NC (city) Durham County	32	0.02
Nanakuli, HI (cdp) Honolulu County	31	0.29
Irving, TX (city) Dallas County	31	0.02
Oceanside, CA (city) San Diego County	31	0.02
Aurora, CO (city) Arapahoe County	31	0.01
Long Beach, CA (city) Los Angeles County	30	0.01
Honalo, HI (cdp) Hawaii County	29	1.46
Riverton-Boulevard Park, WA (cdp) King County	29	0.26
Pittsburg, KS (city) Crawford County	29	0.15
Newport News, VA (independent city) Newport News city	29	0.02
Ainaloa, HI (cdp) Hawaii County	28	1.47
Captain Cook, HI (cdp) Hawaii County	28	0.87
Chico, CA (city) Butte County	28	0.05
Salt Lake City, UT (city) Salt Lake County	28	0.02
Vancouver, WA (city) Clark County	28	0.02
Virginia Beach, VA (independent city) Virginia Beach city	28	0.01
Village Park, HI (cdp) Honolulu County	27	0.28
Dodge City, KS (city) Ford County	27	0.11
Tacoma, WA (city) Pierce County	27	0.01
Waianae, HI (cdp) Honolulu County	26	0.25
Miami, OK (city) Ottawa County	26	0.19
Dubuque, IA (city) Dubuque County	26	0.05
Shoreline, WA (city) King County	26	0.05
Edmond, OK (city) Oklahoma County	26	0.04
Orem, UT (city) Utah County	26	0.03
Colorado Springs, CO (city) El Paso County	26	0.01
Chicago, IL (city) Cook County	26	0.00
Kahaluu-Keauhou, HI (cdp) Hawaii County	25	1.04
Killeen, TX (city) Bell County	25	0.03
Charlotte, NC (city) Mecklenburg County	25	0.00
Waimea, HI (cdp) Hawaii County	24	0.34
Eureka, CA (city) Humboldt County	24	0.09
Keizer, OR (city) Marion County	24	0.07
San Mateo, CA (city) San Mateo County	24	0.03
Westminster, CA (city) Orange County	24	0.03
Vallejo, CA (city) Solano County	24	0.02
Paradise, NV (cdp) Clark County	24	0.01
Schofield Barracks, HI (cdp) Honolulu County	23	0.16
Marina, CA (city) Monterey County	23	0.09
Altadena, CA (cdp) Los Angeles County	23	0.05
Sparks, NV (city) Washoe County	23	0.03
Greensboro, NC (city) Guilford County	23	0.01
Clearfield, UT (city) Davis County	22	0.08
Tualatin, OR (city) Washington County	21	0.09
Lacey, WA (city) Thurston County	21	0.07
Monterey, CA (city) Monterey County	21	0.07
Provo, UT (city) Utah County	21	0.02

Notes: (cdp) census designated place; Refer to the Explanation of Data in the front of the book for more detailed information.

Hawaii Native/Pacific Islander: Other Micronesian

Top 150 Places Sorted by Percent

(Based on all places, regardless of population)

Place	Number	%
Haliimaile, HI (cdp) Maui County	89	9.94
Adair Village, OR (city) Benton County	16	2.99
Cavour, SD (town) Beadle County	4	2.84
Retreat, TX (town) Navarro County	9	2.65
Alto Bonito, TX (cdp) Starr County	15	2.64
Kapalua, HI (cdp) Maui County	12	2.57
Honaunau-Napoopoo, HI (cdp) Hawaii County	60	2.49
Keene, TX (city) Johnson County	113	2.26
Eden Roc, HI (cdp) Hawaii County	10	2.22
Kahului, HI (cdp) Maui County	432	2.14
Orchidlands Estates, HI (cdp) Hawaii County	36	2.08
Hauula, HI (cdp) Honolulu County	75	2.05
Hawaiian Ocean View, HI (cdp) Hawaii County	44	2.02
Springdale, AR (city) Washington County	719	1.57
Waikoloa Village, HI (cdp) Hawaii County	73	1.52
Waikapu, HI (cdp) Maui County	17	1.52
Laupahoehoe, HI (cdp) Hawaii County	7	1.48
Ainaloa, HI (cdp) Hawaii County	28	1.47
Honalo, HI (cdp) Hawaii County	29	1.46
Waipahu, HI (cdp) Honolulu County	443	1.34
Nanawale Estates, HI (cdp) Hawaii County	14	1.30
Papaikou, HI (cdp) Hawaii County	18	1.27
Hilo, HI (cdp) Hawaii County	469	1.15
Pepeekeo, HI (cdp) Hawaii County	19	1.12
Medicine Lake, MT (town) Sheridan County	3	1.12
Honolulu, HI (cdp) Honolulu County	4,106	1.10
Waipio Acres, HI (cdp) Honolulu County	55	1.04
Kahaluu-Keauhou, HI (cdp) Hawaii County	25	1.04
Halawa, HI (cdp) Honolulu County	142	1.02
Parkville, MO (city) Platte County	39	0.96
Kailua, HI (cdp) Hawaii County	94	0.95
Butler, MN (township) Otter Tail County	3	0.95
Wahiawa, HI (cdp) Honolulu County	151	0.93
Honomu, HI (cdp) Hawaii County	5	0.92
Jadis, MN (township) Roseau County	5	0.89
Neosho, MO (city) Newton County	92	0.88
Captain Cook, HI (cdp) Hawaii County	28	0.87
Kealakekua, HI (cdp) Hawaii County	14	0.85
Wailuku, HI (cdp) Maui County	101	0.82
Valley Hi, OH (village) Logan County	2	0.82
Waimalu, HI (cdp) Honolulu County	238	0.81
Wainaku, HI (cdp) Hawaii County	10	0.81
Dunkerton, IA (city) Black Hawk County	6	0.80
Lowell, AR (city) Benton County	39	0.78
Pahoa, HI (cdp) Hawaii County	7	0.73
Norwich, MI (township) Newaygo County	4	0.72
Four Corners, OR (cdp) Marion County	97	0.70
Watson, AR (city) Desha County	2	0.69
Garrett, TX (town) Ellis County	3	0.67
Albion, WA (town) Whitman County	4	0.65
La Grande, OR (city) Union County	78	0.63
Adak, AK (cdp) Aleutians West Census Area	2	0.63
Lanai City, HI (cdp) Maui County	19	0.60
Mulberry Grove, IL (village) Bond County	4	0.60
Angus, TX (city) Navarro County	2	0.60
Holualoa, HI (cdp) Hawaii County	34	0.56
Enid, OK (city) Garfield County	256	0.54
Kalaoa, HI (cdp) Hawaii County	37	0.54
Beulah, ND (city) Mercer County	17	0.54
Honokaa, HI (cdp) Hawaii County	12	0.54
Medicine Park, OK (town) Comanche County	2	0.54
Susanville, CA (city) Lassen County	72	0.53
Paradise, UT (town) Cache County	4	0.53
Hawaiian Paradise Park, HI (cdp) Hawaii County	37	0.52
Sandnes, MN (township) Yellow Medicine County	1	0.51
Waihee-Waiehu, HI (cdp) Maui County	35	0.48
Pine Lake, GA (city) De Kalb County	3	0.48
Saint Francis, KS (city) Cheyenne County	7	0.47
Waimanalo, HI (cdp) Honolulu County	17	0.46
Monmouth, OR (city) Polk County	35	0.45
Kaaawa, HI (cdp) Honolulu County	6	0.45
Punaluu, HI (cdp) Honolulu County	4	0.45
Scranton, AR (city) Logan County	1	0.45
Pearl City, HI (cdp) Honolulu County	134	0.43
Bayou La Batre, AL (city) Mobile County	10	0.43
Panora, IA (city) Guthrie County	5	0.43
Altoona, IA (city) Polk County	43	0.42
Ewa Beach, HI (cdp) Honolulu County	60	0.41
Willow, WI (town) Richland County	2	0.41
Paia, HI (cdp) Maui County	10	0.40
Leola, AR (town) Grant County	2	0.39
Hayesville, OR (cdp) Marion County	70	0.38
Laie, HI (cdp) Honolulu County	17	0.37
Anahola, HI (cdp) Kauai County	7	0.36
Bergland, MI (township) Ontonagon County	2	0.36
Watson, NY (town) Lewis County	7	0.35
Echo Lake, WA (cdp) Snohomish County	3	0.35
Waipio, HI (cdp) Honolulu County	40	0.34
Waimea, HI (cdp) Hawaii County	24	0.34
Donnelsville, OH (village) Clark County	1	0.34
Wells, MI (township) Marquette County	1	0.34
Tigard, OR (city) Washington County	136	0.33
Elk Ridge, UT (town) Utah County	6	0.33
Milburn, OK (town) Johnston County	2	0.32
Taconite, MN (city) Itasca County	1	0.32
Salem, OR (city) Marion County	418	0.31
Corsicana, TX (city) Navarro County	75	0.31
Fairview, NY (cdp) Westchester County	9	0.31
Marshall, MO (city) Saline County	37	0.30
Lyons, OR (city) Linn County	3	0.30
Galena, AK (city) Yukon-Koyukuk Census Area	2	0.30
Nanakuli, HI (cdp) Honolulu County	31	0.29
Maili, HI (cdp) Honolulu County	17	0.29
Baldwin, GA (city) Habersham County	7	0.29
Eleele, HI (cdp) Kauai County	6	0.29
Kilauea, HI (cdp) Kauai County	6	0.29
Leilani Estates, HI (cdp) Hawaii County	3	0.29
Bronson, KS (city) Bourbon County	1	0.29
Marshall, AK (city) Wade Hampton Census Area	1	0.29
Stanton, ND (city) Mercer County	1	0.29
Costa Mesa, CA (city) Orange County	301	0.28
Village Park, HI (cdp) Honolulu County	27	0.28
Williamstown, KY (city) Grant County	9	0.28
Hawaiian Acres, HI (cdp) Hawaii County	5	0.28
Waimea, HI (cdp) Kauai County	5	0.28
Hana, HI (cdp) Maui County	2	0.28
Waikane, HI (cdp) Honolulu County	2	0.28
Fort Lewis, WA (cdp) Pierce County	52	0.27
Makakilo City, HI (cdp) Honolulu County	35	0.27
Volcano, HI (cdp) Hawaii County	6	0.27
Bell Hill, WA (cdp) Clallam County	2	0.27
Kaneohe, HI (cdp) Honolulu County	92	0.26
Riverton-Boulevard Park, WA (cdp) King County	29	0.26
Pukalani, HI (cdp) Maui County	19	0.26
Johnson, AR (city) Washington County	6	0.26
Sandstone, MN (city) Pine County	4	0.26
Waianae, HI (cdp) Honolulu County	26	0.25
Maquoketa, IA (city) Jackson County	15	0.25
Keaau, HI (cdp) Hawaii County	5	0.25
Omao, HI (cdp) Kauai County	3	0.25
Edgewater, FL (cdp) Broward County	2	0.25
East Porterville, CA (cdp) Tulare County	16	0.24
Hanamaulu, HI (cdp) Kauai County	8	0.24
Kahuku, HI (cdp) Honolulu County	5	0.24
Elk Rapids, MI (village) Antrim County	4	0.24
Dafter, MI (township) Chippewa County	3	0.23
Pella, WI (town) Shawano County	2	0.23
Selmer, TN (town) McNairy County	10	0.22
Hawaiian Beaches, HI (cdp) Hawaii County	8	0.22
Kaunakakai, HI (cdp) Maui County	6	0.22
Saint George, MN (township) Benton County	2	0.22
Fort Riley North, KS (cdp) Geary County	17	0.21
Haiku-Pauwela, HI (cdp) Maui County	14	0.21
Belle Plaine, IA (city) Benton County	6	0.21
Mountain View, HI (cdp) Hawaii County	6	0.21
Leupp, AZ (cdp) Coconino County	2	0.21
Sand Point, AK (city) Aleutians East Borough	2	0.21
Pakala Village, HI (cdp) Kauai County	1	0.21
Kihei, HI (cdp) Maui County	33	0.20
Kapaa, HI (cdp) Kauai County	19	0.20

Notes: (cdp) census designated place; Refer to the Explanation of Data in the front of the book for more detailed information.

Hawaii Native/Pacific Islander: Other Micronesian

Top 150 Places Sorted by Percent

(Based on places with populations of 10,000 or more)

Place	Number	%
Kahului, HI (cdp) Maui County	432	2.14
Springdale, AR (city) Washington County	719	1.57
Waipahu, HI (cdp) Honolulu County	443	1.34
Hilo, HI (cdp) Hawaii County	469	1.15
Honolulu, HI (cdp) Honolulu County	4,106	1.10
Halawa, HI (cdp) Honolulu County	142	1.02
Wahiawa, HI (cdp) Honolulu County	151	0.93
Neosho, MO (city) Newton County	92	0.88
Wailuku, HI (cdp) Maui County	101	0.82
Waimalu, HI (cdp) Honolulu County	238	0.81
Four Corners, OR (cdp) Marion County	97	0.70
La Grande, OR (city) Union County	78	0.63
Enid, OK (city) Garfield County	256	0.54
Susanville, CA (city) Lassen County	72	0.53
Pearl City, HI (cdp) Honolulu County	134	0.43
Altoona, IA (city) Polk County	43	0.42
Ewa Beach, HI (cdp) Honolulu County	60	0.41
Hayesville, OR (cdp) Marion County	70	0.38
Waipio, HI (cdp) Honolulu County	40	0.34
Tigard, OR (city) Washington County	136	0.33
Salem, OR (city) Marion County	418	0.31
Corsicana, TX (city) Navarro County	75	0.31
Marshall, MO (city) Saline County	37	0.30
Nanakuli, HI (cdp) Honolulu County	31	0.29
Costa Mesa, CA (city) Orange County	301	0.28
Fort Lewis, WA (cdp) Pierce County	52	0.27
Makakilo City, HI (cdp) Honolulu County	35	0.27
Kaneohe, HI (cdp) Honolulu County	92	0.26
Riverton-Boulevard Park, WA (cdp) King County	29	0.26
Waianae, HI (cdp) Honolulu County	26	0.25
Kihei, HI (cdp) Maui County	33	0.20
Miami, OK (city) Ottawa County	26	0.19
Fort Bragg, NC (cdp) Cumberland County	47	0.16
Mililani Town, HI (cdp) Honolulu County	45	0.16
Gladstone, MO (city) Clay County	41	0.16
Schofield Barracks, HI (cdp) Honolulu County	23	0.16
SeaTac, WA (city) King County	38	0.15
Pittsburg, KS (city) Crawford County	29	0.15
Kailua, HI (cdp) Honolulu County	51	0.14
Cleburne, TX (city) Johnson County	36	0.14
Kaneohe Station, HI (cdp) Honolulu County	16	0.14
Fort Hood, TX (cdp) Coryell County	44	0.13
Des Moines, WA (city) King County	39	0.13
Fort Drum, NY (cdp) Jefferson County	16	0.13
Auburn, WA (city) King County	47	0.12
Fort Carson, CO (cdp) El Paso County	13	0.12
Portland, OR (city) Multnomah County	588	0.11
West Valley City, UT (city) Salt Lake County	117	0.11
Springfield, OR (city) Lane County	57	0.11
Raytown, MO (city) Jackson County	32	0.11
Dodge City, KS (city) Ford County	27	0.11
Fort Benning South, GA (cdp) Chattahoochee County	13	0.11
Fayetteville, AR (city) Washington County	58	0.10
Gladstone, OR (city) Clackamas County	12	0.10
Fort Madison, IA (city) Lee County	11	0.10
Bremerton, WA (city) Kitsap County	32	0.09
Eureka, CA (city) Humboldt County	24	0.09
Marina, CA (city) Monterey County	23	0.09
Tualatin, OR (city) Washington County	21	0.09
Brent, FL (cdp) Escambia County	20	0.09
Port Angeles, WA (city) Clallam County	16	0.09
Aberdeen, WA (city) Grays Harbor County	15	0.09
Fort Polk South, LA (cdp) Vernon Parish	10	0.09
Federal Way, WA (city) King County	69	0.08
Clearfield, UT (city) Davis County	22	0.08
Le Ray, NY (town) Jefferson County	16	0.08
Mountlake Terrace, WA (city) Snohomish County	16	0.08
Fort Campbell North, KY (cdp) Christian County	12	0.08
Clinton, UT (city) Davis County	10	0.08
Lea Hill, WA (cdp) King County	9	0.08
Halfway, MD (cdp) Washington County	8	0.08
Lakewood, WA (city) Pierce County	39	0.07
Keizer, OR (city) Marion County	24	0.07
Lacey, WA (city) Thurston County	21	0.07
Monterey, CA (city) Monterey County	21	0.07
Sun Valley, NV (cdp) Washoe County	14	0.07
Newton, IA (city) Jasper County	11	0.07
Dallas, OR (city) Polk County	9	0.07
Conning Towers-Nautilus Park, CT (cdp) New London County	7	0.07
Tempe, AZ (city) Maricopa County	99	0.06
Everett, WA (city) Snohomish County	59	0.06
Millcreek, UT (cdp) Salt Lake County	19	0.06
University Place, WA (city) Pierce County	19	0.06
Parkland, WA (cdp) Pierce County	14	0.06
South Salt Lake, UT (city) Salt Lake County	14	0.06
Ashland, CA (cdp) Alameda County	13	0.06
Spanaway, WA (cdp) Pierce County	12	0.06
Montclair, VA (cdp) Prince William County	10	0.06
Enterprise, NV (cdp) Clark County	9	0.06
Walnut Park, CA (cdp) Los Angeles County	9	0.06
Alpena, MI (city) Alpena County	7	0.06
La Riviera, CA (cdp) Sacramento County	6	0.06
Reno, NV (city) Washoe County	94	0.05
Gresham, OR (city) Multnomah County	49	0.05
Chico, CA (city) Butte County	28	0.05
Dubuque, IA (city) Dubuque County	26	0.05
Shoreline, WA (city) King County	26	0.05
Altadena, CA (cdp) Los Angeles County	23	0.05
West Sacramento, CA (city) Yolo County	16	0.05
Hinesville, GA (city) Liberty County	15	0.05
Coronado, CA (city) San Diego County	13	0.05
Summerville, SC (town) Dorchester County	13	0.05
Altus, OK (city) Jackson County	11	0.05
Magna, UT (cdp) Salt Lake County	11	0.05
Oak Ridge, FL (cdp) Orange County	11	0.05
Oak Harbor, WA (city) Island County	10	0.05
Sherrelwood, CO (cdp) Adams County	9	0.05
Coos Bay, OR (city) Coos County	7	0.05
Kaukauna, WI (city) Outagamie County	6	0.05
Moss Bluff, LA (cdp) Calcasieu Parish	5	0.05
Shiloh, PA (cdp) York County	5	0.05
South Lyon, MI (city) Oakland County	5	0.05
Spring Creek, NV (cdp) Elko County	5	0.05
Spokane, WA (city) Spokane County	70	0.04
Kent, WA (city) King County	35	0.04
Beaverton, OR (city) Washington County	34	0.04
Lawton, OK (city) Comanche County	34	0.04
San Leandro, CA (city) Alameda County	34	0.04
Edmond, OK (city) Oklahoma County	26	0.04
Fountain Valley, CA (city) Orange County	20	0.04
Highland, CA (city) San Bernardino County	17	0.04
Edmonds, WA (city) Snohomish County	16	0.04
Hillsborough, NJ (township) Somerset County	15	0.04
Laguna, CA (cdp) Sacramento County	14	0.04
Englewood, CO (city) Arapahoe County	13	0.04
Riverton, UT (city) Salt Lake County	11	0.04
Marshalltown, IA (city) Marshall County	10	0.04
Hudson, NH (town) Hillsborough County	9	0.04
Morristown, TN (city) Hamblen County	9	0.04
Pullman, WA (city) Whitman County	9	0.04
Grand Chute, WI (town) Outagamie County	8	0.04
Holiday, FL (cdp) Pasco County	8	0.04
Port Hueneme, CA (city) Ventura County	8	0.04
Homewood, IL (village) Cook County	7	0.04
Loma Linda, CA (city) San Bernardino County	7	0.04
Newberg, OR (city) Yamhill County	7	0.04
Tukwila, WA (city) King County	7	0.04
Arlington, WA (city) Snohomish County	5	0.04
Cornelius, NC (town) Mecklenburg County	5	0.04
Highlands, NY (town) Orange County	5	0.04
Patton, PA (township) Centre County	5	0.04
Pineville, LA (city) Rapides Parish	5	0.04
Beaumont, CA (city) Riverside County	4	0.04
Berkley, CO (cdp) Adams County	4	0.04
Fort Stewart, GA (cdp) Liberty County	4	0.04
Lexington Park, MD (cdp) Saint Mary's County	4	0.04
Ontario, OR (city) Malheur County	4	0.04
Kansas City, MO (city) Jackson County	130	0.03
Tampa, FL (city) Hillsborough County	96	0.03
Hayward, CA (city) Alameda County	47	0.03

Notes: (cdp) census designated place; Refer to the Explanation of Data in the front of the book for more detailed information.

Hawaii Native/Pacific Islander: Polynesian

Top 150 Places Sorted by Number

(Based on all places, regardless of population)

Place	Number	%
Honolulu, HI (cdp) Honolulu County	53,905	14.50
Hilo, HI (cdp) Hawaii County	13,514	33.16
Kaneohe, HI (cdp) Honolulu County	10,918	31.22
Kailua, HI (cdp) Honolulu County	9,008	24.67
Nanakuli, HI (cdp) Honolulu County	8,559	79.15
Waipahu, HI (cdp) Honolulu County	7,226	21.83
Los Angeles, CA (city) Los Angeles County	6,994	0.19
Waianae, HI (cdp) Honolulu County	6,701	63.78
Long Beach, CA (city) Los Angeles County	6,016	1.30
Pearl City, HI (cdp) Honolulu County	5,386	17.39
San Diego, CA (city) San Diego County	5,311	0.43
Mililani Town, HI (cdp) Honolulu County	4,993	17.45
Kahului, HI (cdp) Maui County	4,986	24.75
Wahiawa, HI (cdp) Honolulu County	4,577	28.34
Waimalu, HI (cdp) Honolulu County	4,430	15.08
San Francisco, CA (city) San Francisco County	4,363	0.56
Ewa Beach, HI (cdp) Honolulu County	4,310	29.42
Makaha, HI (cdp) Honolulu County	4,274	55.13
Salt Lake City, UT (city) Salt Lake County	4,005	2.20
San Jose, CA (city) Santa Clara County	3,851	0.43
Makakilo City, HI (cdp) Honolulu County	3,757	28.56
West Valley City, UT (city) Salt Lake County	3,645	3.35
Wailuku, HI (cdp) Maui County	3,630	29.52
Maili, HI (cdp) Honolulu County	3,429	57.70
Waimanalo Beach, HI (cdp) Honolulu County	3,359	78.65
New York, NY (city) New York City	3,253	0.04
Kailua, HI (cdp) Hawaii County	3,230	32.73
Halawa, HI (cdp) Honolulu County	3,221	23.19
Las Vegas, NV (city) Clark County	3,170	0.66
Anchorage, AK (municipality) Anchorage Borough	3,118	1.20
Seattle, WA (city) King County	3,110	0.55
Laie, HI (cdp) Honolulu County	3,043	66.37
Carson, CA (city) Los Angeles County	3,025	3.37
Kihei, HI (cdp) Maui County	2,929	17.49
Sacramento, CA (city) Sacramento County	2,894	0.71
Waimea, HI (cdp) Hawaii County	2,794	39.76
Hauula, HI (cdp) Honolulu County	2,736	74.94
Kapaa, HI (cdp) Kauai County	2,725	28.77
Ahuimanu, HI (cdp) Honolulu County	2,630	30.92
Oceanside, CA (city) San Diego County	2,450	1.52
Waihee-Waiehu, HI (cdp) Maui County	2,399	32.82
Oakland, CA (city) Alameda County	2,294	0.57
Hawaiian Paradise Park, HI (cdp) Hawaii County	2,228	31.60
East Palo Alto, CA (city) San Mateo County	2,086	7.07
Waipio, HI (cdp) Honolulu County	2,073	17.76
Waimanalo, HI (cdp) Honolulu County	2,046	55.84
Tacoma, WA (city) Pierce County	2,024	1.05
Phoenix, AZ (city) Maricopa County	2,023	0.15
Lahaina, HI (cdp) Maui County	1,969	21.59
Pukalani, HI (cdp) Maui County	1,896	25.69
Village Park, HI (cdp) Honolulu County	1,888	19.62
Kalaoa, HI (cdp) Hawaii County	1,884	27.73
Makawao, HI (cdp) Maui County	1,854	29.30
Hayward, CA (city) Alameda County	1,779	1.27
Portland, OR (city) Multnomah County	1,740	0.33
Paradise, NV (cdp) Clark County	1,660	0.89
Anaheim, CA (city) Orange County	1,654	0.50
Hawaiian Beaches, HI (cdp) Hawaii County	1,599	43.11
Kaunakakai, HI (cdp) Maui County	1,590	58.33
Haiku-Pauwela, HI (cdp) Maui County	1,493	22.70
San Mateo, CA (city) San Mateo County	1,493	1.61
Provo, UT (city) Utah County	1,488	1.41
Aiea, HI (cdp) Honolulu County	1,428	15.83
Anahola, HI (cdp) Kauai County	1,402	72.57
Kualapuu, HI (cdp) Maui County	1,374	70.97
Chicago, IL (city) Cook County	1,303	0.04
Waipio Acres, HI (cdp) Honolulu County	1,280	24.16
Waikoloa Village, HI (cdp) Hawaii County	1,262	26.26
Kahaluu, HI (cdp) Honolulu County	1,260	42.93
Mesa, AZ (city) Maricopa County	1,259	0.32
Maunawili, HI (cdp) Honolulu County	1,224	25.14
Garden Grove, CA (city) Orange County	1,221	0.74
Henderson, NV (city) Clark County	1,216	0.69
Kahuku, HI (cdp) Honolulu County	1,209	57.65
Santa Ana, CA (city) Orange County	1,198	0.35
Heeia, HI (cdp) Honolulu County	1,190	24.07
Riverside, CA (city) Riverside County	1,157	0.45
Lakewood, WA (city) Pierce County	1,154	1.98
Daly City, CA (city) San Mateo County	1,145	1.10
Mountain View, HI (cdp) Hawaii County	1,131	40.41
Reno, NV (city) Washoe County	1,110	0.62
Holualoa, HI (cdp) Hawaii County	1,101	18.03
Napili-Honokowai, HI (cdp) Maui County	1,091	16.07
Orem, UT (city) Utah County	1,090	1.29
Taylorsville, UT (city) Salt Lake County	1,084	1.89
Lihue, HI (cdp) Kauai County	1,066	18.79
Compton, CA (city) Los Angeles County	1,046	1.12
Wailua Homesteads, HI (cdp) Kauai County	1,032	22.60
Stockton, CA (city) San Joaquin County	1,003	0.41
Fremont, CA (city) Alameda County	995	0.49
San Bruno, CA (city) San Mateo County	968	2.41
Kekaha, HI (cdp) Kauai County	965	30.39
Vallejo, CA (city) Solano County	965	0.83
Sunrise Manor, NV (cdp) Clark County	952	0.61
Federal Way, WA (city) King County	934	1.12
Euless, TX (city) Tarrant County	925	2.01
South San Francisco, CA (city) San Mateo County	921	1.52
Colorado Springs, CO (city) El Paso County	915	0.25
Ewa Gentry, HI (cdp) Honolulu County	909	18.40
San Antonio, TX (city) Bexar County	896	0.08
Ewa Villages, HI (cdp) Honolulu County	878	18.52
Houston, TX (city) Harris County	877	0.04
Kearns, UT (cdp) Salt Lake County	867	2.58
Honaunau-Napoopoo, HI (cdp) Hawaii County	864	35.79
Waialua, HI (cdp) Honolulu County	847	22.52
Moreno Valley, CA (city) Riverside County	847	0.59
West Jordan, UT (city) Salt Lake County	843	1.23
Whitmore Village, HI (cdp) Honolulu County	836	20.61
Torrance, CA (city) Los Angeles County	834	0.60
Concord, CA (city) Contra Costa County	832	0.68
Hawthorne, CA (city) Los Angeles County	809	0.96
Spring Valley, NV (cdp) Clark County	809	0.69
Captain Cook, HI (cdp) Hawaii County	800	24.95
Oxnard, CA (city) Ventura County	796	0.47
Makaha Valley, HI (cdp) Honolulu County	788	61.13
Haleiwa, HI (cdp) Honolulu County	773	34.74
Chula Vista, CA (city) San Diego County	770	0.44
Vancouver, WA (city) Clark County	768	0.53
Vista, CA (city) San Diego County	766	0.85
Tucson, AZ (city) Pima County	765	0.16
Pupukea, HI (cdp) Honolulu County	762	17.93
Ainaloa, HI (cdp) Hawaii County	756	39.58
North Las Vegas, NV (city) Clark County	740	0.64
San Bernardino, CA (city) San Bernardino County	718	0.39
Redwood City, CA (city) San Mateo County	716	0.95
Fairfield, CA (city) Solano County	707	0.74
SeaTac, WA (city) King County	705	2.77
Fresno, CA (city) Fresno County	701	0.16
Denver, CO (city) Denver County	701	0.13
Paia, HI (cdp) Maui County	696	27.85
Volcano, HI (cdp) Hawaii County	695	31.15
Huntington Beach, CA (city) Orange County	692	0.36
Kent, WA (city) King County	680	0.86
Ontario, CA (city) San Bernardino County	676	0.43
Kalaheo, HI (cdp) Kauai County	674	17.22
Independence, MO (city) Jackson County	665	0.59
Hanamaulu, HI (cdp) Kauai County	662	20.23
Gardena, CA (city) Los Angeles County	658	1.14
Modesto, CA (city) Stanislaus County	654	0.35
Aurora, CO (city) Arapahoe County	639	0.23
San Leandro, CA (city) Alameda County	637	0.80
Lanai City, HI (cdp) Maui County	635	20.07
Philadelphia, PA (city) Philadelphia County	629	0.04
Waimea, HI (cdp) Kauai County	625	34.97
Kaaawa, HI (cdp) Honolulu County	618	46.68
White Center, WA (cdp) King County	592	2.82
Honalo, HI (cdp) Hawaii County	589	29.64
Union City, CA (city) Alameda County	586	0.88
Albuquerque, NM (city) Bernalillo County	572	0.13
Santa Rosa, CA (city) Sonoma County	571	0.39

Notes: (cdp) census designated place; Refer to the Explanation of Data in the front of the book for more detailed information.

Hawaii Native/Pacific Islander: Polynesian

Top 150 Places Sorted by Percent

(Based on all places, regardless of population)

Place	Number	%
Nanakuli, HI (cdp) Honolulu County	8,559	79.15
Waimanalo Beach, HI (cdp) Honolulu County	3,359	78.65
Hana, HI (cdp) Maui County	545	76.87
Hauula, HI (cdp) Honolulu County	2,736	74.94
Anahola, HI (cdp) Kauai County	1,402	72.57
Kualapuu, HI (cdp) Maui County	1,374	70.97
Laie, HI (cdp) Honolulu County	3,043	66.37
Waianae, HI (cdp) Honolulu County	6,701	63.78
Maunaloa, HI (cdp) Maui County	142	61.74
Makaha Valley, HI (cdp) Honolulu County	788	61.13
Kaunakakai, HI (cdp) Maui County	1,590	58.33
Waikane, HI (cdp) Honolulu County	419	57.71
Maili, HI (cdp) Honolulu County	3,429	57.70
Kahuku, HI (cdp) Honolulu County	1,209	57.65
Waimanalo, HI (cdp) Honolulu County	2,046	55.84
Makaha, HI (cdp) Honolulu County	4,274	55.13
Punaluu, HI (cdp) Honolulu County	472	53.58
Kaaawa, HI (cdp) Honolulu County	618	46.68
Kukuihaele, HI (cdp) Hawaii County	139	43.85
Pakala Village, HI (cdp) Kauai County	209	43.72
Hawaiian Beaches, HI (cdp) Hawaii County	1,599	43.11
Kahaluu, HI (cdp) Honolulu County	1,260	42.93
Hawi, HI (cdp) Hawaii County	391	41.68
Mountain View, HI (cdp) Hawaii County	1,131	40.41
Naalehu, HI (cdp) Hawaii County	367	39.93
Waimea, HI (cdp) Hawaii County	2,794	39.76
Nanawale Estates, HI (cdp) Hawaii County	426	39.70
Ainaloa, HI (cdp) Hawaii County	756	39.58
Halaula, HI (cdp) Hawaii County	185	37.37
Honaunau-Napoopoo, HI (cdp) Hawaii County	864	35.79
Waimea, HI (cdp) Kauai County	625	34.97
Pahala, HI (cdp) Hawaii County	481	34.91
Haleiwa, HI (cdp) Honolulu County	773	34.74
Kapaau, HI (cdp) Hawaii County	399	34.43
Hilo, HI (cdp) Hawaii County	13,514	33.16
Waihee-Waiehu, HI (cdp) Maui County	2,399	32.82
Kailua, HI (cdp) Hawaii County	3,230	32.73
Hawaiian Paradise Park, HI (cdp) Hawaii County	2,228	31.60
Kaneohe, HI (cdp) Honolulu County	10,918	31.22
Fern Acres, HI (cdp) Hawaii County	236	31.22
Volcano, HI (cdp) Hawaii County	695	31.15
Ahuimanu, HI (cdp) Honolulu County	2,630	30.92
Kekaha, HI (cdp) Kauai County	965	30.39
Pahoa, HI (cdp) Hawaii County	288	29.94
Paauilo, HI (cdp) Hawaii County	170	29.77
Honalo, HI (cdp) Hawaii County	589	29.64
Wailuku, HI (cdp) Maui County	3,630	29.52
Ewa Beach, HI (cdp) Honolulu County	4,310	29.42
Makawao, HI (cdp) Maui County	1,854	29.30
Eden Roc, HI (cdp) Hawaii County	132	29.27
Kapaa, HI (cdp) Kauai County	2,725	28.77
Makakilo City, HI (cdp) Honolulu County	3,757	28.56
Wahiawa, HI (cdp) Honolulu County	4,577	28.34
Kealakekua, HI (cdp) Hawaii County	463	28.15
Paia, HI (cdp) Maui County	696	27.85
Kalaoa, HI (cdp) Hawaii County	1,884	27.73
Orchidlands Estates, HI (cdp) Hawaii County	475	27.44
Kurtistown, HI (cdp) Hawaii County	306	26.45
Waikoloa Village, HI (cdp) Hawaii County	1,262	26.26
Fern Forest, HI (cdp) Hawaii County	124	25.83
Pukalani, HI (cdp) Maui County	1,896	25.69
Waikapu, HI (cdp) Maui County	286	25.65
Laupahoehoe, HI (cdp) Hawaii County	121	25.58
Maunawili, HI (cdp) Honolulu County	1,224	25.14
Captain Cook, HI (cdp) Hawaii County	800	24.95
Kahului, HI (cdp) Maui County	4,986	24.75
Kailua, HI (cdp) Honolulu County	9,008	24.67
Hanapepe, HI (cdp) Kauai County	527	24.48
Papaikou, HI (cdp) Hawaii County	345	24.40
Waipio Acres, HI (cdp) Honolulu County	1,280	24.16
Heeia, HI (cdp) Honolulu County	1,190	24.07
Haliimaile, HI (cdp) Maui County	215	24.02
Hawaiian Acres, HI (cdp) Hawaii County	424	23.87
Wailua, HI (cdp) Kauai County	497	23.86
Hawaiian Ocean View, HI (cdp) Hawaii County	509	23.37
Halawa, HI (cdp) Honolulu County	3,221	23.19
Koloa, HI (cdp) Kauai County	447	23.02
Honomu, HI (cdp) Hawaii County	123	22.74
Haiku-Pauwela, HI (cdp) Maui County	1,493	22.70
Wailua Homesteads, HI (cdp) Kauai County	1,032	22.60
Waialua, HI (cdp) Honolulu County	847	22.52
Kapalua, HI (cdp) Maui County	104	22.27
Honokaa, HI (cdp) Hawaii County	488	21.85
Waipahu, HI (cdp) Honolulu County	7,226	21.83
Lahaina, HI (cdp) Maui County	1,969	21.59
Wainaku, HI (cdp) Hawaii County	259	21.11
Lawai, HI (cdp) Kauai County	417	21.02
Whitmore Village, HI (cdp) Honolulu County	836	20.61
Mokuleia, HI (cdp) Honolulu County	374	20.34
Hanamaulu, HI (cdp) Kauai County	662	20.23
Lanai City, HI (cdp) Maui County	635	20.07
Eleele, HI (cdp) Kauai County	409	20.05
Village Park, HI (cdp) Honolulu County	1,888	19.62
Keaau, HI (cdp) Hawaii County	392	19.50
Omao, HI (cdp) Kauai County	237	19.41
Pepeekeo, HI (cdp) Hawaii County	329	19.39
Lihue, HI (cdp) Kauai County	1,066	18.79
Ewa Villages, HI (cdp) Honolulu County	878	18.52
Leilani Estates, HI (cdp) Hawaii County	193	18.45
Ewa Gentry, HI (cdp) Honolulu County	909	18.40
Holualoa, HI (cdp) Hawaii County	1,101	18.03
Hanalei, HI (cdp) Kauai County	86	17.99
Pupukea, HI (cdp) Honolulu County	762	17.93
Waipio, HI (cdp) Honolulu County	2,073	17.76
Kihei, HI (cdp) Maui County	2,929	17.49
Mililani Town, HI (cdp) Honolulu County	4,993	17.45
Pearl City, HI (cdp) Honolulu County	5,386	17.39
Kalaheo, HI (cdp) Kauai County	674	17.22
Napili-Honokowai, HI (cdp) Maui County	1,091	16.07
Aiea, HI (cdp) Honolulu County	1,428	15.83
Kahaluu-Keauhou, HI (cdp) Hawaii County	375	15.53
Waimalu, HI (cdp) Honolulu County	4,430	15.08
Paukaa, HI (cdp) Hawaii County	73	14.75
Honolulu, HI (cdp) Honolulu County	53,905	14.50
Kilauea, HI (cdp) Kauai County	303	14.48
Puhi, HI (cdp) Kauai County	161	13.58
Kaumakani, HI (cdp) Kauai County	81	13.34
Puako, HI (cdp) Hawaii County	50	11.66
Kalihiwai, HI (cdp) Kauai County	78	10.88
Appleton, MN (city) Swift County	283	9.86
Kawela Bay, HI (cdp) Honolulu County	35	8.54
Leon, OK (town) Love County	8	8.33
Princeville, HI (cdp) Kauai County	125	7.36
East Palo Alto, CA (city) San Mateo County	2,086	7.07
Poipu, HI (cdp) Kauai County	76	7.07
Tampa, KS (city) Marion County	10	6.94
Elfin Cove, AK (cdp) Skagway-Hoonah-Angoon Census Area	2	6.25
Wailea-Makena, HI (cdp) Maui County	351	6.19
Kirkwood, CA (cdp) Alpine County	5	5.21
Doran, MN (city) Wilkin County	3	5.08
Mulhall, OK (town) Logan County	11	4.60
Watonga, OK (city) Blaine County	208	4.47
Kaanapali, HI (cdp) Maui County	56	4.07
Ranchette Estates, TX (cdp) Willacy County	5	3.76
Petersville, AK (cdp) Matanuska-Susitna Borough	1	3.70
Avon, UT (cdp) Cache County	11	3.59
Kirby, WY (town) Hot Springs County	2	3.51
Morken, MN (township) Clay County	7	3.45
Arkoe, MO (town) Nodaway County	2	3.45
Carson, CA (city) Los Angeles County	3,025	3.37
West Valley City, UT (city) Salt Lake County	3,645	3.35
Maalaea, HI (cdp) Maui County	15	3.30
Roosevelt, OK (town) Kiowa County	9	3.21
Indian Beach, NC (town) Carteret County	3	3.16
Padroni, CO (cdp) Logan County	3	3.09
Barbers Point Housing, HI (cdp) Honolulu County	2	2.99
Brandonville, WV (town) Preston County	3	2.94
White Center, WA (cdp) King County	592	2.82
Seney, MI (township) Schoolcraft County	5	2.78
SeaTac, WA (city) King County	705	2.77

Notes: (cdp) census designated place; Refer to the Explanation of Data in the front of the book for more detailed information.

Hawaii Native/Pacific Islander: Polynesian

Top 150 Places Sorted by Percent

(Based on places with populations of 10,000 or more)

Place	Number	%
Nanakuli, HI (cdp) Honolulu County	8,559	79.15
Waianae, HI (cdp) Honolulu County	6,701	63.78
Hilo, HI (cdp) Hawaii County	13,514	33.16
Kaneohe, HI (cdp) Honolulu County	10,918	31.22
Wailuku, HI (cdp) Maui County	3,630	29.52
Ewa Beach, HI (cdp) Honolulu County	4,310	29.42
Makakilo City, HI (cdp) Honolulu County	3,757	28.56
Wahiawa, HI (cdp) Honolulu County	4,577	28.34
Kahului, HI (cdp) Maui County	4,986	24.75
Kailua, HI (cdp) Honolulu County	9,008	24.67
Halawa, HI (cdp) Honolulu County	3,221	23.19
Waipahu, HI (cdp) Honolulu County	7,226	21.83
Waipio, HI (cdp) Honolulu County	2,073	17.76
Kihei, HI (cdp) Maui County	2,929	17.49
Mililani Town, HI (cdp) Honolulu County	4,993	17.45
Pearl City, HI (cdp) Honolulu County	5,386	17.39
Waimalu, HI (cdp) Honolulu County	4,430	15.08
Honolulu, HI (cdp) Honolulu County	53,905	14.50
East Palo Alto, CA (city) San Mateo County	2,086	7.07
Carson, CA (city) Los Angeles County	3,025	3.37
West Valley City, UT (city) Salt Lake County	3,645	3.35
White Center, WA (cdp) King County	592	2.82
SeaTac, WA (city) King County	705	2.77
Kearns, UT (cdp) Salt Lake County	867	2.58
San Bruno, CA (city) San Mateo County	968	2.41
Salt Lake City, UT (city) Salt Lake County	4,005	2.20
Schofield Barracks, HI (cdp) Honolulu County	293	2.03
Euless, TX (city) Tarrant County	925	2.01
Lakewood, WA (city) Pierce County	1,154	1.98
Twentynine Palms, CA (city) San Bernardino County	282	1.91
Oquirrh, UT (cdp) Salt Lake County	198	1.91
Taylorsville, UT (city) Salt Lake County	1,084	1.89
Kaneohe Station, HI (cdp) Honolulu County	217	1.83
Marina, CA (city) Monterey County	456	1.82
Riverton-Boulevard Park, WA (cdp) King County	204	1.82
Tukwila, WA (city) King County	309	1.80
West Carson, CA (cdp) Los Angeles County	355	1.68
Magna, UT (cdp) Salt Lake County	373	1.64
San Mateo, CA (city) San Mateo County	1,493	1.61
Lennox, CA (cdp) Los Angeles County	355	1.55
Oceanside, CA (city) San Diego County	2,450	1.52
South San Francisco, CA (city) San Mateo County	921	1.52
Fort Lewis, WA (cdp) Pierce County	281	1.47
Provo, UT (city) Utah County	1,488	1.41
South Salt Lake, UT (city) Salt Lake County	310	1.41
Burien, WA (city) King County	430	1.35
Des Moines, WA (city) King County	392	1.34
Menlo Park, CA (city) San Mateo County	409	1.33
Long Beach, CA (city) Los Angeles County	6,016	1.30
Orem, UT (city) Utah County	1,090	1.29
Cherryland, CA (cdp) Alameda County	178	1.29
Hayward, CA (city) Alameda County	1,779	1.27
West Jordan, UT (city) Salt Lake County	843	1.23
Ashland, CA (cdp) Alameda County	255	1.23
North Fair Oaks, CA (cdp) San Mateo County	190	1.23
Anchorage, AK (municipality) Anchorage Borough	3,118	1.20
Parkland, WA (cdp) Pierce County	288	1.20
Gardena, CA (city) Los Angeles County	658	1.14
Spanaway, WA (cdp) Pierce County	247	1.14
Millbrae, CA (city) San Mateo County	237	1.14
Compton, CA (city) Los Angeles County	1,046	1.12
Federal Way, WA (city) King County	934	1.12
Stanton, CA (city) Orange County	417	1.11
Daly City, CA (city) San Mateo County	1,145	1.10
Tacoma, WA (city) Pierce County	2,024	1.05
Elk Plain, WA (cdp) Pierce County	157	1.00
Saint George, UT (city) Washington County	494	0.99
La Presa, CA (cdp) San Diego County	321	0.98
Fort Campbell North, KY (cdp) Christian County	139	0.97
Hawthorne, CA (city) Los Angeles County	809	0.96
Pacifica, CA (city) San Mateo County	368	0.96
Redwood City, CA (city) San Mateo County	716	0.95
Lawndale, CA (city) Los Angeles County	301	0.95
Silverdale, WA (cdp) Kitsap County	150	0.95
Millcreek, UT (cdp) Salt Lake County	282	0.93
Suisun City, CA (city) Solano County	236	0.90
Paradise, NV (cdp) Clark County	1,660	0.89
Union City, CA (city) Alameda County	586	0.88
Pittsburg, CA (city) Contra Costa County	495	0.87
Kent, WA (city) King County	680	0.86
Seaside, CA (city) Monterey County	272	0.86
Vista, CA (city) San Diego County	766	0.85
Paramount, CA (city) Los Angeles County	467	0.85
Newark, CA (city) Alameda County	359	0.85
Bay Point, CA (cdp) Contra Costa County	182	0.85
Bryn Mawr-Skyway, WA (cdp) King County	119	0.85
City of The Dalles, OR (city) Wasco County	103	0.85
Vallejo, CA (city) Solano County	965	0.83
Lomita, CA (city) Los Angeles County	165	0.82
Lacey, WA (city) Thurston County	253	0.81
Hawaiian Gardens, CA (city) Los Angeles County	120	0.81
San Leandro, CA (city) Alameda County	637	0.80
Lemon Grove, CA (city) San Diego County	200	0.80
Fort Bragg, NC (cdp) Cumberland County	232	0.79
East Hill-Meridian, WA (cdp) King County	231	0.79
San Lorenzo, CA (cdp) Alameda County	173	0.79
Belmont, CA (city) San Mateo County	193	0.77
Pleasant Grove, UT (city) Utah County	178	0.76
Bellflower, CA (city) Los Angeles County	547	0.75
University Place, WA (city) Pierce County	224	0.75
Garden Grove, CA (city) Orange County	1,221	0.74
Fairfield, CA (city) Solano County	707	0.74
Fort Hood, TX (cdp) Coryell County	245	0.73
Midvale, UT (city) Salt Lake County	198	0.73
Sacramento, CA (city) Sacramento County	2,894	0.71
Fort Carson, CO (cdp) El Paso County	75	0.71
South Jordan, UT (city) Salt Lake County	206	0.70
Sun Valley, NV (cdp) Washoe County	136	0.70
Henderson, NV (city) Clark County	1,216	0.69
Spring Valley, NV (cdp) Clark County	809	0.69
Imperial Beach, CA (city) San Diego County	187	0.69
Lehi, UT (city) Utah County	131	0.69
Concord, CA (city) Contra Costa County	832	0.68
Alameda, CA (city) Alameda County	489	0.68
Lakewood, CA (city) Los Angeles County	528	0.67
Tracy, CA (city) San Joaquin County	381	0.67
Whitney, NV (cdp) Clark County	123	0.67
Las Vegas, NV (city) Clark County	3,170	0.66
Killeen, TX (city) Bell County	565	0.65
Forest Grove, OR (city) Washington County	115	0.65
North Las Vegas, NV (city) Clark County	740	0.64
Fort Drum, NY (cdp) Jefferson County	77	0.64
Auburn, WA (city) King County	254	0.63
Fairbanks, AK (city) Fairbanks North Star Borough	189	0.63
Draper, UT (city) Salt Lake County	159	0.63
Reno, NV (city) Washoe County	1,110	0.62
Florin, CA (cdp) Sacramento County	172	0.62
Sunrise Manor, NV (cdp) Clark County	952	0.61
Buena Park, CA (city) Orange County	479	0.61
Sparks, NV (city) Washoe County	403	0.61
Rancho Cordova, CA (cdp) Sacramento County	334	0.61
Rohnert Park, CA (city) Sonoma County	257	0.61
Bremerton, WA (city) Kitsap County	228	0.61
Burlingame, CA (city) San Mateo County	172	0.61
Oakley, CA (city) Contra Costa County	155	0.61
Barstow, CA (city) San Bernardino County	129	0.61
Enterprise, NV (cdp) Clark County	89	0.61
Torrance, CA (city) Los Angeles County	834	0.60
Copperas Cove, TX (city) Coryell County	177	0.60
Spring Valley, CA (cdp) San Diego County	160	0.60
Oak Harbor, WA (city) Island County	119	0.60
Moreno Valley, CA (city) Riverside County	847	0.59
Independence, MO (city) Jackson County	665	0.59
Oakland, CA (city) Alameda County	2,294	0.57
Cascade-Fairwood, WA (cdp) King County	198	0.57
Murray, UT (city) Salt Lake County	193	0.57
Juneau, AK (city and borough) Juneau Borough	174	0.57
Foothill Farms, CA (cdp) Sacramento County	100	0.57
Lathrop, CA (city) San Joaquin County	60	0.57
San Francisco, CA (city) San Francisco County	4,363	0.56

Notes: (cdp) census designated place; Refer to the Explanation of Data in the front of the book for more detailed information.

Hawaii Native/Pacific Islander: Native Hawaiian

Top 150 Places Sorted by Number

(Based on all places, regardless of population)

Place	Number	%
Honolulu, HI (cdp) Honolulu County	43,363	11.67
Hilo, HI (cdp) Hawaii County	12,951	31.77
Kaneohe, HI (cdp) Honolulu County	10,067	28.79
Kailua, HI (cdp) Honolulu County	8,390	22.98
Nanakuli, HI (cdp) Honolulu County	7,171	66.31
Waianae, HI (cdp) Honolulu County	6,021	57.31
Pearl City, HI (cdp) Honolulu County	4,596	14.84
Kahului, HI (cdp) Maui County	4,566	22.66
Mililani Town, HI (cdp) Honolulu County	4,483	15.67
Waipahu, HI (cdp) Honolulu County	4,006	12.10
Los Angeles, CA (city) Los Angeles County	3,788	0.10
Wahiawa, HI (cdp) Honolulu County	3,776	23.38
Waimalu, HI (cdp) Honolulu County	3,746	12.75
Makaha, HI (cdp) Honolulu County	3,714	47.90
Ewa Beach, HI (cdp) Honolulu County	3,473	23.71
Wailuku, HI (cdp) Maui County	3,453	28.08
Waimanalo Beach, HI (cdp) Honolulu County	3,229	75.60
Makakilo City, HI (cdp) Honolulu County	3,188	24.23
Kailua, HI (cdp) Hawaii County	2,970	30.09
Maili, HI (cdp) Honolulu County	2,899	48.78
Waimea, HI (cdp) Hawaii County	2,701	38.43
San Diego, CA (city) San Diego County	2,671	0.22
Kapaa, HI (cdp) Kauai County	2,592	27.36
Kihei, HI (cdp) Maui County	2,487	14.85
Ahuimanu, HI (cdp) Honolulu County	2,439	28.67
Las Vegas, NV (city) Clark County	2,396	0.50
Waihee-Waiehu, HI (cdp) Maui County	2,327	31.83
Halawa, HI (cdp) Honolulu County	2,245	16.16
Hawaiian Paradise Park, HI (cdp) Hawaii County	2,099	29.77
Waimanalo, HI (cdp) Honolulu County	1,893	51.66
New York, NY (city) New York City	1,864	0.02
San Jose, CA (city) Santa Clara County	1,848	0.21
Pukalani, HI (cdp) Maui County	1,828	24.77
Waipio, HI (cdp) Honolulu County	1,799	15.41
Hauula, HI (cdp) Honolulu County	1,797	49.22
Makawao, HI (cdp) Maui County	1,770	27.98
Kalaoa, HI (cdp) Hawaii County	1,742	25.64
Lahaina, HI (cdp) Maui County	1,686	18.49
Kaunakakai, HI (cdp) Maui County	1,534	56.27
Hawaiian Beaches, HI (cdp) Hawaii County	1,488	40.12
Haiku-Pauwela, HI (cdp) Maui County	1,450	22.04
Village Park, HI (cdp) Honolulu County	1,438	14.94
San Francisco, CA (city) San Francisco County	1,420	0.18
Anahola, HI (cdp) Kauai County	1,385	71.69
Kualapuu, HI (cdp) Maui County	1,337	69.06
Paradise, NV (cdp) Clark County	1,332	0.72
Aiea, HI (cdp) Honolulu County	1,289	14.29
Phoenix, AZ (city) Maricopa County	1,185	0.09
Waikoloa Village, HI (cdp) Hawaii County	1,180	24.55
Kahaluu, HI (cdp) Honolulu County	1,175	40.03
Seattle, WA (city) King County	1,162	0.21
Maunawili, HI (cdp) Honolulu County	1,149	23.60
Laie, HI (cdp) Honolulu County	1,135	24.75
Waipio Acres, HI (cdp) Honolulu County	1,118	21.10
Heeia, HI (cdp) Honolulu County	1,099	22.23
Mountain View, HI (cdp) Hawaii County	1,082	38.66
Anchorage, AK (municipality) Anchorage Borough	1,055	0.41
Lihue, HI (cdp) Kauai County	1,020	17.98
Holualoa, HI (cdp) Hawaii County	998	16.34
Wailua Homesteads, HI (cdp) Kauai County	986	21.59
Henderson, NV (city) Clark County	957	0.55
Kekaha, HI (cdp) Kauai County	944	29.73
Portland, OR (city) Multnomah County	944	0.18
Sacramento, CA (city) Sacramento County	877	0.22
Long Beach, CA (city) Los Angeles County	876	0.19
Hayward, CA (city) Alameda County	847	0.60
Honaunau-Napoopoo, HI (cdp) Hawaii County	836	34.63
Tacoma, WA (city) Pierce County	812	0.42
Ewa Gentry, HI (cdp) Honolulu County	793	16.06
Fremont, CA (city) Alameda County	792	0.39
Waialua, HI (cdp) Honolulu County	789	20.98
Captain Cook, HI (cdp) Hawaii County	773	24.11
Napili-Honokowai, HI (cdp) Maui County	761	11.21
Haleiwa, HI (cdp) Honolulu County	731	32.85
Ainaloa, HI (cdp) Hawaii County	728	38.12
Ewa Villages, HI (cdp) Honolulu County	708	14.93
Makaha Valley, HI (cdp) Honolulu County	700	54.31
Sunrise Manor, NV (cdp) Clark County	693	0.44
Paia, HI (cdp) Maui County	673	26.93
Oceanside, CA (city) San Diego County	668	0.41
Pupukea, HI (cdp) Honolulu County	664	15.62
San Antonio, TX (city) Bexar County	663	0.06
Whitmore Village, HI (cdp) Honolulu County	660	16.27
Volcano, HI (cdp) Hawaii County	656	29.40
Kalaheo, HI (cdp) Kauai County	650	16.61
Spring Valley, NV (cdp) Clark County	648	0.55
Hanamaulu, HI (cdp) Kauai County	646	19.74
Chicago, IL (city) Cook County	643	0.02
Kahuku, HI (cdp) Honolulu County	641	30.57
Lanai City, HI (cdp) Maui County	625	19.75
Waimea, HI (cdp) Kauai County	606	33.91
Colorado Springs, CO (city) El Paso County	590	0.16
Honalo, HI (cdp) Hawaii County	579	29.14
Anaheim, CA (city) Orange County	570	0.17
Oakland, CA (city) Alameda County	547	0.14
Hana, HI (cdp) Maui County	537	75.74
North Las Vegas, NV (city) Clark County	530	0.46
Stockton, CA (city) San Joaquin County	529	0.22
Kaaawa, HI (cdp) Honolulu County	522	39.43
Hanapepe, HI (cdp) Kauai County	518	24.06
Fairfield, CA (city) Solano County	514	0.53
Huntington Beach, CA (city) Orange County	514	0.27
Torrance, CA (city) Los Angeles County	512	0.37
Houston, TX (city) Harris County	511	0.03
Tucson, AZ (city) Pima County	509	0.10
Vallejo, CA (city) Solano County	490	0.42
Wailua, HI (cdp) Kauai County	485	23.28
Hawaiian Ocean View, HI (cdp) Hawaii County	483	22.18
Mesa, AZ (city) Maricopa County	481	0.12
Honokaa, HI (cdp) Hawaii County	480	21.50
Chula Vista, CA (city) San Diego County	470	0.27
Pahala, HI (cdp) Hawaii County	467	33.89
Provo, UT (city) Utah County	466	0.44
Kealakekua, HI (cdp) Hawaii County	458	27.84
Lakewood, WA (city) Pierce County	449	0.77
Koloa, HI (cdp) Kauai County	435	22.40
Albuquerque, NM (city) Bernalillo County	431	0.10
Orchidlands Estates, HI (cdp) Hawaii County	427	24.67
Riverside, CA (city) Riverside County	425	0.17
Denver, CO (city) Denver County	412	0.07
Reno, NV (city) Washoe County	411	0.23
Lawai, HI (cdp) Kauai County	406	20.46
Eleele, HI (cdp) Kauai County	400	19.61
Vancouver, WA (city) Clark County	398	0.28
Fresno, CA (city) Fresno County	398	0.09
Modesto, CA (city) Stanislaus County	396	0.21
Hawaiian Acres, HI (cdp) Hawaii County	395	22.24
Carson, CA (city) Los Angeles County	393	0.44
Nanawale Estates, HI (cdp) Hawaii County	391	36.44
Kapaau, HI (cdp) Hawaii County	390	33.65
Keaau, HI (cdp) Hawaii County	390	19.40
Waikane, HI (cdp) Honolulu County	385	53.03
Hawi, HI (cdp) Hawaii County	385	41.04
Philadelphia, PA (city) Philadelphia County	384	0.03
Punaluu, HI (cdp) Honolulu County	380	43.13
Aurora, CO (city) Arapahoe County	374	0.14
Federal Way, WA (city) King County	372	0.45
Vacaville, CA (city) Solano County	371	0.42
Moreno Valley, CA (city) Riverside County	371	0.26
Santa Rosa, CA (city) Sonoma County	370	0.25
Jacksonville, FL (special city) Duval County	369	0.05
Concord, CA (city) Contra Costa County	363	0.30
Naalehu, HI (cdp) Hawaii County	362	39.39
Gardena, CA (city) Los Angeles County	358	0.62
Kahaluu-Keauhou, HI (cdp) Hawaii County	353	14.62
Garden Grove, CA (city) Orange County	350	0.21
Mokuleia, HI (cdp) Honolulu County	346	18.81
Austin, TX (city) Travis County	345	0.05
Papaikou, HI (cdp) Hawaii County	341	24.12
San Leandro, CA (city) Alameda County	341	0.43

Notes: (cdp) census designated place; Refer to the Explanation of Data in the front of the book for more detailed information.

Hawaii Native/Pacific Islander: Native Hawaiian

Top 150 Places Sorted by Percent

(Based on places with populations of 10,000 or more)

Place	Number	%
Nanakuli, HI (cdp) Honolulu County	7,171	66.31
Waianae, HI (cdp) Honolulu County	6,021	57.31
Hilo, HI (cdp) Hawaii County	12,951	31.77
Kaneohe, HI (cdp) Honolulu County	10,067	28.79
Wailuku, HI (cdp) Maui County	3,453	28.08
Makakilo City, HI (cdp) Honolulu County	3,188	24.23
Ewa Beach, HI (cdp) Honolulu County	3,473	23.71
Wahiawa, HI (cdp) Honolulu County	3,776	23.38
Kailua, HI (cdp) Honolulu County	8,390	22.98
Kahului, HI (cdp) Maui County	4,566	22.66
Halawa, HI (cdp) Honolulu County	2,245	16.16
Mililani Town, HI (cdp) Honolulu County	4,483	15.67
Waipio, HI (cdp) Honolulu County	1,799	15.41
Kihei, HI (cdp) Maui County	2,487	14.85
Pearl City, HI (cdp) Honolulu County	4,596	14.84
Waimalu, HI (cdp) Honolulu County	3,746	12.75
Waipahu, HI (cdp) Honolulu County	4,006	12.10
Honolulu, HI (cdp) Honolulu County	43,363	11.67
Kaneohe Station, HI (cdp) Honolulu County	171	1.45
Schofield Barracks, HI (cdp) Honolulu County	171	1.19
Marina, CA (city) Monterey County	208	0.83
Lakewood, WA (city) Pierce County	449	0.77
Paradise, NV (cdp) Clark County	1,332	0.72
Ashland, CA (cdp) Alameda County	143	0.69
Cherryland, CA (cdp) Alameda County	94	0.68
Spanaway, WA (cdp) Pierce County	143	0.66
Suisun City, CA (city) Solano County	168	0.64
Silverdale, WA (cdp) Kitsap County	100	0.63
Gardena, CA (city) Los Angeles County	358	0.62
Hayward, CA (city) Alameda County	847	0.60
Forest Grove, OR (city) Washington County	105	0.59
Lacey, WA (city) Thurston County	178	0.57
Whitney, NV (cdp) Clark County	102	0.56
Henderson, NV (city) Clark County	957	0.55
Spring Valley, NV (cdp) Clark County	648	0.55
San Lorenzo, CA (cdp) Alameda County	121	0.55
Elk Plain, WA (cdp) Pierce County	86	0.55
Fairfield, CA (city) Solano County	514	0.53
West Carson, CA (cdp) Los Angeles County	109	0.52
University Place, WA (city) Pierce County	152	0.51
Las Vegas, NV (city) Clark County	2,396	0.50
Pacifica, CA (city) San Mateo County	191	0.50
Parkland, WA (cdp) Pierce County	119	0.49
Fort Lewis, WA (cdp) Pierce County	91	0.48
North Las Vegas, NV (city) Clark County	530	0.46
Union City, CA (city) Alameda County	306	0.46
Enterprise, NV (cdp) Clark County	68	0.46
Federal Way, WA (city) King County	372	0.45
Manteca, CA (city) San Joaquin County	222	0.45
Newark, CA (city) Alameda County	189	0.45
Belmont, CA (city) San Mateo County	113	0.45
Fort Campbell North, KY (cdp) Christian County	65	0.45
Sunrise Manor, NV (cdp) Clark County	693	0.44
Provo, UT (city) Utah County	466	0.44
Carson, CA (city) Los Angeles County	393	0.44
San Leandro, CA (city) Alameda County	341	0.43
Tracy, CA (city) San Joaquin County	244	0.43
Spring Valley, CA (cdp) San Diego County	114	0.43
Oakley, CA (city) Contra Costa County	111	0.43
Tacoma, WA (city) Pierce County	812	0.42
Vallejo, CA (city) Solano County	490	0.42
Vacaville, CA (city) Solano County	371	0.42
La Presa, CA (cdp) San Diego County	137	0.42
East Hill-Meridian, WA (cdp) King County	122	0.42
Winchester, NV (cdp) Clark County	113	0.42
Anchorage, AK (municipality) Anchorage Borough	1,055	0.41
Oceanside, CA (city) San Diego County	668	0.41
Alameda, CA (city) Alameda County	294	0.41
Aloha, OR (cdp) Washington County	172	0.41
San Bruno, CA (city) San Mateo County	163	0.41
Tukwila, WA (city) King County	71	0.41
Kent, WA (city) King County	320	0.40
Bremerton, WA (city) Kitsap County	150	0.40
SeaTac, WA (city) King County	101	0.40
Alderwood Manor, WA (cdp) Snohomish County	62	0.40
Fremont, CA (city) Alameda County	792	0.39
Castro Valley, CA (cdp) Alameda County	222	0.39
Dublin, CA (city) Alameda County	116	0.39
Fort Bragg, NC (cdp) Cumberland County	114	0.39
Lomita, CA (city) Los Angeles County	79	0.39
Lathrop, CA (city) San Joaquin County	41	0.39
Orem, UT (city) Utah County	322	0.38
South San Francisco, CA (city) San Mateo County	228	0.38
Fort Hood, TX (cdp) Coryell County	127	0.38
Morgan Hill, CA (city) Santa Clara County	127	0.38
Salmon Creek, WA (cdp) Clark County	64	0.38
El Segundo, CA (city) Los Angeles County	61	0.38
Troutdale, OR (city) Multnomah County	53	0.38
Patterson, CA (city) Stanislaus County	44	0.38
Torrance, CA (city) Los Angeles County	512	0.37
Campbell, CA (city) Santa Clara County	142	0.37
Imperial Beach, CA (city) San Diego County	100	0.37
Benicia, CA (city) Solano County	99	0.37
Marysville, WA (city) Snohomish County	93	0.37
Oak Harbor, WA (city) Island County	73	0.37
Clearlake, CA (city) Lake County	48	0.37
Fort Drum, NY (cdp) Jefferson County	45	0.37
Vista, CA (city) San Diego County	323	0.36
Beaverton, OR (city) Washington County	272	0.36
Fort Leonard Wood, MO (cdp) Pulaski County	49	0.36
Riverton-Boulevard Park, WA (cdp) King County	40	0.36
Killeen, TX (city) Bell County	302	0.35
Seaside, CA (city) Monterey County	112	0.35
Security-Widefield, CO (cdp) El Paso County	103	0.35
Lemon Grove, CA (city) San Diego County	87	0.35
Twentynine Palms, CA (city) San Bernardino County	52	0.35
Pullman, WA (city) Whitman County	85	0.34
Picnic Point-North Lynnwood, WA (cdp) Snohomish County	79	0.34
La Riviera, CA (cdp) Sacramento County	35	0.34
Redondo Beach, CA (city) Los Angeles County	207	0.33
Rancho Cordova, CA (cdp) Sacramento County	182	0.33
Saint George, UT (city) Washington County	165	0.33
Cascade-Fairwood, WA (cdp) King County	115	0.33
Antioch, CA (city) Contra Costa County	291	0.32
Corvallis, OR (city) Benton County	157	0.32
Rohnert Park, CA (city) Sonoma County	136	0.32
Stanton, CA (city) Orange County	119	0.32
Fairbanks, AK (city) Fairbanks North Star Borough	98	0.32
Hercules, CA (city) Contra Costa County	63	0.32
Pinole, CA (city) Contra Costa County	61	0.32
Livermore, CA (city) Alameda County	224	0.31
Laguna, CA (cdp) Sacramento County	105	0.31
Puyallup, WA (city) Pierce County	101	0.31
South Hill, WA (cdp) Pierce County	98	0.31
Pahrump, NV (cdp) Nye County	77	0.31
Cottage Lake, WA (cdp) King County	76	0.31
Atwater, CA (city) Merced County	72	0.31
Bay Point, CA (cdp) Contra Costa County	67	0.31
Port Hueneme, CA (city) Ventura County	67	0.31
Winter Gardens, CA (cdp) San Diego County	62	0.31
Loma Linda, CA (city) San Bernardino County	57	0.31
Mukilteo, WA (city) Snohomish County	56	0.31
Fountain, CO (city) El Paso County	47	0.31
Tumwater, WA (city) Thurston County	39	0.31
Foothill Ranch, CA (cdp) Orange County	34	0.31
Concord, CA (city) Contra Costa County	363	0.30
Daly City, CA (city) San Mateo County	308	0.30
Santee, CA (city) San Diego County	157	0.30
Aliso Viejo, CA (cdp) Orange County	122	0.30
Des Moines, WA (city) King County	88	0.30
El Cerrito, CA (city) Contra Costa County	70	0.30
Orchards, WA (cdp) Clark County	53	0.30
Martha Lake, WA (cdp) Snohomish County	38	0.30
Fort Carson, CO (cdp) El Paso County	32	0.30
San Mateo, CA (city) San Mateo County	271	0.29
Lakewood, CA (city) Los Angeles County	227	0.29
Hillsboro, OR (city) Washington County	204	0.29
Pittsburg, CA (city) Contra Costa County	163	0.29
Poway, CA (city) San Diego County	139	0.29
North Highlands, CA (cdp) Sacramento County	128	0.29

Notes: (cdp) census designated place; Refer to the Explanation of Data in the front of the book for more detailed information.

Hawaii Native/Pacific Islander: Samoan

Top 150 Places Sorted by Number

(Based on all places, regardless of population)

Place	Number	%
Honolulu, HI (cdp) Honolulu County	8,474	2.28
Long Beach, CA (city) Los Angeles County	4,617	1.00
Waipahu, HI (cdp) Honolulu County	2,845	8.59
San Francisco, CA (city) San Francisco County	2,689	0.35
Carson, CA (city) Los Angeles County	2,575	2.87
Los Angeles, CA (city) Los Angeles County	2,404	0.07
San Diego, CA (city) San Diego County	2,380	0.19
Anchorage, AK (municipality) Anchorage Borough	1,760	0.68
San Jose, CA (city) Santa Clara County	1,721	0.19
Oceanside, CA (city) San Diego County	1,720	1.07
Seattle, WA (city) King County	1,685	0.30
West Valley City, UT (city) Salt Lake County	1,343	1.23
New York, NY (city) New York City	1,279	0.02
Laie, HI (cdp) Honolulu County	1,256	27.39
Nanakuli, HI (cdp) Honolulu County	1,224	11.32
Tacoma, WA (city) Pierce County	1,155	0.60
Compton, CA (city) Los Angeles County	959	1.03
Sacramento, CA (city) Sacramento County	937	0.23
Halawa, HI (cdp) Honolulu County	894	6.44
Anaheim, CA (city) Orange County	888	0.27
Garden Grove, CA (city) Orange County	810	0.49
Ewa Beach, HI (cdp) Honolulu County	751	5.13
Santa Ana, CA (city) Orange County	746	0.22
Daly City, CA (city) San Mateo County	744	0.72
Salt Lake City, UT (city) Salt Lake County	722	0.40
Lakewood, WA (city) Pierce County	672	1.15
Pearl City, HI (cdp) Honolulu County	669	2.16
Wahiawa, HI (cdp) Honolulu County	668	4.14
Kaneohe, HI (cdp) Honolulu County	649	1.86
Waimalu, HI (cdp) Honolulu County	619	2.11
Chicago, IL (city) Cook County	618	0.02
Las Vegas, NV (city) Clark County	610	0.13
Hayward, CA (city) Alameda County	556	0.40
Waianae, HI (cdp) Honolulu County	555	5.28
Independence, MO (city) Jackson County	536	0.47
Phoenix, AZ (city) Maricopa County	534	0.04
Oakland, CA (city) Alameda County	514	0.13
Hauula, HI (cdp) Honolulu County	511	14.00
Makakilo City, HI (cdp) Honolulu County	509	3.87
Makaha, HI (cdp) Honolulu County	503	6.49
Oxnard, CA (city) Ventura County	498	0.29
Taylorsville, UT (city) Salt Lake County	497	0.87
SeaTac, WA (city) King County	493	1.93
Riverside, CA (city) Riverside County	487	0.19
Federal Way, WA (city) King County	486	0.58
East Palo Alto, CA (city) San Mateo County	479	1.62
Maili, HI (cdp) Honolulu County	475	7.99
South San Francisco, CA (city) San Mateo County	469	0.77
White Center, WA (cdp) King County	438	2.09
Mililani Town, HI (cdp) Honolulu County	434	1.52
Provo, UT (city) Utah County	425	0.40
Vista, CA (city) San Diego County	422	0.47
Kearns, UT (cdp) Salt Lake County	421	1.25
Moreno Valley, CA (city) Riverside County	393	0.28
Paramount, CA (city) Los Angeles County	392	0.71
Village Park, HI (cdp) Honolulu County	391	4.06
Stockton, CA (city) San Joaquin County	378	0.16
Vallejo, CA (city) Solano County	375	0.32
San Bernardino, CA (city) San Bernardino County	360	0.19
Bellflower, CA (city) Los Angeles County	358	0.49
Portland, OR (city) Multnomah County	352	0.07
Kailua, HI (cdp) Honolulu County	349	0.96
Orem, UT (city) Utah County	347	0.41
Kent, WA (city) King County	321	0.40
Houston, TX (city) Harris County	319	0.02
Hilo, HI (cdp) Hawaii County	307	0.75
Burien, WA (city) King County	296	0.93
Rialto, CA (city) San Bernardino County	294	0.32
Westminster, CA (city) Orange County	286	0.32
Vancouver, WA (city) Clark County	285	0.20
Des Moines, WA (city) King County	283	0.97
Colorado Springs, CO (city) El Paso County	282	0.08
Kahuku, HI (cdp) Honolulu County	279	13.30
Gardena, CA (city) Los Angeles County	277	0.48
West Jordan, UT (city) Salt Lake County	277	0.41

Place	Number	%
Torrance, CA (city) Los Angeles County	275	0.20
Fresno, CA (city) Fresno County	271	0.06
Lakewood, CA (city) Los Angeles County	268	0.34
Kansas City, MO (city) Jackson County	265	0.06
Stanton, CA (city) Orange County	258	0.69
Paradise, NV (cdp) Clark County	256	0.14
San Bruno, CA (city) San Mateo County	253	0.63
Killeen, TX (city) Bell County	245	0.28
Lynwood, CA (city) Los Angeles County	241	0.35
Nashville-Davidson, TN (special city) Davidson County	237	0.04
Chula Vista, CA (city) San Diego County	235	0.14
Modesto, CA (city) Stanislaus County	235	0.12
Saint George, UT (city) Washington County	234	0.47
West Carson, CA (cdp) Los Angeles County	231	1.09
Marina, CA (city) Monterey County	231	0.92
Reno, NV (city) Washoe County	230	0.13
Santa Clara, CA (city) Santa Clara County	229	0.22
San Leandro, CA (city) Alameda County	223	0.28
Buena Park, CA (city) Orange County	222	0.28
Richmond, CA (city) Contra Costa County	222	0.22
Twentynine Palms, CA (city) San Bernardino County	220	1.49
Mesa, AZ (city) Maricopa County	217	0.05
Denver, CO (city) Denver County	216	0.04
San Antonio, TX (city) Bexar County	214	0.02
Philadelphia, PA (city) Philadelphia County	214	0.01
Waipio, HI (cdp) Honolulu County	210	1.80
Lawton, OK (city) Comanche County	206	0.22
Tukwila, WA (city) King County	203	1.18
Pomona, CA (city) Los Angeles County	198	0.13
Sunrise Manor, NV (cdp) Clark County	193	0.12
Dallas, TX (city) Dallas County	192	0.02
Tucson, AZ (city) Pima County	191	0.04
El Paso, TX (city) El Paso County	187	0.03
Santa Rosa, CA (city) Sonoma County	186	0.13
Columbus, OH (city) Franklin County	186	0.03
North Las Vegas, NV (city) Clark County	185	0.16
Fort Lewis, WA (cdp) Pierce County	183	0.96
Norwalk, CA (city) Los Angeles County	183	0.18
San Mateo, CA (city) San Mateo County	180	0.19
Corona, CA (city) Riverside County	179	0.14
Henderson, NV (city) Clark County	179	0.10
La Presa, CA (cdp) San Diego County	175	0.53
Kahului, HI (cdp) Maui County	174	0.86
Fairfield, CA (city) Solano County	168	0.17
Ontario, CA (city) San Bernardino County	167	0.11
Aurora, CO (city) Arapahoe County	161	0.06
Fontana, CA (city) San Bernardino County	160	0.12
Minneapolis, MN (city) Hennepin County	160	0.04
National City, CA (city) San Diego County	157	0.29
Alameda, CA (city) Alameda County	157	0.22
Arlington, TX (city) Tarrant County	157	0.05
Parkland, WA (cdp) Pierce County	155	0.64
Sandy, UT (city) Salt Lake County	154	0.17
Signal Hill, CA (city) Los Angeles County	152	1.63
Sunnyvale, CA (city) Santa Clara County	149	0.11
Hawthorne, CA (city) Los Angeles County	146	0.17
Whitmore Village, HI (cdp) Honolulu County	145	3.57
Ewa Villages, HI (cdp) Honolulu County	142	3.00
Concord, CA (city) Contra Costa County	141	0.12
Kihei, HI (cdp) Maui County	140	0.84
Fremont, CA (city) Alameda County	134	0.07
Kailua, HI (cdp) Hawaii County	133	1.35
Magna, UT (cdp) Salt Lake County	133	0.58
Lawndale, CA (city) Los Angeles County	132	0.42
Ahuimanu, HI (cdp) Honolulu County	131	1.54
Pacifica, CA (city) San Mateo County	130	0.34
Renton, WA (city) King County	129	0.26
Waipio Acres, HI (cdp) Honolulu County	126	2.38
Auburn, WA (city) King County	124	0.31
Milpitas, CA (city) Santa Clara County	124	0.20
Spring Valley, NV (cdp) Clark County	123	0.10
Aiea, HI (cdp) Honolulu County	122	1.35
Huntington Beach, CA (city) Orange County	121	0.06
Boston, MA (city) Suffolk County	121	0.02
Oquirrh, UT (cdp) Salt Lake County	120	1.15

Notes: (cdp) census designated place; Refer to the Explanation of Data in the front of the book for more detailed information.

Hawaii Native/Pacific Islander: Samoan

Top 150 Places Sorted by Percent

(Based on all places, regardless of population)

Place	Number	%
Laie, HI (cdp) Honolulu County	1,256	27.39
Hauula, HI (cdp) Honolulu County	511	14.00
Kahuku, HI (cdp) Honolulu County	279	13.30
Nanakuli, HI (cdp) Honolulu County	1,224	11.32
Waipahu, HI (cdp) Honolulu County	2,845	8.59
Maili, HI (cdp) Honolulu County	475	7.99
Punaluu, HI (cdp) Honolulu County	69	7.83
Makaha Valley, HI (cdp) Honolulu County	85	6.59
Makaha, HI (cdp) Honolulu County	503	6.49
Halawa, HI (cdp) Honolulu County	894	6.44
Kaaawa, HI (cdp) Honolulu County	78	5.89
Waianae, HI (cdp) Honolulu County	555	5.28
Ewa Beach, HI (cdp) Honolulu County	751	5.13
Wahiawa, HI (cdp) Honolulu County	668	4.14
Village Park, HI (cdp) Honolulu County	391	4.06
Makakilo City, HI (cdp) Honolulu County	509	3.87
Petersville, AK (cdp) Matanuska-Susitna Borough	1	3.70
Whitmore Village, HI (cdp) Honolulu County	145	3.57
Arkoe, MO (town) Nodaway County	2	3.45
Waimanalo, HI (cdp) Honolulu County	118	3.22
Padroni, CO (cdp) Logan County	3	3.09
Ewa Villages, HI (cdp) Honolulu County	142	3.00
Carson, CA (city) Los Angeles County	2,575	2.87
Nanawale Estates, HI (cdp) Hawaii County	30	2.80
Bickleton, WA (cdp) Klickitat County	3	2.65
Hawaiian Beaches, HI (cdp) Hawaii County	94	2.53
Waikane, HI (cdp) Honolulu County	18	2.48
Willow Creek, MT (cdp) Gallatin County	5	2.39
Waipio Acres, HI (cdp) Honolulu County	126	2.38
Waimanalo Beach, HI (cdp) Honolulu County	98	2.29
Honolulu, HI (cdp) Honolulu County	8,474	2.28
Orchidlands Estates, HI (cdp) Hawaii County	38	2.20
Pearl City, HI (cdp) Honolulu County	669	2.16
Waimalu, HI (cdp) Honolulu County	619	2.11
Red Mesa, AZ (cdp) Apache County	5	2.11
White Center, WA (cdp) King County	438	2.09
Kirkwood, CA (cdp) Alpine County	2	2.08
Lake McMurray, WA (cdp) Skagit County	4	2.00
Ewa Gentry, HI (cdp) Honolulu County	96	1.94
SeaTac, WA (city) King County	493	1.93
Kaneohe, HI (cdp) Honolulu County	649	1.86
Waipio, HI (cdp) Honolulu County	210	1.80
Creswell, NC (town) Washington County	5	1.80
Belville, NC (town) Brunswick County	5	1.75
Kirby, WY (town) Hot Springs County	1	1.75
Maunaloa, HI (cdp) Maui County	4	1.74
Mountain View, HI (cdp) Hawaii County	47	1.68
Pupukea, HI (cdp) Honolulu County	71	1.67
Pope, MS (village) Panola County	4	1.66
Signal Hill, CA (city) Los Angeles County	152	1.63
East Palo Alto, CA (city) San Mateo County	479	1.62
Burlington, WY (town) Big Horn County	4	1.60
Ahuimanu, HI (cdp) Honolulu County	131	1.54
Mililani Town, HI (cdp) Honolulu County	434	1.52
Twentynine Palms, CA (city) San Bernardino County	220	1.49
Waialua, HI (cdp) Honolulu County	54	1.44
Kahaluu, HI (cdp) Honolulu County	42	1.43
Pine Hollow, OR (cdp) Wasco County	6	1.42
Appleton, MN (city) Swift County	39	1.36
Mokuleia, HI (cdp) Honolulu County	25	1.36
Kailua, HI (cdp) Hawaii County	133	1.35
Aiea, HI (cdp) Honolulu County	122	1.35
March AFB, CA (cdp) Riverside County	5	1.35
Clark's Point, AK (city) Dillingham Census Area	1	1.33
Hawaiian Acres, HI (cdp) Hawaii County	23	1.30
Kearns, UT (cdp) Salt Lake County	421	1.25
Maunawili, HI (cdp) Honolulu County	61	1.25
Fern Forest, HI (cdp) Hawaii County	6	1.25
West Valley City, UT (city) Salt Lake County	1,343	1.23
Amber, OK (town) Grady County	6	1.22
Waikoloa Village, HI (cdp) Hawaii County	58	1.21
Ainaloa, HI (cdp) Hawaii County	23	1.20
Kualapuu, HI (cdp) Maui County	23	1.19
Fern Acres, HI (cdp) Hawaii County	9	1.19
Tukwila, WA (city) King County	203	1.18
Elm River, MI (township) Houghton County	2	1.18
Lakewood, WA (city) Pierce County	672	1.15
Oquirrh, UT (cdp) Salt Lake County	120	1.15
Hawaiian Paradise Park, HI (cdp) Hawaii County	81	1.15
Kalaoa, HI (cdp) Hawaii County	78	1.15
Athens, LA (village) Claiborne Parish	3	1.15
Kaunakakai, HI (cdp) Maui County	30	1.10
Thorp, WA (cdp) Kittitas County	3	1.10
West Carson, CA (cdp) Los Angeles County	231	1.09
Haleiwa, HI (cdp) Honolulu County	24	1.08
Volcano, HI (cdp) Hawaii County	24	1.08
Oceanside, CA (city) San Diego County	1,720	1.07
Waimea, HI (cdp) Kauai County	19	1.06
Compton, CA (city) Los Angeles County	959	1.03
East Compton, CA (cdp) Los Angeles County	96	1.03
Riverton-Boulevard Park, WA (cdp) King County	114	1.02
Halifax, VT (town) Windham County	8	1.02
Calhoun, MO (city) Henry County	5	1.02
Kodiak, AK (city) Kodiak Island Borough	64	1.01
Long Beach, CA (city) Los Angeles County	4,617	1.00
Zwingle, IA (city) Dubuque County	1	1.00
Mosier, OR (city) Wasco County	4	0.98
Ramah, NM (cdp) McKinley County	4	0.98
Sportsmen Acres, OK (town) Mayes County	2	0.98
Des Moines, WA (city) King County	283	0.97
Chignik Lagoon, AK (cdp) Lake and Peninsula Borough	1	0.97
Kailua, HI (cdp) Honolulu County	349	0.96
Fort Lewis, WA (cdp) Pierce County	183	0.96
Tenakee Springs, AK (city) Skagway-Hoonah-Angoon Census Area	1	0.96
Melrose, WI (village) Jackson County	5	0.95
Marty, SD (cdp) Charles Mix County	4	0.95
Adak, AK (cdp) Aleutians West Census Area	3	0.95
Rockland, ID (city) Power County	3	0.95
Pahoa, HI (cdp) Hawaii County	9	0.94
Belmont, OH (village) Belmont County	5	0.94
Burien, WA (city) King County	296	0.93
Marina, CA (city) Monterey County	231	0.92
Enigma, GA (town) Berrien County	8	0.92
Leeds, UT (town) Washington County	5	0.91
Waco, NC (town) Cleveland County	3	0.91
Wales, UT (town) Sanpete County	2	0.91
Wainaku, HI (cdp) Hawaii County	11	0.90
Heeia, HI (cdp) Honolulu County	44	0.89
Eden Roc, HI (cdp) Hawaii County	4	0.89
Fife, WA (city) Pierce County	42	0.88
Taylorsville, UT (city) Salt Lake County	497	0.87
Kahului, HI (cdp) Maui County	174	0.86
Richford, WI (town) Waushara County	5	0.85
Kihei, HI (cdp) Maui County	140	0.84
McDonald, NC (town) Robeson County	1	0.84
Waimea, HI (cdp) Hawaii County	58	0.83
Barrow, AK (city) North Slope Borough	38	0.83
De Witt, MO (city) Carroll County	1	0.83
Bayview, WI (town) Bayfield County	4	0.81
Manton, CA (cdp) Tehama County	3	0.81
Zenda, KS (city) Kingman County	1	0.81
Napili-Honokowai, HI (cdp) Maui County	54	0.80
Creede, CO (town) Mineral County	3	0.80
Odanah, WI (cdp) Ashland County	2	0.79
South San Francisco, CA (city) San Mateo County	469	0.77
Pepeekeo, HI (cdp) Hawaii County	13	0.77
Pink Hill, NC (town) Lenoir County	4	0.77
Hilo, HI (cdp) Hawaii County	307	0.75
City of The Dalles, OR (city) Wasco County	91	0.75
Bear Valley, CA (cdp) Alpine County	1	0.75
Schofield Barracks, HI (cdp) Honolulu County	107	0.74
Honomu, HI (cdp) Hawaii County	4	0.74
Comstock, MN (township) Marshall County	1	0.74
Kawela Bay, HI (cdp) Honolulu County	3	0.73
Daly City, CA (city) San Mateo County	744	0.72
Broadmoor, CA (cdp) San Mateo County	29	0.72
Waikapu, HI (cdp) Maui County	8	0.72
Roswell, OH (village) Tuscarawas County	2	0.72
La Russell, MO (city) Jasper County	1	0.72
Paramount, CA (city) Los Angeles County	392	0.71

Notes: (cdp) census designated place; Refer to the Explanation of Data in the front of the book for more detailed information.

Hawaii Native/Pacific Islander: Samoan

Top 150 Places Sorted by Percent

(Based on places with populations of 10,000 or more)

Place	Number	%
Nanakuli, HI (cdp) Honolulu County	1,224	11.32
Waipahu, HI (cdp) Honolulu County	2,845	8.59
Halawa, HI (cdp) Honolulu County	894	6.44
Waianae, HI (cdp) Honolulu County	555	5.28
Ewa Beach, HI (cdp) Honolulu County	751	5.13
Wahiawa, HI (cdp) Honolulu County	668	4.14
Makakilo City, HI (cdp) Honolulu County	509	3.87
Carson, CA (city) Los Angeles County	2,575	2.87
Honolulu, HI (cdp) Honolulu County	8,474	2.28
Pearl City, HI (cdp) Honolulu County	669	2.16
Waimalu, HI (cdp) Honolulu County	619	2.11
White Center, WA (cdp) King County	438	2.09
SeaTac, WA (city) King County	493	1.93
Kaneohe, HI (cdp) Honolulu County	649	1.86
Waipio, HI (cdp) Honolulu County	210	1.80
East Palo Alto, CA (city) San Mateo County	479	1.62
Mililani Town, HI (cdp) Honolulu County	434	1.52
Twentynine Palms, CA (city) San Bernardino County	220	1.49
Kearns, UT (cdp) Salt Lake County	421	1.25
West Valley City, UT (city) Salt Lake County	1,343	1.23
Tukwila, WA (city) King County	203	1.18
Lakewood, WA (city) Pierce County	672	1.15
Oquirrh, UT (cdp) Salt Lake County	120	1.15
West Carson, CA (cdp) Los Angeles County	231	1.09
Oceanside, CA (city) San Diego County	1,720	1.07
Compton, CA (city) Los Angeles County	959	1.03
Riverton-Boulevard Park, WA (cdp) King County	114	1.02
Long Beach, CA (city) Los Angeles County	4,617	1.00
Des Moines, WA (city) King County	283	0.97
Kailua, HI (cdp) Honolulu County	349	0.96
Fort Lewis, WA (cdp) Pierce County	183	0.96
Burien, WA (city) King County	296	0.93
Marina, CA (city) Monterey County	231	0.92
Taylorsville, UT (city) Salt Lake County	497	0.87
Kahului, HI (cdp) Maui County	174	0.86
Kihei, HI (cdp) Maui County	140	0.84
South San Francisco, CA (city) San Mateo County	469	0.77
Hilo, HI (cdp) Hawaii County	307	0.75
City of The Dalles, OR (city) Wasco County	91	0.75
Schofield Barracks, HI (cdp) Honolulu County	107	0.74
Daly City, CA (city) San Mateo County	744	0.72
Paramount, CA (city) Los Angeles County	392	0.71
Stanton, CA (city) Orange County	258	0.69
Anchorage, AK (municipality) Anchorage Borough	1,760	0.68
Parkland, WA (cdp) Pierce County	155	0.64
San Bruno, CA (city) San Mateo County	253	0.63
Tacoma, WA (city) Pierce County	1,155	0.60
Wailuku, HI (cdp) Maui County	74	0.60
Federal Way, WA (city) King County	486	0.58
Magna, UT (cdp) Salt Lake County	133	0.58
La Presa, CA (cdp) San Diego County	175	0.53
Fort Campbell North, KY (cdp) Christian County	74	0.52
Bryn Mawr-Skyway, WA (cdp) King County	70	0.50
Garden Grove, CA (city) Orange County	810	0.49
Bellflower, CA (city) Los Angeles County	358	0.49
South Salt Lake, UT (city) Salt Lake County	108	0.49
Gardena, CA (city) Los Angeles County	277	0.48
Independence, MO (city) Jackson County	536	0.47
Vista, CA (city) San Diego County	422	0.47
Saint George, UT (city) Washington County	234	0.47
Spanaway, WA (cdp) Pierce County	102	0.47
Hawaiian Gardens, CA (city) Los Angeles County	68	0.46
Lemon Grove, CA (city) San Diego County	113	0.45
Elk Plain, WA (cdp) Pierce County	70	0.45
Lawndale, CA (city) Los Angeles County	132	0.42
Orem, UT (city) Utah County	347	0.41
West Jordan, UT (city) Salt Lake County	277	0.41
Salt Lake City, UT (city) Salt Lake County	722	0.40
Hayward, CA (city) Alameda County	556	0.40
Provo, UT (city) Utah County	425	0.40
Kent, WA (city) King County	321	0.40
Lomita, CA (city) Los Angeles County	80	0.40
Fort Carson, CO (cdp) El Paso County	41	0.39
Ashland, CA (cdp) Alameda County	76	0.37
Kaneohe Station, HI (cdp) Honolulu County	42	0.36
San Francisco, CA (city) San Francisco County	2,689	0.35
Lynwood, CA (city) Los Angeles County	241	0.35
Millcreek, UT (cdp) Salt Lake County	107	0.35
Copperas Cove, TX (city) Coryell County	103	0.35
Fort Bragg, NC (cdp) Cumberland County	101	0.35
Midvale, UT (city) Salt Lake County	94	0.35
Lakewood, CA (city) Los Angeles County	268	0.34
Pacifica, CA (city) San Mateo County	130	0.34
Lehi, UT (city) Utah County	64	0.34
Barstow, CA (city) San Bernardino County	69	0.33
Cherryland, CA (cdp) Alameda County	45	0.33
Vallejo, CA (city) Solano County	375	0.32
Rialto, CA (city) San Bernardino County	294	0.32
Westminster, CA (city) Orange County	286	0.32
Fort Hood, TX (cdp) Coryell County	107	0.32
Auburn, WA (city) King County	124	0.31
Hinesville, GA (city) Liberty County	95	0.31
South San Jose Hills, CA (cdp) Los Angeles County	63	0.31
Foothill Farms, CA (cdp) Sacramento County	54	0.31
Seattle, WA (city) King County	1,685	0.30
East Hill-Meridian, WA (cdp) King County	89	0.30
Oxnard, CA (city) Ventura County	498	0.29
National City, CA (city) San Diego County	157	0.29
Shelbyville, KY (city) Shelby County	29	0.29
Moreno Valley, CA (city) Riverside County	393	0.28
Killeen, TX (city) Bell County	245	0.28
San Leandro, CA (city) Alameda County	223	0.28
Buena Park, CA (city) Orange County	222	0.28
Lake Elsinore, CA (city) Riverside County	80	0.28
Silverdale, WA (cdp) Kitsap County	45	0.28
Anaheim, CA (city) Orange County	888	0.27
Seaside, CA (city) Monterey County	84	0.27
Renton, WA (city) King County	129	0.26
South Jordan, UT (city) Salt Lake County	77	0.26
Imperial Beach, CA (city) San Diego County	71	0.26
Newark, CA (city) Alameda County	108	0.25
Ridgecrest, CA (city) Kern County	63	0.25
Five Corners, WA (cdp) Clark County	31	0.25
Fort Drum, NY (cdp) Jefferson County	30	0.25
Murray, UT (city) Salt Lake County	82	0.24
Fairbanks, AK (city) Fairbanks North Star Borough	74	0.24
Menlo Park, CA (city) San Mateo County	73	0.24
Cimarron Hills, CO (cdp) El Paso County	37	0.24
Fort Benning South, GA (cdp) Chattahoochee County	28	0.24
Fort Polk South, LA (cdp) Vernon Parish	26	0.24
Sacramento, CA (city) Sacramento County	937	0.23
Rohnert Park, CA (city) Sonoma County	97	0.23
Santa Ana, CA (city) Orange County	746	0.22
Santa Clara, CA (city) Santa Clara County	229	0.22
Richmond, CA (city) Contra Costa County	222	0.22
Lawton, OK (city) Comanche County	206	0.22
Alameda, CA (city) Alameda County	157	0.22
Bountiful, UT (city) Davis County	91	0.22
Lacey, WA (city) Thurston County	70	0.22
Draper, UT (city) Salt Lake County	55	0.22
Artesia, CA (city) Los Angeles County	36	0.22
Pittsburg, CA (city) Contra Costa County	119	0.21
Rowland Heights, CA (cdp) Los Angeles County	102	0.21
University Place, WA (city) Pierce County	62	0.21
Port Hueneme, CA (city) Ventura County	46	0.21
Oak Harbor, WA (city) Island County	41	0.21
South Ogden, UT (city) Weber County	30	0.21
Alum Rock, CA (cdp) Santa Clara County	28	0.21
Vancouver, WA (city) Clark County	285	0.20
Torrance, CA (city) Los Angeles County	275	0.20
Milpitas, CA (city) Santa Clara County	124	0.20
Pleasant Grove, UT (city) Utah County	47	0.20
Fort Stewart, GA (cdp) Liberty County	22	0.20
Capitola, CA (city) Santa Cruz County	20	0.20
San Diego, CA (city) San Diego County	2,380	0.19
San Jose, CA (city) Santa Clara County	1,721	0.19
Riverside, CA (city) Riverside County	487	0.19
San Bernardino, CA (city) San Bernardino County	360	0.19
San Mateo, CA (city) San Mateo County	180	0.19
Rancho Cordova, CA (cdp) Sacramento County	107	0.19

Notes: (cdp) census designated place; Refer to the Explanation of Data in the front of the book for more detailed information.

Hawaii Native/Pacific Islander: Tongan

Top 150 Places Sorted by Number

(Based on all places, regardless of population)

Place	Number	%
Salt Lake City, UT (city) Salt Lake County	2,745	1.51
West Valley City, UT (city) Salt Lake County	1,880	1.73
East Palo Alto, CA (city) San Mateo County	1,497	5.07
Honolulu, HI (cdp) Honolulu County	1,381	0.37
Oakland, CA (city) Alameda County	1,129	0.28
Sacramento, CA (city) Sacramento County	970	0.24
San Mateo, CA (city) San Mateo County	946	1.02
Euless, TX (city) Tarrant County	710	1.54
Los Angeles, CA (city) Los Angeles County	541	0.01
San Bruno, CA (city) San Mateo County	513	1.28
Mesa, AZ (city) Maricopa County	493	0.12
Hawthorne, CA (city) Los Angeles County	448	0.53
Provo, UT (city) Utah County	439	0.42
Taylorsville, UT (city) Salt Lake County	436	0.76
Laie, HI (cdp) Honolulu County	428	9.33
Reno, NV (city) Washoe County	427	0.24
West Jordan, UT (city) Salt Lake County	396	0.58
Redwood City, CA (city) San Mateo County	384	0.51
Portland, OR (city) Multnomah County	378	0.07
Kearns, UT (cdp) Salt Lake County	377	1.12
Long Beach, CA (city) Los Angeles County	373	0.08
Orem, UT (city) Utah County	341	0.40
Hayward, CA (city) Alameda County	335	0.24
Hauula, HI (cdp) Honolulu County	333	9.12
Ontario, CA (city) San Bernardino County	308	0.19
Waipahu, HI (cdp) Honolulu County	302	0.91
Menlo Park, CA (city) San Mateo County	290	0.94
Concord, CA (city) Contra Costa County	287	0.24
Lennox, CA (cdp) Los Angeles County	273	1.19
Kihei, HI (cdp) Maui County	266	1.59
Napili-Honokowai, HI (cdp) Maui County	264	3.89
Kahuku, HI (cdp) Honolulu County	248	11.83
Inglewood, CA (city) Los Angeles County	247	0.22
Phoenix, AZ (city) Maricopa County	235	0.02
Anchorage, AK (municipality) Anchorage Borough	231	0.09
Lahaina, HI (cdp) Maui County	223	2.45
Kahului, HI (cdp) Maui County	220	1.09
Magna, UT (cdp) Salt Lake County	214	0.94
South San Francisco, CA (city) San Mateo County	210	0.35
Riverside, CA (city) Riverside County	208	0.08
San Jose, CA (city) Santa Clara County	199	0.02
Pittsburg, CA (city) Contra Costa County	189	0.33
San Francisco, CA (city) San Francisco County	182	0.02
Fontana, CA (city) San Bernardino County	180	0.14
Hilo, HI (cdp) Hawaii County	172	0.42
Seattle, WA (city) King County	165	0.03
North Fair Oaks, CA (cdp) San Mateo County	164	1.06
Kailua, HI (cdp) Honolulu County	160	0.44
Rancho Cucamonga, CA (city) San Bernardino County	160	0.13
Sandy, UT (city) Salt Lake County	153	0.17
Union City, CA (city) Alameda County	145	0.22
Anaheim, CA (city) Orange County	141	0.04
South Salt Lake, UT (city) Salt Lake County	136	0.62
Millbrae, CA (city) San Mateo County	134	0.65
Sparks, NV (city) Washoe County	134	0.20
San Diego, CA (city) San Diego County	125	0.01
Kaneohe, HI (cdp) Honolulu County	108	0.31
San Bernardino, CA (city) San Bernardino County	104	0.06
Millcreek, UT (cdp) Salt Lake County	103	0.34
Nanakuli, HI (cdp) Honolulu County	102	0.94
Las Vegas, NV (city) Clark County	100	0.02
SeaTac, WA (city) King County	96	0.38
Santa Ana, CA (city) Orange County	91	0.03
Wailuku, HI (cdp) Maui County	85	0.69
White Center, WA (cdp) King County	85	0.41
Vallejo, CA (city) Solano County	84	0.07
Kailua, HI (cdp) Hawaii County	82	0.83
Aurora, CO (city) Arapahoe County	82	0.03
South Jordan, UT (city) Salt Lake County	80	0.27
Fort Worth, TX (city) Tarrant County	80	0.01
Lawndale, CA (city) Los Angeles County	79	0.25
Arlington, TX (city) Tarrant County	79	0.02
Richmond, CA (city) Contra Costa County	78	0.08
Bay Point, CA (cdp) Contra Costa County	77	0.36
Waianae, HI (cdp) Honolulu County	75	0.71
Seaside, CA (city) Monterey County	71	0.22
Saint George, UT (city) Washington County	71	0.14
Stockton, CA (city) San Joaquin County	71	0.03
Moreno Valley, CA (city) Riverside County	69	0.05
Florin, CA (cdp) Sacramento County	68	0.25
Kapaa, HI (cdp) Kauai County	67	0.71
Bedford, TX (city) Tarrant County	65	0.14
Sun Valley, NV (cdp) Washoe County	64	0.33
Logan, UT (city) Cache County	64	0.15
North Richland Hills, TX (city) Tarrant County	64	0.12
Vancouver, WA (city) Clark County	62	0.04
Bountiful, UT (city) Davis County	61	0.15
Hurst, TX (city) Tarrant County	60	0.17
Midvale, UT (city) Salt Lake County	59	0.22
Daly City, CA (city) San Mateo County	59	0.06
Burlingame, CA (city) San Mateo County	58	0.21
Murray, UT (city) Salt Lake County	58	0.17
Fremont, CA (city) Alameda County	58	0.03
Spanish Fork, UT (city) Utah County	57	0.28
Pearl City, HI (cdp) Honolulu County	57	0.18
Newark, CA (city) Alameda County	57	0.13
San Leandro, CA (city) Alameda County	57	0.07
Henderson, NV (city) Clark County	57	0.03
Ewa Beach, HI (cdp) Honolulu County	56	0.38
San Carlos, CA (city) San Mateo County	56	0.20
Belmont, CA (city) San Mateo County	55	0.22
Nampa, ID (city) Canyon County	55	0.11
Federal Way, WA (city) King County	55	0.07
Arden-Arcade, CA (cdp) Sacramento County	55	0.06
Compton, CA (city) Los Angeles County	55	0.06
Sunnyvale, CA (city) Santa Clara County	55	0.04
Holualoa, HI (cdp) Hawaii County	52	0.85
Oquirrh, UT (cdp) Salt Lake County	51	0.49
Norwalk, CA (city) Los Angeles County	51	0.05
Riverton-Boulevard Park, WA (cdp) King County	50	0.45
Rialto, CA (city) San Bernardino County	50	0.05
Chula Vista, CA (city) San Diego County	50	0.03
Buena Park, CA (city) Orange County	49	0.06
Draper, UT (city) Salt Lake County	46	0.18
Parkway-South Sacramento, CA (cdp) Sacramento County	46	0.13
Springville, UT (city) Utah County	45	0.22
Rancho Cordova, CA (cdp) Sacramento County	45	0.08
Juneau, AK (city and borough) Juneau Borough	44	0.14
Pacifica, CA (city) San Mateo County	44	0.11
Palo Alto, CA (city) Santa Clara County	44	0.08
East Millcreek, UT (cdp) Salt Lake County	43	0.20
Foster City, CA (city) San Mateo County	43	0.15
Denver, CO (city) Denver County	43	0.01
Village Park, HI (cdp) Honolulu County	41	0.43
Pleasant Grove, UT (city) Utah County	41	0.17
Tempe, AZ (city) Maricopa County	41	0.03
South Whittier, CA (cdp) Los Angeles County	40	0.07
Orange, CA (city) Orange County	40	0.03
Tacoma, WA (city) Pierce County	40	0.02
Heeia, HI (cdp) Honolulu County	39	0.79
Chandler, AZ (city) Maricopa County	39	0.02
Garden Grove, CA (city) Orange County	39	0.02
Kalaoa, HI (cdp) Hawaii County	38	0.56
Cherryland, CA (cdp) Alameda County	38	0.27
Riverton, UT (city) Salt Lake County	38	0.15
Tucson, AZ (city) Pima County	38	0.01
Hawaiian Paradise Park, HI (cdp) Hawaii County	37	0.52
Ahuimanu, HI (cdp) Honolulu County	37	0.43
Bellflower, CA (city) Los Angeles County	37	0.05
Muscoy, CA (cdp) San Bernardino County	36	0.40
Montclair, CA (city) San Bernardino County	36	0.11
Mountain View, CA (city) Santa Clara County	36	0.05
Cottonwood Heights, UT (cdp) Salt Lake County	35	0.13
Kahaluu, HI (cdp) Honolulu County	34	1.16
Santa Clara, CA (city) Santa Clara County	34	0.03
Torrance, CA (city) Los Angeles County	34	0.02
Waipio, HI (cdp) Honolulu County	33	0.28
Kent, WA (city) King County	33	0.04
Santa Barbara, CA (city) Santa Barbara County	33	0.04
Saint Petersburg, FL (city) Pinellas County	33	0.01

Notes: (cdp) census designated place; Refer to the Explanation of Data in the front of the book for more detailed information.

Hawaii Native/Pacific Islander: Tongan

Top 150 Places Sorted by Percent

(Based on all places, regardless of population)

Place	Number	%
Kahuku, HI (cdp) Honolulu County	248	11.83
Laie, HI (cdp) Honolulu County	428	9.33
Hauula, HI (cdp) Honolulu County	333	9.12
East Palo Alto, CA (city) San Mateo County	1,497	5.07
Napili-Honokowai, HI (cdp) Maui County	264	3.89
Avon, UT (cdp) Cache County	11	3.59
Lahaina, HI (cdp) Maui County	223	2.45
Haliimaile, HI (cdp) Maui County	19	2.12
Waikane, HI (cdp) Honolulu County	13	1.79
West Valley City, UT (city) Salt Lake County	1,880	1.73
Punaluu, HI (cdp) Honolulu County	15	1.70
Kaanapali, HI (cdp) Maui County	22	1.60
Kihei, HI (cdp) Maui County	266	1.59
Euless, TX (city) Tarrant County	710	1.54
Salt Lake City, UT (city) Salt Lake County	2,745	1.51
San Bruno, CA (city) San Mateo County	513	1.28
Lennox, CA (cdp) Los Angeles County	273	1.19
Kahaluu, HI (cdp) Honolulu County	34	1.16
Hana, HI (cdp) Maui County	8	1.13
Kearns, UT (cdp) Salt Lake County	377	1.12
Rush Valley, UT (town) Tooele County	5	1.10
Kahului, HI (cdp) Maui County	220	1.09
North Fair Oaks, CA (cdp) San Mateo County	164	1.06
San Mateo, CA (city) San Mateo County	946	1.02
Menlo Park, CA (city) San Mateo County	290	0.94
Magna, UT (cdp) Salt Lake County	214	0.94
Nanakuli, HI (cdp) Honolulu County	102	0.94
Waipahu, HI (cdp) Honolulu County	302	0.91
Holualoa, HI (cdp) Hawaii County	52	0.85
Kailua, HI (cdp) Hawaii County	82	0.83
Kaunakakai, HI (cdp) Maui County	22	0.81
Waikapu, HI (cdp) Maui County	9	0.81
Heeia, HI (cdp) Honolulu County	39	0.79
Taylorsville, UT (city) Salt Lake County	436	0.76
Koosharem, UT (town) Sevier County	2	0.72
Waianae, HI (cdp) Honolulu County	75	0.71
Kapaa, HI (cdp) Kauai County	67	0.71
Waimanalo, HI (cdp) Honolulu County	26	0.71
Parachute, CO (town) Garfield County	7	0.70
Saratoga Springs, UT (town) Utah County	7	0.70
Wailuku, HI (cdp) Maui County	85	0.69
Hawaiian Ocean View, HI (cdp) Hawaii County	15	0.69
Millbrae, CA (city) San Mateo County	134	0.65
South Salt Lake, UT (city) Salt Lake County	136	0.62
Wailua Homesteads, HI (cdp) Kauai County	28	0.61
Kaaawa, HI (cdp) Honolulu County	8	0.60
Riverside, UT (cdp) Box Elder County	4	0.59
West Jordan, UT (city) Salt Lake County	396	0.58
Orchidlands Estates, HI (cdp) Hawaii County	10	0.58
Kalaoa, HI (cdp) Hawaii County	38	0.56
Hawthorne, CA (city) Los Angeles County	448	0.53
Boronda, CA (cdp) Monterey County	7	0.53
Hawaiian Paradise Park, HI (cdp) Hawaii County	37	0.52
Redwood City, CA (city) San Mateo County	384	0.51
Metzger, OR (cdp) Washington County	17	0.51
Oquirrh, UT (cdp) Salt Lake County	51	0.49
Wainaku, HI (cdp) Hawaii County	6	0.49
Moroni, UT (city) Sanpete County	6	0.47
Nanawale Estates, HI (cdp) Hawaii County	5	0.47
Kahaluu-Keauhou, HI (cdp) Hawaii County	11	0.46
San Geronimo, CA (cdp) Marin County	2	0.46
Riverton-Boulevard Park, WA (cdp) King County	50	0.45
Kailua, HI (cdp) Honolulu County	160	0.44
Levan, UT (town) Juab County	3	0.44
Maalaea, HI (cdp) Maui County	2	0.44
Village Park, HI (cdp) Honolulu County	41	0.43
Ahuimanu, HI (cdp) Honolulu County	37	0.43
Fairview, UT (city) Sanpete County	5	0.43
Kapaau, HI (cdp) Hawaii County	5	0.43
Provo, UT (city) Utah County	439	0.42
Hilo, HI (cdp) Hawaii County	172	0.42
White Center, WA (cdp) King County	85	0.41
Lakeside, IA (city) Buena Vista County	2	0.41
Orem, UT (city) Utah County	341	0.40
Muscoy, CA (cdp) San Bernardino County	36	0.40
Enoch, UT (city) Iron County	14	0.40
Bolinas, CA (cdp) Marin County	5	0.40
Lake Shore, UT (cdp) Utah County	3	0.40
Halaula, HI (cdp) Hawaii County	2	0.40
Benjamin, UT (cdp) Utah County	4	0.39
SeaTac, WA (city) King County	96	0.38
Ewa Beach, HI (cdp) Honolulu County	56	0.38
Pupukea, HI (cdp) Honolulu County	16	0.38
Blanding, UT (city) San Juan County	12	0.38
Loa, UT (town) Wayne County	2	0.38
Honolulu, HI (cdp) Honolulu County	1,381	0.37
Barrow, AK (city) North Slope Borough	17	0.37
Honaunau-Napoopoo, HI (cdp) Hawaii County	9	0.37
Bay Point, CA (cdp) Contra Costa County	77	0.36
Manti, UT (city) Sanpete County	11	0.36
Haleiwa, HI (cdp) Honolulu County	8	0.36
Monticello, UT (city) San Juan County	7	0.36
Pahala, HI (cdp) Hawaii County	5	0.36
South San Francisco, CA (city) San Mateo County	210	0.35
Makaha, HI (cdp) Honolulu County	27	0.35
Pukalani, HI (cdp) Maui County	26	0.35
Makawao, HI (cdp) Maui County	22	0.35
Maili, HI (cdp) Honolulu County	21	0.35
Lihue, HI (cdp) Kauai County	20	0.35
Millcreek, UT (cdp) Salt Lake County	103	0.34
Pittsburg, CA (city) Contra Costa County	189	0.33
Sun Valley, NV (cdp) Washoe County	64	0.33
Alhambra, IL (village) Madison County	2	0.32
Pleasant Valley, AK (cdp) Fairbanks North Star Borough	2	0.32
Kaneohe, HI (cdp) Honolulu County	108	0.31
West Bountiful, UT (city) Davis County	14	0.31
Kualapuu, HI (cdp) Maui County	6	0.31
Swans Island, ME (town) Hancock County	1	0.31
Waihee-Waiehu, HI (cdp) Maui County	22	0.30
Honalo, HI (cdp) Hawaii County	6	0.30
Ephraim, UT (city) Sanpete County	13	0.29
Las Lomas, CA (cdp) Monterey County	9	0.29
Gunnison, UT (city) Sanpete County	7	0.29
Wailua, HI (cdp) Kauai County	6	0.29
Oakland, CA (city) Alameda County	1,129	0.28
Spanish Fork, UT (city) Utah County	57	0.28
Waipio, HI (cdp) Honolulu County	33	0.28
Wailea-Makena, HI (cdp) Maui County	16	0.28
South Jordan, UT (city) Salt Lake County	80	0.27
Cherryland, CA (cdp) Alameda County	38	0.27
August, CA (cdp) San Joaquin County	21	0.27
Hildale, UT (city) Washington County	5	0.26
Nebo Center, CA (cdp) San Bernardino County	3	0.26
Lawndale, CA (city) Los Angeles County	79	0.25
Florin, CA (cdp) Sacramento County	68	0.25
Glenmore, WI (town) Brown County	3	0.25
Sacramento, CA (city) Sacramento County	970	0.24
Reno, NV (city) Washoe County	427	0.24
Hayward, CA (city) Alameda County	335	0.24
Concord, CA (city) Contra Costa County	287	0.24
Del Aire, CA (cdp) Los Angeles County	22	0.24
Hanamaulu, HI (cdp) Kauai County	8	0.24
Princeville, HI (cdp) Kauai County	4	0.24
Purple Sage, WY (cdp) Sweetwater County	1	0.24
Halawa, HI (cdp) Honolulu County	32	0.23
Canyon Rim, UT (cdp) Salt Lake County	24	0.23
Sitka, AK (city and borough) Sitka Borough	20	0.23
Richland Hills, TX (city) Tarrant County	19	0.23
Waimea, HI (cdp) Hawaii County	16	0.23
Waikoloa Village, HI (cdp) Hawaii County	11	0.23
Shingle Springs, CA (cdp) El Dorado County	6	0.23
Zillah, WA (city) Yakima County	5	0.23
Inglewood, CA (city) Los Angeles County	247	0.22
Union City, CA (city) Alameda County	145	0.22
Seaside, CA (city) Monterey County	71	0.22
Midvale, UT (city) Salt Lake County	59	0.22
Belmont, CA (city) San Mateo County	55	0.22
Springville, UT (city) Utah County	45	0.22
Delta, UT (city) Millard County	7	0.22
East Carbon, UT (city) Carbon County	3	0.22

Notes: (cdp) census designated place; Refer to the Explanation of Data in the front of the book for more detailed information.

Hawaii Native/Pacific Islander: Tongan

Top 150 Places Sorted by Percent

(Based on places with populations of 10,000 or more)

Place	Number	%
East Palo Alto, CA (city) San Mateo County	1,497	5.07
West Valley City, UT (city) Salt Lake County	1,880	1.73
Kihei, HI (cdp) Maui County	266	1.59
Euless, TX (city) Tarrant County	710	1.54
Salt Lake City, UT (city) Salt Lake County	2,745	1.51
San Bruno, CA (city) San Mateo County	513	1.28
Lennox, CA (cdp) Los Angeles County	273	1.19
Kearns, UT (cdp) Salt Lake County	377	1.12
Kahului, HI (cdp) Maui County	220	1.09
North Fair Oaks, CA (cdp) San Mateo County	164	1.06
San Mateo, CA (city) San Mateo County	946	1.02
Menlo Park, CA (city) San Mateo County	290	0.94
Magna, UT (cdp) Salt Lake County	214	0.94
Nanakuli, HI (cdp) Honolulu County	102	0.94
Waipahu, HI (cdp) Honolulu County	302	0.91
Taylorsville, UT (city) Salt Lake County	436	0.76
Waianae, HI (cdp) Honolulu County	75	0.71
Wailuku, HI (cdp) Maui County	85	0.69
Millbrae, CA (city) San Mateo County	134	0.65
South Salt Lake, UT (city) Salt Lake County	136	0.62
West Jordan, UT (city) Salt Lake County	396	0.58
Hawthorne, CA (city) Los Angeles County	448	0.53
Redwood City, CA (city) San Mateo County	384	0.51
Oquirrh, UT (cdp) Salt Lake County	51	0.49
Riverton-Boulevard Park, WA (cdp) King County	50	0.45
Kailua, HI (cdp) Honolulu County	160	0.44
Provo, UT (city) Utah County	439	0.42
Hilo, HI (cdp) Hawaii County	172	0.42
White Center, WA (cdp) King County	85	0.41
Orem, UT (city) Utah County	341	0.40
SeaTac, WA (city) King County	96	0.38
Ewa Beach, HI (cdp) Honolulu County	56	0.38
Honolulu, HI (cdp) Honolulu County	1,381	0.37
Bay Point, CA (cdp) Contra Costa County	77	0.36
South San Francisco, CA (city) San Mateo County	210	0.35
Millcreek, UT (cdp) Salt Lake County	103	0.34
Pittsburg, CA (city) Contra Costa County	189	0.33
Sun Valley, NV (cdp) Washoe County	64	0.33
Kaneohe, HI (cdp) Honolulu County	108	0.31
Oakland, CA (city) Alameda County	1,129	0.28
Spanish Fork, UT (city) Utah County	57	0.28
Waipio, HI (cdp) Honolulu County	33	0.28
South Jordan, UT (city) Salt Lake County	80	0.27
Cherryland, CA (cdp) Alameda County	38	0.27
Lawndale, CA (city) Los Angeles County	79	0.25
Florin, CA (cdp) Sacramento County	68	0.25
Sacramento, CA (city) Sacramento County	970	0.24
Reno, NV (city) Washoe County	427	0.24
Hayward, CA (city) Alameda County	335	0.24
Concord, CA (city) Contra Costa County	287	0.24
Halawa, HI (cdp) Honolulu County	32	0.23
Canyon Rim, UT (cdp) Salt Lake County	24	0.23
Inglewood, CA (city) Los Angeles County	247	0.22
Union City, CA (city) Alameda County	145	0.22
Seaside, CA (city) Monterey County	71	0.22
Midvale, UT (city) Salt Lake County	59	0.22
Belmont, CA (city) San Mateo County	55	0.22
Springville, UT (city) Utah County	45	0.22
Burlingame, CA (city) San Mateo County	58	0.21
Sparks, NV (city) Washoe County	134	0.20
San Carlos, CA (city) San Mateo County	56	0.20
East Millcreek, UT (cdp) Salt Lake County	43	0.20
Wahiawa, HI (cdp) Honolulu County	32	0.20
Ontario, CA (city) San Bernardino County	308	0.19
Pearl City, HI (cdp) Honolulu County	57	0.18
Draper, UT (city) Salt Lake County	46	0.18
Sandy, UT (city) Salt Lake County	153	0.17
Hurst, TX (city) Tarrant County	60	0.17
Murray, UT (city) Salt Lake County	58	0.17
Pleasant Grove, UT (city) Utah County	41	0.17
Lehi, UT (city) Utah County	31	0.16
Hawaiian Gardens, CA (city) Los Angeles County	23	0.16
Montecito, CA (cdp) Santa Barbara County	16	0.16
Logan, UT (city) Cache County	64	0.15
Bountiful, UT (city) Davis County	61	0.15
Foster City, CA (city) San Mateo County	43	0.15
Riverton, UT (city) Salt Lake County	38	0.15
Tukwila, WA (city) King County	26	0.15
Sheridan, WY (city) Sheridan County	24	0.15
Hillsborough, CA (town) San Mateo County	16	0.15
Fontana, CA (city) San Bernardino County	180	0.14
Saint George, UT (city) Washington County	71	0.14
Bedford, TX (city) Tarrant County	65	0.14
Juneau, AK (city and borough) Juneau Borough	44	0.14
Oak Ridge, FL (cdp) Orange County	31	0.14
Cedar City, UT (city) Iron County	29	0.14
Rancho Cucamonga, CA (city) San Bernardino County	160	0.13
Newark, CA (city) Alameda County	57	0.13
Parkway-South Sacramento, CA (cdp) Sacramento County	46	0.13
Cottonwood Heights, UT (cdp) Salt Lake County	35	0.13
Holladay, UT (city) Salt Lake County	19	0.13
Payson, UT (city) Utah County	16	0.13
Mesa, AZ (city) Maricopa County	493	0.12
North Richland Hills, TX (city) Tarrant County	64	0.12
Bryn Mawr-Skyway, WA (cdp) King County	17	0.12
Makakilo City, HI (cdp) Honolulu County	16	0.12
Nampa, ID (city) Canyon County	55	0.11
Pacifica, CA (city) San Mateo County	44	0.11
Montclair, CA (city) San Bernardino County	36	0.11
American Fork, UT (city) Utah County	25	0.11
Watauga, TX (city) Tarrant County	24	0.11
Franklin Park, PA (borough) Allegheny County	13	0.11
Burien, WA (city) King County	32	0.10
Centerville, UT (city) Davis County	15	0.10
Susanville, CA (city) Lassen County	13	0.10
Anchorage, AK (municipality) Anchorage Borough	231	0.09
Rubidoux, CA (cdp) Riverside County	26	0.09
Ardmore, PA (cdp) Montgomery County	11	0.09
Long Beach, CA (city) Los Angeles County	373	0.08
Riverside, CA (city) Riverside County	208	0.08
Richmond, CA (city) Contra Costa County	78	0.08
Rancho Cordova, CA (cdp) Sacramento County	45	0.08
Palo Alto, CA (city) Santa Clara County	44	0.08
Stanton, CA (city) Orange County	30	0.08
Fallbrook, CA (cdp) San Diego County	24	0.08
Waimalu, HI (cdp) Honolulu County	24	0.08
Mililani Town, HI (cdp) Honolulu County	23	0.08
Aberdeen, SD (city) Brown County	19	0.08
Pacific Grove, CA (city) Monterey County	13	0.08
Vineyard, CA (cdp) Sacramento County	8	0.08
Portland, OR (city) Multnomah County	378	0.07
Vallejo, CA (city) Solano County	84	0.07
San Leandro, CA (city) Alameda County	57	0.07
Federal Way, WA (city) King County	55	0.07
South Whittier, CA (cdp) Los Angeles County	40	0.07
East Hill-Meridian, WA (cdp) King County	20	0.07
Tooele, UT (city) Tooele County	16	0.07
Ashland, CA (cdp) Alameda County	15	0.07
Alamo, CA (cdp) Contra Costa County	11	0.07
Lakeland North, WA (cdp) King County	11	0.07
Valle Vista, CA (cdp) Riverside County	7	0.07
San Bernardino, CA (city) San Bernardino County	104	0.06
Daly City, CA (city) San Mateo County	59	0.06
Arden-Arcade, CA (cdp) Sacramento County	55	0.06
Compton, CA (city) Los Angeles County	55	0.06
Buena Park, CA (city) Orange County	49	0.06
North Highlands, CA (cdp) Sacramento County	27	0.06
Spring, TX (cdp) Harris County	22	0.06
Santa Paula, CA (city) Ventura County	18	0.06
Clearfield, UT (city) Davis County	16	0.06
Cottonwood West, UT (cdp) Salt Lake County	12	0.06
Hercules, CA (city) Contra Costa County	12	0.06
Newberg, OR (city) Yamhill County	10	0.06
Farmington, UT (city) Davis County	7	0.06
Rio Linda, CA (cdp) Sacramento County	6	0.06
Moreno Valley, CA (city) Riverside County	69	0.05
Norwalk, CA (city) Los Angeles County	51	0.05
Rialto, CA (city) San Bernardino County	50	0.05
Bellflower, CA (city) Los Angeles County	37	0.05
Mountain View, CA (city) Santa Clara County	36	0.05

Notes: (cdp) census designated place; Refer to the Explanation of Data in the front of the book for more detailed information.

Hawaii Native/Pacific Islander: Other Polynesian

Top 150 Places Sorted by Number

(Based on all places, regardless of population)

Place	Number	%
Honolulu, HI (cdp) Honolulu County	687	0.18
Los Angeles, CA (city) Los Angeles County	261	0.01
Salt Lake City, UT (city) Salt Lake County	235	0.13
Laie, HI (cdp) Honolulu County	224	4.89
Provo, UT (city) Utah County	158	0.15
West Valley City, UT (city) Salt Lake County	157	0.14
Long Beach, CA (city) Los Angeles County	150	0.03
San Diego, CA (city) San Diego County	135	0.01
Sacramento, CA (city) Sacramento County	110	0.03
Kailua, HI (cdp) Honolulu County	109	0.30
Oakland, CA (city) Alameda County	104	0.03
Wahiawa, HI (cdp) Honolulu County	101	0.63
Seattle, WA (city) King County	98	0.02
San Mateo, CA (city) San Mateo County	96	0.10
Hauula, HI (cdp) Honolulu County	95	2.60
Kaneohe, HI (cdp) Honolulu County	94	0.27
Hilo, HI (cdp) Hawaii County	84	0.21
New York, NY (city) New York City	84	0.00
San Jose, CA (city) Santa Clara County	83	0.01
Orem, UT (city) Utah County	80	0.09
Waipahu, HI (cdp) Honolulu County	73	0.22
Anchorage, AK (municipality) Anchorage Borough	72	0.03
San Francisco, CA (city) San Francisco County	72	0.01
Phoenix, AZ (city) Maricopa County	69	0.01
Mesa, AZ (city) Maricopa County	68	0.02
Taylorsville, UT (city) Salt Lake County	66	0.11
Portland, OR (city) Multnomah County	66	0.01
Hawthorne, CA (city) Los Angeles County	65	0.08
Pearl City, HI (cdp) Honolulu County	64	0.21
Las Vegas, NV (city) Clark County	64	0.01
Rancho Cucamonga, CA (city) San Bernardino County	63	0.05
Nanakuli, HI (cdp) Honolulu County	62	0.57
East Palo Alto, CA (city) San Mateo County	59	0.20
Euless, TX (city) Tarrant County	58	0.13
Anaheim, CA (city) Orange County	55	0.02
West Jordan, UT (city) Salt Lake County	54	0.08
Mililani Town, HI (cdp) Honolulu County	53	0.19
Waianae, HI (cdp) Honolulu County	50	0.48
Halawa, HI (cdp) Honolulu County	50	0.36
Paradise, NV (cdp) Clark County	48	0.03
Carson, CA (city) Los Angeles County	47	0.05
Kailua, HI (cdp) Hawaii County	45	0.46
Makakilo City, HI (cdp) Honolulu County	44	0.33
Sunrise Manor, NV (cdp) Clark County	44	0.03
Redwood City, CA (city) San Mateo County	43	0.06
Reno, NV (city) Washoe County	42	0.02
Kahuku, HI (cdp) Honolulu County	41	1.96
Waimalu, HI (cdp) Honolulu County	41	0.14
Concord, CA (city) Contra Costa County	41	0.03
Hayward, CA (city) Alameda County	41	0.03
Lennox, CA (cdp) Los Angeles County	39	0.17
San Bruno, CA (city) San Mateo County	39	0.10
Sandy, UT (city) Salt Lake County	39	0.04
Riverside, CA (city) Riverside County	37	0.01
Kihei, HI (cdp) Maui County	36	0.21
Santa Ana, CA (city) Orange County	36	0.01
South Salt Lake, UT (city) Salt Lake County	35	0.16
Chicago, IL (city) Cook County	35	0.00
Maili, HI (cdp) Honolulu County	34	0.57
Kearns, UT (cdp) Salt Lake County	34	0.10
Daly City, CA (city) San Mateo County	34	0.03
Colorado Springs, CO (city) El Paso County	34	0.01
Waipio Acres, HI (cdp) Honolulu County	33	0.62
Oceanside, CA (city) San Diego County	33	0.02
Waipio, HI (cdp) Honolulu County	31	0.27
Makaha, HI (cdp) Honolulu County	30	0.39
Ewa Beach, HI (cdp) Honolulu County	30	0.20
Denver, CO (city) Denver County	30	0.01
San Bernardino, CA (city) San Bernardino County	29	0.02
Waimanalo Beach, HI (cdp) Honolulu County	28	0.66
Bedford, TX (city) Tarrant County	27	0.06
Costa Mesa, CA (city) Orange County	27	0.02
Huntington Beach, CA (city) Orange County	27	0.01
Kansas City, MO (city) Jackson County	27	0.01
Tucson, AZ (city) Pima County	27	0.01
Philadelphia, PA (city) Philadelphia County	27	0.00
Kalaoa, HI (cdp) Hawaii County	26	0.38
Kahului, HI (cdp) Maui County	26	0.13
Fountain Valley, CA (city) Orange County	26	0.05
Sparks, NV (city) Washoe County	26	0.04
Pomona, CA (city) Los Angeles County	25	0.02
Spring Valley, NV (cdp) Clark County	25	0.02
Stockton, CA (city) San Joaquin County	25	0.01
Pleasant Grove, UT (city) Utah County	24	0.10
Saint George, UT (city) Washington County	24	0.05
Pittsburg, CA (city) Contra Costa County	24	0.04
Whitmore Village, HI (cdp) Honolulu County	23	0.57
Ewa Villages, HI (cdp) Honolulu County	23	0.49
Waihee-Waiehu, HI (cdp) Maui County	23	0.31
Ahuimanu, HI (cdp) Honolulu County	23	0.27
Signal Hill, CA (city) Los Angeles County	23	0.25
Vancouver, WA (city) Clark County	23	0.02
Henderson, NV (city) Clark County	23	0.01
Saint Petersburg, FL (city) Pinellas County	23	0.01
Oquirrh, UT (cdp) Salt Lake County	22	0.21
Independence, MO (city) Jackson County	22	0.02
Richmond, CA (city) Contra Costa County	22	0.02
Aurora, CO (city) Arapahoe County	22	0.01
Garden Grove, CA (city) Orange County	22	0.01
Makawao, HI (cdp) Maui County	21	0.33
Ashland, CA (cdp) Alameda County	21	0.10
Hurst, TX (city) Tarrant County	21	0.06
Beaverton, OR (city) Washington County	21	0.03
Federal Way, WA (city) King County	21	0.03
Santa Clara, CA (city) Santa Clara County	21	0.02
Oxnard, CA (city) Ventura County	21	0.01
Ewa Gentry, HI (cdp) Honolulu County	20	0.40
Modesto, CA (city) Stanislaus County	20	0.01
Ontario, CA (city) San Bernardino County	20	0.01
Waimea, HI (cdp) Hawaii County	19	0.27
Union City, CA (city) Alameda County	19	0.03
Dallas, TX (city) Dallas County	19	0.00
Village Park, HI (cdp) Honolulu County	18	0.19
Wailuku, HI (cdp) Maui County	18	0.15
Layton, UT (city) Davis County	18	0.03
Redondo Beach, CA (city) Los Angeles County	18	0.03
Bellevue, WA (city) King County	18	0.02
Fresno, CA (city) Fresno County	18	0.00
Alpine, UT (city) Utah County	17	0.24
Burlingame, CA (city) San Mateo County	17	0.06
Castro Valley, CA (cdp) Alameda County	17	0.03
Fontana, CA (city) San Bernardino County	17	0.01
Glendale, AZ (city) Maricopa County	17	0.01
Irving, TX (city) Dallas County	17	0.01
Tacoma, WA (city) Pierce County	17	0.01
Hempstead, NY (town) Nassau County	17	0.00
Jacksonville, FL (special city) Duval County	17	0.00
Memphis, TN (city) Shelby County	17	0.00
Hesperia, CA (city) San Bernardino County	16	0.03
Killeen, TX (city) Bell County	16	0.02
Lakewood, CA (city) Los Angeles County	16	0.02
San Leandro, CA (city) Alameda County	16	0.02
Inglewood, CA (city) Los Angeles County	16	0.01
Irvine, CA (city) Orange County	16	0.01
Scottsdale, AZ (city) Maricopa County	16	0.01
Sunnyvale, CA (city) Santa Clara County	16	0.01
Vallejo, CA (city) Solano County	16	0.01
Baltimore, MD (independent city) Baltimore city	16	0.00
Houston, TX (city) Harris County	16	0.00
Minneapolis, MN (city) Hennepin County	16	0.00
Volcano, HI (cdp) Hawaii County	15	0.67
Aiea, HI (cdp) Honolulu County	15	0.17
Kapaa, HI (cdp) Kauai County	15	0.16
SeaTac, WA (city) King County	15	0.06
Millcreek, UT (cdp) Salt Lake County	15	0.05
Boise City, ID (city) Ada County	15	0.01
Chula Vista, CA (city) San Diego County	15	0.01
Columbus, GA (special city) Muscogee County	15	0.01
Corona, CA (city) Riverside County	15	0.01
Gilbert, AZ (town) Maricopa County	15	0.01

Notes: (cdp) census designated place; Refer to the Explanation of Data in the front of the book for more detailed information.

Hawaii Native/Pacific Islander: Other Polynesian

Top 150 Places Sorted by Percent

(Based on all places, regardless of population)

Place	Number	%
Laie, HI (cdp) Honolulu County	224	4.89
Maunaloa, HI (cdp) Maui County	7	3.04
Hauula, HI (cdp) Honolulu County	95	2.60
Taylor, WY (cdp) Lincoln County	2	2.22
Kahuku, HI (cdp) Honolulu County	41	1.96
Glennallen, AK (cdp) Valdez-Cordova Census Area	8	1.44
Hollis, AK (cdp) Prince of Wales-Outer Ketchikan Census Area	2	1.44
Yakutat, AK (cdp) Yakutat City and Borough	8	1.18
Maryhill Estates, KY (city) Jefferson County	2	1.14
Richards, MO (town) Vernon County	1	1.05
Mountain View, WY (cdp) Natrona County	1	0.97
Punaluu, HI (cdp) Honolulu County	8	0.91
Paauilo, HI (cdp) Hawaii County	5	0.88
Kurtistown, HI (cdp) Hawaii County	9	0.78
Kaaawa, HI (cdp) Honolulu County	10	0.76
Charleston Park, FL (cdp) Lee County	3	0.73
Clyde, CA (cdp) Contra Costa County	5	0.72
Volcano, HI (cdp) Hawaii County	15	0.67
Waimanalo Beach, HI (cdp) Honolulu County	28	0.66
Alpine Northwest, WY (cdp) Lincoln County	1	0.66
Crouch, ID (city) Boise County	1	0.65
Wahiawa, HI (cdp) Honolulu County	101	0.63
Waipio Acres, HI (cdp) Honolulu County	33	0.62
Nanakuli, HI (cdp) Honolulu County	62	0.57
Maili, HI (cdp) Honolulu County	34	0.57
Whitmore Village, HI (cdp) Honolulu County	23	0.57
Blythe, GA (city) Richmond County	4	0.56
Fairview, UT (city) Sanpete County	6	0.52
Sandnes, MN (township) Yellow Medicine County	1	0.51
Ewa Villages, HI (cdp) Honolulu County	23	0.49
Waianae, HI (cdp) Honolulu County	50	0.48
Puako, HI (cdp) Hawaii County	2	0.47
Kailua, HI (cdp) Hawaii County	45	0.46
Haleiwa, HI (cdp) Honolulu County	10	0.45
Honaunau-Napoopoo, HI (cdp) Hawaii County	10	0.41
Kualapuu, HI (cdp) Maui County	8	0.41
Waikane, HI (cdp) Honolulu County	3	0.41
Ewa Gentry, HI (cdp) Honolulu County	20	0.40
Tenhassen, MN (township) Martin County	1	0.40
Makaha, HI (cdp) Honolulu County	30	0.39
Kalaoa, HI (cdp) Hawaii County	26	0.38
Soda Springs, ID (city) Caribou County	13	0.38
Halawa, HI (cdp) Honolulu County	50	0.36
Koloa, HI (cdp) Kauai County	7	0.36
Makakilo City, HI (cdp) Honolulu County	44	0.33
Makawao, HI (cdp) Maui County	21	0.33
Elk Ridge, UT (town) Utah County	6	0.33
Lonaconing, MD (town) Allegany County	4	0.33
Hawaiian Beaches, HI (cdp) Hawaii County	12	0.32
Paia, HI (cdp) Maui County	8	0.32
Moapa Town, NV (cdp) Clark County	3	0.32
Waihee-Waiehu, HI (cdp) Maui County	23	0.31
Kahaluu, HI (cdp) Honolulu County	9	0.31
Kailua, HI (cdp) Honolulu County	109	0.30
Seven Trees, CA (cdp) Santa Clara County	5	0.30
Mariposa, CA (cdp) Mariposa County	4	0.29
Pahala, HI (cdp) Hawaii County	4	0.29
Hawaiian Ocean View, HI (cdp) Hawaii County	6	0.28
Hawaiian Acres, HI (cdp) Hawaii County	5	0.28
Kaneohe, HI (cdp) Honolulu County	94	0.27
Waipio, HI (cdp) Honolulu County	31	0.27
Ahuimanu, HI (cdp) Honolulu County	23	0.27
Waimea, HI (cdp) Hawaii County	19	0.27
Waikoloa Village, HI (cdp) Hawaii County	13	0.27
March AFB, CA (cdp) Riverside County	1	0.27
Pupukea, HI (cdp) Honolulu County	11	0.26
Signal Hill, CA (city) Los Angeles County	23	0.25
Maunawili, HI (cdp) Honolulu County	12	0.25
Waimanalo, HI (cdp) Honolulu County	9	0.25
Eleele, HI (cdp) Kauai County	5	0.25
Virgin, UT (town) Washington County	1	0.25
Alpine, UT (city) Utah County	17	0.24
Quail Valley, CA (cdp) Riverside County	4	0.24
Ekalaka, MT (town) Carter County	1	0.24
Tyrone, OK (town) Texas County	2	0.23
Gustavus, AK (cdp) Skagway-Hoonah-Angoon Census Area	1	0.23
Waipahu, HI (cdp) Honolulu County	73	0.22
Eden Roc, HI (cdp) Hawaii County	1	0.22
Hilo, HI (cdp) Hawaii County	84	0.21
Pearl City, HI (cdp) Honolulu County	64	0.21
Kihei, HI (cdp) Maui County	36	0.21
Oquirrh, UT (cdp) Salt Lake County	22	0.21
Valentine, NE (city) Cherry County	6	0.21
Anahola, HI (cdp) Kauai County	4	0.21
Hildale, UT (city) Washington County	4	0.21
Hanalei, HI (cdp) Kauai County	1	0.21
East Palo Alto, CA (city) San Mateo County	59	0.20
Ewa Beach, HI (cdp) Honolulu County	30	0.20
Point Lookout, NY (cdp) Nassau County	3	0.20
Mililani Town, HI (cdp) Honolulu County	53	0.19
Village Park, HI (cdp) Honolulu County	18	0.19
Sky Lake, FL (cdp) Orange County	11	0.19
Meredith, NY (town) Delaware County	3	0.19
Grayson, CA (cdp) Stanislaus County	2	0.19
Honolulu, HI (cdp) Honolulu County	687	0.18
Haiku-Pauwela, HI (cdp) Maui County	12	0.18
Napili-Honokowai, HI (cdp) Maui County	12	0.18
Metzger, OR (cdp) Washington County	6	0.18
Glenrock, WY (town) Converse County	4	0.18
Hatch, NM (village) Dona Ana County	3	0.18
Princeville, HI (cdp) Kauai County	3	0.18
Arcadia, MO (city) Iron County	1	0.18
Lennox, CA (cdp) Los Angeles County	39	0.17
Aiea, HI (cdp) Honolulu County	15	0.17
West Longview, WA (cdp) Cowlitz County	5	0.17
South Salt Lake, UT (city) Salt Lake County	35	0.16
Kapaa, HI (cdp) Kauai County	15	0.16
Hawaiian Paradise Park, HI (cdp) Hawaii County	11	0.16
Heeia, HI (cdp) Honolulu County	8	0.16
Captain Cook, HI (cdp) Hawaii County	5	0.16
Iroquois Point, HI (cdp) Honolulu County	4	0.16
Dunsmuir, CA (city) Siskiyou County	3	0.16
Mokuleia, HI (cdp) Honolulu County	3	0.16
Arbon Valley, ID (cdp) Power County	1	0.16
Provo, UT (city) Utah County	158	0.15
Wailuku, HI (cdp) Maui County	18	0.15
Kaunakakai, HI (cdp) Maui County	4	0.15
Berry Hill, TN (city) Davidson County	1	0.15
West Valley City, UT (city) Salt Lake County	157	0.14
Waimalu, HI (cdp) Honolulu County	41	0.14
Sitka, AK (city and borough) Sitka Borough	12	0.14
Valley Center, CA (cdp) San Diego County	10	0.14
Franklin, MI (township) Lenawee County	4	0.14
Fiskdale, MA (cdp) Worcester County	3	0.14
Kilauea, HI (cdp) Kauai County	3	0.14
Mount Olive, IL (city) Macoupin County	3	0.14
Markesan, WI (city) Green Lake County	2	0.14
Kalihiwai, HI (cdp) Kauai County	1	0.14
Salt Lake City, UT (city) Salt Lake County	235	0.13
Euless, TX (city) Tarrant County	58	0.13
Kahului, HI (cdp) Maui County	26	0.13
Holualoa, HI (cdp) Hawaii County	8	0.13
Ivins, UT (town) Washington County	6	0.13
Kalaheo, HI (cdp) Kauai County	5	0.13
Acton, CA (cdp) Los Angeles County	3	0.13
Dalton Gardens, ID (city) Kootenai County	3	0.13
Deltana, AK (cdp) Southeast Fairbanks Census Area	2	0.13
Smokey Point, WA (cdp) Snohomish County	2	0.13
Southside, MN (township) Wright County	2	0.13
Monticello, ME (town) Aroostook County	1	0.13
Paradise, UT (town) Cache County	1	0.13
Cornville, AZ (cdp) Yavapai County	4	0.12
Minoa, NY (village) Onondaga County	4	0.12
Saint Johns, AZ (city) Apache County	4	0.12
Ira, NY (town) Cayuga County	3	0.12
Kahaluu-Keauhou, HI (cdp) Hawaii County	3	0.12
Bradbury, CA (city) Los Angeles County	1	0.12
Mendocino, CA (cdp) Mendocino County	1	0.12
Mona, UT (town) Juab County	1	0.12
Oljato-Monument Valley, UT (cdp) San Juan County	1	0.12

Notes: (cdp) census designated place; Refer to the Explanation of Data in the front of the book for more detailed information.

Hawaii Native/Pacific Islander: Other Polynesian

Top 150 Places Sorted by Percent

(Based on places with populations of 10,000 or more)

Place	Number	%
Wahiawa, HI (cdp) Honolulu County	101	0.63
Nanakuli, HI (cdp) Honolulu County	62	0.57
Waianae, HI (cdp) Honolulu County	50	0.48
Halawa, HI (cdp) Honolulu County	50	0.36
Makakilo City, HI (cdp) Honolulu County	44	0.33
Kailua, HI (cdp) Honolulu County	109	0.30
Kaneohe, HI (cdp) Honolulu County	94	0.27
Waipio, HI (cdp) Honolulu County	31	0.27
Waipahu, HI (cdp) Honolulu County	73	0.22
Hilo, HI (cdp) Hawaii County	84	0.21
Pearl City, HI (cdp) Honolulu County	64	0.21
Kihei, HI (cdp) Maui County	36	0.21
Oquirrh, UT (cdp) Salt Lake County	22	0.21
East Palo Alto, CA (city) San Mateo County	59	0.20
Ewa Beach, HI (cdp) Honolulu County	30	0.20
Mililani Town, HI (cdp) Honolulu County	53	0.19
Honolulu, HI (cdp) Honolulu County	687	0.18
Lennox, CA (cdp) Los Angeles County	39	0.17
South Salt Lake, UT (city) Salt Lake County	35	0.16
Provo, UT (city) Utah County	158	0.15
Wailuku, HI (cdp) Maui County	18	0.15
West Valley City, UT (city) Salt Lake County	157	0.14
Waimalu, HI (cdp) Honolulu County	41	0.14
Salt Lake City, UT (city) Salt Lake County	235	0.13
Euless, TX (city) Tarrant County	58	0.13
Kahului, HI (cdp) Maui County	26	0.13
Taylorsville, UT (city) Salt Lake County	66	0.11
San Mateo, CA (city) San Mateo County	96	0.10
San Bruno, CA (city) San Mateo County	39	0.10
Kearns, UT (cdp) Salt Lake County	34	0.10
Pleasant Grove, UT (city) Utah County	24	0.10
Ashland, CA (cdp) Alameda County	21	0.10
Orem, UT (city) Utah County	80	0.09
Payson, UT (city) Utah County	11	0.09
Hawthorne, CA (city) Los Angeles County	65	0.08
West Jordan, UT (city) Salt Lake County	54	0.08
Redwood City, CA (city) San Mateo County	43	0.06
Bedford, TX (city) Tarrant County	27	0.06
Hurst, TX (city) Tarrant County	21	0.06
Burlingame, CA (city) San Mateo County	17	0.06
SeaTac, WA (city) King County	15	0.06
Millbrae, CA (city) San Mateo County	12	0.06
White Center, WA (cdp) King County	12	0.06
Schofield Barracks, HI (cdp) Honolulu County	9	0.06
Clinton, UT (city) Davis County	8	0.06
Rio Linda, CA (cdp) Sacramento County	6	0.06
Rancho Cucamonga, CA (city) San Bernardino County	63	0.05
Carson, CA (city) Los Angeles County	47	0.05
Fountain Valley, CA (city) Orange County	26	0.05
Saint George, UT (city) Washington County	24	0.05
Millcreek, UT (cdp) Salt Lake County	15	0.05
Imperial Beach, CA (city) San Diego County	13	0.05
Draper, UT (city) Salt Lake County	12	0.05
Parkland, WA (cdp) Pierce County	12	0.05
Sun Valley, NV (cdp) Washoe County	10	0.05
Glassboro, NJ (borough) Gloucester County	9	0.05
Tukwila, WA (city) King County	9	0.05
Magalia, CA (cdp) Butte County	5	0.05
Montecito, CA (cdp) Santa Barbara County	5	0.05
Plover, WI (village) Portage County	5	0.05
Sandy, UT (city) Salt Lake County	39	0.04
Sparks, NV (city) Washoe County	26	0.04
Pittsburg, CA (city) Contra Costa County	24	0.04
Murray, UT (city) Salt Lake County	14	0.04
Fort Bragg, NC (cdp) Cumberland County	12	0.04
Montclair, CA (city) San Bernardino County	12	0.04
Clearfield, UT (city) Davis County	11	0.04
Riverton, UT (city) Salt Lake County	10	0.04
Cottonwood West, UT (cdp) Salt Lake County	8	0.04
Artesia, CA (city) Los Angeles County	7	0.04
Ashland, OR (city) Jackson County	7	0.04
Lehi, UT (city) Utah County	7	0.04
Loma Linda, CA (city) San Bernardino County	7	0.04
Sanger, CA (city) Fresno County	7	0.04
Centerville, UT (city) Davis County	6	0.04

Place	Number	%
Middle, NJ (township) Cape May County	6	0.04
Susanville, CA (city) Lassen County	6	0.04
West Norriton, PA (cdp) Montgomery County	6	0.04
Fort Leonard Wood, MO (cdp) Pulaski County	5	0.04
Coatesville, PA (city) Chester County	4	0.04
Lathrop, CA (city) San Joaquin County	4	0.04
Meadow Woods, FL (cdp) Orange County	4	0.04
Mountain Home, ID (city) Elmore County	4	0.04
Long Beach, CA (city) Los Angeles County	150	0.03
Sacramento, CA (city) Sacramento County	110	0.03
Oakland, CA (city) Alameda County	104	0.03
Anchorage, AK (municipality) Anchorage Borough	72	0.03
Paradise, NV (cdp) Clark County	48	0.03
Sunrise Manor, NV (cdp) Clark County	44	0.03
Concord, CA (city) Contra Costa County	41	0.03
Hayward, CA (city) Alameda County	41	0.03
Daly City, CA (city) San Mateo County	34	0.03
Beaverton, OR (city) Washington County	21	0.03
Federal Way, WA (city) King County	21	0.03
Union City, CA (city) Alameda County	19	0.03
Layton, UT (city) Davis County	18	0.03
Redondo Beach, CA (city) Los Angeles County	18	0.03
Castro Valley, CA (cdp) Alameda County	17	0.03
Hesperia, CA (city) San Bernardino County	16	0.03
Bountiful, UT (city) Davis County	12	0.03
Dana Point, CA (city) Orange County	11	0.03
Delano, CA (city) Kern County	11	0.03
Rohnert Park, CA (city) Sonoma County	11	0.03
San Juan Capistrano, CA (city) Orange County	11	0.03
Burien, WA (city) King County	10	0.03
Menlo Park, CA (city) San Mateo County	10	0.03
Stanton, CA (city) Orange County	10	0.03
Des Moines, WA (city) King County	9	0.03
La Presa, CA (cdp) San Diego County	9	0.03
Moorpark, CA (city) Ventura County	9	0.03
Roseville, MN (city) Ramsey County	9	0.03
Fairbanks, AK (city) Fairbanks North Star Borough	8	0.03
Franconia, VA (cdp) Fairfax County	8	0.03
Lafayette, CA (city) Contra Costa County	8	0.03
East Millcreek, UT (cdp) Salt Lake County	7	0.03
Florin, CA (cdp) Sacramento County	7	0.03
Gallup, NM (city) McKinley County	7	0.03
Prescott Valley, AZ (town) Yavapai County	7	0.03
Savage, MN (city) Scott County	7	0.03
Xenia, OH (city) Greene County	7	0.03
Bainbridge Island, WA (city) Kitsap County	6	0.03
Magna, UT (cdp) Salt Lake County	6	0.03
Mountlake Terrace, WA (city) Snohomish County	6	0.03
Oak Ridge, FL (cdp) Orange County	6	0.03
Valinda, CA (cdp) Los Angeles County	6	0.03
West Carson, CA (cdp) Los Angeles County	6	0.03
Boulder City, NV (city) Clark County	5	0.03
Casa de Oro-Mount Helix, CA (cdp) San Diego County	5	0.03
Fort Lewis, WA (cdp) Pierce County	5	0.03
Holladay, UT (city) Salt Lake County	5	0.03
Mira Loma, CA (cdp) Riverside County	5	0.03
Pinole, CA (city) Contra Costa County	5	0.03
Santa Fe Springs, CA (city) Los Angeles County	5	0.03
Silverdale, WA (cdp) Kitsap County	5	0.03
Twentynine Palms, CA (city) San Bernardino County	5	0.03
Warrensville Heights, OH (city) Cuyahoga County	5	0.03
West Whiteland, PA (township) Chester County	5	0.03
Carpinteria, CA (city) Santa Barbara County	4	0.03
Las Vegas, NM (city) San Miguel County	4	0.03
Middleburg Heights, OH (city) Cuyahoga County	4	0.03
Mokena, IL (village) Will County	4	0.03
Winter Garden, FL (city) Orange County	4	0.03
Azalea Park, FL (cdp) Orange County	3	0.03
Capitola, CA (city) Santa Cruz County	3	0.03
Enumclaw, WA (city) King County	3	0.03
Grand Terrace, CA (city) San Bernardino County	3	0.03
Hillsborough, CA (town) San Mateo County	3	0.03
Lakeside, VA (cdp) Henrico County	3	0.03
Ripon, CA (city) San Joaquin County	3	0.03
South Lyon, MI (city) Oakland County	3	0.03

Notes: (cdp) census designated place; Refer to the Explanation of Data in the front of the book for more detailed information.

Hawaii Native/Pacific Islander: Other Pacific Islander, specified

Top 150 Places Sorted by Number

(Based on all places, regardless of population)

Place	Number	%
New York, NY (city) New York City	639	0.01
Houston, TX (city) Harris County	172	0.01
Los Angeles, CA (city) Los Angeles County	157	0.00
Chicago, IL (city) Cook County	132	0.00
Detroit, MI (city) Wayne County	96	0.01
Dallas, TX (city) Dallas County	95	0.01
Philadelphia, PA (city) Philadelphia County	84	0.01
Atlanta, GA (city) Fulton County	79	0.02
Baltimore, MD (independent city) Baltimore city	76	0.01
New Orleans, LA (city) Orleans Parish	71	0.01
Seattle, WA (city) King County	68	0.01
Saint Louis, MO (independent city) Saint Louis city	65	0.02
Jacksonville, FL (special city) Duval County	59	0.01
Boston, MA (city) Suffolk County	58	0.01
San Francisco, CA (city) San Francisco County	55	0.01
San Diego, CA (city) San Diego County	54	0.00
Indianapolis, IN (special city) Marion County	53	0.01
Augusta-Richmond County, GA (special city) Richmond County	51	0.03
Shreveport, LA (city) Caddo Parish	48	0.02
Fort Worth, TX (city) Tarrant County	46	0.01
Phoenix, AZ (city) Maricopa County	45	0.00
Memphis, TN (city) Shelby County	43	0.01
San Antonio, TX (city) Bexar County	41	0.00
Portland, OR (city) Multnomah County	39	0.01
Birmingham, AL (city) Jefferson County	38	0.02
Rochester, NY (city) Monroe County	38	0.02
Jersey City, NJ (city) Hudson County	37	0.02
Charlotte, NC (city) Mecklenburg County	36	0.01
Cleveland, OH (city) Cuyahoga County	34	0.01
Denver, CO (city) Denver County	34	0.01
Newark, NJ (city) Essex County	34	0.01
Hempstead, NY (town) Nassau County	33	0.00
Oakland, CA (city) Alameda County	32	0.01
Pittsburgh, PA (city) Allegheny County	31	0.01
Tucson, AZ (city) Pima County	31	0.01
Tulsa, OK (city) Tulsa County	31	0.01
Kansas City, MO (city) Jackson County	30	0.01
Virginia Beach, VA (independent city) Virginia Beach city	30	0.01
Austin, TX (city) Travis County	30	0.00
Jackson, MS (city) Hinds County	29	0.02
Louisville, KY (city) Jefferson County	29	0.01
Fresno, CA (city) Fresno County	28	0.01
Savannah, GA (city) Chatham County	27	0.02
Berkeley, CA (city) Alameda County	26	0.03
Saint Petersburg, FL (city) Pinellas County	26	0.01
Columbus, OH (city) Franklin County	26	0.00
Washington, DC (city) District of Columbia	26	0.00
Griffin, GA (city) Spalding County	25	0.11
Baton Rouge, LA (city) East Baton Rouge Parish	25	0.01
Colorado Springs, CO (city) El Paso County	25	0.01
Honolulu, HI (cdp) Honolulu County	25	0.01
Tampa, FL (city) Hillsborough County	25	0.01
Winston-Salem, NC (city) Forsyth County	25	0.01
San Jose, CA (city) Santa Clara County	25	0.00
Durham, NC (city) Durham County	23	0.01
Las Vegas, NV (city) Clark County	23	0.00
North Little Rock, AR (city) Pulaski County	22	0.04
Mobile, AL (city) Mobile County	22	0.01
Montgomery, AL (city) Montgomery County	22	0.01
Milwaukee, WI (city) Milwaukee County	22	0.00
Miami, FL (city) Miami-Dade County	21	0.01
Tallahassee, FL (city) Leon County	21	0.01
Albuquerque, NM (city) Bernalillo County	21	0.00
Oxnard, CA (city) Ventura County	20	0.01
Albany, GA (city) Dougherty County	19	0.02
Boise City, ID (city) Ada County	19	0.01
Waco, TX (city) McLennan County	18	0.02
Akron, OH (city) Summit County	18	0.01
Arlington, TX (city) Tarrant County	18	0.01
Cincinnati, OH (city) Hamilton County	18	0.01
Islip, NY (town) Suffolk County	18	0.01
Raleigh, NC (city) Wake County	18	0.01
Reno, NV (city) Washoe County	18	0.01
Saint Paul, MN (city) Ramsey County	18	0.01
Brookhaven, NY (town) Suffolk County	18	0.00

Place	Number	%
Garden City, GA (city) Chatham County	17	0.15
Buffalo, NY (city) Erie County	17	0.01
Corpus Christi, TX (city) Nueces County	17	0.01
East Palo Alto, CA (city) San Mateo County	16	0.05
Randolph, MA (cdp) Norfolk County	16	0.05
Gainesville, FL (city) Alachua County	16	0.02
Macon, GA (city) Bibb County	16	0.02
Tuscaloosa, AL (city) Tuscaloosa County	16	0.02
Chattanooga, TN (city) Hamilton County	16	0.01
Hartford, CT (city) Hartford County	16	0.01
Lubbock, TX (city) Lubbock County	16	0.01
Richmond, CA (city) Contra Costa County	15	0.02
Union City, NJ (city) Hudson County	15	0.02
Alexandria, VA (independent city) Alexandria city	15	0.01
Little Rock, AR (city) Pulaski County	15	0.01
Yonkers, NY (city) Westchester County	15	0.01
Minneapolis, MN (city) Hennepin County	15	0.00
Toledo, OH (city) Lucas County	15	0.00
Moultrie, GA (city) Colquitt County	14	0.10
La Grange, GA (city) Troup County	14	0.05
Delray Beach, FL (city) Palm Beach County	14	0.02
Lauderhill, FL (city) Broward County	14	0.02
Port Arthur, TX (city) Jefferson County	14	0.02
Reading, PA (city) Berks County	14	0.02
Tyler, TX (city) Smith County	14	0.02
Arlington, VA (cdp) Arlington County	14	0.01
Grand Rapids, MI (city) Kent County	14	0.01
Paterson, NJ (city) Passaic County	14	0.01
Tacoma, WA (city) Pierce County	14	0.01
Nashville-Davidson, TN (special city) Davidson County	14	0.00
Wichita, KS (city) Sedgwick County	14	0.00
New Rochelle, NY (city) Westchester County	13	0.02
Beaumont, TX (city) Jefferson County	13	0.01
Chesapeake, VA (independent city) Chesapeake city	13	0.01
Modesto, CA (city) Stanislaus County	13	0.01
Orlando, FL (city) Orange County	13	0.01
Salt Lake City, UT (city) Salt Lake County	13	0.01
El Paso, TX (city) El Paso County	13	0.00
Long Beach, CA (city) Los Angeles County	13	0.00
Omaha, NE (city) Douglas County	13	0.00
New Eagle, PA (borough) Washington County	12	0.53
Spanaway, WA (cdp) Pierce County	12	0.06
Albany, OR (city) Linn County	12	0.03
Bellingham, WA (city) Whatcom County	12	0.02
Hamilton, OH (city) Butler County	12	0.02
Kent, WA (city) King County	12	0.02
Wheaton-Glenmont, MD (cdp) Montgomery County	12	0.02
Columbia, SC (city) Richland County	12	0.01
Denton, TX (city) Denton County	12	0.01
Eugene, OR (city) Lane County	12	0.01
Santa Clarita, CA (city) Los Angeles County	12	0.01
Loris, SC (city) Horry County	11	0.53
Marion, VA (town) Smyth County	11	0.17
West Point, MS (city) Clay County	11	0.09
Fremont, NE (city) Dodge County	11	0.04
Mililani Town, HI (cdp) Honolulu County	11	0.04
Dover, DE (city) Kent County	11	0.03
Anderson, IN (city) Madison County	11	0.02
Dayton, OH (city) Montgomery County	11	0.01
High Point, NC (city) Guilford County	11	0.01
Madison, WI (city) Dane County	11	0.01
Providence, RI (city) Providence County	11	0.01
Simi Valley, CA (city) Ventura County	11	0.01
Syracuse, NY (city) Onondaga County	11	0.01
Mesa, AZ (city) Maricopa County	11	0.00
Norfolk, VA (independent city) Norfolk city	11	0.00
Frankfort, OH (village) Ross County	10	0.99
Waverly, VA (town) Sussex County	10	0.43
Homer, MI (township) Calhoun County	10	0.33
Willow Oak, FL (cdp) Polk County	10	0.20
Cartersville, GA (city) Bartow County	10	0.06
Bedford, NH (town) Hillsborough County	10	0.05
Milledgeville, GA (city) Baldwin County	10	0.05
Muscatine, IA (city) Muscatine County	10	0.04
Neptune, NJ (township) Monmouth County	10	0.04

Notes: (cdp) census designated place; Refer to the Explanation of Data in the front of the book for more detailed information.

Hawaii Native/Pacific Islander: Other Pacific Islander, specified

Top 150 Places Sorted by Percent

(Based on all places, regardless of population)

Place	Number	%
Mount Carmel, SC (cdp) McCormick County	8	3.38
Eldora, CO (cdp) Boulder County	3	1.76
Warren City, TX (city) Gregg County	6	1.75
Trenton, KY (city) Todd County	7	1.67
Yantis, TX (town) Wood County	5	1.56
Rockleigh, NJ (borough) Bergen County	6	1.53
Hickory Hill, KY (city) Jefferson County	2	1.39
Crown Point, AK (cdp) Kenai Peninsula Borough	1	1.33
Kirby, VT (town) Caledonia County	6	1.32
Elizabeth, LA (town) Allen Parish	7	1.22
Oconee, GA (city) Washington County	3	1.07
Harleyville, SC (town) Dorchester County	6	1.01
Greenview, CA (cdp) Siskiyou County	2	1.00
Arco, MN (city) Lincoln County	1	1.00
Frankfort, OH (village) Ross County	10	0.99
Coram, MT (cdp) Flathead County	3	0.89
Shorter, AL (town) Macon County	3	0.85
Rosser, TX (village) Kaufman County	3	0.79
Wealthwood, MN (township) Aitkin County	2	0.76
San Isidro, TX (cdp) Starr County	2	0.74
Beseman, MN (township) Carlton County	1	0.67
Washington, PA (township) Cambria County	6	0.65
Parrott, GA (town) Terrell County	1	0.64
Paoli, OK (town) Garvin County	4	0.62
Bassett, AR (town) Mississippi County	1	0.60
Thornton, AR (city) Calhoun County	3	0.58
Springville, CA (cdp) Tulare County	6	0.54
New Eagle, PA (borough) Washington County	12	0.53
Loris, SC (city) Horry County	11	0.53
Carrollton, AL (town) Pickens County	5	0.51
Buckner, AR (city) Lafayette County	2	0.51
Braselton, GA (town) Jackson County	6	0.50
Aloha, MI (township) Cheboygan County	5	0.48
Summerton, SC (town) Clarendon County	5	0.47
Sweet Home, AR (cdp) Pulaski County	5	0.47
Flippin, AR (city) Marion County	6	0.44
Linn, MO (city) Osage County	6	0.44
Chinook, WA (cdp) Pacific County	2	0.44
Waverly, VA (town) Sussex County	10	0.43
Olney, MN (township) Nobles County	1	0.43
Minonk, IL (city) Woodford County	9	0.42
Ridgway, CO (town) Ouray County	3	0.42
Marlow, NH (town) Cheshire County	3	0.40
Algoma, MS (town) Pontotoc County	2	0.39
Copperhill, TN (city) Polk County	2	0.39
Philadelphia, TN (city) Loudon County	2	0.38
Ellaville, GA (city) Schley County	6	0.37
Burns, WY (town) Laramie County	1	0.35
West Harrison, IN (town) Dearborn County	1	0.35
Homer, MI (township) Calhoun County	10	0.33
Pineville, KY (city) Bell County	7	0.33
Buffalo, TX (city) Leon County	6	0.33
Richland, GA (city) Stewart County	6	0.33
Moclips, WA (cdp) Grays Harbor County	2	0.33
Elliston-Lafayette, VA (cdp) Montgomery County	4	0.32
Rich Square, NC (town) Northampton County	3	0.32
Halstad, MN (city) Norman County	2	0.32
Macarthur, WV (cdp) Raleigh County	5	0.30
Bergen, WI (town) Vernon County	4	0.30
Saxis, VA (town) Accomack County	1	0.30
Garyville, LA (cdp) Saint John the Baptist Parish	8	0.29
Stigler, OK (city) Haskell County	8	0.29
Derma, MS (town) Calhoun County	3	0.29
Scott, WI (town) Sheboygan County	5	0.28
Springfield, KY (city) Washington County	7	0.27
Newtown, CT (borough) Fairfield County	5	0.27
McCormick, SC (town) McCormick County	4	0.27
Elsinboro, NJ (township) Salem County	3	0.27
Bancroft, WV (town) Putnam County	1	0.27
Parkdale, AR (city) Ashley County	1	0.27
Wyatt, MO (city) Mississippi County	1	0.27
Woodbine, IA (city) Harrison County	4	0.26
De Leon Springs, FL (cdp) Volusia County	6	0.25
Lytle, TX (city) Atascosa County	6	0.25
Greensburg, KS (city) Kiowa County	4	0.25
Woodbury, GA (city) Meriwether County	3	0.25
Fairfield, ID (city) Camas County	1	0.25
Saint Petersburg, PA (borough) Clarion County	1	0.25
Southern Shops, SC (cdp) Spartanburg County	9	0.24
Colorado City, AZ (town) Mohave County	8	0.24
Jay, OK (city) Delaware County	6	0.24
Absarokee, MT (cdp) Stillwater County	3	0.24
Crown City, OH (village) Gallia County	1	0.24
Trapper Creek, AK (cdp) Matanuska-Susitna Borough	1	0.24
Moline Acres, MO (city) Saint Louis County	6	0.23
Natalbany, LA (cdp) Tangipahoa Parish	4	0.23
White Sands, NM (cdp) Dona Ana County	3	0.23
Lake Arthur, NM (town) Chaves County	1	0.23
Tehama, CA (city) Tehama County	1	0.23
Burnett, WI (town) Dodge County	2	0.22
McRoberts, KY (cdp) Letcher County	2	0.22
Maalaea, HI (cdp) Maui County	1	0.22
Dermott, AR (city) Chicot County	7	0.21
Cedar Grove, WI (village) Sheboygan County	4	0.21
Kensington, MD (town) Montgomery County	4	0.21
Pelahatchie, MS (town) Rankin County	3	0.21
Willow Oak, FL (cdp) Polk County	10	0.20
Franklin, MI (village) Oakland County	6	0.20
Pipestone, MI (township) Berrien County	5	0.20
Hillsdale, MO (village) Saint Louis County	3	0.20
Calico Rock, AR (city) Izard County	2	0.20
Rome, ME (town) Kennebec County	2	0.20
Clarksville, MO (city) Pike County	1	0.20
Meadow Lakes, AK (cdp) Matanuska-Susitna Borough	9	0.19
Leet, PA (township) Allegheny County	3	0.19
Lucasville, OH (cdp) Scioto County	3	0.19
Manassa, CO (town) Conejos County	2	0.19
McConnellsburg, PA (borough) Fulton County	2	0.19
Bruin, PA (borough) Butler County	1	0.19
Grayson, LA (village) Caldwell Parish	1	0.19
Lake Nacimiento, CA (cdp) San Luis Obispo County	4	0.18
Mountain Home, NC (cdp) Henderson County	4	0.18
Cresson, PA (borough) Cambria County	3	0.18
Kershaw, SC (town) Lancaster County	3	0.18
Morrison, WI (town) Brown County	3	0.18
Peach Lake, NY (cdp) Putnam County	3	0.18
Baudette, MN (city) Lake of the Woods County	2	0.18
Marion, VA (town) Smyth County	11	0.17
East Flat Rock, NC (cdp) Henderson County	7	0.17
Madison, GA (city) Morgan County	6	0.17
North East, NY (town) Dutchess County	5	0.17
West Terre Haute, IN (town) Vigo County	4	0.17
Burkesville, KY (city) Cumberland County	3	0.17
Kalamo, MI (township) Eaton County	3	0.17
Woodville, MS (town) Wilkinson County	2	0.17
Wescott, WI (town) Shawano County	6	0.16
Bel-Ridge, MO (village) Saint Louis County	5	0.16
Iuka, MS (city) Tishomingo County	5	0.16
Delmont, PA (borough) Westmoreland County	4	0.16
Harris, MI (township) Menominee County	3	0.16
McAlmont, AR (cdp) Pulaski County	3	0.16
Quincy, CA (cdp) Plumas County	3	0.16
Taylor, AL (town) Houston County	3	0.16
Clarkesville, GA (city) Habersham County	2	0.16
Hewlett Harbor, NY (village) Nassau County	2	0.16
Brighton, WI (town) Marathon County	1	0.16
Garden City, GA (city) Chatham County	17	0.15
Sandersville, GA (city) Washington County	9	0.15
China, MI (township) Saint Clair County	5	0.15
Highgrove, CA (cdp) Riverside County	5	0.15
Verona, MS (city) Lee County	5	0.15
White Creek, NY (town) Washington County	5	0.15
Greensboro, AL (city) Hale County	4	0.15
White Hall, IL (city) Greene County	4	0.15
Manattee Road, FL (cdp) Levy County	3	0.15
Shamrock, TX (city) Wheeler County	3	0.15
Cortland West, NY (cdp) Cortland County	2	0.15
Fort Loramie, OH (village) Shelby County	2	0.15
Whitewater, KS (city) Butler County	1	0.15
Edna, TX (city) Jackson County	8	0.14

Notes: (cdp) census designated place; Refer to the Explanation of Data in the front of the book for more detailed information.

Hawaii Native/Pacific Islander: Other Pacific Islander, specified

Top 150 Places Sorted by Percent

(Based on places with populations of 10,000 or more)

Place	Number	%
Garden City, GA (city) Chatham County	17	0.15
Griffin, GA (city) Spalding County	25	0.11
Moultrie, GA (city) Colquitt County	14	0.10
West Point, MS (city) Clay County	11	0.09
McComb, MS (city) Pike County	9	0.07
Raceland, LA (cdp) Lafourche Parish	7	0.07
Spanaway, WA (cdp) Pierce County	12	0.06
Cartersville, GA (city) Bartow County	10	0.06
Springboro, OH (city) Warren County	8	0.06
Berwick, PA (borough) Columbia County	7	0.06
Fort Gratiot, MI (township) Saint Clair County	6	0.06
Leicester, MA (town) Worcester County	6	0.06
East Palo Alto, CA (city) San Mateo County	16	0.05
Randolph, MA (cdp) Norfolk County	16	0.05
La Grange, GA (city) Troup County	14	0.05
Bedford, NH (town) Hillsborough County	10	0.05
Milledgeville, GA (city) Baldwin County	10	0.05
Golden, CO (city) Jefferson County	8	0.05
Cameron Park, CA (cdp) El Dorado County	7	0.05
Crowley, LA (city) Acadia Parish	7	0.05
New Territory, TX (cdp) Fort Bend County	7	0.05
Talladega, AL (city) Talladega County	7	0.05
University Heights, OH (city) Cuyahoga County	7	0.05
Commerce, CA (city) Los Angeles County	6	0.05
El Campo, TX (city) Wharton County	6	0.05
Jefferson, LA (cdp) Jefferson Parish	6	0.05
Kewanee, IL (city) Henry County	6	0.05
Parlier, CA (city) Fresno County	6	0.05
East Rockaway, NY (village) Nassau County	5	0.05
North Little Rock, AR (city) Pulaski County	22	0.04
Fremont, NE (city) Dodge County	11	0.04
Mililani Town, HI (cdp) Honolulu County	11	0.04
Muscatine, IA (city) Muscatine County	10	0.04
Neptune, NJ (township) Monmouth County	10	0.04
Opelousas, LA (city) Saint Landry Parish	10	0.04
West Memphis, AR (city) Crittenden County	10	0.04
Carlisle, PA (borough) Cumberland County	7	0.04
Natchez, MS (city) Adams County	7	0.04
Asbury Park, NJ (city) Monmouth County	6	0.04
Bogalusa, LA (city) Washington Parish	6	0.04
Desert Hot Springs, CA (city) Riverside County	6	0.04
Dixon, IL (city) Lee County	6	0.04
Elizabethton, TN (city) Carter County	6	0.04
Godfrey, IL (village) Madison County	6	0.04
Southfield, MI (township) Oakland County	6	0.04
Sunnyside, WA (city) Yakima County	6	0.04
Beaufort, SC (city) Beaufort County	5	0.04
Ecorse, MI (city) Wayne County	5	0.04
Elizabeth, PA (township) Allegheny County	5	0.04
Fayetteville, GA (city) Fayette County	5	0.04
Fort Stewart, GA (cdp) Liberty County	5	0.04
Goodlettsville, TN (city) Davidson County	5	0.04
Grover Beach, CA (city) San Luis Obispo County	5	0.04
Kings Point, FL (cdp) Palm Beach County	5	0.04
Manorville, NY (cdp) Suffolk County	5	0.04
Susanville, CA (city) Lassen County	5	0.04
Wilton Manors, FL (city) Broward County	5	0.04
Beach Park, IL (village) Lake County	4	0.04
Jeannette, PA (city) Westmoreland County	4	0.04
Lexington Park, MD (cdp) Saint Mary's County	4	0.04
Middleburg, FL (cdp) Clay County	4	0.04
Red Hill, SC (cdp) Horry County	4	0.04
Spring Creek, NV (cdp) Elko County	4	0.04
Tyngsborough, MA (town) Middlesex County	4	0.04
Vineyard, CA (cdp) Sacramento County	4	0.04
Augusta-Richmond County, GA (special city) Richmond County	51	0.03
Berkeley, CA (city) Alameda County	26	0.03
Albany, OR (city) Linn County	12	0.03
Dover, DE (city) Kent County	11	0.03
Juneau, AK (city and borough) Juneau Borough	10	0.03
La Presa, CA (cdp) San Diego County	10	0.03
Prichard, AL (city) Mobile County	10	0.03
University City, MO (city) Saint Louis County	10	0.03
Bartlesville, OK (city) Washington County	9	0.03
Columbus, MS (city) Lowndes County	9	0.03

Place	Number	%
East Cleveland, OH (city) Cuyahoga County	9	0.03
Batavia, IL (city) Kane County	8	0.03
Lochearn, MD (cdp) Baltimore County	8	0.03
Port Chester, NY (village) Westchester County	8	0.03
Riviera Beach, FL (city) Palm Beach County	8	0.03
Frankfort, KY (city) Franklin County	7	0.03
Rockaway, NJ (township) Morris County	7	0.03
Arnold, MD (cdp) Anne Arundel County	6	0.03
Avenel, NJ (cdp) Middlesex County	6	0.03
Bridgeton, NJ (city) Cumberland County	6	0.03
El Dorado, AR (city) Union County	6	0.03
Fort Walton Beach, FL (city) Okaloosa County	6	0.03
Greenville, TX (city) Hunt County	6	0.03
Greenwood, SC (city) Greenwood County	6	0.03
Hazleton, PA (city) Luzerne County	6	0.03
Kenmore, WA (city) King County	6	0.03
Lindenwold, NJ (borough) Camden County	6	0.03
Muskego, WI (city) Waukesha County	6	0.03
New Lenox, IL (village) Will County	6	0.03
Raritan, NJ (township) Hunterdon County	6	0.03
Ronkonkoma, NY (cdp) Suffolk County	6	0.03
Selma, AL (city) Dallas County	6	0.03
Valinda, CA (cdp) Los Angeles County	6	0.03
Webster Groves, MO (city) Saint Louis County	6	0.03
Colleyville, TX (city) Tarrant County	5	0.03
Cudahy, WI (city) Milwaukee County	5	0.03
Idylwood, VA (cdp) Fairfax County	5	0.03
Rye, NY (city) Westchester County	5	0.03
Sayville, NY (cdp) Suffolk County	5	0.03
Schertz, TX (city) Guadalupe County	5	0.03
Shelby, NC (city) Cleveland County	5	0.03
Socastee, SC (cdp) Horry County	5	0.03
Thomasville, GA (city) Thomas County	5	0.03
Beacon, NY (city) Dutchess County	4	0.03
Beekman, NY (town) Dutchess County	4	0.03
Bixby, OK (city) Tulsa County	4	0.03
Brookside, DE (cdp) New Castle County	4	0.03
Brunswick, GA (city) Glynn County	4	0.03
Carpinteria, CA (city) Santa Barbara County	4	0.03
Coos Bay, OR (city) Coos County	4	0.03
Dublin, GA (city) Laurens County	4	0.03
East Highland Park, VA (cdp) Henrico County	4	0.03
Exeter, NH (town) Rockingham County	4	0.03
Hereford, TX (city) Deaf Smith County	4	0.03
North Wantagh, NY (cdp) Nassau County	4	0.03
Orangeburg, SC (city) Orangeburg County	4	0.03
Riverbank, CA (city) Stanislaus County	4	0.03
Roosevelt, NY (cdp) Nassau County	4	0.03
Setauket-East Setauket, NY (cdp) Suffolk County	4	0.03
Silverdale, WA (cdp) Kitsap County	4	0.03
Tillmans Corner, AL (cdp) Mobile County	4	0.03
Bedford Heights, OH (city) Cuyahoga County	3	0.03
Benton Harbor, MI (city) Berrien County	3	0.03
Cambridge, OH (city) Guernsey County	3	0.03
Douglas, GA (city) Coffee County	3	0.03
Evanston, WY (city) Uinta County	3	0.03
Hamptons at Boca Raton, FL (cdp) Palm Beach County	3	0.03
Joppatowne, MD (cdp) Harford County	3	0.03
Neosho, MO (city) Newton County	3	0.03
Panthersville, GA (cdp) De Kalb County	3	0.03
Silver Spring, PA (township) Cumberland County	3	0.03
Somers, CT (town) Tolland County	3	0.03
Timberlake, VA (cdp) Campbell County	3	0.03
Atlanta, GA (city) Fulton County	79	0.02
Saint Louis, MO (independent city) Saint Louis city	65	0.02
Shreveport, LA (city) Caddo Parish	48	0.02
Birmingham, AL (city) Jefferson County	38	0.02
Rochester, NY (city) Monroe County	38	0.02
Jersey City, NJ (city) Hudson County	37	0.02
Jackson, MS (city) Hinds County	29	0.02
Savannah, GA (city) Chatham County	27	0.02
Albany, GA (city) Dougherty County	19	0.02
Waco, TX (city) McLennan County	18	0.02
Gainesville, FL (city) Alachua County	16	0.02
Macon, GA (city) Bibb County	16	0.02

Notes: (cdp) census designated place; Refer to the Explanation of Data in the front of the book for more detailed information.

Hawaii Native/Pacific Islander: Other Pacific Islander, not specified

Top 150 Places Sorted by Number

(Based on all places, regardless of population)

Place	Number	%
New York, NY (city) New York City	13,530	0.17
Los Angeles, CA (city) Los Angeles County	4,308	0.12
Chicago, IL (city) Cook County	2,540	0.09
Sacramento, CA (city) Sacramento County	2,282	0.56
San Diego, CA (city) San Diego County	1,846	0.15
San Jose, CA (city) Santa Clara County	1,817	0.20
Philadelphia, PA (city) Philadelphia County	1,474	0.10
Houston, TX (city) Harris County	1,338	0.07
Hayward, CA (city) Alameda County	1,305	0.93
San Francisco, CA (city) San Francisco County	1,237	0.16
Honolulu, HI (cdp) Honolulu County	1,199	0.32
Boston, MA (city) Suffolk County	1,124	0.19
Long Beach, CA (city) Los Angeles County	1,117	0.24
Saint Paul, MN (city) Ramsey County	1,023	0.36
Stockton, CA (city) San Joaquin County	996	0.41
Seattle, WA (city) King County	957	0.17
Modesto, CA (city) Stanislaus County	952	0.50
Portland, OR (city) Multnomah County	867	0.16
Phoenix, AZ (city) Maricopa County	803	0.06
Fresno, CA (city) Fresno County	680	0.16
Oakland, CA (city) Alameda County	679	0.17
Las Vegas, NV (city) Clark County	650	0.14
Dallas, TX (city) Dallas County	643	0.05
Springfield, MA (city) Hampden County	633	0.42
San Antonio, TX (city) Bexar County	579	0.05
Minneapolis, MN (city) Hennepin County	544	0.14
Fremont, CA (city) Alameda County	531	0.26
Miami, FL (city) Miami-Dade County	509	0.14
Hempstead, NY (town) Nassau County	509	0.07
Anaheim, CA (city) Orange County	456	0.14
Anchorage, AK (municipality) Anchorage Borough	453	0.17
San Bruno, CA (city) San Mateo County	447	1.11
Jacksonville, FL (special city) Duval County	437	0.06
Columbus, OH (city) Franklin County	436	0.06
Jersey City, NJ (city) Hudson County	426	0.18
Newark, NJ (city) Essex County	420	0.15
San Mateo, CA (city) San Mateo County	409	0.44
Paterson, NJ (city) Passaic County	407	0.27
Austin, TX (city) Travis County	393	0.06
Hartford, CT (city) Hartford County	388	0.32
Milwaukee, WI (city) Milwaukee County	385	0.06
Vallejo, CA (city) Solano County	384	0.33
Detroit, MI (city) Wayne County	380	0.04
Daly City, CA (city) San Mateo County	378	0.36
Providence, RI (city) Providence County	365	0.21
Denver, CO (city) Denver County	360	0.06
Virginia Beach, VA (independent city) Virginia Beach city	359	0.08
Tacoma, WA (city) Pierce County	352	0.18
Baltimore, MD (independent city) Baltimore city	342	0.05
Salt Lake City, UT (city) Salt Lake County	338	0.19
Riverside, CA (city) Riverside County	336	0.13
Washington, DC (city) District of Columbia	328	0.06
Union City, CA (city) Alameda County	327	0.49
Bridgeport, CT (city) Fairfield County	321	0.23
South San Francisco, CA (city) San Mateo County	318	0.53
Santa Ana, CA (city) Orange County	303	0.09
Indianapolis, IN (special city) Marion County	303	0.04
Tucson, AZ (city) Pima County	292	0.06
Elk Grove, CA (cdp) Sacramento County	286	0.48
Colorado Springs, CO (city) El Paso County	286	0.08
East Palo Alto, CA (city) San Mateo County	283	0.96
Worcester, MA (city) Worcester County	281	0.16
Henderson, NV (city) Clark County	280	0.16
Hilo, HI (cdp) Hawaii County	279	0.68
Tempe, AZ (city) Maricopa County	276	0.17
Tampa, FL (city) Hillsborough County	260	0.09
Irvine, CA (city) Orange County	257	0.18
Orlando, FL (city) Orange County	251	0.13
Pawtucket, RI (city) Providence County	250	0.34
Paradise, NV (cdp) Clark County	250	0.13
San Leandro, CA (city) Alameda County	248	0.31
New Haven, CT (city) New Haven County	248	0.20
Yonkers, NY (city) Westchester County	248	0.13
Huntington Beach, CA (city) Orange County	245	0.13
Mesa, AZ (city) Maricopa County	243	0.06
Fall River, MA (city) Bristol County	242	0.26
Norfolk, VA (independent city) Norfolk city	242	0.10
Lowell, MA (city) Middlesex County	241	0.23
Reno, NV (city) Washoe County	237	0.13
Rochester, NY (city) Monroe County	237	0.11
Santa Clara, CA (city) Santa Clara County	236	0.23
Glendale, CA (city) Los Angeles County	236	0.12
White Plains, NY (city) Westchester County	235	0.44
Salinas, CA (city) Monterey County	235	0.16
Charlotte, NC (city) Mecklenburg County	235	0.04
Nashville-Davidson, TN (special city) Davidson County	234	0.04
Oceanside, CA (city) San Diego County	232	0.14
Cleveland, OH (city) Cuyahoga County	228	0.05
Carson, CA (city) Los Angeles County	226	0.25
Sunrise Manor, NV (cdp) Clark County	221	0.14
Kansas City, MO (city) Jackson County	220	0.05
Oklahoma City, OK (city) Oklahoma County	220	0.04
North Las Vegas, NV (city) Clark County	219	0.19
Torrance, CA (city) Los Angeles County	218	0.16
Garden Grove, CA (city) Orange County	218	0.13
Oxnard, CA (city) Ventura County	218	0.13
Fairfield, CA (city) Solano County	215	0.22
West Valley City, UT (city) Salt Lake County	214	0.20
Parkway-South Sacramento, CA (cdp) Sacramento County	213	0.58
New Bedford, MA (city) Bristol County	213	0.23
Fort Worth, TX (city) Tarrant County	213	0.04
North Miami, FL (city) Miami-Dade County	209	0.35
Miramar, FL (city) Broward County	209	0.29
Vancouver, WA (city) Clark County	209	0.15
Chula Vista, CA (city) San Diego County	207	0.12
Arlington, TX (city) Tarrant County	207	0.06
Concord, CA (city) Contra Costa County	206	0.17
Seaside, CA (city) Monterey County	205	0.65
El Paso, TX (city) El Paso County	203	0.04
Pittsburg, CA (city) Contra Costa County	202	0.36
Milpitas, CA (city) Santa Clara County	200	0.32
San Bernardino, CA (city) San Bernardino County	199	0.11
Aurora, CO (city) Arapahoe County	198	0.07
Newark, CA (city) Alameda County	197	0.46
West Sacramento, CA (city) Yolo County	194	0.61
Albuquerque, NM (city) Bernalillo County	194	0.04
Islip, NY (town) Suffolk County	193	0.06
Arcadia, CA (city) Los Angeles County	192	0.36
Pomona, CA (city) Los Angeles County	192	0.13
Brockton, MA (city) Plymouth County	191	0.20
Spring Valley, NV (cdp) Clark County	191	0.16
Moreno Valley, CA (city) Riverside County	188	0.13
Wichita, KS (city) Sedgwick County	188	0.05
Elizabeth, NJ (city) Union County	184	0.15
Delray Beach, FL (city) Palm Beach County	183	0.30
Lakewood, CA (city) Los Angeles County	182	0.23
Glendale, AZ (city) Maricopa County	182	0.08
Trenton, NJ (city) Mercer County	181	0.21
Richmond, CA (city) Contra Costa County	181	0.18
Sunnyvale, CA (city) Santa Clara County	181	0.14
Federal Way, WA (city) King County	180	0.22
Fullerton, CA (city) Orange County	178	0.14
Brookhaven, NY (town) Suffolk County	178	0.04
Irving, TX (city) Dallas County	177	0.09
Fontana, CA (city) San Bernardino County	175	0.14
Sunrise, FL (city) Broward County	174	0.20
West Covina, CA (city) Los Angeles County	174	0.17
Richmond, VA (independent city) Richmond city	174	0.09
Everett, WA (city) Snohomish County	173	0.19
Alameda, CA (city) Alameda County	171	0.24
Corona, CA (city) Riverside County	170	0.14
Camden, NJ (city) Camden County	167	0.21
Antioch, CA (city) Contra Costa County	167	0.18
Merced, CA (city) Merced County	166	0.26
Rowland Heights, CA (cdp) Los Angeles County	165	0.34
Turlock, CA (city) Stanislaus County	165	0.30
Kaneohe, HI (cdp) Honolulu County	164	0.47
Cerritos, CA (city) Los Angeles County	164	0.32
Corpus Christi, TX (city) Nueces County	164	0.06
Atlanta, GA (city) Fulton County	163	0.04

Notes: (cdp) census designated place; Refer to the Explanation of Data in the front of the book for more detailed information.

Hawaii Native/Pacific Islander: Other Pacific Islander, not specified

Top 150 Places Sorted by Percent

(Based on all places, regardless of population)

Place	Number	%
Kimmswick, MO (city) Jefferson County	6	6.38
Shoshone, CA (cdp) Inyo County	2	3.85
Egegik, AK (city) Lake and Peninsula Borough	4	3.45
Pringle, SD (town) Custer County	4	3.20
Randsburg, CA (cdp) Kern County	2	2.60
Center, TX (city) Shelby County	125	2.20
Clarksville, PA (borough) Greene County	5	2.14
Fairchild, WI (town) Eau Claire County	7	1.99
Belmont, OH (village) Belmont County	10	1.88
Bannockburn, IL (village) Lake County	26	1.82
Plymouth, IL (village) Hancock County	10	1.78
Cromwell, IN (town) Noble County	8	1.77
Billingsley, AL (town) Autauga County	2	1.72
Appleton, MN (city) Swift County	46	1.60
Honomu, HI (cdp) Hawaii County	8	1.48
Chehalis Village, WA (cdp) Grays Harbor County	5	1.45
Santa Cruz, NM (cdp) Santa Fe County	6	1.42
Beaver, OR (cdp) Tillamook County	2	1.38
Zinc, AR (town) Boone County	1	1.32
Omao, HI (cdp) Kauai County	16	1.31
College Station, AR (cdp) Pulaski County	10	1.31
Strasburg, ND (city) Emmons County	7	1.28
Bonanza, OR (town) Klamath County	5	1.20
Fern Acres, HI (cdp) Hawaii County	9	1.19
Northport, WA (town) Stevens County	4	1.19
Hawaiian Acres, HI (cdp) Hawaii County	21	1.18
Coolidge, KS (city) Hamilton County	1	1.16
Encino, TX (cdp) Brooks County	2	1.13
San Bruno, CA (city) San Mateo County	447	1.11
Martin, KY (city) Floyd County	7	1.11
Coleridge, NE (village) Cedar County	6	1.11
Cairo, MN (township) Renville County	3	1.11
Gregg, PA (township) Union County	51	1.09
Laie, HI (cdp) Honolulu County	50	1.09
Kekaha, HI (cdp) Kauai County	34	1.07
Allegheny, PA (township) Venango County	3	1.07
Goessel, KS (city) Marion County	6	1.06
Pine Mountain, GA (town) Harris County	12	1.05
Kirkwood, CA (cdp) Alpine County	1	1.04
Lake Harbor, FL (cdp) Palm Beach County	2	1.03
Country Homes, WA (cdp) Spokane County	53	1.02
Haliimaile, HI (cdp) Maui County	9	1.01
Snoqualmie Pass, WA (cdp) Kittitas County	2	1.00
Hillsboro Pines, FL (cdp) Broward County	4	0.99
Gun Club Estates, FL (cdp) Palm Beach County	7	0.98
Central City, CO (city) Gilpin County	5	0.97
Mountain View, WY (cdp) Natrona County	1	0.97
East Palo Alto, CA (city) San Mateo County	283	0.96
Hayward, CA (city) Alameda County	1,305	0.93
Belle Glade, FL (city) Palm Beach County	138	0.93
Koloa, HI (cdp) Kauai County	18	0.93
Beaulieu, MN (township) Mahnomen County	1	0.93
Summitville, OH (village) Columbiana County	1	0.93
Lisman, AL (town) Choctaw County	6	0.92
Tallulah, LA (city) Madison Parish	83	0.90
Lake Lillian, MN (township) Kandiyohi County	2	0.90
Hawaiian Beaches, HI (cdp) Hawaii County	33	0.89
Center Hill, FL (city) Sumter County	8	0.88
Stratford, CA (cdp) Kings County	11	0.87
Lawai, HI (cdp) Kauai County	17	0.86
Leilani Estates, HI (cdp) Hawaii County	9	0.86
Saint Libory, IL (village) Saint Clair County	5	0.86
Lost Creek, WV (town) Harrison County	4	0.86
Hawi, HI (cdp) Hawaii County	8	0.85
Bluffton, GA (town) Clay County	1	0.85
Mount Gretna Heights, PA (cdp) Lebanon County	3	0.83
Orchidlands Estates, HI (cdp) Hawaii County	14	0.81
Bethany, WV (town) Brooke County	8	0.81
Zoar, WI (cdp) Menominee County	1	0.81
Linwood, KS (city) Leavenworth County	3	0.80
Ebro, FL (town) Washington County	2	0.80
Makawao, HI (cdp) Maui County	50	0.79
Hauula, HI (cdp) Honolulu County	29	0.79
Apolacon, PA (township) Susquehanna County	4	0.79
La Crosse, WA (town) Whitman County	3	0.79
South Hill, NY (cdp) Tompkins County	47	0.78
Hawaiian Ocean View, HI (cdp) Hawaii County	17	0.78
Allardt, TN (city) Fentress County	5	0.78
Buckland, OH (village) Auglaize County	2	0.78
Pukalani, HI (cdp) Maui County	57	0.77
Spring Creek, PA (township) Elk County	2	0.77
Colusa, CA (city) Colusa County	41	0.76
Central, AK (cdp) Yukon-Koyukuk Census Area	1	0.75
Coal Center, PA (borough) Washington County	1	0.75
Hanapepe, HI (cdp) Kauai County	16	0.74
Oakville, WA (city) Grays Harbor County	5	0.74
Wahiawa, HI (cdp) Honolulu County	118	0.73
Waikoloa Village, HI (cdp) Hawaii County	35	0.73
Ainaloa, HI (cdp) Hawaii County	14	0.73
Holland, TX (town) Bell County	8	0.73
Sunshine Acres, FL (cdp) Broward County	6	0.73
Oaks, OK (town) Delaware County	3	0.73
Wilma, MN (township) Pine County	1	0.73
Ewa Villages, HI (cdp) Honolulu County	34	0.72
Camp Three, MT (cdp) Musselshell County	1	0.72
Momeyer, NC (town) Nash County	2	0.69
Sodaville, OR (city) Linn County	2	0.69
Hilo, HI (cdp) Hawaii County	279	0.68
Alta Vista, KS (city) Wabaunsee County	3	0.68
Cross Village, MI (township) Emmet County	2	0.68
Cannonville, UT (town) Garfield County	1	0.68
Kilauea, HI (cdp) Kauai County	14	0.67
Puhi, HI (cdp) Kauai County	8	0.67
Eden Roc, HI (cdp) Hawaii County	3	0.67
Beseman, MN (township) Carlton County	1	0.67
Waianae, HI (cdp) Honolulu County	69	0.66
Williamstown, MA (town) Berkshire County	56	0.66
Seaside, CA (city) Monterey County	205	0.65
Schwenksville, PA (borough) Montgomery County	11	0.65
Poipu, HI (cdp) Kauai County	7	0.65
Fort Greely, AK (cdp) Southeast Fairbanks Census Area	3	0.65
Breckinridge Center, KY (cdp) Union County	12	0.64
Maywood Park, OR (city) Multnomah County	5	0.64
Desert Shores, CA (cdp) Imperial County	5	0.63
Malin, OR (city) Klamath County	4	0.63
Cragsmoor, NY (cdp) Ulster County	3	0.63
Makaha, HI (cdp) Honolulu County	48	0.62
Haiku-Pauwela, HI (cdp) Maui County	41	0.62
Tracy, MN (city) Lyon County	14	0.62
Wabasso, MN (city) Redwood County	4	0.62
Lisbon, LA (village) Claiborne Parish	1	0.62
West Sacramento, CA (city) Yolo County	194	0.61
Kapaa, HI (cdp) Kauai County	58	0.61
Raisin City, CA (cdp) Fresno County	1	0.61
West Point, AR (town) White County	1	0.61
Poplar-Cotton Center, CA (cdp) Tulare County	9	0.60
Sparland, IL (village) Marshall County	3	0.60
Bay View, WA (cdp) Skagit County	2	0.60
Bingham Lake, MN (city) Cottonwood County	1	0.60
Christie, OK (cdp) Adair County	1	0.60
Summit, WI (town) Langlade County	1	0.60
Waimanalo Beach, HI (cdp) Honolulu County	25	0.59
Rollingwood, CA (cdp) Contra Costa County	17	0.59
Delleker, CA (cdp) Plumas County	4	0.59
Cedar Fort, UT (town) Utah County	2	0.59
Mitchell, OR (city) Wheeler County	1	0.59
Parkway-South Sacramento, CA (cdp) Sacramento County	213	0.58
Hanamaulu, HI (cdp) Kauai County	19	0.58
Nissequogue, NY (village) Suffolk County	9	0.58
Burnsville, MS (town) Tishomingo County	6	0.58
Iron Mountain Lake, MO (city) Saint Francois County	4	0.58
Kirkersville, OH (village) Licking County	3	0.58
Kihei, HI (cdp) Maui County	96	0.57
Waihee-Waiehu, HI (cdp) Maui County	42	0.57
Whitmore Village, HI (cdp) Honolulu County	23	0.57
Carson River Valley, WA (cdp) Skamania County	12	0.57
Kahuku, HI (cdp) Honolulu County	12	0.57
Le Grand, CA (cdp) Merced County	10	0.57
Lawn, TX (town) Taylor County	2	0.57
Springport, IN (town) Henry County	1	0.57

Notes: (cdp) census designated place; Refer to the Explanation of Data in the front of the book for more detailed information.

Hawaii Native/Pacific Islander: Other Pacific Islander, not specified

Top 150 Places Sorted by Percent

(Based on places with populations of 10,000 or more)

Place	Number	%
San Bruno, CA (city) San Mateo County	447	1.11
East Palo Alto, CA (city) San Mateo County	283	0.96
Hayward, CA (city) Alameda County	1,305	0.93
Belle Glade, FL (city) Palm Beach County	138	0.93
Wahiawa, HI (cdp) Honolulu County	118	0.73
Hilo, HI (cdp) Hawaii County	279	0.68
Waianae, HI (cdp) Honolulu County	69	0.66
Seaside, CA (city) Monterey County	205	0.65
West Sacramento, CA (city) Yolo County	194	0.61
Parkway-South Sacramento, CA (cdp) Sacramento County	213	0.58
Kihei, HI (cdp) Maui County	96	0.57
Sacramento, CA (city) Sacramento County	2,282	0.56
South San Francisco, CA (city) San Mateo County	318	0.53
Madison, NJ (borough) Morris County	87	0.53
Modesto, CA (city) Stanislaus County	952	0.50
Ashland, CA (cdp) Alameda County	103	0.50
Union City, CA (city) Alameda County	327	0.49
Florin, CA (cdp) Sacramento County	136	0.49
Tukwila, WA (city) King County	84	0.49
Elk Grove, CA (cdp) Sacramento County	286	0.48
Ewa Beach, HI (cdp) Honolulu County	70	0.48
Kaneohe, HI (cdp) Honolulu County	164	0.47
Nanakuli, HI (cdp) Honolulu County	51	0.47
Newark, CA (city) Alameda County	197	0.46
Kahului, HI (cdp) Maui County	93	0.46
San Mateo, CA (city) San Mateo County	409	0.44
White Plains, NY (city) Westchester County	235	0.44
San Pablo, CA (city) Contra Costa County	131	0.43
Springfield, MA (city) Hampden County	633	0.42
Stockton, CA (city) San Joaquin County	996	0.41
Pearl City, HI (cdp) Honolulu County	126	0.41
Mililani Town, HI (cdp) Honolulu County	116	0.41
Suisun City, CA (city) Solano County	107	0.41
Riverton-Boulevard Park, WA (cdp) King County	46	0.41
Halawa, HI (cdp) Honolulu County	55	0.40
Wailuku, HI (cdp) Maui County	49	0.40
Marina, CA (city) Monterey County	97	0.39
Spanaway, WA (cdp) Pierce County	83	0.38
Pinole, CA (city) Contra Costa County	71	0.37
Makakilo City, HI (cdp) Honolulu County	49	0.37
Lathrop, CA (city) San Joaquin County	39	0.37
Saint Paul, MN (city) Ramsey County	1,023	0.36
Daly City, CA (city) San Mateo County	378	0.36
Pittsburg, CA (city) Contra Costa County	202	0.36
Arcadia, CA (city) Los Angeles County	192	0.36
Kailua, HI (cdp) Honolulu County	131	0.36
Spring Valley, NY (village) Rockland County	91	0.36
North Miami, FL (city) Miami-Dade County	209	0.35
Laguna, CA (cdp) Sacramento County	119	0.35
Ithaca, NY (city) Tompkins County	103	0.35
Lake Forest, IL (city) Lake County	71	0.35
Loma Linda, CA (city) San Bernardino County	66	0.35
Vineyard, CA (cdp) Sacramento County	35	0.35
Pawtucket, RI (city) Providence County	250	0.34
Rowland Heights, CA (cdp) Los Angeles County	165	0.34
Waipahu, HI (cdp) Honolulu County	111	0.34
Ithaca, NY (town) Tompkins County	62	0.34
Artesia, CA (city) Los Angeles County	56	0.34
Vallejo, CA (city) Solano County	384	0.33
Pine Hills, FL (cdp) Orange County	138	0.33
Pacifica, CA (city) San Mateo County	126	0.33
State College, PA (borough) Centre County	126	0.33
Walnut, CA (city) Los Angeles County	98	0.33
Palmetto Estates, FL (cdp) Miami-Dade County	45	0.33
Waipio, HI (cdp) Honolulu County	38	0.33
Honolulu, HI (cdp) Honolulu County	1,199	0.32
Hartford, CT (city) Hartford County	388	0.32
Milpitas, CA (city) Santa Clara County	200	0.32
Cerritos, CA (city) Los Angeles County	164	0.32
Rosemont, CA (cdp) Sacramento County	73	0.32
San Leandro, CA (city) Alameda County	248	0.31
Adelphi, MD (cdp) Prince George's County	46	0.31
Schofield Barracks, HI (cdp) Honolulu County	45	0.31
Chowchilla, CA (city) Madera County	34	0.31
Delray Beach, FL (city) Palm Beach County	183	0.30
Turlock, CA (city) Stanislaus County	165	0.30
Norland, FL (cdp) Miami-Dade County	70	0.30
Fort Lewis, WA (cdp) Pierce County	57	0.30
Cherryland, CA (cdp) Alameda County	42	0.30
San Marino, CA (city) Los Angeles County	39	0.30
Miramar, FL (city) Broward County	209	0.29
Golden Glades, FL (cdp) Miami-Dade County	93	0.29
Mountlake Terrace, WA (city) Snohomish County	59	0.29
La Palma, CA (city) Orange County	45	0.29
Orange, NJ (cdp) Essex County	92	0.28
East Hill-Meridian, WA (cdp) King County	81	0.28
Waimalu, HI (cdp) Honolulu County	81	0.28
Millbrae, CA (city) San Mateo County	58	0.28
Pinewood, FL (cdp) Miami-Dade County	46	0.28
Suffern, NY (village) Rockland County	31	0.28
Paterson, NJ (city) Passaic County	407	0.27
Revere, MA (city) Suffolk County	128	0.27
North Miami Beach, FL (city) Miami-Dade County	110	0.27
North Lauderdale, FL (city) Broward County	87	0.27
Cudahy, CA (city) Los Angeles County	65	0.27
Silverdale, WA (cdp) Kitsap County	43	0.27
Fremont, CA (city) Alameda County	531	0.26
Fall River, MA (city) Bristol County	242	0.26
Merced, CA (city) Merced County	166	0.26
Irvington, NJ (cdp) Essex County	159	0.26
Lauderhill, FL (city) Broward County	152	0.26
Ceres, CA (city) Stanislaus County	90	0.26
Lauderdale Lakes, FL (city) Broward County	84	0.26
Foster City, CA (city) San Mateo County	74	0.26
Imperial Beach, CA (city) San Diego County	69	0.26
San Lorenzo, CA (cdp) Alameda County	58	0.26
Langley Park, MD (cdp) Prince George's County	42	0.26
Linda, CA (cdp) Yuba County	35	0.26
Salida, CA (cdp) Stanislaus County	33	0.26
El Sobrante, CA (cdp) Contra Costa County	32	0.26
Fort Carson, CO (cdp) El Paso County	27	0.26
La Riviera, CA (cdp) Sacramento County	27	0.26
Neosho, MO (city) Newton County	27	0.26
Carson, CA (city) Los Angeles County	226	0.25
Bowling Green, KY (city) Warren County	121	0.25
Springdale, AR (city) Washington County	114	0.25
Elmont, NY (cdp) Nassau County	81	0.25
Scott Lake, FL (cdp) Miami-Dade County	36	0.25
Union Park, FL (cdp) Orange County	25	0.25
Long Beach, CA (city) Los Angeles County	1,117	0.24
Alameda, CA (city) Alameda County	171	0.24
Oak Ridge, FL (cdp) Orange County	53	0.24
Hercules, CA (city) Contra Costa County	47	0.24
Asbury Park, NJ (city) Monmouth County	41	0.24
Hawaiian Gardens, CA (city) Los Angeles County	36	0.24
Fort Campbell North, KY (cdp) Christian County	34	0.24
Oroville, CA (city) Butte County	31	0.24
Bridgeport, CT (city) Fairfield County	321	0.23
Lowell, MA (city) Middlesex County	241	0.23
Santa Clara, CA (city) Santa Clara County	236	0.23
New Bedford, MA (city) Bristol County	213	0.23
Lakewood, CA (city) Los Angeles County	182	0.23
Rancho Cordova, CA (cdp) Sacramento County	128	0.23
Rohnert Park, CA (city) Sonoma County	98	0.23
Oak Harbor, WA (city) Island County	45	0.23
Lake Worth Corridor, FL (cdp) Palm Beach County	42	0.23
Ives Estates, FL (cdp) Miami-Dade County	40	0.23
East San Gabriel, CA (cdp) Los Angeles County	33	0.23
New Cassel, NY (cdp) Nassau County	31	0.23
Fairfield, CA (city) Solano County	215	0.22
Federal Way, WA (city) King County	180	0.22
Lawrence, MA (city) Essex County	158	0.22
Castro Valley, CA (cdp) Alameda County	127	0.22
Hacienda Heights, CA (cdp) Los Angeles County	119	0.22
Bremerton, WA (city) Kitsap County	83	0.22
Lynnwood, WA (city) Snohomish County	76	0.22
Burien, WA (city) King County	69	0.22
Stevens Point, WI (city) Portage County	54	0.22
West Carson, CA (cdp) Los Angeles County	47	0.22
North Fair Oaks, CA (cdp) San Mateo County	34	0.22

Notes: (cdp) census designated place; Refer to the Explanation of Data in the front of the book for more detailed information.

Hispanic or Latino

Top 150 Places Sorted by Number

(Based on all places, regardless of population)

Place	Number	%
New York, NY (city) New York City	2,160,554	26.98
Los Angeles, CA (city) Los Angeles County	1,719,073	46.53
Chicago, IL (city) Cook County	753,644	26.02
Houston, TX (city) Harris County	730,865	37.41
San Antonio, TX (city) Bexar County	671,394	58.66
Phoenix, AZ (city) Maricopa County	449,972	34.06
El Paso, TX (city) El Paso County	431,875	76.62
Dallas, TX (city) Dallas County	422,587	35.55
San Diego, CA (city) San Diego County	310,752	25.40
San Jose, CA (city) Santa Clara County	269,989	30.17
Santa Ana, CA (city) Orange County	257,097	76.07
Miami, FL (city) Miami-Dade County	238,351	65.76
Hialeah, FL (city) Miami-Dade County	204,543	90.34
Austin, TX (city) Travis County	200,579	30.55
Albuquerque, NM (city) Bernalillo County	179,075	39.92
Denver, CO (city) Denver County	175,704	31.68
Tucson, AZ (city) Pima County	173,868	35.72
Fresno, CA (city) Fresno County	170,520	39.87
Laredo, TX (city) Webb County	166,216	94.13
Long Beach, CA (city) Los Angeles County	165,092	35.77
Fort Worth, TX (city) Tarrant County	159,368	29.81
Anaheim, CA (city) Orange County	153,374	46.76
Corpus Christi, TX (city) Nueces County	150,737	54.33
Philadelphia, PA (city) Philadelphia County	128,928	8.50
Brownsville, TX (city) Cameron County	127,535	91.28
East Los Angeles, CA (cdp) Los Angeles County	120,307	96.80
Las Vegas, NV (city) Clark County	112,962	23.61
Oxnard, CA (city) Ventura County	112,807	66.22
San Francisco, CA (city) San Francisco County	109,504	14.10
Riverside, CA (city) Riverside County	97,315	38.14
Salinas, CA (city) Monterey County	96,880	64.13
Pomona, CA (city) Los Angeles County	96,370	64.47
Ontario, CA (city) San Bernardino County	94,610	59.88
South Gate, CA (city) Los Angeles County	88,669	92.00
San Bernardino, CA (city) San Bernardino County	88,022	47.48
Sacramento, CA (city) Sacramento County	87,974	21.61
Oakland, CA (city) Alameda County	87,467	21.89
Hempstead, NY (town) Nassau County	86,657	11.46
Chula Vista, CA (city) San Diego County	86,073	49.59
McAllen, TX (city) Hidalgo County	85,427	80.28
Boston, MA (city) Suffolk County	85,089	14.44
El Monte, CA (city) Los Angeles County	83,945	72.39
Newark, NJ (city) Essex County	80,622	29.47
Bakersfield, CA (city) Kern County	80,170	32.45
Stockton, CA (city) San Joaquin County	79,217	32.50
Mesa, AZ (city) Maricopa County	78,281	19.75
Paterson, NJ (city) Passaic County	74,774	50.11
Fontana, CA (city) San Bernardino County	74,424	57.72
Milwaukee, WI (city) Milwaukee County	71,646	12.00
Pasadena, TX (city) Harris County	68,348	48.24
Jersey City, NJ (city) Hudson County	67,952	28.31
Cicero, IL (town) Cook County	66,299	77.44
Islip, NY (town) Suffolk County	65,031	20.16
Norwalk, CA (city) Los Angeles County	64,965	62.89
Downey, CA (city) Los Angeles County	62,089	57.85
Arlington, TX (city) Tarrant County	60,817	18.27
Irving, TX (city) Dallas County	59,838	31.23
Baldwin Park, CA (city) Los Angeles County	59,660	78.67
Elizabeth, NJ (city) Union County	59,627	49.46
Huntington Park, CA (city) Los Angeles County	58,636	95.58
Tampa, FL (city) Hillsborough County	58,522	19.29
Lynwood, CA (city) Los Angeles County	57,503	82.33
Pico Rivera, CA (city) Los Angeles County	56,000	88.29
Union City, NJ (city) Hudson County	55,226	82.32
Garland, TX (city) Dallas County	55,192	25.58
Lubbock, TX (city) Lubbock County	54,786	27.45
Aurora, CO (city) Arapahoe County	54,764	19.81
Moreno Valley, CA (city) Riverside County	54,689	38.41
Glendale, AZ (city) Maricopa County	54,343	24.84
Garden Grove, CA (city) Orange County	53,608	32.45
Compton, CA (city) Los Angeles County	53,143	56.84
Providence, RI (city) Providence County	52,146	30.03
Fountainbleau, FL (cdp) Miami-Dade County	51,948	87.24
Inglewood, CA (city) Los Angeles County	51,829	46.04
Florence-Graham, CA (cdp) Los Angeles County	51,712	85.90
Escondido, CA (city) San Diego County	51,693	38.70
Oklahoma City, OK (city) Oklahoma County	51,368	10.15
Yonkers, NY (city) Westchester County	50,852	25.93
Hartford, CT (city) Hartford County	49,260	40.52
Oceanside, CA (city) San Diego County	48,691	30.24
Modesto, CA (city) Stanislaus County	48,310	25.58
West Covina, CA (city) Los Angeles County	48,051	45.73
Hayward, CA (city) Alameda County	47,850	34.17
Tamiami, FL (cdp) Miami-Dade County	47,654	86.98
Detroit, MI (city) Wayne County	47,167	4.96
Rialto, CA (city) San Bernardino County	47,050	51.21
Miami Beach, FL (city) Miami-Dade County	47,000	53.45
Whittier, CA (city) Los Angeles County	46,765	55.89
Aurora, IL (city) Kane County	46,557	32.56
Montebello, CA (city) Los Angeles County	46,347	74.57
Santa Maria, CA (city) Santa Barbara County	46,196	59.67
Pueblo, CO (city) Pueblo County	45,066	44.13
Washington, DC (city) District of Columbia	44,953	7.86
Pasadena, CA (city) Los Angeles County	44,734	33.40
Corona, CA (city) Riverside County	44,569	35.66
Bridgeport, CT (city) Fairfield County	44,478	31.88
Palmdale, CA (city) Los Angeles County	43,991	37.71
Paradise, NV (cdp) Clark County	43,663	23.47
Kendale Lakes, FL (cdp) Miami-Dade County	43,574	76.58
North Las Vegas, NV (city) Clark County	43,435	37.61
Colorado Springs, CO (city) El Paso County	43,330	12.01
Lawrence, MA (city) Essex County	43,019	59.71
Edinburg, TX (city) Hidalgo County	42,981	88.68
Passaic, NJ (city) Passaic County	42,387	62.46
Pharr, TX (city) Hidalgo County	42,282	90.62
Grand Prairie, TX (city) Dallas County	42,038	32.99
Harlingen, TX (city) Cameron County	41,881	72.76
Orange, CA (city) Orange County	41,434	32.16
Springfield, MA (city) Hampden County	41,343	27.18
Bell Gardens, CA (city) Los Angeles County	41,132	93.37
Sunrise Manor, NV (cdp) Clark County	40,619	26.02
Paramount, CA (city) Los Angeles County	39,945	72.28
Charlotte, NC (city) Mecklenburg County	39,800	7.36
Waukegan, IL (city) Lake County	39,396	44.82
Pembroke Pines, FL (city) Broward County	38,700	28.16
Glendale, CA (city) Los Angeles County	38,452	19.72
Las Cruces, NM (city) Dona Ana County	38,421	51.73
South Whittier, CA (cdp) Los Angeles County	38,256	69.31
Fullerton, CA (city) Orange County	38,014	30.17
Amarillo, TX (city) Potter County	37,947	21.86
Odessa, TX (city) Ector County	37,671	41.42
Kendall, FL (cdp) Miami-Dade County	37,549	49.91
Hawthorne, CA (city) Los Angeles County	37,227	44.26
Chandler, AZ (city) Maricopa County	37,059	20.99
Indio, CA (city) Riverside County	37,028	75.39
Mission, TX (city) Hidalgo County	36,794	81.03
Portland, OR (city) Multnomah County	36,058	6.81
Brookhaven, NY (town) Suffolk County	36,041	8.04
West New York, NJ (town) Hudson County	36,038	78.74
Rancho Cucamonga, CA (city) San Bernardino County	35,491	27.78
Yuma, AZ (city) Yuma County	35,400	45.67
Arlington, VA (cdp) Arlington County	35,268	18.62
Vista, CA (city) San Diego County	34,990	38.94
Cleveland, OH (city) Cuyahoga County	34,728	7.26
Reno, NV (city) Washoe County	34,616	19.18
Costa Mesa, CA (city) Orange County	34,523	31.75
Salt Lake City, UT (city) Salt Lake County	34,254	18.85
La Puente, CA (city) Los Angeles County	34,122	83.10
Bell, CA (city) Los Angeles County	33,328	90.90
North Bergen, NJ (township) Hudson County	33,260	57.25
Watsonville, CA (city) Santa Cruz County	33,254	75.12
Wichita, KS (city) Sedgwick County	33,112	9.62
Perth Amboy, NJ (city) Middlesex County	33,033	69.83
Visalia, CA (city) Tulare County	32,619	35.62
Orlando, FL (city) Orange County	32,510	17.48
Elgin, IL (city) Kane County	32,430	34.32
Santa Barbara, CA (city) Santa Barbara County	32,330	35.02
National City, CA (city) San Diego County	32,053	59.07
Chino, CA (city) San Bernardino County	31,830	47.39
Bellflower, CA (city) Los Angeles County	31,503	43.23

Notes: (cdp) census designated place; Refer to the Explanation of Data in the front of the book for more detailed information.

Hispanic or Latino

Top 150 Places Sorted by Percent

(Based on all places, regardless of population)

Place	Number	%
Roma Creek, TX (cdp) Starr County	610	100.00
New Falcon, TX (cdp) Zapata County	184	100.00
Concepcion, TX (cdp) Duval County	61	100.00
Cuevitas, TX (cdp) Hidalgo County	37	100.00
Willamar, TX (cdp) Willacy County	15	100.00
Santa Maria, TX (cdp) Cameron County	844	99.76
West Pearsall, TX (cdp) Frio County	348	99.71
Santa Cruz, TX (cdp) Starr County	628	99.68
Lago, TX (cdp) Cameron County	245	99.59
Mila Doce, TX (cdp) Hidalgo County	4,884	99.53
Sparks, TX (cdp) El Paso County	2,958	99.46
Los Alvarez, TX (cdp) Starr County	1,426	99.44
Las Lomas, TX (cdp) Starr County	2,667	99.37
Granjeno, TX (city) Hidalgo County	311	99.36
Salineno, TX (cdp) Starr County	302	99.34
Cameron Park, TX (cdp) Cameron County	5,918	99.28
South Point, TX (cdp) Cameron County	1,110	99.28
La Rosita, TX (cdp) Starr County	1,716	99.25
Scissors, TX (cdp) Hidalgo County	2,783	99.22
El Camino Angosto, TX (cdp) Cameron County	252	99.21
Doffing, TX (cdp) Hidalgo County	4,222	99.20
Faysville, TX (cdp) Hidalgo County	345	99.14
La Casita-Garciasville, TX (cdp) Starr County	2,158	99.13
Tornillo, TX (cdp) El Paso County	1,595	99.13
La Victoria, TX (cdp) Starr County	1,668	99.11
El Refugio, TX (cdp) Starr County	219	99.10
Progreso, TX (city) Hidalgo County	4,803	99.01
Las Quintas Fronterizas, TX (cdp) Maverick County	2,010	99.01
Muniz, TX (cdp) Hidalgo County	1,095	99.01
Midway North, TX (cdp) Hidalgo County	3,905	98.96
El Cenizo, TX (city) Webb County	3,506	98.90
Lyford South, TX (cdp) Willacy County	170	98.84
Laguna Seca, TX (cdp) Hidalgo County	248	98.80
Escobares, TX (cdp) Starr County	1,929	98.72
La Puerta, TX (cdp) Starr County	1,615	98.72
Citrus City, TX (cdp) Hidalgo County	929	98.72
North San Pedro, TX (cdp) Nueces County	908	98.70
Havana, TX (cdp) Hidalgo County	446	98.67
Sullivan City, TX (city) Hidalgo County	3,944	98.65
Roma, TX (city) Starr County	9,477	98.54
San Isidro, TX (cdp) Starr County	266	98.52
Ranchitos Las Lomas, TX (cdp) Webb County	329	98.50
Lozano, TX (cdp) Cameron County	319	98.46
Eidson Road, TX (cdp) Maverick County	9,202	98.44
South Alamo, TX (cdp) Hidalgo County	3,051	98.39
Encantada-Ranchito El Calaboz, TX (cdp) Cameron County	2,064	98.29
Huron, CA (city) Fresno County	6,197	98.27
Lopezville, TX (cdp) Hidalgo County	4,395	98.19
Rosita North, TX (cdp) Maverick County	3,337	98.15
Arroyo Alto, TX (cdp) Cameron County	314	98.13
West Sharyland, TX (cdp) Hidalgo County	2,891	98.10
La Villa, TX (city) Hidalgo County	1,280	98.08
Laureles, TX (cdp) Cameron County	3,221	98.05
Penitas, TX (city) Hidalgo County	1,144	98.03
Mecca, CA (cdp) Riverside County	5,295	98.02
Los Ebanos, TX (cdp) Hidalgo County	395	98.01
Alton, TX (city) Hidalgo County	4,292	97.90
San Elizario, TX (cdp) El Paso County	10,812	97.88
Hidalgo, TX (city) Hidalgo County	7,157	97.75
La Homa, TX (cdp) Hidalgo County	10,196	97.73
Garceno, TX (cdp) Starr County	1,405	97.71
Rio Bravo, TX (city) Webb County	5,425	97.69
La Grulla, TX (city) Starr County	1,182	97.61
Heber, CA (cdp) Imperial County	2,914	97.52
Alton North, TX (cdp) Hidalgo County	4,925	97.51
Westway, TX (cdp) El Paso County	3,732	97.47
Coachella, CA (city) Riverside County	22,132	97.39
La Blanca, TX (cdp) Hidalgo County	2,289	97.36
Alto Bonito, TX (cdp) Starr County	554	97.36
Indian Hills, TX (cdp) Hidalgo County	1,982	97.35
Elsa, TX (city) Hidalgo County	5,398	97.28
Olivarez, TX (cdp) Hidalgo County	2,377	97.22
La Joya, TX (city) Hidalgo County	3,210	97.18
Elm Creek, TX (cdp) Maverick County	1,873	97.15
Edcouch, TX (city) Hidalgo County	3,246	97.13

Place	Number	%
Spring Garden-Terra Verde, TX (cdp) Nueces County	673	97.11
Taft Southwest, TX (cdp) San Patricio County	1,671	97.09
San Carlos, TX (cdp) Hidalgo County	2,572	97.06
Flowella, TX (cdp) Brooks County	130	97.01
Parlier, CA (city) Fresno County	10,807	96.97
El Indio, TX (cdp) Maverick County	255	96.96
San Diego, TX (city) Duval County	4,604	96.87
Green Valley Farms, TX (cdp) Cameron County	697	96.81
East Los Angeles, CA (cdp) Los Angeles County	120,307	96.80
Monte Alto, TX (cdp) Hidalgo County	1,559	96.77
Larga Vista, TX (cdp) Webb County	718	96.77
Lost Hills, CA (cdp) Kern County	1,875	96.75
Nurillo, TX (cdp) Hidalgo County	4,889	96.70
Villa Verde, TX (cdp) Hidalgo County	861	96.63
Arroyo Colorado Estates, TX (cdp) Cameron County	729	96.56
San Pedro, TX (cdp) Cameron County	645	96.56
Del Mar Heights, TX (cdp) Cameron County	250	96.53
Olmito, TX (cdp) Cameron County	1,156	96.49
Los Villareales, TX (cdp) Starr County	897	96.45
Sunland Park, NM (city) Dona Ana County	12,835	96.44
Anthony, NM (cdp) Dona Ana County	7,623	96.44
Socorro, TX (city) El Paso County	26,183	96.43
Laredo Ranchettes, TX (cdp) Webb County	1,778	96.37
Maywood, CA (city) Los Angeles County	27,051	96.33
Morning Glory, TX (cdp) El Paso County	604	96.33
Cutler, CA (cdp) Tulare County	4,322	96.24
Homestead Meadows South, TX (cdp) El Paso County	6,546	96.17
Fabens, TX (cdp) El Paso County	7,734	96.16
Relampago, TX (cdp) Hidalgo County	100	96.15
Cactus, TX (city) Moore County	2,439	96.10
Las Palmas-Juarez, TX (cdp) Cameron County	1,601	96.10
Fronton, TX (cdp) Starr County	575	95.99
Doolittle, TX (cdp) Hidalgo County	2,263	95.97
Rio Grande City, TX (city) Starr County	11,433	95.89
Los Indios, TX (town) Cameron County	1,101	95.82
Lasara, TX (cdp) Willacy County	981	95.80
Walnut Park, CA (cdp) Los Angeles County	15,496	95.77
La Presa, TX (cdp) Webb County	486	95.67
Santa Rosa, TX (town) Cameron County	2,710	95.66
Huntington Park, CA (city) Los Angeles County	58,636	95.58
Benavides, TX (city) Duval County	1,611	95.55
Sebastian, TX (cdp) Willacy County	1,780	95.49
Calexico, CA (city) Imperial County	25,832	95.29
Midway South, TX (cdp) Hidalgo County	1,630	95.27
Reid Hope King, TX (cdp) Cameron County	764	95.26
Arroyo Gardens-La Tina Ranch, TX (cdp) Cameron County	697	95.22
Somerton, AZ (city) Yuma County	6,915	95.17
Cienegas Terrace, TX (cdp) Val Verde County	2,739	95.17
San Juan, TX (city) Hidalgo County	24,950	95.12
Agua Dulce, TX (cdp) El Paso County	702	95.12
Villa Pancho, TX (cdp) Cameron County	367	95.08
Vadito, NM (cdp) Taos County	230	95.04
Pirtleville, AZ (cdp) Cochise County	1,473	95.03
Heidelberg, TX (cdp) Hidalgo County	1,507	95.02
Vado, NM (cdp) Dona Ana County	2,853	95.00
Tierra Bonita, TX (cdp) Cameron County	152	95.00
Crystal City, TX (city) Zavala County	6,828	94.97
Falcon Heights, TX (cdp) Starr County	318	94.93
Encino, TX (cdp) Brooks County	168	94.92
Alice Acres, TX (cdp) Jim Wells County	466	94.91
Eagle Pass, TX (city) Maverick County	21,269	94.90
Loma Linda East, TX (cdp) Jim Wells County	203	94.86
Mesquite, NM (cdp) Dona Ana County	899	94.83
Lasana, TX (cdp) Cameron County	128	94.81
Asherton, TX (city) Dimmit County	1,272	94.78
Ranchette Estates, TX (cdp) Willacy County	126	94.74
Mendota, CA (city) Fresno County	7,468	94.65
Gregory, TX (city) San Patricio County	2,194	94.65
Calwa, CA (cdp) Fresno County	721	94.62
Cantu Addition, TX (cdp) Brooks County	205	94.47
North Escobares, TX (cdp) Starr County	1,598	94.44
Pajaro, CA (cdp) Monterey County	3,189	94.24
Ranchos Penitas West, TX (cdp) Webb County	490	94.23
Los Angeles Subdivision, TX (cdp) Willacy County	81	94.19
Cudahy, CA (city) Los Angeles County	22,790	94.14

Notes: (cdp) census designated place; Refer to the Explanation of Data in the front of the book for more detailed information.

Hispanic or Latino

Top 150 Places Sorted by Percent

(Based on places with populations of 10,000 or more)

Place	Number	%
San Elizario, TX (cdp) El Paso County	10,812	97.88
La Homa, TX (cdp) Hidalgo County	10,196	97.73
Coachella, CA (city) Riverside County	22,132	97.39
Parlier, CA (city) Fresno County	10,807	96.97
East Los Angeles, CA (cdp) Los Angeles County	120,307	96.80
Sunland Park, NM (city) Dona Ana County	12,835	96.44
Socorro, TX (city) El Paso County	26,183	96.43
Maywood, CA (city) Los Angeles County	27,051	96.33
Rio Grande City, TX (city) Starr County	11,433	95.89
Walnut Park, CA (cdp) Los Angeles County	15,496	95.77
Huntington Park, CA (city) Los Angeles County	58,636	95.58
Calexico, CA (city) Imperial County	25,832	95.29
San Juan, TX (city) Hidalgo County	24,950	95.12
Eagle Pass, TX (city) Maverick County	21,269	94.90
Cudahy, CA (city) Los Angeles County	22,790	94.14
Laredo, TX (city) Webb County	166,216	94.13
Commerce, CA (city) Los Angeles County	11,765	93.61
Nogales, AZ (city) Santa Cruz County	19,539	93.59
Bell Gardens, CA (city) Los Angeles County	41,132	93.37
Sweetwater, FL (city) Miami-Dade County	13,253	93.16
Robstown, TX (city) Nueces County	11,848	93.09
South Gate, CA (city) Los Angeles County	88,669	92.00
Brownsville, TX (city) Cameron County	127,535	91.28
Bell, CA (city) Los Angeles County	33,328	90.90
Pharr, TX (city) Hidalgo County	42,282	90.62
Hialeah, FL (city) Miami-Dade County	204,543	90.34
Mercedes, TX (city) Hidalgo County	12,286	90.01
Hialeah Gardens, FL (city) Miami-Dade County	17,324	89.78
Lennox, CA (cdp) Los Angeles County	20,602	89.77
San Fernando, CA (city) Los Angeles County	21,038	89.28
San Luis, AZ (city) Yuma County	13,657	89.13
Lamont, CA (cdp) Kern County	11,814	88.85
Edinburg, TX (city) Hidalgo County	42,981	88.68
Pico Rivera, CA (city) Los Angeles County	56,000	88.29
Greenfield, CA (city) Monterey County	11,055	87.86
Arvin, CA (city) Kern County	11,341	87.53
Donna, TX (city) Hidalgo County	12,886	87.26
Fountainbleau, FL (cdp) Miami-Dade County	51,948	87.24
Tamiami, FL (cdp) Miami-Dade County	47,654	86.98
San Benito, TX (city) Cameron County	20,380	86.93
Soledad, CA (city) Monterey County	9,779	86.82
South El Monte, CA (city) Los Angeles County	18,190	86.03
Douglas, AZ (city) Cochise County	12,306	85.98
Florence-Graham, CA (cdp) Los Angeles County	51,712	85.90
Westchester, FL (cdp) Miami-Dade County	25,824	85.31
Weslaco, TX (city) Hidalgo County	22,560	83.76
South San Jose Hills, CA (cdp) Los Angeles County	16,868	83.43
La Puente, CA (city) Los Angeles County	34,122	83.10
West Whittier-Los Nietos, CA (cdp) Los Angeles County	20,874	83.07
Las Vegas, NM (city) San Miguel County	12,080	82.94
University Park, FL (cdp) Miami-Dade County	21,945	82.69
Lynwood, CA (city) Los Angeles County	57,503	82.33
Union City, NJ (city) Hudson County	55,226	82.32
Coral Terrace, FL (cdp) Miami-Dade County	20,015	82.10
West Puente Valley, CA (cdp) Los Angeles County	18,416	81.53
Del Rio, TX (city) Val Verde County	27,446	81.04
Mission, TX (city) Hidalgo County	36,794	81.03
Sanger, CA (city) Fresno County	15,319	80.92
King City, CA (city) Monterey County	8,922	80.42
McAllen, TX (city) Hidalgo County	85,427	80.28
Kendall West, FL (cdp) Miami-Dade County	30,060	79.03
West New York, NJ (town) Hudson County	36,038	78.74
Baldwin Park, CA (city) Los Angeles County	59,660	78.67
Alamo, TX (city) Hidalgo County	11,528	78.10
Alice, TX (city) Jim Wells County	14,837	78.05
Lindsay, CA (city) Tulare County	8,029	77.97
South Houston, TX (city) Harris County	12,338	77.93
Avocado Heights, CA (cdp) Los Angeles County	11,776	77.74
South Valley, NM (cdp) Bernalillo County	30,307	77.59
Cicero, IL (town) Cook County	66,299	77.44
El Paso, TX (city) El Paso County	431,875	76.62
Kendale Lakes, FL (cdp) Miami-Dade County	43,574	76.58
Olympia Heights, FL (cdp) Miami-Dade County	10,268	76.33
Westwood Lakes, FL (cdp) Miami-Dade County	9,164	76.33
Santa Ana, CA (city) Orange County	257,097	76.07
Uvalde, TX (city) Uvalde County	11,268	75.48
Indio, CA (city) Riverside County	37,028	75.39
Jacinto City, TX (city) Harris County	7,767	75.39
Watsonville, CA (city) Santa Cruz County	33,254	75.12
Dinuba, CA (city) Tulare County	12,647	75.08
Valinda, CA (cdp) Los Angeles County	16,271	74.72
El Centro, CA (city) Imperial County	28,219	74.58
Montebello, CA (city) Los Angeles County	46,347	74.57
Eloy, AZ (city) Pinal County	7,717	74.38
Brawley, CA (city) Imperial County	16,280	73.83
Hawaiian Gardens, CA (city) Los Angeles County	10,869	73.54
Sunnyside, WA (city) Yakima County	10,158	73.05
Harlingen, TX (city) Cameron County	41,881	72.76
El Monte, CA (city) Los Angeles County	83,945	72.39
Paramount, CA (city) Los Angeles County	39,945	72.28
Livingston, CA (city) Merced County	7,521	71.81
Selma, CA (city) Fresno County	13,952	71.75
Santa Fe Springs, CA (city) Los Angeles County	12,447	71.38
Santa Paula, CA (city) Ventura County	20,360	71.19
Immokalee, FL (cdp) Collier County	14,027	70.98
Richmond West, FL (cdp) Miami-Dade County	19,663	70.02
Perth Amboy, NJ (city) Middlesex County	33,033	69.83
Sunset, FL (cdp) Miami-Dade County	11,952	69.69
North Fair Oaks, CA (cdp) San Mateo County	10,741	69.57
Galena Park, TX (city) Harris County	7,343	69.33
South Whittier, CA (cdp) Los Angeles County	38,256	69.31
Delano, CA (city) Kern County	26,584	68.47
Shafter, CA (city) Kern County	8,667	68.05
Madera, CA (city) Madera County	29,274	67.75
Beeville, TX (city) Bee County	8,884	67.67
Reedley, CA (city) Fresno County	14,028	67.59
Doral, FL (cdp) Miami-Dade County	13,784	67.44
Kingsville, TX (city) Kleberg County	17,151	67.06
Alum Rock, CA (cdp) Santa Clara County	9,029	66.99
Wasco, CA (city) Kern County	14,187	66.72
Fillmore, CA (city) Ventura County	9,090	66.63
Miami Lakes, FL (cdp) Miami-Dade County	15,083	66.52
Oxnard, CA (city) Ventura County	112,807	66.22
Avenal, CA (city) Kings County	9,667	65.88
Miami, FL (city) Miami-Dade County	238,351	65.76
The Hammocks, FL (cdp) Miami-Dade County	30,953	65.33
Leisure City, FL (cdp) Miami-Dade County	14,465	65.30
Citrus, CA (cdp) Los Angeles County	6,861	64.84
Deming, NM (city) Luna County	9,116	64.58
Pomona, CA (city) Los Angeles County	96,370	64.47
Vincent, CA (cdp) Los Angeles County	9,724	64.41
Bloomington, CA (cdp) San Bernardino County	12,436	64.38
Salinas, CA (city) Monterey County	96,880	64.13
Azusa, CA (city) Los Angeles County	28,522	63.79
Langley Park, MD (cdp) Prince George's County	10,294	63.49
Norwalk, CA (city) Los Angeles County	64,965	62.89
Passaic, NJ (city) Passaic County	42,387	62.46
Hereford, TX (city) Deaf Smith County	8,958	61.37
Colton, CA (city) San Bernardino County	28,934	60.71
Country Club, FL (cdp) Miami-Dade County	21,903	60.32
Drexel Heights, AZ (cdp) Pima County	14,327	60.07
Montclair, CA (city) San Bernardino County	19,823	59.98
Ontario, CA (city) San Bernardino County	94,610	59.88
Lawrence, MA (city) Essex County	43,019	59.71
Santa Maria, CA (city) Santa Barbara County	46,196	59.67
Corcoran, CA (city) Kings County	8,618	59.61
Miami Springs, FL (city) Miami-Dade County	8,173	59.60
Haverstraw, NY (village) Rockland County	5,998	59.29
National City, CA (city) San Diego County	32,053	59.07
East Palo Alto, CA (city) San Mateo County	17,346	58.79
Los Lunas, NM (village) Valencia County	5,894	58.74
Richmond, TX (city) Fort Bend County	6,506	58.71
San Antonio, TX (city) Bexar County	671,394	58.66
Dover, NJ (town) Morris County	10,539	57.94
Downey, CA (city) Los Angeles County	62,089	57.85
Fontana, CA (city) San Bernardino County	74,424	57.72
North Bergen, NJ (township) Hudson County	33,260	57.25
Patterson, CA (city) Stanislaus County	6,611	56.96
Compton, CA (city) Los Angeles County	53,143	56.84
North Valley, NM (cdp) Bernalillo County	6,773	56.81

Notes: (cdp) census designated place; Refer to the Explanation of Data in the front of the book for more detailed information.

Hispanic: Central American

Top 150 Places Sorted by Number

(Based on all places, regardless of population)

Place	Number	%
Los Angeles, CA (city) Los Angeles County	238,191	6.45
New York, NY (city) New York City	99,099	1.24
Houston, TX (city) Harris County	60,642	3.10
Miami, FL (city) Miami-Dade County	40,158	11.08
San Francisco, CA (city) San Francisco County	23,367	3.01
Chicago, IL (city) Cook County	23,339	0.81
Hempstead, NY (town) Nassau County	22,455	2.97
Washington, DC (city) District of Columbia	15,803	2.76
Dallas, TX (city) Dallas County	14,972	1.26
Islip, NY (town) Suffolk County	14,851	4.60
Hialeah, FL (city) Miami-Dade County	14,668	6.48
Boston, MA (city) Suffolk County	11,532	1.96
Arlington, VA (cdp) Arlington County	11,323	5.98
Long Beach, CA (city) Los Angeles County	8,924	1.93
Hempstead, NY (village) Nassau County	8,382	14.82
Brentwood, NY (cdp) Suffolk County	8,221	15.25
Providence, RI (city) Providence County	8,011	4.61
Santa Ana, CA (city) Orange County	7,559	2.24
San Jose, CA (city) Santa Clara County	7,390	0.83
Fountainbleau, FL (cdp) Miami-Dade County	7,342	12.33
Alexandria, VA (independent city) Alexandria city	7,241	5.64
Silver Spring, MD (cdp) Montgomery County	6,973	9.11
Oakland, CA (city) Alameda County	6,759	1.69
North Hempstead, NY (town) Nassau County	6,571	2.95
Daly City, CA (city) San Mateo County	6,426	6.20
Irving, TX (city) Dallas County	6,225	3.25
South Gate, CA (city) Los Angeles County	6,164	6.40
Elizabeth, NJ (city) Union County	6,126	5.08
Phoenix, AZ (city) Maricopa County	6,085	0.46
Chelsea, MA (city) Suffolk County	6,010	17.13
Langley Park, MD (cdp) Prince George's County	5,970	36.82
Union City, NJ (city) Hudson County	5,750	8.57
Las Vegas, NV (city) Clark County	5,669	1.18
Wheaton-Glenmont, MD (cdp) Montgomery County	5,350	9.27
Inglewood, CA (city) Los Angeles County	5,083	4.52
San Diego, CA (city) San Diego County	5,077	0.41
Glendale, CA (city) Los Angeles County	5,056	2.59
Anaheim, CA (city) Orange County	5,016	1.53
Charlotte, NC (city) Mecklenburg County	5,001	0.92
Jersey City, NJ (city) Hudson County	4,752	1.98
Hawthorne, CA (city) Los Angeles County	4,681	5.57
Huntington Park, CA (city) Los Angeles County	4,334	7.06
Austin, TX (city) Travis County	4,290	0.65
Downey, CA (city) Los Angeles County	4,276	3.98
Freeport, NY (village) Nassau County	4,249	9.70
Stamford, CT (city) Fairfield County	4,097	3.50
West New York, NJ (town) Hudson County	3,978	8.69
Trenton, NJ (city) Mercer County	3,902	4.57
Plainfield, NJ (city) Union County	3,846	8.04
Gaithersburg, MD (city) Montgomery County	3,838	7.29
Pomona, CA (city) Los Angeles County	3,823	2.56
Newark, NJ (city) Essex County	3,785	1.38
Pasadena, CA (city) Los Angeles County	3,687	2.75
Kendale Lakes, FL (cdp) Miami-Dade County	3,640	6.40
Chillum, MD (cdp) Prince George's County	3,635	10.61
Huntington, NY (town) Suffolk County	3,623	1.86
Palmdale, CA (city) Los Angeles County	3,579	3.07
Bailey's Crossroads, VA (cdp) Fairfax County	3,567	15.40
Babylon, NY (town) Suffolk County	3,552	1.68
San Antonio, TX (city) Bexar County	3,492	0.31
New Orleans, LA (city) Orleans Parish	3,485	0.72
San Rafael, CA (city) Marin County	3,471	6.19
Tamiami, FL (cdp) Miami-Dade County	3,451	6.30
Lynwood, CA (city) Los Angeles County	3,441	4.93
Metairie, LA (cdp) Jefferson Parish	3,418	2.34
Hayward, CA (city) Alameda County	3,401	2.43
Yonkers, NY (city) Westchester County	3,374	1.72
Kenner, LA (city) Jefferson Parish	3,364	4.77
Kendall, FL (cdp) Miami-Dade County	3,310	4.40
Garland, TX (city) Dallas County	3,212	1.49
South San Francisco, CA (city) San Mateo County	3,145	5.19
Fontana, CA (city) San Bernardino County	3,141	2.44
Miami Beach, FL (city) Miami-Dade County	3,096	3.52
El Monte, CA (city) Los Angeles County	3,030	2.61
East Los Angeles, CA (cdp) Los Angeles County	3,020	2.43
Lake Worth, FL (city) Palm Beach County	2,965	8.44
Ontario, CA (city) San Bernardino County	2,958	1.87
Huntington Station, NY (cdp) Suffolk County	2,851	9.53
Philadelphia, PA (city) Philadelphia County	2,846	0.19
Burbank, CA (city) Los Angeles County	2,833	2.82
San Mateo, CA (city) San Mateo County	2,826	3.06
Central Islip, NY (cdp) Suffolk County	2,821	8.83
Sweetwater, FL (city) Miami-Dade County	2,818	19.81
West Palm Beach, FL (city) Palm Beach County	2,745	3.34
Bell, CA (city) Los Angeles County	2,742	7.48
North Bergen, NJ (township) Hudson County	2,739	4.71
Norwalk, CA (city) Los Angeles County	2,728	2.64
New Cassel, NY (cdp) Nassau County	2,688	20.21
Herndon, VA (town) Fairfax County	2,687	12.41
Paradise, NV (cdp) Clark County	2,657	1.43
Somerville, MA (city) Middlesex County	2,636	3.40
Oyster Bay, NY (town) Nassau County	2,608	0.89
Brookhaven, NY (town) Suffolk County	2,604	0.58
Homestead, FL (city) Miami-Dade County	2,595	8.13
Nashville-Davidson, TN (special city) Davidson County	2,563	0.47
Concord, CA (city) Contra Costa County	2,543	2.09
West Little River, FL (cdp) Miami-Dade County	2,528	7.78
Richmond, CA (city) Contra Costa County	2,528	2.55
Kendall West, FL (cdp) Miami-Dade County	2,511	6.60
Reno, NV (city) Washoe County	2,509	1.39
Carol City, FL (cdp) Miami-Dade County	2,460	4.14
Riverside, CA (city) Riverside County	2,438	0.96
Bell Gardens, CA (city) Los Angeles County	2,429	5.51
Redwood City, CA (city) San Mateo County	2,381	3.16
Tampa, FL (city) Hillsborough County	2,362	0.78
Florence-Graham, CA (cdp) Los Angeles County	2,345	3.90
The Hammocks, FL (cdp) Miami-Dade County	2,324	4.91
Durham, NC (city) Durham County	2,305	1.23
Baldwin Park, CA (city) Los Angeles County	2,297	3.03
Cudahy, CA (city) Los Angeles County	2,288	9.45
Paterson, NJ (city) Passaic County	2,284	1.53
West Covina, CA (city) Los Angeles County	2,212	2.11
Aspen Hill, MD (cdp) Montgomery County	2,209	4.40
New Brunswick, NJ (city) Middlesex County	2,198	4.53
Compton, CA (city) Los Angeles County	2,191	2.34
Grand Rapids, MI (city) Kent County	2,191	1.11
Costa Mesa, CA (city) Orange County	2,160	1.99
North Bay Shore, NY (cdp) Suffolk County	2,152	14.35
Norwalk, CT (city) Fairfield County	2,117	2.55
Uniondale, NY (cdp) Nassau County	2,114	9.19
Waukegan, IL (city) Lake County	2,082	2.37
Jefferson, VA (cdp) Fairfax County	2,054	7.49
Portland, OR (city) Multnomah County	2,051	0.39
Annandale, VA (cdp) Fairfax County	2,049	3.73
Springfield, VA (cdp) Fairfax County	2,039	6.70
Hollywood, FL (city) Broward County	2,021	1.45
Rye, NY (town) Westchester County	2,016	4.59
Garden Grove, CA (city) Orange County	2,014	1.22
Denver, CO (city) Denver County	1,997	0.36
Seattle, WA (city) King County	1,987	0.35
Lennox, CA (cdp) Los Angeles County	1,980	8.63
Bakersfield, CA (city) Kern County	1,964	0.79
Richmond West, FL (cdp) Miami-Dade County	1,963	6.99
Lynn, MA (city) Essex County	1,963	2.20
Fort Lauderdale, FL (city) Broward County	1,927	1.26
Raleigh, NC (city) Wake County	1,926	0.70
Santa Clarita, CA (city) Los Angeles County	1,922	1.27
Pasadena, TX (city) Harris County	1,900	1.34
Pembroke Pines, FL (city) Broward County	1,896	1.38
Sacramento, CA (city) Sacramento County	1,891	0.46
Aurora, CO (city) Arapahoe County	1,888	0.68
South Miami Heights, FL (cdp) Miami-Dade County	1,868	5.57
Alhambra, CA (city) Los Angeles County	1,849	2.15
Rialto, CA (city) San Bernardino County	1,835	2.00
San Bernardino, CA (city) San Bernardino County	1,832	0.99
Westmont, CA (cdp) Los Angeles County	1,826	5.77
Port Chester, NY (village) Westchester County	1,819	6.53
Reston, VA (cdp) Fairfax County	1,810	3.21
Lawndale, CA (city) Los Angeles County	1,785	5.63
Indianapolis, IN (special city) Marion County	1,770	0.23

Notes: (cdp) census designated place; Refer to the Explanation of Data in the front of the book for more detailed information.

Hispanic: Central American

Top 150 Places Sorted by Percent

(Based on all places, regardless of population)

Place	Number	%
Langley Park, MD (cdp) Prince George's County	5,970	36.82
Georgetown, DE (town) Sussex County	1,018	21.93
New Cassel, NY (cdp) Nassau County	2,688	20.21
Sweetwater, FL (city) Miami-Dade County	2,818	19.81
Indiantown, FL (cdp) Martin County	985	17.63
Ellijay, GA (city) Gilmer County	277	17.49
Chelsea, MA (city) Suffolk County	6,010	17.13
Brewster, NY (village) Putnam County	360	16.65
East Ellijay, GA (city) Gilmer County	117	16.55
Seven Corners, VA (cdp) Fairfax County	1,413	16.24
Bailey's Crossroads, VA (cdp) Fairfax County	3,567	15.40
Brentwood, NY (cdp) Suffolk County	8,221	15.25
Hempstead, NY (village) Nassau County	8,382	14.82
North Bay Shore, NY (cdp) Suffolk County	2,152	14.35
Chamblee, GA (city) De Kalb County	1,206	12.63
Herndon, VA (town) Fairfax County	2,687	12.41
Fountainbleau, FL (cdp) Miami-Dade County	7,342	12.33
Bound Brook, NJ (borough) Somerset County	1,202	11.84
Wallace, NC (town) Duplin County	382	11.42
Mendota, CA (city) Fresno County	892	11.31
Adelphi, MD (cdp) Prince George's County	1,665	11.10
Miami, FL (city) Miami-Dade County	40,158	11.08
Colma, CA (town) San Mateo County	132	11.08
West Gate, VA (cdp) Prince William County	805	10.74
Chillum, MD (cdp) Prince George's County	3,635	10.61
Inwood, NY (cdp) Nassau County	948	10.17
Freeport, NY (village) Nassau County	4,249	9.70
Fairview, NJ (borough) Bergen County	1,283	9.68
Huntington Station, NY (cdp) Suffolk County	2,851	9.53
Canal Point, FL (cdp) Palm Beach County	50	9.52
Cudahy, CA (city) Los Angeles County	2,288	9.45
Wheaton-Glenmont, MD (cdp) Montgomery County	5,350	9.27
Uniondale, NY (cdp) Nassau County	2,114	9.19
Silver Spring, MD (cdp) Montgomery County	6,973	9.11
Brentwood, MD (town) Prince George's County	257	9.04
Magnolia, NC (town) Duplin County	83	8.91
Central Islip, NY (cdp) Suffolk County	2,821	8.83
West New York, NJ (town) Hudson County	3,978	8.69
Lennox, CA (cdp) Los Angeles County	1,980	8.63
Green Forest, AR (city) Carroll County	233	8.58
Union City, NJ (city) Hudson County	5,750	8.57
Lake Worth, FL (city) Palm Beach County	2,965	8.44
Mount Kisco, NY (village) Westchester County	836	8.37
Bayview-Montalvin, CA (cdp) Contra Costa County	417	8.33
Roosevelt, NY (cdp) Nassau County	1,290	8.14
Homestead, FL (city) Miami-Dade County	2,595	8.13
Plainfield, NJ (city) Union County	3,846	8.04
Schuyler, NE (city) Colfax County	425	7.91
Quioque, NY (cdp) Suffolk County	63	7.88
Siler City, NC (town) Chatham County	547	7.85
Buena Vista, GA (city) Marion County	130	7.81
West Little River, FL (cdp) Miami-Dade County	2,528	7.78
Hialeah Gardens, FL (city) Miami-Dade County	1,472	7.63
Rollingwood, CA (cdp) Contra Costa County	221	7.62
Octavia, NE (village) Butler County	11	7.59
Lincolnia, VA (cdp) Fairfax County	1,192	7.55
Grand Pass, MO (village) Saline County	4	7.55
Collinsville, AL (town) De Kalb County	124	7.54
Central Falls, RI (city) Providence County	1,420	7.50
Jefferson, VA (cdp) Fairfax County	2,054	7.49
Bell, CA (city) Los Angeles County	2,742	7.48
Danville, AR (city) Yell County	175	7.32
Gaithersburg, MD (city) Montgomery County	3,838	7.29
Boger City, NC (cdp) Lincoln County	40	7.22
Groveton, VA (cdp) Fairfax County	1,520	7.14
Broadview Park, FL (cdp) Broward County	481	7.08
Huntington Park, CA (city) Los Angeles County	4,334	7.06
Richmond West, FL (cdp) Miami-Dade County	1,963	6.99
Lexington, NE (city) Dawson County	698	6.97
West Smithfield, NC (cdp) Johnston County	4	6.78
Springfield, VA (cdp) Fairfax County	2,039	6.70
Kendall West, FL (cdp) Miami-Dade County	2,511	6.60
Niotaze, KS (city) Chautauqua County	8	6.56
Port Chester, NY (village) Westchester County	1,819	6.53
Hyattsville, MD (city) Prince George's County	960	6.52

Place	Number	%
Hialeah, FL (city) Miami-Dade County	14,668	6.48
Manorhaven, NY (village) Nassau County	397	6.47
Los Angeles, CA (city) Los Angeles County	238,191	6.45
South Gate, CA (city) Los Angeles County	6,164	6.40
Kendale Lakes, FL (cdp) Miami-Dade County	3,640	6.40
Rose Hill, NC (town) Duplin County	84	6.32
Rogers, NE (village) Colfax County	6	6.32
Tamiami, FL (cdp) Miami-Dade County	3,451	6.30
Walnut Park, CA (cdp) Los Angeles County	1,016	6.28
Virginia Gardens, FL (village) Miami-Dade County	146	6.22
North Plainfield, NJ (borough) Somerset County	1,311	6.21
Hybla Valley, VA (cdp) Fairfax County	1,038	6.21
Daly City, CA (city) San Mateo County	6,426	6.20
San Rafael, CA (city) Marin County	3,471	6.19
Trion, GA (town) Chattooga County	123	6.17
Ola, AR (city) Yell County	74	6.15
Morristown, NJ (town) Morris County	1,139	6.14
Westgate-Belvedere Homes, FL (cdp) Palm Beach County	499	6.13
Morganton, NC (city) Burke County	1,052	6.08
Lincolnton, NC (city) Lincoln County	606	6.08
Gladeview, FL (cdp) Miami-Dade County	876	6.05
Arlington, VA (cdp) Arlington County	11,323	5.98
Baxter Estates, NY (village) Nassau County	60	5.96
Bull Run, VA (cdp) Prince William County	657	5.80
Canton, GA (city) Cherokee County	446	5.79
Westmont, CA (cdp) Los Angeles County	1,826	5.77
Doraville, GA (city) De Kalb County	568	5.76
Cedartown, GA (city) Polk County	538	5.68
Loch Lomond, FL (cdp) Broward County	201	5.68
Alexandria, VA (independent city) Alexandria city	7,241	5.64
Mount Vernon, VA (cdp) Fairfax County	1,612	5.64
Lawndale, CA (city) Los Angeles County	1,785	5.63
Lake Worth Corridor, FL (cdp) Palm Beach County	1,051	5.63
Mount Rainier, MD (city) Prince George's County	477	5.61
Hawthorne, CA (city) Los Angeles County	4,681	5.57
South Miami Heights, FL (cdp) Miami-Dade County	1,868	5.57
Bell Gardens, CA (city) Los Angeles County	2,429	5.51
Webster, TX (city) Harris County	500	5.50
Wyandanch, NY (cdp) Suffolk County	576	5.46
Medley, FL (town) Miami-Dade County	60	5.46
Colmar Manor, MD (town) Prince George's County	68	5.41
Maywood, CA (city) Los Angeles County	1,517	5.40
Glen Cove, NY (city) Nassau County	1,434	5.39
Guttenberg, NJ (town) Hudson County	582	5.39
Perry, IA (city) Dallas County	410	5.37
Westbury, NY (village) Nassau County	765	5.36
West Miami, FL (city) Miami-Dade County	313	5.34
Locust Valley, NY (cdp) Nassau County	187	5.31
Princeton, FL (cdp) Miami-Dade County	533	5.28
El Jebel, CO (cdp) Eagle County	236	5.26
Loch Lomond, VA (cdp) Prince William County	179	5.25
Leisure City, FL (cdp) Miami-Dade County	1,154	5.21
South San Francisco, CA (city) San Mateo County	3,145	5.19
Takoma Park, MD (city) Montgomery County	895	5.17
Woodbridge, VA (cdp) Prince William County	1,646	5.15
Idylwood, VA (cdp) Fairfax County	820	5.12
Edmonston, MD (town) Prince George's County	49	5.11
Elizabeth, NJ (city) Union County	6,126	5.08
North Fair Oaks, CA (cdp) San Mateo County	785	5.08
Monterey, TN (town) Putnam County	138	5.08
Henderson, MD (town) Caroline County	6	5.08
Huntington, VA (cdp) Fairfax County	419	5.03
Desert View Highlands, CA (cdp) Los Angeles County	117	5.01
Lynwood, CA (city) Los Angeles County	3,441	4.93
Palmetto Estates, FL (cdp) Miami-Dade County	673	4.92
The Hammocks, FL (cdp) Miami-Dade County	2,324	4.91
Yorkshire, VA (cdp) Prince William County	330	4.90
Pimmit Hills, VA (cdp) Fairfax County	301	4.89
Clewiston, FL (city) Hendry County	315	4.88
San Pablo, CA (city) Contra Costa County	1,467	4.86
Doral, FL (cdp) Miami-Dade County	990	4.84
Redland, MD (cdp) Montgomery County	821	4.83
Greenport, NY (village) Suffolk County	99	4.83
Kenner, LA (city) Jefferson Parish	3,364	4.77
Marydel, MD (town) Caroline County	7	4.76

Notes: (cdp) census designated place; Refer to the Explanation of Data in the front of the book for more detailed information.

Hispanic: Central American

Top 150 Places Sorted by Percent

(Based on places with populations of 10,000 or more)

Place	Number	%
Langley Park, MD (cdp) Prince George's County	5,970	36.82
New Cassel, NY (cdp) Nassau County	2,688	20.21
Sweetwater, FL (city) Miami-Dade County	2,818	19.81
Chelsea, MA (city) Suffolk County	6,010	17.13
Bailey's Crossroads, VA (cdp) Fairfax County	3,567	15.40
Brentwood, NY (cdp) Suffolk County	8,221	15.25
Hempstead, NY (village) Nassau County	8,382	14.82
North Bay Shore, NY (cdp) Suffolk County	2,152	14.35
Herndon, VA (town) Fairfax County	2,687	12.41
Fountainbleau, FL (cdp) Miami-Dade County	7,342	12.33
Bound Brook, NJ (borough) Somerset County	1,202	11.84
Adelphi, MD (cdp) Prince George's County	1,665	11.10
Miami, FL (city) Miami-Dade County	40,158	11.08
Chillum, MD (cdp) Prince George's County	3,635	10.61
Freeport, NY (village) Nassau County	4,249	9.70
Fairview, NJ (borough) Bergen County	1,283	9.68
Huntington Station, NY (cdp) Suffolk County	2,851	9.53
Cudahy, CA (city) Los Angeles County	2,288	9.45
Wheaton-Glenmont, MD (cdp) Montgomery County	5,350	9.27
Uniondale, NY (cdp) Nassau County	2,114	9.19
Silver Spring, MD (cdp) Montgomery County	6,973	9.11
Central Islip, NY (cdp) Suffolk County	2,821	8.83
West New York, NJ (town) Hudson County	3,978	8.69
Lennox, CA (cdp) Los Angeles County	1,980	8.63
Union City, NJ (city) Hudson County	5,750	8.57
Lake Worth, FL (city) Palm Beach County	2,965	8.44
Roosevelt, NY (cdp) Nassau County	1,290	8.14
Homestead, FL (city) Miami-Dade County	2,595	8.13
Plainfield, NJ (city) Union County	3,846	8.04
West Little River, FL (cdp) Miami-Dade County	2,528	7.78
Hialeah Gardens, FL (city) Miami-Dade County	1,472	7.63
Lincolnia, VA (cdp) Fairfax County	1,192	7.55
Central Falls, RI (city) Providence County	1,420	7.50
Jefferson, VA (cdp) Fairfax County	2,054	7.49
Bell, CA (city) Los Angeles County	2,742	7.48
Gaithersburg, MD (city) Montgomery County	3,838	7.29
Groveton, VA (cdp) Fairfax County	1,520	7.14
Huntington Park, CA (city) Los Angeles County	4,334	7.06
Richmond West, FL (cdp) Miami-Dade County	1,963	6.99
Lexington, NE (city) Dawson County	698	6.97
Springfield, VA (cdp) Fairfax County	2,039	6.70
Kendall West, FL (cdp) Miami-Dade County	2,511	6.60
Port Chester, NY (village) Westchester County	1,819	6.53
Hyattsville, MD (city) Prince George's County	960	6.52
Hialeah, FL (city) Miami-Dade County	14,668	6.48
Los Angeles, CA (city) Los Angeles County	238,191	6.45
South Gate, CA (city) Los Angeles County	6,164	6.40
Kendale Lakes, FL (cdp) Miami-Dade County	3,640	6.40
Tamiami, FL (cdp) Miami-Dade County	3,451	6.30
Walnut Park, CA (cdp) Los Angeles County	1,016	6.28
North Plainfield, NJ (borough) Somerset County	1,311	6.21
Hybla Valley, VA (cdp) Fairfax County	1,038	6.21
Daly City, CA (city) San Mateo County	6,426	6.20
San Rafael, CA (city) Marin County	3,471	6.19
Morristown, NJ (town) Morris County	1,139	6.14
Morganton, NC (city) Burke County	1,052	6.08
Gladeview, FL (cdp) Miami-Dade County	876	6.05
Arlington, VA (cdp) Arlington County	11,323	5.98
Bull Run, VA (cdp) Prince William County	657	5.80
Westmont, CA (cdp) Los Angeles County	1,826	5.77
Alexandria, VA (independent city) Alexandria city	7,241	5.64
Mount Vernon, VA (cdp) Fairfax County	1,612	5.64
Lawndale, CA (city) Los Angeles County	1,785	5.63
Lake Worth Corridor, FL (cdp) Palm Beach County	1,051	5.63
Hawthorne, CA (city) Los Angeles County	4,681	5.57
South Miami Heights, FL (cdp) Miami-Dade County	1,868	5.57
Bell Gardens, CA (city) Los Angeles County	2,429	5.51
Wyandanch, NY (cdp) Suffolk County	576	5.46
Maywood, CA (city) Los Angeles County	1,517	5.40
Glen Cove, NY (city) Nassau County	1,434	5.39
Guttenberg, NJ (town) Hudson County	582	5.39
Westbury, NY (village) Nassau County	765	5.36
Princeton, FL (cdp) Miami-Dade County	533	5.28
Leisure City, FL (cdp) Miami-Dade County	1,154	5.21
South San Francisco, CA (city) San Mateo County	3,145	5.19
Takoma Park, MD (city) Montgomery County	895	5.17
Woodbridge, VA (cdp) Prince William County	1,646	5.15
Idylwood, VA (cdp) Fairfax County	820	5.12
Elizabeth, NJ (city) Union County	6,126	5.08
North Fair Oaks, CA (cdp) San Mateo County	785	5.08
Lynwood, CA (city) Los Angeles County	3,441	4.93
Palmetto Estates, FL (cdp) Miami-Dade County	673	4.92
The Hammocks, FL (cdp) Miami-Dade County	2,324	4.91
San Pablo, CA (city) Contra Costa County	1,467	4.86
Doral, FL (cdp) Miami-Dade County	990	4.84
Redland, MD (cdp) Montgomery County	821	4.83
Kenner, LA (city) Jefferson Parish	3,364	4.77
North Bergen, NJ (township) Hudson County	2,739	4.71
Immokalee, FL (cdp) Collier County	930	4.71
Manassas Park, VA (independent city) Manassas Park city	485	4.71
Spring Valley, NY (village) Rockland County	1,193	4.69
Miami Springs, FL (city) Miami-Dade County	643	4.69
University Park, FL (cdp) Miami-Dade County	1,240	4.67
Somerville, NJ (borough) Somerset County	578	4.65
Carthage, MO (city) Jasper County	588	4.64
Providence, RI (city) Providence County	8,011	4.61
Islip, NY (town) Suffolk County	14,851	4.60
Rye, NY (town) Westchester County	2,016	4.59
Trenton, NJ (city) Mercer County	3,902	4.57
New Brunswick, NJ (city) Middlesex County	2,198	4.53
Inglewood, CA (city) Los Angeles County	5,083	4.52
Kendall, FL (cdp) Miami-Dade County	3,310	4.40
Aspen Hill, MD (cdp) Montgomery County	2,209	4.40
Coral Terrace, FL (cdp) Miami-Dade County	1,057	4.34
Pinewood, FL (cdp) Miami-Dade County	715	4.33
Fairfax, VA (independent city) Fairfax city	927	4.31
The Crossings, FL (cdp) Miami-Dade County	1,004	4.26
Westwood Lakes, FL (cdp) Miami-Dade County	512	4.26
Mamaroneck, NY (village) Westchester County	783	4.18
Carol City, FL (cdp) Miami-Dade County	2,460	4.14
North Amityville, NY (cdp) Suffolk County	685	4.13
Westchester, FL (cdp) Miami-Dade County	1,230	4.06
Manassas, VA (independent city) Manassas city	1,410	4.01
Downey, CA (city) Los Angeles County	4,276	3.98
Opa-locka, FL (city) Miami-Dade County	594	3.97
White Oak, MD (cdp) Montgomery County	827	3.94
Florence-Graham, CA (cdp) Los Angeles County	2,345	3.90
San Bruno, CA (city) San Mateo County	1,562	3.89
Country Club, FL (cdp) Miami-Dade County	1,398	3.85
Newburgh, NY (city) Orange County	1,085	3.84
Sunset, FL (cdp) Miami-Dade County	644	3.76
Annandale, VA (cdp) Fairfax County	2,049	3.73
South San Jose Hills, CA (cdp) Los Angeles County	732	3.62
Mineola, NY (village) Nassau County	688	3.58
East Riverdale, MD (cdp) Prince George's County	536	3.58
Merrifield, VA (cdp) Fairfax County	400	3.58
La Puente, CA (city) Los Angeles County	1,466	3.57
Miami Beach, FL (city) Miami-Dade County	3,096	3.52
East Palo Alto, CA (city) San Mateo County	1,037	3.51
Summit, NJ (city) Union County	742	3.51
Stamford, CT (city) Fairfield County	4,097	3.50
Glenvar Heights, FL (cdp) Miami-Dade County	569	3.50
Cliffside Park, NJ (borough) Bergen County	798	3.47
Copiague, NY (cdp) Suffolk County	760	3.47
Port Washington, NY (cdp) Nassau County	528	3.47
Country Walk, FL (cdp) Miami-Dade County	364	3.42
Somerville, MA (city) Middlesex County	2,636	3.40
Dover, NJ (town) Morris County	618	3.40
West Palm Beach, FL (city) Palm Beach County	2,745	3.34
Rockville, MD (city) Montgomery County	1,577	3.33
Commerce, CA (city) Los Angeles County	419	3.33
Farmers Branch, TX (city) Dallas County	909	3.30
Irving, TX (city) Dallas County	6,225	3.25
Bay Point, CA (cdp) Contra Costa County	699	3.25
Palisades Park, NJ (borough) Bergen County	549	3.22
Reston, VA (cdp) Fairfax County	1,810	3.21
Olympia Heights, FL (cdp) Miami-Dade County	432	3.21
Redwood City, CA (city) San Mateo County	2,381	3.16
Everett, MA (city) Middlesex County	1,201	3.16
Valinda, CA (cdp) Los Angeles County	684	3.14

Notes: (cdp) census designated place; Refer to the Explanation of Data in the front of the book for more detailed information.

Hispanic: Costa Rican

Top 150 Places Sorted by Number

(Based on all places, regardless of population)

Place	Number	%
New York, NY (city) New York City	4,939	0.06
Los Angeles, CA (city) Los Angeles County	2,125	0.06
Bound Brook, NJ (borough) Somerset County	941	9.27
Trenton, NJ (city) Mercer County	795	0.93
Paterson, NJ (city) Passaic County	789	0.53
Miami, FL (city) Miami-Dade County	775	0.21
Norwalk, CT (city) Fairfield County	694	0.84
Summit, NJ (city) Union County	640	3.03
Chicago, IL (city) Cook County	609	0.02
Lincolnton, NC (city) Lincoln County	578	5.80
Houston, TX (city) Harris County	567	0.03
Philadelphia, PA (city) Philadelphia County	501	0.03
Hialeah, FL (city) Miami-Dade County	473	0.21
Somerville, NJ (borough) Somerset County	464	3.74
San Diego, CA (city) San Diego County	462	0.04
Hempstead, NY (town) Nassau County	445	0.06
Boston, MA (city) Suffolk County	437	0.07
Dallas, TX (city) Dallas County	418	0.04
San Francisco, CA (city) San Francisco County	326	0.04
Elizabeth, NJ (city) Union County	323	0.27
Bridgewater, NJ (township) Somerset County	316	0.74
Southampton, NY (town) Suffolk County	306	0.56
Miami Beach, FL (city) Miami-Dade County	293	0.33
Charlotte, NC (city) Mecklenburg County	284	0.05
Newark, NJ (city) Essex County	282	0.10
Long Beach, CA (city) Los Angeles County	278	0.06
Jacksonville, FL (special city) Duval County	259	0.04
Hollywood, FL (city) Broward County	256	0.18
Bridgeport, CT (city) Fairfield County	246	0.18
Dover, NJ (town) Morris County	239	1.31
Tampa, FL (city) Hillsborough County	233	0.08
Pembroke Pines, FL (city) Broward County	227	0.17
Phoenix, AZ (city) Maricopa County	212	0.02
Hillsborough, NJ (township) Somerset County	210	0.57
Anaheim, CA (city) Orange County	205	0.06
Bloomfield, NJ (cdp) Essex County	197	0.41
Downey, CA (city) Los Angeles County	197	0.18
Raritan, NJ (borough) Somerset County	194	3.06
Hampton Bays, NY (cdp) Suffolk County	193	1.58
Jersey City, NJ (city) Hudson County	188	0.08
San Jose, CA (city) Santa Clara County	188	0.02
Islip, NY (town) Suffolk County	187	0.06
East Hampton, NY (town) Suffolk County	178	0.90
Kendall, FL (cdp) Miami-Dade County	171	0.23
Washington, DC (city) District of Columbia	167	0.03
Milwaukee, WI (city) Milwaukee County	161	0.03
Las Vegas, NV (city) Clark County	158	0.03
Chelsea, MA (city) Suffolk County	156	0.44
Fountainbleau, FL (cdp) Miami-Dade County	153	0.26
Nashville-Davidson, TN (special city) Davidson County	153	0.03
Union, NJ (cdp) Union County	150	0.28
Lakewood, NJ (township) Ocean County	150	0.25
Burbank, CA (city) Los Angeles County	149	0.15
San Antonio, TX (city) Bexar County	143	0.01
Riverside, CA (city) Riverside County	142	0.06
Hilton Head Island, SC (town) Beaufort County	140	0.41
Glendale, CA (city) Los Angeles County	140	0.07
Yonkers, NY (city) Westchester County	135	0.07
Austin, TX (city) Travis County	134	0.02
Kenner, LA (city) Jefferson Parish	133	0.19
Norwalk, CA (city) Los Angeles County	130	0.13
Manville, NJ (borough) Somerset County	128	1.24
Amsterdam, NY (city) Montgomery County	128	0.70
Carol City, FL (cdp) Miami-Dade County	128	0.22
The Hammocks, FL (cdp) Miami-Dade County	126	0.27
South Gate, CA (city) Los Angeles County	123	0.13
Torrance, CA (city) Los Angeles County	123	0.09
Miramar, FL (city) Broward County	122	0.17
Ontario, CA (city) San Bernardino County	121	0.08
Berea, SC (cdp) Greenville County	119	0.84
Pasadena, CA (city) Los Angeles County	119	0.09
Arlington, VA (cdp) Arlington County	119	0.06
Orlando, FL (city) Orange County	119	0.06
Coral Springs, FL (city) Broward County	118	0.10
North Bergen, NJ (township) Hudson County	116	0.20

Place	Number	%
West Palm Beach, FL (city) Palm Beach County	116	0.14
North Miami, FL (city) Miami-Dade County	115	0.19
Moreno Valley, CA (city) Riverside County	113	0.08
New Orleans, LA (city) Orleans Parish	112	0.02
Hamilton, NJ (township) Mercer County	111	0.13
Miami Springs, FL (city) Miami-Dade County	109	0.79
Springfield, NJ (cdp) Union County	108	0.75
Kendale Lakes, FL (cdp) Miami-Dade County	108	0.19
Hawthorne, CA (city) Los Angeles County	106	0.13
Kendall West, FL (cdp) Miami-Dade County	105	0.28
West Covina, CA (city) Los Angeles County	105	0.10
Rancho Cucamonga, CA (city) San Bernardino County	105	0.08
Reno, NV (city) Washoe County	100	0.06
Country Club, FL (cdp) Miami-Dade County	99	0.27
North Hempstead, NY (town) Nassau County	99	0.04
Berkeley Heights, NJ (cdp) Union County	98	0.73
Coral Gables, FL (city) Miami-Dade County	98	0.23
Tamiami, FL (cdp) Miami-Dade County	97	0.18
Sunrise, FL (city) Broward County	97	0.11
Woodbridge, NJ (township) Middlesex County	97	0.10
Seattle, WA (city) King County	97	0.02
Simi Valley, CA (city) Ventura County	96	0.09
Metairie, LA (cdp) Jefferson Parish	95	0.07
Arlington, TX (city) Tarrant County	95	0.03
Sacramento, CA (city) Sacramento County	95	0.02
Paradise, NV (cdp) Clark County	94	0.05
Ramapo, NY (town) Rockland County	93	0.09
Fort Lauderdale, FL (city) Broward County	93	0.06
Portland, OR (city) Multnomah County	92	0.02
Town 'n' Country, FL (cdp) Hillsborough County	91	0.13
Alhambra, CA (city) Los Angeles County	91	0.11
West Orange, NJ (cdp) Essex County	89	0.20
Irvington, NJ (cdp) Essex County	89	0.15
Union City, NJ (city) Hudson County	89	0.13
Mesa, AZ (city) Maricopa County	89	0.02
South Bound Brook, NJ (borough) Somerset County	88	1.96
Saint Petersburg, FL (city) Pinellas County	88	0.04
Clifton, NJ (city) Passaic County	87	0.11
Santa Ana, CA (city) Orange County	87	0.03
Babylon, NY (town) Suffolk County	85	0.04
Deerfield Beach, FL (city) Broward County	84	0.13
Fontana, CA (city) San Bernardino County	83	0.06
Richmond West, FL (cdp) Miami-Dade County	82	0.29
Hackensack, NJ (city) Bergen County	82	0.19
West New York, NJ (town) Hudson County	82	0.18
Santa Clarita, CA (city) Los Angeles County	82	0.05
Brookhaven, NY (town) Suffolk County	82	0.02
Perth Amboy, NJ (city) Middlesex County	81	0.17
Lakewood, CA (city) Los Angeles County	81	0.10
South Miami Heights, FL (cdp) Miami-Dade County	80	0.24
Springs, NY (cdp) Suffolk County	79	1.60
Stamford, CT (city) Fairfield County	79	0.07
Garland, TX (city) Dallas County	79	0.04
Danbury, CT (city) Fairfield County	78	0.10
Corona, CA (city) Riverside County	78	0.06
Chula Vista, CA (city) San Diego County	75	0.04
North Miami Beach, FL (city) Miami-Dade County	74	0.18
Davie, FL (town) Broward County	74	0.10
Linden, NJ (city) Union County	73	0.19
Palmdale, CA (city) Los Angeles County	73	0.06
San Bernardino, CA (city) San Bernardino County	73	0.04
Ridgewood, NJ (village) Bergen County	72	0.29
Brentwood, NY (cdp) Suffolk County	72	0.13
Rialto, CA (city) San Bernardino County	72	0.08
Springfield, MA (city) Hampden County	72	0.05
Chandler, AZ (city) Maricopa County	72	0.04
Egypt Lake-Leto, FL (cdp) Hillsborough County	71	0.22
Freeport, NY (village) Nassau County	71	0.16
Pomona, CA (city) Los Angeles County	71	0.05
Whittier, CA (city) Los Angeles County	70	0.08
Fullerton, CA (city) Orange County	70	0.06
Inglewood, CA (city) Los Angeles County	70	0.06
Lancaster, CA (city) Los Angeles County	70	0.06
Worcester, MA (city) Worcester County	70	0.04
Hackettstown, NJ (town) Warren County	69	0.66

Notes: (cdp) census designated place; Refer to the Explanation of Data in the front of the book for more detailed information.

Hispanic: Costa Rican

Top 150 Places Sorted by Percent

(Based on all places, regardless of population)

Place	Number	%
Bound Brook, NJ (borough) Somerset County	941	9.27
Boger City, NC (cdp) Lincoln County	37	6.68
Lincolnton, NC (city) Lincoln County	578	5.80
Somerville, NJ (borough) Somerset County	464	3.74
Raritan, NJ (borough) Somerset County	194	3.06
Summit, NJ (city) Union County	640	3.03
Kent, MN (city) Wilkin County	3	2.50
Woodloch, TX (town) Montgomery County	5	2.02
South Bound Brook, NJ (borough) Somerset County	88	1.96
Redings Mill, MO (village) Newton County	3	1.89
Maiden, NC (town) Catawba County	53	1.61
Springs, NY (cdp) Suffolk County	79	1.60
Hampton Bays, NY (cdp) Suffolk County	193	1.58
East Hampton, NY (village) Suffolk County	21	1.57
Clinton, NJ (town) Hunterdon County	39	1.48
Spillertown, IL (village) Williamson County	3	1.36
Dover, NJ (town) Morris County	239	1.31
Lincolnshire, KY (city) Jefferson County	2	1.30
Manville, NJ (borough) Somerset County	128	1.24
Keystone, CO (cdp) Summit County	10	1.21
Grandin, ND (city) Cass County	2	1.10
Prospect Park, NJ (borough) Passaic County	61	1.06
Huetter, ID (city) Kootenai County	1	1.04
Godley, IL (village) Will County	6	1.01
Frenchtown, NJ (borough) Hunterdon County	14	0.94
Trenton, NJ (city) Mercer County	795	0.93
East Hampton North, NY (cdp) Suffolk County	33	0.92
Medley, FL (town) Miami-Dade County	10	0.91
East Hampton, NY (town) Suffolk County	178	0.90
Linn Valley, KS (city) Linn County	5	0.89
Norwalk, CT (city) Fairfield County	694	0.84
Berea, SC (cdp) Greenville County	119	0.84
Sun Valley, ID (city) Blaine County	12	0.84
Miami Springs, FL (city) Miami-Dade County	109	0.79
Wendover, UT (city) Tooele County	12	0.78
Virginia Gardens, FL (village) Miami-Dade County	18	0.77
Flemington, NJ (borough) Hunterdon County	32	0.76
Golden Beach, FL (town) Miami-Dade County	7	0.76
Springfield, NJ (cdp) Union County	108	0.75
Northwest Harbor, NY (cdp) Suffolk County	23	0.75
Hillcrest Heights, FL (town) Polk County	2	0.75
Bridgewater, NJ (township) Somerset County	316	0.74
Bellerose Terrace, NY (cdp) Nassau County	16	0.74
Berkeley Heights, NJ (cdp) Union County	98	0.73
Callahan, FL (town) Nassau County	7	0.73
Bridgehampton, NY (cdp) Suffolk County	10	0.72
Amsterdam, NY (city) Montgomery County	128	0.70
Sans Souci, SC (cdp) Greenville County	53	0.68
Hackettstown, NJ (town) Warren County	69	0.66
Cooperstown, PA (borough) Venango County	3	0.65
Wainscott, NY (cdp) Suffolk County	4	0.64
Thornburg, PA (borough) Allegheny County	3	0.64
Scio, OR (city) Linn County	4	0.58
Washington Grove, MD (town) Montgomery County	3	0.58
Hillsborough, NJ (township) Somerset County	210	0.57
Southampton, NY (town) Suffolk County	306	0.56
Beatyestown, NJ (cdp) Warren County	18	0.56
Glendale, UT (town) Kane County	2	0.56
Keyport, NJ (borough) Monmouth County	42	0.55
Electric City, WA (town) Grant County	5	0.54
Paterson, NJ (city) Passaic County	789	0.53
Kirkland, NC (cdp) New Hanover County	3	0.52
McKean, PA (borough) Erie County	2	0.51
Rice, TX (city) Navarro County	4	0.50
Naples Park, FL (cdp) Collier County	33	0.49
Haledon, NJ (borough) Passaic County	40	0.48
Midland Park, NJ (borough) Bergen County	33	0.48
Lake of the Woods, CA (cdp) Kern County	4	0.48
Cherryville, NC (city) Gaston County	25	0.47
West Pelzer, SC (town) Anderson County	4	0.46
New Providence, NJ (borough) Union County	54	0.45
Spring Valley, KY (city) Jefferson County	3	0.45
Chelsea, MA (city) Suffolk County	156	0.44
Dovre, WI (town) Barron County	3	0.44
Rolfe, IA (city) Pocahontas County	3	0.44
Spurr, MI (township) Baraga County	1	0.44
Desert View Highlands, CA (cdp) Los Angeles County	10	0.43
Georgetown, CT (cdp) Fairfield County	7	0.42
Manor, TX (city) Travis County	5	0.42
Utopia, FL (cdp) Broward County	3	0.42
Arden, DE (village) New Castle County	2	0.42
Bloomfield, NJ (cdp) Essex County	197	0.41
Hilton Head Island, SC (town) Beaufort County	140	0.41
Garland, UT (city) Box Elder County	8	0.41
Morse, MN (township) Saint Louis County	5	0.41
North Beach, FL (cdp) Indian River County	1	0.41
Long Hill, NJ (township) Morris County	35	0.40
Chatham, NJ (borough) Morris County	34	0.40
El Portal, FL (village) Miami-Dade County	10	0.40
Sherwood, WI (town) Clark County	1	0.40
East Quogue, NY (cdp) Suffolk County	16	0.38
Ellisburg, NY (village) Jefferson County	1	0.37
Middlesex, NJ (borough) Middlesex County	49	0.36
East Thermopolis, WY (town) Hot Springs County	1	0.36
Hawthorne, NJ (borough) Passaic County	63	0.35
North Haledon, NJ (borough) Passaic County	28	0.35
East Palatka, FL (cdp) Putnam County	6	0.35
Pompano Beach Highlands, FL (cdp) Broward County	22	0.34
Atlantic Highlands, NJ (borough) Monmouth County	16	0.34
Garwood, NJ (borough) Union County	14	0.34
Biscayne Park, FL (village) Miami-Dade County	11	0.34
Tedder, FL (cdp) Broward County	7	0.34
Godley, TX (city) Johnson County	3	0.34
Haileyville, OK (city) Pittsburg County	3	0.34
Fairmont, MN (township) Martin County	1	0.34
Miami Beach, FL (city) Miami-Dade County	293	0.33
Mansfield, NJ (township) Warren County	22	0.33
Ashland City, TN (town) Cheatham County	12	0.33
Noyack, NY (cdp) Suffolk County	9	0.33
Keating, PA (township) Potter County	1	0.33
Doral, FL (cdp) Miami-Dade County	66	0.32
Glenvar Heights, FL (cdp) Miami-Dade County	52	0.32
Dunellen, NJ (borough) Middlesex County	22	0.32
New Salem, MA (town) Franklin County	3	0.32
Westwood Lakes, FL (cdp) Miami-Dade County	37	0.31
Surfside, FL (town) Miami-Dade County	15	0.31
Montauk, NY (cdp) Suffolk County	12	0.31
Greenvale, NY (cdp) Nassau County	7	0.31
Rio Communities North, NM (cdp) Valencia County	5	0.31
Matteson, WI (town) Waupaca County	3	0.31
Montgomery, MA (town) Hampden County	2	0.31
Bostwick, GA (town) Morgan County	1	0.31
Princeton, FL (cdp) Miami-Dade County	30	0.30
Waldwick, NJ (borough) Bergen County	29	0.30
Washington, NJ (borough) Warren County	20	0.30
Manasquan, NJ (borough) Monmouth County	19	0.30
Lake Forest, FL (cdp) Broward County	15	0.30
Lincoln, WI (town) Forest County	3	0.30
Campbell Hill, IL (village) Jackson County	1	0.30
Richmond West, FL (cdp) Miami-Dade County	82	0.29
Ridgewood, NJ (village) Bergen County	72	0.29
Newton, NC (city) Catawba County	36	0.29
Westwood, NJ (borough) Bergen County	32	0.29
Key Biscayne, FL (village) Miami-Dade County	30	0.29
Kenilworth, NJ (borough) Union County	22	0.29
Senoia, GA (city) Coweta County	5	0.29
Holly, CO (town) Prowers County	3	0.29
Marvin, NC (village) Union County	3	0.29
Williston, TN (city) Fayette County	1	0.29
Union, NJ (cdp) Union County	150	0.28
Kendall West, FL (cdp) Miami-Dade County	105	0.28
White, NJ (township) Warren County	12	0.28
Minisink, NY (town) Orange County	10	0.28
Silverthorne, CO (town) Summit County	9	0.28
Haverhill, FL (town) Palm Beach County	4	0.28
Arizona Village, AZ (cdp) Mohave County	1	0.28
Elizabeth, NJ (city) Union County	323	0.27
The Hammocks, FL (cdp) Miami-Dade County	126	0.27
Country Club, FL (cdp) Miami-Dade County	99	0.27
Ridgefield Park, NJ (village) Bergen County	35	0.27

Notes: (cdp) census designated place; Refer to the Explanation of Data in the front of the book for more detailed information.

Hispanic: Costa Rican

Top 150 Places Sorted by Percent

(Based on places with populations of 10,000 or more)

Place	Number	%
Bound Brook, NJ (borough) Somerset County	941	9.27
Somerville, NJ (borough) Somerset County	464	3.74
Summit, NJ (city) Union County	640	3.03
Hampton Bays, NY (cdp) Suffolk County	193	1.58
Dover, NJ (town) Morris County	239	1.31
Manville, NJ (borough) Somerset County	128	1.24
Trenton, NJ (city) Mercer County	795	0.93
East Hampton, NY (town) Suffolk County	178	0.90
Norwalk, CT (city) Fairfield County	694	0.84
Berea, SC (cdp) Greenville County	119	0.84
Miami Springs, FL (city) Miami-Dade County	109	0.79
Springfield, NJ (cdp) Union County	108	0.75
Bridgewater, NJ (township) Somerset County	316	0.74
Berkeley Heights, NJ (cdp) Union County	98	0.73
Amsterdam, NY (city) Montgomery County	128	0.70
Hackettstown, NJ (town) Warren County	69	0.66
Hillsborough, NJ (township) Somerset County	210	0.57
Southampton, NY (town) Suffolk County	306	0.56
Paterson, NJ (city) Passaic County	789	0.53
New Providence, NJ (borough) Union County	54	0.45
Chelsea, MA (city) Suffolk County	156	0.44
Bloomfield, NJ (cdp) Essex County	197	0.41
Hilton Head Island, SC (town) Beaufort County	140	0.41
Middlesex, NJ (borough) Middlesex County	49	0.36
Hawthorne, NJ (borough) Passaic County	63	0.35
Miami Beach, FL (city) Miami-Dade County	293	0.33
Doral, FL (cdp) Miami-Dade County	66	0.32
Glenvar Heights, FL (cdp) Miami-Dade County	52	0.32
Westwood Lakes, FL (cdp) Miami-Dade County	37	0.31
Princeton, FL (cdp) Miami-Dade County	30	0.30
Richmond West, FL (cdp) Miami-Dade County	82	0.29
Ridgewood, NJ (village) Bergen County	72	0.29
Newton, NC (city) Catawba County	36	0.29
Westwood, NJ (borough) Bergen County	32	0.29
Key Biscayne, FL (village) Miami-Dade County	30	0.29
Union, NJ (cdp) Union County	150	0.28
Kendall West, FL (cdp) Miami-Dade County	105	0.28
Elizabeth, NJ (city) Union County	323	0.27
The Hammocks, FL (cdp) Miami-Dade County	126	0.27
Country Club, FL (cdp) Miami-Dade County	99	0.27
Ridgefield Park, NJ (village) Bergen County	35	0.27
Hillsdale, NJ (borough) Bergen County	27	0.27
Fountainbleau, FL (cdp) Miami-Dade County	153	0.26
Ives Estates, FL (cdp) Miami-Dade County	45	0.26
Lakewood, NJ (township) Ocean County	150	0.25
Coral Terrace, FL (cdp) Miami-Dade County	62	0.25
South Miami Heights, FL (cdp) Miami-Dade County	80	0.24
Pinecrest, FL (village) Miami-Dade County	45	0.24
Palm River-Clair Mel, FL (cdp) Hillsborough County	43	0.24
Kendall, FL (cdp) Miami-Dade County	171	0.23
Coral Gables, FL (city) Miami-Dade County	98	0.23
Leisure City, FL (cdp) Miami-Dade County	52	0.23
Sweetwater, FL (city) Miami-Dade County	33	0.23
Carol City, FL (cdp) Miami-Dade County	128	0.22
Egypt Lake-Leto, FL (cdp) Hillsborough County	71	0.22
Westchester, FL (cdp) Miami-Dade County	68	0.22
Artesia, CA (city) Los Angeles County	36	0.22
Country Walk, FL (cdp) Miami-Dade County	23	0.22
Miami, FL (city) Miami-Dade County	775	0.21
Hialeah, FL (city) Miami-Dade County	473	0.21
Hillside, NJ (cdp) Union County	46	0.21
South Miami, FL (city) Miami-Dade County	23	0.21
North Bergen, NJ (township) Hudson County	116	0.20
West Orange, NJ (cdp) Essex County	89	0.20
Spring Valley, NY (village) Rockland County	51	0.20
The Crossings, FL (cdp) Miami-Dade County	46	0.20
Ojus, FL (cdp) Miami-Dade County	34	0.20
Madison, NJ (borough) Morris County	33	0.20
Sunny Isles Beach, FL (city) Miami-Dade County	31	0.20
Palmetto Estates, FL (cdp) Miami-Dade County	28	0.20
Kenner, LA (city) Jefferson Parish	133	0.19
North Miami, FL (city) Miami-Dade County	115	0.19
Kendale Lakes, FL (cdp) Miami-Dade County	108	0.19
Hackensack, NJ (city) Bergen County	82	0.19
Linden, NJ (city) Union County	73	0.19
Aventura, FL (city) Miami-Dade County	47	0.19
Cutler Ridge, FL (cdp) Miami-Dade County	47	0.19
Uniondale, NY (cdp) Nassau County	43	0.19
Pequannock, NJ (township) Morris County	26	0.19
Key Largo, FL (cdp) Monroe County	23	0.19
Red Bank, NJ (borough) Monmouth County	23	0.19
Chatham, NJ (township) Morris County	19	0.19
Hollywood, FL (city) Broward County	256	0.18
Bridgeport, CT (city) Fairfield County	246	0.18
Downey, CA (city) Los Angeles County	197	0.18
Tamiami, FL (cdp) Miami-Dade County	97	0.18
West New York, NJ (town) Hudson County	82	0.18
North Miami Beach, FL (city) Miami-Dade County	74	0.18
Hallandale, FL (city) Broward County	63	0.18
Maplewood, NJ (cdp) Essex County	44	0.18
North Plainfield, NJ (borough) Somerset County	39	0.18
Elmwood Park, NJ (borough) Bergen County	34	0.18
North Bay Shore, NY (cdp) Suffolk County	27	0.18
Addison, TX (town) Dallas County	25	0.18
Little Ferry, NJ (borough) Bergen County	19	0.18
Miami Shores, FL (village) Miami-Dade County	19	0.18
Pembroke Pines, FL (city) Broward County	227	0.17
Miramar, FL (city) Broward County	122	0.17
Perth Amboy, NJ (city) Middlesex County	81	0.17
Yeehaw Junction, FL (cdp) Osceola County	36	0.17
Fords, NJ (cdp) Middlesex County	25	0.17
Harrison, NJ (town) Hudson County	25	0.17
Meadow Woods, FL (cdp) Orange County	19	0.17
Freeport, NY (village) Nassau County	71	0.16
Lawndale, CA (city) Los Angeles County	52	0.16
University Park, FL (cdp) Miami-Dade County	43	0.16
Glen Cove, NY (city) Nassau County	42	0.16
Cudahy, CA (city) Los Angeles County	39	0.16
Miami Lakes, FL (cdp) Miami-Dade County	37	0.16
Dania Beach, FL (city) Broward County	33	0.16
Hialeah Gardens, FL (city) Miami-Dade County	30	0.16
Olympia Heights, FL (cdp) Miami-Dade County	22	0.16
River Edge, NJ (borough) Bergen County	18	0.16
Citrus, CA (cdp) Los Angeles County	17	0.16
Burbank, CA (city) Los Angeles County	149	0.15
Irvington, NJ (cdp) Essex County	89	0.15
Lake Worth, FL (city) Palm Beach County	51	0.15
Montclair, CA (city) San Bernardino County	48	0.15
Orange, NJ (cdp) Essex County	48	0.15
Homestead, FL (city) Miami-Dade County	47	0.15
Mission Bend, TX (cdp) Fort Bend County	47	0.15
Scotch Plains, NJ (cdp) Union County	34	0.15
North Augusta, SC (city) Aiken County	27	0.15
Santa Fe Springs, CA (city) Los Angeles County	26	0.15
Sunset, FL (cdp) Miami-Dade County	25	0.15
Phillipsburg, NJ (town) Warren County	23	0.15
West Paterson, NJ (borough) Passaic County	17	0.15
West Palm Beach, FL (city) Palm Beach County	116	0.14
Kissimmee, FL (city) Osceola County	69	0.14
Plainfield, NJ (city) Union County	69	0.14
Carteret, NJ (borough) Middlesex County	29	0.14
Millburn, NJ (cdp) Essex County	27	0.14
Longwood, FL (city) Seminole County	19	0.14
Roselle Park, NJ (borough) Union County	19	0.14
Azalea Park, FL (cdp) Orange County	15	0.14
Norwalk, CA (city) Los Angeles County	130	0.13
South Gate, CA (city) Los Angeles County	123	0.13
Hamilton, NJ (township) Mercer County	111	0.13
Hawthorne, CA (city) Los Angeles County	106	0.13
Town 'n' Country, FL (cdp) Hillsborough County	91	0.13
Union City, NJ (city) Hudson County	89	0.13
Deerfield Beach, FL (city) Broward County	84	0.13
Brentwood, NY (cdp) Suffolk County	72	0.13
Peachtree City, GA (city) Fayette County	42	0.13
Long Branch, NJ (city) Monmouth County	41	0.13
Bergenfield, NJ (borough) Bergen County	33	0.13
East Windsor, NJ (township) Mercer County	33	0.13
Key West, FL (city) Monroe County	33	0.13
Mount Olive, NJ (township) Morris County	31	0.13
Ossining, NY (village) Westchester County	31	0.13

Notes: (cdp) census designated place; Refer to the Explanation of Data in the front of the book for more detailed information.

Hispanic: Guatemalan

Top 150 Places Sorted by Number

(Based on all places, regardless of population)

Place	Number	%
Los Angeles, CA (city) Los Angeles County	65,922	1.78
New York, NY (city) New York City	15,212	0.19
Chicago, IL (city) Cook County	13,610	0.47
Houston, TX (city) Harris County	7,220	0.37
Providence, RI (city) Providence County	6,396	3.68
San Francisco, CA (city) San Francisco County	3,196	0.41
Stamford, CT (city) Fairfield County	3,067	2.62
Trenton, NJ (city) Mercer County	2,644	3.10
Boston, MA (city) Suffolk County	2,554	0.43
Miami, FL (city) Miami-Dade County	2,475	0.68
Long Beach, CA (city) Los Angeles County	2,443	0.53
Phoenix, AZ (city) Maricopa County	2,397	0.18
Hempstead, NY (town) Nassau County	2,094	0.28
San Rafael, CA (city) Marin County	2,090	3.73
Dallas, TX (city) Dallas County	1,950	0.16
Santa Ana, CA (city) Orange County	1,931	0.57
Hawthorne, CA (city) Los Angeles County	1,879	2.23
West Palm Beach, FL (city) Palm Beach County	1,841	2.24
Langley Park, MD (cdp) Prince George's County	1,825	11.26
Inglewood, CA (city) Los Angeles County	1,806	1.60
Grand Rapids, MI (city) Kent County	1,762	0.89
Lake Worth, FL (city) Palm Beach County	1,711	4.87
Arlington, VA (cdp) Arlington County	1,703	0.90
Anaheim, CA (city) Orange County	1,638	0.50
Oakland, CA (city) Alameda County	1,549	0.39
South Gate, CA (city) Los Angeles County	1,488	1.54
Plainfield, NJ (city) Union County	1,443	3.02
Lynn, MA (city) Essex County	1,442	1.62
Washington, DC (city) District of Columbia	1,350	0.24
Islip, NY (town) Suffolk County	1,347	0.42
San Diego, CA (city) San Diego County	1,320	0.11
Las Vegas, NV (city) Clark County	1,263	0.26
Central Falls, RI (city) Providence County	1,202	6.35
Chelsea, MA (city) Suffolk County	1,177	3.36
Rye, NY (town) Westchester County	1,143	2.60
Glendale, CA (city) Los Angeles County	1,142	0.59
Ramapo, NY (town) Rockland County	1,116	1.02
Oklahoma City, OK (city) Oklahoma County	1,068	0.21
Homestead, FL (city) Miami-Dade County	1,059	3.32
Port Chester, NY (village) Westchester County	1,037	3.72
Portland, OR (city) Multnomah County	1,014	0.19
Downey, CA (city) Los Angeles County	1,007	0.94
Georgetown, DE (town) Sussex County	1,003	21.60
Huntington Park, CA (city) Los Angeles County	995	1.62
Rome, GA (city) Floyd County	992	2.84
Riverside, CA (city) Riverside County	978	0.38
Spring Valley, NY (village) Rockland County	960	3.77
Lynwood, CA (city) Los Angeles County	959	1.37
Morganton, NC (city) Burke County	945	5.46
Waltham, MA (city) Middlesex County	928	1.57
Indiantown, FL (cdp) Martin County	923	16.52
San Jose, CA (city) Santa Clara County	917	0.10
San Mateo, CA (city) San Mateo County	913	0.99
Pomona, CA (city) Los Angeles County	883	0.59
Santa Clarita, CA (city) Los Angeles County	879	0.58
Immokalee, FL (cdp) Collier County	861	4.36
Silver Spring, MD (cdp) Montgomery County	852	1.11
Hialeah, FL (city) Miami-Dade County	823	0.36
Garland, TX (city) Dallas County	813	0.38
Lennox, CA (cdp) Los Angeles County	811	3.53
Lawrence, MA (city) Essex County	794	1.10
Burbank, CA (city) Los Angeles County	792	0.79
Lawndale, CA (city) Los Angeles County	791	2.49
Newark, NJ (city) Essex County	776	0.28
Palmdale, CA (city) Los Angeles County	767	0.66
Austin, TX (city) Travis County	748	0.11
Reno, NV (city) Washoe County	744	0.41
Ontario, CA (city) San Bernardino County	743	0.47
Fairview, NJ (borough) Bergen County	722	5.45
Pasadena, CA (city) Los Angeles County	712	0.53
Chamblee, GA (city) De Kalb County	711	7.44
Brentwood, NY (cdp) Suffolk County	710	1.32
East Los Angeles, CA (cdp) Los Angeles County	701	0.56
Nashville-Davidson, TN (special city) Davidson County	679	0.12
El Monte, CA (city) Los Angeles County	667	0.58

Place	Number	%
Bailey's Crossroads, VA (cdp) Fairfax County	660	2.85
Mount Kisco, NY (village) Westchester County	657	6.58
Bell, CA (city) Los Angeles County	655	1.79
Alexandria, VA (independent city) Alexandria city	644	0.50
Fontana, CA (city) San Bernardino County	638	0.49
Wheaton-Glenmont, MD (cdp) Montgomery County	626	1.09
Pawtucket, RI (city) Providence County	618	0.85
Costa Mesa, CA (city) Orange County	618	0.57
Compton, CA (city) Los Angeles County	617	0.66
Paradise, NV (cdp) Clark County	609	0.33
San Antonio, TX (city) Bexar County	584	0.05
Grand Island, NE (city) Hall County	571	1.33
Cudahy, CA (city) Los Angeles County	570	2.35
Chattanooga, TN (city) Hamilton County	556	0.36
Norwalk, CA (city) Los Angeles County	555	0.54
North Hempstead, NY (town) Nassau County	550	0.25
Bell Gardens, CA (city) Los Angeles County	547	1.24
Mamaroneck, NY (village) Westchester County	544	2.90
Elizabeth, NJ (city) Union County	537	0.45
Freeport, NY (village) Nassau County	535	1.22
Daly City, CA (city) San Mateo County	533	0.51
Cedartown, GA (city) Polk County	529	5.59
Union City, NJ (city) Hudson County	525	0.78
Jersey City, NJ (city) Hudson County	520	0.22
Philadelphia, PA (city) Philadelphia County	518	0.03
Westmont, CA (cdp) Los Angeles County	515	1.63
Carthage, MO (city) Jasper County	514	4.06
Redwood City, CA (city) San Mateo County	508	0.67
Thousand Oaks, CA (city) Ventura County	504	0.43
Paramount, CA (city) Los Angeles County	497	0.90
Florence-Graham, CA (cdp) Los Angeles County	493	0.82
Lexington, NE (city) Dawson County	490	4.89
Attleboro, MA (city) Bristol County	489	1.16
Garden Grove, CA (city) Orange County	488	0.30
Hayward, CA (city) Alameda County	486	0.35
Hempstead, NY (village) Nassau County	482	0.85
Cicero, IL (town) Cook County	478	0.56
Fort Lauderdale, FL (city) Broward County	477	0.31
Fort Myers, FL (city) Lee County	475	0.99
Marietta, GA (city) Cobb County	473	0.81
Mamaroneck, NY (town) Westchester County	471	1.63
Denver, CO (city) Denver County	469	0.08
North Bergen, NJ (township) Hudson County	467	0.80
Baldwin Park, CA (city) Los Angeles County	466	0.61
Paterson, NJ (city) Passaic County	464	0.31
Lake Worth Corridor, FL (cdp) Palm Beach County	459	2.46
West Covina, CA (city) Los Angeles County	459	0.44
Brookhaven, NY (town) Suffolk County	457	0.10
Framingham, MA (cdp) Middlesex County	454	0.68
Mesa, AZ (city) Maricopa County	452	0.11
Palisades Park, NJ (borough) Bergen County	451	2.64
Sioux City, IA (city) Woodbury County	449	0.53
Charlotte, NC (city) Mecklenburg County	449	0.08
Southampton, NY (town) Suffolk County	446	0.82
Salt Lake City, UT (city) Salt Lake County	439	0.24
Seattle, WA (city) King County	439	0.08
North Plainfield, NJ (borough) Somerset County	431	2.04
Cleveland, OH (city) Cuyahoga County	431	0.09
San Bernardino, CA (city) San Bernardino County	430	0.23
Jupiter, FL (town) Palm Beach County	427	1.09
Richmond, VA (independent city) Richmond city	425	0.21
Hillsboro, OR (city) Washington County	412	0.59
Canton, GA (city) Cherokee County	399	5.18
Kenner, LA (city) Jefferson Parish	399	0.57
Alhambra, CA (city) Los Angeles County	395	0.46
Bonita Springs, FL (city) Lee County	393	1.20
West Little River, FL (cdp) Miami-Dade County	391	1.20
Aurora, CO (city) Arapahoe County	389	0.14
Gardena, CA (city) Los Angeles County	388	0.67
Rialto, CA (city) San Bernardino County	387	0.42
Sioux Falls, SD (city) Minnehaha County	387	0.31
Orange, CA (city) Orange County	386	0.30
Marlborough, MA (city) Middlesex County	384	1.06
Bakersfield, CA (city) Kern County	384	0.16
Minneapolis, MN (city) Hennepin County	384	0.10

Notes: (cdp) census designated place; Refer to the Explanation of Data in the front of the book for more detailed information.

Hispanic: Guatemalan

Top 150 Places Sorted by Percent

(Based on all places, regardless of population)

Place	Number	%
Georgetown, DE (town) Sussex County	1,003	21.60
Ellijay, GA (city) Gilmer County	272	17.17
Indiantown, FL (cdp) Martin County	923	16.52
East Ellijay, GA (city) Gilmer County	114	16.12
Brewster, NY (village) Putnam County	325	15.03
Langley Park, MD (cdp) Prince George's County	1,825	11.26
Green Forest, AR (city) Carroll County	227	8.35
Chamblee, GA (city) De Kalb County	711	7.44
Buena Vista, GA (city) Marion County	121	7.27
Collinsville, AL (town) De Kalb County	117	7.12
Mount Kisco, NY (village) Westchester County	657	6.58
Central Falls, RI (city) Providence County	1,202	6.35
Quioque, NY (cdp) Suffolk County	50	6.25
Trion, GA (town) Chattooga County	123	6.17
Schuyler, NE (city) Colfax County	313	5.83
Cedartown, GA (city) Polk County	529	5.59
Morganton, NC (city) Burke County	945	5.46
Fairview, NJ (borough) Bergen County	722	5.45
Canton, GA (city) Cherokee County	399	5.18
Monterey, TN (town) Putnam County	138	5.08
Henderson, MD (town) Caroline County	6	5.08
Lexington, NE (city) Dawson County	490	4.89
Lake Worth, FL (city) Palm Beach County	1,711	4.87
Marydel, MD (town) Caroline County	7	4.76
Immokalee, FL (cdp) Collier County	861	4.36
Tice, FL (cdp) Lee County	191	4.21
Octavia, NE (village) Butler County	6	4.14
Carthage, MO (city) Jasper County	514	4.06
Siler City, NC (town) Chatham County	276	3.96
Jamesport, NY (cdp) Suffolk County	59	3.87
Cheswold, DE (town) Kent County	12	3.83
Mangonia Park, FL (town) Palm Beach County	49	3.82
Spring Valley, NY (village) Rockland County	960	3.77
San Rafael, CA (city) Marin County	2,090	3.73
Port Chester, NY (village) Westchester County	1,037	3.72
Atlantic Beach, SC (town) Horry County	13	3.70
Providence, RI (city) Providence County	6,396	3.68
Lennox, CA (cdp) Los Angeles County	811	3.53
Russellville, AL (city) Franklin County	304	3.39
Chelsea, MA (city) Suffolk County	1,177	3.36
Alamosa East, CO (cdp) Alamosa County	51	3.34
Homestead, FL (city) Miami-Dade County	1,059	3.32
Westgate-Belvedere Homes, FL (cdp) Palm Beach County	265	3.26
Robbins, NC (city) Moore County	38	3.18
Trenton, NJ (city) Mercer County	2,644	3.10
Plainfield, NJ (city) Union County	1,443	3.02
Jennings, FL (town) Hamilton County	25	3.00
Flanders, NY (cdp) Suffolk County	107	2.93
Greenport, NY (village) Suffolk County	60	2.93
Mamaroneck, NY (village) Westchester County	544	2.90
Fort Payne, AL (city) De Kalb County	374	2.89
Kingston, NJ (cdp) Middlesex County	37	2.86
Bailey's Crossroads, VA (cdp) Fairfax County	660	2.85
Rome, GA (city) Floyd County	992	2.84
Goff, KS (city) Nemaha County	5	2.76
Seven Corners, VA (cdp) Fairfax County	233	2.68
Peconic, NY (cdp) Suffolk County	29	2.68
Palisades Park, NJ (borough) Bergen County	451	2.64
Stamford, CT (city) Fairfield County	3,067	2.62
Rye, NY (town) Westchester County	1,143	2.60
Saluda, SC (town) Saluda County	79	2.58
Stone Park, IL (village) Cook County	129	2.52
Lawndale, CA (city) Los Angeles County	791	2.49
Lake Worth Corridor, FL (cdp) Palm Beach County	459	2.46
Doraville, GA (city) De Kalb County	238	2.41
Cudahy, CA (city) Los Angeles County	570	2.35
Fanning Springs, FL (city) Levy County	17	2.31
Manorhaven, NY (village) Nassau County	141	2.30
Meigs, GA (city) Thomas County	25	2.29
Grattan, MN (township) Itasca County	1	2.27
Optima, OK (town) Texas County	6	2.26
West Palm Beach, FL (city) Palm Beach County	1,841	2.24
Hawthorne, CA (city) Los Angeles County	1,879	2.23
Watts Mills, SC (cdp) Laurens County	33	2.23
Westhampton Beach, NY (village) Suffolk County	41	2.16
Calhoun, GA (city) Gordon County	227	2.13
Conesville, IA (city) Muscatine County	9	2.12
Southeast, NY (town) Putnam County	361	2.08
Cutchogue, NY (cdp) Suffolk County	59	2.07
North Plainfield, NJ (borough) Somerset County	431	2.04
Perry, IA (city) Dallas County	156	2.04
Remsenburg-Speonk, NY (cdp) Suffolk County	54	2.02
Ames, OK (town) Major County	4	2.01
Milano, TX (city) Milam County	8	2.00
Norcross, GA (city) Gwinnett County	163	1.94
Eastport, NY (cdp) Suffolk County	28	1.93
Parksley, VA (town) Accomack County	16	1.91
Eton, GA (city) Murray County	6	1.88
Broadview Park, FL (cdp) Broward County	127	1.87
Saint Leonard, MD (cdp) Calvert County	10	1.87
Princeton, NJ (borough) Mercer County	264	1.86
Selbyville, DE (town) Sussex County	30	1.82
Cove, UT (cdp) Cache County	8	1.81
Bell, CA (city) Los Angeles County	655	1.79
Los Angeles, CA (city) Los Angeles County	65,922	1.78
Albertville, AL (city) Marshall County	306	1.77
Faison, NC (town) Duplin County	13	1.75
Inwood, NY (cdp) Nassau County	162	1.74
Keller, VA (town) Accomack County	3	1.73
Wimauma, FL (cdp) Hillsborough County	72	1.70
Guymon, OK (city) Texas County	177	1.69
Decatur, AR (city) Benton County	22	1.67
West Gate, VA (cdp) Prince William County	124	1.65
Moore Haven, FL (city) Glades County	27	1.65
Westmont, CA (cdp) Los Angeles County	515	1.63
Mamaroneck, NY (town) Westchester County	471	1.63
Lynn, MA (city) Essex County	1,442	1.62
Huntington Park, CA (city) Los Angeles County	995	1.62
Inglewood, CA (city) Los Angeles County	1,806	1.60
Waltham, MA (city) Middlesex County	928	1.57
Hanley Falls, MN (city) Yellow Medicine County	5	1.55
South Gate, CA (city) Los Angeles County	1,488	1.54
East Windsor, NJ (township) Mercer County	383	1.54
Bull Run, VA (cdp) Prince William County	175	1.54
Greenport West, NY (cdp) Suffolk County	25	1.49
New Suffolk, NY (cdp) Suffolk County	5	1.48
Stacey Street, FL (cdp) Palm Beach County	14	1.46
Fort Morgan, CO (city) Morgan County	160	1.45
Cornelia, GA (city) Habersham County	52	1.42
Industry, CA (city) Los Angeles County	11	1.42
North Fair Oaks, CA (cdp) San Mateo County	218	1.41
Morristown, NJ (town) Morris County	259	1.40
Lincolnia, VA (cdp) Fairfax County	220	1.39
Pawling, NY (village) Dutchess County	31	1.39
Baxter Estates, NY (village) Nassau County	14	1.39
Lynwood, CA (city) Los Angeles County	959	1.37
Lincoln Park, TX (town) Denton County	7	1.35
Grand Island, NE (city) Hall County	571	1.33
Dixville, NH (township) Coos County	1	1.33
Brentwood, NY (cdp) Suffolk County	710	1.32
Winterhaven, CA (cdp) Imperial County	7	1.32
Chester, NJ (borough) Morris County	21	1.28
Wakefield, NE (city) Dixon County	18	1.28
Holiday Lakes, TX (town) Brazoria County	14	1.28
Stuart, FL (city) Martin County	186	1.27
Crossville, AL (town) De Kalb County	18	1.26
Colma, CA (town) San Mateo County	15	1.26
Frankford, DE (town) Sussex County	9	1.26
Adelphi, MD (cdp) Prince George's County	187	1.25
Simpsonville, KY (city) Shelby County	16	1.25
Bell Gardens, CA (city) Los Angeles County	547	1.24
Netcong, NJ (borough) Morris County	32	1.24
Freeport, NY (village) Nassau County	535	1.22
Elmsford, NY (village) Westchester County	57	1.22
Clarksville, MO (city) Pike County	6	1.22
Bonita Springs, FL (city) Lee County	393	1.20
West Little River, FL (cdp) Miami-Dade County	391	1.20
Cookeville, TN (city) Putnam County	288	1.20
Shelbyville, KY (city) Shelby County	121	1.20
Walnut Park, CA (cdp) Los Angeles County	192	1.19

Notes: (cdp) census designated place; Refer to the Explanation of Data in the front of the book for more detailed information.

Hispanic: Guatemalan

Top 150 Places Sorted by Percent

(Based on places with populations of 10,000 or more)

Place	Number	%
Langley Park, MD (cdp) Prince George's County	1,825	11.26
Central Falls, RI (city) Providence County	1,202	6.35
Morganton, NC (city) Burke County	945	5.46
Fairview, NJ (borough) Bergen County	722	5.45
Lexington, NE (city) Dawson County	490	4.89
Lake Worth, FL (city) Palm Beach County	1,711	4.87
Immokalee, FL (cdp) Collier County	861	4.36
Carthage, MO (city) Jasper County	514	4.06
Spring Valley, NY (village) Rockland County	960	3.77
San Rafael, CA (city) Marin County	2,090	3.73
Port Chester, NY (village) Westchester County	1,037	3.72
Providence, RI (city) Providence County	6,396	3.68
Lennox, CA (cdp) Los Angeles County	811	3.53
Chelsea, MA (city) Suffolk County	1,177	3.36
Homestead, FL (city) Miami-Dade County	1,059	3.32
Trenton, NJ (city) Mercer County	2,644	3.10
Plainfield, NJ (city) Union County	1,443	3.02
Mamaroneck, NY (village) Westchester County	544	2.90
Fort Payne, AL (city) De Kalb County	374	2.89
Bailey's Crossroads, VA (cdp) Fairfax County	660	2.85
Rome, GA (city) Floyd County	992	2.84
Palisades Park, NJ (borough) Bergen County	451	2.64
Stamford, CT (city) Fairfield County	3,067	2.62
Rye, NY (town) Westchester County	1,143	2.60
Lawndale, CA (city) Los Angeles County	791	2.49
Lake Worth Corridor, FL (cdp) Palm Beach County	459	2.46
Cudahy, CA (city) Los Angeles County	570	2.35
West Palm Beach, FL (city) Palm Beach County	1,841	2.24
Hawthorne, CA (city) Los Angeles County	1,879	2.23
Calhoun, GA (city) Gordon County	227	2.13
Southeast, NY (town) Putnam County	361	2.08
North Plainfield, NJ (borough) Somerset County	431	2.04
Princeton, NJ (borough) Mercer County	264	1.86
Bell, CA (city) Los Angeles County	655	1.79
Los Angeles, CA (city) Los Angeles County	65,922	1.78
Albertville, AL (city) Marshall County	306	1.77
Guymon, OK (city) Texas County	177	1.69
Westmont, CA (cdp) Los Angeles County	515	1.63
Mamaroneck, NY (town) Westchester County	471	1.63
Lynn, MA (city) Essex County	1,442	1.62
Huntington Park, CA (city) Los Angeles County	995	1.62
Inglewood, CA (city) Los Angeles County	1,806	1.60
Waltham, MA (city) Middlesex County	928	1.57
South Gate, CA (city) Los Angeles County	1,488	1.54
East Windsor, NJ (township) Mercer County	383	1.54
Bull Run, VA (cdp) Prince William County	175	1.54
Fort Morgan, CO (city) Morgan County	160	1.45
North Fair Oaks, CA (cdp) San Mateo County	218	1.41
Morristown, NJ (town) Morris County	259	1.40
Lincolnia, VA (cdp) Fairfax County	220	1.39
Lynwood, CA (city) Los Angeles County	959	1.37
Grand Island, NE (city) Hall County	571	1.33
Brentwood, NY (cdp) Suffolk County	710	1.32
Stuart, FL (city) Martin County	186	1.27
Adelphi, MD (cdp) Prince George's County	187	1.25
Bell Gardens, CA (city) Los Angeles County	547	1.24
Freeport, NY (village) Nassau County	535	1.22
Bonita Springs, FL (city) Lee County	393	1.20
West Little River, FL (cdp) Miami-Dade County	391	1.20
Cookeville, TN (city) Putnam County	288	1.20
Shelbyville, KY (city) Shelby County	121	1.20
Walnut Park, CA (cdp) Los Angeles County	192	1.19
Marathon, FL (city) Monroe County	120	1.17
Attleboro, MA (city) Bristol County	489	1.16
Fallbrook, CA (cdp) San Diego County	339	1.16
Peekskill, NY (city) Westchester County	261	1.16
North Bay Shore, NY (cdp) Suffolk County	174	1.16
Southold, NY (town) Suffolk County	232	1.13
Silver Spring, MD (cdp) Montgomery County	852	1.11
Cliffside Park, NJ (borough) Bergen County	256	1.11
Lawrence, MA (city) Essex County	794	1.10
Maywood, CA (city) Los Angeles County	309	1.10
Worthington, MN (city) Nobles County	124	1.10
Wheaton-Glenmont, MD (cdp) Montgomery County	626	1.09
Jupiter, FL (town) Palm Beach County	427	1.09
Leisure City, FL (cdp) Miami-Dade County	236	1.07
Marlborough, MA (city) Middlesex County	384	1.06
Riverhead, NY (town) Suffolk County	292	1.05
Ramapo, NY (town) Rockland County	1,116	1.02
Dalton, GA (city) Whitfield County	279	1.00
San Mateo, CA (city) San Mateo County	913	0.99
Fort Myers, FL (city) Lee County	475	0.99
Lamont, CA (cdp) Kern County	131	0.99
Downey, CA (city) Los Angeles County	1,007	0.94
Jefferson, VA (cdp) Fairfax County	258	0.94
Northlake, IL (city) Cook County	112	0.94
Chillum, MD (cdp) Prince George's County	314	0.92
Port Washington, NY (cdp) Nassau County	140	0.92
Arlington, VA (cdp) Arlington County	1,703	0.90
Paramount, CA (city) Los Angeles County	497	0.90
Bensenville, IL (village) Du Page County	187	0.90
Grand Rapids, MI (city) Kent County	1,762	0.89
Pawtucket, RI (city) Providence County	618	0.85
Hempstead, NY (village) Nassau County	482	0.85
Lake Elsinore, CA (city) Riverside County	246	0.85
South San Jose Hills, CA (cdp) Los Angeles County	169	0.84
Bedford, NY (town) Westchester County	152	0.84
Vincent, CA (cdp) Los Angeles County	127	0.84
Florence-Graham, CA (cdp) Los Angeles County	493	0.82
Southampton, NY (town) Suffolk County	446	0.82
Marietta, GA (city) Cobb County	473	0.81
North Bergen, NJ (township) Hudson County	467	0.80
West New York, NJ (town) Hudson County	364	0.80
Burbank, CA (city) Los Angeles County	792	0.79
Cathedral City, CA (city) Riverside County	339	0.79
Union City, NJ (city) Hudson County	525	0.78
Princeton, FL (cdp) Miami-Dade County	79	0.78
Valinda, CA (cdp) Los Angeles County	168	0.77
Takoma Park, MD (city) Montgomery County	134	0.77
Centreville, VA (cdp) Fairfax County	372	0.76
Melrose Park, IL (village) Cook County	177	0.76
Easton, MD (town) Talbot County	89	0.76
Herndon, VA (town) Fairfax County	162	0.75
Cocoa, FL (city) Brevard County	123	0.75
Central Islip, NY (cdp) Suffolk County	236	0.74
Hyattsville, MD (city) Prince George's County	108	0.73
San Pablo, CA (city) Contra Costa County	218	0.72
Glendale Heights, IL (village) Du Page County	219	0.69
Chambersburg, PA (borough) Franklin County	124	0.69
Miami, FL (city) Miami-Dade County	2,475	0.68
Framingham, MA (cdp) Middlesex County	454	0.68
La Puente, CA (city) Los Angeles County	278	0.68
Sanford, NC (city) Lee County	158	0.68
Redwood City, CA (city) San Mateo County	508	0.67
Gardena, CA (city) Los Angeles County	388	0.67
Fairfax, VA (independent city) Fairfax city	145	0.67
Manassas Park, VA (independent city) Manassas Park city	69	0.67
Palmdale, CA (city) Los Angeles County	767	0.66
Compton, CA (city) Los Angeles County	617	0.66
Idylwood, VA (cdp) Fairfax County	106	0.66
Hampton Bays, NY (cdp) Suffolk County	81	0.66
Gaithersburg, MD (city) Montgomery County	342	0.65
Franklin Park, IL (village) Cook County	127	0.65
Monsey, NY (cdp) Rockland County	95	0.65
Novato, CA (city) Marin County	307	0.64
Doral, FL (cdp) Miami-Dade County	130	0.64
Princeton, NJ (township) Mercer County	102	0.64
Hawaiian Gardens, CA (city) Los Angeles County	94	0.64
Commerce, CA (city) Los Angeles County	80	0.64
East Palo Alto, CA (city) San Mateo County	185	0.63
Bound Brook, NJ (borough) Somerset County	64	0.63
Port Salerno, FL (cdp) Martin County	63	0.62
Baldwin Park, CA (city) Los Angeles County	466	0.61
Chantilly, VA (cdp) Fairfax County	252	0.61
Culver City, CA (city) Los Angeles County	235	0.61
Eloy, AZ (city) Pinal County	63	0.61
Mayfield, KY (city) Graves County	63	0.61
Montclair, CA (city) San Bernardino County	199	0.60
Glendale, CA (city) Los Angeles County	1,142	0.59
Pomona, CA (city) Los Angeles County	883	0.59

Notes: (cdp) census designated place; Refer to the Explanation of Data in the front of the book for more detailed information.

Hispanic: Honduran

Top 150 Places Sorted by Number

(Based on all places, regardless of population)

Place	Number	%
New York, NY (city) New York City	25,600	0.32
Miami, FL (city) Miami-Dade County	12,118	3.34
Los Angeles, CA (city) Los Angeles County	12,030	0.33
Houston, TX (city) Harris County	10,284	0.53
Chicago, IL (city) Cook County	3,049	0.11
Dallas, TX (city) Dallas County	2,637	0.22
Hialeah, FL (city) Miami-Dade County	2,593	1.15
Hempstead, NY (town) Nassau County	2,452	0.32
Jersey City, NJ (city) Hudson County	2,192	0.91
New Orleans, LA (city) Orleans Parish	1,958	0.40
Boston, MA (city) Suffolk County	1,822	0.31
Kenner, LA (city) Jefferson Parish	1,774	2.52
Metairie, LA (cdp) Jefferson Parish	1,741	1.19
Chelsea, MA (city) Suffolk County	1,582	4.51
Charlotte, NC (city) Mecklenburg County	1,577	0.29
Union City, NJ (city) Hudson County	1,541	2.30
New Brunswick, NJ (city) Middlesex County	1,451	2.99
Hempstead, NY (village) Nassau County	1,450	2.56
Alexandria, VA (independent city) Alexandria city	1,326	1.03
Waukegan, IL (city) Lake County	1,287	1.46
Long Beach, CA (city) Los Angeles County	1,230	0.27
Islip, NY (town) Suffolk County	1,211	0.38
Elizabeth, NJ (city) Union County	1,094	0.91
Durham, NC (city) Durham County	1,086	0.58
Austin, TX (city) Travis County	1,065	0.16
Miami Beach, FL (city) Miami-Dade County	1,062	1.21
San Francisco, CA (city) San Francisco County	934	0.12
Washington, DC (city) District of Columbia	853	0.15
Plainfield, NJ (city) Union County	779	1.63
Tampa, FL (city) Hillsborough County	778	0.26
Newburgh, NY (city) Orange County	750	2.65
Yonkers, NY (city) Westchester County	736	0.38
San Jose, CA (city) Santa Clara County	733	0.08
Springfield, VA (cdp) Fairfax County	713	2.34
West Little River, FL (cdp) Miami-Dade County	709	2.18
Arlington, VA (cdp) Arlington County	686	0.36
San Diego, CA (city) San Diego County	685	0.06
Newark, NJ (city) Essex County	657	0.24
Fountainbleau, FL (cdp) Miami-Dade County	650	1.09
San Antonio, TX (city) Bexar County	641	0.06
Morristown, NJ (town) Morris County	638	3.44
Phoenix, AZ (city) Maricopa County	624	0.05
North Hempstead, NY (town) Nassau County	594	0.27
North Miami, FL (city) Miami-Dade County	565	0.94
Lake Worth, FL (city) Palm Beach County	559	1.59
Brentwood, NY (cdp) Suffolk County	546	1.01
West New York, NJ (town) Hudson County	542	1.18
Nashville-Davidson, TN (special city) Davidson County	535	0.10
Stamford, CT (city) Fairfield County	527	0.45
North Bergen, NJ (township) Hudson County	509	0.88
Indianapolis, IN (special city) Marion County	495	0.06
Raleigh, NC (city) Wake County	476	0.17
Irving, TX (city) Dallas County	470	0.25
Philadelphia, PA (city) Philadelphia County	466	0.03
Pasadena, CA (city) Los Angeles County	463	0.35
Oakland, CA (city) Alameda County	459	0.11
Atlantic City, NJ (city) Atlantic County	450	1.11
North Atlanta, GA (cdp) De Kalb County	447	1.16
Carol City, FL (cdp) Miami-Dade County	428	0.72
Conroe, TX (city) Montgomery County	426	1.16
Herndon, VA (town) Fairfax County	424	1.96
Las Vegas, NV (city) Clark County	424	0.09
Hollywood, FL (city) Broward County	418	0.30
Norwalk, CT (city) Fairfield County	417	0.50
Silver Spring, MD (cdp) Montgomery County	397	0.52
North Miami Beach, FL (city) Miami-Dade County	394	0.97
Kendall, FL (cdp) Miami-Dade County	387	0.51
Fort Lauderdale, FL (city) Broward County	381	0.25
Babylon, NY (town) Suffolk County	377	0.18
South Miami Heights, FL (cdp) Miami-Dade County	366	1.09
Wallace, NC (town) Duplin County	361	10.80
Tamiami, FL (cdp) Miami-Dade County	358	0.65
Providence, RI (city) Providence County	355	0.20
Pasadena, TX (city) Harris County	354	0.25
Huntington, NY (town) Suffolk County	354	0.18
Fort Worth, TX (city) Tarrant County	350	0.07
Homestead, FL (city) Miami-Dade County	343	1.07
Pomona, CA (city) Los Angeles County	342	0.23
Gaithersburg, MD (city) Montgomery County	336	0.64
Bridgeport, CT (city) Fairfield County	332	0.24
Seattle, WA (city) King County	332	0.06
Orlando, FL (city) Orange County	329	0.18
Langley Park, MD (cdp) Prince George's County	328	2.02
Memphis, TN (city) Shelby County	320	0.05
Oyster Bay, NY (town) Nassau County	318	0.11
Aurora, CO (city) Arapahoe County	312	0.11
West Palm Beach, FL (city) Palm Beach County	308	0.38
Inglewood, CA (city) Los Angeles County	307	0.27
Garland, TX (city) Dallas County	306	0.14
Terrytown, LA (cdp) Jefferson Parish	305	1.20
Anaheim, CA (city) Orange County	305	0.09
Passaic, NJ (city) Passaic County	301	0.44
Central Islip, NY (cdp) Suffolk County	300	0.94
Oklahoma City, OK (city) Oklahoma County	298	0.06
Kansas City, MO (city) Jackson County	295	0.07
Ontario, CA (city) San Bernardino County	291	0.18
Denver, CO (city) Denver County	289	0.05
Miramar, FL (city) Broward County	287	0.39
Kendale Lakes, FL (cdp) Miami-Dade County	284	0.50
New Cassel, NY (cdp) Nassau County	280	2.11
Santa Ana, CA (city) Orange County	280	0.08
Baltimore, MD (independent city) Baltimore city	278	0.04
Pinewood, FL (cdp) Miami-Dade County	276	1.67
Pembroke Pines, FL (city) Broward County	273	0.20
Compton, CA (city) Los Angeles County	269	0.29
Atlanta, GA (city) Fulton County	267	0.06
Jacksonville, FL (special city) Duval County	267	0.04
South Gate, CA (city) Los Angeles County	264	0.27
Kendall West, FL (cdp) Miami-Dade County	259	0.68
Glendale, CA (city) Los Angeles County	259	0.13
Freeport, NY (village) Nassau County	254	0.58
Huntington Station, NY (cdp) Suffolk County	252	0.84
Bailey's Crossroads, VA (cdp) Fairfax County	244	1.05
Hilton Head Island, SC (town) Beaufort County	239	0.71
North Plainfield, NJ (borough) Somerset County	237	1.12
The Hammocks, FL (cdp) Miami-Dade County	233	0.49
Huntington Park, CA (city) Los Angeles County	230	0.37
Richmond West, FL (cdp) Miami-Dade County	229	0.82
Perth Amboy, NJ (city) Middlesex County	227	0.48
Allentown, PA (city) Lehigh County	226	0.21
Gladeview, FL (cdp) Miami-Dade County	223	1.54
Hialeah Gardens, FL (city) Miami-Dade County	223	1.16
University, FL (cdp) Hillsborough County	222	0.72
Coral Terrace, FL (cdp) Miami-Dade County	219	0.90
Country Club, FL (cdp) Miami-Dade County	219	0.60
Lake Worth Corridor, FL (cdp) Palm Beach County	216	1.16
Wheaton-Glenmont, MD (cdp) Montgomery County	216	0.37
Plano, TX (city) Collin County	216	0.10
Hybla Valley, VA (cdp) Fairfax County	215	1.29
Richardson, TX (city) Dallas County	214	0.23
Paradise, NV (cdp) Clark County	214	0.12
Leisure City, FL (cdp) Miami-Dade County	213	0.96
Harrisonburg, VA (independent city) Harrisonburg city	213	0.53
East Los Angeles, CA (cdp) Los Angeles County	212	0.17
Bayonne, NJ (city) Hudson County	207	0.33
Detroit, MI (city) Wayne County	207	0.02
Portland, OR (city) Multnomah County	203	0.04
El Monte, CA (city) Los Angeles County	202	0.17
Golden Glades, FL (cdp) Miami-Dade County	199	0.61
Rockville, MD (city) Montgomery County	197	0.42
Chamblee, GA (city) De Kalb County	195	2.04
Manassas, VA (independent city) Manassas city	195	0.56
Reston, VA (cdp) Fairfax County	195	0.35
Fontana, CA (city) San Bernardino County	195	0.15
North Bay Shore, NY (cdp) Suffolk County	194	1.29
Lynwood, CA (city) Los Angeles County	189	0.27
Downey, CA (city) Los Angeles County	189	0.18
Sweetwater, FL (city) Miami-Dade County	187	1.31
Long Beach, NY (city) Nassau County	183	0.52
Kansas City, KS (city) Wyandotte County	183	0.12

Notes: (cdp) census designated place; Refer to the Explanation of Data in the front of the book for more detailed information.

Hispanic: Honduran

Top 150 Places Sorted by Percent

(Based on all places, regardless of population)

Place	Number	%
Wallace, NC (town) Duplin County	361	10.80
Magnolia, NC (town) Duplin County	80	8.58
West Smithfield, NC (cdp) Johnston County	4	6.78
Rogers, NE (village) Colfax County	6	6.32
Rose Hill, NC (town) Duplin County	78	5.86
Chelsea, MA (city) Suffolk County	1,582	4.51
Newton, TX (city) Newton County	104	4.23
Gray Court, SC (town) Laurens County	38	3.72
Loch Lomond, FL (cdp) Broward County	128	3.62
Morristown, NJ (town) Morris County	638	3.44
Miami, FL (city) Miami-Dade County	12,118	3.34
Dundarrach, NC (cdp) Hoke County	2	3.23
New Brunswick, NJ (city) Middlesex County	1,451	2.99
Delway, NC (cdp) Sampson County	8	2.96
Dennis Acres, MO (village) Newton County	2	2.94
Broadview Park, FL (cdp) Broward County	182	2.68
Newburgh, NY (city) Orange County	750	2.65
Rest Haven, GA (town) Gwinnett County	4	2.65
Hempstead, NY (village) Nassau County	1,450	2.56
Kenner, LA (city) Jefferson Parish	1,774	2.52
Canal Point, FL (cdp) Palm Beach County	13	2.48
Sodus, MN (township) Lyon County	7	2.48
Teachey, NC (town) Duplin County	6	2.45
Springfield, VA (cdp) Fairfax County	713	2.34
Union City, NJ (city) Hudson County	1,541	2.30
West Little River, FL (cdp) Miami-Dade County	709	2.18
Fossum, MN (township) Norman County	4	2.14
New Cassel, NY (cdp) Nassau County	280	2.11
Kenton, DE (town) Kent County	5	2.11
Ranchitos Las Lomas, TX (cdp) Webb County	7	2.10
Willow Springs, WI (town) Lafayette County	13	2.06
Chamblee, GA (city) De Kalb County	195	2.04
Langley Park, MD (cdp) Prince George's County	328	2.02
Herndon, VA (town) Fairfax County	424	1.96
Greenevers, NC (town) Duplin County	11	1.96
Turkey, NC (town) Sampson County	5	1.91
Creston, NE (village) Platte County	4	1.86
Bonnie Lock-Woodsetter North, FL (cdp) Broward County	73	1.71
North Springfield, VA (cdp) Fairfax County	156	1.70
Pinewood, FL (cdp) Miami-Dade County	276	1.67
Plainfield, NJ (city) Union County	779	1.63
Selma, NC (town) Johnston County	96	1.62
Galax, VA (independent city) Galax city	110	1.61
Dublin, NC (town) Bladen County	4	1.60
Lake Worth, FL (city) Palm Beach County	559	1.59
Spencer, NC (town) Rowan County	52	1.55
Medley, FL (town) Miami-Dade County	17	1.55
Woodridge, NY (village) Sullivan County	14	1.55
Gladeview, FL (cdp) Miami-Dade County	223	1.54
Milton Center, OH (village) Wood County	3	1.54
Springdale, SC (cdp) Lancaster County	43	1.50
Waukegan, IL (city) Lake County	1,287	1.46
Holly Ridge, NC (town) Onslow County	12	1.44
Biscayne Park, FL (village) Miami-Dade County	45	1.38
Farmingdale, NY (village) Nassau County	115	1.37
Benson, MN (township) Swift County	5	1.36
Milbridge, ME (town) Washington County	17	1.33
Seven Corners, VA (cdp) Fairfax County	115	1.32
Louisville, MN (township) Scott County	18	1.32
Sweetwater, FL (city) Miami-Dade County	187	1.31
Hybla Valley, VA (cdp) Fairfax County	215	1.29
North Bay Shore, NY (cdp) Suffolk County	194	1.29
Avon, CO (town) Eagle County	72	1.29
Remington, VA (town) Fauquier County	8	1.28
West Miami, FL (city) Miami-Dade County	73	1.25
Stacey Street, FL (cdp) Palm Beach County	12	1.25
El Portal, FL (village) Miami-Dade County	31	1.24
Mentone, IN (town) Kosciusko County	11	1.22
Fanning Springs, FL (city) Levy County	9	1.22
Miami Beach, FL (city) Miami-Dade County	1,062	1.21
Terrytown, LA (cdp) Jefferson Parish	305	1.20
Metairie, LA (cdp) Jefferson Parish	1,741	1.19
Shawnee Hills, OH (village) Delaware County	5	1.19
West New York, NJ (town) Hudson County	542	1.18
North Atlanta, GA (cdp) De Kalb County	447	1.16
Conroe, TX (city) Montgomery County	426	1.16
Hialeah Gardens, FL (city) Miami-Dade County	223	1.16
Lake Worth Corridor, FL (cdp) Palm Beach County	216	1.16
East Perrine, FL (cdp) Miami-Dade County	82	1.16
Hialeah, FL (city) Miami-Dade County	2,593	1.15
Estelle, LA (cdp) Jefferson Parish	181	1.14
Liberty, NY (village) Sullivan County	45	1.13
North Plainfield, NJ (borough) Somerset County	237	1.12
Village Park, FL (cdp) Broward County	10	1.12
Mifflin, PA (borough) Juniata County	7	1.12
Atlantic City, NJ (city) Atlantic County	450	1.11
Timberlane, LA (cdp) Jefferson Parish	127	1.11
Virginia Gardens, FL (village) Miami-Dade County	26	1.11
Micro, NC (town) Johnston County	5	1.10
Wyandotte, OK (town) Ottawa County	4	1.10
Fountainbleau, FL (cdp) Miami-Dade County	650	1.09
South Miami Heights, FL (cdp) Miami-Dade County	366	1.09
Koosharem, UT (town) Sevier County	3	1.09
Pine Manor, FL (cdp) Lee County	41	1.08
Homestead, FL (city) Miami-Dade County	343	1.07
Nunn, CO (town) Weld County	5	1.06
Bailey's Crossroads, VA (cdp) Fairfax County	244	1.05
Broadview-Pompano Park, FL (cdp) Broward County	56	1.05
Westgate-Belvedere Homes, FL (cdp) Palm Beach County	85	1.04
Kirkwood, CA (cdp) Alpine County	1	1.04
Alexandria, VA (independent city) Alexandria city	1,326	1.03
Palmetto Estates, FL (cdp) Miami-Dade County	141	1.03
Siler City, NC (town) Chatham County	71	1.02
Brentwood, NY (cdp) Suffolk County	546	1.01
Guttenberg, NJ (town) Hudson County	109	1.01
Island Park, NY (village) Nassau County	48	1.01
Falcon Mesa, TX (cdp) Zapata County	5	0.99
Selma, MN (township) Cottonwood County	2	0.98
North Miami Beach, FL (city) Miami-Dade County	394	0.97
Dover, NJ (town) Morris County	176	0.97
Deep River Center, CT (cdp) Middlesex County	24	0.97
Tavernier, FL (cdp) Monroe County	21	0.97
Leisure City, FL (cdp) Miami-Dade County	213	0.96
Princeton, FL (cdp) Miami-Dade County	96	0.95
North Miami, FL (city) Miami-Dade County	565	0.94
Central Islip, NY (cdp) Suffolk County	300	0.94
Miami Springs, FL (city) Miami-Dade County	129	0.94
Edgewater Park, NJ (township) Burlington County	73	0.93
Kahlotus, WA (city) Franklin County	2	0.93
Jefferson, LA (cdp) Jefferson Parish	109	0.92
Smithfield, NC (town) Johnston County	106	0.92
Jersey City, NJ (city) Hudson County	2,192	0.91
Elizabeth, NJ (city) Union County	1,094	0.91
Gretna, LA (city) Jefferson Parish	158	0.91
Doraville, GA (city) De Kalb County	90	0.91
Valdese, NC (town) Burke County	41	0.91
Victory Gardens, NJ (borough) Morris County	14	0.91
Cylinder, IA (city) Palo Alto County	1	0.91
Coral Terrace, FL (cdp) Miami-Dade County	219	0.90
Gypsum, CO (town) Eagle County	33	0.90
Prescott, MN (township) Faribault County	2	0.90
Opa-locka, FL (city) Miami-Dade County	133	0.89
Miami Gardens, FL (cdp) Broward County	24	0.89
North Bergen, NJ (township) Hudson County	509	0.88
North Andrews Gardens, FL (cdp) Broward County	85	0.88
Ventnor City, NJ (city) Atlantic County	112	0.87
Woodmere, LA (cdp) Jefferson Parish	112	0.86
Mendota, CA (city) Fresno County	68	0.86
Edinburg, VA (town) Shenandoah County	7	0.86
North Chevy Chase, MD (village) Montgomery County	4	0.86
West Gate, VA (cdp) Prince William County	64	0.85
Indian Point, MO (village) Stone County	5	0.85
Huntington Station, NY (cdp) Suffolk County	252	0.84
Pompano Beach Highlands, FL (cdp) Broward County	54	0.83
Oakboro, NC (town) Stanly County	10	0.83
Schall Circle, FL (cdp) Palm Beach County	8	0.83
Ingold, NC (cdp) Sampson County	4	0.83
Richmond West, FL (cdp) Miami-Dade County	229	0.82
North Bay Village, FL (city) Miami-Dade County	55	0.82
Stock Island, FL (cdp) Monroe County	36	0.82

Notes: (cdp) census designated place; Refer to the Explanation of Data in the front of the book for more detailed information.

Hispanic: Honduran

Top 150 Places Sorted by Percent

(Based on places with populations of 10,000 or more)

Place	Number	%
Chelsea, MA (city) Suffolk County	1,582	4.51
Morristown, NJ (town) Morris County	638	3.44
Miami, FL (city) Miami-Dade County	12,118	3.34
New Brunswick, NJ (city) Middlesex County	1,451	2.99
Newburgh, NY (city) Orange County	750	2.65
Hempstead, NY (village) Nassau County	1,450	2.56
Kenner, LA (city) Jefferson Parish	1,774	2.52
Springfield, VA (cdp) Fairfax County	713	2.34
Union City, NJ (city) Hudson County	1,541	2.30
West Little River, FL (cdp) Miami-Dade County	709	2.18
New Cassel, NY (cdp) Nassau County	280	2.11
Langley Park, MD (cdp) Prince George's County	328	2.02
Herndon, VA (town) Fairfax County	424	1.96
Pinewood, FL (cdp) Miami-Dade County	276	1.67
Plainfield, NJ (city) Union County	779	1.63
Lake Worth, FL (city) Palm Beach County	559	1.59
Gladeview, FL (cdp) Miami-Dade County	223	1.54
Waukegan, IL (city) Lake County	1,287	1.46
Sweetwater, FL (city) Miami-Dade County	187	1.31
Hybla Valley, VA (cdp) Fairfax County	215	1.29
North Bay Shore, NY (cdp) Suffolk County	194	1.29
Miami Beach, FL (city) Miami-Dade County	1,062	1.21
Terrytown, LA (cdp) Jefferson Parish	305	1.20
Metairie, LA (cdp) Jefferson Parish	1,741	1.19
West New York, NJ (town) Hudson County	542	1.18
North Atlanta, GA (cdp) De Kalb County	447	1.16
Conroe, TX (city) Montgomery County	426	1.16
Hialeah Gardens, FL (city) Miami-Dade County	223	1.16
Lake Worth Corridor, FL (cdp) Palm Beach County	216	1.16
Hialeah, FL (city) Miami-Dade County	2,593	1.15
Estelle, LA (cdp) Jefferson Parish	181	1.14
North Plainfield, NJ (borough) Somerset County	237	1.12
Atlantic City, NJ (city) Atlantic County	450	1.11
Timberlane, LA (cdp) Jefferson Parish	127	1.11
Fountainbleau, FL (cdp) Miami-Dade County	650	1.09
South Miami Heights, FL (cdp) Miami-Dade County	366	1.09
Homestead, FL (city) Miami-Dade County	343	1.07
Bailey's Crossroads, VA (cdp) Fairfax County	244	1.05
Alexandria, VA (independent city) Alexandria city	1,326	1.03
Palmetto Estates, FL (cdp) Miami-Dade County	141	1.03
Brentwood, NY (cdp) Suffolk County	546	1.01
Guttenberg, NJ (town) Hudson County	109	1.01
North Miami Beach, FL (city) Miami-Dade County	394	0.97
Dover, NJ (town) Morris County	176	0.97
Leisure City, FL (cdp) Miami-Dade County	213	0.96
Princeton, FL (cdp) Miami-Dade County	96	0.95
North Miami, FL (city) Miami-Dade County	565	0.94
Central Islip, NY (cdp) Suffolk County	300	0.94
Miami Springs, FL (city) Miami-Dade County	129	0.94
Jefferson, LA (cdp) Jefferson Parish	109	0.92
Smithfield, NC (town) Johnston County	106	0.92
Jersey City, NJ (city) Hudson County	2,192	0.91
Elizabeth, NJ (city) Union County	1,094	0.91
Gretna, LA (city) Jefferson Parish	158	0.91
Coral Terrace, FL (cdp) Miami-Dade County	219	0.90
Opa-locka, FL (city) Miami-Dade County	133	0.89
North Bergen, NJ (township) Hudson County	509	0.88
Ventnor City, NJ (city) Atlantic County	112	0.87
Woodmere, LA (cdp) Jefferson Parish	112	0.86
Huntington Station, NY (cdp) Suffolk County	252	0.84
Richmond West, FL (cdp) Miami-Dade County	229	0.82
Wyandanch, NY (cdp) Suffolk County	80	0.76
Groveton, VA (cdp) Fairfax County	157	0.74
Berea, SC (cdp) Greenville County	105	0.74
Palm Springs, FL (village) Palm Beach County	87	0.74
Carol City, FL (cdp) Miami-Dade County	428	0.72
University, FL (cdp) Hillsborough County	222	0.72
Carrollton, GA (city) Carroll County	143	0.72
Hilton Head Island, SC (town) Beaufort County	239	0.71
Kendall West, FL (cdp) Miami-Dade County	259	0.68
Golden Gate, FL (cdp) Collier County	143	0.68
Doral, FL (cdp) Miami-Dade County	135	0.66
Tamiami, FL (cdp) Miami-Dade County	358	0.65
Greenacres, FL (city) Palm Beach County	180	0.65
Harvey, LA (cdp) Jefferson Parish	145	0.65
Gaithersburg, MD (city) Montgomery County	336	0.64
Glenvar Heights, FL (cdp) Miami-Dade County	102	0.63
Sanford, NC (city) Lee County	144	0.62
Miami Shores, FL (village) Miami-Dade County	64	0.62
Golden Glades, FL (cdp) Miami-Dade County	199	0.61
Weehawken, NJ (township) Hudson County	83	0.61
Country Club, FL (cdp) Miami-Dade County	219	0.60
Salisbury, NC (city) Rowan County	160	0.60
Lenoir, NC (city) Caldwell County	101	0.60
Lincolnia, VA (cdp) Fairfax County	94	0.60
Destrehan, LA (cdp) Saint Charles Parish	66	0.59
Durham, NC (city) Durham County	1,086	0.58
Freeport, NY (village) Nassau County	254	0.58
Manassas, VA (independent city) Manassas city	195	0.56
Cudahy, CA (city) Los Angeles County	136	0.56
Sunset, FL (cdp) Miami-Dade County	96	0.56
University Park, FL (cdp) Miami-Dade County	147	0.55
Ojus, FL (cdp) Miami-Dade County	91	0.55
Mount Vernon, VA (cdp) Fairfax County	155	0.54
Houston, TX (city) Harris County	10,284	0.53
Harrisonburg, VA (independent city) Harrisonburg city	213	0.53
Oakland Park, FL (city) Broward County	163	0.53
Westchester, FL (cdp) Miami-Dade County	159	0.53
Glen Cove, NY (city) Nassau County	140	0.53
Ives Estates, FL (cdp) Miami-Dade County	94	0.53
Silver Spring, MD (cdp) Montgomery County	397	0.52
Long Beach, NY (city) Nassau County	183	0.52
Laplace, LA (cdp) Saint John the Baptist Parish	145	0.52
Cutler Ridge, FL (cdp) Miami-Dade County	129	0.52
Uniondale, NY (cdp) Nassau County	120	0.52
Brownsville, FL (cdp) Miami-Dade County	75	0.52
Kendall, FL (cdp) Miami-Dade County	387	0.51
Chalmette, LA (cdp) Saint Bernard Parish	165	0.51
Norwalk, CT (city) Fairfield County	417	0.50
Kendale Lakes, FL (cdp) Miami-Dade County	284	0.50
Roosevelt, NY (cdp) Nassau County	79	0.50
Westbury, NY (village) Nassau County	72	0.50
Aldine, TX (cdp) Harris County	70	0.50
The Hammocks, FL (cdp) Miami-Dade County	233	0.49
Marrero, LA (cdp) Jefferson Parish	177	0.49
Middletown, NY (city) Orange County	124	0.49
Somerset, NJ (cdp) Somerset County	114	0.49
Perth Amboy, NJ (city) Middlesex County	227	0.48
Oak Ridge, FL (cdp) Orange County	107	0.48
Country Walk, FL (cdp) Miami-Dade County	51	0.48
Olympia Heights, FL (cdp) Miami-Dade County	63	0.47
Westwego, LA (city) Jefferson Parish	51	0.47
Chillum, MD (cdp) Prince George's County	159	0.46
Lennox, CA (cdp) Los Angeles County	106	0.46
Stamford, CT (city) Fairfield County	527	0.45
North Lauderdale, FL (city) Broward County	145	0.45
Westwood Lakes, FL (cdp) Miami-Dade County	54	0.45
Passaic, NJ (city) Passaic County	301	0.44
Jefferson, VA (cdp) Fairfax County	122	0.44
Cloverleaf, TX (cdp) Harris County	104	0.44
Pinecrest, FL (village) Miami-Dade County	83	0.44
Adelphi, MD (cdp) Prince George's County	66	0.44
Rockville, MD (city) Montgomery County	197	0.42
Bell, CA (city) Los Angeles County	154	0.42
The Crossings, FL (cdp) Miami-Dade County	98	0.42
South Houston, TX (city) Harris County	66	0.42
Vienna, VA (town) Fairfax County	60	0.42
New Orleans, LA (city) Orleans Parish	1,958	0.40
Hallandale, FL (city) Broward County	136	0.40
Brigantine, NJ (city) Atlantic County	50	0.40
Miramar, FL (city) Broward County	287	0.39
South Bradenton, FL (cdp) Manatee County	84	0.39
Bull Run, VA (cdp) Prince William County	44	0.39
Freehold, NJ (borough) Monmouth County	43	0.39
Islip, NY (town) Suffolk County	1,211	0.38
Yonkers, NY (city) Westchester County	736	0.38
West Palm Beach, FL (city) Palm Beach County	308	0.38
White Oak, MD (cdp) Montgomery County	80	0.38
Lindenwold, NJ (borough) Camden County	67	0.38
Huntington Park, CA (city) Los Angeles County	230	0.37

Notes: (cdp) census designated place; Refer to the Explanation of Data in the front of the book for more detailed information.

Hispanic: Nicaraguan

Top 150 Places Sorted by Number

(Based on all places, regardless of population)

Place	Number	%
Miami, FL (city) Miami-Dade County	20,543	5.67
Hialeah, FL (city) Miami-Dade County	9,211	4.07
Los Angeles, CA (city) Los Angeles County	8,792	0.24
New York, NY (city) New York City	6,451	0.08
Fountainbleau, FL (cdp) Miami-Dade County	5,624	9.44
San Francisco, CA (city) San Francisco County	5,459	0.70
Kendale Lakes, FL (cdp) Miami-Dade County	2,612	4.59
Tamiami, FL (cdp) Miami-Dade County	2,551	4.66
Sweetwater, FL (city) Miami-Dade County	2,366	16.63
Houston, TX (city) Harris County	2,196	0.11
Daly City, CA (city) San Mateo County	2,052	1.98
Kendall, FL (cdp) Miami-Dade County	1,869	2.48
San Jose, CA (city) Santa Clara County	1,705	0.19
Kendall West, FL (cdp) Miami-Dade County	1,670	4.39
The Hammocks, FL (cdp) Miami-Dade County	1,364	2.88
Carol City, FL (cdp) Miami-Dade County	1,305	2.20
Richmond West, FL (cdp) Miami-Dade County	1,178	4.19
West Little River, FL (cdp) Miami-Dade County	1,163	3.58
Hayward, CA (city) Alameda County	1,045	0.75
South San Francisco, CA (city) San Mateo County	945	1.56
Hialeah Gardens, FL (city) Miami-Dade County	939	4.87
South Miami Heights, FL (cdp) Miami-Dade County	936	2.79
Miami Beach, FL (city) Miami-Dade County	905	1.03
Metairie, LA (cdp) Jefferson Parish	806	0.55
Chicago, IL (city) Cook County	778	0.03
University Park, FL (cdp) Miami-Dade County	767	2.89
Westchester, FL (cdp) Miami-Dade County	682	2.25
Oakland, CA (city) Alameda County	652	0.16
Kenner, LA (city) Jefferson Parish	638	0.90
Downey, CA (city) Los Angeles County	636	0.59
Camden, NJ (city) Camden County	607	0.76
Washington, DC (city) District of Columbia	594	0.10
The Crossings, FL (cdp) Miami-Dade County	592	2.51
Miramar, FL (city) Broward County	589	0.81
Country Club, FL (cdp) Miami-Dade County	585	1.61
South Gate, CA (city) Los Angeles County	581	0.60
Coral Terrace, FL (cdp) Miami-Dade County	553	2.27
North Miami, FL (city) Miami-Dade County	553	0.92
Philadelphia, PA (city) Philadelphia County	544	0.04
Gladeview, FL (cdp) Miami-Dade County	536	3.70
Pembroke Pines, FL (city) Broward County	533	0.39
Long Beach, CA (city) Los Angeles County	509	0.11
San Bruno, CA (city) San Mateo County	508	1.26
Hollywood, FL (city) Broward County	501	0.36
Silver Spring, MD (cdp) Montgomery County	500	0.65
Las Vegas, NV (city) Clark County	493	0.10
New Orleans, LA (city) Orleans Parish	488	0.10
Arlington, VA (cdp) Arlington County	481	0.25
San Diego, CA (city) San Diego County	473	0.04
Charlotte, NC (city) Mecklenburg County	459	0.08
Concord, CA (city) Contra Costa County	457	0.38
Austin, TX (city) Travis County	456	0.07
Fontana, CA (city) San Bernardino County	436	0.34
Port Arthur, TX (city) Jefferson County	432	0.75
Richmond, CA (city) Contra Costa County	416	0.42
Dallas, TX (city) Dallas County	407	0.03
Coral Gables, FL (city) Miami-Dade County	400	0.95
San Antonio, TX (city) Bexar County	395	0.03
Yonkers, NY (city) Westchester County	391	0.20
West Covina, CA (city) Los Angeles County	383	0.36
Glendale, CA (city) Los Angeles County	383	0.20
Pittsburg, CA (city) Contra Costa County	381	0.67
North Miami Beach, FL (city) Miami-Dade County	374	0.92
Wheaton-Glenmont, MD (cdp) Montgomery County	371	0.64
Sunset, FL (cdp) Miami-Dade County	370	2.16
San Mateo, CA (city) San Mateo County	363	0.39
Pomona, CA (city) Los Angeles County	360	0.24
Cutler Ridge, FL (cdp) Miami-Dade County	355	1.43
Jersey City, NJ (city) Hudson County	351	0.15
Hawthorne, CA (city) Los Angeles County	349	0.41
Doral, FL (cdp) Miami-Dade County	346	1.69
Huntington Park, CA (city) Los Angeles County	334	0.54
Antioch, CA (city) Contra Costa County	334	0.37
Opa-locka, FL (city) Miami-Dade County	332	2.22
Pinewood, FL (cdp) Miami-Dade County	331	2.00

Place	Number	%
Palmetto Estates, FL (cdp) Miami-Dade County	326	2.38
Bell Gardens, CA (city) Los Angeles County	325	0.74
Sacramento, CA (city) Sacramento County	321	0.08
Alhambra, CA (city) Los Angeles County	319	0.37
Milwaukee, WI (city) Milwaukee County	318	0.05
Ontario, CA (city) San Bernardino County	315	0.20
Fremont, CA (city) Alameda County	315	0.15
Norwalk, CA (city) Los Angeles County	314	0.30
Anaheim, CA (city) Orange County	313	0.10
Key West, FL (city) Monroe County	311	1.22
Westwood Lakes, FL (cdp) Miami-Dade County	305	2.54
Phoenix, AZ (city) Maricopa County	305	0.02
Leisure City, FL (cdp) Miami-Dade County	304	1.37
El Monte, CA (city) Los Angeles County	295	0.25
Redwood City, CA (city) San Mateo County	285	0.38
Miami Springs, FL (city) Miami-Dade County	283	2.06
Elizabeth, NJ (city) Union County	277	0.23
Glenvar Heights, FL (cdp) Miami-Dade County	274	1.69
Vallejo, CA (city) Solano County	270	0.23
Tampa, FL (city) Hillsborough County	267	0.09
West Palm Beach, FL (city) Palm Beach County	265	0.32
Jacksonville, FL (special city) Duval County	263	0.04
New Brunswick, NJ (city) Middlesex County	258	0.53
Baldwin Park, CA (city) Los Angeles County	258	0.34
San Pablo, CA (city) Contra Costa County	257	0.85
Pacifica, CA (city) San Mateo County	253	0.66
Bell, CA (city) Los Angeles County	247	0.67
Rialto, CA (city) San Bernardino County	247	0.27
Boston, MA (city) Suffolk County	247	0.04
Indianapolis, IN (special city) Marion County	247	0.03
Modesto, CA (city) Stanislaus County	246	0.13
Miami Lakes, FL (cdp) Miami-Dade County	243	1.07
Olympia Heights, FL (cdp) Miami-Dade County	242	1.80
Burbank, CA (city) Los Angeles County	242	0.24
Alexandria, VA (independent city) Alexandria city	240	0.19
Gaithersburg, MD (city) Montgomery County	239	0.45
Cudahy, CA (city) Los Angeles County	236	0.97
Stockton, CA (city) San Joaquin County	232	0.10
Pinecrest, FL (village) Miami-Dade County	228	1.20
Homestead, FL (city) Miami-Dade County	228	0.71
Inglewood, CA (city) Los Angeles County	221	0.20
Golden Glades, FL (cdp) Miami-Dade County	219	0.67
Bailey's Crossroads, VA (cdp) Fairfax County	218	0.94
Princeton, FL (cdp) Miami-Dade County	217	2.15
Carson City, NV (special city) Carson City city	216	0.41
Palmdale, CA (city) Los Angeles County	213	0.18
Moreno Valley, CA (city) Riverside County	198	0.14
Union City, NJ (city) Hudson County	196	0.29
Maywood, CA (city) Los Angeles County	195	0.69
Bellflower, CA (city) Los Angeles County	195	0.27
San Leandro, CA (city) Alameda County	193	0.24
San Bernardino, CA (city) San Bernardino County	192	0.10
Davie, FL (town) Broward County	190	0.25
Paradise, NV (cdp) Clark County	190	0.10
Santa Ana, CA (city) Orange County	190	0.06
Pasadena, CA (city) Los Angeles County	187	0.14
Hempstead, NY (town) Nassau County	187	0.02
Fairfield, CA (city) Solano County	186	0.19
Country Walk, FL (cdp) Miami-Dade County	185	1.74
Aspen Hill, MD (cdp) Montgomery County	184	0.37
Riverside, CA (city) Riverside County	184	0.07
Torrance, CA (city) Los Angeles County	182	0.13
Norwalk, CT (city) Fairfield County	180	0.22
Rancho Cucamonga, CA (city) San Bernardino County	179	0.14
Montebello, CA (city) Los Angeles County	178	0.29
Langley Park, MD (cdp) Prince George's County	177	1.09
Pennsauken, NJ (cdp) Camden County	177	0.50
Danbury, CT (city) Fairfield County	177	0.24
Paterson, NJ (city) Passaic County	177	0.12
West Miami, FL (city) Miami-Dade County	175	2.98
Lynwood, CA (city) Los Angeles County	175	0.25
Newark, NJ (city) Essex County	174	0.06
Fresno, CA (city) Fresno County	172	0.04
Union City, CA (city) Alameda County	169	0.25
Lawndale, CA (city) Los Angeles County	164	0.52

Notes: (cdp) census designated place; Refer to the Explanation of Data in the front of the book for more detailed information.

Hispanic: Nicaraguan

Top 150 Places Sorted by Percent

(Based on all places, regardless of population)

Place	Number	%
Sweetwater, FL (city) Miami-Dade County	2,366	16.63
Fountainbleau, FL (cdp) Miami-Dade County	5,624	9.44
Canal Point, FL (cdp) Palm Beach County	32	6.10
Miami, FL (city) Miami-Dade County	20,543	5.67
Hialeah Gardens, FL (city) Miami-Dade County	939	4.87
Tamiami, FL (cdp) Miami-Dade County	2,551	4.66
Kendale Lakes, FL (cdp) Miami-Dade County	2,612	4.59
Kendall West, FL (cdp) Miami-Dade County	1,670	4.39
Richmond West, FL (cdp) Miami-Dade County	1,178	4.19
Hialeah, FL (city) Miami-Dade County	9,211	4.07
Gladeview, FL (cdp) Miami-Dade County	536	3.70
West Little River, FL (cdp) Miami-Dade County	1,163	3.58
West Miami, FL (city) Miami-Dade County	175	2.98
Brighton, MN (township) Nicollet County	5	2.96
Colma, CA (town) San Mateo County	35	2.94
University Park, FL (cdp) Miami-Dade County	767	2.89
The Hammocks, FL (cdp) Miami-Dade County	1,364	2.88
South Miami Heights, FL (cdp) Miami-Dade County	936	2.79
Westwood Lakes, FL (cdp) Miami-Dade County	305	2.54
The Crossings, FL (cdp) Miami-Dade County	592	2.51
Virginia Gardens, FL (village) Miami-Dade County	59	2.51
Kendall, FL (cdp) Miami-Dade County	1,869	2.48
Cloud Lake, FL (town) Palm Beach County	4	2.40
Palmetto Estates, FL (cdp) Miami-Dade County	326	2.38
Rollingwood, CA (cdp) Contra Costa County	68	2.34
Coral Terrace, FL (cdp) Miami-Dade County	553	2.27
Westchester, FL (cdp) Miami-Dade County	682	2.25
Opa-locka, FL (city) Miami-Dade County	332	2.22
Carol City, FL (cdp) Miami-Dade County	1,305	2.20
Sunset, FL (cdp) Miami-Dade County	370	2.16
Princeton, FL (cdp) Miami-Dade County	217	2.15
Miami Springs, FL (city) Miami-Dade County	283	2.06
Pinewood, FL (cdp) Miami-Dade County	331	2.00
Medley, FL (town) Miami-Dade County	22	2.00
Daly City, CA (city) San Mateo County	2,052	1.98
Olympia Heights, FL (cdp) Miami-Dade County	242	1.80
Three Lakes, FL (cdp) Miami-Dade County	125	1.80
Country Walk, FL (cdp) Miami-Dade County	185	1.74
Delta, IA (city) Keokuk County	7	1.71
Mount Crested Butte, CO (town) Gunnison County	12	1.70
Doral, FL (cdp) Miami-Dade County	346	1.69
Glenvar Heights, FL (cdp) Miami-Dade County	274	1.69
Bayview-Montalvin, CA (cdp) Contra Costa County	81	1.62
Country Club, FL (cdp) Miami-Dade County	585	1.61
Broadmoor, CA (cdp) San Mateo County	65	1.61
Westview, FL (cdp) Miami-Dade County	154	1.59
North Haven, ME (town) Knox County	6	1.57
South San Francisco, CA (city) San Mateo County	945	1.56
East Perrine, FL (cdp) Miami-Dade County	103	1.46
Stock Island, FL (cdp) Monroe County	64	1.45
Cutler Ridge, FL (cdp) Miami-Dade County	355	1.43
El Portal, FL (village) Miami-Dade County	35	1.40
Leisure City, FL (cdp) Miami-Dade County	304	1.37
Marathon, FL (city) Monroe County	133	1.30
Gun Club Estates, FL (cdp) Palm Beach County	9	1.27
San Bruno, CA (city) San Mateo County	508	1.26
Naranja, FL (cdp) Miami-Dade County	51	1.26
Stacey Street, FL (cdp) Palm Beach County	12	1.25
Key West, FL (city) Monroe County	311	1.22
Pinecrest, FL (village) Miami-Dade County	228	1.20
Broadview Park, FL (cdp) Broward County	79	1.16
Lake Forest, FL (cdp) Broward County	58	1.16
Goulds, FL (cdp) Miami-Dade County	86	1.15
Belle Glade Camp, FL (cdp) Palm Beach County	13	1.14
Morton, MS (city) Scott County	39	1.12
Homestead Base, FL (cdp) Miami-Dade County	5	1.12
Moffett, OK (town) Sequoyah County	2	1.12
Langley Park, MD (cdp) Prince George's County	177	1.09
Miami Lakes, FL (cdp) Miami-Dade County	243	1.07
Harveysburg, OH (village) Warren County	6	1.07
Brownsville, FL (cdp) Miami-Dade County	151	1.05
Independence, CA (cdp) Inyo County	6	1.05
Limestone Creek, FL (cdp) Palm Beach County	6	1.05
South Miami, FL (city) Miami-Dade County	112	1.04
Richmond Heights, FL (cdp) Miami-Dade County	88	1.04
Lake Butler, FL (city) Union County	20	1.04
Miami Beach, FL (city) Miami-Dade County	905	1.03
Key Biscayne, FL (village) Miami-Dade County	107	1.02
Sasser, GA (town) Terrell County	4	1.02
Tara Hills, CA (cdp) Contra Costa County	54	1.01
Brewster, MN (city) Nobles County	5	1.00
Cudahy, CA (city) Los Angeles County	236	0.97
Coral Gables, FL (city) Miami-Dade County	400	0.95
Bailey's Crossroads, VA (cdp) Fairfax County	218	0.94
North Miami, FL (city) Miami-Dade County	553	0.92
North Miami Beach, FL (city) Miami-Dade County	374	0.92
Kenner, LA (city) Jefferson Parish	638	0.90
Royal Palm Estates, FL (cdp) Palm Beach County	31	0.87
Westgate-Belvedere Homes, FL (cdp) Palm Beach County	70	0.86
San Pablo, CA (city) Contra Costa County	257	0.85
Lake Lucerne, FL (cdp) Miami-Dade County	78	0.85
Lakes by the Bay, FL (cdp) Miami-Dade County	76	0.84
West Perrine, FL (cdp) Miami-Dade County	72	0.84
Opa-locka North, FL (cdp) Miami-Dade County	52	0.84
Wade, NC (town) Cumberland County	4	0.83
Centerville, WA (cdp) Klickitat County	1	0.83
Miramar, FL (city) Broward County	589	0.81
Cherryland, CA (cdp) Alameda County	112	0.81
Lake Belvedere Estates, FL (cdp) Palm Beach County	12	0.79
Miami Gardens, FL (cdp) Broward County	21	0.78
Milton, WI (town) Buffalo County	4	0.77
Camden, NJ (city) Camden County	607	0.76
Hayward, CA (city) Alameda County	1,045	0.75
Port Arthur, TX (city) Jefferson County	432	0.75
Bell Gardens, CA (city) Los Angeles County	325	0.74
Stratton, VT (town) Windham County	1	0.74
Miami Shores, FL (village) Miami-Dade County	76	0.73
North Bay Village, FL (city) Miami-Dade County	49	0.73
Ashland, CA (cdp) Alameda County	150	0.72
Chandler, MN (city) Murray County	2	0.72
Homestead, FL (city) Miami-Dade County	228	0.71
Norland, FL (cdp) Miami-Dade County	163	0.71
San Francisco, CA (city) San Francisco County	5,459	0.70
Maywood, CA (city) Los Angeles County	195	0.69
Cutler, FL (cdp) Miami-Dade County	120	0.69
Ives Estates, FL (cdp) Miami-Dade County	120	0.68
Pittsburg, CA (city) Contra Costa County	381	0.67
Bell, CA (city) Los Angeles County	247	0.67
Golden Glades, FL (cdp) Miami-Dade County	219	0.67
Poplar-Cotton Center, CA (cdp) Tulare County	10	0.67
Pacifica, CA (city) San Mateo County	253	0.66
Silver Spring, MD (cdp) Montgomery County	500	0.65
Fort Greely, AK (cdp) Southeast Fairbanks Census Area	3	0.65
Wheaton-Glenmont, MD (cdp) Montgomery County	371	0.64
Palm Springs North, FL (cdp) Miami-Dade County	35	0.64
Bay Harbor Islands, FL (town) Miami-Dade County	33	0.64
Colmar Manor, MD (town) Prince George's County	8	0.64
Bay Point, CA (cdp) Contra Costa County	136	0.63
Edgewater, FL (cdp) Broward County	5	0.62
South Gate, CA (city) Los Angeles County	581	0.60
Downey, CA (city) Los Angeles County	636	0.59
Ashley Heights, NC (cdp) Hoke County	2	0.59
Fenwick Island, DE (town) Sussex County	2	0.58
Trondhjem, MN (township) Otter Tail County	1	0.58
Millbrae, CA (city) San Mateo County	115	0.56
Ojus, FL (cdp) Miami-Dade County	93	0.56
Green Valley Farms, TX (cdp) Cameron County	4	0.56
Metairie, LA (cdp) Jefferson Parish	806	0.55
Mayflower Village, CA (cdp) Los Angeles County	28	0.55
Biscayne Park, FL (village) Miami-Dade County	18	0.55
Washington, VA (town) Rappahannock County	1	0.55
Huntington Park, CA (city) Los Angeles County	334	0.54
Lennox, CA (cdp) Los Angeles County	123	0.54
Summit Lake, MN (township) Nobles County	2	0.54
New Brunswick, NJ (city) Middlesex County	258	0.53
Lincolnia, VA (cdp) Fairfax County	83	0.53
Lawndale, CA (city) Los Angeles County	164	0.52
Lake Worth Corridor, FL (cdp) Palm Beach County	97	0.52
Santa Fe Springs, CA (city) Los Angeles County	91	0.52
Takoma Park, MD (city) Montgomery County	88	0.51

Notes: (cdp) census designated place; Refer to the Explanation of Data in the front of the book for more detailed information.

Hispanic: Nicaraguan

Top 150 Places Sorted by Percent

(Based on places with populations of 10,000 or more)

Place	Number	%
Sweetwater, FL (city) Miami-Dade County	2,366	16.63
Fountainbleau, FL (cdp) Miami-Dade County	5,624	9.44
Miami, FL (city) Miami-Dade County	20,543	5.67
Hialeah Gardens, FL (city) Miami-Dade County	939	4.87
Tamiami, FL (cdp) Miami-Dade County	2,551	4.66
Kendale Lakes, FL (cdp) Miami-Dade County	2,612	4.59
Kendall West, FL (cdp) Miami-Dade County	1,670	4.39
Richmond West, FL (cdp) Miami-Dade County	1,178	4.19
Hialeah, FL (city) Miami-Dade County	9,211	4.07
Gladeview, FL (cdp) Miami-Dade County	536	3.70
West Little River, FL (cdp) Miami-Dade County	1,163	3.58
University Park, FL (cdp) Miami-Dade County	767	2.89
The Hammocks, FL (cdp) Miami-Dade County	1,364	2.88
South Miami Heights, FL (cdp) Miami-Dade County	936	2.79
Westwood Lakes, FL (cdp) Miami-Dade County	305	2.54
The Crossings, FL (cdp) Miami-Dade County	592	2.51
Kendall, FL (cdp) Miami-Dade County	1,869	2.48
Palmetto Estates, FL (cdp) Miami-Dade County	326	2.38
Coral Terrace, FL (cdp) Miami-Dade County	553	2.27
Westchester, FL (cdp) Miami-Dade County	682	2.25
Opa-locka, FL (city) Miami-Dade County	332	2.22
Carol City, FL (cdp) Miami-Dade County	1,305	2.20
Sunset, FL (cdp) Miami-Dade County	370	2.16
Princeton, FL (cdp) Miami-Dade County	217	2.15
Miami Springs, FL (city) Miami-Dade County	283	2.06
Pinewood, FL (cdp) Miami-Dade County	331	2.00
Daly City, CA (city) San Mateo County	2,052	1.98
Olympia Heights, FL (cdp) Miami-Dade County	242	1.80
Country Walk, FL (cdp) Miami-Dade County	185	1.74
Doral, FL (cdp) Miami-Dade County	346	1.69
Glenvar Heights, FL (cdp) Miami-Dade County	274	1.69
Country Club, FL (cdp) Miami-Dade County	585	1.61
South San Francisco, CA (city) San Mateo County	945	1.56
Cutler Ridge, FL (cdp) Miami-Dade County	355	1.43
Leisure City, FL (cdp) Miami-Dade County	304	1.37
Marathon, FL (city) Monroe County	133	1.30
San Bruno, CA (city) San Mateo County	508	1.26
Key West, FL (city) Monroe County	311	1.22
Pinecrest, FL (village) Miami-Dade County	228	1.20
Langley Park, MD (cdp) Prince George's County	177	1.09
Miami Lakes, FL (cdp) Miami-Dade County	243	1.07
Brownsville, FL (cdp) Miami-Dade County	151	1.05
South Miami, FL (city) Miami-Dade County	112	1.04
Miami Beach, FL (city) Miami-Dade County	905	1.03
Key Biscayne, FL (village) Miami-Dade County	107	1.02
Cudahy, CA (city) Los Angeles County	236	0.97
Coral Gables, FL (city) Miami-Dade County	400	0.95
Bailey's Crossroads, VA (cdp) Fairfax County	218	0.94
North Miami, FL (city) Miami-Dade County	553	0.92
North Miami Beach, FL (city) Miami-Dade County	374	0.92
Kenner, LA (city) Jefferson Parish	638	0.90
San Pablo, CA (city) Contra Costa County	257	0.85
Miramar, FL (city) Broward County	589	0.81
Cherryland, CA (cdp) Alameda County	112	0.81
Camden, NJ (city) Camden County	607	0.76
Hayward, CA (city) Alameda County	1,045	0.75
Port Arthur, TX (city) Jefferson County	432	0.75
Bell Gardens, CA (city) Los Angeles County	325	0.74
Miami Shores, FL (village) Miami-Dade County	76	0.73
Ashland, CA (cdp) Alameda County	150	0.72
Homestead, FL (city) Miami-Dade County	228	0.71
Norland, FL (cdp) Miami-Dade County	163	0.71
San Francisco, CA (city) San Francisco County	5,459	0.70
Maywood, CA (city) Los Angeles County	195	0.69
Cutler, FL (cdp) Miami-Dade County	120	0.69
Ives Estates, FL (cdp) Miami-Dade County	120	0.68
Pittsburg, CA (city) Contra Costa County	381	0.67
Bell, CA (city) Los Angeles County	247	0.67
Golden Glades, FL (cdp) Miami-Dade County	219	0.67
Pacifica, CA (city) San Mateo County	253	0.66
Silver Spring, MD (cdp) Montgomery County	500	0.65
Wheaton-Glenmont, MD (cdp) Montgomery County	371	0.64
Bay Point, CA (cdp) Contra Costa County	136	0.63
South Gate, CA (city) Los Angeles County	581	0.60
Downey, CA (city) Los Angeles County	636	0.59
Millbrae, CA (city) San Mateo County	115	0.56
Ojus, FL (cdp) Miami-Dade County	93	0.56
Metairie, LA (cdp) Jefferson Parish	806	0.55
Huntington Park, CA (city) Los Angeles County	334	0.54
Lennox, CA (cdp) Los Angeles County	123	0.54
New Brunswick, NJ (city) Middlesex County	258	0.53
Lincolnia, VA (cdp) Fairfax County	83	0.53
Lawndale, CA (city) Los Angeles County	164	0.52
Lake Worth Corridor, FL (cdp) Palm Beach County	97	0.52
Santa Fe Springs, CA (city) Los Angeles County	91	0.52
Takoma Park, MD (city) Montgomery County	88	0.51
Belle Glade, FL (city) Palm Beach County	76	0.51
Scott Lake, FL (cdp) Miami-Dade County	74	0.51
Pennsauken, NJ (cdp) Camden County	177	0.50
Jefferson, VA (cdp) Fairfax County	131	0.48
Gaithersburg, MD (city) Montgomery County	239	0.45
Vincent, CA (cdp) Los Angeles County	68	0.45
Walnut Park, CA (cdp) Los Angeles County	71	0.44
Adelphi, MD (cdp) Prince George's County	66	0.44
Chillum, MD (cdp) Prince George's County	146	0.43
Montclair, CA (city) San Bernardino County	142	0.43
Richmond, CA (city) Contra Costa County	416	0.42
Timberlane, LA (cdp) Jefferson Parish	48	0.42
Hawthorne, CA (city) Los Angeles County	349	0.41
Carson City, NV (special city) Carson City city	216	0.41
Greenacres, FL (city) Palm Beach County	112	0.41
Freeport, TX (city) Brazoria County	52	0.41
North Fair Oaks, CA (cdp) San Mateo County	61	0.40
Hyattsville, MD (city) Prince George's County	59	0.40
Pembroke Pines, FL (city) Broward County	533	0.39
San Mateo, CA (city) San Mateo County	363	0.39
Concord, CA (city) Contra Costa County	457	0.38
Redwood City, CA (city) San Mateo County	285	0.38
La Puente, CA (city) Los Angeles County	156	0.38
Asbury Park, NJ (city) Monmouth County	64	0.38
Antioch, CA (city) Contra Costa County	334	0.37
Alhambra, CA (city) Los Angeles County	319	0.37
Aspen Hill, MD (cdp) Montgomery County	184	0.37
San Lorenzo, CA (cdp) Alameda County	82	0.37
El Sobrante, CA (cdp) Contra Costa County	45	0.37
Hollywood, FL (city) Broward County	501	0.36
West Covina, CA (city) Los Angeles County	383	0.36
Newark, CA (city) Alameda County	153	0.36
North Atlanta, GA (cdp) De Kalb County	140	0.36
Suisun City, CA (city) Solano County	94	0.36
White Oak, MD (cdp) Montgomery County	76	0.36
Lake Worth, FL (city) Palm Beach County	122	0.35
Terrytown, LA (cdp) Jefferson Parish	90	0.35
West Whittier-Los Nietos, CA (cdp) Los Angeles County	88	0.35
Pinole, CA (city) Contra Costa County	67	0.35
Alum Rock, CA (cdp) Santa Clara County	47	0.35
Citrus, CA (cdp) Los Angeles County	37	0.35
Fontana, CA (city) San Bernardino County	436	0.34
Baldwin Park, CA (city) Los Angeles County	258	0.34
East San Gabriel, CA (cdp) Los Angeles County	49	0.34
Beltsville, MD (cdp) Prince George's County	51	0.33
West Palm Beach, FL (city) Palm Beach County	265	0.32
San Gabriel, CA (city) Los Angeles County	129	0.32
Hallandale, FL (city) Broward County	111	0.32
Woodbridge, VA (cdp) Prince William County	102	0.32
Belmont, CA (city) San Mateo County	81	0.32
Carrollton, GA (city) Carroll County	64	0.32
Commerce, CA (city) Los Angeles County	40	0.32
Guttenberg, NJ (town) Hudson County	35	0.32
Kissimmee, FL (city) Osceola County	148	0.31
Oakley, CA (city) Contra Costa County	80	0.31
Herndon, VA (town) Fairfax County	68	0.31
Yeehaw Junction, FL (cdp) Osceola County	68	0.31
Hercules, CA (city) Contra Costa County	61	0.31
Redland, MD (cdp) Montgomery County	52	0.31
Worthington, MN (city) Nobles County	35	0.31
Norwalk, CA (city) Los Angeles County	314	0.30
West Puente Valley, CA (cdp) Los Angeles County	68	0.30
Union City, NJ (city) Hudson County	196	0.29
Montebello, CA (city) Los Angeles County	178	0.29

Notes: (cdp) census designated place; Refer to the Explanation of Data in the front of the book for more detailed information.

Hispanic: Panamanian

Top 150 Places Sorted by Number

(Based on all places, regardless of population)

Place	Number	%
New York, NY (city) New York City	16,847	0.21
Los Angeles, CA (city) Los Angeles County	1,415	0.04
San Antonio, TX (city) Bexar County	853	0.07
Houston, TX (city) Harris County	792	0.04
San Diego, CA (city) San Diego County	682	0.06
Miami, FL (city) Miami-Dade County	657	0.18
Chicago, IL (city) Cook County	637	0.02
Hempstead, NY (town) Nassau County	597	0.08
Killeen, TX (city) Bell County	596	0.69
Boston, MA (city) Suffolk County	527	0.09
Fayetteville, NC (city) Cumberland County	483	0.40
Columbus, GA (special city) Muscogee County	480	0.26
Jacksonville, FL (special city) Duval County	461	0.06
Washington, DC (city) District of Columbia	437	0.08
Colorado Springs, CO (city) El Paso County	429	0.12
Virginia Beach, VA (independent city) Virginia Beach city	422	0.10
Tampa, FL (city) Hillsborough County	407	0.13
Newport News, VA (independent city) Newport News city	381	0.21
Hialeah, FL (city) Miami-Dade County	379	0.17
Philadelphia, PA (city) Philadelphia County	378	0.02
El Paso, TX (city) El Paso County	369	0.07
Pembroke Pines, FL (city) Broward County	367	0.27
Austin, TX (city) Travis County	345	0.05
Miramar, FL (city) Broward County	336	0.46
Clarksville, TN (city) Montgomery County	333	0.32
Dallas, TX (city) Dallas County	319	0.03
Augusta-Richmond County, GA (special city) Richmond County	306	0.16
Islip, NY (town) Suffolk County	298	0.09
Fountainbleau, FL (cdp) Miami-Dade County	293	0.49
Kendall, FL (cdp) Miami-Dade County	268	0.36
San Francisco, CA (city) San Francisco County	261	0.03
Tucson, AZ (city) Pima County	256	0.05
Hollywood, FL (city) Broward County	241	0.17
Country Club, FL (cdp) Miami-Dade County	240	0.66
Hinesville, GA (city) Liberty County	239	0.79
Jersey City, NJ (city) Hudson County	236	0.10
Orlando, FL (city) Orange County	230	0.12
The Hammocks, FL (cdp) Miami-Dade County	226	0.48
Miami Beach, FL (city) Miami-Dade County	224	0.25
Kendale Lakes, FL (cdp) Miami-Dade County	221	0.39
Long Beach, CA (city) Los Angeles County	221	0.05
Lawton, OK (city) Comanche County	220	0.24
Richmond West, FL (cdp) Miami-Dade County	210	0.75
Carol City, FL (cdp) Miami-Dade County	206	0.35
Phoenix, AZ (city) Maricopa County	203	0.02
Hampton, VA (independent city) Hampton city	198	0.14
Las Vegas, NV (city) Clark County	194	0.04
Doral, FL (cdp) Miami-Dade County	192	0.94
San Jose, CA (city) Santa Clara County	187	0.02
Tacoma, WA (city) Pierce County	183	0.09
Babylon, NY (town) Suffolk County	173	0.08
Columbus, OH (city) Franklin County	173	0.02
Fort Bragg, NC (cdp) Cumberland County	165	0.57
Arlington, VA (cdp) Arlington County	159	0.08
Seattle, WA (city) King County	156	0.03
Oakland, CA (city) Alameda County	153	0.04
Sacramento, CA (city) Sacramento County	153	0.04
Newark, NJ (city) Essex County	152	0.06
Aurora, CO (city) Arapahoe County	152	0.05
Oceanside, CA (city) San Diego County	150	0.09
Fort Hood, TX (cdp) Coryell County	148	0.44
Norfolk, VA (independent city) Norfolk city	148	0.06
New Orleans, LA (city) Orleans Parish	146	0.03
Kendall West, FL (cdp) Miami-Dade County	143	0.38
Coral Springs, FL (city) Broward County	143	0.12
Fort Worth, TX (city) Tarrant County	143	0.03
Tamiami, FL (cdp) Miami-Dade County	142	0.26
Albuquerque, NM (city) Bernalillo County	141	0.03
Indianapolis, IN (special city) Marion County	138	0.02
Brentwood, NY (cdp) Suffolk County	137	0.25
Sunrise, FL (city) Broward County	135	0.16
Denver, CO (city) Denver County	135	0.02
Brookhaven, NY (town) Suffolk County	134	0.03
Oklahoma City, OK (city) Oklahoma County	134	0.03
Charlotte, NC (city) Mecklenburg County	133	0.02

Place	Number	%
Town 'n' Country, FL (cdp) Hillsborough County	132	0.18
Copperas Cove, TX (city) Coryell County	131	0.44
Tallahassee, FL (city) Leon County	130	0.09
Palm Bay, FL (city) Brevard County	127	0.16
Lakewood, WA (city) Pierce County	124	0.21
Savannah, GA (city) Chatham County	124	0.09
Silver Spring, MD (cdp) Montgomery County	123	0.16
Brandon, FL (cdp) Hillsborough County	122	0.16
Arlington, TX (city) Tarrant County	122	0.04
Chula Vista, CA (city) San Diego County	121	0.07
Anchorage, AK (municipality) Anchorage Borough	120	0.05
Riverside, CA (city) Riverside County	120	0.05
Hempstead, NY (village) Nassau County	119	0.21
Atlanta, GA (city) Fulton County	119	0.03
Yonkers, NY (city) Westchester County	115	0.06
Saint Petersburg, FL (city) Pinellas County	115	0.05
Raleigh, NC (city) Wake County	114	0.04
Coral Gables, FL (city) Miami-Dade County	113	0.27
Alexandria, VA (independent city) Alexandria city	110	0.09
Pasadena, CA (city) Los Angeles County	110	0.08
Springfield, MA (city) Hampden County	110	0.07
Pemberton, NJ (township) Burlington County	107	0.37
Jacksonville, NC (city) Onslow County	107	0.16
Chesapeake, VA (independent city) Chesapeake city	105	0.05
Baltimore, MD (independent city) Baltimore city	105	0.02
Dale City, VA (cdp) Prince William County	104	0.19
Providence, RI (city) Providence County	103	0.06
Deltona, FL (city) Volusia County	101	0.15
Plantation, FL (city) Broward County	100	0.12
Inglewood, CA (city) Los Angeles County	100	0.09
South Miami Heights, FL (cdp) Miami-Dade County	98	0.29
Honolulu, HI (cdp) Honolulu County	98	0.03
Bayonne, NJ (city) Hudson County	97	0.16
North Miami, FL (city) Miami-Dade County	97	0.16
Fontana, CA (city) San Bernardino County	97	0.08
North Las Vegas, NV (city) Clark County	97	0.08
Fort Lewis, WA (cdp) Pierce County	94	0.49
Davie, FL (town) Broward County	94	0.12
Memphis, TN (city) Shelby County	94	0.01
Minneapolis, MN (city) Hennepin County	93	0.02
Fort Lauderdale, FL (city) Broward County	92	0.06
Nashville-Davidson, TN (special city) Davidson County	92	0.02
Sierra Vista, AZ (city) Cochise County	91	0.24
Kissimmee, FL (city) Osceola County	91	0.19
Fairfield, CA (city) Solano County	91	0.09
Irving, TX (city) Dallas County	91	0.05
San Bernardino, CA (city) San Bernardino County	91	0.05
Fort Campbell North, KY (cdp) Christian County	90	0.63
Anaheim, CA (city) Orange County	90	0.03
Freeport, NY (village) Nassau County	89	0.20
The Crossings, FL (cdp) Miami-Dade County	88	0.37
Elmont, NY (cdp) Nassau County	87	0.27
Milwaukee, WI (city) Milwaukee County	87	0.01
Central Islip, NY (cdp) Suffolk County	85	0.27
North Miami Beach, FL (city) Miami-Dade County	84	0.21
Weston, FL (city) Broward County	84	0.17
Junction City, KS (city) Geary County	83	0.44
Paradise, NV (cdp) Clark County	83	0.04
Corona, CA (city) Riverside County	82	0.07
Gainesville, FL (city) Alachua County	81	0.08
Columbia, SC (city) Richland County	81	0.07
Rochester, NY (city) Monroe County	81	0.04
Palmetto Estates, FL (cdp) Miami-Dade County	80	0.59
Port Saint Lucie, FL (city) Saint Lucie County	80	0.09
Hayward, CA (city) Alameda County	79	0.06
Corpus Christi, TX (city) Nueces County	79	0.03
Fort Stewart, GA (cdp) Liberty County	78	0.70
Detroit, MI (city) Wayne County	78	0.01
Huntsville, AL (city) Madison County	77	0.05
University Park, FL (cdp) Miami-Dade County	76	0.29
Willingboro, NJ (township) Burlington County	76	0.23
Lauderhill, FL (city) Broward County	76	0.13
Moreno Valley, CA (city) Riverside County	76	0.05
Santa Clarita, CA (city) Los Angeles County	76	0.05
Fremont, CA (city) Alameda County	75	0.04

Notes: (cdp) census designated place; Refer to the Explanation of Data in the front of the book for more detailed information.

Hispanic: Panamanian

Top 150 Places Sorted by Percent

(Based on all places, regardless of population)

Place	Number	%
Indian Creek, FL (village) Miami-Dade County	1	3.03
Lisbon, FL (cdp) Lake County	5	1.83
Pinckard, AL (town) Dale County	12	1.80
Trail, MN (city) Polk County	1	1.61
Fort Greely, AK (cdp) Southeast Fairbanks Census Area	7	1.52
Lucky, LA (village) Bienville Parish	5	1.41
Bohemia, MI (township) Ontonagon County	1	1.30
Pemberton Heights, NJ (cdp) Burlington County	31	1.23
Spring Creek, MN (township) Norman County	1	1.20
Toco, TX (city) Lamar County	1	1.12
Taft, WI (town) Taylor County	4	1.11
Miami Gardens, FL (cdp) Broward County	29	1.07
Whitesboro-Burleigh, NJ (cdp) Cape May County	19	1.03
Kenny Lake, AK (cdp) Valdez-Cordova Census Area	4	0.98
Elmira, CA (cdp) Solano County	2	0.98
Millington, MD (town) Kent County	4	0.96
Doral, FL (cdp) Miami-Dade County	192	0.94
Gruver, IA (city) Emmet County	1	0.94
Brokaw, WI (village) Marathon County	1	0.93
Saint Anthony, IA (city) Marshall County	1	0.92
Maple Creek, WI (town) Outagamie County	6	0.87
Morningside, MD (town) Prince George's County	11	0.85
Wabedo, MN (township) Cass County	3	0.80
Hinesville, GA (city) Liberty County	239	0.79
Fort Belvoir, VA (cdp) Fairfax County	56	0.78
Nebo Center, CA (cdp) San Bernardino County	9	0.77
Fort Rucker, AL (cdp) Dale County	46	0.76
Fort Polk North, LA (cdp) Vernon Parish	25	0.76
Richmond West, FL (cdp) Miami-Dade County	210	0.75
Spring Lake, NC (town) Cumberland County	61	0.75
Pine, PA (township) Crawford County	4	0.75
Liverpool, TX (city) Brazoria County	3	0.74
Lakes by the Bay, FL (cdp) Miami-Dade County	65	0.72
East Garden City, NY (cdp) Nassau County	7	0.72
Aberdeen Proving Ground, MD (cdp) Harford County	22	0.71
Fort Stewart, GA (cdp) Liberty County	78	0.70
Moose Lake, MN (township) Cass County	1	0.70
Killeen, TX (city) Bell County	596	0.69
Tyndall AFB, FL (cdp) Bay County	19	0.69
Indian Village, IN (town) Saint Joseph County	1	0.69
Strong City, KS (city) Chase County	4	0.68
Alta Vista, KS (city) Wabaunsee County	3	0.68
Country Club, FL (cdp) Miami-Dade County	240	0.66
Watha, NC (town) Pender County	1	0.66
Dalton, NH (town) Coos County	6	0.65
Ormsby, MN (city) Watonwan County	1	0.65
Fort Campbell North, KY (cdp) Christian County	90	0.63
Cashion, OK (town) Kingfisher County	4	0.63
Maysville, IA (city) Scott County	1	0.61
White Sands, NM (cdp) Dona Ana County	8	0.60
Groton Long Point, CT (borough) New London County	4	0.60
Milford, KS (city) Geary County	3	0.60
Palmetto Estates, FL (cdp) Miami-Dade County	80	0.59
Oak Grove, KY (city) Christian County	41	0.58
Pope AFB, NC (cdp) Cumberland County	15	0.58
Fort Bragg, NC (cdp) Cumberland County	165	0.57
Huachuca City, AZ (town) Cochise County	10	0.57
Saint Paul, OR (city) Marion County	2	0.56
Pomaria, SC (town) Newberry County	1	0.56
Lakeview, NY (cdp) Nassau County	31	0.55
Fort Benning South, GA (cdp) Chattahoochee County	63	0.54
Fort Leonard Wood, MO (cdp) Pulaski County	72	0.53
Andrews AFB, MD (cdp) Prince George's County	42	0.53
Woodfield, SC (cdp) Richland County	48	0.52
Bonney, TX (village) Brazoria County	2	0.52
Eglin AFB, FL (cdp) Okaloosa County	41	0.51
Redstone Arsenal, AL (cdp) Madison County	12	0.51
Fort Lee, VA (cdp) Prince George County	36	0.50
Moody AFB, GA (cdp) Lowndes County	5	0.50
Edgewater, FL (cdp) Broward County	4	0.50
Palm Shores, FL (town) Brevard County	4	0.50
O'Kean, AR (town) Randolph County	1	0.50
Fountainbleau, FL (cdp) Miami-Dade County	293	0.49
Fort Lewis, WA (cdp) Pierce County	94	0.49
East Perrine, FL (cdp) Miami-Dade County	35	0.49
Boys Town, NE (village) Douglas County	4	0.49
Westwood, KY (city) Jefferson County	3	0.49
Ulm, AR (town) Prairie County	1	0.49
The Hammocks, FL (cdp) Miami-Dade County	226	0.48
Schofield Barracks, HI (cdp) Honolulu County	69	0.48
West Perrine, FL (cdp) Miami-Dade County	41	0.48
Geronimo, TX (cdp) Guadalupe County	3	0.48
Newtown, MO (town) Sullivan County	1	0.48
Fort Drum, NY (cdp) Jefferson County	57	0.47
Oakland, SC (cdp) Sumter County	6	0.47
Geuda Springs, KS (city) Sumner County	1	0.47
Miramar, FL (city) Broward County	336	0.46
Fort Meade, MD (cdp) Anne Arundel County	45	0.46
Walthourville, GA (city) Liberty County	18	0.45
Patagonia, AZ (town) Santa Cruz County	4	0.45
Fort Hood, TX (cdp) Coryell County	148	0.44
Copperas Cove, TX (city) Coryell County	131	0.44
Junction City, KS (city) Geary County	83	0.44
Woodridge, NY (village) Sullivan County	4	0.44
Lincoln, MN (township) Blue Earth County	1	0.44
Poinciana, FL (cdp) Osceola County	58	0.43
Fort Polk South, LA (cdp) Vernon Parish	47	0.43
Savoy, MA (town) Berkshire County	3	0.43
Ferndale, FL (cdp) Lake County	1	0.43
Andover, FL (cdp) Miami-Dade County	36	0.42
Bal Harbour, FL (village) Miami-Dade County	14	0.42
Dalzell, IL (village) Bureau County	3	0.42
Shalimar, FL (town) Okaloosa County	3	0.42
New Llano, LA (town) Vernon Parish	10	0.41
Fayetteville, NC (city) Cumberland County	483	0.40
Ives Estates, FL (cdp) Miami-Dade County	70	0.40
Browns Mills, NJ (cdp) Burlington County	45	0.40
Country Walk, FL (cdp) Miami-Dade County	43	0.40
Three Lakes, FL (cdp) Miami-Dade County	28	0.40
McGuire AFB, NJ (cdp) Burlington County	26	0.40
Lake Forest, FL (cdp) Broward County	20	0.40
Pumpkin Center, NC (cdp) Onslow County	9	0.40
Juno Ridge, FL (cdp) Palm Beach County	3	0.40
Bentonia, MS (town) Yazoo County	2	0.40
Forest Hills, KY (city) Jefferson County	2	0.40
Kendale Lakes, FL (cdp) Miami-Dade County	221	0.39
Meadow Woods, FL (cdp) Orange County	44	0.39
Level Plains, AL (town) Dale County	6	0.39
Hanna City, IL (village) Peoria County	4	0.39
McLaughlin, SD (city) Corson County	3	0.39
Kendall West, FL (cdp) Miami-Dade County	143	0.38
West Point, NY (cdp) Orange County	27	0.38
Ocean City, FL (cdp) Okaloosa County	21	0.38
Palm Springs North, FL (cdp) Miami-Dade County	21	0.38
Rockfish, NC (cdp) Hoke County	9	0.38
Dixon, MO (city) Pulaski County	6	0.38
Indian Springs, NV (cdp) Clark County	5	0.38
Ronald, WA (cdp) Kittitas County	1	0.38
Pemberton, NJ (township) Burlington County	107	0.37
The Crossings, FL (cdp) Miami-Dade County	88	0.37
Le Ray, NY (town) Jefferson County	73	0.37
Vandenberg AFB, CA (cdp) Santa Barbara County	23	0.37
Bedford, IA (city) Taylor County	6	0.37
Humphrey, AR (city) Arkansas County	3	0.37
Kendall, FL (cdp) Miami-Dade County	268	0.36
Offutt AFB, NE (cdp) Sarpy County	32	0.36
Calcium, NY (cdp) Jefferson County	12	0.36
Mount Pocono, PA (borough) Monroe County	10	0.36
Sonoita, AZ (cdp) Santa Cruz County	3	0.36
Quantico, VA (town) Prince William County	2	0.36
Dedham, IA (city) Carroll County	1	0.36
Carol City, FL (cdp) Miami-Dade County	206	0.35
North Amityville, NY (cdp) Suffolk County	58	0.35
Piney Green, NC (cdp) Onslow County	41	0.35
Princeton, FL (cdp) Miami-Dade County	35	0.35
Windcrest, TX (city) Bexar County	18	0.35
Meade, MI (township) Mason County	1	0.35
Waynesville, MO (city) Pulaski County	12	0.34
Seligman, MO (city) Barry County	3	0.34
North Bonneville, WA (city) Skamania County	2	0.34

Notes: (cdp) census designated place; Refer to the Explanation of Data in the front of the book for more detailed information.

Hispanic: Panamanian

Top 150 Places Sorted by Percent

(Based on places with populations of 10,000 or more)

Place	Number	%
Doral, FL (cdp) Miami-Dade County	192	0.94
Hinesville, GA (city) Liberty County	239	0.79
Richmond West, FL (cdp) Miami-Dade County	210	0.75
Fort Stewart, GA (cdp) Liberty County	78	0.70
Killeen, TX (city) Bell County	596	0.69
Country Club, FL (cdp) Miami-Dade County	240	0.66
Fort Campbell North, KY (cdp) Christian County	90	0.63
Palmetto Estates, FL (cdp) Miami-Dade County	80	0.59
Fort Bragg, NC (cdp) Cumberland County	165	0.57
Fort Benning South, GA (cdp) Chattahoochee County	63	0.54
Fort Leonard Wood, MO (cdp) Pulaski County	72	0.53
Fountainbleau, FL (cdp) Miami-Dade County	293	0.49
Fort Lewis, WA (cdp) Pierce County	94	0.49
The Hammocks, FL (cdp) Miami-Dade County	226	0.48
Schofield Barracks, HI (cdp) Honolulu County	69	0.48
Fort Drum, NY (cdp) Jefferson County	57	0.47
Miramar, FL (city) Broward County	336	0.46
Fort Hood, TX (cdp) Coryell County	148	0.44
Copperas Cove, TX (city) Coryell County	131	0.44
Junction City, KS (city) Geary County	83	0.44
Poinciana, FL (cdp) Osceola County	58	0.43
Fort Polk South, LA (cdp) Vernon Parish	47	0.43
Fayetteville, NC (city) Cumberland County	483	0.40
Ives Estates, FL (cdp) Miami-Dade County	70	0.40
Browns Mills, NJ (cdp) Burlington County	45	0.40
Country Walk, FL (cdp) Miami-Dade County	43	0.40
Kendale Lakes, FL (cdp) Miami-Dade County	221	0.39
Meadow Woods, FL (cdp) Orange County	44	0.39
Kendall West, FL (cdp) Miami-Dade County	143	0.38
Pemberton, NJ (township) Burlington County	107	0.37
The Crossings, FL (cdp) Miami-Dade County	88	0.37
Le Ray, NY (town) Jefferson County	73	0.37
Kendall, FL (cdp) Miami-Dade County	268	0.36
Carol City, FL (cdp) Miami-Dade County	206	0.35
North Amityville, NY (cdp) Suffolk County	58	0.35
Piney Green, NC (cdp) Onslow County	41	0.35
Princeton, FL (cdp) Miami-Dade County	35	0.35
Clarksville, TN (city) Montgomery County	333	0.32
Miami Lakes, FL (cdp) Miami-Dade County	68	0.30
Radcliff, KY (city) Hardin County	66	0.30
South Miami Heights, FL (cdp) Miami-Dade County	98	0.29
University Park, FL (cdp) Miami-Dade County	76	0.29
Harker Heights, TX (city) Bell County	51	0.29
Sweetwater, FL (city) Miami-Dade County	41	0.29
Hialeah Gardens, FL (city) Miami-Dade County	54	0.28
Glenvar Heights, FL (cdp) Miami-Dade County	46	0.28
Fort Knox, KY (cdp) Hardin County	35	0.28
Pembroke Pines, FL (city) Broward County	367	0.27
Coral Gables, FL (city) Miami-Dade County	113	0.27
Elmont, NY (cdp) Nassau County	87	0.27
Central Islip, NY (cdp) Suffolk County	85	0.27
Riverview, FL (cdp) Hillsborough County	32	0.27
Hope Mills, NC (town) Cumberland County	30	0.27
South Miami, FL (city) Miami-Dade County	29	0.27
Columbus, GA (special city) Muscogee County	480	0.26
Tamiami, FL (cdp) Miami-Dade County	142	0.26
Aventura, FL (city) Miami-Dade County	66	0.26
Sunset, FL (cdp) Miami-Dade County	45	0.26
Fountain, CO (city) El Paso County	39	0.26
Miami Beach, FL (city) Miami-Dade County	224	0.25
Brentwood, NY (cdp) Suffolk County	137	0.25
Wright, FL (cdp) Okaloosa County	54	0.25
Lawton, OK (city) Comanche County	220	0.24
Sierra Vista, AZ (city) Cochise County	91	0.24
Middletown, NY (city) Orange County	60	0.24
North Bay Shore, NY (cdp) Suffolk County	36	0.24
Willingboro, NJ (township) Burlington County	76	0.23
Adelphi, MD (cdp) Prince George's County	35	0.23
Highlands, NY (town) Orange County	29	0.23
Miami Shores, FL (village) Miami-Dade County	24	0.23
Egypt Lake-Leto, FL (cdp) Hillsborough County	73	0.22
Greater Carrollwood, FL (cdp) Hillsborough County	73	0.22
Seaside, CA (city) Monterey County	69	0.22
Cutler Ridge, FL (cdp) Miami-Dade County	55	0.22
Montclair, VA (cdp) Prince William County	35	0.22
Mount Holly, NJ (township) Burlington County	24	0.22
New York, NY (city) New York City	16,847	0.21
Newport News, VA (independent city) Newport News city	381	0.21
Lakewood, WA (city) Pierce County	124	0.21
Hempstead, NY (village) Nassau County	119	0.21
North Miami Beach, FL (city) Miami-Dade County	84	0.21
New London, CT (city) New London County	55	0.21
Cutler, FL (cdp) Miami-Dade County	36	0.21
Eatontown, NJ (borough) Monmouth County	30	0.21
Freeport, NY (village) Nassau County	89	0.20
Golden Glades, FL (cdp) Miami-Dade County	66	0.20
Woodbridge, VA (cdp) Prince William County	64	0.20
Norland, FL (cdp) Miami-Dade County	45	0.20
Burlington, NJ (township) Burlington County	40	0.20
South Laurel, MD (cdp) Prince George's County	40	0.20
Pinecrest, FL (village) Miami-Dade County	39	0.20
Aberdeen, MD (city) Harford County	27	0.20
Lumberton, NJ (township) Burlington County	21	0.20
Wyandanch, NY (cdp) Suffolk County	21	0.20
Dale City, VA (cdp) Prince William County	104	0.19
Kissimmee, FL (city) Osceola County	91	0.19
North Lauderdale, FL (city) Broward County	60	0.19
Westchester, FL (cdp) Miami-Dade County	58	0.19
Savage-Guilford, MD (cdp) Howard County	24	0.19
Converse, TX (city) Bexar County	22	0.19
Fort Carson, CO (cdp) El Paso County	20	0.19
Miami, FL (city) Miami-Dade County	657	0.18
Town 'n' Country, FL (cdp) Hillsborough County	132	0.18
Chillum, MD (cdp) Prince George's County	61	0.18
Security-Widefield, CO (cdp) El Paso County	55	0.18
Fairbanks, AK (city) Fairbanks North Star Borough	54	0.18
Greater Upper Marlboro, MD (cdp) Prince George's County	34	0.18
Takoma Park, MD (city) Montgomery County	32	0.18
North Valley Stream, NY (cdp) Nassau County	29	0.18
Miami Springs, FL (city) Miami-Dade County	25	0.18
Hialeah, FL (city) Miami-Dade County	379	0.17
Hollywood, FL (city) Broward County	241	0.17
Weston, FL (city) Broward County	84	0.17
Altamonte Springs, FL (city) Seminole County	70	0.17
Uniondale, NY (cdp) Nassau County	40	0.17
Oak Ridge, FL (cdp) Orange County	38	0.17
Ojus, FL (cdp) Miami-Dade County	28	0.17
Georgetown, GA (cdp) Chatham County	18	0.17
Augusta-Richmond County, GA (special city) Richmond County	306	0.16
Sunrise, FL (city) Broward County	135	0.16
Palm Bay, FL (city) Brevard County	127	0.16
Silver Spring, MD (cdp) Montgomery County	123	0.16
Brandon, FL (cdp) Hillsborough County	122	0.16
Jacksonville, NC (city) Onslow County	107	0.16
Bayonne, NJ (city) Hudson County	97	0.16
North Miami, FL (city) Miami-Dade County	97	0.16
Oviedo, FL (city) Seminole County	43	0.16
Altus, OK (city) Jackson County	35	0.16
Fairland, MD (cdp) Montgomery County	34	0.16
Evans, GA (cdp) Columbia County	28	0.16
Middle, NJ (township) Cape May County	27	0.16
Langley Park, MD (cdp) Prince George's County	26	0.16
Roosevelt, NY (cdp) Nassau County	25	0.16
Coolbaugh, PA (township) Monroe County	24	0.16
Malone, NY (town) Franklin County	24	0.16
Atlantic Beach, FL (city) Duval County	21	0.16
Dentsville, SC (cdp) Richland County	21	0.16
Goldenrod, FL (cdp) Seminole County	21	0.16
Riverdale, GA (city) Clayton County	20	0.16
Deltona, FL (city) Volusia County	101	0.15
Sanford, FL (city) Seminole County	57	0.15
Severn, MD (cdp) Anne Arundel County	52	0.15
University, FL (cdp) Hillsborough County	45	0.15
Watertown, NY (city) Jefferson County	40	0.15
Leisure City, FL (cdp) Miami-Dade County	34	0.15
Yeehaw Junction, FL (cdp) Osceola County	33	0.15
Enterprise, AL (city) Coffee County	31	0.15
Lorton, VA (cdp) Fairfax County	27	0.15
Myrtle Grove, FL (cdp) Escambia County	26	0.15
Hybla Valley, VA (cdp) Fairfax County	25	0.15

Notes: (cdp) census designated place; Refer to the Explanation of Data in the front of the book for more detailed information.

Hispanic: Salvadoran

Top 150 Places Sorted by Number

(Based on all places, regardless of population)

Place	Number	%
Los Angeles, CA (city) Los Angeles County	126,197	3.42
Houston, TX (city) Harris County	36,799	1.88
New York, NY (city) New York City	24,516	0.31
Hempstead, NY (town) Nassau County	15,659	2.07
Washington, DC (city) District of Columbia	11,741	2.05
Islip, NY (town) Suffolk County	11,046	3.42
San Francisco, CA (city) San Francisco County	10,655	1.37
Dallas, TX (city) Dallas County	8,582	0.72
Arlington, VA (cdp) Arlington County	7,630	4.03
Brentwood, NY (cdp) Suffolk County	6,387	11.85
Hempstead, NY (village) Nassau County	5,949	10.52
Boston, MA (city) Suffolk County	5,333	0.91
Irving, TX (city) Dallas County	5,102	2.66
North Hempstead, NY (town) Nassau County	4,993	2.24
Silver Spring, MD (cdp) Montgomery County	4,764	6.22
Alexandria, VA (independent city) Alexandria city	4,477	3.49
Santa Ana, CA (city) Orange County	4,131	1.22
Wheaton-Glenmont, MD (cdp) Montgomery County	3,770	6.53
Elizabeth, NJ (city) Union County	3,518	2.92
Langley Park, MD (cdp) Prince George's County	3,483	21.48
Chicago, IL (city) Cook County	3,468	0.12
Long Beach, CA (city) Los Angeles County	3,418	0.74
Oakland, CA (city) Alameda County	3,207	0.80
Union City, NJ (city) Hudson County	3,099	4.62
Freeport, NY (village) Nassau County	3,094	7.07
South Gate, CA (city) Los Angeles County	3,040	3.15
San Jose, CA (city) Santa Clara County	2,963	0.33
Daly City, CA (city) San Mateo County	2,896	2.79
Las Vegas, NV (city) Clark County	2,832	0.59
Chillum, MD (cdp) Prince George's County	2,778	8.11
Huntington, NY (town) Suffolk County	2,747	1.41
Chelsea, MA (city) Suffolk County	2,711	7.73
Gaithersburg, MD (city) Montgomery County	2,662	5.06
Glendale, CA (city) Los Angeles County	2,564	1.32
Babylon, NY (town) Suffolk County	2,549	1.20
West New York, NJ (town) Hudson County	2,491	5.44
Miami, FL (city) Miami-Dade County	2,482	0.68
New Cassel, NY (cdp) Nassau County	2,322	17.46
Huntington Station, NY (cdp) Suffolk County	2,304	7.70
Huntington Park, CA (city) Los Angeles County	2,258	3.68
Bailey's Crossroads, VA (cdp) Fairfax County	2,243	9.68
Inglewood, CA (city) Los Angeles County	2,091	1.86
Somerville, MA (city) Middlesex County	2,075	2.68
Palmdale, CA (city) Los Angeles County	2,067	1.77
Anaheim, CA (city) Orange County	1,992	0.61
Central Islip, NY (cdp) Suffolk County	1,967	6.16
Oyster Bay, NY (town) Nassau County	1,898	0.65
Charlotte, NC (city) Mecklenburg County	1,891	0.35
Phoenix, AZ (city) Maricopa County	1,856	0.14
Herndon, VA (town) Fairfax County	1,853	8.56
Downey, CA (city) Los Angeles County	1,834	1.71
Lynwood, CA (city) Los Angeles County	1,775	2.54
Garland, TX (city) Dallas County	1,737	0.81
Pomona, CA (city) Los Angeles County	1,688	1.13
Pasadena, CA (city) Los Angeles County	1,686	1.26
Hawthorne, CA (city) Los Angeles County	1,673	1.99
Uniondale, NY (cdp) Nassau County	1,648	7.16
North Bay Shore, NY (cdp) Suffolk County	1,630	10.87
East Los Angeles, CA (cdp) Los Angeles County	1,607	1.29
Brookhaven, NY (town) Suffolk County	1,581	0.35
Newark, NJ (city) Essex County	1,565	0.57
Yonkers, NY (city) Westchester County	1,518	0.77
South San Francisco, CA (city) San Mateo County	1,514	2.50
El Monte, CA (city) Los Angeles County	1,504	1.30
Concord, CA (city) Contra Costa County	1,431	1.18
Jefferson, VA (cdp) Fairfax County	1,428	5.21
Bell, CA (city) Los Angeles County	1,407	3.84
Annandale, VA (cdp) Fairfax County	1,407	2.56
Aspen Hill, MD (cdp) Montgomery County	1,384	2.76
Reno, NV (city) Washoe County	1,351	0.75
Hayward, CA (city) Alameda County	1,349	0.96
Norwalk, CA (city) Los Angeles County	1,346	1.30
Richmond, CA (city) Contra Costa County	1,340	1.35
Florence-Graham, CA (cdp) Los Angeles County	1,335	2.22
Austin, TX (city) Travis County	1,331	0.20
Paradise, NV (cdp) Clark County	1,315	0.71
Fontana, CA (city) San Bernardino County	1,310	1.02
North Bergen, NJ (township) Hudson County	1,273	2.19
Burbank, CA (city) Los Angeles County	1,262	1.26
Plainfield, NJ (city) Union County	1,260	2.63
Reston, VA (cdp) Fairfax County	1,260	2.23
Redwood City, CA (city) San Mateo County	1,260	1.67
Adelphi, MD (cdp) Prince George's County	1,253	8.35
Bakersfield, CA (city) Kern County	1,223	0.50
Baldwin Park, CA (city) Los Angeles County	1,160	1.53
San Mateo, CA (city) San Mateo County	1,156	1.25
Costa Mesa, CA (city) Orange County	1,144	1.05
Mount Vernon, VA (cdp) Fairfax County	1,133	3.96
Glen Cove, NY (city) Nassau County	1,131	4.25
Bell Gardens, CA (city) Los Angeles County	1,124	2.55
Woodbridge, VA (cdp) Prince William County	1,123	3.52
Pasadena, TX (city) Harris County	1,109	0.78
Groveton, VA (cdp) Fairfax County	1,107	5.20
Ontario, CA (city) San Bernardino County	1,104	0.70
Cudahy, CA (city) Los Angeles County	1,081	4.47
San Rafael, CA (city) Marin County	1,072	1.91
Roosevelt, NY (cdp) Nassau County	1,064	6.71
Rockville, MD (city) Montgomery County	1,046	2.21
San Diego, CA (city) San Diego County	1,034	0.08
Compton, CA (city) Los Angeles County	1,024	1.10
Garden Grove, CA (city) Orange County	1,011	0.61
Worcester, MA (city) Worcester County	1,000	0.58
Springfield, VA (cdp) Fairfax County	990	3.25
Manassas, VA (independent city) Manassas city	963	2.74
Seven Corners, VA (cdp) Fairfax County	955	10.98
West Covina, CA (city) Los Angeles County	936	0.89
Westmont, CA (cdp) Los Angeles County	932	2.95
Jersey City, NJ (city) Hudson County	932	0.39
Sunrise Manor, NV (cdp) Clark County	919	0.59
Vallejo, CA (city) Solano County	893	0.76
Everett, MA (city) Middlesex County	888	2.33
Carrollton, TX (city) Denton County	885	0.81
North Las Vegas, NV (city) Clark County	876	0.76
Providence, RI (city) Providence County	871	0.50
Montebello, CA (city) Los Angeles County	864	1.39
Homestead, FL (city) Miami-Dade County	859	2.69
Nashville-Davidson, TN (special city) Davidson County	855	0.16
Aurora, CO (city) Arapahoe County	853	0.31
Raleigh, NC (city) Wake County	837	0.30
Dale City, VA (cdp) Prince William County	836	1.49
Pico Rivera, CA (city) Los Angeles County	824	1.30
Annapolis, MD (city) Anne Arundel County	821	2.29
San Pablo, CA (city) Contra Costa County	820	2.71
Denver, CO (city) Denver County	811	0.15
Fresno, CA (city) Fresno County	799	0.19
La Puente, CA (city) Los Angeles County	790	1.92
Rialto, CA (city) San Bernardino County	781	0.85
Maywood, CA (city) Los Angeles County	768	2.73
Hialeah, FL (city) Miami-Dade County	763	0.34
Riverside, CA (city) Riverside County	763	0.30
Sacramento, CA (city) Sacramento County	762	0.19
Pittsburg, CA (city) Contra Costa County	758	1.34
Hicksville, NY (cdp) Nassau County	756	1.83
Arlington, TX (city) Tarrant County	755	0.23
Lennox, CA (cdp) Los Angeles County	751	3.27
Mendota, CA (city) Fresno County	742	9.40
Lancaster, CA (city) Los Angeles County	742	0.63
Paramount, CA (city) Los Angeles County	725	1.31
Alhambra, CA (city) Los Angeles County	723	0.84
Lincolnia, VA (cdp) Fairfax County	722	4.57
Durham, NC (city) Durham County	717	0.38
San Bernardino, CA (city) San Bernardino County	700	0.38
Farmers Branch, TX (city) Dallas County	692	2.52
Seattle, WA (city) King County	690	0.12
Hyattsville, MD (city) Prince George's County	678	4.60
Springdale, AR (city) Washington County	676	1.48
Bellflower, CA (city) Los Angeles County	674	0.92
Fort Lauderdale, FL (city) Broward County	674	0.44
Inwood, NY (cdp) Nassau County	670	7.18
San Antonio, TX (city) Bexar County	665	0.06

Notes: (cdp) census designated place; Refer to the Explanation of Data in the front of the book for more detailed information.

Hispanic: Salvadoran

Top 150 Places Sorted by Percent

(Based on all places, regardless of population)

Place	Number	%
Langley Park, MD (cdp) Prince George's County	3,483	21.48
New Cassel, NY (cdp) Nassau County	2,322	17.46
Brentwood, NY (cdp) Suffolk County	6,387	11.85
Seven Corners, VA (cdp) Fairfax County	955	10.98
North Bay Shore, NY (cdp) Suffolk County	1,630	10.87
Hempstead, NY (village) Nassau County	5,949	10.52
Bailey's Crossroads, VA (cdp) Fairfax County	2,243	9.68
Mendota, CA (city) Fresno County	742	9.40
Herndon, VA (town) Fairfax County	1,853	8.56
Adelphi, MD (cdp) Prince George's County	1,253	8.35
Chillum, MD (cdp) Prince George's County	2,778	8.11
Chelsea, MA (city) Suffolk County	2,711	7.73
Huntington Station, NY (cdp) Suffolk County	2,304	7.70
West Gate, VA (cdp) Prince William County	568	7.58
Grand Pass, MO (village) Saline County	4	7.55
Inwood, NY (cdp) Nassau County	670	7.18
Uniondale, NY (cdp) Nassau County	1,648	7.16
Freeport, NY (village) Nassau County	3,094	7.07
Roosevelt, NY (cdp) Nassau County	1,064	6.71
Brentwood, MD (town) Prince George's County	190	6.68
Niotaze, KS (city) Chautauqua County	8	6.56
Wheaton-Glenmont, MD (cdp) Montgomery County	3,770	6.53
Silver Spring, MD (cdp) Montgomery County	4,764	6.22
Central Islip, NY (cdp) Suffolk County	1,967	6.16
Danville, AR (city) Yell County	141	5.89
Colma, CA (town) San Mateo County	67	5.63
West New York, NJ (town) Hudson County	2,491	5.44
Jefferson, VA (cdp) Fairfax County	1,428	5.21
Groveton, VA (cdp) Fairfax County	1,107	5.20
Gaithersburg, MD (city) Montgomery County	2,662	5.06
El Jebel, CO (cdp) Eagle County	218	4.86
Locust Valley, NY (cdp) Nassau County	171	4.86
Union City, NJ (city) Hudson County	3,099	4.62
Hyattsville, MD (city) Prince George's County	678	4.60
Lincolnia, VA (cdp) Fairfax County	722	4.57
Ola, AR (city) Yell County	55	4.57
Bayview-Montalvin, CA (cdp) Contra Costa County	227	4.54
Cudahy, CA (city) Los Angeles County	1,081	4.47
Westbury, NY (village) Nassau County	621	4.35
Glen Cove, NY (city) Nassau County	1,131	4.25
Loch Lomond, VA (cdp) Prince William County	145	4.25
Wyandanch, NY (cdp) Suffolk County	445	4.22
Webster, TX (city) Harris County	381	4.19
Mount Rainier, MD (city) Prince George's County	352	4.14
Arlington, VA (cdp) Arlington County	7,630	4.03
Piermont, NY (village) Rockland County	105	4.03
Pimmit Hills, VA (cdp) Fairfax County	244	3.97
Mount Vernon, VA (cdp) Fairfax County	1,133	3.96
Edmonston, MD (town) Prince George's County	37	3.86
Bell, CA (city) Los Angeles County	1,407	3.84
Hybla Valley, VA (cdp) Fairfax County	636	3.80
Walnut Park, CA (cdp) Los Angeles County	608	3.76
Mecca, CA (cdp) Riverside County	203	3.76
Huntington Park, CA (city) Los Angeles County	2,258	3.68
Redland, MD (cdp) Montgomery County	621	3.65
Huntington, VA (cdp) Fairfax County	301	3.62
North Brentwood, MD (town) Prince George's County	17	3.62
Colmar Manor, MD (town) Prince George's County	45	3.58
Woodbridge, VA (cdp) Prince William County	1,123	3.52
Monon, IN (town) White County	61	3.52
Bull Run, VA (cdp) Prince William County	398	3.51
Alexandria, VA (independent city) Alexandria city	4,477	3.49
Baxter Estates, NY (village) Nassau County	35	3.48
Octavia, NE (village) Butler County	5	3.45
Fairview, NJ (borough) Bergen County	456	3.44
Idylwood, VA (cdp) Fairfax County	549	3.43
Los Angeles, CA (city) Los Angeles County	126,197	3.42
Islip, NY (town) Suffolk County	11,046	3.42
Cottage City, MD (town) Prince George's County	38	3.35
Forest Glen, MD (cdp) Montgomery County	244	3.32
Manorhaven, NY (village) Nassau County	203	3.31
Rollingwood, CA (cdp) Contra Costa County	95	3.28
Lennox, CA (cdp) Los Angeles County	751	3.27
Springfield, VA (cdp) Fairfax County	990	3.25
Takoma Park, MD (city) Montgomery County	561	3.24
Manassas Park, VA (independent city) Manassas Park city	329	3.20
Desert View Highlands, CA (cdp) Los Angeles County	74	3.17
South Gate, CA (city) Los Angeles County	3,040	3.15
North Amityville, NY (cdp) Suffolk County	515	3.11
Clewiston, FL (city) Hendry County	200	3.10
Perry, IA (city) Dallas County	232	3.04
Glenwood, AR (city) Pike County	53	3.03
Kemp Mill, MD (cdp) Montgomery County	301	3.02
Baywood, NY (cdp) Suffolk County	229	3.02
Yorkshire, VA (cdp) Prince William County	203	3.02
Westmont, CA (cdp) Los Angeles County	932	2.95
Dunn Loring, VA (cdp) Fairfax County	232	2.95
Guttenberg, NJ (town) Hudson County	318	2.94
Elizabeth, NJ (city) Union County	3,518	2.92
Kodiak, AK (city) Kodiak Island Borough	182	2.87
Bensley, VA (cdp) Chesterfield County	155	2.85
Hillandale, MD (cdp) Montgomery County	87	2.85
East Farmingdale, NY (cdp) Suffolk County	153	2.83
Daly City, CA (city) San Mateo County	2,896	2.79
Mineola, NY (village) Nassau County	532	2.77
Aspen Hill, MD (cdp) Montgomery County	1,384	2.76
Fairfax, VA (independent city) Fairfax city	594	2.76
Farmingdale, NY (village) Nassau County	232	2.76
Manassas, VA (independent city) Manassas city	963	2.74
Maywood, CA (city) Los Angeles County	768	2.73
San Pablo, CA (city) Contra Costa County	820	2.71
Homestead, FL (city) Miami-Dade County	859	2.69
Somerville, MA (city) Middlesex County	2,075	2.68
Irving, TX (city) Dallas County	5,102	2.66
Copiague, NY (cdp) Suffolk County	581	2.65
Chamblee, GA (city) De Kalb County	253	2.65
Plainfield, NJ (city) Union County	1,260	2.63
North Fair Oaks, CA (cdp) San Mateo County	406	2.63
Siler City, NC (town) Chatham County	181	2.60
Annandale, VA (cdp) Fairfax County	1,407	2.56
Bell Gardens, CA (city) Los Angeles County	1,124	2.55
Mobile City, TX (city) Rockwall County	5	2.55
Lynwood, CA (city) Los Angeles County	1,775	2.54
Farmers Branch, TX (city) Dallas County	692	2.52
South San Francisco, CA (city) San Mateo County	1,514	2.50
East Riverdale, MD (cdp) Prince George's County	374	2.50
Dardanelle, AR (city) Yell County	104	2.46
Buttonwillow, CA (cdp) Kern County	31	2.45
North Kensington, MD (cdp) Montgomery County	215	2.40
Patchogue, NY (village) Suffolk County	285	2.39
Huntingburg, IN (city) Dubois County	134	2.39
White Oak, MD (cdp) Montgomery County	493	2.35
Everett, MA (city) Middlesex County	888	2.33
North Plainfield, NJ (borough) Somerset County	488	2.31
Goodell, IA (city) Hancock County	4	2.30
Annapolis, MD (city) Anne Arundel County	821	2.29
Thomaston, NY (village) Nassau County	59	2.26
North Hempstead, NY (town) Nassau County	4,993	2.24
Reston, VA (cdp) Fairfax County	1,260	2.23
Florence-Graham, CA (cdp) Los Angeles County	1,335	2.22
Rockville, MD (city) Montgomery County	1,046	2.21
Dumfries, VA (town) Prince William County	109	2.21
North Bergen, NJ (township) Hudson County	1,273	2.19
East Palo Alto, CA (city) San Mateo County	643	2.18
Merrifield, VA (cdp) Fairfax County	244	2.18
Broadmoor, CA (cdp) San Mateo County	86	2.14
Medo, MN (township) Blue Earth County	8	2.14
Conesville, IA (city) Muscatine County	9	2.12
South San Jose Hills, CA (cdp) Los Angeles County	424	2.10
Rose Hill, VA (cdp) Fairfax County	316	2.10
North Bellport, NY (cdp) Suffolk County	189	2.10
South Hempstead, NY (cdp) Nassau County	67	2.10
Hempstead, NY (town) Nassau County	15,659	2.07
Orange Cove, CA (city) Fresno County	159	2.06
Keystone, CO (cdp) Summit County	17	2.06
Washington, DC (city) District of Columbia	11,741	2.05
Lake Barcroft, VA (cdp) Fairfax County	183	2.05
Port Washington, NY (cdp) Nassau County	310	2.04
Cliffside Park, NJ (borough) Bergen County	467	2.03
Port Chester, NY (village) Westchester County	558	2.00

Notes: (cdp) census designated place; Refer to the Explanation of Data in the front of the book for more detailed information.

Hispanic: Salvadoran

Top 150 Places Sorted by Percent

(Based on places with populations of 10,000 or more)

Place	Number	%
Langley Park, MD (cdp) Prince George's County	3,483	21.48
New Cassel, NY (cdp) Nassau County	2,322	17.46
Brentwood, NY (cdp) Suffolk County	6,387	11.85
North Bay Shore, NY (cdp) Suffolk County	1,630	10.87
Hempstead, NY (village) Nassau County	5,949	10.52
Bailey's Crossroads, VA (cdp) Fairfax County	2,243	9.68
Herndon, VA (town) Fairfax County	1,853	8.56
Adelphi, MD (cdp) Prince George's County	1,253	8.35
Chillum, MD (cdp) Prince George's County	2,778	8.11
Chelsea, MA (city) Suffolk County	2,711	7.73
Huntington Station, NY (cdp) Suffolk County	2,304	7.70
Uniondale, NY (cdp) Nassau County	1,648	7.16
Freeport, NY (village) Nassau County	3,094	7.07
Roosevelt, NY (cdp) Nassau County	1,064	6.71
Wheaton-Glenmont, MD (cdp) Montgomery County	3,770	6.53
Silver Spring, MD (cdp) Montgomery County	4,764	6.22
Central Islip, NY (cdp) Suffolk County	1,967	6.16
West New York, NJ (town) Hudson County	2,491	5.44
Jefferson, VA (cdp) Fairfax County	1,428	5.21
Groveton, VA (cdp) Fairfax County	1,107	5.20
Gaithersburg, MD (city) Montgomery County	2,662	5.06
Union City, NJ (city) Hudson County	3,099	4.62
Hyattsville, MD (city) Prince George's County	678	4.60
Lincolnia, VA (cdp) Fairfax County	722	4.57
Cudahy, CA (city) Los Angeles County	1,081	4.47
Westbury, NY (village) Nassau County	621	4.35
Glen Cove, NY (city) Nassau County	1,131	4.25
Wyandanch, NY (cdp) Suffolk County	445	4.22
Arlington, VA (cdp) Arlington County	7,630	4.03
Mount Vernon, VA (cdp) Fairfax County	1,133	3.96
Bell, CA (city) Los Angeles County	1,407	3.84
Hybla Valley, VA (cdp) Fairfax County	636	3.80
Walnut Park, CA (cdp) Los Angeles County	608	3.76
Huntington Park, CA (city) Los Angeles County	2,258	3.68
Redland, MD (cdp) Montgomery County	621	3.65
Woodbridge, VA (cdp) Prince William County	1,123	3.52
Bull Run, VA (cdp) Prince William County	398	3.51
Alexandria, VA (independent city) Alexandria city	4,477	3.49
Fairview, NJ (borough) Bergen County	456	3.44
Idylwood, VA (cdp) Fairfax County	549	3.43
Los Angeles, CA (city) Los Angeles County	126,197	3.42
Islip, NY (town) Suffolk County	11,046	3.42
Lennox, CA (cdp) Los Angeles County	751	3.27
Springfield, VA (cdp) Fairfax County	990	3.25
Takoma Park, MD (city) Montgomery County	561	3.24
Manassas Park, VA (independent city) Manassas Park city	329	3.20
South Gate, CA (city) Los Angeles County	3,040	3.15
North Amityville, NY (cdp) Suffolk County	515	3.11
Westmont, CA (cdp) Los Angeles County	932	2.95
Guttenberg, NJ (town) Hudson County	318	2.94
Elizabeth, NJ (city) Union County	3,518	2.92
Daly City, CA (city) San Mateo County	2,896	2.79
Mineola, NY (village) Nassau County	532	2.77
Aspen Hill, MD (cdp) Montgomery County	1,384	2.76
Fairfax, VA (independent city) Fairfax city	594	2.76
Manassas, VA (independent city) Manassas city	963	2.74
Maywood, CA (city) Los Angeles County	768	2.73
San Pablo, CA (city) Contra Costa County	820	2.71
Homestead, FL (city) Miami-Dade County	859	2.69
Somerville, MA (city) Middlesex County	2,075	2.68
Irving, TX (city) Dallas County	5,102	2.66
Copiague, NY (cdp) Suffolk County	581	2.65
Plainfield, NJ (city) Union County	1,260	2.63
North Fair Oaks, CA (cdp) San Mateo County	406	2.63
Annandale, VA (cdp) Fairfax County	1,407	2.56
Bell Gardens, CA (city) Los Angeles County	1,124	2.55
Lynwood, CA (city) Los Angeles County	1,775	2.54
Farmers Branch, TX (city) Dallas County	692	2.52
South San Francisco, CA (city) San Mateo County	1,514	2.50
East Riverdale, MD (cdp) Prince George's County	374	2.50
Patchogue, NY (village) Suffolk County	285	2.39
White Oak, MD (cdp) Montgomery County	493	2.35
Everett, MA (city) Middlesex County	888	2.33
North Plainfield, NJ (borough) Somerset County	488	2.31
Annapolis, MD (city) Anne Arundel County	821	2.29
North Hempstead, NY (town) Nassau County	4,993	2.24
Reston, VA (cdp) Fairfax County	1,260	2.23
Florence-Graham, CA (cdp) Los Angeles County	1,335	2.22
Rockville, MD (city) Montgomery County	1,046	2.21
North Bergen, NJ (township) Hudson County	1,273	2.19
East Palo Alto, CA (city) San Mateo County	643	2.18
Merrifield, VA (cdp) Fairfax County	244	2.18
South San Jose Hills, CA (cdp) Los Angeles County	424	2.10
Rose Hill, VA (cdp) Fairfax County	316	2.10
Hempstead, NY (town) Nassau County	15,659	2.07
Washington, DC (city) District of Columbia	11,741	2.05
Port Washington, NY (cdp) Nassau County	310	2.04
Cliffside Park, NJ (borough) Bergen County	467	2.03
Port Chester, NY (village) Westchester County	558	2.00
Hawthorne, CA (city) Los Angeles County	1,673	1.99
La Puente, CA (city) Los Angeles County	790	1.92
San Rafael, CA (city) Marin County	1,072	1.91
Marshall, MO (city) Saline County	237	1.91
Houston, TX (city) Harris County	36,799	1.88
Inglewood, CA (city) Los Angeles County	2,091	1.86
Hicksville, NY (cdp) Nassau County	756	1.83
Bay Point, CA (cdp) Contra Costa County	390	1.81
Siloam Springs, AR (city) Benton County	196	1.81
Seaside, CA (city) Monterey County	566	1.79
Palmdale, CA (city) Los Angeles County	2,067	1.77
Bay Shore, NY (cdp) Suffolk County	420	1.76
Downey, CA (city) Los Angeles County	1,834	1.71
Rogers, AR (city) Benton County	661	1.70
Redwood City, CA (city) San Mateo County	1,260	1.67
Commerce, CA (city) Los Angeles County	210	1.67
Lawndale, CA (city) Los Angeles County	527	1.66
Beltsville, MD (cdp) Prince George's County	259	1.65
Oakton, VA (cdp) Fairfax County	473	1.61
South Houston, TX (city) Harris County	255	1.61
San Bruno, CA (city) San Mateo County	639	1.59
Mission Bend, TX (cdp) Fort Bend County	489	1.59
Valinda, CA (cdp) Los Angeles County	345	1.58
Lexington, NE (city) Dawson County	157	1.57
Montgomery Village, MD (cdp) Montgomery County	592	1.56
West Hempstead, NY (cdp) Nassau County	291	1.56
Aldine, TX (cdp) Harris County	218	1.56
Baldwin Park, CA (city) Los Angeles County	1,160	1.53
Dale City, VA (cdp) Prince William County	836	1.49
Springdale, AR (city) Washington County	676	1.48
Addison, TX (town) Dallas County	208	1.47
Vienna, VA (town) Fairfax County	209	1.45
Richmond, TX (city) Fort Bend County	160	1.44
Rye, NY (town) Westchester County	622	1.42
Sanford, NC (city) Lee County	329	1.42
Huntington, NY (town) Suffolk County	2,747	1.41
Rosenberg, TX (city) Fort Bend County	338	1.41
Montebello, CA (city) Los Angeles County	864	1.39
San Francisco, CA (city) San Francisco County	10,655	1.37
Oakland Park, FL (city) Broward County	425	1.37
Falls Church, VA (independent city) Falls Church city	142	1.37
Van Buren, AR (city) Crawford County	259	1.36
Richmond, CA (city) Contra Costa County	1,340	1.35
Pittsburg, CA (city) Contra Costa County	758	1.34
West Puente Valley, CA (cdp) Los Angeles County	302	1.34
Glendale, CA (city) Los Angeles County	2,564	1.32
Paramount, CA (city) Los Angeles County	725	1.31
Leesburg, VA (town) Loudoun County	371	1.31
Lorton, VA (cdp) Fairfax County	233	1.31
El Monte, CA (city) Los Angeles County	1,504	1.30
Norwalk, CA (city) Los Angeles County	1,346	1.30
Pico Rivera, CA (city) Los Angeles County	824	1.30
Willowbrook, CA (cdp) Los Angeles County	444	1.30
Weehawken, NJ (township) Hudson County	176	1.30
East Los Angeles, CA (cdp) Los Angeles County	1,607	1.29
Leisure City, FL (cdp) Miami-Dade County	286	1.29
Bound Brook, NJ (borough) Somerset County	131	1.29
Emporia, KS (city) Lyon County	343	1.28
San Fernando, CA (city) Los Angeles County	301	1.28
Pasadena, CA (city) Los Angeles County	1,686	1.26
Burbank, CA (city) Los Angeles County	1,262	1.26

Notes: (cdp) census designated place; Refer to the Explanation of Data in the front of the book for more detailed information.

Hispanic: Other Central American

Top 150 Places Sorted by Number

(Based on all places, regardless of population)

Place	Number	%
Los Angeles, CA (city) Los Angeles County	21,710	0.59
New York, NY (city) New York City	5,534	0.07
Houston, TX (city) Harris County	2,784	0.14
San Francisco, CA (city) San Francisco County	2,536	0.33
Chicago, IL (city) Cook County	1,188	0.04
Miami, FL (city) Miami-Dade County	1,108	0.31
Hempstead, NY (town) Nassau County	1,021	0.14
Santa Ana, CA (city) Orange County	891	0.26
Long Beach, CA (city) Los Angeles County	825	0.18
Daly City, CA (city) San Mateo County	745	0.72
San Jose, CA (city) Santa Clara County	697	0.08
Oakland, CA (city) Alameda County	673	0.17
Washington, DC (city) District of Columbia	661	0.12
Dallas, TX (city) Dallas County	659	0.06
Islip, NY (town) Suffolk County	657	0.20
South Gate, CA (city) Los Angeles County	650	0.67
Boston, MA (city) Suffolk County	612	0.10
Arlington, VA (cdp) Arlington County	545	0.29
Glendale, CA (city) Los Angeles County	512	0.26
Inglewood, CA (city) Los Angeles County	488	0.43
Phoenix, AZ (city) Maricopa County	488	0.04
Anaheim, CA (city) Orange County	473	0.14
Huntington Park, CA (city) Los Angeles County	436	0.71
Hawthorne, CA (city) Los Angeles County	431	0.51
Pomona, CA (city) Los Angeles County	426	0.29
Hialeah, FL (city) Miami-Dade County	426	0.19
San Diego, CA (city) San Diego County	421	0.03
Pasadena, CA (city) Los Angeles County	410	0.31
Alexandria, VA (independent city) Alexandria city	402	0.31
Fontana, CA (city) San Bernardino County	382	0.30
Downey, CA (city) Los Angeles County	362	0.34
West New York, NJ (town) Hudson County	351	0.77
Brentwood, NY (cdp) Suffolk County	337	0.63
Ontario, CA (city) San Bernardino County	335	0.21
Jersey City, NJ (city) Hudson County	333	0.14
East Los Angeles, CA (cdp) Los Angeles County	329	0.26
Hempstead, NY (village) Nassau County	324	0.57
Elizabeth, NJ (city) Union County	320	0.27
South San Francisco, CA (city) San Mateo County	315	0.52
Palmdale, CA (city) Los Angeles County	311	0.27
Chelsea, MA (city) Suffolk County	308	0.88
Las Vegas, NV (city) Clark County	305	0.06
Silver Spring, MD (cdp) Montgomery County	293	0.38
Lynwood, CA (city) Los Angeles County	291	0.42
El Monte, CA (city) Los Angeles County	281	0.24
Hayward, CA (city) Alameda County	281	0.20
Burbank, CA (city) Los Angeles County	275	0.27
Bell Gardens, CA (city) Los Angeles County	268	0.61
San Mateo, CA (city) San Mateo County	259	0.28
Richmond, CA (city) Contra Costa County	256	0.26
Baldwin Park, CA (city) Los Angeles County	254	0.33
North Hempstead, NY (town) Nassau County	252	0.11
Norwalk, CA (city) Los Angeles County	249	0.24
Florence-Graham, CA (cdp) Los Angeles County	248	0.41
Union City, NJ (city) Hudson County	242	0.36
Bell, CA (city) Los Angeles County	240	0.65
Wheaton-Glenmont, MD (cdp) Montgomery County	237	0.41
Redwood City, CA (city) San Mateo County	231	0.31
Cudahy, CA (city) Los Angeles County	225	0.93
Alhambra, CA (city) Los Angeles County	224	0.26
New Orleans, LA (city) Orleans Parish	213	0.04
Austin, TX (city) Travis County	211	0.03
San Antonio, TX (city) Bexar County	211	0.02
Garden Grove, CA (city) Orange County	210	0.13
Charlotte, NC (city) Mecklenburg County	208	0.04
Irving, TX (city) Dallas County	207	0.11
Rialto, CA (city) San Bernardino County	201	0.22
Concord, CA (city) Contra Costa County	200	0.16
West Covina, CA (city) Los Angeles County	198	0.19
Norwalk, CT (city) Fairfield County	194	0.23
Metairie, LA (cdp) Jefferson Parish	194	0.13
Montebello, CA (city) Los Angeles County	191	0.31
San Bernardino, CA (city) San Bernardino County	189	0.10
Compton, CA (city) Los Angeles County	188	0.20
Trenton, NJ (city) Mercer County	185	0.22
Plainfield, NJ (city) Union County	183	0.38
Kenner, LA (city) Jefferson Parish	183	0.26
Freeport, NY (village) Nassau County	180	0.41
Providence, RI (city) Providence County	179	0.10
Newark, NJ (city) Essex County	179	0.07
Riverside, CA (city) Riverside County	177	0.07
Central Islip, NY (cdp) Suffolk County	176	0.55
Westmont, CA (cdp) Los Angeles County	169	0.53
North Bergen, NJ (township) Hudson County	169	0.29
Whittier, CA (city) Los Angeles County	169	0.20
Garland, TX (city) Dallas County	168	0.08
Nashville-Davidson, TN (special city) Davidson County	168	0.03
San Bruno, CA (city) San Mateo County	167	0.42
Pico Rivera, CA (city) Los Angeles County	166	0.26
Orange, CA (city) Orange County	166	0.13
Moreno Valley, CA (city) Riverside County	166	0.12
Lennox, CA (cdp) Los Angeles County	165	0.72
Chillum, MD (cdp) Prince George's County	165	0.48
Gaithersburg, MD (city) Montgomery County	164	0.31
Bailey's Crossroads, VA (cdp) Fairfax County	163	0.70
Costa Mesa, CA (city) Orange County	162	0.15
Aspen Hill, MD (cdp) Montgomery County	160	0.32
Denver, CO (city) Denver County	157	0.03
Herndon, VA (town) Fairfax County	156	0.72
Antioch, CA (city) Contra Costa County	156	0.17
Rancho Cucamonga, CA (city) San Bernardino County	156	0.12
Sacramento, CA (city) Sacramento County	155	0.04
Somerville, MA (city) Middlesex County	154	0.20
Fresno, CA (city) Fresno County	154	0.04
Maywood, CA (city) Los Angeles County	152	0.54
Paradise, NV (cdp) Clark County	152	0.08
Annandale, VA (cdp) Fairfax County	151	0.27
Lawndale, CA (city) Los Angeles County	150	0.47
Santa Clarita, CA (city) Los Angeles County	150	0.10
Lancaster, CA (city) Los Angeles County	148	0.12
New Brunswick, NJ (city) Middlesex County	147	0.30
La Puente, CA (city) Los Angeles County	146	0.36
Paramount, CA (city) Los Angeles County	146	0.26
Vallejo, CA (city) Solano County	144	0.12
Fountainbleau, FL (cdp) Miami-Dade County	143	0.24
Springfield, VA (cdp) Fairfax County	142	0.47
San Rafael, CA (city) Marin County	142	0.25
Reno, NV (city) Washoe County	139	0.08
Uniondale, NY (cdp) Nassau County	136	0.59
Yonkers, NY (city) Westchester County	136	0.07
Huntington, NY (town) Suffolk County	134	0.07
Seattle, WA (city) King County	132	0.02
Mount Vernon, VA (cdp) Fairfax County	131	0.46
Brookhaven, NY (town) Suffolk County	131	0.03
Gardena, CA (city) Los Angeles County	127	0.22
Langley Park, MD (cdp) Prince George's County	126	0.78
Pittsburg, CA (city) Contra Costa County	125	0.22
Bellflower, CA (city) Los Angeles County	123	0.17
Waukegan, IL (city) Lake County	123	0.14
Fremont, CA (city) Alameda County	123	0.06
San Pablo, CA (city) Contra Costa County	121	0.40
Raleigh, NC (city) Wake County	121	0.04
Oyster Bay, NY (town) Nassau County	119	0.04
Paterson, NJ (city) Passaic County	116	0.08
South Whittier, CA (cdp) Los Angeles County	114	0.21
Stamford, CT (city) Fairfield County	113	0.10
Bakersfield, CA (city) Kern County	111	0.04
Oxnard, CA (city) Ventura County	110	0.06
Sunnyvale, CA (city) Santa Clara County	109	0.08
Walnut Park, CA (cdp) Los Angeles County	107	0.66
Modesto, CA (city) Stanislaus County	107	0.06
Woodbridge, VA (cdp) Prince William County	104	0.33
Philadelphia, PA (city) Philadelphia County	102	0.01
Pasadena, TX (city) Harris County	101	0.07
Tustin, CA (city) Orange County	99	0.15
Babylon, NY (town) Suffolk County	99	0.05
Azusa, CA (city) Los Angeles County	98	0.22
Corona, CA (city) Riverside County	98	0.08
Altadena, CA (cdp) Los Angeles County	96	0.23
Rosemead, CA (city) Los Angeles County	96	0.18

Notes: (cdp) census designated place; Refer to the Explanation of Data in the front of the book for more detailed information.

Hispanic: Other Central American

Top 150 Places Sorted by Percent

(Based on all places, regardless of population)

Place	Number	%
Los Angeles Subdivision, TX (cdp) Willacy County	2	2.33
Colma, CA (town) San Mateo County	15	1.26
Rollingwood, CA (cdp) Contra Costa County	36	1.24
Delway, NC (cdp) Sampson County	3	1.11
Valley Ranch, CA (cdp) Plumas County	1	1.09
Bayview-Montalvin, CA (cdp) Contra Costa County	52	1.04
Cudahy, CA (city) Los Angeles County	225	0.93
Chelsea, MA (city) Suffolk County	308	0.88
Francis, UT (town) Summit County	6	0.86
Faison, NC (town) Duplin County	6	0.81
Langley Park, MD (cdp) Prince George's County	126	0.78
West New York, NJ (town) Hudson County	351	0.77
Del Mar Heights, TX (cdp) Cameron County	2	0.77
Mendota, CA (city) Fresno County	58	0.74
Greenport, NY (village) Suffolk County	15	0.73
Daly City, CA (city) San Mateo County	745	0.72
Lennox, CA (cdp) Los Angeles County	165	0.72
Herndon, VA (town) Fairfax County	156	0.72
Chandler, MN (city) Murray County	2	0.72
Huntington Park, CA (city) Los Angeles County	436	0.71
Bailey's Crossroads, VA (cdp) Fairfax County	163	0.70
South Gate, CA (city) Los Angeles County	650	0.67
Walnut Park, CA (cdp) Los Angeles County	107	0.66
Bell, CA (city) Los Angeles County	240	0.65
Seven Corners, VA (cdp) Fairfax County	56	0.64
Colmar Manor, MD (town) Prince George's County	8	0.64
Brentwood, NY (cdp) Suffolk County	337	0.63
Metolius, OR (city) Jefferson County	4	0.63
Weston, VT (town) Windsor County	4	0.63
Wade, NC (town) Cumberland County	3	0.63
Bell Gardens, CA (city) Los Angeles County	268	0.61
Prestonville, KY (city) Carroll County	1	0.61
Broadmoor, CA (cdp) San Mateo County	24	0.60
Los Angeles, CA (city) Los Angeles County	21,710	0.59
Uniondale, NY (cdp) Nassau County	136	0.59
West Athens, CA (cdp) Los Angeles County	53	0.58
Green Valley, MN (township) Becker County	2	0.58
Godfrey Road, FL (cdp) Broward County	4	0.58
Hempstead, NY (village) Nassau County	324	0.57
Inwood, NY (cdp) Nassau County	53	0.57
North Bay Shore, NY (cdp) Suffolk County	84	0.56
Village Park, FL (cdp) Broward County	5	0.56
Central Islip, NY (cdp) Suffolk County	176	0.55
North Fair Oaks, CA (cdp) San Mateo County	85	0.55
Maywood, CA (city) Los Angeles County	152	0.54
Merrifield, VA (cdp) Fairfax County	60	0.54
Manorhaven, NY (village) Nassau County	33	0.54
Westmont, CA (cdp) Los Angeles County	169	0.53
Broadview Park, FL (cdp) Broward County	36	0.53
South San Francisco, CA (city) San Mateo County	315	0.52
Hawthorne, CA (city) Los Angeles County	431	0.51
Chaumont, NY (village) Jefferson County	3	0.51
Baxter Estates, NY (village) Nassau County	5	0.50
South Fork, CO (town) Rio Grande County	3	0.50
Copper Canyon, TX (town) Denton County	6	0.49
Woolstock, IA (city) Wright County	1	0.49
Chillum, MD (cdp) Prince George's County	165	0.48
Sweetwater, FL (city) Miami-Dade County	68	0.48
Millington, MD (town) Kent County	2	0.48
Lawndale, CA (city) Los Angeles County	150	0.47
Springfield, VA (cdp) Fairfax County	142	0.47
Santa Maria, TX (cdp) Cameron County	4	0.47
Mount Vernon, VA (cdp) Fairfax County	131	0.46
Citrus, CA (cdp) Los Angeles County	48	0.45
Homestead Base, FL (cdp) Miami-Dade County	2	0.45
Miami Gardens, FL (cdp) Broward County	12	0.44
Belle Glade Camp, FL (cdp) Palm Beach County	5	0.44
Byron, CA (cdp) Contra Costa County	4	0.44
Elk Park, NC (town) Avery County	2	0.44
Inglewood, CA (city) Los Angeles County	488	0.43
Del Aire, CA (cdp) Los Angeles County	39	0.43
Yorkshire, VA (cdp) Prince William County	29	0.43
Tara Hills, CA (cdp) Contra Costa County	23	0.43
Halesite, NY (cdp) Suffolk County	11	0.43
Lynwood, CA (city) Los Angeles County	291	0.42
San Bruno, CA (city) San Mateo County	167	0.42
Groveton, VA (cdp) Fairfax County	89	0.42
Brentwood, MD (town) Prince George's County	12	0.42
Bellerose Terrace, NY (cdp) Nassau County	9	0.42
East Ellijay, GA (city) Gilmer County	3	0.42
Florence-Graham, CA (cdp) Los Angeles County	248	0.41
Wheaton-Glenmont, MD (cdp) Montgomery County	237	0.41
Freeport, NY (village) Nassau County	180	0.41
Indiantown, FL (cdp) Martin County	23	0.41
Val Verde, CA (cdp) Los Angeles County	6	0.41
San Pablo, CA (city) Contra Costa County	121	0.40
Lincolnia, VA (cdp) Fairfax County	63	0.40
Laguna Heights, TX (cdp) Cameron County	8	0.40
Bay Point, CA (cdp) Contra Costa County	83	0.39
Mangonia Park, FL (town) Palm Beach County	5	0.39
Whitestown, WI (town) Vernon County	2	0.39
Silver Spring, MD (cdp) Montgomery County	293	0.38
Plainfield, NJ (city) Union County	183	0.38
Morristown, NJ (town) Morris County	70	0.38
Vincent, CA (cdp) Los Angeles County	58	0.38
Loch Lomond, VA (cdp) Prince William County	13	0.38
Idylwood, VA (cdp) Fairfax County	59	0.37
Guttenberg, NJ (town) Hudson County	40	0.37
Chamblee, GA (city) De Kalb County	35	0.37
Loch Lomond, FL (cdp) Broward County	13	0.37
Union City, NJ (city) Hudson County	242	0.36
La Puente, CA (city) Los Angeles County	146	0.36
Commerce, CA (city) Los Angeles County	45	0.36
Mountain View, CA (cdp) Contra Costa County	9	0.36
Boger City, NC (cdp) Lincoln County	2	0.36
Elberta, AL (town) Baldwin County	2	0.36
Webster, TX (city) Harris County	32	0.35
Chula Vista, FL (cdp) Broward County	2	0.35
Downey, CA (city) Los Angeles County	362	0.34
Valinda, CA (cdp) Los Angeles County	73	0.34
Manassas Park, VA (independent city) Manassas Park city	35	0.34
Schuyler, NE (city) Colfax County	18	0.34
Glenwood Landing, NY (cdp) Nassau County	12	0.34
Eastport, NY (cdp) Suffolk County	5	0.34
Arrowsmith, IL (village) McLean County	1	0.34
San Francisco, CA (city) San Francisco County	2,536	0.33
Baldwin Park, CA (city) Los Angeles County	254	0.33
Woodbridge, VA (cdp) Prince William County	104	0.33
Adelphi, MD (cdp) Prince George's County	50	0.33
Cherryland, CA (cdp) Alameda County	46	0.33
Dorchester, NE (village) Saline County	2	0.33
Aspen Hill, MD (cdp) Montgomery County	160	0.32
Gladeview, FL (cdp) Miami-Dade County	47	0.32
New Cassel, NY (cdp) Nassau County	43	0.32
Mountain View Acres, CA (cdp) San Bernardino County	8	0.32
Dolan Springs, AZ (cdp) Mohave County	6	0.32
Miami, FL (city) Miami-Dade County	1,108	0.31
Pasadena, CA (city) Los Angeles County	410	0.31
Alexandria, VA (independent city) Alexandria city	402	0.31
Redwood City, CA (city) San Mateo County	231	0.31
Montebello, CA (city) Los Angeles County	191	0.31
Gaithersburg, MD (city) Montgomery County	164	0.31
North Plainfield, NJ (borough) Somerset County	65	0.31
Cheverly, MD (town) Prince George's County	20	0.31
Hatfield, MA (town) Hampshire County	10	0.31
Piermont, NY (village) Rockland County	8	0.31
Pixley, CA (cdp) Tulare County	8	0.31
South Hackensack, NJ (township) Bergen County	7	0.31
Lakeview, CA (cdp) Riverside County	5	0.31
Saucier, MS (cdp) Harrison County	4	0.31
Fontana, CA (city) San Bernardino County	382	0.30
New Brunswick, NJ (city) Middlesex County	147	0.30
Jefferson, VA (cdp) Fairfax County	82	0.30
Hyattsville, MD (city) Prince George's County	44	0.30
North Kensington, MD (cdp) Montgomery County	27	0.30
Basye-Bryce Mountain, VA (cdp) Shenandoah County	3	0.30
Carroll, NH (town) Coos County	2	0.30
Arlington, VA (cdp) Arlington County	545	0.29
Pomona, CA (city) Los Angeles County	426	0.29
North Bergen, NJ (township) Hudson County	169	0.29

Notes: (cdp) census designated place; Refer to the Explanation of Data in the front of the book for more detailed information.

Hispanic: Other Central American

Top 150 Places Sorted by Percent

(Based on places with populations of 10,000 or more)

Place	Number	%
Cudahy, CA (city) Los Angeles County	225	0.93
Chelsea, MA (city) Suffolk County	308	0.88
Langley Park, MD (cdp) Prince George's County	126	0.78
West New York, NJ (town) Hudson County	351	0.77
Daly City, CA (city) San Mateo County	745	0.72
Lennox, CA (cdp) Los Angeles County	165	0.72
Herndon, VA (town) Fairfax County	156	0.72
Huntington Park, CA (city) Los Angeles County	436	0.71
Bailey's Crossroads, VA (cdp) Fairfax County	163	0.70
South Gate, CA (city) Los Angeles County	650	0.67
Walnut Park, CA (cdp) Los Angeles County	107	0.66
Bell, CA (city) Los Angeles County	240	0.65
Brentwood, NY (cdp) Suffolk County	337	0.63
Bell Gardens, CA (city) Los Angeles County	268	0.61
Los Angeles, CA (city) Los Angeles County	21,710	0.59
Uniondale, NY (cdp) Nassau County	136	0.59
Hempstead, NY (village) Nassau County	324	0.57
North Bay Shore, NY (cdp) Suffolk County	84	0.56
Central Islip, NY (cdp) Suffolk County	176	0.55
North Fair Oaks, CA (cdp) San Mateo County	85	0.55
Maywood, CA (city) Los Angeles County	152	0.54
Merrifield, VA (cdp) Fairfax County	60	0.54
Westmont, CA (cdp) Los Angeles County	169	0.53
South San Francisco, CA (city) San Mateo County	315	0.52
Hawthorne, CA (city) Los Angeles County	431	0.51
Chillum, MD (cdp) Prince George's County	165	0.48
Sweetwater, FL (city) Miami-Dade County	68	0.48
Lawndale, CA (city) Los Angeles County	150	0.47
Springfield, VA (cdp) Fairfax County	142	0.47
Mount Vernon, VA (cdp) Fairfax County	131	0.46
Citrus, CA (cdp) Los Angeles County	48	0.45
Inglewood, CA (city) Los Angeles County	488	0.43
Lynwood, CA (city) Los Angeles County	291	0.42
San Bruno, CA (city) San Mateo County	167	0.42
Groveton, VA (cdp) Fairfax County	89	0.42
Florence-Graham, CA (cdp) Los Angeles County	248	0.41
Wheaton-Glenmont, MD (cdp) Montgomery County	237	0.41
Freeport, NY (village) Nassau County	180	0.41
San Pablo, CA (city) Contra Costa County	121	0.40
Lincolnia, VA (cdp) Fairfax County	63	0.40
Bay Point, CA (cdp) Contra Costa County	83	0.39
Silver Spring, MD (cdp) Montgomery County	293	0.38
Plainfield, NJ (city) Union County	183	0.38
Morristown, NJ (town) Morris County	70	0.38
Vincent, CA (cdp) Los Angeles County	58	0.38
Idylwood, VA (cdp) Fairfax County	59	0.37
Guttenberg, NJ (town) Hudson County	40	0.37
Union City, NJ (city) Hudson County	242	0.36
La Puente, CA (city) Los Angeles County	146	0.36
Commerce, CA (city) Los Angeles County	45	0.36
Downey, CA (city) Los Angeles County	362	0.34
Valinda, CA (cdp) Los Angeles County	73	0.34
Manassas Park, VA (independent city) Manassas Park city	35	0.34
San Francisco, CA (city) San Francisco County	2,536	0.33
Baldwin Park, CA (city) Los Angeles County	254	0.33
Woodbridge, VA (cdp) Prince William County	104	0.33
Adelphi, MD (cdp) Prince George's County	50	0.33
Cherryland, CA (cdp) Alameda County	46	0.33
Aspen Hill, MD (cdp) Montgomery County	160	0.32
Gladeview, FL (cdp) Miami-Dade County	47	0.32
New Cassel, NY (cdp) Nassau County	43	0.32
Miami, FL (city) Miami-Dade County	1,108	0.31
Pasadena, CA (city) Los Angeles County	410	0.31
Alexandria, VA (independent city) Alexandria city	402	0.31
Redwood City, CA (city) San Mateo County	231	0.31
Montebello, CA (city) Los Angeles County	191	0.31
Gaithersburg, MD (city) Montgomery County	164	0.31
North Plainfield, NJ (borough) Somerset County	65	0.31
Fontana, CA (city) San Bernardino County	382	0.30
New Brunswick, NJ (city) Middlesex County	147	0.30
Jefferson, VA (cdp) Fairfax County	82	0.30
Hyattsville, MD (city) Prince George's County	44	0.30
Arlington, VA (cdp) Arlington County	545	0.29
Pomona, CA (city) Los Angeles County	426	0.29
North Bergen, NJ (township) Hudson County	169	0.29
Huntington Station, NY (cdp) Suffolk County	87	0.29
Oakton, VA (cdp) Fairfax County	85	0.29
Port Chester, NY (village) Westchester County	82	0.29
Hybla Valley, VA (cdp) Fairfax County	48	0.29
Fairview, NJ (borough) Bergen County	38	0.29
San Mateo, CA (city) San Mateo County	259	0.28
West Little River, FL (cdp) Miami-Dade County	90	0.28
Elizabeth, NJ (city) Union County	320	0.27
Palmdale, CA (city) Los Angeles County	311	0.27
Burbank, CA (city) Los Angeles County	275	0.27
Annandale, VA (cdp) Fairfax County	151	0.27
West Puente Valley, CA (cdp) Los Angeles County	62	0.27
White Oak, MD (cdp) Montgomery County	57	0.27
Santa Fe Springs, CA (city) Los Angeles County	47	0.27
Port Washington, NY (cdp) Nassau County	41	0.27
Santa Ana, CA (city) Orange County	891	0.26
Glendale, CA (city) Los Angeles County	512	0.26
East Los Angeles, CA (cdp) Los Angeles County	329	0.26
Richmond, CA (city) Contra Costa County	256	0.26
Alhambra, CA (city) Los Angeles County	224	0.26
Kenner, LA (city) Jefferson Parish	183	0.26
Pico Rivera, CA (city) Los Angeles County	166	0.26
Paramount, CA (city) Los Angeles County	146	0.26
Montclair, CA (city) San Bernardino County	87	0.26
San Rafael, CA (city) Marin County	142	0.25
Willowbrook, CA (cdp) Los Angeles County	86	0.25
Hialeah Gardens, FL (city) Miami-Dade County	48	0.25
Bound Brook, NJ (borough) Somerset County	25	0.25
El Monte, CA (city) Los Angeles County	281	0.24
Norwalk, CA (city) Los Angeles County	249	0.24
Fountainbleau, FL (cdp) Miami-Dade County	143	0.24
Burlingame, CA (city) San Mateo County	67	0.24
Fairfax, VA (independent city) Fairfax city	52	0.24
Adelanto, CA (city) San Bernardino County	44	0.24
Takoma Park, MD (city) Montgomery County	42	0.24
Rose Hill, VA (cdp) Fairfax County	36	0.24
Norwalk, CT (city) Fairfield County	194	0.23
Altadena, CA (cdp) Los Angeles County	96	0.23
Mission Bend, TX (cdp) Fort Bend County	72	0.23
Dover, NJ (town) Morris County	42	0.23
Rialto, CA (city) San Bernardino County	201	0.22
Trenton, NJ (city) Mercer County	185	0.22
Gardena, CA (city) Los Angeles County	127	0.22
Pittsburg, CA (city) Contra Costa County	125	0.22
Azusa, CA (city) Los Angeles County	98	0.22
Richmond West, FL (cdp) Miami-Dade County	63	0.22
Doral, FL (cdp) Miami-Dade County	44	0.22
Pinole, CA (city) Contra Costa County	42	0.22
Westwood Lakes, FL (cdp) Miami-Dade County	26	0.22
Princeton, FL (cdp) Miami-Dade County	22	0.22
Ontario, CA (city) San Bernardino County	335	0.21
South Whittier, CA (cdp) Los Angeles County	114	0.21
Lake Worth, FL (city) Palm Beach County	75	0.21
Avocado Heights, CA (cdp) Los Angeles County	32	0.21
East Riverdale, MD (cdp) Prince George's County	31	0.21
Westbury, NY (village) Nassau County	30	0.21
Lamont, CA (cdp) Kern County	28	0.21
Islip, NY (town) Suffolk County	657	0.20
Hayward, CA (city) Alameda County	281	0.20
Compton, CA (city) Los Angeles County	188	0.20
Whittier, CA (city) Los Angeles County	169	0.20
Somerville, MA (city) Middlesex County	154	0.20
Rye, NY (town) Westchester County	86	0.20
South San Jose Hills, CA (cdp) Los Angeles County	40	0.20
Mineola, NY (village) Nassau County	39	0.20
Middlesex, NJ (borough) Middlesex County	27	0.20
Lexington, NE (city) Dawson County	20	0.20
Hialeah, FL (city) Miami-Dade County	426	0.19
West Covina, CA (city) Los Angeles County	198	0.19
Covina, CA (city) Los Angeles County	87	0.19
San Gabriel, CA (city) Los Angeles County	74	0.19
Pacifica, CA (city) San Mateo County	72	0.19
Suisun City, CA (city) Solano County	50	0.19
Bloomington, CA (cdp) San Bernardino County	37	0.19
Redland, MD (cdp) Montgomery County	32	0.19

Notes: (cdp) census designated place; Refer to the Explanation of Data in the front of the book for more detailed information.

Hispanic: Cuban

Top 150 Places Sorted by Number

(Based on all places, regardless of population)

Place	Number	%
Hialeah, FL (city) Miami-Dade County	140,651	62.12
Miami, FL (city) Miami-Dade County	123,763	34.14
New York, NY (city) New York City	41,123	0.51
Tamiami, FL (cdp) Miami-Dade County	31,029	56.63
Fountainbleau, FL (cdp) Miami-Dade County	22,206	37.29
Kendale Lakes, FL (cdp) Miami-Dade County	21,953	38.58
Westchester, FL (cdp) Miami-Dade County	19,886	65.69
Miami Beach, FL (city) Miami-Dade County	18,038	20.51
Kendall, FL (cdp) Miami-Dade County	16,029	21.31
University Park, FL (cdp) Miami-Dade County	15,871	59.80
Coral Terrace, FL (cdp) Miami-Dade County	15,084	61.87
Tampa, FL (city) Hillsborough County	14,674	4.84
Los Angeles, CA (city) Los Angeles County	12,431	0.34
Coral Gables, FL (city) Miami-Dade County	12,136	28.72
Pembroke Pines, FL (city) Broward County	11,901	8.66
Carol City, FL (cdp) Miami-Dade County	11,146	18.75
Kendall West, FL (cdp) Miami-Dade County	11,092	29.16
Hialeah Gardens, FL (city) Miami-Dade County	10,480	54.31
Union City, NJ (city) Hudson County	10,296	15.35
Miami Lakes, FL (cdp) Miami-Dade County	9,588	42.28
West New York, NJ (town) Hudson County	8,991	19.64
South Miami Heights, FL (cdp) Miami-Dade County	8,616	25.70
The Hammocks, FL (cdp) Miami-Dade County	8,334	17.59
Richmond West, FL (cdp) Miami-Dade County	8,227	29.30
Chicago, IL (city) Cook County	8,084	0.28
Sunset, FL (cdp) Miami-Dade County	7,989	46.58
Olympia Heights, FL (cdp) Miami-Dade County	7,755	57.65
North Bergen, NJ (township) Hudson County	7,635	13.14
Country Club, FL (cdp) Miami-Dade County	7,251	19.97
Sweetwater, FL (city) Miami-Dade County	7,101	49.92
Elizabeth, NJ (city) Union County	7,069	5.86
Westwood Lakes, FL (cdp) Miami-Dade County	6,730	56.06
Miramar, FL (city) Broward County	6,377	8.77
Egypt Lake-Leto, FL (cdp) Hillsborough County	5,977	18.23
Hollywood, FL (city) Broward County	5,891	4.23
West Little River, FL (cdp) Miami-Dade County	5,452	16.78
Town 'n' Country, FL (cdp) Hillsborough County	5,146	7.10
Houston, TX (city) Harris County	4,970	0.25
The Crossings, FL (cdp) Miami-Dade County	4,821	20.47
Glenvar Heights, FL (cdp) Miami-Dade County	4,693	28.89
Miami Springs, FL (city) Miami-Dade County	4,364	31.83
West Palm Beach, FL (city) Palm Beach County	4,343	5.29
Leisure City, FL (cdp) Miami-Dade County	3,799	17.15
West Miami, FL (city) Miami-Dade County	3,612	61.61
Las Vegas, NV (city) Clark County	3,393	0.71
Cutler Ridge, FL (cdp) Miami-Dade County	3,312	13.37
Davie, FL (town) Broward County	3,275	4.33
Jacksonville, FL (special city) Duval County	3,229	0.44
Doral, FL (cdp) Miami-Dade County	3,106	15.20
Newark, NJ (city) Essex County	2,962	1.08
Hempstead, NY (town) Nassau County	2,934	0.39
Philadelphia, PA (city) Philadelphia County	2,730	0.18
Orlando, FL (city) Orange County	2,696	1.45
Paradise, NV (cdp) Clark County	2,684	1.44
North Miami, FL (city) Miami-Dade County	2,655	4.43
Pinecrest, FL (village) Miami-Dade County	2,613	13.71
Fort Lauderdale, FL (city) Broward County	2,576	1.69
Palm Springs North, FL (cdp) Miami-Dade County	2,380	43.59
Country Walk, FL (cdp) Miami-Dade County	2,366	22.21
Dallas, TX (city) Dallas County	2,283	0.19
Boston, MA (city) Suffolk County	2,221	0.38
Homestead, FL (city) Miami-Dade County	2,171	6.80
South Miami, FL (city) Miami-Dade County	2,103	19.58
Downey, CA (city) Los Angeles County	2,100	1.96
Plantation, FL (city) Broward County	2,043	2.46
Coral Springs, FL (city) Broward County	2,017	1.72
North Miami Beach, FL (city) Miami-Dade County	2,008	4.92
Weston, FL (city) Broward County	1,995	4.05
Key West, FL (city) Monroe County	1,977	7.76
Sunrise, FL (city) Broward County	1,965	2.29
Phoenix, AZ (city) Maricopa County	1,952	0.15
San Diego, CA (city) San Diego County	1,922	0.16
Jersey City, NJ (city) Hudson County	1,860	0.77
Glendale, CA (city) Los Angeles County	1,838	0.94
Cutler, FL (cdp) Miami-Dade County	1,824	10.49
Albuquerque, NM (city) Bernalillo County	1,694	0.38
Golden Gate, FL (cdp) Collier County	1,660	7.92
Key Biscayne, FL (village) Miami-Dade County	1,632	15.53
San Francisco, CA (city) San Francisco County	1,632	0.21
New Orleans, LA (city) Orleans Parish	1,615	0.33
Saint Petersburg, FL (city) Pinellas County	1,560	0.63
Sunny Isles Beach, FL (city) Miami-Dade County	1,493	9.75
San Antonio, TX (city) Bexar County	1,491	0.13
Lakes by the Bay, FL (cdp) Miami-Dade County	1,487	16.42
Cooper City, FL (city) Broward County	1,477	5.29
Louisville, KY (city) Jefferson County	1,461	0.57
Yonkers, NY (city) Westchester County	1,450	0.74
Opa-locka, FL (city) Miami-Dade County	1,432	9.58
Austin, TX (city) Travis County	1,425	0.22
Cape Coral, FL (city) Lee County	1,408	1.38
Stock Island, FL (cdp) Monroe County	1,401	31.77
Sunrise Manor, NV (cdp) Clark County	1,342	0.86
Tallahassee, FL (city) Leon County	1,338	0.89
Portland, OR (city) Multnomah County	1,329	0.25
Golden Glades, FL (cdp) Miami-Dade County	1,317	4.04
Hallandale, FL (city) Broward County	1,308	3.82
Princeton, FL (cdp) Miami-Dade County	1,306	12.94
Gainesville, FL (city) Alachua County	1,278	1.34
Wellington, FL (village) Palm Beach County	1,248	3.27
Lake Worth, FL (city) Palm Beach County	1,218	3.47
Marathon, FL (city) Monroe County	1,212	11.82
Guttenberg, NJ (town) Hudson County	1,203	11.13
Weehawken, NJ (township) Hudson County	1,182	8.75
Palmetto Estates, FL (cdp) Miami-Dade County	1,180	8.63
Rochester, NY (city) Monroe County	1,177	0.54
Metairie, LA (cdp) Jefferson Parish	1,163	0.80
Key Largo, FL (cdp) Monroe County	1,160	9.76
Greater Carrollwood, FL (cdp) Hillsborough County	1,128	3.37
Ojus, FL (cdp) Miami-Dade County	1,126	6.77
Washington, DC (city) District of Columbia	1,101	0.19
Boca Raton, FL (city) Palm Beach County	1,099	1.47
Charlotte, NC (city) Mecklenburg County	1,098	0.20
Burbank, CA (city) Los Angeles County	1,082	1.08
Brandon, FL (cdp) Hillsborough County	1,078	1.38
Long Beach, CA (city) Los Angeles County	1,067	0.23
Three Lakes, FL (cdp) Miami-Dade County	1,047	15.05
Brookhaven, NY (town) Suffolk County	1,032	0.23
Gladeview, FL (cdp) Miami-Dade County	1,003	6.93
San Jose, CA (city) Santa Clara County	1,001	0.11
Bridgeport, CT (city) Fairfield County	994	0.71
Surfside, FL (town) Miami-Dade County	989	20.15
Kenner, LA (city) Jefferson Parish	985	1.40
Hawthorne, CA (city) Los Angeles County	954	1.13
Citrus Park, FL (cdp) Hillsborough County	944	4.67
Bell, CA (city) Los Angeles County	939	2.56
Islip, NY (town) Suffolk County	929	0.29
Perth Amboy, NJ (city) Middlesex County	918	1.94
Palm River-Clair Mel, FL (cdp) Hillsborough County	914	5.20
Anaheim, CA (city) Orange County	897	0.27
Spring Valley, NV (cdp) Clark County	892	0.76
Palm Springs, FL (village) Palm Beach County	891	7.62
Belle Glade, FL (city) Palm Beach County	891	5.98
Atlanta, GA (city) Fulton County	887	0.21
Pinewood, FL (cdp) Miami-Dade County	881	5.33
Detroit, MI (city) Wayne County	871	0.09
Paterson, NJ (city) Passaic County	858	0.57
North Bay Village, FL (city) Miami-Dade County	853	12.67
Kearny, NJ (town) Hudson County	847	2.09
Kissimmee, FL (city) Osceola County	817	1.71
Nashville-Davidson, TN (special city) Davidson County	799	0.15
Margate, FL (city) Broward County	796	1.48
Lansing, MI (city) Ingham County	793	0.67
Tamarac, FL (city) Broward County	790	1.42
Henderson, NV (city) Clark County	787	0.45
Kansas City, MO (city) Jackson County	787	0.18
Port Saint Lucie, FL (city) Saint Lucie County	786	0.89
Broadview Park, FL (cdp) Broward County	774	11.39
South Gate, CA (city) Los Angeles County	761	0.79
Seattle, WA (city) King County	759	0.13
Oyster Bay, NY (town) Nassau County	747	0.25

Notes: (cdp) census designated place; Refer to the Explanation of Data in the front of the book for more detailed information.

Hispanic: Cuban

Top 150 Places Sorted by Percent

(Based on all places, regardless of population)

Place	Number	%
Westchester, FL (cdp) Miami-Dade County	19,886	65.69
Hialeah, FL (city) Miami-Dade County	140,651	62.12
Coral Terrace, FL (cdp) Miami-Dade County	15,084	61.87
West Miami, FL (city) Miami-Dade County	3,612	61.61
University Park, FL (cdp) Miami-Dade County	15,871	59.80
Olympia Heights, FL (cdp) Miami-Dade County	7,755	57.65
Tamiami, FL (cdp) Miami-Dade County	31,029	56.63
Westwood Lakes, FL (cdp) Miami-Dade County	6,730	56.06
Hialeah Gardens, FL (city) Miami-Dade County	10,480	54.31
Medley, FL (town) Miami-Dade County	570	51.91
Sweetwater, FL (city) Miami-Dade County	7,101	49.92
Sunset, FL (cdp) Miami-Dade County	7,989	46.58
Palm Springs North, FL (cdp) Miami-Dade County	2,380	43.59
Miami Lakes, FL (cdp) Miami-Dade County	9,588	42.28
Kendale Lakes, FL (cdp) Miami-Dade County	21,953	38.58
Fountainbleau, FL (cdp) Miami-Dade County	22,206	37.29
Miami, FL (city) Miami-Dade County	123,763	34.14
Miami Springs, FL (city) Miami-Dade County	4,364	31.83
Stock Island, FL (cdp) Monroe County	1,401	31.77
Richmond West, FL (cdp) Miami-Dade County	8,227	29.30
Kendall West, FL (cdp) Miami-Dade County	11,092	29.16
Glenvar Heights, FL (cdp) Miami-Dade County	4,693	28.89
Coral Gables, FL (city) Miami-Dade County	12,136	28.72
Virginia Gardens, FL (village) Miami-Dade County	613	26.11
South Miami Heights, FL (cdp) Miami-Dade County	8,616	25.70
Country Walk, FL (cdp) Miami-Dade County	2,366	22.21
Kendall, FL (cdp) Miami-Dade County	16,029	21.31
Miami Beach, FL (city) Miami-Dade County	18,038	20.51
The Crossings, FL (cdp) Miami-Dade County	4,821	20.47
Surfside, FL (town) Miami-Dade County	989	20.15
Country Club, FL (cdp) Miami-Dade County	7,251	19.97
West New York, NJ (town) Hudson County	8,991	19.64
South Miami, FL (city) Miami-Dade County	2,103	19.58
Carol City, FL (cdp) Miami-Dade County	11,146	18.75
Egypt Lake-Leto, FL (cdp) Hillsborough County	5,977	18.23
The Hammocks, FL (cdp) Miami-Dade County	8,334	17.59
Leisure City, FL (cdp) Miami-Dade County	3,799	17.15
West Little River, FL (cdp) Miami-Dade County	5,452	16.78
Lakes by the Bay, FL (cdp) Miami-Dade County	1,487	16.42
Key Biscayne, FL (village) Miami-Dade County	1,632	15.53
Union City, NJ (city) Hudson County	10,296	15.35
Doral, FL (cdp) Miami-Dade County	3,106	15.20
Gun Club Estates, FL (cdp) Palm Beach County	108	15.19
Three Lakes, FL (cdp) Miami-Dade County	1,047	15.05
Ivanhoe Estates, FL (cdp) Broward County	42	15.05
Chula Vista, FL (cdp) Broward County	84	14.66
Pinecrest, FL (village) Miami-Dade County	2,613	13.71
Tavernier, FL (cdp) Monroe County	298	13.71
Cutler Ridge, FL (cdp) Miami-Dade County	3,312	13.37
North Bergen, NJ (township) Hudson County	7,635	13.14
Princeton, FL (cdp) Miami-Dade County	1,306	12.94
Rolling Oaks, FL (cdp) Broward County	164	12.70
North Bay Village, FL (city) Miami-Dade County	853	12.67
Green Meadow, FL (cdp) Broward County	235	12.54
McGrath, MN (city) Aitkin County	8	12.31
Country Estates, FL (cdp) Broward County	226	11.83
Marathon, FL (city) Monroe County	1,212	11.82
Broadview Park, FL (cdp) Broward County	774	11.39
Guttenberg, NJ (town) Hudson County	1,203	11.13
Homestead Base, FL (cdp) Miami-Dade County	48	10.76
Cutler, FL (cdp) Miami-Dade County	1,824	10.49
Lake Clarke Shores, FL (town) Palm Beach County	348	10.08
Clewiston, FL (city) Hendry County	650	10.06
Big Coppitt Key, FL (cdp) Monroe County	258	9.94
Key Largo, FL (cdp) Monroe County	1,160	9.76
Miami Gardens, FL (cdp) Broward County	264	9.76
Sunny Isles Beach, FL (city) Miami-Dade County	1,493	9.75
Opa-locka, FL (city) Miami-Dade County	1,432	9.58
East Perrine, FL (cdp) Miami-Dade County	678	9.58
Sunshine Ranches, FL (cdp) Broward County	160	9.39
Riverland Village, FL (cdp) Broward County	194	9.20
Miramar, FL (city) Broward County	6,377	8.77
Weehawken, NJ (township) Hudson County	1,182	8.75
Pembroke Pines, FL (city) Broward County	11,901	8.66
Palmetto Estates, FL (cdp) Miami-Dade County	1,180	8.63

Place	Number	%
Opa-locka North, FL (cdp) Miami-Dade County	533	8.56
Bay Harbor Islands, FL (town) Miami-Dade County	438	8.51
Royal Palm Estates, FL (cdp) Palm Beach County	284	7.93
Golden Gate, FL (cdp) Collier County	1,660	7.92
Key West, FL (city) Monroe County	1,977	7.76
Rio en Medio, NM (cdp) Santa Fe County	10	7.63
Palm Springs, FL (village) Palm Beach County	891	7.62
Jefferson, SC (town) Chesterfield County	53	7.53
Royal Palm Ranches, FL (cdp) Broward County	21	7.14
Town 'n' Country, FL (cdp) Hillsborough County	5,146	7.10
Lake Forest, FL (cdp) Broward County	352	7.05
Naples Manor, FL (cdp) Collier County	362	6.98
Gladeview, FL (cdp) Miami-Dade County	1,003	6.93
Homestead, FL (city) Miami-Dade County	2,171	6.80
Ojus, FL (cdp) Miami-Dade County	1,126	6.77
Golden Beach, FL (town) Miami-Dade County	62	6.75
Biscayne Park, FL (village) Miami-Dade County	217	6.64
Westview, FL (cdp) Miami-Dade County	641	6.61
Haverhill, FL (town) Palm Beach County	92	6.33
Miami Shores, FL (village) Miami-Dade County	651	6.27
Lake Minchumina, AK (cdp) Yukon-Koyukuk Census Area	2	6.25
Country Life Acres, MO (village) Saint Louis County	5	6.17
Cloud Lake, FL (town) Palm Beach County	10	5.99
Belle Glade, FL (city) Palm Beach County	891	5.98
Naranja, FL (cdp) Miami-Dade County	238	5.90
Elizabeth, NJ (city) Union County	7,069	5.86
North Andrews Gardens, FL (cdp) Broward County	556	5.76
Bal Harbour, FL (village) Miami-Dade County	185	5.60
Ullin, IL (village) Pulaski County	42	5.39
Pinewood, FL (cdp) Miami-Dade County	881	5.33
West Palm Beach, FL (city) Palm Beach County	4,343	5.29
Cooper City, FL (city) Broward County	1,477	5.29
West Perrine, FL (cdp) Miami-Dade County	448	5.21
Palm River-Clair Mel, FL (cdp) Hillsborough County	914	5.20
Florida City, FL (city) Miami-Dade County	397	5.06
North Miami Beach, FL (city) Miami-Dade County	2,008	4.92
Tampa, FL (city) Hillsborough County	14,674	4.84
Goulds, FL (cdp) Miami-Dade County	350	4.70
Citrus Park, FL (cdp) Hillsborough County	944	4.67
Sky Lake, FL (cdp) Orange County	261	4.62
Lima, MN (township) Cass County	5	4.50
North Miami, FL (city) Miami-Dade County	2,655	4.43
Orangetree, FL (cdp) Collier County	42	4.42
Davie, FL (town) Broward County	3,275	4.33
West Buechel, KY (city) Jefferson County	56	4.30
Fairview, NJ (borough) Bergen County	562	4.24
Hollywood, FL (city) Broward County	5,891	4.23
Lake Belvedere Estates, FL (cdp) Palm Beach County	64	4.20
El Portal, FL (village) Miami-Dade County	105	4.19
Naples Park, FL (cdp) Collier County	280	4.15
Glen Allen, MO (town) Bollinger County	6	4.14
Stacey Street, FL (cdp) Palm Beach County	39	4.07
Weston, FL (city) Broward County	1,995	4.05
Golden Glades, FL (cdp) Miami-Dade County	1,317	4.04
Pitkin, CO (town) Gunnison County	4	4.03
Ridgefield Park, NJ (village) Bergen County	513	3.99
Lake Lucerne, FL (cdp) Miami-Dade County	359	3.93
Utopia, FL (cdp) Broward County	28	3.92
Hallandale, FL (city) Broward County	1,308	3.82
Pine Castle, FL (cdp) Orange County	336	3.82
Sunshine Acres, FL (cdp) Broward County	31	3.75
Westgate-Belvedere Homes, FL (cdp) Palm Beach County	301	3.70
Hillman, MN (township) Morrison County	6	3.66
Venedy, IL (village) Washington County	5	3.65
Big Pine Key, FL (cdp) Monroe County	180	3.58
Greater Northdale, FL (cdp) Hillsborough County	731	3.57
Key Colony Beach, FL (city) Monroe County	28	3.55
Ives Estates, FL (cdp) Miami-Dade County	617	3.51
Kirby, WY (town) Hot Springs County	2	3.51
Lake Worth, FL (city) Palm Beach County	1,218	3.47
Azalea Park, FL (cdp) Orange County	383	3.46
Greater Carrollwood, FL (cdp) Hillsborough County	1,128	3.37
Elaine, AR (city) Phillips County	29	3.35
Seminole Manor, FL (cdp) Palm Beach County	85	3.34
Ridgefield, NJ (borough) Bergen County	361	3.33

Notes: (cdp) census designated place; Refer to the Explanation of Data in the front of the book for more detailed information.

Hispanic: Cuban

Top 150 Places Sorted by Percent

(Based on places with populations of 10,000 or more)

Place	Number	%
Westchester, FL (cdp) Miami-Dade County	19,886	65.69
Hialeah, FL (city) Miami-Dade County	140,651	62.12
Coral Terrace, FL (cdp) Miami-Dade County	15,084	61.87
University Park, FL (cdp) Miami-Dade County	15,871	59.80
Olympia Heights, FL (cdp) Miami-Dade County	7,755	57.65
Tamiami, FL (cdp) Miami-Dade County	31,029	56.63
Westwood Lakes, FL (cdp) Miami-Dade County	6,730	56.06
Hialeah Gardens, FL (city) Miami-Dade County	10,480	54.31
Sweetwater, FL (city) Miami-Dade County	7,101	49.92
Sunset, FL (cdp) Miami-Dade County	7,989	46.58
Miami Lakes, FL (cdp) Miami-Dade County	9,588	42.28
Kendale Lakes, FL (cdp) Miami-Dade County	21,953	38.58
Fountainbleau, FL (cdp) Miami-Dade County	22,206	37.29
Miami, FL (city) Miami-Dade County	123,763	34.14
Miami Springs, FL (city) Miami-Dade County	4,364	31.83
Richmond West, FL (cdp) Miami-Dade County	8,227	29.30
Kendall West, FL (cdp) Miami-Dade County	11,092	29.16
Glenvar Heights, FL (cdp) Miami-Dade County	4,693	28.89
Coral Gables, FL (city) Miami-Dade County	12,136	28.72
South Miami Heights, FL (cdp) Miami-Dade County	8,616	25.70
Country Walk, FL (cdp) Miami-Dade County	2,366	22.21
Kendall, FL (cdp) Miami-Dade County	16,029	21.31
Miami Beach, FL (city) Miami-Dade County	18,038	20.51
The Crossings, FL (cdp) Miami-Dade County	4,821	20.47
Country Club, FL (cdp) Miami-Dade County	7,251	19.97
West New York, NJ (town) Hudson County	8,991	19.64
South Miami, FL (city) Miami-Dade County	2,103	19.58
Carol City, FL (cdp) Miami-Dade County	11,146	18.75
Egypt Lake-Leto, FL (cdp) Hillsborough County	5,977	18.23
The Hammocks, FL (cdp) Miami-Dade County	8,334	17.59
Leisure City, FL (cdp) Miami-Dade County	3,799	17.15
West Little River, FL (cdp) Miami-Dade County	5,452	16.78
Key Biscayne, FL (village) Miami-Dade County	1,632	15.53
Union City, NJ (city) Hudson County	10,296	15.35
Doral, FL (cdp) Miami-Dade County	3,106	15.20
Pinecrest, FL (village) Miami-Dade County	2,613	13.71
Cutler Ridge, FL (cdp) Miami-Dade County	3,312	13.37
North Bergen, NJ (township) Hudson County	7,635	13.14
Princeton, FL (cdp) Miami-Dade County	1,306	12.94
Marathon, FL (city) Monroe County	1,212	11.82
Guttenberg, NJ (town) Hudson County	1,203	11.13
Cutler, FL (cdp) Miami-Dade County	1,824	10.49
Key Largo, FL (cdp) Monroe County	1,160	9.76
Sunny Isles Beach, FL (city) Miami-Dade County	1,493	9.75
Opa-locka, FL (city) Miami-Dade County	1,432	9.58
Miramar, FL (city) Broward County	6,377	8.77
Weehawken, NJ (township) Hudson County	1,182	8.75
Pembroke Pines, FL (city) Broward County	11,901	8.66
Palmetto Estates, FL (cdp) Miami-Dade County	1,180	8.63
Golden Gate, FL (cdp) Collier County	1,660	7.92
Key West, FL (city) Monroe County	1,977	7.76
Palm Springs, FL (village) Palm Beach County	891	7.62
Town 'n' Country, FL (cdp) Hillsborough County	5,146	7.10
Gladeview, FL (cdp) Miami-Dade County	1,003	6.93
Homestead, FL (city) Miami-Dade County	2,171	6.80
Ojus, FL (cdp) Miami-Dade County	1,126	6.77
Miami Shores, FL (village) Miami-Dade County	651	6.27
Belle Glade, FL (city) Palm Beach County	891	5.98
Elizabeth, NJ (city) Union County	7,069	5.86
Pinewood, FL (cdp) Miami-Dade County	881	5.33
West Palm Beach, FL (city) Palm Beach County	4,343	5.29
Cooper City, FL (city) Broward County	1,477	5.29
Palm River-Clair Mel, FL (cdp) Hillsborough County	914	5.20
North Miami Beach, FL (city) Miami-Dade County	2,008	4.92
Tampa, FL (city) Hillsborough County	14,674	4.84
Citrus Park, FL (cdp) Hillsborough County	944	4.67
North Miami, FL (city) Miami-Dade County	2,655	4.43
Davie, FL (town) Broward County	3,275	4.33
Fairview, NJ (borough) Bergen County	562	4.24
Hollywood, FL (city) Broward County	5,891	4.23
Weston, FL (city) Broward County	1,995	4.05
Golden Glades, FL (cdp) Miami-Dade County	1,317	4.04
Ridgefield Park, NJ (village) Bergen County	513	3.99
Hallandale, FL (city) Broward County	1,308	3.82
Greater Northdale, FL (cdp) Hillsborough County	731	3.57
Ives Estates, FL (cdp) Miami-Dade County	617	3.51
Lake Worth, FL (city) Palm Beach County	1,218	3.47
Azalea Park, FL (cdp) Orange County	383	3.46
Greater Carrollwood, FL (cdp) Hillsborough County	1,128	3.37
Ridgefield, NJ (borough) Bergen County	361	3.33
Forest City, FL (cdp) Seminole County	416	3.30
Wellington, FL (village) Palm Beach County	1,248	3.27
Lake Worth Corridor, FL (cdp) Palm Beach County	608	3.26
Oak Ridge, FL (cdp) Orange County	707	3.16
Brownsville, FL (cdp) Miami-Dade County	446	3.10
Harrison, NJ (town) Hudson County	438	3.04
Royal Palm Beach, FL (village) Palm Beach County	635	2.95
Aventura, FL (city) Miami-Dade County	731	2.89
Winchester, NV (cdp) Clark County	737	2.73
Westchase, FL (cdp) Hillsborough County	290	2.61
Bell, CA (city) Los Angeles County	939	2.56
Plantation, FL (city) Broward County	2,043	2.46
Cliffside Park, NJ (borough) Bergen County	565	2.46
Greenacres, FL (city) Palm Beach County	665	2.41
Secaucus, NJ (town) Hudson County	376	2.36
Lake Magdalene, FL (cdp) Hillsborough County	665	2.31
Sunrise, FL (city) Broward County	1,965	2.29
Kearny, NJ (town) Hudson County	847	2.09
Roselle Park, NJ (borough) Union County	275	2.07
Oakland Park, FL (city) Broward County	629	2.03
Meadow Woods, FL (cdp) Orange County	225	1.99
Norland, FL (cdp) Miami-Dade County	456	1.98
Keystone, FL (cdp) Hillsborough County	288	1.97
Downey, CA (city) Los Angeles County	2,100	1.96
Perth Amboy, NJ (city) Middlesex County	918	1.94
Yeehaw Junction, FL (cdp) Osceola County	420	1.93
Tarrytown, NY (village) Westchester County	213	1.92
Hillside, NJ (cdp) Union County	402	1.85
Little Ferry, NJ (borough) Bergen County	199	1.84
Coral Springs, FL (city) Broward County	2,017	1.72
Kissimmee, FL (city) Osceola County	817	1.71
Fort Lauderdale, FL (city) Broward County	2,576	1.69
Dania Beach, FL (city) Broward County	340	1.69
Parkland, FL (city) Broward County	234	1.69
Port Chester, NY (village) Westchester County	465	1.67
Palisades Park, NJ (borough) Bergen County	279	1.63
North Arlington, NJ (borough) Bergen County	241	1.59
Wilton Manors, FL (city) Broward County	201	1.58
Hasbrouck Heights, NJ (borough) Bergen County	184	1.58
Union Park, FL (cdp) Orange County	160	1.57
Rutherford, NJ (borough) Bergen County	280	1.55
Scott Lake, FL (cdp) Miami-Dade County	221	1.53
Goldenrod, FL (cdp) Seminole County	195	1.52
Linden, NJ (city) Union County	593	1.51
Melrose Park, IL (village) Cook County	345	1.49
Lutz, FL (cdp) Hillsborough County	255	1.49
Margate, FL (city) Broward County	796	1.48
Boca Raton, FL (city) Palm Beach County	1,099	1.47
Orlando, FL (city) Orange County	2,696	1.45
Hoboken, NJ (city) Hudson County	560	1.45
Conway, FL (cdp) Orange County	209	1.45
Paradise, NV (cdp) Clark County	2,684	1.44
Temple Terrace, FL (city) Hillsborough County	302	1.44
Tamarac, FL (city) Broward County	790	1.42
Sandalfoot Cove, FL (cdp) Palm Beach County	235	1.42
Lyndhurst, NJ (cdp) Bergen County	273	1.41
Kenner, LA (city) Jefferson Parish	985	1.40
Whitney, NV (cdp) Clark County	255	1.40
Cape Coral, FL (city) Lee County	1,408	1.38
Brandon, FL (cdp) Hillsborough County	1,078	1.38
Gainesville, FL (city) Alachua County	1,278	1.34
Northlake, IL (city) Cook County	158	1.33
University, FL (cdp) Hillsborough County	403	1.31
Lakeland Highlands, FL (cdp) Polk County	162	1.29
Belleville, NJ (cdp) Essex County	454	1.26
Lockhart, FL (cdp) Orange County	163	1.26
Elmwood Park, NJ (borough) Bergen County	237	1.25
Sarasota, FL (city) Sarasota County	656	1.24
Rye, NY (town) Westchester County	540	1.23
Union, NJ (cdp) Union County	666	1.22

Notes: (cdp) census designated place; Refer to the Explanation of Data in the front of the book for more detailed information.

Hispanic: Dominican Republic

Top 150 Places Sorted by Number

(Based on all places, regardless of population)

Place	Number	%
New York, NY (city) New York City	406,806	5.08
Lawrence, MA (city) Essex County	16,186	22.47
Paterson, NJ (city) Passaic County	15,331	10.27
Providence, RI (city) Providence County	14,638	8.43
Boston, MA (city) Suffolk County	12,981	2.20
Jersey City, NJ (city) Hudson County	9,186	3.83
Perth Amboy, NJ (city) Middlesex County	8,897	18.81
Passaic, NJ (city) Passaic County	8,865	13.06
Hempstead, NY (town) Nassau County	8,433	1.12
Yonkers, NY (city) Westchester County	7,838	4.00
Union City, NJ (city) Hudson County	7,688	11.46
Miami, FL (city) Miami-Dade County	6,370	1.76
Newark, NJ (city) Essex County	6,266	2.29
Lynn, MA (city) Essex County	5,517	6.20
Islip, NY (town) Suffolk County	4,792	1.49
Philadelphia, PA (city) Philadelphia County	4,337	0.29
Hialeah, FL (city) Miami-Dade County	4,106	1.81
West New York, NJ (town) Hudson County	3,847	8.41
Haverstraw, NY (town) Rockland County	3,764	11.13
Elizabeth, NJ (city) Union County	3,629	3.01
North Bergen, NJ (township) Hudson County	3,228	5.56
Freeport, NY (village) Nassau County	3,226	7.37
Babylon, NY (town) Suffolk County	3,188	1.51
New Brunswick, NJ (city) Middlesex County	2,855	5.88
Brentwood, NY (cdp) Suffolk County	2,744	5.09
Haverstraw, NY (village) Rockland County	2,727	26.95
Salem, MA (city) Essex County	2,176	5.39
Brookhaven, NY (town) Suffolk County	2,132	0.48
Danbury, CT (city) Fairfield County	2,033	2.72
Camden, NJ (city) Camden County	1,874	2.35
Clifton, NJ (city) Passaic County	1,853	2.36
Carol City, FL (cdp) Miami-Dade County	1,785	3.00
Fountainbleau, FL (cdp) Miami-Dade County	1,779	2.99
Allentown, PA (city) Lehigh County	1,729	1.62
Reading, PA (city) Berks County	1,696	2.09
Hollywood, FL (city) Broward County	1,681	1.21
Chicago, IL (city) Cook County	1,651	0.06
Pembroke Pines, FL (city) Broward County	1,637	1.19
Worcester, MA (city) Worcester County	1,611	0.93
Hackensack, NJ (city) Bergen County	1,573	3.69
Washington, DC (city) District of Columbia	1,496	0.26
Copiague, NY (cdp) Suffolk County	1,440	6.57
Miramar, FL (city) Broward County	1,439	1.98
Tampa, FL (city) Hillsborough County	1,397	0.46
Waterbury, CT (city) New Haven County	1,336	1.25
Country Club, FL (cdp) Miami-Dade County	1,309	3.61
Methuen, MA (city) Essex County	1,308	2.99
Mount Pleasant, NY (town) Westchester County	1,241	2.87
Orlando, FL (city) Orange County	1,191	0.64
Haverhill, MA (city) Essex County	1,179	2.00
Sleepy Hollow, NY (village) Westchester County	1,167	12.67
The Hammocks, FL (cdp) Miami-Dade County	1,167	2.46
Miami Beach, FL (city) Miami-Dade County	1,084	1.23
Bayonne, NJ (city) Hudson County	1,072	1.73
North Miami, FL (city) Miami-Dade County	1,032	1.72
Lowell, MA (city) Middlesex County	1,024	0.97
Hartford, CT (city) Hartford County	1,013	0.83
Houston, TX (city) Harris County	990	0.05
Kendall West, FL (cdp) Miami-Dade County	982	2.58
North Miami Beach, FL (city) Miami-Dade County	976	2.39
Kissimmee, FL (city) Osceola County	964	2.02
Hempstead, NY (village) Nassau County	887	1.57
Bridgeport, CT (city) Fairfield County	886	0.63
Town 'n' Country, FL (cdp) Hillsborough County	876	1.21
North Hempstead, NY (town) Nassau County	864	0.39
Grand Rapids, MI (city) Kent County	863	0.44
Kendale Lakes, FL (cdp) Miami-Dade County	858	1.51
South Miami Heights, FL (cdp) Miami-Dade County	851	2.54
West Haverstraw, NY (village) Rockland County	841	8.17
Atlantic City, NJ (city) Atlantic County	840	2.07
Tamiami, FL (cdp) Miami-Dade County	836	1.53
Kendall, FL (cdp) Miami-Dade County	821	1.09
Rochester, NY (city) Monroe County	808	0.37
Pawtucket, RI (city) Providence County	804	1.10
Mount Vernon, NY (city) Westchester County	792	1.16

Place	Number	%
Anchorage, AK (municipality) Anchorage Borough	792	0.30
West Little River, FL (cdp) Miami-Dade County	786	2.42
Teaneck, NJ (cdp) Bergen County	780	1.99
Weehawken, NJ (township) Hudson County	775	5.74
Cranston, RI (city) Providence County	734	0.93
Central Islip, NY (cdp) Suffolk County	711	2.23
Los Angeles, CA (city) Los Angeles County	706	0.02
Plainfield, NJ (city) Union County	702	1.47
Richmond West, FL (cdp) Miami-Dade County	696	2.48
Woodbridge, NJ (township) Middlesex County	679	0.70
Oak Ridge, FL (cdp) Orange County	677	3.03
Silver Spring, MD (cdp) Montgomery County	669	0.87
White Plains, NY (city) Westchester County	667	1.26
Stamford, CT (city) Fairfield County	656	0.56
Peabody, MA (city) Essex County	639	1.33
Bergenfield, NJ (borough) Bergen County	638	2.43
Coral Springs, FL (city) Broward County	630	0.54
Nashua, NH (city) Hillsborough County	624	0.72
Garfield, NJ (city) Bergen County	623	2.09
Rockville Centre, NY (village) Nassau County	617	2.51
Englewood, NJ (city) Bergen County	617	2.35
Springfield, MA (city) Hampden County	614	0.40
Yeehaw Junction, FL (cdp) Osceola County	609	2.80
Jacksonville, FL (special city) Duval County	601	0.08
East Orange, NJ (city) Essex County	582	0.83
Greenburgh, NY (town) Westchester County	579	0.67
Central Falls, RI (city) Providence County	575	3.04
Sunrise, FL (city) Broward County	573	0.67
Franklin, NJ (township) Somerset County	567	1.11
Golden Glades, FL (cdp) Miami-Dade County	560	1.72
Hialeah Gardens, FL (city) Miami-Dade County	551	2.86
Guttenberg, NJ (town) Hudson County	550	5.09
Pleasantville, NJ (city) Atlantic County	548	2.88
Cleveland, OH (city) Cuyahoga County	542	0.11
Doral, FL (cdp) Miami-Dade County	540	2.64
Hoboken, NJ (city) Hudson County	536	1.39
Chelsea, MA (city) Suffolk County	533	1.52
Lancaster, PA (city) Lancaster County	531	0.94
Chillum, MD (cdp) Prince George's County	510	1.49
Somerset, NJ (cdp) Somerset County	508	2.20
North Bay Shore, NY (cdp) Suffolk County	505	3.37
Oyster Bay, NY (town) Nassau County	492	0.17
Huntington, NY (town) Suffolk County	489	0.25
Charlotte, NC (city) Mecklenburg County	472	0.09
Egypt Lake-Leto, FL (cdp) Hillsborough County	471	1.44
Kearny, NJ (town) Hudson County	469	1.16
New Haven, CT (city) New Haven County	460	0.37
Trenton, NJ (city) Mercer County	458	0.54
Baldwin, NY (cdp) Nassau County	453	1.93
Ossining, NY (town) Westchester County	451	1.23
Buffalo, NY (city) Erie County	445	0.15
Davie, FL (town) Broward County	441	0.58
New Bedford, MA (city) Bristol County	430	0.46
Cambridge, MA (city) Middlesex County	424	0.42
Ossining, NY (village) Westchester County	423	1.76
West Palm Beach, FL (city) Palm Beach County	418	0.51
Valley Stream, NY (village) Nassau County	416	1.14
Pine Hills, FL (cdp) Orange County	412	0.99
Cutler Ridge, FL (cdp) Miami-Dade County	411	1.66
Belleville, NJ (cdp) Essex County	409	1.14
Fairview, NJ (borough) Bergen County	405	3.06
Ridgefield Park, NJ (village) Bergen County	404	3.14
Brockton, MA (city) Plymouth County	403	0.43
Elmont, NY (cdp) Nassau County	402	1.23
Framingham, MA (cdp) Middlesex County	402	0.60
Bloomfield, NJ (cdp) Essex County	399	0.84
Virginia Beach, VA (independent city) Virginia Beach city	397	0.09
Irvington, NJ (cdp) Essex County	396	0.65
North Brunswick Township, NJ (cdp) Middlesex County	392	1.08
San Diego, CA (city) San Diego County	392	0.03
Opa-locka, FL (city) Miami-Dade County	387	2.59
Plantation, FL (city) Broward County	387	0.47
Detroit, MI (city) Wayne County	386	0.04
Ramapo, NY (town) Rockland County	385	0.35
New Rochelle, NY (city) Westchester County	381	0.53

Notes: (cdp) census designated place; Refer to the Explanation of Data in the front of the book for more detailed information.

Hispanic: Dominican Republic

Top 150 Places Sorted by Percent

(Based on all places, regardless of population)

Place	Number	%
Haverstraw, NY (village) Rockland County	2,727	26.95
Lawrence, MA (city) Essex County	16,186	22.47
Perth Amboy, NJ (city) Middlesex County	8,897	18.81
Passaic, NJ (city) Passaic County	8,865	13.06
Sleepy Hollow, NY (village) Westchester County	1,167	12.67
Union City, NJ (city) Hudson County	7,688	11.46
Haverstraw, NY (town) Rockland County	3,764	11.13
Paterson, NJ (city) Passaic County	15,331	10.27
Providence, RI (city) Providence County	14,638	8.43
West New York, NJ (town) Hudson County	3,847	8.41
West Haverstraw, NY (village) Rockland County	841	8.17
Freeport, NY (village) Nassau County	3,226	7.37
Copiague, NY (cdp) Suffolk County	1,440	6.57
Lynn, MA (city) Essex County	5,517	6.20
New Brunswick, NJ (city) Middlesex County	2,855	5.88
Weehawken, NJ (township) Hudson County	775	5.74
North Bergen, NJ (township) Hudson County	3,228	5.56
Salem, MA (city) Essex County	2,176	5.39
Prospect Park, NJ (borough) Passaic County	305	5.28
Brentwood, NY (cdp) Suffolk County	2,744	5.09
Guttenberg, NJ (town) Hudson County	550	5.09
New York, NY (city) New York City	406,806	5.08
Attu Station, AK (cdp) Aleutians West Census Area	1	5.00
Miami Gardens, FL (cdp) Broward County	125	4.62
Yonkers, NY (city) Westchester County	7,838	4.00
Lake Forest, FL (cdp) Broward County	198	3.96
Jersey City, NJ (city) Hudson County	9,186	3.83
Hackensack, NJ (city) Bergen County	1,573	3.69
Country Club, FL (cdp) Miami-Dade County	1,309	3.61
Allegheny, PA (township) Cambria County	87	3.48
North Bay Shore, NY (cdp) Suffolk County	505	3.37
Bogota, NJ (borough) Bergen County	275	3.33
Foster, PA (township) Schuylkill County	37	3.29
Terryville, NY (cdp) Suffolk County	335	3.16
Port Jefferson Station, NY (cdp) Suffolk County	238	3.16
Ridgefield Park, NJ (village) Bergen County	404	3.14
Fairview, NJ (borough) Bergen County	405	3.06
Central Falls, RI (city) Providence County	575	3.04
Oak Ridge, FL (cdp) Orange County	677	3.03
Elizabeth, NJ (city) Union County	3,629	3.01
Carol City, FL (cdp) Miami-Dade County	1,785	3.00
Fountainbleau, FL (cdp) Miami-Dade County	1,779	2.99
Methuen, MA (city) Essex County	1,308	2.99
Pleasantville, NJ (city) Atlantic County	548	2.88
Mount Pleasant, NY (town) Westchester County	1,241	2.87
Hialeah Gardens, FL (city) Miami-Dade County	551	2.86
Yeehaw Junction, FL (cdp) Osceola County	609	2.80
Danbury, CT (city) Fairfield County	2,033	2.72
New Paltz, NY (village) Ulster County	162	2.68
Doral, FL (cdp) Miami-Dade County	540	2.64
Opa-locka, FL (city) Miami-Dade County	387	2.59
Kendall West, FL (cdp) Miami-Dade County	982	2.58
Milan, NY (town) Dutchess County	117	2.57
South Miami Heights, FL (cdp) Miami-Dade County	851	2.54
Rockville Centre, NY (village) Nassau County	617	2.51
Dannemora, NY (village) Clinton County	103	2.49
Richmond West, FL (cdp) Miami-Dade County	696	2.48
The Hammocks, FL (cdp) Miami-Dade County	1,167	2.46
Tarrytown, NY (village) Westchester County	271	2.44
Bergenfield, NJ (borough) Bergen County	638	2.43
West Little River, FL (cdp) Miami-Dade County	786	2.42
Gregg, PA (township) Union County	113	2.41
North Miami Beach, FL (city) Miami-Dade County	976	2.39
Virginia Gardens, FL (village) Miami-Dade County	56	2.39
Clifton, NJ (city) Passaic County	1,853	2.36
Camden, NJ (city) Camden County	1,874	2.35
Englewood, NJ (city) Bergen County	617	2.35
Newark, NJ (city) Essex County	6,266	2.29
Cape Vincent, NY (town) Jefferson County	75	2.24
Greenvale, NY (cdp) Nassau County	50	2.24
Utopia, FL (cdp) Broward County	16	2.24
Homestead Base, FL (cdp) Miami-Dade County	10	2.24
Central Islip, NY (cdp) Suffolk County	711	2.23
Boston, MA (city) Suffolk County	12,981	2.20
Somerset, NJ (cdp) Somerset County	508	2.20

Place	Number	%
Irwin, IL (village) Kankakee County	2	2.17
Westview, FL (cdp) Miami-Dade County	209	2.16
Country Walk, FL (cdp) Miami-Dade County	228	2.14
El Portal, FL (village) Miami-Dade County	53	2.12
Marcy, NY (town) Oneida County	200	2.11
East Hampton, NY (village) Suffolk County	28	2.10
Reading, PA (city) Berks County	1,696	2.09
Garfield, NJ (city) Bergen County	623	2.09
Collins, NY (town) Erie County	174	2.09
Atlantic City, NJ (city) Atlantic County	840	2.07
Little Ferry, NJ (borough) Bergen County	223	2.06
Groveland, NY (town) Livingston County	79	2.05
Dannemora, NY (town) Clinton County	105	2.04
Three Lakes, FL (cdp) Miami-Dade County	141	2.03
Kissimmee, FL (city) Osceola County	964	2.02
Meadow Woods, FL (cdp) Orange County	228	2.02
Haverhill, MA (city) Essex County	1,179	2.00
South Hackensack, NJ (township) Bergen County	45	2.00
Teaneck, NJ (cdp) Bergen County	780	1.99
Miramar, FL (city) Broward County	1,439	1.98
Sky Lake, FL (cdp) Orange County	111	1.96
Bellerose Terrace, NY (cdp) Nassau County	42	1.95
Southchase, FL (cdp) Orange County	90	1.94
Baldwin, NY (cdp) Nassau County	453	1.93
North Amityville, NY (cdp) Suffolk County	314	1.89
North Bay Village, FL (city) Miami-Dade County	124	1.84
Portland, NY (town) Chautauqua County	101	1.84
Amityville, NY (village) Suffolk County	173	1.83
Hialeah, FL (city) Miami-Dade County	4,106	1.81
Old Westbury, NY (village) Nassau County	76	1.80
Mount Ivy, NY (cdp) Rockland County	117	1.79
Miami, FL (city) Miami-Dade County	6,370	1.76
Ossining, NY (village) Westchester County	423	1.76
North Lynbrook, NY (cdp) Nassau County	13	1.75
Port Graham, AK (cdp) Kenai Peninsula Borough	3	1.75
Bayonne, NJ (city) Hudson County	1,072	1.73
Winsted, CT (cdp) Litchfield County	127	1.73
North Miami, FL (city) Miami-Dade County	1,032	1.72
Golden Glades, FL (cdp) Miami-Dade County	560	1.72
East Newark, NJ (borough) Hudson County	41	1.72
Malone, NY (town) Franklin County	256	1.71
Haledon, NJ (borough) Passaic County	141	1.71
Baywood, NY (cdp) Suffolk County	128	1.69
Azalea Park, FL (cdp) Orange County	186	1.68
Wheatley Heights, NY (cdp) Suffolk County	84	1.68
North Lindenhurst, NY (cdp) Suffolk County	196	1.67
Cutler Ridge, FL (cdp) Miami-Dade County	411	1.66
Palisades Park, NJ (borough) Bergen County	283	1.66
Miami Lakes, FL (cdp) Miami-Dade County	375	1.65
Clinton, MA (town) Worcester County	221	1.64
Highland Falls, NY (village) Orange County	60	1.63
Allentown, PA (city) Lehigh County	1,729	1.62
Coxsackie, NY (town) Greene County	143	1.61
Montauk, NY (cdp) Suffolk County	62	1.61
Lakes by the Bay, FL (cdp) Miami-Dade County	145	1.60
Edgewater, NJ (borough) Bergen County	123	1.60
Poinciana, FL (cdp) Osceola County	217	1.59
Saugerties, NY (village) Ulster County	79	1.59
Andover, FL (cdp) Miami-Dade County	134	1.58
Hempstead, NY (village) Nassau County	887	1.57
The Crossings, FL (cdp) Miami-Dade County	371	1.57
Harrison, NJ (town) Hudson County	225	1.56
Pinewood, FL (cdp) Miami-Dade County	254	1.54
Tamiami, FL (cdp) Miami-Dade County	836	1.53
Dover, NJ (town) Morris County	279	1.53
Ives Estates, FL (cdp) Miami-Dade County	269	1.53
Adelphi, MD (cdp) Prince George's County	229	1.53
Chelsea, MA (city) Suffolk County	533	1.52
Lodi, NJ (borough) Bergen County	365	1.52
Babylon, NY (town) Suffolk County	3,188	1.51
Kendale Lakes, FL (cdp) Miami-Dade County	858	1.51
Maywood, NJ (borough) Bergen County	143	1.50
Islip, NY (town) Suffolk County	4,792	1.49
Chillum, MD (cdp) Prince George's County	510	1.49
Plainfield, NJ (city) Union County	702	1.47

Notes: (cdp) census designated place; Refer to the Explanation of Data in the front of the book for more detailed information.

Hispanic: Dominican Republic

Top 150 Places Sorted by Percent

(Based on places with populations of 10,000 or more)

Place	Number	%
Haverstraw, NY (village) Rockland County	2,727	26.95
Lawrence, MA (city) Essex County	16,186	22.47
Perth Amboy, NJ (city) Middlesex County	8,897	18.81
Passaic, NJ (city) Passaic County	8,865	13.06
Union City, NJ (city) Hudson County	7,688	11.46
Haverstraw, NY (town) Rockland County	3,764	11.13
Paterson, NJ (city) Passaic County	15,331	10.27
Providence, RI (city) Providence County	14,638	8.43
West New York, NJ (town) Hudson County	3,847	8.41
West Haverstraw, NY (village) Rockland County	841	8.17
Freeport, NY (village) Nassau County	3,226	7.37
Copiague, NY (cdp) Suffolk County	1,440	6.57
Lynn, MA (city) Essex County	5,517	6.20
New Brunswick, NJ (city) Middlesex County	2,855	5.88
Weehawken, NJ (township) Hudson County	775	5.74
North Bergen, NJ (township) Hudson County	3,228	5.56
Salem, MA (city) Essex County	2,176	5.39
Brentwood, NY (cdp) Suffolk County	2,744	5.09
Guttenberg, NJ (town) Hudson County	550	5.09
New York, NY (city) New York City	406,806	5.08
Yonkers, NY (city) Westchester County	7,838	4.00
Jersey City, NJ (city) Hudson County	9,186	3.83
Hackensack, NJ (city) Bergen County	1,573	3.69
Country Club, FL (cdp) Miami-Dade County	1,309	3.61
North Bay Shore, NY (cdp) Suffolk County	505	3.37
Terryville, NY (cdp) Suffolk County	335	3.16
Ridgefield Park, NJ (village) Bergen County	404	3.14
Fairview, NJ (borough) Bergen County	405	3.06
Central Falls, RI (city) Providence County	575	3.04
Oak Ridge, FL (cdp) Orange County	677	3.03
Elizabeth, NJ (city) Union County	3,629	3.01
Carol City, FL (cdp) Miami-Dade County	1,785	3.00
Fountainbleau, FL (cdp) Miami-Dade County	1,779	2.99
Methuen, MA (city) Essex County	1,308	2.99
Pleasantville, NJ (city) Atlantic County	548	2.88
Mount Pleasant, NY (town) Westchester County	1,241	2.87
Hialeah Gardens, FL (city) Miami-Dade County	551	2.86
Yeehaw Junction, FL (cdp) Osceola County	609	2.80
Danbury, CT (city) Fairfield County	2,033	2.72
Doral, FL (cdp) Miami-Dade County	540	2.64
Opa-locka, FL (city) Miami-Dade County	387	2.59
Kendall West, FL (cdp) Miami-Dade County	982	2.58
South Miami Heights, FL (cdp) Miami-Dade County	851	2.54
Rockville Centre, NY (village) Nassau County	617	2.51
Richmond West, FL (cdp) Miami-Dade County	696	2.48
The Hammocks, FL (cdp) Miami-Dade County	1,167	2.46
Tarrytown, NY (village) Westchester County	271	2.44
Bergenfield, NJ (borough) Bergen County	638	2.43
West Little River, FL (cdp) Miami-Dade County	786	2.42
North Miami Beach, FL (city) Miami-Dade County	976	2.39
Clifton, NJ (city) Passaic County	1,853	2.36
Camden, NJ (city) Camden County	1,874	2.35
Englewood, NJ (city) Bergen County	617	2.35
Newark, NJ (city) Essex County	6,266	2.29
Central Islip, NY (cdp) Suffolk County	711	2.23
Boston, MA (city) Suffolk County	12,981	2.20
Somerset, NJ (cdp) Somerset County	508	2.20
Country Walk, FL (cdp) Miami-Dade County	228	2.14
Reading, PA (city) Berks County	1,696	2.09
Garfield, NJ (city) Bergen County	623	2.09
Atlantic City, NJ (city) Atlantic County	840	2.07
Little Ferry, NJ (borough) Bergen County	223	2.06
Kissimmee, FL (city) Osceola County	964	2.02
Meadow Woods, FL (cdp) Orange County	228	2.02
Haverhill, MA (city) Essex County	1,179	2.00
Teaneck, NJ (cdp) Bergen County	780	1.99
Miramar, FL (city) Broward County	1,439	1.98
Baldwin, NY (cdp) Nassau County	453	1.93
North Amityville, NY (cdp) Suffolk County	314	1.89
Hialeah, FL (city) Miami-Dade County	4,106	1.81
Miami, FL (city) Miami-Dade County	6,370	1.76
Ossining, NY (village) Westchester County	423	1.76
Bayonne, NJ (city) Hudson County	1,072	1.73
North Miami, FL (city) Miami-Dade County	1,032	1.72
Golden Glades, FL (cdp) Miami-Dade County	560	1.72
Malone, NY (town) Franklin County	256	1.71
Azalea Park, FL (cdp) Orange County	186	1.68
North Lindenhurst, NY (cdp) Suffolk County	196	1.67
Cutler Ridge, FL (cdp) Miami-Dade County	411	1.66
Palisades Park, NJ (borough) Bergen County	283	1.66
Miami Lakes, FL (cdp) Miami-Dade County	375	1.65
Clinton, MA (town) Worcester County	221	1.64
Allentown, PA (city) Lehigh County	1,729	1.62
Poinciana, FL (cdp) Osceola County	217	1.59
Hempstead, NY (village) Nassau County	887	1.57
The Crossings, FL (cdp) Miami-Dade County	371	1.57
Harrison, NJ (town) Hudson County	225	1.56
Pinewood, FL (cdp) Miami-Dade County	254	1.54
Tamiami, FL (cdp) Miami-Dade County	836	1.53
Dover, NJ (town) Morris County	279	1.53
Ives Estates, FL (cdp) Miami-Dade County	269	1.53
Adelphi, MD (cdp) Prince George's County	229	1.53
Chelsea, MA (city) Suffolk County	533	1.52
Lodi, NJ (borough) Bergen County	365	1.52
Babylon, NY (town) Suffolk County	3,188	1.51
Kendale Lakes, FL (cdp) Miami-Dade County	858	1.51
Islip, NY (town) Suffolk County	4,792	1.49
Chillum, MD (cdp) Prince George's County	510	1.49
Plainfield, NJ (city) Union County	702	1.47
Egypt Lake-Leto, FL (cdp) Hillsborough County	471	1.44
Ojus, FL (cdp) Miami-Dade County	237	1.42
Hazleton, PA (city) Luzerne County	329	1.41
Carteret, NJ (borough) Middlesex County	291	1.41
Cliffside Park, NJ (borough) Bergen County	323	1.40
Hoboken, NJ (city) Hudson County	536	1.39
Ventnor City, NJ (city) Atlantic County	180	1.39
Peabody, MA (city) Essex County	639	1.33
Princeton, FL (cdp) Miami-Dade County	134	1.33
North Valley Stream, NY (cdp) Nassau County	209	1.32
New Paltz, NY (town) Ulster County	166	1.29
Miami Shores, FL (village) Miami-Dade County	133	1.28
White Plains, NY (city) Westchester County	667	1.26
Bay Shore, NY (cdp) Suffolk County	301	1.26
Waterbury, CT (city) New Haven County	1,336	1.25
Langley Park, MD (cdp) Prince George's County	202	1.25
Miami Beach, FL (city) Miami-Dade County	1,084	1.23
Ossining, NY (town) Westchester County	451	1.23
Elmont, NY (cdp) Nassau County	402	1.23
Winchester, CT (town) Litchfield County	130	1.22
Hollywood, FL (city) Broward County	1,681	1.21
Town 'n' Country, FL (cdp) Hillsborough County	876	1.21
Palm Springs, FL (village) Palm Beach County	140	1.20
Norfolk, MA (town) Norfolk County	125	1.20
Pembroke Pines, FL (city) Broward County	1,637	1.19
Wyandanch, NY (cdp) Suffolk County	124	1.18
Mount Vernon, NY (city) Westchester County	792	1.16
Kearny, NJ (town) Hudson County	469	1.16
Miami Springs, FL (city) Miami-Dade County	158	1.15
Valley Stream, NY (village) Nassau County	416	1.14
Belleville, NJ (cdp) Essex County	409	1.14
Hempstead, NY (town) Nassau County	8,433	1.12
Ridgefield, NJ (borough) Bergen County	121	1.12
Franklin, NJ (township) Somerset County	567	1.11
Pawtucket, RI (city) Providence County	804	1.10
Palmetto Estates, FL (cdp) Miami-Dade County	150	1.10
Kendall, FL (cdp) Miami-Dade County	821	1.09
New London, CT (city) New London County	280	1.09
North Brunswick Township, NJ (cdp) Middlesex County	392	1.08
Norland, FL (cdp) Miami-Dade County	249	1.08
Union Park, FL (cdp) Orange County	110	1.08
Uniondale, NY (cdp) Nassau County	247	1.07
University Park, FL (cdp) Miami-Dade County	280	1.06
Ogdensburg, NY (city) Saint Lawrence County	131	1.06
Westchester, FL (cdp) Miami-Dade County	317	1.05
Coram, NY (cdp) Suffolk County	360	1.03
Oceanside, NY (cdp) Nassau County	332	1.01
Fishkill, NY (town) Dutchess County	204	1.01
New Milford, NJ (borough) Bergen County	166	1.01
Leisure City, FL (cdp) Miami-Dade County	221	1.00
Elmwood Park, NJ (borough) Bergen County	189	1.00

Notes: (cdp) census designated place; Refer to the Explanation of Data in the front of the book for more detailed information.

Hispanic: Mexican

Top 150 Places Sorted by Number

(Based on all places, regardless of population)

Place	Number	%
Los Angeles, CA (city) Los Angeles County	1,091,686	29.55
Chicago, IL (city) Cook County	530,462	18.32
Houston, TX (city) Harris County	527,442	27.00
San Antonio, TX (city) Bexar County	473,420	41.36
Phoenix, AZ (city) Maricopa County	375,096	28.39
El Paso, TX (city) El Paso County	359,699	63.81
Dallas, TX (city) Dallas County	350,491	29.49
San Diego, CA (city) San Diego County	259,219	21.19
Santa Ana, CA (city) Orange County	222,719	65.90
San Jose, CA (city) Santa Clara County	221,148	24.71
New York, NY (city) New York City	186,872	2.33
Austin, TX (city) Travis County	153,868	23.44
Tucson, AZ (city) Pima County	145,234	29.84
Fresno, CA (city) Fresno County	144,772	33.85
Laredo, TX (city) Webb County	133,185	75.43
Fort Worth, TX (city) Tarrant County	132,894	24.85
Long Beach, CA (city) Los Angeles County	127,129	27.55
Anaheim, CA (city) Orange County	126,017	38.42
Denver, CO (city) Denver County	120,664	21.76
East Los Angeles, CA (cdp) Los Angeles County	104,223	83.86
Brownsville, TX (city) Cameron County	103,297	73.93
Oxnard, CA (city) Ventura County	101,264	59.44
Corpus Christi, TX (city) Nueces County	98,146	35.37
Salinas, CA (city) Monterey County	84,815	56.15
Las Vegas, NV (city) Clark County	83,490	17.45
Pomona, CA (city) Los Angeles County	79,757	53.36
Riverside, CA (city) Riverside County	79,041	30.98
Ontario, CA (city) San Bernardino County	77,476	49.03
Chula Vista, CA (city) San Diego County	74,867	43.14
San Bernardino, CA (city) San Bernardino County	71,891	38.78
Sacramento, CA (city) Sacramento County	70,758	17.38
McAllen, TX (city) Hidalgo County	69,931	65.72
El Monte, CA (city) Los Angeles County	69,880	60.26
Albuquerque, NM (city) Bernalillo County	68,537	15.28
South Gate, CA (city) Los Angeles County	68,181	70.75
Stockton, CA (city) San Joaquin County	66,900	27.44
Oakland, CA (city) Alameda County	65,094	16.29
Bakersfield, CA (city) Kern County	64,700	26.19
Mesa, AZ (city) Maricopa County	63,519	16.02
Fontana, CA (city) San Bernardino County	59,386	46.06
Cicero, IL (town) Cook County	58,542	68.38
Pasadena, TX (city) Harris County	54,725	38.63
Norwalk, CA (city) Los Angeles County	52,652	50.97
Baldwin Park, CA (city) Los Angeles County	49,046	64.67
San Francisco, CA (city) San Francisco County	48,935	6.30
Pico Rivera, CA (city) Los Angeles County	48,033	75.73
Arlington, TX (city) Tarrant County	46,766	14.05
Lynwood, CA (city) Los Angeles County	46,491	66.56
Huntington Park, CA (city) Los Angeles County	44,948	73.27
Escondido, CA (city) San Diego County	44,726	33.49
Compton, CA (city) Los Angeles County	43,839	46.89
Garden Grove, CA (city) Orange County	43,576	26.38
Moreno Valley, CA (city) Riverside County	43,485	30.54
Milwaukee, WI (city) Milwaukee County	43,300	7.25
Downey, CA (city) Los Angeles County	43,241	40.29
Glendale, AZ (city) Maricopa County	42,874	19.59
Garland, TX (city) Dallas County	42,452	19.67
Irving, TX (city) Dallas County	42,318	22.08
Florence-Graham, CA (cdp) Los Angeles County	41,897	69.60
Oklahoma City, OK (city) Oklahoma County	40,997	8.10
Oceanside, CA (city) San Diego County	40,729	25.29
Santa Maria, CA (city) Santa Barbara County	40,719	52.59
Aurora, IL (city) Kane County	39,351	27.52
Montebello, CA (city) Los Angeles County	38,881	62.56
Modesto, CA (city) Stanislaus County	38,819	20.55
Whittier, CA (city) Los Angeles County	38,565	46.09
Aurora, CO (city) Arapahoe County	38,276	13.85
Rialto, CA (city) San Bernardino County	37,589	40.91
Inglewood, CA (city) Los Angeles County	37,272	33.11
West Covina, CA (city) Los Angeles County	37,206	35.41
Pharr, TX (city) Hidalgo County	36,574	78.38
Corona, CA (city) Riverside County	36,212	28.98
North Las Vegas, NV (city) Clark County	34,848	30.17
Edinburg, TX (city) Hidalgo County	34,655	71.51
Orange, CA (city) Orange County	34,329	26.65
Hayward, CA (city) Alameda County	34,035	24.31
Detroit, MI (city) Wayne County	33,143	3.48
Paramount, CA (city) Los Angeles County	33,129	59.94
Indio, CA (city) Riverside County	32,985	67.16
Bell Gardens, CA (city) Los Angeles County	32,875	74.62
Lubbock, TX (city) Lubbock County	32,404	16.24
Pasadena, CA (city) Los Angeles County	32,276	24.10
Grand Prairie, TX (city) Dallas County	32,209	25.28
Harlingen, TX (city) Cameron County	31,922	55.45
South Whittier, CA (cdp) Los Angeles County	31,690	57.42
Fullerton, CA (city) Orange County	31,252	24.80
Waukegan, IL (city) Lake County	30,717	34.94
Yuma, AZ (city) Yuma County	30,512	39.36
Mission, TX (city) Hidalgo County	30,495	67.16
Palmdale, CA (city) Los Angeles County	30,117	25.81
Watsonville, CA (city) Santa Cruz County	29,953	67.67
Sunrise Manor, NV (cdp) Clark County	29,891	19.15
Vista, CA (city) San Diego County	29,802	33.17
Chandler, AZ (city) Maricopa County	29,334	16.61
Paradise, NV (cdp) Clark County	28,936	15.55
Odessa, TX (city) Ector County	28,753	31.62
National City, CA (city) San Diego County	28,544	52.61
La Puente, CA (city) Los Angeles County	28,108	68.45
Visalia, CA (city) Tulare County	27,918	30.49
Santa Barbara, CA (city) Santa Barbara County	27,529	29.82
Elgin, IL (city) Kane County	27,444	29.05
Wichita, KS (city) Sedgwick County	26,954	7.83
Amarillo, TX (city) Potter County	26,760	15.41
Rancho Cucamonga, CA (city) San Bernardino County	26,537	20.77
Chino, CA (city) San Bernardino County	26,232	39.05
Costa Mesa, CA (city) Orange County	26,133	24.04
Reno, NV (city) Washoe County	25,601	14.18
Madera, CA (city) Madera County	25,562	59.16
Salt Lake City, UT (city) Salt Lake County	25,430	13.99
Carson, CA (city) Los Angeles County	25,275	28.17
El Centro, CA (city) Imperial County	25,251	66.74
Portland, OR (city) Multnomah County	25,136	4.75
Bell, CA (city) Los Angeles County	24,558	66.98
Bellflower, CA (city) Los Angeles County	24,433	33.53
La Habra, CA (city) Orange County	24,195	41.03
Las Cruces, NM (city) Dona Ana County	24,155	32.52
Kansas City, MO (city) Jackson County	24,042	5.44
Azusa, CA (city) Los Angeles County	23,836	53.31
Colton, CA (city) San Bernardino County	23,813	49.96
Calexico, CA (city) Imperial County	23,781	87.72
Del Rio, TX (city) Val Verde County	23,474	69.31
Delano, CA (city) Kern County	23,428	60.34
Omaha, NE (city) Douglas County	23,290	5.97
Colorado Springs, CO (city) El Paso County	22,991	6.37
Alhambra, CA (city) Los Angeles County	22,857	26.64
Santa Rosa, CA (city) Sonoma County	22,779	15.43
Merced, CA (city) Merced County	22,616	35.40
Socorro, TX (city) El Paso County	22,438	82.64
Hawthorne, CA (city) Los Angeles County	22,385	26.61
San Angelo, TX (city) Tom Green County	22,337	25.26
Tempe, AZ (city) Maricopa County	22,178	13.98
San Juan, TX (city) Hidalgo County	22,175	84.54
Charlotte, NC (city) Mecklenburg County	22,168	4.10
Santa Clarita, CA (city) Los Angeles County	21,603	14.30
Maywood, CA (city) Los Angeles County	21,556	76.76
Waco, TX (city) McLennan County	21,450	18.86
Tulsa, OK (city) Tulsa County	21,110	5.37
Indianapolis, IN (special city) Marion County	21,053	2.69
Huntington Beach, CA (city) Orange County	20,894	11.02
Buena Park, CA (city) Orange County	20,893	26.69
Yakima, WA (city) Yakima County	20,825	28.99
Glendale, CA (city) Los Angeles County	20,810	10.67
Midland, TX (city) Midland County	20,726	21.82
Kansas City, KS (city) Wyandotte County	20,597	14.02
Lancaster, CA (city) Los Angeles County	20,120	16.95
San Buenaventura, CA (city) Ventura County	19,968	19.79
Minneapolis, MN (city) Hennepin County	19,835	5.18
Coachella, CA (city) Riverside County	19,824	87.24
Pueblo, CO (city) Pueblo County	19,523	19.12
Gilroy, CA (city) Santa Clara County	19,226	46.37

Notes: (cdp) census designated place; Refer to the Explanation of Data in the front of the book for more detailed information.

Hispanic: Mexican

Top 150 Places Sorted by Percent

(Based on all places, regardless of population)

Place	Number	%
Roma Creek, TX (cdp) Starr County	606	99.34
El Refugio, TX (cdp) Starr County	219	99.10
Santa Cruz, TX (cdp) Starr County	619	98.25
Las Lomas, TX (cdp) Starr County	2,636	98.21
Granjeno, TX (city) Hidalgo County	306	97.76
South Alamo, TX (cdp) Hidalgo County	3,029	97.68
Lozano, TX (cdp) Cameron County	315	97.22
Alto Bonito, TX (cdp) Starr County	553	97.19
Sparks, TX (cdp) El Paso County	2,888	97.11
Muniz, TX (cdp) Hidalgo County	1,070	96.75
Lago, TX (cdp) Cameron County	238	96.75
Laureles, TX (cdp) Cameron County	3,177	96.71
South Point, TX (cdp) Cameron County	1,080	96.60
Mila Doce, TX (cdp) Hidalgo County	4,739	96.58
Morning Glory, TX (cdp) El Paso County	604	96.33
Doffing, TX (cdp) Hidalgo County	4,089	96.08
West Sharyland, TX (cdp) Hidalgo County	2,828	95.96
Arroyo Colorado Estates, TX (cdp) Cameron County	724	95.89
Westway, TX (cdp) El Paso County	3,640	95.06
Los Ebanos, TX (cdp) Hidalgo County	383	95.04
San Elizario, TX (cdp) El Paso County	10,496	95.02
La Victoria, TX (cdp) Starr County	1,599	95.01
La Puerta, TX (cdp) Starr County	1,553	94.93
Tornillo, TX (cdp) El Paso County	1,525	94.78
Santa Maria, TX (cdp) Cameron County	801	94.68
Citrus City, TX (cdp) Hidalgo County	884	93.94
Olmito, TX (cdp) Cameron County	1,124	93.82
Los Alvarez, TX (cdp) Starr County	1,344	93.72
Lopezville, TX (cdp) Hidalgo County	4,189	93.59
Progreso, TX (city) Hidalgo County	4,539	93.57
Falcon Heights, TX (cdp) Starr County	313	93.43
Alton North, TX (cdp) Hidalgo County	4,716	93.37
Las Palmas-Juarez, TX (cdp) Cameron County	1,555	93.34
La Homa, TX (cdp) Hidalgo County	9,666	92.65
Cuevitas, TX (cdp) Hidalgo County	34	91.89
Faysville, TX (cdp) Hidalgo County	319	91.67
Del Mar Heights, TX (cdp) Cameron County	237	91.51
Midway North, TX (cdp) Hidalgo County	3,600	91.23
Indian Hills, TX (cdp) Hidalgo County	1,855	91.11
Encantada-Ranchito El Calaboz, TX (cdp) Cameron County	1,912	91.05
Agua Dulce, TX (cdp) El Paso County	671	90.92
Cameron Park, TX (cdp) Cameron County	5,412	90.79
Scissors, TX (cdp) Hidalgo County	2,536	90.41
Doolittle, TX (cdp) Hidalgo County	2,129	90.29
North Escobares, TX (cdp) Starr County	1,524	90.07
La Casita-Garciasville, TX (cdp) Starr County	1,958	89.94
Presidio, TX (city) Presidio County	3,747	89.92
Alton, TX (city) Hidalgo County	3,929	89.62
Hidalgo, TX (city) Hidalgo County	6,548	89.43
Cactus, TX (city) Moore County	2,269	89.40
Penitas, TX (city) Hidalgo County	1,043	89.37
Homestead Meadows South, TX (cdp) El Paso County	6,073	89.22
Palmview, TX (city) Hidalgo County	3,662	89.16
Gadsden, AZ (cdp) Yuma County	848	88.98
El Camino Angosto, TX (cdp) Cameron County	226	88.98
Roma, TX (city) Starr County	8,536	88.76
Arroyo Alto, TX (cdp) Cameron County	284	88.75
Fort Hancock, TX (cdp) Hudspeth County	1,511	88.21
San Isidro, TX (cdp) Starr County	238	88.15
Midway South, TX (cdp) Hidalgo County	1,508	88.14
Olivarez, TX (cdp) Hidalgo County	2,149	87.89
Redford, TX (cdp) Presidio County	116	87.88
Heber, CA (cdp) Imperial County	2,623	87.78
Calexico, CA (city) Imperial County	23,781	87.72
Los Villareales, TX (cdp) Starr County	815	87.63
Somerton, AZ (city) Yuma County	6,352	87.42
Coachella, CA (city) Riverside County	19,824	87.24
North Alamo, TX (cdp) Hidalgo County	1,796	87.14
Huron, CA (city) Fresno County	5,481	86.92
Vernon, CA (city) Los Angeles County	79	86.81
Las Quintas Fronterizas, TX (cdp) Maverick County	1,757	86.55
Laguna Seca, TX (cdp) Hidalgo County	217	86.45
Parlier, CA (city) Fresno County	9,631	86.42
Del Rey, CA (cdp) Fresno County	821	86.42
Lost Hills, CA (cdp) Kern County	1,672	86.27
Pajaro, CA (cdp) Monterey County	2,919	86.26
Escobares, TX (cdp) Starr County	1,678	85.88
Mecca, CA (cdp) Riverside County	4,627	85.65
Heidelberg, TX (cdp) Hidalgo County	1,353	85.31
Eidson Road, TX (cdp) Maverick County	7,965	85.21
Cantua Creek, CA (cdp) Fresno County	557	85.04
Tierra Bonita, TX (cdp) Cameron County	136	85.00
Coyanosa, TX (cdp) Pecos County	117	84.78
Rosita North, TX (cdp) Maverick County	2,882	84.76
Cutler, CA (cdp) Tulare County	3,804	84.70
Arroyo Gardens-La Tina Ranch, TX (cdp) Cameron County	620	84.70
Cienegas Terrace, TX (cdp) Val Verde County	2,436	84.64
Relampago, TX (cdp) Hidalgo County	88	84.62
San Juan, TX (city) Hidalgo County	22,175	84.54
La Presa, TX (cdp) Webb County	429	84.45
Kettleman City, CA (cdp) Kings County	1,265	84.39
Calwa, CA (cdp) Fresno County	643	84.38
Salem, NM (cdp) Dona Ana County	670	84.28
San Carlos, TX (cdp) Hidalgo County	2,228	84.08
Llano Grande, TX (cdp) Hidalgo County	2,800	84.01
Chualar, CA (cdp) Monterey County	1,213	84.00
La Joya, TX (city) Hidalgo County	2,772	83.92
Salineno, TX (cdp) Starr County	255	83.88
East Los Angeles, CA (cdp) Los Angeles County	104,223	83.86
Las Colonias, TX (cdp) Zavala County	237	83.75
Bluetown-Iglesia Antigua, TX (cdp) Cameron County	579	83.67
Villa Verde, TX (cdp) Hidalgo County	744	83.50
San Joaquin, CA (city) Fresno County	2,722	83.24
Vinton, TX (village) El Paso County	1,574	83.19
San Luis, AZ (city) Yuma County	12,717	83.00
Havana, TX (cdp) Hidalgo County	375	82.96
Monte Alto, TX (cdp) Hidalgo County	1,335	82.87
Mattawa, WA (town) Grant County	2,161	82.83
Palmview South, TX (cdp) Hidalgo County	5,149	82.79
Sunland Park, NM (city) Dona Ana County	11,009	82.72
Palmhurst, TX (city) Hidalgo County	4,029	82.70
El Cenizo, TX (city) Webb County	2,931	82.68
Socorro, TX (city) El Paso County	22,438	82.64
La Grulla, TX (city) Starr County	1,000	82.58
La Blanca, TX (cdp) Hidalgo County	1,937	82.39
Planada, CA (cdp) Merced County	3,596	82.31
Laredo Ranchettes, TX (cdp) Webb County	1,516	82.17
Canutillo, TX (cdp) El Paso County	4,194	81.77
Richgrove, CA (cdp) Tulare County	2,222	81.60
Ranchitos Las Lomas, TX (cdp) Webb County	272	81.44
Los Angeles Subdivision, TX (cdp) Willacy County	70	81.40
Nogales, AZ (city) Santa Cruz County	16,989	81.37
Los Indios, TX (town) Cameron County	934	81.29
Fabens, TX (cdp) El Paso County	6,521	81.08
Elsa, TX (city) Hidalgo County	4,484	80.81
La Paloma, TX (cdp) Cameron County	286	80.79
Green Valley Farms, TX (cdp) Cameron County	581	80.69
El Indio, TX (cdp) Maverick County	212	80.61
Mabton, WA (city) Yakima County	1,523	80.54
Clint, TX (town) El Paso County	788	80.41
La Rosita, TX (cdp) Starr County	1,387	80.22
Eagle Pass, TX (city) Maverick County	17,965	80.15
Nurillo, TX (cdp) Hidalgo County	4,030	79.71
Chula Vista-Orason, TX (cdp) Cameron County	314	79.70
Granger, WA (town) Yakima County	2,012	79.53
Laguna Heights, TX (cdp) Cameron County	1,579	79.35
Commerce, CA (city) Los Angeles County	9,941	79.10
Sullivan City, TX (city) Hidalgo County	3,148	78.74
London, CA (cdp) Tulare County	1,454	78.68
Woodville, CA (cdp) Tulare County	1,320	78.67
Mojave Ranch Estates, AZ (cdp) Mohave County	22	78.57
San Fernando, CA (city) Los Angeles County	18,504	78.53
Fronton, TX (cdp) Starr County	470	78.46
Pharr, TX (city) Hidalgo County	36,574	78.38
Castroville, CA (cdp) Monterey County	5,265	78.30
Weedpatch, CA (cdp) Kern County	2,130	78.14
Soledad, CA (city) Monterey County	8,798	78.11
Edcouch, TX (city) Hidalgo County	2,610	78.10
Greenfield, CA (city) Monterey County	9,814	77.99
Firebaugh, CA (city) Fresno County	4,477	77.96

Notes: (cdp) census designated place; Refer to the Explanation of Data in the front of the book for more detailed information.

Hispanic: Mexican

Top 150 Places Sorted by Percent

(Based on places with populations of 10,000 or more)

Place	Number	%
San Elizario, TX (cdp) El Paso County	10,496	95.02
La Homa, TX (cdp) Hidalgo County	9,666	92.65
Calexico, CA (city) Imperial County	23,781	87.72
Coachella, CA (city) Riverside County	19,824	87.24
Parlier, CA (city) Fresno County	9,631	86.42
San Juan, TX (city) Hidalgo County	22,175	84.54
East Los Angeles, CA (cdp) Los Angeles County	104,223	83.86
San Luis, AZ (city) Yuma County	12,717	83.00
Sunland Park, NM (city) Dona Ana County	11,009	82.72
Socorro, TX (city) El Paso County	22,438	82.64
Nogales, AZ (city) Santa Cruz County	16,989	81.37
Eagle Pass, TX (city) Maverick County	17,965	80.15
Commerce, CA (city) Los Angeles County	9,941	79.10
San Fernando, CA (city) Los Angeles County	18,504	78.53
Pharr, TX (city) Hidalgo County	36,574	78.38
Soledad, CA (city) Monterey County	8,798	78.11
Greenfield, CA (city) Monterey County	9,814	77.99
Rio Grande City, TX (city) Starr County	9,241	77.51
Maywood, CA (city) Los Angeles County	21,556	76.76
Walnut Park, CA (cdp) Los Angeles County	12,309	76.08
Arvin, CA (city) Kern County	9,826	75.84
Pico Rivera, CA (city) Los Angeles County	48,033	75.73
Laredo, TX (city) Webb County	133,185	75.43
Lamont, CA (cdp) Kern County	9,964	74.94
Bell Gardens, CA (city) Los Angeles County	32,875	74.62
South El Monte, CA (city) Los Angeles County	15,687	74.19
Brownsville, TX (city) Cameron County	103,297	73.93
Huntington Park, CA (city) Los Angeles County	44,948	73.27
Donna, TX (city) Hidalgo County	10,596	71.75
Douglas, AZ (city) Cochise County	10,253	71.64
Edinburg, TX (city) Hidalgo County	34,655	71.51
Sanger, CA (city) Fresno County	13,418	70.88
South Gate, CA (city) Los Angeles County	68,181	70.75
West Whittier-Los Nietos, CA (cdp) Los Angeles County	17,773	70.73
King City, CA (city) Monterey County	7,828	70.56
Florence-Graham, CA (cdp) Los Angeles County	41,897	69.60
Lindsay, CA (city) Tulare County	7,140	69.34
Del Rio, TX (city) Val Verde County	23,474	69.31
South San Jose Hills, CA (cdp) Los Angeles County	13,994	69.22
La Puente, CA (city) Los Angeles County	28,108	68.45
Cicero, IL (town) Cook County	58,542	68.38
Mercedes, TX (city) Hidalgo County	9,325	68.32
Cudahy, CA (city) Los Angeles County	16,520	68.24
Alamo, TX (city) Hidalgo County	10,067	68.20
West Puente Valley, CA (cdp) Los Angeles County	15,403	68.19
Watsonville, CA (city) Santa Cruz County	29,953	67.67
Weslaco, TX (city) Hidalgo County	18,157	67.41
Indio, CA (city) Riverside County	32,985	67.16
Mission, TX (city) Hidalgo County	30,495	67.16
Bell, CA (city) Los Angeles County	24,558	66.98
El Centro, CA (city) Imperial County	25,251	66.74
Lynwood, CA (city) Los Angeles County	46,491	66.56
Brawley, CA (city) Imperial County	14,606	66.23
Avocado Heights, CA (cdp) Los Angeles County	9,985	65.92
Santa Ana, CA (city) Orange County	222,719	65.90
McAllen, TX (city) Hidalgo County	69,931	65.72
Lennox, CA (cdp) Los Angeles County	15,080	65.71
Dinuba, CA (city) Tulare County	11,052	65.61
Livingston, CA (city) Merced County	6,852	65.43
Hawaiian Gardens, CA (city) Los Angeles County	9,577	64.80
Baldwin Park, CA (city) Los Angeles County	49,046	64.67
South Houston, TX (city) Harris County	10,190	64.36
Jacinto City, TX (city) Harris County	6,584	63.91
El Paso, TX (city) El Paso County	359,699	63.81
San Benito, TX (city) Cameron County	14,893	63.53
Santa Paula, CA (city) Ventura County	18,069	63.18
Eloy, AZ (city) Pinal County	6,554	63.17
Montebello, CA (city) Los Angeles County	38,881	62.56
Selma, CA (city) Fresno County	11,953	61.47
Sunnyside, WA (city) Yakima County	8,539	61.41
Valinda, CA (cdp) Los Angeles County	13,364	61.37
Delano, CA (city) Kern County	23,428	60.34
El Monte, CA (city) Los Angeles County	69,880	60.26
Paramount, CA (city) Los Angeles County	33,129	59.94
Avenal, CA (city) Kings County	8,780	59.83

Place	Number	%
Galena Park, TX (city) Harris County	6,334	59.80
Reedley, CA (city) Fresno County	12,379	59.64
Fillmore, CA (city) Ventura County	8,134	59.62
Oxnard, CA (city) Ventura County	101,264	59.44
Madera, CA (city) Madera County	25,562	59.16
Wasco, CA (city) Kern County	12,538	58.97
Alum Rock, CA (cdp) Santa Clara County	7,861	58.32
Santa Fe Springs, CA (city) Los Angeles County	10,059	57.68
Robstown, TX (city) Nueces County	7,334	57.63
Immokalee, FL (cdp) Collier County	11,354	57.45
South Whittier, CA (cdp) Los Angeles County	31,690	57.42
Shafter, CA (city) Kern County	7,169	56.29
Salinas, CA (city) Monterey County	84,815	56.15
North Fair Oaks, CA (cdp) San Mateo County	8,569	55.50
Harlingen, TX (city) Cameron County	31,922	55.45
Corcoran, CA (city) Kings County	7,866	54.41
Bloomington, CA (cdp) San Bernardino County	10,368	53.67
Pomona, CA (city) Los Angeles County	79,757	53.36
Azusa, CA (city) Los Angeles County	23,836	53.31
National City, CA (city) San Diego County	28,544	52.61
Santa Maria, CA (city) Santa Barbara County	40,719	52.59
Uvalde, TX (city) Uvalde County	7,818	52.37
Vincent, CA (cdp) Los Angeles County	7,888	52.25
Citrus, CA (cdp) Los Angeles County	5,500	51.98
Drexel Heights, AZ (cdp) Pima County	12,309	51.61
Norwalk, CA (city) Los Angeles County	52,652	50.97
Colton, CA (city) San Bernardino County	23,813	49.96
East Palo Alto, CA (city) San Mateo County	14,550	49.31
Ontario, CA (city) San Bernardino County	77,476	49.03
Patterson, CA (city) Stanislaus County	5,577	48.05
Montclair, CA (city) San Bernardino County	15,851	47.96
Hollister, CA (city) San Benito County	16,381	47.60
Pasco, WA (city) Franklin County	15,256	47.58
Deming, NM (city) Luna County	6,659	47.17
Compton, CA (city) Los Angeles County	43,839	46.89
Perris, CA (city) Riverside County	16,783	46.38
Gilroy, CA (city) Santa Clara County	19,226	46.37
Kingsville, TX (city) Kleberg County	11,838	46.29
Whittier, CA (city) Los Angeles County	38,565	46.09
Fontana, CA (city) San Bernardino County	59,386	46.06
Rubidoux, CA (cdp) Riverside County	13,271	45.48
Melrose Park, IL (village) Cook County	10,500	45.32
West Chicago, IL (city) Du Page County	10,550	44.95
Aldine, TX (cdp) Harris County	6,266	44.82
Woodburn, OR (city) Marion County	8,945	44.50
Summit, IL (village) Cook County	4,717	44.35
Richmond, TX (city) Fort Bend County	4,853	43.80
Alice, TX (city) Jim Wells County	8,296	43.64
Willowbrook, CA (cdp) Los Angeles County	14,834	43.45
Porterville, CA (city) Tulare County	17,148	43.29
Hereford, TX (city) Deaf Smith County	6,317	43.28
Chula Vista, CA (city) San Diego County	74,867	43.14
Coalinga, CA (city) Fresno County	5,015	42.98
Cathedral City, CA (city) Riverside County	17,791	41.72
Los Banos, CA (city) Merced County	10,753	41.57
Stanton, CA (city) Orange County	15,496	41.43
San Antonio, TX (city) Bexar County	473,420	41.36
Mira Loma, CA (cdp) Riverside County	7,281	41.33
Rosenberg, TX (city) Fort Bend County	9,930	41.30
La Habra, CA (city) Orange County	24,195	41.03
Freeport, TX (city) Brazoria County	5,202	40.93
Rialto, CA (city) San Bernardino County	37,589	40.91
Downey, CA (city) Los Angeles County	43,241	40.29
Riverbank, CA (city) Stanislaus County	6,334	40.02
Blythe, CA (city) Riverside County	4,800	39.49
Beeville, TX (city) Bee County	5,175	39.42
Yuma, AZ (city) Yuma County	30,512	39.36
Port Lavaca, TX (city) Calhoun County	4,736	39.35
Clute, TX (city) Brazoria County	4,092	39.26
Chino, CA (city) San Bernardino County	26,232	39.05
Avondale, AZ (city) Maricopa County	13,987	38.98
Glen Avon, CA (cdp) Riverside County	5,785	38.95
San Bernardino, CA (city) San Bernardino County	71,891	38.78
Tulare, CA (city) Tulare County	17,006	38.66
Pasadena, TX (city) Harris County	54,725	38.63

Notes: (cdp) census designated place; Refer to the Explanation of Data in the front of the book for more detailed information.

Hispanic: Puerto Rican

Top 150 Places Sorted by Number

(Based on all places, regardless of population)

Place	Number	%
New York, NY (city) New York City	789,172	9.85
Chicago, IL (city) Cook County	113,055	3.90
Philadelphia, PA (city) Philadelphia County	91,527	6.03
Newark, NJ (city) Essex County	39,650	14.49
Hartford, CT (city) Hartford County	39,586	32.56
Springfield, MA (city) Hampden County	35,251	23.18
Bridgeport, CT (city) Fairfield County	32,177	23.06
Jersey City, NJ (city) Hudson County	29,777	12.40
Boston, MA (city) Suffolk County	27,442	4.66
Cleveland, OH (city) Cuyahoga County	25,385	5.31
Paterson, NJ (city) Passaic County	24,013	16.09
Camden, NJ (city) Camden County	23,051	28.85
Islip, NY (town) Suffolk County	22,298	6.91
Rochester, NY (city) Monroe County	21,897	9.96
Milwaukee, WI (city) Milwaukee County	19,613	3.29
Reading, PA (city) Berks County	19,054	23.46
Waterbury, CT (city) New Haven County	18,149	16.92
Yonkers, NY (city) Westchester County	18,097	9.23
New Haven, CT (city) New Haven County	17,683	14.30
Allentown, PA (city) Lehigh County	17,682	16.58
Tampa, FL (city) Hillsborough County	17,527	5.78
Buffalo, NY (city) Erie County	17,250	5.89
Worcester, MA (city) Worcester County	17,091	9.90
Orlando, FL (city) Orange County	17,029	9.16
Brookhaven, NY (town) Suffolk County	16,438	3.67
Lawrence, MA (city) Essex County	15,816	21.95
Hempstead, NY (town) Nassau County	15,779	2.09
New Britain, CT (city) Hartford County	15,693	21.94
Holyoke, MA (city) Hampden County	14,539	36.50
Lancaster, PA (city) Lancaster County	13,717	24.34
Los Angeles, CA (city) Los Angeles County	13,427	0.36
Vineland, NJ (city) Cumberland County	13,284	23.61
Perth Amboy, NJ (city) Middlesex County	13,145	27.79
Elizabeth, NJ (city) Union County	12,989	10.77
Providence, RI (city) Providence County	12,712	7.32
Kissimmee, FL (city) Osceola County	11,312	23.66
Jacksonville, FL (special city) Duval County	11,066	1.50
Lorain, OH (city) Lorain County	10,536	15.35
Miami, FL (city) Miami-Dade County	10,257	2.83
Bethlehem, PA (city) Northampton County	10,096	14.15
Meriden, CT (city) New Haven County	9,637	16.55
Lowell, MA (city) Middlesex County	9,604	9.13
Deltona, FL (city) Volusia County	9,136	13.14
Passaic, NJ (city) Passaic County	9,122	13.44
Trenton, NJ (city) Mercer County	8,952	10.48
Brentwood, NY (cdp) Suffolk County	8,254	15.31
Yeehaw Junction, FL (cdp) Osceola County	7,980	36.64
San Antonio, TX (city) Bexar County	7,774	0.68
Town 'n' Country, FL (cdp) Hillsborough County	7,505	10.35
Hollywood, FL (city) Broward County	7,463	5.36
Union City, NJ (city) Hudson County	7,388	11.01
Houston, TX (city) Harris County	6,906	0.35
Pembroke Pines, FL (city) Broward County	6,887	5.01
New Bedford, MA (city) Bristol County	6,657	7.10
Detroit, MI (city) Wayne County	6,615	0.70
Hialeah, FL (city) Miami-Dade County	6,584	2.91
Virginia Beach, VA (independent city) Virginia Beach city	6,273	1.48
Babylon, NY (town) Suffolk County	6,170	2.91
San Diego, CA (city) San Diego County	5,938	0.49
Chelsea, MA (city) Suffolk County	5,363	15.29
East Hartford, CT (cdp) Hartford County	5,121	10.33
Phoenix, AZ (city) Maricopa County	5,089	0.39
York, PA (city) York County	4,977	12.18
Syracuse, NY (city) Onondaga County	4,885	3.32
Hoboken, NJ (city) Hudson County	4,660	12.08
Honolulu, HI (cdp) Honolulu County	4,607	1.24
Brandon, FL (cdp) Hillsborough County	4,599	5.90
Brockton, MA (city) Plymouth County	4,545	4.82
North Bergen, NJ (township) Hudson County	4,535	7.81
Killeen, TX (city) Bell County	4,499	5.18
Windham, CT (town) Windham County	4,462	19.52
Wilmington, DE (city) New Castle County	4,328	5.96
Oak Ridge, FL (cdp) Orange County	4,249	19.01
Bayonne, NJ (city) Hudson County	4,244	6.86
Fitchburg, MA (city) Worcester County	4,199	10.74
Coral Springs, FL (city) Broward County	4,163	3.54
San Jose, CA (city) Santa Clara County	4,072	0.46
Central Islip, NY (cdp) Suffolk County	4,050	12.68
Harrisburg, PA (city) Dauphin County	3,984	8.14
Chicopee, MA (city) Hampden County	3,932	7.19
Clifton, NJ (city) Passaic County	3,923	4.99
Woodbridge, NJ (township) Middlesex County	3,838	3.95
Haverstraw, NY (town) Rockland County	3,812	11.27
Miramar, FL (city) Broward County	3,800	5.22
Poinciana, FL (cdp) Osceola County	3,789	27.76
Meadow Woods, FL (cdp) Orange County	3,772	33.42
Lynn, MA (city) Essex County	3,769	4.23
Palm Bay, FL (city) Brevard County	3,767	4.74
San Francisco, CA (city) San Francisco County	3,758	0.48
Lakewood, NJ (township) Ocean County	3,730	6.18
El Paso, TX (city) El Paso County	3,660	0.65
Atlantic City, NJ (city) Atlantic County	3,635	8.97
Pennsauken, NJ (cdp) Camden County	3,629	10.15
Miami Beach, FL (city) Miami-Dade County	3,596	4.09
Saint Petersburg, FL (city) Pinellas County	3,574	1.44
Egypt Lake-Leto, FL (cdp) Hillsborough County	3,559	10.86
Oyster Bay, NY (town) Nassau County	3,506	1.19
Huntington, NY (town) Suffolk County	3,465	1.77
Belleville, NJ (cdp) Essex County	3,430	9.55
New London, CT (city) New London County	3,382	13.17
Willimantic, CT (cdp) Windham County	3,310	20.92
Pawtucket, RI (city) Providence County	3,298	4.52
Davie, FL (town) Broward County	3,285	4.34
Sunrise, FL (city) Broward County	3,223	3.76
Youngstown, OH (city) Mahoning County	3,222	3.93
New Brunswick, NJ (city) Middlesex County	3,178	6.54
Stamford, CT (city) Fairfield County	3,167	2.70
Newport News, VA (independent city) Newport News city	3,144	1.75
Albany, NY (city) Albany County	3,094	3.23
East Chicago, IN (city) Lake County	3,088	9.53
Newburgh, NY (city) Orange County	3,069	10.86
Spring Hill, FL (cdp) Hernando County	3,067	4.44
Middletown, NY (city) Orange County	3,066	12.08
Lebanon, PA (city) Lebanon County	3,053	12.48
Southbridge, MA (town) Worcester County	3,033	17.62
Altamonte Springs, FL (city) Seminole County	3,007	7.30
Norwalk, CT (city) Fairfield County	2,978	3.59
Waukegan, IL (city) Lake County	2,976	3.39
Pine Hills, FL (cdp) Orange County	2,958	7.08
Norfolk, VA (independent city) Norfolk city	2,916	1.24
Erie, PA (city) Erie County	2,911	2.81
Framingham, MA (cdp) Middlesex County	2,903	4.34
Las Vegas, NV (city) Clark County	2,866	0.60
Leominster, MA (city) Worcester County	2,843	6.88
Port Saint Lucie, FL (city) Saint Lucie County	2,811	3.17
Fort Lauderdale, FL (city) Broward County	2,801	1.84
Woonsocket, RI (city) Providence County	2,798	6.47
West New York, NJ (town) Hudson County	2,791	6.10
Columbus, OH (city) Franklin County	2,790	0.39
Long Branch, NJ (city) Monmouth County	2,778	8.86
The Hammocks, FL (cdp) Miami-Dade County	2,763	5.83
Azalea Park, FL (cdp) Orange County	2,745	24.79
Carol City, FL (cdp) Miami-Dade County	2,745	4.62
Bloomfield, NJ (cdp) Essex County	2,724	5.71
Utica, NY (city) Oneida County	2,721	4.49
Cape Coral, FL (city) Lee County	2,715	2.65
University, FL (cdp) Hillsborough County	2,699	8.78
Colorado Springs, CO (city) El Paso County	2,685	0.74
Columbus, GA (special city) Muscogee County	2,682	1.44
North Miami, FL (city) Miami-Dade County	2,660	4.44
Ramapo, NY (town) Rockland County	2,636	2.42
Aurora, IL (city) Kane County	2,611	1.83
Clarkstown, NY (town) Rockland County	2,609	3.18
North Bay Shore, NY (cdp) Suffolk County	2,578	17.20
Austin, TX (city) Travis County	2,529	0.39
West Haven, CT (city) New Haven County	2,510	4.79
Fayetteville, NC (city) Cumberland County	2,488	2.06
Schenectady, NY (city) Schenectady County	2,422	3.92
Charlotte, NC (city) Mecklenburg County	2,415	0.45
Dover, NJ (town) Morris County	2,413	13.27

Notes: (cdp) census designated place; Refer to the Explanation of Data in the front of the book for more detailed information.

Hispanic: Puerto Rican

Top 150 Places Sorted by Percent

(Based on all places, regardless of population)

Place	Number	%
Harlem Heights, FL (cdp) Lee County	396	37.18
Yeehaw Junction, FL (cdp) Osceola County	7,980	36.64
Holyoke, MA (city) Hampden County	14,539	36.50
Meadow Woods, FL (cdp) Orange County	3,772	33.42
Hartford, CT (city) Hartford County	39,586	32.56
Elwood-Magnolia, NJ (cdp) Atlantic County	428	30.75
Camden, NJ (city) Camden County	23,051	28.85
Perth Amboy, NJ (city) Middlesex County	13,145	27.79
Poinciana, FL (cdp) Osceola County	3,789	27.76
Azalea Park, FL (cdp) Orange County	2,745	24.79
Lancaster, PA (city) Lancaster County	13,717	24.34
Kissimmee, FL (city) Osceola County	11,312	23.66
Vineland, NJ (city) Cumberland County	13,284	23.61
Reading, PA (city) Berks County	19,054	23.46
Springfield, MA (city) Hampden County	35,251	23.18
Bridgeport, CT (city) Fairfield County	32,177	23.06
Lawrence, MA (city) Essex County	15,816	21.95
New Britain, CT (city) Hartford County	15,693	21.94
Willimantic, CT (cdp) Windham County	3,310	20.92
Windham, CT (town) Windham County	4,462	19.52
Egg Harbor City, NJ (city) Atlantic County	880	19.36
Oak Ridge, FL (cdp) Orange County	4,249	19.01
Southchase, FL (cdp) Orange County	880	18.99
Ellenville, NY (village) Ulster County	737	17.85
Southbridge, MA (town) Worcester County	3,033	17.62
Woodbine, NJ (borough) Cape May County	478	17.60
North Bay Shore, NY (cdp) Suffolk County	2,578	17.20
Interlachen, FL (town) Putnam County	252	17.08
Dunkirk, NY (city) Chautauqua County	2,238	17.04
Buena, NJ (borough) Atlantic County	660	17.04
Union Park, FL (cdp) Orange County	1,730	16.98
Waterbury, CT (city) New Haven County	18,149	16.92
Allentown, PA (city) Lehigh County	17,682	16.58
Meriden, CT (city) New Haven County	9,637	16.55
Sky Lake, FL (cdp) Orange County	931	16.47
Pine Castle, FL (cdp) Orange County	1,444	16.40
Woodlynne, NJ (borough) Camden County	456	16.31
Paterson, NJ (city) Passaic County	24,013	16.09
Washington, NJ (township) Burlington County	96	15.46
Lorain, OH (city) Lorain County	10,536	15.35
Brentwood, NY (cdp) Suffolk County	8,254	15.31
Chelsea, MA (city) Suffolk County	5,363	15.29
Haverstraw, NY (village) Rockland County	1,494	14.77
Newark, NJ (city) Essex County	39,650	14.49
New Haven, CT (city) New Haven County	17,683	14.30
West Haverstraw, NY (village) Rockland County	1,464	14.22
Bethlehem, PA (city) Northampton County	10,096	14.15
Halaula, HI (cdp) Hawaii County	69	13.94
Victory Gardens, NJ (borough) Morris County	213	13.78
Woodridge, NY (village) Sullivan County	123	13.64
Passaic, NJ (city) Passaic County	9,122	13.44
Dover, NJ (town) Morris County	2,413	13.27
New London, CT (city) New London County	3,382	13.17
Deltona, FL (city) Volusia County	9,136	13.14
Mullica, NJ (township) Atlantic County	766	12.96
Central Islip, NY (cdp) Suffolk County	4,050	12.68
Lebanon, PA (city) Lebanon County	3,053	12.48
Jersey City, NJ (city) Hudson County	29,777	12.40
Wildwood, NJ (city) Cape May County	668	12.29
Prospect Park, NJ (borough) Passaic County	706	12.22
York, PA (city) York County	4,977	12.18
Hoboken, NJ (city) Hudson County	4,660	12.08
Middletown, NY (city) Orange County	3,066	12.08
Warminster Heights, PA (cdp) Bucks County	503	12.00
Central Falls, RI (city) Providence County	2,249	11.88
Penns Grove, NJ (borough) Salem County	580	11.87
Fort Dix, NJ (cdp) Burlington County	875	11.72
Monticello, NY (village) Sullivan County	755	11.59
Amsterdam, NY (city) Montgomery County	2,124	11.57
Freemansburg, PA (borough) Northampton County	215	11.33
Ainaloa, HI (cdp) Hawaii County	216	11.31
Haverstraw, NY (town) Rockland County	3,812	11.27
Miami Gardens, FL (cdp) Broward County	303	11.20
Union City, NJ (city) Hudson County	7,388	11.01
North Bellport, NY (cdp) Suffolk County	992	11.01
Pleasantville, NJ (city) Atlantic County	2,085	10.97
Plattekill, NY (town) Ulster County	1,084	10.96
Mechanicstown, NY (cdp) Orange County	660	10.89
Kapaau, HI (cdp) Hawaii County	126	10.87
Egypt Lake-Leto, FL (cdp) Hillsborough County	3,559	10.86
Newburgh, NY (city) Orange County	3,069	10.86
Elizabeth, NJ (city) Union County	12,989	10.77
Fitchburg, MA (city) Worcester County	4,199	10.74
Wawarsing, NY (town) Ulster County	1,383	10.73
Carteret, NJ (borough) Middlesex County	2,216	10.70
Seabrook Farms, NJ (cdp) Cumberland County	184	10.70
Gun Club Estates, FL (cdp) Palm Beach County	75	10.55
Fort Myers Shores, FL (cdp) Lee County	608	10.50
Trenton, NJ (city) Mercer County	8,952	10.48
Beacon, NY (city) Dutchess County	1,436	10.40
Dannemora, NY (village) Clinton County	428	10.37
Town 'n' Country, FL (cdp) Hillsborough County	7,505	10.35
East Hartford, CT (cdp) Hartford County	5,121	10.33
Pennsauken, NJ (cdp) Camden County	3,629	10.15
Scotchtown, NY (cdp) Orange County	903	10.08
Princeton, FL (cdp) Miami-Dade County	1,009	10.00
Attu Station, AK (cdp) Aleutians West Census Area	2	10.00
Rochester, NY (city) Monroe County	21,897	9.96
Worcester, MA (city) Worcester County	17,091	9.90
New York, NY (city) New York City	789,172	9.85
Mountain View, HI (cdp) Hawaii County	275	9.82
Groveland, NY (town) Livingston County	378	9.81
Belleville, NJ (cdp) Essex County	3,430	9.55
East Chicago, IN (city) Lake County	3,088	9.53
New Hanover, NJ (township) Burlington County	928	9.52
Bristol, PA (borough) Bucks County	940	9.47
Coolbaugh, PA (township) Monroe County	1,431	9.41
Pine Manor, FL (cdp) Lee County	353	9.33
Maybrook, NY (village) Orange County	287	9.31
Hawaiian Beaches, HI (cdp) Hawaii County	345	9.30
Yonkers, NY (city) Westchester County	18,097	9.23
Campbell, OH (city) Mahoning County	873	9.23
Makaha Valley, HI (cdp) Honolulu County	119	9.23
Orlando, FL (city) Orange County	17,029	9.16
Lowell, MA (city) Middlesex County	9,604	9.13
Baywood, NY (cdp) Suffolk County	687	9.07
Dannemora, NY (town) Clinton County	467	9.07
Tice, FL (cdp) Lee County	411	9.06
Atlantic City, NJ (city) Atlantic County	3,635	8.97
Livingston Manor, NY (cdp) Sullivan County	121	8.93
Millville, NJ (city) Cumberland County	2,392	8.91
Vails Gate, NY (cdp) Orange County	295	8.89
Long Branch, NJ (city) Monmouth County	2,778	8.86
Chambers Estates, FL (cdp) Broward County	315	8.86
Leisure City, FL (cdp) Miami-Dade County	1,960	8.85
Haledon, NJ (borough) Passaic County	729	8.83
University, FL (cdp) Hillsborough County	2,699	8.78
Milan, NY (town) Dutchess County	398	8.73
Makaha, HI (cdp) Honolulu County	674	8.69
Lockhart, FL (cdp) Orange County	1,123	8.68
Goldenrod, FL (cdp) Seminole County	1,106	8.59
Citrus Ridge, FL (cdp) Lake County	1,027	8.55
Liberty, NY (village) Sullivan County	339	8.53
Islandia, NY (village) Suffolk County	260	8.51
Palm River-Clair Mel, FL (cdp) Hillsborough County	1,462	8.31
Casselberry, FL (city) Seminole County	1,869	8.26
Marcy, NY (town) Oneida County	781	8.25
Saint Cloud, FL (city) Osceola County	1,653	8.23
Harrisburg, PA (city) Dauphin County	3,984	8.14
Wallkill, NY (town) Orange County	2,004	8.13
Broadview Park, FL (cdp) Broward County	552	8.12
Cape Vincent, NY (town) Jefferson County	271	8.10
Chesterfield, NJ (township) Burlington County	478	8.03
Lakes by the Bay, FL (cdp) Miami-Dade County	723	7.98
Hammonton, NJ (town) Atlantic County	994	7.89
Maili, HI (cdp) Honolulu County	465	7.82
North Bergen, NJ (township) Hudson County	4,535	7.81
Bay Shore, NY (cdp) Suffolk County	1,855	7.78
Washingtonville, NY (village) Orange County	451	7.71
Orlovista, FL (cdp) Orange County	465	7.69

Notes: (cdp) census designated place; Refer to the Explanation of Data in the front of the book for more detailed information.

Hispanic: Puerto Rican

Top 150 Places Sorted by Percent

(Based on places with populations of 10,000 or more)

Place	Number	%
Yeehaw Junction, FL (cdp) Osceola County	7,980	36.64
Holyoke, MA (city) Hampden County	14,539	36.50
Meadow Woods, FL (cdp) Orange County	3,772	33.42
Hartford, CT (city) Hartford County	39,586	32.56
Camden, NJ (city) Camden County	23,051	28.85
Perth Amboy, NJ (city) Middlesex County	13,145	27.79
Poinciana, FL (cdp) Osceola County	3,789	27.76
Azalea Park, FL (cdp) Orange County	2,745	24.79
Lancaster, PA (city) Lancaster County	13,717	24.34
Kissimmee, FL (city) Osceola County	11,312	23.66
Vineland, NJ (city) Cumberland County	13,284	23.61
Reading, PA (city) Berks County	19,054	23.46
Springfield, MA (city) Hampden County	35,251	23.18
Bridgeport, CT (city) Fairfield County	32,177	23.06
Lawrence, MA (city) Essex County	15,816	21.95
New Britain, CT (city) Hartford County	15,693	21.94
Willimantic, CT (cdp) Windham County	3,310	20.92
Windham, CT (town) Windham County	4,462	19.52
Oak Ridge, FL (cdp) Orange County	4,249	19.01
Southbridge, MA (town) Worcester County	3,033	17.62
North Bay Shore, NY (cdp) Suffolk County	2,578	17.20
Dunkirk, NY (city) Chautauqua County	2,238	17.04
Union Park, FL (cdp) Orange County	1,730	16.98
Waterbury, CT (city) New Haven County	18,149	16.92
Allentown, PA (city) Lehigh County	17,682	16.58
Meriden, CT (city) New Haven County	9,637	16.55
Paterson, NJ (city) Passaic County	24,013	16.09
Lorain, OH (city) Lorain County	10,536	15.35
Brentwood, NY (cdp) Suffolk County	8,254	15.31
Chelsea, MA (city) Suffolk County	5,363	15.29
Haverstraw, NY (village) Rockland County	1,494	14.77
Newark, NJ (city) Essex County	39,650	14.49
New Haven, CT (city) New Haven County	17,683	14.30
West Haverstraw, NY (village) Rockland County	1,464	14.22
Bethlehem, PA (city) Northampton County	10,096	14.15
Passaic, NJ (city) Passaic County	9,122	13.44
Dover, NJ (town) Morris County	2,413	13.27
New London, CT (city) New London County	3,382	13.17
Deltona, FL (city) Volusia County	9,136	13.14
Central Islip, NY (cdp) Suffolk County	4,050	12.68
Lebanon, PA (city) Lebanon County	3,053	12.48
Jersey City, NJ (city) Hudson County	29,777	12.40
York, PA (city) York County	4,977	12.18
Hoboken, NJ (city) Hudson County	4,660	12.08
Middletown, NY (city) Orange County	3,066	12.08
Central Falls, RI (city) Providence County	2,249	11.88
Amsterdam, NY (city) Montgomery County	2,124	11.57
Haverstraw, NY (town) Rockland County	3,812	11.27
Union City, NJ (city) Hudson County	7,388	11.01
Pleasantville, NJ (city) Atlantic County	2,085	10.97
Egypt Lake-Leto, FL (cdp) Hillsborough County	3,559	10.86
Newburgh, NY (city) Orange County	3,069	10.86
Elizabeth, NJ (city) Union County	12,989	10.77
Fitchburg, MA (city) Worcester County	4,199	10.74
Wawarsing, NY (town) Ulster County	1,383	10.73
Carteret, NJ (borough) Middlesex County	2,216	10.70
Trenton, NJ (city) Mercer County	8,952	10.48
Beacon, NY (city) Dutchess County	1,436	10.40
Town 'n' Country, FL (cdp) Hillsborough County	7,505	10.35
East Hartford, CT (cdp) Hartford County	5,121	10.33
Pennsauken, NJ (cdp) Camden County	3,629	10.15
Princeton, FL (cdp) Miami-Dade County	1,009	10.00
Rochester, NY (city) Monroe County	21,897	9.96
Worcester, MA (city) Worcester County	17,091	9.90
New York, NY (city) New York City	789,172	9.85
Belleville, NJ (cdp) Essex County	3,430	9.55
East Chicago, IN (city) Lake County	3,088	9.53
Coolbaugh, PA (township) Monroe County	1,431	9.41
Yonkers, NY (city) Westchester County	18,097	9.23
Orlando, FL (city) Orange County	17,029	9.16
Lowell, MA (city) Middlesex County	9,604	9.13
Atlantic City, NJ (city) Atlantic County	3,635	8.97
Millville, NJ (city) Cumberland County	2,392	8.91
Long Branch, NJ (city) Monmouth County	2,778	8.86
Leisure City, FL (cdp) Miami-Dade County	1,960	8.85
University, FL (cdp) Hillsborough County	2,699	8.78
Lockhart, FL (cdp) Orange County	1,123	8.68
Goldenrod, FL (cdp) Seminole County	1,106	8.59
Citrus Ridge, FL (cdp) Lake County	1,027	8.55
Palm River-Clair Mel, FL (cdp) Hillsborough County	1,462	8.31
Casselberry, FL (city) Seminole County	1,869	8.26
Saint Cloud, FL (city) Osceola County	1,653	8.23
Harrisburg, PA (city) Dauphin County	3,984	8.14
Wallkill, NY (town) Orange County	2,004	8.13
Hammonton, NJ (town) Atlantic County	994	7.89
North Bergen, NJ (township) Hudson County	4,535	7.81
Bay Shore, NY (cdp) Suffolk County	1,855	7.78
Mastic, NY (cdp) Suffolk County	1,166	7.55
Fallsburg, NY (town) Sullivan County	916	7.49
Providence, RI (city) Providence County	12,712	7.32
Thompson, NY (town) Sullivan County	1,038	7.32
Altamonte Springs, FL (city) Seminole County	3,007	7.30
Richmond West, FL (cdp) Miami-Dade County	2,045	7.28
Lake Worth Corridor, FL (cdp) Palm Beach County	1,356	7.27
Lancaster, PA (township) Lancaster County	1,011	7.25
Chicopee, MA (city) Hampden County	3,932	7.19
Citrus Park, FL (cdp) Hillsborough County	1,442	7.13
New Bedford, MA (city) Bristol County	6,657	7.10
Pine Hills, FL (cdp) Orange County	2,958	7.08
Islip, NY (town) Suffolk County	22,298	6.91
Leominster, MA (city) Worcester County	2,843	6.88
Oviedo, FL (city) Seminole County	1,807	6.87
Bayonne, NJ (city) Hudson County	4,244	6.86
Bridgeton, NJ (city) Cumberland County	1,558	6.84
South Miami Heights, FL (cdp) Miami-Dade County	2,285	6.82
Mastic Beach, NY (cdp) Suffolk County	779	6.75
Shirley, NY (cdp) Suffolk County	1,689	6.65
Cutler Ridge, FL (cdp) Miami-Dade County	1,625	6.56
New Brunswick, NJ (city) Middlesex County	3,178	6.54
Homestead, FL (city) Miami-Dade County	2,084	6.53
Peekskill, NY (city) Westchester County	1,454	6.48
Woonsocket, RI (city) Providence County	2,798	6.47
Chester, NY (town) Orange County	779	6.42
Apopka, FL (city) Orange County	1,704	6.40
Malone, NY (town) Franklin County	954	6.37
Somers, CT (town) Tolland County	656	6.30
Lehigh Acres, FL (cdp) Lee County	2,098	6.28
Patchogue, NY (village) Suffolk County	748	6.28
Browns Mills, NJ (cdp) Burlington County	701	6.23
Lakewood, NJ (township) Ocean County	3,730	6.18
West New York, NJ (town) Hudson County	2,791	6.10
Weehawken, NJ (township) Hudson County	822	6.09
New Windsor, NY (town) Orange County	1,382	6.04
Philadelphia, PA (city) Philadelphia County	91,527	6.03
Asbury Park, NJ (city) Monmouth County	1,021	6.03
Fishkill, NY (town) Dutchess County	1,214	5.99
Wilmington, DE (city) New Castle County	4,328	5.96
Mount Holly, NJ (township) Burlington County	638	5.95
Country Club, FL (cdp) Miami-Dade County	2,152	5.93
Newburgh, NY (town) Orange County	1,631	5.92
Brandon, FL (cdp) Hillsborough County	4,599	5.90
Buffalo, NY (city) Erie County	17,250	5.89
Geneva, NY (city) Ontario County	801	5.88
Fort Bragg, NC (cdp) Cumberland County	1,711	5.86
Blooming Grove, NY (town) Orange County	1,013	5.84
The Hammocks, FL (cdp) Miami-Dade County	2,763	5.83
Forest City, FL (cdp) Seminole County	735	5.83
Greater Carrollwood, FL (cdp) Hillsborough County	1,942	5.79
Tampa, FL (city) Hillsborough County	17,527	5.78
Lake Station, IN (city) Lake County	798	5.72
Bloomfield, NJ (cdp) Essex County	2,724	5.71
Freehold, NJ (borough) Monmouth County	627	5.71
Waianae, HI (cdp) Honolulu County	600	5.71
Conway, FL (cdp) Orange County	819	5.69
Kendall West, FL (cdp) Miami-Dade County	2,142	5.63
Clinton, MA (town) Worcester County	757	5.63
Guttenberg, NJ (town) Hudson County	608	5.63
Ludlow, MA (town) Hampden County	1,182	5.57
Winter Springs, FL (city) Seminole County	1,762	5.56
Country Walk, FL (cdp) Miami-Dade County	589	5.53

Notes: (cdp) census designated place; Refer to the Explanation of Data in the front of the book for more detailed information.

Hispanic: South American

Top 150 Places Sorted by Number

(Based on all places, regardless of population)

Place	Number	%
New York, NY (city) New York City	236,374	2.95
Los Angeles, CA (city) Los Angeles County	31,518	0.85
Chicago, IL (city) Cook County	20,828	0.72
Miami, FL (city) Miami-Dade County	15,076	4.16
Elizabeth, NJ (city) Union County	14,831	12.30
Paterson, NJ (city) Passaic County	13,852	9.28
Houston, TX (city) Harris County	13,214	0.68
Hialeah, FL (city) Miami-Dade County	12,510	5.53
Miami Beach, FL (city) Miami-Dade County	11,589	13.18
Hempstead, NY (town) Nassau County	11,430	1.51
Newark, NJ (city) Essex County	11,134	4.07
Union City, NJ (city) Hudson County	10,080	15.03
The Hammocks, FL (cdp) Miami-Dade County	9,494	20.04
Pembroke Pines, FL (city) Broward County	8,292	6.03
Fountainbleau, FL (cdp) Miami-Dade County	8,100	13.60
Kendall, FL (cdp) Miami-Dade County	7,961	10.58
Jersey City, NJ (city) Hudson County	7,807	3.25
North Bergen, NJ (township) Hudson County	7,781	13.39
Islip, NY (town) Suffolk County	7,398	2.29
Arlington, VA (cdp) Arlington County	7,083	3.74
Kendale Lakes, FL (cdp) Miami-Dade County	7,076	12.44
Kendall West, FL (cdp) Miami-Dade County	7,073	18.60
Boston, MA (city) Suffolk County	7,004	1.19
Hollywood, FL (city) Broward County	6,952	4.99
Weston, FL (city) Broward County	6,620	13.43
West New York, NJ (town) Hudson County	6,237	13.63
Coral Springs, FL (city) Broward County	5,261	4.48
Stamford, CT (city) Fairfield County	5,160	4.41
San Francisco, CA (city) San Francisco County	5,007	0.64
Doral, FL (cdp) Miami-Dade County	4,989	24.41
Country Club, FL (cdp) Miami-Dade County	4,843	13.34
Philadelphia, PA (city) Philadelphia County	4,761	0.31
Brookhaven, NY (town) Suffolk County	4,746	1.06
San Diego, CA (city) San Diego County	4,410	0.36
Tamiami, FL (cdp) Miami-Dade County	4,322	7.89
Sunrise, FL (city) Broward County	4,320	5.04
Clifton, NJ (city) Passaic County	4,305	5.47
Hackensack, NJ (city) Bergen County	4,266	10.00
Yonkers, NY (city) Westchester County	3,944	2.01
Rye, NY (town) Westchester County	3,842	8.76
Passaic, NJ (city) Passaic County	3,796	5.59
Washington, DC (city) District of Columbia	3,721	0.65
North Hempstead, NY (town) Nassau County	3,707	1.67
Miramar, FL (city) Broward County	3,696	5.08
White Plains, NY (city) Westchester County	3,641	6.86
Port Chester, NY (village) Westchester County	3,516	12.62
Orlando, FL (city) Orange County	3,494	1.88
Dover, NJ (town) Morris County	3,440	18.91
San Jose, CA (city) Santa Clara County	3,377	0.38
The Crossings, FL (cdp) Miami-Dade County	3,326	14.12
Kearny, NJ (town) Hudson County	3,235	7.99
Brentwood, NY (cdp) Suffolk County	3,139	5.82
Plantation, FL (city) Broward County	3,137	3.78
Oyster Bay, NY (town) Nassau County	3,052	1.04
Danbury, CT (city) Fairfield County	3,049	4.07
Davie, FL (town) Broward County	2,984	3.94
Norwalk, CT (city) Fairfield County	2,959	3.57
Ossining, NY (town) Westchester County	2,942	8.05
North Miami Beach, FL (city) Miami-Dade County	2,936	7.20
Richmond West, FL (cdp) Miami-Dade County	2,906	10.35
Dallas, TX (city) Dallas County	2,895	0.24
Ossining, NY (village) Westchester County	2,819	11.74
Tampa, FL (city) Hillsborough County	2,791	0.92
Charlotte, NC (city) Mecklenburg County	2,732	0.51
Glendale, CA (city) Los Angeles County	2,691	1.38
Coral Gables, FL (city) Miami-Dade County	2,586	6.12
Babylon, NY (town) Suffolk County	2,514	1.19
Tamarac, FL (city) Broward County	2,496	4.49
Downey, CA (city) Los Angeles County	2,478	2.31
Minneapolis, MN (city) Hennepin County	2,457	0.64
Fort Lauderdale, FL (city) Broward County	2,449	1.61
New Rochelle, NY (city) Westchester County	2,435	3.37
Hartford, CT (city) Hartford County	2,430	2.00
Anaheim, CA (city) Orange County	2,406	0.73
Pawtucket, RI (city) Providence County	2,397	3.29
Alexandria, VA (independent city) Alexandria city	2,325	1.81
Aventura, FL (city) Miami-Dade County	2,289	9.06
San Antonio, TX (city) Bexar County	2,288	0.20
North Plainfield, NJ (borough) Somerset County	2,249	10.66
Providence, RI (city) Providence County	2,241	1.29
Long Beach, CA (city) Los Angeles County	2,228	0.48
Carol City, FL (cdp) Miami-Dade County	2,210	3.72
Phoenix, AZ (city) Maricopa County	2,199	0.17
Austin, TX (city) Travis County	2,161	0.33
Sunny Isles Beach, FL (city) Miami-Dade County	2,150	14.04
Annandale, VA (cdp) Fairfax County	2,149	3.91
Englewood, NJ (city) Bergen County	2,130	8.13
Kissimmee, FL (city) Osceola County	2,047	4.28
Jacksonville, FL (special city) Duval County	2,037	0.28
Harrison, NJ (town) Hudson County	2,034	14.10
Margate, FL (city) Broward County	2,029	3.76
North Miami, FL (city) Miami-Dade County	2,009	3.36
Town 'n' Country, FL (cdp) Hillsborough County	2,008	2.77
Central Falls, RI (city) Providence County	1,999	10.56
Bridgeport, CT (city) Fairfield County	1,996	1.43
Perth Amboy, NJ (city) Middlesex County	1,955	4.13
Belleville, NJ (cdp) Essex County	1,939	5.40
Miami Lakes, FL (cdp) Miami-Dade County	1,879	8.29
Garfield, NJ (city) Bergen County	1,868	6.27
Las Vegas, NV (city) Clark County	1,850	0.39
Burbank, CA (city) Los Angeles County	1,835	1.83
Plainfield, NJ (city) Union County	1,826	3.82
Morristown, NJ (town) Morris County	1,814	9.78
Key Biscayne, FL (village) Miami-Dade County	1,793	17.06
Greenburgh, NY (town) Westchester County	1,787	2.06
Wheaton-Glenmont, MD (cdp) Montgomery County	1,784	3.09
East Hampton, NY (town) Suffolk County	1,757	8.91
Santa Ana, CA (city) Orange County	1,742	0.52
Hallandale, FL (city) Broward County	1,731	5.05
North Lauderdale, FL (city) Broward County	1,713	5.31
Greenwich, CT (town) Fairfield County	1,697	2.78
Seattle, WA (city) King County	1,668	0.30
Mount Pleasant, NY (town) Westchester County	1,667	3.86
Boca Raton, FL (city) Palm Beach County	1,662	2.22
New Haven, CT (city) New Haven County	1,630	1.32
Ojus, FL (cdp) Miami-Dade County	1,609	9.67
West Orange, NJ (cdp) Essex County	1,585	3.53
Glenvar Heights, FL (cdp) Miami-Dade County	1,567	9.65
University Park, FL (cdp) Miami-Dade County	1,560	5.88
Huntington, NY (town) Suffolk County	1,535	0.79
Lodi, NJ (borough) Bergen County	1,524	6.36
Torrance, CA (city) Los Angeles County	1,521	1.10
Aspen Hill, MD (cdp) Montgomery County	1,489	2.96
Linden, NJ (city) Union County	1,479	3.75
Pasadena, CA (city) Los Angeles County	1,474	1.10
Hialeah Gardens, FL (city) Miami-Dade County	1,471	7.62
Pompano Beach, FL (city) Broward County	1,461	1.87
Santa Clarita, CA (city) Los Angeles County	1,451	0.96
South Miami Heights, FL (cdp) Miami-Dade County	1,441	4.30
Guttenberg, NJ (town) Hudson County	1,410	13.05
Coconut Creek, FL (city) Broward County	1,402	3.22
Woodbridge, NJ (township) Middlesex County	1,390	1.43
Gaithersburg, MD (city) Montgomery County	1,378	2.62
Lowell, MA (city) Middlesex County	1,336	1.27
Westchester, FL (cdp) Miami-Dade County	1,329	4.39
Sleepy Hollow, NY (village) Westchester County	1,321	14.34
Peekskill, NY (city) Westchester County	1,314	5.86
San Mateo, CA (city) San Mateo County	1,313	1.42
Deerfield Beach, FL (city) Broward County	1,309	2.03
Bloomfield, NJ (cdp) Essex County	1,291	2.71
Provo, UT (city) Utah County	1,273	1.21
Jefferson, VA (cdp) Fairfax County	1,269	4.63
Denver, CO (city) Denver County	1,265	0.23
Burke, VA (cdp) Fairfax County	1,264	2.19
Cambridge, MA (city) Middlesex County	1,251	1.23
Paradise, NV (cdp) Clark County	1,245	0.67
Country Walk, FL (cdp) Miami-Dade County	1,243	11.67
Silver Spring, MD (cdp) Montgomery County	1,242	1.62
Hawthorne, CA (city) Los Angeles County	1,230	1.46
Miami Springs, FL (city) Miami-Dade County	1,228	8.96

Notes: (cdp) census designated place; Refer to the Explanation of Data in the front of the book for more detailed information.

Hispanic: South American

Top 150 Places Sorted by Percent

(Based on all places, regardless of population)

Place	Number	%
Doral, FL (cdp) Miami-Dade County	4,989	24.41
Victory Gardens, NJ (borough) Morris County	331	21.41
East Newark, NJ (borough) Hudson County	490	20.61
The Hammocks, FL (cdp) Miami-Dade County	9,494	20.04
Dover, NJ (town) Morris County	3,440	18.91
Montauk, NY (cdp) Suffolk County	721	18.72
Kendall West, FL (cdp) Miami-Dade County	7,073	18.60
Key Biscayne, FL (village) Miami-Dade County	1,793	17.06
North Bay Village, FL (city) Miami-Dade County	1,087	16.14
Union City, NJ (city) Hudson County	10,080	15.03
Virginia Gardens, FL (village) Miami-Dade County	345	14.69
Sleepy Hollow, NY (village) Westchester County	1,321	14.34
The Crossings, FL (cdp) Miami-Dade County	3,326	14.12
Harrison, NJ (town) Hudson County	2,034	14.10
Sunny Isles Beach, FL (city) Miami-Dade County	2,150	14.04
West New York, NJ (town) Hudson County	6,237	13.63
Fountainbleau, FL (cdp) Miami-Dade County	8,100	13.60
Bay Harbor Islands, FL (town) Miami-Dade County	699	13.58
Weston, FL (city) Broward County	6,620	13.43
North Bergen, NJ (township) Hudson County	7,781	13.39
Country Club, FL (cdp) Miami-Dade County	4,843	13.34
Miami Beach, FL (city) Miami-Dade County	11,589	13.18
Guttenberg, NJ (town) Hudson County	1,410	13.05
Port Chester, NY (village) Westchester County	3,516	12.62
Kendale Lakes, FL (cdp) Miami-Dade County	7,076	12.44
Elizabeth, NJ (city) Union County	14,831	12.30
Ossining, NY (village) Westchester County	2,819	11.74
Surfside, FL (town) Miami-Dade County	575	11.71
Country Walk, FL (cdp) Miami-Dade County	1,243	11.67
Three Lakes, FL (cdp) Miami-Dade County	793	11.40
North Plainfield, NJ (borough) Somerset County	2,249	10.66
Kendall, FL (cdp) Miami-Dade County	7,961	10.58
Central Falls, RI (city) Providence County	1,999	10.56
Richmond West, FL (cdp) Miami-Dade County	2,906	10.35
Corral City, TX (town) Denton County	9	10.11
Hackensack, NJ (city) Bergen County	4,266	10.00
Morristown, NJ (town) Morris County	1,814	9.78
Ojus, FL (cdp) Miami-Dade County	1,609	9.67
Glenvar Heights, FL (cdp) Miami-Dade County	1,567	9.65
Fisher Island, FL (cdp) Miami-Dade County	44	9.42
East Hampton North, NY (cdp) Suffolk County	334	9.31
Paterson, NJ (city) Passaic County	13,852	9.28
Springs, NY (cdp) Suffolk County	450	9.09
Aventura, FL (city) Miami-Dade County	2,289	9.06
Miami Springs, FL (city) Miami-Dade County	1,228	8.96
East Hampton, NY (town) Suffolk County	1,757	8.91
Rye, NY (town) Westchester County	3,842	8.76
Bal Harbour, FL (village) Miami-Dade County	288	8.71
Broadview-Pompano Park, FL (cdp) Broward County	447	8.41
Golden Beach, FL (town) Miami-Dade County	77	8.38
Miami Lakes, FL (cdp) Miami-Dade County	1,879	8.29
Englewood, NJ (city) Bergen County	2,130	8.13
Patchogue, NY (village) Suffolk County	968	8.12
Ossining, NY (town) Westchester County	2,942	8.05
Kearny, NJ (town) Hudson County	3,235	7.99
Weehawken, NJ (township) Hudson County	1,074	7.95
Tamiami, FL (cdp) Miami-Dade County	4,322	7.89
Prospect Park, NJ (borough) Passaic County	456	7.89
Wharton, NJ (borough) Morris County	495	7.86
Hightstown, NJ (borough) Mercer County	407	7.80
Hialeah Gardens, FL (city) Miami-Dade County	1,471	7.62
Elmsford, NY (village) Westchester County	340	7.27
North Miami Beach, FL (city) Miami-Dade County	2,936	7.20
Seven Corners, VA (cdp) Fairfax County	609	7.00
White Plains, NY (city) Westchester County	3,641	6.86
Sunset, FL (cdp) Miami-Dade County	1,162	6.78
Ives Estates, FL (cdp) Miami-Dade County	1,175	6.68
Drummond, ID (city) Fremont County	1	6.67
Fairview, NJ (borough) Bergen County	876	6.61
Chambers Estates, FL (cdp) Broward County	233	6.55
Lodi, NJ (borough) Bergen County	1,524	6.36
Meadow Woods, FL (cdp) Orange County	714	6.33
Ramblewood East, FL (cdp) Broward County	88	6.31
Garfield, NJ (city) Bergen County	1,868	6.27
Manorhaven, NY (village) Nassau County	377	6.14
Coral Gables, FL (city) Miami-Dade County	2,586	6.12
Biscayne Park, FL (village) Miami-Dade County	199	6.09
Pembroke Pines, FL (city) Broward County	8,292	6.03
North Andrews Gardens, FL (cdp) Broward County	576	5.97
Lakes by the Bay, FL (cdp) Miami-Dade County	540	5.96
Mount Kisco, NY (village) Westchester County	588	5.89
University Park, FL (cdp) Miami-Dade County	1,560	5.88
Peekskill, NY (city) Westchester County	1,314	5.86
Brentwood, NY (cdp) Suffolk County	3,139	5.82
Cutler, FL (cdp) Miami-Dade County	978	5.62
Passaic, NJ (city) Passaic County	3,796	5.59
Hialeah, FL (city) Miami-Dade County	12,510	5.53
Clifton, NJ (city) Passaic County	4,305	5.47
Belleville, NJ (cdp) Essex County	1,939	5.40
Napeague, NY (cdp) Suffolk County	12	5.38
Bellerose Terrace, NY (cdp) Nassau County	115	5.33
North Lauderdale, FL (city) Broward County	1,713	5.31
Pinecrest, FL (village) Miami-Dade County	1,006	5.28
Haledon, NJ (borough) Passaic County	434	5.26
Bound Brook, NJ (borough) Somerset County	532	5.24
Hughes, AK (city) Yukon-Koyukuk Census Area	4	5.13
Miramar, FL (city) Broward County	3,696	5.08
Hallandale, FL (city) Broward County	1,731	5.05
Sunrise, FL (city) Broward County	4,320	5.04
Hollywood, FL (city) Broward County	6,952	4.99
Ridgefield Park, NJ (village) Bergen County	636	4.94
North Bay Shore, NY (cdp) Suffolk County	737	4.92
Twin Rivers, NJ (cdp) Mercer County	362	4.88
Brewster, NY (village) Putnam County	105	4.86
West Miami, FL (city) Miami-Dade County	283	4.83
East Windsor, NJ (township) Mercer County	1,197	4.80
Village Park, FL (cdp) Broward County	42	4.69
Jefferson, VA (cdp) Fairfax County	1,269	4.63
Glen Cove, NY (city) Nassau County	1,208	4.54
East Perrine, FL (cdp) Miami-Dade County	319	4.51
Tamarac, FL (city) Broward County	2,496	4.49
Coral Springs, FL (city) Broward County	5,261	4.48
Homestead Base, FL (cdp) Miami-Dade County	20	4.48
Elmwood Park, NJ (borough) Bergen County	845	4.46
Fairview, NY (cdp) Westchester County	128	4.43
Southchase, FL (cdp) Orange County	205	4.42
Stamford, CT (city) Fairfield County	5,160	4.41
Northwest Harbor, NY (cdp) Suffolk County	135	4.41
Sandalfoot Cove, FL (cdp) Palm Beach County	729	4.40
Westchester, FL (cdp) Miami-Dade County	1,329	4.39
Miami Gardens, FL (cdp) Broward County	118	4.36
Forest Home, NY (cdp) Tompkins County	41	4.36
South Miami Heights, FL (cdp) Miami-Dade County	1,441	4.30
Tarrytown, NY (village) Westchester County	477	4.30
Westwood Lakes, FL (cdp) Miami-Dade County	515	4.29
Kissimmee, FL (city) Osceola County	2,047	4.28
Coral Terrace, FL (cdp) Miami-Dade County	1,043	4.28
Bergenfield, NJ (borough) Bergen County	1,121	4.27
South Hackensack, NJ (township) Bergen County	96	4.27
Bogota, NJ (borough) Bergen County	351	4.26
Cutler Ridge, FL (cdp) Miami-Dade County	1,051	4.24
Olympia Heights, FL (cdp) Miami-Dade County	570	4.24
Broadview Park, FL (cdp) Broward County	287	4.22
Lincolnia, VA (cdp) Fairfax County	663	4.20
Roselle Park, NJ (borough) Union County	558	4.20
Medley, FL (town) Miami-Dade County	46	4.19
Cloud Lake, FL (town) Palm Beach County	7	4.19
Dunellen, NJ (borough) Middlesex County	285	4.18
South Miami, FL (city) Miami-Dade County	448	4.17
Miami, FL (city) Miami-Dade County	15,076	4.16
Bailey's Crossroads, VA (cdp) Fairfax County	961	4.15
Perth Amboy, NJ (city) Middlesex County	1,955	4.13
Sweetwater, FL (city) Miami-Dade County	582	4.09
Newark, NJ (city) Essex County	11,134	4.07
Danbury, CT (city) Fairfield County	3,049	4.07
Pimmit Hills, VA (cdp) Fairfax County	248	4.03
Lake Forest, FL (cdp) Broward County	200	4.00
Davie, FL (town) Broward County	2,984	3.94
South Bound Brook, NJ (borough) Somerset County	176	3.92
Annandale, VA (cdp) Fairfax County	2,149	3.91

Notes: (cdp) census designated place; Refer to the Explanation of Data in the front of the book for more detailed information.

Hispanic: South American

Top 150 Places Sorted by Percent

(Based on places with populations of 10,000 or more)

Place	Number	%
Doral, FL (cdp) Miami-Dade County	4,989	24.41
The Hammocks, FL (cdp) Miami-Dade County	9,494	20.04
Dover, NJ (town) Morris County	3,440	18.91
Kendall West, FL (cdp) Miami-Dade County	7,073	18.60
Key Biscayne, FL (village) Miami-Dade County	1,793	17.06
Union City, NJ (city) Hudson County	10,080	15.03
The Crossings, FL (cdp) Miami-Dade County	3,326	14.12
Harrison, NJ (town) Hudson County	2,034	14.10
Sunny Isles Beach, FL (city) Miami-Dade County	2,150	14.04
West New York, NJ (town) Hudson County	6,237	13.63
Fountainbleau, FL (cdp) Miami-Dade County	8,100	13.60
Weston, FL (city) Broward County	6,620	13.43
North Bergen, NJ (township) Hudson County	7,781	13.39
Country Club, FL (cdp) Miami-Dade County	4,843	13.34
Miami Beach, FL (city) Miami-Dade County	11,589	13.18
Guttenberg, NJ (town) Hudson County	1,410	13.05
Port Chester, NY (village) Westchester County	3,516	12.62
Kendale Lakes, FL (cdp) Miami-Dade County	7,076	12.44
Elizabeth, NJ (city) Union County	14,831	12.30
Ossining, NY (village) Westchester County	2,819	11.74
Country Walk, FL (cdp) Miami-Dade County	1,243	11.67
North Plainfield, NJ (borough) Somerset County	2,249	10.66
Kendall, FL (cdp) Miami-Dade County	7,961	10.58
Central Falls, RI (city) Providence County	1,999	10.56
Richmond West, FL (cdp) Miami-Dade County	2,906	10.35
Hackensack, NJ (city) Bergen County	4,266	10.00
Morristown, NJ (town) Morris County	1,814	9.78
Ojus, FL (cdp) Miami-Dade County	1,609	9.67
Glenvar Heights, FL (cdp) Miami-Dade County	1,567	9.65
Paterson, NJ (city) Passaic County	13,852	9.28
Aventura, FL (city) Miami-Dade County	2,289	9.06
Miami Springs, FL (city) Miami-Dade County	1,228	8.96
East Hampton, NY (town) Suffolk County	1,757	8.91
Rye, NY (town) Westchester County	3,842	8.76
Miami Lakes, FL (cdp) Miami-Dade County	1,879	8.29
Englewood, NJ (city) Bergen County	2,130	8.13
Patchogue, NY (village) Suffolk County	968	8.12
Ossining, NY (town) Westchester County	2,942	8.05
Kearny, NJ (town) Hudson County	3,235	7.99
Weehawken, NJ (township) Hudson County	1,074	7.95
Tamiami, FL (cdp) Miami-Dade County	4,322	7.89
Hialeah Gardens, FL (city) Miami-Dade County	1,471	7.62
North Miami Beach, FL (city) Miami-Dade County	2,936	7.20
White Plains, NY (city) Westchester County	3,641	6.86
Sunset, FL (cdp) Miami-Dade County	1,162	6.78
Ives Estates, FL (cdp) Miami-Dade County	1,175	6.68
Fairview, NJ (borough) Bergen County	876	6.61
Lodi, NJ (borough) Bergen County	1,524	6.36
Meadow Woods, FL (cdp) Orange County	714	6.33
Garfield, NJ (city) Bergen County	1,868	6.27
Coral Gables, FL (city) Miami-Dade County	2,586	6.12
Pembroke Pines, FL (city) Broward County	8,292	6.03
University Park, FL (cdp) Miami-Dade County	1,560	5.88
Peekskill, NY (city) Westchester County	1,314	5.86
Brentwood, NY (cdp) Suffolk County	3,139	5.82
Cutler, FL (cdp) Miami-Dade County	978	5.62
Passaic, NJ (city) Passaic County	3,796	5.59
Hialeah, FL (city) Miami-Dade County	12,510	5.53
Clifton, NJ (city) Passaic County	4,305	5.47
Belleville, NJ (cdp) Essex County	1,939	5.40
North Lauderdale, FL (city) Broward County	1,713	5.31
Pinecrest, FL (village) Miami-Dade County	1,006	5.28
Bound Brook, NJ (borough) Somerset County	532	5.24
Miramar, FL (city) Broward County	3,696	5.08
Hallandale, FL (city) Broward County	1,731	5.05
Sunrise, FL (city) Broward County	4,320	5.04
Hollywood, FL (city) Broward County	6,952	4.99
Ridgefield Park, NJ (village) Bergen County	636	4.94
North Bay Shore, NY (cdp) Suffolk County	737	4.92
East Windsor, NJ (township) Mercer County	1,197	4.80
Jefferson, VA (cdp) Fairfax County	1,269	4.63
Glen Cove, NY (city) Nassau County	1,208	4.54
Tamarac, FL (city) Broward County	2,496	4.49
Coral Springs, FL (city) Broward County	5,261	4.48
Elmwood Park, NJ (borough) Bergen County	845	4.46
Stamford, CT (city) Fairfield County	5,160	4.41
Sandalfoot Cove, FL (cdp) Palm Beach County	729	4.40
Westchester, FL (cdp) Miami-Dade County	1,329	4.39
South Miami Heights, FL (cdp) Miami-Dade County	1,441	4.30
Tarrytown, NY (village) Westchester County	477	4.30
Westwood Lakes, FL (cdp) Miami-Dade County	515	4.29
Kissimmee, FL (city) Osceola County	2,047	4.28
Coral Terrace, FL (cdp) Miami-Dade County	1,043	4.28
Bergenfield, NJ (borough) Bergen County	1,121	4.27
Cutler Ridge, FL (cdp) Miami-Dade County	1,051	4.24
Olympia Heights, FL (cdp) Miami-Dade County	570	4.24
Lincolnia, VA (cdp) Fairfax County	663	4.20
Roselle Park, NJ (borough) Union County	558	4.20
South Miami, FL (city) Miami-Dade County	448	4.17
Miami, FL (city) Miami-Dade County	15,076	4.16
Bailey's Crossroads, VA (cdp) Fairfax County	961	4.15
Perth Amboy, NJ (city) Middlesex County	1,955	4.13
Sweetwater, FL (city) Miami-Dade County	582	4.09
Newark, NJ (city) Essex County	11,134	4.07
Danbury, CT (city) Fairfield County	3,049	4.07
Davie, FL (town) Broward County	2,984	3.94
Annandale, VA (cdp) Fairfax County	2,149	3.91
Miami Shores, FL (village) Miami-Dade County	405	3.90
Oak Ridge, FL (cdp) Orange County	865	3.87
Mount Pleasant, NY (town) Westchester County	1,667	3.86
Plainfield, NJ (city) Union County	1,826	3.82
Roselle, NJ (borough) Union County	809	3.80
Plantation, FL (city) Broward County	3,137	3.78
Margate, FL (city) Broward County	2,029	3.76
Linden, NJ (city) Union County	1,479	3.75
Arlington, VA (cdp) Arlington County	7,083	3.74
Yeehaw Junction, FL (cdp) Osceola County	812	3.73
Mamaroneck, NY (village) Westchester County	699	3.73
Carol City, FL (cdp) Miami-Dade County	2,210	3.72
Palmetto Estates, FL (cdp) Miami-Dade County	501	3.66
Carteret, NJ (borough) Middlesex County	756	3.65
Palm Springs, FL (village) Palm Beach County	425	3.63
Central Islip, NY (cdp) Suffolk County	1,156	3.62
Norwalk, CT (city) Fairfield County	2,959	3.57
Palisades Park, NJ (borough) Bergen County	604	3.54
West Orange, NJ (cdp) Essex County	1,585	3.53
Little Ferry, NJ (borough) Bergen County	379	3.51
Orange, NJ (cdp) Essex County	1,134	3.45
Princeton, FL (cdp) Miami-Dade County	345	3.42
New Rochelle, NY (city) Westchester County	2,435	3.37
North Miami, FL (city) Miami-Dade County	2,009	3.36
Cliffside Park, NJ (borough) Bergen County	769	3.34
Bay Shore, NY (cdp) Suffolk County	795	3.33
Egypt Lake-Leto, FL (cdp) Hillsborough County	1,087	3.32
Cooper City, FL (city) Broward County	922	3.30
Pawtucket, RI (city) Providence County	2,397	3.29
Jersey City, NJ (city) Hudson County	7,807	3.25
Greenacres, FL (city) Palm Beach County	893	3.24
Idylwood, VA (cdp) Fairfax County	519	3.24
Coconut Creek, FL (city) Broward County	1,402	3.22
Wheaton-Glenmont, MD (cdp) Montgomery County	1,784	3.09
Ridgefield, NJ (borough) Bergen County	332	3.07
Oakland Park, FL (city) Broward County	930	3.00
Hillside, NJ (cdp) Union County	646	2.97
Aspen Hill, MD (cdp) Montgomery County	1,489	2.96
Elmont, NY (cdp) Nassau County	966	2.96
New York, NY (city) New York City	236,374	2.95
Rahway, NJ (city) Union County	780	2.94
North Bethesda, MD (cdp) Montgomery County	1,114	2.89
West Paterson, NJ (borough) Passaic County	316	2.88
Boca Del Mar, FL (cdp) Palm Beach County	626	2.87
Hampton Bays, NY (cdp) Suffolk County	345	2.82
Valley Stream, NY (village) Nassau County	1,023	2.81
Port Washington, NY (cdp) Nassau County	428	2.81
Greenwich, CT (town) Fairfield County	1,697	2.78
Town 'n' Country, FL (cdp) Hillsborough County	2,008	2.77
Ventnor City, NJ (city) Atlantic County	356	2.76
Mineola, NY (village) Nassau County	527	2.74
Montgomery Village, MD (cdp) Montgomery County	1,034	2.72
Bloomfield, NJ (cdp) Essex County	1,291	2.71

Notes: (cdp) census designated place; Refer to the Explanation of Data in the front of the book for more detailed information.

Hispanic: Argentinean

Top 150 Places Sorted by Number

(Based on all places, regardless of population)

Place	Number	%
New York, NY (city) New York City	9,578	0.12
Los Angeles, CA (city) Los Angeles County	5,126	0.14
Miami Beach, FL (city) Miami-Dade County	2,680	3.05
Miami, FL (city) Miami-Dade County	1,669	0.46
Houston, TX (city) Harris County	1,256	0.06
Chicago, IL (city) Cook County	908	0.03
Hempstead, NY (town) Nassau County	859	0.11
San Diego, CA (city) San Diego County	642	0.05
Hialeah, FL (city) Miami-Dade County	632	0.28
Kendall, FL (cdp) Miami-Dade County	605	0.80
San Francisco, CA (city) San Francisco County	540	0.07
Philadelphia, PA (city) Philadelphia County	531	0.03
Fountainbleau, FL (cdp) Miami-Dade County	518	0.87
Washington, DC (city) District of Columbia	510	0.09
Coral Springs, FL (city) Broward County	498	0.42
Pembroke Pines, FL (city) Broward County	463	0.34
Hollywood, FL (city) Broward County	456	0.33
Aventura, FL (city) Miami-Dade County	424	1.68
Boston, MA (city) Suffolk County	421	0.07
North Bergen, NJ (township) Hudson County	414	0.71
Glendale, CA (city) Los Angeles County	408	0.21
Union City, NJ (city) Hudson County	404	0.60
The Hammocks, FL (cdp) Miami-Dade County	401	0.85
Arlington, VA (cdp) Arlington County	382	0.20
Las Vegas, NV (city) Clark County	378	0.08
Sunny Isles Beach, FL (city) Miami-Dade County	371	2.42
Downey, CA (city) Los Angeles County	350	0.33
Kendale Lakes, FL (cdp) Miami-Dade County	346	0.61
Orem, UT (city) Utah County	344	0.41
San Jose, CA (city) Santa Clara County	327	0.04
Elizabeth, NJ (city) Union County	312	0.26
Provo, UT (city) Utah County	308	0.29
Weston, FL (city) Broward County	306	0.62
North Miami Beach, FL (city) Miami-Dade County	304	0.75
Jersey City, NJ (city) Hudson County	300	0.12
Islip, NY (town) Suffolk County	300	0.09
Coral Gables, FL (city) Miami-Dade County	297	0.70
North Hempstead, NY (town) Nassau County	297	0.13
Kendall West, FL (cdp) Miami-Dade County	294	0.77
Fort Lauderdale, FL (city) Broward County	289	0.19
Key Biscayne, FL (village) Miami-Dade County	282	2.68
Anaheim, CA (city) Orange County	277	0.08
Long Beach, CA (city) Los Angeles County	275	0.06
Paradise, NV (cdp) Clark County	270	0.15
Pasadena, CA (city) Los Angeles County	267	0.20
Brookhaven, NY (town) Suffolk County	265	0.06
Doral, FL (cdp) Miami-Dade County	262	1.28
Santa Clarita, CA (city) Los Angeles County	253	0.17
North Bay Village, FL (city) Miami-Dade County	252	3.74
Tamiami, FL (cdp) Miami-Dade County	251	0.46
Phoenix, AZ (city) Maricopa County	251	0.02
Rancho Cucamonga, CA (city) San Bernardino County	250	0.20
Ojus, FL (cdp) Miami-Dade County	249	1.50
Cambridge, MA (city) Middlesex County	243	0.24
Oyster Bay, NY (town) Nassau County	242	0.08
Austin, TX (city) Travis County	242	0.04
Irving, TX (city) Dallas County	240	0.13
The Crossings, FL (cdp) Miami-Dade County	233	0.99
Sunrise, FL (city) Broward County	233	0.27
North Miami, FL (city) Miami-Dade County	223	0.37
San Antonio, TX (city) Bexar County	223	0.02
Huntington Beach, CA (city) Orange County	222	0.12
Dallas, TX (city) Dallas County	222	0.02
Burbank, CA (city) Los Angeles County	215	0.21
Paterson, NJ (city) Passaic County	213	0.14
Newark, NJ (city) Essex County	213	0.08
Hallandale, FL (city) Broward County	205	0.60
Seattle, WA (city) King County	204	0.04
Salt Lake City, UT (city) Salt Lake County	200	0.11
Santa Ana, CA (city) Orange County	196	0.06
Davie, FL (town) Broward County	190	0.25
Yonkers, NY (city) Westchester County	190	0.10
Torrance, CA (city) Los Angeles County	189	0.14
Irvine, CA (city) Orange County	189	0.13
Santa Monica, CA (city) Los Angeles County	186	0.22
West Covina, CA (city) Los Angeles County	185	0.18
Spring Valley, NV (cdp) Clark County	185	0.16
Henderson, NV (city) Clark County	185	0.11
Ives Estates, FL (cdp) Miami-Dade County	183	1.04
Mission Viejo, CA (city) Orange County	181	0.19
West New York, NJ (town) Hudson County	179	0.39
Orlando, FL (city) Orange County	179	0.10
Plantation, FL (city) Broward County	177	0.21
Country Club, FL (cdp) Miami-Dade County	175	0.48
Simi Valley, CA (city) Ventura County	174	0.16
Greenwich, CT (town) Fairfield County	172	0.28
Riverside, CA (city) Riverside County	169	0.07
Perth Amboy, NJ (city) Middlesex County	166	0.35
Fontana, CA (city) San Bernardino County	166	0.13
Potomac, MD (cdp) Montgomery County	164	0.37
Clifton, NJ (city) Passaic County	160	0.20
Palmdale, CA (city) Los Angeles County	160	0.14
Huntington, NY (town) Suffolk County	160	0.08
Boca Raton, FL (city) Palm Beach County	159	0.21
Ontario, CA (city) San Bernardino County	158	0.10
Bay Harbor Islands, FL (town) Miami-Dade County	157	3.05
Redondo Beach, CA (city) Los Angeles County	156	0.25
Chino, CA (city) San Bernardino County	150	0.22
Miramar, FL (city) Broward County	149	0.20
Babylon, NY (town) Suffolk County	149	0.07
Costa Mesa, CA (city) Orange County	147	0.14
Thousand Oaks, CA (city) Ventura County	147	0.13
Oakland, CA (city) Alameda County	147	0.04
Berkeley, CA (city) Alameda County	146	0.14
Bethesda, MD (cdp) Montgomery County	144	0.26
El Paso, TX (city) El Paso County	134	0.02
Pittsburgh, PA (city) Allegheny County	132	0.04
Culver City, CA (city) Los Angeles County	130	0.33
Garfield, NJ (city) Bergen County	128	0.43
North Bethesda, MD (cdp) Montgomery County	128	0.33
Denver, CO (city) Denver County	127	0.02
University Park, FL (cdp) Miami-Dade County	126	0.47
Upland, CA (city) San Bernardino County	123	0.18
Chula Vista, CA (city) San Diego County	123	0.07
Charlotte, NC (city) Mecklenburg County	123	0.02
Corona, CA (city) Riverside County	118	0.09
Surfside, FL (town) Miami-Dade County	117	2.38
Tampa, FL (city) Hillsborough County	117	0.04
Jacksonville, FL (special city) Duval County	117	0.02
Fullerton, CA (city) Orange County	116	0.09
Orange, CA (city) Orange County	116	0.09
Stamford, CT (city) Fairfield County	115	0.10
New Haven, CT (city) New Haven County	114	0.09
Tucson, AZ (city) Pima County	114	0.02
Pinecrest, FL (village) Miami-Dade County	113	0.59
Arcadia, CA (city) Los Angeles County	113	0.21
Tamarac, FL (city) Broward County	112	0.20
Garden Grove, CA (city) Orange County	112	0.07
Richmond West, FL (cdp) Miami-Dade County	111	0.40
Covina, CA (city) Los Angeles County	109	0.23
Cutler, FL (cdp) Miami-Dade County	107	0.62
West Hollywood, CA (city) Los Angeles County	105	0.29
Kearny, NJ (town) Hudson County	105	0.26
Chino Hills, CA (city) San Bernardino County	105	0.16
South Gate, CA (city) Los Angeles County	105	0.11
Woodbridge, NJ (township) Middlesex County	105	0.11
El Monte, CA (city) Los Angeles County	105	0.09
Rockville, MD (city) Montgomery County	104	0.22
Wellington, FL (village) Palm Beach County	103	0.27
Sunrise Manor, NV (cdp) Clark County	103	0.07
Deerfield Beach, FL (city) Broward County	102	0.16
Miami Lakes, FL (cdp) Miami-Dade County	100	0.44
Glendora, CA (city) Los Angeles County	100	0.20
Greenburgh, NY (town) Westchester County	100	0.12
Atlanta, GA (city) Fulton County	100	0.02
Yorba Linda, CA (city) Orange County	99	0.17
Newton, MA (city) Middlesex County	99	0.12
Linden, NJ (city) Union County	98	0.25
Providence, RI (city) Providence County	98	0.06
Lodi, NJ (borough) Bergen County	97	0.40

Notes: (cdp) census designated place; Refer to the Explanation of Data in the front of the book for more detailed information.

Hispanic: Argentinean

Top 150 Places Sorted by Percent

(Based on all places, regardless of population)

Place	Number	%
North Bay Village, FL (city) Miami-Dade County	252	3.74
Miami Beach, FL (city) Miami-Dade County	2,680	3.05
Bay Harbor Islands, FL (town) Miami-Dade County	157	3.05
Key Biscayne, FL (village) Miami-Dade County	282	2.68
Beseman, MN (township) Carlton County	4	2.68
Sunny Isles Beach, FL (city) Miami-Dade County	371	2.42
Surfside, FL (town) Miami-Dade County	117	2.38
Bal Harbour, FL (village) Miami-Dade County	74	2.24
Chiniak, AK (cdp) Kodiak Island Borough	1	2.00
Fisher Island, FL (cdp) Miami-Dade County	8	1.71
Aventura, FL (city) Miami-Dade County	424	1.68
Biscayne Park, FL (village) Miami-Dade County	52	1.59
Ojus, FL (cdp) Miami-Dade County	249	1.50
Tabiona, UT (town) Duchesne County	2	1.34
Doral, FL (cdp) Miami-Dade County	262	1.28
Forest Home, NY (cdp) Tompkins County	11	1.17
Golden Beach, FL (town) Miami-Dade County	10	1.09
Glen Ridge, FL (town) Palm Beach County	3	1.09
Ives Estates, FL (cdp) Miami-Dade County	183	1.04
Lake Aluma, OK (town) Oklahoma County	1	1.03
The Crossings, FL (cdp) Miami-Dade County	233	0.99
Friendship Village, MD (cdp) Montgomery County	43	0.95
Mount Aetna, MD (cdp) Washington County	8	0.95
Fountainbleau, FL (cdp) Miami-Dade County	518	0.87
The Hammocks, FL (cdp) Miami-Dade County	401	0.85
Three Lakes, FL (cdp) Miami-Dade County	58	0.83
Plantation Mobile Home Park, FL (cdp) Palm Beach County	10	0.82
Kendall, FL (cdp) Miami-Dade County	605	0.80
Hyde Park, PA (borough) Westmoreland County	4	0.78
Kendall West, FL (cdp) Miami-Dade County	294	0.77
North Miami Beach, FL (city) Miami-Dade County	304	0.75
Whiteash, IL (village) Williamson County	2	0.75
North Bergen, NJ (township) Hudson County	414	0.71
Thornton, IA (city) Cerro Gordo County	3	0.71
Unity Village, MO (village) Jackson County	1	0.71
Coral Gables, FL (city) Miami-Dade County	297	0.70
Guttenberg, NJ (town) Hudson County	76	0.70
Scottsburg, VA (town) Halifax County	1	0.69
Village Park, FL (cdp) Broward County	6	0.67
Timblin, PA (borough) Jefferson County	1	0.66
Russell Gardens, NY (village) Nassau County	7	0.65
Hidden Hills, CA (city) Los Angeles County	12	0.64
Malverne Park Oaks, NY (cdp) Nassau County	3	0.64
Weston, FL (city) Broward County	306	0.62
Cutler, FL (cdp) Miami-Dade County	107	0.62
Country Walk, FL (cdp) Miami-Dade County	66	0.62
North El Monte, CA (cdp) Los Angeles County	23	0.62
Islandia, NY (village) Suffolk County	19	0.62
Chevy Chase Section Five, MD (village) Montgomery County	4	0.62
Barnesville, MD (town) Montgomery County	1	0.62
Kendale Lakes, FL (cdp) Miami-Dade County	346	0.61
Weybridge, VT (town) Addison County	5	0.61
Union City, NJ (city) Hudson County	404	0.60
Hallandale, FL (city) Broward County	205	0.60
Cloud Lake, FL (town) Palm Beach County	1	0.60
East New Market, MD (town) Dorchester County	1	0.60
Pinecrest, FL (village) Miami-Dade County	113	0.59
Palm Aire, FL (cdp) Broward County	9	0.58
Rome, MN (township) Faribault County	1	0.58
Sea Ranch Lakes, FL (village) Broward County	8	0.56
El Portal, FL (village) Miami-Dade County	14	0.56
Fetters Hot Springs-Agua Caliente, CA (cdp) Sonoma County	14	0.56
Millbrook, NY (village) Dutchess County	8	0.56
Story, WY (cdp) Sheridan County	5	0.56
Unionville, NY (village) Orange County	3	0.56
Virginia Gardens, FL (village) Miami-Dade County	13	0.55
West Ocean City, MD (cdp) Worcester County	18	0.54
Thomaston, NY (village) Nassau County	14	0.54
Hunting Valley, OH (village) Cuyahoga County	4	0.54
Miami Springs, FL (city) Miami-Dade County	73	0.53
Harbor Hills, NY (cdp) Nassau County	3	0.53
Spring Mill, KY (city) Jefferson County	2	0.53
Riverland Village, FL (cdp) Broward County	11	0.52
Spring City, UT (city) Sanpete County	5	0.52
Sunset, FL (cdp) Miami-Dade County	88	0.51

Place	Number	%
Glenvar Heights, FL (cdp) Miami-Dade County	81	0.50
Silver Plume, CO (town) Clear Creek County	1	0.49
Country Club, FL (cdp) Miami-Dade County	175	0.48
University Park, FL (cdp) Miami-Dade County	126	0.47
Lakes by the Bay, FL (cdp) Miami-Dade County	43	0.47
Kenilworth, NJ (borough) Union County	36	0.47
Laurel Hollow, NY (village) Nassau County	9	0.47
Elsah, IL (village) Jersey County	3	0.47
Morrison, CO (town) Jefferson County	2	0.47
Miami, FL (city) Miami-Dade County	1,669	0.46
Tamiami, FL (cdp) Miami-Dade County	251	0.46
Miami Shores, FL (village) Miami-Dade County	48	0.46
Avondale, PA (borough) Chester County	5	0.45
Centre Island, NY (village) Nassau County	2	0.45
Homestead Base, FL (cdp) Miami-Dade County	2	0.45
Miami Lakes, FL (cdp) Miami-Dade County	100	0.44
Weehawken, NJ (township) Hudson County	59	0.44
East Perrine, FL (cdp) Miami-Dade County	31	0.44
Brookmont, MD (cdp) Montgomery County	14	0.44
Gilmore, MI (township) Isabella County	6	0.44
Clark, MN (township) Faribault County	2	0.44
Crystal Lake Park, MO (city) Saint Louis County	2	0.44
Micro, NC (town) Johnston County	2	0.44
Richlawn, KY (city) Jefferson County	2	0.44
Garfield, NJ (city) Bergen County	128	0.43
Goodsprings, NV (cdp) Clark County	1	0.43
Hays, TX (city) Hays County	1	0.43
Timberlane, IL (village) Boone County	1	0.43
Coral Springs, FL (city) Broward County	498	0.42
Prospect Park, NJ (borough) Passaic County	24	0.42
Bentleyville, OH (village) Cuyahoga County	4	0.42
Thurman, IA (city) Fremont County	1	0.42
Orem, UT (city) Utah County	344	0.41
Clear Lake Shores, TX (city) Galveston County	5	0.41
Plandome Heights, NY (village) Nassau County	4	0.41
Buffalo, IL (village) Sangamon County	2	0.41
Richmond West, FL (cdp) Miami-Dade County	111	0.40
Lodi, NJ (borough) Bergen County	97	0.40
Hiram, OH (village) Portage County	5	0.40
Caledonia, WI (town) Trempealeau County	3	0.40
Megargel, TX (town) Archer County	1	0.40
West New York, NJ (town) Hudson County	179	0.39
Vails Gate, NY (cdp) Orange County	13	0.39
Oak Park, CA (cdp) Ventura County	9	0.39
Chevy Chase Section Three, MD (village) Montgomery County	3	0.39
Terra Mar, FL (cdp) Broward County	10	0.38
Fieldsboro, NJ (borough) Burlington County	2	0.38
North Miami, FL (city) Miami-Dade County	223	0.37
Potomac, MD (cdp) Montgomery County	164	0.37
Basalt, CO (town) Eagle County	10	0.37
Lake Junaluska, NC (cdp) Haywood County	10	0.37
Diamond, MO (town) Newton County	3	0.37
Doctor Phillips, FL (cdp) Orange County	34	0.36
Holden Heights, FL (cdp) Orange County	14	0.36
Nixon, PA (cdp) Butler County	5	0.36
Keystone, CO (cdp) Summit County	3	0.36
Round Grove, MN (township) McLeod County	1	0.36
Perth Amboy, NJ (city) Middlesex County	166	0.35
South River, NJ (borough) Middlesex County	54	0.35
North Andrews Gardens, FL (cdp) Broward County	34	0.35
Pembroke Park, FL (town) Broward County	22	0.35
Doyle, TX (cdp) San Patricio County	1	0.35
Fishers Island, NY (cdp) Suffolk County	1	0.35
Mount Charleston, NV (cdp) Clark County	1	0.35
Pembroke Pines, FL (city) Broward County	463	0.34
West Miami, FL (city) Miami-Dade County	20	0.34
University Gardens, NY (cdp) Nassau County	14	0.34
Cayuga Heights, NY (village) Tompkins County	11	0.34
Hillside, NY (cdp) Ulster County	3	0.34
Patagonia, AZ (town) Santa Cruz County	3	0.34
Sagaponack, NY (cdp) Suffolk County	2	0.34
Two Rivers, MN (township) Morrison County	2	0.34
Casper Mountain, WY (cdp) Natrona County	1	0.34
Hollywood, FL (city) Broward County	456	0.33
Downey, CA (city) Los Angeles County	350	0.33

Notes: (cdp) census designated place; Refer to the Explanation of Data in the front of the book for more detailed information.

Hispanic: Argentinean

Top 150 Places Sorted by Percent

(Based on places with populations of 10,000 or more)

Place	Number	%
Miami Beach, FL (city) Miami-Dade County	2,680	3.05
Key Biscayne, FL (village) Miami-Dade County	282	2.68
Sunny Isles Beach, FL (city) Miami-Dade County	371	2.42
Aventura, FL (city) Miami-Dade County	424	1.68
Ojus, FL (cdp) Miami-Dade County	249	1.50
Doral, FL (cdp) Miami-Dade County	262	1.28
Ives Estates, FL (cdp) Miami-Dade County	183	1.04
The Crossings, FL (cdp) Miami-Dade County	233	0.99
Fountainbleau, FL (cdp) Miami-Dade County	518	0.87
The Hammocks, FL (cdp) Miami-Dade County	401	0.85
Kendall, FL (cdp) Miami-Dade County	605	0.80
Kendall West, FL (cdp) Miami-Dade County	294	0.77
North Miami Beach, FL (city) Miami-Dade County	304	0.75
North Bergen, NJ (township) Hudson County	414	0.71
Coral Gables, FL (city) Miami-Dade County	297	0.70
Guttenberg, NJ (town) Hudson County	76	0.70
Weston, FL (city) Broward County	306	0.62
Cutler, FL (cdp) Miami-Dade County	107	0.62
Country Walk, FL (cdp) Miami-Dade County	66	0.62
Kendale Lakes, FL (cdp) Miami-Dade County	346	0.61
Union City, NJ (city) Hudson County	404	0.60
Hallandale, FL (city) Broward County	205	0.60
Pinecrest, FL (village) Miami-Dade County	113	0.59
Miami Springs, FL (city) Miami-Dade County	73	0.53
Sunset, FL (cdp) Miami-Dade County	88	0.51
Glenvar Heights, FL (cdp) Miami-Dade County	81	0.50
Country Club, FL (cdp) Miami-Dade County	175	0.48
University Park, FL (cdp) Miami-Dade County	126	0.47
Miami, FL (city) Miami-Dade County	1,669	0.46
Tamiami, FL (cdp) Miami-Dade County	251	0.46
Miami Shores, FL (village) Miami-Dade County	48	0.46
Miami Lakes, FL (cdp) Miami-Dade County	100	0.44
Weehawken, NJ (township) Hudson County	59	0.44
Garfield, NJ (city) Bergen County	128	0.43
Coral Springs, FL (city) Broward County	498	0.42
Orem, UT (city) Utah County	344	0.41
Richmond West, FL (cdp) Miami-Dade County	111	0.40
Lodi, NJ (borough) Bergen County	97	0.40
West New York, NJ (town) Hudson County	179	0.39
North Miami, FL (city) Miami-Dade County	223	0.37
Potomac, MD (cdp) Montgomery County	164	0.37
Perth Amboy, NJ (city) Middlesex County	166	0.35
South River, NJ (borough) Middlesex County	54	0.35
Pembroke Pines, FL (city) Broward County	463	0.34
Hollywood, FL (city) Broward County	456	0.33
Downey, CA (city) Los Angeles County	350	0.33
Culver City, CA (city) Los Angeles County	130	0.33
North Bethesda, MD (cdp) Montgomery County	128	0.33
Cliffside Park, NJ (borough) Bergen County	77	0.33
Westwood Lakes, FL (cdp) Miami-Dade County	40	0.33
Cutler Ridge, FL (cdp) Miami-Dade County	80	0.32
Harrison, NJ (town) Hudson County	46	0.32
Palmetto Estates, FL (cdp) Miami-Dade County	44	0.32
Secaucus, NJ (town) Hudson County	50	0.31
South Miami, FL (city) Miami-Dade County	33	0.31
Westchester, FL (cdp) Miami-Dade County	91	0.30
Sandalfoot Cove, FL (cdp) Palm Beach County	49	0.30
Fairview, NJ (borough) Bergen County	40	0.30
Provo, UT (city) Utah County	308	0.29
West Hollywood, CA (city) Los Angeles County	105	0.29
Rutherford, NJ (borough) Bergen County	52	0.29
Hamptons at Boca Raton, FL (cdp) Palm Beach County	33	0.29
West Paterson, NJ (borough) Passaic County	32	0.29
Hialeah, FL (city) Miami-Dade County	632	0.28
Greenwich, CT (town) Fairfield County	172	0.28
Lomita, CA (city) Los Angeles County	57	0.28
Saddle Brook, NJ (cdp) Bergen County	37	0.28
Sunrise, FL (city) Broward County	233	0.27
Wellington, FL (village) Palm Beach County	103	0.27
Boca Del Mar, FL (cdp) Palm Beach County	60	0.27
Elizabeth, NJ (city) Union County	312	0.26
Bethesda, MD (cdp) Montgomery County	144	0.26
Kearny, NJ (town) Hudson County	105	0.26
Elmont, NY (cdp) Nassau County	86	0.26
Coral Terrace, FL (cdp) Miami-Dade County	64	0.26
Dover, NJ (town) Morris County	48	0.26
Davie, FL (town) Broward County	190	0.25
Redondo Beach, CA (city) Los Angeles County	156	0.25
Linden, NJ (city) Union County	98	0.25
Mamaroneck, NY (town) Westchester County	71	0.25
Greenacres, FL (city) Palm Beach County	69	0.25
Jefferson, VA (cdp) Fairfax County	69	0.25
Mamaroneck, NY (village) Westchester County	47	0.25
Adelphi, MD (cdp) Prince George's County	38	0.25
Cambridge, MA (city) Middlesex County	243	0.24
Cooper City, FL (city) Broward County	67	0.24
Duarte, CA (city) Los Angeles County	51	0.24
Agoura Hills, CA (city) Los Angeles County	50	0.24
Hialeah Gardens, FL (city) Miami-Dade County	47	0.24
Ridgefield, NJ (borough) Bergen County	26	0.24
Covina, CA (city) Los Angeles County	109	0.23
Monrovia, CA (city) Los Angeles County	85	0.23
Yeehaw Junction, FL (cdp) Osceola County	51	0.23
La Palma, CA (city) Orange County	35	0.23
Olympia Heights, FL (cdp) Miami-Dade County	31	0.23
Stanford, CA (cdp) Santa Clara County	31	0.23
Santa Monica, CA (city) Los Angeles County	186	0.22
Chino, CA (city) San Bernardino County	150	0.22
Rockville, MD (city) Montgomery County	104	0.22
Coconut Creek, FL (city) Broward County	95	0.22
Hilton Head Island, SC (town) Beaufort County	73	0.22
North Lauderdale, FL (city) Broward County	72	0.22
La Verne, CA (city) Los Angeles County	70	0.22
West Carson, CA (cdp) Los Angeles County	46	0.22
Tysons Corner, VA (cdp) Fairfax County	41	0.22
El Segundo, CA (city) Los Angeles County	36	0.22
Sweetwater, FL (city) Miami-Dade County	32	0.22
Glendale, CA (city) Los Angeles County	408	0.21
Burbank, CA (city) Los Angeles County	215	0.21
Plantation, FL (city) Broward County	177	0.21
Boca Raton, FL (city) Palm Beach County	159	0.21
Arcadia, CA (city) Los Angeles County	113	0.21
Aliso Viejo, CA (cdp) Orange County	86	0.21
McLean, VA (cdp) Fairfax County	82	0.21
Valley Stream, NY (village) Nassau County	76	0.21
Laguna Hills, CA (city) Orange County	65	0.21
Casselberry, FL (city) Seminole County	47	0.21
Dania Beach, FL (city) Broward County	43	0.21
Princeton, NJ (township) Mercer County	33	0.21
East San Gabriel, CA (cdp) Los Angeles County	31	0.21
Kiryas Joel, NY (village) Orange County	27	0.21
Arlington, VA (cdp) Arlington County	382	0.20
Pasadena, CA (city) Los Angeles County	267	0.20
Rancho Cucamonga, CA (city) San Bernardino County	250	0.20
Clifton, NJ (city) Passaic County	160	0.20
Miramar, FL (city) Broward County	149	0.20
Tamarac, FL (city) Broward County	112	0.20
Glendora, CA (city) Los Angeles County	100	0.20
Mission Bend, TX (cdp) Fort Bend County	62	0.20
Newburgh, NY (city) Orange County	57	0.20
Elmwood Park, IL (village) Cook County	52	0.20
Bailey's Crossroads, VA (cdp) Fairfax County	47	0.20
Colesville, MD (cdp) Montgomery County	40	0.20
Roselle Park, NJ (borough) Union County	27	0.20
Fort Lauderdale, FL (city) Broward County	289	0.19
Mission Viejo, CA (city) Orange County	181	0.19
Rancho Santa Margarita, CA (city) Orange County	90	0.19
Long Beach, NY (city) Nassau County	67	0.19
San Dimas, CA (city) Los Angeles County	67	0.19
Central Islip, NY (cdp) Suffolk County	62	0.19
Wekiwa Springs, FL (cdp) Seminole County	45	0.19
North Potomac, MD (cdp) Montgomery County	43	0.19
Calabasas, CA (city) Los Angeles County	38	0.19
West Covina, CA (city) Los Angeles County	185	0.18
Upland, CA (city) San Bernardino County	123	0.18
Belleville, NJ (cdp) Essex County	66	0.18
Fort Lee, NJ (borough) Bergen County	64	0.18
Lake Worth, FL (city) Palm Beach County	62	0.18
Beverly Hills, CA (city) Los Angeles County	60	0.18
South Miami Heights, FL (cdp) Miami-Dade County	60	0.18

Notes: (cdp) census designated place; Refer to the Explanation of Data in the front of the book for more detailed information.

Hispanic: Bolivian

Top 150 Places Sorted by Number

(Based on all places, regardless of population)

Place	Number	%
Arlington, VA (cdp) Arlington County	3,532	1.86
New York, NY (city) New York City	2,942	0.04
Los Angeles, CA (city) Los Angeles County	1,301	0.04
Annandale, VA (cdp) Fairfax County	962	1.75
Jefferson, VA (cdp) Fairfax County	703	2.56
Providence, RI (city) Providence County	634	0.37
Alexandria, VA (independent city) Alexandria city	609	0.47
Houston, TX (city) Harris County	480	0.02
Bailey's Crossroads, VA (cdp) Fairfax County	474	2.05
Chicago, IL (city) Cook County	414	0.01
Miami, FL (city) Miami-Dade County	355	0.10
Wheaton-Glenmont, MD (cdp) Montgomery County	349	0.60
Seven Corners, VA (cdp) Fairfax County	344	3.95
Washington, DC (city) District of Columbia	310	0.05
Aspen Hill, MD (cdp) Montgomery County	290	0.58
Silver Spring, MD (cdp) Montgomery County	287	0.37
Burke, VA (cdp) Fairfax County	283	0.49
Santa Ana, CA (city) Orange County	269	0.08
Springfield, VA (cdp) Fairfax County	260	0.85
San Francisco, CA (city) San Francisco County	258	0.03
San Jose, CA (city) Santa Clara County	249	0.03
Lincolnia, VA (cdp) Fairfax County	245	1.55
Jersey City, NJ (city) Hudson County	244	0.10
Idylwood, VA (cdp) Fairfax County	238	1.49
Hempstead, NY (town) Nassau County	228	0.03
Reston, VA (cdp) Fairfax County	215	0.38
Gaithersburg, MD (city) Montgomery County	188	0.36
Rye, NY (town) Westchester County	180	0.41
Oakton, VA (cdp) Fairfax County	177	0.60
Miami Beach, FL (city) Miami-Dade County	176	0.20
Fairfax, VA (independent city) Fairfax city	170	0.79
Kendall, FL (cdp) Miami-Dade County	170	0.23
Tustin, CA (city) Orange County	166	0.25
North Bethesda, MD (cdp) Montgomery County	164	0.42
Centreville, VA (cdp) Fairfax County	164	0.34
Port Chester, NY (village) Westchester County	163	0.58
Rockville, MD (city) Montgomery County	160	0.34
Burbank, CA (city) Los Angeles County	159	0.16
San Diego, CA (city) San Diego County	154	0.01
Fountainbleau, FL (cdp) Miami-Dade County	153	0.26
Franconia, VA (cdp) Fairfax County	149	0.47
Lake Barcroft, VA (cdp) Fairfax County	142	1.59
West Springfield, VA (cdp) Fairfax County	135	0.48
Groveton, VA (cdp) Fairfax County	129	0.61
Montgomery Village, MD (cdp) Montgomery County	122	0.32
Germantown, MD (cdp) Montgomery County	122	0.22
Elizabeth, NJ (city) Union County	121	0.10
Dallas, TX (city) Dallas County	119	0.01
Clifton, NJ (city) Passaic County	118	0.15
Boston, MA (city) Suffolk County	115	0.02
Hialeah, FL (city) Miami-Dade County	113	0.05
Anaheim, CA (city) Orange County	110	0.03
Austin, TX (city) Travis County	109	0.02
Newington, VA (cdp) Fairfax County	108	0.55
Islip, NY (town) Suffolk County	107	0.03
Merrifield, VA (cdp) Fairfax County	105	0.94
Passaic, NJ (city) Passaic County	103	0.15
Hollywood, FL (city) Broward County	100	0.07
Falls Church, VA (independent city) Falls Church city	99	0.95
Bethesda, MD (cdp) Montgomery County	99	0.18
Cranston, RI (city) Providence County	98	0.12
Kendale Lakes, FL (cdp) Miami-Dade County	96	0.17
The Hammocks, FL (cdp) Miami-Dade County	93	0.20
Waltham, MA (city) Middlesex County	89	0.15
Chantilly, VA (cdp) Fairfax County	88	0.21
Herndon, VA (town) Fairfax County	85	0.39
Riverside, CA (city) Riverside County	85	0.03
Tamiami, FL (cdp) Miami-Dade County	82	0.15
Tysons Corner, VA (cdp) Fairfax County	80	0.43
Kendall West, FL (cdp) Miami-Dade County	79	0.21
Lake Ridge, VA (cdp) Prince William County	77	0.25
San Mateo, CA (city) San Mateo County	77	0.08
White Oak, MD (cdp) Montgomery County	76	0.36
Dale City, VA (cdp) Prince William County	75	0.13
Downey, CA (city) Los Angeles County	75	0.07
Pimmit Hills, VA (cdp) Fairfax County	74	1.20
McLean, VA (cdp) Fairfax County	74	0.19
San Antonio, TX (city) Bexar County	73	0.01
North Springfield, VA (cdp) Fairfax County	72	0.78
Sunnyvale, CA (city) Santa Clara County	72	0.05
Union City, NJ (city) Hudson County	71	0.11
Provo, UT (city) Utah County	71	0.07
Glendale, CA (city) Los Angeles County	70	0.04
The Crossings, FL (cdp) Miami-Dade County	69	0.29
Skokie, IL (village) Cook County	69	0.11
Denver, CO (city) Denver County	68	0.01
Brookhaven, NY (town) Suffolk County	67	0.01
Olney, MD (cdp) Montgomery County	66	0.21
Fayetteville, AR (city) Washington County	66	0.11
Pembroke Pines, FL (city) Broward County	66	0.05
Phoenix, AZ (city) Maricopa County	65	0.00
Tampa, FL (city) Hillsborough County	64	0.02
Lake Worth, FL (city) Palm Beach County	63	0.18
Paterson, NJ (city) Passaic County	63	0.04
Seattle, WA (city) King County	63	0.01
Santa Clarita, CA (city) Los Angeles County	61	0.04
North Providence, RI (cdp) Providence County	60	0.19
Stamford, CT (city) Fairfield County	59	0.05
Garden Grove, CA (city) Orange County	59	0.04
Oyster Bay, NY (town) Nassau County	59	0.02
Redland, MD (cdp) Montgomery County	57	0.34
Woodbridge, VA (cdp) Prince William County	57	0.18
Mount Vernon, VA (cdp) Fairfax County	56	0.20
Jacksonville, FL (special city) Duval County	55	0.01
Philadelphia, PA (city) Philadelphia County	55	0.00
Framingham, MA (cdp) Middlesex County	54	0.08
Davie, FL (town) Broward County	54	0.07
Coral Springs, FL (city) Broward County	54	0.05
Garfield, NJ (city) Bergen County	53	0.18
Orange, NJ (cdp) Essex County	52	0.16
Brentwood, NY (cdp) Suffolk County	51	0.09
Oakland, CA (city) Alameda County	51	0.01
Albuquerque, NM (city) Bernalillo County	50	0.01
Hackensack, NJ (city) Bergen County	49	0.11
Mountain View, CA (city) Santa Clara County	49	0.07
Hayward, CA (city) Alameda County	49	0.03
Rose Hill, VA (cdp) Fairfax County	48	0.32
West New York, NJ (town) Hudson County	48	0.10
Redwood City, CA (city) San Mateo County	47	0.06
Mission Viejo, CA (city) Orange County	47	0.05
Johnston, RI (town) Providence County	46	0.16
Lake Forest, CA (city) Orange County	46	0.08
Cambridge, MA (city) Middlesex County	46	0.05
Pasadena, CA (city) Los Angeles County	46	0.03
Doral, FL (cdp) Miami-Dade County	45	0.22
Salt Lake City, UT (city) Salt Lake County	45	0.02
Fontana, CA (city) San Bernardino County	44	0.03
Saint Petersburg, FL (city) Pinellas County	44	0.02
Lorton, VA (cdp) Fairfax County	43	0.24
Long Beach, CA (city) Los Angeles County	43	0.01
Tulsa, OK (city) Tulsa County	43	0.01
Mantua, VA (cdp) Fairfax County	42	0.56
White Plains, NY (city) Westchester County	42	0.08
Daly City, CA (city) San Mateo County	42	0.04
Portland, OR (city) Multnomah County	42	0.01
Colesville, MD (cdp) Montgomery County	41	0.21
Country Club, FL (cdp) Miami-Dade County	41	0.11
Garland, TX (city) Dallas County	41	0.02
Vienna, VA (town) Fairfax County	40	0.28
Fairland, MD (cdp) Montgomery County	40	0.18
Coral Gables, FL (city) Miami-Dade County	40	0.09
Sunrise, FL (city) Broward County	40	0.05
Gainesville, FL (city) Alachua County	40	0.04
Columbus, GA (special city) Muscogee County	40	0.02
Fremont, CA (city) Alameda County	40	0.02
Las Vegas, NV (city) Clark County	40	0.01
Potomac, MD (cdp) Montgomery County	39	0.09
Concord, CA (city) Contra Costa County	39	0.03
Richmond West, FL (cdp) Miami-Dade County	38	0.14
University Park, FL (cdp) Miami-Dade County	38	0.14

Notes: (cdp) census designated place; Refer to the Explanation of Data in the front of the book for more detailed information.

Hispanic: Bolivian

Top 150 Places Sorted by Percent

(Based on all places, regardless of population)

Place	Number	%
Seven Corners, VA (cdp) Fairfax County	344	3.95
Jefferson, VA (cdp) Fairfax County	703	2.56
Sherrill, IA (city) Dubuque County	4	2.15
Bailey's Crossroads, VA (cdp) Fairfax County	474	2.05
Arlington, VA (cdp) Arlington County	3,532	1.86
Annandale, VA (cdp) Fairfax County	962	1.75
Lake Barcroft, VA (cdp) Fairfax County	142	1.59
Lincolnia, VA (cdp) Fairfax County	245	1.55
Idylwood, VA (cdp) Fairfax County	238	1.49
Pimmit Hills, VA (cdp) Fairfax County	74	1.20
Red Butte, WY (cdp) Natrona County	5	1.14
Urbancrest, OH (village) Franklin County	9	1.04
Falls Church, VA (independent city) Falls Church city	99	0.95
Merrifield, VA (cdp) Fairfax County	105	0.94
Springfield, VA (cdp) Fairfax County	260	0.85
Cooke, PA (township) Cumberland County	1	0.85
Martin's Additions, MD (village) Montgomery County	7	0.80
Fairfax, VA (independent city) Fairfax city	170	0.79
North Springfield, VA (cdp) Fairfax County	72	0.78
Brentwood, MD (town) Prince George's County	22	0.77
Burlington, OH (cdp) Lawrence County	21	0.75
Clyde, CA (cdp) Contra Costa County	5	0.72
Big Water, UT (town) Kane County	3	0.72
Queenstown, MD (town) Queen Anne's County	4	0.65
Groveton, VA (cdp) Fairfax County	129	0.61
Wheaton-Glenmont, MD (cdp) Montgomery County	349	0.60
Oakton, VA (cdp) Fairfax County	177	0.60
Coronaca, SC (cdp) Greenwood County	1	0.59
Aspen Hill, MD (cdp) Montgomery County	290	0.58
Port Chester, NY (village) Westchester County	163	0.58
Mantua, VA (cdp) Fairfax County	42	0.56
Newington, VA (cdp) Fairfax County	108	0.55
Virgin, UT (town) Washington County	2	0.51
Burke, VA (cdp) Fairfax County	283	0.49
West Springfield, VA (cdp) Fairfax County	135	0.48
Matinecock, NY (village) Nassau County	4	0.48
Alexandria, VA (independent city) Alexandria city	609	0.47
Franconia, VA (cdp) Fairfax County	149	0.47
North Bay Village, FL (city) Miami-Dade County	31	0.46
Medley, FL (town) Miami-Dade County	5	0.46
Tysons Corner, VA (cdp) Fairfax County	80	0.43
Dunn Loring, VA (cdp) Fairfax County	34	0.43
North Bethesda, MD (cdp) Montgomery County	164	0.42
Rye, NY (town) Westchester County	180	0.41
South Hackensack, NJ (township) Bergen County	9	0.40
Herndon, VA (town) Fairfax County	85	0.39
Fletcher, OH (village) Miami County	2	0.39
Reston, VA (cdp) Fairfax County	215	0.38
Allenhurst, GA (town) Liberty County	3	0.38
Providence, RI (city) Providence County	634	0.37
Silver Spring, MD (cdp) Montgomery County	287	0.37
Deal, NJ (borough) Monmouth County	4	0.37
Moose Creek, AK (cdp) Fairbanks North Star Borough	2	0.37
Gaithersburg, MD (city) Montgomery County	188	0.36
White Oak, MD (cdp) Montgomery County	76	0.36
Lely Resort, FL (cdp) Collier County	5	0.35
Centreville, VA (cdp) Fairfax County	164	0.34
Rockville, MD (city) Montgomery County	160	0.34
Redland, MD (cdp) Montgomery County	57	0.34
Inwood, NY (cdp) Nassau County	32	0.34
Golden Beach, FL (town) Miami-Dade County	3	0.33
Montgomery Village, MD (cdp) Montgomery County	122	0.32
Rose Hill, VA (cdp) Fairfax County	48	0.32
Naples Park, FL (cdp) Collier County	21	0.31
Kemp Mill, MD (cdp) Montgomery County	30	0.30
White Lake, WI (village) Langlade County	1	0.30
The Crossings, FL (cdp) Miami-Dade County	69	0.29
Grand Meadow, MN (township) Mower County	1	0.29
Platte, MI (township) Benzie County	1	0.29
Vienna, VA (town) Fairfax County	40	0.28
Pennsbury Village, PA (borough) Allegheny County	2	0.27
Fountainbleau, FL (cdp) Miami-Dade County	153	0.26
Key Biscayne, FL (village) Miami-Dade County	27	0.26
Dumfries, VA (town) Prince William County	13	0.26
Westhampton Beach, NY (village) Suffolk County	5	0.26
Tustin, CA (city) Orange County	166	0.25
Lake Ridge, VA (cdp) Prince William County	77	0.25
Bay Harbor Islands, FL (town) Miami-Dade County	13	0.25
Greenfield, IL (city) Greene County	3	0.25
Shoals, IN (town) Martin County	2	0.25
Lorton, VA (cdp) Fairfax County	43	0.24
Mill Neck, NY (village) Nassau County	2	0.24
Kendall, FL (cdp) Miami-Dade County	170	0.23
Miami Springs, FL (city) Miami-Dade County	31	0.23
Islandia, NY (village) Suffolk County	7	0.23
Germantown, MD (cdp) Montgomery County	122	0.22
Doral, FL (cdp) Miami-Dade County	45	0.22
Sunset, FL (cdp) Miami-Dade County	37	0.22
Hybla Valley, VA (cdp) Fairfax County	36	0.22
Middleton, WI (city) Dane County	35	0.22
Fairbanks Ranch, CA (cdp) San Diego County	5	0.22
Chantilly, VA (cdp) Fairfax County	88	0.21
Kendall West, FL (cdp) Miami-Dade County	79	0.21
Olney, MD (cdp) Montgomery County	66	0.21
Colesville, MD (cdp) Montgomery County	41	0.21
Great Falls, VA (cdp) Fairfax County	18	0.21
East Perrine, FL (cdp) Miami-Dade County	15	0.21
Westhampton, NY (cdp) Suffolk County	6	0.21
Sienna Plantation, TX (cdp) Fort Bend County	4	0.21
Miami Beach, FL (city) Miami-Dade County	176	0.20
The Hammocks, FL (cdp) Miami-Dade County	93	0.20
Mount Vernon, VA (cdp) Fairfax County	56	0.20
Ojus, FL (cdp) Miami-Dade County	33	0.20
Friendship Village, MD (cdp) Montgomery County	9	0.20
Moss Beach, CA (cdp) San Mateo County	4	0.20
McLean, VA (cdp) Fairfax County	74	0.19
North Providence, RI (cdp) Providence County	60	0.19
Cutler, FL (cdp) Miami-Dade County	33	0.19
East Rockaway, NY (village) Nassau County	20	0.19
Huntington, VA (cdp) Fairfax County	16	0.19
South Amboy, NJ (city) Middlesex County	15	0.19
Sudley, VA (cdp) Prince William County	15	0.19
Middletown, KY (city) Jefferson County	11	0.19
Bellerose Terrace, NY (cdp) Nassau County	4	0.19
Southside Place, TX (city) Harris County	3	0.19
Benjamin, UT (cdp) Utah County	2	0.19
Wells, WI (town) Monroe County	1	0.19
Bethesda, MD (cdp) Montgomery County	99	0.18
Lake Worth, FL (city) Palm Beach County	63	0.18
Woodbridge, VA (cdp) Prince William County	57	0.18
Garfield, NJ (city) Bergen County	53	0.18
Fairland, MD (cdp) Montgomery County	40	0.18
Lake Worth Corridor, FL (cdp) Palm Beach County	33	0.18
Glenvar Heights, FL (cdp) Miami-Dade County	30	0.18
Bull Run, VA (cdp) Prince William County	20	0.18
Bogota, NJ (borough) Bergen County	15	0.18
Villa Park, CA (city) Orange County	11	0.18
Biscayne Park, FL (village) Miami-Dade County	6	0.18
Kendale Lakes, FL (cdp) Miami-Dade County	96	0.17
Sunny Isles Beach, FL (city) Miami-Dade County	26	0.17
Country Walk, FL (cdp) Miami-Dade County	18	0.17
North Kensington, MD (cdp) Montgomery County	15	0.17
Southchase, FL (cdp) Orange County	8	0.17
Chambers Estates, FL (cdp) Broward County	7	0.17
Bemidji, MN (township) Beltrami County	5	0.17
Berwyn Heights, MD (town) Prince George's County	5	0.17
Hillsmere Shores, MD (cdp) Anne Arundel County	5	0.17
Portland, ND (city) Traill County	1	0.17
Burbank, CA (city) Los Angeles County	159	0.16
Orange, NJ (cdp) Essex County	52	0.16
Johnston, RI (town) Providence County	46	0.16
Forest Glen, MD (cdp) Montgomery County	12	0.16
Three Lakes, FL (cdp) Miami-Dade County	11	0.16
Yorkshire, VA (cdp) Prince William County	11	0.16
Belle Haven, VA (cdp) Fairfax County	10	0.16
Bunker Hill Village, TX (city) Harris County	6	0.16
Brookmont, MD (cdp) Montgomery County	5	0.16
El Portal, FL (village) Miami-Dade County	4	0.16
Burlington, MI (township) Calhoun County	3	0.16
Endicott, WA (town) Whitman County	1	0.16

Notes: (cdp) census designated place; Refer to the Explanation of Data in the front of the book for more detailed information.

Hispanic: Bolivian

Top 150 Places Sorted by Percent

(Based on places with populations of 10,000 or more)

Place	Number	%
Jefferson, VA (cdp) Fairfax County	703	2.56
Bailey's Crossroads, VA (cdp) Fairfax County	474	2.05
Arlington, VA (cdp) Arlington County	3,532	1.86
Annandale, VA (cdp) Fairfax County	962	1.75
Lincolnia, VA (cdp) Fairfax County	245	1.55
Idylwood, VA (cdp) Fairfax County	238	1.49
Falls Church, VA (independent city) Falls Church city	99	0.95
Merrifield, VA (cdp) Fairfax County	105	0.94
Springfield, VA (cdp) Fairfax County	260	0.85
Fairfax, VA (independent city) Fairfax city	170	0.79
Groveton, VA (cdp) Fairfax County	129	0.61
Wheaton-Glenmont, MD (cdp) Montgomery County	349	0.60
Oakton, VA (cdp) Fairfax County	177	0.60
Aspen Hill, MD (cdp) Montgomery County	290	0.58
Port Chester, NY (village) Westchester County	163	0.58
Newington, VA (cdp) Fairfax County	108	0.55
Burke, VA (cdp) Fairfax County	283	0.49
West Springfield, VA (cdp) Fairfax County	135	0.48
Alexandria, VA (independent city) Alexandria city	609	0.47
Franconia, VA (cdp) Fairfax County	149	0.47
Tysons Corner, VA (cdp) Fairfax County	80	0.43
North Bethesda, MD (cdp) Montgomery County	164	0.42
Rye, NY (town) Westchester County	180	0.41
Herndon, VA (town) Fairfax County	85	0.39
Reston, VA (cdp) Fairfax County	215	0.38
Providence, RI (city) Providence County	634	0.37
Silver Spring, MD (cdp) Montgomery County	287	0.37
Gaithersburg, MD (city) Montgomery County	188	0.36
White Oak, MD (cdp) Montgomery County	76	0.36
Centreville, VA (cdp) Fairfax County	164	0.34
Rockville, MD (city) Montgomery County	160	0.34
Redland, MD (cdp) Montgomery County	57	0.34
Montgomery Village, MD (cdp) Montgomery County	122	0.32
Rose Hill, VA (cdp) Fairfax County	48	0.32
The Crossings, FL (cdp) Miami-Dade County	69	0.29
Vienna, VA (town) Fairfax County	40	0.28
Fountainbleau, FL (cdp) Miami-Dade County	153	0.26
Key Biscayne, FL (village) Miami-Dade County	27	0.26
Tustin, CA (city) Orange County	166	0.25
Lake Ridge, VA (cdp) Prince William County	77	0.25
Lorton, VA (cdp) Fairfax County	43	0.24
Kendall, FL (cdp) Miami-Dade County	170	0.23
Miami Springs, FL (city) Miami-Dade County	31	0.23
Germantown, MD (cdp) Montgomery County	122	0.22
Doral, FL (cdp) Miami-Dade County	45	0.22
Sunset, FL (cdp) Miami-Dade County	37	0.22
Hybla Valley, VA (cdp) Fairfax County	36	0.22
Middleton, WI (city) Dane County	35	0.22
Chantilly, VA (cdp) Fairfax County	88	0.21
Kendall West, FL (cdp) Miami-Dade County	79	0.21
Olney, MD (cdp) Montgomery County	66	0.21
Colesville, MD (cdp) Montgomery County	41	0.21
Miami Beach, FL (city) Miami-Dade County	176	0.20
The Hammocks, FL (cdp) Miami-Dade County	93	0.20
Mount Vernon, VA (cdp) Fairfax County	56	0.20
Ojus, FL (cdp) Miami-Dade County	33	0.20
McLean, VA (cdp) Fairfax County	74	0.19
North Providence, RI (cdp) Providence County	60	0.19
Cutler, FL (cdp) Miami-Dade County	33	0.19
East Rockaway, NY (village) Nassau County	20	0.19
Bethesda, MD (cdp) Montgomery County	99	0.18
Lake Worth, FL (city) Palm Beach County	63	0.18
Woodbridge, VA (cdp) Prince William County	57	0.18
Garfield, NJ (city) Bergen County	53	0.18
Fairland, MD (cdp) Montgomery County	40	0.18
Lake Worth Corridor, FL (cdp) Palm Beach County	33	0.18
Glenvar Heights, FL (cdp) Miami-Dade County	30	0.18
Bull Run, VA (cdp) Prince William County	20	0.18
Kendale Lakes, FL (cdp) Miami-Dade County	96	0.17
Sunny Isles Beach, FL (city) Miami-Dade County	26	0.17
Country Walk, FL (cdp) Miami-Dade County	18	0.17
Burbank, CA (city) Los Angeles County	159	0.16
Orange, NJ (cdp) Essex County	52	0.16
Johnston, RI (town) Providence County	46	0.16
Clifton, NJ (city) Passaic County	118	0.15
Passaic, NJ (city) Passaic County	103	0.15
Waltham, MA (city) Middlesex County	89	0.15
Tamiami, FL (cdp) Miami-Dade County	82	0.15
North Potomac, MD (cdp) Montgomery County	34	0.15
Lanham-Seabrook, MD (cdp) Prince George's County	27	0.15
Salisbury, NY (cdp) Nassau County	19	0.15
Richmond West, FL (cdp) Miami-Dade County	38	0.14
University Park, FL (cdp) Miami-Dade County	38	0.14
Lodi, NJ (borough) Bergen County	33	0.14
Dale City, VA (cdp) Prince William County	75	0.13
Coral Terrace, FL (cdp) Miami-Dade County	31	0.13
Hialeah Gardens, FL (city) Miami-Dade County	25	0.13
Cranston, RI (city) Providence County	98	0.12
College Park, MD (city) Prince George's County	29	0.12
Pinecrest, FL (village) Miami-Dade County	22	0.12
Union City, NJ (city) Hudson County	71	0.11
Skokie, IL (village) Cook County	69	0.11
Fayetteville, AR (city) Washington County	66	0.11
Hackensack, NJ (city) Bergen County	49	0.11
Country Club, FL (cdp) Miami-Dade County	41	0.11
Miami Lakes, FL (cdp) Miami-Dade County	24	0.11
Mamaroneck, NY (village) Westchester County	20	0.11
River Forest, IL (village) Cook County	13	0.11
Manassas Park, VA (independent city) Manassas Park city	11	0.11
Miami, FL (city) Miami-Dade County	355	0.10
Jersey City, NJ (city) Hudson County	244	0.10
Elizabeth, NJ (city) Union County	121	0.10
West New York, NJ (town) Hudson County	48	0.10
Leisure City, FL (cdp) Miami-Dade County	23	0.10
Golden Gate, FL (cdp) Collier County	20	0.10
Lynbrook, NY (village) Nassau County	19	0.10
Elmwood Park, NJ (borough) Bergen County	18	0.10
Takoma Park, MD (city) Montgomery County	17	0.10
Langley Park, MD (cdp) Prince George's County	16	0.10
Adelphi, MD (cdp) Prince George's County	15	0.10
Fort Hunt, VA (cdp) Fairfax County	13	0.10
North Wantagh, NY (cdp) Nassau County	12	0.10
Brentwood, NY (cdp) Suffolk County	51	0.09
Coral Gables, FL (city) Miami-Dade County	40	0.09
Potomac, MD (cdp) Montgomery County	39	0.09
Laguna Hills, CA (city) Orange County	27	0.09
Greenacres, FL (city) Palm Beach County	26	0.09
Carteret, NJ (borough) Middlesex County	19	0.09
Highland Park, NJ (borough) Middlesex County	12	0.09
Lincolnwood, IL (village) Cook County	11	0.09
Union Park, FL (cdp) Orange County	9	0.09
Santa Ana, CA (city) Orange County	269	0.08
San Mateo, CA (city) San Mateo County	77	0.08
Framingham, MA (cdp) Middlesex County	54	0.08
Lake Forest, CA (city) Orange County	46	0.08
White Plains, NY (city) Westchester County	42	0.08
League City, TX (city) Galveston County	37	0.08
Newark, CA (city) Alameda County	34	0.08
North Miami Beach, FL (city) Miami-Dade County	34	0.08
Long Beach, NY (city) Nassau County	29	0.08
Central Islip, NY (cdp) Suffolk County	27	0.08
Mamaroneck, NY (town) Westchester County	23	0.08
Aventura, FL (city) Miami-Dade County	19	0.08
Central Falls, RI (city) Providence County	16	0.08
Asbury Park, NJ (city) Monmouth County	14	0.08
South River, NJ (borough) Middlesex County	12	0.08
Westbury, NY (village) Nassau County	11	0.08
Calverton, MD (cdp) Montgomery County	10	0.08
San Anselmo, CA (town) Marin County	10	0.08
Westwood Lakes, FL (cdp) Miami-Dade County	10	0.08
Lea Hill, WA (cdp) King County	9	0.08
Pelham, NY (town) Westchester County	9	0.08
Hollywood, FL (city) Broward County	100	0.07
Downey, CA (city) Los Angeles County	75	0.07
Provo, UT (city) Utah County	71	0.07
Davie, FL (town) Broward County	54	0.07
Mountain View, CA (city) Santa Clara County	49	0.07
Bowie, MD (city) Prince George's County	36	0.07
Weston, FL (city) Broward County	34	0.07
East Hartford, CT (cdp) Hartford County	33	0.07

Notes: (cdp) census designated place; Refer to the Explanation of Data in the front of the book for more detailed information.

Hispanic: Chilean

Top 150 Places Sorted by Number

(Based on all places, regardless of population)

Place	Number	%
New York, NY (city) New York City	5,014	0.06
Los Angeles, CA (city) Los Angeles County	2,736	0.07
Miami, FL (city) Miami-Dade County	939	0.26
Hempstead, NY (town) Nassau County	893	0.12
Chicago, IL (city) Cook County	640	0.02
Miami Beach, FL (city) Miami-Dade County	623	0.71
Hialeah, FL (city) Miami-Dade County	611	0.27
Houston, TX (city) Harris County	591	0.03
Fountainbleau, FL (cdp) Miami-Dade County	550	0.92
North Hempstead, NY (town) Nassau County	521	0.23
Kendall, FL (cdp) Miami-Dade County	479	0.64
San Diego, CA (city) San Diego County	449	0.04
San Jose, CA (city) Santa Clara County	412	0.05
The Hammocks, FL (cdp) Miami-Dade County	409	0.86
Oyster Bay, NY (town) Nassau County	409	0.14
San Francisco, CA (city) San Francisco County	405	0.05
Kendale Lakes, FL (cdp) Miami-Dade County	381	0.67
Washington, DC (city) District of Columbia	359	0.06
Union City, NJ (city) Hudson County	352	0.52
North Bergen, NJ (township) Hudson County	315	0.54
Boston, MA (city) Suffolk County	315	0.05
Hollywood, FL (city) Broward County	302	0.22
Pembroke Pines, FL (city) Broward County	298	0.22
Dover, NJ (town) Morris County	275	1.51
Jersey City, NJ (city) Hudson County	269	0.11
Seattle, WA (city) King County	263	0.05
Tamiami, FL (cdp) Miami-Dade County	262	0.48
Kendall West, FL (cdp) Miami-Dade County	249	0.65
Islip, NY (town) Suffolk County	249	0.08
Doral, FL (cdp) Miami-Dade County	224	1.10
The Crossings, FL (cdp) Miami-Dade County	212	0.90
Elizabeth, NJ (city) Union County	209	0.17
Provo, UT (city) Utah County	206	0.20
Arlington, VA (cdp) Arlington County	204	0.11
Alexandria, VA (independent city) Alexandria city	199	0.16
West New York, NJ (town) Hudson County	196	0.43
Stamford, CT (city) Fairfield County	194	0.17
Mount Pleasant, NY (town) Westchester County	193	0.45
Las Vegas, NV (city) Clark County	193	0.04
Salt Lake City, UT (city) Salt Lake County	188	0.10
North Miami Beach, FL (city) Miami-Dade County	186	0.46
Sleepy Hollow, NY (village) Westchester County	185	2.01
Long Beach, CA (city) Los Angeles County	182	0.04
Philadelphia, PA (city) Philadelphia County	182	0.01
Orem, UT (city) Utah County	177	0.21
Dallas, TX (city) Dallas County	170	0.01
Allentown, PA (city) Lehigh County	169	0.16
Brookhaven, NY (town) Suffolk County	168	0.04
Austin, TX (city) Travis County	168	0.03
Glendale, CA (city) Los Angeles County	165	0.08
Manorhaven, NY (village) Nassau County	164	2.67
Tucson, AZ (city) Pima County	163	0.03
Coral Springs, FL (city) Broward County	162	0.14
Ossining, NY (town) Westchester County	159	0.44
Coral Gables, FL (city) Miami-Dade County	155	0.37
Ossining, NY (village) Westchester County	152	0.63
San Antonio, TX (city) Bexar County	150	0.01
San Mateo, CA (city) San Mateo County	148	0.16
Lancaster, CA (city) Los Angeles County	144	0.12
Miramar, FL (city) Broward County	143	0.20
Bethesda, MD (cdp) Montgomery County	142	0.26
Oakland, CA (city) Alameda County	141	0.04
Greenburgh, NY (town) Westchester County	140	0.16
Torrance, CA (city) Los Angeles County	140	0.10
Charlotte, NC (city) Mecklenburg County	140	0.03
Rye, NY (town) Westchester County	139	0.32
Country Club, FL (cdp) Miami-Dade County	138	0.38
North Bethesda, MD (cdp) Montgomery County	138	0.36
Greenwich, CT (town) Fairfield County	134	0.22
Sunrise, FL (city) Broward County	134	0.16
Cambridge, MA (city) Middlesex County	133	0.13
Albuquerque, NM (city) Bernalillo County	133	0.03
Denver, CO (city) Denver County	133	0.02
Glen Cove, NY (city) Nassau County	132	0.50
Yonkers, NY (city) Westchester County	132	0.07
Cutler, FL (cdp) Miami-Dade County	129	0.74
Richmond West, FL (cdp) Miami-Dade County	129	0.46
Aspen Hill, MD (cdp) Montgomery County	129	0.26
Bayonne, NJ (city) Hudson County	128	0.21
Stockton, CA (city) San Joaquin County	128	0.05
Phoenix, AZ (city) Maricopa County	126	0.01
Rockville, MD (city) Montgomery County	125	0.26
Portland, OR (city) Multnomah County	124	0.02
Wheaton-Glenmont, MD (cdp) Montgomery County	121	0.21
Paradise, NV (cdp) Clark County	121	0.07
Pinecrest, FL (village) Miami-Dade County	119	0.62
Valley Stream, NY (village) Nassau County	118	0.32
Davie, FL (town) Broward County	117	0.15
Anaheim, CA (city) Orange County	117	0.04
Jacksonville, FL (special city) Duval County	117	0.02
Glenvar Heights, FL (cdp) Miami-Dade County	116	0.71
Weston, FL (city) Broward County	116	0.24
Berkeley, CA (city) Alameda County	116	0.11
Huntington, NY (town) Suffolk County	115	0.06
New Haven, CT (city) New Haven County	112	0.09
Minneapolis, MN (city) Hennepin County	112	0.03
Port Chester, NY (village) Westchester County	111	0.40
Potomac, MD (cdp) Montgomery County	110	0.25
Santa Clarita, CA (city) Los Angeles County	110	0.07
Elmont, NY (cdp) Nassau County	107	0.33
Port Washington, NY (cdp) Nassau County	106	0.70
Pasadena, CA (city) Los Angeles County	106	0.08
Babylon, NY (town) Suffolk County	105	0.05
Sacramento, CA (city) Sacramento County	105	0.03
Fremont, CA (city) Alameda County	101	0.05
Madison, WI (city) Dane County	101	0.05
Annandale, VA (cdp) Fairfax County	99	0.18
Hallandale, FL (city) Broward County	98	0.29
Fort Lauderdale, FL (city) Broward County	97	0.06
Burbank, CA (city) Los Angeles County	96	0.10
Miami Lakes, FL (cdp) Miami-Dade County	95	0.42
Brentwood, NY (cdp) Suffolk County	95	0.18
Boca Raton, FL (city) Palm Beach County	95	0.13
Paterson, NJ (city) Passaic County	95	0.06
Gainesville, FL (city) Alachua County	94	0.10
Sunny Isles Beach, FL (city) Miami-Dade County	93	0.61
Redondo Beach, CA (city) Los Angeles County	93	0.15
Carol City, FL (cdp) Miami-Dade County	92	0.15
Huntington Beach, CA (city) Orange County	92	0.05
Oakland Park, FL (city) Broward County	90	0.29
Spring Valley, NV (cdp) Clark County	88	0.07
Irvine, CA (city) Orange County	86	0.06
West Valley City, UT (city) Salt Lake County	85	0.08
Malden, MA (city) Middlesex County	84	0.15
Clifton, NJ (city) Passaic County	84	0.11
Orlando, FL (city) Orange County	84	0.05
Milwaukee, WI (city) Milwaukee County	84	0.01
Country Walk, FL (cdp) Miami-Dade County	83	0.78
Rancho Cucamonga, CA (city) San Bernardino County	83	0.06
Fort Worth, TX (city) Tarrant County	82	0.02
Inwood, NY (cdp) Nassau County	80	0.86
Redwood City, CA (city) San Mateo County	80	0.11
Riverside, CA (city) Riverside County	80	0.03
Pittsburgh, PA (city) Allegheny County	80	0.02
Nashville-Davidson, TN (special city) Davidson County	80	0.01
Hayward, CA (city) Alameda County	78	0.06
Ann Arbor, MI (city) Washtenaw County	77	0.07
Mesa, AZ (city) Maricopa County	77	0.02
Virginia Beach, VA (independent city) Virginia Beach city	77	0.02
Key Biscayne, FL (village) Miami-Dade County	76	0.72
Gaithersburg, MD (city) Montgomery County	76	0.14
Westchester, FL (cdp) Miami-Dade County	74	0.24
North Miami, FL (city) Miami-Dade County	74	0.12
Newark, NJ (city) Essex County	74	0.03
Coral Terrace, FL (cdp) Miami-Dade County	72	0.30
Plantation, FL (city) Broward County	72	0.09
Anchorage, AK (municipality) Anchorage Borough	72	0.03
Guttenberg, NJ (town) Hudson County	71	0.66
Burke, VA (cdp) Fairfax County	71	0.12
Santa Monica, CA (city) Los Angeles County	71	0.08

Notes: (cdp) census designated place; Refer to the Explanation of Data in the front of the book for more detailed information.

Hispanic: Chilean

Top 150 Places Sorted by Percent

(Based on all places, regardless of population)

Place	Number	%
Briarwood, ND (city) Cass County	3	3.85
Manorhaven, NY (village) Nassau County	164	2.67
Sleepy Hollow, NY (village) Westchester County	185	2.01
Grand Acres, TX (cdp) Cameron County	4	1.97
North Lynbrook, NY (cdp) Nassau County	14	1.89
Locust Valley, NY (cdp) Nassau County	56	1.59
Dover, NJ (town) Morris County	275	1.51
Baxter Estates, NY (village) Nassau County	14	1.39
Tajique, NM (cdp) Torrance County	2	1.35
Victory Gardens, NJ (borough) Morris County	20	1.29
Amalga, UT (town) Cache County	5	1.17
Doral, FL (cdp) Miami-Dade County	224	1.10
Mill Neck, NY (village) Nassau County	9	1.09
North Bay Village, FL (city) Miami-Dade County	68	1.01
Fountainbleau, FL (cdp) Miami-Dade County	550	0.92
The Crossings, FL (cdp) Miami-Dade County	212	0.90
Worley, ID (city) Kootenai County	2	0.90
Hawk Creek, MN (township) Renville County	2	0.88
Chula Vista, FL (cdp) Broward County	5	0.87
The Hammocks, FL (cdp) Miami-Dade County	409	0.86
Inwood, NY (cdp) Nassau County	80	0.86
Poquott, NY (village) Suffolk County	8	0.82
Country Walk, FL (cdp) Miami-Dade County	83	0.78
Ellenville, NY (village) Ulster County	32	0.77
Cutler, FL (cdp) Miami-Dade County	129	0.74
Perry, MN (township) Lac qui Parle County	2	0.73
Key Biscayne, FL (village) Miami-Dade County	76	0.72
Miami Beach, FL (city) Miami-Dade County	623	0.71
Glenvar Heights, FL (cdp) Miami-Dade County	116	0.71
Auburn, KS (city) Shawnee County	8	0.71
Port Washington, NY (cdp) Nassau County	106	0.70
Island Park, NY (village) Nassau County	33	0.70
Lake Forest, FL (cdp) Broward County	34	0.68
Todd Mission, TX (city) Grimes County	1	0.68
Kendale Lakes, FL (cdp) Miami-Dade County	381	0.67
Guttenberg, NJ (town) Hudson County	71	0.66
Dewey Beach, DE (town) Sussex County	2	0.66
Kendall West, FL (cdp) Miami-Dade County	249	0.65
Timberlake, OH (village) Lake County	5	0.65
Kendall, FL (cdp) Miami-Dade County	479	0.64
Virginia Gardens, FL (village) Miami-Dade County	15	0.64
Ossining, NY (village) Westchester County	152	0.63
Pinecrest, FL (village) Miami-Dade County	119	0.62
Sunny Isles Beach, FL (city) Miami-Dade County	93	0.61
Youngsville, NC (town) Franklin County	4	0.61
Matinecock, NY (village) Nassau County	5	0.60
Glenview Hills, KY (city) Jefferson County	2	0.59
Three Lakes, FL (cdp) Miami-Dade County	40	0.58
Hewlett, NY (cdp) Nassau County	39	0.55
Miami Gardens, FL (cdp) Broward County	15	0.55
Monico, WI (town) Oneida County	2	0.55
North Bergen, NJ (township) Hudson County	315	0.54
East Hampton North, NY (cdp) Suffolk County	19	0.53
Forest Home, NY (cdp) Tompkins County	5	0.53
Wampsville, NY (village) Madison County	3	0.53
Edgar Springs, MO (city) Phelps County	1	0.53
Union City, NJ (city) Hudson County	352	0.52
Northwest Harbor, NY (cdp) Suffolk County	16	0.52
Genola, UT (town) Utah County	5	0.52
Hilltop, MN (city) Anoka County	4	0.52
Glenwood, AL (town) Crenshaw County	1	0.52
Port Royal, PA (borough) Juniata County	5	0.51
Dunes Road, FL (cdp) Palm Beach County	2	0.51
Glen Cove, NY (city) Nassau County	132	0.50
Tarrytown, NY (village) Westchester County	54	0.49
Wharton, NJ (borough) Morris County	31	0.49
Tamiami, FL (cdp) Miami-Dade County	262	0.48
North Miami Beach, FL (city) Miami-Dade County	186	0.46
Richmond West, FL (cdp) Miami-Dade County	129	0.46
Milford, PA (township) Juniata County	8	0.46
Millville, UT (city) Cache County	7	0.46
Rolling Oaks, FL (cdp) Broward County	6	0.46
Mifflintown, PA (borough) Juniata County	4	0.46
Mount Pleasant, NY (town) Westchester County	193	0.45
Waikapu, HI (cdp) Maui County	5	0.45
Ossining, NY (town) Westchester County	159	0.44
Friendship Village, MD (cdp) Montgomery County	20	0.44
Port Washington North, NY (village) Nassau County	12	0.44
West New York, NJ (town) Hudson County	196	0.43
West Miami, FL (city) Miami-Dade County	25	0.43
Surfside, FL (town) Miami-Dade County	21	0.43
Netcong, NJ (borough) Morris County	11	0.43
Hawi, HI (cdp) Hawaii County	4	0.43
Belgium, IL (village) Vermilion County	2	0.43
Arrowhead, MN (township) Saint Louis County	1	0.43
Miami Lakes, FL (cdp) Miami-Dade County	95	0.42
Weehawken, NJ (township) Hudson County	57	0.42
Woodfin, NC (town) Buncombe County	13	0.41
Glover, VT (town) Orleans County	4	0.41
Port Chester, NY (village) Westchester County	111	0.40
Bolinas, CA (cdp) Marin County	5	0.40
Taos Pueblo, NM (cdp) Taos County	5	0.40
Saratoga Springs, UT (town) Utah County	4	0.40
Juno Ridge, FL (cdp) Palm Beach County	3	0.40
Sunfish Lake, MN (city) Dakota County	2	0.40
Cedarhurst, NY (village) Nassau County	24	0.39
Carlstadt, NJ (borough) Bergen County	23	0.39
Bay Park, NY (cdp) Nassau County	9	0.39
Hendren, WI (town) Clark County	2	0.39
Washington Grove, MD (town) Montgomery County	2	0.39
Country Club, FL (cdp) Miami-Dade County	138	0.38
Coral Gables, FL (city) Miami-Dade County	155	0.37
Wawarsing, NY (town) Ulster County	48	0.37
North Bethesda, MD (cdp) Montgomery County	138	0.36
West Bountiful, UT (city) Davis County	16	0.36
Clancy, MT (cdp) Jefferson County	5	0.36
Ivanhoe Estates, FL (cdp) Broward County	1	0.36
Sweetwater, FL (city) Miami-Dade County	50	0.35
Lakes by the Bay, FL (cdp) Miami-Dade County	32	0.35
Towner, ND (city) McHenry County	2	0.35
Miami Springs, FL (city) Miami-Dade County	46	0.34
North Kensington, MD (cdp) Montgomery County	30	0.34
Montauk, NY (cdp) Suffolk County	13	0.34
Beatyestown, NJ (cdp) Warren County	11	0.34
Hamilton Branch, CA (cdp) Plumas County	2	0.34
Ogle, PA (township) Somerset County	2	0.34
Elmont, NY (cdp) Nassau County	107	0.33
Garrett Park, MD (town) Montgomery County	3	0.33
Fox, AK (cdp) Fairbanks North Star Borough	1	0.33
Rye, NY (town) Westchester County	139	0.32
Valley Stream, NY (village) Nassau County	118	0.32
Morenci, AZ (cdp) Greenlee County	6	0.32
New Milford, PA (township) Susquehanna County	6	0.32
Moore, MI (township) Sanilac County	4	0.32
Corinne, UT (city) Box Elder County	2	0.32
Sunset, FL (cdp) Miami-Dade County	54	0.31
Ojus, FL (cdp) Miami-Dade County	51	0.31
Palm Springs North, FL (cdp) Miami-Dade County	17	0.31
Guilford Center, CT (cdp) New Haven County	8	0.31
Brownsboro Village, KY (city) Jefferson County	1	0.31
Wishram, WA (cdp) Klickitat County	1	0.31
Coral Terrace, FL (cdp) Miami-Dade County	72	0.30
Olympia Heights, FL (cdp) Miami-Dade County	41	0.30
Budd Lake, NJ (cdp) Morris County	24	0.30
Bal Harbour, FL (village) Miami-Dade County	10	0.30
Ester, AK (cdp) Fairbanks North Star Borough	5	0.30
Selbyville, DE (town) Sussex County	5	0.30
Bingen, WA (city) Klickitat County	2	0.30
Moro, OR (city) Sherman County	1	0.30
Hallandale, FL (city) Broward County	98	0.29
Oakland Park, FL (city) Broward County	90	0.29
Morton, MS (city) Scott County	10	0.29
Louisburg, NC (town) Franklin County	9	0.29
Bridgehampton, NY (cdp) Suffolk County	4	0.29
Loughman, FL (cdp) Polk County	4	0.29
Woodacre, CA (cdp) Marin County	4	0.29
Long Lake, MN (township) Watonwan County	1	0.29
Staley, NC (town) Randolph County	1	0.29
East Hampton, NY (town) Suffolk County	56	0.28
Bayville, NY (village) Nassau County	20	0.28

Notes: (cdp) census designated place; Refer to the Explanation of Data in the front of the book for more detailed information.

Hispanic: Chilean

Top 150 Places Sorted by Percent

(Based on places with populations of 10,000 or more)

Place	Number	%
Dover, NJ (town) Morris County	275	1.51
Doral, FL (cdp) Miami-Dade County	224	1.10
Fountainbleau, FL (cdp) Miami-Dade County	550	0.92
The Crossings, FL (cdp) Miami-Dade County	212	0.90
The Hammocks, FL (cdp) Miami-Dade County	409	0.86
Country Walk, FL (cdp) Miami-Dade County	83	0.78
Cutler, FL (cdp) Miami-Dade County	129	0.74
Key Biscayne, FL (village) Miami-Dade County	76	0.72
Miami Beach, FL (city) Miami-Dade County	623	0.71
Glenvar Heights, FL (cdp) Miami-Dade County	116	0.71
Port Washington, NY (cdp) Nassau County	106	0.70
Kendale Lakes, FL (cdp) Miami-Dade County	381	0.67
Guttenberg, NJ (town) Hudson County	71	0.66
Kendall West, FL (cdp) Miami-Dade County	249	0.65
Kendall, FL (cdp) Miami-Dade County	479	0.64
Ossining, NY (village) Westchester County	152	0.63
Pinecrest, FL (village) Miami-Dade County	119	0.62
Sunny Isles Beach, FL (city) Miami-Dade County	93	0.61
North Bergen, NJ (township) Hudson County	315	0.54
Union City, NJ (city) Hudson County	352	0.52
Glen Cove, NY (city) Nassau County	132	0.50
Tarrytown, NY (village) Westchester County	54	0.49
Tamiami, FL (cdp) Miami-Dade County	262	0.48
North Miami Beach, FL (city) Miami-Dade County	186	0.46
Richmond West, FL (cdp) Miami-Dade County	129	0.46
Mount Pleasant, NY (town) Westchester County	193	0.45
Ossining, NY (town) Westchester County	159	0.44
West New York, NJ (town) Hudson County	196	0.43
Miami Lakes, FL (cdp) Miami-Dade County	95	0.42
Weehawken, NJ (township) Hudson County	57	0.42
Port Chester, NY (village) Westchester County	111	0.40
Country Club, FL (cdp) Miami-Dade County	138	0.38
Coral Gables, FL (city) Miami-Dade County	155	0.37
Wawarsing, NY (town) Ulster County	48	0.37
North Bethesda, MD (cdp) Montgomery County	138	0.36
Sweetwater, FL (city) Miami-Dade County	50	0.35
Miami Springs, FL (city) Miami-Dade County	46	0.34
Elmont, NY (cdp) Nassau County	107	0.33
Rye, NY (town) Westchester County	139	0.32
Valley Stream, NY (village) Nassau County	118	0.32
Sunset, FL (cdp) Miami-Dade County	54	0.31
Ojus, FL (cdp) Miami-Dade County	51	0.31
Coral Terrace, FL (cdp) Miami-Dade County	72	0.30
Olympia Heights, FL (cdp) Miami-Dade County	41	0.30
Hallandale, FL (city) Broward County	98	0.29
Oakland Park, FL (city) Broward County	90	0.29
East Hampton, NY (town) Suffolk County	56	0.28
Hialeah, FL (city) Miami-Dade County	611	0.27
Miami, FL (city) Miami-Dade County	939	0.26
Bethesda, MD (cdp) Montgomery County	142	0.26
Aspen Hill, MD (cdp) Montgomery County	129	0.26
Rockville, MD (city) Montgomery County	125	0.26
Miami Shores, FL (village) Miami-Dade County	27	0.26
Potomac, MD (cdp) Montgomery County	110	0.25
Cutler Ridge, FL (cdp) Miami-Dade County	63	0.25
North Bay Shore, NY (cdp) Suffolk County	38	0.25
Weston, FL (city) Broward County	116	0.24
Westchester, FL (cdp) Miami-Dade County	74	0.24
University Park, FL (cdp) Miami-Dade County	64	0.24
North Hempstead, NY (town) Nassau County	521	0.23
Elmwood Park, NJ (borough) Bergen County	43	0.23
Dumas, TX (city) Moore County	31	0.23
Westwood Lakes, FL (cdp) Miami-Dade County	28	0.23
South Miami, FL (city) Miami-Dade County	25	0.23
Hackettstown, NJ (town) Warren County	24	0.23
Hollywood, FL (city) Broward County	302	0.22
Pembroke Pines, FL (city) Broward County	298	0.22
Greenwich, CT (town) Fairfield County	134	0.22
Hialeah Gardens, FL (city) Miami-Dade County	43	0.22
Mamaroneck, NY (village) Westchester County	41	0.22
Salisbury, NY (cdp) Nassau County	27	0.22
Orem, UT (city) Utah County	177	0.21
Bayonne, NJ (city) Hudson County	128	0.21
Wheaton-Glenmont, MD (cdp) Montgomery County	121	0.21
Harrison, NJ (town) Hudson County	30	0.21
Provo, UT (city) Utah County	206	0.20
Miramar, FL (city) Broward County	143	0.20
Aventura, FL (city) Miami-Dade County	50	0.20
Ives Estates, FL (cdp) Miami-Dade County	36	0.20
Albany, CA (city) Alameda County	33	0.20
Rye, NY (city) Westchester County	30	0.20
Fairview, NJ (borough) Bergen County	27	0.20
Roselle Park, NJ (borough) Union County	27	0.20
Millcreek, UT (cdp) Salt Lake County	57	0.19
Oak Ridge, FL (cdp) Orange County	42	0.19
Lynbrook, NY (village) Nassau County	38	0.19
Ridgefield Park, NJ (village) Bergen County	25	0.19
Palm Springs, FL (village) Palm Beach County	22	0.19
Annandale, VA (cdp) Fairfax County	99	0.18
Brentwood, NY (cdp) Suffolk County	95	0.18
Montgomery Village, MD (cdp) Montgomery County	69	0.18
Oceanside, NY (cdp) Nassau County	59	0.18
Long Branch, NJ (city) Monmouth County	55	0.18
Greenacres, FL (city) Palm Beach County	51	0.18
Cooper City, FL (city) Broward County	50	0.18
Jefferson, VA (cdp) Fairfax County	49	0.18
Magna, UT (cdp) Salt Lake County	41	0.18
Fairfax, VA (independent city) Fairfax city	38	0.18
Mineola, NY (village) Nassau County	34	0.18
New Cassel, NY (cdp) Nassau County	24	0.18
Elizabeth, NJ (city) Union County	209	0.17
Stamford, CT (city) Fairfield County	194	0.17
South Miami Heights, FL (cdp) Miami-Dade County	56	0.17
Bergenfield, NJ (borough) Bergen County	45	0.17
Mount Olive, NJ (township) Morris County	41	0.17
Cliffside Park, NJ (borough) Bergen County	39	0.17
Guilford, CT (town) New Haven County	37	0.17
Hillside, NJ (cdp) Union County	37	0.17
Summit, NJ (city) Union County	36	0.17
Sandalfoot Cove, FL (cdp) Palm Beach County	29	0.17
Palmetto Estates, FL (cdp) Miami-Dade County	23	0.17
Alexandria, VA (independent city) Alexandria city	199	0.16
Allentown, PA (city) Lehigh County	169	0.16
San Mateo, CA (city) San Mateo County	148	0.16
Greenburgh, NY (town) Westchester County	140	0.16
Sunrise, FL (city) Broward County	134	0.16
Kearny, NJ (town) Hudson County	64	0.16
Seymour, CT (town) New Haven County	24	0.16
Davie, FL (town) Broward County	117	0.15
Redondo Beach, CA (city) Los Angeles County	93	0.15
Carol City, FL (cdp) Miami-Dade County	92	0.15
Malden, MA (city) Middlesex County	84	0.15
Pullman, WA (city) Whitman County	36	0.15
Bailey's Crossroads, VA (cdp) Fairfax County	35	0.15
Carteret, NJ (borough) Middlesex County	32	0.15
South Laurel, MD (cdp) Prince George's County	30	0.15
Lorton, VA (cdp) Fairfax County	26	0.15
Druid Hills, GA (cdp) De Kalb County	19	0.15
Storrs, CT (cdp) Tolland County	17	0.15
Oyster Bay, NY (town) Nassau County	409	0.14
Coral Springs, FL (city) Broward County	162	0.14
Gaithersburg, MD (city) Montgomery County	76	0.14
McLean, VA (cdp) Fairfax County	55	0.14
Palm Beach Gardens, FL (city) Palm Beach County	48	0.14
Mamaroneck, NY (town) Westchester County	41	0.14
Oakton, VA (cdp) Fairfax County	40	0.14
Nutley, NJ (cdp) Essex County	37	0.14
Pleasant Grove, UT (city) Utah County	32	0.14
Mansfield, CT (town) Tolland County	30	0.14
North Plainfield, NJ (borough) Somerset County	30	0.14
North Laurel, MD (cdp) Howard County	29	0.14
North New Hyde Park, NY (cdp) Nassau County	20	0.14
Cherryland, CA (cdp) Alameda County	19	0.14
Stanford, CA (cdp) Santa Clara County	19	0.14
Greenlawn, NY (cdp) Suffolk County	18	0.14
Greenwood Village, CO (city) Arapahoe County	16	0.14
Falls Church, VA (independent city) Falls Church city	15	0.14
Ridgefield, NJ (borough) Bergen County	15	0.14
Princeton, FL (cdp) Miami-Dade County	14	0.14
Cambridge, MA (city) Middlesex County	133	0.13

Notes: (cdp) census designated place; Refer to the Explanation of Data in the front of the book for more detailed information.

Hispanic: Colombian

Top 150 Places Sorted by Number

(Based on all places, regardless of population)

Place	Number	%
New York, NY (city) New York City	77,154	0.96
Elizabeth, NJ (city) Union County	7,793	6.46
Hialeah, FL (city) Miami-Dade County	7,152	3.16
Houston, TX (city) Harris County	5,821	0.30
Los Angeles, CA (city) Los Angeles County	5,819	0.16
Miami, FL (city) Miami-Dade County	5,784	1.60
Chicago, IL (city) Cook County	5,625	0.19
Paterson, NJ (city) Passaic County	5,110	3.42
The Hammocks, FL (cdp) Miami-Dade County	4,749	10.02
Hempstead, NY (town) Nassau County	4,403	0.58
Pembroke Pines, FL (city) Broward County	4,124	3.00
Boston, MA (city) Suffolk County	4,065	0.69
Miami Beach, FL (city) Miami-Dade County	3,872	4.40
Kendall West, FL (cdp) Miami-Dade County	3,778	9.93
Kendale Lakes, FL (cdp) Miami-Dade County	3,619	6.36
Kendall, FL (cdp) Miami-Dade County	3,429	4.56
North Bergen, NJ (township) Hudson County	3,351	5.77
Fountainbleau, FL (cdp) Miami-Dade County	3,153	5.29
Hollywood, FL (city) Broward County	3,152	2.26
Country Club, FL (cdp) Miami-Dade County	3,134	8.63
Weston, FL (city) Broward County	3,052	6.19
Union City, NJ (city) Hudson County	3,039	4.53
Islip, NY (town) Suffolk County	2,951	0.91
West New York, NJ (town) Hudson County	2,664	5.82
Philadelphia, PA (city) Philadelphia County	2,414	0.16
Coral Springs, FL (city) Broward County	2,408	2.05
Tamiami, FL (cdp) Miami-Dade County	2,161	3.94
Pawtucket, RI (city) Providence County	2,143	2.94
Sunrise, FL (city) Broward County	2,090	2.44
Dover, NJ (town) Morris County	2,050	11.27
Norwalk, CT (city) Fairfield County	1,969	2.37
Stamford, CT (city) Fairfield County	1,937	1.65
Central Falls, RI (city) Providence County	1,882	9.94
Englewood, NJ (city) Bergen County	1,878	7.17
Miramar, FL (city) Broward County	1,827	2.51
Doral, FL (cdp) Miami-Dade County	1,780	8.71
Jersey City, NJ (city) Hudson County	1,683	0.70
Orlando, FL (city) Orange County	1,663	0.89
Hackensack, NJ (city) Bergen County	1,634	3.83
Clifton, NJ (city) Passaic County	1,581	2.01
Tamarac, FL (city) Broward County	1,523	2.74
Plantation, FL (city) Broward County	1,502	1.81
Morristown, NJ (town) Morris County	1,479	7.98
White Plains, NY (city) Westchester County	1,458	2.75
The Crossings, FL (cdp) Miami-Dade County	1,454	6.17
Richmond West, FL (cdp) Miami-Dade County	1,441	5.13
Tampa, FL (city) Hillsborough County	1,401	0.46
Brookhaven, NY (town) Suffolk County	1,400	0.31
Brentwood, NY (cdp) Suffolk County	1,357	2.52
Davie, FL (town) Broward County	1,304	1.72
Carol City, FL (cdp) Miami-Dade County	1,279	2.15
Passaic, NJ (city) Passaic County	1,260	1.86
North Hempstead, NY (town) Nassau County	1,219	0.55
Margate, FL (city) Broward County	1,199	2.22
Lowell, MA (city) Middlesex County	1,167	1.11
North Miami Beach, FL (city) Miami-Dade County	1,154	2.83
San Diego, CA (city) San Diego County	1,152	0.09
Aventura, FL (city) Miami-Dade County	1,075	4.25
North Lauderdale, FL (city) Broward County	1,071	3.32
New Rochelle, NY (city) Westchester County	1,071	1.48
Babylon, NY (town) Suffolk County	1,071	0.51
Newark, NJ (city) Essex County	1,071	0.39
Oyster Bay, NY (town) Nassau County	1,066	0.36
Town 'n' Country, FL (cdp) Hillsborough County	1,057	1.46
Miami Lakes, FL (cdp) Miami-Dade County	1,005	4.43
Yonkers, NY (city) Westchester County	991	0.51
Fort Lauderdale, FL (city) Broward County	988	0.65
Coral Gables, FL (city) Miami-Dade County	961	2.27
Kissimmee, FL (city) Osceola County	960	2.01
Sunny Isles Beach, FL (city) Miami-Dade County	930	6.07
Jacksonville, FL (special city) Duval County	924	0.13
Hialeah Gardens, FL (city) Miami-Dade County	892	4.62
San Antonio, TX (city) Bexar County	888	0.08
Dallas, TX (city) Dallas County	862	0.07
Washington, DC (city) District of Columbia	859	0.15
North Miami, FL (city) Miami-Dade County	858	1.43
Linden, NJ (city) Union County	852	2.16
East Hampton, NY (town) Suffolk County	850	4.31
Bergenfield, NJ (borough) Bergen County	850	3.24
Bridgeport, CT (city) Fairfield County	850	0.61
Charlotte, NC (city) Mecklenburg County	835	0.15
Hartford, CT (city) Hartford County	829	0.68
San Francisco, CA (city) San Francisco County	817	0.11
South Miami Heights, FL (cdp) Miami-Dade County	798	2.38
Key Biscayne, FL (village) Miami-Dade County	743	7.07
Rye, NY (town) Westchester County	739	1.68
Parsippany-Troy Hills, NJ (township) Morris County	739	1.46
Phoenix, AZ (city) Maricopa County	722	0.05
North Plainfield, NJ (borough) Somerset County	704	3.34
Lodi, NJ (borough) Bergen County	704	2.94
University Park, FL (cdp) Miami-Dade County	701	2.64
Port Chester, NY (village) Westchester County	696	2.50
Piscataway, NJ (township) Middlesex County	693	1.37
Providence, RI (city) Providence County	693	0.40
Boca Raton, FL (city) Palm Beach County	685	0.92
Hallandale, FL (city) Broward County	669	1.95
Greenwich, CT (town) Fairfield County	659	1.08
Chelsea, MA (city) Suffolk County	658	1.88
Glendale, CA (city) Los Angeles County	632	0.32
Arlington, VA (cdp) Arlington County	630	0.33
Revere, MA (city) Suffolk County	622	1.32
Ojus, FL (cdp) Miami-Dade County	618	3.71
Plainfield, NJ (city) Union County	616	1.29
Egypt Lake-Leto, FL (cdp) Hillsborough County	608	1.85
San Jose, CA (city) Santa Clara County	597	0.07
Austin, TX (city) Travis County	596	0.09
Country Walk, FL (cdp) Miami-Dade County	594	5.58
Long Beach, CA (city) Los Angeles County	594	0.13
West Palm Beach, FL (city) Palm Beach County	587	0.71
Cape Coral, FL (city) Lee County	576	0.56
Deerfield Beach, FL (city) Broward County	575	0.89
Guttenberg, NJ (town) Hudson County	571	5.28
Glenvar Heights, FL (cdp) Miami-Dade County	563	3.47
Freeport, NY (village) Nassau County	562	1.28
Coconut Creek, FL (city) Broward County	557	1.28
Garfield, NJ (city) Bergen County	542	1.82
Westchester, FL (cdp) Miami-Dade County	536	1.77
Miami Springs, FL (city) Miami-Dade County	533	3.89
Burbank, CA (city) Los Angeles County	502	0.50
Lauderhill, FL (city) Broward County	497	0.86
Cooper City, FL (city) Broward County	496	1.78
Danbury, CT (city) Fairfield County	491	0.66
Anaheim, CA (city) Orange County	491	0.15
Huntington, NY (town) Suffolk County	489	0.25
Las Vegas, NV (city) Clark County	489	0.10
Ives Estates, FL (cdp) Miami-Dade County	486	2.76
Ossining, NY (town) Westchester County	486	1.33
Edison, NJ (cdp) Middlesex County	486	0.50
Pompano Beach, FL (city) Broward County	479	0.61
Yeehaw Junction, FL (cdp) Osceola County	476	2.19
Cutler Ridge, FL (cdp) Miami-Dade County	472	1.90
Downey, CA (city) Los Angeles County	472	0.44
Fairview, NJ (borough) Bergen County	463	3.49
Greenacres, FL (city) Palm Beach County	461	1.67
Sunset, FL (cdp) Miami-Dade County	459	2.68
Altamonte Springs, FL (city) Seminole County	459	1.11
Mission Bend, TX (cdp) Fort Bend County	458	1.49
Ossining, NY (village) Westchester County	456	1.90
Greater Carrollwood, FL (cdp) Hillsborough County	444	1.32
Atlantic City, NJ (city) Atlantic County	444	1.10
Woodbridge, NJ (township) Middlesex County	434	0.45
Oak Ridge, FL (cdp) Orange County	431	1.93
Roselle, NJ (borough) Union County	428	2.01
Elmont, NY (cdp) Nassau County	427	1.31
Greenburgh, NY (town) Westchester County	419	0.48
Coral Terrace, FL (cdp) Miami-Dade County	414	1.70
Three Lakes, FL (cdp) Miami-Dade County	412	5.92
Southampton, NY (town) Suffolk County	409	0.75
Meadow Woods, FL (cdp) Orange County	408	3.62
Palisades Park, NJ (borough) Bergen County	406	2.38

Notes: (cdp) census designated place; Refer to the Explanation of Data in the front of the book for more detailed information.

Hispanic: Colombian

Top 150 Places Sorted by Percent

(Based on all places, regardless of population)

Place	Number	%
Victory Gardens, NJ (borough) Morris County	236	15.27
Dover, NJ (town) Morris County	2,050	11.27
The Hammocks, FL (cdp) Miami-Dade County	4,749	10.02
Central Falls, RI (city) Providence County	1,882	9.94
Kendall West, FL (cdp) Miami-Dade County	3,778	9.93
Montauk, NY (cdp) Suffolk County	367	9.53
Doral, FL (cdp) Miami-Dade County	1,780	8.71
Country Club, FL (cdp) Miami-Dade County	3,134	8.63
Morristown, NJ (town) Morris County	1,479	7.98
Englewood, NJ (city) Bergen County	1,878	7.17
Virginia Gardens, FL (village) Miami-Dade County	168	7.16
Key Biscayne, FL (village) Miami-Dade County	743	7.07
Drummond, ID (city) Fremont County	1	6.67
Elizabeth, NJ (city) Union County	7,793	6.46
Kendale Lakes, FL (cdp) Miami-Dade County	3,619	6.36
Weston, FL (city) Broward County	3,052	6.19
The Crossings, FL (cdp) Miami-Dade County	1,454	6.17
Sunny Isles Beach, FL (city) Miami-Dade County	930	6.07
Three Lakes, FL (cdp) Miami-Dade County	412	5.92
West New York, NJ (town) Hudson County	2,664	5.82
North Bergen, NJ (township) Hudson County	3,351	5.77
Broadview-Pompano Park, FL (cdp) Broward County	297	5.59
Country Walk, FL (cdp) Miami-Dade County	594	5.58
Fountainbleau, FL (cdp) Miami-Dade County	3,153	5.29
North Bay Village, FL (city) Miami-Dade County	356	5.29
Guttenberg, NJ (town) Hudson County	571	5.28
Richmond West, FL (cdp) Miami-Dade County	1,441	5.13
Hughes, AK (city) Yukon-Koyukuk Census Area	4	5.13
East Hampton North, NY (cdp) Suffolk County	173	4.82
Bay Harbor Islands, FL (town) Miami-Dade County	243	4.72
Surfside, FL (town) Miami-Dade County	229	4.66
Hialeah Gardens, FL (city) Miami-Dade County	892	4.62
Kendall, FL (cdp) Miami-Dade County	3,429	4.56
Union City, NJ (city) Hudson County	3,039	4.53
Ramblewood East, FL (cdp) Broward County	62	4.44
Miami Lakes, FL (cdp) Miami-Dade County	1,005	4.43
Miami Beach, FL (city) Miami-Dade County	3,872	4.40
East Hampton, NY (town) Suffolk County	850	4.31
Aventura, FL (city) Miami-Dade County	1,075	4.25
Springs, NY (cdp) Suffolk County	197	3.98
Tamiami, FL (cdp) Miami-Dade County	2,161	3.94
Miami Springs, FL (city) Miami-Dade County	533	3.89
Hackensack, NJ (city) Bergen County	1,634	3.83
Ojus, FL (cdp) Miami-Dade County	618	3.71
Meadow Woods, FL (cdp) Orange County	408	3.62
Chambers Estates, FL (cdp) Broward County	128	3.60
Fairview, NJ (borough) Bergen County	463	3.49
Glenvar Heights, FL (cdp) Miami-Dade County	563	3.47
Wharton, NJ (borough) Morris County	216	3.43
Paterson, NJ (city) Passaic County	5,110	3.42
Homestead Base, FL (cdp) Miami-Dade County	15	3.36
North Plainfield, NJ (borough) Somerset County	704	3.34
North Lauderdale, FL (city) Broward County	1,071	3.32
Bal Harbour, FL (village) Miami-Dade County	108	3.27
Golden Beach, FL (town) Miami-Dade County	30	3.26
Bergenfield, NJ (borough) Bergen County	850	3.24
Hialeah, FL (city) Miami-Dade County	7,152	3.16
Prospect Park, NJ (borough) Passaic County	179	3.10
Pembroke Pines, FL (city) Broward County	4,124	3.00
Pawtucket, RI (city) Providence County	2,143	2.94
Lodi, NJ (borough) Bergen County	704	2.94
Keller, VA (town) Accomack County	5	2.89
Ivanhoe Estates, FL (cdp) Broward County	8	2.87
North Miami Beach, FL (city) Miami-Dade County	1,154	2.83
Bellerose Terrace, NY (cdp) Nassau County	60	2.78
Ives Estates, FL (cdp) Miami-Dade County	486	2.76
White Plains, NY (city) Westchester County	1,458	2.75
Tamarac, FL (city) Broward County	1,523	2.74
Ridgefield Park, NJ (village) Bergen County	347	2.70
Sunset, FL (cdp) Miami-Dade County	459	2.68
Bound Brook, NJ (borough) Somerset County	270	2.66
University Park, FL (cdp) Miami-Dade County	701	2.64
Allegheny, PA (township) Cambria County	66	2.64
Ellenville, NY (village) Ulster County	106	2.57
Berea, SC (cdp) Greenville County	361	2.55
Brentwood, NY (cdp) Suffolk County	1,357	2.52
Miramar, FL (city) Broward County	1,827	2.51
Port Chester, NY (village) Westchester County	696	2.50
Lakes by the Bay, FL (cdp) Miami-Dade County	222	2.45
Sunrise, FL (city) Broward County	2,090	2.44
Weehawken, NJ (township) Hudson County	330	2.44
South Miami Heights, FL (cdp) Miami-Dade County	798	2.38
Palisades Park, NJ (borough) Bergen County	406	2.38
Norwalk, CT (city) Fairfield County	1,969	2.37
Palm Springs North, FL (cdp) Miami-Dade County	129	2.36
Coral Gables, FL (city) Miami-Dade County	961	2.27
Hollywood, FL (city) Broward County	3,152	2.26
Mount Kisco, NY (village) Westchester County	226	2.26
Napeague, NY (cdp) Suffolk County	5	2.24
Margate, FL (city) Broward County	1,199	2.22
Monticello, NY (village) Sullivan County	144	2.21
Yeehaw Junction, FL (cdp) Osceola County	476	2.19
Madison, NJ (borough) Morris County	362	2.19
Linden, NJ (city) Union County	852	2.16
Northwest Harbor, NY (cdp) Suffolk County	66	2.16
Shoreham, NY (village) Suffolk County	9	2.16
Carol City, FL (cdp) Miami-Dade County	1,279	2.15
Elmsford, NY (village) Westchester County	100	2.14
Westwood Lakes, FL (cdp) Miami-Dade County	253	2.11
Medley, FL (town) Miami-Dade County	23	2.09
Red Devil, AK (cdp) Bethel Census Area	1	2.08
Coral Springs, FL (city) Broward County	2,408	2.05
Biscayne Park, FL (village) Miami-Dade County	67	2.05
North Andrews Gardens, FL (cdp) Broward County	196	2.03
Naples Park, FL (cdp) Collier County	136	2.02
Rockaway, NJ (borough) Morris County	131	2.02
Clifton, NJ (city) Passaic County	1,581	2.01
Kissimmee, FL (city) Osceola County	960	2.01
Roselle, NJ (borough) Union County	428	2.01
Southchase, FL (cdp) Orange County	93	2.01
Olympia Heights, FL (cdp) Miami-Dade County	268	1.99
Cutler, FL (cdp) Miami-Dade County	343	1.97
Oakwood, GA (city) Hall County	53	1.97
Hallandale, FL (city) Broward County	669	1.95
Sandalfoot Cove, FL (cdp) Palm Beach County	324	1.95
Roselle Park, NJ (borough) Union County	259	1.95
Estates of Fort Lauderdale, FL (cdp) Broward County	35	1.95
Oak Ridge, FL (cdp) Orange County	431	1.93
Hampton Bays, NY (cdp) Suffolk County	235	1.92
Lake Forest, FL (cdp) Broward County	96	1.92
Palm Springs, FL (village) Palm Beach County	223	1.91
West Miami, FL (city) Miami-Dade County	112	1.91
Mission Bay, FL (cdp) Palm Beach County	56	1.91
Cutler Ridge, FL (cdp) Miami-Dade County	472	1.90
Ossining, NY (village) Westchester County	456	1.90
Palmetto Estates, FL (cdp) Miami-Dade County	258	1.89
Chelsea, MA (city) Suffolk County	658	1.88
Elmwood Park, NJ (borough) Bergen County	353	1.87
Pine Island Ridge, FL (cdp) Broward County	97	1.87
Passaic, NJ (city) Passaic County	1,260	1.86
Sky Lake, FL (cdp) Orange County	105	1.86
Egypt Lake-Leto, FL (cdp) Hillsborough County	608	1.85
Garfield, NJ (city) Bergen County	542	1.82
Ventnor City, NJ (city) Atlantic County	235	1.82
Bonnie Lock-Woodsetter North, FL (cdp) Broward County	78	1.82
Lely Resort, FL (cdp) Collier County	26	1.82
Plantation, FL (city) Broward County	1,502	1.81
Greenport, NY (village) Suffolk County	37	1.81
Sunshine Acres, FL (cdp) Broward County	15	1.81
Brewster, NY (village) Putnam County	39	1.80
North Bay Shore, NY (cdp) Suffolk County	269	1.79
New Holland, PA (borough) Lancaster County	91	1.79
Village Park, FL (cdp) Broward County	16	1.79
Cooper City, FL (city) Broward County	496	1.78
Pinecrest, FL (village) Miami-Dade County	340	1.78
South Bound Brook, NJ (borough) Somerset County	80	1.78
Westchester, FL (cdp) Miami-Dade County	536	1.77
South Miami, FL (city) Miami-Dade County	190	1.77
Princeton, FL (cdp) Miami-Dade County	179	1.77
Little Ferry, NJ (borough) Bergen County	190	1.76

Notes: (cdp) census designated place; Refer to the Explanation of Data in the front of the book for more detailed information.

Hispanic: Colombian

Top 150 Places Sorted by Percent

(Based on places with populations of 10,000 or more)

Place	Number	%
Dover, NJ (town) Morris County	2,050	11.27
The Hammocks, FL (cdp) Miami-Dade County	4,749	10.02
Central Falls, RI (city) Providence County	1,882	9.94
Kendall West, FL (cdp) Miami-Dade County	3,778	9.93
Doral, FL (cdp) Miami-Dade County	1,780	8.71
Country Club, FL (cdp) Miami-Dade County	3,134	8.63
Morristown, NJ (town) Morris County	1,479	7.98
Englewood, NJ (city) Bergen County	1,878	7.17
Key Biscayne, FL (village) Miami-Dade County	743	7.07
Elizabeth, NJ (city) Union County	7,793	6.46
Kendale Lakes, FL (cdp) Miami-Dade County	3,619	6.36
Weston, FL (city) Broward County	3,052	6.19
The Crossings, FL (cdp) Miami-Dade County	1,454	6.17
Sunny Isles Beach, FL (city) Miami-Dade County	930	6.07
West New York, NJ (town) Hudson County	2,664	5.82
North Bergen, NJ (township) Hudson County	3,351	5.77
Country Walk, FL (cdp) Miami-Dade County	594	5.58
Fountainbleau, FL (cdp) Miami-Dade County	3,153	5.29
Guttenberg, NJ (town) Hudson County	571	5.28
Richmond West, FL (cdp) Miami-Dade County	1,441	5.13
Hialeah Gardens, FL (city) Miami-Dade County	892	4.62
Kendall, FL (cdp) Miami-Dade County	3,429	4.56
Union City, NJ (city) Hudson County	3,039	4.53
Miami Lakes, FL (cdp) Miami-Dade County	1,005	4.43
Miami Beach, FL (city) Miami-Dade County	3,872	4.40
East Hampton, NY (town) Suffolk County	850	4.31
Aventura, FL (city) Miami-Dade County	1,075	4.25
Tamiami, FL (cdp) Miami-Dade County	2,161	3.94
Miami Springs, FL (city) Miami-Dade County	533	3.89
Hackensack, NJ (city) Bergen County	1,634	3.83
Ojus, FL (cdp) Miami-Dade County	618	3.71
Meadow Woods, FL (cdp) Orange County	408	3.62
Fairview, NJ (borough) Bergen County	463	3.49
Glenvar Heights, FL (cdp) Miami-Dade County	563	3.47
Paterson, NJ (city) Passaic County	5,110	3.42
North Plainfield, NJ (borough) Somerset County	704	3.34
North Lauderdale, FL (city) Broward County	1,071	3.32
Bergenfield, NJ (borough) Bergen County	850	3.24
Hialeah, FL (city) Miami-Dade County	7,152	3.16
Pembroke Pines, FL (city) Broward County	4,124	3.00
Pawtucket, RI (city) Providence County	2,143	2.94
Lodi, NJ (borough) Bergen County	704	2.94
North Miami Beach, FL (city) Miami-Dade County	1,154	2.83
Ives Estates, FL (cdp) Miami-Dade County	486	2.76
White Plains, NY (city) Westchester County	1,458	2.75
Tamarac, FL (city) Broward County	1,523	2.74
Ridgefield Park, NJ (village) Bergen County	347	2.70
Sunset, FL (cdp) Miami-Dade County	459	2.68
Bound Brook, NJ (borough) Somerset County	270	2.66
University Park, FL (cdp) Miami-Dade County	701	2.64
Berea, SC (cdp) Greenville County	361	2.55
Brentwood, NY (cdp) Suffolk County	1,357	2.52
Miramar, FL (city) Broward County	1,827	2.51
Port Chester, NY (village) Westchester County	696	2.50
Sunrise, FL (city) Broward County	2,090	2.44
Weehawken, NJ (township) Hudson County	330	2.44
South Miami Heights, FL (cdp) Miami-Dade County	798	2.38
Palisades Park, NJ (borough) Bergen County	406	2.38
Norwalk, CT (city) Fairfield County	1,969	2.37
Coral Gables, FL (city) Miami-Dade County	961	2.27
Hollywood, FL (city) Broward County	3,152	2.26
Margate, FL (city) Broward County	1,199	2.22
Yeehaw Junction, FL (cdp) Osceola County	476	2.19
Madison, NJ (borough) Morris County	362	2.19
Linden, NJ (city) Union County	852	2.16
Carol City, FL (cdp) Miami-Dade County	1,279	2.15
Westwood Lakes, FL (cdp) Miami-Dade County	253	2.11
Coral Springs, FL (city) Broward County	2,408	2.05
Clifton, NJ (city) Passaic County	1,581	2.01
Kissimmee, FL (city) Osceola County	960	2.01
Roselle, NJ (borough) Union County	428	2.01
Olympia Heights, FL (cdp) Miami-Dade County	268	1.99
Cutler, FL (cdp) Miami-Dade County	343	1.97
Hallandale, FL (city) Broward County	669	1.95
Sandalfoot Cove, FL (cdp) Palm Beach County	324	1.95
Roselle Park, NJ (borough) Union County	259	1.95
Oak Ridge, FL (cdp) Orange County	431	1.93
Hampton Bays, NY (cdp) Suffolk County	235	1.92
Palm Springs, FL (village) Palm Beach County	223	1.91
Cutler Ridge, FL (cdp) Miami-Dade County	472	1.90
Ossining, NY (village) Westchester County	456	1.90
Palmetto Estates, FL (cdp) Miami-Dade County	258	1.89
Chelsea, MA (city) Suffolk County	658	1.88
Elmwood Park, NJ (borough) Bergen County	353	1.87
Passaic, NJ (city) Passaic County	1,260	1.86
Egypt Lake-Leto, FL (cdp) Hillsborough County	608	1.85
Garfield, NJ (city) Bergen County	542	1.82
Ventnor City, NJ (city) Atlantic County	235	1.82
Plantation, FL (city) Broward County	1,502	1.81
North Bay Shore, NY (cdp) Suffolk County	269	1.79
Cooper City, FL (city) Broward County	496	1.78
Pinecrest, FL (village) Miami-Dade County	340	1.78
Westchester, FL (cdp) Miami-Dade County	536	1.77
South Miami, FL (city) Miami-Dade County	190	1.77
Princeton, FL (cdp) Miami-Dade County	179	1.77
Little Ferry, NJ (borough) Bergen County	190	1.76
Davie, FL (town) Broward County	1,304	1.72
Sweetwater, FL (city) Miami-Dade County	244	1.72
Coral Terrace, FL (cdp) Miami-Dade County	414	1.70
Rye, NY (town) Westchester County	739	1.68
Greenacres, FL (city) Palm Beach County	461	1.67
Stamford, CT (city) Fairfield County	1,937	1.65
Miami Shores, FL (village) Miami-Dade County	170	1.64
Miami, FL (city) Miami-Dade County	5,784	1.60
Wawarsing, NY (town) Ulster County	206	1.60
Cliffside Park, NJ (borough) Bergen County	350	1.52
Mission Bend, TX (cdp) Fort Bend County	458	1.49
New Rochelle, NY (city) Westchester County	1,071	1.48
Town 'n' Country, FL (cdp) Hillsborough County	1,057	1.46
Parsippany-Troy Hills, NJ (township) Morris County	739	1.46
North Miami, FL (city) Miami-Dade County	858	1.43
Valley Falls, RI (cdp) Providence County	165	1.42
Piscataway, NJ (township) Middlesex County	693	1.37
Ridgefield, NJ (borough) Bergen County	148	1.37
Ossining, NY (town) Westchester County	486	1.33
West Paterson, NJ (borough) Passaic County	146	1.33
Revere, MA (city) Suffolk County	622	1.32
Greater Carrollwood, FL (cdp) Hillsborough County	444	1.32
Thompson, NY (town) Sullivan County	187	1.32
Elmont, NY (cdp) Nassau County	427	1.31
Plainfield, NJ (city) Union County	616	1.29
Freeport, NY (village) Nassau County	562	1.28
Coconut Creek, FL (city) Broward County	557	1.28
Central Islip, NY (cdp) Suffolk County	406	1.27
Azalea Park, FL (cdp) Orange County	136	1.23
Mineola, NY (village) Nassau County	232	1.21
Boca Del Mar, FL (cdp) Palm Beach County	262	1.20
Union Park, FL (cdp) Orange County	122	1.20
Harrison, NJ (town) Hudson County	172	1.19
Bay Shore, NY (cdp) Suffolk County	282	1.18
Golden Gate, FL (cdp) Collier County	240	1.15
Citrus Park, FL (cdp) Hillsborough County	228	1.13
Oakland Park, FL (city) Broward County	347	1.12
North Valley Stream, NY (cdp) Nassau County	177	1.12
Lowell, MA (city) Middlesex County	1,167	1.11
Altamonte Springs, FL (city) Seminole County	459	1.11
Dania Beach, FL (city) Broward County	223	1.11
Atlantic City, NJ (city) Atlantic County	444	1.10
South Plainfield, NJ (borough) Middlesex County	239	1.10
Greenwich, CT (town) Fairfield County	659	1.08
Poinciana, FL (cdp) Osceola County	147	1.08
Parkland, FL (city) Broward County	148	1.07
New Milford, NJ (borough) Bergen County	173	1.05
Leisure City, FL (cdp) Miami-Dade County	224	1.01
Citrus Ridge, FL (cdp) Lake County	121	1.01
Rahway, NJ (city) Union County	266	1.00
Lilburn, GA (city) Gwinnett County	112	0.99
Teaneck, NJ (cdp) Bergen County	382	0.97
Hillside, NJ (cdp) Union County	212	0.97
Somerville, NJ (borough) Somerset County	120	0.97

Notes: (cdp) census designated place; Refer to the Explanation of Data in the front of the book for more detailed information.

Hispanic: Ecuadorian

Top 150 Places Sorted by Number

(Based on all places, regardless of population)

Place	Number	%
New York, NY (city) New York City	101,005	1.26
Chicago, IL (city) Cook County	8,941	0.31
Newark, NJ (city) Essex County	7,611	2.78
Los Angeles, CA (city) Los Angeles County	4,692	0.13
Union City, NJ (city) Hudson County	3,984	5.94
Jersey City, NJ (city) Hudson County	3,920	1.63
Hempstead, NY (town) Nassau County	2,343	0.31
North Bergen, NJ (township) Hudson County	2,334	4.02
Danbury, CT (city) Fairfield County	2,183	2.92
Elizabeth, NJ (city) Union County	2,135	1.77
Brookhaven, NY (town) Suffolk County	2,055	0.46
Islip, NY (town) Suffolk County	2,052	0.64
Hackensack, NJ (city) Bergen County	2,040	4.78
West New York, NJ (town) Hudson County	2,035	4.45
Yonkers, NY (city) Westchester County	1,839	0.94
Ossining, NY (town) Westchester County	1,818	4.98
Ossining, NY (village) Westchester County	1,796	7.48
Minneapolis, MN (city) Hennepin County	1,639	0.43
Miami, FL (city) Miami-Dade County	1,408	0.39
Rye, NY (town) Westchester County	1,394	3.18
Port Chester, NY (village) Westchester County	1,366	4.90
Stamford, CT (city) Fairfield County	1,170	1.00
Hialeah, FL (city) Miami-Dade County	1,159	0.51
North Plainfield, NJ (borough) Somerset County	1,138	5.39
Mount Pleasant, NY (town) Westchester County	1,119	2.59
Belleville, NJ (cdp) Essex County	1,098	3.06
Sleepy Hollow, NY (village) Westchester County	991	10.76
Peekskill, NY (city) Westchester County	970	4.32
Houston, TX (city) Harris County	864	0.04
Plainfield, NJ (city) Union County	863	1.80
Kearny, NJ (town) Hudson County	856	2.11
East Windsor, NJ (township) Mercer County	846	3.39
Patchogue, NY (village) Suffolk County	845	7.09
North Hempstead, NY (town) Nassau County	815	0.37
Charlotte, NC (city) Mecklenburg County	800	0.15
Brentwood, NY (cdp) Suffolk County	798	1.48
Paterson, NJ (city) Passaic County	778	0.52
East Hampton, NY (town) Suffolk County	752	3.81
Pembroke Pines, FL (city) Broward County	734	0.53
New Haven, CT (city) New Haven County	660	0.53
Ramapo, NY (town) Rockland County	631	0.58
Dover, NJ (town) Morris County	613	3.37
Hollywood, FL (city) Broward County	592	0.42
Greenburgh, NY (town) Westchester County	566	0.65
Fountainbleau, FL (cdp) Miami-Dade County	564	0.95
Harrison, NJ (town) Hudson County	562	3.90
Babylon, NY (town) Suffolk County	540	0.25
The Hammocks, FL (cdp) Miami-Dade County	522	1.10
Bloomfield, NJ (cdp) Essex County	514	1.08
Passaic, NJ (city) Passaic County	512	0.75
Spring Valley, NY (village) Rockland County	500	1.96
Miami Beach, FL (city) Miami-Dade County	493	0.56
White Plains, NY (city) Westchester County	452	0.85
Bridgeport, CT (city) Fairfield County	450	0.32
Coral Springs, FL (city) Broward County	441	0.38
Oyster Bay, NY (town) Nassau County	441	0.15
Irvington, NJ (cdp) Essex County	438	0.72
Philadelphia, PA (city) Philadelphia County	420	0.03
Guttenberg, NJ (town) Hudson County	419	3.88
Kendall West, FL (cdp) Miami-Dade County	417	1.10
Kendall, FL (cdp) Miami-Dade County	415	0.55
Worcester, MA (city) Worcester County	413	0.24
Glendale, CA (city) Los Angeles County	411	0.21
Clifton, NJ (city) Passaic County	406	0.52
Hempstead, NY (village) Nassau County	395	0.70
Sunrise, FL (city) Broward County	392	0.46
Boston, MA (city) Suffolk County	385	0.07
San Diego, CA (city) San Diego County	383	0.03
Weehawken, NJ (township) Hudson County	382	2.83
Orlando, FL (city) Orange County	376	0.20
Kendale Lakes, FL (cdp) Miami-Dade County	372	0.65
Lawrence, MA (city) Essex County	372	0.52
Bay Shore, NY (cdp) Suffolk County	369	1.55
Downey, CA (city) Los Angeles County	362	0.34
Allentown, PA (city) Lehigh County	349	0.33
Washington, DC (city) District of Columbia	348	0.06
Long Beach, CA (city) Los Angeles County	339	0.07
Huntington, NY (town) Suffolk County	334	0.17
Norwalk, CT (city) Fairfield County	330	0.40
Hightstown, NJ (borough) Mercer County	329	6.31
San Francisco, CA (city) San Francisco County	329	0.04
Country Club, FL (cdp) Miami-Dade County	326	0.90
Central Islip, NY (cdp) Suffolk County	324	1.01
Tamiami, FL (cdp) Miami-Dade County	322	0.59
Weston, FL (city) Broward County	319	0.65
Carol City, FL (cdp) Miami-Dade County	318	0.53
Montauk, NY (cdp) Suffolk County	311	8.08
Tampa, FL (city) Hillsborough County	311	0.10
Hoboken, NJ (city) Hudson County	309	0.80
Trenton, NJ (city) Mercer County	309	0.36
Davie, FL (town) Broward County	307	0.41
Arlington, VA (cdp) Arlington County	305	0.16
Miramar, FL (city) Broward County	297	0.41
Providence, RI (city) Providence County	297	0.17
Bayonne, NJ (city) Hudson County	294	0.48
Orange, NJ (cdp) Essex County	290	0.88
Burbank, CA (city) Los Angeles County	274	0.27
Phoenix, AZ (city) Maricopa County	272	0.02
Tarrytown, NY (village) Westchester County	267	2.41
Garfield, NJ (city) Bergen County	260	0.87
Plantation, FL (city) Broward County	256	0.31
Doral, FL (cdp) Miami-Dade County	241	1.18
Lodi, NJ (borough) Bergen County	238	0.99
Waterbury, CT (city) New Haven County	238	0.22
Freeport, NY (village) Nassau County	230	0.53
Union, NJ (cdp) Union County	230	0.42
Dallas, TX (city) Dallas County	229	0.02
Mount Kisco, NY (village) Westchester County	228	2.28
Town 'n' Country, FL (cdp) Hillsborough County	226	0.31
Twin Rivers, NJ (cdp) Mercer County	224	3.02
Anaheim, CA (city) Orange County	222	0.07
Springs, NY (cdp) Suffolk County	221	4.46
Southampton, NY (town) Suffolk County	218	0.40
South Gate, CA (city) Los Angeles County	217	0.23
West Covina, CA (city) Los Angeles County	217	0.21
Cortlandt, NY (town) Westchester County	213	0.55
Cicero, IL (town) Cook County	208	0.24
Coral Gables, FL (city) Miami-Dade County	206	0.49
Valley Stream, NY (village) Nassau County	203	0.56
Fairview, NJ (borough) Bergen County	201	1.52
Jacksonville, FL (special city) Duval County	201	0.03
Clarkstown, NY (town) Rockland County	199	0.24
Richmond West, FL (cdp) Miami-Dade County	197	0.70
Las Vegas, NV (city) Clark County	196	0.04
East Patchogue, NY (cdp) Suffolk County	194	0.93
Haverstraw, NY (town) Rockland County	192	0.57
New Brunswick, NJ (city) Middlesex County	192	0.40
San Jose, CA (city) Santa Clara County	191	0.02
Hawthorne, CA (city) Los Angeles County	188	0.22
East Newark, NJ (borough) Hudson County	187	7.87
North Bay Shore, NY (cdp) Suffolk County	186	1.24
Ridgefield Park, NJ (village) Bergen County	185	1.44
Kissimmee, FL (city) Osceola County	179	0.37
Ansonia, CT (city) New Haven County	176	0.95
Wheaton-Glenmont, MD (cdp) Montgomery County	175	0.30
Greenwich, CT (town) Fairfield County	175	0.29
Norwalk, CA (city) Los Angeles County	175	0.17
Shelton, CT (city) Fairfield County	173	0.45
Derby, CT (city) New Haven County	171	1.38
North Miami Beach, FL (city) Miami-Dade County	171	0.42
Miami Lakes, FL (cdp) Miami-Dade County	170	0.75
Perth Amboy, NJ (city) Middlesex County	166	0.35
Morristown, NJ (town) Morris County	165	0.89
New Rochelle, NY (city) Westchester County	165	0.23
North Brunswick Township, NJ (cdp) Middlesex County	163	0.45
Torrance, CA (city) Los Angeles County	163	0.12
Hialeah Gardens, FL (city) Miami-Dade County	161	0.83
West Orange, NJ (cdp) Essex County	160	0.36
Cape Coral, FL (city) Lee County	159	0.16
Woodbridge, NJ (township) Middlesex County	158	0.16

Notes: (cdp) census designated place; Refer to the Explanation of Data in the front of the book for more detailed information.

Hispanic: Ecuadorian

Top 150 Places Sorted by Percent

(Based on all places, regardless of population)

Place	Number	%
Sleepy Hollow, NY (village) Westchester County	991	10.76
Corral City, TX (town) Denton County	9	10.11
Montauk, NY (cdp) Suffolk County	311	8.08
East Newark, NJ (borough) Hudson County	187	7.87
Ossining, NY (village) Westchester County	1,796	7.48
Patchogue, NY (village) Suffolk County	845	7.09
Hightstown, NJ (borough) Mercer County	329	6.31
Union City, NJ (city) Hudson County	3,984	5.94
North Plainfield, NJ (borough) Somerset County	1,138	5.39
Ossining, NY (town) Westchester County	1,818	4.98
Port Chester, NY (village) Westchester County	1,366	4.90
Hackensack, NJ (city) Bergen County	2,040	4.78
Springs, NY (cdp) Suffolk County	221	4.46
West New York, NJ (town) Hudson County	2,035	4.45
Peekskill, NY (city) Westchester County	970	4.32
North Bergen, NJ (township) Hudson County	2,334	4.02
Harrison, NJ (town) Hudson County	562	3.90
Guttenberg, NJ (town) Hudson County	419	3.88
East Hampton, NY (town) Suffolk County	752	3.81
East Hampton North, NY (cdp) Suffolk County	122	3.40
East Windsor, NJ (township) Mercer County	846	3.39
Dover, NJ (town) Morris County	613	3.37
Rye, NY (town) Westchester County	1,394	3.18
Belleville, NJ (cdp) Essex County	1,098	3.06
Dillard, GA (city) Rabun County	6	3.03
Twin Rivers, NJ (cdp) Mercer County	224	3.02
Danbury, CT (city) Fairfield County	2,183	2.92
Weehawken, NJ (township) Hudson County	382	2.83
Newark, NJ (city) Essex County	7,611	2.78
Folsom, NM (village) Union County	2	2.67
Mount Pleasant, NY (town) Westchester County	1,119	2.59
Birch, MN (township) Beltrami County	3	2.59
Elmsford, NY (village) Westchester County	116	2.48
Tarrytown, NY (village) Westchester County	267	2.41
Mount Kisco, NY (village) Westchester County	228	2.28
Napeague, NY (cdp) Suffolk County	5	2.24
Brewster, NY (village) Putnam County	48	2.22
Victory Gardens, NJ (borough) Morris County	33	2.13
Kearny, NJ (town) Hudson County	856	2.11
Davis, MN (township) Kittson County	1	2.08
Mobile City, TX (city) Rockwall County	4	2.04
Spring Valley, NY (village) Rockland County	500	1.96
Plainfield, NJ (city) Union County	863	1.80
Elizabeth, NJ (city) Union County	2,135	1.77
Croton-on-Hudson, NY (village) Westchester County	132	1.74
Jersey City, NJ (city) Hudson County	3,920	1.63
Fairview, NY (cdp) Westchester County	47	1.63
Bay Shore, NY (cdp) Suffolk County	369	1.55
Northwest Harbor, NY (cdp) Suffolk County	47	1.54
Fairview, NJ (borough) Bergen County	201	1.52
Baxter Estates, NY (village) Nassau County	15	1.49
Brentwood, NY (cdp) Suffolk County	798	1.48
Manorhaven, NY (village) Nassau County	91	1.48
Millbourne, PA (borough) Delaware County	14	1.48
Bogota, NJ (borough) Bergen County	121	1.47
South Hackensack, NJ (township) Bergen County	33	1.47
Ridgefield Park, NJ (village) Bergen County	185	1.44
Centerville, NY (town) Allegany County	11	1.44
Wainscott, NY (cdp) Suffolk County	9	1.43
Derby, CT (city) New Haven County	171	1.38
Wappingers Falls, NY (village) Dutchess County	67	1.36
Virginia Gardens, FL (village) Miami-Dade County	31	1.32
Wharton, NJ (borough) Morris County	80	1.27
New York, NY (city) New York City	101,005	1.26
North Bay Shore, NY (cdp) Suffolk County	186	1.24
Little Ferry, NJ (borough) Bergen County	132	1.22
Bingham Lake, MN (city) Cottonwood County	2	1.20
Doral, FL (cdp) Miami-Dade County	241	1.18
Ashley Heights, NC (cdp) Hoke County	4	1.17
Haverstraw, NY (village) Rockland County	116	1.15
Pleasantville, NY (village) Westchester County	81	1.13
Yosemite Valley, CA (cdp) Mariposa County	3	1.13
East Hampton, NY (village) Suffolk County	15	1.12
Amagansett, NY (cdp) Suffolk County	12	1.12
The Hammocks, FL (cdp) Miami-Dade County	522	1.10
Kendall West, FL (cdp) Miami-Dade County	417	1.10
Bloomfield, NJ (cdp) Essex County	514	1.08
Nelsonville, NY (village) Putnam County	6	1.06
Norway, MN (township) Kittson County	1	1.06
Central Islip, NY (cdp) Suffolk County	324	1.01
Port Washington, NY (cdp) Nassau County	154	1.01
Stamford, CT (city) Fairfield County	1,170	1.00
Lodi, NJ (borough) Bergen County	238	0.99
Key Biscayne, FL (village) Miami-Dade County	102	0.97
Dunellen, NJ (borough) Middlesex County	66	0.97
Southampton, NY (village) Suffolk County	38	0.96
Fountainbleau, FL (cdp) Miami-Dade County	564	0.95
Ansonia, CT (city) New Haven County	176	0.95
Yonkers, NY (city) Westchester County	1,839	0.94
Bound Brook, NJ (borough) Somerset County	95	0.94
East Patchogue, NY (cdp) Suffolk County	194	0.93
Country Club, FL (cdp) Miami-Dade County	326	0.90
Gordon Heights, NY (cdp) Suffolk County	28	0.90
Morristown, NJ (town) Morris County	165	0.89
Orange, NJ (cdp) Essex County	290	0.88
Garfield, NJ (city) Bergen County	260	0.87
Country Walk, FL (cdp) Miami-Dade County	93	0.87
White Plains, NY (city) Westchester County	452	0.85
Westbrook Center, CT (cdp) Middlesex County	19	0.85
Sunshine Acres, FL (cdp) Broward County	7	0.85
Meadow Woods, FL (cdp) Orange County	95	0.84
Ridgefield, NJ (borough) Bergen County	91	0.84
Perry Lake, MN (township) Crow Wing County	2	0.84
Hialeah Gardens, FL (city) Miami-Dade County	161	0.83
Broadview-Pompano Park, FL (cdp) Broward County	44	0.83
North Haven, NY (village) Suffolk County	6	0.81
Hoboken, NJ (city) Hudson County	309	0.80
South Bound Brook, NJ (borough) Somerset County	35	0.78
North Bellport, NY (cdp) Suffolk County	69	0.77
Verplanck, NY (cdp) Westchester County	6	0.77
Dunes Road, FL (cdp) Palm Beach County	3	0.77
Moonachie, NJ (borough) Bergen County	21	0.76
Passaic, NJ (city) Passaic County	512	0.75
Miami Lakes, FL (cdp) Miami-Dade County	170	0.75
Miami Springs, FL (city) Miami-Dade County	101	0.74
Arion, IA (city) Crawford County	1	0.74
Stratton, VT (town) Windham County	1	0.74
Baywood, NY (cdp) Suffolk County	55	0.73
North Sea, NY (cdp) Suffolk County	33	0.73
Irvington, NJ (cdp) Essex County	438	0.72
Hillside, NJ (cdp) Union County	156	0.72
Secaucus, NJ (town) Hudson County	114	0.72
Otisville, NY (village) Orange County	7	0.71
Hempstead, NY (village) Nassau County	395	0.70
Richmond West, FL (cdp) Miami-Dade County	197	0.70
Dover Plains, NY (cdp) Dutchess County	14	0.70
Copenhagen, NY (village) Lewis County	6	0.69
North Arlington, NJ (borough) Bergen County	103	0.68
Flanders, NY (cdp) Suffolk County	24	0.66
East Marion, NY (cdp) Suffolk County	5	0.66
Greenburgh, NY (town) Westchester County	566	0.65
Kendale Lakes, FL (cdp) Miami-Dade County	372	0.65
Weston, FL (city) Broward County	319	0.65
Uniondale, NY (cdp) Nassau County	150	0.65
Medford, NY (cdp) Suffolk County	142	0.65
North Patchogue, NY (cdp) Suffolk County	51	0.65
Bernardsville, NJ (borough) Somerset County	48	0.65
Hilltop, MN (city) Anoka County	5	0.65
Islip, NY (town) Suffolk County	2,052	0.64
Hackettstown, NJ (town) Warren County	66	0.63
Carle Place, NY (cdp) Nassau County	33	0.63
North Bay Village, FL (city) Miami-Dade County	42	0.62
Red River, NM (town) Taos County	3	0.62
Shrub Oak, NY (cdp) Westchester County	11	0.61
Maywood, NJ (borough) Bergen County	57	0.60
Rockaway, NJ (borough) Morris County	39	0.60
Tamiami, FL (cdp) Miami-Dade County	322	0.59
Sandalfoot Cove, FL (cdp) Palm Beach County	98	0.59
Glenvar Heights, FL (cdp) Miami-Dade County	96	0.59
Westbrook, CT (town) Middlesex County	37	0.59

Notes: (cdp) census designated place; Refer to the Explanation of Data in the front of the book for more detailed information.

Hispanic: Ecuadorian

Top 150 Places Sorted by Percent

(Based on places with populations of 10,000 or more)

Place	Number	%
Ossining, NY (village) Westchester County	1,796	7.48
Patchogue, NY (village) Suffolk County	845	7.09
Union City, NJ (city) Hudson County	3,984	5.94
North Plainfield, NJ (borough) Somerset County	1,138	5.39
Ossining, NY (town) Westchester County	1,818	4.98
Port Chester, NY (village) Westchester County	1,366	4.90
Hackensack, NJ (city) Bergen County	2,040	4.78
West New York, NJ (town) Hudson County	2,035	4.45
Peekskill, NY (city) Westchester County	970	4.32
North Bergen, NJ (township) Hudson County	2,334	4.02
Harrison, NJ (town) Hudson County	562	3.90
Guttenberg, NJ (town) Hudson County	419	3.88
East Hampton, NY (town) Suffolk County	752	3.81
East Windsor, NJ (township) Mercer County	846	3.39
Dover, NJ (town) Morris County	613	3.37
Rye, NY (town) Westchester County	1,394	3.18
Belleville, NJ (cdp) Essex County	1,098	3.06
Danbury, CT (city) Fairfield County	2,183	2.92
Weehawken, NJ (township) Hudson County	382	2.83
Newark, NJ (city) Essex County	7,611	2.78
Mount Pleasant, NY (town) Westchester County	1,119	2.59
Tarrytown, NY (village) Westchester County	267	2.41
Kearny, NJ (town) Hudson County	856	2.11
Spring Valley, NY (village) Rockland County	500	1.96
Plainfield, NJ (city) Union County	863	1.80
Elizabeth, NJ (city) Union County	2,135	1.77
Jersey City, NJ (city) Hudson County	3,920	1.63
Bay Shore, NY (cdp) Suffolk County	369	1.55
Fairview, NJ (borough) Bergen County	201	1.52
Brentwood, NY (cdp) Suffolk County	798	1.48
Ridgefield Park, NJ (village) Bergen County	185	1.44
Derby, CT (city) New Haven County	171	1.38
New York, NY (city) New York City	101,005	1.26
North Bay Shore, NY (cdp) Suffolk County	186	1.24
Little Ferry, NJ (borough) Bergen County	132	1.22
Doral, FL (cdp) Miami-Dade County	241	1.18
Haverstraw, NY (village) Rockland County	116	1.15
The Hammocks, FL (cdp) Miami-Dade County	522	1.10
Kendall West, FL (cdp) Miami-Dade County	417	1.10
Bloomfield, NJ (cdp) Essex County	514	1.08
Central Islip, NY (cdp) Suffolk County	324	1.01
Port Washington, NY (cdp) Nassau County	154	1.01
Stamford, CT (city) Fairfield County	1,170	1.00
Lodi, NJ (borough) Bergen County	238	0.99
Key Biscayne, FL (village) Miami-Dade County	102	0.97
Fountainbleau, FL (cdp) Miami-Dade County	564	0.95
Ansonia, CT (city) New Haven County	176	0.95
Yonkers, NY (city) Westchester County	1,839	0.94
Bound Brook, NJ (borough) Somerset County	95	0.94
East Patchogue, NY (cdp) Suffolk County	194	0.93
Country Club, FL (cdp) Miami-Dade County	326	0.90
Morristown, NJ (town) Morris County	165	0.89
Orange, NJ (cdp) Essex County	290	0.88
Garfield, NJ (city) Bergen County	260	0.87
Country Walk, FL (cdp) Miami-Dade County	93	0.87
White Plains, NY (city) Westchester County	452	0.85
Meadow Woods, FL (cdp) Orange County	95	0.84
Ridgefield, NJ (borough) Bergen County	91	0.84
Hialeah Gardens, FL (city) Miami-Dade County	161	0.83
Hoboken, NJ (city) Hudson County	309	0.80
Passaic, NJ (city) Passaic County	512	0.75
Miami Lakes, FL (cdp) Miami-Dade County	170	0.75
Miami Springs, FL (city) Miami-Dade County	101	0.74
Irvington, NJ (cdp) Essex County	438	0.72
Hillside, NJ (cdp) Union County	156	0.72
Secaucus, NJ (town) Hudson County	114	0.72
Hempstead, NY (village) Nassau County	395	0.70
Richmond West, FL (cdp) Miami-Dade County	197	0.70
North Arlington, NJ (borough) Bergen County	103	0.68
Greenburgh, NY (town) Westchester County	566	0.65
Kendale Lakes, FL (cdp) Miami-Dade County	372	0.65
Weston, FL (city) Broward County	319	0.65
Uniondale, NY (cdp) Nassau County	150	0.65
Medford, NY (cdp) Suffolk County	142	0.65
Islip, NY (town) Suffolk County	2,052	0.64
Hackettstown, NJ (town) Warren County	66	0.63
Tamiami, FL (cdp) Miami-Dade County	322	0.59
Sandalfoot Cove, FL (cdp) Palm Beach County	98	0.59
Glenvar Heights, FL (cdp) Miami-Dade County	96	0.59
Ramapo, NY (town) Rockland County	631	0.58
Cliffside Park, NJ (borough) Bergen County	133	0.58
Haverstraw, NY (town) Rockland County	192	0.57
Nutley, NJ (cdp) Essex County	155	0.57
Miami Beach, FL (city) Miami-Dade County	493	0.56
Valley Stream, NY (village) Nassau County	203	0.56
Roselle Park, NJ (borough) Union County	75	0.56
Kendall, FL (cdp) Miami-Dade County	415	0.55
Cortlandt, NY (town) Westchester County	213	0.55
Pembroke Pines, FL (city) Broward County	734	0.53
New Haven, CT (city) New Haven County	660	0.53
Carol City, FL (cdp) Miami-Dade County	318	0.53
Freeport, NY (village) Nassau County	230	0.53
Sunny Isles Beach, FL (city) Miami-Dade County	81	0.53
Paterson, NJ (city) Passaic County	778	0.52
Clifton, NJ (city) Passaic County	406	0.52
Lawrence, MA (city) Essex County	372	0.52
The Crossings, FL (cdp) Miami-Dade County	122	0.52
Bedford, NY (town) Westchester County	95	0.52
Palm Springs, FL (village) Palm Beach County	61	0.52
Hialeah, FL (city) Miami-Dade County	1,159	0.51
Sunset, FL (cdp) Miami-Dade County	88	0.51
Hasbrouck Heights, NJ (borough) Bergen County	59	0.51
West Haverstraw, NY (village) Rockland County	53	0.51
Rutherford, NJ (borough) Bergen County	90	0.50
Palisades Park, NJ (borough) Bergen County	85	0.50
North New Hyde Park, NY (cdp) Nassau County	73	0.50
Westbury, NY (village) Nassau County	71	0.50
Coral Gables, FL (city) Miami-Dade County	206	0.49
Yeehaw Junction, FL (cdp) Osceola County	107	0.49
Mineola, NY (village) Nassau County	95	0.49
Southeast, NY (town) Putnam County	84	0.49
Bayonne, NJ (city) Hudson County	294	0.48
Huntington Station, NY (cdp) Suffolk County	141	0.47
Brookhaven, NY (town) Suffolk County	2,055	0.46
Sunrise, FL (city) Broward County	392	0.46
Bergenfield, NJ (borough) Bergen County	120	0.46
Shelton, CT (city) Fairfield County	173	0.45
North Brunswick Township, NJ (cdp) Middlesex County	163	0.45
Cutler, FL (cdp) Miami-Dade County	78	0.45
North Valley Stream, NY (cdp) Nassau County	71	0.45
South Plainfield, NJ (borough) Middlesex County	97	0.44
Minneapolis, MN (city) Hennepin County	1,639	0.43
Ojus, FL (cdp) Miami-Dade County	71	0.43
Hampton Bays, NY (cdp) Suffolk County	53	0.43
Azalea Park, FL (cdp) Orange County	48	0.43
Hillsdale, NJ (borough) Bergen County	43	0.43
Hollywood, FL (city) Broward County	592	0.42
Union, NJ (cdp) Union County	230	0.42
North Miami Beach, FL (city) Miami-Dade County	171	0.42
Elmwood Park, NJ (borough) Bergen County	79	0.42
South River, NJ (borough) Middlesex County	64	0.42
Saddle Brook, NJ (cdp) Bergen County	55	0.42
Davie, FL (town) Broward County	307	0.41
Miramar, FL (city) Broward County	297	0.41
Franklin Square, NY (cdp) Nassau County	121	0.41
Wappinger, NY (town) Dutchess County	107	0.41
Oak Ridge, FL (cdp) Orange County	91	0.41
Lyndhurst, NJ (cdp) Bergen County	79	0.41
Nanuet, NY (cdp) Rockland County	69	0.41
New Cassel, NY (cdp) Nassau County	54	0.41
Norwalk, CT (city) Fairfield County	330	0.40
Southampton, NY (town) Suffolk County	218	0.40
New Brunswick, NJ (city) Middlesex County	192	0.40
Lynbrook, NY (village) Nassau County	79	0.40
Middlesex, NJ (borough) Middlesex County	55	0.40
Miami, FL (city) Miami-Dade County	1,408	0.39
Elmont, NY (cdp) Nassau County	126	0.39
Westchester, FL (cdp) Miami-Dade County	119	0.39
Sweetwater, FL (city) Miami-Dade County	56	0.39
Coral Springs, FL (city) Broward County	441	0.38

Notes: (cdp) census designated place; Refer to the Explanation of Data in the front of the book for more detailed information.

Hispanic: Paraguayan

Top 150 Places Sorted by Number

(Based on all places, regardless of population)

Place	Number	%
New York, NY (city) New York City	1,658	0.02
White Plains, NY (city) Westchester County	171	0.32
Bernardsville, NJ (borough) Somerset County	145	1.97
Los Angeles, CA (city) Los Angeles County	105	0.00
Harrison, NY (village) Westchester County	94	0.39
Washington, DC (city) District of Columbia	86	0.02
Arlington, VA (cdp) Arlington County	82	0.04
Chicago, IL (city) Cook County	68	0.00
Miami Beach, FL (city) Miami-Dade County	64	0.07
Greenwich, CT (town) Fairfield County	63	0.10
Hempstead, NY (town) Nassau County	62	0.01
Mount Vernon, NY (city) Westchester County	61	0.09
Rockville, MD (city) Montgomery County	53	0.11
Rye, NY (town) Westchester County	51	0.12
Somerville, NJ (borough) Somerset County	49	0.39
North Hempstead, NY (town) Nassau County	48	0.02
Houston, TX (city) Harris County	48	0.00
Miami, FL (city) Miami-Dade County	45	0.01
Oyster Bay, NY (town) Nassau County	42	0.01
Huntington, NY (town) Suffolk County	40	0.02
Mamaroneck, NY (village) Westchester County	39	0.21
Wheaton-Glenmont, MD (cdp) Montgomery County	38	0.07
Philadelphia, PA (city) Philadelphia County	38	0.00
Greenburgh, NY (town) Westchester County	37	0.04
Peapack and Gladstone, NJ (borough) Somerset County	35	1.44
Warren, NJ (township) Somerset County	31	0.22
Kendall, FL (cdp) Miami-Dade County	31	0.04
Lawrence, KS (city) Douglas County	31	0.04
New Rochelle, NY (city) Westchester County	29	0.04
Aspen Hill, MD (cdp) Montgomery County	28	0.06
Stamford, CT (city) Fairfield County	28	0.02
Norwalk, CT (city) Fairfield County	27	0.03
Islip, NY (town) Suffolk County	27	0.01
Mineola, NY (village) Nassau County	26	0.14
Coral Gables, FL (city) Miami-Dade County	26	0.06
San Diego, CA (city) San Diego County	26	0.00
Bedminster, NJ (township) Somerset County	25	0.30
Stafford, TX (city) Fort Bend County	24	0.15
Boston, MA (city) Suffolk County	24	0.00
Bridgewater, NJ (township) Somerset County	23	0.05
Bethesda, MD (cdp) Montgomery County	23	0.04
Fountainbleau, FL (cdp) Miami-Dade County	23	0.04
Jersey City, NJ (city) Hudson County	23	0.01
Madison, WI (city) Dane County	22	0.01
Doral, FL (cdp) Miami-Dade County	21	0.10
Mount Pleasant, NY (town) Westchester County	21	0.05
Silver Spring, MD (cdp) Montgomery County	21	0.03
Minneapolis, MN (city) Hennepin County	21	0.01
Bridgeport, CT (city) Fairfield County	20	0.01
Overland Park, KS (city) Johnson County	20	0.01
Pembroke Pines, FL (city) Broward County	20	0.01
Austin, TX (city) Travis County	20	0.00
Brookhaven, NY (town) Suffolk County	20	0.00
Germantown, MD (cdp) Montgomery County	19	0.03
Las Vegas, NV (city) Clark County	19	0.00
San Antonio, TX (city) Bexar County	19	0.00
The Crossings, FL (cdp) Miami-Dade County	18	0.08
Saint Paul, MN (city) Ramsey County	18	0.01
Mendham, NJ (borough) Morris County	17	0.33
Port Chester, NY (village) Westchester County	17	0.06
Yonkers, NY (city) Westchester County	17	0.01
Far Hills, NJ (borough) Somerset County	16	1.86
Bernards, NJ (township) Somerset County	16	0.07
North Bergen, NJ (township) Hudson County	16	0.03
Hialeah, FL (city) Miami-Dade County	16	0.01
San Francisco, CA (city) San Francisco County	16	0.00
Bedford, NY (town) Westchester County	15	0.08
Upper Darby, PA (township) Delaware County	15	0.02
Hollywood, FL (city) Broward County	15	0.01
Dallas, TX (city) Dallas County	15	0.00
San Jose, CA (city) Santa Clara County	15	0.00
South Farmingdale, NY (cdp) Nassau County	14	0.09
New Castle, NY (town) Westchester County	14	0.08
Emporia, KS (city) Lyon County	14	0.05
Tucson, AZ (city) Pima County	14	0.00
Key Biscayne, FL (village) Miami-Dade County	13	0.12
Springfield, VA (cdp) Fairfax County	13	0.04
North Bethesda, MD (cdp) Montgomery County	13	0.03
North Miami Beach, FL (city) Miami-Dade County	13	0.03
Bend, OR (city) Deschutes County	13	0.02
Delray Beach, FL (city) Palm Beach County	13	0.02
Gaithersburg, MD (city) Montgomery County	13	0.02
Fort Lauderdale, FL (city) Broward County	13	0.01
Richardson, TX (city) Dallas County	13	0.01
Manville, NJ (borough) Somerset County	12	0.12
Greenlawn, NY (cdp) Suffolk County	12	0.09
Sunny Isles Beach, FL (city) Miami-Dade County	12	0.08
Cutler Ridge, FL (cdp) Miami-Dade County	12	0.05
Ossining, NY (village) Westchester County	12	0.05
Mamaroneck, NY (town) Westchester County	12	0.04
Ossining, NY (town) Westchester County	12	0.03
Davie, FL (town) Broward County	12	0.02
Milford, CT (special city) New Haven County	12	0.02
Milford, CT (town) New Haven County	12	0.02
Ann Arbor, MI (city) Washtenaw County	12	0.01
Cambridge, MA (city) Middlesex County	12	0.01
Tallahassee, FL (city) Leon County	12	0.01
Anchorage, AK (municipality) Anchorage Borough	12	0.00
Aurora, CO (city) Arapahoe County	12	0.00
Valhalla, NY (cdp) Westchester County	11	0.20
Raritan, NJ (borough) Somerset County	11	0.17
Elwood, NY (cdp) Suffolk County	11	0.10
Jefferson, VA (cdp) Fairfax County	11	0.04
Annandale, VA (cdp) Fairfax County	11	0.02
Lower Merion, PA (township) Montgomery County	11	0.02
Manhattan, KS (city) Riley County	11	0.02
Middletown, NJ (township) Monmouth County	11	0.02
Weston, FL (city) Broward County	11	0.02
Glendale, CA (city) Los Angeles County	11	0.01
Simi Valley, CA (city) Ventura County	11	0.01
Milwaukee, WI (city) Milwaukee County	11	0.00
Wichita, KS (city) Sedgwick County	11	0.00
Madison, NJ (borough) Morris County	10	0.06
Highland Park, IL (city) Lake County	10	0.03
Lehigh Acres, FL (cdp) Lee County	10	0.03
Yorktown, NY (town) Westchester County	10	0.03
Brentwood, NY (cdp) Suffolk County	10	0.02
Fairfield, CT (town) Fairfield County	10	0.02
Oak Park, IL (village) Cook County	10	0.02
Potomac, MD (cdp) Montgomery County	10	0.02
Southampton, NY (town) Suffolk County	10	0.02
Boca Raton, FL (city) Palm Beach County	10	0.01
Modesto, CA (city) Stanislaus County	10	0.01
Palm Bay, FL (city) Brevard County	10	0.01
Topeka, KS (city) Shawnee County	10	0.01
Atlanta, GA (city) Fulton County	10	0.00
Long Beach, CA (city) Los Angeles County	10	0.00
North Bay Village, FL (city) Miami-Dade County	9	0.13
Long Hill, NJ (township) Morris County	9	0.10
Sandalfoot Cove, FL (cdp) Palm Beach County	9	0.05
Ridgefield, CT (town) Fairfield County	9	0.04
Monterey, CA (city) Monterey County	9	0.03
Brookline, MA (cdp) Norfolk County	9	0.02
Cortlandt, NY (town) Westchester County	9	0.02
North Miami, FL (city) Miami-Dade County	9	0.02
Alexandria, VA (independent city) Alexandria city	9	0.01
Bloomington, MN (city) Hennepin County	9	0.01
Carrollton, TX (city) Denton County	9	0.01
Columbia, MD (cdp) Howard County	9	0.01
Pasadena, TX (city) Harris County	9	0.01
Babylon, NY (town) Suffolk County	9	0.00
Charlotte, NC (city) Mecklenburg County	9	0.00
Mobile, AL (city) Mobile County	9	0.00
Plano, TX (city) Collin County	9	0.00
Seattle, WA (city) King County	9	0.00
Bound Brook, NJ (borough) Somerset County	8	0.08
Pinecrest, FL (village) Miami-Dade County	8	0.04
Scotch Plains, NJ (cdp) Union County	8	0.04
East Meadow, NY (cdp) Nassau County	8	0.02
Elmhurst, IL (city) Du Page County	8	0.02

Notes: (cdp) census designated place; Refer to the Explanation of Data in the front of the book for more detailed information.

Hispanic: Paraguayan

Top 150 Places Sorted by Percent

(Based on all places, regardless of population)

Place	Number	%
Bernardsville, NJ (borough) Somerset County	145	1.97
Far Hills, NJ (borough) Somerset County	16	1.86
Peapack and Gladstone, NJ (borough) Somerset County	35	1.44
Center Junction, IA (city) Jones County	1	0.76
Josephville, MO (village) Saint Charles County	2	0.74
Fisher Island, FL (cdp) Miami-Dade County	3	0.64
Koliganek, AK (cdp) Dillingham Census Area	1	0.55
Golden Beach, FL (town) Miami-Dade County	5	0.54
Bethel, DE (town) Sussex County	1	0.54
Corn, OK (town) Washita County	3	0.51
Ramblewood East, FL (cdp) Broward County	7	0.50
Good Hope, GA (town) Walton County	1	0.48
Chester, NJ (borough) Morris County	7	0.43
Harrison, NY (village) Westchester County	94	0.39
Somerville, NJ (borough) Somerset County	49	0.39
Partridge, KS (city) Reno County	1	0.39
Shinnecock Hills, NY (cdp) Suffolk County	6	0.34
Mendham, NJ (borough) Morris County	17	0.33
Dewey Beach, DE (town) Sussex County	1	0.33
Westbrook, MN (township) Cottonwood County	1	0.33
White Plains, NY (city) Westchester County	171	0.32
Jamestown, MN (township) Blue Earth County	2	0.32
Bedminster, NJ (township) Somerset County	25	0.30
Fairmont, NE (village) Fillmore County	2	0.29
Mount Aetna, MD (cdp) Washington County	2	0.24
Peru, VT (town) Bennington County	1	0.24
Bellerose Terrace, NY (cdp) Nassau County	5	0.23
Milford, PA (township) Pike County	3	0.23
Warren, NJ (township) Somerset County	31	0.22
Mamaroneck, NY (village) Westchester County	39	0.21
Brentwood, MD (town) Prince George's County	6	0.21
Fairview, NY (cdp) Westchester County	6	0.21
Olivet, NJ (cdp) Salem County	3	0.21
Fillmore, MN (township) Fillmore County	1	0.21
Valhalla, NY (cdp) Westchester County	11	0.20
Cross Mountain, TX (cdp) Bexar County	3	0.20
Todd, PA (township) Huntingdon County	2	0.20
Waldwick, WI (town) Iowa County	1	0.20
Oxford, NY (village) Chenango County	3	0.19
Hill Country Village, TX (city) Bexar County	2	0.19
Lake Marshall, MN (township) Lyon County	1	0.19
Anchorage, KY (city) Jefferson County	4	0.18
Dalworthington Gardens, TX (city) Tarrant County	4	0.18
Raritan, NJ (borough) Somerset County	11	0.17
Sea Bright, NJ (borough) Monmouth County	3	0.17
Newlin, PA (township) Chester County	2	0.17
Gillford, MN (township) Wabasha County	1	0.17
Harding, NJ (township) Morris County	5	0.16
Hillandale, MD (cdp) Montgomery County	5	0.16
Valley, MI (township) Allegan County	3	0.16
Halsey, WI (town) Marathon County	1	0.16
Maple Rapids, MI (village) Clinton County	1	0.16
Scotts Corners, NY (cdp) Westchester County	1	0.16
Stafford, TX (city) Fort Bend County	24	0.15
Chevy Chase, MD (town) Montgomery County	4	0.15
Hypoluxo, FL (town) Palm Beach County	4	0.15
Morris, PA (township) Tioga County	1	0.15
Mineola, NY (village) Nassau County	26	0.14
Verona, WI (town) Dane County	3	0.14
Middleburg, PA (borough) Snyder County	2	0.14
North Bay Village, FL (city) Miami-Dade County	9	0.13
South Bound Brook, NJ (borough) Somerset County	6	0.13
South Floral Park, NY (village) Nassau County	2	0.13
Big Delta, AK (cdp) Southeast Fairbanks Census Area	1	0.13
Cape Vincent, NY (village) Jefferson County	1	0.13
Forest View, IL (village) Cook County	1	0.13
Stinson Beach, CA (cdp) Marin County	1	0.13
Rye, NY (town) Westchester County	51	0.12
Key Biscayne, FL (village) Miami-Dade County	13	0.12
Manville, NJ (borough) Somerset County	12	0.12
Ashton-Sandy Spring, MD (cdp) Montgomery County	4	0.12
Brimfield, OH (cdp) Portage County	4	0.12
Cabin John, MD (cdp) Montgomery County	2	0.12
Shorewood Hills, WI (village) Dane County	2	0.12
Greenwich, NJ (township) Cumberland County	1	0.12

Place	Number	%
Manchester, WI (town) Green Lake County	1	0.12
Pittsville, WI (city) Wood County	1	0.12
Stamford, VT (town) Bennington County	1	0.12
Rockville, MD (city) Montgomery County	53	0.11
Northville, MI (city) Oakland County	7	0.11
Friendship Village, MD (cdp) Montgomery County	5	0.11
Hidden Valley, IN (cdp) Dearborn County	5	0.11
Kingstree, SC (town) Williamsburg County	4	0.11
Clinton, NJ (town) Hunterdon County	3	0.11
Sands Point, NY (village) Nassau County	3	0.11
Bridgewater, MN (township) Rice County	2	0.11
Como, WI (cdp) Walworth County	2	0.11
Alban, WI (town) Portage County	1	0.11
Beavertown, PA (borough) Snyder County	1	0.11
Brooksville, ME (town) Hancock County	1	0.11
Elmdale, MN (township) Morrison County	1	0.11
Old Field, NY (village) Suffolk County	1	0.11
San Francisco, MN (township) Carver County	1	0.11
Village Park, FL (cdp) Broward County	1	0.11
Greenwich, CT (town) Fairfield County	63	0.10
Doral, FL (cdp) Miami-Dade County	21	0.10
Elwood, NY (cdp) Suffolk County	11	0.10
Long Hill, NJ (township) Morris County	9	0.10
Pleasantville, NY (village) Westchester County	7	0.10
Lake Mohegan, NY (cdp) Westchester County	6	0.10
Harbour Heights, FL (cdp) Charlotte County	3	0.10
Cold Spring, NY (village) Putnam County	2	0.10
Mount Vernon, NY (city) Westchester County	61	0.09
South Farmingdale, NY (cdp) Nassau County	14	0.09
Greenlawn, NY (cdp) Suffolk County	12	0.09
Rhinebeck, NY (town) Dutchess County	7	0.09
Bryn Mawr, PA (cdp) Montgomery County	4	0.09
Bal Harbour, FL (village) Miami-Dade County	3	0.09
Avon, MN (township) Stearns County	2	0.09
Crosby, MN (city) Crow Wing County	2	0.09
East Ithaca, NY (cdp) Tompkins County	2	0.09
Kimberling City, MO (city) Stone County	2	0.09
Melville, RI (cdp) Newport County	2	0.09
Bellerose, NY (village) Nassau County	1	0.09
Clarksville, NY (town) Allegany County	1	0.09
Germantown, WI (town) Juneau County	1	0.09
Gibraltar, WI (town) Door County	1	0.09
Hebron, WI (town) Jefferson County	1	0.09
Rafter J Ranch, WY (cdp) Teton County	1	0.09
Taghkanic, NY (town) Columbia County	1	0.09
The Crossings, FL (cdp) Miami-Dade County	18	0.08
Bedford, NY (town) Westchester County	15	0.08
New Castle, NY (town) Westchester County	14	0.08
Sunny Isles Beach, FL (city) Miami-Dade County	12	0.08
Bound Brook, NJ (borough) Somerset County	8	0.08
Lake Barcroft, VA (cdp) Fairfax County	7	0.08
Lawrence, NY (village) Nassau County	5	0.08
Blooming Grove, PA (township) Pike County	3	0.08
Oxford, NY (town) Chenango County	3	0.08
East Williston, NY (village) Nassau County	2	0.08
Excelsior, MN (city) Hennepin County	2	0.08
Hassan, MN (township) Hennepin County	2	0.08
Wyomissing Hills, PA (borough) Berks County	2	0.08
Buena Vista, WI (town) Portage County	1	0.08
Friendship, ME (town) Knox County	1	0.08
Hayfield, MN (city) Dodge County	1	0.08
Meggett, SC (town) Charleston County	1	0.08
Northport, ME (town) Waldo County	1	0.08
Roland, IA (city) Story County	1	0.08
Sterling, PA (township) Wayne County	1	0.08
Miami Beach, FL (city) Miami-Dade County	64	0.07
Wheaton-Glenmont, MD (cdp) Montgomery County	38	0.07
Bernards, NJ (township) Somerset County	16	0.07
Rye Brook, NY (village) Westchester County	7	0.07
Forest Glen, MD (cdp) Montgomery County	6	0.07
Islamorada, FL (village) Monroe County	5	0.07
Pimmit Hills, VA (cdp) Fairfax County	5	0.07
Tewksbury, NJ (township) Hunterdon County	4	0.07
Middleton, WI (town) Dane County	4	0.07
Wailua Homesteads, HI (cdp) Kauai County	3	0.07

Notes: (cdp) census designated place; Refer to the Explanation of Data in the front of the book for more detailed information.

Hispanic: Paraguayan

Top 150 Places Sorted by Percent

(Based on places with populations of 10,000 or more)

Place	Number	%
Harrison, NY (village) Westchester County	94	0.39
Somerville, NJ (borough) Somerset County	49	0.39
White Plains, NY (city) Westchester County	171	0.32
Warren, NJ (township) Somerset County	31	0.22
Mamaroneck, NY (village) Westchester County	39	0.21
Stafford, TX (city) Fort Bend County	24	0.15
Mineola, NY (village) Nassau County	26	0.14
Rye, NY (town) Westchester County	51	0.12
Key Biscayne, FL (village) Miami-Dade County	13	0.12
Manville, NJ (borough) Somerset County	12	0.12
Rockville, MD (city) Montgomery County	53	0.11
Greenwich, CT (town) Fairfield County	63	0.10
Doral, FL (cdp) Miami-Dade County	21	0.10
Elwood, NY (cdp) Suffolk County	11	0.10
Mount Vernon, NY (city) Westchester County	61	0.09
South Farmingdale, NY (cdp) Nassau County	14	0.09
Greenlawn, NY (cdp) Suffolk County	12	0.09
The Crossings, FL (cdp) Miami-Dade County	18	0.08
Bedford, NY (town) Westchester County	15	0.08
New Castle, NY (town) Westchester County	14	0.08
Sunny Isles Beach, FL (city) Miami-Dade County	12	0.08
Bound Brook, NJ (borough) Somerset County	8	0.08
Miami Beach, FL (city) Miami-Dade County	64	0.07
Wheaton-Glenmont, MD (cdp) Montgomery County	38	0.07
Bernards, NJ (township) Somerset County	16	0.07
Aspen Hill, MD (cdp) Montgomery County	28	0.06
Coral Gables, FL (city) Miami-Dade County	26	0.06
Port Chester, NY (village) Westchester County	17	0.06
Madison, NJ (borough) Morris County	10	0.06
New Carrollton, MD (city) Prince George's County	7	0.06
Bridgewater, NJ (township) Somerset County	23	0.05
Mount Pleasant, NY (town) Westchester County	21	0.05
Emporia, KS (city) Lyon County	14	0.05
Cutler Ridge, FL (cdp) Miami-Dade County	12	0.05
Ossining, NY (village) Westchester County	12	0.05
Sandalfoot Cove, FL (cdp) Palm Beach County	9	0.05
Miami Springs, FL (city) Miami-Dade County	7	0.05
Pacific Grove, CA (city) Monterey County	7	0.05
North Castle, NY (town) Westchester County	5	0.05
South Miami, FL (city) Miami-Dade County	5	0.05
Arlington, VA (cdp) Arlington County	82	0.04
Greenburgh, NY (town) Westchester County	37	0.04
Kendall, FL (cdp) Miami-Dade County	31	0.04
Lawrence, KS (city) Douglas County	31	0.04
New Rochelle, NY (city) Westchester County	29	0.04
Bethesda, MD (cdp) Montgomery County	23	0.04
Fountainbleau, FL (cdp) Miami-Dade County	23	0.04
Springfield, VA (cdp) Fairfax County	13	0.04
Mamaroneck, NY (town) Westchester County	12	0.04
Jefferson, VA (cdp) Fairfax County	11	0.04
Ridgefield, CT (town) Fairfield County	9	0.04
Pinecrest, FL (village) Miami-Dade County	8	0.04
Scotch Plains, NJ (cdp) Union County	8	0.04
East Massapequa, NY (cdp) Nassau County	7	0.04
Lincolnia, VA (cdp) Fairfax County	7	0.04
Berkeley Heights, NJ (cdp) Union County	6	0.04
Druid Hills, GA (cdp) De Kalb County	5	0.04
Merrifield, VA (cdp) Fairfax County	5	0.04
Lumberton, NJ (township) Burlington County	4	0.04
Port Salerno, FL (cdp) Martin County	4	0.04
Norwalk, CT (city) Fairfield County	27	0.03
Silver Spring, MD (cdp) Montgomery County	21	0.03
Germantown, MD (cdp) Montgomery County	19	0.03
North Bergen, NJ (township) Hudson County	16	0.03
North Bethesda, MD (cdp) Montgomery County	13	0.03
North Miami Beach, FL (city) Miami-Dade County	13	0.03
Ossining, NY (town) Westchester County	12	0.03
Highland Park, IL (city) Lake County	10	0.03
Lehigh Acres, FL (cdp) Lee County	10	0.03
Yorktown, NY (town) Westchester County	10	0.03
Monterey, CA (city) Monterey County	9	0.03
Coral Terrace, FL (cdp) Miami-Dade County	7	0.03
Fairland, MD (cdp) Montgomery County	7	0.03
North Potomac, MD (cdp) Montgomery County	7	0.03
Brookfield, IL (village) Cook County	6	0.03
Hillside, NJ (cdp) Union County	6	0.03
Merrick, NY (cdp) Nassau County	6	0.03
Newington, VA (cdp) Fairfax County	6	0.03
North Bay Shore, NY (cdp) Suffolk County	5	0.03
Pittsburg, KS (city) Crawford County	5	0.03
Port Washington, NY (cdp) Nassau County	5	0.03
Princeton, NJ (township) Mercer County	5	0.03
South River, NJ (borough) Middlesex County	5	0.03
Whitpain, PA (township) Montgomery County	5	0.03
Ardmore, PA (cdp) Montgomery County	4	0.03
Centerville, UT (city) Davis County	4	0.03
Glens Falls, NY (city) Warren County	4	0.03
Hanover, MA (town) Plymouth County	4	0.03
Keystone, FL (cdp) Hillsborough County	4	0.03
North Arlington, NJ (borough) Bergen County	4	0.03
Rye, NY (city) Westchester County	4	0.03
Setauket-East Setauket, NY (cdp) Suffolk County	4	0.03
Shively, KY (city) Jefferson County	4	0.03
Whitefish Bay, WI (village) Milwaukee County	4	0.03
Wolf Trap, VA (cdp) Fairfax County	4	0.03
Morris, IL (city) Grundy County	3	0.03
North Myrtle Beach, SC (city) Horry County	3	0.03
Palm Beach, FL (town) Palm Beach County	3	0.03
Spring Garden, PA (township) York County	3	0.03
Tarrytown, NY (village) Westchester County	3	0.03
New York, NY (city) New York City	1,658	0.02
Washington, DC (city) District of Columbia	86	0.02
North Hempstead, NY (town) Nassau County	48	0.02
Huntington, NY (town) Suffolk County	40	0.02
Stamford, CT (city) Fairfield County	28	0.02
Upper Darby, PA (township) Delaware County	15	0.02
Bend, OR (city) Deschutes County	13	0.02
Delray Beach, FL (city) Palm Beach County	13	0.02
Gaithersburg, MD (city) Montgomery County	13	0.02
Davie, FL (town) Broward County	12	0.02
Milford, CT (special city) New Haven County	12	0.02
Milford, CT (town) New Haven County	12	0.02
Annandale, VA (cdp) Fairfax County	11	0.02
Lower Merion, PA (township) Montgomery County	11	0.02
Manhattan, KS (city) Riley County	11	0.02
Middletown, NJ (township) Monmouth County	11	0.02
Weston, FL (city) Broward County	11	0.02
Brentwood, NY (cdp) Suffolk County	10	0.02
Fairfield, CT (town) Fairfield County	10	0.02
Oak Park, IL (village) Cook County	10	0.02
Potomac, MD (cdp) Montgomery County	10	0.02
Southampton, NY (town) Suffolk County	10	0.02
Brookline, MA (cdp) Norfolk County	9	0.02
Cortlandt, NY (town) Westchester County	9	0.02
North Miami, FL (city) Miami-Dade County	9	0.02
East Meadow, NY (cdp) Nassau County	8	0.02
Elmhurst, IL (city) Du Page County	8	0.02
Jupiter, FL (town) Palm Beach County	8	0.02
Montgomery Village, MD (cdp) Montgomery County	8	0.02
Wellington, FL (village) Palm Beach County	8	0.02
Blacksburg, VA (town) Montgomery County	7	0.02
Coram, NY (cdp) Suffolk County	7	0.02
Walnut, CA (city) Los Angeles County	7	0.02
Westchester, FL (cdp) Miami-Dade County	7	0.02
Carmel, NY (town) Putnam County	6	0.02
Falmouth, MA (town) Barnstable County	6	0.02
Glen Cove, NY (city) Nassau County	6	0.02
Kendall West, FL (cdp) Miami-Dade County	6	0.02
Manlius, NY (town) Onondaga County	6	0.02
Montclair, NJ (cdp) Essex County	6	0.02
Olney, MD (cdp) Montgomery County	6	0.02
Acton, MA (town) Middlesex County	5	0.02
Bay Shore, NY (cdp) Suffolk County	5	0.02
Cliffside Park, NJ (borough) Bergen County	5	0.02
Duluth, GA (city) Gwinnett County	5	0.02
Lisle, IL (village) Du Page County	5	0.02
Naples, FL (city) Collier County	5	0.02
Oakton, VA (cdp) Fairfax County	5	0.02
Pikesville, MD (cdp) Baltimore County	5	0.02
Randolph, NJ (township) Morris County	5	0.02

Notes: (cdp) census designated place; Refer to the Explanation of Data in the front of the book for more detailed information.

Hispanic: Peruvian

Top 150 Places Sorted by Number

(Based on all places, regardless of population)

Place	Number	%
New York, NY (city) New York City	23,567	0.29
Los Angeles, CA (city) Los Angeles County	7,565	0.20
Paterson, NJ (city) Passaic County	7,038	4.72
Elizabeth, NJ (city) Union County	2,830	2.35
Chicago, IL (city) Cook County	2,737	0.09
Miami, FL (city) Miami-Dade County	2,447	0.68
Clifton, NJ (city) Passaic County	1,788	2.27
San Francisco, CA (city) San Francisco County	1,769	0.23
Hempstead, NY (town) Nassau County	1,724	0.23
Union City, NJ (city) Hudson County	1,694	2.53
Houston, TX (city) Harris County	1,656	0.08
Passaic, NJ (city) Passaic County	1,643	2.42
Miami Beach, FL (city) Miami-Dade County	1,630	1.85
The Hammocks, FL (cdp) Miami-Dade County	1,591	3.36
Kearny, NJ (town) Hudson County	1,549	3.82
Kendall, FL (cdp) Miami-Dade County	1,512	2.01
Hollywood, FL (city) Broward County	1,466	1.05
Hialeah, FL (city) Miami-Dade County	1,418	0.63
Newark, NJ (city) Essex County	1,405	0.51
Stamford, CT (city) Fairfield County	1,268	1.08
White Plains, NY (city) Westchester County	1,266	2.39
Islip, NY (town) Suffolk County	1,244	0.39
Hartford, CT (city) Hartford County	1,184	0.97
Arlington, VA (cdp) Arlington County	1,171	0.62
Kendale Lakes, FL (cdp) Miami-Dade County	1,157	2.03
Kendall West, FL (cdp) Miami-Dade County	1,084	2.85
Pembroke Pines, FL (city) Broward County	1,082	0.79
San Jose, CA (city) Santa Clara County	1,068	0.12
Fountainbleau, FL (cdp) Miami-Dade County	1,044	1.75
Perth Amboy, NJ (city) Middlesex County	1,041	2.20
Rye, NY (town) Westchester County	1,021	2.33
Harrison, NJ (town) Hudson County	1,011	7.01
San Diego, CA (city) San Diego County	987	0.08
Port Chester, NY (village) Westchester County	919	3.30
Downey, CA (city) Los Angeles County	891	0.83
Anaheim, CA (city) Orange County	876	0.27
Coral Springs, FL (city) Broward County	869	0.74
Dallas, TX (city) Dallas County	853	0.07
North Bergen, NJ (township) Hudson County	848	1.46
New Rochelle, NY (city) Westchester County	791	1.10
Jersey City, NJ (city) Hudson County	786	0.33
West New York, NJ (town) Hudson County	771	1.68
Garfield, NJ (city) Bergen County	761	2.55
Boston, MA (city) Suffolk County	759	0.13
North Miami Beach, FL (city) Miami-Dade County	733	1.80
Washington, DC (city) District of Columbia	708	0.12
Sunrise, FL (city) Broward County	688	0.80
Glen Cove, NY (city) Nassau County	659	2.48
Alexandria, VA (independent city) Alexandria city	646	0.50
The Crossings, FL (cdp) Miami-Dade County	634	2.69
Glendale, CA (city) Los Angeles County	630	0.32
San Mateo, CA (city) San Mateo County	623	0.67
Miramar, FL (city) Broward County	614	0.84
Doral, FL (cdp) Miami-Dade County	602	2.95
Weston, FL (city) Broward County	588	1.19
West Orange, NJ (cdp) Essex County	577	1.28
Concord, CA (city) Contra Costa County	566	0.46
Long Beach, CA (city) Los Angeles County	556	0.12
Annandale, VA (cdp) Fairfax County	545	0.99
Brentwood, NY (cdp) Suffolk County	544	1.01
Gaithersburg, MD (city) Montgomery County	542	1.03
Oyster Bay, NY (town) Nassau County	538	0.18
Tamiami, FL (cdp) Miami-Dade County	526	0.96
Torrance, CA (city) Los Angeles County	514	0.37
Woodbridge, NJ (township) Middlesex County	508	0.52
Richmond West, FL (cdp) Miami-Dade County	506	1.80
Wheaton-Glenmont, MD (cdp) Montgomery County	499	0.86
Daly City, CA (city) San Mateo County	496	0.48
Plantation, FL (city) Broward County	484	0.58
Davie, FL (town) Broward County	482	0.64
Fort Lauderdale, FL (city) Broward County	476	0.31
Philadelphia, PA (city) Philadelphia County	471	0.03
San Antonio, TX (city) Bexar County	470	0.04
Burke, VA (cdp) Fairfax County	468	0.81
Yonkers, NY (city) Westchester County	464	0.24
North Hempstead, NY (town) Nassau County	457	0.21
Country Club, FL (cdp) Miami-Dade County	454	1.25
Hawthorne, CA (city) Los Angeles County	447	0.53
Seattle, WA (city) King County	423	0.08
Hayward, CA (city) Alameda County	421	0.30
Santa Ana, CA (city) Orange County	420	0.12
Centreville, VA (cdp) Fairfax County	419	0.86
Carteret, NJ (borough) Middlesex County	417	2.01
Charlotte, NC (city) Mecklenburg County	417	0.08
Brookhaven, NY (town) Suffolk County	415	0.09
Phoenix, AZ (city) Maricopa County	411	0.03
Aspen Hill, MD (cdp) Montgomery County	406	0.81
Babylon, NY (town) Suffolk County	402	0.19
Aurora, CO (city) Arapahoe County	395	0.14
Orange, NJ (cdp) Essex County	391	1.19
Hallandale, FL (city) Broward County	391	1.14
Greenburgh, NY (town) Westchester County	388	0.45
Burbank, CA (city) Los Angeles County	385	0.38
North Miami, FL (city) Miami-Dade County	384	0.64
Belleville, NJ (cdp) Essex County	382	1.06
Ojus, FL (cdp) Miami-Dade County	381	2.29
South Gate, CA (city) Los Angeles County	380	0.39
East Hartford, CT (cdp) Hartford County	378	0.76
Denver, CO (city) Denver County	373	0.07
Lodi, NJ (borough) Bergen County	365	1.52
Tampa, FL (city) Hillsborough County	365	0.12
West Hartford, CT (cdp) Hartford County	363	0.57
Garden Grove, CA (city) Orange County	362	0.22
Santa Clarita, CA (city) Los Angeles County	359	0.24
Austin, TX (city) Travis County	359	0.05
Town 'n' Country, FL (cdp) Hillsborough County	356	0.49
Salt Lake City, UT (city) Salt Lake County	356	0.20
Oakland, CA (city) Alameda County	351	0.09
Tamarac, FL (city) Broward County	342	0.62
Pasadena, CA (city) Los Angeles County	340	0.25
Rockville, MD (city) Montgomery County	336	0.71
Orlando, FL (city) Orange County	336	0.18
Las Vegas, NV (city) Clark County	334	0.07
Newburgh, NY (city) Orange County	330	1.17
Bridgeport, CT (city) Fairfield County	327	0.23
Redwood City, CA (city) San Mateo County	325	0.43
Margate, FL (city) Broward County	315	0.58
Montgomery Village, MD (cdp) Montgomery County	308	0.81
Herndon, VA (town) Fairfax County	303	1.40
Jacksonville, FL (special city) Duval County	303	0.04
Bloomfield, NJ (cdp) Essex County	297	0.62
Hackensack, NJ (city) Bergen County	296	0.69
Sunnyvale, CA (city) Santa Clara County	295	0.22
Fremont, CA (city) Alameda County	293	0.14
Glenvar Heights, FL (cdp) Miami-Dade County	292	1.80
Rahway, NJ (city) Union County	290	1.09
Paradise, NV (cdp) Clark County	290	0.16
Germantown, MD (cdp) Montgomery County	289	0.52
Coral Gables, FL (city) Miami-Dade County	286	0.68
Silver Spring, MD (cdp) Montgomery County	286	0.37
Greenwich, CT (town) Fairfield County	285	0.47
Rancho Cucamonga, CA (city) San Bernardino County	284	0.22
Provo, UT (city) Utah County	283	0.27
Coconut Creek, FL (city) Broward County	279	0.64
Elmwood Park, NJ (borough) Bergen County	273	1.44
Riverside, CA (city) Riverside County	272	0.11
Sunny Isles Beach, FL (city) Miami-Dade County	271	1.77
Long Beach, NY (city) Nassau County	270	0.76
Irvine, CA (city) Orange County	267	0.19
North Plainfield, NJ (borough) Somerset County	266	1.26
Athens-Clarke County, GA (special city) Clarke County	266	0.27
Linden, NJ (city) Union County	263	0.67
Key Biscayne, FL (village) Miami-Dade County	261	2.48
Miami Springs, FL (city) Miami-Dade County	260	1.90
Mamaroneck, NY (village) Westchester County	260	1.39
Oakton, VA (cdp) Fairfax County	257	0.88
Reston, VA (cdp) Fairfax County	256	0.45
West Covina, CA (city) Los Angeles County	256	0.24
Simi Valley, CA (city) Ventura County	255	0.23
Carol City, FL (cdp) Miami-Dade County	253	0.43

Notes: (cdp) census designated place; Refer to the Explanation of Data in the front of the book for more detailed information.

Hispanic: Peruvian

Top 150 Places Sorted by Percent

(Based on all places, regardless of population)

Place	Number	%
East Newark, NJ (borough) Hudson County	240	10.10
Harrison, NJ (town) Hudson County	1,011	7.01
Paterson, NJ (city) Passaic County	7,038	4.72
Kearny, NJ (town) Hudson County	1,549	3.82
The Hammocks, FL (cdp) Miami-Dade County	1,591	3.36
Port Chester, NY (village) Westchester County	919	3.30
Virginia Gardens, FL (village) Miami-Dade County	76	3.24
Prospect Park, NJ (borough) Passaic County	186	3.22
Bay Harbor Islands, FL (town) Miami-Dade County	160	3.11
Doral, FL (cdp) Miami-Dade County	602	2.95
Kendall West, FL (cdp) Miami-Dade County	1,084	2.85
Haledon, NJ (borough) Passaic County	224	2.71
The Crossings, FL (cdp) Miami-Dade County	634	2.69
Garfield, NJ (city) Bergen County	761	2.55
Union City, NJ (city) Hudson County	1,694	2.53
Glen Cove, NY (city) Nassau County	659	2.48
Key Biscayne, FL (village) Miami-Dade County	261	2.48
Passaic, NJ (city) Passaic County	1,643	2.42
White Plains, NY (city) Westchester County	1,266	2.39
Elizabeth, NJ (city) Union County	2,830	2.35
Rye, NY (town) Westchester County	1,021	2.33
Ojus, FL (cdp) Miami-Dade County	381	2.29
Clifton, NJ (city) Passaic County	1,788	2.27
Elmsford, NY (village) Westchester County	105	2.25
Perth Amboy, NJ (city) Middlesex County	1,041	2.20
North Bay Village, FL (city) Miami-Dade County	146	2.17
Kendale Lakes, FL (cdp) Miami-Dade County	1,157	2.03
Kendall, FL (cdp) Miami-Dade County	1,512	2.01
Carteret, NJ (borough) Middlesex County	417	2.01
Miami Springs, FL (city) Miami-Dade County	260	1.90
Miami, MO (city) Saline County	3	1.88
Miami Beach, FL (city) Miami-Dade County	1,630	1.85
North Miami Beach, FL (city) Miami-Dade County	733	1.80
Richmond West, FL (cdp) Miami-Dade County	506	1.80
Glenvar Heights, FL (cdp) Miami-Dade County	292	1.80
Oxbow, ME (plantation) Aroostook County	1	1.79
Sunny Isles Beach, FL (city) Miami-Dade County	271	1.77
Fountainbleau, FL (cdp) Miami-Dade County	1,044	1.75
Fairview, NY (cdp) Westchester County	50	1.73
Country Walk, FL (cdp) Miami-Dade County	183	1.72
West New York, NJ (town) Hudson County	771	1.68
Pine Island, FL (cdp) Hernando County	1	1.56
North Bay, WI (village) Racine County	4	1.54
Lodi, NJ (borough) Bergen County	365	1.52
North Andrews Gardens, FL (cdp) Broward County	146	1.51
Surfside, FL (town) Miami-Dade County	72	1.47
North Bergen, NJ (township) Hudson County	848	1.46
Island Park, NY (village) Nassau County	69	1.46
Sunset, FL (cdp) Miami-Dade County	248	1.45
Elmwood Park, NJ (borough) Bergen County	273	1.44
Gold Hill, CO (cdp) Boulder County	3	1.43
Dunellen, NJ (borough) Middlesex County	97	1.42
Golden Beach, FL (town) Miami-Dade County	13	1.41
Herndon, VA (town) Fairfax County	303	1.40
Mamaroneck, NY (village) Westchester County	260	1.39
Three Lakes, FL (cdp) Miami-Dade County	97	1.39
Muir Beach, CA (cdp) Marin County	4	1.36
Cannonville, UT (town) Garfield County	2	1.35
Guttenberg, NJ (town) Hudson County	144	1.33
Lincolnia, VA (cdp) Fairfax County	209	1.32
Ives Estates, FL (cdp) Miami-Dade County	230	1.31
West Orange, NJ (cdp) Essex County	577	1.28
East Perrine, FL (cdp) Miami-Dade County	90	1.27
North Plainfield, NJ (borough) Somerset County	266	1.26
Miami Gardens, FL (cdp) Broward County	34	1.26
Country Club, FL (cdp) Miami-Dade County	454	1.25
Broadview Park, FL (cdp) Broward County	82	1.21
Bellerose Terrace, NY (cdp) Nassau County	26	1.21
Pimmit Hills, VA (cdp) Fairfax County	74	1.20
Weston, FL (city) Broward County	588	1.19
Orange, NJ (cdp) Essex County	391	1.19
Meservey, IA (city) Cerro Gordo County	3	1.19
Bound Brook, NJ (borough) Somerset County	120	1.18
Struble, IA (city) Plymouth County	1	1.18
Newburgh, NY (city) Orange County	330	1.17
Dover, NJ (town) Morris County	212	1.17
Palm Aire, FL (cdp) Broward County	18	1.17
Max Meadows, VA (cdp) Wythe County	6	1.17
Hallandale, FL (city) Broward County	391	1.14
Weehawken, NJ (township) Hudson County	154	1.14
Central City, AR (town) Sebastian County	6	1.13
Snowville, UT (town) Box Elder County	2	1.13
North Bay Shore, NY (cdp) Suffolk County	166	1.11
Seven Corners, VA (cdp) Fairfax County	97	1.11
Wharton, NJ (borough) Morris County	70	1.11
Highland Falls, NY (village) Orange County	41	1.11
Vails Gate, NY (cdp) Orange County	37	1.11
Glacier, WA (cdp) Whatcom County	1	1.11
New Rochelle, NY (city) Westchester County	791	1.10
Rahway, NJ (city) Union County	290	1.09
Bliss, ID (city) Gooding County	3	1.09
Stamford, CT (city) Fairfield County	1,268	1.08
South Bound Brook, NJ (borough) Somerset County	48	1.07
Bellevue, ID (city) Blaine County	20	1.07
Fisher Island, FL (cdp) Miami-Dade County	5	1.07
Belleville, NJ (cdp) Essex County	382	1.06
Hollywood, FL (city) Broward County	1,466	1.05
Locust Valley, NY (cdp) Nassau County	37	1.05
Canyon City, OR (town) Grant County	7	1.05
West Miami, FL (city) Miami-Dade County	61	1.04
Keddie, CA (cdp) Plumas County	1	1.04
Gaithersburg, MD (city) Montgomery County	542	1.03
Victory Gardens, NJ (borough) Morris County	16	1.03
Lake Harbor, FL (cdp) Palm Beach County	2	1.03
Natural Bridge, NY (cdp) Jefferson County	4	1.02
Brentwood, NY (cdp) Suffolk County	544	1.01
North Kensington, MD (cdp) Montgomery County	90	1.01
Sea Ranch Lakes, FL (village) Broward County	14	1.01
Broadview-Pompano Park, FL (cdp) Broward County	53	1.00
Bal Harbour, FL (village) Miami-Dade County	33	1.00
Medley, FL (town) Miami-Dade County	11	1.00
Annandale, VA (cdp) Fairfax County	545	0.99
Lakes by the Bay, FL (cdp) Miami-Dade County	90	0.99
Lisle, NY (village) Broome County	3	0.99
Hartford, CT (city) Hartford County	1,184	0.97
Byers, TX (city) Clay County	5	0.97
Carey, ID (city) Blaine County	5	0.97
Tamiami, FL (cdp) Miami-Dade County	526	0.96
Miami Lakes, FL (cdp) Miami-Dade County	215	0.95
Meadowview Estates, KY (city) Jefferson County	4	0.95
Jeffrey City, WY (cdp) Fremont County	1	0.94
Aventura, FL (city) Miami-Dade County	236	0.93
North Springfield, VA (cdp) Fairfax County	85	0.93
Chambers Estates, FL (cdp) Broward County	33	0.93
Sandalfoot Cove, FL (cdp) Palm Beach County	152	0.92
Pinecrest, FL (village) Miami-Dade County	173	0.91
Carlstadt, NJ (borough) Bergen County	54	0.91
Southchase, FL (cdp) Orange County	42	0.91
Napeague, NY (cdp) Suffolk County	2	0.90
Bailey's Crossroads, VA (cdp) Fairfax County	206	0.89
Ouzinkie, AK (city) Kodiak Island Borough	2	0.89
Oakton, VA (cdp) Fairfax County	257	0.88
Mount Kisco, NY (village) Westchester County	88	0.88
Morristown, NY (village) Saint Lawrence County	4	0.88
Coral Terrace, FL (cdp) Miami-Dade County	213	0.87
Wheaton-Glenmont, MD (cdp) Montgomery County	499	0.86
Centreville, VA (cdp) Fairfax County	419	0.86
University Park, FL (cdp) Miami-Dade County	227	0.86
Glen Head, NY (cdp) Nassau County	40	0.86
West Paterson, NJ (borough) Passaic County	93	0.85
Foyil, OK (town) Rogers County	2	0.85
Miramar, FL (city) Broward County	614	0.84
Avenel, NJ (cdp) Middlesex County	147	0.84
Barnum Island, NY (cdp) Nassau County	21	0.84
Downey, CA (city) Los Angeles County	891	0.83
Freehold, NJ (borough) Monmouth County	91	0.83
Biscayne Park, FL (village) Miami-Dade County	27	0.83
Burke, VA (cdp) Fairfax County	468	0.81
Aspen Hill, MD (cdp) Montgomery County	406	0.81
Montgomery Village, MD (cdp) Montgomery County	308	0.81

Notes: (cdp) census designated place; Refer to the Explanation of Data in the front of the book for more detailed information.

Hispanic: Peruvian

Top 150 Places Sorted by Percent

(Based on places with populations of 10,000 or more)

Place	Number	%
Harrison, NJ (town) Hudson County	1,011	7.01
Paterson, NJ (city) Passaic County	7,038	4.72
Kearny, NJ (town) Hudson County	1,549	3.82
The Hammocks, FL (cdp) Miami-Dade County	1,591	3.36
Port Chester, NY (village) Westchester County	919	3.30
Doral, FL (cdp) Miami-Dade County	602	2.95
Kendall West, FL (cdp) Miami-Dade County	1,084	2.85
The Crossings, FL (cdp) Miami-Dade County	634	2.69
Garfield, NJ (city) Bergen County	761	2.55
Union City, NJ (city) Hudson County	1,694	2.53
Glen Cove, NY (city) Nassau County	659	2.48
Key Biscayne, FL (village) Miami-Dade County	261	2.48
Passaic, NJ (city) Passaic County	1,643	2.42
White Plains, NY (city) Westchester County	1,266	2.39
Elizabeth, NJ (city) Union County	2,830	2.35
Rye, NY (town) Westchester County	1,021	2.33
Ojus, FL (cdp) Miami-Dade County	381	2.29
Clifton, NJ (city) Passaic County	1,788	2.27
Perth Amboy, NJ (city) Middlesex County	1,041	2.20
Kendale Lakes, FL (cdp) Miami-Dade County	1,157	2.03
Kendall, FL (cdp) Miami-Dade County	1,512	2.01
Carteret, NJ (borough) Middlesex County	417	2.01
Miami Springs, FL (city) Miami-Dade County	260	1.90
Miami Beach, FL (city) Miami-Dade County	1,630	1.85
North Miami Beach, FL (city) Miami-Dade County	733	1.80
Richmond West, FL (cdp) Miami-Dade County	506	1.80
Glenvar Heights, FL (cdp) Miami-Dade County	292	1.80
Sunny Isles Beach, FL (city) Miami-Dade County	271	1.77
Fountainbleau, FL (cdp) Miami-Dade County	1,044	1.75
Country Walk, FL (cdp) Miami-Dade County	183	1.72
West New York, NJ (town) Hudson County	771	1.68
Lodi, NJ (borough) Bergen County	365	1.52
North Bergen, NJ (township) Hudson County	848	1.46
Sunset, FL (cdp) Miami-Dade County	248	1.45
Elmwood Park, NJ (borough) Bergen County	273	1.44
Herndon, VA (town) Fairfax County	303	1.40
Mamaroneck, NY (village) Westchester County	260	1.39
Guttenberg, NJ (town) Hudson County	144	1.33
Lincolnia, VA (cdp) Fairfax County	209	1.32
Ives Estates, FL (cdp) Miami-Dade County	230	1.31
West Orange, NJ (cdp) Essex County	577	1.28
North Plainfield, NJ (borough) Somerset County	266	1.26
Country Club, FL (cdp) Miami-Dade County	454	1.25
Weston, FL (city) Broward County	588	1.19
Orange, NJ (cdp) Essex County	391	1.19
Bound Brook, NJ (borough) Somerset County	120	1.18
Newburgh, NY (city) Orange County	330	1.17
Dover, NJ (town) Morris County	212	1.17
Hallandale, FL (city) Broward County	391	1.14
Weehawken, NJ (township) Hudson County	154	1.14
North Bay Shore, NY (cdp) Suffolk County	166	1.11
New Rochelle, NY (city) Westchester County	791	1.10
Rahway, NJ (city) Union County	290	1.09
Stamford, CT (city) Fairfield County	1,268	1.08
Belleville, NJ (cdp) Essex County	382	1.06
Hollywood, FL (city) Broward County	1,466	1.05
Gaithersburg, MD (city) Montgomery County	542	1.03
Brentwood, NY (cdp) Suffolk County	544	1.01
Annandale, VA (cdp) Fairfax County	545	0.99
Hartford, CT (city) Hartford County	1,184	0.97
Tamiami, FL (cdp) Miami-Dade County	526	0.96
Miami Lakes, FL (cdp) Miami-Dade County	215	0.95
Aventura, FL (city) Miami-Dade County	236	0.93
Sandalfoot Cove, FL (cdp) Palm Beach County	152	0.92
Pinecrest, FL (village) Miami-Dade County	173	0.91
Bailey's Crossroads, VA (cdp) Fairfax County	206	0.89
Oakton, VA (cdp) Fairfax County	257	0.88
Coral Terrace, FL (cdp) Miami-Dade County	213	0.87
Wheaton-Glenmont, MD (cdp) Montgomery County	499	0.86
Centreville, VA (cdp) Fairfax County	419	0.86
University Park, FL (cdp) Miami-Dade County	227	0.86
West Paterson, NJ (borough) Passaic County	93	0.85
Miramar, FL (city) Broward County	614	0.84
Avenel, NJ (cdp) Middlesex County	147	0.84
Downey, CA (city) Los Angeles County	891	0.83
Freehold, NJ (borough) Monmouth County	91	0.83
Burke, VA (cdp) Fairfax County	468	0.81
Aspen Hill, MD (cdp) Montgomery County	406	0.81
Montgomery Village, MD (cdp) Montgomery County	308	0.81
West Springfield, VA (cdp) Fairfax County	230	0.81
Hawthorne, NJ (borough) Passaic County	147	0.81
Sunrise, FL (city) Broward County	688	0.80
Pembroke Pines, FL (city) Broward County	1,082	0.79
Jefferson, VA (cdp) Fairfax County	218	0.79
Springfield, VA (cdp) Fairfax County	236	0.78
Westchester, FL (cdp) Miami-Dade County	236	0.78
Mamaroneck, NY (town) Westchester County	226	0.78
Newington, VA (cdp) Fairfax County	154	0.78
Middlesex, NJ (borough) Middlesex County	105	0.77
East Hartford, CT (cdp) Hartford County	378	0.76
Long Beach, NY (city) Nassau County	270	0.76
Hialeah Gardens, FL (city) Miami-Dade County	146	0.76
Westwood Lakes, FL (cdp) Miami-Dade County	91	0.76
Cutler, FL (cdp) Miami-Dade County	131	0.75
Olympia Heights, FL (cdp) Miami-Dade County	101	0.75
Roselle Park, NJ (borough) Union County	99	0.75
Coral Springs, FL (city) Broward County	869	0.74
North Lauderdale, FL (city) Broward County	240	0.74
Central Islip, NY (cdp) Suffolk County	238	0.74
Lawndale, CA (city) Los Angeles County	236	0.74
Fairfax, VA (independent city) Fairfax city	160	0.74
Lorton, VA (cdp) Fairfax County	131	0.74
Idylwood, VA (cdp) Fairfax County	119	0.74
Roselle, NJ (borough) Union County	155	0.73
South Miami Heights, FL (cdp) Miami-Dade County	243	0.72
Redland, MD (cdp) Montgomery County	123	0.72
Rockville, MD (city) Montgomery County	336	0.71
South Miami, FL (city) Miami-Dade County	75	0.70
Hackensack, NJ (city) Bergen County	296	0.69
Merrifield, VA (cdp) Fairfax County	77	0.69
Miami, FL (city) Miami-Dade County	2,447	0.68
Coral Gables, FL (city) Miami-Dade County	286	0.68
San Mateo, CA (city) San Mateo County	623	0.67
Linden, NJ (city) Union County	263	0.67
New London, CT (city) New London County	169	0.66
Palmetto Estates, FL (cdp) Miami-Dade County	90	0.66
Sweetwater, FL (city) Miami-Dade County	92	0.65
Miami Shores, FL (village) Miami-Dade County	67	0.65
Davie, FL (town) Broward County	482	0.64
North Miami, FL (city) Miami-Dade County	384	0.64
Coconut Creek, FL (city) Broward County	279	0.64
Fairview, NJ (borough) Bergen County	85	0.64
Ventnor City, NJ (city) Atlantic County	83	0.64
Meadow Woods, FL (cdp) Orange County	72	0.64
Hialeah, FL (city) Miami-Dade County	1,418	0.63
Oakland Park, FL (city) Broward County	196	0.63
Arlington, VA (cdp) Arlington County	1,171	0.62
Tamarac, FL (city) Broward County	342	0.62
Bloomfield, NJ (cdp) Essex County	297	0.62
Cutler Ridge, FL (cdp) Miami-Dade County	147	0.59
Plantation, FL (city) Broward County	484	0.58
Margate, FL (city) Broward County	315	0.58
Golden Glades, FL (cdp) Miami-Dade County	189	0.58
Suffern, NY (village) Rockland County	64	0.58
West Hartford, CT (cdp) Hartford County	363	0.57
North Bethesda, MD (cdp) Montgomery County	219	0.57
North Arlington, NJ (borough) Bergen County	86	0.57
Somerville, NJ (borough) Somerset County	71	0.57
Manassas Park, VA (independent city) Manassas Park city	59	0.57
Lake Ridge, VA (cdp) Prince William County	167	0.55
Beltsville, MD (cdp) Prince George's County	85	0.54
Rose Hill, VA (cdp) Fairfax County	82	0.54
Hawthorne, CA (city) Los Angeles County	447	0.53
Valley Stream, NY (village) Nassau County	193	0.53
Boca Del Mar, FL (cdp) Palm Beach County	116	0.53
Woodbridge, NJ (township) Middlesex County	508	0.52
Germantown, MD (cdp) Montgomery County	289	0.52
Kissimmee, FL (city) Osceola County	250	0.52
Rye, NY (city) Westchester County	78	0.52
Hyattsville, MD (city) Prince George's County	76	0.52

Notes: (cdp) census designated place; Refer to the Explanation of Data in the front of the book for more detailed information.

Hispanic: Uruguayan

Top 150 Places Sorted by Number

(Based on all places, regardless of population)

Place	Number	%
New York, NY (city) New York City	1,907	0.02
Elizabeth, NJ (city) Union County	772	0.64
West Orange, NJ (cdp) Essex County	384	0.85
Los Angeles, CA (city) Los Angeles County	320	0.01
Leominster, MA (city) Worcester County	265	0.64
Newark, NJ (city) Essex County	239	0.09
Houston, TX (city) Harris County	230	0.01
Miami Beach, FL (city) Miami-Dade County	222	0.25
Miami, FL (city) Miami-Dade County	221	0.06
Ossining, NY (town) Westchester County	205	0.56
Orange, NJ (cdp) Essex County	190	0.58
Hempstead, NY (town) Nassau County	185	0.02
Ossining, NY (village) Westchester County	179	0.75
Dover, NJ (town) Morris County	157	0.86
Fitchburg, MA (city) Worcester County	142	0.36
Stamford, CT (city) Fairfield County	138	0.12
Chicago, IL (city) Cook County	134	0.00
Rye, NY (town) Westchester County	122	0.28
Manchester, NH (city) Hillsborough County	121	0.11
Hialeah, FL (city) Miami-Dade County	118	0.05
Hollywood, FL (city) Broward County	113	0.08
North Bergen, NJ (township) Hudson County	104	0.18
Kendale Lakes, FL (cdp) Miami-Dade County	100	0.18
Union City, NJ (city) Hudson County	100	0.15
Washington, DC (city) District of Columbia	100	0.02
Coral Springs, FL (city) Broward County	99	0.08
Kearny, NJ (town) Hudson County	98	0.24
Port Chester, NY (village) Westchester County	95	0.34
North Andrews Gardens, FL (cdp) Broward County	93	0.96
Sunrise, FL (city) Broward County	92	0.11
Islip, NY (town) Suffolk County	88	0.03
Philadelphia, PA (city) Philadelphia County	86	0.01
The Hammocks, FL (cdp) Miami-Dade County	79	0.17
Pembroke Pines, FL (city) Broward County	78	0.06
Greenwich, CT (town) Fairfield County	74	0.12
New Rochelle, NY (city) Westchester County	72	0.10
Fountainbleau, FL (cdp) Miami-Dade County	71	0.12
Paterson, NJ (city) Passaic County	71	0.05
Arlington, VA (cdp) Arlington County	68	0.04
Harrison, NJ (town) Hudson County	66	0.46
Kendall, FL (cdp) Miami-Dade County	65	0.09
San Diego, CA (city) San Diego County	65	0.01
Woodbridge, NJ (township) Middlesex County	60	0.06
Hillside, NJ (cdp) Union County	59	0.27
Potomac, MD (cdp) Montgomery County	58	0.13
Country Club, FL (cdp) Miami-Dade County	56	0.15
Tamiami, FL (cdp) Miami-Dade County	56	0.10
West Palm Beach, FL (city) Palm Beach County	56	0.07
Fort Lauderdale, FL (city) Broward County	54	0.04
Boston, MA (city) Suffolk County	54	0.01
Wharton, NJ (borough) Morris County	53	0.84
Union, NJ (cdp) Union County	52	0.10
Belleville, NJ (cdp) Essex County	50	0.14
Plantation, FL (city) Broward County	50	0.06
Babylon, NY (town) Suffolk County	50	0.02
Peekskill, NY (city) Westchester County	49	0.22
The Crossings, FL (cdp) Miami-Dade County	48	0.20
Greenacres, FL (city) Palm Beach County	48	0.17
Kendall West, FL (cdp) Miami-Dade County	48	0.13
North Hempstead, NY (town) Nassau County	47	0.02
Linden, NJ (city) Union County	46	0.12
Parsippany-Troy Hills, NJ (township) Morris County	45	0.09
Miramar, FL (city) Broward County	45	0.06
Salt Lake City, UT (city) Salt Lake County	45	0.02
Roselle, NJ (borough) Union County	44	0.21
Coral Gables, FL (city) Miami-Dade County	44	0.10
Weston, FL (city) Broward County	44	0.09
Old Bridge, NJ (township) Middlesex County	44	0.07
Jersey City, NJ (city) Hudson County	44	0.02
Oakland Park, FL (city) Broward County	43	0.14
West New York, NJ (town) Hudson County	42	0.09
Oyster Bay, NY (town) Nassau County	42	0.01
Phoenix, AZ (city) Maricopa County	42	0.00
North Miami Beach, FL (city) Miami-Dade County	40	0.10
Roselle Park, NJ (borough) Union County	39	0.29
Huntington, NY (town) Suffolk County	38	0.02
San Francisco, CA (city) San Francisco County	38	0.00
Carteret, NJ (borough) Middlesex County	37	0.18
Cambridge, MA (city) Middlesex County	37	0.04
Brentwood, NY (cdp) Suffolk County	36	0.07
Doral, FL (cdp) Miami-Dade County	35	0.17
Cortlandt, NY (town) Westchester County	35	0.09
Bethesda, MD (cdp) Montgomery County	33	0.06
Brookhaven, NY (town) Suffolk County	33	0.01
Tamarac, FL (city) Broward County	32	0.06
Austin, TX (city) Travis County	32	0.00
Ojus, FL (cdp) Miami-Dade County	31	0.19
Mamaroneck, NY (village) Westchester County	31	0.17
Wellington, FL (village) Palm Beach County	31	0.08
Perth Amboy, NJ (city) Middlesex County	31	0.07
Minneapolis, MN (city) Hennepin County	31	0.01
Santa Ana, CA (city) Orange County	31	0.01
Coral Terrace, FL (cdp) Miami-Dade County	30	0.12
Hackensack, NJ (city) Bergen County	30	0.07
Rockville, MD (city) Montgomery County	30	0.06
Davie, FL (town) Broward County	30	0.04
Huntington Beach, CA (city) Orange County	30	0.02
Sunny Isles Beach, FL (city) Miami-Dade County	29	0.19
Westchester, FL (cdp) Miami-Dade County	29	0.10
Deerfield Beach, FL (city) Broward County	29	0.04
Yonkers, NY (city) Westchester County	29	0.01
Mount Olive, NJ (township) Morris County	28	0.12
Hallandale, FL (city) Broward County	28	0.08
Lake Worth, FL (city) Palm Beach County	28	0.08
Santa Monica, CA (city) Los Angeles County	28	0.03
Atlanta, GA (city) Fulton County	28	0.01
Madison Park, NJ (cdp) Middlesex County	27	0.39
Weehawken, NJ (township) Hudson County	27	0.20
Harrison, NY (village) Westchester County	27	0.11
Maplewood, NJ (cdp) Essex County	27	0.11
Rahway, NJ (city) Union County	27	0.10
University Park, FL (cdp) Miami-Dade County	27	0.10
Long Beach, NY (city) Nassau County	27	0.08
Bloomfield, NJ (cdp) Essex County	27	0.06
Passaic, NJ (city) Passaic County	27	0.04
Alexandria, VA (independent city) Alexandria city	27	0.02
Las Vegas, NV (city) Clark County	27	0.01
Coconut Creek, FL (city) Broward County	26	0.06
Lauderhill, FL (city) Broward County	26	0.05
North Miami, FL (city) Miami-Dade County	26	0.04
San Antonio, TX (city) Bexar County	26	0.00
Seattle, WA (city) King County	26	0.00
Ives Estates, FL (cdp) Miami-Dade County	25	0.14
Garfield, NJ (city) Bergen County	25	0.08
Edison, NJ (cdp) Middlesex County	25	0.03
Pompano Beach, FL (city) Broward County	25	0.03
Sandy, UT (city) Salt Lake County	25	0.03
Glendale, CA (city) Los Angeles County	25	0.01
Glenvar Heights, FL (cdp) Miami-Dade County	24	0.15
Aventura, FL (city) Miami-Dade County	24	0.09
Margate, FL (city) Broward County	24	0.04
West Jordan, UT (city) Salt Lake County	24	0.04
Greenburgh, NY (town) Westchester County	24	0.03
Jacksonville, FL (special city) Duval County	24	0.00
New Milford, NJ (borough) Bergen County	23	0.14
North Bethesda, MD (cdp) Montgomery County	23	0.06
Gaithersburg, MD (city) Montgomery County	23	0.04
Clifton, NJ (city) Passaic County	23	0.03
North Bay Village, FL (city) Miami-Dade County	22	0.33
Guttenberg, NJ (town) Hudson County	22	0.20
Cutler Ridge, FL (cdp) Miami-Dade County	22	0.09
Livingston, NJ (cdp) Essex County	22	0.08
Palm Coast, FL (city) Flagler County	22	0.07
South Miami Heights, FL (cdp) Miami-Dade County	22	0.07
Kissimmee, FL (city) Osceola County	22	0.05
White Plains, NY (city) Westchester County	22	0.04
Cape Coral, FL (city) Lee County	22	0.02
Provo, UT (city) Utah County	22	0.02
West Valley City, UT (city) Salt Lake County	22	0.02
Charlotte, NC (city) Mecklenburg County	22	0.00

Notes: (cdp) census designated place; Refer to the Explanation of Data in the front of the book for more detailed information.

Hispanic: Uruguayan

Top 150 Places Sorted by Percent

(Based on all places, regardless of population)

Place	Number	%
Cloud Lake, FL (town) Palm Beach County	2	1.20
North Andrews Gardens, FL (cdp) Broward County	93	0.96
Dover, NJ (town) Morris County	157	0.86
West Orange, NJ (cdp) Essex County	384	0.85
Wharton, NJ (borough) Morris County	53	0.84
Lawrence Creek, OK (town) Creek County	1	0.84
Victory Gardens, NJ (borough) Morris County	12	0.78
Ossining, NY (village) Westchester County	179	0.75
Elizabeth, NJ (city) Union County	772	0.64
Leominster, MA (city) Worcester County	265	0.64
East Newark, NJ (borough) Hudson County	14	0.59
Orange, NJ (cdp) Essex County	190	0.58
Fieldsboro, NJ (borough) Burlington County	3	0.57
Ossining, NY (town) Westchester County	205	0.56
Twin Lakes, FL (cdp) Broward County	10	0.53
Verplanck, NY (cdp) Westchester County	4	0.51
Harrison, NJ (town) Hudson County	66	0.46
Golden Beach, FL (town) Miami-Dade County	4	0.44
Plandome Heights, NY (village) Nassau County	4	0.41
University Heights, IA (city) Johnson County	4	0.41
Crugers, NY (cdp) Westchester County	7	0.40
Madison Park, NJ (cdp) Middlesex County	27	0.39
Evansville, WI (city) Rock County	15	0.37
Newton Hamilton, PA (borough) Mifflin County	1	0.37
Fitchburg, MA (city) Worcester County	142	0.36
Sunshine Acres, FL (cdp) Broward County	3	0.36
Glen Ridge, FL (town) Palm Beach County	1	0.36
Covington, TX (city) Hill County	1	0.35
Port Chester, NY (village) Westchester County	95	0.34
North Bay Village, FL (city) Miami-Dade County	22	0.33
Bay Harbor Islands, FL (town) Miami-Dade County	17	0.33
Otselic, NY (town) Chenango County	3	0.30
Roselle Park, NJ (borough) Union County	39	0.29
Ship Bottom, NJ (borough) Ocean County	4	0.29
Rye, NY (town) Westchester County	122	0.28
Beatyestown, NJ (cdp) Warren County	9	0.28
Muscoda, WI (village) Grant County	4	0.28
West Jefferson, NC (town) Ashe County	3	0.28
Hillside, NJ (cdp) Union County	59	0.27
Glendon, PA (borough) Northampton County	1	0.27
Montauk, NY (cdp) Suffolk County	10	0.26
Palm Aire, FL (cdp) Broward County	4	0.26
Miami Beach, FL (city) Miami-Dade County	222	0.25
Kearny, NJ (town) Hudson County	98	0.24
Riverland Village, FL (cdp) Broward County	5	0.24
Aldrich, MN (township) Wadena County	1	0.24
Timberville, VA (town) Rockingham County	4	0.23
Peekskill, NY (city) Westchester County	49	0.22
Darnestown, MD (cdp) Montgomery County	14	0.22
Flagler Beach, FL (city) Flagler County	11	0.22
Surfside, FL (town) Miami-Dade County	11	0.22
Oak Park, CA (cdp) Ventura County	5	0.22
University Park, MD (town) Prince George's County	5	0.22
Burke, NY (town) Franklin County	3	0.22
Homestead Base, FL (cdp) Miami-Dade County	1	0.22
Roselle, NJ (borough) Union County	44	0.21
Village of the Branch, NY (village) Suffolk County	4	0.21
The Crossings, FL (cdp) Miami-Dade County	48	0.20
Weehawken, NJ (township) Hudson County	27	0.20
Guttenberg, NJ (town) Hudson County	22	0.20
Crompond, NY (cdp) Westchester County	4	0.20
South Ashburnham, MA (cdp) Worcester County	2	0.20
Ojus, FL (cdp) Miami-Dade County	31	0.19
Sunny Isles Beach, FL (city) Miami-Dade County	29	0.19
Brewster, NY (village) Putnam County	4	0.19
North Bergen, NJ (township) Hudson County	104	0.18
Kendale Lakes, FL (cdp) Miami-Dade County	100	0.18
Carteret, NJ (borough) Middlesex County	37	0.18
Lakes by the Bay, FL (cdp) Miami-Dade County	16	0.18
Biscayne Park, FL (village) Miami-Dade County	6	0.18
Wilmington, NY (town) Essex County	2	0.18
The Hammocks, FL (cdp) Miami-Dade County	79	0.17
Greenacres, FL (city) Palm Beach County	48	0.17
Doral, FL (cdp) Miami-Dade County	35	0.17
Mamaroneck, NY (village) Westchester County	31	0.17
Mansfield, NJ (township) Warren County	11	0.17
Broadview-Pompano Park, FL (cdp) Broward County	9	0.17
Lacona, NY (village) Oswego County	1	0.17
Roxbury, NY (town) Delaware County	4	0.16
Seminole Manor, FL (cdp) Palm Beach County	4	0.16
Baldwinville, MA (cdp) Worcester County	3	0.16
Sugar City, ID (city) Madison County	2	0.16
Elsah, IL (village) Jersey County	1	0.16
Union City, NJ (city) Hudson County	100	0.15
Country Club, FL (cdp) Miami-Dade County	56	0.15
Glenvar Heights, FL (cdp) Miami-Dade County	24	0.15
Saint Armand, NY (town) Essex County	2	0.15
Belleville, NJ (cdp) Essex County	50	0.14
Oakland Park, FL (city) Broward County	43	0.14
Ives Estates, FL (cdp) Miami-Dade County	25	0.14
New Milford, NJ (borough) Bergen County	23	0.14
Edgewater, NJ (borough) Bergen County	11	0.14
Lake Clarke Shores, FL (town) Palm Beach County	5	0.14
Royal Palm Estates, FL (cdp) Palm Beach County	5	0.14
Bonanza, GA (cdp) Clayton County	4	0.14
San Luis, CO (town) Costilla County	1	0.14
Seneca Gardens, KY (city) Jefferson County	1	0.14
Potomac, MD (cdp) Montgomery County	58	0.13
Kendall West, FL (cdp) Miami-Dade County	48	0.13
Lilburn, GA (city) Gwinnett County	15	0.13
Falcon Heights, MN (city) Ramsey County	7	0.13
Hubbardston, MA (town) Worcester County	5	0.13
Maybrook, NY (village) Orange County	4	0.13
Haleiwa, HI (cdp) Honolulu County	3	0.13
Lake Belvedere Estates, FL (cdp) Palm Beach County	2	0.13
Occoquan, VA (town) Prince William County	1	0.13
Stamford, CT (city) Fairfield County	138	0.12
Greenwich, CT (town) Fairfield County	74	0.12
Fountainbleau, FL (cdp) Miami-Dade County	71	0.12
Linden, NJ (city) Union County	46	0.12
Coral Terrace, FL (cdp) Miami-Dade County	30	0.12
Mount Olive, NJ (township) Morris County	28	0.12
Palm Springs, FL (village) Palm Beach County	14	0.12
Putnam Valley, NY (town) Putnam County	13	0.12
Princeton, FL (cdp) Miami-Dade County	12	0.12
Lunenburg, MA (town) Worcester County	11	0.12
Kenilworth, NJ (borough) Union County	9	0.12
Golden Lakes, FL (cdp) Palm Beach County	8	0.12
Yorkshire, VA (cdp) Prince William County	8	0.12
Bonnie Lock-Woodsetter North, FL (cdp) Broward County	5	0.12
Balmville, NY (cdp) Orange County	4	0.12
Mentz, NY (town) Cayuga County	3	0.12
Emmet, WI (town) Marathon County	1	0.12
Manchester, NH (city) Hillsborough County	121	0.11
Sunrise, FL (city) Broward County	92	0.11
Harrison, NY (village) Westchester County	27	0.11
Maplewood, NJ (cdp) Essex County	27	0.11
Elmwood Park, NJ (borough) Bergen County	21	0.11
Chappaqua, NY (cdp) Westchester County	10	0.11
Maywood, NJ (borough) Bergen County	10	0.11
Budd Lake, NJ (cdp) Morris County	9	0.11
Palm Springs North, FL (cdp) Miami-Dade County	6	0.11
Suncook, NH (cdp) Merrimack County	6	0.11
Valhalla, NY (cdp) Westchester County	6	0.11
Island Park, NY (village) Nassau County	5	0.11
Stanhope, NJ (borough) Sussex County	4	0.11
Leonardo, NJ (cdp) Monmouth County	3	0.11
Moonachie, NJ (borough) Bergen County	3	0.11
Roanoke, TX (city) Denton County	3	0.11
Terra Mar, FL (cdp) Broward County	3	0.11
Forest Home, NY (cdp) Tompkins County	1	0.11
Rural Valley, PA (borough) Armstrong County	1	0.11
New Rochelle, NY (city) Westchester County	72	0.10
Tamiami, FL (cdp) Miami-Dade County	56	0.10
Union, NJ (cdp) Union County	52	0.10
Coral Gables, FL (city) Miami-Dade County	44	0.10
North Miami Beach, FL (city) Miami-Dade County	40	0.10
Westchester, FL (cdp) Miami-Dade County	29	0.10
Rahway, NJ (city) Union County	27	0.10
University Park, FL (cdp) Miami-Dade County	27	0.10

Notes: (cdp) census designated place; Refer to the Explanation of Data in the front of the book for more detailed information.

Hispanic: Uruguayan

Top 150 Places Sorted by Percent

(Based on places with populations of 10,000 or more)

Place	Number	%
Dover, NJ (town) Morris County	157	0.86
West Orange, NJ (cdp) Essex County	384	0.85
Ossining, NY (village) Westchester County	179	0.75
Elizabeth, NJ (city) Union County	772	0.64
Leominster, MA (city) Worcester County	265	0.64
Orange, NJ (cdp) Essex County	190	0.58
Ossining, NY (town) Westchester County	205	0.56
Harrison, NJ (town) Hudson County	66	0.46
Fitchburg, MA (city) Worcester County	142	0.36
Port Chester, NY (village) Westchester County	95	0.34
Roselle Park, NJ (borough) Union County	39	0.29
Rye, NY (town) Westchester County	122	0.28
Hillside, NJ (cdp) Union County	59	0.27
Miami Beach, FL (city) Miami-Dade County	222	0.25
Kearny, NJ (town) Hudson County	98	0.24
Peekskill, NY (city) Westchester County	49	0.22
Roselle, NJ (borough) Union County	44	0.21
The Crossings, FL (cdp) Miami-Dade County	48	0.20
Weehawken, NJ (township) Hudson County	27	0.20
Guttenberg, NJ (town) Hudson County	22	0.20
Ojus, FL (cdp) Miami-Dade County	31	0.19
Sunny Isles Beach, FL (city) Miami-Dade County	29	0.19
North Bergen, NJ (township) Hudson County	104	0.18
Kendale Lakes, FL (cdp) Miami-Dade County	100	0.18
Carteret, NJ (borough) Middlesex County	37	0.18
The Hammocks, FL (cdp) Miami-Dade County	79	0.17
Greenacres, FL (city) Palm Beach County	48	0.17
Doral, FL (cdp) Miami-Dade County	35	0.17
Mamaroneck, NY (village) Westchester County	31	0.17
Union City, NJ (city) Hudson County	100	0.15
Country Club, FL (cdp) Miami-Dade County	56	0.15
Glenvar Heights, FL (cdp) Miami-Dade County	24	0.15
Belleville, NJ (cdp) Essex County	50	0.14
Oakland Park, FL (city) Broward County	43	0.14
Ives Estates, FL (cdp) Miami-Dade County	25	0.14
New Milford, NJ (borough) Bergen County	23	0.14
Potomac, MD (cdp) Montgomery County	58	0.13
Kendall West, FL (cdp) Miami-Dade County	48	0.13
Lilburn, GA (city) Gwinnett County	15	0.13
Stamford, CT (city) Fairfield County	138	0.12
Greenwich, CT (town) Fairfield County	74	0.12
Fountainbleau, FL (cdp) Miami-Dade County	71	0.12
Linden, NJ (city) Union County	46	0.12
Coral Terrace, FL (cdp) Miami-Dade County	30	0.12
Mount Olive, NJ (township) Morris County	28	0.12
Palm Springs, FL (village) Palm Beach County	14	0.12
Putnam Valley, NY (town) Putnam County	13	0.12
Princeton, FL (cdp) Miami-Dade County	12	0.12
Manchester, NH (city) Hillsborough County	121	0.11
Sunrise, FL (city) Broward County	92	0.11
Harrison, NY (village) Westchester County	27	0.11
Maplewood, NJ (cdp) Essex County	27	0.11
Elmwood Park, NJ (borough) Bergen County	21	0.11
New Rochelle, NY (city) Westchester County	72	0.10
Tamiami, FL (cdp) Miami-Dade County	56	0.10
Union, NJ (cdp) Union County	52	0.10
Coral Gables, FL (city) Miami-Dade County	44	0.10
North Miami Beach, FL (city) Miami-Dade County	40	0.10
Westchester, FL (cdp) Miami-Dade County	29	0.10
Rahway, NJ (city) Union County	27	0.10
University Park, FL (cdp) Miami-Dade County	27	0.10
New Castle, NY (town) Westchester County	17	0.10
Sandalfoot Cove, FL (cdp) Palm Beach County	16	0.10
Newark, NJ (city) Essex County	239	0.09
Kendall, FL (cdp) Miami-Dade County	65	0.09
Parsippany-Troy Hills, NJ (township) Morris County	45	0.09
Weston, FL (city) Broward County	44	0.09
West New York, NJ (town) Hudson County	42	0.09
Cortlandt, NY (town) Westchester County	35	0.09
Aventura, FL (city) Miami-Dade County	24	0.09
Cutler Ridge, FL (cdp) Miami-Dade County	22	0.09
Avenel, NJ (cdp) Middlesex County	16	0.09
North Bay Shore, NY (cdp) Suffolk County	14	0.09
Fords, NJ (cdp) Middlesex County	13	0.09
South Miami, FL (city) Miami-Dade County	10	0.09

Place	Number	%
West Paterson, NJ (borough) Passaic County	10	0.09
Hollywood, FL (city) Broward County	113	0.08
Coral Springs, FL (city) Broward County	99	0.08
Wellington, FL (village) Palm Beach County	31	0.08
Hallandale, FL (city) Broward County	28	0.08
Lake Worth, FL (city) Palm Beach County	28	0.08
Long Beach, NY (city) Nassau County	27	0.08
Garfield, NJ (city) Bergen County	25	0.08
Livingston, NJ (cdp) Essex County	22	0.08
Roxbury, NJ (township) Morris County	19	0.08
Cutler, FL (cdp) Miami-Dade County	14	0.08
Tysons Corner, VA (cdp) Fairfax County	14	0.08
North Valley Stream, NY (cdp) Nassau County	12	0.08
Springfield, NJ (cdp) Union County	12	0.08
Clark, NJ (cdp) Union County	11	0.08
Tarrytown, NY (village) Westchester County	9	0.08
Country Walk, FL (cdp) Miami-Dade County	8	0.08
West Palm Beach, FL (city) Palm Beach County	56	0.07
Old Bridge, NJ (township) Middlesex County	44	0.07
Brentwood, NY (cdp) Suffolk County	36	0.07
Perth Amboy, NJ (city) Middlesex County	31	0.07
Hackensack, NJ (city) Bergen County	30	0.07
Palm Coast, FL (city) Flagler County	22	0.07
South Miami Heights, FL (cdp) Miami-Dade County	22	0.07
East Hampton, NY (town) Suffolk County	14	0.07
Lake Worth Corridor, FL (cdp) Palm Beach County	13	0.07
Rutherford, NJ (borough) Bergen County	13	0.07
Hopatcong, NJ (borough) Sussex County	11	0.07
Lincolnia, VA (cdp) Fairfax County	11	0.07
Fairview, NJ (borough) Bergen County	9	0.07
Miami Springs, FL (city) Miami-Dade County	9	0.07
Westwood Lakes, FL (cdp) Miami-Dade County	9	0.07
Hooksett, NH (town) Merrimack County	8	0.07
Meadow Woods, FL (cdp) Orange County	8	0.07
North Castle, NY (town) Westchester County	8	0.07
Miami, FL (city) Miami-Dade County	221	0.06
Pembroke Pines, FL (city) Broward County	78	0.06
Woodbridge, NJ (township) Middlesex County	60	0.06
Plantation, FL (city) Broward County	50	0.06
Miramar, FL (city) Broward County	45	0.06
Bethesda, MD (cdp) Montgomery County	33	0.06
Tamarac, FL (city) Broward County	32	0.06
Rockville, MD (city) Montgomery County	30	0.06
Bloomfield, NJ (cdp) Essex County	27	0.06
Coconut Creek, FL (city) Broward County	26	0.06
North Bethesda, MD (cdp) Montgomery County	23	0.06
West Springfield, VA (cdp) Fairfax County	18	0.06
Melrose Park, IL (village) Cook County	13	0.06
Lynbrook, NY (village) Nassau County	12	0.06
Morris, NJ (township) Morris County	12	0.06
Pinecrest, FL (village) Miami-Dade County	12	0.06
North New Hyde Park, NY (cdp) Nassau County	8	0.06
North Lindenhurst, NY (cdp) Suffolk County	7	0.06
Richmond Heights, OH (city) Cuyahoga County	7	0.06
Key Biscayne, FL (village) Miami-Dade County	6	0.06
Hialeah, FL (city) Miami-Dade County	118	0.05
Paterson, NJ (city) Passaic County	71	0.05
Lauderhill, FL (city) Broward County	26	0.05
Kissimmee, FL (city) Osceola County	22	0.05
Sayreville, NJ (borough) Middlesex County	21	0.05
Valley Stream, NY (village) Nassau County	20	0.05
McLean, VA (cdp) Fairfax County	19	0.05
North Atlanta, GA (cdp) De Kalb County	19	0.05
Mission Bend, TX (cdp) Fort Bend County	16	0.05
Oakton, VA (cdp) Fairfax County	16	0.05
Mamaroneck, NY (town) Westchester County	15	0.05
Deer Park, NY (cdp) Suffolk County	14	0.05
Richmond West, FL (cdp) Miami-Dade County	14	0.05
West Warwick, RI (cdp) Kent County	14	0.05
Duluth, GA (city) Gwinnett County	12	0.05
Miami Lakes, FL (cdp) Miami-Dade County	12	0.05
Hialeah Gardens, FL (city) Miami-Dade County	10	0.05
Jefferson, NJ (township) Morris County	10	0.05
Morristown, NJ (town) Morris County	10	0.05
Mineola, NY (village) Nassau County	9	0.05

Notes: (cdp) census designated place; Refer to the Explanation of Data in the front of the book for more detailed information.

Hispanic: Venezuelan

Top 150 Places Sorted by Number

(Based on all places, regardless of population)

Place	Number	%
New York, NY (city) New York City	6,713	0.08
Weston, FL (city) Broward County	2,020	4.10
Miami, FL (city) Miami-Dade County	1,959	0.54
Fountainbleau, FL (cdp) Miami-Dade County	1,868	3.14
Doral, FL (cdp) Miami-Dade County	1,680	8.22
Houston, TX (city) Harris County	1,592	0.08
Miami Beach, FL (city) Miami-Dade County	1,572	1.79
The Hammocks, FL (cdp) Miami-Dade County	1,488	3.14
Pembroke Pines, FL (city) Broward County	1,242	0.90
Hialeah, FL (city) Miami-Dade County	1,117	0.49
Kendall, FL (cdp) Miami-Dade County	1,108	1.47
Kendall West, FL (cdp) Miami-Dade County	1,015	2.67
Kendale Lakes, FL (cdp) Miami-Dade County	875	1.54
Los Angeles, CA (city) Los Angeles County	790	0.02
Orlando, FL (city) Orange County	674	0.36
Boston, MA (city) Suffolk County	638	0.11
Chicago, IL (city) Cook County	600	0.02
Tamiami, FL (cdp) Miami-Dade County	583	1.06
Coral Springs, FL (city) Broward County	568	0.48
Hollywood, FL (city) Broward County	568	0.41
Sunrise, FL (city) Broward County	543	0.63
Miramar, FL (city) Broward County	499	0.69
Coral Gables, FL (city) Miami-Dade County	496	1.17
Pompano Beach, FL (city) Broward County	496	0.63
Plantation, FL (city) Broward County	468	0.56
Country Club, FL (cdp) Miami-Dade County	456	1.26
Kissimmee, FL (city) Osceola County	454	0.95
The Crossings, FL (cdp) Miami-Dade County	453	1.92
Philadelphia, PA (city) Philadelphia County	409	0.03
Austin, TX (city) Travis County	390	0.06
Davie, FL (town) Broward County	389	0.51
Richmond West, FL (cdp) Miami-Dade County	381	1.36
Tampa, FL (city) Hillsborough County	353	0.12
Glenvar Heights, FL (cdp) Miami-Dade County	332	2.04
Aventura, FL (city) Miami-Dade County	331	1.31
Fort Lauderdale, FL (city) Broward County	315	0.21
Sunny Isles Beach, FL (city) Miami-Dade County	300	1.96
Elizabeth, NJ (city) Union County	296	0.25
Saint Petersburg, FL (city) Pinellas County	284	0.11
Dallas, TX (city) Dallas County	275	0.02
San Diego, CA (city) San Diego County	268	0.02
University Park, FL (cdp) Miami-Dade County	264	0.99
Tulsa, OK (city) Tulsa County	261	0.07
Key Biscayne, FL (village) Miami-Dade County	248	2.36
Paterson, NJ (city) Passaic County	248	0.17
Arlington, VA (cdp) Arlington County	247	0.13
Washington, DC (city) District of Columbia	247	0.04
Newark, NJ (city) Essex County	246	0.09
Gainesville, FL (city) Alachua County	244	0.26
Boca Raton, FL (city) Palm Beach County	242	0.32
Miami Lakes, FL (cdp) Miami-Dade County	240	1.06
Hempstead, NY (town) Nassau County	235	0.03
San Francisco, CA (city) San Francisco County	234	0.03
Charlotte, NC (city) Mecklenburg County	230	0.04
North Miami Beach, FL (city) Miami-Dade County	222	0.54
Union City, NJ (city) Hudson County	218	0.32
Coconut Creek, FL (city) Broward County	216	0.50
North Miami, FL (city) Miami-Dade County	215	0.36
Jacksonville, FL (special city) Duval County	209	0.03
West Valley City, UT (city) Salt Lake County	203	0.19
Tamarac, FL (city) Broward County	195	0.35
San Jose, CA (city) Santa Clara County	191	0.02
Norwalk, CT (city) Fairfield County	183	0.22
Westchester, FL (cdp) Miami-Dade County	182	0.60
Columbus, OH (city) Franklin County	180	0.03
Country Walk, FL (cdp) Miami-Dade County	178	1.67
San Antonio, TX (city) Bexar County	169	0.01
Jersey City, NJ (city) Hudson County	165	0.07
Nashville-Davidson, TN (special city) Davidson County	165	0.03
Town 'n' Country, FL (cdp) Hillsborough County	160	0.22
Egypt Lake-Leto, FL (cdp) Hillsborough County	159	0.49
Deerfield Beach, FL (city) Broward County	158	0.24
Pinecrest, FL (village) Miami-Dade County	156	0.82
Phoenix, AZ (city) Maricopa County	155	0.01
Indianapolis, IN (special city) Marion County	152	0.02
North Bergen, NJ (township) Hudson County	150	0.26
West New York, NJ (town) Hudson County	148	0.32
Hallandale, FL (city) Broward County	147	0.43
Altamonte Springs, FL (city) Seminole County	147	0.36
Providence, RI (city) Providence County	147	0.08
Fort Worth, TX (city) Tarrant County	147	0.03
Sunset, FL (cdp) Miami-Dade County	146	0.85
North Bay Village, FL (city) Miami-Dade County	145	2.15
Coral Terrace, FL (cdp) Miami-Dade County	144	0.59
Clearwater, FL (city) Pinellas County	140	0.13
Miami Springs, FL (city) Miami-Dade County	139	1.01
Islip, NY (town) Suffolk County	139	0.04
Hialeah Gardens, FL (city) Miami-Dade County	138	0.72
Margate, FL (city) Broward County	136	0.25
Salt Lake City, UT (city) Salt Lake County	132	0.07
Ojus, FL (cdp) Miami-Dade County	131	0.79
Carol City, FL (cdp) Miami-Dade County	131	0.22
Cutler, FL (cdp) Miami-Dade County	130	0.75
Alexandria, VA (independent city) Alexandria city	129	0.10
Atlanta, GA (city) Fulton County	129	0.03
Provo, UT (city) Utah County	126	0.12
Yonkers, NY (city) Westchester County	126	0.06
Pittsburgh, PA (city) Allegheny County	121	0.04
Ives Estates, FL (cdp) Miami-Dade County	120	0.68
Three Lakes, FL (cdp) Miami-Dade County	119	1.71
Irving, TX (city) Dallas County	118	0.06
Cutler Ridge, FL (cdp) Miami-Dade County	117	0.47
Wellington, FL (village) Palm Beach County	117	0.31
Brookline, MA (cdp) Norfolk County	116	0.20
Sandy Springs, GA (cdp) Fulton County	116	0.14
Oak Ridge, FL (cdp) Orange County	115	0.51
Cambridge, MA (city) Middlesex County	112	0.11
Lauderhill, FL (city) Broward County	111	0.19
Raleigh, NC (city) Wake County	111	0.04
Denver, CO (city) Denver County	108	0.02
South Miami Heights, FL (cdp) Miami-Dade County	106	0.32
Orem, UT (city) Utah County	106	0.13
Seattle, WA (city) King County	106	0.02
Oakland Park, FL (city) Broward County	104	0.34
Greater Carrollwood, FL (cdp) Hillsborough County	104	0.31
Brookhaven, NY (town) Suffolk County	103	0.02
North Lauderdale, FL (city) Broward County	102	0.32
Stamford, CT (city) Fairfield County	99	0.08
Wichita, KS (city) Sedgwick County	99	0.03
Oklahoma City, OK (city) Oklahoma County	99	0.02
West Palm Beach, FL (city) Palm Beach County	98	0.12
Mesa, AZ (city) Maricopa County	97	0.02
Madison, WI (city) Dane County	95	0.05
Norman, OK (city) Cleveland County	94	0.10
Tallahassee, FL (city) Leon County	92	0.06
College Station, TX (city) Brazos County	90	0.13
Oakland, CA (city) Alameda County	90	0.02
Tucson, AZ (city) Pima County	90	0.02
Sweetwater, FL (city) Miami-Dade County	89	0.63
Taylorsville, UT (city) Salt Lake County	89	0.15
Brandon, FL (cdp) Hillsborough County	89	0.11
Ann Arbor, MI (city) Washtenaw County	88	0.08
Germantown, MD (cdp) Montgomery County	87	0.16
Boca Del Mar, FL (cdp) Palm Beach County	85	0.39
Plano, TX (city) Collin County	85	0.04
Arlington, TX (city) Tarrant County	85	0.03
Saint Paul, MN (city) Ramsey County	85	0.03
Aurora, CO (city) Arapahoe County	84	0.03
Lexington-Fayette, KY (special city) Fayette County	84	0.03
New Orleans, LA (city) Orleans Parish	83	0.02
South Miami, FL (city) Miami-Dade County	81	0.75
Metairie, LA (cdp) Jefferson Parish	81	0.06
Greensboro, NC (city) Guilford County	81	0.04
North Hempstead, NY (town) Nassau County	81	0.04
Baltimore, MD (independent city) Baltimore city	81	0.01
Meadow Woods, FL (cdp) Orange County	79	0.70
Palm Bay, FL (city) Brevard County	79	0.10
The Woodlands, TX (cdp) Montgomery County	78	0.14
Roswell, GA (city) Fulton County	78	0.10
Columbus, GA (special city) Muscogee County	76	0.04

Notes: (cdp) census designated place; Refer to the Explanation of Data in the front of the book for more detailed information.

Hispanic: Venezuelan

Top 150 Places Sorted by Percent

(Based on all places, regardless of population)

Place	Number	%
Doral, FL (cdp) Miami-Dade County	1,680	8.22
Weston, FL (city) Broward County	2,020	4.10
Fisher Island, FL (cdp) Miami-Dade County	19	4.07
Fountainbleau, FL (cdp) Miami-Dade County	1,868	3.14
The Hammocks, FL (cdp) Miami-Dade County	1,488	3.14
Kendall West, FL (cdp) Miami-Dade County	1,015	2.67
Lazy Lake, FL (village) Broward County	1	2.63
Key Biscayne, FL (village) Miami-Dade County	248	2.36
North Bay Village, FL (city) Miami-Dade County	145	2.15
Glenvar Heights, FL (cdp) Miami-Dade County	332	2.04
Hillsboro Pines, FL (cdp) Broward County	8	1.97
Sunny Isles Beach, FL (city) Miami-Dade County	300	1.96
The Crossings, FL (cdp) Miami-Dade County	453	1.92
Miami Beach, FL (city) Miami-Dade County	1,572	1.79
Three Lakes, FL (cdp) Miami-Dade County	119	1.71
Country Walk, FL (cdp) Miami-Dade County	178	1.67
Sandyville, IA (city) Warren County	1	1.64
Virginia Gardens, FL (village) Miami-Dade County	37	1.58
Kendale Lakes, FL (cdp) Miami-Dade County	875	1.54
Kendall, FL (cdp) Miami-Dade County	1,108	1.47
Dawson, NE (village) Richardson County	3	1.44
Surfside, FL (town) Miami-Dade County	69	1.41
Richmond West, FL (cdp) Miami-Dade County	381	1.36
Aventura, FL (city) Miami-Dade County	331	1.31
Golden Beach, FL (town) Miami-Dade County	12	1.31
Country Club, FL (cdp) Miami-Dade County	456	1.26
Bal Harbour, FL (village) Miami-Dade County	40	1.21
Branchville, AL (town) Saint Clair County	10	1.21
Cloud Lake, FL (town) Palm Beach County	2	1.20
Coral Gables, FL (city) Miami-Dade County	496	1.17
Forest Home, NY (cdp) Tompkins County	11	1.17
Bay Harbor Islands, FL (town) Miami-Dade County	59	1.15
Tamiami, FL (cdp) Miami-Dade County	583	1.06
Miami Lakes, FL (cdp) Miami-Dade County	240	1.06
Estates of Fort Lauderdale, FL (cdp) Broward County	19	1.06
Halcott, NY (town) Greene County	2	1.04
Miami Springs, FL (city) Miami-Dade County	139	1.01
University Park, FL (cdp) Miami-Dade County	264	0.99
Kissimmee, FL (city) Osceola County	454	0.95
Pembroke Pines, FL (city) Broward County	1,242	0.90
Chambers Estates, FL (cdp) Broward County	31	0.87
Sunset, FL (cdp) Miami-Dade County	146	0.85
Babson Park, FL (cdp) Polk County	10	0.85
Lakes by the Bay, FL (cdp) Miami-Dade County	75	0.83
Pinecrest, FL (village) Miami-Dade County	156	0.82
Ojus, FL (cdp) Miami-Dade County	131	0.79
Ramblewood East, FL (cdp) Broward County	11	0.79
Village Park, FL (cdp) Broward County	7	0.78
Sky Lake, FL (cdp) Orange County	43	0.76
Hickory Hills, MS (cdp) Jackson County	23	0.76
Haverhill, FL (town) Palm Beach County	11	0.76
Cutler, FL (cdp) Miami-Dade County	130	0.75
South Miami, FL (city) Miami-Dade County	81	0.75
Langley, OK (town) Mayes County	5	0.75
Boca Pointe, FL (cdp) Palm Beach County	24	0.73
Hialeah Gardens, FL (city) Miami-Dade County	138	0.72
Unity Village, MO (village) Jackson County	1	0.71
Meadow Woods, FL (cdp) Orange County	79	0.70
Biscayne Park, FL (village) Miami-Dade County	23	0.70
Miramar, FL (city) Broward County	499	0.69
Ives Estates, FL (cdp) Miami-Dade County	120	0.68
Mission Bay, FL (cdp) Palm Beach County	19	0.65
Fox Lake, MT (cdp) Richland County	1	0.64
Sunrise, FL (city) Broward County	543	0.63
Pompano Beach, FL (city) Broward County	496	0.63
Sweetwater, FL (city) Miami-Dade County	89	0.63
Coldstream, KY (city) Jefferson County	6	0.63
Hunters Creek, FL (cdp) Orange County	58	0.62
Westchester, FL (cdp) Miami-Dade County	182	0.60
West Miami, FL (city) Miami-Dade County	35	0.60
Barton Hills, MI (village) Washtenaw County	2	0.60
Coral Terrace, FL (cdp) Miami-Dade County	144	0.59
Palm Aire, FL (cdp) Broward County	9	0.58
East Ellijay, GA (city) Gilmer County	4	0.57
Johannesburg, CA (cdp) Kern County	1	0.57
Plantation, FL (city) Broward County	468	0.56
Miami, FL (city) Miami-Dade County	1,959	0.54
North Miami Beach, FL (city) Miami-Dade County	222	0.54
Richmond Heights, FL (cdp) Miami-Dade County	44	0.52
Pine Island Ridge, FL (cdp) Broward County	27	0.52
Hancock, VT (town) Addison County	2	0.52
Davie, FL (town) Broward County	389	0.51
Oak Ridge, FL (cdp) Orange County	115	0.51
Coconut Creek, FL (city) Broward County	216	0.50
Olympia Heights, FL (cdp) Miami-Dade County	67	0.50
Hialeah, FL (city) Miami-Dade County	1,117	0.49
Egypt Lake-Leto, FL (cdp) Hillsborough County	159	0.49
Miami Shores, FL (village) Miami-Dade County	51	0.49
Coral Springs, FL (city) Broward County	568	0.48
Cutler Ridge, FL (cdp) Miami-Dade County	117	0.47
Wesley Chapel, FL (cdp) Pasco County	27	0.47
Southchase, FL (cdp) Orange County	22	0.47
Friendship Village, MD (cdp) Montgomery County	21	0.47
Keene, TX (city) Johnson County	23	0.46
Tierra Verde, FL (cdp) Pinellas County	16	0.45
Lakeside Park, KY (city) Kenton County	13	0.45
Stuart, OK (town) Hughes County	1	0.45
Goldenrod, FL (cdp) Seminole County	57	0.44
Westwood Lakes, FL (cdp) Miami-Dade County	53	0.44
Madisonville, LA (town) Saint Tammany Parish	3	0.44
Notus, ID (city) Canyon County	2	0.44
Goshen, VT (town) Addison County	1	0.44
Hallandale, FL (city) Broward County	147	0.43
Guttenberg, NJ (town) Hudson County	47	0.43
North Andrews Gardens, FL (cdp) Broward County	42	0.43
Gulf Park Estates, MS (cdp) Jackson County	18	0.42
Norwood, MI (township) Charlevoix County	3	0.42
Cragsmoor, NY (cdp) Ulster County	2	0.42
Hollywood, FL (city) Broward County	568	0.41
East Perrine, FL (cdp) Miami-Dade County	29	0.41
Wilder, ID (city) Canyon County	6	0.41
Occoquan, VA (town) Prince William County	3	0.40
Worden, MT (cdp) Yellowstone County	2	0.40
Boca Del Mar, FL (cdp) Palm Beach County	85	0.39
South Ashburnham, MA (cdp) Worcester County	4	0.39
Cheval, FL (cdp) Hillsborough County	29	0.38
Watkinsville, GA (town) Oconee County	8	0.38
Laurelville, OH (village) Hocking County	2	0.38
Page Park, FL (cdp) Lee County	2	0.38
Rosston, AR (town) Nevada County	1	0.38
Pine Castle, FL (cdp) Orange County	33	0.37
Broadview Park, FL (cdp) Broward County	25	0.37
Egremont, MA (town) Berkshire County	5	0.37
Jamaica Beach, TX (city) Galveston County	4	0.37
McCalmont, PA (township) Jefferson County	4	0.37
Albany, OH (village) Athens County	3	0.37
Milroy, MN (city) Redwood County	1	0.37
Orlando, FL (city) Orange County	674	0.36
North Miami, FL (city) Miami-Dade County	215	0.36
Altamonte Springs, FL (city) Seminole County	147	0.36
Princeton, FL (cdp) Miami-Dade County	36	0.36
Broadview-Pompano Park, FL (cdp) Broward County	19	0.36
Medley, FL (town) Miami-Dade County	4	0.36
Wynnedale, IN (town) Marion County	1	0.36
Tamarac, FL (city) Broward County	195	0.35
Andover, FL (cdp) Miami-Dade County	30	0.35
Lauderdale-by-the-Sea, FL (town) Broward County	9	0.35
Wright City, OK (town) McCurtain County	3	0.35
Fishers Island, NY (cdp) Suffolk County	1	0.35
Oakland Park, FL (city) Broward County	104	0.34
Cinco Ranch, TX (cdp) Fort Bend County	38	0.34
Delhi, MN (township) Redwood County	1	0.34
South River, NJ (borough) Middlesex County	50	0.33
Parkland, FL (city) Broward County	46	0.33
Bishopville, SC (city) Lee County	12	0.33
Saint Regis Park, KY (city) Jefferson County	5	0.33
Kensington, NY (village) Nassau County	4	0.33
Dewey Beach, DE (town) Sussex County	1	0.33
Boca Raton, FL (city) Palm Beach County	242	0.32
Union City, NJ (city) Hudson County	218	0.32

Notes: (cdp) census designated place; Refer to the Explanation of Data in the front of the book for more detailed information.

Hispanic: Venezuelan

Top 150 Places Sorted by Percent

(Based on places with populations of 10,000 or more)

Place	Number	%
Doral, FL (cdp) Miami-Dade County	1,680	8.22
Weston, FL (city) Broward County	2,020	4.10
Fountainbleau, FL (cdp) Miami-Dade County	1,868	3.14
The Hammocks, FL (cdp) Miami-Dade County	1,488	3.14
Kendall West, FL (cdp) Miami-Dade County	1,015	2.67
Key Biscayne, FL (village) Miami-Dade County	248	2.36
Glenvar Heights, FL (cdp) Miami-Dade County	332	2.04
Sunny Isles Beach, FL (city) Miami-Dade County	300	1.96
The Crossings, FL (cdp) Miami-Dade County	453	1.92
Miami Beach, FL (city) Miami-Dade County	1,572	1.79
Country Walk, FL (cdp) Miami-Dade County	178	1.67
Kendale Lakes, FL (cdp) Miami-Dade County	875	1.54
Kendall, FL (cdp) Miami-Dade County	1,108	1.47
Richmond West, FL (cdp) Miami-Dade County	381	1.36
Aventura, FL (city) Miami-Dade County	331	1.31
Country Club, FL (cdp) Miami-Dade County	456	1.26
Coral Gables, FL (city) Miami-Dade County	496	1.17
Tamiami, FL (cdp) Miami-Dade County	583	1.06
Miami Lakes, FL (cdp) Miami-Dade County	240	1.06
Miami Springs, FL (city) Miami-Dade County	139	1.01
University Park, FL (cdp) Miami-Dade County	264	0.99
Kissimmee, FL (city) Osceola County	454	0.95
Pembroke Pines, FL (city) Broward County	1,242	0.90
Sunset, FL (cdp) Miami-Dade County	146	0.85
Pinecrest, FL (village) Miami-Dade County	156	0.82
Ojus, FL (cdp) Miami-Dade County	131	0.79
Cutler, FL (cdp) Miami-Dade County	130	0.75
South Miami, FL (city) Miami-Dade County	81	0.75
Hialeah Gardens, FL (city) Miami-Dade County	138	0.72
Meadow Woods, FL (cdp) Orange County	79	0.70
Miramar, FL (city) Broward County	499	0.69
Ives Estates, FL (cdp) Miami-Dade County	120	0.68
Sunrise, FL (city) Broward County	543	0.63
Pompano Beach, FL (city) Broward County	496	0.63
Sweetwater, FL (city) Miami-Dade County	89	0.63
Westchester, FL (cdp) Miami-Dade County	182	0.60
Coral Terrace, FL (cdp) Miami-Dade County	144	0.59
Plantation, FL (city) Broward County	468	0.56
Miami, FL (city) Miami-Dade County	1,959	0.54
North Miami Beach, FL (city) Miami-Dade County	222	0.54
Davie, FL (town) Broward County	389	0.51
Oak Ridge, FL (cdp) Orange County	115	0.51
Coconut Creek, FL (city) Broward County	216	0.50
Olympia Heights, FL (cdp) Miami-Dade County	67	0.50
Hialeah, FL (city) Miami-Dade County	1,117	0.49
Egypt Lake-Leto, FL (cdp) Hillsborough County	159	0.49
Miami Shores, FL (village) Miami-Dade County	51	0.49
Coral Springs, FL (city) Broward County	568	0.48
Cutler Ridge, FL (cdp) Miami-Dade County	117	0.47
Goldenrod, FL (cdp) Seminole County	57	0.44
Westwood Lakes, FL (cdp) Miami-Dade County	53	0.44
Hallandale, FL (city) Broward County	147	0.43
Guttenberg, NJ (town) Hudson County	47	0.43
Hollywood, FL (city) Broward County	568	0.41
Boca Del Mar, FL (cdp) Palm Beach County	85	0.39
Orlando, FL (city) Orange County	674	0.36
North Miami, FL (city) Miami-Dade County	215	0.36
Altamonte Springs, FL (city) Seminole County	147	0.36
Princeton, FL (cdp) Miami-Dade County	36	0.36
Tamarac, FL (city) Broward County	195	0.35
Oakland Park, FL (city) Broward County	104	0.34
Cinco Ranch, TX (cdp) Fort Bend County	38	0.34
South River, NJ (borough) Middlesex County	50	0.33
Parkland, FL (city) Broward County	46	0.33
Boca Raton, FL (city) Palm Beach County	242	0.32
Union City, NJ (city) Hudson County	218	0.32
West New York, NJ (town) Hudson County	148	0.32
South Miami Heights, FL (cdp) Miami-Dade County	106	0.32
North Lauderdale, FL (city) Broward County	102	0.32
Wellington, FL (village) Palm Beach County	117	0.31
Greater Carrollwood, FL (cdp) Hillsborough County	104	0.31
Sandalfoot Cove, FL (cdp) Palm Beach County	49	0.30
Harrison, NJ (town) Hudson County	41	0.28
Forest City, FL (cdp) Seminole County	35	0.28
South Salt Lake, UT (city) Salt Lake County	60	0.27
Yeehaw Junction, FL (cdp) Osceola County	58	0.27
Gainesville, FL (city) Alachua County	244	0.26
North Bergen, NJ (township) Hudson County	150	0.26
Cooper City, FL (city) Broward County	73	0.26
Greater Northdale, FL (cdp) Hillsborough County	54	0.26
Union Park, FL (cdp) Orange County	27	0.26
Elizabeth, NJ (city) Union County	296	0.25
Margate, FL (city) Broward County	136	0.25
Millcreek, UT (cdp) Salt Lake County	75	0.25
Deerfield Beach, FL (city) Broward County	158	0.24
Temple Terrace, FL (city) Hillsborough County	51	0.24
Citrus Park, FL (cdp) Hillsborough County	49	0.24
Dania Beach, FL (city) Broward County	49	0.24
Palmetto Estates, FL (cdp) Miami-Dade County	33	0.24
Homestead, FL (city) Miami-Dade County	74	0.23
Central Falls, RI (city) Providence County	44	0.23
New Territory, TX (cdp) Fort Bend County	32	0.23
Citrus Ridge, FL (cdp) Lake County	28	0.23
Norwalk, CT (city) Fairfield County	183	0.22
Town 'n' Country, FL (cdp) Hillsborough County	160	0.22
Carol City, FL (cdp) Miami-Dade County	131	0.22
Palm Springs, FL (village) Palm Beach County	26	0.22
Azalea Park, FL (cdp) Orange County	24	0.22
Fort Lauderdale, FL (city) Broward County	315	0.21
Clinton, MA (town) Worcester County	28	0.21
Brookline, MA (cdp) Norfolk County	116	0.20
Kearns, UT (cdp) Salt Lake County	66	0.20
Casselberry, FL (city) Seminole County	46	0.20
Fairview, NJ (borough) Bergen County	27	0.20
Wilton Manors, FL (city) Broward County	25	0.20
West Valley City, UT (city) Salt Lake County	203	0.19
Lauderhill, FL (city) Broward County	111	0.19
Montgomery Village, MD (cdp) Montgomery County	74	0.19
Ocean, NJ (township) Monmouth County	50	0.19
Stafford, TX (city) Fort Bend County	30	0.19
Poinciana, FL (cdp) Osceola County	26	0.19
Greenacres, FL (city) Palm Beach County	50	0.18
Leisure City, FL (cdp) Miami-Dade County	40	0.18
Paterson, NJ (city) Passaic County	248	0.17
Apopka, FL (city) Orange County	44	0.17
Lake Worth Corridor, FL (cdp) Palm Beach County	31	0.17
Lincolnia, VA (cdp) Fairfax County	27	0.17
Menomonie, WI (city) Dunn County	25	0.17
Weehawken, NJ (township) Hudson County	23	0.17
Sugar Hill, GA (city) Gwinnett County	19	0.17
Germantown, MD (cdp) Montgomery County	87	0.16
Oviedo, FL (city) Seminole County	42	0.16
Royal Palm Beach, FL (village) Palm Beach County	34	0.16
North Druid Hills, GA (cdp) De Kalb County	31	0.16
Palm River-Clair Mel, FL (cdp) Hillsborough County	29	0.16
West University Place, TX (city) Harris County	23	0.16
Lilburn, GA (city) Gwinnett County	18	0.16
Marathon, FL (city) Monroe County	16	0.16
Taylorsville, UT (city) Salt Lake County	89	0.15
Kearny, NJ (town) Hudson County	59	0.15
Golden Glades, FL (cdp) Miami-Dade County	48	0.15
Mission Bend, TX (cdp) Fort Bend County	46	0.15
Magna, UT (cdp) Salt Lake County	35	0.15
Golden Gate, FL (cdp) Collier County	32	0.15
East Hampton, NY (town) Suffolk County	30	0.15
Sandy Springs, GA (cdp) Fulton County	116	0.14
The Woodlands, TX (cdp) Montgomery County	78	0.14
North Bethesda, MD (cdp) Montgomery County	55	0.14
Cliffside Park, NJ (borough) Bergen County	33	0.14
Lodi, NJ (borough) Bergen County	33	0.14
Kennesaw, GA (city) Cobb County	31	0.14
Redland, MD (cdp) Montgomery County	23	0.14
Lockhart, FL (cdp) Orange County	18	0.14
Maitland, FL (city) Orange County	17	0.14
Bound Brook, NJ (borough) Somerset County	14	0.14
Arlington, VA (cdp) Arlington County	247	0.13
Clearwater, FL (city) Pinellas County	140	0.13
Orem, UT (city) Utah County	106	0.13
College Station, TX (city) Brazos County	90	0.13
Palm Beach Gardens, FL (city) Palm Beach County	45	0.13

Notes: (cdp) census designated place; Refer to the Explanation of Data in the front of the book for more detailed information.

Hispanic: Other South American

Top 150 Places Sorted by Number

(Based on all places, regardless of population)

Place	Number	%
New York, NY (city) New York City	6,836	0.09
Los Angeles, CA (city) Los Angeles County	3,064	0.08
Chicago, IL (city) Cook County	761	0.03
Houston, TX (city) Harris County	676	0.03
San Francisco, CA (city) San Francisco County	601	0.08
Hempstead, NY (town) Nassau County	498	0.07
Arlington, VA (cdp) Arlington County	462	0.24
Jersey City, NJ (city) Hudson County	373	0.16
Elizabeth, NJ (city) Union County	356	0.30
San Jose, CA (city) Santa Clara County	313	0.03
San Diego, CA (city) San Diego County	284	0.02
Glendale, CA (city) Los Angeles County	278	0.14
Miami Beach, FL (city) Miami-Dade County	257	0.29
Miami, FL (city) Miami-Dade County	249	0.07
Islip, NY (town) Suffolk County	241	0.07
Newark, NJ (city) Essex County	240	0.09
Anaheim, CA (city) Orange County	237	0.07
Paterson, NJ (city) Passaic County	230	0.15
Boston, MA (city) Suffolk County	228	0.04
Brookhaven, NY (town) Suffolk County	220	0.05
Union City, NJ (city) Hudson County	213	0.32
North Bergen, NJ (township) Hudson County	212	0.36
Washington, DC (city) District of Columbia	194	0.03
Hollywood, FL (city) Broward County	188	0.13
Downey, CA (city) Los Angeles County	187	0.17
North Hempstead, NY (town) Nassau County	186	0.08
Pembroke Pines, FL (city) Broward County	185	0.13
Santa Ana, CA (city) Orange County	183	0.05
Santa Clarita, CA (city) Los Angeles County	182	0.12
Annandale, VA (cdp) Fairfax County	176	0.32
Hialeah, FL (city) Miami-Dade County	174	0.08
Torrance, CA (city) Los Angeles County	168	0.12
Burbank, CA (city) Los Angeles County	166	0.17
San Mateo, CA (city) San Mateo County	164	0.18
Long Beach, CA (city) Los Angeles County	163	0.04
Oyster Bay, NY (town) Nassau County	159	0.05
The Hammocks, FL (cdp) Miami-Dade County	157	0.33
San Antonio, TX (city) Bexar County	157	0.01
Fountainbleau, FL (cdp) Miami-Dade County	156	0.26
Coral Springs, FL (city) Broward County	156	0.13
Pasadena, CA (city) Los Angeles County	156	0.12
Philadelphia, PA (city) Philadelphia County	155	0.01
West New York, NJ (town) Hudson County	154	0.34
Stamford, CT (city) Fairfield County	152	0.13
Kendall, FL (cdp) Miami-Dade County	147	0.20
Phoenix, AZ (city) Maricopa County	147	0.01
Yonkers, NY (city) Westchester County	141	0.07
Alexandria, VA (independent city) Alexandria city	137	0.11
Weston, FL (city) Broward County	130	0.26
South Gate, CA (city) Los Angeles County	128	0.13
Dallas, TX (city) Dallas County	128	0.01
Huntington Beach, CA (city) Orange County	125	0.07
Kendale Lakes, FL (cdp) Miami-Dade County	123	0.22
Wheaton-Glenmont, MD (cdp) Montgomery County	123	0.21
Charlotte, NC (city) Mecklenburg County	120	0.02
Orlando, FL (city) Orange County	119	0.06
Las Vegas, NV (city) Clark County	115	0.02
Kearny, NJ (town) Hudson County	114	0.28
West Covina, CA (city) Los Angeles County	109	0.10
Passaic, NJ (city) Passaic County	108	0.16
Daly City, CA (city) San Mateo County	107	0.10
Harrison, NJ (town) Hudson County	106	0.73
Seattle, WA (city) King County	106	0.02
Miramar, FL (city) Broward County	105	0.14
Sunrise, FL (city) Broward County	105	0.12
Oakland, CA (city) Alameda County	105	0.03
Kendall West, FL (cdp) Miami-Dade County	103	0.27
Rye, NY (town) Westchester County	103	0.23
Brentwood, NY (cdp) Suffolk County	102	0.19
Austin, TX (city) Travis County	102	0.02
Irvine, CA (city) Orange County	101	0.07
Hayward, CA (city) Alameda County	100	0.07
Ontario, CA (city) San Bernardino County	100	0.06
Babylon, NY (town) Suffolk County	100	0.05
Fremont, CA (city) Alameda County	100	0.05
Doral, FL (cdp) Miami-Dade County	99	0.48
Burke, VA (cdp) Fairfax County	99	0.17
Davie, FL (town) Broward County	99	0.13
Norwalk, CT (city) Fairfield County	98	0.12
Hawthorne, CA (city) Los Angeles County	96	0.11
Hartford, CT (city) Hartford County	96	0.08
Port Chester, NY (village) Westchester County	95	0.34
Plantation, FL (city) Broward County	95	0.11
Concord, CA (city) Contra Costa County	95	0.08
Tampa, FL (city) Hillsborough County	95	0.03
Mission Viejo, CA (city) Orange County	94	0.10
Orange, CA (city) Orange County	89	0.07
Rancho Cucamonga, CA (city) San Bernardino County	89	0.07
Boca Raton, FL (city) Palm Beach County	88	0.12
Palmdale, CA (city) Los Angeles County	88	0.08
Bridgeport, CT (city) Fairfield County	88	0.06
Clifton, NJ (city) Passaic County	87	0.11
New Rochelle, NY (city) Westchester County	85	0.12
Silver Spring, MD (cdp) Montgomery County	85	0.11
Richmond West, FL (cdp) Miami-Dade County	84	0.30
The Crossings, FL (cdp) Miami-Dade County	83	0.35
Gaithersburg, MD (city) Montgomery County	83	0.16
Paradise, NV (cdp) Clark County	82	0.04
Jacksonville, FL (special city) Duval County	81	0.01
Fontana, CA (city) San Bernardino County	80	0.06
North Miami Beach, FL (city) Miami-Dade County	79	0.19
White Plains, NY (city) Westchester County	78	0.15
Sunnyvale, CA (city) Santa Clara County	78	0.06
Garden Grove, CA (city) Orange County	78	0.05
Tamarac, FL (city) Broward County	77	0.14
Tustin, CA (city) Orange County	77	0.11
Redwood City, CA (city) San Mateo County	76	0.10
Fullerton, CA (city) Orange County	76	0.06
Coral Gables, FL (city) Miami-Dade County	75	0.18
Simi Valley, CA (city) Ventura County	75	0.07
Ossining, NY (town) Westchester County	74	0.20
Aspen Hill, MD (cdp) Montgomery County	74	0.15
Alhambra, CA (city) Los Angeles County	74	0.09
Worcester, MA (city) Worcester County	74	0.04
Tamiami, FL (cdp) Miami-Dade County	72	0.13
Minneapolis, MN (city) Hennepin County	72	0.02
Jefferson, VA (cdp) Fairfax County	71	0.26
Lakewood, CA (city) Los Angeles County	71	0.09
Pomona, CA (city) Los Angeles County	71	0.05
Berkeley, CA (city) Alameda County	70	0.07
Montgomery Village, MD (cdp) Montgomery County	69	0.18
North Miami, FL (city) Miami-Dade County	69	0.12
Somerville, MA (city) Middlesex County	69	0.09
Providence, RI (city) Providence County	68	0.04
Ossining, NY (village) Westchester County	67	0.28
West Orange, NJ (cdp) Essex County	67	0.15
Reston, VA (cdp) Fairfax County	67	0.12
Chino Hills, CA (city) San Bernardino County	67	0.10
Fort Lauderdale, FL (city) Broward County	67	0.04
Corona, CA (city) Riverside County	66	0.05
Moreno Valley, CA (city) Riverside County	66	0.05
Riverside, CA (city) Riverside County	66	0.03
Virginia Beach, VA (independent city) Virginia Beach city	66	0.02
North Bethesda, MD (cdp) Montgomery County	65	0.17
Santa Monica, CA (city) Los Angeles County	65	0.08
Sacramento, CA (city) Sacramento County	65	0.02
Tucson, AZ (city) Pima County	65	0.01
Hallandale, FL (city) Broward County	64	0.19
Chula Vista, CA (city) San Diego County	64	0.04
Germantown, MD (cdp) Montgomery County	63	0.11
Greenwich, CT (town) Fairfield County	63	0.10
Westminster, CA (city) Orange County	63	0.07
Lincolnia, VA (cdp) Fairfax County	62	0.39
Belleville, NJ (cdp) Essex County	62	0.17
Hackensack, NJ (city) Bergen County	62	0.15
Town 'n' Country, FL (cdp) Hillsborough County	62	0.09
Plano, TX (city) Collin County	62	0.03
Country Club, FL (cdp) Miami-Dade County	61	0.17
Greenburgh, NY (town) Westchester County	61	0.07
Albuquerque, NM (city) Bernalillo County	61	0.01

Notes: (cdp) census designated place; Refer to the Explanation of Data in the front of the book for more detailed information.

Hispanic: Other South American

Top 150 Places Sorted by Percent

(Based on all places, regardless of population)

Place	Number	%
East Newark, NJ (borough) Hudson County	26	1.09
Cottage Grove, TN (town) Henry County	1	1.03
Upper Brookville, NY (village) Nassau County	15	0.83
Forest Home, NY (cdp) Tompkins County	7	0.74
Harrison, NJ (town) Hudson County	106	0.73
Victory Gardens, NJ (borough) Morris County	10	0.65
High Falls, NY (cdp) Ulster County	4	0.64
Surfside, FL (town) Miami-Dade County	30	0.61
Wharton, NJ (borough) Morris County	36	0.57
Village Park, FL (cdp) Broward County	5	0.56
Danube, NY (town) Herkimer County	6	0.55
Seven Corners, VA (cdp) Fairfax County	43	0.49
Doral, FL (cdp) Miami-Dade County	99	0.48
Fairview, NY (cdp) Westchester County	14	0.48
Good Hope, GA (town) Walton County	1	0.48
Guttenberg, NJ (town) Hudson County	51	0.47
Russell Gardens, NY (village) Nassau County	5	0.47
Mineral Hills, MI (village) Iron County	1	0.47
Bellerose Terrace, NY (cdp) Nassau County	10	0.46
Lake Barcroft, VA (cdp) Fairfax County	39	0.44
Biscayne Park, FL (village) Miami-Dade County	14	0.43
Nehawka, NE (village) Cass County	1	0.43
East Garden City, NY (cdp) Nassau County	4	0.41
North Lynbrook, NY (cdp) Nassau County	3	0.40
Lincolnia, VA (cdp) Fairfax County	62	0.39
Dover Beaches South, NJ (cdp) Ocean County	6	0.38
Quioque, NY (cdp) Suffolk County	3	0.38
Richmondville, NY (village) Schoharie County	3	0.38
Patchogue, NY (village) Suffolk County	44	0.37
Round Lake Heights, IL (village) Lake County	5	0.37
North Bergen, NJ (township) Hudson County	212	0.36
Stockton, NJ (borough) Hunterdon County	2	0.36
Fort Ritchie, MD (cdp) Washington County	1	0.36
The Crossings, FL (cdp) Miami-Dade County	83	0.35
Kangley, IL (village) La Salle County	1	0.35
West New York, NJ (town) Hudson County	154	0.34
Port Chester, NY (village) Westchester County	95	0.34
The Hammocks, FL (cdp) Miami-Dade County	157	0.33
Key Biscayne, FL (village) Miami-Dade County	35	0.33
Manorhaven, NY (village) Nassau County	20	0.33
Bay Harbor Islands, FL (town) Miami-Dade County	17	0.33
Lavaca, AR (city) Sebastian County	6	0.33
Staatsburg, NY (cdp) Dutchess County	3	0.33
Moss Landing, CA (cdp) Monterey County	1	0.33
Union City, NJ (city) Hudson County	213	0.32
Annandale, VA (cdp) Fairfax County	176	0.32
Dover, NJ (town) Morris County	58	0.32
Iroquois Point, HI (cdp) Honolulu County	8	0.32
Sleepy Hollow, NY (village) Westchester County	29	0.31
Bronson, FL (town) Levy County	3	0.31
Elizabeth, NJ (city) Union County	356	0.30
Richmond West, FL (cdp) Miami-Dade County	84	0.30
Belford, NJ (cdp) Monmouth County	4	0.30
Miami Beach, FL (city) Miami-Dade County	257	0.29
Kearny, NJ (town) Hudson County	114	0.28
Ossining, NY (village) Westchester County	67	0.28
Bonnie Lock-Woodsetter North, FL (cdp) Broward County	12	0.28
Gravette, AR (city) Benton County	5	0.28
Shalimar, FL (town) Okaloosa County	2	0.28
Kendall West, FL (cdp) Miami-Dade County	103	0.27
New Hempstead, NY (village) Rockland County	13	0.27
Bal Harbour, FL (village) Miami-Dade County	9	0.27
Kensington, MD (town) Montgomery County	5	0.27
Concow, CA (cdp) Butte County	3	0.27
Fountainbleau, FL (cdp) Miami-Dade County	156	0.26
Weston, FL (city) Broward County	130	0.26
Jefferson, VA (cdp) Fairfax County	71	0.26
Ojus, FL (cdp) Miami-Dade County	43	0.26
Weehawken, NJ (township) Hudson County	35	0.26
Three Lakes, FL (cdp) Miami-Dade County	18	0.26
Prospect Park, NJ (borough) Passaic County	15	0.26
La Crosse, WA (town) Whitman County	1	0.26
North Plainfield, NJ (borough) Somerset County	53	0.25
Pebble Creek, FL (cdp) Hillsborough County	12	0.25
Catawissa, PA (borough) Columbia County	4	0.25
Touchet, WA (cdp) Walla Walla County	1	0.25
Arlington, VA (cdp) Arlington County	462	0.24
Mineola, NY (village) Nassau County	46	0.24
Sunny Isles Beach, FL (city) Miami-Dade County	37	0.24
Inwood, NY (cdp) Nassau County	22	0.24
Garden City Park, NY (cdp) Nassau County	18	0.24
North Bay Village, FL (city) Miami-Dade County	16	0.24
Mount Arlington, NJ (borough) Morris County	11	0.24
Gang Mills, NY (cdp) Steuben County	8	0.24
Newport, NC (town) Carteret County	8	0.24
Riverdale, NJ (borough) Morris County	6	0.24
Escalante, UT (city) Garfield County	2	0.24
Matinecock, NY (village) Nassau County	2	0.24
Otto, NY (town) Cattaraugus County	2	0.24
Wharton, OH (village) Wyandot County	1	0.24
Rye, NY (town) Westchester County	103	0.23
Morristown, NJ (town) Morris County	43	0.23
Loch Lomond, FL (cdp) Broward County	8	0.23
South Windham, CT (cdp) Windham County	3	0.23
Punaluu, HI (cdp) Honolulu County	2	0.23
Barwick, GA (town) Thomas County	1	0.23
Duck Key, FL (cdp) Monroe County	1	0.23
Kendale Lakes, FL (cdp) Miami-Dade County	123	0.22
Falls Church, VA (independent city) Falls Church city	23	0.22
Lakes by the Bay, FL (cdp) Miami-Dade County	20	0.22
Great Neck Plaza, NY (village) Nassau County	14	0.22
Wheatley Heights, NY (cdp) Suffolk County	11	0.22
Westbrook Center, CT (cdp) Middlesex County	5	0.22
Newtown, CT (borough) Fairfield County	4	0.22
Byron, CA (cdp) Contra Costa County	2	0.22
Green Grove, WI (town) Clark County	2	0.22
Hayfield, MN (township) Dodge County	1	0.22
Whiteface, TX (town) Cochran County	1	0.22
Wheaton-Glenmont, MD (cdp) Montgomery County	123	0.21
Burlingame, CA (city) San Mateo County	59	0.21
Idylwood, VA (cdp) Fairfax County	33	0.21
Miami Springs, FL (city) Miami-Dade County	29	0.21
Meadow Woods, FL (cdp) Orange County	24	0.21
Bogota, NJ (borough) Bergen County	17	0.21
Cedarhurst, NY (village) Nassau County	13	0.21
Vails Gate, NY (cdp) Orange County	7	0.21
Indian Hills, KY (city) Jefferson County	6	0.21
Acton, CA (cdp) Los Angeles County	5	0.21
Haverhill, FL (town) Palm Beach County	3	0.21
Ravenswood Estates, FL (cdp) Broward County	2	0.21
Cragsmoor, NY (cdp) Ulster County	1	0.21
Malverne Park Oaks, NY (cdp) Nassau County	1	0.21
Kendall, FL (cdp) Miami-Dade County	147	0.20
Ossining, NY (town) Westchester County	74	0.20
West Springfield, VA (cdp) Fairfax County	57	0.20
Bailey's Crossroads, VA (cdp) Fairfax County	46	0.20
Middlesex, NJ (borough) Middlesex County	27	0.20
Poinciana, FL (cdp) Osceola County	27	0.20
Cloverly, MD (cdp) Montgomery County	16	0.20
Mantua, VA (cdp) Fairfax County	15	0.20
Pimmit Hills, VA (cdp) Fairfax County	12	0.20
Fairmont, IL (cdp) Will County	5	0.20
Ponce Inlet, FL (town) Volusia County	5	0.20
East Pepperell, MA (cdp) Middlesex County	4	0.20
Sperry, OK (town) Tulsa County	2	0.20
Andover, VT (town) Windsor County	1	0.20
Sunfish Lake, MN (city) Dakota County	1	0.20
Brentwood, NY (cdp) Suffolk County	102	0.19
North Miami Beach, FL (city) Miami-Dade County	79	0.19
Hallandale, FL (city) Broward County	64	0.19
Sunset, FL (cdp) Miami-Dade County	32	0.19
Hill Country Village, TX (city) Bexar County	2	0.19
Saxtons River, VT (village) Windham County	1	0.19
San Mateo, CA (city) San Mateo County	164	0.18
Coral Gables, FL (city) Miami-Dade County	75	0.18
Montgomery Village, MD (cdp) Montgomery County	69	0.18
El Cerrito, CA (city) Contra Costa County	42	0.18
Hillside, NJ (cdp) Union County	40	0.18
Roselle, NJ (borough) Union County	39	0.18
Newington, VA (cdp) Fairfax County	35	0.18

Notes: (cdp) census designated place; Refer to the Explanation of Data in the front of the book for more detailed information.

Hispanic: Other South American

Top 150 Places Sorted by Percent

(Based on places with populations of 10,000 or more)

Place	Number	%
Harrison, NJ (town) Hudson County	106	0.73
Doral, FL (cdp) Miami-Dade County	99	0.48
Guttenberg, NJ (town) Hudson County	51	0.47
Lincolnia, VA (cdp) Fairfax County	62	0.39
Patchogue, NY (village) Suffolk County	44	0.37
North Bergen, NJ (township) Hudson County	212	0.36
The Crossings, FL (cdp) Miami-Dade County	83	0.35
West New York, NJ (town) Hudson County	154	0.34
Port Chester, NY (village) Westchester County	95	0.34
The Hammocks, FL (cdp) Miami-Dade County	157	0.33
Key Biscayne, FL (village) Miami-Dade County	35	0.33
Union City, NJ (city) Hudson County	213	0.32
Annandale, VA (cdp) Fairfax County	176	0.32
Dover, NJ (town) Morris County	58	0.32
Elizabeth, NJ (city) Union County	356	0.30
Richmond West, FL (cdp) Miami-Dade County	84	0.30
Miami Beach, FL (city) Miami-Dade County	257	0.29
Kearny, NJ (town) Hudson County	114	0.28
Ossining, NY (village) Westchester County	67	0.28
Kendall West, FL (cdp) Miami-Dade County	103	0.27
Fountainbleau, FL (cdp) Miami-Dade County	156	0.26
Weston, FL (city) Broward County	130	0.26
Jefferson, VA (cdp) Fairfax County	71	0.26
Ojus, FL (cdp) Miami-Dade County	43	0.26
Weehawken, NJ (township) Hudson County	35	0.26
North Plainfield, NJ (borough) Somerset County	53	0.25
Arlington, VA (cdp) Arlington County	462	0.24
Mineola, NY (village) Nassau County	46	0.24
Sunny Isles Beach, FL (city) Miami-Dade County	37	0.24
Rye, NY (town) Westchester County	103	0.23
Morristown, NJ (town) Morris County	43	0.23
Kendale Lakes, FL (cdp) Miami-Dade County	123	0.22
Falls Church, VA (independent city) Falls Church city	23	0.22
Wheaton-Glenmont, MD (cdp) Montgomery County	123	0.21
Burlingame, CA (city) San Mateo County	59	0.21
Idylwood, VA (cdp) Fairfax County	33	0.21
Miami Springs, FL (city) Miami-Dade County	29	0.21
Meadow Woods, FL (cdp) Orange County	24	0.21
Kendall, FL (cdp) Miami-Dade County	147	0.20
Ossining, NY (town) Westchester County	74	0.20
West Springfield, VA (cdp) Fairfax County	57	0.20
Bailey's Crossroads, VA (cdp) Fairfax County	46	0.20
Middlesex, NJ (borough) Middlesex County	27	0.20
Poinciana, FL (cdp) Osceola County	27	0.20
Brentwood, NY (cdp) Suffolk County	102	0.19
North Miami Beach, FL (city) Miami-Dade County	79	0.19
Hallandale, FL (city) Broward County	64	0.19
Sunset, FL (cdp) Miami-Dade County	32	0.19
San Mateo, CA (city) San Mateo County	164	0.18
Coral Gables, FL (city) Miami-Dade County	75	0.18
Montgomery Village, MD (cdp) Montgomery County	69	0.18
El Cerrito, CA (city) Contra Costa County	42	0.18
Hillside, NJ (cdp) Union County	40	0.18
Roselle, NJ (borough) Union County	39	0.18
Newington, VA (cdp) Fairfax County	35	0.18
Glenvar Heights, FL (cdp) Miami-Dade County	29	0.18
Country Walk, FL (cdp) Miami-Dade County	19	0.18
Downey, CA (city) Los Angeles County	187	0.17
Burbank, CA (city) Los Angeles County	166	0.17
Burke, VA (cdp) Fairfax County	99	0.17
North Bethesda, MD (cdp) Montgomery County	65	0.17
Belleville, NJ (cdp) Essex County	62	0.17
Country Club, FL (cdp) Miami-Dade County	61	0.17
Albany, CA (city) Alameda County	28	0.17
North Bay Shore, NY (cdp) Suffolk County	25	0.17
Roselle Park, NJ (borough) Union County	23	0.17
Salisbury, NY (cdp) Nassau County	21	0.17
Westchase, FL (cdp) Hillsborough County	19	0.17
Manassas Park, VA (independent city) Manassas Park city	18	0.17
Jersey City, NJ (city) Hudson County	373	0.16
Passaic, NJ (city) Passaic County	108	0.16
Gaithersburg, MD (city) Montgomery County	83	0.16
Aventura, FL (city) Miami-Dade County	41	0.16
Palisades Park, NJ (borough) Bergen County	28	0.16
Kings Park, NY (cdp) Suffolk County	26	0.16
Paterson, NJ (city) Passaic County	230	0.15
White Plains, NY (city) Westchester County	78	0.15
Aspen Hill, MD (cdp) Montgomery County	74	0.15
West Orange, NJ (cdp) Essex County	67	0.15
Hackensack, NJ (city) Bergen County	62	0.15
Orange, NJ (cdp) Essex County	48	0.15
Garfield, NJ (city) Bergen County	46	0.15
Oakland Park, FL (city) Broward County	46	0.15
Springfield, VA (cdp) Fairfax County	45	0.15
Englewood, NJ (city) Bergen County	38	0.15
Lodi, NJ (borough) Bergen County	36	0.15
Ives Estates, FL (cdp) Miami-Dade County	26	0.15
North Fair Oaks, CA (cdp) San Mateo County	23	0.15
Somerville, NJ (borough) Somerset County	19	0.15
Merrifield, VA (cdp) Fairfax County	17	0.15
Suffern, NY (village) Rockland County	16	0.15
Glendale, CA (city) Los Angeles County	278	0.14
Miramar, FL (city) Broward County	105	0.14
Tamarac, FL (city) Broward County	77	0.14
Linden, NJ (city) Union County	57	0.14
North Lauderdale, FL (city) Broward County	46	0.14
Oak Ridge, FL (cdp) Orange County	32	0.14
Duarte, CA (city) Los Angeles County	30	0.14
South El Monte, CA (city) Los Angeles County	30	0.14
Carteret, NJ (borough) Middlesex County	29	0.14
Wallington, NJ (borough) Bergen County	16	0.14
Hollywood, FL (city) Broward County	188	0.13
Pembroke Pines, FL (city) Broward County	185	0.13
Coral Springs, FL (city) Broward County	156	0.13
Stamford, CT (city) Fairfield County	152	0.13
South Gate, CA (city) Los Angeles County	128	0.13
Davie, FL (town) Broward County	99	0.13
Tamiami, FL (cdp) Miami-Dade County	72	0.13
Perth Amboy, NJ (city) Middlesex County	60	0.13
Potomac, MD (cdp) Montgomery County	57	0.13
Long Beach, NY (city) Nassau County	47	0.13
Woodbridge, VA (cdp) Prince William County	43	0.13
Central Islip, NY (cdp) Suffolk County	40	0.13
Oakton, VA (cdp) Fairfax County	38	0.13
Glen Cove, NY (city) Nassau County	34	0.13
Cudahy, CA (city) Los Angeles County	32	0.13
Fairview, NJ (borough) Bergen County	17	0.13
Palm Springs, FL (village) Palm Beach County	15	0.13
Cinco Ranch, TX (cdp) Fort Bend County	14	0.13
Little Ferry, NJ (borough) Bergen County	14	0.13
Miami Shores, FL (village) Miami-Dade County	14	0.13
Santa Clarita, CA (city) Los Angeles County	182	0.12
Torrance, CA (city) Los Angeles County	168	0.12
Pasadena, CA (city) Los Angeles County	156	0.12
Sunrise, FL (city) Broward County	105	0.12
Norwalk, CT (city) Fairfield County	98	0.12
Boca Raton, FL (city) Palm Beach County	88	0.12
New Rochelle, NY (city) Westchester County	85	0.12
North Miami, FL (city) Miami-Dade County	69	0.12
Reston, VA (cdp) Fairfax County	67	0.12
Centreville, VA (cdp) Fairfax County	59	0.12
Covina, CA (city) Los Angeles County	54	0.12
Altamonte Springs, FL (city) Seminole County	48	0.12
Culver City, CA (city) Los Angeles County	48	0.12
Brea, CA (city) Orange County	42	0.12
Westchester, FL (cdp) Miami-Dade County	37	0.12
Cutler Ridge, FL (cdp) Miami-Dade County	29	0.12
Boca Del Mar, FL (cdp) Palm Beach County	26	0.12
Citrus Park, FL (cdp) Hillsborough County	25	0.12
Greater Northdale, FL (cdp) Hillsborough County	24	0.12
Loma Linda, CA (city) San Bernardino County	23	0.12
Lyndhurst, NJ (cdp) Bergen County	23	0.12
Santa Fe Springs, CA (city) Los Angeles County	21	0.12
El Segundo, CA (city) Los Angeles County	19	0.12
Hampton Bays, NY (cdp) Suffolk County	15	0.12
Ridgefield Park, NJ (village) Bergen County	15	0.12
Oquirrh, UT (cdp) Salt Lake County	12	0.12
Alexandria, VA (independent city) Alexandria city	137	0.11
Hawthorne, CA (city) Los Angeles County	96	0.11
Plantation, FL (city) Broward County	95	0.11

Notes: (cdp) census designated place; Refer to the Explanation of Data in the front of the book for more detailed information.

Hispanic: Other

Top 150 Places Sorted by Number

(Based on all places, regardless of population)

Place	Number	%
New York, NY (city) New York City	401,108	5.01
Los Angeles, CA (city) Los Angeles County	331,114	8.96
San Antonio, TX (city) Bexar County	182,662	15.96
Houston, TX (city) Harris County	116,701	5.97
Albuquerque, NM (city) Bernalillo County	105,381	23.49
El Paso, TX (city) El Paso County	65,939	11.70
Phoenix, AZ (city) Maricopa County	59,239	4.48
Chicago, IL (city) Cook County	56,225	1.94
Corpus Christi, TX (city) Nueces County	50,633	18.25
Denver, CO (city) Denver County	49,402	8.91
Dallas, TX (city) Dallas County	49,358	4.15
Miami, FL (city) Miami-Dade County	39,058	10.78
Austin, TX (city) Travis County	36,177	5.51
San Diego, CA (city) San Diego County	33,794	2.76
San Jose, CA (city) Santa Clara County	32,924	3.68
Laredo, TX (city) Webb County	32,137	18.20
San Francisco, CA (city) San Francisco County	26,657	3.43
Pueblo, CO (city) Pueblo County	25,017	24.50
Hialeah, FL (city) Miami-Dade County	24,305	10.73
Santa Ana, CA (city) Orange County	23,777	7.04
Tucson, AZ (city) Pima County	23,538	4.84
Long Beach, CA (city) Los Angeles County	23,323	5.05
Brownsville, TX (city) Cameron County	23,296	16.67
Hempstead, NY (town) Nassau County	22,655	3.00
Fresno, CA (city) Fresno County	22,209	5.19
Lubbock, TX (city) Lubbock County	21,590	10.82
Fort Worth, TX (city) Tarrant County	21,385	4.00
Santa Fe, NM (city) Santa Fe County	20,727	33.32
Boston, MA (city) Suffolk County	19,783	3.36
South Valley, NM (cdp) Bernalillo County	17,827	45.64
Anaheim, CA (city) Orange County	17,658	5.38
Philadelphia, PA (city) Philadelphia County	16,507	1.09
Colorado Springs, CO (city) El Paso County	15,658	4.34
Washington, DC (city) District of Columbia	15,406	2.69
Las Vegas, NV (city) Clark County	15,401	3.22
Newark, NJ (city) Essex County	14,530	5.31
McAllen, TX (city) Hidalgo County	14,253	13.39
Las Cruces, NM (city) Dona Ana County	13,736	18.50
Tampa, FL (city) Hillsborough County	13,499	4.45
Paterson, NJ (city) Passaic County	13,432	9.00
Elizabeth, NJ (city) Union County	13,371	11.09
Islip, NY (town) Suffolk County	13,353	4.14
San Bernardino, CA (city) San Bernardino County	12,522	6.75
Riverside, CA (city) Riverside County	12,515	4.90
East Los Angeles, CA (cdp) Los Angeles County	12,446	10.01
Ontario, CA (city) San Bernardino County	12,090	7.65
Jersey City, NJ (city) Hudson County	12,075	5.03
Arlington, VA (cdp) Arlington County	12,050	6.36
Sacramento, CA (city) Sacramento County	12,050	2.96
Bakersfield, CA (city) Kern County	11,906	4.82
South Gate, CA (city) Los Angeles County	11,881	12.33
Providence, RI (city) Providence County	11,839	6.82
Aurora, CO (city) Arapahoe County	11,726	4.24
Oakland, CA (city) Alameda County	11,466	2.87
Union City, NJ (city) Hudson County	11,272	16.80
Pomona, CA (city) Los Angeles County	11,068	7.40
Mesa, AZ (city) Maricopa County	10,816	2.73
Amarillo, TX (city) Potter County	10,525	6.06
Salinas, CA (city) Monterey County	10,445	6.91
Pasadena, TX (city) Harris County	10,395	7.34
Las Vegas, NM (city) San Miguel County	10,106	69.39
Fountainbleau, FL (cdp) Miami-Dade County	9,962	16.73
El Monte, CA (city) Los Angeles County	9,899	8.54
Fontana, CA (city) San Bernardino County	9,796	7.60
Stockton, CA (city) San Joaquin County	9,553	3.92
Rio Rancho, NM (city) Sandoval County	9,477	18.31
Oxnard, CA (city) Ventura County	9,477	5.56
Harlingen, TX (city) Cameron County	9,445	16.41
Downey, CA (city) Los Angeles County	9,295	8.66
Irving, TX (city) Dallas County	9,251	4.83
Arlington, TX (city) Tarrant County	9,148	2.75
Glendale, AZ (city) Maricopa County	9,096	4.16
Yonkers, NY (city) Westchester County	8,855	4.52
Odessa, TX (city) Ector County	8,703	9.57
Lawrence, MA (city) Essex County	8,567	11.89
Miami Beach, FL (city) Miami-Dade County	8,414	9.57
Inglewood, CA (city) Los Angeles County	8,193	7.28
Lakewood, CO (city) Jefferson County	8,154	5.66
Edinburg, TX (city) Hidalgo County	8,036	16.58
Norwalk, CA (city) Los Angeles County	8,033	7.78
Palmdale, CA (city) Los Angeles County	8,030	6.88
Huntington Park, CA (city) Los Angeles County	7,992	13.03
Victoria, TX (city) Victoria County	7,908	13.05
Chula Vista, CA (city) San Diego County	7,899	4.55
Garland, TX (city) Dallas County	7,870	3.65
Roswell, NM (city) Chaves County	7,646	16.88
Grand Prairie, TX (city) Dallas County	7,612	5.97
Kendale Lakes, FL (cdp) Miami-Dade County	7,479	13.14
Thornton, CO (city) Adams County	7,442	9.03
Baldwin Park, CA (city) Los Angeles County	7,411	9.77
Glendale, CA (city) Los Angeles County	7,388	3.79
Moreno Valley, CA (city) Riverside County	7,282	5.11
Hawthorne, CA (city) Los Angeles County	7,236	8.60
West New York, NJ (town) Hudson County	7,212	15.76
Florence-Graham, CA (cdp) Los Angeles County	7,206	11.97
Pembroke Pines, FL (city) Broward County	7,127	5.19
Hayward, CA (city) Alameda County	7,127	5.09
Modesto, CA (city) Stanislaus County	7,071	3.74
Brookhaven, NY (town) Suffolk County	7,071	1.58
Lynwood, CA (city) Los Angeles County	7,062	10.11
Espanola, NM (city) Rio Arriba County	6,840	70.60
North Bergen, NJ (township) Hudson County	6,789	11.69
Compton, CA (city) Los Angeles County	6,779	7.25
Paradise, NV (cdp) Clark County	6,589	3.54
Honolulu, HI (cdp) Honolulu County	6,572	1.77
Midland, TX (city) Midland County	6,565	6.91
San Angelo, TX (city) Tom Green County	6,553	7.41
Kendall, FL (cdp) Miami-Dade County	6,548	8.70
Alice, TX (city) Jim Wells County	6,472	34.05
West Covina, CA (city) Los Angeles County	6,444	6.13
The Hammocks, FL (cdp) Miami-Dade County	6,367	13.44
Pasadena, CA (city) Los Angeles County	6,328	4.72
Rialto, CA (city) San Bernardino County	6,288	6.84
Oklahoma City, OK (city) Oklahoma County	6,278	1.24
Daly City, CA (city) San Mateo County	6,274	6.05
Tamiami, FL (cdp) Miami-Dade County	6,257	11.42
Brentwood, NY (cdp) Suffolk County	6,219	11.53
Hollywood, FL (city) Broward County	6,096	4.37
Abilene, TX (city) Taylor County	6,066	5.23
Garden Grove, CA (city) Orange County	6,052	3.66
Mission, TX (city) Hidalgo County	6,013	13.24
Westminster, CO (city) Adams County	5,952	5.90
Jacksonville, FL (special city) Duval County	5,934	0.81
Milwaukee, WI (city) Milwaukee County	5,932	0.99
Alexandria, VA (independent city) Alexandria city	5,925	4.62
Charlotte, NC (city) Mecklenburg County	5,914	1.09
Chandler, AZ (city) Maricopa County	5,889	3.34
Sunrise Manor, NV (cdp) Clark County	5,872	3.76
Salt Lake City, UT (city) Salt Lake County	5,854	3.22
Silver Spring, MD (cdp) Montgomery County	5,848	7.64
Seattle, WA (city) King County	5,834	1.04
Greeley, CO (city) Weld County	5,819	7.56
Kendall West, FL (cdp) Miami-Dade County	5,815	15.29
Passaic, NJ (city) Passaic County	5,795	8.54
Wheaton-Glenmont, MD (cdp) Montgomery County	5,777	10.01
Pico Rivera, CA (city) Los Angeles County	5,662	8.93
Clovis, NM (city) Curry County	5,627	17.23
North Hempstead, NY (town) Nassau County	5,592	2.51
Hempstead, NY (village) Nassau County	5,550	9.81
Pharr, TX (city) Hidalgo County	5,547	11.89
Portland, OR (city) Multnomah County	5,545	1.05
Whittier, CA (city) Los Angeles County	5,541	6.62
San Benito, TX (city) Cameron County	5,394	23.01
Bell Gardens, CA (city) Los Angeles County	5,394	12.24
North Las Vegas, NV (city) Clark County	5,387	4.66
Lancaster, CA (city) Los Angeles County	5,342	4.50
Corona, CA (city) Riverside County	5,321	4.26
Rancho Cucamonga, CA (city) San Bernardino County	5,259	4.12
Reno, NV (city) Washoe County	5,235	2.90
New Orleans, LA (city) Orleans Parish	5,201	1.07

Notes: (cdp) census designated place; Refer to the Explanation of Data in the front of the book for more detailed information.

Hispanic: Other

Top 150 Places Sorted by Percent

(Based on all places, regardless of population)

Place	Number	%
Vadito, NM (cdp) Taos County	222	91.74
Rio Lucio, NM (cdp) Taos County	346	91.29
Manzano, NM (cdp) Torrance County	47	87.04
Chamisal, NM (cdp) Taos County	259	86.05
Penasco, NM (cdp) Taos County	488	85.31
Alcalde, NM (cdp) Rio Arriba County	313	83.02
Rio Chiquito, NM (cdp) Santa Fe County	82	79.61
Chimayo, NM (cdp) Rio Arriba County	2,326	79.55
Wagon Mound, NM (village) Mora County	293	79.40
Cuyamungue, NM (cdp) Santa Fe County	326	77.43
Santa Cruz, NM (cdp) Santa Fe County	325	76.83
Cundiyo, NM (cdp) Santa Fe County	71	74.74
Questa, NM (village) Taos County	1,352	72.53
Pena Blanca, NM (cdp) Sandoval County	477	72.16
Espanola, NM (city) Rio Arriba County	6,840	70.60
La Jara, NM (cdp) Sandoval County	147	70.33
Encino, NM (village) Torrance County	66	70.21
Casa Colorada, NM (cdp) Valencia County	39	69.64
San Luis, CO (town) Costilla County	514	69.55
Rio en Medio, NM (cdp) Santa Fe County	91	69.47
Las Vegas, NM (city) San Miguel County	10,106	69.39
Vaughn, NM (town) Guadalupe County	372	69.02
La Puebla, NM (cdp) Santa Fe County	885	68.29
Antonito, CO (town) Conejos County	593	67.93
Cuartelez, NM (cdp) Santa Fe County	304	67.26
Santa Rosa, NM (city) Guadalupe County	1,812	66.03
Willard, NM (village) Torrance County	155	64.58
San Ysidro, NM (village) Sandoval County	153	64.29
El Rancho, NM (cdp) Santa Fe County	512	62.67
Guerra, TX (cdp) Jim Hogg County	5	62.50
Ranchos de Taos, NM (cdp) Taos County	1,493	62.47
Mosquero, NM (village) Harding County	73	60.83
Chama, NM (village) Rio Arriba County	729	60.80
Loma Linda East, TX (cdp) Jim Wells County	129	60.28
Romeo, CO (town) Conejos County	223	59.47
Pecos, NM (village) San Miguel County	852	59.13
Jaconita, NM (cdp) Santa Fe County	202	58.89
Springer, NM (town) Colfax County	742	57.74
Bernalillo, NM (town) Sandoval County	3,807	57.59
Chilili, NM (cdp) Bernalillo County	65	57.52
El Valle de Arroyo Seco, NM (cdp) Santa Fe County	655	57.01
Torreon, NM (cdp) Torrence County	138	56.56
Ponderosa, NM (cdp) Sandoval County	172	55.48
Agua Fria, NM (cdp) Santa Fe County	1,134	55.29
Tome-Adelino, NM (cdp) Valencia County	1,199	54.23
Hilltop, TX (cdp) Frio County	161	53.67
Willamar, TX (cdp) Willacy County	8	53.33
Belen, NM (city) Valencia County	3,663	53.08
Freer, TX (city) Duval County	1,712	52.82
San Diego, TX (city) Duval County	2,501	52.62
Cimarron, NM (village) Colfax County	477	52.02
Owl Ranch-Amargosa, TX (cdp) Jim Wells County	272	51.61
Los Trujillos-Gabaldon, NM (cdp) Valencia County	1,116	51.52
Ardoch, ND (city) Walsh County	31	50.82
Tajique, NM (cdp) Torrance County	75	50.68
Pojoaque, NM (cdp) Santa Fe County	626	49.64
La Cienega, NM (cdp) Santa Fe County	1,478	49.15
Maxwell, NM (village) Colfax County	134	48.91
Jarales, NM (cdp) Valencia County	698	48.68
Rancho Banquete, TX (cdp) Nueces County	228	48.61
Algodones, NM (cdp) Sandoval County	334	48.55
Fort Garland, CO (cdp) Costilla County	209	48.38
Benavides, TX (city) Duval County	775	45.97
Mountainair, NM (town) Torrance County	513	45.97
South Valley, NM (cdp) Bernalillo County	17,827	45.64
Starkville, CO (town) Las Animas County	58	45.31
Pawnee, TX (cdp) Bee County	90	44.78
Sombrillo, NM (cdp) Santa Fe County	220	44.62
La Jara, CO (town) Conejos County	391	44.58
Taos, NM (town) Taos County	2,080	44.26
Glorieta, NM (cdp) Santa Fe County	380	44.24
Loving, NM (village) Eddy County	586	44.19
Raton, NM (city) Colfax County	3,200	43.94
Cuba, NM (village) Sandoval County	259	43.90
Poteet, TX (city) Atascosa County	1,442	43.63
Los Lunas, NM (village) Valencia County	4,377	43.62
Mathis, TX (city) San Patricio County	2,195	43.60
Roy, NM (village) Harding County	132	43.42
Chupadero, NM (cdp) Santa Fe County	138	43.40
Ignacio, CO (town) La Plata County	290	43.35
Tijeras, NM (village) Bernalillo County	203	42.83
Del Norte, CO (town) Rio Grande County	730	42.82
Grants, NM (city) Cibola County	3,653	41.48
Milan, NM (village) Cibola County	784	41.46
Villa Pancho, TX (cdp) Cameron County	160	41.45
Salt Creek, CO (cdp) Pueblo County	268	41.36
Hebbronville, TX (cdp) Jim Hogg County	1,841	40.93
Magdalena, NM (village) Socorro County	373	40.85
Los Chaves, NM (cdp) Valencia County	2,054	40.81
Carnuel, NM (cdp) Bernalillo County	353	40.48
Canada de los Alamos, NM (cdp) Santa Fe County	144	40.22
North Valley, NM (cdp) Bernalillo County	4,793	40.20
Lamy, NM (cdp) Santa Fe County	55	40.15
Charlotte, TX (city) Atascosa County	649	39.65
Cantu Addition, TX (cdp) Brooks County	86	39.63
Concepcion, TX (cdp) Duval County	24	39.34
Manassa, CO (town) Conejos County	404	38.77
Realitos, TX (cdp) Duval County	81	38.76
Asherton, TX (city) Dimmit County	520	38.75
Las Lomitas, TX (cdp) Jim Hogg County	103	38.58
Fort Sumner, NM (village) De Baca County	481	38.51
Edgewater-Paisano, TX (cdp) San Patricio County	70	38.46
Peralta, NM (cdp) Valencia County	1,437	38.32
South Fork Estates, TX (cdp) Jim Hogg County	18	38.30
Los Cerrillos, NM (cdp) Santa Fe County	87	37.99
Bruni, TX (cdp) Webb County	156	37.86
Monte Vista, CO (city) Rio Grande County	1,714	37.84
Coyote Acres, TX (cdp) Jim Wells County	144	37.02
Carrizo Hill, TX (cdp) Dimmit County	202	36.86
Socorro, NM (city) Socorro County	3,263	36.76
Chula Vista-River Spur, TX (cdp) Zavala County	147	36.75
Avondale, CO (cdp) Pueblo County	277	36.74
Tucumcari, NM (city) Quay County	2,193	36.62
K-Bar Ranch, TX (cdp) Jim Wells County	128	36.57
Lopeno, TX (cdp) Zapata County	51	36.43
Valencia, NM (cdp) Valencia County	1,639	36.42
Gregory, TX (city) San Patricio County	844	36.41
North San Pedro, TX (cdp) Nueces County	335	36.41
Clayton, NM (town) Union County	908	35.97
New Falcon, TX (cdp) Zapata County	66	35.87
Santa Clara, NM (village) Grant County	694	35.70
Walsenburg, CO (city) Huerfano County	1,490	35.63
Ranchette Estates, TX (cdp) Willacy County	47	35.34
Trinidad, CO (city) Las Animas County	3,205	35.31
Robstown, TX (city) Nueces County	4,490	35.28
Dilley, TX (city) Frio County	1,296	35.27
Alamosa East, CO (cdp) Alamosa County	538	35.21
Rancho Alegre, TX (cdp) Jim Wells County	617	34.76
Morales-Sanchez, TX (cdp) Zapata County	33	34.74
Pagosa Springs, CO (town) Archuleta County	552	34.70
Alfred-South La Paloma, TX (cdp) Jim Wells County	155	34.37
Botines, TX (cdp) Webb County	45	34.09
Alice, TX (city) Jim Wells County	6,472	34.05
Ratamosa, TX (cdp) Cameron County	74	33.94
Corona, NM (village) Lincoln County	56	33.94
Center, CO (town) Saguache County	811	33.90
Odem, TX (city) San Patricio County	843	33.73
Mirando City, TX (cdp) Webb County	166	33.67
Red Cliff, CO (town) Eagle County	97	33.56
Santa Fe, NM (city) Santa Fe County	20,727	33.32
Premont, TX (city) Jim Wells County	916	33.04
West Pearsall, TX (cdp) Frio County	115	32.95
Quemado, TX (cdp) Maverick County	80	32.92
Pearsall, TX (city) Frio County	2,352	32.86
Flowella, TX (cdp) Brooks County	44	32.84
Falfurrias, TX (city) Brooks County	1,729	32.64
Tierra Grande, TX (cdp) Nueces County	118	32.60
Tesuque, NM (cdp) Santa Fe County	296	32.56
Sanford, CO (town) Conejos County	266	32.56
Aguilar, CO (town) Las Animas County	191	32.21

Notes: (cdp) census designated place; Refer to the Explanation of Data in the front of the book for more detailed information.

Hispanic: Other

Top 150 Places Sorted by Percent

(Based on places with populations of 10,000 or more)

Place	Number	%
Las Vegas, NM (city) San Miguel County	10,106	69.39
South Valley, NM (cdp) Bernalillo County	17,827	45.64
Los Lunas, NM (village) Valencia County	4,377	43.62
North Valley, NM (cdp) Bernalillo County	4,793	40.20
Robstown, TX (city) Nueces County	4,490	35.28
Alice, TX (city) Jim Wells County	6,472	34.05
Santa Fe, NM (city) Santa Fe County	20,727	33.32
Beeville, TX (city) Bee County	3,669	27.95
Pueblo, CO (city) Pueblo County	25,017	24.50
Albuquerque, NM (city) Bernalillo County	105,381	23.49
San Benito, TX (city) Cameron County	5,394	23.01
Uvalde, TX (city) Uvalde County	3,413	22.86
Silver City, NM (town) Grant County	2,404	22.80
Mercedes, TX (city) Hidalgo County	2,924	21.42
Kingsville, TX (city) Kleberg County	5,141	20.10
Portales, NM (city) Roosevelt County	2,131	19.14
Las Cruces, NM (city) Dona Ana County	13,736	18.50
Rio Rancho, NM (city) Sandoval County	9,477	18.31
Corpus Christi, TX (city) Nueces County	50,633	18.25
Laredo, TX (city) Webb County	32,137	18.20
Rio Grande City, TX (city) Starr County	2,154	18.07
Langley Park, MD (cdp) Prince George's County	2,923	18.03
Hereford, TX (city) Deaf Smith County	2,621	17.96
Clovis, NM (city) Curry County	5,627	17.23
Plainview, TX (city) Hale County	3,838	17.18
Deming, NM (city) Luna County	2,420	17.14
Roswell, NM (city) Chaves County	7,646	16.88
Union City, NJ (city) Hudson County	11,272	16.80
Fountainbleau, FL (cdp) Miami-Dade County	9,962	16.73
Carlsbad, NM (city) Eddy County	4,273	16.68
Brownsville, TX (city) Cameron County	23,296	16.67
Edinburg, TX (city) Hidalgo County	8,036	16.58
Commerce City, CO (city) Adams County	3,447	16.42
Harlingen, TX (city) Cameron County	9,445	16.41
Levelland, TX (city) Hockley County	2,106	16.37
Gallup, NM (city) McKinley County	3,227	15.97
San Antonio, TX (city) Bexar County	182,662	15.96
Weslaco, TX (city) Hidalgo County	4,286	15.91
Sweetwater, FL (city) Miami-Dade County	2,264	15.91
West New York, NJ (town) Hudson County	7,212	15.76
Artesia, NM (city) Eddy County	1,678	15.69
Seguin, TX (city) Guadalupe County	3,396	15.43
Kendall West, FL (cdp) Miami-Dade County	5,815	15.29
Sherrelwood, CO (cdp) Adams County	2,694	15.26
Donna, TX (city) Hidalgo County	2,251	15.24
Cudahy, CA (city) Los Angeles County	3,425	14.15
Eagle Pass, TX (city) Maverick County	3,167	14.13
Hobbs, NM (city) Lea County	4,045	14.12
Douglas, AZ (city) Cochise County	1,992	13.92
Welby, CO (cdp) Adams County	1,805	13.91
Berkley, CO (cdp) Adams County	1,472	13.70
Socorro, TX (city) El Paso County	3,696	13.61
Sunland Park, NM (city) Dona Ana County	1,797	13.50
Lennox, CA (cdp) Los Angeles County	3,094	13.48
The Hammocks, FL (cdp) Miami-Dade County	6,367	13.44
McAllen, TX (city) Hidalgo County	14,253	13.39
Doral, FL (cdp) Miami-Dade County	2,727	13.34
Hialeah Gardens, FL (city) Miami-Dade County	2,571	13.32
Mission, TX (city) Hidalgo County	6,013	13.24
Kendale Lakes, FL (cdp) Miami-Dade County	7,479	13.14
Victoria, TX (city) Victoria County	7,908	13.05
Huntington Park, CA (city) Los Angeles County	7,992	13.03
Richmond, TX (city) Fort Bend County	1,439	12.99
Bailey's Crossroads, VA (cdp) Fairfax County	2,977	12.85
Maywood, CA (city) Los Angeles County	3,588	12.78
Bell, CA (city) Los Angeles County	4,680	12.76
Lockhart, TX (city) Caldwell County	1,480	12.74
Richmond West, FL (cdp) Miami-Dade County	3,557	12.67
Country Club, FL (cdp) Miami-Dade County	4,563	12.57
South Gate, CA (city) Los Angeles County	11,881	12.33
Bell Gardens, CA (city) Los Angeles County	5,394	12.24
Port Lavaca, TX (city) Calhoun County	1,462	12.15
El Campo, TX (city) Wharton County	1,319	12.05
Florence-Graham, CA (cdp) Los Angeles County	7,206	11.97
Nogales, AZ (city) Santa Cruz County	2,486	11.91
Lawrence, MA (city) Essex County	8,567	11.89
Pharr, TX (city) Hidalgo County	5,547	11.89
Guttenberg, NJ (town) Hudson County	1,285	11.89
Brighton, CO (city) Adams County	2,470	11.82
Rosenberg, TX (city) Fort Bend County	2,820	11.73
Dover, NJ (town) Morris County	2,134	11.73
El Paso, TX (city) El Paso County	65,939	11.70
North Bergen, NJ (township) Hudson County	6,789	11.69
Harrison, NJ (town) Hudson County	1,666	11.55
Brentwood, NY (cdp) Suffolk County	6,219	11.53
Tamiami, FL (cdp) Miami-Dade County	6,257	11.42
Del Rio, TX (city) Val Verde County	3,815	11.26
Key Biscayne, FL (village) Miami-Dade County	1,182	11.25
Shafter, CA (city) Kern County	1,415	11.11
Snyder, TX (city) Scurry County	1,197	11.10
Elizabeth, NJ (city) Union County	13,371	11.09
Walnut Park, CA (cdp) Los Angeles County	1,781	11.01
Central Falls, RI (city) Providence County	2,083	11.00
The Crossings, FL (cdp) Miami-Dade County	2,584	10.97
Sunnyside, WA (city) Yakima County	1,515	10.90
West Odessa, TX (cdp) Ector County	1,930	10.84
Lubbock, TX (city) Lubbock County	21,590	10.82
Miami, FL (city) Miami-Dade County	39,058	10.78
Arvin, CA (city) Kern County	1,392	10.74
Hialeah, FL (city) Miami-Dade County	24,305	10.73
South Houston, TX (city) Harris County	1,673	10.57
Country Walk, FL (cdp) Miami-Dade County	1,112	10.44
Farmington, NM (city) San Juan County	3,908	10.33
Parlier, CA (city) Fresno County	1,150	10.32
Port Chester, NY (village) Westchester County	2,861	10.27
Haverstraw, NY (village) Rockland County	1,037	10.25
Pueblo West, CO (cdp) Pueblo County	1,728	10.23
Freeport, TX (city) Brazoria County	1,292	10.17
Lynwood, CA (city) Los Angeles County	7,062	10.11
San Juan, TX (city) Hidalgo County	2,634	10.04
East Los Angeles, CA (cdp) Los Angeles County	12,446	10.01
Wheaton-Glenmont, MD (cdp) Montgomery County	5,777	10.01
Big Spring, TX (city) Howard County	2,502	9.92
Commerce, CA (city) Los Angeles County	1,247	9.92
Barstow, CA (city) San Bernardino County	2,090	9.90
North Bay Shore, NY (cdp) Suffolk County	1,476	9.85
Hempstead, NY (village) Nassau County	5,550	9.81
Baldwin Park, CA (city) Los Angeles County	7,411	9.77
La Puente, CA (city) Los Angeles County	4,000	9.74
West Puente Valley, CA (cdp) Los Angeles County	2,195	9.72
Selma, CA (city) Fresno County	1,890	9.72
San Marcos, TX (city) Hays County	3,345	9.63
Lamont, CA (cdp) Kern County	1,280	9.63
Dumas, TX (city) Moore County	1,322	9.62
Sanger, CA (city) Fresno County	1,817	9.60
Alamo, TX (city) Hidalgo County	1,417	9.60
Jacinto City, TX (city) Harris County	989	9.60
Westmont, CA (cdp) Los Angeles County	3,028	9.58
Odessa, TX (city) Ector County	8,703	9.57
Miami Beach, FL (city) Miami-Dade County	8,414	9.57
Coachella, CA (city) Riverside County	2,173	9.56
Eloy, AZ (city) Pinal County	990	9.54
South San Jose Hills, CA (cdp) Los Angeles County	1,925	9.52
Lawndale, CA (city) Los Angeles County	3,009	9.49
Greenfield, CA (city) Monterey County	1,188	9.44
Chelsea, MA (city) Suffolk County	3,286	9.37
North Plainfield, NJ (borough) Somerset County	1,966	9.32
Sweetwater, TX (city) Nolan County	1,049	9.19
Perth Amboy, NJ (city) Middlesex County	4,294	9.08
Thornton, CO (city) Adams County	7,442	9.03
Paterson, NJ (city) Passaic County	13,432	9.00
Northglenn, CO (city) Adams County	2,834	8.98
Los Angeles, CA (city) Los Angeles County	331,114	8.96
Dinuba, CA (city) Tulare County	1,509	8.96
Pico Rivera, CA (city) Los Angeles County	5,662	8.93
Adelphi, MD (cdp) Prince George's County	1,339	8.93
Fairview, NJ (borough) Bergen County	1,184	8.93
Denver, CO (city) Denver County	49,402	8.91
Avocado Heights, CA (cdp) Los Angeles County	1,334	8.81
Valinda, CA (cdp) Los Angeles County	1,916	8.80

Notes: (cdp) census designated place; Refer to the Explanation of Data in the front of the book for more detailed information.

Hungarian

Top 150 Places Sorted by Number

(Based on all places, regardless of population)

Place	Number	%
New York, NY (city) New York City	48,879	0.61
Los Angeles, CA (city) Los Angeles County	19,612	0.53
Chicago, IL (city) Cook County	9,418	0.33
Cleveland, OH (city) Cuyahoga County	8,385	1.75
Hempstead, NY (town) Nassau County	7,004	0.93
Toledo, OH (city) Lucas County	6,188	1.97
Phoenix, AZ (city) Maricopa County	5,925	0.45
Columbus, OH (city) Franklin County	5,889	0.83
Philadelphia, PA (city) Philadelphia County	5,848	0.39
San Diego, CA (city) San Diego County	5,737	0.47
Woodbridge, NJ (township) Middlesex County	5,000	5.14
Parma, OH (city) Cuyahoga County	4,514	5.27
Brookhaven, NY (town) Suffolk County	4,122	0.92
Akron, OH (city) Summit County	4,025	1.85
Pittsburgh, PA (city) Allegheny County	3,961	1.18
San Francisco, CA (city) San Francisco County	3,711	0.48
Hamilton, NJ (township) Mercer County	3,648	4.18
South Bend, IN (city) Saint Joseph County	3,605	3.37
Oyster Bay, NY (town) Nassau County	3,453	1.17
Houston, TX (city) Harris County	3,161	0.16
Edison, NJ (cdp) Middlesex County	3,121	3.19
Fairfield, CT (town) Fairfield County	3,088	5.39
Lorain, OH (city) Lorain County	3,078	4.48
Las Vegas, NV (city) Clark County	2,985	0.62
Bethlehem, PA (city) Northampton County	2,907	4.08
Milwaukee, WI (city) Milwaukee County	2,798	0.47
Ramapo, NY (town) Rockland County	2,708	2.49
Lakewood, OH (city) Cuyahoga County	2,674	4.72
Monroe, NY (town) Orange County	2,620	8.32
Seattle, WA (city) King County	2,547	0.45
Jacksonville, FL (special city) Duval County	2,485	0.34
North Hempstead, NY (town) Nassau County	2,470	1.11
San Jose, CA (city) Santa Clara County	2,436	0.27
Elyria, OH (city) Lorain County	2,342	4.19
Virginia Beach, VA (independent city) Virginia Beach city	2,316	0.54
Indianapolis, IN (special city) Marion County	2,281	0.29
Norwalk, CT (city) Fairfield County	2,259	2.72
Mentor, OH (city) Lake County	2,253	4.48
Dearborn, MI (city) Wayne County	2,232	2.28
Portland, OR (city) Multnomah County	2,231	0.42
Lincoln Park, MI (city) Wayne County	2,225	5.56
Allentown, PA (city) Lehigh County	2,216	2.08
Buffalo, NY (city) Erie County	2,190	0.75
Bridgeport, CT (city) Fairfield County	2,176	1.56
Taylor, MI (city) Wayne County	2,146	3.26
Washington, DC (city) District of Columbia	2,048	0.36
Denver, CO (city) Denver County	2,039	0.37
Allen Park, MI (city) Wayne County	2,020	6.88
Tucson, AZ (city) Pima County	2,016	0.41
Kiryas Joel, NY (village) Orange County	2,010	15.21
Huntington, NY (town) Suffolk County	1,955	1.00
Islip, NY (town) Suffolk County	1,931	0.60
Strongsville, OH (city) Cuyahoga County	1,885	4.30
Livonia, MI (city) Wayne County	1,839	1.83
North Olmsted, OH (city) Cuyahoga County	1,815	5.32
Dover, NJ (township) Ocean County	1,808	2.01
East Brunswick, NJ (cdp) Middlesex County	1,779	3.80
Toms River, NJ (cdp) Ocean County	1,755	2.03
Austin, TX (city) Travis County	1,741	0.27
Franklin, NJ (township) Somerset County	1,717	3.37
Hollywood, FL (city) Broward County	1,703	1.22
Dallas, TX (city) Dallas County	1,703	0.14
Scottsdale, AZ (city) Maricopa County	1,697	0.84
Youngstown, OH (city) Mahoning County	1,692	2.06
Southgate, MI (city) Wayne County	1,691	5.61
Clifton, NJ (city) Passaic County	1,688	2.15
Albuquerque, NM (city) Bernalillo County	1,686	0.38
Milford, CT (town) New Haven County	1,684	3.22
Saint Petersburg, FL (city) Pinellas County	1,673	0.68
Colorado Springs, CO (city) El Paso County	1,669	0.46
Charlotte, NC (city) Mecklenburg County	1,660	0.31
Milford, CT (special city) New Haven County	1,659	3.28
Brunswick, OH (city) Medina County	1,590	4.76
North Brunswick Township, NJ (cdp) Middlesex County	1,581	4.36
Stratford, CT (cdp) Fairfield County	1,559	3.12
Detroit, MI (city) Wayne County	1,527	0.16
Smithtown, NY (town) Suffolk County	1,499	1.30
Long Beach, CA (city) Los Angeles County	1,491	0.32
Farmington Hills, MI (city) Oakland County	1,490	1.81
Euclid, OH (city) Cuyahoga County	1,475	2.80
Brick, NJ (township) Ocean County	1,463	1.92
Cincinnati, OH (city) Hamilton County	1,455	0.44
West Mifflin, PA (borough) Allegheny County	1,452	6.46
Hammond, IN (city) Lake County	1,436	1.73
Santa Clarita, CA (city) Los Angeles County	1,435	0.95
Mesa, AZ (city) Maricopa County	1,434	0.36
Mishawaka, IN (city) Saint Joseph County	1,428	3.05
Shelton, CT (city) Fairfield County	1,423	3.73
Oregon, OH (city) Lucas County	1,412	7.29
Tonawanda, NY (town) Erie County	1,403	1.80
Babylon, NY (town) Suffolk County	1,402	0.66
Ann Arbor, MI (city) Washtenaw County	1,401	1.23
North Royalton, OH (city) Cuyahoga County	1,372	4.79
Greenburgh, NY (town) Westchester County	1,356	1.56
Lakewood, NJ (township) Ocean County	1,354	2.24
Westland, MI (city) Wayne County	1,351	1.56
Westlake, OH (city) Cuyahoga County	1,348	4.23
Granger, IN (cdp) Saint Joseph County	1,343	4.76
Yonkers, NY (city) Westchester County	1,327	0.68
Solon, OH (city) Cuyahoga County	1,325	6.08
Trumbull, CT (cdp) Fairfield County	1,322	3.86
Sterling Heights, MI (city) Macomb County	1,322	1.06
Amherst, NY (town) Erie County	1,316	1.13
Garfield Heights, OH (city) Cuyahoga County	1,310	4.28
Huntington Beach, CA (city) Orange County	1,305	0.69
Boardman, OH (cdp) Mahoning County	1,284	3.45
San Antonio, TX (city) Bexar County	1,272	0.11
West Bloomfield, MI (township) Oakland County	1,271	1.96
Arlington, VA (cdp) Arlington County	1,269	0.67
Bethlehem, PA (township) Northampton County	1,262	5.96
Baltimore, MD (independent city) Baltimore city	1,245	0.19
Canton, MI (cdp) Wayne County	1,236	1.62
Boston, MA (city) Suffolk County	1,236	0.21
Simi Valley, CA (city) Ventura County	1,224	1.10
Tampa, FL (city) Hillsborough County	1,218	0.40
Barberton, OH (city) Summit County	1,215	4.34
Cuyahoga Falls, OH (city) Summit County	1,211	2.45
Wyandotte, MI (city) Wayne County	1,204	4.30
Willoughby, OH (city) Lake County	1,190	5.27
South Brunswick, NJ (township) Middlesex County	1,186	3.14
North Ridgeville, OH (city) Lorain County	1,183	5.30
Minneapolis, MN (city) Hennepin County	1,181	0.31
Henderson, NV (city) Clark County	1,177	0.67
Aurora, CO (city) Arapahoe County	1,172	0.42
Sayreville, NJ (borough) Middlesex County	1,162	2.88
Fort Lauderdale, FL (city) Broward County	1,161	0.76
Stow, OH (city) Summit County	1,159	3.61
Paradise, NV (cdp) Clark County	1,137	0.61
Oakland, CA (city) Alameda County	1,137	0.28
Coral Springs, FL (city) Broward County	1,134	0.97
Saint Paul, MN (city) Ramsey County	1,130	0.39
Warren, MI (city) Macomb County	1,129	0.82
Dayton, OH (city) Montgomery County	1,129	0.68
Lyndhurst, OH (city) Cuyahoga County	1,127	7.38
Parma Heights, OH (city) Cuyahoga County	1,123	5.18
Anchorage, AK (municipality) Anchorage Borough	1,123	0.43
Omaha, NE (city) Douglas County	1,118	0.29
Mercerville-Hamilton Square, NJ (cdp) Mercer County	1,117	4.22
Nashville-Davidson, TN (special city) Davidson County	1,093	0.20
Stamford, CT (city) Fairfield County	1,082	0.92
Old Bridge, NJ (township) Middlesex County	1,071	1.77
Plantation, FL (city) Broward County	1,070	1.28
Dearborn Heights, MI (city) Wayne County	1,060	1.82
Brook Park, OH (city) Cuyahoga County	1,059	4.99
Boca Raton, FL (city) Palm Beach County	1,054	1.39
Pembroke Pines, FL (city) Broward County	1,052	0.77
Warren, OH (city) Trumbull County	1,044	2.23
Monroe, NJ (township) Middlesex County	1,043	3.73
Jackson, NJ (township) Ocean County	1,042	2.43
Naperville, IL (city) Du Page County	1,042	0.81

Notes: (cdp) census designated place; Refer to the Explanation of Data in the front of the book for more detailed information.

Hungarian

Top 150 Places Sorted by Percent

(Based on all places, regardless of population)

Place	Number	%
Hobart Bay, AK (cdp) Skagway-Hoonah-Angoon Census Area	2	50.00
Diamond Beach, NJ (cdp) Cape May County	34	25.19
Bonanza, CO (town) Saguache County	5	21.74
Godfrey Road, FL (cdp) Broward County	38	17.84
Balfour, ND (city) McHenry County	2	15.38
Kiryas Joel, NY (village) Orange County	2,010	15.21
Fairport Harbor, OH (village) Lake County	448	14.09
Regent, ND (city) Hettinger County	31	13.60
Walpack, NJ (township) Sussex County	5	13.51
Kupreanof, AK (city) Wrangell-Petersburg Census Area	4	12.50
Twin Bridges, MO (village) Laclede County	3	12.50
Orienta, WI (town) Bayfield County	12	11.65
West Pike Run, PA (township) Washington County	230	11.47
Ronald, WA (cdp) Kittitas County	20	11.30
Gulivoire Park, IN (cdp) Saint Joseph County	333	11.29
Grand River, OH (village) Lake County	38	11.24
Oneida, PA (cdp) Schuylkill County	20	10.93
Rayland, OH (village) Jefferson County	49	10.86
Freemansburg, PA (borough) Northampton County	199	10.49
Lake View, ME (plantation) Piscataquis County	3	10.34
Fieldsboro, NJ (borough) Burlington County	54	10.23
Taylor, ND (city) Stark County	15	10.07
Middletown, PA (cdp) Northampton County	749	10.06
Layton, FL (city) Monroe County	24	10.00
Sandy Ridge, PA (cdp) Centre County	28	9.89
Sewaren, NJ (cdp) Middlesex County	278	9.85
Paint, PA (borough) Somerset County	108	9.79
Tiltonsville, OH (village) Jefferson County	124	9.55
Vintondale, PA (borough) Cambria County	50	9.45
Fountain Hill, PA (borough) Lehigh County	435	9.43
Alpha, NJ (borough) Warren County	232	9.35
Albany, LA (village) Livingston Parish	80	9.30
Brownsville, PA (township) Fayette County	72	9.30
Tightwad, MO (village) Henry County	5	9.26
Port Reading, NJ (cdp) Middlesex County	326	8.92
Coppock, IA (city) Henry County	6	8.70
Herndon, KS (city) Rawlins County	15	8.38
West Brownsville, PA (borough) Washington County	90	8.37
Loch Arbour, NJ (village) Monmouth County	23	8.36
Monroe, NY (town) Orange County	2,620	8.32
Reminderville, OH (village) Summit County	193	8.25
Slickville, PA (cdp) Westmoreland County	30	8.17
Scalp Level, PA (borough) Cambria County	69	8.11
Florence-Roebling, NJ (cdp) Burlington County	646	7.87
Yankee Lake, OH (village) Trumbull County	7	7.87
Yorkville, OH (village) Jefferson County	98	7.83
Mantua, OH (village) Portage County	85	7.79
Greig, NY (town) Lewis County	102	7.77
Benson, PA (borough) Somerset County	15	7.73
Smithboro, IL (village) Bond County	15	7.69
Spirit, WI (town) Price County	20	7.66
Munhall, PA (borough) Allegheny County	938	7.65
Pepper Pike, OH (city) Cuyahoga County	458	7.58
Milltown, NJ (borough) Middlesex County	526	7.51
Sheffield, OH (village) Lorain County	221	7.49
Florence, NJ (township) Burlington County	802	7.46
Lyndhurst, OH (city) Cuyahoga County	1,127	7.38
Kaser, NY (village) Rockland County	243	7.37
Aquilla, OH (village) Geauga County	27	7.36
Abbott, PA (township) Potter County	17	7.36
West Homestead, PA (borough) Allegheny County	161	7.33
Hellertown, PA (borough) Northampton County	411	7.32
Oregon, OH (city) Lucas County	1,412	7.29
Hilltop, OH (cdp) Trumbull County	41	7.22
White Horse, NJ (cdp) Mercer County	687	7.19
Ellport, PA (borough) Lawrence County	82	7.16
Central City, PA (borough) Somerset County	90	7.15
Perryopolis, PA (borough) Fayette County	126	7.14
Northampton, PA (borough) Northampton County	671	7.13
Bombay Beach, CA (cdp) Imperial County	28	7.09
Sheffield Lake, OH (city) Lorain County	661	7.05
Grindstone-Rowes Run, PA (cdp) Fayette County	77	7.04
Ward, CO (town) Boulder County	5	7.04
Richfield, OH (village) Summit County	230	6.97
Dravosburg, PA (borough) Allegheny County	140	6.95
Kelleys Island, OH (village) Erie County	24	6.92
Allen Park, MI (city) Wayne County	2,020	6.88
Windber, PA (borough) Somerset County	300	6.83
Chesterland, OH (cdp) Geauga County	187	6.82
Beachwood, OH (city) Cuyahoga County	830	6.81
Pigeon Creek, OH (cdp) Summit County	60	6.71
Put-in-Bay, OH (village) Ottawa County	10	6.71
New Square, NY (village) Rockland County	315	6.69
Mayfield, OH (village) Cuyahoga County	232	6.67
Viking, MN (township) Marshall County	10	6.67
Glen Ullin, ND (city) Morton County	57	6.64
Port Vue, PA (borough) Allegheny County	279	6.60
Calumet-Norvelt, PA (cdp) Westmoreland County	110	6.59
Rivesville, WV (town) Marion County	60	6.59
Helmetta, NJ (borough) Middlesex County	120	6.58
Spring Hill, PA (cdp) Cambria County	61	6.58
Hebron, ND (city) Morton County	52	6.51
Roscoe, PA (borough) Washington County	55	6.49
Leechburg, PA (borough) Armstrong County	154	6.48
West Mifflin, PA (borough) Allegheny County	1,452	6.46
Blacklick, PA (township) Cambria County	141	6.41
Plainfield, OH (village) Coshocton County	10	6.41
Orange, OH (village) Cuyahoga County	206	6.37
Bordentown, NJ (township) Burlington County	533	6.36
Allen, PA (township) Northampton County	167	6.35
Lower Saucon, PA (township) Northampton County	627	6.34
Northwood, OH (city) Wood County	347	6.34
Centerville, PA (borough) Washington County	215	6.34
Moreland Hills, OH (village) Cuyahoga County	207	6.27
New Salem-Buffington, PA (cdp) Fayette County	49	6.27
Avon, OH (city) Lorain County	708	6.19
Elmore, OH (village) Ottawa County	90	6.19
Fords, NJ (cdp) Middlesex County	934	6.17
Garrettsville, OH (village) Portage County	141	6.17
Pohatcong, NJ (township) Warren County	210	6.15
Hiram, OH (village) Portage County	74	6.12
Brownstown, PA (borough) Cambria County	54	6.12
Norfolk, NY (town) Saint Lawrence County	279	6.11
East Kingston, NY (cdp) Ulster County	16	6.11
South Amherst, OH (village) Lorain County	117	6.09
Granville, WV (town) Monongalia County	48	6.09
Solon, OH (city) Cuyahoga County	1,325	6.08
Miller Landing, AK (cdp) Kenai Peninsula Borough	4	6.06
Ong, NE (village) Clay County	4	6.06
Reserve, MT (cdp) Sheridan County	2	6.06
Gilpin, PA (township) Armstrong County	156	6.03
Walton Hills, OH (village) Cuyahoga County	144	6.02
New Centerville, PA (borough) Somerset County	11	6.01
Twinsburg, OH (city) Summit County	1,012	5.99
Amherst, OH (city) Lorain County	711	5.98
Lagrange, OH (village) Lorain County	110	5.98
Bethlehem, PA (township) Northampton County	1,262	5.96
Burgoon, OH (village) Sandusky County	11	5.95
East Side, PA (borough) Carbon County	16	5.93
Coal Center, PA (borough) Washington County	8	5.93
Bedford, OH (city) Cuyahoga County	841	5.92
Twilight, PA (borough) Washington County	18	5.92
Everton, MO (city) Dade County	18	5.90
Monongahela, PA (township) Greene County	100	5.88
Mount Gretna Heights, PA (cdp) Lebanon County	21	5.88
Indian Creek, FL (village) Miami-Dade County	2	5.88
Streetsboro, OH (city) Portage County	721	5.85
Macedonia, OH (city) Summit County	540	5.85
McDonald, OH (village) Trumbull County	202	5.83
Orwell, OH (village) Ashtabula County	89	5.81
Riverview, MI (city) Wayne County	770	5.80
Nanty-Glo, PA (borough) Cambria County	177	5.80
Perry, PA (township) Fayette County	161	5.78
Perry, OH (village) Lake County	69	5.77
Genoa, OH (village) Ottawa County	129	5.76
Sharpsville, PA (borough) Mercer County	260	5.74
South Canal, OH (cdp) Trumbull County	77	5.72
Canton City, ND (city) Pembina County	2	5.71
Clark, PA (borough) Mercer County	36	5.70
Yardville-Groveville, NJ (cdp) Mercer County	512	5.65

Notes: (cdp) census designated place; Refer to the Explanation of Data in the front of the book for more detailed information.

Hungarian

Top 150 Places Sorted by Percent

(Based on places with populations of 10,000 or more)

Place	Number	%
Kiryas Joel, NY (village) Orange County	2,010	15.21
Monroe, NY (town) Orange County	2,620	8.32
Munhall, PA (borough) Allegheny County	938	7.65
Florence, NJ (township) Burlington County	802	7.46
Lyndhurst, OH (city) Cuyahoga County	1,127	7.38
Oregon, OH (city) Lucas County	1,412	7.29
Allen Park, MI (city) Wayne County	2,020	6.88
Beachwood, OH (city) Cuyahoga County	830	6.81
West Mifflin, PA (borough) Allegheny County	1,452	6.46
Avon, OH (city) Lorain County	708	6.19
Fords, NJ (cdp) Middlesex County	934	6.17
Solon, OH (city) Cuyahoga County	1,325	6.08
Twinsburg, OH (city) Summit County	1,012	5.99
Amherst, OH (city) Lorain County	711	5.98
Bethlehem, PA (township) Northampton County	1,262	5.96
Bedford, OH (city) Cuyahoga County	841	5.92
Streetsboro, OH (city) Portage County	721	5.85
Riverview, MI (city) Wayne County	770	5.80
Middleburg Heights, OH (city) Cuyahoga County	875	5.63
Southgate, MI (city) Wayne County	1,691	5.61
Lincoln Park, MI (city) Wayne County	2,225	5.56
Manville, NJ (borough) Somerset County	568	5.51
Woodhaven, MI (city) Wayne County	688	5.49
Metuchen, NJ (borough) Middlesex County	694	5.40
Fairfield, CT (town) Fairfield County	3,088	5.39
Salisbury, PA (township) Lehigh County	725	5.37
North Olmsted, OH (city) Cuyahoga County	1,815	5.32
North Ridgeville, OH (city) Lorain County	1,183	5.30
Broadview Heights, OH (city) Cuyahoga County	846	5.30
Parma, OH (city) Cuyahoga County	4,514	5.27
Willoughby, OH (city) Lake County	1,190	5.27
Parma Heights, OH (city) Cuyahoga County	1,123	5.18
Woodbridge, NJ (township) Middlesex County	5,000	5.14
Monsey, NY (cdp) Rockland County	752	5.12
Trenton, MI (city) Wayne County	990	5.06
Rocky River, OH (city) Cuyahoga County	1,039	5.01
Brook Park, OH (city) Cuyahoga County	1,059	4.99
Brooklyn, OH (city) Cuyahoga County	576	4.97
Mayfield Heights, OH (city) Cuyahoga County	957	4.94
Fairview Park, OH (city) Cuyahoga County	866	4.93
Seven Hills, OH (city) Cuyahoga County	592	4.90
North Royalton, OH (city) Cuyahoga County	1,372	4.79
Brunswick, OH (city) Medina County	1,590	4.76
Granger, IN (cdp) Saint Joseph County	1,343	4.76
Lakewood, OH (city) Cuyahoga County	2,674	4.72
Avon Lake, OH (city) Lorain County	852	4.70
Highland Park, NJ (borough) Middlesex County	655	4.68
Grosse Ile, MI (cdp) Wayne County	508	4.66
Carteret, NJ (borough) Middlesex County	958	4.63
Aurora, OH (city) Portage County	626	4.62
Painesville, OH (city) Lake County	796	4.55
Willowick, OH (city) Lake County	652	4.53
Wickliffe, OH (city) Lake County	611	4.53
Brecksville, OH (city) Cuyahoga County	601	4.51
Elizabeth, PA (township) Allegheny County	623	4.50
Lorain, OH (city) Lorain County	3,078	4.48
Mentor, OH (city) Lake County	2,253	4.48
Brownstown, MI (township) Wayne County	1,026	4.46
Phillipsburg, NJ (town) Warren County	671	4.42
South Euclid, OH (city) Cuyahoga County	1,039	4.41
North Brunswick Township, NJ (cdp) Middlesex County	1,581	4.36
Barberton, OH (city) Summit County	1,215	4.34
Strongsville, OH (city) Cuyahoga County	1,885	4.30
Wyandotte, MI (city) Wayne County	1,204	4.30
Garfield Heights, OH (city) Cuyahoga County	1,310	4.28
University Heights, OH (city) Cuyahoga County	603	4.26
Westlake, OH (city) Cuyahoga County	1,348	4.23
Eastlake, OH (city) Lake County	853	4.23
Mercerville-Hamilton Square, NJ (cdp) Mercer County	1,117	4.22
Elyria, OH (city) Lorain County	2,342	4.19
Hamilton, NJ (township) Mercer County	3,648	4.18
South River, NJ (borough) Middlesex County	638	4.16
Green, OH (city) Summit County	948	4.15
Bethlehem, PA (city) Northampton County	2,907	4.08
Monroe, CT (town) Fairfield County	766	3.98

Place	Number	%
Conneaut, OH (city) Ashtabula County	498	3.98
Norton, OH (city) Summit County	454	3.94
McKeesport, PA (city) Allegheny County	945	3.93
Trumbull, CT (cdp) Fairfield County	1,322	3.86
Melvindale, MI (city) Wayne County	412	3.84
East Brunswick, NJ (cdp) Middlesex County	1,779	3.80
Maple Heights, OH (city) Cuyahoga County	992	3.79
Bay Village, OH (city) Cuyahoga County	604	3.75
Shelton, CT (city) Fairfield County	1,423	3.73
Monroe, NJ (township) Middlesex County	1,043	3.73
Berea, OH (city) Cuyahoga County	702	3.69
Stow, OH (city) Summit County	1,159	3.61
Highland, IN (town) Lake County	846	3.59
Grand Island, NY (town) Erie County	660	3.54
North Huntingdon, PA (township) Westmoreland County	1,031	3.53
Ravenna, OH (city) Portage County	425	3.53
Medina, OH (city) Medina County	872	3.48
Boardman, OH (cdp) Mahoning County	1,284	3.45
Rostraver, PA (township) Westmoreland County	399	3.43
Whitehall, PA (township) Lehigh County	845	3.39
South Bend, IN (city) Saint Joseph County	3,605	3.37
Franklin, NJ (township) Somerset County	1,717	3.37
Newtown, CT (town) Fairfield County	843	3.37
Niles, OH (city) Trumbull County	692	3.31
Milford, CT (special city) New Haven County	1,659	3.28
Taylor, MI (city) Wayne County	2,146	3.26
Austintown, OH (cdp) Mahoning County	1,032	3.26
Perrysburg, OH (city) Wood County	554	3.24
Milford, CT (town) New Haven County	1,684	3.22
North Versailles, PA (cdp) Allegheny County	358	3.22
Tonawanda, NY (city) Erie County	516	3.20
Edison, NJ (cdp) Middlesex County	3,121	3.19
Branchburg, NJ (township) Somerset County	463	3.18
South Brunswick, NJ (township) Middlesex County	1,186	3.14
Avenel, NJ (cdp) Middlesex County	551	3.14
Vermilion, OH (city) Lorain County	340	3.13
Stratford, CT (cdp) Fairfield County	1,559	3.12
Hermitage, PA (city) Mercer County	503	3.12
Iselin, NJ (cdp) Middlesex County	511	3.08
Wadsworth, OH (city) Medina County	567	3.06
Mount Pleasant, PA (township) Westmoreland County	343	3.06
Mishawaka, IN (city) Saint Joseph County	1,428	3.05
Barnegat, NJ (township) Ocean County	463	3.03
Upper Saucon, PA (township) Lehigh County	362	3.03
Griffith, IN (town) Lake County	519	2.99
Niles, MI (township) Berrien County	395	2.94
Huron charter, MI (township) Wayne County	401	2.92
Sayreville, NJ (borough) Middlesex County	1,162	2.88
South Plainfield, NJ (borough) Middlesex County	615	2.82
Euclid, OH (city) Cuyahoga County	1,475	2.80
Schererville, IN (town) Lake County	694	2.80
Dobbs Ferry, NY (village) Westchester County	297	2.80
Palmer, PA (township) Northampton County	469	2.79
South Fayette, PA (township) Allegheny County	340	2.77
Kings Point, FL (cdp) Palm Beach County	341	2.75
Norwalk, CT (city) Fairfield County	2,259	2.72
Flushing, MI (township) Genesee County	278	2.72
Readington, NJ (township) Hunterdon County	428	2.71
Somerset, NJ (cdp) Somerset County	619	2.69
Seymour, CT (town) New Haven County	416	2.69
South Whitehall, PA (township) Lehigh County	484	2.68
Kent, OH (city) Portage County	748	2.67
Fullerton, PA (cdp) Lehigh County	379	2.67
Colonia, NJ (cdp) Middlesex County	471	2.65
Richmond Heights, OH (city) Cuyahoga County	289	2.64
Shaker Heights, OH (city) Cuyahoga County	768	2.61
Ashtabula, OH (city) Ashtabula County	539	2.58
Van Buren, MI (township) Wayne County	602	2.55
Phoenixville, PA (borough) Chester County	376	2.54
North Whitehall, PA (township) Lehigh County	374	2.54
Derby, CT (city) New Haven County	315	2.54
Washington, NJ (township) Mercer County	261	2.54
Sumpter, MI (township) Wayne County	299	2.52
Munster, IN (town) Lake County	541	2.51
Dickinson, ND (city) Stark County	397	2.51

Notes: (cdp) census designated place; Refer to the Explanation of Data in the front of the book for more detailed information.

Icelander

Top 150 Places Sorted by Number

(Based on all places, regardless of population)

Place	Number	%
Seattle, WA (city) King County	906	0.16
Spanish Fork, UT (city) Utah County	548	2.70
New York, NY (city) New York City	541	0.01
Los Angeles, CA (city) Los Angeles County	405	0.01
Orem, UT (city) Utah County	299	0.35
Grand Forks, ND (city) Grand Forks County	288	0.58
Fargo, ND (city) Cass County	265	0.29
Minneapolis, MN (city) Hennepin County	245	0.06
San Diego, CA (city) San Diego County	244	0.02
Bellingham, WA (city) Whatcom County	238	0.36
Springville, UT (city) Utah County	226	1.10
Tulsa, OK (city) Tulsa County	221	0.06
Portland, OR (city) Multnomah County	210	0.04
Grafton, ND (city) Walsh County	192	4.28
Bellevue, WA (city) King County	192	0.18
Chicago, IL (city) Cook County	176	0.01
Salt Lake City, UT (city) Salt Lake County	174	0.10
Phoenix, AZ (city) Maricopa County	158	0.01
Reno, NV (city) Washoe County	156	0.09
Denver, CO (city) Denver County	150	0.03
Everett, WA (city) Snohomish County	149	0.16
Burnsville, MN (city) Dakota County	147	0.24
Colorado Springs, CO (city) El Paso County	147	0.04
Virginia Beach, VA (independent city) Virginia Beach city	147	0.03
Cavalier, ND (city) Pembina County	138	8.96
San Francisco, CA (city) San Francisco County	134	0.02
Saint Paul, MN (city) Ramsey County	129	0.04
Overland Park, KS (city) Johnson County	127	0.09
Sandy, UT (city) Salt Lake County	125	0.14
Fort Collins, CO (city) Larimer County	121	0.10
Long Beach, CA (city) Los Angeles County	120	0.03
Shoreline, WA (city) King County	117	0.22
Provo, UT (city) Utah County	116	0.11
San Jose, CA (city) Santa Clara County	116	0.01
Lynnwood, WA (city) Snohomish County	115	0.34
Apple Valley, MN (city) Dakota County	115	0.25
Torrance, CA (city) Los Angeles County	112	0.08
Edmonds, WA (city) Snohomish County	107	0.27
Somerville, MA (city) Middlesex County	106	0.14
Maltby, WA (cdp) Snohomish County	99	1.17
Boise City, ID (city) Ada County	99	0.05
Minot, ND (city) Ward County	97	0.27
Hempstead, NY (town) Nassau County	97	0.01
Madison, WI (city) Dane County	96	0.05
Memphis, TN (city) Shelby County	96	0.01
Saint George, UT (city) Washington County	95	0.19
San Antonio, TX (city) Bexar County	95	0.01
Bloomington, MN (city) Hennepin County	92	0.11
Orlando, FL (city) Orange County	91	0.05
Albuquerque, NM (city) Bernalillo County	91	0.02
Mesa, AZ (city) Maricopa County	91	0.02
Tallahassee, FL (city) Leon County	90	0.06
Bismarck, ND (city) Burleigh County	87	0.16
Norfolk, VA (independent city) Norfolk city	87	0.04
Houston, TX (city) Harris County	87	0.00
Blaine, WA (city) Whatcom County	86	2.32
Carson City, NV (special city) Carson City city	86	0.16
Santa Rosa, CA (city) Sonoma County	86	0.06
Spokane, WA (city) Spokane County	85	0.04
Kent, WA (city) King County	83	0.10
Boulder, CO (city) Boulder County	83	0.09
Seattle Hill-Silver Firs, WA (cdp) Snohomish County	82	0.23
Federal Way, WA (city) King County	82	0.10
Walhalla, ND (city) Pembina County	80	7.66
Redlands, CA (city) San Bernardino County	79	0.12
Moreno Valley, CA (city) Riverside County	79	0.06
Scottsdale, AZ (city) Maricopa County	79	0.04
Indianapolis, IN (special city) Marion County	79	0.01
Henderson, NV (city) Clark County	78	0.04
Mountain, ND (city) Pembina County	76	51.70
East Grand Forks, MN (city) Polk County	76	1.01
Babylon, NY (town) Suffolk County	76	0.04
Pasadena, CA (city) Los Angeles County	75	0.06
Eden Prairie, MN (city) Hennepin County	74	0.13
Dallas, TX (city) Dallas County	71	0.01
Park River, ND (city) Walsh County	69	4.48
Elk Plain, WA (cdp) Pierce County	69	0.44
Kenmore, WA (city) King County	69	0.37
Coon Rapids, MN (city) Anoka County	69	0.11
San Mateo, CA (city) San Mateo County	69	0.07
Inglewood-Finn Hill, WA (cdp) King County	68	0.30
Minnetonka, MN (city) Hennepin County	68	0.13
Ogden, UT (city) Weber County	68	0.09
Naperville, IL (city) Du Page County	68	0.05
Tucson, AZ (city) Pima County	68	0.01
The Woodlands, TX (cdp) Montgomery County	67	0.12
Puyallup, WA (city) Pierce County	66	0.20
West Lake Stevens, WA (cdp) Snohomish County	65	0.36
Columbus, GA (special city) Muscogee County	65	0.03
Plymouth, MN (city) Hennepin County	64	0.10
Jacksonville, FL (special city) Duval County	64	0.01
Lake Forest Park, WA (city) King County	63	0.47
Brookhaven, NY (town) Suffolk County	63	0.01
Havre de Grace, MD (city) Harford County	62	0.55
Draper, UT (city) Salt Lake County	62	0.24
Saint Louis Park, MN (city) Hennepin County	62	0.14
Eugene, OR (city) Lane County	62	0.04
Washington, WI (town) Door County	61	9.27
Chesapeake, VA (independent city) Chesapeake city	61	0.03
Tacoma, WA (city) Pierce County	61	0.03
Santa Ana, CA (city) Orange County	61	0.02
Aurora, CO (city) Arapahoe County	60	0.02
Omaha, NE (city) Douglas County	60	0.02
Baltimore, MD (independent city) Baltimore city	60	0.01
Las Vegas, NV (city) Clark County	60	0.01
Salem, UT (city) Utah County	58	1.32
Davis, CA (city) Yolo County	58	0.10
Stamford, CT (city) Fairfield County	58	0.05
Vancouver, WA (city) Clark County	58	0.04
Spring Valley, CA (cdp) San Diego County	57	0.21
Spring Valley, NV (cdp) Clark County	57	0.05
Arlington, VA (cdp) Arlington County	57	0.03
Oyster Bay, NY (town) Nassau County	56	0.02
Mapleton, UT (city) Utah County	55	0.94
Ferndale, WA (city) Whatcom County	55	0.62
Juneau, AK (city and borough) Juneau Borough	55	0.18
Arvada, CO (city) Jefferson County	54	0.05
Oakland, CA (city) Alameda County	54	0.01
SeaTac, WA (city) King County	53	0.21
Maple Grove, MN (city) Hennepin County	53	0.11
Eagan, MN (city) Dakota County	53	0.08
Irvine, CA (city) Orange County	53	0.04
El Paso, TX (city) El Paso County	53	0.01
Neenah, WI (city) Winnebago County	52	0.21
Meridian, ID (city) Ada County	52	0.15
El Cajon, CA (city) San Diego County	52	0.05
Boston, MA (city) Suffolk County	52	0.01
San Bernardino, CA (city) San Bernardino County	51	0.03
Langdon, ND (city) Cavalier County	50	2.35
Valley City, ND (city) Barnes County	50	0.73
Nashville-Davidson, TN (special city) Davidson County	50	0.01
Edinburg, ND (city) Walsh County	49	18.08
Lodi, MI (township) Washtenaw County	49	0.86
Picnic Point-North Lynnwood, WA (cdp) Snohomish County	49	0.21
Hurricane, UT (city) Washington County	48	0.58
Layton, UT (city) Davis County	48	0.08
Rochester, MN (city) Olmsted County	48	0.06
Tustin Foothills, CA (cdp) Orange County	47	0.20
Berkeley, CA (city) Alameda County	47	0.05
Sioux Falls, SD (city) Minnehaha County	47	0.04
Durham, NC (city) Durham County	47	0.03
Newport News, VA (independent city) Newport News city	47	0.03
Sacramento, CA (city) Sacramento County	47	0.01
Amityville, NY (village) Suffolk County	46	0.49
Tysons Corner, VA (cdp) Fairfax County	46	0.25
North Marysville, WA (cdp) Snohomish County	46	0.22
Wellesley, MA (cdp) Norfolk County	46	0.17
Kearns, UT (cdp) Salt Lake County	46	0.14
San Buenaventura, CA (city) Ventura County	46	0.05
North Las Vegas, NV (city) Clark County	46	0.04

Notes: (cdp) census designated place; Refer to the Explanation of Data in the front of the book for more detailed information.

Icelander

Top 150 Places Sorted by Percent

(Based on all places, regardless of population)

Place	Number	%
Mountain, ND (city) Pembina County	76	51.70
Milton, ND (city) Cavalier County	21	23.86
Edinburg, ND (city) Walsh County	49	18.08
Canton City, ND (city) Pembina County	5	14.29
Prairie Rose, ND (city) Cass County	7	10.29
Donaldson, MN (city) Kittson County	5	9.62
Washington, WI (town) Door County	61	9.27
Cavalier, ND (city) Pembina County	138	8.96
Limestone, MN (township) Lincoln County	12	8.28
Hamilton, ND (city) Pembina County	6	8.11
Inkster, ND (city) Grand Forks County	8	7.77
Walhalla, ND (city) Pembina County	80	7.66
Roberts, MN (township) Wilkin County	10	7.63
Point Baker, AK (cdp) Prince of Wales-Outer Ketchikan Census Area	3	7.32
Crystal, ND (city) Pembina County	11	6.96
Alta Vista, MN (township) Lincoln County	11	5.73
Keystone, MN (township) Polk County	5	5.10
Park River, ND (city) Walsh County	69	4.48
Musselshell, MT (cdp) Musselshell County	3	4.41
Grafton, ND (city) Walsh County	192	4.28
Eden, MN (township) Polk County	8	4.23
Pohlitz, MN (township) Roseau County	2	4.17
Westerheim, MN (township) Lyon County	12	4.11
Y, AK (cdp) Matanuska-Susitna Borough	36	3.92
Arthur, ND (city) Cass County	17	3.81
Bancroft, ID (city) Caribou County	14	3.39
Upham, ND (city) McHenry County	6	3.23
Vega, MN (township) Marshall County	5	3.23
Pick City, ND (city) Mercer County	5	2.98
Grand Forks, MN (township) Polk County	6	2.97
Hamlin, MN (township) Lac qui Parle County	5	2.94
Swede Prairie, MN (township) Yellow Medicine County	5	2.94
Benjamin, UT (cdp) Utah County	27	2.91
Cohassett Beach, WA (cdp) Grays Harbor County	18	2.90
Logan, MN (township) Grant County	3	2.88
Taunton, MN (city) Lyon County	5	2.86
Hoople, ND (city) Walsh County	8	2.78
Spanish Fork, UT (city) Utah County	548	2.70
Marietta, MN (city) Lac qui Parle County	4	2.70
Willow Lake, SD (city) Clark County	8	2.65
Dieter, MN (township) Roseau County	4	2.63
Eidsvold, MN (township) Lyon County	6	2.54
South Prairie, WA (town) Pierce County	11	2.43
Kent Narrows, MD (cdp) Queen Anne's County	14	2.39
Langdon, ND (city) Cavalier County	50	2.35
Blaine, WA (city) Whatcom County	86	2.32
Havana, ND (city) Sargent County	2	2.22
Bowbells, ND (city) Burke County	9	2.21
Annabella, UT (town) Sevier County	13	2.18
Minto, ND (city) Walsh County	14	2.14
Huntsville, MN (township) Polk County	13	2.09
Bygland, MN (township) Polk County	6	2.08
Higdem, MN (township) Polk County	2	2.06
Durand, MN (township) Beltrami County	3	2.00
Drayton, ND (city) Pembina County	18	1.97
Elbridge, MI (township) Oceana County	24	1.94
Mentor, MN (city) Polk County	3	1.92
Northwest Snohomish, WA (cdp) Snohomish County	38	1.79
Upper Lake, CA (cdp) Lake County	17	1.79
Scraper, OK (cdp) Cherokee County	9	1.79
Soler, MN (township) Roseau County	2	1.71
Euclid, MN (township) Polk County	3	1.69
Osnabrock, ND (city) Cavalier County	3	1.67
Minneota, MN (city) Lyon County	24	1.65
Deerhorn, MN (township) Wilkin County	2	1.65
Golden Valley, ND (city) Mercer County	3	1.60
Mohall, ND (city) Renville County	13	1.59
Golden Valley, MN (township) Roseau County	3	1.58
Leavenworth, WA (city) Chelan County	32	1.57
Hallock, MN (city) Kittson County	19	1.57
Bynum, AL (cdp) Calhoun County	28	1.56
Cromwell, MN (city) Carlton County	2	1.56
Lincolndale, NY (cdp) Westchester County	29	1.53
Moose Wilson Road, WY (cdp) Teton County	23	1.53
Bottineau, ND (city) Bottineau County	36	1.51
Malung, MN (township) Roseau County	7	1.51
Adams, ND (city) Walsh County	3	1.51
Porter, MN (city) Yellow Medicine County	3	1.49
Vadito, NM (cdp) Taos County	3	1.49
Stallion Springs, CA (cdp) Kern County	24	1.47
Industrial, MN (township) Saint Louis County	9	1.47
South Heart, ND (city) Stark County	5	1.47
Collins, MN (township) McLeod County	7	1.42
Huss, MN (township) Roseau County	2	1.42
Island Lake, MN (township) Lyon County	3	1.39
Yellow Bank, MN (township) Lac qui Parle County	2	1.39
Skippers Corner, NC (cdp) New Hanover County	16	1.36
Manvel, ND (city) Grand Forks County	5	1.35
Salem, UT (city) Utah County	58	1.32
Ellsworth, MI (village) Antrim County	6	1.27
Rio Dell, CA (city) Humboldt County	40	1.26
Lake Stay, MN (township) Lincoln County	2	1.26
Neche, ND (city) Pembina County	5	1.24
Satsop, WA (cdp) Grays Harbor County	8	1.23
Laona, MN (township) Roseau County	7	1.23
Towner, ND (city) McHenry County	7	1.20
Manzanita, OR (city) Tillamook County	6	1.20
Falun, MN (township) Roseau County	3	1.20
Liberty Grove, WI (town) Door County	22	1.18
Elmo, UT (town) Emery County	4	1.18
Maltby, WA (cdp) Snohomish County	99	1.17
Cormorant, MN (township) Becker County	11	1.15
Foyil, OK (town) Rogers County	3	1.15
Blomkest, MN (city) Kandiyohi County	2	1.14
Roome, MN (township) Polk County	2	1.14
Placid Lakes, FL (cdp) Highlands County	34	1.13
Burton, MN (township) Yellow Medicine County	2	1.13
Bellevue, MI (village) Eaton County	15	1.12
Springville, UT (city) Utah County	226	1.10
Chevy Chase Section Five, MD (village) Montgomery County	7	1.10
Leeds, ND (city) Benson County	5	1.09
Garvin, MN (city) Lyon County	2	1.09
Moorcroft, WY (town) Crook County	9	1.08
Buzzle, MN (township) Beltrami County	3	1.07
Acton, CA (cdp) Los Angeles County	23	1.06
Roseau, MN (city) Roseau County	29	1.05
Grimstad, MN (township) Roseau County	2	1.05
Ross, MN (township) Roseau County	5	1.04
Rio Verde, AZ (cdp) Maricopa County	15	1.03
Elliott, IA (city) Montgomery County	4	1.03
Tyro, MN (township) Yellow Medicine County	2	1.03
Nora, MN (township) Clearwater County	4	1.02
Shaokatan, MN (township) Lincoln County	2	1.02
East Grand Forks, MN (city) Polk County	76	1.01
Woodruff, UT (town) Rich County	2	1.01
Gosport, IN (town) Owen County	7	1.00
Woodbury, VT (town) Washington County	8	0.98
Plains, MT (town) Sanders County	11	0.97
Turtle Lake, MN (township) Beltrami County	11	0.97
Hendricks, MN (city) Lincoln County	7	0.97
Cleveland, UT (town) Emery County	5	0.96
Wildwood, MN (township) Itasca County	2	0.96
Page, ND (city) Cass County	2	0.95
Mapleton, UT (city) Utah County	55	0.94
West Glendive, MT (cdp) Dawson County	17	0.94
Lyons, MN (township) Lyon County	2	0.93
Westline, MN (township) Redwood County	2	0.93
Hustler, WI (village) Juneau County	1	0.93
Nezperce, ID (city) Lewis County	5	0.92
Royal, MN (township) Lincoln County	2	0.92
Highland, WI (town) Iowa County	7	0.91
Jadis, MN (township) Roseau County	5	0.91
Hitterdal, MN (city) Clay County	2	0.91
Muncy, PA (borough) Lycoming County	24	0.90
Greenfield, MN (city) Hennepin County	23	0.90
Buffalo Soapstone, AK (cdp) Matanuska-Susitna Borough	6	0.89
Vermilion Lake, MN (township) Saint Louis County	3	0.89
East Troy, WI (village) Walworth County	31	0.88
Cando, ND (city) Towner County	12	0.88
Maine, MN (township) Otter Tail County	6	0.88

Notes: (cdp) census designated place; Refer to the Explanation of Data in the front of the book for more detailed information.

Icelander

Top 150 Places Sorted by Percent

(Based on places with populations of 10,000 or more)

Place	Number	%
Spanish Fork, UT (city) Utah County	548	2.70
Springville, UT (city) Utah County	226	1.10
Grand Forks, ND (city) Grand Forks County	288	0.58
Havre de Grace, MD (city) Harford County	62	0.55
Lake Forest Park, WA (city) King County	63	0.47
Elk Plain, WA (cdp) Pierce County	69	0.44
Kenmore, WA (city) King County	69	0.37
Bellingham, WA (city) Whatcom County	238	0.36
West Lake Stevens, WA (cdp) Snohomish County	65	0.36
Orem, UT (city) Utah County	299	0.35
Lynnwood, WA (city) Snohomish County	115	0.34
Williston, ND (city) Williams County	42	0.33
Tumwater, WA (city) Thurston County	41	0.32
Cornelius, NC (town) Mecklenburg County	37	0.32
Inglewood-Finn Hill, WA (cdp) King County	68	0.30
North Mankato, MN (city) Nicollet County	35	0.30
Fargo, ND (city) Cass County	265	0.29
Payson, UT (city) Utah County	37	0.29
Arlington, WA (city) Snohomish County	35	0.29
Vermilion, OH (city) Lorain County	31	0.29
Oxford charter, MI (township) Oakland County	45	0.28
Edmonds, WA (city) Snohomish County	107	0.27
Minot, ND (city) Ward County	97	0.27
Elko, NV (city) Elko County	44	0.27
Garden City, ID (city) Ada County	30	0.27
Joppatowne, MD (cdp) Harford County	30	0.27
West Haverstraw, NY (village) Rockland County	28	0.27
Dickinson, ND (city) Stark County	41	0.26
Longwood, FL (city) Seminole County	35	0.26
Brunswick, NY (town) Rensselaer County	30	0.26
Apple Valley, MN (city) Dakota County	115	0.25
Tysons Corner, VA (cdp) Fairfax County	46	0.25
Salmon Creek, WA (cdp) Clark County	41	0.25
Burnsville, MN (city) Dakota County	147	0.24
Draper, UT (city) Salt Lake County	62	0.24
Indianola, IA (city) Warren County	31	0.24
Solana Beach, CA (city) San Diego County	31	0.24
El Sobrante, CA (cdp) Contra Costa County	28	0.24
Hewitt, TX (city) McLennan County	26	0.24
Seattle Hill-Silver Firs, WA (cdp) Snohomish County	82	0.23
Farmington, UT (city) Davis County	28	0.23
Shoreline, WA (city) King County	117	0.22
North Marysville, WA (cdp) Snohomish County	46	0.22
Spring Valley, CA (cdp) San Diego County	57	0.21
SeaTac, WA (city) King County	53	0.21
Neenah, WI (city) Winnebago County	52	0.21
Picnic Point-North Lynnwood, WA (cdp) Snohomish County	49	0.21
Casa de Oro-Mount Helix, CA (cdp) San Diego County	40	0.21
Jamestown, ND (city) Stutsman County	33	0.21
Westwood, MA (town) Norfolk County	29	0.21
Wildomar, CA (cdp) Riverside County	29	0.21
Puyallup, WA (city) Pierce County	66	0.20
Tustin Foothills, CA (cdp) Orange County	47	0.20
Somers, NY (town) Westchester County	36	0.20
Rye, NY (city) Westchester County	30	0.20
Washington, NJ (township) Mercer County	21	0.20
Vashon, WA (cdp) King County	20	0.20
Saint George, UT (city) Washington County	95	0.19
Bainbridge Island, WA (city) Kitsap County	39	0.19
Port Angeles, WA (city) Clallam County	35	0.19
Oshtemo, MI (township) Kalamazoo County	32	0.19
Clayton, CA (city) Contra Costa County	21	0.19
Bellevue, WA (city) King County	192	0.18
Juneau, AK (city and borough) Juneau Borough	55	0.18
South Salt Lake, UT (city) Salt Lake County	39	0.18
Miami Springs, FL (city) Miami-Dade County	24	0.18
Sun Lakes, AZ (cdp) Maricopa County	21	0.18
Wellesley, MA (cdp) Norfolk County	46	0.17
Lutherville-Timonium, MD (cdp) Baltimore County	26	0.17
Wolf Trap, VA (cdp) Fairfax County	24	0.17
Rancho Mirage, CA (city) Riverside County	22	0.17
Seattle, WA (city) King County	906	0.16
Everett, WA (city) Snohomish County	149	0.16
Bismarck, ND (city) Burleigh County	87	0.16
Carson City, NV (special city) Carson City city	86	0.16
San Lorenzo, CA (cdp) Alameda County	36	0.16
Golden Valley, MN (city) Hennepin County	33	0.16
Kernersville, NC (town) Forsyth County	27	0.16
West Fargo, ND (city) Cass County	23	0.16
New Fairfield, CT (town) Fairfield County	22	0.16
Camano, WA (cdp) Island County	21	0.16
Coto de Caza, CA (cdp) Orange County	21	0.16
Metuchen, NJ (borough) Middlesex County	21	0.16
Vadnais Heights, MN (city) Ramsey County	21	0.16
Meridian, ID (city) Ada County	52	0.15
Orcutt, CA (cdp) Santa Barbara County	44	0.15
Marysville, WA (city) Snohomish County	38	0.15
Elkridge, MD (cdp) Howard County	32	0.15
Garden City, NY (village) Nassau County	32	0.15
Mountlake Terrace, WA (city) Snohomish County	31	0.15
Cottonwood West, UT (cdp) Salt Lake County	28	0.15
Mandan, ND (city) Morton County	25	0.15
Montclair, VA (cdp) Prince William County	24	0.15
Rose Hill, VA (cdp) Fairfax County	22	0.15
Carpinteria, CA (city) Santa Barbara County	21	0.15
Ferguson, PA (township) Centre County	21	0.15
Miami, OK (city) Ottawa County	21	0.15
Brainerd, MN (city) Crow Wing County	19	0.15
Sandy, UT (city) Salt Lake County	125	0.14
Somerville, MA (city) Middlesex County	106	0.14
Saint Louis Park, MN (city) Hennepin County	62	0.14
Kearns, UT (cdp) Salt Lake County	46	0.14
Peachtree City, GA (city) Fayette County	45	0.14
Bensenville, IL (village) Du Page County	29	0.14
Cedar City, UT (city) Iron County	28	0.14
Lakeside, CA (cdp) San Diego County	28	0.14
Deerfield, IL (village) Lake County	26	0.14
Willmar, MN (city) Kandiyohi County	25	0.14
Sayville, NY (cdp) Suffolk County	24	0.14
Alderwood Manor, WA (cdp) Snohomish County	22	0.14
Flowing Wells, AZ (cdp) Pima County	21	0.14
Stanford, CA (cdp) Santa Clara County	19	0.14
Lebanon, NH (city) Grafton County	18	0.14
Marshall, MN (city) Lyon County	18	0.14
Kingsgate, WA (cdp) King County	17	0.14
Green River, WY (city) Sweetwater County	16	0.14
Lincoln, CA (city) Placer County	15	0.14
Eden Prairie, MN (city) Hennepin County	74	0.13
Minnetonka, MN (city) Hennepin County	68	0.13
Moorhead, MN (city) Clay County	41	0.13
University Place, WA (city) Pierce County	39	0.13
Benicia, CA (city) Solano County	35	0.13
Batavia, IL (city) Kane County	31	0.13
Tooele, UT (city) Tooele County	29	0.13
Hauppauge, NY (cdp) Suffolk County	26	0.13
Ramsey, MN (city) Anoka County	24	0.13
Enumclaw, WA (city) King County	15	0.13
Leicester, MA (town) Worcester County	14	0.13
Redlands, CA (city) San Bernardino County	79	0.12
The Woodlands, TX (cdp) Montgomery County	67	0.12
Cascade-Fairwood, WA (cdp) King County	41	0.12
Vernon, CT (town) Tolland County	35	0.12
Cleburne, TX (city) Johnson County	32	0.12
Paine Field-Lake Stickney, WA (cdp) Snohomish County	29	0.12
Parker, CO (town) Douglas County	28	0.12
Kaysville, UT (city) Davis County	25	0.12
Ashland, OR (city) Jackson County	24	0.12
Northfield, MN (city) Rice County	21	0.12
Depew, NY (village) Erie County	20	0.12
Bemidji, MN (city) Beltrami County	15	0.12
Lynn Haven, FL (city) Bay County	15	0.12
Corinth, TX (city) Denton County	14	0.12
Lakewood Park, FL (cdp) Saint Lucie County	13	0.12
Lighthouse Point, FL (city) Broward County	13	0.12
Provo, UT (city) Utah County	116	0.11
Bloomington, MN (city) Hennepin County	92	0.11
Coon Rapids, MN (city) Anoka County	69	0.11
Maple Grove, MN (city) Hennepin County	53	0.11
Bountiful, UT (city) Davis County	44	0.11
Manassas, VA (independent city) Manassas city	40	0.11

Notes: (cdp) census designated place; Refer to the Explanation of Data in the front of the book for more detailed information.

Iranian

Top 150 Places Sorted by Number

(Based on all places, regardless of population)

Place	Number	%
Los Angeles, CA (city) Los Angeles County	44,521	1.20
New York, NY (city) New York City	8,506	0.11
North Hempstead, NY (town) Nassau County	7,622	3.42
San Diego, CA (city) San Diego County	7,241	0.59
San Jose, CA (city) Santa Clara County	6,728	0.75
Beverly Hills, CA (city) Los Angeles County	6,260	18.50
Glendale, CA (city) Los Angeles County	5,612	2.88
Irvine, CA (city) Orange County	5,307	3.71
Houston, TX (city) Harris County	4,436	0.23
Santa Monica, CA (city) Los Angeles County	2,590	3.08
Laguna Niguel, CA (city) Orange County	2,276	3.67
Plano, TX (city) Collin County	2,152	0.97
Great Neck, NY (village) Nassau County	2,061	21.60
Mission Viejo, CA (city) Orange County	2,033	2.19
Dallas, TX (city) Dallas County	1,994	0.17
Chicago, IL (city) Cook County	1,944	0.07
San Francisco, CA (city) San Francisco County	1,662	0.21
Anaheim, CA (city) Orange County	1,597	0.49
Kings Point, NY (village) Nassau County	1,486	29.28
Fremont, CA (city) Alameda County	1,485	0.73
Austin, TX (city) Travis County	1,369	0.21
Torrance, CA (city) Los Angeles County	1,271	0.92
Thousand Oaks, CA (city) Ventura County	1,241	1.06
Aliso Viejo, CA (cdp) Orange County	1,220	3.03
Huntington Beach, CA (city) Orange County	1,192	0.63
Lake Forest, CA (city) Orange County	1,170	1.99
Newport Beach, CA (city) Orange County	1,128	1.61
Potomac, MD (cdp) Montgomery County	1,116	2.49
Calabasas, CA (city) Los Angeles County	1,096	5.45
Phoenix, AZ (city) Maricopa County	1,055	0.08
Long Beach, CA (city) Los Angeles County	1,043	0.23
Oklahoma City, OK (city) Oklahoma County	1,014	0.20
Rancho Palos Verdes, CA (city) Los Angeles County	1,004	2.43
Arlington, TX (city) Tarrant County	1,000	0.30
Sunnyvale, CA (city) Santa Clara County	981	0.74
Hempstead, NY (town) Nassau County	954	0.13
San Antonio, TX (city) Bexar County	954	0.08
Gaithersburg, MD (city) Montgomery County	922	1.75
Bellevue, WA (city) King County	897	0.82
Walnut Creek, CA (city) Contra Costa County	895	1.39
Burbank, CA (city) Los Angeles County	892	0.89
Tysons Corner, VA (cdp) Fairfax County	879	4.75
Rockville, MD (city) Montgomery County	858	1.82
Santa Clarita, CA (city) Los Angeles County	849	0.56
Fresno, CA (city) Fresno County	833	0.19
Berkeley, CA (city) Alameda County	799	0.78
Cupertino, CA (city) Santa Clara County	761	1.50
Santa Clara, CA (city) Santa Clara County	758	0.74
Oyster Bay, NY (town) Nassau County	751	0.26
Washington, DC (city) District of Columbia	746	0.13
Columbus, OH (city) Franklin County	725	0.10
San Mateo, CA (city) San Mateo County	723	0.78
Seattle, WA (city) King County	719	0.13
Montgomery Village, MD (cdp) Montgomery County	705	1.86
Beaverton, OR (city) Washington County	700	0.92
Fullerton, CA (city) Orange County	691	0.55
North Bethesda, MD (cdp) Montgomery County	688	1.78
Orange, CA (city) Orange County	688	0.54
Rancho Santa Margarita, CA (city) Orange County	672	1.41
Pasadena, CA (city) Los Angeles County	671	0.50
Boston, MA (city) Suffolk County	649	0.11
West Hollywood, CA (city) Los Angeles County	647	1.81
Oakland, CA (city) Alameda County	642	0.16
Bethesda, MD (cdp) Montgomery County	636	1.15
Charlotte, NC (city) Mecklenburg County	633	0.12
Denver, CO (city) Denver County	625	0.11
Campbell, CA (city) Santa Clara County	623	1.63
Saratoga, CA (city) Santa Clara County	622	2.08
Mountain View, CA (city) Santa Clara County	620	0.88
Scottsdale, AZ (city) Maricopa County	620	0.31
Albuquerque, NM (city) Bernalillo County	617	0.14
Los Gatos, CA (town) Santa Clara County	614	2.14
Philadelphia, PA (city) Philadelphia County	613	0.04
Laguna Hills, CA (city) Orange County	610	1.95
Arlington, VA (cdp) Arlington County	608	0.32
Reston, VA (cdp) Fairfax County	600	1.06
Portland, OR (city) Multnomah County	586	0.11
Tustin, CA (city) Orange County	582	0.86
Great Neck Plaza, NY (village) Nassau County	580	9.15
McLean, VA (cdp) Fairfax County	580	1.49
Chantilly, VA (cdp) Fairfax County	574	1.40
San Ramon, CA (city) Contra Costa County	570	1.28
Redondo Beach, CA (city) Los Angeles County	561	0.89
Folsom, CA (city) Sacramento County	554	1.07
Alexandria, VA (independent city) Alexandria city	550	0.43
Germantown, MD (cdp) Montgomery County	543	0.98
Spring Valley, NV (cdp) Clark County	536	0.46
Colorado Springs, CO (city) El Paso County	532	0.15
Belmont, CA (city) San Mateo County	529	2.10
Concord, CA (city) Contra Costa County	528	0.43
Pleasanton, CA (city) Alameda County	522	0.82
Carrollton, TX (city) Denton County	519	0.48
Nashville-Davidson, TN (special city) Davidson County	515	0.09
Overland Park, KS (city) Johnson County	512	0.34
Sacramento, CA (city) Sacramento County	511	0.13
San Rafael, CA (city) Marin County	510	0.91
Palo Alto, CA (city) Santa Clara County	505	0.86
Paradise, NV (cdp) Clark County	505	0.27
Danville, CA (town) Contra Costa County	493	1.17
North Potomac, MD (cdp) Montgomery County	487	2.12
Naperville, IL (city) Du Page County	479	0.37
Arden-Arcade, CA (cdp) Sacramento County	475	0.49
Huntington, NY (town) Suffolk County	464	0.24
Baltimore, MD (independent city) Baltimore city	458	0.07
Columbia, MD (cdp) Howard County	457	0.52
Costa Mesa, CA (city) Orange County	453	0.42
Las Vegas, NV (city) Clark County	453	0.09
Yorba Linda, CA (city) Orange County	443	0.76
Davis, CA (city) Yolo County	440	0.73
Burlingame, CA (city) San Mateo County	437	1.56
Tulsa, OK (city) Tulsa County	432	0.11
Tucson, AZ (city) Pima County	426	0.09
Paramus, NJ (borough) Bergen County	425	1.65
Wichita, KS (city) Sedgwick County	425	0.12
Kansas City, MO (city) Jackson County	425	0.10
Sugar Land, TX (city) Fort Bend County	423	0.67
Chandler, AZ (city) Maricopa County	423	0.24
Upland, CA (city) San Bernardino County	412	0.60
Jacksonville, FL (special city) Duval County	407	0.06
Corona, CA (city) Riverside County	406	0.32
Indianapolis, IN (special city) Marion County	399	0.05
Lexington-Fayette, KY (special city) Fayette County	398	0.15
Los Altos, CA (city) Santa Clara County	395	1.43
Citrus Heights, CA (city) Sacramento County	394	0.46
Tempe, AZ (city) Maricopa County	394	0.25
Virginia Beach, VA (independent city) Virginia Beach city	388	0.09
Wolf Trap, VA (cdp) Fairfax County	385	2.77
Rancho Cucamonga, CA (city) San Bernardino County	383	0.30
Ann Arbor, MI (city) Washtenaw County	380	0.33
Turlock, CA (city) Stanislaus County	378	0.68
Burke, VA (cdp) Fairfax County	378	0.66
Raleigh, NC (city) Wake County	376	0.14
Kirkland, WA (city) King County	372	0.83
Carlsbad, CA (city) San Diego County	370	0.47
Brookline, MA (cdp) Norfolk County	369	0.65
Richardson, TX (city) Dallas County	369	0.40
Flower Hill, NY (village) Nassau County	367	8.14
Marina del Rey, CA (cdp) Los Angeles County	367	4.49
Diamond Bar, CA (city) Los Angeles County	365	0.65
Great Falls, VA (cdp) Fairfax County	364	4.25
Santa Rosa, CA (city) Sonoma County	364	0.25
Edmond, OK (city) Oklahoma County	363	0.53
Irving, TX (city) Dallas County	361	0.19
Carmichael, CA (cdp) Sacramento County	359	0.72
Orinda, CA (city) Contra Costa County	353	2.02
Brea, CA (city) Orange County	346	0.99
Simi Valley, CA (city) Ventura County	343	0.31
Santa Ana, CA (city) Orange County	341	0.10
Newton, MA (city) Middlesex County	336	0.40
Brookhaven, NY (town) Suffolk County	325	0.07

Notes: (cdp) census designated place; Refer to the Explanation of Data in the front of the book for more detailed information.

Iranian

Top 150 Places Sorted by Percent

(Based on all places, regardless of population)

Place	Number	%
Kings Point, NY (village) Nassau County	1,486	29.28
Great Neck, NY (village) Nassau County	2,061	21.60
Harbor Hills, NY (cdp) Nassau County	113	19.72
Beverly Hills, CA (city) Los Angeles County	6,260	18.50
Saddle Rock, NY (village) Nassau County	123	15.55
Kensington, NY (village) Nassau County	182	14.98
Great Neck Gardens, NY (cdp) Nassau County	147	13.16
Great Neck Estates, NY (village) Nassau County	304	10.76
Newport Coast, CA (cdp) Orange County	285	10.72
Great Neck Plaza, NY (village) Nassau County	580	9.15
Fisher Island, FL (cdp) Miami-Dade County	30	8.85
Flower Hill, NY (village) Nassau County	367	8.14
Thomaston, NY (village) Nassau County	149	5.74
Roslyn, NY (village) Nassau County	147	5.69
Calabasas, CA (city) Los Angeles County	1,096	5.45
Morongo Valley, CA (cdp) San Bernardino County	105	5.16
Oak Park, CA (cdp) Ventura County	125	5.10
Roslyn Harbor, NY (village) Nassau County	48	4.80
Tysons Corner, VA (cdp) Fairfax County	879	4.75
Roslyn Heights, NY (cdp) Nassau County	299	4.75
Norwood, KY (city) Jefferson County	21	4.60
Marina del Rey, CA (cdp) Los Angeles County	367	4.49
Rogers, MN (township) Cass County	2	4.44
Saddle Rock Estates, NY (cdp) Nassau County	19	4.33
Loyola, CA (cdp) Santa Clara County	148	4.28
Great Falls, VA (cdp) Fairfax County	364	4.25
Searingtown, NY (cdp) Nassau County	207	4.10
Lake View, TX (cdp) Val Verde County	6	3.87
North Hills, NY (village) Nassau County	160	3.72
Irvine, CA (city) Orange County	5,307	3.71
Roslyn Estates, NY (village) Nassau County	45	3.69
Laguna Niguel, CA (city) Orange County	2,276	3.67
Westlake Village, CA (city) Los Angeles County	309	3.57
North Hempstead, NY (town) Nassau County	7,622	3.42
Taos Ski Valley, NM (village) Taos County	3	3.33
Fairbanks Ranch, CA (cdp) San Diego County	61	3.25
Santa Monica, CA (city) Los Angeles County	2,590	3.08
San Joaquin Hills, CA (cdp) Orange County	94	3.05
Aliso Viejo, CA (cdp) Orange County	1,220	3.03
Dunn Loring, VA (cdp) Fairfax County	238	3.03
Carriage Club, CO (cdp) Douglas County	30	2.98
Fairmont, OK (town) Garfield County	4	2.92
East Hills, NY (village) Nassau County	199	2.90
Glendale, CA (city) Los Angeles County	5,612	2.88
Oak Brook, IL (village) Du Page County	239	2.83
Pennsbury Village, PA (borough) Allegheny County	21	2.83
Ann Arbor, MI (township) Washtenaw County	133	2.80
Wolf Trap, VA (cdp) Fairfax County	385	2.77
Bethania, NC (town) Forsyth County	10	2.75
Lucas Valley-Marinwood, CA (cdp) Marin County	173	2.74
Hunting Valley, OH (village) Cuyahoga County	20	2.71
Friendship Village, MD (cdp) Montgomery County	117	2.64
Potomac, MD (cdp) Montgomery County	1,116	2.49
Rancho Palos Verdes, CA (city) Los Angeles County	1,004	2.43
Laytonsville, MD (town) Montgomery County	7	2.41
South Barrington, IL (village) Cook County	88	2.36
Tiburon, CA (town) Marin County	201	2.30
Strawberry, CA (cdp) Marin County	123	2.30
Albertson, NY (cdp) Nassau County	119	2.30
Lightstreet, PA (cdp) Columbia County	18	2.29
Travilah, MD (cdp) Montgomery County	170	2.25
Seven Corners, VA (cdp) Fairfax County	199	2.24
University Gardens, NY (cdp) Nassau County	92	2.22
Las Flores, CA (cdp) Orange County	125	2.21
Mission Viejo, CA (city) Orange County	2,033	2.19
Pinehurst, GA (city) Dooly County	7	2.17
Old Westbury, NY (village) Nassau County	91	2.15
Plandome Manor, NY (village) Nassau County	18	2.15
Los Gatos, CA (town) Santa Clara County	614	2.14
Blackhawk-Camino Tassajara, CA (cdp) Contra Costa County	212	2.13
North Potomac, MD (cdp) Montgomery County	487	2.12
Ailey, GA (city) Montgomery County	8	2.11
Belmont, CA (city) San Mateo County	529	2.10
Lake Barcroft, VA (cdp) Fairfax County	190	2.10
Hunters Creek Village, TX (city) Harris County	92	2.10
Saratoga, CA (city) Santa Clara County	622	2.08
Vienna, VA (town) Fairfax County	300	2.06
Palos Verdes Estates, CA (city) Los Angeles County	275	2.06
Grasonville, MD (cdp) Queen Anne's County	45	2.06
Old Brookville, NY (village) Nassau County	45	2.06
Orinda, CA (city) Contra Costa County	353	2.02
Lake Forest, CA (city) Orange County	1,170	1.99
Alpine, NJ (borough) Bergen County	43	1.97
Piperton, TN (city) Fayette County	11	1.97
Parkersburg, IL (village) Richland County	4	1.96
Laguna Hills, CA (city) Orange County	610	1.95
Laupahoehoe, HI (cdp) Hawaii County	9	1.95
Bell, OK (cdp) Adair County	13	1.93
Idylwood, VA (cdp) Fairfax County	307	1.91
Berkeley Lake, GA (city) Gwinnett County	33	1.88
Westwood, KY (city) Jefferson County	12	1.87
Montgomery Village, MD (cdp) Montgomery County	705	1.86
Rockville, MD (city) Montgomery County	858	1.82
University Heights, IA (city) Johnson County	18	1.82
West Hollywood, CA (city) Los Angeles County	647	1.81
North Bethesda, MD (cdp) Montgomery County	688	1.78
El Valle de Arroyo Seco, NM (cdp) Santa Fe County	15	1.76
Gaithersburg, MD (city) Montgomery County	922	1.75
Lake Success, NY (village) Nassau County	49	1.75
Eidsvold, MN (township) Lyon County	4	1.69
Paramus, NJ (borough) Bergen County	425	1.65
Alamo, CA (cdp) Contra Costa County	250	1.65
Bulverde, TX (city) Comal County	62	1.65
Clifton, VA (town) Fairfax County	3	1.64
Campbell, CA (city) Santa Clara County	623	1.63
Newport Beach, CA (city) Orange County	1,128	1.61
Paragonah, UT (town) Iron County	8	1.61
Hillsborough, CA (town) San Mateo County	173	1.60
Burlingame, CA (city) San Mateo County	437	1.56
Del Monte Forest, CA (cdp) Monterey County	71	1.56
Waite Hill, OH (village) Lake County	7	1.55
Agoura Hills, CA (city) Los Angeles County	314	1.54
Cupertino, CA (city) Santa Clara County	761	1.50
Naranja, FL (cdp) Miami-Dade County	63	1.50
McLean, VA (cdp) Fairfax County	580	1.49
Russell Gardens, NY (village) Nassau County	16	1.49
Bath, WV (town) Morgan County	10	1.49
South Abington, PA (township) Lackawanna County	129	1.48
Hillandale, MD (cdp) Montgomery County	44	1.48
Waldon, CA (cdp) Contra Costa County	74	1.47
Dasher, GA (town) Lowndes County	13	1.47
Village Saint George, LA (cdp) East Baton Rouge Parish	100	1.46
Los Altos Hills, CA (town) Santa Clara County	116	1.45
Rosebud, SD (cdp) Todd County	24	1.45
Malibu, CA (city) Los Angeles County	180	1.44
Emeryville, CA (city) Alameda County	99	1.44
Hewlett Bay Park, NY (village) Nassau County	7	1.44
Los Altos, CA (city) Santa Clara County	395	1.43
Sewickley Heights, PA (borough) Allegheny County	14	1.43
Collins, MN (township) McLeod County	7	1.42
Rancho Santa Margarita, CA (city) Orange County	574	1.41
Chantilly, VA (cdp) Fairfax County	574	1.40
Walnut Creek, CA (city) Contra Costa County	895	1.39
Asharoken, NY (village) Suffolk County	9	1.39
Stagecoach, TX (town) Montgomery County	7	1.39
West Dundee, IL (village) Kane County	74	1.38
Parker, PA (township) Butler County	10	1.38
El Cerrito, CA (city) Contra Costa County	317	1.37
Spearsville, LA (village) Union Parish	2	1.37
Redland, MD (cdp) Montgomery County	231	1.34
Albany, CA (city) Alameda County	221	1.34
Alturas, CA (city) Modoc County	40	1.34
Sands Point, NY (village) Nassau County	37	1.34
Morrisonville, NY (cdp) Clinton County	22	1.33
Lambertville, NJ (city) Hunterdon County	51	1.32
Granite, UT (cdp) Salt Lake County	29	1.32
Atlantic Beach, NY (village) Nassau County	26	1.32
Darnestown, MD (cdp) Montgomery County	83	1.30
Brookville, NY (village) Nassau County	28	1.30
Mentor, WI (town) Clark County	7	1.29

Notes: (cdp) census designated place; Refer to the Explanation of Data in the front of the book for more detailed information.

Iranian

Top 150 Places Sorted by Percent

(Based on places with populations of 10,000 or more)

Place	Number	%
Beverly Hills, CA (city) Los Angeles County	6,260	18.50
Calabasas, CA (city) Los Angeles County	1,096	5.45
Tysons Corner, VA (cdp) Fairfax County	879	4.75
Irvine, CA (city) Orange County	5,307	3.71
Laguna Niguel, CA (city) Orange County	2,276	3.67
North Hempstead, NY (town) Nassau County	7,622	3.42
Santa Monica, CA (city) Los Angeles County	2,590	3.08
Aliso Viejo, CA (cdp) Orange County	1,220	3.03
Glendale, CA (city) Los Angeles County	5,612	2.88
Wolf Trap, VA (cdp) Fairfax County	385	2.77
Potomac, MD (cdp) Montgomery County	1,116	2.49
Rancho Palos Verdes, CA (city) Los Angeles County	1,004	2.43
Mission Viejo, CA (city) Orange County	2,033	2.19
Los Gatos, CA (town) Santa Clara County	614	2.14
North Potomac, MD (cdp) Montgomery County	487	2.12
Belmont, CA (city) San Mateo County	529	2.10
Saratoga, CA (city) Santa Clara County	622	2.08
Vienna, VA (town) Fairfax County	300	2.06
Palos Verdes Estates, CA (city) Los Angeles County	275	2.06
Orinda, CA (city) Contra Costa County	353	2.02
Lake Forest, CA (city) Orange County	1,170	1.99
Laguna Hills, CA (city) Orange County	610	1.95
Idylwood, VA (cdp) Fairfax County	307	1.91
Montgomery Village, MD (cdp) Montgomery County	705	1.86
Rockville, MD (city) Montgomery County	858	1.82
West Hollywood, CA (city) Los Angeles County	647	1.81
North Bethesda, MD (cdp) Montgomery County	688	1.78
Gaithersburg, MD (city) Montgomery County	922	1.75
Paramus, NJ (borough) Bergen County	425	1.65
Alamo, CA (cdp) Contra Costa County	250	1.65
Campbell, CA (city) Santa Clara County	623	1.63
Newport Beach, CA (city) Orange County	1,128	1.61
Hillsborough, CA (town) San Mateo County	173	1.60
Burlingame, CA (city) San Mateo County	437	1.56
Agoura Hills, CA (city) Los Angeles County	314	1.54
Cupertino, CA (city) Santa Clara County	761	1.50
McLean, VA (cdp) Fairfax County	580	1.49
Malibu, CA (city) Los Angeles County	180	1.44
Los Altos, CA (city) Santa Clara County	395	1.43
Rancho Santa Margarita, CA (city) Orange County	672	1.41
Chantilly, VA (cdp) Fairfax County	574	1.40
Walnut Creek, CA (city) Contra Costa County	895	1.39
El Cerrito, CA (city) Contra Costa County	317	1.37
Redland, MD (cdp) Montgomery County	231	1.34
Albany, CA (city) Alameda County	221	1.34
San Ramon, CA (city) Contra Costa County	570	1.28
Mill Creek, WA (city) Snohomish County	146	1.28
Moraga, CA (town) Contra Costa County	210	1.26
Larkspur, CA (city) Marin County	149	1.24
La Canada Flintridge, CA (city) Los Angeles County	246	1.21
Los Angeles, CA (city) Los Angeles County	44,521	1.20
Parkland, FL (city) Broward County	167	1.19
Danville, CA (town) Contra Costa County	493	1.17
North New Hyde Park, NY (cdp) Nassau County	170	1.17
Bethesda, MD (cdp) Montgomery County	636	1.15
Oakton, VA (cdp) Fairfax County	324	1.10
Foster City, CA (city) San Mateo County	314	1.09
Folsom, CA (city) Sacramento County	554	1.07
Thousand Oaks, CA (city) Ventura County	1,241	1.06
Reston, VA (cdp) Fairfax County	600	1.06
San Carlos, CA (city) San Mateo County	291	1.05
Franklin Lakes, NJ (borough) Bergen County	109	1.05
Laguna Beach, CA (city) Orange County	243	1.04
Foothill Ranch, CA (cdp) Orange County	112	1.03
Mukilteo, WA (city) Snohomish County	183	1.01
Brea, CA (city) Orange County	346	0.99
Merrifield, VA (cdp) Fairfax County	110	0.99
Germantown, MD (cdp) Montgomery County	543	0.98
Plano, TX (city) Collin County	2,152	0.97
Dublin, CA (city) Alameda County	291	0.97
Bernards, NJ (township) Somerset County	234	0.95
Mineola, NY (village) Nassau County	179	0.93
Torrance, CA (city) Los Angeles County	1,271	0.92
Beaverton, OR (city) Washington County	700	0.92
San Rafael, CA (city) Marin County	510	0.91

Place	Number	%
Town and Country, MO (city) Saint Louis County	98	0.90
Burbank, CA (city) Los Angeles County	892	0.89
Redondo Beach, CA (city) Los Angeles County	561	0.89
Mountain View, CA (city) Santa Clara County	620	0.88
Lake Oswego, OR (city) Clackamas County	308	0.87
Tustin, CA (city) Orange County	582	0.86
Palo Alto, CA (city) Santa Clara County	505	0.86
Tustin Foothills, CA (cdp) Orange County	206	0.86
The Crossings, FL (cdp) Miami-Dade County	202	0.86
Morris, NJ (township) Morris County	182	0.84
Westwood, MA (town) Norfolk County	119	0.84
San Marino, CA (city) Los Angeles County	109	0.84
Wanaque, NJ (borough) Passaic County	86	0.84
Kirkland, WA (city) King County	372	0.83
Cockeysville, MD (cdp) Baltimore County	163	0.83
North Valley Stream, NY (cdp) Nassau County	131	0.83
Coto de Caza, CA (cdp) Orange County	108	0.83
Bellevue, WA (city) King County	897	0.82
Pleasanton, CA (city) Alameda County	522	0.82
Holmdel, NJ (township) Monmouth County	129	0.82
Cedar Mill, OR (cdp) Washington County	105	0.82
La Verne, CA (city) Los Angeles County	257	0.81
Manhattan Beach, CA (city) Los Angeles County	272	0.80
Bailey's Crossroads, VA (cdp) Fairfax County	183	0.80
Cliffside Park, NJ (borough) Bergen County	182	0.79
Millbrae, CA (city) San Mateo County	164	0.79
Lomita, CA (city) Los Angeles County	157	0.79
Hockessin, DE (cdp) New Castle County	102	0.79
Berkeley, CA (city) Alameda County	799	0.78
San Mateo, CA (city) San Mateo County	723	0.78
Isla Vista, CA (cdp) Santa Barbara County	142	0.77
Yorba Linda, CA (city) Orange County	443	0.76
San Jose, CA (city) Santa Clara County	6,728	0.75
Cutler, FL (cdp) Miami-Dade County	132	0.75
Sunnyvale, CA (city) Santa Clara County	981	0.74
Santa Clara, CA (city) Santa Clara County	758	0.74
Watertown, MA (city) Middlesex County	245	0.74
Colesville, MD (cdp) Montgomery County	146	0.74
New Canaan, CT (town) Fairfield County	144	0.74
Greenwood Village, CO (city) Arapahoe County	82	0.74
Fremont, CA (city) Alameda County	1,485	0.73
Davis, CA (city) Yolo County	440	0.73
Orangevale, CA (cdp) Sacramento County	196	0.73
West Carson, CA (cdp) Los Angeles County	155	0.73
Carmichael, CA (cdp) Sacramento County	359	0.72
Sugar Hill, GA (city) Gwinnett County	80	0.71
Menlo Park, CA (city) San Mateo County	217	0.70
Fort Lee, NJ (borough) Bergen County	244	0.69
Lexington, MA (cdp) Middlesex County	208	0.69
Turlock, CA (city) Stanislaus County	378	0.68
Livingston, NJ (cdp) Essex County	185	0.68
La Crescenta-Montrose, CA (cdp) Los Angeles County	126	0.68
Piedmont, CA (city) Alameda County	74	0.68
Sugar Land, TX (city) Fort Bend County	423	0.67
Redmond, WA (city) King County	304	0.67
Moorpark, CA (city) Ventura County	208	0.67
Fair Oaks, CA (cdp) Sacramento County	189	0.67
Glen Cove, NY (city) Nassau County	179	0.67
South Pasadena, CA (city) Los Angeles County	163	0.67
El Segundo, CA (city) Los Angeles County	107	0.67
Suffern, NY (village) Rockland County	74	0.67
Burke, VA (cdp) Fairfax County	378	0.66
Brookline, MA (cdp) Norfolk County	369	0.65
Diamond Bar, CA (city) Los Angeles County	365	0.65
Inglewood-Finn Hill, WA (cdp) King County	145	0.64
Huntington Beach, CA (city) Orange County	1,192	0.63
Olney, MD (cdp) Montgomery County	198	0.63
Brentwood, TN (city) Williamson County	151	0.63
Coralville, IA (city) Johnson County	96	0.63
Upper Macungie, PA (township) Lehigh County	88	0.63
Bull Run, VA (cdp) Prince William County	71	0.62
Tarrytown, NY (village) Westchester County	69	0.62
Upland, CA (city) San Bernardino County	412	0.60
Claremont, CA (city) Los Angeles County	205	0.60
Mayfield Heights, OH (city) Cuyahoga County	117	0.60

Notes: (cdp) census designated place; Refer to the Explanation of Data in the front of the book for more detailed information.

Irish

Top 150 Places Sorted by Number

(Based on all places, regardless of population)

Place	Number	%
New York, NY (city) New York City	420,810	5.25
Philadelphia, PA (city) Philadelphia County	206,350	13.60
Chicago, IL (city) Cook County	191,729	6.62
Los Angeles, CA (city) Los Angeles County	138,379	3.75
Hempstead, NY (town) Nassau County	133,307	17.63
Phoenix, AZ (city) Maricopa County	123,592	9.36
Brookhaven, NY (town) Suffolk County	112,354	25.06
San Diego, CA (city) San Diego County	105,547	8.63
Boston, MA (city) Suffolk County	93,198	15.82
Houston, TX (city) Harris County	83,633	4.28
Columbus, OH (city) Franklin County	83,226	11.69
Indianapolis, IN (special city) Marion County	79,838	10.20
Islip, NY (town) Suffolk County	69,514	21.55
San Francisco, CA (city) San Francisco County	68,307	8.79
Seattle, WA (city) King County	66,326	11.77
Jacksonville, FL (special city) Duval County	66,148	8.99
Portland, OR (city) Multnomah County	64,086	12.11
Omaha, NE (city) Douglas County	62,349	15.98
Oyster Bay, NY (town) Nassau County	60,453	20.57
San Antonio, TX (city) Bexar County	59,637	5.21
Dallas, TX (city) Dallas County	58,746	4.94
Austin, TX (city) Travis County	55,063	8.39
San Jose, CA (city) Santa Clara County	54,056	6.05
Denver, CO (city) Denver County	52,989	9.55
Pittsburgh, PA (city) Allegheny County	52,845	15.80
Virginia Beach, VA (independent city) Virginia Beach city	52,692	12.39
Nashville-Davidson, TN (special city) Davidson County	48,414	8.87
Tucson, AZ (city) Pima County	46,811	9.62
Las Vegas, NV (city) Clark County	46,617	9.73
Oklahoma City, OK (city) Oklahoma County	46,591	9.21
Kansas City, MO (city) Jackson County	45,655	10.35
Colorado Springs, CO (city) El Paso County	44,871	12.44
Babylon, NY (town) Suffolk County	43,411	20.50
Mesa, AZ (city) Maricopa County	42,830	10.78
Charlotte, NC (city) Mecklenburg County	42,394	7.82
Huntington, NY (town) Suffolk County	41,599	21.30
Albuquerque, NM (city) Bernalillo County	41,090	9.16
Tulsa, OK (city) Tulsa County	40,850	10.39
Cleveland, OH (city) Cuyahoga County	38,986	8.15
Baltimore, MD (independent city) Baltimore city	38,980	5.99
Minneapolis, MN (city) Hennepin County	38,670	10.11
Milwaukee, WI (city) Milwaukee County	37,726	6.32
Saint Paul, MN (city) Ramsey County	36,699	12.78
Buffalo, NY (city) Erie County	35,608	12.17
Cincinnati, OH (city) Hamilton County	34,226	10.35
Toledo, OH (city) Lucas County	33,738	10.76
Wichita, KS (city) Sedgwick County	33,723	9.80
Fort Worth, TX (city) Tarrant County	33,209	6.20
Worcester, MA (city) Worcester County	32,733	18.96
Memphis, TN (city) Shelby County	31,924	4.91
Lexington-Fayette, KY (special city) Fayette County	31,113	11.94
Saint Petersburg, FL (city) Pinellas County	30,759	12.41
Madison, WI (city) Dane County	30,141	14.52
Saint Louis, MO (independent city) Saint Louis city	30,092	8.64
Smithtown, NY (town) Suffolk County	30,091	26.00
Quincy, MA (city) Norfolk County	30,036	34.12
Anchorage, AK (municipality) Anchorage Borough	30,031	11.54
North Hempstead, NY (town) Nassau County	28,740	12.91
Louisville, KY (city) Jefferson County	28,695	11.19
Lincoln, NE (city) Lancaster County	28,602	12.69
Arlington, TX (city) Tarrant County	28,487	8.56
Scottsdale, AZ (city) Maricopa County	28,482	14.05
Aurora, CO (city) Arapahoe County	28,267	10.24
Washington, DC (city) District of Columbia	28,081	4.91
Upper Darby, PA (township) Delaware County	27,905	34.10
Sacramento, CA (city) Sacramento County	27,663	6.80
Long Beach, CA (city) Los Angeles County	27,575	5.98
Spokane, WA (city) Spokane County	26,966	13.75
Tampa, FL (city) Hillsborough County	25,499	8.40
Huntington Beach, CA (city) Orange County	25,309	13.32
Yonkers, NY (city) Westchester County	25,213	12.86
Des Moines, IA (city) Polk County	25,184	12.68
Akron, OH (city) Summit County	24,889	11.46
Warwick, RI (city) Kent County	24,403	28.44
Arlington, VA (cdp) Arlington County	24,102	12.72
Overland Park, KS (city) Johnson County	24,001	16.12
Plano, TX (city) Collin County	23,979	10.79
Naperville, IL (city) Du Page County	23,688	18.46
Syracuse, NY (city) Onondaga County	23,375	15.87
Scranton, PA (city) Lackawanna County	23,171	30.32
Boise City, ID (city) Ada County	23,146	12.45
Raleigh, NC (city) Wake County	23,117	8.36
Henderson, NV (city) Clark County	23,090	13.12
Fresno, CA (city) Fresno County	22,970	5.38
New Orleans, LA (city) Orleans Parish	22,944	4.73
Reno, NV (city) Washoe County	22,897	12.67
Glendale, AZ (city) Maricopa County	22,682	10.38
Colonie, NY (town) Albany County	22,194	28.00
Brick, NJ (township) Ocean County	22,022	28.93
Dover, NJ (township) Ocean County	21,766	24.25
Middletown, NJ (township) Monmouth County	21,756	32.80
Fort Wayne, IN (city) Allen County	21,601	10.49
Weymouth, MA (cdp) Norfolk County	21,420	39.68
Rochester, NY (city) Monroe County	21,011	9.56
Metairie, LA (cdp) Jefferson Parish	20,904	14.33
Toms River, NJ (cdp) Ocean County	20,815	24.08
Chandler, AZ (city) Maricopa County	20,634	11.70
Cedar Rapids, IA (city) Linn County	20,591	17.08
Lowell, MA (city) Middlesex County	20,467	19.46
Riverside, CA (city) Riverside County	20,181	7.91
Lakewood, CO (city) Jefferson County	20,170	14.00
Tacoma, WA (city) Pierce County	19,843	10.27
Anaheim, CA (city) Orange County	19,691	6.02
Springfield, MO (city) Greene County	19,438	12.80
Manchester, NH (city) Hillsborough County	19,368	18.10
Amherst, NY (town) Erie County	19,215	16.49
Springfield, MA (city) Hampden County	19,143	12.59
Bakersfield, CA (city) Kern County	19,049	7.70
Santa Rosa, CA (city) Sonoma County	19,008	12.88
Norfolk, VA (independent city) Norfolk city	18,925	8.07
Tempe, AZ (city) Maricopa County	18,902	11.93
Chesapeake, VA (independent city) Chesapeake city	18,765	9.42
Santa Clarita, CA (city) Los Angeles County	18,642	12.31
Atlanta, GA (city) Fulton County	18,503	4.44
Paradise, NV (cdp) Clark County	18,033	9.70
Corpus Christi, TX (city) Nueces County	17,977	6.48
Nashua, NH (city) Hillsborough County	17,958	20.74
Eugene, OR (city) Lane County	17,938	13.02
Plymouth, MA (town) Plymouth County	17,701	34.24
Springfield, IL (city) Sangamon County	17,457	15.56
Greece, NY (town) Monroe County	17,425	18.51
Albany, NY (city) Albany County	17,209	17.99
Levittown, PA (cdp) Bucks County	17,123	31.89
Haverford, PA (township) Delaware County	17,096	35.25
Knoxville, TN (city) Knox County	17,050	9.82
Oakland, CA (city) Alameda County	17,021	4.26
Grand Rapids, MI (city) Kent County	16,984	8.58
Oak Lawn, IL (village) Cook County	16,841	30.40
Tonawanda, NY (town) Erie County	16,819	21.52
Rockford, IL (city) Winnebago County	16,786	11.21
Fort Collins, CO (city) Larimer County	16,756	14.15
Providence, RI (city) Providence County	16,748	9.65
Brockton, MA (city) Plymouth County	16,690	17.70
Modesto, CA (city) Stanislaus County	16,588	8.76
Gloucester, NJ (township) Camden County	16,582	25.78
El Paso, TX (city) El Paso County	16,469	2.92
Livonia, MI (city) Wayne County	16,435	16.35
Woodbridge, NJ (township) Middlesex County	16,323	16.79
Cape Coral, FL (city) Lee County	16,271	15.92
Lynn, MA (city) Essex County	16,252	18.24
Orlando, FL (city) Orange County	16,241	8.73
Levittown, NY (cdp) Nassau County	16,106	30.35
Garland, TX (city) Dallas County	16,092	7.45
Vancouver, WA (city) Clark County	15,998	11.17
Hamilton, NJ (township) Mercer County	15,948	18.28
Warren, MI (city) Macomb County	15,820	11.44
Bristol, PA (township) Bucks County	15,737	28.33
Fort Lauderdale, FL (city) Broward County	15,639	10.28
Thousand Oaks, CA (city) Ventura County	15,582	13.35
Lubbock, TX (city) Lubbock County	15,569	7.80

Notes: (cdp) census designated place; Refer to the Explanation of Data in the front of the book for more detailed information.

Irish

Top 150 Places Sorted by Percent

(Based on all places, regardless of population)

Place	Number	%
Champ, MO (village) Saint Louis County	21	100.00
Lost Springs, WY (town) Converse County	6	100.00
Tolsona, AK (cdp) Valdez-Cordova Census Area	2	100.00
La Porte, CA (cdp) Plumas County	32	80.00
Walpack, NJ (township) Sussex County	28	75.68
Alcova, WY (cdp) Natrona County	23	74.19
Ronneby, MN (city) Benton County	8	66.67
North Red River, MN (township) Kittson County	4	66.67
Randsburg, CA (cdp) Kern County	38	64.41
Crookston, NE (village) Cherry County	54	62.07
Hart's Location, NH (town) Carroll County	20	60.61
Bay Lake, FL (city) Orange County	23	58.97
Kendall, WA (cdp) Whatcom County	38	57.58
Tavistock, NJ (borough) Camden County	13	56.52
Heckscherville, PA (cdp) Schuylkill County	40	56.34
Washam, WY (cdp) Sweetwater County	27	56.25
Valley Ranch, CA (cdp) Plumas County	46	54.12
Rickreall, OR (cdp) Polk County	40	52.63
Bancroft, ME (town) Aroostook County	21	52.50
Barada, NE (village) Richardson County	13	52.00
Green Harbor-Cedar Crest, MA (cdp) Plymouth County	1,252	51.99
Fountain Springs, PA (cdp) Schuylkill County	51	51.00
Huntley, WY (cdp) Goshen County	26	50.98
Spring Lake, NJ (borough) Monmouth County	1,807	50.66
Hope, NM (village) Eddy County	57	50.00
Belden, CA (cdp) Plumas County	11	50.00
Rapid River, MN (township) Lake of the Woods County	7	50.00
Nenzel, NE (village) Cherry County	6	50.00
Franktown, CO (cdp) Douglas County	46	49.46
Ocean Bluff-Brant Rock, MA (cdp) Plymouth County	2,515	49.44
Jeffrey City, WY (cdp) Fremont County	42	49.41
Powder River, WY (cdp) Natrona County	19	48.72
Melrose, IA (city) Monroe County	62	48.44
Highland, ME (plantation) Somerset County	33	47.83
Allagash, ME (town) Aroostook County	129	47.60
Tagg Flats, OK (cdp) Delaware County	9	47.37
Farmer, SD (town) Hanson County	8	47.06
Lupus, MO (town) Moniteau County	8	47.06
West Wildwood, NJ (borough) Cape May County	211	46.99
Pearl River, NY (cdp) Rockland County	7,256	46.60
Emmet, NE (village) Holt County	34	46.58
Harmon, IL (village) Lee County	73	46.50
Point Lookout, NY (cdp) Nassau County	705	46.38
Edgerton, WY (town) Natrona County	64	46.04
Avon-by-the-Sea, NJ (borough) Monmouth County	1,019	45.55
Grenville, NM (village) Union County	10	45.45
Sea Girt, NJ (borough) Monmouth County	972	45.25
Slater, WY (cdp) Platte County	28	45.16
Collingdale, PA (borough) Delaware County	3,912	45.15
Marshfield, MA (town) Plymouth County	10,932	44.94
Albany, WY (cdp) Albany County	34	44.74
North Pembroke, MA (cdp) Plymouth County	1,307	44.70
Briarwood, ND (city) Cass County	50	44.64
Scituate, MA (town) Plymouth County	7,877	44.10
Belford, NJ (cdp) Monmouth County	627	43.97
Teterboro, NJ (borough) Bergen County	7	43.75
North Scituate, MA (cdp) Plymouth County	2,250	43.19
Milton, MA (cdp) Norfolk County	11,198	42.97
Weldon Spring Heights, MO (town) Saint Charles County	35	42.68
Greeley Center, NE (village) Greeley County	224	42.50
Folsom, PA (cdp) Delaware County	3,512	42.47
Gloucester City, NJ (city) Camden County	4,859	42.34
Spring Lake Heights, NJ (borough) Monmouth County	2,204	42.17
Green Hills, PA (borough) Washington County	8	42.11
Drexel Hill, PA (cdp) Delaware County	12,267	41.87
Hersey, ME (town) Aroostook County	28	41.79
Imogene, IA (city) Fremont County	20	41.67
Elfin Cove, AK (cdp) Skagway-Hoonah-Angoon Census Area	15	41.67
Pioneer, IA (city) Humboldt County	10	41.67
Jackson, NE (village) Dakota County	89	41.20
Pembroke, MA (town) Plymouth County	6,971	41.18
Long Beach, IN (town) La Porte County	649	41.18
Esterbrook, WY (cdp) Converse County	7	41.18
Braintree, MA (town) Norfolk County	13,869	41.00
Peach Lake, NY (cdp) Putnam County	694	40.73

Place	Number	%
Westvale, NY (cdp) Onondaga County	2,082	40.45
Glenolden, PA (borough) Delaware County	3,022	40.42
Prospect Park, PA (borough) Delaware County	2,663	40.39
Cohasset, MA (town) Norfolk County	2,931	40.37
South Duxbury, MA (cdp) Plymouth County	1,237	40.36
Verplanck, NY (cdp) Westchester County	299	40.35
Phoenicia, NY (cdp) Ulster County	162	40.30
Plandome, NY (village) Nassau County	512	40.25
Murphys Estates, SC (cdp) Edgefield County	566	40.11
Vining, KS (city) Clay County	18	40.00
Brightwaters, NY (village) Suffolk County	1,299	39.99
Walpole, MA (town) Norfolk County	9,097	39.86
Norwood, PA (borough) Delaware County	2,380	39.77
Glenside, PA (cdp) Montgomery County	3,198	39.76
Weymouth, MA (cdp) Norfolk County	21,420	39.68
Evergreen Park, IL (village) Cook County	8,250	39.62
Ivesdale, IL (village) Champaign County	126	39.62
Hanover, MA (town) Plymouth County	5,208	39.56
Clifton Heights, PA (borough) Delaware County	2,682	39.56
Whitman, MA (town) Plymouth County	5,470	39.40
Saint James, MI (township) Charlevoix County	132	39.40
Norwell, MA (town) Plymouth County	3,844	39.37
Port Monmouth, NJ (cdp) Monmouth County	1,439	39.37
Pinehurst, MA (cdp) Middlesex County	2,729	39.35
Ryan, IA (city) Delaware County	162	39.32
Abington, MA (cdp) Plymouth County	5,741	39.31
Aldan, PA (borough) Delaware County	1,694	39.28
Loch Arbour, NJ (village) Monmouth County	108	39.27
Stewart Manor, NY (village) Nassau County	761	39.23
Zwingle, IA (city) Dubuque County	29	39.19
Duxbury, MA (town) Plymouth County	5,566	39.07
Folcroft, PA (borough) Delaware County	2,717	38.94
Sea Isle City, NJ (city) Cape May County	1,099	38.92
Eddystone, PA (borough) Delaware County	949	38.86
West Millgrove, OH (village) Wood County	40	38.83
Springfield, PA (cdp) Delaware County	9,000	38.01
Girardville, PA (borough) Schuylkill County	659	37.83
Renningers, PA (cdp) Schuylkill County	171	37.83
Chugwater, WY (town) Platte County	101	37.83
Deer Grove, IL (village) Whiteside County	20	37.74
Hanson, MA (town) Plymouth County	3,579	37.69
Mount Carbon, PA (borough) Schuylkill County	32	37.65
Cornwells Heights-Eddington, PA (cdp) Bucks County	1,248	37.64
Tinicum Township, PA (cdp) Delaware County	1,635	37.56
Brooklawn, NJ (borough) Camden County	884	37.55
Huetter, ID (city) Kootenai County	36	37.50
Millville, IA (city) Clayton County	12	37.50
Wamic, OR (cdp) Wasco County	12	37.50
Seconsett Island, MA (cdp) Barnstable County	9	37.50
West Hampton Dunes, NY (village) Suffolk County	3	37.50
Norwood, MA (cdp) Norfolk County	10,680	37.36
Hingham, MA (town) Plymouth County	7,406	37.25
Elmira, CA (cdp) Solano County	32	37.21
Ridley, PA (township) Delaware County	11,455	37.20
Rodney, IA (city) Monona County	26	37.14
Hillman, MN (city) Morrison County	10	37.04
Rockland, MA (town) Plymouth County	6,525	36.93
East Lansdowne, PA (borough) Delaware County	955	36.93
Frankfort Springs, PA (borough) Beaver County	48	36.92
Ridley Park, PA (borough) Delaware County	2,655	36.90
Medfield, MA (town) Norfolk County	4,527	36.89
Dedham, MA (cdp) Norfolk County	8,661	36.84
Saint Bonaventure, NY (cdp) Cattaraugus County	792	36.82
Harding-Birch Lakes, AK (cdp) Fairbanks North Star Borough	64	36.78
Dry Creek, AK (cdp) Southeast Fairbanks Census Area	54	36.73
Bernard, IA (city) Dubuque County	36	36.73
Rosalie, NE (village) Thurston County	69	36.70
Point Baker, AK (cdp) Prince of Wales-Outer Ketchikan C.A.	15	36.59
Monmouth Beach, NJ (borough) Monmouth County	1,314	36.55
Minerva, NY (town) Essex County	287	36.38
Long, OK (cdp) Sequoyah County	136	36.36
North Wildwood, NJ (city) Cape May County	1,790	36.27
Floral Park, NY (village) Nassau County	5,771	36.10
National Park, NJ (borough) Gloucester County	1,157	36.10
Allenhurst, NJ (borough) Monmouth County	261	36.10

Notes: (cdp) census designated place; Refer to the Explanation of Data in the front of the book for more detailed information.

Irish

Top 150 Places Sorted by Percent

(Based on places with populations of 10,000 or more)

Place	Number	%
Pearl River, NY (cdp) Rockland County	7,256	46.60
Marshfield, MA (town) Plymouth County	10,932	44.94
Scituate, MA (town) Plymouth County	7,877	44.10
Milton, MA (cdp) Norfolk County	11,198	42.97
Gloucester City, NJ (city) Camden County	4,859	42.34
Drexel Hill, PA (cdp) Delaware County	12,267	41.87
Pembroke, MA (town) Plymouth County	6,971	41.18
Braintree, MA (town) Norfolk County	13,869	41.00
Walpole, MA (town) Norfolk County	9,097	39.86
Weymouth, MA (cdp) Norfolk County	21,420	39.68
Evergreen Park, IL (village) Cook County	8,250	39.62
Hanover, MA (town) Plymouth County	5,208	39.56
Whitman, MA (town) Plymouth County	5,470	39.40
Abington, MA (cdp) Plymouth County	5,741	39.31
Duxbury, MA (town) Plymouth County	5,566	39.07
Springfield, PA (cdp) Delaware County	9,000	38.01
Norwood, MA (cdp) Norfolk County	10,680	37.36
Hingham, MA (town) Plymouth County	7,406	37.25
Ridley, PA (township) Delaware County	11,455	37.20
Rockland, MA (town) Plymouth County	6,525	36.93
Medfield, MA (town) Norfolk County	4,527	36.89
Dedham, MA (cdp) Norfolk County	8,661	36.84
Floral Park, NY (village) Nassau County	5,771	36.10
Hull, MA (cdp) Plymouth County	3,986	36.07
Woburn, MA (city) Middlesex County	13,434	36.06
Stony Point, NY (town) Rockland County	5,104	35.83
Sayville, NY (cdp) Suffolk County	5,967	35.65
Melrose, MA (city) Middlesex County	9,588	35.34
Haverford, PA (township) Delaware County	17,096	35.25
Holbrook, MA (cdp) Norfolk County	3,787	35.22
Garden City, NY (village) Nassau County	7,627	35.21
Kingston, MA (town) Plymouth County	4,147	35.20
Tewksbury, MA (town) Middlesex County	10,158	35.16
Wrentham, MA (town) Norfolk County	3,686	34.93
Wall, NJ (township) Monmouth County	8,809	34.87
Medway, MA (town) Norfolk County	4,341	34.87
Keansburg, NJ (borough) Monmouth County	3,710	34.57
Plymouth, MA (town) Plymouth County	17,701	34.24
Quincy, MA (city) Norfolk County	30,036	34.12
Upper Darby, PA (township) Delaware County	27,905	34.10
Norfolk, MA (town) Norfolk County	3,552	33.96
Woodlyn, PA (cdp) Delaware County	3,386	33.83
Kent, NY (town) Putnam County	4,733	33.79
Billerica, MA (town) Middlesex County	13,157	33.78
Wilmington, MA (cdp) Middlesex County	7,201	33.71
Westwood, MA (town) Norfolk County	4,744	33.60
Croydon, PA (cdp) Bucks County	3,370	33.55
Rockville Centre, NY (village) Nassau County	8,214	33.43
Winthrop, MA (cdp) Suffolk County	6,117	33.42
West Deptford, NJ (township) Gloucester County	6,423	33.16
Canton, MA (town) Norfolk County	6,862	33.03
Wakefield, MA (cdp) Middlesex County	8,185	33.00
Hazlet, NJ (township) Monmouth County	7,033	32.90
Middletown, NJ (township) Monmouth County	21,756	32.80
Reading, MA (cdp) Middlesex County	7,776	32.80
Easton, MA (town) Bristol County	7,310	32.78
Newtown, PA (township) Delaware County	3,833	32.76
Point Pleasant, NJ (borough) Ocean County	6,317	32.72
Foxborough, MA (town) Norfolk County	5,316	32.72
Upper, NJ (township) Cape May County	3,933	32.46
East Bridgewater, MA (town) Plymouth County	4,210	32.45
Miller Place, NY (cdp) Suffolk County	3,459	32.43
Aston, PA (township) Delaware County	5,234	32.30
Mansfield, MA (town) Bristol County	7,233	32.27
Franklin, MA (city) Norfolk County	9,496	32.12
Brunswick, NY (town) Rensselaer County	3,757	32.06
Lower, NJ (township) Cape May County	7,350	32.03
Chelmsford, MA (town) Middlesex County	10,803	31.91
Levittown, PA (cdp) Bucks County	17,123	31.89
Hopkinton, MA (town) Middlesex County	4,253	31.87
New Fairfield, CT (town) Fairfield County	4,437	31.80
Sandwich, MA (town) Barnstable County	6,400	31.77
Narragansett, RI (town) Washington County	5,197	31.76
Manorville, NY (cdp) Suffolk County	3,515	31.48
East Islip, NY (cdp) Suffolk County	4,404	31.27
Mastic, NY (cdp) Suffolk County	4,849	31.23
Massapequa Park, NY (village) Nassau County	5,463	31.22
Bellmawr, NJ (borough) Camden County	3,515	31.21
Westtown, PA (township) Chester County	3,201	31.08
Stoneham, MA (town) Middlesex County	6,871	30.92
Cinnaminson, NJ (township) Burlington County	4,513	30.92
West Islip, NY (cdp) Suffolk County	8,990	30.89
Horsham, PA (township) Montgomery County	7,475	30.85
River Forest, IL (village) Cook County	3,586	30.82
Tyngsborough, MA (town) Middlesex County	3,409	30.76
Bridgewater, MA (town) Plymouth County	7,734	30.73
Babylon, NY (village) Suffolk County	3,877	30.73
Lansdowne, PA (borough) Delaware County	3,378	30.69
Kings Park, NY (cdp) Suffolk County	4,944	30.64
Carver, MA (town) Plymouth County	3,414	30.58
West Goshen, PA (township) Chester County	6,257	30.53
Newburyport, MA (city) Essex County	5,256	30.48
Watervliet, NY (city) Albany County	3,111	30.48
Oak Lawn, IL (village) Cook County	16,841	30.40
North Andover, MA (town) Essex County	8,266	30.39
Middletown, PA (township) Bucks County	13,406	30.37
Bourne, MA (town) Barnstable County	5,683	30.37
Levittown, NY (cdp) Nassau County	16,106	30.35
Scranton, PA (city) Lackawanna County	23,171	30.32
Brewster, MA (town) Barnstable County	3,056	30.28
Haddonfield, NJ (borough) Camden County	3,523	30.21
Orangetown, NY (town) Rockland County	14,379	30.08
North Reading, MA (town) Middlesex County	4,155	30.03
Haddon, NJ (township) Camden County	4,394	29.97
Western Springs, IL (village) Cook County	3,770	29.87
Blooming Grove, NY (town) Orange County	5,166	29.77
Warrington, PA (township) Bucks County	5,226	29.73
Saint James, NY (cdp) Suffolk County	3,912	29.48
East Greenbush, NY (town) Rensselaer County	4,601	29.47
Stafford, NJ (township) Ocean County	6,627	29.43
Crestwood, IL (village) Cook County	3,301	29.42
Mokena, IL (village) Will County	4,316	29.41
East Goshen, PA (township) Chester County	4,947	29.40
Holden, MA (town) Worcester County	4,591	29.39
Dennis, MA (town) Barnstable County	4,693	29.38
Holliston, MA (town) Middlesex County	4,055	29.38
East Northport, NY (cdp) Suffolk County	6,098	29.30
La Grange, NY (town) Dutchess County	4,366	29.29
Arlington, MA (cdp) Middlesex County	12,394	29.24
Lake Ronkonkoma, NY (cdp) Suffolk County	5,753	29.24
Maynard, MA (cdp) Middlesex County	3,045	29.19
Harwich, MA (town) Barnstable County	3,609	29.14
Warminster, PA (township) Bucks County	9,143	29.11
Dracut, MA (town) Middlesex County	8,299	29.06
Holtsville, NY (cdp) Suffolk County	4,929	29.04
Somers Point, NJ (city) Atlantic County	3,373	29.04
Washington, NJ (township) Gloucester County	13,639	28.95
Brick, NJ (township) Ocean County	22,022	28.93
Bellingham, MA (town) Norfolk County	4,428	28.91
Seaford, NY (cdp) Nassau County	4,564	28.90
Burlington, MA (cdp) Middlesex County	6,604	28.87
Marlton, NJ (cdp) Burlington County	2,951	28.79
Willistown, PA (township) Chester County	2,882	28.79
Massapequa, NY (cdp) Nassau County	6,520	28.78
Dunmore, PA (borough) Lackawanna County	4,028	28.73
Upper Southampton, PA (township) Bucks County	4,520	28.67
Marple, PA (township) Delaware County	6,796	28.63
Norton, MA (town) Bristol County	5,162	28.62
Southeast, NY (town) Putnam County	4,955	28.62
Onondaga, NY (town) Onondaga County	6,008	28.59
Newport East, RI (cdp) Newport County	3,336	28.57
Broomall, PA (cdp) Delaware County	3,186	28.51
Waterford, NJ (township) Camden County	2,989	28.51
Warwick, RI (city) Kent County	24,403	28.44
Raynham, MA (town) Bristol County	3,338	28.44
Winchester, MA (cdp) Middlesex County	5,916	28.43
Danvers, MA (cdp) Essex County	7,163	28.41
Vernon, NJ (township) Sussex County	7,005	28.38
Upper Providence Township, PA (cdp) Delaware County	2,978	28.34
Bristol, PA (township) Bucks County	15,737	28.33

Notes: (cdp) census designated place; Refer to the Explanation of Data in the front of the book for more detailed information.

Israeli

Top 150 Places Sorted by Number

(Based on all places, regardless of population)

Place	Number	%
New York, NY (city) New York City	20,946	0.26
Los Angeles, CA (city) Los Angeles County	11,480	0.31
Hempstead, NY (town) Nassau County	1,877	0.25
North Hempstead, NY (town) Nassau County	1,348	0.61
Chicago, IL (city) Cook County	1,033	0.04
Sunnyvale, CA (city) Santa Clara County	1,003	0.76
San Diego, CA (city) San Diego County	942	0.08
Philadelphia, PA (city) Philadelphia County	931	0.06
Fair Lawn, NJ (borough) Bergen County	926	2.93
Ramapo, NY (town) Rockland County	917	0.84
Oyster Bay, NY (town) Nassau County	821	0.28
Hollywood, FL (city) Broward County	742	0.53
Dallas, TX (city) Dallas County	736	0.06
Houston, TX (city) Harris County	661	0.03
San Francisco, CA (city) San Francisco County	615	0.08
Brookline, MA (cdp) Norfolk County	605	1.06
Aventura, FL (city) Miami-Dade County	580	2.30
Beverly Hills, CA (city) Los Angeles County	534	1.58
Cupertino, CA (city) Santa Clara County	518	1.02
Newton, MA (city) Middlesex County	483	0.58
Boston, MA (city) Suffolk County	483	0.08
Woodmere, NY (cdp) Nassau County	450	2.74
Plantation, FL (city) Broward County	439	0.53
Sunrise, FL (city) Broward County	434	0.51
San Jose, CA (city) Santa Clara County	399	0.04
North Bethesda, MD (cdp) Montgomery County	389	1.01
Rockville, MD (city) Montgomery County	383	0.81
Plainview, NY (cdp) Nassau County	381	1.49
Phoenix, AZ (city) Maricopa County	372	0.03
Brookhaven, NY (town) Suffolk County	360	0.08
Lower Merion, PA (township) Montgomery County	353	0.59
Cambridge, MA (city) Middlesex County	353	0.35
Denver, CO (city) Denver County	346	0.06
Monsey, NY (cdp) Rockland County	330	2.25
Coral Springs, FL (city) Broward County	320	0.27
West Bloomfield, MI (township) Oakland County	314	0.48
Ann Arbor, MI (city) Washtenaw County	311	0.27
Monroe, NY (town) Orange County	305	0.97
Palo Alto, CA (city) Santa Clara County	298	0.51
Ojus, FL (cdp) Miami-Dade County	295	1.77
Teaneck, NJ (cdp) Bergen County	291	0.74
Greenburgh, NY (town) Westchester County	279	0.32
Berkeley, CA (city) Alameda County	279	0.27
Kiryas Joel, NY (village) Orange County	274	2.07
Sunny Isles Beach, FL (city) Miami-Dade County	260	1.70
Huntington, NY (town) Suffolk County	260	0.13
Long Beach, CA (city) Los Angeles County	260	0.06
Highland Park, IL (city) Lake County	251	0.80
Skokie, IL (village) Cook County	251	0.40
New Haven, CT (city) New Haven County	251	0.20
West Hollywood, CA (city) Los Angeles County	250	0.70
Seattle, WA (city) King County	249	0.04
Lawrence, NY (village) Nassau County	248	3.80
Pittsburgh, PA (city) Allegheny County	248	0.07
Spring Valley, NV (cdp) Clark County	241	0.20
Paradise, NV (cdp) Clark County	239	0.13
Las Vegas, NV (city) Clark County	238	0.05
Boca Raton, FL (city) Palm Beach County	237	0.31
Miami Beach, FL (city) Miami-Dade County	237	0.27
Stamford, CT (city) Fairfield County	237	0.20
Buffalo Grove, IL (village) Lake County	234	0.55
Cooper City, FL (city) Broward County	233	0.84
Washington, DC (city) District of Columbia	229	0.04
Austin, TX (city) Travis County	226	0.03
Columbus, OH (city) Franklin County	226	0.03
Cherry Hill, NJ (township) Camden County	225	0.32
Great Neck, NY (village) Nassau County	224	2.35
Santa Monica, CA (city) Los Angeles County	221	0.26
Scottsdale, AZ (city) Maricopa County	221	0.11
Potomac, MD (cdp) Montgomery County	217	0.48
Huntington Beach, CA (city) Orange County	215	0.11
Agoura Hills, CA (city) Los Angeles County	201	0.99
Myrtle Beach, SC (city) Horry County	201	0.89
Tenafly, NJ (borough) Bergen County	200	1.45
Millburn, NJ (cdp) Essex County	199	1.01
Jersey City, NJ (city) Hudson County	197	0.08
Lakewood, NJ (township) Ocean County	191	0.32
Oceanside, NY (cdp) Nassau County	190	0.58
San Antonio, TX (city) Bexar County	188	0.02
Irvine, CA (city) Orange County	187	0.13
Islip, NY (town) Suffolk County	187	0.06
Wesley Hills, NY (village) Rockland County	182	3.69
Walnut Creek, CA (city) Contra Costa County	182	0.28
Englewood, NJ (city) Bergen County	181	0.69
Baltimore, MD (independent city) Baltimore city	181	0.03
Bethesda, MD (cdp) Montgomery County	179	0.32
Beachwood, OH (city) Cuyahoga County	178	1.46
Calabasas, CA (city) Los Angeles County	178	0.89
East Brunswick, NJ (cdp) Middlesex County	178	0.38
Voorhees, NJ (township) Camden County	177	0.63
Livingston, NJ (cdp) Essex County	176	0.64
Clearwater, FL (city) Pinellas County	173	0.16
Springfield, MA (city) Hampden County	162	0.11
Mountain View, CA (city) Santa Clara County	160	0.23
Clarkstown, NY (town) Rockland County	160	0.19
Princeton, NJ (township) Mercer County	157	0.98
Oakland, CA (city) Alameda County	156	0.04
Worcester, MA (city) Worcester County	155	0.09
Paramus, NJ (borough) Bergen County	153	0.59
Albuquerque, NM (city) Bernalillo County	153	0.03
Madison, WI (city) Dane County	152	0.07
Aspen Hill, MD (cdp) Montgomery County	150	0.30
Santa Clarita, CA (city) Los Angeles County	150	0.10
Cliffside Park, NJ (borough) Bergen County	143	0.62
Miami, FL (city) Miami-Dade County	142	0.04
Manalapan, NJ (township) Monmouth County	141	0.42
Lauderhill, FL (city) Broward County	141	0.25
Thousand Oaks, CA (city) Ventura County	140	0.12
Henderson, NV (city) Clark County	139	0.08
De Witt, NY (town) Onondaga County	138	0.57
Redmond, WA (city) King County	137	0.30
Closter, NJ (borough) Bergen County	136	1.62
Smithtown, NY (town) Suffolk County	136	0.12
Great Neck Estates, NY (village) Nassau County	133	4.71
Coconut Creek, FL (city) Broward County	130	0.30
Oak Park, CA (cdp) Ventura County	129	5.26
Portland, OR (city) Multnomah County	129	0.02
North Miami Beach, FL (city) Miami-Dade County	128	0.31
Needham, MA (cdp) Norfolk County	127	0.44
Hallandale, FL (city) Broward County	126	0.36
Deerfield Beach, FL (city) Broward County	126	0.19
Merrick, NY (cdp) Nassau County	125	0.55
Lexington, MA (cdp) Middlesex County	124	0.41
Southfield, MI (city) Oakland County	124	0.16
Fort Lee, NJ (borough) Bergen County	122	0.34
Tamarac, FL (city) Broward County	122	0.22
Wayne, NJ (cdp) Passaic County	121	0.22
Bellevue, WA (city) King County	121	0.11
Pikesville, MD (cdp) Baltimore County	120	0.41
Deerfield, IL (village) Lake County	119	0.64
South Euclid, OH (city) Cuyahoga County	119	0.51
Wilmette, IL (village) Cook County	118	0.43
Ives Estates, FL (cdp) Miami-Dade County	116	0.67
Highland Park, NJ (borough) Middlesex County	114	0.81
Urbana, IL (city) Champaign County	113	0.31
Long Beach, NY (city) Nassau County	111	0.31
Yorba Linda, CA (city) Orange County	111	0.19
Erlton-Ellisburg, NJ (cdp) Camden County	109	1.36
Mount Pleasant, NY (town) Westchester County	109	0.25
Ocean, NJ (township) Monmouth County	108	0.40
Tulsa, OK (city) Tulsa County	108	0.03
New City, NY (cdp) Rockland County	107	0.31
Bloomington, IN (city) Monroe County	107	0.15
Columbia, MD (cdp) Howard County	107	0.12
Edison, NJ (cdp) Middlesex County	107	0.11
Echelon, NJ (cdp) Camden County	106	1.02
Iowa City, IA (city) Johnson County	106	0.17
Scarsdale, NY (village) Westchester County	105	0.59
Plano, TX (city) Collin County	104	0.05
Waltham, MA (city) Middlesex County	103	0.17

Notes: (cdp) census designated place; Refer to the Explanation of Data in the front of the book for more detailed information.

Israeli

Top 150 Places Sorted by Percent

(Based on all places, regardless of population)

Place	Number	%
Galatia, KS (city) Barton County	6	12.00
Kensington, NY (village) Nassau County	78	6.42
Saddle Rock, NY (village) Nassau County	45	5.69
Oak Park, CA (cdp) Ventura County	129	5.26
Great Neck Estates, NY (village) Nassau County	133	4.71
Saratoga Springs, UT (town) Utah County	42	4.52
Golden Beach, FL (town) Miami-Dade County	46	4.39
Amador City, CA (city) Amador County	8	3.98
Lawrence, NY (village) Nassau County	248	3.80
Wesley Hills, NY (village) Rockland County	182	3.69
Deal, NJ (borough) Monmouth County	36	3.36
Estates of Fort Lauderdale, FL (cdp) Broward County	61	3.31
Fair Lawn, NJ (borough) Bergen County	926	2.93
Kaser, NY (village) Rockland County	95	2.88
Woodmere, NY (cdp) Nassau County	450	2.74
Hewlett Bay Park, NY (village) Nassau County	12	2.47
Great Neck, NY (village) Nassau County	224	2.35
Aventura, FL (city) Miami-Dade County	580	2.30
Monsey, NY (cdp) Rockland County	330	2.25
Kiryas Joel, NY (village) Orange County	274	2.07
Russell Gardens, NY (village) Nassau County	22	2.05
Twin Oaks, MO (village) Saint Louis County	7	1.96
Kings Point, NY (village) Nassau County	96	1.89
Fairbanks Ranch, CA (cdp) San Diego County	35	1.86
Ojus, FL (cdp) Miami-Dade County	295	1.77
Grand View-on-Hudson, NY (village) Rockland County	5	1.77
Sunny Isles Beach, FL (city) Miami-Dade County	260	1.70
Mission Bay, FL (cdp) Palm Beach County	50	1.63
Closter, NJ (borough) Bergen County	136	1.62
Pepper Pike, OH (city) Cuyahoga County	98	1.62
Springvale, WI (town) Columbia County	9	1.60
Beverly Hills, CA (city) Los Angeles County	534	1.58
Ponder, TX (town) Denton County	7	1.54
Roslyn Heights, NY (cdp) Nassau County	95	1.51
Plainview, NY (cdp) Nassau County	381	1.49
East Hills, NY (village) Nassau County	101	1.47
Woodside, PA (cdp) Bucks County	40	1.47
Beachwood, OH (city) Cuyahoga County	178	1.46
Tenafly, NJ (borough) Bergen County	200	1.45
Hanalei, HI (cdp) Kauai County	7	1.45
Great Neck Gardens, NY (cdp) Nassau County	16	1.43
New Square, NY (village) Rockland County	66	1.40
University Gardens, NY (cdp) Nassau County	58	1.40
Oakhurst, NJ (cdp) Monmouth County	57	1.38
Erlton-Ellisburg, NJ (cdp) Camden County	109	1.36
University Heights, IA (city) Johnson County	13	1.31
Orange, OH (village) Cuyahoga County	40	1.24
Ardsley, NY (village) Westchester County	51	1.19
Hewlett Harbor, NY (village) Nassau County	15	1.18
George, WA (city) Grant County	6	1.18
Port Washington North, NY (village) Nassau County	32	1.17
Viola, NY (cdp) Rockland County	67	1.13
Huntington Woods, MI (city) Oakland County	68	1.11
Lake Success, NY (village) Nassau County	31	1.11
Forest Home, NY (cdp) Tompkins County	11	1.08
Brookline, MA (cdp) Norfolk County	605	1.06
Tigerton, WI (village) Shawano County	8	1.06
Cedarhurst, NY (village) Nassau County	65	1.05
Old Field, NY (village) Suffolk County	10	1.03
Cupertino, CA (city) Santa Clara County	518	1.02
Echelon, NJ (cdp) Camden County	106	1.02
Pomona, NY (village) Rockland County	28	1.02
North Bethesda, MD (cdp) Montgomery County	389	1.01
Millburn, NJ (cdp) Essex County	199	1.01
Roslyn Harbor, NY (village) Nassau County	10	1.00
Agoura Hills, CA (city) Los Angeles County	201	0.99
Princeton, NJ (township) Mercer County	157	0.98
Monroe, NY (town) Orange County	305	0.97
Woodbury, NY (cdp) Nassau County	85	0.94
Puako, HI (cdp) Hawaii County	4	0.94
Clyde Hill, WA (city) King County	27	0.93
Inkom, ID (city) Bannock County	7	0.93
Kemp Mill, MD (cdp) Montgomery County	91	0.92
Oyster Bay Cove, NY (village) Nassau County	20	0.92
Kingston, RI (cdp) Washington County	50	0.91
Del Mar, CA (city) San Diego County	40	0.91
Roslyn Estates, NY (village) Nassau County	11	0.90
Hunts Point, WA (town) King County	4	0.90
Myrtle Beach, SC (city) Horry County	201	0.89
Calabasas, CA (city) Los Angeles County	178	0.89
Greenville, NY (cdp) Westchester County	75	0.88
Penn Wynne, PA (cdp) Montgomery County	48	0.88
Englewood Cliffs, NJ (borough) Bergen County	47	0.88
Princeville, HI (cdp) Kauai County	15	0.88
Callisburg, TX (city) Cooke County	3	0.88
Harbor Hills, NY (cdp) Nassau County	5	0.87
Muttontown, NY (village) Nassau County	29	0.86
South Valley Stream, NY (cdp) Nassau County	48	0.85
Salem, PA (township) Wayne County	31	0.85
Spruce Hill, PA (township) Juniata County	6	0.85
Lutsen, MN (township) Cook County	3	0.85
Ramapo, NY (town) Rockland County	917	0.84
Cooper City, FL (city) Broward County	233	0.84
Hamptons at Boca Raton, FL (cdp) Palm Beach County	96	0.84
Bayside, WI (village) Milwaukee County	38	0.84
Forestburgh, NY (town) Sullivan County	7	0.84
Watermill, NY (cdp) Suffolk County	14	0.83
Pleasantville, NY (village) Westchester County	59	0.82
Rockville, MD (city) Montgomery County	383	0.81
Highland Park, NJ (borough) Middlesex County	114	0.81
Highland Park, IL (city) Lake County	251	0.80
Demarest, NJ (borough) Bergen County	39	0.80
Stanhope, NJ (borough) Sussex County	28	0.80
Matinecock, NY (village) Nassau County	7	0.79
Eldorado Springs, CO (cdp) Boulder County	4	0.78
North Hills, NY (village) Nassau County	33	0.77
Roslyn, NY (village) Nassau County	20	0.77
South Padre Island, TX (town) Cameron County	19	0.77
Sunnyvale, CA (city) Santa Clara County	1,003	0.76
Plainsboro Center, NJ (cdp) Middlesex County	18	0.76
Hawaiian Acres, HI (cdp) Hawaii County	13	0.75
Jackson, PA (township) Mercer County	9	0.75
Teaneck, NJ (cdp) Bergen County	291	0.74
Manhasset Hills, NY (cdp) Nassau County	27	0.74
Hartsville, TN (town) Trousdale County	17	0.71
Ramblewood East, FL (cdp) Broward County	9	0.71
West Hollywood, CA (city) Los Angeles County	250	0.70
Upper Saddle River, NJ (borough) Bergen County	54	0.70
Englewood, NJ (city) Bergen County	181	0.69
Ives Estates, FL (cdp) Miami-Dade County	116	0.67
Harrison, WI (town) Calumet County	40	0.67
Redington Beach, FL (town) Pinellas County	11	0.67
Naples Park, FL (cdp) Collier County	44	0.65
Herriman, UT (town) Salt Lake County	11	0.65
Livingston, NJ (cdp) Essex County	176	0.64
Deerfield, IL (village) Lake County	119	0.64
Voorhees, NJ (township) Camden County	177	0.63
Westlake Village, CA (city) Los Angeles County	55	0.63
Woodcliff Lake, NJ (borough) Bergen County	36	0.63
Meshoppen, PA (borough) Wyoming County	3	0.63
Cliffside Park, NJ (borough) Bergen County	143	0.62
Melville, NY (cdp) Suffolk County	90	0.62
Heuvelton, NY (village) Saint Lawrence County	5	0.62
North Hempstead, NY (town) Nassau County	1,348	0.61
Herricks, NY (cdp) Nassau County	25	0.61
Heathrow, FL (cdp) Seminole County	24	0.61
Atlantic Beach, NY (village) Nassau County	12	0.61
Briarcliff Manor, NY (village) Westchester County	46	0.60
Orangeburg, NY (cdp) Rockland County	21	0.60
Baldwin, WI (village) Saint Croix County	16	0.60
Lower Merion, PA (township) Montgomery County	353	0.59
Paramus, NJ (borough) Bergen County	153	0.59
Scarsdale, NY (village) Westchester County	105	0.59
Newton, MA (city) Middlesex County	483	0.58
Oceanside, NY (cdp) Nassau County	190	0.58
Collinsville, CT (cdp) Hartford County	15	0.58
Whately, MA (town) Franklin County	9	0.58
Peninsula, OH (village) Summit County	3	0.58
De Witt, NY (town) Onondaga County	138	0.57
Jericho, NY (cdp) Nassau County	74	0.57

Notes: (cdp) census designated place; Refer to the Explanation of Data in the front of the book for more detailed information.

Israeli

Top 150 Places Sorted by Percent

(Based on places with populations of 10,000 or more)

Place	Number	%
Fair Lawn, NJ (borough) Bergen County	926	2.93
Woodmere, NY (cdp) Nassau County	450	2.74
Aventura, FL (city) Miami-Dade County	580	2.30
Monsey, NY (cdp) Rockland County	330	2.25
Kiryas Joel, NY (village) Orange County	274	2.07
Ojus, FL (cdp) Miami-Dade County	295	1.77
Sunny Isles Beach, FL (city) Miami-Dade County	260	1.70
Beverly Hills, CA (city) Los Angeles County	534	1.58
Plainview, NY (cdp) Nassau County	381	1.49
Beachwood, OH (city) Cuyahoga County	178	1.46
Tenafly, NJ (borough) Bergen County	200	1.45
Brookline, MA (cdp) Norfolk County	605	1.06
Cupertino, CA (city) Santa Clara County	518	1.02
Echelon, NJ (cdp) Camden County	106	1.02
North Bethesda, MD (cdp) Montgomery County	389	1.01
Millburn, NJ (cdp) Essex County	199	1.01
Agoura Hills, CA (city) Los Angeles County	201	0.99
Princeton, NJ (township) Mercer County	157	0.98
Monroe, NY (town) Orange County	305	0.97
Myrtle Beach, SC (city) Horry County	201	0.89
Calabasas, CA (city) Los Angeles County	178	0.89
Ramapo, NY (town) Rockland County	917	0.84
Cooper City, FL (city) Broward County	233	0.84
Hamptons at Boca Raton, FL (cdp) Palm Beach County	96	0.84
Rockville, MD (city) Montgomery County	383	0.81
Highland Park, NJ (borough) Middlesex County	114	0.81
Highland Park, IL (city) Lake County	251	0.80
Sunnyvale, CA (city) Santa Clara County	1,003	0.76
Teaneck, NJ (cdp) Bergen County	291	0.74
West Hollywood, CA (city) Los Angeles County	250	0.70
Englewood, NJ (city) Bergen County	181	0.69
Ives Estates, FL (cdp) Miami-Dade County	116	0.67
Livingston, NJ (cdp) Essex County	176	0.64
Deerfield, IL (village) Lake County	119	0.64
Voorhees, NJ (township) Camden County	177	0.63
Cliffside Park, NJ (borough) Bergen County	143	0.62
Melville, NY (cdp) Suffolk County	90	0.62
North Hempstead, NY (town) Nassau County	1,348	0.61
Lower Merion, PA (township) Montgomery County	353	0.59
Paramus, NJ (borough) Bergen County	153	0.59
Scarsdale, NY (village) Westchester County	105	0.59
Newton, MA (city) Middlesex County	483	0.58
Oceanside, NY (cdp) Nassau County	190	0.58
De Witt, NY (town) Onondaga County	138	0.57
Jericho, NY (cdp) Nassau County	74	0.57
Buffalo Grove, IL (village) Lake County	234	0.55
Merrick, NY (cdp) Nassau County	125	0.55
Hollywood, FL (city) Broward County	742	0.53
Plantation, FL (city) Broward County	439	0.53
Sunrise, FL (city) Broward County	434	0.51
Palo Alto, CA (city) Santa Clara County	298	0.51
South Euclid, OH (city) Cuyahoga County	119	0.51
Springfield, NJ (cdp) Union County	74	0.51
Lakewood Park, FL (cdp) Saint Lucie County	52	0.50
West Bloomfield, MI (township) Oakland County	314	0.48
Potomac, MD (cdp) Montgomery County	217	0.48
Franklin Lakes, NJ (borough) Bergen County	50	0.48
West Hempstead, NY (cdp) Nassau County	88	0.47
Bellmore, NY (cdp) Nassau County	78	0.47
Albany, CA (city) Alameda County	75	0.46
Stanford, CA (cdp) Santa Clara County	60	0.45
Needham, MA (cdp) Norfolk County	127	0.44
El Cerrito, CA (city) Contra Costa County	102	0.44
Wilmette, IL (village) Cook County	118	0.43
Palos Verdes Estates, CA (city) Los Angeles County	58	0.43
Manalapan, NJ (township) Monmouth County	141	0.42
North Druid Hills, GA (cdp) De Kalb County	79	0.42
Eatontown, NJ (borough) Monmouth County	59	0.42
Lighthouse Point, FL (city) Broward County	45	0.42
Doraville, GA (city) De Kalb County	43	0.42
Lexington, MA (cdp) Middlesex County	124	0.41
Pikesville, MD (cdp) Baltimore County	120	0.41
North Bellmore, NY (cdp) Nassau County	82	0.41
Setauket-East Setauket, NY (cdp) Suffolk County	66	0.41
Skokie, IL (village) Cook County	251	0.40
Ocean, NJ (township) Monmouth County	108	0.40
Springdale, NJ (cdp) Camden County	58	0.40
Glendale, WI (city) Milwaukee County	54	0.40
Suffern, NY (village) Rockland County	44	0.40
Wantage, NJ (township) Sussex County	42	0.40
East Hanover, NJ (township) Morris County	45	0.39
East Brunswick, NJ (cdp) Middlesex County	178	0.38
Dobbs Ferry, NY (village) Westchester County	40	0.38
Amherst Center, MA (cdp) Hampshire County	64	0.37
Hallandale, FL (city) Broward County	126	0.36
Plainsboro, NJ (township) Middlesex County	73	0.36
North New Hyde Park, NY (cdp) Nassau County	53	0.36
Cambridge, MA (city) Middlesex County	353	0.35
Fort Lee, NJ (borough) Bergen County	122	0.34
Massapequa, NY (cdp) Nassau County	78	0.34
Creve Coeur, MO (city) Saint Louis County	54	0.33
Stony Brook, NY (cdp) Suffolk County	45	0.33
Ardmore, PA (cdp) Montgomery County	41	0.33
Greenburgh, NY (town) Westchester County	279	0.32
Cherry Hill, NJ (township) Camden County	225	0.32
Lakewood, NJ (township) Ocean County	191	0.32
Bethesda, MD (cdp) Montgomery County	179	0.32
Los Altos, CA (city) Santa Clara County	89	0.32
Sharon, MA (town) Norfolk County	56	0.32
Bethpage, NY (cdp) Nassau County	53	0.32
Los Angeles, CA (city) Los Angeles County	11,480	0.31
Boca Raton, FL (city) Palm Beach County	237	0.31
North Miami Beach, FL (city) Miami-Dade County	128	0.31
Urbana, IL (city) Champaign County	113	0.31
Long Beach, NY (city) Nassau County	111	0.31
New City, NY (cdp) Rockland County	107	0.31
Los Gatos, CA (town) Santa Clara County	90	0.31
Foster City, CA (city) San Mateo County	88	0.31
New Castle, NY (town) Westchester County	54	0.31
Lower Moreland, PA (township) Montgomery County	35	0.31
North Castle, NY (town) Westchester County	34	0.31
Lake Grove, NY (village) Suffolk County	32	0.31
Aspen Hill, MD (cdp) Montgomery County	150	0.30
Redmond, WA (city) King County	137	0.30
Coconut Creek, FL (city) Broward County	130	0.30
White Oak, MD (cdp) Montgomery County	63	0.30
Palm Valley, FL (cdp) Saint Johns County	59	0.30
Westbury, NY (village) Nassau County	43	0.30
Boone, NC (town) Watauga County	41	0.30
North Andover, MA (town) Essex County	80	0.29
Dix Hills, NY (cdp) Suffolk County	76	0.29
Glen Cove, NY (city) Nassau County	76	0.29
Susquehanna, PA (township) Dauphin County	62	0.29
Sandalfoot Cove, FL (cdp) Palm Beach County	48	0.29
Mill Valley, CA (city) Marin County	40	0.29
Princeton Meadows, NJ (cdp) Middlesex County	38	0.29
Oyster Bay, NY (town) Nassau County	821	0.28
Walnut Creek, CA (city) Contra Costa County	182	0.28
Vestal, NY (town) Broome County	73	0.28
Port Washington, NY (cdp) Nassau County	42	0.28
Coral Springs, FL (city) Broward County	320	0.27
Ann Arbor, MI (city) Washtenaw County	311	0.27
Berkeley, CA (city) Alameda County	279	0.27
Miami Beach, FL (city) Miami-Dade County	237	0.27
Winter Park, FL (city) Orange County	65	0.27
Boca Del Mar, FL (cdp) Palm Beach County	58	0.27
Winchester, MA (cdp) Middlesex County	57	0.27
Bellaire, TX (city) Harris County	42	0.27
Vidor, TX (city) Orange County	31	0.27
Freehold, NJ (borough) Monmouth County	30	0.27
Hackettstown, NJ (town) Warren County	28	0.27
New York, NY (city) New York City	20,946	0.26
Santa Monica, CA (city) Los Angeles County	221	0.26
Scotch Plains, NJ (cdp) Union County	59	0.26
Wilton, CT (town) Fairfield County	46	0.26
Winnetka, IL (village) Cook County	32	0.26
Larkspur, CA (city) Marin County	31	0.26
Glen Rock, NJ (borough) Bergen County	30	0.26
Hempstead, NY (town) Nassau County	1,877	0.25
Lauderhill, FL (city) Broward County	141	0.25

Notes: (cdp) census designated place; Refer to the Explanation of Data in the front of the book for more detailed information.

Italian

Top 150 Places Sorted by Number

(Based on all places, regardless of population)

Place	Number	%
New York, NY (city) New York City	692,739	8.65
Hempstead, NY (town) Nassau County	179,140	23.70
Brookhaven, NY (town) Suffolk County	147,077	32.81
Philadelphia, PA (city) Philadelphia County	140,139	9.23
Chicago, IL (city) Cook County	101,903	3.52
Los Angeles, CA (city) Los Angeles County	95,263	2.58
Oyster Bay, NY (town) Nassau County	87,807	29.87
Islip, NY (town) Suffolk County	83,408	25.85
Babylon, NY (town) Suffolk County	63,967	30.20
Phoenix, AZ (city) Maricopa County	58,578	4.43
San Diego, CA (city) San Diego County	55,764	4.56
Huntington, NY (town) Suffolk County	51,869	26.56
Boston, MA (city) Suffolk County	49,017	8.32
San Jose, CA (city) Santa Clara County	43,165	4.83
Smithtown, NY (town) Suffolk County	40,891	35.34
North Hempstead, NY (town) Nassau County	39,788	17.87
Pittsburgh, PA (city) Allegheny County	39,632	11.85
San Francisco, CA (city) San Francisco County	39,144	5.04
Yonkers, NY (city) Westchester County	36,907	18.82
Columbus, OH (city) Franklin County	35,236	4.95
Buffalo, NY (city) Erie County	34,379	11.75
Las Vegas, NV (city) Clark County	32,124	6.71
Houston, TX (city) Harris County	31,899	1.63
Dover, NJ (township) Ocean County	28,261	31.48
Cranston, RI (city) Providence County	27,359	34.51
Toms River, NJ (cdp) Ocean County	27,250	31.52
Greece, NY (town) Monroe County	26,253	27.89
Jacksonville, FL (special city) Duval County	25,385	3.45
Waterbury, CT (city) New Haven County	24,476	22.82
Providence, RI (city) Providence County	23,960	13.80
Virginia Beach, VA (independent city) Virginia Beach city	23,949	5.63
Metairie, LA (cdp) Jefferson Parish	23,259	15.95
Brick, NJ (township) Ocean County	23,161	30.43
Hamilton, NJ (township) Mercer County	22,684	26.00
Rochester, NY (city) Monroe County	22,077	10.05
Cleveland, OH (city) Cuyahoga County	22,053	4.61
Seattle, WA (city) King County	21,754	3.86
San Antonio, TX (city) Bexar County	21,697	1.90
Syracuse, NY (city) Onondaga County	20,778	14.10
Amherst, NY (town) Erie County	20,696	17.76
Worcester, MA (city) Worcester County	19,950	11.56
Stamford, CT (city) Fairfield County	19,873	16.97
Portland, OR (city) Multnomah County	19,810	3.74
Tucson, AZ (city) Pima County	19,636	4.04
Warwick, RI (city) Kent County	19,549	22.78
Denver, CO (city) Denver County	19,333	3.49
Middletown, NJ (township) Monmouth County	19,142	28.86
Tonawanda, NY (town) Erie County	18,881	24.16
Gloucester, NJ (township) Camden County	18,860	29.32
Omaha, NE (city) Douglas County	18,716	4.80
Clarkstown, NY (town) Rockland County	18,611	22.67
Baltimore, MD (independent city) Baltimore city	18,492	2.84
Levittown, NY (cdp) Nassau County	18,020	33.96
Woodbridge, NJ (township) Middlesex County	17,734	18.24
Mesa, AZ (city) Maricopa County	17,724	4.46
Charlotte, NC (city) Mecklenburg County	17,676	3.26
Revere, MA (city) Suffolk County	17,662	37.35
Milwaukee, WI (city) Milwaukee County	17,499	2.93
Indianapolis, IN (special city) Marion County	17,442	2.23
Medford, MA (city) Middlesex County	17,390	31.18
Scottsdale, AZ (city) Maricopa County	17,283	8.52
Tampa, FL (city) Hillsborough County	17,096	5.63
Saint Petersburg, FL (city) Pinellas County	16,736	6.75
Albuquerque, NM (city) Bernalillo County	16,721	3.73
Coral Springs, FL (city) Broward County	16,709	14.22
Colorado Springs, CO (city) El Paso County	16,692	4.63
Sterling Heights, MI (city) Macomb County	16,556	13.30
Norwalk, CT (city) Fairfield County	16,397	19.77
Austin, TX (city) Travis County	16,185	2.47
Wayne, NJ (cdp) Passaic County	16,166	29.87
Colonie, NY (town) Albany County	16,064	20.27
Dallas, TX (city) Dallas County	16,058	1.35
Upper Darby, PA (township) Delaware County	16,035	19.60
Washington, NJ (township) Gloucester County	15,966	33.89
Hamden, CT (town) New Haven County	15,953	28.03
Henderson, NV (city) Clark County	15,863	9.01
Utica, NY (city) Oneida County	15,831	26.09
Kansas City, MO (city) Jackson County	15,818	3.58
West Babylon, NY (cdp) Suffolk County	15,785	36.33
Jersey City, NJ (city) Hudson County	15,731	6.55
New Orleans, LA (city) Orleans Parish	15,695	3.24
Sacramento, CA (city) Sacramento County	15,643	3.84
Greenburgh, NY (town) Westchester County	15,494	17.86
Clinton, MI (cdp) Macomb County	15,285	15.98
Johnston, RI (town) Providence County	15,114	53.56
Clifton, NJ (city) Passaic County	15,108	19.20
Cheektowaga, NY (town) Erie County	15,047	16.00
Howell, NJ (township) Monmouth County	15,020	30.71
Irondequoit, NY (cdp) Monroe County	14,968	28.59
Scranton, PA (city) Lackawanna County	14,833	19.41
Old Bridge, NJ (township) Middlesex County	14,722	24.35
Akron, OH (city) Summit County	14,705	6.77
Warren, MI (city) Macomb County	14,700	10.63
Edison, NJ (cdp) Middlesex County	14,431	14.77
New Rochelle, NY (city) Westchester County	14,404	19.96
West Haven, CT (city) New Haven County	14,395	27.49
East Haven, CT (cdp) New Haven County	14,248	50.54
Springfield, MA (city) Hampden County	14,093	9.27
Franklin Square, NY (cdp) Nassau County	13,970	47.61
Port Saint Lucie, FL (city) Saint Lucie County	13,966	15.73
Erie, PA (city) Erie County	13,937	13.44
North Providence, RI (cdp) Providence County	13,924	42.96
Fresno, CA (city) Fresno County	13,914	3.26
Naperville, IL (city) Du Page County	13,611	10.61
Long Beach, CA (city) Los Angeles County	13,576	2.94
Huntington Beach, CA (city) Orange County	13,455	7.08
Cape Coral, FL (city) Lee County	13,437	13.15
Paradise, NV (cdp) Clark County	13,395	7.21
Hollywood, FL (city) Broward County	13,206	9.48
Clay, NY (town) Onondaga County	13,040	22.17
New Haven, CT (city) New Haven County	13,038	10.55
Niagara Falls, NY (city) Niagara County	12,879	23.13
Pembroke Pines, FL (city) Broward County	12,850	9.37
Vineland, NJ (city) Cumberland County	12,847	22.83
Bristol, CT (city) Hartford County	12,595	20.97
Bloomfield, NJ (cdp) Essex County	12,590	26.40
Washington, DC (city) District of Columbia	12,587	2.20
Saint Louis, MO (independent city) Saint Louis city	12,579	3.61
Mount Pleasant, NY (town) Westchester County	12,467	28.84
Santa Rosa, CA (city) Sonoma County	12,445	8.44
Spring Hill, FL (cdp) Hernando County	12,431	17.96
Bayonne, NJ (city) Hudson County	12,416	20.08
Yorktown, NY (town) Westchester County	12,407	34.16
Nutley, NJ (cdp) Essex County	12,183	44.53
Schenectady, NY (city) Schenectady County	12,168	19.65
Commack, NY (cdp) Suffolk County	12,124	33.37
Milford, CT (town) New Haven County	12,071	23.08
Bridgeport, CT (city) Fairfield County	12,051	8.64
Everett, MA (city) Middlesex County	11,963	31.45
Reno, NV (city) Washoe County	11,948	6.61
Quincy, MA (city) Norfolk County	11,919	13.54
Deer Park, NY (cdp) Suffolk County	11,899	42.10
Danbury, CT (city) Fairfield County	11,869	15.86
Malden, MA (city) Middlesex County	11,828	20.99
Albany, NY (city) Albany County	11,816	12.35
Cherry Hill, NJ (township) Camden County	11,780	16.84
Berkeley, NJ (township) Ocean County	11,757	29.40
Santa Clarita, CA (city) Los Angeles County	11,757	7.77
Wallingford, CT (town) New Haven County	11,704	27.20
Milford, CT (special city) New Haven County	11,660	23.04
Carmel, NY (town) Putnam County	11,655	35.31
Hicksville, NY (cdp) Nassau County	11,616	28.15
Parma, OH (city) Cuyahoga County	11,603	13.55
Valley Stream, NY (village) Nassau County	11,559	31.76
Fort Lauderdale, FL (city) Broward County	11,512	7.57
Haverford, PA (township) Delaware County	11,494	23.70
Southington, CT (town) Hartford County	11,474	28.88
Spring Valley, NV (cdp) Clark County	11,377	9.67
Jackson, NJ (township) Ocean County	11,311	26.42
Fairfield, CT (town) Fairfield County	11,290	19.69

Notes: (cdp) census designated place; Refer to the Explanation of Data in the front of the book for more detailed information.

Italian

Top 150 Places Sorted by Percent

(Based on all places, regardless of population)

Place	Number	%
Saltaire, NY (village) Suffolk County	51	75.00
Teterboro, NJ (borough) Bergen County	11	68.75
East Brooklyn, IL (village) Grundy County	56	54.90
Hammonton, NJ (town) Atlantic County	6,841	54.28
Popponesset Island, MA (cdp) Barnstable County	7	53.85
Johnston, RI (town) Providence County	15,114	53.56
Edgewood, CA (cdp) Siskiyou County	34	53.13
Malverne Park Oaks, NY (cdp) Nassau County	259	52.01
East Haven, CT (cdp) New Haven County	14,248	50.54
Rapid River, MN (township) Lake of the Woods County	7	50.00
Yatesville, PA (borough) Luzerne County	323	49.77
Roseto, PA (borough) Northampton County	816	49.36
Frankfort, NY (village) Herkimer County	1,239	48.93
North Massapequa, NY (cdp) Nassau County	9,368	48.91
Lowellville, OH (village) Mahoning County	615	48.01
Franklin Square, NY (cdp) Nassau County	13,970	47.61
Ramtown, NJ (cdp) Monmouth County	2,914	46.78
Fairfield, NJ (cdp) Essex County	3,235	45.80
Frankfort, NY (town) Herkimer County	3,349	44.78
Nutley, NJ (cdp) Essex County	12,183	44.53
Totowa, NJ (borough) Passaic County	4,381	44.50
Pence, WI (town) Iron County	88	44.44
Standard, IL (village) Putnam County	114	44.19
Hawthorne, NY (cdp) Westchester County	2,227	44.07
North Lynbrook, NY (cdp) Nassau County	287	43.82
Holiday Heights, NJ (cdp) Ocean County	1,017	43.07
North Providence, RI (cdp) Providence County	13,924	42.96
Shrub Oak, NY (cdp) Westchester County	791	42.94
Jessup, PA (borough) Lackawanna County	2,005	42.50
Old Forge, PA (borough) Lackawanna County	3,723	42.32
Deer Park, NY (cdp) Suffolk County	11,899	42.10
East Hanover, NJ (township) Morris County	4,759	41.77
Dover Beaches South, NJ (cdp) Ocean County	682	41.26
Thornwood, NY (cdp) Westchester County	2,459	41.20
North Branford, CT (town) New Haven County	5,717	41.11
Lyncourt, NY (cdp) Onondaga County	1,789	41.11
Massapequa Park, NY (village) Nassau County	7,169	40.97
Lyndhurst, NJ (cdp) Bergen County	7,914	40.83
Lake Grove, NY (village) Suffolk County	4,236	40.74
Pittston, PA (township) Luzerne County	1,400	40.58
West Paterson, NJ (borough) Passaic County	4,452	40.52
Wood-Ridge, NJ (borough) Bergen County	3,082	40.32
Holiday City South, NJ (cdp) Ocean County	1,634	40.30
North Haven, CT (town) New Haven County	9,271	40.25
Islip Terrace, NY (cdp) Suffolk County	2,269	40.22
Garden City South, NY (cdp) Nassau County	1,597	40.19
South Hackensack, NJ (township) Bergen County	905	40.19
Holtsville, NY (cdp) Suffolk County	6,821	40.18
Selden, NY (cdp) Suffolk County	8,748	40.10
River Bend, MO (village) Jackson County	4	40.00
Valhalla, NY (cdp) Westchester County	2,107	39.91
Holbrook, NY (cdp) Suffolk County	10,982	39.89
Milton, NY (cdp) Ulster County	512	39.78
Ronkonkoma, NY (cdp) Suffolk County	7,963	39.73
Oakville, CT (cdp) Litchfield County	3,411	39.61
Farmingville, NY (cdp) Suffolk County	6,530	39.60
Massapequa, NY (cdp) Nassau County	8,969	39.59
Carlstadt, NJ (borough) Bergen County	2,342	39.58
North Great River, NY (cdp) Suffolk County	1,548	39.40
Bethpage, NY (cdp) Nassau County	6,507	39.33
Dunmore, PA (borough) Lackawanna County	5,501	39.24
Casa Colorada, NM (cdp) Valencia County	20	39.22
Manorville, NY (cdp) Suffolk County	4,374	39.17
Homewood, PA (borough) Beaver County	65	38.92
Brewster Hill, NY (cdp) Putnam County	850	38.90
Netcong, NJ (borough) Morris County	1,003	38.88
Lindenhurst, NY (village) Suffolk County	10,831	38.77
Cardwell, MT (cdp) Jefferson County	12	38.71
Roseland, NJ (borough) Essex County	2,050	38.69
Shirley, NY (cdp) Suffolk County	9,797	38.58
Bohemia, NY (cdp) Suffolk County	3,796	38.54
Hasbrouck Heights, NJ (borough) Bergen County	4,486	38.47
North Patchogue, NY (cdp) Suffolk County	3,009	38.44
Lincolndale, NY (cdp) Westchester County	729	38.43
Brinckerhoff, NY (cdp) Dutchess County	1,059	38.41
West Islip, NY (cdp) Suffolk County	11,177	38.40
Nesconset, NY (cdp) Suffolk County	4,599	38.35
Mechanicville, NY (city) Saratoga County	1,924	38.33
South Wilmington, IL (village) Grundy County	247	38.24
Marlborough, NY (town) Ulster County	3,196	38.23
Belford, NJ (cdp) Monmouth County	545	38.22
Wolcott, CT (town) New Haven County	5,804	38.15
Mount Sinai, NY (cdp) Suffolk County	3,283	38.07
Harrison, NY (village) Westchester County	9,185	38.04
Malverne, NY (village) Nassau County	3,419	38.02
Crompond, NY (cdp) Westchester County	781	37.99
South Farmingdale, NY (cdp) Nassau County	5,700	37.85
Hughestown, PA (borough) Luzerne County	583	37.83
Seaford, NY (cdp) Nassau County	5,960	37.74
Newfield, NJ (borough) Gloucester County	609	37.69
Turnersville, NJ (cdp) Gloucester County	1,451	37.57
Hauppauge, NY (cdp) Suffolk County	7,556	37.54
Mylo, ND (city) Rolette County	9	37.50
Seconsett Island, MA (cdp) Barnstable County	9	37.50
Plainedge, NY (cdp) Nassau County	3,448	37.48
Glendora, NJ (cdp) Camden County	1,815	37.40
Koppel, PA (borough) Beaver County	320	37.38
Revere, MA (city) Suffolk County	17,662	37.35
Rocky Point, NY (cdp) Suffolk County	3,803	37.15
Island Park, NY (village) Nassau County	1,757	37.13
Lewis Run, PA (borough) McKean County	217	37.03
North Babylon, NY (cdp) Suffolk County	6,572	36.99
Terryville, NY (cdp) Suffolk County	3,908	36.90
Jefferson Valley-Yorktown, NY (cdp) Westchester County	5,485	36.83
Centereach, NY (cdp) Suffolk County	9,983	36.73
Glen Head, NY (cdp) Nassau County	1,696	36.67
Kings Park, NY (cdp) Suffolk County	5,910	36.63
Saugus, MA (cdp) Essex County	9,518	36.60
West Babylon, NY (cdp) Suffolk County	15,785	36.33
West Long Branch, NJ (borough) Monmouth County	2,984	36.13
Gates-North Gates, NY (cdp) Monroe County	5,454	36.03
Sharpsburg, PA (borough) Allegheny County	1,295	36.03
Pittston, PA (city) Luzerne County	2,918	36.01
Lynbrook, NY (village) Nassau County	7,140	35.91
Bay Park, NY (cdp) Nassau County	808	35.90
Lake Ronkonkoma, NY (cdp) Suffolk County	7,061	35.89
Follansbee, WV (city) Brooke County	1,082	35.79
Saddle Brook, NJ (cdp) Bergen County	4,700	35.73
Gibbstown, NJ (cdp) Gloucester County	1,341	35.72
Dalzell, IL (village) Bureau County	252	35.69
Hillside Lake, NY (cdp) Dutchess County	735	35.59
Glasco, NY (cdp) Ulster County	606	35.48
Head of the Harbor, NY (village) Suffolk County	512	35.38
Lavallette, NJ (borough) Ocean County	942	35.35
Smithtown, NY (town) Suffolk County	40,891	35.34
Taylor, PA (township) Lawrence County	424	35.33
Carmel, NY (town) Putnam County	11,655	35.31
West Caldwell, NJ (cdp) Essex County	3,958	35.24
Highland, NY (cdp) Ulster County	1,779	35.16
Saint James, NY (cdp) Suffolk County	4,662	35.14
East Islip, NY (cdp) Suffolk County	4,942	35.09
Mastic, NY (cdp) Suffolk County	5,435	35.01
Oceanport, NJ (borough) Monmouth County	2,026	34.84
Greenwich, NJ (township) Gloucester County	1,700	34.84
Cedar Grove, NJ (cdp) Essex County	4,278	34.78
Knight, WI (town) Iron County	93	34.70
Solvay, NY (village) Onondaga County	2,374	34.67
Eastchester, NY (town) Westchester County	10,844	34.63
Port Reading, NJ (cdp) Middlesex County	1,265	34.60
Little Falls, NJ (cdp) Passaic County	3,755	34.59
Buena, NJ (borough) Atlantic County	1,339	34.57
North Wantagh, NY (cdp) Nassau County	4,200	34.55
North Merrick, NY (cdp) Nassau County	4,092	34.55
Orange, CT (cdp) New Haven County	4,571	34.54
Shenorock, NY (cdp) Westchester County	680	34.54
Cranston, RI (city) Providence County	27,359	34.51
Farmingdale, NY (village) Nassau County	2,881	34.29
Verona, NJ (cdp) Essex County	4,638	34.27
Lloyd, NY (town) Ulster County	3,406	34.26
Westerly, RI (town) Washington County	7,863	34.24

Notes: (cdp) census designated place; Refer to the Explanation of Data in the front of the book for more detailed information.

Italian

Top 150 Places Sorted by Percent

(Based on places with populations of 10,000 or more)

Place	Number	%
Hammonton, NJ (town) Atlantic County	6,841	54.28
Johnston, RI (town) Providence County	15,114	53.56
East Haven, CT (cdp) New Haven County	14,248	50.54
North Massapequa, NY (cdp) Nassau County	9,368	48.91
Franklin Square, NY (cdp) Nassau County	13,970	47.61
Nutley, NJ (cdp) Essex County	12,183	44.53
North Providence, RI (cdp) Providence County	13,924	42.96
Deer Park, NY (cdp) Suffolk County	11,899	42.10
East Hanover, NJ (township) Morris County	4,759	41.77
North Branford, CT (town) New Haven County	5,717	41.11
Massapequa Park, NY (village) Nassau County	7,169	40.97
Lyndhurst, NJ (cdp) Bergen County	7,914	40.83
Lake Grove, NY (village) Suffolk County	4,236	40.74
West Paterson, NJ (borough) Passaic County	4,452	40.52
North Haven, CT (town) New Haven County	9,271	40.25
Holtsville, NY (cdp) Suffolk County	6,821	40.18
Selden, NY (cdp) Suffolk County	8,748	40.10
Holbrook, NY (cdp) Suffolk County	10,982	39.89
Ronkonkoma, NY (cdp) Suffolk County	7,963	39.73
Farmingville, NY (cdp) Suffolk County	6,530	39.60
Massapequa, NY (cdp) Nassau County	8,969	39.59
Bethpage, NY (cdp) Nassau County	6,507	39.33
Dunmore, PA (borough) Lackawanna County	5,501	39.24
Manorville, NY (cdp) Suffolk County	4,374	39.17
Lindenhurst, NY (village) Suffolk County	10,831	38.77
Shirley, NY (cdp) Suffolk County	9,797	38.58
Hasbrouck Heights, NJ (borough) Bergen County	4,486	38.47
West Islip, NY (cdp) Suffolk County	11,177	38.40
Nesconset, NY (cdp) Suffolk County	4,599	38.35
Wolcott, CT (town) New Haven County	5,804	38.15
Harrison, NY (village) Westchester County	9,185	38.04
South Farmingdale, NY (cdp) Nassau County	5,700	37.85
Seaford, NY (cdp) Nassau County	5,960	37.74
Hauppauge, NY (cdp) Suffolk County	7,556	37.54
Revere, MA (city) Suffolk County	17,662	37.35
Rocky Point, NY (cdp) Suffolk County	3,803	37.15
North Babylon, NY (cdp) Suffolk County	6,572	36.99
Terryville, NY (cdp) Suffolk County	3,908	36.90
Jefferson Valley-Yorktown, NY (cdp) Westchester County	5,485	36.83
Centereach, NY (cdp) Suffolk County	9,983	36.73
Kings Park, NY (cdp) Suffolk County	5,910	36.63
Saugus, MA (cdp) Essex County	9,518	36.60
West Babylon, NY (cdp) Suffolk County	15,785	36.33
Gates-North Gates, NY (cdp) Monroe County	5,454	36.03
Lynbrook, NY (village) Nassau County	7,140	35.91
Lake Ronkonkoma, NY (cdp) Suffolk County	7,061	35.89
Saddle Brook, NJ (cdp) Bergen County	4,700	35.73
Smithtown, NY (town) Suffolk County	40,891	35.34
Carmel, NY (town) Putnam County	11,655	35.31
West Caldwell, NJ (cdp) Essex County	3,958	35.24
Saint James, NY (cdp) Suffolk County	4,662	35.14
East Islip, NY (cdp) Suffolk County	4,942	35.09
Mastic, NY (cdp) Suffolk County	5,435	35.01
Cedar Grove, NJ (cdp) Essex County	4,278	34.78
Eastchester, NY (town) Westchester County	10,844	34.63
Little Falls, NJ (cdp) Passaic County	3,755	34.59
North Wantagh, NY (cdp) Nassau County	4,200	34.55
North Merrick, NY (cdp) Nassau County	4,092	34.55
Orange, CT (cdp) New Haven County	4,571	34.54
Cranston, RI (city) Providence County	27,359	34.51
Verona, NJ (cdp) Essex County	4,638	34.27
Westerly, RI (town) Washington County	7,863	34.24
Yorktown, NY (town) Westchester County	12,407	34.16
Watertown, CT (town) Litchfield County	7,378	34.06
Levittown, NY (cdp) Nassau County	18,020	33.96
Washington, NJ (township) Gloucester County	15,966	33.89
Mastic Beach, NY (cdp) Suffolk County	3,877	33.59
Hawthorne, NJ (borough) Passaic County	6,096	33.46
Derby, CT (city) New Haven County	4,143	33.44
Commack, NY (cdp) Suffolk County	12,124	33.37
Lodi, NJ (borough) Bergen County	7,986	33.32
Ridge, NY (cdp) Suffolk County	4,399	33.18
Stoneham, MA (town) Middlesex County	7,350	33.08
Rotterdam, NY (town) Schenectady County	9,364	32.99
Beekman, NY (town) Dutchess County	3,764	32.92

Place	Number	%
East Patchogue, NY (cdp) Suffolk County	6,867	32.91
Hazlet, NJ (township) Monmouth County	7,032	32.89
Brookhaven, NY (town) Suffolk County	147,077	32.81
Medford, NY (cdp) Suffolk County	7,186	32.69
Gates, NY (town) Monroe County	9,541	32.57
Miller Place, NY (cdp) Suffolk County	3,452	32.36
Hazleton, PA (city) Luzerne County	7,477	32.14
North Bellmore, NY (cdp) Nassau County	6,429	32.02
Valley Stream, NY (village) Nassau County	11,559	31.76
Wethersfield, CT (cdp) Hartford County	8,333	31.76
Coram, NY (cdp) Suffolk County	11,086	31.69
Toms River, NJ (cdp) Ocean County	27,250	31.52
Southeast, NY (town) Putnam County	5,457	31.51
Clark, NJ (cdp) Union County	4,599	31.51
Dover, NJ (township) Ocean County	28,261	31.48
Everett, MA (city) Middlesex County	11,963	31.45
Kent, NY (town) Putnam County	4,386	31.31
Medford, MA (city) Middlesex County	17,390	31.18
Wantagh, NY (cdp) Nassau County	5,910	31.15
Smithfield, RI (town) Providence County	6,411	31.14
Bellmawr, NJ (borough) Camden County	3,501	31.09
Lacey, NJ (township) Ocean County	7,872	31.06
North Lindenhurst, NY (cdp) Suffolk County	3,652	31.04
Belleville, NJ (cdp) Essex County	11,115	30.94
New Castle, PA (city) Lawrence County	8,127	30.89
Copiague, NY (cdp) Suffolk County	6,765	30.86
Sayville, NY (cdp) Suffolk County	5,160	30.82
Howell, NJ (township) Monmouth County	15,020	30.71
Stony Point, NY (town) Rockland County	4,375	30.71
Floral Park, NY (village) Nassau County	4,887	30.57
Somers, NY (town) Westchester County	5,599	30.52
Brick, NJ (township) Ocean County	23,161	30.43
Hanover, NJ (township) Morris County	3,917	30.37
Garden City, NY (village) Nassau County	6,552	30.25
Babylon, NY (town) Suffolk County	63,967	30.20
Branford, CT (town) New Haven County	8,659	30.19
Holiday City-Berkeley, NJ (cdp) Ocean County	4,195	30.16
Babylon, NY (village) Suffolk County	3,803	30.15
East Fishkill, NY (town) Dutchess County	7,705	30.04
Milford, MA (town) Worcester County	8,025	29.95
Oyster Bay, NY (town) Nassau County	87,807	29.87
Wayne, NJ (cdp) Passaic County	16,166	29.87
Franklin Lakes, NJ (borough) Bergen County	3,110	29.84
Pelham, NY (town) Westchester County	3,537	29.81
Rocky Hill, CT (town) Hartford County	5,344	29.78
Winthrop, MA (cdp) Suffolk County	5,439	29.72
East Norriton, PA (cdp) Montgomery County	3,895	29.64
East Massapequa, NY (cdp) Nassau County	5,785	29.57
Trumbull, CT (cdp) Fairfield County	10,107	29.52
Girard, OH (city) Trumbull County	3,285	29.46
Berkeley, NJ (township) Ocean County	11,757	29.40
Gloucester, NJ (township) Camden County	18,860	29.32
Monroe, CT (town) Fairfield County	5,642	29.31
Elwood, NY (cdp) Suffolk County	3,179	29.31
Putnam Valley, NY (town) Putnam County	3,122	29.22
Pequannock, NJ (township) Morris County	4,049	29.15
Mercerville-Hamilton Square, NJ (cdp) Mercer County	7,710	29.11
Ansonia, CT (city) New Haven County	5,386	29.03
Oceanside, NY (cdp) Nassau County	9,488	28.99
Berlin, CT (town) Hartford County	5,276	28.97
Southington, CT (town) Hartford County	11,474	28.88
Middletown, NJ (township) Monmouth County	19,142	28.86
Mount Pleasant, NY (town) Westchester County	12,467	28.84
Patterson, NY (town) Putnam County	3,248	28.73
Elmwood Park, IL (village) Cook County	7,293	28.71
Torrington, CT (city) Litchfield County	10,094	28.67
Irondequoit, NY (cdp) Monroe County	14,968	28.59
Mamaroneck, NY (village) Westchester County	5,354	28.53
Wakefield, MA (cdp) Middlesex County	7,069	28.50
Wappinger, NY (town) Dutchess County	7,488	28.46
East Meadow, NY (cdp) Nassau County	10,662	28.43
Shelton, CT (city) Fairfield County	10,816	28.39
Succasunna-Kenvil, NJ (cdp) Morris County	3,553	28.36
Struthers, OH (city) Mahoning County	3,332	28.34
Beachwood, NJ (borough) Ocean County	2,917	28.28

Notes: (cdp) census designated place; Refer to the Explanation of Data in the front of the book for more detailed information.

Latvian

Top 150 Places Sorted by Number

(Based on all places, regardless of population)

Place	Number	%
New York, NY (city) New York City	3,777	0.05
Los Angeles, CA (city) Los Angeles County	1,687	0.05
Chicago, IL (city) Cook County	1,383	0.05
San Francisco, CA (city) San Francisco County	629	0.08
Seattle, WA (city) King County	624	0.11
Hempstead, NY (town) Nassau County	490	0.06
Minneapolis, MN (city) Hennepin County	479	0.13
Philadelphia, PA (city) Philadelphia County	466	0.03
Portland, OR (city) Multnomah County	428	0.08
Boston, MA (city) Suffolk County	428	0.07
Indianapolis, IN (special city) Marion County	392	0.05
Grand Rapids, MI (city) Kent County	378	0.19
Phoenix, AZ (city) Maricopa County	378	0.03
San Diego, CA (city) San Diego County	367	0.03
Saint Petersburg, FL (city) Pinellas County	350	0.14
Washington, DC (city) District of Columbia	336	0.06
Lincoln, NE (city) Lancaster County	315	0.14
Columbus, OH (city) Franklin County	290	0.04
Milwaukee, WI (city) Milwaukee County	285	0.05
Denver, CO (city) Denver County	283	0.05
Oyster Bay, NY (town) Nassau County	275	0.09
Baltimore, MD (independent city) Baltimore city	268	0.04
Brookhaven, NY (town) Suffolk County	261	0.06
Houston, TX (city) Harris County	255	0.01
Arlington, VA (cdp) Arlington County	235	0.12
North Hempstead, NY (town) Nassau County	234	0.11
Kalamazoo, MI (city) Kalamazoo County	228	0.30
Cleveland, OH (city) Cuyahoga County	213	0.04
San Jose, CA (city) Santa Clara County	207	0.02
Tacoma, WA (city) Pierce County	197	0.10
Omaha, NE (city) Douglas County	191	0.05
Brookline, MA (cdp) Norfolk County	183	0.32
Berkeley, CA (city) Alameda County	179	0.17
Newton, MA (city) Middlesex County	177	0.21
Palatine, IL (village) Cook County	172	0.26
Des Moines, IA (city) Polk County	172	0.09
Saint Paul, MN (city) Ramsey County	172	0.06
Long Beach, CA (city) Los Angeles County	172	0.04
Babylon, NY (town) Suffolk County	170	0.08
Huntington, NY (town) Suffolk County	167	0.09
Colorado Springs, CO (city) El Paso County	165	0.05
Mesa, AZ (city) Maricopa County	159	0.04
Las Vegas, NV (city) Clark County	158	0.03
San Antonio, TX (city) Bexar County	158	0.01
East Brunswick, NJ (cdp) Middlesex County	155	0.33
Bellevue, WA (city) King County	155	0.14
Austin, TX (city) Travis County	153	0.02
Oak Park, IL (village) Cook County	146	0.28
Ann Arbor, MI (city) Washtenaw County	144	0.13
Buffalo, NY (city) Erie County	144	0.05
Lakewood, OH (city) Cuyahoga County	141	0.25
Greenwich, CT (town) Fairfield County	139	0.23
De Witt, NY (town) Onondaga County	135	0.56
Islip, NY (town) Suffolk County	135	0.04
Columbia, MD (cdp) Howard County	132	0.15
Parma, OH (city) Cuyahoga County	131	0.15
Madison, WI (city) Dane County	129	0.06
Tempe, AZ (city) Maricopa County	128	0.08
Bloomington, MN (city) Hennepin County	125	0.15
Evanston, IL (city) Cook County	124	0.17
Brick, NJ (township) Ocean County	123	0.16
Thousand Oaks, CA (city) Ventura County	123	0.11
Spokane, WA (city) Spokane County	122	0.06
Oakland, CA (city) Alameda County	122	0.03
Charlotte, NC (city) Mecklenburg County	120	0.02
Tucson, AZ (city) Pima County	120	0.02
Scottsdale, AZ (city) Maricopa County	117	0.06
Nashville-Davidson, TN (special city) Davidson County	116	0.02
Reston, VA (cdp) Fairfax County	115	0.20
Cambridge, MA (city) Middlesex County	114	0.11
Sacramento, CA (city) Sacramento County	114	0.03
Stamford, CT (city) Fairfield County	112	0.10
Dallas, TX (city) Dallas County	111	0.01
Manchester, NJ (township) Ocean County	109	0.28
Syracuse, NY (city) Onondaga County	109	0.07
Fair Lawn, NJ (borough) Bergen County	107	0.34
Des Plaines, IL (city) Cook County	105	0.18
Kalamazoo, MI (township) Kalamazoo County	103	0.47
Memphis, TN (city) Shelby County	103	0.02
Jacksonville, FL (special city) Duval County	103	0.01
Highlands Ranch, CO (cdp) Douglas County	102	0.14
Ramapo, NY (town) Rockland County	102	0.09
Cincinnati, OH (city) Hamilton County	102	0.03
Pikesville, MD (cdp) Baltimore County	101	0.35
Manhattan Beach, CA (city) Los Angeles County	101	0.30
Greenburgh, NY (town) Westchester County	101	0.12
Pittsburgh, PA (city) Allegheny County	101	0.03
Virginia Beach, VA (independent city) Virginia Beach city	101	0.02
Mount Prospect, IL (village) Cook County	100	0.18
Reno, NV (city) Washoe County	100	0.06
Meridian charter, MI (township) Ingham County	99	0.25
Coral Springs, FL (city) Broward County	99	0.08
Kenmore, WA (city) King County	98	0.53
Aspen Hill, MD (cdp) Montgomery County	98	0.20
Atlanta, GA (city) Fulton County	98	0.02
Fabius, MI (township) Saint Joseph County	97	2.93
Saint Pete Beach, FL (city) Pinellas County	97	0.98
Windham, CT (town) Windham County	97	0.42
Buffalo Grove, IL (village) Lake County	97	0.23
Castro Valley, CA (cdp) Alameda County	96	0.17
Miami Beach, FL (city) Miami-Dade County	96	0.11
Dedham, MA (cdp) Norfolk County	95	0.40
Okemos, MI (cdp) Ingham County	94	0.41
Wyoming, MI (city) Kent County	94	0.14
Minnetonka, MN (city) Hennepin County	93	0.18
Cherry Hill, NJ (township) Camden County	92	0.13
Walnut Creek, CA (city) Contra Costa County	91	0.14
Amherst, NY (town) Erie County	91	0.08
North Miami, FL (city) Miami-Dade County	89	0.15
Silver Spring, MD (cdp) Montgomery County	89	0.12
Edison, NJ (cdp) Middlesex County	89	0.09
Hollywood, FL (city) Broward County	89	0.06
Roxbury, NJ (township) Morris County	88	0.37
Northbrook, IL (village) Cook County	88	0.26
Chapel Hill, NC (town) Orange County	88	0.18
Somerville, MA (city) Middlesex County	88	0.11
Albuquerque, NM (city) Bernalillo County	88	0.02
Laguna Beach, CA (city) Orange County	87	0.37
Natick, MA (town) Middlesex County	87	0.27
Quincy, MA (city) Norfolk County	87	0.10
Farmington Hills, MI (city) Oakland County	86	0.10
Plano, TX (city) Collin County	86	0.04
Abington, PA (township) Montgomery County	85	0.15
Irvine, CA (city) Orange County	85	0.06
Louisville, KY (city) Jefferson County	85	0.03
White Bear, MN (township) Ramsey County	84	0.75
Joppatowne, MD (cdp) Harford County	84	0.74
Northampton, PA (township) Bucks County	84	0.21
West Bloomfield, MI (township) Oakland County	84	0.13
Lombard, IL (village) Du Page County	83	0.20
Rockville, MD (city) Montgomery County	83	0.18
Redondo Beach, CA (city) Los Angeles County	83	0.13
Whitefish Bay, WI (village) Milwaukee County	82	0.58
North Bethesda, MD (cdp) Montgomery County	82	0.21
Redford, MI (cdp) Wayne County	81	0.16
Bethesda, MD (cdp) Montgomery County	81	0.15
Boulder, CO (city) Boulder County	81	0.09
Miami, FL (city) Miami-Dade County	81	0.02
Mamaroneck, NY (town) Westchester County	80	0.28
Watertown, MA (city) Middlesex County	80	0.24
Bloomfield, MI (township) Oakland County	80	0.19
Arden-Arcade, CA (cdp) Sacramento County	80	0.08
Franklin, MA (city) Norfolk County	79	0.27
West Allis, WI (city) Milwaukee County	79	0.13
Plymouth, MN (city) Hennepin County	79	0.12
Davie, FL (town) Broward County	79	0.10
Brockton, MA (city) Plymouth County	79	0.08
Santa Clarita, CA (city) Los Angeles County	79	0.05
La Grange, NY (town) Dutchess County	78	0.52
Worcester, MA (city) Worcester County	78	0.05

Notes: (cdp) census designated place; Refer to the Explanation of Data in the front of the book for more detailed information.

Latvian

Top 150 Places Sorted by Percent

(Based on all places, regardless of population)

Place	Number	%
New Hudson, NY (town) Allegany County	40	5.45
Roberts, MN (township) Wilkin County	7	5.34
Radisson, WI (village) Sawyer County	13	5.10
Crestone, CO (town) Saguache County	3	4.55
Seabrook, MA (cdp) Barnstable County	19	3.56
Hill, WI (town) Price County	13	3.40
Arpin, WI (village) Wood County	12	3.39
Lee, IL (village) Lee County	9	3.31
Wetherington, OH (cdp) Butler County	33	3.24
Hooppole, IL (village) Henry County	5	3.07
Lake, MI (township) Menominee County	17	3.06
South Windham, CT (cdp) Windham County	39	2.96
Mantador, ND (city) Richland County	2	2.94
Fabius, MI (township) Saint Joseph County	97	2.93
Grant, WI (town) Monroe County	14	2.85
Cedar Glen West, NJ (cdp) Ocean County	39	2.81
Russell, WI (town) Lincoln County	19	2.77
Holyoke, MN (township) Carlton County	5	2.75
Winnebago, MN (township) Houston County	7	2.68
Ophir, CO (town) San Miguel County	3	2.61
Hartly, DE (town) Kent County	2	2.60
Vandiver, MO (village) Audrain County	2	2.56
Morris, PA (township) Tioga County	16	2.45
Withee, WI (village) Clark County	10	2.35
Orchid, FL (town) Indian River County	3	2.17
Blue Springs, AL (town) Barbour County	2	2.17
Beverly Shores, IN (town) Porter County	14	2.08
Medo, MN (township) Blue Earth County	8	2.05
Big Falls, MN (city) Koochiching County	5	1.98
La Barge, WY (town) Lincoln County	8	1.95
Glenview Hills, KY (city) Jefferson County	6	1.76
Shafer, MN (city) Chisago County	6	1.71
Julian, CA (cdp) San Diego County	29	1.70
Haycock, PA (township) Bucks County	37	1.69
Cascade, MN (township) Olmsted County	50	1.60
Berlin, WI (town) Marathon County	14	1.58
Mifflin, OH (village) Ashland County	2	1.52
Makanda, IL (village) Jackson County	6	1.47
Lakehead-Lakeshore, CA (cdp) Shasta County	9	1.45
Punaluu, HI (cdp) Honolulu County	12	1.42
Lolo, MT (cdp) Missoula County	46	1.38
Harris, WI (town) Marquette County	10	1.38
Thurman, IA (city) Fremont County	3	1.36
Okauchee Lake, WI (cdp) Waukesha County	51	1.35
Knapp, WI (town) Jackson County	4	1.32
Odessa, MN (township) Big Stone County	2	1.30
Shepherdstown, WV (town) Jefferson County	10	1.26
Johnstown, WI (town) Rock County	10	1.24
Westby, MT (town) Sheridan County	2	1.24
Edisto Beach, SC (town) Colleton County	8	1.23
Hulett, WY (town) Crook County	5	1.23
Pelham, MA (town) Hampshire County	17	1.21
Lorraine, NY (town) Jefferson County	11	1.20
Eau Pleine, WI (town) Marathon County	9	1.20
Easton, NH (town) Grafton County	3	1.20
Kilkenny, MN (city) Le Sueur County	2	1.20
Tully, NY (village) Onondaga County	11	1.19
South Duxbury, MA (cdp) Plymouth County	36	1.17
Lavallette, NJ (borough) Ocean County	31	1.16
Fort Montgomery, NY (cdp) Orange County	16	1.16
Deer Park, IL (village) Lake County	37	1.15
Sherman, NY (village) Chautauqua County	8	1.15
Chatham, NH (town) Carroll County	3	1.15
Henniker, NH (town) Merrimack County	50	1.13
Glover, VT (town) Orleans County	11	1.13
Pine Grove Mills, PA (cdp) Centre County	13	1.12
Hubbard, WI (town) Rusk County	2	1.12
Clifton, VA (town) Fairfax County	2	1.09
Hunter, NY (town) Greene County	29	1.07
Palm Beach Shores, FL (town) Palm Beach County	13	1.07
Crystal Lake, CT (cdp) Tolland County	15	1.05
Morristown, MN (township) Rice County	7	1.04
Stockbridge, VT (town) Windsor County	7	1.04
Esperance, NY (village) Schoharie County	4	1.04
Lizton, IN (town) Hendricks County	4	1.04

Place	Number	%
Argyle, NY (village) Washington County	3	1.04
Bradley Beach, NJ (borough) Monmouth County	49	1.02
Rossmoor, NJ (cdp) Middlesex County	32	1.02
Caroline, NY (town) Tompkins County	29	1.02
Woodridge, NY (village) Sullivan County	9	1.01
Westbrook Center, CT (cdp) Middlesex County	22	1.00
Amherst, WI (village) Portage County	10	0.99
New Seabury, MA (cdp) Barnstable County	8	0.99
Saint Pete Beach, FL (city) Pinellas County	97	0.98
South Valley Stream, NY (cdp) Nassau County	55	0.98
Holmes, MI (township) Menominee County	3	0.97
Schley, WI (town) Lincoln County	9	0.96
Belle Terre, NY (village) Suffolk County	8	0.96
Manila, UT (town) Daggett County	3	0.94
Brookfield, WI (town) Waukesha County	58	0.93
Skaneateles, NY (village) Onondaga County	25	0.93
Dillsboro, NC (town) Jackson County	2	0.93
Liberty, PA (borough) Tioga County	2	0.93
Waterford, WI (village) Racine County	38	0.92
Eagle, MI (township) Clinton County	21	0.91
New Hartford Center, CT (cdp) Litchfield County	9	0.91
Home Lake, MN (township) Norman County	2	0.91
Eastwood, MI (cdp) Kalamazoo County	55	0.90
Dresden, NY (town) Washington County	6	0.90
Yarrow Point, WA (town) King County	9	0.89
Rusk, WI (town) Burnett County	4	0.89
Trout Lake, WA (cdp) Klickitat County	4	0.88
Warner, NH (town) Merrimack County	24	0.87
Sharon, NH (town) Hillsborough County	3	0.87
Barton Hills, MI (village) Washtenaw County	3	0.86
Delavan Lake, WI (cdp) Walworth County	20	0.85
Gold River, CA (cdp) Sacramento County	70	0.84
Bentleyville, OH (village) Cuyahoga County	8	0.84
San Mar, MD (cdp) Washington County	6	0.84
Byron, MI (village) Shiawassee County	5	0.84
Rhodhiss, NC (town) Caldwell County	3	0.84
Scandinavia, WI (village) Waupaca County	3	0.84
Lanark, WI (town) Portage County	12	0.82
Fox Point, WI (village) Milwaukee County	57	0.81
Grafton, WI (town) Ozaukee County	34	0.81
Shaver Lake, CA (cdp) Fresno County	6	0.81
Monroe, NY (village) Orange County	62	0.80
Lattingtown, NY (village) Nassau County	15	0.80
Norman, MN (township) Pine County	2	0.80
Peshtigo, WI (city) Marinette County	26	0.79
Scotland, SD (city) Bon Homme County	7	0.79
Mesa, CA (cdp) Inyo County	2	0.79
Ridgway, PA (borough) Elk County	36	0.78
Myrtletown, CA (cdp) Humboldt County	34	0.78
Algona, WA (city) King County	19	0.78
Ross, CA (town) Marin County	18	0.78
Richford, NY (town) Tioga County	9	0.78
Philip, SD (city) Haakon County	7	0.78
Winter Park, CO (town) Grand County	5	0.78
Gretna, NE (city) Sarpy County	18	0.77
Asharoken, NY (village) Suffolk County	5	0.77
Wilson, WY (cdp) Teton County	10	0.76
Wild Rose, WI (village) Waushara County	6	0.76
White Bear, MN (township) Ramsey County	84	0.75
Carson, WI (town) Portage County	10	0.75
Dixmont, ME (town) Penobscot County	8	0.75
Hodges, MN (township) Stevens County	2	0.75
Joppatowne, MD (cdp) Harford County	84	0.74
Liberty, NY (village) Sullivan County	29	0.74
Ben Lomond, CA (cdp) Santa Cruz County	17	0.74
Hiram, OH (village) Portage County	9	0.74
Verona, ME (town) Hancock County	4	0.74
Springfield, PA (township) Bucks County	36	0.73
Elkland, PA (borough) Tioga County	13	0.73
Monument Beach, MA (cdp) Barnstable County	18	0.72
Pine Mountain Club, CA (cdp) Kern County	12	0.72
Bodega Bay, CA (cdp) Sonoma County	11	0.72
Dahlgren, VA (cdp) King George County	7	0.72
Easton, WA (cdp) Kittitas County	3	0.72
Westwood, MO (village) Saint Louis County	2	0.72

Notes: (cdp) census designated place; Refer to the Explanation of Data in the front of the book for more detailed information.

Latvian

Top 150 Places Sorted by Percent

(Based on places with populations of 10,000 or more)

Place	Number	%
White Bear, MN (township) Ramsey County	84	0.75
Joppatowne, MD (cdp) Harford County	84	0.74
Texas, MI (township) Kalamazoo County	73	0.67
Wrentham, MA (town) Norfolk County	62	0.59
Whitefish Bay, WI (village) Milwaukee County	82	0.58
De Witt, NY (town) Onondaga County	135	0.56
Kenmore, WA (city) King County	98	0.53
Lyons, IL (village) Cook County	54	0.53
La Grange, NY (town) Dutchess County	78	0.52
Medfield, MA (town) Norfolk County	61	0.50
Piedmont, CA (city) Alameda County	54	0.49
Cedarburg, WI (city) Ozaukee County	52	0.48
Kalamazoo, MI (township) Kalamazoo County	103	0.47
Highland Park, NJ (borough) Middlesex County	62	0.44
Windham, CT (town) Windham County	97	0.42
Okemos, MI (cdp) Ingham County	94	0.41
Dedham, MA (cdp) Norfolk County	95	0.40
Hamptons at Boca Raton, FL (cdp) Palm Beach County	46	0.40
Leisure Village West-Pine Lake Park, NJ (cdp) Ocean County	44	0.40
Roxbury, NJ (township) Morris County	88	0.37
Laguna Beach, CA (city) Orange County	87	0.37
Deerfield, IL (village) Lake County	69	0.37
Willimantic, CT (cdp) Windham County	58	0.37
Port Washington, NY (cdp) Nassau County	55	0.36
Pikesville, MD (cdp) Baltimore County	101	0.35
Milford, MI (township) Oakland County	54	0.35
Oldsmar, FL (city) Pinellas County	41	0.35
Greenwood Village, CO (city) Arapahoe County	39	0.35
Fair Lawn, NJ (borough) Bergen County	107	0.34
Duxbury, MA (town) Plymouth County	48	0.34
Mashpee, MA (town) Barnstable County	44	0.34
East Brunswick, NJ (cdp) Middlesex County	155	0.33
North Potomac, MD (cdp) Montgomery County	75	0.33
Rockland, MA (town) Plymouth County	58	0.33
Western Springs, IL (village) Cook County	42	0.33
Brookline, MA (cdp) Norfolk County	183	0.32
Oshtemo, MI (township) Kalamazoo County	55	0.32
Broadview Heights, OH (city) Cuyahoga County	51	0.32
Ukiah, CA (city) Mendocino County	49	0.32
Shorewood, WI (village) Milwaukee County	44	0.32
Hampton Bays, NY (cdp) Suffolk County	39	0.32
White Bear Lake, MN (city) Ramsey County	76	0.31
Mercer Island, WA (city) King County	68	0.31
Brook Park, OH (city) Cuyahoga County	65	0.31
Oxford charter, MI (township) Oakland County	50	0.31
Brooklyn Park, MD (cdp) Anne Arundel County	34	0.31
Kalamazoo, MI (city) Kalamazoo County	228	0.30
Manhattan Beach, CA (city) Los Angeles County	101	0.30
Whitemarsh, PA (township) Montgomery County	50	0.30
Wayland, MA (town) Middlesex County	39	0.30
Medway, MA (town) Norfolk County	37	0.30
Grand Haven, MI (city) Ottawa County	33	0.30
Morris, NJ (township) Morris County	64	0.29
Arroyo Grande, CA (city) San Luis Obispo County	46	0.29
Haddonfield, NJ (borough) Camden County	34	0.29
Freehold, NJ (borough) Monmouth County	32	0.29
Oak Park, IL (village) Cook County	146	0.28
Manchester, NJ (township) Ocean County	109	0.28
Mamaroneck, NY (town) Westchester County	80	0.28
Louisville, CO (city) Boulder County	52	0.28
Plymouth, PA (township) Montgomery County	45	0.28
Lower Salford, PA (township) Montgomery County	36	0.28
Brown Deer, WI (village) Milwaukee County	34	0.28
Elma, NY (town) Erie County	32	0.28
Lower Gwynedd, PA (township) Montgomery County	29	0.28
Natick, MA (town) Middlesex County	87	0.27
Franklin, MA (city) Norfolk County	79	0.27
East Hempfield, PA (township) Lancaster County	57	0.27
Montville, NJ (township) Morris County	56	0.27
Saugerties, NY (town) Ulster County	54	0.27
Middleborough, MA (town) Plymouth County	53	0.27
Grand Rapids charter, MI (township) Kent County	38	0.27
Ellington, CT (town) Tolland County	35	0.27
Ipswich, MA (town) Essex County	35	0.27
Winnetka, IL (village) Cook County	34	0.27
Hanover, NH (town) Grafton County	29	0.27
Palatine, IL (village) Cook County	172	0.26
Northbrook, IL (village) Cook County	88	0.26
Westchester, IL (village) Cook County	44	0.26
Laguna Woods, CA (city) Orange County	42	0.26
Berkley, MI (city) Oakland County	41	0.26
Sunny Isles Beach, FL (city) Miami-Dade County	39	0.26
Clive, IA (city) Polk County	33	0.26
Raynham, MA (town) Bristol County	30	0.26
Lakewood, OH (city) Cuyahoga County	141	0.25
Meridian charter, MI (township) Ingham County	99	0.25
Fridley, MN (city) Anoka County	69	0.25
McHenry, IL (city) McHenry County	54	0.25
Mountlake Terrace, WA (city) Snohomish County	50	0.25
Birmingham, MI (city) Oakland County	48	0.25
Sharon, MA (town) Norfolk County	43	0.25
South Farmingdale, NY (cdp) Nassau County	37	0.25
Cherry Hill Mall, NJ (cdp) Camden County	34	0.25
Glendale, WI (city) Milwaukee County	34	0.25
Beachwood, OH (city) Cuyahoga County	31	0.25
Middle Smithfield, PA (township) Monroe County	29	0.25
Willistown, PA (township) Chester County	25	0.25
Watertown, MA (city) Middlesex County	80	0.24
Highland Park, IL (city) Lake County	76	0.24
New Milford, CT (town) Litchfield County	66	0.24
Randolph, NJ (township) Morris County	60	0.24
Millburn, NJ (cdp) Essex County	48	0.24
Syosset, NY (cdp) Nassau County	44	0.24
Scarsdale, NY (village) Westchester County	42	0.24
Carrboro, NC (town) Orange County	40	0.24
Willow Grove, PA (cdp) Montgomery County	39	0.24
Aurora, NY (town) Erie County	34	0.24
Stony Brook, NY (cdp) Suffolk County	33	0.24
Greenwich, CT (town) Fairfield County	139	0.23
Buffalo Grove, IL (village) Lake County	97	0.23
New Brighton, MN (city) Ramsey County	51	0.23
Burleson, TX (city) Johnson County	48	0.23
Springdale, NJ (cdp) Camden County	33	0.23
Stanford, CA (cdp) Santa Clara County	31	0.23
Tarrytown, NY (village) Westchester County	26	0.23
Holbrook, MA (cdp) Norfolk County	25	0.23
Monroe, NY (town) Orange County	68	0.22
Seal Beach, CA (city) Orange County	54	0.22
Walpole, MA (town) Norfolk County	50	0.22
Bourbonnais, IL (village) Kankakee County	34	0.22
Gates-North Gates, NY (cdp) Monroe County	34	0.22
San Anselmo, CA (town) Marin County	27	0.22
South Yarmouth, MA (cdp) Barnstable County	26	0.22
Lea Hill, WA (cdp) King County	24	0.22
Vashon, WA (cdp) King County	22	0.22
Newton, MA (city) Middlesex County	177	0.21
Northampton, PA (township) Bucks County	84	0.21
North Bethesda, MD (cdp) Montgomery County	82	0.21
Long Beach, NY (city) Nassau County	76	0.21
Brighton, NY (town) Monroe County	74	0.21
Deer Park, NY (cdp) Suffolk County	60	0.21
West Islip, NY (cdp) Suffolk County	60	0.21
Ocean, NJ (township) Monmouth County	57	0.21
Stoughton, MA (town) Norfolk County	57	0.21
Muskego, WI (city) Waukesha County	45	0.21
Menomonie, WI (city) Dunn County	31	0.21
Springfield, NJ (cdp) Union County	31	0.21
Westwood, MA (town) Norfolk County	29	0.21
Hanover, MA (town) Plymouth County	28	0.21
Franklin Park, PA (borough) Allegheny County	24	0.21
Port Washington, WI (city) Ozaukee County	22	0.21
Tamalpais-Homestead Valley, CA (cdp) Marin County	22	0.21
Reston, VA (cdp) Fairfax County	115	0.20
Aspen Hill, MD (cdp) Montgomery County	98	0.20
Lombard, IL (village) Du Page County	83	0.20
Cheltenham, PA (township) Montgomery County	73	0.20
Fort Lee, NJ (borough) Bergen County	72	0.20
Greenfield, WI (city) Milwaukee County	72	0.20
Morgan Hill, CA (city) Santa Clara County	66	0.20
Mayfield Heights, OH (city) Cuyahoga County	38	0.20

Notes: (cdp) census designated place; Refer to the Explanation of Data in the front of the book for more detailed information.

Lithuanian

Top 150 Places Sorted by Number

(Based on all places, regardless of population)

Place	Number	%
Chicago, IL (city) Cook County	15,383	0.53
New York, NY (city) New York City	13,847	0.17
Los Angeles, CA (city) Los Angeles County	6,800	0.18
Philadelphia, PA (city) Philadelphia County	5,681	0.37
Worcester, MA (city) Worcester County	3,812	2.21
Boston, MA (city) Suffolk County	2,778	0.47
San Diego, CA (city) San Diego County	2,707	0.22
Hempstead, NY (town) Nassau County	2,517	0.33
Waterbury, CT (city) New Haven County	2,475	2.31
Phoenix, AZ (city) Maricopa County	2,467	0.19
Pittsburgh, PA (city) Allegheny County	2,413	0.72
Oak Lawn, IL (village) Cook County	2,101	3.79
San Francisco, CA (city) San Francisco County	2,038	0.26
Scranton, PA (city) Lackawanna County	1,880	2.46
Brookhaven, NY (town) Suffolk County	1,800	0.40
Omaha, NE (city) Douglas County	1,761	0.45
Wilkes-Barre, PA (city) Luzerne County	1,644	3.81
Baltimore, MD (independent city) Baltimore city	1,519	0.23
Grand Rapids, MI (city) Kent County	1,509	0.76
Orland Park, IL (village) Cook County	1,500	2.94
Seattle, WA (city) King County	1,469	0.26
Cleveland, OH (city) Cuyahoga County	1,444	0.30
Oyster Bay, NY (town) Nassau County	1,389	0.47
Brockton, MA (city) Plymouth County	1,370	1.45
Naperville, IL (city) Du Page County	1,291	1.01
Tinley Park, IL (village) Cook County	1,250	2.59
Denver, CO (city) Denver County	1,213	0.22
Houston, TX (city) Harris County	1,202	0.06
Washington, DC (city) District of Columbia	1,156	0.20
Tucson, AZ (city) Pima County	1,148	0.24
North Hempstead, NY (town) Nassau County	1,128	0.51
Springfield, IL (city) Sangamon County	1,091	0.97
Portland, OR (city) Multnomah County	1,034	0.20
Columbus, OH (city) Franklin County	1,028	0.14
Jacksonville, FL (special city) Duval County	1,014	0.14
Watertown, CT (town) Litchfield County	1,002	4.63
Islip, NY (town) Suffolk County	967	0.30
Huntington, NY (town) Suffolk County	962	0.49
Burbank, IL (city) Cook County	960	3.45
San Antonio, TX (city) Bexar County	938	0.08
Goodings Grove, IL (cdp) Will County	934	5.46
Colorado Springs, CO (city) El Paso County	929	0.26
San Jose, CA (city) Santa Clara County	919	0.10
Virginia Beach, VA (independent city) Virginia Beach city	917	0.22
Downers Grove, IL (village) Du Page County	911	1.87
Kenosha, WI (city) Kenosha County	890	0.98
Indianapolis, IN (special city) Marion County	875	0.11
Saint Petersburg, FL (city) Pinellas County	873	0.35
Oak Forest, IL (city) Cook County	869	3.11
Dallas, TX (city) Dallas County	867	0.07
Newton, MA (city) Middlesex County	853	1.02
Scottsdale, AZ (city) Maricopa County	838	0.41
Rockford, IL (city) Winnebago County	829	0.55
Milwaukee, WI (city) Milwaukee County	821	0.14
Bristol, CT (city) Hartford County	812	1.35
Nashua, NH (city) Hillsborough County	812	0.94
Euclid, OH (city) Cuyahoga County	811	1.54
Shenandoah, PA (borough) Schuylkill County	802	14.26
Austin, TX (city) Travis County	791	0.12
Arlington, VA (cdp) Arlington County	782	0.41
Santa Monica, CA (city) Los Angeles County	780	0.93
Back Mountain, PA (cdp) Luzerne County	775	2.90
New Britain, CT (city) Hartford County	775	1.08
Darien, IL (city) Du Page County	770	3.35
Palos Hills, IL (city) Cook County	759	4.27
Aurora, IL (city) Kane County	753	0.52
Naugatuck, CT (borough) New Haven County	751	2.42
Joliet, IL (city) Will County	749	0.71
Las Vegas, NV (city) Clark County	743	0.16
Woodbridge, NJ (township) Middlesex County	738	0.76
Charlotte, NC (city) Mecklenburg County	735	0.14
Livonia, MI (city) Wayne County	728	0.72
Westmont, IL (village) Du Page County	727	2.99
Huntington Beach, CA (city) Orange County	726	0.38
Mesa, AZ (city) Maricopa County	707	0.18
Mahanoy City, PA (borough) Schuylkill County	705	15.17
Hickory Hills, IL (city) Cook County	685	4.92
Oakland, CA (city) Alameda County	685	0.17
Madison, WI (city) Dane County	684	0.33
Hanover, PA (township) Luzerne County	682	5.95
West Hartford, CT (cdp) Hartford County	682	1.07
Albuquerque, NM (city) Bernalillo County	663	0.15
Cherry Hill, NJ (township) Camden County	656	0.94
Woodridge, IL (village) Du Page County	654	2.10
Enfield, CT (town) Hartford County	653	1.44
Pottsville, PA (city) Schuylkill County	649	4.18
Farmington Hills, MI (city) Oakland County	649	0.79
Quincy, MA (city) Norfolk County	630	0.72
Cambridge, MA (city) Middlesex County	614	0.61
Shrewsbury, MA (town) Worcester County	611	1.93
Minneapolis, MN (city) Hennepin County	606	0.16
Detroit, MI (city) Wayne County	597	0.06
Evanston, IL (city) Cook County	590	0.79
Dearborn, MI (city) Wayne County	590	0.60
Minersville, PA (borough) Schuylkill County	589	12.94
Smithtown, NY (town) Suffolk County	583	0.50
Warren, MI (city) Macomb County	581	0.42
Manchester, NH (city) Hillsborough County	579	0.54
Brick, NJ (township) Ocean County	575	0.76
Saint Paul, MN (city) Ramsey County	575	0.20
Middletown, PA (township) Bucks County	573	1.30
West Mahanoy, PA (township) Schuylkill County	571	9.26
Evergreen Park, IL (village) Cook County	570	2.74
Norwood, MA (cdp) Norfolk County	568	1.99
Manchester, CT (town) Hartford County	566	1.03
Levittown, PA (cdp) Bucks County	559	1.04
Berwyn, IL (city) Cook County	556	1.03
Henderson, NV (city) Clark County	552	0.31
Kingston, PA (borough) Luzerne County	550	3.97
Southington, CT (town) Hartford County	548	1.38
Carol Stream, IL (village) Du Page County	542	1.36
Millbury, MA (town) Worcester County	541	4.23
Lemont, IL (village) Cook County	539	4.09
Chicago Ridge, IL (village) Cook County	534	3.85
Bolingbrook, IL (village) Will County	533	0.94
Providence, RI (city) Providence County	532	0.31
Amsterdam, NY (city) Montgomery County	530	2.89
Parma, OH (city) Cuyahoga County	527	0.62
Waukegan, IL (city) Lake County	525	0.60
Plano, TX (city) Collin County	525	0.24
Westfield, MA (city) Hampden County	522	1.30
Skokie, IL (village) Cook County	517	0.82
Dover, NJ (township) Ocean County	517	0.58
Schaumburg, IL (village) Cook County	514	0.69
Toms River, NJ (cdp) Ocean County	510	0.59
Ann Arbor, MI (city) Washtenaw County	510	0.45
Atlanta, GA (city) Fulton County	509	0.12
New Lenox, IL (village) Will County	508	2.88
Lakewood, NJ (township) Ocean County	508	0.84
Berkeley, CA (city) Alameda County	508	0.49
Pittston, PA (city) Luzerne County	506	6.24
Babylon, NY (town) Suffolk County	505	0.24
Brookfield, IL (village) Cook County	503	2.65
Cincinnati, OH (city) Hamilton County	496	0.15
Bridgewater, MA (town) Plymouth County	490	1.95
Hollywood, FL (city) Broward County	490	0.35
Frackville, PA (borough) Schuylkill County	489	11.21
Framingham, MA (cdp) Middlesex County	488	0.73
Somerville, MA (city) Middlesex County	486	0.63
Troy, MI (city) Oakland County	482	0.60
Saint Louis, MO (independent city) Saint Louis city	478	0.14
Abington, PA (township) Montgomery County	477	0.85
Alsip, IL (village) Cook County	476	2.40
Plains, PA (township) Luzerne County	473	4.34
Berlin, CT (town) Hartford County	473	2.60
Wallingford, CT (town) New Haven County	468	1.09
Weymouth, MA (cdp) Norfolk County	465	0.86
Anchorage, AK (municipality) Anchorage Borough	465	0.18
Auburn, MA (town) Worcester County	464	2.92
Plymouth, MA (town) Plymouth County	463	0.90

Notes: (cdp) census designated place; Refer to the Explanation of Data in the front of the book for more detailed information.

Lithuanian

Top 150 Places Sorted by Percent

(Based on all places, regardless of population)

Place	Number	%
Sunrise, AK (cdp) Kenai Peninsula Borough	7	100.00
Centralia, PA (borough) Columbia County	4	66.67
Seltzer, PA (cdp) Schuylkill County	114	40.28
New Philadelphia, PA (borough) Schuylkill County	296	25.76
Diamond Beach, NJ (cdp) Cape May County	32	23.70
Shenandoah Heights, PA (cdp) Schuylkill County	251	17.33
Girardville, PA (borough) Schuylkill County	287	16.48
Marlin, PA (cdp) Schuylkill County	103	16.17
Mahanoy City, PA (borough) Schuylkill County	705	15.17
Beverly Shores, IN (town) Porter County	99	14.73
Middleport, PA (borough) Schuylkill County	66	14.54
Locustdale, PA (cdp) Columbia County	12	14.29
Shenandoah, PA (borough) Schuylkill County	802	14.26
Grier City-Park Crest, PA (cdp) Schuylkill County	132	13.89
Norwegian, PA (township) Schuylkill County	292	13.46
Ryan, PA (township) Schuylkill County	191	13.17
Minersville, PA (borough) Schuylkill County	589	12.94
Gilberton, PA (borough) Schuylkill County	112	12.92
Union, PA (township) Schuylkill County	159	12.17
Blythe, PA (township) Schuylkill County	110	12.10
Shoal Creek Estates, MO (town) Newton County	5	11.36
Frackville, PA (borough) Schuylkill County	489	11.21
Cherry Valley, PA (borough) Butler County	7	10.61
Ringtown, PA (borough) Schuylkill County	85	10.27
West Abington, PA (township) Lackawanna County	30	10.07
East Norwegian, PA (township) Schuylkill County	85	9.88
Monomoscoy Island, MA (cdp) Barnstable County	12	9.68
Mahanoy, PA (township) Schuylkill County	107	9.61
Branch, PA (township) Schuylkill County	177	9.46
Brandonville, PA (cdp) Schuylkill County	21	9.42
West Mahanoy, PA (township) Schuylkill County	571	9.26
Port Carbon, PA (borough) Schuylkill County	186	9.19
Butler, PA (township) Schuylkill County	320	8.92
Delano, PA (township) Schuylkill County	43	8.78
Michiana, MI (village) Berrien County	16	8.70
Bonanza, CO (town) Saguache County	2	8.70
East Union, PA (township) Schuylkill County	118	8.32
Bethlehem, CT (town) Litchfield County	281	8.21
Bethlehem Village, CT (cdp) Litchfield County	170	8.21
New Castle, PA (township) Schuylkill County	34	8.13
New Boston-Morea, PA (cdp) Schuylkill County	37	8.08
Swoyersville, PA (borough) Luzerne County	403	7.81
Callimont, PA (borough) Somerset County	4	7.69
Fairview Beach, VA (cdp) King George County	19	7.66
Goshen, VT (town) Addison County	14	7.25
Luzerne, PA (borough) Luzerne County	213	7.22
Sugar Notch, PA (borough) Luzerne County	72	7.11
Mechanicsville, PA (borough) Schuylkill County	39	7.07
Byron, ME (town) Oxford County	6	6.98
Fort Johnson, NY (village) Montgomery County	34	6.81
Jenkins, PA (township) Luzerne County	311	6.78
Timber Lakes, UT (cdp) Wasatch County	20	6.76
Michiana Shores, IN (town) La Porte County	19	6.76
Gold Hill, CO (cdp) Boulder County	14	6.70
Brass Castle, NJ (cdp) Warren County	100	6.49
Elk, MI (township) Lake County	58	6.42
Rohrsburg, PA (cdp) Columbia County	10	6.41
Beurys Lake, PA (cdp) Schuylkill County	7	6.36
Dover, IL (village) Bureau County	10	6.33
Wyoming, PA (borough) Luzerne County	203	6.30
Buck Run, PA (cdp) Schuylkill County	15	6.30
Pringle, PA (borough) Luzerne County	62	6.26
Forty Fort, PA (borough) Luzerne County	286	6.25
Pittston, PA (city) Luzerne County	506	6.24
West Pittston, PA (borough) Luzerne County	316	6.23
Englewood, PA (cdp) Schuylkill County	27	6.21
Ashland, PA (borough) Schuylkill County	201	6.12
Wright, MN (city) Carlton County	7	6.03
Hanover, PA (township) Luzerne County	682	5.95
Campus, IL (village) Livingston County	7	5.88
Slabtown, PA (cdp) Columbia County	6	5.88
West Hazleton, PA (borough) Luzerne County	208	5.87
Bulpitt, IL (village) Christian County	12	5.85
Shooks, MN (township) Beltrami County	11	5.85
Ross, PA (township) Luzerne County	160	5.84
Westville, IL (village) Vermilion County	180	5.60
Hagaman, NY (village) Montgomery County	75	5.57
Huntleigh, MO (city) Saint Louis County	17	5.57
Gurney, WI (town) Iron County	9	5.56
West Wyoming, PA (borough) Luzerne County	156	5.51
Sheppton, PA (cdp) Schuylkill County	13	5.51
Lowell Point, AK (cdp) Kenai Peninsula Borough	6	5.50
Saddle Rock Estates, NY (cdp) Nassau County	24	5.47
Goodings Grove, IL (cdp) Will County	934	5.46
Juno Ridge, FL (cdp) Palm Beach County	41	5.44
Fraser, CO (town) Grand County	50	5.42
Wilburton Number Two, PA (cdp) Columbia County	4	5.41
Exeter, PA (township) Wyoming County	40	5.37
Sherman, MI (township) Mason County	59	5.32
Palo Alto, PA (borough) Schuylkill County	54	5.32
Forest City, PA (borough) Susquehanna County	98	5.28
Wilkes-Barre Township, PA (cdp) Luzerne County	170	5.26
Hookstown, PA (borough) Beaver County	8	5.26
Yatesville, PA (borough) Luzerne County	34	5.24
Alta, UT (town) Salt Lake County	18	5.22
Doylestown, WI (village) Columbia County	16	5.19
Hartly, DE (town) Kent County	4	5.19
Schuylkill, PA (township) Schuylkill County	58	5.16
Edwardsville, PA (borough) Luzerne County	256	5.14
Grand Island, MI (township) Alger County	2	5.13
Branchdale, PA (cdp) Schuylkill County	22	5.06
Exeter, PA (borough) Luzerne County	299	5.02
Mount Carmel, PA (borough) Northumberland County	317	4.96
Custer, MI (township) Mason County	62	4.93
Hickory Hills, IL (city) Cook County	685	4.92
Moodus, CT (cdp) Middlesex County	68	4.92
Canton Valley, CT (cdp) Hartford County	80	4.90
Tamaqua, PA (borough) Schuylkill County	351	4.89
Saint Clair, PA (borough) Schuylkill County	159	4.87
Cass, PA (township) Schuylkill County	114	4.83
Harveys Lake, PA (borough) Luzerne County	139	4.81
Pittston, PA (township) Luzerne County	165	4.78
Hughestown, PA (borough) Luzerne County	72	4.67
New Buffalo, MI (township) Berrien County	115	4.66
Dune Acres, IN (town) Porter County	9	4.66
Exeter, PA (township) Luzerne County	119	4.65
Watertown, CT (town) Litchfield County	1,002	4.63
Duryea, PA (borough) Luzerne County	213	4.60
Brooklyn, IL (village) Saint Clair County	30	4.56
Wellington, ME (town) Piscataquis County	11	4.55
Rush, PA (township) Dauphin County	8	4.52
Rush, PA (township) Schuylkill County	178	4.51
Rumford, ME (town) Oxford County	288	4.45
Dallas, ME (plantation) Franklin County	11	4.45
Franklin, PA (township) Luzerne County	71	4.43
Plymouth, PA (borough) Luzerne County	287	4.41
Oyehut-Hogans Corner, WA (cdp) Grays Harbor County	9	4.37
Plains, PA (township) Luzerne County	473	4.34
Middlebury, CT (town) New Haven County	283	4.33
Forrestville, PA (cdp) Schuylkill County	17	4.33
Oakville, CT (cdp) Litchfield County	371	4.31
Mexico, ME (town) Oxford County	127	4.29
Palos Hills, IL (city) Cook County	759	4.27
Conyngham, PA (township) Columbia County	34	4.27
Tuscarora, PA (cdp) Schuylkill County	39	4.26
Glen Lyn, VA (town) Giles County	6	4.26
Millbury, MA (town) Worcester County	541	4.23
Ashville, PA (borough) Cambria County	11	4.23
Thornhurst, PA (township) Lackawanna County	33	4.20
Pottsville, PA (city) Schuylkill County	649	4.18
Todd Mission, TX (city) Grimes County	6	4.17
Mount Carmel, PA (township) Northumberland County	112	4.15
Amsterdam, NY (town) Montgomery County	240	4.12
Donnelsville, OH (village) Clark County	10	4.12
Custer, MI (village) Mason County	12	4.11
Lemont, IL (village) Cook County	539	4.09
Barre, MA (town) Worcester County	209	4.09
Hardwick, MA (town) Worcester County	107	4.08
Courtdale, PA (borough) Luzerne County	32	4.05
Manley Hot Springs, AK (cdp) Yukon-Koyukuk Census Area	3	4.05

Notes: (cdp) census designated place; Refer to the Explanation of Data in the front of the book for more detailed information.

Lithuanian

Top 150 Places Sorted by Percent

(Based on places with populations of 10,000 or more)

Place	Number	%
Hanover, PA (township) Luzerne County	682	5.95
Goodings Grove, IL (cdp) Will County	934	5.46
Hickory Hills, IL (city) Cook County	685	4.92
Watertown, CT (town) Litchfield County	1,002	4.63
Plains, PA (township) Luzerne County	473	4.34
Palos Hills, IL (city) Cook County	759	4.27
Millbury, MA (town) Worcester County	541	4.23
Pottsville, PA (city) Schuylkill County	649	4.18
Lemont, IL (village) Cook County	539	4.09
Kingston, PA (borough) Luzerne County	550	3.97
Worth, IL (village) Cook County	433	3.88
Chicago Ridge, IL (village) Cook County	534	3.85
Wilkes-Barre, PA (city) Luzerne County	1,644	3.81
Oak Lawn, IL (village) Cook County	2,101	3.79
Athol, MA (town) Worcester County	399	3.53
Leicester, MA (town) Worcester County	370	3.53
Burbank, IL (city) Cook County	960	3.45
Darien, IL (city) Du Page County	770	3.35
Palos Heights, IL (city) Cook County	360	3.18
Oak Forest, IL (city) Cook County	869	3.11
Westmont, IL (village) Du Page County	727	2.99
Orland Park, IL (village) Cook County	1,500	2.94
Auburn, MA (town) Worcester County	464	2.92
Back Mountain, PA (cdp) Luzerne County	775	2.90
Nanticoke, PA (city) Luzerne County	318	2.90
Amsterdam, NY (city) Montgomery County	530	2.89
New Lenox, IL (village) Will County	508	2.88
Evergreen Park, IL (village) Cook County	570	2.74
Brookfield, IL (village) Cook County	503	2.65
Midlothian, IL (village) Cook County	371	2.61
Berlin, CT (town) Hartford County	473	2.60
Tinley Park, IL (village) Cook County	1,250	2.59
Hanover, MA (town) Plymouth County	340	2.58
Westchester, IL (village) Cook County	422	2.53
Beachwood, OH (city) Cuyahoga County	308	2.53
Bridgeview, IL (village) Cook County	386	2.51
Frankfort, IL (village) Will County	255	2.49
Western Springs, IL (village) Cook County	313	2.48
Scranton, PA (city) Lackawanna County	1,880	2.46
Naugatuck, CT (borough) New Haven County	751	2.42
Alsip, IL (village) Cook County	476	2.40
Spencer, MA (town) Worcester County	275	2.35
Sharon, MA (town) Norfolk County	406	2.33
Waterbury, CT (city) New Haven County	2,475	2.31
Mountain Top, PA (cdp) Luzerne County	350	2.29
Tolland, CT (town) Tolland County	300	2.28
Ellington, CT (town) Tolland County	289	2.24
Worcester, MA (city) Worcester County	3,812	2.21
Sandy, PA (township) Clearfield County	254	2.20
Wolcott, CT (town) New Haven County	328	2.16
Holden, MA (town) Worcester County	334	2.14
Woodridge, IL (village) Du Page County	654	2.10
Crestwood, IL (village) Cook County	236	2.10
La Grange Park, IL (village) Cook County	276	2.08
Mansfield, MA (town) Bristol County	456	2.03
Plymouth, CT (town) Litchfield County	236	2.03
Charlton, MA (town) Worcester County	229	2.03
Oxford, MA (town) Worcester County	268	2.01
Norwood, MA (cdp) Norfolk County	568	1.99
Hinsdale, IL (village) Du Page County	345	1.97
Raynham, MA (town) Bristol County	231	1.97
Dudley, MA (town) Worcester County	198	1.97
Bridgewater, MA (town) Plymouth County	490	1.95
Shrewsbury, MA (town) Worcester County	611	1.93
Ansonia, CT (city) New Haven County	348	1.88
Mokena, IL (village) Will County	276	1.88
Downers Grove, IL (village) Du Page County	911	1.87
Willowick, OH (city) Lake County	270	1.87
Greentree, NJ (cdp) Camden County	213	1.85
Lockport, IL (city) Will County	269	1.82
Cranford, NJ (cdp) Union County	406	1.80
Croydon, PA (cdp) Bucks County	180	1.79
Whitehall, PA (borough) Allegheny County	254	1.76
Justice, IL (village) Cook County	211	1.75
La Grange, IL (village) Cook County	274	1.74

Place	Number	%
Deerfield, IL (village) Lake County	317	1.71
Warrenville, IL (city) Du Page County	226	1.71
South Windsor, CT (town) Hartford County	413	1.69
Lisle, IL (village) Du Page County	355	1.68
Windsor Locks, CT (cdp) Hartford County	202	1.68
Waterford, NJ (township) Camden County	174	1.66
Oswego, IL (village) Kendall County	217	1.63
Walker, MI (city) Kent County	354	1.62
Dunmore, PA (borough) Lackawanna County	227	1.62
Richmond Heights, OH (city) Cuyahoga County	173	1.58
Brewster, MA (town) Barnstable County	159	1.58
Seymour, CT (town) New Haven County	243	1.57
South Fayette, PA (township) Allegheny County	193	1.57
Euclid, OH (city) Cuyahoga County	811	1.54
Glen Ellyn, IL (village) Du Page County	415	1.53
Coventry, CT (town) Tolland County	176	1.53
Stoughton, MA (town) Norfolk County	412	1.52
Gardner, MA (city) Worcester County	311	1.50
Palm Beach, FL (town) Palm Beach County	155	1.49
Windsor, CT (town) Hartford County	419	1.48
Needham, MA (cdp) Norfolk County	426	1.47
Hudson, NH (town) Hillsborough County	338	1.47
Arbutus, MD (cdp) Baltimore County	296	1.47
Foxborough, MA (town) Norfolk County	239	1.47
Grafton, MA (town) Worcester County	217	1.46
Brockton, MA (city) Plymouth County	1,370	1.45
Branford, CT (town) New Haven County	417	1.45
Chesterton, IN (town) Porter County	151	1.45
Enfield, CT (town) Hartford County	653	1.44
Wethersfield, CT (cdp) Hartford County	378	1.44
Whitman, MA (town) Plymouth County	200	1.44
Newington, CT (cdp) Hartford County	418	1.43
Romeoville, IL (village) Will County	301	1.42
Old Saybrook, CT (town) Middlesex County	147	1.42
Lower Salford, PA (township) Montgomery County	182	1.41
Pikesville, MD (cdp) Baltimore County	404	1.40
Southington, CT (town) Hartford County	548	1.38
Glastonbury, CT (town) Hartford County	440	1.38
Middleborough, MA (town) Plymouth County	275	1.38
Wrentham, MA (town) Norfolk County	146	1.38
Burr Ridge, IL (village) Du Page County	143	1.38
Lyons, IL (village) Cook County	140	1.38
Holbrook, MA (cdp) Norfolk County	147	1.37
Summit, IL (village) Cook County	146	1.37
Carol Stream, IL (village) Du Page County	542	1.36
Collinsville, IL (city) Madison County	333	1.36
Pembroke, MA (town) Plymouth County	231	1.36
Coal, PA (township) Northumberland County	145	1.36
Bristol, CT (city) Hartford County	812	1.35
Monroe, CT (town) Fairfield County	260	1.35
Pelham, NH (town) Hillsborough County	144	1.32
Villa Park, IL (village) Du Page County	291	1.31
Northborough, MA (town) Worcester County	184	1.31
North Branford, CT (town) New Haven County	182	1.31
Middletown, PA (township) Bucks County	573	1.30
Westfield, MA (city) Hampden County	522	1.30
Canton, MA (town) Norfolk County	271	1.30
Eastlake, OH (city) Lake County	262	1.30
Bexley, OH (city) Franklin County	172	1.30
Westwood, MA (town) Norfolk County	182	1.29
East Bridgewater, MA (town) Plymouth County	168	1.29
Torrington, CT (city) Litchfield County	452	1.28
Easton, MA (town) Bristol County	286	1.28
Colchester, CT (town) New London County	186	1.28
Plainfield, IL (village) Will County	167	1.28
New Providence, NJ (borough) Union County	152	1.28
Highland Park, IL (city) Lake County	398	1.27
Springfield, PA (township) Montgomery County	248	1.27
Scituate, MA (town) Plymouth County	227	1.27
Suffield, CT (town) Hartford County	172	1.27
Munhall, PA (borough) Allegheny County	156	1.27
Dyer, IN (town) Lake County	174	1.26
Pleasant Prairie, WI (village) Kenosha County	198	1.25
Clinton, CT (town) Middlesex County	164	1.25
Walpole, MA (town) Norfolk County	284	1.24

Notes: (cdp) census designated place; Refer to the Explanation of Data in the front of the book for more detailed information.

Luxemburger

Top 150 Places Sorted by Number

(Based on all places, regardless of population)

Place	Number	%
Chicago, IL (city) Cook County	756	0.03
Dubuque, IA (city) Dubuque County	740	1.29
Aurora, IL (city) Kane County	597	0.42
Port Washington, WI (city) Ozaukee County	551	5.32
Minneapolis, MN (city) Hennepin County	397	0.10
Saint Paul, MN (city) Ramsey County	389	0.14
Sioux Falls, SD (city) Minnehaha County	350	0.28
Milwaukee, WI (city) Milwaukee County	328	0.05
Belgium, WI (town) Ozaukee County	303	19.89
Remsen, IA (city) Plymouth County	283	16.30
Le Mars, IA (city) Plymouth County	272	2.95
Belgium, WI (village) Ozaukee County	271	16.25
Sioux City, IA (city) Woodbury County	252	0.30
New York, NY (city) New York City	233	0.00
Omaha, NE (city) Douglas County	230	0.06
Portland, OR (city) Multnomah County	216	0.04
Phoenix, AZ (city) Maricopa County	202	0.02
Fredonia, WI (town) Ozaukee County	194	6.67
West Bend, WI (city) Washington County	188	0.67
Lincoln, NE (city) Lancaster County	179	0.08
San Diego, CA (city) San Diego County	177	0.01
Winona, MN (city) Winona County	174	0.64
Northbrook, IL (village) Cook County	169	0.51
Los Angeles, CA (city) Los Angeles County	163	0.00
Random Lake, WI (village) Sheboygan County	161	10.33
Fredonia, WI (village) Ozaukee County	155	8.04
Denver, CO (city) Denver County	155	0.03
Schaumburg, IL (village) Cook County	154	0.21
Port Washington, WI (town) Ozaukee County	152	8.77
Rochester, MN (city) Olmsted County	149	0.17
Arlington Heights, IL (village) Cook County	141	0.19
Skokie, IL (village) Cook County	138	0.22
Sheboygan, WI (city) Sheboygan County	137	0.27
Palatine, IL (village) Cook County	131	0.20
Des Plaines, IL (city) Cook County	129	0.22
Seattle, WA (city) King County	125	0.02
Des Moines, IA (city) Polk County	123	0.06
Clearwater, FL (city) Pinellas County	122	0.11
Eagan, MN (city) Dakota County	121	0.19
Alton, IA (city) Sioux County	117	10.62
Minnetonka, MN (city) Hennepin County	117	0.23
Shakopee, MN (city) Scott County	114	0.56
Plymouth, MN (city) Hennepin County	114	0.17
Colorado Springs, CO (city) El Paso County	114	0.03
Glenview, IL (village) Cook County	112	0.27
Naperville, IL (city) Du Page County	108	0.08
Scottsdale, AZ (city) Maricopa County	108	0.05
San Francisco, CA (city) San Francisco County	105	0.01
Maquoketa, IA (city) Jackson County	104	1.70
Sherman, WI (town) Sheboygan County	103	6.89
Bellevue, IA (city) Jackson County	102	4.33
Indianapolis, IN (special city) Marion County	99	0.01
Bloomington, MN (city) Hennepin County	94	0.11
Madison, WI (city) Dane County	93	0.04
Morton Grove, IL (village) Cook County	87	0.39
Mount Prospect, IL (village) Cook County	86	0.15
Cedar Grove, WI (village) Sheboygan County	85	4.51
Tucson, AZ (city) Pima County	84	0.02
Park Ridge, IL (city) Cook County	83	0.22
Waterloo, IA (city) Black Hawk County	83	0.12
Iowa City, IA (city) Johnson County	82	0.13
North Aurora, IL (village) Kane County	81	0.76
Rolling Meadows, IL (city) Cook County	81	0.33
Wheaton, IL (city) Du Page County	81	0.15
Wilmette, IL (village) Cook County	80	0.29
Wauwatosa, WI (city) Milwaukee County	79	0.17
West Des Moines, IA (city) Polk County	79	0.17
Cedarburg, WI (city) Ozaukee County	78	0.72
New Berlin, WI (city) Waukesha County	78	0.20
Overland Park, KS (city) Johnson County	77	0.05
Eugene, OR (city) Lane County	76	0.06
Ames, IA (city) Story County	72	0.14
Fargo, ND (city) Cass County	71	0.08
Mitchell, SD (city) Davison County	69	0.47
Batavia, IL (city) Kane County	69	0.29
Marion, IA (city) Linn County	68	0.26
Cedar Rapids, IA (city) Linn County	68	0.06
Saukville, WI (village) Ozaukee County	66	1.59
Saint Cloud, MN (city) Stearns County	66	0.11
Evanston, IL (city) Cook County	66	0.09
Cincinnati, OH (city) Hamilton County	66	0.02
Holland, WI (town) Sheboygan County	65	2.71
Grafton, WI (village) Ozaukee County	65	0.63
Albuquerque, NM (city) Bernalillo County	65	0.01
Davenport, IA (city) Scott County	63	0.06
Montgomery, IL (village) Kane County	62	1.23
Monett, MO (city) Barry County	61	0.82
Brookfield, WI (city) Waukesha County	61	0.16
West Saint Paul, MN (city) Dakota County	60	0.31
Elk Grove Village, IL (village) Cook County	60	0.17
Elgin, IL (city) Kane County	60	0.06
Mendota Heights, MN (city) Dakota County	59	0.52
Sauk Rapids, MN (city) Benton County	58	0.57
Greendale, WI (village) Milwaukee County	58	0.40
Hopkins, MN (city) Hennepin County	58	0.34
De Kalb, IL (city) De Kalb County	58	0.15
Fort Collins, CO (city) Larimer County	58	0.05
Franklin, WI (city) Milwaukee County	57	0.19
Plano, TX (city) Collin County	57	0.03
Storm Lake, IA (city) Buena Vista County	56	0.55
Mequon, WI (city) Ozaukee County	56	0.26
Fond du Lac, WI (city) Fond du Lac County	56	0.13
Eden Prairie, MN (city) Hennepin County	55	0.10
Rollingstone, MN (township) Winona County	54	4.81
Madison, SD (city) Lake County	54	0.81
New Brighton, MN (city) Ramsey County	54	0.24
La Crosse, WI (city) La Crosse County	54	0.10
Burnsville, MN (city) Dakota County	54	0.09
Santa Rosa, CA (city) Sonoma County	54	0.04
Cascade, IA (city) Dubuque County	53	2.70
Germantown, WI (village) Washington County	53	0.29
Owatonna, MN (city) Steele County	53	0.24
Mesa, AZ (city) Maricopa County	53	0.01
Trenton, WI (town) Washington County	52	1.16
Ankeny, IA (city) Polk County	52	0.19
Greenfield, WI (city) Milwaukee County	52	0.15
Edina, MN (city) Hennepin County	52	0.11
Kenosha, WI (city) Kenosha County	51	0.06
Oakland, CA (city) Alameda County	51	0.01
Sammamish, WA (city) King County	50	0.15
Pearland, TX (city) Brazoria County	50	0.13
Lafayette, IN (city) Tippecanoe County	50	0.09
Arlington, VA (cdp) Arlington County	50	0.03
Austin, TX (city) Travis County	50	0.01
Asbury, IA (city) Dubuque County	49	1.98
Oakdale, MN (city) Washington County	49	0.18
Niles, IL (village) Cook County	49	0.16
Livermore, CA (city) Alameda County	49	0.07
Mason City, IA (city) Cerro Gordo County	48	0.16
Cedarburg, WI (town) Ozaukee County	47	0.81
Bee Ridge, FL (cdp) Sarasota County	47	0.53
Great Bend, KS (city) Barton County	47	0.31
Bellevue, NE (city) Sarpy County	47	0.11
Coral Gables, FL (city) Miami-Dade County	47	0.11
Concord, CA (city) Contra Costa County	47	0.04
Boise City, ID (city) Ada County	47	0.03
Algona, IA (city) Kossuth County	46	0.80
Brown Deer, WI (village) Milwaukee County	46	0.38
Whitefish Bay, WI (village) Milwaukee County	46	0.32
Prescott, AZ (city) Yavapai County	46	0.13
Rapid City, SD (city) Pennington County	46	0.08
Edmond, OK (city) Oklahoma County	46	0.07
Houston, TX (city) Harris County	46	0.00
Marcus, IA (city) Cherokee County	45	3.95
Sun City, AZ (cdp) Maricopa County	45	0.12
Buffalo Grove, IL (village) Lake County	45	0.11
Maple Grove, MN (city) Hennepin County	45	0.09
Chandler, AZ (city) Maricopa County	45	0.03
Lewiston, MN (city) Winona County	44	2.92
Elmhurst, IL (city) Du Page County	44	0.10

Notes: (cdp) census designated place; Refer to the Explanation of Data in the front of the book for more detailed information.

Luxemburger

Top 150 Places Sorted by Percent

(Based on all places, regardless of population)

Place	Number	%
Saint Donatus, IA (city) Jackson County	29	21.48
Belgium, WI (town) Ozaukee County	303	19.89
Nenzel, NE (village) Cherry County	2	16.67
Remsen, IA (city) Plymouth County	283	16.30
Belgium, WI (village) Ozaukee County	271	16.25
Springbrook, IA (city) Jackson County	24	12.63
Woodstock, MN (city) Pipestone County	16	12.60
Elba, MN (township) Winona County	33	12.27
Mount Vernon, MN (township) Winona County	35	11.51
La Motte, IA (city) Jackson County	31	11.15
Alton, IA (city) Sioux County	117	10.62
Random Lake, WI (village) Sheboygan County	161	10.33
Amo, MN (township) Cottonwood County	14	9.72
Cameron, MN (township) Murray County	13	9.22
Port Washington, WI (town) Ozaukee County	152	8.77
Fredonia, WI (village) Ozaukee County	155	8.04
Mayville, MN (township) Houston County	32	7.90
Granville, IA (city) Sioux County	23	7.77
North Buena Vista, IA (city) Clayton County	9	7.32
Steamboat River, MN (township) Hubbard County	9	7.20
Norton, MN (township) Winona County	38	6.91
Sherman, WI (town) Sheboygan County	103	6.89
Fredonia, WI (town) Ozaukee County	194	6.67
Rollingstone, MN (city) Winona County	43	6.38
Bellechester, MN (city) Goodhue County	10	5.78
Port Washington, WI (city) Ozaukee County	551	5.32
Elba, MN (city) Winona County	11	5.26
Oyens, IA (city) Plymouth County	8	5.23
Vermillion, MN (city) Dakota County	23	5.22
Mount Charleston, NV (cdp) Clark County	13	5.16
Lane, SD (town) Jerauld County	2	5.00
Craig, IA (city) Plymouth County	5	4.95
Spragueville, IA (city) Jackson County	4	4.88
Rollingstone, MN (township) Winona County	54	4.81
Luxemburg, IA (city) Dubuque County	13	4.81
Randolph, MO (village) Clay County	2	4.76
Livermore, IA (city) Humboldt County	21	4.73
Avoca, MN (city) Murray County	7	4.73
Cedar Grove, WI (village) Sheboygan County	85	4.51
Southbrook, MN (township) Cottonwood County	6	4.51
Emery, SD (city) Hanson County	20	4.37
Bellevue, IA (city) Jackson County	102	4.33
Centralia, IA (city) Dubuque County	5	4.03
Altura, MN (city) Winona County	15	4.02
Knierim, IA (city) Calhoun County	3	4.00
La Crosse, MN (township) Jackson County	8	3.96
Marcus, IA (city) Cherokee County	45	3.95
Estelline, SD (city) Hamlin County	28	3.90
Rosendale, MN (township) Watonwan County	13	3.88
Elmer, MN (township) Pipestone County	12	3.86
Merrill, IA (city) Plymouth County	28	3.80
Caledonia, MN (township) Houston County	25	3.79
Brislet, MN (township) Polk County	2	3.77
Palermo, ND (city) Mountrail County	3	3.66
Sentinel Butte, ND (city) Golden Valley County	2	3.64
Whitewater, MN (township) Winona County	8	3.59
Nordland, MN (township) Lyon County	10	3.57
Adell, WI (village) Sheboygan County	19	3.56
Pine Lake, MN (township) Cass County	6	3.47
Hospers, IA (city) Sioux County	24	3.46
New Munich, MN (city) Stearns County	7	3.40
Adrian, MN (city) Nobles County	42	3.37
Malta, MN (township) Big Stone County	3	3.37
Lismore, MN (township) Nobles County	7	3.27
Fremont, MN (township) Winona County	12	3.17
Mason, MN (township) Murray County	9	3.09
Marshfield, MN (township) Lincoln County	6	3.08
Eden, SD (town) Marshall County	3	3.00
Le Mars, IA (city) Plymouth County	272	2.95
Lewiston, MN (city) Winona County	44	2.92
Saint Charles, MN (township) Winona County	16	2.77
Roosevelt, WI (town) Taylor County	11	2.73
Minneiska, MN (city) Wabasha County	3	2.73
Holland, WI (town) Sheboygan County	65	2.71
Inman, MN (township) Otter Tail County	9	2.71
Larkin, MN (township) Nobles County	6	2.71
Cascade, IA (city) Dubuque County	53	2.70
Riverton, MN (city) Crow Wing County	3	2.65
Patch Grove, WI (town) Grant County	12	2.62
Hope, ND (city) Steele County	8	2.62
Superior, IA (city) Dickinson County	4	2.61
Kranzburg, SD (town) Codington County	5	2.60
Farmington, MN (township) Olmsted County	13	2.59
Glasgow, MN (township) Wabasha County	8	2.57
Bellwood, NE (village) Butler County	12	2.56
Struble, IA (city) Plymouth County	2	2.56
McKinley, WI (town) Polk County	8	2.54
Opheim, MT (town) Valley County	2	2.41
Weimer, MN (township) Jackson County	4	2.31
Beaver, MN (township) Aitkin County	2	2.30
Currie, MN (city) Murray County	4	2.22
Beckwourth, CA (cdp) Plumas County	9	2.15
Gully, MN (city) Polk County	2	2.11
Saukville, WI (town) Ozaukee County	35	2.09
Mineral Point, WI (town) Iowa County	19	2.07
Rock, MN (township) Pipestone County	4	2.07
Worthington, IA (city) Dubuque County	8	2.06
Reine, MN (township) Roseau County	2	2.02
Sheldon, ND (city) Ransom County	3	2.01
Graf, IA (city) Dubuque County	2	2.00
Asbury, IA (city) Dubuque County	49	1.98
Richmond, MN (township) Winona County	14	1.98
Elmira, MN (township) Olmsted County	7	1.97
The Lakes, MN (cdp) Murray County	12	1.96
Greenfield, MN (township) Wabasha County	24	1.95
Orienta, WI (town) Bayfield County	2	1.94
Alexandria, SD (city) Hanson County	10	1.92
Chester, MN (township) Wabasha County	9	1.91
Whitten, IA (city) Hardin County	3	1.90
Caswell, WI (town) Forest County	2	1.90
Saint Leo, MN (city) Yellow Medicine County	2	1.90
Hodges, MN (township) Stevens County	5	1.89
Colman, SD (city) Moody County	10	1.85
Lac La Belle, WI (village) Waukesha County	6	1.79
Preston, IA (city) Jackson County	17	1.78
Conger, MN (city) Freeborn County	3	1.78
Dover, MN (township) Olmsted County	8	1.72
Andrew, IA (city) Jackson County	8	1.71
Kellogg, MN (city) Wabasha County	8	1.71
Maquoketa, IA (city) Jackson County	104	1.70
Quincy, MN (township) Olmsted County	6	1.70
Slayton, MN (township) Murray County	6	1.70
Wesley, IA (city) Kossuth County	8	1.69
Sageville, IA (city) Dubuque County	4	1.69
Kensal, ND (city) Stutsman County	2	1.67
West Albany, MN (township) Wabasha County	8	1.65
Wabana, MN (township) Itasca County	8	1.63
Odin, MN (city) Watonwan County	2	1.60
Warrenton, MN (township) Marshall County	2	1.60
Saukville, WI (village) Ozaukee County	66	1.59
Cushing, IA (city) Woodbury County	4	1.58
Deerfield, MN (township) Steele County	11	1.57
Keene, MN (township) Clay County	2	1.57
David City, NE (city) Butler County	41	1.55
Rutledge, MN (city) Pine County	3	1.55
Montrose, SD (city) McCook County	7	1.54
Wilson, WI (town) Lincoln County	4	1.54
Ephraim, WI (village) Door County	5	1.52
Warren, MN (township) Winona County	10	1.51
Plover, WI (town) Portage County	33	1.50
Molitor, WI (town) Taylor County	4	1.49
Roscoe, MN (township) Goodhue County	12	1.48
Clover, MN (township) Hubbard County	2	1.45
Sharon, MN (township) Le Sueur County	10	1.44
Brownsville, MN (city) Houston County	7	1.44
Utica, MN (city) Winona County	3	1.44
Ledyard, IA (city) Kossuth County	2	1.44
Utica, MN (township) Winona County	9	1.42
Bedford Park, IL (village) Cook County	8	1.42
Parker, MN (township) Morrison County	7	1.40

Notes: (cdp) census designated place; Refer to the Explanation of Data in the front of the book for more detailed information.

Luxemburger

Top 150 Places Sorted by Percent

(Based on places with populations of 10,000 or more)

Place	Number	%
Port Washington, WI (city) Ozaukee County	551	5.32
Dubuque, IA (city) Dubuque County	740	1.29
North Aurora, IL (village) Kane County	81	0.76
Cedarburg, WI (city) Ozaukee County	78	0.72
West Bend, WI (city) Washington County	188	0.67
Winona, MN (city) Winona County	174	0.64
Grafton, WI (village) Ozaukee County	65	0.63
Sauk Rapids, MN (city) Benton County	58	0.57
Shakopee, MN (city) Scott County	114	0.56
Storm Lake, IA (city) Buena Vista County	56	0.55
Mendota Heights, MN (city) Dakota County	59	0.52
Northbrook, IL (village) Cook County	169	0.51
Mitchell, SD (city) Davison County	69	0.47
Aurora, IL (city) Kane County	597	0.42
Greendale, WI (village) Milwaukee County	58	0.40
Morton Grove, IL (village) Cook County	87	0.39
Brown Deer, WI (village) Milwaukee County	46	0.38
Gages Lake, IL (cdp) Lake County	38	0.36
Hopkins, MN (city) Hennepin County	58	0.34
Rolling Meadows, IL (city) Cook County	81	0.33
Whitefish Bay, WI (village) Milwaukee County	46	0.32
Richfield, WI (town) Washington County	33	0.32
West Saint Paul, MN (city) Dakota County	60	0.31
Great Bend, KS (city) Barton County	47	0.31
Worthington, MN (city) Nobles County	35	0.31
Sioux City, IA (city) Woodbury County	252	0.30
Wilmette, IL (village) Cook County	80	0.29
Batavia, IL (city) Kane County	69	0.29
Germantown, WI (village) Washington County	53	0.29
Sioux Falls, SD (city) Minnehaha County	350	0.28
Escanaba, MI (city) Delta County	37	0.28
Altoona, IA (city) Polk County	29	0.28
Sheboygan, WI (city) Sheboygan County	137	0.27
Glenview, IL (village) Cook County	112	0.27
Cary, IL (village) McHenry County	42	0.27
Farmington, MN (city) Dakota County	34	0.27
Winnetka, IL (village) Cook County	33	0.27
Marion, IA (city) Linn County	68	0.26
Mequon, WI (city) Ozaukee County	56	0.26
Pierre, SD (city) Hughes County	36	0.26
Oswego, IL (village) Kendall County	34	0.26
Yankton, SD (city) Yankton County	33	0.25
North Mankato, MN (city) Nicollet County	29	0.25
New Brighton, MN (city) Ramsey County	54	0.24
Owatonna, MN (city) Steele County	53	0.24
Onalaska, WI (city) La Crosse County	36	0.24
Dover, OH (city) Tuscarawas County	29	0.24
Minnetonka, MN (city) Hennepin County	117	0.23
Skokie, IL (village) Cook County	138	0.22
Des Plaines, IL (city) Cook County	129	0.22
Park Ridge, IL (city) Cook County	83	0.22
Plainfield, IL (village) Will County	29	0.22
Schaumburg, IL (village) Cook County	154	0.21
Hastings, MN (city) Dakota County	38	0.21
Ocean Acres, NJ (cdp) Ocean County	28	0.21
Carroll, IA (city) Carroll County	21	0.21
Palatine, IL (village) Cook County	131	0.20
New Berlin, WI (city) Waukesha County	78	0.20
Forest Park, IL (village) Cook County	32	0.20
Arlington Heights, IL (village) Cook County	141	0.19
Eagan, MN (city) Dakota County	121	0.19
Franklin, WI (city) Milwaukee County	57	0.19
Ankeny, IA (city) Polk County	52	0.19
Munster, IN (town) Lake County	41	0.19
Grayslake, IL (village) Lake County	35	0.19
Hinsdale, IL (village) Du Page County	33	0.19
Shorewood, WI (village) Milwaukee County	26	0.19
Vermilion, OH (city) Lorain County	21	0.19
Oakdale, MN (city) Washington County	49	0.18
Villa Park, IL (village) Du Page County	40	0.18
Clinton, NJ (township) Hunterdon County	23	0.18
Landen, OH (cdp) Warren County	23	0.18
Warren, RI (town) Bristol County	21	0.18
Rochester, MN (city) Olmsted County	149	0.17
Plymouth, MN (city) Hennepin County	114	0.17
Wauwatosa, WI (city) Milwaukee County	79	0.17
West Des Moines, IA (city) Polk County	79	0.17
Elk Grove Village, IL (village) Cook County	60	0.17
Roselle, IL (village) Du Page County	39	0.17
Crystal, MN (city) Hennepin County	38	0.17
Lake Zurich, IL (village) Lake County	31	0.17
Coralville, IA (city) Johnson County	25	0.17
Norridge, IL (village) Cook County	25	0.17
Oconomowoc, WI (city) Waukesha County	21	0.17
Palos Heights, IL (city) Cook County	19	0.17
Brookfield, WI (city) Waukesha County	61	0.16
Niles, IL (village) Cook County	49	0.16
Mason City, IA (city) Cerro Gordo County	48	0.16
Columbia Heights, MN (city) Anoka County	30	0.16
Hickory Hills, IL (city) Cook County	22	0.16
Hutchinson, MN (city) McLeod County	21	0.16
Sedona, AZ (city) Yavapai County	16	0.16
Mount Prospect, IL (village) Cook County	86	0.15
Wheaton, IL (city) Du Page County	81	0.15
De Kalb, IL (city) De Kalb County	58	0.15
Greenfield, WI (city) Milwaukee County	52	0.15
Sammamish, WA (city) King County	50	0.15
Mamaroneck, NY (town) Westchester County	43	0.15
Okemos, MI (cdp) Ingham County	34	0.15
Columbus, NE (city) Platte County	31	0.15
South Milwaukee, WI (city) Milwaukee County	31	0.15
Chaska, MN (city) Carver County	27	0.15
Greenfield, IN (city) Hancock County	22	0.15
Keystone, FL (cdp) Hillsborough County	22	0.15
Fostoria, OH (city) Seneca County	21	0.15
Saint Augustine, FL (city) Saint Johns County	17	0.15
Saint Paul, MN (city) Ramsey County	389	0.14
Ames, IA (city) Story County	72	0.14
Saratoga, CA (city) Santa Clara County	42	0.14
Chanhassen, MN (city) Carver County	29	0.14
Bellingham, MA (town) Norfolk County	22	0.14
Allouez, WI (village) Brown County	21	0.14
West Fargo, ND (city) Cass County	20	0.14
Iowa City, IA (city) Johnson County	82	0.13
Fond du Lac, WI (city) Fond du Lac County	56	0.13
Pearland, TX (city) Brazoria County	50	0.13
Prescott, AZ (city) Yavapai County	46	0.13
Mundelein, IL (village) Lake County	40	0.13
Fort Dodge, IA (city) Webster County	33	0.13
Helena, MT (city) Lewis and Clark County	32	0.13
Stevens Point, WI (city) Portage County	32	0.13
North Platte, NE (city) Lincoln County	30	0.13
Picnic Point-North Lynnwood, WA (cdp) Snohomish County	30	0.13
McHenry, IL (city) McHenry County	27	0.13
Deerfield, IL (village) Lake County	24	0.13
Madison, NJ (borough) Morris County	22	0.13
Prior Lake, MN (city) Scott County	20	0.13
Stillwater, MN (city) Washington County	19	0.13
La Grange Park, IL (village) Cook County	17	0.13
New Ulm, MN (city) Brown County	17	0.13
Waterloo, IA (city) Black Hawk County	83	0.12
Sun City, AZ (cdp) Maricopa County	45	0.12
Richfield, MN (city) Hennepin County	41	0.12
Stafford, NJ (township) Ocean County	28	0.12
Northville, MI (township) Wayne County	25	0.12
Bentonville, AR (city) Benton County	24	0.12
Golden Valley, MN (city) Hennepin County	24	0.12
Washington, MI (township) Macomb County	22	0.12
Beltsville, MD (cdp) Prince George's County	19	0.12
Middleton, WI (city) Dane County	19	0.12
Red Wing, MN (city) Goodhue County	19	0.12
Springdale, NJ (cdp) Camden County	18	0.12
Universal City, TX (city) Bexar County	18	0.12
Lemont, IL (village) Cook County	16	0.12
Fort Atkinson, WI (city) Jefferson County	14	0.12
La Vista, NE (city) Sarpy County	14	0.12
Vineyard, CA (cdp) Sacramento County	12	0.12
Clearwater, FL (city) Pinellas County	122	0.11
Bloomington, MN (city) Hennepin County	94	0.11
Saint Cloud, MN (city) Stearns County	66	0.11

Notes: (cdp) census designated place; Refer to the Explanation of Data in the front of the book for more detailed information.

Macedonian

Top 150 Places Sorted by Number

(Based on all places, regardless of population)

Place	Number	%
New York, NY (city) New York City	1,736	0.02
Sterling Heights, MI (city) Macomb County	887	0.71
Garfield, NJ (city) Bergen County	834	2.80
Dearborn Heights, MI (city) Wayne County	705	1.21
Crown Point, IN (city) Lake County	613	3.13
Shelby, MI (cdp) Macomb County	486	0.75
Columbus, OH (city) Franklin County	471	0.07
Merrillville, IN (town) Lake County	466	1.52
Macomb, MI (township) Macomb County	454	0.90
Chicago, IL (city) Cook County	450	0.02
Fort Wayne, IN (city) Allen County	432	0.21
Livonia, MI (city) Wayne County	421	0.42
Schererville, IN (town) Lake County	384	1.55
Los Angeles, CA (city) Los Angeles County	341	0.01
Irondequoit, NY (cdp) Monroe County	319	0.61
Elmwood Park, NJ (borough) Bergen County	306	1.62
Clifton, NJ (city) Passaic County	298	0.38
Gahanna, OH (city) Franklin County	284	0.87
Paterson, NJ (city) Passaic County	281	0.19
Canton, MI (cdp) Wayne County	257	0.34
Indianapolis, IN (special city) Marion County	233	0.03
Hobart, IN (city) Lake County	230	0.91
Chili, NY (town) Monroe County	220	0.80
Clay, NY (town) Onondaga County	215	0.37
Akron, OH (city) Summit County	214	0.10
Troy, MI (city) Oakland County	211	0.26
Hamburg, NY (town) Erie County	198	0.35
Parsippany-Troy Hills, NJ (township) Morris County	193	0.38
Dearborn, MI (city) Wayne County	193	0.20
Warren, MI (city) Macomb County	191	0.14
Granite City, IL (city) Madison County	173	0.55
Phoenix, AZ (city) Maricopa County	171	0.01
Plymouth Township, MI (cdp) Wayne County	153	0.55
Winfield, IN (town) Lake County	148	6.52
Clinton, MI (cdp) Macomb County	147	0.15
Lincoln Park, NJ (borough) Morris County	140	1.28
Syracuse, NY (city) Onondaga County	139	0.09
Westland, MI (city) Wayne County	134	0.15
West Seneca, NY (town) Erie County	127	0.28
Hamtramck, MI (city) Wayne County	125	0.54
Detroit, MI (city) Wayne County	124	0.01
Lackawanna, NY (city) Erie County	113	0.59
San Diego, CA (city) San Diego County	113	0.01
San Francisco, CA (city) San Francisco County	113	0.01
Portland, OR (city) Multnomah County	111	0.02
Southgate, MI (city) Wayne County	109	0.36
Salina, NY (town) Onondaga County	109	0.33
Rochester, NY (city) Monroe County	108	0.05
Portage, IN (city) Porter County	107	0.32
Hackensack, NJ (city) Bergen County	106	0.25
Mount Prospect, IL (village) Cook County	105	0.19
Lorain, OH (city) Lorain County	105	0.15
Cleveland, OH (city) Cuyahoga County	101	0.02
Waterbury, CT (city) New Haven County	100	0.09
Escondido, CA (city) San Diego County	100	0.07
Saint Louis, MO (independent city) Saint Louis city	96	0.03
Philadelphia, PA (city) Philadelphia County	96	0.01
Bloomfield, MI (township) Oakland County	93	0.22
Massillon, OH (city) Stark County	92	0.29
Lakewood, OH (city) Cuyahoga County	92	0.16
Ann Arbor, MI (city) Washtenaw County	91	0.08
Flint, MI (city) Genesee County	90	0.07
Rochester Hills, MI (city) Oakland County	89	0.13
Portage, MI (city) Kalamazoo County	87	0.19
Lemont, IL (village) Cook County	83	0.63
Lake Station, IN (city) Lake County	82	0.59
Pequannock, NJ (township) Morris County	82	0.59
Novi, MI (city) Oakland County	81	0.17
Green, OH (city) Summit County	79	0.35
Chesterfield, MI (township) Macomb County	77	0.21
Pittsburgh, PA (city) Allegheny County	77	0.02
Summit, MI (township) Jackson County	76	0.35
Valparaiso, IN (city) Porter County	76	0.28
Whitehall, OH (city) Franklin County	75	0.39
Perinton, NY (town) Monroe County	75	0.16

Place	Number	%
Secaucus, NJ (town) Hudson County	74	0.47
Henrietta, NY (town) Monroe County	74	0.19
Hollywood, FL (city) Broward County	73	0.05
Lansing, IL (village) Cook County	71	0.25
Gates, NY (town) Monroe County	71	0.24
Northville, MI (township) Wayne County	70	0.33
Royal Oak, MI (city) Oakland County	70	0.12
Boca Raton, FL (city) Palm Beach County	70	0.09
Cincinnati, OH (city) Hamilton County	70	0.02
Farmington Hills, MI (city) Oakland County	69	0.08
Ira, MI (township) Saint Clair County	68	0.97
Greece, NY (town) Monroe County	68	0.07
Ontario, OH (village) Richland County	66	1.26
Lincoln Park, MI (city) Wayne County	66	0.16
Wayne, NJ (cdp) Passaic County	66	0.12
Fort Lauderdale, FL (city) Broward County	66	0.04
Onondaga, NY (town) Onondaga County	65	0.31
Highland, IN (town) Lake County	65	0.28
Grand Blanc, MI (township) Genesee County	64	0.21
Fairfield, CT (town) Fairfield County	64	0.11
Fairlawn, OH (city) Summit County	63	0.86
New Baltimore, MI (city) Macomb County	62	0.84
Lodi, NJ (borough) Bergen County	62	0.26
Bristol, CT (city) Hartford County	62	0.10
Tustin, CA (city) Orange County	62	0.09
Bloomingdale, NJ (borough) Passaic County	61	0.80
Toledo, OH (city) Lucas County	61	0.02
Summit, IL (village) Cook County	60	0.56
Washington, MI (township) Macomb County	60	0.31
Cuyahoga Falls, OH (city) Summit County	60	0.12
Bridgeport, CT (city) Fairfield County	60	0.04
Barberton, OH (city) Summit County	59	0.21
Blackman, MI (township) Jackson County	58	0.26
Seattle, WA (city) King County	58	0.01
Parma Heights, OH (city) Cuyahoga County	57	0.26
Santa Monica, CA (city) Los Angeles County	56	0.07
Woodstock, IL (city) McHenry County	55	0.27
Manlius, NY (town) Onondaga County	55	0.17
Anchorage, AK (municipality) Anchorage Borough	55	0.02
East Lansing, MI (city) Ingham County	54	0.12
Countryside, IL (city) Cook County	53	0.89
Lakes of the Four Seasons, IN (cdp) Lake County	53	0.73
Ridgewood, NJ (village) Bergen County	53	0.21
Gary, IN (city) Lake County	53	0.05
Amherst, OH (city) Lorain County	52	0.44
Kearny, NJ (town) Hudson County	52	0.13
Houston, TX (city) Harris County	52	0.00
Fairfield, NJ (cdp) Essex County	51	0.72
De Witt, NY (town) Onondaga County	51	0.21
Meridian charter, MI (township) Ingham County	51	0.13
Taylor, MI (city) Wayne County	51	0.08
Mesa, AZ (city) Maricopa County	51	0.01
Broadview Heights, OH (city) Cuyahoga County	50	0.31
Springfield, OH (city) Clark County	50	0.08
Waukegan, IL (city) Lake County	50	0.06
Long Beach, CA (city) Los Angeles County	49	0.01
Brookfield, IL (village) Cook County	48	0.25
Hasbrouck Heights, NJ (borough) Bergen County	47	0.40
Mahwah, NJ (township) Bergen County	47	0.20
Boardman, OH (cdp) Mahoning County	47	0.13
Webster, NY (town) Monroe County	47	0.12
Berwyn, IL (city) Cook County	47	0.09
Jackson, MI (city) Jackson County	46	0.13
Columbia, MD (cdp) Howard County	46	0.05
Parma, OH (city) Cuyahoga County	46	0.05
San Jose, CA (city) Santa Clara County	46	0.01
North Salem, NY (town) Westchester County	45	0.87
Plantation, FL (city) Broward County	45	0.05
Denver, CO (city) Denver County	45	0.01
Cromwell, CT (town) Middlesex County	44	0.34
Saddle Brook, NJ (cdp) Bergen County	44	0.33
Roxbury, NJ (township) Morris County	44	0.18
Lower Paxton, PA (township) Dauphin County	44	0.10
Cary, NC (town) Wake County	44	0.05
Swatara, PA (township) Dauphin County	43	0.19

Notes: (cdp) census designated place; Refer to the Explanation of Data in the front of the book for more detailed information.

Macedonian

Top 150 Places Sorted by Percent

(Based on all places, regardless of population)

Place	Number	%
Winfield, IN (town) Lake County	148	6.52
Brock, NE (village) Nemaha County	10	5.68
Crown Point, IN (city) Lake County	613	3.13
Hindsboro, IL (village) Douglas County	10	2.81
Garfield, NJ (city) Bergen County	834	2.80
New Haven, WI (town) Adams County	17	2.71
Teton Village, WY (cdp) Teton County	6	2.34
Broadview, MT (town) Yellowstone County	4	2.17
Frenchtown, MT (cdp) Missoula County	14	2.01
Boswell, IN (town) Benton County	16	1.89
Newton Hamilton, PA (borough) Mifflin County	5	1.81
Elmwood Park, NJ (borough) Bergen County	306	1.62
Schererville, IN (town) Lake County	384	1.55
Merrillville, IN (town) Lake County	466	1.52
Brookfield Center, OH (cdp) Trumbull County	17	1.46
Lenape Heights, PA (cdp) Armstrong County	17	1.45
Shirleysburg, PA (borough) Huntingdon County	2	1.43
Bloomingdale, OH (village) Jefferson County	3	1.29
Lincoln Park, NJ (borough) Morris County	140	1.28
Ontario, OH (village) Richland County	66	1.26
Washington, WI (town) Vilas County	19	1.23
Dearborn Heights, MI (city) Wayne County	705	1.21
Bromley, KY (city) Kenton County	9	1.07
Culbertson, MT (town) Roosevelt County	7	1.02
Lake Telemark, NJ (cdp) Morris County	13	1.01
Ira, MI (township) Saint Clair County	68	0.97
Ellport, PA (borough) Lawrence County	11	0.96
Burleigh, MI (township) Iosco County	7	0.92
Hobart, IN (city) Lake County	230	0.91
Macomb, MI (township) Macomb County	454	0.90
Elma Center, NY (cdp) Erie County	22	0.90
Iona, MN (township) Todd County	4	0.90
Countryside, IL (city) Cook County	53	0.89
Blasdell, NY (village) Erie County	24	0.88
Gahanna, OH (city) Franklin County	284	0.87
North Salem, NY (town) Westchester County	45	0.87
Coal City, IL (village) Grundy County	42	0.87
Sloatsburg, NY (village) Rockland County	27	0.87
Fairlawn, OH (city) Summit County	63	0.86
New Baltimore, MI (city) Macomb County	62	0.84
Des Lacs, ND (city) Ward County	2	0.84
Mount Eaton, OH (village) Wayne County	2	0.83
Galeville, NY (cdp) Onondaga County	36	0.82
Mogadore, OH (village) Summit County	30	0.81
Marshall, MI (township) Calhoun County	24	0.81
Chili, NY (town) Monroe County	220	0.80
Bloomingdale, NJ (borough) Passaic County	61	0.80
Bridgewater, PA (borough) Beaver County	6	0.80
Wyomissing Hills, PA (borough) Berks County	20	0.78
Cutler, ME (town) Washington County	5	0.78
Shelby, MI (cdp) Macomb County	486	0.75
Pine Ridge, FL (cdp) Collier County	14	0.75
Indian Springs, NV (cdp) Clark County	10	0.75
Lakes of the Four Seasons, IN (cdp) Lake County	53	0.73
Fairfield, NJ (cdp) Essex County	51	0.72
Sterling Heights, MI (city) Macomb County	887	0.71
Obetz, OH (village) Franklin County	27	0.71
Wormleysburg, PA (borough) Cumberland County	19	0.71
Geraldine, MT (town) Chouteau County	2	0.68
Prairie Grove, IL (village) McHenry County	7	0.66
Pottawattamie Park, IN (town) La Porte County	2	0.66
Huntington Woods, MI (city) Oakland County	40	0.65
Steelton, PA (borough) Dauphin County	37	0.64
Lemont, IL (village) Cook County	83	0.63
Leighton, MI (township) Allegan County	23	0.63
Chevy Chase Section Five, MD (village) Montgomery County	4	0.63
Irondequoit, NY (cdp) Monroe County	319	0.61
Shoreham, MI (village) Berrien County	5	0.60
Lackawanna, NY (city) Erie County	113	0.59
Lake Station, IN (city) Lake County	82	0.59
Pequannock, NJ (township) Morris County	82	0.59
Bearinger, MI (township) Presque Isle County	2	0.59
Peapack and Gladstone, NJ (borough) Somerset County	14	0.58
Coolspring, PA (township) Mercer County	13	0.57
Barton Hills, MI (village) Washtenaw County	2	0.57

Place	Number	%
Summit, IL (village) Cook County	60	0.56
Granite City, IL (city) Madison County	173	0.55
Plymouth Township, MI (cdp) Wayne County	153	0.55
Pontoon Beach, IL (village) Madison County	31	0.55
Hamtramck, MI (city) Wayne County	125	0.54
Pennville, PA (cdp) York County	11	0.54
Toro Canyon, CA (cdp) Santa Barbara County	9	0.54
Sauget, IL (village) Saint Clair County	1	0.54
Churchill, PA (borough) Allegheny County	19	0.53
Meyers Lake, OH (village) Stark County	3	0.53
Empire, MI (village) Leelanau County	2	0.53
Cumberland, IN (town) Marion County	28	0.52
Utica, MI (city) Macomb County	24	0.52
Bart, PA (township) Lancaster County	16	0.52
Lynn, MI (township) Saint Clair County	6	0.51
Manorville, PA (borough) Armstrong County	2	0.51
Lake Elmo, MN (city) Washington County	34	0.50
Prospect Park, NJ (borough) Passaic County	29	0.50
Lexington, OH (village) Richland County	21	0.50
Lucas, OH (village) Richland County	3	0.50
Orleans, IN (town) Orange County	11	0.49
Stambaugh, MI (city) Iron County	6	0.49
Arona, PA (borough) Westmoreland County	2	0.49
Vandercook Lake, MI (cdp) Jackson County	23	0.48
Secaucus, NJ (town) Hudson County	74	0.47
Edgewater, NJ (borough) Bergen County	36	0.47
Fanwood, NJ (borough) Union County	34	0.47
Hedwig Village, TX (city) Harris County	11	0.47
Tawas, MI (township) Iosco County	8	0.47
Orbisonia, PA (borough) Huntingdon County	2	0.47
Myrtletown, CA (cdp) Humboldt County	20	0.46
Forsyth, IL (village) Macon County	11	0.46
Wayne, PA (township) Mifflin County	11	0.46
Athens, WI (village) Marathon County	5	0.46
Rives, MI (township) Jackson County	21	0.45
Knox, IN (city) Starke County	17	0.45
Ohioville, PA (borough) Beaver County	17	0.45
Aberdeen Proving Ground, MD (cdp) Harford County	14	0.45
Guerneville, CA (cdp) Sonoma County	11	0.45
Amherst, OH (city) Lorain County	52	0.44
Sodus, NY (town) Wayne County	39	0.44
North Buffalo, PA (township) Armstrong County	13	0.44
Grabill, IN (town) Allen County	5	0.44
Rosenhayn, NJ (cdp) Cumberland County	5	0.44
Boston, NY (town) Erie County	34	0.43
Cohoctah, MI (township) Livingston County	15	0.43
Wickerham Manor-Fisher, PA (cdp) Washington County	7	0.43
Viola, IL (village) Mercer County	4	0.43
Bull Valley, IL (village) McHenry County	3	0.43
Livonia, MI (city) Wayne County	421	0.42
Shenango, PA (township) Mercer County	17	0.42
Rutherford, PA (cdp) Dauphin County	16	0.42
Springdale, MI (township) Manistee County	3	0.42
Lucas Valley-Marinwood, CA (cdp) Marin County	26	0.41
Schuyler, NY (town) Herkimer County	14	0.41
Berlin, MI (township) Saint Clair County	13	0.41
Winter, WI (town) Sawyer County	4	0.41
Hasbrouck Heights, NJ (borough) Bergen County	47	0.40
Macedonia, OH (city) Summit County	37	0.40
Powell, OH (village) Delaware County	25	0.40
Rochelle Park, NJ (cdp) Bergen County	22	0.40
Silverton, OH (city) Hamilton County	21	0.40
Manor, PA (township) Armstrong County	17	0.40
Tekonsha, MI (village) Calhoun County	3	0.40
Mesa, CA (cdp) Inyo County	1	0.40
Whitehall, OH (city) Franklin County	75	0.39
Fairmount, NY (cdp) Onondaga County	42	0.39
Winsted, CT (cdp) Litchfield County	28	0.39
Laurel Hollow, NY (village) Nassau County	8	0.39
Loveland Park, OH (cdp) Warren County	7	0.39
Saline, MI (township) Washtenaw County	5	0.39
Clifton, NJ (city) Passaic County	298	0.38
Parsippany-Troy Hills, NJ (township) Morris County	193	0.38
Alanson, MI (village) Emmet County	3	0.38
Clay, NY (town) Onondaga County	215	0.37

Notes: (cdp) census designated place; Refer to the Explanation of Data in the front of the book for more detailed information.

Macedonian

Top 150 Places Sorted by Percent

(Based on places with populations of 10,000 or more)

Place	Number	%
Crown Point, IN (city) Lake County	613	3.13
Garfield, NJ (city) Bergen County	834	2.80
Elmwood Park, NJ (borough) Bergen County	306	1.62
Schererville, IN (town) Lake County	384	1.55
Merrillville, IN (town) Lake County	466	1.52
Lincoln Park, NJ (borough) Morris County	140	1.28
Dearborn Heights, MI (city) Wayne County	705	1.21
Hobart, IN (city) Lake County	230	0.91
Macomb, MI (township) Macomb County	454	0.90
Gahanna, OH (city) Franklin County	284	0.87
Chili, NY (town) Monroe County	220	0.80
Shelby, MI (cdp) Macomb County	486	0.75
Sterling Heights, MI (city) Macomb County	887	0.71
Lemont, IL (village) Cook County	83	0.63
Irondequoit, NY (cdp) Monroe County	319	0.61
Lackawanna, NY (city) Erie County	113	0.59
Lake Station, IN (city) Lake County	82	0.59
Pequannock, NJ (township) Morris County	82	0.59
Summit, IL (village) Cook County	60	0.56
Granite City, IL (city) Madison County	173	0.55
Plymouth Township, MI (cdp) Wayne County	153	0.55
Hamtramck, MI (city) Wayne County	125	0.54
Secaucus, NJ (town) Hudson County	74	0.47
Amherst, OH (city) Lorain County	52	0.44
Livonia, MI (city) Wayne County	421	0.42
Hasbrouck Heights, NJ (borough) Bergen County	47	0.40
Whitehall, OH (city) Franklin County	75	0.39
Fairmount, NY (cdp) Onondaga County	42	0.39
Clifton, NJ (city) Passaic County	298	0.38
Parsippany-Troy Hills, NJ (township) Morris County	193	0.38
Clay, NY (town) Onondaga County	215	0.37
Southgate, MI (city) Wayne County	109	0.36
Hamburg, NY (town) Erie County	198	0.35
Green, OH (city) Summit County	79	0.35
Summit, MI (township) Jackson County	76	0.35
Canton, MI (cdp) Wayne County	257	0.34
Cromwell, CT (town) Middlesex County	44	0.34
Wantage, NJ (township) Sussex County	35	0.34
Salina, NY (town) Onondaga County	109	0.33
Northville, MI (township) Wayne County	70	0.33
Saddle Brook, NJ (cdp) Bergen County	44	0.33
Munhall, PA (borough) Allegheny County	40	0.33
Bound Brook, NJ (borough) Somerset County	34	0.33
Portage, IN (city) Porter County	107	0.32
Brigantine, NJ (city) Atlantic County	40	0.32
Onondaga, NY (town) Onondaga County	65	0.31
Washington, MI (township) Macomb County	60	0.31
Broadview Heights, OH (city) Cuyahoga County	50	0.31
Ringwood, NJ (borough) Passaic County	38	0.31
Hartland, MI (township) Livingston County	34	0.31
Mundy, MI (township) Genesee County	37	0.30
Massillon, OH (city) Stark County	92	0.29
West Seneca, NY (town) Erie County	127	0.28
Valparaiso, IN (city) Porter County	76	0.28
Highland, IN (town) Lake County	65	0.28
Woodstock, IL (city) McHenry County	55	0.27
North Smithfield, RI (town) Providence County	29	0.27
Troy, MI (city) Oakland County	211	0.26
Lodi, NJ (borough) Bergen County	62	0.26
Blackman, MI (township) Jackson County	58	0.26
Parma Heights, OH (city) Cuyahoga County	57	0.26
Bridgeview, IL (village) Cook County	40	0.26
Chicago Ridge, IL (village) Cook County	36	0.26
Speedway, IN (town) Marion County	33	0.26
Melvindale, MI (city) Wayne County	28	0.26
Winchester, CT (town) Litchfield County	28	0.26
Hackensack, NJ (city) Bergen County	106	0.25
Lansing, IL (village) Cook County	71	0.25
Brookfield, IL (village) Cook County	48	0.25
Owosso, MI (city) Shiawassee County	39	0.25
Gates, NY (town) Monroe County	71	0.24
Somers Point, NJ (city) Atlantic County	28	0.24
Elma, NY (town) Erie County	27	0.24
Bloomfield, MI (township) Oakland County	93	0.22
Morrisville, PA (borough) Bucks County	22	0.22
Fort Wayne, IN (city) Allen County	432	0.21
Chesterfield, MI (township) Macomb County	77	0.21
Grand Blanc, MI (township) Genesee County	64	0.21
Barberton, OH (city) Summit County	59	0.21
Ridgewood, NJ (village) Bergen County	53	0.21
De Witt, NY (town) Onondaga County	51	0.21
North Canton, OH (city) Stark County	35	0.21
Westchester, IL (village) Cook County	35	0.21
Wheatfield, NY (town) Niagara County	29	0.21
Hutchinson, MN (city) McLeod County	27	0.21
Dearborn, MI (city) Wayne County	193	0.20
Mahwah, NJ (township) Bergen County	47	0.20
Springfield, NJ (cdp) Union County	29	0.20
Woodbury, NJ (city) Gloucester County	21	0.20
Paterson, NJ (city) Passaic County	281	0.19
Mount Prospect, IL (village) Cook County	105	0.19
Portage, MI (city) Kalamazoo County	87	0.19
Henrietta, NY (town) Monroe County	74	0.19
Swatara, PA (township) Dauphin County	43	0.19
Lockport, IL (city) Will County	28	0.19
Oakland charter, MI (township) Oakland County	25	0.19
Sycamore, IL (city) De Kalb County	23	0.19
Healdsburg, CA (city) Sonoma County	20	0.19
Roxbury, NJ (township) Morris County	44	0.18
Camillus, NY (town) Onondaga County	42	0.18
Watertown, CT (town) Litchfield County	38	0.18
Greater Sun Center, FL (cdp) Hillsborough County	29	0.18
Forestville, OH (cdp) Hamilton County	20	0.18
Novi, MI (city) Oakland County	81	0.17
Manlius, NY (town) Onondaga County	55	0.17
Middletown, NY (city) Orange County	42	0.17
Montville, NJ (township) Morris County	35	0.17
Norton, OH (city) Summit County	20	0.17
Lakewood, OH (city) Cuyahoga County	92	0.16
Perinton, NY (town) Monroe County	75	0.16
Lincoln Park, MI (city) Wayne County	66	0.16
Pittsford, NY (town) Monroe County	43	0.16
Ferndale, MI (city) Oakland County	35	0.16
Dyer, IN (town) Lake County	22	0.16
Lincolnwood, IL (village) Cook County	20	0.16
Lyons, IL (village) Cook County	16	0.16
Clinton, MI (cdp) Macomb County	147	0.15
Westland, MI (city) Wayne County	134	0.15
Lorain, OH (city) Lorain County	105	0.15
Genesee, MI (township) Genesee County	36	0.15
Westmont, IL (village) Du Page County	36	0.15
Okemos, MI (cdp) Ingham County	34	0.15
Hamburg, MI (township) Livingston County	31	0.15
Wayne, MI (city) Wayne County	28	0.15
Middleburg Heights, OH (city) Cuyahoga County	24	0.15
La Grange, IL (village) Cook County	23	0.15
White Oak, OH (cdp) Hamilton County	20	0.15
North Myrtle Beach, SC (city) Horry County	17	0.15
Urbana, OH (city) Champaign County	17	0.15
Warren, MI (city) Macomb County	191	0.14
Gurnee, IL (village) Lake County	39	0.14
Saint Charles, IL (city) Kane County	38	0.14
West Milford, NJ (cdp) Passaic County	38	0.14
Ossining, NY (village) Westchester County	34	0.14
Southfield, MI (township) Oakland County	20	0.14
Wawarsing, NY (town) Ulster County	18	0.14
Wixom, MI (city) Oakland County	18	0.14
West Deer, PA (township) Allegheny County	16	0.14
East Grand Rapids, MI (city) Kent County	15	0.14
Rochester Hills, MI (city) Oakland County	89	0.13
Kearny, NJ (town) Hudson County	52	0.13
Meridian charter, MI (township) Ingham County	51	0.13
Boardman, OH (cdp) Mahoning County	47	0.13
Jackson, MI (city) Jackson County	46	0.13
Garden City, MI (city) Wayne County	40	0.13
Sandusky, OH (city) Erie County	37	0.13
North Ridgeville, OH (city) Lorain County	29	0.13
Grosse Pointe Woods, MI (city) Wayne County	23	0.13
Farmington, NY (town) Ontario County	14	0.13
Royal Oak, MI (city) Oakland County	70	0.12

Notes: (cdp) census designated place; Refer to the Explanation of Data in the front of the book for more detailed information.

Maltese

Top 150 Places Sorted by Number

(Based on all places, regardless of population)

Place	Number	%
New York, NY (city) New York City	3,082	0.04
Livonia, MI (city) Wayne County	942	0.94
Hempstead, NY (town) Nassau County	730	0.10
Dearborn Heights, MI (city) Wayne County	656	1.13
Dearborn, MI (city) Wayne County	626	0.64
San Francisco, CA (city) San Francisco County	610	0.08
Canton, MI (cdp) Wayne County	592	0.78
Brookhaven, NY (town) Suffolk County	587	0.13
Westland, MI (city) Wayne County	519	0.60
Detroit, MI (city) Wayne County	473	0.05
Sterling Heights, MI (city) Macomb County	418	0.34
Oyster Bay, NY (town) Nassau County	390	0.13
Islip, NY (town) Suffolk County	388	0.12
Taylor, MI (city) Wayne County	296	0.45
San Bruno, CA (city) San Mateo County	285	0.71
South San Francisco, CA (city) San Mateo County	279	0.46
San Mateo, CA (city) San Mateo County	279	0.30
Allen Park, MI (city) Wayne County	265	0.90
San Jose, CA (city) Santa Clara County	261	0.03
Warren, MI (city) Macomb County	258	0.19
Redford, MI (cdp) Wayne County	251	0.49
Commerce, MI (township) Oakland County	230	0.66
Babylon, NY (town) Suffolk County	218	0.10
Millbrae, CA (city) San Mateo County	212	1.02
Garden City, MI (city) Wayne County	211	0.70
Clinton, MI (cdp) Macomb County	210	0.22
Macomb, MI (township) Macomb County	207	0.41
Southgate, MI (city) Wayne County	184	0.61
Novi, MI (city) Oakland County	171	0.36
White Lake, MI (township) Oakland County	170	0.60
Royal Oak, MI (city) Oakland County	166	0.28
Shelby, MI (cdp) Macomb County	162	0.25
Los Angeles, CA (city) Los Angeles County	161	0.00
Wixom, MI (city) Oakland County	159	1.20
North Hempstead, NY (town) Nassau County	158	0.07
Petaluma, CA (city) Sonoma County	153	0.28
Saint Clair Shores, MI (city) Macomb County	151	0.24
San Diego, CA (city) San Diego County	150	0.01
Smithtown, NY (town) Suffolk County	149	0.13
Farmington Hills, MI (city) Oakland County	145	0.18
Milford, MI (township) Oakland County	144	0.94
Cape Coral, FL (city) Lee County	141	0.14
Huntington, NY (town) Suffolk County	140	0.07
Grosse Ile, MI (cdp) Wayne County	131	1.20
Rochester Hills, MI (city) Oakland County	129	0.19
Phoenix, AZ (city) Maricopa County	128	0.01
Woodhaven, MI (city) Wayne County	123	0.98
Franklin Square, NY (cdp) Nassau County	123	0.42
Orion, MI (township) Oakland County	118	0.35
Concord, CA (city) Contra Costa County	118	0.10
West Bloomfield, MI (township) Oakland County	115	0.18
Campbell, CA (city) Santa Clara County	113	0.30
Wyandotte, MI (city) Wayne County	111	0.40
Plano, TX (city) Collin County	111	0.05
Lincoln Park, MI (city) Wayne County	110	0.27
Hazel Park, MI (city) Oakland County	108	0.57
Plymouth Township, MI (cdp) Wayne County	108	0.39
Troy, MI (city) Oakland County	104	0.13
Trenton, MI (city) Wayne County	103	0.53
Roseville, MI (city) Macomb County	103	0.21
Ronkonkoma, NY (cdp) Suffolk County	102	0.51
Antioch, CA (city) Contra Costa County	102	0.11
South Lyon, MI (city) Oakland County	100	1.00
Brownstown, MI (township) Wayne County	100	0.43
Pacifica, CA (city) San Mateo County	100	0.26
Virginia Beach, VA (independent city) Virginia Beach city	99	0.02
Burlingame, CA (city) San Mateo County	97	0.35
Hamburg, MI (township) Livingston County	96	0.47
Chicago, IL (city) Cook County	96	0.00
Redwood City, CA (city) San Mateo County	95	0.13
Brighton, MI (township) Livingston County	92	0.52
Rose, MI (township) Oakland County	91	1.47
West Babylon, NY (cdp) Suffolk County	90	0.21
Northville, MI (township) Wayne County	89	0.42
San Carlos, CA (city) San Mateo County	89	0.32

Place	Number	%
Mastic Beach, NY (cdp) Suffolk County	88	0.76
Ormond Beach, FL (city) Volusia County	87	0.24
Henderson, NV (city) Clark County	87	0.05
Green Haven, MD (cdp) Anne Arundel County	86	0.50
Seattle, WA (city) King County	85	0.02
Shirley, NY (cdp) Suffolk County	84	0.33
Huntington Beach, CA (city) Orange County	81	0.04
Houston, TX (city) Harris County	81	0.00
Highland, MI (township) Oakland County	80	0.42
Modesto, CA (city) Stanislaus County	80	0.04
Bridgewater, NJ (township) Somerset County	79	0.18
Riverview, MI (city) Wayne County	77	0.58
Sebastopol, CA (city) Sonoma County	74	0.92
Lake Charles, LA (city) Calcasieu Parish	74	0.10
Chesterfield, MI (township) Macomb County	72	0.19
Washington, MI (township) Macomb County	71	0.37
Wayne, MI (city) Wayne County	71	0.37
Bloomfield, MI (township) Oakland County	70	0.16
Scottsdale, AZ (city) Maricopa County	70	0.03
Saint Clair, MI (city) Saint Clair County	69	1.19
Addison, MI (township) Oakland County	67	1.04
Birmingham, MI (city) Oakland County	67	0.35
Ash, MI (township) Monroe County	66	0.87
New Windsor, NY (town) Orange County	65	0.28
Flint, MI (township) Genesee County	65	0.19
Rancho Cordova, CA (cdp) Sacramento County	64	0.12
Old Bridge, NJ (township) Middlesex County	64	0.11
New Rochelle, NY (city) Westchester County	64	0.09
Sacramento, CA (city) Sacramento County	64	0.02
Farmingdale, NY (village) Nassau County	63	0.75
North Bellmore, NY (cdp) Nassau County	62	0.31
Pleasant Hill, CA (city) Contra Costa County	61	0.19
East Brunswick, NJ (cdp) Middlesex County	61	0.13
Yonkers, NY (city) Westchester County	61	0.03
Harrison, MI (cdp) Macomb County	60	0.25
Santa Rosa, CA (city) Sonoma County	59	0.04
Fremont, CA (city) Alameda County	59	0.03
Northfield, MI (township) Washtenaw County	58	0.70
Blooming Grove, NY (town) Orange County	58	0.33
Brighton, MI (city) Livingston County	57	0.85
Shady Hills, FL (cdp) Pasco County	57	0.73
Rohnert Park, CA (city) Sonoma County	57	0.13
Dallas, TX (city) Dallas County	57	0.00
Belleville, MI (city) Wayne County	56	1.40
Berlin charter, MI (township) Monroe County	56	0.81
Massapequa, NY (cdp) Nassau County	56	0.25
Novato, CA (city) Marin County	56	0.12
Van Buren, MI (township) Wayne County	55	0.23
Bayonne, NJ (city) Hudson County	55	0.09
Ann Arbor, MI (city) Washtenaw County	55	0.05
Stamford, CT (city) Fairfield County	55	0.05
Belmont, CA (city) San Mateo County	54	0.21
Southampton, NY (town) Suffolk County	54	0.10
Thousand Oaks, CA (city) Ventura County	54	0.05
Philadelphia, PA (city) Philadelphia County	54	0.00
Rochester, MI (city) Oakland County	53	0.51
Clawson, MI (city) Oakland County	53	0.42
Hazlet, NJ (township) Monmouth County	53	0.25
Inkster, MI (city) Wayne County	53	0.18
Elmont, NY (cdp) Nassau County	53	0.16
Martinez, CA (city) Contra Costa County	53	0.15
Folsom, CA (city) Sacramento County	53	0.10
Albany, NY (city) Albany County	53	0.06
Clearwater, FL (city) Pinellas County	53	0.05
Santa Clara, CA (city) Santa Clara County	51	0.05
Tucson, AZ (city) Pima County	51	0.01
Schuylkill, PA (township) Chester County	50	0.72
Oxford charter, MI (township) Oakland County	50	0.31
Lansing, IL (village) Cook County	50	0.18
Elk Grove, CA (cdp) Sacramento County	50	0.08
Mount Vernon, NY (city) Westchester County	50	0.07
Waterford, MI (cdp) Oakland County	50	0.07
Clarkstown, NY (town) Rockland County	50	0.06
Albuquerque, NM (city) Bernalillo County	50	0.01
Coconut Creek, FL (city) Broward County	49	0.11

Notes: (cdp) census designated place; Refer to the Explanation of Data in the front of the book for more detailed information.

Maltese

Top 150 Places Sorted by Percent

(Based on all places, regardless of population)

Place	Number	%
Aspen Park, CO (cdp) Jefferson County	35	4.24
Felsenthal, AR (town) Union County	6	3.61
Mount Lena, MD (cdp) Washington County	15	3.19
Belvue, KS (city) Pottawatomie County	7	2.86
Eyers Grove, PA (cdp) Columbia County	2	2.11
Ludlow, ME (town) Aroostook County	8	2.00
Bemus Point, NY (village) Chautauqua County	6	1.75
Magnolia, DE (town) Kent County	4	1.69
Tuolumne City, CA (cdp) Tuolumne County	32	1.67
Lexington, MI (village) Sanilac County	18	1.63
Rose, MI (township) Oakland County	91	1.47
Townsend, DE (town) New Castle County	5	1.41
Belleville, MI (city) Wayne County	56	1.40
Wixom, MI (city) Oakland County	159	1.20
Grosse Ile, MI (cdp) Wayne County	131	1.20
Saint Clair, MI (city) Saint Clair County	69	1.19
Dearborn Heights, MI (city) Wayne County	656	1.13
Mason, WI (town) Bayfield County	4	1.13
Grand View-on-Hudson, NY (village) Rockland County	3	1.06
Addison, MI (township) Oakland County	67	1.04
Calvert Beach-Long Beach, MD (cdp) Calvert County	25	1.03
Millbrae, CA (city) San Mateo County	212	1.02
South Lyon, MI (city) Oakland County	100	1.00
Woodhaven, MI (city) Wayne County	123	0.98
Worth, MI (township) Sanilac County	38	0.97
Livonia, MI (city) Wayne County	942	0.94
Milford, MI (township) Oakland County	144	0.94
Sebastopol, CA (city) Sonoma County	74	0.92
Richmond, MI (city) Macomb County	45	0.92
Cuba, KS (city) Republic County	2	0.91
Allen Park, MI (city) Wayne County	265	0.90
Hooper, UT (cdp) Weber County	35	0.90
Forester, MI (township) Sanilac County	10	0.90
Ash, MI (township) Monroe County	66	0.87
Gladwin, MI (city) Gladwin County	26	0.87
Brighton, MI (city) Livingston County	57	0.85
Manhasset Hills, NY (cdp) Nassau County	30	0.82
Berlin charter, MI (township) Monroe County	56	0.81
Edmore, MI (village) Montcalm County	10	0.79
Canton, MI (cdp) Wayne County	592	0.78
Lake Fenton, MI (cdp) Genesee County	38	0.78
Speaker, MI (township) Sanilac County	11	0.78
Cottrellville, MI (township) Saint Clair County	29	0.77
Mastic Beach, NY (cdp) Suffolk County	88	0.76
Farmingdale, NY (village) Nassau County	63	0.75
East Quogue, NY (cdp) Suffolk County	32	0.75
Shady Hills, FL (cdp) Pasco County	57	0.73
Amboy, MI (township) Hillsdale County	9	0.73
Schuylkill, PA (township) Chester County	50	0.72
Plandome Manor, NY (village) Nassau County	6	0.72
Applegate, MI (village) Sanilac County	2	0.72
San Bruno, CA (city) San Mateo County	285	0.71
Dryden, MI (township) Lapeer County	33	0.71
Walton Park, NY (cdp) Orange County	17	0.71
Garden City, MI (city) Wayne County	211	0.70
Northfield, MI (township) Washtenaw County	58	0.70
White Oak, MI (township) Ingham County	8	0.69
Marine City, MI (city) Saint Clair County	33	0.68
East Williston, NY (village) Nassau County	17	0.68
Allis, MI (township) Presque Isle County	7	0.68
Commerce, MI (township) Oakland County	230	0.66
Blackhoof, MN (township) Carlton County	5	0.66
Gerrish, MI (township) Roscommon County	20	0.65
Bengal, MI (township) Clinton County	8	0.65
Dearborn, MI (city) Wayne County	626	0.64
Waxhaw, NC (town) Union County	17	0.64
Ellsworth, MI (village) Antrim County	3	0.64
Lake Ann, MI (village) Benzie County	2	0.64
Kalamo, MI (township) Eaton County	11	0.63
Reklaw, TX (city) Cherokee County	2	0.63
Milford, MI (village) Oakland County	39	0.62
Southgate, MI (city) Wayne County	184	0.61
Tioga, PA (township) Tioga County	6	0.61
Foster, MI (township) Ogemaw County	5	0.61
Bear Lake, MI (village) Manistee County	2	0.61
Westland, MI (city) Wayne County	519	0.60
White Lake, MI (township) Oakland County	170	0.60
Salem, CT (town) New London County	23	0.60
Cathcart, WA (cdp) Snohomish County	17	0.60
Hancock, VT (town) Addison County	2	0.60
Verdi-Mogul, NV (cdp) Washoe County	17	0.59
Wilson, MI (township) Charlevoix County	12	0.59
Riverview, MI (city) Wayne County	77	0.58
Highland Mills, NY (cdp) Orange County	20	0.58
Peaceful Valley, WA (cdp) Whatcom County	15	0.58
Marlboro, NY (cdp) Ulster County	14	0.58
Norwood, MI (township) Charlevoix County	4	0.58
Hazel Park, MI (city) Oakland County	108	0.57
Sawgrass, FL (cdp) Saint Johns County	28	0.57
Monroe, NY (village) Orange County	44	0.56
Silver Lake, OH (village) Summit County	17	0.56
Northville, MI (city) Oakland County	35	0.55
Mendon, MI (village) Saint Joseph County	5	0.55
Pound, WI (village) Marinette County	2	0.55
Unionville, NC (town) Union County	26	0.54
Franklin, MI (village) Oakland County	16	0.54
Moonachie, NJ (borough) Bergen County	15	0.54
Glen Ellen, CA (cdp) Sonoma County	5	0.54
Trenton, MI (city) Wayne County	103	0.53
Ailey, GA (city) Montgomery County	2	0.53
Newry, ME (town) Oxford County	2	0.53
Brighton, MI (township) Livingston County	92	0.52
Pebble Creek, FL (cdp) Hillsborough County	25	0.52
Nissequogue, NY (village) Suffolk County	8	0.52
Memphis, MI (city) Macomb County	6	0.52
Torch Lake, MI (township) Antrim County	6	0.52
Amity, AR (city) Clark County	4	0.52
Ronkonkoma, NY (cdp) Suffolk County	102	0.51
Rochester, MI (city) Oakland County	53	0.51
Allegheny, PA (township) Cambria County	13	0.51
Frederic, MI (township) Crawford County	7	0.51
Green Haven, MD (cdp) Anne Arundel County	86	0.50
Montebello, NY (village) Rockland County	18	0.50
Unadilla, GA (city) Dooly County	14	0.50
Redford, MI (cdp) Wayne County	251	0.49
Center Moriches, NY (cdp) Suffolk County	32	0.49
Imlay City, MI (city) Lapeer County	19	0.49
Lexington, MI (township) Sanilac County	18	0.49
Thiensville, WI (village) Ozaukee County	16	0.49
Saint George, SC (town) Dorchester County	10	0.49
Weippe, ID (city) Clearwater County	2	0.49
Bayville, NY (village) Nassau County	34	0.48
Acme, MI (township) Grand Traverse County	21	0.48
Ross, CA (town) Marin County	11	0.48
North Woodbridge, CA (cdp) San Joaquin County	6	0.48
Hamburg, MI (township) Livingston County	96	0.47
Windsor, WI (town) Dane County	25	0.47
Aptos Hills-Larkin Valley, CA (cdp) Santa Cruz County	10	0.47
South San Francisco, CA (city) San Mateo County	279	0.46
Flat Rock, MI (city) Wayne County	39	0.46
Pittston, PA (township) Luzerne County	16	0.46
Iosco, MI (township) Livingston County	14	0.46
Ortonville, MI (village) Oakland County	7	0.46
Orwell, OH (village) Ashtabula County	7	0.46
Norwich, MI (township) Missaukee County	3	0.46
Taylor, MI (city) Wayne County	296	0.45
Monte Sereno, CA (city) Santa Clara County	16	0.45
Riverton, MI (township) Mason County	6	0.45
Farmington, MI (city) Oakland County	46	0.44
Putnam Lake, NY (cdp) Putnam County	17	0.44
Unadilla, MI (township) Livingston County	14	0.44
Conway, MI (township) Livingston County	12	0.44
Laurel Hollow, NY (village) Nassau County	9	0.44
North De Land, FL (cdp) Volusia County	6	0.44
Mecosta, MI (village) Mecosta County	2	0.44
Brownstown, MI (township) Wayne County	100	0.43
York charter, MI (township) Washtenaw County	32	0.43
Country Estates, FL (cdp) Broward County	8	0.43
Los Alamos, CA (cdp) Santa Barbara County	6	0.43
Franklin Square, NY (cdp) Nassau County	123	0.42

Notes: (cdp) census designated place; Refer to the Explanation of Data in the front of the book for more detailed information.

Maltese

Top 150 Places Sorted by Percent

(Based on places with populations of 10,000 or more)

Place	Number	%
Wixom, MI (city) Oakland County	159	1.20
Grosse Ile, MI (cdp) Wayne County	131	1.20
Dearborn Heights, MI (city) Wayne County	656	1.13
Millbrae, CA (city) San Mateo County	212	1.02
South Lyon, MI (city) Oakland County	100	1.00
Woodhaven, MI (city) Wayne County	123	0.98
Livonia, MI (city) Wayne County	942	0.94
Milford, MI (township) Oakland County	144	0.94
Allen Park, MI (city) Wayne County	265	0.90
Canton, MI (cdp) Wayne County	592	0.78
Mastic Beach, NY (cdp) Suffolk County	88	0.76
San Bruno, CA (city) San Mateo County	285	0.71
Garden City, MI (city) Wayne County	211	0.70
Commerce, MI (township) Oakland County	230	0.66
Dearborn, MI (city) Wayne County	626	0.64
Southgate, MI (city) Wayne County	184	0.61
Westland, MI (city) Wayne County	519	0.60
White Lake, MI (township) Oakland County	170	0.60
Riverview, MI (city) Wayne County	77	0.58
Hazel Park, MI (city) Oakland County	108	0.57
Trenton, MI (city) Wayne County	103	0.53
Brighton, MI (township) Livingston County	92	0.52
Ronkonkoma, NY (cdp) Suffolk County	102	0.51
Rochester, MI (city) Oakland County	53	0.51
Green Haven, MD (cdp) Anne Arundel County	86	0.50
Redford, MI (cdp) Wayne County	251	0.49
Hamburg, MI (township) Livingston County	96	0.47
South San Francisco, CA (city) San Mateo County	279	0.46
Taylor, MI (city) Wayne County	296	0.45
Farmington, MI (city) Oakland County	46	0.44
Brownstown, MI (township) Wayne County	100	0.43
Franklin Square, NY (cdp) Nassau County	123	0.42
Northville, MI (township) Wayne County	89	0.42
Highland, MI (township) Oakland County	80	0.42
Clawson, MI (city) Oakland County	53	0.42
Macomb, MI (township) Macomb County	207	0.41
Wyandotte, MI (city) Wayne County	111	0.40
Lake Grove, NY (village) Suffolk County	42	0.40
Rocky Point, NY (cdp) Suffolk County	41	0.40
Plymouth Township, MI (cdp) Wayne County	108	0.39
Washington, MI (township) Macomb County	71	0.37
Wayne, MI (city) Wayne County	71	0.37
Hartland, MI (township) Livingston County	40	0.37
Novi, MI (city) Oakland County	171	0.36
Scotts Valley, CA (city) Santa Cruz County	42	0.36
Orion, MI (township) Oakland County	118	0.35
Burlingame, CA (city) San Mateo County	97	0.35
Birmingham, MI (city) Oakland County	67	0.35
Springfield, MI (township) Oakland County	46	0.35
Sterling Heights, MI (city) Macomb County	418	0.34
Fort Polk South, LA (cdp) Vernon Parish	37	0.34
Shirley, NY (cdp) Suffolk County	84	0.33
Blooming Grove, NY (town) Orange County	58	0.33
San Carlos, CA (city) San Mateo County	89	0.32
North Bellmore, NY (cdp) Nassau County	62	0.31
Oxford charter, MI (township) Oakland County	50	0.31
San Mateo, CA (city) San Mateo County	279	0.30
Campbell, CA (city) Santa Clara County	113	0.30
Seaford, NY (cdp) Nassau County	47	0.30
Cameron Park, CA (cdp) El Dorado County	44	0.30
Manorville, NY (cdp) Suffolk County	34	0.30
Secaucus, NJ (town) Hudson County	46	0.29
Green Oak, MI (township) Livingston County	45	0.29
Fenton, MI (township) Genesee County	38	0.29
Royal Oak, MI (city) Oakland County	166	0.28
Petaluma, CA (city) Sonoma County	153	0.28
New Windsor, NY (town) Orange County	65	0.28
Mastic, NY (cdp) Suffolk County	43	0.28
Beacon, NY (city) Dutchess County	39	0.28
Lincoln Park, MI (city) Wayne County	110	0.27
Washington, NJ (township) Morris County	48	0.27
Kings Park, NY (cdp) Suffolk County	44	0.27
Pacifica, CA (city) San Mateo County	100	0.26
Somers, NY (town) Westchester County	48	0.26
Holtsville, NY (cdp) Suffolk County	44	0.26
Berkley, MI (city) Oakland County	40	0.26
Jericho, NY (cdp) Nassau County	34	0.26
West Freehold, NJ (cdp) Monmouth County	32	0.26
Piedmont, CA (city) Alameda County	29	0.26
Shelby, MI (cdp) Macomb County	162	0.25
Harrison, MI (cdp) Macomb County	60	0.25
Massapequa, NY (cdp) Nassau County	56	0.25
Hazlet, NJ (township) Monmouth County	53	0.25
Saint Clair Shores, MI (city) Macomb County	151	0.24
Ormond Beach, FL (city) Volusia County	87	0.24
Genoa, MI (township) Livingston County	38	0.24
Melvindale, MI (city) Wayne County	26	0.24
Van Buren, MI (township) Wayne County	55	0.23
West Hempstead, NY (cdp) Nassau County	43	0.23
Conning Towers-Nautilus Park, CT (cdp) New London County	24	0.23
Clinton, MI (cdp) Macomb County	210	0.22
Harper Woods, MI (city) Wayne County	31	0.22
Roseville, MI (city) Macomb County	103	0.21
West Babylon, NY (cdp) Suffolk County	90	0.21
Belmont, CA (city) San Mateo County	54	0.21
Grosse Pointe Woods, MI (city) Wayne County	36	0.21
Ocean Springs, MS (city) Jackson County	36	0.21
Melville, NY (cdp) Suffolk County	30	0.21
Fort Benning South, GA (cdp) Chattahoochee County	25	0.21
North Wantagh, NY (cdp) Nassau County	25	0.21
Syosset, NY (cdp) Nassau County	38	0.20
Huron charter, MI (township) Wayne County	27	0.20
Warren, MI (city) Macomb County	258	0.19
Rochester Hills, MI (city) Oakland County	129	0.19
Chesterfield, MI (township) Macomb County	72	0.19
Flint, MI (township) Genesee County	65	0.19
Pleasant Hill, CA (city) Contra Costa County	61	0.19
Oakley, CA (city) Contra Costa County	48	0.19
Windsor, CA (town) Sonoma County	43	0.19
Edwardsville, IL (city) Madison County	39	0.19
Lynbrook, NY (village) Nassau County	37	0.19
North Lindenhurst, NY (cdp) Suffolk County	22	0.19
Clayton, CA (city) Contra Costa County	20	0.19
Fenton, MI (city) Genesee County	20	0.19
Farmington Hills, MI (city) Oakland County	145	0.18
West Bloomfield, MI (township) Oakland County	115	0.18
Bridgewater, NJ (township) Somerset County	79	0.18
Inkster, MI (city) Wayne County	53	0.18
Lansing, IL (village) Cook County	50	0.18
Cutler, FL (cdp) Miami-Dade County	31	0.18
Fraser, MI (city) Macomb County	28	0.18
Saddle Brook, NJ (cdp) Bergen County	24	0.18
North New Hyde Park, NY (cdp) Nassau County	24	0.17
Somerville, NJ (borough) Somerset County	21	0.17
Bloomfield, MI (township) Oakland County	70	0.16
Elmont, NY (cdp) Nassau County	53	0.16
Ferndale, MI (city) Oakland County	35	0.16
Hillside, NJ (cdp) Union County	35	0.16
North Merrick, NY (cdp) Nassau County	19	0.16
Jensen Beach, FL (cdp) Martin County	18	0.16
Barclay-Kingston, NJ (cdp) Camden County	17	0.16
Lighthouse Point, FL (city) Broward County	17	0.16
Martinez, CA (city) Contra Costa County	53	0.15
Holbrook, NY (cdp) Suffolk County	40	0.15
Plainview, NY (cdp) Nassau County	39	0.15
Garden City, NY (village) Nassau County	33	0.15
Farmingville, NY (cdp) Suffolk County	25	0.15
Patterson, NY (town) Putnam County	17	0.15
Hillsborough, CA (town) San Mateo County	16	0.15
Terryville, NY (cdp) Suffolk County	16	0.15
Cape Coral, FL (city) Lee County	141	0.14
Monroe, NY (town) Orange County	44	0.14
Lindenhurst, NY (village) Suffolk County	40	0.14
Bay Shore, NY (cdp) Suffolk County	34	0.14
Bayonet Point, FL (cdp) Pasco County	34	0.14
Morris, NJ (township) Morris County	31	0.14
Wantagh, NY (cdp) Nassau County	27	0.14
Mount Clemens, MI (city) Macomb County	24	0.14
Southeast, NY (town) Putnam County	24	0.14
Upper Chichester, PA (township) Delaware County	24	0.14

Notes: (cdp) census designated place; Refer to the Explanation of Data in the front of the book for more detailed information.

New Zealander

Top 150 Places Sorted by Number

(Based on all places, regardless of population)

Place	Number	%
New York, NY (city) New York City	559	0.01
Los Angeles, CA (city) Los Angeles County	476	0.01
San Francisco, CA (city) San Francisco County	219	0.03
San Diego, CA (city) San Diego County	210	0.02
Seattle, WA (city) King County	142	0.03
Little Rock, AR (city) Pulaski County	133	0.07
San Jose, CA (city) Santa Clara County	125	0.01
Mount Pleasant, SC (town) Charleston County	120	0.25
Houston, TX (city) Harris County	102	0.01
Menomonie, WI (city) Dunn County	95	0.63
Phoenix, AZ (city) Maricopa County	91	0.01
Hempstead, NY (town) Nassau County	86	0.01
Denver, CO (city) Denver County	83	0.01
Irvine, CA (city) Orange County	81	0.06
Oakland, CA (city) Alameda County	79	0.02
Boston, MA (city) Suffolk County	78	0.01
Travilah, MD (cdp) Montgomery County	75	0.99
Austin, TX (city) Travis County	73	0.01
Arlington, VA (cdp) Arlington County	71	0.04
Las Vegas, NV (city) Clark County	71	0.01
Berkeley, CA (city) Alameda County	68	0.07
Portland, OR (city) Multnomah County	66	0.01
Mountain View, CA (city) Santa Clara County	65	0.09
Washington, DC (city) District of Columbia	63	0.01
Chicago, IL (city) Cook County	62	0.00
Menlo Park, CA (city) San Mateo County	59	0.19
Fort Lauderdale, FL (city) Broward County	59	0.04
Huntington Beach, CA (city) Orange County	59	0.03
Davis, CA (city) Yolo County	58	0.10
Scottsdale, AZ (city) Maricopa County	57	0.03
Dallas, TX (city) Dallas County	57	0.00
Dover, MA (town) Norfolk County	56	1.01
Levittown, NY (cdp) Nassau County	56	0.11
Arlington, TX (city) Tarrant County	56	0.02
Plano, TX (city) Collin County	55	0.02
Aztec, NM (city) San Juan County	54	0.82
Castro Valley, CA (cdp) Alameda County	53	0.09
Pittsburgh, PA (city) Allegheny County	53	0.02
Sacramento, CA (city) Sacramento County	53	0.01
Leesburg, VA (town) Loudoun County	52	0.18
New Haven, CT (city) New Haven County	52	0.04
Fort Worth, TX (city) Tarrant County	52	0.01
Walnut Creek, CA (city) Contra Costa County	51	0.08
Orem, UT (city) Utah County	51	0.06
Honolulu, HI (cdp) Honolulu County	50	0.01
Fair Lawn, NJ (borough) Bergen County	48	0.15
Palm Coast, FL (city) Flagler County	48	0.14
Tucson, AZ (city) Pima County	48	0.01
Cary, NC (town) Wake County	47	0.05
Fresno, CA (city) Fresno County	47	0.01
Manteca, CA (city) San Joaquin County	45	0.09
Long Beach, CA (city) Los Angeles County	45	0.01
Tulsa, OK (city) Tulsa County	45	0.01
Alpine, UT (city) Utah County	44	0.60
Encinitas, CA (city) San Diego County	44	0.08
Naperville, IL (city) Du Page County	44	0.03
Saint Petersburg, FL (city) Pinellas County	43	0.02
Philadelphia, PA (city) Philadelphia County	43	0.00
Petaluma, CA (city) Sonoma County	42	0.08
San Marcos, CA (city) San Diego County	42	0.08
Durham, NC (city) Durham County	42	0.02
Stockton, CA (city) San Joaquin County	42	0.02
Anaheim, CA (city) Orange County	42	0.01
Lower Merion, PA (township) Montgomery County	41	0.07
Champlin, MN (city) Hennepin County	40	0.18
Saratoga, CA (city) Santa Clara County	40	0.13
Yorba Linda, CA (city) Orange County	40	0.07
Anchorage, AK (municipality) Anchorage Borough	40	0.02
Oakville, MO (cdp) Saint Louis County	39	0.11
Kirkland, WA (city) King County	39	0.09
Layton, UT (city) Davis County	39	0.07
Bellingham, WA (city) Whatcom County	39	0.06
Glendale, CA (city) Los Angeles County	39	0.02
San Antonio, TX (city) Bexar County	39	0.00
San Rafael, CA (city) Marin County	38	0.07
Southampton, NY (town) Suffolk County	37	0.07
Sandy, UT (city) Salt Lake County	37	0.04
Mapleton, UT (city) Utah County	36	0.61
Pleasant Hill, CA (city) Contra Costa County	36	0.11
Tracy, CA (city) San Joaquin County	35	0.06
Wilmington, NC (city) New Hanover County	35	0.05
Huntsville, AL (city) Madison County	35	0.02
Salt Lake City, UT (city) Salt Lake County	35	0.02
Molalla, OR (city) Clackamas County	34	0.61
San Anselmo, CA (town) Marin County	34	0.27
Hampden, PA (township) Cumberland County	34	0.14
Manhattan, KS (city) Riley County	34	0.08
Ogden, UT (city) Weber County	34	0.04
Laie, HI (cdp) Honolulu County	33	0.72
Bend, OR (city) Deschutes County	33	0.06
Beaverton, OR (city) Washington County	33	0.04
High Point, NC (city) Guilford County	33	0.04
Costa Mesa, CA (city) Orange County	33	0.03
Vancouver, WA (city) Clark County	32	0.02
Santa Ana, CA (city) Orange County	32	0.01
Des Peres, MO (city) Saint Louis County	31	0.35
Jenks, OK (city) Tulsa County	31	0.33
McLean, VA (cdp) Fairfax County	31	0.08
Rancho Palos Verdes, CA (city) Los Angeles County	31	0.08
Bellevue, WA (city) King County	31	0.03
Escondido, CA (city) San Diego County	31	0.02
Savannah, GA (city) Chatham County	31	0.02
Oklahoma City, OK (city) Oklahoma County	31	0.01
Saint Paul, MN (city) Ramsey County	31	0.01
Jacksonville, FL (special city) Duval County	31	0.00
Killingworth, CT (town) Middlesex County	30	0.50
New Providence, NJ (borough) Union County	30	0.25
Cottonwood West, UT (cdp) Salt Lake County	30	0.16
Oakton, VA (cdp) Fairfax County	30	0.10
San Juan Capistrano, CA (city) Orange County	30	0.09
Streamwood, IL (village) Cook County	30	0.08
Somerville, MA (city) Middlesex County	30	0.04
Aurora, IL (city) Kane County	30	0.02
Salem, OR (city) Marion County	30	0.02
Avon, CT (town) Hartford County	29	0.18
Big Spring, TX (city) Howard County	29	0.11
East Palo Alto, CA (city) San Mateo County	29	0.10
Minnetonka, MN (city) Hennepin County	29	0.06
Rapid City, SD (city) Pennington County	29	0.05
El Cajon, CA (city) San Diego County	29	0.03
Eldorado at Santa Fe, NM (cdp) Santa Fe County	28	0.49
Wolf Trap, VA (cdp) Fairfax County	28	0.20
Westminster, CA (city) Orange County	28	0.03
Lubbock, TX (city) Lubbock County	28	0.01
Riverside, CA (city) Riverside County	28	0.01
Spokane, WA (city) Spokane County	28	0.01
Cornville, AZ (cdp) Yavapai County	27	0.76
Bothell, WA (city) King County	27	0.09
Hopkinsville, KY (city) Christian County	27	0.09
Yorktown, NY (town) Westchester County	27	0.07
San Buenaventura, CA (city) Ventura County	27	0.03
Toledo, OH (city) Lucas County	27	0.01
Southampton, NY (village) Suffolk County	26	0.66
McCook, NE (city) Red Willow County	26	0.33
Malibu, CA (city) Los Angeles County	26	0.21
South Hill, WA (cdp) Pierce County	26	0.08
Pasadena, CA (city) Los Angeles County	26	0.02
West Valley City, UT (city) Salt Lake County	26	0.02
Madison, WI (city) Dane County	26	0.01
Modesto, CA (city) Stanislaus County	26	0.01
Charlotte, NC (city) Mecklenburg County	26	0.00
Upper Freehold, NJ (township) Monmouth County	25	0.58
Laconia, NH (city) Belknap County	25	0.15
Aiken, SC (city) Aiken County	25	0.10
Livermore, CA (city) Alameda County	25	0.03
Redwood City, CA (city) San Mateo County	25	0.03
Cambridge, MA (city) Middlesex County	25	0.02
Orange, CA (city) Orange County	25	0.02
Santa Clarita, CA (city) Los Angeles County	25	0.02
Sulphur, OK (city) Murray County	24	0.50

Notes: (cdp) census designated place; Refer to the Explanation of Data in the front of the book for more detailed information.

New Zealander

Top 150 Places Sorted by Percent

(Based on all places, regardless of population)

Place	Number	%
Tulsita, TX (cdp) Bee County	4	16.00
Varina, IA (city) Pocahontas County	6	5.77
Gosnold, MA (town) Dukes County	3	3.70
Atqasuk, AK (city) North Slope Borough	5	2.46
Sagaponack, NY (cdp) Suffolk County	11	2.03
Chokoloskee, FL (cdp) Collier County	8	1.55
San Geronimo, CA (cdp) Marin County	6	1.55
Chinese Camp, CA (cdp) Tuolumne County	2	1.42
Skandia, MN (township) Murray County	2	1.35
Condon, OR (city) Gilliam County	10	1.28
Alma, CO (town) Park County	2	1.23
Echo, MN (city) Yellow Medicine County	3	1.18
Geraldine, MT (town) Chouteau County	3	1.02
Dover, MA (town) Norfolk County	56	1.01
Poipu, HI (cdp) Kauai County	11	1.01
Travilah, MD (cdp) Montgomery County	75	0.99
Pine Mountain Club, CA (cdp) Kern County	16	0.96
Punaluu, HI (cdp) Honolulu County	8	0.95
Snoqualmie Pass, WA (cdp) Kittitas County	2	0.94
Hancock, NH (town) Hillsborough County	16	0.92
Ore City, TX (city) Upshur County	10	0.88
Oakley, UT (city) Summit County	8	0.84
Darnen, MN (township) Stevens County	3	0.83
Aztec, NM (city) San Juan County	54	0.82
Northeast Ithaca, NY (cdp) Tompkins County	22	0.81
Morrill, ME (town) Waldo County	6	0.78
Anchorage, KY (city) Jefferson County	17	0.77
Cornville, AZ (cdp) Yavapai County	27	0.76
Dalton Gardens, ID (city) Kootenai County	17	0.75
Stark, NH (town) Coos County	4	0.75
Laie, HI (cdp) Honolulu County	33	0.72
Frisco, CO (town) Summit County	17	0.72
Arcadia, MO (city) Iron County	4	0.69
Deep River Center, CT (cdp) Middlesex County	16	0.67
Southampton, NY (village) Suffolk County	26	0.66
Sterling, CT (town) Windham County	20	0.65
Cherry, MN (township) Saint Louis County	6	0.65
Leilani Estates, HI (cdp) Hawaii County	6	0.65
Newport Coast, CA (cdp) Orange County	17	0.64
Elsah, IL (village) Jersey County	4	0.64
Menomonie, WI (city) Dunn County	95	0.63
Point Arena, CA (city) Mendocino County	3	0.62
Mapleton, UT (city) Utah County	36	0.61
Molalla, OR (city) Clackamas County	34	0.61
Alpine, UT (city) Utah County	44	0.60
Hedwig Village, TX (city) Harris County	14	0.60
Lewisville, ID (city) Jefferson County	3	0.59
Upper Freehold, NJ (township) Monmouth County	25	0.58
Temelec, CA (cdp) Sonoma County	8	0.55
Dorchester, NH (town) Grafton County	2	0.55
Driggs, ID (city) Teton County	6	0.53
South Woodstock, CT (cdp) Windham County	6	0.53
Houserville, PA (cdp) Centre County	9	0.52
Keystone, CO (cdp) Summit County	4	0.52
Killingworth, CT (town) Middlesex County	30	0.50
Sulphur, OK (city) Murray County	24	0.50
Cross Plains, WI (town) Dane County	7	0.50
Eldorado at Santa Fe, NM (cdp) Santa Fe County	28	0.49
Dunbar, WI (town) Marinette County	6	0.49
White, PA (township) Cambria County	4	0.48
Blanca, CO (town) Costilla County	2	0.48
Aurelius, MI (township) Ingham County	15	0.45
Borrego Springs, CA (cdp) San Diego County	11	0.43
North Snyderville Basin, UT (cdp) Summit County	8	0.43
Nassau, NY (town) Rensselaer County	20	0.42
Canaan, NH (town) Grafton County	14	0.42
Hudson Bend, TX (cdp) Travis County	10	0.42
Linden, IN (town) Montgomery County	3	0.42
South Deerfield, MA (cdp) Franklin County	8	0.41
University Park, NM (cdp) Dona Ana County	11	0.40
Stanhope, IA (city) Hamilton County	2	0.40
Warm Beach, WA (cdp) Snohomish County	8	0.39
Avon, IN (town) Hendricks County	22	0.38
Manheim, PA (township) York County	12	0.38
Mountain View, CA (cdp) Contra Costa County	9	0.38

Place	Number	%
Dollar Point, CA (cdp) Placer County	6	0.38
Hillandale, MD (cdp) Montgomery County	11	0.37
Strawberry, AR (town) Lawrence County	1	0.37
Esperance, WA (cdp) Snohomish County	13	0.36
Clinton, NY (village) Oneida County	7	0.36
Des Peres, MO (city) Saint Louis County	31	0.35
Boyes Hot Springs, CA (cdp) Sonoma County	22	0.35
Deep River, CT (town) Middlesex County	16	0.35
Wilkinson Heights, SC (cdp) Orangeburg County	10	0.35
Swansboro, NC (town) Onslow County	5	0.35
Ester, AK (cdp) Fairbanks North Star Borough	6	0.34
Jenks, OK (city) Tulsa County	31	0.33
McCook, NE (city) Red Willow County	26	0.33
Surfside, FL (town) Miami-Dade County	17	0.33
Glendale, CO (city) Arapahoe County	15	0.33
Lincoln Beach, OR (cdp) Lincoln County	7	0.33
Franklin, GA (city) Heard County	3	0.33
Waddington, NY (village) Saint Lawrence County	3	0.33
Mira Monte, CA (cdp) Ventura County	22	0.32
Hidden Hills, CA (city) Los Angeles County	6	0.32
Chapman, KS (city) Dickinson County	4	0.32
Grove City, MN (city) Meeker County	2	0.32
Minnetonka Beach, MN (city) Hennepin County	2	0.32
Lower Alsace, PA (township) Berks County	14	0.31
Lexington, IL (city) McLean County	6	0.31
Rosalia, WA (town) Whitman County	2	0.31
Winter Park, CO (town) Grand County	2	0.31
Nokomis, FL (cdp) Sarasota County	10	0.30
Shamrock, TX (city) Wheeler County	6	0.30
Eagle Butte, SD (city) Dewey County	2	0.30
Woodside, CA (town) San Mateo County	15	0.29
Sherborn, MA (town) Middlesex County	12	0.29
Rochester, MN (township) Olmsted County	9	0.29
Guilford, VT (town) Windham County	6	0.29
Woodstock, VT (town) Windsor County	9	0.28
Bloomfield, PA (borough) Perry County	3	0.28
Scobey, MT (city) Daniels County	3	0.28
Waikane, HI (cdp) Honolulu County	2	0.28
San Anselmo, CA (town) Marin County	34	0.27
Biscayne Park, FL (village) Miami-Dade County	9	0.27
Farmington, IL (city) Fulton County	7	0.27
Medary, WI (town) La Crosse County	4	0.27
Indian Hills, CO (cdp) Jefferson County	3	0.27
Edgewood, WA (city) Pierce County	24	0.26
Portola Valley, CA (town) San Mateo County	12	0.26
Meeme, WI (town) Manitowoc County	4	0.26
Grafton, NH (town) Grafton County	3	0.26
Mount Pleasant, SC (town) Charleston County	120	0.25
New Providence, NJ (borough) Union County	30	0.25
Fairfield, IA (city) Jefferson County	24	0.25
Oxford, ME (town) Oxford County	10	0.25
New Albany, OH (village) Franklin County	9	0.25
Mayo, MD (cdp) Anne Arundel County	8	0.25
Lake Success, NY (village) Nassau County	7	0.25
Blaine, ME (town) Aroostook County	2	0.25
Hardin, TX (city) Liberty County	2	0.25
Treasure Island, FL (city) Pinellas County	18	0.24
White Oak, TX (city) Gregg County	13	0.24
Hadley, MI (township) Lapeer County	11	0.24
West Tisbury, MA (town) Dukes County	6	0.24
Dighton, KS (city) Lane County	3	0.24
Wailua Homesteads, HI (cdp) Kauai County	10	0.23
Becket, MA (town) Berkshire County	4	0.23
Vail, CO (town) Eagle County	10	0.22
South Weber, UT (city) Davis County	9	0.22
Conway, MI (township) Livingston County	6	0.22
Dennison, PA (township) Luzerne County	2	0.22
Malibu, CA (city) Los Angeles County	26	0.21
California, MD (cdp) Saint Mary's County	20	0.21
Oak View, CA (cdp) Ventura County	9	0.21
Lauderdale, MN (city) Ramsey County	5	0.21
Langdon Place, KY (city) Jefferson County	2	0.21
Wolf Trap, VA (cdp) Fairfax County	28	0.20
Rendon, TX (cdp) Tarrant County	18	0.20
Mammoth Lakes, CA (town) Mono County	14	0.20

Notes: (cdp) census designated place; Refer to the Explanation of Data in the front of the book for more detailed information.

New Zealander

Top 150 Places Sorted by Percent

(Based on places with populations of 10,000 or more)

Place	Number	%
Menomonie, WI (city) Dunn County	95	0.63
San Anselmo, CA (town) Marin County	34	0.27
Mount Pleasant, SC (town) Charleston County	120	0.25
New Providence, NJ (borough) Union County	30	0.25
Malibu, CA (city) Los Angeles County	26	0.21
Wolf Trap, VA (cdp) Fairfax County	28	0.20
Menlo Park, CA (city) San Mateo County	59	0.19
Canyon Rim, UT (cdp) Salt Lake County	20	0.19
Leesburg, VA (town) Loudoun County	52	0.18
Champlin, MN (city) Hennepin County	40	0.18
Avon, CT (town) Hartford County	29	0.18
Five Corners, WA (cdp) Clark County	22	0.18
Texas, MI (township) Kalamazoo County	20	0.18
Upper, NJ (township) Cape May County	21	0.17
Cottonwood West, UT (cdp) Salt Lake County	30	0.16
Winfield, KS (city) Cowley County	20	0.16
Guttenberg, NJ (town) Hudson County	17	0.16
Lincoln, CA (city) Placer County	17	0.16
Fair Lawn, NJ (borough) Bergen County	48	0.15
Laconia, NH (city) Belknap County	25	0.15
Healdsburg, CA (city) Sonoma County	16	0.15
Plover, WI (village) Portage County	16	0.15
Palm Coast, FL (city) Flagler County	48	0.14
Hampden, PA (township) Cumberland County	34	0.14
Saratoga, CA (city) Santa Clara County	40	0.13
Ramsey, NJ (borough) Bergen County	19	0.13
Rye, NY (city) Westchester County	19	0.13
Canby, OR (city) Clackamas County	17	0.13
Ithaca, NY (town) Tompkins County	22	0.12
El Segundo, CA (city) Los Angeles County	19	0.12
Belchertown, MA (town) Hampshire County	15	0.12
Gardnerville Ranchos, NV (cdp) Douglas County	13	0.12
Levittown, NY (cdp) Nassau County	56	0.11
Oakville, MO (cdp) Saint Louis County	39	0.11
Pleasant Hill, CA (city) Contra Costa County	36	0.11
Big Spring, TX (city) Howard County	29	0.11
Calabasas, CA (city) Los Angeles County	23	0.11
New Castle, NY (town) Westchester County	19	0.11
Windham, NH (town) Rockingham County	12	0.11
Davis, CA (city) Yolo County	58	0.10
Oakton, VA (cdp) Fairfax County	30	0.10
East Palo Alto, CA (city) San Mateo County	29	0.10
Aiken, SC (city) Aiken County	25	0.10
Magna, UT (cdp) Salt Lake County	22	0.10
Americus, GA (city) Sumter County	16	0.10
Lutherville-Timonium, MD (cdp) Baltimore County	16	0.10
Pacific Grove, CA (city) Monterey County	16	0.10
Granby, CT (town) Hartford County	10	0.10
Mountain View, CA (city) Santa Clara County	65	0.09
Castro Valley, CA (cdp) Alameda County	53	0.09
Manteca, CA (city) San Joaquin County	45	0.09
Kirkland, WA (city) King County	39	0.09
San Juan Capistrano, CA (city) Orange County	30	0.09
Bothell, WA (city) King County	27	0.09
Hopkinsville, KY (city) Christian County	27	0.09
Spring Valley, CA (cdp) San Diego County	24	0.09
Lyndhurst, NJ (cdp) Bergen County	18	0.09
Bedford, NY (town) Westchester County	17	0.09
Rexburg, ID (city) Madison County	15	0.09
Lewiston, NY (town) Niagara County	14	0.09
Princeton, NJ (township) Mercer County	14	0.09
Durango, CO (city) La Plata County	13	0.09
Lebanon, NH (city) Grafton County	11	0.09
New Paltz, NY (town) Ulster County	11	0.09
Lakeland South, WA (cdp) King County	10	0.09
Wrentham, MA (town) Norfolk County	10	0.09
Weigelstown, PA (cdp) York County	9	0.09
Walnut Creek, CA (city) Contra Costa County	51	0.08
Encinitas, CA (city) San Diego County	44	0.08
Petaluma, CA (city) Sonoma County	42	0.08
San Marcos, CA (city) San Diego County	42	0.08
Manhattan, KS (city) Riley County	34	0.08
McLean, VA (cdp) Fairfax County	31	0.08
Rancho Palos Verdes, CA (city) Los Angeles County	31	0.08
Streamwood, IL (village) Cook County	30	0.08

Place	Number	%
South Hill, WA (cdp) Pierce County	26	0.08
Grayslake, IL (village) Lake County	14	0.08
New Kensington, PA (city) Westmoreland County	12	0.08
Carpinteria, CA (city) Santa Barbara County	11	0.08
Coto de Caza, CA (cdp) Orange County	11	0.08
Riverview, FL (cdp) Hillsborough County	10	0.08
Grass Valley, CA (city) Nevada County	9	0.08
Greentree, NJ (cdp) Camden County	9	0.08
Pompton Lakes, NJ (borough) Passaic County	9	0.08
Scotts Valley, CA (city) Santa Cruz County	9	0.08
Weston, CT (town) Fairfield County	8	0.08
Little Rock, AR (city) Pulaski County	133	0.07
Berkeley, CA (city) Alameda County	68	0.07
Lower Merion, PA (township) Montgomery County	41	0.07
Yorba Linda, CA (city) Orange County	40	0.07
Layton, UT (city) Davis County	39	0.07
San Rafael, CA (city) Marin County	38	0.07
Southampton, NY (town) Suffolk County	37	0.07
Yorktown, NY (town) Westchester County	27	0.07
Fairbanks, AK (city) Fairbanks North Star Borough	20	0.07
Upper Dublin, PA (township) Montgomery County	17	0.07
Hudson, NH (town) Hillsborough County	15	0.07
La Canada Flintridge, CA (city) Los Angeles County	14	0.07
Loma Linda, CA (city) San Bernardino County	13	0.07
Manor, PA (township) Lancaster County	11	0.07
Port Washington, NY (cdp) Nassau County	10	0.07
Storrs, CT (cdp) Tolland County	8	0.07
Kirkland, NY (town) Oneida County	7	0.07
Irvine, CA (city) Orange County	81	0.06
Orem, UT (city) Utah County	51	0.06
Bellingham, WA (city) Whatcom County	39	0.06
Tracy, CA (city) San Joaquin County	35	0.06
Bend, OR (city) Deschutes County	33	0.06
Minnetonka, MN (city) Hennepin County	29	0.06
Brookfield, WI (city) Waukesha County	23	0.06
Kailua, HI (cdp) Honolulu County	23	0.06
Fort Lee, NJ (borough) Bergen County	21	0.06
Stanton, CA (city) Orange County	21	0.06
Newport, RI (city) Newport County	16	0.06
Pullman, WA (city) Whitman County	16	0.06
Morgantown, WV (city) Monongalia County	15	0.06
Laguna Beach, CA (city) Orange County	14	0.06
Prairie Village, KS (city) Johnson County	14	0.06
South Salt Lake, UT (city) Salt Lake County	14	0.06
Oak Harbor, WA (city) Island County	11	0.06
Bella Vista, AR (cdp) Benton County	10	0.06
Lorton, VA (cdp) Fairfax County	10	0.06
Post Falls, ID (city) Kootenai County	10	0.06
South Hadley, MA (town) Hampshire County	10	0.06
Dublin, GA (city) Laurens County	9	0.06
Lancaster, PA (township) Lancaster County	9	0.06
Central Point, OR (city) Jackson County	8	0.06
Stanford, CA (cdp) Santa Clara County	8	0.06
Lancaster, NY (village) Erie County	7	0.06
Newton, NC (city) Catawba County	7	0.06
Pelham, NY (town) Westchester County	7	0.06
Saint Augustine, FL (city) Saint Johns County	7	0.06
Oquirrh, UT (cdp) Salt Lake County	6	0.06
Richfield, WI (town) Washington County	6	0.06
Cary, NC (town) Wake County	47	0.05
Wilmington, NC (city) New Hanover County	35	0.05
Rapid City, SD (city) Pennington County	29	0.05
Fond du Lac, WI (city) Fond du Lac County	21	0.05
Hoboken, NJ (city) Hudson County	19	0.05
Seattle Hill-Silver Firs, WA (cdp) Snohomish County	18	0.05
Monterey, CA (city) Monterey County	16	0.05
Randallstown, MD (cdp) Baltimore County	16	0.05
University Place, WA (city) Pierce County	15	0.05
Vestal, NY (town) Broome County	14	0.05
Atwater, CA (city) Merced County	12	0.05
Key West, FL (city) Monroe County	12	0.05
Lemon Grove, CA (city) San Diego County	12	0.05
Belton, MO (city) Cass County	11	0.05
Pleasant Grove, UT (city) Utah County	11	0.05
Tarpon Springs, FL (city) Pinellas County	11	0.05

Notes: (cdp) census designated place; Refer to the Explanation of Data in the front of the book for more detailed information.

Northern European

Top 150 Places Sorted by Number

(Based on all places, regardless of population)

Place	Number	%
Seattle, WA (city) King County	2,597	0.46
New York, NY (city) New York City	1,917	0.02
San Diego, CA (city) San Diego County	1,571	0.13
Portland, OR (city) Multnomah County	1,466	0.28
Los Angeles, CA (city) Los Angeles County	1,389	0.04
San Francisco, CA (city) San Francisco County	1,033	0.13
San Jose, CA (city) Santa Clara County	859	0.10
Minneapolis, MN (city) Hennepin County	843	0.22
Austin, TX (city) Travis County	823	0.13
Chicago, IL (city) Cook County	783	0.03
Denver, CO (city) Denver County	667	0.12
Eugene, OR (city) Lane County	626	0.45
Phoenix, AZ (city) Maricopa County	584	0.04
Houston, TX (city) Harris County	582	0.03
Oakland, CA (city) Alameda County	560	0.14
Dallas, TX (city) Dallas County	559	0.05
Sacramento, CA (city) Sacramento County	550	0.14
Saint Paul, MN (city) Ramsey County	528	0.18
Mesa, AZ (city) Maricopa County	496	0.12
San Antonio, TX (city) Bexar County	492	0.04
Colorado Springs, CO (city) El Paso County	467	0.13
Salt Lake City, UT (city) Salt Lake County	457	0.25
Arlington, VA (cdp) Arlington County	431	0.23
Anchorage, AK (municipality) Anchorage Borough	426	0.16
Kansas City, MO (city) Jackson County	423	0.10
Indianapolis, IN (special city) Marion County	422	0.05
Washington, DC (city) District of Columbia	420	0.07
Bellevue, WA (city) King County	412	0.38
Boston, MA (city) Suffolk County	406	0.07
Philadelphia, PA (city) Philadelphia County	392	0.03
Santa Rosa, CA (city) Sonoma County	378	0.26
Madison, WI (city) Dane County	367	0.18
Albuquerque, NM (city) Bernalillo County	364	0.08
Charlotte, NC (city) Mecklenburg County	360	0.07
Vancouver, WA (city) Clark County	359	0.25
Cambridge, MA (city) Middlesex County	348	0.34
Hillsboro, OR (city) Washington County	337	0.48
Boulder, CO (city) Boulder County	333	0.35
Tacoma, WA (city) Pierce County	331	0.17
Boise City, ID (city) Ada County	330	0.18
Tucson, AZ (city) Pima County	327	0.07
Berkeley, CA (city) Alameda County	299	0.29
Ann Arbor, MI (city) Washtenaw County	297	0.26
Reno, NV (city) Washoe County	296	0.16
Columbus, OH (city) Franklin County	293	0.04
Spokane, WA (city) Spokane County	287	0.15
Davis, CA (city) Yolo County	269	0.45
Fort Collins, CO (city) Larimer County	265	0.22
Atlanta, GA (city) Fulton County	265	0.06
Walnut Creek, CA (city) Contra Costa County	263	0.41
Beaverton, OR (city) Washington County	256	0.34
Eagan, MN (city) Dakota County	255	0.40
Sunnyvale, CA (city) Santa Clara County	245	0.19
Santa Cruz, CA (city) Santa Cruz County	244	0.45
Provo, UT (city) Utah County	243	0.23
Huntington Beach, CA (city) Orange County	239	0.13
Saint Louis, MO (independent city) Saint Louis city	235	0.07
Fresno, CA (city) Fresno County	227	0.05
Grand Rapids, MI (city) Kent County	223	0.11
Fort Worth, TX (city) Tarrant County	223	0.04
Oklahoma City, OK (city) Oklahoma County	222	0.04
Tulsa, OK (city) Tulsa County	219	0.06
Nashville-Davidson, TN (special city) Davidson County	219	0.04
Omaha, NE (city) Douglas County	218	0.06
Concord, CA (city) Contra Costa County	217	0.18
Alexandria, VA (independent city) Alexandria city	217	0.17
University Place, WA (city) Pierce County	214	0.71
Salem, OR (city) Marion County	213	0.16
Bellingham, WA (city) Whatcom County	206	0.31
Everett, WA (city) Snohomish County	206	0.23
Long Beach, CA (city) Los Angeles County	206	0.04
Corvallis, OR (city) Benton County	204	0.41
Highlands Ranch, CO (cdp) Douglas County	202	0.29
Lakewood, CO (city) Jefferson County	202	0.14
Overland Park, KS (city) Johnson County	201	0.14

Place	Number	%
Wichita, KS (city) Sedgwick County	200	0.06
Apple Valley, MN (city) Dakota County	198	0.43
Raleigh, NC (city) Wake County	198	0.07
Edina, MN (city) Hennepin County	197	0.41
Aurora, CO (city) Arapahoe County	193	0.07
Tigard, OR (city) Washington County	190	0.46
Durham, NC (city) Durham County	190	0.10
Pasadena, CA (city) Los Angeles County	189	0.14
Jacksonville, FL (special city) Duval County	188	0.03
Lansing, MI (city) Ingham County	187	0.16
Roseville, CA (city) Placer County	185	0.23
Los Gatos, CA (town) Santa Clara County	184	0.64
Santa Fe, NM (city) Santa Fe County	184	0.30
Novato, CA (city) Marin County	182	0.38
Lake Oswego, OR (city) Clackamas County	181	0.51
Mercer Island, WA (city) King County	178	0.81
Palo Alto, CA (city) Santa Clara County	178	0.30
Bloomington, MN (city) Hennepin County	178	0.21
Fremont, CA (city) Alameda County	177	0.09
Kirkland, WA (city) King County	176	0.39
Annandale, VA (cdp) Fairfax County	172	0.31
Scottsdale, AZ (city) Maricopa County	172	0.08
Iowa City, IA (city) Johnson County	171	0.27
Rochester, MN (city) Olmsted County	171	0.20
Torrance, CA (city) Los Angeles County	171	0.12
Bethesda, MD (cdp) Montgomery County	170	0.31
Riverside, CA (city) Riverside County	170	0.07
Henderson, NV (city) Clark County	169	0.10
Des Moines, IA (city) Polk County	169	0.09
Lincoln, NE (city) Lancaster County	169	0.07
Edmonds, WA (city) Snohomish County	168	0.42
McKinleyville, CA (cdp) Humboldt County	167	1.23
Cincinnati, OH (city) Hamilton County	167	0.05
Petaluma, CA (city) Sonoma County	164	0.30
San Buenaventura, CA (city) Ventura County	164	0.16
Bothell, WA (city) King County	162	0.54
Santa Clarita, CA (city) Los Angeles County	162	0.11
Montgomery, AL (city) Montgomery County	161	0.08
Cottage Lake, WA (cdp) King County	160	0.66
Sunrise Manor, NV (cdp) Clark County	159	0.10
Modesto, CA (city) Stanislaus County	158	0.08
Livermore, CA (city) Alameda County	156	0.21
New Orleans, LA (city) Orleans Parish	156	0.03
Hempstead, NY (town) Nassau County	156	0.02
Pleasanton, CA (city) Alameda County	155	0.24
Sandy Springs, GA (cdp) Fulton County	154	0.18
Claremont, CA (city) Los Angeles County	153	0.45
Shoreline, WA (city) King County	152	0.29
Layton, UT (city) Davis County	152	0.26
Mission Viejo, CA (city) Orange County	151	0.16
Federal Way, WA (city) King County	150	0.18
Winters, CA (city) Yolo County	149	2.44
Richmond, VA (independent city) Richmond city	149	0.08
Arden-Arcade, CA (cdp) Sacramento County	148	0.15
Coppell, TX (city) Dallas County	147	0.41
Turlock, CA (city) Stanislaus County	147	0.26
Menlo Park, CA (city) San Mateo County	145	0.47
Oceanside, CA (city) San Diego County	145	0.09
Olathe, KS (city) Johnson County	144	0.15
Baltimore, MD (independent city) Baltimore city	144	0.02
Glendale, CA (city) Los Angeles County	142	0.07
Louisville, KY (city) Jefferson County	142	0.06
Stockton, CA (city) San Joaquin County	142	0.06
McLean, VA (cdp) Fairfax County	141	0.36
Ames, IA (city) Story County	141	0.28
San Rafael, CA (city) Marin County	141	0.25
Newport Beach, CA (city) Orange County	141	0.20
Bainbridge Island, WA (city) Kitsap County	140	0.69
El Cajon, CA (city) San Diego County	140	0.15
Thousand Oaks, CA (city) Ventura County	140	0.12
Cupertino, CA (city) Santa Clara County	139	0.27
Kent, WA (city) King County	139	0.18
Redmond, WA (city) King County	138	0.30
Norman, OK (city) Cleveland County	138	0.14
Darien, CT (cdp) Fairfield County	137	0.70

Notes: (cdp) census designated place; Refer to the Explanation of Data in the front of the book for more detailed information.

Northern European

Top 150 Places Sorted by Percent

(Based on all places, regardless of population)

Place	Number	%
Long Island, KS (city) Phillips County	31	20.39
La Porte, CA (cdp) Plumas County	8	20.00
Hegne, MN (township) Norman County	6	12.24
Cundiyo, NM (cdp) Santa Fe County	13	10.83
Scarville, IA (city) Winnebago County	11	10.78
Maryhill, WA (cdp) Klickitat County	9	10.59
Shiloh, NJ (borough) Cumberland County	51	9.51
Metaline Falls, WA (town) Pend Oreille County	18	9.05
Deming, WA (cdp) Whatcom County	16	8.84
Crystal Lakes, MO (city) Ray County	36	8.53
Willow Valley, AZ (cdp) Mohave County	44	7.96
Monhegan, ME (plantation) Lincoln County	6	7.59
Eschbach, WA (cdp) Yakima County	32	7.55
Shelocta, PA (borough) Indiana County	9	7.09
Edison, WA (cdp) Skagit County	10	7.04
Holt, MN (township) Marshall County	10	6.71
Springport, IN (town) Henry County	10	6.37
Homestead, MO (village) Ray County	14	6.22
Amo, MN (township) Cottonwood County	8	5.56
Pleasant Valley, AK (cdp) Fairbanks North Star Borough	32	5.33
Patterson, IA (city) Madison County	7	5.07
Franklin, ID (city) Franklin County	30	4.97
Tonsina, AK (cdp) Valdez-Cordova Census Area	5	4.81
Hampden Sydney, VA (cdp) Prince Edward County	58	4.70
Kevin, MT (town) Toole County	7	4.64
Metaline, WA (town) Pend Oreille County	8	4.47
White Earth, ND (city) Mountrail County	2	4.44
Portage, UT (town) Box Elder County	11	4.35
Julian, NE (village) Nemaha County	3	4.23
Altamont, UT (town) Duchesne County	8	4.21
Meadow Valley, CA (cdp) Plumas County	23	4.04
Steamboat River, MN (township) Hubbard County	5	4.00
Muir Beach, CA (cdp) Marin County	11	3.99
Ottosen, IA (city) Humboldt County	2	3.77
Underwood, MN (township) Redwood County	8	3.76
Winona, KS (city) Logan County	9	3.75
McDonaldsville, MN (township) Norman County	7	3.68
Wharton, PA (township) Potter County	4	3.67
Blacksville, WV (town) Monongalia County	6	3.61
Trent, TX (town) Taylor County	11	3.58
Belle Rive, IL (village) Jefferson County	13	3.46
Clay Banks, WI (town) Door County	13	3.40
Ward, PA (township) Tioga County	5	3.40
Barronett, WI (town) Washburn County	13	3.23
Iroquois, IL (village) Iroquois County	6	3.23
Cabot, VT (village) Washington County	8	3.21
Pine Springs, MN (city) Washington County	12	3.08
Koosharem, UT (town) Sevier County	8	3.08
New Suffolk, NY (cdp) Suffolk County	10	3.07
Riverside, WY (town) Carbon County	2	3.03
Cabin John, MD (cdp) Montgomery County	51	3.02
Wild Rice, MN (township) Norman County	10	3.02
Dunkirk, MD (cdp) Calvert County	70	2.99
Union, IL (village) McHenry County	17	2.93
Port Alexander, AK (city) Wrangell-Petersburg Census Area	2	2.86
Fall River Mills, CA (cdp) Shasta County	19	2.73
Eaton, NH (town) Carroll County	8	2.70
Lostine, OR (city) Wallowa County	7	2.70
Sweet, MN (township) Pipestone County	12	2.69
Crooked Creek, MN (township) Houston County	8	2.61
Cross Roads, PA (borough) York County	14	2.59
Springdale, MN (township) Redwood County	5	2.58
Nichols, IA (city) Muscatine County	9	2.54
Fairbanks, MN (township) Saint Louis County	2	2.53
Cobb, WI (village) Iowa County	12	2.51
Amador City, CA (city) Amador County	5	2.49
New Trier, MN (city) Dakota County	3	2.46
Wells River, VT (village) Orange County	8	2.45
Winters, CA (city) Yolo County	149	2.44
South Solon, OH (village) Madison County	10	2.43
Marengo, WI (town) Ashland County	9	2.42
Fulshear, TX (city) Fort Bend County	17	2.41
Loghill Village, CO (cdp) Ouray County	7	2.33
Clarkston, UT (town) Cache County	16	2.31
Plum Grove, TX (city) Liberty County	20	2.30
Union, WI (town) Burnett County	8	2.30
North Snyderville Basin, UT (cdp) Summit County	43	2.29
Chignik, AK (city) Lake and Peninsula Borough	2	2.25
Newfane, VT (village) Windham County	3	2.24
Haverhill, MN (township) Olmsted County	36	2.21
Galena, AK (city) Yukon-Koyukuk Census Area	15	2.21
Sheldon, MN (township) Houston County	7	2.15
Wilder, MN (city) Jackson County	2	2.15
Fayetteville, TX (city) Fayette County	6	2.14
Riverdale, IA (city) Scott County	13	2.09
Gladstone, MI (city) Delta County	104	2.06
Lund, MN (township) Douglas County	8	2.04
Allenspark, CO (cdp) Boulder County	10	2.03
Swink, OK (town) Choctaw County	2	2.00
Lakeview, WA (cdp) Grant County	15	1.99
Malcom, IA (city) Poweshiek County	7	1.96
Mendota, MN (city) Dakota County	3	1.95
Maple Plain, WI (town) Barron County	17	1.94
Sergeant, PA (township) McKean County	4	1.93
Terrebonne, OR (cdp) Deschutes County	30	1.91
Greenwood, PA (township) Clearfield County	8	1.89
Victor, MT (cdp) Ravalli County	14	1.88
McIntosh, FL (town) Marion County	8	1.86
Basin, MT (cdp) Jefferson County	4	1.86
Gildford, MT (cdp) Hill County	3	1.84
Arctander, MN (township) Kandiyohi County	8	1.83
Wilsall, MT (cdp) Park County	4	1.83
Lizton, IN (town) Hendricks County	7	1.81
Blountville, TN (cdp) Sullivan County	54	1.79
Latham, IL (village) Logan County	7	1.79
Lawrence, MN (township) Grant County	2	1.79
Big Lake, WA (cdp) Skagit County	24	1.76
Cambridge, KS (city) Cowley County	2	1.75
Roosevelt, WI (town) Taylor County	7	1.74
Williams Creek, IN (town) Marion County	7	1.71
Gilby, ND (city) Grand Forks County	4	1.69
White Bird, ID (city) Idaho County	2	1.69
Meridian Hills, IN (town) Marion County	29	1.68
Primrose, WI (town) Dane County	11	1.68
Brandon, NY (town) Franklin County	9	1.68
Owens, MN (township) Saint Louis County	5	1.66
Todd Creek, CO (cdp) Adams County	22	1.65
Kingman, MN (township) Renville County	4	1.65
Corralitos, CA (cdp) Santa Cruz County	47	1.64
Superior, MT (town) Mineral County	15	1.62
Carmel Valley Village, CA (cdp) Monterey County	76	1.61
Pleasant Gap, PA (cdp) Centre County	28	1.60
Park Ridge, WI (village) Portage County	8	1.60
Fairbanks, MI (township) Delta County	5	1.58
Merkel, TX (town) Taylor County	40	1.57
Bell Center, WI (village) Crawford County	2	1.57
Mantua, UT (town) Box Elder County	12	1.56
Osakis, MN (township) Douglas County	9	1.56
Comstock, NE (village) Custer County	2	1.56
Perry, IL (village) Pike County	6	1.55
Hagerstown, IN (town) Wayne County	27	1.52
Arlington Heights, WA (cdp) Snohomish County	38	1.51
Parchment, MI (city) Kalamazoo County	29	1.50
Woodway, WA (city) Snohomish County	14	1.49
Karthaus, PA (township) Clearfield County	12	1.49
Ben Lomond, CA (cdp) Santa Cruz County	34	1.48
Park Lake, KY (city) Oldham County	8	1.48
Waterville, KS (city) Marshall County	10	1.47
Westfield, WI (town) Marquette County	10	1.47
Martin's Additions, MD (village) Montgomery County	13	1.46
Harrisburg, OH (village) Franklin County	5	1.45
Gas, KS (city) Allen County	8	1.44
McKinley Park, AK (cdp) Denali Census Area	2	1.44
Cambrian Park, CA (cdp) Santa Clara County	48	1.43
Sverdrup, MN (township) Otter Tail County	8	1.43
Gotebo, OK (town) Kiowa County	4	1.43
Indianola, WA (cdp) Kitsap County	43	1.42
Saint David, AZ (cdp) Cochise County	23	1.41
Glorieta, NM (cdp) Santa Fe County	10	1.41
Everglade, MN (township) Stevens County	2	1.41

Notes: (cdp) census designated place; Refer to the Explanation of Data in the front of the book for more detailed information.

Northern European

Top 150 Places Sorted by Percent

(Based on places with populations of 10,000 or more)

Place	Number	%
McKinleyville, CA (cdp) Humboldt County	167	1.23
Vashon, WA (cdp) King County	99	0.98
Monroe, WA (city) Snohomish County	119	0.88
Mercer Island, WA (city) King County	178	0.81
Hillsdale, NJ (borough) Bergen County	81	0.80
Ripon, CA (city) San Joaquin County	80	0.79
San Anselmo, CA (town) Marin County	97	0.77
Coos Bay, OR (city) Coos County	116	0.75
Cedar Mill, OR (cdp) Washington County	96	0.75
University Place, WA (city) Pierce County	214	0.71
Darien, CT (cdp) Fairfield County	137	0.70
Ladson, SC (cdp) Berkeley County	93	0.70
Bainbridge Island, WA (city) Kitsap County	140	0.69
Montgomery, NJ (township) Somerset County	118	0.68
Cottage Lake, WA (cdp) King County	160	0.66
Bonita, CA (cdp) San Diego County	79	0.66
Los Gatos, CA (town) Santa Clara County	184	0.64
Holladay, UT (city) Salt Lake County	91	0.63
Hillsborough, CA (town) San Mateo County	68	0.63
Montecito, CA (cdp) Santa Barbara County	64	0.63
Camano, WA (cdp) Island County	84	0.62
Nether Providence Township, PA (cdp) Delaware County	84	0.62
Palos Verdes Estates, CA (city) Los Angeles County	83	0.62
Winnetka, IL (village) Cook County	77	0.62
Chanhassen, MN (city) Carver County	123	0.61
Goodlettsville, TN (city) Davidson County	83	0.60
West Linn, OR (city) Clackamas County	129	0.58
Poquoson, VA (independent city) Poquoson city	67	0.58
Newton, IA (city) Jasper County	89	0.57
Ardmore, PA (cdp) Montgomery County	70	0.56
Bothell, WA (city) King County	162	0.54
Alpine, CA (cdp) San Diego County	71	0.54
Haslett, MI (cdp) Ingham County	59	0.52
Lake Oswego, OR (city) Clackamas County	181	0.51
Springville, UT (city) Utah County	104	0.51
Ashland, OR (city) Jackson County	99	0.51
Alderwood Manor, WA (cdp) Snohomish County	77	0.50
Baywood-Los Osos, CA (cdp) San Luis Obispo County	71	0.50
Clinton, MS (city) Hinds County	115	0.49
Mukilteo, WA (city) Snohomish County	89	0.49
Texas, MI (township) Kalamazoo County	54	0.49
Hillsboro, OR (city) Washington County	337	0.48
Lafayette, CA (city) Contra Costa County	113	0.48
Larkspur, CA (city) Marin County	58	0.48
Menlo Park, CA (city) San Mateo County	145	0.47
Takoma Park, MD (city) Montgomery County	81	0.47
Stephenville, TX (city) Erath County	70	0.47
Kingsgate, WA (cdp) King County	56	0.47
Healdsburg, CA (city) Sonoma County	50	0.47
Seattle, WA (city) King County	2,597	0.46
Tigard, OR (city) Washington County	190	0.46
Orinda, CA (city) Contra Costa County	81	0.46
Eugene, OR (city) Lane County	626	0.45
Davis, CA (city) Yolo County	269	0.45
Santa Cruz, CA (city) Santa Cruz County	244	0.45
Claremont, CA (city) Los Angeles County	153	0.45
Riverton-Boulevard Park, WA (cdp) King County	51	0.45
Albany, CA (city) Alameda County	73	0.44
Fort Payne, AL (city) De Kalb County	58	0.44
Bedford, MA (town) Middlesex County	55	0.44
Apple Valley, MN (city) Dakota County	198	0.43
Clearfield, UT (city) Davis County	111	0.43
Middleton, WI (city) Dane County	67	0.43
Fort Hunt, VA (cdp) Fairfax County	55	0.43
Clinton, UT (city) Davis County	54	0.43
Sherwood, OR (city) Washington County	51	0.43
Lea Hill, WA (cdp) King County	46	0.43
Edmonds, WA (city) Snohomish County	168	0.42
East Lake, FL (cdp) Pinellas County	124	0.42
Lehi, UT (city) Utah County	81	0.42
Madison, NJ (borough) Morris County	70	0.42
Piedmont, CA (city) Alameda County	46	0.42
Walnut Creek, CA (city) Contra Costa County	263	0.41
Corvallis, OR (city) Benton County	204	0.41
Edina, MN (city) Hennepin County	197	0.41
Coppell, TX (city) Dallas County	147	0.41
Pike Creek, DE (cdp) New Castle County	80	0.41
Kenmore, WA (city) King County	76	0.41
Burkburnett, TX (city) Wichita County	45	0.41
Eagan, MN (city) Dakota County	255	0.40
Burien, WA (city) King County	128	0.40
Orangevale, CA (cdp) Sacramento County	107	0.40
Winchester, MA (cdp) Middlesex County	83	0.40
Five Corners, WA (cdp) Clark County	48	0.40
Kirkland, WA (city) King County	176	0.39
Laguna Beach, CA (city) Orange County	92	0.39
Mill Valley, CA (city) Marin County	53	0.39
Bellevue, WA (city) King County	412	0.38
Novato, CA (city) Marin County	182	0.38
University Park, TX (city) Dallas County	88	0.38
Adrian, MI (city) Lenawee County	81	0.38
Half Moon Bay, CA (city) San Mateo County	45	0.38
Simsbury, CT (town) Hartford County	85	0.37
Moraga, CA (town) Contra Costa County	62	0.37
Ballenger Creek, MD (cdp) Frederick County	50	0.37
Hewitt, TX (city) McLennan County	40	0.37
Sierra Madre, CA (city) Los Angeles County	39	0.37
McLean, VA (cdp) Fairfax County	141	0.36
New Brighton, MN (city) Ramsey County	81	0.36
New Hope, MN (city) Hennepin County	75	0.36
Rexburg, ID (city) Madison County	62	0.36
Daphne, AL (city) Baldwin County	60	0.36
Middle, NJ (township) Cape May County	59	0.36
North Decatur, GA (cdp) De Kalb County	55	0.36
Moses Lake, WA (city) Grant County	54	0.36
Mohave Valley, AZ (cdp) Mohave County	49	0.36
Troutdale, OR (city) Multnomah County	49	0.36
Gardnerville Ranchos, NV (cdp) Douglas County	40	0.36
Leeds, AL (city) Jefferson County	39	0.36
Boulder, CO (city) Boulder County	333	0.35
White Bear Lake, MN (city) Ramsey County	86	0.35
Golden, CO (city) Jefferson County	61	0.35
Warrensburg, MO (city) Johnson County	58	0.35
Westwood, MA (town) Norfolk County	49	0.35
Wilbraham, MA (town) Hampden County	47	0.35
Spencer, IA (city) Clay County	40	0.35
Cambridge, MA (city) Middlesex County	348	0.34
Beaverton, OR (city) Washington County	256	0.34
Los Altos, CA (city) Santa Clara County	95	0.34
Winter Park, FL (city) Orange County	82	0.34
Arcata, CA (city) Humboldt County	56	0.34
Malibu, CA (city) Los Angeles County	43	0.34
Cloquet, MN (city) Carlton County	38	0.34
Carmel, IN (city) Hamilton County	126	0.33
Gloucester, MA (city) Essex County	101	0.33
Saratoga, CA (city) Santa Clara County	99	0.33
Golden Valley, MN (city) Hennepin County	67	0.33
Anoka, MN (city) Anoka County	59	0.33
Indianola, IA (city) Warren County	43	0.33
Fort Stewart, GA (cdp) Liberty County	38	0.33
Greenwood Village, CO (city) Arapahoe County	37	0.33
Putnam Valley, NY (town) Putnam County	35	0.33
Westtown, PA (township) Chester County	34	0.33
Wheeling, WV (city) Ohio County	100	0.32
Pullman, WA (city) Whitman County	80	0.32
Aurora, OH (city) Portage County	43	0.32
Clive, IA (city) Polk County	41	0.32
Clemson, SC (city) Pickens County	39	0.32
East Rockaway, NY (village) Nassau County	33	0.32
Bellingham, WA (city) Whatcom County	206	0.31
Annandale, VA (cdp) Fairfax County	172	0.31
Bethesda, MD (cdp) Montgomery County	170	0.31
Cascade-Fairwood, WA (cdp) King County	107	0.31
Roseville, MN (city) Ramsey County	103	0.31
Peachtree City, GA (city) Fayette County	100	0.31
North Potomac, MD (cdp) Montgomery County	71	0.31
Kaysville, UT (city) Davis County	64	0.31
Woodburn, OR (city) Marion County	63	0.31
West Odessa, TX (cdp) Ector County	56	0.31
Dumont, NJ (borough) Bergen County	55	0.31

Notes: (cdp) census designated place; Refer to the Explanation of Data in the front of the book for more detailed information.

Norwegian

Top 150 Places Sorted by Number

(Based on all places, regardless of population)

Place	Number	%
Minneapolis, MN (city) Hennepin County	41,917	10.96
Fargo, ND (city) Cass County	32,515	35.81
Seattle, WA (city) King County	32,018	5.68
Portland, OR (city) Multnomah County	24,064	4.55
Saint Paul, MN (city) Ramsey County	24,035	8.37
New York, NY (city) New York City	23,849	0.30
Sioux Falls, SD (city) Minnehaha County	23,218	18.71
Phoenix, AZ (city) Maricopa County	22,052	1.67
Madison, WI (city) Dane County	21,487	10.35
Los Angeles, CA (city) Los Angeles County	21,111	0.57
San Diego, CA (city) San Diego County	18,681	1.53
Grand Forks, ND (city) Grand Forks County	17,945	36.41
Bloomington, MN (city) Hennepin County	15,600	18.31
Eau Claire, WI (city) Eau Claire County	15,377	25.00
Chicago, IL (city) Cook County	14,890	0.51
Rochester, MN (city) Olmsted County	14,772	17.30
Duluth, MN (city) Saint Louis County	14,601	16.82
Moorhead, MN (city) Clay County	12,855	39.97
Milwaukee, WI (city) Milwaukee County	12,144	2.03
Spokane, WA (city) Spokane County	12,013	6.12
Minot, ND (city) Ward County	11,805	32.27
Tacoma, WA (city) Pierce County	11,169	5.78
Coon Rapids, MN (city) Anoka County	11,159	18.11
Mesa, AZ (city) Maricopa County	10,709	2.70
Burnsville, MN (city) Dakota County	10,603	17.63
Plymouth, MN (city) Hennepin County	10,577	16.05
La Crosse, WI (city) La Crosse County	10,570	20.47
Billings, MT (city) Yellowstone County	10,492	11.74
Bismarck, ND (city) Burleigh County	10,121	18.31
Anchorage, AK (municipality) Anchorage Borough	9,988	3.84
Colorado Springs, CO (city) El Paso County	9,960	2.76
Brooklyn Park, MN (city) Hennepin County	9,712	14.41
Eagan, MN (city) Dakota County	9,558	15.02
San Jose, CA (city) Santa Clara County	9,506	1.06
Omaha, NE (city) Douglas County	9,233	2.37
Eden Prairie, MN (city) Hennepin County	9,185	16.73
Janesville, WI (city) Rock County	9,106	15.34
Maple Grove, MN (city) Hennepin County	8,946	17.77
Denver, CO (city) Denver County	8,643	1.56
Minnetonka, MN (city) Hennepin County	8,445	16.46
Lakeville, MN (city) Dakota County	8,436	19.56
Tucson, AZ (city) Pima County	8,435	1.73
Saint Cloud, MN (city) Stearns County	8,030	13.62
Edina, MN (city) Hennepin County	7,951	16.74
Blaine, MN (city) Anoka County	7,910	17.60
San Francisco, CA (city) San Francisco County	7,830	1.01
Apple Valley, MN (city) Dakota County	7,828	17.19
Des Moines, IA (city) Polk County	7,473	3.76
Vancouver, WA (city) Clark County	7,413	5.18
Houston, TX (city) Harris County	7,367	0.38
Everett, WA (city) Snohomish County	7,203	7.89
Las Vegas, NV (city) Clark County	7,125	1.49
Saint Louis Park, MN (city) Hennepin County	7,082	16.05
Boise City, ID (city) Ada County	6,957	3.74
Eugene, OR (city) Lane County	6,676	4.84
Albuquerque, NM (city) Bernalillo County	6,528	1.46
Rapid City, SD (city) Pennington County	6,496	10.92
Great Falls, MT (city) Cascade County	6,488	11.45
Scottsdale, AZ (city) Maricopa County	6,401	3.16
Albert Lea, MN (city) Freeborn County	6,369	34.68
Woodbury, MN (city) Washington County	6,359	13.69
Cedar Rapids, IA (city) Linn County	6,145	5.10
Richfield, MN (city) Hennepin County	6,030	17.51
Williston, ND (city) Williams County	5,978	47.52
Aurora, CO (city) Arapahoe County	5,964	2.16
West Fargo, ND (city) Cass County	5,938	40.58
Mankato, MN (city) Blue Earth County	5,646	17.45
Brookhaven, NY (town) Suffolk County	5,636	1.26
Dallas, TX (city) Dallas County	5,596	0.47
Austin, MN (city) Mower County	5,584	23.98
Austin, TX (city) Travis County	5,544	0.84
Fergus Falls, MN (city) Otter Tail County	5,497	40.78
Lincoln, NE (city) Lancaster County	5,477	2.43
Sioux City, IA (city) Woodbury County	5,473	6.44
Missoula, MT (city) Missoula County	5,400	9.48
Rockford, IL (city) Winnebago County	5,394	3.60
Salem, OR (city) Marion County	5,282	3.86
Long Beach, CA (city) Los Angeles County	5,217	1.13
Bellevue, WA (city) King County	5,149	4.72
Roseville, MN (city) Ramsey County	5,026	14.89
Bellingham, WA (city) Whatcom County	5,024	7.52
Watertown, SD (city) Codington County	4,926	24.26
San Antonio, TX (city) Bexar County	4,914	0.43
Jacksonville, FL (special city) Duval County	4,816	0.65
Reno, NV (city) Washoe County	4,775	2.64
Salt Lake City, UT (city) Salt Lake County	4,770	2.63
Mason City, IA (city) Cerro Gordo County	4,763	16.32
Andover, MN (city) Anoka County	4,656	17.51
Chandler, AZ (city) Maricopa County	4,655	2.64
Willmar, MN (city) Kandiyohi County	4,631	25.18
Sacramento, CA (city) Sacramento County	4,601	1.13
Brookings, SD (city) Brookings County	4,580	24.68
Inver Grove Heights, MN (city) Dakota County	4,541	15.28
Fridley, MN (city) Anoka County	4,428	16.13
Lakewood, CO (city) Jefferson County	4,410	3.06
Federal Way, WA (city) King County	4,404	5.29
Owatonna, MN (city) Steele County	4,384	19.56
Cottage Grove, MN (city) Washington County	4,374	14.31
Ames, IA (city) Story County	4,365	8.62
Shoreline, WA (city) King County	4,364	8.24
Maplewood, MN (city) Ramsey County	4,352	12.45
Hempstead, NY (town) Nassau County	4,339	0.57
Fort Collins, CO (city) Larimer County	4,302	3.63
Gresham, OR (city) Multnomah County	4,277	4.74
Champlin, MN (city) Hennepin County	4,248	19.00
Winona, MN (city) Winona County	4,192	15.53
Virginia Beach, VA (independent city) Virginia Beach city	4,192	0.99
Thief River Falls, MN (city) Pennington County	4,187	50.02
Superior, WI (city) Douglas County	4,171	15.23
Shoreview, MN (city) Ramsey County	4,119	15.89
Kent, WA (city) King County	4,100	5.17
Tempe, AZ (city) Maricopa County	4,098	2.59
Savage, MN (city) Scott County	4,075	19.24
Brooklyn Center, MN (city) Hennepin County	4,009	13.80
Crystal, MN (city) Hennepin County	3,952	17.30
Santa Rosa, CA (city) Sonoma County	3,943	2.67
Edmonds, WA (city) Snohomish County	3,900	9.85
Appleton, WI (city) Outagamie County	3,889	5.55
Waukesha, WI (city) Waukesha County	3,888	6.04
Huntington Beach, CA (city) Orange County	3,874	2.04
Oakdale, MN (city) Washington County	3,804	14.26
Racine, WI (city) Racine County	3,796	4.64
Kenosha, WI (city) Kenosha County	3,787	4.18
Indianapolis, IN (special city) Marion County	3,756	0.48
Glendale, AZ (city) Maricopa County	3,743	1.71
Green Bay, WI (city) Brown County	3,682	3.60
Aberdeen, SD (city) Brown County	3,681	14.96
Stoughton, WI (city) Dane County	3,675	29.56
Chanhassen, MN (city) Carver County	3,671	18.06
Beaverton, OR (city) Washington County	3,592	4.73
Ramsey, MN (city) Anoka County	3,586	19.39
White Bear Lake, MN (city) Ramsey County	3,544	14.49
Jamestown, ND (city) Stutsman County	3,475	22.46
Kansas City, MO (city) Jackson County	3,462	0.78
Golden Valley, MN (city) Hennepin County	3,457	17.08
Northfield, MN (city) Rice County	3,425	20.01
Onalaska, WI (city) La Crosse County	3,407	22.93
Henderson, NV (city) Clark County	3,400	1.93
Sandy, UT (city) Salt Lake County	3,363	3.81
Waterloo, IA (city) Black Hawk County	3,303	4.81
New Brighton, MN (city) Ramsey County	3,293	14.80
Tulsa, OK (city) Tulsa County	3,259	0.83
Red Wing, MN (city) Goodhue County	3,241	20.09
Iowa City, IA (city) Johnson County	3,222	5.17
Oklahoma City, OK (city) Oklahoma County	3,169	0.63
Cedar Falls, IA (city) Black Hawk County	3,167	8.73
Fresno, CA (city) Fresno County	3,151	0.74
Wichita, KS (city) Sedgwick County	3,125	0.91
Westminster, CO (city) Adams County	3,098	3.06
Anaheim, CA (city) Orange County	3,093	0.94

Notes: (cdp) census designated place; Refer to the Explanation of Data in the front of the book for more detailed information.

Norwegian

Top 150 Places Sorted by Percent

(Based on all places, regardless of population)

Place	Number	%
Rawson, ND (city) McKenzie County	3	100.00
Ambrose, ND (city) Divide County	16	84.21
Espelie, MN (township) Marshall County	55	83.33
Hill River, MN (township) Polk County	160	82.47
Winsor, MN (township) Clearwater County	96	82.05
Strathcona, MN (city) Roseau County	22	81.48
Onstad, MN (township) Polk County	47	79.66
Goodridge, MN (township) Pennington County	40	78.43
Calpet, WY (cdp) Sublette County	7	77.78
New Folden, MN (township) Marshall County	152	77.55
Big Woods, MN (township) Marshall County	74	77.08
Alamo, ND (city) Williams County	37	77.08
Soler, MN (township) Roseau County	90	76.92
Good Hope, MN (township) Norman County	32	76.19
Trail, MN (city) Polk County	41	75.93
Keene, MN (township) Clay County	96	75.59
Whalan, MN (city) Fillmore County	49	75.38
Bear Park, MN (township) Norman County	138	75.00
Hubbard, MN (township) Polk County	69	75.00
Rollis, MN (township) Marshall County	94	74.02
Roome, MN (township) Polk County	130	73.86
Columbus, ND (city) Burke County	117	73.13
Scandia, MN (township) Polk County	68	73.12
Dieter, MN (township) Roseau County	111	73.03
Lincoln, MN (township) Marshall County	92	73.02
Kragero, MN (township) Chippewa County	116	72.96
Reiner, MN (township) Pennington County	70	72.92
Nereson, MN (township) Roseau County	64	72.73
Big Bend, MN (township) Chippewa County	181	72.69
Rolling Forks, MN (township) Pope County	122	72.62
Marsh Grove, MN (township) Marshall County	95	72.52
Fortuna, ND (city) Divide County	36	72.00
Oak Park, MN (township) Marshall County	112	71.79
Cerro Gordo, MN (township) Lac qui Parle County	175	71.72
Eckvoll, MN (township) Marshall County	65	71.43
York, ND (city) Benson County	10	71.43
Pohlitz, MN (township) Roseau County	34	70.83
Souris, ND (city) Bottineau County	48	70.59
Landa, ND (city) Bottineau County	24	70.59
Winger, MN (township) Polk County	115	70.55
Shelly, MN (township) Norman County	89	70.08
Larson, ND (city) Burke County	21	70.00
Rulien, MN (township) Lake of the Woods County	14	70.00
Garfield, MN (township) Polk County	274	69.72
Fertile, MN (city) Polk County	618	69.67
Deer, MN (township) Roseau County	55	69.62
Veldt, MN (township) Marshall County	41	69.49
Godfrey, MN (township) Polk County	218	69.43
Norway, MN (township) Fillmore County	244	69.32
Halstad, MN (township) Norman County	88	69.29
Star, MN (township) Pennington County	88	69.29
Hickory, MN (township) Pennington County	63	69.23
Huntly, MN (township) Marshall County	51	68.92
Norway Lake, MN (township) Kandiyohi County	192	68.82
Sundal, MN (township) Norman County	114	68.67
Riverside, MN (township) Lac qui Parle County	214	68.59
Wheatland, ND (cdp) Cass County	26	68.42
Kratka, MN (township) Pennington County	88	68.22
Gary, MN (city) Norman County	152	68.16
Chester, MN (township) Polk County	66	68.04
Friendship, MN (township) Yellow Medicine County	184	67.90
Liberty, MN (township) Polk County	112	67.88
Silverton, MN (township) Pennington County	138	67.65
Hegne, MN (township) Norman County	33	67.35
Hampden, ND (city) Ramsey County	35	67.31
Sunburg, MN (city) Kandiyohi County	72	67.29
Lind, MN (township) Roseau County	39	67.24
Pleasant View, MN (township) Norman County	94	67.14
Clover Leaf, MN (township) Pennington County	47	67.14
Higdem, MN (township) Polk County	65	67.01
Ten Mile Lake, MN (township) Lac qui Parle County	117	66.86
Baxter, MN (township) Lac qui Parle County	147	66.82
Northwood, ND (city) Grand Forks County	630	66.67
Hantho, MN (township) Lac qui Parle County	118	66.67
Linsell, MN (township) Marshall County	18	66.67
Garden, MN (township) Polk County	145	66.51
Buxton, ND (city) Traill County	226	66.47
Lignite, ND (city) Burke County	111	66.47
Reis, MN (township) Polk County	53	66.25
Waukon, MN (township) Norman County	102	66.23
Seely, MN (township) Faribault County	115	66.09
Ulen, MN (city) Clay County	354	65.92
Astoria, SD (town) Deuel County	106	65.84
Garnes, MN (township) Red Lake County	131	65.83
Knox, ND (city) Benson County	25	65.79
Holt, MN (township) Marshall County	98	65.77
Edinburg, ND (city) Walsh County	178	65.68
Hendrum, MN (city) Norman County	223	65.59
Spring Grove, MN (township) Houston County	247	65.52
Leal, ND (city) Barnes County	36	65.45
Strum, WI (village) Trempealeau County	612	65.31
Gardena, ND (city) Bottineau County	15	65.22
Humboldt, MN (township) Clay County	158	65.02
Lee, MN (township) Beltrami County	24	64.86
Hammond, MN (township) Polk County	35	64.81
Swedes Forest, MN (township) Redwood County	68	64.76
Averill, VT (town) Essex County	11	64.71
Twin Valley, MN (city) Norman County	557	64.62
Johnson, MN (township) Polk County	31	64.58
Spring Grove, MN (city) Houston County	840	64.52
King, MN (township) Polk County	128	64.32
West Valley, MN (township) Marshall County	90	64.29
Equality, MN (township) Red Lake County	72	64.29
Almont, ND (city) Morton County	70	64.22
Portland, ND (city) Traill County	418	64.21
Deer Park, MN (township) Pennington County	82	64.06
Newburg, MN (township) Fillmore County	293	63.70
Norwegian Grove, MN (township) Otter Tail County	214	63.69
Langhei, MN (township) Pope County	138	63.59
New Solum, MN (township) Marshall County	196	63.43
Brandsvold, MN (township) Polk County	149	63.40
Borup, MN (city) Norman County	57	63.33
Loraine, ND (city) Renville County	19	63.33
Mandt, MN (township) Chippewa County	113	63.13
Hawk Creek, MN (township) Renville County	123	63.08
Rockwell, MN (township) Norman County	41	63.08
Hitterdal, MN (city) Clay County	138	63.01
Climax, MN (city) Polk County	154	62.86
Black Hammer, MN (township) Houston County	208	62.65
Eleva, WI (village) Trempealeau County	399	62.64
Finley, ND (city) Steele County	322	62.52
Vining, MN (city) Otter Tail County	40	62.50
Palmville, MN (township) Roseau County	30	62.50
Tolna, ND (city) Nelson County	133	62.44
Black River, MN (township) Pennington County	63	62.38
Moose, MN (township) Roseau County	74	62.18
Tanberg, MN (township) Wilkin County	41	62.12
Gully, MN (city) Polk County	59	62.11
Leeds, ND (city) Benson County	285	62.09
Crosby, ND (city) Divide County	697	62.01
Preble, MN (township) Fillmore County	166	61.94
Vineland, MN (township) Polk County	83	61.94
Shelly, MN (city) Norman County	159	61.87
Garfield, MN (township) Lac qui Parle County	115	61.83
McVille, ND (city) Nelson County	288	61.67
Coon, WI (town) Vernon County	394	61.66
Ann, MN (township) Cottonwood County	119	61.66
Pine Lake, MN (township) Clearwater County	192	61.54
Strand, MN (township) Norman County	64	61.54
Viking, MN (city) Marshall County	56	61.54
Leonard, MN (city) Clearwater County	24	61.54
Eglon, MN (township) Clay County	283	61.52
Blair, WI (city) Trempealeau County	766	61.48
Gully, MN (township) Polk County	65	61.32
Antelope, MT (cdp) Sheridan County	30	61.22
Hazel Run, MN (city) Yellow Medicine County	41	61.19
Westby, WI (city) Vernon County	1,231	61.12
Sharon, ND (city) Steele County	66	61.11
Dazey, ND (city) Barnes County	44	61.11
Calio, ND (city) Cavalier County	11	61.11

Notes: (cdp) census designated place; Refer to the Explanation of Data in the front of the book for more detailed information.

Norwegian

Top 150 Places Sorted by Percent

(Based on places with populations of 10,000 or more)

Place	Number	%
Williston, ND (city) Williams County	5,978	47.52
Fergus Falls, MN (city) Otter Tail County	5,497	40.78
West Fargo, ND (city) Cass County	5,938	40.58
Moorhead, MN (city) Clay County	12,855	39.97
Grand Forks, ND (city) Grand Forks County	17,945	36.41
Fargo, ND (city) Cass County	32,515	35.81
Albert Lea, MN (city) Freeborn County	6,369	34.68
Minot, ND (city) Ward County	11,805	32.27
Stoughton, WI (city) Dane County	3,675	29.56
Willmar, MN (city) Kandiyohi County	4,631	25.18
Eau Claire, WI (city) Eau Claire County	15,377	25.00
Brookings, SD (city) Brookings County	4,580	24.68
Watertown, SD (city) Codington County	4,926	24.26
Austin, MN (city) Mower County	5,584	23.98
Onalaska, WI (city) La Crosse County	3,407	22.93
Bemidji, MN (city) Beltrami County	2,732	22.63
Jamestown, ND (city) Stutsman County	3,475	22.46
River Falls, WI (city) Pierce County	2,617	20.74
La Crosse, WI (city) La Crosse County	10,570	20.47
Ham Lake, MN (city) Anoka County	2,587	20.30
Red Wing, MN (city) Goodhue County	3,241	20.09
Northfield, MN (city) Rice County	3,425	20.01
Lakeville, MN (city) Dakota County	8,436	19.56
Owatonna, MN (city) Steele County	4,384	19.56
Ramsey, MN (city) Anoka County	3,586	19.39
Menomonie, WI (city) Dunn County	2,899	19.33
Savage, MN (city) Scott County	4,075	19.24
Chippewa Falls, WI (city) Chippewa County	2,471	19.04
Champlin, MN (city) Hennepin County	4,248	19.00
Sioux Falls, SD (city) Minnehaha County	23,218	18.71
Robbinsdale, MN (city) Hennepin County	2,605	18.45
Bloomington, MN (city) Hennepin County	15,600	18.31
Bismarck, ND (city) Burleigh County	10,121	18.31
Coon Rapids, MN (city) Anoka County	11,159	18.11
Buffalo, MN (city) Wright County	1,833	18.09
Chanhassen, MN (city) Carver County	3,671	18.06
Maple Grove, MN (city) Hennepin County	8,946	17.77
Marshall, MN (city) Lyon County	2,260	17.72
Burnsville, MN (city) Dakota County	10,603	17.63
Prior Lake, MN (city) Scott County	2,808	17.62
Blaine, MN (city) Anoka County	7,910	17.60
Richfield, MN (city) Hennepin County	6,030	17.51
Andover, MN (city) Anoka County	4,656	17.51
Mankato, MN (city) Blue Earth County	5,646	17.45
Rochester, MN (city) Olmsted County	14,772	17.30
Crystal, MN (city) Hennepin County	3,952	17.30
Apple Valley, MN (city) Dakota County	7,828	17.19
Elk River, MN (city) Sherburne County	2,828	17.19
Golden Valley, MN (city) Hennepin County	3,457	17.08
Anoka, MN (city) Anoka County	3,084	17.06
East Bethel, MN (city) Anoka County	1,845	16.86
Rosemount, MN (city) Dakota County	2,459	16.83
Duluth, MN (city) Saint Louis County	14,601	16.82
Brainerd, MN (city) Crow Wing County	2,185	16.75
Edina, MN (city) Hennepin County	7,951	16.74
Eden Prairie, MN (city) Hennepin County	9,185	16.73
Farmington, MN (city) Dakota County	2,076	16.64
Minnetonka, MN (city) Hennepin County	8,445	16.46
North Mankato, MN (city) Nicollet County	1,941	16.44
Mason City, IA (city) Cerro Gordo County	4,763	16.32
Columbia Heights, MN (city) Anoka County	3,011	16.27
Lino Lakes, MN (city) Anoka County	2,727	16.26
Fridley, MN (city) Anoka County	4,428	16.13
Plymouth, MN (city) Hennepin County	10,577	16.05
Saint Louis Park, MN (city) Hennepin County	7,082	16.05
Shoreview, MN (city) Ramsey County	4,119	15.89
Hastings, MN (city) Dakota County	2,890	15.87
Cloquet, MN (city) Carlton County	1,764	15.81
Hutchinson, MN (city) McLeod County	2,053	15.72
Hopkins, MN (city) Hennepin County	2,659	15.59
Chaska, MN (city) Carver County	2,710	15.54
Winona, MN (city) Winona County	4,192	15.53
Fairmont, MN (city) Martin County	1,671	15.35
Janesville, WI (city) Rock County	9,106	15.34
Mandan, ND (city) Morton County	2,567	15.34

Place	Number	%
Inver Grove Heights, MN (city) Dakota County	4,541	15.28
Superior, WI (city) Douglas County	4,171	15.23
Mounds View, MN (city) Ramsey County	1,932	15.20
Monroe, WI (city) Green County	1,642	15.19
Eagan, MN (city) Dakota County	9,558	15.02
Aberdeen, SD (city) Brown County	3,681	14.96
Roseville, MN (city) Ramsey County	5,026	14.89
New Brighton, MN (city) Ramsey County	3,293	14.80
Faribault, MN (city) Rice County	3,079	14.78
Stillwater, MN (city) Washington County	2,238	14.74
White Bear Lake, MN (city) Ramsey County	3,544	14.49
New Hope, MN (city) Hennepin County	3,020	14.48
Brooklyn Park, MN (city) Hennepin County	9,712	14.41
Cottage Grove, MN (city) Washington County	4,374	14.31
Dickinson, ND (city) Stark County	2,266	14.30
Oakdale, MN (city) Washington County	3,804	14.26
Vadnais Heights, MN (city) Ramsey County	1,860	14.24
White Bear, MN (township) Ramsey County	1,594	14.24
Grand Rapids, MN (township) Itasca County	1,664	14.22
Pierre, SD (city) Hughes County	1,985	14.21
Huron, SD (city) Beadle County	1,683	14.05
Brooklyn Center, MN (city) Hennepin County	4,009	13.80
Woodbury, MN (city) Washington County	6,359	13.69
Saint Cloud, MN (city) Stearns County	8,030	13.62
Shakopee, MN (city) Scott County	2,767	13.50
Yankton, SD (city) Yankton County	1,815	13.49
Sun Prairie, WI (city) Dane County	2,719	13.46
Morris, IL (city) Grundy County	1,595	13.36
Hibbing, MN (city) Saint Louis County	2,192	12.84
Maplewood, MN (city) Ramsey County	4,352	12.45
North Saint Paul, MN (city) Ramsey County	1,457	12.21
Anacortes, WA (city) Skagit County	1,770	12.04
New Ulm, MN (city) Brown County	1,602	11.82
Kalispell, MT (city) Flathead County	1,667	11.77
Billings, MT (city) Yellowstone County	10,492	11.74
South Saint Paul, MN (city) Dakota County	2,360	11.69
Mitchell, SD (city) Davison County	1,711	11.65
Worthington, MN (city) Nobles County	1,305	11.56
Great Falls, MT (city) Cascade County	6,488	11.45
Camano, WA (cdp) Island County	1,548	11.44
Sauk Rapids, MN (city) Benton County	1,158	11.37
Fitchburg, WI (city) Dane County	2,285	11.18
Minneapolis, MN (city) Hennepin County	41,917	10.96
Rapid City, SD (city) Pennington County	6,496	10.92
Arlington, WA (city) Snohomish County	1,294	10.89
West Lake Stevens, WA (cdp) Snohomish County	1,932	10.81
Middleton, WI (city) Dane County	1,655	10.63
Mendota Heights, MN (city) Dakota County	1,186	10.44
Mukilteo, WA (city) Snohomish County	1,874	10.39
Madison, WI (city) Dane County	21,487	10.35
Spencer, IA (city) Clay County	1,168	10.23
Helena, MT (city) Lewis and Clark County	2,550	9.98
Edmonds, WA (city) Snohomish County	3,900	9.85
Marysville, WA (city) Snohomish County	2,454	9.73
West Saint Paul, MN (city) Dakota County	1,866	9.62
North Marysville, WA (cdp) Snohomish County	2,049	9.61
Fort Dodge, IA (city) Webster County	2,406	9.58
Prairie Ridge, WA (cdp) Pierce County	1,097	9.53
Missoula, MT (city) Missoula County	5,400	9.48
Bozeman, MT (city) Gallatin County	2,632	9.40
Maple Valley, WA (city) King County	1,334	9.30
Whitewater, WI (city) Walworth County	1,207	8.99
East Renton Highlands, WA (cdp) King County	1,171	8.93
Enumclaw, WA (city) King County	990	8.85
Cedar Falls, IA (city) Black Hawk County	3,167	8.73
Lake Forest Park, WA (city) King County	1,171	8.71
Seattle Hill-Silver Firs, WA (cdp) Snohomish County	3,075	8.65
Ames, IA (city) Story County	4,365	8.62
Beloit, WI (city) Rock County	3,071	8.61
Picnic Point-North Lynnwood, WA (cdp) Snohomish County	1,956	8.57
Bothell, WA (city) King County	2,555	8.55
Kenmore, WA (city) King County	1,572	8.48
Saint Paul, MN (city) Ramsey County	24,035	8.37
Shoreline, WA (city) King County	4,364	8.24
Fort Atkinson, WI (city) Jefferson County	963	8.23

Notes: (cdp) census designated place; Refer to the Explanation of Data in the front of the book for more detailed information.

Pennsylvania German

Top 150 Places Sorted by Number

(Based on all places, regardless of population)

Place	Number	%
Allentown, PA (city) Lehigh County	5,614	5.26
Reading, PA (city) Berks County	2,472	3.04
Bethlehem, PA (city) Northampton County	2,437	3.42
Philadelphia, PA (city) Philadelphia County	1,857	0.12
North Whitehall, PA (township) Lehigh County	1,421	9.65
Whitehall, PA (township) Lehigh County	1,311	5.27
South Whitehall, PA (township) Lehigh County	1,036	5.75
Emmaus, PA (borough) Lehigh County	988	8.79
Lower Macungie, PA (township) Lehigh County	951	4.95
Moore, PA (township) Northampton County	937	10.80
Upper Macungie, PA (township) Lehigh County	883	6.35
Northampton, PA (borough) Northampton County	851	9.05
Lehigh, PA (township) Northampton County	826	8.49
Washington, PA (township) Lehigh County	795	12.07
Muhlenberg, PA (township) Berks County	761	4.67
Easton, PA (city) Northampton County	741	2.82
Salisbury, PA (township) Lehigh County	730	5.41
Fullerton, PA (cdp) Lehigh County	704	4.95
Nazareth, PA (borough) Northampton County	669	11.11
Exeter, PA (township) Berks County	664	3.13
Palmerton, PA (borough) Carbon County	625	11.91
Palmer, PA (township) Northampton County	574	3.41
Upper Saucon, PA (township) Lehigh County	569	4.77
Altoona, PA (city) Blair County	557	1.12
Douglass, PA (township) Montgomery County	556	6.08
Berwick, PA (borough) Columbia County	556	5.20
Bethlehem, PA (township) Northampton County	550	2.60
Williamsport, PA (city) Lycoming County	535	1.74
Cumru, PA (township) Berks County	529	3.83
Richland, PA (township) Bucks County	524	5.28
Pottstown, PA (borough) Montgomery County	514	2.36
Phoenix, AZ (city) Maricopa County	514	0.04
Lower Saucon, PA (township) Northampton County	512	5.18
Spring, PA (township) Berks County	510	2.34
Los Angeles, CA (city) Los Angeles County	505	0.01
Longswamp, PA (township) Berks County	501	8.93
Hempfield, PA (township) Westmoreland County	500	1.23
Columbus, OH (city) Franklin County	487	0.07
Catasauqua, PA (borough) Lehigh County	481	7.30
Upper Milford, PA (township) Lehigh County	467	6.71
Wilkes-Barre, PA (city) Luzerne County	464	1.08
Bushkill, PA (township) Northampton County	456	6.53
Colebrookdale, PA (township) Berks County	441	8.37
Hellertown, PA (borough) Northampton County	437	7.78
Heidelberg, PA (township) Lehigh County	435	12.64
Plainfield, PA (township) Northampton County	412	7.27
Slatington, PA (borough) Lehigh County	406	9.16
Akron, OH (city) Summit County	405	0.19
Franconia, PA (township) Montgomery County	404	3.51
Lower Paxton, PA (township) Dauphin County	400	0.90
Lebanon, PA (city) Lebanon County	399	1.63
Mountain Top, PA (cdp) Luzerne County	396	2.60
Boyertown, PA (borough) Berks County	393	9.97
Lower Towamensing, PA (township) Carbon County	386	12.12
Wichita, KS (city) Sedgwick County	376	0.11
Quakertown, PA (borough) Bucks County	371	4.15
Maidencreek, PA (township) Berks County	367	5.60
Lynn, PA (township) Lehigh County	365	9.90
Polk, PA (township) Monroe County	365	5.59
West Penn, PA (township) Schuylkill County	355	9.30
Wilson, PA (borough) Northampton County	355	4.62
Weisenberg, PA (township) Lehigh County	353	8.52
New York, NY (city) New York City	350	0.00
Tilden, PA (township) Berks County	345	9.62
Pottsville, PA (city) Schuylkill County	337	2.17
Omaha, NE (city) Douglas County	334	0.09
Milford, PA (township) Bucks County	329	3.73
Oley, PA (township) Berks County	328	9.15
North Lebanon, PA (township) Lebanon County	327	3.08
Perkasie, PA (borough) Bucks County	320	3.62
Schuylkill Haven, PA (borough) Schuylkill County	317	5.71
Back Mountain, PA (cdp) Luzerne County	317	1.19
North Catasauqua, PA (borough) Northampton County	315	11.19
Coplay, PA (borough) Lehigh County	315	9.30
Johnstown, PA (city) Cambria County	312	1.31
Alburtis, PA (borough) Lehigh County	310	14.64
Bensalem, PA (township) Bucks County	310	0.53
York, PA (city) York County	307	0.75
East Lampeter, PA (township) Lancaster County	303	2.23
Sunbury, PA (city) Northumberland County	302	2.85
East Pennsboro, PA (township) Cumberland County	302	1.66
Swatara, PA (township) Dauphin County	302	1.33
Conemaugh, PA (township) Somerset County	301	4.00
Washington, PA (township) Berks County	299	8.90
Portland, OR (city) Multnomah County	299	0.06
East Allen, PA (township) Northampton County	298	6.08
Honey Brook, PA (township) Chester County	294	4.68
Souderton, PA (borough) Montgomery County	294	4.42
Hereford, PA (township) Berks County	293	9.25
South Lebanon, PA (township) Lebanon County	293	3.50
Upper Nazareth, PA (township) Northampton County	286	6.46
Towamensing, PA (township) Carbon County	284	8.20
Franklin, PA (township) Carbon County	282	6.65
Maxatawny, PA (township) Berks County	280	4.64
Gilbertsville, PA (cdp) Montgomery County	279	6.57
Levittown, PA (cdp) Bucks County	279	0.52
Lower Nazareth, PA (township) Northampton County	276	5.25
Hanover, PA (township) Northampton County	275	2.88
Greenwich, PA (township) Berks County	274	8.09
Colorado Springs, CO (city) El Paso County	274	0.08
Wayne, PA (township) Schuylkill County	273	5.78
Leacock, PA (township) Lancaster County	273	5.60
West Rockhill, PA (township) Bucks County	269	6.35
Ross, PA (township) Monroe County	269	4.95
Lower Pottsgrove, PA (township) Montgomery County	268	2.37
San Diego, CA (city) San Diego County	267	0.02
Strasburg, PA (township) Lancaster County	266	6.62
Norristown, PA (borough) Montgomery County	265	0.85
Mahoning, PA (township) Carbon County	262	6.58
East Rockhill, PA (township) Bucks County	261	5.02
Amity, PA (township) Berks County	259	2.93
Lehighton, PA (borough) Carbon County	258	4.66
Hamburg, PA (borough) Berks County	256	6.22
Chestnuthill, PA (township) Monroe County	256	1.78
Goshen, IN (city) Elkhart County	252	0.86
Bart, PA (township) Lancaster County	251	8.19
Phillipsburg, NJ (town) Warren County	251	1.66
Upper Leacock, PA (township) Lancaster County	249	3.03
Tamaqua, PA (borough) Schuylkill County	246	3.43
New Hanover, PA (township) Montgomery County	246	3.34
Eldred, PA (township) Monroe County	245	9.19
Bath, PA (borough) Northampton County	243	9.07
Windsor, PA (township) Berks County	241	10.08
East Penn, PA (township) Carbon County	241	9.80
Indianapolis, IN (special city) Marion County	241	0.03
Middletown, PA (cdp) Northampton County	240	3.22
Allen, PA (township) Northampton County	237	9.01
Upper Mount Bethel, PA (township) Northampton County	237	3.90
Seattle, WA (city) King County	236	0.04
Bristol, PA (township) Bucks County	235	0.42
Upper Darby, PA (township) Delaware County	235	0.29
Lincoln, NE (city) Lancaster County	235	0.10
Falls, PA (township) Bucks County	232	0.67
Rockford, IL (city) Winnebago County	232	0.15
Eastlawn Gardens, PA (cdp) Northampton County	231	8.05
Limerick, PA (township) Montgomery County	229	1.69
Rockland, PA (township) Berks County	226	6.00
Stroud, PA (township) Monroe County	226	1.62
Sellersville, PA (borough) Bucks County	225	4.90
Mesa, AZ (city) Maricopa County	225	0.06
Canton, OH (city) Stark County	224	0.28
Binghamton, NY (city) Broome County	223	0.47
Union, NY (town) Broome County	223	0.40
Toledo, OH (city) Lucas County	223	0.07
Lancaster, PA (city) Lancaster County	222	0.39
Virginia Beach, VA (independent city) Virginia Beach city	222	0.05
Sparta, PA (township) Crawford County	221	12.81
Earl, PA (township) Berks County	221	7.21
Fairview, PA (township) York County	221	1.54
Hamilton, PA (township) Monroe County	220	2.67

Notes: (cdp) census designated place; Refer to the Explanation of Data in the front of the book for more detailed information.

Pennsylvania German

Top 150 Places Sorted by Percent

(Based on all places, regardless of population)

Place	Number	%
Atlantic, PA (cdp) Crawford County	9	31.03
Klingerstown, PA (cdp) Schuylkill County	18	18.75
Lyons, PA (borough) Berks County	85	18.72
Jerseytown, PA (cdp) Columbia County	21	18.26
Rupert, PA (cdp) Columbia County	27	15.25
Upper Mahantongo, PA (township) Schuylkill County	97	14.65
Alburtis, PA (borough) Lehigh County	310	14.64
Renningers, PA (cdp) Schuylkill County	64	14.16
Lenhartsville, PA (borough) Berks County	24	13.87
Bowmanstown, PA (borough) Carbon County	120	13.41
Sparta, PA (township) Crawford County	221	12.81
Heidelberg, PA (township) Lehigh County	435	12.64
Yale, SD (town) Beadle County	15	12.50
Lower Towamensing, PA (township) Carbon County	386	12.12
Washington, PA (township) Lehigh County	795	12.07
Chapman, PA (borough) Northampton County	28	12.07
Palmerton, PA (borough) Carbon County	625	11.91
Eldred, PA (township) Schuylkill County	84	11.85
Arvada, WY (cdp) Sheridan County	2	11.76
Millstone, PA (township) Elk County	9	11.54
Foundryville, PA (cdp) Columbia County	30	11.32
Greene, PA (township) Clinton County	164	11.26
North Catasauqua, PA (borough) Northampton County	315	11.19
Nazareth, PA (borough) Northampton County	669	11.11
Grugan, PA (township) Clinton County	4	11.11
Summit Station, PA (cdp) Schuylkill County	23	10.85
Moore, PA (township) Northampton County	937	10.80
Rush, PA (township) Dauphin County	19	10.73
Taiwah, OK (cdp) Rogers County	14	10.61
Albany, PA (township) Berks County	171	10.29
Walnutport, PA (borough) Northampton County	209	10.23
Windsor, PA (township) Berks County	241	10.08
Boyertown, PA (borough) Berks County	393	9.97
Auburn, PA (borough) Schuylkill County	83	9.95
Lynn, PA (township) Lehigh County	365	9.90
Belfast, PA (cdp) Northampton County	130	9.83
East Penn, PA (township) Carbon County	241	9.80
North Whitehall, PA (township) Lehigh County	1,421	9.65
Tilden, PA (township) Berks County	345	9.62
Bally, PA (borough) Berks County	100	9.42
West Penn, PA (township) Schuylkill County	355	9.30
Coplay, PA (borough) Lehigh County	315	9.30
Hereford, PA (township) Berks County	293	9.25
Eldred, PA (township) Monroe County	245	9.19
Centerport, PA (borough) Berks County	30	9.17
Slatington, PA (borough) Lehigh County	406	9.16
Oley, PA (township) Berks County	328	9.15
Bath, PA (borough) Northampton County	243	9.07
Freemansburg, PA (borough) Northampton County	172	9.07
Northampton, PA (borough) Northampton County	851	9.05
Saint Michael-Sidman, PA (cdp) Cambria County	86	9.03
Allen, PA (township) Northampton County	237	9.01
Longswamp, PA (township) Berks County	501	8.93
Washington, PA (township) Berks County	299	8.90
Roaring Creek, PA (township) Columbia County	43	8.88
Schnecksville, PA (cdp) Lehigh County	191	8.80
Emmaus, PA (borough) Lehigh County	988	8.79
Leon, NY (town) Cattaraugus County	124	8.74
Weisenberg, PA (township) Lehigh County	353	8.52
Lehigh, PA (township) Northampton County	826	8.49
Colebrookdale, PA (township) Berks County	441	8.37
Tatamy, PA (borough) Northampton County	77	8.27
Towamensing, PA (township) Carbon County	284	8.20
Bart, PA (township) Lancaster County	251	8.19
Wilburton Number Two, PA (cdp) Columbia County	6	8.11
Greenwich, PA (township) Berks County	274	8.09
Eastlawn Gardens, PA (cdp) Northampton County	231	8.05
Clifton, WI (town) Monroe County	57	7.94
Freehold, PA (township) Warren County	112	7.92
Strausstown, PA (borough) Berks County	24	7.92
Landingville, PA (borough) Schuylkill County	15	7.85
Henderson, PA (township) Jefferson County	137	7.84
Mifflin, PA (township) Columbia County	176	7.82
Hellertown, PA (borough) Northampton County	437	7.78
Clinton, WI (town) Vernon County	107	7.78
East Bangor, PA (borough) Northampton County	76	7.76
Coopersburg, PA (borough) Lehigh County	199	7.71
Mifflinville, PA (cdp) Columbia County	90	7.71
Mainville, PA (cdp) Columbia County	5	7.69
Lowhill, PA (township) Lehigh County	140	7.49
East Side, PA (borough) Carbon County	20	7.41
Monument, PA (cdp) Centre County	8	7.41
East Cameron, PA (township) Northumberland County	50	7.35
Marseilles, OH (village) Wyandot County	10	7.35
Port Clinton, PA (borough) Schuylkill County	21	7.34
West Mahoning, PA (township) Indiana County	82	7.33
Catasauqua, PA (borough) Lehigh County	481	7.30
Pennsburg, PA (borough) Montgomery County	199	7.28
Plainfield, PA (township) Northampton County	412	7.27
New Ringgold, PA (borough) Schuylkill County	20	7.27
Earl, PA (township) Berks County	221	7.21
Randall, KS (city) Jewell County	7	7.14
Wolford, ND (city) Pierce County	3	7.14
Gray, PA (township) Greene County	16	7.11
Cressona, PA (borough) Schuylkill County	116	7.10
Friedensburg, PA (cdp) Schuylkill County	51	7.10
Thornburg, IA (city) Keokuk County	6	7.06
Macungie, PA (borough) Lehigh County	214	7.04
Eden, PA (township) Lancaster County	130	7.00
District, PA (township) Berks County	101	6.97
East Greenville, PA (borough) Montgomery County	214	6.90
Wiconisco, PA (township) Dauphin County	81	6.88
Burnside, PA (borough) Clearfield County	20	6.80
Topton, PA (borough) Berks County	132	6.79
Barry, PA (township) Schuylkill County	65	6.72
Upper Milford, PA (township) Lehigh County	467	6.71
Hollenback, PA (township) Luzerne County	83	6.68
Driftwood, PA (borough) Cameron County	6	6.67
Franklin, PA (township) Carbon County	282	6.65
Strasburg, PA (township) Lancaster County	266	6.62
Hooversville, PA (borough) Somerset County	52	6.59
Weissport, PA (borough) Carbon County	29	6.59
Mahoning, PA (township) Carbon County	262	6.58
Gilbertsville, PA (cdp) Montgomery County	279	6.57
Mount Union, IA (city) Henry County	9	6.57
Bushkill, PA (township) Northampton County	456	6.53
Verdon, MN (township) Aitkin County	3	6.52
Upper Bern, PA (township) Berks County	96	6.49
Hanover, PA (township) Lehigh County	124	6.48
Upper Nazareth, PA (township) Northampton County	286	6.46
Halfway House, PA (cdp) Montgomery County	109	6.45
Kenhorst, PA (borough) Berks County	170	6.39
Harmony, WI (town) Vernon County	47	6.39
Grapeville, PA (cdp) Westmoreland County	43	6.39
Green Lane, PA (borough) Montgomery County	37	6.39
Upper Macungie, PA (township) Lehigh County	883	6.35
West Rockhill, PA (township) Bucks County	269	6.35
Ogle, PA (township) Somerset County	37	6.25
Hamburg, PA (borough) Berks County	256	6.22
Lykens, PA (borough) Dauphin County	119	6.17
Nescopeck, PA (borough) Luzerne County	94	6.15
Bechtelsville, PA (borough) Berks County	57	6.13
Shoemakersville, PA (borough) Berks County	130	6.12
Douglass, PA (township) Montgomery County	556	6.08
East Allen, PA (township) Northampton County	298	6.08
East Brunswick, PA (township) Schuylkill County	98	6.06
Hartleton, PA (borough) Union County	16	6.02
Rockland, PA (township) Berks County	226	6.00
Landisburg, PA (borough) Perry County	12	6.00
Sand Hill, PA (cdp) Lebanon County	139	5.97
Locustdale, PA (cdp) Columbia County	5	5.95
Pike, PA (township) Berks County	99	5.90
South Mahoning, PA (township) Indiana County	112	5.89
Leesport, PA (borough) Berks County	106	5.87
Gratz, PA (borough) Dauphin County	38	5.83
Brown, PA (township) Lycoming County	6	5.83
East Fallowfield, PA (township) Crawford County	80	5.81
Conewango, NY (town) Cattaraugus County	98	5.79
Wayne, PA (township) Schuylkill County	273	5.78
Rohrsburg, PA (cdp) Columbia County	9	5.77

Notes: (cdp) census designated place; Refer to the Explanation of Data in the front of the book for more detailed information.

Pennsylvania German

Top 150 Places Sorted by Percent

(Based on places with populations of 10,000 or more)

Place	Number	%
North Whitehall, PA (township) Lehigh County	1,421	9.65
Emmaus, PA (borough) Lehigh County	988	8.79
Upper Macungie, PA (township) Lehigh County	883	6.35
South Whitehall, PA (township) Lehigh County	1,036	5.75
Salisbury, PA (township) Lehigh County	730	5.41
Whitehall, PA (township) Lehigh County	1,311	5.27
Allentown, PA (city) Lehigh County	5,614	5.26
Berwick, PA (borough) Columbia County	556	5.20
Lower Macungie, PA (township) Lehigh County	951	4.95
Fullerton, PA (cdp) Lehigh County	704	4.95
Upper Saucon, PA (township) Lehigh County	569	4.77
Muhlenberg, PA (township) Berks County	761	4.67
Cumru, PA (township) Berks County	529	3.83
Franconia, PA (township) Montgomery County	404	3.51
Bethlehem, PA (city) Northampton County	2,437	3.42
Palmer, PA (township) Northampton County	574	3.41
Exeter, PA (township) Berks County	664	3.13
North Lebanon, PA (township) Lebanon County	327	3.08
Reading, PA (city) Berks County	2,472	3.04
Sunbury, PA (city) Northumberland County	302	2.85
Easton, PA (city) Northampton County	741	2.82
Bethlehem, PA (township) Northampton County	550	2.60
Mountain Top, PA (cdp) Luzerne County	396	2.60
Lower Pottsgrove, PA (township) Montgomery County	268	2.37
Pottstown, PA (borough) Montgomery County	514	2.36
Spring, PA (township) Berks County	510	2.34
East Lampeter, PA (township) Lancaster County	303	2.23
Pottsville, PA (city) Schuylkill County	337	2.17
Coal, PA (township) Northumberland County	197	1.85
Chestnuthill, PA (township) Monroe County	256	1.78
Williamsport, PA (city) Lycoming County	535	1.74
Limerick, PA (township) Montgomery County	229	1.69
Southport, NY (town) Chemung County	189	1.69
East Pennsboro, PA (township) Cumberland County	302	1.66
Phillipsburg, NJ (town) Warren County	251	1.66
Lebanon, PA (city) Lebanon County	399	1.63
Stroud, PA (township) Monroe County	226	1.62
Bloomsburg, PA (town) Columbia County	194	1.56
Fairview, PA (township) York County	221	1.54
Salisbury, PA (township) Lancaster County	144	1.44
Nanticoke, PA (city) Luzerne County	150	1.37
Hilltown, PA (township) Bucks County	162	1.34
Swatara, PA (township) Dauphin County	302	1.33
Lower Salford, PA (township) Montgomery County	170	1.32
Johnstown, PA (city) Cambria County	312	1.31
Lansdale, PA (borough) Montgomery County	210	1.31
Newberry, PA (township) York County	186	1.30
Hempfield, PA (township) Westmoreland County	500	1.23
Towamencin, PA (township) Montgomery County	216	1.23
Back Mountain, PA (cdp) Luzerne County	317	1.19
Phoenixville, PA (borough) Chester County	177	1.19
Hanover, PA (township) Luzerne County	134	1.17
New Britain, PA (township) Bucks County	123	1.15
Altoona, PA (city) Blair County	557	1.12
Wilkes-Barre, PA (city) Luzerne County	464	1.08
North Middleton, PA (township) Cumberland County	110	1.08
Hatfield, PA (township) Montgomery County	178	1.07
Southampton, NJ (township) Burlington County	111	1.07
Richland, PA (township) Cambria County	128	1.02
Elizabethtown, PA (borough) Lancaster County	117	0.98
Silver Spring, PA (township) Cumberland County	102	0.96
Ephrata, PA (borough) Lancaster County	126	0.95
Ferguson, PA (township) Centre County	132	0.94
South Middleton, PA (township) Cumberland County	122	0.94
Windsor, PA (township) York County	119	0.93
Mount Pleasant, PA (township) Westmoreland County	104	0.93
Lower Paxton, PA (township) Dauphin County	400	0.90
Upper Allen, PA (township) Cumberland County	135	0.88
Middle Smithfield, PA (township) Monroe County	100	0.87
Goshen, IN (city) Elkhart County	252	0.86
Norristown, PA (borough) Montgomery County	265	0.85
Sandy, PA (township) Clearfield County	98	0.85
York, PA (township) York County	196	0.83
Wadsworth, OH (city) Medina County	154	0.83
Susquehanna, PA (township) Dauphin County	178	0.82
Derry, PA (township) Dauphin County	168	0.79
New Kensington, PA (city) Westmoreland County	113	0.77
Kingston, PA (borough) Luzerne County	107	0.77
Woodlyn, PA (cdp) Delaware County	76	0.76
York, PA (city) York County	307	0.75
Upper Providence, PA (township) Montgomery County	115	0.75
Mantua, NJ (township) Gloucester County	104	0.73
Guilford, PA (township) Franklin County	95	0.73
Hazleton, PA (city) Luzerne County	167	0.72
North Union, PA (township) Fayette County	102	0.72
Meadville, PA (city) Crawford County	99	0.72
Hershey, PA (cdp) Dauphin County	91	0.71
Greene, PA (township) Franklin County	85	0.69
Falls, PA (township) Bucks County	232	0.67
Lower Providence, PA (township) Montgomery County	150	0.67
King of Prussia, PA (cdp) Montgomery County	124	0.67
West Chester, PA (borough) Chester County	119	0.67
Upper Chichester, PA (township) Delaware County	112	0.67
Elmira, NY (city) Chemung County	203	0.66
Buckingham, PA (township) Bucks County	109	0.66
Lansdowne, PA (borough) Delaware County	73	0.66
Croydon, PA (cdp) Bucks County	66	0.66
Oil City, PA (city) Venango County	75	0.65
Ridley, PA (township) Delaware County	190	0.62
West Norriton, PA (cdp) Montgomery County	92	0.62
Niles, MI (city) Berrien County	75	0.62
Montgomeryville, PA (cdp) Montgomery County	73	0.61
Plymouth, PA (township) Montgomery County	96	0.60
Hampden, PA (township) Cumberland County	142	0.59
Shiloh, PA (cdp) York County	60	0.59
Lower Southampton, PA (township) Bucks County	111	0.58
West Manchester, PA (township) York County	99	0.58
Austintown, OH (cdp) Mahoning County	179	0.57
Derry, PA (township) Westmoreland County	83	0.56
White, PA (township) Indiana County	78	0.56
Manheim, PA (township) Lancaster County	187	0.55
Springettsbury, PA (township) York County	130	0.54
Niles, MI (township) Berrien County	73	0.54
Bensalem, PA (township) Bucks County	310	0.53
East Moline, IL (city) Rock Island County	107	0.53
Lower Allen, PA (township) Cumberland County	92	0.53
Endwell, NY (cdp) Broome County	62	0.53
Willistown, PA (township) Chester County	53	0.53
Levittown, PA (cdp) Bucks County	279	0.52
Horseheads, NY (town) Chemung County	102	0.52
Whitpain, PA (township) Montgomery County	97	0.52
Aston, PA (township) Delaware County	83	0.51
Logan, PA (township) Blair County	61	0.51
Upper Merion, PA (township) Montgomery County	135	0.50
Jeannette, PA (city) Westmoreland County	53	0.50
Morrisville, PA (borough) Bucks County	50	0.50
North Huntingdon, PA (township) Westmoreland County	144	0.49
Greensburg, PA (city) Westmoreland County	78	0.49
Dover, OH (city) Tuscarawas County	59	0.48
Binghamton, NY (city) Broome County	223	0.47
Deptford, NJ (township) Gloucester County	125	0.47
Ashland, OH (city) Ashland County	100	0.47
West Whiteland, PA (township) Chester County	77	0.47
Hopewell, NJ (township) Mercer County	75	0.47
Butler, PA (city) Butler County	70	0.47
East Norriton, PA (cdp) Montgomery County	62	0.47
Pennsville, NJ (township) Salem County	62	0.47
Harrison Township, PA (cdp) Allegheny County	51	0.47
Granger, IN (cdp) Saint Joseph County	131	0.46
Warwick, PA (township) Lancaster County	71	0.46
Colonial Park, PA (cdp) Dauphin County	61	0.46
Manchester, PA (township) York County	59	0.46
Caln, PA (township) Chester County	55	0.46
Corning, NY (city) Steuben County	50	0.46
Columbia, PA (borough) Lancaster County	47	0.46
West Goshen, PA (township) Chester County	93	0.45
Bear, DE (cdp) New Castle County	79	0.45
Manor, PA (township) Lancaster County	74	0.45
Coolbaugh, PA (township) Monroe County	68	0.45
Brookside, DE (cdp) New Castle County	66	0.45

Notes: (cdp) census designated place; Refer to the Explanation of Data in the front of the book for more detailed information.

Polish

Top 150 Places Sorted by Number

(Based on all places, regardless of population)

Place	Number	%
New York, NY (city) New York City	213,447	2.67
Chicago, IL (city) Cook County	210,421	7.27
Philadelphia, PA (city) Philadelphia County	65,508	4.32
Milwaukee, WI (city) Milwaukee County	57,485	9.63
Los Angeles, CA (city) Los Angeles County	56,670	1.53
Hempstead, NY (town) Nassau County	38,256	5.06
Cheektowaga, NY (town) Erie County	37,560	39.95
Buffalo, NY (city) Erie County	34,254	11.70
Phoenix, AZ (city) Maricopa County	32,050	2.43
Toledo, OH (city) Lucas County	31,802	10.14
Warren, MI (city) Macomb County	29,075	21.03
Pittsburgh, PA (city) Allegheny County	28,178	8.42
Brookhaven, NY (town) Suffolk County	26,848	5.99
Sterling Heights, MI (city) Macomb County	26,123	20.99
San Diego, CA (city) San Diego County	25,207	2.06
Cleveland, OH (city) Cuyahoga County	22,978	4.80
Oyster Bay, NY (town) Nassau County	19,752	6.72
Houston, TX (city) Harris County	19,297	0.99
Detroit, MI (city) Wayne County	18,992	2.00
Omaha, NE (city) Douglas County	18,447	4.73
Baltimore, MD (independent city) Baltimore city	18,400	2.83
Livonia, MI (city) Wayne County	18,131	18.03
Clinton, MI (cdp) Macomb County	17,532	18.33
Minneapolis, MN (city) Hennepin County	15,785	4.13
Parma, OH (city) Cuyahoga County	15,503	18.10
Grand Rapids, MI (city) Kent County	15,442	7.81
Amherst, NY (town) Erie County	15,136	12.99
Erie, PA (city) Erie County	14,718	14.19
Columbus, OH (city) Franklin County	14,510	2.04
San Antonio, TX (city) Bexar County	14,475	1.26
San Francisco, CA (city) San Francisco County	14,332	1.85
New Britain, CT (city) Hartford County	14,257	19.93
West Seneca, NY (town) Erie County	14,236	30.95
Islip, NY (town) Suffolk County	14,034	4.35
Naperville, IL (city) Du Page County	13,936	10.86
Lancaster, NY (town) Erie County	13,903	35.63
Boston, MA (city) Suffolk County	13,704	2.33
North Hempstead, NY (town) Nassau County	13,130	5.90
Hamburg, NY (town) Erie County	12,779	22.74
Seattle, WA (city) King County	12,622	2.24
Shelby, MI (cdp) Macomb County	12,462	19.15
Chicopee, MA (city) Hampden County	12,448	22.78
West Allis, WI (city) Milwaukee County	12,364	20.17
Las Vegas, NV (city) Clark County	12,188	2.55
Dearborn Heights, MI (city) Wayne County	12,058	20.70
Westland, MI (city) Wayne County	11,905	13.74
Dearborn, MI (city) Wayne County	11,555	11.82
Babylon, NY (town) Suffolk County	11,519	5.44
Clifton, NJ (city) Passaic County	11,451	14.56
Huntington, NY (town) Suffolk County	11,435	5.86
South Bend, IN (city) Saint Joseph County	11,417	10.67
Scranton, PA (city) Lackawanna County	11,311	14.80
Madison, WI (city) Dane County	11,144	5.37
Schaumburg, IL (village) Cook County	11,109	14.91
Bayonne, NJ (city) Hudson County	11,095	17.94
Denver, CO (city) Denver County	11,055	1.99
Arlington Heights, IL (village) Cook County	11,001	14.46
Tonawanda, NY (town) Erie County	10,969	14.03
Tucson, AZ (city) Pima County	10,967	2.25
Saint Paul, MN (city) Ramsey County	10,868	3.78
Virginia Beach, VA (independent city) Virginia Beach city	10,781	2.54
Saint Clair Shores, MI (city) Macomb County	10,776	17.07
San Jose, CA (city) Santa Clara County	10,766	1.20
Hamilton, NJ (township) Mercer County	10,751	12.32
Des Plaines, IL (city) Cook County	10,703	18.23
Woodbridge, NJ (township) Middlesex County	10,694	11.00
Oak Lawn, IL (village) Cook County	10,667	19.26
Indianapolis, IN (special city) Marion County	10,643	1.36
Canton, MI (cdp) Wayne County	10,506	13.77
Jacksonville, FL (special city) Duval County	10,500	1.43
Worcester, MA (city) Worcester County	10,482	6.07
Hammond, IN (city) Lake County	10,190	12.27
Green Bay, WI (city) Brown County	10,058	9.83
Portland, OR (city) Multnomah County	10,042	1.90
Mesa, AZ (city) Maricopa County	9,974	2.51
Macomb, MI (township) Macomb County	9,909	19.63
Dallas, TX (city) Dallas County	9,642	0.81
Roseville, MI (city) Macomb County	9,549	19.84
Tinley Park, IL (village) Cook County	9,540	19.74
Austin, TX (city) Travis County	9,466	1.44
Orland Park, IL (village) Cook County	9,430	18.45
Greenfield, WI (city) Milwaukee County	9,310	26.24
Mount Prospect, IL (village) Cook County	9,216	16.25
Colorado Springs, CO (city) El Paso County	9,154	2.54
Springfield, MA (city) Hampden County	9,094	5.98
Farmington Hills, MI (city) Oakland County	9,011	10.97
Troy, MI (city) Oakland County	8,928	11.03
Scottsdale, AZ (city) Maricopa County	8,905	4.39
Wilkes-Barre, PA (city) Luzerne County	8,547	19.82
Rochester Hills, MI (city) Oakland County	8,482	12.32
Burbank, IL (city) Cook County	8,427	30.29
Joliet, IL (city) Will County	8,153	7.68
Sayreville, NJ (borough) Middlesex County	8,133	20.14
Charlotte, NC (city) Mecklenburg County	8,090	1.49
Dover, NJ (township) Ocean County	8,088	9.01
Garfield Heights, OH (city) Cuyahoga County	7,983	26.07
Meriden, CT (city) New Haven County	7,970	13.68
Smithtown, NY (town) Suffolk County	7,970	6.89
Bay City, MI (city) Bay County	7,968	21.64
Washington, DC (city) District of Columbia	7,910	1.38
Park Ridge, IL (city) Cook County	7,855	20.82
Palatine, IL (village) Cook County	7,846	12.04
Redford, MI (cdp) Wayne County	7,787	15.08
Bristol, CT (city) Hartford County	7,696	12.81
Toms River, NJ (cdp) Ocean County	7,691	8.90
Dundalk, MD (cdp) Baltimore County	7,682	12.33
Kenosha, WI (city) Kenosha County	7,663	8.45
Saint Petersburg, FL (city) Pinellas County	7,542	3.04
Oak Creek, WI (city) Milwaukee County	7,485	26.30
Franklin, WI (city) Milwaukee County	7,480	25.31
Albuquerque, NM (city) Bernalillo County	7,468	1.66
Garfield, NJ (city) Bergen County	7,431	24.95
Syracuse, NY (city) Onondaga County	7,424	5.04
Ann Arbor, MI (city) Washtenaw County	7,288	6.39
Edison, NJ (cdp) Middlesex County	7,251	7.42
Downers Grove, IL (village) Du Page County	7,247	14.90
Jersey City, NJ (city) Hudson County	7,215	3.01
Taylor, MI (city) Wayne County	7,143	10.84
Linden, NJ (city) Union County	7,098	18.02
New Berlin, WI (city) Waukesha County	7,025	18.31
Millcreek, PA (township) Erie County	7,000	13.43
Royal Oak, MI (city) Oakland County	6,987	11.63
Brick, NJ (township) Ocean County	6,973	9.16
North Tonawanda, NY (city) Niagara County	6,949	20.89
Niles, IL (village) Cook County	6,880	22.82
Chesterfield, MI (township) Macomb County	6,877	18.34
Coral Springs, FL (city) Broward County	6,741	5.74
Elk Grove Village, IL (village) Cook County	6,725	19.35
Hoffman Estates, IL (village) Cook County	6,721	13.35
Waukesha, WI (city) Waukesha County	6,708	10.42
Depew, NY (village) Erie County	6,687	40.24
Aurora, IL (city) Kane County	6,644	4.63
Stamford, CT (city) Fairfield County	6,578	5.62
Stevens Point, WI (city) Portage County	6,529	26.66
Colonie, NY (town) Albany County	6,515	8.22
Berwyn, IL (city) Cook County	6,480	12.00
Yonkers, NY (city) Westchester County	6,444	3.29
Southington, CT (town) Hartford County	6,378	16.05
Glendale, AZ (city) Maricopa County	6,329	2.90
Wyandotte, MI (city) Wayne County	6,292	22.47
Westfield, MA (city) Hampden County	6,290	15.70
Eastpointe, MI (city) Macomb County	6,278	18.42
Elmwood Park, IL (village) Cook County	6,270	24.68
Greece, NY (town) Monroe County	6,174	6.56
Henderson, NV (city) Clark County	6,144	3.49
Duluth, MN (city) Saint Louis County	6,128	7.06
Ramapo, NY (town) Rockland County	6,124	5.62
Anchorage, AK (municipality) Anchorage Borough	6,103	2.34
Niagara Falls, NY (city) Niagara County	6,100	10.96
Waterford, MI (cdp) Oakland County	6,070	8.30

Notes: (cdp) census designated place; Refer to the Explanation of Data in the front of the book for more detailed information.

Polish

Top 150 Places Sorted by Percent

(Based on all places, regardless of population)

Place	Number	%
Elbe, WA (cdp) Pierce County	8	100.00
Grenville, SD (town) Day County	47	74.60
Franzen, WI (town) Marathon County	348	66.67
Albee, SD (town) Grant County	6	66.67
Pulawski, MI (township) Presque Isle County	253	65.71
Posen, MI (township) Presque Isle County	652	65.40
Ashton, NE (village) Sherman County	151	65.09
Metz, MI (township) Presque Isle County	217	64.39
Nelson Park, MN (township) Marshall County	91	63.64
Sharon, WI (town) Portage County	1,256	63.50
Royal, MN (township) Lincoln County	135	61.93
Burnside, WI (town) Trempealeau County	333	61.44
Bevent, WI (town) Marathon County	687	60.80
Dewey, WI (town) Portage County	579	60.06
Fork, MN (township) Marshall County	11	57.89
Swan River, MN (township) Morrison County	438	57.78
Dupont, PA (borough) Luzerne County	1,546	56.86
Linwood, WI (town) Portage County	642	56.86
Alban, WI (town) Portage County	460	56.37
Posen, MI (village) Presque Isle County	180	56.07
Sloan, NY (village) Erie County	2,117	55.84
Stockton, WI (town) Portage County	1,621	55.84
Sobieski, MN (city) Morrison County	118	55.66
Armstrong Creek, WI (town) Forest County	267	53.08
Arcadia, WI (town) Trempealeau County	787	51.98
Wallington, NJ (borough) Bergen County	5,967	51.52
Bowlus, MN (city) Morrison County	149	51.38
Strickland, WI (town) Rusk County	161	51.27
Gilman, MN (city) Benton County	114	51.12
Independence, WI (city) Trempealeau County	640	51.00
Du Bois, IL (village) Washington County	107	50.95
Wanger, MN (township) Marshall County	49	50.00
Nanticoke, PA (city) Luzerne County	5,444	49.58
Paris, MI (township) Huron County	281	49.56
Wright, MN (township) Marshall County	67	49.26
Dodge, WI (town) Trempealeau County	206	48.93
Saint Joseph, MN (township) Kittson County	22	48.89
Alberta, MN (township) Benton County	402	48.79
Flensburg, MN (city) Morrison County	124	47.88
Barto, MN (township) Roseau County	66	47.83
Falls City, TX (city) Karnes County	281	47.79
Warrior Run, PA (borough) Luzerne County	302	47.63
Denham, MN (city) Pine County	24	47.06
Guenther, WI (town) Marathon County	137	46.76
Marble, MN (township) Lincoln County	92	46.70
Pulaski, MN (township) Morrison County	157	46.59
Cornlea, NE (village) Platte County	19	46.34
Hatley, WI (village) Marathon County	243	45.94
Krakow, MI (township) Presque Isle County	290	45.60
Rosholt, WI (village) Portage County	260	45.30
Nelsonville, WI (village) Portage County	95	45.24
Reid, WI (town) Marathon County	538	44.91
Two Rivers, MN (township) Morrison County	253	44.70
Aurora, WI (town) Taylor County	168	43.86
Hull, WI (town) Portage County	2,455	43.63
Taft, WI (town) Taylor County	161	43.63
Alma, MN (township) Marshall County	41	43.62
Carson, WI (town) Portage County	579	43.47
Duryea, PA (borough) Luzerne County	1,994	43.03
Lincoln, MI (township) Huron County	378	42.52
Dickson City, PA (borough) Lackawanna County	2,597	41.85
Lublin, WI (village) Taylor County	43	41.75
Maple Grove, WI (town) Shawano County	425	41.46
Amherst Junction, WI (village) Portage County	117	41.34
Pulaski, WI (village) Brown County	1,251	40.50
South Fork, WI (town) Rusk County	55	40.44
Depew, NY (village) Erie County	6,687	40.24
Roosevelt, WI (town) Taylor County	162	40.20
Glen Lyon, PA (cdp) Luzerne County	767	40.12
Kulpmont, PA (borough) Northumberland County	1,195	40.03
Bingham, MI (township) Huron County	697	40.03
Pike Creek, MN (township) Morrison County	361	40.02
Cheektowaga, NY (town) Erie County	37,560	39.95
Cuyahoga Heights, OH (village) Cuyahoga County	239	39.90
Silver Creek, NE (village) Merrick County	170	39.53
Thorp, WI (town) Clark County	295	39.49
Austin, MI (township) Sanilac County	273	39.45
Farwell, NE (village) Howard County	56	39.44
Dwight, MI (township) Huron County	365	39.42
New Hope, WI (town) Portage County	294	39.20
Ubly, MI (village) Huron County	334	38.88
Radom, IL (village) Washington County	162	38.85
Morrill, MN (township) Morrison County	260	38.81
Polonia, MN (township) Roseau County	12	38.71
Harding, MN (city) Morrison County	45	38.46
Avoca, PA (borough) Luzerne County	1,090	38.23
Sigel, MI (township) Huron County	228	37.94
Richardville, MN (township) Kittson County	44	37.93
West Wyoming, PA (borough) Luzerne County	1,069	37.73
West Hampton Dunes, NY (village) Suffolk County	3	37.50
Harwood Heights, IL (village) Cook County	3,079	37.43
Norrie, WI (town) Marathon County	326	37.34
Sugar Notch, PA (borough) Luzerne County	378	37.31
Elderon, WI (town) Marathon County	211	37.08
New York Mills, NY (village) Oneida County	1,190	37.00
Holding, MN (township) Stearns County	408	36.96
Filer charter, MI (township) Manistee County	825	36.86
Rietbrock, WI (town) Marathon County	336	36.84
Knowlton, WI (town) Marathon County	621	36.66
Buena Vista, WI (town) Portage County	443	36.52
Yorkville, NY (village) Oneida County	973	36.31
Larksville, PA (borough) Luzerne County	1,704	36.30
Dunkirk, NY (town) Chautauqua County	510	36.27
Shenandoah, PA (borough) Schuylkill County	2,039	36.26
Duncan, NE (village) Platte County	129	36.24
Tarnov, NE (village) Platte County	25	36.23
Angelica, WI (town) Shawano County	576	36.11
Hume, MI (township) Huron County	292	36.09
Newport, PA (township) Luzerne County	1,803	36.02
Montana, WI (town) Buffalo County	120	35.93
Thorp, WI (city) Clark County	548	35.86
Pringle, PA (borough) Luzerne County	354	35.72
Lancaster, NY (town) Erie County	13,903	35.63
Bondsville, MA (cdp) Hampden County	643	35.52
Forestville, MI (village) Sanilac County	39	35.45
Middle River, MN (township) Marshall County	34	35.42
Loup City, NE (city) Sherman County	346	35.31
Marshallton, PA (cdp) Northumberland County	506	35.09
Minden, MI (township) Sanilac County	215	35.02
East Park, MN (township) Marshall County	7	35.00
Portsmouth, MI (township) Bay County	1,266	34.95
Plymouth, PA (township) Luzerne County	733	34.95
Marion Heights, PA (borough) Northumberland County	257	34.87
Chimney Rock, WI (town) Trempealeau County	99	34.86
City Point, WI (town) Jackson County	61	34.86
Glencoe, WI (town) Buffalo County	166	34.80
Minto, ND (city) Walsh County	227	34.76
Gilmanton, MN (township) Benton County	242	34.72
Mayfield, PA (borough) Lackawanna County	608	34.62
Hatfield, MA (town) Hampshire County	1,118	34.41
Whiting, WI (village) Portage County	593	34.10
Arcadia, WI (city) Trempealeau County	827	33.98
Elderon, WI (village) Marathon County	54	33.96
Fairview-Ferndale, PA (cdp) Northumberland County	821	33.91
Chase, WI (town) Oconto County	705	33.91
Granite Ledge, MN (township) Benton County	220	33.90
Amherst, WI (town) Portage County	470	33.81
Germania, WI (town) Shawano County	122	33.80
Everson, PA (borough) Fayette County	284	33.77
Lausanne, PA (township) Carbon County	76	33.63
Rogers, MI (township) Presque Isle County	328	33.40
Lakin, MN (township) Morrison County	130	33.25
Warner, MI (township) Antrim County	128	33.25
Plains, PA (township) Luzerne County	3,606	33.06
Wilkes-Barre Township, PA (cdp) Luzerne County	1,068	33.01
Junction City, WI (village) Portage County	128	32.99
Slocum, PA (township) Luzerne County	361	32.94
Verona, MI (township) Huron County	450	32.89
Bloomer, MN (township) Marshall County	25	32.89
Lemont, IL (village) Cook County	4,327	32.84

Notes: (cdp) census designated place; Refer to the Explanation of Data in the front of the book for more detailed information.

Polish

Top 150 Places Sorted by Percent

(Based on places with populations of 10,000 or more)

Place	Number	%
Wallington, NJ (borough) Bergen County	5,967	51.52
Nanticoke, PA (city) Luzerne County	5,444	49.58
Depew, NY (village) Erie County	6,687	40.24
Cheektowaga, NY (town) Erie County	37,560	39.95
Lancaster, NY (town) Erie County	13,903	35.63
Plains, PA (township) Luzerne County	3,606	33.06
Lemont, IL (village) Cook County	4,327	32.84
Norridge, IL (village) Cook County	4,673	31.81
River Grove, IL (village) Cook County	3,375	31.79
West Seneca, NY (town) Erie County	14,236	30.95
Burbank, IL (city) Cook County	8,427	30.29
Hanover, PA (township) Luzerne County	3,450	30.10
Lackawanna, NY (city) Erie County	5,656	29.70
Lancaster, NY (village) Erie County	3,317	29.65
Manville, NJ (borough) Somerset County	2,999	29.10
Elma, NY (town) Erie County	3,284	29.05
Goodings Grove, IL (cdp) Will County	4,825	28.21
Plover, WI (village) Portage County	3,002	28.20
Dunkirk, NY (city) Chautauqua County	3,641	27.73
South Milwaukee, WI (city) Milwaukee County	5,826	27.49
Hickory Hills, IL (city) Cook County	3,750	26.91
Stevens Point, WI (city) Portage County	6,529	26.66
Alpena, MI (city) Alpena County	2,963	26.56
Cudahy, WI (city) Milwaukee County	4,889	26.53
Mountain Top, PA (cdp) Luzerne County	4,047	26.53
Oak Creek, WI (city) Milwaukee County	7,485	26.30
Greenfield, WI (city) Milwaukee County	9,310	26.24
Garfield Heights, OH (city) Cuyahoga County	7,983	26.07
Bridgeview, IL (village) Cook County	3,942	25.65
Dudley, MA (town) Worcester County	2,542	25.33
Franklin, WI (city) Milwaukee County	7,480	25.31
Palmer, MA (town) Hampden County	3,132	25.06
Garfield, NJ (city) Bergen County	7,431	24.95
Coal, PA (township) Northumberland County	2,626	24.71
Elmwood Park, IL (village) Cook County	6,270	24.68
Alden, NY (town) Erie County	2,572	24.57
Justice, IL (village) Cook County	2,931	24.24
Muskego, WI (city) Waukesha County	5,106	23.87
Hamtramck, MI (city) Wayne County	5,263	22.91
Niles, IL (village) Cook County	6,880	22.82
Webster, MA (town) Worcester County	3,744	22.81
Chicopee, MA (city) Hampden County	12,448	22.78
Hamburg, NY (town) Erie County	12,779	22.74
Greendale, WI (village) Milwaukee County	3,260	22.63
Seven Hills, OH (city) Cuyahoga County	2,732	22.62
Wyandotte, MI (city) Wayne County	6,292	22.47
Easthampton, MA (city) Hampshire County	3,591	22.45
Monitor, MI (township) Bay County	2,246	22.38
Schiller Park, IL (village) Cook County	2,616	22.20
Bay City, MI (city) Bay County	7,968	21.64
Whitestown, NY (town) Oneida County	3,954	21.25
Warren, MI (city) Macomb County	29,075	21.03
Sterling Heights, MI (city) Macomb County	26,123	20.99
Dyer, IN (town) Lake County	2,903	20.95
Fraser, MI (city) Macomb County	3,203	20.94
North Tonawanda, NY (city) Niagara County	6,949	20.89
Park Ridge, IL (city) Cook County	7,855	20.82
Dearborn Heights, MI (city) Wayne County	12,058	20.70
Wood Dale, IL (city) Du Page County	2,886	20.63
Harrison Township, PA (cdp) Allegheny County	2,246	20.54
Evans, NY (town) Erie County	3,608	20.51
Lockport, IL (city) Will County	3,031	20.48
Prospect Heights, IL (city) Cook County	3,575	20.38
Chicago Ridge, IL (village) Cook County	2,823	20.34
Berlin, CT (town) Hartford County	3,701	20.32
Worth, IL (village) Cook County	2,264	20.30
West Allis, WI (city) Milwaukee County	12,364	20.17
Sayreville, NJ (borough) Middlesex County	8,133	20.14
Amsterdam, NY (city) Montgomery County	3,670	19.99
New Britain, CT (city) Hartford County	14,257	19.93
Washington, MI (township) Macomb County	3,796	19.85
Roseville, MI (city) Macomb County	9,549	19.84
Wilkes-Barre, PA (city) Luzerne County	8,547	19.82
Crestwood, IL (village) Cook County	2,224	19.82
Tinley Park, IL (village) Cook County	9,540	19.74
Macomb, MI (township) Macomb County	9,909	19.63
Franklin Park, IL (village) Cook County	3,812	19.61
Plainville, CT (town) Hartford County	3,382	19.52
Munster, IN (town) Lake County	4,173	19.40
Elk Grove Village, IL (village) Cook County	6,725	19.35
Oak Lawn, IL (village) Cook County	10,667	19.26
Darien, IL (city) Du Page County	4,415	19.22
Bangor, MI (township) Bay County	2,986	19.21
Pomfret, NY (town) Chautauqua County	2,819	19.20
Shelby, MI (cdp) Macomb County	12,462	19.15
Palos Hills, IL (city) Cook County	3,364	18.95
South River, NJ (borough) Middlesex County	2,894	18.89
Orchard Park, NY (town) Erie County	5,165	18.69
Kingston, PA (borough) Luzerne County	2,583	18.64
Back Mountain, PA (cdp) Luzerne County	4,970	18.62
Algonquin, IL (village) McHenry County	4,352	18.58
Mokena, IL (village) Will County	2,710	18.46
Orland Park, IL (village) Cook County	9,430	18.45
Eastpointe, MI (city) Macomb County	6,278	18.42
North Royalton, OH (city) Cuyahoga County	5,278	18.42
Chesterfield, MI (township) Macomb County	6,877	18.34
Clinton, MI (cdp) Macomb County	17,532	18.33
New Berlin, WI (city) Waukesha County	7,025	18.31
Oak Forest, IL (city) Cook County	5,116	18.30
Harborcreek, PA (township) Erie County	2,774	18.28
Brecksville, OH (city) Cuyahoga County	2,436	18.27
Des Plaines, IL (city) Cook County	10,703	18.23
Parma, OH (city) Cuyahoga County	15,503	18.10
Brookfield, IL (village) Cook County	3,430	18.05
Livonia, MI (city) Wayne County	18,131	18.03
Linden, NJ (city) Union County	7,098	18.02
Derby, CT (city) New Haven County	2,228	17.98
Bayonne, NJ (city) Hudson County	11,095	17.94
Weston, WI (village) Marathon County	2,189	17.87
Clark, NJ (cdp) Union County	2,588	17.73
Highland, IN (town) Lake County	4,141	17.59
Fredonia, NY (village) Chautauqua County	1,889	17.52
Schererville, IN (town) Lake County	4,296	17.31
Alsip, IL (village) Cook County	3,434	17.29
Grosse Ile, MI (cdp) Wayne County	1,883	17.28
Roselle, IL (village) Du Page County	3,980	17.10
Saint Clair Shores, MI (city) Macomb County	10,776	17.07
Seymour, CT (town) New Haven County	2,629	17.01
Mount Pleasant, PA (township) Westmoreland County	1,889	16.88
Ludlow, MA (town) Hampden County	3,572	16.84
Allen Park, MI (city) Wayne County	4,939	16.81
New Lenox, IL (village) Will County	2,955	16.77
Garden City, MI (city) Wayne County	5,027	16.73
Plymouth, CT (town) Litchfield County	1,942	16.69
Harrison, MI (cdp) Macomb County	4,073	16.65
Woodhaven, MI (city) Wayne County	2,084	16.63
Wheatfield, NY (town) Niagara County	2,339	16.61
Lake in the Hills, IL (village) McHenry County	3,886	16.56
Lake Zurich, IL (village) Lake County	3,000	16.53
Mount Prospect, IL (village) Cook County	9,216	16.25
Broadview Heights, OH (city) Cuyahoga County	2,565	16.06
La Grange Park, IL (village) Cook County	2,126	16.06
Southington, CT (town) Hartford County	6,378	16.05
Trenton, MI (city) Wayne County	3,126	15.96
Lower Burrell, PA (city) Westmoreland County	1,989	15.75
Lansing, IL (village) Cook County	4,429	15.73
Griswold, CT (town) New London County	1,698	15.71
Westfield, MA (city) Hampden County	6,290	15.70
Romeoville, IL (village) Will County	3,312	15.67
Lyons, IL (village) Cook County	1,580	15.59
Wilbraham, MA (town) Hampden County	2,094	15.54
Plymouth Township, MI (cdp) Wayne County	4,279	15.48
Plainfield, IL (village) Will County	2,006	15.42
Midlothian, IL (village) Cook County	2,190	15.40
Walker, MI (city) Kent County	3,354	15.39
Southold, NY (town) Suffolk County	3,160	15.34
Bartlett, IL (village) Du Page County	5,619	15.25
Southgate, MI (city) Wayne County	4,591	15.23
Howard, WI (village) Brown County	2,051	15.15
Redford, MI (cdp) Wayne County	7,787	15.08

Notes: (cdp) census designated place; Refer to the Explanation of Data in the front of the book for more detailed information.

Portuguese

Top 150 Places Sorted by Number

(Based on all places, regardless of population)

Place	Number	%
Fall River, MA (city) Bristol County	43,253	47.05
New Bedford, MA (city) Bristol County	36,239	38.65
Newark, NJ (city) Essex County	15,801	5.78
Taunton, MA (city) Bristol County	15,370	27.46
San Jose, CA (city) Santa Clara County	15,285	1.71
East Providence, RI (city) Providence County	15,032	30.87
Dartmouth, MA (town) Bristol County	12,408	40.46
New York, NY (city) New York City	11,307	0.14
Pawtucket, RI (city) Providence County	8,463	11.60
Bristol, RI (cdp) Bristol County	8,266	36.79
San Diego, CA (city) San Diego County	8,040	0.66
Honolulu, HI (cdp) Honolulu County	8,033	2.16
Somerset, MA (cdp) Bristol County	7,578	41.56
Providence, RI (city) Providence County	7,002	4.03
Elizabeth, NJ (city) Union County	6,639	5.51
Modesto, CA (city) Stanislaus County	6,477	3.42
Fremont, CA (city) Alameda County	6,475	3.18
Lowell, MA (city) Middlesex County	6,067	5.77
Swansea, MA (town) Bristol County	5,922	37.24
Warwick, RI (city) Kent County	5,867	6.84
Somerville, MA (city) Middlesex County	5,815	7.51
Sacramento, CA (city) Sacramento County	5,414	1.33
Fairhaven, MA (town) Bristol County	5,384	33.32
Los Angeles, CA (city) Los Angeles County	5,228	0.14
San Leandro, CA (city) Alameda County	5,168	6.52
Westport, MA (town) Bristol County	4,918	34.68
Tiverton, RI (town) Newport County	4,783	31.34
Kearny, NJ (town) Hudson County	4,773	11.78
Hayward, CA (city) Alameda County	4,751	3.40
Boston, MA (city) Suffolk County	4,513	0.77
Ludlow, MA (town) Hampden County	4,506	21.25
Fresno, CA (city) Fresno County	4,337	1.02
Cranston, RI (city) Providence County	4,282	5.40
Cumberland, RI (town) Providence County	4,279	13.44
Bridgeport, CT (city) Fairfield County	4,107	2.94
Danbury, CT (city) Fairfield County	4,056	5.42
Turlock, CA (city) Stanislaus County	3,995	7.20
Santa Clara, CA (city) Santa Clara County	3,959	3.88
Attleboro, MA (city) Bristol County	3,851	9.15
Acushnet, MA (town) Bristol County	3,827	37.66
Peabody, MA (city) Essex County	3,816	7.93
Tulare, CA (city) Tulare County	3,760	8.56
Union, NJ (cdp) Union County	3,725	6.85
San Francisco, CA (city) San Francisco County	3,679	0.47
Hilo, HI (cdp) Hawaii County	3,664	8.98
Warren, RI (town) Bristol County	3,537	31.14
Castro Valley, CA (cdp) Alameda County	3,268	5.69
North Hempstead, NY (town) Nassau County	3,259	1.46
Falmouth, MA (town) Barnstable County	3,247	9.94
Plymouth, MA (town) Plymouth County	3,239	6.26
Tracy, CA (city) San Joaquin County	3,217	5.66
Stockton, CA (city) San Joaquin County	3,129	1.29
Cambridge, MA (city) Middlesex County	3,128	3.09
Hanford, CA (city) Kings County	3,123	7.48
Gloucester, MA (city) Essex County	2,977	9.83
Brookhaven, NY (town) Suffolk County	2,972	0.66
West Warwick, RI (cdp) Kent County	2,958	10.00
Seekonk, MA (town) Bristol County	2,947	21.95
Livermore, CA (city) Alameda County	2,947	4.01
Manteca, CA (city) San Joaquin County	2,852	5.80
Bliss Corner, MA (cdp) Bristol County	2,845	52.58
Stoughton, MA (town) Norfolk County	2,794	10.29
Brockton, MA (city) Plymouth County	2,789	2.96
Valley Falls, RI (cdp) Providence County	2,753	23.86
Freetown, MA (town) Bristol County	2,722	32.13
Phoenix, AZ (city) Maricopa County	2,722	0.21
Philadelphia, PA (city) Philadelphia County	2,589	0.17
Yonkers, NY (city) Westchester County	2,558	1.30
Coventry, RI (town) Kent County	2,507	7.45
Oakland, CA (city) Alameda County	2,489	0.62
Portsmouth, RI (town) Newport County	2,452	14.30
Kailua, HI (cdp) Honolulu County	2,425	6.63
Hillside, NJ (cdp) Union County	2,391	10.99
Santa Rosa, CA (city) Sonoma County	2,387	1.62
Concord, CA (city) Contra Costa County	2,374	1.95

Place	Number	%
Pleasanton, CA (city) Alameda County	2,335	3.67
North Providence, RI (cdp) Providence County	2,303	7.11
Hudson, MA (town) Middlesex County	2,290	12.64
Visalia, CA (city) Tulare County	2,253	2.46
Antioch, CA (city) Contra Costa County	2,219	2.44
Rehoboth, MA (town) Bristol County	2,205	21.68
Barnstable Town, MA (city) Barnstable County	2,183	4.56
Hempstead, NY (town) Nassau County	2,111	0.28
Middletown, RI (town) Newport County	2,107	12.16
Milford, MA (town) Worcester County	2,087	7.79
Mineola, NY (village) Nassau County	2,076	10.79
Dighton, MA (town) Bristol County	2,055	33.28
Naugatuck, CT (borough) New Haven County	2,044	6.60
Waterbury, CT (city) New Haven County	2,023	1.89
Newark, CA (city) Alameda County	2,008	4.73
Harrison, NJ (town) Hudson County	1,961	13.60
Newport, RI (city) Newport County	1,934	7.31
North Westport, MA (cdp) Bristol County	1,928	41.01
Springfield, MA (city) Hampden County	1,892	1.24
Smith Mills, MA (cdp) Bristol County	1,872	41.93
Reno, NV (city) Washoe County	1,850	1.02
Wareham, MA (town) Plymouth County	1,820	8.95
Kaneohe, HI (cdp) Honolulu County	1,805	5.16
Los Banos, CA (city) Merced County	1,798	6.95
Islip, NY (town) Suffolk County	1,771	0.55
Seattle, WA (city) King County	1,652	0.29
Medford, MA (city) Middlesex County	1,639	2.94
Lincoln, RI (town) Providence County	1,636	7.83
Newport East, RI (cdp) Newport County	1,635	14.00
Middleborough, MA (town) Plymouth County	1,634	8.19
Central Falls, RI (city) Providence County	1,633	8.63
Portland, OR (city) Multnomah County	1,618	0.31
Raynham, MA (town) Bristol County	1,573	13.40
Union City, CA (city) Alameda County	1,572	2.35
San Ramon, CA (city) Contra Costa County	1,555	3.50
Artesia, CA (city) Los Angeles County	1,539	9.40
Vacaville, CA (city) Solano County	1,533	1.73
Roseville, CA (city) Placer County	1,532	1.91
Sunnyvale, CA (city) Santa Clara County	1,519	1.15
Hilmar-Irwin, CA (cdp) Merced County	1,507	30.93
Mount Vernon, NY (city) Westchester County	1,498	2.19
Gustine, CA (city) Merced County	1,492	30.81
West Hartford, CT (cdp) Hartford County	1,489	2.34
Bridgewater, MA (town) Plymouth County	1,485	5.90
Framingham, MA (cdp) Middlesex County	1,469	2.20
Houston, TX (city) Harris County	1,466	0.07
Redding, CA (city) Shasta County	1,451	1.79
South River, NJ (borough) Middlesex County	1,432	9.35
Hartford, CT (city) Hartford County	1,429	1.18
Ceres, CA (city) Stanislaus County	1,425	4.13
Citrus Heights, CA (city) Sacramento County	1,423	1.67
Arden-Arcade, CA (cdp) Sacramento County	1,417	1.48
San Lorenzo, CA (cdp) Alameda County	1,415	6.45
Las Vegas, NV (city) Clark County	1,411	0.29
Vallejo, CA (city) Solano County	1,384	1.19
Billerica, MA (town) Middlesex County	1,383	3.55
Woodbridge, NJ (township) Middlesex County	1,369	1.41
Nashua, NH (city) Hillsborough County	1,365	1.58
Dracut, MA (town) Middlesex County	1,360	4.76
Oakley, CA (city) Contra Costa County	1,352	5.31
Elk Grove, CA (cdp) Sacramento County	1,342	2.23
San Antonio, TX (city) Bexar County	1,341	0.12
Merced, CA (city) Merced County	1,339	2.09
Bakersfield, CA (city) Kern County	1,330	0.54
Malden, MA (city) Middlesex County	1,298	2.30
Virginia Beach, VA (independent city) Virginia Beach city	1,296	0.30
Napa, CA (city) Napa County	1,295	1.78
Barrington, RI (town) Bristol County	1,291	7.68
Chicopee, MA (city) Hampden County	1,289	2.36
Petaluma, CA (city) Sonoma County	1,279	2.35
Stonington, CT (town) New London County	1,262	7.05
Salinas, CA (city) Monterey County	1,247	0.83
Worcester, MA (city) Worcester County	1,247	0.72
Rohnert Park, CA (city) Sonoma County	1,238	2.92
Berkley, MA (town) Bristol County	1,233	21.45

Notes: (cdp) census designated place; Refer to the Explanation of Data in the front of the book for more detailed information.

Portuguese

Top 150 Places Sorted by Percent

(Based on all places, regardless of population)

Place	Number	%
Bliss Corner, MA (cdp) Bristol County	2,845	52.58
Fall River, MA (city) Bristol County	43,253	47.05
La Porte, CA (cdp) Plumas County	17	42.50
Smith Mills, MA (cdp) Bristol County	1,872	41.93
Somerset, MA (cdp) Bristol County	7,578	41.56
Scottsville, KS (city) Mitchell County	7	41.18
North Westport, MA (cdp) Bristol County	1,928	41.01
Dartmouth, MA (town) Bristol County	12,408	40.46
New Bedford, MA (city) Bristol County	36,239	38.65
Ocean Grove, MA (cdp) Bristol County	1,206	38.37
Acushnet, MA (town) Bristol County	3,827	37.66
Swansea, MA (town) Bristol County	5,922	37.24
Bristol, RI (cdp) Bristol County	8,266	36.79
Westport, MA (town) Bristol County	4,918	34.68
Acushnet Center, MA (cdp) Bristol County	1,110	33.91
Fairhaven, MA (town) Bristol County	5,384	33.32
Dighton, MA (town) Bristol County	2,055	33.28
Rickreall, OR (cdp) Polk County	25	32.89
Freetown, MA (town) Bristol County	2,722	32.13
Tiverton, RI (town) Newport County	4,783	31.34
Warren, RI (town) Bristol County	3,537	31.14
Hilmar-Irwin, CA (cdp) Merced County	1,507	30.93
East Providence, RI (city) Providence County	15,032	30.87
Gustine, CA (city) Merced County	1,492	30.81
Elfin Cove, AK (cdp) Skagway-Hoonah-Angoon Census Area	10	27.78
Taunton, MA (city) Bristol County	15,370	27.46
Truro, MA (town) Barnstable County	537	25.76
Valley Falls, RI (cdp) Providence County	2,753	23.86
Provincetown, MA (town) Barnstable County	783	22.82
Elmira, CA (cdp) Solano County	19	22.09
Seekonk, MA (town) Bristol County	2,947	21.95
Rehoboth, MA (town) Bristol County	2,205	21.68
Berkley, MA (town) Bristol County	1,233	21.45
Ludlow, MA (town) Hampden County	4,506	21.25
Farmington, CA (cdp) San Joaquin County	36	19.05
Laupahoehoe, HI (cdp) Hawaii County	87	18.87
North Plymouth, MA (cdp) Plymouth County	667	18.56
Honokaa, HI (cdp) Hawaii County	404	18.04
Rochester, MA (town) Plymouth County	788	17.20
Moss Landing, CA (cdp) Monterey County	49	16.23
Honomu, HI (cdp) Hawaii County	85	16.19
Renfrow, OK (town) Grant County	3	15.79
Makawao, HI (cdp) Maui County	1,002	15.77
Raynham Center, MA (cdp) Bristol County	542	14.87
Little Compton, RI (town) Newport County	532	14.81
Kalaheo, HI (cdp) Kauai County	580	14.63
Paauilo, HI (cdp) Hawaii County	85	14.63
East Newark, NJ (borough) Hudson County	345	14.51
Portsmouth, RI (town) Newport County	2,452	14.30
Mattapoisett, MA (town) Plymouth County	887	14.15
Mountain View, HI (cdp) Hawaii County	431	14.13
Newport East, RI (cdp) Newport County	1,635	14.00
Carrick, CA (cdp) Siskiyou County	21	13.82
Topeka, IL (village) Mason County	10	13.70
Harrison, NJ (town) Hudson County	1,961	13.60
Papaikou, HI (cdp) Hawaii County	193	13.49
Wainaku, HI (cdp) Hawaii County	165	13.45
Cumberland, RI (town) Providence County	4,279	13.44
Raynham, MA (town) Bristol County	1,573	13.40
East Falmouth, MA (cdp) Barnstable County	882	13.38
Whitehawk, CA (cdp) Plumas County	7	13.21
Teaticket, MA (cdp) Barnstable County	252	13.14
Mattapoisett Center, MA (cdp) Plymouth County	378	12.95
Vineyard Haven, MA (cdp) Dukes County	245	12.73
Hudson, MA (town) Middlesex County	2,290	12.64
Lawai, HI (cdp) Kauai County	250	12.54
West Wareham, MA (cdp) Plymouth County	219	12.21
Oak Bluffs, MA (town) Dukes County	452	12.17
Middletown, RI (town) Newport County	2,107	12.16
Port Costa, CA (cdp) Contra Costa County	29	11.98
Kearny, NJ (town) Hudson County	4,773	11.78
Pawtucket, RI (city) Providence County	8,463	11.60
Pakala Village, HI (cdp) Kauai County	55	11.46
Lakeville, MA (town) Plymouth County	1,118	11.38
Bradford, RI (cdp) Washington County	163	11.23
Pawcatuck, CT (cdp) New London County	614	11.18
Fern Acres, HI (cdp) Hawaii County	88	11.17
Newman, CA (city) Stanislaus County	784	11.08
Hillside, NJ (cdp) Union County	2,391	10.99
Ainaloa, HI (cdp) Hawaii County	213	10.93
Mountain View, CA (cdp) Contra Costa County	256	10.84
Mineola, NY (village) Nassau County	2,076	10.79
Cooperton, OK (town) Kiowa County	3	10.71
Hawaiian Beaches, HI (cdp) Hawaii County	406	10.70
Edgartown, MA (town) Dukes County	404	10.69
Hawaiian Acres, HI (cdp) Hawaii County	185	10.66
Tisbury, MA (town) Dukes County	390	10.39
Wareham Center, MA (cdp) Plymouth County	295	10.38
East Oakdale, CA (cdp) Stanislaus County	284	10.31
Stoughton, MA (town) Norfolk County	2,794	10.29
Pepeekeo, HI (cdp) Hawaii County	180	10.29
Wellfleet, MA (town) Barnstable County	282	10.25
Pukalani, HI (cdp) Maui County	759	10.16
Escalon, CA (city) San Joaquin County	599	10.13
West Warwick, RI (cdp) Kent County	2,958	10.00
Falmouth, MA (town) Barnstable County	3,247	9.94
Gloucester, MA (city) Essex County	2,977	9.83
West River, WY (cdp) Washakie County	32	9.76
White Island Shores, MA (cdp) Plymouth County	223	9.75
Kapaa, HI (cdp) Kauai County	928	9.58
Ellsworth, NH (town) Grafton County	6	9.52
North Seekonk, MA (cdp) Bristol County	250	9.48
Artesia, CA (city) Los Angeles County	1,539	9.40
South River, NJ (borough) Middlesex County	1,432	9.35
Attleboro, MA (city) Bristol County	3,851	9.15
Chickaloon, AK (cdp) Matanuska-Susitna Borough	26	9.12
Hilo, HI (cdp) Hawaii County	3,664	8.98
Armona, CA (cdp) Kings County	302	8.96
Wareham, MA (town) Plymouth County	1,820	8.95
Omao, HI (cdp) Kauai County	109	8.91
Tipton, CA (cdp) Tulare County	155	8.66
Central Falls, RI (city) Providence County	1,633	8.63
Haiku-Pauwela, HI (cdp) Maui County	568	8.61
Tulare, CA (city) Tulare County	3,760	8.56
Byron, CA (cdp) Contra Costa County	75	8.48
Keaau, HI (cdp) Hawaii County	169	8.43
Waimanalo, HI (cdp) Honolulu County	308	8.35
Paukaa, HI (cdp) Hawaii County	39	8.35
Stonington, CT (borough) New London County	86	8.33
Marion, MA (town) Plymouth County	425	8.30
Middleborough, MA (town) Plymouth County	1,634	8.19
Lemon Cove, CA (cdp) Tulare County	25	8.14
Hawaiian Paradise Park, HI (cdp) Hawaii County	568	8.02
Peabody, MA (city) Essex County	3,816	7.93
Beaver, OR (cdp) Tillamook County	13	7.88
Rio Vista, CA (city) Solano County	363	7.86
Lincoln, RI (town) Providence County	1,636	7.83
Milford, MA (town) Worcester County	2,087	7.79
Strang, NE (village) Fillmore County	2	7.69
Barrington, RI (town) Bristol County	1,291	7.68
Middleborough Center, MA (cdp) Plymouth County	530	7.67
Puhi, HI (cdp) Kauai County	91	7.67
Pahala, HI (cdp) Hawaii County	108	7.61
Somerville, MA (city) Middlesex County	5,815	7.51
Hanford, CA (city) Kings County	3,123	7.48
Coventry, RI (town) Kent County	2,507	7.45
Aptos Hills-Larkin Valley, CA (cdp) Santa Cruz County	156	7.38
Naalehu, HI (cdp) Hawaii County	73	7.37
Pine Lakes, FL (cdp) Lake County	44	7.36
Isleton, CA (city) Sacramento County	59	7.35
Newport, RI (city) Newport County	1,934	7.31
Volcano, HI (cdp) Hawaii County	161	7.22
Turlock, CA (city) Stanislaus County	3,995	7.20
Heron, MT (cdp) Sanders County	11	7.14
North Providence, RI (cdp) Providence County	2,303	7.11
Stonington, CT (town) New London County	1,262	7.05
Hanamaulu, HI (cdp) Kauai County	230	7.03
Kapaau, HI (cdp) Hawaii County	82	7.01
Weweantic, MA (cdp) Plymouth County	136	6.98
Los Banos, CA (city) Merced County	1,798	6.95

Notes: (cdp) census designated place; Refer to the Explanation of Data in the front of the book for more detailed information.

Portuguese

Top 150 Places Sorted by Percent

(Based on places with populations of 10,000 or more)

Place	Number	%
Fall River, MA (city) Bristol County	43,253	47.05
Somerset, MA (cdp) Bristol County	7,578	41.56
Dartmouth, MA (town) Bristol County	12,408	40.46
New Bedford, MA (city) Bristol County	36,239	38.65
Acushnet, MA (town) Bristol County	3,827	37.66
Swansea, MA (town) Bristol County	5,922	37.24
Bristol, RI (cdp) Bristol County	8,266	36.79
Westport, MA (town) Bristol County	4,918	34.68
Fairhaven, MA (town) Bristol County	5,384	33.32
Tiverton, RI (town) Newport County	4,783	31.34
Warren, RI (town) Bristol County	3,537	31.14
East Providence, RI (city) Providence County	15,032	30.87
Taunton, MA (city) Bristol County	15,370	27.46
Valley Falls, RI (cdp) Providence County	2,753	23.86
Seekonk, MA (town) Bristol County	2,947	21.95
Rehoboth, MA (town) Bristol County	2,205	21.68
Ludlow, MA (town) Hampden County	4,506	21.25
Portsmouth, RI (town) Newport County	2,452	14.30
Newport East, RI (cdp) Newport County	1,635	14.00
Harrison, NJ (town) Hudson County	1,961	13.60
Cumberland, RI (town) Providence County	4,279	13.44
Raynham, MA (town) Bristol County	1,573	13.40
Hudson, MA (town) Middlesex County	2,290	12.64
Middletown, RI (town) Newport County	2,107	12.16
Kearny, NJ (town) Hudson County	4,773	11.78
Pawtucket, RI (city) Providence County	8,463	11.60
Hillside, NJ (cdp) Union County	2,391	10.99
Mineola, NY (village) Nassau County	2,076	10.79
Stoughton, MA (town) Norfolk County	2,794	10.29
West Warwick, RI (cdp) Kent County	2,958	10.00
Falmouth, MA (town) Barnstable County	3,247	9.94
Gloucester, MA (city) Essex County	2,977	9.83
Artesia, CA (city) Los Angeles County	1,539	9.40
South River, NJ (borough) Middlesex County	1,432	9.35
Attleboro, MA (city) Bristol County	3,851	9.15
Hilo, HI (cdp) Hawaii County	3,664	8.98
Wareham, MA (town) Plymouth County	1,820	8.95
Central Falls, RI (city) Providence County	1,633	8.63
Tulare, CA (city) Tulare County	3,760	8.56
Middleborough, MA (town) Plymouth County	1,634	8.19
Peabody, MA (city) Essex County	3,816	7.93
Lincoln, RI (town) Providence County	1,636	7.83
Milford, MA (town) Worcester County	2,087	7.79
Barrington, RI (town) Bristol County	1,291	7.68
Somerville, MA (city) Middlesex County	5,815	7.51
Hanford, CA (city) Kings County	3,123	7.48
Coventry, RI (town) Kent County	2,507	7.45
Newport, RI (city) Newport County	1,934	7.31
Turlock, CA (city) Stanislaus County	3,995	7.20
North Providence, RI (cdp) Providence County	2,303	7.11
Stonington, CT (town) New London County	1,262	7.05
Los Banos, CA (city) Merced County	1,798	6.95
Union, NJ (cdp) Union County	3,725	6.85
Warwick, RI (city) Kent County	5,867	6.84
Norton, MA (town) Bristol County	1,219	6.76
Kailua, HI (cdp) Honolulu County	2,425	6.63
Naugatuck, CT (borough) New Haven County	2,044	6.60
San Leandro, CA (city) Alameda County	5,168	6.52
San Lorenzo, CA (cdp) Alameda County	1,415	6.45
Plymouth, MA (town) Plymouth County	3,239	6.26
Wailuku, HI (cdp) Maui County	773	6.22
Carver, MA (town) Plymouth County	662	5.93
Bridgewater, MA (town) Plymouth County	1,485	5.90
Manteca, CA (city) San Joaquin County	2,852	5.80
Newark, NJ (city) Essex County	15,801	5.78
Lowell, MA (city) Middlesex County	6,067	5.77
Cherryland, CA (cdp) Alameda County	794	5.76
Castro Valley, CA (cdp) Alameda County	3,268	5.69
Waianae, HI (cdp) Honolulu County	604	5.67
Tracy, CA (city) San Joaquin County	3,217	5.66
Kingston, MA (town) Plymouth County	660	5.60
Ewa Beach, HI (cdp) Honolulu County	809	5.52
Elizabeth, NJ (city) Union County	6,639	5.51
Half Moon Bay, CA (city) San Mateo County	656	5.48
Danbury, CT (city) Fairfield County	4,056	5.42

Place	Number	%
Cranston, RI (city) Providence County	4,282	5.40
Salida, CA (cdp) Stanislaus County	675	5.37
Oakdale, CA (city) Stanislaus County	836	5.34
Ripon, CA (city) San Joaquin County	540	5.33
Oakley, CA (city) Contra Costa County	1,352	5.31
Kahului, HI (cdp) Maui County	1,058	5.28
Kaneohe, HI (cdp) Honolulu County	1,805	5.16
Lathrop, CA (city) San Joaquin County	520	5.03
Lemoore, CA (city) Kings County	964	4.94
Scituate, RI (town) Providence County	504	4.88
North Arlington, NJ (borough) Bergen County	731	4.82
Dracut, MA (town) Middlesex County	1,360	4.76
Newark, CA (city) Alameda County	2,008	4.73
Nanakuli, HI (cdp) Honolulu County	504	4.71
Smithfield, RI (town) Providence County	961	4.67
Barnstable Town, MA (city) Barnstable County	2,183	4.56
Harwich, MA (town) Barnstable County	538	4.34
Johnston, RI (town) Providence County	1,206	4.27
Mililani Town, HI (cdp) Honolulu County	1,218	4.26
Makakilo City, HI (cdp) Honolulu County	557	4.23
Ceres, CA (city) Stanislaus County	1,425	4.13
South Yarmouth, MA (cdp) Barnstable County	482	4.10
Easton, MA (town) Bristol County	904	4.05
Alum Rock, CA (cdp) Santa Clara County	556	4.04
Providence, RI (city) Providence County	7,002	4.03
Livermore, CA (city) Alameda County	2,947	4.01
Santa Clara, CA (city) Santa Clara County	3,959	3.88
Colonia, NJ (cdp) Middlesex County	689	3.88
Mashpee, MA (town) Barnstable County	487	3.76
North Kingstown, RI (town) Washington County	983	3.73
Westerly, RI (town) Washington County	856	3.73
Prunedale, CA (cdp) Monterey County	613	3.68
Pleasanton, CA (city) Alameda County	2,335	3.67
Dublin, CA (city) Alameda County	1,095	3.65
Chowchilla, CA (city) Madera County	406	3.64
Brentwood, CA (city) Contra Costa County	838	3.60
Yarmouth, MA (town) Barnstable County	889	3.58
Billerica, MA (town) Middlesex County	1,383	3.55
Kihei, HI (cdp) Maui County	596	3.54
San Ramon, CA (city) Contra Costa County	1,555	3.50
Benicia, CA (city) Solano County	942	3.49
Newington, CT (cdp) Hartford County	1,014	3.46
North Attleborough, MA (town) Bristol County	931	3.43
Clark, NJ (cdp) Union County	500	3.43
Modesto, CA (city) Stanislaus County	6,477	3.42
Galt, CA (city) Sacramento County	668	3.42
Hayward, CA (city) Alameda County	4,751	3.40
Long Branch, NJ (city) Monmouth County	1,067	3.40
East Bridgewater, MA (town) Plymouth County	437	3.37
Wilmington, MA (cdp) Middlesex County	716	3.35
Tewksbury, MA (town) Middlesex County	962	3.33
North Attleborough Center, MA (cdp) Bristol County	560	3.33
Tyngsborough, MA (town) Middlesex County	369	3.33
Sandwich, MA (town) Barnstable County	662	3.29
Patterson, CA (city) Stanislaus County	375	3.29
Pearl City, HI (cdp) Honolulu County	1,012	3.28
Atwater, CA (city) Merced County	740	3.23
Fortuna, CA (city) Humboldt County	335	3.23
Fremont, CA (city) Alameda County	6,475	3.18
Riverbank, CA (city) Stanislaus County	505	3.18
McKinleyville, CA (cdp) Humboldt County	431	3.17
Wahiawa, HI (cdp) Honolulu County	510	3.16
Narragansett, RI (town) Washington County	516	3.15
East Greenwich, RI (town) Kent County	406	3.14
Burrillville, RI (town) Providence County	493	3.12
Mansfield, MA (town) Bristol County	695	3.10
Arcata, CA (city) Humboldt County	518	3.10
Cambridge, MA (city) Middlesex County	3,128	3.09
Linden, NJ (city) Union County	1,216	3.09
Lincoln, CA (city) Placer County	338	3.09
Martinez, CA (city) Contra Costa County	1,093	3.02
Grass Valley, CA (city) Nevada County	337	3.02
South Kingstown, RI (town) Washington County	837	3.00
Livingston, CA (city) Merced County	308	2.98
Brockton, MA (city) Plymouth County	2,789	2.96

Notes: (cdp) census designated place; Refer to the Explanation of Data in the front of the book for more detailed information.

Romanian

Top 150 Places Sorted by Number

(Based on all places, regardless of population)

Place	Number	%
New York, NY (city) New York City	30,360	0.38
Los Angeles, CA (city) Los Angeles County	10,274	0.28
Chicago, IL (city) Cook County	8,227	0.28
Portland, OR (city) Multnomah County	3,711	0.70
Hempstead, NY (town) Nassau County	3,220	0.43
Philadelphia, PA (city) Philadelphia County	3,009	0.20
Phoenix, AZ (city) Maricopa County	2,975	0.23
San Diego, CA (city) San Diego County	2,063	0.17
Anaheim, CA (city) Orange County	1,617	0.49
Hollywood, FL (city) Broward County	1,613	1.16
Detroit, MI (city) Wayne County	1,510	0.16
Cleveland, OH (city) Cuyahoga County	1,461	0.31
San Francisco, CA (city) San Francisco County	1,455	0.19
Houston, TX (city) Harris County	1,448	0.07
Oyster Bay, NY (town) Nassau County	1,381	0.47
North Hempstead, NY (town) Nassau County	1,317	0.59
Sterling Heights, MI (city) Macomb County	1,282	1.03
Indianapolis, IN (special city) Marion County	1,122	0.14
Troy, MI (city) Oakland County	1,111	1.37
Seattle, WA (city) King County	1,076	0.19
Hallandale, FL (city) Broward County	1,056	3.06
Gresham, OR (city) Multnomah County	1,018	1.13
Columbus, OH (city) Franklin County	954	0.13
Dallas, TX (city) Dallas County	954	0.08
Huntington, NY (town) Suffolk County	951	0.49
Dearborn, MI (city) Wayne County	939	0.96
San Jose, CA (city) Santa Clara County	936	0.10
Las Vegas, NV (city) Clark County	933	0.19
Washington, DC (city) District of Columbia	930	0.16
Brookhaven, NY (town) Suffolk County	919	0.21
Sacramento, CA (city) Sacramento County	876	0.22
Scottsdale, AZ (city) Maricopa County	832	0.41
Glendale, AZ (city) Maricopa County	825	0.38
Ramapo, NY (town) Rockland County	823	0.76
Skokie, IL (village) Cook County	822	1.30
Riverside, CA (city) Riverside County	771	0.30
Warren, MI (city) Macomb County	753	0.54
Boston, MA (city) Suffolk County	743	0.13
Long Beach, CA (city) Los Angeles County	730	0.16
Pittsburgh, PA (city) Allegheny County	727	0.22
Livonia, MI (city) Wayne County	719	0.72
Aurora, IL (city) Kane County	711	0.50
Jacksonville, FL (special city) Duval County	707	0.10
Denver, CO (city) Denver County	692	0.12
Pembroke Pines, FL (city) Broward County	684	0.50
Vancouver, WA (city) Clark County	670	0.47
Citrus Heights, CA (city) Sacramento County	662	0.78
Glendale, CA (city) Los Angeles County	632	0.32
Akron, OH (city) Summit County	623	0.29
Coral Springs, FL (city) Broward County	611	0.52
Fullerton, CA (city) Orange County	593	0.47
West Bloomfield, MI (township) Oakland County	586	0.90
Lakewood, OH (city) Cuyahoga County	582	1.03
Madison Heights, MI (city) Oakland County	577	1.86
Minneapolis, MN (city) Hennepin County	570	0.15
Tucson, AZ (city) Pima County	568	0.12
Sunrise, FL (city) Broward County	559	0.65
Bellevue, WA (city) King County	559	0.51
Clarkstown, NY (town) Rockland County	545	0.66
Huntington Beach, CA (city) Orange County	522	0.27
Dearborn Heights, MI (city) Wayne County	520	0.89
Oakland, CA (city) Alameda County	519	0.13
Canton, OH (city) Stark County	517	0.64
Farmington Hills, MI (city) Oakland County	508	0.62
Parma, OH (city) Cuyahoga County	506	0.59
Westland, MI (city) Wayne County	504	0.58
Baltimore, MD (independent city) Baltimore city	502	0.08
Redmond, WA (city) King County	496	1.09
Austin, TX (city) Travis County	490	0.07
Warren, OH (city) Trumbull County	487	1.04
Ann Arbor, MI (city) Washtenaw County	482	0.42
Arlington, VA (cdp) Arlington County	479	0.25
Buena Park, CA (city) Orange County	478	0.61
Plantation, FL (city) Broward County	469	0.56
Reading, PA (city) Berks County	466	0.57
Shelby, MI (cdp) Macomb County	464	0.71
Stamford, CT (city) Fairfield County	464	0.40
Santa Monica, CA (city) Los Angeles County	459	0.55
Saint Paul, MN (city) Ramsey County	459	0.16
Yonkers, NY (city) Westchester County	456	0.23
North Olmsted, OH (city) Cuyahoga County	453	1.33
Tamarac, FL (city) Broward County	452	0.81
San Antonio, TX (city) Bexar County	449	0.04
Aventura, FL (city) Miami-Dade County	446	1.77
Peoria, AZ (city) Maricopa County	440	0.41
Lower Merion, PA (township) Montgomery County	438	0.73
Arden-Arcade, CA (cdp) Sacramento County	435	0.45
Mesa, AZ (city) Maricopa County	432	0.11
Clinton, MI (cdp) Macomb County	430	0.45
Cherry Hill, NJ (township) Camden County	429	0.61
Boardman, OH (cdp) Mahoning County	414	1.11
Hammond, IN (city) Lake County	412	0.50
Des Plaines, IL (city) Cook County	408	0.70
Davie, FL (town) Broward County	407	0.54
Alliance, OH (city) Stark County	406	1.75
Saint Louis Park, MN (city) Hennepin County	405	0.92
Edison, NJ (cdp) Middlesex County	404	0.41
Thousand Oaks, CA (city) Ventura County	402	0.34
Miami Beach, FL (city) Miami-Dade County	400	0.45
Beaverton, OR (city) Washington County	399	0.53
Corona, CA (city) Riverside County	394	0.32
Rochester Hills, MI (city) Oakland County	393	0.57
San Bernardino, CA (city) San Bernardino County	392	0.21
Brookline, MA (cdp) Norfolk County	391	0.69
Irvine, CA (city) Orange County	391	0.27
Tacoma, WA (city) Pierce County	386	0.20
Albuquerque, NM (city) Bernalillo County	384	0.09
Lincolnwood, IL (village) Cook County	382	3.09
Smithtown, NY (town) Suffolk County	379	0.33
Garden Grove, CA (city) Orange County	377	0.23
Morton Grove, IL (village) Cook County	376	1.67
Bridgeport, CT (city) Fairfield County	376	0.27
Fort Lauderdale, FL (city) Broward County	375	0.25
Marlboro, NJ (township) Monmouth County	373	1.02
Saint Clair Shores, MI (city) Macomb County	372	0.59
Evanston, IL (city) Cook County	372	0.50
Islip, NY (town) Suffolk County	369	0.11
Wayne, NJ (cdp) Passaic County	368	0.68
Charlotte, NC (city) Mecklenburg County	366	0.07
Boca Raton, FL (city) Palm Beach County	365	0.48
Colorado Springs, CO (city) El Paso County	360	0.10
Fairfield, CT (town) Fairfield County	357	0.62
Waterford, MI (cdp) Oakland County	357	0.49
Loma Linda, CA (city) San Bernardino County	351	1.89
Youngstown, OH (city) Mahoning County	350	0.43
Fort Wayne, IN (city) Allen County	344	0.17
Greenburgh, NY (town) Westchester County	341	0.39
Nashville-Davidson, TN (special city) Davidson County	340	0.06
Royal Oak, MI (city) Oakland County	338	0.56
Cincinnati, OH (city) Hamilton County	338	0.10
Strongsville, OH (city) Cuyahoga County	337	0.77
Buffalo, NY (city) Erie County	337	0.12
Omaha, NE (city) Douglas County	337	0.09
Canton, MI (cdp) Wayne County	335	0.44
Novi, MI (city) Oakland County	332	0.70
East Brunswick, NJ (cdp) Middlesex County	331	0.71
Kent, WA (city) King County	330	0.42
Cambridge, MA (city) Middlesex County	330	0.33
Beverly Hills, CA (city) Los Angeles County	328	0.97
Parma Heights, OH (city) Cuyahoga County	327	1.51
Pasadena, CA (city) Los Angeles County	323	0.24
Fremont, CA (city) Alameda County	321	0.16
Modesto, CA (city) Stanislaus County	319	0.17
Newton, MA (city) Middlesex County	318	0.38
Plainview, NY (cdp) Nassau County	317	1.24
Roswell, GA (city) Fulton County	317	0.40
Amherst, NY (town) Erie County	315	0.27
Milwaukee, WI (city) Milwaukee County	315	0.05
Highland Park, IL (city) Lake County	314	1.00
Berkeley, CA (city) Alameda County	314	0.31

Notes: (cdp) census designated place; Refer to the Explanation of Data in the front of the book for more detailed information.

Romanian

Top 150 Places Sorted by Percent

(Based on all places, regardless of population)

Place	Number	%
Alsen, ND (city) Cavalier County	44	42.31
Boulder, WY (cdp) Sublette County	4	33.33
Chupadero, NM (cdp) Santa Fe County	20	6.92
Saddle Rock Estates, NY (cdp) Nassau County	30	6.83
Yankee Lake, OH (village) Trumbull County	6	6.74
Lake McMurray, WA (cdp) Skagit County	11	6.18
Lester, AL (town) Limestone County	6	6.00
Highgrove, CA (cdp) Riverside County	184	5.31
Montgomery Creek, CA (cdp) Shasta County	6	5.22
Hale's, NH (location) Carroll County	3	4.92
Bradley, CA (cdp) Monterey County	7	4.43
Leidy, PA (township) Clinton County	9	4.19
Harbor Hills, NY (cdp) Nassau County	23	4.01
Grand View Estates, CO (cdp) Douglas County	29	3.91
Heritage Hills, CO (cdp) Douglas County	24	3.72
Wooldridge, MO (village) Cooper County	2	3.70
Brookfield Center, OH (cdp) Trumbull County	43	3.69
Hancock, WI (town) Waushara County	20	3.69
Andover, NJ (borough) Sussex County	23	3.50
Emmett, MI (village) Saint Clair County	9	3.50
Copper City, MI (village) Houghton County	7	3.50
Rocky Mound, TX (town) Camp County	3	3.37
Kingston, NJ (cdp) Middlesex County	42	3.36
Zemple, MN (city) Itasca County	2	3.28
Piehl, WI (town) Oneida County	3	3.16
Kaser, NY (village) Rockland County	103	3.12
Lincolnwood, IL (village) Cook County	382	3.09
Eastgate, WA (cdp) King County	143	3.08
Carriage Club, CO (cdp) Douglas County	31	3.08
Hallandale, FL (city) Broward County	1,056	3.06
Elgin, MN (city) Wabasha County	24	3.06
Green Valley, SD (cdp) Pennington County	23	3.04
Concordia, NJ (cdp) Middlesex County	111	3.00
York charter, MI (township) Washtenaw County	215	2.91
Keeler, CA (cdp) Inyo County	2	2.82
Thomaston, NY (village) Nassau County	73	2.81
Sagaponack, NY (cdp) Suffolk County	15	2.77
Deweese, NE (village) Clay County	2	2.74
Levan, UT (town) Juab County	19	2.68
Whittingham, NJ (cdp) Middlesex County	65	2.66
Del Sol-Loma Linda, TX (cdp) San Patricio County	19	2.64
Hewlett Neck, NY (village) Nassau County	13	2.63
Ovando, MT (cdp) Powell County	2	2.63
Keene, TX (city) Johnson County	125	2.56
Limaville, OH (village) Stark County	5	2.49
Mokelumne Hill, CA (cdp) Calaveras County	17	2.47
Marvin, SD (town) Grant County	2	2.44
Wheatland, PA (borough) Mercer County	18	2.43
Yorkville, IL (city) Kendall County	150	2.40
Summerdale, AL (town) Baldwin County	15	2.37
Fisher Island, FL (cdp) Miami-Dade County	8	2.36
Teton Village, WY (cdp) Teton County	6	2.34
Interlaken, NY (village) Seneca County	16	2.33
Tuxedo Park, NY (village) Orange County	17	2.32
Great Neck Estates, NY (village) Nassau County	65	2.30
Bennett, WI (town) Douglas County	15	2.27
Norway, MN (township) Fillmore County	8	2.27
Windsor, MN (township) Traverse County	1	2.27
Villages of Oriole, FL (cdp) Palm Beach County	107	2.26
Lawrence, NY (village) Nassau County	147	2.25
Keego Harbor, MI (city) Oakland County	62	2.24
Lido Beach, NY (cdp) Nassau County	62	2.23
Leitersburg, MD (cdp) Washington County	10	2.11
Mercer, ND (city) McLean County	2	2.11
Century Village, FL (cdp) Palm Beach County	159	2.10
Meshoppen, PA (township) Wyoming County	18	2.09
Newburg, ND (city) Bottineau County	2	2.08
Sheffield, OH (village) Lorain County	61	2.07
Harbor Isle, NY (cdp) Nassau County	29	2.05
Sands Point, NY (village) Nassau County	56	2.03
Grant, MI (township) Keweenaw County	3	2.03
Saint Lawrence, PA (borough) Berks County	36	1.99
Milton, NC (town) Caswell County	3	1.99
Perry Heights, OH (cdp) Stark County	175	1.95
Kings Point, FL (cdp) Palm Beach County	239	1.93
Whisper Walk, FL (cdp) Palm Beach County	99	1.93
Fairchild, WI (town) Eau Claire County	4	1.92
Sims, MI (township) Arenac County	21	1.91
Clearbrook Park, NJ (cdp) Middlesex County	58	1.90
Loma Linda, CA (city) San Bernardino County	351	1.89
Great Neck Gardens, NY (cdp) Nassau County	21	1.88
Madison Heights, MI (city) Oakland County	577	1.86
Great Neck Plaza, NY (village) Nassau County	118	1.86
Tanner, WA (cdp) King County	55	1.86
Henderson, MI (township) Wexford County	3	1.86
Bardonia, NY (cdp) Rockland County	81	1.85
Oakwood Park, MO (village) Clay County	3	1.82
Granville, MN (township) Kittson County	2	1.82
Rio Linda, CA (cdp) Sacramento County	189	1.81
Florence-Roebling, NJ (cdp) Burlington County	149	1.81
Hewlett Harbor, NY (village) Nassau County	23	1.81
Malverne Park Oaks, NY (cdp) Nassau County	9	1.81
Blacksville, WV (town) Monongalia County	3	1.81
La Habra Heights, CA (city) Los Angeles County	97	1.80
Livingston, WI (village) Grant County	11	1.79
Aventura, FL (city) Miami-Dade County	446	1.77
Kiryas Joel, NY (village) Orange County	234	1.77
Closter, NJ (borough) Bergen County	148	1.77
Lausanne, PA (township) Carbon County	4	1.77
Alliance, OH (city) Stark County	406	1.75
Florence, NJ (township) Burlington County	188	1.75
Castle Valley, UT (town) Grand County	6	1.75
Montebello, NY (village) Rockland County	63	1.73
Boca Pointe, FL (cdp) Palm Beach County	57	1.73
Fairview, OR (city) Multnomah County	131	1.71
Zeeland, ND (city) McIntosh County	2	1.71
South Valley Stream, NY (cdp) Nassau County	96	1.70
Aspen Park, CO (cdp) Jefferson County	14	1.70
Chippewa, PA (township) Beaver County	119	1.69
Crugers, NY (cdp) Westchester County	31	1.69
Sandisfield, MA (town) Berkshire County	14	1.68
Morton Grove, IL (village) Cook County	376	1.67
Dacula, GA (city) Gwinnett County	65	1.67
Belfast, PA (cdp) Northampton County	22	1.66
Tofte, MN (township) Cook County	4	1.66
Monsey, NY (cdp) Rockland County	242	1.65
Shenango, PA (township) Lawrence County	126	1.65
Kensington, NY (village) Nassau County	20	1.65
Ellwood City, PA (borough) Lawrence County	142	1.64
Howland Center, OH (cdp) Trumbull County	108	1.64
Bear Creek, TX (village) Hays County	7	1.64
Luther, MI (village) Lake County	6	1.63
Cedarhurst, NY (village) Nassau County	100	1.62
Richmond, MI (township) Macomb County	55	1.62
Berlin, MI (township) Saint Clair County	51	1.61
Bailey, TX (city) Fannin County	4	1.61
Mud Bay, AK (cdp) Haines Borough	2	1.61
Middleburg Heights, OH (city) Cuyahoga County	249	1.60
Hamptons at Boca Raton, FL (cdp) Palm Beach County	183	1.60
Newtonia, MO (town) Newton County	4	1.60
Amherst, WI (village) Portage County	16	1.59
Westwood, IA (city) Henry County	2	1.59
Erwin, MI (township) Gogebic County	6	1.58
Romeo, MI (village) Macomb County	58	1.56
Bolindale, OH (cdp) Trumbull County	38	1.55
Little Falls-South Windham, ME (cdp) Cumberland County	25	1.55
West Leipsic, OH (village) Putnam County	4	1.55
Mettawa, IL (village) Lake County	5	1.54
Valley Hill, NC (cdp) Henderson County	34	1.53
Warren, WI (town) Waushara County	10	1.53
Shandaken, NY (town) Ulster County	50	1.52
Parma Heights, OH (city) Cuyahoga County	327	1.51
Bern, PA (township) Berks County	102	1.51
Pulaski, PA (township) Lawrence County	55	1.50
Kenockee, MI (township) Saint Clair County	36	1.49
Battle Ground, WA (city) Clark County	137	1.47
Walnut Grove, WA (cdp) Clark County	107	1.47
Poland, OH (village) Mahoning County	42	1.47
Myersville, MD (town) Frederick County	20	1.47
Cornwall, VT (town) Addison County	17	1.47

Notes: (cdp) census designated place; Refer to the Explanation of Data in the front of the book for more detailed information.

Romanian

Top 150 Places Sorted by Percent

(Based on places with populations of 10,000 or more)

Place	Number	%
Lincolnwood, IL (village) Cook County	382	3.09
Hallandale, FL (city) Broward County	1,056	3.06
Kings Point, FL (cdp) Palm Beach County	239	1.93
Loma Linda, CA (city) San Bernardino County	351	1.89
Madison Heights, MI (city) Oakland County	577	1.86
Rio Linda, CA (cdp) Sacramento County	189	1.81
Aventura, FL (city) Miami-Dade County	446	1.77
Kiryas Joel, NY (village) Orange County	234	1.77
Alliance, OH (city) Stark County	406	1.75
Florence, NJ (township) Burlington County	188	1.75
Morton Grove, IL (village) Cook County	376	1.67
Monsey, NY (cdp) Rockland County	242	1.65
Middleburg Heights, OH (city) Cuyahoga County	249	1.60
Hamptons at Boca Raton, FL (cdp) Palm Beach County	183	1.60
Parma Heights, OH (city) Cuyahoga County	327	1.51
Sunny Isles Beach, FL (city) Miami-Dade County	219	1.43
Troy, MI (city) Oakland County	1,111	1.37
Clawson, MI (city) Oakland County	174	1.37
North Olmsted, OH (city) Cuyahoga County	453	1.33
Jericho, NY (cdp) Nassau County	171	1.32
Skokie, IL (village) Cook County	822	1.30
Beachwood, OH (city) Cuyahoga County	154	1.26
Plainview, NY (cdp) Nassau County	317	1.24
Hollywood, FL (city) Broward County	1,613	1.16
Salisbury, NY (cdp) Nassau County	143	1.16
Rocky River, OH (city) Cuyahoga County	237	1.14
Cutler, FL (cdp) Miami-Dade County	201	1.14
Gresham, OR (city) Multnomah County	1,018	1.13
Woodmere, NY (cdp) Nassau County	186	1.13
Boardman, OH (cdp) Mahoning County	414	1.11
Redmond, WA (city) King County	496	1.09
North Canton, OH (city) Stark County	177	1.08
South Orange, NJ (cdp) Essex County	180	1.06
Ojus, FL (cdp) Miami-Dade County	177	1.06
Lawrenceville, GA (city) Gwinnett County	236	1.05
Niles, OH (city) Trumbull County	220	1.05
Kingsgate, WA (cdp) King County	126	1.05
Warren, OH (city) Trumbull County	487	1.04
Sterling Heights, MI (city) Macomb County	1,282	1.03
Lakewood, OH (city) Cuyahoga County	582	1.03
Marlboro, NJ (township) Monmouth County	373	1.02
Monroe, NJ (township) Middlesex County	285	1.02
Millburn, NJ (cdp) Essex County	201	1.02
Lower Moreland, PA (township) Montgomery County	115	1.02
Hermitage, PA (city) Mercer County	163	1.01
Highland Park, IL (city) Lake County	314	1.00
Dix Hills, NY (cdp) Suffolk County	262	1.00
Munster, IN (town) Lake County	215	1.00
Morganville, NJ (cdp) Monmouth County	111	1.00
Monroe, NY (town) Orange County	311	0.99
Green, OH (city) Summit County	226	0.99
New Castle, NY (town) Westchester County	174	0.99
Palm Beach, FL (town) Palm Beach County	102	0.98
Beverly Hills, CA (city) Los Angeles County	328	0.97
Boca Del Mar, FL (cdp) Palm Beach County	208	0.97
Agoura Hills, CA (city) Los Angeles County	197	0.97
Mayfield Heights, OH (city) Cuyahoga County	188	0.97
Greentree, NJ (cdp) Camden County	111	0.97
Dearborn, MI (city) Wayne County	939	0.96
Oroville, CA (city) Butte County	124	0.96
Tamalpais-Homestead Valley, CA (cdp) Marin County	102	0.96
Syosset, NY (cdp) Nassau County	177	0.95
Brooklyn, OH (city) Cuyahoga County	110	0.95
Allen Park, MI (city) Wayne County	275	0.94
Vernon Hills, IL (village) Lake County	193	0.94
Melville, NY (cdp) Suffolk County	136	0.94
Highland Park, NJ (borough) Middlesex County	132	0.94
Farragut, TN (town) Knox County	167	0.93
Saint Louis Park, MN (city) Hennepin County	405	0.92
Springdale, NJ (cdp) Camden County	132	0.92
Rockville Centre, NY (village) Nassau County	224	0.91
West Bloomfield, MI (township) Oakland County	586	0.90
Calabasas, CA (city) Los Angeles County	180	0.90
Dearborn Heights, MI (city) Wayne County	520	0.89
Northbrook, IL (village) Cook County	297	0.89
Massillon, OH (city) Stark County	278	0.89
Whitemarsh, PA (township) Montgomery County	149	0.89
Storrs, CT (cdp) Tolland County	99	0.89
Niles, IL (village) Cook County	266	0.88
Farmington, MI (city) Oakland County	91	0.87
New City, NY (cdp) Rockland County	291	0.85
Hobart, IN (city) Lake County	216	0.85
Bay Village, OH (city) Cuyahoga County	137	0.85
Highland, IN (town) Lake County	197	0.84
Riverton-Boulevard Park, WA (cdp) King County	96	0.84
Tamarac, FL (city) Broward County	452	0.81
Hazel Park, MI (city) Oakland County	153	0.81
East Meadow, NY (cdp) Nassau County	301	0.80
Parkland, FL (city) Broward County	112	0.80
Salem, OH (city) Columbiana County	96	0.80
Oceanside, NY (cdp) Nassau County	259	0.79
South Saint Paul, MN (city) Dakota County	160	0.79
Tenafly, NJ (borough) Bergen County	109	0.79
North Aurora, IL (village) Kane County	84	0.79
Citrus Heights, CA (city) Sacramento County	662	0.78
Livingston, NJ (cdp) Essex County	213	0.78
Strongsville, OH (city) Cuyahoga County	337	0.77
Golden Valley, MN (city) Hennepin County	156	0.77
Lakeland North, WA (cdp) King County	117	0.77
Seven Hills, OH (city) Cuyahoga County	93	0.77
Struthers, OH (city) Mahoning County	90	0.77
Ramapo, NY (town) Rockland County	823	0.76
Washington, MI (township) Macomb County	145	0.76
Scarsdale, NY (village) Westchester County	135	0.76
Hillsdale, NJ (borough) Bergen County	77	0.76
Brook Park, OH (city) Cuyahoga County	159	0.75
Orchards, WA (cdp) Clark County	134	0.75
Springfield, MI (township) Oakland County	100	0.75
Port Washington, NY (cdp) Nassau County	112	0.74
Rancho Mirage, CA (city) Riverside County	96	0.74
Grand Terrace, CA (city) San Bernardino County	87	0.74
Suffern, NY (village) Rockland County	81	0.74
Hillsborough, CA (town) San Mateo County	80	0.74
Lower Merion, PA (township) Montgomery County	438	0.73
Schererville, IN (town) Lake County	181	0.73
Granite Bay, CA (cdp) Placer County	142	0.73
Berea, OH (city) Cuyahoga County	139	0.73
Deerfield, IL (village) Lake County	135	0.73
Livonia, MI (city) Wayne County	719	0.72
Yorktown, NY (town) Westchester County	263	0.72
Shelby, MI (cdp) Macomb County	464	0.71
East Brunswick, NJ (cdp) Middlesex County	331	0.71
Buffalo Grove, IL (village) Lake County	302	0.71
West Hollywood, CA (city) Los Angeles County	252	0.71
Nanuet, NY (cdp) Rockland County	119	0.71
Springfield, NJ (cdp) Union County	103	0.71
Joppatowne, MD (cdp) Harford County	80	0.71
Portland, OR (city) Multnomah County	3,711	0.70
Des Plaines, IL (city) Cook County	408	0.70
Novi, MI (city) Oakland County	332	0.70
Chesterfield, MI (township) Macomb County	261	0.70
Westport, CT (cdp) Fairfield County	179	0.70
Rockaway, NJ (township) Morris County	161	0.70
Oakland charter, MI (township) Oakland County	91	0.70
Brookline, MA (cdp) Norfolk County	391	0.69
Merrick, NY (cdp) Nassau County	157	0.69
Oswego, IL (village) Kendall County	92	0.69
Lewisboro, NY (town) Westchester County	85	0.69
Wayne, NJ (cdp) Passaic County	368	0.68
Orion, MI (township) Oakland County	227	0.68
Jefferson Valley-Yorktown, NY (cdp) Westchester County	101	0.68
Brecksville, OH (city) Cuyahoga County	91	0.68
Lindenhurst, IL (village) Lake County	86	0.68
Arlington, NY (cdp) Dutchess County	84	0.68
Loveland, OH (city) Hamilton County	81	0.68
North Royalton, OH (city) Cuyahoga County	191	0.67
Florin, CA (cdp) Sacramento County	186	0.67
Glendale, WI (city) Milwaukee County	89	0.67
Ecorse, MI (city) Wayne County	75	0.67
Clarkstown, NY (town) Rockland County	545	0.66

Notes: (cdp) census designated place; Refer to the Explanation of Data in the front of the book for more detailed information.

Russian

Top 150 Places Sorted by Number

(Based on all places, regardless of population)

Place	Number	%
New York, NY (city) New York City	243,015	3.03
Los Angeles, CA (city) Los Angeles County	87,419	2.37
Hempstead, NY (town) Nassau County	30,246	4.00
Chicago, IL (city) Cook County	28,845	1.00
Philadelphia, PA (city) Philadelphia County	26,375	1.74
San Francisco, CA (city) San Francisco County	21,727	2.80
San Diego, CA (city) San Diego County	16,955	1.39
Oyster Bay, NY (town) Nassau County	14,698	5.00
North Hempstead, NY (town) Nassau County	12,446	5.59
Phoenix, AZ (city) Maricopa County	10,601	0.80
Portland, OR (city) Multnomah County	10,303	1.95
Boston, MA (city) Suffolk County	10,267	1.74
Brookhaven, NY (town) Suffolk County	10,157	2.27
Seattle, WA (city) King County	9,717	1.72
Huntington, NY (town) Suffolk County	8,974	4.60
Houston, TX (city) Harris County	8,423	0.43
Washington, DC (city) District of Columbia	8,338	1.46
Newton, MA (city) Middlesex County	8,055	9.61
Denver, CO (city) Denver County	7,785	1.40
San Jose, CA (city) Santa Clara County	6,930	0.78
Lower Merion, PA (township) Montgomery County	6,737	11.26
Pittsburgh, PA (city) Allegheny County	6,697	2.00
Las Vegas, NV (city) Clark County	6,593	1.38
Buffalo Grove, IL (village) Lake County	6,542	15.36
Dallas, TX (city) Dallas County	6,152	0.52
West Bloomfield, MI (township) Oakland County	6,071	9.37
Santa Monica, CA (city) Los Angeles County	5,774	6.87
Coral Springs, FL (city) Broward County	5,710	4.86
Cherry Hill, NJ (township) Camden County	5,620	8.03
Skokie, IL (village) Cook County	5,609	8.86
Baltimore, MD (independent city) Baltimore city	5,526	0.85
Scottsdale, AZ (city) Maricopa County	5,509	2.72
Clarkstown, NY (town) Rockland County	5,482	6.68
Pikesville, MD (cdp) Baltimore County	5,365	18.54
Brookline, MA (cdp) Norfolk County	5,338	9.35
Islip, NY (town) Suffolk County	5,270	1.63
Highland Park, IL (city) Lake County	5,157	16.43
Ramapo, NY (town) Rockland County	4,997	4.59
Greenburgh, NY (town) Westchester County	4,988	5.75
West Hollywood, CA (city) Los Angeles County	4,871	13.64
Oakland, CA (city) Alameda County	4,760	1.19
Smithtown, NY (town) Suffolk County	4,736	4.09
Tucson, AZ (city) Pima County	4,523	0.93
Hollywood, FL (city) Broward County	4,464	3.21
Berkeley, CA (city) Alameda County	4,359	4.24
Columbus, OH (city) Franklin County	4,333	0.61
Bismarck, ND (city) Burleigh County	4,250	7.69
Minneapolis, MN (city) Hennepin County	4,220	1.10
Pembroke Pines, FL (city) Broward County	4,179	3.05
Austin, TX (city) Travis County	4,168	0.64
Sacramento, CA (city) Sacramento County	4,140	1.02
Northbrook, IL (village) Cook County	4,101	12.27
Boca Raton, FL (city) Palm Beach County	4,066	5.38
Marlboro, NJ (township) Monmouth County	3,914	10.75
Cambridge, MA (city) Middlesex County	3,870	3.82
Potomac, MD (cdp) Montgomery County	3,824	8.53
Farmington Hills, MI (city) Oakland County	3,773	4.59
Jacksonville, FL (special city) Duval County	3,705	0.50
Fair Lawn, NJ (borough) Bergen County	3,699	11.69
Thousand Oaks, CA (city) Ventura County	3,695	3.17
Arlington, VA (cdp) Arlington County	3,685	1.95
West Hartford, CT (cdp) Hartford County	3,662	5.76
East Brunswick, NJ (cdp) Middlesex County	3,627	7.76
Long Beach, CA (city) Los Angeles County	3,626	0.79
Vancouver, WA (city) Clark County	3,611	2.52
Stamford, CT (city) Fairfield County	3,590	3.07
Sunrise, FL (city) Broward County	3,533	4.13
Tamarac, FL (city) Broward County	3,431	6.12
Plantation, FL (city) Broward County	3,428	4.12
Milwaukee, WI (city) Milwaukee County	3,374	0.57
Bethesda, MD (cdp) Montgomery County	3,363	6.08
New City, NY (cdp) Rockland County	3,352	9.82
Manalapan, NJ (township) Monmouth County	3,333	9.97
Miami Beach, FL (city) Miami-Dade County	3,286	3.73
Santa Clarita, CA (city) Los Angeles County	3,246	2.14
Spokane, WA (city) Spokane County	3,244	1.65
Cheltenham, PA (township) Montgomery County	3,236	8.78
Atlanta, GA (city) Fulton County	3,233	0.78
Beverly Hills, CA (city) Los Angeles County	3,184	9.41
Madison, WI (city) Dane County	3,164	1.52
Yonkers, NY (city) Westchester County	3,150	1.61
Aurora, CO (city) Arapahoe County	3,150	1.14
Ann Arbor, MI (city) Washtenaw County	3,149	2.76
Virginia Beach, VA (independent city) Virginia Beach city	3,132	0.74
San Antonio, TX (city) Bexar County	3,126	0.27
Anchorage, AK (municipality) Anchorage Borough	3,098	1.19
Edison, NJ (cdp) Middlesex County	3,097	3.17
Albuquerque, NM (city) Bernalillo County	3,024	0.67
Charlotte, NC (city) Mecklenburg County	3,018	0.56
Aventura, FL (city) Miami-Dade County	2,998	11.87
Babylon, NY (town) Suffolk County	2,973	1.40
Indianapolis, IN (special city) Marion County	2,954	0.38
Northampton, PA (township) Bucks County	2,951	7.50
Amherst, NY (town) Erie County	2,937	2.52
Huntington Beach, CA (city) Orange County	2,925	1.54
Evanston, IL (city) Cook County	2,892	3.90
Fort Lee, NJ (borough) Bergen County	2,858	8.06
Coconut Creek, FL (city) Broward County	2,804	6.47
Plainview, NY (cdp) Nassau County	2,802	10.93
Nashville-Davidson, TN (special city) Davidson County	2,802	0.51
Weston, FL (city) Broward County	2,784	5.67
North Bethesda, MD (cdp) Montgomery County	2,758	7.14
Framingham, MA (cdp) Middlesex County	2,753	4.11
Plano, TX (city) Collin County	2,722	1.22
Irvine, CA (city) Orange County	2,703	1.89
Livingston, NJ (cdp) Essex County	2,693	9.83
Boulder, CO (city) Boulder County	2,693	2.85
Overland Park, KS (city) Johnson County	2,679	1.80
Saint Paul, MN (city) Ramsey County	2,651	0.92
Palo Alto, CA (city) Santa Clara County	2,646	4.50
West Orange, NJ (cdp) Essex County	2,620	5.84
Monroe, NJ (township) Middlesex County	2,597	9.28
Bellevue, WA (city) King County	2,547	2.33
Southfield, MI (city) Oakland County	2,514	3.21
Glenview, IL (village) Cook County	2,510	6.02
Merrick, NY (cdp) Nassau County	2,502	10.99
Sharon, MA (town) Norfolk County	2,490	14.30
Omaha, NE (city) Douglas County	2,487	0.64
Henderson, NV (city) Clark County	2,478	1.41
Deerfield, IL (village) Lake County	2,473	13.37
New Rochelle, NY (city) Westchester County	2,472	3.42
Lincoln, NE (city) Lancaster County	2,454	1.09
Columbia, MD (cdp) Howard County	2,441	2.76
Cleveland, OH (city) Cuyahoga County	2,429	0.51
Tampa, FL (city) Hillsborough County	2,419	0.80
Oceanside, NY (cdp) Nassau County	2,418	7.39
Providence, RI (city) Providence County	2,411	1.39
Chesterfield, MO (city) Saint Louis County	2,410	5.13
Abington, PA (township) Montgomery County	2,409	4.29
Kendall, FL (cdp) Miami-Dade County	2,409	3.20
Fort Lauderdale, FL (city) Broward County	2,408	1.58
Woodmere, NY (cdp) Nassau County	2,391	14.54
Long Beach, NY (city) Nassau County	2,379	6.71
Davie, FL (town) Broward County	2,365	3.12
Sandy Springs, GA (cdp) Fulton County	2,350	2.75
Colorado Springs, CO (city) El Paso County	2,341	0.65
Wheeling, IL (village) Cook County	2,334	6.78
Scranton, PA (city) Lackawanna County	2,325	3.04
Millburn, NJ (cdp) Essex County	2,309	11.68
Calabasas, CA (city) Los Angeles County	2,259	11.24
Upper Dublin, PA (township) Montgomery County	2,243	8.67
Saint Petersburg, FL (city) Pinellas County	2,236	0.90
West Sacramento, CA (city) Yolo County	2,228	7.05
Fresno, CA (city) Fresno County	2,206	0.52
White Plains, NY (city) Westchester County	2,194	4.13
Old Bridge, NJ (township) Middlesex County	2,187	3.62
Mandan, ND (city) Morton County	2,185	13.05
Wayne, NJ (cdp) Passaic County	2,185	4.04
Worcester, MA (city) Worcester County	2,174	1.26
Catalina Foothills, AZ (cdp) Pima County	2,173	4.06

Notes: (cdp) census designated place; Refer to the Explanation of Data in the front of the book for more detailed information.

Russian

Top 150 Places Sorted by Percent

(Based on all places, regardless of population)

Place	Number	%
Chicken, AK (cdp) Southeast Fairbanks Census Area	1	100.00
Fox River, AK (cdp) Kenai Peninsula Borough	488	80.93
Aleneva, AK (cdp) Kodiak Island Borough	66	72.53
Marineland, FL (town) Flagler County	5	71.43
Nikolaevsk, AK (cdp) Kenai Peninsula Borough	281	67.55
Artas, SD (town) Campbell County	3	42.86
Leith, ND (city) Grant County	16	39.02
Voltaire, ND (city) McHenry County	15	32.61
Zeeland, ND (city) McIntosh County	36	30.77
Hewlett Neck, NY (village) Nassau County	144	29.15
Saddle Rock Estates, NY (cdp) Nassau County	112	25.51
Saltaire, NY (village) Suffolk County	17	25.00
New Leipzig, ND (city) Grant County	66	24.18
Streeter, ND (city) Stutsman County	48	23.41
Hewlett Bay Park, NY (village) Nassau County	113	23.30
Venturia, ND (city) McIntosh County	4	22.22
Peaceful Valley, WA (cdp) Whatcom County	572	22.18
Concordia, NJ (cdp) Middlesex County	814	22.02
Mound City, SD (town) Campbell County	19	21.84
Fredonia, ND (city) Logan County	12	20.34
Wishek, ND (city) McIntosh County	223	20.11
Mayfield, PA (borough) Lackawanna County	352	20.05
Lowry, SD (town) Walworth County	2	20.00
Harbor Hills, NY (cdp) Nassau County	114	19.90
Napoleon, ND (city) Logan County	170	19.38
Whittingham, NJ (cdp) Middlesex County	465	19.03
Karlsruhe, ND (city) McHenry County	19	19.00
Egeland, ND (city) Towner County	10	18.87
Clearbrook Park, NJ (cdp) Middlesex County	573	18.74
Pikesville, MD (cdp) Baltimore County	5,365	18.54
Roslyn Estates, NY (village) Nassau County	219	17.95
Hewlett Harbor, NY (village) Nassau County	227	17.89
Keddie, CA (cdp) Plumas County	14	17.72
Boca Pointe, FL (cdp) Palm Beach County	584	17.70
Villages of Oriole, FL (cdp) Palm Beach County	829	17.50
Duck Key, FL (cdp) Monroe County	94	17.38
Penn Wynne, PA (cdp) Montgomery County	941	17.32
Dawson, ND (city) Kidder County	11	17.19
Eola, OR (cdp) Polk County	8	17.02
Kensington, NY (village) Nassau County	205	16.87
Richardton, ND (city) Stark County	100	16.75
East Hills, NY (village) Nassau County	1,147	16.69
Eureka, SD (city) McPherson County	181	16.51
Highland Park, IL (city) Lake County	5,157	16.43
Flasher, ND (city) Morton County	38	16.38
Glen Ullin, ND (city) Morton County	140	16.32
Kings Point, FL (cdp) Palm Beach County	2,005	16.19
Jericho, NY (cdp) Nassau County	2,096	16.14
Pick City, ND (city) Mercer County	27	16.07
Fisher Island, FL (cdp) Miami-Dade County	54	15.93
Ouzinkie, AK (city) Kodiak Island Borough	32	15.92
Hosmer, SD (city) Edmunds County	45	15.73
Stratford, SD (town) Brown County	17	15.60
Beachwood, OH (city) Cuyahoga County	1,894	15.54
Dering Harbor, NY (village) Suffolk County	2	15.38
Buffalo Grove, IL (village) Lake County	6,542	15.36
Lido Beach, NY (cdp) Nassau County	427	15.35
Linton, ND (city) Emmons County	201	15.33
Ashley, ND (city) McIntosh County	133	15.13
High Point, FL (cdp) Palm Beach County	330	14.97
Great Neck Estates, NY (village) Nassau County	421	14.91
Century Village, FL (cdp) Palm Beach County	1,129	14.88
Woodbury, NY (cdp) Nassau County	1,340	14.87
Thomaston, NY (village) Nassau County	386	14.87
Bowdle, SD (city) Edmunds County	83	14.87
Roslyn Harbor, NY (village) Nassau County	147	14.70
Lower Moreland, PA (township) Montgomery County	1,648	14.61
Woodmere, NY (cdp) Nassau County	2,391	14.54
Great Neck Plaza, NY (village) Nassau County	921	14.53
Gackle, ND (city) Logan County	51	14.49
Golden's Bridge, NY (cdp) Westchester County	222	14.33
Sharon, MA (town) Norfolk County	2,490	14.30
Lake Success, NY (village) Nassau County	397	14.19
Great Neck Gardens, NY (cdp) Nassau County	158	14.15
Russell Gardens, NY (village) Nassau County	152	14.15
Springdale, NJ (cdp) Camden County	2,014	13.97
Java, SD (town) Walworth County	24	13.95
Oak Point, FL (cdp) Broward County	22	13.92
Scotts Corners, NY (cdp) Westchester County	80	13.89
Herreid, SD (city) Campbell County	67	13.76
West Hollywood, CA (city) Los Angeles County	4,871	13.64
Hetland, SD (town) Kingsbury County	8	13.56
Deerfield, IL (village) Lake County	2,473	13.37
Hidden Hills, CA (city) Los Angeles County	248	13.23
Garrison, MD (cdp) Baltimore County	1,083	13.18
Mandan, ND (city) Morton County	2,185	13.05
Chappaqua, NY (cdp) Westchester County	1,228	13.04
Ramblewood East, FL (cdp) Broward County	165	13.01
Morganville, NJ (cdp) Monmouth County	1,440	12.93
Mountain, ND (city) Pembina County	19	12.93
Galisteo, NM (cdp) Santa Fe County	43	12.91
Strasburg, ND (city) Emmons County	65	12.75
Butte, ND (city) McLean County	12	12.63
Lublin, WI (village) Taylor County	13	12.62
Whisper Walk, FL (cdp) Palm Beach County	646	12.58
Teterboro, NJ (borough) Bergen County	2	12.50
Huntington Woods, MI (city) Oakland County	760	12.36
Bayside, WI (village) Milwaukee County	554	12.29
Northbrook, IL (village) Cook County	4,101	12.27
Viola, NY (cdp) Rockland County	715	12.04
Bal Harbour, FL (village) Miami-Dade County	399	12.01
Riverwoods, IL (village) Lake County	449	11.90
Marsh Creek, MN (township) Mahnomen County	15	11.90
Aventura, FL (city) Miami-Dade County	2,998	11.87
Glencoe, IL (village) Cook County	1,042	11.80
Atlantic Beach, NY (village) Nassau County	232	11.77
Matinicus Isle, ME (plantation) Knox County	6	11.76
Indian Creek, FL (village) Miami-Dade County	4	11.76
Sands Point, NY (village) Nassau County	324	11.73
Medina, ND (city) Stutsman County	40	11.73
Fair Lawn, NJ (borough) Bergen County	3,699	11.69
Millburn, NJ (cdp) Essex County	2,309	11.68
Scarsdale, NY (village) Westchester County	2,075	11.64
Darwin, CA (cdp) Inyo County	8	11.59
Brookville, NY (village) Nassau County	248	11.56
Hebron, ND (city) Morton County	92	11.51
Highland Beach, FL (town) Palm Beach County	415	11.49
North Hills, NY (village) Nassau County	493	11.46
Pound Ridge, NY (town) Westchester County	540	11.43
Wesley Hills, NY (village) Rockland County	562	11.39
Pomona, NY (village) Rockland County	311	11.37
Hague, ND (city) Emmons County	11	11.34
Lower Merion, PA (township) Montgomery County	6,737	11.26
Calabasas, CA (city) Los Angeles County	2,259	11.24
New Castle, NY (town) Westchester County	1,939	11.09
McIntosh, SD (city) Corson County	22	11.06
Merrick, NY (cdp) Nassau County	2,502	10.99
Plainview, NY (cdp) Nassau County	2,802	10.93
Berlin, ND (city) La Moure County	4	10.81
Marlboro, NJ (township) Monmouth County	3,914	10.75
New Salem, ND (city) Morton County	103	10.75
Utica, KS (city) Ness County	25	10.73
Chevy Chase Section Five, MD (village) Montgomery County	68	10.68
Port Washington North, NY (village) Nassau County	292	10.67
Olivette, MO (city) Saint Louis County	795	10.56
Leola, SD (city) McPherson County	47	10.56
Palm Beach, FL (town) Palm Beach County	1,089	10.50
Cedarhurst, NY (village) Nassau County	647	10.50
Saddle Rock, NY (village) Nassau County	83	10.49
Fort Ransom, ND (city) Ransom County	7	10.45
South Valley Stream, NY (cdp) Nassau County	586	10.39
Springfield, NJ (cdp) Union County	1,493	10.35
Woodsburgh, NY (village) Nassau County	87	10.33
Hewlett, NY (cdp) Nassau County	727	10.30
Longboat Key, FL (town) Sarasota County	779	10.28
Churchs Ferry, ND (city) Ramsey County	8	10.13
Fell, PA (township) Lackawanna County	235	10.04
Moreland Hills, OH (village) Cuyahoga County	331	10.02
Ferry, AK (cdp) Yukon-Koyukuk Census Area	5	10.00
Miltonsburg, OH (village) Monroe County	2	10.00

Notes: (cdp) census designated place; Refer to the Explanation of Data in the front of the book for more detailed information.

Russian

Top 150 Places Sorted by Percent

(Based on places with populations of 10,000 or more)

Place	Number	%
Pikesville, MD (cdp) Baltimore County	5,365	18.54
Highland Park, IL (city) Lake County	5,157	16.43
Kings Point, FL (cdp) Palm Beach County	2,005	16.19
Jericho, NY (cdp) Nassau County	2,096	16.14
Beachwood, OH (city) Cuyahoga County	1,894	15.54
Buffalo Grove, IL (village) Lake County	6,542	15.36
Lower Moreland, PA (township) Montgomery County	1,648	14.61
Woodmere, NY (cdp) Nassau County	2,391	14.54
Sharon, MA (town) Norfolk County	2,490	14.30
Springdale, NJ (cdp) Camden County	2,014	13.97
West Hollywood, CA (city) Los Angeles County	4,871	13.64
Deerfield, IL (village) Lake County	2,473	13.37
Mandan, ND (city) Morton County	2,185	13.05
Morganville, NJ (cdp) Monmouth County	1,440	12.93
Northbrook, IL (village) Cook County	4,101	12.27
Aventura, FL (city) Miami-Dade County	2,998	11.87
Fair Lawn, NJ (borough) Bergen County	3,699	11.69
Millburn, NJ (cdp) Essex County	2,309	11.68
Scarsdale, NY (village) Westchester County	2,075	11.64
Lower Merion, PA (township) Montgomery County	6,737	11.26
Calabasas, CA (city) Los Angeles County	2,259	11.24
New Castle, NY (town) Westchester County	1,939	11.09
Merrick, NY (cdp) Nassau County	2,502	10.99
Plainview, NY (cdp) Nassau County	2,802	10.93
Marlboro, NJ (township) Monmouth County	3,914	10.75
Palm Beach, FL (town) Palm Beach County	1,089	10.50
Springfield, NJ (cdp) Union County	1,493	10.35
Greentree, NJ (cdp) Camden County	1,149	9.99
Manalapan, NJ (township) Monmouth County	3,333	9.97
Livingston, NJ (cdp) Essex County	2,693	9.83
New City, NY (cdp) Rockland County	3,352	9.82
Newton, MA (city) Middlesex County	8,055	9.61
Sunny Isles Beach, FL (city) Miami-Dade County	1,447	9.47
Boca Del Mar, FL (cdp) Palm Beach County	2,027	9.46
Beverly Hills, CA (city) Los Angeles County	3,184	9.41
West Bloomfield, MI (township) Oakland County	6,071	9.37
Brookline, MA (cdp) Norfolk County	5,338	9.35
Agoura Hills, CA (city) Los Angeles County	1,898	9.34
Monroe, NJ (township) Middlesex County	2,597	9.28
Creve Coeur, MO (city) Saint Louis County	1,500	9.21
Hamptons at Boca Raton, FL (cdp) Palm Beach County	1,035	9.06
Swampscott, MA (cdp) Essex County	1,280	8.88
Skokie, IL (village) Cook County	5,609	8.86
Cheltenham, PA (township) Montgomery County	3,236	8.78
Tenafly, NJ (borough) Bergen County	1,208	8.75
Lincolnwood, IL (village) Cook County	1,078	8.72
Upper Dublin, PA (township) Montgomery County	2,243	8.67
Lewisboro, NY (town) Westchester County	1,059	8.59
Potomac, MD (cdp) Montgomery County	3,824	8.53
Whitemarsh, PA (township) Montgomery County	1,386	8.30
Dix Hills, NY (cdp) Suffolk County	2,164	8.29
Melville, NY (cdp) Suffolk County	1,195	8.22
Fort Lee, NJ (borough) Bergen County	2,858	8.06
Cherry Hill, NJ (township) Camden County	5,620	8.03
Westport, CT (cdp) Fairfield County	2,012	7.81
Highland Park, NJ (borough) Middlesex County	1,091	7.79
East Brunswick, NJ (cdp) Middlesex County	3,627	7.76
Bismarck, ND (city) Burleigh County	4,250	7.69
Clayton, MO (city) Saint Louis County	970	7.56
Ojus, FL (cdp) Miami-Dade County	1,256	7.53
Northampton, PA (township) Bucks County	2,951	7.50
Oceanside, NY (cdp) Nassau County	2,418	7.39
Bexley, OH (city) Franklin County	967	7.33
Dickinson, ND (city) Stark County	1,152	7.27
Mamaroneck, NY (town) Westchester County	2,080	7.18
North Bethesda, MD (cdp) Montgomery County	2,758	7.14
West Sacramento, CA (city) Yolo County	2,228	7.05
Wayland, MA (town) Middlesex County	919	7.02
Laguna Woods, CA (city) Orange County	1,137	7.00
Parkland, FL (city) Broward County	976	6.98
Port Washington, NY (cdp) Nassau County	1,057	6.96
Pinecrest, FL (village) Miami-Dade County	1,331	6.94
Syosset, NY (cdp) Nassau County	1,285	6.93
Weston, CT (town) Fairfield County	691	6.88
Santa Monica, CA (city) Los Angeles County	5,774	6.87
Cherry Hill Mall, NJ (cdp) Camden County	924	6.86
Needham, MA (cdp) Norfolk County	1,979	6.85
Malibu, CA (city) Los Angeles County	856	6.84
Mayfield Heights, OH (city) Cuyahoga County	1,318	6.80
Wheeling, IL (village) Cook County	2,334	6.78
Long Beach, NY (city) Nassau County	2,379	6.71
Solon, OH (city) Cuyahoga County	1,464	6.71
North Wantagh, NY (cdp) Nassau County	816	6.71
Clarkstown, NY (town) Rockland County	5,482	6.68
Princeton, NJ (township) Mercer County	1,046	6.53
Coconut Creek, FL (city) Broward County	2,804	6.47
Rockville Centre, NY (village) Nassau County	1,588	6.46
Bellmore, NY (cdp) Nassau County	1,062	6.46
Longmeadow, MA (cdp) Hampden County	1,007	6.44
North Castle, NY (town) Westchester County	695	6.41
River Edge, NJ (borough) Bergen County	698	6.38
Setauket-East Setauket, NY (cdp) Suffolk County	1,009	6.33
Reisterstown, MD (cdp) Baltimore County	1,413	6.28
Dobbs Ferry, NY (village) Westchester County	667	6.28
Marblehead, MA (cdp) Essex County	1,273	6.25
University Heights, OH (city) Cuyahoga County	880	6.22
East Rockaway, NY (village) Nassau County	649	6.20
Tamarac, FL (city) Broward County	3,431	6.12
South Euclid, OH (city) Cuyahoga County	1,439	6.11
Bethesda, MD (cdp) Montgomery County	3,363	6.08
Franklin Lakes, NJ (borough) Bergen County	634	6.08
Montville, NJ (township) Morris County	1,262	6.06
Glenview, IL (village) Cook County	2,510	6.02
North Bellmore, NY (cdp) Nassau County	1,188	5.92
Wilmette, IL (village) Cook County	1,631	5.89
Vernon Hills, IL (village) Lake County	1,214	5.89
Aberdeen, SD (city) Brown County	1,448	5.88
Shorewood, WI (village) Milwaukee County	806	5.86
Mill Valley, CA (city) Marin County	795	5.86
San Anselmo, CA (town) Marin County	733	5.85
West Orange, NJ (cdp) Essex County	2,620	5.84
Lyndhurst, OH (city) Cuyahoga County	893	5.84
Commack, NY (cdp) Suffolk County	2,112	5.81
Metuchen, NJ (borough) Middlesex County	743	5.79
West Hartford, CT (cdp) Hartford County	3,662	5.76
Greenburgh, NY (town) Westchester County	4,988	5.75
East Meadow, NY (cdp) Nassau County	2,155	5.75
Tamalpais-Homestead Valley, CA (cdp) Marin County	608	5.74
Suffern, NY (village) Rockland County	628	5.71
Newtown, PA (township) Bucks County	1,040	5.70
Warren, NJ (township) Somerset County	812	5.69
Weston, MA (town) Middlesex County	652	5.68
Weston, FL (city) Broward County	2,784	5.67
Plains, PA (township) Luzerne County	611	5.60
North Hempstead, NY (town) Nassau County	12,446	5.59
North Potomac, MD (cdp) Montgomery County	1,281	5.58
Brighton, NY (town) Monroe County	1,979	5.56
Bedford, NY (town) Westchester County	1,008	5.56
Lower Southampton, PA (township) Bucks County	1,051	5.45
East Windsor, NJ (township) Mercer County	1,353	5.43
Verona, NJ (cdp) Essex County	733	5.42
Nesconset, NY (cdp) Suffolk County	647	5.40
West Windsor, NJ (township) Mercer County	1,181	5.39
Boca Raton, FL (city) Palm Beach County	4,066	5.38
Lower Gwynedd, PA (township) Montgomery County	559	5.36
Morton Grove, IL (village) Cook County	1,199	5.34
Stony Brook, NY (cdp) Suffolk County	731	5.34
Teaneck, NJ (cdp) Bergen County	2,093	5.33
Scotch Plains, NJ (cdp) Union County	1,211	5.33
Whitpain, PA (township) Montgomery County	987	5.28
Rancho Mirage, CA (city) Riverside County	682	5.26
Cooper City, FL (city) Broward County	1,453	5.25
Ithaca, NY (city) Tompkins County	1,518	5.23
Somers, NY (town) Westchester County	949	5.17
Chesterfield, MO (city) Saint Louis County	2,410	5.13
Shaker Heights, OH (city) Cuyahoga County	1,509	5.13
Randolph, NJ (township) Morris County	1,275	5.13
Hallandale, FL (city) Broward County	1,750	5.06
Larkspur, CA (city) Marin County	607	5.06
West Freehold, NJ (cdp) Monmouth County	632	5.04

Notes: (cdp) census designated place; Refer to the Explanation of Data in the front of the book for more detailed information.

Scandinavian

Top 150 Places Sorted by Number

(Based on all places, regardless of population)

Place	Number	%
Minneapolis, MN (city) Hennepin County	4,239	1.11
Seattle, WA (city) King County	3,524	0.63
Los Angeles, CA (city) Los Angeles County	2,919	0.08
San Diego, CA (city) San Diego County	2,586	0.21
Phoenix, AZ (city) Maricopa County	2,542	0.19
Portland, OR (city) Multnomah County	2,471	0.47
New York, NY (city) New York City	2,129	0.03
Salt Lake City, UT (city) Salt Lake County	2,089	1.15
Saint Paul, MN (city) Ramsey County	1,877	0.65
Provo, UT (city) Utah County	1,723	1.64
Chicago, IL (city) Cook County	1,649	0.06
Spokane, WA (city) Spokane County	1,378	0.70
Denver, CO (city) Denver County	1,367	0.25
Sandy, UT (city) Salt Lake County	1,362	1.54
Bloomington, MN (city) Hennepin County	1,313	1.54
Mesa, AZ (city) Maricopa County	1,233	0.31
Tacoma, WA (city) Pierce County	1,211	0.63
Anchorage, AK (municipality) Anchorage Borough	1,203	0.46
Duluth, MN (city) Saint Louis County	1,146	1.32
Fargo, ND (city) Cass County	1,141	1.26
San Jose, CA (city) Santa Clara County	1,133	0.13
Houston, TX (city) Harris County	1,092	0.06
San Francisco, CA (city) San Francisco County	1,029	0.13
Plymouth, MN (city) Hennepin County	1,014	1.54
Boise City, ID (city) Ada County	975	0.52
Austin, TX (city) Travis County	935	0.14
Tucson, AZ (city) Pima County	927	0.19
Las Vegas, NV (city) Clark County	925	0.19
Madison, WI (city) Dane County	908	0.44
Albuquerque, NM (city) Bernalillo County	873	0.19
Everett, WA (city) Snohomish County	861	0.94
Colorado Springs, CO (city) El Paso County	858	0.24
Omaha, NE (city) Douglas County	845	0.22
West Jordan, UT (city) Salt Lake County	837	1.23
Logan, UT (city) Cache County	832	1.95
Maple Grove, MN (city) Hennepin County	800	1.59
Coon Rapids, MN (city) Anoka County	796	1.29
West Valley City, UT (city) Salt Lake County	789	0.73
Tempe, AZ (city) Maricopa County	774	0.49
Bellevue, WA (city) King County	758	0.69
Orem, UT (city) Utah County	757	0.90
Federal Way, WA (city) King County	739	0.89
Eugene, OR (city) Lane County	726	0.53
Gresham, OR (city) Multnomah County	707	0.78
Burnsville, MN (city) Dakota County	693	1.15
San Antonio, TX (city) Bexar County	691	0.06
Sioux Falls, SD (city) Minnehaha County	685	0.55
Brooklyn Park, MN (city) Hennepin County	680	1.01
Fort Collins, CO (city) Larimer County	678	0.57
Edina, MN (city) Hennepin County	669	1.41
Dallas, TX (city) Dallas County	662	0.06
Salem, OR (city) Marion County	658	0.48
Rochester, MN (city) Olmsted County	650	0.76
Eden Prairie, MN (city) Hennepin County	649	1.18
Santa Rosa, CA (city) Sonoma County	646	0.44
Virginia Beach, VA (independent city) Virginia Beach city	638	0.15
Indianapolis, IN (special city) Marion County	621	0.08
Taylorsville, UT (city) Salt Lake County	614	1.06
Vancouver, WA (city) Clark County	608	0.42
Columbus, OH (city) Franklin County	596	0.08
Eagan, MN (city) Dakota County	589	0.93
Bellingham, WA (city) Whatcom County	574	0.86
Scottsdale, AZ (city) Maricopa County	574	0.28
Jacksonville, FL (special city) Duval County	560	0.08
Long Beach, CA (city) Los Angeles County	558	0.12
Saint Louis Park, MN (city) Hennepin County	554	1.26
Riverton, UT (city) Salt Lake County	548	2.18
Des Moines, IA (city) Polk County	542	0.27
Minnetonka, MN (city) Hennepin County	541	1.05
Woodbury, MN (city) Washington County	537	1.16
Aurora, CO (city) Arapahoe County	534	0.19
Sacramento, CA (city) Sacramento County	534	0.13
Kent, WA (city) King County	528	0.67
Lakeville, MN (city) Dakota County	523	1.21
Nashville-Davidson, TN (special city) Davidson County	519	0.10

Place	Number	%
Saint Cloud, MN (city) Stearns County	517	0.88
Washington, DC (city) District of Columbia	515	0.09
Ogden, UT (city) Weber County	513	0.66
Bountiful, UT (city) Davis County	508	1.23
Apple Valley, MN (city) Dakota County	508	1.12
Brookhaven, NY (town) Suffolk County	505	0.11
Chandler, AZ (city) Maricopa County	501	0.28
Reno, NV (city) Washoe County	501	0.28
Huntington Beach, CA (city) Orange County	498	0.26
Blaine, MN (city) Anoka County	494	1.10
Gilbert, AZ (town) Maricopa County	491	0.45
Murray, UT (city) Salt Lake County	490	1.44
Crystal, MN (city) Hennepin County	489	2.14
Layton, UT (city) Davis County	487	0.83
Tulsa, OK (city) Tulsa County	478	0.12
Pocatello, ID (city) Bannock County	476	0.92
Milwaukee, WI (city) Milwaukee County	476	0.08
Bismarck, ND (city) Burleigh County	463	0.84
Henderson, NV (city) Clark County	459	0.26
Fort Worth, TX (city) Tarrant County	458	0.09
Missoula, MT (city) Missoula County	451	0.79
Beaverton, OR (city) Washington County	444	0.58
Richfield, MN (city) Hennepin County	437	1.27
Draper, UT (city) Salt Lake County	436	1.71
Santa Clarita, CA (city) Los Angeles County	435	0.29
South Jordan, UT (city) Salt Lake County	428	1.45
Charlotte, NC (city) Mecklenburg County	424	0.08
Arden-Arcade, CA (cdp) Sacramento County	422	0.44
Kaysville, UT (city) Davis County	421	2.03
Olympia, WA (city) Thurston County	420	0.99
Grand Forks, ND (city) Grand Forks County	416	0.84
Arlington, TX (city) Tarrant County	416	0.13
Hillsboro, OR (city) Washington County	410	0.59
South Hill, WA (cdp) Pierce County	409	1.28
Fremont, CA (city) Alameda County	409	0.20
Oceanside, CA (city) San Diego County	408	0.25
Redmond, WA (city) King County	406	0.89
Boston, MA (city) Suffolk County	403	0.07
Shoreview, MN (city) Ramsey County	402	1.55
Thousand Oaks, CA (city) Ventura County	400	0.34
Riverside, CA (city) Riverside County	395	0.15
Arlington, VA (cdp) Arlington County	394	0.21
Kirkland, WA (city) King County	393	0.87
Anaheim, CA (city) Orange County	392	0.12
Billings, MT (city) Yellowstone County	385	0.43
Westminster, CO (city) Adams County	385	0.38
Oakland, CA (city) Alameda County	384	0.10
Ramsey, MN (city) Anoka County	382	2.07
Ephraim, UT (city) Sanpete County	380	8.49
Corvallis, OR (city) Benton County	380	0.77
Minot, ND (city) Ward County	378	1.03
Glendale, AZ (city) Maricopa County	378	0.17
Moorhead, MN (city) Clay County	376	1.17
Simi Valley, CA (city) Ventura County	373	0.33
Rapid City, SD (city) Pennington County	370	0.62
Millcreek, UT (cdp) Salt Lake County	368	1.21
Paradise, NV (cdp) Clark County	366	0.20
Seattle Hill-Silver Firs, WA (cdp) Snohomish County	364	1.02
Highlands Ranch, CO (cdp) Douglas County	359	0.51
Escondido, CA (city) San Diego County	359	0.27
Ames, IA (city) Story County	358	0.71
Plano, TX (city) Collin County	356	0.16
Oakdale, MN (city) Washington County	355	1.33
Fridley, MN (city) Anoka County	354	1.29
Naperville, IL (city) Du Page County	347	0.27
Farmington, UT (city) Davis County	346	2.83
Brooklyn Center, MN (city) Hennepin County	346	1.19
Irvine, CA (city) Orange County	346	0.24
Great Falls, MT (city) Cascade County	345	0.61
Canyon Rim, UT (cdp) Salt Lake County	343	3.25
Cottage Grove, MN (city) Washington County	341	1.12
Wichita, KS (city) Sedgwick County	341	0.10
Richland, WA (city) Benton County	339	0.88
Oklahoma City, OK (city) Oklahoma County	339	0.07
Medford, OR (city) Jackson County	338	0.53

Notes: (cdp) census designated place; Refer to the Explanation of Data in the front of the book for more detailed information.

Scandinavian

Top 150 Places Sorted by Percent

(Based on all places, regardless of population)

Place	Number	%
Donaldson, MN (city) Kittson County	15	28.85
Gold Hill, CO (cdp) Boulder County	48	22.97
Boone, MN (township) Lake of the Woods County	20	21.98
Vienna, SD (town) Clark County	12	19.05
Ferry, AK (cdp) Yukon-Koyukuk Census Area	9	18.00
Sawpit, CO (town) San Miguel County	3	17.65
Inverness, MT (cdp) Hill County	16	16.33
Angle, MN (township) Lake of the Woods County	22	15.07
Antler, ND (city) Bottineau County	8	14.55
Beaver, AR (town) Carroll County	10	12.99
Redpath, MN (township) Traverse County	5	12.50
Potamo, MN (township) Lake of the Woods County	16	12.40
Tuttle, ND (city) Kidder County	12	12.37
Gem, KS (city) Thomas County	9	12.16
Viking, MN (city) Marshall County	11	12.09
Port Alexander, AK (city) Wrangell-Petersburg Census Area	8	11.43
Whitehawk, CA (cdp) Plumas County	6	11.32
Saddle Butte, MT (cdp) Hill County	10	10.87
Dwight, ND (city) Richland County	8	10.67
Athelstan, IA (city) Taylor County	2	10.53
Hansonville, MN (township) Lincoln County	9	10.11
New Maine, MN (township) Marshall County	20	10.05
Pomroy, MN (township) Itasca County	4	9.76
River Falls, MN (township) Pennington County	19	9.69
Golva, ND (city) Golden Valley County	9	9.68
Polonia, MN (township) Roseau County	3	9.68
Florida, MN (township) Yellow Medicine County	16	9.64
Barry, MN (city) Big Stone County	2	9.52
Flaxton, ND (city) Burke County	7	9.21
Outlook, MT (town) Sheridan County	8	9.20
Hill, MN (township) Kittson County	2	9.09
Grover, WY (cdp) Lincoln County	8	8.89
White Earth, ND (city) Mountrail County	4	8.89
Ephraim, UT (city) Sanpete County	380	8.49
Leon, MN (township) Clearwater County	27	8.46
Hubbell, NE (village) Thayer County	9	8.41
Tamarac, MN (township) Marshall County	6	8.33
Mason, WI (village) Bayfield County	3	8.33
Akron, MN (township) Wilkin County	13	8.23
Brocket, ND (city) Ramsey County	5	8.20
Bedford, WY (cdp) Lincoln County	9	8.11
Cedar, MN (township) Marshall County	9	8.04
Manley, NE (village) Cass County	15	7.94
Moorhead, MN (township) Clay County	31	7.89
Wendell, MN (city) Grant County	15	7.81
Huss, MN (township) Roseau County	11	7.80
Edison, WA (cdp) Skagit County	11	7.75
Springbrook, ND (city) Williams County	2	7.69
Barney, ND (city) Richland County	5	7.58
Tanberg, MN (township) Wilkin County	5	7.58
Davis, MN (township) Kittson County	4	7.55
Park, MN (township) Pine County	4	7.55
Sandsville, MN (township) Polk County	5	7.46
Eden, MN (township) Polk County	14	7.41
Fairdale, ND (city) Walsh County	4	7.41
Koosharem, UT (town) Sevier County	19	7.31
Hebo, OR (cdp) Tillamook County	20	7.27
Whitestone Logging Camp, AK (cdp) Skagway-Hoonah-Angoon C.A.	8	7.27
Bushnell, SD (town) Brookings County	5	7.25
Arna, MN (township) Pine County	7	7.22
Chignik Lagoon, AK (cdp) Lake and Peninsula Borough	8	7.21
Spring Lake, UT (cdp) Utah County	30	7.19
Lignite, ND (city) Burke County	12	7.19
Percy, MN (township) Kittson County	3	7.14
Linden Grove, MN (township) Saint Louis County	9	7.09
Barnett, MN (township) Roseau County	11	7.05
Wood Lake, MN (township) Yellow Medicine County	17	7.00
Champion, MN (township) Wilkin County	6	6.90
Fountain Green, UT (city) Sanpete County	61	6.59
Kennedy, MN (city) Kittson County	15	6.36
Hampton, MN (city) Dakota County	31	6.34
Wing, ND (city) Burleigh County	9	6.34
Henriette, MN (city) Pine County	6	6.32
Blomkest, MN (city) Kandiyohi County	11	6.25
Indian Beach, NC (town) Carteret County	5	6.25
Alamo, ND (city) Williams County	3	6.25
Clover, WI (town) Bayfield County	13	6.22
Garrison, MN (city) Crow Wing County	10	6.13
Ophir, CO (town) San Miguel County	7	6.09
Gascoyne, ND (city) Bowman County	2	6.06
Sabin, MN (city) Clay County	28	5.96
Fort Peck, MT (town) Valley County	14	5.88
Barnesville, MN (township) Clay County	8	5.88
Denham, MN (city) Pine County	3	5.88
Willernie, MN (city) Washington County	31	5.82
Broaddus, TX (town) San Augustine County	10	5.81
Tonsina, AK (cdp) Valdez-Cordova Census Area	6	5.77
Crosby, MN (township) Pine County	5	5.75
Winton, MN (city) Saint Louis County	11	5.73
Aastad, MN (township) Otter Tail County	11	5.67
Shelby, MN (township) Blue Earth County	16	5.59
North Star, MN (township) Brown County	17	5.48
Fort Ripley, MN (city) Crow Wing County	4	5.48
Polk Centre, MN (township) Pennington County	4	5.48
Louisburg, MO (village) Dallas County	7	5.47
Sherman, MI (township) Keweenaw County	3	5.45
Western, MN (township) Otter Tail County	8	5.44
Crooks, MN (township) Renville County	12	5.43
Hamilton, ND (city) Pembina County	4	5.41
Brookview, MD (town) Dorchester County	5	5.38
Fayette, UT (town) Sanpete County	11	5.37
Leiding, MN (township) Saint Louis County	20	5.36
Sandy, MN (township) Saint Louis County	22	5.34
Manti, UT (city) Sanpete County	161	5.27
Tegner, MN (township) Kittson County	4	5.26
Deerwood, MN (township) Kittson County	10	5.21
Odessa, MN (township) Big Stone County	8	5.19
Slater, MN (township) Cass County	12	5.17
Jefferson City, MT (cdp) Jefferson County	15	5.10
Quamba, MN (city) Kanabec County	5	5.10
Henning, MN (township) Otter Tail County	22	5.08
Rickardsville, IA (city) Dubuque County	11	5.07
Swan Lake, MN (township) Stevens County	11	5.07
Henning, MN (city) Otter Tail County	36	5.04
Glenwood, UT (town) Sevier County	23	5.04
West Valley, MN (township) Marshall County	7	5.00
Grove Lake, MN (township) Pope County	10	4.98
Hallock, MN (city) Kittson County	60	4.95
Ballantine, MT (cdp) Yellowstone County	18	4.92
Eagle Lake, MN (township) Otter Tail County	17	4.86
Minong, WI (village) Washburn County	26	4.85
Pomme de Terre, MN (township) Grant County	7	4.83
Paradise, MT (cdp) Sanders County	8	4.82
Moylan, MN (township) Marshall County	5	4.81
Odin, MN (city) Watonwan County	6	4.80
Sugar Bush, MN (township) Becker County	28	4.78
Tynsid, MN (township) Polk County	3	4.76
Fern, MN (township) Hubbard County	10	4.72
Beaver, MN (township) Roseau County	5	4.72
Lakeside, MN (township) Cottonwood County	12	4.71
Delton, MN (township) Cottonwood County	7	4.70
Kandiyohi, MN (township) Kandiyohi County	29	4.69
Dalton, MN (city) Otter Tail County	13	4.69
Akron, MN (township) Big Stone County	9	4.66
Lake Alice, MN (township) Hubbard County	4	4.65
Thomastown, MN (township) Wadena County	33	4.64
Underwood, MN (city) Otter Tail County	15	4.64
Lavina, MT (town) Golden Valley County	10	4.63
Greenfield, MN (city) Hennepin County	117	4.59
Marble, MN (township) Lincoln County	9	4.57
Vernon, UT (town) Tooele County	10	4.55
Altamont, SD (town) Deuel County	2	4.55
Benjamin, UT (cdp) Utah County	42	4.52
Big Water, UT (town) Kane County	19	4.52
Synnes, MN (township) Stevens County	5	4.50
Kalevala, MN (township) Carlton County	13	4.48
Duluth, MN (township) Saint Louis County	76	4.46
Poplar, MN (township) Cass County	7	4.46
Wood River, WI (town) Burnett County	44	4.42
Ross, MN (township) Roseau County	21	4.38

Notes: (cdp) census designated place; Refer to the Explanation of Data in the front of the book for more detailed information.

Scandinavian

Top 150 Places Sorted by Percent

(Based on places with populations of 10,000 or more)

Place	Number	%
Canyon Rim, UT (cdp) Salt Lake County	343	3.25
Farmington, UT (city) Davis County	346	2.83
Bemidji, MN (city) Beltrami County	320	2.65
White Bear, MN (township) Ramsey County	250	2.23
Riverton, UT (city) Salt Lake County	548	2.18
Crystal, MN (city) Hennepin County	489	2.14
Ramsey, MN (city) Anoka County	382	2.07
Buffalo, MN (city) Wright County	208	2.05
Kaysville, UT (city) Davis County	421	2.03
Rosemount, MN (city) Dakota County	296	2.03
Logan, UT (city) Cache County	832	1.95
Fergus Falls, MN (city) Otter Tail County	256	1.90
Draper, UT (city) Salt Lake County	436	1.71
Anoka, MN (city) Anoka County	307	1.70
Provo, UT (city) Utah County	1,723	1.64
Ham Lake, MN (city) Anoka County	208	1.63
Maple Grove, MN (city) Hennepin County	800	1.59
Prior Lake, MN (city) Scott County	249	1.56
Shoreview, MN (city) Ramsey County	402	1.55
Sandy, UT (city) Salt Lake County	1,362	1.54
Bloomington, MN (city) Hennepin County	1,313	1.54
Plymouth, MN (city) Hennepin County	1,014	1.54
Rexburg, ID (city) Madison County	263	1.53
Fairmont, MN (city) Martin County	166	1.52
Savage, MN (city) Scott County	319	1.51
Cloquet, MN (city) Carlton County	168	1.51
East Millcreek, UT (cdp) Salt Lake County	322	1.50
Mounds View, MN (city) Ramsey County	189	1.49
West Fargo, ND (city) Cass County	214	1.46
South Jordan, UT (city) Salt Lake County	428	1.45
Hibbing, MN (city) Saint Louis County	248	1.45
Murray, UT (city) Salt Lake County	490	1.44
Blackfoot, ID (city) Bingham County	150	1.44
Edina, MN (city) Hennepin County	669	1.41
Pleasant Grove, UT (city) Utah County	324	1.38
Red Wing, MN (city) Goodhue County	222	1.38
Riverton-Boulevard Park, WA (cdp) King County	155	1.36
Golden Valley, MN (city) Hennepin County	271	1.34
Oakdale, MN (city) Washington County	355	1.33
Holladay, UT (city) Salt Lake County	194	1.33
Duluth, MN (city) Saint Louis County	1,146	1.32
Coon Rapids, MN (city) Anoka County	796	1.29
Fridley, MN (city) Anoka County	354	1.29
Cedar City, UT (city) Iron County	266	1.29
Columbia Heights, MN (city) Anoka County	238	1.29
South Hill, WA (cdp) Pierce County	409	1.28
Spanish Fork, UT (city) Utah County	259	1.28
Richfield, MN (city) Hennepin County	437	1.27
Issaquah, WA (city) King County	142	1.27
Fargo, ND (city) Cass County	1,141	1.26
Saint Louis Park, MN (city) Hennepin County	554	1.26
Springville, UT (city) Utah County	257	1.25
New Hope, MN (city) Hennepin County	259	1.24
West Jordan, UT (city) Salt Lake County	837	1.23
Bountiful, UT (city) Davis County	508	1.23
Elk River, MN (city) Sherburne County	203	1.23
Lakeville, MN (city) Dakota County	523	1.21
Millcreek, UT (cdp) Salt Lake County	368	1.21
White Bear Lake, MN (city) Ramsey County	295	1.21
Cottonwood Heights, UT (cdp) Salt Lake County	329	1.20
Brooklyn Center, MN (city) Hennepin County	346	1.19
North Saint Paul, MN (city) Ramsey County	142	1.19
Eden Prairie, MN (city) Hennepin County	649	1.18
Superior, WI (city) Douglas County	323	1.18
Moorhead, MN (city) Clay County	376	1.17
South Ogden, UT (city) Weber County	168	1.17
Woodbury, MN (city) Washington County	537	1.16
Salt Lake City, UT (city) Salt Lake County	2,089	1.15
Burnsville, MN (city) Dakota County	693	1.15
Lea Hill, WA (cdp) King County	122	1.14
Saint Helens, OR (city) Columbia County	116	1.14
Apple Valley, MN (city) Dakota County	508	1.12
Cottage Grove, MN (city) Washington County	341	1.12
Minneapolis, MN (city) Hennepin County	4,239	1.11
Blaine, MN (city) Anoka County	494	1.10
New Brighton, MN (city) Ramsey County	245	1.10
Hopkins, MN (city) Hennepin County	188	1.10
Camano, WA (cdp) Island County	149	1.10
Martha Lake, WA (cdp) Snohomish County	139	1.10
Stillwater, MN (city) Washington County	166	1.09
Lehi, UT (city) Utah County	207	1.08
Alderwood Manor, WA (cdp) Snohomish County	164	1.08
Centerville, UT (city) Davis County	155	1.08
Andover, MN (city) Anoka County	284	1.07
Taylorsville, UT (city) Salt Lake County	614	1.06
Marysville, WA (city) Snohomish County	267	1.06
Tooele, UT (city) Tooele County	238	1.06
Robbinsdale, MN (city) Hennepin County	149	1.06
Union Hill-Novelty Hill, WA (cdp) King County	118	1.06
Minnetonka, MN (city) Hennepin County	541	1.05
Minot, ND (city) Ward County	378	1.03
Seattle Hill-Silver Firs, WA (cdp) Snohomish County	364	1.02
Magna, UT (cdp) Salt Lake County	232	1.02
Brooklyn Park, MN (city) Hennepin County	680	1.01
Chanhassen, MN (city) Carver County	204	1.00
Hutchinson, MN (city) McLeod County	131	1.00
Olympia, WA (city) Thurston County	420	0.99
Williston, ND (city) Williams County	124	0.99
Grand Rapids, MN (township) Itasca County	114	0.97
Cascade-Fairwood, WA (cdp) King County	330	0.96
North Creek, WA (cdp) Snohomish County	250	0.96
South Saint Paul, MN (city) Dakota County	194	0.96
Kenmore, WA (city) King County	176	0.95
Northfield, MN (city) Rice County	162	0.95
Lino Lakes, MN (city) Anoka County	159	0.95
Everett, WA (city) Snohomish County	861	0.94
Shakopee, MN (city) Scott County	193	0.94
Eagan, MN (city) Dakota County	589	0.93
Elk Plain, WA (cdp) Pierce County	146	0.93
Pocatello, ID (city) Bannock County	476	0.92
Lacey, WA (city) Thurston County	282	0.91
Tumwater, WA (city) Thurston County	115	0.91
Mendota Heights, MN (city) Dakota County	103	0.91
Orem, UT (city) Utah County	757	0.90
East Renton Highlands, WA (cdp) King County	118	0.90
Federal Way, WA (city) King County	739	0.89
Redmond, WA (city) King County	406	0.89
Oquirrh, UT (cdp) Salt Lake County	92	0.89
Saint Cloud, MN (city) Stearns County	517	0.88
Richland, WA (city) Benton County	339	0.88
Bozeman, MT (city) Gallatin County	246	0.88
Tualatin, OR (city) Washington County	198	0.88
Kirkland, WA (city) King County	393	0.87
Mankato, MN (city) Blue Earth County	283	0.87
American Fork, UT (city) Utah County	190	0.87
Ontario, OR (city) Malheur County	97	0.87
Bellingham, WA (city) Whatcom County	574	0.86
University Place, WA (city) Pierce County	259	0.86
West Linn, OR (city) Clackamas County	192	0.86
North Marysville, WA (cdp) Snohomish County	183	0.86
Mountain Home, ID (city) Elmore County	97	0.85
Bismarck, ND (city) Burleigh County	463	0.84
Grand Forks, ND (city) Grand Forks County	416	0.84
Bainbridge Island, WA (city) Kitsap County	171	0.84
Hastings, MN (city) Dakota County	153	0.84
Ellensburg, WA (city) Kittitas County	129	0.84
Falmouth, ME (town) Cumberland County	87	0.84
Layton, UT (city) Davis County	487	0.83
Midvale, UT (city) Salt Lake County	224	0.83
Champlin, MN (city) Hennepin County	186	0.83
Barrington, IL (village) Cook County	83	0.83
Roseville, MN (city) Ramsey County	277	0.82
Lynnwood, WA (city) Snohomish County	276	0.82
Fairbanks, AK (city) Fairbanks North Star Borough	248	0.82
Sycamore, IL (city) De Kalb County	98	0.81
Enumclaw, WA (city) King County	91	0.81
Boulder City, NV (city) Clark County	119	0.80
Lake Forest Park, WA (city) King County	108	0.80
Vadnais Heights, MN (city) Ramsey County	104	0.80
Kingsgate, WA (cdp) King County	96	0.80

Notes: (cdp) census designated place; Refer to the Explanation of Data in the front of the book for more detailed information.

Scotch-Irish

Top 150 Places Sorted by Number

(Based on all places, regardless of population)

Place	Number	%
Los Angeles, CA (city) Los Angeles County	22,037	0.60
New York, NY (city) New York City	21,951	0.27
Houston, TX (city) Harris County	21,553	1.10
Charlotte, NC (city) Mecklenburg County	21,114	3.89
San Diego, CA (city) San Diego County	16,552	1.35
Dallas, TX (city) Dallas County	16,308	1.37
Austin, TX (city) Travis County	16,024	2.44
Phoenix, AZ (city) Maricopa County	15,707	1.19
Nashville-Davidson, TN (special city) Davidson County	15,608	2.86
San Antonio, TX (city) Bexar County	14,938	1.31
Jacksonville, FL (special city) Duval County	13,064	1.78
Seattle, WA (city) King County	12,206	2.17
Memphis, TN (city) Shelby County	11,311	1.74
Chicago, IL (city) Cook County	11,142	0.38
Portland, OR (city) Multnomah County	11,032	2.09
Indianapolis, IN (special city) Marion County	10,322	1.32
Columbus, OH (city) Franklin County	9,675	1.36
Raleigh, NC (city) Wake County	9,482	3.43
Virginia Beach, VA (independent city) Virginia Beach city	9,362	2.20
Philadelphia, PA (city) Philadelphia County	9,109	0.60
Oklahoma City, OK (city) Oklahoma County	8,918	1.76
Denver, CO (city) Denver County	8,810	1.59
Fort Worth, TX (city) Tarrant County	8,654	1.62
Tulsa, OK (city) Tulsa County	8,601	2.19
Colorado Springs, CO (city) El Paso County	8,284	2.30
San Francisco, CA (city) San Francisco County	8,129	1.05
Greensboro, NC (city) Guilford County	8,118	3.64
Albuquerque, NM (city) Bernalillo County	7,923	1.77
Tucson, AZ (city) Pima County	7,648	1.57
San Jose, CA (city) Santa Clara County	7,565	0.85
Lexington-Fayette, KY (special city) Fayette County	7,515	2.88
Kansas City, MO (city) Jackson County	6,904	1.56
Knoxville, TN (city) Knox County	6,779	3.90
Wichita, KS (city) Sedgwick County	6,185	1.80
Atlanta, GA (city) Fulton County	6,088	1.46
Arlington, TX (city) Tarrant County	6,023	1.81
Mesa, AZ (city) Maricopa County	5,735	1.44
Las Vegas, NV (city) Clark County	5,616	1.17
Omaha, NE (city) Douglas County	5,565	1.43
Spokane, WA (city) Spokane County	5,223	2.66
Boston, MA (city) Suffolk County	5,138	0.87
Plano, TX (city) Collin County	5,027	2.26
Huntsville, AL (city) Madison County	4,793	3.04
Winston-Salem, NC (city) Forsyth County	4,747	2.56
Lubbock, TX (city) Lubbock County	4,693	2.35
Hempstead, NY (town) Nassau County	4,687	0.62
Little Rock, AR (city) Pulaski County	4,680	2.55
Saint Petersburg, FL (city) Pinellas County	4,625	1.87
Sacramento, CA (city) Sacramento County	4,605	1.13
Aurora, CO (city) Arapahoe County	4,576	1.66
Anchorage, AK (municipality) Anchorage Borough	4,565	1.75
Long Beach, CA (city) Los Angeles County	4,500	0.98
Tampa, FL (city) Hillsborough County	4,497	1.48
Montgomery, AL (city) Montgomery County	4,479	2.22
Arlington, VA (cdp) Arlington County	4,435	2.34
Brookhaven, NY (town) Suffolk County	4,402	0.98
Corpus Christi, TX (city) Nueces County	4,365	1.57
Pittsburgh, PA (city) Allegheny County	4,363	1.30
Shreveport, LA (city) Caddo Parish	4,318	2.15
Boise City, ID (city) Ada County	4,215	2.27
Mobile, AL (city) Mobile County	4,197	2.11
Washington, DC (city) District of Columbia	4,185	0.73
Eugene, OR (city) Lane County	4,064	2.95
Scottsdale, AZ (city) Maricopa County	4,051	2.00
Fresno, CA (city) Fresno County	3,986	0.93
Lincoln, NE (city) Lancaster County	3,943	1.75
El Paso, TX (city) El Paso County	3,933	0.70
Asheville, NC (city) Buncombe County	3,860	5.60
Baton Rouge, LA (city) East Baton Rouge Parish	3,843	1.69
Louisville, KY (city) Jefferson County	3,833	1.49
Columbia, SC (city) Richland County	3,824	3.30
Overland Park, KS (city) Johnson County	3,806	2.56
Huntington Beach, CA (city) Orange County	3,781	1.99
Chesapeake, VA (independent city) Chesapeake city	3,781	1.90
Durham, NC (city) Durham County	3,778	2.02
Jackson, MS (city) Hinds County	3,759	2.04
Minneapolis, MN (city) Hennepin County	3,744	0.98
New Orleans, LA (city) Orleans Parish	3,680	0.76
Amarillo, TX (city) Potter County	3,643	2.10
Springfield, MO (city) Greene County	3,485	2.30
Garland, TX (city) Dallas County	3,455	1.60
Norfolk, VA (independent city) Norfolk city	3,438	1.47
Tacoma, WA (city) Pierce County	3,433	1.78
Chattanooga, TN (city) Hamilton County	3,429	2.21
Lakewood, CO (city) Jefferson County	3,399	2.36
Reno, NV (city) Washoe County	3,375	1.87
Richmond, VA (independent city) Richmond city	3,371	1.70
Tallahassee, FL (city) Leon County	3,309	2.20
Baltimore, MD (independent city) Baltimore city	3,274	0.50
Wilmington, NC (city) New Hanover County	3,248	4.30
Fayetteville, NC (city) Cumberland County	3,222	2.67
Des Moines, IA (city) Polk County	3,212	1.62
Cary, NC (town) Wake County	3,050	3.23
Santa Rosa, CA (city) Sonoma County	3,049	2.07
Charleston, SC (city) Charleston County	3,048	3.17
Newport News, VA (independent city) Newport News city	2,994	1.66
Akron, OH (city) Summit County	2,991	1.38
Cincinnati, OH (city) Hamilton County	2,970	0.90
Tempe, AZ (city) Maricopa County	2,944	1.86
Toledo, OH (city) Lucas County	2,923	0.93
Richardson, TX (city) Dallas County	2,906	3.17
Riverside, CA (city) Riverside County	2,890	1.13
Fort Collins, CO (city) Larimer County	2,852	2.41
Santa Clarita, CA (city) Los Angeles County	2,843	1.88
Henderson, NV (city) Clark County	2,815	1.60
Salem, OR (city) Marion County	2,813	2.06
Boulder, CO (city) Boulder County	2,809	2.97
Bakersfield, CA (city) Kern County	2,809	1.14
Athens-Clarke County, GA (special city) Clarke County	2,787	2.78
Irving, TX (city) Dallas County	2,768	1.44
Saint Paul, MN (city) Ramsey County	2,757	0.96
Independence, MO (city) Jackson County	2,742	2.42
Columbus, GA (special city) Muscogee County	2,742	1.48
Anaheim, CA (city) Orange County	2,705	0.83
Hoover, AL (city) Jefferson County	2,701	4.32
Oakland, CA (city) Alameda County	2,689	0.67
Topeka, KS (city) Shawnee County	2,684	2.20
Oceanside, CA (city) San Diego County	2,682	1.67
Vancouver, WA (city) Clark County	2,678	1.87
Roswell, GA (city) Fulton County	2,655	3.33
Gastonia, NC (city) Gaston County	2,634	3.97
Orlando, FL (city) Orange County	2,634	1.42
Norman, OK (city) Cleveland County	2,615	2.73
Honolulu, HI (cdp) Honolulu County	2,612	0.70
Roanoke, VA (independent city) Roanoke city	2,586	2.72
Alexandria, VA (independent city) Alexandria city	2,581	2.01
Birmingham, AL (city) Jefferson County	2,573	1.06
Greenville, SC (city) Greenville County	2,540	4.51
Glendale, AZ (city) Maricopa County	2,503	1.15
Milwaukee, WI (city) Milwaukee County	2,457	0.41
Concord, CA (city) Contra Costa County	2,437	2.00
Sandy Springs, GA (cdp) Fulton County	2,430	2.84
Saint Louis, MO (independent city) Saint Louis city	2,429	0.70
Islip, NY (town) Suffolk County	2,406	0.75
Livonia, MI (city) Wayne County	2,386	2.37
Rock Hill, SC (city) York County	2,385	4.75
Augusta-Richmond County, GA (special city) Richmond County	2,373	1.21
Chapel Hill, NC (town) Orange County	2,365	4.85
Chandler, AZ (city) Maricopa County	2,361	1.34
Abilene, TX (city) Taylor County	2,337	2.02
Modesto, CA (city) Stanislaus County	2,332	1.23
Cleveland, OH (city) Cuyahoga County	2,319	0.48
Johnson City, TN (city) Washington County	2,313	4.18
Salt Lake City, UT (city) Salt Lake County	2,312	1.27
Billings, MT (city) Yellowstone County	2,310	2.58
San Buenaventura, CA (city) Ventura County	2,309	2.28
High Point, NC (city) Guilford County	2,297	2.67
Madison, WI (city) Dane County	2,292	1.10
Arden-Arcade, CA (cdp) Sacramento County	2,285	2.38
Pasadena, TX (city) Harris County	2,281	1.61

Notes: (cdp) census designated place; Refer to the Explanation of Data in the front of the book for more detailed information.

Scotch-Irish

Top 150 Places Sorted by Percent

(Based on all places, regardless of population)

Place	Number	%
Cottonwood, SD (town) Jackson County	2	100.00
Oak Hill, AL (town) Wilcox County	13	59.09
Lambert, OK (town) Alfalfa County	5	55.56
Kupreanof, AK (city) Wrangell-Petersburg Census Area	13	40.63
Ayr, ND (city) Cass County	7	38.89
Susitna, AK (cdp) Matanuska-Susitna Borough	12	38.71
Whitehawk, CA (cdp) Plumas County	20	37.74
Mountville, SC (cdp) Laurens County	32	35.96
Hill, MN (township) Kittson County	7	31.82
Mound, LA (village) Madison Parish	7	31.82
Codyville, ME (plantation) Washington County	6	31.58
Norwich, OH (village) Muskingum County	32	30.48
Greenwater, WA (cdp) King County	19	28.36
Gold Hill, CO (cdp) Boulder County	58	27.75
Meyers Chuck, AK (cdp) Prince of Wales-Outer Ketchikan C.A.	4	26.67
Bayport, FL (cdp) Hernando County	6	25.00
Alexandria, OH (village) Licking County	4	23.53
Balfour, ND (city) McHenry County	3	23.08
Livengood, AK (cdp) Yukon-Koyukuk Census Area	3	23.08
Balsam, MN (township) Aitkin County	5	22.73
Benton, IA (city) Ringgold County	7	22.58
Deepstep, GA (town) Washington County	27	22.31
Verlot, WA (cdp) Snohomish County	52	22.03
Tar Heel, NC (town) Bladen County	13	22.03
Boxville, MN (township) Marshall County	7	21.21
Woodbury, KY (city) Butler County	19	21.11
Winchester, WY (cdp) Washakie County	8	21.05
Green Hills, PA (borough) Washington County	4	21.05
Rockport, WA (cdp) Skagit County	11	20.75
Elbert, TX (cdp) Throckmorton County	14	20.29
Rockville, SC (town) Charleston County	32	19.88
Vantage, WA (cdp) Kittitas County	4	19.05
Patmos, AR (town) Hempstead County	11	18.97
Madrid, NM (cdp) Santa Fe County	20	18.87
Lake Minchumina, AK (cdp) Yukon-Koyukuk Census Area	6	18.75
Port Alexander, AK (city) Wrangell-Petersburg Census Area	13	18.57
Troy, SC (town) Greenwood County	18	18.56
Nashville, ME (plantation) Aroostook County	10	18.52
Woods Landing-Jelm, WY (cdp) Albany County	24	17.91
Mehama, OR (cdp) Marion County	59	17.82
Carrick, CA (cdp) Siskiyou County	27	17.76
Cayuse, OR (cdp) Umatilla County	11	17.74
Silerton, TN (town) Hardeman County	9	17.65
Crossnore, NC (town) Avery County	41	17.45
McKittrick, MO (town) Montgomery County	10	17.24
Fancy Gap, VA (cdp) Carroll County	38	16.96
Gandy, NE (village) Logan County	4	16.67
Hamlin, KS (city) Brown County	4	16.67
Hammond, ME (town) Aroostook County	15	16.48
Markham, WA (cdp) Grays Harbor County	12	16.44
West Alexander, PA (borough) Washington County	49	16.33
South Fork Estates, TX (cdp) Jim Hogg County	8	16.33
Edmond, KS (city) Norton County	7	16.28
Hitchcock, OK (town) Blaine County	26	16.25
Wenonah, IL (village) Montgomery County	5	16.13
Tarrants, MO (village) Pike County	6	15.79
Smyrna, SC (town) York County	12	15.58
Sugar Mountain, NC (village) Avery County	33	15.42
Donegal, PA (township) Washington County	372	15.20
Forest Hills, NC (village) Jackson County	48	15.14
Cotter, IA (city) Louisa County	8	15.09
McDonald, NC (town) Robeson County	17	14.91
Farson, WY (cdp) Sweetwater County	24	14.81
Mize, MS (town) Smith County	41	14.70
Van Tassell, WY (town) Niobrara County	2	14.29
Glenview Manor, KY (city) Jefferson County	29	14.15
Webster, NC (town) Jackson County	64	14.13
Old Bennington, VT (village) Bennington County	33	14.10
Wallula, WA (cdp) Walla Walla County	32	14.10
Barker Ten Mile, NC (cdp) Robeson County	125	14.08
Hopewell, PA (township) Washington County	138	13.93
Moose Lake, MN (township) Cass County	18	13.85
Blaine, PA (township) Washington County	82	13.83
Port Protection, AK (cdp) Prince of Wales-Outer Ketchikan Census Area	10	13.70
Waldo, KS (city) Russell County	6	13.64
Montreat, NC (town) Buncombe County	93	13.62
Phenix, VA (town) Charlotte County	25	13.44
Cannon, MN (township) Kittson County	4	13.33
Beddington, ME (town) Washington County	2	13.33
East Fork, PA (district) Potter County	2	13.33
Jamestown, OK (town) Rogers County	2	13.33
West Liberty, PA (borough) Butler County	49	13.28
Cumberland Gap, TN (town) Claiborne County	27	13.11
Mineral Springs, NC (town) Union County	135	13.06
Bonanza, CO (town) Saguache County	3	13.04
Hickory Valley, TN (town) Hardeman County	20	12.99
Utica, MO (village) Livingston County	35	12.77
Mooresville, AL (town) Limestone County	6	12.77
Morris, PA (township) Washington County	162	12.74
Sandy Lake, PA (borough) Mercer County	95	12.73
Duffield, VA (town) Scott County	8	12.70
Keeler, CA (cdp) Inyo County	9	12.68
Cameron, NC (town) Moore County	19	12.67
Monhegan, ME (plantation) Lincoln County	10	12.66
West Smithfield, NC (cdp) Johnston County	10	12.66
Five Points, NC (cdp) Hoke County	46	12.64
Clio, IA (city) Wayne County	15	12.50
Frenchtown-Rumbly, MD (cdp) Somerset County	7	12.50
Pine Ridge, NE (cdp) Sheridan County	2	12.50
Reed, ME (plantation) Aroostook County	28	12.44
Lamy, NM (cdp) Santa Fe County	20	12.42
Lonsdale, AR (town) Garland County	15	12.40
Reserve, KS (city) Brown County	12	12.37
Minnesott Beach, NC (town) Pamlico County	38	12.34
Holiday Valley, OH (cdp) Clark County	224	12.33
Bondurant, WY (cdp) Sublette County	18	12.33
Nesbit, MN (township) Polk County	15	12.20
Lake Junaluska, NC (cdp) Haywood County	331	12.17
Cherry Valley, PA (borough) Butler County	8	12.12
Monomoscoy Island, MA (cdp) Barnstable County	15	12.10
Clarkton, NC (town) Bladen County	86	12.01
Spray, OR (town) Wheeler County	18	12.00
Highlands, NC (town) Macon County	108	11.99
Lake Secession, SC (cdp) Abbeville County	90	11.90
Volant, PA (borough) Lawrence County	12	11.88
Cedar Rock, NC (village) Caldwell County	34	11.76
Falcon Village, TX (cdp) Starr County	8	11.76
Goodsprings, NV (cdp) Clark County	28	11.72
Claysville, PA (borough) Washington County	85	11.68
Halibut Cove, AK (cdp) Kenai Peninsula Borough	7	11.67
Murdock, NE (village) Cass County	37	11.64
Briarcliffe Acres, SC (town) Horry County	55	11.63
Edna Bay, AK (cdp) Prince of Wales-Outer Ketchikan Census Area	6	11.54
Preston, KS (city) Pratt County	21	11.48
Heath, PA (township) Jefferson County	16	11.43
Gilbert, AR (town) Searcy County	4	11.43
Donalds, SC (town) Abbeville County	37	11.42
Hyattville, WY (cdp) Big Horn County	7	11.29
Rinard, IA (city) Calhoun County	7	11.29
Prosper, MN (township) Lake of the Woods County	11	11.22
Meta, MO (city) Osage County	28	11.11
Catarina, TX (cdp) Dimmit County	15	11.11
Alger, WA (cdp) Skagit County	9	11.11
Berkley, IA (city) Boone County	3	11.11
Dyer Brook, ME (town) Aroostook County	22	11.06
Cooper, ME (town) Washington County	16	11.03
Lesslie, SC (cdp) York County	263	11.01
Scott, PA (township) Lawrence County	246	11.01
Osborn, ME (town) Hancock County	9	10.98
Amwell, PA (township) Washington County	431	10.88
East Finley, PA (township) Washington County	162	10.88
Saddle Butte, MT (cdp) Hill County	10	10.87
Hamilton, ND (city) Pembina County	8	10.81
Ross, TX (city) McLennan County	27	10.71
Fairview, PA (borough) Butler County	26	10.70
Biltmore Forest, NC (town) Buncombe County	154	10.69
Henry, NE (village) Scotts Bluff County	17	10.69
Bluewater, CA (cdp) San Bernardino County	22	10.68
Vernon, CA (city) Los Angeles County	10	10.64
Atwood, PA (borough) Armstrong County	12	10.62

Notes: (cdp) census designated place; Refer to the Explanation of Data in the front of the book for more detailed information.

Scotch-Irish

Top 150 Places Sorted by Percent

(Based on places with populations of 10,000 or more)

Place	Number	%
Mint Hill, NC (town) Mecklenburg County	1,249	8.49
Forest Acres, SC (city) Richland County	830	7.78
Boone, NC (town) Watauga County	1,039	7.73
Masonboro, NC (cdp) New Hanover County	725	6.06
Clemson, SC (city) Pickens County	728	6.01
Cornelius, NC (town) Mecklenburg County	704	6.01
Mountain Brook, AL (city) Jefferson County	1,250	5.96
Clinton, MS (city) Hinds County	1,355	5.79
Staunton, VA (independent city) Staunton city	1,366	5.73
Maryville, TN (city) Blount County	1,315	5.68
Asheville, NC (city) Buncombe County	3,860	5.60
North Myrtle Beach, SC (city) Horry County	609	5.53
Washington, PA (city) Washington County	844	5.51
Laurinburg, NC (city) Scotland County	859	5.44
Brentwood, TN (city) Williamson County	1,293	5.43
Saint Simons, GA (cdp) Glynn County	728	5.41
Matthews, NC (town) Mecklenburg County	1,201	5.36
Indian Trail, NC (town) Union County	626	5.29
Germantown, TN (city) Shelby County	1,966	5.27
Huntersville, NC (town) Mecklenburg County	1,309	5.25
Madison, MS (city) Madison County	769	5.23
Fairhope, AL (city) Baldwin County	639	5.23
Wade Hampton, SC (cdp) Greenville County	1,046	5.15
Vestavia Hills, AL (city) Jefferson County	1,268	5.10
Decatur, GA (city) De Kalb County	925	5.08
Statesville, NC (city) Iredell County	1,166	5.06
Farragut, TN (town) Knox County	898	5.02
Bon Air, VA (cdp) Chesterfield County	793	4.90
Chapel Hill, NC (town) Orange County	2,365	4.85
Hendersonville, NC (city) Henderson County	499	4.81
Taylors, SC (cdp) Greenville County	952	4.80
Homewood, AL (city) Jefferson County	1,183	4.76
Rock Hill, SC (city) York County	2,385	4.75
Oak Ridge, TN (city) Anderson County	1,296	4.73
Crestline, CA (cdp) San Bernardino County	483	4.73
Anderson, SC (city) Anderson County	1,184	4.69
Green Valley, AZ (cdp) Pima County	810	4.67
Butler, PA (township) Butler County	804	4.67
North Decatur, GA (cdp) De Kalb County	700	4.62
Sevierville, TN (city) Sevier County	546	4.61
Irmo, SC (town) Richland County	511	4.60
Greenville, SC (city) Greenville County	2,540	4.51
Bartlett, TN (city) Shelby County	1,805	4.48
Seven Oaks, SC (cdp) Lexington County	710	4.48
Mount Pleasant, SC (town) Charleston County	2,107	4.45
Kingsport, TN (city) Sullivan County	1,963	4.41
Florence, SC (city) Florence County	1,329	4.39
Butler, PA (city) Butler County	651	4.33
Wilmington Island, GA (cdp) Chatham County	615	4.33
East Brainerd, TN (cdp) Hamilton County	601	4.33
Hoover, AL (city) Jefferson County	2,701	4.32
Wilmington, NC (city) New Hanover County	3,248	4.30
Southern Pines, NC (town) Moore County	481	4.29
North Strabane, PA (township) Washington County	431	4.29
University Park, TX (city) Dallas County	1,000	4.28
East Ridge, TN (city) Hamilton County	889	4.28
Maumelle, AR (city) Pulaski County	447	4.25
Mooresville, NC (town) Iredell County	811	4.24
Mountain Park, GA (cdp) Gwinnett County	484	4.21
Hope Mills, NC (town) Cumberland County	476	4.19
Johnson City, TN (city) Washington County	2,313	4.18
Morganton, NC (city) Burke County	707	4.14
Simpsonville, SC (city) Greenville County	594	4.13
Upper Saint Clair, PA (cdp) Allegheny County	826	4.12
Hermitage, PA (city) Mercer County	658	4.08
Starkville, MS (city) Oktibbeha County	894	4.06
Carlisle, PA (borough) Cumberland County	729	4.06
South Middleton, PA (township) Cumberland County	522	4.03
Waynesboro, VA (independent city) Waynesboro city	785	4.02
Grass Valley, CA (city) Nevada County	448	4.01
Tuckahoe, VA (cdp) Henrico County	1,729	4.00
Black Forest, CO (cdp) El Paso County	528	4.00
Ridgeland, MS (city) Madison County	803	3.99
Easley, SC (city) Pickens County	716	3.99
Gastonia, NC (city) Gaston County	2,634	3.97
Kerrville, TX (city) Kerr County	823	3.96
Fort Hunt, VA (cdp) Fairfax County	505	3.94
Cookeville, TN (city) Putnam County	950	3.93
La Grande, OR (city) Union County	479	3.91
Knoxville, TN (city) Knox County	6,779	3.90
Charlotte, NC (city) Mecklenburg County	21,114	3.89
Brandon, MS (city) Rankin County	636	3.89
Cayce, SC (city) Lexington County	466	3.89
Cave Spring, VA (cdp) Roanoke County	965	3.87
Blacksburg, VA (town) Montgomery County	1,522	3.86
Radford, VA (independent city) Radford city	612	3.86
Concord, NC (city) Cabarrus County	2,153	3.85
Auburn, AL (city) Lee County	1,651	3.85
Bristol, TN (city) Sullivan County	962	3.85
Hanover, MA (town) Plymouth County	504	3.83
Sun City, CA (cdp) Riverside County	678	3.80
West Columbia, SC (city) Lexington County	502	3.79
Auburn, CA (city) Placer County	472	3.79
Cocoa Beach, FL (city) Brevard County	471	3.79
Tucker, GA (cdp) De Kalb County	1,004	3.77
Highland Village, TX (city) Denton County	457	3.76
Vashon, WA (cdp) King County	381	3.76
Aiken, SC (city) Aiken County	951	3.75
Canyon Lake, TX (cdp) Comal County	630	3.73
Bainbridge Island, WA (city) Kitsap County	754	3.71
Elizabethton, TN (city) Carter County	499	3.71
Helena, MT (city) Lewis and Clark County	945	3.70
Ashland, OR (city) Jackson County	722	3.70
Danville, KY (city) Boyle County	572	3.69
Trussville, AL (city) Jefferson County	505	3.68
Center, PA (township) Beaver County	423	3.68
Dunwoody, GA (cdp) De Kalb County	1,200	3.66
Murray, KY (city) Calloway County	552	3.66
Burlington, NC (city) Alamance County	1,656	3.65
Hickory, NC (city) Catawba County	1,369	3.65
Belton, TX (city) Bell County	537	3.65
Greensboro, NC (city) Guilford County	8,118	3.64
Pelham, AL (city) Shelby County	512	3.63
Socastee, SC (cdp) Horry County	515	3.62
Spartanburg, SC (city) Spartanburg County	1,418	3.60
Wake Forest, NC (town) Wake County	452	3.60
Lake Forest Park, WA (city) King County	482	3.59
Myrtle Beach, SC (city) Horry County	808	3.57
Prairie Village, KS (city) Johnson County	786	3.57
Grand Rapids charter, MI (township) Kent County	501	3.57
Valle Vista, CA (cdp) Riverside County	379	3.57
Sanford, NC (city) Lee County	842	3.56
Mount Juliet, TN (city) Wilson County	437	3.56
Garner, NC (town) Wake County	624	3.55
Laguna Woods, CA (city) Orange County	577	3.55
Apex, NC (town) Wake County	710	3.54
Saint Augustine, FL (city) Saint Johns County	407	3.54
Christiansburg, VA (town) Montgomery County	600	3.53
Abington, MA (cdp) Plymouth County	516	3.53
Avon Lake, OH (city) Lorain County	638	3.52
Bella Vista, AR (cdp) Benton County	579	3.52
Druid Hills, GA (cdp) De Kalb County	447	3.52
Ferry Pass, FL (cdp) Escambia County	951	3.50
Clemmons, NC (village) Forsyth County	490	3.50
Lumberton, NC (city) Robeson County	717	3.49
Benbrook, TX (city) Tarrant County	692	3.48
Pacific Grove, CA (city) Monterey County	538	3.48
Collierville, TN (town) Shelby County	1,106	3.47
Falls Church, VA (independent city) Falls Church city	360	3.47
Lakeside, VA (cdp) Henrico County	386	3.46
Willistown, PA (township) Chester County	346	3.46
Manor, PA (township) Lancaster County	567	3.45
Solana Beach, CA (city) San Diego County	445	3.45
Sparta, NJ (township) Sussex County	623	3.44
Bellaire, TX (city) Harris County	536	3.44
Falmouth, ME (town) Cumberland County	355	3.44
Raleigh, NC (city) Wake County	9,482	3.43
Upper Arlington, OH (city) Franklin County	1,153	3.43
Mechanicsville, VA (cdp) Hanover County	1,045	3.43
Weirton, WV (city) Hancock County	698	3.43

Notes: (cdp) census designated place; Refer to the Explanation of Data in the front of the book for more detailed information.

Scottish

Top 150 Places Sorted by Number

(Based on all places, regardless of population)

Place	Number	%
New York, NY (city) New York City	32,024	0.40
Los Angeles, CA (city) Los Angeles County	29,048	0.79
San Diego, CA (city) San Diego County	21,965	1.80
Phoenix, AZ (city) Maricopa County	20,873	1.58
Houston, TX (city) Harris County	20,171	1.03
Seattle, WA (city) King County	19,880	3.53
Portland, OR (city) Multnomah County	17,002	3.21
Austin, TX (city) Travis County	15,382	2.34
Dallas, TX (city) Dallas County	14,482	1.22
Chicago, IL (city) Cook County	14,285	0.49
San Francisco, CA (city) San Francisco County	13,596	1.75
Jacksonville, FL (special city) Duval County	13,558	1.84
Indianapolis, IN (special city) Marion County	13,190	1.69
Charlotte, NC (city) Mecklenburg County	12,846	2.37
San Antonio, TX (city) Bexar County	11,915	1.04
Columbus, OH (city) Franklin County	11,819	1.66
Virginia Beach, VA (independent city) Virginia Beach city	11,175	2.63
Nashville-Davidson, TN (special city) Davidson County	11,108	2.04
San Jose, CA (city) Santa Clara County	11,103	1.24
Denver, CO (city) Denver County	11,046	1.99
Colorado Springs, CO (city) El Paso County	10,314	2.86
Albuquerque, NM (city) Bernalillo County	9,761	2.18
Mesa, AZ (city) Maricopa County	9,469	2.38
Tucson, AZ (city) Pima County	9,397	1.93
Philadelphia, PA (city) Philadelphia County	8,323	0.55
Tulsa, OK (city) Tulsa County	8,035	2.04
Oklahoma City, OK (city) Oklahoma County	7,985	1.58
Fort Worth, TX (city) Tarrant County	7,923	1.48
Las Vegas, NV (city) Clark County	7,916	1.65
Raleigh, NC (city) Wake County	7,915	2.86
Salt Lake City, UT (city) Salt Lake County	7,838	4.32
Memphis, TN (city) Shelby County	7,522	1.16
Boston, MA (city) Suffolk County	7,340	1.25
Boise City, ID (city) Ada County	7,186	3.86
Anchorage, AK (municipality) Anchorage Borough	6,943	2.67
Atlanta, GA (city) Fulton County	6,711	1.61
Kansas City, MO (city) Jackson County	6,667	1.51
Washington, DC (city) District of Columbia	6,536	1.14
Lexington-Fayette, KY (special city) Fayette County	6,375	2.45
Minneapolis, MN (city) Hennepin County	6,354	1.66
Saint Petersburg, FL (city) Pinellas County	6,317	2.55
Arlington, TX (city) Tarrant County	6,042	1.82
Scottsdale, AZ (city) Maricopa County	5,948	2.93
Wichita, KS (city) Sedgwick County	5,896	1.71
Plano, TX (city) Collin County	5,888	2.65
Spokane, WA (city) Spokane County	5,691	2.90
Aurora, CO (city) Arapahoe County	5,481	1.99
Long Beach, CA (city) Los Angeles County	5,359	1.16
Arlington, VA (cdp) Arlington County	5,336	2.82
Tampa, FL (city) Hillsborough County	5,312	1.75
Sacramento, CA (city) Sacramento County	5,248	1.29
Hempstead, NY (town) Nassau County	5,207	0.69
Eugene, OR (city) Lane County	5,172	3.75
Provo, UT (city) Utah County	5,151	4.89
Greensboro, NC (city) Guilford County	5,151	2.31
Omaha, NE (city) Douglas County	5,076	1.30
Brookhaven, NY (town) Suffolk County	4,974	1.11
Fresno, CA (city) Fresno County	4,909	1.15
Huntington Beach, CA (city) Orange County	4,900	2.58
Reno, NV (city) Washoe County	4,697	2.60
Oakland, CA (city) Alameda County	4,547	1.14
Overland Park, KS (city) Johnson County	4,429	2.98
Knoxville, TN (city) Knox County	4,360	2.51
Santa Clarita, CA (city) Los Angeles County	4,318	2.85
Baltimore, MD (independent city) Baltimore city	4,306	0.66
Fort Collins, CO (city) Larimer County	4,277	3.61
Livonia, MI (city) Wayne County	4,245	4.22
Orem, UT (city) Utah County	4,230	5.02
Sandy, UT (city) Salt Lake County	4,198	4.76
Pittsburgh, PA (city) Allegheny County	4,189	1.25
Chesapeake, VA (independent city) Chesapeake city	4,133	2.07
Tacoma, WA (city) Pierce County	4,126	2.14
Cincinnati, OH (city) Hamilton County	4,086	1.24
Lakewood, CO (city) Jefferson County	4,011	2.78
Santa Rosa, CA (city) Sonoma County	4,007	2.72
Boulder, CO (city) Boulder County	4,003	4.24
Riverside, CA (city) Riverside County	3,904	1.53
Salem, OR (city) Marion County	3,894	2.85
Vancouver, WA (city) Clark County	3,888	2.71
Norfolk, VA (independent city) Norfolk city	3,881	1.66
Richmond, VA (independent city) Richmond city	3,861	1.95
Henderson, NV (city) Clark County	3,810	2.16
Tempe, AZ (city) Maricopa County	3,805	2.40
Madison, WI (city) Dane County	3,780	1.82
Ann Arbor, MI (city) Washtenaw County	3,770	3.30
Winston-Salem, NC (city) Forsyth County	3,740	2.02
Lincoln, NE (city) Lancaster County	3,675	1.63
Montgomery, AL (city) Montgomery County	3,674	1.82
Louisville, KY (city) Jefferson County	3,603	1.41
Saint Paul, MN (city) Ramsey County	3,564	1.24
Bakersfield, CA (city) Kern County	3,546	1.43
Little Rock, AR (city) Pulaski County	3,529	1.92
Tallahassee, FL (city) Leon County	3,513	2.33
Anaheim, CA (city) Orange County	3,500	1.07
El Paso, TX (city) El Paso County	3,492	0.62
Garland, TX (city) Dallas County	3,460	1.60
Chandler, AZ (city) Maricopa County	3,431	1.95
Fort Wayne, IN (city) Allen County	3,423	1.66
Toledo, OH (city) Lucas County	3,419	1.09
Thousand Oaks, CA (city) Ventura County	3,402	2.91
Durham, NC (city) Durham County	3,378	1.80
Bellevue, WA (city) King County	3,372	3.09
Oceanside, CA (city) San Diego County	3,353	2.08
Huntsville, AL (city) Madison County	3,336	2.11
Glendale, AZ (city) Maricopa County	3,327	1.52
Alexandria, VA (independent city) Alexandria city	3,255	2.54
Lubbock, TX (city) Lubbock County	3,238	1.62
Honolulu, HI (cdp) Honolulu County	3,222	0.87
Portland, ME (city) Cumberland County	3,218	5.01
New Orleans, LA (city) Orleans Parish	3,213	0.66
West Valley City, UT (city) Salt Lake County	3,205	2.95
Charleston, SC (city) Charleston County	3,168	3.30
Springfield, MO (city) Greene County	3,167	2.09
Orlando, FL (city) Orange County	3,164	1.70
Des Moines, IA (city) Polk County	3,141	1.58
Akron, OH (city) Summit County	3,134	1.44
Manchester, NH (city) Hillsborough County	3,088	2.89
Bellingham, WA (city) Whatcom County	3,086	4.62
Corpus Christi, TX (city) Nueces County	3,072	1.11
West Jordan, UT (city) Salt Lake County	3,046	4.47
Cary, NC (town) Wake County	3,034	3.21
Ogden, UT (city) Weber County	3,016	3.90
Mobile, AL (city) Mobile County	3,014	1.52
Arvada, CO (city) Jefferson County	2,977	2.90
Chattanooga, TN (city) Hamilton County	2,956	1.90
Gilbert, AZ (town) Maricopa County	2,944	2.68
Irvine, CA (city) Orange County	2,933	2.05
Amarillo, TX (city) Potter County	2,931	1.69
Milwaukee, WI (city) Milwaukee County	2,889	0.48
Paradise, NV (cdp) Clark County	2,880	1.55
Islip, NY (town) Suffolk County	2,878	0.89
Costa Mesa, CA (city) Orange County	2,876	2.64
Newport News, VA (independent city) Newport News city	2,830	1.57
Canton, MI (cdp) Wayne County	2,793	3.66
Sandy Springs, GA (cdp) Fulton County	2,775	3.24
Sterling Heights, MI (city) Macomb County	2,765	2.22
Irving, TX (city) Dallas County	2,751	1.44
Augusta-Richmond County, GA (special city) Richmond County	2,749	1.41
Royal Oak, MI (city) Oakland County	2,738	4.56
Richardson, TX (city) Dallas County	2,734	2.98
Berkeley, CA (city) Alameda County	2,731	2.66
Billings, MT (city) Yellowstone County	2,729	3.05
Concord, CA (city) Contra Costa County	2,729	2.24
Norman, OK (city) Cleveland County	2,718	2.84
San Buenaventura, CA (city) Ventura County	2,706	2.68
Athens-Clarke County, GA (special city) Clarke County	2,695	2.69
Fort Lauderdale, FL (city) Broward County	2,689	1.77
Modesto, CA (city) Stanislaus County	2,681	1.42
Mission Viejo, CA (city) Orange County	2,673	2.88
Fayetteville, NC (city) Cumberland County	2,666	2.21

Notes: (cdp) census designated place; Refer to the Explanation of Data in the front of the book for more detailed information.

Scottish

Top 150 Places Sorted by Percent

(Based on all places, regardless of population)

Place	Number	%
Averill, VT (town) Essex County	11	64.71
Magalloway, ME (plantation) Oxford County	17	60.71
Jamestown, OK (town) Rogers County	9	60.00
Halibut Cove, AK (cdp) Kenai Peninsula Borough	29	48.33
Port Clarence, AK (cdp) Nome Census Area	9	42.86
Lutak, AK (cdp) Haines Borough	14	38.89
Excursion Inlet, AK (cdp) Haines Borough	6	37.50
Codyville, ME (plantation) Washington County	7	36.84
Conway, WA (cdp) Skagit County	18	36.73
South Fork Estates, TX (cdp) Jim Hogg County	18	36.73
Grandfather, NC (village) Avery County	30	36.59
Long Island, ME (town) Cumberland County	60	29.85
Matinicus Isle, ME (plantation) Knox County	15	29.41
McKinnon, WY (cdp) Sweetwater County	16	27.59
Spring Garden, CA (cdp) Plumas County	7	26.92
Darwin, CA (cdp) Inyo County	18	26.09
Masardis, ME (town) Aroostook County	69	25.37
Owl Creek, WY (cdp) Hot Springs County	13	24.53
Harrison City, PA (cdp) Westmoreland County	31	23.31
Dering Harbor, NY (village) Suffolk County	3	23.08
Kicking Horse, MT (cdp) Lake County	18	22.78
South Bend, NE (village) Cass County	18	22.78
Halls Crossing, UT (cdp) San Juan County	22	22.22
Oxbow, ME (plantation) Aroostook County	11	21.57
Blairsden, CA (cdp) Plumas County	15	21.43
Lonerock, OR (city) Gilliam County	6	21.43
Ree Heights, SD (town) Hand County	17	21.25
Tenakee Springs, AK (city) Skagway-Hoonah-Angoon Census Area	18	21.18
Pliny, MN (township) Aitkin County	25	20.83
Sarles, ND (city) Cavalier County	5	20.83
Pleasant Ridge, ME (plantation) Somerset County	18	20.22
Upton, ME (town) Oxford County	11	20.00
Chiniak, AK (cdp) Kodiak Island Borough	9	20.00
Fort Indiantown Gap, PA (cdp) Lebanon County	17	19.54
Hannah, ND (city) Cavalier County	5	19.23
Shannon, NC (cdp) Robeson County	39	19.12
North Crows Nest, IN (town) Marion County	8	19.05
Edison, WA (cdp) Skagit County	27	19.01
Tar Heel, NC (town) Bladen County	11	18.64
Lance Creek, WY (cdp) Niobrara County	10	18.52
Laurel Mountain, PA (borough) Westmoreland County	34	18.38
Westview Circle, WY (cdp) Platte County	17	18.28
Latimer, KS (city) Morris County	2	18.18
Bay View, WA (cdp) Skagit County	80	18.10
Eldora, CO (cdp) Boulder County	40	18.02
Lake Santeetlah, NC (town) Graham County	12	17.65
Scottsville, KS (city) Mitchell County	3	17.65
Hillsboro, VA (town) Loudoun County	14	17.50
Highland, ME (plantation) Somerset County	12	17.39
Isle au Haut, ME (town) Knox County	14	17.28
Lonetree, WY (cdp) Uinta County	14	17.28
Palmyra, UT (cdp) Utah County	81	17.27
Ward, CO (town) Boulder County	12	16.90
Pointe Aux Barques, MI (township) Huron County	2	16.67
Swans Island, ME (town) Hancock County	56	16.62
Glacier, WA (cdp) Whatcom County	12	16.44
Wentworth, NH (location) Coos County	8	16.33
Slater, WY (cdp) Platte County	10	16.13
Raynham, NC (town) Robeson County	12	15.79
Green Hills, PA (borough) Washington County	3	15.79
Fenwick, CT (borough) Middlesex County	8	15.69
Brunswick, VT (town) Essex County	17	15.45
Peacham, VT (town) Caledonia County	103	15.24
Monhegan, ME (plantation) Lincoln County	12	15.19
Byron, ME (town) Oxford County	13	15.12
The Forks, ME (plantation) Somerset County	9	15.00
Lonaconing, MD (town) Allegany County	181	14.96
Bettles, AK (city) Yukon-Koyukuk Census Area	7	14.89
Landgrove, VT (town) Bennington County	15	14.71
Uniontown, KS (city) Bourbon County	37	14.62
Washam, WY (cdp) Sweetwater County	7	14.58
Mud Bay, AK (cdp) Haines Borough	18	14.52
Spanish Valley, UT (cdp) San Juan County	26	14.44
Woodbury, KY (city) Butler County	13	14.44
Frenchtown, MT (cdp) Missoula County	100	14.39
House, NM (village) Quay County	8	14.29
Dresden, KS (city) Decatur County	6	14.29
Brinsmade, ND (city) Benson County	3	14.29
Van Tassell, WY (town) Niobrara County	2	14.29
Paisley, OR (city) Lake County	32	14.22
Brookfield, NH (town) Carroll County	86	14.21
Moorefield, NE (village) Frontier County	6	13.95
Islesboro, ME (town) Waldo County	85	13.93
Mount Charleston, NV (cdp) Clark County	35	13.89
Lake View, ME (plantation) Piscataquis County	4	13.79
Randolph, UT (city) Rich County	65	13.74
Weston, ME (town) Aroostook County	27	13.71
Barton, MD (town) Allegany County	58	13.68
Teton Village, WY (cdp) Teton County	35	13.67
Lamy, NM (cdp) Santa Fe County	22	13.66
Johannesburg, CA (cdp) Kern County	18	13.64
Franconia, NH (town) Grafton County	125	13.56
Highland Park, FL (village) Polk County	32	13.56
Toivola, MN (township) Saint Louis County	24	13.56
McClellanville, SC (town) Charleston County	62	13.51
Goshen, VT (town) Addison County	26	13.47
Coolidge, KS (city) Hamilton County	9	13.43
Washington, VA (town) Rappahannock County	24	13.41
North Haven, ME (town) Knox County	52	13.40
Fairview, WY (cdp) Lincoln County	34	13.33
Eaton, NH (town) Carroll County	44	13.21
Placerville, ID (city) Boise County	7	13.21
Thayne, WY (town) Lincoln County	54	13.14
Cimarron City, OK (town) Logan County	16	13.11
Bowerbank, ME (town) Piscataquis County	14	13.08
Grand Ronde, OR (cdp) Polk County	26	13.07
Brownsboro Village, KY (city) Jefferson County	41	13.02
Stow, ME (town) Oxford County	32	13.01
Sandy River, ME (plantation) Franklin County	10	12.82
Carrabassett Valley, ME (town) Franklin County	48	12.80
Mooresville, AL (town) Limestone County	6	12.77
Greensboro, VT (town) Orleans County	97	12.75
Dallas, ME (plantation) Franklin County	31	12.55
Bovina, NY (town) Delaware County	83	12.54
Mission Woods, KS (city) Johnson County	19	12.50
Girdletree, MD (cdp) Worcester County	17	12.50
Ellston, IA (city) Ringgold County	10	12.50
Cabot, VT (village) Washington County	31	12.45
Abbot, ME (town) Piscataquis County	78	12.42
Andes, NY (village) Delaware County	39	12.38
Carrier, OK (town) Garfield County	10	12.35
Hyden, KY (city) Leslie County	27	12.33
Plano, IA (city) Appanoose County	8	12.31
Lone Oak, GA (town) Meriwether County	14	12.17
McCarthy, AK (cdp) Valdez-Cordova Census Area	4	12.12
Ryegate, VT (town) Caledonia County	139	12.09
Kittery Point, ME (cdp) York County	135	12.08
Henrieville, UT (town) Garfield County	21	12.07
Strafford, VT (town) Orange County	126	12.06
Stannard, VT (town) Caledonia County	24	12.06
Topsham, VT (town) Orange County	137	12.00
Cameron, NC (town) Moore County	18	12.00
Plainfield, VT (town) Washington County	154	11.98
Port Hope, MI (village) Huron County	34	11.97
Saint Joe, AR (town) Searcy County	12	11.88
The Plains, VA (town) Fauquier County	35	11.78
Hooper, CO (town) Alamosa County	14	11.76
Leonard, MO (village) Shelby County	6	11.76
Hendley, NE (village) Furnas County	4	11.76
Arvada, WY (cdp) Sheridan County	2	11.76
Bishop, GA (town) Oconee County	17	11.72
Sebec, ME (town) Piscataquis County	72	11.69
Dillon Beach, CA (cdp) Marin County	35	11.59
Itasca, MN (township) Clearwater County	16	11.59
Cumberland Center, ME (cdp) Cumberland County	301	11.58
Deblois, ME (town) Washington County	4	11.43
Hardenburgh, NY (town) Ulster County	25	11.42
Avon, MT (cdp) Powell County	13	11.40
Crossgate, KY (city) Jefferson County	29	11.37
Broadwater, NE (village) Morrill County	17	11.26

Notes: (cdp) census designated place; Refer to the Explanation of Data in the front of the book for more detailed information.

Scottish

Top 150 Places Sorted by Percent

(Based on places with populations of 10,000 or more)

Place	Number	%
Cottonwood West, UT (cdp) Salt Lake County	1,456	7.82
Centerville, UT (city) Davis County	1,014	7.06
Carver, MA (town) Plymouth County	756	6.77
Bainbridge Island, WA (city) Kitsap County	1,372	6.76
Falmouth, ME (town) Cumberland County	688	6.67
Holladay, UT (city) Salt Lake County	963	6.62
Mountain Brook, AL (city) Jefferson County	1,367	6.51
Kennebunk, ME (town) York County	676	6.45
Scarborough, ME (town) Cumberland County	1,062	6.26
Birmingham, MI (city) Oakland County	1,202	6.20
South Portland, ME (city) Cumberland County	1,415	6.07
Brewster, MA (town) Barnstable County	612	6.06
Cedar City, UT (city) Iron County	1,196	5.81
South Lyon, MI (city) Oakland County	581	5.79
Amherst, NH (town) Hillsborough County	622	5.78
Hanover, NH (town) Grafton County	624	5.75
Falls Church, VA (independent city) Falls Church city	595	5.73
Rochester, MI (city) Oakland County	599	5.72
Druid Hills, GA (cdp) De Kalb County	710	5.60
Vashon, WA (cdp) King County	565	5.58
Tooele, UT (city) Tooele County	1,245	5.53
Kaysville, UT (city) Davis County	1,143	5.52
Boone, NC (town) Watauga County	740	5.50
South Ogden, UT (city) Weber County	790	5.48
Wilmington Island, GA (cdp) Chatham County	779	5.48
Cottonwood Heights, UT (cdp) Salt Lake County	1,496	5.47
Mill Valley, CA (city) Marin County	742	5.47
South Jordan, UT (city) Salt Lake County	1,602	5.44
Bountiful, UT (city) Davis County	2,235	5.40
Harwich, MA (town) Barnstable County	668	5.39
Lake Oswego, OR (city) Clackamas County	1,884	5.35
Windham, ME (town) Cumberland County	793	5.32
Canyon Rim, UT (cdp) Salt Lake County	561	5.31
Alamo, CA (cdp) Contra Costa County	802	5.30
Roy, UT (city) Weber County	1,725	5.27
Oxford, MS (city) Lafayette County	621	5.27
Darien, CT (cdp) Fairfield County	1,029	5.25
Clawson, MI (city) Oakland County	668	5.25
Montecito, CA (cdp) Santa Barbara County	530	5.25
Grosse Pointe Woods, MI (city) Wayne County	885	5.18
Amesbury, MA (town) Essex County	848	5.17
Southern Pines, NC (town) Moore County	579	5.17
Concord, NH (city) Merrimack County	2,094	5.15
Pleasant Grove, UT (city) Utah County	1,213	5.15
Logan, UT (city) Cache County	2,196	5.14
Gorham, ME (town) Cumberland County	727	5.14
Camano, WA (cdp) Island County	692	5.11
Westbrook, ME (city) Cumberland County	822	5.09
Winter Park, FL (city) Orange County	1,229	5.07
American Fork, UT (city) Utah County	1,112	5.07
Vestavia Hills, AL (city) Jefferson County	1,257	5.06
York, ME (town) York County	650	5.06
Fort Hunt, VA (cdp) Fairfax County	649	5.06
North Ogden, UT (city) Weber County	753	5.04
Fort Gratiot, MI (township) Saint Clair County	537	5.03
Orem, UT (city) Utah County	4,230	5.02
Portland, ME (city) Cumberland County	3,218	5.01
Portsmouth, NH (city) Rockingham County	1,040	5.00
San Anselmo, CA (town) Marin County	623	4.98
Evanston, WY (city) Uinta County	569	4.98
Rexburg, ID (city) Madison County	855	4.97
Yarmouth, MA (town) Barnstable County	1,231	4.96
Farmington, UT (city) Davis County	604	4.95
Berkley, MI (city) Oakland County	768	4.94
Provo, UT (city) Utah County	5,151	4.89
Ashland, OR (city) Jackson County	954	4.89
Newberg, OR (city) Yamhill County	886	4.89
Kingsgate, WA (cdp) King County	588	4.89
Saint George, UT (city) Washington County	2,423	4.88
Hampton, NH (town) Rockingham County	729	4.88
South Yarmouth, MA (cdp) Barnstable County	573	4.87
Forest Acres, SC (city) Richland County	517	4.84
Commerce, MI (township) Oakland County	1,682	4.81
Springville, UT (city) Utah County	985	4.80
Issaquah, WA (city) King County	538	4.80
East Millcreek, UT (cdp) Salt Lake County	1,023	4.78
Sandy, UT (city) Salt Lake County	4,198	4.76
Essex, VT (town) Chittenden County	885	4.75
Merrimack, NH (town) Hillsborough County	1,184	4.71
Saint Simons, GA (cdp) Glynn County	634	4.71
Massena, NY (village) Saint Lawrence County	525	4.68
New Canaan, CT (town) Fairfield County	905	4.67
Sandwich, MA (town) Barnstable County	937	4.65
Lehi, UT (city) Utah County	891	4.65
Bellingham, WA (city) Whatcom County	3,086	4.62
Grosse Pointe Park, MI (city) Wayne County	575	4.62
Farmington, MI (city) Oakland County	482	4.62
Arcata, CA (city) Humboldt County	771	4.61
Scotts Valley, CA (city) Santa Cruz County	531	4.61
Uxbridge, MA (town) Worcester County	513	4.61
University Park, TX (city) Dallas County	1,072	4.59
Lafayette, CA (city) Contra Costa County	1,075	4.58
Clinton, UT (city) Davis County	580	4.58
Oakland charter, MI (township) Oakland County	597	4.57
Royal Oak, MI (city) Oakland County	2,738	4.56
Chapel Hill, NC (town) Orange County	2,224	4.56
Dover, NH (city) Strafford County	1,225	4.56
Cave Spring, VA (cdp) Roanoke County	1,138	4.56
Cottage Lake, WA (cdp) King County	1,108	4.56
Atlantic Beach, FL (city) Duval County	613	4.55
Mount Pleasant, SC (town) Charleston County	2,151	4.54
Anacortes, WA (city) Skagit County	667	4.54
Westerly, RI (town) Washington County	1,037	4.52
Baywood-Los Osos, CA (cdp) San Luis Obispo County	640	4.52
Lake Forest Park, WA (city) King County	607	4.52
Brunswick, ME (town) Cumberland County	953	4.50
Milford, NH (town) Hillsborough County	609	4.50
Wrentham, MA (town) Norfolk County	475	4.50
Highlands, NY (town) Orange County	560	4.49
West Jordan, UT (city) Salt Lake County	3,046	4.47
East Brainerd, TN (cdp) Hamilton County	621	4.47
Whitman, MA (town) Plymouth County	621	4.47
Concord, MA (town) Middlesex County	756	4.45
Saco, ME (city) York County	748	4.45
Barnstable Town, MA (city) Barnstable County	2,114	4.42
Solana Beach, CA (city) San Diego County	569	4.42
Vienna, WV (city) Wood County	475	4.42
Newburyport, MA (city) Essex County	758	4.40
Naples, FL (city) Collier County	921	4.39
Avon Lake, OH (city) Lorain County	794	4.38
Golden, CO (city) Jefferson County	763	4.38
Tustin Foothills, CA (cdp) Orange County	1,046	4.36
Port Angeles, WA (city) Clallam County	803	4.35
Holbrook, MA (cdp) Norfolk County	468	4.35
Northville, MI (township) Wayne County	913	4.34
Redmond, OR (city) Deschutes County	600	4.34
Murray, UT (city) Salt Lake County	1,470	4.33
Kingston, MA (town) Plymouth County	510	4.33
Salt Lake City, UT (city) Salt Lake County	7,838	4.32
Palm Valley, FL (cdp) Saint Johns County	858	4.32
Hartford, VT (town) Windsor County	448	4.32
Moscow, ID (city) Latah County	913	4.31
Spanish Fork, UT (city) Utah County	874	4.31
Rock Springs, WY (city) Sweetwater County	817	4.31
Greenwood Village, CO (city) Arapahoe County	477	4.31
Cascade, MI (township) Kent County	650	4.30
West Valley, WA (cdp) Yakima County	433	4.30
Bend, OR (city) Deschutes County	2,222	4.29
Beverly, MA (city) Essex County	1,706	4.28
Marblehead, MA (cdp) Essex County	873	4.28
Wakefield, MA (cdp) Middlesex County	1,058	4.27
Scio, MI (township) Washtenaw County	669	4.27
Lebanon, NH (city) Grafton County	537	4.27
Idaho Falls, ID (city) Bonneville County	2,151	4.26
Acton, MA (town) Middlesex County	864	4.25
Boulder, CO (city) Boulder County	4,003	4.24
Prescott, AZ (city) Yavapai County	1,460	4.24
Stonington, CT (town) New London County	760	4.24
North Decatur, GA (cdp) De Kalb County	642	4.24
Destin, FL (city) Okaloosa County	477	4.24

Notes: (cdp) census designated place; Refer to the Explanation of Data in the front of the book for more detailed information.

Serbian

Top 150 Places Sorted by Number

(Based on all places, regardless of population)

Place	Number	%
Chicago, IL (city) Cook County	5,044	0.17
New York, NY (city) New York City	2,652	0.03
Milwaukee, WI (city) Milwaukee County	1,750	0.29
Phoenix, AZ (city) Maricopa County	1,645	0.12
Los Angeles, CA (city) Los Angeles County	1,214	0.03
Schererville, IN (town) Lake County	1,137	4.58
Akron, OH (city) Summit County	1,135	0.52
Pittsburgh, PA (city) Allegheny County	1,002	0.30
Parma, OH (city) Cuyahoga County	941	1.10
Cleveland, OH (city) Cuyahoga County	721	0.15
Columbus, OH (city) Franklin County	651	0.09
San Diego, CA (city) San Diego County	631	0.05
Hammond, IN (city) Lake County	567	0.68
Weirton, WV (city) Hancock County	489	2.40
Munster, IN (town) Lake County	479	2.23
Sterling Heights, MI (city) Macomb County	476	0.38
Hopewell, PA (township) Beaver County	466	3.50
Merrillville, IN (town) Lake County	462	1.50
Crown Point, IN (city) Lake County	458	2.34
Niles, IL (village) Cook County	439	1.46
North Huntingdon, PA (township) Westmoreland County	427	1.46
Hobart, IN (city) Lake County	415	1.63
Omaha, NE (city) Douglas County	407	0.10
Hibbing, MN (city) Saint Louis County	401	2.35
San Francisco, CA (city) San Francisco County	396	0.05
Lansing, IL (village) Cook County	385	1.37
Aliquippa, PA (city) Beaver County	378	3.24
Center, PA (township) Beaver County	362	3.15
Berwyn, IL (city) Cook County	357	0.66
Las Vegas, NV (city) Clark County	350	0.07
Barberton, OH (city) Summit County	334	1.19
West Mifflin, PA (borough) Allegheny County	332	1.48
Indianapolis, IN (special city) Marion County	332	0.04
Mesa, AZ (city) Maricopa County	326	0.08
Seattle, WA (city) King County	325	0.06
Lorain, OH (city) Lorain County	324	0.47
Broadview Heights, OH (city) Cuyahoga County	314	1.97
Bethel Park, PA (borough) Allegheny County	310	0.92
Johnstown, PA (city) Cambria County	304	1.27
Highland, IN (town) Lake County	298	1.27
West Allis, WI (city) Milwaukee County	298	0.49
Lakewood, OH (city) Cuyahoga County	296	0.52
Duluth, MN (city) Saint Louis County	292	0.34
Warren, MI (city) Macomb County	287	0.21
Naperville, IL (city) Du Page County	286	0.22
Philadelphia, PA (city) Philadelphia County	286	0.02
Greenfield, WI (city) Milwaukee County	281	0.79
Buffalo, NY (city) Erie County	278	0.09
Minneapolis, MN (city) Hennepin County	278	0.07
Spring Valley, NV (cdp) Clark County	277	0.24
Strongsville, OH (city) Cuyahoga County	266	0.61
Hempfield, PA (township) Westmoreland County	265	0.65
Houston, TX (city) Harris County	264	0.01
Elmhurst, IL (city) Du Page County	262	0.61
Charlotte, NC (city) Mecklenburg County	257	0.05
Brunswick, OH (city) Medina County	255	0.76
Youngstown, OH (city) Mahoning County	253	0.31
Scottsdale, AZ (city) Maricopa County	253	0.12
Lyons, IL (village) Cook County	248	2.45
Kenosha, WI (city) Kenosha County	238	0.26
Austin, TX (city) Travis County	237	0.04
Washington, DC (city) District of Columbia	237	0.04
Penn, PA (township) Westmoreland County	236	1.20
Portage, IN (city) Porter County	231	0.69
North Royalton, OH (city) Cuyahoga County	229	0.80
Brighton, PA (township) Beaver County	228	2.84
Racine, WI (city) Racine County	224	0.27
Nashville-Davidson, TN (special city) Davidson County	223	0.04
Massillon, OH (city) Stark County	222	0.71
East Chicago, IN (city) Lake County	220	0.68
Ann Arbor, MI (city) Washtenaw County	219	0.19
San Jose, CA (city) Santa Clara County	218	0.02
South Bend, IN (city) Saint Joseph County	217	0.20
Dallas, TX (city) Dallas County	216	0.02
Oak Creek, WI (city) Milwaukee County	207	0.73
Tempe, AZ (city) Maricopa County	207	0.13
Saint Clair Shores, MI (city) Macomb County	206	0.33
Saint Petersburg, FL (city) Pinellas County	206	0.08
Saint Louis, MO (independent city) Saint Louis city	202	0.06
Clinton, MI (cdp) Macomb County	201	0.21
Paradise, NV (cdp) Clark County	201	0.11
Detroit, MI (city) Wayne County	198	0.02
Municipality of Monroeville, PA (borough) Allegheny County	195	0.66
Midland, PA (borough) Beaver County	192	6.12
Steubenville, OH (city) Jefferson County	192	1.01
Cuyahoga Falls, OH (city) Summit County	192	0.39
Tucson, AZ (city) Pima County	191	0.04
Kansas City, MO (city) Jackson County	190	0.04
Butte-Silver Bow, MT (special city) Silver Bow County	189	0.56
Portland, OR (city) Multnomah County	185	0.03
Escondido, CA (city) San Diego County	184	0.14
Boston, MA (city) Suffolk County	181	0.03
Dyer, IN (town) Lake County	180	1.30
Muskego, WI (city) Waukesha County	180	0.84
Carol Stream, IL (village) Du Page County	180	0.45
Denver, CO (city) Denver County	180	0.03
McKeesport, PA (city) Allegheny County	177	0.74
Troy, MI (city) Oakland County	177	0.22
Countryside, IL (city) Cook County	174	2.91
Canton, OH (city) Stark County	172	0.21
Sacramento, CA (city) Sacramento County	171	0.04
Monaca, PA (borough) Beaver County	169	2.69
Ohioville, PA (borough) Beaver County	168	4.47
Westmont, IL (village) Du Page County	167	0.69
Santa Monica, CA (city) Los Angeles County	167	0.20
Carlsbad, CA (city) San Diego County	161	0.21
Livonia, MI (city) Wayne County	161	0.16
Henderson, NV (city) Clark County	161	0.09
Madison, WI (city) Dane County	160	0.08
Irwin, PA (borough) Westmoreland County	159	3.64
Skokie, IL (village) Cook County	159	0.25
Albuquerque, NM (city) Bernalillo County	159	0.04
Norton, OH (city) Summit County	158	1.37
Valparaiso, IN (city) Porter County	158	0.57
South Holland, IL (village) Cook County	157	0.70
South Milwaukee, WI (city) Milwaukee County	155	0.73
Swatara, PA (township) Dauphin County	155	0.68
Jacksonville, FL (special city) Duval County	155	0.02
Wheaton, IL (city) Du Page County	153	0.28
South Saint Paul, MN (city) Dakota County	152	0.75
Gary, IN (city) Lake County	152	0.15
Lackawanna, NY (city) Erie County	151	0.79
Streamwood, IL (village) Cook County	151	0.41
Rockford, IL (city) Winnebago County	151	0.10
Cranberry, PA (township) Butler County	150	0.63
Royal Oak, MI (city) Oakland County	150	0.25
Waukesha, WI (city) Waukesha County	149	0.23
Lower Paxton, PA (township) Dauphin County	148	0.33
Anchorage, AK (municipality) Anchorage Borough	148	0.06
Villa Park, IL (village) Du Page County	147	0.66
Arlington Heights, IL (village) Cook County	147	0.19
Parma Heights, OH (city) Cuyahoga County	146	0.67
Mount Lebanon, PA (cdp) Allegheny County	146	0.44
Mentor, OH (city) Lake County	145	0.29
Irvine, CA (city) Orange County	145	0.10
Clifton, NJ (city) Passaic County	144	0.18
North Versailles, PA (cdp) Allegheny County	143	1.29
Franklin, WI (city) Milwaukee County	143	0.48
Long Beach, CA (city) Los Angeles County	143	0.03
Baldwin, PA (borough) Allegheny County	142	0.71
Gurnee, IL (village) Lake County	140	0.49
Stow, OH (city) Summit County	140	0.44
New Berlin, WI (city) Waukesha County	140	0.36
Lakes of the Four Seasons, IN (cdp) Lake County	139	1.90
Brookfield, WI (city) Waukesha County	139	0.36
Westland, MI (city) Wayne County	138	0.16
Dearborn, MI (city) Wayne County	136	0.14
Arlington, VA (cdp) Arlington County	136	0.07
White Oak, PA (borough) Allegheny County	135	1.59
Campbell, OH (city) Mahoning County	135	1.43

Notes: (cdp) census designated place; Refer to the Explanation of Data in the front of the book for more detailed information.

Serbian

Top 150 Places Sorted by Percent

(Based on all places, regardless of population)

Place	Number	%
Kingston, WI (town) Juneau County	18	23.08
North Crows Nest, IN (town) Marion County	5	11.90
Wall, PA (borough) Allegheny County	61	8.24
East Brooklyn, IL (village) Grundy County	8	7.84
Export, PA (borough) Westmoreland County	70	7.83
Lake Village, IN (cdp) Newton County	59	7.33
Bovey, MN (city) Itasca County	44	7.04
Franklin, PA (borough) Cambria County	28	6.38
Midland, PA (borough) Beaver County	192	6.12
Industry, PA (borough) Beaver County	111	5.78
Calumet, MN (city) Itasca County	20	5.08
Zippel, MN (township) Lake of the Woods County	5	4.85
Wilmerding, PA (borough) Allegheny County	102	4.76
Glasgow, PA (borough) Beaver County	3	4.76
Schererville, IN (town) Lake County	1,137	4.58
Ohioville, PA (borough) Beaver County	168	4.47
Jette, MT (cdp) Lake County	16	4.46
Trommald, MN (city) Crow Wing County	6	4.38
Julian, PA (cdp) Centre County	8	4.32
Shippingport, PA (borough) Beaver County	10	4.17
Marble, MN (city) Itasca County	27	3.95
Greenway, MN (township) Itasca County	77	3.84
Buhl, MN (city) Saint Louis County	38	3.83
Lynnwood-Pricedale, PA (cdp) Westmoreland County	76	3.71
Maple Ridge, OH (cdp) Mahoning County	34	3.71
Ogden Dunes, IN (town) Porter County	48	3.66
Irwin, PA (borough) Westmoreland County	159	3.64
Hopewell, PA (township) Beaver County	466	3.50
Raccoon, PA (township) Beaver County	119	3.50
Pisek, ND (city) Walsh County	3	3.45
Coleraine, MN (city) Itasca County	38	3.38
Goodland, MN (township) Itasca County	15	3.36
Dauphin, PA (borough) Dauphin County	26	3.35
Aliquippa, PA (city) Beaver County	378	3.24
Center, PA (township) Beaver County	362	3.15
La Prairie, MN (city) Itasca County	18	3.07
East Taylor, PA (township) Cambria County	81	2.97
Cross Creek, PA (township) Washington County	50	2.97
Splithand, MN (township) Itasca County	8	2.94
Countryside, IL (city) Cook County	174	2.91
Brighton, PA (township) Beaver County	228	2.84
Winfield, IN (town) Lake County	63	2.78
Dougherty, IA (city) Cerro Gordo County	2	2.78
Stokes, MN (township) Itasca County	2	2.76
Deerfield, PA (township) Warren County	9	2.74
Monaca, PA (borough) Beaver County	169	2.69
Keewatin, MN (city) Itasca County	31	2.66
Mingo Junction, OH (village) Jefferson County	97	2.65
Harmony Township, PA (cdp) Beaver County	88	2.61
Bearville, MN (township) Itasca County	4	2.61
Burlington, IL (village) Kane County	12	2.60
Cuyuna, MN (city) Crow Wing County	6	2.60
Burbank, OH (village) Wayne County	7	2.48
Conemaugh, PA (township) Cambria County	53	2.47
Lyons, IL (village) Cook County	248	2.45
East Rochester, PA (borough) Beaver County	15	2.45
Weirton, WV (city) Hancock County	489	2.40
Lorimor, IA (city) Union County	10	2.40
Agar, SD (town) Sully County	2	2.38
Conway, PA (borough) Beaver County	54	2.36
Hibbing, MN (city) Saint Louis County	401	2.35
Crown Point, IN (city) Lake County	458	2.34
Nashwauk, MN (city) Itasca County	21	2.30
Kinney, MN (city) Saint Louis County	4	2.27
Trafford, PA (borough) Westmoreland County	73	2.26
Greene, PA (township) Beaver County	61	2.26
Stockdale, PA (borough) Washington County	12	2.26
Yankee Lake, OH (village) Trumbull County	2	2.25
Cokeburg, PA (borough) Washington County	16	2.24
Munster, IN (town) Lake County	479	2.23
Chisholm, MN (city) Saint Louis County	108	2.18
Wakefield, MI (city) Gogebic County	45	2.17
Downieville-Lawson-Dumont, CO (cdp) Clear Creek County	8	2.17
Port Sheldon, MI (township) Ottawa County	95	2.16
Melstone, MT (town) Musselshell County	3	2.16
Freedom, PA (borough) Beaver County	38	2.15
Cascade Valley, WA (cdp) Grant County	38	2.13
Remer, MN (township) Cass County	4	2.12
Rices Landing, PA (borough) Greene County	9	2.05
Granville, IL (village) Putnam County	29	2.03
Steelton, PA (borough) Dauphin County	116	2.00
Broadview Heights, OH (city) Cuyahoga County	314	1.97
Jefferson, PA (township) Washington County	24	1.97
Nashwauk, MN (township) Itasca County	32	1.96
Forward, PA (township) Allegheny County	73	1.94
Poppleton, MN (township) Kittson County	2	1.92
Lakes of the Four Seasons, IN (cdp) Lake County	139	1.90
Independence, PA (township) Beaver County	52	1.88
Buckner, IL (village) Franklin County	9	1.88
Shadyside, OH (village) Belmont County	68	1.87
Bridgewater, PA (borough) Beaver County	14	1.87
French, MN (township) Saint Louis County	6	1.85
Warm Mineral Springs, FL (cdp) Sarasota County	90	1.83
Princeton, IA (city) Scott County	18	1.83
Ball Bluff, MN (township) Aitkin County	6	1.83
Lower Yoder, PA (township) Cambria County	55	1.82
Hidden Meadows, CA (cdp) San Diego County	62	1.81
Southmont, PA (borough) Cambria County	41	1.81
Ferndale, PA (borough) Cambria County	33	1.80
Bellaire, OH (city) Belmont County	88	1.78
Willow Springs, IL (village) Cook County	88	1.78
East Side, MN (township) Mille Lacs County	13	1.78
Iron Range, MN (township) Itasca County	12	1.77
Smith, PA (township) Washington County	79	1.73
Hiller, PA (cdp) Fayette County	21	1.72
Bloomingdale, OH (village) Jefferson County	4	1.72
Old Bennington, VT (village) Bennington County	4	1.71
Ambridge, PA (borough) Beaver County	132	1.70
Dunkard, PA (township) Greene County	40	1.70
McDonald, OH (village) Trumbull County	58	1.68
Calumet-Norvelt, PA (cdp) Westmoreland County	28	1.68
Diamond Springs, CA (cdp) El Dorado County	81	1.66
North Barrington, IL (village) Lake County	48	1.66
Balsam, MN (township) Itasca County	10	1.66
Follansbee, WV (city) Brooke County	50	1.65
Manor, PA (borough) Westmoreland County	46	1.65
Darlington, PA (borough) Beaver County	5	1.65
Morristown, OH (village) Belmont County	5	1.64
Hobart, IN (city) Lake County	415	1.63
Wintersville, OH (village) Jefferson County	65	1.62
Tontogany, OH (village) Wood County	6	1.61
White Oak, PA (borough) Allegheny County	135	1.59
Blackhoof, MN (township) Carlton County	12	1.59
Washington, PA (township) Fayette County	71	1.58
Gordonville, MO (village) Cape Girardeau County	7	1.58
Woodville, ME (town) Penobscot County	4	1.58
Tripp, WI (town) Bayfield County	3	1.58
Uniontown, OH (cdp) Stark County	45	1.57
Beaver, PA (borough) Beaver County	74	1.55
Walkertown, NC (town) Forsyth County	60	1.52
Wakefield, MI (township) Gogebic County	6	1.52
Whitestown, IN (town) Boone County	8	1.51
Merrillville, IN (town) Lake County	462	1.50
Taconite, MN (city) Itasca County	5	1.50
Vanport, PA (township) Beaver County	22	1.49
West Mifflin, PA (borough) Allegheny County	332	1.48
Saint Michael-Sidman, PA (cdp) Cambria County	14	1.47
Niles, IL (village) Cook County	439	1.46
North Huntingdon, PA (township) Westmoreland County	427	1.46
Elim, PA (cdp) Cambria County	64	1.46
Wickerham Manor-Fisher, PA (cdp) Washington County	24	1.46
Coloma, WI (village) Waushara County	7	1.44
Edgerton, WY (town) Natrona County	2	1.44
Campbell, OH (city) Mahoning County	135	1.43
Stony Point, MI (cdp) Monroe County	24	1.43
Harmony, WI (town) Price County	3	1.42
Hilltop, OH (cdp) Trumbull County	8	1.41
Blooming Valley, PA (borough) Crawford County	6	1.41
Carthage, SD (city) Miner County	3	1.41
Springlake, TX (town) Lamb County	2	1.40

Notes: (cdp) census designated place; Refer to the Explanation of Data in the front of the book for more detailed information.

Serbian

Top 150 Places Sorted by Percent

(Based on places with populations of 10,000 or more)

Place	Number	%
Schererville, IN (town) Lake County	1,137	4.58
Hopewell, PA (township) Beaver County	466	3.50
Aliquippa, PA (city) Beaver County	378	3.24
Center, PA (township) Beaver County	362	3.15
Lyons, IL (village) Cook County	248	2.45
Weirton, WV (city) Hancock County	489	2.40
Hibbing, MN (city) Saint Louis County	401	2.35
Crown Point, IN (city) Lake County	458	2.34
Munster, IN (town) Lake County	479	2.23
Broadview Heights, OH (city) Cuyahoga County	314	1.97
Hobart, IN (city) Lake County	415	1.63
Merrillville, IN (town) Lake County	462	1.50
West Mifflin, PA (borough) Allegheny County	332	1.48
Niles, IL (village) Cook County	439	1.46
North Huntingdon, PA (township) Westmoreland County	427	1.46
Lansing, IL (village) Cook County	385	1.37
Norton, OH (city) Summit County	158	1.37
Dyer, IN (town) Lake County	180	1.30
North Versailles, PA (cdp) Allegheny County	143	1.29
Johnstown, PA (city) Cambria County	304	1.27
Highland, IN (town) Lake County	298	1.27
Penn, PA (township) Westmoreland County	236	1.20
Barberton, OH (city) Summit County	334	1.19
Seven Hills, OH (city) Cuyahoga County	135	1.12
Parma, OH (city) Cuyahoga County	941	1.10
Grosse Ile, MI (cdp) Wayne County	119	1.09
Steubenville, OH (city) Jefferson County	192	1.01
Lincolnwood, IL (village) Cook County	123	1.00
Jeannette, PA (city) Westmoreland County	106	0.99
Burr Ridge, IL (village) Du Page County	96	0.93
Bethel Park, PA (borough) Allegheny County	310	0.92
Brooklyn, OH (city) Cuyahoga County	105	0.91
Brentwood, PA (borough) Allegheny County	95	0.91
Fernway, PA (cdp) Butler County	109	0.89
Muskego, WI (city) Waukesha County	180	0.84
Lake Station, IN (city) Lake County	118	0.84
North Royalton, OH (city) Cuyahoga County	229	0.80
Greenfield, WI (city) Milwaukee County	281	0.79
Lackawanna, NY (city) Erie County	151	0.79
Elizabeth, PA (township) Allegheny County	110	0.79
Brunswick, OH (city) Medina County	255	0.76
South Saint Paul, MN (city) Dakota County	152	0.75
McKeesport, PA (city) Allegheny County	177	0.74
Norridge, IL (village) Cook County	109	0.74
Oak Creek, WI (city) Milwaukee County	207	0.73
South Milwaukee, WI (city) Milwaukee County	155	0.73
Massillon, OH (city) Stark County	222	0.71
Baldwin, PA (borough) Allegheny County	142	0.71
South Holland, IL (village) Cook County	157	0.70
Chesterton, IN (town) Porter County	73	0.70
Portage, IN (city) Porter County	231	0.69
Westmont, IL (village) Du Page County	167	0.69
Hammond, IN (city) Lake County	567	0.68
East Chicago, IN (city) Lake County	220	0.68
Swatara, PA (township) Dauphin County	155	0.68
Parma Heights, OH (city) Cuyahoga County	146	0.67
Tallmadge, OH (city) Summit County	110	0.67
Berwyn, IL (city) Cook County	357	0.66
Municipality of Monroeville, PA (borough) Allegheny County	195	0.66
Villa Park, IL (village) Du Page County	147	0.66
Hempfield, PA (township) Westmoreland County	265	0.65
Ramona, CA (cdp) San Diego County	102	0.65
North Fayette, PA (township) Allegheny County	80	0.65
Girard, OH (city) Trumbull County	72	0.65
Cranberry, PA (township) Butler County	150	0.63
Brecksville, OH (city) Cuyahoga County	82	0.62
Strongsville, OH (city) Cuyahoga County	266	0.61
Elmhurst, IL (city) Du Page County	262	0.61
Western Springs, IL (village) Cook County	76	0.60
Grand Rapids, MN (township) Itasca County	70	0.60
North College Hill, OH (city) Hamilton County	60	0.60
Green, OH (city) Summit County	135	0.59
Morton Grove, IL (village) Cook County	130	0.58
Munhall, PA (borough) Allegheny County	71	0.58
Amherst, OH (city) Lorain County	69	0.58
Upper Saucon, PA (township) Lehigh County	69	0.58
Holt, MI (cdp) Ingham County	65	0.58
Gages Lake, IL (cdp) Lake County	61	0.58
Valparaiso, IN (city) Porter County	158	0.57
Brook Park, OH (city) Cuyahoga County	121	0.57
South Park Township, PA (cdp) Allegheny County	82	0.57
Butte-Silver Bow, MT (special city) Silver Bow County	189	0.56
Monroe charter, MI (township) Monroe County	75	0.56
Mount Pleasant, WI (town) Racine County	128	0.55
Griffith, IN (town) Lake County	91	0.53
Akron, OH (city) Summit County	1,135	0.52
Lakewood, OH (city) Cuyahoga County	296	0.52
Wadsworth, OH (city) Medina County	94	0.51
Prospect Heights, IL (city) Cook County	90	0.51
Mokena, IL (village) Will County	75	0.51
East Liverpool, OH (city) Columbiana County	66	0.51
Franklin Park, PA (borough) Allegheny County	58	0.51
Whitehall, PA (borough) Allegheny County	72	0.50
West Allis, WI (city) Milwaukee County	298	0.49
Gurnee, IL (village) Lake County	140	0.49
Plum, PA (borough) Allegheny County	132	0.49
Shorewood, WI (village) Milwaukee County	68	0.49
Franklin, WI (city) Milwaukee County	143	0.48
Municipality of Murrysville, PA (borough) Westmoreland County	90	0.48
Robinson Township, PA (cdp) Allegheny County	59	0.48
Sun Lakes, AZ (cdp) Maricopa County	57	0.48
Lorain, OH (city) Lorain County	324	0.47
Pleasant Prairie, WI (village) Kenosha County	75	0.47
Uniontown, PA (city) Fayette County	58	0.47
Rostraver, PA (township) Westmoreland County	55	0.47
Manville, NJ (borough) Somerset County	48	0.47
Cudahy, WI (city) Milwaukee County	85	0.46
Ocean City, NJ (city) Cape May County	70	0.46
Carol Stream, IL (village) Du Page County	180	0.45
Monroe, MI (city) Monroe County	100	0.45
Grand Island, NY (town) Erie County	84	0.45
Struthers, OH (city) Mahoning County	53	0.45
Avon, OH (city) Lorain County	52	0.45
Mount Lebanon, PA (cdp) Allegheny County	146	0.44
Stow, OH (city) Summit County	140	0.44
Wolf Trap, VA (cdp) Fairfax County	61	0.44
Upper Allen, PA (township) Cumberland County	66	0.43
Libertyville, IL (village) Lake County	87	0.42
Streamwood, IL (village) Cook County	151	0.41
Herndon, VA (town) Fairfax County	88	0.41
Washington, PA (city) Washington County	63	0.41
Lockport, IL (city) Will County	60	0.41
Peters, PA (township) Washington County	71	0.40
Hermitage, PA (city) Mercer County	65	0.40
Altoona, IA (city) Polk County	41	0.40
Cuyahoga Falls, OH (city) Summit County	192	0.39
Moon, PA (township) Allegheny County	86	0.39
Pflugerville, TX (city) Travis County	64	0.39
Princeton Meadows, NJ (cdp) Middlesex County	51	0.39
Sterling Heights, MI (city) Macomb County	476	0.38
Caledonia, WI (town) Racine County	91	0.38
Derry, PA (township) Dauphin County	80	0.38
Frenchtown, MI (township) Monroe County	78	0.38
Woodhaven, MI (city) Wayne County	47	0.38
North Ridgeville, OH (city) Lorain County	82	0.37
Alsip, IL (village) Cook County	73	0.37
Greendale, WI (village) Milwaukee County	53	0.37
Colonial Park, PA (cdp) Dauphin County	49	0.37
Streetsboro, OH (city) Portage County	45	0.37
North Saint Paul, MN (city) Ramsey County	44	0.37
New Berlin, WI (city) Waukesha County	140	0.36
Brookfield, WI (city) Waukesha County	139	0.36
Shaler Township, PA (cdp) Allegheny County	107	0.36
Grosse Pointe Woods, MI (city) Wayne County	62	0.36
Twinsburg, OH (city) Summit County	60	0.36
Sierra Madre, CA (city) Los Angeles County	38	0.36
Austintown, OH (cdp) Mahoning County	111	0.35
Vernon Hills, IL (village) Lake County	73	0.35
Plainsboro, NJ (township) Middlesex County	70	0.35
Palm Beach, FL (town) Palm Beach County	36	0.35

Notes: (cdp) census designated place; Refer to the Explanation of Data in the front of the book for more detailed information.

Slavic

Top 150 Places Sorted by Number

(Based on all places, regardless of population)

Place	Number	%
New York, NY (city) New York City	2,025	0.03
Los Angeles, CA (city) Los Angeles County	962	0.03
Chicago, IL (city) Cook County	846	0.03
Phoenix, AZ (city) Maricopa County	590	0.04
San Diego, CA (city) San Diego County	581	0.05
Pittsburgh, PA (city) Allegheny County	517	0.15
San Francisco, CA (city) San Francisco County	482	0.06
Philadelphia, PA (city) Philadelphia County	391	0.03
Bayonne, NJ (city) Hudson County	383	0.62
Columbus, OH (city) Franklin County	374	0.05
Pueblo, CO (city) Pueblo County	365	0.36
Indianapolis, IN (special city) Marion County	361	0.05
Minneapolis, MN (city) Hennepin County	354	0.09
Erie, PA (city) Erie County	344	0.33
Portland, OR (city) Multnomah County	344	0.07
Seattle, WA (city) King County	340	0.06
Hamilton, NJ (township) Mercer County	339	0.39
Houston, TX (city) Harris County	306	0.02
Milwaukee, WI (city) Milwaukee County	303	0.05
Tucson, AZ (city) Pima County	285	0.06
Duluth, MN (city) Saint Louis County	271	0.31
Colorado Springs, CO (city) El Paso County	267	0.07
Hempstead, NY (town) Nassau County	263	0.03
Austin, TX (city) Travis County	255	0.04
Tacoma, WA (city) Pierce County	254	0.13
Woodbridge, NJ (township) Middlesex County	234	0.24
Long Beach, CA (city) Los Angeles County	233	0.05
Albuquerque, NM (city) Bernalillo County	230	0.05
Jacksonville, FL (special city) Duval County	227	0.03
San Antonio, TX (city) Bexar County	224	0.02
San Jose, CA (city) Santa Clara County	223	0.02
Saint Louis, MO (independent city) Saint Louis city	212	0.06
Dallas, TX (city) Dallas County	211	0.02
Hibbing, MN (city) Saint Louis County	198	1.16
Cleveland, OH (city) Cuyahoga County	189	0.04
Las Vegas, NV (city) Clark County	188	0.04
Martinez, CA (city) Contra Costa County	187	0.52
Rock Springs, WY (city) Sweetwater County	186	0.98
Millcreek, PA (township) Erie County	184	0.35
Irvine, CA (city) Orange County	183	0.13
Virginia Beach, VA (independent city) Virginia Beach city	180	0.04
Livonia, MI (city) Wayne County	178	0.18
Edison, NJ (cdp) Middlesex County	174	0.18
Arlington, VA (cdp) Arlington County	174	0.09
Yonkers, NY (city) Westchester County	173	0.09
Madison, WI (city) Dane County	171	0.08
Charlotte, NC (city) Mecklenburg County	169	0.03
Mesa, AZ (city) Maricopa County	167	0.04
Buffalo, NY (city) Erie County	165	0.06
Huntington, NY (town) Suffolk County	161	0.08
Trenton, NJ (city) Mercer County	159	0.19
Naperville, IL (city) Du Page County	157	0.12
South Bend, IN (city) Saint Joseph County	151	0.14
Kansas City, MO (city) Jackson County	148	0.03
Municipality of Monroeville, PA (borough) Allegheny County	140	0.48
Oyster Bay, NY (town) Nassau County	139	0.05
Union, NY (town) Broome County	137	0.24
Independence, MO (city) Jackson County	137	0.12
Boston, MA (city) Suffolk County	136	0.02
Denver, CO (city) Denver County	136	0.02
Clifton, NJ (city) Passaic County	134	0.17
Joliet, IL (city) Will County	134	0.13
Punxsutawney, PA (borough) Jefferson County	132	2.10
Lower Paxton, PA (township) Dauphin County	132	0.30
Saint Paul, MN (city) Ramsey County	131	0.05
Omaha, NE (city) Douglas County	131	0.03
Salt Lake City, UT (city) Salt Lake County	130	0.07
Virginia, MN (city) Saint Louis County	128	1.40
Oakland, CA (city) Alameda County	128	0.03
West Allis, WI (city) Milwaukee County	127	0.21
Henderson, NV (city) Clark County	127	0.07
Spokane, WA (city) Spokane County	127	0.06
Madison, CT (town) New Haven County	126	0.71
North Royalton, OH (city) Cuyahoga County	126	0.44
Alexandria, VA (independent city) Alexandria city	126	0.10
Johnstown, PA (city) Cambria County	125	0.52
Milford, CT (town) New Haven County	123	0.24
Milford, CT (special city) New Haven County	123	0.24
Smithtown, NY (town) Suffolk County	122	0.11
Paradise, NV (cdp) Clark County	122	0.07
Biloxi, MS (city) Harrison County	121	0.24
Anchorage, AK (municipality) Anchorage Borough	121	0.05
Bethlehem, PA (city) Northampton County	120	0.17
Islip, NY (town) Suffolk County	120	0.04
Hempfield, PA (township) Westmoreland County	118	0.29
Saint Cloud, MN (city) Stearns County	117	0.20
Saint Petersburg, FL (city) Pinellas County	116	0.05
Brooklyn Park, MN (city) Hennepin County	115	0.17
Hammond, IN (city) Lake County	115	0.14
Lincoln, NE (city) Lancaster County	115	0.05
Arvada, CO (city) Jefferson County	114	0.11
Tampa, FL (city) Hillsborough County	114	0.04
New Castle, PA (city) Lawrence County	113	0.43
Dearborn, MI (city) Wayne County	113	0.12
Santa Rosa, CA (city) Sonoma County	113	0.08
Linden, NJ (city) Union County	112	0.28
Bridgewater, NJ (township) Somerset County	112	0.26
Parma, OH (city) Cuyahoga County	112	0.13
Aurora, CO (city) Arapahoe County	112	0.04
Franklin, NJ (township) Somerset County	111	0.22
Sayreville, NJ (borough) Middlesex County	110	0.27
Altoona, PA (city) Blair County	110	0.22
Canton, MI (cdp) Wayne County	110	0.14
Allentown, PA (city) Lehigh County	110	0.10
Hudson, FL (cdp) Pasco County	109	0.86
Eagan, MN (city) Dakota County	108	0.17
Baltimore, MD (independent city) Baltimore city	108	0.02
Shawnee, KS (city) Johnson County	107	0.22
Dover, NJ (township) Ocean County	107	0.12
Jersey City, NJ (city) Hudson County	107	0.04
Walden, NY (village) Orange County	106	1.72
Montgomery, NY (town) Orange County	106	0.51
Waterford, MI (cdp) Oakland County	106	0.14
Billings, MT (city) Yellowstone County	106	0.12
Cincinnati, OH (city) Hamilton County	106	0.03
Babylon, NY (town) Suffolk County	105	0.05
Lakewood, CO (city) Jefferson County	104	0.07
Mercerville-Hamilton Square, NJ (cdp) Mercer County	103	0.39
Gurnee, IL (village) Lake County	103	0.36
North Huntingdon, PA (township) Westmoreland County	103	0.35
Farmington Hills, MI (city) Oakland County	103	0.13
Arlington, TX (city) Tarrant County	103	0.03
Brookhaven, NY (town) Suffolk County	103	0.02
Severna Park, MD (cdp) Anne Arundel County	102	0.36
Sterling Heights, MI (city) Macomb County	102	0.08
Penn, PA (township) Westmoreland County	101	0.52
Alameda, CA (city) Alameda County	100	0.14
Oxnard, CA (city) Ventura County	100	0.06
Tempe, AZ (city) Maricopa County	100	0.06
Akron, OH (city) Summit County	100	0.05
Anaheim, CA (city) Orange County	100	0.03
Santa Ana, CA (city) Orange County	100	0.03
Sandy, PA (township) Clearfield County	99	0.86
Garfield, NJ (city) Bergen County	99	0.33
State College, PA (borough) Centre County	99	0.26
Warren, MI (city) Macomb County	98	0.07
Glendale, AZ (city) Maricopa County	98	0.04
Sharon, PA (city) Mercer County	97	0.59
Apple Valley, MN (city) Dakota County	97	0.21
Penn Hills, PA (cdp) Allegheny County	97	0.21
Blue Springs, MO (city) Jackson County	97	0.20
Middletown, NJ (township) Monmouth County	97	0.15
Boulder, CO (city) Boulder County	97	0.10
Torrance, CA (city) Los Angeles County	97	0.07
Hazleton, PA (city) Luzerne County	95	0.41
Fresno, CA (city) Fresno County	95	0.02
Sheboygan, WI (city) Sheboygan County	94	0.19
Saint Charles, MO (city) Saint Charles County	94	0.16
Sacramento, CA (city) Sacramento County	94	0.02
Canon City, CO (city) Fremont County	93	0.61

Notes: (cdp) census designated place; Refer to the Explanation of Data in the front of the book for more detailed information.

Slavic

Top 150 Places Sorted by Percent

(Based on all places, regardless of population)

Place	Number	%
Fort Ritchie, MD (cdp) Washington County	21	10.05
Callimont, PA (borough) Somerset County	4	7.69
Alger, WA (cdp) Skagit County	6	7.41
Chickamaw Beach, MN (city) Cass County	11	7.38
Breitung, MN (township) Saint Louis County	42	6.10
Lake Hattie, MN (township) Hubbard County	8	5.88
Willow Valley, MN (township) Saint Louis County	7	5.65
Gildford, MT (cdp) Hill County	9	5.52
Aguilar, CO (town) Las Animas County	37	5.49
Sherman, MI (township) Keweenaw County	3	5.45
Chillicothe, IA (city) Wapello County	4	5.00
Red House, NY (town) Cattaraugus County	2	4.76
Englewood, PA (cdp) Schuylkill County	20	4.60
Cloverland, WI (town) Douglas County	11	4.56
Brookfield Center, OH (cdp) Trumbull County	52	4.47
Clifton, VA (town) Fairfax County	8	4.37
Wilson, WI (village) Saint Croix County	8	4.26
Colver, PA (cdp) Cambria County	42	4.15
Granger, WY (town) Sweetwater County	6	4.11
Portage, MN (township) Saint Louis County	7	4.05
Eden, WY (cdp) Sweetwater County	20	3.95
Ramey, PA (borough) Clearfield County	18	3.56
Chapman, PA (borough) Northampton County	8	3.45
East New Market, MD (town) Dorchester County	6	3.41
Bureau Junction, IL (village) Bureau County	12	3.32
Fisher Island, FL (cdp) Miami-Dade County	11	3.24
Sandy Ridge, PA (cdp) Centre County	9	3.18
French, MN (township) Saint Louis County	10	3.09
Judith Gap, MT (city) Wheatland County	4	2.82
Fort Ann, NY (village) Washington County	13	2.77
Mountain Iron, MN (city) Saint Louis County	82	2.71
Haysville, PA (borough) Allegheny County	2	2.67
Alder, MT (cdp) Madison County	3	2.65
Prue, OK (town) Osage County	11	2.56
Lilly, PA (borough) Cambria County	24	2.55
Keams Canyon, AZ (cdp) Navajo County	5	2.50
Wildwood, KY (city) Jefferson County	6	2.45
Nesbit, MN (township) Polk County	3	2.44
North Rock Springs, WY (cdp) Sweetwater County	45	2.40
Washington, PA (township) Cambria County	22	2.37
Schroeder, MN (township) Cook County	5	2.37
Tower, MN (city) Saint Louis County	11	2.35
Weyerhaeuser, WI (village) Rusk County	8	2.35
Parrish, WI (town) Langlade County	2	2.35
Pike, MN (township) Saint Louis County	11	2.34
Hiller, PA (cdp) Fayette County	28	2.30
Wall, PA (borough) Allegheny County	17	2.30
Coal Creek, CO (town) Fremont County	8	2.28
Silver City, IA (city) Mills County	6	2.25
Cokeburg, PA (borough) Washington County	16	2.24
Deersville, OH (village) Harrison County	2	2.22
Bushong, KS (city) Lyon County	1	2.22
Matlacha Isles-Matlacha Shores, FL (cdp) Lee County	6	2.21
Iron Junction, MN (city) Saint Louis County	2	2.17
Jefferson Heights, NY (cdp) Greene County	24	2.13
Punxsutawney, PA (borough) Jefferson County	132	2.10
Beallsville, PA (borough) Washington County	11	2.09
Aurora, WI (town) Taylor County	8	2.09
Fayal, MN (township) Saint Louis County	39	2.05
Oliver, WI (village) Douglas County	7	2.05
Ely, MN (city) Saint Louis County	76	2.04
Babbitt, MN (city) Saint Louis County	34	2.04
Houtzdale, PA (borough) Clearfield County	19	2.02
Glacier View, AK (cdp) Matanuska-Susitna Borough	5	2.02
Lone Pine, MN (township) Itasca County	11	2.00
Mountainhome, PA (cdp) Monroe County	25	1.99
Roosevelt, WI (town) Taylor County	8	1.99
Kaibab, AZ (cdp) Mohave County	5	1.97
McDavitt, MN (township) Saint Louis County	9	1.94
Ripley, MN (township) Dodge County	4	1.94
Gulich, PA (township) Clearfield County	25	1.93
Amity, PA (township) Erie County	22	1.93
Slickville, PA (cdp) Westmoreland County	7	1.91
Gilbert, MN (city) Saint Louis County	35	1.89
Rosemont, IL (village) Cook County	78	1.87
Columbus AFB, MS (cdp) Lowndes County	40	1.86
Bigler, PA (township) Clearfield County	25	1.86
Ogle, PA (township) Somerset County	11	1.86
Fort Shaw, MT (cdp) Cascade County	5	1.84
White, MN (township) Saint Louis County	64	1.83
North Utica, IL (village) La Salle County	17	1.82
Wheeler, MN (township) Lake of the Woods County	6	1.81
Fall Lake, MN (township) Lake County	10	1.80
McCook, IL (village) Cook County	4	1.76
Rossiter, PA (cdp) Indiana County	13	1.75
Ann Lake, MN (township) Kanabec County	7	1.75
North Granby, CT (cdp) Hartford County	30	1.74
Bridgewater, PA (borough) Beaver County	13	1.74
Peeksville, WI (town) Ashland County	3	1.74
Saint Helena, NC (village) Pender County	7	1.73
Walden, NY (village) Orange County	106	1.72
Brodheadsville, PA (cdp) Monroe County	25	1.72
Northwest Ithaca, NY (cdp) Tompkins County	19	1.72
Wedgefield, FL (cdp) Orange County	48	1.71
Diamondville, WY (town) Lincoln County	12	1.71
Biwabik, MN (city) Saint Louis County	16	1.69
Corvallis, MT (cdp) Ravalli County	7	1.69
Drake, ND (city) McHenry County	5	1.69
Cassville, MO (city) Barry County	49	1.68
Kugler, MN (township) Saint Louis County	3	1.68
Port Alsworth, AK (cdp) Lake and Peninsula Borough	2	1.67
Sheffield, PA (township) Warren County	39	1.66
Allegany, NY (village) Cattaraugus County	30	1.64
Mansfield, MI (township) Iron County	4	1.64
Round Valley, CA (cdp) Inyo County	4	1.63
Frankfort, SD (city) Spink County	3	1.63
Ault, MN (township) Saint Louis County	2	1.63
Iron Range, MN (township) Itasca County	11	1.62
Julian, PA (cdp) Centre County	3	1.62
Clam Gulch, AK (cdp) Kenai Peninsula Borough	3	1.61
Guy, AR (town) Faulkner County	3	1.61
Morrisville, PA (cdp) Greene County	23	1.60
Winslow, PA (township) Jefferson County	41	1.58
Clifford, MI (village) Lapeer County	6	1.58
Plymouth, CA (city) Amador County	15	1.57
Pleasantville, PA (borough) Bedford County	3	1.57
Pillager, MN (city) Cass County	6	1.56
Beaver Meadows, PA (borough) Carbon County	15	1.55
South Prairie, WA (town) Pierce County	7	1.55
Foster, PA (township) Luzerne County	52	1.53
Biwabik, MN (township) Saint Louis County	14	1.53
Rose, WI (town) Waushara County	9	1.53
Central City, PA (borough) Somerset County	19	1.51
Allen, MI (village) Hillsdale County	3	1.51
East Taylor, PA (township) Cambria County	41	1.50
Hopwood, PA (cdp) Fayette County	30	1.50
McCalmont, PA (township) Jefferson County	16	1.50
Krain, MN (township) Stearns County	14	1.49
Gilman, WI (village) Taylor County	7	1.48
Happy Valley, AK (cdp) Kenai Peninsula Borough	7	1.47
Arona, PA (borough) Westmoreland County	6	1.47
Mansfield, MN (township) Freeborn County	4	1.47
Union Star, MO (town) De Kalb County	6	1.46
Trommald, MN (city) Crow Wing County	2	1.46
Bethlehem Village, CT (cdp) Litchfield County	30	1.45
Akron, NY (village) Erie County	45	1.44
Iola, WI (town) Waupaca County	12	1.44
New Castle, PA (township) Schuylkill County	6	1.44
Buena Vista, CO (town) Chaffee County	30	1.43
Marianna, PA (borough) Washington County	9	1.43
Springfield, PA (township) Erie County	48	1.42
Sugar Bush Knolls, OH (village) Portage County	3	1.42
Genesee, CO (cdp) Jefferson County	51	1.41
Virginia, MN (city) Saint Louis County	128	1.40
Bovina, WI (town) Outagamie County	17	1.40
Vernon Valley, NJ (cdp) Sussex County	24	1.38
Long Branch, PA (borough) Washington County	7	1.38
Maeystown, IL (village) Monroe County	2	1.38
Eveleth, MN (city) Saint Louis County	53	1.37
Esperance, WA (cdp) Snohomish County	49	1.37

Notes: (cdp) census designated place; Refer to the Explanation of Data in the front of the book for more detailed information.

Slavic

Top 150 Places Sorted by Percent

(Based on places with populations of 10,000 or more)

Place	Number	%
Hibbing, MN (city) Saint Louis County	198	1.16
Rock Springs, WY (city) Sweetwater County	186	0.98
Hudson, FL (cdp) Pasco County	109	0.86
Sandy, PA (township) Clearfield County	99	0.86
North Versailles, PA (cdp) Allegheny County	92	0.83
Florence, NJ (township) Burlington County	79	0.74
Manville, NJ (borough) Somerset County	74	0.72
Madison, CT (town) New Haven County	126	0.71
Center, PA (township) Beaver County	72	0.63
Bayonne, NJ (city) Hudson County	383	0.62
Canon City, CO (city) Fremont County	93	0.61
Sharon, PA (city) Mercer County	97	0.59
Derry, PA (township) Westmoreland County	86	0.58
Munhall, PA (borough) Allegheny County	69	0.56
Martinez, CA (city) Contra Costa County	187	0.52
Johnstown, PA (city) Cambria County	125	0.52
Penn, PA (township) Westmoreland County	101	0.52
Montgomery, NY (town) Orange County	106	0.51
Chenango, NY (town) Broome County	57	0.50
Harrison Township, PA (cdp) Allegheny County	55	0.50
New Britain, PA (township) Bucks County	53	0.50
Municipality of Monroeville, PA (borough) Allegheny County	140	0.48
Elizabeth, PA (township) Allegheny County	67	0.48
North Royalton, OH (city) Cuyahoga County	126	0.44
Mount Pleasant, PA (township) Westmoreland County	49	0.44
White Bear, MN (township) Ramsey County	49	0.44
New Castle, PA (city) Lawrence County	113	0.43
Coventry, CT (town) Tolland County	50	0.43
Gardnerville Ranchos, NV (cdp) Douglas County	47	0.42
Hazleton, PA (city) Luzerne County	95	0.41
Fernway, PA (cdp) Butler County	50	0.41
Nanticoke, PA (city) Luzerne County	45	0.41
Woodburn, OR (city) Marion County	80	0.40
Avon, CT (town) Hartford County	64	0.40
Brooklyn, OH (city) Cuyahoga County	46	0.40
Little Falls, NJ (cdp) Passaic County	43	0.40
Hamilton, NJ (township) Mercer County	339	0.39
Mercerville-Hamilton Square, NJ (cdp) Mercer County	103	0.39
Unity, PA (township) Westmoreland County	81	0.39
Pottsville, PA (city) Schuylkill County	57	0.37
Pewaukee, WI (city) Waukesha County	44	0.37
Pueblo, CO (city) Pueblo County	365	0.36
Gurnee, IL (village) Lake County	103	0.36
Severna Park, MD (cdp) Anne Arundel County	102	0.36
Gallup, NM (city) McKinley County	74	0.36
Steubenville, OH (city) Jefferson County	69	0.36
Melville, NY (cdp) Suffolk County	53	0.36
Branchburg, NJ (township) Somerset County	52	0.36
Granby, CT (town) Hartford County	37	0.36
Millcreek, PA (township) Erie County	184	0.35
North Huntingdon, PA (township) Westmoreland County	103	0.35
Moon, PA (township) Allegheny County	78	0.35
Spring, PA (township) Berks County	76	0.35
Bethlehem, PA (township) Northampton County	75	0.35
Lino Lakes, MN (city) Anoka County	59	0.35
Berkley, MI (city) Oakland County	54	0.35
Fairview, PA (township) York County	50	0.35
Pottstown, PA (borough) Montgomery County	73	0.34
Painesville, OH (city) Lake County	59	0.34
New River, AZ (cdp) Maricopa County	37	0.34
Erie, PA (city) Erie County	344	0.33
Garfield, NJ (city) Bergen County	99	0.33
McKeesport, PA (city) Allegheny County	79	0.33
New Kensington, PA (city) Westmoreland County	49	0.33
Crest Hill, IL (city) Will County	43	0.33
Loveland, OH (city) Hamilton County	39	0.33
Lansing, NY (town) Tompkins County	34	0.33
Avenel, NJ (cdp) Middlesex County	57	0.32
Johnson City, NY (village) Broome County	49	0.32
Kaneohe Station, HI (cdp) Honolulu County	38	0.32
South Union, PA (township) Fayette County	36	0.32
Woodlyn, PA (cdp) Delaware County	32	0.32
Duluth, MN (city) Saint Louis County	271	0.31
Lebanon, PA (city) Lebanon County	76	0.31
West Mifflin, PA (borough) Allegheny County	70	0.31
Bainbridge Island, WA (city) Kitsap County	63	0.31
Birmingham, MI (city) Oakland County	60	0.31
Butler, PA (township) Butler County	54	0.31
Green Haven, MD (cdp) Anne Arundel County	54	0.31
Rosemount, MN (city) Dakota County	46	0.31
Greendale, WI (village) Milwaukee County	45	0.31
Lower Burrell, PA (city) Westmoreland County	39	0.31
Linganore-Bartonsville, MD (cdp) Frederick County	38	0.31
North Palm Beach, FL (village) Palm Beach County	37	0.31
Superior, MI (township) Washtenaw County	33	0.31
Lower Paxton, PA (township) Dauphin County	132	0.30
Lodi, NJ (borough) Bergen County	71	0.30
Lafayette, CO (city) Boulder County	69	0.30
Parma Heights, OH (city) Cuyahoga County	66	0.30
Palm City, FL (cdp) Martin County	60	0.30
Upper Saint Clair, PA (cdp) Allegheny County	60	0.30
Avon Lake, OH (city) Lorain County	55	0.30
Indiana, PA (borough) Indiana County	45	0.30
South Park Township, PA (cdp) Allegheny County	43	0.30
Thomas, MI (township) Saginaw County	36	0.30
Saint Augustine, FL (city) Saint Johns County	35	0.30
Berwick, PA (borough) Columbia County	32	0.30
Hempfield, PA (township) Westmoreland County	118	0.29
Brighton, MI (township) Livingston County	52	0.29
Phoenixville, PA (borough) Chester County	43	0.29
East Bridgewater, MA (town) Plymouth County	37	0.29
Falls Church, VA (independent city) Falls Church city	30	0.29
Linden, NJ (city) Union County	112	0.28
Columbine, CO (cdp) Jefferson County	67	0.28
York, PA (township) York County	67	0.28
Scottsboro, AL (city) Jackson County	42	0.28
Holiday City-Berkeley, NJ (cdp) Ocean County	39	0.28
Endicott, NY (village) Broome County	37	0.28
Lakeland Highlands, FL (cdp) Polk County	36	0.28
Middle Smithfield, PA (township) Monroe County	32	0.28
Wallington, NJ (borough) Bergen County	32	0.28
Beachwood, NJ (borough) Ocean County	29	0.28
Halfway, MD (cdp) Washington County	28	0.28
Sayreville, NJ (borough) Middlesex County	110	0.27
Wheeling, WV (city) Ohio County	83	0.27
Monroe, MI (city) Monroe County	61	0.27
Brighton, CO (city) Adams County	56	0.27
Raritan, NJ (township) Hunterdon County	54	0.27
Colonia, NJ (cdp) Middlesex County	48	0.27
Peters, PA (township) Washington County	48	0.27
Pleasant Prairie, WI (village) Kenosha County	43	0.27
Plymouth, PA (township) Montgomery County	43	0.27
Great Bend, KS (city) Barton County	42	0.27
Upper Southampton, PA (township) Bucks County	42	0.27
Warren, NJ (township) Somerset County	39	0.27
Dunmore, PA (borough) Lackawanna County	38	0.27
Saddle Brook, NJ (cdp) Bergen County	35	0.27
Uniontown, PA (city) Fayette County	33	0.27
Franklin Park, PA (borough) Allegheny County	31	0.27
Corning, NY (city) Steuben County	29	0.27
Jeannette, PA (city) Westmoreland County	29	0.27
Monitor, MI (township) Bay County	27	0.27
Bridgewater, NJ (township) Somerset County	112	0.26
State College, PA (borough) Centre County	99	0.26
New Milford, CT (town) Litchfield County	71	0.26
Slidell, LA (city) Saint Tammany Parish	66	0.26
Owosso, MI (city) Shiawassee County	41	0.26
Willowick, OH (city) Lake County	37	0.26
San Marino, CA (city) Los Angeles County	34	0.26
West Lampeter, PA (township) Lancaster County	34	0.26
Catskill, NY (town) Greene County	31	0.26
Falls, PA (township) Bucks County	87	0.25
Trumbull, CT (cdp) Fairfield County	87	0.25
Ridley, PA (township) Delaware County	78	0.25
Shaler Township, PA (cdp) Allegheny County	73	0.25
Monroe, NJ (township) Middlesex County	71	0.25
Bel Air North, MD (cdp) Harford County	65	0.25
Homewood, AL (city) Jefferson County	63	0.25
Cranberry, PA (township) Butler County	59	0.25
Villa Park, IL (village) Du Page County	56	0.25

Notes: (cdp) census designated place; Refer to the Explanation of Data in the front of the book for more detailed information.

Slovak

Top 150 Places Sorted by Number

(Based on all places, regardless of population)

Place	Number	%
Cleveland, OH (city) Cuyahoga County	8,402	1.76
Parma, OH (city) Cuyahoga County	7,940	9.27
Pittsburgh, PA (city) Allegheny County	6,566	1.96
New York, NY (city) New York City	6,459	0.08
Chicago, IL (city) Cook County	6,238	0.22
Youngstown, OH (city) Mahoning County	4,345	5.30
West Mifflin, PA (borough) Allegheny County	3,607	16.06
Boardman, OH (cdp) Mahoning County	3,552	9.53
Hammond, IN (city) Lake County	3,259	3.92
Stratford, CT (cdp) Fairfield County	3,173	6.35
Union, NY (town) Broome County	3,039	5.40
Lakewood, OH (city) Cuyahoga County	3,006	5.31
Bethlehem, PA (city) Northampton County	2,830	3.97
Hazleton, PA (city) Luzerne County	2,662	11.44
Allentown, PA (city) Lehigh County	2,639	2.47
Lorain, OH (city) Lorain County	2,618	3.81
Columbus, OH (city) Franklin County	2,491	0.35
Akron, OH (city) Summit County	2,479	1.14
Strongsville, OH (city) Cuyahoga County	2,467	5.62
North Huntingdon, PA (township) Westmoreland County	2,446	8.38
Austintown, OH (cdp) Mahoning County	2,411	7.62
Philadelphia, PA (city) Philadelphia County	2,388	0.16
Munhall, PA (borough) Allegheny County	2,363	19.27
Brunswick, OH (city) Medina County	2,335	6.99
Wilkes-Barre, PA (city) Luzerne County	2,281	5.29
North Royalton, OH (city) Cuyahoga County	2,276	7.94
Hempfield, PA (township) Westmoreland County	2,261	5.55
North Olmsted, OH (city) Cuyahoga County	1,990	5.83
Phoenix, AZ (city) Maricopa County	1,914	0.14
Struthers, OH (city) Mahoning County	1,887	16.05
Johnstown, PA (city) Cambria County	1,862	7.79
Mentor, OH (city) Lake County	1,851	3.68
Woodbridge, NJ (township) Middlesex County	1,833	1.89
Los Angeles, CA (city) Los Angeles County	1,792	0.05
Hamilton, NJ (township) Mercer County	1,785	2.05
Binghamton, NY (city) Broome County	1,704	3.60
Parma Heights, OH (city) Cuyahoga County	1,690	7.80
Unity, PA (township) Westmoreland County	1,662	7.90
Streator, IL (city) La Salle County	1,653	11.70
Warren, OH (city) Trumbull County	1,594	3.40
Shelton, CT (city) Fairfield County	1,588	4.17
Milwaukee, WI (city) Milwaukee County	1,577	0.26
Bridgeport, CT (city) Fairfield County	1,569	1.12
Westlake, OH (city) Cuyahoga County	1,551	4.87
Milford, CT (special city) New Haven County	1,520	3.00
Milford, CT (town) New Haven County	1,520	2.91
Garfield Heights, OH (city) Cuyahoga County	1,485	4.85
North Union, PA (township) Fayette County	1,476	10.44
Penn Hills, PA (cdp) Allegheny County	1,473	3.15
Hermitage, PA (city) Mercer County	1,470	9.11
Whitehall, PA (township) Lehigh County	1,470	5.90
Scranton, PA (city) Lackawanna County	1,458	1.91
Joliet, IL (city) Will County	1,456	1.37
Brook Park, OH (city) Cuyahoga County	1,444	6.81
Bethel Park, PA (borough) Allegheny County	1,398	4.17
San Diego, CA (city) San Diego County	1,360	0.11
McKeesport, PA (city) Allegheny County	1,340	5.58
Municipality of Monroeville, PA (borough) Allegheny County	1,297	4.42
Plum, PA (borough) Allegheny County	1,294	4.80
Mount Pleasant, PA (township) Westmoreland County	1,270	11.35
Euclid, OH (city) Cuyahoga County	1,259	2.39
Erie, PA (city) Erie County	1,235	1.19
Lower Burrell, PA (city) Westmoreland County	1,226	9.71
Middleburg Heights, OH (city) Cuyahoga County	1,226	7.89
Elyria, OH (city) Lorain County	1,216	2.18
Campbell, OH (city) Mahoning County	1,207	12.76
Ross Township, PA (cdp) Allegheny County	1,199	3.68
Penn, PA (township) Westmoreland County	1,194	6.09
Maple Heights, OH (city) Cuyahoga County	1,179	4.51
Broadview Heights, OH (city) Cuyahoga County	1,177	7.37
Clifton, NJ (city) Passaic County	1,163	1.48
Harrison Township, PA (cdp) Allegheny County	1,150	10.52
Elizabeth, PA (township) Allegheny County	1,145	8.27
Back Mountain, PA (cdp) Luzerne County	1,135	4.25
Trumbull, CT (cdp) Fairfield County	1,121	3.27
Edison, NJ (cdp) Middlesex County	1,097	1.12
Brooklyn, OH (city) Cuyahoga County	1,090	9.41
Hazle, PA (township) Luzerne County	1,089	12.11
Seven Hills, OH (city) Cuyahoga County	1,081	8.95
South Union, PA (township) Fayette County	1,068	9.46
Johnson City, NY (village) Broome County	1,044	6.72
Torrington, CT (city) Litchfield County	1,041	2.96
Swoyersville, PA (borough) Luzerne County	1,025	19.88
Merrillville, IN (town) Lake County	1,025	3.34
Hubbard, OH (city) Trumbull County	1,024	12.42
Baldwin, PA (borough) Allegheny County	1,017	5.09
Charlotte, NC (city) Mecklenburg County	1,006	0.19
North Ridgeville, OH (city) Lorain County	1,004	4.49
Niles, OH (city) Trumbull County	1,003	4.79
Warren, MI (city) Macomb County	1,002	0.72
Toledo, OH (city) Lucas County	1,001	0.32
Fairview Park, OH (city) Cuyahoga County	992	5.65
Rocky River, OH (city) Cuyahoga County	991	4.78
Virginia Beach, VA (independent city) Virginia Beach city	989	0.23
Willoughby, OH (city) Lake County	976	4.32
Highland, IN (town) Lake County	969	4.12
Avon Lake, OH (city) Lorain County	962	5.30
Derry, PA (township) Westmoreland County	958	6.51
Lansford, PA (borough) Carbon County	949	22.43
Sterling Heights, MI (city) Macomb County	937	0.75
Yonkers, NY (city) Westchester County	931	0.47
Millcreek, PA (township) Erie County	928	1.78
Linden, NJ (city) Union County	927	2.35
Whiting, IN (city) Lake County	926	18.03
Houston, TX (city) Harris County	922	0.05
Eastlake, OH (city) Lake County	916	4.54
Hempstead, NY (town) Nassau County	908	0.12
Stow, OH (city) Summit County	903	2.81
Rostraver, PA (township) Westmoreland County	895	7.69
Sharon, PA (city) Mercer County	895	5.48
Monessen, PA (city) Westmoreland County	892	10.29
Munster, IN (town) Lake County	883	4.10
Solon, OH (city) Cuyahoga County	878	4.03
Municipality of Murrysville, PA (borough) Westmoreland County	876	4.65
North Versailles, PA (cdp) Allegheny County	875	7.87
Bethlehem, PA (township) Northampton County	870	4.11
Richland, PA (township) Cambria County	862	6.84
Jefferson Hills, PA (borough) Allegheny County	859	8.89
Bayonne, NJ (city) Hudson County	857	1.39
Minneapolis, MN (city) Hennepin County	847	0.22
Medina, OH (city) Medina County	845	3.37
White Oak, PA (borough) Allegheny County	844	9.96
South Park Township, PA (cdp) Allegheny County	843	5.88
Berea, OH (city) Cuyahoga County	838	4.41
Scottsdale, AZ (city) Maricopa County	838	0.41
Wickliffe, OH (city) Lake County	826	6.13
McCandless Township, PA (cdp) Allegheny County	824	2.84
Barberton, OH (city) Summit County	817	2.92
Twinsburg, OH (city) Summit County	815	4.83
Cranberry, PA (township) Butler County	814	3.44
Naperville, IL (city) Du Page County	809	0.63
Willowick, OH (city) Lake County	805	5.59
Tucson, AZ (city) Pima County	791	0.16
Moon, PA (township) Allegheny County	788	3.54
New Kensington, PA (city) Westmoreland County	781	5.30
Colorado Springs, CO (city) El Paso County	779	0.22
Brecksville, OH (city) Cuyahoga County	775	5.81
Schererville, IN (town) Lake County	775	3.12
Las Vegas, NV (city) Clark County	771	0.16
Fullerton, PA (cdp) Lehigh County	758	5.33
Salisbury, PA (township) Lehigh County	755	5.59
Mount Lebanon, PA (cdp) Allegheny County	750	2.27
Indianapolis, IN (special city) Marion County	743	0.09
Canfield, OH (city) Mahoning County	741	9.89
Clinton, MI (cdp) Macomb County	736	0.77
Center, PA (township) Beaver County	734	6.39
San Francisco, CA (city) San Francisco County	734	0.09
Portage, IN (city) Porter County	727	2.17
Plains, PA (township) Luzerne County	725	6.65
Hanover, PA (township) Luzerne County	720	6.28

Notes: (cdp) census designated place; Refer to the Explanation of Data in the front of the book for more detailed information.

Slovak

Top 150 Places Sorted by Percent

(Based on all places, regardless of population)

Place	Number	%
Clarence, PA (cdp) Centre County	185	31.04
Susitna, AK (cdp) Matanuska-Susitna Borough	9	29.03
Marblehead, OH (village) Ottawa County	206	27.14
Banks, PA (township) Carbon County	320	23.24
Brownstown, PA (borough) Cambria County	203	22.99
Tresckow, PA (cdp) Carbon County	221	22.93
Lansford, PA (borough) Carbon County	949	22.43
Whitaker, PA (borough) Allegheny County	297	22.20
East Vandergrift, PA (borough) Westmoreland County	163	21.53
Snow Shoe, PA (township) Centre County	368	21.10
Beaver Meadows, PA (borough) Carbon County	202	20.87
New Boston-Morea, PA (cdp) Schuylkill County	95	20.74
Vintondale, PA (borough) Cambria County	107	20.23
Swoyersville, PA (borough) Luzerne County	1,025	19.88
Munhall, PA (borough) Allegheny County	2,363	19.27
Calumet-Norvelt, PA (cdp) Westmoreland County	319	19.10
West Homestead, PA (borough) Allegheny County	407	18.53
Nesquehoning, PA (borough) Carbon County	579	18.08
Whiting, IN (city) Lake County	926	18.03
Wilburton Number Two, PA (cdp) Columbia County	13	17.57
Lower Yoder, PA (township) Cambria County	529	17.46
Yankee Lake, OH (village) Trumbull County	15	16.85
Jeddo, PA (borough) Luzerne County	24	16.67
Cassandra, PA (borough) Cambria County	18	16.36
West Mifflin, PA (borough) Allegheny County	3,607	16.06
Struthers, OH (city) Mahoning County	1,887	16.05
Lenape Heights, PA (cdp) Armstrong County	183	15.65
Freeland, PA (borough) Luzerne County	561	15.40
West Wyoming, PA (borough) Luzerne County	435	15.35
Perryopolis, PA (borough) Fayette County	269	15.25
Harrison City, PA (cdp) Westmoreland County	20	15.04
Wall, PA (borough) Allegheny County	110	14.86
Seltzer, PA (cdp) Schuylkill County	42	14.84
Dravosburg, PA (borough) Allegheny County	294	14.59
Keystone, WI (town) Bayfield County	61	14.56
West Leechburg, PA (borough) Westmoreland County	187	14.50
Summit Hill, PA (borough) Carbon County	440	14.38
Perry, PA (township) Fayette County	397	14.25
Oneida, PA (cdp) Schuylkill County	26	14.21
Hyde Park, PA (borough) Westmoreland County	72	14.09
Menallen, PA (township) Fayette County	652	14.04
Crabtree, PA (cdp) Westmoreland County	51	13.75
Coaldale, PA (borough) Schuylkill County	316	13.57
Middle Taylor, PA (township) Cambria County	106	13.50
South Canal, OH (cdp) Trumbull County	181	13.44
Springdale, PA (borough) Allegheny County	514	13.43
Fawn, PA (township) Allegheny County	331	13.22
Poland, OH (village) Mahoning County	372	12.98
Allenport, PA (borough) Washington County	75	12.98
Olyphant, PA (borough) Lackawanna County	645	12.96
Kline, PA (township) Schuylkill County	206	12.92
Tuscarora, PA (cdp) Schuylkill County	118	12.88
McAdoo, PA (borough) Schuylkill County	291	12.80
Morris, PA (township) Clearfield County	391	12.79
Campbell, OH (city) Mahoning County	1,207	12.76
Port Vue, PA (borough) Allegheny County	538	12.72
Susquehanna, PA (township) Cambria County	279	12.69
Glassport, PA (borough) Allegheny County	628	12.58
New Salem-Buffington, PA (cdp) Fayette County	98	12.53
Hubbard, OH (city) Trumbull County	1,024	12.42
Branchdale, PA (cdp) Schuylkill County	54	12.41
East Pittsburgh, PA (borough) Allegheny County	249	12.35
Oliver, PA (cdp) Fayette County	371	12.28
Scalp Level, PA (borough) Cambria County	104	12.22
Hazle, PA (township) Luzerne County	1,089	12.11
East Deer, PA (township) Allegheny County	165	12.11
Clymer, PA (borough) Indiana County	185	12.10
Ramey, PA (borough) Clearfield County	61	12.08
Fredericktown-Millsboro, PA (cdp) Washington County	133	11.89
Windber, PA (borough) Somerset County	521	11.85
Hilltop, OH (cdp) Trumbull County	67	11.80
McChesneytown-Loyalhanna, PA (cdp) Westmoreland County	407	11.72
Streator, IL (city) La Salle County	1,653	11.70
Stockdale, PA (borough) Washington County	62	11.65
Cheswick, PA (borough) Allegheny County	221	11.64
Franklin, PA (township) Fayette County	303	11.53
Central City, PA (borough) Somerset County	145	11.53
East Norwegian, PA (township) Schuylkill County	99	11.51
Heilwood, PA (cdp) Indiana County	93	11.51
Northern Cambria, PA (borough) Cambria County	481	11.46
Hazleton, PA (city) Luzerne County	2,662	11.44
Shenango, PA (township) Mercer County	459	11.37
Mount Pleasant, PA (township) Westmoreland County	1,270	11.35
Schuylkill, PA (township) Schuylkill County	126	11.22
Franklin, PA (borough) Cambria County	49	11.16
New Washington, PA (borough) Clearfield County	7	11.11
Liberty, PA (borough) Allegheny County	295	11.05
East Conemaugh, PA (borough) Cambria County	143	11.05
Roscoe, PA (borough) Washington County	93	10.97
Masontown, PA (borough) Fayette County	377	10.91
Larksville, PA (borough) Luzerne County	511	10.89
Cooper, PA (township) Clearfield County	297	10.88
Farley, MN (township) Polk County	4	10.81
Ashley, PA (borough) Luzerne County	306	10.68
Donora, PA (borough) Washington County	603	10.66
Hastings, PA (borough) Cambria County	149	10.66
West Hazleton, PA (borough) Luzerne County	375	10.58
Foster, PA (township) Luzerne County	358	10.54
Patton, PA (borough) Cambria County	213	10.53
Harrison Township, PA (cdp) Allegheny County	1,150	10.52
North Catasauqua, PA (borough) Northampton County	296	10.52
Mahanoy, PA (township) Schuylkill County	117	10.51
North Union, PA (township) Fayette County	1,476	10.44
Republic, PA (cdp) Fayette County	146	10.40
Flambeau, WI (town) Price County	58	10.36
Lincoln, PA (borough) Allegheny County	124	10.32
Monessen, PA (city) Westmoreland County	892	10.29
Exeter, PA (borough) Luzerne County	613	10.29
Edwardsville, PA (borough) Luzerne County	511	10.25
Throop, PA (borough) Lackawanna County	409	10.20
East Bethlehem, PA (township) Washington County	256	10.14
Spring Hill, PA (cdp) Cambria County	94	10.14
Middleport, PA (borough) Schuylkill County	46	10.13
Pringle, PA (borough) Luzerne County	100	10.09
Saint Michael-Sidman, PA (cdp) Cambria County	96	10.08
Daisytown, PA (borough) Cambria County	36	10.08
East Uniontown, PA (cdp) Fayette County	272	10.06
Speers, PA (borough) Washington County	118	10.02
Brackenridge, PA (borough) Allegheny County	354	9.99
White Oak, PA (borough) Allegheny County	844	9.96
Jefferson, PA (township) Fayette County	225	9.95
West Brownsville, PA (borough) Washington County	107	9.95
Elco, PA (borough) Washington County	39	9.95
East Union, PA (township) Schuylkill County	141	9.94
Packer, PA (township) Carbon County	96	9.92
Canfield, OH (city) Mahoning County	741	9.89
Blakely, PA (borough) Lackawanna County	695	9.89
Tarentum, PA (borough) Allegheny County	493	9.87
North Braddock, PA (borough) Allegheny County	631	9.84
Snow Shoe, PA (borough) Centre County	76	9.77
Lausanne, PA (township) Carbon County	22	9.73
Lower Burrell, PA (city) Westmoreland County	1,226	9.71
Leith-Hatfield, PA (cdp) Fayette County	276	9.71
Zippel, MN (township) Lake of the Woods County	10	9.71
Portage, PA (borough) Cambria County	274	9.66
Carrolltown, PA (borough) Cambria County	101	9.65
McDonald, OH (village) Trumbull County	333	9.62
South Greensburg, PA (borough) Westmoreland County	218	9.56
Boardman, OH (cdp) Mahoning County	3,552	9.53
Paint, PA (township) Somerset County	314	9.53
Braddock Hills, PA (borough) Allegheny County	190	9.51
Portage, PA (township) Cambria County	371	9.50
Courtdale, PA (borough) Luzerne County	75	9.48
South Union, PA (township) Fayette County	1,068	9.46
Conemaugh, PA (township) Cambria County	202	9.42
Brooklyn, OH (city) Cuyahoga County	1,090	9.41
Tiffany, WI (town) Dunn County	54	9.38
Lawson Heights, PA (cdp) Westmoreland County	214	9.32
Chalfant, PA (borough) Allegheny County	81	9.31
Gilpin, PA (township) Armstrong County	240	9.28

Notes: (cdp) census designated place; Refer to the Explanation of Data in the front of the book for more detailed information.

Slovak

Top 150 Places Sorted by Percent

(Based on places with populations of 10,000 or more)

Place	Number	%
Munhall, PA (borough) Allegheny County	2,363	19.27
West Mifflin, PA (borough) Allegheny County	3,607	16.06
Struthers, OH (city) Mahoning County	1,887	16.05
Streator, IL (city) La Salle County	1,653	11.70
Hazleton, PA (city) Luzerne County	2,662	11.44
Mount Pleasant, PA (township) Westmoreland County	1,270	11.35
Harrison Township, PA (cdp) Allegheny County	1,150	10.52
North Union, PA (township) Fayette County	1,476	10.44
Lower Burrell, PA (city) Westmoreland County	1,226	9.71
Boardman, OH (cdp) Mahoning County	3,552	9.53
South Union, PA (township) Fayette County	1,068	9.46
Brooklyn, OH (city) Cuyahoga County	1,090	9.41
Parma, OH (city) Cuyahoga County	7,940	9.27
Hermitage, PA (city) Mercer County	1,470	9.11
Seven Hills, OH (city) Cuyahoga County	1,081	8.95
North Huntingdon, PA (township) Westmoreland County	2,446	8.38
Elizabeth, PA (township) Allegheny County	1,145	8.27
North Royalton, OH (city) Cuyahoga County	2,276	7.94
Unity, PA (township) Westmoreland County	1,662	7.90
Middleburg Heights, OH (city) Cuyahoga County	1,226	7.89
North Versailles, PA (cdp) Allegheny County	875	7.87
Parma Heights, OH (city) Cuyahoga County	1,690	7.80
Johnstown, PA (city) Cambria County	1,862	7.79
Rostraver, PA (township) Westmoreland County	895	7.69
Austintown, OH (cdp) Mahoning County	2,411	7.62
Broadview Heights, OH (city) Cuyahoga County	1,177	7.37
Brunswick, OH (city) Medina County	2,335	6.99
Richland, PA (township) Cambria County	862	6.84
Brook Park, OH (city) Cuyahoga County	1,444	6.81
Johnson City, NY (village) Broome County	1,044	6.72
Plains, PA (township) Luzerne County	725	6.65
Derry, PA (township) Westmoreland County	958	6.51
Center, PA (township) Beaver County	734	6.39
Stratford, CT (cdp) Fairfield County	3,173	6.35
Hanover, PA (township) Luzerne County	720	6.28
Wickliffe, OH (city) Lake County	826	6.13
Penn, PA (township) Westmoreland County	1,194	6.09
Whitehall, PA (township) Lehigh County	1,470	5.90
South Park Township, PA (cdp) Allegheny County	843	5.88
North Olmsted, OH (city) Cuyahoga County	1,990	5.83
Brecksville, OH (city) Cuyahoga County	775	5.81
Fairview Park, OH (city) Cuyahoga County	992	5.65
Strongsville, OH (city) Cuyahoga County	2,467	5.62
Willowick, OH (city) Lake County	805	5.59
Salisbury, PA (township) Lehigh County	755	5.59
McKeesport, PA (city) Allegheny County	1,340	5.58
Hempfield, PA (township) Westmoreland County	2,261	5.55
Sharon, PA (city) Mercer County	895	5.48
Endwell, NY (cdp) Broome County	634	5.41
Union, NY (town) Broome County	3,039	5.40
Fullerton, PA (cdp) Lehigh County	758	5.33
Nanticoke, PA (city) Luzerne County	585	5.33
Lakewood, OH (city) Cuyahoga County	3,006	5.31
Youngstown, OH (city) Mahoning County	4,345	5.30
Avon Lake, OH (city) Lorain County	962	5.30
New Kensington, PA (city) Westmoreland County	781	5.30
Wilkes-Barre, PA (city) Luzerne County	2,281	5.29
Baldwin, PA (borough) Allegheny County	1,017	5.09
Hopewell, PA (township) Beaver County	668	5.02
Bedford, OH (city) Cuyahoga County	711	5.00
Kingston, PA (borough) Luzerne County	676	4.88
Westlake, OH (city) Cuyahoga County	1,551	4.87
Uniontown, PA (city) Fayette County	605	4.87
Avon, OH (city) Lorain County	556	4.86
Garfield Heights, OH (city) Cuyahoga County	1,485	4.85
Twinsburg, OH (city) Summit County	815	4.83
North Strabane, PA (township) Washington County	486	4.83
Plum, PA (borough) Allegheny County	1,294	4.80
Niles, OH (city) Trumbull County	1,003	4.79
Rocky River, OH (city) Cuyahoga County	991	4.78
Robinson Township, PA (cdp) Allegheny County	587	4.78
West Deer, PA (township) Allegheny County	543	4.70
Municipality of Murrysville, PA (borough) Westmoreland County	876	4.65
White, PA (township) Indiana County	638	4.55
Eastlake, OH (city) Lake County	916	4.54
Aliquippa, PA (city) Beaver County	527	4.52
Maple Heights, OH (city) Cuyahoga County	1,179	4.51
Chenango, NY (town) Broome County	517	4.51
Emmaus, PA (borough) Lehigh County	507	4.51
North Ridgeville, OH (city) Lorain County	1,004	4.49
Municipality of Monroeville, PA (borough) Allegheny County	1,297	4.42
Berea, OH (city) Cuyahoga County	838	4.41
North Whitehall, PA (township) Lehigh County	638	4.33
Willoughby, OH (city) Lake County	976	4.32
Back Mountain, PA (cdp) Luzerne County	1,135	4.25
Mountain Top, PA (cdp) Luzerne County	649	4.25
Shelton, CT (city) Fairfield County	1,588	4.17
Bethel Park, PA (borough) Allegheny County	1,398	4.17
Brentwood, PA (borough) Allegheny County	433	4.14
Highland, IN (town) Lake County	969	4.12
Bethlehem, PA (township) Northampton County	870	4.11
Munster, IN (town) Lake County	883	4.10
Whitehall, PA (borough) Allegheny County	586	4.06
Solon, OH (city) Cuyahoga County	878	4.03
Upper Macungie, PA (township) Lehigh County	557	4.01
Bethlehem, PA (city) Northampton County	2,830	3.97
Greensburg, PA (city) Westmoreland County	628	3.95
Bay Village, OH (city) Cuyahoga County	634	3.94
Amherst, OH (city) Lorain County	468	3.94
Hammond, IN (city) Lake County	3,259	3.92
Phoenixville, PA (borough) Chester County	567	3.82
Lorain, OH (city) Lorain County	2,618	3.81
Manville, NJ (borough) Somerset County	388	3.76
Norton, OH (city) Summit County	432	3.75
Mentor, OH (city) Lake County	1,851	3.68
Ross Township, PA (cdp) Allegheny County	1,199	3.68
Fernway, PA (cdp) Butler County	442	3.63
Binghamton, NY (city) Broome County	1,704	3.60
Girard, OH (city) Trumbull County	399	3.58
Moon, PA (township) Allegheny County	788	3.54
Lyndhurst, OH (city) Cuyahoga County	538	3.52
Endicott, NY (village) Broome County	457	3.51
Cranberry, PA (township) Butler County	814	3.44
Crown Point, IN (city) Lake County	668	3.41
Warren, OH (city) Trumbull County	1,594	3.40
Pottsville, PA (city) Schuylkill County	528	3.40
Medina, OH (city) Medina County	845	3.37
Monroe, CT (town) Fairfield County	646	3.36
Merrillville, IN (town) Lake County	1,025	3.34
Trumbull, CT (cdp) Fairfield County	1,121	3.27
Aurora, OH (city) Portage County	441	3.25
Dunmore, PA (borough) Lackawanna County	443	3.16
Penn Hills, PA (cdp) Allegheny County	1,473	3.15
Schererville, IN (town) Lake County	775	3.12
Weirton, WV (city) Hancock County	629	3.09
Carteret, NJ (borough) Middlesex County	635	3.07
Butler, PA (township) Butler County	526	3.05
South Whitehall, PA (township) Lehigh County	544	3.02
Franklin Park, PA (borough) Allegheny County	342	3.01
Milford, CT (special city) New Haven County	1,520	3.00
Indiana, PA (borough) Indiana County	445	2.99
Torrington, CT (city) Litchfield County	1,041	2.96
North Fayette, PA (township) Allegheny County	362	2.96
Barberton, OH (city) Summit County	817	2.92
Milford, CT (town) New Haven County	1,520	2.91
Griffith, IN (town) Lake County	499	2.88
South Fayette, PA (township) Allegheny County	354	2.88
McCandless Township, PA (cdp) Allegheny County	824	2.84
Peters, PA (township) Washington County	497	2.83
Stow, OH (city) Summit County	903	2.81
Chesterton, IN (town) Porter County	282	2.70
Hobart, IN (city) Lake County	680	2.68
Scott Township, PA (cdp) Allegheny County	461	2.67
Cambridge, OH (city) Guernsey County	305	2.64
Mayfield Heights, OH (city) Cuyahoga County	507	2.62
Streetsboro, OH (city) Portage County	320	2.60
Coal, PA (township) Northumberland County	276	2.60
Readington, NJ (township) Hunterdon County	401	2.54
Owego, NY (town) Tioga County	516	2.53
Vermilion, OH (city) Lorain County	272	2.50

Notes: (cdp) census designated place; Refer to the Explanation of Data in the front of the book for more detailed information.

Slovene

Top 150 Places Sorted by Number

(Based on all places, regardless of population)

Place	Number	%
Euclid, OH (city) Cuyahoga County	4,640	8.80
Cleveland, OH (city) Cuyahoga County	3,828	0.80
Mentor, OH (city) Lake County	3,652	7.26
Joliet, IL (city) Will County	1,770	1.67
Eastlake, OH (city) Lake County	1,558	7.72
Chicago, IL (city) Cook County	1,555	0.05
Parma, OH (city) Cuyahoga County	1,477	1.72
Willowick, OH (city) Lake County	1,387	9.63
Willoughby, OH (city) Lake County	1,346	5.96
Wickliffe, OH (city) Lake County	1,336	9.91
Pueblo, CO (city) Pueblo County	1,298	1.27
New York, NY (city) New York City	1,162	0.01
Milwaukee, WI (city) Milwaukee County	1,145	0.19
Willoughby Hills, OH (city) Lake County	1,060	12.23
Strongsville, OH (city) Cuyahoga County	979	2.23
West Allis, WI (city) Milwaukee County	786	1.28
Indianapolis, IN (special city) Marion County	734	0.09
Columbus, OH (city) Franklin County	733	0.10
Garfield Heights, OH (city) Cuyahoga County	720	2.35
Los Angeles, CA (city) Los Angeles County	699	0.02
Sheboygan, WI (city) Sheboygan County	697	1.37
Lakewood, OH (city) Cuyahoga County	662	1.17
North Olmsted, OH (city) Cuyahoga County	657	1.93
Brunswick, OH (city) Medina County	644	1.93
Pittsburgh, PA (city) Allegheny County	624	0.19
Richmond Heights, OH (city) Cuyahoga County	613	5.60
Highland Heights, OH (city) Cuyahoga County	591	7.31
Lyndhurst, OH (city) Cuyahoga County	583	3.82
San Francisco, CA (city) San Francisco County	559	0.07
Duluth, MN (city) Saint Louis County	558	0.64
North Royalton, OH (city) Cuyahoga County	555	1.94
Hibbing, MN (city) Saint Louis County	544	3.19
Lorain, OH (city) Lorain County	544	0.79
Akron, OH (city) Summit County	535	0.25
Broadview Heights, OH (city) Cuyahoga County	515	3.23
Mayfield Heights, OH (city) Cuyahoga County	507	2.62
Westlake, OH (city) Cuyahoga County	498	1.56
San Diego, CA (city) San Diego County	478	0.04
Denver, CO (city) Denver County	474	0.09
Chisholm, MN (city) Saint Louis County	467	9.42
Ely, MN (city) Saint Louis County	464	12.46
South Euclid, OH (city) Cuyahoga County	459	1.95
Minneapolis, MN (city) Hennepin County	447	0.12
Waukegan, IL (city) Lake County	444	0.50
Kirtland, OH (city) Lake County	440	6.59
Phoenix, AZ (city) Maricopa County	425	0.03
Maple Heights, OH (city) Cuyahoga County	424	1.62
Twinsburg, OH (city) Summit County	407	2.41
Mentor-on-the-Lake, OH (city) Lake County	403	4.96
Solon, OH (city) Cuyahoga County	395	1.81
Barberton, OH (city) Summit County	393	1.40
Hempfield, PA (township) Westmoreland County	387	0.95
North Madison, OH (cdp) Lake County	381	4.46
Eveleth, MN (city) Saint Louis County	366	9.47
Virginia, MN (city) Saint Louis County	366	4.00
North Strabane, PA (township) Washington County	359	3.57
Naperville, IL (city) Du Page County	351	0.27
Crest Hill, IL (city) Will County	349	2.68
Austin, TX (city) Travis County	348	0.05
Penn, PA (township) Westmoreland County	338	1.72
Painesville, OH (city) Lake County	336	1.92
Fairview Park, OH (city) Cuyahoga County	334	1.90
Seattle, WA (city) King County	329	0.06
Saint Paul, MN (city) Ramsey County	324	0.11
Shorewood, IL (village) Will County	323	4.15
Stow, OH (city) Summit County	320	1.00
Parma Heights, OH (city) Cuyahoga County	306	1.41
Rock Springs, WY (city) Sweetwater County	304	1.60
Middleburg Heights, OH (city) Cuyahoga County	300	1.93
Hudson, OH (city) Summit County	299	1.34
Elyria, OH (city) Lorain County	299	0.54
Houston, TX (city) Harris County	297	0.02
Bedford, OH (city) Cuyahoga County	289	2.03
Brecksville, OH (city) Cuyahoga County	283	2.12
Aurora, OH (city) Portage County	278	2.05
Colorado Springs, CO (city) El Paso County	276	0.08
Shaler Township, PA (cdp) Allegheny County	275	0.92
Gilbert, MN (city) Saint Louis County	274	14.83
Canonsburg, PA (borough) Washington County	269	3.13
Rocky River, OH (city) Cuyahoga County	268	1.29
Franklin, WI (city) Milwaukee County	266	0.90
Bethlehem, PA (city) Northampton County	264	0.37
Cecil, PA (township) Washington County	263	2.71
Brook Park, OH (city) Cuyahoga County	262	1.23
La Salle, IL (city) La Salle County	258	2.63
North Huntingdon, PA (township) Westmoreland County	256	0.88
Cleveland Heights, OH (city) Cuyahoga County	247	0.49
Kansas City, KS (city) Wyandotte County	247	0.17
Chartiers, PA (township) Washington County	242	3.38
Greenfield, WI (city) Milwaukee County	242	0.68
Seven Hills, OH (city) Cuyahoga County	240	1.99
Portland, OR (city) Multnomah County	240	0.05
Macedonia, OH (city) Summit County	239	2.59
Toledo, OH (city) Lucas County	238	0.08
Independence, OH (city) Cuyahoga County	236	3.28
Charlotte, NC (city) Mecklenburg County	236	0.04
Municipality of Murrysville, PA (borough) Westmoreland County	233	1.24
Olmsted Falls, OH (city) Cuyahoga County	231	2.95
Medina, OH (city) Medina County	228	0.91
Avon Lake, OH (city) Lorain County	226	1.25
Berea, OH (city) Cuyahoga County	223	1.17
Scottsdale, AZ (city) Maricopa County	221	0.11
White, MN (township) Saint Louis County	217	6.22
Tucson, AZ (city) Pima County	215	0.04
Mesa, AZ (city) Maricopa County	214	0.05
North Ridgeville, OH (city) Lorain County	213	0.95
South Huntingdon, PA (township) Westmoreland County	211	3.42
Aurora, CO (city) Arapahoe County	209	0.08
San Jose, CA (city) Santa Clara County	209	0.02
Brooklyn, OH (city) Cuyahoga County	208	1.80
Downers Grove, IL (village) Du Page County	206	0.42
Lakewood, CO (city) Jefferson County	206	0.14
Plum, PA (borough) Allegheny County	204	0.76
San Antonio, TX (city) Bexar County	204	0.02
Wauwatosa, WI (city) Milwaukee County	201	0.43
South Fayette, PA (township) Allegheny County	199	1.62
Albuquerque, NM (city) Bernalillo County	198	0.04
Las Vegas, NV (city) Clark County	193	0.04
Sewickley, PA (township) Westmoreland County	192	3.08
New Berlin, WI (city) Waukesha County	191	0.50
Lockport, IL (city) Will County	190	1.28
Fayal, MN (township) Saint Louis County	187	9.82
Washington, DC (city) District of Columbia	186	0.03
Kent, OH (city) Portage County	184	0.66
Penn Hills, PA (cdp) Allegheny County	183	0.39
Forest City, PA (borough) Susquehanna County	182	9.81
Mountain Iron, MN (city) Saint Louis County	182	6.02
Avon, OH (city) Lorain County	182	1.59
Eagan, MN (city) Dakota County	178	0.28
Channahon, IL (village) Will County	177	2.42
Bay Village, OH (city) Cuyahoga County	177	1.10
Waukesha, WI (city) Waukesha County	177	0.27
Hempstead, NY (town) Nassau County	176	0.02
Fairport Harbor, OH (village) Lake County	175	5.50
Peru, IL (city) La Salle County	174	1.77
Streetsboro, OH (city) Portage County	174	1.41
Fairfield, CT (town) Fairfield County	173	0.30
Rostraver, PA (township) Westmoreland County	172	1.48
Aurora, IL (city) Kane County	171	0.12
Cuyahoga Falls, OH (city) Summit County	169	0.34
Aurora, MN (city) Saint Louis County	168	9.08
Norton, OH (city) Summit County	168	1.46
Johnstown, PA (city) Cambria County	167	0.70
Saint Cloud, MN (city) Stearns County	164	0.28
Jacksonville, FL (special city) Duval County	163	0.02
McGovern, PA (cdp) Washington County	160	6.34
Amherst, OH (city) Lorain County	159	1.34
Bethel Park, PA (borough) Allegheny County	159	0.47
Wadsworth, OH (city) Medina County	157	0.85
Orland Park, IL (village) Cook County	157	0.31

Notes: (cdp) census designated place; Refer to the Explanation of Data in the front of the book for more detailed information.

Slovene

Top 150 Places Sorted by Percent

(Based on all places, regardless of population)

Place	Number	%
Point of Rocks, WY (cdp) Sweetwater County	10	50.00
Hendren, WI (town) Clark County	89	17.32
Gilbert, MN (city) Saint Louis County	274	14.83
McKinley, MN (city) Saint Louis County	12	14.63
Herminie, PA (cdp) Westmoreland County	94	13.11
Bassett, MN (township) Saint Louis County	6	12.77
Ely, MN (city) Saint Louis County	464	12.46
Willoughby Hills, OH (city) Lake County	1,060	12.23
Harrietta, MI (village) Wexford County	17	11.81
Leonidas, MN (city) Saint Louis County	4	11.43
Vandling, PA (borough) Lackawanna County	83	11.32
Wickliffe, OH (city) Lake County	1,336	9.91
Fayal, MN (township) Saint Louis County	187	9.82
Forest City, PA (borough) Susquehanna County	182	9.81
Great Scott, MN (township) Saint Louis County	59	9.74
Willowick, OH (city) Lake County	1,387	9.63
Eveleth, MN (city) Saint Louis County	366	9.47
Chisholm, MN (city) Saint Louis County	467	9.42
Aurora, MN (city) Saint Louis County	168	9.08
Saint Stephen, MN (city) Stearns County	77	9.02
Euclid, OH (city) Cuyahoga County	4,640	8.80
Iron Junction, MN (city) Saint Louis County	8	8.70
Breitung, MN (township) Saint Louis County	59	8.58
Morse, MN (township) Saint Louis County	104	8.52
Timberlake, OH (village) Lake County	65	8.46
Winton, MN (city) Saint Louis County	16	8.33
Kirtland Hills, OH (village) Lake County	49	8.18
French, MN (township) Saint Louis County	26	8.02
Balkan, MN (township) Saint Louis County	63	7.83
Pershing, WI (town) Taylor County	12	7.74
Eastlake, OH (city) Lake County	1,558	7.72
Rocky Point, MT (cdp) Lake County	10	7.41
Highland Heights, OH (city) Cuyahoga County	591	7.31
Mentor, OH (city) Lake County	3,652	7.26
Clinton, PA (township) Wayne County	136	7.17
Biwabik, MN (city) Saint Louis County	68	7.17
Tower, MN (city) Saint Louis County	33	7.04
Fall Lake, MN (township) Lake County	39	7.03
Moro, ME (plantation) Aroostook County	4	6.90
Waite Hill, OH (village) Lake County	30	6.65
Brookside, CO (town) Fremont County	15	6.64
Lakeline, OH (village) Lake County	11	6.63
Kirtland, OH (city) Lake County	440	6.59
Eden, WY (cdp) Sweetwater County	33	6.52
Roseland, KS (city) Cherokee County	5	6.49
McGovern, PA (cdp) Washington County	160	6.34
White, MN (township) Saint Louis County	217	6.22
Mountain Iron, MN (city) Saint Louis County	182	6.02
Willoughby, OH (city) Lake County	1,346	5.96
Eaton, WI (town) Clark County	43	5.93
Richmond Heights, OH (city) Cuyahoga County	613	5.60
Fairport Harbor, OH (village) Lake County	175	5.50
Valley View, OH (village) Cuyahoga County	114	5.24
Mentor-on-the-Lake, OH (city) Lake County	403	4.96
McKinley, WI (town) Taylor County	22	4.94
Leadville, CO (city) Lake County	140	4.92
Decatur, NY (town) Otsego County	19	4.90
Foster, WI (town) Clark County	4	4.82
Bratenahl, OH (village) Cuyahoga County	64	4.79
Mead, WI (town) Clark County	14	4.75
Sugar Bush Knolls, OH (village) Portage County	10	4.74
Greenwood, WI (city) Clark County	48	4.61
Chesterland, OH (cdp) Geauga County	126	4.60
Gates Mills, OH (village) Cuyahoga County	112	4.58
Cherry, MN (township) Saint Louis County	42	4.58
Buhl, MN (city) Saint Louis County	45	4.54
North Madison, OH (cdp) Lake County	381	4.46
Sandy, MN (township) Saint Louis County	18	4.37
Wayne, IL (village) Kane County	90	4.29
Perry, OH (village) Lake County	51	4.27
Warner, WI (town) Clark County	26	4.24
Boon, MI (township) Wexford County	28	4.19
Shorewood, IL (village) Will County	323	4.15
Babbitt, MN (city) Saint Louis County	68	4.07
Virginia, MN (city) Saint Louis County	366	4.00

Place	Number	%
Rockdale, IL (village) Will County	75	3.93
Reddick, IL (village) Kankakee County	10	3.91
Vermilion Lake, MN (township) Saint Louis County	13	3.86
Lyndhurst, OH (city) Cuyahoga County	583	3.82
Keewatin, MN (city) Itasca County	44	3.78
Conemaugh, PA (township) Cambria County	80	3.73
Sturgeon, MN (township) Saint Louis County	5	3.73
Heritage Hills, CO (cdp) Douglas County	24	3.72
Walton Hills, OH (village) Cuyahoga County	88	3.68
Lorain, PA (borough) Cambria County	29	3.68
Limestone, MI (township) Alger County	15	3.67
Embarrass, MN (township) Saint Louis County	25	3.64
Summit, PA (township) Potter County	4	3.64
Biwabik, MN (township) Saint Louis County	33	3.61
Jerome, PA (cdp) Somerset County	41	3.60
North Strabane, PA (township) Washington County	359	3.57
Persia, NY (town) Cattaraugus County	89	3.52
Burgettstown, PA (borough) Washington County	55	3.49
Stonycreek, PA (township) Cambria County	110	3.48
Oglesby, IL (city) La Salle County	124	3.44
South Huntingdon, PA (township) Westmoreland County	211	3.42
Kinney, MN (city) Saint Louis County	6	3.41
Chartiers, PA (township) Washington County	242	3.38
Alaska, MN (township) Beltrami County	7	3.33
Union Dale, PA (borough) Susquehanna County	13	3.30
Independence, OH (city) Cuyahoga County	236	3.28
Madison, OH (village) Lake County	95	3.25
Bessemer, PA (borough) Lawrence County	38	3.25
Broadview Heights, OH (city) Cuyahoga County	515	3.23
Worcester, NY (town) Otsego County	71	3.22
North Perry, OH (village) Lake County	27	3.22
Hibbing, MN (city) Saint Louis County	544	3.19
Canonsburg, PA (borough) Washington County	269	3.13
Brockway, MN (township) Stearns County	80	3.11
Sewickley, PA (township) Westmoreland County	192	3.08
Mayfield, OH (village) Cuyahoga County	107	3.07
Gowanda, NY (village) Cattaraugus County	85	3.06
De Borgia, MT (cdp) Mineral County	2	3.03
Greenwood, MN (township) Saint Louis County	27	2.99
Franklin, PA (borough) Cambria County	13	2.96
Olmsted Falls, OH (city) Cuyahoga County	231	2.95
Ehrenfeld, PA (borough) Cambria County	7	2.95
Arma, KS (city) Crawford County	45	2.94
Wuori, MN (township) Saint Louis County	15	2.92
Clinton, MN (township) Saint Louis County	30	2.89
Little Falls, NY (town) Herkimer County	44	2.86
Indian Village, IN (town) Saint Joseph County	4	2.86
West Branch, MI (township) Dickinson County	2	2.86
Toivola, MN (township) Saint Louis County	5	2.82
Kugler, MN (township) Saint Louis County	5	2.79
Highland, PA (township) Elk County	15	2.75
Nelchina, AK (cdp) Valdez-Cordova Census Area	2	2.74
Millston, WI (town) Jackson County	4	2.72
Cecil, PA (township) Washington County	263	2.71
East Taylor, PA (township) Cambria County	74	2.71
Crest Hill, IL (city) Will County	349	2.68
Cross Creek, PA (township) Washington County	45	2.67
Sherman, WI (town) Clark County	22	2.67
La Salle, IL (city) La Salle County	258	2.63
Nashwauk, MN (city) Itasca County	24	2.63
Pilsen, WI (town) Bayfield County	5	2.63
Mayfield Heights, OH (city) Cuyahoga County	507	2.62
Fern Forest, HI (cdp) Hawaii County	12	2.62
Reminderville, OH (village) Summit County	61	2.61
Bearville, MN (township) Itasca County	4	2.61
Macedonia, OH (city) Summit County	239	2.59
Wilson, WY (cdp) Teton County	34	2.59
Taylor, WI (village) Jackson County	13	2.59
South Russell, OH (village) Geauga County	102	2.54
Leadville North, CO (cdp) Lake County	49	2.52
Burton, OH (village) Geauga County	36	2.48
Beaverdale-Lloydell, PA (cdp) Cambria County	30	2.48
Bainbridge, OH (cdp) Geauga County	86	2.47
Arona, PA (borough) Westmoreland County	10	2.46
East Prospect, PA (borough) York County	19	2.44

Notes: (cdp) census designated place; Refer to the Explanation of Data in the front of the book for more detailed information.

Slovene

Top 150 Places Sorted by Percent

(Based on places with populations of 10,000 or more)

Place	Number	%
Wickliffe, OH (city) Lake County	1,336	9.91
Willowick, OH (city) Lake County	1,387	9.63
Euclid, OH (city) Cuyahoga County	4,640	8.80
Eastlake, OH (city) Lake County	1,558	7.72
Mentor, OH (city) Lake County	3,652	7.26
Willoughby, OH (city) Lake County	1,346	5.96
Richmond Heights, OH (city) Cuyahoga County	613	5.60
Lyndhurst, OH (city) Cuyahoga County	583	3.82
North Strabane, PA (township) Washington County	359	3.57
Broadview Heights, OH (city) Cuyahoga County	515	3.23
Hibbing, MN (city) Saint Louis County	544	3.19
Crest Hill, IL (city) Will County	349	2.68
Mayfield Heights, OH (city) Cuyahoga County	507	2.62
Twinsburg, OH (city) Summit County	407	2.41
Garfield Heights, OH (city) Cuyahoga County	720	2.35
Strongsville, OH (city) Cuyahoga County	979	2.23
Brecksville, OH (city) Cuyahoga County	283	2.12
Aurora, OH (city) Portage County	278	2.05
Bedford, OH (city) Cuyahoga County	289	2.03
Seven Hills, OH (city) Cuyahoga County	240	1.99
South Euclid, OH (city) Cuyahoga County	459	1.95
North Royalton, OH (city) Cuyahoga County	555	1.94
North Olmsted, OH (city) Cuyahoga County	657	1.93
Brunswick, OH (city) Medina County	644	1.93
Middleburg Heights, OH (city) Cuyahoga County	300	1.93
Painesville, OH (city) Lake County	336	1.92
Fairview Park, OH (city) Cuyahoga County	334	1.90
Solon, OH (city) Cuyahoga County	395	1.81
Brooklyn, OH (city) Cuyahoga County	208	1.80
Parma, OH (city) Cuyahoga County	1,477	1.72
Penn, PA (township) Westmoreland County	338	1.72
Joliet, IL (city) Will County	1,770	1.67
Maple Heights, OH (city) Cuyahoga County	424	1.62
South Fayette, PA (township) Allegheny County	199	1.62
Rock Springs, WY (city) Sweetwater County	304	1.60
Avon, OH (city) Lorain County	182	1.59
Westlake, OH (city) Cuyahoga County	498	1.56
Rostraver, PA (township) Westmoreland County	172	1.48
Norton, OH (city) Summit County	168	1.46
Parma Heights, OH (city) Cuyahoga County	306	1.41
Streetsboro, OH (city) Portage County	174	1.41
Barberton, OH (city) Summit County	393	1.40
Sheboygan, WI (city) Sheboygan County	697	1.37
Hudson, OH (city) Summit County	299	1.34
Amherst, OH (city) Lorain County	159	1.34
Rocky River, OH (city) Cuyahoga County	268	1.29
West Allis, WI (city) Milwaukee County	786	1.28
Lockport, IL (city) Will County	190	1.28
Pueblo, CO (city) Pueblo County	1,298	1.27
Avon Lake, OH (city) Lorain County	226	1.25
Municipality of Murrysville, PA (borough) Westmoreland County	233	1.24
Brook Park, OH (city) Cuyahoga County	262	1.23
Lakewood, OH (city) Cuyahoga County	662	1.17
Berea, OH (city) Cuyahoga County	223	1.17
Richland, PA (township) Cambria County	145	1.15
Girard, OH (city) Trumbull County	127	1.14
Robinson Township, PA (cdp) Allegheny County	139	1.13
North Fayette, PA (township) Allegheny County	138	1.13
Bay Village, OH (city) Cuyahoga County	177	1.10
Conneaut, OH (city) Ashtabula County	134	1.07
West Deer, PA (township) Allegheny County	121	1.05
Lindenhurst, IL (village) Lake County	131	1.04
Stow, OH (city) Summit County	320	1.00
Hempfield, PA (township) Westmoreland County	387	0.95
North Ridgeville, OH (city) Lorain County	213	0.95
University Heights, OH (city) Cuyahoga County	135	0.95
Shaler Township, PA (cdp) Allegheny County	275	0.92
Medina, OH (city) Medina County	228	0.91
Franklin, WI (city) Milwaukee County	266	0.90
North Huntingdon, PA (township) Westmoreland County	256	0.88
Wadsworth, OH (city) Medina County	157	0.85
South Park Township, PA (cdp) Allegheny County	122	0.85
Cleveland, OH (city) Cuyahoga County	3,828	0.80
Lorain, OH (city) Lorain County	544	0.79
Hermitage, PA (city) Mercer County	128	0.79

Place	Number	%
New Lenox, IL (village) Will County	137	0.78
Plum, PA (borough) Allegheny County	204	0.76
Pueblo West, CO (cdp) Pueblo County	127	0.75
Shorewood, WI (village) Milwaukee County	101	0.73
Lemont, IL (village) Cook County	94	0.71
Johnstown, PA (city) Cambria County	167	0.70
Greenfield, WI (city) Milwaukee County	242	0.68
Black Forest, CO (cdp) El Paso County	88	0.67
Kent, OH (city) Portage County	184	0.66
Vermilion, OH (city) Lorain County	72	0.66
Duluth, MN (city) Saint Louis County	558	0.64
Ashtabula, OH (city) Ashtabula County	133	0.64
Center, PA (township) Beaver County	72	0.63
Moon, PA (township) Allegheny County	135	0.61
Baldwin, PA (borough) Allegheny County	122	0.61
Greensburg, PA (city) Westmoreland County	97	0.61
Derry, PA (township) Westmoreland County	90	0.61
Cloquet, MN (city) Carlton County	68	0.61
Scott Township, PA (cdp) Allegheny County	103	0.60
Oconomowoc, WI (city) Waukesha County	71	0.58
Pleasant Prairie, WI (village) Kenosha County	91	0.57
Peters, PA (township) Washington County	96	0.55
Plainfield, IL (village) Will County	71	0.55
Sauk Rapids, MN (city) Benton County	56	0.55
Elyria, OH (city) Lorain County	299	0.54
Unity, PA (township) Westmoreland County	113	0.54
Hampton Township, PA (cdp) Allegheny County	90	0.51
Waukegan, IL (city) Lake County	444	0.50
New Berlin, WI (city) Waukesha County	191	0.50
Cleveland Heights, OH (city) Cuyahoga County	247	0.49
Affton, MO (cdp) Saint Louis County	103	0.49
Bethel Park, PA (borough) Allegheny County	159	0.47
Upper Saint Clair, PA (cdp) Allegheny County	95	0.47
Greendale, WI (village) Milwaukee County	67	0.47
Mendota Heights, MN (city) Dakota County	53	0.47
Indiana, PA (borough) Indiana County	69	0.46
Speedway, IN (town) Marion County	59	0.46
Libertyville, IL (village) Lake County	93	0.45
Grand Rapids, MN (township) Itasca County	53	0.45
Whitehall, PA (borough) Allegheny County	63	0.44
Wauwatosa, WI (city) Milwaukee County	201	0.43
Maumee, OH (city) Lucas County	66	0.43
New Kensington, PA (city) Westmoreland County	63	0.43
Jeannette, PA (city) Westmoreland County	46	0.43
Brentwood, PA (borough) Allegheny County	45	0.43
Port Washington, WI (city) Ozaukee County	45	0.43
Downers Grove, IL (village) Du Page County	206	0.42
Caledonia, WI (town) Racine County	100	0.42
Mokena, IL (village) Will County	61	0.42
Wooster, OH (city) Wayne County	103	0.41
Darien, IL (city) Du Page County	95	0.41
Canon City, CO (city) Fremont County	63	0.41
North Versailles, PA (cdp) Allegheny County	46	0.41
Lyons, IL (village) Cook County	42	0.41
Brownsburg, IN (town) Hendricks County	58	0.40
Winnetka, IL (village) Cook County	49	0.40
Enumclaw, WA (city) King County	45	0.40
Penn Hills, PA (cdp) Allegheny County	183	0.39
Lino Lakes, MN (city) Anoka County	65	0.39
Saint Marys, PA (city) Elk County	56	0.39
White, PA (township) Indiana County	55	0.39
Fernway, PA (cdp) Butler County	47	0.39
Brookfield, WI (city) Waukesha County	148	0.38
Swatara, PA (township) Dauphin County	85	0.38
Struthers, OH (city) Mahoning County	45	0.38
Bethlehem, PA (city) Northampton County	264	0.37
Ross Township, PA (cdp) Allegheny County	122	0.37
McCandless Township, PA (cdp) Allegheny County	106	0.37
Westchester, IL (village) Cook County	62	0.37
Sharon, PA (city) Mercer County	60	0.37
Paradise Valley, AZ (town) Maricopa County	50	0.37
La Grange Park, IL (village) Cook County	49	0.37
Westerville, OH (city) Franklin County	126	0.36
Municipality of Monroeville, PA (borough) Allegheny County	105	0.36
Champlin, MN (city) Hennepin County	80	0.36

Notes: (cdp) census designated place; Refer to the Explanation of Data in the front of the book for more detailed information.

Soviet Union

Top 138 Places Sorted by Number

(Based on all places, regardless of population)

Place	Number	%
New York, NY (city) New York City	550	0.01
Chicago, IL (city) Cook County	60	0.00
Brookline, MA (cdp) Norfolk County	59	0.10
San Francisco, CA (city) San Francisco County	54	0.01
Hempstead, NY (town) Nassau County	51	0.01
West Nyack, NY (cdp) Rockland County	45	1.39
Clarkstown, NY (town) Rockland County	45	0.05
Philadelphia, PA (city) Philadelphia County	43	0.00
Kachina Village, AZ (cdp) Coconino County	37	1.33
Boston, MA (city) Suffolk County	37	0.01
Northbrook, IL (village) Cook County	34	0.10
Providence, RI (city) Providence County	34	0.02
Oceanside, NY (cdp) Nassau County	32	0.10
Rockville, MD (city) Montgomery County	31	0.07
West Hollywood, CA (city) Los Angeles County	29	0.08
Swampscott, MA (cdp) Essex County	28	0.19
Highland Park, IL (city) Lake County	28	0.09
Nether Providence Township, PA (cdp) Delaware County	27	0.20
Southfield, MI (city) Oakland County	27	0.03
Belmont, CA (city) San Mateo County	26	0.10
Lynnwood, WA (city) Snohomish County	25	0.07
Los Angeles, CA (city) Los Angeles County	25	0.00
Tenafly, NJ (borough) Bergen County	21	0.15
New Milford, NJ (borough) Bergen County	21	0.13
Valley Stream, NY (village) Nassau County	19	0.05
Beverly Hills, CA (city) Los Angeles County	16	0.05
New Haven, CT (city) New Haven County	16	0.01
Milwaukee, WI (city) Milwaukee County	16	0.00
Boca Del Mar, FL (cdp) Palm Beach County	15	0.07
Morton Grove, IL (village) Cook County	15	0.07
Minnetonka, MN (city) Hennepin County	15	0.03
Roseville, CA (city) Placer County	15	0.02
Somerville, MA (city) Middlesex County	15	0.02
Corona, CA (city) Riverside County	15	0.01
Garland, TX (city) Dallas County	15	0.01
Spokane, WA (city) Spokane County	14	0.01
Silverton, OR (city) Marion County	13	0.17
Pikesville, MD (cdp) Baltimore County	13	0.04
North Bethesda, MD (cdp) Montgomery County	13	0.03
Royal Oak charter, MI (township) Oakland County	12	0.22
Framingham, MA (cdp) Middlesex County	12	0.02
Santa Clara, CA (city) Santa Clara County	12	0.01
Fairview, NJ (borough) Bergen County	11	0.08
Millbrae, CA (city) San Mateo County	11	0.05
Madison, WI (city) Dane County	11	0.01
Rancho Cucamonga, CA (city) San Bernardino County	11	0.01
Washington, DC (city) District of Columbia	11	0.00
Cocoa Beach, FL (city) Brevard County	10	0.08
Foothill Farms, CA (cdp) Sacramento County	10	0.06
Ridgewood, NJ (village) Bergen County	10	0.04
Burke, VA (cdp) Fairfax County	10	0.02
Marietta, GA (city) Cobb County	10	0.02
Lakewood, CO (city) Jefferson County	10	0.01
Kansas City, MO (city) Jackson County	10	0.00
Mesa, AZ (city) Maricopa County	10	0.00
Newark, NJ (city) Essex County	10	0.00
Linn, WI (town) Walworth County	9	0.41
Chester, NY (village) Orange County	9	0.25
Beachwood, OH (city) Cuyahoga County	9	0.07
Chester, NY (town) Orange County	9	0.07
Phillipsburg, NJ (town) Warren County	9	0.06
Novi, MI (city) Oakland County	9	0.02
Parsippany-Troy Hills, NJ (township) Morris County	9	0.02
Naperville, IL (city) Du Page County	9	0.01
Norwalk, CT (city) Fairfield County	9	0.01
Santa Clarita, CA (city) Los Angeles County	9	0.01
Tucson, AZ (city) Pima County	9	0.00
Rossmoor, MD (cdp) Montgomery County	8	0.11
Malibu, CA (city) Los Angeles County	8	0.06
Ronkonkoma, NY (cdp) Suffolk County	8	0.04
Apple Valley, MN (city) Dakota County	8	0.02
Cortlandt, NY (town) Westchester County	8	0.02
San Dimas, CA (city) Los Angeles County	8	0.02
Smyrna, GA (city) Cobb County	8	0.02
Cambridge, MA (city) Middlesex County	8	0.01
Passaic, NJ (city) Passaic County	8	0.01
Colorado Springs, CO (city) El Paso County	8	0.00
Islip, NY (town) Suffolk County	8	0.00
Glendale, CO (city) Arapahoe County	7	0.15
Boone, NC (town) Watauga County	7	0.05
Metuchen, NJ (borough) Middlesex County	7	0.05
Aventura, FL (city) Miami-Dade County	7	0.03
Reisterstown, MD (cdp) Baltimore County	7	0.03
Saint Andrews, SC (cdp) Richland County	7	0.03
Tustin Foothills, CA (cdp) Orange County	7	0.03
Dover, DE (city) Kent County	7	0.02
Fair Lawn, NJ (borough) Bergen County	7	0.02
Lake Magdalene, FL (cdp) Hillsborough County	7	0.02
North Highlands, CA (cdp) Sacramento County	7	0.02
Westfield, MA (city) Hampden County	7	0.02
Buena Park, CA (city) Orange County	7	0.01
Dearborn Heights, MI (city) Wayne County	7	0.01
Hartford, CT (city) Hartford County	7	0.01
Lowell, MA (city) Middlesex County	7	0.01
Durham, NC (city) Durham County	7	0.00
Vancouver, WA (city) Clark County	7	0.00
La Paz, IN (town) Marshall County	6	1.19
Brandywine, MD (cdp) Prince George's County	6	0.41
Summit, PA (township) Erie County	6	0.11
Washington Township, NJ (cdp) Bergen County	6	0.07
Arnold, MD (cdp) Anne Arundel County	6	0.03
Peekskill, NY (city) Westchester County	6	0.03
Montclair, NJ (cdp) Essex County	6	0.02
Plainview, NY (cdp) Nassau County	6	0.02
Amherst, NY (town) Erie County	6	0.01
Newton, MA (city) Middlesex County	6	0.01
Arlington, VA (cdp) Arlington County	6	0.00
Columbus, OH (city) Franklin County	6	0.00
Indianapolis, IN (special city) Marion County	6	0.00
Oyster Bay, NY (town) Nassau County	6	0.00
Benton, MI (township) Eaton County	5	0.18
Great Neck Estates, NY (village) Nassau County	5	0.18
Lansing, NY (village) Tompkins County	5	0.17
Kaser, NY (village) Rockland County	5	0.15
Lansing, NY (town) Tompkins County	5	0.05
Saint Pete Beach, FL (city) Pinellas County	5	0.05
Lincolnwood, IL (village) Cook County	5	0.04
Myrtle Grove, FL (cdp) Escambia County	5	0.03
Rutherford, NJ (borough) Bergen County	5	0.03
La Mesa, CA (city) San Diego County	5	0.01
Santa Fe, NM (city) Santa Fe County	5	0.01
Jersey City, NJ (city) Hudson County	5	0.00
North Hempstead, NY (town) Nassau County	5	0.00
Ramapo, NY (town) Rockland County	5	0.00
San Jose, CA (city) Santa Clara County	5	0.00
Galatia, IL (village) Saline County	4	0.38
Weston, WI (town) Clark County	3	0.51
Ogden, KS (city) Riley County	3	0.17
Kailua, HI (cdp) Honolulu County	3	0.01
Riverwood, KY (city) Jefferson County	2	0.44
Garwin, IA (city) Tama County	2	0.34
Upton, KY (city) Hardin County	2	0.31
Newark, MI (township) Gratiot County	2	0.18
Orwell, PA (township) Bradford County	2	0.18
Lewisboro, NY (town) Westchester County	2	0.02
Millbrook, NY (village) Dutchess County	1	0.07
Ely, MN (city) Saint Louis County	1	0.03
Washington, NY (town) Dutchess County	1	0.02

Notes: (cdp) census designated place; Refer to the Explanation of Data in the front of the book for more detailed information.

Soviet Union

Top 138 Places Sorted by Percent

(Based on all places, regardless of population)

Place	Number	%
West Nyack, NY (cdp) Rockland County	45	1.39
Kachina Village, AZ (cdp) Coconino County	37	1.33
La Paz, IN (town) Marshall County	6	1.19
Weston, WI (town) Clark County	3	0.51
Riverwood, KY (city) Jefferson County	2	0.44
Linn, WI (town) Walworth County	9	0.41
Brandywine, MD (cdp) Prince George's County	6	0.41
Galatia, IL (village) Saline County	4	0.38
Garwin, IA (city) Tama County	2	0.34
Upton, KY (city) Hardin County	2	0.31
Chester, NY (village) Orange County	9	0.25
Royal Oak charter, MI (township) Oakland County	12	0.22
Nether Providence Township, PA (cdp) Delaware County	27	0.20
Swampscott, MA (cdp) Essex County	28	0.19
Benton, MI (township) Eaton County	5	0.18
Great Neck Estates, NY (village) Nassau County	5	0.18
Newark, MI (township) Gratiot County	2	0.18
Orwell, PA (township) Bradford County	2	0.18
Silverton, OR (city) Marion County	13	0.17
Lansing, NY (village) Tompkins County	5	0.17
Ogden, KS (city) Riley County	3	0.17
Tenafly, NJ (borough) Bergen County	21	0.15
Glendale, CO (city) Arapahoe County	7	0.15
Kaser, NY (village) Rockland County	5	0.15
New Milford, NJ (borough) Bergen County	21	0.13
Rossmoor, MD (cdp) Montgomery County	8	0.11
Summit, PA (township) Erie County	6	0.11
Brookline, MA (cdp) Norfolk County	59	0.10
Northbrook, IL (village) Cook County	34	0.10
Oceanside, NY (cdp) Nassau County	32	0.10
Belmont, CA (city) San Mateo County	26	0.10
Highland Park, IL (city) Lake County	28	0.09
West Hollywood, CA (city) Los Angeles County	29	0.08
Fairview, NJ (borough) Bergen County	11	0.08
Cocoa Beach, FL (city) Brevard County	10	0.08
Rockville, MD (city) Montgomery County	31	0.07
Lynnwood, WA (city) Snohomish County	25	0.07
Boca Del Mar, FL (cdp) Palm Beach County	15	0.07
Morton Grove, IL (village) Cook County	15	0.07
Beachwood, OH (city) Cuyahoga County	9	0.07
Chester, NY (town) Orange County	9	0.07
Washington Township, NJ (cdp) Bergen County	9	0.07
Millbrook, NY (village) Dutchess County	1	0.07
Foothill Farms, CA (cdp) Sacramento County	10	0.06
Phillipsburg, NJ (town) Warren County	9	0.06
Malibu, CA (city) Los Angeles County	8	0.06
Clarkstown, NY (town) Rockland County	45	0.05
Valley Stream, NY (village) Nassau County	19	0.05
Beverly Hills, CA (city) Los Angeles County	16	0.05
Millbrae, CA (city) San Mateo County	11	0.05
Boone, NC (town) Watauga County	7	0.05
Metuchen, NJ (borough) Middlesex County	7	0.05
Lansing, NY (town) Tompkins County	5	0.05
Saint Pete Beach, FL (city) Pinellas County	5	0.05
Pikesville, MD (cdp) Baltimore County	13	0.04
Ridgewood, NJ (village) Bergen County	10	0.04
Ronkonkoma, NY (cdp) Suffolk County	8	0.04
Lincolnwood, IL (village) Cook County	5	0.04
Southfield, MI (city) Oakland County	27	0.03
Minnetonka, MN (city) Hennepin County	15	0.03
North Bethesda, MD (cdp) Montgomery County	13	0.03
Aventura, FL (city) Miami-Dade County	7	0.03
Reisterstown, MD (cdp) Baltimore County	7	0.03
Saint Andrews, SC (cdp) Richland County	7	0.03
Tustin Foothills, CA (cdp) Orange County	7	0.03
Arnold, MD (cdp) Anne Arundel County	6	0.03
Peekskill, NY (city) Westchester County	6	0.03
Myrtle Grove, FL (cdp) Escambia County	5	0.03
Rutherford, NJ (borough) Bergen County	5	0.03
Ely, MN (city) Saint Louis County	1	0.03
Providence, RI (city) Providence County	34	0.02
Roseville, CA (city) Placer County	15	0.02
Somerville, MA (city) Middlesex County	15	0.02
Framingham, MA (cdp) Middlesex County	12	0.02
Burke, VA (cdp) Fairfax County	10	0.02

Place	Number	%
Marietta, GA (city) Cobb County	10	0.02
Novi, MI (city) Oakland County	9	0.02
Parsippany-Troy Hills, NJ (township) Morris County	9	0.02
Apple Valley, MN (city) Dakota County	8	0.02
Cortlandt, NY (town) Westchester County	8	0.02
San Dimas, CA (city) Los Angeles County	8	0.02
Smyrna, GA (city) Cobb County	8	0.02
Dover, DE (city) Kent County	7	0.02
Fair Lawn, NJ (borough) Bergen County	7	0.02
Lake Magdalene, FL (cdp) Hillsborough County	7	0.02
North Highlands, CA (cdp) Sacramento County	7	0.02
Westfield, MA (city) Hampden County	7	0.02
Montclair, NJ (cdp) Essex County	6	0.02
Plainview, NY (cdp) Nassau County	6	0.02
Lewisboro, NY (town) Westchester County	2	0.02
Washington, NY (town) Dutchess County	1	0.02
New York, NY (city) New York City	550	0.01
San Francisco, CA (city) San Francisco County	54	0.01
Hempstead, NY (town) Nassau County	51	0.01
Boston, MA (city) Suffolk County	37	0.01
New Haven, CT (city) New Haven County	16	0.01
Corona, CA (city) Riverside County	15	0.01
Garland, TX (city) Dallas County	15	0.01
Spokane, WA (city) Spokane County	14	0.01
Santa Clara, CA (city) Santa Clara County	12	0.01
Madison, WI (city) Dane County	11	0.01
Rancho Cucamonga, CA (city) San Bernardino County	11	0.01
Lakewood, CO (city) Jefferson County	10	0.01
Naperville, IL (city) Du Page County	9	0.01
Norwalk, CT (city) Fairfield County	9	0.01
Santa Clarita, CA (city) Los Angeles County	9	0.01
Cambridge, MA (city) Middlesex County	8	0.01
Passaic, NJ (city) Passaic County	8	0.01
Buena Park, CA (city) Orange County	7	0.01
Dearborn Heights, MI (city) Wayne County	7	0.01
Hartford, CT (city) Hartford County	7	0.01
Lowell, MA (city) Middlesex County	7	0.01
Amherst, NY (town) Erie County	6	0.01
Newton, MA (city) Middlesex County	6	0.01
La Mesa, CA (city) San Diego County	5	0.01
Santa Fe, NM (city) Santa Fe County	5	0.01
Kailua, HI (cdp) Honolulu County	3	0.01
Chicago, IL (city) Cook County	60	0.00
Philadelphia, PA (city) Philadelphia County	43	0.00
Los Angeles, CA (city) Los Angeles County	25	0.00
Milwaukee, WI (city) Milwaukee County	16	0.00
Washington, DC (city) District of Columbia	11	0.00
Kansas City, MO (city) Jackson County	10	0.00
Mesa, AZ (city) Maricopa County	10	0.00
Newark, NJ (city) Essex County	10	0.00
Tucson, AZ (city) Pima County	9	0.00
Colorado Springs, CO (city) El Paso County	8	0.00
Islip, NY (town) Suffolk County	8	0.00
Durham, NC (city) Durham County	7	0.00
Vancouver, WA (city) Clark County	7	0.00
Arlington, VA (cdp) Arlington County	6	0.00
Columbus, OH (city) Franklin County	6	0.00
Indianapolis, IN (special city) Marion County	6	0.00
Oyster Bay, NY (town) Nassau County	6	0.00
Jersey City, NJ (city) Hudson County	5	0.00
North Hempstead, NY (town) Nassau County	5	0.00
Ramapo, NY (town) Rockland County	5	0.00
San Jose, CA (city) Santa Clara County	5	0.00

Notes: (cdp) census designated place; Refer to the Explanation of Data in the front of the book for more detailed information.

Soviet Union

Top 110 Places Sorted by Percent

(Based on places with populations of 10,000 or more)

Place	Number	%
Nether Providence Township, PA (cdp) Delaware County	27	0.20
Swampscott, MA (cdp) Essex County	28	0.19
Tenafly, NJ (borough) Bergen County	21	0.15
New Milford, NJ (borough) Bergen County	21	0.13
Brookline, MA (cdp) Norfolk County	59	0.10
Northbrook, IL (village) Cook County	34	0.10
Oceanside, NY (cdp) Nassau County	32	0.10
Belmont, CA (city) San Mateo County	26	0.10
Highland Park, IL (city) Lake County	28	0.09
West Hollywood, CA (city) Los Angeles County	29	0.08
Fairview, NJ (borough) Bergen County	11	0.08
Cocoa Beach, FL (city) Brevard County	10	0.08
Rockville, MD (city) Montgomery County	31	0.07
Lynnwood, WA (city) Snohomish County	25	0.07
Boca Del Mar, FL (cdp) Palm Beach County	15	0.07
Morton Grove, IL (village) Cook County	15	0.07
Beachwood, OH (city) Cuyahoga County	9	0.07
Chester, NY (town) Orange County	9	0.07
Foothill Farms, CA (cdp) Sacramento County	10	0.06
Phillipsburg, NJ (town) Warren County	9	0.06
Malibu, CA (city) Los Angeles County	8	0.06
Clarkstown, NY (town) Rockland County	45	0.05
Valley Stream, NY (village) Nassau County	19	0.05
Beverly Hills, CA (city) Los Angeles County	16	0.05
Millbrae, CA (city) San Mateo County	11	0.05
Boone, NC (town) Watauga County	7	0.05
Metuchen, NJ (borough) Middlesex County	7	0.05
Lansing, NY (town) Tompkins County	5	0.05
Pikesville, MD (cdp) Baltimore County	13	0.04
Ridgewood, NJ (village) Bergen County	10	0.04
Ronkonkoma, NY (cdp) Suffolk County	8	0.04
Lincolnwood, IL (village) Cook County	5	0.04
Southfield, MI (city) Oakland County	27	0.03
Minnetonka, MN (city) Hennepin County	15	0.03
North Bethesda, MD (cdp) Montgomery County	13	0.03
Aventura, FL (city) Miami-Dade County	7	0.03
Reisterstown, MD (cdp) Baltimore County	7	0.03
Saint Andrews, SC (cdp) Richland County	7	0.03
Tustin Foothills, CA (cdp) Orange County	7	0.03
Arnold, MD (cdp) Anne Arundel County	6	0.03
Peekskill, NY (city) Westchester County	6	0.03
Myrtle Grove, FL (cdp) Escambia County	5	0.03
Rutherford, NJ (borough) Bergen County	5	0.03
Providence, RI (city) Providence County	34	0.02
Roseville, CA (city) Placer County	15	0.02
Somerville, MA (city) Middlesex County	15	0.02
Framingham, MA (cdp) Middlesex County	12	0.02
Burke, VA (cdp) Fairfax County	10	0.02
Marietta, GA (city) Cobb County	10	0.02
Novi, MI (city) Oakland County	9	0.02
Parsippany-Troy Hills, NJ (township) Morris County	9	0.02
Apple Valley, MN (city) Dakota County	8	0.02
Cortlandt, NY (town) Westchester County	8	0.02
San Dimas, CA (city) Los Angeles County	8	0.02
Smyrna, GA (city) Cobb County	8	0.02
Dover, DE (city) Kent County	7	0.02
Fair Lawn, NJ (borough) Bergen County	7	0.02
Lake Magdalene, FL (cdp) Hillsborough County	7	0.02
North Highlands, CA (cdp) Sacramento County	7	0.02
Westfield, MA (city) Hampden County	7	0.02
Montclair, NJ (cdp) Essex County	6	0.02
Plainview, NY (cdp) Nassau County	6	0.02
Lewisboro, NY (town) Westchester County	2	0.02
New York, NY (city) New York City	550	0.01
San Francisco, CA (city) San Francisco County	54	0.01
Hempstead, NY (town) Nassau County	51	0.01
Boston, MA (city) Suffolk County	37	0.01
New Haven, CT (city) New Haven County	16	0.01
Corona, CA (city) Riverside County	15	0.01
Garland, TX (city) Dallas County	15	0.01
Spokane, WA (city) Spokane County	14	0.01
Santa Clara, CA (city) Santa Clara County	12	0.01
Madison, WI (city) Dane County	11	0.01
Rancho Cucamonga, CA (city) San Bernardino County	11	0.01
Lakewood, CO (city) Jefferson County	10	0.01
Naperville, IL (city) Du Page County	9	0.01
Norwalk, CT (city) Fairfield County	9	0.01
Santa Clarita, CA (city) Los Angeles County	9	0.01
Cambridge, MA (city) Middlesex County	8	0.01
Passaic, NJ (city) Passaic County	8	0.01
Buena Park, CA (city) Orange County	7	0.01
Dearborn Heights, MI (city) Wayne County	7	0.01
Hartford, CT (city) Hartford County	7	0.01
Lowell, MA (city) Middlesex County	7	0.01
Amherst, NY (town) Erie County	6	0.01
Newton, MA (city) Middlesex County	6	0.01
La Mesa, CA (city) San Diego County	5	0.01
Santa Fe, NM (city) Santa Fe County	5	0.01
Kailua, HI (cdp) Honolulu County	3	0.01
Chicago, IL (city) Cook County	60	0.00
Philadelphia, PA (city) Philadelphia County	43	0.00
Los Angeles, CA (city) Los Angeles County	25	0.00
Milwaukee, WI (city) Milwaukee County	16	0.00
Washington, DC (city) District of Columbia	11	0.00
Kansas City, MO (city) Jackson County	10	0.00
Mesa, AZ (city) Maricopa County	10	0.00
Newark, NJ (city) Essex County	10	0.00
Tucson, AZ (city) Pima County	9	0.00
Colorado Springs, CO (city) El Paso County	8	0.00
Islip, NY (town) Suffolk County	8	0.00
Durham, NC (city) Durham County	7	0.00
Vancouver, WA (city) Clark County	7	0.00
Arlington, VA (cdp) Arlington County	6	0.00
Columbus, OH (city) Franklin County	6	0.00
Indianapolis, IN (special city) Marion County	6	0.00
Oyster Bay, NY (town) Nassau County	6	0.00
Jersey City, NJ (city) Hudson County	5	0.00
North Hempstead, NY (town) Nassau County	5	0.00
Ramapo, NY (town) Rockland County	5	0.00
San Jose, CA (city) Santa Clara County	5	0.00

Notes: (cdp) census designated place; Refer to the Explanation of Data in the front of the book for more detailed information.

Swedish

Top 150 Places Sorted by Number

(Based on all places, regardless of population)

Place	Number	%
Minneapolis, MN (city) Hennepin County	30,518	7.98
Chicago, IL (city) Cook County	24,882	0.86
Los Angeles, CA (city) Los Angeles County	23,026	0.62
New York, NY (city) New York City	20,644	0.26
Seattle, WA (city) King County	19,413	3.45
Phoenix, AZ (city) Maricopa County	19,294	1.46
Saint Paul, MN (city) Ramsey County	18,394	6.41
San Diego, CA (city) San Diego County	17,644	1.44
Portland, OR (city) Multnomah County	17,378	3.28
Rockford, IL (city) Winnebago County	14,720	9.83
Omaha, NE (city) Douglas County	14,061	3.60
Duluth, MN (city) Saint Louis County	13,253	15.27
Lincoln, NE (city) Lancaster County	11,296	5.01
Bloomington, MN (city) Hennepin County	10,368	12.17
Denver, CO (city) Denver County	10,158	1.83
San Francisco, CA (city) San Francisco County	9,748	1.26
San Jose, CA (city) Santa Clara County	9,350	1.05
Mesa, AZ (city) Maricopa County	9,152	2.30
Houston, TX (city) Harris County	8,798	0.45
Colorado Springs, CO (city) El Paso County	8,486	2.35
Coon Rapids, MN (city) Anoka County	8,022	13.02
Tucson, AZ (city) Pima County	7,792	1.60
Austin, TX (city) Travis County	7,553	1.15
Spokane, WA (city) Spokane County	7,294	3.72
Plymouth, MN (city) Hennepin County	7,222	10.96
Las Vegas, NV (city) Clark County	6,808	1.42
Dallas, TX (city) Dallas County	6,748	0.57
Anchorage, AK (municipality) Anchorage Borough	6,707	2.58
Salt Lake City, UT (city) Salt Lake County	6,424	3.54
Maple Grove, MN (city) Hennepin County	6,417	12.75
Brooklyn Park, MN (city) Hennepin County	6,371	9.45
Des Moines, IA (city) Polk County	6,285	3.16
Eagan, MN (city) Dakota County	6,179	9.71
Boise City, ID (city) Ada County	6,140	3.30
Jamestown, NY (city) Chautauqua County	6,062	19.10
Burnsville, MN (city) Dakota County	6,026	10.02
Edina, MN (city) Hennepin County	6,023	12.68
Tacoma, WA (city) Pierce County	5,930	3.07
Aurora, CO (city) Arapahoe County	5,918	2.14
Fargo, ND (city) Cass County	5,910	6.51
Scottsdale, AZ (city) Maricopa County	5,907	2.91
Sioux Falls, SD (city) Minnehaha County	5,822	4.69
Minnetonka, MN (city) Hennepin County	5,746	11.20
Eden Prairie, MN (city) Hennepin County	5,735	10.45
Albuquerque, NM (city) Bernalillo County	5,708	1.27
Milwaukee, WI (city) Milwaukee County	5,693	0.95
Wichita, KS (city) Sedgwick County	5,661	1.65
Blaine, MN (city) Anoka County	5,609	12.48
Madison, WI (city) Dane County	5,603	2.70
Brookhaven, NY (town) Suffolk County	5,546	1.24
Worcester, MA (city) Worcester County	5,535	3.21
Kansas City, MO (city) Jackson County	5,368	1.22
San Antonio, TX (city) Bexar County	5,322	0.46
Indianapolis, IN (special city) Marion County	5,192	0.66
Fort Collins, CO (city) Larimer County	4,795	4.05
Lakewood, CO (city) Jefferson County	4,776	3.31
Jacksonville, FL (special city) Duval County	4,774	0.65
Sandy, UT (city) Salt Lake County	4,773	5.41
Richfield, MN (city) Hennepin County	4,758	13.81
Hempstead, NY (town) Nassau County	4,688	0.62
Long Beach, CA (city) Los Angeles County	4,658	1.01
Naperville, IL (city) Du Page County	4,529	3.53
Overland Park, KS (city) Johnson County	4,512	3.03
Apple Valley, MN (city) Dakota County	4,476	9.83
Huntington Beach, CA (city) Orange County	4,466	2.35
Saint Cloud, MN (city) Stearns County	4,407	7.47
Eugene, OR (city) Lane County	4,396	3.19
Vancouver, WA (city) Clark County	4,355	3.04
Lakeville, MN (city) Dakota County	4,322	10.02
Sacramento, CA (city) Sacramento County	4,317	1.06
Provo, UT (city) Utah County	4,316	4.10
Rochester, MN (city) Olmsted County	4,299	5.03
Columbus, OH (city) Franklin County	4,254	0.60
Sioux City, IA (city) Woodbury County	4,234	4.98
Boston, MA (city) Suffolk County	4,211	0.71
Saint Louis Park, MN (city) Hennepin County	4,177	9.47
Superior, WI (city) Douglas County	4,175	15.25
Glendale, AZ (city) Maricopa County	4,113	1.88
Arvada, CO (city) Jefferson County	4,095	3.99
Maplewood, MN (city) Ramsey County	4,087	11.70
Moline, IL (city) Rock Island County	4,073	9.32
Woodbury, MN (city) Washington County	4,067	8.75
Roseville, MN (city) Ramsey County	4,045	11.98
Chandler, AZ (city) Maricopa County	4,045	2.29
Tulsa, OK (city) Tulsa County	4,032	1.03
Fresno, CA (city) Fresno County	4,032	0.94
Henderson, NV (city) Clark County	4,016	2.28
Virginia Beach, VA (independent city) Virginia Beach city	3,987	0.94
Bellevue, WA (city) King County	3,874	3.55
Oklahoma City, OK (city) Oklahoma County	3,841	0.76
Reno, NV (city) Washoe County	3,808	2.11
Salem, OR (city) Marion County	3,690	2.70
Orem, UT (city) Utah County	3,672	4.35
Shoreview, MN (city) Ramsey County	3,614	13.94
Andover, MN (city) Anoka County	3,613	13.59
Philadelphia, PA (city) Philadelphia County	3,597	0.24
Tempe, AZ (city) Maricopa County	3,573	2.26
Fridley, MN (city) Anoka County	3,472	12.65
Charlotte, NC (city) Mecklenburg County	3,417	0.63
Santa Clarita, CA (city) Los Angeles County	3,400	2.25
Galesburg, IL (city) Knox County	3,374	9.97
Everett, WA (city) Snohomish County	3,370	3.69
Arlington Heights, IL (village) Cook County	3,307	4.35
Santa Rosa, CA (city) Sonoma County	3,302	2.24
Davenport, IA (city) Scott County	3,293	3.35
Modesto, CA (city) Stanislaus County	3,276	1.73
Gresham, OR (city) Multnomah County	3,212	3.56
Plano, TX (city) Collin County	3,201	1.44
Wheaton, IL (city) Du Page County	3,197	5.77
West Valley City, UT (city) Salt Lake County	3,192	2.93
Cedar Rapids, IA (city) Linn County	3,179	2.64
Westminster, CO (city) Adams County	3,159	3.12
West Jordan, UT (city) Salt Lake County	3,153	4.62
Saint Petersburg, FL (city) Pinellas County	3,150	1.27
Aurora, IL (city) Kane County	3,129	2.18
Oakland, CA (city) Alameda County	3,117	0.78
Anaheim, CA (city) Orange County	3,095	0.95
Topeka, KS (city) Shawnee County	3,058	2.51
Washington, DC (city) District of Columbia	3,013	0.53
Fremont, CA (city) Alameda County	2,981	1.47
Elgin, IL (city) Kane County	2,978	3.17
Fort Worth, TX (city) Tarrant County	2,971	0.55
Moorhead, MN (city) Clay County	2,966	9.22
Grand Rapids, MI (city) Kent County	2,966	1.50
Nashville-Davidson, TN (special city) Davidson County	2,923	0.54
White Bear Lake, MN (city) Ramsey County	2,918	11.93
Arlington, TX (city) Tarrant County	2,917	0.88
Bellingham, WA (city) Whatcom County	2,913	4.36
Boulder, CO (city) Boulder County	2,907	3.08
Brooklyn Center, MN (city) Hennepin County	2,905	10.00
Riverside, CA (city) Riverside County	2,904	1.14
Grand Forks, ND (city) Grand Forks County	2,886	5.86
Thousand Oaks, CA (city) Ventura County	2,864	2.45
New Brighton, MN (city) Ramsey County	2,780	12.49
Irvine, CA (city) Orange County	2,773	1.94
Warwick, RI (city) Kent County	2,759	3.22
Crystal, MN (city) Hennepin County	2,741	12.00
Paradise, NV (cdp) Clark County	2,695	1.45
Bakersfield, CA (city) Kern County	2,679	1.08
Kenosha, WI (city) Kenosha County	2,677	2.95
Highlands Ranch, CO (cdp) Douglas County	2,674	3.77
Billings, MT (city) Yellowstone County	2,668	2.99
Cottage Grove, MN (city) Washington County	2,662	8.71
Honolulu, HI (cdp) Honolulu County	2,651	0.71
Joliet, IL (city) Will County	2,645	2.49
Oakdale, MN (city) Washington County	2,634	9.88
Olathe, KS (city) Johnson County	2,623	2.82
Arlington, VA (cdp) Arlington County	2,615	1.38
Oceanside, CA (city) San Diego County	2,603	1.62
Mission Viejo, CA (city) Orange County	2,585	2.79

Notes: (cdp) census designated place; Refer to the Explanation of Data in the front of the book for more detailed information.

Swedish

Top 150 Places Sorted by Percent

(Based on all places, regardless of population)

Place	Number	%
South Red River, MN (township) Kittson County	10	83.33
North Red River, MN (township) Kittson County	4	66.67
Leonidas, MN (city) Saint Louis County	23	65.71
Whiteford, MN (township) Marshall County	27	60.00
Hangaard, MN (township) Clearwater County	3	60.00
Granville, MN (township) Kittson County	61	55.45
Eagle Point, MN (township) Marshall County	16	55.17
Stockholm, WI (town) Pepin County	35	53.85
Jupiter, MN (township) Kittson County	61	48.41
Hazelton, MN (township) Kittson County	43	47.25
Vilas, SD (town) Miner County	8	47.06
Skane, MN (township) Kittson County	22	46.81
Popponesset Island, MA (cdp) Barnstable County	6	46.15
Hallock, MN (township) Kittson County	41	46.07
Tegner, MN (township) Kittson County	35	46.05
Lancaster, MN (city) Kittson County	159	45.17
Grattan, MN (township) Itasca County	23	44.23
Lake Bronson, MN (city) Kittson County	130	44.07
Leonard, MN (city) Clearwater County	17	43.59
Lincoln, MN (township) Marshall County	54	42.86
Sinnott, MN (township) Marshall County	23	42.59
West Valley, MN (township) Marshall County	59	42.14
Palmyra, MN (township) Renville County	86	41.75
Falun, MN (township) Roseau County	104	41.60
Rio, IL (village) Knox County	101	40.40
Wausa, NE (village) Knox County	258	39.88
Spruce Grove, MN (township) Beltrami County	18	39.13
Elliott, ND (city) Ransom County	5	38.46
Norway, MN (township) Kittson County	38	38.38
Vasa, MN (township) Goodhue County	318	37.77
Kennedy, MN (city) Kittson County	89	37.71
Amador, MN (township) Chisago County	271	37.53
New Sweden, MN (township) Nicollet County	120	37.04
Westview Circle, WY (cdp) Platte County	34	36.56
Balsam, MN (township) Aitkin County	8	36.36
Breen, MI (township) Dickinson County	170	36.32
New Sweden, ME (town) Aroostook County	225	36.00
Foldahl, MN (township) Marshall County	36	36.00
Thief Lake, MN (township) Marshall County	18	36.00
Maple Ridge, MN (township) Isanti County	256	35.90
Cedar, MN (township) Martin County	89	35.89
Park, MN (township) Pine County	19	35.85
Svea, MN (township) Kittson County	24	35.82
Stockholm, ME (town) Aroostook County	100	35.59
Saronville, NE (village) Clay County	21	35.59
Sturgeon, MN (township) Saint Louis County	47	35.07
Comstock, MN (township) Marshall County	48	35.04
Rulien, MN (township) Lake of the Woods County	7	35.00
Karlstad, MN (city) Kittson County	280	34.78
Donnelly, MN (township) Marshall County	8	34.78
Felch, MI (township) Dickinson County	251	34.15
Funk, NE (village) Phelps County	62	33.88
Cannon, MN (township) Kittson County	10	33.33
Hallock, MN (city) Kittson County	402	33.20
Viking, MN (city) Marshall County	30	32.97
Stromsburg, NE (city) Polk County	404	32.50
Alvarado, MN (city) Marshall County	111	32.46
Olsburg, KS (city) Pottawatomie County	71	32.42
Vega, MN (township) Marshall County	50	32.26
Trade Lake, WI (town) Burnett County	267	32.17
Walhalla, MN (township) Lake of the Woods County	46	32.17
Mahtowa, MN (township) Carlton County	162	31.95
Bassett, MN (township) Saint Louis County	15	31.91
Springvale, MN (township) Isanti County	439	31.90
Altona, IL (village) Knox County	176	31.88
Hill View Heights, WY (cdp) Weston County	58	31.69
Gennessee, MN (township) Kandiyohi County	134	31.53
Third River, MN (township) Itasca County	25	31.25
Ford, MN (township) Kanabec County	56	31.11
Rogers, MN (township) Cass County	14	31.11
Norcross, MN (city) Grant County	18	31.03
Loma, ND (city) Cavalier County	9	31.03
Percy, MN (township) Kittson County	13	30.95
Hill, WI (town) Price County	118	30.89
Bessemer Bend, WY (cdp) Natrona County	63	30.88
Cambridge, MN (township) Isanti County	721	30.81
Westmanland, ME (town) Aroostook County	22	30.56
Shafer, MN (township) Chisago County	212	30.50
Pillsbury, MN (township) Swift County	82	30.48
Reine, MN (township) Roseau County	30	30.30
Fairview, WY (cdp) Lincoln County	77	30.20
Davis, MN (township) Kittson County	16	30.19
Turnerville, WY (cdp) Lincoln County	34	30.09
Lake Lillian, MN (township) Kandiyohi County	66	30.00
Linden Grove, MN (township) Saint Louis County	38	29.92
Wetmore, PA (township) McKean County	525	29.90
Grass Lake, MN (township) Kanabec County	270	29.77
Thompson, MN (township) Kittson County	55	29.73
Arveson, MN (township) Kittson County	27	29.67
Monson, MN (township) Traverse County	55	29.57
Evansville, MN (township) Douglas County	70	29.54
Harris, MN (city) Chisago County	330	29.49
Danvers, MN (city) Swift County	25	29.41
Laketown, WI (town) Polk County	263	29.39
Wright, MN (city) Carlton County	34	29.31
Lincoln, WI (town) Burnett County	84	29.27
Dalbo, MN (township) Isanti County	187	29.26
Atkinson, MN (township) Carlton County	100	29.24
Palmville, MN (township) Roseau County	14	29.17
Wood River, WI (town) Burnett County	290	29.12
Oxford, MN (township) Isanti County	238	29.10
Fish Lake, MN (township) Chisago County	513	29.08
Augsburg, MN (township) Marshall County	34	29.06
Scandia, KS (city) Republic County	131	28.85
Donaldson, MN (city) Kittson County	15	28.85
Woodhull, IL (village) Henry County	237	28.69
Stockholm, WI (village) Pepin County	30	28.57
Morcom, MN (township) Saint Louis County	39	28.47
Isanti, MN (township) Isanti County	697	28.41
Verdon, MN (township) Aitkin County	13	28.26
Concord, NE (village) Dixon County	47	28.14
Hampden, MN (township) Kittson County	9	28.13
Grantsburg, WI (village) Burnett County	383	28.12
Bungo, MN (township) Cass County	30	28.04
Odin, MN (township) Watonwan County	59	27.96
Marquette, KS (city) McPherson County	150	27.93
Northland, MN (township) Saint Louis County	43	27.92
Spruce Valley, MN (township) Marshall County	62	27.80
Bemus Point, NY (village) Chautauqua County	95	27.78
Cache, UT (cdp) Cache County	5	27.78
Dassel, MN (city) Meeker County	348	27.66
Rickreall, OR (cdp) Polk County	21	27.63
Lindsborg, KS (city) McPherson County	920	27.59
Lost River, ID (city) Custer County	8	27.59
Stratford, IA (city) Hamilton County	205	27.55
Bowstring, MN (township) Itasca County	60	27.52
Fahlun, MN (township) Kandiyohi County	112	27.45
Ellsborough, MN (township) Murray County	62	27.43
Stafford, MN (township) Roseau County	78	27.37
Henriette, MN (city) Pine County	26	27.37
Cambridge, MN (city) Isanti County	1,499	27.36
Grace City, ND (city) Foster County	27	27.27
Boxville, MN (township) Marshall County	9	27.27
McCrea, MN (township) Marshall County	70	27.24
Port Wing, WI (town) Bayfield County	117	27.21
Clow, MN (township) Kittson County	13	27.08
Smoky Hollow, MN (township) Cass County	13	27.08
Jadis, MN (township) Roseau County	149	27.04
Lewis, MN (township) Mille Lacs County	17	26.98
Malta, MN (township) Big Stone County	24	26.97
Poppleton, MN (township) Kittson County	28	26.92
Spring Garden, CA (cdp) Plumas County	7	26.92
Dassel, MN (township) Meeker County	376	26.90
Lac qui Parle, MN (township) Lac qui Parle County	43	26.88
Waskish, MN (township) Beltrami County	33	26.83
Frewsburg, NY (cdp) Chautauqua County	528	26.82
Arna, MN (township) Pine County	26	26.80
Kerkhoven, MN (township) Swift County	82	26.71
Malmo, MN (township) Aitkin County	82	26.62
Stanchfield, MN (township) Isanti County	318	26.61

Notes: (cdp) census designated place; Refer to the Explanation of Data in the front of the book for more detailed information.

Swedish

Top 150 Places Sorted by Percent

(Based on places with populations of 10,000 or more)

Place	Number	%
Jamestown, NY (city) Chautauqua County	6,062	19.10
Ham Lake, MN (city) Anoka County	2,040	16.01
Cloquet, MN (city) Carlton County	1,734	15.54
Duluth, MN (city) Saint Louis County	13,253	15.27
Superior, WI (city) Douglas County	4,175	15.25
East Bethel, MN (city) Anoka County	1,657	15.14
Stillwater, MN (city) Washington County	2,250	14.82
Vadnais Heights, MN (city) Ramsey County	1,924	14.73
Robbinsdale, MN (city) Hennepin County	1,984	14.05
Shoreview, MN (city) Ramsey County	3,614	13.94
Richfield, MN (city) Hennepin County	4,758	13.81
Andover, MN (city) Anoka County	3,613	13.59
Willmar, MN (city) Kandiyohi County	2,487	13.52
Coon Rapids, MN (city) Anoka County	8,022	13.02
Ramsey, MN (city) Anoka County	2,406	13.01
Anoka, MN (city) Anoka County	2,307	12.76
Maple Grove, MN (city) Hennepin County	6,417	12.75
Mounds View, MN (city) Ramsey County	1,618	12.73
Red Wing, MN (city) Goodhue County	2,047	12.69
Edina, MN (city) Hennepin County	6,023	12.68
Fridley, MN (city) Anoka County	3,472	12.65
Buffalo, MN (city) Wright County	1,273	12.57
New Brighton, MN (city) Ramsey County	2,780	12.49
Blaine, MN (city) Anoka County	5,609	12.48
Golden Valley, MN (city) Hennepin County	2,509	12.39
Bloomington, MN (city) Hennepin County	10,368	12.17
Warren, PA (city) Warren County	1,247	12.16
Columbia Heights, MN (city) Anoka County	2,240	12.10
Crystal, MN (city) Hennepin County	2,741	12.00
Chanhassen, MN (city) Carver County	2,437	11.99
Roseville, MN (city) Ramsey County	4,045	11.98
White Bear Lake, MN (city) Ramsey County	2,918	11.93
White Bear, MN (township) Ramsey County	1,318	11.78
Maplewood, MN (city) Ramsey County	4,087	11.70
Lino Lakes, MN (city) Anoka County	1,902	11.34
Minnetonka, MN (city) Hennepin County	5,746	11.20
Escanaba, MI (city) Delta County	1,457	11.09
Plymouth, MN (city) Hennepin County	7,222	10.96
Champlin, MN (city) Hennepin County	2,451	10.96
North Saint Paul, MN (city) Ramsey County	1,305	10.94
Loves Park, IL (city) Winnebago County	2,149	10.80
Elk River, MN (city) Sherburne County	1,756	10.68
Fergus Falls, MN (city) Otter Tail County	1,436	10.65
Savage, MN (city) Scott County	2,227	10.51
Eden Prairie, MN (city) Hennepin County	5,735	10.45
Hutchinson, MN (city) McLeod County	1,355	10.38
Grand Rapids, MN (township) Itasca County	1,201	10.26
Brainerd, MN (city) Crow Wing County	1,327	10.18
Hibbing, MN (city) Saint Louis County	1,728	10.12
Prior Lake, MN (city) Scott County	1,609	10.10
Burnsville, MN (city) Dakota County	6,026	10.02
Lakeville, MN (city) Dakota County	4,322	10.02
Hopkins, MN (city) Hennepin County	1,710	10.02
Brooklyn Center, MN (city) Hennepin County	2,905	10.00
Galesburg, IL (city) Knox County	3,374	9.97
New Hope, MN (city) Hennepin County	2,067	9.91
Oakdale, MN (city) Washington County	2,634	9.88
Rockford, IL (city) Winnebago County	14,720	9.83
Apple Valley, MN (city) Dakota County	4,476	9.83
Eagan, MN (city) Dakota County	6,179	9.71
Hastings, MN (city) Dakota County	1,743	9.57
Saint Louis Park, MN (city) Hennepin County	4,177	9.47
Brooklyn Park, MN (city) Hennepin County	6,371	9.45
Boone, IA (city) Boone County	1,204	9.40
River Falls, WI (city) Pierce County	1,183	9.38
Moline, IL (city) Rock Island County	4,073	9.32
Moorhead, MN (city) Clay County	2,966	9.22
Northfield, MN (city) Rice County	1,533	8.96
Machesney Park, IL (village) Winnebago County	1,847	8.93
McPherson, KS (city) McPherson County	1,217	8.83
Bemidji, MN (city) Beltrami County	1,063	8.80
Woodbury, MN (city) Washington County	4,067	8.75
Cottage Grove, MN (city) Washington County	2,662	8.71
Norton Shores, MI (city) Muskegon County	1,961	8.71
Holladay, UT (city) Salt Lake County	1,263	8.68

Place	Number	%
Chaska, MN (city) Carver County	1,505	8.63
Marquette, MI (city) Marquette County	1,690	8.62
Sycamore, IL (city) De Kalb County	1,030	8.49
Holden, MA (town) Worcester County	1,316	8.42
South Saint Paul, MN (city) Dakota County	1,685	8.34
Auburn, MA (town) Worcester County	1,299	8.17
Kearney, NE (city) Buffalo County	2,202	8.14
Batavia, IL (city) Kane County	1,930	8.07
Oxford, MA (town) Worcester County	1,069	8.01
Minneapolis, MN (city) Hennepin County	30,518	7.98
Inver Grove Heights, MN (city) Dakota County	2,359	7.94
North Mankato, MN (city) Nicollet County	929	7.87
Rosemount, MN (city) Dakota County	1,135	7.77
Millbury, MA (town) Worcester County	993	7.77
Kewanee, IL (city) Henry County	987	7.63
Mendota Heights, MN (city) Dakota County	862	7.59
Geneva, IL (city) Kane County	1,479	7.56
Chalco, NE (cdp) Sarpy County	802	7.49
Saint Cloud, MN (city) Stearns County	4,407	7.47
East Millcreek, UT (cdp) Salt Lake County	1,599	7.47
Farmington, MN (city) Dakota County	926	7.42
West Fargo, ND (city) Cass County	1,083	7.40
Libertyville, IL (village) Lake County	1,516	7.33
West Saint Paul, MN (city) Dakota County	1,403	7.23
Shakopee, MN (city) Scott County	1,459	7.12
Camano, WA (cdp) Island County	956	7.07
Gages Lake, IL (cdp) Lake County	730	6.98
Belvidere, IL (city) Boone County	1,427	6.89
Marinette, WI (city) Marinette County	798	6.81
Oquirrh, UT (cdp) Salt Lake County	701	6.77
Fargo, ND (city) Cass County	5,910	6.51
Murray, UT (city) Salt Lake County	2,192	6.46
Saint Paul, MN (city) Ramsey County	18,394	6.41
Cottonwood Heights, UT (cdp) Salt Lake County	1,754	6.41
East Moline, IL (city) Rock Island County	1,293	6.35
Fremont, NE (city) Dodge County	1,591	6.32
Fort Dodge, IA (city) Webster County	1,589	6.32
Leicester, MA (town) Worcester County	657	6.27
Chesterton, IN (town) Porter County	653	6.26
South Jordan, UT (city) Salt Lake County	1,839	6.24
Marshall, MN (city) Lyon County	786	6.16
Riverton, UT (city) Salt Lake County	1,535	6.11
Anacortes, WA (city) Skagit County	895	6.09
Cottonwood West, UT (cdp) Salt Lake County	1,127	6.06
Grand Forks, ND (city) Grand Forks County	2,886	5.86
Frankfort, IL (village) Will County	599	5.85
Saint Charles, IL (city) Kane County	1,631	5.83
Arlington, WA (city) Snohomish County	692	5.82
Rock Island, IL (city) Rock Island County	2,309	5.81
Windsor, CO (town) Weld County	589	5.81
Wheaton, IL (city) Du Page County	3,197	5.77
Fairmont, MN (city) Martin County	626	5.75
Kenmore, WA (city) King County	1,058	5.71
Mukilteo, WA (city) Snohomish County	1,028	5.70
East Renton Highlands, WA (cdp) King County	743	5.67
Lehi, UT (city) Utah County	1,076	5.62
Martha Lake, WA (cdp) Snohomish County	698	5.52
Merrill, WI (city) Lincoln County	559	5.51
Centerville, UT (city) Davis County	787	5.48
Alderwood Manor, WA (cdp) Snohomish County	832	5.45
Norfolk, NE (city) Madison County	1,278	5.43
Lake Forest Park, WA (city) King County	729	5.42
Clive, IA (city) Polk County	697	5.42
Sandy, UT (city) Salt Lake County	4,773	5.41
Brookings, SD (city) Brookings County	1,001	5.39
Urbandale, IA (city) Polk County	1,565	5.38
Brigham City, UT (city) Box Elder County	930	5.34
Spencer, IA (city) Clay County	610	5.34
Issaquah, WA (city) King County	596	5.32
Moscow, ID (city) Latah County	1,120	5.28
Mankato, MN (city) Blue Earth County	1,701	5.26
Western Springs, IL (village) Cook County	663	5.25
Bountiful, UT (city) Davis County	2,170	5.24
Edmonds, WA (city) Snohomish County	2,076	5.24
Columbine, CO (cdp) Jefferson County	1,245	5.18

Notes: (cdp) census designated place; Refer to the Explanation of Data in the front of the book for more detailed information.

Swiss

Top 150 Places Sorted by Number

(Based on all places, regardless of population)

Place	Number	%
New York, NY (city) New York City	8,108	0.10
Los Angeles, CA (city) Los Angeles County	6,169	0.17
San Diego, CA (city) San Diego County	4,349	0.36
Portland, OR (city) Multnomah County	4,102	0.78
Madison, WI (city) Dane County	3,898	1.88
Phoenix, AZ (city) Maricopa County	3,460	0.26
Seattle, WA (city) King County	3,446	0.61
San Francisco, CA (city) San Francisco County	3,381	0.44
Chicago, IL (city) Cook County	3,008	0.10
San Jose, CA (city) Santa Clara County	2,661	0.30
Columbus, OH (city) Franklin County	2,640	0.37
Monroe, WI (city) Green County	2,582	23.88
Houston, TX (city) Harris County	2,226	0.11
Salt Lake City, UT (city) Salt Lake County	2,105	1.16
Indianapolis, IN (special city) Marion County	1,939	0.25
Fort Wayne, IN (city) Allen County	1,905	0.93
Denver, CO (city) Denver County	1,877	0.34
Dallas, TX (city) Dallas County	1,803	0.15
Colorado Springs, CO (city) El Paso County	1,721	0.48
Provo, UT (city) Utah County	1,718	1.63
Orem, UT (city) Utah County	1,663	1.97
Milwaukee, WI (city) Milwaukee County	1,649	0.28
Austin, TX (city) Travis County	1,633	0.25
Mesa, AZ (city) Maricopa County	1,580	0.40
Goshen, IN (city) Elkhart County	1,577	5.38
Boise City, ID (city) Ada County	1,560	0.84
Minneapolis, MN (city) Hennepin County	1,557	0.41
Kansas City, MO (city) Jackson County	1,554	0.35
Sandy, UT (city) Salt Lake County	1,512	1.71
Tucson, AZ (city) Pima County	1,436	0.30
Sacramento, CA (city) Sacramento County	1,375	0.34
San Antonio, TX (city) Bexar County	1,359	0.12
Albuquerque, NM (city) Bernalillo County	1,320	0.29
Lincoln, NE (city) Lancaster County	1,319	0.59
Saint Paul, MN (city) Ramsey County	1,278	0.45
Louisville, KY (city) Jefferson County	1,277	0.50
Toledo, OH (city) Lucas County	1,245	0.40
Las Vegas, NV (city) Clark County	1,237	0.26
Omaha, NE (city) Douglas County	1,232	0.32
Janesville, WI (city) Rock County	1,219	2.05
Philadelphia, PA (city) Philadelphia County	1,218	0.08
Hempstead, NY (town) Nassau County	1,191	0.16
Berne, IN (city) Adams County	1,184	27.99
Bountiful, UT (city) Davis County	1,181	2.85
Wichita, KS (city) Sedgwick County	1,174	0.34
Washington, DC (city) District of Columbia	1,153	0.20
Logan, UT (city) Cache County	1,132	2.65
Scottsdale, AZ (city) Maricopa County	1,100	0.54
Spokane, WA (city) Spokane County	1,077	0.55
Jacksonville, FL (special city) Duval County	1,064	0.14
Saint George, UT (city) Washington County	1,043	2.10
Modesto, CA (city) Stanislaus County	1,037	0.55
Manheim, PA (township) Lancaster County	1,018	3.01
Anchorage, AK (municipality) Anchorage Borough	1,018	0.39
Charlotte, NC (city) Mecklenburg County	987	0.18
Nashville-Davidson, TN (special city) Davidson County	979	0.18
Akron, OH (city) Summit County	976	0.45
Santa Rosa, CA (city) Sonoma County	974	0.66
Aurora, CO (city) Arapahoe County	954	0.35
Eugene, OR (city) Lane County	946	0.69
Arlington, VA (cdp) Arlington County	934	0.49
Tulsa, OK (city) Tulsa County	920	0.23
Brookhaven, NY (town) Suffolk County	901	0.20
Long Beach, CA (city) Los Angeles County	901	0.20
Oakland, CA (city) Alameda County	899	0.23
Salem, OR (city) Marion County	891	0.65
Tacoma, WA (city) Pierce County	877	0.45
Overland Park, KS (city) Johnson County	876	0.59
Harrisonburg, VA (independent city) Harrisonburg city	873	2.16
Ann Arbor, MI (city) Washtenaw County	827	0.72
Boston, MA (city) Suffolk County	824	0.14
Rochester, MN (city) Olmsted County	804	0.94
Plano, TX (city) Collin County	804	0.36
Cincinnati, OH (city) Hamilton County	800	0.24
Fresno, CA (city) Fresno County	798	0.19

Place	Number	%
Henderson, NV (city) Clark County	790	0.45
Oklahoma City, OK (city) Oklahoma County	783	0.15
Boulder, CO (city) Boulder County	777	0.82
Earl, PA (township) Lancaster County	775	12.53
Canton, OH (city) Stark County	775	0.96
Vancouver, WA (city) Clark County	767	0.54
Glendale, AZ (city) Maricopa County	765	0.35
Reno, NV (city) Washoe County	759	0.42
Salinas, CA (city) Monterey County	757	0.50
Fort Collins, CO (city) Larimer County	755	0.64
Saint Louis, MO (independent city) Saint Louis city	749	0.22
New Glarus, WI (village) Green County	747	35.54
Fremont, CA (city) Alameda County	746	0.37
San Luis Obispo, CA (city) San Luis Obispo County	723	1.64
West Jordan, UT (city) Salt Lake County	723	1.06
Thousand Oaks, CA (city) Ventura County	716	0.61
Lakewood, CO (city) Jefferson County	716	0.50
Sunnyvale, CA (city) Santa Clara County	703	0.53
Huntington Beach, CA (city) Orange County	697	0.37
Lexington-Fayette, KY (special city) Fayette County	684	0.26
Naperville, IL (city) Du Page County	681	0.53
West Earl, PA (township) Lancaster County	677	10.01
East Lampeter, PA (township) Lancaster County	674	4.97
West Valley City, UT (city) Salt Lake County	669	0.61
Virginia Beach, VA (independent city) Virginia Beach city	667	0.16
Topeka, KS (city) Shawnee County	657	0.54
Newport Beach, CA (city) Orange County	656	0.94
Orrville, OH (city) Wayne County	654	7.66
Peoria, IL (city) Peoria County	649	0.57
Rockford, IL (city) Winnebago County	642	0.43
Novato, CA (city) Marin County	633	1.32
Oyster Bay, NY (town) Nassau County	630	0.21
Millcreek, UT (cdp) Salt Lake County	629	2.06
Dover, OH (city) Tuscarawas County	625	5.10
Bakersfield, CA (city) Kern County	623	0.25
Huntington, NY (town) Suffolk County	622	0.32
Atlanta, GA (city) Fulton County	621	0.15
Raleigh, NC (city) Wake County	620	0.22
Irvine, CA (city) Orange County	619	0.43
Waukesha, WI (city) Waukesha County	615	0.96
Saint Petersburg, FL (city) Pinellas County	615	0.25
Dubuque, IA (city) Dubuque County	609	1.06
Eau Claire, WI (city) Eau Claire County	603	0.98
Manor, PA (township) Lancaster County	602	3.66
Pittsburgh, PA (city) Allegheny County	595	0.18
Bellevue, WA (city) King County	592	0.54
Pasadena, CA (city) Los Angeles County	592	0.44
Paradise, NV (cdp) Clark County	591	0.32
Chandler, AZ (city) Maricopa County	590	0.33
Ogden, UT (city) Weber County	589	0.76
Beaverton, OR (city) Washington County	588	0.77
Gresham, OR (city) Multnomah County	586	0.65
Saint Joseph, MO (city) Buchanan County	583	0.79
Concord, CA (city) Contra Costa County	582	0.48
Hillsboro, OR (city) Washington County	576	0.82
Sunrise Manor, NV (cdp) Clark County	574	0.37
Wooster, OH (city) Wayne County	573	2.29
Petaluma, CA (city) Sonoma County	573	1.05
Pocatello, ID (city) Bannock County	571	1.11
Baltimore, MD (independent city) Baltimore city	571	0.09
Berkeley, CA (city) Alameda County	568	0.55
Cedar Rapids, IA (city) Linn County	566	0.47
Santa Clarita, CA (city) Los Angeles County	565	0.37
Riverside, CA (city) Riverside County	563	0.22
Mount Joy, PA (township) Lancaster County	562	7.07
Corvallis, OR (city) Benton County	561	1.14
Bloomington, MN (city) Hennepin County	561	0.66
Arlington, TX (city) Tarrant County	559	0.17
Arden-Arcade, CA (cdp) Sacramento County	554	0.58
Islip, NY (town) Suffolk County	550	0.17
Tampa, FL (city) Hillsborough County	549	0.18
Lancaster, PA (city) Lancaster County	545	0.97
Pleasanton, CA (city) Alameda County	544	0.86
Palo Alto, CA (city) Santa Clara County	543	0.92
Highland, IL (city) Madison County	541	6.46

Notes: (cdp) census designated place; Refer to the Explanation of Data in the front of the book for more detailed information.

Swiss

Top 150 Places Sorted by Percent

(Based on all places, regardless of population)

Place	Number	%
Washington, WI (town) Green County	270	43.06
Mount Pleasant, WI (town) Green County	229	36.01
Monticello, WI (village) Green County	404	35.91
New Glarus, WI (village) Green County	747	35.54
Clarno, WI (town) Green County	395	33.99
Monroe, WI (town) Green County	349	30.53
Jordan, WI (town) Green County	159	28.29
Berne, IN (city) Adams County	1,184	27.99
New Glarus, WI (town) Green County	250	26.65
Argyle, WI (village) Lafayette County	205	24.76
Lincoln, WI (town) Buffalo County	46	24.73
Sylvester, WI (town) Green County	180	24.46
Monroe, WI (city) Green County	2,582	23.88
Jefferson, WI (town) Green County	275	23.63
Wiota, WI (town) Lafayette County	195	23.55
Edgewood, CA (cdp) Siskiyou County	15	23.44
Bern, KS (city) Nemaha County	44	22.45
Warm River, ID (city) Fremont County	2	22.22
Adams, WI (town) Green County	102	21.61
Exeter, WI (town) Green County	262	21.21
Cadiz, WI (town) Green County	171	20.50
Argyle, WI (town) Lafayette County	98	20.29
Spring Grove, WI (town) Green County	178	19.45
Elgin, IA (city) Fayette County	123	19.01
Pandora, OH (village) Putnam County	227	18.64
York, WI (town) Green County	117	18.60
Montrose, WI (town) Dane County	212	18.42
Albany, WI (town) Green County	135	18.24
Primrose, WI (town) Dane County	119	18.17
Conrath, WI (village) Rusk County	11	18.03
Moore, MN (township) Stevens County	45	17.79
Andrea, MN (township) Wilkin County	13	17.33
Alma, WI (town) Buffalo County	60	17.09
Sugarcreek, OH (village) Tuscarawas County	366	16.70
Brooklyn, WI (town) Green County	153	16.35
Decatur, WI (town) Green County	273	16.22
Lester, IA (city) Lyon County	39	16.18
South Wayne, WI (village) Lafayette County	70	15.98
Belleville, WI (village) Dane County	292	15.43
Blanchardville, WI (village) Lafayette County	117	14.90
Fayette, WI (town) Lafayette County	52	14.90
Cross, WI (town) Buffalo County	57	14.50
Wayne, WI (town) Lafayette County	81	14.46
Lower Salem, OH (village) Washington County	20	14.39
Albany, WI (village) Green County	175	14.30
Van Tassell, WY (town) Niobrara County	2	14.29
Wilmot, OH (village) Stark County	50	14.25
Pittman, FL (cdp) Lake County	11	14.10
Gratiot, WI (village) Lafayette County	36	13.64
Hollandale, WI (village) Iowa County	34	13.28
Alma, WI (city) Buffalo County	125	13.27
Graf, IA (city) Dubuque County	13	13.00
Blanchard, WI (town) Lafayette County	33	12.79
Moscow, WI (town) Iowa County	74	12.54
Earl, PA (township) Lancaster County	775	12.53
Monroe, IN (town) Adams County	91	12.45
Montana, WI (town) Buffalo County	41	12.28
Powhattan, KS (city) Brown County	11	12.09
Chugcreek, WY (cdp) Platte County	16	12.03
Conway, IA (city) Taylor County	6	12.00
Brickerville, PA (cdp) Lancaster County	155	11.93
Baltic, OH (village) Tuscarawas County	86	11.75
Congerville, IL (village) Woodford County	52	11.61
Boulder, UT (town) Garfield County	21	11.60
Hoff, MN (township) Pope County	21	11.60
Ramona, SD (town) Lake County	19	11.52
Dalton, OH (village) Wayne County	179	11.44
Lamont, WI (town) Lafayette County	32	11.43
Milton, MN (township) Dodge County	76	11.34
Wasta, SD (town) Pennington County	10	11.24
Dot Lake, AK (cdp) Southeast Fairbanks Census Area	2	11.11
Meteor, WI (town) Sawyer County	17	11.04
Horton, MN (township) Stevens County	30	11.03
Brodhead, WI (city) Green County	348	11.01
Burchard, NE (village) Pawnee County	8	10.96
Darlington, WI (town) Lafayette County	87	10.94
Yosemite Valley, CA (cdp) Mariposa County	24	10.76
Parral, OH (village) Tuscarawas County	26	10.74
Georgetown, ID (city) Bear Lake County	59	10.73
Perry, WI (town) Dane County	75	10.71
Gilmanton, WI (town) Buffalo County	43	10.57
Elbing, KS (city) Butler County	25	10.50
Darnen, MN (township) Stevens County	38	10.47
Bluffton, OH (village) Allen County	385	10.39
Blue Mounds, WI (town) Dane County	83	10.30
Willow Springs, WI (town) Lafayette County	68	10.26
Lazy Lake, FL (village) Broward County	4	10.26
Gratiot, WI (town) Lafayette County	66	10.19
Fairfield, MN (township) Swift County	16	10.19
Olde West Chester, OH (cdp) Butler County	27	10.15
Latty, OH (village) Paulding County	21	10.14
West Earl, PA (township) Lancaster County	677	10.01
Browntown, WI (village) Green County	27	10.00
Mount Eaton, OH (village) Wayne County	24	9.96
Clay, PA (township) Lancaster County	509	9.90
Menno, PA (township) Mifflin County	173	9.81
Turnerville, WY (cdp) Lincoln County	11	9.73
Sabetha, KS (city) Nemaha County	248	9.64
Spring Valley, WI (town) Rock County	74	9.61
Waldwick, WI (town) Iowa County	50	9.43
Jeffrey City, WY (cdp) Fremont County	8	9.41
Monticello, WI (town) Lafayette County	14	9.33
Shipshewana, IN (town) La Grange County	50	9.28
Hixon, WI (town) Clark County	68	9.25
Orangeville, IL (village) Stephenson County	69	9.13
Chickaloon, AK (cdp) Matanuska-Susitna Borough	26	9.12
Fairview, WY (cdp) Lincoln County	23	9.02
Leacock, PA (township) Lancaster County	439	9.00
Montezuma, CO (town) Summit County	3	8.82
Smithville, OH (village) Wayne County	118	8.66
Elizabeth, PA (township) Lancaster County	332	8.59
Fountain City, WI (city) Buffalo County	81	8.55
West Bend, IA (city) Palo Alto County	71	8.48
Johnson, WI (town) Marathon County	84	8.42
Evansville, WI (city) Rock County	334	8.37
Magnolia, WI (town) Rock County	76	8.35
Mylo, ND (city) Rolette County	2	8.33
Springdale, WI (town) Dane County	128	8.27
South Willard, UT (cdp) Box Elder County	49	8.26
Richland, NE (village) Colfax County	7	8.24
Paris, ID (city) Bear Lake County	46	8.20
Elk Lick, PA (township) Somerset County	187	8.14
Du Bois, NE (village) Pawnee County	13	8.13
Brunswick, NE (village) Antelope County	15	8.11
Gilboa, OH (village) Putnam County	14	8.09
Midway, UT (city) Wasatch County	173	8.05
Roanoke, IL (village) Woodford County	159	8.01
Caernarvon, PA (township) Lancaster County	338	7.90
Black Earth, WI (town) Dane County	34	7.89
Santa Clara, UT (city) Washington County	364	7.88
Garden City, UT (town) Rich County	25	7.86
Indian Village, IN (town) Saint Joseph County	11	7.86
Milton, WI (town) Buffalo County	39	7.85
Monroe, NE (village) Platte County	23	7.80
Skwentna, AK (cdp) Matanuska-Susitna Borough	8	7.69
Beaver Cove, ME (town) Piscataquis County	7	7.69
Ferndale, CA (city) Humboldt County	109	7.67
Orrville, OH (city) Wayne County	654	7.66
Lewiston, NE (village) Pawnee County	7	7.53
Govan, SC (town) Bamberg County	5	7.46
Terre Hill, PA (borough) Lancaster County	92	7.42
Woodland, WI (town) Sauk County	57	7.35
Queen Valley, AZ (cdp) Pinal County	53	7.33
Modena, WI (town) Buffalo County	26	7.26
Goodfield, IL (village) Woodford County	49	7.22
Eden, WI (town) Iowa County	27	7.20
Marshallville, OH (village) Wayne County	60	7.17
Hoard, WI (town) Clark County	42	7.17
Vermont, WI (town) Dane County	58	7.16
Brecknock, PA (township) Lancaster County	478	7.14

Notes: (cdp) census designated place; Refer to the Explanation of Data in the front of the book for more detailed information.

Swiss

Top 150 Places Sorted by Percent

(Based on places with populations of 10,000 or more)

Place	Number	%
Monroe, WI (city) Green County	2,582	23.88
Goshen, IN (city) Elkhart County	1,577	5.38
Dover, OH (city) Tuscarawas County	625	5.10
East Lampeter, PA (township) Lancaster County	674	4.97
Salisbury, PA (township) Lancaster County	457	4.56
Ellington, CT (town) Tolland County	517	4.00
Manor, PA (township) Lancaster County	602	3.66
Franconia, PA (township) Montgomery County	360	3.12
Warwick, PA (township) Lancaster County	472	3.05
Morton, IL (village) Tazewell County	456	3.03
Manheim, PA (township) Lancaster County	1,018	3.01
Hilltown, PA (township) Bucks County	346	2.86
Bountiful, UT (city) Davis County	1,181	2.85
Stoughton, WI (city) Dane County	343	2.76
Logan, UT (city) Cache County	1,132	2.65
West Hempfield, PA (township) Lancaster County	391	2.58
New Philadelphia, OH (city) Tuscarawas County	418	2.48
East Hempfield, PA (township) Lancaster County	525	2.47
Brigham City, UT (city) Box Elder County	420	2.41
East Millcreek, UT (cdp) Salt Lake County	506	2.36
Wadsworth, OH (city) Medina County	432	2.33
Alliance, OH (city) Stark County	537	2.31
Wooster, OH (city) Wayne County	573	2.29
Rexburg, ID (city) Madison County	384	2.23
Kaysville, UT (city) Davis County	454	2.19
Middleton, WI (city) Dane County	341	2.19
Harrisonburg, VA (independent city) Harrisonburg city	873	2.16
Centerville, UT (city) Davis County	306	2.13
Saint George, UT (city) Washington County	1,043	2.10
Millcreek, UT (cdp) Salt Lake County	629	2.06
Janesville, WI (city) Rock County	1,219	2.05
Orem, UT (city) Utah County	1,663	1.97
Holladay, UT (city) Salt Lake County	287	1.97
Ephrata, PA (borough) Lancaster County	260	1.97
Farmington, UT (city) Davis County	240	1.97
Antrim, PA (township) Franklin County	243	1.94
Springville, UT (city) Utah County	393	1.92
West Lampeter, PA (township) Lancaster County	251	1.91
Madison, WI (city) Dane County	3,898	1.88
Fitchburg, WI (city) Dane County	380	1.86
Freeport, IL (city) Stephenson County	478	1.81
North Canton, OH (city) Stark County	291	1.78
Cottonwood West, UT (cdp) Salt Lake County	328	1.76
Fortuna, CA (city) Humboldt County	182	1.76
Cottonwood Heights, UT (cdp) Salt Lake County	475	1.74
Sandy, UT (city) Salt Lake County	1,512	1.71
South Jordan, UT (city) Salt Lake County	502	1.70
New Canaan, CT (town) Fairfield County	326	1.68
Cedar City, UT (city) Iron County	344	1.67
Riverton, UT (city) Salt Lake County	415	1.65
San Luis Obispo, CA (city) San Luis Obispo County	723	1.64
Columbus, NE (city) Platte County	344	1.64
Provo, UT (city) Utah County	1,718	1.63
Guilford, PA (township) Franklin County	211	1.61
Massillon, OH (city) Stark County	495	1.58
Mill Valley, CA (city) Marin County	213	1.57
Upper Allen, PA (township) Cumberland County	237	1.55
Whitewater, WI (city) Walworth County	207	1.54
North Lebanon, PA (township) Lebanon County	164	1.54
Oatfield, OR (cdp) Clackamas County	240	1.53
Beaver Dam, WI (city) Dodge County	228	1.52
Pleasant Grove, UT (city) Utah County	356	1.51
Green River, WY (city) Sweetwater County	174	1.48
Lancaster, PA (township) Lancaster County	204	1.47
Canyon Rim, UT (cdp) Salt Lake County	155	1.47
Murray, UT (city) Salt Lake County	494	1.46
Uwchlan, PA (township) Chester County	242	1.46
Chatham, NJ (township) Morris County	140	1.39
Lower Salford, PA (township) Montgomery County	177	1.37
Hillsborough, CA (town) San Mateo County	148	1.37
Whitefish Bay, WI (village) Milwaukee County	192	1.36
Gardnerville Ranchos, NV (cdp) Douglas County	151	1.36
Ripon, CA (city) San Joaquin County	138	1.36
Elizabethtown, PA (borough) Lancaster County	160	1.35
Lebanon, OR (city) Linn County	173	1.34
Oquirrh, UT (cdp) Salt Lake County	139	1.34
North Castle, NY (town) Westchester County	144	1.33
Novato, CA (city) Marin County	633	1.32
Fort Atkinson, WI (city) Jefferson County	155	1.32
Lehi, UT (city) Utah County	251	1.31
Dallas, OR (city) Polk County	160	1.29
Lafayette, CA (city) Contra Costa County	301	1.28
Los Altos, CA (city) Santa Clara County	341	1.24
Stillwater, MN (city) Washington County	189	1.24
Laguna Beach, CA (city) Orange County	286	1.23
North Ogden, UT (city) Weber County	184	1.23
Concord, MO (cdp) Saint Louis County	201	1.21
Baraboo, WI (city) Sauk County	130	1.21
Lake Oswego, OR (city) Clackamas County	421	1.20
Moscow, ID (city) Latah County	252	1.19
Maumee, OH (city) Lucas County	179	1.18
Gladstone, OR (city) Clackamas County	134	1.18
Puyallup, WA (city) Pierce County	384	1.17
Watertown, WI (city) Jefferson County	253	1.17
Salt Lake City, UT (city) Salt Lake County	2,105	1.16
Orinda, CA (city) Contra Costa County	203	1.16
Spring Garden, PA (township) York County	139	1.16
Roy, UT (city) Weber County	378	1.15
Marshfield, WI (city) Wood County	217	1.15
Alamo, CA (cdp) Contra Costa County	174	1.15
Corvallis, OR (city) Benton County	561	1.14
American Fork, UT (city) Utah County	249	1.14
Montville, NJ (township) Morris County	238	1.14
Punta Gorda, FL (city) Charlotte County	164	1.14
Amherst, NH (town) Hillsborough County	123	1.14
Laramie, WY (city) Albany County	308	1.13
Mountain Park, GA (cdp) Gwinnett County	130	1.13
Green Valley, AZ (cdp) Pima County	194	1.12
New Haven, IN (city) Allen County	138	1.12
Pocatello, ID (city) Bannock County	571	1.11
Draper, UT (city) Salt Lake County	283	1.11
Findlay, OH (city) Hancock County	431	1.10
Upper Arlington, OH (city) Franklin County	365	1.09
Perrysburg, OH (city) Wood County	186	1.09
Kingsgate, WA (cdp) King County	131	1.09
Eagle, ID (city) Ada County	120	1.08
Brookfield, WI (city) Waukesha County	417	1.07
Sullivan, NY (town) Madison County	160	1.07
Limerick, PA (township) Montgomery County	145	1.07
Richfield, WI (town) Washington County	111	1.07
West Jordan, UT (city) Salt Lake County	723	1.06
Dubuque, IA (city) Dubuque County	609	1.06
Mequon, WI (city) Ozaukee County	232	1.06
Sherwood, OR (city) Washington County	127	1.06
Raymore, MO (city) Cass County	116	1.06
Petaluma, CA (city) Sonoma County	573	1.05
Arcata, CA (city) Humboldt County	176	1.05
La Crosse, WI (city) La Crosse County	536	1.04
Orcutt, CA (cdp) Santa Barbara County	300	1.04
El Cerrito, CA (city) Contra Costa County	240	1.04
North Saint Paul, MN (city) Ramsey County	124	1.04
Sturgis, MI (city) Saint Joseph County	118	1.04
Sun Prairie, WI (city) Dane County	209	1.03
Tolland, CT (town) Tolland County	136	1.03
Beatrice, NE (city) Gage County	128	1.03
River Forest, IL (village) Cook County	120	1.03
Scotts Valley, CA (city) Santa Cruz County	119	1.03
Crestline, CA (cdp) San Bernardino County	105	1.03
Cranberry, PA (township) Butler County	241	1.02
Athens, OH (city) Athens County	216	1.02
Sylvania, OH (city) Lucas County	192	1.02
Cedar Falls, IA (city) Black Hawk County	365	1.01
Naples, FL (city) Collier County	213	1.01
Cumru, PA (township) Berks County	140	1.01
Cypress Lake, FL (cdp) Lee County	122	1.01
Sun Lakes, AZ (cdp) Maricopa County	121	1.01
Lilburn, GA (city) Gwinnett County	115	1.01
Eureka, CA (city) Humboldt County	258	1.00
Hampton Township, PA (cdp) Allegheny County	176	1.00
Pacific Grove, CA (city) Monterey County	154	1.00

Notes: (cdp) census designated place; Refer to the Explanation of Data in the front of the book for more detailed information.

Turkish

Top 150 Places Sorted by Number

(Based on all places, regardless of population)

Place	Number	%
New York, NY (city) New York City	12,221	0.15
Los Angeles, CA (city) Los Angeles County	2,587	0.07
Hempstead, NY (town) Nassau County	1,424	0.19
Brookhaven, NY (town) Suffolk County	1,182	0.26
Chicago, IL (city) Cook County	1,178	0.04
San Diego, CA (city) San Diego County	930	0.08
Paterson, NJ (city) Passaic County	842	0.56
Clifton, NJ (city) Passaic County	839	1.07
Houston, TX (city) Harris County	764	0.04
Seattle, WA (city) King County	710	0.13
Oyster Bay, NY (town) Nassau County	638	0.22
North Hempstead, NY (town) Nassau County	612	0.27
Boston, MA (city) Suffolk County	612	0.10
Philadelphia, PA (city) Philadelphia County	595	0.04
Rochester, NY (city) Monroe County	593	0.27
Islip, NY (town) Suffolk County	585	0.18
San Francisco, CA (city) San Francisco County	565	0.07
Babylon, NY (town) Suffolk County	544	0.26
Irondequoit, NY (cdp) Monroe County	459	0.88
Columbus, OH (city) Franklin County	454	0.06
Washington, DC (city) District of Columbia	435	0.08
Huntington, NY (town) Suffolk County	432	0.22
Arlington, VA (cdp) Arlington County	430	0.23
Raleigh, NC (city) Wake County	416	0.15
San Jose, CA (city) Santa Clara County	391	0.04
Tucson, AZ (city) Pima County	358	0.07
Austin, TX (city) Travis County	355	0.05
Phoenix, AZ (city) Maricopa County	350	0.03
Miami Beach, FL (city) Miami-Dade County	342	0.39
Smithtown, NY (town) Suffolk County	328	0.28
Pittsburgh, PA (city) Allegheny County	327	0.10
Jacksonville, FL (special city) Duval County	324	0.04
Cliffside Park, NJ (borough) Bergen County	306	1.33
Huntington Beach, CA (city) Orange County	306	0.16
Sandy Springs, GA (cdp) Fulton County	305	0.36
Las Vegas, NV (city) Clark County	303	0.06
Dallas, TX (city) Dallas County	300	0.03
Providence, RI (city) Providence County	270	0.16
Minneapolis, MN (city) Hennepin County	261	0.07
Tulsa, OK (city) Tulsa County	260	0.07
West Haven, CT (city) New Haven County	256	0.49
Silver Spring, MD (cdp) Montgomery County	251	0.33
Wayne, NJ (cdp) Passaic County	250	0.46
Ann Arbor, MI (city) Washtenaw County	248	0.22
San Antonio, TX (city) Bexar County	247	0.02
Madison, WI (city) Dane County	245	0.12
Syracuse, NY (city) Onondaga County	241	0.16
North Bethesda, MD (cdp) Montgomery County	240	0.62
Cambridge, MA (city) Middlesex County	238	0.23
Fairview, NJ (borough) Bergen County	230	1.74
Commack, NY (cdp) Suffolk County	229	0.63
Alexandria, VA (independent city) Alexandria city	229	0.18
Greece, NY (town) Monroe County	227	0.24
Delran, NJ (township) Burlington County	226	1.45
Arlington, TX (city) Tarrant County	223	0.07
Sacramento, CA (city) Sacramento County	222	0.05
Long Beach, CA (city) Los Angeles County	220	0.05
Hollywood, FL (city) Broward County	218	0.16
Bethlehem, PA (city) Northampton County	214	0.30
Naperville, IL (city) Du Page County	211	0.16
Irvine, CA (city) Orange County	211	0.15
Tampa, FL (city) Hillsborough County	208	0.07
Long Beach, NY (city) Nassau County	203	0.57
Somerville, MA (city) Middlesex County	202	0.26
Foster City, CA (city) San Mateo County	200	0.69
Monterey, CA (city) Monterey County	200	0.67
Edison, NJ (cdp) Middlesex County	199	0.20
Ramapo, NY (town) Rockland County	198	0.18
Virginia Beach, VA (independent city) Virginia Beach city	198	0.05
Parsippany-Troy Hills, NJ (township) Morris County	196	0.39
Plano, TX (city) Collin County	196	0.09
Greenburgh, NY (town) Westchester County	194	0.22
Coral Springs, FL (city) Broward County	192	0.16
Indianapolis, IN (special city) Marion County	192	0.02
Lexington-Fayette, KY (special city) Fayette County	188	0.07
College Station, TX (city) Brazos County	187	0.28
Coconut Creek, FL (city) Broward County	186	0.43
Evanston, IL (city) Cook County	185	0.25
Sunnyvale, CA (city) Santa Clara County	184	0.14
Tysons Corner, VA (cdp) Fairfax County	183	0.99
Belleville, NJ (cdp) Essex County	183	0.51
Weston, FL (city) Broward County	183	0.37
Santa Monica, CA (city) Los Angeles County	183	0.22
Glendale, CA (city) Los Angeles County	182	0.09
Coram, NY (cdp) Suffolk County	181	0.52
Aurora, CO (city) Arapahoe County	176	0.06
Fort Lee, NJ (borough) Bergen County	172	0.49
Edgewater Park, NJ (township) Burlington County	170	2.16
Methuen, MA (city) Essex County	170	0.39
Bethesda, MD (cdp) Montgomery County	170	0.31
Amherst, NY (town) Erie County	167	0.14
Lyndhurst, NJ (cdp) Bergen County	166	0.86
Pompano Beach, FL (city) Broward County	165	0.21
Mesa, AZ (city) Maricopa County	164	0.04
Gainesville, FL (city) Alachua County	163	0.17
Milwaukee, WI (city) Milwaukee County	163	0.03
Atlanta, GA (city) Fulton County	161	0.04
Miami, FL (city) Miami-Dade County	160	0.04
Jersey City, NJ (city) Hudson County	158	0.07
Knoxville, TN (city) Knox County	157	0.09
West New York, NJ (town) Hudson County	156	0.34
Chula Vista, CA (city) San Diego County	155	0.09
Denver, CO (city) Denver County	155	0.03
West Babylon, NY (cdp) Suffolk County	154	0.35
Dearborn, MI (city) Wayne County	154	0.16
Charlotte, NC (city) Mecklenburg County	154	0.03
Ridgefield, NJ (borough) Bergen County	152	1.40
Cleveland, OH (city) Cuyahoga County	151	0.03
Beaverton, OR (city) Washington County	150	0.20
Portland, OR (city) Multnomah County	149	0.03
Potomac, MD (cdp) Montgomery County	148	0.33
Walnut Creek, CA (city) Contra Costa County	148	0.23
Boca Raton, FL (city) Palm Beach County	147	0.19
Chandler, AZ (city) Maricopa County	147	0.08
Holmdel, NJ (township) Monmouth County	146	0.93
Baltimore, MD (independent city) Baltimore city	144	0.02
Boonton, NJ (town) Morris County	142	1.67
Amherst, MA (town) Hampshire County	141	0.40
Schaumburg, IL (village) Cook County	141	0.19
Aventura, FL (city) Miami-Dade County	140	0.55
Sunrise, FL (city) Broward County	140	0.16
Palisades Park, NJ (borough) Bergen County	139	0.81
Medford, NY (cdp) Suffolk County	138	0.63
Ridgewood, NJ (village) Bergen County	138	0.55
Oakton, VA (cdp) Fairfax County	137	0.47
Blacksburg, VA (town) Montgomery County	137	0.35
Bellevue, WA (city) King County	137	0.13
Gaithersburg, MD (city) Montgomery County	136	0.26
Pembroke Pines, FL (city) Broward County	136	0.10
Teaneck, NJ (cdp) Bergen County	135	0.34
Brookline, MA (cdp) Norfolk County	133	0.23
Worcester, MA (city) Worcester County	133	0.08
Ojus, FL (cdp) Miami-Dade County	132	0.79
McLean, VA (cdp) Fairfax County	132	0.34
Oakland Park, FL (city) Broward County	131	0.42
North Miami Beach, FL (city) Miami-Dade County	130	0.32
Hoffman Estates, IL (village) Cook County	130	0.26
Cary, NC (town) Wake County	129	0.14
Saint Petersburg, FL (city) Pinellas County	129	0.05
Tempe, AZ (city) Maricopa County	128	0.08
Anaheim, CA (city) Orange County	128	0.04
East Meadow, NY (cdp) Nassau County	127	0.34
Newport News, VA (independent city) Newport News city	127	0.07
Yonkers, NY (city) Westchester County	126	0.06
New Rochelle, NY (city) Westchester County	123	0.17
Weehawken, NJ (township) Hudson County	121	0.90
Bloomington, IN (city) Monroe County	121	0.17
Cincinnati, OH (city) Hamilton County	119	0.04
Annandale, VA (cdp) Fairfax County	118	0.21
Costa Mesa, CA (city) Orange County	118	0.11

Notes: (cdp) census designated place; Refer to the Explanation of Data in the front of the book for more detailed information.

Turkish

Top 150 Places Sorted by Percent

(Based on all places, regardless of population)

Place	Number	%
Bushong, KS (city) Lyon County	7	15.56
New Buffalo, PA (borough) Perry County	7	6.42
Bancroft, SD (town) Kingsbury County	2	5.88
Royal Palm Ranches, FL (cdp) Broward County	14	4.65
Springtown, AR (town) Benton County	4	3.70
Denton, NE (village) Lancaster County	6	3.59
Islandia, NY (village) Suffolk County	86	2.81
Salo, MN (township) Aitkin County	6	2.70
Agenda, KS (city) Republic County	2	2.35
Cairo, MN (township) Renville County	6	2.26
Edgewater Park, NJ (township) Burlington County	170	2.16
East Ithaca, NY (cdp) Tompkins County	46	2.01
Benson, IL (village) Woodford County	8	1.95
Dalzell, SC (cdp) Sumter County	43	1.94
Max, MN (township) Itasca County	3	1.92
Palm Shores, FL (town) Brevard County	15	1.90
Dewey Beach, DE (town) Sussex County	5	1.85
Point Lookout, NY (cdp) Nassau County	28	1.84
Fairview, NJ (borough) Bergen County	230	1.74
Richardville, MN (township) Kittson County	2	1.72
Franksville, WI (cdp) Racine County	29	1.71
Golden's Bridge, NY (cdp) Westchester County	26	1.68
Boonton, NJ (town) Morris County	142	1.67
Port Alsworth, AK (cdp) Lake and Peninsula Borough	2	1.67
Jeffersonville, NY (village) Sullivan County	7	1.66
Buffalo Soapstone, AK (cdp) Matanuska-Susitna Borough	11	1.63
Torning, MN (township) Swift County	8	1.51
New Egypt, NJ (cdp) Ocean County	38	1.48
Delran, NJ (township) Burlington County	226	1.45
Fleischmanns, NY (village) Delaware County	5	1.42
Cane Savannah, SC (cdp) Sumter County	22	1.41
Ridgefield, NJ (borough) Bergen County	152	1.40
Bellerose Terrace, NY (cdp) Nassau County	30	1.39
Preston, MD (town) Caroline County	8	1.39
South Amherst, MA (cdp) Hampshire County	69	1.37
Herricks, NY (cdp) Nassau County	56	1.37
Bay Harbor Islands, FL (town) Miami-Dade County	70	1.36
Pemberton Heights, NJ (cdp) Burlington County	34	1.35
Cliffside Park, NJ (borough) Bergen County	306	1.33
Angola on the Lake, NY (cdp) Erie County	23	1.33
Exeland, WI (village) Sawyer County	3	1.33
Fairchild, WI (village) Eau Claire County	7	1.30
Friendship Village, MD (cdp) Montgomery County	57	1.29
Wallins Creek, KY (city) Harlan County	3	1.29
Fountainhead-Orchard Hills, MD (cdp) Washington County	46	1.24
Van Buren, MN (township) Saint Louis County	2	1.24
Highland Beach, FL (town) Palm Beach County	44	1.22
Emmett, KS (city) Pottawatomie County	3	1.22
Peconic, NY (cdp) Suffolk County	14	1.20
Quogue, NY (village) Suffolk County	12	1.19
Woodsburgh, NY (village) Nassau County	10	1.19
Haledon, NJ (borough) Passaic County	95	1.15
Klacking, MI (township) Ogemaw County	7	1.14
Sycamore, KY (city) Jefferson County	2	1.13
Cedar Point, IL (village) La Salle County	3	1.11
Munsey Park, NY (village) Nassau County	29	1.10
Wahkon, MN (city) Mille Lacs County	3	1.09
Clifton, NJ (city) Passaic County	839	1.07
Summit, IL (village) Cook County	112	1.05
Westport, NC (cdp) Lincoln County	19	1.05
Easton, IL (village) Mason County	4	1.04
Oklee, MN (city) Red Lake County	4	1.03
Rutledge, MN (city) Pine County	2	1.03
Montebello, NY (village) Rockland County	37	1.02
Westhampton, NY (cdp) Suffolk County	29	1.02
Englishtown, NJ (borough) Monmouth County	18	1.02
Copper City, MI (village) Houghton County	2	1.00
Tysons Corner, VA (cdp) Fairfax County	183	0.99
North Great River, NY (cdp) Suffolk County	39	0.99
Greene, PA (township) Pike County	31	0.98
Algonquin, MD (cdp) Dorchester County	14	0.98
Marshville, NC (town) Union County	23	0.97
Westlake Corner, VA (cdp) Franklin County	9	0.97
Virgin, UT (town) Washington County	4	0.97
Moose Lake, MN (township) Carlton County	9	0.94
Holmdel, NJ (township) Monmouth County	146	0.93
Piermont, NY (village) Rockland County	24	0.92
Kennard, IN (town) Henry County	4	0.92
Florence-Roebling, NJ (cdp) Burlington County	75	0.91
Weehawken, NJ (township) Hudson County	121	0.90
Barry, IL (city) Pike County	12	0.90
Great Neck Gardens, NY (cdp) Nassau County	10	0.90
Athol, ID (city) Kootenai County	6	0.90
Cloverdale, IN (town) Putnam County	20	0.89
Irondequoit, NY (cdp) Monroe County	459	0.88
Matlacha, FL (cdp) Lee County	7	0.88
Fredon, NJ (township) Sussex County	25	0.87
Lyndhurst, NJ (cdp) Bergen County	166	0.86
Garden City Park, NY (cdp) Nassau County	65	0.86
McLendon-Chisholm, TX (city) Rockwall County	8	0.86
Roslyn, NY (village) Nassau County	22	0.85
Wallace, ID (city) Shoshone County	8	0.85
East Rockaway, NY (village) Nassau County	88	0.84
Caldwell, NJ (borough) Essex County	64	0.84
Berlin, NJ (borough) Camden County	51	0.83
La Harpe, KS (city) Allen County	6	0.83
Haycock, PA (township) Bucks County	18	0.82
Roslyn Estates, NY (village) Nassau County	10	0.82
Point Arena, CA (city) Mendocino County	4	0.82
Mount Gretna, PA (borough) Lebanon County	2	0.82
Palisades Park, NJ (borough) Bergen County	139	0.81
Airmont, NY (village) Rockland County	63	0.81
North Lindenhurst, NY (cdp) Suffolk County	94	0.80
Londontowne, MD (cdp) Anne Arundel County	60	0.80
Boxborough, MA (town) Middlesex County	39	0.80
Ojus, FL (cdp) Miami-Dade County	132	0.79
Edgewood, NM (town) Santa Fe County	16	0.79
Great Neck Plaza, NY (village) Nassau County	49	0.77
Kings Beach, CA (cdp) Placer County	30	0.77
Afton, NY (village) Chenango County	6	0.77
Upper Marlboro, MD (town) Prince George's County	5	0.77
South Hooksett, NH (cdp) Merrimack County	40	0.76
Quioque, NY (cdp) Suffolk County	6	0.76
White Meadow Lake, NJ (cdp) Morris County	68	0.75
Schlusser, PA (cdp) Cumberland County	36	0.75
Quinton, NJ (township) Salem County	21	0.75
Monterey, MA (town) Berkshire County	7	0.75
Tenafly, NJ (borough) Bergen County	102	0.74
Kensington, NY (village) Nassau County	9	0.74
Edgewater, NJ (borough) Bergen County	56	0.73
Walker, MI (township) Cheboygan County	2	0.73
El Sobrante, CA (cdp) Contra Costa County	83	0.72
Sound Beach, NY (cdp) Suffolk County	71	0.72
Massanutten, VA (cdp) Rockingham County	14	0.72
Southampton, NY (village) Suffolk County	28	0.71
Hillsmere Shores, MD (cdp) Anne Arundel County	20	0.71
Red Lodge, MT (city) Carbon County	16	0.71
Buffalo, PA (township) Washington County	15	0.71
Harbor Isle, NY (cdp) Nassau County	10	0.71
Whipps Millgate, KY (city) Jefferson County	3	0.71
Florence, NJ (township) Burlington County	75	0.70
Foster City, CA (city) San Mateo County	200	0.69
West Freehold, NJ (cdp) Monmouth County	86	0.69
Kings Point, FL (cdp) Palm Beach County	85	0.69
West Paterson, NJ (borough) Passaic County	76	0.69
Rocky Point, NY (cdp) Suffolk County	71	0.69
Chatham, NJ (township) Morris County	69	0.68
Whitemarsh Island, GA (cdp) Chatham County	40	0.68
Piney Point Village, TX (city) Harris County	23	0.68
La Puebla, NM (cdp) Santa Fe County	9	0.68
Monterey, CA (city) Monterey County	200	0.67
Lincolnia, VA (cdp) Fairfax County	106	0.67
Sea Cliff, NY (village) Nassau County	34	0.67
Metamora, IL (village) Woodford County	18	0.67
Laurel, NY (cdp) Suffolk County	8	0.67
North Oaks, MN (city) Ramsey County	26	0.66
Port Washington North, NY (village) Nassau County	18	0.66
Woodland Hills, KY (city) Jefferson County	4	0.66
Plumsted, NJ (township) Ocean County	47	0.65
Kingston, NJ (cdp) Middlesex County	8	0.64

Notes: (cdp) census designated place; Refer to the Explanation of Data in the front of the book for more detailed information.

Turkish

Top 150 Places Sorted by Percent

(Based on places with populations of 10,000 or more)

Place	Number	%
Fairview, NJ (borough) Bergen County	230	1.74
Delran, NJ (township) Burlington County	226	1.45
Ridgefield, NJ (borough) Bergen County	152	1.40
Cliffside Park, NJ (borough) Bergen County	306	1.33
Clifton, NJ (city) Passaic County	839	1.07
Summit, IL (village) Cook County	112	1.05
Tysons Corner, VA (cdp) Fairfax County	183	0.99
Holmdel, NJ (township) Monmouth County	146	0.93
Weehawken, NJ (township) Hudson County	121	0.90
Irondequoit, NY (cdp) Monroe County	459	0.88
Lyndhurst, NJ (cdp) Bergen County	166	0.86
East Rockaway, NY (village) Nassau County	88	0.84
Palisades Park, NJ (borough) Bergen County	139	0.81
North Lindenhurst, NY (cdp) Suffolk County	94	0.80
Ojus, FL (cdp) Miami-Dade County	132	0.79
Tenafly, NJ (borough) Bergen County	102	0.74
El Sobrante, CA (cdp) Contra Costa County	83	0.72
Florence, NJ (township) Burlington County	75	0.70
Foster City, CA (city) San Mateo County	200	0.69
West Freehold, NJ (cdp) Monmouth County	86	0.69
Kings Point, FL (cdp) Palm Beach County	85	0.69
West Paterson, NJ (borough) Passaic County	76	0.69
Rocky Point, NY (cdp) Suffolk County	71	0.69
Chatham, NJ (township) Morris County	69	0.68
Monterey, CA (city) Monterey County	200	0.67
Lincolnia, VA (cdp) Fairfax County	106	0.67
Commack, NY (cdp) Suffolk County	229	0.63
Medford, NY (cdp) Suffolk County	138	0.63
Eatontown, NJ (borough) Monmouth County	88	0.63
North Bethesda, MD (cdp) Montgomery County	240	0.62
Ardmore, PA (cdp) Montgomery County	78	0.62
Rolla, MO (city) Phelps County	101	0.61
North Arlington, NJ (borough) Bergen County	91	0.60
Montgomery, OH (city) Hamilton County	59	0.59
Long Beach, NY (city) Nassau County	203	0.57
Paterson, NJ (city) Passaic County	842	0.56
Lincoln, RI (town) Providence County	117	0.56
Aventura, FL (city) Miami-Dade County	140	0.55
Ridgewood, NJ (village) Bergen County	138	0.55
Agoura Hills, CA (city) Los Angeles County	112	0.55
Stanford, CA (cdp) Santa Clara County	72	0.54
Lynbrook, NY (village) Nassau County	105	0.53
Coram, NY (cdp) Suffolk County	181	0.52
Fairfax, VA (independent city) Fairfax city	111	0.52
Port Washington, NY (cdp) Nassau County	79	0.52
Wanaque, NJ (borough) Passaic County	53	0.52
Belleville, NJ (cdp) Essex County	183	0.51
East Massapequa, NY (cdp) Nassau County	99	0.51
Issaquah, WA (city) King County	57	0.51
Ferguson, PA (township) Centre County	70	0.50
West Haven, CT (city) New Haven County	256	0.49
Fort Lee, NJ (borough) Bergen County	172	0.49
Woodmere, NY (cdp) Nassau County	80	0.49
Wolf Trap, VA (cdp) Fairfax County	66	0.48
Oakton, VA (cdp) Fairfax County	137	0.47
Wayne, NJ (cdp) Passaic County	250	0.46
Saddle Brook, NJ (cdp) Bergen County	61	0.46
East Windsor, NJ (township) Mercer County	113	0.45
Springfield, NJ (cdp) Union County	65	0.45
Paradise Valley, AZ (town) Maricopa County	62	0.45
Hopewell, NJ (township) Mercer County	71	0.44
Coconut Creek, FL (city) Broward County	186	0.43
North Bellmore, NY (cdp) Nassau County	86	0.43
Hybla Valley, VA (cdp) Fairfax County	72	0.43
Seymour, CT (town) New Haven County	67	0.43
Little Falls, NJ (cdp) Passaic County	47	0.43
Dobbs Ferry, NY (village) Westchester County	46	0.43
Oakland Park, FL (city) Broward County	131	0.42
Highland Park, NJ (borough) Middlesex County	59	0.42
Chili, NY (town) Monroe County	114	0.41
Plainview, NY (cdp) Nassau County	105	0.41
Ithaca, NY (town) Tompkins County	75	0.41
Schiller Park, IL (village) Cook County	48	0.41
Amherst, MA (town) Hampshire County	141	0.40
Lake Ronkonkoma, NY (cdp) Suffolk County	78	0.40
Setauket-East Setauket, NY (cdp) Suffolk County	64	0.40
New Providence, NJ (borough) Union County	48	0.40
Union Hill-Novelty Hill, WA (cdp) King County	45	0.40
Clayton, CA (city) Contra Costa County	43	0.40
Miami Beach, FL (city) Miami-Dade County	342	0.39
Parsippany-Troy Hills, NJ (township) Morris County	196	0.39
Methuen, MA (city) Essex County	170	0.39
Sunny Isles Beach, FL (city) Miami-Dade County	59	0.39
Larkspur, CA (city) Marin County	47	0.39
Patchogue, NY (village) Suffolk County	47	0.39
Lynnfield, MA (cdp) Essex County	45	0.39
Lake Saint Louis, MO (city) Saint Charles County	39	0.39
Hawthorne, NJ (borough) Passaic County	70	0.38
North Babylon, NY (cdp) Suffolk County	68	0.38
Warrensburg, MO (city) Johnson County	62	0.38
North Palm Beach, FL (village) Palm Beach County	46	0.38
Weston, FL (city) Broward County	183	0.37
Mukilteo, WA (city) Snohomish County	66	0.37
Cutler, FL (cdp) Miami-Dade County	65	0.37
New Milford, NJ (borough) Bergen County	60	0.37
Saint James, NY (cdp) Suffolk County	49	0.37
Clemson, SC (city) Pickens County	45	0.37
Hillsdale, NJ (borough) Bergen County	37	0.37
Sandy Springs, GA (cdp) Fulton County	305	0.36
Riverhead, NY (town) Suffolk County	101	0.36
Mount Olive, NJ (township) Morris County	88	0.36
Roselle, IL (village) Du Page County	83	0.36
Melville, NY (cdp) Suffolk County	53	0.36
Lewisboro, NY (town) Westchester County	44	0.36
West Babylon, NY (cdp) Suffolk County	154	0.35
Blacksburg, VA (town) Montgomery County	137	0.35
Freehold, NJ (township) Monmouth County	111	0.35
Greenlawn, NY (cdp) Suffolk County	47	0.35
North Middleton, PA (township) Cumberland County	36	0.35
West New York, NJ (town) Hudson County	156	0.34
Teaneck, NJ (cdp) Bergen County	135	0.34
McLean, VA (cdp) Fairfax County	132	0.34
East Meadow, NY (cdp) Nassau County	127	0.34
Calabasas, CA (city) Los Angeles County	69	0.34
West Hempstead, NY (cdp) Nassau County	64	0.34
Hooksett, NH (town) Merrimack County	40	0.34
Silver Spring, MD (cdp) Montgomery County	251	0.33
Potomac, MD (cdp) Montgomery County	148	0.33
Griffith, IN (town) Lake County	58	0.33
Druid Hills, GA (cdp) De Kalb County	42	0.33
Lincolnwood, IL (village) Cook County	41	0.33
Salisbury, NY (cdp) Nassau County	40	0.33
Forestville, OH (cdp) Hamilton County	37	0.33
North Miami Beach, FL (city) Miami-Dade County	130	0.32
Franconia, VA (cdp) Fairfax County	102	0.32
Bellmore, NY (cdp) Nassau County	53	0.32
Parkland, FL (city) Broward County	45	0.32
Coto de Caza, CA (cdp) Orange County	42	0.32
Colts Neck, NJ (township) Monmouth County	39	0.32
Upper Grand Lagoon, FL (cdp) Bay County	35	0.32
Bethesda, MD (cdp) Montgomery County	170	0.31
Randolph, NJ (township) Morris County	76	0.31
Laguna Beach, CA (city) Orange County	73	0.31
Copiague, NY (cdp) Suffolk County	68	0.31
Selden, NY (cdp) Suffolk County	67	0.31
Madison, NJ (borough) Morris County	51	0.31
Wyckoff, NJ (cdp) Bergen County	51	0.31
Forest City, FL (cdp) Seminole County	39	0.31
Westwood, NJ (borough) Bergen County	34	0.31
Bethlehem, PA (city) Northampton County	214	0.30
Stillwater, OK (city) Payne County	117	0.30
Garfield, NJ (city) Bergen County	90	0.30
Rockaway, NJ (township) Morris County	68	0.30
West Caldwell, NJ (cdp) Essex County	34	0.30
Town and Country, MO (city) Saint Louis County	33	0.30
Brighton, NY (town) Monroe County	104	0.29
Upper Arlington, OH (city) Franklin County	97	0.29
Kent, OH (city) Portage County	81	0.29
Herndon, VA (town) Fairfax County	62	0.29
New Castle, NY (town) Westchester County	51	0.29

Notes: (cdp) census designated place; Refer to the Explanation of Data in the front of the book for more detailed information.

Ukrainian

Top 150 Places Sorted by Number

(Based on all places, regardless of population)

Place	Number	%
New York, NY (city) New York City	62,695	0.78
Philadelphia, PA (city) Philadelphia County	15,665	1.03
Chicago, IL (city) Cook County	13,579	0.47
Los Angeles, CA (city) Los Angeles County	12,292	0.33
Portland, OR (city) Multnomah County	5,867	1.11
San Francisco, CA (city) San Francisco County	5,516	0.71
Hempstead, NY (town) Nassau County	4,023	0.53
Parma, OH (city) Cuyahoga County	3,692	4.31
Cleveland, OH (city) Cuyahoga County	3,224	0.67
San Diego, CA (city) San Diego County	3,104	0.25
Pittsburgh, PA (city) Allegheny County	3,067	0.92
Vancouver, WA (city) Clark County	2,873	2.01
Phoenix, AZ (city) Maricopa County	2,417	0.18
Warren, MI (city) Macomb County	2,397	1.73
Brookhaven, NY (town) Suffolk County	2,385	0.53
Boston, MA (city) Suffolk County	2,337	0.40
Sacramento, CA (city) Sacramento County	2,287	0.56
Rochester, NY (city) Monroe County	2,179	0.99
Seattle, WA (city) King County	2,091	0.37
Rancho Cordova, CA (cdp) Sacramento County	2,083	3.82
Yonkers, NY (city) Westchester County	1,975	1.01
Columbus, OH (city) Franklin County	1,955	0.27
Oyster Bay, NY (town) Nassau County	1,917	0.65
Woodbridge, NJ (township) Middlesex County	1,848	1.90
Clifton, NJ (city) Passaic County	1,795	2.28
West Hollywood, CA (city) Los Angeles County	1,770	4.96
Greece, NY (town) Monroe County	1,726	1.83
Houston, TX (city) Harris County	1,693	0.09
Tacoma, WA (city) Pierce County	1,681	0.87
Spokane, WA (city) Spokane County	1,661	0.85
Irondequoit, NY (cdp) Monroe County	1,643	3.14
Denver, CO (city) Denver County	1,570	0.28
Baltimore, MD (independent city) Baltimore city	1,567	0.24
North Highlands, CA (cdp) Sacramento County	1,536	3.48
Minneapolis, MN (city) Hennepin County	1,510	0.39
Bensalem, PA (township) Bucks County	1,487	2.54
Kent, WA (city) King County	1,477	1.86
Allentown, PA (city) Lehigh County	1,442	1.35
Buffalo, NY (city) Erie County	1,439	0.49
San Jose, CA (city) Santa Clara County	1,423	0.16
Sterling Heights, MI (city) Macomb County	1,405	1.13
Livonia, MI (city) Wayne County	1,402	1.39
Scranton, PA (city) Lackawanna County	1,373	1.80
Arden-Arcade, CA (cdp) Sacramento County	1,365	1.42
Syracuse, NY (city) Onondaga County	1,361	0.92
Auburn, NY (city) Cayuga County	1,352	4.73
Detroit, MI (city) Wayne County	1,346	0.14
Federal Way, WA (city) King County	1,328	1.60
Babylon, NY (town) Suffolk County	1,323	0.62
Jacksonville, FL (special city) Duval County	1,294	0.18
Virginia Beach, VA (independent city) Virginia Beach city	1,262	0.30
Washington, DC (city) District of Columbia	1,247	0.22
Huntington, NY (town) Suffolk County	1,234	0.63
Citrus Heights, CA (city) Sacramento County	1,212	1.42
Las Vegas, NV (city) Clark County	1,210	0.25
Hamilton, NJ (township) Mercer County	1,208	1.38
Skokie, IL (village) Cook County	1,206	1.90
North Hempstead, NY (town) Nassau County	1,196	0.54
Troy, MI (city) Oakland County	1,179	1.46
Islip, NY (town) Suffolk County	1,168	0.36
Amherst, NY (town) Erie County	1,158	0.99
Northampton, PA (township) Bucks County	1,147	2.92
Dover, NJ (township) Ocean County	1,139	1.27
Union, NY (town) Broome County	1,129	2.01
Youngstown, OH (city) Mahoning County	1,111	1.35
Charlotte, NC (city) Mecklenburg County	1,075	0.20
Toms River, NJ (cdp) Ocean County	1,052	1.22
Scottsdale, AZ (city) Maricopa County	1,049	0.52
Edison, NJ (cdp) Middlesex County	1,048	1.07
Union, NJ (cdp) Union County	1,045	1.92
Mesa, AZ (city) Maricopa County	1,043	0.26
Pikesville, MD (cdp) Baltimore County	1,026	3.55
Strongsville, OH (city) Cuyahoga County	1,019	2.32
Buffalo Grove, IL (village) Lake County	1,017	2.39
Tucson, AZ (city) Pima County	1,017	0.21
Clinton, MI (cdp) Macomb County	1,007	1.05
Smithtown, NY (town) Suffolk County	1,004	0.87
Arlington, VA (cdp) Arlington County	1,002	0.53
Cherry Hill, NJ (township) Camden County	976	1.39
Everett, WA (city) Snohomish County	965	1.06
Webster, NY (town) Monroe County	958	2.53
Dearborn, MI (city) Wayne County	958	0.98
Milwaukee, WI (city) Milwaukee County	948	0.16
Bethlehem, PA (city) Northampton County	947	1.33
Colonie, NY (town) Albany County	943	1.19
Saint Petersburg, FL (city) Pinellas County	943	0.38
Newton, MA (city) Middlesex County	939	1.12
Indianapolis, IN (special city) Marion County	924	0.12
Dallas, TX (city) Dallas County	923	0.08
Dearborn Heights, MI (city) Wayne County	916	1.57
Colorado Springs, CO (city) El Paso County	915	0.25
Fair Lawn, NJ (borough) Bergen County	898	2.84
Westfield, MA (city) Hampden County	881	2.20
New Britain, CT (city) Hartford County	878	1.23
Canton, MI (cdp) Wayne County	863	1.13
Levittown, PA (cdp) Bucks County	856	1.59
Aurora, CO (city) Arapahoe County	856	0.31
Santa Monica, CA (city) Los Angeles County	854	1.02
Austin, TX (city) Travis County	854	0.13
Whitehall, PA (township) Lehigh County	848	3.41
Akron, OH (city) Summit County	844	0.39
North Royalton, OH (city) Cuyahoga County	836	2.92
Cheektowaga, NY (town) Erie County	830	0.88
Camillus, NY (town) Onondaga County	809	3.49
Auburn, WA (city) King County	809	2.01
Ramapo, NY (town) Rockland County	807	0.74
Lincoln, NE (city) Lancaster County	796	0.35
Utica, NY (city) Oneida County	790	1.30
Binghamton, NY (city) Broome County	787	1.66
Palatine, IL (village) Cook County	785	1.20
Bayonne, NJ (city) Hudson County	772	1.25
Stamford, CT (city) Fairfield County	768	0.66
Clay, NY (town) Onondaga County	766	1.30
Carteret, NJ (borough) Middlesex County	764	3.69
San Antonio, TX (city) Bexar County	761	0.07
Fair Oaks, CA (cdp) Sacramento County	755	2.70
Ann Arbor, MI (city) Washtenaw County	755	0.66
Hollywood, FL (city) Broward County	753	0.54
Carmichael, CA (cdp) Sacramento County	750	1.51
Abington, PA (township) Montgomery County	742	1.32
Hamtramck, MI (city) Wayne County	738	3.21
West Bloomfield, MI (township) Oakland County	737	1.14
Geddes, NY (town) Onondaga County	735	4.15
Piscataway, NJ (township) Middlesex County	728	1.44
Middletown, NJ (township) Monmouth County	728	1.10
Gresham, OR (city) Multnomah County	728	0.81
Raleigh, NC (city) Wake County	718	0.26
Albuquerque, NM (city) Bernalillo County	714	0.16
Overland Park, KS (city) Johnson County	712	0.48
Troy, NY (city) Rensselaer County	711	1.45
Renton, WA (city) King County	710	1.42
Perinton, NY (town) Monroe County	709	1.54
East Brunswick, NJ (cdp) Middlesex County	706	1.51
Linden, NJ (city) Union County	697	1.77
Rochester Hills, MI (city) Oakland County	697	1.01
Bridgewater, NJ (township) Somerset County	696	1.62
Saint Paul, MN (city) Ramsey County	691	0.24
Erie, PA (city) Erie County	690	0.67
Jersey City, NJ (city) Hudson County	682	0.28
Bristol, PA (township) Bucks County	679	1.22
Farmington Hills, MI (city) Oakland County	672	0.82
Hillsborough, NJ (township) Somerset County	668	1.82
Lakewood, OH (city) Cuyahoga County	663	1.17
Albany, NY (city) Albany County	662	0.69
West Hartford, CT (cdp) Hartford County	658	1.03
Naperville, IL (city) Du Page County	658	0.51
Hamburg, NY (town) Erie County	652	1.16
Austintown, OH (cdp) Mahoning County	651	2.06
Cambridge, MA (city) Middlesex County	650	0.64
Oakland, CA (city) Alameda County	649	0.16

Notes: (cdp) census designated place; Refer to the Explanation of Data in the front of the book for more detailed information.

Ukrainian

Top 150 Places Sorted by Percent

(Based on all places, regardless of population)

Place	Number	%
Forrestville, PA (cdp) Schuylkill County	140	35.62
Centralia, PA (borough) Columbia County	2	33.33
Oak Point, FL (cdp) Broward County	40	25.32
Bergen, ND (city) McHenry County	1	25.00
Butte, ND (city) McLean County	21	22.11
Percy, MN (township) Kittson County	8	19.05
Seltzer, PA (cdp) Schuylkill County	50	17.67
New Castle, PA (township) Schuylkill County	72	17.22
Belfield, ND (city) Stark County	147	17.01
Gilberton, PA (borough) Schuylkill County	138	15.92
Marion Heights, PA (borough) Northumberland County	111	15.06
Wilburton Number One, PA (cdp) Columbia County	40	15.04
Ramey, PA (borough) Clearfield County	70	13.86
Eagle Point, MN (township) Marshall County	4	13.79
Pine, PA (township) Clearfield County	10	13.70
Cass, PA (township) Schuylkill County	322	13.64
Wilton, ND (city) McLean County	104	12.71
Poppleton, MN (township) Kittson County	13	12.50
Lengby, MN (city) Polk County	11	12.50
Chester, MN (township) Polk County	12	12.37
Gulich, PA (township) Clearfield County	157	12.12
Scandia, MN (township) Polk County	11	11.83
Conyngham, PA (township) Columbia County	93	11.67
Lumberland, NY (town) Sullivan County	219	11.29
Aristes, PA (cdp) Columbia County	23	10.80
Viking, MN (city) Marshall County	9	9.89
Delta Junction, AK (city) Southeast Fairbanks Census Area	82	9.70
Potamo, MN (township) Lake of the Woods County	12	9.30
Olyphant, PA (borough) Lackawanna County	457	9.18
Saint Clair, PA (borough) Schuylkill County	299	9.15
Harrison City, PA (cdp) Westmoreland County	12	9.02
Frackville, PA (borough) Schuylkill County	388	8.90
Norwegian, PA (township) Schuylkill County	191	8.80
Lublin, WI (village) Taylor County	9	8.74
Marlin, PA (cdp) Schuylkill County	55	8.63
Harmony Township, PA (cdp) Beaver County	285	8.45
Smoky Hollow, MN (township) Cass County	4	8.33
Slickville, PA (cdp) Westmoreland County	29	7.90
Deltana, AK (cdp) Southeast Fairbanks Census Area	120	7.71
North Beach, FL (cdp) Indian River County	17	7.69
Tolstoy, SD (town) Potter County	4	7.69
Houtzdale, PA (borough) Clearfield County	72	7.65
Soap Lake, WA (city) Grant County	133	7.64
Englewood, PA (cdp) Schuylkill County	33	7.59
Branch, PA (township) Schuylkill County	140	7.48
Baden, PA (borough) Beaver County	318	7.27
McAdoo, PA (borough) Schuylkill County	165	7.26
Kerhonkson, NY (cdp) Ulster County	130	7.25
Delano, PA (township) Schuylkill County	34	6.94
Spooner, MN (township) Lake of the Woods County	19	6.81
Ehrenfeld, PA (borough) Cambria County	16	6.75
Hallock, MN (township) Kittson County	6	6.74
Rhinehart, MN (township) Polk County	6	6.74
West Leechburg, PA (borough) Westmoreland County	86	6.67
Cannon, MN (township) Kittson County	2	6.67
Jacksonville, PA (cdp) Indiana County	44	6.61
Pleasant Valley, AK (cdp) Fairbanks North Star Borough	39	6.50
Mount Carmel, PA (township) Northumberland County	175	6.48
Warren, NY (town) Herkimer County	76	6.47
Kline, PA (township) Schuylkill County	103	6.46
Granville, MN (township) Kittson County	7	6.36
Lorain, PA (borough) Cambria County	50	6.35
Ambridge, PA (borough) Beaver County	489	6.29
Northampton, PA (borough) Northampton County	591	6.28
Marshallton, PA (cdp) Northumberland County	90	6.24
Little Pine, MN (township) Crow Wing County	6	6.19
Stone Ridge, NY (cdp) Ulster County	76	6.18
Throop, NY (town) Cayuga County	112	6.14
Summit Station, PA (cdp) Schuylkill County	13	6.13
Postville, IA (city) Allamakee County	139	6.09
East Berwick, PA (cdp) Luzerne County	123	6.09
Miller Landing, AK (cdp) Kenai Peninsula Borough	4	6.06
East Norwegian, PA (township) Schuylkill County	52	6.05
Clayville, NY (village) Oneida County	27	6.01
McKees Rocks, PA (borough) Allegheny County	395	5.96
Kulpmont, PA (borough) Northumberland County	176	5.90
Port Carbon, PA (borough) Schuylkill County	119	5.88
Bethany, PA (borough) Wayne County	19	5.85
Halma, MN (city) Kittson County	5	5.75
Minersville, PA (borough) Schuylkill County	259	5.69
Numidia, PA (cdp) Columbia County	15	5.66
Heckscherville, PA (cdp) Schuylkill County	4	5.63
Ward, CO (town) Boulder County	4	5.63
Fleming, NY (town) Cayuga County	148	5.59
Franklin, PA (township) Columbia County	36	5.58
Moses Lake North, WA (cdp) Grant County	234	5.55
Palmerton, PA (borough) Carbon County	290	5.53
Gladstone, ND (city) Stark County	13	5.51
Allen, PA (township) Northampton County	144	5.48
Ocracoke, NC (cdp) Hyde County	40	5.48
New Boston-Morea, PA (cdp) Schuylkill County	25	5.46
Bigler, PA (township) Clearfield County	73	5.44
Wilburton Number Two, PA (cdp) Columbia County	4	5.41
Webster, NY (village) Monroe County	279	5.40
Mount Carmel, PA (borough) Northumberland County	341	5.34
Union Dale, PA (borough) Susquehanna County	21	5.33
Ford City, PA (borough) Armstrong County	183	5.30
Deerfield, NY (town) Oneida County	203	5.20
Richardville, MN (township) Kittson County	6	5.17
East Cameron, PA (township) Northumberland County	35	5.15
Benville, MN (township) Beltrami County	4	5.13
Lexington, NY (town) Greene County	41	5.07
Briar Creek, PA (borough) Columbia County	33	5.07
Middleport, PA (borough) Schuylkill County	23	5.07
Leet, PA (township) Allegheny County	79	5.04
Buck, PA (township) Luzerne County	20	5.04
Fountain Springs, PA (cdp) Schuylkill County	5	5.00
Owasco, NY (town) Cayuga County	187	4.98
Stowe Township, PA (cdp) Allegheny County	333	4.97
West Hollywood, CA (city) Los Angeles County	1,770	4.96
Westvale, NY (cdp) Onondaga County	252	4.90
Peaceful Valley, WA (cdp) Whatcom County	126	4.89
Glendon, PA (borough) Northampton County	18	4.88
Danforth, MN (township) Pine County	3	4.84
Glenfield, PA (borough) Allegheny County	11	4.82
Feasterville-Trevose, PA (cdp) Bucks County	311	4.80
Melrose Park, NY (cdp) Cayuga County	116	4.79
West Easton, PA (borough) Northampton County	55	4.78
Jermyn, PA (borough) Lackawanna County	109	4.77
Auburn, NY (city) Cayuga County	1,352	4.73
Mount Carbon, PA (borough) Schuylkill County	4	4.71
Edge Hill, GA (city) Glascock County	2	4.65
Buck Run, PA (cdp) Schuylkill County	11	4.62
Homa Hills, WY (cdp) Natrona County	12	4.55
Shoal Creek Estates, MO (town) Newton County	2	4.55
Dicksonville, PA (cdp) Indiana County	19	4.52
Rupert, PA (cdp) Columbia County	8	4.52
Saint Joseph, MN (township) Kittson County	2	4.44
Indian Lake, PA (borough) Somerset County	20	4.42
Independence, NJ (township) Warren County	247	4.41
Saint Michael-Sidman, PA (cdp) Cambria County	42	4.41
Coplay, PA (borough) Lehigh County	149	4.40
Homeacre-Lyndora, PA (cdp) Butler County	293	4.35
Shenandoah Heights, PA (cdp) Schuylkill County	63	4.35
Monroe, NY (village) Orange County	338	4.33
Parma, OH (city) Cuyahoga County	3,692	4.31
Wetherington, OH (cdp) Butler County	44	4.31
West Carroll, PA (township) Cambria County	62	4.29
Sharptown, MD (town) Wicomico County	29	4.29
Glenwillow, OH (village) Cuyahoga County	19	4.27
North Whitehall, PA (township) Lehigh County	627	4.26
Fairmount, NY (cdp) Onondaga County	456	4.22
Economy, PA (borough) Beaver County	395	4.22
Carnegie, PA (borough) Allegheny County	352	4.20
Newburg, ND (city) Bottineau County	4	4.17
Geddes, NY (town) Onondaga County	735	4.15
Seven Hills, OH (city) Cuyahoga County	501	4.15
Franklin, CT (town) New London County	76	4.14
Madrid, ME (town) Franklin County	6	4.14
Young, PA (township) Indiana County	72	4.13

Notes: (cdp) census designated place; Refer to the Explanation of Data in the front of the book for more detailed information.

Ukrainian

Top 150 Places Sorted by Percent

(Based on places with populations of 10,000 or more)

Place	Number	%
West Hollywood, CA (city) Los Angeles County	1,770	4.96
Auburn, NY (city) Cayuga County	1,352	4.73
Parma, OH (city) Cuyahoga County	3,692	4.31
North Whitehall, PA (township) Lehigh County	627	4.26
Fairmount, NY (cdp) Onondaga County	456	4.22
Geddes, NY (town) Onondaga County	735	4.15
Seven Hills, OH (city) Cuyahoga County	501	4.15
Rancho Cordova, CA (cdp) Sacramento County	2,083	3.82
Seymour, CT (town) New Haven County	586	3.79
Coal, PA (township) Northumberland County	395	3.72
Carteret, NJ (borough) Middlesex County	764	3.69
Berwick, PA (borough) Columbia County	387	3.62
Pikesville, MD (cdp) Baltimore County	1,026	3.55
Hanover, NJ (township) Morris County	454	3.52
Camillus, NY (town) Onondaga County	809	3.49
North Highlands, CA (cdp) Sacramento County	1,536	3.48
Butler, PA (township) Butler County	600	3.48
Whitehall, PA (township) Lehigh County	848	3.41
Cohoes, NY (city) Albany County	522	3.36
Lower Southampton, PA (township) Bucks County	627	3.25
Hamtramck, MI (city) Wayne County	738	3.21
Johnson City, NY (village) Broome County	492	3.17
Irondequoit, NY (cdp) Monroe County	1,643	3.14
Manville, NJ (borough) Somerset County	318	3.09
Middleburg Heights, OH (city) Cuyahoga County	473	3.04
Hanover, PA (township) Luzerne County	349	3.04
Northampton, PA (township) Bucks County	1,147	2.92
North Royalton, OH (city) Cuyahoga County	836	2.92
Plains, PA (township) Luzerne County	318	2.92
Lakeland North, WA (cdp) King County	436	2.88
Parma Heights, OH (city) Cuyahoga County	622	2.87
Fair Lawn, NJ (borough) Bergen County	898	2.84
Watervliet, NY (city) Albany County	284	2.78
Phoenixville, PA (borough) Chester County	406	2.74
Nanticoke, PA (city) Luzerne County	301	2.74
Pottsville, PA (city) Schuylkill County	422	2.72
Fair Oaks, CA (cdp) Sacramento County	755	2.70
North Port, FL (city) Sarasota County	612	2.69
Ansonia, CT (city) New Haven County	488	2.63
Robinson Township, PA (cdp) Allegheny County	319	2.60
Clark, NJ (cdp) Union County	376	2.58
Bensalem, PA (township) Bucks County	1,487	2.54
Webster, NY (town) Monroe County	958	2.53
North Smithfield, RI (town) Providence County	266	2.51
Lower Macungie, PA (township) Lehigh County	480	2.50
Salisbury, PA (township) Lehigh County	335	2.48
Upper Southampton, PA (township) Bucks County	390	2.47
Broadview Heights, OH (city) Cuyahoga County	393	2.46
Plumstead, PA (township) Bucks County	276	2.42
Springfield, NJ (cdp) Union County	348	2.41
Buffalo Grove, IL (village) Lake County	1,017	2.39
Colonia, NJ (cdp) Middlesex County	425	2.39
Upper Saucon, PA (township) Lehigh County	284	2.38
Brentwood, PA (borough) Allegheny County	249	2.38
Fullerton, PA (cdp) Lehigh County	337	2.37
Nether Providence Township, PA (cdp) Delaware County	319	2.37
Lower Burrell, PA (city) Westmoreland County	298	2.36
Strongsville, OH (city) Cuyahoga County	1,019	2.32
Branchburg, NJ (township) Somerset County	336	2.31
Upper Macungie, PA (township) Lehigh County	320	2.30
Caln, PA (township) Chester County	273	2.30
Clifton, NJ (city) Passaic County	1,795	2.28
Little Falls, NJ (cdp) Passaic County	242	2.23
Dickinson, ND (city) Stark County	350	2.21
Westfield, MA (city) Hampden County	881	2.20
Oakland charter, MI (township) Oakland County	287	2.20
Derry, PA (township) Westmoreland County	320	2.17
Wawarsing, NY (town) Ulster County	279	2.16
Mayfield Heights, OH (city) Cuyahoga County	416	2.15
Richland, PA (township) Cambria County	270	2.14
Butler, PA (city) Butler County	320	2.13
Vernon Hills, IL (village) Lake County	437	2.12
Warwick, PA (township) Bucks County	253	2.11
Cherry Hill Mall, NJ (cdp) Camden County	283	2.10
Reisterstown, MD (cdp) Baltimore County	469	2.09
Roselle Park, NJ (borough) Union County	278	2.09
Girard, OH (city) Trumbull County	233	2.09
Ridley, PA (township) Delaware County	636	2.07
South Whitehall, PA (township) Lehigh County	373	2.07
Brunswick, NY (town) Rensselaer County	242	2.07
Austintown, OH (cdp) Mahoning County	651	2.06
Upper Providence Township, PA (cdp) Delaware County	217	2.06
Vancouver, WA (city) Clark County	2,873	2.01
Union, NY (town) Broome County	1,129	2.01
Auburn, WA (city) King County	809	2.01
Mountain Top, PA (cdp) Luzerne County	305	2.00
Brook Park, OH (city) Cuyahoga County	422	1.99
Woodlyn, PA (cdp) Delaware County	197	1.97
South Plainfield, NJ (borough) Middlesex County	427	1.96
Montgomery, NJ (township) Somerset County	343	1.96
Cumru, PA (township) Berks County	269	1.95
West Sacramento, CA (city) Yolo County	613	1.94
Aston, PA (township) Delaware County	312	1.93
Hopewell, PA (township) Beaver County	257	1.93
Union, NJ (cdp) Union County	1,045	1.92
Derby, CT (city) New Haven County	237	1.91
Woodbridge, NJ (township) Middlesex County	1,848	1.90
Skokie, IL (village) Cook County	1,206	1.90
South River, NJ (borough) Middlesex County	290	1.89
Buckingham, PA (township) Bucks County	309	1.88
Emmaus, PA (borough) Lehigh County	210	1.87
Washington, NJ (township) Mercer County	192	1.87
Kent, WA (city) King County	1,477	1.86
Lower Salford, PA (township) Montgomery County	239	1.85
Brecksville, OH (city) Cuyahoga County	245	1.84
Greece, NY (town) Monroe County	1,726	1.83
Paine Field-Lake Stickney, WA (cdp) Snohomish County	444	1.83
Hillsborough, NJ (township) Somerset County	668	1.82
Cranford, NJ (cdp) Union County	412	1.82
Upper Chichester, PA (township) Delaware County	306	1.82
North Greenbush, NY (town) Rensselaer County	196	1.82
Scranton, PA (city) Lackawanna County	1,373	1.80
Wethersfield, CT (cdp) Hartford County	472	1.80
Woodburn, OR (city) Marion County	359	1.79
Dunmore, PA (borough) Lackawanna County	251	1.79
Baldwin, PA (borough) Allegheny County	355	1.78
Linden, NJ (city) Union County	697	1.77
Wheeling, IL (village) Cook County	608	1.77
Holiday City-Berkeley, NJ (cdp) Ocean County	246	1.77
Iselin, NJ (cdp) Middlesex County	292	1.76
New Providence, NJ (borough) Union County	209	1.76
Endwell, NY (cdp) Broome County	205	1.75
Greentree, NJ (cdp) Camden County	201	1.75
Fairview Park, OH (city) Cuyahoga County	306	1.74
Warren, MI (city) Macomb County	2,397	1.73
Scott Township, PA (cdp) Allegheny County	298	1.72
Elmwood Park, NJ (borough) Bergen County	323	1.71
Welby, CO (cdp) Adams County	223	1.71
Gulfport, FL (city) Pinellas County	216	1.71
Pottstown, PA (borough) Montgomery County	367	1.69
Raritan, NJ (township) Hunterdon County	334	1.69
Horseheads, NY (town) Chemung County	330	1.69
South Park Township, PA (cdp) Allegheny County	243	1.69
Niles, IL (village) Cook County	507	1.68
Binghamton, NY (city) Broome County	787	1.66
Windham, CT (town) Windham County	376	1.65
Penfield, NY (town) Monroe County	567	1.64
Whitehall, PA (borough) Allegheny County	237	1.64
Orchard Park, NY (town) Erie County	450	1.63
Lower Moreland, PA (township) Montgomery County	184	1.63
Lower Pottsgrove, PA (township) Montgomery County	184	1.63
Bridgewater, NJ (township) Somerset County	696	1.62
Warminster, PA (township) Bucks County	508	1.62
Parma, NY (town) Monroe County	241	1.62
Plymouth, CT (town) Litchfield County	189	1.62
Boardman, OH (cdp) Mahoning County	601	1.61
Colchester, CT (town) New London County	234	1.61
Federal Way, WA (city) King County	1,328	1.60
Levittown, PA (cdp) Bucks County	856	1.59
Halfmoon, NY (town) Saratoga County	293	1.59

Notes: (cdp) census designated place; Refer to the Explanation of Data in the front of the book for more detailed information.

United States or American

Top 150 Places Sorted by Number

(Based on all places, regardless of population)

Place	Number	%
New York, NY (city) New York County	238,385	2.98
Los Angeles, CA (city) Los Angeles County	94,294	2.55
Indianapolis, IN (special city) Marion County	72,698	9.29
Houston, TX (city) Harris County	71,531	3.66
Jacksonville, FL (special city) Duval County	68,488	9.31
Nashville-Davidson, TN (special city) Davidson County	59,521	10.91
Phoenix, AZ (city) Maricopa County	53,479	4.05
Columbus, OH (city) Franklin County	51,427	7.23
Dallas, TX (city) Dallas County	48,183	4.06
Oklahoma City, OK (city) Oklahoma County	45,589	9.01
Chicago, IL (city) Cook County	38,779	1.34
San Diego, CA (city) San Diego County	38,557	3.15
Charlotte, NC (city) Mecklenburg County	36,557	6.74
San Antonio, TX (city) Bexar County	36,123	3.16
Fort Worth, TX (city) Tarrant County	34,680	6.48
Hempstead, NY (town) Nassau County	31,416	4.16
Tulsa, OK (city) Tulsa County	31,397	7.99
Virginia Beach, VA (independent city) Virginia Beach city	31,137	7.32
Lexington-Fayette, KY (special city) Fayette County	30,490	11.70
Wichita, KS (city) Sedgwick County	29,266	8.51
Memphis, TN (city) Shelby County	29,105	4.48
Austin, TX (city) Travis County	28,052	4.27
Philadelphia, PA (city) Philadelphia County	27,843	1.83
Arlington, TX (city) Tarrant County	25,940	7.80
Kansas City, MO (city) Jackson County	25,807	5.85
Knoxville, TN (city) Knox County	23,175	13.34
Louisville, KY (city) Jefferson County	22,380	8.73
Mesa, AZ (city) Maricopa County	21,665	5.45
Las Vegas, NV (city) Clark County	21,393	4.47
Portland, OR (city) Multnomah County	20,367	3.85
Colorado Springs, CO (city) El Paso County	19,877	5.51
Boston, MA (city) Suffolk County	19,387	3.29
Chesapeake, VA (independent city) Chesapeake city	19,360	9.72
Chattanooga, TN (city) Hamilton County	19,092	12.28
Montgomery, AL (city) Montgomery County	18,878	9.36
Tampa, FL (city) Hillsborough County	18,834	6.21
Denver, CO (city) Denver County	18,640	3.36
Albuquerque, NM (city) Bernalillo County	18,480	4.12
Amarillo, TX (city) Potter County	18,352	10.58
Lubbock, TX (city) Lubbock County	18,232	9.14
Columbus, GA (special city) Muscogee County	18,200	9.80
Huntsville, AL (city) Madison County	18,157	11.50
Tucson, AZ (city) Pima County	17,944	3.69
Augusta-Richmond County, GA (special city) Richmond County	17,803	9.11
Garland, TX (city) Dallas County	17,564	8.13
Springfield, MO (city) Greene County	17,304	11.40
Raleigh, NC (city) Wake County	17,282	6.25
San Jose, CA (city) Santa Clara County	16,961	1.90
Mobile, AL (city) Mobile County	16,873	8.48
Greensboro, NC (city) Guilford County	16,391	7.34
Baltimore, MD (independent city) Baltimore city	16,056	2.47
Cincinnati, OH (city) Hamilton County	15,919	4.81
Anchorage, AK (municipality) Anchorage Borough	15,614	6.00
Mesquite, TX (city) Dallas County	15,311	12.29
Plano, TX (city) Collin County	15,200	6.84
El Paso, TX (city) El Paso County	15,060	2.67
Fort Wayne, IN (city) Allen County	14,422	7.00
Seattle, WA (city) King County	14,343	2.55
Little Rock, AR (city) Pulaski County	14,281	7.78
Newport News, VA (independent city) Newport News city	14,113	7.83
Saint Petersburg, FL (city) Pinellas County	14,062	5.67
Abilene, TX (city) Taylor County	13,965	12.06
Bakersfield, CA (city) Kern County	13,935	5.63
Akron, OH (city) Summit County	13,911	6.41
Winston-Salem, NC (city) Forsyth County	13,890	7.49
Oyster Bay, NY (town) Nassau County	13,610	4.63
Omaha, NE (city) Douglas County	13,521	3.47
Des Moines, IA (city) Polk County	13,477	6.78
Boise City, ID (city) Ada County	13,208	7.10
Irving, TX (city) Dallas County	13,091	6.83
Shreveport, LA (city) Caddo Parish	13,079	6.52
Evansville, IN (city) Vanderburgh County	13,067	10.72
Cleveland, OH (city) Cuyahoga County	13,063	2.73
Sacramento, CA (city) Sacramento County	12,801	3.14
Dayton, OH (city) Montgomery County	12,783	7.69
Brookhaven, NY (town) Suffolk County	12,588	2.81
San Francisco, CA (city) San Francisco County	12,520	1.61
Orlando, FL (city) Orange County	12,426	6.68
Atlanta, GA (city) Fulton County	12,412	2.98
Aurora, CO (city) Arapahoe County	12,393	4.49
Norfolk, VA (independent city) Norfolk city	12,290	5.24
Toledo, OH (city) Lucas County	12,242	3.90
Roanoke, VA (independent city) Roanoke city	11,855	12.49
Fresno, CA (city) Fresno County	11,686	2.74
Corpus Christi, TX (city) Nueces County	11,641	4.19
Detroit, MI (city) Wayne County	11,574	1.22
Independence, MO (city) Jackson County	11,544	10.20
Miami, FL (city) Miami-Dade County	11,317	3.12
North Hempstead, NY (town) Nassau County	11,272	5.06
Clarksville, TN (city) Montgomery County	11,205	10.80
Milwaukee, WI (city) Milwaukee County	11,106	1.86
Pasadena, TX (city) Harris County	10,965	7.74
Glendale, AZ (city) Maricopa County	10,851	4.96
Saint Louis, MO (independent city) Saint Louis city	10,641	3.06
Long Beach, CA (city) Los Angeles County	10,639	2.31
Hampton, VA (independent city) Hampton city	10,614	7.25
Jonesboro, AR (city) Craighead County	10,538	18.95
Dothan, AL (city) Houston County	10,500	18.21
Anaheim, CA (city) Orange County	10,403	3.18
Spokane, WA (city) Spokane County	10,331	5.27
Owensboro, KY (city) Daviess County	10,253	18.94
Riverside, CA (city) Riverside County	9,981	3.91
Washington, DC (city) District of Columbia	9,919	1.73
Wichita Falls, TX (city) Wichita County	9,844	9.47
Lafayette, LA (city) Lafayette Parish	9,843	8.93
New Orleans, LA (city) Orleans Parish	9,836	2.03
Hollywood, FL (city) Broward County	9,762	7.01
Baton Rouge, LA (city) East Baton Rouge Parish	9,583	4.20
Birmingham, AL (city) Jefferson County	9,529	3.92
Anderson, IN (city) Madison County	9,501	15.93
Fort Smith, AR (city) Sebastian County	9,432	11.73
Fayetteville, NC (city) Cumberland County	9,326	7.72
Henderson, NV (city) Clark County	9,306	5.29
Durham, NC (city) Durham County	9,266	4.95
Hamilton, OH (city) Butler County	9,129	15.05
Gastonia, NC (city) Gaston County	9,128	13.77
Scottsdale, AZ (city) Maricopa County	9,120	4.50
Kansas City, KS (city) Wyandotte County	9,046	6.16
Springfield, OH (city) Clark County	9,036	13.83
Johnson City, TN (city) Washington County	8,981	16.23
Vancouver, WA (city) Clark County	8,934	6.24
Fort Lauderdale, FL (city) Broward County	8,904	5.85
Lincoln, NE (city) Lancaster County	8,895	3.95
Islip, NY (town) Suffolk County	8,893	2.76
Modesto, CA (city) Stanislaus County	8,806	4.65
Murfreesboro, TN (city) Rutherford County	8,782	12.74
Decatur, AL (city) Morgan County	8,668	16.07
Muncie, IN (city) Delaware County	8,603	12.75
Tacoma, WA (city) Pierce County	8,544	4.42
Grand Prairie, TX (city) Dallas County	8,528	6.71
Topeka, KS (city) Shawnee County	8,493	6.96
High Point, NC (city) Guilford County	8,482	9.87
Decatur, IL (city) Macon County	8,418	10.25
Pembroke Pines, FL (city) Broward County	8,380	6.11
Norman, OK (city) Cleveland County	8,354	8.73
Jackson, MS (city) Hinds County	8,353	4.54
Huntington Beach, CA (city) Orange County	8,322	4.38
Carrollton, TX (city) Denton County	8,317	7.62
Overland Park, KS (city) Johnson County	8,191	5.50
West Valley City, UT (city) Salt Lake County	8,182	7.52
Reno, NV (city) Washoe County	8,167	4.52
Lawton, OK (city) Comanche County	8,122	8.73
Lynchburg, VA (independent city) Lynchburg city	8,070	12.36
Tallahassee, FL (city) Leon County	7,976	5.30
Springfield, IL (city) Sangamon County	7,965	7.10
Middletown, OH (city) Butler County	7,955	15.36
Concord, NC (city) Cabarrus County	7,887	14.10
Chandler, AZ (city) Maricopa County	7,881	4.47
Paradise, NV (cdp) Clark County	7,854	4.23
Saint Joseph, MO (city) Buchanan County	7,852	10.64

Notes: (cdp) census designated place; Refer to the Explanation of Data in the front of the book for more detailed information.

United States or American

Top 150 Places Sorted by Percent

(Based on all places, regardless of population)

Place	Number	%
Valley City, IL (village) Pike County	18	100.00
Hawk Springs, WY (cdp) Goshen County	13	100.00
Monowi, NE (village) Boyd County	3	100.00
Hartwell, MO (village) Henry County	23	92.00
Dycusburg, KY (city) Crittenden County	37	86.05
Blandville, KY (city) Ballard County	83	84.69
Fortescue, MO (town) Holt County	51	83.61
Rockwood, IL (village) Randolph County	38	80.85
Weston, GA (town) Webster County	52	77.61
Valeria, IA (city) Jasper County	43	71.67
Rohrersville, MD (cdp) Washington County	136	71.20
Lockhart, SC (town) Union County	29	70.73
Garfield, GA (town) Emanuel County	108	70.13
Orchard Hill, GA (town) Spalding County	139	69.50
River Forest, IN (town) Madison County	20	68.97
Vicco, KY (city) Perry County	197	65.89
Pope-Vannoy Landing, AK (cdp) Lake and Peninsula Borough	5	62.50
Love Valley, NC (town) Iredell County	18	62.07
Talking Rock, GA (town) Pickens County	31	62.00
Edwardsville, AL (town) Cleburne County	136	60.99
Blue Springs, AL (town) Barbour County	56	60.87
Iatan, MO (village) Platte County	37	60.66
Dumas, MS (town) Tippah County	293	60.29
Inez, KY (city) Martin County	261	60.14
Goldville, AL (town) Tallapoosa County	13	59.09
Holiday City, OH (village) Williams County	30	58.82
Wallins Creek, KY (city) Harlan County	135	58.19
Riverside, GA (town) Colquitt County	36	58.06
Hamill, SD (cdp) Tripp County	23	57.50
Passaic, MO (town) Bates County	31	57.41
Nunez, GA (town) Emanuel County	100	57.14
Stotesbury, MO (town) Vernon County	24	57.14
Sale City, GA (town) Mitchell County	181	56.92
Coalmont, TN (city) Grundy County	527	56.61
Knowles, OK (town) Beaver County	13	56.52
Aquilla, TX (city) Hill County	79	56.03
Edge Hill, GA (city) Glascock County	24	55.81
Surrency, GA (town) Appling County	154	55.40
Millican, TX (town) Brazos County	64	55.17
Egypt, AR (town) Craighead County	59	55.14
Scotland, GA (city) Telfair County	167	53.35
Tupelo, AR (town) Jackson County	91	53.22
Camden, MO (city) Ray County	108	52.94
Altamont, TN (town) Grundy County	630	52.81
Mason, WI (village) Bayfield County	19	52.78
Mexico, PA (cdp) Juniata County	174	52.73
Wade, MS (cdp) Jackson County	292	52.71
Blackey, KY (city) Letcher County	78	52.70
Samburg, TN (town) Obion County	128	52.67
South Middletown, OH (cdp) Butler County	91	52.30
Campus, IL (village) Livingston County	62	52.10
Paden, MS (village) Tishomingo County	58	50.88
Seven Devils, NC (town) Watauga County	63	50.81
Ward, SC (town) Saluda County	63	50.81
Albion, OK (town) Pushmataha County	68	50.75
Hambleton, WV (town) Tucker County	122	50.41
Chokoloskee, FL (cdp) Collier County	259	50.29
Rayle, GA (town) Wilkes County	57	50.00
Delphos, IA (city) Ringgold County	12	50.00
Irena, MO (village) Worth County	11	50.00
Mound, LA (village) Madison Parish	11	50.00
Salyersville, KY (city) Magoffin County	802	49.91
Eldred, IL (village) Greene County	109	49.77
Macksburg, OH (village) Washington County	94	49.47
Wayland, KY (city) Floyd County	149	49.34
Braswell, GA (city) Paulding County	34	49.28
White Plains, NC (cdp) Surry County	616	49.16
Cedarville, KY (city) Pike County	24	48.98
Aldora, GA (town) Lamar County	37	48.68
Maramec, OK (town) Pawnee County	53	48.62
O'Kean, AR (town) Randolph County	100	48.54
Woodburn, KY (city) Warren County	146	48.50
Plainville, GA (city) Gordon County	133	48.19
Turkey Creek, LA (village) Evangeline Parish	170	48.02
Beersheba Springs, TN (town) Grundy County	251	47.99
Oak Grove, AL (town) Talladega County	227	47.79
Evarts, KY (city) Harlan County	513	47.41
Brookview, MD (town) Dorchester County	44	47.31
Princeton, SC (cdp) Laurens County	26	47.27
Cash, AR (town) Craighead County	140	47.14
Etowah, OK (town) Cleveland County	66	47.14
Gilbert Creek, WV (cdp) Mingo County	739	47.13
Onycha, AL (town) Covington County	98	47.12
Summertown, GA (town) Emanuel County	65	47.10
Bradshaw, WV (town) McDowell County	134	46.53
Petrey, AL (town) Crenshaw County	26	46.43
Paxson, AK (cdp) Valdez-Cordova Census Area	13	46.43
Lasker, NC (town) Northampton County	32	46.38
Hull, GA (city) Madison County	63	46.32
Riley, IN (town) Vigo County	67	46.21
Watha, NC (town) Pender County	61	46.21
Annada, MO (village) Pike County	18	46.15
Franklin, AR (town) Izard County	87	46.03
Fisk, MO (city) Butler County	169	45.92
Spearsville, LA (village) Union Parish	67	45.89
Kite, GA (town) Johnson County	83	45.86
Radium, KS (city) Stafford County	11	45.83
Harris, MO (town) Sullivan County	49	45.79
Saint Francis, ME (town) Aroostook County	267	45.72
La Due, MO (village) Henry County	21	45.65
Montrose, MS (town) Jasper County	80	45.45
La Prairie, IL (village) Adams County	25	45.45
Ludlow, ME (town) Aroostook County	182	45.39
Haysi, VA (town) Dickenson County	88	45.36
Prestonville, KY (city) Carroll County	80	45.20
Kildare, OK (town) Kay County	46	45.10
East Haven, VT (town) Essex County	132	45.05
Hodges, SC (town) Greenwood County	77	45.03
Monterey, KY (city) Owen County	90	45.00
Sand Rock, AL (town) Cherokee County	218	44.95
Iron City, TN (city) Lawrence County	162	44.88
Ironton, MN (city) Crow Wing County	197	44.87
Saint Charles, KY (city) Hopkins County	141	44.76
Cottage Grove, TN (town) Henry County	46	44.66
Higgston, GA (town) Montgomery County	159	44.54
Nebo, KY (city) Hopkins County	92	44.44
Tinsman, AR (city) Calhoun County	36	44.44
Venturia, ND (city) McIntosh County	8	44.44
Parkerville, KS (city) Morris County	23	44.23
Waltham, ME (town) Hancock County	150	44.12
Avon, ME (town) Franklin County	217	44.11
East Germantown, IN (town) Wayne County	101	44.10
Heflin, LA (village) Webster Parish	104	44.07
Beattyville, KY (city) Lee County	502	44.00
Lester, AL (town) Limestone County	44	44.00
McKee, KY (city) Jackson County	391	43.83
Avon, AL (town) Houston County	188	43.82
Gainesboro, TN (town) Jackson County	378	43.80
Urania, LA (town) La Salle Parish	304	43.80
Saint Charles, VA (town) Lee County	67	43.79
Emington, IL (village) Livingston County	56	43.75
Needham, AL (town) Choctaw County	49	43.75
Branson, CO (town) Las Animas County	42	43.75
Smith Village, OK (town) Oklahoma County	17	43.59
Enville, TN (town) Chester County	98	43.56
Leon, WV (town) Mason County	56	43.08
Elizabeth, IN (town) Harrison County	59	43.07
Saint John, ME (plantation) Aroostook County	121	43.06
Eubank, KY (city) Pulaski County	159	42.97
Doyle, TN (town) White County	229	42.96
Glenwood, IN (town) Rush County	132	42.86
Game Creek, AK (cdp) Skagway-Hoonah-Angoon Census Area	12	42.86
Blodgett, MO (village) Scott County	118	42.75
Bairdstown, OH (village) Wood County	56	42.75
Lima, OK (town) Seminole County	32	42.67
Gilbert, WV (town) Mingo County	176	42.62
Askewville, NC (town) Bertie County	83	42.56
Lockhart, AL (town) Covington County	233	42.44
Woodville, ME (town) Penobscot County	107	42.29
Rives, TN (town) Obion County	158	42.25

Notes: (cdp) census designated place; Refer to the Explanation of Data in the front of the book for more detailed information.

United States or American

Top 150 Places Sorted by Percent

(Based on places with populations of 10,000 or more)

Place	Number	%
Middlesborough, KY (city) Bell County	3,914	37.72
Martinsville, IN (city) Morgan County	3,287	27.96
Campbellsville, KY (city) Taylor County	2,886	27.92
Soddy-Daisy, TN (city) Hamilton County	3,111	27.06
Madison Heights, VA (cdp) Amherst County	2,988	26.32
Glasgow, KY (city) Barren County	3,268	24.89
Athens, TN (city) McMinn County	3,213	24.65
Lebanon, TN (city) Wilson County	5,002	24.64
Fort Payne, AL (city) De Kalb County	3,236	24.60
Bloomingdale, TN (cdp) Sullivan County	2,521	24.28
Gardendale, AL (city) Jefferson County	2,837	24.03
Winchester, KY (city) Clark County	3,944	23.89
Smiths, AL (cdp) Lee County	5,156	23.86
Muscle Shoals, AL (city) Colbert County	2,852	23.74
Parker, SC (cdp) Greenville County	2,526	23.72
Saraland, AL (city) Mobile County	2,800	23.25
Shelbyville, IN (city) Shelby County	4,092	23.13
Corinth, MS (city) Alcorn County	3,246	23.10
Lenoir, NC (city) Caldwell County	3,826	22.97
Shelbyville, TN (city) Bedford County	3,676	22.87
Kennett, MO (city) Dunklin County	2,578	22.87
McMinnville, TN (city) Warren County	2,910	22.84
Lewisburg, TN (city) Marshall County	2,365	22.81
Jasper, AL (city) Walker County	3,193	22.69
Albertville, AL (city) Marshall County	3,939	22.67
Eden, NC (city) Rockingham County	3,615	22.54
Pearl, MS (city) Rankin County	4,941	22.50
Madisonville, KY (city) Hopkins County	4,268	22.33
Middle Valley, TN (cdp) Hamilton County	2,631	22.33
Harrison, AR (city) Boone County	2,729	22.26
Washington, IN (city) Daviess County	2,510	22.26
Paragould, AR (city) Greene County	4,828	21.91
New Castle, IN (city) Henry County	3,900	21.90
Cookeville, TN (city) Putnam County	5,277	21.84
Oxford, AL (city) Calhoun County	3,193	21.77
Front Royal, VA (town) Warren County	2,985	21.66
Franklin, OH (city) Warren County	2,482	21.51
Cullman, AL (city) Cullman County	3,007	21.40
Hartselle, AL (city) Morgan County	2,517	21.40
Lawrenceburg, TN (city) Lawrence County	2,227	21.26
Nicholasville, KY (city) Jessamine County	4,128	21.10
Sylacauga, AL (city) Talladega County	2,586	20.78
Sevierville, TN (city) Sevier County	2,459	20.78
Moss Bluff, LA (cdp) Calcasieu Parish	2,185	20.74
Connersville, IN (city) Fayette County	3,191	20.70
Morristown, TN (city) Hamblen County	5,225	20.67
Florence, AL (city) Lauderdale County	7,465	20.49
Albemarle, NC (city) Stanly County	3,187	20.42
Vidalia, GA (city) Toombs County	2,152	20.29
Graham, NC (city) Alamance County	2,562	20.20
East Ridge, TN (city) Hamilton County	4,194	20.19
Frankfort, KY (city) Franklin County	5,550	20.18
Beech Grove, IN (city) Marion County	2,865	20.18
Bardstown, KY (city) Nelson County	2,096	20.07
Seymour, IN (city) Jackson County	3,612	20.06
Trussville, AL (city) Jefferson County	2,744	20.00
Pleasure Ridge Park, KY (cdp) Jefferson County	5,191	19.98
Waynesboro, VA (independent city) Waynesboro city	3,890	19.93
Mount Juliet, TN (city) Wilson County	2,444	19.89
Henderson, KY (city) Henderson County	5,437	19.85
Somerset, KY (city) Pulaski County	2,262	19.78
Scottsboro, AL (city) Jackson County	2,921	19.76
Timberlake, VA (cdp) Campbell County	2,107	19.35
Gadsden, AL (city) Etowah County	7,492	19.29
Hueytown, AL (city) Jefferson County	2,935	19.29
Mayfield, KY (city) Graves County	1,990	19.26
Lebanon, MO (city) Laclede County	2,359	19.24
Tarboro, NC (town) Edgecombe County	2,140	19.07
Durant, OK (city) Bryan County	2,583	19.06
La Vergne, TN (city) Rutherford County	3,599	19.03
Jonesboro, AR (city) Craighead County	10,538	18.95
Owensboro, KY (city) Daviess County	10,253	18.94
Teays Valley, WV (cdp) Putnam County	2,396	18.90
Monroe, GA (city) Walton County	2,184	18.88
Benton, AR (city) Saline County	4,157	18.86
Elizabethton, TN (city) Carter County	2,527	18.81
Dickson, TN (city) Dickson County	2,352	18.81
Elizabethtown, KY (city) Hardin County	4,213	18.75
Smyrna, TN (town) Rutherford County	4,739	18.67
Thomasville, NC (city) Davidson County	3,662	18.64
Marion, OH (city) Marion County	6,571	18.62
Clarksburg, WV (city) Harrison County	3,079	18.61
Athens, AL (city) Limestone County	3,548	18.59
Columbia, TN (city) Maury County	6,140	18.57
Easley, SC (city) Pickens County	3,333	18.55
Gallatin, TN (city) Sumner County	4,305	18.53
Martin, TN (city) Weakley County	1,954	18.53
Brandon, MS (city) Rankin County	3,017	18.47
Sulphur, LA (city) Calcasieu Parish	3,762	18.44
Saks, AL (cdp) Calhoun County	1,941	18.40
Buford, GA (city) Gwinnett County	1,969	18.39
Bedford, IN (city) Lawrence County	2,541	18.31
Cartersville, GA (city) Bartow County	2,939	18.28
Southaven, MS (city) De Soto County	5,312	18.26
Staunton, VA (independent city) Staunton city	4,350	18.24
Dothan, AL (city) Houston County	10,500	18.21
Goodlettsville, TN (city) Davidson County	2,512	18.14
Horn Lake, MS (city) De Soto County	2,505	18.14
Bristol, VA (independent city) Bristol city	3,147	18.12
Leeds, AL (city) Jefferson County	1,950	18.11
Ironton, OH (city) Lawrence County	2,042	18.09
Salem, VA (independent city) Salem city	4,474	18.08
Richmond, KY (city) Madison County	4,893	18.06
Valley Station, KY (cdp) Jefferson County	4,111	18.02
Tillmans Corner, AL (cdp) Mobile County	2,807	18.01
Washington, OH (city) Fayette County	2,420	18.00
Brownsburg, IN (town) Hendricks County	2,565	17.88
Bristol, TN (city) Sullivan County	4,452	17.82
Auburndale, FL (city) Polk County	1,984	17.69
Maryville, TN (city) Blount County	4,088	17.65
Vidor, TX (city) Orange County	2,008	17.65
Georgetown, KY (city) Scott County	3,185	17.64
Tupelo, MS (city) Lee County	6,066	17.62
Millbrook, AL (city) Elmore County	1,802	17.59
Cleveland, TN (city) Bradley County	6,496	17.49
Vincennes, IN (city) Knox County	3,242	17.45
Sulphur Springs, TX (city) Hopkins County	2,543	17.45
Dyersburg, TN (city) Dyer County	3,031	17.36
Parkersburg, WV (city) Wood County	5,752	17.35
Alexander City, AL (city) Tallapoosa County	2,590	17.32
Springfield, TN (city) Robertson County	2,442	17.23
Plainfield, IN (town) Hendricks County	3,248	17.20
Union City, TN (city) Obion County	1,834	17.13
Hopkinsville, KY (city) Christian County	5,172	17.11
Sikeston, MO (city) Scott County	2,909	17.10
Wylie, TX (city) Collin County	2,558	17.09
Hannibal, MO (city) Marion County	3,053	17.03
Winder, GA (city) Barrow County	1,708	17.01
Chickasha, OK (city) Grady County	2,677	16.86
Kingsport, TN (city) Sullivan County	7,453	16.73
Upper Grand Lagoon, FL (cdp) Bay County	1,822	16.59
Alabaster, AL (city) Shelby County	3,843	16.56
Bellefontaine, OH (city) Logan County	2,155	16.51
Prattville, AL (city) Autauga County	4,009	16.50
Red Bank, TN (city) Hamilton County	2,053	16.38
Galion, OH (city) Crawford County	1,879	16.35
Greer, SC (city) Greenville County	2,701	16.33
Christiansburg, VA (town) Montgomery County	2,768	16.31
Gaffney, SC (city) Cherokee County	2,110	16.30
Circleville, OH (city) Pickaway County	2,206	16.26
Urbana, OH (city) Champaign County	1,889	16.26
Nixa, MO (city) Christian County	1,980	16.24
Kilgore, TX (city) Gregg County	1,814	16.24
Johnson City, TN (city) Washington County	8,981	16.23
Moundsville, WV (city) Marshall County	1,639	16.22
Pampa, TX (city) Gray County	2,880	16.10
Helena, AL (city) Shelby County	1,632	16.08
Decatur, AL (city) Morgan County	8,668	16.07
Kannapolis, NC (city) Cabarrus County	5,896	16.07
Calhoun, GA (city) Gordon County	1,670	16.07

Notes: (cdp) census designated place; Refer to the Explanation of Data in the front of the book for more detailed information.

Welsh

Top 150 Places Sorted by Number

(Based on all places, regardless of population)

Place	Number	%
Los Angeles, CA (city) Los Angeles County	10,233	0.28
Columbus, OH (city) Franklin County	9,969	1.40
New York, NY (city) New York City	8,830	0.11
San Diego, CA (city) San Diego County	7,838	0.64
Phoenix, AZ (city) Maricopa County	7,728	0.59
Portland, OR (city) Multnomah County	6,701	1.27
Seattle, WA (city) King County	6,671	1.18
Houston, TX (city) Harris County	5,325	0.27
Scranton, PA (city) Lackawanna County	5,300	6.94
Chicago, IL (city) Cook County	5,226	0.18
Indianapolis, IN (special city) Marion County	5,008	0.64
Philadelphia, PA (city) Philadelphia County	4,922	0.32
San Francisco, CA (city) San Francisco County	4,487	0.58
Austin, TX (city) Travis County	4,261	0.65
Dallas, TX (city) Dallas County	4,060	0.34
Denver, CO (city) Denver County	4,039	0.73
Albuquerque, NM (city) Bernalillo County	3,728	0.83
Jacksonville, FL (special city) Duval County	3,699	0.50
San Jose, CA (city) Santa Clara County	3,669	0.41
Salt Lake City, UT (city) Salt Lake County	3,598	1.98
San Antonio, TX (city) Bexar County	3,598	0.31
Mesa, AZ (city) Maricopa County	3,516	0.89
Tucson, AZ (city) Pima County	3,447	0.71
Colorado Springs, CO (city) El Paso County	3,434	0.95
Boise City, ID (city) Ada County	3,344	1.80
Charlotte, NC (city) Mecklenburg County	3,208	0.59
Virginia Beach, VA (independent city) Virginia Beach city	3,144	0.74
Kansas City, MO (city) Jackson County	3,001	0.68
Nashville-Davidson, TN (special city) Davidson County	2,865	0.53
Las Vegas, NV (city) Clark County	2,832	0.59
Pittsburgh, PA (city) Allegheny County	2,816	0.84
Tulsa, OK (city) Tulsa County	2,705	0.69
Wilkes-Barre, PA (city) Luzerne County	2,650	6.15
Provo, UT (city) Utah County	2,495	2.37
Oklahoma City, OK (city) Oklahoma County	2,463	0.49
Wichita, KS (city) Sedgwick County	2,413	0.70
Akron, OH (city) Summit County	2,390	1.10
Anchorage, AK (municipality) Anchorage Borough	2,288	0.88
Minneapolis, MN (city) Hennepin County	2,270	0.59
Back Mountain, PA (cdp) Luzerne County	2,247	8.42
Orem, UT (city) Utah County	2,216	2.63
Aurora, CO (city) Arapahoe County	2,207	0.80
Sandy, UT (city) Salt Lake County	2,200	2.49
Spokane, WA (city) Spokane County	2,195	1.12
Scottsdale, AZ (city) Maricopa County	2,175	1.07
Baltimore, MD (independent city) Baltimore city	2,137	0.33
Lexington-Fayette, KY (special city) Fayette County	2,129	0.82
Sacramento, CA (city) Sacramento County	2,080	0.51
Des Moines, IA (city) Polk County	2,074	1.04
Washington, DC (city) District of Columbia	2,067	0.36
Fort Worth, TX (city) Tarrant County	2,061	0.38
Omaha, NE (city) Douglas County	2,054	0.53
Raleigh, NC (city) Wake County	2,052	0.74
Eugene, OR (city) Lane County	1,990	1.44
Saint Petersburg, FL (city) Pinellas County	1,985	0.80
Long Beach, CA (city) Los Angeles County	1,984	0.43
Arlington, TX (city) Tarrant County	1,879	0.56
Arlington, VA (cdp) Arlington County	1,862	0.98
Huntington Beach, CA (city) Orange County	1,795	0.95
Madison, WI (city) Dane County	1,790	0.86
Overland Park, KS (city) Johnson County	1,755	1.18
Lincoln, NE (city) Lancaster County	1,750	0.78
Cincinnati, OH (city) Hamilton County	1,745	0.53
West Valley City, UT (city) Salt Lake County	1,718	1.58
Henderson, NV (city) Clark County	1,648	0.94
Plano, TX (city) Collin County	1,643	0.74
Riverside, CA (city) Riverside County	1,617	0.63
Allentown, PA (city) Lehigh County	1,613	1.51
Salem, OR (city) Marion County	1,612	1.18
Toledo, OH (city) Lucas County	1,611	0.51
Oakland, CA (city) Alameda County	1,579	0.40
Milwaukee, WI (city) Milwaukee County	1,577	0.26
Tacoma, WA (city) Pierce County	1,575	0.82
Santa Rosa, CA (city) Sonoma County	1,552	1.05
Boston, MA (city) Suffolk County	1,544	0.26
Fort Collins, CO (city) Larimer County	1,490	1.26
Fresno, CA (city) Fresno County	1,489	0.35
Atlanta, GA (city) Fulton County	1,472	0.35
Lakewood, CO (city) Jefferson County	1,461	1.01
Reno, NV (city) Washoe County	1,456	0.81
Glendale, AZ (city) Maricopa County	1,453	0.66
Bakersfield, CA (city) Kern County	1,434	0.58
Bethlehem, PA (city) Northampton County	1,411	1.98
Memphis, TN (city) Shelby County	1,391	0.21
West Jordan, UT (city) Salt Lake County	1,379	2.02
Tampa, FL (city) Hillsborough County	1,346	0.44
Ogden, UT (city) Weber County	1,333	1.73
Tempe, AZ (city) Maricopa County	1,319	0.83
Pocatello, ID (city) Bannock County	1,309	2.54
Cleveland, OH (city) Cuyahoga County	1,309	0.27
Bountiful, UT (city) Davis County	1,302	3.15
Saint Paul, MN (city) Ramsey County	1,298	0.45
Modesto, CA (city) Stanislaus County	1,293	0.68
Union, NY (town) Broome County	1,281	2.28
Honolulu, HI (cdp) Honolulu County	1,280	0.34
Chesapeake, VA (independent city) Chesapeake city	1,277	0.64
Chandler, AZ (city) Maricopa County	1,272	0.72
Anaheim, CA (city) Orange County	1,267	0.39
Vancouver, WA (city) Clark County	1,252	0.87
Knoxville, TN (city) Knox County	1,248	0.72
San Buenaventura, CA (city) Ventura County	1,247	1.23
Santa Clarita, CA (city) Los Angeles County	1,245	0.82
Louisville, KY (city) Jefferson County	1,237	0.48
Oceanside, CA (city) San Diego County	1,228	0.76
Layton, UT (city) Davis County	1,223	2.08
Greensboro, NC (city) Guilford County	1,202	0.54
Topeka, KS (city) Shawnee County	1,198	0.98
New Orleans, LA (city) Orleans Parish	1,186	0.24
Stockton, CA (city) San Joaquin County	1,183	0.49
Independence, MO (city) Jackson County	1,181	1.04
Idaho Falls, ID (city) Bonneville County	1,167	2.31
El Paso, TX (city) El Paso County	1,157	0.21
Concord, CA (city) Contra Costa County	1,149	0.94
Taylorsville, UT (city) Salt Lake County	1,146	1.98
Paradise, NV (cdp) Clark County	1,140	0.61
Mountain Top, PA (cdp) Luzerne County	1,133	7.43
Gilbert, AZ (town) Maricopa County	1,131	1.03
Richmond, VA (independent city) Richmond city	1,131	0.57
Utica, NY (city) Oneida County	1,125	1.85
Winston-Salem, NC (city) Forsyth County	1,125	0.61
Norfolk, VA (independent city) Norfolk city	1,119	0.48
Lubbock, TX (city) Lubbock County	1,099	0.55
Arvada, CO (city) Jefferson County	1,076	1.05
Thousand Oaks, CA (city) Ventura County	1,075	0.92
Fort Wayne, IN (city) Allen County	1,073	0.52
Cuyahoga Falls, OH (city) Summit County	1,064	2.16
Tallahassee, FL (city) Leon County	1,061	0.70
Upper Arlington, OH (city) Franklin County	1,060	3.15
Boulder, CO (city) Boulder County	1,057	1.12
Fort Lauderdale, FL (city) Broward County	1,050	0.69
Ann Arbor, MI (city) Washtenaw County	1,048	0.92
Orlando, FL (city) Orange County	1,046	0.56
Mission Viejo, CA (city) Orange County	1,040	1.12
Irvine, CA (city) Orange County	1,034	0.72
Durham, NC (city) Durham County	1,030	0.55
New Hartford, NY (town) Oneida County	1,029	4.86
Everett, WA (city) Snohomish County	1,028	1.13
Olathe, KS (city) Johnson County	1,028	1.11
Brookhaven, NY (town) Suffolk County	1,023	0.23
Springfield, MO (city) Greene County	1,016	0.67
Hempstead, NY (town) Nassau County	1,013	0.13
Canton, OH (city) Stark County	1,012	1.25
Logan, UT (city) Cache County	1,008	2.36
Westminster, CO (city) Adams County	1,007	1.00
Bellingham, WA (city) Whatcom County	1,001	1.50
Lawrence, KS (city) Douglas County	994	1.24
Austintown, OH (cdp) Mahoning County	990	3.13
Billings, MT (city) Yellowstone County	990	1.11
Gresham, OR (city) Multnomah County	986	1.09
Torrance, CA (city) Los Angeles County	985	0.71

Notes: (cdp) census designated place; Refer to the Explanation of Data in the front of the book for more detailed information.

Welsh

Top 150 Places Sorted by Percent

(Based on all places, regardless of population)

Place	Number	%
Marineland, FL (town) Flagler County	2	28.57
Table Rock, WY (cdp) Sweetwater County	23	24.21
Malad City, ID (city) Oneida County	499	22.77
Lowry, SD (town) Walworth County	2	20.00
Nora, NE (village) Nuckolls County	2	20.00
Sedalia, CO (cdp) Douglas County	42	19.72
Haynesville, ME (town) Aroostook County	24	19.35
Venedocia, OH (village) Van Wert County	31	19.02
Shoshone, CA (cdp) Inyo County	15	17.86
Montezuma, CO (town) Summit County	6	17.65
Remsen, NY (town) Oneida County	329	16.97
Biggs Junction, OR (cdp) Sherman County	12	16.90
Smoot, WY (cdp) Lincoln County	31	16.85
Holland Patent, NY (village) Oneida County	74	16.78
Middletown, PA (township) Susquehanna County	53	16.77
Remsen, NY (village) Oneida County	86	16.76
Wales, UT (town) Sanpete County	38	16.31
Lake McMurray, WA (cdp) Skagit County	27	15.17
Unity Village, MO (village) Jackson County	31	14.98
Washam, WY (cdp) Sweetwater County	7	14.58
Cashiers, NC (cdp) Jackson County	24	14.46
Salladasburg, PA (borough) Lycoming County	38	14.02
Cambria, MN (township) Blue Earth County	42	13.68
Steuben, NY (town) Oneida County	160	13.43
East Fork, PA (district) Potter County	2	13.33
Ransom, PA (township) Lackawanna County	188	13.15
Monomoscoy Island, MA (cdp) Barnstable County	16	12.90
Judson, MN (township) Blue Earth County	74	12.74
Barneveld, NY (village) Oneida County	42	12.50
Panola, IL (village) Woodford County	4	12.50
Ophir, UT (town) Tooele County	2	12.50
Lake Bosworth, WA (cdp) Snohomish County	20	12.35
Lumber City, PA (borough) Clearfield County	12	12.24
Parc, NY (cdp) Clinton County	6	12.24
Waverly, WA (town) Spokane County	16	12.21
Madison, NY (village) Madison County	37	11.67
Plymouth, PA (borough) Luzerne County	759	11.66
Benton, PA (township) Lackawanna County	218	11.59
Dalton, PA (borough) Lackawanna County	150	11.59
Alexander, KS (city) Rush County	8	11.59
Alpine Northeast, WY (cdp) Lincoln County	12	11.43
Nuangola, PA (borough) Luzerne County	78	11.37
Henlopen Acres, DE (town) Sussex County	16	11.35
Lake, PA (township) Luzerne County	238	11.28
Louviers, CO (cdp) Douglas County	22	11.17
Kingston, PA (township) Luzerne County	784	10.97
Saint Charles, ID (city) Bear Lake County	15	10.95
Dallas, PA (borough) Luzerne County	279	10.91
Montague, NY (town) Lewis County	11	10.89
Tse Bonito, NM (cdp) McKinley County	30	10.79
Factoryville, PA (borough) Wyoming County	123	10.75
Franktown, CO (cdp) Douglas County	10	10.75
Rupert, PA (cdp) Columbia County	19	10.73
Clarks Summit, PA (borough) Lackawanna County	542	10.71
Frenchtown-Rumbly, MD (cdp) Somerset County	6	10.71
Green Hills, PA (borough) Washington County	2	10.53
Butternut Valley, MN (township) Blue Earth County	38	10.50
Slocum, PA (township) Luzerne County	115	10.49
Nicholson, PA (borough) Wyoming County	73	10.44
Spring Brook, PA (township) Lackawanna County	244	10.43
Johnson, MN (township) Polk County	5	10.42
Oak Hill, OH (village) Jackson County	177	10.41
Gibson, PA (township) Susquehanna County	116	10.27
Overfield, PA (township) Wyoming County	154	10.05
The Forks, ME (plantation) Somerset County	6	10.00
Bangor, PA (borough) Northampton County	531	9.98
Arrowhead Springs, WY (cdp) Sweetwater County	10	9.62
Clarks Green, PA (borough) Lackawanna County	156	9.59
La Plume, PA (township) Lackawanna County	61	9.50
Junction City, WA (cdp) Grays Harbor County	9	9.47
Madrid, NM (cdp) Santa Fe County	10	9.43
Cotter, IA (city) Louisa County	5	9.43
Duane, NY (town) Franklin County	13	9.42
Woodston, KS (city) Rooks County	8	9.41
Silvana, WA (cdp) Snohomish County	9	9.38
New Cambria, MO (city) Macon County	20	9.26
Herrick, PA (township) Susquehanna County	53	9.20
Prompton, PA (borough) Wayne County	25	9.19
Hartline, WA (town) Grant County	13	9.15
Edwardsville, PA (borough) Luzerne County	452	9.07
Poultney, VT (village) Rutland County	143	9.06
Ross, PA (township) Luzerne County	247	9.01
Englewood, PA (cdp) Schuylkill County	39	8.97
Lehman, PA (township) Luzerne County	286	8.92
Franklin, PA (township) Luzerne County	142	8.87
Exeter, PA (township) Wyoming County	66	8.86
Taylor, PA (borough) Lackawanna County	573	8.85
Russia, NY (town) Herkimer County	218	8.82
Buck Run, PA (cdp) Schuylkill County	21	8.82
Harveys Lake, PA (borough) Luzerne County	254	8.80
Waverly, AL (town) Chambers County	15	8.77
Bear Creek, PA (township) Luzerne County	226	8.76
Plainfield, NY (town) Otsego County	86	8.72
Roaring Brook, PA (township) Lackawanna County	140	8.63
Henrieville, UT (town) Garfield County	15	8.62
Winfield, NY (town) Herkimer County	190	8.61
South Abington, PA (township) Lackawanna County	745	8.56
Poultney, VT (town) Rutland County	310	8.53
Lenox, PA (township) Susquehanna County	156	8.52
Courtdale, PA (borough) Luzerne County	67	8.47
Back Mountain, PA (cdp) Luzerne County	2,247	8.42
Nicholson, PA (township) Wyoming County	115	8.36
Elfin Cove, AK (cdp) Skagway-Hoonah-Angoon Census Area	3	8.33
Larksville, PA (borough) Luzerne County	390	8.31
Boulder, UT (town) Garfield County	15	8.29
Rice, PA (township) Luzerne County	203	8.25
Stillwater, PA (borough) Columbia County	15	8.24
Warrior Run, PA (borough) Luzerne County	52	8.20
Clifford, PA (township) Susquehanna County	194	8.15
Matfield Green, KS (city) Chase County	5	8.06
Madisonburg, PA (cdp) Centre County	10	8.00
Broeck Pointe, KY (city) Jefferson County	23	7.99
Hunlock, PA (township) Luzerne County	205	7.98
Elmhurst, PA (township) Lackawanna County	68	7.98
Glenburn, PA (cdp) Lackawanna County	96	7.92
Laurel Run, PA (borough) Luzerne County	57	7.84
West Winfield, NY (village) Herkimer County	68	7.83
Trenton, NY (town) Oneida County	367	7.81
Catawba, OH (village) Clark County	15	7.77
Covington, PA (township) Lackawanna County	154	7.72
Newton, PA (township) Lackawanna County	208	7.71
Harford, PA (township) Susquehanna County	100	7.69
Millstone, PA (township) Elk County	6	7.69
Struble, IA (city) Plymouth County	6	7.69
Oakley, ID (city) Cassia County	49	7.67
Bishop, GA (town) Oconee County	11	7.59
Tanberg, MN (township) Wilkin County	5	7.58
Farmersville, NY (town) Cattaraugus County	78	7.56
Fort Smith, MT (cdp) Big Horn County	8	7.55
Kings Point, MT (cdp) Lake County	8	7.55
Brownville, ME (town) Piscataquis County	96	7.54
Tabiona, UT (town) Duchesne County	14	7.53
Garland, WY (cdp) Park County	6	7.50
Jermyn, PA (borough) Lackawanna County	171	7.48
Rewey, WI (village) Iowa County	21	7.47
Mountain Top, PA (cdp) Luzerne County	1,133	7.43
Moscow, PA (borough) Lackawanna County	140	7.43
Snowville, UT (town) Box Elder County	14	7.41
New Hartford, NY (village) Oneida County	139	7.37
Piehl, WI (town) Oneida County	7	7.37
Plymouth, PA (township) Luzerne County	153	7.30
Lyons Falls, NY (village) Lewis County	41	7.28
Exeter, PA (township) Luzerne County	186	7.27
Metaline, WA (town) Pend Oreille County	13	7.26
Rowan, IA (city) Wright County	15	7.25
Banks Lake South, WA (cdp) Grant County	10	7.25
Clinton, PA (township) Wyoming County	97	7.22
Nelson, NY (town) Madison County	142	7.20
Fairview, PA (township) Luzerne County	286	7.16
Prosser, NE (village) Adams County	7	7.14

Notes: (cdp) census designated place; Refer to the Explanation of Data in the front of the book for more detailed information.

Welsh

Top 150 Places Sorted by Percent

(Based on places with populations of 10,000 or more)

Place	Number	%
Back Mountain, PA (cdp) Luzerne County	2,247	8.42
Mountain Top, PA (cdp) Luzerne County	1,133	7.43
Scranton, PA (city) Lackawanna County	5,300	6.94
Hanover, PA (township) Luzerne County	764	6.67
Kingston, PA (borough) Luzerne County	914	6.60
Nanticoke, PA (city) Luzerne County	702	6.39
Wilkes-Barre, PA (city) Luzerne County	2,650	6.15
New Hartford, NY (town) Oneida County	1,029	4.86
Pottsville, PA (city) Schuylkill County	711	4.58
Kirkland, NY (town) Oneida County	431	4.25
Whitestown, NY (town) Oneida County	781	4.20
Plains, PA (township) Luzerne County	443	4.06
Niles, OH (city) Trumbull County	819	3.91
Sharon, PA (city) Mercer County	617	3.78
Spanish Fork, UT (city) Utah County	739	3.65
German Flatts, NY (town) Herkimer County	472	3.46
Dunmore, PA (borough) Lackawanna County	480	3.42
Chenango, NY (town) Broome County	388	3.39
Cottonwood West, UT (cdp) Salt Lake County	619	3.33
Cedar City, UT (city) Iron County	680	3.30
Woodlyn, PA (cdp) Delaware County	330	3.30
Dover, OH (city) Tuscarawas County	395	3.22
Blackfoot, ID (city) Bingham County	332	3.18
Grove City, OH (city) Franklin County	856	3.17
Bountiful, UT (city) Davis County	1,302	3.15
Upper Arlington, OH (city) Franklin County	1,060	3.15
Austintown, OH (cdp) Mahoning County	990	3.13
Worthington, OH (city) Franklin County	448	3.13
Owego, NY (town) Tioga County	635	3.12
Oneida, NY (city) Madison County	341	3.10
East Millcreek, UT (cdp) Salt Lake County	638	2.98
Holladay, UT (city) Salt Lake County	428	2.94
Springville, UT (city) Utah County	601	2.93
Pleasant Grove, UT (city) Utah County	680	2.89
South Ogden, UT (city) Weber County	417	2.89
Hermitage, PA (city) Mercer County	464	2.88
Kingsgate, WA (cdp) King County	343	2.85
Kaysville, UT (city) Davis County	575	2.78
South Jordan, UT (city) Salt Lake County	812	2.76
Salisbury, PA (township) Lehigh County	371	2.75
Girard, OH (city) Trumbull County	303	2.72
Westerville, OH (city) Franklin County	956	2.70
Hershey, PA (cdp) Dauphin County	344	2.69
North Ogden, UT (city) Weber County	395	2.65
Orem, UT (city) Utah County	2,216	2.63
Vashon, WA (cdp) King County	261	2.58
Boardman, OH (cdp) Mahoning County	950	2.55
Pocatello, ID (city) Bannock County	1,309	2.54
Lehi, UT (city) Utah County	485	2.53
Draper, UT (city) Salt Lake County	642	2.52
New Britain, PA (township) Bucks County	268	2.51
North Whitehall, PA (township) Lehigh County	368	2.50
Sandy, UT (city) Salt Lake County	2,200	2.49
Rome, NY (city) Oneida County	868	2.49
Murray, UT (city) Salt Lake County	844	2.49
North Canton, OH (city) Stark County	406	2.48
Stow, OH (city) Summit County	793	2.47
Patton, PA (township) Centre County	282	2.47
American Fork, UT (city) Utah County	540	2.46
Athens, OH (city) Athens County	515	2.43
Magna, UT (cdp) Salt Lake County	551	2.42
Brigham City, UT (city) Box Elder County	421	2.42
Endwell, NY (cdp) Broome County	283	2.42
Doylestown, PA (township) Bucks County	425	2.41
Ravenna, OH (city) Portage County	290	2.41
Easttown, PA (township) Chester County	248	2.41
Upper Chichester, PA (township) Delaware County	405	2.40
West Whiteland, PA (township) Chester County	395	2.39
Cottonwood Heights, UT (cdp) Salt Lake County	651	2.38
Provo, UT (city) Utah County	2,495	2.37
Logan, UT (city) Cache County	1,008	2.36
Lansing, NY (town) Tompkins County	243	2.36
Rexburg, ID (city) Madison County	405	2.35
White, PA (township) Indiana County	330	2.35
Payson, UT (city) Utah County	302	2.35
Van Wert, OH (city) Van Wert County	252	2.35
Farmington, UT (city) Davis County	286	2.34
Derry, PA (township) Dauphin County	495	2.33
Larkspur, CA (city) Marin County	280	2.33
Idaho Falls, ID (city) Bonneville County	1,167	2.31
Millcreek, UT (cdp) Salt Lake County	704	2.31
Hampden, PA (township) Cumberland County	557	2.30
Union, NY (town) Broome County	1,281	2.28
Mount Lebanon, PA (cdp) Allegheny County	739	2.24
Bothell, WA (city) King County	666	2.23
Susquehanna, PA (township) Dauphin County	485	2.23
Emporia, KS (city) Lyon County	594	2.22
Kalispell, MT (city) Flathead County	314	2.22
Riverton, UT (city) Salt Lake County	551	2.19
Cuyahoga Falls, OH (city) Summit County	1,064	2.16
Centerville, UT (city) Davis County	311	2.16
Massillon, OH (city) Stark County	675	2.15
Delaware, OH (city) Delaware County	543	2.15
Bedford, MA (town) Middlesex County	269	2.14
Kingsbury, NY (town) Washington County	239	2.14
Upper Saint Clair, PA (cdp) Allegheny County	425	2.12
Tumwater, WA (city) Thurston County	268	2.12
Newark, OH (city) Licking County	975	2.11
Dublin, OH (city) Franklin County	665	2.11
West Goshen, PA (township) Chester County	432	2.11
Hilliard, OH (city) Franklin County	509	2.10
Coal, PA (township) Northumberland County	223	2.10
Horseheads, NY (town) Chemung County	407	2.09
Layton, UT (city) Davis County	1,223	2.08
West Deer, PA (township) Allegheny County	241	2.08
Berwick, PA (borough) Columbia County	223	2.08
Middletown, PA (township) Delaware County	332	2.07
San Anselmo, CA (town) Marin County	259	2.07
Ridley, PA (township) Delaware County	634	2.06
Palmer, PA (township) Northampton County	347	2.06
Pacific Grove, CA (city) Monterey County	319	2.06
Pataskala, OH (city) Licking County	211	2.06
Capitola, CA (city) Santa Cruz County	210	2.06
Tooele, UT (city) Tooele County	462	2.05
Colonial Park, PA (cdp) Dauphin County	270	2.05
Damascus, MD (cdp) Montgomery County	232	2.05
Vestal, NY (town) Broome County	538	2.03
Whitehall, PA (township) Lehigh County	505	2.03
Elizabethtown, PA (borough) Lancaster County	241	2.03
Vermilion, OH (city) Lorain County	221	2.03
West Jordan, UT (city) Salt Lake County	1,379	2.02
Exeter, PA (township) Berks County	429	2.02
Gahanna, OH (city) Franklin County	655	2.01
Southampton, NJ (township) Burlington County	207	2.00
Johnson City, NY (village) Broome County	309	1.99
Salt Lake City, UT (city) Salt Lake County	3,598	1.98
Bethlehem, PA (city) Northampton County	1,411	1.98
Taylorsville, UT (city) Salt Lake County	1,146	1.98
Munhall, PA (borough) Allegheny County	243	1.98
Rock Springs, WY (city) Sweetwater County	372	1.96
Middletown, PA (township) Bucks County	852	1.93
Fullerton, PA (cdp) Lehigh County	275	1.93
Kearns, UT (cdp) Salt Lake County	647	1.92
Roy, UT (city) Weber County	629	1.92
Municipality of Murrysville, PA (borough) Westmoreland County	362	1.92
Ardmore, PA (cdp) Montgomery County	241	1.92
Oskaloosa, IA (city) Mahaska County	209	1.92
North Middleton, PA (township) Cumberland County	195	1.91
Cranberry, PA (township) Butler County	449	1.90
North Marysville, WA (cdp) Snohomish County	404	1.90
Scott Township, PA (cdp) Allegheny County	328	1.90
New Philadelphia, OH (city) Tuscarawas County	320	1.89
Westtown, PA (township) Chester County	195	1.89
Reynoldsburg, OH (city) Franklin County	607	1.88
Rossmoor, CA (cdp) Orange County	193	1.88
Muhlenberg, PA (township) Berks County	304	1.87
Caln, PA (township) Chester County	222	1.87
Spring, PA (township) Berks County	406	1.86
Utica, NY (city) Oneida County	1,125	1.85
Bel Air North, MD (cdp) Harford County	481	1.85

Notes: (cdp) census designated place; Refer to the Explanation of Data in the front of the book for more detailed information.

West Indian, excluding Hispanic

Top 150 Places Sorted by Number

(Based on all places, regardless of population)

Place	Number	%
New York, NY (city) New York City	549,664	6.86
Boston, MA (city) Suffolk County	37,614	6.38
Hempstead, NY (town) Nassau County	36,824	4.87
Miami, FL (city) Miami-Dade County	22,904	6.32
North Miami, FL (city) Miami-Dade County	22,034	36.70
Miramar, FL (city) Broward County	18,445	25.38
Philadelphia, PA (city) Philadelphia County	18,376	1.21
Los Angeles, CA (city) Los Angeles County	17,241	0.47
Lauderhill, FL (city) Broward County	16,626	29.04
Fort Lauderdale, FL (city) Broward County	14,964	9.84
Golden Glades, FL (cdp) Miami-Dade County	13,197	41.01
Pembroke Pines, FL (city) Broward County	12,327	8.99
Chicago, IL (city) Cook County	11,698	0.40
Lauderdale Lakes, FL (city) Broward County	11,455	36.35
Mount Vernon, NY (city) Westchester County	11,360	16.61
North Miami Beach, FL (city) Miami-Dade County	11,041	27.15
Sunrise, FL (city) Broward County	11,027	12.88
Hartford, CT (city) Hartford County	10,114	8.32
Ramapo, NY (town) Rockland County	9,716	8.92
Irvington, NJ (cdp) Essex County	9,590	15.82
Norland, FL (cdp) Miami-Dade County	8,976	38.98
Bridgeport, CT (city) Fairfield County	8,665	6.21
Washington, DC (city) District of Columbia	7,861	1.37
East Orange, NJ (city) Essex County	7,743	11.08
Plantation, FL (city) Broward County	7,276	8.74
Delray Beach, FL (city) Palm Beach County	7,220	12.05
Hollywood, FL (city) Broward County	7,171	5.15
Pine Hills, FL (cdp) Orange County	7,145	17.02
Coral Springs, FL (city) Broward County	7,065	6.01
Orlando, FL (city) Orange County	6,955	3.74
Islip, NY (town) Suffolk County	6,903	2.14
North Lauderdale, FL (city) Broward County	6,828	21.12
Baltimore, MD (independent city) Baltimore city	6,597	1.01
Elmont, NY (cdp) Nassau County	6,585	20.16
Houston, TX (city) Harris County	6,543	0.33
Spring Valley, NY (village) Rockland County	6,484	25.55
Newark, NJ (city) Essex County	6,424	2.35
Yonkers, NY (city) Westchester County	6,418	3.27
West Palm Beach, FL (city) Palm Beach County	6,338	7.77
Stamford, CT (city) Fairfield County	6,319	5.40
Hempstead, NY (village) Nassau County	6,264	11.08
Babylon, NY (town) Suffolk County	6,081	2.87
Carol City, FL (cdp) Miami-Dade County	5,829	9.81
Jersey City, NJ (city) Hudson County	5,769	2.40
Brockton, MA (city) Plymouth County	5,732	6.08
Orange, NJ (cdp) Essex County	5,505	16.75
Paterson, NJ (city) Passaic County	5,479	3.67
Pompano Beach, FL (city) Broward County	5,453	6.96
Pinewood, FL (cdp) Miami-Dade County	5,402	32.12
Boynton Beach, FL (city) Palm Beach County	5,221	8.71
Cambridge, MA (city) Middlesex County	5,164	5.09
Uniondale, NY (cdp) Nassau County	5,030	21.86
Jacksonville, FL (special city) Duval County	4,952	0.67
Tampa, FL (city) Hillsborough County	4,748	1.56
Brookhaven, NY (town) Suffolk County	4,646	1.04
North Hempstead, NY (town) Nassau County	4,524	2.03
Margate, FL (city) Broward County	4,094	7.60
Elizabeth, NJ (city) Union County	4,021	3.34
Ives Estates, FL (cdp) Miami-Dade County	3,901	22.40
Tamarac, FL (city) Broward County	3,834	6.84
Rochester, NY (city) Monroe County	3,755	1.71
North Valley Stream, NY (cdp) Nassau County	3,709	23.49
New Rochelle, NY (city) Westchester County	3,552	4.92
Lake Worth, FL (city) Palm Beach County	3,512	9.97
Oakland Park, FL (city) Broward County	3,501	11.22
Palmetto Estates, FL (cdp) Miami-Dade County	3,497	25.57
Deerfield Beach, FL (city) Broward County	3,467	5.36
Evanston, IL (city) Cook County	3,448	4.64
Detroit, MI (city) Wayne County	3,413	0.36
Scott Lake, FL (cdp) Miami-Dade County	3,269	22.72
Saint Petersburg, FL (city) Pinellas County	3,261	1.32
Springfield, MA (city) Hampden County	3,198	2.10
Bloomfield, CT (town) Hartford County	3,143	16.05
Randolph, MA (cdp) Norfolk County	3,111	10.04
Freeport, NY (village) Nassau County	3,076	7.03
Norwalk, CT (city) Fairfield County	3,070	3.70
South Miami Heights, FL (cdp) Miami-Dade County	2,956	8.80
Melrose Park, FL (cdp) Broward County	2,918	41.17
Chillum, MD (cdp) Prince George's County	2,862	8.38
Silver Spring, MD (cdp) Montgomery County	2,862	3.73
Somerville, MA (city) Middlesex County	2,844	3.67
Oak Ridge, FL (cdp) Orange County	2,824	12.60
Providence, RI (city) Providence County	2,821	1.62
Fort Pierce, FL (city) Saint Lucie County	2,816	7.51
Port Saint Lucie, FL (city) Saint Lucie County	2,798	3.15
Palm Bay, FL (city) Brevard County	2,785	3.51
West Orange, NJ (cdp) Essex County	2,674	5.96
The Hammocks, FL (cdp) Miami-Dade County	2,670	5.63
West Little River, FL (cdp) Miami-Dade County	2,654	8.22
New Haven, CT (city) New Haven County	2,602	2.10
Greenburgh, NY (town) Westchester County	2,582	2.98
Baldwin, NY (cdp) Nassau County	2,578	10.99
Country Club, FL (cdp) Miami-Dade County	2,555	7.02
Fort Myers, FL (city) Lee County	2,509	5.22
Clarkstown, NY (town) Rockland County	2,505	3.05
Brentwood, NY (cdp) Suffolk County	2,493	4.63
Teaneck, NJ (cdp) Bergen County	2,469	6.29
Plainfield, NJ (city) Union County	2,465	5.15
Charlotte, NC (city) Mecklenburg County	2,453	0.45
Virginia Beach, VA (independent city) Virginia Beach city	2,445	0.57
Maplewood, NJ (cdp) Essex County	2,423	10.15
Atlanta, GA (city) Fulton County	2,406	0.58
San Diego, CA (city) San Diego County	2,390	0.20
Andover, FL (cdp) Miami-Dade County	2,379	27.48
Roosevelt, NY (cdp) Nassau County	2,343	14.78
Tallahassee, FL (city) Leon County	2,340	1.55
Roselle, NJ (borough) Union County	2,331	10.96
Kendall, FL (cdp) Miami-Dade County	2,298	3.05
Immokalee, FL (cdp) Collier County	2,135	11.00
Huntington, NY (town) Suffolk County	2,103	1.08
Central Islip, NY (cdp) Suffolk County	2,040	6.40
Englewood, NJ (city) Bergen County	2,034	7.76
New Cassel, NY (cdp) Nassau County	2,029	15.26
Oyster Bay, NY (town) Nassau County	2,024	0.69
Trenton, NJ (city) Mercer County	2,019	2.37
Montclair, NJ (cdp) Essex County	2,015	5.16
Belle Glade, FL (city) Palm Beach County	1,988	13.25
Union, NJ (cdp) Union County	1,977	3.63
Franklin, NJ (township) Somerset County	1,925	3.78
Homestead, FL (city) Miami-Dade County	1,923	6.00
North Amityville, NY (cdp) Suffolk County	1,901	11.51
Westview, FL (cdp) Miami-Dade County	1,896	19.76
Lake Park, FL (town) Palm Beach County	1,848	21.93
East Hartford, CT (cdp) Hartford County	1,846	3.72
Dallas, TX (city) Dallas County	1,837	0.15
Waterbury, CT (city) New Haven County	1,830	1.71
Hackensack, NJ (city) Bergen County	1,816	4.26
Malden, MA (city) Middlesex County	1,810	3.21
Redan, GA (cdp) De Kalb County	1,805	5.33
Poughkeepsie, NY (city) Dutchess County	1,795	6.01
Windsor, CT (town) Hartford County	1,794	6.35
Hillcrest, NY (cdp) Rockland County	1,784	25.10
Wheaton-Glenmont, MD (cdp) Montgomery County	1,747	3.03
White Plains, NY (city) Westchester County	1,736	3.25
Columbus, OH (city) Franklin County	1,726	0.24
Linden, NJ (city) Union County	1,723	4.37
Norfolk, VA (independent city) Norfolk city	1,723	0.74
Long Beach, CA (city) Los Angeles County	1,691	0.37
Medford, MA (city) Middlesex County	1,679	3.01
Albany, NY (city) Albany County	1,672	1.75
Oakland, CA (city) Alameda County	1,670	0.42
Cleveland, OH (city) Cuyahoga County	1,651	0.35
Columbia, MD (cdp) Howard County	1,646	1.86
San Francisco, CA (city) San Francisco County	1,639	0.21
Richmond West, FL (cdp) Miami-Dade County	1,635	5.84
Asbury Park, NJ (city) Monmouth County	1,629	9.62
New Orleans, LA (city) Orleans Parish	1,627	0.34
Hallandale, FL (city) Broward County	1,623	4.70
Phoenix, AZ (city) Maricopa County	1,614	0.12
Milwaukee, WI (city) Milwaukee County	1,600	0.27

Notes: (cdp) census designated place; Refer to the Explanation of Data in the front of the book for more detailed information.

West Indian, excluding Hispanic

Top 150 Places Sorted by Percent

(Based on all places, regardless of population)

Place	Number	%
Melrose Park, FL (cdp) Broward County	2,918	41.17
Golden Glades, FL (cdp) Miami-Dade County	13,197	41.01
Norland, FL (cdp) Miami-Dade County	8,976	38.98
North Miami, FL (city) Miami-Dade County	22,034	36.70
Lauderdale Lakes, FL (city) Broward County	11,455	36.35
Pompano Estates, FL (cdp) Broward County	1,172	33.82
El Portal, FL (village) Miami-Dade County	813	32.30
Pinewood, FL (cdp) Miami-Dade County	5,402	32.12
Lauderhill, FL (city) Broward County	16,626	29.04
Belle Glade Camp, FL (cdp) Palm Beach County	355	28.09
South Floral Park, NY (village) Nassau County	434	27.50
Andover, FL (cdp) Miami-Dade County	2,379	27.48
North Miami Beach, FL (city) Miami-Dade County	11,041	27.15
Tedder, FL (cdp) Broward County	537	27.03
Blue Hills, CT (cdp) Hartford County	807	26.17
Bonnie Lock-Woodsetter North, FL (cdp) Broward County	1,123	26.07
Loch Lomond, FL (cdp) Broward County	866	26.07
Palmetto Estates, FL (cdp) Miami-Dade County	3,497	25.57
Spring Valley, NY (village) Rockland County	6,484	25.55
Miramar, FL (city) Broward County	18,445	25.38
Hillcrest, NY (cdp) Rockland County	1,784	25.10
Kendall Green, FL (cdp) Broward County	760	24.19
Lakeview, NY (cdp) Nassau County	1,336	23.83
North Valley Stream, NY (cdp) Nassau County	3,709	23.49
Scott Lake, FL (cdp) Miami-Dade County	3,269	22.72
Ives Estates, FL (cdp) Miami-Dade County	3,901	22.40
Lake Park, FL (town) Palm Beach County	1,848	21.93
Uniondale, NY (cdp) Nassau County	5,030	21.86
North Lauderdale, FL (city) Broward County	6,828	21.12
Utopia, FL (cdp) Broward County	148	20.41
Elmont, NY (cdp) Nassau County	6,585	20.16
Westview, FL (cdp) Miami-Dade County	1,896	19.76
Pine Hills, FL (cdp) Orange County	7,145	17.02
Orange, NJ (cdp) Essex County	5,505	16.75
Mount Vernon, NY (city) Westchester County	11,360	16.61
Bloomfield, CT (town) Hartford County	3,143	16.05
Pembroke Park, FL (town) Broward County	1,010	15.94
Irvington, NJ (cdp) Essex County	9,590	15.82
Stacey Street, FL (cdp) Palm Beach County	128	15.42
New Cassel, NY (cdp) Nassau County	2,029	15.26
Wheatley Heights, NY (cdp) Suffolk County	767	15.24
Mangonia Park, FL (town) Palm Beach County	195	15.07
Roosevelt, NY (cdp) Nassau County	2,343	14.78
Broadview-Pompano Park, FL (cdp) Broward County	708	13.80
Fairview, NY (cdp) Westchester County	398	13.31
Biscayne Park, FL (village) Miami-Dade County	439	13.27
Belle Glade, FL (city) Palm Beach County	1,988	13.25
Miami Shores, FL (village) Miami-Dade County	1,377	13.19
Lake Lucerne, FL (cdp) Miami-Dade County	1,189	13.00
Sunrise, FL (city) Broward County	11,027	12.88
Opa-locka North, FL (cdp) Miami-Dade County	791	12.71
Oak Ridge, FL (cdp) Orange County	2,824	12.60
South Fork Estates, TX (cdp) Jim Hogg County	6	12.24
East Perrine, FL (cdp) Miami-Dade County	834	12.17
East Garden City, NY (cdp) Nassau County	120	12.06
Delray Beach, FL (city) Palm Beach County	7,220	12.05
Gordon Heights, NY (cdp) Suffolk County	370	11.96
Millward, MN (township) Aitkin County	7	11.67
Silver Springs Shores, FL (cdp) Marion County	764	11.66
North Amityville, NY (cdp) Suffolk County	1,901	11.51
West Perrine, FL (cdp) Miami-Dade County	971	11.29
Oakland Park, FL (city) Broward County	3,501	11.22
Lake Forest, FL (cdp) Broward County	552	11.12
East Orange, NJ (city) Essex County	7,743	11.08
Hempstead, NY (village) Nassau County	6,264	11.08
Three Lakes, FL (cdp) Miami-Dade County	773	11.08
Immokalee, FL (cdp) Collier County	2,135	11.00
Baldwin, NY (cdp) Nassau County	2,578	10.99
Roselle, NJ (borough) Union County	2,331	10.96
Gun Club Estates, FL (cdp) Palm Beach County	92	10.86
Nyack, NY (village) Rockland County	711	10.62
Rock Island, FL (cdp) Broward County	333	10.59
Naranja, FL (cdp) Miami-Dade County	444	10.57
South Nyack, NY (village) Rockland County	367	10.57
Miami Gardens, FL (cdp) Broward County	270	10.46
Leisureville, FL (cdp) Broward County	113	10.42
Tangelo Park, FL (cdp) Orange County	241	10.40
Maplewood, NJ (cdp) Essex County	2,423	10.15
Randolph, MA (cdp) Norfolk County	3,111	10.04
Seminole Manor, FL (cdp) Palm Beach County	263	9.98
Lake Worth, FL (city) Palm Beach County	3,512	9.97
Fort Lauderdale, FL (city) Broward County	14,964	9.84
Carol City, FL (cdp) Miami-Dade County	5,829	9.81
Naples Manor, FL (cdp) Collier County	499	9.76
Bunche Park, FL (cdp) Miami-Dade County	387	9.71
Saint Leo, FL (town) Pasco County	59	9.69
Collier Manor-Cresthaven, FL (cdp) Broward County	768	9.67
Saint George, FL (cdp) Broward County	233	9.67
Washington Park, FL (cdp) Broward County	120	9.64
Asbury Park, NJ (city) Monmouth County	1,629	9.62
Fort Devens, MA (cdp) Worcester County	95	9.51
Goulds, FL (cdp) Miami-Dade County	705	9.25
Country Walk, FL (cdp) Miami-Dade County	980	9.20
Harlem, FL (cdp) Hendry County	256	9.04
Pembroke Pines, FL (city) Broward County	12,327	8.99
Ramapo, NY (town) Rockland County	9,716	8.92
Golden Lakes, FL (cdp) Palm Beach County	594	8.87
South Miami Heights, FL (cdp) Miami-Dade County	2,956	8.80
Plantation, FL (city) Broward County	7,276	8.74
Boynton Beach, FL (city) Palm Beach County	5,221	8.71
Westgate-Belvedere Homes, FL (cdp) Palm Beach County	700	8.61
Wilton Manors, FL (city) Broward County	1,082	8.52
Chillum, MD (cdp) Prince George's County	2,862	8.38
Hartford, CT (city) Hartford County	10,114	8.32
West Little River, FL (cdp) Miami-Dade County	2,654	8.22
Estates of Fort Lauderdale, FL (cdp) Broward County	151	8.18
Wyandanch, NY (cdp) Suffolk County	852	8.05
Poinciana, FL (cdp) Osceola County	1,088	8.01
Westbury, NY (village) Nassau County	1,130	7.92
Hillburn, NY (village) Rockland County	61	7.78
West Palm Beach, FL (city) Palm Beach County	6,338	7.77
Englewood, NJ (city) Bergen County	2,034	7.76
Pomona, NY (village) Rockland County	210	7.68
Margate, FL (city) Broward County	4,094	7.60
Florida City, FL (city) Miami-Dade County	609	7.59
Fort Pierce, FL (city) Saint Lucie County	2,816	7.51
Johnstown, NE (village) Brown County	4	7.27
Mount Rainier, MD (city) Prince George's County	611	7.22
Pine Manor, FL (cdp) Lee County	281	7.22
Oronoko charter, MI (township) Berrien County	707	7.18
Broadview Park, FL (cdp) Broward County	487	7.17
Lakes by the Bay, FL (cdp) Miami-Dade County	643	7.15
Opa-locka, FL (city) Miami-Dade County	1,079	7.08
Inwood, FL (cdp) Polk County	477	7.04
Freeport, NY (village) Nassau County	3,076	7.03
Country Club, FL (cdp) Miami-Dade County	2,555	7.02
Greenvale, NY (cdp) Nassau County	155	7.01
Elmer, OK (town) Jackson County	6	6.98
Pompano Beach, FL (city) Broward County	5,453	6.96
South Orange, NJ (cdp) Essex County	1,177	6.94
New York, NY (city) New York City	549,664	6.86
Tamarac, FL (city) Broward County	3,834	6.84
New Hempstead, NY (village) Rockland County	328	6.84
Lantana, FL (town) Palm Beach County	652	6.83
Golden Gate, FL (cdp) Collier County	1,402	6.67
Langley Park, MD (cdp) Prince George's County	1,070	6.60
Broward Estates, FL (cdp) Broward County	229	6.50
Royal Palm Beach, FL (village) Palm Beach County	1,385	6.42
Central Islip, NY (cdp) Suffolk County	2,040	6.40
Boston, MA (city) Suffolk County	37,614	6.38
Windsor, CT (town) Hartford County	1,794	6.35
Miami, FL (city) Miami-Dade County	22,904	6.32
Teaneck, NJ (cdp) Bergen County	2,469	6.29
Meridian, CO (cdp) Douglas County	10	6.29
Roosevelt Gardens, FL (cdp) Broward County	117	6.28
Bridgeport, CT (city) Fairfield County	8,665	6.21
Chambers Estates, FL (cdp) Broward County	221	6.21
Boulevard Gardens, FL (cdp) Broward County	83	6.16
Inwood, NY (cdp) Nassau County	570	6.11
Brockton, MA (city) Plymouth County	5,732	6.08

Notes: (cdp) census designated place; Refer to the Explanation of Data in the front of the book for more detailed information.

West Indian, excluding Hispanic

Top 150 Places Sorted by Percent

(Based on places with populations of 10,000 or more)

Place	Number	%
Golden Glades, FL (cdp) Miami-Dade County	13,197	41.01
Norland, FL (cdp) Miami-Dade County	8,976	38.98
North Miami, FL (city) Miami-Dade County	22,034	36.70
Lauderdale Lakes, FL (city) Broward County	11,455	36.35
Pinewood, FL (cdp) Miami-Dade County	5,402	32.12
Lauderhill, FL (city) Broward County	16,626	29.04
North Miami Beach, FL (city) Miami-Dade County	11,041	27.15
Palmetto Estates, FL (cdp) Miami-Dade County	3,497	25.57
Spring Valley, NY (village) Rockland County	6,484	25.55
Miramar, FL (city) Broward County	18,445	25.38
North Valley Stream, NY (cdp) Nassau County	3,709	23.49
Scott Lake, FL (cdp) Miami-Dade County	3,269	22.72
Ives Estates, FL (cdp) Miami-Dade County	3,901	22.40
Uniondale, NY (cdp) Nassau County	5,030	21.86
North Lauderdale, FL (city) Broward County	6,828	21.12
Elmont, NY (cdp) Nassau County	6,585	20.16
Pine Hills, FL (cdp) Orange County	7,145	17.02
Orange, NJ (cdp) Essex County	5,505	16.75
Mount Vernon, NY (city) Westchester County	11,360	16.61
Bloomfield, CT (town) Hartford County	3,143	16.05
Irvington, NJ (cdp) Essex County	9,590	15.82
New Cassel, NY (cdp) Nassau County	2,029	15.26
Roosevelt, NY (cdp) Nassau County	2,343	14.78
Belle Glade, FL (city) Palm Beach County	1,988	13.25
Miami Shores, FL (village) Miami-Dade County	1,377	13.19
Sunrise, FL (city) Broward County	11,027	12.88
Oak Ridge, FL (cdp) Orange County	2,824	12.60
Delray Beach, FL (city) Palm Beach County	7,220	12.05
North Amityville, NY (cdp) Suffolk County	1,901	11.51
Oakland Park, FL (city) Broward County	3,501	11.22
East Orange, NJ (city) Essex County	7,743	11.08
Hempstead, NY (village) Nassau County	6,264	11.08
Immokalee, FL (cdp) Collier County	2,135	11.00
Baldwin, NY (cdp) Nassau County	2,578	10.99
Roselle, NJ (borough) Union County	2,331	10.96
Maplewood, NJ (cdp) Essex County	2,423	10.15
Randolph, MA (cdp) Norfolk County	3,111	10.04
Lake Worth, FL (city) Palm Beach County	3,512	9.97
Fort Lauderdale, FL (city) Broward County	14,964	9.84
Carol City, FL (cdp) Miami-Dade County	5,829	9.81
Asbury Park, NJ (city) Monmouth County	1,629	9.62
Country Walk, FL (cdp) Miami-Dade County	980	9.20
Pembroke Pines, FL (city) Broward County	12,327	8.99
Ramapo, NY (town) Rockland County	9,716	8.92
South Miami Heights, FL (cdp) Miami-Dade County	2,956	8.80
Plantation, FL (city) Broward County	7,276	8.74
Boynton Beach, FL (city) Palm Beach County	5,221	8.71
Wilton Manors, FL (city) Broward County	1,082	8.52
Chillum, MD (cdp) Prince George's County	2,862	8.38
Hartford, CT (city) Hartford County	10,114	8.32
West Little River, FL (cdp) Miami-Dade County	2,654	8.22
Wyandanch, NY (cdp) Suffolk County	852	8.05
Poinciana, FL (cdp) Osceola County	1,088	8.01
Westbury, NY (village) Nassau County	1,130	7.92
West Palm Beach, FL (city) Palm Beach County	6,338	7.77
Englewood, NJ (city) Bergen County	2,034	7.76
Margate, FL (city) Broward County	4,094	7.60
Fort Pierce, FL (city) Saint Lucie County	2,816	7.51
Opa-locka, FL (city) Miami-Dade County	1,079	7.08
Freeport, NY (village) Nassau County	3,076	7.03
Country Club, FL (cdp) Miami-Dade County	2,555	7.02
Pompano Beach, FL (city) Broward County	5,453	6.96
South Orange, NJ (cdp) Essex County	1,177	6.94
New York, NY (city) New York City	549,664	6.86
Tamarac, FL (city) Broward County	3,834	6.84
Golden Gate, FL (cdp) Collier County	1,402	6.67
Langley Park, MD (cdp) Prince George's County	1,070	6.60
Royal Palm Beach, FL (village) Palm Beach County	1,385	6.42
Central Islip, NY (cdp) Suffolk County	2,040	6.40
Boston, MA (city) Suffolk County	37,614	6.38
Windsor, CT (town) Hartford County	1,794	6.35
Miami, FL (city) Miami-Dade County	22,904	6.32
Teaneck, NJ (cdp) Bergen County	2,469	6.29
Bridgeport, CT (city) Fairfield County	8,665	6.21
Brockton, MA (city) Plymouth County	5,732	6.08
Nanuet, NY (cdp) Rockland County	1,013	6.06
Coral Springs, FL (city) Broward County	7,065	6.01
Poughkeepsie, NY (city) Dutchess County	1,795	6.01
Homestead, FL (city) Miami-Dade County	1,923	6.00
West Orange, NJ (cdp) Essex County	2,674	5.96
Richmond West, FL (cdp) Miami-Dade County	1,635	5.84
West Haverstraw, NY (village) Rockland County	597	5.80
East Massapequa, NY (cdp) Nassau County	1,119	5.72
The Hammocks, FL (cdp) Miami-Dade County	2,670	5.63
Cutler Ridge, FL (cdp) Miami-Dade County	1,374	5.57
Adelphi, MD (cdp) Prince George's County	829	5.52
Stamford, CT (city) Fairfield County	6,319	5.40
Lake Worth Corridor, FL (cdp) Palm Beach County	989	5.38
Deerfield Beach, FL (city) Broward County	3,467	5.36
Redan, GA (cdp) De Kalb County	1,805	5.33
Pleasantville, NJ (city) Atlantic County	1,001	5.24
Fort Myers, FL (city) Lee County	2,509	5.22
Yeehaw Junction, FL (cdp) Osceola County	1,150	5.19
Montclair, NJ (cdp) Essex County	2,015	5.16
Hollywood, FL (city) Broward County	7,171	5.15
Plainfield, NJ (city) Union County	2,465	5.15
Cambridge, MA (city) Middlesex County	5,164	5.09
Riviera Beach, FL (city) Palm Beach County	1,533	5.04
Ojus, FL (cdp) Miami-Dade County	836	5.01
Somerset, NJ (cdp) Somerset County	1,149	4.98
Beltsville, MD (cdp) Prince George's County	776	4.93
New Rochelle, NY (city) Westchester County	3,552	4.92
Leisure City, FL (cdp) Miami-Dade County	1,067	4.90
New Carrollton, MD (city) Prince George's County	627	4.88
Hempstead, NY (town) Nassau County	36,824	4.87
Palm Springs, FL (village) Palm Beach County	575	4.86
Milton, MA (cdp) Norfolk County	1,240	4.76
Hallandale, FL (city) Broward County	1,623	4.70
Evanston, IL (city) Cook County	3,448	4.64
Brentwood, NY (cdp) Suffolk County	2,493	4.63
Fairland, MD (cdp) Montgomery County	970	4.49
Takoma Park, MD (city) Montgomery County	763	4.44
University, FL (cdp) Hillsborough County	1,344	4.38
Linden, NJ (city) Union County	1,723	4.37
Yeadon, PA (borough) Delaware County	507	4.30
Hillside, NJ (cdp) Union County	928	4.27
Hackensack, NJ (city) Bergen County	1,816	4.26
South Miami, FL (city) Miami-Dade County	462	4.22
Meadow Woods, FL (cdp) Orange County	482	4.20
Dania Beach, FL (city) Broward County	839	4.17
Willingboro, NJ (township) Burlington County	1,357	4.11
North Bay Shore, NY (cdp) Suffolk County	617	4.11
Hyattsville, MD (city) Prince George's County	605	4.08
Princeton, FL (cdp) Miami-Dade County	414	4.08
Valley Stream, NY (village) Nassau County	1,452	3.99
Haverstraw, NY (town) Rockland County	1,338	3.97
Calverton, MD (cdp) Montgomery County	499	3.96
Lanham-Seabrook, MD (cdp) Prince George's County	701	3.88
Haines City, FL (city) Polk County	510	3.88
Greenlawn, NY (cdp) Suffolk County	513	3.86
The Crossings, FL (cdp) Miami-Dade County	907	3.85
Peekskill, NY (city) Westchester County	859	3.83
Franklin, NJ (township) Somerset County	1,925	3.78
Neptune, NJ (township) Monmouth County	1,043	3.77
Brownsville, FL (cdp) Miami-Dade County	544	3.76
Orlando, FL (city) Orange County	6,955	3.74
Silver Spring, MD (cdp) Montgomery County	2,862	3.73
Apopka, FL (city) Orange County	974	3.73
East Hartford, CT (cdp) Hartford County	1,846	3.72
Arlington, NY (cdp) Dutchess County	462	3.71
Norwalk, CT (city) Fairfield County	3,070	3.70
Paterson, NJ (city) Passaic County	5,479	3.67
Somerville, MA (city) Middlesex County	2,844	3.67
Union, NJ (cdp) Union County	1,977	3.63
East Riverdale, MD (cdp) Prince George's County	558	3.63
White Oak, MD (cdp) Montgomery County	746	3.57
Everett, MA (city) Middlesex County	1,354	3.56
Palm Bay, FL (city) Brevard County	2,785	3.51
Gladeview, FL (cdp) Miami-Dade County	504	3.48
Elizabeth, NJ (city) Union County	4,021	3.34

Notes: (cdp) census designated place; Refer to the Explanation of Data in the front of the book for more detailed information.

West Indian: Bahamian, excluding Hispanic

Top 150 Places Sorted by Number

(Based on all places, regardless of population)

Place	Number	%
New York, NY (city) New York City	1,658	0.02
Miami, FL (city) Miami-Dade County	1,470	0.41
North Miami, FL (city) Miami-Dade County	675	1.12
Fort Lauderdale, FL (city) Broward County	607	0.40
Miramar, FL (city) Broward County	578	0.80
Golden Glades, FL (cdp) Miami-Dade County	541	1.68
Pembroke Pines, FL (city) Broward County	518	0.38
Norland, FL (cdp) Miami-Dade County	513	2.23
Lauderhill, FL (city) Broward County	473	0.83
North Miami Beach, FL (city) Miami-Dade County	441	1.08
Carol City, FL (cdp) Miami-Dade County	437	0.74
Hollywood, FL (city) Broward County	435	0.31
West Little River, FL (cdp) Miami-Dade County	339	1.05
West Palm Beach, FL (city) Palm Beach County	327	0.40
Country Club, FL (cdp) Miami-Dade County	313	0.86
Pinewood, FL (cdp) Miami-Dade County	304	1.81
Andover, FL (cdp) Miami-Dade County	295	3.41
Lauderdale Lakes, FL (city) Broward County	291	0.92
Delray Beach, FL (city) Palm Beach County	286	0.48
Brownsville, FL (cdp) Miami-Dade County	279	1.93
Key West, FL (city) Monroe County	269	1.06
Jacksonville, FL (special city) Duval County	264	0.04
Tampa, FL (city) Hillsborough County	252	0.08
Lake Lucerne, FL (cdp) Miami-Dade County	237	2.59
Coral Springs, FL (city) Broward County	237	0.20
Sunrise, FL (city) Broward County	227	0.27
Scott Lake, FL (cdp) Miami-Dade County	223	1.55
Plantation, FL (city) Broward County	223	0.27
Hallandale, FL (city) Broward County	210	0.61
Orlando, FL (city) Orange County	207	0.11
Tallahassee, FL (city) Leon County	187	0.12
Los Angeles, CA (city) Los Angeles County	180	0.00
Philadelphia, PA (city) Philadelphia County	175	0.01
Westview, FL (cdp) Miami-Dade County	164	1.71
Houston, TX (city) Harris County	154	0.01
Riviera Beach, FL (city) Palm Beach County	151	0.50
Ives Estates, FL (cdp) Miami-Dade County	146	0.84
Goulds, FL (cdp) Miami-Dade County	140	1.84
Gladeview, FL (cdp) Miami-Dade County	138	0.95
Oakland Park, FL (city) Broward County	138	0.44
Raleigh, NC (city) Wake County	133	0.05
Bunche Park, FL (cdp) Miami-Dade County	131	3.29
Port Saint Lucie, FL (city) Saint Lucie County	130	0.15
South Miami Heights, FL (cdp) Miami-Dade County	124	0.37
Dania Beach, FL (city) Broward County	122	0.61
Washington, DC (city) District of Columbia	114	0.02
Chicago, IL (city) Cook County	114	0.00
The Hammocks, FL (cdp) Miami-Dade County	113	0.24
Daytona Beach, FL (city) Volusia County	113	0.18
Belle Glade, FL (city) Palm Beach County	110	0.73
Pompano Beach, FL (city) Broward County	110	0.14
Carver Ranches, FL (cdp) Broward County	109	2.54
Richmond Heights, FL (cdp) Miami-Dade County	105	1.25
Lakes by the Bay, FL (cdp) Miami-Dade County	103	1.15
Detroit, MI (city) Wayne County	102	0.01
Deerfield Beach, FL (city) Broward County	98	0.15
Palmetto Estates, FL (cdp) Miami-Dade County	97	0.71
Davie, FL (town) Broward County	97	0.13
Fort Pierce, FL (city) Saint Lucie County	94	0.25
Mobile, AL (city) Mobile County	93	0.05
Lake Forest, FL (cdp) Broward County	92	1.85
Nashville-Davidson, TN (special city) Davidson County	88	0.02
Seven Oaks, SC (cdp) Lexington County	87	0.55
Lake Worth Corridor, FL (cdp) Palm Beach County	87	0.47
Florida Ridge, FL (cdp) Indian River County	86	0.56
Fort Pierce North, FL (cdp) Saint Lucie County	84	1.14
Boynton Beach, FL (city) Palm Beach County	84	0.14
Opa-locka, FL (city) Miami-Dade County	79	0.52
Huntsville, AL (city) Madison County	77	0.05
Sanford, FL (city) Seminole County	75	0.20
Charlotte, NC (city) Mecklenburg County	75	0.01
University, FL (cdp) Hillsborough County	71	0.23
Florida City, FL (city) Miami-Dade County	70	0.87
North Lauderdale, FL (city) Broward County	70	0.22
Gifford, FL (cdp) Indian River County	69	0.91
Bradenton, FL (city) Manatee County	68	0.14
Eustis, FL (city) Lake County	67	0.44
Atlanta, GA (city) Fulton County	65	0.02
Virginia Beach, VA (independent city) Virginia Beach city	63	0.01
Princeton, FL (cdp) Miami-Dade County	61	0.60
University Park, FL (cdp) Miami-Dade County	61	0.23
Franconia, VA (cdp) Fairfax County	61	0.19
Gainesville, FL (city) Alachua County	61	0.06
Golden Gate, FL (cdp) Collier County	60	0.29
Galloway, NJ (township) Atlantic County	59	0.19
Pine Hills, FL (cdp) Orange County	59	0.14
Weston, FL (city) Broward County	59	0.12
Lake Magdalene, FL (cdp) Hillsborough County	58	0.20
Tamarac, FL (city) Broward County	58	0.10
Hialeah, FL (city) Miami-Dade County	57	0.03
Baltimore, MD (independent city) Baltimore city	57	0.01
Altamonte Springs, FL (city) Seminole County	56	0.14
Portage, MI (city) Kalamazoo County	56	0.12
Killeen, TX (city) Bell County	56	0.06
Opa-locka North, FL (cdp) Miami-Dade County	55	0.88
Poughkeepsie, NY (city) Dutchess County	55	0.18
Hempstead, NY (town) Nassau County	54	0.01
El Portal, FL (village) Miami-Dade County	53	2.11
Wilton Manors, FL (city) Broward County	53	0.42
Homestead, FL (city) Miami-Dade County	52	0.16
Palm Beach Gardens, FL (city) Palm Beach County	52	0.15
Durham, NC (city) Durham County	52	0.03
Kendall, FL (cdp) Miami-Dade County	51	0.07
Birmingham, AL (city) Jefferson County	51	0.02
Stacey Street, FL (cdp) Palm Beach County	50	6.02
South Miami, FL (city) Miami-Dade County	50	0.46
Fairfax, VA (independent city) Fairfax city	49	0.23
Dayton, OH (city) Montgomery County	49	0.03
Saint Petersburg, FL (city) Pinellas County	49	0.02
Pembroke Park, FL (town) Broward County	48	0.76
Chambers Estates, FL (cdp) Broward County	47	1.32
Boston, MA (city) Suffolk County	47	0.01
Surfside, FL (town) Miami-Dade County	45	0.88
Essex, MD (cdp) Baltimore County	45	0.12
Hampton, VA (independent city) Hampton city	45	0.03
Phoenix, AZ (city) Maricopa County	45	0.00
Golden Lakes, FL (cdp) Palm Beach County	44	0.66
Glenvar Heights, FL (cdp) Miami-Dade County	44	0.27
Kearney, NE (city) Buffalo County	43	0.16
Aurora, CO (city) Arapahoe County	43	0.02
Jersey City, NJ (city) Hudson County	43	0.02
Cleveland, TN (city) Bradley County	41	0.11
Gary, IN (city) Lake County	41	0.04
Loch Lomond, FL (cdp) Broward County	40	1.20
High Point, NC (city) Guilford County	40	0.05
California, MD (cdp) Saint Mary's County	39	0.41
Marathon, FL (city) Monroe County	39	0.38
Lake Worth, FL (city) Palm Beach County	39	0.11
Miami Beach, FL (city) Miami-Dade County	39	0.04
Alexandria, VA (independent city) Alexandria city	39	0.03
Tulsa, OK (city) Tulsa County	38	0.01
Naples, FL (city) Collier County	37	0.18
Yonkers, NY (city) Westchester County	37	0.02
Pensacola, FL (city) Escambia County	36	0.06
Cedar Rapids, IA (city) Linn County	36	0.03
Madison, WI (city) Dane County	36	0.02
Norfolk, VA (independent city) Norfolk city	36	0.02
Pompano Estates, FL (cdp) Broward County	35	1.01
Zephyrhills South, FL (cdp) Pasco County	35	0.75
Superior, MI (township) Washtenaw County	35	0.33
Stuart, FL (city) Martin County	35	0.24
Mauldin, SC (city) Greenville County	35	0.23
Newport News, VA (independent city) Newport News city	35	0.02
Rock Island, FL (cdp) Broward County	34	1.08
Olean, NY (city) Cattaraugus County	34	0.22
New Rochelle, NY (city) Westchester County	34	0.05
Boca Raton, FL (city) Palm Beach County	34	0.04
Arlington, VA (cdp) Arlington County	34	0.02
Coconut Creek, FL (city) Broward County	33	0.08
Strongsville, OH (city) Cuyahoga County	33	0.08

Notes: (cdp) census designated place; Refer to the Explanation of Data in the front of the book for more detailed information.

West Indian: Bahamian, excluding Hispanic

Top 150 Places Sorted by Percent

(Based on all places, regardless of population)

Place	Number	%
Johnstown, NE (village) Brown County	4	7.27
Stacey Street, FL (cdp) Palm Beach County	50	6.02
Andover, FL (cdp) Miami-Dade County	295	3.41
Bunche Park, FL (cdp) Miami-Dade County	131	3.29
Lake Lucerne, FL (cdp) Miami-Dade County	237	2.59
Carver Ranches, FL (cdp) Broward County	109	2.54
Lake Ida, MN (township) Norman County	5	2.49
Norland, FL (cdp) Miami-Dade County	513	2.23
El Portal, FL (village) Miami-Dade County	53	2.11
Brownsville, FL (cdp) Miami-Dade County	279	1.93
Lake Forest, FL (cdp) Broward County	92	1.85
Goulds, FL (cdp) Miami-Dade County	140	1.84
Pinewood, FL (cdp) Miami-Dade County	304	1.81
Ophir, CO (town) San Miguel County	2	1.74
Westview, FL (cdp) Miami-Dade County	164	1.71
Golden Glades, FL (cdp) Miami-Dade County	541	1.68
Scott Lake, FL (cdp) Miami-Dade County	223	1.55
Kent Acres, DE (cdp) Kent County	25	1.44
Green Meadow, FL (cdp) Broward County	25	1.36
Chambers Estates, FL (cdp) Broward County	47	1.32
Richmond Heights, FL (cdp) Miami-Dade County	105	1.25
Loch Lomond, FL (cdp) Broward County	40	1.20
Lakes by the Bay, FL (cdp) Miami-Dade County	103	1.15
Fort Pierce North, FL (cdp) Saint Lucie County	84	1.14
North Miami, FL (city) Miami-Dade County	675	1.12
Crystal Lake, IA (city) Hancock County	3	1.09
North Miami Beach, FL (city) Miami-Dade County	441	1.08
Rock Island, FL (cdp) Broward County	34	1.08
Key West, FL (city) Monroe County	269	1.06
West Little River, FL (cdp) Miami-Dade County	339	1.05
Pompano Estates, FL (cdp) Broward County	35	1.01
Utopia, FL (cdp) Broward County	7	0.97
Washington Park, FL (cdp) Broward County	12	0.96
Gladeview, FL (cdp) Miami-Dade County	138	0.95
Lauderdale Lakes, FL (city) Broward County	291	0.92
Gifford, FL (cdp) Indian River County	69	0.91
Belmont, MN (township) Jackson County	2	0.91
Big Coppitt Key, FL (cdp) Monroe County	23	0.89
Opa-locka North, FL (cdp) Miami-Dade County	55	0.88
Surfside, FL (town) Miami-Dade County	45	0.88
Munford, AL (cdp) Talladega County	18	0.88
Florida City, FL (city) Miami-Dade County	70	0.87
Country Club, FL (cdp) Miami-Dade County	313	0.86
Ives Estates, FL (cdp) Miami-Dade County	146	0.84
Lauderhill, FL (city) Broward County	473	0.83
Rincon, GA (city) Effingham County	32	0.81
Miramar, FL (city) Broward County	578	0.80
Pembroke Park, FL (town) Broward County	48	0.76
Zephyrhills South, FL (cdp) Pasco County	35	0.75
Carol City, FL (cdp) Miami-Dade County	437	0.74
Sturgeon Lake, MN (township) Pine County	3	0.74
Belle Glade, FL (city) Palm Beach County	110	0.73
Palmetto Estates, FL (cdp) Miami-Dade County	97	0.71
Goulding, FL (cdp) Escambia County	31	0.69
Scotts Mills, OR (city) Marion County	2	0.68
Sewaren, NJ (cdp) Middlesex County	19	0.67
Kensington, MN (city) Douglas County	2	0.67
Golden Lakes, FL (cdp) Palm Beach County	44	0.66
June Park, FL (cdp) Brevard County	30	0.64
Cudjoe Key, FL (cdp) Monroe County	11	0.63
Penndel, PA (borough) Bucks County	15	0.62
Hallandale, FL (city) Broward County	210	0.61
Dania Beach, FL (city) Broward County	122	0.61
Princeton, FL (cdp) Miami-Dade County	61	0.60
Harlem, FL (cdp) Hendry County	16	0.57
Florida Ridge, FL (cdp) Indian River County	86	0.56
Tusculum, TN (city) Greene County	11	0.56
Seven Oaks, SC (cdp) Lexington County	87	0.55
Claxton, GA (city) Evans County	13	0.55
Mangonia Park, FL (town) Palm Beach County	7	0.54
Opa-locka, FL (city) Miami-Dade County	79	0.52
Naranja, FL (cdp) Miami-Dade County	22	0.52
Jupiter Inlet Colony, FL (town) Palm Beach County	2	0.52
Riviera Beach, FL (city) Palm Beach County	151	0.50
Stock Island, FL (cdp) Monroe County	22	0.50
Royal Palm Estates, FL (cdp) Palm Beach County	17	0.49
Delray Beach, FL (city) Palm Beach County	286	0.48
Lake Worth Corridor, FL (cdp) Palm Beach County	87	0.47
South Miami, FL (city) Miami-Dade County	50	0.46
Oakland Park, FL (city) Broward County	138	0.44
Eustis, FL (city) Lake County	67	0.44
Helmetta, NJ (borough) Middlesex County	8	0.44
Trimble, MO (city) Clinton County	2	0.44
Broward Estates, FL (cdp) Broward County	15	0.43
Whitewater, KS (city) Butler County	3	0.43
Wilton Manors, FL (city) Broward County	53	0.42
Seminole Manor, FL (cdp) Palm Beach County	11	0.42
Eau Pleine, WI (town) Portage County	4	0.42
Miami, FL (city) Miami-Dade County	1,470	0.41
California, MD (cdp) Saint Mary's County	39	0.41
South Bay, FL (city) Palm Beach County	16	0.41
Fort Lauderdale, FL (city) Broward County	607	0.40
West Palm Beach, FL (city) Palm Beach County	327	0.40
Melrose Park, FL (cdp) Broward County	28	0.40
Willington, CT (town) Tolland County	23	0.39
Pembroke Pines, FL (city) Broward County	518	0.38
Marathon, FL (city) Monroe County	39	0.38
South Miami Heights, FL (cdp) Miami-Dade County	124	0.37
Blountstown, FL (city) Calhoun County	9	0.37
East Perrine, FL (cdp) Miami-Dade County	25	0.36
Tavernier, FL (cdp) Monroe County	8	0.36
Whitesboro-Burleigh, NJ (cdp) Cape May County	7	0.36
Lake Park, FL (town) Palm Beach County	29	0.34
West Perrine, FL (cdp) Miami-Dade County	29	0.34
Superior, MI (township) Washtenaw County	35	0.33
Oronoko charter, MI (township) Berrien County	32	0.33
Kosciusko, MS (city) Attala County	24	0.33
Hollywood, FL (city) Broward County	435	0.31
Broadview-Pompano Park, FL (cdp) Broward County	16	0.31
Greenwood, WI (town) Taylor County	2	0.31
Golden Gate, FL (cdp) Collier County	60	0.29
Collier Manor-Cresthaven, FL (cdp) Broward County	23	0.29
Miami Shores, FL (village) Miami-Dade County	29	0.28
Stone Mountain, GA (city) De Kalb County	19	0.28
Bay Hill, FL (cdp) Orange County	15	0.28
Easton, MI (township) Ionia County	8	0.28
Hudson, IA (city) Black Hawk County	6	0.28
Kimball, SD (city) Brule County	2	0.28
Sunrise, FL (city) Broward County	227	0.27
Plantation, FL (city) Broward County	223	0.27
Glenvar Heights, FL (cdp) Miami-Dade County	44	0.27
North Sarasota, FL (cdp) Sarasota County	19	0.27
Rockbridge, WI (town) Richland County	2	0.27
Mount Vernon, GA (city) Montgomery County	6	0.26
La Farge, WI (village) Vernon County	2	0.26
Fort Pierce, FL (city) Saint Lucie County	94	0.25
Broadview Park, FL (cdp) Broward County	17	0.25
Greenland, NH (town) Rockingham County	8	0.25
Hypoluxo, FL (town) Palm Beach County	5	0.25
The Hammocks, FL (cdp) Miami-Dade County	113	0.24
Stuart, FL (city) Martin County	35	0.24
Avon Park, FL (city) Highlands County	21	0.24
Camp Pendleton North, CA (cdp) San Diego County	19	0.24
Honey Brook, PA (township) Chester County	15	0.24
Athens, NY (village) Greene County	4	0.24
Marvin, NC (village) Union County	3	0.24
University, FL (cdp) Hillsborough County	71	0.23
University Park, FL (cdp) Miami-Dade County	61	0.23
Fairfax, VA (independent city) Fairfax city	49	0.23
Mauldin, SC (city) Greenville County	35	0.23
Thief River Falls, MN (city) Pennington County	19	0.23
The Meadows, FL (cdp) Sarasota County	10	0.23
Hancock, ME (town) Hancock County	5	0.23
Manawa, WI (city) Waupaca County	3	0.23
North Lauderdale, FL (city) Broward County	70	0.22
Olean, NY (city) Cattaraugus County	34	0.22
Lake Mary, FL (city) Seminole County	25	0.22
Caernarvon, PA (township) Berks County	5	0.22
Princeton Meadows, NJ (cdp) Middlesex County	28	0.21
Hasbrouck Heights, NJ (borough) Bergen County	24	0.21

Notes: (cdp) census designated place; Refer to the Explanation of Data in the front of the book for more detailed information.

West Indian: Bahamian, excluding Hispanic

Top 150 Places Sorted by Percent

(Based on places with populations of 10,000 or more)

Place	Number	%
Norland, FL (cdp) Miami-Dade County	513	2.23
Brownsville, FL (cdp) Miami-Dade County	279	1.93
Pinewood, FL (cdp) Miami-Dade County	304	1.81
Golden Glades, FL (cdp) Miami-Dade County	541	1.68
Scott Lake, FL (cdp) Miami-Dade County	223	1.55
North Miami, FL (city) Miami-Dade County	675	1.12
North Miami Beach, FL (city) Miami-Dade County	441	1.08
Key West, FL (city) Monroe County	269	1.06
West Little River, FL (cdp) Miami-Dade County	339	1.05
Gladeview, FL (cdp) Miami-Dade County	138	0.95
Lauderdale Lakes, FL (city) Broward County	291	0.92
Country Club, FL (cdp) Miami-Dade County	313	0.86
Ives Estates, FL (cdp) Miami-Dade County	146	0.84
Lauderhill, FL (city) Broward County	473	0.83
Miramar, FL (city) Broward County	578	0.80
Carol City, FL (cdp) Miami-Dade County	437	0.74
Belle Glade, FL (city) Palm Beach County	110	0.73
Palmetto Estates, FL (cdp) Miami-Dade County	97	0.71
Hallandale, FL (city) Broward County	210	0.61
Dania Beach, FL (city) Broward County	122	0.61
Princeton, FL (cdp) Miami-Dade County	61	0.60
Florida Ridge, FL (cdp) Indian River County	86	0.56
Seven Oaks, SC (cdp) Lexington County	87	0.55
Opa-locka, FL (city) Miami-Dade County	79	0.52
Riviera Beach, FL (city) Palm Beach County	151	0.50
Delray Beach, FL (city) Palm Beach County	286	0.48
Lake Worth Corridor, FL (cdp) Palm Beach County	87	0.47
South Miami, FL (city) Miami-Dade County	50	0.46
Oakland Park, FL (city) Broward County	138	0.44
Eustis, FL (city) Lake County	67	0.44
Wilton Manors, FL (city) Broward County	53	0.42
Miami, FL (city) Miami-Dade County	1,470	0.41
Fort Lauderdale, FL (city) Broward County	607	0.40
West Palm Beach, FL (city) Palm Beach County	327	0.40
Pembroke Pines, FL (city) Broward County	518	0.38
Marathon, FL (city) Monroe County	39	0.38
South Miami Heights, FL (cdp) Miami-Dade County	124	0.37
Superior, MI (township) Washtenaw County	35	0.33
Hollywood, FL (city) Broward County	435	0.31
Golden Gate, FL (cdp) Collier County	60	0.29
Miami Shores, FL (village) Miami-Dade County	29	0.28
Sunrise, FL (city) Broward County	227	0.27
Plantation, FL (city) Broward County	223	0.27
Glenvar Heights, FL (cdp) Miami-Dade County	44	0.27
Fort Pierce, FL (city) Saint Lucie County	94	0.25
The Hammocks, FL (cdp) Miami-Dade County	113	0.24
Stuart, FL (city) Martin County	35	0.24
University, FL (cdp) Hillsborough County	71	0.23
University Park, FL (cdp) Miami-Dade County	61	0.23
Fairfax, VA (independent city) Fairfax city	49	0.23
Mauldin, SC (city) Greenville County	35	0.23
North Lauderdale, FL (city) Broward County	70	0.22
Olean, NY (city) Cattaraugus County	34	0.22
Lake Mary, FL (city) Seminole County	25	0.22
Princeton Meadows, NJ (cdp) Middlesex County	28	0.21
Hasbrouck Heights, NJ (borough) Bergen County	24	0.21
Coral Springs, FL (city) Broward County	237	0.20
Sanford, FL (city) Seminole County	75	0.20
Lake Magdalene, FL (cdp) Hillsborough County	58	0.20
Arlington, NY (cdp) Dutchess County	25	0.20
Franconia, VA (cdp) Fairfax County	61	0.19
Galloway, NJ (township) Atlantic County	59	0.19
Cocoa, FL (city) Brevard County	31	0.19
Daytona Beach, FL (city) Volusia County	113	0.18
Poughkeepsie, NY (city) Dutchess County	55	0.18
Naples, FL (city) Collier County	37	0.18
North Amityville, NY (cdp) Suffolk County	28	0.17
Homestead, FL (city) Miami-Dade County	52	0.16
Kearney, NE (city) Buffalo County	43	0.16
North Valley Stream, NY (cdp) Nassau County	25	0.16
Parkland, FL (city) Broward County	23	0.16
Port Saint Lucie, FL (city) Saint Lucie County	130	0.15
Deerfield Beach, FL (city) Broward County	98	0.15
Palm Beach Gardens, FL (city) Palm Beach County	52	0.15
Leisure City, FL (cdp) Miami-Dade County	32	0.15

Place	Number	%
Sebastian, FL (city) Indian River County	25	0.15
Fernandina Beach, FL (city) Nassau County	15	0.15
Pompano Beach, FL (city) Broward County	110	0.14
Boynton Beach, FL (city) Palm Beach County	84	0.14
Bradenton, FL (city) Manatee County	68	0.14
Pine Hills, FL (cdp) Orange County	59	0.14
Altamonte Springs, FL (city) Seminole County	56	0.14
Temple Terrace, FL (city) Hillsborough County	30	0.14
Plainsboro, NJ (township) Middlesex County	28	0.14
Hanahan, SC (city) Berkeley County	18	0.14
Key Largo, FL (cdp) Monroe County	17	0.14
Mendota Heights, MN (city) Dakota County	16	0.14
Lower Gwynedd, PA (township) Montgomery County	15	0.14
Davie, FL (town) Broward County	97	0.13
Port Saint John, FL (cdp) Brevard County	16	0.13
Tallahassee, FL (city) Leon County	187	0.12
Weston, FL (city) Broward County	59	0.12
Portage, MI (city) Kalamazoo County	56	0.12
Essex, MD (cdp) Baltimore County	45	0.12
Miami Springs, FL (city) Miami-Dade County	16	0.12
Orlando, FL (city) Orange County	207	0.11
Cleveland, TN (city) Bradley County	41	0.11
Lake Worth, FL (city) Palm Beach County	39	0.11
Ojus, FL (cdp) Miami-Dade County	18	0.11
Stafford, TX (city) Fort Bend County	17	0.11
Lake Wales, FL (city) Polk County	11	0.11
Wantage, NJ (township) Sussex County	11	0.11
Tamarac, FL (city) Broward County	58	0.10
Miami Lakes, FL (cdp) Miami-Dade County	22	0.10
Apex, NC (town) Wake County	21	0.10
Royal Palm Beach, FL (village) Palm Beach County	21	0.10
King of Prussia, PA (cdp) Montgomery County	18	0.10
Greeneville, TN (town) Greene County	16	0.10
Glen Rock, NJ (borough) Bergen County	12	0.10
Somerville, NJ (borough) Somerset County	12	0.10
Tuskegee, AL (city) Macon County	12	0.10
Lighthouse Point, FL (city) Broward County	11	0.10
Randallstown, MD (cdp) Baltimore County	27	0.09
Cutler Ridge, FL (cdp) Miami-Dade County	21	0.09
Lockport, NY (city) Niagara County	19	0.09
Palm City, FL (cdp) Martin County	19	0.09
Robbinsdale, MN (city) Hennepin County	13	0.09
Fairview Shores, FL (cdp) Orange County	12	0.09
Beaufort, SC (city) Beaufort County	11	0.09
Lilburn, GA (city) Gwinnett County	10	0.09
Riverton-Boulevard Park, WA (cdp) King County	10	0.09
Easttown, PA (township) Chester County	9	0.09
Tampa, FL (city) Hillsborough County	252	0.08
Coconut Creek, FL (city) Broward County	33	0.08
Strongsville, OH (city) Cuyahoga County	33	0.08
Stillwater, OK (city) Payne County	31	0.08
Ormond Beach, FL (city) Volusia County	29	0.08
Dover, DE (city) Kent County	25	0.08
Lawrence, NJ (township) Mercer County	22	0.08
Rahway, NJ (city) Union County	22	0.08
Statesboro, GA (city) Bulloch County	18	0.08
Burlington, NJ (township) Burlington County	17	0.08
East Patchogue, NY (cdp) Suffolk County	17	0.08
Forest Park, GA (city) Clayton County	16	0.08
Loves Park, IL (city) Winnebago County	16	0.08
Wade Hampton, SC (cdp) Greenville County	16	0.08
East Massapequa, NY (cdp) Nassau County	15	0.08
Immokalee, FL (cdp) Collier County	15	0.08
Pittsburg, KS (city) Crawford County	15	0.08
Asbury Park, NJ (city) Monmouth County	13	0.08
Glen Allen, VA (cdp) Henrico County	10	0.08
South Daytona, FL (city) Volusia County	10	0.08
Lakewood Park, FL (cdp) Saint Lucie County	8	0.08
Kendall, FL (cdp) Miami-Dade County	51	0.07
Tuckahoe, VA (cdp) Henrico County	31	0.07
Coral Gables, FL (city) Miami-Dade County	30	0.07
Hackensack, NJ (city) Bergen County	30	0.07
Jefferson City, MO (city) Cole County	26	0.07
Candler-McAfee, GA (cdp) De Kalb County	21	0.07
Norristown, PA (borough) Montgomery County	21	0.07

Notes: (cdp) census designated place; Refer to the Explanation of Data in the front of the book for more detailed information.

West Indian: Barbadian, excluding Hispanic

Top 150 Places Sorted by Number

(Based on all places, regardless of population)

Place	Number	%
New York, NY (city) New York City	26,816	0.33
Boston, MA (city) Suffolk County	2,165	0.37
Hempstead, NY (town) Nassau County	1,180	0.16
Philadelphia, PA (city) Philadelphia County	568	0.04
Mount Vernon, NY (city) Westchester County	457	0.67
Cambridge, MA (city) Middlesex County	374	0.37
Elmont, NY (cdp) Nassau County	315	0.96
New Rochelle, NY (city) Westchester County	296	0.41
Springfield, MA (city) Hampden County	292	0.19
Hartford, CT (city) Hartford County	278	0.23
Plainfield, NJ (city) Union County	270	0.56
Islip, NY (town) Suffolk County	270	0.08
Los Angeles, CA (city) Los Angeles County	257	0.01
Saint Petersburg, FL (city) Pinellas County	240	0.10
Hempstead, NY (village) Nassau County	239	0.42
Washington, DC (city) District of Columbia	196	0.03
East Orange, NJ (city) Essex County	193	0.28
Freeport, NY (village) Nassau County	186	0.42
Brockton, MA (city) Plymouth County	173	0.18
Lauderhill, FL (city) Broward County	168	0.29
Baltimore, MD (independent city) Baltimore city	167	0.03
Yonkers, NY (city) Westchester County	160	0.08
Orlando, FL (city) Orange County	156	0.08
Rochester, NY (city) Monroe County	155	0.07
North Miami, FL (city) Miami-Dade County	149	0.25
Chicago, IL (city) Cook County	144	0.00
San Diego, CA (city) San Diego County	141	0.01
Miramar, FL (city) Broward County	139	0.19
Bridgeport, CT (city) Fairfield County	138	0.10
Somerville, MA (city) Middlesex County	135	0.17
Medford, MA (city) Middlesex County	116	0.21
Brookhaven, NY (town) Suffolk County	116	0.03
Greenburgh, NY (town) Westchester County	114	0.13
Irvington, NJ (cdp) Essex County	113	0.19
Pine Hills, FL (cdp) Orange County	112	0.27
Virginia Beach, VA (independent city) Virginia Beach city	111	0.03
White Plains, NY (city) Westchester County	109	0.21
Colorado Springs, CO (city) El Paso County	106	0.03
Babylon, NY (town) Suffolk County	105	0.05
North Hempstead, NY (town) Nassau County	103	0.05
Redan, GA (cdp) De Kalb County	102	0.30
Houston, TX (city) Harris County	102	0.01
Ramapo, NY (town) Rockland County	101	0.09
North Valley Stream, NY (cdp) Nassau County	100	0.63
Tampa, FL (city) Hillsborough County	99	0.03
Brentwood, NY (cdp) Suffolk County	98	0.18
Central Islip, NY (cdp) Suffolk County	95	0.30
Stamford, CT (city) Fairfield County	95	0.08
Franklin, NJ (township) Somerset County	92	0.18
Palm Bay, FL (city) Brevard County	92	0.12
Lakeview, NY (cdp) Nassau County	87	1.55
Lynn, MA (city) Essex County	86	0.10
Hollywood, FL (city) Broward County	86	0.06
Detroit, MI (city) Wayne County	86	0.01
Fort Lauderdale, FL (city) Broward County	84	0.06
Davie, FL (town) Broward County	83	0.11
Atlanta, GA (city) Fulton County	83	0.02
Frederick, MD (city) Frederick County	82	0.16
Jersey City, NJ (city) Hudson County	82	0.03
East Hartford, CT (cdp) Hartford County	80	0.16
Albany, NY (city) Albany County	76	0.08
Jacksonville, FL (special city) Duval County	76	0.01
Waterbury, CT (city) New Haven County	75	0.07
Augusta-Richmond County, GA (special city) Richmond County	75	0.04
Uniondale, NY (cdp) Nassau County	74	0.32
Montclair, NJ (cdp) Essex County	74	0.19
Sunrise, FL (city) Broward County	74	0.09
Old Bridge, NJ (township) Middlesex County	71	0.12
Deerfield Beach, FL (city) Broward County	70	0.11
Oakland, CA (city) Alameda County	68	0.02
Maplewood, NJ (cdp) Essex County	67	0.28
Golden Glades, FL (cdp) Miami-Dade County	67	0.21
Boynton Beach, FL (city) Palm Beach County	67	0.11
Delray Beach, FL (city) Palm Beach County	66	0.11
Bloomfield, CT (town) Hartford County	65	0.33
Randolph, MA (cdp) Norfolk County	65	0.21
Willingboro, NJ (township) Burlington County	65	0.20
South Plainfield, NJ (borough) Middlesex County	64	0.29
New Haven, CT (city) New Haven County	64	0.05
Arlington, VA (cdp) Arlington County	63	0.03
San Antonio, TX (city) Bexar County	63	0.01
North Amityville, NY (cdp) Suffolk County	62	0.38
Las Vegas, NV (city) Clark County	62	0.01
Gates, NY (town) Monroe County	61	0.21
Orange, NJ (cdp) Essex County	61	0.19
Ossining, NY (town) Westchester County	61	0.17
Fort Pierce, FL (city) Saint Lucie County	61	0.16
Silver Spring, MD (cdp) Montgomery County	61	0.08
Oyster Bay, NY (town) Nassau County	61	0.02
Fairview, NY (cdp) Westchester County	60	2.01
Columbia, MD (cdp) Howard County	60	0.07
Summit, NJ (city) Union County	59	0.28
Cortlandt, NY (town) Westchester County	59	0.15
Chesapeake, VA (independent city) Chesapeake city	59	0.03
Cheltenham, PA (township) Montgomery County	58	0.16
Hampton, VA (independent city) Hampton city	58	0.04
Norland, FL (cdp) Miami-Dade County	57	0.25
Long Beach, CA (city) Los Angeles County	57	0.01
Phoenix, AZ (city) Maricopa County	56	0.00
Plantation, FL (city) Broward County	55	0.07
Paterson, NJ (city) Passaic County	55	0.04
Melrose Park, FL (cdp) Broward County	54	0.76
Carol City, FL (cdp) Miami-Dade County	54	0.09
West Orange, NJ (cdp) Essex County	53	0.12
Aspen Hill, MD (cdp) Montgomery County	53	0.11
Huntsville, AL (city) Madison County	53	0.03
Newark, NJ (city) Essex County	53	0.02
South Laurel, MD (cdp) Prince George's County	51	0.25
Atlantic City, NJ (city) Atlantic County	51	0.13
Palmetto Estates, FL (cdp) Miami-Dade County	50	0.37
Roosevelt, NY (cdp) Nassau County	50	0.32
Piscataway, NJ (township) Middlesex County	50	0.10
West Palm Beach, FL (city) Palm Beach County	50	0.06
Worcester, MA (city) Worcester County	50	0.03
Linden, NJ (city) Union County	49	0.12
Coral Springs, FL (city) Broward County	49	0.04
Pembroke Pines, FL (city) Broward County	49	0.04
Dallas, TX (city) Dallas County	49	0.00
Raleigh, NC (city) Wake County	48	0.02
Manchester, CT (town) Hartford County	47	0.09
Apex, NC (town) Wake County	46	0.23
Hillside, NJ (cdp) Union County	46	0.21
Port Chester, NY (village) Westchester County	46	0.17
Rye, NY (town) Westchester County	46	0.10
Wheaton-Glenmont, MD (cdp) Montgomery County	46	0.08
Azalea Park, FL (cdp) Orange County	45	0.40
Gates-North Gates, NY (cdp) Monroe County	45	0.30
Asbury Park, NJ (city) Monmouth County	45	0.27
Somerset, NJ (cdp) Somerset County	45	0.20
Sugar Land, TX (city) Fort Bend County	45	0.07
Upper Darby, PA (township) Delaware County	45	0.05
Seattle, WA (city) King County	45	0.01
Poinciana, FL (cdp) Osceola County	44	0.32
Charleston, SC (city) Charleston County	44	0.05
Palm Coast, FL (city) Flagler County	43	0.13
Kissimmee, FL (city) Osceola County	43	0.09
Charlotte, NC (city) Mecklenburg County	43	0.01
Hackettstown, NJ (town) Warren County	42	0.40
Tucker, GA (cdp) De Kalb County	42	0.16
Rome, NY (city) Oneida County	42	0.12
Meadow Woods, FL (cdp) Orange County	41	0.36
Shrub Oak, NY (cdp) Westchester County	40	2.17
North Laurel, MD (cdp) Howard County	40	0.19
Yorktown, NY (town) Westchester County	40	0.11
Norfolk, VA (independent city) Norfolk city	40	0.02
Neptune, NJ (township) Monmouth County	39	0.14
Port Charlotte, FL (cdp) Charlotte County	39	0.08
Berkeley, CA (city) Alameda County	39	0.04
Austin, TX (city) Travis County	39	0.01
New Hempstead, NY (village) Rockland County	38	0.79

Notes: (cdp) census designated place; Refer to the Explanation of Data in the front of the book for more detailed information.

West Indian: Barbadian, excluding Hispanic

Top 150 Places Sorted by Percent

(Based on all places, regardless of population)

Place	Number	%
Shrub Oak, NY (cdp) Westchester County	40	2.17
Fairview, NY (cdp) Westchester County	60	2.01
Lakeview, NY (cdp) Nassau County	87	1.55
Avery, CA (cdp) Calaveras County	8	1.30
Harlem, FL (cdp) Hendry County	34	1.20
Coplin, ME (plantation) Franklin County	2	1.13
Mashpee Neck, MA (cdp) Barnstable County	10	1.08
East Garden City, NY (cdp) Nassau County	10	1.01
Saint George, FL (cdp) Broward County	24	1.00
Elmont, NY (cdp) Nassau County	315	0.96
Mangonia Park, FL (town) Palm Beach County	11	0.85
New Hempstead, NY (village) Rockland County	38	0.79
Melrose Park, FL (cdp) Broward County	54	0.76
Hinsdale, MA (town) Berkshire County	14	0.75
Gordon Heights, NY (cdp) Suffolk County	23	0.74
Mount Vernon, NY (city) Westchester County	457	0.67
North Valley Stream, NY (cdp) Nassau County	100	0.63
Belle Glade Camp, FL (cdp) Palm Beach County	8	0.63
Plainfield, PA (township) Northampton County	35	0.62
Flemington, NJ (borough) Hunterdon County	26	0.62
Brodheadsville, PA (cdp) Monroe County	9	0.62
Tuckahoe, NY (village) Westchester County	38	0.61
Samsula-Spruce Creek, FL (cdp) Volusia County	30	0.61
Linntown, PA (cdp) Union County	9	0.61
Sharon Hill, PA (borough) Delaware County	33	0.60
Millville, MA (town) Worcester County	16	0.59
Blue Hills, CT (cdp) Hartford County	18	0.58
Eutawville, SC (town) Orangeburg County	2	0.57
Plainfield, NJ (city) Union County	270	0.56
Conklin, NY (town) Broome County	33	0.56
Spotsylvania Courthouse, VA (cdp) Spotsylvania County	22	0.55
McGregor, TX (city) McLennan County	25	0.54
Hillandale, MD (cdp) Montgomery County	16	0.54
Newport, DE (town) New Castle County	6	0.54
Bern, PA (township) Berks County	36	0.53
De Land Southwest, FL (cdp) Volusia County	6	0.53
Wagner, WI (town) Marinette County	4	0.53
Indian Head, MD (town) Charles County	17	0.50
Keene, TX (city) Johnson County	24	0.49
Morrow, GA (city) Clayton County	23	0.47
Three Lakes, FL (cdp) Miami-Dade County	31	0.44
Oak Ridge North, TX (city) Montgomery County	13	0.44
Waverly, FL (cdp) Polk County	8	0.43
Hempstead, NY (village) Nassau County	239	0.42
Freeport, NY (village) Nassau County	186	0.42
New Rochelle, NY (city) Westchester County	296	0.41
Indiantown, FL (cdp) Martin County	22	0.41
Azalea Park, FL (cdp) Orange County	45	0.40
Hackettstown, NJ (town) Warren County	42	0.40
Hewlett Neck, NY (village) Nassau County	2	0.40
Hanson, MA (town) Plymouth County	37	0.39
Haverhill, FL (town) Palm Beach County	6	0.39
North Amityville, NY (cdp) Suffolk County	62	0.38
Boston, MA (city) Suffolk County	2,165	0.37
Cambridge, MA (city) Middlesex County	374	0.37
Palmetto Estates, FL (cdp) Miami-Dade County	50	0.37
Rio Communities North, NM (cdp) Valencia County	6	0.37
Meadow Woods, FL (cdp) Orange County	41	0.36
Covington, TN (city) Tipton County	30	0.36
Ellenville, NY (village) Ulster County	15	0.36
Baldwin, LA (town) Saint Mary Parish	9	0.36
Norton Center, MA (cdp) Bristol County	9	0.36
Oronoko charter, MI (township) Berrien County	34	0.35
Dover, NY (town) Dutchess County	29	0.34
Bristol, VT (town) Addison County	13	0.34
New York, NY (city) New York City	26,816	0.33
Bloomfield, CT (town) Hartford County	65	0.33
Chesterton, IN (town) Porter County	34	0.33
Columbus AFB, MS (cdp) Lowndes County	7	0.33
Uniondale, NY (cdp) Nassau County	74	0.32
Roosevelt, NY (cdp) Nassau County	50	0.32
Poinciana, FL (cdp) Osceola County	44	0.32
Middle Island, NY (cdp) Suffolk County	31	0.32
Wyndmoor, PA (cdp) Montgomery County	18	0.32
Millbourne, PA (borough) Delaware County	3	0.32
Shell Point, SC (cdp) Beaufort County	9	0.31
Castleton-on-Hudson, NY (village) Rensselaer County	5	0.31
Moore Haven, FL (city) Glades County	5	0.31
Redan, GA (cdp) De Kalb County	102	0.30
Central Islip, NY (cdp) Suffolk County	95	0.30
Gates-North Gates, NY (cdp) Monroe County	45	0.30
Holiday City South, NJ (cdp) Ocean County	12	0.30
Montgomery, VT (town) Franklin County	3	0.30
Canyon City, OR (town) Grant County	2	0.30
Pembina, ND (city) Pembina County	2	0.30
Lauderhill, FL (city) Broward County	168	0.29
South Plainfield, NJ (borough) Middlesex County	64	0.29
Fair Oaks, GA (cdp) Cobb County	25	0.29
Montrose, VA (cdp) Henrico County	20	0.29
East Orange, NJ (city) Essex County	193	0.28
Maplewood, NJ (cdp) Essex County	67	0.28
Summit, NJ (city) Union County	59	0.28
Pine Hills, FL (cdp) Orange County	112	0.27
Asbury Park, NJ (city) Monmouth County	45	0.27
Lake Park, FL (town) Palm Beach County	23	0.27
Ridgefield, WA (city) Clark County	6	0.27
Waterford, VT (town) Caledonia County	3	0.27
Metzger, OR (cdp) Washington County	9	0.26
Lawnside, NJ (borough) Camden County	7	0.26
Wyoming, DE (town) Kent County	3	0.26
North Miami, FL (city) Miami-Dade County	149	0.25
Norland, FL (cdp) Miami-Dade County	57	0.25
South Laurel, MD (cdp) Prince George's County	51	0.25
Orangeburg, SC (city) Orangeburg County	32	0.25
Cocoa West, FL (cdp) Brevard County	14	0.25
Watchung, NJ (borough) Somerset County	14	0.25
Progress Village, FL (cdp) Hillsborough County	6	0.25
Tullytown, PA (borough) Bucks County	5	0.25
Yemassee, SC (town) Hampton County	2	0.25
Twentynine Palms, CA (city) San Bernardino County	35	0.24
Westbury, NY (village) Nassau County	34	0.24
Glenn Dale, MD (cdp) Prince George's County	31	0.24
Wilder, VT (cdp) Windsor County	4	0.24
Hartford, CT (city) Hartford County	278	0.23
Apex, NC (town) Wake County	46	0.23
Adelphi, MD (cdp) Prince George's County	34	0.23
Yeadon, PA (borough) Delaware County	27	0.23
Lansing charter, MI (township) Ingham County	20	0.23
Lancaster, MA (town) Worcester County	17	0.23
North Hills, NY (village) Nassau County	10	0.23
Harvest, AL (cdp) Madison County	7	0.23
Copenhagen, NY (village) Lewis County	2	0.23
Lincoln, MA (town) Middlesex County	18	0.22
Chestnut Ridge, NY (village) Rockland County	17	0.22
Jefferson City, TN (city) Jefferson County	17	0.22
Feasterville-Trevose, PA (cdp) Bucks County	14	0.22
Goddard, MD (cdp) Prince George's County	12	0.22
Twin Lakes, CA (cdp) Santa Cruz County	12	0.22
Bryans Road, MD (cdp) Charles County	11	0.22
Vassar, MI (city) Tuscola County	6	0.22
Medford, MA (city) Middlesex County	116	0.21
White Plains, NY (city) Westchester County	109	0.21
Golden Glades, FL (cdp) Miami-Dade County	67	0.21
Randolph, MA (cdp) Norfolk County	65	0.21
Gates, NY (town) Monroe County	61	0.21
Hillside, NJ (cdp) Union County	46	0.21
Mountain Home AFB, ID (cdp) Elmore County	19	0.21
Pahokee, FL (city) Palm Beach County	12	0.21
Marion, MA (town) Plymouth County	11	0.21
Ann Arbor, MI (township) Washtenaw County	10	0.21
Del Mar, CA (city) San Diego County	9	0.21
Old Westbury, NY (village) Nassau County	9	0.21
White, NJ (township) Warren County	9	0.21
Dexter, ME (town) Penobscot County	8	0.21
South Bay, FL (city) Palm Beach County	8	0.21
Loch Lomond, FL (cdp) Broward County	7	0.21
Bunnell, FL (city) Flagler County	4	0.21
Willingboro, NJ (township) Burlington County	65	0.20
Somerset, NJ (cdp) Somerset County	45	0.20
Fairview Shores, FL (cdp) Orange County	27	0.20

Notes: (cdp) census designated place; Refer to the Explanation of Data in the front of the book for more detailed information.

West Indian: Barbadian, excluding Hispanic

Top 150 Places Sorted by Percent

(Based on places with populations of 10,000 or more)

Place	Number	%
Elmont, NY (cdp) Nassau County	315	0.96
Mount Vernon, NY (city) Westchester County	457	0.67
North Valley Stream, NY (cdp) Nassau County	100	0.63
Plainfield, NJ (city) Union County	270	0.56
Hempstead, NY (village) Nassau County	239	0.42
Freeport, NY (village) Nassau County	186	0.42
New Rochelle, NY (city) Westchester County	296	0.41
Azalea Park, FL (cdp) Orange County	45	0.40
Hackettstown, NJ (town) Warren County	42	0.40
North Amityville, NY (cdp) Suffolk County	62	0.38
Boston, MA (city) Suffolk County	2,165	0.37
Cambridge, MA (city) Middlesex County	374	0.37
Palmetto Estates, FL (cdp) Miami-Dade County	50	0.37
Meadow Woods, FL (cdp) Orange County	41	0.36
New York, NY (city) New York City	26,816	0.33
Bloomfield, CT (town) Hartford County	65	0.33
Chesterton, IN (town) Porter County	34	0.33
Uniondale, NY (cdp) Nassau County	74	0.32
Roosevelt, NY (cdp) Nassau County	50	0.32
Poinciana, FL (cdp) Osceola County	44	0.32
Redan, GA (cdp) De Kalb County	102	0.30
Central Islip, NY (cdp) Suffolk County	95	0.30
Gates-North Gates, NY (cdp) Monroe County	45	0.30
Lauderhill, FL (city) Broward County	168	0.29
South Plainfield, NJ (borough) Middlesex County	64	0.29
East Orange, NJ (city) Essex County	193	0.28
Maplewood, NJ (cdp) Essex County	67	0.28
Summit, NJ (city) Union County	59	0.28
Pine Hills, FL (cdp) Orange County	112	0.27
Asbury Park, NJ (city) Monmouth County	45	0.27
North Miami, FL (city) Miami-Dade County	149	0.25
Norland, FL (cdp) Miami-Dade County	57	0.25
South Laurel, MD (cdp) Prince George's County	51	0.25
Orangeburg, SC (city) Orangeburg County	32	0.25
Twentynine Palms, CA (city) San Bernardino County	35	0.24
Westbury, NY (village) Nassau County	34	0.24
Glenn Dale, MD (cdp) Prince George's County	31	0.24
Hartford, CT (city) Hartford County	278	0.23
Apex, NC (town) Wake County	46	0.23
Adelphi, MD (cdp) Prince George's County	34	0.23
Yeadon, PA (borough) Delaware County	27	0.23
Medford, MA (city) Middlesex County	116	0.21
White Plains, NY (city) Westchester County	109	0.21
Golden Glades, FL (cdp) Miami-Dade County	67	0.21
Randolph, MA (cdp) Norfolk County	65	0.21
Gates, NY (town) Monroe County	61	0.21
Hillside, NJ (cdp) Union County	46	0.21
Willingboro, NJ (township) Burlington County	65	0.20
Somerset, NJ (cdp) Somerset County	45	0.20
Fairview Shores, FL (cdp) Orange County	27	0.20
Glasgow, DE (cdp) New Castle County	26	0.20
Springfield, MA (city) Hampden County	292	0.19
Miramar, FL (city) Broward County	139	0.19
Irvington, NJ (cdp) Essex County	113	0.19
Montclair, NJ (cdp) Essex County	74	0.19
Orange, NJ (cdp) Essex County	61	0.19
North Laurel, MD (cdp) Howard County	40	0.19
Sandalfoot Cove, FL (cdp) Palm Beach County	31	0.19
Brockton, MA (city) Plymouth County	173	0.18
Brentwood, NY (cdp) Suffolk County	98	0.18
Franklin, NJ (township) Somerset County	92	0.18
Hillcrest Heights, MD (cdp) Prince George's County	29	0.18
Somerville, MA (city) Middlesex County	135	0.17
Ossining, NY (town) Westchester County	61	0.17
Port Chester, NY (village) Westchester County	46	0.17
Dania Beach, FL (city) Broward County	34	0.17
Glen Rock, NJ (borough) Bergen County	20	0.17
Country Walk, FL (cdp) Miami-Dade County	18	0.17
Hempstead, NY (town) Nassau County	1,180	0.16
Frederick, MD (city) Frederick County	82	0.16
East Hartford, CT (cdp) Hartford County	80	0.16
Fort Pierce, FL (city) Saint Lucie County	61	0.16
Cheltenham, PA (township) Montgomery County	58	0.16
Tucker, GA (cdp) De Kalb County	42	0.16
Royal Palm Beach, FL (village) Palm Beach County	34	0.16
Redland, MD (cdp) Montgomery County	28	0.16
East Riverdale, MD (cdp) Prince George's County	25	0.16
Niles, MI (township) Berrien County	22	0.16
Acworth, GA (city) Cobb County	21	0.16
Saint Marys, GA (city) Camden County	21	0.16
Red Hook, NY (town) Dutchess County	17	0.16
Cortlandt, NY (town) Westchester County	59	0.15
New London, CT (city) New London County	38	0.15
Loma Linda, CA (city) San Bernardino County	27	0.15
Upper Chichester, PA (township) Delaware County	26	0.15
Springdale, NJ (cdp) Camden County	21	0.15
Plumstead, PA (township) Bucks County	17	0.15
Neptune, NJ (township) Monmouth County	39	0.14
Greenbelt, MD (city) Prince George's County	31	0.14
Hazlet, NJ (township) Monmouth County	29	0.14
South Orange, NJ (cdp) Essex County	23	0.14
Belle Glade, FL (city) Palm Beach County	21	0.14
Oldsmar, FL (city) Pinellas County	17	0.14
Tarrytown, NY (village) Westchester County	16	0.14
Florence, NJ (township) Burlington County	15	0.14
Freehold, NJ (borough) Monmouth County	15	0.14
Greenburgh, NY (town) Westchester County	114	0.13
Atlantic City, NJ (city) Atlantic County	51	0.13
Palm Coast, FL (city) Flagler County	43	0.13
Baldwin, NY (cdp) Nassau County	30	0.13
Yeehaw Junction, FL (cdp) Osceola County	29	0.13
Lakeside, CA (cdp) San Diego County	25	0.13
Lake Worth Corridor, FL (cdp) Palm Beach County	23	0.13
Rye, NY (city) Westchester County	20	0.13
Excelsior Springs, MO (city) Clay County	14	0.13
Tyngsborough, MA (town) Middlesex County	14	0.13
Rocky Point, NY (cdp) Suffolk County	13	0.13
Palm Bay, FL (city) Brevard County	92	0.12
Old Bridge, NJ (township) Middlesex County	71	0.12
West Orange, NJ (cdp) Essex County	53	0.12
Linden, NJ (city) Union County	49	0.12
Rome, NY (city) Oneida County	42	0.12
Eastchester, NY (town) Westchester County	38	0.12
Windsor, CT (town) Hartford County	35	0.12
Holbrook, NY (cdp) Suffolk County	32	0.12
Jefferson, NJ (township) Morris County	23	0.12
Camp Springs, MD (cdp) Prince George's County	21	0.12
Cimarron Hills, CO (cdp) El Paso County	19	0.12
Muhlenberg, PA (township) Berks County	19	0.12
East Greenwich, RI (town) Kent County	15	0.12
Wawarsing, NY (town) Ulster County	15	0.12
Kingston, MA (town) Plymouth County	14	0.12
Davie, FL (town) Broward County	83	0.11
Deerfield Beach, FL (city) Broward County	70	0.11
Boynton Beach, FL (city) Palm Beach County	67	0.11
Delray Beach, FL (city) Palm Beach County	66	0.11
Aspen Hill, MD (cdp) Montgomery County	53	0.11
Yorktown, NY (town) Westchester County	40	0.11
Manalapan, NJ (township) Monmouth County	36	0.11
Duluth, GA (city) Gwinnett County	25	0.11
Peekskill, NY (city) Westchester County	25	0.11
Forest Park, OH (city) Hamilton County	22	0.11
Aberdeen, NJ (township) Monmouth County	19	0.11
Sharon, MA (town) Norfolk County	19	0.11
Madison, NJ (borough) Morris County	18	0.11
Princeton Meadows, NJ (cdp) Middlesex County	15	0.11
Fort Drum, NY (cdp) Jefferson County	13	0.11
Citrus, CA (cdp) Los Angeles County	12	0.11
East Hanover, NJ (township) Morris County	12	0.11
Lower Pottsgrove, PA (township) Montgomery County	12	0.11
View Park-Windsor Hills, CA (cdp) Los Angeles County	12	0.11
Saint Petersburg, FL (city) Pinellas County	240	0.10
Bridgeport, CT (city) Fairfield County	138	0.10
Lynn, MA (city) Essex County	86	0.10
Piscataway, NJ (township) Middlesex County	50	0.10
Rye, NY (town) Westchester County	46	0.10
Maywood, IL (village) Cook County	26	0.10
Easton, PA (city) Northampton County	25	0.10
Milton, MA (cdp) Norfolk County	25	0.10
Lynbrook, NY (village) Nassau County	20	0.10

Notes: (cdp) census designated place; Refer to the Explanation of Data in the front of the book for more detailed information.

West Indian: Belizean, excluding Hispanic

Top 150 Places Sorted by Number

(Based on all places, regardless of population)

Place	Number	%
Los Angeles, CA (city) Los Angeles County	7,742	0.21
New York, NY (city) New York City	6,487	0.08
Chicago, IL (city) Cook County	2,244	0.08
Inglewood, CA (city) Los Angeles County	581	0.52
Evanston, IL (city) Cook County	488	0.66
Hawthorne, CA (city) Los Angeles County	435	0.52
Houston, TX (city) Harris County	379	0.02
Waukegan, IL (city) Lake County	366	0.42
Gardena, CA (city) Los Angeles County	276	0.48
Long Beach, CA (city) Los Angeles County	254	0.06
Oakland, CA (city) Alameda County	244	0.06
Moreno Valley, CA (city) Riverside County	209	0.15
New Orleans, LA (city) Orleans Parish	209	0.04
Hempstead, NY (town) Nassau County	209	0.03
Rochester, NY (city) Monroe County	195	0.09
Garland, TX (city) Dallas County	188	0.09
Fontana, CA (city) San Bernardino County	179	0.14
Kenner, LA (city) Jefferson Parish	173	0.25
Jersey City, NJ (city) Hudson County	153	0.06
Dallas, TX (city) Dallas County	152	0.01
West Athens, CA (cdp) Los Angeles County	151	1.63
Compton, CA (city) Los Angeles County	151	0.16
San Diego, CA (city) San Diego County	146	0.01
Bellflower, CA (city) Los Angeles County	140	0.19
Lancaster, CA (city) Los Angeles County	133	0.11
Westmont, CA (cdp) Los Angeles County	123	0.39
Jacksonville, FL (special city) Duval County	122	0.02
Pine Manor, FL (cdp) Lee County	119	3.06
Lawndale, CA (city) Los Angeles County	119	0.38
Perris, CA (city) Riverside County	113	0.31
Rialto, CA (city) San Bernardino County	113	0.12
Islip, NY (town) Suffolk County	107	0.03
Miami, FL (city) Miami-Dade County	105	0.03
Riverside, CA (city) Riverside County	103	0.04
San Francisco, CA (city) San Francisco County	97	0.01
San Antonio, TX (city) Bexar County	96	0.01
Elmont, NY (cdp) Nassau County	93	0.28
Ladera Heights, CA (cdp) Los Angeles County	92	1.41
Glendale, CA (city) Los Angeles County	92	0.05
Plantation, FL (city) Broward County	91	0.11
Mesa, AZ (city) Maricopa County	86	0.02
North Miami Beach, FL (city) Miami-Dade County	85	0.21
Carol City, FL (cdp) Miami-Dade County	85	0.14
Zion, IL (city) Lake County	84	0.36
Central Islip, NY (cdp) Suffolk County	84	0.26
Wheeling, IL (village) Cook County	83	0.24
Irving, TX (city) Dallas County	83	0.04
Palmdale, CA (city) Los Angeles County	79	0.07
Ontario, CA (city) San Bernardino County	79	0.05
La Mesa, CA (city) San Diego County	78	0.14
Lakewood, CA (city) Los Angeles County	77	0.10
Arlington, TX (city) Tarrant County	73	0.02
Santa Clarita, CA (city) Los Angeles County	72	0.05
San Bernardino, CA (city) San Bernardino County	72	0.04
Philadelphia, PA (city) Philadelphia County	72	0.00
North Hempstead, NY (town) Nassau County	69	0.03
Las Vegas, NV (city) Clark County	69	0.01
Upland, CA (city) San Bernardino County	68	0.10
Aurora, CO (city) Arapahoe County	68	0.02
San Jose, CA (city) Santa Clara County	67	0.01
Plano, TX (city) Collin County	66	0.03
Adelanto, CA (city) San Bernardino County	65	0.36
Yonkers, NY (city) Westchester County	64	0.03
Azusa, CA (city) Los Angeles County	63	0.14
Buena Park, CA (city) Orange County	63	0.08
View Park-Windsor Hills, CA (cdp) Los Angeles County	62	0.57
Skokie, IL (village) Cook County	62	0.10
Sunrise Manor, NV (cdp) Clark County	62	0.04
Teaneck, NJ (cdp) Bergen County	61	0.16
Berwyn, IL (city) Cook County	60	0.11
Pleasanton, TX (city) Atascosa County	59	0.72
Tamarac, FL (city) Broward County	59	0.11
Huntington Park, CA (city) Los Angeles County	59	0.10
East Orange, NJ (city) Essex County	59	0.08
Lomita, CA (city) Los Angeles County	57	0.29
North Chicago, IL (city) Lake County	56	0.16
North Miami, FL (city) Miami-Dade County	56	0.09
Collier Manor-Cresthaven, FL (cdp) Broward County	55	0.69
South Whittier, CA (cdp) Los Angeles County	55	0.10
Pomona, CA (city) Los Angeles County	55	0.04
Pembroke Pines, FL (city) Broward County	54	0.04
Baldwin Park, CA (city) Los Angeles County	53	0.07
Long Branch, NJ (city) Monmouth County	52	0.17
Richmond, CA (city) Contra Costa County	52	0.05
Santa Ana, CA (city) Orange County	52	0.02
Kansas City, MO (city) Jackson County	52	0.01
Colton, CA (city) San Bernardino County	51	0.11
Danbury, CT (city) Fairfield County	51	0.07
Metairie, LA (cdp) Jefferson Parish	51	0.03
Anaheim, CA (city) Orange County	51	0.02
Standish, ME (town) Cumberland County	50	0.54
Fort Myers, FL (city) Lee County	50	0.10
Pensacola, FL (city) Escambia County	50	0.09
Friendswood, TX (city) Galveston County	49	0.17
Freeport, NY (village) Nassau County	49	0.11
Milwaukee, WI (city) Milwaukee County	49	0.01
Asbury Park, NJ (city) Monmouth County	48	0.28
Maywood, IL (village) Cook County	48	0.18
Brandon, FL (cdp) Hillsborough County	48	0.06
Abilene, TX (city) Taylor County	48	0.04
Pacifica, CA (city) San Mateo County	47	0.12
Coral Springs, FL (city) Broward County	47	0.04
Sauk Village, IL (village) Cook County	46	0.44
Oakland Park, FL (city) Broward County	46	0.15
Lake Worth, FL (city) Palm Beach County	46	0.13
San Leandro, CA (city) Alameda County	46	0.06
Fullerton, CA (city) Orange County	46	0.04
Columbus, GA (special city) Muscogee County	46	0.02
Royal Palm Estates, FL (cdp) Palm Beach County	45	1.30
Alondra Park, CA (cdp) Los Angeles County	45	0.53
Meadow Woods, FL (cdp) Orange County	45	0.39
La Presa, CA (cdp) San Diego County	45	0.14
Diamond Bar, CA (city) Los Angeles County	44	0.08
Saint Petersburg, FL (city) Pinellas County	44	0.02
Miramar, FL (city) Broward County	42	0.06
Carson, CA (city) Los Angeles County	42	0.05
Norwalk, CA (city) Los Angeles County	42	0.04
Raleigh, NC (city) Wake County	42	0.02
Searingtown, NY (cdp) Nassau County	41	0.81
Collingdale, PA (borough) Delaware County	41	0.47
Oceanside, CA (city) San Diego County	41	0.03
Lynwood, IL (village) Cook County	40	0.54
Palmetto Estates, FL (cdp) Miami-Dade County	40	0.29
Passaic, NJ (city) Passaic County	40	0.06
Lawton, OK (city) Comanche County	40	0.04
Dumbarton, VA (cdp) Henrico County	39	0.58
Casselberry, FL (city) Seminole County	39	0.18
Monrovia, CA (city) Los Angeles County	39	0.11
Pasadena, CA (city) Los Angeles County	39	0.03
Palatine, IL (village) Cook County	38	0.06
Hollywood, FL (city) Broward County	38	0.03
Babylon, NY (town) Suffolk County	38	0.02
Glendale, AZ (city) Maricopa County	38	0.02
Tampa, FL (city) Hillsborough County	38	0.01
Joppatowne, MD (cdp) Harford County	37	0.33
Fort Washington, MD (cdp) Prince George's County	37	0.15
San Gabriel, CA (city) Los Angeles County	37	0.09
Arcadia, CA (city) Los Angeles County	37	0.07
Paramount, CA (city) Los Angeles County	37	0.07
Simi Valley, CA (city) Ventura County	37	0.03
Indianapolis, IN (special city) Marion County	37	0.00
Country Club Hills, IL (city) Cook County	36	0.22
Culver City, CA (city) Los Angeles County	36	0.09
Rosemead, CA (city) Los Angeles County	36	0.07
Orlando, FL (city) Orange County	36	0.02
Mission Bend, TX (cdp) Fort Bend County	35	0.11
Freehold, NJ (borough) Monmouth County	34	0.31
Cortlandt, NY (town) Westchester County	34	0.09
The Hammocks, FL (cdp) Miami-Dade County	34	0.07
Berkeley, CA (city) Alameda County	34	0.03

Notes: (cdp) census designated place; Refer to the Explanation of Data in the front of the book for more detailed information.

West Indian: Belizean, excluding Hispanic

Top 150 Places Sorted by Percent

(Based on all places, regardless of population)

Place	Number	%
Industry, TX (city) Austin County	16	5.52
Pine Manor, FL (cdp) Lee County	119	3.06
Seltzer, PA (cdp) Schuylkill County	6	2.12
West Athens, CA (cdp) Los Angeles County	151	1.63
Eastville, VA (town) Northampton County	3	1.55
Ladera Heights, CA (cdp) Los Angeles County	92	1.41
Royal Palm Estates, FL (cdp) Palm Beach County	45	1.30
Searingtown, NY (cdp) Nassau County	41	0.81
Pleasanton, TX (city) Atascosa County	59	0.72
Greenvale, NY (cdp) Nassau County	16	0.72
Lexington, TX (town) Lee County	8	0.70
Collier Manor-Cresthaven, FL (cdp) Broward County	55	0.69
Eagle Nest, NM (village) Colfax County	2	0.67
Evanston, IL (city) Cook County	488	0.66
Hamilton, KS (city) Greenwood County	2	0.65
Elmwood, LA (cdp) Jefferson Parish	26	0.59
Dumbarton, VA (cdp) Henrico County	39	0.58
View Park-Windsor Hills, CA (cdp) Los Angeles County	62	0.57
Wheatley Heights, NY (cdp) Suffolk County	28	0.56
Hubbard, TX (city) Hill County	9	0.55
Standish, ME (town) Cumberland County	50	0.54
Lynwood, IL (village) Cook County	40	0.54
Rock Island, FL (cdp) Broward County	17	0.54
Roosevelt Gardens, FL (cdp) Broward County	10	0.54
Alondra Park, CA (cdp) Los Angeles County	45	0.53
Inglewood, CA (city) Los Angeles County	581	0.52
Hawthorne, CA (city) Los Angeles County	435	0.52
Calhoun Falls, SC (town) Abbeville County	12	0.52
Southwest, PA (township) Warren County	3	0.52
Urbana, IA (city) Benton County	5	0.49
Gardena, CA (city) Los Angeles County	276	0.48
Weisenberg, PA (township) Lehigh County	20	0.48
Pamplin City, VA (town) Appomattox County	1	0.48
Collingdale, PA (borough) Delaware County	41	0.47
Pontotoc, MS (city) Pontotoc County	24	0.47
East Lackawannock, PA (township) Mercer County	8	0.47
Bithlo, FL (cdp) Orange County	20	0.45
Sauk Village, IL (village) Cook County	46	0.44
Yaphank, NY (cdp) Suffolk County	22	0.43
Waukegan, IL (city) Lake County	366	0.42
Golden Lakes, FL (cdp) Palm Beach County	28	0.42
Boyes Hot Springs, CA (cdp) Sonoma County	26	0.41
Alorton, IL (village) Saint Clair County	11	0.40
Washington Park, FL (cdp) Broward County	5	0.40
Westmont, CA (cdp) Los Angeles County	123	0.39
Meadow Woods, FL (cdp) Orange County	45	0.39
Lawndale, CA (city) Los Angeles County	119	0.38
Warrenton, MO (city) Warren County	20	0.38
Munsons Corners, NY (cdp) Cortland County	9	0.37
Allentown, NJ (borough) Monmouth County	7	0.37
Wheatland, MI (township) Sanilac County	2	0.37
Zion, IL (city) Lake County	84	0.36
Adelanto, CA (city) San Bernardino County	65	0.36
Woodfield, SC (cdp) Richland County	33	0.36
Keyport, NJ (borough) Monmouth County	27	0.36
Saluda, NC (city) Polk County	2	0.36
Lancaster, MA (town) Worcester County	26	0.35
Mountain View, WY (town) Uinta County	4	0.35
Cassopolis, MI (village) Cass County	6	0.34
Joppatowne, MD (cdp) Harford County	37	0.33
Opal Cliffs, CA (cdp) Santa Cruz County	21	0.33
Brocton, NY (village) Chautauqua County	5	0.32
Perris, CA (city) Riverside County	113	0.31
Freehold, NJ (borough) Monmouth County	34	0.31
Avondale, LA (cdp) Jefferson Parish	17	0.31
Fresno, TX (cdp) Fort Bend County	20	0.30
Tangelo Park, FL (cdp) Orange County	7	0.30
Lomita, CA (city) Los Angeles County	57	0.29
Palmetto Estates, FL (cdp) Miami-Dade County	40	0.29
Hometown, IL (city) Cook County	13	0.29
Oak Point, TX (city) Denton County	5	0.29
Tonica, IL (village) La Salle County	2	0.29
Elmont, NY (cdp) Nassau County	93	0.28
Asbury Park, NJ (city) Monmouth County	48	0.28
Fern Park, FL (cdp) Seminole County	23	0.28
West Compton, CA (cdp) Los Angeles County	15	0.28
Zephyrhills South, FL (cdp) Pasco County	13	0.28
Atlantis, FL (city) Palm Beach County	6	0.28
Norwegian, PA (township) Schuylkill County	6	0.28
Perryville, AR (city) Perry County	4	0.28
Shell Point, SC (cdp) Beaufort County	8	0.27
Fairmont, IL (cdp) Will County	7	0.27
Sand Lake, WI (town) Sawyer County	2	0.27
Central Islip, NY (cdp) Suffolk County	84	0.26
Browns Mills, NJ (cdp) Burlington County	29	0.26
Andrews AFB, MD (cdp) Prince George's County	21	0.26
Birdsboro, PA (borough) Berks County	13	0.26
Hamilton, NY (village) Madison County	9	0.26
Mount Healthy Heights, OH (cdp) Hamilton County	9	0.26
Westminster, LA (cdp) East Baton Rouge Parish	7	0.26
Gambier, OH (village) Knox County	5	0.26
Cottage City, MD (town) Prince George's County	3	0.26
Kenner, LA (city) Jefferson Parish	173	0.25
Upper Grand Lagoon, FL (cdp) Bay County	28	0.25
Lexington Park, MD (cdp) Saint Mary's County	27	0.25
East Perrine, FL (cdp) Miami-Dade County	17	0.25
Port Monmouth, NJ (cdp) Monmouth County	9	0.25
Wheeling, IL (village) Cook County	83	0.24
Kings Point, NY (village) Nassau County	12	0.24
Forsyth, MO (city) Taney County	4	0.24
Locke, MI (township) Ingham County	4	0.24
Brownsville, FL (cdp) Miami-Dade County	33	0.23
Glen Raven, NC (cdp) Alamance County	6	0.23
Coats, NC (town) Harnett County	4	0.23
Country Club Hills, IL (city) Cook County	36	0.22
Dryden, NY (town) Tompkins County	30	0.22
Calumet Park, IL (village) Cook County	19	0.22
Royal Oak charter, MI (township) Oakland County	12	0.22
Wesley Hills, NY (village) Rockland County	11	0.22
Los Angeles, CA (city) Los Angeles County	7,742	0.21
North Miami Beach, FL (city) Miami-Dade County	85	0.21
Markham, IL (city) Cook County	27	0.21
Apalachicola, FL (city) Franklin County	5	0.21
Larkspur, CA (city) Marin County	24	0.20
Fort Valley, GA (city) Peach County	16	0.20
Bellflower, CA (city) Los Angeles County	140	0.19
Estelle, LA (cdp) Jefferson Parish	31	0.19
Eatontown, NJ (borough) Monmouth County	26	0.19
Merrifield, VA (cdp) Fairfax County	21	0.19
Maywood, IL (village) Cook County	48	0.18
Casselberry, FL (city) Seminole County	39	0.18
Miami Springs, FL (city) Miami-Dade County	25	0.18
Hartsdale, NY (cdp) Westchester County	18	0.18
Westgate-Belvedere Homes, FL (cdp) Palm Beach County	15	0.18
La Grange, MI (township) Cass County	6	0.18
Cuba, NY (village) Allegany County	3	0.18
Picher, OK (city) Ottawa County	3	0.18
Long Branch, NJ (city) Monmouth County	52	0.17
Friendswood, TX (city) Galveston County	49	0.17
Fort Stewart, GA (cdp) Liberty County	19	0.17
Kettering, MD (cdp) Prince George's County	19	0.17
Darby, PA (borough) Delaware County	18	0.17
Chestnut Ridge, NY (village) Rockland County	13	0.17
University Park, IL (village) Will County	11	0.17
Rancho Viejo, TX (town) Cameron County	3	0.17
Compton, CA (city) Los Angeles County	151	0.16
Teaneck, NJ (cdp) Bergen County	61	0.16
North Chicago, IL (city) Lake County	56	0.16
New Fairfield, CT (town) Fairfield County	22	0.16
Hope Mills, NC (town) Cumberland County	18	0.16
Dover, NY (town) Dutchess County	14	0.16
Carrizo Springs, TX (city) Dimmit County	9	0.16
Hamilton, NY (town) Madison County	9	0.16
Colwyn, PA (borough) Delaware County	4	0.16
Columbus Junction, IA (city) Louisa County	3	0.16
Warren, CT (town) Litchfield County	2	0.16
Moreno Valley, CA (city) Riverside County	209	0.15
Oakland Park, FL (city) Broward County	46	0.15
Fort Washington, MD (cdp) Prince George's County	37	0.15
Evergreen Park, IL (village) Cook County	32	0.15

Notes: (cdp) census designated place; Refer to the Explanation of Data in the front of the book for more detailed information.

West Indian: Belizean, excluding Hispanic

Top 150 Places Sorted by Percent

(Based on places with populations of 10,000 or more)

Place	Number	%
Evanston, IL (city) Cook County	488	0.66
View Park-Windsor Hills, CA (cdp) Los Angeles County	62	0.57
Inglewood, CA (city) Los Angeles County	581	0.52
Hawthorne, CA (city) Los Angeles County	435	0.52
Gardena, CA (city) Los Angeles County	276	0.48
Sauk Village, IL (village) Cook County	46	0.44
Waukegan, IL (city) Lake County	366	0.42
Westmont, CA (cdp) Los Angeles County	123	0.39
Meadow Woods, FL (cdp) Orange County	45	0.39
Lawndale, CA (city) Los Angeles County	119	0.38
Zion, IL (city) Lake County	84	0.36
Adelanto, CA (city) San Bernardino County	65	0.36
Joppatowne, MD (cdp) Harford County	37	0.33
Perris, CA (city) Riverside County	113	0.31
Freehold, NJ (borough) Monmouth County	34	0.31
Lomita, CA (city) Los Angeles County	57	0.29
Palmetto Estates, FL (cdp) Miami-Dade County	40	0.29
Elmont, NY (cdp) Nassau County	93	0.28
Asbury Park, NJ (city) Monmouth County	48	0.28
Central Islip, NY (cdp) Suffolk County	84	0.26
Browns Mills, NJ (cdp) Burlington County	29	0.26
Kenner, LA (city) Jefferson Parish	173	0.25
Upper Grand Lagoon, FL (cdp) Bay County	28	0.25
Lexington Park, MD (cdp) Saint Mary's County	27	0.25
Wheeling, IL (village) Cook County	83	0.24
Brownsville, FL (cdp) Miami-Dade County	33	0.23
Country Club Hills, IL (city) Cook County	36	0.22
Dryden, NY (town) Tompkins County	30	0.22
Los Angeles, CA (city) Los Angeles County	7,742	0.21
North Miami Beach, FL (city) Miami-Dade County	85	0.21
Markham, IL (city) Cook County	27	0.21
Larkspur, CA (city) Marin County	24	0.20
Bellflower, CA (city) Los Angeles County	140	0.19
Estelle, LA (cdp) Jefferson Parish	31	0.19
Eatontown, NJ (borough) Monmouth County	26	0.19
Merrifield, VA (cdp) Fairfax County	21	0.19
Maywood, IL (village) Cook County	48	0.18
Casselberry, FL (city) Seminole County	39	0.18
Miami Springs, FL (city) Miami-Dade County	25	0.18
Long Branch, NJ (city) Monmouth County	52	0.17
Friendswood, TX (city) Galveston County	49	0.17
Fort Stewart, GA (cdp) Liberty County	19	0.17
Kettering, MD (cdp) Prince George's County	19	0.17
Darby, PA (borough) Delaware County	18	0.17
Compton, CA (city) Los Angeles County	151	0.16
Teaneck, NJ (cdp) Bergen County	61	0.16
North Chicago, IL (city) Lake County	56	0.16
New Fairfield, CT (town) Fairfield County	22	0.16
Hope Mills, NC (town) Cumberland County	18	0.16
Moreno Valley, CA (city) Riverside County	209	0.15
Oakland Park, FL (city) Broward County	46	0.15
Fort Washington, MD (cdp) Prince George's County	37	0.15
Evergreen Park, IL (village) Cook County	32	0.15
Dickinson, TX (city) Galveston County	25	0.15
Longwood, FL (city) Seminole County	20	0.15
Saddle Brook, NJ (cdp) Bergen County	20	0.15
Fontana, CA (city) San Bernardino County	179	0.14
Carol City, FL (cdp) Miami-Dade County	85	0.14
La Mesa, CA (city) San Diego County	78	0.14
Azusa, CA (city) Los Angeles County	63	0.14
La Presa, CA (cdp) San Diego County	45	0.14
Lake Worth, FL (city) Palm Beach County	46	0.13
El Paso de Robles, CA (city) San Luis Obispo County	31	0.13
Camp Springs, MD (cdp) Prince George's County	23	0.13
Decatur, GA (city) De Kalb County	23	0.13
Iselin, NJ (cdp) Middlesex County	22	0.13
Lakeland Highlands, FL (cdp) Polk County	17	0.13
Fort Carson, CO (cdp) El Paso County	14	0.13
Marathon, FL (city) Monroe County	13	0.13
Rialto, CA (city) San Bernardino County	113	0.12
Pacifica, CA (city) San Mateo County	47	0.12
Whitney, NV (cdp) Clark County	22	0.12
Lutz, FL (cdp) Hillsborough County	21	0.12
Lancaster, CA (city) Los Angeles County	133	0.11
Plantation, FL (city) Broward County	91	0.11
Berwyn, IL (city) Cook County	60	0.11
Tamarac, FL (city) Broward County	59	0.11
Colton, CA (city) San Bernardino County	51	0.11
Freeport, NY (village) Nassau County	49	0.11
Monrovia, CA (city) Los Angeles County	39	0.11
Mission Bend, TX (cdp) Fort Bend County	35	0.11
Clinton, MD (cdp) Prince George's County	28	0.11
Baldwin, NY (cdp) Nassau County	26	0.11
San Fernando, CA (city) Los Angeles County	26	0.11
Yeehaw Junction, FL (cdp) Osceola County	25	0.11
Waipio, HI (cdp) Honolulu County	13	0.11
Lakewood, CA (city) Los Angeles County	77	0.10
Upland, CA (city) San Bernardino County	68	0.10
Skokie, IL (village) Cook County	62	0.10
Huntington Park, CA (city) Los Angeles County	59	0.10
South Whittier, CA (cdp) Los Angeles County	55	0.10
Fort Myers, FL (city) Lee County	50	0.10
Pemberton, NJ (township) Burlington County	29	0.10
Walnut, CA (city) Los Angeles County	29	0.10
Clinton, IA (city) Clinton County	28	0.10
El Cerrito, CA (city) Contra Costa County	23	0.10
La Crescenta-Montrose, CA (cdp) Los Angeles County	19	0.10
Loma Linda, CA (city) San Bernardino County	19	0.10
Palisades Park, NJ (borough) Bergen County	17	0.10
Scott Lake, FL (cdp) Miami-Dade County	15	0.10
Keystone, FL (cdp) Hillsborough County	14	0.10
South Daytona, FL (city) Volusia County	13	0.10
Commerce, CA (city) Los Angeles County	12	0.10
Gonzalez, FL (cdp) Escambia County	12	0.10
Vineyard, CA (cdp) Sacramento County	10	0.10
Rochester, NY (city) Monroe County	195	0.09
Garland, TX (city) Dallas County	188	0.09
North Miami, FL (city) Miami-Dade County	56	0.09
Pensacola, FL (city) Escambia County	50	0.09
San Gabriel, CA (city) Los Angeles County	37	0.09
Culver City, CA (city) Los Angeles County	36	0.09
Cortlandt, NY (town) Westchester County	34	0.09
Dana Point, CA (city) Orange County	33	0.09
Claremont, CA (city) Los Angeles County	32	0.09
Riviera Beach, FL (city) Palm Beach County	27	0.09
University, FL (cdp) Hillsborough County	27	0.09
Dalton, GA (city) Whitfield County	24	0.09
Blue Island, IL (city) Cook County	22	0.09
West Carson, CA (cdp) Los Angeles County	20	0.09
Newberg, OR (city) Yamhill County	17	0.09
New Kingman-Butler, AZ (cdp) Mohave County	14	0.09
Goldenrod, FL (cdp) Seminole County	12	0.09
Lindenhurst, IL (village) Lake County	11	0.09
Matteson, IL (village) Cook County	11	0.09
Red Bank, NJ (borough) Monmouth County	11	0.09
Middle Smithfield, PA (township) Monroe County	10	0.09
New York, NY (city) New York City	6,487	0.08
Chicago, IL (city) Cook County	2,244	0.08
Buena Park, CA (city) Orange County	63	0.08
East Orange, NJ (city) Essex County	59	0.08
Diamond Bar, CA (city) Los Angeles County	44	0.08
Redan, GA (cdp) De Kalb County	26	0.08
Golden Glades, FL (cdp) Miami-Dade County	25	0.08
Lakeside, FL (cdp) Clay County	24	0.08
Harvey, IL (city) Cook County	23	0.08
Burlington, MA (cdp) Middlesex County	18	0.08
Norland, FL (cdp) Miami-Dade County	18	0.08
Hauppauge, NY (cdp) Suffolk County	16	0.08
Homewood, IL (village) Cook County	15	0.08
Rocky Hill, CT (town) Hartford County	14	0.08
Rutherford, NJ (borough) Bergen County	14	0.08
Santa Fe Springs, CA (city) Los Angeles County	14	0.08
El Segundo, CA (city) Los Angeles County	12	0.08
Midlothian, IL (village) Cook County	11	0.08
Clayton, MO (city) Saint Louis County	10	0.08
Tuskegee, AL (city) Macon County	10	0.08
Excelsior Springs, MO (city) Clay County	9	0.08
North Aurora, IL (village) Kane County	8	0.08
Palmdale, CA (city) Los Angeles County	79	0.07
Baldwin Park, CA (city) Los Angeles County	53	0.07

Notes: (cdp) census designated place; Refer to the Explanation of Data in the front of the book for more detailed information.

West Indian: Bermudan, excluding Hispanic

Top 150 Places Sorted by Number

(Based on all places, regardless of population)

Place	Number	%
New York, NY (city) New York City	608	0.01
Hampton, VA (independent city) Hampton city	134	0.09
Boston, MA (city) Suffolk County	105	0.02
Jacksonville, FL (special city) Duval County	90	0.01
Los Angeles, CA (city) Los Angeles County	72	0.00
Brookhaven, NY (town) Suffolk County	56	0.01
Huntsville, AL (city) Madison County	54	0.03
Atlanta, GA (city) Fulton County	50	0.01
Junction City, KS (city) Geary County	48	0.25
Montclair, NJ (cdp) Essex County	48	0.12
Lake Mary, FL (city) Seminole County	46	0.41
Cambridge, MA (city) Middlesex County	45	0.04
Brentwood, CA (city) Contra Costa County	44	0.19
Philadelphia, PA (city) Philadelphia County	40	0.00
Springfield, MA (city) Hampden County	39	0.03
Fern Park, FL (cdp) Seminole County	38	0.46
East Orange, NJ (city) Essex County	37	0.05
Stamford, CT (city) Fairfield County	36	0.03
Plainfield, NJ (city) Union County	35	0.07
Babylon, NY (town) Suffolk County	34	0.02
Burton, SC (cdp) Beaufort County	33	0.47
Irvington, NJ (cdp) Essex County	33	0.05
Greensboro, NC (city) Guilford County	32	0.01
Newark, DE (city) New Castle County	31	0.11
Bessemer, AL (city) Jefferson County	31	0.10
Hanford, CA (city) Kings County	31	0.07
Corpus Christi, TX (city) Nueces County	31	0.01
Oyster Bay, NY (town) Nassau County	31	0.01
Sunrise, FL (city) Broward County	30	0.04
Virginia Beach, VA (independent city) Virginia Beach city	30	0.01
Beckett, NJ (cdp) Gloucester County	29	0.60
Logan, NJ (township) Gloucester County	29	0.48
Columbus, OH (city) Franklin County	28	0.00
San Antonio, TX (city) Bexar County	28	0.00
North Bellport, NY (cdp) Suffolk County	27	0.30
Flint, MI (township) Genesee County	27	0.08
Burke, VA (cdp) Fairfax County	27	0.05
Oakland, CA (city) Alameda County	26	0.01
Hempstead, NY (town) Nassau County	26	0.00
Ogden, NC (cdp) New Hanover County	25	0.45
Hillsborough, NJ (township) Somerset County	25	0.07
Lake Charles, LA (city) Calcasieu Parish	25	0.03
Columbia, SC (city) Richland County	25	0.02
Celebration, FL (cdp) Osceola County	24	0.87
Punta Gorda, FL (city) Charlotte County	24	0.17
North Fair Oaks, CA (cdp) San Mateo County	24	0.16
Eden, NC (city) Rockingham County	24	0.15
Raleigh, NC (city) Wake County	24	0.01
Old Bethpage, NY (cdp) Nassau County	23	0.43
Willingboro, NJ (township) Burlington County	22	0.07
Horn Lake, MS (city) De Soto County	21	0.15
North Marysville, WA (cdp) Snohomish County	21	0.10
Bremerton, WA (city) Kitsap County	21	0.06
Canton, MI (cdp) Wayne County	21	0.03
Glendale, AZ (city) Maricopa County	21	0.01
Olyphant, PA (borough) Lackawanna County	20	0.40
Springfield, FL (city) Bay County	20	0.22
Douglasville, GA (city) Douglas County	20	0.10
Hillside, NJ (cdp) Union County	20	0.09
Somerville, MA (city) Middlesex County	20	0.03
Crestwood Village, NJ (cdp) Ocean County	19	0.22
Milton, MA (cdp) Norfolk County	19	0.07
Manchester, NJ (township) Ocean County	19	0.05
Gainesville, FL (city) Alachua County	19	0.02
Chesapeake, VA (independent city) Chesapeake city	19	0.01
Edwards, CO (cdp) Eagle County	18	0.21
Martinsburg, WV (city) Berkeley County	18	0.12
North Amityville, NY (cdp) Suffolk County	18	0.11
Roosevelt, NY (cdp) Nassau County	18	0.11
Van Buren, MI (township) Wayne County	18	0.08
Huntington Beach, CA (city) Orange County	18	0.01
Baltimore, MD (independent city) Baltimore city	18	0.00
Christopher, IL (city) Franklin County	17	0.62
Edgemoor, DE (cdp) New Castle County	17	0.28
Bowie, MD (city) Prince George's County	17	0.03
Towson, MD (cdp) Baltimore County	17	0.03
Cape Coral, FL (city) Lee County	17	0.02
Silver Spring, MD (cdp) Montgomery County	17	0.02
Augusta-Richmond County, GA (special city) Richmond County	17	0.01
Sioux Falls, SD (city) Minnehaha County	17	0.01
Chicago, IL (city) Cook County	17	0.00
Detroit, MI (city) Wayne County	17	0.00
Houston, TX (city) Harris County	17	0.00
Conway, NH (town) Carroll County	16	0.19
Rye, NY (city) Westchester County	16	0.11
Erlanger, KY (city) Kenton County	16	0.10
Casselberry, FL (city) Seminole County	16	0.07
West Babylon, NY (cdp) Suffolk County	16	0.04
Kenosha, WI (city) Kenosha County	16	0.02
Salinas, CA (city) Monterey County	16	0.01
Allendale, NJ (borough) Bergen County	15	0.22
Prien, LA (cdp) Calcasieu Parish	15	0.21
Lansdowne, PA (borough) Delaware County	15	0.14
Cortlandt, NY (town) Westchester County	15	0.04
Morgan Hill, CA (city) Santa Clara County	15	0.04
Palm Beach Gardens, FL (city) Palm Beach County	15	0.04
Dayton, OH (city) Montgomery County	15	0.01
Providence, RI (city) Providence County	15	0.01
Saint Petersburg, FL (city) Pinellas County	15	0.01
Las Vegas, NV (city) Clark County	15	0.00
Toledo, OH (city) Lucas County	15	0.00
Jackson, CA (city) Amador County	14	0.31
California City, CA (city) Kern County	14	0.17
Willimantic, CT (cdp) Windham County	14	0.09
Laurel, MD (city) Prince George's County	14	0.07
Windham, CT (town) Windham County	14	0.06
Galloway, NJ (township) Atlantic County	14	0.04
Watertown, MA (city) Middlesex County	14	0.04
Smithtown, NY (town) Suffolk County	14	0.01
Yonkers, NY (city) Westchester County	14	0.01
Plain View, NC (cdp) Sampson County	13	0.71
Pinellas Park, FL (city) Pinellas County	13	0.03
Annandale, VA (cdp) Fairfax County	13	0.02
Clifton, NJ (city) Passaic County	13	0.02
Hammond, IN (city) Lake County	13	0.02
Largo, FL (city) Pinellas County	13	0.02
Richmond, VA (independent city) Richmond city	13	0.01
Tallahassee, FL (city) Leon County	13	0.01
Newark, NJ (city) Essex County	13	0.00
Pittsburgh, PA (city) Allegheny County	13	0.00
Seattle, WA (city) King County	13	0.00
West Amwell, NJ (township) Hunterdon County	12	0.50
Chester, NY (town) Warren County	12	0.33
Pepper Pike, OH (city) Cuyahoga County	12	0.20
Mount Healthy, OH (city) Hamilton County	12	0.17
Stafford, TX (city) Fort Bend County	12	0.08
Sebastian, FL (city) Indian River County	12	0.07
North Fort Myers, FL (cdp) Lee County	12	0.03
North Hempstead, NY (town) Nassau County	12	0.01
San Diego, CA (city) San Diego County	12	0.00
Mountain Park, GA (cdp) Gwinnett County	11	0.10
Fort Campbell North, KY (cdp) Christian County	11	0.08
South Park Township, PA (cdp) Allegheny County	11	0.08
Warrensville Heights, OH (city) Cuyahoga County	11	0.07
Waycross, GA (city) Ware County	11	0.07
Greater Upper Marlboro, MD (cdp) Prince George's County	11	0.06
Burlington, NJ (township) Burlington County	11	0.05
Gardner, MA (city) Worcester County	11	0.05
Susquehanna, PA (township) Dauphin County	11	0.05
Merrillville, IN (town) Lake County	11	0.04
Chapel Hill, NC (town) Orange County	11	0.02
Hamden, CT (town) New Haven County	11	0.02
Irondequoit, NY (cdp) Monroe County	11	0.02
Lakewood, NJ (township) Ocean County	11	0.02
Miramar, FL (city) Broward County	11	0.02
Mission Viejo, CA (city) Orange County	11	0.01
Paterson, NJ (city) Passaic County	11	0.01
Plantation, FL (city) Broward County	11	0.01
West Palm Beach, FL (city) Palm Beach County	11	0.01
Honolulu, HI (cdp) Honolulu County	11	0.00

Notes: (cdp) census designated place; Refer to the Explanation of Data in the front of the book for more detailed information.

West Indian: Bermudan, excluding Hispanic

Top 150 Places Sorted by Percent

(Based on all places, regardless of population)

Place	Number	%
Williams, MN (township) Aitkin County	2	1.27
Nespelem, WA (town) Okanogan County	2	1.21
Celebration, FL (cdp) Osceola County	24	0.87
Plain View, NC (cdp) Sampson County	13	0.71
Christopher, IL (city) Franklin County	17	0.62
Beckett, NJ (cdp) Gloucester County	29	0.60
Woodland, NC (town) Northampton County	5	0.56
Lawtey, FL (city) Bradford County	3	0.53
West Amwell, NJ (township) Hunterdon County	12	0.50
Logan, NJ (township) Gloucester County	29	0.48
Burton, SC (cdp) Beaufort County	33	0.47
Fern Park, FL (cdp) Seminole County	38	0.46
Ogden, NC (cdp) New Hanover County	25	0.45
Old Bethpage, NY (cdp) Nassau County	23	0.43
Hopewell, PA (township) Cumberland County	9	0.42
Lake Mary, FL (city) Seminole County	46	0.41
Olyphant, PA (borough) Lackawanna County	20	0.40
Benson, VT (town) Rutland County	4	0.38
Chester, NY (town) Warren County	12	0.33
Jackson, CA (city) Amador County	14	0.31
North Bellport, NY (cdp) Suffolk County	27	0.30
Edgemoor, DE (cdp) New Castle County	17	0.28
Gravel Ridge, AR (cdp) Pulaski County	9	0.28
Wheatfield, PA (township) Perry County	9	0.27
Clinton, MI (village) Lenawee County	6	0.26
Elmer, MI (township) Sanilac County	2	0.26
Junction City, KS (city) Geary County	48	0.25
Henrietta, TX (city) Clay County	8	0.24
Sinking Spring, PA (borough) Berks County	6	0.23
Greenvale, NY (cdp) Nassau County	5	0.23
Rose Hill, NC (town) Duplin County	3	0.23
Springfield, FL (city) Bay County	20	0.22
Crestwood Village, NJ (cdp) Ocean County	19	0.22
Allendale, NJ (borough) Bergen County	15	0.22
Edwards, CO (cdp) Eagle County	18	0.21
Prien, LA (cdp) Calcasieu Parish	15	0.21
Warren, MA (town) Worcester County	10	0.21
Pepper Pike, OH (city) Cuyahoga County	12	0.20
Pompano Estates, FL (cdp) Broward County	7	0.20
Sewickley Heights, PA (borough) Allegheny County	2	0.20
Brentwood, CA (city) Contra Costa County	44	0.19
Conway, NH (town) Carroll County	16	0.19
Port La Belle, FL (cdp) Hendry County	6	0.19
Warren, VT (town) Washington County	3	0.18
Punta Gorda, FL (city) Charlotte County	24	0.17
California City, CA (city) Kern County	14	0.17
Mount Healthy, OH (city) Hamilton County	12	0.17
Nessel, MN (township) Chisago County	3	0.17
North Fair Oaks, CA (cdp) San Mateo County	24	0.16
Jamestown, RI (town) Newport County	9	0.16
Clinton, MI (township) Lenawee County	6	0.16
Barbourmeade, KY (city) Jefferson County	2	0.16
Eden, NC (city) Rockingham County	24	0.15
Horn Lake, MS (city) De Soto County	21	0.15
Pimmit Hills, VA (cdp) Fairfax County	9	0.15
Eatons Neck, NY (cdp) Suffolk County	2	0.15
Lansdowne, PA (borough) Delaware County	15	0.14
Center Moriches, NY (cdp) Suffolk County	9	0.14
Cheshire Village, CT (cdp) New Haven County	8	0.14
West Newbury, MA (town) Essex County	6	0.14
Terryville, CT (cdp) Litchfield County	7	0.13
Sherman, CT (town) Fairfield County	5	0.13
South Bay, FL (city) Palm Beach County	5	0.13
Montclair, NJ (cdp) Essex County	48	0.12
Martinsburg, WV (city) Berkeley County	18	0.12
North Star, DE (cdp) New Castle County	10	0.12
Pine, PA (township) Allegheny County	9	0.12
Half Moon, NC (cdp) Onslow County	8	0.12
Emporia, VA (independent city) Emporia city	7	0.12
Princeton, MA (town) Worcester County	4	0.12
Leverett, MA (town) Franklin County	2	0.12
Newark, DE (city) New Castle County	31	0.11
North Amityville, NY (cdp) Suffolk County	18	0.11
Roosevelt, NY (cdp) Nassau County	18	0.11
Rye, NY (city) Westchester County	16	0.11
Scotchtown, NY (cdp) Orange County	10	0.11
Live Oak, FL (city) Suwannee County	7	0.11
Bessemer, AL (city) Jefferson County	31	0.10
North Marysville, WA (cdp) Snohomish County	21	0.10
Douglasville, GA (city) Douglas County	20	0.10
Erlanger, KY (city) Kenton County	16	0.10
Mountain Park, GA (cdp) Gwinnett County	11	0.10
Chesterfield, NJ (township) Burlington County	6	0.10
Lake Butler, FL (city) Union County	2	0.10
Marlborough, NH (town) Cheshire County	2	0.10
North Norwich, NY (town) Chenango County	2	0.10
Hampton, VA (independent city) Hampton city	134	0.09
Hillside, NJ (cdp) Union County	20	0.09
Willimantic, CT (cdp) Windham County	14	0.09
Collegedale, TN (city) Hamilton County	6	0.09
Goddard, MD (cdp) Prince George's County	5	0.09
Wyndmoor, PA (cdp) Montgomery County	5	0.09
Port Aransas, TX (city) Nueces County	3	0.09
Flint, MI (township) Genesee County	27	0.08
Van Buren, MI (township) Wayne County	18	0.08
Stafford, TX (city) Fort Bend County	12	0.08
Fort Campbell North, KY (cdp) Christian County	11	0.08
South Park Township, PA (cdp) Allegheny County	11	0.08
Glasgow, DE (cdp) New Castle County	10	0.08
Oronoko charter, MI (township) Berrien County	8	0.08
Superior, CO (town) Boulder County	7	0.08
Marlton, MD (cdp) Prince George's County	6	0.08
Thornbury, PA (township) Delaware County	6	0.08
Quantico Station, VA (cdp) Prince William County	6	0.08
Plainfield, NJ (city) Union County	35	0.07
Hanford, CA (city) Kings County	31	0.07
Hillsborough, NJ (township) Somerset County	25	0.07
Willingboro, NJ (township) Burlington County	22	0.07
Milton, MA (cdp) Norfolk County	19	0.07
Casselberry, FL (city) Seminole County	16	0.07
Laurel, MD (city) Prince George's County	14	0.07
Sebastian, FL (city) Indian River County	12	0.07
Warrensville Heights, OH (city) Cuyahoga County	11	0.07
Waycross, GA (city) Ware County	11	0.07
Hyattsville, MD (city) Prince George's County	10	0.07
Hobe Sound, FL (cdp) Martin County	8	0.07
Riverview, FL (cdp) Hillsborough County	8	0.07
Westwood, NJ (borough) Bergen County	8	0.07
Potsdam, NY (village) Saint Lawrence County	7	0.07
Scottdale, GA (cdp) De Kalb County	7	0.07
Byram, NJ (township) Sussex County	6	0.07
Kitty Hawk, NC (town) Dare County	2	0.07
Bremerton, WA (city) Kitsap County	21	0.06
Windham, CT (town) Windham County	14	0.06
Greater Upper Marlboro, MD (cdp) Prince George's County	11	0.06
Readington, NJ (township) Hunterdon County	10	0.06
Redland, MD (cdp) Montgomery County	10	0.06
Rocky Hill, CT (town) Hartford County	10	0.06
Cumru, PA (township) Berks County	8	0.06
Medway, MA (town) Norfolk County	8	0.06
New Fairfield, CT (town) Fairfield County	8	0.06
Plymouth, CT (town) Litchfield County	7	0.06
Holbrook, MA (cdp) Norfolk County	6	0.06
Irondale, GA (cdp) Clayton County	5	0.06
Iola, KS (city) Allen County	4	0.06
Blooming Grove, PA (township) Pike County	2	0.06
East Orange, NJ (city) Essex County	37	0.05
Irvington, NJ (cdp) Essex County	33	0.05
Burke, VA (cdp) Fairfax County	27	0.05
Manchester, NJ (township) Ocean County	19	0.05
Burlington, NJ (township) Burlington County	11	0.05
Gardner, MA (city) Worcester County	11	0.05
Susquehanna, PA (township) Dauphin County	11	0.05
Edwardsville, IL (city) Madison County	10	0.05
Laurel, MS (city) Jones County	10	0.05
Westbury, NY (village) Nassau County	7	0.05
Fort Knox, KY (cdp) Hardin County	6	0.05
Stanford, CA (cdp) Santa Clara County	6	0.05
Red Hook, NY (town) Dutchess County	5	0.05
Timberlake, VA (cdp) Campbell County	5	0.05

Notes: (cdp) census designated place; Refer to the Explanation of Data in the front of the book for more detailed information.

West Indian: Bermudan, excluding Hispanic

Top 150 Places Sorted by Percent

(Based on places with populations of 10,000 or more)

Place	Number	%
Lake Mary, FL (city) Seminole County	46	0.41
Junction City, KS (city) Geary County	48	0.25
Brentwood, CA (city) Contra Costa County	44	0.19
Punta Gorda, FL (city) Charlotte County	24	0.17
North Fair Oaks, CA (cdp) San Mateo County	24	0.16
Eden, NC (city) Rockingham County	24	0.15
Horn Lake, MS (city) De Soto County	21	0.15
Lansdowne, PA (borough) Delaware County	15	0.14
Montclair, NJ (cdp) Essex County	48	0.12
Martinsburg, WV (city) Berkeley County	18	0.12
Newark, DE (city) New Castle County	31	0.11
North Amityville, NY (cdp) Suffolk County	18	0.11
Roosevelt, NY (cdp) Nassau County	18	0.11
Rye, NY (city) Westchester County	16	0.11
Bessemer, AL (city) Jefferson County	31	0.10
North Marysville, WA (cdp) Snohomish County	21	0.10
Douglasville, GA (city) Douglas County	20	0.10
Erlanger, KY (city) Kenton County	16	0.10
Mountain Park, GA (cdp) Gwinnett County	11	0.10
Hampton, VA (independent city) Hampton city	134	0.09
Hillside, NJ (cdp) Union County	20	0.09
Willimantic, CT (cdp) Windham County	14	0.09
Flint, MI (township) Genesee County	27	0.08
Van Buren, MI (township) Wayne County	18	0.08
Stafford, TX (city) Fort Bend County	12	0.08
Fort Campbell North, KY (cdp) Christian County	11	0.08
South Park Township, PA (cdp) Allegheny County	11	0.08
Glasgow, DE (cdp) New Castle County	10	0.08
Plainfield, NJ (city) Union County	35	0.07
Hanford, CA (city) Kings County	31	0.07
Hillsborough, NJ (township) Somerset County	25	0.07
Willingboro, NJ (township) Burlington County	22	0.07
Milton, MA (cdp) Norfolk County	19	0.07
Casselberry, FL (city) Seminole County	16	0.07
Laurel, MD (city) Prince George's County	14	0.07
Sebastian, FL (city) Indian River County	12	0.07
Warrensville Heights, OH (city) Cuyahoga County	11	0.07
Waycross, GA (city) Ware County	11	0.07
Hyattsville, MD (city) Prince George's County	10	0.07
Hobe Sound, FL (cdp) Martin County	8	0.07
Riverview, FL (cdp) Hillsborough County	8	0.07
Westwood, NJ (borough) Bergen County	8	0.07
Bremerton, WA (city) Kitsap County	21	0.06
Windham, CT (town) Windham County	14	0.06
Greater Upper Marlboro, MD (cdp) Prince George's County	11	0.06
Readington, NJ (township) Hunterdon County	10	0.06
Redland, MD (cdp) Montgomery County	10	0.06
Rocky Hill, CT (town) Hartford County	10	0.06
Cumru, PA (township) Berks County	8	0.06
Medway, MA (town) Norfolk County	8	0.06
New Fairfield, CT (town) Fairfield County	8	0.06
Plymouth, CT (town) Litchfield County	7	0.06
Holbrook, MA (cdp) Norfolk County	6	0.06
East Orange, NJ (city) Essex County	37	0.05
Irvington, NJ (cdp) Essex County	33	0.05
Burke, VA (cdp) Fairfax County	27	0.05
Manchester, NJ (township) Ocean County	19	0.05
Burlington, NJ (township) Burlington County	11	0.05
Gardner, MA (city) Worcester County	11	0.05
Susquehanna, PA (township) Dauphin County	11	0.05
Edwardsville, IL (city) Madison County	10	0.05
Laurel, MS (city) Jones County	10	0.05
Westbury, NY (village) Nassau County	7	0.05
Fort Knox, KY (cdp) Hardin County	6	0.05
Stanford, CA (cdp) Santa Clara County	6	0.05
Red Hook, NY (town) Dutchess County	5	0.05
Timberlake, VA (cdp) Campbell County	5	0.05
Cambridge, MA (city) Middlesex County	45	0.04
Sunrise, FL (city) Broward County	30	0.04
West Babylon, NY (cdp) Suffolk County	16	0.04
Cortlandt, NY (town) Westchester County	15	0.04
Morgan Hill, CA (city) Santa Clara County	15	0.04
Palm Beach Gardens, FL (city) Palm Beach County	15	0.04
Galloway, NJ (township) Atlantic County	14	0.04
Watertown, MA (city) Middlesex County	14	0.04
Merrillville, IN (town) Lake County	11	0.04
Neptune, NJ (township) Monmouth County	10	0.04
Statesville, NC (city) Iredell County	10	0.04
Wallkill, NY (town) Orange County	10	0.04
Roxbury, NJ (township) Morris County	9	0.04
Sanford, NC (city) Lee County	9	0.04
Benbrook, TX (city) Tarrant County	8	0.04
East Massapequa, NY (cdp) Nassau County	8	0.04
Aberdeen, NJ (township) Monmouth County	7	0.04
Potsdam, NY (town) Saint Lawrence County	7	0.04
Tanque Verde, AZ (cdp) Pima County	7	0.04
South Ogden, UT (city) Weber County	6	0.04
Hanover, NJ (township) Morris County	5	0.04
Huntsville, AL (city) Madison County	54	0.03
Springfield, MA (city) Hampden County	39	0.03
Stamford, CT (city) Fairfield County	36	0.03
Lake Charles, LA (city) Calcasieu Parish	25	0.03
Canton, MI (cdp) Wayne County	21	0.03
Somerville, MA (city) Middlesex County	20	0.03
Bowie, MD (city) Prince George's County	17	0.03
Towson, MD (cdp) Baltimore County	17	0.03
Pinellas Park, FL (city) Pinellas County	13	0.03
North Fort Myers, FL (cdp) Lee County	12	0.03
Annapolis, MD (city) Anne Arundel County	10	0.03
Central Islip, NY (cdp) Suffolk County	10	0.03
Pennsauken, NJ (cdp) Camden County	10	0.03
Centereach, NY (cdp) Suffolk County	9	0.03
Englewood, NJ (city) Bergen County	9	0.03
Parkville, MD (cdp) Baltimore County	9	0.03
Cheshire, CT (town) New Haven County	8	0.03
Deptford, NJ (township) Gloucester County	8	0.03
Monroe, NC (city) Union County	8	0.03
Oakley, CA (city) Contra Costa County	8	0.03
Ossining, NY (village) Westchester County	8	0.03
Rahway, NJ (city) Union County	7	0.03
Xenia, OH (city) Greene County	7	0.03
Auburn, ME (city) Androscoggin County	6	0.03
Morris, NJ (township) Morris County	6	0.03
Takoma Park, MD (city) Montgomery County	6	0.03
Wilton, CT (town) Fairfield County	6	0.03
Springfield, PA (township) Montgomery County	5	0.03
Boston, MA (city) Suffolk County	105	0.02
Babylon, NY (town) Suffolk County	34	0.02
Columbia, SC (city) Richland County	25	0.02
Gainesville, FL (city) Alachua County	19	0.02
Cape Coral, FL (city) Lee County	17	0.02
Silver Spring, MD (cdp) Montgomery County	17	0.02
Kenosha, WI (city) Kenosha County	16	0.02
Annandale, VA (cdp) Fairfax County	13	0.02
Clifton, NJ (city) Passaic County	13	0.02
Hammond, IN (city) Lake County	13	0.02
Largo, FL (city) Pinellas County	13	0.02
Chapel Hill, NC (town) Orange County	11	0.02
Hamden, CT (town) New Haven County	11	0.02
Irondequoit, NY (cdp) Monroe County	11	0.02
Lakewood, NJ (township) Ocean County	11	0.02
Miramar, FL (city) Broward County	11	0.02
Charlottesville, VA (independent city) Charlottesville city	10	0.02
Margate, FL (city) Broward County	10	0.02
Mount Laurel, NJ (township) Burlington County	10	0.02
Piscataway, NJ (township) Middlesex County	10	0.02
Redlands, CA (city) San Bernardino County	10	0.02
Union, NJ (cdp) Union County	10	0.02
Anderson, IN (city) Madison County	9	0.02
Apple Valley, CA (town) San Bernardino County	9	0.02
Cleveland, TN (city) Bradley County	9	0.02
Germantown, MD (cdp) Montgomery County	9	0.02
Hackensack, NJ (city) Bergen County	9	0.02
Henrietta, NY (town) Monroe County	9	0.02
Golden Glades, FL (cdp) Miami-Dade County	8	0.02
Ossining, NY (town) Westchester County	8	0.02
Palm Coast, FL (city) Flagler County	8	0.02
Coram, NY (cdp) Suffolk County	7	0.02
East Lake, FL (cdp) Pinellas County	7	0.02
Lewiston, ME (city) Androscoggin County	7	0.02

Notes: (cdp) census designated place; Refer to the Explanation of Data in the front of the book for more detailed information.

West Indian: British West Indian, excluding Hispanic

Top 150 Places Sorted by Number

(Based on all places, regardless of population)

Place	Number	%
New York, NY (city) New York City	47,084	0.59
Boston, MA (city) Suffolk County	1,359	0.23
Hempstead, NY (town) Nassau County	1,135	0.15
Philadelphia, PA (city) Philadelphia County	671	0.04
Houston, TX (city) Harris County	450	0.02
Miramar, FL (city) Broward County	428	0.59
Los Angeles, CA (city) Los Angeles County	383	0.01
Jersey City, NJ (city) Hudson County	377	0.16
Mount Vernon, NY (city) Westchester County	365	0.53
Carol City, FL (cdp) Miami-Dade County	327	0.55
Washington, DC (city) District of Columbia	322	0.06
Norland, FL (cdp) Miami-Dade County	305	1.32
Virginia Beach, VA (independent city) Virginia Beach city	304	0.07
Hartford, CT (city) Hartford County	280	0.23
Orlando, FL (city) Orange County	279	0.15
Pembroke Pines, FL (city) Broward County	270	0.20
East Orange, NJ (city) Essex County	260	0.37
Lauderhill, FL (city) Broward County	254	0.44
Yonkers, NY (city) Westchester County	250	0.13
Newark, NJ (city) Essex County	248	0.09
Hempstead, NY (village) Nassau County	247	0.44
North Miami, FL (city) Miami-Dade County	246	0.41
Lauderdale Lakes, FL (city) Broward County	238	0.76
Baytown, TX (city) Harris County	224	0.33
Hollywood, FL (city) Broward County	224	0.16
Fort Lauderdale, FL (city) Broward County	209	0.14
Golden Glades, FL (cdp) Miami-Dade County	197	0.61
Teaneck, NJ (cdp) Bergen County	196	0.50
Brookhaven, NY (town) Suffolk County	195	0.04
Islip, NY (town) Suffolk County	190	0.06
Miami, FL (city) Miami-Dade County	189	0.05
Baltimore, MD (independent city) Baltimore city	187	0.03
Deerfield Beach, FL (city) Broward County	177	0.27
Pine Hills, FL (cdp) Orange County	176	0.42
Sunrise, FL (city) Broward County	172	0.20
North Hempstead, NY (town) Nassau County	170	0.08
Babylon, NY (town) Suffolk County	168	0.08
Long Beach, CA (city) Los Angeles County	166	0.04
Town 'n' Country, FL (cdp) Hillsborough County	163	0.23
Jacksonville, FL (special city) Duval County	161	0.02
Coral Springs, FL (city) Broward County	158	0.13
Greenburgh, NY (town) Westchester County	157	0.18
Irvington, NJ (cdp) Essex County	153	0.25
Hackensack, NJ (city) Bergen County	146	0.34
Elmont, NY (cdp) Nassau County	145	0.44
Chicago, IL (city) Cook County	143	0.00
Freeport, NY (village) Nassau County	139	0.32
Randolph, MA (cdp) Norfolk County	136	0.44
Scott Lake, FL (cdp) Miami-Dade County	134	0.93
South Miami Heights, FL (cdp) Miami-Dade County	133	0.40
Chillum, MD (cdp) Prince George's County	128	0.37
San Francisco, CA (city) San Francisco County	128	0.02
Detroit, MI (city) Wayne County	127	0.01
Silver Spring, MD (cdp) Montgomery County	126	0.16
Bridgeport, CT (city) Fairfield County	116	0.08
Paterson, NJ (city) Passaic County	113	0.08
Saint Petersburg, FL (city) Pinellas County	113	0.05
Tallahassee, FL (city) Leon County	111	0.07
Lake Worth, FL (city) Palm Beach County	110	0.31
New Rochelle, NY (city) Westchester County	110	0.15
Uniondale, NY (cdp) Nassau County	109	0.47
Englewood, NJ (city) Bergen County	106	0.40
West Palm Beach, FL (city) Palm Beach County	106	0.13
Tampa, FL (city) Hillsborough County	106	0.03
Aspen Hill, MD (cdp) Montgomery County	99	0.20
Huntsville, AL (city) Madison County	99	0.06
Titusville, FL (city) Brevard County	98	0.24
Columbus, GA (special city) Muscogee County	98	0.05
Charlotte, NC (city) Mecklenburg County	97	0.02
Fairland, MD (cdp) Montgomery County	95	0.44
Sandalfoot Cove, FL (cdp) Palm Beach County	93	0.56
Cutler Ridge, FL (cdp) Miami-Dade County	93	0.38
Milton, MA (cdp) Norfolk County	93	0.36
Franklin, NJ (township) Somerset County	92	0.18
Windsor, CT (town) Hartford County	91	0.32
Pompano Beach, FL (city) Broward County	91	0.12
Milwaukee, WI (city) Milwaukee County	91	0.02
Lorton, VA (cdp) Fairfax County	90	0.51
Atlanta, GA (city) Fulton County	89	0.02
Country Club, FL (cdp) Miami-Dade County	88	0.24
Kissimmee, FL (city) Osceola County	87	0.18
New Britain, CT (city) Hartford County	86	0.12
Worcester, MA (city) Worcester County	86	0.05
Austin, TX (city) Travis County	86	0.01
San Diego, CA (city) San Diego County	85	0.01
North Valley Stream, NY (cdp) Nassau County	84	0.53
Albany, NY (city) Albany County	84	0.09
North Lauderdale, FL (city) Broward County	82	0.25
Laurel, MD (city) Prince George's County	81	0.40
Rochester, NY (city) Monroe County	81	0.04
Ramapo, NY (town) Rockland County	80	0.07
South Orange, NJ (cdp) Essex County	79	0.47
Waterbury, CT (city) New Haven County	79	0.07
Roosevelt, NY (cdp) Nassau County	78	0.49
Fort Stewart, GA (cdp) Liberty County	77	0.68
The Hammocks, FL (cdp) Miami-Dade County	77	0.16
Deltona, FL (city) Volusia County	76	0.11
Providence, RI (city) Providence County	76	0.04
Norfolk, VA (independent city) Norfolk city	76	0.03
Severn, MD (cdp) Anne Arundel County	75	0.21
Palm Bay, FL (city) Brevard County	75	0.09
East Hartford, CT (cdp) Hartford County	74	0.15
Germantown, MD (cdp) Montgomery County	73	0.13
Dallas, TX (city) Dallas County	73	0.01
Manhasset, NY (cdp) Nassau County	72	0.86
Tamarac, FL (city) Broward County	72	0.13
New Haven, CT (city) New Haven County	72	0.06
Lake Lucerne, FL (cdp) Miami-Dade County	70	0.77
Oakland Park, FL (city) Broward County	70	0.22
Stamford, CT (city) Fairfield County	69	0.06
Oyster Bay, NY (town) Nassau County	69	0.02
Baldwin, NY (cdp) Nassau County	68	0.29
University, FL (cdp) Hillsborough County	67	0.22
Wichita Falls, TX (city) Wichita County	67	0.06
Pembroke Park, FL (town) Broward County	66	1.04
Matthews, NC (town) Mecklenburg County	66	0.29
Orange, NJ (cdp) Essex County	66	0.20
Norwalk, CT (city) Fairfield County	66	0.08
Lawton, OK (city) Comanche County	66	0.07
North Amityville, NY (cdp) Suffolk County	65	0.39
Pinewood, FL (cdp) Miami-Dade County	65	0.39
North Miami Beach, FL (city) Miami-Dade County	64	0.16
Bunche Park, FL (cdp) Miami-Dade County	63	1.58
Manchester, CT (town) Hartford County	63	0.12
West Haven, CT (city) New Haven County	63	0.12
Oronoko charter, MI (township) Berrien County	62	0.63
Maplewood, NJ (cdp) Essex County	62	0.26
Clarksville, TN (city) Montgomery County	62	0.06
Hampton, VA (independent city) Hampton city	62	0.04
Lehigh Acres, FL (cdp) Lee County	61	0.18
Brentwood, NY (cdp) Suffolk County	61	0.11
Ridgefield, NJ (borough) Bergen County	60	0.55
Aurora, CO (city) Arapahoe County	60	0.02
Raleigh, NC (city) Wake County	60	0.02
Hyattsville, MD (city) Prince George's County	59	0.40
North Port, FL (city) Sarasota County	59	0.26
Melbourne, FL (city) Brevard County	59	0.08
Inwood, NY (cdp) Nassau County	58	0.62
Plantation, FL (city) Broward County	58	0.07
Syracuse, NY (city) Onondaga County	58	0.04
Memphis, TN (city) Shelby County	58	0.01
Bloomfield, CT (town) Hartford County	57	0.29
Richmond West, FL (cdp) Miami-Dade County	57	0.20
Piscataway, NJ (township) Middlesex County	57	0.11
Golden Lakes, FL (cdp) Palm Beach County	56	0.84
Peekskill, NY (city) Westchester County	56	0.25
Missouri City, TX (city) Fort Bend County	55	0.10
Grand Prairie, TX (city) Dallas County	55	0.04
Arlington, VA (cdp) Arlington County	55	0.03
Doctor Phillips, FL (cdp) Orange County	54	0.56

Notes: (cdp) census designated place; Refer to the Explanation of Data in the front of the book for more detailed information.

West Indian: British West Indian, excluding Hispanic

Top 150 Places Sorted by Percent

(Based on all places, regardless of population)

Place	Number	%
South Fork Estates, TX (cdp) Jim Hogg County	6	12.24
Utopia, FL (cdp) Broward County	29	4.00
Shrub Oak, NY (cdp) Westchester County	36	1.95
Bunche Park, FL (cdp) Miami-Dade County	63	1.58
Brentwood, MD (town) Prince George's County	45	1.57
Scotts Corners, NY (cdp) Westchester County	9	1.56
Morrisville, NY (village) Madison County	33	1.52
South Floral Park, NY (village) Nassau County	23	1.46
Royal Palm Estates, FL (cdp) Palm Beach County	46	1.33
Norland, FL (cdp) Miami-Dade County	305	1.32
Hughes, WI (town) Bayfield County	5	1.21
Thompson, PA (township) Susquehanna County	5	1.20
Blue Hills, CT (cdp) Hartford County	34	1.10
Gordon Heights, NY (cdp) Suffolk County	34	1.10
Wampsville, NY (village) Madison County	6	1.07
Sherman, MI (township) Iosco County	5	1.05
Pembroke Park, FL (town) Broward County	66	1.04
Scott Lake, FL (cdp) Miami-Dade County	134	0.93
Watermill, NY (cdp) Suffolk County	15	0.89
Manhasset, NY (cdp) Nassau County	72	0.86
Shandaken, NY (town) Ulster County	28	0.85
Golden Lakes, FL (cdp) Palm Beach County	56	0.84
Norwood, NJ (borough) Bergen County	48	0.83
Loch Lomond, FL (cdp) Broward County	26	0.78
Lake Lucerne, FL (cdp) Miami-Dade County	70	0.77
Lauderdale Lakes, FL (city) Broward County	238	0.76
Avon, MA (town) Norfolk County	33	0.74
Fort Stewart, GA (cdp) Liberty County	77	0.68
Eaton, NY (town) Madison County	33	0.68
Castine, ME (town) Hancock County	9	0.67
Oronoko charter, MI (township) Berrien County	62	0.63
Inwood, NY (cdp) Nassau County	58	0.62
Golden Glades, FL (cdp) Miami-Dade County	197	0.61
Mount Rainier, MD (city) Prince George's County	51	0.60
Woodlawn, MD (cdp) Prince George's County	37	0.60
New York, NY (city) New York City	47,084	0.59
Miramar, FL (city) Broward County	428	0.59
Sandalfoot Cove, FL (cdp) Palm Beach County	93	0.56
Doctor Phillips, FL (cdp) Orange County	54	0.56
California, MD (cdp) Saint Mary's County	53	0.56
Carol City, FL (cdp) Miami-Dade County	327	0.55
Ridgefield, NJ (borough) Bergen County	60	0.55
West Perrine, FL (cdp) Miami-Dade County	47	0.55
Atlantic Highlands, NJ (borough) Monmouth County	26	0.55
Mount Vernon, NY (city) Westchester County	365	0.53
North Valley Stream, NY (cdp) Nassau County	84	0.53
South Hempstead, NY (cdp) Nassau County	17	0.53
Shenandoah, VA (town) Page County	10	0.53
Pompano Estates, FL (cdp) Broward County	18	0.52
Lorton, VA (cdp) Fairfax County	90	0.51
Terryville, NY (cdp) Suffolk County	54	0.51
Opa-locka North, FL (cdp) Miami-Dade County	32	0.51
Teaneck, NJ (cdp) Bergen County	196	0.50
Roosevelt, NY (cdp) Nassau County	78	0.49
Riverdale Park, MD (town) Prince George's County	32	0.49
Roslyn Heights, NY (cdp) Nassau County	31	0.49
East Farmingdale, NY (cdp) Suffolk County	27	0.49
East Freehold, NJ (cdp) Monmouth County	25	0.49
Sciota, MI (township) Shiawassee County	9	0.49
Colmar Manor, MD (town) Prince George's County	6	0.48
Uniondale, NY (cdp) Nassau County	109	0.47
South Orange, NJ (cdp) Essex County	79	0.47
Sheridan, MT (town) Madison County	3	0.45
Lauderhill, FL (city) Broward County	254	0.44
Hempstead, NY (village) Nassau County	247	0.44
Elmont, NY (cdp) Nassau County	145	0.44
Randolph, MA (cdp) Norfolk County	136	0.44
Fairland, MD (cdp) Montgomery County	95	0.44
Lower Oxford, PA (township) Chester County	19	0.44
Baywood, NY (cdp) Suffolk County	32	0.43
Weathersfield, VT (town) Windsor County	12	0.43
Silver Lake, FL (cdp) Lake County	8	0.43
Pine Hills, FL (cdp) Orange County	176	0.42
Nevada, IA (city) Story County	28	0.42
West Laurel, MD (cdp) Prince George's County	17	0.42

Place	Number	%
Forest Heights, MD (town) Prince George's County	11	0.42
North Miami, FL (city) Miami-Dade County	246	0.41
Eastport, NY (cdp) Suffolk County	6	0.41
South Miami Heights, FL (cdp) Miami-Dade County	133	0.40
Englewood, NJ (city) Bergen County	106	0.40
Laurel, MD (city) Prince George's County	81	0.40
Hyattsville, MD (city) Prince George's County	59	0.40
North Amityville, NY (cdp) Suffolk County	65	0.39
Pinewood, FL (cdp) Miami-Dade County	65	0.39
Penbrook, PA (borough) Dauphin County	12	0.39
Cutler Ridge, FL (cdp) Miami-Dade County	93	0.38
Kettering, MD (cdp) Prince George's County	42	0.38
Chestnut Ridge, NY (village) Rockland County	29	0.38
White, NJ (township) Warren County	16	0.38
Jacksons' Gap, AL (town) Tallapoosa County	3	0.38
East Orange, NJ (city) Essex County	260	0.37
Chillum, MD (cdp) Prince George's County	128	0.37
Elmsford, NY (village) Westchester County	17	0.37
Port Richey, FL (city) Pasco County	11	0.37
Milton, MA (cdp) Norfolk County	93	0.36
Malabar, FL (town) Brevard County	10	0.36
Norton Center, MA (cdp) Bristol County	9	0.36
Cocoa West, FL (cdp) Brevard County	20	0.35
Kendall Green, FL (cdp) Broward County	11	0.35
Harlem, FL (cdp) Hendry County	10	0.35
Salem, WV (city) Harrison County	7	0.35
Hackensack, NJ (city) Bergen County	146	0.34
Belle Isle, FL (city) Orange County	20	0.34
Feather Sound, FL (cdp) Pinellas County	14	0.34
East Hampton North, NY (cdp) Suffolk County	12	0.34
Progress Village, FL (cdp) Hillsborough County	8	0.34
Baytown, TX (city) Harris County	224	0.33
Lake Arbor, MD (cdp) Prince George's County	28	0.33
Bladensburg, MD (town) Prince George's County	25	0.33
Woodmore, MD (cdp) Prince George's County	20	0.33
Mount Pocono, PA (borough) Monroe County	9	0.33
Freeport, NY (village) Nassau County	139	0.32
Windsor, CT (town) Hartford County	91	0.32
Madison Park, NJ (cdp) Middlesex County	22	0.32
Lake Worth, FL (city) Palm Beach County	110	0.31
Palm Beach, FL (town) Palm Beach County	32	0.31
Lake Park, FL (town) Palm Beach County	26	0.31
Pamelia, NY (town) Jefferson County	9	0.31
Shell Point, SC (cdp) Beaufort County	9	0.31
Lehigh, PA (township) Wayne County	5	0.31
Lake Hamilton, FL (town) Polk County	4	0.31
North Bay Shore, NY (cdp) Suffolk County	45	0.30
Hartsdale, NY (cdp) Westchester County	30	0.30
North Bonneville, WA (city) Skamania County	2	0.30
Baldwin, NY (cdp) Nassau County	68	0.29
Matthews, NC (town) Mecklenburg County	66	0.29
Bloomfield, CT (town) Hartford County	57	0.29
Mahopac, NY (cdp) Putnam County	25	0.29
Lakeview, NY (cdp) Nassau County	16	0.29
Beltsville, MD (cdp) Prince George's County	44	0.28
Timberlane, LA (cdp) Jefferson Parish	32	0.28
Deerpark, NY (town) Orange County	22	0.28
Meadows Place, TX (city) Fort Bend County	14	0.28
Kings Bay Base, GA (cdp) Camden County	7	0.28
Deerfield Beach, FL (city) Broward County	177	0.27
Fairview, PA (township) York County	38	0.27
Friendly, MD (cdp) Prince George's County	30	0.27
West Samoset, FL (cdp) Manatee County	15	0.27
Grand Forks AFB, ND (cdp) Grand Forks County	13	0.27
Newark Valley, NY (town) Tioga County	11	0.27
Folkston, GA (city) Charlton County	6	0.27
Greenvale, NY (cdp) Nassau County	6	0.27
West Point, KY (city) Hardin County	3	0.27
Oregon, PA (township) Wayne County	2	0.27
Wrightstown, NJ (borough) Burlington County	2	0.27
Maplewood, NJ (cdp) Essex County	62	0.26
North Port, FL (city) Sarasota County	59	0.26
Palmetto Estates, FL (cdp) Miami-Dade County	35	0.26
Kenai, AK (city) Kenai Peninsula Borough	18	0.26
Hamilton, NY (village) Madison County	9	0.26

Notes: (cdp) census designated place; Refer to the Explanation of Data in the front of the book for more detailed information.

West Indian: British West Indian, excluding Hispanic

Top 150 Places Sorted by Percent

(Based on places with populations of 10,000 or more)

Place	Number	%
Norland, FL (cdp) Miami-Dade County	305	1.32
Scott Lake, FL (cdp) Miami-Dade County	134	0.93
Lauderdale Lakes, FL (city) Broward County	238	0.76
Fort Stewart, GA (cdp) Liberty County	77	0.68
Golden Glades, FL (cdp) Miami-Dade County	197	0.61
New York, NY (city) New York City	47,084	0.59
Miramar, FL (city) Broward County	428	0.59
Sandalfoot Cove, FL (cdp) Palm Beach County	93	0.56
Carol City, FL (cdp) Miami-Dade County	327	0.55
Ridgefield, NJ (borough) Bergen County	60	0.55
Mount Vernon, NY (city) Westchester County	365	0.53
North Valley Stream, NY (cdp) Nassau County	84	0.53
Lorton, VA (cdp) Fairfax County	90	0.51
Terryville, NY (cdp) Suffolk County	54	0.51
Teaneck, NJ (cdp) Bergen County	196	0.50
Roosevelt, NY (cdp) Nassau County	78	0.49
Uniondale, NY (cdp) Nassau County	109	0.47
South Orange, NJ (cdp) Essex County	79	0.47
Lauderhill, FL (city) Broward County	254	0.44
Hempstead, NY (village) Nassau County	247	0.44
Elmont, NY (cdp) Nassau County	145	0.44
Randolph, MA (cdp) Norfolk County	136	0.44
Fairland, MD (cdp) Montgomery County	95	0.44
Pine Hills, FL (cdp) Orange County	176	0.42
North Miami, FL (city) Miami-Dade County	246	0.41
South Miami Heights, FL (cdp) Miami-Dade County	133	0.40
Englewood, NJ (city) Bergen County	106	0.40
Laurel, MD (city) Prince George's County	81	0.40
Hyattsville, MD (city) Prince George's County	59	0.40
North Amityville, NY (cdp) Suffolk County	65	0.39
Pinewood, FL (cdp) Miami-Dade County	65	0.39
Cutler Ridge, FL (cdp) Miami-Dade County	93	0.38
Kettering, MD (cdp) Prince George's County	42	0.38
East Orange, NJ (city) Essex County	260	0.37
Chillum, MD (cdp) Prince George's County	128	0.37
Milton, MA (cdp) Norfolk County	93	0.36
Hackensack, NJ (city) Bergen County	146	0.34
Baytown, TX (city) Harris County	224	0.33
Freeport, NY (village) Nassau County	139	0.32
Windsor, CT (town) Hartford County	91	0.32
Lake Worth, FL (city) Palm Beach County	110	0.31
Palm Beach, FL (town) Palm Beach County	32	0.31
North Bay Shore, NY (cdp) Suffolk County	45	0.30
Baldwin, NY (cdp) Nassau County	68	0.29
Matthews, NC (town) Mecklenburg County	66	0.29
Bloomfield, CT (town) Hartford County	57	0.29
Beltsville, MD (cdp) Prince George's County	44	0.28
Timberlane, LA (cdp) Jefferson Parish	32	0.28
Deerfield Beach, FL (city) Broward County	177	0.27
Fairview, PA (township) York County	38	0.27
Friendly, MD (cdp) Prince George's County	30	0.27
Maplewood, NJ (cdp) Essex County	62	0.26
North Port, FL (city) Sarasota County	59	0.26
Palmetto Estates, FL (cdp) Miami-Dade County	35	0.26
Irvington, NJ (cdp) Essex County	153	0.25
North Lauderdale, FL (city) Broward County	82	0.25
Peekskill, NY (city) Westchester County	56	0.25
East Massapequa, NY (cdp) Nassau County	49	0.25
Ives Estates, FL (cdp) Miami-Dade County	43	0.25
Country Walk, FL (cdp) Miami-Dade County	27	0.25
Bound Brook, NJ (borough) Somerset County	25	0.25
Titusville, FL (city) Brevard County	98	0.24
Country Club, FL (cdp) Miami-Dade County	88	0.24
Takoma Park, MD (city) Montgomery County	41	0.24
Opa-locka, FL (city) Miami-Dade County	36	0.24
Boston, MA (city) Suffolk County	1,359	0.23
Hartford, CT (city) Hartford County	280	0.23
Town 'n' Country, FL (cdp) Hillsborough County	163	0.23
Smithfield, RI (town) Providence County	48	0.23
Greater Upper Marlboro, MD (cdp) Prince George's County	43	0.23
Oakland Park, FL (city) Broward County	70	0.22
University, FL (cdp) Hillsborough County	67	0.22
Lanham-Seabrook, MD (cdp) Prince George's County	39	0.22
Cedar Mill, OR (cdp) Washington County	28	0.22
Dobbs Ferry, NY (village) Westchester County	23	0.22
Guttenberg, NJ (town) Hudson County	23	0.22
Severn, MD (cdp) Anne Arundel County	75	0.21
Apopka, FL (city) Orange County	54	0.21
Roselle, NJ (borough) Union County	45	0.21
Glenvar Heights, FL (cdp) Miami-Dade County	34	0.21
Pembroke Pines, FL (city) Broward County	270	0.20
Sunrise, FL (city) Broward County	172	0.20
Aspen Hill, MD (cdp) Montgomery County	99	0.20
Orange, NJ (cdp) Essex County	66	0.20
Richmond West, FL (cdp) Miami-Dade County	57	0.20
Bensenville, IL (village) Du Page County	41	0.20
New Cassel, NY (cdp) Nassau County	27	0.20
Yeadon, PA (borough) Delaware County	24	0.20
Lansdowne, PA (borough) Delaware County	22	0.20
Clinton, MD (cdp) Prince George's County	50	0.19
Wappinger, NY (town) Dutchess County	50	0.19
Doral, FL (cdp) Miami-Dade County	39	0.19
Hatfield, PA (township) Montgomery County	31	0.19
Damascus, MD (cdp) Montgomery County	22	0.19
Greenburgh, NY (town) Westchester County	157	0.18
Franklin, NJ (township) Somerset County	92	0.18
Kissimmee, FL (city) Osceola County	87	0.18
Lehigh Acres, FL (cdp) Lee County	61	0.18
College Park, MD (city) Prince George's County	44	0.18
Stafford, TX (city) Fort Bend County	28	0.18
Oviedo, FL (city) Seminole County	47	0.17
Scotch Plains, NJ (cdp) Union County	38	0.17
South Laurel, MD (cdp) Prince George's County	36	0.17
Adelphi, MD (cdp) Prince George's County	25	0.17
Atlantic Beach, FL (city) Duval County	23	0.17
Jersey City, NJ (city) Hudson County	377	0.16
Hollywood, FL (city) Broward County	224	0.16
Silver Spring, MD (cdp) Montgomery County	126	0.16
The Hammocks, FL (cdp) Miami-Dade County	77	0.16
North Miami Beach, FL (city) Miami-Dade County	64	0.16
The Crossings, FL (cdp) Miami-Dade County	37	0.16
Lutz, FL (cdp) Hillsborough County	27	0.16
Warrensburg, MO (city) Johnson County	26	0.16
Westbury, NY (village) Nassau County	23	0.16
Ventnor City, NJ (city) Atlantic County	21	0.16
Hempstead, NY (town) Nassau County	1,135	0.15
Orlando, FL (city) Orange County	279	0.15
New Rochelle, NY (city) Westchester County	110	0.15
East Hartford, CT (cdp) Hartford County	74	0.15
Redan, GA (cdp) De Kalb County	51	0.15
Bergenfield, NJ (borough) Bergen County	39	0.15
Colesville, MD (cdp) Montgomery County	29	0.15
Decatur, GA (city) De Kalb County	27	0.15
Fairview Park, OH (city) Cuyahoga County	27	0.15
Brownsville, FL (cdp) Miami-Dade County	21	0.15
Springfield, NJ (cdp) Union County	21	0.15
Poinciana, FL (cdp) Osceola County	20	0.15
Riverdale, GA (city) Clayton County	19	0.15
Brown Deer, WI (village) Milwaukee County	18	0.15
Fernandina Beach, FL (city) Nassau County	15	0.15
Fort Lauderdale, FL (city) Broward County	209	0.14
Dover, DE (city) Kent County	45	0.14
Copperas Cove, TX (city) Coryell County	42	0.14
Fort Bragg, NC (cdp) Cumberland County	42	0.14
East Fishkill, NY (town) Dutchess County	36	0.14
Opelika, AL (city) Lee County	33	0.14
Reisterstown, MD (cdp) Baltimore County	31	0.14
Temple Terrace, FL (city) Hillsborough County	30	0.14
Bourbonnais, IL (village) Kankakee County	22	0.14
Ardmore, PA (cdp) Montgomery County	18	0.14
Weston, MA (town) Middlesex County	16	0.14
Yonkers, NY (city) Westchester County	250	0.13
Coral Springs, FL (city) Broward County	158	0.13
West Palm Beach, FL (city) Palm Beach County	106	0.13
Germantown, MD (cdp) Montgomery County	73	0.13
Tamarac, FL (city) Broward County	72	0.13
Linden, NJ (city) Union County	53	0.13
Dunedin, FL (city) Pinellas County	46	0.13
Egypt Lake-Leto, FL (cdp) Hillsborough County	44	0.13
Olney, MD (cdp) Montgomery County	40	0.13

Notes: (cdp) census designated place; Refer to the Explanation of Data in the front of the book for more detailed information.

West Indian: Dutch West Indian, excluding Hispanic

Top 150 Places Sorted by Number

(Based on all places, regardless of population)

Place	Number	%
Oklahoma City, OK (city) Oklahoma County	1,092	0.22
New York, NY (city) New York City	994	0.01
Tulsa, OK (city) Tulsa County	870	0.22
Norman, OK (city) Cleveland County	272	0.28
Amarillo, TX (city) Potter County	259	0.15
Dallas, TX (city) Dallas County	234	0.02
San Antonio, TX (city) Bexar County	230	0.02
Ardmore, OK (city) Carter County	227	0.97
Fort Smith, AR (city) Sebastian County	216	0.27
Ada, OK (city) Pontotoc County	214	1.37
Moore, OK (city) Cleveland County	201	0.49
Broken Arrow, OK (city) Tulsa County	196	0.26
Odessa, TX (city) Ector County	196	0.22
Fort Worth, TX (city) Tarrant County	195	0.04
Wichita Falls, TX (city) Wichita County	152	0.15
Duncan, OK (city) Stephens County	146	0.65
Muskogee, OK (city) Muskogee County	144	0.38
Lubbock, TX (city) Lubbock County	142	0.07
Knoxville, TN (city) Knox County	140	0.08
Sapulpa, OK (city) Creek County	137	0.73
Shawnee, OK (city) Pottawatomie County	130	0.45
Houston, TX (city) Harris County	117	0.01
San Angelo, TX (city) Tom Green County	113	0.13
McAlester, OK (city) Pittsburg County	109	0.61
Austin, TX (city) Travis County	109	0.02
Edmond, OK (city) Oklahoma County	107	0.16
Corpus Christi, TX (city) Nueces County	107	0.04
North Richland Hills, TX (city) Tarrant County	105	0.19
Garland, TX (city) Dallas County	102	0.05
Claremore, OK (city) Rogers County	99	0.62
Owasso, OK (city) Tulsa County	98	0.53
Arlington, TX (city) Tarrant County	98	0.03
Checotah, OK (city) McIntosh County	97	2.76
Rogers, AR (city) Benton County	95	0.25
Midland, TX (city) Midland County	95	0.10
Sand Springs, OK (city) Tulsa County	92	0.52
Abilene, TX (city) Taylor County	92	0.08
Hobbs, NM (city) Lea County	91	0.32
Lawton, OK (city) Comanche County	91	0.10
Del City, OK (city) Oklahoma County	89	0.40
Wagoner, OK (city) Wagoner County	86	1.10
Russellville, AR (city) Pope County	86	0.36
Ponca City, OK (city) Kay County	85	0.33
Bartlesville, OK (city) Washington County	79	0.23
Mesquite, TX (city) Dallas County	77	0.06
Phoenix, AZ (city) Maricopa County	77	0.01
Midwest City, OK (city) Oklahoma County	76	0.14
Idabel, OK (city) McCurtain County	74	1.06
Enid, OK (city) Garfield County	73	0.16
Denton, TX (city) Denton County	71	0.09
Springdale, AR (city) Washington County	67	0.15
Grand Prairie, TX (city) Dallas County	66	0.05
Carrollton, TX (city) Denton County	65	0.06
Colorado City, TX (city) Mitchell County	64	1.52
Tahlequah, OK (city) Cherokee County	63	0.43
Modesto, CA (city) Stanislaus County	61	0.03
Pampa, TX (city) Gray County	59	0.33
Oildale, CA (cdp) Kern County	59	0.21
Lewisville, TX (city) Denton County	59	0.08
Palm Bay, FL (city) Brevard County	59	0.07
Henryetta, OK (city) Okmulgee County	58	0.94
Haltom City, TX (city) Tarrant County	58	0.15
Euless, TX (city) Tarrant County	58	0.13
Irving, TX (city) Dallas County	58	0.03
Springfield, MO (city) Greene County	57	0.04
Sulphur, OK (city) Murray County	56	1.17
Sallisaw, OK (city) Sequoyah County	56	0.71
Chickasha, OK (city) Grady County	56	0.35
Paris, TX (city) Lamar County	56	0.22
Longview, TX (city) Gregg County	56	0.08
Guymon, OK (city) Texas County	55	0.52
Durant, OK (city) Bryan County	55	0.41
Waco, TX (city) McLennan County	55	0.05
Fresno, CA (city) Fresno County	55	0.01
Coweta, OK (city) Wagoner County	53	0.73
Wichita, KS (city) Sedgwick County	53	0.02
Hempstead, NY (town) Nassau County	53	0.01
Davis, OK (city) Murray County	52	1.98
Marlow, OK (city) Stephens County	52	1.13
Yukon, OK (city) Canadian County	52	0.25
Colorado Springs, CO (city) El Paso County	52	0.01
Bethany, OK (city) Oklahoma County	51	0.25
Plantation, FL (city) Broward County	50	0.06
Healdton, OK (city) Carter County	49	1.74
Siloam Springs, AR (city) Benton County	49	0.45
Shreveport, LA (city) Caddo Parish	49	0.02
Texarkana, TX (city) Bowie County	48	0.14
Boston, MA (city) Suffolk County	48	0.01
Mesa, AZ (city) Maricopa County	48	0.01
Tecumseh, OK (city) Pottawatomie County	47	0.78
Hurst, TX (city) Tarrant County	47	0.13
Noble, OK (city) Cleveland County	46	0.88
Burleson, TX (city) Johnson County	46	0.22
Paradise, NV (cdp) Clark County	46	0.02
Eastland, TX (city) Eastland County	45	1.14
Balch Springs, TX (city) Dallas County	45	0.23
Big Spring, TX (city) Howard County	45	0.18
Camden, NJ (city) Camden County	45	0.06
Babylon, NY (town) Suffolk County	45	0.02
Saks, AL (cdp) Calhoun County	44	0.42
Apple Valley, CA (town) San Bernardino County	44	0.08
Lorain, OH (city) Lorain County	44	0.06
Greenburgh, NY (town) Westchester County	43	0.05
Nashville-Davidson, TN (special city) Davidson County	43	0.01
Royal Palm Beach, FL (village) Palm Beach County	42	0.19
Denison, TX (city) Grayson County	41	0.18
Pauls Valley, OK (city) Garvin County	40	0.65
Miami, OK (city) Ottawa County	40	0.29
West Odessa, TX (cdp) Ector County	40	0.22
Cedar Hill, TX (city) Dallas County	40	0.12
Kendale Lakes, FL (cdp) Miami-Dade County	40	0.07
Bakersfield, CA (city) Kern County	40	0.02
Los Angeles, CA (city) Los Angeles County	40	0.00
Guthrie, OK (city) Logan County	39	0.38
Gainesville, TX (city) Cooke County	39	0.25
Tishomingo, OK (city) Johnston County	38	1.20
Lake Dallas, TX (city) Denton County	38	0.63
Vernon, TX (city) Wilbarger County	38	0.33
Richardson, TX (city) Dallas County	38	0.04
Visalia, CA (city) Tulare County	38	0.04
Plano, TX (city) Collin County	38	0.02
Forest City, FL (cdp) Seminole County	37	0.29
Glen Burnie, MD (cdp) Anne Arundel County	37	0.10
Manteca, CA (city) San Joaquin County	37	0.08
Jacksonville, FL (special city) Duval County	37	0.01
San Jose, CA (city) Santa Clara County	37	0.00
Kelseyville, CA (cdp) Lake County	36	1.26
Dewey, OK (city) Washington County	36	1.17
Purcell, OK (city) McClain County	36	0.65
Levelland, TX (city) Hockley County	36	0.28
Van Buren, AR (city) Crawford County	36	0.19
Eureka, CA (city) Humboldt County	36	0.14
Akron, OH (city) Summit County	36	0.02
Commerce, OK (city) Ottawa County	35	1.35
Watonga, OK (city) Blaine County	35	0.75
Sherman, TX (city) Grayson County	35	0.10
Winters, TX (city) Runnels County	34	1.13
Dublin, TX (city) Erath County	34	0.89
El Reno, OK (city) Canadian County	34	0.21
La Vergne, TN (city) Rutherford County	34	0.18
Yonkers, NY (city) Westchester County	34	0.02
Tampa, FL (city) Hillsborough County	34	0.01
San Diego, CA (city) San Diego County	34	0.00
Mannford, OK (town) Creek County	33	1.66
Breckenridge, TX (city) Stephens County	33	0.56
Choctaw, OK (city) Oklahoma County	33	0.35
Clovis, NM (city) Curry County	33	0.10
Joplin, MO (city) Jasper County	33	0.07
Brick, NJ (township) Ocean County	33	0.04
Columbus, OH (city) Franklin County	33	0.00

Notes: (cdp) census designated place; Refer to the Explanation of Data in the front of the book for more detailed information.

West Indian: Dutch West Indian, excluding Hispanic

Top 150 Places Sorted by Percent

(Based on all places, regardless of population)

Place	Number	%
Elmer, OK (town) Jackson County	6	6.98
Addington, OK (town) Jefferson County	7	5.60
Stony Point, OK (cdp) Sequoyah County	9	5.49
Pyote, TX (town) Ward County	7	5.34
Zeb, OK (cdp) Cherokee County	25	5.12
Rosston, OK (town) Harper County	5	5.10
Watts Community, OK (cdp) Adair County	25	4.92
Thackerville, OK (town) Love County	23	4.86
Fairfield, OK (cdp) Adair County	19	4.82
Dennis, OK (cdp) Delaware County	11	4.72
Waco, MO (town) Jasper County	4	4.17
Tara, MN (township) Swift County	5	4.07
Mutual, OK (town) Woodward County	3	3.57
Las Colonias, TX (cdp) Zavala County	8	3.49
Yale, IL (village) Jasper County	3	3.49
Hickory, OK (town) Murray County	3	3.45
Rosedale, OK (town) McClain County	2	3.23
Hawk Cove, TX (city) Hunt County	14	3.21
Bridgeport, OK (city) Caddo County	3	3.06
Gene Autry, OK (town) Carter County	3	3.00
Millerton, OK (town) McCurtain County	10	2.89
Bennington, OK (town) Bryan County	8	2.81
Checotah, OK (city) McIntosh County	97	2.76
Zuehl, TX (cdp) Guadalupe County	7	2.75
Wanette, OK (town) Pottawatomie County	3	2.74
Sand Hills, OK (cdp) Muskogee County	10	2.73
Mosquero, NM (village) Harding County	4	2.70
Dewar, OK (town) Okmulgee County	24	2.67
Wainwright, OK (town) Muskogee County	5	2.66
Hope, NM (village) Eddy County	3	2.63
New Alluwe, OK (town) Nowata County	3	2.56
Calhoun, TN (town) McMinn County	13	2.52
Zenda, KS (city) Kingman County	3	2.52
Roff, OK (town) Pontotoc County	17	2.46
Quinton, OK (town) Pittsburg County	26	2.44
Indianola, OK (town) Pittsburg County	5	2.43
Westphalia, KS (city) Anderson County	4	2.34
Porter, OK (town) Wagoner County	12	2.33
Webb City, OK (town) Osage County	2	2.20
Josephine, TX (city) Collin County	13	2.18
Rocky Mountain, OK (cdp) Adair County	10	2.14
Woodall, OK (cdp) Cherokee County	16	2.13
Highfield-Cascade, MD (cdp) Washington County	23	2.06
Atwood, OK (town) Hughes County	2	2.04
Gerty, OK (town) Hughes County	2	2.02
Davis, OK (city) Murray County	52	1.98
Blackwell, TX (city) Nolan County	7	1.92
Hitchita, OK (town) McIntosh County	2	1.89
Grays Prairie, TX (village) Kaufman County	5	1.85
River Bottom, OK (cdp) Muskogee County	5	1.82
Rush Springs, OK (town) Grady County	23	1.76
Tupelo, OK (city) Coal County	7	1.76
Stuart, OK (town) Hughes County	4	1.75
Healdton, OK (city) Carter County	49	1.74
Velma, OK (town) Stephens County	12	1.73
Moran, TX (city) Shackelford County	4	1.72
Box Canyon-Amistad, TX (cdp) Val Verde County	1	1.72
Vian, OK (town) Sequoyah County	23	1.70
Binger, OK (town) Caddo County	12	1.69
Spavinaw, OK (town) Mayes County	9	1.69
Morrison, OK (town) Noble County	11	1.68
Carlile, OK (cdp) Sequoyah County	12	1.67
Mannford, OK (town) Creek County	33	1.66
Flute Springs, OK (cdp) Sequoyah County	4	1.65
Cimarron City, OK (town) Logan County	2	1.64
Wink, TX (city) Winkler County	15	1.62
Alexandria, MO (city) Clark County	3	1.60
Newcastle, TX (city) Young County	10	1.59
Ninnekah, OK (town) Grady County	16	1.57
Bromide, OK (town) Johnston County	3	1.57
Howe, OK (town) Le Flore County	11	1.54
Ponder, TX (town) Denton County	7	1.54
Ringling, OK (town) Jefferson County	17	1.53
Colorado City, TX (city) Mitchell County	64	1.52
Log Cabin, TX (city) Henderson County	12	1.52

Place	Number	%
Tushka, OK (town) Atoka County	5	1.51
Gracemont, OK (town) Caddo County	5	1.47
Elmore City, OK (town) Garvin County	11	1.46
Winchester, OK (town) Okmulgee County	6	1.46
Kingston, OK (town) Marshall County	20	1.44
Shady Grove, OK (cdp) Cherokee County	8	1.44
Brushy, OK (cdp) Sequoyah County	11	1.43
Cleveland, VA (town) Russell County	2	1.42
Hoffman, OK (town) Okmulgee County	2	1.41
Tenkiller, OK (cdp) Cherokee County	7	1.39
Kenefic, OK (town) Bryan County	3	1.38
Ada, OK (city) Pontotoc County	214	1.37
Chelsea, OK (city) Rogers County	30	1.37
Commerce, OK (city) Ottawa County	35	1.35
Hammon, OK (town) Roger Mills County	6	1.35
Allen, OK (town) Pontotoc County	13	1.33
Morgan Farm Area, TX (cdp) San Patricio County	7	1.31
Oktaha, OK (town) Muskogee County	4	1.27
Richland, OR (city) Baker County	2	1.27
Kelseyville, CA (cdp) Lake County	36	1.26
Kibler, AR (city) Crawford County	12	1.26
Braman, OK (town) Kay County	3	1.24
Rockville, SC (town) Charleston County	2	1.24
Braggs, OK (town) Muskogee County	4	1.23
Tillar, AR (city) Drew County	3	1.23
Calumet, OK (town) Canadian County	7	1.22
Sterling, OK (town) Comanche County	9	1.21
Slick, OK (town) Creek County	2	1.21
Tishomingo, OK (city) Johnston County	38	1.20
Crary, ND (city) Ramsey County	2	1.20
Mertens, TX (town) Hill County	2	1.20
Okarche, OK (town) Kingfisher County	14	1.19
Bonanza, AR (town) Sebastian County	6	1.19
Scraper, OK (cdp) Cherokee County	6	1.19
Gold Beach, OR (city) Curry County	22	1.18
Notchietown, OK (cdp) Sequoyah County	5	1.18
Sulphur, OK (city) Murray County	56	1.17
Dewey, OK (city) Washington County	36	1.17
McQueeney, TX (cdp) Guadalupe County	19	1.17
Aspermont, TX (town) Stonewall County	12	1.17
Redbird Smith, OK (cdp) Sequoyah County	5	1.17
Trinity, TX (city) Trinity County	31	1.15
Warner, OK (town) Muskogee County	17	1.15
Jacksons' Gap, AL (town) Tallapoosa County	9	1.15
Eastland, TX (city) Eastland County	45	1.14
West Jefferson, AL (town) Jefferson County	4	1.14
Marlow, OK (city) Stephens County	52	1.13
Winters, TX (city) Runnels County	34	1.13
Earlsboro, OK (town) Pottawatomie County	5	1.13
Akins, OK (cdp) Sequoyah County	5	1.13
Asher, OK (town) Pottawatomie County	5	1.13
Rattan, OK (town) Pushmataha County	3	1.13
Horatio, AR (city) Sevier County	11	1.11
Quapaw, OK (town) Ottawa County	11	1.11
Eastview, TN (town) McNairy County	7	1.11
Wagoner, OK (city) Wagoner County	86	1.10
Austin, AR (city) Lonoke County	7	1.10
Bonaparte, IA (city) Van Buren County	5	1.09
Oakman, AL (town) Walker County	10	1.08
Idabel, OK (city) McCurtain County	74	1.06
Inola, OK (town) Rogers County	17	1.06
Robbinsville, NC (town) Graham County	8	1.06
Collinsville, TX (town) Grayson County	13	1.05
Douglassville, TX (town) Cass County	2	1.05
Bokchito, OK (town) Bryan County	6	1.03
Maud, OK (city) Pottawatomie County	11	1.02
Opdyke West, TX (town) Hockley County	2	1.01
Eufaula, OK (city) McIntosh County	26	1.00
Spiro, OK (town) Le Flore County	23	1.00
Byng, OK (town) Pontotoc County	11	1.00
Oak Ridge, TX (town) Cooke County	2	1.00
Blowers, MN (township) Otter Tail County	3	0.99
Rocky, OK (town) Washita County	2	0.99
Long Creek, OR (city) Grant County	2	0.98
Ardmore, OK (city) Carter County	227	0.97

Notes: (cdp) census designated place; Refer to the Explanation of Data in the front of the book for more detailed information.

West Indian: Dutch West Indian, excluding Hispanic

Top 150 Places Sorted by Percent

(Based on places with populations of 10,000 or more)

Place	Number	%
Ada, OK (city) Pontotoc County	214	1.37
Ardmore, OK (city) Carter County	227	0.97
Sapulpa, OK (city) Creek County	137	0.73
Duncan, OK (city) Stephens County	146	0.65
Claremore, OK (city) Rogers County	99	0.62
McAlester, OK (city) Pittsburg County	109	0.61
Owasso, OK (city) Tulsa County	98	0.53
Sand Springs, OK (city) Tulsa County	92	0.52
Guymon, OK (city) Texas County	55	0.52
Moore, OK (city) Cleveland County	201	0.49
Shawnee, OK (city) Pottawatomie County	130	0.45
Siloam Springs, AR (city) Benton County	49	0.45
Tahlequah, OK (city) Cherokee County	63	0.43
Saks, AL (cdp) Calhoun County	44	0.42
Durant, OK (city) Bryan County	55	0.41
Del City, OK (city) Oklahoma County	89	0.40
Muskogee, OK (city) Muskogee County	144	0.38
Guthrie, OK (city) Logan County	39	0.38
Russellville, AR (city) Pope County	86	0.36
Chickasha, OK (city) Grady County	56	0.35
Ponca City, OK (city) Kay County	85	0.33
Pampa, TX (city) Gray County	59	0.33
Vernon, TX (city) Wilbarger County	38	0.33
Hobbs, NM (city) Lea County	91	0.32
Miami, OK (city) Ottawa County	40	0.29
Forest City, FL (cdp) Seminole County	37	0.29
Norman, OK (city) Cleveland County	272	0.28
Levelland, TX (city) Hockley County	36	0.28
Fort Smith, AR (city) Sebastian County	216	0.27
Elk City, OK (city) Beckham County	29	0.27
Broken Arrow, OK (city) Tulsa County	196	0.26
Rogers, AR (city) Benton County	95	0.25
Yukon, OK (city) Canadian County	52	0.25
Bethany, OK (city) Oklahoma County	51	0.25
Gainesville, TX (city) Cooke County	39	0.25
Snyder, TX (city) Scurry County	27	0.25
Mustang, OK (city) Canadian County	32	0.24
Bartlesville, OK (city) Washington County	79	0.23
Balch Springs, TX (city) Dallas County	45	0.23
Oklahoma City, OK (city) Oklahoma County	1,092	0.22
Tulsa, OK (city) Tulsa County	870	0.22
Odessa, TX (city) Ector County	196	0.22
Paris, TX (city) Lamar County	56	0.22
Burleson, TX (city) Johnson County	46	0.22
West Odessa, TX (cdp) Ector County	40	0.22
Reidsville, NC (city) Rockingham County	31	0.22
Oildale, CA (cdp) Kern County	59	0.21
El Reno, OK (city) Canadian County	34	0.21
Coos Bay, OR (city) Coos County	32	0.21
Westchase, FL (cdp) Hillsborough County	23	0.21
Stephenville, TX (city) Erath County	30	0.20
Bixby, OK (city) Tulsa County	27	0.20
Lebanon, MO (city) Laclede County	25	0.20
Princeton, FL (cdp) Miami-Dade County	20	0.20
North Richland Hills, TX (city) Tarrant County	105	0.19
Royal Palm Beach, FL (village) Palm Beach County	42	0.19
Van Buren, AR (city) Crawford County	36	0.19
Borger, TX (city) Hutchinson County	27	0.19
Grover Beach, CA (city) San Luis Obispo County	25	0.19
Big Spring, TX (city) Howard County	45	0.18
Denison, TX (city) Grayson County	41	0.18
La Vergne, TN (city) Rutherford County	34	0.18
Opa-locka, FL (city) Miami-Dade County	28	0.18
Stony Point, NY (town) Rockland County	26	0.18
Hewitt, TX (city) McLennan County	19	0.18
The Village, OK (city) Oklahoma County	18	0.18
Loma Linda, CA (city) San Bernardino County	32	0.17
Four Corners, OR (cdp) Marion County	24	0.17
Highland Village, TX (city) Denton County	21	0.17
Olivehurst, CA (cdp) Yuba County	19	0.17
Edmond, OK (city) Oklahoma County	107	0.16
Enid, OK (city) Garfield County	73	0.16
Wylie, TX (city) Collin County	24	0.16
White Settlement, TX (city) Tarrant County	23	0.16
Amarillo, TX (city) Potter County	259	0.15
Wichita Falls, TX (city) Wichita County	152	0.15
Springdale, AR (city) Washington County	67	0.15
Haltom City, TX (city) Tarrant County	58	0.15
Bostonia, CA (cdp) San Diego County	23	0.15
Martin, TN (city) Weakley County	16	0.15
Morrisville, PA (borough) Bucks County	15	0.15
Midwest City, OK (city) Oklahoma County	76	0.14
Texarkana, TX (city) Bowie County	48	0.14
Eureka, CA (city) Humboldt County	36	0.14
Rockwall, TX (city) Rockwall County	26	0.14
Bella Vista, AR (cdp) Benton County	23	0.14
San Angelo, TX (city) Tom Green County	113	0.13
Euless, TX (city) Tarrant County	58	0.13
Hurst, TX (city) Tarrant County	47	0.13
Newton, KS (city) Harvey County	22	0.13
Greeneville, TN (town) Greene County	20	0.13
East Lampeter, PA (township) Lancaster County	18	0.13
Okmulgee, OK (city) Okmulgee County	17	0.13
Miami Shores, FL (village) Miami-Dade County	14	0.13
Tehachapi, CA (city) Kern County	14	0.13
Cedar Hill, TX (city) Dallas County	40	0.12
Alvin, TX (city) Brazoria County	25	0.12
Roseburg, OR (city) Douglas County	25	0.12
Brownwood, TX (city) Brown County	23	0.12
Dickinson, TX (city) Galveston County	21	0.12
Mount Vernon, IL (city) Jefferson County	20	0.12
Burkburnett, TX (city) Wichita County	13	0.12
Texarkana, AR (city) Miller County	30	0.11
Sulphur, LA (city) Calcasieu Parish	22	0.11
Weatherford, TX (city) Parker County	22	0.11
Moses Lake, WA (city) Grant County	17	0.11
Elfers, FL (cdp) Pasco County	14	0.11
Villas, FL (cdp) Lee County	12	0.11
Atchison, KS (city) Atchison County	11	0.11
Midland, TX (city) Midland County	95	0.10
Lawton, OK (city) Comanche County	91	0.10
Glen Burnie, MD (cdp) Anne Arundel County	37	0.10
Sherman, TX (city) Grayson County	35	0.10
Clovis, NM (city) Curry County	33	0.10
Maryville, TN (city) Blount County	23	0.10
Altus, OK (city) Jackson County	22	0.10
Searcy, AR (city) White County	19	0.10
Tuskegee, AL (city) Macon County	12	0.10
Denton, TX (city) Denton County	71	0.09
Duncanville, TX (city) Dallas County	31	0.09
Nacogdoches, TX (city) Nacogdoches County	27	0.09
Mansfield, TX (city) Tarrant County	25	0.09
Bentonville, AR (city) Benton County	17	0.09
Arkansas City, KS (city) Cowley County	11	0.09
Saginaw, TX (city) Tarrant County	11	0.09
Sherwood, OR (city) Washington County	11	0.09
Panthersville, GA (cdp) De Kalb County	10	0.09
Georgetown, GA (cdp) Chatham County	9	0.09
Los Lunas, NM (village) Valencia County	9	0.09
Knoxville, TN (city) Knox County	140	0.08
Abilene, TX (city) Taylor County	92	0.08
Lewisville, TX (city) Denton County	59	0.08
Longview, TX (city) Gregg County	56	0.08
Apple Valley, CA (town) San Bernardino County	44	0.08
Manteca, CA (city) San Joaquin County	37	0.08
Orange, NJ (cdp) Essex County	27	0.08
Deer Park, TX (city) Harris County	22	0.08
Coronado, CA (city) San Diego County	19	0.08
Norland, FL (cdp) Miami-Dade County	19	0.08
Ridgecrest, CA (city) Kern County	19	0.08
Tualatin, OR (city) Washington County	19	0.08
Lemoore, CA (city) Kings County	15	0.08
Setauket-East Setauket, NY (cdp) Suffolk County	12	0.08
Tillmans Corner, AL (cdp) Mobile County	12	0.08
Riverdale, GA (city) Clayton County	10	0.08
Katy, TX (city) Harris County	9	0.08
Kilgore, TX (city) Gregg County	9	0.08
Warwick, PA (township) Bucks County	9	0.08
Saint Helens, OR (city) Columbia County	8	0.08
Lubbock, TX (city) Lubbock County	142	0.07

Notes: (cdp) census designated place; Refer to the Explanation of Data in the front of the book for more detailed information.

West Indian: Haitian, excluding Hispanic

Top 150 Places Sorted by Number

(Based on all places, regardless of population)

Place	Number	%
New York, NY (city) New York City	118,769	1.48
Boston, MA (city) Suffolk County	18,979	3.22
North Miami, FL (city) Miami-Dade County	18,656	31.07
Miami, FL (city) Miami-Dade County	18,309	5.05
Hempstead, NY (town) Nassau County	13,599	1.80
Fort Lauderdale, FL (city) Broward County	10,869	7.14
Golden Glades, FL (cdp) Miami-Dade County	10,284	31.95
North Miami Beach, FL (city) Miami-Dade County	7,864	19.33
Ramapo, NY (town) Rockland County	7,559	6.94
Delray Beach, FL (city) Palm Beach County	6,351	10.60
Irvington, NJ (cdp) Essex County	5,812	9.59
Spring Valley, NY (village) Rockland County	5,349	21.08
Lauderhill, FL (city) Broward County	5,034	8.79
Pine Hills, FL (cdp) Orange County	4,817	11.47
Lauderdale Lakes, FL (city) Broward County	4,732	15.01
Brockton, MA (city) Plymouth County	4,720	5.01
Pompano Beach, FL (city) Broward County	4,718	6.03
Miramar, FL (city) Broward County	4,359	6.00
Pinewood, FL (cdp) Miami-Dade County	4,315	25.66
Philadelphia, PA (city) Philadelphia County	4,221	0.28
Boynton Beach, FL (city) Palm Beach County	4,040	6.74
Elmont, NY (cdp) Nassau County	3,572	10.94
Stamford, CT (city) Fairfield County	3,524	3.01
Orlando, FL (city) Orange County	3,514	1.89
West Palm Beach, FL (city) Palm Beach County	3,389	4.16
Cambridge, MA (city) Middlesex County	3,265	3.22
Orange, NJ (cdp) Essex County	3,250	9.89
Chicago, IL (city) Cook County	3,104	0.11
Elizabeth, NJ (city) Union County	3,016	2.50
Coral Springs, FL (city) Broward County	2,856	2.43
East Orange, NJ (city) Essex County	2,852	4.08
Norland, FL (cdp) Miami-Dade County	2,789	12.11
Lake Worth, FL (city) Palm Beach County	2,763	7.84
Newark, NJ (city) Essex County	2,634	0.96
Pembroke Pines, FL (city) Broward County	2,583	1.88
Sunrise, FL (city) Broward County	2,524	2.95
Islip, NY (town) Suffolk County	2,487	0.77
Ives Estates, FL (cdp) Miami-Dade County	2,449	14.06
Deerfield Beach, FL (city) Broward County	2,350	3.63
Plantation, FL (city) Broward County	2,307	2.77
Fort Pierce, FL (city) Saint Lucie County	2,303	6.14
Oakland Park, FL (city) Broward County	2,299	7.37
Oak Ridge, FL (cdp) Orange County	2,240	10.00
North Lauderdale, FL (city) Broward County	2,223	6.88
Fort Myers, FL (city) Lee County	2,202	4.58
Somerville, MA (city) Middlesex County	2,168	2.80
Hollywood, FL (city) Broward County	2,140	1.54
Immokalee, FL (cdp) Collier County	2,095	10.79
Randolph, MA (cdp) Norfolk County	2,060	6.65
North Hempstead, NY (town) Nassau County	2,007	0.90
Bridgeport, CT (city) Fairfield County	1,980	1.42
Jersey City, NJ (city) Hudson County	1,931	0.80
Uniondale, NY (cdp) Nassau County	1,882	8.18
Providence, RI (city) Providence County	1,878	1.08
Margate, FL (city) Broward County	1,853	3.44
Babylon, NY (town) Suffolk County	1,819	0.86
North Valley Stream, NY (cdp) Nassau County	1,792	11.35
Roselle, NJ (borough) Union County	1,709	8.03
West Little River, FL (cdp) Miami-Dade County	1,687	5.23
Tampa, FL (city) Hillsborough County	1,619	0.53
West Orange, NJ (cdp) Essex County	1,618	3.61
Hempstead, NY (village) Nassau County	1,601	2.83
Clarkstown, NY (town) Rockland County	1,586	1.93
Homestead, FL (city) Miami-Dade County	1,531	4.78
Malden, MA (city) Middlesex County	1,508	2.68
Norwalk, CT (city) Fairfield County	1,499	1.81
Belle Glade, FL (city) Palm Beach County	1,476	9.84
Brentwood, NY (cdp) Suffolk County	1,431	2.66
Hillcrest, NY (cdp) Rockland County	1,390	19.56
Linden, NJ (city) Union County	1,360	3.45
Carol City, FL (cdp) Miami-Dade County	1,357	2.28
New Cassel, NY (cdp) Nassau County	1,257	9.45
Golden Gate, FL (cdp) Collier County	1,228	5.84
Huntington, NY (town) Suffolk County	1,220	0.62
Lake Park, FL (town) Palm Beach County	1,211	14.37
Everett, MA (city) Middlesex County	1,208	3.18
Maplewood, NJ (cdp) Essex County	1,181	4.95
Union, NJ (cdp) Union County	1,156	2.12
Melrose Park, FL (cdp) Broward County	1,128	15.92
Medford, MA (city) Middlesex County	1,112	1.99
Country Club, FL (cdp) Miami-Dade County	1,111	3.05
Baldwin, NY (cdp) Nassau County	1,104	4.71
Brookhaven, NY (town) Suffolk County	1,089	0.24
Pompano Estates, FL (cdp) Broward County	1,083	31.26
Orangetown, NY (town) Rockland County	1,026	2.15
Jacksonville, FL (special city) Duval County	996	0.14
Los Angeles, CA (city) Los Angeles County	980	0.03
Waltham, MA (city) Middlesex County	977	1.65
Asbury Park, NJ (city) Monmouth County	974	5.75
Kendall, FL (cdp) Miami-Dade County	974	1.29
Miami Shores, FL (village) Miami-Dade County	969	9.28
Westview, FL (cdp) Miami-Dade County	963	10.04
New Rochelle, NY (city) Westchester County	933	1.29
Boca Raton, FL (city) Palm Beach County	928	1.23
Lynn, MA (city) Essex County	926	1.04
Wilton Manors, FL (city) Broward County	925	7.29
Hamilton, NJ (township) Mercer County	914	1.05
Washington, DC (city) District of Columbia	896	0.16
Yonkers, NY (city) Westchester County	887	0.45
Bonnie Lock-Woodsetter North, FL (cdp) Broward County	872	20.24
The Hammocks, FL (cdp) Miami-Dade County	861	1.82
Evanston, IL (city) Cook County	856	1.15
Hallandale, FL (city) Broward County	849	2.46
Mount Vernon, NY (city) Westchester County	825	1.21
Tamarac, FL (city) Broward County	809	1.44
Haverstraw, NY (town) Rockland County	793	2.35
Scott Lake, FL (cdp) Miami-Dade County	788	5.48
Silver Spring, MD (cdp) Montgomery County	766	1.00
Leisure City, FL (cdp) Miami-Dade County	765	3.51
Trenton, NJ (city) Mercer County	737	0.86
Kendall Green, FL (cdp) Broward County	724	23.04
Oyster Bay, NY (town) Nassau County	721	0.25
Port Saint Lucie, FL (city) Saint Lucie County	702	0.79
Kendale Lakes, FL (cdp) Miami-Dade County	644	1.13
Nanuet, NY (cdp) Rockland County	632	3.78
Lake Worth Corridor, FL (cdp) Palm Beach County	627	3.41
Loch Lomond, FL (cdp) Broward County	618	18.60
Roosevelt, NY (cdp) Nassau County	599	3.78
Houston, TX (city) Harris County	592	0.03
Riviera Beach, FL (city) Palm Beach County	582	1.91
Valley Stream, NY (village) Nassau County	582	1.60
Nyack, NY (village) Rockland County	576	8.60
Westgate-Belvedere Homes, FL (cdp) Palm Beach County	576	7.08
Pleasantville, NJ (city) Atlantic County	575	3.01
Milton, MA (cdp) Norfolk County	574	2.20
Freeport, NY (village) Nassau County	568	1.30
Collier Manor-Cresthaven, FL (cdp) Broward County	564	7.10
El Portal, FL (village) Miami-Dade County	556	22.09
Winter Haven, FL (city) Polk County	550	2.12
Columbia, MD (cdp) Howard County	550	0.62
University, FL (cdp) Hillsborough County	545	1.78
Andover, FL (cdp) Miami-Dade County	543	6.27
Lantana, FL (town) Palm Beach County	542	5.68
Hillside, NJ (cdp) Union County	540	2.48
Tallahassee, FL (city) Leon County	512	0.34
Ojus, FL (cdp) Miami-Dade County	505	3.03
Tedder, FL (cdp) Broward County	499	25.11
East Massapequa, NY (cdp) Nassau County	497	2.54
Rahway, NJ (city) Union County	492	1.86
South Orange, NJ (cdp) Essex County	488	2.88
Wyandanch, NY (cdp) Suffolk County	487	4.60
Kansas City, MO (city) Jackson County	481	0.11
Naples Manor, FL (cdp) Collier County	470	9.19
Central Islip, NY (cdp) Suffolk County	470	1.47
Palmetto Estates, FL (cdp) Miami-Dade County	469	3.43
Florida City, FL (city) Miami-Dade County	468	5.83
Montclair, NJ (cdp) Essex County	468	1.20
Atlanta, GA (city) Fulton County	468	0.11
Wheaton-Glenmont, MD (cdp) Montgomery County	448	0.78
Inwood, FL (cdp) Polk County	442	6.53

Notes: (cdp) census designated place; Refer to the Explanation of Data in the front of the book for more detailed information.

West Indian: Haitian, excluding Hispanic

Top 150 Places Sorted by Percent

(Based on all places, regardless of population)

Place	Number	%
Golden Glades, FL (cdp) Miami-Dade County	10,284	31.95
Pompano Estates, FL (cdp) Broward County	1,083	31.26
North Miami, FL (city) Miami-Dade County	18,656	31.07
Pinewood, FL (cdp) Miami-Dade County	4,315	25.66
Tedder, FL (cdp) Broward County	499	25.11
Kendall Green, FL (cdp) Broward County	724	23.04
Belle Glade Camp, FL (cdp) Palm Beach County	284	22.47
El Portal, FL (village) Miami-Dade County	556	22.09
Spring Valley, NY (village) Rockland County	5,349	21.08
Bonnie Lock-Woodsetter North, FL (cdp) Broward County	872	20.24
Hillcrest, NY (cdp) Rockland County	1,390	19.56
North Miami Beach, FL (city) Miami-Dade County	7,864	19.33
Loch Lomond, FL (cdp) Broward County	618	18.60
Melrose Park, FL (cdp) Broward County	1,128	15.92
Lauderdale Lakes, FL (city) Broward County	4,732	15.01
Lake Park, FL (town) Palm Beach County	1,211	14.37
Ives Estates, FL (cdp) Miami-Dade County	2,449	14.06
Norland, FL (cdp) Miami-Dade County	2,789	12.11
Pine Hills, FL (cdp) Orange County	4,817	11.47
North Valley Stream, NY (cdp) Nassau County	1,792	11.35
Elmont, NY (cdp) Nassau County	3,572	10.94
Immokalee, FL (cdp) Collier County	2,095	10.79
Delray Beach, FL (city) Palm Beach County	6,351	10.60
Biscayne Park, FL (village) Miami-Dade County	340	10.28
Westview, FL (cdp) Miami-Dade County	963	10.04
Oak Ridge, FL (cdp) Orange County	2,240	10.00
Orange, NJ (cdp) Essex County	3,250	9.89
Belle Glade, FL (city) Palm Beach County	1,476	9.84
Irvington, NJ (cdp) Essex County	5,812	9.59
New Cassel, NY (cdp) Nassau County	1,257	9.45
Miami Shores, FL (village) Miami-Dade County	969	9.28
Naples Manor, FL (cdp) Collier County	470	9.19
Mangonia Park, FL (town) Palm Beach County	116	8.96
South Nyack, NY (village) Rockland County	308	8.87
Lauderhill, FL (city) Broward County	5,034	8.79
Nyack, NY (village) Rockland County	576	8.60
Leisureville, FL (cdp) Broward County	93	8.58
Seminole Manor, FL (cdp) Palm Beach County	221	8.38
Uniondale, NY (cdp) Nassau County	1,882	8.18
Roselle, NJ (borough) Union County	1,709	8.03
Lake Worth, FL (city) Palm Beach County	2,763	7.84
Oakland Park, FL (city) Broward County	2,299	7.37
Wilton Manors, FL (city) Broward County	925	7.29
Fort Lauderdale, FL (city) Broward County	10,869	7.14
Collier Manor-Cresthaven, FL (cdp) Broward County	564	7.10
Westgate-Belvedere Homes, FL (cdp) Palm Beach County	576	7.08
Broadview-Pompano Park, FL (cdp) Broward County	361	7.04
Ramapo, NY (town) Rockland County	7,559	6.94
North Lauderdale, FL (city) Broward County	2,223	6.88
Boynton Beach, FL (city) Palm Beach County	4,040	6.74
Randolph, MA (cdp) Norfolk County	2,060	6.65
Inwood, FL (cdp) Polk County	442	6.53
Meridian, CO (cdp) Douglas County	10	6.29
Andover, FL (cdp) Miami-Dade County	543	6.27
Saint Leo, FL (town) Pasco County	38	6.24
Fort Pierce, FL (city) Saint Lucie County	2,303	6.14
Pompano Beach, FL (city) Broward County	4,718	6.03
Miramar, FL (city) Broward County	4,359	6.00
Pomona, NY (village) Rockland County	164	6.00
Whitfield, FL (cdp) Manatee County	181	5.86
Golden Gate, FL (cdp) Collier County	1,228	5.84
Florida City, FL (city) Miami-Dade County	468	5.83
Asbury Park, NJ (city) Monmouth County	974	5.75
South Floral Park, NY (village) Nassau County	90	5.70
Lantana, FL (town) Palm Beach County	542	5.68
Scott Lake, FL (cdp) Miami-Dade County	788	5.48
Wheatley Heights, NY (cdp) Suffolk County	271	5.38
Pembroke Park, FL (town) Broward County	337	5.32
West Little River, FL (cdp) Miami-Dade County	1,687	5.23
Miami, FL (city) Miami-Dade County	18,309	5.05
Lakeview, NY (cdp) Nassau County	283	5.05
Brockton, MA (city) Plymouth County	4,720	5.01
Maplewood, NJ (cdp) Essex County	1,181	4.95
Homestead, FL (city) Miami-Dade County	1,531	4.78
Baldwin, NY (cdp) Nassau County	1,104	4.71
Wyandanch, NY (cdp) Suffolk County	487	4.60
Fort Myers, FL (city) Lee County	2,202	4.58
Rodney Village, DE (cdp) Kent County	60	4.37
Quinebaug, CT (cdp) Windham County	47	4.36
Estates of Fort Lauderdale, FL (cdp) Broward County	79	4.28
West Palm Beach, FL (city) Palm Beach County	3,389	4.16
Pompano Beach Highlands, FL (cdp) Broward County	271	4.16
East Orange, NJ (city) Essex County	2,852	4.08
Naranja, FL (cdp) Miami-Dade County	169	4.02
Lake Belvedere Estates, FL (cdp) Palm Beach County	60	4.02
East Garden City, NY (cdp) Nassau County	40	4.02
Lake Forest, FL (cdp) Broward County	194	3.91
Fairview, NY (cdp) Westchester County	114	3.81
Nanuet, NY (cdp) Rockland County	632	3.78
Roosevelt, NY (cdp) Nassau County	599	3.78
Knik River, AK (cdp) Matanuska-Susitna Borough	23	3.73
Hillburn, NY (village) Rockland County	29	3.70
West Haverstraw, NY (village) Rockland County	380	3.69
Miami Gardens, FL (cdp) Broward County	95	3.68
Deerfield Beach, FL (city) Broward County	2,350	3.63
West Orange, NJ (cdp) Essex County	1,618	3.61
Pine Manor, FL (cdp) Lee County	140	3.60
Leisure City, FL (cdp) Miami-Dade County	765	3.51
Linden, NJ (city) Union County	1,360	3.45
Margate, FL (city) Broward County	1,853	3.44
Palmetto Estates, FL (cdp) Miami-Dade County	469	3.43
Lake Worth Corridor, FL (cdp) Palm Beach County	627	3.41
Tangelo Park, FL (cdp) Orange County	77	3.32
Jewett City, CT (borough) New London County	101	3.27
Boston, MA (city) Suffolk County	18,979	3.22
Cambridge, MA (city) Middlesex County	3,265	3.22
Everett, MA (city) Middlesex County	1,208	3.18
Mount Ivy, NY (cdp) Rockland County	207	3.17
West Perrine, FL (cdp) Miami-Dade County	271	3.15
Palm Springs, FL (village) Palm Beach County	365	3.09
Baldwin Harbor, NY (cdp) Nassau County	252	3.09
Country Club, FL (cdp) Miami-Dade County	1,111	3.05
Lake Lucerne, FL (cdp) Miami-Dade County	279	3.05
Ojus, FL (cdp) Miami-Dade County	505	3.03
Stamford, CT (city) Fairfield County	3,524	3.01
Pleasantville, NJ (city) Atlantic County	575	3.01
Sunrise, FL (city) Broward County	2,524	2.95
Breckinridge Center, KY (cdp) Union County	56	2.95
South Orange, NJ (cdp) Essex County	488	2.88
Broadview Park, FL (cdp) Broward County	195	2.87
Hempstead, NY (village) Nassau County	1,601	2.83
High Point, FL (cdp) Palm Beach County	62	2.81
Somerville, MA (city) Middlesex County	2,168	2.80
Plantation, FL (city) Broward County	2,307	2.77
Avon Park, FL (city) Highlands County	239	2.76
Haines City, FL (city) Polk County	359	2.73
Lake Alfred, FL (city) Polk County	106	2.73
Highland Falls, NY (village) Orange County	100	2.73
Malden, MA (city) Middlesex County	1,508	2.68
Chestnut Ridge, NY (village) Rockland County	206	2.67
Brentwood, NY (cdp) Suffolk County	1,431	2.66
Opa-locka North, FL (cdp) Miami-Dade County	165	2.65
Broward Estates, FL (cdp) Broward County	93	2.64
Westbury, NY (village) Nassau County	366	2.57
Dennis Port, MA (cdp) Barnstable County	92	2.55
Gordon Heights, NY (cdp) Suffolk County	79	2.55
East Massapequa, NY (cdp) Nassau County	497	2.54
Wrightstown, NJ (borough) Burlington County	19	2.54
Blades, DE (town) Sussex County	24	2.53
Elizabeth, NJ (city) Union County	3,016	2.50
Hillside, NJ (cdp) Union County	540	2.48
Georgetown, DE (town) Sussex County	115	2.48
Hallandale, FL (city) Broward County	849	2.46
Pine Castle, FL (cdp) Orange County	201	2.46
Goulds, FL (cdp) Miami-Dade County	187	2.45
Lely Resort, FL (cdp) Collier County	35	2.45
Hampton, FL (city) Bradford County	12	2.44
Coral Springs, FL (city) Broward County	2,856	2.43
Bunche Park, FL (cdp) Miami-Dade County	96	2.41
Opa-locka, FL (city) Miami-Dade County	364	2.39

Notes: (cdp) census designated place; Refer to the Explanation of Data in the front of the book for more detailed information.

West Indian: Haitian, excluding Hispanic

Top 150 Places Sorted by Percent

(Based on places with populations of 10,000 or more)

Place	Number	%
Golden Glades, FL (cdp) Miami-Dade County	10,284	31.95
North Miami, FL (city) Miami-Dade County	18,656	31.07
Pinewood, FL (cdp) Miami-Dade County	4,315	25.66
Spring Valley, NY (village) Rockland County	5,349	21.08
North Miami Beach, FL (city) Miami-Dade County	7,864	19.33
Lauderdale Lakes, FL (city) Broward County	4,732	15.01
Ives Estates, FL (cdp) Miami-Dade County	2,449	14.06
Norland, FL (cdp) Miami-Dade County	2,789	12.11
Pine Hills, FL (cdp) Orange County	4,817	11.47
North Valley Stream, NY (cdp) Nassau County	1,792	11.35
Elmont, NY (cdp) Nassau County	3,572	10.94
Immokalee, FL (cdp) Collier County	2,095	10.79
Delray Beach, FL (city) Palm Beach County	6,351	10.60
Oak Ridge, FL (cdp) Orange County	2,240	10.00
Orange, NJ (cdp) Essex County	3,250	9.89
Belle Glade, FL (city) Palm Beach County	1,476	9.84
Irvington, NJ (cdp) Essex County	5,812	9.59
New Cassel, NY (cdp) Nassau County	1,257	9.45
Miami Shores, FL (village) Miami-Dade County	969	9.28
Lauderhill, FL (city) Broward County	5,034	8.79
Uniondale, NY (cdp) Nassau County	1,882	8.18
Roselle, NJ (borough) Union County	1,709	8.03
Lake Worth, FL (city) Palm Beach County	2,763	7.84
Oakland Park, FL (city) Broward County	2,299	7.37
Wilton Manors, FL (city) Broward County	925	7.29
Fort Lauderdale, FL (city) Broward County	10,869	7.14
Ramapo, NY (town) Rockland County	7,559	6.94
North Lauderdale, FL (city) Broward County	2,223	6.88
Boynton Beach, FL (city) Palm Beach County	4,040	6.74
Randolph, MA (cdp) Norfolk County	2,060	6.65
Fort Pierce, FL (city) Saint Lucie County	2,303	6.14
Pompano Beach, FL (city) Broward County	4,718	6.03
Miramar, FL (city) Broward County	4,359	6.00
Golden Gate, FL (cdp) Collier County	1,228	5.84
Asbury Park, NJ (city) Monmouth County	974	5.75
Scott Lake, FL (cdp) Miami-Dade County	788	5.48
West Little River, FL (cdp) Miami-Dade County	1,687	5.23
Miami, FL (city) Miami-Dade County	18,309	5.05
Brockton, MA (city) Plymouth County	4,720	5.01
Maplewood, NJ (cdp) Essex County	1,181	4.95
Homestead, FL (city) Miami-Dade County	1,531	4.78
Baldwin, NY (cdp) Nassau County	1,104	4.71
Wyandanch, NY (cdp) Suffolk County	487	4.60
Fort Myers, FL (city) Lee County	2,202	4.58
West Palm Beach, FL (city) Palm Beach County	3,389	4.16
East Orange, NJ (city) Essex County	2,852	4.08
Nanuet, NY (cdp) Rockland County	632	3.78
Roosevelt, NY (cdp) Nassau County	599	3.78
West Haverstraw, NY (village) Rockland County	380	3.69
Deerfield Beach, FL (city) Broward County	2,350	3.63
West Orange, NJ (cdp) Essex County	1,618	3.61
Leisure City, FL (cdp) Miami-Dade County	765	3.51
Linden, NJ (city) Union County	1,360	3.45
Margate, FL (city) Broward County	1,853	3.44
Palmetto Estates, FL (cdp) Miami-Dade County	469	3.43
Lake Worth Corridor, FL (cdp) Palm Beach County	627	3.41
Boston, MA (city) Suffolk County	18,979	3.22
Cambridge, MA (city) Middlesex County	3,265	3.22
Everett, MA (city) Middlesex County	1,208	3.18
Palm Springs, FL (village) Palm Beach County	365	3.09
Country Club, FL (cdp) Miami-Dade County	1,111	3.05
Ojus, FL (cdp) Miami-Dade County	505	3.03
Stamford, CT (city) Fairfield County	3,524	3.01
Pleasantville, NJ (city) Atlantic County	575	3.01
Sunrise, FL (city) Broward County	2,524	2.95
South Orange, NJ (cdp) Essex County	488	2.88
Hempstead, NY (village) Nassau County	1,601	2.83
Somerville, MA (city) Middlesex County	2,168	2.80
Plantation, FL (city) Broward County	2,307	2.77
Haines City, FL (city) Polk County	359	2.73
Malden, MA (city) Middlesex County	1,508	2.68
Brentwood, NY (cdp) Suffolk County	1,431	2.66
Westbury, NY (village) Nassau County	366	2.57
East Massapequa, NY (cdp) Nassau County	497	2.54
Elizabeth, NJ (city) Union County	3,016	2.50
Hillside, NJ (cdp) Union County	540	2.48
Hallandale, FL (city) Broward County	849	2.46
Coral Springs, FL (city) Broward County	2,856	2.43
Opa-locka, FL (city) Miami-Dade County	364	2.39
Haverstraw, NY (town) Rockland County	793	2.35
Carol City, FL (cdp) Miami-Dade County	1,357	2.28
Milton, MA (cdp) Norfolk County	574	2.20
Monsey, NY (cdp) Rockland County	317	2.16
Orangetown, NY (town) Rockland County	1,026	2.15
Union, NJ (cdp) Union County	1,156	2.12
Winter Haven, FL (city) Polk County	550	2.12
Greenlawn, NY (cdp) Suffolk County	282	2.12
Medford, MA (city) Middlesex County	1,112	1.99
Yeehaw Junction, FL (cdp) Osceola County	441	1.99
Clarkstown, NY (town) Rockland County	1,586	1.93
Riviera Beach, FL (city) Palm Beach County	582	1.91
Orlando, FL (city) Orange County	3,514	1.89
Pembroke Pines, FL (city) Broward County	2,583	1.88
Rahway, NJ (city) Union County	492	1.86
North Amityville, NY (cdp) Suffolk County	303	1.83
The Hammocks, FL (cdp) Miami-Dade County	861	1.82
Norwalk, CT (city) Fairfield County	1,499	1.81
Hempstead, NY (town) Nassau County	13,599	1.80
University, FL (cdp) Hillsborough County	545	1.78
Country Walk, FL (cdp) Miami-Dade County	190	1.78
Dania Beach, FL (city) Broward County	341	1.69
Waltham, MA (city) Middlesex County	977	1.65
Valley Stream, NY (village) Nassau County	582	1.60
Cutler Ridge, FL (cdp) Miami-Dade County	384	1.56
Hollywood, FL (city) Broward County	2,140	1.54
North Bay Shore, NY (cdp) Suffolk County	232	1.54
Gladeview, FL (cdp) Miami-Dade County	221	1.53
Ocean, NJ (township) Monmouth County	406	1.51
New York, NY (city) New York City	118,769	1.48
Richmond West, FL (cdp) Miami-Dade County	415	1.48
Neptune, NJ (township) Monmouth County	409	1.48
The Crossings, FL (cdp) Miami-Dade County	348	1.48
Central Islip, NY (cdp) Suffolk County	470	1.47
Tamarac, FL (city) Broward County	809	1.44
Poinciana, FL (cdp) Osceola County	195	1.44
Bridgeport, CT (city) Fairfield County	1,980	1.42
Elwood, NY (cdp) Suffolk County	145	1.34
Salisbury, MD (city) Wicomico County	319	1.32
Panthersville, GA (cdp) De Kalb County	154	1.32
Burlington, MA (cdp) Middlesex County	299	1.31
Freeport, NY (village) Nassau County	568	1.30
Kendall, FL (cdp) Miami-Dade County	974	1.29
New Rochelle, NY (city) Westchester County	933	1.29
Huntington Station, NY (cdp) Suffolk County	384	1.28
Boca Raton, FL (city) Palm Beach County	928	1.23
Takoma Park, MD (city) Montgomery County	209	1.22
Mount Vernon, NY (city) Westchester County	825	1.21
Montclair, NJ (cdp) Essex County	468	1.20
South Miami Heights, FL (cdp) Miami-Dade County	403	1.20
Calverton, MD (cdp) Montgomery County	151	1.20
Palm River-Clair Mel, FL (cdp) Hillsborough County	208	1.18
Evanston, IL (city) Cook County	856	1.15
Kendale Lakes, FL (cdp) Miami-Dade County	644	1.13
Meadow Woods, FL (cdp) Orange County	130	1.13
Wellington, FL (village) Palm Beach County	422	1.11
Naples, FL (city) Collier County	234	1.11
Greenacres, FL (city) Palm Beach County	299	1.10
Providence, RI (city) Providence County	1,878	1.08
Norwich, CT (city) New London County	389	1.08
Chillum, MD (cdp) Prince George's County	370	1.08
West Hempstead, NY (cdp) Nassau County	202	1.08
Hamilton, NJ (township) Mercer County	914	1.05
Englewood, NJ (city) Bergen County	274	1.05
Lynn, MA (city) Essex County	926	1.04
Stoughton, MA (town) Norfolk County	281	1.04
Langley Park, MD (cdp) Prince George's County	164	1.01
Silver Spring, MD (cdp) Montgomery County	766	1.00
Newark, NJ (city) Essex County	2,634	0.96
Lanham-Seabrook, MD (cdp) Prince George's County	173	0.96
East Riverdale, MD (cdp) Prince George's County	148	0.96

Notes: (cdp) census designated place; Refer to the Explanation of Data in the front of the book for more detailed information.

West Indian: Jamaican, excluding Hispanic

Top 150 Places Sorted by Number

(Based on all places, regardless of population)

Place	Number	%
New York, NY (city) New York City	212,972	2.66
Hempstead, NY (town) Nassau County	15,339	2.03
Miramar, FL (city) Broward County	11,263	15.50
Lauderhill, FL (city) Broward County	9,723	16.98
Philadelphia, PA (city) Philadelphia County	9,249	0.61
Mount Vernon, NY (city) Westchester County	8,419	12.31
Hartford, CT (city) Hartford County	8,293	6.82
Boston, MA (city) Suffolk County	8,226	1.40
Pembroke Pines, FL (city) Broward County	7,648	5.58
Sunrise, FL (city) Broward County	6,888	8.04
Bridgeport, CT (city) Fairfield County	5,924	4.25
Lauderdale Lakes, FL (city) Broward County	5,646	17.91
Los Angeles, CA (city) Los Angeles County	5,537	0.15
Norland, FL (cdp) Miami-Dade County	4,849	21.06
Chicago, IL (city) Cook County	4,778	0.16
Paterson, NJ (city) Passaic County	4,776	3.20
Washington, DC (city) District of Columbia	4,184	0.73
Yonkers, NY (city) Westchester County	3,822	1.95
North Lauderdale, FL (city) Broward County	3,688	11.41
Plantation, FL (city) Broward County	3,657	4.39
East Orange, NJ (city) Essex County	3,368	4.82
Carol City, FL (cdp) Miami-Dade County	3,111	5.23
Hollywood, FL (city) Broward County	3,105	2.23
Hempstead, NY (village) Nassau County	3,064	5.42
Coral Springs, FL (city) Broward County	3,019	2.57
Baltimore, MD (independent city) Baltimore city	2,979	0.46
Fort Lauderdale, FL (city) Broward County	2,726	1.79
Bloomfield, CT (town) Hartford County	2,588	13.21
Irvington, NJ (cdp) Essex County	2,585	4.26
Rochester, NY (city) Monroe County	2,517	1.15
Babylon, NY (town) Suffolk County	2,491	1.18
Uniondale, NY (cdp) Nassau County	2,430	10.56
Tamarac, FL (city) Broward County	2,398	4.28
Islip, NY (town) Suffolk County	2,379	0.74
Palmetto Estates, FL (cdp) Miami-Dade County	2,359	17.25
Houston, TX (city) Harris County	2,344	0.12
Springfield, MA (city) Hampden County	2,314	1.52
Stamford, CT (city) Fairfield County	2,289	1.96
Detroit, MI (city) Wayne County	2,260	0.24
North Miami Beach, FL (city) Miami-Dade County	2,178	5.35
West Palm Beach, FL (city) Palm Beach County	2,134	2.62
Miami, FL (city) Miami-Dade County	2,080	0.57
Jacksonville, FL (special city) Duval County	2,010	0.27
Newark, NJ (city) Essex County	2,008	0.73
Elmont, NY (cdp) Nassau County	1,962	6.01
Orlando, FL (city) Orange County	1,955	1.05
Evanston, IL (city) Cook County	1,937	2.61
South Miami Heights, FL (cdp) Miami-Dade County	1,909	5.69
Scott Lake, FL (cdp) Miami-Dade County	1,870	13.00
North Miami, FL (city) Miami-Dade County	1,837	3.06
Palm Bay, FL (city) Brevard County	1,756	2.21
Golden Glades, FL (cdp) Miami-Dade County	1,739	5.40
Margate, FL (city) Broward County	1,734	3.22
Ramapo, NY (town) Rockland County	1,684	1.55
Tampa, FL (city) Hillsborough County	1,680	0.55
New Rochelle, NY (city) Westchester County	1,657	2.30
Saint Petersburg, FL (city) Pinellas County	1,649	0.67
Brookhaven, NY (town) Suffolk County	1,649	0.37
Melrose Park, FL (cdp) Broward County	1,596	22.52
New Haven, CT (city) New Haven County	1,591	1.29
Port Saint Lucie, FL (city) Saint Lucie County	1,584	1.78
Chillum, MD (cdp) Prince George's County	1,564	4.58
North Hempstead, NY (town) Nassau County	1,534	0.69
Poughkeepsie, NY (city) Dutchess County	1,524	5.10
Pine Hills, FL (cdp) Orange County	1,472	3.51
Plainfield, NJ (city) Union County	1,450	3.03
Windsor, CT (town) Hartford County	1,442	5.11
Greenburgh, NY (town) Westchester County	1,434	1.65
Andover, FL (cdp) Miami-Dade County	1,433	16.55
The Hammocks, FL (cdp) Miami-Dade County	1,410	2.97
East Hartford, CT (cdp) Hartford County	1,360	2.74
Norwalk, CT (city) Fairfield County	1,358	1.64
Teaneck, NJ (cdp) Bergen County	1,351	3.44
Freeport, NY (village) Nassau County	1,327	3.03
North Valley Stream, NY (cdp) Nassau County	1,319	8.35
Englewood, NJ (city) Bergen County	1,307	4.99
Franklin, NJ (township) Somerset County	1,295	2.54
Orange, NJ (cdp) Essex County	1,238	3.77
Redan, GA (cdp) De Kalb County	1,231	3.64
Hackensack, NJ (city) Bergen County	1,226	2.87
Cleveland, OH (city) Cuyahoga County	1,194	0.25
Atlanta, GA (city) Fulton County	1,189	0.29
Roosevelt, NY (cdp) Nassau County	1,187	7.49
Silver Spring, MD (cdp) Montgomery County	1,185	1.54
Jersey City, NJ (city) Hudson County	1,154	0.48
Milwaukee, WI (city) Milwaukee County	1,152	0.19
Trenton, NJ (city) Mercer County	1,134	1.33
Waterbury, CT (city) New Haven County	1,122	1.05
Charlotte, NC (city) Mecklenburg County	1,116	0.21
Albany, NY (city) Albany County	1,064	1.11
Virginia Beach, VA (independent city) Virginia Beach city	1,062	0.25
Columbus, OH (city) Franklin County	1,058	0.15
Tallahassee, FL (city) Leon County	1,045	0.69
Baldwin, NY (cdp) Nassau County	1,005	4.28
Ives Estates, FL (cdp) Miami-Dade County	1,000	5.74
San Diego, CA (city) San Diego County	981	0.08
Montclair, NJ (cdp) Essex County	978	2.50
Spring Valley, NY (village) Rockland County	974	3.84
North Amityville, NY (cdp) Suffolk County	971	5.88
Royal Palm Beach, FL (village) Palm Beach County	970	4.50
White Plains, NY (city) Westchester County	963	1.81
Richmond West, FL (cdp) Miami-Dade County	947	3.38
Weston, FL (city) Broward County	944	1.92
Cambridge, MA (city) Middlesex County	939	0.93
Norfolk, VA (independent city) Norfolk city	933	0.40
Somerset, NJ (cdp) Somerset County	910	3.95
Kendall, FL (cdp) Miami-Dade County	894	1.19
Wheaton-Glenmont, MD (cdp) Montgomery County	889	1.54
Central Islip, NY (cdp) Suffolk County	874	2.74
Dallas, TX (city) Dallas County	865	0.07
Boynton Beach, FL (city) Palm Beach County	856	1.43
Coconut Creek, FL (city) Broward County	834	1.92
Port Charlotte, FL (cdp) Charlotte County	820	1.76
Aspen Hill, MD (cdp) Montgomery County	802	1.60
Oakland, CA (city) Alameda County	795	0.20
Poughkeepsie, NY (town) Dutchess County	746	1.75
Country Club, FL (cdp) Miami-Dade County	745	2.05
Oakland Park, FL (city) Broward County	743	2.38
Columbia, MD (cdp) Howard County	741	0.84
New Orleans, LA (city) Orleans Parish	741	0.15
San Francisco, CA (city) San Francisco County	738	0.10
Clarkstown, NY (town) Rockland County	737	0.90
Maplewood, NJ (cdp) Essex County	735	3.08
Oyster Bay, NY (town) Nassau County	731	0.25
Syracuse, NY (city) Onondaga County	729	0.49
Indianapolis, IN (special city) Marion County	711	0.09
Buffalo, NY (city) Erie County	710	0.24
Davie, FL (town) Broward County	696	0.92
Phoenix, AZ (city) Maricopa County	696	0.05
Minneapolis, MN (city) Hennepin County	673	0.18
Lakeview, NY (cdp) Nassau County	667	11.90
Westview, FL (cdp) Miami-Dade County	666	6.94
Blue Hills, CT (cdp) Hartford County	658	21.34
Langley Park, MD (cdp) Prince George's County	654	4.03
Deerfield Beach, FL (city) Broward County	652	1.01
Silver Springs Shores, FL (cdp) Marion County	649	9.90
Riviera Beach, FL (city) Palm Beach County	646	2.12
West Orange, NJ (cdp) Essex County	646	1.44
Fort Worth, TX (city) Tarrant County	641	0.12
Cutler Ridge, FL (cdp) Miami-Dade County	634	2.57
Brandon, FL (cdp) Hillsborough County	630	0.81
Inglewood, CA (city) Los Angeles County	630	0.56
Peekskill, NY (city) Westchester County	614	2.74
Willingboro, NJ (township) Burlington County	611	1.85
Seattle, WA (city) King County	598	0.11
New Cassel, NY (cdp) Nassau County	589	4.43
Newport News, VA (independent city) Newport News city	589	0.33
Hampton, VA (independent city) Hampton city	584	0.40
Piscataway, NJ (township) Middlesex County	577	1.14
Pinewood, FL (cdp) Miami-Dade County	576	3.42

Notes: (cdp) census designated place; Refer to the Explanation of Data in the front of the book for more detailed information.

West Indian: Jamaican, excluding Hispanic

Top 150 Places Sorted by Percent

(Based on all places, regardless of population)

Place	Number	%
Melrose Park, FL (cdp) Broward County	1,596	22.52
Blue Hills, CT (cdp) Hartford County	658	21.34
Norland, FL (cdp) Miami-Dade County	4,849	21.06
Lauderdale Lakes, FL (city) Broward County	5,646	17.91
Palmetto Estates, FL (cdp) Miami-Dade County	2,359	17.25
Lauderhill, FL (city) Broward County	9,723	16.98
Andover, FL (cdp) Miami-Dade County	1,433	16.55
South Floral Park, NY (village) Nassau County	259	16.41
Miramar, FL (city) Broward County	11,263	15.50
Bloomfield, CT (town) Hartford County	2,588	13.21
Scott Lake, FL (cdp) Miami-Dade County	1,870	13.00
Utopia, FL (cdp) Broward County	91	12.55
Mount Vernon, NY (city) Westchester County	8,419	12.31
Lakeview, NY (cdp) Nassau County	667	11.90
Millward, MN (township) Aitkin County	7	11.67
North Lauderdale, FL (city) Broward County	3,688	11.41
Uniondale, NY (cdp) Nassau County	2,430	10.56
Silver Springs Shores, FL (cdp) Marion County	649	9.90
Rock Island, FL (cdp) Broward County	272	8.65
Fort Devens, MA (cdp) Worcester County	84	8.41
North Valley Stream, NY (cdp) Nassau County	1,319	8.35
Washington Park, FL (cdp) Broward County	103	8.27
El Portal, FL (village) Miami-Dade County	204	8.10
Sunrise, FL (city) Broward County	6,888	8.04
Pembroke Park, FL (town) Broward County	502	7.92
Roosevelt, NY (cdp) Nassau County	1,187	7.49
Saint George, FL (cdp) Broward County	178	7.39
Fairview, NY (cdp) Westchester County	217	7.26
Three Lakes, FL (cdp) Miami-Dade County	499	7.15
Stacey Street, FL (cdp) Palm Beach County	59	7.11
East Garden City, NY (cdp) Nassau County	70	7.04
Westview, FL (cdp) Miami-Dade County	666	6.94
Hartford, CT (city) Hartford County	8,293	6.82
Harlem, FL (cdp) Hendry County	186	6.57
Miami Gardens, FL (cdp) Broward County	167	6.47
Opa-locka North, FL (cdp) Miami-Dade County	397	6.38
Lake Lucerne, FL (cdp) Miami-Dade County	567	6.20
Tangelo Park, FL (cdp) Orange County	143	6.17
Elmont, NY (cdp) Nassau County	1,962	6.01
East Perrine, FL (cdp) Miami-Dade County	404	5.89
North Amityville, NY (cdp) Suffolk County	971	5.88
Ives Estates, FL (cdp) Miami-Dade County	1,000	5.74
Lake Park, FL (town) Palm Beach County	483	5.73
South Miami Heights, FL (cdp) Miami-Dade County	1,909	5.69
Gordon Heights, NY (cdp) Suffolk County	173	5.59
Pembroke Pines, FL (city) Broward County	7,648	5.58
Hillcrest, NY (cdp) Rockland County	387	5.45
Hempstead, NY (village) Nassau County	3,064	5.42
Golden Glades, FL (cdp) Miami-Dade County	1,739	5.40
North Miami Beach, FL (city) Miami-Dade County	2,178	5.35
Wheatley Heights, NY (cdp) Suffolk County	268	5.32
Carol City, FL (cdp) Miami-Dade County	3,111	5.23
Broadview-Pompano Park, FL (cdp) Broward County	264	5.15
Windsor, CT (town) Hartford County	1,442	5.11
Poughkeepsie, NY (city) Dutchess County	1,524	5.10
Canal Point, FL (cdp) Palm Beach County	28	5.09
Englewood, NJ (city) Bergen County	1,307	4.99
Belle Glade Camp, FL (cdp) Palm Beach County	63	4.98
East Orange, NJ (city) Essex County	3,368	4.82
West Perrine, FL (cdp) Miami-Dade County	410	4.77
Country Walk, FL (cdp) Miami-Dade County	498	4.67
Chillum, MD (cdp) Prince George's County	1,564	4.58
Royal Palm Beach, FL (village) Palm Beach County	970	4.50
New Cassel, NY (cdp) Nassau County	589	4.43
Plantation, FL (city) Broward County	3,657	4.39
Bonnie Lock-Woodsetter North, FL (cdp) Broward County	186	4.32
Boulevard Gardens, FL (cdp) Broward County	58	4.31
Tamarac, FL (city) Broward County	2,398	4.28
Baldwin, NY (cdp) Nassau County	1,005	4.28
Irvington, NJ (cdp) Essex County	2,585	4.26
Bridgeport, CT (city) Fairfield County	5,924	4.25
Langley Park, MD (cdp) Prince George's County	654	4.03
Poinciana, FL (cdp) Osceola County	545	4.01
Somerset, NJ (cdp) Somerset County	910	3.95
Westbury, NY (village) Nassau County	562	3.94

Place	Number	%
Chambers Estates, FL (cdp) Broward County	139	3.90
New Carrollton, MD (city) Prince George's County	496	3.86
Mangonia Park, FL (town) Palm Beach County	50	3.86
Spring Valley, NY (village) Rockland County	974	3.84
Schaghticoke, NY (village) Rensselaer County	26	3.80
Orange, NJ (cdp) Essex County	1,238	3.77
Inwood, NY (cdp) Nassau County	350	3.75
Lake Arbor, MD (cdp) Prince George's County	318	3.73
Cottage City, MD (town) Prince George's County	42	3.70
Goulds, FL (cdp) Miami-Dade County	281	3.69
Lake Forest, FL (cdp) Broward County	183	3.69
Port La Belle, FL (cdp) Hendry County	119	3.68
Redan, GA (cdp) De Kalb County	1,231	3.64
Lakes by the Bay, FL (cdp) Miami-Dade County	324	3.60
Juno Ridge, FL (cdp) Palm Beach County	27	3.59
Shoreham, NY (village) Suffolk County	15	3.59
Adelphi, MD (cdp) Prince George's County	533	3.55
Naranja, FL (cdp) Miami-Dade County	148	3.52
Pine Hills, FL (cdp) Orange County	1,472	3.51
Stone Mountain, GA (city) De Kalb County	237	3.47
Mount Rainier, MD (city) Prince George's County	292	3.45
Teaneck, NJ (cdp) Bergen County	1,351	3.44
Pinewood, FL (cdp) Miami-Dade County	576	3.42
Estates of Fort Lauderdale, FL (cdp) Broward County	63	3.41
Haverhill, FL (town) Palm Beach County	52	3.40
Richmond West, FL (cdp) Miami-Dade County	947	3.38
Broadview Park, FL (cdp) Broward County	225	3.31
Wedgefield, FL (cdp) Orange County	91	3.23
Lake Harbor, FL (cdp) Palm Beach County	3	3.23
Margate, FL (city) Broward County	1,734	3.22
Paterson, NJ (city) Passaic County	4,776	3.20
South Hempstead, NY (cdp) Nassau County	102	3.20
Eldorado, MD (town) Dorchester County	2	3.17
Arlington, NY (cdp) Dutchess County	391	3.14
Golden Lakes, FL (cdp) Palm Beach County	209	3.12
Prospect Park, NJ (borough) Passaic County	180	3.11
Maplewood, NJ (cdp) Essex County	735	3.08
North Miami, FL (city) Miami-Dade County	1,837	3.06
Barton Creek, TX (cdp) Travis County	48	3.05
Plainfield, NJ (city) Union County	1,450	3.03
Freeport, NY (village) Nassau County	1,327	3.03
Brentwood, MD (town) Prince George's County	86	3.00
Biscayne Park, FL (village) Miami-Dade County	99	2.99
Greenvale, NY (cdp) Nassau County	66	2.99
De Land Southwest, FL (cdp) Volusia County	34	2.98
The Hammocks, FL (cdp) Miami-Dade County	1,410	2.97
Hillburn, NY (village) Rockland County	23	2.93
New Hempstead, NY (village) Rockland County	138	2.88
Hackensack, NJ (city) Bergen County	1,226	2.87
South Miami, FL (city) Miami-Dade County	312	2.85
Richmond Heights, FL (cdp) Miami-Dade County	240	2.85
Sunshine Acres, FL (cdp) Broward County	30	2.85
Broward Estates, FL (cdp) Broward County	100	2.84
Lorenz Park, NY (cdp) Columbia County	58	2.83
Victory Gardens, NJ (borough) Morris County	43	2.78
East Hartford, CT (cdp) Hartford County	1,360	2.74
Central Islip, NY (cdp) Suffolk County	874	2.74
Peekskill, NY (city) Westchester County	614	2.74
New York, NY (city) New York City	212,972	2.66
Asbury Park, NJ (city) Monmouth County	449	2.65
Roosevelt Gardens, FL (cdp) Broward County	49	2.63
West Palm Beach, FL (city) Palm Beach County	2,134	2.62
Evanston, IL (city) Cook County	1,937	2.61
Coral Springs, FL (city) Broward County	3,019	2.57
Cutler Ridge, FL (cdp) Miami-Dade County	634	2.57
Opa-locka, FL (city) Miami-Dade County	389	2.55
Franklin, NJ (township) Somerset County	1,295	2.54
Belle Glade, FL (city) Palm Beach County	381	2.54
Yeadon, PA (borough) Delaware County	297	2.52
Burtonsville, MD (cdp) Montgomery County	184	2.52
Montclair, NJ (cdp) Essex County	978	2.50
Crown Heights, NY (cdp) Dutchess County	74	2.47
Colwyn, PA (borough) Delaware County	60	2.45
Pahokee, FL (city) Palm Beach County	142	2.44
Hartsdale, NY (cdp) Westchester County	238	2.42

Notes: (cdp) census designated place; Refer to the Explanation of Data in the front of the book for more detailed information.

West Indian: Jamaican, excluding Hispanic

Top 150 Places Sorted by Percent

(Based on places with populations of 10,000 or more)

Place	Number	%
Norland, FL (cdp) Miami-Dade County	4,849	21.06
Lauderdale Lakes, FL (city) Broward County	5,646	17.91
Palmetto Estates, FL (cdp) Miami-Dade County	2,359	17.25
Lauderhill, FL (city) Broward County	9,723	16.98
Miramar, FL (city) Broward County	11,263	15.50
Bloomfield, CT (town) Hartford County	2,588	13.21
Scott Lake, FL (cdp) Miami-Dade County	1,870	13.00
Mount Vernon, NY (city) Westchester County	8,419	12.31
North Lauderdale, FL (city) Broward County	3,688	11.41
Uniondale, NY (cdp) Nassau County	2,430	10.56
North Valley Stream, NY (cdp) Nassau County	1,319	8.35
Sunrise, FL (city) Broward County	6,888	8.04
Roosevelt, NY (cdp) Nassau County	1,187	7.49
Hartford, CT (city) Hartford County	8,293	6.82
Elmont, NY (cdp) Nassau County	1,962	6.01
North Amityville, NY (cdp) Suffolk County	971	5.88
Ives Estates, FL (cdp) Miami-Dade County	1,000	5.74
South Miami Heights, FL (cdp) Miami-Dade County	1,909	5.69
Pembroke Pines, FL (city) Broward County	7,648	5.58
Hempstead, NY (village) Nassau County	3,064	5.42
Golden Glades, FL (cdp) Miami-Dade County	1,739	5.40
North Miami Beach, FL (city) Miami-Dade County	2,178	5.35
Carol City, FL (cdp) Miami-Dade County	3,111	5.23
Windsor, CT (town) Hartford County	1,442	5.11
Poughkeepsie, NY (city) Dutchess County	1,524	5.10
Englewood, NJ (city) Bergen County	1,307	4.99
East Orange, NJ (city) Essex County	3,368	4.82
Country Walk, FL (cdp) Miami-Dade County	498	4.67
Chillum, MD (cdp) Prince George's County	1,564	4.58
Royal Palm Beach, FL (village) Palm Beach County	970	4.50
New Cassel, NY (cdp) Nassau County	589	4.43
Plantation, FL (city) Broward County	3,657	4.39
Tamarac, FL (city) Broward County	2,398	4.28
Baldwin, NY (cdp) Nassau County	1,005	4.28
Irvington, NJ (cdp) Essex County	2,585	4.26
Bridgeport, CT (city) Fairfield County	5,924	4.25
Langley Park, MD (cdp) Prince George's County	654	4.03
Poinciana, FL (cdp) Osceola County	545	4.01
Somerset, NJ (cdp) Somerset County	910	3.95
Westbury, NY (village) Nassau County	562	3.94
New Carrollton, MD (city) Prince George's County	496	3.86
Spring Valley, NY (village) Rockland County	974	3.84
Orange, NJ (cdp) Essex County	1,238	3.77
Redan, GA (cdp) De Kalb County	1,231	3.64
Adelphi, MD (cdp) Prince George's County	533	3.55
Pine Hills, FL (cdp) Orange County	1,472	3.51
Teaneck, NJ (cdp) Bergen County	1,351	3.44
Pinewood, FL (cdp) Miami-Dade County	576	3.42
Richmond West, FL (cdp) Miami-Dade County	947	3.38
Margate, FL (city) Broward County	1,734	3.22
Paterson, NJ (city) Passaic County	4,776	3.20
Arlington, NY (cdp) Dutchess County	391	3.14
Maplewood, NJ (cdp) Essex County	735	3.08
North Miami, FL (city) Miami-Dade County	1,837	3.06
Plainfield, NJ (city) Union County	1,450	3.03
Freeport, NY (village) Nassau County	1,327	3.03
The Hammocks, FL (cdp) Miami-Dade County	1,410	2.97
Hackensack, NJ (city) Bergen County	1,226	2.87
South Miami, FL (city) Miami-Dade County	312	2.85
East Hartford, CT (cdp) Hartford County	1,360	2.74
Central Islip, NY (cdp) Suffolk County	874	2.74
Peekskill, NY (city) Westchester County	614	2.74
New York, NY (city) New York City	212,972	2.66
Asbury Park, NJ (city) Monmouth County	449	2.65
West Palm Beach, FL (city) Palm Beach County	2,134	2.62
Evanston, IL (city) Cook County	1,937	2.61
Coral Springs, FL (city) Broward County	3,019	2.57
Cutler Ridge, FL (cdp) Miami-Dade County	634	2.57
Opa-locka, FL (city) Miami-Dade County	389	2.55
Franklin, NJ (township) Somerset County	1,295	2.54
Belle Glade, FL (city) Palm Beach County	381	2.54
Yeadon, PA (borough) Delaware County	297	2.52
Montclair, NJ (cdp) Essex County	978	2.50
Greenbelt, MD (city) Prince George's County	514	2.40
Oakland Park, FL (city) Broward County	743	2.38
Hyattsville, MD (city) Prince George's County	352	2.37
Miami Shores, FL (village) Miami-Dade County	242	2.32
New Rochelle, NY (city) Westchester County	1,657	2.30
Beltsville, MD (cdp) Prince George's County	362	2.30
South Orange, NJ (cdp) Essex County	383	2.26
Hollywood, FL (city) Broward County	3,105	2.23
Palm Bay, FL (city) Brevard County	1,756	2.21
Nanuet, NY (cdp) Rockland County	357	2.14
Riviera Beach, FL (city) Palm Beach County	646	2.12
Wyandanch, NY (cdp) Suffolk County	223	2.11
Milford Mill, MD (cdp) Baltimore County	549	2.07
East Massapequa, NY (cdp) Nassau County	403	2.06
Country Club, FL (cdp) Miami-Dade County	745	2.05
Hempstead, NY (town) Nassau County	15,339	2.03
Stamford, CT (city) Fairfield County	2,289	1.96
Yonkers, NY (city) Westchester County	3,822	1.95
Weston, FL (city) Broward County	944	1.92
Coconut Creek, FL (city) Broward County	834	1.92
Lanham-Seabrook, MD (cdp) Prince George's County	340	1.88
Willingboro, NJ (township) Burlington County	611	1.85
Pleasantville, NJ (city) Atlantic County	352	1.84
White Plains, NY (city) Westchester County	963	1.81
Roselle, NJ (borough) Union County	386	1.81
Fort Lauderdale, FL (city) Broward County	2,726	1.79
Neptune, NJ (township) Monmouth County	497	1.79
Port Saint Lucie, FL (city) Saint Lucie County	1,584	1.78
Port Charlotte, FL (cdp) Charlotte County	820	1.76
Poughkeepsie, NY (town) Dutchess County	746	1.75
West Little River, FL (cdp) Miami-Dade County	565	1.75
White Oak, MD (cdp) Montgomery County	366	1.75
Newburgh, NY (city) Orange County	486	1.72
Ossining, NY (village) Westchester County	412	1.72
Yeehaw Junction, FL (cdp) Osceola County	378	1.71
Calverton, MD (cdp) Montgomery County	214	1.70
Princeton, FL (cdp) Miami-Dade County	171	1.69
Lockhart, FL (cdp) Orange County	209	1.67
Randolph, MA (cdp) Norfolk County	515	1.66
Lochearn, MD (cdp) Baltimore County	419	1.66
Greenburgh, NY (town) Westchester County	1,434	1.65
Norwalk, CT (city) Fairfield County	1,358	1.64
Lehigh Acres, FL (cdp) Lee County	545	1.64
Fairland, MD (cdp) Montgomery County	353	1.64
Aspen Hill, MD (cdp) Montgomery County	802	1.60
Apopka, FL (city) Orange County	417	1.60
The Crossings, FL (cdp) Miami-Dade County	369	1.57
Ramapo, NY (town) Rockland County	1,684	1.55
Takoma Park, MD (city) Montgomery County	267	1.55
Silver Spring, MD (cdp) Montgomery County	1,185	1.54
Wheaton-Glenmont, MD (cdp) Montgomery County	889	1.54
Morristown, NJ (town) Morris County	283	1.53
Springfield, MA (city) Hampden County	2,314	1.52
North Laurel, MD (cdp) Howard County	314	1.52
Glenn Dale, MD (cdp) Prince George's County	192	1.50
Valley Stream, NY (village) Nassau County	542	1.49
Deer Park, NY (cdp) Suffolk County	421	1.49
Palm Coast, FL (city) Flagler County	492	1.47
North Port, FL (city) Sarasota County	329	1.45
West Orange, NJ (cdp) Essex County	646	1.44
Randallstown, MD (cdp) Baltimore County	447	1.44
Boynton Beach, FL (city) Palm Beach County	856	1.43
Dania Beach, FL (city) Broward County	285	1.42
Lansdowne, PA (borough) Delaware County	155	1.41
Boston, MA (city) Suffolk County	8,226	1.40
Bay Shore, NY (cdp) Suffolk County	335	1.40
Middletown, NY (city) Orange County	346	1.37
Hallandale, FL (city) Broward County	464	1.34
Trenton, NJ (city) Mercer County	1,134	1.33
Coram, NY (cdp) Suffolk County	466	1.33
Milton, MA (cdp) Norfolk County	346	1.33
View Park-Windsor Hills, CA (cdp) Los Angeles County	146	1.33
Oak Ridge, FL (cdp) Orange County	296	1.32
Darby, PA (borough) Delaware County	136	1.32
East Riverdale, MD (cdp) Prince George's County	201	1.31
New Haven, CT (city) New Haven County	1,591	1.29
Palm Springs, FL (village) Palm Beach County	152	1.29

Notes: (cdp) census designated place; Refer to the Explanation of Data in the front of the book for more detailed information.

West Indian: Trinidadian and Tobagonian, excluding Hispanic

Top 150 Places Sorted by Number

(Based on all places, regardless of population)

Place	Number	%
New York, NY (city) New York City	75,584	0.94
Boston, MA (city) Suffolk County	3,309	0.56
Hempstead, NY (town) Nassau County	2,770	0.37
Baltimore, MD (independent city) Baltimore city	1,804	0.28
Philadelphia, PA (city) Philadelphia County	1,738	0.11
Washington, DC (city) District of Columbia	1,249	0.22
Houston, TX (city) Harris County	1,097	0.06
Jersey City, NJ (city) Hudson County	1,031	0.43
Miramar, FL (city) Broward County	897	1.23
Los Angeles, CA (city) Los Angeles County	800	0.02
Brookhaven, NY (town) Suffolk County	746	0.17
Islip, NY (town) Suffolk County	733	0.23
Hollywood, FL (city) Broward County	727	0.52
Sunrise, FL (city) Broward County	694	0.81
Orange, NJ (cdp) Essex County	630	1.92
Chillum, MD (cdp) Prince George's County	595	1.74
Babylon, NY (town) Suffolk County	595	0.28
Pembroke Pines, FL (city) Broward County	592	0.43
Newark, NJ (city) Essex County	585	0.21
Hempstead, NY (village) Nassau County	583	1.03
East Orange, NJ (city) Essex County	518	0.74
Irvington, NJ (cdp) Essex County	491	0.81
Lauderhill, FL (city) Broward County	480	0.84
Plantation, FL (city) Broward County	461	0.55
Silver Spring, MD (cdp) Montgomery County	455	0.59
Coral Springs, FL (city) Broward County	433	0.37
Palmetto Estates, FL (cdp) Miami-Dade County	413	3.02
Chicago, IL (city) Cook County	407	0.01
Freeport, NY (village) Nassau County	380	0.87
North Hempstead, NY (town) Nassau County	367	0.16
Yonkers, NY (city) Westchester County	359	0.18
Tampa, FL (city) Hillsborough County	359	0.12
North Lauderdale, FL (city) Broward County	357	1.10
Palm Bay, FL (city) Brevard County	356	0.45
Margate, FL (city) Broward County	333	0.62
Elmont, NY (cdp) Nassau County	329	1.01
Long Beach, CA (city) Los Angeles County	329	0.07
Norland, FL (cdp) Miami-Dade County	328	1.42
Central Islip, NY (cdp) Suffolk County	326	1.02
Jacksonville, FL (special city) Duval County	297	0.04
Edison, NJ (cdp) Middlesex County	294	0.30
Carol City, FL (cdp) Miami-Dade County	282	0.47
Saint Petersburg, FL (city) Pinellas County	273	0.11
Roosevelt, NY (cdp) Nassau County	272	1.72
Tamarac, FL (city) Broward County	271	0.48
North Miami, FL (city) Miami-Dade County	267	0.44
Baytown, TX (city) Harris County	267	0.40
Mount Vernon, NY (city) Westchester County	266	0.39
Hartford, CT (city) Hartford County	255	0.21
Woodbridge, NJ (township) Middlesex County	252	0.26
Elizabeth, NJ (city) Union County	252	0.21
Union, NJ (cdp) Union County	250	0.46
New Haven, CT (city) New Haven County	248	0.20
Fairland, MD (cdp) Montgomery County	244	1.13
Uniondale, NY (cdp) Nassau County	242	1.05
San Diego, CA (city) San Diego County	239	0.02
Virginia Beach, VA (independent city) Virginia Beach city	238	0.06
Hampton, VA (independent city) Hampton city	236	0.16
Orlando, FL (city) Orange County	236	0.13
South Laurel, MD (cdp) Prince George's County	235	1.13
Brentwood, NY (cdp) Suffolk County	235	0.44
Maplewood, NJ (cdp) Essex County	234	0.98
Fort Lauderdale, FL (city) Broward County	233	0.15
Wheaton-Glenmont, MD (cdp) Montgomery County	232	0.40
Scotch Plains, NJ (cdp) Union County	231	1.02
South Miami Heights, FL (cdp) Miami-Dade County	229	0.68
Miami, FL (city) Miami-Dade County	229	0.06
Coconut Creek, FL (city) Broward County	226	0.52
Phoenix, AZ (city) Maricopa County	222	0.02
Valley Stream, NY (village) Nassau County	221	0.61
Plainfield, NJ (city) Union County	221	0.46
Lauderdale Lakes, FL (city) Broward County	217	0.69
North Miami Beach, FL (city) Miami-Dade County	215	0.53
Charlotte, NC (city) Mecklenburg County	214	0.04
Detroit, MI (city) Wayne County	213	0.02
Langley Park, MD (cdp) Prince George's County	208	1.28
Bloomfield, CT (town) Hartford County	208	1.06
West Perrine, FL (cdp) Miami-Dade County	207	2.41
North Amityville, NY (cdp) Suffolk County	207	1.25
Kendall, FL (cdp) Miami-Dade County	205	0.27
Cambridge, MA (city) Middlesex County	204	0.20
Atlanta, GA (city) Fulton County	199	0.05
San Antonio, TX (city) Bexar County	199	0.02
Hackensack, NJ (city) Bergen County	197	0.46
Norfolk, VA (independent city) Norfolk city	191	0.08
Country Walk, FL (cdp) Miami-Dade County	190	1.78
North Valley Stream, NY (cdp) Nassau County	188	1.19
Teaneck, NJ (cdp) Bergen County	186	0.47
Cleveland, OH (city) Cuyahoga County	184	0.04
Richmond, VA (independent city) Richmond city	183	0.09
Mount Rainier, MD (city) Prince George's County	182	2.15
Bridgeport, CT (city) Fairfield County	180	0.13
Richmond West, FL (cdp) Miami-Dade County	177	0.63
Beltsville, MD (cdp) Prince George's County	176	1.12
Coolbaugh, PA (township) Monroe County	175	1.15
Nashville-Davidson, TN (special city) Davidson County	175	0.03
Apopka, FL (city) Orange County	174	0.67
Takoma Park, MD (city) Montgomery County	171	1.00
Stamford, CT (city) Fairfield County	171	0.15
Randallstown, MD (cdp) Baltimore County	170	0.55
Indianapolis, IN (special city) Marion County	170	0.02
Bergenfield, NJ (borough) Bergen County	169	0.64
Woodlawn, MD (cdp) Baltimore County	167	0.46
Huntsville, AL (city) Madison County	166	0.11
Woodbridge, VA (cdp) Prince William County	165	0.52
Brandon, FL (cdp) Hillsborough County	165	0.21
Port Saint Lucie, FL (city) Saint Lucie County	165	0.19
Brockton, MA (city) Plymouth County	165	0.17
Clearwater, FL (city) Pinellas County	160	0.15
Oakland, CA (city) Alameda County	160	0.04
Daytona Beach, FL (city) Volusia County	159	0.25
Cutler Ridge, FL (cdp) Miami-Dade County	154	0.62
Chelsea, MA (city) Suffolk County	154	0.44
San Francisco, CA (city) San Francisco County	154	0.02
Greenburgh, NY (town) Westchester County	153	0.18
Englewood, NJ (city) Bergen County	152	0.58
Inglewood, CA (city) Los Angeles County	152	0.14
Severn, MD (cdp) Anne Arundel County	147	0.42
Lakeview, NY (cdp) Nassau County	144	2.57
West Orange, NJ (cdp) Essex County	143	0.32
Redan, GA (cdp) De Kalb County	142	0.42
Roselle, NJ (borough) Union County	141	0.66
Oakland Park, FL (city) Broward County	141	0.45
Bowie, MD (city) Prince George's County	139	0.28
Springfield, MA (city) Hampden County	139	0.09
Adelphi, MD (cdp) Prince George's County	137	0.91
Rochester, NY (city) Monroe County	137	0.06
Oyster Bay, NY (town) Nassau County	136	0.05
East Riverdale, MD (cdp) Prince George's County	134	0.87
Montclair, NJ (cdp) Essex County	134	0.34
Pine Hills, FL (cdp) Orange County	134	0.32
Providence, RI (city) Providence County	133	0.08
West Palm Beach, FL (city) Palm Beach County	132	0.16
Milford Mill, MD (cdp) Baltimore County	130	0.49
Laurel, MD (city) Prince George's County	128	0.64
New Rochelle, NY (city) Westchester County	128	0.18
Austin, TX (city) Travis County	128	0.02
Aspen Hill, MD (cdp) Montgomery County	127	0.25
White Plains, NY (city) Westchester County	127	0.24
Columbia, MD (cdp) Howard County	126	0.14
The Crossings, FL (cdp) Miami-Dade County	124	0.53
Willingboro, NJ (township) Burlington County	123	0.37
Country Club, FL (cdp) Miami-Dade County	123	0.34
Bloomfield, NJ (cdp) Essex County	123	0.26
Lanham-Seabrook, MD (cdp) Prince George's County	122	0.67
East Perrine, FL (cdp) Miami-Dade County	121	1.77
Minneapolis, MN (city) Hennepin County	121	0.03
Oak Ridge, FL (cdp) Orange County	119	0.53
Golden Glades, FL (cdp) Miami-Dade County	119	0.37
Boca Raton, FL (city) Palm Beach County	119	0.16

Notes: (cdp) census designated place; Refer to the Explanation of Data in the front of the book for more detailed information.

West Indian: Trinidadian and Tobagonian, excluding Hispanic

Top 150 Places Sorted by Percent

(Based on all places, regardless of population)

Place	Number	%
McIntyre, GA (town) Wilkinson County	35	4.55
Palmetto Estates, FL (cdp) Miami-Dade County	413	3.02
South Floral Park, NY (village) Nassau County	42	2.66
Lakeview, NY (cdp) Nassau County	144	2.57
Naranja, FL (cdp) Miami-Dade County	105	2.50
West Perrine, FL (cdp) Miami-Dade County	207	2.41
Mount Rainier, MD (city) Prince George's County	182	2.15
Blue Hills, CT (cdp) Hartford County	60	1.95
Orange, NJ (cdp) Essex County	630	1.92
Springdale, MD (cdp) Prince George's County	54	1.92
Loch Lomond, FL (cdp) Broward County	63	1.90
Country Walk, FL (cdp) Miami-Dade County	190	1.78
East Perrine, FL (cdp) Miami-Dade County	121	1.77
Chillum, MD (cdp) Prince George's County	595	1.74
Roosevelt, NY (cdp) Nassau County	272	1.72
Cheverly, MD (town) Prince George's County	108	1.67
Ramblewood East, FL (cdp) Broward County	21	1.66
Pine Lake, GA (city) De Kalb County	9	1.60
Landover Hills, MD (town) Prince George's County	23	1.53
Bonnie Lock-Woodsetter North, FL (cdp) Broward County	65	1.51
Neptune City, NJ (borough) Monmouth County	76	1.46
Norland, FL (cdp) Miami-Dade County	328	1.42
Surfside, FL (town) Miami-Dade County	73	1.42
Harrington Park, NJ (borough) Bergen County	66	1.39
Riverdale Park, MD (town) Prince George's County	88	1.34
Sky Lake, FL (cdp) Orange County	78	1.32
Wheatley Heights, NY (cdp) Suffolk County	65	1.29
Pine Hill, NY (cdp) Ulster County	5	1.29
Langley Park, MD (cdp) Prince George's County	208	1.28
Quioque, NY (cdp) Suffolk County	10	1.26
North Amityville, NY (cdp) Suffolk County	207	1.25
Miramar, FL (city) Broward County	897	1.23
Gordon Heights, NY (cdp) Suffolk County	38	1.23
North Valley Stream, NY (cdp) Nassau County	188	1.19
Kent Narrows, MD (cdp) Queen Anne's County	7	1.19
Coolbaugh, PA (township) Monroe County	175	1.15
Fairland, MD (cdp) Montgomery County	244	1.13
South Laurel, MD (cdp) Prince George's County	235	1.13
Beltsville, MD (cdp) Prince George's County	176	1.12
North Lauderdale, FL (city) Broward County	357	1.10
Bloomfield, CT (town) Hartford County	208	1.06
West Marion, NC (cdp) McDowell County	17	1.06
Cottage City, MD (town) Prince George's County	12	1.06
Millbourne, PA (borough) Delaware County	10	1.06
Berry Hill, TN (city) Davidson County	7	1.06
Uniondale, NY (cdp) Nassau County	242	1.05
Freeborn, MN (city) Freeborn County	3	1.05
Hempstead, NY (village) Nassau County	583	1.03
Central Islip, NY (cdp) Suffolk County	326	1.02
Scotch Plains, NJ (cdp) Union County	231	1.02
North Bellport, NY (cdp) Suffolk County	93	1.02
Edmonston, MD (town) Prince George's County	10	1.02
Elmont, NY (cdp) Nassau County	329	1.01
Takoma Park, MD (city) Montgomery County	171	1.00
Three Lakes, FL (cdp) Miami-Dade County	70	1.00
Greenvale, NY (cdp) Nassau County	22	1.00
Higganum, CT (cdp) Middlesex County	17	1.00
Maplewood, NJ (cdp) Essex County	234	0.98
Polkville, NC (city) Cleveland County	5	0.97
Mitchellville, MD (cdp) Prince George's County	93	0.96
New York, NY (city) New York City	75,584	0.94
Manalapan, FL (town) Palm Beach County	3	0.93
Adelphi, MD (cdp) Prince George's County	137	0.91
Fort Belvoir, VA (cdp) Fairfax County	64	0.90
Freeport, NY (village) Nassau County	380	0.87
East Riverdale, MD (cdp) Prince George's County	134	0.87
Roosevelt Gardens, FL (cdp) Broward County	16	0.86
Ocean Ridge, FL (town) Palm Beach County	14	0.86
Lauderhill, FL (city) Broward County	480	0.84
Thiells, NY (cdp) Rockland County	40	0.84
Chester, NY (village) Orange County	30	0.84
Brentwood, MD (town) Prince George's County	24	0.84
Oronoko charter, MI (township) Berrien County	82	0.83
Lorenz Park, NY (cdp) Columbia County	17	0.83
Utopia, FL (cdp) Broward County	6	0.83
Sunrise, FL (city) Broward County	694	0.81
Irvington, NJ (cdp) Essex County	491	0.81
Princeton, FL (cdp) Miami-Dade County	80	0.79
Brush Prairie, WA (cdp) Clark County	19	0.79
Fairmount Heights, MD (town) Prince George's County	12	0.79
Melrose Park, FL (cdp) Broward County	55	0.78
Colley, PA (township) Sullivan County	5	0.78
Woodside, PA (cdp) Bucks County	21	0.77
Broadview-Pompano Park, FL (cdp) Broward County	39	0.76
Ludowici, GA (city) Long County	11	0.76
Poinciana, FL (cdp) Osceola County	102	0.75
Calverton, MD (cdp) Montgomery County	95	0.75
Minneola, FL (city) Lake County	38	0.75
East Orange, NJ (city) Essex County	518	0.74
Glenn Dale, MD (cdp) Prince George's County	93	0.73
Bunche Park, FL (cdp) Miami-Dade County	29	0.73
Onset, MA (cdp) Plymouth County	10	0.73
Scott Lake, FL (cdp) Miami-Dade County	104	0.72
Manhasset, NY (cdp) Nassau County	60	0.72
Main, PA (township) Columbia County	9	0.71
Portage, NY (town) Livingston County	6	0.71
Lauderdale Lakes, FL (city) Broward County	217	0.69
Collegeville, IN (cdp) Jasper County	6	0.69
South Miami Heights, FL (cdp) Miami-Dade County	229	0.68
Glenarden, MD (city) Prince George's County	43	0.68
Apopka, FL (city) Orange County	174	0.67
Lanham-Seabrook, MD (cdp) Prince George's County	122	0.67
Wilton Manors, FL (city) Broward County	85	0.67
Dayton, NJ (cdp) Middlesex County	43	0.67
Roselle, NJ (borough) Union County	141	0.66
Wyandanch, NY (cdp) Suffolk County	70	0.66
Mount Arlington, NJ (borough) Morris County	31	0.66
Old Westbury, NY (village) Nassau County	28	0.66
Ojus, FL (cdp) Miami-Dade County	108	0.65
Haledon, NJ (borough) Passaic County	54	0.65
Queenstown, MD (town) Queen Anne's County	4	0.65
Bergenfield, NJ (borough) Bergen County	169	0.64
Laurel, MD (city) Prince George's County	128	0.64
Wedgefield, FL (cdp) Orange County	18	0.64
Maytown, PA (cdp) Lancaster County	16	0.64
Hillburn, NY (village) Rockland County	5	0.64
Richmond West, FL (cdp) Miami-Dade County	177	0.63
Orlovista, FL (cdp) Orange County	38	0.63
Woodmore, MD (cdp) Prince George's County	38	0.63
Margate, FL (city) Browârd County	333	0.62
Cutler Ridge, FL (cdp) Miami-Dade County	154	0.62
Ives Estates, FL (cdp) Miami-Dade County	108	0.62
New Cassel, NY (cdp) Nassau County	82	0.62
Whisper Walk, FL (cdp) Palm Beach County	32	0.62
Valley Stream, NY (village) Nassau County	221	0.61
Olga, FL (cdp) Lee County	9	0.61
New Carrollton, MD (city) Prince George's County	77	0.60
Westampton, NJ (township) Burlington County	43	0.60
New Paltz, NY (village) Ulster County	36	0.60
Kingston, NH (town) Rockingham County	35	0.60
Chuluota, FL (cdp) Seminole County	12	0.60
Silver Spring, MD (cdp) Montgomery County	455	0.59
Mechanicstown, NY (cdp) Orange County	36	0.59
Port La Belle, FL (cdp) Hendry County	19	0.59
Englewood, NJ (city) Bergen County	152	0.58
Westbury, NY (village) Nassau County	83	0.58
Andover, FL (cdp) Miami-Dade County	50	0.58
North Caldwell, NJ (borough) Essex County	43	0.58
Colwyn, PA (borough) Delaware County	14	0.57
Boston, MA (city) Suffolk County	3,309	0.56
Walker Mill, MD (cdp) Prince George's County	63	0.56
Silver Springs Shores, FL (cdp) Marion County	37	0.56
Cranbury, NJ (township) Middlesex County	18	0.56
Pemberton Heights, NJ (cdp) Burlington County	14	0.56
Hernando Beach, FL (cdp) Hernando County	12	0.56
Plantation, FL (city) Broward County	461	0.55
Randallstown, MD (cdp) Baltimore County	170	0.55
Woodlawn, MD (cdp) Prince George's County	34	0.55
Tedder, FL (cdp) Broward County	11	0.55
Yeadon, PA (borough) Delaware County	64	0.54

Notes: (cdp) census designated place; Refer to the Explanation of Data in the front of the book for more detailed information.

West Indian: Trinidadian and Tobagonian, excluding Hispanic

Top 150 Places Sorted by Percent

(Based on places with populations of 10,000 or more)

Place	Number	%
Palmetto Estates, FL (cdp) Miami-Dade County	413	3.02
Orange, NJ (cdp) Essex County	630	1.92
Country Walk, FL (cdp) Miami-Dade County	190	1.78
Chillum, MD (cdp) Prince George's County	595	1.74
Roosevelt, NY (cdp) Nassau County	272	1.72
Norland, FL (cdp) Miami-Dade County	328	1.42
Langley Park, MD (cdp) Prince George's County	208	1.28
North Amityville, NY (cdp) Suffolk County	207	1.25
Miramar, FL (city) Broward County	897	1.23
North Valley Stream, NY (cdp) Nassau County	188	1.19
Coolbaugh, PA (township) Monroe County	175	1.15
Fairland, MD (cdp) Montgomery County	244	1.13
South Laurel, MD (cdp) Prince George's County	235	1.13
Beltsville, MD (cdp) Prince George's County	176	1.12
North Lauderdale, FL (city) Broward County	357	1.10
Bloomfield, CT (town) Hartford County	208	1.06
Uniondale, NY (cdp) Nassau County	242	1.05
Hempstead, NY (village) Nassau County	583	1.03
Central Islip, NY (cdp) Suffolk County	326	1.02
Scotch Plains, NJ (cdp) Union County	231	1.02
Elmont, NY (cdp) Nassau County	329	1.01
Takoma Park, MD (city) Montgomery County	171	1.00
Maplewood, NJ (cdp) Essex County	234	0.98
New York, NY (city) New York City	75,584	0.94
Adelphi, MD (cdp) Prince George's County	137	0.91
Freeport, NY (village) Nassau County	380	0.87
East Riverdale, MD (cdp) Prince George's County	134	0.87
Lauderhill, FL (city) Broward County	480	0.84
Sunrise, FL (city) Broward County	694	0.81
Irvington, NJ (cdp) Essex County	491	0.81
Princeton, FL (cdp) Miami-Dade County	80	0.79
Poinciana, FL (cdp) Osceola County	102	0.75
Calverton, MD (cdp) Montgomery County	95	0.75
East Orange, NJ (city) Essex County	518	0.74
Glenn Dale, MD (cdp) Prince George's County	93	0.73
Scott Lake, FL (cdp) Miami-Dade County	104	0.72
Lauderdale Lakes, FL (city) Broward County	217	0.69
South Miami Heights, FL (cdp) Miami-Dade County	229	0.68
Apopka, FL (city) Orange County	174	0.67
Lanham-Seabrook, MD (cdp) Prince George's County	122	0.67
Wilton Manors, FL (city) Broward County	85	0.67
Roselle, NJ (borough) Union County	141	0.66
Wyandanch, NY (cdp) Suffolk County	70	0.66
Ojus, FL (cdp) Miami-Dade County	108	0.65
Bergenfield, NJ (borough) Bergen County	169	0.64
Laurel, MD (city) Prince George's County	128	0.64
Richmond West, FL (cdp) Miami-Dade County	177	0.63
Margate, FL (city) Broward County	333	0.62
Cutler Ridge, FL (cdp) Miami-Dade County	154	0.62
Ives Estates, FL (cdp) Miami-Dade County	108	0.62
New Cassel, NY (cdp) Nassau County	82	0.62
Valley Stream, NY (village) Nassau County	221	0.61
New Carrollton, MD (city) Prince George's County	77	0.60
Silver Spring, MD (cdp) Montgomery County	455	0.59
Englewood, NJ (city) Bergen County	152	0.58
Westbury, NY (village) Nassau County	83	0.58
Boston, MA (city) Suffolk County	3,309	0.56
Walker Mill, MD (cdp) Prince George's County	63	0.56
Plantation, FL (city) Broward County	461	0.55
Randallstown, MD (cdp) Baltimore County	170	0.55
Yeadon, PA (borough) Delaware County	64	0.54
North Miami Beach, FL (city) Miami-Dade County	215	0.53
The Crossings, FL (cdp) Miami-Dade County	124	0.53
Oak Ridge, FL (cdp) Orange County	119	0.53
South Orange, NJ (cdp) Essex County	90	0.53
New Territory, TX (cdp) Fort Bend County	74	0.53
Hollywood, FL (city) Broward County	727	0.52
Coconut Creek, FL (city) Broward County	226	0.52
Woodbridge, VA (cdp) Prince William County	165	0.52
Highland Park, NJ (borough) Middlesex County	72	0.51
Pine Hill, NJ (borough) Camden County	56	0.51
East Rockaway, NY (village) Nassau County	52	0.50
Milford Mill, MD (cdp) Baltimore County	130	0.49
Tamarac, FL (city) Broward County	271	0.48
Baldwin, NY (cdp) Nassau County	113	0.48
Carol City, FL (cdp) Miami-Dade County	282	0.47
Teaneck, NJ (cdp) Bergen County	186	0.47
Dumont, NJ (borough) Bergen County	83	0.47
Union, NJ (cdp) Union County	250	0.46
Plainfield, NJ (city) Union County	221	0.46
Hackensack, NJ (city) Bergen County	197	0.46
Woodlawn, MD (cdp) Baltimore County	167	0.46
Palm Bay, FL (city) Brevard County	356	0.45
Oakland Park, FL (city) Broward County	141	0.45
White Oak, MD (cdp) Montgomery County	93	0.45
Lockhart, FL (cdp) Orange County	57	0.45
Miami Shores, FL (village) Miami-Dade County	47	0.45
North Miami, FL (city) Miami-Dade County	267	0.44
Brentwood, NY (cdp) Suffolk County	235	0.44
Chelsea, MA (city) Suffolk County	154	0.44
Colesville, MD (cdp) Montgomery County	88	0.44
Forestville, MD (cdp) Prince George's County	56	0.44
West Caldwell, NJ (cdp) Essex County	49	0.44
Jersey City, NJ (city) Hudson County	1,031	0.43
Pembroke Pines, FL (city) Broward County	592	0.43
Severn, MD (cdp) Anne Arundel County	147	0.42
Redan, GA (cdp) De Kalb County	142	0.42
Hillside, NJ (cdp) Union County	91	0.42
Lochearn, MD (cdp) Baltimore County	103	0.41
Harvey, LA (cdp) Jefferson Parish	91	0.41
Holtsville, NY (cdp) Suffolk County	69	0.41
Gladeview, FL (cdp) Miami-Dade County	60	0.41
Greenlawn, NY (cdp) Suffolk County	55	0.41
Kettering, MD (cdp) Prince George's County	45	0.41
Guttenberg, NJ (town) Hudson County	44	0.41
Baytown, TX (city) Harris County	267	0.40
Wheaton-Glenmont, MD (cdp) Montgomery County	232	0.40
Mount Vernon, NY (city) Westchester County	266	0.39
Royal Palm Beach, FL (village) Palm Beach County	81	0.38
Hillcrest Heights, MD (cdp) Prince George's County	62	0.38
Fort Drum, NY (cdp) Jefferson County	46	0.38
Hempstead, NY (town) Nassau County	2,770	0.37
Coral Springs, FL (city) Broward County	433	0.37
Willingboro, NJ (township) Burlington County	123	0.37
Golden Glades, FL (cdp) Miami-Dade County	119	0.37
Fort Washington, MD (cdp) Prince George's County	89	0.37
North Bay Shore, NY (cdp) Suffolk County	56	0.37
Carteret, NJ (borough) Middlesex County	75	0.36
Ardmore, PA (cdp) Montgomery County	45	0.36
Pinewood, FL (cdp) Miami-Dade County	59	0.35
Farmingville, NY (cdp) Suffolk County	58	0.35
Douglas, GA (city) Coffee County	36	0.35
Montclair, NJ (cdp) Essex County	134	0.34
Country Club, FL (cdp) Miami-Dade County	123	0.34
College Park, MD (city) Prince George's County	84	0.34
Leisure City, FL (cdp) Miami-Dade County	73	0.34
Lake Worth Corridor, FL (cdp) Palm Beach County	63	0.34
Camp Springs, MD (cdp) Prince George's County	60	0.34
Palm Springs, FL (village) Palm Beach County	40	0.34
Westwood, NJ (borough) Bergen County	37	0.34
Warrensville Heights, OH (city) Cuyahoga County	51	0.33
Longwood, FL (city) Seminole County	45	0.33
Dobbs Ferry, NY (village) Westchester County	35	0.33
West Orange, NJ (cdp) Essex County	143	0.32
Pine Hills, FL (cdp) Orange County	134	0.32
Deer Park, NY (cdp) Suffolk County	90	0.32
Avenel, NJ (cdp) Middlesex County	57	0.32
Aberdeen, NJ (township) Monmouth County	56	0.32
Mastic, NY (cdp) Suffolk County	49	0.32
Opa-locka, FL (city) Miami-Dade County	49	0.32
Lynn Haven, FL (city) Bay County	39	0.32
Olney, MD (cdp) Montgomery County	99	0.31
Callaway, FL (city) Bay County	44	0.31
Sugar Hill, GA (city) Gwinnett County	35	0.31
The Village, OK (city) Oklahoma County	32	0.31
West Haverstraw, NY (village) Rockland County	32	0.31
Edison, NJ (cdp) Middlesex County	294	0.30
Peekskill, NY (city) Westchester County	68	0.30
Hope Mills, NC (town) Cumberland County	34	0.30
Union City, GA (city) Fulton County	34	0.30

Notes: (cdp) census designated place; Refer to the Explanation of Data in the front of the book for more detailed information.

West Indian: U.S. Virgin Islander, excluding Hispanic

Top 150 Places Sorted by Number

(Based on all places, regardless of population)

Place	Number	%
New York, NY (city) New York City	2,790	0.03
Houston, TX (city) Harris County	272	0.01
Boston, MA (city) Suffolk County	232	0.04
Baltimore, MD (independent city) Baltimore city	222	0.03
Miramar, FL (city) Broward County	207	0.28
Saint Petersburg, FL (city) Pinellas County	197	0.08
Odenton, MD (cdp) Anne Arundel County	170	0.82
Orlando, FL (city) Orange County	166	0.09
Lauderdale Lakes, FL (city) Broward County	159	0.50
Chicago, IL (city) Cook County	154	0.01
Tallahassee, FL (city) Leon County	153	0.10
Tacoma, WA (city) Pierce County	135	0.07
Deltona, FL (city) Volusia County	123	0.18
Tampa, FL (city) Hillsborough County	108	0.04
Miami, FL (city) Miami-Dade County	107	0.03
Jacksonville, FL (special city) Duval County	107	0.01
Pine Hills, FL (cdp) Orange County	100	0.24
Virginia Beach, VA (independent city) Virginia Beach city	96	0.02
Opa-locka North, FL (cdp) Miami-Dade County	94	1.51
Los Angeles, CA (city) Los Angeles County	94	0.00
Carrollton, GA (city) Carroll County	89	0.45
Scott Lake, FL (cdp) Miami-Dade County	85	0.59
Hempstead, NY (town) Nassau County	83	0.01
Lauderhill, FL (city) Broward County	82	0.14
Atlanta, GA (city) Fulton County	76	0.02
Savannah, GA (city) Chatham County	74	0.06
Newport News, VA (independent city) Newport News city	72	0.04
Baytown, TX (city) Harris County	71	0.11
Washington, DC (city) District of Columbia	71	0.01
Hollywood, FL (city) Broward County	67	0.05
Decatur, GA (city) De Kalb County	66	0.36
North Lauderdale, FL (city) Broward County	65	0.20
Lawrence, MA (city) Essex County	60	0.08
Plantation, FL (city) Broward County	56	0.07
Everett, MA (city) Middlesex County	55	0.14
Fort Lauderdale, FL (city) Broward County	55	0.04
Country Club, FL (cdp) Miami-Dade County	52	0.14
Philadelphia, PA (city) Philadelphia County	51	0.00
Panthersville, GA (cdp) De Kalb County	50	0.43
Yeehaw Junction, FL (cdp) Osceola County	50	0.23
Killeen, TX (city) Bell County	50	0.06
Aberdeen, MD (city) Harford County	48	0.35
Town 'n' Country, FL (cdp) Hillsborough County	48	0.07
Norfolk, VA (independent city) Norfolk city	48	0.02
Sunrise, FL (city) Broward County	47	0.05
Huntsville, AL (city) Madison County	47	0.03
Pembroke Pines, FL (city) Broward County	46	0.03
Augusta-Richmond County, GA (special city) Richmond County	45	0.02
Fort Worth, TX (city) Tarrant County	45	0.01
San Diego, CA (city) San Diego County	45	0.00
Milford Mill, MD (cdp) Baltimore County	44	0.17
Inglewood, CA (city) Los Angeles County	44	0.04
Sandy Springs, GA (cdp) Fulton County	43	0.05
Columbus, OH (city) Franklin County	43	0.01
Indianapolis, IN (special city) Marion County	41	0.01
Silver Springs Shores, FL (cdp) Marion County	40	0.61
Elizabeth, NJ (city) Union County	40	0.03
Charlotte, NC (city) Mecklenburg County	40	0.01
Westview, FL (cdp) Miami-Dade County	39	0.41
Omaha, NE (city) Douglas County	39	0.01
New London, CT (city) New London County	37	0.14
Redmond, WA (city) King County	37	0.08
Phoenix, AZ (city) Maricopa County	37	0.00
Pembroke Park, FL (town) Broward County	36	0.57
Lake Lucerne, FL (cdp) Miami-Dade County	36	0.39
Aurora, CO (city) Arapahoe County	36	0.01
Newark, NJ (city) Essex County	36	0.01
North Miami Beach, FL (city) Miami-Dade County	35	0.09
Hartford, CT (city) Hartford County	35	0.03
Golden Lakes, FL (cdp) Palm Beach County	34	0.51
Altamonte Springs, FL (city) Seminole County	34	0.08
West Palm Beach, FL (city) Palm Beach County	34	0.04
Nashville-Davidson, TN (special city) Davidson County	34	0.01
University Park, IL (village) Will County	33	0.50
Golden Glades, FL (cdp) Miami-Dade County	33	0.10
South Miami Heights, FL (cdp) Miami-Dade County	33	0.10
Daytona Beach, FL (city) Volusia County	33	0.05
Ives Estates, FL (cdp) Miami-Dade County	32	0.18
North Miami, FL (city) Miami-Dade County	32	0.05
Palm Bay, FL (city) Brevard County	32	0.04
Fountainbleau, FL (cdp) Miami-Dade County	31	0.05
Roswell, GA (city) Fulton County	31	0.04
Birmingham, AL (city) Jefferson County	31	0.01
San Francisco, CA (city) San Francisco County	31	0.00
Parker, CO (town) Douglas County	30	0.13
Cary, NC (town) Wake County	30	0.03
Cleveland, OH (city) Cuyahoga County	30	0.01
Oakland, CA (city) Alameda County	30	0.01
Tucson, AZ (city) Pima County	30	0.01
Port Jefferson, NY (village) Suffolk County	29	0.37
Plainfield, NJ (city) Union County	29	0.06
Schenectady, NY (city) Schenectady County	29	0.05
Silver Spring, MD (cdp) Montgomery County	29	0.04
Brookhaven, NY (town) Suffolk County	29	0.01
Jersey City, NJ (city) Hudson County	29	0.01
Portland, OR (city) Multnomah County	29	0.01
Winter Springs, FL (city) Seminole County	28	0.09
Columbus, GA (special city) Muscogee County	28	0.02
Durham, NC (city) Durham County	28	0.01
Austin, TX (city) Travis County	28	0.00
South Laurel, MD (cdp) Prince George's County	27	0.13
North Brunswick Township, NJ (cdp) Middlesex County	27	0.07
Hawthorne, CA (city) Los Angeles County	27	0.03
Paterson, NJ (city) Passaic County	27	0.02
North Bay Village, FL (city) Miami-Dade County	26	0.39
Shrewsbury, MA (town) Worcester County	26	0.08
Brandon, FL (cdp) Hillsborough County	26	0.03
Springfield, MA (city) Hampden County	26	0.02
Freeport, NY (village) Nassau County	25	0.06
Woonsocket, RI (city) Providence County	25	0.06
Irvington, NJ (cdp) Essex County	25	0.04
Colorado Springs, CO (city) El Paso County	25	0.01
Plano, TX (city) Collin County	25	0.01
Richmond, VA (independent city) Richmond city	25	0.01
Norland, FL (cdp) Miami-Dade County	24	0.10
Mount Pleasant, SC (town) Charleston County	24	0.05
Providence, RI (city) Providence County	24	0.01
San Antonio, TX (city) Bexar County	24	0.00
College Park, GA (city) Fulton County	23	0.11
Oak Ridge, FL (cdp) Orange County	23	0.10
Mount Vernon, VA (cdp) Fairfax County	23	0.08
Germantown, MD (cdp) Montgomery County	23	0.04
West Hartford, CT (cdp) Hartford County	23	0.04
East Orange, NJ (city) Essex County	23	0.03
New Rochelle, NY (city) Westchester County	23	0.03
Somerville, MA (city) Middlesex County	23	0.03
Rochester, NY (city) Monroe County	23	0.01
Naples Manor, FL (cdp) Collier County	22	0.43
North Valley Stream, NY (cdp) Nassau County	22	0.14
Riviera Beach, FL (city) Palm Beach County	22	0.07
San Juan Capistrano, CA (city) Orange County	22	0.06
Mount Vernon, NY (city) Westchester County	22	0.03
Narragansett Pier, RI (cdp) Washington County	21	0.58
Mount Rainier, MD (city) Prince George's County	21	0.25
Narragansett, RI (town) Washington County	21	0.13
Cooper City, FL (city) Broward County	21	0.08
Williamsport, PA (city) Lycoming County	21	0.07
Elizabeth City, NC (city) Pasquotank County	20	0.12
Rosedale, MD (cdp) Baltimore County	20	0.10
North Potomac, MD (cdp) Montgomery County	20	0.09
Englewood, NJ (city) Bergen County	20	0.08
Coral Gables, FL (city) Miami-Dade County	20	0.05
Smyrna, GA (city) Cobb County	20	0.05
Carol City, FL (cdp) Miami-Dade County	20	0.03
Dallas, TX (city) Dallas County	20	0.00
Benton Harbor, MI (city) Berrien County	19	0.17
Fort Stewart, GA (cdp) Liberty County	19	0.17
Orange, NJ (cdp) Essex County	19	0.06
East Point, GA (city) Fulton County	19	0.05
East Lansing, MI (city) Ingham County	19	0.04

Notes: (cdp) census designated place; Refer to the Explanation of Data in the front of the book for more detailed information.

West Indian: U.S. Virgin Islander, excluding Hispanic

Top 150 Places Sorted by Percent

(Based on all places, regardless of population)

Place	Number	%
Utopia, FL (cdp) Broward County	15	2.07
Opa-locka North, FL (cdp) Miami-Dade County	94	1.51
Maalaea, HI (cdp) Maui County	4	0.88
Odenton, MD (cdp) Anne Arundel County	170	0.82
Mulga, AL (town) Jefferson County	7	0.79
Nebo Center, CA (cdp) San Bernardino County	9	0.71
Silver Springs Shores, FL (cdp) Marion County	40	0.61
Scott Lake, FL (cdp) Miami-Dade County	85	0.59
Narragansett Pier, RI (cdp) Washington County	21	0.58
Pembroke Park, FL (town) Broward County	36	0.57
Edgewood, NM (town) Santa Fe County	11	0.54
Golden Lakes, FL (cdp) Palm Beach County	34	0.51
Bicknell, UT (town) Wayne County	2	0.51
Lauderdale Lakes, FL (city) Broward County	159	0.50
University Park, IL (village) Will County	33	0.50
Dane, WI (village) Dane County	4	0.50
Carrollton, GA (city) Carroll County	89	0.45
Murray City, OH (village) Hocking County	2	0.45
Lyon, MS (town) Coahoma County	2	0.44
Panthersville, GA (cdp) De Kalb County	50	0.43
Naples Manor, FL (cdp) Collier County	22	0.43
Frankford, DE (town) Sussex County	3	0.43
Westview, FL (cdp) Miami-Dade County	39	0.41
Nice, CA (cdp) Lake County	10	0.40
Lake Lucerne, FL (cdp) Miami-Dade County	36	0.39
North Bay Village, FL (city) Miami-Dade County	26	0.39
Forest Heights, MD (town) Prince George's County	10	0.38
Port Jefferson, NY (village) Suffolk County	29	0.37
Parksley, VA (town) Accomack County	3	0.37
Decatur, GA (city) De Kalb County	66	0.36
Aberdeen, MD (city) Harford County	48	0.35
Sagamore, MA (cdp) Barnstable County	12	0.34
Brunswick Station, ME (cdp) Cumberland County	5	0.34
Orleans, MI (township) Ionia County	9	0.33
Kingston, NY (town) Ulster County	3	0.33
South Gate Ridge, FL (cdp) Sarasota County	18	0.32
Crystal Lake, FL (cdp) Polk County	16	0.31
Mangonia Park, FL (town) Palm Beach County	4	0.31
Prairie View, TX (city) Waller County	13	0.30
Progress Village, FL (cdp) Hillsborough County	7	0.30
Houghton, NY (cdp) Allegany County	5	0.29
Miramar, FL (city) Broward County	207	0.28
Dalworthington Gardens, TX (city) Tarrant County	6	0.27
Otisco, MI (township) Ionia County	6	0.27
Wayne, OK (town) McClain County	2	0.27
Birch Bay, WA (cdp) Whatcom County	13	0.26
Daleville, AL (city) Dale County	12	0.26
Mount Rainier, MD (city) Prince George's County	21	0.25
Broadview-Pompano Park, FL (cdp) Broward County	13	0.25
Pine Hills, FL (cdp) Orange County	100	0.24
Confluence, PA (borough) Somerset County	2	0.24
Yeehaw Junction, FL (cdp) Osceola County	50	0.23
West Samoset, FL (cdp) Manatee County	13	0.23
Morningside, MD (town) Prince George's County	3	0.23
Abbottstown, PA (borough) Adams County	2	0.23
Pine Castle, FL (cdp) Orange County	18	0.22
Marlton, MD (cdp) Prince George's County	17	0.22
Aberdeen Proving Ground, MD (cdp) Harford County	7	0.22
McGuire AFB, NJ (cdp) Burlington County	14	0.21
Notasulga, AL (town) Macon County	2	0.21
North Lauderdale, FL (city) Broward County	65	0.20
Lansing, KS (city) Leavenworth County	18	0.20
Heathcote, NJ (cdp) Middlesex County	9	0.20
Broward Estates, FL (cdp) Broward County	7	0.20
Caneadea, NY (town) Allegany County	5	0.19
Deltona, FL (city) Volusia County	123	0.18
Ives Estates, FL (cdp) Miami-Dade County	32	0.18
North Sea, NY (cdp) Suffolk County	8	0.18
Delaware, NY (town) Sullivan County	5	0.18
Hahnville, LA (cdp) Saint Charles Parish	5	0.18
Dresden, ME (town) Lincoln County	3	0.18
Leverett, MA (town) Franklin County	3	0.18
Milford Mill, MD (cdp) Baltimore County	44	0.17
Benton Harbor, MI (city) Berrien County	19	0.17
Fort Stewart, GA (cdp) Liberty County	19	0.17
Iva, SC (town) Anderson County	2	0.17
Wyandanch, NY (cdp) Suffolk County	17	0.16
Dumbarton, VA (cdp) Henrico County	11	0.16
Boxborough, MA (town) Middlesex County	8	0.16
Carver Ranches, FL (cdp) Broward County	7	0.16
Porter, PA (township) Huntingdon County	3	0.16
Collinsville, TX (town) Grayson County	2	0.16
Shiloh, PA (cdp) York County	15	0.15
New Hempstead, NY (village) Rockland County	7	0.15
Limington, ME (town) York County	5	0.15
Livingston, AL (city) Sumter County	5	0.15
Greenport, NY (village) Suffolk County	3	0.15
Kaanapali, HI (cdp) Maui County	2	0.15
Lauderhill, FL (city) Broward County	82	0.14
Everett, MA (city) Middlesex County	55	0.14
Country Club, FL (cdp) Miami-Dade County	52	0.14
New London, CT (city) New London County	37	0.14
North Valley Stream, NY (cdp) Nassau County	22	0.14
New Hanover, NJ (township) Burlington County	14	0.14
Canton, NY (village) Saint Lawrence County	8	0.14
Fremont, NY (town) Sullivan County	2	0.14
Horicon, NY (town) Warren County	2	0.14
Parker, CO (town) Douglas County	30	0.13
South Laurel, MD (cdp) Prince George's County	27	0.13
Narragansett, RI (town) Washington County	21	0.13
Maitland, FL (city) Orange County	15	0.13
East Lake-Orient Park, FL (cdp) Hillsborough County	7	0.13
Robinwood, MD (cdp) Washington County	6	0.13
Crump, TN (city) Hardin County	2	0.13
Landover Hills, MD (town) Prince George's County	2	0.13
Elizabeth City, NC (city) Pasquotank County	20	0.12
Highview, KY (cdp) Jefferson County	18	0.12
New Carrollton, MD (city) Prince George's County	15	0.12
Andover, FL (cdp) Miami-Dade County	10	0.12
Garrison, MD (cdp) Baltimore County	10	0.12
Fairlawn, OH (city) Summit County	9	0.12
Milton, FL (city) Santa Rosa County	8	0.12
Fort Rucker, AL (cdp) Dale County	7	0.12
Vivian, LA (town) Caddo Parish	5	0.12
Twin City, GA (city) Emanuel County	2	0.12
Duncan, AZ (town) Greenlee County	1	0.12
Baytown, TX (city) Harris County	71	0.11
College Park, GA (city) Fulton County	23	0.11
Savage-Guilford, MD (cdp) Howard County	14	0.11
Zephyrhills, FL (city) Pasco County	12	0.11
Franklin Lakes, NJ (borough) Bergen County	11	0.11
Greencastle, IN (city) Putnam County	11	0.11
Esopus, NY (town) Ulster County	10	0.11
Fort Bliss, TX (cdp) El Paso County	9	0.11
Lakeview, NY (cdp) Nassau County	6	0.11
Eagleville, PA (cdp) Montgomery County	5	0.11
Belleview, FL (city) Marion County	4	0.11
Tallahassee, FL (city) Leon County	153	0.10
Golden Glades, FL (cdp) Miami-Dade County	33	0.10
South Miami Heights, FL (cdp) Miami-Dade County	33	0.10
Norland, FL (cdp) Miami-Dade County	24	0.10
Oak Ridge, FL (cdp) Orange County	23	0.10
Rosedale, MD (cdp) Baltimore County	20	0.10
Poquoson, VA (independent city) Poquoson city	12	0.10
Colonie, NY (village) Albany County	8	0.10
Bunche Park, FL (cdp) Miami-Dade County	4	0.10
Orlando, FL (city) Orange County	166	0.09
North Miami Beach, FL (city) Miami-Dade County	35	0.09
Winter Springs, FL (city) Seminole County	28	0.09
North Potomac, MD (cdp) Montgomery County	20	0.09
Wilkinsburg, PA (borough) Allegheny County	18	0.09
Belvedere Park, GA (cdp) De Kalb County	17	0.09
West Manchester, PA (township) York County	15	0.09
Webster, MA (town) Worcester County	14	0.09
Highland Park, NJ (borough) Middlesex County	13	0.09
Glen Allen, VA (cdp) Henrico County	12	0.09
Orangeburg, SC (city) Orangeburg County	12	0.09
Palm Springs, FL (village) Palm Beach County	11	0.09
Bacliff, TX (cdp) Galveston County	6	0.09
Phoenix, IL (village) Cook County	2	0.09

Notes: (cdp) census designated place; Refer to the Explanation of Data in the front of the book for more detailed information.

West Indian: U.S. Virgin Islander, excluding Hispanic

Top 150 Places Sorted by Percent

(Based on places with populations of 10,000 or more)

Place	Number	%
Odenton, MD (cdp) Anne Arundel County	170	0.82
Scott Lake, FL (cdp) Miami-Dade County	85	0.59
Lauderdale Lakes, FL (city) Broward County	159	0.50
Carrollton, GA (city) Carroll County	89	0.45
Panthersville, GA (cdp) De Kalb County	50	0.43
Decatur, GA (city) De Kalb County	66	0.36
Aberdeen, MD (city) Harford County	48	0.35
Miramar, FL (city) Broward County	207	0.28
Pine Hills, FL (cdp) Orange County	100	0.24
Yeehaw Junction, FL (cdp) Osceola County	50	0.23
North Lauderdale, FL (city) Broward County	65	0.20
Deltona, FL (city) Volusia County	123	0.18
Ives Estates, FL (cdp) Miami-Dade County	32	0.18
Milford Mill, MD (cdp) Baltimore County	44	0.17
Benton Harbor, MI (city) Berrien County	19	0.17
Fort Stewart, GA (cdp) Liberty County	19	0.17
Wyandanch, NY (cdp) Suffolk County	17	0.16
Shiloh, PA (cdp) York County	15	0.15
Lauderhill, FL (city) Broward County	82	0.14
Everett, MA (city) Middlesex County	55	0.14
Country Club, FL (cdp) Miami-Dade County	52	0.14
New London, CT (city) New London County	37	0.14
North Valley Stream, NY (cdp) Nassau County	22	0.14
Parker, CO (town) Douglas County	30	0.13
South Laurel, MD (cdp) Prince George's County	27	0.13
Narragansett, RI (town) Washington County	21	0.13
Maitland, FL (city) Orange County	15	0.13
Elizabeth City, NC (city) Pasquotank County	20	0.12
Highview, KY (cdp) Jefferson County	18	0.12
New Carrollton, MD (city) Prince George's County	15	0.12
Baytown, TX (city) Harris County	71	0.11
College Park, GA (city) Fulton County	23	0.11
Savage-Guilford, MD (cdp) Howard County	14	0.11
Zephyrhills, FL (city) Pasco County	12	0.11
Franklin Lakes, NJ (borough) Bergen County	11	0.11
Tallahassee, FL (city) Leon County	153	0.10
Golden Glades, FL (cdp) Miami-Dade County	33	0.10
South Miami Heights, FL (cdp) Miami-Dade County	33	0.10
Norland, FL (cdp) Miami-Dade County	24	0.10
Oak Ridge, FL (cdp) Orange County	23	0.10
Rosedale, MD (cdp) Baltimore County	20	0.10
Poquoson, VA (independent city) Poquoson city	12	0.10
Orlando, FL (city) Orange County	166	0.09
North Miami Beach, FL (city) Miami-Dade County	35	0.09
Winter Springs, FL (city) Seminole County	28	0.09
North Potomac, MD (cdp) Montgomery County	20	0.09
Wilkinsburg, PA (borough) Allegheny County	18	0.09
Belvedere Park, GA (cdp) De Kalb County	17	0.09
West Manchester, PA (township) York County	15	0.09
Webster, MA (town) Worcester County	14	0.09
Highland Park, NJ (borough) Middlesex County	13	0.09
Glen Allen, VA (cdp) Henrico County	12	0.09
Orangeburg, SC (city) Orangeburg County	12	0.09
Palm Springs, FL (village) Palm Beach County	11	0.09
Saint Petersburg, FL (city) Pinellas County	197	0.08
Lawrence, MA (city) Essex County	60	0.08
Redmond, WA (city) King County	37	0.08
Altamonte Springs, FL (city) Seminole County	34	0.08
Shrewsbury, MA (town) Worcester County	26	0.08
Mount Vernon, VA (cdp) Fairfax County	23	0.08
Cooper City, FL (city) Broward County	21	0.08
Englewood, NJ (city) Bergen County	20	0.08
Boca Del Mar, FL (cdp) Palm Beach County	17	0.08
Pinewood, FL (cdp) Miami-Dade County	14	0.08
Winthrop, MA (cdp) Suffolk County	14	0.08
Red Bank, NJ (borough) Monmouth County	10	0.08
Canton, NY (town) Saint Lawrence County	8	0.08
Tacoma, WA (city) Pierce County	135	0.07
Plantation, FL (city) Broward County	56	0.07
Town 'n' Country, FL (cdp) Hillsborough County	48	0.07
North Brunswick Township, NJ (cdp) Middlesex County	27	0.07
Riviera Beach, FL (city) Palm Beach County	22	0.07
Williamsport, PA (city) Lycoming County	21	0.07
Salisbury, MD (city) Wicomico County	16	0.07
Cockeysville, MD (cdp) Baltimore County	13	0.07
Bellair-Meadowbrook Terrace, FL (cdp) Clay County	12	0.07
Nanuet, NY (cdp) Rockland County	11	0.07
Fort Drum, NY (cdp) Jefferson County	8	0.07
Fort Carson, CO (cdp) El Paso County	7	0.07
Miami Shores, FL (village) Miami-Dade County	7	0.07
Savannah, GA (city) Chatham County	74	0.06
Killeen, TX (city) Bell County	50	0.06
Plainfield, NJ (city) Union County	29	0.06
Freeport, NY (village) Nassau County	25	0.06
Woonsocket, RI (city) Providence County	25	0.06
San Juan Capistrano, CA (city) Orange County	22	0.06
Orange, NJ (cdp) Essex County	19	0.06
Leesburg, VA (town) Loudoun County	18	0.06
Fort Bragg, NC (cdp) Cumberland County	17	0.06
Mableton, GA (cdp) Cobb County	17	0.06
Apopka, FL (city) Orange County	15	0.06
Fairland, MD (cdp) Montgomery County	13	0.06
Bourne, MA (town) Barnstable County	12	0.06
Forest Park, GA (city) Clayton County	12	0.06
Point Pleasant, NJ (borough) Ocean County	12	0.06
Amherst Center, MA (cdp) Hampshire County	11	0.06
Ansonia, CT (city) New Haven County	11	0.06
Avenel, NJ (cdp) Middlesex County	11	0.06
Gretna, LA (city) Jefferson Parish	10	0.06
Goldenrod, FL (cdp) Seminole County	8	0.06
Okmulgee, OK (city) Okmulgee County	8	0.06
Poinciana, FL (cdp) Osceola County	8	0.06
Princeton Meadows, NJ (cdp) Middlesex County	8	0.06
Robbinsdale, MN (city) Hennepin County	8	0.06
College, AK (cdp) Fairbanks North Star Borough	7	0.06
Hollywood, FL (city) Broward County	67	0.05
Sunrise, FL (city) Broward County	47	0.05
Sandy Springs, GA (cdp) Fulton County	43	0.05
Daytona Beach, FL (city) Volusia County	33	0.05
North Miami, FL (city) Miami-Dade County	32	0.05
Fountainbleau, FL (cdp) Miami-Dade County	31	0.05
Schenectady, NY (city) Schenectady County	29	0.05
Mount Pleasant, SC (town) Charleston County	24	0.05
Coral Gables, FL (city) Miami-Dade County	20	0.05
Smyrna, GA (city) Cobb County	20	0.05
East Point, GA (city) Fulton County	19	0.05
Suitland-Silver Hill, MD (cdp) Prince George's County	18	0.05
Teaneck, NJ (cdp) Bergen County	18	0.05
Trumbull, CT (cdp) Fairfield County	16	0.05
Oviedo, FL (city) Seminole County	14	0.05
Salisbury, NC (city) Rowan County	14	0.05
Bella Vista, AR (cdp) Benton County	9	0.05
Bloomfield, CT (town) Hartford County	9	0.05
New Milford, NJ (borough) Bergen County	9	0.05
Walnut Park, CA (cdp) Los Angeles County	8	0.05
Opa-locka, FL (city) Miami-Dade County	7	0.05
Westbury, NY (village) Nassau County	7	0.05
Wolcott, CT (town) New Haven County	7	0.05
Boston, MA (city) Suffolk County	232	0.04
Tampa, FL (city) Hillsborough County	108	0.04
Newport News, VA (independent city) Newport News city	72	0.04
Fort Lauderdale, FL (city) Broward County	55	0.04
Inglewood, CA (city) Los Angeles County	44	0.04
West Palm Beach, FL (city) Palm Beach County	34	0.04
Palm Bay, FL (city) Brevard County	32	0.04
Roswell, GA (city) Fulton County	31	0.04
Silver Spring, MD (cdp) Montgomery County	29	0.04
Irvington, NJ (cdp) Essex County	25	0.04
Germantown, MD (cdp) Montgomery County	23	0.04
West Hartford, CT (cdp) Hartford County	23	0.04
East Lansing, MI (city) Ingham County	19	0.04
West Orange, NJ (cdp) Essex County	19	0.04
Norwich, CT (city) New London County	16	0.04
Goldsboro, NC (city) Wayne County	15	0.04
Oxon Hill-Glassmanor, MD (cdp) Prince George's County	15	0.04
Pennsauken, NJ (cdp) Camden County	14	0.04
Fairbanks, AK (city) Fairbanks North Star Borough	13	0.04
Lawrence, NJ (township) Mercer County	12	0.04
Cleburne, TX (city) Johnson County	11	0.04
Lake Magdalene, FL (cdp) Hillsborough County	11	0.04

Notes: (cdp) census designated place; Refer to the Explanation of Data in the front of the book for more detailed information.

West Indian: West Indian, excluding Hispanic

Top 150 Places Sorted by Number

(Based on all places, regardless of population)

Place	Number	%
New York, NY (city) New York City	54,585	0.68
Boston, MA (city) Suffolk County	3,101	0.53
Hempstead, NY (town) Nassau County	2,280	0.30
Philadelphia, PA (city) Philadelphia County	1,513	0.10
Los Angeles, CA (city) Los Angeles County	1,121	0.03
Houston, TX (city) Harris County	975	0.05
Jersey City, NJ (city) Hudson County	923	0.38
Mount Vernon, NY (city) Westchester County	895	1.31
Baltimore, MD (independent city) Baltimore city	874	0.13
Newark, NJ (city) Essex County	812	0.30
Washington, DC (city) District of Columbia	794	0.14
Yonkers, NY (city) Westchester County	785	0.40
Jacksonville, FL (special city) Duval County	750	0.10
Babylon, NY (town) Suffolk County	741	0.35
Islip, NY (town) Suffolk County	694	0.22
Brookhaven, NY (town) Suffolk County	635	0.14
Hartford, CT (city) Hartford County	573	0.47
Chicago, IL (city) Cook County	552	0.02
Pembroke Pines, FL (city) Broward County	522	0.38
Miramar, FL (city) Broward County	493	0.68
Hempstead, NY (village) Nassau County	448	0.79
Raleigh, NC (city) Wake County	441	0.16
Tampa, FL (city) Hillsborough County	415	0.14
San Diego, CA (city) San Diego County	414	0.03
Charlotte, NC (city) Mecklenburg County	408	0.08
East Orange, NJ (city) Essex County	406	0.58
New Haven, CT (city) New Haven County	383	0.31
Freeport, NY (village) Nassau County	376	0.86
Orlando, FL (city) Orange County	369	0.20
Lauderhill, FL (city) Broward County	365	0.64
New Rochelle, NY (city) Westchester County	364	0.50
Teaneck, NJ (cdp) Bergen County	363	0.92
Miami, FL (city) Miami-Dade County	350	0.10
Sunrise, FL (city) Broward County	337	0.39
Irvington, NJ (cdp) Essex County	326	0.54
Hollywood, FL (city) Broward County	324	0.23
Waterbury, CT (city) New Haven County	322	0.30
Bridgeport, CT (city) Fairfield County	308	0.22
North Lauderdale, FL (city) Broward County	307	0.95
Virginia Beach, VA (independent city) Virginia Beach city	303	0.07
Huntsville, AL (city) Madison County	298	0.19
Detroit, MI (city) Wayne County	294	0.03
Plantation, FL (city) Broward County	288	0.35
Pine Hills, FL (cdp) Orange County	275	0.65
Uniondale, NY (cdp) Nassau County	270	1.17
Dallas, TX (city) Dallas County	270	0.02
Rochester, NY (city) Monroe County	268	0.12
Saint Petersburg, FL (city) Pinellas County	268	0.11
Cambridge, MA (city) Middlesex County	265	0.26
Montclair, NJ (cdp) Essex County	261	0.67
Phoenix, AZ (city) Maricopa County	260	0.02
Buffalo, NY (city) Erie County	258	0.09
North Hempstead, NY (town) Nassau County	250	0.11
North Amityville, NY (cdp) Suffolk County	247	1.50
Coral Springs, FL (city) Broward County	240	0.20
Randolph, MA (cdp) Norfolk County	238	0.77
Springfield, MA (city) Hampden County	237	0.16
Baldwin, NY (cdp) Nassau County	232	0.99
Willingboro, NJ (township) Burlington County	228	0.69
Plainfield, NJ (city) Union County	227	0.47
Greenburgh, NY (town) Westchester County	227	0.26
Lynn, MA (city) Essex County	225	0.25
Oyster Bay, NY (town) Nassau County	225	0.08
Baytown, TX (city) Harris County	221	0.33
Long Beach, CA (city) Los Angeles County	218	0.05
Franklin, NJ (township) Somerset County	214	0.42
San Francisco, CA (city) San Francisco County	212	0.03
Columbus, OH (city) Franklin County	201	0.03
New London, CT (city) New London County	200	0.78
Brockton, MA (city) Plymouth County	199	0.21
Schenectady, NY (city) Schenectady County	198	0.32
Palm Bay, FL (city) Brevard County	197	0.25
Albany, NY (city) Albany County	197	0.21
Anchorage, AK (municipality) Anchorage Borough	196	0.08
Silver Spring, MD (cdp) Montgomery County	194	0.25
Orange, NJ (cdp) Essex County	191	0.58
Syracuse, NY (city) Onondaga County	186	0.13
Ramapo, NY (town) Rockland County	185	0.17
Pittsburgh, PA (city) Allegheny County	182	0.05
Port Charlotte, FL (cdp) Charlotte County	177	0.38
Colorado Springs, CO (city) El Paso County	175	0.05
Las Vegas, NV (city) Clark County	175	0.04
Huntington, NY (town) Suffolk County	173	0.09
Golden Glades, FL (cdp) Miami-Dade County	172	0.53
Framingham, MA (cdp) Middlesex County	168	0.25
North Valley Stream, NY (cdp) Nassau County	167	1.06
Dale City, VA (cdp) Prince William County	167	0.30
Atlanta, GA (city) Fulton County	166	0.04
San Antonio, TX (city) Bexar County	166	0.01
Apopka, FL (city) Orange County	165	0.63
Worcester, MA (city) Worcester County	164	0.09
Elmont, NY (cdp) Nassau County	163	0.50
Clarkstown, NY (town) Rockland County	163	0.20
Poinciana, FL (cdp) Osceola County	162	1.19
Providence, RI (city) Providence County	162	0.09
Hampton, VA (independent city) Hampton city	160	0.11
Nashville-Davidson, TN (special city) Davidson County	160	0.03
Redan, GA (cdp) De Kalb County	159	0.47
Brentwood, NY (cdp) Suffolk County	158	0.29
New Bedford, MA (city) Bristol County	158	0.17
Newport News, VA (independent city) Newport News city	157	0.09
Yeehaw Junction, FL (cdp) Osceola County	156	0.70
Chesapeake, VA (independent city) Chesapeake city	156	0.08
Windsor, CT (town) Hartford County	155	0.55
Arlington, TX (city) Tarrant County	154	0.05
Cleveland, OH (city) Cuyahoga County	154	0.03
Greensboro, NC (city) Guilford County	152	0.07
Tamarac, FL (city) Broward County	151	0.27
Somerville, MA (city) Middlesex County	148	0.19
Indianapolis, IN (special city) Marion County	148	0.02
Chillum, MD (cdp) Prince George's County	147	0.43
Bloomfield, CT (town) Hartford County	146	0.75
Central Islip, NY (cdp) Suffolk County	146	0.46
Englewood, NJ (city) Bergen County	145	0.55
Lawrence, NJ (township) Mercer County	145	0.50
Newburgh, NY (city) Orange County	143	0.51
Lauderdale Lakes, FL (city) Broward County	141	0.45
White Plains, NY (city) Westchester County	141	0.27
Norfolk, VA (independent city) Norfolk city	141	0.06
Milton, MA (cdp) Norfolk County	140	0.54
West Orange, NJ (cdp) Essex County	139	0.31
Roosevelt, NY (cdp) Nassau County	136	0.86
New Orleans, LA (city) Orleans Parish	136	0.03
Richmond, VA (independent city) Richmond city	134	0.07
Oakland, CA (city) Alameda County	134	0.03
University, FL (cdp) Hillsborough County	133	0.43
West Haven, CT (city) New Haven County	132	0.25
Tallahassee, FL (city) Leon County	132	0.09
Montgomery Village, MD (cdp) Montgomery County	131	0.35
Port Saint Lucie, FL (city) Saint Lucie County	131	0.15
Augusta-Richmond County, GA (special city) Richmond County	131	0.07
Woodbridge, NJ (township) Middlesex County	130	0.13
Palm Coast, FL (city) Flagler County	129	0.39
Minneapolis, MN (city) Hennepin County	129	0.03
Lakeview, NY (cdp) Nassau County	127	2.27
Beltsville, MD (cdp) Prince George's County	127	0.81
Lakeland, FL (city) Polk County	127	0.16
Bay Shore, NY (cdp) Suffolk County	126	0.53
Elizabeth, NJ (city) Union County	126	0.10
Maplewood, NJ (cdp) Essex County	125	0.52
Fort Lauderdale, FL (city) Broward County	124	0.08
Carol City, FL (cdp) Miami-Dade County	122	0.21
Altamonte Springs, FL (city) Seminole County	121	0.29
East Hartford, CT (cdp) Hartford County	121	0.24
Fort Bragg, NC (cdp) Cumberland County	120	0.41
White Oak, MD (cdp) Montgomery County	119	0.57
North Brunswick Township, NJ (cdp) Middlesex County	119	0.33
Davie, FL (town) Broward County	119	0.16
West Palm Beach, FL (city) Palm Beach County	119	0.15
Irving, TX (city) Dallas County	119	0.06

Notes: (cdp) census designated place; Refer to the Explanation of Data in the front of the book for more detailed information.

West Indian: West Indian, excluding Hispanic

Top 150 Places Sorted by Percent

(Based on all places, regardless of population)

Place	Number	%
Gun Club Estates, FL (cdp) Palm Beach County	92	10.86
Chula Vista, FL (cdp) Broward County	20	3.42
Annandale, NJ (cdp) Hunterdon County	44	3.36
Climax, GA (city) Decatur County	8	2.62
Rentiesville, OK (town) McIntosh County	2	2.44
Lakeview, NY (cdp) Nassau County	127	2.27
Kings Bay Base, GA (cdp) Camden County	57	2.26
Grand View-on-Hudson, NY (village) Rockland County	6	2.12
Wheatley Heights, NY (cdp) Suffolk County	104	2.07
Lake Belvedere Estates, FL (cdp) Palm Beach County	27	1.81
East Hampton North, NY (cdp) Suffolk County	63	1.79
Thorndale, PA (cdp) Chester County	61	1.69
Grayson, GA (city) Gwinnett County	13	1.67
Saint Leo, FL (town) Pasco County	10	1.64
Whitesboro-Burleigh, NJ (cdp) Cape May County	31	1.58
Jumpertown, MS (town) Prentiss County	6	1.57
Orlovista, FL (cdp) Orange County	95	1.56
North Amityville, NY (cdp) Suffolk County	247	1.50
Rockleigh, NJ (borough) Bergen County	6	1.50
East Perrine, FL (cdp) Miami-Dade County	102	1.49
Richlawn, KY (city) Jefferson County	7	1.49
Jonestown, PA (borough) Lebanon County	15	1.46
Whiting, KS (city) Jackson County	3	1.46
South Windham, CT (cdp) Windham County	19	1.44
Tobyhanna, PA (township) Monroe County	88	1.43
Calcium, NY (cdp) Jefferson County	44	1.39
Roosevelt Gardens, FL (cdp) Broward County	26	1.39
Sky Lake, FL (cdp) Orange County	81	1.37
Coleman, GA (city) Randolph County	2	1.36
Gordonsville, TN (town) Smith County	14	1.32
Mount Vernon, NY (city) Westchester County	895	1.31
Jacksonville, GA (town) Telfair County	2	1.29
Dunkirk, MD (cdp) Calvert County	29	1.24
Loch Lomond, FL (cdp) Broward County	41	1.23
Blue Hills, CT (cdp) Hartford County	37	1.20
Poinciana, FL (cdp) Osceola County	162	1.19
Uniondale, NY (cdp) Nassau County	270	1.17
Melville, RI (cdp) Newport County	26	1.17
La Grange, WY (town) Goshen County	4	1.17
Cliffwood Beach, NJ (cdp) Monmouth County	41	1.16
Fairton, NJ (cdp) Cumberland County	27	1.16
South Floral Park, NY (village) Nassau County	18	1.14
Royal Lakes, IL (village) Macoupin County	2	1.14
Lake Forest, FL (cdp) Broward County	55	1.11
Penbrook, PA (borough) Dauphin County	33	1.08
Timmonsville, SC (town) Florence County	25	1.08
North Valley Stream, NY (cdp) Nassau County	167	1.06
Wentworth, SD (village) Lake County	2	1.02
Baldwin, NY (cdp) Nassau County	232	0.99
Golden Lakes, FL (cdp) Palm Beach County	65	0.97
North Bellport, NY (cdp) Suffolk County	88	0.96
North Lauderdale, FL (city) Broward County	307	0.95
Millbourne, PA (borough) Delaware County	9	0.95
South Hackensack, NJ (township) Bergen County	21	0.93
Teaneck, NJ (cdp) Bergen County	363	0.92
Fort Myers Shores, FL (cdp) Lee County	53	0.92
Morrow, GA (city) Clayton County	45	0.92
Stone Mountain, GA (city) De Kalb County	62	0.91
Greatwood, TX (cdp) Fort Bend County	60	0.91
Ridgeville, SC (town) Dorchester County	15	0.90
Olivet, NJ (cdp) Salem County	13	0.88
De Land Southwest, FL (cdp) Volusia County	10	0.88
Riverdale Park, MD (town) Prince George's County	57	0.87
Napeague, NY (cdp) Suffolk County	2	0.87
Freeport, NY (village) Nassau County	376	0.86
Roosevelt, NY (cdp) Nassau County	136	0.86
Fayette, MO (city) Howard County	24	0.85
Hope, MI (township) Midland County	11	0.85
Weybridge, VT (town) Addison County	7	0.85
Forestville, CA (cdp) Sonoma County	21	0.84
Layton, FL (city) Monroe County	2	0.83
Islandia, NY (village) Suffolk County	25	0.82
Beltsville, MD (cdp) Prince George's County	127	0.81
Meadow Woods, FL (cdp) Orange County	93	0.81
Oronoko charter, MI (township) Berrien County	80	0.81

Place	Number	%
Goulds, FL (cdp) Miami-Dade County	61	0.80
Highlands, TX (cdp) Harris County	56	0.80
Northwest Harbor, NY (cdp) Suffolk County	25	0.80
Hempstead, NY (village) Nassau County	448	0.79
New London, CT (city) New London County	200	0.78
Colley, PA (township) Sullivan County	5	0.78
Randolph, MA (cdp) Norfolk County	238	0.77
Opa-locka North, FL (cdp) Miami-Dade County	48	0.77
Greenvale, NY (cdp) Nassau County	17	0.77
Bloomfield, CT (town) Hartford County	146	0.75
Gordon Heights, NY (cdp) Suffolk County	23	0.74
Homestead, PA (borough) Allegheny County	26	0.73
Selbyville, DE (town) Sussex County	12	0.73
Gettysburg, OH (village) Darke County	4	0.73
Gibsonia, FL (cdp) Polk County	35	0.72
Greenwich, NJ (township) Warren County	31	0.71
Springdale, MD (cdp) Prince George's County	20	0.71
Beverly, NJ (city) Burlington County	19	0.71
Yeehaw Junction, FL (cdp) Osceola County	156	0.70
University Gardens, NY (cdp) Nassau County	29	0.70
Barrett, TX (cdp) Harris County	19	0.70
Silver Lake, FL (cdp) Lake County	13	0.70
Willingboro, NJ (township) Burlington County	228	0.69
Opa-locka, FL (city) Miami-Dade County	105	0.69
New York, NY (city) New York City	54,585	0.68
Miramar, FL (city) Broward County	493	0.68
Kettering, MD (cdp) Prince George's County	75	0.68
Montclair, NJ (cdp) Essex County	261	0.67
Carlisle, IN (town) Sullivan County	17	0.67
Ocean Breeze Park, FL (town) Martin County	3	0.67
Eastampton, NJ (township) Burlington County	41	0.66
Westfall, PA (township) Pike County	16	0.66
Lometa, TX (city) Lampasas County	5	0.66
Pine Hills, FL (cdp) Orange County	275	0.65
Kemp Mill, MD (cdp) Montgomery County	65	0.65
Mechanicstown, NY (cdp) Orange County	40	0.65
Haverhill, FL (town) Palm Beach County	10	0.65
Forest Park, OK (town) Oklahoma County	7	0.65
Fairmount, MD (cdp) Somerset County	4	0.65
Lauderhill, FL (city) Broward County	365	0.64
North Brentwood, MD (town) Prince George's County	3	0.64
Apopka, FL (city) Orange County	165	0.63
South Orange, NJ (cdp) Essex County	107	0.63
Melrose Park, FL (cdp) Broward County	45	0.63
Huber Ridge, OH (cdp) Franklin County	31	0.63
Broad Brook, CT (cdp) Hartford County	22	0.63
Deerfield, WI (town) Dane County	9	0.63
Nebo Center, CA (cdp) San Bernardino County	8	0.63
Rodessa, LA (village) Caddo Parish	2	0.63
Elwood, NY (cdp) Suffolk County	67	0.62
Richland Hills, TX (city) Tarrant County	50	0.62
Brodheadsville, PA (cdp) Monroe County	9	0.62
Ehrhardt, SC (town) Bamberg County	4	0.62
Glen Haven, WI (town) Grant County	3	0.62
Springdale, WA (town) Stevens County	2	0.62
Caln, PA (township) Chester County	72	0.61
Purcellville, VA (town) Loudoun County	22	0.61
Terryville, NY (cdp) Suffolk County	64	0.60
Mount Ivy, NY (cdp) Rockland County	39	0.60
New Hempstead, NY (village) Rockland County	29	0.60
Manning, SC (city) Clarendon County	24	0.60
Rollingwood, CA (cdp) Contra Costa County	17	0.60
Lewistown, IL (city) Fulton County	15	0.60
Portland, TX (city) San Patricio County	88	0.59
Lake Los Angeles, CA (cdp) Los Angeles County	69	0.59
East Orange, NJ (city) Essex County	406	0.58
Orange, NJ (cdp) Essex County	191	0.58
Ives Estates, FL (cdp) Miami-Dade County	101	0.58
Laurel, VA (cdp) Henrico County	84	0.58
Woodcrest, CA (cdp) Riverside County	48	0.58
Provincetown, MA (town) Barnstable County	20	0.58
White Oak, MD (cdp) Montgomery County	119	0.57
North Bay Shore, NY (cdp) Suffolk County	85	0.57
Oriental, NC (town) Pamlico County	5	0.57
Fleischmanns, NY (village) Delaware County	2	0.57

Notes: (cdp) census designated place; Refer to the Explanation of Data in the front of the book for more detailed information.

West Indian: West Indian, excluding Hispanic

Top 150 Places Sorted by Percent

(Based on places with populations of 10,000 or more)

Place	Number	%
North Amityville, NY (cdp) Suffolk County	247	1.50
Mount Vernon, NY (city) Westchester County	895	1.31
Poinciana, FL (cdp) Osceola County	162	1.19
Uniondale, NY (cdp) Nassau County	270	1.17
North Valley Stream, NY (cdp) Nassau County	167	1.06
Baldwin, NY (cdp) Nassau County	232	0.99
North Lauderdale, FL (city) Broward County	307	0.95
Teaneck, NJ (cdp) Bergen County	363	0.92
Freeport, NY (village) Nassau County	376	0.86
Roosevelt, NY (cdp) Nassau County	136	0.86
Beltsville, MD (cdp) Prince George's County	127	0.81
Meadow Woods, FL (cdp) Orange County	93	0.81
Hempstead, NY (village) Nassau County	448	0.79
New London, CT (city) New London County	200	0.78
Randolph, MA (cdp) Norfolk County	238	0.77
Bloomfield, CT (town) Hartford County	146	0.75
Yeehaw Junction, FL (cdp) Osceola County	156	0.70
Willingboro, NJ (township) Burlington County	228	0.69
Opa-locka, FL (city) Miami-Dade County	105	0.69
New York, NY (city) New York City	54,585	0.68
Miramar, FL (city) Broward County	493	0.68
Kettering, MD (cdp) Prince George's County	75	0.68
Montclair, NJ (cdp) Essex County	261	0.67
Pine Hills, FL (cdp) Orange County	275	0.65
Lauderhill, FL (city) Broward County	365	0.64
Apopka, FL (city) Orange County	165	0.63
South Orange, NJ (cdp) Essex County	107	0.63
Elwood, NY (cdp) Suffolk County	67	0.62
Caln, PA (township) Chester County	72	0.61
Terryville, NY (cdp) Suffolk County	64	0.60
Portland, TX (city) San Patricio County	88	0.59
Lake Los Angeles, CA (cdp) Los Angeles County	69	0.59
East Orange, NJ (city) Essex County	406	0.58
Orange, NJ (cdp) Essex County	191	0.58
Ives Estates, FL (cdp) Miami-Dade County	101	0.58
Laurel, VA (cdp) Henrico County	84	0.58
White Oak, MD (cdp) Montgomery County	119	0.57
North Bay Shore, NY (cdp) Suffolk County	85	0.57
Miami Shores, FL (village) Miami-Dade County	58	0.56
Windsor, CT (town) Hartford County	155	0.55
Englewood, NJ (city) Bergen County	145	0.55
Aberdeen, NJ (township) Monmouth County	95	0.55
Irvington, NJ (cdp) Essex County	326	0.54
Milton, MA (cdp) Norfolk County	140	0.54
Country Walk, FL (cdp) Miami-Dade County	57	0.54
Boston, MA (city) Suffolk County	3,101	0.53
Golden Glades, FL (cdp) Miami-Dade County	172	0.53
Bay Shore, NY (cdp) Suffolk County	126	0.53
East Hampton, NY (town) Suffolk County	105	0.53
Maplewood, NJ (cdp) Essex County	125	0.52
West Haverstraw, NY (village) Rockland County	54	0.52
Newburgh, NY (city) Orange County	143	0.51
Groton, CT (city) New London County	51	0.51
New Rochelle, NY (city) Westchester County	364	0.50
Elmont, NY (cdp) Nassau County	163	0.50
Lawrence, NJ (township) Mercer County	145	0.50
New Cassel, NY (cdp) Nassau County	67	0.50
Rossville, MD (cdp) Baltimore County	58	0.50
Hyattsville, MD (city) Prince George's County	72	0.49
Hartford, CT (city) Hartford County	573	0.47
Plainfield, NJ (city) Union County	227	0.47
Redan, GA (cdp) De Kalb County	159	0.47
Central Islip, NY (cdp) Suffolk County	146	0.46
East Massapequa, NY (cdp) Nassau County	90	0.46
Lauderdale Lakes, FL (city) Broward County	141	0.45
Wallkill, NY (town) Orange County	110	0.45
Oak Ridge, FL (cdp) Orange County	101	0.45
Chillum, MD (cdp) Prince George's County	147	0.43
University, FL (cdp) Hillsborough County	133	0.43
Fort Benning South, GA (cdp) Chattahoochee County	50	0.43
Franklin, NJ (township) Somerset County	214	0.42
Windham, CT (town) Windham County	95	0.42
Fairland, MD (cdp) Montgomery County	90	0.42
Carteret, NJ (borough) Middlesex County	87	0.42
Princeton, NJ (township) Mercer County	68	0.42
Fort Bragg, NC (cdp) Cumberland County	120	0.41
Lochearn, MD (cdp) Baltimore County	103	0.41
Somers, CT (town) Tolland County	43	0.41
Yonkers, NY (city) Westchester County	785	0.40
Somerset, NJ (cdp) Somerset County	92	0.40
Sunrise, FL (city) Broward County	337	0.39
Palm Coast, FL (city) Flagler County	129	0.39
Jersey City, NJ (city) Hudson County	923	0.38
Pembroke Pines, FL (city) Broward County	522	0.38
Port Charlotte, FL (cdp) Charlotte County	177	0.38
Hyde Park, NY (town) Dutchess County	80	0.38
Stafford, TX (city) Fort Bend County	59	0.38
Wyandanch, NY (cdp) Suffolk County	40	0.38
Kingsland, GA (city) Camden County	39	0.37
Clinton, MD (cdp) Prince George's County	95	0.36
Sandalfoot Cove, FL (cdp) Palm Beach County	60	0.36
River Edge, NJ (borough) Bergen County	39	0.36
Babylon, NY (town) Suffolk County	741	0.35
Plantation, FL (city) Broward County	288	0.35
Montgomery Village, MD (cdp) Montgomery County	131	0.35
East Windsor, NJ (township) Mercer County	86	0.35
West Hempstead, NY (cdp) Nassau County	65	0.35
Camp Springs, MD (cdp) Prince George's County	62	0.35
Palm River-Clair Mel, FL (cdp) Hillsborough County	62	0.35
Asbury Park, NJ (city) Monmouth County	59	0.35
Fords, NJ (cdp) Middlesex County	53	0.35
Haverstraw, NY (town) Rockland County	114	0.34
Reidsville, NC (city) Rockingham County	49	0.34
Westbury, NY (village) Nassau County	48	0.34
Clinton, NJ (township) Hunterdon County	44	0.34
Baytown, TX (city) Harris County	221	0.33
North Brunswick Township, NJ (cdp) Middlesex County	119	0.33
Spring Valley, NY (village) Rockland County	83	0.33
College Park, GA (city) Fulton County	69	0.33
Secaucus, NJ (town) Hudson County	53	0.33
Wawarsing, NY (town) Ulster County	42	0.33
Schenectady, NY (city) Schenectady County	198	0.32
Le Ray, NY (town) Jefferson County	63	0.32
Estelle, LA (cdp) Jefferson Parish	51	0.32
Carver, MA (town) Plymouth County	36	0.32
New Haven, CT (city) New Haven County	383	0.31
West Orange, NJ (cdp) Essex County	139	0.31
Newport, RI (city) Newport County	81	0.31
Greenbelt, MD (city) Prince George's County	67	0.31
Forest City, FL (cdp) Seminole County	40	0.31
Middle Smithfield, PA (township) Monroe County	36	0.31
Hempstead, NY (town) Nassau County	2,280	0.30
Newark, NJ (city) Essex County	812	0.30
Waterbury, CT (city) New Haven County	322	0.30
Dale City, VA (cdp) Prince William County	167	0.30
South Miami Heights, FL (cdp) Miami-Dade County	101	0.30
Fort Washington, MD (cdp) Prince George's County	73	0.30
Pinewood, FL (cdp) Miami-Dade County	50	0.30
Northbridge, MA (town) Worcester County	39	0.30
Brentwood, NY (cdp) Suffolk County	158	0.29
Altamonte Springs, FL (city) Seminole County	121	0.29
North Miami Beach, FL (city) Miami-Dade County	117	0.29
New City, NY (cdp) Rockland County	100	0.29
Norland, FL (cdp) Miami-Dade County	66	0.29
South Laurel, MD (cdp) Prince George's County	61	0.29
Gretna, LA (city) Jefferson Parish	50	0.29
Carrboro, NC (town) Orange County	49	0.29
Scott Lake, FL (cdp) Miami-Dade County	42	0.29
Freehold, NJ (borough) Monmouth County	32	0.29
Egypt Lake-Leto, FL (cdp) Hillsborough County	92	0.28
Cutler Ridge, FL (cdp) Miami-Dade County	69	0.28
Owings Mills, MD (cdp) Baltimore County	56	0.28
Takoma Park, MD (city) Montgomery County	48	0.28
Willimantic, CT (cdp) Windham County	45	0.28
Aberdeen, MD (city) Harford County	38	0.28
Mastic Beach, NY (cdp) Suffolk County	32	0.28
Tamarac, FL (city) Broward County	151	0.27
White Plains, NY (city) Westchester County	141	0.27
Cortlandt, NY (town) Westchester County	102	0.27
Long Branch, NJ (city) Monmouth County	86	0.27

Notes: (cdp) census designated place; Refer to the Explanation of Data in the front of the book for more detailed information.

West Indian: Other, excluding Hispanic

Top 150 Places Sorted by Number

(Based on all places, regardless of population)

Place	Number	%
New York, NY (city) New York City	1,317	0.02
Hempstead, NY (town) Nassau County	96	0.01
Saint Petersburg, FL (city) Pinellas County	74	0.03
Brookhaven, NY (town) Suffolk County	63	0.01
Greater Northdale, FL (cdp) Hillsborough County	59	0.29
Philadelphia, PA (city) Philadelphia County	55	0.00
Houston, TX (city) Harris County	44	0.00
Mount Vernon, NY (city) Westchester County	43	0.06
Pendleton, OR (city) Umatilla County	42	0.26
Davie, FL (town) Broward County	42	0.06
Jacksonville, FL (special city) Duval County	42	0.01
Lompoc, CA (city) Santa Barbara County	41	0.10
Jersey City, NJ (city) Hudson County	39	0.02
Centereach, NY (cdp) Suffolk County	38	0.14
Tampa, FL (city) Hillsborough County	38	0.01
Fort Lauderdale, FL (city) Broward County	37	0.02
Orlando, FL (city) Orange County	37	0.02
Hempstead, NY (village) Nassau County	35	0.06
Los Angeles, CA (city) Los Angeles County	35	0.00
Carol City, FL (cdp) Miami-Dade County	34	0.06
Port Arthur, TX (city) Jefferson County	34	0.06
Benner, PA (township) Centre County	32	0.61
University, FL (cdp) Hillsborough County	32	0.10
Rockville, MD (city) Montgomery County	32	0.07
Allentown, PA (city) Lehigh County	32	0.03
Carrollton, TX (city) Denton County	32	0.03
Nederland, TX (city) Jefferson County	31	0.18
New London, CT (city) New London County	30	0.12
Miami Beach, FL (city) Miami-Dade County	29	0.03
Seffner, FL (cdp) Hillsborough County	28	0.50
Valley Stream, NY (village) Nassau County	28	0.08
Mableton, GA (cdp) Cobb County	26	0.09
Coral Springs, FL (city) Broward County	26	0.02
North Miami Beach, FL (city) Miami-Dade County	25	0.06
Miami, FL (city) Miami-Dade County	25	0.01
South Miami Heights, FL (cdp) Miami-Dade County	24	0.07
Lakewood, CO (city) Jefferson County	24	0.02
Virginia Beach, VA (independent city) Virginia Beach city	24	0.01
Orange, NJ (cdp) Essex County	23	0.07
Elizabeth, NJ (city) Union County	23	0.02
Pembroke Pines, FL (city) Broward County	23	0.02
Riverside, CA (city) Riverside County	22	0.01
Saint Rose, LA (cdp) Saint Charles Parish	21	0.32
Hyattsville, MD (city) Prince George's County	19	0.13
Pinewood, FL (cdp) Miami-Dade County	19	0.11
Frisco, TX (city) Collin County	19	0.06
Mansfield, OH (city) Richland County	19	0.04
Palm Bay, FL (city) Brevard County	19	0.02
Plantation, FL (city) Broward County	19	0.02
West Palm Beach, FL (city) Palm Beach County	19	0.02
De Bary, FL (city) Volusia County	18	0.11
College Park, MD (city) Prince George's County	18	0.07
Orion, MI (township) Oakland County	18	0.05
Miramar, FL (city) Broward County	18	0.02
Hollywood, FL (city) Broward County	18	0.01
Tallahassee, FL (city) Leon County	18	0.01
Cold Spring, NY (village) Putnam County	17	0.86
Matawan, NJ (borough) Monmouth County	17	0.19
Philipstown, NY (town) Putnam County	17	0.18
Coram, NY (cdp) Suffolk County	17	0.05
Teaneck, NJ (cdp) Bergen County	17	0.04
Chandler, AZ (city) Maricopa County	17	0.01
San Francisco, CA (city) San Francisco County	17	0.00
Fussels Corner, FL (cdp) Polk County	16	0.31
De Land, FL (city) Volusia County	16	0.08
Hinesville, GA (city) Liberty County	16	0.05
South Brunswick, NJ (township) Middlesex County	16	0.04
Stamford, CT (city) Fairfield County	16	0.01
Takoma Park, MD (city) Montgomery County	15	0.09
Citrus Park, FL (cdp) Hillsborough County	15	0.07
Ankeny, IA (city) Polk County	15	0.06
Grandview, MO (city) Jackson County	15	0.06
Doral, FL (cdp) Miami-Dade County	14	0.07
University Park, FL (cdp) Miami-Dade County	14	0.05
Kendall West, FL (cdp) Miami-Dade County	14	0.04
East Hartford, CT (cdp) Hartford County	14	0.03
Levittown, NY (cdp) Nassau County	14	0.03
Lauderhill, FL (city) Broward County	14	0.02
Washington, DC (city) District of Columbia	14	0.00
Mystic, CT (cdp) New London County	13	0.32
Kettering, MD (cdp) Prince George's County	13	0.12
Atlantic Beach, FL (city) Duval County	13	0.10
Seekonk, MA (town) Bristol County	13	0.10
Stonington, CT (town) New London County	13	0.07
Ithaca, NY (city) Tompkins County	13	0.04
Delray Beach, FL (city) Palm Beach County	13	0.02
Sunrise, FL (city) Broward County	13	0.02
Newport News, VA (independent city) Newport News city	13	0.01
Oyster Bay, NY (town) Nassau County	13	0.00
East Perrine, FL (cdp) Miami-Dade County	12	0.18
Poinciana, FL (cdp) Osceola County	12	0.09
North Valley Stream, NY (cdp) Nassau County	12	0.08
West Bloomfield, MI (township) Oakland County	12	0.02
Alexandria, VA (independent city) Alexandria city	12	0.01
San Bernardino, CA (city) San Bernardino County	12	0.01
Topeka, KS (city) Shawnee County	12	0.01
Portland, OR (city) Multnomah County	12	0.00
Corinth, TX (city) Denton County	11	0.10
Palestine, TX (city) Anderson County	11	0.06
Bessemer, AL (city) Jefferson County	11	0.04
Suisun City, CA (city) Solano County	11	0.04
Franklin, NJ (township) Somerset County	11	0.02
Gaithersburg, MD (city) Montgomery County	11	0.02
Old Bridge, NJ (township) Middlesex County	11	0.02
Evanston, IL (city) Cook County	11	0.01
Richmond, VA (independent city) Richmond city	11	0.01
Tacoma, WA (city) Pierce County	11	0.01
Islip, NY (town) Suffolk County	11	0.00
Kansas City, MO (city) Jackson County	11	0.00
Madeira Beach, FL (city) Pinellas County	10	0.22
Chatham, NJ (borough) Morris County	10	0.12
Park Ridge, NJ (borough) Bergen County	10	0.11
Mount Kisco, NY (village) Westchester County	10	0.10
Hartland, MI (township) Livingston County	10	0.09
Fairhope, AL (city) Baldwin County	10	0.08
Summit, NJ (city) Union County	10	0.05
Country Club, FL (cdp) Miami-Dade County	10	0.03
Lake Magdalene, FL (cdp) Hillsborough County	10	0.03
Randolph, MA (cdp) Norfolk County	10	0.03
Decatur, AL (city) Morgan County	10	0.02
North Bergen, NJ (township) Hudson County	10	0.02
Perth Amboy, NJ (city) Middlesex County	10	0.02
West New York, NJ (town) Hudson County	10	0.02
Lake Charles, LA (city) Calcasieu Parish	10	0.01
Anchorage, AK (municipality) Anchorage Borough	10	0.00
Boston, MA (city) Suffolk County	10	0.00
Memphis, TN (city) Shelby County	10	0.00
Hampden Sydney, VA (cdp) Prince Edward County	9	0.73
Bridgeport, IL (city) Lawrence County	9	0.40
Flagler Beach, FL (city) Flagler County	9	0.18
Dayton, NJ (cdp) Middlesex County	9	0.14
Lakeside, VA (cdp) Henrico County	9	0.08
Upper Grand Lagoon, FL (cdp) Bay County	9	0.08
Parkland, FL (city) Broward County	9	0.06
Kahului, HI (cdp) Maui County	9	0.04
Plainview, NY (cdp) Nassau County	9	0.04
Florin, CA (cdp) Sacramento County	9	0.03
Kaneohe, HI (cdp) Honolulu County	9	0.03
Lauderdale Lakes, FL (city) Broward County	9	0.03
Holyoke, MA (city) Hampden County	9	0.02
Jupiter, FL (town) Palm Beach County	9	0.02
Oak Park, IL (village) Cook County	9	0.02
East Orange, NJ (city) Essex County	9	0.01
Gainesville, FL (city) Alachua County	9	0.01
Hartford, CT (city) Hartford County	9	0.01
Wilmington, DE (city) New Castle County	9	0.01
Chicago, IL (city) Cook County	9	0.00
Oakland, CA (city) Alameda County	9	0.00
San Diego, CA (city) San Diego County	9	0.00
Orleans, MI (township) Ionia County	8	0.29

Notes: (cdp) census designated place; Refer to the Explanation of Data in the front of the book for more detailed information.

West Indian: Other, excluding Hispanic

Top 150 Places Sorted by Percent

(Based on all places, regardless of population)

Place	Number	%
Grandfather, NC (village) Avery County	2	2.44
Buckingham, IL (village) Kankakee County	3	1.29
Cold Spring, NY (village) Putnam County	17	0.86
Hampden Sydney, VA (cdp) Prince Edward County	9	0.73
Benner, PA (township) Centre County	32	0.61
Seffner, FL (cdp) Hillsborough County	28	0.50
Whitsett, NC (town) Guilford County	3	0.44
Bridgeport, IL (city) Lawrence County	9	0.40
Breckinridge Center, KY (cdp) Union County	7	0.37
Kinde, MI (village) Huron County	2	0.37
Saint Rose, LA (cdp) Saint Charles Parish	21	0.32
Mystic, CT (cdp) New London County	13	0.32
Fussels Corner, FL (cdp) Polk County	16	0.31
University Heights, IA (city) Johnson County	3	0.30
Greater Northdale, FL (cdp) Hillsborough County	59	0.29
Orleans, MI (township) Ionia County	8	0.29
Monmouth Junction, NJ (cdp) Middlesex County	7	0.29
Hennepin, IL (village) Putnam County	2	0.29
Douglas, MN (township) Dakota County	2	0.27
Pendleton, OR (city) Umatilla County	42	0.26
Rosiclare, IL (city) Hardin County	3	0.25
Oxoboxo River, CT (cdp) New London County	7	0.24
Shinglehouse, PA (borough) Potter County	3	0.24
Madeira Beach, FL (city) Pinellas County	10	0.22
Lincoln, MI (township) Huron County	2	0.22
Matawan, NJ (borough) Monmouth County	17	0.19
Pennington, NJ (borough) Mercer County	5	0.19
Nederland, TX (city) Jefferson County	31	0.18
Philipstown, NY (town) Putnam County	17	0.18
East Perrine, FL (cdp) Miami-Dade County	12	0.18
Flagler Beach, FL (city) Flagler County	9	0.18
Sherman, MI (township) Huron County	2	0.17
Canterbury, CT (town) Windham County	7	0.15
East Norwich, NY (cdp) Nassau County	4	0.15
Gregory, SD (city) Gregory County	2	0.15
Groton Long Point, CT (borough) New London County	1	0.15
Centereach, NY (cdp) Suffolk County	38	0.14
Dayton, NJ (cdp) Middlesex County	9	0.14
Waimanalo, HI (cdp) Honolulu County	5	0.14
Huntington, TX (city) Angelina County	3	0.14
Hyattsville, MD (city) Prince George's County	19	0.13
Tilton-Northfield, NH (cdp) Belknap County	4	0.13
Southside Place, TX (city) Harris County	2	0.13
New London, CT (city) New London County	30	0.12
Kettering, MD (cdp) Prince George's County	13	0.12
Chatham, NJ (borough) Morris County	10	0.12
West Sayville, NY (cdp) Suffolk County	6	0.12
Pinewood, FL (cdp) Miami-Dade County	19	0.11
De Bary, FL (city) Volusia County	18	0.11
Park Ridge, NJ (borough) Bergen County	10	0.11
Accokeek, MD (cdp) Prince George's County	8	0.11
La Salle, CO (town) Weld County	2	0.11
Ripley, OH (village) Brown County	2	0.11
Lompoc, CA (city) Santa Barbara County	41	0.10
University, FL (cdp) Hillsborough County	32	0.10
Atlantic Beach, FL (city) Duval County	13	0.10
Seekonk, MA (town) Bristol County	13	0.10
Corinth, TX (city) Denton County	11	0.10
Mount Kisco, NY (village) Westchester County	10	0.10
Schuylkill, PA (township) Chester County	7	0.10
Liberty, NY (village) Sullivan County	4	0.10
Pine Beach, NJ (borough) Ocean County	2	0.10
Mableton, GA (cdp) Cobb County	26	0.09
Takoma Park, MD (city) Montgomery County	15	0.09
Poinciana, FL (cdp) Osceola County	12	0.09
Hartland, MI (township) Livingston County	10	0.09
Northfield, NH (town) Merrimack County	4	0.09
Valley Stream, NY (village) Nassau County	28	0.08
De Land, FL (city) Volusia County	16	0.08
North Valley Stream, NY (cdp) Nassau County	12	0.08
Fairhope, AL (city) Baldwin County	10	0.08
Lakeside, VA (cdp) Henrico County	9	0.08
Upper Grand Lagoon, FL (cdp) Bay County	9	0.08
Jacinto City, TX (city) Harris County	8	0.08
Clear Lake Shores, TX (city) Galveston County	1	0.08
Rockville, MD (city) Montgomery County	32	0.07
South Miami Heights, FL (cdp) Miami-Dade County	24	0.07
Orange, NJ (cdp) Essex County	23	0.07
College Park, MD (city) Prince George's County	18	0.07
Citrus Park, FL (cdp) Hillsborough County	15	0.07
Doral, FL (cdp) Miami-Dade County	14	0.07
Stonington, CT (town) New London County	13	0.07
Freehold, NJ (borough) Monmouth County	8	0.07
Ridgefield, NJ (borough) Bergen County	8	0.07
Putnam Valley, NY (town) Putnam County	7	0.07
Baywood, NY (cdp) Suffolk County	5	0.07
Milton, VT (village) Chittenden County	1	0.07
Mount Vernon, NY (city) Westchester County	43	0.06
Davie, FL (town) Broward County	42	0.06
Hempstead, NY (village) Nassau County	35	0.06
Carol City, FL (cdp) Miami-Dade County	34	0.06
Port Arthur, TX (city) Jefferson County	34	0.06
North Miami Beach, FL (city) Miami-Dade County	25	0.06
Frisco, TX (city) Collin County	19	0.06
Ankeny, IA (city) Polk County	15	0.06
Grandview, MO (city) Jackson County	15	0.06
Palestine, TX (city) Anderson County	11	0.06
Parkland, FL (city) Broward County	9	0.06
Miami Springs, FL (city) Miami-Dade County	8	0.06
North Merrick, NY (cdp) Nassau County	7	0.06
Somerville, NJ (borough) Somerset County	7	0.06
Washington Terrace, UT (city) Weber County	5	0.06
Taos, NM (town) Taos County	3	0.06
La Center, WA (city) Clark County	1	0.06
Orion, MI (township) Oakland County	18	0.05
Coram, NY (cdp) Suffolk County	17	0.05
Hinesville, GA (city) Liberty County	16	0.05
University Park, FL (cdp) Miami-Dade County	14	0.05
Summit, NJ (city) Union County	10	0.05
Setauket-East Setauket, NY (cdp) Suffolk County	8	0.05
Keystone, FL (cdp) Hillsborough County	7	0.05
Opa-locka, FL (city) Miami-Dade County	7	0.05
Storrs, CT (cdp) Tolland County	6	0.05
New Britain, PA (township) Bucks County	5	0.05
Mansfield, OH (city) Richland County	19	0.04
Teaneck, NJ (cdp) Bergen County	17	0.04
South Brunswick, NJ (township) Middlesex County	16	0.04
Kendall West, FL (cdp) Miami-Dade County	14	0.04
Ithaca, NY (city) Tompkins County	13	0.04
Bessemer, AL (city) Jefferson County	11	0.04
Suisun City, CA (city) Solano County	11	0.04
Kahului, HI (cdp) Maui County	9	0.04
Plainview, NY (cdp) Nassau County	9	0.04
Groveton, VA (cdp) Fairfax County	8	0.04
O'Fallon, IL (city) Saint Clair County	8	0.04
Elmwood Park, NJ (borough) Bergen County	7	0.04
Loma Linda, CA (city) San Bernardino County	7	0.04
Montville, CT (town) New London County	7	0.04
Whitehall, PA (borough) Allegheny County	6	0.04
Liberty, NY (town) Sullivan County	4	0.04
Blackwell, OK (city) Kay County	3	0.04
Hudson, NY (city) Columbia County	3	0.04
Saint Petersburg, FL (city) Pinellas County	74	0.03
Allentown, PA (city) Lehigh County	32	0.03
Carrollton, TX (city) Denton County	32	0.03
Miami Beach, FL (city) Miami-Dade County	29	0.03
East Hartford, CT (cdp) Hartford County	14	0.03
Levittown, NY (cdp) Nassau County	14	0.03
Country Club, FL (cdp) Miami-Dade County	10	0.03
Lake Magdalene, FL (cdp) Hillsborough County	10	0.03
Randolph, MA (cdp) Norfolk County	10	0.03
Florin, CA (cdp) Sacramento County	9	0.03
Kaneohe, HI (cdp) Honolulu County	9	0.03
Lauderdale Lakes, FL (city) Broward County	9	0.03
Laramie, WY (city) Albany County	8	0.03
Norland, FL (cdp) Miami-Dade County	8	0.03
Casselberry, FL (city) Seminole County	7	0.03
Rosemont, CA (cdp) Sacramento County	7	0.03
Seguin, TX (city) Guadalupe County	7	0.03
Athens, AL (city) Limestone County	6	0.03

Notes: (cdp) census designated place; Refer to the Explanation of Data in the front of the book for more detailed information.

West Indian: Other, excluding Hispanic

Top 150 Places Sorted by Percent

(Based on places with populations of 10,000 or more)

Place	Number	%
Greater Northdale, FL (cdp) Hillsborough County	59	0.29
Pendleton, OR (city) Umatilla County	42	0.26
Nederland, TX (city) Jefferson County	31	0.18
Centereach, NY (cdp) Suffolk County	38	0.14
Hyattsville, MD (city) Prince George's County	19	0.13
New London, CT (city) New London County	30	0.12
Kettering, MD (cdp) Prince George's County	13	0.12
Pinewood, FL (cdp) Miami-Dade County	19	0.11
De Bary, FL (city) Volusia County	18	0.11
Lompoc, CA (city) Santa Barbara County	41	0.10
University, FL (cdp) Hillsborough County	32	0.10
Atlantic Beach, FL (city) Duval County	13	0.10
Seekonk, MA (town) Bristol County	13	0.10
Corinth, TX (city) Denton County	11	0.10
Mableton, GA (cdp) Cobb County	26	0.09
Takoma Park, MD (city) Montgomery County	15	0.09
Poinciana, FL (cdp) Osceola County	12	0.09
Hartland, MI (township) Livingston County	10	0.09
Valley Stream, NY (village) Nassau County	28	0.08
De Land, FL (city) Volusia County	16	0.08
North Valley Stream, NY (cdp) Nassau County	12	0.08
Fairhope, AL (city) Baldwin County	10	0.08
Lakeside, VA (cdp) Henrico County	9	0.08
Upper Grand Lagoon, FL (cdp) Bay County	9	0.08
Jacinto City, TX (city) Harris County	8	0.08
Rockville, MD (city) Montgomery County	32	0.07
South Miami Heights, FL (cdp) Miami-Dade County	24	0.07
Orange, NJ (cdp) Essex County	23	0.07
College Park, MD (city) Prince George's County	18	0.07
Citrus Park, FL (cdp) Hillsborough County	15	0.07
Doral, FL (cdp) Miami-Dade County	14	0.07
Stonington, CT (town) New London County	13	0.07
Freehold, NJ (borough) Monmouth County	8	0.07
Ridgefield, NJ (borough) Bergen County	8	0.07
Putnam Valley, NY (town) Putnam County	7	0.07
Mount Vernon, NY (city) Westchester County	43	0.06
Davie, FL (town) Broward County	42	0.06
Hempstead, NY (village) Nassau County	35	0.06
Carol City, FL (cdp) Miami-Dade County	34	0.06
Port Arthur, TX (city) Jefferson County	34	0.06
North Miami Beach, FL (city) Miami-Dade County	25	0.06
Frisco, TX (city) Collin County	19	0.06
Ankeny, IA (city) Polk County	15	0.06
Grandview, MO (city) Jackson County	15	0.06
Palestine, TX (city) Anderson County	11	0.06
Parkland, FL (city) Broward County	9	0.06
Miami Springs, FL (city) Miami-Dade County	8	0.06
North Merrick, NY (cdp) Nassau County	7	0.06
Somerville, NJ (borough) Somerset County	7	0.06
Orion, MI (township) Oakland County	18	0.05
Coram, NY (cdp) Suffolk County	17	0.05
Hinesville, GA (city) Liberty County	16	0.05
University Park, FL (cdp) Miami-Dade County	14	0.05
Summit, NJ (city) Union County	10	0.05
Setauket-East Setauket, NY (cdp) Suffolk County	8	0.05
Keystone, FL (cdp) Hillsborough County	7	0.05
Opa-locka, FL (city) Miami-Dade County	7	0.05
Storrs, CT (cdp) Tolland County	6	0.05
New Britain, PA (township) Bucks County	5	0.05
Mansfield, OH (city) Richland County	19	0.04
Teaneck, NJ (cdp) Bergen County	17	0.04
South Brunswick, NJ (township) Middlesex County	16	0.04
Kendall West, FL (cdp) Miami-Dade County	14	0.04
Ithaca, NY (city) Tompkins County	13	0.04
Bessemer, AL (city) Jefferson County	11	0.04
Suisun City, CA (city) Solano County	11	0.04
Kahului, HI (cdp) Maui County	9	0.04
Plainview, NY (cdp) Nassau County	9	0.04
Groveton, VA (cdp) Fairfax County	8	0.04
O'Fallon, IL (city) Saint Clair County	8	0.04
Elmwood Park, NJ (borough) Bergen County	7	0.04
Loma Linda, CA (city) San Bernardino County	7	0.04
Montville, CT (town) New London County	7	0.04
Whitehall, PA (borough) Allegheny County	6	0.04
Saint Petersburg, FL (city) Pinellas County	74	0.03
Allentown, PA (city) Lehigh County	32	0.03
Carrollton, TX (city) Denton County	32	0.03
Miami Beach, FL (city) Miami-Dade County	29	0.03
East Hartford, CT (cdp) Hartford County	14	0.03
Levittown, NY (cdp) Nassau County	14	0.03
Country Club, FL (cdp) Miami-Dade County	10	0.03
Lake Magdalene, FL (cdp) Hillsborough County	10	0.03
Randolph, MA (cdp) Norfolk County	10	0.03
Florin, CA (cdp) Sacramento County	9	0.03
Kaneohe, HI (cdp) Honolulu County	9	0.03
Lauderdale Lakes, FL (city) Broward County	9	0.03
Laramie, WY (city) Albany County	8	0.03
Norland, FL (cdp) Miami-Dade County	8	0.03
Casselberry, FL (city) Seminole County	7	0.03
Rosemont, CA (cdp) Sacramento County	7	0.03
Seguin, TX (city) Guadalupe County	7	0.03
Athens, AL (city) Limestone County	6	0.03
Mansfield, CT (town) Tolland County	6	0.03
Millbrae, CA (city) San Mateo County	6	0.03
Waterford, CT (town) New London County	6	0.03
Swampscott, MA (cdp) Essex County	5	0.03
Mamakating, NY (town) Sullivan County	3	0.03
New York, NY (city) New York City	1,317	0.02
Jersey City, NJ (city) Hudson County	39	0.02
Fort Lauderdale, FL (city) Broward County	37	0.02
Orlando, FL (city) Orange County	37	0.02
Coral Springs, FL (city) Broward County	26	0.02
Lakewood, CO (city) Jefferson County	24	0.02
Elizabeth, NJ (city) Union County	23	0.02
Pembroke Pines, FL (city) Broward County	23	0.02
Palm Bay, FL (city) Brevard County	19	0.02
Plantation, FL (city) Broward County	19	0.02
West Palm Beach, FL (city) Palm Beach County	19	0.02
Miramar, FL (city) Broward County	18	0.02
Lauderhill, FL (city) Broward County	14	0.02
Delray Beach, FL (city) Palm Beach County	13	0.02
Sunrise, FL (city) Broward County	13	0.02
West Bloomfield, MI (township) Oakland County	12	0.02
Franklin, NJ (township) Somerset County	11	0.02
Gaithersburg, MD (city) Montgomery County	11	0.02
Old Bridge, NJ (township) Middlesex County	11	0.02
Decatur, AL (city) Morgan County	10	0.02
North Bergen, NJ (township) Hudson County	10	0.02
Perth Amboy, NJ (city) Middlesex County	10	0.02
West New York, NJ (town) Hudson County	10	0.02
Holyoke, MA (city) Hampden County	9	0.02
Jupiter, FL (town) Palm Beach County	9	0.02
Oak Park, IL (village) Cook County	9	0.02
Coconut Creek, FL (city) Broward County	8	0.02
Hoboken, NJ (city) Hudson County	8	0.02
Severn, MD (cdp) Anne Arundel County	8	0.02
West Orange, NJ (cdp) Essex County	8	0.02
Marion, IN (city) Grant County	7	0.02
North Brunswick Township, NJ (cdp) Middlesex County	7	0.02
Temple City, CA (city) Los Angeles County	7	0.02
Spring Valley, NY (village) Rockland County	6	0.02
Carteret, NJ (borough) Middlesex County	5	0.02
Jefferson, VA (cdp) Fairfax County	5	0.02
Olney, MD (cdp) Montgomery County	5	0.02
Slidell, LA (city) Saint Tammany Parish	5	0.02
Barstow, CA (city) San Bernardino County	4	0.02
Hempstead, NY (town) Nassau County	96	0.01
Brookhaven, NY (town) Suffolk County	63	0.01
Jacksonville, FL (special city) Duval County	42	0.01
Tampa, FL (city) Hillsborough County	38	0.01
Miami, FL (city) Miami-Dade County	25	0.01
Virginia Beach, VA (independent city) Virginia Beach city	24	0.01
Riverside, CA (city) Riverside County	22	0.01
Hollywood, FL (city) Broward County	18	0.01
Tallahassee, FL (city) Leon County	18	0.01
Chandler, AZ (city) Maricopa County	17	0.01
Stamford, CT (city) Fairfield County	16	0.01
Newport News, VA (independent city) Newport News city	13	0.01
Alexandria, VA (independent city) Alexandria city	12	0.01
San Bernardino, CA (city) San Bernardino County	12	0.01

Notes: (cdp) census designated place; Refer to the Explanation of Data in the front of the book for more detailed information.

White

Top 150 Places Sorted by Number

(Based on all places, regardless of population)

Place	Number	%
New York, NY (city) New York City	3,806,508	47.53
Los Angeles, CA (city) Los Angeles County	1,891,358	51.19
Chicago, IL (city) Cook County	1,282,320	44.28
Houston, TX (city) Harris County	1,012,413	51.82
Phoenix, AZ (city) Maricopa County	975,418	73.84
San Antonio, TX (city) Bexar County	810,913	70.84
San Diego, CA (city) San Diego County	781,652	63.89
Philadelphia, PA (city) Philadelphia County	703,584	46.36
Dallas, TX (city) Dallas County	630,419	53.04
Hempstead, NY (town) Nassau County	575,620	76.15
Indianapolis, IN (special city) Marion County	550,768	70.44
Columbus, OH (city) Franklin County	496,425	69.77
Jacksonville, FL (special city) Duval County	485,785	66.04
San Jose, CA (city) Santa Clara County	460,772	51.49
Austin, TX (city) Travis County	445,388	67.84
Portland, OR (city) Multnomah County	430,350	81.33
El Paso, TX (city) El Paso County	430,142	76.31
Seattle, WA (city) King County	413,396	73.38
San Francisco, CA (city) San Francisco County	411,427	52.97
Brookhaven, NY (town) Suffolk County	402,768	89.85
Denver, CO (city) Denver County	378,715	68.28
Nashville-Davidson, TN (special city) Davidson County	368,247	67.50
Oklahoma City, OK (city) Oklahoma County	362,788	71.68
Tucson, AZ (city) Pima County	356,783	73.31
Las Vegas, NV (city) Clark County	350,136	73.18
Albuquerque, NM (city) Bernalillo County	337,780	75.30
Boston, MA (city) Suffolk County	334,684	56.81
Mesa, AZ (city) Maricopa County	333,223	84.07
Fort Worth, TX (city) Tarrant County	331,448	61.99
Charlotte, NC (city) Mecklenburg County	321,491	59.44
Virginia Beach, VA (independent city) Virginia Beach city	312,913	73.58
Omaha, NE (city) Douglas County	311,843	79.96
Milwaukee, WI (city) Milwaukee County	310,734	52.05
Colorado Springs, CO (city) El Paso County	302,662	83.87
Tulsa, OK (city) Tulsa County	290,292	73.86
Kansas City, MO (city) Jackson County	276,006	62.51
Oyster Bay, NY (town) Nassau County	269,904	91.83
Wichita, KS (city) Sedgwick County	267,771	77.78
Minneapolis, MN (city) Hennepin County	260,089	67.98
Islip, NY (town) Suffolk County	255,698	79.26
Miami, FL (city) Miami-Dade County	251,993	69.52
Arlington, TX (city) Tarrant County	233,461	70.11
Fresno, CA (city) Fresno County	230,797	53.97
Pittsburgh, PA (city) Allegheny County	230,266	68.83
Memphis, TN (city) Shelby County	228,633	35.17
Toledo, OH (city) Lucas County	227,094	72.41
Long Beach, CA (city) Los Angeles County	225,899	48.95
Lexington-Fayette, KY (special city) Fayette County	214,657	82.40
Sacramento, CA (city) Sacramento County	214,140	52.61
Baltimore, MD (independent city) Baltimore city	212,064	32.57
Hialeah, FL (city) Miami-Dade County	206,539	91.22
Cleveland, OH (city) Cuyahoga County	206,487	43.16
Corpus Christi, TX (city) Nueces County	206,308	74.36
Lincoln, NE (city) Lancaster County	205,351	91.03
Tampa, FL (city) Hillsborough County	201,268	66.33
Anchorage, AK (municipality) Anchorage Borough	200,926	77.20
Saint Paul, MN (city) Ramsey County	199,862	69.60
Aurora, CO (city) Arapahoe County	199,729	72.26
Anaheim, CA (city) Orange County	193,586	59.02
Scottsdale, AZ (city) Maricopa County	189,833	93.65
Washington, DC (city) District of Columbia	184,309	32.22
Saint Petersburg, FL (city) Pinellas County	181,278	73.03
Spokane, WA (city) Spokane County	181,072	92.56
North Hempstead, NY (town) Nassau County	180,100	80.90
Cincinnati, OH (city) Hamilton County	179,453	54.17
Madison, WI (city) Dane County	178,831	85.95
Raleigh, NC (city) Wake County	178,649	64.71
Plano, TX (city) Collin County	178,070	80.20
Boise City, ID (city) Ada County	175,314	94.36
Huntington, NY (town) Suffolk County	174,756	89.49
Glendale, AZ (city) Maricopa County	171,720	78.48
Des Moines, IA (city) Polk County	167,179	84.14
Babylon, NY (town) Suffolk County	165,170	77.99
Louisville, KY (city) Jefferson County	164,602	64.24
Buffalo, NY (city) Erie County	164,588	56.24
Riverside, CA (city) Riverside County	162,256	63.59
Bakersfield, CA (city) Kern County	161,898	65.53
Fort Wayne, IN (city) Allen County	159,264	77.42
Santa Ana, CA (city) Orange County	157,483	46.60
Saint Louis, MO (independent city) Saint Louis city	157,460	45.22
Huntington Beach, CA (city) Orange County	156,886	82.75
Henderson, NV (city) Clark County	153,372	87.45
Akron, OH (city) Summit County	149,577	68.91
Laredo, TX (city) Webb County	149,389	84.60
Salt Lake City, UT (city) Salt Lake County	149,310	82.15
Lubbock, TX (city) Lubbock County	148,853	74.59
Garland, TX (city) Dallas County	146,000	67.67
Reno, NV (city) Washoe County	145,315	80.52
Tacoma, WA (city) Pierce County	143,426	74.10
Glendale, CA (city) Los Angeles County	142,615	73.15
Paradise, NV (cdp) Clark County	142,055	76.34
Springfield, MO (city) Greene County	141,722	93.50
Atlanta, GA (city) Fulton County	141,429	33.96
Knoxville, TN (city) Knox County	140,965	81.07
Chandler, AZ (city) Maricopa County	140,714	79.69
Modesto, CA (city) Stanislaus County	140,170	74.22
New Orleans, LA (city) Orleans Parish	140,168	28.92
Oakland, CA (city) Alameda County	138,593	34.69
Grand Rapids, MI (city) Kent County	138,222	69.88
Amarillo, TX (city) Potter County	138,120	79.55
Worcester, MA (city) Worcester County	137,758	79.79
Arlington, VA (cdp) Arlington County	137,049	72.34
Overland Park, KS (city) Johnson County	137,012	91.91
Chesapeake, VA (independent city) Chesapeake city	135,730	68.14
Detroit, MI (city) Wayne County	131,691	13.84
Warren, MI (city) Macomb County	128,997	93.31
Lakewood, CO (city) Jefferson County	128,953	89.47
Metairie, LA (cdp) Jefferson Parish	128,507	87.94
Irving, TX (city) Dallas County	127,950	66.77
Tempe, AZ (city) Maricopa County	127,293	80.25
Greensboro, NC (city) Guilford County	126,700	56.59
Vancouver, WA (city) Clark County	126,605	88.19
Eugene, OR (city) Lane County	126,225	91.54
Santa Clarita, CA (city) Los Angeles County	125,345	82.96
Yonkers, NY (city) Westchester County	123,920	63.20
Santa Rosa, CA (city) Sonoma County	120,069	81.35
Orlando, FL (city) Orange County	117,957	63.43
Salem, OR (city) Marion County	117,898	86.10
Norfolk, VA (independent city) Norfolk city	117,511	50.13
Brownsville, TX (city) Cameron County	117,048	83.77
Stockton, CA (city) San Joaquin County	116,389	47.75
Sterling Heights, MI (city) Macomb County	115,818	93.05
Sioux Falls, SD (city) Minnehaha County	115,744	93.36
Oceanside, CA (city) San Diego County	113,622	70.56
Cedar Rapids, IA (city) Linn County	112,874	93.47
Rockford, IL (city) Winnebago County	112,487	74.93
Hollywood, FL (city) Broward County	112,460	80.70
Rochester, NY (city) Monroe County	111,891	50.91
Honolulu, HI (cdp) Honolulu County	111,687	30.05
Smithtown, NY (town) Suffolk County	111,298	96.18
Naperville, IL (city) Du Page County	110,648	86.20
Fort Collins, CO (city) Larimer County	109,122	91.97
Sunrise Manor, NV (cdp) Clark County	108,082	69.23
Pembroke Pines, FL (city) Broward County	107,142	77.96
Independence, MO (city) Jackson County	106,517	94.02
Fremont, CA (city) Alameda County	106,512	52.36
Evansville, IN (city) Vanderburgh County	106,366	87.48
Baton Rouge, LA (city) East Baton Rouge Parish	105,691	46.39
Winston-Salem, NC (city) Forsyth County	105,410	56.74
Pasadena, TX (city) Harris County	105,171	74.23
Amherst, NY (town) Erie County	105,096	90.20
Huntsville, AL (city) Madison County	104,278	65.91
Chula Vista, CA (city) San Diego County	103,924	59.88
Little Rock, AR (city) Pulaski County	102,705	56.08
Thousand Oaks, CA (city) Ventura County	102,573	87.67
Mobile, AL (city) Mobile County	101,736	51.15
Aurora, IL (city) Kane County	100,854	70.53
Providence, RI (city) Providence County	100,834	58.08
Fort Lauderdale, FL (city) Broward County	99,898	65.55
Newport News, VA (independent city) Newport News city	99,800	55.40

Notes: (cdp) census designated place; Refer to the Explanation of Data in the front of the book for more detailed information.

White

Top 150 Places Sorted by Percent

(Based on all places, regardless of population)

Place	Number	%
Milroy, PA (cdp) Mifflin County	1,386	100.00
Fort Loramie, OH (village) Shelby County	1,344	100.00
Bremen, OH (village) Fairfield County	1,265	100.00
Victoria, KS (city) Ellis County	1,208	100.00
Wayne, PA (township) Armstrong County	1,117	100.00
Jerome, PA (cdp) Somerset County	1,068	100.00
Meredosia, IL (village) Morgan County	1,041	100.00
Pringle, PA (borough) Luzerne County	991	100.00
North Bibb, AL (town) Bibb County	986	100.00
Barry, PA (township) Schuylkill County	967	100.00
Stonington, IL (village) Christian County	960	100.00
Grier City-Park Crest, PA (cdp) Schuylkill County	954	100.00
Enterprise, WV (cdp) Harrison County	939	100.00
Lorraine, NY (town) Jefferson County	930	100.00
Hopedale, IL (village) Tazewell County	929	100.00
Washington, PA (township) Cambria County	921	100.00
Newhall, IA (city) Benton County	886	100.00
Salisbury, PA (borough) Somerset County	878	100.00
Middlebourne, WV (town) Tyler County	870	100.00
Annawan, IL (town) Henry County	868	100.00
Saint Stephen, MN (city) Stearns County	860	100.00
Southwest Madison, PA (township) Perry County	856	100.00
Highland, WI (village) Iowa County	855	100.00
Hamburg, WI (town) Vernon County	848	100.00
Somerset, MN (township) Steele County	847	100.00
Riceville, IA (city) Mitchell County	840	100.00
Saint Clair, MN (city) Blue Earth County	827	100.00
Foster, MI (township) Ogemaw County	821	100.00
Junction City, OH (village) Perry County	818	100.00
Union, PA (township) Jefferson County	816	100.00
Franklin, MI (township) Clare County	809	100.00
Meade, MI (township) Huron County	799	100.00
Rossiter, PA (cdp) Indiana County	790	100.00
Faulkton, SD (city) Faulk County	785	100.00
Swan River, MN (township) Morrison County	755	100.00
Stratford, IA (city) Hamilton County	746	100.00
Reseburg, WI (town) Clark County	740	100.00
Auburndale, WI (village) Wood County	738	100.00
Elgin, NE (city) Antelope County	735	100.00
Beetown, WI (town) Grant County	734	100.00
Deer Creek, WI (town) Taylor County	733	100.00
Oak Grove Heights, AR (town) Greene County	727	100.00
Greenville, PA (township) Somerset County	718	100.00
Jennerstown, PA (borough) Somerset County	714	100.00
Moravia, IA (city) Appanoose County	713	100.00
Potosi, WI (village) Grant County	711	100.00
Cady, WI (town) Saint Croix County	710	100.00
West Hamlin, WV (town) Lincoln County	696	100.00
Fontanelle, IA (city) Adair County	692	100.00
Round Prairie, MN (township) Todd County	692	100.00
Moe, MN (township) Douglas County	683	100.00
Hopkinton, IA (city) Delaware County	681	100.00
Irvona, PA (borough) Clearfield County	680	100.00
Littlefork, MN (city) Koochiching County	680	100.00
Ivanhoe, MN (city) Lincoln County	679	100.00
East Prospect, PA (borough) York County	678	100.00
Sabula, IA (city) Jackson County	670	100.00
Morristown, MN (township) Rice County	665	100.00
South Fork, MN (township) Kanabec County	662	100.00
New Market, IN (town) Montgomery County	659	100.00
Augusta, IL (village) Hancock County	657	100.00
Upper Mahantongo, PA (township) Schuylkill County	652	100.00
Tell, PA (township) Huntingdon County	648	100.00
Everly, IA (city) Clay County	647	100.00
Murrayville, IL (village) Morgan County	644	100.00
Plymouth, WI (town) Juneau County	639	100.00
Alhambra, IL (village) Madison County	630	100.00
Golden, IL (village) Adams County	629	100.00
Jamestown, MN (township) Blue Earth County	628	100.00
Lowell, OH (village) Washington County	628	100.00
Milford Center, OH (village) Union County	626	100.00
Loretto, KY (city) Marion County	623	100.00
Williamsfield, IL (village) Knox County	620	100.00
Union, WI (town) Pierce County	618	100.00
Dodge City, AL (town) Cullman County	612	100.00
Springfield, PA (township) Huntingdon County	612	100.00
Milton, IN (town) Wayne County	611	100.00
Badger, IA (city) Webster County	610	100.00
Ellenboro, WI (town) Grant County	608	100.00
Havana, MN (township) Steele County	607	100.00
York, WI (town) Green County	605	100.00
Strasburg, IL (village) Shelby County	603	100.00
Gilman, IA (city) Marshall County	600	100.00
Fennimore, WI (town) Grant County	599	100.00
Livingston, WI (village) Grant County	597	100.00
Annville, KY (city) Jackson County	589	100.00
Ogle, PA (township) Somerset County	588	100.00
Nelson, NE (city) Nuckolls County	587	100.00
Richland, IA (city) Keokuk County	587	100.00
Forest, WI (town) Vernon County	583	100.00
Hopkins, MO (city) Nodaway County	579	100.00
Campbellsburg, IN (town) Washington County	578	100.00
Saint Francis, ME (town) Aroostook County	577	100.00
Bastress, PA (township) Lycoming County	574	100.00
Plum City, WI (village) Pierce County	574	100.00
Birch Lake, MN (township) Cass County	573	100.00
Jeffersonville, VT (village) Lamoille County	568	100.00
Grantsville, WV (town) Calhoun County	565	100.00
Medora, IN (town) Jackson County	565	100.00
Arlington, MN (township) Sibley County	562	100.00
Bern, WI (town) Marathon County	562	100.00
Alburnett, IA (city) Linn County	559	100.00
Carmichaels, PA (borough) Greene County	556	100.00
Unity, WI (town) Trempealeau County	556	100.00
Essex, IL (village) Kankakee County	554	100.00
Beersheba Springs, TN (town) Grundy County	553	100.00
Elk, PA (township) Warren County	551	100.00
Frenchburg, KY (city) Menifee County	551	100.00
Midvale, OH (village) Tuscarawas County	547	100.00
Grand Ridge, IL (village) La Salle County	546	100.00
Dayton, PA (borough) Armstrong County	543	100.00
West Shenango, PA (township) Crawford County	541	100.00
Whittemore, IA (city) Kossuth County	530	100.00
Burnside, WI (town) Trempealeau County	529	100.00
Vintondale, PA (borough) Cambria County	528	100.00
Beaver, PA (township) Snyder County	527	100.00
Reedsville, WV (town) Preston County	517	100.00
West Cameron, PA (township) Northumberland County	517	100.00
Dahlgren, IL (village) Hamilton County	514	100.00
Chalmers, IN (town) White County	513	100.00
Pierz, MN (township) Morrison County	513	100.00
Nicollet, MN (township) Nicollet County	511	100.00
Ackley, WI (town) Langlade County	510	100.00
Burbank, MN (township) Kandiyohi County	510	100.00
Marietta, WI (town) Crawford County	510	100.00
Grove, MN (township) Stearns County	505	100.00
Salem, WI (town) Pierce County	505	100.00
Lamont, IA (city) Buchanan County	503	100.00
Perrysville, IN (town) Vermillion County	502	100.00
Maynard, IA (city) Fayette County	500	100.00
Pine, PA (township) Armstrong County	499	100.00
Wayne, WI (town) Lafayette County	496	100.00
Brady, PA (township) Lycoming County	494	100.00
Silver Lake, MN (township) Martin County	494	100.00
Adams, NE (village) Gage County	489	100.00
Riceland, MN (township) Freeborn County	489	100.00
Fredericksburg, OH (village) Wayne County	487	100.00
Goodrich, WI (town) Taylor County	487	100.00
Wabana, MN (township) Itasca County	487	100.00
Plum Lake, WI (town) Vilas County	486	100.00
Englewood, PA (cdp) Schuylkill County	484	100.00
Leaf Valley, MN (township) Douglas County	484	100.00
South Wayne, WI (village) Lafayette County	484	100.00
Jewell, KS (city) Jewell County	483	100.00
Granite, MN (township) Morrison County	480	100.00
Royal, IA (city) Clay County	479	100.00
Glencoe, WI (town) Buffalo County	478	100.00
New Haven, IL (village) Gallatin County	477	100.00
Fox Chase, KY (city) Bullitt County	476	100.00
Adams, MN (township) Mower County	475	100.00

Notes: (cdp) census designated place; Refer to the Explanation of Data in the front of the book for more detailed information.

White

Top 150 Places Sorted by Percent

(Based on places with populations of 10,000 or more)

Place	Number	%
Mount Pleasant, PA (township) Westmoreland County	11,105	99.57
Elma, NY (town) Erie County	11,253	99.55
Kiryas Joel, NY (village) Orange County	13,076	99.53
Kings Point, FL (cdp) Palm Beach County	12,134	99.40
Holiday City-Berkeley, NJ (cdp) Ocean County	13,787	99.30
Aurora, NY (town) Erie County	13,895	99.28
West Deer, PA (township) Allegheny County	11,473	99.22
Nanticoke, PA (city) Luzerne County	10,865	99.18
North Huntingdon, PA (township) Westmoreland County	28,882	99.17
Martinsville, IN (city) Morgan County	11,600	99.16
Greater Sun Center, FL (cdp) Hillsborough County	16,181	99.14
Vermilion, OH (city) Lorain County	10,831	99.12
Bloomingdale, TN (cdp) Sullivan County	10,257	99.10
Burrillville, RI (town) Providence County	15,650	99.08
Lancaster, NY (village) Erie County	11,084	99.07
Warren, PA (city) Warren County	10,164	99.07
Hamburg, NY (village) Erie County	10,022	99.07
Saint Marys, PA (city) Elk County	14,364	99.05
Sandy, PA (township) Clearfield County	11,443	99.02
Kingsbury, NY (town) Washington County	11,061	99.02
Berlin, NH (city) Coos County	10,229	99.01
Sun City West, AZ (cdp) Maricopa County	26,072	98.97
Somerset, MA (cdp) Bristol County	18,046	98.97
Washington, IL (city) Tazewell County	10,728	98.96
Penn, PA (township) Westmoreland County	19,385	98.95
Salem, OH (city) Columbiana County	12,068	98.94
Sullivan, NY (town) Madison County	14,827	98.91
Carroll, IA (city) Carroll County	9,996	98.91
York, ME (town) York County	12,713	98.90
Bridgetown North, OH (cdp) Hamilton County	12,426	98.86
Logan, PA (township) Blair County	11,789	98.86
Sun City, AZ (cdp) Maricopa County	37,870	98.85
Green Valley, AZ (cdp) Pima County	17,082	98.84
Greenfield, IN (city) Hancock County	14,431	98.84
Swansea, MA (town) Bristol County	15,715	98.83
Mountain Brook, AL (city) Jefferson County	20,360	98.82
Arnold, MO (city) Jefferson County	19,729	98.82
Western Springs, IL (village) Cook County	12,345	98.82
Goffstown, NH (town) Hillsborough County	16,728	98.81
Saco, ME (city) York County	16,621	98.81
Boone, IA (city) Boone County	12,651	98.81
Galion, OH (city) Crawford County	11,206	98.81
Richfield, WI (town) Washington County	10,250	98.81
Soddy-Daisy, TN (city) Hamilton County	11,389	98.78
Butler, PA (township) Butler County	16,974	98.77
Westport, MA (town) Bristol County	14,009	98.77
Hartland, MI (township) Livingston County	10,861	98.77
Englewood, FL (cdp) Sarasota County	15,995	98.76
German Flatts, NY (town) Herkimer County	13,459	98.75
Muskego, WI (city) Waukesha County	21,127	98.74
Dunmore, PA (borough) Lackawanna County	13,842	98.74
Cedarburg, WI (city) Ozaukee County	10,770	98.73
North Smithfield, RI (town) Providence County	10,483	98.73
Hanover, PA (township) Luzerne County	11,340	98.71
New Ulm, MN (city) Brown County	13,417	98.70
Uxbridge, MA (town) Worcester County	11,011	98.70
Scituate, RI (town) Providence County	10,190	98.70
Bay Village, OH (city) Cuyahoga County	15,875	98.68
Tiverton, RI (town) Newport County	15,058	98.68
Mountain Home, AR (city) Baxter County	10,865	98.67
Fairview, PA (township) Erie County	10,005	98.67
Newburyport, MA (city) Essex County	16,959	98.66
Monitor, MI (township) Bay County	9,902	98.65
West Seneca, NY (town) Erie County	45,296	98.64
Bella Vista, AR (cdp) Benton County	16,356	98.64
Rutland, VT (city) Rutland County	17,055	98.63
Kennebunk, ME (town) York County	10,333	98.63
Venice, FL (city) Sarasota County	17,519	98.62
Indianola, IA (city) Warren County	12,819	98.62
Windsor, PA (township) York County	12,629	98.61
Sun Lakes, AZ (cdp) Maricopa County	11,770	98.61
Charlton, MA (town) Worcester County	11,104	98.59
Plains, PA (township) Luzerne County	10,752	98.59
Highland, MI (township) Oakland County	18,897	98.58
Pembroke, MA (town) Plymouth County	16,686	98.58

Place	Number	%
Brandon, MI (township) Oakland County	14,556	98.58
Evans, NY (town) Erie County	17,342	98.57
Derry, PA (township) Westmoreland County	14,516	98.57
Paragould, AR (city) Greene County	21,700	98.56
Claremont, NH (city) Sullivan County	12,961	98.56
Windham, ME (town) Cumberland County	14,688	98.55
Lower Burrell, PA (city) Westmoreland County	12,425	98.55
Rehoboth, MA (town) Bristol County	10,024	98.55
Milford, MI (township) Oakland County	15,046	98.53
Alpena, MI (city) Alpena County	11,138	98.53
Wadsworth, OH (city) Medina County	18,164	98.52
Willowick, OH (city) Lake County	14,147	98.51
East Bethel, MN (city) Anoka County	10,778	98.51
North Tonawanda, NY (city) Niagara County	32,762	98.50
Unity, PA (township) Westmoreland County	20,821	98.50
Beatrice, NE (city) Gage County	12,308	98.50
Point Pleasant, NJ (borough) Ocean County	19,015	98.49
Huntington, IN (city) Huntington County	17,187	98.49
Concord, MO (cdp) Saint Louis County	16,437	98.49
Tonawanda, NY (city) Erie County	15,892	98.49
Auburn, IN (city) De Kalb County	11,892	98.49
Hamburg, NY (town) Erie County	55,402	98.48
Lancaster, NY (town) Erie County	38,425	98.48
Coventry, RI (town) Kent County	33,156	98.48
Lacey, NJ (township) Ocean County	24,960	98.48
Depew, NY (village) Erie County	16,377	98.48
Cannon, MI (township) Kent County	11,891	98.48
Spencer, MA (town) Worcester County	11,513	98.48
Oakville, MO (cdp) Saint Louis County	34,770	98.47
Bedford, MI (township) Monroe County	28,165	98.46
Marco Island, FL (city) Collier County	14,650	98.46
Vidor, TX (city) Orange County	11,264	98.46
Shaler Township, PA (cdp) Allegheny County	29,295	98.45
Genoa, MI (township) Livingston County	15,652	98.43
Antrim, PA (township) Franklin County	12,306	98.42
Nixa, MO (city) Christian County	11,932	98.42
Gorham, ME (town) Cumberland County	13,916	98.41
Stillwater, MN (city) Washington County	14,901	98.40
Oil City, PA (city) Venango County	11,320	98.40
Monroe, WI (city) Green County	10,669	98.40
Brentwood, PA (borough) Allegheny County	10,299	98.40
Effingham, IL (city) Effingham County	12,185	98.39
Merrill, WI (city) Lincoln County	9,983	98.39
Keene, NH (city) Cheshire County	22,197	98.38
South Venice, FL (cdp) Sarasota County	13,319	98.38
Ipswich, MA (town) Essex County	12,774	98.36
Chippewa Falls, WI (city) Chippewa County	12,713	98.36
Sandwich, MA (town) Barnstable County	19,803	98.35
New Lenox, IL (village) Will County	17,478	98.35
Washington, MO (city) Franklin County	13,025	98.35
Lancaster, OH (city) Fairfield County	34,748	98.34
Grafton, WI (village) Ozaukee County	10,141	98.34
Hingham, MA (town) Plymouth County	19,549	98.33
Hibbing, MN (city) Saint Louis County	16,786	98.33
Oconomowoc, WI (city) Waukesha County	12,175	98.33
Franklin, OH (city) Warren County	11,204	98.32
Lebanon, IN (city) Boone County	13,982	98.31
Chenango, NY (town) Broome County	11,261	98.31
Pepperell, MA (town) Middlesex County	10,954	98.31
Marshfield, MA (town) Plymouth County	23,911	98.30
Auburn, ME (city) Androscoggin County	22,809	98.30
Acushnet, MA (town) Bristol County	9,988	98.30
Upper, NJ (township) Cape May County	11,908	98.29
Duxbury, MA (town) Plymouth County	14,003	98.28
Falmouth, ME (town) Cumberland County	10,133	98.28
Greenville, OH (city) Darke County	13,064	98.27
Queensbury, NY (town) Warren County	24,998	98.26
Marinette, WI (city) Marinette County	11,545	98.26
Greensburg, IN (city) Decatur County	10,080	98.25
Morton, IL (village) Tazewell County	14,930	98.24
Grand Haven, MI (township) Ottawa County	13,044	98.24
Spring Lake, MI (township) Ottawa County	12,909	98.24
Abington, MA (cdp) Plymouth County	14,346	98.23
Brownsburg, IN (town) Hendricks County	14,263	98.23
Wood River, IL (city) Madison County	11,096	98.23

Notes: (cdp) census designated place; Refer to the Explanation of Data in the front of the book for more detailed information.

White: Not Hispanic

Top 150 Places Sorted by Number

(Based on all places, regardless of population)

Place	Number	%
New York, NY (city) New York City	2,912,995	36.37
Los Angeles, CA (city) Los Angeles County	1,167,030	31.59
Chicago, IL (city) Cook County	943,299	32.57
Phoenix, AZ (city) Maricopa County	754,002	57.08
Philadelphia, PA (city) Philadelphia County	658,721	43.41
San Diego, CA (city) San Diego County	632,533	51.70
Houston, TX (city) Harris County	618,504	31.66
Indianapolis, IN (special city) Marion County	536,689	68.64
Hempstead, NY (town) Nassau County	526,808	69.69
Columbus, OH (city) Franklin County	487,638	68.54
Jacksonville, FL (special city) Duval County	467,111	63.50
Dallas, TX (city) Dallas County	420,044	35.34
Portland, OR (city) Multnomah County	414,564	78.35
Seattle, WA (city) King County	398,409	70.72
Brookhaven, NY (town) Suffolk County	378,052	84.34
San Antonio, TX (city) Bexar County	374,557	32.72
Nashville-Davidson, TN (special city) Davidson County	356,627	65.37
San Francisco, CA (city) San Francisco County	356,374	45.88
Austin, TX (city) Travis County	355,695	54.18
San Jose, CA (city) Santa Clara County	343,088	38.34
Oklahoma City, OK (city) Oklahoma County	340,685	67.31
Virginia Beach, VA (independent city) Virginia Beach city	303,258	71.31
Charlotte, NC (city) Mecklenburg County	302,363	55.91
Boston, MA (city) Suffolk County	300,117	50.94
Omaha, NE (city) Douglas County	298,507	76.54
Denver, CO (city) Denver County	296,074	53.38
Mesa, AZ (city) Maricopa County	295,371	74.52
Las Vegas, NV (city) Clark County	287,272	60.04
Colorado Springs, CO (city) El Paso County	279,961	77.58
Milwaukee, WI (city) Milwaukee County	279,184	46.77
Tulsa, OK (city) Tulsa County	276,741	70.41
Tucson, AZ (city) Pima County	270,941	55.67
Kansas City, MO (city) Jackson County	260,692	59.04
Oyster Bay, NY (town) Nassau County	259,218	88.19
Wichita, KS (city) Sedgwick County	253,386	73.60
Fort Worth, TX (city) Tarrant County	250,412	46.83
Minneapolis, MN (city) Hennepin County	247,853	64.78
Albuquerque, NM (city) Bernalillo County	230,367	51.35
Pittsburgh, PA (city) Allegheny County	227,669	68.05
Islip, NY (town) Suffolk County	220,676	68.40
Memphis, TN (city) Shelby County	220,230	33.88
Toledo, OH (city) Lucas County	217,906	69.48
Lexington-Fayette, KY (special city) Fayette County	209,229	80.31
Baltimore, MD (independent city) Baltimore city	206,940	31.78
Arlington, TX (city) Tarrant County	203,832	61.22
Lincoln, NE (city) Lancaster County	201,485	89.32
Anchorage, AK (municipality) Anchorage Borough	193,246	74.24
Cleveland, OH (city) Cuyahoga County	191,741	40.08
Saint Paul, MN (city) Ramsey County	189,419	65.96
Scottsdale, AZ (city) Maricopa County	180,598	89.09
Cincinnati, OH (city) Hamilton County	177,483	53.57
Spokane, WA (city) Spokane County	177,219	90.59
Sacramento, CA (city) Sacramento County	176,446	43.35
Madison, WI (city) Dane County	173,934	83.60
Saint Petersburg, FL (city) Pinellas County	173,878	70.05
Boise City, ID (city) Ada County	170,284	91.66
Aurora, CO (city) Arapahoe County	169,688	61.39
Raleigh, NC (city) Wake County	169,263	61.31
Fresno, CA (city) Fresno County	167,387	39.14
Huntington, NY (town) Suffolk County	166,630	85.32
North Hempstead, NY (town) Nassau County	165,291	74.25
Plano, TX (city) Collin County	164,535	74.10
Washington, DC (city) District of Columbia	164,520	28.76
Louisville, KY (city) Jefferson County	161,747	63.13
Long Beach, CA (city) Los Angeles County	161,584	35.01
Des Moines, IA (city) Polk County	161,091	81.08
Tampa, FL (city) Hillsborough County	158,426	52.21
Buffalo, NY (city) Erie County	155,570	53.16
Saint Louis, MO (independent city) Saint Louis city	153,721	44.15
Fort Wayne, IN (city) Allen County	153,635	74.68
Babylon, NY (town) Suffolk County	152,316	71.92
Akron, OH (city) Summit County	148,161	68.25
Glendale, AZ (city) Maricopa County	145,107	66.32
Henderson, NV (city) Clark County	140,808	80.29
Huntington Beach, CA (city) Orange County	140,797	74.26
Springfield, MO (city) Greene County	139,565	92.07
Knoxville, TN (city) Knox County	139,473	80.21
Tacoma, WA (city) Pierce County	136,970	70.77
Chesapeake, VA (independent city) Chesapeake city	133,421	66.98
Overland Park, KS (city) Johnson County	133,306	89.42
Atlanta, GA (city) Fulton County	132,645	31.85
New Orleans, LA (city) Orleans Parish	132,133	27.26
Salt Lake City, UT (city) Salt Lake County	131,523	72.37
Bakersfield, CA (city) Kern County	131,024	53.03
Reno, NV (city) Washoe County	128,351	71.12
Warren, MI (city) Macomb County	127,532	92.25
Grand Rapids, MI (city) Kent County	127,058	64.24
Worcester, MA (city) Worcester County	125,264	72.55
Lubbock, TX (city) Lubbock County	123,822	62.05
Chandler, AZ (city) Maricopa County	123,728	70.07
Anaheim, CA (city) Orange County	123,555	37.67
Eugene, OR (city) Lane County	122,465	88.81
Greensboro, NC (city) Guilford County	122,099	54.54
Vancouver, WA (city) Clark County	121,989	84.97
Glendale, CA (city) Los Angeles County	121,608	62.37
Riverside, CA (city) Riverside County	121,595	47.65
Metairie, LA (cdp) Jefferson Parish	120,886	82.72
Amarillo, TX (city) Potter County	120,784	69.57
Arlington, VA (cdp) Arlington County	118,148	62.36
Modesto, CA (city) Stanislaus County	117,806	62.38
Garland, TX (city) Dallas County	117,531	54.47
Lakewood, CO (city) Jefferson County	115,820	80.36
Paradise, NV (cdp) Clark County	115,248	61.94
Sterling Heights, MI (city) Macomb County	114,532	92.02
Sioux Falls, SD (city) Minnehaha County	114,251	92.16
Norfolk, VA (independent city) Norfolk city	113,769	48.54
Tempe, AZ (city) Maricopa County	113,240	71.39
Detroit, MI (city) Wayne County	112,574	11.83
Cedar Rapids, IA (city) Linn County	111,470	92.31
Salem, OR (city) Marion County	109,272	79.80
Corpus Christi, TX (city) Nueces County	109,251	39.38
Smithtown, NY (town) Suffolk County	108,125	93.44
Santa Rosa, CA (city) Sonoma County	108,025	73.19
Santa Clarita, CA (city) Los Angeles County	107,908	71.42
Naperville, IL (city) Du Page County	107,484	83.74
El Paso, TX (city) El Paso County	106,960	18.98
Evansville, IN (city) Vanderburgh County	105,476	86.75
Rockford, IL (city) Winnebago County	104,846	69.84
Independence, MO (city) Jackson County	104,073	91.87
Amherst, NY (town) Erie County	103,945	89.22
Honolulu, HI (cdp) Honolulu County	103,539	27.86
Fort Collins, CO (city) Larimer County	103,324	87.08
Baton Rouge, LA (city) East Baton Rouge Parish	103,223	45.31
Yonkers, NY (city) Westchester County	102,650	52.35
Huntsville, AL (city) Madison County	102,425	64.74
Oakland, CA (city) Alameda County	101,996	25.53
Rochester, NY (city) Monroe County	101,473	46.17
Little Rock, AR (city) Pulaski County	100,532	54.90
Mobile, AL (city) Mobile County	100,266	50.41
Winston-Salem, NC (city) Forsyth County	98,788	53.18
Orlando, FL (city) Orange County	96,921	52.12
Manchester, NH (city) Hillsborough County	96,903	90.56
Newport News, VA (independent city) Newport News city	96,441	53.53
Montgomery, AL (city) Montgomery County	96,137	47.69
Syracuse, NY (city) Onondaga County	95,595	64.90
Livonia, MI (city) Wayne County	95,576	95.06
Irving, TX (city) Dallas County	94,634	49.39
Topeka, KS (city) Shawnee County	94,231	77.00
Shreveport, LA (city) Caddo Parish	93,058	46.50
Chattanooga, TN (city) Hamilton County	93,003	59.79
Thousand Oaks, CA (city) Ventura County	92,891	79.39
Columbus, GA (special city) Muscogee County	92,112	49.58
Dearborn, MI (city) Wayne County	91,715	93.80
Fremont, CA (city) Alameda County	91,403	44.93
Springfield, IL (city) Sangamon County	90,850	81.51
Oceanside, CA (city) San Diego County	90,451	56.17
Cape Coral, FL (city) Lee County	90,436	88.41
Provo, UT (city) Utah County	89,851	85.44
Dayton, OH (city) Montgomery County	89,683	53.97
Gilbert, AZ (town) Maricopa County	89,286	81.39

Notes: (cdp) census designated place; Refer to the Explanation of Data in the front of the book for more detailed information.

White: Not Hispanic

Top 150 Places Sorted by Percent

(Based on all places, regardless of population)

Place	Number	%
Wayne, PA (township) Armstrong County	1,117	100.00
Barry, PA (township) Schuylkill County	967	100.00
Middlebourne, WV (town) Tyler County	870	100.00
Southwest Madison, PA (township) Perry County	856	100.00
Riceville, IA (city) Mitchell County	840	100.00
Auburndale, WI (village) Wood County	738	100.00
Elgin, NE (city) Antelope County	735	100.00
Oak Grove Heights, AR (town) Greene County	727	100.00
Greenville, PA (township) Somerset County	718	100.00
Jennerstown, PA (borough) Somerset County	714	100.00
Round Prairie, MN (township) Todd County	692	100.00
Irvona, PA (borough) Clearfield County	680	100.00
Tell, PA (township) Huntingdon County	648	100.00
Everly, IA (city) Clay County	647	100.00
Murrayville, IL (village) Morgan County	644	100.00
Plymouth, WI (town) Juneau County	639	100.00
Alhambra, IL (village) Madison County	630	100.00
Williamsfield, IL (village) Knox County	620	100.00
Union, WI (town) Pierce County	618	100.00
Forest, WI (town) Vernon County	583	100.00
Saint Francis, ME (town) Aroostook County	577	100.00
Birch Lake, MN (township) Cass County	573	100.00
Arlington, MN (township) Sibley County	562	100.00
Essex, IL (village) Kankakee County	554	100.00
Elk, PA (township) Warren County	551	100.00
Dayton, PA (borough) Armstrong County	543	100.00
West Shenango, PA (township) Crawford County	541	100.00
Whittemore, IA (city) Kossuth County	530	100.00
Beaver, PA (township) Snyder County	527	100.00
Nicollet, MN (township) Nicollet County	511	100.00
Burbank, MN (township) Kandiyohi County	510	100.00
Marietta, WI (town) Crawford County	510	100.00
Grove, MN (township) Stearns County	505	100.00
Perrysville, IN (town) Vermillion County	502	100.00
Plum Lake, WI (town) Vilas County	486	100.00
Englewood, PA (cdp) Schuylkill County	484	100.00
South Wayne, WI (village) Lafayette County	484	100.00
Granite, MN (township) Morrison County	480	100.00
Fox Chase, KY (city) Bullitt County	476	100.00
Adams, MN (township) Mower County	475	100.00
Gilmanton, WI (town) Buffalo County	470	100.00
McVille, ND (city) Nelson County	470	100.00
Benton, WI (town) Lafayette County	469	100.00
Camargo, IL (village) Douglas County	469	100.00
Bay City, WI (village) Pierce County	465	100.00
Barree, PA (township) Huntingdon County	460	100.00
Melbourne, KY (city) Campbell County	457	100.00
Senecaville, OH (village) Guernsey County	453	100.00
Thomas, WV (city) Tucker County	452	100.00
Marion Center, PA (borough) Indiana County	451	100.00
Garrett, PA (borough) Somerset County	449	100.00
Callery, PA (borough) Butler County	444	100.00
Roosevelt, WI (town) Taylor County	444	100.00
Chokio, MN (city) Stevens County	443	100.00
Emery, SD (city) Hanson County	439	100.00
Kellogg, MN (city) Wabasha County	439	100.00
Spring Hill, MN (township) Stearns County	438	100.00
Ewing, NE (village) Holt County	433	100.00
Forrestville, PA (cdp) Schuylkill County	431	100.00
Pelican Lake, MN (township) Grant County	425	100.00
Arenzville, IL (village) Cass County	419	100.00
Commonwealth, WI (town) Florence County	419	100.00
McKinley, WI (town) Taylor County	418	100.00
McHenry, KY (city) Ohio County	417	100.00
New Canton, IL (town) Pike County	417	100.00
Tabor, SD (town) Bon Homme County	417	100.00
Bowerston, OH (village) Harrison County	414	100.00
Colesburg, IA (city) Delaware County	412	100.00
Bellflower, IL (village) McLean County	408	100.00
Dean, PA (township) Cambria County	408	100.00
Western Grove, AR (town) Newton County	407	100.00
Mahaffey, PA (borough) Clearfield County	402	100.00
Melrose, WI (town) Jackson County	402	100.00
Alma, MO (city) Lafayette County	399	100.00
Harmony, MN (township) Fillmore County	396	100.00
Le Roy, MN (township) Mower County	396	100.00
Lewisville, IN (town) Henry County	395	100.00
Readstown, WI (village) Vernon County	395	100.00
Orchard, NE (village) Antelope County	391	100.00
Cadogan, PA (township) Armstrong County	390	100.00
Patch Grove, WI (town) Grant County	390	100.00
Broad Top City, PA (borough) Huntingdon County	384	100.00
Danbury, IA (city) Woodbury County	384	100.00
Markleville, IN (town) Madison County	383	100.00
Bosworth, MO (city) Carroll County	382	100.00
Bristol, SD (city) Day County	377	100.00
Bismarck, MN (township) Sibley County	376	100.00
Lake George, MN (township) Stearns County	371	100.00
Hildreth, NE (village) Franklin County	370	100.00
Salix, IA (city) Woodbury County	370	100.00
Wauzeka, WI (town) Crawford County	369	100.00
Fayette, WI (town) Lafayette County	366	100.00
Burleene, MN (township) Todd County	365	100.00
Loraine, IL (village) Adams County	363	100.00
Marshall, IN (town) Parke County	360	100.00
Frankford, MN (township) Mower County	358	100.00
Applewold, PA (borough) Armstrong County	356	100.00
Bloss, PA (township) Tioga County	354	100.00
French, MN (township) Saint Louis County	354	100.00
Manchester, IL (village) Scott County	354	100.00
Skanawan, WI (town) Lincoln County	354	100.00
Accident, MD (town) Garrett County	353	100.00
Crow River, MN (township) Stearns County	352	100.00
Elmira, MN (township) Olmsted County	352	100.00
Altmar, NY (village) Oswego County	351	100.00
Brainard, NE (village) Butler County	351	100.00
Fairwater, WI (village) Fond du Lac County	350	100.00
Lake Sarah, MN (township) Murray County	348	100.00
Rabbit Lake, MN (township) Crow Wing County	348	100.00
Prairieville, MN (township) Brown County	346	100.00
West Jefferson, AL (town) Jefferson County	344	100.00
Green Camp, OH (village) Marion County	342	100.00
Mount Pleasant Mills, PA (cdp) Snyder County	342	100.00
Sandy Ridge, PA (cdp) Centre County	340	100.00
Waukenabo, MN (township) Aitkin County	340	100.00
Holy Cross, IA (city) Dubuque County	339	100.00
Bondin, MN (township) Murray County	335	100.00
London, MN (township) Freeborn County	334	100.00
Rockport, KY (city) Ohio County	334	100.00
Deerfield, PA (township) Warren County	333	100.00
Spartansburg, PA (borough) Crawford County	333	100.00
Lake Henry, MN (township) Stearns County	330	100.00
Platte, MN (township) Morrison County	329	100.00
Shrewsbury, PA (township) Sullivan County	328	100.00
Godfrey, MN (township) Polk County	327	100.00
Westside, IA (city) Crawford County	327	100.00
Marble Rock, IA (city) Floyd County	326	100.00
Darnen, MN (township) Stevens County	325	100.00
Franklin, WI (town) Jackson County	325	100.00
Brocton, IL (village) Edgar County	322	100.00
Casstown, OH (village) Miami County	322	100.00
Meadow Bridge, WV (town) Fayette County	321	100.00
Junction City, MO (village) Madison County	319	100.00
Middle River, MN (city) Marshall County	319	100.00
Glenwood, IN (town) Rush County	318	100.00
New Holland, IL (village) Logan County	318	100.00
Troy, MN (township) Pipestone County	318	100.00
Vicco, KY (city) Perry County	318	100.00
Dungannon, VA (town) Scott County	317	100.00
Little Rice, WI (town) Oneida County	314	100.00
Rock City, IL (village) Stephenson County	313	100.00
Diagonal, IA (city) Ringgold County	312	100.00
West Abington, PA (township) Lackawanna County	311	100.00
McNabb, IL (village) Putnam County	310	100.00
Popponesset, MA (cdp) Barnstable County	310	100.00
Vail, MN (township) Redwood County	310	100.00
Wyaconda, MO (city) Clark County	310	100.00
Altenburg, MO (city) Perry County	309	100.00
Holt, MN (township) Fillmore County	307	100.00
Seltzer, PA (cdp) Schuylkill County	307	100.00

Notes: (cdp) census designated place; Refer to the Explanation of Data in the front of the book for more detailed information.

White: Not Hispanic

Top 150 Places Sorted by Percent

(Based on places with populations of 10,000 or more)

Place	Number	%
Mount Pleasant, PA (township) Westmoreland County	11,065	99.21
Elma, NY (town) Erie County	11,196	99.04
Saint Marys, PA (city) Elk County	14,342	98.90
Nanticoke, PA (city) Luzerne County	10,833	98.89
West Deer, PA (township) Allegheny County	11,432	98.87
North Huntingdon, PA (township) Westmoreland County	28,774	98.80
Aurora, NY (town) Erie County	13,826	98.79
Kiryas Joel, NY (village) Orange County	12,976	98.77
Warren, PA (city) Warren County	10,132	98.76
Sandy, PA (township) Clearfield County	11,400	98.65
Carroll, IA (city) Carroll County	9,967	98.62
Penn, PA (township) Westmoreland County	19,317	98.60
Bridgetown North, OH (cdp) Hamilton County	12,390	98.58
Kingsbury, NY (town) Washington County	11,011	98.57
Somerset, MA (cdp) Bristol County	17,969	98.55
Logan, PA (township) Blair County	11,750	98.53
Berlin, NH (city) Coos County	10,178	98.52
Sullivan, NY (town) Madison County	14,768	98.51
Salem, OH (city) Columbiana County	12,015	98.51
Washington, IL (city) Tazewell County	10,678	98.50
Bloomingdale, TN (cdp) Sullivan County	10,192	98.47
Sun City West, AZ (cdp) Maricopa County	25,937	98.46
Butler, PA (township) Butler County	16,921	98.46
Hamburg, NY (village) Erie County	9,960	98.46
Burrillville, RI (town) Providence County	15,549	98.44
Martinsville, IN (city) Morgan County	11,515	98.44
Lancaster, NY (village) Erie County	11,012	98.43
Boone, IA (city) Boone County	12,596	98.38
Kings Point, FL (cdp) Palm Beach County	12,007	98.36
Saco, ME (city) York County	16,542	98.34
Mountain Brook, AL (city) Jefferson County	20,255	98.31
Swansea, MA (town) Bristol County	15,632	98.31
North Smithfield, RI (town) Providence County	10,439	98.31
York, ME (town) York County	12,635	98.30
Holiday City-Berkeley, NJ (cdp) Ocean County	13,646	98.29
Westport, MA (town) Bristol County	13,939	98.28
Goffstown, NH (town) Hillsborough County	16,631	98.24
Tiverton, RI (town) Newport County	14,991	98.24
Pembroke, MA (town) Plymouth County	16,626	98.22
Richfield, WI (town) Washington County	10,188	98.22
Hanover, PA (township) Luzerne County	11,282	98.21
Kennebunk, ME (town) York County	10,288	98.21
Windham, ME (town) Cumberland County	14,634	98.19
Unity, PA (township) Westmoreland County	20,753	98.18
Plains, PA (township) Luzerne County	10,705	98.16
Scituate, RI (town) Providence County	10,134	98.16
Derry, PA (township) Westmoreland County	14,453	98.15
Dunmore, PA (borough) Lackawanna County	13,759	98.15
Claremont, NH (city) Sullivan County	12,907	98.14
Lower Burrell, PA (city) Westmoreland County	12,374	98.14
Galion, OH (city) Crawford County	11,130	98.14
Rehoboth, MA (town) Bristol County	9,983	98.14
Soddy-Daisy, TN (city) Hamilton County	11,314	98.13
Greater Sun Center, FL (cdp) Hillsborough County	16,012	98.11
Fairview, PA (township) Erie County	9,947	98.10
Alpena, MI (city) Alpena County	11,084	98.05
Sun City, AZ (cdp) Maricopa County	37,556	98.03
Wadsworth, OH (city) Medina County	18,072	98.02
New Ulm, MN (city) Brown County	13,325	98.02
Shaler Township, PA (cdp) Allegheny County	29,164	98.01
Arnold, MO (city) Jefferson County	19,565	98.00
Cedarburg, WI (city) Ozaukee County	10,689	97.99
Indianola, IA (city) Warren County	12,736	97.98
Depew, NY (village) Erie County	16,292	97.97
Chippewa Falls, WI (city) Chippewa County	12,663	97.97
Newburyport, MA (city) Essex County	16,838	97.96
Antrim, PA (township) Franklin County	12,246	97.94
Hartland, MI (township) Livingston County	10,770	97.94
West Seneca, NY (town) Erie County	44,969	97.93
Lancaster, NY (town) Erie County	38,206	97.92
Gorham, ME (town) Cumberland County	13,847	97.92
Rutland, VT (city) Rutland County	16,931	97.91
Greenfield, IN (city) Hancock County	14,295	97.91
Windsor, PA (township) York County	12,539	97.91
Charlton, MA (town) Worcester County	11,028	97.91
Concord, MO (cdp) Saint Louis County	16,338	97.90
Uxbridge, MA (town) Worcester County	10,922	97.90
Falmouth, ME (town) Cumberland County	10,094	97.90
Beatrice, NE (city) Gage County	12,232	97.89
Franklin, OH (city) Warren County	11,156	97.89
Washington, MO (city) Franklin County	12,960	97.86
Oil City, PA (city) Venango County	11,257	97.85
East Bethel, MN (city) Anoka County	10,706	97.85
Tonawanda, NY (city) Erie County	15,788	97.84
Bay Village, OH (city) Cuyahoga County	15,740	97.84
Willowick, OH (city) Lake County	14,050	97.83
Marshfield, MA (town) Plymouth County	23,793	97.82
Keene, NH (city) Cheshire County	22,072	97.82
Bella Vista, AR (cdp) Benton County	16,221	97.82
Taylorville, IL (city) Christian County	11,178	97.82
Mountain Home, AR (city) Baxter County	10,771	97.81
Brentwood, PA (borough) Allegheny County	10,237	97.81
Hibbing, MN (city) Saint Louis County	16,695	97.80
Paragould, AR (city) Greene County	21,530	97.79
Effingham, IL (city) Effingham County	12,110	97.79
Acushnet, MA (town) Bristol County	9,936	97.79
Merrill, WI (city) Lincoln County	9,922	97.79
Muskego, WI (city) Waukesha County	20,921	97.78
Scarborough, ME (town) Cumberland County	16,593	97.78
Sandwich, MA (town) Barnstable County	19,686	97.77
Green, OH (city) Summit County	22,305	97.76
Cannon, MI (township) Kent County	11,805	97.76
Sun Lakes, AZ (cdp) Maricopa County	11,669	97.76
Greensburg, IN (city) Decatur County	10,030	97.76
Stillwater, MN (city) Washington County	14,802	97.75
Venice, FL (city) Sarasota County	17,360	97.73
Fort Thomas, KY (city) Campbell County	16,120	97.73
Morton, IL (village) Tazewell County	14,853	97.73
Hingham, MA (town) Plymouth County	19,429	97.72
Norton, OH (city) Summit County	11,260	97.72
Hanover, MA (town) Plymouth County	12,862	97.71
Chenango, NY (town) Broome County	11,192	97.71
Lancaster, OH (city) Fairfield County	34,522	97.70
Auburn, ME (city) Androscoggin County	22,669	97.70
Huntington, IN (city) Huntington County	17,045	97.68
Englewood, FL (cdp) Sarasota County	15,819	97.67
Whitman, MA (town) Plymouth County	13,559	97.67
Vermilion, OH (city) Lorain County	10,672	97.67
Coventry, RI (town) Kent County	32,881	97.66
Pepperell, MA (town) Middlesex County	10,881	97.66
North Tonawanda, NY (city) Niagara County	32,482	97.65
Abington, MA (cdp) Plymouth County	14,262	97.65
Ipswich, MA (town) Essex County	12,682	97.65
Oakville, MO (cdp) Saint Louis County	34,474	97.64
Duxbury, MA (town) Plymouth County	13,909	97.62
Genoa, MI (township) Livingston County	15,520	97.60
Eastlake, OH (city) Lake County	19,868	97.59
Hampton, NH (town) Rockingham County	14,575	97.58
Peters, PA (township) Washington County	17,140	97.57
Danvers, MA (cdp) Essex County	24,596	97.56
Evans, NY (town) Erie County	17,164	97.56
German Flatts, NY (town) Herkimer County	13,297	97.56
Marinette, WI (city) Marinette County	11,462	97.56
Milford, MI (township) Oakland County	14,897	97.55
Wrentham, MA (town) Norfolk County	10,295	97.55
Highland, MI (township) Oakland County	18,698	97.54
Harborcreek, PA (township) Erie County	14,804	97.54
Monroe, WI (city) Green County	10,576	97.54
Hempfield, PA (township) Westmoreland County	39,715	97.53
Amesbury, MA (town) Essex County	16,043	97.53
Elizabeth, PA (township) Allegheny County	13,497	97.53
Greenville, OH (city) Darke County	12,964	97.52
Marblehead, MA (cdp) Essex County	19,868	97.50
Monitor, MI (township) Bay County	9,786	97.50
Hampton Township, PA (cdp) Allegheny County	17,084	97.48
Exeter, NH (town) Rockingham County	13,702	97.47
Spencer, MA (town) Worcester County	11,395	97.47
Salisbury, PA (township) Lancaster County	9,759	97.47
Brownsburg, IN (town) Hendricks County	14,150	97.45
Queensbury, NY (town) Warren County	24,787	97.43

Notes: (cdp) census designated place; Refer to the Explanation of Data in the front of the book for more detailed information.

White: Hispanic

Top 150 Places Sorted by Number

(Based on all places, regardless of population)

Place	Number	%
New York, NY (city) New York City	893,513	11.16
Los Angeles, CA (city) Los Angeles County	724,328	19.60
San Antonio, TX (city) Bexar County	436,356	38.12
Houston, TX (city) Harris County	393,909	20.16
Chicago, IL (city) Cook County	339,021	11.71
El Paso, TX (city) El Paso County	323,182	57.34
Phoenix, AZ (city) Maricopa County	221,416	16.76
Dallas, TX (city) Dallas County	210,375	17.70
Miami, FL (city) Miami-Dade County	207,888	57.35
Hialeah, FL (city) Miami-Dade County	187,865	82.97
San Diego, CA (city) San Diego County	149,119	12.19
Laredo, TX (city) Webb County	140,279	79.44
San Jose, CA (city) Santa Clara County	117,684	13.15
Santa Ana, CA (city) Orange County	113,370	33.54
Albuquerque, NM (city) Bernalillo County	107,413	23.94
Brownsville, TX (city) Cameron County	106,012	75.87
Corpus Christi, TX (city) Nueces County	97,057	34.98
Austin, TX (city) Travis County	89,693	13.66
Tucson, AZ (city) Pima County	85,842	17.64
Denver, CO (city) Denver County	82,641	14.90
Fort Worth, TX (city) Tarrant County	81,036	15.16
Anaheim, CA (city) Orange County	70,031	21.35
McAllen, TX (city) Hidalgo County	67,912	63.82
Long Beach, CA (city) Los Angeles County	64,315	13.94
Fresno, CA (city) Fresno County	63,410	14.83
Las Vegas, NV (city) Clark County	62,864	13.14
San Francisco, CA (city) San Francisco County	55,053	7.09
East Los Angeles, CA (cdp) Los Angeles County	50,945	40.99
Hempstead, NY (town) Nassau County	48,812	6.46
Fountainbleau, FL (cdp) Miami-Dade County	47,111	79.11
Chula Vista, CA (city) San Diego County	45,046	25.95
Philadelphia, PA (city) Philadelphia County	44,863	2.96
Tamiami, FL (cdp) Miami-Dade County	44,572	81.35
Tampa, FL (city) Hillsborough County	42,842	14.12
Miami Beach, FL (city) Miami-Dade County	42,181	47.97
Pomona, CA (city) Los Angeles County	41,241	27.59
Oxnard, CA (city) Ventura County	40,882	24.00
Riverside, CA (city) Riverside County	40,661	15.94
Kendale Lakes, FL (cdp) Miami-Dade County	40,249	70.74
Elizabeth, NJ (city) Union County	38,524	31.95
Ontario, CA (city) San Bernardino County	38,302	24.24
South Gate, CA (city) Los Angeles County	38,095	39.53
Newark, NJ (city) Essex County	38,067	13.92
Mesa, AZ (city) Maricopa County	37,852	9.55
Sacramento, CA (city) Sacramento County	37,694	9.26
Pasadena, TX (city) Harris County	37,157	26.23
Oakland, CA (city) Alameda County	36,597	9.16
El Monte, CA (city) Los Angeles County	36,332	31.33
Salinas, CA (city) Monterey County	35,758	23.67
Kendall, FL (cdp) Miami-Dade County	35,083	46.64
Islip, NY (town) Suffolk County	35,022	10.86
San Bernardino, CA (city) San Bernardino County	34,645	18.69
Boston, MA (city) Suffolk County	34,567	5.87
Pharr, TX (city) Hidalgo County	33,794	72.43
Union City, NJ (city) Hudson County	33,741	50.29
Irving, TX (city) Dallas County	33,316	17.39
Pembroke Pines, FL (city) Broward County	33,066	24.06
Harlingen, TX (city) Cameron County	32,076	55.72
Stockton, CA (city) San Joaquin County	31,886	13.08
Edinburg, TX (city) Hidalgo County	31,634	65.27
Milwaukee, WI (city) Milwaukee County	31,550	5.28
Bakersfield, CA (city) Kern County	30,874	12.50
Fontana, CA (city) San Bernardino County	30,848	23.93
Aurora, CO (city) Arapahoe County	30,041	10.87
Paterson, NJ (city) Passaic County	29,860	20.01
Arlington, TX (city) Tarrant County	29,629	8.90
Norwalk, CA (city) Los Angeles County	29,563	28.62
Downey, CA (city) Los Angeles County	29,559	27.54
Pico Rivera, CA (city) Los Angeles County	29,212	46.06
Garland, TX (city) Dallas County	28,469	13.19
Jersey City, NJ (city) Hudson County	28,197	11.75
Mission, TX (city) Hidalgo County	28,063	61.80
Pueblo, CO (city) Pueblo County	27,829	27.25
The Hammocks, FL (cdp) Miami-Dade County	27,479	58.00
Baldwin Park, CA (city) Los Angeles County	27,425	36.16
Kendall West, FL (cdp) Miami-Dade County	27,141	71.36
Cicero, IL (town) Cook County	26,837	31.35
Paradise, NV (cdp) Clark County	26,807	14.41
Garden Grove, CA (city) Orange County	26,626	16.12
Glendale, AZ (city) Maricopa County	26,613	12.16
Huntington Park, CA (city) Los Angeles County	26,365	42.98
Hollywood, FL (city) Broward County	25,034	17.96
Lubbock, TX (city) Lubbock County	25,031	12.54
Aurora, IL (city) Kane County	24,823	17.36
Westchester, FL (cdp) Miami-Dade County	24,773	81.84
Brookhaven, NY (town) Suffolk County	24,716	5.51
Escondido, CA (city) San Diego County	24,416	18.28
West Covina, CA (city) Los Angeles County	24,208	23.04
Montebello, CA (city) Los Angeles County	24,101	38.78
North Las Vegas, NV (city) Clark County	24,023	20.80
Moreno Valley, CA (city) Riverside County	23,900	16.79
Lynwood, CA (city) Los Angeles County	23,877	34.19
Whittier, CA (city) Los Angeles County	23,842	28.49
Sunrise Manor, NV (cdp) Clark County	23,426	15.01
North Bergen, NJ (township) Hudson County	23,319	40.14
Oceanside, CA (city) San Diego County	23,171	14.39
West New York, NJ (town) Hudson County	22,990	50.23
Colorado Springs, CO (city) El Paso County	22,701	6.29
Santa Maria, CA (city) Santa Barbara County	22,583	29.17
Hayward, CA (city) Alameda County	22,551	16.10
Orange, CA (city) Orange County	22,519	17.48
Odessa, TX (city) Ector County	22,373	24.60
Modesto, CA (city) Stanislaus County	22,364	11.84
Oklahoma City, OK (city) Oklahoma County	22,103	4.37
Bridgeport, CT (city) Fairfield County	21,930	15.72
Las Cruces, NM (city) Dona Ana County	21,721	29.25
Pasadena, CA (city) Los Angeles County	21,658	16.17
Corona, CA (city) Riverside County	21,396	17.12
Yonkers, NY (city) Westchester County	21,270	10.85
Del Rio, TX (city) Val Verde County	21,154	62.46
Orlando, FL (city) Orange County	21,036	11.31
Grand Prairie, TX (city) Dallas County	21,035	16.51
Glendale, CA (city) Los Angeles County	21,007	10.77
Bell Gardens, CA (city) Los Angeles County	20,855	47.34
University Park, FL (cdp) Miami-Dade County	20,825	78.47
San Juan, TX (city) Hidalgo County	20,551	78.35
Carol City, FL (cdp) Miami-Dade County	19,975	33.60
Socorro, TX (city) El Paso County	19,902	73.30
Washington, DC (city) District of Columbia	19,789	3.46
Santa Fe, NM (city) Santa Fe County	19,692	31.66
Inglewood, CA (city) Los Angeles County	19,267	17.11
Charlotte, NC (city) Mecklenburg County	19,128	3.54
Coral Terrace, FL (cdp) Miami-Dade County	19,121	78.43
Detroit, MI (city) Wayne County	19,117	2.01
Coral Gables, FL (city) Miami-Dade County	18,960	44.88
Arlington, VA (cdp) Arlington County	18,901	9.98
Rialto, CA (city) San Bernardino County	18,696	20.35
Palmdale, CA (city) Los Angeles County	18,685	16.02
Jacksonville, FL (special city) Duval County	18,674	2.54
Waukegan, IL (city) Lake County	18,468	21.01
Fullerton, CA (city) Orange County	18,444	14.64
Country Club, FL (cdp) Miami-Dade County	18,435	50.77
Providence, RI (city) Providence County	17,926	10.32
Yuma, AZ (city) Yuma County	17,848	23.03
Salt Lake City, UT (city) Salt Lake County	17,787	9.79
Rancho Cucamonga, CA (city) San Bernardino County	17,472	13.68
Richmond West, FL (cdp) Miami-Dade County	17,454	62.15
Santa Clarita, CA (city) Los Angeles County	17,437	11.54
Amarillo, TX (city) Potter County	17,336	9.98
South Whittier, CA (cdp) Los Angeles County	17,167	31.10
Miramar, FL (city) Broward County	17,127	23.55
Elgin, IL (city) Kane County	17,098	18.10
Chandler, AZ (city) Maricopa County	16,986	9.62
Reno, NV (city) Washoe County	16,964	9.40
Bell, CA (city) Los Angeles County	16,949	46.23
Compton, CA (city) Los Angeles County	16,917	18.09
Weslaco, TX (city) Hidalgo County	16,724	62.09
Florence-Graham, CA (cdp) Los Angeles County	16,650	27.66
San Angelo, TX (city) Tom Green County	16,372	18.51
Santa Barbara, CA (city) Santa Barbara County	16,253	17.60

Notes: (cdp) census designated place; Refer to the Explanation of Data in the front of the book for more detailed information.

White: Hispanic

Top 150 Places Sorted by Percent

(Based on all places, regardless of population)

Place	Number	%
Cuevitas, TX (cdp) Hidalgo County	37	100.00
El Refugio, TX (cdp) Starr County	219	99.10
Roma Creek, TX (cdp) Starr County	602	98.69
Lozano, TX (cdp) Cameron County	319	98.46
Granjeno, TX (city) Hidalgo County	305	97.44
Laureles, TX (cdp) Cameron County	3,174	96.62
La Puerta, TX (cdp) Starr County	1,578	96.45
Arroyo Colorado Estates, TX (cdp) Cameron County	726	96.16
Westway, TX (cdp) El Paso County	3,681	96.13
South Alamo, TX (cdp) Hidalgo County	2,981	96.13
South Point, TX (cdp) Cameron County	1,074	96.06
Los Ebanos, TX (cdp) Hidalgo County	386	95.78
La Victoria, TX (cdp) Starr County	1,609	95.60
Alto Bonito, TX (cdp) Starr County	542	95.25
San Isidro, TX (cdp) Starr County	257	95.19
Olmito, TX (cdp) Cameron County	1,140	95.16
Mila Doce, TX (cdp) Hidalgo County	4,663	95.03
Falcon Heights, TX (cdp) Starr County	317	94.63
La Rosita, TX (cdp) Starr County	1,635	94.56
North Escobares, TX (cdp) Starr County	1,591	94.03
Olivarez, TX (cdp) Hidalgo County	2,290	93.66
Lyford South, TX (cdp) Willacy County	161	93.60
San Elizario, TX (cdp) El Paso County	10,323	93.45
Las Palmas-Juarez, TX (cdp) Cameron County	1,556	93.40
Villa Pancho, TX (cdp) Cameron County	360	93.26
Tornillo, TX (cdp) El Paso County	1,500	93.23
Arroyo Gardens-La Tina Ranch, TX (cdp) Cameron County	674	92.08
Salineno, TX (cdp) Starr County	279	91.78
Lopezville, TX (cdp) Hidalgo County	4,066	90.84
Roma, TX (city) Starr County	8,686	90.32
Las Lomas, TX (cdp) Starr County	2,413	89.90
Alton North, TX (cdp) Hidalgo County	4,528	89.65
Relampago, TX (cdp) Hidalgo County	93	89.42
Encantada-Ranchito El Calaboz, TX (cdp) Cameron County	1,872	89.14
Fronton, TX (cdp) Starr County	533	88.98
Midway North, TX (cdp) Hidalgo County	3,499	88.67
Progreso, TX (city) Hidalgo County	4,298	88.60
Escobares, TX (cdp) Starr County	1,731	88.59
La Casita-Garciasville, TX (cdp) Starr County	1,928	88.56
Morales-Sanchez, TX (cdp) Zapata County	84	88.42
Lindsay, TX (cdp) Reeves County	348	88.32
North Alamo, TX (cdp) Hidalgo County	1,808	87.72
Cameron Park, TX (cdp) Cameron County	5,194	87.13
Fort Hancock, TX (cdp) Hudspeth County	1,487	86.81
La Homa, TX (cdp) Hidalgo County	8,974	86.02
Agua Dulce, TX (cdp) El Paso County	633	85.77
Coyanosa, TX (cdp) Pecos County	118	85.51
Morning Glory, TX (cdp) El Paso County	535	85.33
Canutillo, TX (cdp) El Paso County	4,367	85.14
Laredo Ranchettes, TX (cdp) Webb County	1,570	85.09
New Falcon, TX (cdp) Zapata County	156	84.78
Chula Vista-Orason, TX (cdp) Cameron County	334	84.77
Sweetwater, FL (city) Miami-Dade County	12,056	84.75
La Presa, TX (cdp) Webb County	429	84.45
Ranchos Penitas West, TX (cdp) Webb County	439	84.42
West Sharyland, TX (cdp) Hidalgo County	2,472	83.88
Hialeah, FL (city) Miami-Dade County	187,865	82.97
El Cenizo, TX (city) Webb County	2,934	82.76
Rio Grande City, TX (city) Starr County	9,860	82.70
Hialeah Gardens, FL (city) Miami-Dade County	15,954	82.68
Hidalgo, TX (city) Hidalgo County	5,998	81.92
Westchester, FL (cdp) Miami-Dade County	24,773	81.84
Penitas, TX (city) Hidalgo County	955	81.83
Realitos, TX (cdp) Duval County	171	81.82
Santa Cruz, TX (cdp) Starr County	514	81.59
Garceno, TX (cdp) Starr County	1,171	81.43
Tamiami, FL (cdp) Miami-Dade County	44,572	81.35
Benavides, TX (city) Duval County	1,370	81.26
Mirando City, TX (cdp) Webb County	397	80.53
Bluetown-Iglesia Antigua, TX (cdp) Cameron County	554	80.06
Larga Vista, TX (cdp) Webb County	594	80.05
Encino, TX (cdp) Brooks County	141	79.66
Rio Bravo, TX (city) Webb County	4,422	79.63
West Miami, FL (city) Miami-Dade County	4,660	79.48
Laredo, TX (city) Webb County	140,279	79.44
San Carlos, TX (cdp) Hidalgo County	2,099	79.21
Midway South, TX (cdp) Hidalgo County	1,355	79.19
Fountainbleau, FL (cdp) Miami-Dade County	47,111	79.11
Carrizo Hill, TX (cdp) Dimmit County	433	79.01
Concepcion, TX (cdp) Duval County	48	78.69
Alton, TX (city) Hidalgo County	3,446	78.60
Presidio, TX (city) Presidio County	3,271	78.50
University Park, FL (cdp) Miami-Dade County	20,825	78.47
Coral Terrace, FL (cdp) Miami-Dade County	19,121	78.43
San Juan, TX (city) Hidalgo County	20,551	78.35
San Diego, TX (city) Duval County	3,718	78.22
Las Quintas Fronterizas, TX (cdp) Maverick County	1,586	78.13
Scissors, TX (cdp) Hidalgo County	2,189	78.04
Eidson Road, TX (cdp) Maverick County	7,291	78.00
Medina, TX (cdp) Zapata County	2,305	77.87
Heidelberg, TX (cdp) Hidalgo County	1,232	77.68
Vinton, TX (village) El Paso County	1,460	77.17
Reid Hope King, TX (cdp) Cameron County	615	76.68
Redford, TX (cdp) Presidio County	101	76.52
Ranchitos Las Lomas, TX (cdp) Webb County	255	76.35
Tierra Bonita, TX (cdp) Cameron County	122	76.25
Edcouch, TX (city) Hidalgo County	2,547	76.21
Zapata, TX (cdp) Zapata County	3,692	76.03
Brownsville, TX (city) Cameron County	106,012	75.87
Butterfield, TX (cdp) El Paso County	46	75.41
Laguna Seca, TX (cdp) Hidalgo County	189	75.30
San Ignacio, TX (cdp) Zapata County	642	75.26
Owl Ranch-Amargosa, TX (cdp) Jim Wells County	396	75.14
Nurillo, TX (cdp) Hidalgo County	3,798	75.12
Hebbronville, TX (cdp) Jim Hogg County	3,377	75.08
Lopeno, TX (cdp) Zapata County	105	75.00
Guerra, TX (cdp) Jim Hogg County	6	75.00
Nogales, AZ (city) Santa Cruz County	15,634	74.88
Primera, TX (town) Cameron County	2,039	74.88
Elsa, TX (city) Hidalgo County	4,141	74.63
La Grulla, TX (city) Starr County	901	74.40
Ranchette Estates, TX (cdp) Willacy County	98	73.68
Del Mar Heights, TX (cdp) Cameron County	190	73.36
Socorro, TX (city) El Paso County	19,902	73.30
Palmhurst, TX (city) Hidalgo County	3,570	73.28
Los Villareales, TX (cdp) Starr County	681	73.23
Fabens, TX (cdp) El Paso County	5,884	73.16
Olympia Heights, FL (cdp) Miami-Dade County	9,836	73.12
Asherton, TX (city) Dimmit County	980	73.03
Westwood Lakes, FL (cdp) Miami-Dade County	8,741	72.81
Botines, TX (cdp) Webb County	96	72.73
Alice Acres, TX (cdp) Jim Wells County	356	72.51
Rancho Alegre, TX (cdp) Jim Wells County	1,286	72.45
La Blanca, TX (cdp) Hidalgo County	1,703	72.44
Pharr, TX (city) Hidalgo County	33,794	72.43
Bruni, TX (cdp) Webb County	296	71.84
Mercedes, TX (city) Hidalgo County	9,797	71.78
Big Wells, TX (city) Dimmit County	504	71.59
Eagle Pass, TX (city) Maverick County	16,025	71.50
Las Colonias, TX (cdp) Zavala County	202	71.38
Kendall West, FL (cdp) Miami-Dade County	27,141	71.36
Oilton, TX (cdp) Webb County	221	71.29
Sparks, TX (cdp) El Paso County	2,110	70.95
Kendale Lakes, FL (cdp) Miami-Dade County	40,249	70.74
K-Bar Ranch, TX (cdp) Jim Wells County	247	70.57
Cotulla, TX (city) La Salle County	2,546	70.45
Radar Base, TX (cdp) Maverick County	114	70.37
West Pearsall, TX (cdp) Frio County	245	70.20
Falfurrias, TX (city) Brooks County	3,715	70.13
Los Fresnos, TX (city) Cameron County	3,159	70.01
Taft Southwest, TX (cdp) San Patricio County	1,204	69.96
Green Valley Farms, TX (cdp) Cameron County	502	69.72
Sunland Park, NM (city) Dona Ana County	9,243	69.45
San Perlita, TX (city) Willacy County	472	69.41
Las Lomitas, TX (cdp) Jim Hogg County	185	69.29
Llano Grande, TX (cdp) Hidalgo County	2,305	69.16
Del Sol-Loma Linda, TX (cdp) San Patricio County	498	68.60
Sebastian, TX (cdp) Willacy County	1,274	68.35
Hilltop, TX (cdp) Frio County	205	68.33
Rancho Banquete, TX (cdp) Nueces County	320	68.23

Notes: (cdp) census designated place; Refer to the Explanation of Data in the front of the book for more detailed information.

White: Hispanic

Top 150 Places Sorted by Percent

(Based on places with populations of 10,000 or more)

Place	Number	%
San Elizario, TX (cdp) El Paso County	10,323	93.45
La Homa, TX (cdp) Hidalgo County	8,974	86.02
Sweetwater, FL (city) Miami-Dade County	12,056	84.75
Hialeah, FL (city) Miami-Dade County	187,865	82.97
Rio Grande City, TX (city) Starr County	9,860	82.70
Hialeah Gardens, FL (city) Miami-Dade County	15,954	82.68
Westchester, FL (cdp) Miami-Dade County	24,773	81.84
Tamiami, FL (cdp) Miami-Dade County	44,572	81.35
Laredo, TX (city) Webb County	140,279	79.44
Fountainbleau, FL (cdp) Miami-Dade County	47,111	79.11
University Park, FL (cdp) Miami-Dade County	20,825	78.47
Coral Terrace, FL (cdp) Miami-Dade County	19,121	78.43
San Juan, TX (city) Hidalgo County	20,551	78.35
Brownsville, TX (city) Cameron County	106,012	75.87
Nogales, AZ (city) Santa Cruz County	15,634	74.88
Socorro, TX (city) El Paso County	19,902	73.30
Olympia Heights, FL (cdp) Miami-Dade County	9,836	73.12
Westwood Lakes, FL (cdp) Miami-Dade County	8,741	72.81
Pharr, TX (city) Hidalgo County	33,794	72.43
Mercedes, TX (city) Hidalgo County	9,797	71.78
Eagle Pass, TX (city) Maverick County	16,025	71.50
Kendall West, FL (cdp) Miami-Dade County	27,141	71.36
Kendale Lakes, FL (cdp) Miami-Dade County	40,249	70.74
Sunland Park, NM (city) Dona Ana County	9,243	69.45
Sunset, FL (cdp) Miami-Dade County	11,427	66.63
Donna, TX (city) Hidalgo County	9,760	66.09
San Benito, TX (city) Cameron County	15,420	65.77
Robstown, TX (city) Nueces County	8,309	65.29
Edinburg, TX (city) Hidalgo County	31,634	65.27
McAllen, TX (city) Hidalgo County	67,912	63.82
Alamo, TX (city) Hidalgo County	9,412	63.77
Miami Lakes, FL (cdp) Miami-Dade County	14,298	63.05
Del Rio, TX (city) Val Verde County	21,154	62.46
Doral, FL (cdp) Miami-Dade County	12,730	62.29
Richmond West, FL (cdp) Miami-Dade County	17,454	62.15
Weslaco, TX (city) Hidalgo County	16,724	62.09
Mission, TX (city) Hidalgo County	28,063	61.80
Alice, TX (city) Jim Wells County	11,290	59.39
The Hammocks, FL (cdp) Miami-Dade County	27,479	58.00
Miami, FL (city) Miami-Dade County	207,888	57.35
El Paso, TX (city) El Paso County	323,182	57.34
Harlingen, TX (city) Cameron County	32,076	55.72
Miami Springs, FL (city) Miami-Dade County	7,614	55.53
San Luis, AZ (city) Yuma County	8,230	53.71
Douglas, AZ (city) Cochise County	7,644	53.41
The Crossings, FL (cdp) Miami-Dade County	12,425	52.74
Leisure City, FL (cdp) Miami-Dade County	11,648	52.58
Uvalde, TX (city) Uvalde County	7,826	52.42
Glenvar Heights, FL (cdp) Miami-Dade County	8,319	51.22
Country Walk, FL (cdp) Miami-Dade County	5,411	50.79
Country Club, FL (cdp) Miami-Dade County	18,435	50.77
Union City, NJ (city) Hudson County	33,741	50.29
West New York, NJ (town) Hudson County	22,990	50.23
South Houston, TX (city) Harris County	7,805	49.30
Jacinto City, TX (city) Harris County	5,012	48.65
Key Biscayne, FL (village) Miami-Dade County	5,060	48.16
Miami Beach, FL (city) Miami-Dade County	42,181	47.97
Kingsville, TX (city) Kleberg County	12,116	47.37
Bell Gardens, CA (city) Los Angeles County	20,855	47.34
South Miami Heights, FL (cdp) Miami-Dade County	15,807	47.15
Calexico, CA (city) Imperial County	12,721	46.93
Kendall, FL (cdp) Miami-Dade County	35,083	46.64
Walnut Park, CA (cdp) Los Angeles County	7,524	46.50
Beeville, TX (city) Bee County	6,072	46.25
Bell, CA (city) Los Angeles County	16,949	46.23
Pico Rivera, CA (city) Los Angeles County	29,212	46.06
Coral Gables, FL (city) Miami-Dade County	18,960	44.88
Commerce, CA (city) Los Angeles County	5,615	44.68
Maywood, CA (city) Los Angeles County	12,474	44.42
Las Vegas, NM (city) San Miguel County	6,463	44.37
Galena Park, TX (city) Harris County	4,697	44.34
Cudahy, CA (city) Los Angeles County	10,637	43.94
Huntington Park, CA (city) Los Angeles County	26,365	42.98
West Whittier-Los Nietos, CA (cdp) Los Angeles County	10,711	42.62
Avocado Heights, CA (cdp) Los Angeles County	6,421	42.39

Place	Number	%
South Valley, NM (cdp) Bernalillo County	16,095	41.21
East Los Angeles, CA (cdp) Los Angeles County	50,945	40.99
Homestead, FL (city) Miami-Dade County	12,905	40.44
Dover, NJ (town) Morris County	7,310	40.19
North Bergen, NJ (township) Hudson County	23,319	40.14
South El Monte, CA (city) Los Angeles County	8,402	39.74
West Puente Valley, CA (cdp) Los Angeles County	8,973	39.72
Coachella, CA (city) Riverside County	9,005	39.63
South Gate, CA (city) Los Angeles County	38,095	39.53
Eloy, AZ (city) Pinal County	4,101	39.53
Langley Park, MD (cdp) Prince George's County	6,405	39.50
Deming, NM (city) Luna County	5,550	39.32
Montebello, CA (city) Los Angeles County	24,101	38.78
Arvin, CA (city) Kern County	5,009	38.66
Lamont, CA (cdp) Kern County	5,082	38.22
Princeton, FL (cdp) Miami-Dade County	3,849	38.15
San Antonio, TX (city) Bexar County	436,356	38.12
San Fernando, CA (city) Los Angeles County	8,914	37.83
North Valley, NM (cdp) Bernalillo County	4,455	37.36
Meadow Woods, FL (cdp) Orange County	4,212	37.32
Guttenberg, NJ (town) Hudson County	3,930	36.37
Baldwin Park, CA (city) Los Angeles County	27,425	36.16
Egypt Lake-Leto, FL (cdp) Hillsborough County	11,843	36.13
La Puente, CA (city) Los Angeles County	14,817	36.08
Sanger, CA (city) Fresno County	6,801	35.93
Dinuba, CA (city) Tulare County	6,001	35.63
Hereford, TX (city) Deaf Smith County	5,185	35.52
Yeehaw Junction, FL (cdp) Osceola County	7,646	35.11
Corpus Christi, TX (city) Nueces County	97,057	34.98
Port Lavaca, TX (city) Calhoun County	4,178	34.72
South San Jose Hills, CA (cdp) Los Angeles County	7,017	34.71
Santa Fe Springs, CA (city) Los Angeles County	6,037	34.62
Parlier, CA (city) Fresno County	3,839	34.45
Immokalee, FL (cdp) Collier County	6,793	34.37
Lynwood, CA (city) Los Angeles County	23,877	34.19
Greenfield, CA (city) Monterey County	4,290	34.09
Sunny Isles Beach, FL (city) Miami-Dade County	5,216	34.06
Brawley, CA (city) Imperial County	7,489	33.96
Carol City, FL (cdp) Miami-Dade County	19,975	33.60
Santa Ana, CA (city) Orange County	113,370	33.54
Melrose Park, IL (village) Cook County	7,662	33.07
West Chicago, IL (city) Du Page County	7,695	32.79
Santa Paula, CA (city) Ventura County	9,217	32.23
Rosenberg, TX (city) Fort Bend County	7,708	32.06
Valinda, CA (cdp) Los Angeles County	6,980	32.05
Lennox, CA (cdp) Los Angeles County	7,335	31.96
Elizabeth, NJ (city) Union County	38,524	31.95
South Miami, FL (city) Miami-Dade County	3,432	31.95
Seguin, TX (city) Guadalupe County	7,012	31.86
Indio, CA (city) Riverside County	15,639	31.84
Santa Fe, NM (city) Santa Fe County	19,692	31.66
West Little River, FL (cdp) Miami-Dade County	10,288	31.66
Azusa, CA (city) Los Angeles County	14,117	31.57
Citrus, CA (cdp) Los Angeles County	3,324	31.41
Cicero, IL (town) Cook County	26,837	31.35
El Monte, CA (city) Los Angeles County	36,332	31.33
El Centro, CA (city) Imperial County	11,793	31.17
South Whittier, CA (cdp) Los Angeles County	17,167	31.10
Perth Amboy, NJ (city) Middlesex County	14,661	30.99
Cutler Ridge, FL (cdp) Miami-Dade County	7,660	30.91
Vincent, CA (cdp) Los Angeles County	4,647	30.78
North Fair Oaks, CA (cdp) San Mateo County	4,698	30.43
Freeport, TX (city) Brazoria County	3,854	30.33
Hawaiian Gardens, CA (city) Los Angeles County	4,463	30.20
Big Spring, TX (city) Howard County	7,431	29.45
Los Lunas, NM (village) Valencia County	2,950	29.40
Livingston, CA (city) Merced County	3,075	29.36
Las Cruces, NM (city) Dona Ana County	21,721	29.25
Santa Maria, CA (city) Santa Barbara County	22,583	29.17
Silver City, NM (town) Grant County	3,071	29.12
Golden Gate, FL (cdp) Collier County	6,060	28.92
Paramount, CA (city) Los Angeles County	15,877	28.73
Norwalk, CA (city) Los Angeles County	29,563	28.62
Lockhart, TX (city) Caldwell County	3,315	28.54
Whittier, CA (city) Los Angeles County	23,842	28.49

Notes: (cdp) census designated place; Refer to the Explanation of Data in the front of the book for more detailed information.

Yugoslavian

Top 150 Places Sorted by Number

(Based on all places, regardless of population)

Place	Number	%
New York, NY (city) New York City	15,273	0.19
Chicago, IL (city) Cook County	10,130	0.35
Saint Louis, MO (independent city) Saint Louis city	5,128	1.47
Phoenix, AZ (city) Maricopa County	4,559	0.35
Los Angeles, CA (city) Los Angeles County	3,995	0.11
Jacksonville, FL (special city) Duval County	2,655	0.36
Utica, NY (city) Oneida County	2,596	4.28
Hamtramck, MI (city) Wayne County	2,403	10.46
Des Moines, IA (city) Polk County	2,253	1.13
San Jose, CA (city) Santa Clara County	2,222	0.25
Houston, TX (city) Harris County	1,789	0.09
Waterloo, IA (city) Black Hawk County	1,776	2.59
San Diego, CA (city) San Diego County	1,684	0.14
Dallas, TX (city) Dallas County	1,618	0.14
Salt Lake City, UT (city) Salt Lake County	1,535	0.85
Saint Petersburg, FL (city) Pinellas County	1,459	0.59
Boise City, ID (city) Ada County	1,444	0.78
San Francisco, CA (city) San Francisco County	1,367	0.18
Seattle, WA (city) King County	1,348	0.24
Portland, OR (city) Multnomah County	1,286	0.24
Grand Rapids, MI (city) Kent County	1,215	0.61
Bowling Green, KY (city) Warren County	1,123	2.29
Denver, CO (city) Denver County	1,065	0.19
Sterling Heights, MI (city) Macomb County	1,044	0.84
Fort Worth, TX (city) Tarrant County	1,005	0.19
Louisville, KY (city) Jefferson County	978	0.38
Mehlville, MO (cdp) Saint Louis County	942	3.27
Oakland, CA (city) Alameda County	916	0.23
Clinton, MI (cdp) Macomb County	902	0.94
Manchester, NH (city) Hillsborough County	818	0.76
Las Vegas, NV (city) Clark County	804	0.17
Hempstead, NY (town) Nassau County	765	0.10
Indianapolis, IN (special city) Marion County	757	0.10
Spokane, WA (city) Spokane County	744	0.38
Sacramento, CA (city) Sacramento County	743	0.18
Hartford, CT (city) Hartford County	739	0.61
Santa Clara, CA (city) Santa Clara County	723	0.71
Erie, PA (city) Erie County	718	0.69
Rochester, NY (city) Monroe County	703	0.32
Philadelphia, PA (city) Philadelphia County	701	0.05
Burlington, VT (city) Chittenden County	694	1.78
Minneapolis, MN (city) Hennepin County	691	0.18
Tucson, AZ (city) Pima County	685	0.14
Fort Wayne, IN (city) Allen County	683	0.33
Fargo, ND (city) Cass County	660	0.73
Aurora, CO (city) Arapahoe County	660	0.24
Sioux Falls, SD (city) Minnehaha County	648	0.52
Syracuse, NY (city) Onondaga County	634	0.43
Columbus, OH (city) Franklin County	631	0.09
Warren, MI (city) Macomb County	628	0.45
Akron, OH (city) Summit County	626	0.29
Milwaukee, WI (city) Milwaukee County	616	0.10
Millcreek, UT (cdp) Salt Lake County	609	2.00
Austin, TX (city) Travis County	603	0.09
Cleveland, OH (city) Cuyahoga County	599	0.13
Rockford, IL (city) Winnebago County	590	0.39
Clearwater, FL (city) Pinellas County	585	0.54
Chelsea, MA (city) Suffolk County	573	1.63
Nashville-Davidson, TN (special city) Davidson County	570	0.10
Lakewood, CO (city) Jefferson County	554	0.38
Tukwila, WA (city) King County	541	3.14
West Valley City, UT (city) Salt Lake County	540	0.50
Charlotte, NC (city) Mecklenburg County	535	0.10
Mesa, AZ (city) Maricopa County	532	0.13
Lawrenceville, GA (city) Gwinnett County	530	2.35
Reno, NV (city) Washoe County	523	0.29
Oyster Bay, NY (town) Nassau County	518	0.18
Paradise, NV (cdp) Clark County	512	0.28
Huntington Beach, CA (city) Orange County	510	0.27
Long Beach, CA (city) Los Angeles County	504	0.11
Colorado Springs, CO (city) El Paso County	503	0.14
Billings, MT (city) Yellowstone County	496	0.56
Shelby, MI (cdp) Macomb County	495	0.76
Pittsburgh, PA (city) Allegheny County	495	0.15
Anchorage, AK (municipality) Anchorage Borough	493	0.19
Brookhaven, NY (town) Suffolk County	470	0.10
Hibbing, MN (city) Saint Louis County	467	2.74
Tacoma, WA (city) Pierce County	454	0.24
Kentwood, MI (city) Kent County	443	0.98
Tempe, AZ (city) Maricopa County	441	0.28
Clarkston, GA (city) De Kalb County	436	6.39
Rochester, MN (city) Olmsted County	433	0.51
Macomb, MI (township) Macomb County	428	0.85
Vancouver, WA (city) Clark County	423	0.30
Bellevue, WA (city) King County	421	0.39
Duluth, MN (city) Saint Louis County	420	0.48
Omaha, NE (city) Douglas County	417	0.11
Glendale, AZ (city) Maricopa County	415	0.19
Butte-Silver Bow, MT (special city) Silver Bow County	414	1.22
Revere, MA (city) Suffolk County	414	0.88
Albuquerque, NM (city) Bernalillo County	413	0.09
Livonia, MI (city) Wayne County	403	0.40
Twin Falls, ID (city) Twin Falls County	401	1.17
Dearborn Heights, MI (city) Wayne County	395	0.68
Torrance, CA (city) Los Angeles County	393	0.28
Parma, OH (city) Cuyahoga County	383	0.45
Rancho Palos Verdes, CA (city) Los Angeles County	381	0.92
Fresno, CA (city) Fresno County	379	0.09
Biloxi, MS (city) Harrison County	377	0.74
Pueblo, CO (city) Pueblo County	369	0.36
Ankeny, IA (city) Polk County	368	1.37
San Antonio, TX (city) Bexar County	368	0.03
Portland, ME (city) Cumberland County	364	0.57
Roanoke, VA (independent city) Roanoke city	358	0.38
Yonkers, NY (city) Westchester County	358	0.18
Greece, NY (town) Monroe County	354	0.38
Scottsdale, AZ (city) Maricopa County	351	0.17
Skokie, IL (village) Cook County	345	0.54
Santa Rosa, CA (city) Sonoma County	345	0.23
Lincoln, NE (city) Lancaster County	345	0.15
Tampa, FL (city) Hillsborough County	345	0.11
Boston, MA (city) Suffolk County	345	0.06
Henderson, NV (city) Clark County	342	0.19
Pinellas Park, FL (city) Pinellas County	338	0.74
Santa Clarita, CA (city) Los Angeles County	334	0.22
Alameda, CA (city) Alameda County	324	0.45
Mission Viejo, CA (city) Orange County	313	0.34
Affton, MO (cdp) Saint Louis County	309	1.48
Wyoming, MI (city) Kent County	309	0.45
Escondido, CA (city) San Diego County	309	0.23
Wheaton, IL (city) Du Page County	305	0.55
Greensboro, NC (city) Guilford County	304	0.14
Rock Springs, WY (city) Sweetwater County	302	1.59
Berwyn, IL (city) Cook County	301	0.56
Lynn, MA (city) Essex County	297	0.33
Kansas City, MO (city) Jackson County	297	0.07
Babylon, NY (town) Suffolk County	293	0.14
Huntington, NY (town) Suffolk County	290	0.15
Lexington-Fayette, KY (special city) Fayette County	290	0.11
Amarillo, TX (city) Potter County	286	0.16
Chandler, AZ (city) Maricopa County	286	0.16
Madison, WI (city) Dane County	282	0.14
New Orleans, LA (city) Orleans Parish	282	0.06
Redwood City, CA (city) San Mateo County	281	0.37
Saint Paul, MN (city) Ramsey County	280	0.10
Washington, DC (city) District of Columbia	279	0.05
Clifton, NJ (city) Passaic County	278	0.35
Garfield, NJ (city) Bergen County	277	0.93
Whitehall, PA (borough) Allegheny County	275	1.90
Paterson, NJ (city) Passaic County	273	0.18
Dearborn, MI (city) Wayne County	272	0.28
Rancho Cucamonga, CA (city) San Bernardino County	269	0.21
Gilbert, AZ (town) Maricopa County	267	0.24
Metairie, LA (cdp) Jefferson Parish	267	0.18
Virginia Beach, VA (independent city) Virginia Beach city	267	0.06
Pleasanton, CA (city) Alameda County	266	0.42
Arlington, TX (city) Tarrant County	266	0.08
Madison Heights, MI (city) Oakland County	265	0.85
Farmington Hills, MI (city) Oakland County	265	0.32
Irvine, CA (city) Orange County	265	0.19

Notes: (cdp) census designated place; Refer to the Explanation of Data in the front of the book for more detailed information.

Yugoslavian

Top 150 Places Sorted by Percent

(Based on all places, regardless of population)

Place	Number	%
Hangaard, MN (township) Clearwater County	3	60.00
West Buechel, KY (city) Jefferson County	212	16.32
Franktown, CO (cdp) Douglas County	14	15.05
Morcom, MN (township) Saint Louis County	19	13.87
New Rome, OH (village) Franklin County	9	13.85
North Ottawa, MN (township) Grant County	9	11.84
Hamtramck, MI (city) Wayne County	2,403	10.46
Grass Range, MT (town) Fergus County	12	8.45
Kirby, WY (town) Hot Springs County	3	7.32
Pelican, MN (township) Otter Tail County	59	7.02
Camp Three, MT (cdp) Musselshell County	9	6.52
Clarkston, GA (city) De Kalb County	436	6.39
Lynne, WI (town) Oneida County	12	6.35
Logan, MN (township) Aitkin County	16	6.30
Arrowhead Springs, WY (cdp) Sweetwater County	6	5.77
Bearcreek, MT (town) Carbon County	5	5.75
Kings Point, MT (cdp) Lake County	6	5.66
Goodland, FL (cdp) Collier County	11	4.98
Robertson, WY (cdp) Uinta County	3	4.76
Lake Almanor Country Club, CA (cdp) Plumas County	40	4.65
Cisco, NE (cdp) Garden County	3	4.55
Espelie, MN (township) Marshall County	3	4.55
Utica, NY (city) Oneida County	2,596	4.28
Ferguson, IA (city) Marshall County	6	4.26
Deer Park, CA (cdp) Napa County	61	4.19
Sylvania, PA (township) Potter County	2	4.08
Woodcock, PA (borough) Crawford County	6	3.97
Toivola, MN (township) Saint Louis County	7	3.95
Hawkins, WI (village) Rusk County	12	3.92
Woodland, UT (cdp) Summit County	12	3.86
Plantation Island, FL (cdp) Collier County	8	3.76
Ogdensburg, WI (village) Waupaca County	7	3.76
Winooski, VT (city) Chittenden County	243	3.70
North Kansas City, MO (city) Clay County	174	3.69
Pelican Rapids, MN (city) Otter Tail County	84	3.53
Great Meadows-Vienna, NJ (cdp) Warren County	46	3.49
Deerfield, MO (village) Vernon County	3	3.49
Ely, MN (city) Saint Louis County	127	3.41
Faithorn, MI (township) Menominee County	7	3.38
Bath, WV (town) Morgan County	22	3.28
Mehlville, MO (cdp) Saint Louis County	942	3.27
Stone Mountain, GA (city) De Kalb County	222	3.25
Custer, WA (cdp) Whatcom County	6	3.19
Tukwila, WA (city) King County	541	3.14
Westbrook Center, CT (cdp) Middlesex County	69	3.14
Wilson, WI (town) Lincoln County	8	3.09
Ethel, MO (town) Macon County	3	3.09
Huntley, MT (cdp) Yellowstone County	14	2.94
Musselshell, MT (cdp) Musselshell County	2	2.94
Cedar Grove, NM (cdp) Santa Fe County	20	2.93
Carter, MT (cdp) Chouteau County	2	2.90
Highland, ME (plantation) Somerset County	2	2.90
Fayal, MN (township) Saint Louis County	55	2.89
New Morgan, PA (borough) Berks County	1	2.86
Keewatin, MN (city) Itasca County	33	2.84
Winnebago City, MN (township) Faribault County	7	2.82
Alford, MA (town) Berkshire County	11	2.80
Dougherty, IA (city) Cerro Gordo County	2	2.78
Woodland Mills, TN (city) Obion County	8	2.75
Hibbing, MN (city) Saint Louis County	467	2.74
Wormleysburg, PA (borough) Cumberland County	73	2.73
Hudson, WY (town) Fremont County	11	2.72
Millville, CA (cdp) Shasta County	16	2.70
East Gillespie, IL (village) Macoupin County	6	2.64
Waterloo, IA (city) Black Hawk County	1,776	2.59
Tower, MN (city) Saint Louis County	12	2.56
Red Lodge, MT (city) Carbon County	57	2.54
Wilson, WY (cdp) Teton County	33	2.52
Fall Lake, MN (township) Lake County	14	2.52
Eagarville, IL (village) Macoupin County	3	2.50
Port Costa, CA (cdp) Contra Costa County	6	2.48
Morristown, SD (town) Corson County	2	2.47
Halifax, PA (borough) Dauphin County	21	2.43
Corvallis, MT (cdp) Ravalli County	10	2.41
Spring Hill, IN (town) Marion County	3	2.40

Place	Number	%
Countryside, IL (city) Cook County	143	2.39
Lawrenceville, GA (city) Gwinnett County	530	2.35
Fox Island, WA (cdp) Pierce County	66	2.35
Ford, KS (city) Ford County	7	2.33
Bowling Green, KY (city) Warren County	1,123	2.29
Burbank, CA (cdp) Santa Clara County	121	2.27
Courtland, MN (city) Nicollet County	12	2.23
Annandale, NJ (cdp) Hunterdon County	29	2.21
Montcalm, WV (cdp) Mercer County	19	2.21
Vandling, PA (borough) Lackawanna County	16	2.18
Cooper Landing, AK (cdp) Kenai Peninsula Borough	7	2.17
Iron Junction, MN (city) Saint Louis County	2	2.17
Sudley, VA (cdp) Prince William County	172	2.16
Munds Park, AZ (cdp) Coconino County	29	2.16
Marlborough, MO (village) Saint Louis County	48	2.14
Stallion Springs, CA (cdp) Kern County	35	2.14
Perry Lake, MN (township) Crow Wing County	6	2.11
Rail Road Flat, CA (cdp) Calaveras County	12	2.10
Plumas Eureka, CA (cdp) Plumas County	6	2.09
Neola, UT (cdp) Duchesne County	11	2.08
Leilani Estates, HI (cdp) Hawaii County	19	2.05
Stateburg, SC (cdp) Sumter County	26	2.04
Goodland, MN (township) Itasca County	9	2.02
Millcreek, UT (cdp) Salt Lake County	609	2.00
Eden, SD (town) Marshall County	2	2.00
Limestone, MI (township) Alger County	8	1.96
Winthrop Harbor, IL (village) Lake County	128	1.92
Whitehall, PA (borough) Allegheny County	275	1.90
Imlay City, MI (city) Lapeer County	73	1.89
East Helena, MT (town) Lewis and Clark County	30	1.87
Demorest, GA (city) Habersham County	27	1.84
Malden, NY (cdp) Ulster County	9	1.84
Dewey, WI (town) Rusk County	10	1.83
Wharton, PA (township) Potter County	2	1.83
Helena Valley Southeast, MT (cdp) Lewis and Clark County	128	1.80
Fairbanks, WI (town) Shawano County	12	1.80
Denton, NE (village) Lancaster County	3	1.80
Pick City, ND (city) Mercer County	3	1.79
Burlington, VT (city) Chittenden County	694	1.78
Gays Mills, WI (village) Crawford County	11	1.78
Homestead, MO (village) Ray County	4	1.78
Jump River, WI (town) Taylor County	5	1.77
Biwabik, MN (township) Saint Louis County	16	1.75
Charenton, LA (cdp) Saint Mary Parish	32	1.74
Truxton, MO (village) Lincoln County	2	1.74
Fultonham, OH (village) Muskingum County	3	1.73
Barton Hills, MI (village) Washtenaw County	6	1.72
Wisdom, MT (cdp) Beaverhead County	2	1.72
Colorado City, CO (cdp) Pueblo County	34	1.71
Diamondville, WY (town) Lincoln County	12	1.71
Herndon, PA (borough) Northumberland County	6	1.71
Scotts Mills, OR (city) Marion County	5	1.71
Middlebury, VT (town) Addison County	139	1.70
Shoshoni, WY (town) Fremont County	11	1.70
Arlington, IA (city) Fayette County	8	1.70
Webster, NY (village) Monroe County	87	1.69
Ironwood, MI (township) Gogebic County	39	1.69
Rembert, SC (cdp) Sumter County	6	1.69
Roslyn, WA (city) Kittitas County	17	1.68
Clive, IA (city) Polk County	214	1.67
Irondale, MN (township) Crow Wing County	18	1.67
Worthington, WV (town) Marion County	3	1.67
Eveleth, MN (city) Saint Louis County	64	1.66
Roundup, MT (city) Musselshell County	32	1.66
Anaconda-Deer Lodge County, MT (special city) Deer Lodge County	155	1.65
Utica, MI (city) Macomb County	75	1.64
Chelsea, MA (city) Suffolk County	573	1.63
Pittsfield, VT (town) Rutland County	7	1.63
Benton, NH (town) Grafton County	5	1.63
Pine Haven, WY (town) Crook County	4	1.63
Windsor Heights, IA (city) Polk County	77	1.62
Liberty Hill, TX (city) Williamson County	25	1.62
Coleraine, MN (city) Itasca County	18	1.60
Hotchkiss, CO (town) Delta County	16	1.60
Bovey, MN (city) Itasca County	10	1.60

Notes: (cdp) census designated place; Refer to the Explanation of Data in the front of the book for more detailed information.

Yugoslavian

Top 150 Places Sorted by Percent

(Based on places with populations of 10,000 or more)

Place	Number	%
Hamtramck, MI (city) Wayne County	2,403	10.46
Utica, NY (city) Oneida County	2,596	4.28
Mehlville, MO (cdp) Saint Louis County	942	3.27
Tukwila, WA (city) King County	541	3.14
Hibbing, MN (city) Saint Louis County	467	2.74
Waterloo, IA (city) Black Hawk County	1,776	2.59
Lawrenceville, GA (city) Gwinnett County	530	2.35
Bowling Green, KY (city) Warren County	1,123	2.29
Millcreek, UT (cdp) Salt Lake County	609	2.00
Whitehall, PA (borough) Allegheny County	275	1.90
Burlington, VT (city) Chittenden County	694	1.78
Clive, IA (city) Polk County	214	1.67
Chelsea, MA (city) Suffolk County	573	1.63
Rock Springs, WY (city) Sweetwater County	302	1.59
Schiller Park, IL (village) Cook County	187	1.59
Lyons, IL (village) Cook County	160	1.58
Affton, MO (cdp) Saint Louis County	309	1.48
Saint Louis, MO (independent city) Saint Louis city	5,128	1.47
Foothill Farms, CA (cdp) Sacramento County	248	1.43
Ankeny, IA (city) Polk County	368	1.37
Cutlerville, MI (cdp) Kent County	200	1.32
Butte-Silver Bow, MT (special city) Silver Bow County	414	1.22
East Ridge, TN (city) Hamilton County	250	1.20
Twin Falls, ID (city) Twin Falls County	401	1.17
Des Moines, IA (city) Polk County	2,253	1.13
Hackettstown, NJ (town) Warren County	118	1.13
Carlisle, PA (borough) Cumberland County	190	1.06
New Port Richey, FL (city) Pasco County	164	1.05
Gulf Gate Estates, FL (cdp) Sarasota County	121	1.05
Lackawanna, NY (city) Erie County	193	1.01
Cottonwood West, UT (cdp) Salt Lake County	187	1.00
Kentwood, MI (city) Kent County	443	0.98
Lakeside, VA (cdp) Henrico County	109	0.98
Saint Matthews, KY (city) Jefferson County	150	0.95
Clinton, MI (cdp) Macomb County	902	0.94
Garfield, NJ (city) Bergen County	277	0.93
Rancho Palos Verdes, CA (city) Los Angeles County	381	0.92
Columbia Heights, MN (city) Anoka County	171	0.92
Gaines, MI (township) Kent County	182	0.91
Ringwood, NJ (borough) Passaic County	112	0.90
Revere, MA (city) Suffolk County	414	0.88
Spring Creek, NV (cdp) Elko County	96	0.87
Brownsburg, IN (town) Hendricks County	123	0.86
Salt Lake City, UT (city) Salt Lake County	1,535	0.85
Macomb, MI (township) Macomb County	428	0.85
Madison Heights, MI (city) Oakland County	265	0.85
Sterling Heights, MI (city) Macomb County	1,044	0.84
Parma Heights, OH (city) Cuyahoga County	182	0.84
Urbandale, IA (city) Polk County	240	0.83
SeaTac, WA (city) King County	211	0.83
Catskill, NY (town) Greene County	98	0.83
Cliffside Park, NJ (borough) Bergen County	189	0.82
Derby, CT (city) New Haven County	100	0.81
Loves Park, IL (city) Winnebago County	158	0.79
Brookfield, IL (village) Cook County	151	0.79
Lower Allen, PA (township) Cumberland County	138	0.79
Lemay, MO (cdp) Saint Louis County	136	0.79
Boise City, ID (city) Ada County	1,444	0.78
Manchester, NH (city) Hillsborough County	818	0.76
Shelby, MI (cdp) Macomb County	495	0.76
Biloxi, MS (city) Harrison County	377	0.74
Pinellas Park, FL (city) Pinellas County	338	0.74
Green, OH (city) Summit County	168	0.74
Fargo, ND (city) Cass County	660	0.73
Oakland, NJ (borough) Bergen County	91	0.73
Burien, WA (city) King County	228	0.72
Norridge, IL (village) Cook County	106	0.72
Malibu, CA (city) Los Angeles County	90	0.72
Santa Clara, CA (city) Santa Clara County	723	0.71
Niles, IL (village) Cook County	214	0.71
Coto de Caza, CA (cdp) Orange County	93	0.71
Bonita, CA (cdp) San Diego County	85	0.71
Erie, PA (city) Erie County	718	0.69
Dearborn Heights, MI (city) Wayne County	395	0.68
Mayfield Heights, OH (city) Cuyahoga County	131	0.68

Place	Number	%
Pueblo West, CO (cdp) Pueblo County	115	0.68
Lincolnwood, IL (village) Cook County	84	0.68
Hershey, PA (cdp) Dauphin County	86	0.67
Summit, IL (village) Cook County	70	0.66
Guttenberg, NJ (town) Hudson County	69	0.65
Pleasant Prairie, WI (village) Kenosha County	101	0.64
Lynnwood, WA (city) Snohomish County	214	0.63
New Brighton, MN (city) Ramsey County	140	0.63
Streamwood, IL (village) Cook County	227	0.62
Cloquet, MN (city) Carlton County	69	0.62
Grand Rapids, MI (city) Kent County	1,215	0.61
Hartford, CT (city) Hartford County	739	0.61
Tooele, UT (city) Tooele County	137	0.61
Swatara, PA (township) Dauphin County	135	0.60
Saint Petersburg, FL (city) Pinellas County	1,459	0.59
Carol Stream, IL (village) Du Page County	233	0.59
Rocky Hill, CT (town) Hartford County	105	0.59
Warrenville, IL (city) Du Page County	78	0.59
Eureka, CA (city) Humboldt County	150	0.58
Romeoville, IL (village) Will County	122	0.58
Gloversville, NY (city) Fulton County	90	0.58
Greendale, WI (village) Milwaukee County	83	0.58
Cedar Mill, OR (cdp) Washington County	74	0.58
Elma, NY (town) Erie County	66	0.58
Portland, ME (city) Cumberland County	364	0.57
Palm Desert, CA (city) Riverside County	235	0.57
Littleton, CO (city) Arapahoe County	231	0.57
Dublin, CA (city) Alameda County	171	0.57
Mount Olive, NJ (township) Morris County	138	0.57
Birmingham, MI (city) Oakland County	110	0.57
Upper Allen, PA (township) Cumberland County	87	0.57
Fairview, NJ (borough) Bergen County	76	0.57
Billings, MT (city) Yellowstone County	496	0.56
Berwyn, IL (city) Cook County	301	0.56
Glendale Heights, IL (village) Du Page County	176	0.56
Delran, NJ (township) Burlington County	87	0.56
Enterprise, NV (cdp) Clark County	81	0.56
North Lindenhurst, NY (cdp) Suffolk County	66	0.56
Wheaton, IL (city) Du Page County	305	0.55
Hermitage, PA (city) Mercer County	89	0.55
Plainfield, IL (village) Will County	71	0.55
Clearwater, FL (city) Pinellas County	585	0.54
Skokie, IL (village) Cook County	345	0.54
North Royalton, OH (city) Cuyahoga County	155	0.54
Hermosa Beach, CA (city) Los Angeles County	100	0.54
Chesterton, IN (town) Porter County	56	0.54
Novato, CA (city) Marin County	252	0.53
Binghamton, NY (city) Broome County	249	0.53
Munster, IN (town) Lake County	115	0.53
Crown Point, IN (city) Lake County	103	0.53
East Renton Highlands, WA (cdp) King County	70	0.53
Mounds View, MN (city) Ramsey County	67	0.53
Middle Valley, TN (cdp) Hamilton County	62	0.53
Buford, GA (city) Gwinnett County	57	0.53
Sioux Falls, SD (city) Minnehaha County	648	0.52
Lower Paxton, PA (township) Dauphin County	229	0.52
Hobart, IN (city) Lake County	132	0.52
Eastlake, OH (city) Lake County	104	0.52
Laguna Woods, CA (city) Orange County	85	0.52
La Grange Park, IL (village) Cook County	69	0.52
North Saint Paul, MN (city) Ramsey County	62	0.52
Rochester, MN (city) Olmsted County	433	0.51
Richland, WA (city) Benton County	197	0.51
Saratoga, CA (city) Santa Clara County	152	0.51
Fridley, MN (city) Anoka County	141	0.51
Libertyville, IL (village) Lake County	105	0.51
East Pennsboro, PA (township) Cumberland County	92	0.51
Western Springs, IL (village) Cook County	64	0.51
West Valley City, UT (city) Salt Lake County	540	0.50
Helena, MT (city) Lewis and Clark County	127	0.50
Caledonia, WI (town) Racine County	118	0.50
Casselberry, FL (city) Seminole County	110	0.50
Truckee, CA (town) Nevada County	70	0.50
Burr Ridge, IL (village) Du Page County	52	0.50
Saint Charles, IL (city) Kane County	138	0.49

Notes: (cdp) census designated place; Refer to the Explanation of Data in the front of the book for more detailed information.

INDEX

A

B

C

D

E

F

G

H

I

J

K

L

M

N

O

P

Q

R

S

T

U

W

X

Y

Z

America's Top-Rated Cities, 2003

America's Top-Rated Cities provides current, comprehensive statistical information and other essential data in one easy-to-use source on the 100 "top" cities that have been cited as the best for business and living in the U.S. This handbook allows readers to see, at a glance, a concise social, business, economic, demographic and environmental profile of each city, including brief evaluative comments. In addition to detailed data on Cost of Living, Finances, Real Estate, Education, Major Employers, Media, Crime and Climate, city reports now include Housing Vacancies, Tax Audits, Bankruptcy, Presidential Election Results and more. This outstanding source of information will be widely used in any reference collection.

"The only source of its kind that brings together all of this information into one easy-to-use source." –ARBA

2,500 pages, 4 Volume Set; Softcover ISBN 1-891482-79-3, $195.00

America's Top-Rated Smaller Cities, 2002

A perfect companion to *America's Top-Rated Cities, America's Top-Rated Smaller Cities* provides current, comprehensive business and living profiles of smaller cities (population 25,000-99,999) that have been cited as the best for business and living in the United States. Sixty new, never-before profiled cities make up this 2002 edition of *America's Top-Rated Smaller Cities*, all are top-ranked by Population Growth, Median Income, Unemployment Rate and Crime Rate. In addition to this new selection procedure, city reports reflect the most current data available on a wide-range of statistics as well. Each includes a Background of the City, an Overview of the State Finances and statistical details on Employment & Earnings, Household Income, Unemployment Rate, Population Characteristics, Taxes, Cost of Living, Education, Health Care, Public Safety, Recreation, Media, Air & Water Quality and much more. *America's Top-Rated Smaller Cities* offers a reliable, one-stop source for statistical data that, before now, could only be found scattered in hundreds of sources. This volume is designed for a wide range of readers: individuals considering relocating a residence or business; professionals considering expanding their business or changing careers; general and market researchers; real estate consultants; human resource personnel; urban planners and investors.

"Provides current, comprehensive statistical information in one easy-to-use source... Recommended for public and academic libraries and specialized collections." –Library Journal

1,072 pages; Softcover ISBN 1-930956-67-3, $160.00

Crime in America's Top-Rated Cities, 2000

This volume includes over 20 years of crime statistics in all major crime categories: violent crimes, property crimes and total crime. *Crime in America's Top-Rated Cities* is conveniently arranged by city and covers 76 top-rated cities. *Crime in America's Top-Rated Cities* offers details that compare the number of crimes and crime rates for the city, suburbs and metro area along with national crime trends for violent, property and total crimes. Also, this handbook contains important information and statistics on Anti-Crime Programs, Crime Risk, Hate Crimes, Illegal Drugs, Law Enforcement, Correctional Facilities, Death Penalty Laws and much more. A much-needed resource for people who are relocating, business professionals, general researchers, the press, law enforcement officials and students of criminal justice.

"Data is easy to access and will save hours of searching." –Global Enforcement Review

832 pages; Softcover ISBN 1-891482-84-X, $155.00

The Comparative Guide to American Suburbs, 2001

The Comparative Guide to American Suburbs is a one-stop source for Statistics on the 2,000+ suburban communities surrounding the 50 largest metropolitan areas – their population characteristics, income levels, economy, school system and important data on how they compare to one another. Organized into 50 Metropolitan Area chapters, each chapter contains an overview of the Metropolitan Area, a detailed Map followed by a comprehensive Statistical Profile of each Suburban Community, including Contact Information, Physical Characteristics, Population Characteristics, Income, Economy, Unemployment Rate, Cost of Living, Education, Chambers of Commerce and more. Next, statistical data is sorted into Ranking Tables that rank the suburbs by twenty different criteria, including Population, Per Capita Income, Unemployment Rate, Crime Rate, Cost of Living and more. *The Comparative Guide to American Suburbs* is the best source for locating data on suburbs. Those looking to relocate, as well as those doing preliminary market research, will find this an invaluable timesaving resource.

"Public and academic libraries will find this compilation useful... The work draws together figures from many sources and will be especially helpful for job relocation decisions." – Booklist

1,681 pages; Softcover ISBN 1-930956-42-8, $130.00

Working Americans 1880-1999

Volume I: The Working Class, Volume II: The Middle Class, Volume III: The Upper Class

Each of the volumes in the *Working Americans 1880-1999* series focuses on a particular class of Americans, The Working Class, The Middle Class and The Upper Class over the last 120 years. Chapters in each volume focus on one decade and profile three to five families. Family Profiles include real data on Income & Job Descriptions, Selected Prices of the Times, Annual Income, Annual Budgets, Family Finances, Life at Work, Life at Home, Life in the Community, Working Conditions, Cost of Living, Amusements and much more. Each chapter also contains an Economic Profile with Average Wages of other Professions, a selection of Typical Pricing, Key Events & Inventions, News Profiles, Articles from Local Media and Illustrations. The *Working Americans* series captures the lifestyles of each of the classes from the last twelve decades, covers a vast array of occupations and ethnic backgrounds and travels the entire nation. These interesting and useful compilations of portraits of the American Working, Middle and Upper Classes during the last 120 years will be an important addition to any high school, public or academic library reference collection.

"These interesting, unique compilations of economic and social facts, figures and graphs will support multiple research needs. They will engage and enlighten patrons in high school, public and academic library collections." –Booklist (on Volumes I and II)

Volume I: The Working Class ◆ 558 pages; Hardcover ISBN 1-891482-81-5, $135.00
Volume II: The Middle Class ◆ 591 pages; Hardcover ISBN 1-891482-72-6; $135.00
Volume III: The Upper Class ◆ 567 pages; Hardcover ISBN 1-930956-38-X, $135.00

Working Americans 1880-1999 Volume IV: Their Children

This Fourth Volume in the highly successful *Working Americans 1880-1999* series focuses on American children, decade by decade from 1880 to 1999. This interesting and useful volume introduces the reader to three children in each decade, one from each of the Working, Middle and Upper classes. Like the first three volumes in the series, the individual profiles are created from interviews, diaries, statistical studies, biographies and news reports. Profiles cover a broad range of ethnic backgrounds, geographic area and lifestyles – everything from an orphan in Memphis in 1882, following the Yellow Fever epidemic of 1878 to an eleven-year-old nephew of a beer baron and owner of the New York Yankees in New York City in 1921. Chapters also contain important supplementary materials including News Features as well as information on everything from Schools to Parks, Infectious Diseases to Childhood Fears along with Entertainment, Family Life and much more to provide an informative overview of the lifestyles of children from each decade. This interesting account of what life was like for Children in the Working, Middle and Upper Classes will be a welcome addition to the reference collection of any high school, public or academic library.

600 pages; Hardcover ISBN 1-930956-35-5, $135.00
Four Volume Set (Volumes I-IV), Hardcover ISBN 1-59237-017-9, $500.00

Weather America, A Thirty-Year Summary of Statistical Weather Data and Rankings, 2001

This valuable resource provides extensive climatological data for over 4,000 National and Cooperative Weather Stations throughout the United States. *Weather America* begins with a new Major Storms section that details major storm events of the nation and a National Rankings section that details rankings for several data elements, such as Maximum Temperature and Precipitation. The main body of *Weather America* is organized into 50 state sections. Each section provides a Data Table on each Weather Station, organized alphabetically, that provides statistics on Maximum and Minimum Temperatures, Precipitation, Snowfall, Extreme Temperatures, Foggy Days, Humidity and more. State sections contain two brand new features in this edition – a City Index and a narrative Description of the climatic conditions of the state. Each section also includes a revised Map of the State that includes not only weather stations, but cities and towns.

"Best Reference Book of the Year." –Library Journal

2,013 pages; Softcover ISBN 1-891482-29-7, $175.00

The Environmental Resource Handbook, 2004

The Environmental Resource Handbook, now in its second edition, is the most up-to-date and comprehensive source for Environmental Resources and Statistics. Section I: Resources provides detailed contact information for thousands of information sources, including Associations & Organizations, Awards & Honors, Conferences, Foundations & Grants, Environmental Health, Government Agencies, National Parks & Wildlife Refuges, Publications, Research Centers, Educational Programs, Green Product Catalogs, Consultants and much more. Section II: Statistics, provides statistics and rankings on hundreds of important topics, including Children's Environmental Index, Municipal Finances, Toxic Chemicals, Recycling, Climate, Air & Water Quality and more. This kind of up-to-date environmental data, all in one place, is not available anywhere else on the market place today. This vast compilation of resources and statistics is a must-have for all public and academic libraries as well as any organization with a primary focus on the environment.

"...the intrinsic value of the information make it worth consideration by libraries with environmental collections and environmentally concerned users." –Booklist

1,000 pages; Softcover ISBN 1-59237-030-6, $155.00 ◆ Online Database $300.00

Grey House Publishing
Business Directories

The Directory of Business Information Resources, 2003/04

With 100% verification, over 1,000 new listings and more than 12,000 updates, this 2003/04 edition of *The Directory of Business Information Resources* is the most up-to-date source for contacts in over 98 business areas – from advertising and agriculture to utilities and wholesalers. This carefully researched volume details: the Associations representing each industry; the Newsletters that keep members current; the Magazines and Journals - with their "Special Issues" - that are important to the trade, the Conventions that are "must attends," Databases, Directories and Industry Web Sites that provide access to must-have marketing resources. Includes contact names, phone & fax numbers, web sites and e-mail addresses. This one-volume resource is a gold mine of information and would be a welcome addition to any reference collection.

"This is a most useful and easy-to-use addition to any researcher's library." –The Information Professionals Institute

2,500 pages; Softcover ISBN 1-59237-000-4, $250.00 ◆ Online Database $495.00

Nations of the World, 2003 A Political, Economic and Business Handbook

This completely revised Third Edition covers all the nations of the world in an easy-to-use, single volume. Each nation is profiled in a single chapter that includes Key Facts, Political & Economic Issues, a Country Profile and Business Information. This 2003 edition has been completely updated with the latest Political and Economic data including changes since September 11, 2001 and now reflects the most current information on Politics, Travel Advisories, Economics and more. You'll find such vital information as a Country Map, Population Characteristics, Inflation, Agricultural Production, Foreign Debt, Political History, Foreign Policy, Regional Insecurity, Economics, Trade & Tourism, Historical Profile, Political Systems, Ethnicity, Languages, Media, Climate, Hotels, Chambers of Commerce, Banking, Travel Information and more. Five Regional Chapters follow the main text and include a Regional Map, an Introductory Article, Key Indicators and Currencies for the Region. Noted for its sophisticated, up-to-date and reliable compilation of political, economic and business information, this edition will be an important acquisition to any public, academic or special library reference collection.

"A useful addition to both general reference collections and business collections." –RUSQ

1,700 pages; Softcover ISBN 1-930956-00-2, $135.00

The Grey House Performing Arts Directory, 2003

The Grey House Performing Arts Directory is the most comprehensive resource covering the Performing Arts. This important directory provides current information on over 8,500 Dance Companies, Instrumental Music Programs, Opera Companies, Choral Groups, Theater Companies, Performing Arts Series and Performing Arts Facilities. Plus, this edition now contains a brand new section on Artist Management Groups. In addition to mailing address, phone & fax numbers, e-mail addresses and web sites, dozens of other fields of available information include mission statement, key contacts, facilities, seating capacity, season, attendance and more. This directory also provides an important Information Resources section that covers hundreds of Performing Arts Associations, Magazines, Newsletters, Trade Shows, Directories, Databases and Industry Web Sites. Five indexes provide immediate access to this wealth of information: Entry Name, Executive Name, Performance Facilities, Geographic and Information Resources. *The Grey House Performing Arts Directory* pulls together thousands of Performing Arts Organizations, Facilities and Information Resources into an easy-to-use source – this kind of comprehensiveness and extensive detail is not available in any resource on the market place today.

"Recommended for public, academic and certain special library reference collections." –Booklist

1,500 pages; Softcover ISBN 1-930956-87-8, $170.00 ◆ Online Database $335.00

Research Services Directory, 2003/04 Commercial & Corporate Research Centers

This Ninth Edition provides access to well over 8,000 independent Commercial Research Firms, Corporate Research Centers and Laboratories offering contract services for hands-on, basic or applied research. *Research Services Directory* covers the thousands of types of research companies, including Biotechnology & Pharmaceutical Developers, Consumer Product Research, Defense Contractors, Electronics & Software Engineers, Think Tanks, Forensic Investigators, Independent Commercial Laboratories, Information Brokers, Market & Survey Research Companies, Medical Diagnostic Facilities, Product Research & Development Firms and more. Each entry provides the company's name, mailing address, phone & fax numbers, key contacts, web site, e-mail address, as well as a company description and research and technical fields served. Four indexes provide immediate access to this wealth of information: Research Firms Index, Geographic Index, Personnel Name Index and Subject Index.

"An important source for organizations in need of information about laboratories, individuals and other facilities." –ARBA

1,400 pages; Softcover ISBN 1-59237-003-9, $395.00 ◆ Online Database (includes a free copy of the directory) $850.00

To preview any of our Directories Risk-Free for 30 days, call (800) 562-2139 or fax to (518) 789-0556

The Directory of Venture Capital Firms, 2003

This brand new Sixth Edition has been extensively updated and broadly expanded to offer direct access to over 2,800 Domestic and International Venture Capital Firms, including address, phone & fax numbers, e-mail addresses and web sites for both primary and branch locations. Entries include details on the firm's Mission Statement, Industry Group Preferences, Geographic Preferences, Average and Minimum Investments and Investment Criteria. You'll also find details that are available nowhere else, including the Firm's Portfolio Companies and extensive information on each of the firm's Managing Partners, such as Education, Professional Background and Directorships held, along with the Partner's E-mail Address. *The Directory of Venture Capital Firms* offers five important indexes: Geographic Index, Executive Name Index, Portfolio Company Index, Industry Preference Index and College & University Index. With its comprehensive coverage and detailed, extensive information on each company, *The Directory of Venture Capital Firms* is an important addition to any finance collection.

"The sheer number of listings, the descriptive information provided and the outstanding indexing make this directory a better value than its principal competitor, Pratt's Guide to Venture Capital Sources. Recommended for business collections in large public, academic and business libraries." –Choice

1,300 pages; Softcover ISBN 1-930956-77-0, $450.00 ◆ Online Database (includes a free copy of the directory) $889.00

The Directory of Mail Order Catalogs, 2003

Published since 1981, this Seventeenth Edition features 100% verification of data and is the premier source of information on the mail order catalog industry. Details over 12,000 consumer catalog companies with 44 different product chapters from Animals to Toys & Games. Contains detailed contact information including e-mail addresses and web sites along with important business details such as employee size, years in business, sales volume, catalog size, number of catalogs mailed and more. Four indexes provide quick access to information: Catalog & Company Name Index, Geographic Index, Product Index and Web Sites Index.

"This is a godsend for those looking for information." –Reference Book Review

"The scope and arrangement make this directory useful. Certainly the broad coverage of subjects is not available elsewhere in a single-volume format." –Booklist

1,700 pages; Softcover ISBN 1-891482-73-4, $250.00 ◆ Online Database (includes a free copy of the directory) $495.00

The Directory of Business to Business Catalogs, 2003

The completely updated 2003 *Directory of Business to Business Catalogs*, provides details on over 6,000 suppliers of everything from computers to laboratory supplies… office products to office design… marketing resources to safety equipment… landscaping to maintenance suppliers… building construction and much more. Detailed entries offer mailing address, phone & fax numbers, e-mail addresses, web sites, key contacts, sales volume, employee size, catalog printing information and more. Jut about every kind of product a business needs in its day-to-day operations is covered in this carefully-researched volume. Three indexes are provided for at-a-glance access to information: Catalog & Company Name Index, Geographic Index and Web Sites Index.

"Much smaller and easier to use than the Thomas Register or Sweet's Catalog, it is an excellent choice for libraries… wishing to supplement their business supplier resources." –Booklist

800 pages; Softcover ISBN 1-891482-69-6, $165.00 ◆ Online Database (includes a free copy of the directory) $325.00

Thomas Food and Beverage Market Place, 2002/03

Thomas Food and Beverage Market Place is bigger and better than ever with thousands of new companies, thousands of updates to existing companies and two revised and enhanced product category indexes. This comprehensive directory profiles over 18,000 Food & Beverage Manufacturers, 12,000 Equipment & Supply Companies, 2,200 Transportation & Warehouse Companies, 2,000 Brokers & Wholesalers, 8,000 Importers & Exporters, 900 Industry Resources and hundreds of Mail Order Catalogs. Listings include detailed Contact Information, Sales Volumes, Key Contacts, Brand & Product Information, Packaging Details and much more. *Thomas Food and Beverage Market Place* is available as a three-volume printed set, a subscription-based Online Database via the Internet, on CD-ROM, as well as mailing lists and a licensable database.

"An essential purchase for those in the food industry but will also be useful in public libraries where needed. Much of the information will be difficult and time consuming to locate without this handy three-volume ready-reference source." –ARBA

8,500 pages, 3 Volume Set; Softcover ISBN 1-930956-95-9, $495.00 ◆ CD-ROM ISBN 1-930956-33-9, $695.00 ◆ CD-ROM & 3 Volume Set Combo ISBN 1-930956-34-7, $895.00 ◆ Online Database $695.00 ◆ Online Database & 3 Volume Set Combo, $895.00

The Grey House Safety & Security Directory, 2003

The Grey House Safety & Security Directory is the most comprehensive reference tool and buyer's guide for the safety and security industry. Published continuously since 1943 as Best's Safety & Security Directory, Grey House acquired the title in 2002. Arranged by safety topic, each chapter begins with OSHA regulations for the topic, followed by Training Articles written by top professionals in the field and Self-Inspection Checklists. Next, each topic contains Buyer's Guide sections that feature related products and services. Topics include Administration, Loss Control & Consulting, Protective Equipment & Apparel, Facilities Monitoring & Maintenance, Machine Guards, Materials Handling, Workplace Preparation & Maintenance, Electrical Lighting & Safety, Fire & Rescue and Security. The Buyer's Guide sections are carefully indexed within each topic area to ensure that you can find the supplies needed to meet OSHA's regulations. This comprehensive, up-to-date reference will provide every tool necessary to make sure a business is in compliance with OSHA regulations and locate the products and services needed to meet those regulations.

1,500 pages, 2 Volume Set; Softcover ISBN1-930956-71-1, $225.00

International Business and Trade Directories, 2003/04

Completely updated, the Third Edition of *International Business and Trade Directories* now contains more than 10,000 entries, over 2,000 more than the last edition, making this directory the most comprehensive resource of the worlds business and trade directories. Entries include content descriptions, price, publisher's name and address, web site and e-mail addresses, phone and fax numbers and editorial staff. Organized by industry group, and then by region, this resource puts over 10,000 industry-specific business and trade directories at the reader's fingertips. Three indexes are included for quick access to information: Geographic Index, Publisher Index and Title Index. Public, college and corporate libraries, as well as individuals and corporations seeking critical market information will want to add this directory to their marketing collection.

1,800 pages; Softcover ISBN 1-930956-63-0, $225.00 ◆ Online Database (includes a free copy of the directory) $450.00

Sedgwick Press - Education Directories

The Comparative Guide to American Elementary & Secondary Schools, 2002/03

The only guide of its kind, this 2002/03 edition of the award winning Comparative Guide to American Elementary and Secondary Schools has been broadly expanded to offer a snapshot profile of every public school district in the United States serving 1,500 or more students – more than 5,900 districts are covered, that's almost 2,000 more than the previous edition. Organized alphabetically by district within state, each chapter begins with a Statistical Overview of the state. Each district listing includes contact information (name, address, phone number and web site) plus Grades Served, the Numbers of Students and Teachers and the Number of Regular, Special Education, Alternative and Vocational Schools in the district along with statistics on Student/Classroom Teacher Ratios, Drop Out Rates, Ethnicity, the Numbers of Librarians and Guidance Counselors and District Expenditures per student. Brand New to this edition, *The Comparative Guide to American Elementary and Secondary Schools* provides important ranking tables, both by state and nationally, for each data element. For easy navigation through this wealth of information, this handbook contains a useful City Index that lists all districts that operate schools within a city. These important comparative statistics are necessary for anyone considering relocation or doing comparative research on their own district and would be a perfect acquisition for any public library or school district library.

"This straightforward guide is an easy way to find general information. Valuable for academic and large public library collections." –ARBA

2,355 pages; Softcover ISBN 1-930956-93-2, $125.00

Educators Resource Directory, 2003/04

Educators Resource Directory is a comprehensive resource that provides the educational professional with thousands of resources and statistical data for professional development. This directory saves hours of research time by providing immediate access to Associations & Organizations, Conferences & Trade Shows, Educational Research Centers, Employment Opportunities & Teaching Abroad, School Library Services, Scholarships, Financial Resources, Professional Consultants, Computer Software & Testing Resources and much more. Plus, this comprehensive directory also includes a section on Statistics and Rankings with over 100 tables, including statistics on Average Teacher Salaries, SAT/ACT scores, Revenues & Expenditures and more. These important statistics will allow the user to see how their school rates among others, make relocation decisions and so much more. In addition to the Entry & Publisher Index, Geographic Index and Web Sites Index, our editors have added a Subject & Grade Index to this 2003/04 edition – so now it's even quicker and easier to locate information. *Educators Resource Directory* will be a well-used addition to the reference collection of any school district, education department or public library.

"Recommended for all collections that serve elementary and secondary school professionals." –Choice

1,000 pages; Softcover ISBN 1-59237-002-0, $145.00 ◆ Online Database $195.00 ◆ Online Database & Directory Combo $280.00

Sedgwick Press
Health Directories

The Directory of Drug & Alcohol Residential Rehabilitation Facilities, 2004

This brand new directory is the first-ever resource to bring together, all in one place, data on the thousands of drug and alcohol residential rehabilitation facilities in the United States. *The Directory of Drug & Alcohol Residential Rehabilitation Facilities* covers over 6,000 facilities, with detailed contact information for each one, including mailing address, phone and fax numbers, email addresses and web sites, mission statement, type of treatment programs, cost, average length of stay, numbers of residents and counselors, accreditation, insurance plans accepted, type of environment, religious affiliation, education components and much more. It also contains a helpful chapter on General Resources that provides contact information for Associations, Print & Electronic Media, Support Groups and Conferences. Multiple indexes allow the user to pinpoint the facilities that meet very specific criteria. This time-saving tool is what so many counselors, parents and medical professionals have been asking for. *The Directory of Drug & Alcohol Residential Rehabilitation Facilities* will be a helpful tool in locating the right source for treatment for a wide range of individuals. This comprehensive directory will be an important acquisition for all reference collections: public and academic libraries, case managers, social workers, state agencies and many more.

1,000 pages; Softcover ISBN 1-59237-031-4, $165.00

The Complete Directory for People with Disabilities, 2003

A wealth of information, now in one comprehensive sourcebook. Completely updated for 2003, this edition contains more information than ever before, including thousands of new entries and enhancements to existing entries and thousands of additional web sites and e-mail addresses. Plus, the chapters on Camps and Rehabilitation Facilities have been extensively updated and a brand new chapter on Sub-Acute Rehabilitation Facilities has been added to this edition. This up-to-date directory is the most comprehensive resource available for people with disabilities, detailing Independent Living Centers, Rehabilitation Facilities, State & Federal Agencies, Associations, Support Groups, Periodicals & Books, Assistive Devices, Employment & Education Programs, Camps and Travel Groups. Each year, more libraries, schools, colleges, hospitals, rehabilitation centers and individuals add *The Complete Directory for People with Disabilities* to their collections, making sure that this information is readily available to the families, individuals and professionals who can benefit most from the amazing wealth of resources cataloged here.

"No other reference tool exists to meet the special needs of the disabled in one convenient resource for information." –Library Journal

1,200 pages; Softcover ISBN 1-930956-69-X, $165.00 ◆ Online Database $215.00 ◆ Online Database & Directory Combo $300.00

The Complete Directory for People with Chronic Illness, 2003/04

Thousands of hours of research have gone into this completely updated 2003/04 edition – several new chapters have been added along with thousands of new entries and enhancements to existing entries. Plus, each chronic illness chapter has been reviewed by an medical expert in the field. This widely-hailed directory is structured around the 90 most prevalent chronic illnesses – from Asthma to Cancer to Wilson's Disease – and provides a comprehensive overview of the support services and information resources available for people diagnosed with a chronic illness. Each chronic illness has its own chapter and contains a brief description in layman's language, followed by important resources for National & Local Organizations, State Agencies, Newsletters, Books & Periodicals, Libraries & Research Centers, Support Groups & Hotlines, Web Sites and much more. This directory is an important resource for health care professionals, the collections of hospital and health care libraries, as well as an invaluable tool for people with a chronic illness and their support network.

"A must purchase for all hospital and health care libraries and is strongly recommended for all public library reference departments." –ARBA

1,200 pages; Softcover ISBN 1-930956-83-5, $165.00 ◆ Online Database $215.00 ◆ Online Database & Directory Combo $300.00

The Complete Learning Disabilities Directory, 2003/04

The Complete Learning Disabilities Directory is the most comprehensive database of Programs, Services, Curriculum Materials, Professional Meetings & Resources, Camps, Newsletters and Support Groups for teachers, students and families concerned with learning disabilities. This information-packed directory includes information about Associations & Organizations, Schools, Colleges & Testing Materials, Government Agencies, Legal Resources and much more. For quick, easy access to information, this directory contains four indexes: Entry Name Index, Subject Index and Geographic Index. With every passing year, the field of learning disabilities attracts more attention and the network of caring, committed and knowledgeable professionals grows every day. This directory is an invaluable research tool for these parents, students and professionals.

"Due to its wealth and depth of coverage, parents, teachers and others… should find this an invaluable resource." -Booklist

900 pages; Softcover ISBN 1-930956-79-7, $145.00 ◆ Online Database $195.00 ◆ Online Database & Directory Combo $280.00

To preview any of our Directories Risk-Free for 30 days, call (800) 562-2139 or fax to (518) 789-0556

The Complete Mental Health Directory, 2002

This is the most comprehensive resource covering the field of behavioral health, with critical information for both the layman and the mental health professional. For the layman, this directory offers understandable descriptions of 25 Mental Health Disorders as well as detailed information on Associations, Media, Support Groups and Mental Health Facilities. For the professional, *The Complete Mental Health Directory* offers critical and comprehensive information on Managed Care Organizations, Information Systems, Government Agencies and Provider Organizations. This comprehensive volume of needed information will be widely used in any reference collection.

"... the strength of this directory is that it consolidates widely dispersed information into a single volume." –Booklist

800 pages; Softcover ISBN 1-930956-06-1, $165.00 ◆ Online Database $215.00 ◆ Online & Directory Combo $300.00

Older Americans Information Directory, 2002/03

Completely updated for 2002/03, this Fourth Edition has been completely revised and now contains 1,000 new listings, over 8,000 updates to existing listings and over 3,000 brand new e-mail addresses and web sites. You'll find important resources for Older Americans including National, Regional, State & Local Organizations, Government Agencies, Research Centers, Libraries & Information Centers, Legal Resources, Discount Travel Information, Continuing Education Programs, Disability Aids & Assistive Devices, Health, Print Media and Electronic Media. Three indexes: Entry Index, Subject Index and Geographic Index make it easy to find just the right source of information. This comprehensive guide to resources for Older Americans will be a welcome addition to any reference collection.

"Highly recommended for academic, public, health science and consumer libraries..." –Choice

1,200 pages; Softcover ISBN 1-930956-65-7, $165.00 ◆ Online Database $215.00 ◆ Online Database & Directory Combo $300.00

The Complete Directory for Pediatric Disorders, 2002/03

This important directory provides parents and caregivers with information about Pediatric Conditions, Disorders, Diseases and Disabilities, including Blood Disorders, Bone & Spinal Disorders, Brain Defects & Abnormalities, Chromosomal Disorders, Congenital Heart Defects, Movement Disorders, Neuromuscular Disorders and Pediatric Tumors & Cancers. This carefully written directory offers: understandable Descriptions of 15 major bodily systems; Descriptions of more than 200 Disorders and a Resources Section, detailing National Agencies & Associations, State Associations, Online Services, Libraries & Resource Centers, Research Centers, Support Groups & Hotlines, Camps, Books and Periodicals. This resource will provide immediate access to information crucial to families and caregivers when coping with children's illnesses.

"Recommended for public and consumer health libraries." –Library Journal

1,120 pages; Softcover ISBN 1-930956-61-4, $165.00 ◆ Online Database $215.00 ◆ Online Database & Directory Combo $300.00

The Complete Directory for People with Rare Disorders, 2002/03

This outstanding reference is produced in conjunction with the National Organization for Rare Disorders to provide comprehensive and needed access to important information on over 1,000 rare disorders, including Cancers and Muscular, Genetic and Blood Disorders. An informative Disorder Description is provided for each of the 1,100 disorders (rare Cancers and Muscular, Genetic and Blood Disorders) followed by information on National and State Organizations dealing with a particular disorder, Umbrella Organizations that cover a wide range of disorders, the Publications that can be useful when researching a disorder and the Government Agencies to contact. Detailed and up-to-date listings contain mailing address, phone and fax numbers, web sites and e-mail addresses along with a description. For quick, easy access to information, this directory contains two indexes: Entry Name Index and Acronym/Keyword Index along with an informative Guide for Rare Disorder Advocates. The Complete Directory for People with Rare Disorders will be an invaluable tool for the thousands of families that have been struck with a rare or "orphan" disease, who feel that they have no place to turn and will be a much-used addition to the reference collection of any public or academic library.

"Quick access to information... public libraries and hospital patient libraries will find this a useful resource in directing users to support groups or agencies dealing with a rare disorder." –Booklist

726 pages; Softcover ISBN 1-891482-18-1, $165.00

To preview any of our Directories Risk-Free for 30 days, call (800) 562-2139 or fax to (518) 789-0556

Sedgwick Press
Hospital & Health Plan Directories

The Directory of Hospital Personnel, 2003

The Directory of Hospital Personnel is the best resource you can have at your fingertips when researching or marketing a product or service to the hospital market. A "Who's Who" of the hospital universe, this directory puts you in touch with over 150,000 key decision-makers. With 100% verification of data you can rest assured that you will reach the right person with just one call. Every hospital in the U.S. is profiled, listed alphabetically by city within state. *The Directory of Hospital Personnel* is the only complete source for key hospital decision-makers by name. Whether you want to define or restructure sales territories… locate hospitals with the purchasing power to accept your proposals… keep track of important contacts or colleagues… or find information on which insurance plans are accepted, *The Directory of Hospital Personnel* gives you the information you need – easily, efficiently, effectively and accurately.

"Recommended for college, university and medical libraries." -ARBA

2,500 pages; Softcover ISBN 1-930956-72-X, $275.00 ◆ Online Database $545.00 ◆ Online Database & Directory Combo, $650.00

The Directory of Health Care Group Purchasing Organizations, 2003

This comprehensive directory provides the important data you need to get in touch with over 1,000 Group Purchasing Organizations. By providing in-depth information on this growing market and its members, *The Directory of Health Care Group Purchasing Organizations* fills a major need for the most accurate and comprehensive information on over 1,000 GPOs – Mailing Address, Phone & Fax Numbers, E-mail Addresses, Key Contacts, Purchasing Agents, Group Descriptions, Membership Categorization, Standard Vendor Proposal Requirements, Membership Fees & Terms, Expanded Services, Total Member Beds & Outpatient Visits represented and more. With its comprehensive and detailed information on each purchasing organization, *The Directory of Health Care Group Purchasing Organizations* is the go-to source for anyone looking to target this market.

"The information is clearly arranged and easy to access…recommended for those needing this very specialized information." –ARBA

1,000 pages; Softcover ISBN 1-59237-001-2, $325.00 ◆ Online Database, $650.00 ◆ Online Database & Directory Combo, $750.00

The HMO/PPO Directory, 2003

The HMO/PPO Directory is a comprehensive source that provides detailed information about Health Maintenance Organizations and Preferred Provider Organizations nationwide. This comprehensive directory details more information about more managed health care organizations than ever before. Over 1,100 HMOs, PPOs and affiliated companies are listed, arranged alphabetically by state. Detailed listings include Key Contact Information, Prescription Drug Benefits, Enrollment, Geographical Areas served, Affiliated Physicians & Hospitals, Federal Qualifications, Status, Year Founded, Managed Care Partners, Employer References, Fees & Payment Information and more. Plus, five years of historical information is included related to Revenues, Net Income, Medical Loss Ratios, Membership Enrollment and Number of Patient Complaints. *The HMO/PPO Directory* provides the most comprehensive information on the most companies available on the market place today.

"Helpful to individuals requesting certain HMO/PPO issues such as co-payment costs, subscription costs and patient complaints. Individuals concerned (or those with questions) about their insurance may find this text to be of use to them." -ARBA

600 pages; Softcover ISBN 1-930956-91-6, $250.00 ◆ Online Database, $495.00 ◆ Online Database & Directory Combo, $600.00

The Directory of Independent Ambulatory Care Centers, 2002/03

This first edition of *The Directory of Independent Ambulatory Care Centers* provides access to detailed information that, before now, could only be found scattered in hundreds of different sources. This comprehensive and up-to-date directory pulls together a vast array of contact information for over 7,200 Ambulatory Surgery Centers, Ambulatory General and Urgent Care Clinics, and Diagnostic Imaging Centers that are not affiliated with a hospital or major medical center. Detailed listings include Mailing Address, Phone & Fax Numbers, E-mail and Web Site addresses, Contact Name and Phone Numbers of the Medical Director and other Key Executives and Purchasing Agents, Specialties & Services Offered, Year Founded, Numbers of Employees and Surgeons, Number of Operating Rooms, Number of Cases seen per year, Overnight Options, Contracted Services and much more. Listings are arranged by State, by Center Category and then alphabetically by Organization Name. *The Directory of Independent Ambulatory Care Centers* is a must-have resource for anyone marketing a product or service to this important industry and will be an invaluable tool for those searching for a local care center that will meet their specific needs.

"Among the numerous hospital directories, no other provides information on independent ambulatory centers. A handy, well-organized resource that would be useful in medical center libraries and public libraries." –Choice

986 pages; Softcover ISBN 1-930956-90-8, $185.00 ◆ Online Database, $365.00 ◆ Online Database & Directory Combo, $450.00

To preview any of our Directories Risk-Free for 30 days, call (800) 562-2139 or fax to (518) 789-0556